Encyclopedia of Educational Research

BOARD OF EDITORS

Appointed by the American Educational Research Association

T. R. McConnell, Chairman
John B. Carroll
Raymond O. Collier, Jr.
N. L. Gage
John I. Goodlad
Daniel E. Griffiths
B. Othanel Smith
Robert L. Thorndike

Encyclopedia of Educational Research

FOURTH EDITION

A Project of
The American Educational
Research Association

ROBERT L. EBEL, Editor
Victor H. Noll, Associate Editor
Roger M. Bauer, Editorial Assistant

THE MACMILLAN COMPANY
COLLIER-MACMILLAN LIMITED, LONDON

Copyright © American Educational Research Association 1969

All rights reserved. No part of this book may be reproduced or transmitted in any form or by any means, electronic or mechanical, including photocopying, recording, or by any information storage and retrieval system, without permission in writing from the Publisher.

5-K.

Earlier Editions copyright 1941, 1950, © 1960 by American Educational Research Association

The Macmillan Company
Collier-Macmillan Canada Ltd., Toronto, Ontario

Printed in the United States of America

PREFACE

The first Encyclopedia of Educational Research, conceived, developed, and edited by Professor Walter S. Monroe, was published in 1941. A revision, again edited by Professor Monroe, appeared in 1950. The Third Edition, serving the same purposes and retaining the essential features of its predecessors, with Professor Chester W. Harris as Editor, was published in 1960. This Fourth Edition continues the series.

Each of these volumes has been designed to provide a convenient source of information about most of the important aspects of education. They were developed for use by scholars, students, and practitioners of education at all educational levels and in most fields of specialization. The articles provide concise summaries of research and many references for further study. The popularity of the preceding editions testifies to their success in meeting an important educational need.

The editors of the Fourth Edition, like those of the earlier editions, planned its essential features, its content coverage, and its list of contributing authors with the help of a distinguished Board of Editors. One of the guiding principles endorsed by this board was that the Fourth Edition should be essentially new in structure and content, not simply a revision of the Third Edition. This decision called for a review of the content to be covered and the articles to be written. (Pages vii to ix present the outline of content which evolved from this review.) It also called for the selection of a new group of contributors.

Another major guiding principle concerned the definition of educational research for purposes of the Fourth Edition. The Board of Editors concurred in the recommendation that research should be broadly conceived to include all kinds of contributions to educational knowledge, not simply those resulting from experimental studies. As a consequence, the lists of references are likely to include articles presenting analyses of educational problems, critiques of educational practices, and reports of practical experiences, along with more elegantly designed and analyzed experimental studies.

In planning the articles to be included in the Fourth Edition, the Board of Editors sought to include topics dealing with new areas of research interest and activity, to combine related topics into more comprehensive articles, and to delete topics on which interest and activity were waning. But the board did not subscribe to the belief that today's research is discrediting most of yesterday's knowledge about education. Authors were not instructed to limit their references to articles published in the last decade. The articles tend to deal with persistent educational problems and continuing educational concerns, rather than with the latest panacea or the contemporary crisis.

The Board of Editors, thus, played a crucial role in the design and development of the Fourth Edition; the implementation of their directives was left entirely in the hands of the editors and the contributing authors. Accordingly, any shortcomings of this volume should not be attributed to members of the board.

The development of the Fourth Edition began early in 1964 when an editor was selected. A Board of Editors under the chairmanship of Professor T. R. McConnell was nominated by the Editor and appointed by the AERA President. The first meeting of the Board of Editors was held in Chicago in December, 1964. A second meeting was held in the same place in April, 1965.

The first invitations to contribute articles were issued to prospective authors in November, 1965. Some completed manuscripts were received as early as August, 1966. By July 12, 1968, the final manuscript had been received, edited, and forwarded to The Macmillan Company for publication.

Authors who contribute articles to the Encyclopedia of Educational Research receive no honorarium. Their willingness to do the research and the reflection, the writing and the revision, to supervise the typing of the final draft and to proofread it, and to supply revisions and corrections called for by the editors testify to their commitment to scholarship. The merits of the Fourth Edition are largely attributable to the competence and the conscientious efforts of the contributors.

Financial support for preparation of the Fourth Edition came from the Encyclopedia Royalty Account established by the American Educational Research Association. Major items of expenditure were for editorial and secretarial assistance, for meetings of the Board of Editors, and for stationery, postage, and telephone bills. Michigan State University released the Editor for half-time work on the Encyclopedia from September, 1964, to August, 1968. The University also provided office space for the editors. Professional education in the United States owes a debt of gratitude to Michigan State University, and in particular to Professor John E. Ivey, Jr., Dean of the College of Education, and to President John Hannah, for supporting this enterprise wholeheartedly.

Several others deserve special words of appreciation. Mr. Roger Bauer, an advanced graduate student at Michigan State University, played a crucial role in the editorial process by reading the manuscripts critically and checking innumerable details for accuracy and style. His wife, Mary Jane Bauer, checked all references for completeness and consistency. Dr. Richard Dershimer, Executive Officer of the American Educational Research Association, in addition to submitting an article for the Encyclopedia, gave the entire project consistent, sympathetic, and intelligent support. Mr. Robert Rahtz, Editorial Director of the School Division of The Macmillan Company, was a wise, friendly counselor and a considerate watcher of deadlines. Mr. Bernard S. Cayne and his associates at The Macmillan Company reduced by several orders of magnitude the frequency of errors that had escaped our notice. Finally, our secretaries—first, Mrs. Ted Kundevich and, later, Mrs. Terry Powell—handled the typing, the filing, the record keeping, and the other operational details with skill and unfailing good humor.

So, to the Association, the University, the Company, the Board of Editors, the authors, our editorial associates, and our secretarial assistants, may we express deep gratitude for services well and faithfully rendered.

Robert L. Ebel, Editor
Victor H. Noll, Associate Editor
Michigan State University
July 20, 1968

CONTENT OUTLINE

1. **CONTENT AREAS**

   I. **Foundation Areas**
      A. Developmental Psychology
      B. Psychology of Learning
      C. Human Behavior
      D. Social Foundations

   II. **Function Areas**
      E. Curriculum
      F. Instruction
      G. Special Education
      H. Educational Measurement
      I. Research

   III. **Subject Areas**
      J. Tool Subjects
      K. Cultural Subjects
      L. Vocational Subjects

   IV. **Personnel Areas**
      M. Student Personnel
      N. Teacher Education
      O. Teacher Personnel

   V. **Administration Areas**
      P. Levels of Education
      Q. School Systems
      R. School Administration
      S. Educational Finance
      T. Educational Facilities

2. **ARTICLES IN EACH CONTENT AREA**

   A. **Developmental Psychology**
      1. Child Development
      2. Adolescence
      3. Adulthood and Old Age
      4. Physical Development
      5. Social and Emotional Development
      6. Individual Differences
      7. Sex Differences

   B. **Psychology of Learning**
      1. Educational Psychology
      2. Perception
      3. Learning
      4. Transfer of Learning
      5. Motivation
      6. Motor Abilities
      7. Concept Formation
      8. Language Development
      9. Intelligence
      10. Higher Mental Processes
      11. Creativity

   C. **Human Behavior**
      1. Personality
      2. Interests
      3. Group Processes
      4. Leadership
      5. Mental Health
      6. Behavior Problems

   D. **Social Foundations**
      1. History of Education
      2. Philosophy of Education
      3. Sociology of Education
      4. Economics of Education
      5. Comparative Education
      6. Religion and Education

   E. **Curriculum**
      1. Objectives and Outcomes
      2. Curriculum
      3. Curriculum Evaluation
      4. Educational Programs—Elementary Schools
      5. Educational Programs—Secondary Schools
      6. Educational Programs—College and University
      7. General Education
      8. Honors Programs
      9. Student Organizations and Activities— Elementary and Secondary
      10. Student Organizations and Activities— College and University
      11. Education of Women

F. Instruction
1. Teaching Methods
2. Class Size
3. Grouping
4. Readiness
5. Study
6. Pupil Progress
7. Programmed Instruction
8. Educational Communications Media

G. Special Education
1. Special Education
2. Physically Handicapped Children
3. Mentally Retarded Children
4. Gifted Children
5. Educational Handicaps
6. Speech Pathology and Audiology
7. Rehabilitation

H. Educational Measurement
1. Measurement in Education
2. Intelligence and Special Aptitude Tests
3. Achievement Tests
4. Scores and Norms
5. Test Use
6. Measurement Theory
7. Scaling
8. Prediction
9. Marks and Marking Systems

I. Research
1. Research in Education
2. Research Methods
3. Experimental Methods
4. Statistical Methods
5. Survey Research Methods
6. Data Processing and Computing
7. Research Organizations
8. Training Research Workers

J. Tool Subjects
1. Reading
2. Mathematics
3. English Composition
4. Speech
5. Listening
6. Handwriting
7. Spelling

K. Cultural Subjects
1. Classical Languages
2. Modern Languages
3. English Literature
4. Science Education
5. Social Studies Education
6. Citizenship and Political Socialization
7. Religious Education
8. Art Education
9. Music Education
10. Dramatic Arts Education
11. Physical Education
12. Health Education
13. Outdoor Education

L. Vocational Subjects
1. Vocational and Technical Education
2. Agricultural Education
3. Business Education
4. Home Economics
5. Safety Education
6. Professional Education
7. Medical Education
8. Legal Education
9. Engineering Education
10. Military Education

M. Student Personnel
1. Admissions—College and University
2. Student Financial Aid—College and University
3. Attendance
4. Dropout—Causes and Consequences
5. Records and Reports
6. Student Characteristics—Elementary and Secondary
7. Student Characteristics—College and University
8. College Environments
9. Occupational Placement
10. Counseling Theory
11. Counseling—Elementary Schools
12. Counseling—Secondary Schools
13. Counseling—College and University
14. School Health Services
15. Health Services—College and University

N. Teacher Education
1. Teacher Education Programs
2. Student Teaching
3. In-Service Education of Teachers

O. Teacher Personnel
1. Teacher Certification
2. Economic Status of Teachers
3. Tenure of Teachers
4. Teacher Roles
5. Faculty Characteristics—College and University
6. Teacher Effectiveness
7. Professional Educational Organizations
8. Collective Action by Teachers
9. Academic Freedom

P. Levels of Education
1. Early Childhood Education
2. Elementary Education
3. Secondary Education
4. Community College Education
5. Graduate Education
6. Adult Education
7. Correspondence Instruction
8. Extension Education

CONTENT OUTLINE

Q. **School Systems**
1. Local School Systems
2. State Regulation of Education
3. Cooperation, Coordination, and Control in Higher Education
4. Articulation of Educational Units
5. Federal Programs, Relation and Influence
6. Urban Educational Problems
7. Parochial Schools—Roman Catholic
8. Independent Schools
9. Proprietary Schools
10. Education in Developing Nations

R. **School Administration**
1. Administrative Theory
2. Preparation of Administrators
3. Public School Administration
4. School Business Administration
5. College and University Administration
6. School Personnel Administration
7. Improvement in Educational Practice
8. Public Relations
9. Supervision
10. Discipline

S. **Educational Finance**
1. Finance—Public Schools
2. Finance—College and University
3. Foundations

T. **Educational Facilities**
1. Libraries
2. Textbooks
3. Transportation of Students

CONTRIBUTORS TO THE FOURTH EDITION

AUTHOR	ARTICLE
Kathleen Amershek	*Student Teaching*
Margaret Ammons	*Objectives and Outcomes*
Dan W. Andersen	*Handwriting*
Robert H. Anderson	*Pupil Progress*
Gustave O. Arlt	*Graduate Education*
J. Myron Atkin	*Science Education*
David B. Austin	*Secondary Education*
Richard H. Barbe	*Foundations*
S. Howard Bartley	*Perception*
Ernest E. Bayles	*History of Education*
Lois A. Beilin	*Curriculum*
Charles S. Benson	*Finance—College and University*
Ralph F. Berdie	*Counseling—College and University*
Frederick W. Bertolaet	*Urban Educational Problems*
Bruce J. Biddle	*Teacher Roles*
Charles E. Bidwell	*Sociology of Education*
Edward B. Blackman	*General Education*
Benjamin S. Bloom	*Higher Mental Processes*
Carolyn E. Bock	*Classical Languages*
Wallace J. Bonk	*Libraries*
Eli M. Bower	*Mental Health*
Richard Braddock	*English Composition*
George L. Brandon	*Vocational and Technical Education*
William W. Brickman	*Comparative Education*
Conrad Briner	*Leadership*
Leland D. Brokaw	*Military Education*
R. Will Burnett	*Science Education*
John B. Carroll	*Modern Languages*
W. W. Charters, Jr.	*Public Relations*

CONTRIBUTORS TO THE FOURTH EDITION

Jack R. Childress	*In-Service Education of Teachers*
David L. Clark	*Training Research Workers*
Norman Cliff	*Scaling*
William E. Coffman	*Achievement Tests*
William W. Cooley	*Data Processing and Computing*
Dan H. Cooper	*Local School Systems*
Harold F. Cottingham	*Counseling—Elementary Schools*
John O. Crites	*Interests*
David A. Cunningham	*Physical Education*
Edward E. Cureton	*Measurement Theory*
Don Davies	*Student Teaching*
J. Kent Davis	*Transfer of Learning*
Richard A. Dershimer	*Professional Educational Organizations*
Edith M. Dowley	*Early Childhood Education*
Paul L. Dressel	*Faculty Characteristics—College and University*
Sam Duker	*Listening*
Henry S. Dyer	*Admissions—College and University*
Robert L. Ebel	*Educational Programs—Secondary Schools*
	Measurement in Education
Elliott W. Eisner	*Art Education*
Dana L. Farnsworth	*Health Services—College and University*
Nicholas A. Fattu	*Research Organizations*
John C. Flanagan	*Student Characteristics—Elementary and Secondary*
Ned A. Flanders	*Teacher Effectiveness*
Edwin A. Fleishman	*Motor Abilities*
Arthur W. Foshay	*Curriculum*
R. A. Fulton	*Proprietary Schools*
N. L. Gage	*Teaching Methods*
James J. Gallagher	*Gifted Children*
J. W. Getzels	*Creativity*
R. Oliver Gibson	*Attendance*
	School Personnel Administration
Robert Glaser	*Learning*
Ira J. Gordon	*Social and Emotional Development*
D. B. Gowin	*Philosophy of Education*
Grace Graham	*Student Organizations and Activities—Elementary and Secondary*
Russell T. Gregg	*Preparation of Administrators*
Calvin Grieder	*Public School Administration*
Daniel E. Griffiths	*Administrative Theory*
Kenneth J. Groves	*Military Education*
Roy M. Hall	*Foundations*
W. Lee Hansen	*Economics of Education*
John W. Hanson	*Education in Developing Nations*
Melvene D. Hardee	*Education of Women*
Chester W. Harris	*Statistical Methods*

CONTRIBUTORS TO THE FOURTH EDITION

Theodore L. Harris	*Reading*
Robert J. Havighurst	*Adulthood and Old Age*
James E. Heald	*Supervision*
Robert W. Heath	*Curriculum Evaluation*
Glen Heathers	*Grouping*
Hubert C. Heffner	*Dramatic Arts Education*
Paul Heist	*Student Characteristics—College and University*
Robert E. Herriott	*Survey Research Method*
Ernest Hilton	*Textbooks*
Wayne H. Holtzman	*Study*
John E. Hopkins	*Training Research Workers*
Thomas D. Horn	*Spelling*
Cyril O. Houle	*Adult Education*
J. T. Hunt	*Mentally Retarded Children*
Robert M. Isenberg	*Transportation of Students*
John E. Ivey, Jr.	*Improvement in Educational Practice*
H. Thomas James	*Finance—Public Schools*
John X. Jamrich	*Cooperation, Coordination, and Control in Higher Education*
K. Forbis Jordan	*School Business Administration*
Martin R. Katz	*Counseling—Secondary Schools*
Fred N. Kerlinger	*Research in Education*
Norman Key	*Safety Education*
Herbert J. Klausmeier	*Transfer of Learning*
M. Frances Klein	*Educational Programs—Elementary Schools*
Alan B. Knox	*Extension Education*
C. Albert Koob	*Parochial Schools—Roman Catholic*
John F. Latimer	*Classical Languages*
William K. LeBold	*Engineering Education*
Roger T. Lennon	*Scores and Norms*
J. Kenneth Little	*Federal Programs, Relation and Influence*
Sara Little	*Religious Education*
Lloyd H. Lofquist	*Rehabilitation*
Margaret F. Lorimer	*Faculty Characteristics—College and University*
Walter H. MacGinitie	*Language Development*
Romaine P. Mackie	*Physically Handicapped Children*
George F. Madaus	*Creativity*
Byron G. Massialas	*Citizenship and Political Socialization*
Kenneth B. Matheny	*Counseling Theory*
Cyrus Mayshark	*Health Education*
Lewis B. Mayhew	*Educational Programs—College and University*
Boyd R. McCandless	*Child Development*
William J. McGlothlin	*Professional Education*
Sterling M. McMurrin	*Academic Freedom*
Leland L. Medsker	*Community College Education*
Howard V. Meredith	*Physical Development*
William B. Michael	*Prediction*

CONTRIBUTORS TO THE FOURTH EDITION

George E. Miller	*Medical Education*
John D. Millett	*College and University Administration*
Philip I. Mitterling	*Honors Programs*
Henry J. Montoye	*Physical Education*
George J. Mouly	*Research Methods*
Donald A. Myers	*Educational Programs—Elementary Schools*
George Nash	*Student Financial Aid—College and University*
Martin J. Nelson	*Intelligence and Special Aptitude Tests*
Helen Y. Nelson	*Home Economics*
Raphael O. Nystrand	*Urban Educational Problems*
Charles Odell	*Occupational Placement*
Ralph H. Ojemann	*Behavior Problems*
William T. O'Hara	*Legal Education*
Wayne Otto	*Handwriting*
Herbert J. Oyer	*Speech Pathology and Audiology*
C. Robert Pace	*College Environments*
Francis Parkman	*Independent Schools*
Robert P. Parker, Jr.	*Teacher Education Programs*
Robert F. Peck	*Adolescence*
Edgar Persons	*Agricultural Education*
Malcolm Provus	*Collective Action by Teachers*
Ernest A. Rakow	*Higher Mental Processes*
Maynard C. Reynolds	*Special Education*
Herbert Richek	*Adolescence*
Cynthia Ritsher	*Pupil Progress*
William H. Roe	*State Regulation of Education*
Gilbert Sax	*Concept Formation*
Richard A. Schmuck	*Group Processes*
Erwin H. Schneider	*Music Education*
Daniel Schreiber	*Dropout—Causes and Consequences*
Hugh F. Seabury	*Speech*
William M. Seaman	*Classical Languages*
Saul B. Sells	*Personality*
James C. Shelburne	*Military Education*
Anita Simon	*Teacher Effectiveness*
John A. Sivatko	*Correspondence Instruction*
J. R. Skretting	*Social Studies Education*
B. Othanel Smith	*Discipline*
Julian Smith	*Outdoor Education*
James R. Squire	*English Literature*
G. Wesley Sowards	*Elementary Education*
Harry L. Stearns	*Religion and Education*
Buford Stefflre	*Counseling Theory*
Gertrude N. Stieber	*Economic Status of Teachers*
Jo Ann K. Stiles	*Child Development*
Lindley J. Stiles	*Teacher Education Programs*

CONTRIBUTORS TO THE FOURTH EDITION

T. M. Stinnett	Teacher Certification
Lawrence M. Stolurow	Programmed Instruction
James C. Stone	Articulation of Educational Units
Robert Stout	Leadership
James E. Sundeen	Social Studies Education
Gordon Swanson	Agricultural Education
Maurice M. Tatsuoka	Experimental Methods
R. Murray Thomas	Records and Reports
Robert L. Thorndike	Marks and Marking Systems
Robert M. W. Travers	Educational Psychology
Read D. Tuddenham	Intelligence
Frederick T. Tyler	Readiness
Leona E. Tyler	Individual Differences
	Sex Differences
Loren Twyford	Educational Communications Media
William S. Vincent	Class Size
N. Kishor Wahi	Test Use
Helen M. Wallace	School Health Services
Ted W. Ward	Improvement in Educational Practice
Martha L. Ware	Tenure of Teachers
William W. Wattenberg	Educational Handicaps
Bernard Weiner	Motivation
Leonard J. West	Business Education
Morris Wiener	Outdoor Education
E. G. Williamson	Student Organizations and Activities—College and University
Stephen S. Willoughby	Mathematics
Frank B. Womer	Test Use
Donald Zander	Student Organizations and Activities—College and University

CONTRIBUTORS TO EARLIER EDITIONS

Georgia Sachs Adams, 1950
Harold Alberty, 1960
William H. Allen, 1960
C. H. Ammons, 1960
R. B. Ammons, 1960
Anne Anastasi, 1960
Archibald W. Anderson, 1941, 1950
Earl W. Anderson, 1941, 1950, 1960
G. Lester Anderson, 1950, 1960
John E. Anderson, 1941, 1950
Kenneth E. Anderson, 1960
Thomas G. Andrews, 1950
William H. Angoff, 1960
Clifford P. Archer, 1941, 1950, 1960
Willard P. Ashbrook, 1941, 1950
David P. Ausubel, 1960
William V. Badger, 1960
Harold Wood Bailey, 1941, 1950
G. Derwood Baker, 1960
Harry J. Baker, 1950
Evelyn I. Banning, 1960
Roger G. Barker, 1941, 1950
A. S. Barr, 1941, 1950, 1960
Nancy Bayley, 1950, 1960
John D. Beatty, 1941
Kenneth R. Beittel, 1960
Hugh M. Bell, 1941, 1950
Margaret E. Bennett, 1941, 1950
Raymond D. Bennett, 1941, 1950
Ralph F. Berdie, 1950
Emma M. Birkmaier, 1960
W. S. Bittner, 1941, 1950
Earl G. Blackstone, 1941
Thomas E. Blackwell, 1960
Willard W. Blaesser, 1960
Glenn M. Blair, 1950, 1960
Lloyd E. Blauch, 1941, 1950, 1960
Charles W. Boardman, 1941, 1950
Joan Bollenbacher, 1960
Horace M. Bond, 1941, 1950
Merl E. Bonney, 1960
Merle L. Borrowman, 1960
Paul L. Boynton, 1941

Ruth Boynton, 1941, 1950
Francis F. Bradshaw, 1941
Arthur H. Brayfield, 1950
Howard S. Bretsch, 1960
William W. Brickman, 1950, 1960
William G. Brink, 1960
William H. Bristow, 1941, 1950
K. O. Broady, 1941, 1950
Sara Ann Brown, 1960
John S. Brubacher, 1950, 1960
Leo J. Brueckner, 1941, 1950
A. J. Brumbaugh, 1941
Edmund deS. Brunner, 1941, 1950
B. R. Buckingham, 1960
H. O. Burgess, 1941
Arvid J. Burke, 1960
John E. Burke, 1960
Norman Burns, 1960
G. T. Buswell, 1960
J. Donald Butler, 1960
R. L. C. Butsch, 1941
Leo F. Cain, 1941, 1950, 1960
G. Robert Carlsen, 1960
Leon Carnovsky, 1941, 1950
Edwin R. Carr, 1950
W. L. Carr, 1941, 1950
William G. Carr, 1941, 1950
John B. Carroll, 1960
Harold D. Carter, 1941, 1960
Francis P. Cassidy, 1941, 1950
Hester Chadderdon, 1941, 1950
M. M. Chambers, 1941, 1950
W. W. Charters, Jr., 1960
Israel S. Chipkin, 1941, 1950
Harold F. Clark, 1941, 1950
Charles M. Clarke, 1960
A. Stafford Clayton, 1960
John A. Clement, 1941
Algernon Coleman, 1941
Herbert S. Conrad, 1941, 1950
Lloyd Allen Cook, 1941, 1950
Walter W. Cook, 1941, 1950, 1960
Dennis H. Cooke, 1941

Dan H. Cooper, 1960
Russell M. Cooper, 1950
Shirley Cooper, 1950, 1960
Stephen M. Corey, 1941
Francis G. Cornell, 1950, 1960
Warren W. Coxe, 1941, 1950
Frederick W. Cozens, 1941, 1950
Sherman G. Crayton, 1941
Lee J. Cronbach, 1950, 1960
Burns B. Crookston, 1960
Jack Culbertson, 1960
Margaret W. Curti, 1941, 1950
Wesley P. Cushman, 1950
Frank W. Cyr, 1941, 1950
Edgar Dale, 1941, 1950, 1960
Julia I. Dalrymple, 1960
Dora E. Damrin, 1960
John G. Darley, 1941
John F. Dashiell, 1941, 1950
Hazel Davis, 1950, 1960
Howard A. Dawson, 1941, 1960
H. C. De Kock, 1960
Norman J. De Witt, 1960
G. P. Deyoe, 1950
Gwendolen Schneidler Dickson, 1950
Stanley E. Dimond, 1960
John E. Dobbin, 1960
Dan W. Dodson, 1960
James I. Doi, 1960
E. W. Dolch, 1941, 1950
Harl R. Douglass, 1941, 1950
Richard M. Drake, 1950
Paul L. Dressel, 1960
Fannie W. Dunn, 1941
Lloyd M. Dunn, 1960
Margaret J. Early, 1960
Howard Easley, 1941, 1950
Robert W. Eaves, 1950
Robert L. Ebel, 1960
R. H. Eckelberry, 1941, 1950
Ruth E. Eckert, 1950, 1960
Newton Edwards, 1941, 1950
Walter Crosby Eells, 1941, 1950
Willard S. Elsbree, 1941, 1950
Max D. Englehart, 1941, 1950
E. R. Enlow, 1941
Anna Espenschade, 1950
A. A. Esslinger, 1941, 1950
Dwain M. Estes, 1960
William K. Estes, 1960
Alvin C. Eurich, 1941, 1960
Elvin S. Eyster, 1960
Dana L. Farnsworth, 1960
Elwin D. Farwell, 1960
Nicholas A. Fattu, 1960
Roland C. Faunce, 1960
Daniel D. Feder, 1941, 1950, 1960
Norman Fenton, 1950
Warren G. Findley, 1960
James D. Finn, 1950
Cecile White Flemming, 1941, 1950
John Forbes, 1960
Richard R. Foster, 1941
Maurice H. Fouracre, 1950, 1960
Orie I. Frederick, 1941

Frank N. Freeman, 1941
Frank S. Freeman, 1950
Gustav J. Froehlich, 1960
Edgar Fuller, 1960
Elizabeth Mechem Fuller, 1960
N. L. Gage, 1960
Donfred H. Gardner, 1941, 1950
T. R. Garth, 1941
E. Glenadine Gibb, 1960
Ruth B. Glassow, 1960
Lyman A. Glenny, 1960
Goldine C. Gleser, 1960
G. M. Gloss, 1941
Carter V. Good, 1941, 1950, 1960
H. G. Good, 1941, 1950
Florence L. Goodenough, 1941, 1950
John I. Goodlad, 1960
William S. Gray, 1941, 1950, 1960
Harry A. Greene, 1941, 1950
Russell T. Gregg, 1960
E. D. Grizzell, 1941, 1950, 1960
Richard E. Gross, 1960
Harold M. Groves, 1960
William T. Gruhn, 1941, 1950
Elizabeth P. Hagen, 1960
Harlan L. Hagman, 1960
Roy M. Hall, 1960
H. M. Hamlin, 1941, 1950
Paul R. Hanna, 1950
Carl W. Hansen, 1950
Melvene D. Hardee, 1960
Chester W. Harris, 1960
Theodore L. Harris, 1960
Laurence D. Haskew, 1960
Robert J. Havighurst, 1960
Harriet Hayes, 1941, 1950
Wayland J. Hayes, 1941, 1950
Mary O. Hayslip, 1950
Arch O. Heck, 1941, 1950
Fred V. Hein, 1960
Paul A. Heist, 1960
Andrew Hendrickson, 1960
Gordon Hendrickson, 1941, 1950, 1960
Frances Henne, 1950
John H. Herrick, 1950
Virgil E. Herrick, 1960
Gertrude Hildreth, 1941, 1950
Marie A. Hinrichs, 1960
Charles F. Hoban, Jr., 1941
Frederick G. Hochwalt, 1950
Ernest V. Hollis, 1941, 1950, 1960
T. C. Holy, 1941, 1950
Karl J. Holzinger, 1941, 1950
Robert Hoppock, 1941
Ernest Horn, 1941, 1950, 1960
Victor O. Hornbostel, 1960
W. W. Howells, 1960
Cyril J. Hoyt, 1960
Frank W. Hubbard, 1941, 1950, 1960
Lloyd G. Humphreys, 1950
Richard J. Hurley, 1960
C. Robert Hutchcroft, 1960
Clayton D. Hutchins, 1950
H. Clifton Hutchins, 1960
John L. Hutchinson, 1950

Mark E. Hutchinson, 1950
Max L. Hutt, 1960
Grant M. Hyde, 1941, 1950
Robert Isenberg, 1960
David Iwamoto, 1960
Kai Jensen, 1941, 1950, 1960
George Johnson, 1941
Edward S. Jones, 1941, 1950
Harold E. Jones, 1941, 1950
Mary Cover Jones, 1941, 1950
R. Stewart Jones, 1960
Vernon Jones, 1941, 1950, 1960
Walter V. Kaulfers, 1941, 1950
Joseph Kavetsky, 1960
Nolan C. Kearney, 1960
Alice V. Keliher, 1941, 1950
Robert J. Keller, 1960
Janet Agnes Kelley, 1950
Thomas E. Kendig, 1950
Clara Breslove King, 1941
Otto Klineberg, 1950
George F. Kneller, 1960
S. J. Knezevich, 1960
Edgar W. Knight, 1941, 1950
Franklin H. Knower, 1960
Helen L. Koch, 1941, 1950
Clyde F. Kohn, 1950
Henry Kronenberg, 1941
Raymond G. Kuhlen, 1960
William C. Kvaraceus, 1960
Sam M. Lambert, 1960
Arch D. Lang, 1950
Gerald B. Leighbody, 1960
Harold R. Leith, 1950
Joseph Lev, 1950
Irving Lieberman, 1960
Walter M. Lifton, 1960
J. Kenneth Little, 1960
Ester Lloyd-Jones, 1941, 1950
Omer L. Loop, 1941
F. E. Lord, 1941, 1950
Irving Lorge, 1950
Margaret F. Lorimer, 1960
C. M. Louttit, 1941
William H. Lucio, 1960
Dorothea McCarthy, 1941, 1950
T. R. McConnell, 1950, 1960
J. Edward McCracken, 1950
R. S. McElhinney, 1941
Carson McGuire, 1950, 1960
Katherine L. McLaughlin, 1941, 1950
J. B. Maller, 1941, 1950
Herschel T. Manuel, 1950, 1960
Arlyn C. Marks, 1941, 1950
T. D. Martin, 1941, 1950
William E. Martin, 1960
Velorus Martz, 1941
Melvin H. Marx, 1960
Ray C. Maul, 1960
John R. Mayor, 1960
Otto Mayer, 1941, 1950
A. B. Mays, 1941, 1950
Bernard Mehl, 1960
Arthur W. Melton, 1941, 1950
Thornton W. Merriam, 1941, 1950

William B. Michael, 1960
John U. Michaelis, 1950, 1960
Catharine C. Miles, 1941
Harold E. Mitzel, 1960
Edward O. Moe, 1960
Walter S. Monroe, 1941, 1950
Harold E. Moore, 1960
Joseph E. Moore, 1941
Lloyd Morey, 1941
J. Cayce Morrison, 1960
Robert H. Morrison, 1941, 1950
Horace T. Morse, 1950
Milosh Muntyan, 1960
Wilbur F. Murra, 1941
Paul H. Mussen, 1960
T. Ernest Newland, 1960
Victor H. Noll, 1960
Norma I. Noonan, 1941
Dorothy E. Norris, 1941, 1950
Arwood S. Northby, 1941, 1950
John K. Norton, 1960
C. W. Odell, 1941, 1950
Ralph H. Ojemann, 1950, 1960
Edward G. Olsen, 1950
Willard C. Olson, 1941, 1950, 1960
Henry J. Otto, 1941, 1950, 1960
H. W. Paine, 1950
Clyde A. Parker, 1960
Donald G. Paterson, 1941, 1950
Helen M. Patterson, 1941, 1950
Ann Pavan, 1941
W. E. Peik, 1941
Charles C. Peters, 1941
John E. Phay, 1950
Thomas A. Phillips, 1950
Founta Green Pollard, 1950
James Z. Polychrones, 1960
Robert C. Pooley, 1941, 1950, 1960
Samuel Ralph Powers, 1950
Karl C. Pratt, 1941, 1950
Willis E. Pratt, 1950
Sidney L. Pressey, 1960
Ray G. Price, 1941, 1950
Harves C. Rahe, 1950
Theophile Raphael, 1941, 1950
G. Lawrence Rarick, 1960
Walter C. Reckless, 1941, 1950
Fritz Redl, 1941, 1950
Edwin H. Reeder, 1941, 1950
Ward G. Reeder, 1941, 1950
C. E. Reeves, 1941, 1950
William C. Rein, 1950
Wilhelm Reitz, 1941, 1950
Theodore L. Reller, 1941, 1950
Madaline Kinter Remmlein, 1950, 1960
Harold C. Reppert, 1950
James W. Reynolds, 1960
Herman G. Richey, 1960
William McKinley Robinson, 1941, 1950
Stephen Romine, 1950
Frank J. Roos, 1950
Frederick T. Rope, 1950
G. Robert Ross, 1960
Floyd L. Ruch, 1941
Elfreda M. Rusher, 1960

David H. Russell, 1960
John Dale Russell, 1941, 1950, 1960
David G. Ryans, 1960
Peter Sandiford, 1941
Charles W. Sanford, 1941, 1950
Theodore R. Sarbin, 1941
Michael O. Sawyer, 1950
Galen Saylor, 1960
John J. Scanlon, 1960
Douglas E. Scates, 1941, 1950
Dorothy Schaffter, 1950
Norma V. Scheidemann, 1941
Gwendolen G. Schneidler, 1941
William B. Schrader, 1960
Harold A. Schultz, 1950
Gladys C. Schwesinger, 1941
May V. Seagoe, 1960
John R. Searles, 1960
Jesse B. Sears, 1941, 1950
Saul B. Sells, 1960
Harold G. Shane, 1960
Russell T. Sharpe, 1941
C. L. Shartle, 1950
Paul H. Sheats, 1960
Mary Shirley, 1941
Nathan W. Shock, 1941, 1950
Mildred Sikkema, 1950
George W. Sledge, 1960
Ann Z. Smith, 1960
B. Othanel Smith, 1950, 1960
H. L. Smith, 1941
Herbert A. Smith, 1960
W. Ray Smittle, 1941, 1950
Wayne W. Soper, 1950
W. Lloyd Sprouse, 1950
Ross Stagner, 1941, 1950
Edwin Diller Starbuck, 1941
John E. Stecklein, 1960
J. M. Stephens, 1960
Lindley J. Stiles, 1950, 1960
T. M. Stinnett, 1960
Ruth M. Strang, 1941, 1950, 1960
Clara G. Stratemeyer, 1950
Merle R. Sumption, 1941, 1950
Donald E. Super, 1960
Paul W. Terry, 1941
James B. Tharp, 1950
W. W. Theisen, 1950

Robert L. Thorndike, 1950, 1960
Robert D. Thornton, 1960
David V. Tiedeman, 1960
Herbert A. Toops, 1941, 1950
Joseph V. Totaro, 1960
M. R. Trabue, 1950
Lee Edward Travis, 1941, 1950
Arthur E. Traxler, 1941, 1950
Edith Treuenfels, 1960
David K. Trites, 1960
William Clark Trow, 1960
J. Lloyd Trump, 1950, 1960
Fred T. Tyler, 1960
J. G. Umstattd, 1941, 1950, 1960
George E. Van Dyke, 1950
William Van Til, 1960
Fred von Borgersrode, 1941
Antonio M. Vincent, 1960
Helen M. Walker, 1941, 1950
J. E. Wallace Wallin, 1941, 1950
Martha L. Ware, 1960
Robert I. Watson, 1960
William W. Wattenberg, 1950
Beth L. Wellman, 1941, 1950
Ralph C. Wenrich, 1960
Edgar B. Wesley, 1941, 1950
Paul V. West, 1950
Willis A. Whitehead, 1950
Stephen B. Whithey, 1960
Gould Wickey, 1941, 1950
David J. Wiens, 1950
Kimball Wiles, 1960
Harold A. Williams, 1960
E. G. Williamson, 1941, 1950
Betty Wills, 1960
Guy M. Wilson, 1941, 1950
G. Max Wingo, 1960
Robert C. Woellner, 1941, 1950
Kate V. Wofford, 1950
Asahel D. Woodruff, 1960
Thomas Woody, 1941
F. Lynwood Wren, 1941, 1950
C. Gilbert Wrenn, 1941, 1950, 1960
J. Wayne Wrightstone, 1941, 1950, 1960
Doris A. Young, 1960
Paul Thomas Young, 1941, 1950
Leslie Day Zeleny, 1941, 1950
Norah E. Zink, 1941

ABBREVIATIONS

The abbreviations listed below were used for names of organizations and publishers and for the titles of periodicals.

AAAS–American Association for the Advancement of Science
AACRAO–American Association of Collegiate Registrars and Admissions Officers
AACTE–American Association of Colleges for Teacher Education
AAHPER–American Association for Health, Physical Education and Recreation
AAJC–American Association of Junior Colleges
AAPSS–American Academy of Political and Social Science
AASA–American Association of School Administrators
AAUP–American Association of University Professors
Abn–Abnormal
Acad–Academy
Academic–Academic Press, Inc.
ACE–American Council on Education
ACT–American College Testing Program
Addison–Addison-Wesley Publishing Company, Inc.
Adm–Administration, Administrative
AERA–American Educational Research Association
Ag–Agriculture, Agricultural
AGB–Association of Governing Boards
ALA–American Library Association
Allen–George Allen & Unwin, Ltd.
Allyn–Allyn and Bacon, Inc.
Am–America, American
AMA–American Medical Association
American–American Book Company
Anthrop–Anthropology, Anthropologist
APA–American Psychological Association
APGA–American Personnel and Guidance Association
Appleton–Appleton-Century-Crofts, Inc.
ASCD–Association for Supervision and Curriculum Development
Assn–Association(s)

B–Bulletin
Barnes–Barnes & Noble, Inc.
Bd–Board
Biol–Biology, Biological
Bobbs-Merrill–Bobbs-Merrill Company, Inc.
Br–British
Brown–William C. Brown Company
Bruce–Bruce Publishing Company
Bus–Business

Carnegie–Carnegie Foundation for the Advancement of Teaching
Cath–Catholic
CEEB–College Entrance Examination Board
Cen–Central
CGSUS–Council of Graduate Schools in the United States
Chem–Chemistry
Childh–Childhood
Clin–Clinical
Col–College(s), Collegiate
Com–Community
Comp–Comparative
Concordia–Concordia Publishing House
Cons–Consulting
Contr–Contributions
Couns–Counselor, Counseling
Croft–Arthur C. Croft Publications
Crowell–Crowell-Collier Publishing Company
CRP–Cooperative Research Project
Curric–Curriculum

Dept–Department
Develop–Development
Dodd–Dodd, Mead & Company, Inc.
Doubleday–Doubleday & Company, Inc.
Dover–Dover Publications
Duell–Duell, Sloan & Pearce–Meredith Press
Dutton–E. P. Dutton & Co., Inc.

Econ–Economics, Economy
Ed–Education, Educational
El–Elementary
Engl–English
ETS–Educational Testing Service
Excep–Exceptional
Exp–Experimental, Experiment
Ext–Extension

Follett–Follett Publishing Co.
Free Press–Free Press of Glencoe
Funk–Funk & Wagnalls Company

ABBREVIATIONS

Gen–General
Genet–Genetic, Genetics
Geog–Geography
Geront–Gerontology
Ginn–Ginn & Company
GPO–Government Printing Office
Grune–Grune & Stratton, Inc.
Guid–Guidance

H–High, Higher
Harcourt–Harcourt, Brace & World, Inc.
Harper–Harper & Row, Publishers
Heath–D. C. Heath and Company
HEW–United States Department of Health, Education and Welfare
Hist–Historical
Holt–Holt, Rinehart & Winston, Inc.
Houghton–Houghton Mifflin Company
Hum–Human

IBM–International Business Machines, Inc.
Ind–Industry, Industrial
Int–International

J–Journal
Jun–Junior

Knopf–Alfred A. Knopf, Inc.

Lang–Language
Lib–Library(ies)
Lippincott–J. B. Lippincott Company
Little–Little, Brown & Company
Liveright–Liveright Publishing Corporation

M–Magazine
Macmillan–The Macmillan Company
Manag–Management
Math–Mathematics, Mathematical
McGraw-Hill–McGraw-Hill Book Company, Inc.
McKay–David McKay Company, Inc.
Meas–Measurement
Med–Medicine, Medical
Mem–Memoirs, Memorial
Merriam–G. & C. Merriam Company
Meth–Method(s)
MLA–Modern Language Association of America
Mod–Modern
Mon–Monthly
Monogr–Monograph(s)
Morrow–William Morrow & Company, Inc.
Mosby–C. V. Mosby Company

NAEYC–National Association for the Education of Young Children
NAIS–National Association of Independent Schools
NASSP–National Association of Secondary School Principals
Nat–National
NCME–National Council on Measurement in Education
NCTE–National Council of Teachers of English
NEA–National Education Association
Nelson–Thomas Nelson & Sons
NMSC–National Merit Scholarship Corporation
NORC–National Opinion Research Center

Norton–W. W. Norton & Company, Inc.
NSSE–National Society for the Study of Education

Odyssey–Odyssey Press, Inc.
Oliver–Oliver & Boyd, Ltd.
Opin–Opinion

PDK–Phi Delta Kappa
PEA–Progressive Education Association
Ped–Pedagogical
Pers–Personality
Philos–Philosophy
Phys–Physical
Physiol–Physiology, Physiological
Praeger–Frederick A. Praeger, Inc.
Prentice-Hall–Prentice-Hall, Inc.
Prin–Principal(s)
Proc–Proceedings
Prof–Professor(s)
Prog–Progressive
Psychoanal–Psychoanalysis, Psychoanalytic
Psychol–Psychology, Psychological
Psychol Corp–Psychological Corporation
Psychosom–Psychosomatic
PTA–Parent-Teacher Association
Pub–Publication(s)
Putnam–G. P. Putnam's Sons

Q–Quarterly

R–Review
Rand McNally–Rand McNally & Company
Random–Random House, Inc.
Rec–Record
Reg–Registrars
Reinhold–Reinhold Publishing Corporation
Relig–Religious
Res–Research
Ronald–Ronald Press Company
Routledge–Routledge & Kegan Paul, Ltd.
Russell Sage–Russell Sage Foundation

Saunders–W. B. Saunders Company
Sch–School(s)
Sci–Science, Scientific, Scientist
Science–Science Press
Scott–Scott, Foresman and Company
Scribner–Charles Scribner's Sons
SDC–Systems Development Corporation
Sec–Secondary
Sect–Section
Sem–Seminary
Silver–Silver Burdett Company
Simon–Simon and Schuster, Inc.
Soc–Society(ies), Social
Sociol–Sociology, Sociological, Sociologist
SRA–Science Research Associates
SREB–Southern Regional Education Board
Stat–Statistics, Statistical
Stoelting–C. H. Stoelting Company
Stud–Studies
Sup–Supervision

TC–Teachers College, Columbia University
Teach–Teacher(s)
Train–Training
Trans–Transactions

U–University
UCEA–University Council for Educational Administration
UNESCO–United Nations Educational, Scientific and Cultural Organization
USOE–United States Office of Education

Van Nostrand–D. Van Nostrand Company, Inc.
Voc–Vocational

Welf–Welfare
WHO–World Health Organization
WICHE–Western Interstate Commission for Higher Education
WCOTP–World Confederation of Organizations of the Teaching Profession
Wiley–John Wiley & Sons, Inc.
Williams and Wilkins–Williams and Wilkins Company
Wilson–H. W. Wilson Company

ARTICLES AND AUTHORS

Academic Freedom
   Sterling M. McMurrin

Achievement Tests
   William E. Coffman

Administrative Theory
   Daniel E. Griffiths

Admissions—College and University
   Henry S. Dyer

Adolescence
   Robert F. Peck and Herbert Richek

Adult Education
   Cyril O. Houle

Adulthood and Old Age
   Robert J. Havighurst

Agricultural Education
   Gordon Swanson and Edgar Persons

Art Education
   Elliott W. Eisner

Articulation of Educational Units
   James C. Stone

Attendance
   R. Oliver Gibson

Behavior Problems
   Ralph H. Ojemann

Business Education
   Leonard J. West

Child Development
   Boyd R. McCandless and Jo Ann K. Stiles

Citizenship and Political Socialization
   Byron G. Massialas

Class Size
   William S. Vincent

Classical Languages
   John F. Latimer, Carolyn E. Bock, and William M. Seaman

Collective Action by Teachers
   Malcolm Provus

College and University Administration
   John D. Millett

College Environments
   C. Robert Pace

Community College Education
   Leland L. Medsker

Comparative Education
   William W. Brickman

Concept Formation
   Gilbert Sax

Cooperation, Coordination, and Control in Higher Education
   John X. Jamrich

Correspondence Instruction
   John R. Sivatko

Counseling—College and University
   Ralph F. Berdie

Counseling—Elementary Schools
   Harold F. Cottingham

Counseling—Secondary Schools
   Martin R. Katz

Counseling Theory
   Buford Stefflre and Kenneth B. Matheny

Creativity
   J. W. Getzels and George F. Madaus

Curriculum
   Arthur W. Foshay and Lois A. Beilin

Curriculum Evaluation
   Robert W. Heath

Data Processing and Computing
  William W. Cooley
Discipline
  B. Othanel Smith
Dramatic Arts Education
  Hubert C. Heffner
Dropout—Causes and Consequences
  Daniel Schreiber

Early Childhood Education
  Edith M. Dowley
Economic Status of Teachers
  Gertrude N. Stieber
Economics of Education
  W. Lee Hansen
Education in Developing Nations
  John W. Hanson
Education of Women
  Melvene D. Hardee
Educational Communications Media
  Loren Twyford
Educational Handicaps
  William W. Wattenberg
Educational Programs—College and University
  Lewis B. Mayhew
Educational Programs—Elementary Schools
  Donald A. Myers and M. Frances Klein
Educational Programs—Secondary Schools
  Robert L. Ebel
Educational Psychology
  Robert M. W. Travers
Elementary Education
  G. Wesley Sowards
Engineering Education
  William LeBold
English Composition
  Richard Braddock
English Literature
  James R. Squire
Experimental Methods
  Maurice M. Tatsuoka
Extension Education
  Alan B. Knox

Faculty Characteristics—College and University
  Paul L. Dressel and Margaret F. Lorimer
Federal Programs, Relation and Influence
  J. Kenneth Little

Finance—College and University
  Charles S. Benson
Finance—Public Schools
  H. Thomas James
Foundations
  Richard H. Barbe and Roy M. Hall

General Education
  Edward B. Blackman
Gifted Children
  James J. Gallagher
Graduate Education
  Gustav O. Arlt
Group Processes
  Richard A. Schmuck
Grouping
  Glen Heathers

Handwriting
  Dan W. Andersen and Wayne Otto
Health Education
  Cyrus Mayshark
Health Services—College and University
  Dana L. Farnsworth
Higher Mental Processes
  Benjamin S. Bloom and Ernest A. Rakow
History of Education
  Ernest E. Bayles
Home Economics
  Helen Y. Nelson
Honors Programs
  Philip I. Mitterling

Improvement in Educational Practice
  John E. Ivey, Jr., and Ted W. Ward
Independent Schools
  Francis Parkman
Individual Differences
  Leona E. Tyler
In-Service Education of Teachers
  Jack R. Childress
Intelligence
  Read D. Tuddenham
Intelligence and Special Aptitude Tests
  Martin J. Nelson
Interests
  John O. Crites

Language Development
  Walter MacGinitie

Leadership
Conrad Briner and Robert Stout

Learning
Robert Glaser

Legal Education
William T. O'Hara

Libraries
Wallace J. Bonk

Listening
Sam Duker

Local School Systems
Dan H. Cooper

Marks and Marking Systems
Robert L. Thorndike

Mathematics
Stephen S. Willoughby

Measurement in Education
Robert L. Ebel

Measurement Theory
Edward E. Cureton

Medical Education
George E. Miller

Mental Health
Eli M. Bower

Mentally Retarded Children
J. T. Hunt

Military Education
James C. Shelburne, Kenneth J. Groves, and Leland D. Brokaw

Modern Languages
John B. Carroll

Motivation
Bernard Weiner

Motor Abilities
Edwin A. Fleishman

Music Education
Erwin H. Schneider

Objectives and Outcomes
Margaret Ammons

Occupational Placement
Charles O'Dell

Outdoor Education
Julian Smith and Morris Wiener

Parochial Schools—Roman Catholic
C. Albert Koob

Perception
S. Howard Bartley

Personality
Saul B. Sells

Philosophy of Education
D. B. Gowin

Physical Development
Howard W. Meredith

Physical Education
Henry J. Montoye and David Cunningham

Physically Handicapped Children
Romaine P. Mackie

Prediction
William B. Michael

Preparation of Administrators
Russell T. Gregg

Professional Education
William J. McGlothlin

Professional Educational Organizations
Richard A. Dershimer

Programmed Instruction
Lawrence M. Stolurow

Proprietary Schools
R. A. Fulton

Public Relations
W. W. Charters, Jr.

Public School Administration
Calvin Grieder

Pupil Progress
Robert H. Anderson and Cynthia Ritsher

Readiness
Frederick T. Tyler

Reading
Theodore L. Harris

Records and Reports
R. Murray Thomas

Rehabilitation
Lloyd H. Lofquist

Religion and Education
Harry L. Stearns

Religious Education
Sara Little

Research in Education
Fred N. Kerlinger

Research Methods
George Mouley

Research Organizations
Nicholas A. Fattu

Safety Education
Norman Key

Scaling
  Norman Cliff
School Business Administration
  K. Forbis Jordan
School Health Services
  Helen M. Wallace
School Personnel Administration
  R. Oliver Gibson
Science Education
  J. Myron Atkin and R. Will Burnett
Scores and Norms
  Roger T. Lennon
Secondary Education
  David B. Austin
Sex Differences
  Leona E. Tyler
Social and Emotional Development
  Ira J. Gordon
Social Studies Education
  J. R. Skretting and James E. Sundeen
Sociology of Education
  Charles E. Bidwell
Special Education
  Maynard C. Reynolds
Speech
  Hugh Seabury
Speech Pathology and Audiology
  Herbert Oyer
Spelling
  Thomas D. Horn
State Regulation of Education
  William Roe
Statistical Methods
  Chester W. Harris
Student Characteristics—College and University
  Paul Heist
Student Characteristics—Elementary and Secondary
  John C. Flanagan
Student Financial Aid—College and University
  George Nash

Student Organizations and Activities—College and University
  E. G. Williamson and Donald Zander
Student Organizations and Activities—Elementary and Secondary
  Grace Graham
Student Teaching
  Don Davies and Kathleen Amershek
Study
  Wayne H. Holtzman
Supervision
  James E. Heald
Survey Research Method
  Robert E. Herriott
Teacher Certification
  T. M. Stinnett
Teacher Education Programs
  Lindley J. Stiles and Robert P. Parker
Teacher Effectiveness
  Ned A. Flanders and Anita Simon
Teacher Roles
  Bruce J. Biddle
Teaching Methods
  N. L. Gage
Tenure of Teachers
  Martha L. Ware
Test Use
  Frank B. Womer and N. Kishor Wahi
Textbooks
  Ernest Hilton
Training Research Workers
  David L. Clark and John E. Hopkins
Transfer of Learning
  Herbert J. Klausmeier and J. Kent Davis
Transportation of Students
  Robert M. Isenberg
Urban Educational Problems
  Frederick W. Bertolaet and Raphael O. Nystrand
Vocational and Technical Education
  George L. Brandon

Encyclopedia of Educational Research

Encyclopedia of Educational Research

ACADEMIC FREEDOM

MEANING OF ACADEMIC FREEDOM. Academic freedom, the intellectual freedom of persons participating in academic affairs, is now generally recognized as a necessary foundation of education in an open or free society, essential to the effective achievement and dissemination of knowledge and to the strength and integrity of the culture (Popper, 1950; Anshen, 1940). The discussion of academic freedom has most commonly referred to institutions of higher education, where frequent and large controversies have brought attention to the basic issues of academic responsibility and have resulted in policies and practices which are now widely accepted in principle. Its meaning and value, however, extend equally to all levels of education and are relevant to the activities of nonschool educational institutions—e.g., museums and certain kinds of institutes and expositions which serve the public interest (Beale, 1936). The issue of academic freedom is pertinent to private institutions, those not supported by public funds, insofar as these are intended to serve the public good. And it pertains as well, with certain qualifications, to parochial and other specialized schools.

The ideal of academic freedom and the principles and practices associated with it have in the past referred especially to the functions of teaching and research and to the public oral and written statements of academic personnel. University and college professors, acting individually and through their associations, have here been the main fashioners of policy. Much attention is currently given, however, to the matter of academic freedom for students, a concern which is widely shared by administrators and teachers as well as by students. Academic freedom for students is today defined as the absence of restraint upon learning and expression of opinion. It is not irrelevant, moreover, to think in terms of academic freedom for administrators, referring to their responsibilities and prerogatives in matters pertaining to the intellectual life. It is perhaps not useful to formulate a concept of academic freedom for the public, even though the rights of the public in expecting or demanding certain qualities in an institution should be clearly recognized and respected, for the meaning of academic freedom has been shaped largely as a professional ideal within the context of various pressures upon faculties by external individuals or organizations or by the general public directly or through their representatives—i.e., regents and trustees.

Academic freedom in the traditional sense of describing the claims to freedom of teachers and research scientists and scholars refers especially to the question of the professional right of the teacher to be free from external or institutional restraint in the teaching process in the classroom, laboratory, or lecture hall and of the researcher to be free from restraint in his pursuit of knowledge and the development of theory. For the teacher this is primarily a right to speak, for the researcher a right to publish (Lovejoy, 1930). An important element of the claim to academic freedom has been the insistence that the scholar is to be judged by his professional peers when his scholarly pronouncements are at issue.

The principle of academic freedom covers more than speaking and publishing, however. It refers as well to such matters as the exhibition of art or the performance of music, the selection of literature employed for instructional purposes, acquisitions of libraries, and invitations extended to guest lecturers. It clearly involves, therefore, the activities of administrators as well as teachers. When the concept of academic freedom is applied to students, it refers to learning and free expression of knowledge and opinion. Whether it should be regarded as involving such matters as policies governing student organizations, the publication of uncensored student newspapers and magazines, student-invited lecturers, on-campus political activities, and student protests and demonstrations is a matter of debate. The question at issue is whether the concept of academic freedom should be broadened to include every freedom or right desirable on a campus.

JUSTIFICATION OF ACADEMIC FREEDOM. The justification of academic freedom for an open, free society is, first, its intrinsic value and, second, its necessity as an instrument for criticism, the achievement of knowledge, and the improvement of the quality of personal and social life. As a value in itself, intellectual freedom is the primary ingredient of a free society. Academic freedom is central to a general intellectual freedom not only for those in academic life but for the entire community and society. It is especially in academic freedom that the freedom of a people becomes articulate, and it is here that it is matured and tested. The destruction of academic freedom is the destruction of the living center of a free society (Dewey, 1919; Riesman, 1956).

The instrumental value of academic freedom is immediately apparent when it is seen that a university is the primary agency for the cultivation of critical ability and that the successful pursuit of knowledge is possible only in an environment which not only permits but demands uninhibited intellectual exploration. The activities of a university which directly or indirectly eventuate in the critical analysis of society and its values are not properly regarded as simply permitted or tolerated by the society. They are intended by it, even when tensions and open conflict between social agencies and the university result. For the critical function of a university is an essential element in its meaning and purpose. That the quest for knowledge requires the freedom to explore and communicate ideas, to examine and appraise factual evidence, and to criticize and correct established theories is too obvious to require argument. And finally, that freedom of thought and inquiry and expression is relevant to the melioration of the conditions of life, to the strengthening of the value structure of a culture or of the moral and spiritual character of the individual person, is evident to all who believe that knowledge and reason, the two foundations of education, are essential to the achievement of the good life.

Academic freedom, like most other freedoms, is

usually defined in negative terms, as freedom *from* something—from external interference, from imposed restraints, from intellectually inhibiting regulations, from censorship or inordinate or unreasonable criticism. But there are positive as well as negative freedoms, and the positive facet of academic freedom deserves recognition and cultivation. Conceived positively, academic freedom is the encouragement to adventurous, creative, and innovative thought, the condition and inspiration for genuine intellectual and artistic achievement.

CONDITIONS FOR ACADEMIC FREEDOM. No responsible conception of academic freedom intends to encourage license or intellectual and moral anarchy in an educational institution. On the contrary, the academic freedom of a teacher is a professional value, and it incurs a professional responsibility— responsibility to his subject, to his students, and to society—a genuine commitment to truth, intellectual integrity, a personal restraint with due regard for propriety and established usage, a sense of fitness and appropriateness, and wisdom in both statement and action. The claim of academic freedom does not entitle a teacher to convert his schoolroom into a private rostrum from which to declaim his personal views on any and every subject or to propagandize a captive audience on whatever cause he personally supports. It entitles him, rather, to pursue freely the educational tasks for which he was appointed and for which he is judged to have professional competence, and to pursue them within the bounds of recognized professional restraint.

It is generally recognized that although a person does not abrogate his citizenship and the civic rights guaranteed by it when he enters academic life, when he is associated with either a private or a public institution he becomes in certain ways a public servant, and this fact alone may importantly affect his judgments and actions. This does not justify, of course, the exploitation of his private time and energy by the institution or the community, or dictation to his private life, a condition that has often obtained with teachers in small communities. But it does mean, for instance, that in his private utterances he should not presume to speak as if officially for his college, and he should not attempt to implicate his institution in his private pursuits.

It is entirely obvious that much that should be said or done in a university or an elementary school should be said or done not indiscriminately but at an appropriate time or place and in an appropriate manner, with a sensitivity that respects the level of maturity, the knowledge, and the experience of the students. What is quite fitting for a college lecture hall may be entirely inappropriate for the classroom of a secondary school. Works of art that constitute a felicitous exhibit for a university campus may be less proper for the halls of a junior high school, and literature that can be effectively employed in the teaching of college freshmen may be morally destructive if read by eighth graders. To cultivate the judgment requisite to determine when and where and how to best proceed in sensitive matters is a part of the basic responsibility of the educator (McMurrin, 1964).

ACADEMIC FREEDOM AND THE PURPOSES OF EDUCATION. The nature and value of academic freedom cannot be adequately defined apart from a consideration of the purposes of education. There is no academic freedom in general; there are only particular freedoms—freedoms from and freedoms for—especially freedoms from unreasonable or illicit restraints and freedoms for courageous and independent thought (Hook, 1962). The conditions for these specific freedoms are set by the social circumstances, moral philosophies, and aims and goals which describe a society and its culture and determine the purposes of its educational institutions (Adler, 1958; Russell, 1945). It is quite meaningless to think in terms of absolute or unconditional freedom, and it is possible, therefore, to conceive academic freedom in varying degrees. Considering the maturity and intellectual levels of elementary pupils and university students, for instance, it seems wise in constructing normative descriptions to define academic freedom for universities as much less conditioned than academic freedom for elementary schools. This does not mean that in elementary or secondary education intellectual freedom is less important or ideally less real or that it is to be less prized or cultivated. It means simply that here the conditions for freedom properly entail restraints or prohibitions of a different order or magnitude (McMurrin, 1964).

In the same way, though the present discussion refers to academic freedom for what are now commonly called "free societies," it is possible to define academic freedom for societies of a different type— for instance, totalitarian societies. Academic freedom in a totalitarian society may be roughly the equivalent of academic freedom in a free society in matters pertaining to the natural sciences, although this has not always been the case, while freedom may be grossly restricted in social thought or the creative arts.

The concept of academic freedom is a function of the purposes of education as those purposes are a function of the values of the culture. In a closed society education serves large propagandistic purposes that may conflict with the unimpeded search for knowledge or with the honest criticism of established values and institutions. The scope of intellectual freedom is therefore circumscribed and narrowed, and severe strictures are placed upon it.

In an open or free society the purposes of education are ideally critical, conservative, and creative— the criticism of accepted ideas, attitudes and practices; the conservation of whatever proves to be true and good; and the achievement of new, and hopefully better, ways of thinking and acting, the extension of knowledge, the cultivation of reason and reasonableness, and the creation of a more relevant and viable morality, a more profound art, and a more genuine spirituality (Dewey, 1916). In such a society, therefore, academic freedom is properly conceived in generous and liberal terms. It is not a special privilege that is granted the academic profession, a concession of rights to reward their merit and shield them from criticism or censure. It is, rather, a condition which the society imposes upon itself as essential to its own continuing criticism and advancement, the condition of free, creative thought and expression. The teacher who from fear, indifference, or a failure of understanding is unable to grasp that freedom in the moment of decision, preferring the safety of silence and conformity or the anonymity and ambiguity of indecision, may win the approval of the majority, but in so doing he may betray the high responsibility which his society had conferred upon him.

ACADEMIC FREEDOM AND OTHER FREEDOMS. Academic freedom should not be confused with the other freedoms which academic personnel enjoy by reason of their citizenship in a democratic society—the right of privacy and the right to engage as a private citizen in political and civic activities, freedom from espionage in and out of the classroom, the right to protection against aspersion, defamation and false accusation, or the right to seek redress through due process, to speak or write freely on civic issues, or, under specified conditions, to campaign for and hold public office. The problems of conflict of interest and the expenditure of time and energy may necessitate formal understandings under which public office can be sought or held by an educator in institutional employ. Private consultative activities by university professors are in the same category. A claim to the privilege of engaging in such activities may be entirely justified, but the issue is not a matter of academic freedom.

The question of academic freedom, moreover, should not be confused with matters of institutional administrative policy and procedure which are not concerned directly with the support of or restraint upon intellectual activity. A member of a faculty may be justified, for instance, in opposing the established procedures and policies relating to appointment or promotion, but the object of his criticism may have nothing to do with academic freedom. Academic freedom and sound administrative policy are closely related, and the protection of the first commonly depends upon the second, but they are not the same thing. To categorize every academic virtue under the concept of academic freedom, as is sometimes done, can produce nothing but confusion, and may in the long run weaken the case for intellectual freedom.

There are, of course, areas of decision and action where academic freedom and simple administrative policy are more or less closely involved and the distinction between them is difficult or ambiguous. A noteworthy example is the approved practice on the part of governing boards of colleges and universities of delegating to the faculties the responsibility and prerogative for designing and establishing the basic educational policies and curricula of the institutions. Another instance is the establishment of adequate instrumentalities and procedures guaranteeing due process in matters relating to the discharge of faculty personnel. These are administrative matters, but they clearly relate importantly to the creation of a climate of academic freedom on a college or university campus. The case is not essentially different with elementary or secondary schools, though there the role of individual schools in larger school systems and the presence of professional educational supervisory staffs place the matter of educational policy and curriculum in a somewhat different context.

PROTECTION OF ACADEMIC FREEDOM. If academic freedom is to be a reality, it must be supported and protected by policies and procedures establishing academic tenure and guaranteeing against penalties and reprisals relating to such matters as promotion, compensation, teaching loads, and the availability of research funds and publication opportunities. It is especially important that academic personnel have access to instrumentalities of appeal and that institutional authorities and faculty fully respect the right to due process.

Tenure policies and regulations are not intended to protect incompetence or those guilty of moral turpitude, unethical professional conduct, or failure to meet their contractual obligations. Nor do they guarantee employment when financial resources are inadequate or the services to be performed are, for good cause or reason, eliminated. Tenure is intended, rather, to assure stability of employment for those whose professional services are judged satisfactory and to guarantee that academic freedom is not abrogated by the fear or threat of discharge, and to assure that those who have performed within the proper limits of academic freedom are in fact not subjected to the reprisal of discharge. The force of tenure policies in the colleges and universities of the United States is usually simply the bond of moral commitment made by the institutional governing boards. Such policies can be established by statute, however, and even where this has not been done the courts have sometimes given them the force of law. Within the higher educational institutions, and to a lesser degree within school systems, administrative regulations and professional codes are designed to ensure due process and the possibility of appeal in matters pertaining to tenure as well as to ensure fairness and justice in cases of discharge where tenure is not at issue.

Though written policies and procedural regulations ensuring the establishment and protection of academic freedom are necessary and useful, it is clear that academic freedom is difficult to define and that it cannot be reduced to a legal or procedural code. It is quite impossible to develop a catalog prescribing freedom for every occasion, and it is not possible to formulate a definitive statement of academic freedom in principle from which rules governing every relevant instance can be derived. The authority of wisdom, experience, reason, and sensitive judgment is essential to the integrity of academic life even where the most commendable professional codes and procedural rules are observed. And nowhere is this more true than in matters pertaining to intellectual freedom. Often in academic-freedom controversies the issues are obscure, ambiguous, and difficult to define, and the facts may be elusive or inconclusive. Under such conditions experienced judgment, personal restraint, and plain good sense can count for more than absolute principles or rules and regulations.

Because the common conservatism of society may be expected to conflict on occasion with the critical and creative function of the schools and colleges, tensions and controversies referring to academic freedom must be regarded as more or less normal where institutions are engaged in serious work. The mark of maturity in a society and its institutions is not so much that conflicts do not arise as that they are resolved reasonably and on the basis of good will, knowledge, and understanding rather than inflamed by irrational prejudice and passion.

HISTORY OF ACADEMIC FREEDOM. The history of academic freedom is a central element in the story of the intellectual development of Western culture and the rise of its liberal institutions. Where intellectual freedom has existed in the ancient academies and in the medieval and modern universities, it has been won in opposition to the conservative and reactionary forces of folk society, religion, law, politics, and business. Only a close examination of the history of education from the Platonic Academy and the Stoa to the University of California can supply the fascinating data of the struggle, and only a knowledge of the conflict of cultures and ideas, of the subtle relations between theory and practice, and of the psychology of free and authoritarian personality can provide an understanding of the forces which produced it. Academic freedom as it is known today is the product of many centuries; its roots are deep in history. But its mature development is very recent, and perhaps its most exciting era has been the years since World War II.

The immense influence of the ancient academies, especially the Academy of Plato and the Lyceum of Aristotle, is central to the character of the intellectual foundations of Western culture (Jaeger, 1961). The tradition of inquiry and liberal learning that were established by them has persisted, though often precariously, and has been continued by the medieval and Renaissance universities until the present time. The academies were not free from doctrinaire positions in matters of science, religion, ethics, and politics, but a genuine spirit of learning often pervaded them, and their resistance especially to political and ecclesiastical pressures is an important factor in the rudimentary development of free institutions (Bronowski, 1960; Dampier, 1942).

The great medieval universities, especially Paris, Bologna, and Oxford, achieved a powerful influence on contemporary life and thought and enjoyed, especially because of the nature of their material foundations and the social status associated with learning, a quite remarkable autonomy (Rashdall, 1936). This independence, shared by faculties and students, ensured a measure of immunity from intellectual dictation and protected the universities in some degree from political and ecclesiastical reprisals while at the same time providing centers of critical and creative thought. Academic freedom with the guarantees which are now common was quite unknown at this early time, but considering the general temper of mind that was common in the early universities and the social circumstances surrounding them, the degree of freedom and independence was far greater than is commonly supposed. The medieval scholar functioned within comparatively narrow limits which were set by the cultural climate and by ecclesiastical decree, but within those limits he often enjoyed considerable freedom and not infrequently triumphed in his battles with established authority. The intense intellectual interests of the Renaissance centuries served to expand the range of intellectual freedom as well as to cultivate an increased appreciation of its value (Randall, 1926; Lucki, 1963). In early modern Europe the quality of intellectual freedom was often a function of the liberality or tyranny of the national or local sovereign. To some degree it was enhanced by the not uncommon isolation of the universities from the general public and its practical interests.

The early colleges of the United States knew little of what is now called academic freedom in either ideal or practice. They were often instruments for the support of ecclesiastical authority and the propagation of religious dogma as well as of learning, and it was not until after the Civil War that fullfledged intellectual freedom became an issue. In the antebellum period academic controversies were waged within very limited bounds, largely because of the denominational sponsorship of colleges and because a broad conception of the purposes of higher education as relating to criticism and to the expansion of knowledge had not developed. The organization and control of most colleges, where faculties had little or no part in government, discouraged any real emergence of an ideal of freedom, and the general lack of a professional mentality and ideal in teachers made the formulation of an ethic of the intellectual life an impossibility. The main conflicts relating to freedom involved college presidents rather than professors (Hofstadter, 1955).

Nevertheless, the general liberal trend of the eighteenth century both weakened the hold of orthodoxy on the colleges and strengthened the academic appetite for freedom to dissent and to pursue new knowledge. By the close of that century, the advances of secularism and the concern for civic rights and religious toleration had influenced the control of many institutions and had affected both the spirit and the substance of education in a manner conducive to greater freedom. In the early decades of the nineteenth century, however, a proliferation of denominationally controlled and locally oriented colleges, many of them constantly on the edge of poverty, produced an unfortunate mediocrity in American higher education, and the cause of learning and intellectual freedom suffered a severe decline (Hofstadter, 1955).

From the time of the Civil War, the character of American higher education changed importantly, and the modern ideal of academic freedom was born. A conception of education as the pursuit of new knowledge gave rise to the universities, with their disdain for a purely conservative role and their commitment to criticism and research. In particular, the rapid spread of Darwinian thought and the attendant controversies weakened the grip of religion upon education and strengthened the scientific interests and therefore the open-ended attitudes of the institutions. As clerical control declined, a genuine educational professionalism took root in the faculties, and, because large numbers of American students studied in Germany, German university ideals and practices relating to research and academic freedom produced an explosive impact. German academic freedom differed importantly from the American ideal, conforming as it did to the German cultural and political environment, which had little in common with American democracy, but the German idea that a university must enjoy a kind of neutral independence was a powerful influence in the United States (Metzger, 1955).

As the universities developed as research institutions a new form of conflict arose to replace the old struggle with religion and the church—the conflict between professors and presidents who held liberal or radical economic views, on the one hand, and conservative groups or wealthy donors, on the other, whose gifts endowed some of the nation's leading institutions and professorial chairs. The decades at the turn of the century produced a number of celebrated cases of such conflict, cases that were the inevitable outcome of a nation involved in rapid economic advance, an educational system feeling its way toward something other than simply a conserving role, and a teaching profession becoming articulate, self-conscious, and at times militant (Metzger, 1955).

In this century the discussion of academic freedom in the United States has centered especially on political, social, and economic issues. The great wars, economic failure, the rise of communism and its threat to world peace, and the development of domestic political confusion and hysteria have provided the conditions for a set of new problems which have combined the issue of national loyalty with that of social and economic heresy. The central controversies have concerned technical questions of law and ethics and the establishment of due process and sound tenure principles as safeguards of academic freedom.

In the United States the wars inevitably generated problems relating to the loyalty of dissenters and critics of governmental policy, but it was especially the aftermath of World War II which produced the setting for the most dramatic events and most important arguments.

In the face of a general fear of Soviet aggression and nuclear war, official attempts to guarantee national security produced special loyalty oaths and disclaimers for teachers, aggressive hunts for subversives by legislative committees, extensive censorship of texts and libraries, censorship of campus speakers, and what many have regarded as unnecessary restrictions on the publication of certain kinds of scientific research (MacIver, 1955; Fidler, 1965). Official action complemented and encouraged numerous private and semipublic groups in their efforts to police the schools and colleges. The climax of the hysteria was the discharge of 36 members of the University of California faculty for their refusal to sign a Regent-imposed oath which not only affirmed loyalty but also disavowed affiliation with communist or communist-front organizations. The California courts upheld the complaints of the professors, some of whom were world-famous scholars and none of whom had been accused of communism, disloyalty, or professional unfitness (Gardner, 1967).

Recent discussions have been concerned with distinguishing academic freedom from general intellectual freedom and from civil rights and with analyzing the moral responsibilities of persons required to testify before investigative committees or in courts of law (Boas, 1953; Hook, 1953a, 1953b). In the matter of claiming constitutional immunity under the fifth amendment, for instance, it has been effectively argued that it is morally reprehensible for a teacher to refuse to answer questions relating to his professional fitness where the truth would be incriminating, even though the law protects him in his refusal (Hook, 1953a, 1953b). Another argument of interest has been whether membership in the Communist party professionally disqualifies a person on the ground that by such membership he compromises his intellectual integrity.

The student protests and campus rebellions which attracted wide attention during the decade of the 1960's have had complex causes and important results for academic organization and policies governing student rights and discipline. For the most part, however, they have not been grounded in considerations of academic freedom (Hook, 1965).

ACADEMIC FREEDOM AND THE COURTS. Although cases involving academic freedom have appeared in the courts for many decades, the number has increased since the development of professional codes of ethics and policies on tenure and academic freedom. Among important legal disputes producing different resolutions by court action has been the question of the validity of tenure regulations and the enforcement of institutional contractual commitments under those regulations. Those courts which have denied the validity of tenure regulations have commonly done so on the ground that where institutional control is derived from the state constitution, that control cannot be subordinated to institutional regulation. Tenure laws which are legally enforceable as public statutes are not uncommon as protection for public school teachers, but they are unusual in relation to higher schools (Beale, 1941; Edwards, 1933). Private institutions, of course, have a different status before the law from that of public institutions. Nevertheless, recent decisions have implied that private-institutional tenure plans are legally valid. Tenure violations in private institutions have generally been treated as contract violations where redress can be sought through action for damages. It is of major importance that there is no recognized ground for the legal validity of tenure plans which is compelling to the generality of American courts. Many decisions, moreover, have clearly demonstrated the failure of some courts to appreciate the importance of academic freedom and the necessity of its protection (Murphy, 1963).

In recent years several Supreme Court decisions have indicated a trend toward the recognition of the legal protection of academic freedom under the first and fourteenth amendments to the constitution, those amendments which guarantee freedom of speech and due process. In *Sweezy* v. *New Hampshire*, in 1957, the Supreme Court handed down its first decision, six justices concurring, in which the violation of academic freedom was declared to be unconstitutional. Earlier dissenting statements issued by individual justices had supported this position in principle. It is generally assumed that constitutional protection of academic freedom pertains only to public institutions (Byse & Joughin, 1959; Van Alstyne, 1965; Davis, 1961).

OFFICIAL STATEMENTS ON ACADEMIC FREEDOM. Since its organization in 1915 by a group of leading scholars, the American Association of University Professors (AAUP) has been the central agency in the development of a code for academic freedom and tenure. The AAUP's first committee on academic freedom and tenure was formed primarily to formulate principles and procedures relating to intellectual freedom in higher institutions, but it became involved almost immediately in the investigation of complaints and ensuing recommendations. The committee, known as Committee A, recommends censure by the AAUP of institutions which are judged guilty of serious infraction of accepted principles. Censure actions by the AAUP are published, as are actions removing censure (American Association of University Professors, 1966).

The AAUP published, in 1915, a "General Declaration of Principles" (American Association of University Professors, 1954), which was the basis for the "1925 Conference Statement on Academic Freedom and Tenure" of the American Council on Education (1941) and several other national educational organizations. In 1940 the AAUP and the Association of American Colleges (AAC) agreed upon a restatement of the principles enunciated in the 1925 conference statement. This document, known as the 1940 statement of principles on academic freedom and tenure, is the main basis for official action on academic freedom cases at the present time (American Association of University Professors, 1941). It has been officially endorsed by the major national and regional educational and scholarly associations and by the trustees and faculties of large numbers of American colleges and universities.

The "Statement on Procedural Standards in Faculty Dismissal Proceedings" was approved in 1958 by the AAUP and the AAC as a supplement to the 1940 statement of principles on academic freedom and tenure (American Association of University Professors, 1964). This statement was intended as a procedural guide, while the "1940 Statement" was intended to establish norms in academic freedom. In 1965 the AAUP established a new standing committee known as Committee S on Faculty Responsibility for the Academic Freedom of Students. In 1965 the association's Council approved a report of Committee S entitled "Statement on the Academic Freedom of Students" (American Association of University Professors, 1965). This statement became on approval a *tentative* policy of the association. The statement is concerned with freedom in the classroom, the privacy and disclosure of student records, freedom in student affairs, including government, publication, and campus speakers, freedom from discrimination, off-campus freedom of students, and disciplinary procedures (Williamson & Cowan, 1965).

Sterling M. McMurrin
The University of Utah

References

Adler, Mortimer J. *The Idea of Freedom.* 2 vols. Doubleday, 1958, 1961.

American Association of University Professors. "Academic Freedom and Tenure: 1940 Statement of Principles." *B Am Assn U Prof* 27:40–3; 1941.

American Association of University Professors. "The 1915 Declaration of Principles: Academic Freedom and Tenure." *B Am Assn U Prof* 40:90–112; 1954.

American Association of University Professors. "Academic Freedom and Tenure; Statements of Principles." *B Am Assn U Prof* 42:41–6; 1956.

American Association of University Professors. "Statement on Procedural Standards in Faculty Dismissal Proceedings." *B Am Assn U Prof* 50:69–71; 1964.

American Association of University Professors. "Statement on the Academic Freedom of Students." *B Am Assn U Prof* 51:447–9; 1965.

American Association of University Professors. "Report of Committee A, 1965–66." *B Am Assn U Prof* Summer:115–30; 1966.

American Council on Education. "1925 Conference Statement on Academic Freedom and Tenure." *B Am Assn U Prof* 27:43–5; 1941.

Anshen, Ruth Nanda. (Ed.) *Freedom: Its Meaning.* Harcourt, 1940.

Beale, Howard K. *Are American Teachers Free?* Scribner, 1936. 855p.

Beale, Howard K. *A History of Freedom of Teaching in American Schools.* Scribner, 1941. 343p.

Boas, George. "The Ethics of Academic Freedom." In White, Morton. (Ed.) *Academic Freedom, Logic and Religion.* U Pennsylvania Press, 1953. p. 1–17.

Bronowski, J., and Mazlish, Bruce. *The Western Intellectual Tradition.* Harper, 1960.

Byse, Clark, and Joughin, Louis. *Tenure in American Higher Education.* Cornell U Press, 1959.

Dampier, William Cecil. *A History of Science,* 3rd ed. Macmillan, 1942.

Davis, Frederick. "Enforcing Academic Tenure: Reflections and Suggestions." *Wisconsin Law R* 200; 1961.
Dewey, John. *Democracy and Education*. Macmillan, 1916.
Dewey, John. "Academic Freedom." In Monroe, Paul. (Ed.) *Cyclopedia of Education*. Vol. 2. Macmillan, 1919. p. 700-5.
Edwards, Newton. *The Courts and the Public Schools*. U Chicago Press, 1933. 591p.
Fidler, William P. "Academic Freedom in the South Today." *B Am Assn U Prof* 51:413-21; 1965.
Gardner, David P. *The California Oath Controversy*. U California Press, 1967.
Hofstadter, Richard. *Academic Freedom in the Age of the College*. Columbia U Press, 1955. 274p.
Hofstadter, Richard, and Metzger, Walter P. *The Development of Academic Freedom in the United States*. Columbia U Press, 1955. 527p.
Hook, Sidney. "The Ethics of Academic Freedom." In White, Morton. (Ed.) *Academic Freedom, Logic and Religion*. U Pennsylvania Press, 1953(a). p. 19-37.
Hook, Sidney. *Heresy, Yes—Conspiracy, No*. The John Day Company, Inc. 1953 (b). 283p.
Hook, Sidney. *Paradoxes of Freedom*. U California Press, 1962.
Hook, Sidney. "Freedom to Learn But Not to Riot." *New York Times*, Section 6; January 3, 1965.
Hook, Sidney, and Konvitz, Milton R. (Eds.) *Freedom and Experience*. Cornell U Press, 1947.
Jaeger, Werner. *Paideia: The Ideals of Greek Culture*, Vol. 3. Oxford U Press, 1961.
Lovejoy, Arthur O. "Academic Freedom." In *Encyclopedia of the Social Sciences*. Vol 1. Macmillan, 1930. p. 384-8.
Lucki, Emil. *History of the Renaissance*, Book III, *Education, Learning, and Thought*. U Utah Press, 1963.
MacIver, Robert M. *Academic Freedom in Our Time*. Columbia U Press, 1955. 329p.
McMurrin, Sterling M. "Academic Freedom in the Schools." *Teach Col Rec* 65:658-63; 1964.
Metzger, Walter P. *Academic Freedom in the Age of the University*. Columbia U Press, 1955.
Murphy, William P. "Educational Freedom in the Courts." *B Am Assn U Prof* 49; 1963.
Popper, Karl R. *The Open Society and Its Enemies*. Princeton U Press, 1950. 732p.
Randall, John Herman, Jr. *The Making of the Modern Mind*. Houghton, 1926.
Rashdall, Hastings. *The Universities of Europe in the Middle Ages*. 3 vols. New ed. Oxford U Press, 1936. 558p.
Riesman, David. *Constraint and Variety in American Education*. U Nebraska Press, 1956.
Russell, Bertrand. *A History of Western Philosophy*. Simon, 1945.
Russell, Bertrand. *Authority and the Individual*. Simon, 1949.
Van Alstyne, William W. "Student Academic Freedom and the Rule Making Powers of Public Universities; Some Constitutional Considerations." *Law in Transition Q* Winter:1-34; 1965.
White, Morton. (Ed.) *Academic Freedom, Logic and Religion*. U Pennsylvania Press, 1953.
Williamson, E. G., and Cowan, John L. "The Role of the President in the Desirable Enactment of Academic Freedom for Students." *Ed Rec* Fall; 1965.

ACHIEVEMENT TESTS

This discussion is concerned with what has been learned through systematic research and accumulated practical experience about how to measure the outcomes of formal instruction in schools and colleges. According to Adkins (1958) we may think of achievement as consisting of (1) increases in the variety of stimulus dimensions to which the learner will be sensitive and responsive, (2) increases in the number of new responses that will be made in the presence of familiar, or already discriminated, stimulus components, or (3) increases in the number of new responses to be made in novel stimulus situations. The emphasis on change which Adkins makes calls attention to the fact that, although an achievement test can provide only a measure of status at a particular time, interpretation of achievement-test scores in relation to educational programs must of necessity involve, either explicitly or implicitly, the collection of data at two points in time. A single sample taken at a point in time can give no evidence of an "increase" in any attribute unless one is willing to make an assumption regarding the status of the student at some prior point in time. If there is any single limitation which more than any other characterizes the evaluation practices of educators at all stages of the educational system it is the tendency to accept as evidence of achievement the performance of students at a single point in time without regard to differences in achievement at some defined previous point in time. The result is that schools are credited with producing high-quality output when the output depends primarily on high-quality input, and pupils are charged with deficiencies in effort when they are actually achieving at normal levels in relation to their abilities and backgrounds.

Not all types of relevant data regarding achievement can be obtained through formal tests. According to Dyer (1965) it is necessary (1) that test situations be chosen with a reasonable expectation that they may be repeatable from one occasion to another and (2) that they be identical for all students in the group whose learning is being measured. Thus, such techniques as observing the naturally occurring behavior of students and making value judgments based on these observations or examining term papers or other products created by individual students in response to stimuli generated by instructional activity, while important to any comprehensive assessment of an educational program, will not be treated here. On the other hand, the discussion is intended to range somewhat wider than that of Ebel and Damrin (1960), which was limited to essay and objective paper-and-pencil tests of achievement. For purposes of this discussion, any stimulus which is relevant to an educational objective and which may be presented systematically to members of a group for the purpose of eliciting responses which may be ordered along a value continuum will be considered appropriate for an achievement test. To be of practical significance, however, it must also be feasible in terms of time and cost.

The references cited have been chosen as illustrative of the relevant literature rather than exhaustive. Where several equally appropriate references were available, the more general or more recent or less well-known has been included in the reference list. The reader may wish to examine individual references for leads into the rich literature on the subject. He may also wish to consider this discussion in the light of related entries which provide a general discussion of the context (MEASUREMENT IN EDUCATION), details with respect to applications of test results (TEST USE, MARKING SYSTEMS AND REPORTS), and a comprehensive treatment of technical aspects of testing (MEASUREMENT THEORY, SCORES AND NORMS, PREDICTION).

HISTORY OF ACHIEVEMENT TESTING. The history of achievement testing can be traced back to antiquity, but it is only in the present century that testing methods themselves have been subjected to systematic, critical investigations using scientific methods. Modern achievement testing is generally considered to have begun with the publication of J. M. Rice's study of achievement in spelling in 1897 (Scates, 1947). By presenting systematic data which called into question certain widely held assumptions about teaching and learning, Rice initiated a research movement that was to have a profound effect on American education.

This does not mean, however, that there had been no systematic evaluation of learning prior to that time. Undoubtedly, teachers have used more or less systematic methods of evaluating learning as long as there have been teachers and as long as those who would occupy positions of responsibility in a society have been required to demonstrate their competence in one way or another. The most dramatic use of formal testing in the service of society is the 3,000-year history of civil service examinations in Imperial China (DuBois, 1965), but there is little doubt that a systematic search would turn up similar, if less persistent, practices in other areas of the world. The testing system in China was formal and explicit, the learning informal and individual. By creating a succession of hurdles within a competitive system and requiring candidates to demonstrate not only ability to learn but also willingness to exert effort toward a formal if not necessarily relevant goal, the system ensured that only intelligent and dedicated individuals would rise to the top of the civil service system.

The parallel to the requirement of a college degree for entry into many positions at the present time will not be lost on the alert observer. Often it is not the particular knowledge required by an examination or implied by a diploma but rather the ability to acquire new knowledge implicit in the examination grade or in the degree that marks the individual as competent to undertake a new responsibility. Thus, where the selection ratio is low, an inefficient and irrelevant educational system may nevertheless provide a means of screening out the required leadership. However, in a complex industrial society where general competence on the part of a high proportion of the population is required if the system is to operate effectively, efficiency and relevance become of critical importance. Achievement testing can no longer follow the Chinese pattern.

The need for comparative data such as common written examinations might provide was recognized in this country by Horace Mann as early as 1845 (Caldwell & Courtis, 1924). The recognition that a system of common examinations could be a means of raising standards within a state system of education led to the establishment, in 1865, of the Regents Examinations in the State of New York, and the system, continuing into the present, has participated actively in efforts to advance testing techniques over the years (Tinkelman, 1966). In fact, many of the significant advances in testing have grown out of efforts to apply common measures over a wide range of schools and school systems. The College Entrance Examination Board (CEEB), founded in 1900, has pioneered in the field of measurement at the point of transition from school to college (Fuess, 1950). Learned and Wood (1938) with financial support from the Carnegie Foundation, applied objective testing techniques to the problem of comparing the knowledge of students in the various colleges in the state of Pennsylvania and demonstrated that the wide individual differences which had been observed among public school students could also be found at the college level. The data reported by Learned and Wood clearly demonstrated that it was inaccurate to assume that entering college students were essentially alike in prior achievement or that a bachelor's degree represented a single level of achievement. The Eight-year Study of the Progressive Education Association (E. Smith and others, 1942) applied objective measurement techniques to a wide variety of educational objectives other than knowledge. The study provided convincing evidence that specific subject-matter courses were not a necessary requirement in college preparatory programs but that individuals with a wide variety of experiences in secondary school could perform successfully in college. The critical requirement was not that they had studied particular courses, only that they had been successful in whatever they had studied. The Cooperative Study of Evaluation in General Education (Dressel & Mayhew, 1954) applied a variety of testing procedures to the evaluation of outcomes of education at the college level.

The broad advances achieved by these large-scale studies would have been impossible, however, had it not been for the contributions of individuals who provided the break-through insights. E. L. Thorndike (Scates, 1947), following close on the heels of Rice, developed standardized tests in a wide variety of subject-matter and skills areas. Starch and Eliott in the United States (Ebel & Damrin, 1960) and Hartog and Rhodes in England (1936) presented convincing evidence that grades which students received on essay tests of achievement often depended more on which particular set of questions were included on a particular test and on which particular person happened to read the paper than on the students' true level of achievement. Such evidence gave a strong impetus to efforts to develop more objective methods of measuring student achievement. Tyler (1934) called attention to the fact that the specific information learned in a course might be quickly forgotten while the broad understandings and skills developed through dealing with the specifics of a course remained and even increased with the passage of time. Lindquist (1951) argued that the final validation of a test of achievement rests in the demonstration that the sample of responses called for by the test is representative of those which constitute the goals of instruction. Since the achievement test used to evaluate the student's learning serves to define for the student the goals of instruction, it becomes essential that all important outcomes of instruction be measured. If success on a test can be achieved simply by learning facts from a textbook, then the student will learn facts, regardless of what other goals the instructor may assume he is striving for.

From time to time as developments in the field have warranted, systematic summaries of principles and practices have been compiled by scholars. Recent ones include *Improving Classroom Testing* (Engelhart, 1964), which provides for the classroom teacher a general overview of principles for constructing tests together with examples; *Constructing Evaluation Instruments* (Furst, 1958), which emphasizes the rational and philosophical bases of test construction with particular emphasis on testing at the college level; and *Measuring Educational Achievement* (Ebel, 1965), which is particularly strong in reporting the accumulated professional judgment when specific research evidence is lacking. The educator looking for specific guides to the art of test construction will find these and similar volumes a rich source of guidance.

There appears to be general agreement that achievement tests serve a number of purposes. Historically, they have been recognized as motivators of students and as one basis for assigning grades. Their use in providing teachers with feedback regarding the effects of instructional procedures has also been recognized, in principle if not often in practice. Their use in certification and in selection both in the United States and in other countries has been well established for many years. Recently two additional uses have received attention. Barnette (1957) has reported that students who entered college with advanced standing based on performance on achievement tests have generally had better records in college than students admitted under regular procedures. More recently a national program of advanced-standing and placement examinations has been established by the CEEB under which thousands of secondary school students are demonstrating their eligibility for advanced standing when they enter college (College Entrance Examination Board, 1966). A second recent development is an attempt to establish a systematic base for a continuous study of the progress of education within the United States by administering samples of test questions to samples of age groups within the population of the United States (Tyler, 1966). The approach differs markedly from the typical one involving standardized achievement tests in that the test item itself becomes the unit of interpretation in a manner similar to that of the polling studies, and generalizations are related to the achievement of broad subclasses of the population rather than to individual students, specific schools, or identifiable school systems. The conception is so different from the typical one that there has been widespread misunderstanding. The development, if successful, should provide educational policy makers with significant information for decisions of broad significance.

Finally, as systematic testing has become a significant element in American education there has been growing concern about the effects of misuses of tests (Goslin, 1963). A standardized test readily takes on an aura of scientific precision far beyond that which its creator would claim. Sarason and his associates (1960) have examined the contribution of tests, both standardized and informal, to anxiety in elementary school children. Ebel (1964) has pointed to the dangers of overinterpretation of test scores and has called on educators to consider at every point the social consequences as well as the advantages in terms of useful information whenever they use tests. Clearly, it is not enough simply to have mastered the technical aspects of scientific testing. It is also necessary to develop an understanding of the context within which tests are used, to be aware of limitations and possible misuses, and to weigh a broad range of possible effects before deciding to use a particular context.

TYPES OF ACHIEVEMENT TESTS. As the historical survey indicates, it was the demonstration of serious limitations in the traditional essay examinations which sparked the development of other methods of testing and the conducting of a host of studies designed to compare the relative merits of the old and the new types of examinations. The claims on both sides have been vigorous and the "research" studies extensive if not always definitive. As data have accumulated, it has become clear that the variability to be found within any one type of examination is likely to outweigh any systematic differences between types. There is little profit in comparing types per se.

It is much more important to determine, for any type of examination, the quality of the individual questions or problems and the appropriateness of the particular type to the behavior one is trying to measure. In general, when well-constructed selection-type questions (in which the student chooses from among alternative answers presented with the question) have been compared with well-constructed supply-type questions (in which the student composes his own response), the two have been shown to provide essentially the same information whether the content be mathematics (Plumlee, 1947), science (Cook, 1955), reading skills (Vernon, 1962), or English composition (Godshalk & others, 1966). In some cases where it seemed that only supply-type items would do the job, it has proved possible to develop parallel selection-type items (Thomas, 1956; Coffman & Papachristou, 1955). It seems safe to conclude that the decision to use a particular type of test question ought to be made on the basis of the efficiency of the type for the particular situation and the skills of the test writer rather than in terms of any supposed uniqueness of the data to be obtained. An item type appropriate for use in a large-scale testing program may be inappropriate for use by an individual teacher who is planning to examine a class of ten students. On the other hand, a procedure which the individual teacher may find highly appropriate for the single class could easily prove unmanageable in a large-scale testing program.

The Essay Examination. It has often been said that essay tests are easy to prepare and difficult to grade reliably, while objective tests are difficult to prepare and easy to grade. This may account, at least in part, for the fact that over the past fifty years there has been a marked reduction in the use of essay examinations in large-scale testing programs while essay questions or problems requiring the student to create his own responses continue to be widely used by individual teachers for measuring the results of instruction. The problem of scoring free-response answers is large compared to that of preparing questions for an objective test if the number of students to be examined is large; the reverse is true if the number to be examined is small.

It is doubtful, however, if such a simple answer to the question of when essay examinations are appropriate can be accepted without qualification. There are many different kinds of essay or problem-type examinations, each having its peculiar advantages and limitations. In its simplest form an essay question may require the student only to recall and record what he has memorized under the direction of a teacher, just as the simplest multiple-choice question may require only that the student recognize specific information previously learned. In contrast, an essay question may be presented which requires the student to analyze a complex set of relationships involving a setting which he has not previously studied, to recall from various similar settings which have been studied a variety of relevant data, and to draw conclusions regarding the probability that a particular course of action he proposes will lead to the desired results. Similarly, a complex multiple-choice question may require the student to recognize the points of similarity between a situation described in the item and different situations studied in class and to assess the relative probability of success of several alternative courses of action which might be taken in relation to the situation. There is, therefore, sound justification for excluding the simple supply-type question from the category of essay questions. At the same time, to classify such questions together with all choice-type items in a single category of *objective* questions is to suggest that choice-type questions are inherently superficial. It is not possible to make categorical statements about either essay or choice-type examinations in general apart from the types of questions included, the context in which the examination is used, and the qualifications of the individual or individuals who prepare and grade the examinations.

There is no doubt that reading reliability can be a problem, but the problem is much more severe with questions designed to measure complex analytical, integrative, or evaluative skills or the even more complex composition skills than with those intended to assess substantive knowledge. Studies can be found which report reading reliability coefficients ranging from as low as .32 to as high as .98 depending on the number of different questions included in the test, the types of questions, the extent of training given the readers, and the number of independent ratings combined in the score. One can say, however, that well-constructed essay questions of all types can be graded with an acceptable degree of reliability whether the grading method is analytical (Stalnaker & Stalnaker, 1934) or global (Godshalk & others, 1966). The reading is more likely to be satisfactory if small numbers of readers and papers are involved, but success has been achieved even in large-scale testing programs and with many readers involved (Myers & others, 1966). In most cases, however, reliable reading is achieved only at considerable cost in time and effort (Swineford, 1956; Finlayson, 1951). There is some evidence that in many cases essays have proved difficult to grade, at least in part, because too little effort went into the preparation of questions (Solomon, 1965). On the other hand, since a major portion of the error variance is contributed by differences in the ordering of papers by different readers, a high reliability of reading almost always involves the summing of ratings of a number of different readers.

There is some evidence that the differences in reader judgment can be attributed to stable differences in value orientation rather than simply to random error (J. W. French, 1962). To the extent that this is the case, the differences need to be isolated and reported rather than to be hidden in a single composition mark. More research is needed on this question. It does seem clear, however, that it may prove easier to identify clusters of readers with different value systems than to train readers holding different values to identify and report evaluations of different factors characterizing students' essays. Pearson (1955) reported that even experienced readers were unable to differentiate among characteristics of English composition. Scannell and Marshall (1966) found that student teachers directed to grade history papers on the basis of content alone were unable to ignore mistakes in English composition. Of particular significance was the fact that lower grades were given to papers with spelling errors than to those with errors in grammar or in punctuation even though one might expect the latter to show greater interaction with content.

There has been a tendency to emphasize the problem of reading reliability to the exclusion of other aspects of reliability. The major limitation of the essay examination is not that it is difficult to grade reliably but rather that in comparison to short-answer or choice-type tests it permits only a limited sample of the student's achievement to be collected. "Students spend most of their time in thinking and writing when taking an essay test. They spend most of their time reading and thinking when taking an objective test" (Ebel, 1965). Since reading is much more rapid than writing, more material can be covered in an objective than in an essay examination, and since students differ in their ability to answer different questions, the reliability of a test is a function of the number of questions rather than of the time involved. An inadequate sample, even if it is read with high reliability, cannot provide a reliable score. It is to be hoped that recent developments in conceptualization of the problem of test reliability in terms of variance components will lead to greater clarification of the relative importance of the several sources of error in tests (Gleser & others, 1965). Pidgeon and Yates (1957) have provided some indication of the possibilities of variance analysis for clarifying the relationships among various sources of error in essay examinations, but the experimental designs and the frame of reference for interpretation of experimental results which Gleser and her associates propose seem superior to any so far reported in the literature.

Critics of essay examinations have not limited their attacks to considerations of reliability alone. They have argued that the low reliability leads directly to low validity. Studies of the relationship of test scores to teacher judgments or to grades have generally supported such a position. Essay tests have generally lost out in competition with well-constructed objective tests whether the criterion was judgment of writing skill (Huddleston, 1954) or substantive knowledge (Cowles & Hubbard, 1952). However, these results may be attributable to the fact that the criterion measures were inappropriate or that they were of low reliability. Coffman (1966) has shown that if the criterion measure is both relevant and of high reliability, an essay test which is relatively low in reliability can correlate with the criterion as highly as a much more reliable objective test. Interpretation of research findings are made more difficult by the high relationships which all measures have with the underlying scholastic aptitude. As Adkins (1958) says, ". . . scores on an achievement test also may be affected by aptitude differentials, because those with higher native potentialities for learning will have acquired more in a uniform period of practice or study. Hence relative differences in achievement, real though they may be, depend in part upon aptitude variability."

Defenders of the use of essay examinations have argued that the exclusive use of objective tests may have an undesirable effect on teaching and learning practices and that therefore essay examinations should be used even at the expense of low reliability. They explain that the ability to assemble relevant facts and ideas and to communicate a synthesis is the distinguishing mark of an educated man. To substitute a check-off procedure in evaluating learning is to change the basic context within which the student works and to remove a major force motivating the development of communication skills. To the extent that the ability being tested is the ability to compose answers to relevant questions in a limited period of time, Coffman's data (1966) would support the use of essay examinations. It must be recognized, however, that the typical essay examination presents a highly artificial task in comparison with the typical real-life communication situation. There would appear to be better contexts for the development of writing skills than a restricted examination situation which precludes the careful checking of facts and revision of a succession of drafts which characterize most writing of high quality. The published research offers little support for the proposition that essay examinations are required to motivate students or teachers (Vallance, 1947; J. W. French, 1957). Although earlier studies suggested that students adopt better study procedures when preparing for essay examinations than when preparing for objective examinations, the results appear to reflect more the relative qualities of the objective and essay examinations to which the students had been exposed than any inherently greater motivating force for essay examinations.

It must also be recognized that what has been learned can be applied to discrimination situations as well as to communication situations. In everyday life the individual quite often finds himself required to make choices from among a number of alternatives, a situation not unlike the one he faces in taking a multiple-choice examination.

Choice-type Questions. Of the many choice-type questions which have been developed and used, clearly the most popular is the multiple-choice question. The examinee is presented with a situation or problem described in the first part of the question, called the "stem," and with a number of different answers or solutions among which he is to discriminate. Conceptually, all choice-type questions can be subsumed under the multiple-choice type, since all involve making choices among alternatives. The experienced test writer recognizes that the basic consideration is the objective to be achieved by the question rather than the mechanics of presenting the problem. In particular cases, however, a special format such as the true-false question, which is basically a two-choice, multiple-choice question, or the key list, which is a series of question stems with the same set of responses, may be more efficient than the standard multiple-choice format.

Research findings testify to the flexibility of choice-type items. Two-choice questions have been shown to be highly efficient (Ebel, 1965; K. Smith, 1958).

In particular cases, scoring both best and worst among three or more possibilities may provide additional information over that provided by scoring only the best answer (Nedelsky, 1954). Dressel and Schmid (1953) tried a variety of different ways of administering and scoring multiple-choice questions and concluded: "It seems that a great deal of liberty may be taken in modifying the multiple-choice item without impairing its efficiency as a measuring instrument, and with the possibility that the measuring efficiency may actually be improved." The productive variations which may be developed seem to be limited only by the ingenuity of the item writer. Examples of a variety of different objective test questions have been provided by Engelhart (1942), Diederich and others (1958), and the Educational Testing Service (1963).

All that the item writer produces, however, cannot be taken at face value. It is necessary to examine each new idea rigorously. For example, Gega and Karlsen (1962) report that there was no difference between students' performances on the regular form of *STEP Elementary Science* in which the questions were based on realistic problem situations and on experimental form in which items were recast in a self-contained form unrelated to the situations. Holland (1967) described a "blackout" technique in which portions of a programmed text judged to be unnecessary to obtaining the answer to questions are removed by being covered with black crayon. The remaining text is then administered to one sample of students and the original text to a parallel sample. If the blacking out has been properly performed, there should be no significant difference in the number of errors made by students in the two samples. If this is the case, the proportion of text blacked out provides a measure of the efficiency of the program. The technique might be applied to test items as well as to programmed texts.

Researchers have been concerned with what seem to be limitations of the choice-type question. Three, in particular, have been studied: correct answers may be obtained by guessing; an examinee who does not know the right answer may proceed by eliminating wrong answers; there is evidence that individuals, in the absence of information, may respond in terms of personal response tendencies which are irrelevant to the achievement being measured. The influence of such factors as guessing and answering by eliminating wrong answers appears to vary with the quality of the questions. Rapaport and Berg (1955) found little evidence of response sets even with very difficult items and concluded that for the usual achievement items, responses were made on the basis of direct information, formal characteristics of items, and response set, in that order. Gustav (1963), however, reported evidence that response set could affect test scores significantly. There is need for additional research in which the variables of guessing, answering by elimination, and response set are related to quality and appropriateness of test items for the population being tested.

Special Types of Examinations. The field of achievement testing is not limited to the traditional essay or objective tests. Findley (1953) has described an interlinear exercise for measuring English composition skills which appears to combine the characteristics of free response with the advantages of reliable scoring. The student is required to study a text, presumably a student essay, which is printed with spaces between the lines, and to make corrections as he might in revising his own manuscript. Trained readers can mark the revised papers with reliabilities in excess of .95. Glaser and his associates (1954) devised a tab item as a means of measuring proficiency in diagnostic problem-solving tasks. The tab item is a multiple-choice item with provision for feedback by placing the feedback information under a tab corresponding to each choice. By making provision for recording the sequence in which tabs are removed, the tester is enabled to infer the thought processes of the examinee. Damrin (1959) reported on the development of *The Russell Sage Social Relations Test*, a group problem-solving situation designed to measure the extent to which a classroom group has developed the capacity to work together effectively in accomplishing a complex perceptual and motor task.

These examples of the test writer's ability to create test situations which are appropriate in relation to particular educational objectives and which meet Dyer's criteria should provide encouragement to teachers or test developers faced with new areas of behavior to measure. There seems to be no reason, for example, why the interlinear exercise could not be adapted to the measurement of achievement in content areas, although no examples of such adaptation have been found in the literature. A student who could evaluate and correct a series of faulty statements about subject-matter content would surely have demonstrated his knowledge as well as a student who evaluated and corrected an English composition had demonstrated his composition skill. The critical requirements for creative test development appear to be (1) a clear understanding of what is to be measured, (2) the creation of a situation in which the relevant behavior can be observed, and (3) a hierarchy of value categories for classifying the responses of the students.

TEST CONSTRUCTION. A major criticism of formal testing procedures in education is that they tend to concentrate on those achievements which are easy to measure and to ignore the rest. The magnitude of the task facing one who proposes to overcome this criticism may be grasped by examining published statements of educational goals. Kearney (1953) provided such a statement at the elementary-school level, J. W. French and his associates (1957) at the secondary-school level, and H. Smith (1955) at the college level. Their statements represent relatively successful attempts to deal with educational outcomes in terms of behavior rather than abstraction, but the detail tends to be overwhelming. A committee of specialists in evaluation provided a classification system for organizing educational objectives within the cognitive domain (Bloom, 1956), and Stoker and Kropp (1964) and McGuire (1963) have produced evidence that the system may be applied effectively to actual test construction. More recently Krathwohl and his associates (1965) have attempted to accomplish in the affective domain what Bloom and his associates accomplished in the cognitive domain. It is too early yet to assess the degree of success which they have achieved.

Tests developed in relation to statements of educational objectives or taxonomies of the type cited above rest essentially on an authoritative base where the authority is the expert in the field that the test is intended to measure. In large-scale testing programs, the authority is generally exercised by a committee rather than by a single individual. But the judgment of the committee is generally subjected to an empirical check by administering the questions on an experimental basis and carrying out an item analysis. The procedure of constructing tests using committees of examiners has been described by Dyer and Coffman (1957) and by Epstein and Myers (1958). The item analysis provides information with respect to two sorts of judgments made by the item writer (or committee). The difficulty index confirms or negates the judgment that the item is appropriate in difficulty for the intended group. The discrimination index confirms or negates the judgment that the question is not ambiguous. Depending on the context, it may also confirm or negate the judgment that the item forms a cluster with other items of similar content. Thus, professional judgment and empirical try-out complement each other. Fan (1954) has described the construction of a table which facilitates item analysis when large-scale data-processing equipment is not available. Ebel (1954) and Diederich (1960) have suggested procedures which make it feasible for the teacher to apply item analysis to classroom tests.

Dr. John Flanagan has proposed the development of measurement objectives through a process involving a much wider judgment base than that which can be provided by a working committee (American Institute for Research, 1949, 1950), and Dressel and Mayhew (1954) have described the application of the procedure to the development of objectives for English composition. The procedure involves collecting from a representative sample of experts in a field (for example, English teachers) descriptions of particularly effective or ineffective performances which they have observed. Thus, each of a number of English teachers might be asked to describe in detail what it was about a particular student's writing which led him to the judgment that the writing was particularly effective or particularly ineffective. These "critical incidents"—all except critical behaviors which differentiate sharply between effective and ineffective behavior are ignored by the procedure—when collected and classified lead to a description of the domain to be measured. The categories may turn out to be the same as those which might be generated by a working committee. Sometimes, however, they include unanticipated characteristics. In any case, the broad sampling of judgments on which the conclusions rest is easier to defend than the narrower sampling which might be provided by a small committee regardless of the status of its individual members.

Another suggestion for establishing a broad base for the judgments which must underlie any achievement testing has been offered by Tucker (1962). Whereas Flanagan begins with critical incidents and generates items only after the domain has been described in an exhaustive manner, Tucker begins with a pool of test items which are submitted to experts for judgments regarding their relevance for measurement in a particular area. A factor analysis of the judgments of relevance provides insight into the extent and kind of different interpretations which experts in a field may hold. One limitation of Tucker's approach is that the characteristics of the item pool determine the factors which are generated. To provide some check on the adequacy of the item pool, Tucker asked his judges to suggest additional categories of items which would be considered appropriate but which were not included in the judgment pool.

By and large, the writing of test questions or the creation of problem situations designed to elicit relevant responses from groups of students remains largely an art rather than a science, and the inexperienced test maker must look to examples rather than to research reports for inspiration. Research studies have provided some guidance with respect to procedures which are likely to prove helpful. Rimland and Zwerski (1962) report that free-response answers to arithmetic problems may be used to generate options for a multiple-choice format, but they caution that parallel procedures might not work effectively in other subject-matter areas. Lorge and Diamond (1954) have demonstrated that experienced item writers develop the ability to make reasonably accurate estimates of the difficulty of newly written items for populations with which they have had experience. Gruber and Weitman (1962) have called attention to the fact that items may discriminate effectively or not, depending on whether they appear in a test administered at the beginning of a period of instruction or at the end. Ebel (1953) has shown that maximum validity may be expected per unit of time if an achievement test is so long that nobody finishes and if scores are expressed as a percentage of the number of items tried. Brenner (1964) reports that there is little effect on test scores attributable to differences in the order of item difficulty. He concludes that classroom instructors gain little from the time and effort spent in arranging items of a power test of facts and principles in order of item difficulty. Such findings, however, constitute guidance for refining the items and for assembling them into tests; they do not reduce the responsibility of the test writer to supply the essential underlying creative insights.

Traditionally, educational programs have tended to remain reasonably stable over long periods of time. The typical secondary-school first-year course in algebra remained very much the same during the period from 1920 to 1950, for example. The same standardized achievement test in algebra might therefore have been appropriate over a considerable period of time and for a wide range of schools. In recent years, however, there have been dramatic changes in course content and methods. Tests which in former years were clearly appropriate were suddenly found to be of questionable value. In the changing situation, research studies have provided the test developer with considerable assistance in building tests appropriate to the changing context (Douglas, 1957; Coffman, 1965).

The development of electronic data-processing equipment promises to have much wider influences than were at first anticipated. Whereas the early effects of large-scale data-processing developments were to reduce sharply the formats available to the test specialist, recent developments appear to encourage flexibility. For example, Page (1966) has already succeeded in programming a computer to produce grades on essay tests of composition ability which are indistinguishable from those produced by trained readers. As electronic document readers become more generally available and more flexible, one may expect to find less need to think in terms of test items with responses limited to choosing and checking the preferred among several alternatives. The test writer who fails to be alert to the possibilities of such developments is likely to find himself becoming an anachronism.

EVALUATION OF TEST QUALITY. To a considerable extent, the evaluation of the quality of an achievement test rests on a careful examination of the procedures by which the test was constructed and on a judgment regarding the adequacy of those procedures. In the case of a psychological test designed to predict future behavior, one can always conduct an experiment to see how good the prediction is. But an achievement test is typically intended to assess the extent to which a student, at a given point in time, has acquired the knowledges and skills a particular course of instruction was intended to develop. If the test is a good one, it is unlikely that a better measure of the particular achievement exists; otherwise, why has the test been built at all? The first question which ought to be asked about an achievement test is, then, "Have acceptable procedures been followed in constructing the test?"

The steps for following up on such a question are implicit in the preceding section on test construction. In the first place, one needs to determine that the objectives to be assessed have been systematically set forth in a test plan. If the plan has been approved by a number of different competent people, it is more likely to be acceptable than if it has been the work of a single individual. In any case, the plan should be available for examination by the critic. Second, one needs to determine that the individual test questions are relevant to the plan and that they are well constructed. Procedures of the type proposed by Ebel (1954) are highly appropriate for the evaluation of classroom tests. Those described by Tucker (1962) and Malcolm (1965) are applicable to tests designed for wider use. A joint committee of the APA, AERA, and NCME has prepared a booklet entitled *Standards for Educational and Psychological Tests and Manuals* (American Psychological Association & others, 1966). Buros (1965) has provided professional reviews of most published tests in common use.

Essential to a sound evaluation of test questions is an item analysis. It must be understood, however, that item-analysis procedures cannot replace professional judgment in the selection of questions for an achievement test. Rather, the item analysis provides a check on professional judgment, particularly with respect to ambiguity. Often a question which looks satisfactory to the professional test writer turns out to elicit unexpected response patterns from students, patterns which assist the professional in locating a defect previously overlooked (Educational Testing Service, 1963).

Since any particular achievement test is only a sample of questions from a much larger pool of potential questions, it is possible to evaluate a particular test by comparing scores on it with scores on a much longer test of the same sort or by building a series of parallel forms and demonstrating that they are related in the manner predicted by test theory. It was by such procedures that Godshalk and others (1966) evaluated short essays as measures of English composition ability. The practice has not been applied widely, however, because of the great expense and the requirement of long periods of experimental testing time.

Even if test questions appear appropriate to professional judges and produce the anticipated response patterns when subjected to item analysis, there is no guarantee that they have elicited the particular types of responses from students which the test writer anticipated. Questions designed to elicit analytical thinking may be answered on the basis of simple memory or through giving attention to irrelevant cues. To develop a better understanding of the mental processes elicited by test questions, Connolly and Wantman (1964) asked students to "think out loud" as they formulated answers. Kropp (1956) reported that the procedure might very well lead to incorrect inferences about problem-solving processes. It was effective, however, for revealing ambiguities, hidden clues, and the like.

It is surprising that there has been so little in the way of rigorous experimentation as a means of developing principles of item writing. By presenting to experimental subjects a series of test questions designed to measure the same thing but varied in systematic ways, one should be able to determine the effects of particular variations. The blackout technique described by Holland (1967) and described in the section on choice-type questions offers one possible technique for producing desirable variations.

The educator concerned with keeping up on developments in the field of achievement testing will wish to examine the periodic reviews published in the

Review of Educational Research and relevant articles to be found in *Educational and Psychological Measurement* and the *Journal of Educational Measurement*. Articles on achievement tests appearing in a variety of journals are listed under the heading "Tests and Examinations" in the *Education Index*.

William E. Coffman
Educational Testing Service

References

Adkins, Dorothy C. "Measurement in Relation to the Educational Process." *Ed Psychol Meas* 18:221–40; 1958.

American Institute for Research. *Critical Requirements for Research Personnel, A Study of Observed Behavior of Personnel in Research Laboratories*. The Institute, 1949. 66p.

American Institute for Research. *The Development of a Test for Selecting Research Personnel*. The Institute, 1950. 33p.

American Psychological Association and others. *Standards for Educational and Psychological Tests and Manuals*. APA, 1966. 40p.

Barnette, W. Leslie, Jr. "Advanced Credit for the Superior High School Student." *J H Ed* 28:15–20; 1957.

Bloom, Benjamin S. (Ed.) *Taxonomy of Educational Objectives: The Classification of Educational Goals. Handbook I: Cognitive Domain*. McKay, 1956. 207p.

Brenner, Marshall H. "Test Difficulty, Reliability, and Discrimination as Functions of Item Difficulty Order." *J Applied Psychol* 48:98–100; 1964.

Buros, Oscar K. (Ed.) *The Sixth Mental Measurements Yearbook*. Gryphon Press, 1965. 1,714p.

Caldwell, Otis W., and Courtis, S. A. *Then and Now in Education, 1845–1923*. Harcourt, 1924. 400p.

Coffman, W. E. "Developing Tests for the Culturally Different." *Sch Soc* 93:420–33; 1965.

Coffman, W. E. "On the Validity of Essay Tests of Achievement." *J Ed Meas* 3:151–6; 1966.

Coffman, W. E., and Papachristou, Judith. "Experimental Objective Tests of Writing Ability for the Law School Admission Test." *J Legal Ed* 7:388–94; 1955.

College Entrance Examination Board. *Advanced Placement Program: 1966–68 Course Descriptions*. CEEB, 1966. 160p.

Connolly, John A., and Wantman, M. J. "An Exploration of Oral Reasoning Processes in Responding to Objective Test Items." *J Ed Meas* 1:59–64; 1964.

Cook, Desmond L. *An Investigation of Three Aspects of Free Response and Choice Type Tests at the College Level*. Doctoral Dissertation. State U Iowa, 1955. 377p.

Cowles, John T., and Hubbard, John P. "A Comparative Study of Essay and Objective Examinations for Medical Students." *J Med Ed* 27:14–7; 1952.

Damrin, Dora E. "The Russell Sage Social Relations Test: A Technique for Measuring Group Problem Solving Skills in Elementary School Children." *J Exp Ed* 28:85–99; 1959.

Diederich, Paul. *Short-cut Statistics for Teacher-made Tests*. ETS, 1960. 37p.

Diederich, Paul, and others. "Exercise Writing in the Humanities, Natural Sciences, and Social Sciences." In *Proceedings of the 1957 Individual Conference on Testing Problems*. ETS, 1958. p. 36–67.

Douglas, Edwin C. "College Board Examinations and Curriculum Change." *Math Teach* 50:305–8; 1957.

Dressel, Paul L., and Mayhew, Lewis B. *General Education: Explorations in Evaluation*. ACE, 1954. 302p.

Dressel, Paul L., and Schmid, John. "Some Modifications of the Multiple-choice Items." *Ed Psychol Meas* 13:574–95; 1953.

DuBois, P. H. "A Test-dominated Society: China, 1115 B.C.–1905 A.D." In *Proceedings of the 1964 Invitational Conference on Testing Problems*. ETS, 1965. p. 3–11.

Dyer, H. S. "Educational Measurement—Its Nature and Its Problems." In Berg, H. D. (Ed.) *Evaluation in Social Studies*. National Council for Social Studies, 1965. p. 21–46.

Dyer, Henry S., and Coffman, W. E. "The Tests of Developed Abilities." *Col Bd R* 31:5–10; 1957.

Ebel, Robert L. "Maximizing Test Validity in Fixed Time Limits." *Ed Psychol Meas* 13:347–57; 1953.

Ebel, Robert L. "Procedures for the Analysis of Classroom Tests." *Ed Psychol Meas* 14:352–64; 1954.

Ebel, Robert L. "The Social Consequences of Educational Testing." *Sch Soc* 92:331–4; 1964.

Ebel, Robert L. *Measuring Educational Achievement*. Prentice-Hall, 1965. 481p.

Ebel, Robert L., and Damrin, Dora E. "Tests and Examinations." In Harris, Chester W. (Ed.) *Encyclopedia of Educational Research*, 3rd ed. Macmillan, 1960. p. 1502–17.

Educational Testing Service. *Multiple-choice Questions: A Close Look*. ETS, 1963. 43p.

Engelhart, Max D. "Unique Types of Achievement Test Exercises." *Psychometrika* 7:103–15; 1942.

Engelhart, Max D. "Improving Classroom Testing." In *What Research Says to the Teacher*. NEA, 1964.

Epstein, Marion, and Myers, Sheldon S. "How a Mathematics Test Is Born." *Math Teach* 51:299–302; 1958.

Fan, C. T. "Note on Construction of an Item Analysis Table for the High-Low-27-Per-cent Group Method." *Psychometrika* 19:231–7; 1954.

Findley, Warren G. "How Objective Can Free-style Measures of Writing Ability be Made?" *Engl Rec* 4:19–25; 1953.

Finlayson, Douglas S. "The Reliability of the Marking of Essays." *Br J Ed Psychol* 21:126–34; 1951.

French, J. W. "What English Teachers Think of Early Testing." *Engl J* 46:196–201; 1957.

French, J. W. "Schools of Thought in Judging Excellence of English Themes." In *Proceedings of the 1961 Invitational Conference on Testing Problems*. ETS, 1962. p. 19–28.

French, Will, and others. *Behavioral Outcomes of General Education in High School.* Russell Sage, 1957. 247p.

Fuess, Claude M. *The College Board: Its First Fifty Years.* Columbia U Press, 1950. 222p.

Furst, Edward J. *Constructing Evaluation Instruments.* McKay, 1958. 334p.

Gega, Peter C., and Karlsen, Bjorn. "Situational vs. Non-situational Casting of Items in the STEP . . . Elementary Science." *California J Ed Res* 13:99–104; 1962.

Glaser, Robert, and others. "The Tab Item: A Technique for the Measurement of Proficiency in Diagnostic Problem-solving Tasks." *Ed Psychol Meas* 14:283–93; 1954.

Gleser, Goldine C., and others. "Generalizability of Scores Influenced by Multiple Sources of Variance." *Psychometrika* 30:395–418; 1965.

Godshalk, Fred, and others. *The Measurement of Writing Ability.* CEEB, 1966. 84p.

Goslin, David A. "Testing in Education." In *The Search for Ability; Standardized Testing in Social Perspective.* Russell Sage, 1963. p. 55–94.

Gruber, Howard E., and Weitman, Morris. "Item Analysis and the Measurement of Change." *J Ed Res* 55:287–9; 1962.

Gustav, Alice. "Response Set in Objective Achievement Tests." *J Psychol* 56:421–7; 1963.

Hartog, P., and Rhodes, E. C. *The Marks of Examiners.* Macmillan, 1936. 344p.

Holland, James G. "A Quantitative Measure for Programmed Instruction." *Am Ed Res J* 4:87–101; 1967.

Huddleston, Edith M. "Measurement of Writing Ability at the College-entrance Level: Objective vs. Subjective Testing Techniques." *J Exp Ed* 22:165–213; 1954.

Kearney, Nolan C. *Elementary School Objectives.* Russell Sage, 1953. 189p.

Krathwohl, D. R., and Others. (Eds.) *Taxonomy of Educational Objectives. Handbook II: Affective Domain.* McKay, 1965. 196p.

Kropp, Russell P. "The Relationship Between Process and Correct Item Response." *J Ed Res* 49:385–8; 1956.

Learned, William S., and Wood, Ben D. *The Student and His Knowledge.* Carnegie, 1938. 406p.

Lindquist, E. F. (Ed.) *Educational Measurement.* ACE, 1951. 819p.

Lorge, Irving, and Diamond, Lorraine K. "Prediction of Absolute Item Difficulty by Ranking and Estimating Techniques." *Ed Psychol Meas* 14:365–72; 1954.

Malcolm, Donald J. "Content Validity of Achievement Tests as Judged by Teachers." In *ETS Annual Report, 1963–64.* ETS, 1965. p. 147.

McGuire, Christine. "Research in the Process Approach to the Construction and Analysis of Medical Examinations." In *Twentieth Yearbook of the National Council on Measurement in Education.* Michigan State U Press, 1963. p. 7–16.

Myers, A. E., and Others. "Simplex Structure in the Grading of Essay Tests." *Ed Psychol Meas* 26:41–54; 1966.

Nedelsky, Leo. "Ability to Avoid Gross Error as a Measure of Achievement." *Ed Psychol Meas* 14:459–72; 1954.

Page, Ellis B. "The Imminence of Grading Essays by Computer." *Phi Delta Kappan* 47:238–43; 1966.

Pearson, Richard. "The Test Fails as an Entrance Examination." *Col Bd R* 25:2–9; 1955.

Pidgeon, D. A., and Yates, A. "Symposium: The Use of Essays in Selection at 11+. IV: Experimental Inquiries into the Use of Essay-type English Papers." *Br J Ed Psychol* 27:37–61; 1957.

Plumlee, Lynette B. "Comparison of Problem Types in the Comprehensive Mathematics Test." *Col Bd R* 1:17, 29–31; 1947.

Rapaport, Gerald M., and Berg, Irwin A. "Response Sets in a Multiple-choice Test." *Ed Psychol Meas* 15:58–62; 1955.

Rimland, Bernard, and Zwerski, Edwin. "The Use of Open-end Data as an Aid in Writing Multiple-choice Distracters: An Evaluation with Arithmetic Reasoning and Computation Items." *J Applied Psychol* 46:31–3; 1962.

Sarason, S. B., and Others. *Anxiety in Elementary School Children.* Wiley, 1960. 351p.

Scannell, Dale P., and Marshall, Jon C. "The Effect of Selected Composition Errors on Grades Assigned to Essay Examinations." *Am Ed Res J* 3:125–30; 1966.

Scates, Douglas E. "Fifty Years of Objective Measurement and Research in Education." *J Ed Res* 41:241–64; 1947.

Smith, Eugene R., and others. *Appraising and Recording Student Progress.* Harper, 1942. 550p.

Smith, H. *The Purposes of Higher Education,* 1st ed. Harper, 1955. 218p.

Smith, Kendon. "An Investigation of the Use of 'Double-choice' Items in Testing Achievement." *J Ed Res* 51:387–9; 1958.

Solomon, R. J. "Improving the Essay Test in the Social Studies." In Berg, H. D. (Ed.) *Evaluation in Social Studies.* National Council for Social Studies, 1965. p. 137–53.

Stalnaker, John M., and Stalnaker, R. C. "Reliable Reading of Essay Tests." *Sch R* 42:599–605; 1934.

Stoker, H. W., and Kropp, R. P. "Measurement of Cognitive Processes." *J Ed Meas* 1:39–42; 1964.

Swineford, Frances. *Test Analysis of the CEEB Advanced Placement Tests, Form EBP.* ETS, 1956. 56p.

Thomas, Macklin. "Construction Shift Exercises in Objective Form." *Ed Psychol Meas* 16:181–6; 1956.

Tinkelman, S. N. "Regents Examinations in New York State after 100 Years." In *Proceedings of the 1965 Invitational Conference on Testing Problems.* ETS, 1966. p. 85–94.

Tucker, L. R. "Factor Analysis of Relevance Judgments: An Approach to Content Validity." In *Proceedings of the 1961 Invitational Conference on Testing Problems.* ETS, 1962. p. 29–38.

Tyler, R. W. *Constructing Achievement Tests.* Ohio State U Press, 1934. 110p.

Tyler, R. W. "The Development of Instruments for Assessing Educational Progress." In *Proceedings of the 1965 Invitational Conference on Testing Problems*. ETS, 1966. p. 95–105.

Vallance, Theodore R. "A Comparison of Essay and Objective Examination as Learning Experience." *J Ed Res* 41:279–88; 1947.

Vernon, Philip E. "The Determinants of Reading Comprehension." *Ed Psychol Meas* 22:269–86; 1962.

ADMINISTRATIVE THEORY

The predominantly practical posture of educational administration came under severe and continuing criticism in the early 1950's, which resulted in a more theoretical attitude on the part of those who study administration. The extent to which practitioners have been influenced by administrative theory has not been determined. The shift from "very practical" to "somewhat theoretical" has been described by Griffiths (1959a), and the present status of theory has also been described by Griffiths (1968).

The first attempt at a full-fledged theory of educational administration is generally conceded to have been undertaken by Mort (1946, rev. ed., Mort & Ross, 1957) although some credit Cubberly (1916) with a try. Cubberly presented some fundamental principles which he thought would serve as guides to action. Mort undertook a more ambitious task, the development of a system of principles. He started with some common-sense value statements and derived, in a manner that is not at all clear, 14 principles grouped into three categories. Mort acknowledged that the principles were contradictory and not all equally applicable in a given situation. A concept, balanced judgment, was invented as a solution to this dilemma. Although not a theory in any intellectual sense, Mort's work was a pioneering effort.

Sears' book (1950) is also considered to be one of the first volumes of administrative theory. He claimed a direct relationship to the classical writers in administration, Taylor, Fayol, Gulick, and Urwick, yet his modifications of their basic ideas were such as to produce an approach to theory that was different in kind. He held that the administrative function derives its nature from the nature of the services it directs. In modern terminology, he would hold that administration is primarily adjectival, a view that is now held by few writers.

Concurrent with the publication of these two books were two developments which were very influential in the theory movement in educational administration: the formation of the National Conference of Professors of Educational Administration (NCPEA) and of the Cooperative Program in Educational Administration (CPEA), the Kellogg Foundation project. These two organizations brought professors together and stimulated much discussion and critical analysis. The CPEA also provided funds for consultants and, to some extent, research; it was described by Moore (1957). Though little of theoretical substance can be found in its list of publications, a change in the prevailing modes of inquiry can be discerned. The major changes were an increase in the emphasis upon empirical research, an interest in conceptual thinking, and an infusion of behavioral scientists into educational administration.

In retrospect it would appear that the major force toward a more theoretical orientation was the group of behavioral scientists which began to attend conferences, write, and, in general, challenge the thinking of professors of educational administration. In spite of this, the first genuinely critical article to appear was by Walton (1955), an ex-superintendent of schools and a professor of education. He expressed eloquent dismay at the primitive state of theory development in educational administration and turned to other fields of administration for guidance; in so doing he set a pattern followed by many in subsequent years. A provocative and highly critical monograph by Coladarci and Getzels (1955) appeared almost simultaneously with Walton's article. In addition, the Coladarci and Getzels volume offered a version of role theory which was to be used in various forms in a number of studies reported by Chase and Guba (1955), Griffiths and Iannaccone (1958), R. Campbell and Faber (1961), Lipham (1964), and Erickson (1967).

Three seminal volumes appeared in 1957 and 1958 written by R. Campbell and Gregg (1957), Halpin (1958), and Gross (1958). The only report of empirical research was that of Gross, but it appears to have had much more of an impact on sociologists than on educators.

Halpin's work (1958) was the product of the first research seminar held by the University Council for Education Administration (UCEA). Four of the chapters could be termed "announcements" to professors of educational administration of lines of inquiry. Getzels (in Halpin, 1958) described administration as a social process in which behavior was conceived as a function of both the nomothetic and the idiographic dimensions of a social system and reported on two studies which employed his model. Hemphill (in Halpin, 1958) described administration as a process of solving mutual problems. He introduced the concept of a leader as one who initiates structure-in-interaction in a group, a concept which he had developed earlier. Griffiths (in Halpin, 1958) developed the idea that decision making is the central function of the administrator. Parsons (in Halpin, 1958) presented some ideas relevant to a theory of formal organizations. The four lines of inquiry, which had been begun prior to the publication of Halpin's book, were to be the major focuses of research attention in subsequent years.

Halpin laid out the ground rules for acceptable theory. He advocated the use of Feigl's definition (1951) which, while rather narrow, is relatively clear and concise: "a set of assumptions from which can be derived by purely locio-mathematical procedures, a larger set of empirical laws." The use of this definition was supported by Griffiths (1959a, 1964).

SOCIAL SYSTEMS THEORY. The Midwest Administration Center at the University of Chicago is noted for its contribution to theory-based research. Studies done in the 1950's and early 1960's established the value of social systems theory in the investigation of problems of school administration. Getzels (1952) and Getzels and Guba (1954, 1955a, 1955b) established the now well-known two-dimensional theory of organizational behavior described briefly above. Fourteen studies were done at the Midwest Administration Center and reported in the journal *Administrator's Notebook*. Hills (1960) summarized the studies done up to 1960 and related them to the Getzels-Guba model. Hills contended that work with the social systems model provides the administrator with a framework in which he could systematize his observations and experiences, provides him with clear, precise concepts, and reveals blind spots to him.

Later studies at the Midwest Center explored particular aspects of the Getzels-Guba model. Hencley (1960) developed a typology of administrator–reference-group conflict. He found that while some conflicts result from real differences between the beliefs and values of superintendents and others, most differences arise from superintendents' misperceptions of reality. Lipham (1960) related certain personal variables to the judged effectiveness of public school principals. Abbott (1960) found that superintendent–school-board relationships were dependent upon agreement on basic issues and on how each member of the relationship perceived the position of the other. Powers (1966) showed that the model was capable of broader use in his study of the mobility of assistant principals. He found that organization-oriented behavior was not uniquely characteristic of upward-mobile personnel.

The model was used at other universities as well as at Chicago, notably by Willower (1960). Willower found that principals employing an idiographic style tended to regard teachers as professionals to a greater extent than did principals who employ a nomothetic style.

The number of studies done using the Getzels-Guba model has fallen off sharply in recent years. It would appear that the model is due for a revision which would incorporate the research of the past 17 years. The model served the purpose well of moving research in educational administration away from naked empiricism toward theory. The fact that the model encompasses such a narrow range of organizational behavior was a strength when it was conceived, but the narrowness is now a weakness.

LEADERSHIP THEORY. The term "leadership theory" is used here to mean the line of inquiry initiated by the Personnel Research Board at Ohio State. This work began with the development of the *Leader Behavior Description Questionnaire (LBDQ)* by Hemphill and Coons (1950). The theory of leadership basic to the questionnaire was published by Hemphill (in Halpin, 1958). It is interesting to note that the theory and the questionnaire parted company soon after birth and are practically never related by researchers. Without question, the *LBDQ* has been the most widely used research instrument in the past two decades. As late as 1966, 17 years after the *LBDQ* was first used, it was employed in at least seven doctoral studies in educational administration. Its popularity is due, no doubt, to the ease of administration. Copies can be purchased, the reliability is substantial, and the two factors, consideration and initiating structure, are well known. All that is needed is a population and a measure with which to correlate results, and the basis for another doctoral dissertation has been laid.

The value of the *LBDQ* was developed by Halpin in a number of studies. Halpin and Winer (1952) factor analyzed the responses of 300 aircrew members, reporting on the behavior of their 52 aircraft commanders. Two factors, initiating structure and consideration, accounted for approximately 34 and 50 percent, respectively, of the common variance. Halpin (1955) reported a comparative study of aircraft commanders and superintendents of Ohio schools in which the two types differed significantly in their leadership styles and ideologies. Both Halpin (1953) and Hemphill (1955) had previously reported that "effective" leaders were those who scored high on both dimensions. Halpin reported that school administrators showed more consideration and less initiating structure than the aircraft commanders. He accounted for this in part by pointing out the marked situational differences between the two positions and in part by remarking on the influence of the "human relations" movement on school superintendents. Halpin called for research which would relate specific aspects of the situation to differences in *LBDQ* scores. This research has not yet been done. He also called for objective criteria of "effective" school administration, and this, too, is yet to come.

In spite of the wide use of the *LBDQ* there have been repeated criticisms of the instrument. In many of his writings (e.g., Halpin, 1956) Halpin advocates the study of leader *behavior,* yet the *LBDQ* records only self-perceptions and the perceptions of others about the behavior of the leader. Griffiths (1959b) warned against the dangers of confusing perceptions with behavior. Hills (1959) protested that leadership as seen through the *LBDQ* was completely internal to the organization. He developed two dimensions relating to the "outside" of an organization and recommended that they be incorporated into the *LBDQ*. Erickson (1967) used critical discussions of the *LBDQ*, particularly those of Charters (1964) and Brown (1967), in a penetrating analysis of the methodology of leader research. Charters' study (1964) of factors influencing teacher perceptions of administrative behavior is perhaps the most comprehensive to date. He found that superintendents rarely have more than fleeting contact with teachers regardless of the size of the school district. Charters questioned the validity in the bureaucratic setting of the school of instruments developed from small-group research. He pointed out that many of the leadership functions which are performed by people in small groups are executed in bureaucracies by rules and regulations, bells and clocks, etc. He concluded that since many leadership functions in schools are served by impersonal mechanisms of the organization, their consequences cannot be attributed to the behavioral acts of any given person.

Brown's contribution (1967) to the critical analysis of the *LBDQ* and similar instruments resulted from a study in which he used the *LBDQ-12*, which was developed by Stogdill (1959, 1963). He argues that the statements in such questionnaires are not valid revelations of leader behavior regardless of the titles of the questionnaires or uses to which researchers have put them. Brown further contends that leadership is a transaction rather than a behavior and that if this is so the "description questionnaire" is useful in assessing leadership. Brown therefore defines leadership as "a state of the total group" that is determined by both the leader's and the followers' behavior.

If to this discussion is added the Hemphill study (Hemphill & others, 1962) in which initiating structure and consideration, along with a large number of other measures, were correlated with behavior in simulated situations and found to be virtually irrelevant, one wonders if the large number of studies done with the *LBDQ* were worth the effort.

The major question concerning the *LBDQ* is What does it measure? The object of the instrument appears to be a person who fills the official role of head of an organization, but it may well be that the members of the organization are responding according to how they feel about the school at that particular time. Brown is probably correct, but one would feel more comfortable with a bit more precision on his part. Charters' conclusion that the respondents are not reporting on the head's behavior but rather on an institutionalized leadership makes it urgent that the job of definition be taken more seriously than in the past. Lipham (in Griffiths, 1964) laid the groundwork for clarifying the issue by clearly differentiating leadership from administration. Leadership research would profit from operational definitions and a return to theory.

DECISION THEORY. A third line of inquiry begun by Halpin (1958) has been research with a decision-theory base. As in the two previous lines of inquiry the theme of the research was taken from the social sciences and from types of organizations other than education. The two major sources used by Griffiths in his contribution to Halpin's book (1958) were the works of Barnard (1938) and of Simon (1950).

Research in decision making proceeded more slowly than did the other three lines of inquiry. From 1956 through 1962 an average of only one dissertation a year was written using decision making as a basis. However, an average of six per year were completed from 1963 through 1966. The same pattern is apparent in projects funded by the U.S. Office of Education extramural research program. Only eight decision research projects have been funded, and six of these had yet to be completed by October 1966 (Boerrigter & Williams, 1966).

Griffiths (1959a) identified four assumptions, described a set of concepts, and formulated several propositions in a step toward developing a decision-based theory of administration. In a study of administrative performance in a simulated situation, Hemphill and others (1962) found that of two secondary or underlying factors, one could be called preparation for decision and the second could be identified as amount of work. The significance of this finding for decision theory is in the nature of validation of an assumption, but the significance must be discounted to some extent because the study was not designed as a test and the nature of the study was such that it was unlikely that other theories could account for the findings. Panttaja (1966) verified two hypotheses derived from Griffiths' proposition: First, if the administrator confines his behavior to making decisions on the decision-making process rather than making terminal decisions for the organization, his behavior will be more acceptable to his subordinates. Second, Panttaja found that, nevertheless, the style of decision making overrode the effect of the type of decision employed by the administrator. Thomas (1963) employed the stages in decision making described by Griffiths and Iannaccone (1958) and found that secondary-school principals used them all but gave most of their attention to putting the decision into action.

One of the major contributions to decision research was that of Gross (1958), the basic work for which was reported by Gross and others (1958). Gross attempted to find answers to questions concerning why school-board members and superintendents made the decisions that they did make. Gross listed 19 groups which exerted pressure (requests or demands accompanied by an apparent threat in case of failure to conform to them) on superintendents and school-board members. The groups included virtually everyone in the community! He also studied attitudes of board members and superintendents toward important educational issues and pointed out that these affected the kind of decision made. Gross demonstrated the reciprocal value of research on practical school problems and contributions to theoretical knowledge.

Fogarty and Gregg (1966) reported an interesting study in which an instrument developed by Eye and others (1966) was used to determine the degree of centralization of decision making in school districts. They found that the degree of centralization varied with functional areas of administration. Decision making was most centralized in community relations and least centralized in pupil personnel. No significant relationships were found between centralization of decision making and the superintendents' personalities or scores on the *LBDQ*.

In a major study of decision making Eye and others (1966) attempted to answer the question "To what extent do administrators and teachers in a given school system tend to agree or disagree in their perceptions of decision-making roles and responsibilities?" The investigators employed social systems theory as the vehicle for the study, but decision making was selected as a focus of study for a number of reasons, the most cogent of which was that it bridged conceptually the rational systems model and the natural systems model. The Decision Point Analysis Instrument was developed, enabling the researchers to determine who made a decision, who participated in that decision, and the extent of the respondent's participation in the decision. In systems of high congruence of perception of decision points there was a high incidence of planned instructional change, and the opposite occurred in systems of low congruence of perceptions. The *LBDQ* was used to relate measures of leader behavior to other variables, with considerable success. One of the most significant findings was that consideration is a more valuable behavior for the superintendent to exhibit than initiating-structure behavior is if curriculum change is the goal.

Bowman (1963) and Ziegler (1964) studied the decision making of superintendents. Bowman was able to establish three modes of decision making which described the behavior of superintendents in decision-making situations with their boards of education. He was also able to associate variations in the modes with position, size of district, tenure in position, and age.

Bridges (1967) accepted the premise that principals should share decision making with their teachers but raised several questions, the answers to which would bring specificity to what is usually considered general advice. One of his propositions dealt with Barnard's "zone of indifference" (1938) and related this to teachers' acceptance of the principals' decisions. Bridges (1964) went farther in his study of teacher participation in decision making. Teachers did, he found, prefer principals who involved them in decision making, but teachers with a high need for independence expressed less favorable attitudes toward such a principal than did teachers with a low need for independence. Teachers' attitudes were also influenced by the support which principals had given teachers. Bridges has moved conclusions concerning decision making well out of the cliché stage and has pointed to the kind of research that is needed.

Research in decision theory has just gotten under way and, as yet, has not been the subject of critical analysis.

ORGANIZATION THEORY. Much of the most significant and useful research of the past two decades can be classified under the heading "organization theory." This is an omnibus heading and normally includes all theory concerning the study of the structure and functioning of organizations and of the behavior of the people within them. Since the practice in educational administration varies somewhat from that in other fields it is used here in a residual manner to include role theory and research and theory pertinent to organizations not discussed under social systems theory, leadership theory, or decision theory.

Parsons (in Halpin, 1958) set out some issues that must be resolved before a general theory of organization can be devised. He was particularly interested in factors which differentiated among types of organizations. Some of his ideas have generated fruitful research studies—e.g., that of Hills (1959), who recommended adding the dimensions of procurement and disposal to the *LBDQ*, and that of Campbell (in Griffiths, 1964).

Relatively little of a theoretical or research nature has been done on the structure of organizations. The Cooperative Development of Public School Administration, a Kellogg Foundation project in New York State, was probably the most ambitious undertaking reported. The research studies on functions of various administrative roles and on the structure of local districts were published in several pamphlets, but all were combined in a volume by Griffiths and others (1962). A subsequent study by Bell (1965) confirmed the finding that superintendents perceived the flat structure of a school district to be more effective than the tall. One of the basic concepts of structure, span of control, was critically analyzed by Lehto (1966). The topic of school size was analyzed by W. J. Campbell (1965) and Faber (1966). They found school districts tending to become larger and that researchers recommended even larger districts. Two researchers, Bloom (1966) and Heathers (1967), offered recommendations for the organization of schools based upon studies of learning—a rather novel development.

A notable difference between the study of educational administration and the study of other adjectival types of administration lies in the study of concepts. While this is common in other fields (Pugh, 1966), it is relatively rare in education. Lehto's study, mentioned above, Anderson's study of authority (1960), and studies of power by Briner and Iannaccone (1966) and Kimbrough (1964) appear to be the sole examples. While these studies helped to clarify important concepts, many more such studies are needed.

Another type of research that is rare in educational administration is the comprehensive review; only one case of this was noted (Davies & Iannaccone, 1958). Again, this is a type of research which should be stimulated.

Bidwell (in March 1965, Ch. 23) has made a significant contribution to theorizing about administration by conceptualizing the school as a formal organization. While a thorough review of his essay belongs in another section of this encyclopedia, his description of the setting in which administrators work is of great value. Of particular importance is the specification of four organizational attributes of the school. It would certainly appear that theoretical studies of administrative behavior would have to take into account the involuntary nature of the student role, the professionalization of staff roles, the combination of bureaucracy and structural looseness present in schools, and the power of local constituents and higher governmental agencies. Past efforts at theory building have too often been concerned with only one or two of the attributes listed by Bidwell.

A number of studies in organization theory employing the concepts and structure of role theory have been completed. The most comprehensive and significant role study was that of Gross (1958). According to Pugh (1966) the studies by Gross and by Kahn and others (1964) demonstrated for the first time the usefulness of role theory. Prior to these studies, role theory had been virtually sterile as a source of research.

The major purpose of the Gross study (1958) was, in his words, to forge a "closer link between theoretical and empirical analyses concerned with the study of roles." This purpose was in large part accomplished through operationally defining concepts which had previously been only described, by collecting data systematically, and by subjecting the data to careful statistical analysis. Problems of dealing with the lengthy interviews employed to collect data were reported by Gross and Mason (1953).

Gross's study of superintendents was followed by a national study of principals reported by Gross and Herriott (1965) and Gross and Trask (1964). The Gross and Herriott report was the subject of a critical analysis by Erickson (1965) on the grounds that the central variable may not be valid, the study's conceptual scheme is oversimplified, and the researchers were attracted to "obvious" interpretations.

Other contributions to role theory are those in administrator and teacher relationships by Bidwell (1955, 1956, 1957) and Brookover (1955). Griffiths and others (1965) presented a typology of teacher roles constructed with data collected during a study of New York City teachers. Bridges (1965) reported a carefully devised study of a single administrative role.

The development of the *Organizational Climate Description Questionnaire* (*OCDQ*) by Halpin and Croft (1963) has had a quantitative impact upon research related to administrative theory. Since all administrative behavior takes place in a situation, the lack of proper instrumentation has made the measurement of situations impossible. The *OCDQ* is a step toward remedying this problem. The *OCDQ* has had a reception similar to that enjoyed by the *LBDQ*. Brown (1967) estimates that it has been used in at least 100 studies. The studies are empirical and are generally correlational in nature.

OTHER THEORETICAL RESEARCH. A number of interesting studies have opened up new avenues to administrative theory, although none has resulted in a full-blown theory.

There has been a lack of historical studies of educational administration which is now beginning to be alleviated. Callahan (1962) studied the social forces which shaped the administration of American schools from 1900 to 1930. He concluded that much of what has happened in American education since 1900 can be explained on the basis of the extreme vulnerability of schoolmen to public criticism and pressure. He further argued that the prevailing pattern of local support and control perpetuated this vulnerability. Callahan (1964) expanded his interest in the history of the superintendency and established four descriptive-historical categories to describe the development of the school superintendent. Callahan and Button (in Griffiths, 1964) traced the superintendency from 1865 to 1950 and noted the changes both in incumbents and in concepts used to discuss administration. Kelley (1961) studied the period from approximately 1910 to 1915, the start of the scientific movement in educational administration. In a study which used secondary sources Griffiths (1966) categorized the historical development of the superintendent's role as initially that of (1) instructor, then (2) business man, and currently (3) professional administrator. Historical research is one of several types of research which are introducing extraorganizational variables into the development of administrative theory.

An even richer lode for extraorganizational variables is the research in the politics of education. Bailey (1962) studied the Northeastern states to determine how schoolmen organized to influence state legislatures. Masters and others (1964) did a similar study in three central states. These studies presented several hypotheses which should be rigorously tested. Iannaccone (1967) summarized both his own work and the work of his students in a seminal volume. His is the most theoretical work of the three to date. Masters and Pettit (1966) noted changes in the way in which educational policies are being made. Variables at both the state and the local levels have been isolated which must be considered in future theory building.

Dye's study (1967) is an interesting exploration of a number of economic, political, social, and professional variables and their relation to educational outcomes. He reported that socioeconomic variables account for most of the variance among the states in educational policies. As a result of his study Dye warns against making simple generalizations about the policy consequences of political variables. They are apparently much less significant than political scientists have believed.

THE PRESENT CONDITION. Griffiths (1968) has attempted to assess the state of affairs in administration as of 1966. He pointed out that there had been little formal theory construction in educational administration since Halpin's 1958 study. Two books, by Graff and others (1966) and by Saunders and others (1966), have titles which appear to be presentations of theory but which do not fall within the definition given above. A third, by Halpin (1966), is a collection of previously published papers. Griffiths quoted the Trow review (1959) of the theories presented in Halpin. Trow was critical of the lack of theoretically guided research, the lack of empirical study of substantive problems, and the lack of discovery and interrelation of empirical uniformities. In other words, he deplored the lack of theorizing, the work that should precede the construction of formal theory. Griffiths documented the fact that numerous studies now under way or recently completed are of the theorizing variety and that they are not subject to the valid criticisms of Trow. It is probably a fair appraisal of the field to state that while theory building has declined, the work necessary for theory building in the future is under way. Of particular note are the studies by Iannaccone (1967), Carlson

(1965, and in Griffiths, 1964), and Bridges (1967). These illustrate the careful work under way in concept development and in the testing of relationships among concepts. Formal theory building may well begin anew when the knowledge built through theorizing reaches the critical mass.

Recent years have seen the introduction of a new set of problems which need to be described and explained by administrative theorists. This is the arena of collective negotiations with teachers. Two texts have been published, one by Stinnett and others (1966) and one by Lieberman and Moskow (1966). These are a good start for the literature of collective negotiations but do little to build a theory base. Two volumes which contain several theoretical papers have also appeared, by Lutz and Azzarelli (1966) and by Lutz and others (1967). Lutz's paper, in the second volume, on a bureaucratic theory of grievance resolution offers some interesting leads to hypothesizing in this area. Evans (1966) was the first to gather data to test hypotheses concerning collective-negotiations behavior. Corwin (1965) reported research data relevant to understanding why teachers are becoming more militant.

A major methodological problem is now becoming apparent. Walton (1955) set in motion a powerful trend when he suggested that administration students in education should look to other fields for models. The influx of behavioral scientists into education further accentuated the idea that educational theorists should use the substance of sociology, psychology, anthropology, and studies done in business, industrial, military, and governmental settings. Griffiths and others (1965), however, found that it was not possible to use, without serious modification, the typology of members of large organizations developed by Presthus (1962). As a result they warned against the uncritical transfer of content from the behavioral sciences and studies of noneducational organizations to educational administration. Dye (1967) issued a warning against the use of generalizations about political variables. Both Lipham (1964) and Erickson (1967) warned against the use of instruments which lack veridicality, which may be another way of stating the problem raised by Griffiths. If instruments have been developed from research done on informal small groups (as many have), they may well lack validity for use in school districts.

In spite of difficulties noted throughout this paper it would be highly improper to close on a note of pessimism. The condition of the theoretical study of educational administration has never been better. Interest in research is at an all-time high. The basic work which leads to sound theory is being done, and the future is bright indeed.

Daniel E. Griffiths
New York University

References

Abbott, Max G. "Values and Value Perceptions in Superintendent-School Board Relationships." *Administrator's Notebook* 9:4; 1960.

Anderson, James G. "Bureaucratic Rules: Bearers of Organizational Authority." *Ed Adm Q* 2:7–31; 1960.

Bailey, Stephen K. *Schoolmen and Politics.* Syracuse U Press, 1962. 111p.

Barnard, Chester I. *The Functions of the Executive.* Harvard U Press, 1938. 334p.

Bell, Dennis D. "Superintendents' Perceptions of the Effectiveness of Their Administrative Organizations." Doctoral dissertation. Ohio State U, 1965.

Bidwell, Charles E. "The Administrative Role and Satisfaction in Teaching." *J Ed Sociol* 29:41–7; 1955.

Bidwell, Charles E. "Administration and Teacher Satisfaction." *Phi Delta Kappan* 37:285–8; 1956.

Bidwell, Charles E. "Some Effects of Administrative Behavior: A Study in Role Theory." *Adm Sch Q* 2:163–81; 1957.

Bloom, Benjamin S. "Stability and Change in Human Characteristics: Implications for School Reorganization." *Ed Adm Q* 2:35–49; 1966.

Boerrigter, Glenn C., and Williams, Jeanne. *School Administration Research.* USOE, 1966.

Bowman, Thomas R. "Participation of Superintendents in School Board Decision Making." *Administrator's Notebook* 11:5; 1963.

Bridges, Edwin M. "Teacher Participation in Decision Making." *Administrator's Notebook* 12:9; 1964.

Bridges, Edwin M. "Bureaucratic Role and Socialization: The Influence of Experience on the Elementary Principal." *Ed Adm Q* 1:19–28; 1965.

Bridges, Edwin M. "A Model for Shared Decision Making in the School Principalship." *Ed Adm Q* 3:49–61; 1967.

Briner, Conrad, and Iannaccone, Laurence. "Selected Power Relationships in Education." *Ed Adm Q* 2:190–203; 1966.

Brookover, W. B. "Research on Teacher and Administrator Roles." *J Ed Sociol* 29:2–13; 1955.

Brown, Alan F. "How Administrators View Teachers." *Canadian Ed Res Digest* 6:34–52; 1966(*a*).

Brown, Alan F. "A Perceptual Taxonomy of the Effective-rated Teacher." *J Exp Ed* 35:1–10; 1966(*b*).

Brown, Alan F. "Reactions to Leadership." *Ed Adm Q* 3:62–73; 1967.

Callahan, Raymond E. *Education and the Cult of Efficiency.* U Chicago Press, 1962. 273p.

Callahan, Raymond E. *Changing Conceptions of the Superintendency of Public Instruction, 1865–1964.* New England School Development Council, 1964. 32p.

Campbell, Roald F., and Faber, Charles F. "Administrative Behavior: Theory and Research." *R Ed Res* 31:352–67; 1961.

Campbell, Roald F., and Gregg, Russell T. (Eds.) *Administrative Behavior in Education.* Harper, 1957. 547p.

Campbell, W. J. "School Size: Its Influence on Pupils." *J Ed Adm* 3:3–17; 1965.

Carlson, Richard O. *Adoption of Educational Innovation.* Center for the Advanced Study of Educational Administration, 1965. 84p.

Charters, W. W., Jr. *Teacher Perceptions of Administrator Behavior.* Cooperative Research Project No. 929. USOE, 1964. 205p.

Chase, Francis, and Guba, Egon. "Administrative Roles and Behavior." *R Ed Res* 25:281–98; 1955.

Coladarci, Arthur P., and Getzels, Jacob W. *The Use of Theory in Educational Administration.* Stanford U Press, 1955. 28p.

Corwin, Ronald G. "Professional Persons in Public Organizations." *Ed Adm Q* 1:1–22; 1965.

Cubberly, Ellwood P. *Public School Administration.* Houghton, 1916.

Davies, Daniel R., and Iannaccone, Laurence. "Ferment in the Study of Organization." *Teach Col Rec* 60:61–72; 1958.

Dye, Thomas R. "Politics, Economics, and Educational Outcomes in the States." *Ed Adm Q* 3:28–48; 1967.

Erickson, Donald A. "Essay Review: Some Misgivings Concerning a Study of Leadership." *Ed Adm Q* 1:52–9; 1965.

Erickson, Donald A. "The School Administrator." *R Ed Res* 37:417–32; 1967.

Evans, Seymour. "Toward a Theory of Teacher Collective Organizational Behavior." Doctoral dissertation. New York U, 1966.

Eye, Glen G., and others. *Relationship Between Instructional Change and the Extent to Which School Administrators and Teachers Agree on the Location of Responsibilities for Administrative Decisions.* Cooperative Research Project No. 5–0443. USOE, 1966. 240p.

Faber, Charles F. "The Size of a School District." *Phi Delta Kappan* 48:33–5; 1966.

Feigl, Herbert. "Principles and Problems of Theory Construction in Psychology." In *Current Trends in Psychological Theory.* U Pittsburgh Press, 1951.

Fogarty, Bryce M., and Gregg, Russell T. "Centralization of Decision Making and Selected Characteristics of Superintendents of Schools." *Ed Adm Q* 2:62–71; 1966.

Getzels, Jacob W. "A Psycho-sociological Framework for the Study of Educational Administration." *Harvard Ed R* 22:235–46; 1952.

Getzels, Jacob W., and Guba, Egon G. "Role, Role Conflict, and Effectiveness: An Emperical Study." *Am Sociol R* 19:1964–75; 1954.

Getzels, Jacob W., and Guba, Egon G. "Role Conflict and Personality." *J Pers* 24:74–86; 1955(a).

Getzels, Jacob W., and Guba, Egon G. "The Structure of Roles and Role Conflict in the Teaching Situation." *J Ed Sociol* 29:30–40; 1955(b).

Graff, Orin B., and others. *Philosophic Theory and Practice in Educational Administration.* Wadsworth Publishing Co., Inc., 1966. 314p.

Griffiths, Daniel E. *Administrative Theory.* Appleton, 1959(a). 124p.

Griffiths, Daniel E. *Research in Educational Administration.* Teachers College, Columbia University, 1959(b). 59p.

Griffiths, Daniel E. *The School Superintendent.* Center for Applied Research in Education, 1966. 115p.

Griffiths, Daniel E. "Theory in Educational Administration: 1966." In Baron, George, and others. (Eds.) *Educational Administration: International Perspectives.* Rand McNally, 1968.

Griffiths, Daniel E., and Iannaccone, Laurence. "Administrative Theory, Relationships, and Preparation." *R Ed Res* 28:334–57; 1958.

Griffiths, Daniel E., and others. *Organizing Schools for Effective Education.* Interstate, 1962. 338p.

Griffiths, Daniel E., and others. "Teacher Mobility in New York City." *Ed Adm Q* 1:15–31; 1965.

Griffiths, Daniel W. (Ed.) *Behavioral Science and Educational Administration.* 63rd Yearbook, NSSE. U Chicago Press, 1964. 360p.

Gross, Neal. *Who Runs Our Schools?* Wiley, 1958. 195p.

Gross, Neal, and Herriott, Robert E. *Staff Leadership in Public Schools: A Sociological Inquiry.* Wiley, 1965. 247p.

Gross, Neal, and Mason, Ward S. "Some Methodological Problems of Eight Hour Interviews." *Am J Sociol* 59:197–204; 1953.

Gross, Neal, and Trask, Anne E. *Men and Women as Elementary School Principals.* Cooperative Research Project No. 853. USOE, 1964. 389p.

Gross, Neal, and others. *Explorations in Role Analysis.* Wiley, 1958. 379p.

Halpin, Andrew W. *Studies in Aircrew Composition.* III: *The Combat Leader Behavior of B-29 Aircraft Commanders* HFORL Memo. No. TN-54-7. 1953.

Halpin, Andrew W. "The Leader Behavior and Leadership Ideology of Educational Administrators and Aircraft Commanders." *Harvard Ed R* 25:19–32; 1955.

Halpin, Andrew W. "The Behavior of Leaders." *Ed Leadership* 14:172–6; 1956.

Halpin, Andrew W. (Ed.) *Administrative Theory in Education.* Midwest Administrative Center, 1958. 188p.

Halpin, Andrew W. *Theory and Research in Administration.* Macmillan, 1966. 352p.

Halpin, Andrew W., and Croft, Don B. *The Organizational Climate of Schools.* Midwest Administrative Center, 1963. 130p.

Halpin, Andrew W., and Winer, B. J. *The Leadership Behavior of the Airplane Commander.* Ohio State U Press, 1952.

Heathers, Glenn. *Organizing Schools Through the Dual Progress Plan.* Interstate, 1967. 228p.

Hemphill, John K. "Leadership Behavior Associated with the Administrative Reputation of College Department." *J Ed Psych* 46:385–401; 1955.

Hemphill, John K., and Coons, Alvin E. *Leader Behavior Description*. Ohio State U Press, 1950.

Hemphill, John K., and others. *Administrative Performance and Personality*. Teachers College, Columbia U, 1962. 432p.

Hencley, Stephen P. "The Conflict Patterns of School Superintendents." *Administrator's Notebook* 7:9; 1960.

Hills, R. Jean. "The Representative Function: Neglected Dimension of Leadership Behavior." *Adm Sci Q* 4:83-93; 1959.

Hills, R. Jean. "A New Concept of Staff Relations." *Administrator's Notebook* 8:7; 1960.

Iannaccone, Laurence. *Politics in Education*. Center for Applied Research in Education, 1967. 112p.

Kahn, R. L., and others. *Organizational Stress*. Wiley, 1964.

Kelley, Charles R. "Toward an Interpretation of the New Movement of 1915 in Educational Administration." Doctoral dissertation. Teachers College, Columbia U, 1961. 252p.

Kimbrough, Ralph B. *Political Power and Educational Decision Making*. Rand McNally, 1964. 307p.

Lehto, Paul N. "Span of Control: A Critical Review and Some New Considerations." Doctoral dissertation. Michigan State U, 1966.

Lieberman, Myron, and Moskow, Michael H. *Collective Negotiations for Teachers*. Rand McNally, 1966. 745p.

Lipham, James M. "Personal Variables of Effective Administrators." *Administrator's Notebook* 9:1; 1960.

Lipham, James M. "Organizational Charactor of Education: Administrative Behavior." *R Ed Res* 34: 435-54; 1964.

Lutz, Frank, and Azzarelli, Joseph J. *Struggle for Power in Education*. Center for Applied Research in Education, 1966. 120p.

Lutz, Frank, and others. *Grievances and Their Resolution*. Interstate, 1967. 108p.

March, James G. (Ed.) *Handbook of Organizations*. Rand McNally, 1965. 1247p.

Masters, Nicholas A., and Pettit, Lawrence K. "Some Changing Patterns in Educational Policy Making." *Ed Adm Q* 2:81-100; 1966.

Masters, Nicholas A., and others. *State Politics and the Public Schools: An Exploratory Analysis*. Knopf, 1964. 319p.

Moore, Hollis A., Jr. *Studies in School Administration*. AASA, 1957. 202p.

Mort, Paul R. *Principles of School Administration*. McGraw-Hill, 1946. 388p.

Mort, Paul R., and Ross, Donald H. *Principles of School Administration*, rev. ed. McGraw-Hill, 1957. 451p.

Panttaja, Leon A. "Subordinates' Perceptions of the Decision-making Behavior of Their Chief Administrator." Doctoral dissertation. U Southern California, 1966.

Powers, Thomas E. "Administrative Behavior and Upward Mobility." *Administrator's Notebook* 15:1; 1966.

Presthus, Robert. *The Organizational Society*. Knopf, 1962. 323p.

Pugh, D. S. "Modern Organizational Theory: A Psychological and Sociological Study." *Psychol B* 66:235-51; 1966.

Saunders, Robert L., and others. *A Theory of Educational Leadership*. Charles E. Merrill, Inc., 1966. 174p.

Sears, Jesse B. *The Nature of the Administrative Process*. McGraw-Hill, 1950. 623p.

Simon, Herbert A. *Administrative Behavior*. Macmillan, 1950. 259p.

Stinnett, T. M., and others. *Professional Negotiation in Public Education*. Macmillan, 1966.

Stogdill, Ralph M. *Individual Behavior and Group Achievement*, Oxford U Press, 1959.

Stogdill, Ralph M. *Manual for the Leader Behavior Description Questionnaire-Form XII*. Ohio State U Press, 1963.

Thomas, Lawrence F. "An Analysis of the Instructional Leadership of the Secondary School Principal in the Decision-making Process." Doctoral dissertation. U Arizona, 1963. 157p.

Trow, Martin. "Administrative Theory in Educational Administration." *Adm Sc Q* 4:122-6; 1959.

Walton, John. "The Theoretical Study of Educational Administration." *Harvard Ed R* 25:169-78; 1955.

Willower, Donald J. "Leadership Styles and Leaders' Perceptions of Subordinates." *J Ed Sociol* 34:58-64; 1960.

Ziegler, Walter J. "The Bases and Process for Decision-making by the Superintendent of Schools." Doctoral dissertation. U Southern California, 1964. 301p.

ADMISSIONS—COLLEGE AND UNIVERSITY

THE NATURE AND SCOPE OF THE ADMISSIONS PROCESS. In a report on university admissions in the world at large, Frank Bowles (1963) has suggested that the admissions process can be regarded as a "series of selections" that begins in the primary grades and continues into graduate and professional school. It is a process that has large consequences for the careers of individuals and for the character of the society of which those individuals are a part. The selections may be deliberate decisions by parents, students, and institutions, or they may be the result of social, cultural, and economic forces outside the range of individual human choice. The manner in which an admission system operates is thus partly a product and partly a determinant of these forces. It has three principal focuses: the transition from secondary school to college, the transition from college to college, and the transition from college to graduate school. What happens at these points can have a profound influence on the educational systems in which they occur.

Transition from Secondary School to College. In most countries educational systems are so structured that the main determination of whether or where a student goes to college is made upon entry into secondary school. The English grammar school, the French lycée, and the German gymnasium, for example, are highly selective schools, and whether a student is successful in getting admitted to one of them largely determines whether he can eventually become a candidate for one of the universities. The same general pattern holds for most educational systems outside the United States.

The typical American college candidate, on the other hand, goes to a nonselective public high school, and the main determination of which college he will enter, or whether he will go to college at all, does not usually take place until his secondary-school studies are almost over. He may get a certain amount of guidance about college plans in the early years of high school, and he may elect a pattern of courses labeled "college preparatory," but the critical decisions that will carry him into some form of postsecondary education are usually not made until he is about ready to graduate. In his last year of high school a student may or may not undergo a formal screening for college, depending on whether the requirements of the colleges at which he applies are nominal or based upon specific academic requirements, possibly buttressed by entrance examinations (West, 1965).

American high schools and colleges have great freedom in designing the courses they offer, and American students have a large measure of freedom in choosing the courses they take and the colleges they enter. This freedom to choose and the concomitant diversity among high schools and colleges are perhaps the salient characteristics of college admissions in the United States. They are characteristics that pose special problems for both secondary schools and colleges in the organization of curricula and of programs for the educational guidance and placement of students.

The role of the secondary school in this situation consists of three kinds of tasks: (1) providing probable college candidates with programs of study that will lead into college work at whatever college the student may finally elect to enter, (2) giving the student guidance in the choice of particular courses and in deciding on colleges at which to apply, and (3) handling a variety of administrative details involved in transmitting needed information to candidates about colleges and to colleges about candidates. Schools vary widely in their performance of these tasks, depending on their resources, the quality of their staffs, the expectations of students and parents, the size of the enrollment, and a number of community factors, such as the presence or absence in the community of a college or university.

The impact of this combination of factors on the flow of candidates into colleges is not well understood. High schools in isolated and depressed areas, where resources are severely limited, send a very small percentage of their students on to college; independent schools and public schools in affluent suburbs send nearly all of their students on to college. Thus far, no study has successfully disentangled all the factors in the school, the community, and the students themselves that account for these differences.

The part played by the colleges in the transition process varies widely from one college to another. Much of this variability is a function of the degree to which colleges are or can be selective. Hawes (1966) places all the colleges in the United States in four categories according to the degree to which they are selective in admissions. In the top category are colleges with "highly competitive" admissions. These are the colleges that, because of a surplus of applicants, customarily reject many who have superior high school records. In the bottom category are the colleges with "open-admission" policies; they accept practically any applicant who can submit a high school diploma. In his 1965–66 survey of 2,960 colleges, Hawes found them about evenly distributed among the four categories. Other factors that help to determine how a college handles admissions are its size and location, the nature of its offerings, its traditions and resources, and, probably most importantly, the form of its support and control.

In most colleges the admissions process extends beyond the actual matriculation of the entering class and includes procedures for steering freshmen into the courses best suited to their interests and level of preparation. Because of the diversity of secondary schools from which the students come, the considerable amount of discontinuity between high school and college curricula, and the heterogeneity in the abilities, interests, and preparation of the entering class, the problem of initial academic adjustment is usually severe. The success with which colleges deal with the problem varies according to the flexibility and variety of their freshman course offerings, the adequacy of their course placement procedures, and the effectiveness of their counseling services. The heavy attrition certain colleges experience in the freshman year may be attributed in part at least to failures to cope with this problem of the initial adjustment of entering freshmen.

Admission by Transfer. The practice of transferring from college to college is rooted in a tradition that goes back to the Middle Ages, when it was commonplace for wandering scholars to go from one university to another in order to study under the great lecturers of their time. Nowadays, in the United States, the motivations for similar student wanderings are, to say the least, usually different from those of the medieval scholar, and considerably more various (Gummere, 1961). The reasons underlying the mobility of the American college student grow out of complex personal, social, academic, and economic considerations (Iffert, 1958).

Perhaps the largest single element in the transfer situation is that which has been occasioned by the rise of two-year colleges—the junior and community colleges and technical institutes. These colleges perform three functions in the "series of selections" that constitute the admissions process. They provide a form of terminal postsecondary education for those who, for a variety of reasons, are unable or unwilling to enter four-year colleges upon completion of secondary school. For many students they serve as a stepping-stone into a four-year college. And for a significant proportion of the entire college-bound population, they are, in effect, a device for sorting out those who will continue toward the bachelor's degree from those who will not. The majority of students entering junior colleges do so with the intention of subsequently transferring to a senior college even though only a minority of them actually do so (Knoell & Medsker, 1965).

The problems surrounding the admission of students by transfer are not unlike those that accompany the transition from secondary school to college—problems in guidance, in articulation of curricula, in exchange of information, and in getting the student properly placed once he arrives on the new campus. In the case of transfers, however, the problem is further complicated by the necessity for evaluating the student's previous record in order to determine how much of it can be credited toward the degree. The variety of institutions from which transfer students come and the variety of credit-granting practices in the institutions to which they go tends to make this aspect of admission by transfer the most vexing part of the operation for students and colleges alike (Holmes, 1961; Wise & Gummere, 1962; Knoell & Medsker, 1965).

Admission to Graduate and Professional Schools. In 1965 the proportion of the age group 14 to 18 in American secondary schools was 93 percent; the proportion of the age group 18 to 21 attending college was 35 percent; and the proportion 23 years old and up that was in some form of graduate education was 3 percent. The ratios of these percentages, if taken successively, are 1 to 3 and 1 to 10, respectively; they give a rough idea of the sharp increase in selectivity as one moves up the academic ladder of the American educational system. It is important to remember, however, that the selective factors operating in the system include many that have nothing to do with academic requirements or the abilities of candidates. The difference between the proportions engaged in undergraduate and graduate study can be accounted for in large part by the availability of funds, by the aspirations and interests of students, and by the limited number of graduate-level institutions.

Nevertheless, there is hardly a doubt that, on balance, the characteristic that most sharply distinguishes graduate from undergraduate admissions is the greater insistence by the former on the meeting of specific academic prerequisites. This is true of both the professional graduate schools—law, medicine, education, theology, and the like—and the graduate schools of arts and sciences. The degree of specificity of requirements varies from school to school and from field to field. Medical schools, for instance, generally require satisfactory work in certain undergraduate science courses. Law schools, on the other hand, usually pay little attention to the specifics of the undergraduate record, only to its overall quality.

Another characteristic that distinguishes graduate from undergraduate admissions is the prevalence of two levels of graduate degrees: the master of arts and the doctor of philosophy, for instance, or the bachelor of laws and the doctor of jurisprudence, or the master of arts in teaching and the doctor of education. The field of medicine is the major exception to this rule. In some fields—engineering, business, and law, for example—the first graduate degree is, for most students, the final degree; in other fields—the sciences and humanities, for example—the tendency is to take the master's degree en route to the Ph.D. These differences in the patterns of study affect the admissions process in two ways: they determine the number of hurdles the candidate will have to clear before settling into his final degree program; and in certain fields, they may generate a considerable amount of interinstitutional mobility among aspirants for the doctorate. In education, for instance, a candidate for the Ph.D. may well have received a master's degree in education at an institution different from the one at which he is studying for the doctorate.

A third characteristic of graduate admissions is the timing of student decisions to enter graduate study. Candidates for medical schools, for instance, generally make up their minds well before receiving the bachelor's degree, while Ph.D. candidates tend to postpone the decision until after they have finished college (Berelson, 1960).

Within a single complex university with a number of different graduate schools the problem of administering the variety of rules and regulations for admission which have been promulgated by the several faculties and departments can become extremely complicated. And the complications can be further increased, in some fields, by the intense competition among candidates for the most remunerative fellowships.

The Role of Accreditation and Educational Associations. The extent to which both students and institutions have traditionally been given freedom of choice in the admissions process has always been, and continues to be, a threat to the viability of the system. It is precisely this sort of threat that, over the years, has brought into being a number of state, regional, and national mechanisms having as their purpose the promotion of orderly relations between secondary schools and colleges. Probably the earliest effort in this direction was the development of the New York Regents Examination system, which was inaugurated in 1865 to ensure that entrants into secondary school were of potential college caliber and which later became a means for defining and setting standards for college preparatory courses throughout the state (University of the State of New York, 1964; Tinkelman, 1965).

The state of California has followed a different system for regularizing the college preparatory curriculum. There the State University prescribes in detail the patterns of study to be followed and the level of performance to be attained in terms of the grades assigned by the schools. The university admits automatically any student whose record shows he has obtained the required grades in the required courses (University of California at Berkeley, 1966). Students failing to meet these requirements may be admitted to the California state colleges or the junior colleges.

A third pattern for maintaining standards of college preparatory study is found in the operations of the North Central Association, which embraces the schools and colleges of 19 states in the Middle West. Among its many activities, the North Central Association accredits secondary schools after evaluating their academic programs, facilities, teacher preparation, and the like (North Central Association . . ., 1965–66), and admission to most colleges in the Middle West has depended primarily on whether the candidate has graduated from a school so accredited. Thus, for purposes of college admission, the focus here has been more on establishing the credentials of the school that is preparing candidates than on assessing the credentials of the candidates themselves.

Perhaps the most clear-cut response to the threat of chaos in college admissions was the establishment of the College Entrance Examination Board (CEEB) in 1900 (Fuess, 1950). This organization, now national in scope and purpose, was originally an offshoot of the Association of Colleges and Secondary Schools of the Middle States and Maryland. Each of the old-line colleges in the Northeast at that time had tended to set its own requirements and administer its own examinations for admission without regard for the requirements and examinations of other colleges. As a result, the secondary schools were faced with an impossible problem in providing curricula suited to the needs of students heading for different colleges. What the CEEB provided, in its early days, was a common definition of course requirements and a common set of entrance examinations based upon them and administered according to a single schedule throughout the country.

These common requirements and examinations were abandoned at the beginning of World War II as the CEEB's membership expanded to include colleges in all parts of the nation. They have been replaced by the CEEB's *Scholastic Aptitude Test* and a battery of largely objective achievement tests which purport to avoid putting any constraints on secondary school curricula. This move toward greater flexibility, however, has generated countermoves toward closer articulation of school-college curricula nationally. One such move, aimed at reducing the waste motion and loss of time of gifted students, was contained in the Blackmer Report (Blackmer & others, 1952). This report recommended a plan by which such students could anticipate college-level work in high school by taking prescribed courses and being examined on them. The recommended plan, known as the Advanced Placement Program, was sponsored by the CEEB in 1955 and is now an established feature of the admissions process (College Entrance Examination Board, 1966a). The CEEB is now proposing additional measures to close still further the curricular gaps that exist nationally between grades 12 and 13 (Pearson, 1966a, 1966b).

Although there are a number of associations concerned with graduate and professional education— the Council of Graduate Schools, the Association of American Medical Colleges, and the like—these associations have thus far developed no comparable concern for the regulation of graduate-school admissions, though some ground rules have been established for the handling of graduate fellowships.

The Role of Student Financial Aid. Although Americans have long accepted the idea that elementary and secondary education should be tuition-free as a matter of right, they have traditionally expected students to pay for the privilege of a college education. This tradition has been a barrier to higher education for many academically qualified students who could not pay their own way. In recent years there have been increasing efforts to remedy the situation by aiding needy students with scholarships, loans, and jobs from private and public funds (Moon, 1963; Haven & Smith, 1965). The state system in California and the colleges in the City University of New York have been tuition-free for some time. New York and other states have generous scholarship programs that have the effect of essentially cancelling tuition in state institutions for students who cannot afford to pay. Despite these developments to remove the financial barrier, however, the present writer has elsewhere estimated that, nationwide, the total cash currently available from all forms of financial aid— jobs, loans, and scholarships, both publicly and privately underwritten—pays only one-tenth of the amount actually billed to enrolled students each year (Dyer, 1966).

It has been argued in some quarters that lack of money has never constituted the most serious barrier to higher education. The claim has been made that any student with a sufficiently strong desire for a college education could find some way to finance it, and the principal drawback in the case of the potential students who have never arrived in college has been the low level of parental expectation and lack of motivation on the part of the students themselves (Stouffer, 1955, 1960; Havighurst & Neugarten, 1962; Gordon, 1965). The evidence for this position is strong, but the level of financial strength of a family over the period when the children are growing up may itself be, at least in part, determinative of the educational aspirations that are conveyed to their children. A family history of limited means may have much to do with the habitual motivations that adolescents carry into adult life.

The Nature of Admissions Research. It should be apparent from the foregoing that the processes by which students move into and through college and into graduate schools of various kinds are enormously complex and that they vary from one country to another and, within the United States, from one region or one state to another. It is for this reason that research on the process of college and university admissions takes—and has taken—many different forms. It may focus on the social implications and effects of the process, on its economics, on its impact on individuals and institutions, on the operational problems it entails, and on the very practical problems of picking the "right" college for a student and the "right" students for a college. In short, college and university admissions, like any phenomenon involving great masses of human beings, have many frames of reference within which they can be studied. It is important for their full understanding that no one of these frames of reference be neglected.

THE DEMOGRAPHIC CHARACTERISTICS OF ADMISSIONS. The first comprehensive attempt to bring together worldwide data on the demographic characteristics of admissions was made by Bowles (1963). In 1959, according to his estimates, the world enrollment in all forms of education stood slightly over 400 million, which was about 35 percent of the total school-age population 5 to 24 years old. Of the 400 million, less than 3 percent were in institutions of higher education. These numbers, however, represent very considerable increases for the decade 1950–1959. While the school-age population of the world was increasing 16 percent, enrollments at all educational levels went up 61 percent, and enrollment in higher education went up 71 percent.

Using Bowles's estimates and data from the U.S. Census for 1960 one can compare the severity of educational selection in the world at large with its severity in the American system (Table 1). Table 1 highlights the fact that, despite some changes in the situation since 1950, the selective processes come into play at much earlier ages and far more rigorously in other parts of the world than they do in the American system.

The Flow of the American Student Population. Although statistics on college and university admissions are notoriously inadequate and untrustworthy for a number of reasons, it is nevertheless possible, by drawing on different sources, to piece together in some detail a reasonable picture of the flow of the American student population through the educational system from elementary school to graduate school.

Of the total number of American children who entered the fifth grade in 1956, 36 percent entered college in 1964 by normal progression through the system (U.S. Bureau of the Census, 1965). Of those

TABLE 1

WORLD AND U.S. SCHOOL ENROLLMENTS EXPRESSED AS PERCENTAGES OF AGE GROUPS

Educational Level	World 1950	U.S. 1950	World 1959	U.S. 1960
Primary	37	93	50	95
Secondary	18	75	27	85
Higher	3	15	5	24

a. Adapted from Bowles (1963), p. 7, and from U.S. Bureau of the Census (1965), p. 106–107. The age groups used for the world percentages are not strictly comparable to those used for the U.S. percentages. For the world they are: primary, 5–14; secondary, 15–19; higher, 20–24. For the United States they are: primary, 5–13; secondary, 14–17; higher, 18–24.

who started the fifth grade in 1942, only 21 percent entered college when their time came in 1950. The jump of 15 percentage points between 1950 and 1964 is accounted for largely by the increased holding power of the schools all the way through the grades. That is, a considerably larger proportion of the later group entered high school (930 per 1,000 versus 807), more got to grade 12 (724 per 1,000 versus 539), and more graduated from high school (667 versus 505).

In 1964, 54 percent of the high school graduates went directly on to some form of college work, compared to only 41 percent of the earlier group. This rate increase probably reflects, to some extent at least, both the greater pulling power of higher education and greater accessibility of its institutions. Jaffe and Adams (1965), however, have shown that, over the period 1880–1950, the percentage of high school graduates who eventually went to college at some time in their lives has stood consistently at 50 percent with only minor fluctuations. Other studies have shown that the number involved in delayed admissions is a significant element in the total picture. A study of the college-going plans of high-aptitude high school students in the middle 1950's showed that approximately 30 percent of the boys and 20 percent of the girls planned to postpone entrance into college for a year or more, while 55 percent of the boys and nearly 50 percent of the girls planned to go to college directly from high school (Stice & others, 1956).

Whatever relative weights one may place on the several factors that have produced the increasing influx of college students—the rise in the birth rate, the greater holding power of precollege education, and the greater accessibility of the colleges—there can be no doubt about the fact of the increase. Since 1950 the college admissions curve has become steadily steeper: 517,000 entered in 1950, 690,000 entered in 1955, 929,800 entered in 1960, 1,453,000 entered in 1965, and conservative projections say that the number of new freshman in 1975 will be something over 3,000,000 (Thompson, 1961; U.S. Office of Education, 1965a). The problems growing out of this massive population shift from school to college each year are somewhat less than they might be because of the fact that four-fifths of the new freshmen go to college in their home states (U.S. Office of Education, 1965a). The export–import balance varies considerably, however, from one state to another. For example, as of 1963 only 57 percent of New Jersey high school graduates went to college in New Jersey. In New York the comparable figure was 79 percent, in Michigan, 89 percent, and in California, 94 percent.

In 1965 the ratio of men to women among the entering students was about 4 to 3; students entering publicly controlled colleges outnumbered those entering privately controlled colleges by a ratio of a little more than 2 to 1; and twice as many students entered four-year institutions as entered two-year institutions. The last ratio is based on published U.S. Office of Education estimates (1965a) adjusted for about 160,000 students entering non-degree-granting programs. With the increasing pressure for technical-vocational training beyond high school and with the rising number of community colleges, the chances are that new enrollments in two-year institutions will increase to the point where they may equal, if not exceed, the numbers entering four-year colleges.

In New England and the Middle Atlantic states the majority of students, by a considerable margin, enter privately controlled colleges. In the middle parts of the country the situation is reversed: about three times as many enter publicly controlled institutions as enter those under private control. In the Far West the public colleges outstrip the private colleges in this respect by more than 8 to 1 (U.S. Office of Education, 1966). This change in the ratios as one moves from East to West reflects historic differences in both academic traditions and admission policies (Rudolph, 1962).

The types of educational programs students enter when they get to college vary widely. According to Flanagan and Cooley (1966) the majority of the men entering colleges of all types over the four-year period 1960–1963 were expecting to major in four fields in order of popularity as follows: business, the natural sciences, engineering, and the social sciences. The majority of women freshmen chose, in order, education, business, English, and the social sciences.

The selective process continues to operate on students who have actually entered college. In a study of a national sample of students entering in 1950, Iffert (1958) found that during or at the end of the first year, 27 percent of those in four-year institutions and 28 percent of those in two-year institutions had left. Iffert's estimate showed slightly under 40 percent getting their degrees four years after entering the freshman class, but this figure does not account for "drop-outs who come back." In a ten-year follow-up study of dropouts at the University of Illinois, Eckland (1964) found that, of 1,952 entrants 21 percent had left by the end of the freshman year, but he also found that over three-fifths of these first-year dropouts picked up their studies again after a year or more, and, for the entering class as a whole, 70 to 75 percent got their degrees at Illinois or elsewhere within the ten-year period.

Gummere in his essay "America's Wandering Scholars" (1961) notes the fact that about one-fifth of the "new" students each year have transferred from one college to another. Wise and Gummere (1962), in a study of the attitudes of college officials to acceptance of transfers, found that the requirements were not overrigorous but that colleges are generally uncomfortable about transfer students—both those they get and those they lose.

In their study of junior-college transfers, Knoell and Medsker (1965) found that, except for the economic condition of their parents, the students transferring into senior colleges from junior colleges were strikingly like the students who had begun their work in the four-year institutions.

They note also, as Wise and Gummere had discovered before them, that an average junior college student—one with at least a C average in his junior college—is not likely to have much trouble finding a four-year college somewhere that will accept him. They further note that the four-year institutions were finding the major problem in the admission of junior-college transfer students to be that of working out with the junior colleges course programs that run reasonably parallel to those in the first two years of the senior college, so as to provide some measure of articulation between the work of the two types of institutions. In their sample, 62 percent of the junior-college transfers got their bachelor's degrees on schedule, and they estimate that 75 percent will eventually get their degrees. These percentages are about the same as those for a comparison group that had completed two years at four-year institutions.

The final major step in the series of selections that constitutes the admissions process occurs at the graduate and professional level. By combining and manipulating data from three different sources (Johnson, 1964; U.S. Office of Education, 1965b; Hervey, 1966) one can put together the rough estimate that 300,000 students entered some form of graduate study in the fall of 1963—9,000 in medicine, 21,000 in law, 270,000 in other fields. This total, very roughly, is 65 percent of the number that graduated from college in that year, 30 percent of the number that entered some sort of postsecondary study four years previously, and 10 percent of the students who entered high school four years before that.

Factors Related to the Flow. Why do some students move out of the educational system at certain points while others continue? There is no easy answer. It is well known that the ability of students, the quality of their performance in secondary school, the economic and educational level of their parents, and their race, their religion, and their sex all have a bearing on where or whether they will go to college (Educational Testing Service, 1957; Havighurst & Neugarten, 1962; Medsker & Trent, 1965). It is also well known that all of these factors are interrelated in complicated ways: ability with economic level with school performance with religion, and so on. These interrelationships, however, can vary from one situation to another depending on the degree of accessibility of higher education to the students involved (Medsker *Plan for Higher Education in Illinois*. The Depart- & Trent, 1965). In short, it is not yet possible to pin down any one factor and assert that, for all kinds and conditions of students, that one factor is, to some ascertainable extent, determinative of their educational careers.

Nevertheless, certain factors stand out. An important one is the degree of availability of higher educational opportunities in the locality where the student lives. The Bowles study (1963) shows how this varies across the world. Data collected by Medsker and Trent (1965) suggest that within the United States the presence or absence of a college in the student's home community is positively related to the proportion of high school graduates in the community who go to college anywhere.

A second factor of major importance is academic ability. According to Havighurst and Neugarten

(1962) 60 percent of the ablest quarter of the adolescent population entered college in 1960, while practically none of those in the lowest quarter did so. An Educational Testing Service survey (1957) found that 75 percent of the boys and 60 percent of the girls who scored among the top 10 percent on a test of academic ability went to college, while only 17 percent of the boys and 14 percent of the girls who scored among the lowest 40 percent did so. Medsker and Trent (1965) show that within ability groups the occupational level of the student's parents makes a great difference in whether the students will go to college. For example, among the ablest two-fifths of their sample the college attendance rate was 87 percent of those with fathers at the highest occupational level, 65 percent for those at the middle level, and 49 percent for those at the lowest level. Among the least able two-fifths, the comparable rates were 63 percent, 32 percent and 27 percent.

A third factor is sex. Whereas the number of boys and the number of girls graduating from high school are about equal (the girls have a small edge), the ratio of boys to girls among college entrants is approximately 3 to 2 (Havighurst & Neugarten, 1962). Even with ability held constant, the same relationship tends to hold (Educational Testing Service, 1957).

Finally, a very powerful factor in college-going is the socioeconomic status of the student's family. In their study of California students, for instance, Sanders and Palmer (1965) show that only 22 percent of all 18-year-olds from families with incomes under $2,000 were in college, compared to 72 percent of those whose family income was $14,000 or over. The educational status of the student's family is also important. The Educational Testing Service study (1957) found that among low-ability boys, the likelihood of going to college was almost three times greater for those whose fathers had been to college than it was for those whose fathers had not gone to college (41 percent as against 14 percent); the same held for low-ability girls (33 percent as against 12 percent). Among high-ability students the ratio for boys was 8 to 5 and for girls 2 to 1.

International Exchange of Students. Relative to the total number of students in higher education, the number studying outside their native country is small but increasing. According to information gathered by the Institute of International Education (1966), approximately 30,000 foreign students entered American colleges and universities in 1965, bringing the total number of such students to over 90,000. This total represents a threefold increase during the preceding ten years. About two-fifths of the students were in graduate or professional schools. The preferred fields of study were, in order: engineering, the humanities, the physical and natural sciences, and the social sciences. Their length of stay in this country is, on the average, about three years. Over three-quarters of the students were men, and about half were from Far Eastern and Latin American countries. Typically, over 150 countries send students to institutions of higher education in the United States.

In 1964–65, 22,000 American students were studying abroad—twice as many as had been doing so in 1954–55. Over half of them were at European universities, and over three-fifths were in the humanities and social sciences.

Although the number of foreign students in American universities is something under 2 percent of the total enrollment, these students tend to be concentrated in relatively few institutions. In 1965, for example, 11 universities enrolled over 1,000 foreign students each, and at 4 institutions the foreign contingent accounted for over 10 percent of the student body.

The acceleration, since World War II, in the international exchange of students has introduced some unfamiliar and peculiarly difficult problems into the admissions process. These problems have become the special concern of such organizations as the Institute of International Education, Education in World Affairs, and the National Association for Foreign Student Affairs. One of the principal needs of these organizations, as is the case with many other aspects of admissions, is more adequate demographic data so that the scope and dimensions of the problems can be better understood.

THE CHOOSING OF INSTITUTIONS BY STUDENTS. One may view the movement of students through the educational system as the outcome of an interplay of demographic variables; or one may view it as a succession of decisions that students make as they move into a career. The latter view, focusing on the choice process itself, has been the concern of a considerable amount of recent theorizing and research (e.g., Ginzberg & others, 1951; Super, 1957; Tiedeman, 1962; Katz, 1963). Katz, for instance, sees the process by which high school students ultimately arrive in college (or in a job) as a sequence of choices that might be regarded as the obverse of the series of selections by which Bowles characterizes the admissions process as a whole. There are two periods when the choices a student makes are crucial: at the beginning of high school and at the end. In the earlier period the student makes *curricular* choices that may considerably reduce his freedom of choice in the later period. If he does not start algebra, for instance, he may foreclose his chances of picking an engineering school later on. In the last years of high school the student makes *institutional* choices which, although not absolutely irrevocable, are nevertheless major factors in determining his field of undergraduate study. Katz takes the position that the kinds of decisions the student makes are products of his value system, which is itself a product of the home, the school, and the community conditions in which he has developed.

Whether to Go to College. Most students appear to have made a fairly firm decision on whether to go to college early in their high school careers. Medsker and Trent (1965) found in a 1959 sample of 4,206 college freshmen in California that 65 percent said they had definitely decided to go to college no later than grade 10. Rossi and Coleman (1964) in a 1957–58 survey of 10,000 northern Illinois students in grades 9 to 13 found that 54 percent of the grade 9 boys and 58 percent of the girls were reasonably certain they would be going to college. Stice and his collaborators (1956) found that in a national sample of high-ability high school sophomores 71 percent of the boys and 60 percent of the girls thought they would eventually get to college. The amount of tentativeness in decisions about college-going for some students, however, may be considerable. Rossi and Coleman (1964) found that 14 percent of the students in their sample changed their minds between fall and spring about whether college should be in their educational plans.

The influence of the student's parents on his decisions to attend college is probably paramount. In all three studies mentioned above, students were asked to indicate how much discussion about college plans they had had with their parents, teachers, counselors, and friends, and in all three the data support the not surprising conclusion that, for most students who are considering college at all, the discussion of the subject most frequently begins and ends in the home. However, the school, also not surprisingly, plays a part in the decision process. Medsker and Trent (1965), for instance, found 90 percent of their college freshman sample recalling that their high school teachers and counselors had "encouraged" them to go to college, but only two-thirds of the same students were willing to admit that the encouragement "influenced" their decision.

The pull of the peer group is also of importance: if most of a student's friends are going to college, he tends to follow suit. The Medsker-Trent data, for instance, showed that 78 percent of the college freshman sample had at least two friends in high school who also went to college, whereas in a noncollege sample the comparable percentage was 58. An interesting additional finding from the same study shows that among the college-going group 70 percent of those in the *lowest* quintile on an academic ability test had close friends in college, while in the noncollege group only 40 percent in the two *top* quintiles had close friends in college.

The vocational motive is a strong determinant in the decision to go to college both in the students themselves and in their parents. Douvan and Kaye (1962), in an intensive study of the students at a single institution, found that the boys in their group tended to think of college primarily as a way to a good job. Girls tended to think of college as not just as a place to find a husband but as an enriching experience that would make them better wives and mothers. In Michigan a survey of the parents of college students found 90 percent mentioning job benefits as a reason for sending their sons to college, and 76 percent mentioned the same reason for daughters (Withey & others, 1959). Thus, insofar as college-going is concerned, the aspirations of students, contrary to popular mythology, tend to coincide with the aspirations their parents have for them.

Which College to Attend. For most students, whether they realize it or not, the choosing of a particular college to attend is far more difficult than simply deciding whether to keep going beyond grade 12. The difficulty has three elements. One is the enormous variety of postsecondary educational opportunities open to the American high school student. A second is the scarcity of adequate ways of describing and communicating to the student those characteristics of colleges that will enable him to form a realistic picture of what he will find there and how it will affect him. The third is the problem the student has of getting an objective view of himself and what he wants out of life and trying to relate this view to the opportunities available.

Data on how well students cope with these difficulties are scarce. Rossi and Coleman (1964) suggest that the "images" students have of colleges change very little from the time they enter high school to the time they enter college. Thus, even though during his high school years a student may accumulate a considerable amount of information about colleges from reading their literature, visiting their campuses, and talking with their representatives, the stereotypes of colleges formed by grade 9 tend to be the same stereotypes the student carries around in his head at grade 12. The Rossi-Coleman data also suggest that for a good many students any correspondence between the images they have of themselves and the images of the colleges they hope to attend are hardly more than coincidental. For example, quite a few of the students in their northern Illinois sample who were aiming at Ivy League colleges in the East tended to see these colleges as emphasizing intellectual demands but saw themselves *not* as "brilliant students" but as socially "most popular" types. This sort of logical disjunction turns up in other forms among other college candidates. Flanagan and Cooley (1966) present data which suggest a similar disjunction between a student's career plans and his choice of college. They found, for instance, that even in grade 12 the number of boys who thought they would become engineers was far greater than the number that could ever reasonably expect to get into an engineering school.

The factors that become involved in choosing which college to attend are about the same as those that seem to bear on whether the student chooses to go to college at all. Parental educational backgrounds, the quality and amount of reading that goes on in the home, the socioeconomic status of the family, the family's religion, the presence or absence of different types of colleges in the home community, the level of the student's academic performance in secondary school, the size of the school he attends, distance from home, cost, and scholarship opportunities—all such matters enter into the choosing of the particular college, or the particular type of college, a student finally decides to enter.

The many subtleties in the choice process, and how they operate in various types of students, remain to be studied. For many students whose parents went to college, there is undoubtedly a tendency to give more than a passing thought to following in the parental tradition by going to the same place. A student who has made an outstanding record in athletics is not likely to go unnoticed by coaches and alumni in search of athletic talent. The chance of making a particular fraternity in a particular college may be decisive. The stream of college literature, films, and recruiters moving through the high schools is probably also not without some effect on some students. In view of the many influences playing upon the student, exceptional strength of mind would seem to be required of him if he is to stay in charge of his own college choices rather than be pushed by a thousand external pressures into choices that are not really his own.

The Question of Going Beyond the Baccalaureate. After a student arrives in college, his decision process takes on new dimensions. Gropper and Fitzpatrick (1959) surveyed a national sample of 2,037 graduate students and of 1,544 college seniors judged by their professors to be of graduate-school caliber. They found a strong contrast between the reasons their students gave for going to college and for going to graduate school: in the decision to go to college the modal influence was the home; in the decision to go to graduate school, the modal influence was the furtherance of specific vocational objectives already formed in college. Among the group of able college seniors who had decided not to attend graduate school, the reason most frequently given was lack of any real interest or sense of need for further education (52 percent); another 34 percent ascribed their discontinuance to lack of the necessary ability or money to see them through. The reason students most frequently gave for choosing a particular graduate school had to do with its academic quality. Financial considerations came second, and the nature of the university environment came third.

The time at which students in the Gropper-Fitzpatrick sample decided to go on to graduate study seemed to depend on what field the student was interested in. Forty-six percent of those going to law school had made up their minds to do so before the end of the sophomore year in college; only 21 percent heading for the academic fields of graduate study had similarly decided. Berelson (1960) found the contrast still more striking: most medical-school students had made the choice about graduate education *before* they got to college; most law-school students had made it *during* college; and most Ph.D. candidates made it *after* they got the bachelor's degree. Astin (1965) has data based on a sample of 248 colleges which confirm the same trends.

According to Berelson, the decision to undertake study toward the Ph.D. is considerably less affected by the socioeconomic status of the student's family than is true of students looking toward law and medicine. He estimates that 50 percent of the Ph.D. students, 75 percent of the law students, and 67 percent of the medical students come from upper-middle-class and upper-class families. Law-school and medical-school students are more often than Ph.D. candidates motivated by job considerations. One factor that does *not* operate strongly in the choice of graduate school is that of distance from home: only 25 percent of graduate students, in contrast to 80 percent of undergraduates, are enrolled at institutions in the same state where they attended high school.

Generally speaking, a student makes up his own mind about whether and where to do graduate work. The college experience is one in which he experiments to discover the field in which he wants to spend his later life (Iffert, 1958; Beardslee & O'Dowd, 1962), and his decision with respect to further study relates largely to how the experiment turns out. There may be a sex difference in this matter, however: a larger percentage of women than of men in the Gropper-Fitzpatrick survey attributed their decision to go on with graduate study to educational experiences in college. Family influence is minimal. Few students in medicine and law are following in the footsteps of their fathers, and even fewer professorial fathers have children planning on Ph.D.'s (Berelson, 1960).

Aids to the Choice Process. As noted above, one of the main difficulties for the student in choosing a college or graduate school is the lack of usable information about them. In recent years there have been attempts to remedy this deficiency. The effort has taken three principal forms: (1) the production of handbooks describing the surface characteristics of institutions with possibly some inferential assessments of their quality, (2) prediction systems for helping potential applicants assess their chances of doing satisfactory academic work at any college they may choose to enter, and (3) procedures for measuring the "climate" of a college in such fashion that the student can get an idea of whether he will find it congenial.

Descriptive Handbooks. A pamphlet published by the College Entrance Examination Board (1966c) lists the titles of 48 college directories and guides, 26 of them issued by educational and government agencies and 22 by commercial publishers. Two of the directories, published by the American Council on Education, are probably the most comprehensive standard works: *Accredited Institutions of Higher Education,* (revised semiannually) and *American Universities and Colleges* (Cartter, 1964), which at this writing has gone through nine editions. More specialized works are represented by such titles as *American Junior Colleges* (Gleazer, 1963), *The College Handbook* (College Entrance Examination Board, 1965), which describes the colleges belonging to the CEEB, and *A Guide to Graduate Study: Programs Leading to the Ph.D. Degree* (Ness, 1965). Two of the commercially published guides (Cass & Birnbaum, 1965; Hawes, 1966) not only describe the leading characteristics of every college in the United States but also attempt to rate each one with respect to its quality and selectivity.

The information available from these sources is deficient in two main respects for purposes of guidance. First, in no case has there been any serious empirical attempt to determine whether or to what extent each type of information used to differentiate among colleges is needed for the decision-making process. Second, in the publications that attempt to

dent who has made an outstanding record in athletics is not likely to go unnoticed by coaches and alumni in search of athletic talent. The chance of making a particular fraternity in a particular college may be decisive. The stream of college literature, films, and recruiters moving through the high schools is probably also not without some effect on some students. In view of the many influences playing upon the student, exceptional strength of mind would seem to be required of him if he is to stay in charge of his own college choices rather than be pushed by a thousand external pressures into choices that are not really his own.

The Question of Going Beyond the Baccalaureate. After a student arrives in college, his decision process takes on new dimensions. Gropper and Fitzpatrick (1959) surveyed a national sample of 2,037 graduate students and of 1,544 college seniors judged by their professors to be of graduate-school caliber. They found a strong contrast between the reasons their students gave for going to college and for going to graduate school: in the decision to go to college the modal influence was the home; in the decision to go to graduate school, the modal influence was the furtherance of specific vocational objectives already formed in college. Among the group of able college seniors who had decided not to attend graduate school, the reason most frequently given was lack of any real interest or sense of need for further education (52 percent); another 34 percent ascribed their discontinuance to lack of the necessary ability or money to see them through. The reason students most frequently gave for choosing a particular graduate school had to do with its academic quality. Financial considerations came second, and the nature of the university environment came third.

The time at which students in the Gropper-Fitzpatrick sample decided to go on to graduate study seemed to depend on what field the student was interested in. Forty-six percent of those going to law school had made up their minds to do so before the end of the sophomore year in college; only 21 percent heading for the academic fields of graduate study had similarly decided. Berelson (1960) found the contrast still more striking: most medical-school students had made the choice about graduate education *before* they got to college; most law-school students had made it *during* college; and most Ph.D. candidates made it *after* they got the bachelor's degree. Astin (1965) has data based on a sample of 248 colleges which confirm the same trends.

According to Berelson, the decision to undertake study toward the Ph.D. is considerably less affected by the socioeconomic status of the student's family than is true of students looking toward law and medicine. He estimates that 50 percent of the Ph.D. students, 75 percent of the law students, and 67 percent of the medical students come from upper-middle-class and upper-class families. Law-school and medical-school students are more often than Ph.D. candidates motivated by job considerations. One factor that does *not* operate strongly in the choice of graduate school is that of distance from home: only 25 percent of graduate students, in contrast to 80 percent of undergraduates, are enrolled at institutions in the same state where they attended high school.

Generally speaking, a student makes up his own mind about whether and where to do graduate work. The college experience is one in which he experiments to discover the field in which he wants to spend his later life (Iffert, 1958; Beardslee & O'Dowd, 1962), and his decision with respect to further study relates largely to how the experiment turns out. There may be a sex difference in this matter, however: a larger percentage of women than of men in the Gropper-Fitzpatrick survey attributed their decision to go on with graduate study to educational experiences in college. Family influence is minimal. Few students in medicine and law are following in the footsteps of their fathers, and even fewer professorial fathers have children planning on Ph.D.'s (Berelson, 1960).

Aids to the Choice Process. As noted above, one of the main difficulties for the student in choosing a college or graduate school is the lack of usable information about them. In recent years there have been attempts to remedy this deficiency. The effort has taken three principal forms: (1) the production of handbooks describing the surface characteristics of institutions with possibly some inferential assessments of their quality, (2) prediction systems for helping potential applicants assess their chances of doing satisfactory academic work at any college they may choose to enter, and (3) procedures for measuring the "climate" of a college in such fashion that the student can get an idea of whether he will find it congenial.

Descriptive Handbooks. A pamphlet published by the College Entrance Examination Board (1966c) lists the titles of 48 college directories and guides, 26 of them issued by educational and government agencies and 22 by commercial publishers. Two of the directories, published by the American Council on Education, are probably the most comprehensive standard works: *Accredited Institutions of Higher Education,* (revised semiannually) and *American Universities and Colleges* (Cartter, 1964), which at this writing has gone through nine editions. More specialized works are represented by such titles as *American Junior Colleges* (Gleazer, 1963), *The College Handbook* (College Entrance Examination Board, 1965), which describes the colleges belonging to the CEEB, and *A Guide to Graduate Study: Programs Leading to the Ph.D. Degree* (Ness, 1965). Two of the commercially published guides (Cass & Birnbaum, 1965; Hawes, 1966) not only describe the leading characteristics of every college in the United States but also attempt to rate each one with respect to its quality and selectivity.

The information available from these sources is deficient in two main respects for purposes of guidance. First, in no case has there been any serious empirical attempt to determine whether or to what extent each type of information used to differentiate among colleges is needed for the decision-making process. Second, in the publications that attempt to

in a 1957–58 survey of 10,000 northern Illinois students in grades 9 to 13 found that 54 percent of the grade 9 boys and 58 percent of the girls were reasonably certain they would be going to college. Stice and his collaborators (1956) found that in a national sample of high-ability high school sophomores 71 percent of the boys and 60 percent of the girls thought they would eventually get to college. The amount of tentativeness in decisions about college-going for some students, however, may be considerable. Rossi and Coleman (1964) found that 14 percent of the students in their sample changed their minds between fall and spring about whether college should be in their educational plans.

The influence of the student's parents on his decisions to attend college is probably paramount. In all three studies mentioned above, students were asked to indicate how much discussion about college plans they had had with their parents, teachers, counselors, and friends, and in all three the data support the not surprising conclusion that, for most students who are considering college at all, the discussion of the subject most frequently begins and ends in the home. However, the school, also not surprisingly, plays a part in the decision process. Medsker and Trent (1965), for instance, found 90 percent of their college freshman sample recalling that their high school teachers and counselors had "encouraged" them to go to college, but only two-thirds of the same students were willing to admit that the encouragement "influenced" their decision.

The pull of the peer group is also of importance: if most of a student's friends are going to college, he tends to follow suit. The Medsker-Trent data, for instance, showed that 78 percent of the college freshman sample had at least two friends in high school who also went to college, whereas in a non-college sample the comparable percentage was 58. An interesting additional finding from the same study shows that among the college-going group 70 percent of those in the *lowest* quintile on an academic ability test had close friends in college, while in the non-college group only 40 percent in the two *top* quintiles had close friends in college.

The vocational motive is a strong determinant in the decision to go to college both in the students themselves and in their parents. Douvan and Kaye (1962), in an intensive study of the students at a single institution, found that the boys in their group tended to think of college primarily as a way to a good job. Girls tended to think of college as not just as a place to find a husband but as an enriching experience that would make them better wives and mothers. In Michigan a survey of the parents of college students found 90 percent mentioning job benefits as a reason for sending their sons to college, and 76 percent mentioned the same reason for daughters (Withey & others, 1959). Thus, insofar as college-going is concerned, the aspirations of students, contrary to popular mythology, tend to coincide with the aspirations their parents have for them.

Which College to Attend. For most students, whether they realize it or not, the choosing of a particular college to attend is far more difficult than simply deciding whether to keep going beyond grade 12. The difficulty has three elements. One is the enormous variety of postsecondary educational opportunities open to the American high school student. A second is the scarcity of adequate ways of describing and communicating to the student those characteristics of colleges that will enable him to form a realistic picture of what he will find there and how it will affect him. The third is the problem the student has of getting an objective view of himself and what he wants out of life and trying to relate this view to the opportunities available.

Data on how well students cope with these difficulties are scarce. Rossi and Coleman (1964) suggest that the "images" students have of colleges change very little from the time they enter high school to the time they enter college. Thus, even though during his high school years a student may accumulate a considerable amount of information about colleges from reading their literature, visiting their campuses, and talking with their representatives, the stereotypes of colleges formed by grade 9 tend to be the same stereotypes the student carries around in his head at grade 12. The Rossi-Coleman data also suggest that for a good many students any correspondence between the images they have of themselves and the images of the colleges they hope to attend are hardly more than coincidental. For example, quite a few of the students in their northern Illinois sample who were aiming at Ivy League colleges in the East tended to see these colleges as emphasizing intellectual demands but saw themselves *not* as "brilliant students" but as socially "most popular" types. This sort of logical disjunction turns up in other forms among other college candidates. Flanagan and Cooley (1966) present data which suggest a similar disjunction between a student's career plans and his choice of college. They found, for instance, that even in grade 12 the number of boys who thought they would become engineers was far greater than the number that could ever reasonably expect to get into an engineering school.

The factors that become involved in choosing which college to attend are about the same as those that seem to bear on whether the student chooses to go to college at all. Parental educational backgrounds, the quality and amount of reading that goes on in the home, the socioeconomic status of the family, the family's religion, the presence or absence of different types of colleges in the home community, the level of the student's academic performance in secondary school, the size of the school he attends, distance from home, cost, and scholarship opportunities—all such matters enter into the choosing of the particular college, or the particular type of college, a student finally decides to enter.

The many subtleties in the choice process, and how they operate in various types of students, remain to be studied. For many students whose parents went to college, there is undoubtedly a tendency to give more than a passing thought to following in the parental tradition by going to the same place. A stu-

rate institutions, the ratings given are based on inferences and value judgments that are unvalidated. To rate an institution as "very selective" or "extremely selective" on the ratio of acceptances to applicants having a certain reported level of measured aptitude and grade-getting ability has a good deal of "face validity." But it is not known how well a different group of raters, working independently on the same set of data and using the same set of categories, would agree in their categorization of the 2,900-plus colleges of the United States.

There have been some efforts to make the masses of data on American colleges more readily accessible to students. Probably the first such effort of any practical consequence has been the College Admissions Data Service run by the Educational Research Corporation (1966). The distinctive feature of this service is a procedure by which a student, through his school counselor, submits a set of characteristics he wants in the college of his choice, and the service sorts out by computer all the colleges that meet these specifications. Research with computers and other devices is now under way to build on and elaborate these procedures. Thus far the research has turned up some promising notions about *systems* for helping students sort out what they need to know to arrive at a choice of college, but most of the information (the "software") to be programmed into the systems is still lacking.

Academic Prediction Systems. One exception to this general state of affairs has been the development of academic prediction systems, i.e., the organization of data to give the student a preview of how he is likely to do at one college as compared with others. The earliest effort of this kind was undertaken by Horst at the University of Washington in 1949 (Horst, 1956a, 1957a, 1957b). Horst's system has since grown into the Washington Pre-College Testing Program in which 32 of the colleges and universities and practically all of the high schools in the state of Washington participate (Washington Pre-College Testing Program, 1965-66). Horst's work is grounded in two techniques that he calls multiple absolute prediction and differential prediction (Horst, 1954, 1955, 1956b). The underlying notion on which the program operates is that what a college-bound student most needs in the decision process is a set of predictions as to how well he is likely to meet the specific subject-matter requirements in each of the major fields in each of the colleges available to him.

The University System of Georgia provides a similar service. This service, inaugurated by Davis and his associates in 1957 with prediction studies in 16 colleges in the Georgia system (Franz & others, 1958), has since been expanded by Hills to include nearly all of the colleges in the state, both public and private (Hills, 1964a, 1964b; Hills & others, 1965). The main differences between the Georgia prediction system and the one in Washington is that the Georgia program concentrates on the prediction of overall grade-point average at each of the several colleges in the state while the Washington program concentrates on the differential prediction of success in major fields *within* the colleges. The relative utility of the two approaches from the standpoint of the high school guidance counselor and the college candidates he serves is unknown.

A third type of prediction service has been developed in Indiana under the auspices of the CEEB (Educational Testing Service, 1965). The Indiana program is similar to the Georgia program in that it provides predictions of overall performance in each of the colleges in the state. Through the use of a set of predictive composites and expectancy tables a guidance counselor in Indiana can compute for any student his probable chances of making a satisfactory record at any college in the state.

All three prediction systems justify their existence on the basis of three assumptions: (1) that the academic demands of different colleges are measurably different in kind as well as in level, (2) that students are measurably different in their ability to meet these different kinds of intellectual demands, and (3) that the degree of accuracy in the differential predictions is sufficiently great to warrant their use in secondary-school guidance. There is not much question that the differences in general intellectual *level* among the colleges are measurable and that it is possible, with a prediction equation incorporating aptitude-test scores and average grade (or rank in class) in high school, to get a reasonably reliable indication of the relative chances of making good grades in the freshman year at a "hard" college as compared with an "easy" one. It is still questionable, however, whether the instruments and techniques now available are capable of telling a student how much his chances of success may differ in one *type* of institution, or one field, as compared with another (French, 1961). The differential prediction problem is clouded by the many unpredictable contingencies that are an inevitable part of the school-to-college transition, by the as-yet unknown impact of different kinds of colleges on different kinds of students, and by the unsolved problem of devising for intraindividual differences measures that are lengthy enough to be adequately reliable and short enough to be practicable.

Measurement of College Climates. The first major research on the measurement of college climates was that of Pace and Stern in the development of the College Characteristics Index (CCI) (Pace & Stern, 1958; Pace, 1960; Stern, 1963). Their work stems from the dynamic theory of personality formulated by Murray in the 1930's. Murray conceived of the functioning of the human organism as an interaction between two sets of variables: the *press* of the environment and the *needs* of the individual (Murray & others, 1938). Following this theory, the CCI provides a method for characterizing the psychological environments of colleges by purporting to measure 30 kinds of press that may or may not be associated with a particular campus—e.g., press for orderliness, understanding, and achievement. The CCI is a questionnaire on which students report the kinds of press in the college they attend by giving their observations of such matters as the strictness of its rules and regulations, the kinds of nonacademic activities that predominate, and the degree to which students take their studies seriously.

From these kinds of data, Stern (1963) has developed six variables to characterize a college. Pace (1960, 1963), taking a somewhat different tack, has constructed a shorter instrument, called College and University Environment Scales (CUES), which characterizes a college along five dimensions.

It seems reasonably clear from the data developed by Pace and Stern on a fairly large group of institutions that college environments do indeed differ to a very high degree with respect to the environmental press measured by these instruments. In some colleges, for instance, the press for "intellectual orientation" or "scholarship" is dominant; in others it is practically nonexistent. Similarly, some colleges, typically certain small liberal arts colleges, are characterized by a strong press for "friendliness" or "community" in the student body, while others, typically urban universities with large numbers of commuting students, exhibit no such press at all.

A quite different approach to the assessment of the academic climate of colleges has been taken by Davis, who has tried to order colleges in accordance with the perceptions college faculties have of what constitutes the "desirable" as contrasted with the "undesirable" student (Davis, 1964, 1965a, 1965b, 1966). Using two types of instruments, the *Student Nomination Form* and the *Student Rating Form*, Davis has identified 16 dimensions in the faculty perceptions of students. Although he finds that faculties at different colleges perceive students differently and attach different values to the qualities they perceive, perhaps his most important finding is that colleges differ markedly in the degree to which different traits in students are *visible* to their instructors. From the standpoint of the high school student considering a particular college, it may be important for him to know not only what qualities in him are likely to be approved or disapproved by his professors but also whether the professors will pay any attention at all to his distinguishing characteristics.

A sociological approach to the analysis of college environments has been taken by Clark and Trow (1966). The Clark-Trow hypothesis is that there are two dimensions that determine student subcultures: involvement with ideas and affiliation with the institution. From these two dimensions they generate four subcultures, as shown in the accompanying diagram:

Involvement with ideas

	+	−
Affiliation + with the college −	Academic student subculture	Collegiate subculture
	Nonconformist subculture	Consumer-vocational subculture

According to this scheme a college may contain within it all four subcultures, though one or two may predominate. Peterson has incorporated this scheme in a series of college student questionnaires (Peterson, 1965; Educational Testing Service, 1963). By subscribing to one of four statements of personal philosophy of higher education a student indicates the subculture to which he is oriented. Application of this procedure to freshmen in 23 colleges has provided data showing the degree of dominance of each of the four subcultures in each college. The descriptions of colleges so obtained have high face validity, but Clark and Trow, among others, insist that to "type" institutions or students along the lines suggested can result in serious oversimplification and such "typing" must be handled with care. Nonetheless, the approach produces some useful broad insights for purposes of institutional research.

The three methods so far described for depicting the college environment all depend on student or faculty reports. Astin (1964a, 1964b, 1965) has proposed techniques which bypass such first-hand reports by attempting to find correlates in standard directories and compendiums. One of Astin's principal hypotheses (Astin and Holland, 1961; Astin, 1963) is that the personal orientation of college students can be inferred from the major fields they enter, and hence the environmental press or subcultures of a college can be determined in part simply by calculating the proportion of students in each major field. This technique provides six personal orientations to which are added two environmental variables and five so-called freshman input factors. Since these input factors, however, depend on many of the same institutional data used to assess the eight other variables (Astin, 1965), there is likely to be so much redundancy in the 13 measures used to characterize colleges according to this scheme that there is considerable risk of confusion in the interpretation of the college profiles.

Presumably there will emerge from the present research on college environments a reasonably valid set of measures capable of giving college candidates a somewhat clearer picture than is now obtainable of the ways of life, the pressures, and the types of stimulation and frustration that students are likely to find at any particular college. How these measures can be made interpretable by the ordinary college candidate and how he and his counselor can incorporate into the college decision process the types of information they may some day provide are massive problems that have yet to receive any serious or sustained attention.

THE CHOOSING OF STUDENTS BY INSTITUTIONS. Riesman and Jencks (1962) have suggested that going to college can be usefully looked at as an "initiation rite . . . for changing the semi-amorphous adolescent into a semi-identified adult." If so, the rite achieves its most intense focus in the mystique of the college admissions office. What goes on there is a matter for grave conjecture among schools, candidates, college faculties, alumni, and others—including admissions officers.

Because of the tremendous variety of institutions of higher education, only very few, not very helpful, generalizations are capable of encompassing all the procedures by which they admit students. They all have some sort of *policy* on admissions. Each of them has an *administrative organization* of some kind to handle the work. All *give some attention to their relations with the institutions that feed them*—high school in the case of colleges, colleges in the case of graduate and professional schools. And all of them have a *method for deciding* which applicants to accept and which to reject.

Policies, administrative setups, external relations, and decision methods are all of course intimately interrelated and all are largely, but not absolutely, conditioned by the size, type, traditions, and purposes of the institutions that admissions offices are supposed to serve. Some part of the differences in the functioning of such offices, however, is due to the differing perceptions and predilections of the people who run them. Very little is objectively known about how all these institutional and personal factors interact with one another or about how they bear on the actual choosing of students. Hauser and Lazarsfeld (1964) have made a beginning on the problem in their study of the job of the admissions officer in undergraduate colleges, and Whitla (in press) has traced the evolution of policy as expressed in the decision processes of a single college admissions committee over a ten-year period. Beyond these, the literature on the subject is mostly hortatory.

Admission Policies. All colleges are to some extent selective. A public community college may be required by law to accept any high school graduate in its district who cares to apply. The decision to accept or reject is thus preordained: residents of the district qualify, nonresidents do not; high school graduates are acceptable, high school dropouts are not. The *degree* of selection in such a case is minimal, but the *policy* is nevertheless selective since some kinds of people are excluded.

In general an admissions policy is a description, written or implied, of the number and kinds of candidates who will be accepted. The policy on numbers may be stringent or expansible. The University of California, for instance, took in upwards of 14,000 new freshman and 7,000 transfer students on all its campuses in 1966, and it is committed to a long-term policy of accepting as many applicants as can meet its requirements. It sees its mission as one of estimating the future educational needs of the community and building to accommodate them. At the opposite extreme are small liberal arts colleges that are committed to slow growth and that have to limit acceptance to one or two hundred students.

The variety of ways in which students can be and are categorized for purposes of selection is the salient factor that characterizes differences among institutions in their admission policies. Some ways of categorizing applicants—for example, by sex, by home address, by amount and kind of previous schooling, by religious affiliation, by ability to pay tuition—are obvious and relatively uncomplicated determinants of policy. Other bases for classification may be equally obvious, but some of them are not so easy to define or apply: quality of previous academic performance, future promise, soundness of character, seriousness of purpose, and the like. Admission policies that incorporate terms as vague as some of these may be doubtful guides for the actual selection of students, but their presence or absence in policy statements and the amount of serious effort institutions put out in trying to apply them unquestionably make for vast differences in the approaches institutions take to the task of selection.

For the most part, the criteria for admission to publicly supported institutions are such that they can be more or less automatically applied, particularly at the undergraduate level. Criteria for admission to privately supported institutions depend more on personal judgment in the selection process and may therefore be considerably less uniform from year to year or even from candidate to candidate in the same year.

There is a point of view on admission policy that has been associated in the past particularly with the land-grant colleges and the least selective state universities. It is that in a democracy every high school graduate has the right to enter college, even though there may be, in some cases, every expectation that he will fail. Therefore the decision regarding admission must be left to the student himself; it is not for the college to make. The main principle underlying this policy is that since no prediction of an individual's performance in college or in his later life can be perfect, every candidate should be given an opportunity to prove himself. This policy raises complicated psychological, economic, and philosophical issues concerning the relations between the rights of the individual and the requirements of society. These issues have been variously resolved, usually less by debate than by the amount of population and political pressure and the ability of the public institutions to meet the demands generated thereby.

Administrative Organization. In an earlier time the registrar or some similar official of a college or university was usually responsible for handling admissions. The job was regarded mainly as a routine matter of comparing candidate records with admission requirements to see which candidates qualified. The registrar's original function is still part of the admissions operation, but so many other responsibilities have become associated with it that the admissions office in a majority of the larger institutions has been spun off from the registrar's office. The director or dean of admissions is now seen, especially in large and highly selective institutions, as a specialist who is at least coordinate with the registrar in the administrative hierarchy. The reasons for this shift are fairly obvious: the sheer increase, over the past fifty years, in the number of applicants and in the number and variety of schools and colleges from which they come; the growing complexity in most colleges and universities themselves; and the increasing expectation, as a consequence of technical developments in personnel selection, that the officer in charge of admitting students shall have some special expertise in that field.

The survey by Hauser and Lazarsfeld (1964) found that the conduct of admissions in the large majority of undergraduate colleges is under the general surveillance of an admissions committee on which both the faculty and the administration are usually represented. In some instances such committees are concerned only with general policy; in other instances they are working committees that go over the material on applicants and decide each case by majority vote. In large, complex institutions there may be several admissions committees, one for each unit of the institution (agriculture, education, engineering, liberal arts, etc.) and an overall committee with representatives from each of the unit committees. How the director of admissions works within the committee structure of his institution varies widely: he may use the committee as a rubber stamp to legalize his own unaided decisions; he may use it for aid and comfort in deciding "hard cases"; and he may function primarily in a staff capacity, preparing case dockets carrying recommendations which a committee may accept or vote down.

In some large universities the administrative responsibility for admissions at the graduate level may be vested in the same official who administers undergraduate admissions. In others this work is handled by each of the graduate colleges or divisions or departments on its own. In nearly all cases, whatever the logistical arrangements may be for processing applications at the graduate level, the power of decision as well as the determination of admission policy is closely held by each of the graduate faculties and is rarely delegated to an admissions officer serving in a purely administrative capacity.

External Relations. A shift in the focus of undergraduate admissions is reflected in the names of the two professional organizations to which admissions officers ordinarily belong. The older of the two is the American Association of Collegiate Registrars and Admissions Officers; the younger is the Association of College Admissions Counselors. The use of the word "counselor" in the newer organization has a significant implication: it suggests that the new breed is more concerned with face-to-face contact with candidates. The data collected by Hauser and Lazarsfeld (1964) tend to bear this out: admissions "specialists" as contrasted with "registrars" spend much more of their time in the field visiting schools and talking to prospective students.

This kind of activity has a number of different purposes which vary with the character of the colleges. In the case of the small liberal arts college that has to struggle to get enough students to stay alive, the field operations of the admissions counselor are almost solely recruiting operations—outright efforts to sell students on coming to his particular college. In the case of the prestigious college that typically has many more candidates than it can possibly accept, the field work has a fourfold purpose: (1) to recruit the *best* candidates, that is, those with special talents, athletic and otherwise, (2) to provide as many candidates as possible with accurate information about the college, so that they will know what to expect if admitted, (3) to size up their personal characteristics by seeing them face-to-face and by talking with their teachers and their school counselors, and (4) to enlist, encourage, and attempt to control the continuing efforts of local alumni in the performance of these same functions.

The field activities of the admissions officers in state university systems tend to take on a somewhat different cast. There is generally less direct recruiting of individuals—though this is not unknown—and much more emphasis on keeping schools up-to-date about the state colleges and universities and on keeping the state system au courant with what is happening in the schools. The general aim is to maintain smooth working relations among the institutions involved, so that the students passing between them will be somewhat less likely to lose their way. College admissions counseling in these circumstances is often done by bringing the candidates to the campus, either singly or in groups, and giving them a firsthand briefing on the array of higher educational opportunities available there. One intended effect of such preadmission counseling, especially at institutions with so-called "open admissions" policies, is to discourage the completion of applications from students for whom the academic demands of the institution are obviously too difficult or the types of available offerings inappropriate.

The Decision Process. The majority of institutions of higher education, public and private, undergraduate and graduate, now require their candidates to take entrance tests of some kind. The results of such tests may be variously employed. In rare instances the scores on the tests may be the sole determiners of admission. In many cases, perhaps most, the test scores are used in conjunction with the previous academic records to get an assessment of the applicant's general competence. Such an assessment may form the basis for acceptance or rejection or may be used only for counseling the student subsequent to his admission or for placing him in courses and programs at an appropriate level of difficulty. In some cases the entrance tests are merely a pro forma requirement, and the results are never consulted for any purpose whatever. Thus test scores may figure more or less prominently, or not at all, in the process by which an admissions office staff or an admissions committee or the two combined reach the decision whether a candidate will be allowed to matriculate.

In American institutions the school or college transcript, on the other hand, is of universal importance in the decision process. The least selective and the most selective colleges and universities rely heavily on it for determining whether the candidate has accumulated course credits of the right amount and kind and quality to be favorably considered or, in many cases, for seeing whether he has met specified prerequisites—the necessary mathematics and physics for a start at engineering, for instance, or the right courses in chemistry and biology for entrance into medical school. The uses of the transcript are many and varied, but it is afflicted with a curious difficulty: although it has achieved universality as a form of interinstitutional communication, it is far from having achieved uniformity in design or content. As a consequence a not inconsiderable part of the decision process consists of trying to decode the messages that transcripts are attempting to convey. Transcripts having become symbols of institutional autonomy, and efforts to computerize them have foundered because of the failure to get general agreement on a common language or a common format. The miscellaneous character of transcripts is particularly apparent at the college level. A good many secondary schools, on the other hand, have adopted the common transcript form published by the National Association of Secondary School Principals (American Association of College Registrars . . ., 1964) and have thus somewhat reduced the burden of interpretation for the colleges.

At the graduate level, because of the much smaller numbers involved, the process of deciding on admission tends in most instances to be highly personalized, with much reliance on interviews and personal recommendations. Scores on tests may carry considerable weight in judging candidates, especially in the case of fellowship applicants, but their use is informal and far less decisive than letters of recommendation from known colleagues at undergraduate institutions. As the pressure of numbers in the graduate schools builds up, however, the tendency is to adopt more formalized procedures similar to those in use by large and highly selective colleges at the undergraduate level. This greater formalization of selection methods is already apparent in the admissions procedures of many law schools.

At the undergraduate level the manner of deciding on applicants in the least selective public institutions is essentially a clerical operation: candidates are cleared for admission upon routine certification of their eligibility. At colleges where the ability of the candidate, his background, and the quality of his preparation are factors in the choice, the decision to admit or reject may follow either of two general patterns. Under one pattern, sometimes called "rolling admissions," the decision is made as soon as the candidate's qualifications have been satisfactorily established. According to this arrangement a candidate may be admitted before he graduates from secondary school and so notified, or he may be given an advance promise of admission contingent upon satisfactory completion of his twelfth-grade work. Under a second pattern, the decision to admit or reject is postponed until evidence on all the qualifications of all the candidates has been accumulated, reviewed, and evaluated. The applicants are then ranked in order of merit and the most meritorious accepted. Merit, however, may have several dimensions; that is, it may include social, personal, and demographic as well as several kinds of intellectual qualities.

Whitla's painstaking analysis of the determinants of the decision process at Harvard College (in press) shows how this conception of merit can actually function. By using factor analysis and multiple regression techniques, he has been able to display the subtle changes in the criteria employed by the Harvard College Committee on Admission over a ten-year period as the applicant pool has changed in character and grown in size. The differences between the factors operating for two subgroups of applicants and the changes of emphasis that have taken place under changing conditions are exemplified in Table 2.

These data, together with other data in Whitla's ten-year study, illuminate some intriguing characteristics of the committee process at Harvard which may or may not be discernible elsewhere: (1) as the academic ability of the applicant pool goes up, the committee tends to put greater weight on the personal attributes of candidates; (2) the criteria the committee applies may vary from one subgroup of applicants to another, depending on the nature of the data obtainable; and (3) the richer the data on an applicant, the more complex and unpredictable the committee's decision becomes.

One of the perennial and unresolved controversies in connection with selective admissions is whether the choice of an entering class shall rest on actuarial or

TABLE 2

CONTRIBUTIONS OF FACTORS TO ADMISSIONS DECISIONS OF THE HARVARD COLLEGE COMMITTEE ON ADMISSIONS, IN PERCENTAGES

Class	Academic Ability	Personal Attributes	Principal's Report	Athletics	Total
Candidates interviewed by staff					
Class of 1958	33	52	14	1	100
Class of 1968	16	60	21	3	100
Candidates not interviewed by staff					
Class of 1958	51	28	20	1	100
Class of 1968	23	51	24	2	100

a. Adopted from Whitla (in press).

clinical predictions. The debate has taken a good many twists and turns since Allport delivered his famous address on the subject in 1939 (Allport, 1940). Insofar as the prediction of grade-point averages is concerned, the unencumbered actuarial approach has usually turned out to be a shade more accurate than the clinical approach (Sarbin, 1942; Melton, 1952; Meehl, 1954; Fricke, 1958; Gough, 1962). There is little question that if most probable grade-point average is the only basis for deciding which candidates to admit, the actuarial approach is by far the more efficient and, in view of the unknown variability of individual human judgments, more dependable. The principal counterargument is that probable grade-point average is not the only criterion for admission, and not a very satisfactory one at that, since the grade-point average reflects only a small, and possibly a relatively unimportant, part of the benefit a student derives from his educational experience and no part at all of what he contributes to the college or university he attends. There are counterarguments to this counterargument, but it is unlikely that the debate has had any appreciable effect on practice either way. Under circumstances where intuitive judgment is permitted in the decision process, such judgments tend to predominate; under circumstances where intuitive judgments are not permitted, a straight actuarial approach in the setting of admission standards is or is not used, depending on the statistical sophistication of the officers responsible for admission operations

The Relevance of Tests and Other Measures. There are currently nine major national admissions testing programs in the United States. These programs and the tests offered in them are shown in Table 3.

The increasing use of tests for admission since World War II has probably come about because of the very great increase in the numbers of applicants, the diversity of grading standards in the feeder schools and colleges, and the consequent need for some common measures on which to align candidates. From the time of the introduction of the College Board Scholastic Aptitude Test in 1926 (Brigham, 1932) there has been a continuing preoccupation, especially among testers, with the predictive power of the tests, and this has led to literally thousands of studies of their predictive validity.

This research has been directed primarily at the question of what tests of what types best predict grades at particular institutions. It has also customarily been concerned with showing the incremental value of the test scores when combined with some sort of quantification of the previous academic record (e.g., Lannholm & Schrader, 1951; Dyer & King, 1955; Fishman, 1957; Shane & others, 1964; Munday, 1965). At an increasing number of institutions the prediction studies have become an annual routine, aimed not only at creating general confidence in the data available but also at providing best-weighted combinations of grades and test scores which can be used in actuarial fashion for assessing each candidate's chances of getting good grades (Duggan & Hazlett, 1961; American College Testing Program, 1965; College Entrance Examination Board, 1966*b*).

The typical prediction study at the college level has consisted of regressing freshman grade-point averages on high school grade-point averages (or rank in class) and test scores. Innumerable refinements on this basic pattern have been investigated in an effort to increase the accuracy of prediction. In complex institutions, separate regression equations are developed for different groupings of students: liberal arts majors, engineering majors, and so on. In coeducational colleges it is usually found that there are enough differences in the standard regression weights for men and for women to make separate regression equations useful.

In view of the obvious differences among secondary schools in quality and marking standards, it has long been supposed that some method of adjusting their grade-point averages to take account of the differences among them would produce a useful amount of improvement in the predictive accuracy of composites of marks and scores. Various proposals have been made for developing such adjustments (e.g., Bloom & Peters, 1961), but thus far these proposals have proved to be will-o'-the-wisps (e.g., Willingham, 1963; Lindquist, 1963). The reduction in error variance that comes of incorporating the test scores in ordinary prediction formulas appears to account for about all of the variance across schools that can be accounted for.

Multiple correlations with freshman grade-point averages usually run from about .50 to slightly above .60, depending on the type of institution and the homogeneity of the student body, and these correlations seem to represent the upper limits of accuracy with which presently available criterion measures of academic performance can be predicted. Attempts to improve the situation by using personality measures of the self-report type have produced no practically useful increases in validity and have raised questions about the ethics of employing such measures (Messick, 1963; Lavin, 1965). Certain types of biographical and demographic information about candidates show some promise of raising predictive accuracy for specified institutions—particularly information that pertains to the student's socioeconomic background and to activities for which he has received special recognition (e.g., Anastasi & others, 1960; Lavin, 1965; Skager & others, 1965; Freeberg, 1966). Correlations with longer-term criteria, such as persistence in college or honors at graduation, tend to run lower than the correlations with freshman grade-point average (French, 1958). Combinations of test data and undergraduate grades tend to produce correlations with success in graduate school that are typically somewhat lower (about .40 to above .50) than those obtained in predictions of college achievement (e.g., Lannholm & Schrader, 1951; Shane & others, 1964). The lower coefficients in this case may, of course, be due to a narrowing in the range of talent.

There have been attempts to predict nonacademic accomplishments in college as measured by students'

TABLE 3
MAJOR NATIONAL ADMISSIONS TESTINGS PROGRAMS[a]

Programs	Tests Offered
UNDERGRADUATE PROGRAMS	
American College Testing Program	Subtests: English usage, mathematics, natural sciences reading, social studies reading.
College Entrance Examination Board	*Preliminary Scholastic Aptitude Test.* Subtests: verbal and mathematical ability—eleventh grade.
	Scholastic Aptitude Test. Subtests: verbal and mathematical ability—twelfth grade.
	Spanish Scholastic Aptitude Test.
	Achievement tests (14 subject fields).
	Supplementary achievement tests (7 subject fields).
	Advanced-placement examinations (9 subject fields).
College Qualification Tests	Subtests: Verbal ability, numerical ability, science information, social studies information.
National Merit Scholarship Qualifying Test	Subtests: English usage, mathematics usage, social studies reading, natural sciences reading, word usage.
GRADUATE PROGRAMS	
Admission Test for Graduate Study in Business	Subtests: verbal and quantitative ability.
Graduate Record Examinations	Aptitude test (Subtests: verbal and quantitative ability). Advanced tests (20 major subject fields).
Law School Admission Test	Subtests: reading comprehension, data interpretation, principles and cases, figure classification, writing ability, general background.
Medical College Admission Test	Subtests: verbal and quantitative ability, general information, science.
Miller Analogies Test	Verbal analogies.

a. See Buros (1965) for a description of each of these testing programs.

reports of their extracurricular activities. There appears to be a small relationship (somewhat above or below .40) between the favorable things students say about their nonacademic accomplishments in high school and the favorable things the same students say about their accomplishments in college (Richards & others, 1966).

Some people have expressed serious doubts about what seems to be an excessive preoccupation with prediction studies and their uses in the decision process. From the standpoint of a behavioral scientist, Fishman (1962)—after taking a look at the several kinds of institutional and environmental variables that have been, or might be, or ought to be involved in predicting performance in college, both academic and nonacademic—has concluded that a moratorium on prediction studies might be useful. His main point is that there has been too much blind empiricism in the development of prediction systems and too little effort to understand the variables involved before putting numbers on them. Lavin's work, referred to above, is a step in the direction Fishman advocates.

Ebel (1964) has expressed even more profound doubts. He suggests that the use of statistically produced predictive composites in the selection of students may tempt the deciders "to overlook the gross inadequacies that plague our measurements and the great uncertainties that bedevil our predictions . . . and attempt to play God with the lives of other human beings." The temptation is unquestionably real, and cases can be found of individuals who have fallen into it, but the prevalence of such aberrations is unknown.

The Admission of Disadvantaged Students. The concern expressed by Ebel has been shared especially by those who suspect that the typical tests and prediction equations developed on white middle-class students may underpredict or fail to predict the college success of members of minority groups and thereby prejudice their chances of admission. Clark and Plotkin (1963) studied this question by surveying Negroes and whites attending a miscellaneous group of integrated colleges during the 1950's. Their data suggest that the CEEB *Scholastic Aptitude Test* (*SAT*) scores generally fail to predict the college performance of Negro students and probably underestimate it as compared to the performance of white students. A number of uncontrolled variables in their sample, however, make their findings inconclusive and possibly misleading.

There have been several other more carefully controlled studies (e.g., Roberts, 1962; Stanley & others, 1966) showing that the predictive power of the *SAT*–high school grade combination is just as great in predominantly Negro colleges as it is in predominantly white colleges, possibly greater.

Cleary (1966) has investigated in particular the question of whether Negro students' academic success tends to be underpredicted by test scores and high school data. In each of three integrated colleges she compared the regressions of college grades on *SAT* scores and high school grades of Negroes and whites separately and for the two groups combined. At two of the colleges she found no significant differences between the Negro and white regression lines and no underprediction of Negroes when the common regression line was used. At the third college she found that the regression line common to Negroes and whites significantly *over*predicted the academic success of Negroes. Cleary's findings, however, are also inconclusive for two reasons: (1) three colleges are clearly insufficient as a sample on which to generalize to all integrated colleges, and (2) the very fact that the Negro groups studied had already gained admission to these colleges probably makes them atypical of potential Negro college candidates generally.

The college admission problem in the case of disadvantaged groups, however, is not so much in the possible bias of tests and other measures used to predict future academic success as it is in the deficiencies the disadvantaged groups show by the time they reach grade 12. The evidence is overwhelming that students coming out of schools in the urban ghettos and rural slums, even if they manage to complete high school, are far behind the white majority in academic achievement and the basic tools for learning (e.g., Coleman & others, 1966; Karpinos, 1966).

The response of higher education to this problem has been direct, but highly tentative and far from massive. In a questionnaire addressed in 1964 to the 2,131 institutions listed in the U.S. Office of Education's *Education Directory 1962–63: Higher Education,* Gordon and Wilkerson (1966) asked the colleges what they were doing about compensatory education for potentially able college students from socially disadvantaged environments. They heard from 610 institutions, of which 224 said they were doing something and 386 confessed they were doing nothing. Presumably the vast majority of the nonrespondents would also have fallen in the negative column.

The findings of the study are nevertheless important in that they show some of the general directions a considerable number of colleges are taking toward this aspect of the admissions situation. There are four general approaches: (1) special help to schools and individuals with precollege education, (2) special recruiting procedures coupled with special financial aid programs and relaxed admission standards, (3) special counseling, tutoring, and remedial courses following entrance into college, and (4) development of special curricula, sometimes involving lengthened time for completing the degree (Gordon & Wilkerson, 1966). The effort is not focused solely on admission from secondary school to college; a few professional schools at the graduate level are also investigating ways to broaden their student bodies so that the professions eventually will have a more balanced representation from minority groups.

The movement of higher education toward direct involvement in the preparation of students whom they would otherwise be unable to admit has a hopeful precedent. At the time when the land-grant colleges were getting organized in the 1860's and 1870's, most of them found themselves in rural areas where public secondary education was still unavailable. To generate a supply of entering students, they had to find some way to close the gap between elementary and higher education. They succeeded in doing so by organizing their own college preparatory departments (Rudolph, 1962). Closing the educational-opportunity gap in the 1960's and 1970's so that higher education can meet the needs of the disadvantaged is a problem of a somewhat different order. The solutions are not yet clear, nor will they be simple and easy. But the fact that some colleges and universities are beginning to address themselves to the problem enlarges the possibility of an eventual solution.

Henry S. Dyer
Educational Testing Service

References

Allport, Gordon W. "The Psychologist's Frame of Reference." *Psychol B* 37:1–27; 1940.

American Association of Collegiate Registrars and Admissions Officers–National Association of Secondary School Principals Joint Committee. *Manual for the Secondary-school Record.* National Association of Secondary School Principals, 1964.

American College Testing Program. *ACT Technical Report.* ACT, 1965.

American Council on Education. *Accredited Institutions of Higher Education.* ACE, revised semiannually.

Anastasi, Anne, and others. *The Validation of a Biographical Inventory as a Predictor of College Success.* CEEB, 1960. 87p.

Astin, Alexander W. "Further Validation of the Environmental Assessment Technique." *J Ed Psychol* 54:217–26; 1963.

Astin, Alexander W. "Distribution of Students Among Higher Educational Institutions." *J Ed Psychol* 55:276–87; 1964(*a*).

Astin, Alexander W. "Some Characteristics of Student Bodies Entering Higher Educational Institutions." *J Ed Psychol* 55:267–75; 1964(*b*).

Astin, Alexander W. *Who Goes Where to College?* SRA, 1965. 125p.

Astin, Alexander W., and Holland, John L. "The Environmental Assessment Technique: A Way to Measure College Environments." *J Ed Psychol* 52:308–16; 1961.

Beardslee, David C., and O'Dowd, Donald D. "Students and the Occupational World." In Sanford, Nevitt. (Ed.) *The American College.* Wiley, 1962. p. 597–626.

Berelson, Bernard. *Graduate Education in the United States.* McGraw-Hill, 1960. 346p.

Blackmer, A. R., and others. *General Education in School and College.* Harvard Press, 1952. 142p.

Bloom, Benjamin S., and Peters, Frank R. *The Use of Academic Prediction Scales for Counseling and Selecting College Entrants.* Crowell-Collier and Macmillan, Inc., 1961. 145p.

Bowles, Frank. *Access to Higher Education: The International Study of University Admissions,* Vol. 1. UNESCO and the International Association of Universities, 1963. 212p.

Brigham, Carl C. *A Study of Error.* CEEB, 1932. 384p.

Buros, Oscar K. (Ed.) *The Sixth Mental Measurements Yearbook.* Gryphon Press, 1965. 1714p.

Cartter, Allan M. (Ed.) *American Universities and Colleges,* 9th ed. ACE, 1964. 1339p.

Cass, James, and Birnbaum, Max. *Comparative Guide to American Colleges for Students, Parents, and Counselors.* Harper, 1965. 556p.

Clark, Burton R., and Trow, Martin. "Organizational Context." In *College Peer Groups.* Aldine Publishing Co., 1966. p. 17–70.

Clark, K. B., and Plotkin, L. *The Negro Student at Integrated Colleges.* National Scholarship Service and Fund for Negro Students, 1963. 59p.

Cleary, T. A. *Test Bias: Validity of the Scholastic Aptitude Test for Negro and White Students in Integrated Colleges.* ETS, 1966. 23p.

Coleman, J. S., and others. *Equality of Educational Opportunity.* USOE, 1966. 737p.

College Entrance Examination Board. *The College Handbook.* CEEB, 1965. Published biennially. 716p.

College Entrance Examination Board. *Advanced Placement Program: 1966–68 Course Descriptions.* CEEB, 1966(*a*). 160p.

College Entrance Examination Board. *Data Analysis: Validity Service.* CEEB, 1966(*b*). 17p.

College Entrance Examination Board. *Educational Information and Guidance: A Selected Bibliography.* CEEB, 1966(*c*). 32p.

Davis, Junius A. *Faculty Perceptions of Students: Research and Development Reports.* Numbers 7, 8, 9, 10, 14, and 15. ETS, 1964, 1965(*a*), 1966.

Davis, Junius A. "What College Teachers Value in Students." *Col Bd R* 56:15–8; 1965(*b*).

Douvan, Elizabeth, and Kaye, Carol. "Motivational Factors in College Entrance." In Sanford, Nevitt. (Ed.) *The American College.* Wiley, 1962. p. 199–224.

Duggan, John M., and Hazlett, Paul H., Jr. *Predicting College Grades.* CEEB, 1961.

Dyer, Henry S. "The Squeeze in College Admissions." *PTA M* 60:19–20; 1966.

Dyer, Henry S., and King, Richard G. *College Board Scores, Their Use and Interpretation, No. 2.* CEEB, 1955. 192p.

Ebel, Robert L. "The Social Consequences of Educational Testing." *Col Bd R* 52:10–6; 1964.

Eckland, Bruce K. "College Dropouts Who Came Back." *Harvard Ed R* 34:402–20; 1964.

Educational Research Corporation. *College Admission Data Service.* Educational Research Corporation, 1966. Revised annually.

Educational Testing Service. *Background Factors Relating to College Plans and College Enrollment Among Public High School Students.* ETS, 1957. 84p.

Educational Testing Service. *College Student Questionnaires.* ETS, 1963. 60p.

Educational Testing Service. *Manual of Freshman Class Profiles for Indiana Colleges.* CEEB, 1965. 93p.

Fishman, Joshua A. *1957 Supplement to College Board Scores No. 2.* CEEB, 1957. 206p.

Fishman, Joshua A. "Some Social-psychological Theory for Selecting and Guiding College Students." In Sanford, Nevitt. (Ed.) *The American College.* Wiley, 1962. p. 666–89.

Flanagan, John C., and Cooley, William W. *Project Talent: One-year Follow-up Studies.* U Pittsburgh Press, 1966.

Franz, Gretchen, and others. "Prediction of Grades from Pre-admission Indices in Georgia Tax-supported Colleges." *Ed and Psychol Meas* 18:841–4; 1958.

Freeberg, Norman E. *The Biographical Information Blank as a Predictor of Student Achievement and Vocational Choice: A Review.* ETS, 1966.

French, John W. "Validation of New Item Types Against Four-year Academic Criteria." *J Ed Psychol* 49:67–76; 1958.

French, John W. *Comparative Prediction of Success and Satisfaction in College Major Fields.* ETS, 1961.

Fricke, Benno G. "How Colleges Should Pick Their Students." *Col Bd R* 34:17–22; 1958.

Fuess, Claude M. *The College Board: Its First Fifty Years.* Columbia U Press, 1950. 222p.

Ginzberg, E., and others. *Occupational Choice.* Columbia U Press, 1951. 271p.

Gleazer, Edmund J., Jr. (Ed.) *American Junior Colleges,* 6th ed. ACE, 1963. 551p.

Gordon, Edmund W. "Opportunities in Higher Education for Socially Disadvantaged Youth." In *From High School to College: Readings for Counselors.* CEEB, 1965. p. 53–61.

Gordon, Edmund W., and Wilkerson, D. A. *Compensatory Education for the Disadvantaged: Programs and Practices Preschool Through College.* CEEB, 1966. 298p.

Gough, Harrison. "Clinical vs. Statistical Prediction in Psychology." In Postman, Leo. (Ed.) *Psychology in the Making*. Knopf, 1962.

Gropper, George L., and Fitzpatrick, Robert. *Who Goes to Graduate School?* American Institute for Research, 1959. 66p.

Gummere, Richard M., Jr. "America's Wandering Scholars." *Harper's Magazine* 222:73–76; May 1961.

Hauser, J. Z., and Lazarsfeld, P. F. *The Admissions Officer*. CEEB, 1964.

Haven, Elizabeth W., and Smith, Robert E. *Financial Aid to College Students, 1963–64*. ETS, 1965. 81p.

Havighurst, Robert J., and Neugarten, Bernice L. *Society and Education*, 2nd Ed. Allyn, 1962. 585p.

Hawes, Gene R. *The New American Guide to Colleges*. Columbia U Press, 1966. 332p.

Hervey, John G. "Law School Registration, 1965." *J Legal Ed* 18:197–211; 1966.

Hills, John R. "College Expectancy Tables for High School Counselors." *Personnel Guid J* 42:479–83; 1964(a).

Hills, John R. "Prediction of College Grades for All Public Colleges of a State." *J Ed Meas* 1:155–9; 1964(b).

Hills, John R., and Others. *Counselor's Guide to Georgia Colleges*. Board of Regents, University System of Georgia, 1965. 60p.

Holmes, C. H. "A Case Study of the Four-year Transfer Student." *Col and U* Spring: 322–9; 1961.

Horst, Paul. "A Technique for the Development of a Differential Prediction Battery." *Psychol Monogr* No. 380, 1954. 31p.

Horst, Paul. "A Technique for the Development of a Multiple Absolute Prediction Battery." *Psychol Monogr* No. 390, 1955. 22p.

Horst, Paul. "The Differential Prediction of Success in Various College Course Areas." *Col and U* 31:456–71; 1956(a).

Horst, Paul. "Optimal Test Length for Maximum Differential Prediction." *Psychometrika* 21:51–66; 1956(b).

Horst, Paul. "Differential Prediction in College Admissions." *Col Bd R* 33:19–23; 1957(a).

Horst, Paul. "The Differential Prediction of College Course Grades as a Basis for Academic Guidance." In *The Effective Use of Measurement in Guidance: Proceedings of the Sixth Annual Western Regional Conference on Testing Problems*. ETS, 1957(b). p. 28–37.

Iffert, Robert E. *Retention and Withdrawal of College Students*. USOE, 1958.

Institute of International Education. *Open Doors, 1966: Report on International Exchange*. Institute of International Education, 1966. 64p.

Jaffe, A. J., and Adams, Walter. "Trends in College Enrollments." *Col Bd R* 55:27–32; 1965.

Johnson, Davis G. "The Study of Applicants, 1963–64." *J Med Ed* 39:899–975; 1964.

Karpinos, B. D. *The Mental Qualification of American Youths for Military Service and Its Relationship to Educational Attainment*. Proceedings of the Social Statistics Section, American Statistical Association, 1966.

Katz, Martin. *Decisions and Values: A Rationale for Secondary School Guidance*. CEEB, 1963. 67p.

Knoell, Dorothy M., and Medsker, Leland L. *Factors Affecting Performance of Transfer Students from Two- to Four-year Colleges; With Implications for Coordination and Articulation*. U California Press, 1965. 193p.

Lannholm, G. V., and Schrader, W. B. *Prediction of Graduate School Success: An Evaluation of the Effectiveness of the Graduate Record Examinations*. ETS, 1951. 50p.

Lavin, David E. *The Prediction of Academic Performance*. Russell Sage, 1965. 182p.

Lindquist, E. F. "An Evaluation of a Technique for Scaling High School Grades to Improve Prediction of College Success." *Ed and Psychol* 23:623–46; 1963.

Medsker, Leland L., and Trent, James W. *The Influence of Different Types of Public Higher Institutions on College Attendance From Varying Socioeconomic and Ability Levels*. Center for Higher Education, 1965. 110p.

Meehl, Paul E. *Clinical vs. Statistical Prediction*. U Minnesota Press, 1954. 149p.

Melton, Richard S. *A Comparison of Clinical and Actuarial Methods of Prediction with an Assessment of the Relative Accuracy of Different Clinicians*. Doctoral dissertation, U Minnesota Press, 1952. 124p.

Messick, Samuel. "Personality Measurement and College Performance." *Proceedings of the 1963 Invitational Conference on Testing Problems*. ETS, 1963.

Moon, Rexford G., Jr. *Student Financial Aid in the United States: Administration and Resources*. CEEB, 1963. 53p.

Munday, Leo. *Comparative Predictive Validities of the American College Tests and Two Other Scholastic Aptitude Tests: ACT Research Reports*. ACT, 1965.

Murray, Henry A., and others. *Explorations in Personality*. Oxford U Press, 1938. 761p.

Ness, Frederic W. (Ed.) *A Guide to Graduate Study: Programs Leading to the Ph.D. Degree*, 2nd ed. ACE, 1965. 609p.

North Central Association of Colleges and Secondary Schools. *Policies and Criteria for the Approval of Secondary Schools*. Commission on Secondary Schools, 1965–66. 38p.

Pace, C. Robert. "Five College Environments." *Col Bd R* 41:24–8; 1960.

Pace, C. Robert. *CUES: College and University Environment Scales, Preliminary Technical Manual*. ETS, 1963. 79p.

Pace, C. Robert, and Stern, George G. "An Approach to the Measurement of College Environments." *J Ed Psychol* 49:269–77; 1958.

Pearson, Richard. "Admission to College." In McGrath, E. J. (Ed.) *Universal Higher Education*. McGraw-Hill, 1966(a).

Pearson, Richard. "Proposed: A Commission on General Education in School and College." In Schwilck,

Gene L. (Ed.) *The Challenge of Curricular Change.* CEEB, 1966(*b*).

Peterson, Richard E. *A Typology of College Students: Research Bulletin.* ETS, 1965.

Richards, James M., Jr., and others. *The Prediction of Student Accomplishment in College.* ACT, 1966.

Riesman, David, and Jencks, Christopher. "The Viability of the American College." In Sanford, Nevitt. (Ed.) *The American College.* Wiley, 1962. p. 74–192.

Roberts, S. O. *Studies in Identification of College Potential.* Fisk U, 1962. (Mimeographed.)

Rossi, Peter, and Coleman, James S. *Determinants and Consequences of College Choice.* NORC and Johns Hopkins U, 1964. (Mimeographed.)

Rudolph, Frederick. *The American College and University: A History.* Knopf, 1962. 516p.

Sanders, J. Edward, and Palmer, Hans C. *The Barrier to Higher Education in California.* Pomona Col Press, 1965. 295p.

Sarbin, T. R. "A Contribution to the Study of Actuarial and Individual Methods of Prediction." *Am J Sociol* 48:593–602; 1942.

Shane, William R., and others. *LSAT Handbook: The Law School Admission Test—Its Nature, Uses, and Limitations.* ETS, 1964. 69p.

Skager, R. W., and others. "Quality and Quantity of Accomplishments as Measures of Creativity." *J Ed Psychol* 56:31–9; 1965.

Stanley, J. C., and others. *Relative Predictability of Freshman Grade-Point Averages from SAT Scores in Negro and White Southern Colleges.* Laboratory of Experimental Design, 1966. (Mimeographed.)

Stern, George G. "Characteristics of the Intellectual Climate in College Environments." *Harvard Ed R* 33:5–41; 1963.

Stice, Glen, and others. *Background Factors and College-going Plans Among High-aptitude Public High School Seniors.* ETS, 1956.

Stouffer, Samuel A. "Social Forces That Produce the Great Sorting." In *College Admissions No. 2.* CEEB, 1955. p. 1–7.

Stouffer, Samuel A. "Breaking Down Barriers to the Development of Talent." In *College Admissions, No. 7: The Search for Talent.* CEEB, 1960. p. 93–100.

Super, Donald. *The Psychology of Careers.* Harper, 1957. 362p.

Thompson, Ronald B. *Enrollment Projections for Higher Education, 1961–1978.* American Association of Collegiate Registrars and Admissions Officers, 1961. 36p.

Tiedeman, David. "Decision and Vocational Development: A Paradigm and Its Implications." *Personnel Guid J* 40:15–21, 1962.

Tinkelman, Sherman N. "Regents Examinations in New York State after 100 Years." In *Proceedings of the 1965 Invitational Conference on Testing Problems.* ETS, 1965. p. 85–94.

U.S. Bureau of the Census. *Statistical Abstract of the United States: 1965.* GPO, 1965.

U.S. Office of Education. *Digest of Educational Statistics.* USOE, 1965(*a*).

U.S. Office of Education. *Enrollment for Advanced Degrees: Fall 1963.* USOE, 1965(*b*).

U.S. Office of Education. *Opening Fall Enrollment in Higher Education, 1965.* USOE, 1966.

University of California at Berkeley. *General Catalogue, 1966–1967.* U California Press, 1966.

University of the State of New York. *Handbook on Examinations and Scholarships.* New York State Education Department, 1964.

Washington Pre-College Testing Program. *Student Instruction Booklet.* U Washington Press, 1965–66.

West, Elmer D. "United States of America." In *Access to Higher Education,* Vol. 2, *National Studies.* UNESCO and the International Association of Universities, 1965. p. 594–612.

Whitla, Dean K. "A Statistical Study of Admissions Policy." In Whitla, Dean K. (Ed.) *Handbook of Measurement.* Addison-Wesley (in press).

Willingham, W. W. "Adjusting College Predictions on the Basis of Academic Origins." In Katz, Martin. (Ed.) *The 20th Yearbook of the National Council on Measurement in Education.* NCME, 1963.

Wise, W. M., and Gummere, R., Jr. "College Transfer: A Study of the Reactions of Colleges and Universities to Eight Candidates." *Ed Rec* 43:228–34; 1962.

Withey, S. B., and others. *The Public Picture of Higher Education in the State of Michigan.* U of Michigan Press, 1959.

ADOLESCENCE

Adolescence is a period of interest to researchers for a variety of reasons not necessarily related to one another: (1) Adolescence is a period of major change, physically, psychologically, and socially. As such, it offers a chance to study the processes of development and change in human beings who are already quite complex and capable of initiating much of their own behavior. (2) Adolescence is preparation for adulthood. Consequently, to explain successes and failures in later life, it is necessary to discover how adolescent events and developments facilitate or hinder later coping behavior. (3) In many specific areas of behavior we need much more solid knowledge in order to improve the weighty social decisions we make, as regards (*a*) selective educational retention and placement; (*b*) vocational guidance and training, in its many informal as well as formal guises; (*c*) dealing with delinquents and juvenile criminals, some acting individually, some in gangs—this is actually a subfacet of the broad problem of training children and youth in ethical behavior; (*d*) some psychological developments and some health problems which may be partially unique to adolescence and which require practical action; (*e*) the large number of adolescents who suffer from neurotic or psychotic illness and who require much better informed, more effective handling than we currently give; (*f*) the problem of motivating, training, and unleashing our most gifted young people for maximum productivity and maximum realization of their capacities—the quantity of academic dropouts and of gifted youth who "slide by" in school and in life testify to the need for much more knowledge, put to effective use in family and school education; (g) preparing young people for marriage—for whatever our theoretical knowledge, our practical social mechanisms are notably haphazard and often illogical. (4) There have been some major historical changes in adolescent behavior which call for understandings we do not now possess. One of the more dramatic is the post-World War II, worldwide rise in juvenile delinquency; but there are others which may be as important, such as the long-term effect of postponing adult responsibilities and freedoms, for many more youth, through prolonging their years of schooling. The rapid rise in teen-age marriages is another new phenomenon, at least in the United States. (5) In most cultures, at least, youth is the time to capture passionate interest and loyalty to a specific ideology—political, economic, or religious. Revolutionaries appeal to the young. How this happens, why, and how it can be rationally dealt with calls for more knowledge than we now possess. (6) Wars may now be started by the old, but they are still fought by the young. Why are youth so willing, in the last analysis, to go to war? What inner needs compel it, or at least permit it? Are these forces susceptible to constructive diversion? This is only one facet of the problem of war, but it certainly is not yet understood. (7) School and college populations have been and continue to be popular subjects for research for the extremely practical reason that they are more available and controllable than any other group of normal, near-adult people. It is both easy and cheap to study almost-adults in captive populations. This is usually done in academic settings, but also in such nonpowerful groups (viewed in the total society) as youthful gangs, especially lower-class ones with very little political, economic, or social leverage.

Turning to the research that has already been done, it develops that adolescence is seldom rigorously defined in the psychological literature. In general, psychological rather than chronological divisions of the developmental stages seem to be preferred. With regard to the chronology of adolescence, however, most writers seem to agree that adolescence begins approximately at the first manifestations of puberty (Jersild, 1963; McCandless, 1961). An exact span of years is not linked with adolescence: McCandless (1961) states that some authors extend the period to age 24; Jersild (1963) considers that adolescence continues through sexual maturity, achievement of maximum growth in height, and full mental growth as measured by tests of intelligence and that these take place between ages 12 and 20. Mussen and his associates (1963) use ages 11 to 18. Hurlock (1964) suggests that for purposes of definition adolescence be considered as terminating at the age of legal maturity (21). Further, she divides the period (which begins at approximately age 13 for girls and age 14 for boys) into "early" and "late," with age 17 as the dividing line. This emphasis on the chronology of adolescence is of some importance in the light of Erikson's construct (1959) of the "psychosocial moratorium" wherein societies are said to offer, in accordance with individual requirements, a sanctioned transitional period between childhood and adulthood. Previously Kuhlen (1960) noted that educators at the high school level (both junior and senior) were considered to be especially concerned with adolescent phenomena. There is now consensus (Group for the Advancement of Psychiatry, 1962) that the college years, in whole or part, compose a part of adolescence. Thus, prolongation of adolescence would be in accord with Erikson's concept.

Developmental Trends in Adolescence. Adolescents have been said to require the achievement of certain developmental tasks (Havighurst, 1953). Various theorists have stressed, in accordance with their predilections, varying developmental tasks. Thus, in psychoanalytic theory, major tasks of adolescence include establishment of a new balance between id and ego forces (Freud, 1958), inevitably necessary because of the quantitative and qualitative changes in drive activity concomitant with puberty. Erikson (1959), also a psychoanalytic theorist but one who stresses ego development, contends that the special unique task of adolescence is the establishment of "ego identity." This idea has enjoyed great vogue in psychological writings since it was first set forth. Virtually all recent texts on introductory psychology and educational psychology refer in their exposition of adolescence to the "ego identity" or "ego diffusion" crisis of this stage. Ross (1962) and Bronson (1959) report empirical evidence to support this concept. White (1952) identifies four major growth trends specific to this stage in life: stabilizing of ego identity (taken from Erikson), deepening of interests, freeing of personal relationships (from mere transference of reactions to people known in childhood), and humanizing of values (instead of literal rule conformity). Sanford (1966) adds a fifth: general development and strengthening of ego. He adds that in the Vassar study, senior women showed greater uncertainty about identity than did freshmen women; but he reports that the seniors had given up their earlier, narrower self-definitions, were striving to achieve a wider, more complex identity, and had given up much of their earlier dependence on external definition and support. So little research has been done on the psychological aspects of the transition from adolescence to adulthood that few firm assertions can be made. Nonetheless, it seems clear that the "crystallization" of adult identity does not occur in many people—perhaps, especially, in college students—until the early or middle twenties. It may only be when a firm, purposeful career choice is evolved and executed, when a purposefully chosen mate is found and married (with allowances for sex-role differences), or both, that adolescence can truly be said to end. The question of adolescent "storm and stress" was well reviewed by Kuhlen (1960). Little new evidence exists to contradict his conclusion that adolescence is probably no more or less stressful than other periods of life. Bandura and Walters (1959) question the hypotheses of inevitable storm and stress, increased parental restrictiveness at adolescence, increased parent–peer-group conflicts, and intensified dependence–independence conflicts. In this last instance, Bandura (1964) holds that emancipation from parents has been virtually completed rather than begun at adolescence. This view is at variance with that of the Group for Advancement of Psychiatry. Based on their review of the literature on personality development during the college years, the Group for the Advancement of Psychiatry Report No. 32 (1955) listed resolution of the dependence–independence problem as the first of five aspects of personality development especially crucial during college years (ages 17–22). The contradictions, the inconsistent findings, could be cited ad infinitum. They sum up to what has been regarded as the current state of adolescent psychology—one in which studies are highly diversified and do not add up to any specific, coherent whole. Nonetheless, if all these studies are viewed in context with recent studies of psychological adjustment in adult populations (e.g., Neugarten, 1964), it begins to look as though the inner storms and stresses which most adolescents are thought to experience are the lot they share with people of all ages. Adolescence is certainly no idyll for most people (Lorand & Schneer, 1961), but neither is childhood or adulthood. While the voluble unrest of some college students makes headlines (Dennis & Kauffman, 1966), a psychiatrist functioning in a college setting comments that even the students with problems whom he has studied are the most intelligent and healthy there have been (Blaine, 1966; see also Meredith, 1963).

Biological Changes. The biological changes of adolescence, including body-image changes and intensified sexual impulses (Bosselman & others, 1965), bring inevitable psychological reactions (Ausubel, 1954). Both the biological changes and the psychobiological phenomena have been well described (Ausubel, 1954; Tanner, 1963). The Gesell work (Gesell & others, 1956) describes typical, major manifestations, both biological and psychological, of each year from 10 to 16. The phenomena characteristic of each year are categorized under nine headings: (1) total action system, which includes also health, tensional outlets, physical development, and sex awareness (for both boys and girls), (2) self-care and routines covering eating (appetite, preferences and refusals, snacks, and table behavior), sleep, bathing and care of hair, clothes and care of room, money, and work, (3) emotions, (4) the growing self, (5) interpersonal relationships, (6) activities and interests, (7) school life, (8) ethical sense, and (9) philosophical outlook, which involves conceptions of time and space and death and Deity. The authors caution that their data do not constitute psychometric norms but may, nonetheless, be used in estimating maturity levels. Tanner's findings (1963) on growth changes in British children confirm the studies reported by Kuhlen (1960). Menarche occurs in British girls at an average age of 13.1 years; full reproductive function is not achieved with this first menstrual period, the period of infertility being said to endure for a year and a half. Growth of breasts in girls and of testes in boys is considered the first sign of imminent pubescence, although growth of pubic hair in both sexes is usually regarded as an early sign. Contrary to many popular assumptions—and fears—premarital sexual codes of teen-agers of the past decade have been found to be more conservative and restrained than those of their older siblings. Reiss, in "Sexual Codes in Teen Age Culture" (1961), using his own data as well as those of the Kinsey studies (1948, 1953), states that (1) the coitus rate for females doubles between the ages of 20 and 25; (2) petting with affection is a most popular code with teen-age girls; however, religion and social class are important variables in the control of this sexual behavior; (3) among teen-age boys, the double standard still remains dominant, although a trend toward equalitarian sexual attitudes (similar to those in the Scandinavian countries) is perceived; (4) when venereal disease and pregnancy statistics are analyzed, older groups have, in the former regard, almost three times the incidence compared to later teen-age groups; (5) while 40 percent of the unwed mothers are teen-agers, most of the reported cases are Negro and/or lower class rather than middle class. Reiss's paper appears in the volume *Teen Age Culture* (Bernard, 1961); in this collection of papers both sexual and other aspects of special teen-age cultures (i.e., rural, ethnic, bicultural) are discussed by Mays, in "Teen Age Culture in Contemporary Britain and Europe"; by Bealer and Willets, in "Rural Youth"; by Ianni, in "The Italo-American Teenager"; by Boroff, in "Jewish Teen Age Culture"; and by Himes, in "Negro Teen Age Culture." Their essays also cover much more than just the sexual behavior of these groups.

There are, of course, psychological concomitants of the various biological changes. Mussen and Jones (1963) found that late-maturing boys showed higher drives for social acceptance than the early maturers. In girls (Jones & Mussen, 1963) the group differences are not so clear-cut, but the conclusion of these authors is that physical retardation may have adverse personality effects for both sexes: early maturation appears to favor more adequate psychological and social adjustment. Faust (1960) found developmental maturity in girls to be an asset in prestige status in the seventh and eighth grades, although it constituted a detriment to prestige among sixth graders.

Intellectual Abilities, Interests, and Performance. The work of Piaget, Inhelder, and their associates (Inhelder & Piaget, 1958) ascribes to early adolescence (ages 11–15) the realization of the end stage in intellectual development—i.e., the stage of *formal operations*. In contrast to the stage of *concrete operations*, which prevails during the years 7–11, they say that the adolescent who has adopted formal thinking is now capable of reasoning and of arriving at conclusions without assistance from objects actually present. In general, the adolescent achieves the capability of all characteristics of thought ordinarily associated with human maturity: critical evaluation of one's own thinking, theory construction, capacity for abstraction, and so forth. An excellent exposition of

Piaget's theory is given by Flavell (1963). By and large, there has been empirical confirmation of many of Piaget's formulations (e.g., Elkind, 1963). Thurstone's analysis (1955) indicated that of the primary mental abilities, the space and reasoning factors mature at approximately 14, memory and number at about age 16, and verbal comprehension and word fluency even beyond age 16. Mental age, as measured by the Wechsler scales, rises during the years up to 16, stabilizes until the mid-twenties, and then declines slightly (Wechsler, 1958). Data from the California Growth Study (Bayley, 1957) indicate, however, that there may be exceptions to this pattern; some individuals show IQ gains during ages 16–21. There are, as might be predicted, adolescents whose IQ's continue to gain in college. Sontag and Kagan (1963) have demonstrated relationships between independent behavior, achievement motivation, and efficient intellectual performance which agree with Bayley's report. Ausubel's research (1954) on intellectual growth in adolescence remains pertinent. Recent research has not contradicted his findings that intellectual growth in adolescence proceeds smoothly from earlier stages; this is in marked contrast to other components of growth—physiological, personality, and social—where there are accelerated periods of development. Bloom's analysis (1964) of longitudinal studies indicates that there is a significant amount of growth in scholastic aptitude between the ages of 18 and 22 in students attending college. The major growth appears to take place between 18 and 20.

Interests and Performance. Lucas and Horrocks (1960) extracted approximately 70 stated needs of adolescents from a survey of the literature and constructed a questionnaire covering these needs. Factor analysis of the responses of over 725 adolescents to the questionnaire revealed five factors: (1) need for recognition-acceptance, (2) need for heterosexual affection and attention, (3) need for independence and dominance in relationships with adults, (4) need to conform to adult expectations, and (5) need for achievement related primarily to school achievement. A desire for academic achievement clearly characterizes most adolescents, and a number of studies have provided data on such school-related interests. Harris' data (1959) revealed that "study habits" were high on the list of problems of adolescent boys and girls in 1937 and 1957 but were ranked quite low by both sexes in terms of interest. Hess (1963) found that high school scholastic performance was the best and most consistent simple predictor of adult success (as defined by level of occupation, social mobility, and salary). This finding held for both sexes, but particularly for males. Personality and family variables bore some relationship to adult achievement, but this was slight in comparison to the relationship between high school academic performance and adult achievement. Sontag and Kagan (1963) maintain that there is a critical period in the development of the desire for intellectual achievement: the period between six and ten, when the child is in the first to the fourth grades. Achievement in the academic arena does not make for popularity, however, among many adolescents. In Coleman's studies (1961a), the attributes of "high grades, honor roll" ranked fourth out of six in terms of their contribution toward making a boy popular. Jones (1963) found that there were no significant correlations between high IQ and "high mention" status (as measured by the frequency with which names appeared in high school newspapers). In Australia, "cognitive abilities" are traits more closely associated with adolescent popularity than they are in the United States, but even there, Wheeler (1963) found that "sporting abilities" are far more contributory to popularity among Australian youth than intellectual capacity and performance. The report of Project Talent (1964) on the American high school student is a large-scale contribution. Over 400,000 students (grades 9–12) in approximately 1,300 public, private, and parochial schools all over the United States completed a battery of tests and questionnaires which explored ability, personality, interest, family, vocational, socioeconomic, and other characteristics. Specifically with regard to interests, those of the male students were found to focus on three themes: (1) the appeal of the masculine hero, (2) a drive for power and self, and (3) science and technology. Interests of girls related to four themes: (1) homemaking and motherhood, (2) glamour and adventure, (3) social service, and (4) making a living. In terms of occupational preferences, boys were partial to aviation, professional athletics, engineering, science, military service, and business; girls enjoyed social work, secretarial duties, being airline hostesses, and being housewives. Boys also favor sports and the desire to become "millionaires." (At the ninth-grade level, this drive for money ranks third—by the eleventh grade it is tied for first with "save money.") Cultural pursuits—e.g., symphony concerts, art galleries, poetry are ranked quite low by boys. Girls seem to be preoccupied with saving money (ranked first throughout ninth to twelfth grades), but they also like to "help the poor" and to "help parents."

Personality characteristics of this enormous adolescent sample were related to characteristics of the home, cultural activities, aptitude and achievement variables, and social activities. Of interest to educators are such findings as those that "mature personality" and "leadership" scores were more closely related to school marks than were other personality variables. The variables of mature personality, self-confidence, social sensitivity, and calmness correlated most highly (of the 20 personality measures) with aptitude and achievement test scores. While participation in athletics correlated significantly with scores on leadership, the correlation with school marks was low. Follow-up studies of over 60,000 students yield data of considerable importance to those concerned with the entry of the adolescent into the world of work and the world of college. In the Project Talent sample, 53 percent of the boys and 35 percent of the girls went on to college. Of the students who went on to college, 80 percent attended four-year colleges, while 20 percent entered junior colleges. There was a marked relationship between aptitude level and the tendency to remain in college. In the top 2 percent of the aptitude distribution, almost 93 percent of the boys and 91 percent of the girls were still enrolled one year after college entrance, while in the bottom 25 percent of the distribution, 85 percent of the boys and 89 percent of the girls had dropped out. Considering all college dropouts, 21 percent of the girls dropped out because of marriage, while 28 percent of the boys did so because of financial difficulties or to take good jobs. Assuming that many reasons could be subsumed under "emotional disturbance"— "failure" (22 percent of boy dropouts), "didn't enjoy social life" (0.9 percent), "college work was boring" (2.7 percent), "had to work too hard" (1.7 percent), "was afraid of failing" (3.1 percent), "became ill" (1.9 percent)—the total (32.3 percent) still falls short of the estimate made by Farnsworth (1959) that 50 percent of all college students who drop out of college do so for emotional causes.

Values and Attitudes. Reiss (1961) reported that with regard to sexual codes, there is not a "youth culture" with its own values, separate, apart, and antipathetic to the larger adult culture, nor is there inevitably a conflict of generations on their values and attitudes. Coleman (1961a), Friedenberg (1965), and Smith (1962) subscribe to the thesis that disparate adult and youth cultures exist; Bandura (1964) and Elkin and Westley (1955) do not find this to be true. Setting aside the issue whether the two cultures are disparate and in conflict (Smith, 1962), or whether the teen-age culture is an adaptation of the adult culture (Reiss, 1961; Matza, 1961), Bernard (1961) has suggested that a highly visible teen-age culture continues because ours is an affluent society, highlighting an adolescent emphasis on fun and popularity. Materially, clothes, records, cosmetics, and automobiles are basic preoccupations in the teen-age culture (Bernard, 1961). McFarland and Moore (1961) estimate that approximately 18.5 percent of licensed drivers in the United States are under 24 years of age and that by age 19, four or five out of every six boys and two or three girls out of every six are licensed drivers. The implications of the automobile for adolescent behavior and culture are well known. Automobile driving has been found to be positively related to dropping out of school and absenteeism and inversely related to grade-point average and to school achievement in general. Twenty-five percent of the motor vehicle deaths in 1957 occurred in the 15-to-24-year age group. Some kind of improved education for driving would seem to be literally a life-and-death necessity for many adolescents.

Adolescent values and attitudes are related to social class (e.g., Coster, 1963; Kohn, 1963; Rosen, 1963). Coster found that high school students of families of middle- and high-income groups participated more in extracurricular activities, had higher grade-point averages, and went on to higher education. In Rosen's study, social class was consistently associated with achievement motivation. Havighurst and his associates (1962) emphasize that the dropouts (largely lower class) among River City youth had the greatest difficulty in moving on to adulthood —they obtained the worst jobs, were most vulnerable to delinquency, and had the most marital problems. They conclude that "school provides the only pathway to adolescence in River City, and high school is the only easily traveled route through adolescence to adulthood." The implication here is that participation in adolescent society and high school attendance are closely intertwined. Social class is also related to social leadership and social participation; i.e., social leaders tend to originate in the higher socioeconomic strata.

Social Relations. Many theorists are in accord that peer relations play a major role in adolescence, though perhaps they hold this for differing reasons. Ausubel (1954) states that these interactions serve, among other functions, the facilitation of emancipation from the home and the transmission of social class values. Sullivan (1953) posits certain crucial interpersonal needs during each developmental stage, with "chumship" (i.e., intimate relationships with a like-sexed person) being the crucial need during preadolescence and the patterning of heterosexual object relationships prepotent in adolescence. With regard to deviant adolescents, such as delinquents and emotionally ill teen-agers, the presence of distorted, unhealthy parent-child relationships is a common finding (Lichter & others, 1962; Bennett, 1960). Glueck and Glueck (1962) studied 500 delinquent adolescents and 500 proved nondelinquent adolescents, carefully matched in terms of age, general intelligence (IQ), ethnic-racial derivation, and residence in depressed areas of Greater Boston. The incidence of 44 social factors (all related to home and family) was compared in the two groups. Significant differences in the incidence of 40 out of the 44 parental-family factors were found between the two groups. Slocum and Stone (1963) investigated the relationship between family culture patterns (fairness of discipline, degree of affection, family democracy, and intrafamily cooperation) and delinquent-type behavior among 3,000 adolescents. Delinquent behavior was found to be associated with low scores on the four family variables. McCord and his associates (1963), investigating *antisocial* as opposed to *socialized* aggressiveness, found that extreme neglect and punitiveness, along with a deviant, aggressive paternal model, produce antisocial aggressiveness; on the other hand, moderate neglect, moderate punitiveness, and ineffective control produce socialized aggressiveness. Even in nonachieving societies, lack or limitation of opportunity for the young boy to form an identification with his father was associated with theft and personal crime (e.g., assault, murder, and rape) in adolescence. This finding emerged from a study by Bacon and others (1963) of the correlates of crime in 48 nonliterate societies. Peck and his associates (1960) experimented with a scheme of developmental levels of character formation and reported systematic relationships of character structure to several aspects of parental behavior, to relations with age mates, and to school achievement. Their theoretical scheme is allied to the ideas of Piaget and of neoanalytic psychologists such as Erikson and Fromm. In emotionally disturbed adolescents, it seems rather definitively established that unhealthy parent-child relations have been antecedent to the emotional illness (Heilbrun & McKinley, 1962; Garmezy & others, 1961; Vogel & Lauterbach, 1963). Carlson (1963) studied the role of parental identification in the development of the child's self-image and social relationships in preadolescence. One of her findings of pertinence here was that children whose identification is based on parental support show greater self-esteem and greater acceptance by peers as compared with those children who either identify with nonsupporting parents or do not identify. Bath and Lewis (1962) studied conflict between parents and adolescent girls in a sample of college students. They found that (1) conflict is more likely to occur when parents' practices are inconsistent and restrictive, (2) the major determinant of attitudes held by the subjects was the particular set of practices within their own families, and (3) very few of the subjects would be less strict with their own teen-age daughters than their parents had been with them. The authors hypothesize that conflict between parents and adolescents may have little effect on the long-term attitudes of the latter and that with maturity the individual female incorporates the attitudes of her parents into her own behavior. Elder (1962) concludes that strong parental control which does not change in response to increasing age of the adolescent weakens the affectional ties between the child and parent. "Democratic" parents make more attractive models for their adolescent children than do "aristocratic" or "permissive" parents (Elder, 1963). Simpson (1962) studied parental versus peer-group influences on ambition and aspirations to mobility among both middle- and working-class boys. Subjects were classified as "high" or "low" regarding the extent to which they had been subjected to parental influence and to peer influence toward high occupational aspiration. The influence of parents was found to be greater than that of peers. Middleton and Putney (1963), studying the political expression of adolescent rebellion in 1,440 college students, found that political rebellion appears most likely to occur when parent and child are emotionally estranged, when the parent is interested in politics, and when the child believes paternal discipline is either too strict or too permissive.

The weight of recent evidence seems to indicate that the vast majority of adolescents remain more under parental than peer influence. As the Bernard essay (1961a) has shown, teen-age culture is more conservative and closer to adult culture than it is popularly thought to be. Sanford's *American College* (1962) provides an excellent overview of the college experience and its impact on late adolescents. Ausubel (1954), in his chapter "Adolescents and the School," summarizes the influence the school exercises on adolescents in intellectual, moral, personal, and social respects.

Implications for Education. Since ego identity is so urgent and preoccupying a subject in adolescence, it would seem sensible to introduce junior high school students to those parts of the behavioral sciences that can help them identify, understand, and develop their own natures. Their deepening capacity for dedication to intrinsically valuable tasks could undoubtedly be more frequently enlisted in projects of genuine human value, as the Peace Corps amply demonstrates. The organization of the high school in terms of subject-matter areas, whatever its original purpose, seems in tune with the need for numerous, diversified adult models at this stage. The growth of rationality suggests a need for many opportunities for adolescents to discuss and debate issues and learn facts for themselves, during much of the school day. The biological changes, and their preoccupying power, suggest some changes in the content of junior high school and high school courses—and college courses, too—to deal more directly and relevantly with the issues central to the several stages in this period. Honest education about the several aspects of boy-girl behavior captures the eager attraction of adolescents, from 12 through 21, at least. Biological aspects should be taught earlier and considered as only part of the story. The evidence on intellectual growth and interests suggests several points: (1) junior high school education should be adapted to the emergent theory-building and testing capacities of early adolescents. Didactic teaching should yield increasing proportions of time to student exploration of issues and facts; (2) even college students who do not think or study effectively can be taught to do so; but (3) the growth of an inner desire to achieve must occur in the first four grades; junior high school may be too late to start; hence (4) deficiently motivated high school and college students may have to be identified, so that the external pressure they require can be maintained, if they are to achieve at all. With money so fascinating a subject to adolescents (as to their parents), schools might earn more respect and more attention if they would frankly and honestly go into the natural attractions of money: how education can help to get it (for the boys) and how to manage it (for the girls). Realism here might salvage some of the 28 percent of male dropouts, for example, who leave school to make some money. Not only is driver education not a "frill," judging by the accident statistics, but automobiles are hypnotically attractive to many youth. It would seem that cars need not be a taboo subject in courses in mathematics, English, or economics. Family relations play so dominant a role in creating ambition, mental illness, antisocial behavior, and moral maturity that schools can hardly afford to surrender to pressure groups who would outlaw any study of a student's family experiences as being an "invasion of privacy." Confidentiality must always be protected, but as long as schools are charged with the responsibility for fostering effective learning and healthy, ethical conduct, educators can not reasonably be forbidden to consider those family influences which outweigh all others in their potency.

Robert F. Peck
Herbert Richek
University of Texas

References

Ausubel, D. P. *Theory and Problems of Adolescent Development.* Grune, 1954. 580p.

Bacon, Margaret K., and others. "A cross-cultural study of correlates of crime." *Social Psychol* 66:291–300; 1963.

Bandura, A. "The Stormy Decade: Fact or Fiction." *Psychol Schs* 1:224–31; 1964.

Bandura, A., and Walters, R. H. *Adolescent Aggression.* Ronald, 1959. 475p.

Bath, J. A., and Lewis, E. C. "Attitudes of Young Female Adults Toward Some Areas of Parent-adolescent Conflict." *Genet Psychol* 100:241–53; 1962.

Bayley, Nancy. "Data on the Growth of Intelligence Between 16 and 21 Years." *Genet Psychol* 90:3–15; 1957.

Bealer, R. C., and Willets, Fern. "Rural Youth: A Case Study in the Rebelliousness of Adolescents." In Bernard, Jessie. (Ed.) *Teen Age Culture.* The Annals of the American Academy of Political and Social Science, 1961. p. 63–69.

Bennett, Ivy. *Delinquent and Neurotic Children: A Comparative Study.* Basic Books, Inc., Publishers, 1960. 532p.

Bernard, Jessie (Ed.) *Teen Age Culture.* The Annals of the American Academy of Political and Social Science. 1961(a). 210p.

Bernard, Jessie. "Teen Age Culture: An Overview." In Bernard, Jessie. (Ed.) *Teen Age Culture.* The Annals of the American Academy of Political and Social Science, 1961(b). p. 1–12.

Blaine, G. B., Jr. "College Students and Moral Values." In Dennis, L., and Kauffman, J. F. (Eds.) *The College and the Student.* ACE, 1966. p. 372–6.

Bloom, B. S. *Stability and Change in Human Characteristics.* Wiley, 1964. 237p.

Boroff, D. "Jewish Teen Age Culture." In Bernard, Jessie. (Ed.) *Teen Age Culture.* The Annals of the American Academy of Political and Social Science, 1961. p. 79–90.

Bosselman, Beulah C., and others. *Introduction to Developmental Psychiatry.* Thomas, 1965. 139p.

Bronson, G. W. "Identity Diffusion in Late Adolescents." *Social Psychol* 59:414–7; 1959.

Carlson, Rae. "Identification and Personality Structure in Preadolescence." *Psychol* 67:566–73; 1963.

Coleman, J. S. *The Adolescent Society.* Free, 1961(a). 368p.

Coleman, J. S. "Athletics in High School." In Bernard, Jessie. (Ed.) *Teen Age Culture.* The Annals of the American Academy of Political and Social Science, 1961(b). p. 33–43.

Coster, J. K. "Some Characteristics of High School Pupils From Three Income Groups." In Grinder, R. (Ed.) *Studies in Adolescence.* Macmillan, 1963. p. 208–18.

Dansereau, H. K. "Work and the Teen-ager." In Bernard, Jessie. (Ed.) *Teen Age Culture.* The Annals of the American Academy of Political and Social Science, 1961. p. 44–52.

Dennis, L., and Kauffman, J. F. (Eds.) *The College and the Student.* ACE, 1966. 390p.

Elder, Glen H., Jr. "Structural Variations in the Child Rearing Relationship." *Sociometry* 25:241–62; 1962.

Elder, Glen H., Jr. "Parental Power Legitimation and Its Effect on the Adolescent." *Sociometry* 26:50–65; 1963.

Elkin, F., and Westley, W. A. "The Myth of Adolescent Culture." *Am Soc Rev* 20:680–4; 1955.

Elkind, D. "Quantity Conceptions in Junior and Senior High School Students." In Grinder, R. (Ed.) *Studies in Adolescence.* Macmillan, 1963. p. 474–83.

Erikson, Erik H. "Identity and the Life Cycle: Selected Papers." *Psychol Issues* 1:18–171; 1959.

Farnsworth, D. S. "We're Wasting Brainpower." *NEA J* 48:42; 1959.

Faust, M. S. "Developmental Maturity as a Determinant of Prestige in Adolescent Girls." *Child Develop* 31:173–84; 1960.

Flavell, J. H. *The Developmental Psychology of Jean Piaget.* Van Nostrand, 1963. 472p.

Freud, Anna. "Adolescence." In *Psychoanalytic Study of the Child*, Vol. 13. International Universities Press, Inc., 1958. p. 255–78.

Friedenberg, Edgar Z. *Coming of Age in America.* Random, 1965. 300p.

Garmezy, N., and others. "Child Rearing Attitudes of Mothers and Fathers as Reported by Schizophrenic and Normal Patients." *J Abn Social Psychol* 63:176–82; 1961.

Gesell, Arnold, and others. *Youth: The Years from Ten to Sixteen.* Harper, 1956. 542p.

Ginzberg, E. (Ed.) *Values and Ideals of American Youth.* Columbia U Press, 1961. 338p.

Glueck, Sheldon, and Glueck, Eleanor. *Family Environment and Delinquency.* Houghton, 1962. 328p.

Grinder, R. (Ed.) *Studies in Adolescence.* Macmillan, 1963. 524p.

Group for the Advancement of Psychiatry. *Considerations on Personality Development in College Students.* Group Report No. 32. The Group, 1955. 11p.

Group for the Advancement of Psychiatry. *The College Experience: A Focus for Psychiatric Research.* Group Report No. 52. The Group, 1962. 48p.

Harris, D. B. "Sex Differences in the Life Problems and Interests of Adolescents, 1935 and 1957." *Child Develop* 30:453–9; 1959.

Havighurst, R. J. *Human Development and Education.* McKay, 1953. 338p.

Havighurst, R. J., and Taba, Hilda. *Adolescent Character and Personality.* Wiley, 1949. 315p.

Havighurst, Robert J., and others. *Growing Up in River City.* Wiley, 1962. 189p.

Heilbrun, A. B., Jr., and McKinley, R. "Perception of Maternal Childrearing Attitudes, Personality of the Perceiver, and Incipient Psychopathology." *Child Develop* 33:73–83; 1962.

Himes, J. S. "Negro Teen Age Culture." In Bernard, Jessie. (Ed.) *Teen Age Culture.* The Annals of the American Academy of Political and Social Science, 1961. p. 91–101.

Hess, R. D. "High School Antecedents of Young

Adult Achievement." in Grinder, R. (Ed.) *Studies in Adolescence*. Macmillan, 1963. p. 401–14.

Hurlock, Elizabeth B. *Child Development*, 4th ed. McGraw-Hill, 1964. 776p.

Ianni, F. A. J. "The Italo-American Teenager." In Bernard, Jessie. (Ed.) *Teen Age Culture*. The Annals of the American Academy of Political and Social Science, 1961. p. 70–8.

Inhelder, B., and Piaget, Jean. *The Growth of Logical Thinking from Childhood to Adolescence*. Basic Books, Inc., Publishers, 1958. 356p.

Jersild, A. *The Psychology of Adolescence*, 2nd ed. Macmillan, 1963. 468p.

Jones, Mary C. "A Study of Socialization Patterns at the High School Level." In Grinder, R. (Ed.) *Studies in Adolescence*. Macmillan, 1963. p. 349–73.

Jones, Mary C., and Mussen, P. H. "Self-conceptions, Motivations, and Interpersonal Attitudes of Early- and Late-maturing Girls." In Grinder, R. (Ed.) *Studies in Adolescence*. Macmillan, 1963. p. 354–65.

Kinsey, A. C., and others. *Sexual Behavior in the Human Male*. Saunders, 1948. 804p.

Kinsey, A. C., and others. *Sexual Behavior in the Human Female*. Saunders, 1953. 842p.

Kohn, M. L. "Social Class and Parental Values." In Grinder, R. (Ed.) *Studies in Adolescence*. Macmillan, 1963. p. 187–207.

Kuhlen, Raymond G. "Adolescence." In *Encyclopedia of Educational Research*. Macmillan, 1960. p. 24–30.

Lichter, S. O., and others. *The Dropouts*. Free, 1962. 802p.

Lorand, S., and Schneer, H. (Eds.) *Adolescents: Psychoanalytic Approach to Problems and Therapy*. Harper, 1961. 378p.

Lucas, C. M., and Horrocks, J. E. "An Experimental Approach to the Analysis of Adolescent Needs." *Child Develop* 31:479–87; 1960.

Matza, D. "Subterranean Traditions of Youth." In Bernard, Jessie. (Ed.) *Teen Age Culture*. The Annals of the American Academy of Political and Social Science, 1961. p. 102–17.

Mays, J. B. "Teen Age Culture in Contemporary Britain and Europe." In Bernard, Jessie. (Ed.) *Teen Age Culture*. The Annals of the American Academy of Political and Social Science, 1961. p. 22–32.

McCandless, B. R. *Children and Adolescents: Behavior and Development*. Holt, 1961. 521p.

McCord, J., and others. "Family Interaction as Antecedent to the Direction of Male Aggressiveness." *J Abn Social Psychol* 66:239–42; 1963.

McFarland and Moore. "Automobiles and Adolescence." In Ginzberg, E. (Ed.) *Values and Ideals of American Youth*. Columbia U Press, 1961. p. 169–191.

Meredith, H. V. "Change in the Stature and Body Weight of North American Boys During the Last 80 Years." In Lipsett, L. P., and Spiker, C. C. (Eds.) *Advances in Child Development and Behavior*, Vol. 1. Academic, 1963. p. 69–114.

Middleton, R., and Putney, S. "Student Rebellion Against Parental Political Beliefs." *Social Forces* 41:377–83; 1963.

Mussen, P. H., and Jones, Mary C. "The Behavior Inferred Motivations of Late- and Early-maturing Boys." In Grinder, R. (Ed.) *Studies in Adolescence*. Macmillan, 1963. p. 446–53.

Mussen, P. H., and others. *Child Development and Personality*, 2nd ed. Harper, 1963. 625p.

Neugarten, Bernice L. (Ed.) *Personality in Middle and Later Life*. Atherton Press, 1964. 231p.

Peck, Robert F., and others. *The Psychology of Character Development*. Wiley, 1960. 267p.

Project Talent. *The American High School Student*. U Pittsburg Press, 1964.

Reiss, I. L. "Sexual Codes in Teen Age Culture." In Bernard, Jessie, (Ed.) *Teen Age Culture*. The Annals of the American Academy of Political and Social Science, 1961. p. 53–62.

Rosen, B. C. "Family Structure and Achievement Motivation." In Grinder, R. (Ed.) *Studies in Adolescence*. Macmillan, 1963. p. 169–86.

Ross, A. O. "Ego Identity and the Social Order: A Psychosocial Analysis of Six Indonesians." *Psychol Monogr* 76 (Whole No. 542); 1962.

Sanford, Nevitt. (Ed.) *The American College*. Wiley, 1962. 1084p.

Sanford, Nevitt. *Self and Society*. Atherton Press, 1966. 381p.

Simpson, R. L. "Parental Influence, Anticipatory Socialization and Social Mobility." *Am Social Rev* 27:517–22; 1962.

Slocum, W. L., and Stone, Carol L. "Family Culture Patterns and Delinquent-type Behavior." *Marriage and Family Living* 25:202–8; 1963.

Smith, E. A. *American Youth Culture: Group Life in Teenage Society*. Free, 1962. 264p.

Sontag, L. W., and Kagan, J. "The Emergence of Intellectual Achievement Motives." *Am J Orthopsychiatry* 33:532–5; 1963.

Sullivan, Harry Stack. *The Interpersonal Theory of Psychiatry*. W. A. White Psychiatric Foundation, 1953. 393p.

Tanner, J. M. "The Course of Children's Growth." In Grinder, R. (Ed.) *Studies in Adolescence*. Macmillan, 1963. 417–32.

Thurstone, L. L. *The Differential Growth of Mental Ability*. U North Carolina Press, 1955.

Vogel, W., and Lauterbach, C. G. "Relationships Between Normal and Disturbed Sons' Percepts of Their Parents' Behavior, and Personality Attributes of the Parents and Sons." *J Clin Psychol* 19:52–6; 1963.

Wechsler, D. *The Measurement and Appraisal of Adult Intelligence*, 4th ed. Williams and Wilkins, 1958. 297p.

Wheeler, D. K. "Popularity Among Adolescents in Western Australia and in the United States of America." In Grinder, R. (Ed.) *Studies in Adolescence*. Macmillan, 1963. p. 297–308.

White, R. W. *Lives in Progress*. The Dryden Press, Inc., 1952. 376p.

ADULT EDUCATION

In its largest sense, the education of an adult (like that of a child) may be said to be the result of all of his experiences, since any act can, theoretically at least, have an influence on the reinforcement or change of his ability to know, to do, or to feel. While recognizing this largest application of the term, most writers limit their investigation to those activities of men and women which are guided and shaped for an appreciable period of time by the desire to learn or to teach. The element of purpose may be in the mind of the student, of the would-be teacher, or of both. The frequent and casual expression of curiosity (such as glancing at an item in an encyclopedia, walking rapidly through a museum, or asking someone the meaning of a word) would logically, perhaps, fall within the definition of adult education, as would the passing along of information in conversations. For practical purposes, however, some limitation of persistence or endurance is usually imposed to avoid the unmanageable task of trying to cope with the myriad and fleeting ways by which men and women seek or convey knowledge, skills, or attitudes.

GROWTH OF THE FIELD. Cultural history is rich with references to the need of adults to learn throughout life and with accounts of their efforts to do so. Some expression of this idea may usually be found in the traditions, lore, or written records of almost any society. Until the early years of the nineteenth century, however, learning at any age was usually restricted to an elite or to those few people, in monasteries or elsewhere, who could devote themselves to lives of scholarship. As the idea of cultural democracy was gradually established, the first aim of society was to extend the benefits of education to all children and youth. The concentration on this task created such an intense interest and required so much expenditure of time and effort that it almost wholly absorbed the attention which both the lay public and the teaching professions could give to education and caused the meaning of learning as a lifelong activity to be forgotten or ignored. Meanwhile, however, countless new institutions of adult education were created, particularly in Europe and the United States. While many died or survive only in an enfeebled condition, others have flourished and now provide some of the strongest programs in existence. Among them are public evening schools, general university extension divisions, agricultural extension services, folk high schools, evening colleges, public libraries, people's colleges, workers' educational groups, museums, settlement houses, social centers, correspondence schools, and voluntary associations.

In the twentieth century, adult education has grown so rapidly that it has challenged the imagination of many people and required the reassessment of the idea that education is an activity solely of childhood and youth. This idea was always more implicit than explicit in educational writings. For example, few, if any, psychologists would deny that adults can learn, but books on educational psychology have tended to ignore or to give only a cursory glance at research on the learning of men and women, and most such books suggest few applications to adult educational practice. This situation is changing, but only slowly.

The growth of adult educational activities may be attributed to numerous factors. It has come to be generally realized that many social problems can be solved only by the education of those who are already mature; among the best-known campaigns of the present century in the United States have been those devoted to literacy, Americanization, more effective parenthood, the training of civilians for the military service, education for employment (particularly during the depression years), a multifaceted attack on the causes and effects of poverty, and the efforts by which minority groups of various kinds have learned their rights and obligations. Certain basic social trends have also had powerful influences on the growth of adult education. Among them are the increasing number and proportion of adults in the population of the highly developed nations, the shortening of the work week, the migration of people both within a nation and to other nations, the growth of knowledge, the increase of transportation and communication, and the insistence of colonies on independence. An important element in this complex of causes has been the rising level of education in the more fully developed nations and the recognition of the importance of education in the less fully developed ones.

THE LITERATURE OF ADULT EDUCATION. Both the growth of adult education and the attention devoted to it have produced a literature of almost bewildering magnitude and variety. Now in print are thousands of books and even more journal articles which bear directly or tangentially on the learning activities of adults, most of this literature lying outside the study of education as it is ordinarily defined. The field of adult education is a lively one, full of different theoretical and methodological approaches, and has its full share of controversies on many points. This complexity of viewpoint is certain to endure in a field of work which includes so many diverse institutions, deals with learning activities which occur during the long span of the years of maturity, and is closely connected to the highly variable conditions of adult life. But amid this diversity there has grown up a body of central conceptions and data which, far too slowly but nonetheless certainly, is giving some structure to the thought and practice which guides this aspect of man's life. This development of tested knowledge and accepted principles has been greatly stimulated by the growth of adult education as a graduate field of study in the universities of several countries, most notably the United States.

The most profound difference of viewpoint among those who study adult education lies in the fundamental conception they hold of the field. One group believes that education is a single basic process which varies at the different stages of life; it is important, therefore, to study both the fundamental activity itself and its special applications in the lives of men and women. The other group believes that adult education is inherently different from the education of children, using an entirely separate stock of ideas and principles and proceeding in completely distinctive ways. In the United States this second view prevailed (in the literature at least) during the early major growth of the field (from about 1922 to about 1940), though never without dissent. In recent years there has been a gradual shift to the first point of view, though it is by no means unanimously held. The separatist conception of adult education is now chiefly found on the continent of Europe, where the established schools and universities have resisted efforts to broaden their scope to serve adults, so that new institutions have had to be set up for that purpose. In the middle European countries, in fact, the term "androgogy" (from *andros,* meaning "man") has been developed to parallel "pedagogy," and a special literature on the subject has grown up, one summary statement of which is provided by Hanselmann (1951).

Most of the items in the literature of adult education use one of six different basic approaches, outlined below.

The Institutional Approach. The most evident manifestation of adult education is its varied institutional structure, which differs profoundly from that of childhood-youth education. The latter is characterized by relatively few dominant and sequential forms, progressing from the day nursery through the graduate school. In contrast, many kinds of adult educational institutions exist side by side and often overlap. They can be divided (though only very generally) into four groups on the basis of their conception of purpose.

The first type of institution is that in which the central purpose is the education of adults. Other functions, if present at all, are subsidiary. The best-known American example is the Cooperative Extension Service, in which agriculture, home economics, and related subjects have long been taught by precept and practice to men and women, particularly those who live in rural areas. This service is supported jointly by the federal, state, and local governments and has developed a program of great size and substantial achievement. A biography of its major founder, Seaman Knapp (Bailey, 1945), gives a graphic account of its early days, and the point of view of its current leaders is provided by Sanders (Sanders & others, 1966). Other outstanding institutions primarily designed to educate adults are the proprietary school (teaching either directly or by correspondence), vocational rehabilitational services and other similar casework agencies, the folk high school of Denmark, and the Workers' Educational Association of Great Britain.

The second type of institution is that in which the education of adults is combined with other educational purposes which ordinarily have come first historically and are still dominant. In the public school system, for example, evening schools appeared soon after the day schools but have always been a secondary and, to some extent, peripheral activity. Clark (1956) has shown graphically how this marginality has influenced the conceptions of the program held by both the school authorities and the public. A similar conception has often been significant in the growth of general university extension (as distinguished from the Cooperative Extension Service), though it has long provided a wide variety of services, such as off-campus classes, evening colleges and instructional centers, radio and television and correspondence courses, residential conference centers, and specialized programs for client groups. Eddy (1957) has dealt historically with the growth of extension services in the land-grant institutions, and McMahon (1960) has explored the future directions which might be undertaken by the evening college. A general symposium on the nature of change in the modern university was edited by Ingham (1966). Most public school systems and universities have clusters of differently organized services scattered throughout their organizations, but there is now a tendency toward the coordination of such services by a single, highly placed administrator. If this trend continues, the adult educational function in this type of institution will become less marginal than in the past.

The third type of institution is that in which the education of adults is one of a group of objectives. In the public library, for example, the purposefully educational and sequential reading of books or the pursuit of other forms of education is paralleled by the use of the library to satisfy other desires, such as recreation, aesthetic appreciation, or the seeking out of specific facts. In all institutions of this type, it is hard to assess which activities are educational and which are not. However, both Monroe (1963) and Lee (1966) have explored the historical development of the conception of adult education within the public library. Another institution which falls in this category is the museum, where research and custodianship parallel education. Other examples are the various kinds of voluntary associations, most of which assert that the education of their membership is an important function, though their programs may often seem to be devoted chiefly to other goals, such as community service, fellowship, and the advancement of professional or other special interests.

The fourth type of institution is that in which the education of adults is a subordinate function. In the armed services, for example, the development of a strong and disciplined military force requires not only that officers and men be trained throughout their careers but also that large groups of civilians must sometimes be given sufficient training to enable them to carry out military duties. Shelburne and Groves (1965) have given the most extended account of this broad program. Industry and commerce have somewhat analogous needs, which Clark and Sloan have investigated in two volumes (1958, 1962). Other major social institutions which use the education of their own members, their staff, or the public as a means to achieve their basic purposes are churches and other religious institutions, labor unions, government departments, prisons, sanitariums, the commercial mass media, and cooperatives.

Although general institutional forms tend to fall within the categories suggested, some examples of each form may be found in other categories. In most churches, for instance, education as here defined is but one means to the deeper end of salvation, but the members of at least some liberal and humanistic denominations consider education their chief end. The founders of the cooperative movement clearly saw self-education of the membership as the central purpose of their activity, but today in most cooperatives this goal seems a secondary one. When any such change occurs, adult educational conceptions are strongly influenced, and this fact tends to confirm the practical significance of this theoretical distinction among institutions.

In the past, each agency of adult education has tended to regard itself as unique, but the application of general organizational theory has demonstrated the fundamental similarities of organizations and associations which appear, on the surface, to be highly different. Griffith (1965) has shown, for example, that five remarkably different institutions (representing all four of the above-mentioned categories) all proceeded through the same steps in their process of development. Griffith concludes, therefore, that there is a basic model, whose nature and structure he describes.

Since institutions of all types usually exist side by side, a comprehensive survey of adult education in a community, a state, or a nation must ordinarily include descriptions of all major programs. A large number of such surveys are now in existence. Two of the earliest were provided by Hudson (1851), of English programs, and Adams (1901), of United States programs. An excellent example of the modern community survey is that conducted in Oakland, California, by London and others (1963). Johnstone and Rivera (1965) have also made a comparative survey of two cities in the Midwestern United States.

The Social Approach. A second major approach to adult education is taken by all those who start with a conception of man as a social being. It is clear, for example, that any given milieu has problems that can be solved only by the education of the people who are now in control of political and economic processes. Consequently the literature of adult education is replete with works which analyze either society in general or a single social entity (ranging from a neighborhood to the world community) and then suggest how the quality of life may be perfected by some campaign which uses the broad instrument of adult education. Thus, one man may espouse liberal education as the greatest present need of mankind; another may say that a country should both improve its vocational education and heighten the quality of its cultural life; a third may point out that mankind will destroy itself unless it has massive campaigns designed to create international understanding.

Some social needs are so widespread, persistent, and difficult that efforts to meet them have become established as significant fields of endeavor, each with a literature of its own which is too voluminous to cite here. Among the most prominent of these fields are the acculturation and naturalization of immigrants (often called "Americanization" in the United States); education for home life and family relationships, particularly those between parents and children; literacy and other remedial training for adults who did not secure adequate schooling in youth; vocational education; continuing education for each of the professions; public affairs education; human relations training; health education; and safety education.

A number of the major research themes of the social sciences have had important consequences for both the theory and practice of adult education, though such consequences are often incidental to the major intent of the authors of these studies. Cultural history, for example, illuminates the past of adult education even though it was often carried out under other names. Curti (1964) has provided an excellent treatment of this sort as far as the United States is concerned.

Sociology and social psychology have been particularly fruitful in providing insights into topics which have important implications for adult education. Much of adult education occurs, for example, in tutorial, casework, counseling, or other face-to-face contacts to which the generalized study of interpersonal relationships has much meaning. Bennis and others (1964) have reviewed and excerpted this literature. Much of the work on the study of small groups was first carried out in adult educational settings, and this literature is reviewed by Hare and others (1965). Throughout the world, communities must find ways of achieving a better life for themselves. The realization of this fact has brought forth many programs, some of which have been described (Du Sautoy, 1958) and analyzed (Batten, 1957). The question how innovations of all kinds are diffused through society has been intensively studied in agriculture, health, education, and other fields; the results of many of these studies have been brought together by Rogers (1962). The great significance of adult education in the diffusion process was revealed in a study by Verner and Millerd (1966). The nature and effect of mass communication in the spread of ideas and practices has also been extensively investigated; Schramm (1964) has dealt with the worldwide needs for systems of communication. Such themes as these are touched on in a general symposium on the sociological aspects of adult education edited by Burns (1964).

In the field of economics, a number of interesting approaches have also been made. Machlup (1962) has established a comprehensive framework for the analysis of the methods by which knowledge is produced and distributed in the United States. The concept of education as a process of capital formation has given rise to a number of studies, which have been summarized by Schultz (1963). A pioneer investigation dealing with the implications of this idea for adult education is that by Mincer (1962). Harbison and Myers (1964), adopting a worldwide view, have looked into the whole question of education, manpower, and economic growth and have pointed out at many places the implications for adult education.

The Individual Approach. To another very large group of investigators the individual appears to be the proper focus for any study of adult education, for although social factors influence the goals, nature, and results of learning, learning must ultimately be measured in the change of the individual who is the one enduring element amidst all the diversity of social change.

Perhaps the most important question raised in the development of modern adult education has to do with the effect of increasing age upon the ability to learn. The first studies on this subject by Thorndike (Thorndike & others, 1928) had profound consequences, since they seemed to suggest that age was no barrier to learning. Suggestive though these studies were, they had major methodological flaws, as is only natural in pioneering research. These were corrected in more sophisticated studies by Ruch (1934) and others, however, and Thorndike's general findings still seemed to be applicable. The matter has since been studied in many different ways: in the laboratory by Welford (1958) and by Eisdorfer (1965); in industry by the U.S. Department of Labor (1963); in terms of outstanding creativity by Lehman (1953); in terms of various subcategories of "intelligence" by Wechsler (1958); in the comparison of campus and extension classes (summarized by DeCrow, 1959); and in the relative performance of mature women and their young fellow classmates in degree programs at two universities by Halfter (1962). The results may be summarized overbriefly as follows: some kinds of learning abilities (chiefly those which have to do with neuromuscular skill) decline after the age of 40; some do not decline (and may even increase) up to the onset of senility; individual variation is very great, some people retaining their learning skills to an advanced age; most people do show a gradual general decline in learning abilities in their later years; and a great deal of this decline is considered to be due not to age itself but to the disuse of learning habits and the increasing sense of strain which the aging adult feels in educational situations.

Another question, a double-barreled one, important throughout the history of the field, has been: How many adults participate and how much do they do so? In the United States, various well-informed investigators have made estimates on this matter through the years, usually adding up the reported or probable enrollment figures for various programs and taking no account of duplicate registrations. While this technique was far from reliable, the successive estimates indicated that the number of persons involved was growing rapidly.

Another method of estimating the extent of participation was initiated by the United States Bureau of the Census and later used more systematically in a study undertaken by the National Opinion Research Center and reported by Johnstone and Rivera (1965). Using a sample of 23,950 adults chosen, by sophisticated sampling techniques, to be representative of the total population, the investigators and their associates conducted interviews to discover both the extent and the nature of adult educational participation. When the resulting figures were projected nationally, it was estimated that approximately 25 million American adults had been active in at least one form of sequential learning during the 12-month period preceding June 1962. The total report of this study, going into great detail concerning the scope and nature of these learning activities, is the largest and most complex single investigation yet conducted in the field of adult education.

Another way of studying participation requires individuals to respond to a lengthy inventory which lists many kinds of educational activities. Three introductory studies of this sort have been reported in a volume edited by Solomon (1964), and other more refined investigations are now under way. If such an inventory can be perfected and used to establish national norms, the measurement of the extent and nature of adult educational participation will gain a precision which it now lacks. Also, it will be possible to relate such participation to various other personal and social factors.

Johnstone and Rivera (1965) and the developers of the self-report inventory have all included in their measurement the self-directed learning activities of adults which they undertake on their own initiative either independently or in autonomous groups. Cawelti (1965) has shown how self-improvement is an essential element in the American conception of the self-made man, and many other people have speculated on the nature, scope, and value of this form of independent study, but as yet it remains an ill-defined and poorly understood (though obviously very important) aspect of adult education.

The motivation which impels adults to learn has been studied in many different ways. Perhaps the most common method has been to infer motivation by analyzing enrollment figures to see what courses are chosen, a dangerous procedure, since every experienced practitioner knows that adults undertake a learning activity for a variety of reasons which may not be related in any way to the announced purpose of the course. A second technique has been simply to ask people why they came; such a study was reported by Nicholson (1955). A somewhat different effort has been the attempt to discover whether people have basic orientations toward learning which lie deeper than their reasons for undertaking a particular activity. Two of the studies in the Solomon book (1964) deal in varying ways with this matter. Some attempts have also been made to relate motivation for learning with broader motivational or personality theories, but as yet most such efforts are in the realm of speculation.

The individual approach to adult education has benefited greatly from basic psychological writings. Hebb (1949), for example, has presented an essentially neurological conception of learning abilities, suggesting that the highest kinds of learning cannot be achieved until maturity. The effects of age upon the physical and psychological human organism have become the subject of an extensive literature. Four useful summaries of this literature are given by Anderson (1956), Pressey and Kuhlen (1957), and Birren (1959, 1964). Kuhlen has edited a symposium (1963) which relates this literature directly to adult education, and other specific analyses have been made by Knox and Videbeck (1963) and Knox and Sjogren (1965).

Of all the ages of adulthood, old age has been more thoroughly studied than any other, and most of the references just cited include reports on such investigations. Other basic volumes which report on various aspects of middle or old age and which are of particular relevance to adult learning are those of Chown (1961), Cumming and Henry (1961), and Neugarten and others (1964). Havighurst and Orr (1956) have suggested a number of implications for adult education, and Wolfe (1963) has demonstrated that those adults who continue learning throughout life are more likely than other adults to have a well-adjusted old age.

The Contemplative Approach. Throughout history many writers have been led to speculate on the nature of adult education as an essential or significant activity in which man must engage if he is to realize his fullest human potential. With the rise of adult education to prominence a great many people—at all levels of sophistication—have adopted a contemplative approach, using logical inquiry or some other method of philosophy to establish their points of view. The single most influential work of this sort in recent years is that of Livingstone (1945).

The Methodological Approach. Perhaps the greatest total volume of literature in the field, at least in the United States, is that which has to do with the analysis or promulgation of particular methods of or approaches to teaching and learning. Much of this work parallels, overlaps, or borrows from the methods or principles of program design also used with children and young people, though usually stressing the need for adaptation to adults. For example, Gray's study of reading and writing (1956) is so written as to have relevance to all ages of life, though with due attention to each. Other studies, however, focus directly on adults. Thus, adult reading has been analyzed in one of the yearbooks of the National Society for the Study of Education (1956), and Barnes and Hendrickson (1965) have appraised literacy programs in the United States.

The nature of community-based adult learning is such as often to require fresh approaches to the technology of adult education, not merely the adaptation of school and college practice. Liveright (1959), for example, developed a typology of the various kinds of strategy required in the leadership of adult groups. Some of the theoretical students of group dynamics have perfected practical techniques for developing greater personal sensitivity and understanding of group relationships; Bradford and his colleagues (1964) describe one main thrust of this effort. The effort to conceptualize the processes of individual and social change—sometimes called "change theory" —has made much use of programs and institutions of adult education (Lippitt & others, 1958).

Miller (1964) has provided the best review of the methodology of adult education, and the most comprehensive view of the literature is that of Aker (1965).

The Eclectic Approach. Many authors so define their inquiry into adult education as to use two or more of the five distinctive approaches just defined. One common combination is that in which an institution is accepted as a basic frame of reference but the subsequent inquiry is essentially individualistic. Thus, Berelson (1949) summarized the literature dealing with the characteristics of public library users, and Davis (Davis & others, 1961) studied the men and women who participate in the nationwide Great Books program.

Those books which aim at a comprehensive treatment of the field are a combination or blending of several or all of the five approaches. Perhaps the most influential single book ever published in adult education is the Final Report of the Adult Education Committee of the British Ministry of Reconstruction (Great Britain . . . , 1919), since it defined and described adult education with a sweep and brilliance never previously (or subsequently) achieved and set in motion programs which are now worldwide in their significance. Much of the early and most eloquent American writing on the subject is brought together in an anthology edited by Ely (1936). Several comprehensive American handbooks have been issued, the most recent edited by Knowles (1960). Brunner (1959) surveyed the research literature in the field, Jensen and others (1964) described the nature of graduate study in adult education, and Verner and Booth (1964) prepared a brief comprehensive account. Most of these books provide extended treatment of the topics which can only be mentioned in the present brief overview of the field.

General historical treatments of adult education have largely been restricted to the programs of particular countries. There are two excellent English accounts, one by Kelly (1962a) and one by Harrison (1961). As yet there is no satisfactory American history of the field, though the closest approximation is that of Knowles (1962), which concentrates heavily on recent developments and current issues.

Many comprehensive bibliographies exist, most of them essentially based on the literature of the country represented by the bibliographer. At their best, these volumes go far beyond a mere listing of sources to a grouping and evaluation of related items in such a way as to indicate the scope and dimensions of the whole field. An excellent older book of this sort is that by Beals and Brody (1941), but the most illuminating and masterful recent analysis of the literature (though oriented to British sources and practice) is that of Kelly (1962b).

Cyril O. Houle
University of Chicago

References

Adams, Herbert B. "Educational Extension in the United States." In *Report of the Commissioner of Education for the Year 1899–1900*, GPO, 1901. p. 275–379.

Aker, George F. *Adult Education Procedures, Methods and Techniques.* Syracuse U Press, 1965. 163p.

Anderson, John E. (Ed.) *Psychological Aspects of Aging.* APA, 1956. 323p.

Bailey, Joseph Cannon. *Seaman A. Knapp: Schoolmaster of American Agriculture.* Columbia U Press, 1945. 307p.

Barnes, Robert F., and Hendrickson, Andrew. *A Review and Appraisal of Adult Literacy Materials and Programs.* Cooporative Research Project No. G-029. Center for Adult Education, Ohio State U, 1965. 207p.

Batten, T. R. *Communities and Their Development.* Oxford U Press, 1957. 248p.

Beals, Ralph A., and Brody, Leon. *The Literature of Adult Education.* American Association for Adult Education, 1941. 493p.

Bennis, Warren G., and others. *Interpersonal Dynamics.* Dorsey Press, Inc., 1964. 763p.

Berelson, Bernard. *The Library's Public.* Columbia U Press, 1949. 174p.

Birren, James E. (Ed.) *Handbook of Aging and the Individual.* U Chicago Press, 1959. 939p.

Birren, James E. *The Psychology of Aging.* Prentice-Hall, 1964. 303p.

Bradford, Leland P., and others. (Eds.) *T-group Theory and Laboratory Method.* Wiley, 1964. 498p.

Brunner, Edmund DeS., and others. *An Overview of Adult Education Research.* Adult Education Association of the United States of America, 1959. 274p.

Burns, Hobert W. (Ed.) *Sociological Backgrounds of Adult Education.* Notes and Essays on Education for Adults, No. 41. Center for the Study of Liberal Education for Adults, 1964. 169p.

Cawelti, John G. *Apostles of the Self-made Man.* U Chicago Press, 1965. 279p.

Chown, Sheila M. "Âge and the Rigidities." *J Geront* 16:353–62; 1961.

Clark, Burton R. "Adult Education in Transition." *University of California Publications in Society and Social Institutions* 1, No. 2:43–202; 1956.

Clark, Harold F., and Sloan, Harold S. *Classrooms in the Factories.* New York U Press, 1958. 139p.

Clark, Harold F., and Sloan, Harold S. *Classrooms in the Stores.* Roxbury Press, 1962. 123p.

Cumming, Elaine, and Henry, William E. *Growing Old.* Basic Books, Inc., Publishers, 1961. 293p.

Curti, Merle. *The Growth of American Thought*, 3rd ed. Harper, 1964. 939p.

Davis, James A., and others. *Great Books and Small Groups.* Macmillan, 1961. 237p.

DeCrow, Roger. *Ability and Achievement of Evening College and Extension Students.* Center for the Study of Liberal Education for Adults, 1959. 13p.

Du Sautoy, Peter. *Community Development in Ghana.* Oxford U Press, 1958. 209p.

Eddy, Edward Danforth, Jr. *Colleges for Our Land and Time.* Harper, 1957. 328p.

Eisdorfer, Carl. "Verbal Learning and Response Time in the Aged." *J Genet Psychol* 107:15–22; 1965.

Ely, Mary L. (Ed.) *Adult Education in Action.* American Association for Adult Education, 1936. 480p.

Gray, William S. *The Teaching of Reading and Writing.* UNESCO, 1956. 286p.

Great Britain, Ministry of Reconstruction, Adult Education Committee. *Final Report.* H.M. Stationery Office, 1919. 409p.

Griffith, William S. "Implications for Administrators in the Changing Adult Education Agency." *Adult Ed* 15:138–44; 1965.

Halfter, Irma T. "Aging and Learning: An Achievement Study." *Sch R* 70:287–302; 1962.

Hanselmann, Heinrich. *Andragogik.* Rotapfel, 1951. 160p.

Harbison, Frederick, and Myers, Charles A. *Education, Manpower and Economic Growth.* McGraw-Hill, 1964. 229p.

Hare, A. Paul, and others (Eds.) *Small Groups*, rev. ed. Knopf, 1965. 705p.

Harrison, J. F. C. *Learning and Living, 1790–1960.* U Toronto Press, 1961. 404p.

Havighurst, Robert J., and Orr, Betty. *Adult Education and Adult Needs.* Center for the Study of Liberal Education for Adults, 1956. 66p.

Hebb, D. O. *The Organization of Behavior.* Wiley, 1949. 335p.

Hudson, J. W. *The History of Adult Education.* McKay, 1851. 238p.

Ingham, R. J. (Ed.) *Institutional Backgrounds of Adult Education.* Notes and Essays on Education for Adults, No. 50. Center for the Study of Liberal Education for Adults, 1966. 115p.

Jensen, Gale, and others. (Eds.) *Adult Education: Outlines of an Emerging Field of University Study.* Adult Education Association of the United States of America, 1964. 334p.

Johnstone, John W. C., and Rivera, Ramon J. *Volunteers for Learning.* Aldine Publishing Co., 1965. 624p.

Kelly, Thomas. *A History of Adult Education in Great Britain.* Liverpool U Press, 1962(a). 352p.

Kelly, Thomas (Ed.) *A Select Bibliography of Adult Education in Great Britain.* National Institute of Adult Education, 1962(b), 126p.

Knowles, Malcolm S. (Ed.) *Handbook of Adult Education in the United States.* Adult Education Association of the United States of America, 1960. 624p.

Knowles, Malcolm S. *The Adult Education Movement in the United States.* Holt, 1962. 335p.

Knox, Alan B., and Sjogren, Douglas. "Research on Adult Learning." *Adult Ed* 15:133–7; 1965.

Knox, Alan B., and Videbeck, Richard. "Adult Education and Adult Life Cycle." *Adult Ed* 13:102–21; 1963.

Kuhlen, Raymond G. (Ed.) *Psychological Backgrounds of Adult Education.* Notes and Essays on Education for Adults, No. 40. Center for the Study of Liberal Education for Adults, 1963. 148p.

Lee, Robert Ellis. *Continuing Education for Adults through the American Public Library, 1833–1964.* ALA, 1966. 158p.

Lehman, Harvey C. *Age and Achievement.* Princeton U Press, 1953. 359p.

Lippitt, Ronald, and others. *The Dynamics of Planned Change.* Harcourt, 1958. 312p.

Liveright, A. A. *Strategies of Leadership,* 1st ed. Harper, 1959. 140p.

Livingstone, Richard. "The Future in Education." In *On Education.* Macmillan, 1945. 127p.

London, Jack, and others. *Adult Education and Social Class.* Survey Research Center, U California, 1963. 246p.

Machlup, Fritz. *The Production and Distribution of Knowledge in the United States.* Princeton U Press, 1962. 416p.

McMahon, Ernest E. *The Emerging Evening College.* Columbia U Press, 1960. 163p.

Miller, Harry L. *Teaching and Learning in Adult Education.* Macmillan, 1964. 340p.

Mincer, Jacob. "On-the-job Training: Costs, Returns, and Some Implications." *J Political Econ* 70 (Suppl.) No. 5:50–79; 1962.

Monroe, Margaret E. *Library Adult Education.* Scarecrow Press, 1963. 550p.

National Society for the Study of Education. *Adult Reading.* 55th Yearbook. U Chicago Press, 1956. 279p.

Neugarten, Bernice L., and Others. *Personality in Middle and Late Life.* Atherton Press, 1964. 231p.

Nicholson, David Hull. "Why Adults Attend School." *U Missouri Bulletin 56.* Education Series No. 57, 1955. 23p.

Pressey, Sidney L., and Kuhlen, Raymond G. *Psychological Development Through the Life Span.* Harper, 1957. 654p.

Rogers, Everett M. *Diffusion of Innovations.* Free, 1962. 367p.

Ruch, Floyd L. "The Differentiative Effects of Age Upon Human Learning." *J Gen Psychol* 11:261–86; 1934.

Sanders, H. C., and others (Eds.) *The Cooperative Extension Service.* Prentice-Hall, 1966. 436p.

Schramm, Wilbur L. *Mass Media and National Development.* Stanford U Press, 1964. 333p.

Schultz, Theodore W. *The Economic Value of Education.* Columbia U Press, 1963. 92p.

Shelburne, James C., and Groves, Kenneth J. *Education in the Armed Forces.* Center for Applied Research in Education, Inc., 1965. 118p.

Solomon, Daniel (Ed.) *The Continuing Learner.* Center for the Study of Liberal Education for Adults, 1964. 95p.

Thorndike, Edward L., and Others. *Adult Learning.* Macmillan, 1928. 335p.

U.S. Department of Labor, Bureau of Labor Statistics. *Industrial Retraining Programs for Technological Change.* Bulletin No. 1368, GPO, 1963. 34p.

Verner, Coolie, and Booth, Alan. *Adult Education.* Center for Applied Research in Education, 1964. 118p.

Verner, Coolie, and Millerd, Frank W. *Adult Education and the Adoption of Innovation By Orchardists in the Okanagan Valley of British Columbia.* Rural Sociological Monograph No. 1. U British Columbia Press, 1966. 92p.

Wechsler, David. *The Measurement and Appraisal of Adult Intelligence,* 4th ed. Williams and Wilkins, 1958. 297p.

Welford, Alan T. *Ageing and Human Skill.* Oxford U Press, 1958. 300p.

Wolfe, Lloyd M. "Lifelong Learning and Adjustment in the Later Years." *Adult Ed* 14:26–32; 1963.

ADULTHOOD AND OLD AGE

The long segment of the human life span after adolescence is not very well known to science. In spite of a considerable amount of research in the current century, we cannot claim to have gone far beyond Shakespeare's insight by which he was able to describe the seven ages of man.

BODY CHANGES IN THE ADULT LIFE CYCLE. Physical strength and speed of body movement reach a peak at about 30 years of age, after which there is a slow decline. Between 40 and 50 there is a noticeable loss in attractiveness of the body, because of skin wrinkles, fat around the middle of the body, and thinning hair. The eye lens slowly loses elasticity until in the forties many people must use reading glasses in order to see fine print clearly. Also, as people go into their sixties, they lose acuity of vision at night. The sense of hearing holds out without loss until the sixties, generally, though men tend to lose their hearing earlier than women do.

The sex glands of women atrophy around the age of 50, at the time of the menopause. In men, there is a gradual reduction in glandular activity after about 50. Both sexes continue sexual activity after this age, but there is a substantial decrease in the frequency of sexual intercourse.

There is loss of teeth throughout the adult years for some people, and in the 1950's in the United States, a dental survey found that 56 percent of people aged 65–74 had no natural teeth. There is also a shrinkage of most muscles, possibly due to disuse.

Thus, the middle and later years bring insults to the body, but a very large proportion of people maintain robust health in spite of them. The variability of the population increases with age. That is, the range of health status becomes broader and broader with time, and people are more "spread out" on a health scale.

Studies of the extent of illness and the number of days of disability due to illness show a sharp increase of disability after age 50, but the great majority of people feel quite well and go about their work quite actively.

The average person in the United States lives to the age 70, according to the mortality rates of the 1960's. The average 60-year-old lives for another 18 years, and the average 70-year-old lives another 11 years. There is some evidence that those who survive beyond 70 are especially "hardy" and have less illness than those who die in their fifties and sixties.

There is a relatively high incidence of mental disease loosely called "senility" after about age 70.

After about 50, the death rate due to chronic and degenerative diseases goes up, while that due to acute diseases does not change very much. Heart disease and cancer are the two principal causes of death after age 50. Not until medical science gains control over these diseases will the death rate be appreciably reduced.

Thus, the general picture of the changes undergone by the body during the adult life cycle of present-day Americans is one of decrement; but the great majority of people live in fairly good health and feel physiologically comfortable throughout their adult years. They adapt easily to the physiological changes of maturing and aging.

The biological aspects of aging are summarized in several handbooks, the most complete and authoritative being that of Birren (1959), while the chapter by Confrey and Goldstein (1960) on health status gives a convenient overview.

BODY, SELF, AND SOCIETY. The behavior of children and adolescents is very closely tied to the development of their bodies. Their maturation gives them new powers and opens up new aspects of life to them as they grow older. But the behavior of adults is much less defined and limited by their physical and physiological condition. Charlotte Buehler pointed this out more than 30 years ago in her book on the course of human life (1959). She distinguished between the "biological" curve of the life span and the "biographical" or "psychological" curve.

The biological life curve rises steeply in childhood and adolescence to a peak at about 30, when the biological resources of the body are at a maximum. After a plateau lasting about 20 years, this curve slopes downward from age 50, reflecting the decreasing physical vigor and decreasing body efficiency. Manual workers have a biographical life curve very similar to this. However, people who work with their brains and many highly skilled craftsmen start slowly in the biographical curve because they have a long period of preparation, and then their biographical curve stays on a high plateau after the biological curve commences to decline. In other words, the curve of functioning as workers and citizens and social beings builds to its adult maximum after the structure of the body begins to decrease its effectiveness and power. Havighurst (1958) has described this as the principle of the separation of function from structure in the later part of life. The older person is able to function efficiently through his stored-up experience and knowledge in spite of his loss of physical strength and skill.

What the older person accomplishes is determined by his self-concept, his aspirations, and by the society around him, which encourages him in certain activities and discourages him in others. His body is a limiting factor, particularly if he is in poor health. But self and society are more influential in his behavior than body is.

Even in such a biological event as the menopause in women, the self seems to determine the reaction of the woman. Kraines (1963), in studying women who had recently passed through the menopause, found that those who complained of body tensions and other symptoms of malaise at the time of the menopause were less well-adjusted socially and personally than women who took the menopause in their stride and reported minimal ill effects. In other words, one could predict with considerable confidence that women who before the menopause were well adjusted to their lives would have less difficulty with body symptoms at the time of the menopause than women who had been relatively poorly adjusted.

The relation of the state of the body to the state of the self is not at all clear, nor has it been clarified much by recent research. All we can say for certain is that drastic changes in the body—such things as heart attacks, crippling illness, and profound loss of physical vigor have some influence on the self-concept of a person, or on his personal-social adjustment. On the other hand, a person's self-concept tends to determine his reaction to physical disability.

In this connection an interesting set of researches has been reported on the relation of illness to aging. One speculative hypothesis is that aging is a kind of illness, and illness is a kind of aging. If this is so, then middle-aged people who are sick should feel old and appear old, while old people who are in good health should feel young and appear young. In order to test this hypothesis, Schwartz and Kleemeier (1965) compared a group of healthy men in the adult range with another group who were in a hospital for acute (not chronic) conditions such as fractures, ulcers, and back trouble. The two groups were given tests of their feelings about themselves (self concept). The two groups were divided again into two groups by age. It was hypothesized that the chronologically old but well men would see themselves in a more favorable light than the chronologically old but ill men. Similarly, the young ill men would have less favorable self concepts than the young and well men. There was some tendency in this direction, but it was not statistically significant. And the young but ill men had more favorable self-concepts than the old but well men. Evidence on this matter was also obtained by Birren and his colleagues (1963b) in a comparison of older men (65 to 90) in average health with older men in very good health. The older men in very good health did act and feel as though they were younger than the older men in average health. The men in very good health showed low or negligible correlations between age and intelligence, and between age and symptoms of senility; but the old men of only average health did show decreased intellectual efficiency with greater age. Birren wrote that "health status is more significant in determining various aspects of functioning than the unspecified consequences of advanced chronological age."

ABILITIES AND THE LIFE CYCLE. The abilities and skills that are measured by psychologists have been explored through the adult years for a number of variously selected samples. Sampling is a weakness of research in this area, since the researcher did not make repeated studies of the same persons but compared people of diverse ages, assuming that his sample of a given age was equivalent to his samples of other ages and that therefore the observed age changes were truly changes that occur in people as they grow older. However, in a cross-sectional research, the group which is older in age is generally a "better" group than one which is younger in average age, because the older group has already lost some of its "weaker" members by death. Furthermore, the psychological tests of ability have generally been made on samples of people who were in relatively good health. Thus, those who are in poor health are left out, and there are more of these in the older groups.

Nevertheless, there are some facts about changes of ability with age which are quite thoroughly documented in spite of the sampling problem just mentioned. For instance, acuity of hearing, seeing, feeling, and tasting all decrease after middle age. The decrease is not extremely rapid or severe in most people, and they adjust to this decline with relatively little difficulty. The range of performance and the standard deviation generally increase with increasing age of the group. This seems to mean that there is a more rapid and extended decrease in some people than in others.

The scientific studies of human ability have been well organized and summarized by seven or eight people in Birren's *Handbook* (1959), each person reviewing his own area of special competence as a psychologist. Welford (1959, 1961) has established the fact that sensorimotor performance decreases in speed and accuracy with greater age in the adult period of life. He interprets this to mean that as impulses come into the central nervous system from the sense organs, the central mechanisms take longer to act in older than in younger people. If the older person is not forced to hurry but can take his time, his accuracy is not impaired. The more complex the task is, the more fully this finding of Welford applies. Jerome (1959) has demonstrated that the performance of people in situations where they need to learn is poorer in older people than in younger ones. He is not sure whether there is something about the aging process per se that reduces learning ability or whether the reduction is due to decreased speed, decreased motivation, or decreased health.

Creativity. One quality which may not be generally considered an "ability" is that of creativity. Since Lehman's monumental work (1953), there have been other studies in this field, with somewhat contradictory results. Lehman, studying the ages at which prominent people have done their best work, found that the decades from 20 to 40 were far more productive than those from 40 to 60. Artists, poets, and mathematicians were earlier in reaching their creative peaks than philosophers, historians, and social scientists. But Dennis (1966) has used a different method of study and believes that Lehman has exaggerated the relation of age and creativity. For instance, if only people who lived to be 75–80 are studied, the inverse relation of age and quality of creative work is much less marked than when the work of people who died rather young is included. Obviously, those who died young must have done their best work while they were young. There is some reason to accept Lehman's findings in general, after applying Dennis' critique. If this is done, it appears likely that one cause for decreasing productivity and creativity after age 40 is the fact that many successful leaders in the arts and sciences accept positions of administrative power and responsibility as they grow older, and they have less time to devote to their own scholarly and artistic work.

Sexual Power. Another area of "ability" is that of sexual activity. Not much had been known scientifically about the relation of sexual activity to age until the publications of Kinsey's books (Kinsey & others, 1948, 1953). Males and females decrease in their frequency of achieving physical sexual outlet after their early adult years. Men decrease more rapidly than women after the age of 50. The fact that women also decrease after the age of 50 may be attributed to the fact that male sexual partners are less active and less available to women after this age. In any case, it is generally believed that sexual activity decreases substantially in both sexes after 70, but the samples of people studied in that age group are small, and the evidence is scanty. It is supposed that the decrease of sexual activity after about age 50 may be due partly to decreased physiological (gonadal) activity, but also partly to a kind of satiation, and, to quote Kinsey (1948), "by psychological fatigue, a loss of interest in repetition of the same sort of experience, an exhaustion of the possibilities for exploring new techniques, new types of contacts, new situations."

Capacity to Learn. There has been a dramatic change in our notions of the capacity of adults to learn. Until as recently as 1950 it was generally supposed that people lost much of their learning ability after age 40 and that 50 was nearly the limit for useful learning. Yet since that time the Federal Aeronautics Authority decided to permit commercial airline pilots up to the age of 55 to shift from flying piston airplanes to jet planes—a formidable learning task (Birren, 1963a). Professor Ross McFarland of the Harvard University School of Public Health says, "In general, it may be concluded that the older pilots can be utilized very effectively until they reach 60 years of age. This observation would not have been acceptable or predictable in the earlier history of the air transport industry." (McFarland & O'Doherty, 1959).

Learning the new skills that go with automation in industry has been studied with respect to age of employees in several industries. When the level of education is taken into account, there is very little difference in learning ability related to age among adult employees. Birren (1963a) summed up the evidence on learning ability of adults within the 25–65 age range with the conclusion that there is very little relation to age. For many if not for most tasks, the amount of education a person has is more significant than his age in predicting his ability to learn a new job.

The data on the relation of intelligence-test scores to age show decreases with age in scores on tests that require speed and perception, while tests which allow for accumulated experience such as vocabulary show increasing scores with age.

The longitudinal studies of mental ability which have included people over 60 generally show a significant decline beginning about 70 years of age.

From the longitudinal study by Owens (Owens & Charles, 1963) of men from about 20 to 60, it appears that there is no appreciable change of intelligence with age until after 60.

PERSONALITY AND MOTIVATION. The motives, or needs and values, of people change through their adult years. These changes reflect changes in the life situation rather than changes in basic personality. The interests and choices of where to focus one's energy and how to allocate one's time depend on such matters as marriage, the birth of children and their presence in the home, the possibility of advancement in one's work career, the possession of a nice home, the existence of a group of congenial friends, the opportunity to take a responsible role in local civic affairs, the existence of a local theater group, the existence of good hunting or camping nearby, and so on.

There are two broad types of motivation in adult life. One is a *growth-expansion* motive and the other, opposed to it, is a motive resulting from *anxiety and sense of threat*. These have been summarized by Kuhlen (1963). There seems to be a continuing need for expansion, through achievement, power, self-actualization, and generativity in Erikson's sense (1959). This need continues at least until age 60 in most people but may die down in some toward the close of middle age and decrease even more later on. Family and work constitute the major areas of expansion in the first half of adult life. Then civic activity, home beautification, sociability, and various forms of creativity may become the theater for these needs in the latter half of adult life, after 50 or 55.

The opposite form of motivation, due to anxiety, presumably arises from the inevitable losses of physical strength and attractiveness after 40 or 50, coupled with increasing responsibilities and commitments to family and work. Thus, in a national interview study on mental health status, Gurin and others (1960) found the following five factors of subjective maladjustment: (1) felt psychological disturbances, (2) unhappiness, (3) social inadequacy, (4) lack of identity, and (5) physical distress. Both sexes showed the first four factors, but women did not show the physical-distress factor. There are losses in these areas in the middle and later years.

Incidentally, how one classifies oneself with respect to age appears to be a reflection of good and poor self-concept. Studies made by several different researchers indicate that many people over 70 or 75 classify themselves as middle-aged when asked on a questionnaire "In which age group do you feel that you belong—elderly, young, or middle-aged?" As many as 50 percent of persons over 65 rate themselves as middle-aged, and one study found that this subgroup was better adjusted in measure of personal-social adjustment than those who rated themselves in the other two groups (Havighurst & Albrecht, 1953).

There is a socioeconomic factor in the way people perceive the appropriate ages for such concepts as "prime of life," "good-looking" (for women), "most competent," "middle-aged," and "old." People in the upper middle class place these at later ages than do people of working-class status. This is probably related to the actual fact that working-class people are more dependent on physical strength and physique for competence in their lives than are middle-class people. It may also be due to a tendency for middle-class people to have a more favorable perception of middle age and old age than working-class people have.

There is really no integrated body of psychological theory concerning the development of human personality during the adult years, as Neugarten has pointed out (1966). However, there are orderly and sequential changes that occur with the passage of time as individuals move from adolescence through adulthood, and students of adult psychology are beginning to trace these changes. We shall look at the research and the findings when we come to the subject of stages or phases in the adult life cycle.

COMPETENCE. "Competence" is a global term which denotes and contains much of what we consider desirable in human behavior. It includes skill, determination, and judgment. It is what Buehler (1959) intends to discuss when she differentiates between the biographical curve and the biological curve of adult life. It is what the adult brings to bear on the tasks and roles of his life, and it is measured in terms of his effectiveness.

Wilensky (1961) made a study of what he called "orderly careers," in relation to the extent and quality of social-civic participation of people. He found that people who were competent in their work careers were more active in social and civic roles in the community than were those who had less "orderly" work careers. This finding of a kind of g factor of adult competence has been confirmed in other studies. For instance, in the Kansas City Study of Adult Life, Havighurst (1957) rated people aged 40 to 70 on their competence in performing nine common social roles: worker, parent, spouse, homemaker, citizen, club and association member, church member, friend, and user of leisure time. He found a positive intercorrelation among all the roles, which was taken as evidence of a g competence factor. He also found no change with age up to 65, when certain roles, such as spouse and worker, are often lost to a person through no act of his own. Some people compensate for these losses by increasing their activity in other roles. Other people simply drop these roles and carry on the other roles with relatively little change.

Subgroups of people move up or down the socioeconomic scale during their adulthood. This motion might be interpreted as competence or incompetence. Coleman and Neugarten (1967) reported on the social mobility of a sample of men in Kansas City, aged 40 to 70. Compared with the socioeconomic status of their fathers, 36 percent had moved up at least one step on a five-class scale, and 13 percent had moved down.

SOCIETY AND THE ADULT LIFE CYCLE. Up to this point, attention has here been directed to the individual as he progresses through the life cycle. Although it is understood that society and its social institutions form the framework within which a person lives his life, very little attention is paid to the influence of society in the psychological and biological analyses of the life cycles that have been reported. Now the focus will be shifted to the society which surrounds the individual and to the ways by which it shapes the adult life cycle.

The Economy. The economy or the system of producing and distributing goods and services provides employment, purchasing power, and income during retirement. The economy also deprives a person of employment under certain conditions. The economy is the principal source of nonfinancial as well as financial rewards to the person who is employed. As noted by Friedmann and Havighurst (1954), work gives people a sense of achievement, a feeling of being creative, a feeling of being of service, and a place to make good friends and to enjoy human companionship. At the very least, the economy structures many of the waking hours and helps the person without much individual initiative to organize his life and to make time pass in a tolerable way.

In return, the economy asks the adult as a worker to do his job conscientiously and to support the economic system intelligently and critically. The economy also asks the worker to give up his life work and accept retirement status, generally in his mid-sixties, whether he likes it or not.

For women the American economy has been increasingly hospitable during the twentieth century. Most young women are employed before their marriages. After age 45, women enter or reenter the labor force in large numbers. In effect, a woman makes a choice, after her childbearing and childrearing years are over, whether she will take on a worker role or will put more time and energy into various social-civic roles outside the family and outside the economy.

The trend of retirement policy and practice is toward earlier retirement. While rules for compulsory retirement in most large organizations have not been changed in the past decade, there has been a policy of encouraging voluntary retirement for wage workers through liberalized pension plans on the part of many large enterprises, and this has been supported by most labor unions. The reason for this is that industry and commerce have been using automated production and service machinery to an increasing degree, thus eliminating certain jobs and forcing the necessity of reducing the working force. In order to protect jobs for younger and middle-aged workers, older workers have been encouraged to retire voluntarily.

In connection with the tendency toward earlier retirement, employers have given more attention to the preparation of their employees for retirement through counseling and through short educational courses on preparations for retirement.

The State. The government differentiates with regard to age in its relations with adult citizens perhaps less than most other social institutions do. The right and the obligation to vote is independent of age in adults. Certain government offices have minimum ages attached to them, but very few have compulsory retirement related to age. Taxes are assessed independent of age, except for minor concessions to people over 65. Military service is related to age and to sex.

Through government-operated social security and medical-care programs, the government pays special attention to the economic and health needs of its older citizens. This is balanced, partially at least, by the provision of education at state expense which goes mainly to young adults.

For all ages the government increasingly supplies such cultural goods as subsidized theater and music, recreation in national parks, and educational television.

The Church. The role of the church member changes very little through the adult life cycle. Those who do not invest much of themselves in this role may attend church services more or less regularly and send their children to church school. Those who are more involved in this role may take positions of responsibility open to laymen, and they may continue in these positions generally beyond the normal age of retirement from employment. Some elderly people increase their church activities as they become free of other responsibilities, and they get great satisfaction from active church work.

The church itself recognizes some of the special needs of old age and attempts to give assistance. Many clergymen study problems of the aging so as to be able to counsel their older parishioners. Most church groups provide homes for elderly members whose families cannot look after their welfare.

The Family. While people's participation in most social roles tends to decrease as they get older, the family roles generally increase in importance for them. The role of parent is central throughout adulthood but takes somewhat less time and energy after about the age of 50. However, the man or woman of 50 to 60 generally finds himself involved in assisting his aging parents to work out some of their problems. Also the role of grandparent enters and provides many satisfactions together with responsibilities, especially for women. The role of homemaker continues in full force for most women, and many men become more involved in the physical upkeep of their houses and gardens as they grow older. Studies of family interaction through the life cycle (Shanas & Streib, 1965) indicate that the relations among the generations in the family are active and well maintained in the contemporary urban family, much more than would be expected from some of the sociological essays which portray a decrease of family activity and a narrowing of family function in this century.

The Social Environment. There are fairly definite expectations on the part of society concerning the social behavior of people at various stages of the adult life cycle. People in their thirties and forties are expected to be most interested in their children, in schools, and in the building of a secure and stable family. In their fifties they are expected to extend their interests to the wider community, since their children are now growing up and leaving home. In their sixties, and more in the seventies, they are expected to "slow down," to take life more easily. In their personal-social lives they are expected to become less active—to go out less often at night, to be less interested in the opposite sex, and to exert less authority over others in their family, at their place of work, and in other roles where they have been leaders.

These expectations on the part of society are documented in several studies of what people expect of other people at various age periods (Neugarten, 1966; Havighurst & Albrecht, 1953). People thus know in a general way what is expected of them by society, and they may conform to these expectations or they may resist them more or less successfully (Kuhlen, 1964).

The social policy with respect to adult behavior is mainly implicit in these general social expectations but becomes more explicit in such things as the age of eligibility for social security benefits, the age of eligibility for private company pensions and for government pensions, the age of eligibility for membership in retirement communities, etc. In general, this social policy seems to be based more on the needs and convenience of the American economy than on the biological capability of the individual or any kind of ideology about what is good or bad for the human personality.

ADULT EDUCATION AND THE ADULT LIFE CYCLE. In 1962 about 15 percent of the adult population took part in some formal adult education program. What kinds of people are these "volunteers for learning," to use the phrase of Johnstone and Rivera (1965)? Their study and two others (Knox & Videbeck, 1963; London & others, 1963) give a good idea of the characteristics of adult education students. They cluster mainly in the age group 25 to 45, with relatively few over 50. They tend to be middle-class rather than working-class people. The people with most education are likely to continue with adult education, and those who participate after age 50 are definitely higher in educational level than the average of those who participate below this age.

Until now the stress in adult education has been upon *instrumental* rather than *expressive* educational activity. The instrumental educational activity has as a goal something beyond the immediate activity. That is, it may lead to a better job, to better cooking on the part of a young wife, to better care of children, etc. The expressive educational activity is largely done for its own sake. It is done for the value of the immediate experience. Courses in painting, art, foreign language, "great books," photography, etc., are in the expressive category for most people, though they may also have an instrumental value for a minority of students.

The older people in adult education tend to elect expressive activities aimed at helping them enjoy leisure time more fully. An example of the trend to be expected is the programs of the Institute for Lifetime Learning, in Washington, D.C. Affiliated with the American Association of Retired Persons, the Institute in 1966 offered about 50 courses, most of them of an expressive type. This may herald a major development of expressive forms of adult education as more people have more leisure time at all ages. It may also foretell an increase in the proportion of students past 50 years of age.

STAGES AND DEVELOPMENTAL PHASES OF THE ADULT LIFE CYCLE. Considering the normal progression in the situation of adults in a modern society, with concomitant changes in their social roles, the expectations that society lays upon them, and their expectations of themselves, a scheme of three stages with transition periods preceding each stage seems to fit the facts reasonably well.

Transition period from adolescence to (1) *early adulthood* (20–30 to 40–45). Duration of stage: 15 years.

Transition period to (2) *plateau of adulthood* (40–45 to 60–70). Duration of stage: 25 years.

Transition period to (3) *later maturity* (60–70 to 85–90). Duration of stage: 20 years.

The transition periods vary in length for different persons. For example, a young man who enters college and then goes on to medical school and to a hospital residency in a specialty requires a full ten years to make the transition into early adulthood. By contrast, a young man who goes right to work upon graduation from high school, gets married at once, and starts a family requires only two or three years to make the transition. Also, a person who tapers off from full-time employment to a leisurely retirement by working part-time for several years during his sixties may take eight or ten years for the transition to later maturity.

Generally, people of lower socioeconomic status make the transitions at younger ages than those of higher socioeconomic status.

Each stage of the adult life cycle has its characteristic developmental tasks. For *early adulthood* these are finding a mate; establishing a stable marriage; raising a family; and getting well established in an occupation. The tasks of the *plateau of adulthood* are setting adolescent children free; establishing a comfortable home; maintaining a peak of occupational effectiveness; adjusting to unfavorable changes in body status; and (for women who have concentrated on raising children) working into new civic-social-occupational roles. For *later maturity* the developmental tasks are working out a new pattern of social roles that suits one's personality; accepting one's status as an elderly person; adjusting to loss of employment and/or loss of spouse; relating to one's grown children on an adult-to-adult level; finding satisfactory housing and living arrangements.

Stage or Phase Theories. Several students of adult psychology have defined stages or phases of adult life. Erikson (1959) has proposed that the ego or self goes through eight stages of development from birth to death. The last three stages are similar in timing to the three stages noted above. Dominating the stage of early adulthood is the psychosocial need for *intimacy*—the ability to merge one's own self with that of another person, to share love and life intimately with another person. Next comes the phase of *generativity*. This is investment in the next generation and in the community. It is an altruistic preoccupation. Normally it involves getting children ready for their adult life, and it may also consist of improving one's land and one's house and working for the betterment of one's community.

Finally comes the stage of *integrity*. One's active life has nearly been completed; one looks over it and accepts it as meaningful and in a sense inevitable. One does not make excuses for it, even though it has not been all that one hoped for. Therefore one has no fear of death, because one does not feel a need to make something different of one's life.

Other formulations of adult life in terms of stages have been given by Buehler (1959) and by Havighurst (1964). Buehler organized the total life cycle into ten stages and applied a theory of *basic tendencies* to the description of these stages. Havighurst took each decade of life as a unit and described its "dominant concerns."

LONGITUDINAL STUDIES OF ADULT LIFE. All of these stage or phase theories suffer from the lack of evidence provided by longitudinal studies—studies of one and the same person through an extended period of time. This kind of study has given us our most valuable information on childhood and adolescence. Longitudinal studies of children and adolescents have established the fact that while all persons go through the stages of development, the actual timing and the detailed characteristics of each person's career are unique to him. Thus, it is not sufficient to study groups of people at various ages on the supposition that each person at a given age will be like the others at that age.

The life career is the proper subject of study if we are to learn the most about adulthood and old age. There are several semilongitudinal studies in existence. The study of gifted children started by Terman about 1920 has been continued with a publication by Terman and Oden (1959), when the subjects were in their forties. The University of California Study of Adolescents, which began in 1932 with a sample of ten-year-olds, has been continued with reports by Jones and others (1960), Mussen (1961), and Tuddenham (1959) when the subjects were in their thirties. A biological study of men in their early middle age was commenced by Keys in 1947, with a psychological panel which has been reported from time to time by Brozek (1955). Specific studies made on a group of subjects at a given time have been repeated on the same subjects as far as possible at later times. One of the most valuable of these is the study of intelligence of men averaging about 21 who were inducted into the Army in World War I. A substantial number of these men have been retested twice by Owens and Charles (1963), the latest study being made when the men were an average of 61 years old. Useful as these studies are, none of them has been continued long enough with the kind of measurements and assessments that can answer the most interesting question of all—to what extent is human personality constant through time?

Studies of this question can start with the personality in childhood or adolescence and trace it into adulthood, or they may start in early or middle adulthood and follow through a decade or more of adult life.

In the studies made at the Institute of Human Development at the University of California at Berkeley it proved very difficult to predict personality characteristics of young adults from data obtained about them in their adolescence. Jones and his associates (1960) concluded that the myriad changes in life situations to which the adolescents were exposed as they grew older would produce changes in behavior that would be difficult to predict from the kinds of information obtainable about personality in childhood and adolescence.

This view was also confirmed by Rohner and Edmonson (1960) in their study of 20 young Negro adults who had been studied 20 years earlier and described by Davis and Dollard in their book *Children of Bondage* (1940).

A study made by Kelly (1955) reported on a group of 300 young couples engaged to be married who were studied in the 1930's and then retested with many of the same instruments about 1955 when they were in their forties. Kelly found correlation coefficients of about .50 in the areas of values and vocational interests and coefficients of about .30 on paper-and-pencil tests of personality between scores in the 1930's and those in 1955. He concludes: "Our findings indicate that significant changes in the human personality may continue to occur in the years of adulthood."

From middle to old age there have been no longitudinal studies reported, but there have been several studies of personality of middle-aged and older people in which age was treated as a variable. Among these studies the Kansas City Studies of Adult Life are especially useful because they were made with normal people, drawn by random-sampling techniques from the community at large. There were three main lines of study. The first dealt with social competence and social interaction. Havighurst's study (1957) dealt with competence in the common social roles. He found that the quality of role performance did not vary with age between 40 and 65. At about 65, there was indication of gross changes in social interaction.

The second dealt with personal-social adjustment or life satisfaction. Peck and Berkowitz (1964) rated 120 persons in the Kansas City sample, aged 40 to 64 and from all social class levels, and found no relationship to chronological age. Similarly, Neugarten and her associates (1961) rated more than 200 persons, aged 50 to 85, on life satisfaction, and found no correlation with age.

The third type of study concentrated on the "inner" personality and was made with projective tests. Here it was found that there are changes with age in the modes of dealing with impulse life and of relating in fantasy to the environment (Neugarten, 1964). Beginning as early as age 40, there is a decrease in active manipulation and attempts to dominate the environment. The person is seen increasingly as a passive object manipulated by the environment. By the sixties the heroes in the Thematic Apperception Test are conforming, meek, and friendly. They no longer try to dominate the situation by taking the initiative through aggressive action. In another study using the Thematic Apperception Test, the amount of "ego energy" was measured, defined as energy available to the self to respond to events in the outer world. Scores on ego energy decreased regularly with age from 40 to 71. These studies do not necessarily mean that people become overtly more passive as they grow older, although they would be expected to change in this direction eventually. Rather, it means that people become more preoccupied with themselves, more concerned with the control or satisfaction of their personal needs, and more likely to take a reflective stance with respect to the world around them (Neugarten, 1964).

PERSONALITY AND PATTERNS OF AGING.
It appears, from the best evidence we have today, that there are no gross changes in personality after the individual reaches the plateau of adulthood which are attributable to the process of aging alone. Such changes as do take place are at the covert level. The observable life style of the individual persists with relatively little change as long as he maintains the physical and mental ability to look after his personal needs.

Consequently, the patterns of behavior in the latter half of life should be systematically related to personality. There should be distinct personality types which lead to distinct behavior patterns. A search for such personality types was made at the University of California at Berkeley by Else Frenkel-Brunswik and her colleagues, who studied a group of 87 elderly men, 42 of them retired and 45 not retired. They reported finding five personality types (Reichard & others, 1962) which were systematically related to patterns of successful and unsuccessful aging.

The Kansas City Study of Adult Life made a study of 159 men and women aged 50 to 90, who were interviewed a total of seven times between 1956 and 1962. They were rated on 45 personality variables reflecting both the cognitive and the affective aspects of personality. Types of personality were extracted from the data by means of factor analysis. There were four major types, which were called the integrated, armored-defended, passive-dependent, and unintegrated personalities.

Patterns of behavior were defined on the basis of a rating of *activity* in 11 common social roles: worker, parent, grandparent, kin-group member, spouse, homemaker, citizen, friend, neighbor, club and association member, and church member. Ratings were made by judges on each of the 11 roles, based on a reading of the seven interviews with each person. The sum of the role-activity scores was used to divide the respondents into three activity levels, high, medium, and low.

A third component of the patterns of aging was a measure of *life satisfaction* or psychological well-being, which was a composite rating based on five scales recording the extent to which a person (1) finds gratification in the activities of his everyday life, (2) regards his life as meaningful and accepts both the good and the bad in it, (3) feels that he has succeeded in achieving his major goals, (4) has a positive image of himself; and (5) maintains happy and optimistic moods and attitudes. Scores on life satisfaction were grouped into high, medium, and low categories.

The analysis based on these three dimensions (personality, role activity, and life satisfaction) was applied to the 59 men and women in the study who were aged 70 to 79. This is the group in which the transition from middle age to old age has presumably been accomplished. Fifty of these people fell clearly into one or another of eight patterns of aging, which are presented in the following scheme (Neugarten, 1965).

A. integrated personality, high role activity (RA), high life satisfaction (LS); 9 persons.
B. integrated personality, medium RA, high LS; 5 cases.
C. integrated personality, low RA, high LS; 3 cases.
D. armored-defended personality, high or medium RA, high LS; 11 cases.
E. armored-defended personality, low or medium RA, high or medium LS; 4 cases.
F. passive-dependent personality, high or medium RA, high or medium LS; 6 cases.
G. passive-dependent personality, low RA, medium or low LS; 5 cases.
H. unintegrated personality, low RA, medium or low LS; 7 cases.

Group A, called the *reorganizers*, are competent people engaged in a wide variety of activity. They are the optimal agers in terms of the American ideal of "keeping active, staying young." They reorganize their lives to substitute new activities for lost ones.

Group B were called the *focused*. They are well-integrated personalities with medium levels of activity. They tend to be selective about their activities, devoting their time and energy to gaining satisfaction in one or two role areas.

Group C were called the *successful disengaged*. They have low activity levels and high life satisfaction. They have voluntarily moved away from role commitments as they have grown older. They have high feelings of self-regard, with a contented "rocking-chair" position in life.

Group D exhibit the *holding-on* pattern. They hold as long as possible to the activities of middle age. As long as they are successful in this, they have high life satisfaction.

Group E are *constricted*. They have reduced their role activity, presumably as a defense against aging. They constrict their social interactions and maintain a medium to high level of satisfaction. They differ from the focused in having less-integrated personalities.

Group F are *succorance-seeking*. They are successful in getting emotional support from others and thus maintain a medium level of role activity and of life satisfaction.

Group G are *apathetic*. They have low role activity combined with medium or low life satisfaction. Presumably, they are people who have never given much to life and never expected much from it.

Group H are *disorganized*. They have deteriorated thought processes and poor control over their emotions. They barely maintain themselves in the community and have low or at the most medium life satisfaction.

These eight patterns of aging probably are established and predictable by middle age, though we do not have longitudinal studies to prove this proposition. It seems reasonable to suppose that a person's underlying personality needs become consonant with his overt behavior patterns in a social environment that permits wide variation.

ORGANIZATIONS FOR SCIENTIFIC STUDY OF ADULTHOOD. There are several organizations intended primarily to study adulthood or to promote education for adults. The Adult Education Association has become an effective organization for the promotion and improvement of educational practices and has sponsored a number of useful researches and reports on the status of adult education. The Division on Maturity and Old Age of the American Psychological Association has been a stimulant to psychological research. The Gerontological Society is an interdisciplinary group consisting of psychologists, sociologists, social workers, and medical and biological scientists devoted to the study of aging. The International Gerontological Association has held congresses every third year since 1948, to bring together representatives of gerontological societies from about twenty countries.

Robert J. Havighurst
University of Chicago

References

Birren, James E. *Handbook of Aging and the Individual.* U Chicago Press, 1959. 939p.

Birren, James E. "Adult Capacities to Learn." In Kuhlen, R. G. (Ed.) *Psychological Backgrounds of Adult Education.* Center for the Study of Liberal Education for Adults, 1963(a).

Birren, James E., and others. *Human Aging: A Biological and Behavioral Study.* US Public Health Service, National Institutes of Mental Health, 1963(b).

Brozek, J. "Personality Changes with Age." *J Geront* 10:194–206; 1955.

Buehler, Charlotte. *Der menschliche Lebenslauf als psychologisches Problem,* 2d ed. Verlag für Psychologie, 1959. For an English version see Buehler, C. "The Course of Life as Studied in Biographies." *J Applied Psychol* 19:405–9; 1933.

Coleman, Richard, and Neugarten, Bernice L. "Social Mobility in a Midwestern City." In Havighurst, Robert J., and others. (Eds.) *Society and Education.* Allyn and Bacon, 1967. p. 38–49.

Confrey, Eugene A., and Goldstein, Marcus S. "The Health Status of Aging People." In Tibbitts, Clark. (Ed.) *Handbook of Social Gerontology.* U Chicago Press, 1960. p. 165–207.

Davis, Allison, and Dollard, John. *Children of Bondage.* ACE, 1940.

Dennis, Wayne. "Creative Productivity Between Ages of 20 and 80 Years." *J Geront* 21:1–8; 1966.

Erikson, Erik H. "Identity and the Life Cycle: Selected Papers." *Psychol Issues* 1; 1959.

Friedmann, Eugene, and Havighurst, Robert J. *The Meaning of Work and Retirement.* U Chicago Press, 1954. 197p.

Gordon, Margaret S. "Work and Patterns of Retirement." In Kleemeier, Robert W. (Ed.) *Aging and Leisure.* Oxford U Press, 1961. p. 15–53.

Gurin, Gerald and others. *Americans View Their Mental Health.* Basic Books, Inc., Publishers, 1960. 444p.

Havighurst, Robert J. "The Social Competence of Middle-aged People." *Genet Psychol Monogr* 56:297–375; 1957.

Havighurst, Robert J. "The Sociological Meaning of Aging." *Geriatrics* 13:43–50; 1958.

Havighurst, Robert J. "Dominant Concerns in the Life Cycle." In *Gegenwartsprobleme der Entwicklungspsychologie: Festschrift für Charlotte Buehler.* Verlag für Psychologie, 1964.

Havighurst, Robert J., and Albrecht, Ruth. *Older People.* McKay, 1953. 415p.

Jerome, Edward A. "Age and Learning—Experimental Studies." In Birren, James E. (Ed.) *Handbook of*

Aging and the Individual. U Chicago Press, 1959. p. 655–99.

Johnstone, John W. C., and Rivera, Ramon J. *Volunteers for Learning.* Aldine Publishing Co., 1965. 624p.

Jones, Harold E., and others. "Progress Report on Growth Studies at the University of California." *Vita Humana* 3:17–31; 1960.

Kelly, E. L. "Consistency of the Adult Personality." *Am Psychologist* 10:659–81; 1955.

Kinsey, A. C., and others. *Sexual Behavior in the Human Male.* Saunders, 1948. 804p.

Kinsey, A. C., and others. *Sexual Behavior in the Human Female,* Saunders, 1953. 842p.

Knox, Alan B., and Videbeck, Richard. "Adult Education and the Adult Life Cycle." *Adult Ed* 13: 102–21; 1963.

Kraines, Ruth. "The Menopause and Evaluations of the Self: A Study of Women in the Climacteric Years." Unpublished doctoral dissertation. U Chicago, 1963.

Kuhlen, Raymond G. "Motivational Changes During the Adult Years." In Kuhlen, Raymond G. (Ed.) *Psychological Backgrounds of Adult Education.* Center for the Study of Liberal Education for Adults, 1963. p. 77–113.

Kuhlen, Raymond G. "Developmental Changes in Motivation During the Adult Years." In Birren, James E. (Ed.) *Relations of Development and Aging.* Charles C Thomas, Publisher, 1964. p. 209–46.

Lehman, Harvey C. *Age and Achievement.* Princeton U Press, 1953.

London, Jack, and others. *Adult Education and Social Class.* Survey Research Center, U California, 1963.

Maves, Paul B. "Aging, Religion, and the Church." In Tibbitts, Clark. (Ed.) *Handbook of Social Gerontology.* U Chicago Press, 1960. p. 698–749.

McFarland, Ross, and O'Doherty, Brian. "Work and Occupational Skills." In Birren, James E. (Ed.) *Handbook of Aging and the Individual.* U Chicago Press, 1959. p. 477.

Mussen, Paul. "Some Antecedents and Consequents of Masculine Sex Typing in Adolescent Boys." *Psychol Monogr* 75:No. 2 (Whole No. 506); 1961.

Neugarten, Bernice L. "Personality Changes During the Adult Years." In Kuhlen, Raymond G. (Ed.) *Psychological Backgrounds of Adult Education.* Center for the Study of Liberal Education for Adults, 1963. p. 43–76.

Neugarten, Bernice L. "Personality Change over the Adult Years." In Birren, James E. (Ed.) *Relations of Development and Aging.* Charles C Thomas, Publisher, 1964. p. 176–208.

Neugarten, Bernice L. "Personality and Patterns of Aging." *Gawein* 13:249–56; 1965.

Neugarten, Bernice L. "Adult Personality: Toward a Psychology of the Life Cycle." Paper presented at annual meeting of the APA. New York, September 1966.

Neugarten, Bernice L., and others. "The Measurement of Life Satisfaction." *J Geront* 16:134–43; 1961.

Owens, W. A., and Charles, D. C. *Life History Correlates of Age Changes in Mental Abilities.* Purdue U Press, 1963. 200p.

Peck, Robert F., and Berkowitz, H. "Personality and Adjustment in Middle Age." In Neugarten, B. L. (Ed.) *Personality in Middle and Late Life.* Atherton Press, 1964. p. 15–43.

Reichard, Suzanne, and others. *Aging and Personality.* Wiley, 1962. 237p.

Rohner, J. H., and Edmonson, M. S. (Eds.) *The Eighth Generation.* Harper, 1960.

Schwartz, Arthur N., and Kleemeier, Robert W. "The Effects of Illness and Age upon Some Aspects of Personality." *J Geront* 20:85–91; 1965.

Shanas, Ethel, and Streib, Gordon F. *Social Structure and the Family: Generational Relations.* Prentice-Hall, 1965.

Terman, Lewis, and Oden, Melita H. *The Gifted Group at Mid-Life.* Stanford U Press, 1959.

Tuddenham, R. D. "Constancy of Personality Ratings over Two Decades." *Genet Psychol Monogr* 60: 3–29; 1959.

Welford, Alan T. "Psychomotor Performance." In Birren, James E. (Ed.) *Handbook of Aging and the Individual.* U Chicago Press, 1959. p. 562–613.

Welford, Alan T. *Skill and Age.* Oxford U Press, 1961. 121p.

Wilensky, Harold. "Orderly Careers and Social Participation." *Am Sociol R* 26:521–39; 1961.

AGRICULTURAL EDUCATION

During the decade represented by the Fourth Edition of the *Encyclopedia of Educational Research,* research in agricultural education began to reflect a revolutionary transition within the field. At the beginning of the decade there was apprehension arising from domestic agricultural surpluses and the fear that surpluses of agricultural manpower, including teachers, would become chronic. Toward the end of the decade the surpluses had vanished and the problem of sustaining a flow of qualified agricultural manpower became an important part of the national legislative intent. It was included in legislation specified for area redevelopment, economic opportunity, manpower development, and vocational education.

This transition was also characterized by a shift in attention from natural resources to human resources and from a domestic context to an international context. Most important, perhaps, was a new commitment to research in agricultural education. This commitment, also a part of the legislative intent, was more programmatic than episodic. It began at about the midpoint of the decade, and, thus, timing does not allow an adequate representation of the new research emphasis. Other aspects of the transition are, however, represented in this review.

ORGANIZATION AND ADMINISTRATION. Research in agricultural education arises from the technology of agriculture and from the advancement of behavioral science. Each plays a part in the broad task of reacting to the needs of rural people and in improving the product and process of the agricultural industry. The research dealing with technological aspects of agriculture is beyond the scope of this discussion except as such advancement may stimulate a change in educational objectives, products, or processes.

This chapter reflects on institutionalized agricultural education typical of the elementary, secondary, and postsecondary schools. The more pertinent research in international agricultural education is included to reflect the broad scope of the literature and to provide a measure of the significance of agricultural education to mankind.

Supply and Demand. While the numbers of persons engaged in production agriculture declined markedly during the decade from 1954 to 1964 (U.S. Office of Education, 1964), the number of agricultural workers employed in agricultural service and in marketing of farm products has increased sharply.

Agriculture usually provides more employment opportunities than its reservoir of skilled manpower can supply. Many positions at all levels must be filled by workers with limited agricultural competencies. Numerous studies have been made to assist in defining the need for trained personnel in farm and off-farm occupations.

The Role of Postsecondary Education. An emerging system of postsecondary education in agriculture is centered in the junior or community college and in area vocational-technical schools. Much of this education is for the preparation of workers in off-farm agricultural occupations rather than in production phases of agriculture.

While the transfer of credit from the junior college to a four-year degree program has been the principal concern of many junior colleges, more emphasis is being placed on the role of these institutions in terminal education (Vorhies, 1964). Little attention has been focused on adult education in agriculture by the junior colleges (Snepp, 1963).

Enrollment in agriculture at all levels of instruction has continued to grow. Emerging programs in off-farm agricultural occupations has increased the scope of interest in agriculture and provided new employment opportunities for youth and adults who would have no opportunity to become established in production agriculture.

Staff and Facilities. Increased secondary enrollments and the consolidation of smaller schools into larger units have added to the increased numbers of multiple-teacher vocational agricultural departments. Emphasis on the off-farm phases of agriculture has also prompted the addition of staff with competencies in off-farm specialties. Often new staff contribute to the concept of specialization by sharing the teaching responsibility.

While there appears to be desire to continue a democratic approach to department administration among administrators and vocational agriculture teachers, department heads continue to have strong administrative roles. These often include (1) attendance at meetings of the board of education, (2) suggestions for change in administrative policy and practices, (3) classroom visits, and (4) authorization of departmental expenditure. School administrators should be expected to participate freely in working with the agricultural advisory committee, reviewing the curriculum, and deciding upon the kinds of programs to be offered for beginning and adult farmers (Jacoby, 1961).

The number of teachers who devote full time to educational programs for adults has increased. While most of these staff members have general competencies in production agriculture, there is a tendency for them to become more specialized in the management aspects of the farm business.

Facilities correspond to the type of agricultural program offered in the school. While the classroom, laboratory, and farm shop remain as the usual facility requirements for a comprehensive program, laboratories and shops have been expanded to accommodate the increased emphasis on off-farm agriculture and the farm-mechanics phase of production agriculture. A typical shop would include space and facilities for instruction in (1) farm buildings and conveniences, (2) farm power and machinery, (3) soil and water conservation, (4) electricity, and (5) general shop practices. The size of the school shop for agriculture is determined by the number of students enrolled and the kinds of jobs performed. The size of each work station is dependent upon (1) the work performed at the station, (2) the size of the material on which the work is performed, (3) the anatomical dimensions of the workers, (4) the working habits of the individual, and (5) the number of people using the station at one time (H. Henderson, 1958).

The field laboratory and greenhouse in teaching vocational agriculture are used increasingly to provide opportunity for practicing a variety of skills and acquiring experiences that the student may not gain at home or in the classroom, shop, or traditional laboratory. The principal uses are (1) to provide useful agricultural experiences, (2) to develop cooperation, (3) to provide facilities for demonstration and (4) to provide publicity for the programs (McComas, 1962).

Planning and Management. Planning and management of agricultural education in the public schools are guided by laws which provide for federal sharing of program costs. Programs prior to 1963 were established under the guide lines initiated by the passage of the Smith-Hughes Act of 1917 and the George-Barden Act of 1946 (U.S. Office of Education, 1965a). States also contribute to the operation of local programs by providing services to programs as well as financial aids.

The state supervisors are most often perceived in the role of stimulators in the five functions of their office: administration, improvement of instruction, research and evaluation, and public relations (Schroeder, 1962). Supervisors perceive a strong need for in-service education for themselves in (1) evaluation of the supervisory program, (2) encouraging and assisting in the evaluation of local vocational agriculture programs, (3) cooperatively developing a public relations program and (4) providing leadership in educational planning (Taylor, 1961).

The manner in which costs of the agricultural education program in local schools are shared by the federal, state, and local governments is usually determined by individual states acting within the guide lines established by federal law. Some states use a program of differential cost sharing as a means of stimulating participation in various phases of the total agricultural education program. Warmbrod (1962) found four methods of reimbursement in common use: (1) a percentage of the incurred costs; (2) flat grants per school, student, or adult or young farmer class, or hours of out-of-school instruction; (3) sliding scales with newer departments having higher reimbursement rates; (4) additional reimbursement for summer work, and (5) reimbursement on the basis of an excess-cost formula.

The Morris-Perkins Act of 1963 (P.L. 88–210) provided additional support for vocational education but gave states more responsibility for fund distribution. The bill authorized $225-million annually after 1967. It continued the necessity for each state to have a state plan outlining the general policies under which vocational education would be administered. Vocational agriculture gained new flexibility by provisions that removed the directed or supervised practice on the farm as an adjunct to student enrollment at the secondary level and which permitted expenditure of vocational agriculture funds for instruction in any occupation involving knowledge and skills in agricultural subjects (U.S. Office of Education, 1965b).

STUDIES OF AGRICULTURAL MANPOWER.

Changing Occupational Structure. Agricultural education has been affected by changes in agricultural technology and by the migration of the rural population. The interaction of these changes has had a marked effect upon the occupational structure of agriculture. The impact of technological change has increased the demand for services by those agencies and industries that supply and supplement the work of the farmer or aid in the distribution, processing, and marketing of his products. Agricultural educators often refer to the work force serving in this capacity as the "off-farm agriculture occupation" sector.

The steady increase in the dependence on the off-farm occupation sector does not reflect a decline in the importance of production or on-farm agriculture. In the decade of the 1950's national farm output increased 2.5 percent per year. At the same time, farm employment declined by about 4.9 percent per year (J. Henderson & Krueger, 1965). Some of the decline in farm employment was balanced by gains in employment in the off-farm agricultural occupations. Educators began to look more closely at the role of agricultural education in training for employment in the full range of agricultural occupations rather than limiting educational goals to production farming. The Vocational Education Act of 1963 gave impetus to this changing role by broadening the objectives of agricultural education (U.S. Office of Education, 1965b).

Early investigation of off-farm occupational training showed the need for (1) modification of state plans and policies, (2) more adequate teacher training in such off-farm occupational skill areas as human relations, economics, English, and mathematics, and (3) a better understanding by administrators and supervisors of the merit of an expanded agricultural training program (Clark, 1963; Barwick, 1965). Identification of individual job opportunities sometimes led to the conclusion that there was too little employment opportunity to warrant the establishment of specific vocational training programs by the local school district (Frederick & others, 1961; Hoover, 1957). Other investigators attempted to determine the number of persons needed and the kinds of job entry skills employers were looking for when hiring new employees (Morrison, 1964; Thompson & others, 1963). The Vocational Education Act of 1963 triggered a veritable explosion of new studies aimed at determining the number of people to be served and the kinds of skills and competencies needed.

Assessment of Educational Needs. Pennsylvania reported that approximately 3.5 percent of the persons employed in the state (excluding farmers) needed special competencies in agriculture (Barwick, 1965). About 50 percent of those employed in businesses with an agricultural base needed special agricultural skills (Hoover & others, 1965), and those needing agricultural skills used agricultural competencies most of the time on the job (Cushman & others, 1965). Training programs for the off-farm sector should emphasize competencies in (1) agricultural business and agricultural mechanics for employees in all occupational groups, (2) plant science for workers in crop marketing and processing, forestry and soil conservation, wildlife and recreation, and ornamental horticulture and agricultural service occupations, (3) animal science for prospective workers in dairy manufacturing and processing, livestock marketing and processing, and other livestock-industry and farm-service occupations and (4) forestry, conservation, outdoor recreation, and ornamental horticulture for workers in these fields (Barwick, 1965; Cushman & others, 1965; Hoover & others, 1965; Judge, 1965). Workers in off-farm occupations are needed at all levels of competency. Hoover and his associates (1965) reported that of the 13,668 off-farm persons needing agricultural competencies in a 17-county Pennsylvania area, 10 percent were classified as professional, 10 percent as managerial, 12 percent as sales, and 58 percent as skilled or semi-skilled workers.

Agriculture in a Changing Context. Attention is also focused on the problems associated with entry into farming. As farm size increases, farm operation as an entry occupation becomes more difficult and more risky. There is a need for instructional programs in agriculture in order that beginning farmers can minimize financial risks and maximize the possibilities of success as they move toward farming as a business career. Program needs vary among farmers in the same way that there is variation in the educational attainment of prospective farmers. Reading habits, for example, appear to have some relationship to educational need. There is evidence that a substitution effect exists between capital required for a beginning farmer and the amount of education he brings to the occupation (Pearce, 1964; Persons & Swanson, 1966). In-service education for production agriculture should emphasize farm management instruction, farm mechanics, and technical assistance in specific enterprises (Pearce, 1964; Jensen, 1961).

CURRICULUM DEVELOPMENT. Secondary Education. Traditionally, the curriculum for agricultural education in the secondary school has been designed to deal with problems found in the local community. A common curricular pattern includes agriculture in grades 9, 10, 11, and 12. A student may elect to take all four units of vocational agriculture. Some schools offer one or more additional course units in farm mechanics.

The responsibility for organizing a curriculum in agriculture for the community often resides with the teacher of vocational agriculture. Certain units of instruction dealing with the general physical and biological aspects of agriculture are important in all areas of the nation, and they often form a common element in secondary agricultural curricula. Other agricultural units may have application only within certain regions or localities (Coupland, 1962).

The inclusion or exclusion of areas of instruction in a secondary curriculum may be determined by comprehensive study of the needs described by the educational clientele. In New York, for example, dairy farmers rated the importance of six areas of farm-mechanics instruction. The rank order was (1) farm machinery, (2) farm power, (3) farm shop, (4) farm buildings and conveniences, (5) electricity, and (6) soil and water management. They indicated the kinds of jobs they expected to be able to perform in the several instructional areas. It resulted in a curriculum and a training program based upon the number of farmers performing the job, its value to farmers, and the desire of farmers to do the job themselves (Annis, 1961). Wisconsin farmers also responded to questions regarding their use of 143 farm-mechanics skills. They saw need for some training in 95 of the skills listed, thus giving a basis for developing a farm-mechanics curriculum (Jensen, 1961). Other methods of determining agricultural education curriculum needs are enumerated by James (1953) in an early study of three Illinois communities. As the concept of "community" changes, it may be necessary to devise new ways to more accurately assess the current and projected needs of the broader community. Attention to the off-farm occupation sector has provided a model for assessing curriculum needs for larger geographic communities (Frederick & others, 1961; Barwick, 1965; Hoover & others, 1965).

With general responsibility for the curriculum residing with teachers of agriculture, it is not surprising that much of the innovation in curriculum is of teacher origin. Teachers usually concentrate developmental efforts upon a single subject area within the curriculum and attempt to develop a comprehensive course of study and supporting procedures for implementation of the new curriculum (Oren, 1963; Anderson, 1960).

With a rapidly changing technology giving impetus to curriculum patterns which are more adaptable to change and less subject to obsolescence, some attention has been focused on curricula based on a study of principles. Sutherland developed content and teaching suggestions for integrating biological principles with instruction in agriculture. This integrated subject matter can be effectively introduced into the agricultural curriculum, although some traditionally included content might have to be eliminated in order to allow sufficient instructional time (Sutherland & Sams, 1963). A later experiment in Ohio showed the "principle" approach to be effective in increasing achievement in agriculture and biology as measured by standardized tests. A concentration on teaching principles also seemed effective in making vocational agriculture more challenging to students (Starling, 1964; Krueger, 1965).

Curriculum development in the off-farm agricultural occupations has been more direct. Curriculum development has often originated at the state or regional level. Identification of common elements in groups of job titles has led to the discovery of clusters of jobs with similar training needs. Curriculum units have been developed for use in training for the occupational clusters (Center for Research . . ., 1965). A unit on business communication, for example, may be readily adaptable for inclusion in training for a number of off-farm agriculture occupational clusters of job titles.

In spite of the success of a regional approach to curriculum development for off-farm agricultural occupations, little progress has been made in similar approaches to curriculum development for on-farm production agriculture. Identification of curriculum elements that transcend agriculture and the identification of elements that have regional significance would suggest that it is feasible to develop a core course of agricultural subject content that can improve agricultural curricula (Coupland, 1962; Trammel, 1964).

Post-High School Education. The post-high school agricultural curriculum of less-than-baccalaureate level is generally in the category of off-farm agricultural occupations, beginning farmer instruction, or instruction for adults. Institutions offering such instruction are secondary schools, technical institutes, junior colleges, comprehensive community colleges, and area vocational-technical schools (Clary, 1964).

A significant addition to beginning farmer and adult farm education was made when curriculums were developed to systematize farm management instruction. A farm management program is characterized by (1) regular enrollment, (2) specific instructional units within each course, (3) a definite and regular sequence of courses, and (4) continuity between courses with progression toward farm business reorganization or improved efficiency (Palan, 1962). Individualized on-farm instruction plays an important role in adult and beginning farm education. Francis (1966) outlined a curriculum to be followed during the on-farm visit by making a complete monthly list of the kinds of problems with which farmers might be most concerned.

Higher Education. The rise in numbers of junior and community colleges offering transfer credit in agriculture has required greater coordination between institutions of higher learning. Simultaneously, a gradual rise in admission requirements has affected the nature of the technical agricultural courses. It has allowed greater flexibility and more depth in course offerings. Many colleges with agricultural curricula have adapted some minimal requirements for general education and have broadened their curriculum to allow a more liberal education. Little research has been done to assess the effect of the broadened curriculum on the performance of graduates.

INSTRUCTION. Agricultural education takes advantage of many of the methods and media of instruction commonly used in the public school. The extension of the classroom to include the farms and businesses in the community provides a unique opportunity to maximize use of a variety of methods of instruction including field trips, demonstrations, experimental plots, individualized on-farm instruction, field laboratories, and work experience.

Methods and Techniques of Instruction. Some types of subject materials are more easily adapted to presentation with teaching aids than others are. A topic dealing with specific facts and illustrations, such as the use of herbicides and insecticides in coffee production, is often more effectively taught with the aid of visual materials. The learning of more general topics, such as farm management, may not be appreciably affected when teaching aids are utilized. The aids must be specific to the topic and prepared to illustrate methods, facts, or concepts that are not so effectively presented by conventional means (Gonzalez, 1962; Madison, 1962).

Programmed instruction has been tried experimentally with a variety of agricultural subjects. Legg found the lecture-discussion method to be superior to the programmed-instruction method in teaching agricultural finance. Programmed instruction may be most helpful to students exploring areas of special interest or in filling in areas of knowledge not included by other methods (Legg, 1962). When time used in study was carefully controlled, the differences in learning between programmed instruction and lecture-discussion were negligible (Legg, 1962; McClay, 1964; Zarraga, 1963).

Experimental Approaches to Improved Instruction. In subject matter that is not based upon a known body of facts but deals in concepts and ideas, the sequence in which programmed materials are presented may be important. Hull (1965) found that the effect of sequence in instructional materials is related to the achievement level of the students and the difficulty of the material. Material organized according to psychological sequence or human developmental stages was superior for low-achievement students when the criterion measure involved questions regarding subject content. The psychological sequence was superior for high-ability students when the criterion measure related to concept generalizations.

The intensity of instruction and the specific patterns of supervision and instruction have varying effects on learning. Love and Stevens (1964) found that three-day workshops or weekly sessions were more effective than monthly sessions for the in-service training of teachers. Qualified teachers or educational specialists were also more effective as teachers than other types of specialists were.

Laboratory and On-farm Instruction. The use of special laboratory facilities and a specifically organized teaching plan were shown to be of value in teaching greenhouse management and plant science principles. Students also exhibited significant transfer of learning in applying the principles learned to other growing things, although knowledge of specific factors such as light and nutrients transferred to a greater degree than did knowledge of temperature, moisture, and aeration. The latter observation cautions against the assumption of uniform transfer of all types of knowledge (Drawbaugh, 1963). Land laboratories for studying crops and livestock may also provide desirable agricultural experiences. In addition, they aid in the development of teaching demonstrations and individualized instruction (McComas & others, 1962). On-farm instruction is utilized very effectively in agricultural education. Moeckel pointed out several kinds of activities where on-farm instruction could be used to advantage with adult farmers: (1) to assist farmers in conducting trial and demonstration plots, (2) to analyze the instruction of a previous adult class as it relates to the farm, (3) to analyze Dairy Herd Improvement Association, soil-test, or other farm records, (4) to use local production standards to assist the farmer in evaluating his farm business, (5) to use farms as a source of visual materials to illustrate principles and practices (Moeckel, 1960). The specific tasks and questions that should be explored in on-farm instruction for adults in farm management programs cover all facets of the farm business (Francis, 1966).

Work Experience Programs. Designed especially for students studying for employment in off-farm agricultural occupations, the work experience program provides for practical on-the-job experience in a variety of occupations (USOE, 1965b). The work experience program in agriculture is comparable to the supervised farming program for learning skills and competencies and practicing management abilities (U.S. Office of Education, 1965b).

Hull (1966) and his associates developed a comprehensive series of curriculum materials for use in cooperative experience programs in horticulture, agricultural supply, and farm machinery. The two-year course contained learning areas common to all types of businesses as well as those based upon the competencies needed for the specific occupational groups. Developments in the occupational experience field have been the result of cooperative efforts between teacher educators, state supervisors, and practicing teachers (Benson, 1966). An effective program in off-farm agricultural occupations would include opportunities for exploration of occupational choices suited to student interests and capabilities as well as actual work experience in a single industry (Agan, 1967).

TEACHER EDUCATION. Teacher Supply and Demand. Effective programs of agricultural education are dependent upon an adequate supply of qualified teachers. Teacher supply has not been stable. A few years of oversupply have been followed by years of teacher shortage. The 1950–1960 decade revealed an increasing shortage of vocational agriculture teachers. There has been an increased demand for teachers in off-farm agricultural occupations, for expanded programs of adult education, and as teachers of agriculture in vocational-technical schools.

There were a total of 10,325 teaching positions in agriculture in 1966. Projections based upon increasing demands for vocational agriculture teachers during the first half of the 1950–1960 decade indicate a need for 11,257 teachers by 1970 (Woodin, 1967). The turnover rate of vocational agriculture teachers, about 10.4 percent per year, appears to be greater than that of other kinds of teachers, although beginning agriculture teachers entered teaching with good perceptions of their teaching roles (Woodin, 1967; Todd, 1965). Woodin (1967) found that only 61.4 percent of the 1965–66 graduates in agricultural education were employed in teaching agriculture the following year. Greater chance for personal achievement was given most frequently as a reason for entering nonteaching positions (Shoup, 1965).

Curriculum in Teacher Education. The curriculum in agricultural education is reasonably uniform among training institutions. A survey of 43 teacher training institutions showed institutional medians of 56.5 to 59 semester credits in general education for graduation. Technical agricultural requirements varied from 35 to 67 credits with institutional medians of 55 to 58 credits. Schools required from 15 to 38 credits in professional education, with institutional medians of 21 to 26 credits. Farm experience is a requirement in a large number of institutions (Jabro, 1962). Self-evaluation of teacher education programs in the United States shows the strongest areas of the total program in agriculture to be (1) the staff, (2) the curriculum, and (3) the institutional facilities. The weakest areas in the total program of agricultural education departments are (1) research, (2) recruiting trainees, and (3) public relations activities (Bronson, 1963).

One method of determining the areas of curriculum needing stress was utilized by Horner (1960) when he surveyed first-year teachers in Nebraska. Twelve activities were ranked by teachers and identified as areas where there was need for assistance. Competencies least adequately developed were described by Gadda (1963) as those pertaining to (1) performing guidance services, (2) teaching young and adult farmers, (3) conducting a public relations program, (4) teaching in-school classes, and (5) supervised farming program. Little research has been done to test the effects of change in the teacher training curriculum.

Student Teaching. Many attempts have been made to predict the teaching success of prospective teachers of agriculture. Investigators have found only minor relationships between undergraduate academic achievement and teaching performance. Cardozier (1965) found the relationship between achievement and performance closest in the cases of biological sciences, agricultural education, and student teaching.

Hutchinson (1961) reports that student-teaching assignments range from 3 to 48 weeks with an average of 10.5 weeks. Two students are often assigned to the same teacher center. Teacher trainers rate exceptionally highly the participating experiences in the areas of (1) teaching all-day students, (2) supervised farming programs, and (3) adult and beginning farmer instruction. Promoting and publicizing the "vo-ag" program, understanding the objectives and philosophy of the school, and experience in non-school activities were rated lowest in importance by the same group.

Predictions of student-teaching success have been based both on undergraduate achievement and on personal characteristics. In New York, close relationships were found between student-teaching success and (1) second-year cumulative college grade average, (2) number of farm practice credits, (3) average grade in vocational agriculture, and (4) Regent's grade in high school physics (Jarmin, 1963). Student teachers in agricultural education exhibit characteristics which may be used to evaluate student-teaching performance and which are conditioned by other behaviors observed during their participation in student teaching. Behaviors most closely related to effective student teaching were fairness, kindness, alertness, attractiveness, responsibility, steadiness, and poise. Behaviors associated with below-average student teaching were evasiveness, dullness, being stereotyped, uncertainty, disorganization, inflexibility, and narrowness. The correlation of predicted and actual student-teaching effectiveness was numerically four times greater when based upon student characteristics than when based upon predictions of teacher educators (Fuller, 1963).

Effective supervising teachers are important to the student-teaching experience. Rogers (1965) corroborated the work of earlier researchers when he found that effectiveness of the supervising teacher was influenced by (1) previous experience as a supervising teacher, (2) academic degree held, (3) reading of professional literature, and (4) participation in local community organizations. Employment mobility and the age of the teacher were also important factors.

SPECIAL EMPHASIS STUDIES. Studies of some of the social variables that affect agricultural education have attracted considerable attention. Teacher morale has been shown to be a significant factor in student attitude. Attitudes of students as measured by the Minnesota Student Attitude Inventory were significantly better when students were under the direction of high-morale teachers rather than teachers who scored low on the Purdue Teacher Morale Inventory. Greatest differences occurred for items pertaining to teacher planning, control, and general climate in the classroom (Bentley, 1963).

Social Variables. The socioeconomic status of agriculture students does not seem to be related to reading scores even when the reading material is agricultural in context (Hayes, 1966). This finding reinforces those of other inquiries showing that neither the school achievement of rural children nor their scholastic aptitude is related to measures of parental farm income (Persons & Swanson, 1966). Socioeconomic level was related, however, to the meaning that students placed upon the words "leadership" and "cooperation." Students of low socioeconomic status placed higher values on the word "leadership" than did students in other status groups. Middle socioeconomic groups placed more value on the word "cooperation" than did the low-status or the high-status groups (McMillion, 1966). It is important to observe that social-status studies dealing with rural farm people produce results that are generally inconsistent with similar studies conducted in urban areas. This is a subject of considerable research interest in the field of agricultural education.

There is concern for the value patterns and aspiration levels of students of agriculture. Personal and occupational values appear to be already established by the time students enroll in senior high school and are not to be influenced appreciably by school personnel or activities (Thompson & Carr, 1966). Aspiration levels do not appear amenable to change by exposure to occupational information given during a short period of time. (Wolf, 1966). Research is not adequate to define the effects of long-range programs of exposure to occupational information on the aspiration level of students in rural areas.

Guidance in Agriculture. The unusually close relationship of student to teacher, teacher knowledge of the student's home and family, and a common agricultural interest are factors that contribute to a successful guidance relationship.

College students in agriculture indicate that vocational agriculture teachers ranked second to parents as a positive influence in choosing agriculture as a career. Experiences in high school in vocational agriculture and the Future Farmers of America outranked other high school experiences in career influence (Bentley, 1963).

Input-Output Cost Analyses. Agricultural education has been the vehicle for a special series of studies aimed at assessing the economic return to investment in adult education. These are among the very few microeconomic studies in the field of education. Returns from adult farm management instruction have been about $500 in added gross income per farmer for each year of the first three years the farmer was enrolled in farm management instruction. A declining return for the third year of instruction suggests that the principle of diminishing marginal return is operative (Cvancara, 1964). The relationship of years of general education to measures of farm earnings was not significant, although attendance at adult classes was significantly related to increases in income (Persons & Swanson, 1966). The return on investment in adult education in farm management is very high. Ohio farmers reported an increase of $53.16 in net farm income for each dollar invested in the instructional program by the public school. Instruction also resulted in an increase in student understanding of profit-maximizing economic principles (Rolloff, 1966). Research is needed to assess some of the noneconomic benefits that may accrue as a result of organized adult education.

Future Farmers of America. Many facets of the program of the Future Farmers of America and New Farmers of America have been examined. However, almost all studies have been at a community or state level. Topics that have been examined are (1) the FFA and NFA awards and contests program, (2) summer activities and program of work, (3) leadership activities, and (4) establishment in farming and other occupations. No recent studies have been completed on a regional or national level to evaluate the program of the FFA or to improve the impact of the organization on the successful occupational establishment of vocational agricultural students.

MEASUREMENT AND EVALUATION. Follow-up Studies. A common way of evaluating a program of agricultural education is through follow-up of former students. The effectiveness of the program is gauged by the number of students who are employed in the occupation for which they were trained or in closely related occupations. Note is also taken of the number unemployed or employed only part time. Byram (1965b) lists uses of follow-up information as (1) a measure of the needs of business and industry, (2) a guide for changing curriculum, (3) a study of desired employee characteristics, (4) information valuable for guidance and counseling personnel, (5) insight into employee mobility, (6) a guide for studying program effectiveness in the business community, and (7) a guide for establishing the training needs of employees.

Follow-up studies of agricultural education students have produced widely diverse results. Of Louisiana graduates from high school vocational agriculture, 30.3 percent were engaged in on-farm agriculture or related occupations. These graduates placed high values on all phases of the vocational agriculture program in assisting them to make an occupational choice (Hayles, 1963). A study of 8,000 Minnesota students of vocational agriculture showed that almost three-fourths of the former students employed in the civilian labor force were engaged in farming, off-farm agricultural occupations, or mechanical trades related to farm-mechanics instruction. Over 40 percent of the total group were engaged in farming or related occupations. Less than 1 percent of all former students studied were unemployed (Johnson, 1965). Of 9,792 Virginia former students of vocational agriculture, 62 percent were employed in some phase of off-farm agricultural occupations or mechanical occupations related to training. Less than 1 percent of the Virginia students who had studied vocational agriculture for four years were unemployed (Campbell & others, 1963).

There are some inherent weaknesses in many of the efforts to evaluate agricultural education programs through follow-up studies of graduates. First, the decision to enter the business of farming may be either assisted or restricted by the general level of employment and by current labor-force participation rates at the time the decision occurs. Second, the exit requirements of instructional programs are often quite different from entrance requirements for any occupation requiring self-employment and entrepreneurial skill.

While many follow-up studies deal with the employment status of graduates, a few concentrate on the variations in occupational performances which accrue from agricultural instruction. An experimental study in Georgia revealed that farmers who had studied vocational agriculture in high school were significantly more willing to adopt new farm practices than those who had not engaged in such study (O'Kelley & Lester, 1965).

The development and use of evaluative instruments for agricultural education is a continuing process. In general, they are of three types. Most common is the type used to evaluate a total instructional program within a school setting employing national criteria. Such criteria have been developed by the National Study of Secondary School Standards (National Study . . . , 1960) and have been used frequently for evaluation and for research. A second type involves the evaluation of statewide programs. An example was the Florida inquiry (Eaddy, 1965) which included a critique of direction as well as performance. The critique included the observations that research was insufficient and that follow-up studies were too infrequent. A third type of evaluation instrument is the kind developed to measure a specific teaching objective. McCormick (1964) developed such an instrument for measuring the understanding of profit-maximizing principles.

Attainment of Vocational Goals. Since agricultural education is a part of the offerings in public school vocational education, its evaluation is often included in procedures employed to assess vocational goals within the total educational process. Methodological inquiries have been undertaken to establish principles and guide lines for this process. A Michigan study has contributed to this effort by working in pilot communities (Byram, 1965a), and a further inquiry in Michigan has produced a manual for evaluating programs of vocational education in local communities (Byram, 1965b). This manual, an outline of a demonstration project, includes many practical suggestions and many checklists which may be used in gathering relevant data.

INTERNATIONAL AGRICULTURAL EDUCATION. With the alarming estimates of world food shortages and possible famine within the next several decades, attention has turned to agricultural education as a way to promote production and to alleviate the crisis.

Advanced countries have relied heavily on secondary-level school-oriented agricultural training programs to meet development objectives. Less-developed countries have relied mainly on extension services and university-level agricultural training programs. Attention to a full range of institutional emphasis has been unexpectedly tardy, and research on these development problems is only in its beginning stages. Much of it has been prompted by a lack of success in reaching agricultural development objectives in the less-developed countries.

Research studies have been of three types. The first arises from increasing numbers of exchange students. Dissertation inquiries have focused on some of the problems of the student's homeland. The second is typified by general studies which examine the capacity to accommodate agricultural and educational change. Included are the capacities inherent in individual farmers which have been described as including mental ability, values, attitudes, customs, and individual farming goals (Hirsch, 1963) Also included are the capacities of teachers and administrators to acquire and adopt training methods to cope with the instructional objectives of agricultural development (Batten, 1962). A few countries have made dramatic progress toward agricultural and economic development. Some of the research has chronicled the role of agricultural education in this progress (Meaders, 1966).

The third type of research involves planning and pilot projects. They underline the principle that rural development goes hand in hand with the development of rural education and that in the processes of planning, development and education must be integral (Malassis, 1966a).

At the secondary and higher education levels, nationwide pilot projects have been undertaken in France and in Sweden. Both emphasize the need for an intellectual investment at the agricultural secondary level in order to achieve national development goals. The French model (Malassis, 1966b) emphasizes general economic principles. The Swedish model (Ericson & Petrini, 1966) gives more emphasis to objectives, data analysis, and long-term planning. Both of the pilot projects are planning models for actual use in agricultural development within their respective countries. The impact of these studies is likely to be widespread. For both the more and the less-developed countries, these pilot studies may come to be regarded as among the most important agricultural inquiries of the decade. They focus on the importance of human resources and the important role of the school systems as institutional mechanisms for developing human and agricultural productivity.

In the United States as well as in other countries, education has acquired a new economic and social relevance. It has come to be regarded as an essential vehicle for achieving both individual and national goals. During the past decade, research in agricultural education has mirrored the shifting emphasis toward the heightened role of human resources in agricultural development and the educational problems associated with its demand, supply, and flow.

Gordon I. Swanson
University of Minnesota

Edgar Persons
University of Minnesota

References

Agan, R. J. *A Coordinated and Integrated Program of Occupational Information, Selection and Preparation in a Secondary School.* Kansas State U Press, 1967.

Anderson, Glenn Myron. *A Reference Unit for Teaching Cooperatives.* Master's thesis. U Minnesota, 1960.

Annis, William H. *The Needs of Dairy Farmers in Agricultural Mechanics in Selected Dairy Counties in New York.* Doctoral dissertation. Cornell U, 1961.

Barwick, Ralph P. *Identification of Off-farm Agricultural Occupations and the Education Needed for Employment in these Occupations in Delaware.* Doctoral dissertation. Pennsylvania State U, 1965.

Batten, T. R. *Training for Community Development: A Critical Study of Method.* Oxford U Press, 1962. 200p.

Benson, Herbert. *A One-week Workshop for Supervising Teachers in Agricultural Occupations.* Colorado State U Press, 1966.

Bentley, Ralph R. *Factors Influencing the Vocational Choices of Agricultural College Freshmen.* Purdue U Press, 1963. 51p.

Bentley, Ralph R., and Rempel, Averno M. *Vocational Agriculture Teacher Morale Study.* Purdue U Press, 1963.

Bronson, Clement Alphonso. *An Evaluation of Selected Aspects of Agricultural Education Programs in the Inter-regional Land-grant Institutions of the United States.* Ohio State U Press, 1963.

Byram, H. *Evaluating Vocational Education in the Public Schools.* Bureau of Educational and Research Services, Michigan State U, 1965(a).

Byram, H. *Evaluation of Local Vocational Education Programs.* Bureau of Education and Research Services, Michigan State U, 1965(b).

Campbell, Julian M., and others. *A Follow-up Study of Former Students of Vocational Agriculture in Virginia Who Were Graduated From or Dropped Out of High School During 1954, 1960 and 1963.* Virginia State Department of Education, 1963.

Cardozier, V. R. *Undergraduate Academic Achievement and Teaching Performance.* U Maryland Press, 1965.

Center for Research and Leadership Development in Vocational and Technical Education. *Course Outline for Agricultural Machinery-service Occupations.* Ohio State U Press, 1965.

Clark, Raymond M. *Training for Off-farm Agricultural Occupations.* Michigan State U Press, 1963.

Clary, Joseph Ray. *Guidelines for the Development of Training Programs for Agricultural Technicians.* Doctoral dissertation. Ohio State U Press, 1964.

Coupland, Joe. *The Importance of Units of Instruction in the High School Vocational Agriculture Curriculum.* Doctoral dissertation. Ohio State U, 1962.

Cushman, Harold R., and others. *A Study of Off-farm Agricultural Occupations in New York State.* Cornell U Press, 1965.

Cvancara, Joseph G. *Input-output Relationships Among Selected Intellectual Investments in Agriculture.* Doctoral dissertation. U Minnesota, 1964.

Drawbaugh, Charles C. *A Teaching Experiment in the Use of Greenhouse Facilities in Vocational Agriculture.* Doctoral dissertation. Pennsylvania State U, 1963.

Eaddy, Kenneth M. *A Critique of the Agricultural Education Program in Florida.* Doctoral dissertation. U Florida, 1965.

Ericson, G., and Petrini, F. "Pilot Study on Sweden." In *Training Manpower for Tomorrow's Agriculture.* Organization for Economic Cooperation and Development Pub. No. 80. Paris, 1966. p. 13–62.

Francis, Eugene U. *A Course of Study for On-the-farm Instruction and Farm Business Analysis.* Master's thesis. U Minnesota, 1966.

Frederick, Tom, and others. *Employment Opportunities in Certain Occupations Related to Farming in the Syracuse Economic Area.* Cornell U Press, 1961.

Fuller, G. R. *The Relationship of Characteristics of Prospective Student Teachers and Student Teaching Effectiveness in Agricultural Education.* U Illinois Press, 1963.

Gadda, Hilding W. *An Evaluation of the Pre-service Program of Teacher Education in Agriculture at South Dakota State College.* Doctoral dissertation. Michigan State U, 1963.

Gonzalez, Crescenciano. *A Comparison of Methods of Instruction Utilized in Adult Farmer Classes for Teaching the Proper Use of Insecticides, Fungicides and Herbicides in Coffee Production in Puerto Rico.* Master's thesis. Pennsylvania State U, 1962.

Hayes, Glenn Warren. *The Relationship of Socio-economic Status of Pupils to Their Comprehension of Reference Materials Written at Different Levels of Readability.* U Illinois Press, 1966.

Hayles, Jasper Asbury, Jr. *Occupational Experiences of High School Graduates Who Completed Four Years of Vocational Agriculture in Louisiana.* Doctoral dissertation. Louisiana State U, 1963.

Henderson, Harry D. *Spatial Requirements for a Farm*

Mechanics Laboratory. Doctoral dissertation. U Minnesota, 1958.

Henderson, James M., and Krueger, Anne O. *National Growth and Economic Change in the Upper Midwest.* Upper Midwest Research and Development Council, U Minnesota Press, 1965.

Hirsch, G. P. *Incentives for Rural Development and the Agricultural Population.* Proceedings of the Rehovoth [Israel] Conference on Comprehensive Planning of Agriculture in Developing Countries, 1963.

Hoover, Norman Kurtz. *Factors Associated with Establishment in Related Agricultural Occupations and Their Relationship to the High School Curriculum in Vocational Agriculture.* Doctoral dissertation. Pennsylvania State U, 1957.

Hoover, Norman Kurtz, and others. *Technical Education Needs of Persons Engaged in Agricultural Occupations.* Pennsylvania State U Press, 1965.

Horner, James T. *A Followup Study of First-Year Instructors of Vocational Agriculture in Nebraska.* U Nebraska Press, 1960. 40p.

Hull, William Lee. *A Procedure for Sequencing Self-instructional Materials for Concept Attainment of Human Relations Abilities in Agricultural Business Occupations.* Doctoral dissertation. Pennsylvania State U, 1965.

Hull, William Lee. *Developing Curriculum Materials for Cooperative Experience Programs in Agriculture.* Oklahoma State U, 1966

Hutchinson, James Herman. *A Study of the Participating Experiences of Student Teachers of Vocational Agriculture.* Doctoral dissertation. Louisiana State U, 1961.

Jabro, Salim Hanna. *Curricula in Agricultural Education at the Land-grant Colleges and State Universities in the United States.* Doctoral dissertation. Iowa State U, 1962.

Jacoby, Walter. *Policies and Practices in the Administration of Multiple Teacher Vocational Agriculture Departments in the United States.* Doctoral dissertation. U Connecticut, 1961.

James, Gerald B. *A Redefinition of the Clientele for Agricultural Education in the Public Schools.* Doctoral dissertation. U Illinois, 1953.

Jarmin, Martin V. *Prediction of Success in the Student Teaching Program for Prospective Teachers of Vocational Agriculture at the New York State College of Agriculture at Cornell University.* Doctoral dissertation. Cornell U, 1963.

Jensen, Arthur K. *An Analysis of Farm Mechanics Knowledge and Skills Needed by Wisconsin Farmers.* Doctoral dissertation. U Wisconsin, 1961.

Johnson, Donald G. *Employment Status of Former High School Students of Vocational Agriculture in Minnesota.* Master's thesis. U Minnesota, 1965.

Judge, Homer V. *Employment Opportunities and Needed Competencies in Off-farm Agricultural Occupations in Massachusetts.* Massachusetts Department of Education, 1965.

Krueger, August W., Jr. *The Principle Approach in Teaching Mechanical Technology in Agriculture.* Master's thesis. Oregon State U, 1965.

Legg, Otto Pearl. *Programmed-instruction and Lecture-discussion Methods Compared for Effectiveness in Teaching Agriculture Finance to Vocational Agriculture Students.* Doctoral dissertation. Pennsylvania State U, 1962.

Love, Gene M., and Stevens, Glenn Z. *Educational Effectiveness of Three Sequences of Scheduling Classes and of Three Patterns of Supervision and Instruction in an In-service Course for Teachers.* Pennsylvania State U Press, 1964.

Madison, Eldon H. *The Effectiveness of Visual Aids in Presenting an Analysis of Selected Farm Management Factors.* Doctoral dissertation. U Minnesota, 1962.

Malassis, L. *Développement économique et programmation de l'education rurale.* UNESCO, 1966(a).

Malassis, L. "Pilot Study on France." In *Trained Manpower for Tomorrow's Agriculture.* Organization for Economic Cooperation and Development Pub. No. 80, 1966(b). p. 63–142.

McClay, David R. *A Comparison of Programmed and Lecture-discussion Methods of Teaching Farm Credit to High School and Adult Students.* Pennsylvania State U, 1964.

McComas, James Douglas. *Land and Livestock Laboratories in New Mexico and West Texas.* New Mexico State U Press, 1962.

McComas, James Douglas, and Others. *Land and Livestock Laboratories in New Mexico and Texas.* New Mexico State U Press, 1962.

McCormick, Floyd G. *The Development of an Instrument for Measuring the Understanding of Profit-maximizing Principles.* Doctoral dissertation. Ohio State U, 1964.

McMillion, Martin B. *A Study in Communication Between High School Teachers of Vocational Agriculture and Socio-economically Disadvantaged Youth by the Use of the Semantic Differential.* U Illinois Press, 1966. 133p.

Meaders, O. Donald. *Educational and Occupational Attainments of Taiwan Vocational Agriculture Graduates.* Michigan State U Press, 1966. 114p.

Moeckel, Rolf E. *The Effectiveness of Practices of Individual On-farm Instruction Used by Teachers of Adult Farmer Courses in Michigan.* Doctoral dissertation. Michigan State U, 1960.

Morrison, Richard G. *Development and Application of Techniques and Procedures for Determining Training Needs and Educational Opportunities for Students of Vocational Agriculture Within the Baton Rouge Agri-business Complex.* Doctoral dissertation. Louisiana State U, 1964.

National Study of Secondary School Evaluation. *Evaluative Criteria, 1960.* GPO, 1960. p. 61–8.

O'Kelley, G., and Lester, H. *A Comparison of Farmers Who Studied Vocational Agriculture in High School and Those Who Did Not in Terms of Their Tendencies to Adopt Improved Farming Practices.* U Georgia, 1965.

Oren, John William, Jr. *The Development of a Horticultural Program in Vocational Agriculture.* Master's thesis. Ohio State U, 1963.

Palan, Ralph L. *A Program of Instruction for Adult*

Farmers in Agriculture. Master's thesis. U Minnesota, 1962.

Pearce, Frank C. *The Educational Needs of Beginning Farm Operators in Becoming Established in Farming in New York.* Doctoral dissertation. Cornell U, 1964.

Persons, Edgar A., and Swanson, Gordon I. *Educational Restrictions to Agricultural Success and the Relationship of Education to Income Among Farmers.* U Minnesota Press, 1966.

Rogers, Charles Herman. *Factors Associated with Supervising Teacher Effectiveness.* Doctoral dissertation. Cornell U, 1965.

Rolloff, John A. *The Development of a Model Design to Assess Instruction in Farm Management in Terms of Economic Returns and Understanding of Economic Principles.* Doctoral dissertation. Ohio State U, 1966.

Schroeder, Wayne E. *Role Expectations of State Supervision in Vocational Agriculture.* Doctoral dissertation. Ohio State U, 1962.

Shoup, Charles A. *Factors Affecting the Occupational Choice of Agricultural Education Graduates.* Master's thesis. Cornell U, 1965.

Snepp, Neil Owen. *Agricultural Offerings in Community Colleges in the United States.* Doctoral dissertation. Ohio State U, 1963.

Starling, John Tull. *Integrating Biological Principles with Instruction in Vocational Agriculture.* Ohio State U Press, 1964.

Sutherland, Sidney S., and Sams, W. Earn. *Biological Principles in Agriculture.* U California Press, 1963.

Taylor, Robert E. *An In-service Education Program for State Supervisors of Vocational Education in Agriculture.* Doctoral dissertation. Ohio State U, 1961.

Thompson, Evans G., and others. *A Survey to Determine the Opportunities and Training Needs for Career Persons in Agriculturally Related Distributive Business in the Geographical Area Served by George Wythe High School, Wytheville, Virginia.* Virginia Polytechnic Institute, 1963.

Thompson, O. E., and Carr, S. G. *Values of High School Students and Their Teachers.* U California Press, 1966.

Todd, Hollis Elbert. *A Role Analysis of the Perceptions of the Beginning Vocational Agriculture Teachers and Their Professional Difficulties in Role Performance.* Ohio State U Press, 1965.

Trammel, Joe Allen. *Criteria to Use in Selecting Content for a Vocational Agriculture Curriculum and Determining the Grade in Which Material Should Be Taught.* Master's thesis. U Minnesota, 1964.

U.S. Office of Education. *Agricultural Statistics, 1964.* USOE, 1964.

U.S. Office of Education. *A Compendium of Statutes Administered by, Delegating Authority to, or Under Which Authority has been Delegated to the USOE, Dept. of HEW.* GPO, 1965(a).

U.S. Office of Education. *A Compendium of Statutes.* GPO, 1965(b).

Vorhies, Ralph M. *Status and Role of the Non-transfer Agricultural Education Program in California Junior Colleges.* Doctoral dissertation. Missouri, 1964.

Warmbrod, J. R. *State Policies for Distributing State and Federal Funds for Vocational Education in Agriculture to Local School Districts.* Doctoral dissertation. U Illinois, 1962.

Wolf, Jimmie Darrell. *An Experimental Study Investigating the Effects of Teaching Occupational Information on the Level of Aspiration of Oklahoma Vocational Agriculture Students.* Doctoral dissertation. Oklahoma State U, 1966.

Woodin, Ralph J. *Supply and Demand for Teachers of Vocational Agriculture in the United States for the 1966–1967 School Year.* Ohio State U Press, 1967.

Zarraga, José Cruz. *The Development and Experimental Trail of Programmed Learning Material in Teaching Farm Business Management to Vocational Agriculture Students.* Doctoral dissertation. U Minnesota, 1963.

ART EDUCATION

This article is intended to perform two functions: first, to describe the scope and history of the field of art education and, second, to present a summary of research having significant bearing on problems in the field.

THE SCOPE OF ART EDUCATION. Art education, like other fields within education, may be viewed as having two major aspects. One aspect, of more importance to those concerned primarily with teaching, supervision, and curriculum construction, is technological in nature. The second aspect is theoretical and occupies those whose primary concerns rest in establishing, through systematic study, knowledge necessary for improving the technology of art education. These distinctions have been elaborated by a number of writers, perhaps first by Aristotle in his distinctions between the theoretical, practical, and productive forms of knowing, later by writers such as Charles Morris (1939) in his effort to distinguish between science, art, and technology and by Eisner (1965c) in an attempt to differentiate professional functions within art education and to make distinctions among the ways in which graduate students might be prepared.

The technological aspect occupies most members of the field and is concerned not with the production of knowledge primarily but with the improvement of the human's ability to experience and produce art, with the improvement of professional effectiveness in day-to-day situations, and with facilitating the construction of programs and methods that are instrumental to the achievement of objectives within the field. The technological roles filled by the teacher, the supervisor, and the curriculum specialist are aimed at the improvement of particular situations relative to normative ends within the field.

The theoretical aspect of the field deals with the production of knowledge in a variety of modes, scientific and otherwise, and is carried forth by those conducting research. Thus, problems in the field of art education—problems dealing with the means of instruction and with the ends to which they are directed, with understanding the development of the field and its relationship to education and to culture generally—may be considered as subject matters that can be studied through a variety of disciplines.

This view of the field and of the relationship of disciplines to it is not uniformly accepted by scholars. Whether art education is and must be essentially a practical, normatively directed enterprise or whether it is capable of becoming a discipline has been debated. Addressing themselves to the question "Is there a discipline in art education?" Barkan (1963), Logan (1963), and Kaufman (1963) arrived at different answers.

Barkan believes that although there is not at the present time a discipline of art education, there can be. The major lack at present, according to Barkan, is that of adequate strategies for inquiry into problems in the field. The concepts are available, but the methods are not.

Logan believes there is a discipline in art education and that great teachers and theoreticians of art and learning in it have provided tools that exemplify that discipline.

Kaufman, however, believes not only that there is no discipline of art education but also that there cannot be. The nature of both teaching and art precludes the possibility of art education's becoming a discipline in the sense that psychology is a discipline.

Irrespective of the disagreements which have arisen regarding the nature of art education, it is clear from the literature that methods and theories from a variety of disciplines have been used to inquire into problems within its domain. Historical studies have illuminated the growth of the field in the context of a developing nation; psychological inquiry has yielded important generalizations about artistic learning and creativity; sociopsychological studies have been useful in identifying sources of aesthetic judgment; and philosophical research has explicated concepts and theories that have previously gone relatively unexamined.

Although a modern comprehensive history of the field has yet to be written, a number of studies describe some of the more significant developments. Belsche's dissertation (1946) reports some of the major episodes in the growth of the field since Revolutionary days. And Green's dissertation (1948) traces the influence of world expositions of the middle and late nineteenth century upon the growth of art education through the first half of the twentieth century. Logan's *Growth of Art in American Schools* (1955) is one of the few more recent book-length treatments of the history of art education, and Eisner and Ecker (1966) provide brief descriptions of some of the more significant historical developments in their work.

HISTORICAL DEVELOPMENTS IN ART EDUCATION. What is apparent from all of the historical studies is the extent to which goals and practices in the field have shifted over the years. Art education, like the larger scheme of education of which it is a part, has responded to demands of the social order. During the mid-nineteenth century, art was taught in the schools unsystematically and was justified in the name of cultural refinement and because it was thought to develop the penmanship skills of the general school population—a belief that rested upon the assumption that by coordinating the hand and eye in drawing better penmanship would result.

With the growth of industry, especially in the eastern seaboard states, and with increased economic competition from France and England, efforts were made in Massachusetts in the 1870's to improve the artistic skills of students who subsequently would use them in the textile and hardware industries. To achieve this end, Walter Smith, an art master from Leeds, England, was invited to direct art education for the state of Massachusetts and to establish art normal schools for the training of art teachers (W. Smith, 1873). Art education during this period was in the service of industry (Belsche, 1946; Green, 1948; W. Smith, 1873).

The development of the child-study movement under G. Stanley Hall's influence in the 1880's, the availability of colored crayons and paints, the growing concern with the child and his development, all effected a shift toward the use of art for the ends of self-expression and self-realization. The progressive spirit in education which developed during the early part of the twentieth century and the increased importance of Freud's work among the intellectual elite in the East, combined with other intellectual, ideological, economic, and social developments, strengthened the position and values of those who were a part of the child-study movement. By the late 1920's and early 1930's providing for "creative self-expression" became a major goal for the teaching of art in the public schools. Some progressive theorists urged teachers to avoid intervening in the child's work in the belief that art was caught rather than taught. Art education in some circles during this period was in the service of creativity and mental health.

Except for brief interludes such as the depression, in which art was called upon to serve practical aesthetic needs in the home and community, and during World War II, when art at the secondary-school level was used to contribute to the war effort by having students make posters, creative development through art continued to hold high priority, at least in the literature if not always in practice. Lowenfeld's work (1957) as well as that of D'Amico (1942) stressed the importance of the process over the product, although these two writers recognized that product and process were not unrelated. Art education during the late 1940's and the 1950's continued the tradition initiated twenty years earlier which subscribed to the belief that the primary function of art in education was to develop the creative and mental powers of the child.

By the early 1960's art educators had become increasingly concerned with the development of art appreciation skills. Ecker (1963), Lanier (1963), Ralph Smith (1966), and others argued that a most important, if not the primary, goal of education in art for the average student ought to be that of developing his powers of art appreciation. Although they use different terms to describe this goal, their writings reflect a recognition on the part of art educators that work with art media does not automatically yield skills necessary for viewing works of art in aesthetically relevant ways. The emerging theme in the field of art education during the mid-1960's appears to be a concern for the development of what Eisner (1965b) has called the critical and historical as well as the productive skills of the general student in art.

The general and growing interest in art appreciation and art history among art educators appears to be related to developments in American society at large. During the latter half of the 1950's and the first half of the 1960's, cultural developments and awareness of visual art forms among the general public appear to have increased. Museum attendance has risen dramatically, the sale of art books and art reproductions has grown remarkably, and the national government has provided financial support for the arts and humanities on a scale never before available. Nevertheless, empirical data gathered by Downey (1960) and by Dressel and his associates (1959) indicate that the public still does not assign the arts high priority among school subjects. Downey conducted an extensive survey to determine educational priorities assigned to various subject matters by various reference groups. In his survey he asked people from various parts of the country to rank in order of importance 16 tasks typically undertaken by the school. Aesthetic education as the development of artistic capacities and skills was ranked fourteenth by lay people and twelfth by educators. Although the value assigned to aesthetic education increased with the amount of schooling individuals had, in no group did it break into the upper half of the ranking.

In a survey of views of college faculty members regarding the importance of the arts in higher education, Dressel and others (1959) found that about 13 percent thought that study in the arts should be required of all students in college. Although the status of the visual arts in public education appears to be low, there is some evidence to suggest that greater concern for education in the arts is beginning to emerge. The national government and the private foundations have begun to support research and program development, and hopefully the schools, from kindergarten through college, will begin to make adequate provision for meaningful and systematic programs.

Although art education, broadly conceived, is not limited to the artistic education of children and youth, the largest part of the field's concern has been devoted to this population, and most of the research that has been conducted has been directed toward people in these age groups.

THEORIES OF ARTISTIC LEARNING. A persistent interest among those concerned with artistic learning has been with the problem of constructing theory adequate to account for the perception of art and for its production by children. Arnheim (1954), whose view of child art grows out of Gestalt theory, holds that perception proceeds from the simple to the complex and that children draw pictures which are simplifications of visual phenomena because of the way in which those phenomena are perceived. The child, according to Arnheim, draws not what he knows but what he sees; simplification is a result of perceptual skills which have not yet matured.

McFee (1961) holds that four factors affect the child's perception and work in art. These factors are the readiness of the child, the psychological environment in which he is to work, his ability to handle and process visual information, and delineation skills (skills which are directly involved in art production). Any adequate understanding of the child's ability to produce drawings and paintings must, she believes, take into account all four of these factors and their effects upon one another.

Lowenfeld (1957) argues that the child goes through ordered stages of development in drawing and that, in general, these stages unfold naturally if the child's development is not coerced or hampered. In addition to the stage theory that Lowenfeld articulates, he also holds that by the time children reach adolescence they move toward either a visual or a haptic orientation in their perceptual development and hence in their drawing. Visually oriented individuals tend to make contact with the world through visual means primarily; their pictures and sculptures are "realistic." Haptic individuals deal with the world in terms of kinesthetic cues and through their feelings about the phenomena they encounter; their work in art tends, in general, to be more expressionistic in character.

In a major revision and restandardization of Goodenough's *Draw a Man Test,* Harris (1963) developed separate norms for girls and boys, restandardized the old scale which was originally constructed in 1926, and developed a short scoring form. According to Goodenough and Harris the qualities a child draws are related directly to the conceptual maturity he has attained. Since concepts represent the child's ability to recognize differences and similarities among a group of particulars, the amount of detail a child produces in a drawing is an index of the extent to which such classes have been formed. These classes or details, in turn, are related empirically to his measured intelligence. Goodenough and Harris report correlations between the *Draw a Man Test* and the Stanford-Binet of an order of magnitude that is well beyond chance.

The validity of the *Draw a Man Test* has been questioned by Medinnus and others (1966), who, in an experimental study, demonstrated that scores on the *Draw a Man Test* could be altered through training. Fourteen kindergartners and 20 first graders were divided into experimental and control groups, and the experimental group was asked to assemble a jigsaw puzzle of a male figure four times. Scores on pre- and posttests of experimental and control groups indicated a mean increase of about four points on the *Draw a Man Test* for the experimental group, a difference in scores well beyond chance.

Desmond Morris (1962) has attempted to study the evolution of art forms by studying the ways in which monkeys go about the task of using graphic media. Morris finds a systematic development in the use and exploration of formal qualities in drawings made by monkeys and suggests relationships between these drawings and those of young children. Janson (1966), however, believes that Morris does not adequately recognize that the distinctive difference between the drawings of monkeys and those of young children is that the latter use symbols while the former do not.

Although there are a number of issues on which investigators disagree regarding the explanation of child art, consensus appears on a number of important points. First, investigators agree that children's drawings tend to become more complex and highly differentiated as the children mature. Second, there is general agreement that greater differentiation in drawing is related to the child's general perceptual development and hence to his developing cognitive abilities. Third, there is some agreement that the child's personality and his specific needs at the time he is working affect the form and content he creates in his art work.

Investigators differ significantly, however, in their conception of appropriate conditions for developing ability in art. Some, like Read (1945) and Kellogg (1959), believe that the child should be left to develop naturally—development proceeds essentially from the inside out. Others, such as Eisner (1967), hold that much can be done through instruction to develop perception and art skills even with very young children.

THE ASSESSMENT OF ARTISTIC LEARNING. Tools appropriate for assessing artistic learning are scarce relative to assessment instruments available in other fields. Nevertheless some instruments have been published. One of the most widely used has been the *Meier Art Judgment Test* (Meier, 1940). This test attempts to assess one of the most significant abilities in the field of art—the ability to respond to aesthetic quality. Other tests, such as the *Graves Design Judgment Test* (Graves, 1948), attempt to measure similar abilities using as stimulus material not representational works but work of an abstract character.

The *Horn Art Aptitude Inventory* (Horn, 1944) and the *Selective Art Aptitude Test* (Varnum, 1946) are designed to predict artistic talent by assessing the subject's ability to perform on a specific array of art tools, but, as is characteristic of other tests in this field, these tests tend to have low predictive validity and tend to have low correlations with tests purporting to assess similar abilities. Thus, most investigators have tended to construct their own instruments when attempting to measure artistic learning.

Some evidence bearing upon the consequences of art instruction in preschool children was acquired by Dubin (1946). In an effort to foster artistic development, Dubin employed a conception of artistic stages used by Monroe (1929) and attempted to compare the effects of instruction on 52 preschool children equally divided into experimental and control groups. Dubin attempted to help children in the experimental group move up to the stage in painting that was one level higher than the one in which they were working. By verbal instructions and questions Dubin was able to demonstrate that the experimental subjects progressed significantly beyond the level achieved by subjects in the control group.

Although there have been many anecdotal descriptions of the characteristics of children's art, until recently no objective scales have been published to assess the ways in which children create space in drawing. Lewis (1962, 1963) and Eisner (1967) have produced and published such scales. Lewis formulated visual scales describing three types of spatial representation: spherical space, cubic space, and spatial depth. Twenty-seven intact classes of children enrolled in kindergarten through the eighth grade in five public schools were asked to make five drawings of each type of space. Lewis found that relationships existed between the characteristics drawn in each of the types of spatial drawing and the grade level of the subjects and that children tended to prefer pictures in which the characteristics of objects were revealed with great clarity. No differences in drawing characteristics or picture preference were found between the sexes.

In another attempt to assess objectively children's representation of space in drawing, Eisner constructed a scale containing 14 categories of spatial treatment used by 1,300 students in grades one, three, five and seven. Half of the subjects were upper-middle-class children attending suburban schools, the other half of the population was composed of culturally disadvantaged students living in a slum area of a large city. Subjects were asked to create a colored crayon drawing under controlled conditions, and the scale was then used to determine (1) if it could be employed reliably, (2) if differences between the two populations existed with respect to their treatment of space, and (3) the relationship between drawing development as measured by the scale and reading vocabulary. In addition, performance by sex was compared.

Eisner found that the scale could be reliably employed by judges working independently. He also found that children from culturally disadvantaged communities were so far behind their culturally advantaged contemporaries at the first-grade level that it took until the fifth grade for the disadvantaged groups to reach the level attained by the advantaged group at grade one. By the time both groups reached the seventh grade, however, the culturally disadvantaged group's performance approximated that of the advantaged group.

In addition, Eisner found that reading vocabulary was significantly correlated with drawing scores. No differences were found between the sexes, a finding similar to Lewis' earlier finding.

In another study of the relationship between drawing and cultural deprivation, Lourenso and his associates (1965) analyzed drawings of the family made by 111 children from five fourth-grade classes in a severely depressed urban area. By asking the child to circle his "self" in the drawing and by analyzing the presence of hands, the proportion of the head to the body, the clothing drawn, and the facial expression, they were able to compare differences between students grouped by sex in relation to good, average, and poor *Metropolitan Primary Reading Test* scores. The striking finding of the study was that poor-achieving boys, unlike poor-achieving girls, drew a "self" in which some major part of the body, such as the head, trunk, limbs, hands with fingers, or feet, is omitted. Ninety-three percent of the boys omitted one or more of these parts, as compared to 70 percent of the poor-achieving girls. The authors explain this difference in relation to the research evidence which indicates that Negro girls have better opportunities to develop a positive self concept than do boys. And in general girls, for all groups, had higher scores, indicating more positive personality development.

In an effort to use artistic data to assess the child's development, Boyer and Wilson (1959) attempted to use Lanz's *Easel Age Scale* to evaluate not easel paintings but crayon drawings, since crayon is used more frequently in elementary-school classrooms. Twenty-four first-grade and 21 second-grade students were tested with the *Draw a Man Test* and the *California Reading Test*, and correlations were computed between the *Easel Age Scale* scores derived from crayon drawings and the other tests. Coefficients were considerably lower for crayon drawings than those for tempera paintings but were significantly related to *Draw a Man Test* scores.

Other efforts to construct instruments for assessing artistic learning are represented by Flick's attempts (1963) to construct measures of visual and haptical aptitudes. Using Lowenfeld's haptic-visual continuum (1945) as a basis for their construction, Flick developed ten tests which proved reliable on 63 randomly selected college students.

Krathwohl and his associates (1964) have constructed a taxonomy of educational objectives in the affective domain. This taxonomy, which parallels Bloom's cognitive taxonomy published earlier (1956), provides a hierarchy of affective objectives designed to guide the curriculum builder and test constructor in the affective domain. This area of human behavior is very closely related to the concerns of those in art education and might prove useful in developing measures of artistic learning.

The taxonomy identifies five levels of affective response beginning with receiving and ending with a value or value complex. Sample objectives at each level of affective behavior are provided along with suggestions for appropriate test items.

Recognizing the growing interest in developing students' understanding and appreciation of art, Eisner (1966) constructed three instruments, the first designed to measure information about art; the second, attitudes toward art; and a third, ability to analyze works of art. In a series of studies of about 4,000 students from grade 7 through the senior year in college, Eisner found that students' information about art increases very slowly—students are able to answer about three more questions each additional year. Eisner also found that girls know more about art than boys and that their attitudes toward art are more positive, a finding that supports previous findings on the aesthetic values of males and females.

The study also indicated that during the high school years attitudes toward art and artists remain fairly stable but that during the college years attitudes in this area become more positive. Although students enrolled in art courses know more about art and have more positive attitudes toward it than do randomly selected students, the increase in art information scores of those enrolled in art courses per year is about the same as those who are not enrolled.

The efforts made to construct valid and reliable instruments to assess artistic learning represent a growing interest in research among members of the field of art education as well as a recognition of the scarcity of such tools. Instruments designed by Beittel and Burkhart (1963), Lewis (1963), Flick (1963), Eisner (1966), and others are beginning to provide a modest array of tools researchers and teachers can use in their work. These new instruments take on even greater significance when one recognizes that of the 2,126 tests listed in *Tests in Print* (Buros, 1961) only 1.4 percent, or 29, are in the fine arts. Of those in the fine arts, only 10 are in the visual arts, and of the 10 in the visual arts, 3 were constructed in the 1920's or 1930's.

Thus far the scope, history and nature of the field of art education have been discussed, and theories of children's development in art have been presented. In addition, some of the newer testing procedures and instruments have been identified. Now we turn to experimental research as it relates to artistic learning.

RESEARCH ON ARTISTIC LEARNING. Experimental research may be described as inquiries designed to measure the effects of certain treatments intended to bring about behavioral change in human beings. Descriptive research reports conditions as they are—no effort at intervention or treatment is made. Experimental research induces and assesses change.

One of the important problems in the field is one of determining how best to organize the art curriculum, a prime element for inducing change. In an effort to identify the effects of a breadth versus a depth curriculum in art, Beittel and others (1961) devised a depth curriculum, one in which students worked for several months with a limited array of media, and compared the creativity, satisfaction, and aesthetic quality of products made in this program to those made by junior high school students who had worked with a breadth curriculum—one in which a wide variety of media were used for the same period of time. The study indicated that students in the depth curriculum produced products having higher aesthetic quality than those in the breadth program but that students found greater satisfaction in the breadth program.

Because perceptual skills are thought to play such an important part in the production and appreciation of art their study has occupied theoreticians and experimentalists alike. Kensler (1965) attempted to measure the effects of perceptual training upon seventh graders' ability to learn perspective drawing. Two experimental groups and one control group were used. Experimental group 1 received formal training in the rules of perspective; experimental group 2 received similar training, but in addition they received perceptual training. The control group received art training that was unrelated to perspective. Five drawing tests were used on a pre- and posttest basis to measure the various effects. No differences were found between the two groups receiving training in perspective, even though one group received perceptual training as well.

In another experimental study dealing with the development of perception Salome (1965) found that perceptual training which directed children's attention to those areas of the figure that reveal the greatest amount of visual information—curved areas or areas in which the form changes most markedly—did have an effect in increasing fifth-grade children's ability to draw as measured by closure-clarity, proportion, and what Salome calls communicative symbol, "the degree to which a drawing was judged to communicate the characteristics of a given stimulus object . . . ." The experimental groups received exercises in locating and differentiating between points of maximal contour information prior to drawing. The control sections were given conventional instruction in drawing the same stimulus objects presented in the experimental classes. Salome concluded that improved visual perception may be not a naturally occurring by-product of art activities but a specific form of behavior that one must teach.

Because research by Rosen (1955) has indicated that preference for complexity over simplicity is related to inventive behavior and is a characteristic preference of creative people in the arts and sciences, McWhinnie (1966) attempted to develop preferences for complexity and symmetry experimentally. Two populations, one at the college level, the other at the sixth-grade level, were treated by a method which was designed to enable them to resist preference for simplicity and symmetry in favor of a preference for complexity and asymmetry. McWhinnie found no differences between groups that was due to treatment at the college level but did find significant differences in favor of experimental over control groups for males at the sixth-grade level. This study provides some evidence, as does the study by Eisner (1966), that sex or attitudes associated with sex may have an influence on learning in art.

Related to the growing amount of research evidence which indicates that highly creative individuals as well as those trained in the arts tend to prefer visual complexity to simplicity is Pyron's study (1966) of college students' preference for types of art. Pyron asked 40 college students to accept or reject three art forms (visual, literary, and musical) in three different art styles (classical, popular, and avant-garde). It was found that acceptance of avant-garde art is significantly related to the acceptance of complexity and change and negatively related to rigidity as measured by a variety of attitude and personality tests.

In a similar vein Linderman's (1962) study of the relation of picture preference to personality traits of college students indicated that graduate students in art education prefer abstract to realistic paintings as contrasted to non-art education graduate students and that judges with similar personality traits, in general, tend to have similar picture preferences.

Linderman's research is consonant with Doerter's (1966) findings that college art students tend to paint in the style of their college art professors and that the professors consider work in their own style more creative than work which deviates drastically from their style.

Because the development of the students' general creativity through art has for many years been a major objective in the field of art education it is not surprising that a great many research efforts have attempted to define creativity, to measure it, and to identify personality traits related to it.

FOSTERING AND ASSESSING CREATIVE BEHAVIOR IN ART. Of the approaches that have been taken three have been prominent. Guilford (1957) has attempted to identify the types of behaviors that constitute the complex behavior called creativity and has constructed tests to measure these behaviors. He identifies creativity in the visual arts with behaviors displayed in the figural rather than conceptual or structural domain. The "structure of intellect" he has created has been useful to a variety of investigators studying creativity in art education as well as in other fields.

Other research workers have attempted to identify creative individuals through patents, awards, prizes, and other indexes of creative accomplishments. Once these individuals have been identified various test situations have been used to assess a variety of characteristics that might be related to their creativity. Barron (1953), McKinnon (1961), and Blatt and Stein (1957) have used such an approach in their work.

A third approach used to study creativity has been one of identifying and describing the various ways in which individuals go about the task of making a painting or a drawing. By studying the process through which such works are created, as can be done through time-lapse photography, it becomes possible to assess the products after they are completed with respect to their creative status and to identify the relationship existing between the processes used and the characteristics of the products. Work by Beittel and Burkhart (1963) and Csikszentmihalyi (1965) employed the latter approach.

A fourth approach taken to study creative behavior has been employed by Eisner (1965a). Instead of using a general conception of creativity, Eisner formulated four types of creativity that children can display in the visual arts. In addition, these four types of creativity may be displayed in either the treatment of form or the use of subject matter. By formulating types of creativity and their loci it becomes possible to determine relationships existing among the several types and to construct a profile of creative behavior for individuals or groups.

The development of empirical methods and test instruments for assessing creative behavior has been one of the most important research contributions during the past twenty-year period. The instruments that have been constructed, the conceptions that have been formulated, and the methods of study that have been created have made it possible to use procedures other than introspection for studying an exceedingly important aspect of human behavior. These contributions become even more important when one considers that prior to the early 1950's psychologists paid relatively little attention to creativity as a subject matter to be studied through the tools and concepts of psychology.

In an effort to identify the ways in which college art students work in the creation of a painting, Beittel and Burkhart, in the study referred to above (1963), used time-lapse photography to study their working strategies. They were able to identify three distinct strategies that students employed. One strategy is called spontaneous, another, divergent, and the third, academic. Beittel and Burkhart found that spontaneous and divergent strategies tend to yield the most highly creative products. In the spontaneous strategy the student alters the working procedures until he arrives at a solution to a goal that has been predetermined. The divergent student may vary the goal while the academic student tends to use known procedures to arrive at known goals. According to Beittel and Burkhart the strategies that students employ are related to personality traits that determine their orientation to problem-solving generally.

There is evidence from a variety of studies that creative individuals as well as individuals working in the visual arts tend to be less conforming and more tolerant of ambiguity. Hoffa (1960) found, for example, that art experience is negatively related to measures of conformity. And Barron (1953) has found that artists and creative individuals prefer complexity to simplicity: they tend to prefer questions over answers. Personal traits that were found to be related to preference for complexity were verbal fluency, effeminacy, sentience, and sensuality. These traits are not unrelated to aesthetic values generally as measured by the Allport-Vernon-Lindzey Study of Values.

Whether higher creativity scores are a result of work in the arts or whether creative people tend to go into the arts is a question for which at present there is no adequate answer. McFee (1965) found that students at the junior high school level who are academically superior and who were given systematic instruction in design, creative problem solving, and perceptual training scored higher on standardized measures of creativity than did a control group of students similar in academic achievement and other relevant variables.

Getzels and Jackson (1962), however, found that the home life of highly creative but not so highly intelligent adolescents differed significantly from the home life of their contemporaries who were highly intelligent and not so highly creative. The high creatives came from homes in which the mothers paid less attention to neatness and order than did the mothers of the highly intelligent. In addition, the values of the high creatives were acquired in homes that did not place great emphasis on conformity, togetherness, or usual standards of academic or vocational achievement. In view of research by Bloom (1964), Dave (1963), and Wolf (1964), as well as by Hunt (1961), it appears that the home environment is most important in fostering or hampering a disposition toward creativity during the crucial early years of the child's development. It appears that creativity will be more difficult to develop the later one begins to foster or nurture such behavior. The evidence, however, to support such a view is tenuous.

In an effort to differentiate the ways in which creativity may be displayed in the visual arts, Eisner (1965a) distinguished between four types of creativity. These types are called boundary pushing, inventing, boundary breaking, and aesthetic organizing. Boundary pushing is defined as extending the use or function of an ordinary object, form or subject matter; inventing is the combination of forms, objects, or subject matters in such a way that an essentially new form, object, or subject matter is created; and boundary breaking is a result of making the given problematic and creating, therefore, a form, object, or subject matter that is radically new. Aesthetic organizing is defined as forming in an aesthetic way the forms that constitute an object.

Using these categories as criteria to analyze the two and three dimensional art products of sixth-grade children, Eisner found that some types of creativity such as boundary pushing and inventing were more common than boundary breaking and that creativity displayed in two-dimensional art products did not necessarily indicate that high degrees of creativity would be displayed in three-dimensional art products. There was a tendency, however, for subjects who displayed high levels of creativity in either form or subject matter in two-dimensional products to display creativity in these loci in three-dimensional products as well.

Jones (1963) found a small but positive relationship between creative writing and creative drawing. One hundred and fifty sixth-grade children were motivated to write a series of imaginative stories and to produce a series of imaginary drawings. In addition, a variety of tests developed by Guilford was used to measure semantic and figural creativity. Jones found significant correlations between scores for drawing and writing as well as between scores from Guilford's tests of creativity and the semantic and figural domains.

In a study of the way in which creative processes

are employed in problematic situations, Csikszentmihalyi (1965) used a model developed by Getzels (1964) which differentiates between problems that are presented and those which are discovered. A presented problem is one which is both known and solved through known methods. A discovered problem is one in which the problem as well as the method of solution have to be discovered. Thirty-one male third- and fourth-year art students attending a private art school were asked to make drawings in task situations described as presented and discovered. The quality of the drawings was compared as well as the methods the subject used in each task and his recollection of his working processes.

One major finding of the study indicated that students who in their verbal reports claimed they were seeking to discover new relationships or meanings in reality tended to also engage in discovery-oriented activity, activity which manifests itself as a high degree of exploration of materials and forms drawn. In addition, it was found that highly significant correlations existed between the originality of the drawings produced and a discovery-oriented strategy, a finding consonant with the findings of Beittel and Burkhart.

In general, research on creativity during the past decade has been most useful in operationalizing concepts that have been, more often than not, both ambiguous and vague. Guilford's work has produced both useful conceptualizations of the intellect and a variety of important instruments. Getzels' has formulated some useful distinctions between the presented and discovered problem as well as the various places in which the problem can be located. Barron's work, as well as the work of Beittel and his associates, has underscored the relationship between creative behavior and personality and perception. And Eisner has differentiated between types of creativity as displayed in the art products of children.

Theoretical argument, especially by Schachtel (1959) and Kubie (1958), and some empirical experimental evidence indicate that creative behavior can be developed by the environment's being controlled in appropriate ways. Maltzman and associates (1958) and Parnes and Meadow (1959) have both provided evidence that creativity scores can be increased through experimental treatment. In sum, when compared with previous decades, the decades of the 1950's and the 1960's have yielded important contributions to the measurement and understanding of creativity in art.

AESTHETIC JUDGMENT AND PREFERENCE. One of the most intriguing and difficult areas of study in art education deals with understanding the effect of culture upon artistic performance and aesthetic judgment. For years aestheticians have attempted to formulate real definitions of art, definitions which in their views were independent of culture. Weitz (1966) has argued that such definitions are logically impossible to formulate since art is an open concept, one for which no necessary *and* sufficient conditions can be identified. The function and contribution of the aesthetician, according to Weitz, is not to lay down the necessary and sufficient conditions of art but to call to the viewer's attention what is important to look for in the art product.

Not all attempts to identify the bases of art and aesthetic judgment have been made by aestheticians. Child (1964, 1965) and Child and Siroto (1965) have conducted a series of inquiries on the relationships existing between culture, aesthetic judgment, and personality. In a study of the aesthetic judgment of American art experts and Japanese potters, Iwao and Child (1966) found that Japanese potters—even ones who had little contact with Western art—agreed more with the aesthetic judgments of American art experts than did American high school students. In another study of aesthetic judgment, this one by Ford and others (1966), the general findings of Child's previous study were supported; craftsmen and artisans in a remote Fijian village and in the Cycladic Islands of Greece generally agreed with the aesthetic judgments of American experts. The findings of these studies as well as that of Child and Siroto (1965) indicate strongly that while cultural differences may have some effects upon diversifying aesthetic judgments, individuals from different cultures who have an interest in art and who actively engage in art activities tend to agree more highly than do those within the same culture who are not engaged or interested in art.

Child (1964) has attempted to distinguish between aesthetic preference and aesthetic judgment as a basis of conducting research in these areas. Aesthetic preference relates simply to the aesthetic qualities in a work, taste, or aroma that people like. Aesthetic judgment is defined as the degree to which a person's judgment of a work, taste, or aroma corresponds to the judgment of experts. Child goes further to distinguish these concepts from aesthetic sensitivity, which "refers to the extent to which a person gives evidence of responding to relevant stimuli in some consistent and appropriate relation to the external standard."

In a study of personal preferences as an expression of aesthetic sensitivity Child (1966) found that the extent of agreement between one's aesthetic preference and one's conception of the value of a work of art was significantly related to information about art. Aesthetic sensitivity, he also found, was related to high scores on the *Barron-Welsh Art Scale*, a scale designed to measure creativity. The evidence that Child has collected together with that from studies conducted by others suggests that aesthetic sensitivity and the ability to make discriminating judgments are related to the values one holds and the general way in which one orients oneself to the world.

In an attempt to use drawings to understand the values displayed by people in various cultures, Dennis (1966) analyzed the form and content of children's drawings for value preferences. Using drawings made by children in 27 different cultural groups, Dennis found that the types of dress portrayed, the physical features of the people drawn, the religious content of the drawings, if any, and the demeanor of the people drawn provide evidence useful for understanding children's social values. Although children's drawings have been used as indexes of intelligence, conceptual maturity, personality, and creativity, they have seldom been used to assess social values. Dennis' work in this area provides a promising beginning.

Cross-cultural research on art performance and artistic preference is beginning to provide valuable insights into the sources of aesthetic preferences and the effect of values upon artistic behavior.

Because the practice of education is a normative enterprise, the problem of justifying in normative terms the place of the visual arts in education remains an important one. Although scientific research can provide knowledge useful for understanding, predicting, and at times controlling human behavior, it cannot provide or justify the values toward which the educational enterprise is directed. For this we must turn to philosophical research.

PHILOSOPHICAL RESEARCH IN ART EDUCATION. Philosophers concerned with art have attempted to identify not only its unique characteristics but also its relationship to education. Champlin (1966), Ecker (1963), and Villemain (1964) have, through their work, extended Dewey's conception of qualitative thought in an effort to indicate how intelligence is exercised in the production of aesthetic qualities. Villemain argues that art, as a type of human experience, represents a quality of life that characterizes a democratic civilization functioning at its supreme level. Champlin argues that qualities not only can serve as means or ends in problematic situations but also can serve as controls through which the use of qualities is directed and through which qualitative ends are realized. And Ecker has used Dewey's steps in scientific problem solving as an analogue through which he constructed a model of qualitative problem solving, the type of problem solving used in the production of art. Champlin, Ecker, and Villemain have not only argued eloquently the case for the place of art in education but have also formed concepts useful for thinking about the process through which it comes into being.

Read (1960), a long-standing student of education, art, and aesthetics, has pointed out that it is through artistic activity that men can remain or become human and that unless art is used to maintain man's humanity the technological society will rob him of this unique trait. For Read, art is a product of the play instinct that Schiller (1916) described, and through it not only is his selfhood realized, but also his society is saved. An education through art, says Read, is an education for peace.

Broudy (1960), however, views the contribution and significance of art differently. For Broudy the case for art education is that it enables the student to learn how life *might* feel and thereby provides a source of experience beyond his own limited geographical spheres. In so doing art shapes values, and hence, for Broudy, it ought not be ignored by those responsible for building school programs.

Ralph Smith (1965) shares this view and argues that art provides a source for acquiring meanings that lie beyond the pale of science, a view also advanced by Eisner (1963) in his distinctions between knowing and knowledge.

One of the few efforts to use an existential aesthetic theory to argue a place for art in education has been advanced by Kaelin (1966). He argues that art provides an important vehicle through which the student can express himself and thereby understand and experience his situation. Kaelin holds further that both teacher and student should be allowed to make their own educational decisions so that openness to experience can be maintained.

Relatively few efforts have been made to understand the dynamics of classroom activity in art from the standpoint of teacher behavior. Two efforts to frame concepts and gather empirical data on teaching behavior in art have been made by B. Othanel Smith (1961) and Clements (1964). Smith has formulated concepts that distinguish between various instructional goals in art, and Clements has collected data on the type of questions teachers ask in art at various grade levels. One of the most interesting of his findings is the extreme brevity of student answers.

Perhaps the most significant development in research in art education during the decade of the 1960's is the increase in the number of young and relatively sophisticated researchers in the field. The volume of research has increased considerably compared to previous decades. The scope of research has broadened, and the goals of art education have begun to include the development of the critical and historical competences of the student as well as competences necessary for producing products having high degrees of aesthetic quality.

Elliot W. Eisner
Stanford University

References

Arnheim, Rudolph. *Art and Visual Perception.* U California Press, 1954. 408p.

Barkan, Manuel. "Is There a Discipline of Art Education?" *Stud Art Ed* 4:4–9; 1963.

Barron, Frank. "Complexity-simplicity as a Personality Dimension." *J. Abn Soc Psychol* 48:163–72; 1953.

Beittel, Kenneth. "Molesting or Meeting the Muse: A Look at Research on the 'Creativity' in the Visual Arts." *Stud Art Ed* 1:26–34; 1959.

Beittel, Kenneth, and Burkhart, Robert C. "Strategies of Spontaneous, Divergent and Academic Art Students." *Stud Art Ed* 5:20–41; 1963.

Beittel, Kenneth, and others. "The Effect of a 'Depth' Versus a 'Breadth' Method of Art Instruction at the Ninth Grade Level." *Stud Art Ed* 3:75–87; 1961.

Belsche, Francis B. "A History of Art Education in the Public Schools of the United States." Unpublished doctoral dissertation. Yale U, 1946.

Blatt, Sidney J., and Stein, Morris. *Some Personality, Value, and Cognitive Characteristics of the Creative*

Person. Paper presented to the APA, September 1957.

Bloom, Benjamin. *Stability and Change in Human Characteristics*. Wiley, 1964. 237p.

Bloom, Benjamin. (Ed.) *Taxonomy of Educational Objectives*. Handbook I: *Cognitive Domain*. McKay, 1956. 207p.

Boyer, Roscoe, and Wilson, Cleora. "Use of the Easel Age Scale to Evaluate Crayon Drawings." *El Sch J* 59:228–32; 1959.

Broudy, Harry. "The Case for Art Education." *Art Ed* 3:7–8, 19; 1960.

Buros, Oscar K. (Ed.) *Tests in Print*. Gryphon Press, 1961. 479p.

Champlin, Nathaniel. "Methodological Inquiry and Educational Research." In *A Seminar in Art Education for Research and Curriculum Development*. Cooperative Research Project No. V-022, 1966. p. 291–338.

Child, Irvin L. "Observations on the Meaning of Some Measures of Esthetic Sensitivity." *J Psychol* 57:49–64; 1964.

Child, Irvin L. "Personality Correlates of Esthetic Judgment in College Students." *J Pers* 33:476–511; 1965.

Child, Irvin L. "Personal Preferences as an Expression of Aesthetic Sensitivity." *J Pers* 30:469–512; 1966.

Child, Irvin L., and Siroto, Leon. "Bakwele and American Aesthetic Evaluations Compared." *Ethnology* 4:349–60; 1965.

Clements, Robert D. *Question Types, Patterns, and Sequences Used by Art Teachers in the Classroom*. Cooperative Research Project No. S-161, 1964.

Csikszentmihalyi, Mihaly. *Artistic Problems and Their Solutions*. Unpublished doctoral dissertation. U Chicago, 1965.

D'Amico, Victor. *Creative Teaching in Art*. International Textbook Company, 1942. 261p.

Dave, R. H. *The Identification and Measurement of Environmental Process Variables That Are Related to Educational Achievement*. Unpublished doctoral dissertation. U Chicago, 1963.

Dennis, Wayne, *Group Values Through Children's Drawings*. Wiley, 1966. 211p.

Doerter, James. "Influences of College Art Instructors Upon Their Students' Painting Styles." *Stud Art Ed* 7:46–53; 1966.

Downey, Lawrence. *The Task of Public Education: The Perceptions of People*. Midwest Administration Center, U Chicago, 1960.

Dressel, Paul, and others. *The Liberal Arts as Viewed by Faculty Members in Professional Schools*. Teachers College, Columbia U, 1959.

Dubin, Elizabeth. "The Effect of Training on the Tempo of Development of Graphic Representation in Preschool Children." *J Exp Ed* 15:166–73; 1946.

Ecker, David. "The Artistic Process as Qualitative Problem-solving." *J Aesthetics Art Criticism* 21:283–90; 1963.

Ecker, David. "Some Problems of Art Education: A Methodological Definition." In *Seminar in Art Education for Research and Curriculum Development*. Cooperative Research Project No. V-022, 1966. p. 24–37.

Eisner, Elliot W. "The Loci of Creativity in Art." *Stud Art Ed* 2:22–42; 1960.

Eisner, Elliot W. "A Typology of Creativity in the Visual Arts." *Stud Art Ed* 4:11–22; 1962.

Eisner, Elliot W. "Knowledge, Knowing, and the Visual Arts." *Harvard Ed R* 33:208–18; 1963.

Eisner, Elliot W. "Children's Creativity in Art: A Study of Types." *Am Ed Res J* 2:125–36; 1965(*a*).

Eisner, Elliot W. "Curriculum Ideas in Time of Crisis." *Art Ed* 18:7–12; 1965(*b*).

Eisner, Elliot W. "Graduate Study and the Preparation of Scholars in Art Education." In *Art Education*. 64th Yearbook, NSSE. U Chicago Press, 1965(*c*). p. 274–98.

Eisner, Elliot W. "The Development of Information and Attitudes Toward Art at the Secondary and College Levels." *Stud Art Ed* 8:43–58; 1966.

Eisner, Elliot W. *The Developmental Drawing Characteristics of Culturally Advantaged and Disadvantaged Children*. Cooperative Research Project No. OE 6-10-027, 1967.

Eisner, Elliot W., and Ecker, David W. "What Is Art Education?" In Eisner, Elliot W., and Ecker, David W. *Readings in Art Education*. Blaisdell Publishing Company, 1966. p. 1–27.

Flick, Paul B. "Ten Tests of the Visual Haptic Aptitude." *Stud Art Ed* 4:24–34; 1963.

Ford, C. S., and others. "Some Transcultural Comparisons of Aesthetic Judgment." *J Social Psychol* 68:19–26; 1966.

Getzels, Jacob. "Creative Thinking, Problem Solving and Instruction." In Hilgard, Ernest. (Ed.) *Theories of Learning and Instruction*. 63rd Yearbook, NSSE, U Chicago Press, 1964. p. 240–67.

Getzels, Jacob and Jackson, Philip. *Creativity and Intelligence*. Wiley, 1962. 293p.

Graves, Maitland. *Graves Design Judgment Test*. Psych Corp, 1948.

Green, Harry. *The Introduction of Art as a General Education Subject in American Schools*. Unpublished doctoral dissertation. Stanford U, 1948.

Guilford, J. P. "Creative Ability in the Arts." *Psychol R* 64:110–8; 1957.

Harris, Dale. *Children's Drawing as Measures of Intellectual Maturity*. Harcourt, 1963. 367p.

Hoffa, Harlan. "The Relationship of Art Experience to Conformity." *Stud Art Ed* 1:35–41; 1960.

Horn, Charles C. *Horn Art Aptitude Inventory: Preliminary Form, 1944 Revision*. Rochester Institute of Technology, 1944.

Hunt, J. McV. *Intelligence and Experience*. Ronald, 1961. 416p.

Iwao, Fumiko, and Child, Irvin L. "Comparison of Esthetic Judgments by American Experts and by Japanese Potters." *J Social Psychol* 68:27–33; 1966.

Janson, H. W. "After Betsy, What?" In Eisner, Elliot W., and Ecker, David W. (Eds.) *Readings in Art Education*. Blaisdell Publishing Company, 1966. p. 370–8.

Jones, Clyde A. "Relationships Between Creative

Writing and Creative Drawing of Sixth Grade Children." *Stud Art Ed* 3:34–43; 1963.
Kaelin, Eugene. "The Existential Ground for Aesthetic Education." *Stud Art Ed* 8:3–12; 1966.
Kaufman, Irving. "Is There a Discipline of Art Education?" *Stud Art Ed* 4:15–23; 1963.
Kellogg, Rhoda. *What Children Scribble and Why.* N-P Publications, 1959. 137p.
Kensler, Gordon L. "The Effects of Perceptual Training and Modes of Perceiving Upon Individual Differences in Ability to Learn Perspective Drawing." *Stud Art Ed* 7:34–41; 1965.
Krathwohl, David, and others. *Taxonomy of Educational Objectives.* Handbook II: *Affective Domain.* McKay, 1964. 196p.
Kubie, Lawrence. *Neurotic Distortion of the Creative Process.* U Kansas Press, 1958. 151p.
Lanier, Vincent. "Schizmogenesis in Contemporary Art Education." *Stud Art Ed* 5:10–9; 1963.
Lewis, Hilda P. "Developmental Stages in Children's Representation of Spatial Relations in Drawing." *Stud Art Ed* 3:67–76; 1962.
Lewis, Hilda P. "Spatial Representation in Drawing as a Correlate of Development and a Basis for Picture Preference." *J Genet Psychol* 102:95–107; 1963.
Linderman, Earl W. "The Relation of Art Picture Judgment to Judge Personality." *Stud Art Ed* 3:46–51; 1962.
Logan, Fred. *The Growth of Art in American Schools.* Harper, 1955. 310p.
Logan, Fred. "Is There a Discipline of Art Education?" *Stud Art Ed* 4:10–4; 1963.
Lourenso, S. V., and others. "Personality Characteristics Revealed in Drawings of Deprived Children Who Differ in School Achievement." *J Ed Res* 59:63–7; 1965.
Lowenfeld, Viktor. "Tests for Visual and Haptical Aptitudes." *Am J Psychol* 58:100–11; 1945.
Lowenfeld, Viktor. *Creative and Mental Growth,* 3rd ed. Macmillan, 1957. 541p.
Maltzman, I., and others. "A Procedure for Increasing Word Association Originality and Its Transfer-effects." *J Exp Psychol* 56:392–8; 1958.
McFee, June. *Preparation for Art.* Wadsworth Publishing Co., 1961. 341p.
McFee, June. *Creative Problem-solving Abilities of Academically Superior Adolescents.* Mimeographed. U Oregon, 1965. 31p.
McKinnon, Donald W. "Creativity in Architects." In *The Creative Person.* U California Press, 1961. p. 5–22.
McWhinnie, Harold J. "The Effects of a Learning Experience Upon the Preference for Complexity and Asymmetry." *Psychol in Sch* 3:253–5; 1966.
Medinnus, Gene R., and others. "Effects of Training on the 'Draw a Man' Test." *J Exp Ed* 35:62–3; 1966.
Meier, Norman Charles. *Meier Art Tests.* I: *Art Judgment.* State U Iowa, 1940.
Monroe, Marian. *The Drawings and Color Preferences of Young Children.* Unpublished doctoral dissertation. U Chicago, 1929.

Morris, Charles. "Science, Art, and Technology." *Kenyon R* 1:409–23; 1939.
Morris, Desmond. *The Biology of Art.* Knopf, 1962.
Parnes, Sidney, and Meadow, A. "Effects of 'Brainstorming' Instructions on Creative Problem-solving by Trained and Untrained Subjects." *J Ed Psychol* 50:171–6; 1959.
Pyron, Bernard. "Rejection of Avant-garde Art and the Need for Simple Order." *J Psychol* 63:159–78; 1966.
Read, Herbert. *Education through Art,* 2nd ed. Pantheon Books, 1945.
Read, Herbert. "The Third Realm of Education." In *The Creative Arts in American Education.* Harvard U Press, 1960. p. 35–60.
Rosen, J. D. "The Barron-Welsh Art Scale as a Predictor of Originality and Level of Ability in Art." *J Applied Psychol* 39:366–7; 1955.
Salome, R. A. "The Effects of Perceptual Training on the Two-dimensional Drawings of Children." *Stud Art Ed* 7:18–33; 1965.
Schachtel, Ernest. *Metamorphosis: On the Development of Affect, Perception, Attention and Memory.* Basic Books, Inc., Publishers, 1959. 344p.
Schiller, Friedrich. *Essays, Aesthetical and Philosophical.* G. Bell & Sons, Ltd., 1916.
Smith, B. Othanel. "The Logic of Teaching in The Arts." *Teach Col Rec* 63:176–83; 1961.
Smith, Ralph. "Patterns of Meanings in Aesthetic Education." In *Council for Research in Music Education.* U Illinois, 1965. p. 1–12.
Smith, Ralph. "Editorial." *J Aesthetic Ed* 1; 1966.
Smith, Walter. *Teachers Manual of Free Hand Drawing and Designing.* Charles Osgood and Company, 1873.
Varnum, William Harrison. *Selective Art Aptitude Tests,* 2nd ed. International Textbook Company, 1946.
Villemain, Francis. "Democracy, Education, and Art." *Ed Theory* 14:1–15; 1964.
Weitz, Morris. "The Nature of Art." In Eisner, Elliot W., and Ecker, David W. (Eds.) *Readings in Art Education.* Blaisdell Publishing Company, 1966. p. 49–56.
Wolf, R. M. *The Identification and Measurement of Environmental Process Variables Related to Intelligence.* Unpublished doctoral dissertation. U Chicago, 1964.

ARTICULATION OF EDUCATIONAL UNITS

Our present educational establishment is an anachronistic reflection of its antecedent development. Pervading its modern organizational structure are the vestigial remains of the influence of and accommodation to historical expediency and imported innovation. Particularly, the educational units into which the system is divided (or, perhaps more properly, from which it was assembled) were drawn from widely dissimilar philosophical positions and geographical areas. The American child begins his formal education in a German kindergarten, then moves up into the Prussian elementary school, from which he progresses to the essentially American junior or junior and senior high school, and possibly on to the originally English college and finally the German graduate school (Russell & Judd, 1940).

Moreover, these separately conceived and independently developed institutional entities have been further reorganized and rearranged in this country into such sequences as the eight-four, the six-two-four, the six-three-three, and the six-five year units, each with various names. To these are being added the junior college, the senior college, the university entities, and an increasing array of special and terminal curricula. Certainly, this eclectic character of the American educational evolution is not without great advantage; applicable and desirable qualities of established and tested systems can be selected and refined, presumably without precluding divergence in response to unique and developing conditions.

NATURE AND EXTENT OF THE PROBLEM. The resultant assemblage of schools is not necessarily a system of education; to the multiplicity of considerations essential to producing educational units must be added the increasingly significant problem of their articulation. Inadequate or improper articulation between and within this aggregate of derived educational units amplifies the discontinuity already inherent in its organization and produces an irregular transition which prevents the student from moving smoothly from one phase to another. For in a very real sense, that student must undertake transition in our school system almost continuously, at the end of each school term and, most importantly, each school unit. Each division is arbitrary. Each was developed to fulfill collective, rather than individual, needs of students in a program of universal education. Many exist simply to meet institutional necessities of faculty size, physical space, and curricular specialization. And in the interest of that mass education and of that expedient functioning of its institutions, the individual student's needs are very frequently subordinated (cf. Foshay, 1956).

Significant in this connection is a concomitant development in American education. With a national commitment to the concept and practice of universal education is a national objection to centralized planning for and administration of that education. To the somewhat alien and frequently anachronistic educational structure inherited and adapted from abroad is added a domestic ideological aversion to centralization, particularly at the national level. Although the concept of the national curriculum was occasionally considered during the past several centuries, it was seldom significant in the development of American education (Spain, 1956), and it is only beginning to emerge as an important factor.

Horizontal and Vertical Inconsistency. Notwithstanding the many abuses inherent in centralized curricula, and without minimizing their gravity, some overall planning might be particularly instrumental in improving horizontal articulation (between schools and school systems) as well as vertical continuity (between grade levels and educational units). With the increasing geographical mobility of our population, the former is highly significant; with the developing socioeconomic mobility offered through education, the latter is of unprecedented urgency. Indeed, of the two, this vertical articulation of educational units has received the greater attention in recent research as students aspire to more advanced and more varied educational objectives.

Philosophical and Functional Diversity. As each student moves from class to class, building to building, or campus to campus, he also encounters varying educational philosophies, missions, and approaches. Profound philosophical differences confront him as he progresses through school systems; perhaps his elementary-school teacher was concerned with the child as he has been, or possibly as he is, whereas his secondary-school teacher was concerned with preparing him for what he will be. College presents an entirely new emphasis, centered upon individual effort and relatively independent achievement. Similarly, school missions differ on several levels, as well as in different ways, in their multiplicity of purpose, in their more or less selective nature, in their diverse viewpoints toward function, and in their physical conduct of the school situation. The elementary-school class, a somewhat self-contained entity, with one teacher responsible for a particular group of students throughout the day, differs from the secondary-school class, which is typically and increasingly highly departmentalized and where the teacher must know and teach a large number of students as well as a specialized subject area (Campbell, 1958).

For many children this stratification of educational processes into class units and grades injects obstacles into the normal, essentially continuous, pattern of their natural intellectual growth—and this is done by the very organization designed to facilitate their education. There remains the goal of establishing a student-centered rather than a school-centered organization.

Consequences of Poor Articulation. The only common, singular, and dynamic element persisting before, throughout, and beyond the 12-year program is the learner (Romine, 1961). Complications in articulation of educational units arise because this learner simply does not develop socially, biologically, and intellectually at a single and uniform rate (Kirksey, 1959). Traditional educational structure interferes with the continuity of learning experiences when these fundamental characteristics of the learner are neglected, ignored, or, more commonly, overridden by pragmatic considerations, as suggested above.

Human learning is a continuous process, and the pattern of learning is seldom represented by the form of school organization. When the natural, continuous processes of learning are divided by the neat gridiron pattern of school structure so expedient in the management of large numbers of students, an artificial stratification of education develops and injects obstacles into the normal process of development. There remains, perhaps, to discover a form of school organization congruous with the nature of the human mind and its manner of growth and development (Committee on Educational Research, 1937).

Improper or Inadequate Preparation. Basic to much of this interference with the natural continuity of learning is the traditional, seemingly indispensable, and, recently, widely assailed (Varner, 1962) presupposition by curriculum planners that each student has mastered the content of the preceding grade level. Accordingly, the graduate school continues to blame the college, the college the high school, the high school elementary education, and so on, presumably back to some prenatal causality, thereby relieving everyone of responsibility for inadequate educational preparation—everyone but the student (Gow, 1960). Inadequate or improper preparation for entry to a higher educational unit is at once a consequence of and a perpetuating reason for faulty articulation. As the student arrives at a higher educational unit unprepared for its curriculum, this unit, too, frequently accommodates itself by the repetition of subject matter and duplication of study effort, thereby producing another extreme of poor articulation. Rather than improving articulation between schools in order to remove the cause of inadequate or improper preparation, each educational unit looks to its own remedial program to alleviate the effect.

Duplication of Study. Cases of duplication in course content are widely reported, particularly between the secondary and higher education levels (Blackmer, 1952), in the subjects of English, beginning science (Fox, 1962), and history (Hochman, 1959). The resulting double exposure in education, which produces little additional subject comprehension (Learned & Wood, 1938), often contributes to the exclusion of important and significant depth of study and wastes student and institutional time and effort. The quality of the student's educational experience depends upon the extent to which his learning is cumulative, and to make it cumulative, institutional programs must cooperate and collaborate to articulate their curricula and coordinate their efforts. Moreover, the above-mentioned articulation simply on a vertical scale is not sufficient; perhaps more difficult, and certainly increasingly important, is provision for horizontal continuity, in order that all the subjects a student takes be correlated, that the units of organization be consistent within a school system, and that transfer between systems be conducted effectively. Finally, undue concern for and emphasis upon these problems of vertical and horizontal articulation, of omission of material and of student unpreparedness, and of duplication and repetition of material can result in impairment of curricular flexibility and instructional creativity.

Efforts to Improve Articulation. Historically, inadequate or improper articulation has concerned primarily the college admissions officer. Perhaps from the founding of Harvard College until the period between the Civil War and the turn of this century, there has been a traditionally close, if somewhat unilateral, relationship between secondary-school and college programs. Accordingly, secondary schools assumed an essentially college preparatory function. College admission requirements were highly specific, and efforts to improve articulation between educational units were motivated by and directed toward the need for improved preparation of entering college students. As late as 1893 the function of the secondary school was defined simply as college preparatory, and the various studies undertaken to improve articulation were in this spirit and at these levels.

With the development of the comprehensive high school and the extension of secondary education to include vocational, terminal, and otherwise non-college preparatory curricula, objections arose to the traditional standardization of the secondary program to conform to collegiate standards for admission. Concern for the establishment of secondary-school autonomy, in which the secondary school would be free of the domination of higher education, has been evident since the early years of this century.

Preschool to Elementary Level. Accordingly, and properly, in recent years the problem of faulty articulation has become a major consideration in the development of the entire educational sequence, from kindergarten to graduate school and, still more recently, before and beyond. The preschool to elementary-school transition, particularly for the socio-economically disadvantaged child, is increasingly facilitated by preparatory programs directed toward providing a social and intellectual background for school attendance. Among these programs is Project Head Start (Osborn, 1965), which seeks to utilize all resources—parental, social, and professional—to provide a community facility as well as an educational institution. Moreover, it is suggested by Heffernan (1965) that recent legislation, notably the Economic Opportunity Act of 1964, may provide the means for preparing children for school.

Recent developments in elementary-school articulation include the abolition of grade placement in favor of "interage grouping" (Spain, 1956), whereby a growing percentage of the nation's urban schools has begun to place students according to individual ability and development, rather than by chronological time in school, for grades 1, 2, and 3. Some schools have extended the nongraded approach to grade 6, involving the entire elementary sequence.

The Intermediate Level. The intermediate school has blurred the conventional division between elementary and secondary school, and anticipated (Elliott, 1961) are high schools which not only will offer a number of curricula but which also will be entirely nongraded. At long last an educational structure is being tried which pays attention to the learner, not simply to the organization.

In philosophical orientation as well as practical organization, significant advances are reported in overcoming the traditional divisive nature of educational units. The junior high school, itself created in an early effort to ease the transition between elementary and secondary education, is in some areas designated and regarded as a "middle school" in order to avoid the tendency for it to imitate the high school (Isacksen, 1959). With over 80 percent of our total secondary-school population enrolled in systems which include junior high schools, careful attention has been devoted to its concept, to guard against its becoming neither a glorified elementary school or a miniature high school (McKeehan, 1961). Advance to secondary education should be carefully directed to emphasize continuity. Hearn (1956) discusses the elimination of formal, culminating elementary graduation ceremonies in favor of a more natural transition. Moreover, at the beginning of grade 9 the student must make important educational decisions which influence his entire life and for which he needs expert professional guidance. Hearn (1956) recommends more counseling, regularly scheduled and carefully conducted visiting days to the secondary institution, and conscious effort to emphasize welcoming, assisting, and orienting activities by the secondary-school students rather than the hazing and initiating practices currently widespread. Such organizations as the Future Teachers of America can be most helpful in guiding students entering junior or senior high school. Homework throughout elementary school, as preparation for secondary studies, is suggested by St. Mary (1961).

Within the secondary-school structure, a new student typology is proposed (Lessinger, 1965) based upon the recognition of four distinct post-high school patterns. The high school student may graduate to the university or four-year college, to junior college, to vocational school, or to modified high school studies. Preparatory programs are proposed in direct relation to these four-, two-, and one-year courses for an increasing percentage of occupations. Belanger (1965) recommends the proposed typology to replace the simple dichotomy of the college preparatory and non-college preparatory classification and emphasizes its purpose of recognizing students' similarities and differences.

School to College Articulation. There are, perhaps, at least three levels of articulation between secondary school and college. The college admits students with deficient preparation and provides remedial opportunities; the gifted student is offered college course work while still in high school and is admitted to advanced standing in college; Meder (1956) maintains that the student at the average level of ability, while numerically most significant, receives relatively little attention in his transition from school to college.

Antman (1963) suggests that articulation between school and college for the average student can be improved through the development of a simulated college environment within the high school for the college-bound, organized in a manner similar to that of the college, including lectures, large reading assignments, and schedules of only 15 or so hours of instruction weekly, in order to inculcate in the student the habits of independent study and inquiry, the prime requisites for college success.

Widespread experimentation has been conducted in recent years in an effort to allow the academically superior student to progress as fast and as far as his abilities will permit and to release him from an unchallenging environment which often promotes duplication of effort and waste of time. Advanced-standing examinations are now widely utilized and growing in popularity every year; in 1960, 10,500 students from 850 high schools participated in advanced standing examinations (Fox, 1962). When combined with improvements in college admission procedures and uniformity of records and transcripts, as suggested by Cook (1957), such examinations offer the possibility of greatly improved high-school-to-college articulation. Notable success is reported by Bernstein (1958) and Michael (1959) with advanced-placement and early-admission programs, although Meister (1956) has reported somewhat negative reactions by some professional groups, and Myers (1956) notes that colleges have been hostile toward the granting of college credit or advanced standing to high school graduates on these bases. It is perhaps significant in this connection that the early-admission program seeks to improve articulation by shifting the responsibility for articulating the studies of the able student from the high school to the college, while the advanced placement program accords the responsibility for challenging the gifted student to the secondary school (Fels, 1958).

Other efforts to improve high-school-to-college articulation have included subject-matter committees of secondary-school and college teachers which have developed syllabi and examinations for courses generally offered to college freshmen for use by gifted high school students (Sanders, 1961). Experimentation with new media has produced four units of open-circuit television courses, offered during the summer to recent high school graduates bound for college in the fall, which have proved to be in some ways advantageous in improving articulation (Head & Philips, 1961).

Greatly significant in high-school-to-college articulation is the development of the junior college. Serving a student population with widely different levels of aspiration, ability, or both, both terminal and transfer (Medsker, 1958), these schools have made notable advances in providing at once an efficient transition to college or university work and, further, terminal educational opportunities for high school graduates. Again, it is emphasized (President's Committee on Education . . ., 1957) that the planning and development of junior, or community, colleges, should be coordinated with the planning for upper-division and graduate facilities in the state or area.

From the research and experimentation conducted throughout the history of concern for articulation of educational units, and particularly from that of recent years, have emerged not simply advanced and improved procedures and techniques but the realization that the experience of the individual must be a continuous and cumulative process. The evolutionary process through which our modern educational establishment has developed has left our schools with the remnants of earlier and obsolete systems. Encouragingly, this traditional structure is continually and increasingly submitted to careful and critical scrutiny, and it promises to develop in the direction of providing for each child the opportunity to progress through his educational experience at his own social and intellectual pace. As more students pursue higher-educational aspirations, the frontier of this articulation has moved on to questions of articulation between college and graduate or professional school (Wilson, 1958) and to the life and work situation beyond. With the application of recent research findings, as briefly reviewed here, to positive and practical programs for the enhancement of articulation, the present, frequently uncoordinated assemblage of schools can emerge as a continuous educational system, conceived and organized as a unified entity.

James C. Stone
University of California (Berkeley)

References

Antman, David. "An Ounce of Prevention." *High Points* 45:60–2; 1963.

Belanger, Laurence L. "Lessinger's Typology Revisited." *J Sec Ed* 40:247–51; 1965.

Bernstein, Jacob L. "Midwood High School's Advanced Placement Program." *Nat Assn Sec Sch Prin B* 42:22–3; 1958.

Blackmer, Alan H. *General Education in School and College.* Harvard U Press, 1952. 142p.

Campbell, Roald F. "Articulating Elementary and Secondary Schools." *El Sch J* 58:257–63; 1958.

Committee on Educational Research. *Minnesota Studies in Articulation.* U Minn Press, 1937, 128p.

Cook, Denton L. "High School and College: Some Problems in Articulation." *Clearing House* 32:167–8; 1957.

Elliott, Richard W. "New Problems in Articulation." *Am Sch Bd J* 142:11; 1961.

Fels, William C. "Articulation Between School and College." *Ed Rec* 39:110–2; 1958.

Foshay, Arthur W. "A Note on Articulation." *Ed Res B* (Ohio State U) 35:187–90; 1956.

Fox, Raymond B. "Improving Relations between High School and College." *Clearing House* 36:323–6; 1962.

Gow, J. Steele, Jr. "Articulation Between Secondary Schools and Colleges." *Nat Assn Women Deans Counselors* 24:11–5; 1960.

Head, Sydney W., and Philips, C. Lee. *A Field Experiment in the Summertime Use of Open Circuit Television Instruction to Bridge the Gap Between High School and College.* U Miami Press, 1961. 39p.

Hearn, Arthur C. "Increasing the School's Holding Power Through Improved Articulation." *Ed Adm Sup* 42:214–8; 1956.

Heffernan, Helen. "New Opportunity for the Preschool Child." *Childh Ed* 41:227–30; 1965.

Hochman, William Russell, "Double Exposure in Education." *NEA J* 48:61–2; 1959.

Isacksen, Roy O. "Assessing New Issues in Junior High School Organization." *Nat Assn Sec Sch Prin B* 45:104–6; 1961.

Kirksey, Howard G. "Articulation in the Junior-senior High School." *Nat Assn Sec Sch Prin B* 43:87–8; 1959.

Learned, W. S., and Wood, B. D. *The Student and His Knowledge.* Carnegie, 1938. 406p.

Lessinger, Leon M. "Toward a More Adequate High School Student Typology." *J Sec Ed* 40:243–6; 1965.

McKeehan, Rollin. "Assessing New Issues in Junior High School Organization." *Nat Assn Sec Sch Prin B* 45:101–2; 1961.

Meder, Albert E., Jr. "Articulation of General Education Programs." *J Ed Sociol* 29:202–8; 1956.

Medsker, Leland L. "Cooperative Action among Two-year and Four-year Colleges: Opportunities and Obstacles." *Ed Rec* 39:114–21; 1958.

Meister, Morris. "Cooperation of Secondary School and Colleges in Acceleration of Gifted Students." *J Ed Sociol* 29:220–7; 1956.

Myers, Alonzo F. "A Time for Action." *J Ed Sociol* 29:193–4; 1956.

Michael, Lloyd S. "Articulation Problems with Lower Schools and Higher Education." *Nat Assn Sec Sch Prin B* 43:51–5; 1959.

Osborn, Keith. "Project Head Start—An Assessment." *Ed Leadership* 23:98–102; 1965.

President's Committee on Education Beyond the High School. *Second Report to the President.* GPO, 1957. 65p.

Romine, Stephen A. "Articulation: A Look at the Twelve Year Program." *North Cen Assn Q* 35:274–7; 1961.

Russell, John Dale, and Judd, Charles H. *The American Educational System.* Houghton-Mifflin, 1940. 554p.

Sanders, Edward. "The Independent Colleges and the High Schools." *J Sec Ed* 36:157–62; 1961.

Spain, Clarence H. "Continuity in the Whole School Program." *Clearing House* 31:195–9; 1956.

St. Mary, M. E. "Bridging the Gap." *Ed* 81:486–8; 1961.

Varner, Glenn F. "How May We Achieve Better Articulation with the Elementary School and the Senior High School?" *Nat Assn Sec Sch Prin B* 46:30–1; 1962.

Wilson, O. Meredith. "The Next Problem of Articulation: The Undergraduate College and the Professional and Graduate Schools." *Ed Rec* 39:124–8; 1958.

ATTENDANCE

CONCEPT OF ATTENDANCE. Attendance can be seen as a form of the social behavior of people. In its broadest sense "attendance" means the behavior of a person, involving that person's being present at an event, occasion, undertaking, or the like. Thus, people speak of attendance at weddings, parties, commencements, and so forth. The concern here is with school attendance for the purpose of obtaining an education. This does not include the attendance of employed staff in the performance of their duties at school or the attendance of people simply to observe an event, such as a commencement, or to observe an educational activity. Rather, it includes people in the act of being formally present at school for the purpose of getting an education as provided by the school.

Education may be seen as a social institution along with a number of other institutions, including the family and religious and economic institutions. While each of those institutions has a concern for socialization and influences educational attendance, socialization per se is seen here as more particularly a *school* function. The "school" is viewed as that social institution the primary function of which is education (socialization).

The school, as a social institution, regularly has social sanction for its function, expressed in a constitution, legislation, or the pronouncements of social leaders. Those expectations may vary widely. Northern climates, such as those that prevail in the United States, Canada, and much of Europe, make a physical structure for the school almost a necessity. The Greek Academy and Lyceum emphasized education out-of-doors. With the increasing speed and facility of movement from place to place, the assumption of attendance at a particular building in a particular place becomes more subject to question. It may well be that some of the traditional notions of attendance will be greatly modified by mobility. However, in the past, and at present also, school attendance can be thought of, for the large part, as presence within a physical educational institution, including its extensions, for the purpose of participating in its educational program.

This concept of attendance involves other social dimensions. Time and space are relevant. How much of a unit of time, such as a day, week, or year, is spent in attendance at school? Let us refer to this time dimension as the *totality* of attendance; *full-time* versus *part-time* attendance will be the major distinction. How long—from what age to what age—is a person to attend school? Let the period be the *duration* of attendance and the beginning and ending ages the *entrance* and *withdrawal* ages. Attendance may or may not be obligatory; i.e., attendance at school may be *compulsory* (required by law), it may be *required* for entrance into certain parts of society —e.g., the professions—or it may be *discretionary* (a matter of choice). From the point of view of society we may say that attendance is *permissive,* and the individual's use of the opportunity may be called *voluntary* attendance.

We may think, then, of school attendance as primarily an institutional device for transition from childhood or youth to adulthood. Such attendance is seen in three stages with attendant characteristics:

Duration: Entrance–attendance–withdrawal
Totality: full-time or part-time
Obligation: Compulsory, required, or discretionary

a. Permissive
b. Voluntary

School attendance, largely as a result of historical development, has come to be thought of at three levels; namely, at childhood (primary), which developed first; at adolescence and youth (secondary), which developed second; and at youth and adulthood (tertiary), including higher and adult education, which developed recently. The school may be either public or private. Attendance at a private school at primary, elementary, or tertiary level, as long as the school meets public requirements, is regularly both permissive and voluntary. In recent decades primary education has become almost universally compulsory in the United States, and secondary education is becoming increasingly so, and both are generally required in occupational life. Tertiary education remains, for the most part, discretionary, although required by an increasing number of occupations.

HISTORICAL AND SOCIAL PERSPECTIVES. Overview. In primitive society, education was for the most part carried on in the home and was given social sanction through coming-of-age ceremonies (Hart, 1963). Eventually these rites of passage (Van Gennep, 1960) to adulthood were institutionalized in the school. However, the early schools were designed primarily for the socialization of elite groups responsible for religious, governmental, and other leadership activities. Such schools served both to prepare the elite group for its adult functions and to set the group off as a preferred class. School attendance was, therefore, an instrument of a class society and, typically, an institutional complement to religious organizations.

Requirements of school attendance were, under the above circumstances, reflections of the belief and value systems of the social groups supporting the schools. Thus, in a system in which belief in a class or caste system was combined with low value ascribed to an individual apart from benefit of class, it was quite sensible that school attendance be limited to those who derived such a "right" by benefit of class or status. Such assumptions were generally characteristic of Eastern and European societies in ancient times and on down through the feudal age.

Already in feudal times new trends were becoming operative which are still at work, changing the nature of school attendance throughout the world. The critical changes involved a different set of beliefs concerning the individual in society and a new basis for the value of the human individual. Out of the Judeo-Christian tradition developed a view of the individual as a person of inherent worth in and of himself, quite apart from his status in society. If not all society, an increasing sector of the nonelite, particularly those near to the elite or experiencing deprivation because of it, was coming to believe in the inherent worth of each individual in society. Once this new set of social postulates began to gain acceptance, a number of corollaries began to develop. For example, the individual had as much right to his ideas as members of the elite had to theirs. Therefore he had as much right to access to ideas, i.e., attendance at school. Another corollary was the equal right of each person to have a hand in determining the course of society. Once the principle of self-government was accepted, it was a short step to the duty to be prepared to participate both equally and responsibly in society. Consequently a new conception of the adult role in society in modern times has brought about new conceptions of the rights and duties of school attendance.

Concomitantly, the social pattern of institutional relationships has been changing. The earlier close association and, at times, domination of schools by religious institutions has been decreasing. In recent centuries, schools have been coming into closer association with, and at times under the domination of, national governmental institutions. National ideology, as it emphasizes general social welfare or special privilege, may shape education in various ways. Thus, Nazism made much use of schools for indoctrination in Nazi ideology; schools are regularly seen as proper vehicles of democratic ideology; and schools may be made instruments of special privilege (Curle, 1965). National control continues to pose a number of educational issues.

These broad trends of modern times are further reinforced by the expansion of knowledge stemming from the scientific revolution. A new elite of scholars, scientists, technologists, and professionals has emerged. Because of the high level of knowledge and skill mastery necessary for successful performance in such positions, school attendance for a specified time is becoming more commonly a condition of entry into the field. The greater the critical importance of these positions to the development of a society, the greater the national significance of school attendance. In this connection may be noted the growing emphasis upon compulsory school attendance in developing countries (Rosenblum, 1966).

Early Development. Against the background of general trends affecting school attendance policy and procedure, a more detailed view is now appropriate. In the early stages of social development, education was carried on primarily in the family, and security and conformity to social norms were emphasized. Consequently, attendance at school did not become an issue; presence in the home was automatically associated with socialization (Kluckhohn & Leighton, 1946; Leighton & Adair, 1963; Leighton & Kluckhohn, 1947; McIlwraith, 1948). Early education among the Hebrews, Chinese, and Hindus as well as among primitive tribes was centered in the family (Wilds, 1936).

Separation of the school from the family was brought about through other institutional interests. The need to transmit religious beliefs and ceremonies resulted in religion-connected schools. The need for security of the state resulted in military schools. As the school became institutionalized apart from the home, school attendance became separated, in varying degrees, from the home (Kneale, 1950).

Spartan and Athenian education provide interesting contrasts with respect to attendance. For the Spartans the school was very much tied up with the militarism of the state. The primacy of the state's goals over those of the family resulted almost in the suppression of the family. The child was taken from the mother at the age of 8 years, and he lived at the school in full-time attendance until 18 and for much of his later life. On the other hand, for the Athenians school attendance was very much a matter of family responsibility, and the child, while in attendance, was accompanied by a family slave, the *pædagogus*.

These schools served class societies, and attendance was almost wholly confined to elite social groups, such as priests, military leaders, and government, scholarly, and leisure groups. Since those roles were regularly allocated to males, female attendance at school was uncommon. A similar situation still persists today in a number of developing countries (Bereday & Lauwreys, 1965).

Renaissance. During the Middle Ages almost all schools (cathedral, parish, and monastic) were church-connected. The feudal gentlemen learned at home and at court. There were also mercantile and guild schools. At the same time another trend was taking shape through the revival of learning. The new spirit of freedom of inquiry and conscience gave an impetus toward universal education and compulsory attendance at school for all.

The Reformation was a direct outgrowth of the Renaissance. The emphasis upon individual freedom of conscience and responsibility, in matters of both religion and citizenship, pointed toward significant adult roles for all. Thus, attendance at school as preparation for those roles took on new and critical importance for society. Hence, compulsory education took on new justification.

Religious reformers emphasized attendance at school. Luther, in his *Letter to The Mayors and Aldermen of the Cities of Germany in behalf of Christian Schools* of 1524, argued for compulsory education for all on grounds of both religious activity and civil government. The first German state school system at elementary, secondary, and tertiary levels was organized in Württemberg in 1559. The first compulsory-attendance law was passed in Weimar in 1617 (Kandel, 1951). Calvin, in plans published in 1538, outlined universal elementary education for Geneva. In Scotland a statute of James IV in 1494 required all freeholders of substance to send their heirs to school. John Knox, in his *Book of Discipline for the Scottish Church* issued by the church assembly in 1560, contended that every town of "any reputation" should have its school. In 1696, under an act of the Scottish parliament, parish schools were set up in connection with the Established Church of Scotland. It seems safe to say that the statements of Luther and Knox helped to create the climate of public opinion which made possible early acceptance of the principle of compulsory school attendance in Prussia and Scotland.

National and Economic Welfare. The dual threads of religion and government appeared in the thinking of Luther. At the same time nationalism was spreading. Prussia provides an example of a state in which compulsory attendance was developed as a national policy. With the rising spirit of patriotism after the battle of Jena, von Stein in 1807 transferred authority for schools from the church-connected Oberschulkollegium to a special section of the Ministry of the Interior. In 1825 the compulsory-attendance law was strengthened, and in 1834 candidates for the learned professions, the civil service, and university studies were required to have passed the leaving examinations of the gymnasiums. Thus, attendance at secondary schools was made more important, and the state achieved wider control of entry into careers.

Another example of an association between the idea of compulsory education and national spirit appears in the French constitution of 1791 (though not carried into effect), which enunciated the principle that primary education should be compulsory and free.

Nationalism, as already suggested, promoted compulsory attendance as a means of inculcating national ideologies and for military security. Economic development and security were also closely related to compulsory attendance. In marginal and less-developed countries economic factors tended to prevent school attendance. The Navaho parent was concerned with having the child attend school, but not for so long that it reduced too greatly the earning power of the child as a member of the family (Kneale, 1950). Attendance at school meant absence from the home and the nonperformance of the many tasks that children can undertake. Thus, school attendance had an economic cost.

A relationship between school attendance and economic productivity has long been recognized. The medieval guild schools serve as examples of schools aimed at economic development. Reference has already been made to the growing importance of education for entry into careers. As a society becomes more future-oriented, school attendance can more readily be viewed as an investment in future productivity. As the standard of living rises, postponement of present gratification for future advantage becomes more feasible. When the chief activities of the majority of occupations involved primarily manual dexterity and some reading, writing, and arithmetic, it was reasonable to require only seven or eight years of school between the ages of about 6 and 13 or 14 (Kandel, 1951). A less-developed country might have a shorter period of school attendance, while one more developed might require a longer period. As the development of science and technology has increased, the level of preparation necessary for occupations has risen, and thus pressure is exerted to lengthen the period of compulsory school attendance.

Horace Mann contended in his "Report for 1841" and "Report for 1848" that education had great importance for human welfare and productivity. School attendance as a form of investment in human capital has been supported by such economists as Marshall, Taussig, and Tawney. The contention has been further endorsed by the United States Chamber of Commerce in the pamphlet *Education: An Investment in People*, published in 1945. More recently Schultz has strengthened the economic analysis supporting the concept of education as investment in human capital (Schultz, 1960, 1964). With an increasing intellectual component in most occupations, the period of compulsory school attendance can be expected to increase, by either a lowering of the school-entry age or a raising of the school-leaving age or both.

In the United States in 1840 only 40 percent of the children between the ages of 6 and 18 years attended schools of any kind for any length of time (Brinkley, 1957). The percentage of the age group 5 to 17 years attending school in 1910 was 69.3. By 1930 it had gone up to 80 percent, and in 1960 it was about 90 percent (U.S. Department of Health, Education, and Welfare, 1963). There are now few countries in which children are permitted to leave school before the age of 14 (Kneller, 1965).

Compulsory Attendance and Labor Laws. Long tradition made the transfer of education from the church to the state difficult in Europe. The United States, in making a new start, was able to separate church and state, placing responsibility for education with the state. Also, the country was founded upon the assumption of an informed and responsible populace. The citizens of Massachusetts had already provided schools under laws of 1642 and 1647. While compulsory provision of school services did much to encourage school attendance, it was not compulsory attendance as such. Action on compulsory attendance was much slower in coming in the United States, with the first legislation dating from the Rhode Island child-labor law of 1840. The first compulsory-attendance law was enacted by Massachusetts in 1852 (Knight, 1953).

The slowness of the spread of compulsory attendance is, in some ways, understandable. It involved entry of the state into the family. English law has never recognized the sovereign authority of the head of the family that was accorded the paterfamilias under Roman law (Winter & Rosenheim, 1966). In theory, at least, English law has made available to children the same remedies for ill-usage as were made to adults. What constitutes ill-usage has certainly changed over time as social and moral standards have changed and as different insights into human welfare have developed (Craies & Ingram, 1911). Such a shift in social standards is reflected in the emergence of legislation on child labor and school attendance during the latter part of the nineteenth century. While public opinion and the law had come to endorse the principle of intervention in the family in cases of ill-usage, public action through legislation had major obstacles to overcome. Nonintervention by the state was supported by belief in the governmental policy of laissez-faire. To many, intervention appeared to strike at the very roots of individual liberty. There was, however, in the United States a basic commitment to the importance of the parents' obligation to ensure their children's education (Rosenheim, 1966).

Child labor emerged as a social issue in association with the development of the factory system, first in England and subsequently in other countries. Public attention in England seems first to have been drawn to overwork of children and unwholesome working conditions as a result of a serious outbreak of fever in 1784 in cotton mills near Manchester (A. Anderson & Horr, 1911). The first really effective factory act, in 1833, prohibited the employment of children under nine years of age in certain types of factories and required that a child have a document from a schoolmaster stating that he was receiving a specified minimum of education as a condition of employment. In this way, laws on child labor and school attendance come into direct contact. That contact may be either sequential or overlapping; namely, (1) provision for school leaving and then entry into employment or (2) provision for school attendance as a condition of employment, as in the case of the factory act mentioned above. The second amounts to part-time and the first to full-time compulsory education. If there is a gap between the legislated ages of school leaving and entry into employment, a period of uncertainty is created for youth. The International Labor Organization has continued to urge that the upper age limit of compulsory school attendance and the lower age limit for employment be the same (International Labor Office, 1951).

The Massachusetts law of 1866 included the first legislation on child labor and school attendance in the United States. The minimum employment age was set at 10 years, and school attendance for six months a year was made a condition of employment between ages 10 and 14. Already in 1852 Massachusetts had passed the first compulsory school attendance law in the United States, requiring that all children between the ages of 8 and 14 attend school for 12 weeks each year. The first compulsory-attendance act in New York State, in 1874, requiring 14 weeks' attendance each year between ages 8 and 14, also required that no child at that age level be employed unless school attendance was a condition of employment.

In the United States the lowest age for compulsory school attendance is now 6 years in 6 states; 7 in 38 states; and 8 in 4 states. The top compulsory attendance age is 16 years in 39 states, the District of Columbia, and Puerto Rico; 17 years in 5 states; and 18 in 4 states (National Education Association, 1966).

As already indicated, the first compulsory-attendance law in Massachusetts in 1852 specified 12 weeks of school attendance per year. In 1869-70 the average length of the school term was 132 days; the length had increased to 173 days in 1929-30 and to 178 in 1959-60 (U.S. Department of Health, Education, and Welfare, 1963). While children were formerly needed at home in a rural economy to help with work during part of the year, that need has largely disappeared. With the disappearance of chores and work about the home, the portion of the year spent in voluntary school attendance has increased (American Association of School Administrators, 1960). Indicative of this trend have been the increased enrollments in summer schools and provisions for full-year study in colleges and universities.

ATTENDANCE AND SOCIAL AND ECONOMIC CHANGE. The 1954 Supreme Court decision *Brown* v. *Board of Education* made provision for attendance at racially integrated schools. Compulsory-attendance laws have since been repealed in Mississippi and South Carolina, and Virginia has made its law dependent upon local option (Blaustein & Ferguson, 1962; National Education Association, 1966). Many other consequences for school attendance follow from *Brown* v. *Board of Education*. Basic is the assumption that our society should be an integrated one and that preparation for life in that society should occur through attendance at an integrated school. How may attendance districts be drawn in order to bring about integration? How may transportation be used to increase integration? When it is community conditions that basically are in need of change, to what extent should school attendance be made a vehicle of change or a palliative? Evident again is the conflict of beliefs and values about the kinds of societies to be preferred. Since attendance at school provides for socialization, it is most natural that social conflicts have in the past affected school attendance policy. They continue to have such effects and will in the future. Overriding such differences, on the whole, has been a belief in the importance of school attendance for the economic and cultural welfare of the state and for the well-being of the individual.

The economically developed countries have transformed that belief in the economic value of attendance into performance more completely than the developing countries have. A rough gauge of the world situation is given by the United Nations (1963), which has reported 29 countries with a lower age limit of 14 for employment, 27 with age 10, and 17 with age 15. Of the 29 countries with age 14, 19 were in North America and Europe; of the 27 with age 10, 12 were in North America, 4 in South America, 10 in Africa and Asia, and 1 in Europe. Differences in employment age are associated with differences in attendance; for example, with respect to the percent of children aged 5–14 enrolled in primary education, in Africa 45 countries had less than one-half of this age group enrolled in school, while 6 countries had more. In North America 8 countries had less than one-half and 18 had more than one-half of this age group enrolled.

Similar differences occur at the tertiary or higher level of education. A striking contrast is that between Africa and Europe in terms of enrollment per 100,000 total population. While in Africa 19 countries had less than 100 enrolled per 100,000 total population and 2 had more, in Europe 1 country had less than 100 and 27 had more (United Nations, 1963).

School-leaving ages are being raised throughout the world. In England the school-leaving age was raised from 14 to 15 in 1947. Some of the sociological phenomena related to that change have been reported (Carter, 1962). Those countries which have not yet raised their school-leaving ages to 14 are, for the most part, prevented from doing so by financial and material limitations. Economic development combined with an increasing intellectual component in most occupations and continued application of egalitarian principles in societies throughout the world will serve to increase the extent of school attendance and the length of compulsory education. This trend may raise the upper age limit of compulsory education to age 18 or even 20. The upper age limit can be expected to reflect supply in the labor force; raising the upper age limit of compulsory education can serve to delay entry into the labor force.

If, on the other hand, the desire is to increase compulsory education without affecting supply of the labor force, it would be sensible to reduce the lower age limit. In 1966 the Educational Policies Commission of the National Education Association of the United States recommended that free public schooling at the age of four be made available to all children. The proposal of permissive school attendance from age four reflects in part already existing voluntary attendance at nursery schools and head-start programs.

With increasing economic production and efficiency, more leisure time has become available, and further increase can be expected, resulting in a still broader social significance for school attendance, especially at the adult level. Required, if not compulsory, adult attendance at schools for job retraining is expanding. There will be some extension of upper and lower compulsory school-attendance age limits, particularly in developing countries; voluntary attendance has been increasing both at the lower and upper age limits; and increased voluntary attendance will tend toward legislation extending the range of permissive school attendance. Economic change and need for occupational reorientation as well as adult avocational interests have extended permissive school attendance throughout the adult period. Therefore, there have been developing (and apparently will continue to develop) both social norms which sanction more school attendance and economic realities which make such attendance of practical importance. Within the total complex, perhaps the greatest influence toward expanded school attendance will be the raising of educational standards for various occupations, thus increasing the extent of required school attendance.

ATTENDANCE BEHAVIOR. School attendance has been considered in its social and historical perspectives. A pervasive trend of expanding school attendance has been identified. Yet school attendance in general is measured in terms of the individuals who go to school or stay away. What is the nature of the behavior of those who stay away? From a study of factors associated with absenteeism from school it was concluded that absence was related to a number of variables each of which is "symptomatic of an unfavorable adjustment between the learner and the educational and social environment in which he is operating" (Greene, 1963). Social acceptance has been found to make an important difference between dropouts and those who stay in school (Cady, 1964). Gibson (1966) has concluded that employees' absence from work is a matter of "behavioral exchange" between the individual and the organization in relation to their beliefs and values. If such is the case, school attendance becomes tied to internalized beliefs and values as they come to shape behavior. One has the impression that the traditional conception of school attendance as a necessary drudgery from which one escapes when and as soon as possible has diminished greatly. Such ideological negativism provided a social sanction for absence and dropping out and increased the need for punitive action through attendance and court procedures. A trend toward a more positive conception of the school as meaningfully related to future opportunities would be expected to create a more positive disposition toward school attendance. One comes to a sort of "push-pull" view of the individual as he comes to favor or avoid school attendance.

A number of situational and personal factors involving the school, the family, peers, and personal orientation have been identified (Cervantes, 1965; Paolucci, 1964). Cervantes concluded that the greater the number of negative factors, the greater the chances of dropping out. However, he concluded, if there was "a primary relationship favorable to his remaining in school, all disadvantages are fairly readily overcome." This finding suggests the basic importance of *primary reference groups*, including the family, favorable toward school attendance in shaping attendance behavior (Roberts, 1965).

Such a favorable attitude could be expected to have a relationship to perceived enhancement of life chances through school attendance. These chances are related to social class (Barber, 1961). The change from a class-dominated to an egalitarian society (McCain, 1960) tends to advance lower-class life chances and to expand lower-class primary reference groups supportive of school attendance. In those societies in which life chances are still dominated by a hereditary elite class, extension of school attendance is slower than in countries with less class domination (Curle, 1965).

The above findings at the level of microanalysis, emphasizing, as they do, the importance of the individual's beliefs and values in shaping school attendance, support the earlier macroanalysis. There the emphasis was upon historical-social trends in beliefs and values related to social status, the individual human being, and social welfare. As the trend is away from an elitist, closed society toward a more liberal and open society, school attendance becomes more universal and of greater duration.

Research concerned with attendance behavior and school integration is still limited. St. John (1966) suggests that the variables may be many and complex and speculates that attendance at a desegregated, as compared with a segregated, school in some ways may be the more harmful unless wholesome environmental conditions exist. Rentsch (1967) found that pupils in an open-enrollment program were less often tardy and had better attendance records than pupils in other types of programs. In Seattle, transferred Negroes were found to have improved attendance (Hammond and others, 1964), a finding similar to those in New York regarding Puerto Ricans and Negroes who were bussed to integrated schools (East Harlem Project . . . , 1962).

Proposals are being advanced (American Association of School Administrators, 1966; Center for Field Studies, 1965) for racially mixed attendance units. Often these must be formulated on premises about what is desirable with limited knowledge of the variables at work and probable outcomes.

ORGANIZATION AND ADMINISTRATION OF ATTENDANCE. Once a state has committed itself to permissive or compulsory school attendance, or both, the means to the accomplishment of its objective and control of the process become necessary. The ineffectiveness of many early attendance laws stems from the fact that the law was a statement of intent without there being any organizational and administrative machinery to carry it out. Indeed, it would appear that some of the early policy statements and legislation were more statements of belief and values aimed at moving the public conscience ahead to the point where the intent could be effectively implemented than programs for action.

Some important aspects of the structure for implementation are district organization and control, school census, and enrollment accounting.

District Organization and Control. Organization and control, depending upon geography and culture (such as traditions of government and experience with attendance), may range from highly centralized to highly decentralized. The UNESCO studies of compulsory education illustrate the range of organizational patterns (UNESCO, 1951———).

The political tradition of decentralization in the United States has set a general pattern of local attendance administration. Connecticut, which for some time was an exception to the general pattern and had state control of attendance, has moved, in recent years, to a more decentralized system (Umbeck & Flynt, 1960).

Attendance laws in the United States have regularly placed responsibility for enforcement of attendance with the board of the local school district. Normally, residence and school are different places for the student. Consequently, the distance and means of travel from residence to school must be considered. As districts have been reorganized and enlarged, attendance has come to involve more travel, necessitating the introduction of an extensive bussing program. The local board has wide authority in determining which school the child will attend, as long as it acts with reasonable discretion. Life and safety take priority over education as a necessary condition for education; hence, local decisions on attendance make very explicit provision for safety.

Unless the local ideas and norms provide reasonable support for those assumed by the attendance legislation, the law has proved to be almost unenforceable. Reference has already been made to the earlier class-society system which held that education was for the elite. Change to a more egalitarian society has meant that two changes have had to take place, (1) the elite had to accept the right of and need for education for all, and (2) the lower classes had to accept their own right of and need for education.

When local beliefs and values are in conflict with those of legislated school attendance, some critical problems can arise. This conflict is strikingly illustrated in the case of the Amish in Pennsylvania and the Dukobors in British Columbia, Canada.

Ethnic as well as social-class difference from the elite group have tended to restrict school attendance. In early attendance legislation it appears that the Negro was the person passed over (Boskin, 1966). Indians received much more attention. The 1954 decision in *Brown* v. *Board of Education* has involved differences in beliefs and values and has been followed by changes in attendance laws in Mississippi, South Carolina, and Virginia. Administrative control needs, therefore, a base of popular understanding in order to bring about compliance and the sanctions which promote that compliance. Normally both the standards and sanctions have been established in state legislation, thus providing the local school system, as administrative agent, with the means of enforcing attendance. Once the constitutionality of state enforcement of attendance had been established through cases in Indiana, New Hampshire, Ohio, and Pennsylvania, the way was opened to further improvements in state laws and local procedures. As state laws have become more specific, local administrative discretion has decreased. With growing public acceptance and support, administrative control can assume a more socially constructive approach. With growing public support and district reorganization, bus transportation, improved supportive staff, and the related advances in the census and in enrollment accounting have made possible more efficient and effective administrative control of school attendance. However, the problems of attendance areas and integration are likely to persist for some time (Campbell & others, 1965), combined with the negativism toward education of lower-class children (Roucek, 1965).

School Census and Enrollment Accounting. The census is one of the major tools in control of school attendance. The census provides data on those people who may be expected to attend school. Thus, it provides a means of identification and action with respect to those who must attend school. Originally the census tended to be a count, taken periodically, of young people between certain ages. The trend is toward continuous census-taking for all young people from the time of birth. Thus the scope and usefulness of the census in control and planning are broadening.

In recent years school systems have been adapting their census data-collection procedures to data-processing facilities. This trend is apparent in all areas of attendance accounting. Some of the advantages are rather evident. Routine clerical tasks performed by teachers are reduced. Data are made more conveniently available. For example, if desired, a printed list of absentee pupils within a school related to the census can be had shortly after the opening of the day.

What effect does the introduction of data processing have on school attendance? This question is posed as one facet of the more general question concerning the impact of the introduction of automated procedures into social systems. There has been some study of this question, largely in business and industrial organizations (Silverman, 1966). Reports concerning schools appear, for the most part, to be speculative so far, although reports of experience are beginning to appear (G. Anderson, 1965; Furno & Kiser, 1963; Lindquist, 1966).

Since attendance data for data processing must be collected according to general rules anticipated for processing, it is reasonable to expect that automated procedures will tend to increase rule making. It is not clear how it is that the processors and the users of the data affect the rule-making process.

Some final observations seem to be in order. It appears that the *totality* and *duration* of attendance, as defined earlier, are increasing. The totality is reflected in rising attendance rates during the regular school year and, more strikingly, during the summer. Duration is increasing in terms of both earlier entrance and later withdrawal. Recent increases have tended at first to take the form of *voluntary* attendance, reflecting rising educational expectations in society. Subsequently, as in the nursery school and junior college, the rising expectation is expressed through legislation providing for *permissive* attendance. There appears to be growing impetus to extend the compulsory-attendance age; recently the concern has been with the younger age limit, but the upper age limit is also relevant to increasing leisure and a shift in the composition of the labor force. During the nineteenth and early twentieth centuries economic growth, social importance of education, and broad humanization of schools have been associated with public beliefs and values that sanction school attendance, reducing legalistic and punitive control of attendance. Illustrative of a changing view is that which sees nonattendance as a symptom for clinical study, not as an infraction of law (Ferguson, 1965). Increasing social sanction of school attendance from childhood to adulthood tends to establish more firmly in society the *compulsory* attendance base and to expand the *discretionary* sector.

Growing school attendance in the discretionary sector is intimately related to social changes, particularly in the occupational field. With growing professionalism there tends to be a concomitant escalation of educational standards leading to greater school attendance. Occupational obsolescence results in adult school attendance in order to prepare for new jobs. The social changes themselves create new interests and needs for knowledge which motivate individuals toward *voluntary* school attendance at almost all ages.

Some of the discretionary expansion in school attendance is not purely voluntary. When a job is eliminated, job retraining is much less a matter of choice. Such economic and social constraints can be expected to continue and, in all probability, to increase. If this is the case, it is reasonable to expect that the expanding sector of discretionary school attendance will tend to draw out the boundary of the compulsory-attendance sector. While duration is likely to increase, it may be that age as a criterion for compulsory attendance will in an increasing degree be supplemented by functional criteria such as skill obsolescence or new knowledge. Such attendance is often *required* by the employer or by occupational standards. It may be that the major future expansion in school attendance will be in functionally required areas of education extending throughout the life span.

R. Oliver Gibson
State University of New York

References

American Association of School Administrators. *Year-round School*. The Association, 1960.

American Association of School Administrators. *School Racial Policy*. The Association, 1966.

Anderson, Adelaide Mary, and Horr, Carroll Davidson. "Labor Legislation." *Encyclopaedia Britannica*, Vol. 16, 11th ed. 1911. p. 7–27.

Anderson, G. Ernest, Jr. "New Directions in Attendance Accounting." In Goodman, Edith Harwith. (Ed.) *Automated Education Handbook*. Automated Education Center, 1965. p. VA27–38.

Barber, Bernard. "Social Class Differences in Educational Life Chances." *Teach Col Rec* 63:102–13; 1961.

Bereday, George Z. F., and Lauwreys, Joseph A. (Eds.) *The Education Explosion*. Harcourt, 1965.

Blaustein, Albert P., and Ferguson, Clarence Clyde, Jr. *Desegregation and the Law*, 2nd ed. Vintage Books, Inc., Knopf, 1962.

Boskin, Joseph. "The Origins of American Slavery: Education as an Index of Early Differentiation." *J Negro Ed* 35:125–33; 1966.

Brinkley, Sterling G. "Growth of School Attendance and Literacy in the United States Since 1840." *J Exp Ed* 26:51–66; 1957.

Cady, Lillian Vernitta. "An Analysis of Relatedness Needs, Relatedness Imagery, and Sociometric Factors Associated with School Dropouts." Unpublished doctoral dissertation. Washington State U, 1964.

Campbell, Roald F., and others. *The Organization and Control of American Schools*. Charles E. Merrill, Inc., 1965.

Carter, M. P. *Home, School and Work*. Macmillan, 1962.

Center for Field Studies. *Schools for Hartford*. The President and Fellows of Harvard College, 1965.

Cervantes, Lucius F. *The Dropout*. U Michigan Press, 1965.

Craies, William Feilden, and Ingram, Thomas Allan. "Law Relating to Children." *Encyclopaedia Britannica*, Vol. 6, 11th ed. 1911. p. 138–40.

Curle, Adam. "Political Implications of the Educational Explosion in Developing Countries." In Bereday, George Z. F., and Lauwreys, Joseph A. *The Education Explosion*. Harcourt, 1965. p. 178–84.

East Harlem Project and City Commission on Human Rights. *Releasing Human Potential, A Study of East Harlem–Yorkville School Bus Transfer.* New York City Commission on Human Rights, 1962.

Ferguson, Donald G. "Critical Issues in Pupil Personnel Work." *Theory into Practice* 4:140–4; 1965.

Furno, O. F., and Kiser, C. L. "Automated Pupil Attendance Procedures." *Baltimore B Ed* 40:1–24; 1963.

Gibson, R. Oliver. "Toward a Conceptualization of Absence Behavior of Personnel in Organizations." *Adm Sci Q* 11:107–33; 1966.

Greene, James E., Sr. "Factors Associated with Absenteeism Among Students in Two Metropolitan High Schools." *J Exp Ed* 31:389–94; 1963.

Hammond, Alpha, and others. "A Survey of the Adjustment of the Negro Students Who Transferred to Schools Outside Their Neighborhoods During 1963–64 Under the New Seattle School Board Ruling." Unpublished Master's thesis. U Washington, 1964.

Hart, C. W. M. "Contrasts Between Prepubertal and Postpubertal Education." In Spindler, George D. (Ed.) *Education and Culture.* Holt, 1963. p. 400–25.

International Labor Office. *Child Labour in Relation to Compulsory Education.* Columbia U Press, 1951.

Kandel, I. L. *Raising the School-leaving Age.* Columbia U Press, 1951.

Kluckhohn, Clyde, and Leighton, Dorothea. *The Navaho.* Harvard U Press, 1946.

Kneale, Albert H. *Indian Agent.* The Caxton Printers, Ltd., 1950.

Kneller, George Frederick. "School Administration." *Encyclopaedia Britannica*, Vol. 20. 1965. p. 89.

Knight, Edgar W. *Readings in Educational Administration.* Holt, 1953.

Leighton, Dorothea, and Adair, John. "People of the Middle Place: A Study of the Zuñi Indians." Unpublished manuscript on file at the Human Relations Area Files, Inc., New Haven, Conn., 1963.

Leighton, Dorothea, and Kluckhohn, Clyde. *Children of the People.* Harvard U Press, 1947.

Lindquist, E. F. "Implications and Potential of Information Systems in Public Schools." In Marker, Robert W., and others. (Eds.) *Computer Concepts and Educational Administration.* U Iowa and U Council for Educational Administration, 1966. p. 41–57.

McCain, James A. "The Expansion of Educational Opportunity in Europe." *J H Ed* 31:75–80; 1960.

McIlwraith, Thomas F. *The Bella Coola Indians*, Vol. 1. U Toronto Press, 1948.

National Education Association. *NEA Res B* 44:No. 2; 1966.

Paolucci, Thomas Daniel. "A Comparative Study of Factors Relating to Lack of School Persistence at the High School Level." Unpublished doctoral dissertation. Cornell U, 1964.

Rentsch, George J. "Open Enrollment: An Appraisal." Unpublished doctoral dissertation. State U New York at Buffalo, 1967.

Roberts, Tommy Lee. "A Comparative Analysis of the Achievement and Training Success of High School Dropouts." Unpublished doctoral dissertation. Oklahoma, 1965.

Rosenblum, Lila. "Child Labor." *Encyclopaedia Britannica*, Vol. 5. 1966. p. 503–4.

Rosenheim, Margaret Keeney. "Laws Concerning Children: United States." *Encyclopaedia Britannica*, Vol. 5. 1966. p. 514–6.

Roucek, Joseph S. "The Role of Educational Institutions with Special Reference to Highly Industrialized Areas." In Bereday, George Z. F., and Lauwreys, Joseph A. (Eds.) *The Education Explosion.* Harcourt, 1965. p. 137–61.

St. John, Nancy Hoyt. "The Effect of Segregation on the Aspirations of Negro Youth." *Harvard Ed R* 36:284–94; 1966.

Schultz, Theodore W. "Capital Formation by Education." *J Political Econ* 68:571–83; 1960.

Schultz, Theodore W. "Investment in Human Capital." In Gutmann, Peter M. (Ed.) *Economic Growth, An American Problem.* Prentice-Hall, 1964. p. 125–42.

Silverman, William. "The Economic and Social Effects of Automation in an Organization." *Am Behavioral Sci* 9:3–8; 1966.

Umbeck, Nelda, and Flynt, Ralph C. M. *State Legislation on School Attendance and Related Matters—School Census and Child Labor.* GPO, 1960.

UNESCO. *Studies on Compulsory Education.* Columbia U Press, 1951——.

United Nations. *United Nations Compendium of Social Statistics, 1963.* UN Publishing Service, 1963.

U.S. Department of Health, Education, and Welfare. *Statistics of State School Systems, 1959–60.* GPO, 1963.

Van Gennep, Arnold. *Les Rites de passage.* Translated by Monika B. Vizedom and Gabrielle L. Chaffee. Phoenix Books, U Chicago Press, 1960.

Wilds, Elmer Harrison. *The Foundations of Modern Education.* Wiley, 1936.

Winter, Charles, and Rosenheim, Margaret Keeney. "Laws Concerning Children." *Encyclopaedia Britannica*, Vol. 5. 1966. p. 512–4.

BEHAVIOR PROBLEMS

The term "behavior problem" is used to designate a deviation in behavior from that which is expected or approved by the group making the designation. This is a rather broad definition. It includes, for example, delinquency as well as social deviance. When a deviation in behavior constitutes a violation of the ordinances of the community (city, state, or nation) it is commonly classified as a delinquency, and if (in most states) the child is 18 years of age or younger he is classified as a juvenile delinquent. In previous editions of the Encyclopedia separate entries were provided for "behavior problems" and "delinquency." It has been difficult to distinguish between these categories except on an arbitrary age and legal basis. Numerous studies of behavior deviations which constitute direct violations of legal statutes and those which do not have revealed so great a similarity in causes that the distinction, except for legal purposes, has not proved very useful.

This trend in thinking is reflected in the recent yearbook of the National Society for the Study of Education (1966), which does not bear the title *Juvenile Delinquency*, as did the earlier yearbook of that society (1948), but rather the title *Social Deviancy*. In the introduction to the more recent yearbook it is pointed out that delinquency as seen in its broad social context is regarded as one form of a cluster of problems which have many basic characteristics in common.

Another complication in the definition of behavior problems centers in their relation to emotional disturbance. Sometimes the student with a behavior problem shows considerable emotional reaction along with the deviant behavior. There may be anger, fear, worry, etc. This seems to happen so frequently that it has become difficult to distinguish a child who presents a "behavior problem" from one who is also emotionally disturbed. Thus, Bower (1955), Bower and others (1958), and Lambert and Bower (1961), in discussing their method of screening to locate emotionally disturbed children, point out that behavior deviations without a high degree of emotional disturbance tend to occur along with those accompanied by a high degree of emotional disturbance and that it is difficult to separate them.

> Children identified by this screening process will be "different"; not all, however, will be suffering from emotional problems. It may be difficult to distinguish the child who behaves differently but has a relatively healthy personality from the child who behaves differently because of compelling emotional problems.

Yet another difficulty in defining behavior problems is a result of their cultural relativism. A particular pattern of behavior may be approved in one group but not in another. But the acceptance or rejection of a given form of behavior is not entirely an arbitrary matter. Behavior has effects, both short and long term. Some forms of behavior are developmental in the sense that they tend to facilitate the continued development of those experiencing them; other forms tend to be detrimental to human development; and still others are relatively neutral. Stealing in any culture limits the amount of mutual confidence and thus makes impossible those forms of social organization which depend on a high degree of mutual trust. On the other hand, whether one wears a necktie or not is largely a matter of attitude; this is an example of a form of behavior that is more or less neutral insofar as its effects on the subsequent development of people is concerned.

Finally, there is the difficulty of distinguishing behavior problems that reflect mainly the immaturity of the child from those that are primarily a result of environmental stresses. When a child does not behave in the approved or expected way a very common reaction is to assume that it is the child who is the problem. This assumption tends to be implied in such statements as "He is a behavior problem," and "There are many behavior problems in this class."

Suppose, however, we consider the situation in which a teacher manages his class in an arbitrary and autocratic way and makes his decisions with little reference to class members. There is experimental evidence to indicate that such a procedure tends to increase the incidence of overaggressiveness and other forms of noncooperative behavior (Lewin & others, 1938).

Let us suppose that a careful analysis of this situation shows that there are some students in the class who, as a result of the autocratic procedures of the teacher, feel that their abilities are not recognized and that they will be arbitrarily discriminated against. It is well known that a student under such conditions in his eagerness to overcome the feeling of inferiority may overreact by trying to prove to himself and others that he still possesses some ability. If he has had no help in understanding his feelings, he may not be fully aware that he is using such methods as overaggression in trying to resolve his difficulty.

In such a situation who is the "problem"? One could say that there is as much of a behavior problem with the teacher as with the student. This possibility has to be taken into account in interpreting the label "behavior problem." The usual use of the label does not differentiate between deviations in behavior which represent an immaturity of the child and those which are the result in large part of excessive stresses placed on the child by others.

These considerations suggest that the term "behavior problem" is not one to which specific, precise meaning can be ascribed. It designates a general area—deviations in behavior from some reference point. Such deviations may be of great variety in (1) the overt form, (2) the motivational forces that underlie the behavior, (3) the reference point from which the deviation is measured, and (4) the amount of emotional disturbance or pathology that accompanies or characterizes the behavior.

In order to come to grips with the meaning of "behavior problems" it is necessary, therefore, to specify in detail the kind of behavior that is under consideration, such as thumb sucking, stealing, fighting, and shyness. It is also essential to describe the behavior not only in its outward form but also in terms of the factors that underlie it or produce it. Thus, shy or withdrawal behavior representing a loss of confidence in one's ability to make a respected contribution to the group is different from shy or withdrawal behavior which is the result of one's having been taught by the culture that this is the "right" thing to do. Overaggressive behavior by a child in an autocratic classroom may be more often "teacher produced" than aggressive behavior in a democratic classroom is (Anderson and Brewer, 1946).

Examples such as these point out the great importance of considering underlying structure of the behavior in attempting to classify it. Knowledge of the underlying structure also is the foundation on which a program of redevelopment is logically based.

The suggestion from this discussion of the definition of the term "behavior problem" is that the term be considered as representing the general area of deviations in behavior and that more precise definition be obtained by considering (1) the reference point from which the deviation is measured (thus there will be as many terms or qualifiers of a term as there are reference points), (2) the amount of emotional disturbance that accompanies the behavior, and (3) the underlying structure of the behavior, thus separating those forms arising from stresses which are within the capacity of the child to meet from those that are beyond his capacity (Ojemann, 1957). The latter will include those representing more of a deviation by the teacher, parent, or other person in authority than one by the child.

In the subsequent discussion the term "behavior problems" will include deviations in behavior represented by both of the former terms "behavior problems" and "delinquency" as they were used in previous editions of the Encyclopedia, and it will consider for the most part those deviations which are not accompanied by such severe emotional disturbances as to be considered a mental breakdown. These are considered under "mental health."

KINDS AND INCIDENCE. Since behavior has both an outward or overt form and an underlying structure, some classifications of kinds of deviance have been based on the underlying structure or "mental mechanisms" and some on the overt form. Thus, Redl and Wattenberg, in *Mental Hygiene in Teaching* (1959), identify 15 "mechanisms" which they group into three major divisions: (1) ignoring or overlooking important aspects of the situation (mechanisms of denial), (2) attempting to escape or evade (mechanisms of escape), and (3) substituting or shifting the form (mechanisms of shift and substitution). Such a classification has been useful in giving an indication of the variety of processes that may underlie behavior deviance.

Another approach to classification has been to group behavior deviances in terms of their overt form. This procedure was used by Lapouse and Monk (1964) in their study of behavior deviations in children 6 to 12 years of age. They developed four major groups, with subsections in each group. The four groups are (1) problems of body control (including body management, tics, tension phenomena, etc.—five subsections); (2) problems of behavior control (four subsections); (3) combined habits (two subsections), and (4) miscellaneous (includes physical inactivity, daydreaming, etc.).

A refinement of classifications based on overt form has been to factor analyze data obtained through the use of a check list of problems. Representative of recent studies of this type are those by Fanshel and others (1963) and Quay and others (1966). From data obtained through the use of a problem-behavior rating scale developed by Peterson (1961), Quay and his associates found that three factorially independent dimensions accounted for 76 percent of the variance of the interrelationships. The three dimensions were (1) aggressive, hostile; (2) anxious, withdrawn; and (3) preoccupied, daydreaming.

A classification which emphasized social desirability was developed by Havighurst (1966). It consists of three major categories: (1) undesirable forms of deviance (including such forms as hostile, aggressive behavior, stealing, illegitimate motherhood, withdrawn-apathetic behavior, etc.—eight subgroups), (2) desirable forms of deviance (including highly intelligent behavior, creative behavior in the arts, highly developed skill in socially approved areas, and physical attractiveness), and (3) forms of deviance about which people are ambivalent (including highly developed masculine skills among girls, highly developed feminine skills and interests among boys, skeptical and critical social attitudes and privatist or "beatnik" behavior).

A classification which is confined primarily to delinquent behavior was developed by Hewitt and Jenkins (1946). It includes three major categories: the socialized delinquent, the unsocialized aggressive, and the neurotic. A somewhat similar classification was developed by Reiss (1952).

A recent classification using five groups to encompass the various types of disturbed deviants has been developed by Bower (1966).

Data on incidence are highly variable, as would be expected from the discussion of difficulty of definition and variations in classification. Lapouse and Monk (1964) in a study of 482 children 6 to 12 years of age in Buffalo considered the highest quartile of deviant scores as representing behavior problems. Using this cutoff point they found children aged 6 to 8 to have a significantly higher proportion of deviant scores (30 percent) than children 9 to 12 (19 percent).

The *Uniform Crime Reports* of the U.S. Federal Bureau of Investigation (1966) and the U.S. Children's Bureau's *Juvenile Court Statistics* (1963) provide extensive data concerning the total number of offenses and arrests, the variation of rate by age groups, the incidence of types of delinquent behavior as represented by arrests, and the kinds of cases handled by the juvenile courts. According to the data gathered by these agencies, and using their definitions, juvenile-court cases in the United States in 1962 represented 1.8 percent of all children 10 to 17 years of age. There was a 225 percent increase in juvenile-court cases from 1940 to 1959. During the same time the population aged 10 to 17 increased approximately 30 percent.

CAUSES. In the discussion of the definition of "behavior problem" it was indicated that the causes may be of great variety. A reading of the results of the analyses of behavior problems reported in the literature will soon convince the reader of this (Orthopsychiatry, 1965 and 1966). There is now general agreement that behavior deviances are produced by a multiplicity of factors. When we consider a given form of behavior it appears to be a product of several immediate antecedents, such as the conscious and unconscious motives the individual is attempting to work out and the ideas, skills, etc. he had available for working them out. If we consider the development of these antecedents we find that they are the product of the past interactions of organism and environment, and these interactions may be of great variety.

A good illustration of what is meant by "multiple-caused" and the significance of this conception is furnished by the history of investigations into the causes of delinquency. During the 1920's and 1930's investigators such as Shaw and McKay (1931, 1942) provided data indicating that there is a relationship between urban delinquency rates and distance from the center of the city. The highest rates were found near the center of the city, with rates decreasing gradually as one moved away from the center. Although there was a significant correlation, it was not high. There were many exceptions. This led Healy and Bronner (1936) to pose the question why, of two children living in the same home and under the *same* environmental conditions, one becomes delinquent and the other does not. Their inquiry, involving 105 delinquents paired with 105 sibling controls, indicated that a variety of blocked emotional forces, such as feeling rejected, deprived, or thwarted, internal mental conflict, or a sense of guilt, characterized 96 of the 105 cases. The remaining 9 without marked emotional stress revealed such factors as various social pressures, lack of supervision, and poor family standards. A similar study by Scott (1950) of delinquents in English culture revealed a comparable network of factors. In both studies a detailed inquiry into the process through which the delinquent behavior developed revealed a complex network of factors.

When the Gluecks (Glueck & Glueck, 1950) organized their study of the development of predictive factors in the 1940's they felt that an "eclectic approach" to the study of the causes of delinquency was necessary, involving at least four levels of inquiry —the sociocultural level, the somatic level, the intellectual level, and the emotional-temperamental level. The prediction tables resulting from this study were three in number—one constructed from social factors, one from Rorschach test results, and one from personality traits as determined in psychiatric interviews. The social-factors prediction table was refined after extensive study into a three-factor scale including supervision of boy by his father, supervision of boy by his mother, and family cohesiveness. This three-factor table "yielded approximately a 70% accuracy in predicting delinquents and an 85% accuracy in predicting nondelinquents" (Craig & Glick, 1963) when tested with youth in an urban area. Another example of the testing of the Glueck social prediction scale is the study by Michael and Houck (1965). An improvement of the Glueck Social Prediction Table has been reported by E. Glueck (1966*a*). A predictive instrument for identifying potential delinquents at school entrance (Glueck, 1966*c*) and one for identification at age two to three years (Glueck, 1966*b*) have also been reported.

Other predictive instruments such as those by Stott (1950) and Kvaraceus (1966) are based on a similar sensitivity to a multiplicity of factors.

Recent studies of the role in delinquency of the self concept (Lively & others, 1962; S. Smith, 1965; Scarpitti, 1965; Fannin, 1965), attitudes engendered by social status (Robins & others, 1962), opportunities to achieve (Cloward & Ohlin, 1960; Landis & Scarpitti, 1965), and difficulty in developing an ego identity (Erikson, 1959) further extend the list of factors suspected of having causative roles in deviant behavior.

PREVENTION AND CONTROL. In the development of programs for the prevention and control of deviance some basic considerations are presently emerging. First, since the findings of studies on causes have indicated that a complex variety of factors may be involved, more attention is being given to the development of diagnostic facilities so that the deviance can be carefully studied. The development of community child-guidance clinics from the stimulus provided by the National Institute of Mental Health, the development of residential receiving centers for juvenile delinquents, and the increase in school psychological and guidance services are examples of this trend (Eckerson & Smith, 1966).

Second, there is a developing recognition of the distinction between the several levels of prevention. In the public health literature it has been found helpful to recognize the differences between secondary prevention, which seeks to locate the deviant individual early in his life cycle to "prevent" the deviation from becoming more serious, and primary prevention, which seeks to remove the noxious influences which produced the difficulty (Caplan, 1964). Programs for the early detection and redevelopment of deviant cases have been suggested as preventive programs. They are essentially secondary preventive procedures. Similarly special programs for the identification and redevelopment of young delinquents also fall in this category.

When we inquire into the causes of the deviance and ask how the forces producing the deviance can be removed or controlled we become concerned with primary prevention. Thus, primary prevention seeks to prevent the deviance from occurring in the first place. Such procedures might include helping teachers, parents, judges, and community citizens generally and the child himself to develop a greater sensitivity to the needs of the human personality so as to enable them to develop homes, schools, churches, and communities where the needs of the growing child are met more adequately.

Sometimes a program may represent a mixture of secondary and primary preventive procedures. Thus, the program for the early identification and education of emotionally handicapped children developed by Bower and his associates (Lambert & Bower, 1961) included such procedures as mental health counseling for teachers, providing child study meetings for teachers, group counseling for parents, group counseling for adolescents, and the organization of special classes at the elementary and secondary levels. Although the mental health consultations with teachers were concerned with teacher attitudes and behavior toward the deviant child, nevertheless the insight the teacher gained from these consultations could be helpful in his attitudes and behavior toward all children. A similar effect could accrue from the work with parents and pupils themselves.

Development of Child-guidance Clinics and Related Diagnostic Facilities. One of the best known early child-guidance clinics in the United States was the Juvenile Psychopathic Institute, later renamed the Institute for Juvenile Research. It was organized in Chicago in 1909 under the leadership of Healy (Healy & Bronner, 1948). An earlier guidance clinic was organized in 1896 by Lightner as the Psychological Clinic of the University of Pennsylvania. A brief history of these developments can be found in the studies by Shakow (1945), Stevenson and Smith (1934), Watson (1953), and Witmer (1907). A history of child-guidance clinics in Britain (beginning with the first child-guidance clinic in 1913) and in France is given by Keir (1952).

In the United States during the 1920's the Commonwealth Fund stimulated the development of a number of child-guidance clinics (Stevenson & Smith, 1934).

Recently, child-guidance clinics have become more closely identified with mental health. Under the influence of the National Institute of Mental Health an extensive program of community mental health centers in the various states has been developed. The Community Mental Health Centers legislation of 1963 authorized Congress to appropriate $150-million over a three-year period beginning in July 1964 for the construction of Community Mental Health Centers (Chandler, 1965). It is estimated that by 1970 there will be around 500 such centers in operation throughout the country.

Recent thinking also has suggested that the outpatient departments of general hospitals having psychiatric departments can be developed as community diagnostic centers (Chandler, 1965).

Because recent legislation has been under mental health auspices a more complete discussion of Mental Health Centers is found in MENTAL HEALTH.

An indication of the growth of diagnostic facilities involving the school is furnished by data provided in the Digest of Educational Statistics of the U.S. Department of Health, Education, and Welfare (1963, 1965). The number of guidance personnel in public elementary and secondary schools rose from 13,119 in 1959–60 to 21,152 in 1961–62. During the same period the number of psychological personnel increased from 2,054 to 2,409. An extended discussion of these developments is given by Eckerson and Smith (1966).

Programs. A wide variety of programs has been developed in past decades for both deviant children in school and delinquents in the community. Some of these programs have emphasized a single or small cluster of factors—for example, the early Cambridge-Somerville study (Powers & Witmer, 1951), which sought to provide an interested adult adviser for the delinquent. Most of the programs, especially those recently organized, have been designed with multiple factors in mind. In recent literature such phrases as "total-push," "multidimensional," and "multi-ingredient" have appeared to indicate the more comprehensive approach involving community clinics, schools, churches, homes, employment facilities, recreational opportunities, and health agencies, all with their respective personnel.

In a number of cases, such as the Cambridge-Somerville Youth Study (Powers & Witmer, 1951), the Boston "Total-community" Delinquency Project (Miller, 1962), the Massimo and Shore project (Massimo & Shore, 1963), and the Schwitzgebel project (Schwitzgebel, 1964), an experimental group and a control group were employed to test the effectiveness of the program, and the experiment was continued for a varying number of years. In general the results have indicated few or no differences between the experimental and control groups. Such results indicate the difficulty of the problem of redevelopment and the inadequacy of present knowledge and skill to deal with this difficulty.

A variety of programs emphasizing work experience and career development has been described by Ahlstrom (1966) and by Schreiber (1966). Programs emphasizing changes in school experiences have been summarized by Byerly (1966). A recent study of the use of psychodramatic techniques has been reported by Pancratz and Buchan (1965).

A frequently suggested plan for dealing with problem cases in school is to use special classes. An extensive discussion of this plan is found in Long and Morse (1966). The child's behavior is interpreted as indicating that he has difficulty in "fitting into" the regular classes and that therefore a special class is needed.

For children who are overstimulated by being in a group this appears a logical procedure. But for children whose deviance is produced at least in part by a misunderstanding of other children or by not having had an opportunity to learn the simpler procedures for resolving differences with other children, removal from the group is not very likely to help them learn how to work and play with others. Similarly, if the deviance has resulted from conditions in the home environment, a special class is not likely to alter the home situation.

These considerations suggest again that in any program of secondary prevention and control it appears from the findings of the complex multicausation of deviance that the first requirement after the deviance has been located is a careful diagnosis of the difficulty. Since behavior problems may arise from various combinations of experiences in the home, school, and community and organic deficiencies in the child, the diagnostic facility would have to be one which can make a study of the child in his total setting, including his home, school, and community relationships. This conception has given impetus to the development of the community clinic appearing as a separate agency, as a community child-guidance clinic, a mental health center, or an outpatient department of a general hospital. The importance of the availability of a comprehensive diagnostic facility cannot be overemphasized.

Primary Prevention. Recently there has developed a clear realization that programs involving work with the child in difficulty are essentially secondary prevention and that more concern needs to be given to the forces, conditions, or influences which originally produced the difficulty (Lemkau, 1955; Caplan, 1964; Ojemann, 1954). Thus, one could provide the deviant child with a counselor and a job, but if much of his difficulty arose from being subjected to arbitrary discrimination or neglect at home or at school, these forces remain at work unless the child is taken into another home and school or unless a change can be made in parent and teacher. Similarly, the deviant can be supplied with a counselor and a job, but if the area in which his talents lie is one that is not valued by the community in which he lives, it will be difficult for him to overcome his feeling of discrimination or alienation (Schreiber, 1966).

Again, in providing for the education of children from poverty areas or the "disadvantaged" child, it has been found that such children often lack the basic experiences that readiness for school implies. Silberman (1965), for example, reports that the child from the slums often lacks much of the sensory development that ordinary experience provides. Providing such experiences in school or community programs is most helpful, but as the child goes on through school the home influence continues to fail to provide the experiences that will help the child to profit most from his school experiences unless some change is made in the home.

Identifying and seeking to change the noxious forces which produced the difficulty is the role of primary prevention. A thoroughgoing primary preventive program requires a recognition of the many influences that affect the growing child. These include parents in the home, the teachers and other personnel at school, the mass media, the various aspects of the legal and law-enforcing agencies in the community (Fahr & Ojemann, 1962), the employer, and the opportunities used to develop one's abilities to make a contribution as a person of significance (Ojemann, 1958).

The basic problem in the prevention of deviant behavior is one of providing what every child needs as a growing human personality to develop into a constructive, cooperative, contributing member of society. This means that the various environments in which the child lives—the family, school, church, employment situation, and the community—are to be shaped by persons who appreciate the needs of the growing personality (Ojemann, 1960). This suggests an extensive education of parents, teachers, employers, religious personnel, judges, policemen, youth leaders, social workers, and community citizens generally—all who have a responsibility in shaping the environment of the growing child. Such a conception of the nature of primary prevention also includes the cultivation in the child himself of an appreciation of the effect of various experiences on his own growth and development (Ojemann, 1955).

Much effort is expended to describe the ills of the current scene. Relatively little has been done in the past to help youth gain some insight into how community attitudes and behavior came about, the meaning and source of the inconsistency in adults as well as youth, and the common struggle of all men against ignorance and human limitations (Ojemann, 1962). If the growing child were helped to understand and appreciate the nature and origin of community attitudes, it appears he would be in a better position to consider them for what they are—namely, the attitudes and behavior of a generation many of whose members did not have an opportunity to learn what is presently known concerning the needs of the human personality and how such needs can be supplied.

These considerations suggest that a comprehensive approach to the problem of behavior deviance is needed. When the deviance occurs, the child has to be helped through redevelopment (secondary prevention), but if the goal is to prevent the development of deviance a removal of the "sources of infection" and their replacement by influences which promote the constructive development of the personality are indicated. The development of these conceptions of primary prevention is still in its infancy (Caplan, 1964).

Ralph H. Ojemann
Educational Research Council
of Greater Cleveland

References

Ahlstrom, Winton N. "Masculine Identity and Career Problems for Boys." In *Social Deviancy Among Youth*, 65th Yearbook, Part I, NSSE, 1966. p. 135–63.

Anderson, H. H., and Brewer, Joseph E. "Studies of Teachers' Classroom Personalities. II: Effects of Teachers' Dominative and Integrative Contacts on Children's Classroom Behavior." *Applied Psychol Monogr* 8: No. 128; 1946.

Bower, Eli M. "Early Identification of Maladjusted School Children." *B California State Dept Ed* 26:232–6; 1955.

Bower, Eli M. "A Conceptual Framework for the Development of Programs for Emotionally Disturbed Children." In Landy, Edward, and Kroll, Arthur M. (Eds.) *Guidance in American Education*. Vol. 3: *Needs and Influencing Forces*. Harvard U Press, 1966. p. 131–44.

Bower, Eli M., and others. "A Process for Early Identification of Emotionally Disturbed Children." *B California State Dept Ed* 27:1–111; 1958.

Byerly, Carl L. "A School Curriculum for Prevention and Remediation of Deviancy." In *Social Deviancy*

Among Youth, 65th Yearbook, Part I, NSSE, 1966. p. 221–57.

Caplan, Gerald. *Principles of Preventive Psychiatry*. Basic Books, 1964. 304p.

Chandler, Caroline A. "The Role of the Community Treatment Facility in Prevention." In Ojemann, Ralph H. (Ed.) *The School and the Community Treatment Facility in Preventive Psychiatry*, Proceedings of the Fifth Institute on Preventive Psychiatry, U Iowa, 1965. p. 78–98.

Cloward, Richard A., and Ohlin, Lloyd E. *Delinquency and Opportunity*. Free, 1960, 220p.

Craig, Maude M., and Glick, Selma J. "Ten Years' Experience with the Glueck Social Prediction Table." *Crime and Delinquency* 9–10:249–61; 1963.

Eckerson, Louise Omwake, and Smith, Hyrum M. (Coordinators) *Scope of Pupil Personnel Services*. GPO, 1966. 95p.

Erikson, Erik H. "Identity and the Life Cycle: Selected Papers." *Psychol Issues* 1:18–164; 1959.

Fahr, Samuel M., and Ojemann, Ralph H. "The Use of Social and Behavioral Science Knowledge in Law." *Iowa Law R* 48:59–75; 1962.

Fannin, Leon F., and Clinard, Marshall B. "Differences in the Conception of Self as a Male Among Lower and Middle-class Delinquents." *Social Problems* 13:205–14; 1965.

Fanshel, David, and others. "A Study of Behavior Disorders of Children in Residential Treatment Centers." *J Psychol Stud* 14:1–23; 1963.

Glueck, Eleanor T. "Distinguishing Delinquents from Pseudodelinquents." *Harvard Ed R* 36:119–30; 1966(*a*).

Glueck, Eleanor T. "Identification of Potential Delinquents at Age 2–3 Years." *Int J Social Psychiatry*. 12:5–16; 1966(*b*).

Glueck, Eleanor T. "A More Discriminative Instrument for the Identification of Potential Delinquents at School Entrance." *J Criminal Law, Criminology, Police Sci* 57:27–30; 1966(*c*).

Glueck, Sheldon, and Glueck, Eleanor, *Unraveling Juvenile Delinquency*. The Commonwealth Fund, 1950. 399p.

Havighurst, Robert J. "Social Deviancy Among Youth: Types and Significance." In *Social Deviancy Among Youth*, 65th Yearbook, Part I, NSSE, 1966. p. 59–77.

Healy, William, and Bronner, Augusta F. *New Light on Delinquency and Its Treatment*. Yale U Press, 1936. 226p.

Healy, William, and Bronner, Augusta F. "The Child Guidance Clinic: Birth and Growth of an Idea." In Lowrey, Lawson G. (Ed.) *Orthopsychiatry, 1923–1948: Retrospect and Prospect*. American Orthopsychiatric Association, 1948. p. 14–49.

Hewitt, Lester E., and Jenkins, Richard L. *Fundamental Patterns of Maladjustment: The Dynamics of Their Origin*. State of Illinois, Springfield, 1946. 110p.

Journal of Orthopsychiatry; 1965–1966. Numerous case studies.

Keir, Gertrude. "Symposium on Psychologists and Psychiatrists in the Child Guidance Service. 3: A History of Child Guidance." *Br J Ed Psychol* 22:5–29; 1952.

Kvaraceus, William C. "Programs of Early Identification and Prevention of Delinquency." In *Social Deviancy Among Youth*, 65th Yearbook, Part I, NSSE, 1966. p. 189–220.

Lambert, Nadine M., and Bower, Eli M. *A Process for In-school Screening of Children with Emotional Handicaps*. ETS, 1961. 72p.

Landis, Judson R., and Scarpitti, Frank R. "Perceptions Regarding Value Orientation and Legitimate Opportunity: Delinquents and Nondelinquents." *Social Forces* 44:83–91; 1965.

Lapouse, Rema, and Monk, Mary A. "Behavior Deviations in a Representative Sample of Children: Variation by Sex, Age, Race, Social Class, and Family Size." *Am J. Orthopsychiatry* 34:436–46; 1964.

Lemkau, Paul V. *Mental Hygiene in Public Health*, 2nd ed. McGraw-Hill, 1955. 450p.

Lewin, Kurt, and others. "An Experimental Approach to the Study of Autocracy and Democracy." *Sociometry* 1:292–300; 1938.

Lively, Edwin L., and others. "Self-concept as a Predictor of Juvenile Delinquency." *Am J Orthopsychiatry* 32:159–69; 1962.

Long, Nicholas J., and Morse, William C. "Special Classes for Children with Social and Emotional Problems in the Public Schools." In *Social Deviancy Among Youth*, 65th Yearbook, Part I, NSSE, 1966. p. 315–43.

Massimo, Joseph L., and Shore, Milton F. "The Effectiveness of a Comprehensive, Vocationally Oriented Psychotherapeutic Program for Delinquent Boys." *Am J Orthopsychiatry* 33:635; 1963.

Michael, Carmen M., and Houck, Frances C. "Use of the Glueck Prediction Scale in Identification of Potential Delinquents." *Corrective Psychiatry and J Social Therapy* 11:66–71; 1965.

Miller, Walter B. "The Impact of a 'Total Community' Delinquency Control Project." *Social Problems* 10:168–91; 1962.

National Society for the Study of Education. *Juvenile Delinquency and the Schools*. 47th Yearbook, Part I, NSSE, 1948. 397p.

National Society for the Study of Education. *Social Deviancy Among Youth*. 65th Yearbook, Part I, NSSE, 1966. 434p.

Ojemann, Ralph H. *Personality Adjustment of Individual Children*. Research Pamphlet Series No. 5. NEA, 1954, 32p.

Ojemann, Ralph H. "The Role of the Community in the Mental-health Program of the School." In *Mental Health in Modern Education*, 54th Yearbook, Part II, NSSE, 1955. p. 125–41.

Ojemann, Ralph H. (Ed.) *Four Basic Aspects of Preventive Psychiatry*. Report of the First Institute on Preventive Psychiatry. State U Iowa, 1957. 122p.

Ojemann, Ralph H. "The Human Relations Program at the State University of Iowa." *Personnel Guid J* 37:199–206; 1958.

Ojemann, Ralph H. "Sources of Infection Revealed in Preventive Psychiatry Research." *Am J Public Health.* 50:329–35; 1960.

Ojemann, Ralph H. "The Significance of Education in Human Behavior for the Social Development of Children." *Int R Educ* 8:61–73; 1962.

Pancratz, L. D., and Buchan, G. "Exploring Psychodramatic Techniques with Defective Delinquents." *Group Psychotherapy* 18:136–41; 1965.

Peterson, D. R. "Behavior Problems of Middle Childhood." *J Cons Psychol* 25:205–9; 1961.

Powers, Edwin, and Witmer, Helen L. *An Experiment in the Prevention of Delinquency.* Columbia U Press, 1951. 649p.

Quay, Herbert C., and others. "Personality Patterns of Pupils in Special Classes for the Emotionally Disturbed." *Exceptional Children* 32:297–301; 1966.

Redl, Fritz, and Wattenberg, W. W. *Mental Hygiene in Teaching.* Harcourt, 1959. 562p.

Reiss, Albert John. "Social Correlates of Psychological Types of Delinquency." *Am Sociol R* 17:710–8; 1952.

Robins, Lee N., and others. "The Interaction of Social Class and Deviant Behavior." *Am Sociol R* 27:480–91; 1962.

Scarpitti, Frank R. "Delinquent and Nondelinquent Perceptions of Self, Values and Opportunity." *Mental Hygiene* 49:399–404; 1965.

Schreiber, Daniel. "Work-experience Programs." In *Social Deviancy Among Youth,* 65th Yearbook, Part I, NSSE, 1966. p. 280–314.

Schwitzgebel, Ralph. *Street-corner Research: An Experimental Approach to the Juvenile Delinquent.* Harvard U Press, 1964. 163p.

Shakow, David. "One Hundred Years of American Psychiatry: A Special Review." *Psychol B* 42:423–32; 1945.

Shaw, Clifford R., and McKay, Henry D. *Social Factors in Juvenile Delinquency.* Vol. 2 of National Commission on Law Observance and Enforcement, *Report on the Causes of Crime.* GPO, 1931. 196p.

Shaw, Clifford R., and McKay, Henry D. *Juvenile Delinquency and Urban Areas.* U Chicago Press, 1942. 451p.

Silberman, Charles E. *Crisis in Black and White.* Random, 1965. 370p.

Smith, M. Brewster. "Recent Contributions of Research to Development of the Concept of 'Creative Mental Health.'" In Ojemann, Ralph H. (Ed.) *Recent Contributions of Biological and Psychosocial Investigations to Preventive Psychiatry,* Proceedings of the Second Institute on Preventive Psychiatry, U Iowa, 1959. p. 12–45.

Smith, M. Brewster. "'Mental Health' Reconsidered. A Special Case of the Problem of Values in Psychology." *Am Psychologist* 16:299–306; 1961.

Smith, Sydney. "The Adolescent Murderer." *Archives of Gen Psychiatry* 13:310–9; 1965.

Stevenson, George S., and Smith, Geddes. *Child Guidance Clinics.* The Commonwealth Fund, 1934. 186p.

Stott, D. H. *Delinquency and Human Nature.* Carnegie United Kingdom Trust, 1950. 460p.

U.S. Children's Bureau. *Juvenile Court Statistics, 1962.* GPO, 1963. 23p.

U.S. Department of Health, Education, and Welfare. *Digest of Educational Statistics.* GPO, 1963. 135p.

U.S. Department of Health, Education, and Welfare. *Digest of Educational Statistics.* GPO, 1965. 174p.

U.S. Federal Bureau of Investigation. *Uniform Crime Reports for the United States and Its Possessions, 1966.* GPO, 1966. 192p.

Watson, Robert I. "A Brief History of Clinical Psychology." *Psychol B* 50:321–46; 1953.

Witmer, Lightner. "Clinical Psychology." *Psychol Clinic* 1:1–9; 1907.

BUSINESS EDUCATION

The term "Business education" has several meanings. At collegiate levels the term refers, on the one hand, to preparation for professional careers in the broad area of business management and administration and, on the other, to the preparation of teachers of business subjects at collegiate and secondary-school levels. In the secondary schools the term refers both to vocational objectives—preparation for initial office or distributive occupations; and to nonvocational objectives—general or basic business, consumer, and economic information and understandings applicable to all persons as part of general education, as well as beginning typewriting and, in the view of some, beginning bookkeeping.

Collegiate business education is here treated first and then, in turn, the series of subject-matter areas within secondary-school business education. At some small sacrifice of breadth, major attention is given to those researches and trends that appear to have important implications for the content and conduct of instruction—not seldom, ones that provide a basis for important correctives to conventional practices and understandings.

COLLEGIATE EDUCATION FOR MANAGEMENT. From modest beginnings in the late decades of the nineteenth century, there were by the late 1950's 581 collegiate divisions, departments, and schools for undergraduate business studies (Pierson & others, 1959). Among 1,964 graduates, the 65,614 recipients of degrees in business and commerce accounted for 10.6 percent of all earned degrees (P. Wright, 1966), a decrease from a peak of 15.5 percent in 1949 and from the 12 to 13 percent levels of the 1950's (Gordon & Howell, 1959).

Curriculum and Objectives. A major purpose of collegiate education for business has been professional training for business leadership and of the specialists who serve management: accountants, statisticians, economists, and others. However, the curricula in accounting and business administration of early years rapidly proliferated into a number of discrete specializations oriented toward initial job preparation (Lee, 1956). That orientation, among other things, has been attacked in two searching and highly critical studies of collegiate business education: that of Gordon and Howell (1959) for the Ford Foundation, evaluatively summarized by Silk (1960), and that of Pierson and (thirteen) others (1959), descriptively summarized by Finberg (1960). The two studies also criticize the narrowly descriptive treatment of subject matter and recommend an analytic treatment bearing on managerial decision making as proper for lifetime careers in business. Specific preparation for narrowly defined entry jobs, they say, should be relegated to the junior college and the high school. The two studies point to the emergence of a systematic body of knowledge applicable to business problems that should form the core of collegiate education for business. As a spokesman for the contrary view, Gallagher has suggested that managerial ability is best developed through experience, with "additional study and training at strategic points of advancement," and has insisted that "the primary target of undergraduate schools of business, as well as the overriding concern of graduate schools of business, must be the area of first employment upon conclusion of the degree" (1963).

A number of later studies have been carried out that bear on some of the recommendations and implications of the Ford and Carnegie reports. One implication—that business careers are not notably tied to specific collegiate preparation—was corroborated in a survey of the occupational history of graduates of one reasonably typical collegiate school of business from one through ten years after graduation (West, 1960a). It was found that five-sixths of the accountants and those in educational positions had been specifically prepared for their occupations as undergraduates. For all other business occupations, on the other hand, only 3.5 of every 6 persons (58 percent) had majored in directly relevant undergraduate specializations, such as marketing, economics, and management (general, financial, personnel). Secretarial training is an instance of specific job preparation that the Ford and Carnegie reports recommended for removal from senior college offerings. Lowe (1966) canvassed deans of collegiate business schools (mostly in Texas) and found some discarding of secretarial programs, some offering of credit only for advanced-skill courses, and a trend toward increased management orientation in secretarial programs. However, despite a variety of pressures in the other direction, the majority of deans reported retention of these programs.

BUSINESS-TEACHER EDUCATION. While alternatives to collegiate programs do exist for the training of secretaries, Lowe's findings (1966) suggest that there are no viable alternatives to collegiate secretarial programs for that part of the preparation of teachers of secretarial skills designed to produce sufficient proficiency in the subjects to be taught.

Concerning collegiate curricula in the light of certification requirements for high school business teachers, Hohbach (1962) found a trend toward requiring specific preparation for the subject(s) taught, toward several-subject rather than one-subject preparation, an increase in general education requirements, and numerous discrepancies between state certification requirements and those recommended by the National Association for Business Teacher Education (NABTE). On the continuous need to bring general instructional practices into closer accord with best practices, college teacher education staffs are presumably more closely conversant with recent research findings and their implications than are high school classroom teachers. If so, it is disturbing that the attitudes toward instructional practices among student teachers were found to be in closer accord with those of their supervising teachers than with those of their professors in college methods courses (Cooper, 1962). In a study of "critical incidents" among distributive occupations students and teacher coordinators, Samson (1964) identified particular effective and ineffective behaviors pertaining to instruction in and coordination of distributive education programs and found a higher percentage of effective behaviors among younger and less experienced teacher-coordinators than among their older colleagues.

SECONDARY SCHOOL ENROLLMENTS AND STUDENT CHARACTERISTICS. In business education more than in any other field pupils take two or more subjects simultaneously (e.g., shorthand and typewriting). Including these duplications, business education enrollments in 1961 were 57 percent of total enrollments in grades 9–12. Of these, 39.3 percent were in nonvocational subjects (general or basic business, business arithmetic and English, business law, economic geography, beginning typewriting) and 17.5 percent in vocational office education subjects (advanced typewriting and bookkeeping, shorthand, office machines and office practice, cooperative office training, and clerical practice) (G. Wright, 1965). A handful of others were in distributive education.

Applying the arithmetic that follows from the assumption of normally distributed scores to the findings of Poindexter (1963), who surveyed the IQ's of 5,200 graduates of 33 high schools, it appears that the median IQ of business majors was six points lower than that of other majors; 7.9 percent of business majors and 11.7 percent of other majors had IQ's above 120; among business graduates, the median IQ of stenographic majors was four points higher than that of clerical majors.

Implications for Objectives. Poindexter's results (1963) corroborate general opinion and are not unrelated to Kennedy's finding (1963) that a business background in high school did not lead to higher achievement in college business subjects than did an academic high school background. A correlation of only .18 was found between high school bookkeeping grades and achievement in elementary college accounting (Cannon, 1964). Findings such as those of Kennedy and Cannon call into question the purported college preparatory function of some aspects of conventional high school business programs and suggest that these programs are not sufficiently challenging to attract bright students. Suggestions for attracting more of the academically talented to business subjects (Olson & Swearingen, 1961) necessarily focus on upgrading of curricula, and studies by Scriven and Surina are suggestive. Scriven (1965) found that high school students who have college-level abilities learned as much from a college-level course in elementary economic principles as college students did. Although probable differences in motivation were not controlled, Surina (1963) found that supplementary units in college accounting added to high school bookkeeping instruction led to scores on a college accounting test greatly superior to those of bookkeeping students not given the supplementary units. Although it is not surprising that those who are taught more outscore those who are taught less, these findings suggest the directions curricular revision could successfully take on behalf of the college-bound high school student.

For students for whom high school education is terminal, profound implications for clerical and office-occupations curricula arise from occupational trends, which suggest that some aspects of conventional high school programs are tending toward obsolescence.

OCCUPATIONAL TRENDS. With few exceptions, the occupations represented by the vocational objectives of secondary-school business education fit within the federal occupational census designations of "sales" and of "clerical and kindred" workers. From 1950 to 1960 sales work held steady, and it is not expected to be notably affected by technological developments (Diebold, 1963). Office occupations present a rather different picture. While decennial census data show steady increases in clerical workers, with further increases expected in the coming years (U.S. Department of Labor, 1963), the trends and expectations are not uniform across all office occupations. From 1950 to 1960 the percentage of bookkeepers in the labor force decreased slightly, and, except for the small office in which the bookkeeper does other things as well, bookkeepers are expected to be hit heavily by automation (Diebold, 1963; Hoos, 1961; Rosenberg, 1966). More generally, in her even-handed treatment of automation in the office Hoos (1961) points to increased specialization of function, to the eventual elimination of those low-grade, repetitive clerical tasks most susceptible to automation (already apparent in banks, insurance companies, and other substantial employers of clerks); to clerical work becoming more routine, monotonous, pressurized, and confining; to the office becoming more like a factory as automation makes possible precise measurement of output (with attendant effects on middle-class ideas about the gentility of white collar jobs); and to the increasing obsolescence of key-punch operators with the rapid development of point-of-origin recording devices, permitting direct tape-to-card conversion and requiring only ordinary typing skill. In support of Hoos's prediction, Cook and Lanham (1966), in a massive study of entry employment among high school graduates (plus a small handful of senior dropouts) in office and retail occupations in Detroit, found that clerical entrants decreased to 39 percent in 1964–65 from the 46-percent levels for 1962–1964 —the offsetting increase being among the unskilled. At the same time, clerical positions greatly outnumbered any others as entry positions for high school graduates. In connection with the possibility that automatic data processing itself creates jobs for those with a high school education, Jones (1966), in a questionnaire survey of 69 computer installations, reported that of 54 job titles within the field of digital computers, 27 were first-level occupations for which there were no experience, educational, or training requirements exceeding six months beyond high school graduation. While programming and procedures analysis appear to require mathematical and logical skills (Hoos, 1961) not commonly found among high school clerical trainees and while the total need for computer personnel surely will not approach the legions of displaced clerks (Hoos, 1961), many of the other computer jobs among the 27 represent at least one direction for curricular innovation in clerical training. In any event Rosenberg (1966) points to the need for the continuous collection of evidence that could either support or refute the numerous predictions about the effects of automation and, in particular, asks whether the schools have become sufficiently concerned about the pertinence of their instruction to present occupational facts and probable future developments.

TYPEWRITING. In 1961, typewriting accounted for one-fourth of all high school enrollments, including more than half of all ninth-grade pupils. Seventy percent of typing enrollments were for one year, an amount of training generally considered insufficient for the development of high occupational skill (as contrasted with that adequate for a "general clerk"). Another 2.6 percent were in avowedly personal typing courses of a half or full year (G. Wright, 1964, 1965).

Curriculum and Objectives. Several lines of evidence point to a vastly greater market for personal than for vocational typing skills, with attendant curricular implications. For one thing, the number of high school students taught to type each year greatly exceeds the 2.3 million employed typists, stenographers, and secretaries in 1960 (Rutzick & Swerdloff, 1962). Second, in 1966 the ratio of domestic sales of portable to standard typewriters was 7 to 5 (U.S. Bureau of the Census, 1967). Third, there is increasing recognition of typewriting as an ordinary writing tool for all—as illustrated by Rowe's skillful work with third and fourth graders (1958) and by the intent to teach typewriting to all "intermediate school" (fifth to eighth grades) students in the New York City school system (Hofmann, 1966). Changes in secondary-school typing curricula will have to follow from the expected entry into the high schools in the coming years of increasing numbers of students with some prior typing skill. Problems of appropriate instructional materials and of staffing "intermediate school" typing instruction will also have to be met. Modern technology, as represented in Pask's fully adaptive computerized device for training key-punch operators (1958), could readily permit an automated typing-training device on a one-station-per-classroom basis, at which students take turns. That is, automated instruction represents at least one possibility for teaching fifth graders to type. Among seventh and eighth graders, the need is to devote to their training the same seriousness of purpose and careful consideration of appropriate materials and procedures that have been given to high school vocational typing.

Personal typewriting notwithstanding, the prominence of typing as a vocational skill across nearly all office occupations is patent. For example, the study, mentioned earlier, of initial employment among 16- to 20-year-olds in Detroit (Cook & Lanham, 1966) found that 44 percent of all office and retail jobs demanded typing skill, as did 85 percent of all jobs that were not for the unskilled. Typewriting was overwhelmingly the skill most often required for initial office and retail positions among high school graduates, and the investigators recommended that it be taught to all office and retail job seekers.

Instruction. A substantial body of early and more recent experimental and correlational evidence permits specification of findings on the major instructional considerations that apply to (1) the acquisition of ordinary stroking skill and to (2) the application of stroking skill to realistic typing activities, i.e., to production typing.

Ordinary Copying Skill. With respect to practice materials, holding other relevant features constant, West (1956) found the use of ordinary language materials to result in an early advantage over the use of nonsense sequences for keyboard learning. At later stages, ordinary unselected English prose covering a wide vocabulary is preferable to a focus on the commonest words in the language (Green, 1932) and to practice on specially contrived materials representing various types of letter or motion sequences. The rule on practice materials from first to last is ordinary prose over a wide vocabulary.

On procedures, the advantage of a dominant stress on speed, not on accuracy, has been shown in numerous classroom experiments (e.g., Du Frain, 1945; Smith, 1943), and the necessity of initial stress on speed for skills involving ballistic motions was established in the tightly designed and controlled laboratory study of Fulton (1945). More recent evidence, showing reliabilities in the .80's and .90's for measures of speed but in the .30's and .40's for measures of errors (Eckert, 1960; Martin, 1954; West, 1956), further demonstrates the advantage of dominant attention to speed and, as well, the impropriety of giving errors more than nominal weight in the evaluation of ordinary copying skill.

Concerning stroking accuracy per se, nothing by way of conventional procedures has had the faintest merit: not retyping of mistyped words (Lukenbach, 1938), not the use of particular drill materials aimed at particular errors (Holmes, 1954), not "perfect copy" practice (Fraser, 1942; Nicholson, 1934), not rhythm drills or records or typing to music (e.g., McDermott, 1938). Rhythm is not teachable (Weitz & Fair, 1951); the most efficient typing rhythms are the *least* metronomic (Harding, 1933) and are "dis-covered" by the typing during the course of practice aimed at ever-increasing rates (Seashore, 1951). In general, accuracy development is not a matter of specialized practice materials, but appears to depend instead on stroking at the right speed. The dependence of accuracy on the timing of responses calls for procedures (or devices) that pace the typist at a speed a little below his normal speed. Further, the typically near-zero correlations between speed and error measures—one of .14 for typists throughout the range of skill from 9 to 108 words per minute (wpm) (West, 1967b), of −.17 among second-year typists (Ackerson, 1926), of −.07 among novices (West, 1956)—demonstrate the need for speed practice with lenient error standards separate from accuracy practice in which no attempt is made to maintain high, forced speeds. Studies by Kamnetz (1955) and Smith (1943) showed large and rapid increments in speed from long-duration focus on speed alone and swift reduction of errors when followed by short-duration equal emphasis on speed and accuracy together. That is, good overall performance, rather than high accuracy alone, should be aimed at during the short-duration practice that follows extended speed practice. Concerning distribution of practice in the light of the conventional snail's pace move toward uninterrupted practice durations of five minutes or more, West (1967a) found that typing is not a notably fatiguing task. For 30 minutes of continuous typing among 9–108-wpm typists, speed was wholly unaffected, while errors increased very gradually as the work period progressed (e.g., four more errors in minutes 26–30 than in minutes 1–5). Further, faster typists were significantly more consistent than slower typists with respect to speed, while variability in errors during the 30-minute work period did not vary with skill level.

Despite the almost religious faith in repetitive drill, Temple's finding (1963) of no advantage for it as contrasted with nonrepetitive practice over a larger body of varied materials has provocative and pervasive implications for materials and procedures throughout training. Bearing on repetitive practice and on electromechanical pacing devices (as contrasted with self-paced practice), the findings of Tranquill (1965) and of Bryson (1965), considered in the light of what is known about skill-acquisition processes, demonstrate disadvantages for highly repetitive practice aimed at errorless copy and confirm the need to set small-step, not large-step, speed goals during practice. Concerning the development of proficiency on both electric and manual typewriters, Schmale's finding (1956) that manual-then-electric is superior to the reverse order of instruction is in accord with the generalization from laboratory studies that positive transfer is greater from a task requiring more force to one requiring less force than from the reverse situation. Also, within the skill levels ordinarily developed in school training, there were no differences in proficiency between manual and electric typists (Di Loreto, 1956).

As a final but crucial point on the acquisition of ordinary stroking skill, West (1967b) demonstrated that the conventional insistence on touch (i.e., nonvisual) operation at the outset is wrong. Kinesthetic or muscular sensations were found to be undependable among novice typists and did not reach their (40–45 percent) maximum levels of dependability until 30-wpm skill levels were attained. Beyond doubt, insistence on touch operation at the start denies the novice guidance for making responses, sufficiently prompt information about wrong responses, and immediate reinforcement for correct responses. Among novices (for decidedly longer than the first few days of practice), free visual access to typewriter and typescript is indicated, visual giving way to kinesthetic cues as skill develops.

Production Typing. The ultimate objective of instruction is the development of a useful level of skill at the realistic typing activities of later life (whether for vocational or personal purposes). It has tacitly been assumed for years that high stroking skill makes a significant contribution to proficiency at real-life typing tasks. The facts show otherwise and dictate direct practice at production tasks beginning rather earlier in training than has been characteristic. Straight-copy speed correlates in the .70's with speed at what is called "problem" or production typing, whereas error correlations are in the .20's and .30's (Muhich, 1967; West, 1960b; West & Bolanovich, 1963). Production speeds tend to range from one-twelfth to one-half of straight-copy speeds (varying with the complexity of the task), while production errors are one-fourth to one-tenth of straight-copy errors (Banner, 1953; Crawford, 1956; Muhich, 1967; Peterson, 1952; West & Bolanovich, 1963). All of third-semester training devoted to production typing resulted in greatly superior production performance and equal straight-copy performance compared to those who gave two-thirds of their training to straight-copy skills (Crawford, 1956). There was no stable increase in production output among employed typists who devoted 10 minutes daily at their work stations to ordinary drill work aimed at improving copying skill (Christensen, 1957). Equal copying skill was found among first-semester students who (after the first six weeks) spent their time at "problem" typing, as contrasted with those who did the substantial amounts of ordinary drill work characteristic of first-semester instruction (Hill, 1957). These various lines of evidence, experimental and correlational, point overwhelmingly to the disadvantage of the traditional focus on ordinary copying skills and on stroking errors in straight-copy work and to the merit of early and continuous attention thereafter to "problem" or production typing on realistic tasks done under realistic conditions. This recommendation is further supported by McCoy's finding (1959) that students after two years of conventional instruction were still below initial employment standards for production tasks. Applicable to instruction in production typing is the general principle about the decreasing effectiveness of guidance as it moves further away from early stages of learning (Stolurow, 1959)—a principle that mandates early movement toward wholly unarranged copy requiring the learner to make his own placement decisions, without prior help from teacher or textbook.

Testing. Average straight-copy gross speeds after each of four semesters of training of 31, 40, 46, and 50 wpm are typical (Balsley, 1956; DeHamer, 1956). However, the common practice of recording the best of several tries at the test copy or the use of error cutoffs (which ignore all performance beyond some maximum number of errors) makes a travesty of reliability. The flat requirement is for the averaging of a student's entire performance over different copy on any given testing occasion and the scoring of entire performance—good, bad, or indifferent, e.g., gross speed and number of errors on a pair of 5-minute timings on different copy of equal difficulty. Despite the gross impropriety of giving more than nominal weight to straight-copy skills and to stroking errors in ordinary copying, many employers still mainly use straight-copy tests (Anderson & Pullis, 1965), and they and teachers would do well to throw them out and test on realistic typing tasks under realistic conditions. Because of the traditional focus on artificial copy work among teachers and in employment testing, standards and norms for real-life typing tasks are in too small supply to justify specifications as of mid-1966. Besides, the reliability of those production typing standards that have been reported is open to question. The concept of typewriting as an ordinary writing tool for all makes aptitude testing inapplicable. However, when the demand for vocational training exceeds facilities, Flanagan's *Tapping Test* (Flanagan & Fivars, 1964) should prove useful. In a small-scale study Natale (1963) found the typing subtest of the *National Business Entrance Test* battery to have a test-retest reliability of .86 and a validity coefficient (against employers' ratings) of .68.

A final word on instructional materials, whether for practice or testing purposes, is that the conventional assumptions of 5.0 typewriter strokes and 1.40 syllables in the average word are gross underestimates. Dewey (1926) long ago found 5.7 to be the mean number of typewriter strokes per word for samples of English prose from various sources, while West (1967c), in a reanalysis of Silverthorn's vocabulary of written business communication, reported 1.54 as mean syllabic intensity (average number of syllables per word) and 6.0 as mean stroke intensity (average number of typewriter strokes per word)—4.67 letters plus 1.0 spaces plus .3 for the incidence of punctuation. A swift move toward these latter values in practice and in test materials is indicated if typists and stenographers are not to be underprepared for the vocabulary of later-life uses of their skills or if their proficiency is not to be overestimated.

SHORTHAND. In 1961, shorthand accounted for 7 percent of all secondary-school enrollments and 30 percent of typing enrollments in grades 9–12; four of every ten first-year enrollees took a second year of shorthand, which was offered by half the schools offering first-year shorthand (G. Wright, 1965).

Curriculum and Objectives. Two years of instruction are commonly thought to be desirable for the development of marketable skill with a symbolic system capable of high writing speeds. Presumably, less skill is developed in the one-year courses that predominate. In recognition of that, numerous simpler alphabetic systems and less complex symbolic systems have been developed, for which it is claimed that writing speeds of about 80 wpm can readily be attained in from one to two semesters of instruction. These simpler systems are sometimes designated "personal shorthand" in the public schools. Some of these simpler systems are taught in proprietary business schools and have presumably been found adequate for initial stenographic employment and for less demanding stenographic activities. In this connection, Green's findings on dictation speeds of employers (1950) suggest that while most jobs require writing speeds of 80 to 100 wpm and higher, some 10 to 15 percent of stenographic positions can be satisfactorily filled by those who write at 80 and even fewer wpm.

Instruction. Special impetus toward modification of the content and conduct of instruction in stenographic skills has been provided by the notoriously high attrition rates that have for years been characteristic of shorthand students (Frink, 1961). School administrators seem not to have been aware that shorthand is on a par with many academic subjects in its correlations with the usual indexes of academic aptitude, e.g., correlations between shorthand achievement and IQ scores in the .50's and .60's (Frink, 1961). Better selection of students is one avenue toward minimizing human waste through reduction of attrition rates, and the prognostic tests of Turse for two-year students (see Buros, 1961) and of Byers for one-year students (1958) are applicable.

Better selection aside, a body of studies of dictation and transcription error rates, of difficulty indexes for stenographic materials, and of the consequences of two revisions of Gregg shorthand (the system most widely taught in this country), taken together, shed revealing light on (1) the nature of the stenographic task, (2) desirable instructional procedures, and on (3) optimum directions for system revision in any shorthand system whatever.

First, the finding of large percentages of incorrectly written outlines during dictation, but even larger percentages of correct transcription of these wrong outlines (Lusk, 1959; Frye, 1965) shows (1) that in an absolute sense shorthand is not regularly well written and, more important, (2) that successful stenographic performance depends at least as much on what might be called "word sense" (size of vocabulary and the ability to infer missing words or to interpret poorly written shorthand outlines from contextual clues) as one of the characteristics of the shorthand system. The focus of the difficulties has been pinpointed by Hillestad and Palmer, among others. Examining note errors in ordinary matter dictated to students completing a second year of training, Hillestad (1960) found a 2.6-percent error rate on brief forms (arbitrary outlines for the very common words), but a 15.6-percent error rate on constructed words (those requiring the application of system principles). To put it another way, three-fourths of all errors in the notes were on constructed words and only 15 percent on brief forms (with another 9 percent on brief-form derivatives). Palmer (1965) selected for examination the unfamiliar words (those not among the 5,000 commonest in the language) in dictation and found error rates in the notes of 39 and 45 percent on these words among 80- and 120-wpm writers (accompanied by transcription error rates on these words of 38 percent by both groups of writers). These findings (of Lusk, Frye, Hillestad, and Palmer) clearly point to reducing the conventional focus on brief forms in favor of early use of new-matter dictation over an increasingly wider vocabulary. Extensive practice in outline construction under dictation conditions is required. In this connection, Danielson's finding (1959) that shorthand theory (i.e., vocabulary) scores are correlated with dictation rates may *not* be taken to mean that heavy focus on shorthand theory per se is in order. For one thing, the majority of wrong outlines are correctly transcribed; for another, the conditions of vocabulary testing and of dictation are quite different, the former being untimed. There is nothing to show that outlines are written identically under both conditions. The better route to correctly written shorthand would appear to lie not in mastery of complex shorthand system principles but in reducing system complexities.

Reduction of system complexities has been the objective of two recent revisions of Gregg shorthand, the Simplified, in 1949, and the Diamond Jubilee, in 1963. On the one hand, the memory load has been reduced by eliminating many brief forms, which are now written out in full rather than arbitrarily abbreviated. More consequentially, severe problems in unwanted stimulus-and-response generalization have been reduced through providing one, rather than several, ways to represent the same pattern of sounds and by eliminating selected abbreviating principles. In general, Gregg shorthand has been made more fully phonetic. Young's finding (1965), for both Pitman and Gregg writers, of marked hesitancy at choice points offered by the theory of the system confirms the propriety of the second of the two directions system revision has taken. At the same time, Iannizzi's finding (1967) of no differences in dictation and in transcription error rates between writers of the Simplified and the Jubilee versions of Gregg shorthand calls into question the merit of the particular changes made in the Jubilee edition. Perhaps there are more important changes yet to be made. On the other hand, perhaps system revision has gone nearly as far as it can go, leaving better selection and improved instructional procedures as more promising avenues for increasing the supply of competent stenographers. Iannizzi's other finding—of relatively small improvement in percentage of correctly written outlines among second-year students as compared to first-year students—has also been found in other studies and makes it apparent that in a second year of training students learn to write faster, if not appreciably better, shorthand.

Suggestive support for the greater prominence of instructional over shorthand-system variables has been furnished by a number of studies. In deriving a regression equation to predict the difficulty of dictation materials, Hillestad (1960) found that vocabulary characteristics were much more influential than shorthand-system features in accounting for dictation errors among second-year students. Moreover, of several measures of vocabulary resulting in a multiple correlation of .88 with predicted note errors, vocabulary level (frequency of occurrence of the words in the language) was substantially more powerful than a syllabic index. That finding points to the serious fallacy of the conventional assumption that difficulty of materials is equalized by considering every 28 syllables as equal to 20 words and by pacing dictation rates accordingly. It is the proportion of unfamiliar or lightly practiced words in the materials that mainly accounts for dictation difficulty, and syllabic intensity (average number of syllables per word) is a relatively weak measure of that factor. (It is, by the way, the shorthand outline, not the meaning of the word, that is "unfamiliar.") The implication is evident: plentiful practice in outline construction through early new-matter dictation over an increasingly wider vocabulary is necessary. One small-scale study contrasted early new-matter dictation combined with a stress on system principles (as a basis for outline construction) with deferring of new-matter dictation and no particular attention to system principles (McKenna, 1966). No differences in dictation or transcription errors were found after 20 weeks of training. However, attention to system principles is not a necessary concomitant of early new-matter dictation. More important, the criterion measures appear to have used a conventional and presumably heavily practiced vocabulary of words. The important issue—that of a sufficiently different spread of vocabulary in the training and the test materials that could be built into an experimental contrast—was not tested in McKenna's investigation.

As with dictation, so with transcription. Transcription of new-matter dictation on the typewriter is commonly deferred until relatively late stages of training. However, Condon (1945), in combining early transcription with other features, found this combination to be generally superior to a combination of more conventional instructional procedures that did not include early transcription. In a small-scale study of a single class Jester (1959) found that three-fifths of transcription time was spent at non-typing activities and that transcription rates were typically one-fifth of ordinary typing rates. Transcription is patently more than ordinary typing skill brought to dictation skill. Any expectation that good proficiency at the central objective of the training (usable transcript) can follow from modest amounts of transcription practice is naive, and early typewritten transcription is required. It follows that the student must bring some typing skill to shorthand instruction. A semester or a year of typing instruction should precede shorthand instruction.

On closer accounting for individual differences, Lensing (1961) found small but not significant advantages for the availability of dictation tapes at a variety of speeds, from which the student may choose —as contrasted with live dictation at a single speed for all at any given time. Firmer results must await the establishment of criteria for identifying optimum dictation speeds and speed goals for individuals.

Psychological analysis of dictation and transcription behaviors (West, 1963) suggests that the factors governing note errors (dictation speed aside) ought to overlap substantially with those governing transcript errors for any shorthand system whatever. This expectation has received good support in two studies. Applying Hillestad's regression equation originally developed for note errors to the prediction of transcript errors, for six letters whose predicted order of difficulty was 1–6, the obtained order was 2–3–4–1–6–5 (Baggett, 1964). Applying the same Gregg-based formula to the prediction of transcript errors from Pitman shorthand notes, Farmer (1961) found the formula to discriminate high- from low-difficulty materials. Its failure to discriminate between low- and medium-difficulty materials was attributed by the investigator (despite the random assignment of materials to classes) to a posteriori finding of differences between classes assigned the different materials. However, this could have been prevented had all the materials at the various difficulty levels been dictated to and transcribed by all classes. In any event, Hillestad's regression equation (1960) provides a means of estimating the difficulty of stenographic materials.

The various routes to higher stenographic proficiency notwithstanding (through improved selection, further system revision, better instruction), personnel managers were reported to base both hiring and promotion of beginning stenographic-secretarial workers more on personal than on skill factors (James, 1963). First-level office supervisors, on the other hand, are selected primarily on the basis of past performance (with particular focus on communications and human relations skills), rather than on the basis of educational qualifications (Deihl, 1964).

Testing. Although the publishers of the *National Business Entrance Test* battery have for years maintained a studious silence, Natale (1963) found for the stenographic subtest a test-retest reliability (over a ten-day interval) of .97 and a validity coefficient of .60 against a criterion of employers' ratings. Natale's findings for shorthand and her previously mentioned ones for typewriting are in marked contrast to those of earlier studies, which showed nearly no validity for these tests against employers' ratings. However, employer's ratings are notoriously susceptible to personal factors that the proficiency tests do not attempt to measure. For example, Zaugg (1960) found low validity for the secretarial-procedures section of the *Certified Professional Secretaries Test* against employers' ratings.

BOOKKEEPING. In 1961, 8 percent of high school enrollments were in bookkeeping, almost wholly for one year of study (G. Wright, 1965). Devine (1962), in surveying the field, identified the "balance sheet" approach as most popular and mentioned the absence of good predictors of bookkeeping achievement. Although there was no control for other (and probably interacting) variables, Maier (1957) found higher bookkeeping achievement among students whose teachers presented new units with books closed and who gave oral drill. Insofar as these tactics can be considered to be indicative of the focusing of student attention and of active student responding susceptible to immediate reinforcement, they are good prescriptions for any and all instruction.

Punch-card and other machine and automated bookkeeping and accounting systems have led many to question the pertinence of traditional bookkeeping curricula. In general, there has been much wringing of hands and soul-searching about bookkeeping instruction. There is no shortage of opinion about numerous objectives—e.g., vocational, general understandings, personal use, college preparatory (Devine, 1962); but there is more special pleading than evidence on the validity of these objectives. For example, Joice (1962), in canvassing the judgments of employed bookkeeping-machine operators, their supervisors, and teachers of machine bookkeeping, reported their advice to be that the high schools should not teach machine bookkeeping. It is readily learned on the job, and the need is for good instructional materials for on-the-job training.

Sweatt (1962), while inevitably finding fundamental accounting concepts unchanged by mechanization of accounting procedures, identified particular concepts relating to payroll, inventory, sales, etc., in which mechanization has wrought changes, ones that should be reflected in accounting instruction.

CLERICAL AND OFFICE PRACTICE AND MACHINES. As broadly defined by Cook and Lanham (1966) in accordance with census usage, clerical occupations run the gamut from less than office boy to more than executive secretary. Thus broadly defined, it was found that among non-college-bound high school graduates in Detroit (aged 16–21), 54 percent of the high-intelligence group entered clerical occupations, whereas only 17 percent of the low-intelligence group did so. The investigators point to this finding as being contrary to common belief, and they urge school personnel, especially counselors, not to counsel bright students out of an office curriculum but to discourage those of low intelligence. That advice presumably applies to secretarial and comparable high-order skills, not to routine clerical tasks making little demand on intelligence. They also found, contrary to earlier studies, that inadequate skills (including basic language and arithmetic skills), not personal factors, were the primary causes of dismissal among 16-to-21-year-olds.

Concerning "general clerical" activities (apart from ones performed by those whose job title is typist, stenographer or secretary), based on job analysis and observation of workers, Van Derveer (1951), in a study whose findings have not been made less applicable by technological developments, has furnished a breakdown of six major classes of clerical duties into 69 subclasses, for each of which step-by-step operation is given (e.g., the sequence of steps for cutting a stencil, labeling file folders, etc.). Concerning general clerical activities of the sort treated by Van Derveer, Berry (1963), in examining employers' practices in relation to office practice instruction, found formal training to be necessary for typing, key-punch, and stenographic activities; for all other general office work, on-the-job training was found to be adequate. The adequacy of on-the-job training was also in evidence for operators of some office machines. Cook and Maliche (1966), in a survey of 239 firms (half with fewer than four employees) in a Michigan area of 100,000 population, found that typewriters and adding/calculating machines greatly outnumbered any others; that no previous training or experience is required for adding/calculating machine operation; that companies prefer to train their own machine operators; and that pre-employment determination of proficiency is more often applied to typists than to operators of any other machine.

BASIC BUSINESS EDUCATION. The objective of basic or general business education is the providing of general business information of value to everyone in conducting his business affairs (Sluder, 1965). Besides its economic and consumer literacy function, its "introduction to business" function encompasses exploratory or prevocational objectives. Some two dozen topics commonly treated include such areas as banking, communications, transportation, consumer buying, occupational information, money management, and business organization. Sluder also reported that interest in teaching the course is low but that it tends to increase with educational preparation, experience in teaching the subject, and work experience in business.

Paralleling the efforts on behalf of economic literacy and the massive nationwide student and adult testing of knowledge of "extremely elementary" economic understandings carried out under the auspices of the Joint Council on Economic Education (Bach & Saunders, 1965), comparable studies on a smaller scale have corroborated the findings of the larger study: disappointingly low average scores. For example, high school seniors understood about half the concepts deemed minimal for effective economic citizenship; those with an economics course outscored others; while the finding that business majors and those with a general business course did less well than those with an economics course (Deitz, 1963) suggests that "general business" instruction is mainly on a factual rather than on a conceptual level and that economics enrollees have higher academic abilities.

Testing. Reflecting the increasing focus on economic and consumer literacy, a number of tests in specified subject areas have been developed and validated: on money-management understandings by Jelley (1958), who found achievement scores among high school seniors to be related to socioeconomic status of parents; on personal finance (attitudes and achievement) by Beattie (1962), who found no relationship between achievement and attitudes but a positive relationship between test scores and parental occupation rankings; and on personal business knowledges and understandings (parallel forms of a 50-item achievement test) by Forkner (1963).

DISTRIBUTIVE EDUCATION. Distributive education is a federally supported program of vocational instruction to qualify persons for full-time employment in the sale, distribution, and marketing of goods and services. Under earlier federal legislation the program required half-time school attendance and half-time employment, with a teacher-coordinator acting as liaison between school and employer. Programs of that kind had enrollments of 38.2 thousand secondary-school students in 1961 (Wright, 1965), and 92.6 thousand students in 1965. A survey of the academic status of 2,700 such secondary-school enrollees in 85 high schools in 37 states revealed that at least two-thirds of the students ranked in the lower halves of their graduating classes, with a grade-point average at the lower border of a C grade (Mills, 1963).

The relatively undemanding nature of the program, as may be inferred from the academic capacities of enrollees, appears to be undergoing substantial upgrading as a consequence of the Vocational Education Act of 1963, which for the first time provides federal support for office education programs as well. The new legislation removes the previous restrictions on cooperative (schoolwork) programs for in-school youth and on part-time or evening classes for employed adults. In-school, preparatory training for high school students, without accompanying employment, is now permissible. In secondary-school programs the emphasis continues to be on employee training, but the U.S. Office of Education (personal communication, 1966) has reported a strong trend toward the installation of programs at junior college levels, aimed at middle management and providing for increasingly specialized training. Kunsemiller's identification (1961) of knowledge and personality factors that discriminated successful from unsuccessful operators of small retail businesses provides useful information for junior-college distributive education programs. The impact of the new legislation in the 1965–66 school year has been descriptively reported in a nationwide survey (*Business Education World*, 1966).

Among workers in distributive occupations who did and did not receive formal high school training for such occupations, only small and probably not significant differences have been found between the two groups in their self-reported judgments of the extent to which their jobs required or involved knowledge and experience, judgment, initiative and ingenuity, supervisory activities and responsibility for sales volume (Mason, 1961). If it is proper to assume that the two groups of employees were comparable in other relevant background factors (formal school training aside), then it would appear that high school distributive-occupations instruction has not been a necessary condition for employment; on-the-job, post-high school training seems adequate. This inference is further supported by the finding of the Cook and Lanham study of Detroit employment of 16-to-21-year-olds (1966) that retail occupations at the levels available to such persons have no apparent prerequisites other than high school graduation.

Leonard J. West
City University of New York

References

Ackerson, Luton. "A Correlational Analysis of Proficiency in Typing." *Archives Psychol* 13 (No. 82); 1926.

Anderson, Ruth I., and Pullis, Joe. "Measurement and Evaluation in Typewriting." In Rowe, John L. (Ed.) *Methods of Teaching Typewriting*, 38th Yearbook, Eastern Business Teachers Association, 1965. p. 183–201.

Bach, G. L., and Saunders, Phillip. "Economic Education: Aspirations and Achievements." *Am Economic R* 55:329–56; 1965.

Baggett, Harry W., Jr. "The Validity of a Measure of the Difficulty of Gregg Shorthand Dictation Materials." Doctoral dissertation. U Minnesota, 1964.

Balsley, Irol W. *A Study of the Validity of Some Methods of Measuring Straight-copy Skill.* Louisiana Polytechnic Institute, Department of Business and Economic Research, 1956.

Banner, Mary R. "A Study of the Relationship Between Letter-production Test Rates and Straight-copy Test Rates in High School Typewriting (Virginia)." Master's thesis. U Tennessee, 1953.

Beattie, A. Donald. "Relationships Between Information and Attitudes of High School Pupils Toward Personal Finance." Doctoral dissertation. U Minnesota, 1962.

Berry, Doris A. "The Role of Office Practice in the Training for General Office Assignments." Doctoral dissertation. Indiana U, 1963.

Bryson, Jewell. "The Effectiveness of an Individualized Mechanical Pacing Device, the Strong Pacer, in College Typewriting." Doctoral dissertation. U Tennessee, 1965.

Buros, Oscar K. (Ed.) *Tests in Print*. The Gryphon Press, 1961. 479p.

Byers, Edward E. "Construction of Tests Predictive of Success in First-year Shorthand." Doctoral dissertation. Boston U, 1958.

Cannon, Harold. "Prediction of Success in College Elementary Accounting." Doctoral dissertation. U Minnesota, 1964.

Christensen, Opal. "The Value of Speed-forcing Drills Administered at the Work Station in Improving Typewriting Proficiency and Production." Doctoral dissertation. New York U, 1957.

Condon, Arnold. "A Comparative Study of the Transcription and Functional Methods of Teaching Elementary Shorthand." Doctoral dissertation. New York U, 1945.

Cook, Fred S., and Lanham, Frank W. *Opportunities and Requirements for Initial Employment of School Leavers with Emphasis on Office and Retail Jobs.* USOE, Cooperative Research Project No. 2378, 1966. 133p.

Cook, Fred S., and Maliche, Eleanor. "Office Machines Used in Business." *Delta Pi Epsilon J* 8(3):1–16; 1966.

Cooper, George K. "A Study of Attitudes Held by Methods Teachers, Supervising Teachers, and Student Teachers of Business Subjects." Doctoral dissertation. U Michigan, 1962.

Crawford, T. James. "The Effect of Emphasizing Production Typewriting Contrasted with Speed Typewriting in Developing Production Typewriting Ability." Doctoral dissertation. U Pittsburgh, 1956.

Danielson, Harriet. "The Relationship Between Competency in Shorthand Vocabulary and Achievement in Shorthand Dictation." Doctoral dissertation. Indiana U, 1959.

DeHamer, Dorothy J. *A Study of the Performances of First-year Typing Students on Straight-copy Writings."* Master's thesis. U Iowa, 1956.

Deihl, Lincoln W. "Factors Contributing to the Selection of First-level Office Supervisors with Implications for Business Education." Doctoral dissertation. Ohio State U, 1964.

Deitz, James E. "Economic Understandings of Senior Students in Selected California High Schools." Doctoral dissertation. U California Los Angeles, 1963.

Devine, John W. "A Comprehensive Analysis, Classification, and Synthesis of Research Findings and Thought on the Teaching of Bookkeeping and Accounting, 1950–1960." Doctoral dissertation. Indiana U, 1962.

Dewey, Godfrey. "A System of Shorthand for General Use." Doctoral dissertation. Harvard U, 1926.

Diebold, John. "When Will Your Husband Be Obsolete?" *McCall's* 90:64–5, 118–9; 1963.

Di Loreto, Antonette E. "An Experimental Study to Determine the Effectiveness of Using the Electric Typewriter as Compared with the Manual Typewriter in Typing Straight-copy Material, Numbers, and Other Selected Typing Jobs." Doctoral dissertation. Boston U, 1956.

"Distributive Education: A Nationwide Survey." *Bus Ed World* 47(1):19–39; 1966.

Du Frain, Viola. "The Practicability of Emphasizing Speed Before Accuracy in Elementary Typewriting." *J Bus, U Chicago* 19 (No. 3, Part 2); 1945.

Eckert, Sidney W. "A Comparison of Intelligence and Reading Ability with Speed and Accuracy in Typewriting." Master's thesis. U Minnesota, 1960.

Farmer, Geraldine M. "An Experiment to Test the Validity of a Measure of the Difficulty of Shorthand Dictation Materials." Doctoral dissertation. U Minnesota, 1961.

Finberg, Barbara D. *The Education of American Businessmen.* Carnegie Corporation, 1960. 71p.

Flanagan, John C., and Fivars, Grace. "The Tapping Test—A New Tool to Predict Aptitude for Typing." *Delta Pi Epsilon J* 6(2):33–9; 1964.

Forkner, Irvine H. "An Achievement Test of Personal Business Knowledges and Understandings." Doctoral dissertation. Columbia U Teachers College, 1963.

Fraser, Marjorie A. "An Investigation of First Semester Speed and Accuracy in Typewriting." Master's thesis. U Southern California, 1942.

Frink, Inez. "A Comprehensive Analysis and Synthesis of Research and Thought Pertaining to Shorthand and Transcription." Doctoral dissertation. Indiana U, 1961.

Frye, Carolyn F. "An Error Analysis of Dictation Notes of Second-semester High School Students of Gregg Shorthand Simplified." Master's thesis. U Tennessee, 1965.

Fulton, Ruth E. "Speed and Accuracy in Learning Movements." *Archives Psychol* 41 (No. 300); 1945.

Gallagher, Buell G. "One President's Views on Schools of Business." *Collegiate News and Views* (South-Western Pub. Co.) 16(3):1–6; 1963.

Gordon, Robert A., and Howell, James E. *Higher Education for Business.* Columbia U Press, 1959. 191p.

Green, Harold H. "The Relative Effectiveness of the Thousand Commonest Words in the Teaching of Typewriting." *U Iowa Monogr Ed, Res Stud Commercial Ed* 5:167–78; 1932.

Green, Harold H. "The Nature of Business Dictation." Doctoral dissertation. U Pittsburgh, 1950.

Harding, D. W. "Rhythmization and Speed of Work." *Br J Psychol* 23:262–78; 1933.

Hill, Dorothy J. "A Study of the Effects of Drill Upon Typewriting." Master's thesis. U Michigan, 1957.

Hillestad, Mildred. "Factors Which Contribute to the Difficulty of Shorthand Dictation Materials." Doctoral dissertation. U Minnesota, 1960.

Hofmann, Paul. "All Pupils in City to Study Typing." *New York Times,* May 8, 1966; p. 1, 43.

Hohbach, Ardith O. "A Study of Business Teacher Certification Practices in the Fifty States with a Comparison of the National Association for Business Teacher Education Recommended Course Study for Business Teachers to the Minimum State Requirements for Business Teachers." Master's thesis. U Wisconsin, 1962.

Holmes, Helen M. "A Study of the Frequency of Keystroking and Reading Errors in Typewriting, Their Probable Causes, and the Effect of Remedial Drills." Master's thesis. U Wisconsin, 1954.

Hoos, Ida R. *Automation in the Office.* Public Affairs Press, 1961. 138p.

Iannizzi, Elizabeth. "Transcription and Shorthand Errors Among Elementary and Advanced High School Writers of Simplified and Diamond Jubilee Gregg Shorthand." Doctoral dissertation. New York U, 1967.

James, Thomas. "A Comparison of Criteria Utilized by Employers in Employing and Promoting Beginning Stenographic-secretarial Workers." Doctoral dissertation. New York U, 1963.

Jelley, Herbert M. "A Measurement and Interpretation of Money Management Understandings of Twelfth-grade Students." Doctoral dissertation. U Cincinnati, 1958.

Jester, Donald. "A Time Study of Shorthand Transcription Problems with Implications for the Improvement of Transcription Training." Doctoral dissertation. Northwestern U, 1959.

Joice, Paul W. "The Training, Duties, and Personal Traits of Bookkeeping Machine Operators." Doctoral dissertation. U Nebraska Teachers College, 1962.

Jones, Adaline D. S. "The Knowledges and Skills Needed by Clerical Workers in First-level Entry Occupations in Digital Computer Installations." *Delta Pi Epsilon J* 8(4):18–27; 1966.

Kamnetz, Harvey. "The Relative Importance of Emphasis on Speed and Accuracy in Beginning Typewriting." Master's thesis. U Minnesota, 1955.

Kennedy, Calvin E. "Differences in Academic Achievement in an Undergraduate College of Business Among Students Having Different Backgrounds of High School Preparation." Doctoral dissertation. U Nebraska, 1963.

Kunsemiller, Charles F. "Recognized Educational Needs of Independent Retail Store Owners in Selected Cities in California." Doctoral dissertation. U Southern California, 1961.

Lee, Dorothy. "Changing Objectives in Business Education on the Collegiate Level in the United States from 1889 to 1954." Doctoral dissertation. New York U, 1956.

Lensing, Ellen L. "An Experiment to Compare Terminal Achievement in Second-Semester Shorthand Classes Taking Dictation from the Teacher and Classes Taking Dictation from a Range of Tape-recorded Material." Doctoral dissertation. U Wisconsin, 1961.

Lowe, Helen. "A Study of Prospects for Secretarial and Business Education Curricula in Four-year Colleges." *Delta Pi Epsilon J* 8(4): 28–32; 1966.

Lukenbach, Walter E. "A Study to Determine the Effectiveness of Corrective Drills in Improving Accuracy in First-semester Typewriting." Master's thesis. U Iowa, 1938.

Lusk, Norman M. "A Study of the Comparison Between Construction of Shorthand Outlines According to Theory and the Accuracy of Transcription." Master's thesis. U Washington, 1959.

Maier, Thomas B. "Bookkeeping Achievement as Related to Instructional Methodology." Doctoral dissertation. Temple U, 1957.

Martin, George E. "The Effects of Continuous and Interval Speed-forcing in Learning to Typewrite." Doctoral dissertation. U Pittsburgh, 1954.

Mason, Ralph. "An Analysis of Related Instruction for Cooperative Part-time Programs in Distributive Education in Illinois." Doctoral dissertation. U Illinois, 1961.

McCoy, Carl. "A Study of Achievement in Second-year Typewriting." Doctoral dissertation. U Oklahoma, 1959.

McDermott, Sister Mary S. "An Experimental Study of the Use of Rhythm in Learning Typewriting." Master's thesis. Catholic U America, 1938.

McKenna, Margaret A. "An Experiment to Determine the Effect of Early Introduction of New-matter Dictation in the Teaching of Beginning Shorthand to College Students." Doctoral dissertation. Michigan State U, 1966.

Mills, Chester O. "Academic Status of High School Distributive Education Cooperative Students." Doctoral dissertation. Ohio State U, 1963.

Muhich, Dolores M. "Key-stroking vs. Decision-making Factors in Proficiency at Office-typing Tasks." Master's thesis. Southern Illinois U, 1967.

Natale, Gloria. "Measurement Aspects of the Shorthand and Typewriting Forms of the National Business Entrance Tests." Doctoral dissertation. Columbia U Teachers College, 1963.

Nicholson, George L. "Comparative Attainment in Typewriting Skill Under Two Methods of Conducting Practice." Master's thesis. Kansas State Teachers College (Pittsburg), 1934.

Olson, Milton C., and Swearingen, Eugene L. (Eds.) *Business and Economic Education for the Academic Student*. NEA and the United Business Education Association, 1961. 80p.

Palmer, Rose. "A Comparison Between Two Groups of Shorthand Writers." Doctoral dissertation. New York U, 1965.

Pask, G. "Electronic Keyboard Teaching Machines." *Ed Commerce* 24:16–26; 1958.

Peterson, Charles. "A Study of the Relationship Between Straight-copy Rates and Production Rates in College Typewriting." Master's thesis. U Tennessee, 1952.

Pierson, Frank C., and Others. *The Education of American Businessmen*. McGraw-Hill, 1959. 740p.

Poindexter, Meada G. "A Comparison of the Intelligence Quotient of Business Education Students with that of All High School Students in Thirty-three Selected Schools." Master's thesis. U Wisconsin, 1963.

Porter, Sylvia, "Typewriter Boom." *New York Post Magazine*, June 22, 1966, p. 2.

Rosenberg, Jerry M. *Automation, Manpower, and Education*. Random, 1966. 179p.

Rowe, John L. "An Experimental Project in Teaching Touch Typewriting to Third and Fourth Grade Children to Promote the Learning Process." *U North Dakota Col Ed Rec* 44:21–32; 1958.

Rutzick, Max, and Swerdloff, Sol. "The Occupational Structure of U.S. Employment." *Mon Labor R* 85:1209–13; 1962.

Samson, Harland E. "Critical Requirements for Distributive Education Teacher-coordinators." Doctoral dissertation. U Minnesota, 1964.

Schmale, Verne E. "A Comparison of Achievement of Students Using Electric and Manual Typewriters." Master's thesis. U Wisconsin, 1956.

Scriven, Donald. "Economic Education: A Development of Teaching Materials and Comparison of Related Achievement." Doctoral dissertation. U Iowa, 1965.

Seashore, Robert H. "Work and Motor Performance." In Stevens, S. S. (Ed.) *Handbook of Experimental Psychology*. Wiley, 1951. p. 1341–62.

Silk, Leonard. *The Education of Businessmen.* Committee for Economic Development (New York), Suppl. Paper No. 11, 1960. 44p.

Sluder, Lester I. "An Analysis and Synthesis of Research Findings Pertaining to General Business." Doctoral dissertation. Indiana U, 1965.

Smith, Nellie M. "Teaching Emphasis on Speed in Typewriting Compared with Emphasis on Accuracy, in the Green Bank High School of West Virginia." Master's thesis. Colorado State College of Education, 1943.

Stolurow, Lawrence M. "The Psychology of Skills. II: Analysis and Implications." *Delta Pi Epsilon J* 2(3):16–31; 1959.

Surina, Martin W. "The Effect of Supplementary College Accounting Units in High School Bookkeeping Courses." Doctoral dissertation. U Minnesota, 1963.

Sweatt, Basil O. "Concept Changes Related to Mechanization of Accounting Procedures." Doctoral dissertation. Indiana U, 1962.

Temple, Pat. "A Comparison of Two Methods of Teaching Typewriting." Master's thesis. U Minnesota, 1963.

Tranquill, C. J. "The Effectiveness of Individualized Pacing in Improving Typewriting Speed and Accuracy." Doctoral dissertation. U Pittsburgh, 1965.

U.S. Bureau of the Census. "Typewriters, Summary for 1966." In *Current Industrial Reports,* Series M35C(66)–13. GPO, June 8, 1967.

U.S. Department of Labor. "Employment Projections by Industry and Occupation, 1960–1975." *Mon Labor R* 86:240–8; 1963.

Van Derveer, Elizabeth. "A Study of Patterns of Performance for the Most Frequent Duties of Beginning Clerical Employees." Doctoral dissertation. New York U, 1951.

Weitz, J., and Fair, K. L. "A Survey of Studies of Rhythm." Air Force Personnel and Training Research Center (Lackland Air Force Base, Texas). *Res B* 51–4, 1951.

West, Leonard J. "An Experimental Comparison of Nonsense, Word, and Sentence Materials in Early Typing Training." *J Ed Psychol* 47:481–9; 1956.

West, Leonard J. "Education for Business—A Survey of Southern's Alumni, 1949–1958." *Southern Illinois Bus B* 10(4):1–12; 1960(a).

West, Leonard J. "Some Relationships Between Straight-copy Typing Skill and Performance on Job-type Activities." *Delta Pi Epsilon J* 3(1):17–27; 1960(b).

West, Leonard J. "Acquisition of Stenographic Skills: A Psychological Analysis." *Bus Ed Forum* 18(1):7–8; 1963.

West, Leonard J. *Fatigue and Performance Variability Among Typists.* Research Report 67–16. City U of New York, 1967(a).

West, Leonard J. "Vision and Kinesthesis in the Acquisition of Typewriting Skill." *J Applied Psychol* 51:161–6, 1967(b).

West, Leonard J. *The Vocabulary of Instructional Materials for Typing and Stenographic Training–Research Findings and Implications.* Research Report 67–10. City U of New York, 1967 (c).

West, Leonard J., and Bolanovich, D. J. "Evaluation of Typewriting Proficiency Training: Preliminary Test Development." *J Applied Psychol* 47:403–7; 1963.

Wright, Grace S. *Summary of Offerings and Enrollments in High School Subjects, 1960–61.* USOE, 1964.

Wright, Grace S. *Subject Offerings and Enrollments in Public Secondary Schools.* USOE, 1965.

Wright, Patricia. *Earned Degrees Conferred, 1963–64.* USOE, 1966. 371p.

Young, Israel. "An Analytical Study of the Effect of Choice Making on the Speed of Writing Symbol Combinations in Gregg and Pitman Shorthand." Doctoral dissertation. New York U, 1965.

Zaugg, Margaret. "A Study to Determine the Validity of Part VI, Secretarial Procedures, of the Certified Professional Secretaries Examination." Doctoral dissertation. U Michigan, 1960.

CHILD DEVELOPMENT

At times the terms "child development" and "developmental psychology" are used interchangeably (Mussen, 1963). Some developmentalists make careful distinctions between the two, pointing out that developmental psychology stresses the theory and experimental evidence of psychology, whereas child development includes contributions from many disciplines: physiology, anthropology, sociology, pediatrics, etc. (Olson, 1963). Actually, the developmental psychologist, like all developmentalists, should be a specialist and a generalist. He will specialize in what he knows best, the psychological approach; but as a perennial student of child development, his continued reading must span the scholarly contributions from all applicable sources. Any comprehensive review of the literature relevant to development contains a bibliography representative of diverse disciplines (Kagan & Henker, 1966; Brackbill, 1964).

A developmentalist is interested in changes in behavioral and physical dimensions as a function of age. He is interested in describing these dimensions; and, more importantly, he searches for possible explainers or predictors of physiological and behavioral change. He studies the life span—the continuum of time from conception through senescence. As a focus of convenience, this expanse of time is frequently divided into overlapping developmental periods. The prenatal period will not be covered in this article, although this is assuredly an all-important subject worthy of its own chapter (Collaborative Perinatal Research Project, 1963). This article will emphasize the neonatal period (first two weeks of life), infancy (the first two years of life), and childhood (the period from infancy to puberty). Generally, the onset of puberty in our culture occurs between the eleventh and thirteenth years for females and the twelfth to fourteenth years for males.

HISTORY OF DEVELOPMENTAL STUDY. Preyer is considered by some to be the "father" of child psychology. In diary form, he recorded the behavior of his own infant (1888). This autobiographical approach served as the impetus for later and more systematic observations and research upon large numbers of children as exemplified in Binet's study of mental growth (Binet & Simson, 1916).

G. Stanley Hall was the pioneer of child study in the United States. He founded one of the first centers for child study, and his students soon became famous in their own right: Gesell, Goddard, Kuhlmann, Mateer, Terman, and others. In his research, Hall used the questionnaire method of data gathering and amassed extensive normative data: norms for sensorimotor development, intelligence, language development, etc. However, adults were frequently asked to recall their childhood experiences in these questionnaires, and this technique of reconstruction through retrospection made others suspicious of Hall's findings. Hall realized the need for a multidisciplinary approach to the study of development as early as 1904, as shown in his book *Adolescence: Its Psychology, and Its Relations to Physiology, Anthropology, Sociology, Sex, Crime, and Education* (Hall, 1904).

During the 1920's, centers for the study of children were established throughout the country. At the Iowa Child Welfare Research Station, B. T. Baldwin charted a number of physical growth curves based on measures of large samples of children. Dissatisfied with the grossness of chronological age as the sole measure of development, he found that the degree of ossification in the carpal bones of the wrist was a more sensitive measure of differences in physical maturity (1921). Others who have followed him have found that a useful supplement to skeletal age is that of dental age (Moorrees & others, 1963).

At Harvard, Dearborn and Rothney annually measured the mental and physical characteristics of a large sample of students during their years in public school (1941). The Samuel Fels Research Institute in Yellow Springs, Ohio, tested and observed a sample of subjects from their birth to maturity (Kagan & Moss, 1962). This research is continuing and exemplifies the growing interest in the interrelationships of many developmental variables and their subtle changes and predictive values as the child matures. This study illustrates the recent move from purely descriptive studies toward a search for predictors of development. Among the many variables measured, the researchers studied the possible effects of different parental attitudes and child-rearing practices in relation to the child's age, sex, personality characteristics, later social and emotional development, academic interests and achievements, and so on.

Research in child development continues at the Iowa, Harvard, and Fels centers, as it does at the University of California, Purdue University, the University of Minnesota, Yale University, The Merrill-Palmer Institute, Stanford University, Cornell University, and many others. In fact, centers for child study exist throughout the world. The international flavor is reflected in the rosters of attendants at world conferences (Tanner & Inhelder, 1960). Even national conferences include reviews of research from other countries such as the Soviet Union (Wright & Kagan, 1963).

INFANCY. According to William James, the infant's world is a "big, blooming, buzzing confusion" (1890). This general and anthropomorphic statement is open to debate. The neonatal period witnesses an important transition from the confines and shelter of intrauterine environment to the necessary adaptation to this world. During these early days of life the infant is a relatively poor learner but an efficient adapter (Bell, 1965). Although research with the neonate indicates some success at establishing simple learning in the form of conditioned responses (Lipsitt, 1963), the stability and permanence of these responses is highly variable (Thompson, 1962).

During early infancy, most specific responses are reflexive in nature: the Moro reflex, sucking reflex, plantar reflex, tonic-neck reflex, etc. Gesell indicates that such responses can be considered important foundations for the far more complex responses that will follow (1954). Measures of reflexive responses in relation to auditory, olfactory, and tactile stimulation indicate that the neonate of three to four days is far more responsive to stimulation than the neonate of one to two days (Kagan & Henker, 1966; Bell, 1965). Neonatal evaluation at the later age produces a better relationship to behaviors at four and eight months, indicating greater prognostic utility (Rosenblith, 1964).

At no other period in life is the formula "development equals maturation plus learning" more dramatically in evidence than during infancy. Maturation involves biochemical-physiological changes across time, whereas learning involves relatively permanent changes in behavior brought about by experience or practice. The neonate's nervous system is neither mature enough nor experienced enough to localize the sources of stimulation appropriately. Development has not progressed sufficiently to inhibit inappropriate and excite only appropriate neuromuscular responses (Schiebel & Schiebel, 1964).

Although the neonate's response to stimulation seems generalized and almost purposeless (Delman, 1935), some expert observers note that the young infant is more active and competent than we give him credit for being (Kessen, 1963; Peiper, 1963). No matter how one classifies these responses during infancy, they are *the* foundation for all the infant's future behavior (McCandless, in press). For this reason, the history of child development is replete with experimental attempts to assess norms for infant sensorimotor development accurately (Pratt, 1954; Munn, 1955; Lipsitt & Spiker, 1963).

The infant is not born knowing how to perceive depth. For him this is a problem in complex and long-term learning (Goodenough, 1934). Extensive learning is required to perceive and discriminate forms (von Senden, as reported in Hebb, 1949). Further, the infant must learn to distinguish himself as an object separate from other objects in his world (Sullivan, 1947). He must learn that his arms, hands, and feet are extensions of himself, not objects separate from him (Piaget, as presented in Flavell, 1963). Although the infant is not considered truly human before he can communicate with others (Thompson, 1962), infancy is certainly the stage of "becoming human."

At birth, normal neonates possess organically complete visual equipment, but it is not until the sixth month that ocular responses are comparable to those of the adult (Zubek & Solberg, 1954). Typically, by the third day of life the infant can fixate on a source of light (Zubek & Solberg, 1954). When he is approximately a month old, he can fixate on an object (Gesell & Thompson, 1934). He normally develops the ability to visually track a horizontally moving object at 4½ weeks of age, then a vertical one (9 weeks) and finally tracks a rotating stimulus at about 10 weeks (Shirley, 1931). What kind of visual information the infant attains from these responses can only be conjectured. During the first three months of life the infant has not developed the ability to fuse the images entering the two eyes, and double vision is common (Ashley, 1961).

Carefully controlled research by Staples (1932) with infants of 2 to 4½ months produced significant results indicating that infants of these ages could differentiate colored from colorless stimuli. Spears, too, has found (1964) that infants of 4 months prefer colored stimuli (red and blue) to colorless (gray) ones.

Visual preference for pattern seems to move from relatively simple to complex designs. Fantz (1958) found that subjects before the age of seven weeks preferred a rather simple striped design to a bull's-eye pattern, and all subjects showed a preference for the more complex pattern by the age of eight weeks. Berlyne's research (1958) with infants of three to nine months also indicated a preference for the greater stimulation of complex patterns.

By the sixth month the infant may begin to show signs of useful depth perception (Walk & Gibson, 1961). Really efficient depth perception as required in reaching for and attaining an object occurs nearer the end of the first year (Goodenough, 1934).

Visual sensations, perceptions, and discriminations are continually being coordinated with information obtained through the infant's other sense modalities. Without accompanying tactile experiences—the chance to feel, hold, and manipulate objects—and without the chance to kinesthetically explore through head movements, crawling, walking, visual discriminations may not develop properly (Goodenough, 1934).

Recent research on the development of audition is fragmentary and, in part, conflicting. There is evidence that the neonate is capable of gross discriminations of pitch (Leventhal & Lipsitt, 1964) and loudness of sound (Bartoshuk, 1964). Casler (1965) found that infants from 19 weeks of age on attend to the sound of the human voice. This finding complements Gesell's statement (1925) that the infant of 20 weeks can locate the source of a sound.

The most necessary source of auditory stimulation is that of the human voice. The infant must receive proper auditory feedback from his own voice (Sortini, 1959). He needs appropriate vocal models to imitate (McCarthy, 1953). Hearing one's own voice and hearing and imitating the vocalizations of others is an important foundation for the development of language. In turn, it is language that so dramatically affects intellectual functioning (Whorf, 1956).

There is evidence of a rapid development of sensitivity to certain odors (asafetida) during the first few days after birth (Lipsitt & others, 1963). Because taste preferences are closely linked to the odors and textures of foods, research on gustation is problematic. Research does indicate that infants have taste preferences, with sweet substances most preferred, then sour, and last salty or bitter tastes (Pratt, 1954).

Accompanied by visual stimulation, tactile and kinesthetic stimulation give the human organism valuable sensory information necessary for learning to discriminate depth, form, shape, size, etc. A study done with institutionalized infants from seven months to 1½ years of age allowed one group of subjects a month of brief daily supplementary experiences in viewing and manipulating objects. A second group received experience typical of the institution. Tests at the end of the month indicated that the group given the extra stimulation was far superior in developmental age (Sayegh & Dennis, 1965). Such seemingly simple experiences as manipulating a cube, placing it in the mouth, dropping it and watching it fall through space, crawling to it, etc., may appear irrelevant or cute to the parent. These are the child's first valuable "reading" exercises. Early practice in motor movements and manipulating objects are crucial "prereading" exercises. Deficiencies in such experiencing may be related to some of the reading problems which emerge when children are introduced to the complex process of learning to decipher written symbols.

Advice given by experts on how new parents should raise their children can vary considerably from one generation to another (McCandless, 1961). In the seventeenth century, John Locke stressed the need to curb the child's natural impulses. In the eighteenth century, Rousseau emphasized the need to allow the child freedom in expressing himself, giving vent to his impulses, developing without restrictions. Neither philosophy was in error unless carried to the extreme. Unfortunately, an idea that appears new may appeal because of its novelty and be accepted with such vigor that its application is overdone.

No comprehensive theory of child-rearing practices denies the all-important relationship between mother (or mother substitute) and child. Erikson, a psychoanalytic theorist, postulates that the kind of maternal care administered during early infancy will determine whether the child will grow to generally trust or mistrust others. Physical comforting, frequent bodily contact with the mother, and a general feeling of physical contentment give the child a sense of security which will allow him to seek and accept new experiences.

Erikson makes clear that the infant is an active influence in determining the outcome of his own life. Just as his family relates to him, he is also an important influence on his family. In agreement, Sears speaks of the "diadic" relationship between child and parent (see Erikson and Sears in Maier, 1965).

No relationship with another human being is a one-way street. As much as a mother may wish to be a cuddling and fondling parent, she may find that her newborn is not a "cuddler." Although it might be assumed that all infants enjoy the kinesthetic stimulation of being held and stroked, this does not seem to be the case. Some infants are cuddlers, and some are not with an indication that more infant girls than boys like this contact (Schaffer & Emerson, 1964).

Hebb is typical of those theorists who view infancy as an important critical period for all learning that will follow. He stresses the need for "optimal" stimulation during infancy. Either inadequate stimulation and experiencing or a bombardment of excessive stimulation can adversely affect sensory development. This, in turn, will limit percepts and concepts that normally follow (Hebb, 1949). The question remains of what is optimal stimulation and what is the optimal time for introducing new experiences to each individual infant (Denenberg, 1964). Even during the neonatal period there are distinct differences in the kinds of external stimuli that the human organism prefers. Also, some neonates respond much more intensely to stimulation, in general, than others do (Birns, 1965). Thus, the research indicates that what is optimal stimulation for one infant might well be inadequate or excessive stimulation for others. Even during the earliest days of life there is a need to respect the constitutional uniqueness of the individual and his concomitant preferences.

CHILD REARING AND DEPRIVATION. The term "maternal instinct" implies that each female is born not only knowing how to but also wanting to mother her young. This is not the case with human beings. In fact, in some existing primitive cultures, it is the male who mothers the children. The female gives birth and then returns to the fields or to the hunt in her role as the provider for the family (Mead, 1935).

Research with monkeys indicates that they learn to be mothers by observing their own mothers and others and by later imitating the observed behaviors. Female monkeys raised in isolation make very inadequate mothers with their firstborn but seem to learn from this first experience and are more competent with their second children (Seay & others, 1964). Mothering is an attribute that is learned.

The culture in which one lives influences the method of maternal care that will be exhibited. Whether the human female is a permissive or a restrictive parent, an explaining or a dictatorial parent is determined, in part, by her culture (Whiting & Child, 1953). Also, mothers from the various socioeconomic levels in the United States show some differences in child-rearing methods. In general, the lower-class mother tends to expect obedience to her commands, though she seldom explains why her child should behave in a prescribed manner. If her demands are not met, she frequently uses physical punishment. The middle-class mother tends to explain the reason for her requests. She frequently gives her child alternatives—he may consider her request and obey; he may discuss his reasons for not wishing to do as requested. The middle-class mother tends to use verbal reprimands and, at times, implies that she does not love her child as much when he misbehaves—she threatens a withdrawal of affection (Hess & Shipman, 1965). Such distinctions between maternal styles may exist generally between social classes, but there are exceptions too. Studies of mothering patterns within the middle class indicate that there are a number of child-rearing dimensions, and middle-class parents may vary considerably along these dimensions: permissive-restrictive; autocratic-democratic; punitive-nonpunitive; warm or affectionate-cold or rejecting; etc. (Sears & others, 1957; Crandall & Preston, 1955).

Until the late 1950's there was relatively little research on the effects a father had on his children. A few studies were conducted during World War II which indicated that male children were more affected and more adversely affected by their father's absence than were females. Such boys exhibited less aggressive behavior than comparable boys whose fathers remained at home (Bach, 1946). Although this can be looked upon as favorable by some, our culture and others expect the male to become competitive, dominant, and assertive—to behave in ways that can be considered socially acceptable for exhibiting aggression.

Even the father's presence in the home cannot assure that his influence will be a positive one. A father who is described as passive, uninterested, or rejecting may represent a sex model that the son finds a confusing, nebulous, or unacceptable guide for his imitative behaviors. The boy may be considerably hampered in his development of conscience and masculine mannerisms (Mussen & Distler, 1960). He may have difficulty later in life assuming a normal sex role (Marmor, 1965). Certainly, father influence is not the only factor in determining the son's future behavior; however, it can be an important contributor.

The effects of separation from a parent or the parents are dependent upon a number of variables, among them the child's individual interpretation. This is strongly influenced by parental attitudes before, during, and after the separation. However, maternal employment cannot be equated with deprivation of maternal care. Regardless of whether the mother works or remains at home, the woman who is satisfied with her role will exhibit positive attitudes in her child-rearing practices. Dissatisfaction will be accompanied by undesirable attitudes and methods of child rearing (M. Yarrow, 1961). In a recent review L. J. Yarrow (1964) pointed out that separation may involve brief periods of hospitalization to the finality of separation through death. He concludes that any form of separation will vary in its effect, depending upon the child's age, the quality of mothering before and after the separation, the relationship between the parents, length of separation, the child's constitutional makeup, etc.

SOCIAL LEARNING. We are social beings, and our learnings typically take place within social situations. According to social learning theory the child learns that some of his responses are pleasing to his parents and receive their obvious approval. This approval of others acquires strong positive reinforcement value. The child also learns that many of his responses which please him are considered inappropriate by others. He will incur parental disapproval or punishment for these and begin to learn what is expected of him and how to meet these expectations. Thus, the child gradually learns to behave in a social way acceptable to his "significant others" (Sullivan, 1947).

During the lengthy process of socialization, the child selects models to imitate: parents, siblings, peers, and teachers. Much of the child's imitative behavior is easily observable in his play. Also, through successive approximations, the development of language indicates the child's gradual acquisition of verbalizations which are imitative of models around him (Skinner, 1957).

Not all imitative behavior is necessarily overt and thus observable. If a child has a very powerful figure who represents a certain role to him, he may internalize the cues presented by that figure and manifest the observed behavior only later in life, when he deems it safe or acceptable (Maccoby, 1959). The parent who serves as a model of aggressive behavior by using physical punishment extensively may or may not note aggressive behavior in his child at home. Children with such parents are more likely to be aggressive within the school setting, especially children of the lower socioeconomic class (Eron & others, 1963).

Generally speaking, the male model more strongly influences the behavior of boys than the female model influences the behavior of girls (Rosenblith, 1959; Gray, 1959). However, the degree of influence is partially determined by the age of the child. Also, there are complicated same-sex and cross-sex influences between parent and child which vary according to the specific kind of role under consideration. Research findings are conflicting, but they do show agreement in pointing out the important role of both parents as the socializers and models for their children.

ACHIEVEMENT MOTIVATION IN THE SCHOOL. Many middle-class children view their teachers as parent substitutes. In fact, this perception may continue into college (McCandless, 1961).

When interviewed, children in the primary grades express a liking for school and school activities. They rate their teacher highly, and they are sensitive to the reinforcements she uses to motivate them (Sechrest, 1962). Thus, the social reinforcers of approval or threat of disapproval which first emanated from the parents are also used by the teacher. This history of reinforcement is more frequently true for middle-class children, and their transition from home to school is a relatively easy one because of this similarity. Unfortunately, the home environment of the lower-class child can be almost traumatically different from that of the middle-class oriented school (Reisman, 1962).

A child's unique interpretation of a social reinforcer is determined by a multiplicity of factors. If he makes a correct response to a teacher's question and the teacher unintentionally ignores this, he may interpret the lack of reinforcement as an implied affirmation of his correctness *or* as an indication that his answer was not correct (Crandall, 1963). This depends upon his personality and the degree to which he has been positively or negatively reinforced in the past. The age of a child is relevant too. Young children prefer immediate rewards rather than the promise of some later, postponed reward, even when the postponed reward is obviously of greater value (Mischel, 1958; Abel, 1936). This preference also relates to intellectual levels and personality characteristics like impulsiveness (Kagan & others, 1963).

Even before the child starts school, he is an astute observer, noting the behavior and interests of his parents. Many of these interests he will begin to internalize as his own. He will be developing the motivation to achieve success in activities of value to his parents. Since he is, in part, a self-decider, his achievement behaviors will also indicate those areas of activity in which success will give him another important positive reinforcement, approval of self.

Mothers and fathers who value intellectual attainment for themselves value this for their children too. These parental values relate closely to the intellectual achievement values of daughters but not sons (Katkovsky & others, 1964). This might well be because parents and children regard schoolwork at the elementary level, especially reading, as a feminine kind of activity (Kagan, 1964), perhaps because boys are expected to be more physically expressive and active at this age. The fact that elementary schools are dominated by females might also be relevant.

The child's achievement efforts will be influenced by the potential approval from others or himself and by the kind and amount of independence training he receives. Children who are dependent upon their mothers when at home are found to be relatively dependent upon their teachers in the nursery-school setting. Mothers who frequently reward achievement efforts of their children and seldom reward dependent behavior tend to have children who exhibit independence in their achievement efforts in the school. Such children do not seek help or support in their actual achievement efforts, though they do seek approval from others for exhibiting this independent striving. These statements hold true for male and female children up to the age of six. From approximately the age of six on, there are interesting changes. Throughout elementary school, girls more often seek help, emotional support, and approval from others for their achievement behaviors. Increasingly, boys become independent of others and strive less for other approval than for self-approval (Crandall & others, 1960; Crandall & Rabson, 1960).

In essence, the achievement efforts of elementary-school girls seem aimed toward the goal of affection and approval from others. This may be one of the reasons why the female elementary-school teacher cannot control the behavior of boys as easily as she can that of girls. Boys value teacher and parental approval, but they tend to serve as their own critical evaluators of their efforts.

Vicarious reinforcement can be very motivating to children. Often a teacher will praise one child or group of children and be overheard by other children in the classroom. Although the second group of children was not directly reinforced, it may identify with those who were and feel just as strongly rewarded as their praised peers (Auble & Mech, 1953). Whether or not this transfer effect will occur depends upon the child's history of success and failure and his unique personality.

Generally speaking, the lower-class child has not learned to value the approval of adults since he has so seldom experienced it in his home. Teacher praise may have little meaning and thus little value to him. Young children, and many lower-class children regardless of age, learn faster when rewarded with something material than they do when rewarded with praise (Terrell & Kennedy, 1957; Terrell & others, 1959). An acceptable grade may be motivating to the middle-class child but have little or no incentive value to the psychosocially deprived child of the lower class. Rather than assuming that what the educator views as a reward and incentive is viewed in the same manner by each child in the classroom, learning might be enhanced by determining early in the school year what each child personally defines as an incentive (Brackbill & Jack, 1958).

Generally, children learn most effectively when their correct responses are rewarded *and* their incorrect responses are not rewarded or are actually penalized (Cantor & Spiker, 1954; Stevenson & others, 1959). It is not enough merely to let a child know when his response is correct. In fact, older children in more complex learning situations can learn as much or more from knowledge of the incorrectness of their responses. Although this is generally true, the child who lacks confidence or is fairly young might do better under as little negative reinforcement as possible.

COGNITION. In the child's early school years, he is limited in his learning to those things he can perceive. He operates on a concrete level (Piaget, in Flavell, 1963). He learns more from experiences with three-dimensional objects than from their two-dimensional representations (Stevenson & McBee, 1958). Even in coping with problems on the concrete level, the kindergarten child can be misled by his perceptions. A row of seven pennies placed close together is not as "big" as a row of seven pennies spaced farther apart, even when the child counts and knows that there are seven in each row. He has perceived the space between the first and last penny, and the longer row leads him to believe that there must be more in that row. When he sees the water from a tall beaker poured into a shallow tank, the difference in perceived water levels directs his thinking, and he concludes that there was more water in the beaker (Gordon, 1966). However, kindergarten children who are carefully instructed and given appropriate experiences can learn to "conserve" number and amount. They learn through training not to be deceived by their perceptions (Bruner, 1964; Wohlwill & Lowe, 1962).

Children learn to think logically, to be consistent, to see relations, to analyze, and to be abstract thinkers rather than concrete thinkers (Gordon, 1966). In Piaget's terms, children move through the intellectual stage of sensorimotor operations to that of concrete operations to that of formal thought (Piaget, in Flavell, 1963). Formal thinking involves, among other things, deductive logic and the making and testing of hypotheses based on some theory. Simple forms of formal thinking can be attained by the ages of eight or nine *if* instruction and experiences have been appropriate (Gordon, 1966). Methods are being devised and refined for assessing a child's level of cognitive functioning. These scoring systems have operationalized Piaget's theory in a manner applicable to our culture (Goldman, 1964). With appropriate modifications, Piaget's theory can be used to evaluate learning and can also be used as an instructional guide (Educational Testing Service, 1965).

From birth on, there are measurable individual differences in general amount of reactivity and speed of reactivity to stimulation. These response differences might be reflections of true physiological differences, with some nervous systems being more sensitive to, and thus more reactive to, stimulation in general. Observations of children indicate the possibility that they have different modes of intellectual responding to very similar situations.

Of recent theoretical and empirical interest has been the topic of cognitive styles. Some children are "analytic," whereas some are "nonanalytic" or relational in problem-solving situations that require them to categorize stimuli (Kagan & others, 1963) A child with an analytic cognitive style groups stimuli according to their similarities. When shown a card with many human figures he may group them into "people with hats" and "people without hats." The child with a "nonanalytic," or relational, cognitive style would view the same set of figures and group them according to "people I like" and "people I don't like." An analytic approach is considered more efficient, for it groups stimuli according to one or very few common elements. With increase in age, analytic responses tend to increase and nonanalytic to decrease. Generally, males are more analytic than females. As Gordon points out, this could be of considerable importance to a teacher. Analytic thinkers "differentiate the stimulus environment." "They tend to be able to separate relevant from irrelevant cues" (Gordon, 1966). The nonanalytic child is more "field dependent" (Witkin & others, 1962). He tends to be more impulsive and more susceptible to immediate perceptual experiences. He is rather impatient for his answers. The analytic thinker is more independent. The implication is that differing "personality styles" accompany these cognitive styles.

Other important research continues in the role of verbal mediators in the child's learning and cognition and the related investigations in concept attainment (Kendler, 1961).

The complex subtleties of behavior required to operate effectively and the need for one to make rapid and dramatic shifts in attitude and behavior are evident in the world of this generation. Even the world of the child is one of continual change and paradoxical demands: to conform, yet be independent; to compete, yet to cooperate; to discover the new, yet realize there is nothing new under the sun. There is little chance that life will become less complex. There is little chance that the study of human development will soon, or indeed, ever, be completed.

Jo Ann Stiles
Boyd McCandless
Indiana University

References

Abel, L. B. "The Effects of Shift in Motivation upon the Learning of a Sensori-motor Task." *Archives Psychol* 29 (No. 205); 1936.

Ashley, C. "Eye Problems in Early Childhood." *Sight-saving R* 31:25–8; 1961.

Auble, D., and Mech, E. V. "Quantitative Studies of Verbal Reinforcement in Classroom Situations. I: Differential Reinforcement Related to the Frequency of Error and Correct Responses." *J Psychol* 35:307–12; 1953.

Bach, G. R. "Father-fantasies and Father-typing in Father-separated Children." *Child Develop* 17:63–80; 1946.

Baldwin, B. T. "Physical Growth of Children From Birth to Maturity." *U Iowa Stud Child Welf* 1 (No. 1): 1–411; 1921.

Bartoshuk, A. "Human Neonatal Cardiac Response to Sound: A Power Function." *Psychon Sci* 1:151–2; 1964.

Bell, R. Q. "Developmental Psychology." In *Annual Review of Psychology*, Vol. 16. Annual Reviews, Inc., 1965. p. 1–38.

Berlyne, D. E. "The Influence of the Albedo and Complexity of Stimuli on Visual Fixation in the Human Infant." *Br J Psychol* 49:315–8; 1958.

Binet, A. and Simon, T. *The Development of Intelligence in Children*. Translated by Elizabeth S. Kite. Williams and Wilkins, 1916. 336p.

Birns, Beverly. "Individual Differences in Human Neonate's Responses to Stimulation." *Child Develop* 36:249–56; 1965.

Brackbill, Y. *Research in Infant Behavior: A Cross-indexed Bibliography*. Williams and Wilkins, 1964. 281p.

Brackbill, Y. and Jack D. "Discrimination Learning in Children as a Function of Reinforcement Value." *Child Develop* 29:185–90; 1958.

Bruner, Jerome S. "The Course of Cognitive Growth." *Am Psychologist* 19:1–15; 1964.

Cantor, G. N., and Spiker, C. C. "Effects of Nonreinforced Trials on Discrimination Learning in Preschool Children." *J Exp Psychol* 47:256–8; 1954.

Casler, L. "The Effects of Extratactile Stimulation on a Group of Institutionalized Infants." *Genet Psychol Monogr* 71:137–75; 1965.

Collaborative Perinatal Research Project, *Five Years of Progress*. National Institute of Neurological Diseases and Blindness, National Institutes of Health, 1963. 22p.

Crandall, V. J. "Reinforcement Effects of Adult Reactions and Nonreactions on Children's Achievement Expectations." *Child Develop* 34:335–54; 1963.

Crandall, V. J., and Preston, Anne. "Patterns and Levels of Maternal Behavior." *Child Develop* 26:267–77; 1955.

Crandall, V. J., and Rabson, Alice. "Children's Repetition Choices in an Intellectual Achievement Situation Following Success and Failure." *J Genet Psychol* 97:161–8; 1960.

Crandall, V. J., and others. "Maternal Reactions and the Development of Independence and Achievement Behavior in Young Children." *Child Develop* 31:243–51; 1960.

Dearborn, W. F., and Rothney, J. W. M. *Predicting the Child's Development*. Sci-Art, 1941. 360p.

Delman, L. "The Order of Participation of Limbs in Responses to Tactual Stimulation of the Newborn Infant." *Child Develop* 6:98–109; 1935.

Denenberg, V. H. "Critical Periods, Stimulus Input, and Emotional Reactivity: A Theory of Infantile Stimulation." *Psychol R* 71:335–51; 1964.

Educational Testing Service. *Instructional and Assessment Materials for First Graders, Manual of Directions*. Board of Education of New York, 1965. 27p.

Eron, Leonard D., and others. "Social Class, Parental Punishment for Aggression, and Child Aggression." *Child Develop* 34:849–67; 1963.

Fantz, R. L. "Pattern Vision in Young Infants." *Psychol Rec* 8:43–7; 1958.

Flavell, J. H. *The Developmental Psychology of Jean Piaget*. Van Nostrand, 1963. 472p.

Gesell, A. *The Mental Growth of the Preschool Child*. Macmillan, 1925. 447p.

Gesell, A. "The Ontogenesis of Infant Behavior." In *Manual of Child Psychology*, Wiley, 1954. p. 335–73.

Gesell, A., and Thompson, H. *Infant Behavior*. McGraw-Hill, 1934. 343p.

Goldman, R. *Religious Thinking from Childhood to Adolescence*. Routledge & Kegan Paul, Ltd., 1964. 276p.

Goodenough, Florence. *Developmental Psychology*. Appleton, 1934. 619p.

Gordon, Ira J. *Studying the Child in the Classroom*. Wiley, 1966. 145p.

Gray, Susan W. "Perceived Similarity to Parents and Adjustment." *Child Develop* 30:91–107; 1959.

Hall, G. Stanley *Adolescence: Its Psychology, and Its Relations to Physiology, Anthropology, Sociology, Sex, Crime, and Education.* 2 vols. Appleton, 1904.

Hebb, D. O. *The Organization of Behavior.* Science Editions, Inc., 1949. 335p.

Hess, R., and Shipman, V. "Early Experience and the Socialization of Cognitive Modes in Children." *Child Develop* 36:869–87; 1965.

Inhelder, Barbel, and Piaget, Jean. *The Growth of Logical Thinking from Childhood to Adolescence.* Basic Books, Inc., Publishers, 1958. 356p.

James, William. *The Principles of Psychology.* 2 vols. Holt, 1890.

Kagan, Jerome. "The Child's Sex Role Classification of School Objects." *Child Develop* 35:1051–6; 1964.

Kagan, Jerome, and Henker, B. A. "Developmental Psychology." In *Annual Review of Psychology,* Vol. 17. Annual Reviews, Inc., 1966. p. 1–50.

Kagan, Jerome, and Moss, H. A. *Birth to Maturity.* Wiley, 1962. 381p.

Kagan, Jerome, and others. "Psychological Significance of Styles of Conceptualization." *Society for Research in Child Development, Monographs,* Serial #36, 28:73–112; 1963.

Katkovsky, W., and others. "Parents' Attitudes Toward their Personal Achievements and Toward the Achievement Behaviors of Their Children." *J Genet Psychol* 104:67–82; 1964.

Kendler, Tracy. "Concept Formation." In *Annual Review of Psychology,* Vol. 12. Annual Review Publications, 1961. p. 447–72.

Kessen, W. "Research in the Psychological Development of Infants: An Overview." *Merrill-Palmer Q* 9:83–94; 1963.

Kessen, W. *The Child.* Wiley, 1965. 301p.

Leventhal, A. S., and Lipsitt, L. P. "Adaptation, Pitch Discrimination, and Sound Vocalization in the Neonate." *Child Develop* 35:759–67; 1964.

Lipsitt, L. P. "Learning in the First Year of Life." In Lipsitt, L. P., and Spiker, C. C. *Advances in Child Development and Behavior.* Academic, 1963. p. 147–95.

Lipsitt, L. P., and Spiker, C. C. *Advances in Child Development and Behavior.* Academic, 1963. 387p.

Lipsitt, L. P., and others. "Developmental Changes in the Olfactory Threshold of the Neonate." *Child Develop* 34:371–6; 1963.

Maccoby, Eleanor E. "Role Taking in Childhood and Its Consequences for Social Learning." *Child Develop* 30:239–52; 1959.

Maier, H. W. *Three Theories of Child Development —The Contributions of Erik Erikson, Jean Piaget, and Robert Sears and Their Applications.* Harper, 1965. 314p.

Marmor, Judd. *Sexual Inversion.* Basic Books, Inc., Publishers. 1965. 358p.

McCandless, B. *Childhood and Adolescence.* Holt, 1961.

McCandless, B. *Child Behavior and Development.* Holt (in press).

McCarthy, Dorothea. "Some Possible Explanations of Sex Differences in Language Development and Disorders. *J Psychol* 35:155–60; 1953.

Mead, Margaret. *Sex and Temperament in Three Primitive Societies.* Morrow, 1935. 335p.

Mischel, W. "Preference for Delayed Reinforcement: An Experimental Study of a Cultural Observation." *J Abn Social Psychol* 56:57–61; 1958.

Moorrees, C. F. A., and others. "Formation and Resorption of Three Deciduous Teeth in Children." *Am J Phys Anthrop* 21:205–13; 1963.

Munn, N. L. *The Evolution and Growth of Human Behavior.* Houghton, 1955. 525p.

Mussen, Paul H. *The Psychological Development of the Child.* Prentice-Hall, 1963. 109p.

Mussen, Paul H., and Distler, Luther. "Child-rearing Antecedents of Masculine Identification in Kindergarten Boys." *Child Develop* 31:89–100; 1960.

Olson, W. C. "Developmental Psychology" In *Encyclopedia of Educational Research,* Vol. 3. 1960. p. 370–6.

Peiper, A. *Cerebral Function in Infancy and Childhood.* Consultants Bureau, Plenum Publishing Corp., 1963. 683p.

Pratt, Karl C. "The Neonate." In *Manual of Child Psychology.* Wiley, 1954. p. 215–91.

Preyer, W. *The Mind of the Child.* Appleton, 1888. 346p.

Reisman, Frank. *The Culturally Deprived Child.* Harper, 1962. 140p.

Rheingold, H. L. *Maternal Behavior in Mammals.* Wiley, 1963. 349p.

Rosenblith, Judy F. "Learning by Imitation in Kindergarten Children." *Child Develop* 30:69–80; 1959.

Rosenblith, Judy F. "Prognostic Value of Behavioral Assessments of Neonates." *Biol Neonat* 6:76–103; 1964.

Sayegh, Y., and Dennis, W. "The Effects of Supplementary Experiences Upon the Behavioral Development of Infants in Institutions." *Child Develop* 36:89–90; 1965.

Schaffer, H. R., and Emerson, P. E. "The Development of Social Attachments in Infancy." *Monogr Social Res Child Develop* 29(3):1–77; 1964.

Schiebel, M., and Schiebel, A. "Some Neural Substrates of Postnatal Development." In *Review of Child Development Research.* Russell Sage, 1964. p. 481–520.

Sears, R. R., and others. *Patterns of Child Rearing.* Harper, 1957. 549p.

Seay, B., and others. "Maternal Behavior of Socially Deprived Rhesus Monkeys." *J Abn Soc Psychol* 69:345–54; 1964.

Sechrest, Lee B. "The Motivation in School of Young Children: Some Interview Data." *J Exp Ed* 30 327–35; 1962.

Shirley, Mary M. "The Sequential Method for the Study of Maturing Behavior Patterns." *Psychol R* 38:507–528; 1931.

Skinner, B. F. *Verbal Behavior.* Appleton, 1957. 478p.

Sortini, A. J. "Importance of Individual Hearing Aids and Early Therapy for Preschool Children." *J Speech Hearing Disorders* 24:346–53; 1959.

Spears, W. C. "Assessment of Visual Preference and Discrimination in the Four Month Old Infant." *J Compar Physiol Psychol* 57:381–6; 1964.

Staples, R. "The Responses of Infants to Color." *J Exp Psychol* 15:119–41; 1932.

Stevenson, H. W., and McBee, G. "The Learning of Object and Pattern Discriminations by Children." *J Compar Physiol Psychol* 51:752–4; 1958.

Stevenson, H. W., and others. "Discrimination Learning in Children as a Function of Motive-incentive Conditions." *Psychol Reports* 5:95–8; 1959.

Sullivan, H. S. "Conceptions of Modern Psychiatry." William Alanson White Psychiatric Foundation, 1947. 147p.

Tanner, J. M., and Inhelder, Barbel. (Eds.) *Discussions on Child Development.* Tavistock Publications, 1960. 186p.

Terrell, G., Jr., and Kennedy, W. A. "Discrimination Learning and Transposition in Children as a Function of the Nature of the Reward." *J Exp Psychol* 53:257–60. 1957.

Terrell, G., Jr., and others. "Social Class and the Nature of the Incentive in Discrimination Learning." *J Abn Social Psychol* 59:270–2; 1959.

Thompson, G. *Child Psychology.* Houghton, 1962. 714p.

Walk, R. D., and Gibson, E. J. "A Comparative and Analytical Study of Visual Depth Perception." *Psychol Monogr* No. 15 (75):1–44; 1961.

Whiting, J. W. M., and Child, I. L. *Child Training and Personality.* Yale U Press, 1953. 353p.

Whorf, B. L. *Language, Thought, and Reality.* MIT, 1956. 278p.

Witkin, H. A., and others. *Psychological Differentiation.* Wiley, 1962. 418p.

Wohlwill, J. F., and Lowe, R. C. "Experimental Analysis of the Development of the Conservative Number." *Child Develop* 33:153–67; 1962.

Wright, J. C., and Kagan, Jerome. (Eds.) "Basic Cognitive Processes in Children." *Monogr Soc Res Child Develop* 28; 1963.

Yarrow, L. J. "Separation from Parents During Early Childhood." In *Review of Child Development Research*, Vol. 1. Russell Sage, 1964. p. 89–136.

Yarrow, M. R. "Maternal Employment and Child Rearing." *Children* 8:223–8; 1961.

Zubek, J. P., and Solberg, P. A. *Human Development.* McGraw-Hill, 1964. 476p.

CITIZENSHIP AND POLITICAL SOCIALIZATION

From time immemorial, statesmen, scholars, philosophers, and educators have shown a concern for and tried to answer questions about citizenship. Some of the perennial questions have been: (1) What is citizenship and how does one identify its basic features? (2) What are the positive as well as the negative aspects of citizenship and how do they relate to the functioning of the state? (3) How do children and youth acquire citizenship qualities? (4) What are the significant factors—biological, personal, and social—in the acquisition of citizenship norms? and (5) What are the similarities and differences among generations with regard to civic and political values?

Beginning with the classical period questions such as the above were raised by Plato, Aristotle, Machiavelli, Rousseau, Locke, and others. The search for thoughtful and valid answers to these questions persisted through the years and resulted in a number of empirical studies executed in the late 1950's and in the 1960's in the United States. It was difficult to provide grounded and fruitful responses to the perennial questions about citizenship, largely for the following reasons.

(1) Implicit in the concept of citizenship education or character training as popularly held was an assumption that political and civic learnings are acquired deliberately through instruction in the school or in other educational institutions. It was implied that good citizenship was the product of rational and systematic instructional processes. In spite of some scattered statements to the contrary, it was commonly held that formal school training, especially courses in social studies—civics, American history, problems of democracy, etc.—does have a major impact on the formation of basic civic attitudes among youth (Patterson, 1960). There was very little consideration for the total school milieu, the out-of-school activities, and the influence of other socialization agents—e.g., the family, the church, and the peer group. As one author put it, ". . . the independent variables open to manipulation and change which have been used to produce increased citizenship have been sorely conservative in centering around curriculum, method, and student activities" (Chin, 1960).

(2) The notion of citizenship education or character training was quite ambiguous. The term "citizenship" had both descriptive and normative (melioristic) aspects, and there have been no major efforts to separate the two. Several earlier projects—e.g., "The New York Regents' Inquiry on Citizenship Education" (Wilson, 1938), "The Stanford Investigations" (Quillen & Lavone, 1948), "The Kansas Study of Education for Citizenship" (Edgar, 1951), "The Citizenship Education Project of Teachers College, Columbia University" (Citizenship Education Project, 1955)—had not been very careful in distinguishing between citizenship as a process through which one internalizes the sociopolitical beliefs and values of the system and citizenship as the ideal state of being which each member of a civilized society ought to achieve. Citizenship, in several of these projects, could mean either a process or a desirable human quality. Thus, the descriptive-explanatory usages of citizenship were mingled with the valuative-prescriptive and the applicative.

(3) In most of the earlier studies and in the popular professional journals citizenship was defined in terms of broad human qualities assumed a priori to be desirable and acceptable to all. A good citizen must possess knowledge; he must be friendly and cooperative; and generally he should demonstrate so-

cially desirable attitudes and habits. The person who does not exhibit these or similar qualities is not regarded as a well-functioning member of society. As one author observed, "'good citizenship' was equated with 'good conduct and behavior,' by either implicit understanding or explicit regulation. Non-conforming behavior was generally identified as 'poor citizenship,' and punished directly or indirectly" (Patterson, 1960). The main difficulties with citizenship defined in terms of a list of human attributes are (a) attributes are often stated in idealistic language, removed from the realities of society, (b) there is no consensus on what civic qualities a person should possess—different groups emphasize different and often conflicting qualities—and (c) these attributes are expressed in such vague and ambiguous terms that it is virtually impossible to determine whether they can be exemplified in behavior.

(4) Until recently citizenship studies have been largely nontheoretical. That is, the studies have made loose references to the relationship between citizenship and society, or they have defined citizenship as a desirable form of behavior, but they have not systematically elaborated on a theory of personality, society, or the political system under which hypotheses and data about citizenship could be subsumed. In addition to the failure to link citizenship studies to a broad theoretical framework, the earlier studies suffered from unsophisticated design and survey research tools. Perhaps these weaknesses were not peculiar to studies of citizenship but reflected the state of educational research in general.

THEORETICAL FRAMEWORK AND DEFINITION. In recent years the term "citizenship" has been replaced by the concept of political socialization, or politicization. The new concept is generally defined as a process by which a person internalizes the norms and values of the political system or, to give a slightly different definition, as the process through which political and social values are transmitted from one generation to the next. The main focuses of the political socialization studies have been the following:

(1) An attempt to explain how children and youth acquire their political orientations from their environment. Rather than suggesting what young people ought to value, these studies concentrated on figuring out how these values come about. Thus, the social system is presented as a system of actions performed by actors in real rather than ideal world situations.

(2) Instead of focusing exclusively on the influence of formal schooling, especially on the curriculum, the textbooks, and civic education programs, as was the case of the earlier citizenship studies, the new approach considers additional social agents—e.g., the family, the church, the job, and the peer group— and their roles in inducting youth into the civic culture. Furthermore, the inclusion of such mediating factors as personality, intelligence, sex, ethnic-group membership, and social class has provided a larger scope to study membership in the polity. While formal and deliberate learning environments continued to be investigated, it was realized that informal, casual, and unplanned sociopolitical learning was taking place among youth. Several investigations began to explore ways in which nonpolitical settings, on one hand, and political behavior, on the other, could be related (Almond & Verba, 1963; Sigel, 1965).

(3) The studies reviewed here have by and large attempted to assess through fairly rigorous empirical procedures the role of each socialization agent. A number of these studies were based on carefully selected samples and used sophisticated statistical techniques in the analysis of data. However, since most of these studies explored only limited aspects of political socialization and since most of the investigations could not build on the earlier literature, which was mostly nonempirical, their findings have often been inconclusive or somewhat inconsistent.

(4) Theoretical frames of reference have received concentrated attention in an effort to link empirical findings in the political realm with a body of generalizations about man in society. One such effort (Litt, 1965) resulted in the identification of three historical models of civic education in the United States: "rational-activist," "integrative-consensual," and "segmental-organizational." The first model, primarily provided by the liberal arts college or preparatory school, stressed "the mastery of the political environment by the application of reasoned, voluntary effort," and it strongly suggested that "harmony and political compromise are fundamental to civic education." The second model, provided through civic literacy and Americanization programs of the public schools, sought to "create an allegiant and integrated citizenry." Finally, the citizen represented by the third model has been the person with highly technical and analytical skills who can perform managerial functions. Instruction for this type of model citizen has been provided in "the national federal-grant university and the highly developed or prototype research institute." This particular study of historical models suggests relationships between educational institutions, the dominant social ethos, and politically relevant learning. It is asserted that the rational-activist and the integrative-consensual models have monopolized school curricula and teaching materials in the past (Litt, 1965).

Another, more fruitful theoretical setting for civic training and political socialization is proposed in terms of a political system which is demarcated from other social systems by two distinctive features: (a) the authoritative allocation of values in a society effected by the regulation, through various mechanisms, of the flow of demands from the electorate, and (b) the existence of compliance mechanisms in political life (Easton, 1965). It is postulated that a political system cannot function and persist without support from the populace. The younger generation, through the various agents and processes of socialization, develops supportive attitudes toward the regime, the political community, and the authorities. The support that accrues to the political system may be specific or diffuse—specific if it is the consequence of a particular satisfaction obtained in the system and diffuse if the system stores up over a period of time a reservoir of approval and favorable predisposition toward it. Diffuse support for the system enables the system to survive during periods of unrest and frustration (strikes, marches, acts of civil disobedience, etc.). It is hypothesized that mechanisms of socialization of political attitudes toward the system are very important in building up a store of diffuse support. Loyalty to and acceptance of the symbols and laws of government are important factors in system maintenance. The studies and proposals mentioned earlier may provide the necessary theoretical background to conduct investigations of political socialization patterns.

(5) There has been an effort in recent projects in this particular field to include subjects from other countries (e.g., Almond & Verba, 1963; Hess, 1963; Inglehart, 1967; Langton, 1966; Pinner, 1965). The fact that the samples from which the data were drawn extended beyond the national boundaries of one country partly accounted for the development of a broader conceptual framework and for the search to construct cross-culturally valid categories to compare political attitudes and behaviors. While there is a consensus that the specific historical and cultural context of a country is important, there is an increasing belief that cross-nationally relevant indexes can be constructed for comparative purposes.

THE ROLE OF THE FAMILY. The family's pivotal role in children's acquisition of social norms and role expectations has been discussed extensively in the social science literature (Hyman, 1959). While many students of personality and human behavior support the view that the family is the most important agent of socialization into the general value and behavioral system of society, recent studies raise some questions about the function of the family particularly in the development of political attitudes and expectations for political participation (Hess & Torney, 1965). Enlarging upon and somewhat revising notions about the family presented in an earlier study (Easton & Hess, 1966), Hess and Torney (1965) suggested that the role of the parents in political socialization is largely circumstantial and its influence is not based on any special effort to engage in such an activity as a social unit. The sample upon which the interview data were based included 10,165 children in grades 2 through 8, and an attempt was made to control or account for such factors as age, geographic region, socioeconomic status, intelligence, reading achievement, social participation, and religious affiliation. It was concluded that the main role of the family in political socialization or the acquisition of norms of citizenship, in addition to transmitting partisanship preferences, was in the transmission of consensus toward the government and in reinforcing other institutions to develop a system of compliance with law and a loyalty and attachment to the nation and its symbols. It appears that specific cognitive and affective perceptions about his family, e.g., the father vis-à-vis the president, the child does not tend to generalize or make the transfer from the nonpolitical (the family figure) to the political (the president). It is also important to note that children of low socioeconomic status tend to look upon their schools (especially their teachers) rather than their homes as potential sources of information about citizenship. In families where the father is perceived as powerful, children tend to show more interest in and are more informed about political matters. If there is no active male in the family, or if the parents are politically insensitive, children do not develop their political orientations rapidly.

A study of secondary-school students in Jamaica (Langton, 1966) revealed that those who came from maternal rather than nuclear families (those in which the mother is the head of the family rather than ones in which a married couple live with their children) were more authoritarian, less interested in political life, and less efficacious. (Political efficacy, or civic competence, is the belief that one can affect political outcomes.) With the exception of the dimension of political efficacy, the relationships above, as measured by an index of political efficacy, are stronger among male than female youth, and they are not affected by social class. The differential socialization influence of family structure remains with the student through the twelfth grade of the high school and constitutes a significant factor in explaining his political perceptions as he enters adulthood.

A relationship between parental overprotection and political distrust and disaffection was posited in a recent study of Belgian, Dutch, and French high school and university students (Pinner, 1965). By "overprotection" was meant the practice of parents to narrow down the outside contacts of their children and control rather closely their general emotional and intellectual development. By "political disaffection" was meant a belief that politicians were immoral and that political parties were useless. Political distrust related to the belief that the world of politics is "conflicting, compromising, and threatening." Each of the national samples showed statistically significant but fairly low correlations between parental overprotection and political distrust. Dutch students were less distrustful and disaffected than Belgian and French students. It is suggested that more detailed and refined explanations of the relationships under study will have to consider the more specific cultural conditions prevailing in each of the three societies.

The Almond and Verba study (1963) of citizenship in the United States, Britain, West Germany, Italy, and Mexico sought, among other things, to explore the relationship between participation in family decisions and subjective competence. Subjective competence is the self-perception of the individual citizen's power to influence governmental decisions. Their findings, based on a thousand interviews of a cross section of the population in each nation, indicated a connection between remembered participation in family affairs and a feeling of political competence. The relationship between family participation and political participation is apparent among those with eighth-grade education or less but not among those with secondary education or more. Also, in the United States, Britain, and Germany the relationship is strongest among the respondents over 50 years of age. While the investigators pointed to a general connection between democracy in the family and democratic participation in the system, they warned the reader against oversimplification, especially since "a number of intervening variables can blunt the impact of this democratic training on political attitudes."

With regard to the transmission of particular values from parent to offspring, a study based on a national probability sample of 1,699 seniors in 97 public and nonpublic secondary schools concluded that parent-student value correspondence differed widely depending on the particular political value being considered (Jennings & Niemi, 1968). While there was substantial agreement between parents and students on party identification, students showed less political cynicism than their parents. Although one-fifth of the student sample was higher on the cynicism scale than their parents, three-fifths of the parents were higher than their offspring on the same scale. It is suggested that this difference may be explained by a trusting attitude imparted by other socialization agents, especially the school. As on the scale of cynicism, on the scale of cosmopolitanism-localism the students scored higher than their parents. That is, the students were more cosmopolitan in their political orientations than their parents. In conclusion, it is asserted that "parental values are an extremely variable and often feeble guide as to what the pre-adult's values will be."

PEER GROUP AND EXTRA-CURRICULAR INFLUENCES. While there have been some studies which deal specifically with the "adolescent subculture," the influence of peer group on school achievement, social status, social aspirations, vocational goals, etc., very little empirical research has been conducted on the direct relationship between peer group and citizenship (Coleman, 1961; Hollingshead, 1949). Therefore, much of what is offered in this area is hypothetical or conjectural (Levine, 1963).

While not directly applicable to our specific concerns, the Coleman study (1961) of the life of the teen-ager provides several insights into peer-group influence. After surveying ten high schools in northern Illinois through questionnaires administered to students, teachers, and parents, Coleman concluded that there is indeed an adolescent subculture which has certain norms, values, and aspirations that are different from, and at times in conflict with, those of the adult culture. The adolescent subculture relies heavily on the values and aspirations of the peer group rather than of the family or the teacher. The athlete, among boys, and the activities leader, among girls, emerge as the basic behavioral models of adolescents. Intellectual or scholarly pursuits were given lower priority among the majority of the respondents. It is asserted that "the relative unimportance of academic achievement . . . suggests that the adolescent sub-cultures in these schools exert a rather strong deterrent to academic achievement." It is obvious that a substantial number of students in secondary schools look primarily to the norms and values of their friends, but the extent of reliance on their counsel varies with the specific issue at hand. On some issues the peer group is most influential, e.g., what course to enroll in; on some, the advice of parents is respected, e.g., which of the two boys asking for a date to choose (Coleman, 1961).

A composite index of group activities in such areas as (1) service organizations, YMCA, Boy Scouts, Campfire Girls, etc., (2) school-sponsored clubs, sports, band, etc., and (3) leadership positions in these groups provided the basis for linking peer-group membership to political orientations (Hess & Torney, 1965). It was found that students who shared in these activities had higher scores in participating in conversations about political issues and events, defending their stand on these issues, and expressing high interest in political affairs than those who did not. There was no indication of any influence that social or peer participation may have on compliance, basic attachment to the system, or acceptance of citizenship norms.

Somewhat different results from those above were reported in a recent investigation of the extracurricular influences on attitude toward politics (Ziblatt, 1965). The study, which was conducted in Springfield, Oregon, attempted to assess the importance of participation in extraclass activities in high school on a dimension of favorable or unfavorable disposition toward politics. After securing 526 responses to a questionnaire it was found that there was no direct relationship between the rate of participation and attitude toward politics as measured by a five-item evaluative factor of the semantic differential, i.e., harmful-beneficial, wise-foolish, dirty-clean, good-bad, and positive-negative. The same observation was made when such factors as age, sex, and party affiliations were considered. On the other hand, it was found that the teen-ager who is more integrated into the informal status system of the school has a high degree of social trust (as measured by a five-item index), which in turn produces a more positive attitude toward politics. The chain of factors which issues in a positive attitude toward the political system begins with teen-agers whose frequency of extraclass participation correlates with fathers' education, all leading to a feeling of integration into the status hierarchy of the school and to social trust. It is social trust rather than extracurricular participation per se that makes the difference.

Jamaican students who conceive of themselves as participants in a homogeneous class peer group (as opposed to those who fraternize with peers who represent higher, lower, or the same social class) with a working-class background tend to reinforce the political and economic attitudes of their class and accentuate existing social-class cleavages (Langton, 1967). Students who identify with a heterogeneous peer group, on the other hand, are resocialized into the political norms of the higher classes, i.e., students of working-class background in a heterogeneous social environment are more politicized and more democratic, give stronger endorsement to civil liberties, have more positive attitudes toward voting, and are more conservative on economic matters than those in a homogeneous class environment. Heterogeneous peers of working-class origin show less support for the system and are more ambivalent toward the system's claim to legitimacy, contrary to the Jamaican "civics" textbooks, which tend to emphasize support. On the basis of the data it is suggested that this informal acquisition of the political values of the "real" world is more significant than the information students receive from the formal educational system. As we shall see later, the formal school curriculum and the instructional methods and materials in the United States do not present a realistic picture of the political world.

SCHOOL INFLUENCES. Curricular. How does the formal school curriculum influence citizenship values that students have? What particular aspects of the curriculum are more directly related to sociopolitical learnings? These are some of the questions raised by recent investigations.

Hess and Torney (1965), whose findings on political socialization patterns among American children in grades 2 through 8 have been reported under different headings in this review, unequivocally stated: "The public school is the most important and effective instrument of political socialization in the United States." In support of this claim they provided questionnaire data on curriculum practices and various indexes of politicization. On the socialization of loyalty it was found that the school reinforced an early attachment to the nation through formal classroom rituals—e.g., displaying the American flag, pledging allegiance to the flag, and singing patriotic songs. There are some minor differences on the emphases given to these activities: patriotic songs are sung daily in 58.3 percent of the second-grade classrooms, in contrast to 14.3 percent of the seventh- and eighth-grade classrooms. On the whole, however, about 100 percent of the teachers in grades 2 through 8 have flags on permanent display, and almost all of them (86.9 percent of the combined seventh- and eighth-grade teachers and 95.7 percent of the second-grade teachers) perform the ritual of pledging allegiance to the flag daily. The investigators suggest that these "indoctrinating acts" result in an emotional attachment and unquestioning loyalty and patriotism to the country. Even though many children do not understand the meaning and the function of national symbols and rituals, the adult goals of fostering respect and awe for government are admired.

In comparison with other subjects, such as reading and arithmetic, elementary-school teachers give increasing importance to such topics as parties, institutions, and persons in government, importance varying with the grade: generally the higher the grade, the more important the political topic vis-à-vis other subjects. While, for example, the topic of political parties is not given any rating by second-year teachers, it is considered "equally, more, or much more important" (than other subjects) by approximately 74 percent of seventh- and eighth-grade teachers. The topic "duties of citizens" was consistently rated high in importance among teachers— approximately 62, 85, and 81 percent of the second- fifth- and sixth-, and seventh- and eighth-grade teachers, respectively, considered it an important item, comparatively speaking. There was some disparity on importance attached to political institutions and governmental persons between teachers and students. In contrast to teachers, students as they grow older, attach less importance to persons and greater importance to institutions. Possibly the influence of other social agents on these topics may be stronger than that of the teacher and the school. The high importance given by teachers to inculcating the duties and obligations of citizens through discussion of the law, the policeman, and the obligations to conform to school and societal rules reinforces compliant behavior among young children.

Summarizing their findings regarding the influence of the school, Hess and Torney (1965) state the following (emphasis is theirs):

1. "*Compliance to rules and authority is the major focus of civic education in elementary schools.*"
2. "*The citizen's right to participate in government is underemphasized in the school's curriculum.*"
3. "*The role of political parties and partisanship receives less attention in the elementary school than any other topic.*"

The authors also point out that the curriculum generally ignores the unpleasant and ugly aspects of political life in the United States, and it emphasizes ideal norms and myths about government responsiveness to the demands of the average citizen. The unrealistic picture that the curriculum presents about American social and political life is confirmed by investigations of civics textbooks, which we will review in another section. It is suggested that the curriculum is doing a disservice to the American child and future voter because it gives him a distorted view of his capabilities.

One of the relationships examined by Almond and Verba (1963) in their five-nation study was the connection between manifest teaching about government and subjective political competence. Seventy-two percent of those who remembered being taught about government in the United States had the highest scores on the subjective competence scale. In Britain, Germany, Italy, and Mexico the corresponding percentages were 73, 52, 45, and 44, respectively. Although data were limited, the authors of the study suggested that direct teaching about politics can have an impact on the individual's perceived competence, but the impact may vary with the content of what is being taught.

Results somewhat contradictory to these were reported in a recent study of attitudes of high school youth (Horton, 1963). The study, based on a representative sample of high school seniors obtained through the Purdue Opinion Panel, pointed to the lack of any relationship between the completion of a high school course in civics or U.S. government and liberal attitudes, which were defined as high agreement with the Bill of Rights, rejection or low scores on fascist ideology and Marxism, less extreme anticommunist feelings, and disagreement with "superpatriotic" statements. It was found that liberal attitudes characterized certain geographical regions (the Midwest and South being the least liberal, the East and Mountain-Pacific regions being the most liberal) and were related to place of residence (urban students were more liberal than rural), mother's education, student's knowledge score, absence of political-party preference, and low intensity of religious belief. It is certainly striking to note that "those who have had a course in civics tend to be *less* in agreement with the Bill of Rights." These findings lend themselves to different interpretations. To begin with, in addition to some possible flaws in the research design and the statistical analysis, it is possible that the measuring instruments are not sensitive enough to detect underlying relations between variables. On the other hand, one might possibly accept the absence of any relationship between formal instruction and the formulation of liberal attitudes—also, as reported in earlier studies of citizenship (Patterson, 1960)—if one considers the way courses in this field are organized and taught. Generally, courses in government or civics, in addition to giving an unrealistic picture of society, mainly describe or narrate historically functions performed by the government, how a bill becomes a law, the branches and the levels of government, the articles of the constitution, etc. If these courses were more analytical and functional, they would give a true picture of life, and they would support an inquiring frame of mind; both the cognitive and the affective student outcomes would perhaps be more positive. The limited experimental research on the effectiveness of social studies courses in developing critical skills among students generally suggests a strong relationship between the quality of instructional procedure, on the one hand, and skills of critical inquiry, open-mindedness, and effective decision-making, on the other (Massialas, 1963). Certainly this critical educational area needs to be explored more thoroughly through analysis of classroom interaction and follow-up behavioral studies. Litt, who administered questionnaires to three "matched" secondary-school groups in the Boston metropolitan area, found that students who took a semester-long course in civic education "were more likely to endorse aspects of the democratic creed and less likely to hold chauvinistic political sentiments than students not exposed to the program" (1963). However, there was no higher preference for political participation among those who were exposed to civic education than those who were not. It was concluded that "training in the tenets of democratic fair-play and tolerance is sustained by civic education courses within a supporting educational and political milieu." But it was also indicated that "civic education does not affect the varying positive attitudes toward citizen political participation manifested by the school population of the three communities." Apparently in order for a school program to be effective in citizenship training, especially in the formation of attitudes toward the political process, there must be concomitant support from textbooks and materials used in the schools and a congenial community climate.

The most significant study to date on the effect of the formal civics curriculum on student politicization has been conducted by Langton and Jennings (1967). The study, based on a national probability sample of 1,669 seniors in 97 secondary schools, identified eight dependent variables and tried to relate them to the number of government or civics courses taken by the respondents (none, one, two, or more). The eight dependent variables were: political knowledge, political interest, spectator politicization, political discourse, political efficacy, political cynicism, civic tolerance, and participative orientation. The investigators found that the civics curriculum had very little, if any, impact on most of the foregoing behavioral outcomes. The increments were "so miniscule as to raise serious questions about the utility of investing in government courses in the senior high school, at least as these courses are presently constituted." It was also pointed out that history courses had as low or lower impact on student politicization.

On the other hand, the Negro subsample in the study exhibited some interesting differences from that of the white sample. For example, while civics courses had very little effect on the political knowledge of whites, they did have a significant effect on the knowledge of Negroes. The school government and civics courses constituted a significant source of political information for the Negro. Generally, the political efficacy level of Negroes was lower than that of whites (i.e., they felt less able to influence the government), but the civics curriculum seemed to have a strong effect on the Negro. For middle- and low-status Negroes in particular, the civics curriculum acted to bring their measured efficacy level up to that of their higher-status cohorts. A similar relationship prevailed when the civics curriculum was juxtaposed with the respondents' measured civic tolerance (tolerance for diverse views about, for example, religion and politics). On citizenship behavior among Negroes more civics courses involved higher loyalty orientation toward the system than to participation in it. That is, these courses appear "to inculcate in Negroes the role expectation that a good citizen is above all a loyal citizen, rather than an active one." Little course effect was observed among white students.

In general, it appears that courses in civics and government have a greater impact on the political socialization of the Negro student than on the white student. Langton and Jennings attribute this to information redundancy (repetition of instruction and duplication of information cues from the mass media, formal organizations, and primary groups) which appears to be higher among whites. It is pointed out that until changes take place in instructional objectives and methods, course context, timing of exposure, teacher education, and the school milieu, "one must continue to expect little contribution from the formal curriculum in the political socialization of American pre-adults."

With regard to curriculum offerings in political education, a comparative study of school programs based on official and unofficial documents (Bereday & Stretch, 1963) concluded that the amount of political exposure in schools in the United States was greater than that in the Soviet Union. The total percentage of time in the United States and the Soviet Union given to political education (defined by the authors as courses in language arts, social studies, and homeroom and school-life activities) in grades 5 to 8 was 50 and 47, respectively. In grades 9 to 12 the percentage of time allotted was 41.9 and 26.8, respectively. Total exposure to political education for grades 5 to 12 was approximately 46 percent in the United States and 38 percent in the Soviet Union. From these data it becomes apparent that exposure to political and social ideas and issues decreased with age in both countries, but more markedly in the Soviet Union. It is possible that Soviet officials operate under the assumption that the formative years in the internalization of the political world are those spent in elementary school and that political orientations and moral beliefs and attitudes are firmly established before children leave the eighth grade. Nevertheless, it should be understood that mere exposure, calculated on the basis of the distribution of subjects in the curriculum, does not necessarily indicate the degree of depth and intensity of treatment. It is conceivable that a short but well-planned program of civic education, presented by highly qualified and enthusiastic teachers, might be more effective than a long program taught unsystematically by incompetent and apathetic teachers. According to Bereday and Stretch, the differences in political "exposure" between the two systems (especially the fact that more time is given to political education in the United States than in the Soviet Union) are reasonable, because it takes more time to elicit allegiance to the nation in a pluralistic and free society than in a more traditional, monolithic, and controlled society. In addition to this explanation, one could maintain that the Soviet system does not generally emphasize the humanities and social sciences because of its present commitment to school offerings that contribute directly to industrial and scientific development.

An index of the quality of civic education in the classroom is the teacher's perception of his role in dealing with contemporary social and political issues and his actual classroom behavior. Earlier studies indicated that the majority of the American teenagers favored teachers who express their own opinions on political and economic problems confronting the nation. A study conducted in Oregon based on 803 interviews with high school teachers revealed that teacher perception of expression of controversial issues in the classroom was not close to that of the American teen-agers (Ziegler, 1966). That is, on selected possible teacher behaviors (eight out of ten) the majority of teachers chose to remain quiet. The behaviors ranged from "speaking in favor of the United Nations" (81 percent) to "allowing the distribution of anticommunist literature put out by the National Association of Manufacturers" (46 percent) and "in a presidential election, explaining to the class reasons for preferring a candidate" (27 percent). It is suggested that expressive behavior is in part a function of the nature of the topic; the "safer" the topic is, the more willing the teacher is to deal with it in the classroom. When similar behaviors were suggested in out-of-class situations, the majority of the teachers in seven out of nine such behaviors indicated that a given behavior was proper. It is pointed out that the more active, liberal, and youthful the teacher is, the more expressive his behavior is.

On the relationship between expressive role orientation and discussion of political topics in the classroom the same study indicated that the higher the index of expressive orientation is, the more talk about politics there is (Ziegler, 1966). This relationship notwithstanding, the classroom is the last place where teachers discuss politics and related issues. The overwhelming majority of them talk about politics with friends, other teachers, or their families, but not with students. The nature of the subject matter makes a difference in the frequency of the classroom political discussion. For example, 97 percent of social studies teachers, as opposed to 34 percent of teachers of art or music, "always," "often," or "sometimes" talk about politics in class. Ziegler points out that "the social studies and English and foreign languages are characterized by the liberal teachers who talk a lot about politics in class and who think that this is the proper sort of thing for them to do."

In spite of the willingness of selected groups of teachers to talk about issues in the classroom, Ziegler holds that there is some indication that high school teachers are not intellectually equipped to do so. On a simple question asking teachers to distinguish between fact and opinion the study indicated that the distinction made by the teachers in the sample was very obscure. To the statement that "the American form of government may not be perfect, but it is the best type of government yet devised by man" 42 percent of the teachers indicated that it was a statement of fact and 50 percent that it was an opinion. Those who agreed with the statement tended to identify it as fact. Interestingly, 51 percent of the social studies teachers thought that the statement was factual.

A study which sought to analyze the effect of an introductory political science course on political participation concluded that the approach used in teaching the course had no impact on the attitudes of students (Somit & others, 1958). This conclusion was obtained by comparing one course, fundamentally "traditional" in approach, which stressed American government with three "participation-oriented" courses which were part of an integrated social science sequence and in which a conscious effort was made to expose students to practical politics and to provide them with the opportunity to discuss politics with local party officials. It is interesting also to note that the typical undergraduate in the four-course sample was close to neutral or indifferent toward political participation. Although it is based on a limited sample and does not control for some important demographic and personal factors, the study challenges some of the findings of Almond and Verba (1963) on the positive relationship between manifest teaching about politics and subjective political competence. Perhaps more sophisticated longitudinal studies in the future will give us better grounds to make generalizations on the outcomes of different courses and on the way they are taught.

A nonempirical but carefully documented study of contemporary Soviet education concluded that much like the Americans, the Soviets used their schools as agents of political socialization of children and youth although the political role of the school in the U.S.S.R. has been much more explicit than in the United States (Azrael, 1965). The main goals of Soviet education were to create an "all-inclusive, monolithic, and homogeneous political culture" characterized by total compliance to the rules of the party and the regime. Beginning with the primary grades the school curriculum (especially courses in the social sciences and the humanities), the printed materials, the teachers, and the general school and extraschool milieus tried to instill Soviet patriotism and develop an identification with the fatherland and its leaders. "Primary school readers were replete with tales of the careers of political leaders (above all Lenin and Stalin), valiant soldiers, famous scientists, and production heroes." Soviet accomplishments were juxtaposed with Western failures to bring a hatred for the "exploiters" of the masses. At the higher educational levels—i.e., secondary schools and universities—the indoctrinational themes continued to be emphasized but were treated in a more sophisticated way. The concept of "socialist legality" and "scientific theories" of Marxism-Leninism were introduced along with courses on the constitution of the U.S.S.R. and the history of the Communist party. Along with the indoctrinational nature of the atmosphere prevailing in the schools was one that fostered unquestionable compliance with the rules of the school and the regime. Through strict discipline and an external system of rewards and punishments the teachers were to introduce early in the student's life such fundamental Soviet institutions as criticism and self-criticism, denunciation, confession, and recantation. Youth organizations such as the Octobrists, Young Pioneers, and the Komsomol reinforced the political and social values imparted by the formal educational system.

How successful have the Soviet schools been in politicizing the youth into regime norms? Azrael points out that the educational system accomplished several important tasks, such as developing mass literacy, eliminating traditional church influences, acculturating the populace into the tempo of an industrial society, and pioneering new developments in a variety of scientific fields (1965). Furthermore, the system was able to produce what Easton has called "diffuse support" for the regime to allow it to survive crises from within and without. In the words of the author, "The system . . . was instrumental in producing enough highly motivated, ideologically committed, and politically active young people that the regime was able to institutionalize tremendously rapid social and economic change. . . ." These apparent successes notwithstanding, the educational system has had its share in creating or perpetuating acute social problems. For example, in the polyglot culture of the U.S.S.R. non-Russian youth has had difficulty in developing a loyalty to the Russian-dominated Soviet state. Also, the school has in many cases operated as an obstacle to social mobility—children of working-class parents or those living in rural areas did not receive the same amount and quality of education as those whose parents belonged to the managerial class living in urban communities. Contrary to the ideological commitment to "classlessness" there was a growth of "'class consciousness' which the schools seemed powerless to prevent and often subtly encouraged." Finally, there have been problems of disaffection and apathy. Some forms of disaffection involved a protest against Soviet puritanical life and an acceptance of Western styles and tastes. A larger segment of students was politically apathetic and indifferent. Some of those students substituted a sense of professionalism and technocracy for that of political sensitivity. Some were simply bored with "the dogmatism and repetitiveness of all political communication sponsored by the regime, whether in the classroom, the Komsomol, or the mass media." Finally, another group saw political involvement as an instrument for access into the higher strata of society rather than something to which they were personally or ideologically committed.

The school reform initiated by Khrushchev in 1958 tried in part to solve these problems by revising the curriculum and by making provisions for "polytechnical education." Students now were supposed to get an understanding of and an appreciation for socially useful work and to combine the work of the mind with menial work. Students were to have technical training along with academic work throughout the various school levels, by taking courses in shop and related subjects in the lower grades, and by actual factory assignments while in the secondary school or upon graduation from it. The establishment of boarding schools for lower-class children, polytechnization, and intensified political-education programs in secondary schools were meant to create the "new Soviet man," the man who has a high respect for labor, is an enthusiastic supporter of the economic objectives of the regime, understands the meaning of socialist ownership, and works against the growth of class and status consciousness. How successful Khrushchev and those who succeeded him have been in using education as an agent of political socialization in meeting the goals of the regime is very difficult to determine. In the absence of studies based on survey research, any generalizations about training for citizenship and relevant student beliefs and values in the Soviet Union will continue to be largely conjectural.

A more recent study which included the influence on youth (aged 9–14) of the Young Pioneer organization in Uzbekistan indicated that the agency performed important social, moral, and educational roles (Medlin & others, 1965). The study, based on field observations, challenged the all-too-common claim by Western visitors that the Pioneer movement is a parapolitical organization the main purpose of which is the political indoctrination of youth. While ideological indoctrination is part of the activities, the organization is functioning as (1) an extension of the school in terms of special knowledges and skills, (2) a talent-discovering and personal development unit, (3) a collectivizing agency, (4) an ideological encampment, (5) a substitute moral and spiritual system, and (5) a social system. It is asserted that the Young Pioneers is a very influential agent of cultural change and that its activities foster creativity and student self-expression. The organization instills the "pioneer" spirit in youth as well as faith in the future. It also provides experience in interpersonal relations, and it develops a "noticeable *esprit de corps.*" The Pioneer groups in Uzbekistan are characterized by an openness and a participatory climate, but at the same time emphasize specific models to be emulated. The "new Soviet man" is created not by brutal force and harsh punishments but by encouragement in developing and cultivating personal and group interests. Perhaps the Young Pioneer movement in the Soviet Union provides a unique institution in citizenship and character training which needs to be studied more thoroughly in the future.

Textbook. How do textbooks and other classroom materials contribute to the politicization of student attitudes? How is the political system represented? How do authors present the United States vis-à-vis other countries? How do they treat minority groups? These are some of the questions that one may ask on the influence of printed material used in schools. Actually, there is very little or no research on the role of the textbook in the development of beliefs and attitudes about the social and political world. At best, it is purported to exert minimal influence (Massialas, 1967). Most investigations in this area concentrate on the content of the textbook and the images of the political and social systems it conveys. Most of these investigations seem to operate on the implicit assumption that the specific messages in each textbook will have an impact on the reader and his pattern of socialization.

Litt, in his study of major secondary schools in three Boston communities (1963), which varied in socioeconomic and political factors, included a content analysis of textbooks used in the civic education programs. The text evaluation was based on a random sample of paragraphs which were read and classified by three judges along five dimensions: emphasis on citizen political participation, political chauvinism, the democratic creed, emphasis on political process, and emphasis on politics as the resolution of group conflict. The study, which found no significant differences in the school textbooks in references to the democratic creed and political chauvinism, pointed out that "few references in the material connoted an insular view of American politics." It was also concluded that the "isolationist and jingoist orientation" of civics texts of earlier years was absent in this sampling and that the support of the democratic creed outweighed all other political dimensions. However, differences exist on the values relating to political participation, politics as a process, and the functions of the political system. The texts from the working-class community as opposed to those in the middle and upper classes make few attempts to encourage people to vote or to instill in them a sense of civic duty and political effectiveness. Also absent from the texts of this community (working-class) are references to the actual process of politics and the use of political power, rather than the workings of an invisible hand of government. The reviewed textbooks, in general, supported the school and community influences in the development of student attitudes toward the political system and their potential participation in it. Students of the affluent community were oriented "toward a 'realistic' and active view of the political process, stressing political conflict." Students in the working-class community received training in the elements of democratic government, but the main emphasis was on duties and responsibilities of citizens, not on the process of influencing the government through political participation. In the words of the investigator, "In the working-class community students were oriented toward a more 'idealistic' and passive view, stressing political harmony."

A report for the Anti-Defamation League of B'nai B'rith in 1961 on the treatment of minorities in secondary-school textbooks concluded that the texts in question were presenting "a largely white, Protestant, Anglo-Saxon view of history and the current social scene" and that the problems of minority groups in America were "still very largely neglected" (Marcus, 1961). The report was based on a study of 48 textbooks in American history, world history, and social problems and civics, and its findings were elaborately documented. On the treatment of Negroes, the study concluded:

> In most cases, the 1954 Supreme Court decision on public school desegregation is presented without any consideration of the underlying principles and of the subsequent, ongoing attempts at compliance and evasion. The achievements of living Negro Americans are mentioned in very few books. Residential segregation by race is seldom discussed. American Negroes are portrayed, for the most part, in the eras of slavery and of Reconstruction. What comes through in most books is a stereotype of a simple, child-like superstitious people.

The study further indicated the lack of scientific information about race and about the historic achievements of American Negroes. With few exceptions, the textbooks did not include photographs or other illustrations of Negroes.

Another study of citizenship education based on a

subjective examination of three popular civics textbooks concluded that (1) textbooks, while readable and attractive in appearance, do not deal adequately with controversial social issues, (2) many crucial issues such as segregation and racial discrimination in housing and voting are either excluded altogether or they are treated with "detached objectivity," and (3) the books are written in such a way that they do not encourage commitment to the democratic way of life and system of government (Krug, 1960). The investigator related the comments of a foreign student who observed that the textbook authors, their scholarship notwithstanding, "failed to point even to one mistake or blunder committed by the United States in all its history."

A more sophisticated and comprehensive study than the one mentioned above dealt with the relative emphasis given to reflective thinking or intelligent decision making and to human values by social studies textbooks (Shaver, 1965). After examining 93 current secondary-school textbooks in the fields of American government, American problems, and citizenship or civics, the investigator drew a number of conclusions, the most important of which were the following: (1) Although appeals to critical or mature thinking about problems of society were made in practically all of the books, none gave the reader a conceptual framework which would contribute to the development of critical skills. Most of the critical thinking material was presented in an exhortative manner. (2) Several statements about American democracy presented an "incredibly naive" picture of society which may lead the student either to be "unrealistically optimistic" about his social world or to wonder about the discrepancies between textbooks and what newspapers and other communication media report. Textbooks tended to confuse the ideals of democracy with the realities of the political system; in several instances the reader was given the impression that the "ideals" were indeed operant in daily life. (3) Textbooks generally failed to give the student an intellectual scheme or strategy that could be used to resolve intelligently problems created by the clash of values in society. Most textbooks do not deal with the cognitive and affective components of the decision-making process in the resolution of conflict—there is no attempt to help the reader clarify his own value position and assume a defensible posture. In many instances the emphasis regarding controversial issues and social cleavages is given to the factual rather than the value basis of the disputes. Often, it is erroneously and naively assumed that when all the facts are in, then warranted value judgments will be made.

Two more recent critical reviews of civics texts confirmed some of the earlier findings and concluded that if the student were to receive information about the political system and his potential role in it solely from textbooks, he would not be a very effective citizen (Massialas, 1967; Smith & Patrick, 1967). The main reason for this is that texts present an unrealistic picture of American society, a picture which conveniently excludes pressing problems of life from careful consideration and makes the student feel that he has a priori the capability to influence major governmental decisions. Smith and Patrick (1967), who reviewed junior high school civics texts, pointed to this trend of perpetuating misconceptions and inculcating values through moralizing prescriptions. Massialas (1967), who reviewed senior high school textbooks on government, found basic ethnocentric tendencies in them—e.g., the United States is always presented as the champion of freedom, good will, and rationality while other sovereign states are either aggressors or second-raters. It was concluded that textbook authors generally underestimate the ability of young people to order their own learning experiences and to develop plausible explanations of natural and social phenomena in their environment. The materials and the level of questions in them are often an insult to the intelligence of adolescents as well as to their teachers (Massialas, 1967). In spite of the textbooks, however, the typical American teen-ager develops some sensitivity to the real political world. Perhaps the new mass communication media play an important part in this.

The School Milieu. In what ways does the particular culture of the school affect the civic socialization of youth? Can any differences in attitudes be attributed to the differences in the type of school— e.g., private versus public, city versus suburban, academic versus vocational schools? What students are recruited into the different types of schools and on what bases?

Almond and Verba (1963), in the study cited earlier, found that Americans participate more in decisions at school than the nationals of the other countries studied. A higher percentage of Americans reported that they felt free to discuss unfair treatment in school or to disagree with their teachers. Likewise, 40 percent of the Americans responded that they "could and did participate" in the debates of political and social issues in school. Responses on school participation in the other nations ranged from 16 percent among the British to 11 percent among the Italians. As the authors pointed out, "clearly, the amount of explicit training for political participation in the schools is much higher in the United States than elsewhere." Generally, the frequency of formal or informal participation in discussion relates to the amount of education of the respondent; participation is three or four times greater among those with secondary education than among those with only primary education.

A review of several studies conducted in the United States and abroad revealed that the type of school a child attends is important in the development of his role in society (Kazamias & Massialas, 1965). In England, for example, a student enrolled in a secondary grammar school, as contrasted with one who is enrolled in a technical or a secondary modern school, has much better chances of becoming a member of the elite group. "The secondary grammar school is the pride of the English, and the most sought-after school by parents for their children." This type of school is, by tradition, the training ground for leadership and emphasizes such personal qualities as "character and spirit." As Rose (1964) observed, "nearly all the schools, within their own school community, stress a hierarchical system of authority, training youths for different but complementary roles as leader and follower." This dual system of education, one catering to the "elites" and the other to the "masses," is present in several other nations. For example, in France the elites attend the lycée, in Germany the gymnasium, in the Soviet Union the senior or complete secondary school. Even in the United States, which purport not to discriminate on the basis of sex, status, ethnic-group membership, or race, there is sufficient research to indicate tant factor in social and political recruitment. For example, a student attending a small rural secondary that the type and location of the school is an important factor in social and political recruitment. For example, a student attending a small rural secondary school has fewer chances of achieving social and political mobility than one attending a large school in a metropolitan area. The same principle would hold for children who attended ghetto schools or schools in poverty-stricken areas. Generally speaking, students in suburban schools have higher aspirations for participation in the political, social, and economic life of their society than their counterparts in city or rural schools do. Their aspirations tend to reflect the realities of the system (Kazamias & Massialas, 1965). Litt's study (1963) of schools in three communities which differed in wealth and status confirmed the proposition that different schools train for the performance of different roles in society. The working-class school fosters passive acceptance of government rules and regulations. The affluent community stresses political participation and critical evaluation of governmental policy.

MEDIATORS OF POLITICAL SOCIALIZATION. Sex. In what ways do such factors as sex, intelligence, social class, ethnic-group membership, race, and religion relate to the internalization of political values? What is the evidence from the literature on each factor?

In a study of children in grades 4 through 8 in New Haven, Connecticut, Greenstein (1965) reported sex differences on specifically political responses. For example, fourth-grade boys were significantly better informed about politics than girls were. To the question "If you could change the world in any way you wanted, what change would you make?" boys' responses were more "political" than girls'. It is suggested that while early childhood experiences and personality traits may account for the sex differences, the children turn to the father rather than the mother for political advice, and hence the development and perpetuation of the idea from generation to generation that "politics is the man's business."

Hess and Torney (1965) generally corroborated earlier ideas about male dominance in political life. Their study suggests that sex differences begin early in life and that they are constant across the grades. Boys acquire their political attitudes more rapidly than girls, and they show more interest in political affairs. Girls view government as a personal figure, whereas boys tend to identify it as an institution.

Girls have more faith in the fairness of the laws and view the legal authorities as more responsive to citizens' demands than boys do. There were no differences between the sexes on the question of loyalty, attachment, and support of the regime and the political system. Also, there were no differences between boys and girls on knowledge of the process and norms of the political system. However, political parties appear to be more salient for boys, who also report more political activity (in grades 3 through 5) than girls do.

The five-country study by Almond and Verba (1963) confirmed some of the claimed sex differences on such indexes as obligation to participate in community affairs and sense of civic competence. "Males in all countries are more likely to say they can influence the local government." The male-female differences, however, are less apparent in the United States than in the other countries.

Social Class. Although some items in the questionnaire used by Greenstein in the New Haven study (1965) failed to reveal differences in response between upper and lower socioeconomic groups of children, there was class differentiation on capacity and motivation for political participation. On issues that would distinguish between parties 32 percent of the upper-class children made references to such issues. Both groups showed tendencies to identify with a political party, but the upper-class group had more grounded information about their party choice. On information about formal governmental institutions, on the whole, there are no significant differences relative to socioeconomic status. This lack of difference is attributed to classroom teaching, which "tends to equalize the information about formal aspects of government among upper- and lower-status children." Also, on questions about personal willingness to participate in politics and the "importance" of politics there are no differences between the groups. On the other hand, the data generally reinforce the belief that upper-class children are more politicized than lower-class children. Lower-class children show more deference toward political leaders—there is reluctance Regarding the source of political learning, references on their part to name politicians as negative models. to parents are dominant, especially in the lower grades, but the older upper-class children volunteer the statement that they would want to make their *own* choices. The lower-class children do not volunteer this alternative, but they refer to the schoolteacher as a source of information. "The teacher is probably the one emissary of middle-class sub-culture with whom many lower status children are acquainted."

Greenstein's findings above are confirmed and expanded by Hess and Torney (1965). When intelligence is controlled, there are no differences among high-, middle-, and low-status children with respect to their loyalty to the nation. However, children from working-class backgrounds show a higher regard for the policeman and for the president than do those from middle-class backgrounds. Higher-class children report more frequent participation in political discussion and more concern for national issues than lower-class children. The most striking difference is that lower-class children are less politically efficacious (that is, have little belief in their ability to affect political outcomes) than higher-status children. The lower-class children have a rather limited view of themselves and their ability to influence governmental policy. These children tend to accept authority figures as trustworthy and benign, and there is little motivation on their part to question the government and its policies. While the school appears to be effective in providing information about the political structure, it is "not doing an adequate job in socializing children in active participation." Children from lower socioeconomic origin who largely depend on their teachers and the curriculum to acquire the basic concepts of government and political behavior are at a great disadvantage because schools are neither equipped nor inclined to examine systematically the relevant political concepts and skills. The main inference from these findings is that schools which enroll children and youth from working-class environments need to address themselves to developing a curriculum and a school milieu that facilitate the process of socialization into the mainstream of American life.

Intelligence. The most significant research on the relationship between intelligence and political socialization is that reported by Hess and Torney (1965). On the basis of the data it is suggested that, in general, the active and initiatory aspects of political participation are related to IQ and, as we have seen, to a lesser degree to social class. Intelligence helps accelerate the process of political socialization. Although loyalty and devotion to the nation are found in all children, the higher the child's IQ is, the more capable he is of conceptualizing the institution of government in abstract terms. The more intelligent children tend to view the political system and the laws of the government in less absolute terms, and they are more reserved in assessing governmental competence and intentions. Also, higher-IQ children have a more realistic picture of the political system and how it operates, are more willing to accept change in the system, and are more interested in governmental matters than lower-IQ children. In sum, the more intelligent child is more politically efficacious and exhibits more interest in political involvement. The school is a powerful agent in introducing participant political norms, or norms which instill a propensity toward involvement in public life, to children, especially of elementary and junior high school age. However, unevenness in civic competence of children is associated with such factors as IQ, social class, and ethnic-group membership. If the school is to bring about greater evenness in the politicization of the populace, it will have to pay more explicit attention to civic programs designed for children with relatively low IQ scores. Compensatory civic education programs may provide an avenue in bridging the gap between the various groups of children.

Race and Ethnicity. There is virtually no empirical research on the political socialization of ethnic and racial minorities. An exception is a study of limited scope on the American Negro reported by Marvick (1965). It is claimed that historically the Negro has been excluded from the mainstream of American political life. Consequently, such terms as "protest," "alienation," "reconciliation," and "reintegration" are most relevant in understanding political socialization or resocialization patterns among Negroes. The study was based on the national survey conducted by the National Opinion Research Center (NORC) in 1960 (the same data were used by Almond and Verba in their 1963 study *The Civic Culture*) and included the responses of 100 Negroes and their white counterparts. (The Negroes and their white counterparts were matched on five variables.) A national, white cross section of 870 was also used for comparative purposes. On the question whether the government would give them "equal treatment" in housing or taxes 49 percent of the Negroes, as opposed to 90 percent of the white counterparts, answered in the affirmative. Similarly, only 60 percent of the Negroes, as contrasted to 85 percent of the whites, expected equal treatment from the police. Of the national, white cross section 88 percent gave a vote of confidence to the police. It is also interesting to note that there are attitudinal differences among Negroes. For example, only 40 percent of the Negroes in the South expect equal treatment from the police. Of the national, white with 60 percent in the North. Only 18 percent of the Southern group, as contrasted with 44 percent of the Northern group, expected officials to listen and take their views seriously. On generational factors— e.g., younger versus older persons—Negroes under forty exhibited more confidence in the government and the police, and on some items they came close to the response registered by their white counterparts. On expectations about the local government 50 percent of the Negroes as against 72 percent of their white counterparts felt that "local government actions are usually helpful." Also, 86 percent of the Negroes, compared to 73 percent of the white counterparts, said that they had never tried to influence local policy decisions. Among Southern Negroes 53 percent felt that changing a bad local law was almost impossible, but only 20 percent of the Northern Negroes shared this feeling. The younger Negroes were less pessimistic about the possibility of changing a bad law than older Negroes were—28 percent and 47 percent, respectively.

Years of oppression and discrimination have left a mark on Negro citizens, that of passivity and alienation. Younger Negroes, especially those in the urban communities of the North, are attempting to break with the past and become more involved in the mainstream of American political life. What their views are and how they differ from those of their white counterparts should be the focus of several studies in the future.

THE CONTENT OF POLITICAL ATTITUDES. What are some basic attitudes of American children and youth toward the political system? Are they politically efficacious? Are they alienated? How do they view authority? Do they expect to participate actively in political life? In what ways are they similar or different from youth in other countries?

The reports by Easton and Dennis (1965, 1967) regarding the political images of and attitudes toward government of children in grades 2 through 8 suggested the following: (1) Children form political orientations toward their environment early in life, especially the sense of political efficacy, which is formed by the third grade. (2) Children regard the government as being very benevolent, one which helps, protects, and cares for people. When asked to associate government with ten United States symbols, 39.47 percent and 46.26 percent of the second graders, as opposed to 1.72 and 22.9 percent of the eighth graders, on a two-answer question associated it with George Washington and President Kennedy, respectively. On the other hand, 4.32 percent and 5.93 percent of the second graders, as contrasted with 46.77 percent and 49.14 percent of the eighth graders, associated government with voting and the Congress, respectively. From these data it is concluded that as he grows older the child moves cognitively from a personal to an impersonal or institutional image of government. As children advance through the elementary grades, they deal with the concept of government in abstract terms, and they begin to develop an awareness of "the regime rules associated with popular democracy and the role of ordinary people in it." Teachers also tend to endorse an institutional view of government. The overall affective response of the children toward the government is that they approve of it, and they reject propositions claiming that the government is getting too large and that it meddles too much in the private lives of citizens. Children generally have a deep sympathy and affection toward government, even before they have much information about it.

Sigel (1966), who examined 1,349 primary- and secondary-school children for their reactions to the assassination of President Kennedy, concluded that (1) children were greatly moved by the event; (2) their reactions were similar to those of adults; (3) Negro children and those who anticipated voting Democratic were more upset than were white children who intended to vote Republican; (4) while there was a slight decrease in the perception of the overall power of the Presidency, the office is still presented in a highly positive light. Children seemed to be more upset than adults about the death of the president, since to them, as pointed out previously by Easton and Dennis (1965), he was the symbol of governmental authority and the central power figure. To the question of whether they hoped that the man who killed the president "would be shot or beat up" two-thirds of the fourth graders and 53 percent of the sixth graders answered in the affirmative. Through the grades, however, there was a constant decline of youth sharing this sentiment; by grade 12 only 17 percent felt this way. It appears that the younger children are not sufficiently socialized to reject violence as a means of retribution. Also, children from lower socioeconomic backgrounds in all age groups approved of aggression more readily than those from upper classes. In general, while children were worried about the future of the country in view of the assassination, they expressed faith in the stability of the system. This belief in the power of the system to survive even under critical conditions is part of the American rational-legal system, which is based in large part on diffuse rather than specific support. Had this happened in a country where legitimacy is established through charisma, the consequences would have probably been different.

Jennings (1967), who examined the orientations of high school seniors toward multiple systems of government (international, national, state, and local), pointed out that "in the aggregate the students lean . . . more toward a cosmopolitan rather than a provincial orientation." A person with a pure cosmopolitan outlook orders his orientations as international, national, state, and local, whereas one with a pure local outlook uses the reverse ordering. On a seven-point scale of cosmopolitanism, 54 percent of the students ($N = 1837$) were on the two highest rankings (most cosmopolitan), as contrasted with 6 percent in the lowest rankings (least cosmopolitan or most local). However, it should be noted that the ordering of political orientations in this form does not, in and of itself, imply qualitative aspects of the preferences. As Jennings indicated, a cosmopolitan may be a pacifist seeking world peace or a superpatriot contemplating dropping the atomic bomb. However, when students were confronted with the statement "The American system of government is one that all nations should have," those who were oriented toward cosmopolitanism tended to disagree with the proposition. It seems that political chauvinism is not compatible with cosmopolitanism among preadults. Other items among the data indicate that the more cosmopolitan the student is, the more likely he is to know more about and have a greater interest in world affairs. Also, the cosmopolitan tends to deal with the international and national aspects of public affairs. In terms of affective evaluations of various levels of government (national, state, local, or combinations of these) the more the student is oriented toward cosmopolitanism, the less is his trust in the lower levels of government.

It is interesting to note the topics of political conversations and the emphasis given to each one (Jennings, 1966). Among high school seniors 49 percent of those responding identified domestic national affairs as a topic of conversation. This was followed by civil rights, 47 percent; specific international problems, 34 percent; general news of government and politics, 21 percent; general international problems, 17 percent; local domestic problems, 8 percent; and state domestic problems, 4 percent. It appears that national and international problems and civil rights issues are popular political conversation topics among youth who are ready to enter adulthood. In the category "specific international problems" 30 percent of the students pointed to Vietnam as the topic of conversation. The saliency of civil rights is also indicated from the response to an open-ended question on "the things [you are] least proud of as an American."

Sixty-four percent of the students in this category, as contrasted with 49 percent of the parents and 51 percent of the teachers, indicated civil rights and race relations as the area which made them least proud of being Americans. Other student identifications on the same question were the following: political system properties, 17 percent; non-civil rights social problems, 15 percent; world leadership and United States image, 14 percent; moral, ethical, and religious matters, 6 percent. On civil rights, 31 percent indicated no clear affect, 31 percent fell into the pro-Negro and anti-bigotry category, and 6 percent were in the anti-civil rights group. On "things they were most proud of as Americans," 67 percent of the students, as compared with 76 percent of the parents and 66 percent of the teachers, identified "freedoms and rights." Among students, "freedoms and rights" is followed by "forms and processes of political system," 51 percent; "world leadership and the U.S. image," 18 percent; "opportunity structure," 5 percent; and "scientific and technical progress," 4 percent. On the strength of these figures Jennings concluded that the belief in freedom and rights of citizens has been internalized by American youth—since early childhood youth have been impressed with the idea that America is the land of the free. While actual practice may often contradict these assumptions about the system and the citizen's rights in it, the ideals of American democracy are accepted mostly on faith.

A study based on a national sample by Remmers and Franklin (1963) of the Purdue Opinion Panel on attitudes of high school students with regard to certain freedoms guaranteed by the first amendment of the United States constitution revealed some interesting findings. On a question about freedom of the press ("Newspapers and magazines should be allowed to print anything they want except military secrets") 41 percent in 1951 and 51 percent of the sample in 1960 disagreed with the statement. When the question was asked whether objectionable material defined as "sexy, profane, obscene, immoral, filthy, etc." should be presented only 11 percent of the teen-agers voted for not prohibiting or limiting the material. Also, only 8 percent voted for no prohibition of "objectionable" movies. (In examining these results one wonders whether the negative teen-age response is in part a function of the loaded and certainly pejorative terms in the questions.) The general attitude of the teen-ager toward constitutional freedoms is perhaps better revealed by this question: "Police and other groups have sometimes banned or censored certain books and movies in their cities. Should they or should they not have power to do this?" Both in 1951 and 1960, 60 percent felt that police *should* have this power. On printing or selling communist literature 66 percent in 1951 and 61 percent in 1960 said that laws should be passed to prohibit printing or selling such literature. An overwhelming majority of the teen-agers both in 1951 and 1960 (79 percent and 83 percent, respectively) agreed with the proposition that "religious belief and worship should not be restricted by laws." Also, a majority, 69 percent in 1951 and 57 percent in 1960, disagreed with the statement that in some cases the police should search a person or his home without a warrant. There was also strong acceptance on the part of teen-agers in the sample of trial by jury and protection against arrest without formal charge. There is considerable decline since 1951 on agreement with the statement "The police or F.B.I. may sometimes be right in giving a man the 'third degree' to make him talk." While in 1951 58 percent agreed with the statement, in 1960 only 42 percent agreed. The reader should be extremely cautious in generalizing from these and similar polls of American youth because of limited procedural and contextual information included in most reports of this kind. Perhaps fewer questions but more careful analyses should become the pattern of future reports taken by national polls.

The Almond and Verba study of citizenship in five nations (1963) indicated that Americans have the highest scores on obligation to participate in governmental affairs and on sense of civic competence. For example, 51 percent of the respondents in the United States, followed by 39 percent in the United Kingdom, 26 percent in Mexico, 22 percent in Germany, and 10 percent in Italy, said that the ordinary man should be active in his community. It appears that Americans have the highest participatory norms. As we have seen before, the amount of education is related to participatory standards—the more education a person has, the higher is his norm of active citizenship. On subjective competence or the ability to influence the government (national and local) the United States sample provides the highest score (67 percent), followed by the United Kingdom, Germany, Mexico, and Italy, in that order. The investigators concluded that "the sense of local and national civic competence is widely distributed among the American and British populations." In Germany and Italy competence in influencing the local government rather than the national is widely distributed. Subjective competence is also related to participation and allegiance. For example, those who are higher on the subjective-competence scale (those who believe they can participate in political decisions) are also high on exposure to political communications, participation in political discussion, and the belief that elections are necessary. The United States again emerges as the country having the most self-confident and active citizens. It is suggested that "the belief in one's competence is a key political attitude. The self-confident citizen appears to be the democratic citizen." This citizen has high expectations for participation; he is also a "more satisfied and loyal citizen."

A recent study of Western European youth concludes that there is a strong feeling among them for European integration. In 1964–65 the overall percentage of youth, aged 13–19, who were for European unification was as follows: the Netherlands, 95 percent; France, 93 percent; Germany, 95 percent; Britain, 72 percent (Inglehart, 1967). A poll of adults in these countries taken in 1962 indicated a strong feeling for unification, but not as high as that of the teen-age group. The age group of 55 and over is "markedly less European" than all others. The younger adults, especially in France and Germany, exhibit a more stable commitment to European integration than older adults. It is hypothesized that these differences are due to the early socialization patterns in the different age groups. In any case, the prospects for a United States of Europe are good.

We shall briefly identify some ideas and generalizations that issue from the studies reviewed in this essay. These should be thought of as tentative and open to additional research.

Theoretical Framework and Definition:
1. Until recently, the concept of citizenship has been ambiguous, and it has encompassed descriptive, melioristic, and prescriptive elements.

2. In recent years the global concept of citizenship has been refined by selecting specific aspects for investigation. One of the most important of these is the concept of political socialization.

3. Political socialization is the process of inducting youth into the political culture of their society.

4. Institutions which directly relate to political socialization are the family, school, church, peer group, and job. Race, ethnic-group membership, religion, social status, sex, and personality are also important factors to consider in studying political socialization.

5. Most recent studies of the process have been characterized by an empirical orientation. A cross-national perspective has also been introduced.

The Role of the Family:
1. The role of the family in the socialization of children has been reconsidered recently. It appears that the key role of the family is in the training of very young children and in the socialization of sex roles.

2. The family's major role in political socialization is to impart partisanship preference and consensus toward the government.

3. Children from low-income groups tend to look to their teachers rather than their parents for political information.

4. Students from maternal rather than nuclear families tend to be more authoritarian, less interested in political life, and less efficacious politically.

5. Participation in family decisions is strongly related to political participation and a feeling of political competence.

6. The political beliefs of parents, e.g., political trust and cosmopolitan tendencies, do not necessarily provide reliable guides for predicting the political beliefs of their offspring.

Peer-group and Extracurricular Influences:
1. Adolescents rely heavily on peer-group influences with regard to values and aspirations.

2. Children and youth who participate in group activities also have an interest in politics, defend their stand on issues, and participate in conversations on political issues.

3. There is no direct relationship between the rate of participation in extraclass activities and attitude toward politics as measured by a five-item evaluative factor of the semantic differential. However, the teen-ager who is well integrated into the informal status system of his school exhibits a relatively high degree of social trust and has a more positive attitude toward politics.

4. Students with a working-class background in a homogeneous-class peer group tend to reinforce the political and economic attitudes of their class. Students who identify with a heterogeneous-class peer group are socialized into the political norms of the higher classes.

School Influences:
1. The school is emerging as an important agent in political socialization.

2. The major function of the elementary school in politicization is to foster compliance with governmental rules and authority.

3. The elementary-school curriculum underemphasizes the citizen's right to participate in government. Political parties and partisanship also do not receive much attention.

4. The relationship between manifest teaching about politics and knowledge about and attitudes toward the political system among high school youth is not very clear. Although the research evidence is not very conclusive, it is claimed that civic education in the schools is not very effective in civic training. The civics curriculum seems to have a greater impact on the Negro and low-social-status student.

5. While teen-agers favor politically expressive teachers, teachers tend to remain quiet on controversial social issues.

6. The more active, liberal, and youthful the teacher is, the more expressive his behavior is. The higher the level of expressive orientation, the more talk there is about politics.

7. High school teachers are not intellectually equipped to deal judiciously with social issues. Possibly a more sophisticated and analytical curriculum taught by teachers who have had inquiry-training experience may produce better results.

8. It is observed that Soviet schools and youth organizations perform political socialization functions similar to those performed by American schools. The lack of field data makes it difficult to figure out the actual relationship between education and the creation of the "new Soviet man."

9. School textbooks generally present an unrealistic picture of society, and they conceal social problems from youth. Textbooks tend to perpetuate misconceptions, and they are biased in their treatment of other cultures. Textbook authors tend to underestimate the ability of children and youth to deal with social problems intelligently.

10. Students from all social strata receive formal training in the elements of democratic government. However, students from working-class backgrounds are encouraged both by the formal instructional program and by the textbooks used in it to emphasize the duties and responsibilities of citizens. Working-class students, as opposed to students from affluent communities, are oriented toward an idealistic view of the political process, and they have a passive view of themselves.

11. A major cross-cultural study of the United States, England, Germany, Italy, and Mexico indicates that there is more freedom in the United States to participate in school decisions and in debates of social and political problems.

12. Throughout the world the school operates as an agent of recruitment for political leadership. Students attending a small rural secondary school as compared with those attending a large school in a suburb have fewer chances for membership in the political elites. Children from ghetto schools or from schools in poverty-stricken areas neither have the opportunity for nor aspire to political leadership. In many cases, schools tend to perpetuate and even accentuate political and economic inequalities.

Mediators of Political Socialization:

1. Boys tend to be somewhat more knowledgeable and more sensitive to political affairs than girls. Girls perceive government on a personal rather than an institutional basis. Girls have more faith in the fairness of the laws, and they believe authorities to be more responsive to the demands of citizens than boys do. There are no differences between the sexes on loyalty to and support for the government.

2. Male-female differences in political life are more apparent in countries other than the United States.

3. Social status makes a difference in capacity and motivation for political participation among children.

4. Both low- and high-status children show a tendency to identify with a political party, but the high-status group has more grounded information about its preferred party.

5. Generally, social status makes no significant difference in information about governmental institutions.

6. Low-status children show more deference toward political leaders; they tend to show high regard for the president and the policeman. These children tend to accept authority figures as trustworthy and benign.

7. Lower-class children largely depend on their teachers in acquiring the basic concepts about government.

8. Low-status children are less politically efficacious than high-status children.

9. The higher the child's intelligence, the higher is his capability to conceptualize the institution of government in abstract terms.

10. Children with high intelligence are more politically efficacious and they exhibit more interest in political involvement than children with low intelligence.

11. Whites have more faith in the government and its agencies than Negroes do. Younger Negroes who live in the North have greater confidence in the government than older Negroes in the South.

The Content of Political Attitudes:

1. Children view government as being very benevolent.

2. With increasing age children tend to move from an image of government as a person, such as George Washington, to that of government as an institution, such as voting or the Congress. Teachers tend to endorse an institutional rather than a personal view of government.

3. Children are greatly moved when something such as the assassination of President Kennedy happens to the symbols of government. The younger the child is, the more he is inclined to accept violence as a means of retribution for that assassination. In spite of catastrophic events such as this, children have faith in the stability of the system to survive.

4. High school seniors tend toward a cosmopolitan rather than a parochial orientation.

5. The more cosmopolitan a student is, the greater is his tendency to know more about and have a greater interest in world affairs.

6. National affairs, civil rights, and specific international problems are the three topics which are listed high among conversational subjects among high school seniors. Local and state domestic problems rarely constitute topics of discussion.

7. Problems connected with civil rights and race relations make high school seniors least proud of being Americans. Freedoms and rights—e.g., freedom of speech, religion, movement and action, and job choice make them most proud.

8. In a five-nation study Americans had the highest scores on obligation to participate in governmental affairs and on sense of civic competence.

9. Among the five nations studied Americans and Britons showed the greatest confidence in their ability to influence government. Responses of Americans suggest that they are the most self-confident and active citizens of the five nations studied.

10. Western European youth have strong feelings in favor of European integration. The age group of 55 and over is markedly less in favor of European integration than all others.

Byron G. Massialas
The University of Michigan

References

Almond, Gabriel A., and Verba, Sidney. *The Civic Culture: Political Attitudes and Democracy in Five Nations.* Princeton U Press, 1963. 562p.

Azrael, Jeremy R. "Patterns of Polity-directed Educational Development: The Soviet Union." In Coleman, James S. (Ed.) *Education and Political Development.* Princeton U Press, 1965. p. 233–71.

Bereday, George Z. F., and Stretch, Bonnie B. "Political Education in the U.S.A. and the U.S.S.R." *Compar Ed R* 7:1–16; 1963.

Chin, Robert. "Research Approaches to the Problem of Civic Training." In Patterson, Franklin, and others. (Eds.) *The Adolescent Citizen.* Free, 1960. p. 247–68.

Citizenship Education Project. *Improving Citizenship Education.* Teachers College, Columbia U, 1952. 44p.

Citizenship Education Project. *Resources for Citizenship.* Teachers College, Columbia U, 1955. 328p.

Coleman, James S. *The Adolescent Society.* Free, 1961. 368p.

Easton, David. *A Systems Analysis of Political Life.* Wiley, 1965. 507p.

Easton, David, and Dennis, Jack. "The Child's Image of Government." *Annals Am Acad Political Social Sci* 361:40–57; 1965.

Easton, David, and Dennis, Jack. "The Child's Acquisition of Regime Norms: Political Efficacy." *Am Political Sci R* 61:25–38; 1967.

Easton, David, and Hess, Robert D. "The Child's Political World." In Dreyer, Edward C., and Rosenbaum, Walter A. (Eds.) *Political Opinion and Electoral Behavior: Essays and Studies.* Wadsworth Publishing Co., Inc., 1966. p. 151–65.

Edgar, Earl E. "Kansas Study of Education for Citizenship." *Phi Delta Kappan* 33:177–8; 1951.

Greenstein, Fred I. *Children and Politics.* Yale U Press, 1965. 199p.

Hess, Robert D. "The Socialization of Attitudes Toward Political Authority: Some Cross-national Comparisons." *Int Social Sci J* 15:542–59; 1963.

Hess, Robert D., and Torney, Judith V. *The Development of Basic Attitudes and Values Toward Government and Citizenship During the Elementary School Years*, Part I. Cooperative Research Project No. 1078. U Chicago Press, 1965. 499p.

Hollingshead, August B. *Elmtown's Youth.* Wiley, 1949. 480p.

Horton, Roy E., Jr. "American Freedom and the Values of Youth." In Remmers, H. H. (Ed.) *Antidemocratic Attitudes in American Schools.* Northwestern U Press, 1963. p. 18–60.

Hyman, Herbert. *Political Socialization.* Free, 1959. 175p.

Inglehart, Ronald. "An End to European Integration?" *Am Political Sci R* 61:91–105; 1967.

Jennings, M. Kent. *Observations on the Study of Political Values Among Pre-adults.* Unpublished informal paper prepared for Center for Res and Ed in Am Liberties, TC October 21–3, 1966. (Mimeographed.) 25p.

Jennings, M. Kent. *Pre-adult Orientations to Multiple Systems of Government. Midwest J Political Sci* 9:291–317; 1967.

Jennings, M. Kent, and Niemi, Richard G. *Family Structure and the Transmission of Political Values. Am Political Sci R* March 1968.

Kazamias, Andreas M., and Massialas, Byron G. *Tradition and Change in Education: A Comparative Study.* Prentice-Hall, 1965. 182p.

Krug, Mark M. "'Safe' Textbooks and Citizenship Education." *Sch R* 68:463–80; 1960.

Lambert, W. E., and Klineberg, O. "A Pilot Study of the Origin and Development of National Stereotypes." *Int Social Sci J* 11:221–38; 1959.

Langton, Kenneth P. *Conjugal Power Structure and Political Socialization.* Paper delivered to the American Political Science Association, September 6–10, 1966. (Mimeographed.) 25p.

Langton, Kenneth P. "Peer Group and School and the Political Socialization Process." *Am Political Sci R* September 1967.

Langton, Kenneth P., and Jennings, M. Kent. "Political Socialization and the High School Curriculum in the United States," 1967. (Mimeographed.) 42p.

Levine, Robert. "Political Socialization and Cultural Change." In Geertz, Clifford. (Ed.) *Old Societies and New States.* Free, 1963. p. 280–303.

Litt, Edgar. "Civic Education, Community Norms, and Political Indoctrination." *Am Sociol R* 28:69–75; 1963.

Litt, Edgar. "Education and Political Enlightenment in America." *Annals Acad Political Social Sci* 361: 32–9; 1965.

Marcus, Lloyd. *The Treatment of Minorities in Secondary School Textbooks.* B'nai B'rith Anti-Defamation League, 1961. 63p.

Marvick, Dwaine. "The Political Socialization of the American Negro." *Annals Acad Political Social Sci* 361:112–27; 1965.

Massialas, Byron G. "Government: We Are the Greatest!" In Cox, C. B., and Massialas, Byron G. (Eds.) *Social Studies in the United States: A Critical Appraisal.* Harcourt, 1967. p. 167–95.

Massialas, Byron G. (Ed.). "The Indiana Experiments in Inquiry." *B Sch Ed: Indiana U* 39:1–139; 1963.

Medlin, William K., and others. "The Young Pioneers: Social, Moral, and Learning Agency for

Youth Outside the School." (Dittographed.) 27p. Revised section of Medlin and others. *Education and Social Change: A Study of the Role of the School in a Technically Developing Society in Central Asia.* CRP Nos. 1414, 2620. U Michigan Press, 1965. 457p.

Patterson, Franklin. "Citizenship and the High School: Representative Current Practices." In Patterson, Franklin and others. (Eds.) *The Adolescent Citizen.* Free, 1960. p. 100–75.

Pinner, Frank A. "Parental Overprotection and Political Distrust." *Annals Am Acad Political Social Sci* 361:58–70; 1965.

Quillen, I. James, and Lavone, A. Hanna. *Education for Social Competence: Curriculum and Instruction in Secondary School Social Studies.* Scott, 1948. 572p.

Remmers, H. H., and Franklin, Richard D. "Sweet Land of Liberty." In Remmers, H. H. (Ed.) *Antidemocratic Attitudes in American Schools.* Northwestern U Press, 1963. p. 61–72.

Rose, Richard. *Politics in England.* Little, 1964. 266p.

Shaver, James P. "Reflective Thinking, Values and Social Studies Textbooks." *Sch R* 73:226–57; 1965.

Sigel, Roberta. "Assumptions about the Learning of Political Values." *Annals Am Acad Political Social Sci* 361:1–9; 1965.

Sigel, Roberta. "An Exploration into Some Aspects of Political Socialization: School Children's Reactions to the Death of a President." In Wolfenstein, Martha, and Kliman, Gilbert. (Eds.) *Children and the Death of a President.* Doubleday, 1966. p. 34–69.

Smith, Frederick R., and Patrick, John J. "Civics: Relating Social Study to Social Reality." In Cox, C. B., and Massialas, Byron G. (Eds.) *Social Studies in the United States: A Critical Appraisal.* Harcourt, 1967. p. 105–27.

Somit, Albert, and others. "The Effect of Introductory Political Science Course on Student Attitudes Toward Personal Political Participation." *Am Political Sci R* 12:1129–32; 1958.

Wilson, Howard E. *Education for Citizenship.* McGraw-Hill, 1938. 272p.

Zeigler, Harmon. *The Political World of the High School Teacher.* U Oregon, 1966. 160p.

Ziblatt, David. "High School Extracurricular Activities and Political Socialization." *Annals Am Acad Political and Social Sci* 361:20–31; 1965.

CLASS SIZE

Some 80 percent of the current budget for the operation of public elementary and secondary schools goes for the employment of personnel. Hence the answer to the question of how many teachers must be employed to teach a given number of pupils can have an important influence on the ultimate size of the budget. This, it would appear, is the principal reason for interest in the subject. It was not until the period of rapidly increasing enrollments in public schools, beginning about the turn of the century, that serious efforts were made to research the function of class size. J. M. Rice is generally credited with being the first in the field, and according to Blake (1954) his two published studies do not meet criteria of scientific rigor. Nearly 70 years and many studies later it must be admitted that even yet very few studies do. Consequently the question of class size remains in that limbo of educational concern where definitive and categorical answers are elusive. Even the terms "small class" and "large class" have not been numerically defined, and their limits vary greatly in the studies which have been reported.

DIMENSIONS OF THE CLASS SIZE QUESTION. Class size may be broadly defined, for present purposes, as the relative amount of instructional service, in terms of professional personnel, that is brought to bear upon the educational task. It is clear that instructional service can be packaged in a number of different ways for a given financial input. Administration can concentrate its staff dollars in the classroom, with the result that the more personnel who are employed, the smaller will be the classes. Or the choice may be to concentrate as much as possible on extra-class services performed by administrators, supervisors, guidance counselors, health personnel, and other subject-matter and functional specialists. In the latter case many professionals could be added to the school staff without any reduction in class size. But it is hard to presume that the employment of extra-class personnel has no effect upon the total educational enterprise. Thus a measure of class size per se is not a fully relevant dimension of staff deployment. For this reason McKenna (1965) derived a measure to replace pupil-teacher ratio, average class size, and other such measures of personnel adequacy. He termed his measure "numerical staff adequacy" (NSA) and defined it as the number of professionals of all kinds employed per 1,000 pupils. Few of the studies extant control the variable under investigation in terms of the total staff available in the educational setting. A few studies admit the presence of additional staff, such as graduate assistants, leaders of question-and-discussion sessions, readers, etc., without any attempt to quantify their presence or to account for their influence upon the criterion. Thus, the first dimension of the class-size question is the measure of the variable itself, the control of all personnel resources contributing to achievement, or some other criterion, being measured. The studies noted generally fail to do this.

The second dimension relates not to the quantity but to the quality of staff. Almost without exception the studies done appear to adopt the mythical view that all teachers are equivalent. This is not to say that certain studies do not attempt to "control" the teacher variable by age, sex, years of training, experience, and the like. However, the problem is somewhat more complex and relates to the balance between the quantity and the quality of staff. It is elementary that for the same cost one cannot buy as many items of high quality as can be afforded if one will settle for lower quality. Thus, in most instances the choices open to administrators are alternatives between fewer staff members at higher salaries or more staff members at lower salaries. Binion (1955) showed that staff adequacy is related to staff salaries. NSA deviating too markedly from an expected figure based upon net current expenditure has a negative relationship to a criterion of school system adaptability. Other evidence (Vincent & others, 1960) shows that it is possible for a school district to have classes that are too small in relation to its overall expenditure and salary policy, just as it is possible to have classes that are too large in relation to these financial factors. Swanson (1961) showed that a school district's competitive position, regionally and economically, influences its capacity to attract quality staff as measured by the relationship between staff age and staff training when average salary is controlled. A given district may enjoy an excellent competitive position among its neighbors within the boundaries of a single state but suffer markedly in its ability to attract teachers in competition with districts of neighboring states. This suggests that staff studies confined to single states are rarely applicable to other locales.

Thus, these two dimensions of the class-size problem must qualify any answer that can be given to the question whether smaller classes really make a difference. First, the issue is not one of class size per se but one of numerical staff adequacy. Second, the answer depends upon the kind of staff as measured by some criterion which reflects the competitive economics of staff recruitment policies—staff selection, retention, training, age, and salaries (Vincent & Swanson, 1961).

A third dimension concerns materials and equipment—the tools of teaching. No study that has come to the attention of this writer injects any such control into the analysis of the relative effectiveness of large and small classes. It is clear that in some instances additionally prepared materials are integral to the large class variable (Trathen, 1960). Yet neither this component nor the effect of its contribution is measured. Furthermore, no indication is given of what materials were integral to the small-class variable. Under the circumstances the general inconclusiveness of results of investigations in the area of class size is understandable.

CLASS SIZE AND METHOD. Some indication of the laxness of approach to research in class size may be seen in the designations employed—for example, referring to "methods of instruction" when what is meant is "size of group or class." Trathen (1960) states, for example: "Three *methods* (emphasis added) of instruction were employed: small sections, lecture-discussion, and an experimental approach to be used with large classes." Haziness regarding the function of method and its particular influence upon the class-size variable appears to be rather typical of the researches examined, particularly at the college level. Trathen goes on to state: "The first two formats are rather standard in institutions of higher learning and *descriptions at this point would appear to serve no useful purpose*" (emphasis added).

On the contrary, it would appear that descriptions of method are of vital importance to the research. The variable under study, it may be observed, is in two parts: (1) a classification of pupils into groups of a stated size, (2) teaching by a method of specified characteristics. Without control of both parts of the variable very little of meaning can be discerned from an investigation. Proponents of small classes have consistently maintained that the advantage lies in the methods that may be employed, such as variety of experiences, exploration, personal attention, teacher knowledge of individuals, social amenities, and interpersonal relations (Little, 1951). Any criterion employed to assess the effect of class size is in actuality assessing the accomplishments of some method—the method of teaching which was used in the study in question. Whether it appears to better advantage in large classes or in small classes depends upon the compatibility of the method with the size of the groups being investigated. One is at a loss to know, with respect to virtually all of the class-size literature, whether the research design specifies a method for either or both of the class-size categories and whether the method specified was actually consistently employed. It can be inferred from most of the studies at the college level that the method which predominates in both large and small groups is the lecture method (i.e., the instructor uses the greater portion of the time speaking out loud). For example Roberson (1959) quotes an instructor in a large-class experiment: "It seemed the handling of the large section was no more difficult so far as lecture presentation was concerned than a small class." This is one of the few indications of what the method was. It is probable that the principal finding of most college-level studies (see below) is that the lecture method is as compatible with large groups as with small groups.

McKenna and Pugh (1964) state that not all teachers, given a small group, will automatically adopt a method of optimum compatibility with the group size. They cite more individualized instruction in small classes, yet a considerable amount of instruction (43 percent) in small classes was still mass oriented. Danowski (1965) developed an instrument to measure individualization of instruction and applied it in 132 small classes (20 pupils or fewer). His purpose was to investigate differences between teachers who do and those who do not take advantage of the opportunity afforded in small classes for individualization of instruction. His sample of 132 fell roughly into equal halves, 68 teachers of small classes who employed individualized teaching and 64 who did not, despite the supposed opportunity afforded by the small class.

THE CRITERION VARIABLE. Five general types of criteria have been employed in the assessment of class size: (1) cost and related expediencies, including efficiency, ease of administration, and availability of personnel, which is frequently the principal motivation in the investigation (Stover, 1954); (2) working conditions, such as teacher load, which has had relatively little attention in the literature (Anderson, 1950); (3) opinion of teachers, administrators, or both, which has had widespread use and which almost invariably favors small classes (National Education Association, 1961); (4) effect on pupils, as measured by achievement or adjustment, some achievement measure being the criterion most frequently used (see below); (5) class activities made possible, or prohibited, by the particular size of the group intervals under investigation, the assumption being that appraisal of educational processes discriminates among potential outcomes (Newell, 1943).

The difficulties inherent in the employment of a criterion are the same as those which confront any measurement of school quality, namely, the necessity to establish the thing measured by the criterion as important, significant, or necessary to the educational enterprise. Thus, a study which employs one type of criterion can be faulted because of its failure to measure other outcomes. The majority of recent studies employ standardized achievement tests or class marks. Granted other purposes in education, it would appear that growth in measurable knowledge is a universal objective, and thus such a criterion can be defended, though no study examined by the present writer undertakes to do so. The other criterion principally employed, professional or pupil opinion, is less defensible on grounds of reliability (although no great case can be made on this score for class marks). Where more than one type of criterion is employed the results are frequently contradictory. For example, Siegel and his colleagues (1959) found college students in large groups obtaining class marks as high as those obtained in small groups, though attitudes of students in general expressed preference for small-class instruction.

Half a Century of Evidence. The decade of the 1920's, with the advent of reliable instruments for testing, appears to have been the period of greatest interest in the subject of class size at the elementary and secondary school levels, judging from the volume of published literature. After 1930 interest fell off, and comparatively few experimental studies are to be found in the reference guides. Rather, compendiums of data on the status of class size appear as the most frequent type of study in recent years (National Education Association 1964, 1965). Otto and his colleagues (1954) present a comprehensive review of the class-size literature, both experimental and conjectural, from the earliest writings (c. 1890) to the early 1950's.

ELEMENTARY AND SECONDARY CLASS SIZE. In 1954 Blake made an important analysis which was never published. He subjected the studies reported up to that time to six criteria of scientific adequacy and stated that of 267 reports in print only 22 met the requirements of these evaluative criteria (Blake, 1954). Of the 22, exactly half had employed some achievement measure as the criterion variable. Of these, 5 found small classes superior (Anderson, 1950; Lundberg, 1947; Wasson, 1929; Whitney, 1932; Wingfield, 1931); three found large classes superior (Eastburn, 1937; Smith, 1931; Stevenson, 1925); and three were inconclusive (Eastburn, 1936; Ewan, 1934; Metzner, 1926). Among Blake's 22 were 8 studies which had employed teacher or administrator opinion as the criterion variable. All of these found small classes to be superior. One of the studies cited by Blake, that of Baker (1936), employed teacher knowledge of individual pupils as the criterion variable; 2 studies—those of Pertsch (1943) and Newell (1943) employed class activities and teacher practices as criteria. All three of these found small classes superior.

This writer has found four studies subsequent to Blake's report in which an evaluation of the educational process was employed as the criterion variable. Three of them showed smaller classes to be superior in terms of a greater variety of activities, greater enrichment of materials, greater individualization of the teacher's communication and attention to pupils, and the like. Richman (1955) studied the middle elementary grades and found that in locations where class size had been reduced, practices designed to produce greater teacher understanding of individuals were increasingly used. He found the converse where class size was increased. Whitsitt (1955) observed large (34 pupils and more) and small (24 pupils and fewer) high school social studies and English classes in 35 schools. In small classes he found more use of enrichment materials, more detailed and current subject matter, more group work, more informality, and more opportunity for personal interaction. Pugh (1965) found in 90 small classes (20 or fewer), compared to 90 large classes (30 or more), a greater number of activities taking place in a given period of time, a greater variety of activities, a greater percentage of activities involving individual pupils and small groups within the class, and the following cognitive activities occurring significantly more frequently: listening, outlining, generalizing, analyzing and creating, in addition to greater use of motor skills and reading skills.

Otto (1954) used an observation check list supplemented by a teacher questionnaire to study 50 large elementary classes (35 pupils or more) and 50 small classes (25 pupils or fewer), and concludes that the findings "do not reveal small classes as possessing the expected distinctive advantages over large classes." The large-size category was favored by differences observed in practices, such as the following: mean total hours spent by teacher in the work week, total floor area devoted to seating, pupils hitting, punching, and fighting with others, and pupils participating in school safety patrol and in selected classroom activities. The small-size category was favored by differences observed in practices such as the following: mean per-pupil floor area, prevalence of desk chairs, pupils discourteous to teacher or fellow pupils, and all pupils in art classes receiving hectographed copies to color.

Three recent studies employ achievement as the

criterion variable. Spitzer (1954) tested the achievement of third-grade pupils enrolled in 50 small classes (26 and fewer) and 26 large classes (30 or more) and of sixth-grade pupils enrolled in 55 small classes and 17 large classes similarly defined. In general, the differences observed were not significant. Johnson and Lobb (1961) report an experiment with classes of 10, 20, 35, 60, and 70 pupils in academic senior high school subjects as part of a team-teaching program and state that "size of class did not in itself make any significant difference." Frymier (1964) compared reading achievement of 249 first graders enrolled in nine classes of fewer than 30 and 238 enrolled in six classes of more than 35. The two groups were closely comparable with regard to sex, age, and incidence of visual and hearing defects. Though the group in the large classes scored significantly higher initially on a test of reading readiness, spring testing on a standardized reading achievement test showed the group enrolled in the small classes approximately one month in advance of the large-class group, a difference significant at the .001 level.

Thus, as in the earlier studies, the evidence adduced by means of an achievement criterion is mixed, and it is not likely to become more nearly conclusive until studies are undertaken in which clearly specified characteristics of method and objective measures of teacher competence to deal with the methods specified are introduced as controls. The evidence adduced by means of an appraisal of the educational process is almost completely favorable to small classes. Such a criterion emphasizes method, whereas the achievement criterion does not. It is unfortunate that no study, so far, has combined both criteria in the same investigation.

COLLEGE AND UNIVERSITY CLASSES. Although interest in the subject has flagged among investigators of elementary- and secondary-school classes, interest at the college level has increased with the increasing enrollments in higher education. Nearly a dozen studies have been published since 1957. Practically all of these employ some achievement criterion, either tests or class marks. Bosley (1962), who reviews the bulk of the literature pertaining to college classes published since the 1920's, observes, "A majority of the small-class versus large-class investigations has not been overwhelmingly conclusive. . . . Most experiments have used subject fields in which the lecture technique is the major instructional approach." The college investigators appear to be interested in the practicality of exceptionally large groups for reasons of economy (Stempel, 1963). Nelson (1959) summarizes comparisons of classes numbering 309 and 332 students with classes numbering 23 and 31 in American government, sections of 125 with sections of fewer than 30 in geography, and a section of 109 with a section of 45 in a course in education. Statistically significant differences were not obtained.

Siegel (1959) tested achievement in a variety of college subjects taught in large groups (most of them over 100) by television and live lecture. He found achievement in small groups (19 to 32) not significantly better, except in second-semester geography. Macomber and Siegel (1957) studied a variety of large college classes (generally upwards of 77 to 183) taught by television, live lecture, and "case study" procedures. They compared the achievement of students in these with that of small classes (generally 20 to 30) taught by "small-group instructional procedures" that are unspecified. Among 27 pairings examined, statistically significant differences favoring small classes were obtained only in human biology and geology.

Cammarosano and Santopolo (1958) compared classes of 60 and 30 in freshman economics, government, and sociology using (1) semester averages of routine quizzes, written assignments, and examinations, some of the examinations having essay-type answers; (2) a "social-awareness" test of objective questions drawn from recent news accounts, and (3) a test of "principled synthesis of social outlook" based upon objective responses to hypothetical situations. Only in the principled-synthesis test for sociology were significant differences obtained, and these favored the smaller group. Nelson (1959) compared achievement of students in elementary economics in large classes (85–141) and small classes (16–20) and found no significant differences.

The only college-level study seen by this writer which shows achievement superior in small groups is also one which specifies differences in method applicable to the groups of different sizes. Simmons (1959) compared achievement of students in intermediate algebra by drawing a sample of 200 students from a control group where class size averaged 21.4 and a similar sample from an experimental group where class size averaged 84.6. He reports that the small classes were taught by "informal short lectures, the solving of illustrative examples, class discussion and recitation, unannounced short quizzes, and blackboard drill." The large classes were taught by "formal lecture interspersed with many illustrative examples" with a five-minute question period at the end. In addition, special conference hours were scheduled for large class students six times per week at which attendance was optional. After final letter marks were converted to numerical values the small-class average was 1.325 and the large class average .825, a difference significant at the .01 level.

CLASS-SIZE POLICY. Presumably the reason for investigating class size is that the results may influence administrative policies. However, there is scant evidence to show that there is any such thing as a class-size policy, if by "policy" is meant a relatively stable principle to which instant decisions are consciously referred. Mort and Furno (1960) suggest that class size appears to be more closely related to the community and its setting external to the school than to any single set of factors within the school. Ross and McKenna (1955) note that communities in general are willing to build new buildings, rent church basements, and even go on half sessions before departing too markedly from a class size to which they are accustomed. Stover (1954) observes that class size appears to be determined by such factors as expediency, birth rate, financial considerations, and the availability of physical facilities. There is ample evidence of excessive overcrowding. It is estimated that if all elementary-school children in classes of more than 25 were regrouped into classes of 25, 17 percent more classroom space would be needed (National Education Association, 1965). Thus it might be hypothesized that class size, as we find it, is determined by space availability rather than any conscious class-size policy. At the secondary level it is reported that the larger the school system, the larger the classes in both junior and senior high schools (National Education Association, 1964). Furthermore, there is enormous variability; class size ranges from under 16 to over 45. The range is so great within individual districts that median class size means little. Modal class size in home economics and industrial arts runs about half that in the academic subjects. This, it would appear, results from the practice of dividing girls and boys out of the full-size academic class in order to make up the smaller groups rather than from a particular class-size policy for these subjects. Among the academic subjects like English, mathematics, and science more of the classes are large classes (35 and more) in the junior high school, while more of these classes are small classes (21 or fewer) in the senior high school. This is probably a function of pupil attrition.

Whatever the cause, numerical staff adequacy has increased constantly and progressively for the past several decades. According to Danowski and Finch (1966) in the nation at large the average number of professionals per 1,000 pupils (NSA) stood at 25 in 1920. By 1950 it was 36, and by 1964 it was 43. In a group of relatively well-financed suburban school districts average NSA stood at 39 in 1921. By 1966 it was 62. Of the 62, 50 staff members per 1,000 pupils were in the classrooms, the remaining 12 filling administrative, supervisory, and other specialist positions. This figures out to an average class size of 20. Thus, in the schools of the nation at large, and in well-financed schools particularly, class size has decreased even in a period of rising enrollments and increasing salaries.

William S. Vincent
Columbia University

References

Anderson, Kenneth E. "The Relationship Between Teacher Load and Student Achievement." *Sch Sci Math* 50:468–70; 1950.

Baker, H. Leigh. "A Study of Five Connecticut High Schools and 250 Pupils in Relation to Class Size." Doctoral dissertation. Yale U, 1935. Abstract in "Class Size Does Make a Difference." *Nation's Sch* 17:27–28; 1936.

Binion, Stuart, "An Analysis of the Relationship of Pupil-Teacher Ratio to School Quality." Doctoral dissertation. Teachers College, Columbia U, 1955.

Blake, Howard E. "Class Size: A Summary of Selected Studies in Elementary and Secondary Public Schools." Doctoral dissertation. Teachers College, Columbia U, 1954.

Bosley, Howard E. "Class Sizes and Faculty-Student Ratios in American Colleges." *Ed Rec* 43:148–53; 1962.

Cammarosano, Joseph R., and Santopolo, Frank A. "Teaching Efficiency and Class Size." *Sch Soc* 86:338–41; 1958.

Danowski, Charles E. *Teachers Who Individualize Instruction*. Teachers College, Columbia U, 1965.

Danowski, Charles E., and Finch, James N. "Teacher Preparation and Numerical Adequacy." In *Research Bulletin No. 6* Institute Adm Res, 1966. p. 7–10.

Eastburn, Lacey A. "The Relative Efficiency of Instruction in Large and Small Classes on Three Ability Levels." *Exp Ed* 5:17–22; 1936.

Eastburn, Lacey A., and Garretson, O. K. "A Report of Class Size Investigations in the Phoenix Union High School, 1933–34 to 1935–36." *J Ed Res* 31:107–17; 1937.

Ewan, Stacy N., Jr. *The Relation of Class Size and Selected Teaching Methods*. The author, 1934. 100p.

Frymier, Jack R. "The Effect of Class Size upon Reading Achievement in First Grade." *Reading Teach* 18:90–3; 1964.

Johnson, Robert H., and Lobb, M. Delbert. "Jefferson County, Colorado, Completes Three Year Study of Staffing, Changing Class Size, Programming, and Scheduling." *Nat Assn Sec Sch Prin B* 45:57–78; 1961.

Little, Ruth C. "Effect of Class Size on Learning." *NEA J* 40:215–6; 1951.

Lundberg, Lawrence D. "Effects of Smaller Classes." *Nation's Sch* 39:20–2; 1947.

Macomber, F. G., and Siegel, Laurence. "Study in Large Group Teaching Procedures." *Ed Rec*, 38:220–9; 1957.

McKenna, Bernard H. *Staffing the Schools*. Teachers College, Columbia U, 1965. 120p.

McKenna, Bernard H., and Pugh, James B., Jr. "Performance of Pupils and Teachers in Small Classes Compared to Large." *IAR Res B*, 4(2):1–4; 1964.

Metzner, Alice B., and Berry, Charles S. "Size of Class for Mentally Retarded Children." *Training Sch B* 23:241–51; 1926.

Mort, Paul R., and Furno, Orlando F. *Theory and Synthesis of A Sequential Simplex: A Model for Assessing the Effectiveness of Administrative Policies*. Institute Research Study No. 12. Teachers College, Columbia U, 1960. 104p.

National Education Association. "Teachers and Principals Agree on Best Class Size." *NEA Res B* 39:107; 1961.

National Education Association. *Class Size in Secondary Schools*. Research Report 1964–R16. NEA, 1964, 30p.

National Education Association. *Class Size in Kinder-*

gartens and Elementary Schools. Research Report 1965–R11. NEA, 1965.

Newell, Clarence A. *Class Size and Adaptability.* Contributions to Education, No. 894. Teachers College, Columbia U, 1943. 99p.

Nelson, Wallace B. "An Experiment with Class Size in the Teaching of Elementary Economics." *Ed Rec* 40:330–41; 1959.

Otto, Henry J., and others. *Class Size Factors in Elementary Schools.* U Texas Press, 1954. 178p.

Pertsch, C. Frederick. "Some Effect of Class Size on the Educational Program in New York City Elementary Schools." In *The Advancing Front of Education,* 8th Yearbook, New York Society for the Experimental Study of Education. Thesis Publishing Company, 1943.

Pugh, James B., Jr. *Performance of Teachers and Pupils in Small Classes.* Teachers College, Columbia U, 1965.

Richman, Harold, "Educational Practices as Affected by Class Size." Doctoral dissertation. Teachers College, Columbia U, 1955.

Roberson, John A. "Teaching Efficiency and Class Size." *J Engineering Ed* 50:37–40; 1959.

Ross, Donald H., and McKenna, Bernard H. *Class Size: The Multi-million Dollar Question.* Teachers College, Columbia U, 1955. 24p.

Siegel, Laurence, and others. "Effectiveness of Large Group Instruction at the University Level." *Harvard Ed Res* 29(3):216–26; 1959.

Simmons, Harold F. "Achievement in Intermediate Algebra Associated with Class Size at the University of Wichita." *Col U* 34:309–15; 1959.

Smith, Dora V. *Class Size in High School English.* Minnesota Press, 1931. 309p.

Spitzer, Herbert F. "Class Size and Pupil Achievement in Elementary Schools." *El Sch J* 55:82–6; 1954.

Stempel, Guido H. "Relationship of Cost of Instruction and Attitudes toward Instruction." *J Ed Res* 57:207–9; 1963.

Stevenson, Paul R. *Class-size in the Elementary School.* Ohio State U Press, 1925. 35p.

Stover, Frank B. "Administrator Policies in Class Size." Doctoral dissertation. Teachers College, Columbia U, 1954.

Swanson, Austin D. *Effective Administrative Strategy.* Teachers College, Columbia U, 1961. 80p.

Trathen, Ronald H. "Two Years of Experimental Work on Various Teaching Methods and Class Sizes." *J Engineering Ed* 50:380–7; 1960.

Vincent, William S., and Swanson, Austin D. "Regional Variations in Educational Cost and Their Potential Influence Upon Staff Recruitment Policies." *IAR Res B* 1(3):5–7; 1961.

Vincent, William S., and others. "The Question of Class Size." *IAR Res B* 1(1):1–4; 1960.

Wasson, William H. "A Controlled Experiment in the Size of Classes." Master's thesis. U Chicago, 1929.

Whitney, Frederick L., and Willey, Gilbert S. "Advantages of Small Classes." *Sch Executives M* 51:504–6; 1932.

Whitsitt, Robert C. "Comparing the Individualities of Large Secondary School Classes with Small Secondary School Classes Through the Use of a Structured Observation Schedule." Doctoral dissertation. Teachers College, Columbia U, 1955.

Wingfield, Robert C. "An Experimental Study of the Determination of Relative Efficiency of Instruction in Large and Small Classes of Elementary Algebra." Master's thesis. U Virginia, 1930. Abstract in *U Virginia Rec Extension Series, Sec Ed Virginia* 15:3–13; 1931.

CLASSICAL LANGUAGES

For an excellent summary of the historical background and development of the study and teaching of Latin and Greek in the United States, the reader is referred to the article CLASSICAL LANGUAGES by DeWitt in the third edition of this encyclopedia. In that account DeWitt divided the history of teaching the classical languages into two periods, the traditional and the contemporary. For the sake of convenience he set the dividing line at 1925, a date which he regarded as marking the end of the classical tradition in American education.

Larudee (1964), in surveying the same pedagogical terrain, puts the evolution of language in a slightly different way. He notes two significant periods, the lexical and the structural. In the first, extending down to the nineteenth century, language was viewed as consisting of words; memorization was the primary goal of language instruction and intuition the principal source of methodological changes. In the second period, since the nineteenth century, emphasis has been on structural patterns of language; the goal of instruction has been habit formation; and the development of method has been based on what are believed to be scientifically sound pedagogical principles.

CONTEMPORARY TRENDS. Although, as Jones (1966) points out, the structural approach appeared very early in the history of grammar, Sweet (1953, 1954) was the first American to make practical application available in the form of two textbooks for beginning students in Latin. Each of these has gone through several editions and revisions by Sweet himself, some of his workshop teacher-students, or both. Several articles by Sweet had earlier aroused considerable interest and controversy among Latin teachers throughout the country. Through his publications and workshops the structural or linguistic approach to the teaching of Latin has had a strong impact on the profession as a whole, especially on instruction in the secondary schools. For a complete bibliography of his texts and an account of his method and its development between 1953 and 1967, see Sweet (1967).

The emergence of the structural approach to the study of Latin has brought into focus the contrast between this and the traditional method, which is commonly referred to as the reading or functional method. Since the principal aim of all "methods" and texts is to help students to learn to read Latin as Latin, as stated in the Classical Investigation of 1924 (American Classical League, 1924), the problem becomes one of determining how this can best be accomplished. Answers to this question will naturally vary with individual teachers, many of whom find that an eclectic approach is best. Some of the choices therefore are considered in the following discussion.

Oral-aural Practice. The psychology of learning long ago demonstrated that a child hears and speaks his native language before he learns to read it. The application of this principle to learning Latin has taken two forms which are often confused with each other. One is generally called the "direct method," attributed to the noted British scholar Rouse (Rouse, 1910; Rouse & Appleton, 1925). Intensive use of this method for teaching languages in World War II revived educational interest in it, and another British scholar, Peckett (1963) advocated its application to Latin once more, on the common-sense ground that sound adds to sense, particularly in poetry. This method, however, is *not* to be identified with the linguistic approach, in which the core lies in the pursuit of language as language, in the reading of Latin as Latin in the Latin word order. Oral practice, necessarily associated with aural experience, in the interrelation of Teacher and student in the classroom, is reinforced by the use of tapes and disks inside or outside the language laboratory. These facilities combine oral-aural practice and lead to correct habits of pronunciation and intonation and to comprehension of language patterns. Carr (1963) stresses the necessity of reading Latin as Latin to appreciate the niceties of Latin word order as an aid to comprehension. Ward (1962) affirms that bringing out quantitive differences between syllables, both for vowels and consonants, will make Latin come alive and give it the ring and accent of a real language.

Word Order. Structural linguists emphasize the contrast between Latin and English as shown by the different role that word order plays in each. In English it is the key to meaning. In Latin it is the inflection which serves that purpose; word order reflects emphasis. Ullman (1960), however, warns against the idea of "fixed" rules for Latin word order and denies that there is a "normal" order based on frequency of occurrence. He points out that important words in a group are likely to come first and that separation of grammatically related words, such as nouns and adjectives, often tends to give greater emphasis to the word preceding. A sample of run-on lines from familiar authors shows no consistent pattern for the position of nouns versus adjectives, or for verbs in a clause. He concludes therefore that flexibility of the Latin word order gives almost endless variety to Latin speech and writing and makes possible subtle distinctions of emphasis that are most difficult, if not impossible, to attain in English.

Another aspect of word order, the position of the direct object in relation to its verb, was investigated by Carr (1961). In Vergil the direct object precedes the verb 60 percent of the time, in contrast to 88 percent of the time in Cicero and 98 percent in Caesar. Comparable figures for Catullus are 51 percent, for Ovid 52 percent, for Horace (*Satires*) 66 percent, and for Lucretius 67 percent. One advantage that advocates of the "translation method" claim for such word order is that it compels the student to put the Latin verb and its object into normal English word order. Those who belong to the "direct-reading" school warn that students who are allowed to transpose Latin words into the more familiar English word order will never learn to comprehend Latin as Latin; nor will they come to appreciate the various rhetorical and rhythmical effects which the Latin writer achieves through a word order that inflectional forms make possible. There is little question that word order is one of the most difficult problems the young Latin student has to master, and the final word on the matter has not yet been said.

Cunningham (1965), in presenting a theoretical model or framework for basic syntactical structures characteristic of the Latin sentence, specifies two types: the simple verbal sentence and the simple predicate sentence. The presence of a finite verb characterizes the former. It includes, however, clauses with a narrative infinitive, clauses with accusative and infinitive, and clauses in which a finite form of a verb is "understood." In the simple predicate type of sentence the verb is neither expressed nor understood. Cunningham also points out that the meaning of a given sentence depends upon a number of factors, important among which is the social and situational character of the syntactical unit. He suggests that linguistics deals primarily with the audible elements in a speech situation, whereas grammar embraces the total speech situation.

Grammar Via Structure. Traditional texts present grammar by the deductive method; that is, a certain "rule" is stated and sentences are given to illustrate the principle. In the structural approach grammar is presented inductively; that is, many examples of a given grammatical construction are presented in the context of Latin phrases and sentences. Questions are then asked or written in Latin about the phrase or sentence which must be answered by the student in Latin. This sort of repetition, known as "pattern practice," develops a technique for the learning of grammatical principles by "doing." The "utterance," as the phrase or clause is termed, may be written in a text, spoken by the teacher, or put on a tape. Often all three presentations are used in a class period or drill.

The basic utterance usually consists of five or six words, or it may be longer. Since nouns and adjectives are given in horizontal paradigms, that is, in all five declensions at once, in the three most common case-forms (nominative, accusative, and ablative), great variety is possible. Paradigms of verbs are presented in the same way for all four conjugations, first the third person singular of the present tense active, then the perfect tense. In due time the other tenses, voices and moods follow.

Variations of the basic pattern come from three types of drill: (1) expansion, by addition or omission of such items as pronouns, adjectives, or ablatival phrases; (2) substitution of vocabulary items or phrases; and (3) transformation, in which the verb is changed in number, tense, voice, or mood, and nouns and pronouns are changed in case, number, or both, as desired.

In each drill only one grammatical item is changed at a time, and drill is continued until that particular item is presumably learned. Continued as part of a daily routine, with corresponding time saving in class, the response should eventually become automatic through a saturation process. Sweet (1961) carries the technique to the extreme by the use of "clozes" (a term derived from "closure," to describe "what occurs when an organism connects two events in a series when one or more of the intermediate steps have been omitted") in a passage from a literary work. This method guarantees such control of the passage that a student can reproduce it with only the suggestion of a clue. It differs from total recall in putting the premium not on memorization but on such comprehension of the patterns shown by the Latin writer that the student can reproduce the missing links.

Critique of the Structural Approach. Classicists have received Sweet's structural approach with varying degrees of approval and disapproval. Among the early professional reactions was a symposium at the spring 1956 meeting of the Classical Association of the Middle West and South, at which four prepared papers supported the structural approach (Fowler & others, 1957). The first opponent to appear in print (Johnson, 1958) based his objections on the loss of the humane values of Latin and on the insistence on the differences between Latin and English. To him one of the great strengths of Latin study was its "training in exactness, subtlety, discrimination, sensitivity in word and thought." Corcoran (1961) objected to the overuse of Latin questions and answers, the proliferation of technical terms, and the lack of connected discourse for translation.

Because of the growing uneasiness among members of the profession concerning the new approach, the American Philological Association devoted one session of its 1959 meeting to the topic (Levy, 1962). Five classicists presented different aspects, theoretical and practical, in prepared papers. The general discussion showed that opinion was divided. For a summary of the various points of view, see Jones (1966; the article was written in 1961).

Whatever method is used, one of the essentials in learning a second language is knowledge of the grammar of that language. Carroll (1966) describes research to determine what kind of practice in sentence construction is most effective. Method I was analogous to "pattern practice" used in language laboratories in which the learner repeats the utterance heard. This is termed "passive" practice. Method II was similar to Method I except that a language master card with a pictorial representation enabled the student to *see* the "action" described in the sentence he was repeating. In Method III the student looked at the picture on the card and tried to compose a sentence describing the action *before* listening to the sentence. This is termed "active" practice. Method III was found definitely superior to Method II and Method II definitely superior to Method I. Results of other experiments showed that explanation of grammatical features preceding drill (deductive method) produced better results than omission of such explanations (inductive method).

In commenting on the contributions of linguistic theory to second-language learning, Chomsky (1966) recommends that teachers should not accept ideas or proposals on faith without attempting to validate or refute them. He points out that the principles of phonemic analysis and even the status of the concept "phoneme" are much in doubt. (A phoneme is a "cluster of closely related sounds that are never contrasted with each other.") He also questions the notion that linguistic behavior consists of "responses" to "stimuli," or that it is a "matter of habit and generalization." Normal language use has the "property of being innovative and stimulus-free." Native speakers have "internalized a 'generative grammar'— a system of rules that can be used in new and untried combinations to form new sentences." Chomsky doubts very much whether such a generative grammar can be acquired by experience or training.

Although the science of linguistics, as Ferguson (1966) indicates, does not say directly how grammatical systems should be taught, Ferguson examines four principles that have come to be regarded as basic in any application of linguistics to language teaching.

Principle 1 is that language is patterned human behavior subject to systematic, objective analysis. This principle has resulted in the development of pattern drills used in language laboratories. It has also given rise to the serious misunderstanding that the setting aside of value judgments for linguistic analysis meant the scrapping of standards in grammar. This is not the case.

Principle 2 holds that every language presents a unique structure which must be analyzed on its own terms. The provision of reliable language data and descriptions, in Ferguson's opinion, will probably be the most important single contribution of linguistics to language teaching for some time to come.

Principle 3 holds that speech has primacy over writing. This principle has resulted in several misconceptions. Chief among them is the idea that the acquisition of a reading knowledge was improved and accelerated by concentration on oral competence first. The idea that linguists are concerned only with speech and not with written language seems strange in view of the fact that much of their work has been involved with the analysis of written texts. It is expected that linguists will contribute substantially to improvement of language teaching by investigating more thoroughly the relationship between speech and writing.

Principle 4 is that language behavior is part of a communication process and takes place within social and situational contexts. This is an area in which more research needs to be done and one which will require the cooperation of other social scientists, language teachers, and humanistic scholars. It holds much promise for the improvement of language teaching in this country.

Considerations such as those indicated above had already influenced the development of Latin texts and programs. In 1956 Sweet revised his *Latin Workshop Experimental Materials,* first published in 1953. It was revised again by Crawford and others (1963). In 1957 Sweet published *Latin: A Structural Approach* (revised by Craig and Seligson in 1966). This differed from traditional texts in several ways but chiefly in having the text and readings taken from Latin authors, pattern practice and questions on the text and readings mostly in Latin, and tapes for optional pattern practice drills. This was followed by *Vergil's Aeneid: A Structural Approach* in 1960, and in 1961 by *Clozes and Vocabulary Exercises for Books I and II of the Aeneid.*

Programmed Learning. By this time, however, Sweet was gradually becoming convinced that pattern-practice techniques had several weaknesses. The student mimicked the teacher's taped recording or studied the text until he had memorized the drill. The follow-up self tests showed a serious gap between echoing a drill and constructing responses. Errors made in this way or in answering questions on the texts or readings remained uncorrected until the student came to class. Sweet sought to overcome this difficulty by adapting his material for programming on the technique of the "teaching machine" as described by Skinner (1958). After examining the self-corrected responses Sweet revised the drills radically. He proceeded gradually from easy "clues" to the correct answer to the point where few or no clues were given. This technique makes it possible to control the rate of error and to determine that the program is more important than the machine. As a result, after several years of work and five revisions, *Latin: Level One* (Sweet, 1966) appeared in 1966 as the core of what is called the *Artes Latinae* Program. *Latin: Level Two* will soon be published.

Level One is a linear program in book form of about 10,000 frames divided into 30 units, covering about the same structures usually covered in American high schools in the ninth grade. The program is multisensory in that it employs aural-oral and written work, with the addition of visual stimuli. The drills are massive and varied, requiring Latin responses to Latin texts or pictures. Use of a tape recorder for oral-aural work is optional.

Other components of the *Artes Latinae* Program include filmstrips, study prints, a reader, a reference notebook, and tests, all closely integrated with the basic text. Motion picture films dealing with various aspects of the Roman world and civilization are available for enrichment.

Classics and Computers. The flexibility of Latin (and Greek) structure makes it particularly adaptable for piecemeal or small-step learning, which is the essence of programming. Barrutia (1965) has studied the relationship between machine teaching and the linguistic theory of language learning. He notes that linguistic science analyzes language by describing the distribution of minimal contrasts, while programmed learning involves a behavioristic approach to learning, its basic principle of reinforced minimal steps making it a logical vehicle of language instruction.

Such characteristics of Latin make computer use of its material very promising. The IBM 705 computer, for example, has been used for literary data processing in the preparation of a concordance to such literary works as those of Thomas Aquinas. McDonough (1959), a pioneer in such studies, demonstrates the versatility of the computer for the emendation of texts, the autoabstraction of learned articles, and the collation of manuscripts. He unveils the potential for a new era in scholarship when the electronic computer is made to perform the servile secretarial tasks of machine processing that will free the scholar for the important function of humanistic evaluation and interpretation.

Translation. In the *Classical Investigation* (American Classical League, 1924) the primary teaching objective in the study of Latin was given as a "progressive development of the power to read and understand Latin." This was considered "indispensable for the attainment of long range objectives," which were listed as instrumental (direct use of the ability to read and understand Latin), application (the use of facts or methods acquired in the study of Latin in the acquisition of other facts in the linguistic experience of the pupil outside the immediate field of Latin), disciplinary, and cultural.

Although the *Classical Investigation* placed emphasis on the reading of Latin and understanding it in Latin, the practical result was that the student was expected to translate into English to demonstrate his understanding of the original. Textbooks after 1924 show many changes in format, with Latin reading usually placed first, vocabulary and word study next, forms and syntax later. Among the various texts there was a great variety in the order of presentation of material, less learning of paradigms. Questions on the text were introduced, there was much word study, and large sections of cultural background in English were to be found, together with attractive photographs. Yet, perhaps because of the training and experience of teachers, the study of Latin remained largely one of translation from Latin to English.

The salient features of the structural approach tend to minimize translation of Latin into English. Emphasis is, rather, on interpretation of a given passage in simpler Latin. Poetry, for example, is paraphrased in prose; notes to selections of poetry and prose are given in Latin, and questions and answers on content of a Latin passage are given in Latin.

It is still a debatable point, however, to what extent this method will develop real facility in reading and understanding Latin prose and poetry in appreciable amounts without the intellectual exercise and stimulation of interpreting Latin in one's own language. A kind of compromise between the literal and the literary translation is possibly represented by Seligson's metaphrasing (1960): a technique for observing the signals of Latin syntax to arrive at meaning in English.

The views of Johnson (1958) and Corcoran (1961) on this matter have been cited above. Levy (1959) makes a cogent plea for virile translation into English on two counts: that one may learn from the difference between Latin and English about the patterns of English in its more formal aspects and that Latin and Greek classrooms may soon be the only places in which translation from a foreign language into English will be part of the school curriculum. They may be the only places in which the American student will be required to compare and contrast another idiom with his own in long, connected contexts. Such juxtaposition of literary material is still considered a valid avenue of self-discovery and development. The smooth transition from mastery of language elements to proficiency in reading and understanding the sophisticated literature of Latin (and Greek) authors remains yet to be worked out to reach a level of competency deemed adequate for the majority of Latin students in secondary schools.

Almost by way of parenthesis it might be added here that, since the study of Greek is almost nonexistent in public and private secondary schools of the country, the situation just mentioned pertains primarily to Latin. At the college level, however, Greek study is reviving. For this reason, as the wording indicates, the title of this article implies the inclusion of Greek.

Writing Latin. The ability to write Latin comes only after extensive study to gain familiarity with the idioms and patterns of the language. Such knowledge must be based on the writings of Latin authors. For these reasons Latin composition is the last skill to be practiced and attained. More often than not it is used as a test for comprehension of the pattern rather than as a means of learning it. Completion exercises and sentence writing may help fix morphology and syntax, but free composition or stylistic exercises have largely given way to headline writing or paraphrase when original work is required.

Texts. There is little doubt that the writings and textbooks of Sweet have had a pronounced influence on the production of Latin textbooks for secondary schools since the early 1950's. Several inductive or reading-method texts have been revised, with the addition of tapes for drill. The number of new texts linguistically oriented, with excerpts from Latin authors rather than from "made" Latin, is noteworthy; they are those of O'Brien and Twombley (1964), Burns and others (1964), Distler (1963), Most (1961), Towey and Akielascek (1966), Stephens and Springhetti (1967), and Ashley and Lashbrook (1967). Two texts for use in grades 7 and 8 may soon be ready for publication: one by Richard T. Urban, of Saint John Fisher College, Rochester, N.Y.; the other by Gerald F. Erickson, of the University of Minnesota. Still another text in manuscript form is that of J. D. Sadler, of Austin College, Sherman, Texas. In the last the linguistic approach is modified in favor of emphasis on etymology. Other materials for use in grade 6 are in preparation in Washington, D.C., and possibly in other places not known to the writers.

Readers. The program of automated language instruction has produced a need for supplementary reading materials. Among the readers there are several types: composite work from the same Latin author, selections from different authors on a single theme, and anthologies arranged chronologically or by genre. Drake (1964, 1965) has produced two readers with a wide variety of selections. A plastic grid for covering interlinear vocabulary helps has the double advantage of being novel and of having self-instructing value. British writers and publishers have been alert to current needs and have been providing readers, described by Bateman (1963, 1964, 1965), that are being widely used in the United States.

In addition to their use as supplements to a given text, the readers may serve to enrich an honors class and provide special assignments for gifted students, summer reading for the more serious students, and extra practice in preparation for Regents' examinations and College Board examinations. They have also given teachers an added incentive to extend the reading horizon both for their students and for themselves.

Cultural Enrichment. The new emphasis on language learning places another responsibility on the teacher, that of integrating for the student the values that may accrue from an early and intensive experience with literature that reflects the classical tradition. The 1960 Northeast Conference on the Teaching of Foreign Languages explored this pedagogical obligation. As chairman of Working Committee IV, Kibbe (1960) showed the degree to which adaptation and assimilation of the classical ingredients have helped to mold our cultural history. The task of integration becomes greater with the increased presence of the classical influence and consequently the increased need for the classics student to develop and express critical judgment in discerning authentic reproductions or adaptations of the classical elements in our culture. Else (1965a) has suggested construction of curricula that focus on active engagement of the student in the treatment of people, their actions, and the implications of their actions. Such curricula will help to guide the student toward imaginative structuring of experience into an aesthetically ordered whole. Else (1965b) has also made an eloquent plea for greater emphasis, in the education of teachers of the classics, on the historical, philosophical, literary, and humane significance of the ancient writers and on the interdisciplinary nature of classical studies.

In the populace at large many factors contribute to the creation of a climate favorable to the classics. Among these may be mentioned the educational activities of museums, diffusion of the arts through commercial and educational television, and numerous translations of the classics by reputable scholars, published at popular prices. Gifted specialists and amateurs reveal the treasures of such special fields as numismatics and archaeology as visual corroboration of literature and as irrefutable records of the Greco-Roman world.

Testing. A decided shift in emphasis has taken place in testing: from recognition and recall to application of the known to the unknown, from memory to logic and reason. The real test of the linguistic proficiency of a student is his ability to solve new problems comparable to those he has mastered. In the absence of national examinations to establish norms in teaching-learning, the New York State Regents' examinations, Advanced Placement tests, and the College Board examinations are the most widely used and recognized yardsticks. Many state classical associations and colleges and universities conduct competitive examinations to broaden the testing experience and to give recognition to superior students. Among others, Hogan (1964) offers good rationale and concrete examples for testing language skills. Eder and Summerlin (1960) enumerate and give examples of objective type questions appropriate to Latin testing. Vocabulary, for example, may be tested by multiple-choice, completion, and matching tests. Comprehension may be tested by multiple-choice, completion, true-false, and essay tests. The same elements enter into testing for cultural background and aural-oral facility.

PRESENT STATUS. Teacher Training. The new methods of language teaching, with emphasis on the aural-oral and pattern practice, and the increasing use of such tools as tape recorders, language laboratories, and projectors of several types require special training of teachers of Latin. Often the classics departments in colleges and universities are quite unprepared or unwilling to provide Latin teachers with training adequate for the current situation. To meet this need summer workshops and institutes have been established, some with financial aid from foundations and some with federal support. Special MAT programs for Latin which have been established in several universities are also excellent answers to the problem. Since there are many older women returning to Latin teaching because of a shortage of personnel, special courses for "retooling" are being offered. Textbooks on methods typically lag behind current research and trends. Those by Hall (1966) and Lado (1964) are useful for the general field of language teaching; more practical for Latin are the methods texts of Distler (1962) and Morris (1966). To keep abreast of current methods, theory and techniques, the best source is to be found in the classical publications—e.g., *Classical Bulletin, Classical Journal, Classical Outlook,* and *Classical World.* Recent conferences on the problems of the classical profession have stimulated serious studies of standards for certification of Latin teachers and standards for courses in teacher training.

Classics in the Curriculum. Despite the competition of other courses in the secondary curriculum, which has cut into Latin enrollments for some years, Latin has held its own until the past decade, both in numbers and percentages. But the lack of teachers in some instances has caused the dropping of courses. The traditional Latin program of four years has gradually diminished to a two-year sequence, partly because of the idea that two years of a language are enough, partly because college requirements usually specify two years of language for entrance. There has also been a mistaken idea that Latin is not accepted for college entrance, perhaps because of the term "foreign language," which is interpreted to mean "modern language." An unexpected competition to Latin in the past decade has been the growth of the FLES program, which begins foreign languages in the elementary schools. Students are then urged to continue with the same language and are not encouraged to change to Latin or to study two languages at the same time. Parker (1964), who was largely responsible for initiating the FLES program, has issued a plea for the maintaining of Latin study along with modern languages.

To meet the situation the classicists are devising courses for the institution of Latin in the sixth grade. Courses in Latin at this level are already in operation in several school systems. The linguistically talented high school student, who is most likely to be attracted to classical studies, can carry on Latin study under such programs as provided by honors classes, independent study, and summer study, especially under the Advanced Placement program (Taylor, 1962).

Increased interest in area studies from elementary school through college provides the Latin teacher with an opportunity to participate in a team-teaching program in the humanities for which the Latin course, since 1924, has often been an introduction. An important aspect of Latin study may well lie in the direction of a general course in classical studies. This trend may already be noted on the college level, where classics in translation, mythology, classical civilization, archaeology, art, and history are often combined in the humanities program. Urbanization and the rise of the so-called inner-city school present the problem of exposing the underprivileged segment of the school population to the humanities through direct language experience or indirectly through secondary or auxiliary objectives of language study—e.g., etymology, mythology, literary allusion, ancient civilization. Such a course in Washington, D.C., is described by Hayden (1966) and in Detroit, Michigan, by Kovach (1966). Schoenheim's (1967) annual listing of texts and inexpensive books for teaching all aspects of the classics indicates the great volume of material appearing regularly. Although Greek has almost disappeared from the high school curriculum, advanced students are asking for it and are in many places studying Greek along with Latin 3 and 4, or in extracurricular study.

Professional Activities. Because of the need for unifying the classics teachers on all levels and the need for articulation of college and secondary programs, in 1962 Latimer proposed the formation of a new organization to be called CAUSA (Classical Association of the United States of America). This proposal was not acceptable to the various regional groups, but it was pointed out that the American Classical League (ACL) was already a national representative body, since its council was made up of delegates from all classical organizations. Accordingly, in 1966, ACL, with the financial support of the American Philological Association and other classical organizations, established in Washington, D.C., the National

Office with Latimer as its executive secretary. This office, a center for collecting and distributing information, is now engaged in compiling a master roster of all classics teachers in the country, the gathering of statistics on enrollments, and the coordination of classics programs at all levels. It publishes a newsletter, *Classical Action, USA.*

Several conferences since 1959 dealing with the status of the classics are evidence of the scholarly interest in improving course content and methodology, as well as the relevance of classical studies in the present-day curriculum. The first of these was the Classics Panel sponsored by the American Council of Learned Societies (ACLS) for its Committee on the Secondary Schools, reported by Pratt (1959). ACLS again sponsored a colloquium on the classics in education on the program of the Fourth International Congress of Classical Studies in Philadelphia in 1964, with papers on the teaching of classical languages, classical literature, and ancient history and civilization (Else, 1965b). This was followed in 1965 by the Planning Conference to Examine the Role of Classical Studies in American Education and to Make Recommendations for Needed Research and Development, supported by the Cooperative Research Projects of the U.S. Office of Education. The report of the four study groups (Latimer, 1965), known as the Airlie Report, after the conference site, provides a valuable inventory of the contemporary situation of the classics. More practical results are to be expected from a conference held at Oxford, Ohio, in June, 1967 under a grant from the National Endowment for the Humanities (NEH). Study groups at this conference, dealing with Latin in grades 6, 7, and 8, Latin I and II, teacher training, and public relations, produced essential guidelines for improving the classics programs. A report of the Conference will be published in the fall of 1967. The NEH grant for a Latin Institute at the University of Minnesota in the summer of 1966 for training Latin teachers for grades 7 and 8 marked the first federal support for preparation of materials and teachers in Latin. This was followed by a similar NEH program in the summer of 1967 at the same institution. Recent federal legislation on the support of education makes provision for the training of Latin teachers on terms similar to those authorized under the National Defense Education Act of 1958 and its subsequent revisions.

General Situation in 1967. Between 1958 and 1962 there was a consistent and gradual increase of Latin students in the public high schools of the country. Between 1962 and 1963, however, there was a drop of about 6 percent, with the decreases where it hurt most, in Latin I and II. In the following year there was an even sharper drop of 13 percent, with Latin III joining Latin I and II in the downward swing.

In 1965 this trend was reversed for the key points, Latin I and III; Latin II and IV showed slight further losses.

College majors in classics show a slow but steady increase. The latest figures, for June 1965, as given in a report by the U.S. Office of Education (1966),

indicate about 1,100 graduates who majored in classics. In 1963–64 college undergraduates in Latin numbered about 30,000; graduate students, about 1300. In 1964–65, according to a study made by the Modern Language Association of America (1966), these figures had increased to 36,200 and 1,677, respectively. In 1964–65 undergraduates studying Greek numbered about 15,600 and graduates 2,630. The excess of graduate students in Greek over those in Latin explains the relative scarcity of Latinists as compared with Hellenists for college teaching positions. Since Greek has long been all but nonexistent in public high schools and greatly diminished in private schools, it seems clear that college teaching is the goal of most graduate students of Greek. The ranks of graduate students of Latin are undoubtedly thinned by those who respond to the need for teachers in the secondary schools.

The exact situation in these schools is uncertain. In many large urban areas there is probably a surplus of Latin teachers. In smaller communities, particularly those too far from a college or university to permit graduate study, there is often a shortage, and Latin is dropped for lack of a teacher. How to solve this problem is one of the most serious questions facing the profession.

Perhaps an even greater problem, however, is the number of teachers who have not kept pace with the changing methods of language teaching. Although the figures are far from complete, on the basis of replies received to a brief questionnaire sent out by the National Office of the ACL, it is estimated that only a little more than one-third of the Latin teachers in public and private secondary schools have attended a summer institute or workshop. The change in federal legislation to include Latin for summer institutes makes the situation brighter for the teachers and for the 750,000–800,000 Latin students in our secondary schools.

Carolyn E. Bock
Montclair State College
John F. Latimer
The George Washington University
William M. Seaman
Michigan State University

References

American Classical League. *The Classical Investigation.* Princeton U Press, 1924. 305p.

Ashley, Clara, and Lashbrook, Austin. *Living Latin: A Contemporary Approach.* 2 vols. Ginn, 1967. Vol. 1, 304p., Vol. 2, 360p.

Barrutia, R. *Linguistic Theory of Language Learning as Related to Machine Teaching.* Doctoral dissertation (microfilm). U Texas, 1965. 301p.

Bateman, John. "A Survey of Latin Readers for High School Use." *Classical J* 58:296–311; 1963.

Bateman, John. "Latin Readers for High School Use." *Classical J* 59:350–4; 1964.

Bateman, John. "More Latin Readers for High School Use." *Classical J* 60:306–7; 1965.

Burns, Mary Ann, and others. *Lingua Latina*. Bruce, 1964. 502p.

Carr, W. L. "The Direct Object Is Where You Find It." *Classical Outlook* 38:53–6; 1961.

Carr, W. L. "O See Can You Say?" *Classical Outlook* 41:1–2; 1963.

Carroll, John B. "Research in Foreign Language Teaching: the Last Five Years." In *Northeast Conference on the Teaching of Foreign Languages. Reports of the Working Committees*. The Conference, 1966. p. 12–42.

Chomsky, Noam. "Linguistic Theory." In *Northeast Conference on the Teaching of Foreign Languages. Reports of the Working Committees*. The Conference, 1966. p. 43–9.

Corcoran, Thomas. "The Structural Approach: A Hostile Criticism." *Classical Outlook* 38:77–9; 1961.

Crawford, Grace A., and others. *Elementary Latin: the Basic Structures*. U Michigan Press, 1963. 438p.

Cunningham, Maurice P. "A Theory of the Latin Sentence." *Classical Philology* 60:24–8; 1965.

Distler, Paul F., S.J. *Teach the Latin, I Pray You*. Loyola U Press, 1962. 254p.

Distler, Paul F., S.J. *Beginning Reading and Progress in Reading*. Loyola U Press, 1963. 510p.

Drake, Gertrude. *Latin Readings*. Scott, 1964. 109p.

Drake, Gertrude. *More Latin Readings*. Scott, 1965. 112p.

Eder, Michael D., and Summerlin, Benjamin A. "Construction of Achievement Tests in Latin." *Classical J* 56:110–3; 1960.

Else, Gerald F. "New Classical Curricula." *Classical J* 61:58–60; 1965(a).

Else, Gerald F. (Ed.) *Colloquium on the Classics in Education 1965*. American Council of Learned Societies, 1965(b). 65p.

Ferguson, Charles A. "Applied Linguistics." In *Northeast Conference on the Teaching of Foreign Languages. Reports of the Working Committees*. The Conference, 1966. p. 50–8.

Fowler, Murray, and others. "Linguistics and the Classical Languages." *Classical J* 52:259–78; 1957.

Hall, Robert A., Jr. *New Ways To Learn a Foreign Language*. Bantam Books, Inc., 1966. 180p.

Hayden, Hilary, O.S.B. "Classics in the Inner-city School—Experiments and Proposals." *Classical World* 60:93–8; 1966.

Hogan, Edward D., S.J. *Testing Latin Structure*. Georgetown U, Institute of Languages and Linguistics, 1964. 73p.

Johnson, Van L. "Latin Is More Than Linguistics." *Classical J* 53:290–301; 1958.

Jones, Frank P. "Structural Linguistics." *Classical Outlook* 44:29–32; 1966.

Kibbe, Doris E. "Teaching of Classical Cultures—Culture in Language Learning." In *Northeast Conference on the Teaching of Foreign Languages. Reports of the Working Committees*. The Conference, 1960. p. 62–76.

Kovach, Edith M. A. "Ten Master Teacher and Program Award Programs." *Classical World* 60:37–47; 1966.

Lado, Robert. *Language Teaching, A Scientific Approach*. McGraw-Hill, 1964. 239p.

Larudee, Faze. *Language Teaching in Historical Perspective*. Doctoral dissertation. U Michigan, 1964. 167p.

Latimer, John F. (Ed.) *Planning Conference to Examine the Role of Classical Studies in American Education and to Make Recommendations for Needed Research and Development*. George Washington U Press, 1965. 48p.

Levy, Harry L. "Disciplina Mores Facit." *Classical J* 55:15–21; 1959.

Levy, Harry L. "Teaching Latin and Greek: New Approaches." *Classical J* 57:202–30; 1962.

McDonough, James T., Jr. "Computers and Classics." *Classical World* 53:44–50; 1959.

Modern Language Association of America. *Foreign Language Enrollments in Institutions of Higher Education, Fall 1965*. MLA, 1966. 88p.

Morris, Sidney. *Viae Novae: New Techniques in Latin Teaching*. Hulton Educational Publishers, 1966. 93p.

Most, William G. "Latin by the Natural Method." *Classical Outlook* 38:42–5; 1961.

O'Brien, Richard J., S.J., and Twombly, Neil J., S.J. *An Intermediate Course in Latin*. Loyola U Press, 1964. 432p.

Parker, William R. "A Case for Latin." *Proc MLA* 79:3–10; 1964.

Peckett, C. W. E. "Modern Methods of Teaching Latin." *Classical J* 59:58–62; 1963.

Pratt, Norman T. "The ACLS Classics Panel." *Classical J* 54:346–9; 1959.

Rouse, William H. D. *The Teaching of Latin at the Perse School*. Great Britain Board of Education Ed. Pamphlets No. 20. H.M. Stationery Office, 1910. 42p.

Rouse, William H. D., and Appleton, R. B. *Latin on the Direct Method*. U London Press, 1925. 226p.

Schoenheim, Ursula. "Textbooks in Greek and Latin: 1967 List." *Classical World* 60:329–44; 1967.

Schoenheim, Ursula. "Inexpensive Books for Teaching the Classics." *Classical World* 60:189–206; 1967.

Seligson, Gerda M. "Rules for Metaphrase." *Classical J* 56:61–3; 1960.

Skinner, B. F. "Teaching Machines." *Sci* October: 969–77; 1958.

Stephens, Wade C., and Springhetti, Emilio, S.J. *Lingua Latina Viva II*. McGraw-Hill, 1967. 401p.

Sweet, Waldo E. "The Horizontal Approach." *Classical World* 43:118–21; 1950.

Sweet, Waldo E. *Latin Workshop Experimental Materials*, Book 1. U Michigan Press, 1953. 304p.

Sweet, Waldo E. *Latin Workshop Experimental Materials*, Book 2. U Michigan Press, 1954. 306p.

Sweet, Waldo E. *Latin Workshop Experimental Materials*, Book 1, rev. ed. U Michigan Press, 1956(a). 247p.

Sweet, Waldo E. *Latin Workshop Experimental Ma-*

terials, Book 2, rev. ed. U Michigan Press, 1956(*b*). 296p.

Sweet, Waldo E. *Latin: A Structural Approach.* U Michigan Press, 1957. 520p.

Sweet, Waldo E. *Vergil's Aeneid: A Structural Approach.* Vol. 1: *The Aeneid, Books I and II.* U Michigan Press, 1960. 163p.

Sweet, Waldo E. *Clozes and Vocabulary Exercises for Books I and II of the Aeneid.* U Michigan Press, 1961. 102p.

Sweet, Waldo E. *Latin: Level One.* Encyclopaedia Britannica Films, Incorporated, 1966.

Sweet, Waldo E. "The Continued Development of the Structural Approach." *Didaskalos* 2:141–59; 1967.

Taylor, Margaret E. "The Advanced Placement Program in Latin." *Classical World* 56:33–9; 1962.

Towey, Cyprian, C.B., and Akielascek, Stanislaus. *Lingua Latina Viva I.* McGraw-Hill, 1966. 375p.

Ullman, B. L. "What Should We Teach About Latin Word Order?" *Classical J* 55:346–7; 1960.

U.S. Office of Education. *Summary Report on Bachelor's and Higher Degrees Conferred during the Year 1964–1965.* USOE, 1966. 9p.

Ward, Ralph L. "Evidence for the Pronunciation of Latin." *Classical World* 55:273–5; 1962.

COLLECTIVE ACTION BY TEACHERS

Collective action by teachers generally is interpreted to mean the pursuit of group benefits by a formal organization representing teacher members. For the past few decades, benefits sought have been higher wages and better conditions of work. More recently, groups of teachers organized both formally and informally have sought a voice in the determination of school-system programs and organization. It is likely that in the future the major purpose of collective action in public schools will be to obtain control of management functions.

Until the twentieth century in America, there was a tradition of independent decision making on the part of classroom teachers. More recently, however, centralized administration of increasingly large school districts has tended to limit this freedom. Consequently compensating activity has been employed by teachers, their organizations, and their school administrators.

This article seeks to describe the forces which have advanced the collective interests of teachers in pursuit of professional and personal fulfillment through the enlargement of their decision-making authority. For the most part these forces have not been subject to the control of individuals or groups. As modern man has been recast ever more sharply in the mold of urban life, large and centralized institutions such as government, business, and education have come to shape his behavior. The struggle to seize or at least to share control of these goliathan enterprises is, after all, the dominant theme of the history of industrial society. Now, as the scientific revolution moves us from the industrial age into the electronic age, the forces which place large and complex organizations in control of man's affairs continue unchecked.

Education, as the handmaiden of social, scientific, and economic progress, has for the past century been under increasing pressure to reconcile man's need for personal expression with his dependence on impersonal and all-powerful organizations. Historically, public education served the purpose of socializing each new member of society while leaving to individual and family personal forms of expression. Recently, we have, as a society, recognized the need to use education to cultivate the self as well as the socially acceptable man to insure a balance between conformity and eccentricity.

As technology has exploded, so also has man's expectation and desire for change in his social institutions. America's schools, long the instruments for conserving tradition and value, are now being seen as a mechanism for change. Whereas in 1936 Counts could ask, "Dare the schools build a new social order?" (Counts, 1936), and remain unanswered, the same question today goes without asking. In the decade of space flight and the great society, the only question is, "How?"

As the purposes of education have been redefined, so the role of its practitioners also has been under revision. The purpose of teaching has changed from the inculcation of truths to the determination of relevance. The demands of this job establish new teacher qualifications, training, and professional experience. As teachers learn their new role, they gain for themselves and project to others a new image which is at the same time a throwback to the autonomy of the one-room rural teacher and a prediction of future self-determination based on collective professional strength.

Public-school educators, aware of their responsibility to change society and hence aware of the need to change themselves, have popularized the word *innovation.* Connoting the unsettlement of the established, the word *innovative* is used to describe persons who are experimentally minded or are just smitten with newness for its own sake. Teaching in America's schools today takes place in a climate of pressure for innovation.

As teachers strive for self-realization through creative teaching, they may find themselves at odds with school systems employing a strategy of directed change (Wiles, 1965). Conflict between teaching strategy and administrative "strategy for innovation" can produce severe intraorganizational tensions (Lortie, 1961; American Society . . . , 1965). When a well-established communication system does not exist for the reconciliation of differences in conflicting strategies, teachers may seek adjustment through some form of collective action.

As teachers respond to societal and administrative pressures for change, another pressure for innovative teacher behavior can be traced to new definitions of mental health and human well being by behavioral scientists. Lawrence Kubie states,

The measure of health is flexibility, the freedom to learn through experience, the freedom to change with changing internal and external circumstances, to be influenced by reasonable argument, admonitions, exhortation, and the appeal to emotions; the freedom to respond appropriately to the stimulus of reward and punishment, and especially the freedom to cease when sated. The essence of normality is flexibility in all of these vital ways.

The essence of illness is the freezing of behavior into unalterable and insatiable patterns. It is this which characterizes every manifestation of psychopathology, whether in impulse, purpose, act, thought, or feeling. (Kubie, 1961)

The concept of mental health in education prescribes the ability to cope with stress as the major goal of every educational program (Bower & Hollister, 1967). The process of "experiential" learning, as it is called by Rogers (1966), permits every student to learn value while at the same time learning information so that the consequence of his learning will be the capacity to act to adjust himself and the real world in accordance with his own expectations.

Individual and group therapy has been viewed as a basic form of education for personal adjustment (Rogers, 1959). Problem solving as educational methodology for societal and personal development is another product of behavioral-science research which leads to autonomous behavior in both students and teachers.

Suchman's "inquiry" method of teaching (1964) defines educational purpose and method as the discovery of phenomena, relationships, and a method of learning which prepare children for adult life in a world of cause and effect relationships.

Provus (1966a) describes teaching as the establishment of conditions under which unlimited options are made available to test the consequences of continuous self-directed problem solving.

These approaches to teaching and those of many others—Torrance (1965), Beberman (1959), Gordon (1959), emphasize the importance of the teacher's own spontaneity and judgment. The problem-solving skills to be taught to children are precisely those to be practiced by their teachers (Chicago Public Schools, 1965).

Research which treats teaching behavior as problem-solving behavior (Fattu, 1965) is beginning to have some influence on teacher training programs in colleges and universities, for example, that of Fenton (1966), Joyce and Hodges (1966), and Hughes (1959).

New definitions of the teaching act have, therefore, placed a premium on the independent decision-making abilities of teachers—precisely those skills which teachers must have to advance their own collective interests with the organizations which employ them.

The conditions surrounding a teacher's work can be viewed as the context in which problem solving takes place. The literature of problem solving emphasizes the importance of context or situation as a determinant factor in outcome (Moreno, 1953; Wertheimer, 1945). It is, therefore, not surprising that in the last few years considerable attention has been given by researchers to teacher's working conditions and perceived working conditions and in particular to the climate in which teacher and administrator relations function. Many of these studies (Hemphill & others, 1962; Huggett, 1956; Lieberman, 1956) have been made to provide administrators with a better understanding of teacher-administrator interpersonal relations, but all shed light on the causes and objectives of teacher militancy.

Callahan (1964) traces the history of training for educational administration and documents the domination of public schools and training institutions by persons inculcated with the value of tangible goods over intangible human processes. Gross (1958) finds in Massachusetts that superintendents admit that they are doing their poorest job in instructional leadership. Charters (1964) finds that superintendents have only fleeting contacts with teachers, leaving the functions of management to an impersonal bureaucratic mechanism.

It is no wonder then that Steinhoff and Stern (n.d.) report that the broad achievement needs of secondary-school teachers are not being satisfied in the schools studied. Taylor (n.d.) reports findings that suggest many principals actually reward dependent and subordinate behavior. Corwin (1963) reports evidence that teachers are constantly struggling to gain control over their work in such areas as status and responsibility as well as in matters of income and seniority.

A national study of local education association grievances by Provus (1966b) revealed five major areas of teacher frustration: poor organization of the instructional program, inadequate curriculum planning and material selection, excessive nonteaching duties, insufficient time for working with individual students, and administrative interference. The conclusion of this study is that teachers want authority to determine for themselves how to allocate time during the working day. A study of California school districts (McLaughlin & Shea, 1960) revealed that important sources of teacher job dissatisfaction were excessive class size, number of classes, and number of preparations imposed on teachers.

Hagstrom's job analysis of the teachers' work day (1962) leads him to the conclusion that about 30 percent of the teachers' time is spent in nonprofessional duties. Data of this sort tend to support the view of Wayland (1961) that the teacher is not a professional but a bureaucratic functionary.

It seems likely that the new teachers' self-image may diminish from that of an enthusiastic innovator to that of an enforcer of codes determined by higher authority. Studies of role perception by new teachers and experienced teachers suggest considerable naïveté among first-year teachers (Biddle & others, 1962). Moeller (1962) found that first-year teachers have extremely high "sense of power" scores compared with scores for teachers in their second and third years of teaching.

What happens to the teacher under such constrictive conditions of work? What happens to his sense of judgment and personal security?

Stimbert and Dykes (1964) state:

A large, highly centralized organization, with its hierarchies of authority and corollary bureaucracy, contributes to a sense of frustration and powerlessness on the part of teachers in regard to their ability to influence matters of concern to them. When administration is decentralized and the number of intermediaries is reduced, teachers can speak more effectively. With teacher organizations competing strenuously for teacher loyalties, such a consideration may be a crucial factor in determining where teachers shall look for leadership.

Keene (1962) suggests that informal colleague groups among teachers interpose themselves between the individual and the organization to protect him from loss of autonomy.

The socioeconomic status of the school population is a factor apparently related to teacher satisfaction—perhaps more because of its effect on the principals' leadership than its direct effect on the teacher. Nicholas and her associates found that principals are so harassed by community demands in central-city schools that there is little opportunity for teachers and principals to set common goals and share responsibility for their realization (Nicholas & others, 1965).

Campbell (1964) sees a major administrative problem posed by the growing conflict between professional and hierarchical control of America's schools. He recognizes the need and desirability of superintendents' relinquishing aspects of control in exchange for responsible teachers' decisions in the realm of their expert knowledge, but he cannot foresee how this accommodation will be effected in the years ahead.

It seems safe to conclude that the desire of teachers to secure control over management functions is more an expression of need for self-realization than a desire to seize the master-control lever of America's institutional life.

Research suggests that at the most general level the issue is the same as that affecting workers everywhere: the personal meaningfulness of work. For example, the findings of Frederick Herzberg and his colleagues in a study at Texas Instruments, Incorporated, appeared as revelant to teachers as to the factory employees to whom the findings refer:

What motivates employees to work effectively? A challenging job which allows a feeling of achievement, responsibility, growth, advancement, enjoyment of work of itself, and earned recognition.

What dissatisfies workers? Mostly factors which are peripheral to the job—work rules, lighting, coffee breaks, titles, seniority rights, wages, fringe benefits, and the like.

When do workers become dissatisfied? When opportunities for meaningful achievement are eliminated and they become sensitized to their environment and begin to find fault. (Myers, 1964)

Group problem-solving behavior, its products and processes, and its relevance for education as means and end have been the subject of research and speculation for Dewey (1916), Lewin (1953), and Corey (1953), to mention but a few luminaries in this field. More recently, group problem-solving techniques have been used to train teachers and solve problems of pressing interest to teachers (Bradford & others, 1964; Miles, 1959). Corey's concept of problem solving as research and his conviction that everyone can experience both the excitement and the advantages of research methodology are only gradually being assimilated by teachers. Shumsky (1958) recommends in-service training experience for teachers which forces them to question their own values as well as the stated goals of the institutions which employ them as they explore the assumptions of their own microcosms for psychologically relevant research projects. The effect of such practices is to create an ever larger number of teachers who believe that a change for the better in their work situation is possible through their own experimentation and evaluation.

Griffiths (1959) has persuaded school people that the school is an organization which can benefit from the same theories of human management that apply to industry. Bennis (1962), on the basis of his work in noneducational settings, argues that large hierarchical organizations designed around strict division of labor, accountability, and limited span of control can no longer be successful.

Miles, drawing on the industrial work of Bennis and Argyris, describes the conditions of existence essential to the mental health of members of an organization. These conditions for him define in turn the health of the organization:

The inhabitants of an educational organization must have reasonably clear perceptions of the goal or goals to which the system is devoted; these in turn affect the role specifications and performance for the inhabitants. Systems of reward and penalty regulate role performance as do the norms governing the style of interpersonal transactions in the system. (Miles, 1965)

In summarizing the seminar *Change Processes in the Public Schools,* Tope (1965) states that there was agreement by the seminar participants that the school administrator is more effective when he acts as the mediator rather than the advocate of change. As mediator, his role is to support the development of interest and capacity for change in teachers. The encouragement of a new teaching role which includes such management functions as goal setting and decisions concerning the allocation of resources and evaluation in effect establishes administrative practice based on sound theory in support of collective action by teachers.

It must be remembered, however, that these behavioral scientists are talking about teachers in very special kinds of groups: work groups, small groups, or, as Miles (1965) has called them, "temporary systems" groups.

Argyris (1964) has suggested that "temporary product teams" created for a limited but specific purpose may be able to compensate for the inability of large hierarchical organizations to tap their employees' reserves of ingenuity and sustained creative endeavor. Likert (1961) also has shown that when small work teams share status and power in pursuit of a common task, they appear to be more effective than when organized in line and staff relationships.

In a major contribution to the literature, Miles (1964) has compiled and edited works dealing with the theory, practice and context of planned change in American education. In one chapter of his book Miles explains the utility of deliberately designing temporary groups for the purpose of introducing change. The productive power of the temporary system is derived from its ego-maintenance and -protection functions, its communication efficiency, and its utilitarian norms, which make possible a dynamic reward system. The norms of the temporary system, which have value for participants in and of themselves are the value of equal status, trust, inquiry, newness, and the completion of work with efficient dispatch. Miles points out that the output of such groups includes, in addition to tangible acts or products, the modification of people, their relationships, and work styles. Miles concludes his chapter with the following:

> Educational administrators may see how thoroughgoing adaptation of their institutions to the stresses of external demands and internal disequilibria can occur without violent revolution, major surgery or collapse. Without increased sophistication in the management of change, those responsible for the leadership of educational institutions are almost certainly headed for a very difficult time in the next few decades. (Miles, 1964)

Clearly, teachers have either read and understood or have intuitively sensed the relevance of Matthew Miles's position for their own professional existence.

Lortie (1961) makes much of the invisibility of the teacher's role. Like a medieval craftsman, the teacher is cut off from feedback information about the immediate effects of his work and therefore develops and maintains his own standards of performance. The creation of individualistic norms tends, in Lortie's opinion, to restrict the effective interdependent work of teachers.

There is some evidence that the resistance of individual teachers to group work stems from a craft attitude. However, as teachers feel, on the one hand, increased pressure to account to higher authority for their everyday professional activity and, on the other hand, a need for self-realization, it is likely that the forces making for teacher syndicalism will outweigh those making for diffusive activity. The use of membership organizations as bargaining agents constitutes one major method of collective activity by teachers as they seek the benefits of shared power. As has already been suggested, the union movement among public-school employees is clearly an effort toward collective attainment of professional rights as well as pecuniary benefits.

State governments and local boards as well as the major national employee organizations generally agree on the value to the school program of formalized effective employee-employer relationships. These relationships are held to be most productive when every employee has an internal apparatus available to him for the expression of personal and professional concerns. For example, the Final Report of the Governor's Committee on Public Employee Relations (New York State, 1966) states:

> [E]mployers soon discovered that no package of unilaterally-developed procedures, no matter how good in detail, could be effective in satisfying the employees' desire for participation in the determination of their working conditions. . . . It was soon found, however, that even the best procedures and the most carefully developed policy fail to achieve results in the absence of effective organization within the human structure of the enterprise.

Employers, however, are not in agreement about the form and power base of an adjudication apparatus. And employees still lack agreement about who shall represent their interests. As of June 1965 the National Education Association (NEA) represented 943,581 educators, or about 52 percent of the nation's instructional staffs, as compared to about 110,500, or 6.1 percent, members in the American Federation of Teachers (AFT). Since 1960, however, the rate with which the AFT has gained new members has surpassed slightly that of the NEA (Provus, 1965). It is interesting to note that teachers' unions have experienced their greatest success in cities where teacher frustrations can, at least in part, be traced to the size and bureaucratic structure of school districts.

Wildman (1964) lists other factors causing teacher militancy in urban America: the existence of other highly organized and powerful groups in the community, the greater number of career-committed males in teaching, the desire of unions to demonstrate the feasibility of organizing white collar workers, and the desire of the NEA to demonstrate its leadership capacity in securing teacher benefits. Stinnett and others (1966) lists additional causes: hunger for recognition, status related to higher training requirements, and societal repugnance for paternalism and oppression.

Both NEA and AFT are now committed to winning for teachers a share in the determination of educational policy. The success of the AFT in securing contracts which have progressively expanded teacher policy-making influence is impressive. In New York City, their first contract established the union as the bargaining agent for teachers. Their third contract recognized teacher policy-making discretion in such matters as recruitment, class size, curriculum, and "problem" schools (Rosenthal, 1966).

It is evident that collective bargaining as a method of achieving managerial influence for teachers is an established reality in America. Doherty (1966) traces changes in state statutes to accommodate such negotiation. There is, however, still some question whether the desire of teachers to share in management functions at the level of their own school building can be satisfied by recourse to a large centralized employee organization or an emerging body of contractual law. Wildman and Perry (1966) warn that there is as yet no clear-cut evidence that the interests of teachers will be better served by confrontation between labor- and management-oriented agents than by teachers and administrators sharing a common goal and an effective problem-solving methodology.

It should be recognized, however, that it is not common practice in public schools to solve problems of concern to teachers by means of group-process techniques. On the other hand, problems identified by administrators are often tossed to teachers to be chewed over in small groups. Even nonurban, local teacher associations affiliated with traditionally conservative state educational associations generally use forms of collective pressure on management to solve teachers' problems in preference to the participation of all parties in honest confrontation and problem resolution through the use of group dynamics techniques. Davidson provides an example of this (1966).

Only one national study has investigated the effect of negotiation consisting of personalized, teacher-administrator confrontation and reconciliation through joint effort and responsibility. Because this effort occurred at the level of the smallest unit of organization in a school district, the school building, it tested the strength of group process for building faculty unity and role satisfaction for both teachers and administrators (Provus, 1964).

In essence, the project provided guide lines whereby superintendents and principals could share with teachers the responsibility for allocating time, personnel, and existing funds in return for a sustained effort to creatively use these resources to solve problems identified by teachers themselves. The results of this research showed that although many administrators are able to recognize the benefits of shared authority with teachers, most are unable to relinquish control of either resources or the processes for allocating resources in sufficient degree to provide teachers with meaningful choices for decision making. When administrators do share power, however, teacher decisions, though initially naïve, are ultimately responsible, creative solutions to real and pressing school problems (Provus, 1966b).

Although few superintendents or school boards are as yet willing to take the initiative in sharing with teachers such basic management functions as determining priorities and the allocation of resources, there are discernible trends in that direction.

Widely publicized procedures such as team teaching (Trump & Baynham, 1961), the establishment of nongraded schools (Goodlad & Anderson, 1959), and flexible scheduling (Manlowe & Beggs, 1965) have the effect of putting administrators in the position of sanctioning teacher determination of educational program ends and means, at least for short periods of time in specific locations. National professional societies such as the Association for Supervision and Curriculum Development (ASCD) and Teacher Education and Professional Standards (TEPS) have used their publications (*Educational Leadership*, December 1964, and *Journal of Teacher Education*, December 1965) to advocate the greater involvement of all members of the professional staff in crucial management decisions. A series of proposals for the improvement of teacher training, invited and published by the TEPS Commission (National Education Association, 1966) suggests many ways in which teachers and student teachers may participate in program planning and stand responsible for deciding how to maintain programs.

Training programs for school principals aimed at improving staff communication and developing interpersonal competence inevitably produce in administrators an increased sensitivity to the teachers' need to participate in management decisions (Jacobson, 1965).

Some nonprofit regional organizations appear concerned with achieving greater teacher involvement in new program development—for example, the Center for Coordinated Education (publishers of the bulletin *Remaking the Educational Order*) and Bill Rogge's Co-op Educational Research Laboratories, Inc.

At least one state department, that of Michigan, has published material advising teachers on how to use a problem-solving approach to instructional problems (Curriculum Research Committee, 1962). In the same state, not by coincidence, a major university research center is providing teachers with small-group work skills (Kaufman & others, 1963) invaluable to the solution of classroom problems, interpersonal problems, and collective professional problems.

The training and use of teachers for program construction work and creative problem solving is not new in American education. Summaries of unpublished research on CORE programs from 1956–1962 (U.S. Office of Education, 1963) reveal considerable administrative support of independent teacher judgment and activity. And a perusal of educational journals shows that similar activity has been encouraged for decades. However, there is clearly an increase in administrative awareness of the central nature of policy decision making by teachers as an essential part of good teaching.

Emphasis on teacher classroom experimentation has contributed to the teacher's ability and appetite for exercising judgment. After all, the execution of a research project—no matter how limited in scope—involves the same kind of decision making in the face of known constraints and unknown consequences as confronts a school superintendent managing far-flung school affairs. It is likely that when teachers experience success as decision-making experimenters, they realize the power at their individual and collective disposal to change school programs for the better.

Fay's work (1958) is an example of such teacher-determined research.

Universities have in some instances taken active roles in encouraging teacher participation in the formulation of school policy. The Bureau of Educational Research of the University of Oregon is a case in point, as are the University of Utah, which sponsors the Salt Lake City Schools' Winter Institutes, and the University of Rhode Island, which sponsors labor-management training programs each summer.

The federal government, through enactment of Public Law 89-10, has contributed to the trend. Titles I and III of the act call for broadly based surveys of educational needs. Many school districts are taking care to include teachers in decisions which establish programs for federal support. The use of nonprofessionals in the classroom and out of the classroom as tutors is heavily endorsed by the Office of Education (Provus, 1967). The successful employment of such persons is ultimately contingent on their being responsible to teachers who must thereby enlarge their own management capacity. At least one school district urges that, despite state laws to the contrary, nonprofessionals be permitted to teach in order to free teachers to diagnose and prescribe (Esbensen, 1966).

It is entirely possible that in the next decade teachers will exercise many management functions now performed by school principals. Teachers may very well exercise these functions as part of a school council headed by an executive appointed by them and responsible to them for the execution of their commitment to the board of education and its designated officers.

Such speculation may be rash. However, any projection of the forces described in this article leads to the conclusion that teachers will become increasingly more active in collectively attaining their professional ends—whether their instruments be formal bargaining agents or informal, administrator-supported committees.

Malcolm Provus
The Board of Public Education
Pittsburgh, Pennsylvania

References

American Society for Supervision and Curriculum Development, 1965 Yearbook Committee. *Role of Supervisor and Curriculum Director in a Climate of Change*. ASCD, 1965.

Argyris, C. *Integrating the Individual and the Organization*. Wiley, 1964.

Beberman, Max. "Improving High School Mathematics Teaching." *Ed Leadership* 17:162–6; 1959.

Bennis, W. G. "Towards a 'Truly' Scientific Management: The Concept of Organization Health." In Rapoport, A. (Ed.) *General Systems*. Yearbook of the Society for the Advancement of General Systems Theory, 1962.

Biddle, Bruce J., and others. "The Role of the Teacher and Occupational Choice." *Sch R* 70:191–206; 1962.

Bower, Eli M., and Hollister, William G. *Behavioral Science and Frontiers in Education*. Wiley, 1967.

Bradford, Leland P., and others. (Eds.) *Teacher Group Theory and Laboratory Method*. Wiley, 1964.

Callahan, Raymond E. *Education and the Cult of Efficiency*. U Chicago Press, 1964.

Campbell, Roald F. "The Control of American Schools." *El Sch J* 65:120–9; 1964.

Charters, Werrett W., Jr. *Teacher Perceptions of Administrator Behavior*. Washington U Press, 1964.

Chicago Public Schools. *In-Service Training Program for the Promotion of Creative Problem-solving*. The Schools, 1965.

Corey, Stephen M. *Action Research to Improve School Practices*. Teachers College, Columbia U, 1953.

Corwin, Ronald G. *The Development of an Instrument for Examining Staff Conflicts in the Public School*. Ohio State U Press, 1963.

Counts, George. *Dare the Schools Build a New Social Order?* The John Day Company, Inc., 1936.

Curriculum Research Committee. *Solving Classroom Problems Through Systematic Study*. Bulletin No. 433. Department of Public Instruction, Lansing, Michigan, 1962.

Davidson, Shirley B. "A Study of Procedures in Teacher-board Relations." Master's thesis. Adelphi U, 1966.

Dewey, John. *Democracy in Education*. Macmillan, 1916.

Doherty, Robert E. "The Law and Collective Bargaining for Teachers." *Teach Col Rec* 68:1–12; 1966.

Esbensen, Thorwald. "Should Teacher Aides Be More Than Clerks?" *Phi Delta Kappan* 47:237; 1966.

Fattu, N. A. "A Model of Teaching as Problem Solving." In *Theories of Instruction*. ASCD, 1965.

Fay, Leo C. *Improving the Teaching of Reading by Teacher Experimentation*. Bulletin of the School of Education, Indiana U, 1958.

Fenton, Edwin. *Teaching the New Social Studies in Secondary Schools*. Holt, 1966.

Goodlad, John I., and Anderson, Robert H. *The Nongraded Elementary School*. Harcourt, 1959.

Gordon, Ira Jay. "Observing From a Perceptual Viewpoint; Teaching Teachers to See Children as Children See Themselves." *J Teach Ed* 10:280–4; 1959.

Griffiths, Daniel E. *Research in Educational Administration: An Appraisal and a Plan*. Teachers College, Columbia U, 1959.

Gross, Neal. *Who Runs Our Schools?* Wiley, 1958.

Hagstrom, Ellis A. "The Teacher's Day." *El Sch J* 62:422–31; 1962.

Hemphill, J. K., and others. *Administrative Performance and Personality: A Study of the Principal in a Simulated Elementary School*. Teachers College, Columbia U, 1962.

Huggett, Albert John. *Professional Problems of Teachers*. Macmillan, 1956.

Hughes, Marie M., and others. "Assessment of the

Quality of Teaching in Elementary Schools." Unpublished research report. U Utah, 1959.

Jacobson, Stanley. "When School People Get Together." *Nat El Prin* 44:25–9; 1965.

Joyce, Bruce R., and Hodges, Richard E. "Instructional Flexibility Training." *J Teach Ed* Winter: 409–16; 1966.

Kaufman, Mabel, and others. "Creative Practices Developed by Teachers for Improving Classroom Atmospheres." In *Studies in Children, Youth and Family Life*. Institute for Social Research, U Michigan, 1963.

Keene, Roland. "Operational Freedom in Complex Organizations." Doctoral dissertation. Washington U, 1962.

Kubie, Lawrence S. *Neurotic Distortion of the Creative Process*. U Kansas Press, 1961.

Lewin, Kurt. "Studies in Group Decision." In Cartwright, D., and Zander, A. (Eds.) *Group Dynamics*. Harper, 1953.

Lieberman, Myron. *Education as a Profession*. Prentice-Hall, 1956.

Likert, R. *New Patterns of Management*. McGraw-Hill, 1961.

Lortie, D. C. "Craftsmen and Colleagueship, A Frame for the Investigation of Work Values Among Public School Teachers." Paper presented to the American Sociological Association, 1961.

Manlowe, Donald C., and Beggs, David W. *Flexible Scheduling*. Indiana U Press, 1965.

McLaughlin, Jack W., and Shea, John T. "California Teacher's Job Dissatisfactions." *California J Ed Res* 11:216–24; 1960.

Miles, Matthew B. *Learning to Work in Groups*. Teachers College, Columbia U, 1959.

Miles, Matthew B. (Ed.) *Innovation in Education*. Teachers College, Columbia U, 1964.

Miles, Matthew B. "Planned Change and Organizational Health: Figure and Ground." *Change Processes in the Public Schools*. U Oregon Press, 1965.

Miller, William C. "Curricular Implications of Negotiation." *Ed Leadership* 23:533–6; 1966.

Moeller, Gerald H. "The Relationship Between Bureaucracy in School System Organization and Teachers' Sense of Power." Doctoral dissertation. Washington U, 1962.

Moreno, J. L. *Who Shall Survive?* Beacon House, Inc., 1953.

Myers, M. Scott. "Who Are Your Motivated Workers?" *Harvard Bus R* 42:73; 1964.

National Education Association, Commission on Professional Rights and Responsibilities. *AFT Membership and Affiliated Locals 1963–65*. NEA, n.d.

National Education Association, National Commission on Teacher Education and Professional Standards. *Remaking the World of the Career Teacher*. NEA, 1966.

New York State. "Organization for Collective Negotiations." In *Governor's Committee on Public Employee Relations Final Report*. New York State, 1966.

Nicholas, Lynn N., and others. *Effects of Socioeconomic Setting and Organizational Climate on Problems Brought to Elementary School Offices*. Wayne State U Press, 1965.

Provus, Malcolm M. "Project: Time to Teach." *Nat El Prin* 44:52–7; 1964.

Provus, Malcolm M. *Problems in Perspective*. NEA, 1965.

Provus, Malcolm M. "Some Personal Observations on Creativity." In Taylor, C. W. (Ed.) *Instructional Media and Creativity*. Wiley, 1966(*a*).

Provus, Malcolm M. *Time to Teach: Action Report*. NEA, 1966(*b*).

Provus, Malcolm M. *Staffing for Better Schools*. USOE, 1967.

Rogers, Carl. *Client Centered Therapy*. Houghton, 1959.

Rogers, Carl. "To Facilitate Learning." In Provus, Malcolm M. (Ed.) *Innovations for Time to Teach*. NEA, 1966.

Rosenthal, Alan. "New Voices in Public Education." *Teach Col Rec* 68:1–12; 1966.

Shumsky, Abraham. *The Action Research Way of Learning*. Teachers College, Columbia U, 1958.

Steinhoff, Carl R., and Stern, George B. *Organizational Climate in a Public School System*. Syracuse U Press, n.d.

Stimbert, E. C., and Dykes, Archie R. "Decentralization of Administration." *Phi Delta Kappan* 47: 174–7; 1964.

Stinnett, F. M., and others. *Professional Negotiation in Public Education*. Macmillan, 1966.

Suchman, J. Richard. "The Child and the Inquiry Process." In *Intellectual Development: Another Look*. Papers from ASCD Eighth Curriculum Research Institute, 1964.

Taylor, Calvin. "A Tentative Description of the Creative Individual." The Author, n.d. (Mimeographed.)

Tope, Donald E. "Summary of Seminar." In *Change Processes in the Public Schools*. U Oregon, 1965.

Torrance, Ellis Paul. *Rewarding Creative Behavior*. Prentice-Hall, 1965.

Trump, J. Lloyd, and Baynham, Dorsey. *Focus on Change*. Rand McNally, 1961.

U.S. Office of Education. *The Core Program Unpublished Research 1956–1962*. GPO, 1963.

Wayland, S. R. "The Teacher as a Member of a Bureaucracy." In "Work Conference in Supervision and Curriculum." Teachers College, Columbia U, 1961. (Mimeographed.)

Wertheimer, Max. *Productive Thinking*. Harper, 1945.

Wildman, Wesley A. "Implications of Teacher Bargaining for School Administration." *Phi Delta Kappan* 46:152–8; 1964.

Wildman, Wesley A., and Perry, Charles R. "Group Conflict and School Organization." *Phi Delta Kappan* 48:244–51; 1966.

Wiles, Kimball. "Contrasts in Strategies of Change." In *Strategy for Curriculum Change*. Papers from ASCD Seminar on Strategy for Curriculum Change, 1965.

COLLEGE AND UNIVERSITY ADMINISTRATION

Administration is the component part of an organized enterprise concerned with facilitating and supporting the accomplishment of the operations or end purposes of that enterprise. The goal of administration is to direct the utilization of limited resources of time, people, space, equipment, supplies, and work technique in the realization of coherent operation of an enterprise. Necessarily, in any particular organized enterprise, administration is conditioned by the nature of the operation itself, whether it be a product or a service, and by the history or traditions of the enterprise. This circumstance is especially evident in the instance of college and university administration.

Administration involves activities and processes which require specialization of effort and sophistication in use. These have frequently been identified as including such activities as planning, programming, budgeting, staffing, constructing, supplying, servicing, and evaluating and such processes as leadership, organization, communication, and coordination. Administration as a set of more or less well-defined activities and processes occurs in every organized enterprise. In a college or university, administration is performed within the context of an enterprise devoted to the preservation, transmission, and advancement of learning and within the tradition of a free society. Such constituent groups of the college or university as faculty, students, and alumni do not readily fit the usual pattern of an organized enterprise, economic or governmental, which recognizes ownership or executive-legislative direction, management, employees, and customers or clientele. College or university administration must fit the particular set of purposes and operating procedures of higher education.

In one important respect, college and university administration resembles the circumstances of private business enterprise in the United States. As higher education has become more important to the national well-being and security of the nation, individual colleges and universities have come more and more to operate under the policy and financial direction of government. College and university administration has thus become increasingly subject to various external restraints which circumscribe the operation of the enterprise.

Although administration is properly described in terms of both activities and processes, administration is also a structure of decision making. Organizing an enterprise means more than the recognition of specialized activities performed by individuals; it means establishing also a framework of power. Organization brings people together in a common endeavor in accordance with a more or less explicit system of authority. Organization implies purposeful endeavor, or direction. Purposeful endeavor depends upon leadership and decisions. No discussion of administration is complete without some consideration of the structure of authority in an enterprise.

Administrative activity tends to increase under conditions of growing size and greater complexity of operation. More students, enlarged programs of study as at the graduate level, expanding activities of research and public service, varied resources of financial support, increased governmental interest in higher education—all of these and other influences as well have tended to increase the administrative activity of colleges and universities. For example, the data required to be submitted to a state commission and to the U.S. Office of Education in an application for a federal government facilities grant are quite extensive. Administrative effort must be devoted on a sizable scale simply to file such an application for funds.

The several good histories of higher education produced in the United States in recent years give only incidental attention to the development of administrative activity in various colleges and universities. Major discussions about the policy issues of higher education also treat administrative activity as a subordinate, almost unimportant phase of the college or university enterprise (Harris, 1960, 1965a, 1965b; Henderson, 1960; McConnell, 1962). There is need for more systematic historical data about college and university administration.

LEADERSHIP. In recent years a great deal of attention has been given to the subject of leadership and authority within the individual college or university. Traditionally and legally, the authority of governance within a college or university has been vested in a board of trustees (there may be other designations). Most discussions of the role of trustees tend to emphasize the formal nature of board authority. Except in the selection of a president and on questions involving the investment of funds and the management of property, boards serve primarily as devices to arbitrate academic conflict and to express general public reaction to academic policies (Bolman, (1965; Burns, 1966; Martorana, 1963; Rauh, 1959).

The role of academic leadership has fallen principally upon the college or university president. This fact is evident in presidential memoirs and in other volumes (Dodds, 1962; Stoke, 1959; Wriston, 1959). Yet the authority and responsibility of academic leadership have undergone subtle and far-reaching changes in recent years (Study of Academic Administration, 1963).

Leadership in higher education must look in two quite different directions. Externally, colleges and universities must look in large part to government appropriations and to philanthropy for their financial well-being. Internally, an academic community involves various groups such as faculty, students, and alumni, who have their own interests to advance and who insist that academic leadership help to achieve their particular goals.

The external environment upon which higher education is so largely dependent continually preoccupies the attention of academic leadership. Colleges and universities must justify their desires or requests for financial assistance upon the broad grounds of an educated citizenry or upon the more specific grounds of the manpower requirements of society, the contributions of education to economic growth, and the importance of research to national security (Harbison & Myers, 1964; Mushkin, 1962; Schultz, 1963; Vaizey, 1962; Wolfle, 1959; *Manpower Report of the President*, 1966). In turn, public attitudes, or the attitudes of influential persons and groups, intrude upon the academic community with the expectation that colleges and universities shall conform to certain standards of acceptable or desirable conduct (Perkins, 1966).

This external situation must compete for the attention of academic leadership with a rapidly changing internal situation. The faculties of colleges and universities are restive, and student bodies are demanding important changes. These two forces present new challenges to boards of trustees, to presidents, and to their administrative associates.

Faculty restiveness centers in two conditions. Scholars expect recognition as members of a learned profession and will not accept a status which suggests a role of subordination to trustees or academic administrators. Many faculty members believe that academic administrators are too slow in according proper deference to a faculty role in formulating or deciding issues of educational policy or that academic administrators are too closely allied with particular power groups in society and do not protect faculty members in their role of social criticism (Lazarsfeld & Thielens, 1958; Long, 1966; Weber, 1966). In addition, faculty members of colleges and universities carry heavier tasks of instruction, of research, and of public service than ever before in history. Faculty members are in demand as consultants to government agencies, business corporations, professional groups, and other groups. Many faculty members find other colleges and universities, as well as business enterprise, government, and professions, competing for their services. Such faculty members expect their contribution to society to be recognized by appropriate compensation and appropriate status.

A great deal has been written recently about the changing position of students in higher education. Only a sampling of such writing can be cited. Hawes (1966); Sanford (1962); *Order and Freedom on the Campus* (1965); "Student Discontent Today" (1965); and *The Student in Higher Education* (1965). Much has been said about the so-called civil liberties or the academic freedom of students. Much also has been said about the response of students to the instructional activity of colleges, and especially of universities. It has been suggested that on residential campuses in particular, colleges and universities have been slow to emulate the permissive relationships which have come to characterize family life in the more affluent families whence college students tend to come. In their role *in loco parentis*, colleges and universities are accused of establishing unreasonable or unduly restrictive standards of personal conduct for students, especially with respect to such matters as drinking, social gatherings, and personal relationships. The whole concept of parental supervision on the part of colleges and universities has come under severe attack; it is uncertain whether this concept needs modification or elimination. Moreover, many students have become much interested in various social and political problems, such as race relations and foreign policy. Here the academic issues revolve around the conduct of student groups in holding meetings, inviting speakers, and staging demonstrations on campus.

Some students have also protested the kind of instruction provided them. Faculty members have been accused of a "flight from teaching." Instruction has been left, it is said, to inexperienced graduate students. Or some faculty members are charged with providing instruction which is outdated, irrelevant to present concerns, or boring. Students have requested the opportunity to participate in formulation of the curriculum in various fields of study and in evaluation of the instructional performance of faculty members.

These problems of faculty and student status within colleges and universities have raised some far-reaching questions about leadership and decision making. (J. Brown, 1966). If leadership and decision making are based primarily upon the expectation of a "command-response" relationship between superiors and subordinates, then this concept of relationship clearly appears to be inappropriate to an academic community. On the other hand, presidential leadership can scarcely be relegated to a "caretaker" position in a college or university. It has been suggested that colleges and universities need a new sense of their "human environment," with greater emphasis upon their role in meeting urgent social exigencies, in facilitating the growth of knowledge, in providing informed judgments about public policy alternatives, in monitoring "man's image of reality," and in strengthening the foundations for social consensus (Caldwell, 1966).

It has been argued that the individual college or university is unique among organizational enterprises in the United States and that in reality the academic community is composed of four different constituent groups: faculty, students, alumni, and administration, including the board of trustees (Millett, 1962). The relation among these constituent groups should be thought of not as a hierarchy of subordination but rather as one of mutually shared power. Decision making in the academic community then becomes a process of arriving at a consensus in which all four groups participate. Presidential leadership is essential in facilitating this consensus and in effecting the decisions based upon it.

This concept of the academic community as a structure of shared power is not acceptable to those who would uphold or assert the primacy of a particular person or group. It is asserted that the primary need in a college or university today is for effective leadership and that such leadership can be provided only by the president, sustained and reinforced by a sympathetic board of trustees (Corson, 1960). There are faculty members who insist that the faculty should provide the leadership of a university, but such proposals almost never outline a structure of organization for such leadership or suggest how essential administrative activities are to be directed and supervised.

The same observation may be made about proposals for student or alumni leadership. Furthermore, decisions about academic problems must be timely if they are to meet external requirements.

American colleges and universities are caught in a fateful dilemma at a time when they are expanding and when their social role is more important than ever before in history (Wilson, 1965). Faculty members insist that they have professional competence which transcends administrative competence, and students argue that they have rights which university rules and administrative surveillance violate. Faculty members tend to seek authority over administrators, and students tend to seek an elimination of administrative authority. Yet there are still scarce resources to manage, purposes to be kept in some degree of balance, bills to be collected and paid, buildings to construct and manage, endowment funds to supervise, students to be housed and fed, coherence to be achieved (Perkins, 1966). Administration is becoming a much more highly specialized activity (Rourke & Brooks, 1964). The dilemma is how to keep a college or university effective as an enterprise which requires administration—and viable as an enterprise in which faculties, students, alumni, and others have some influence upon decision making.

PLANNING. In a college, the primary objective is the instruction of students in undergraduate programs, usually in the arts and sciences, but often also in teacher education, business administration, music, and fine arts. Some colleges add a master's-degree program in some or all of these fields. A university provides extensive graduate as well as undergraduate instruction in a variety of fields and performs important research and public service work. All of this academic activity must be undertaken in accordance with some prevailing concept of the public good (Phenix, 1961). Planning within individual colleges and universities is usually concerned with particular levels of learning (lower division, upper division, graduate, and graduate professional) and with improvements in particular fields of study such as general education, international affairs, teacher education, business administration, engineering, and medicine (Medsker, 1960; Bell, 1966; Bidwell, 1962; Thomas, 1962; Conant, 1963; Woodring, 1957; Gordon & Howell, 1959; Pierson, 1959; Estrin, 1963; Coggeshall, 1965).

For a long time research tended to be a relatively minor activity of a university. Since the end of World War II, research has become a major university endeavor (Keenan, 1966; *Administration of Government Supported Research . . .* , 1966; *Federal Support of Basic Research . . .* , 1964). Public service demands upon colleges and universities have also increased, especially for overseas activities, for general and specialized continuing education, and for hospital service (Weidner, 1962; Burch, 1961; Fletcher, 1961). The university has been labeled a "multiversity" and an instrument for national goals (Hanna, 1962; Kerr, 1963).

One of the major characteristics of our time is the extent to which planning is now being undertaken external to individual colleges and universities. The president of the United States may designate a special body to make a study of government policy affecting higher education, and the subsequent recommendations may influence legislative action (Babbidge & Rosenzweig, 1962; Orlans, 1962; *President's Committee . . .* , 1957; *Technology and the American Economy*, 1966). Federal government agencies may make special studies, or special inquiries may be made by Congressional committees; these may affect subsequent legislative or administrative action. The same procedure may be followed within state governments (Chambers, 1965; Glenny, 1959; Moos & Rourke, 1959). Moreover, many states have established official agencies to prepare and publish master plans for public policy on higher education (California State Department of Education, 1960; Illinois Board of Higher Education, 1964; Ohio Board of Regents, 1966; University of the State of New York . . . , 1965).

The most important subjects of concern to higher education planning in recent years have been the quality of instruction, the increasing demand for educated talent, access to higher education, advancing enrollments, the scope of undergraduate programs of instruction, the scope of graduate study, the extent of continuing education activity, and the extent of research activity (Gardner, 1961; Machlup, 1962; Bowles, 1963; Brown, 1960; Berelson, 1960; Carmichael, 1961). Necessarily, all such issues have their financial limitations, with corresponding appeals for "planning" and coordination (Conant, 1964; McGrath, 1964).

PROGRAMMING. The translation of general policies and plans into specific programs of instruction and of other activity has received little attention within higher education. Some suggestions have been made about how programs should be formulated, especially in budgetary terms, and the importance of programming as the center of all academic administration has been underlined (Tickton, 1961; H. Williams, 1966; R. Williams, 1965). There is a need for more careful study of the preparation of instructional and other programs and of the relation of these programs to the general objectives of individual colleges and universities.

ORGANIZATION. Although numerous organizational surveys of particular colleges and universities have been undertaken in recent years, little has been accomplished in the systematic analysis of internal organizational structure. Studies made by outside consultants are usually restricted to the committee structure and decision-making activities of boards of trustees, to the so-called top-management of a college or university, and to the "business" functions of a college or university. Usually, boards of trustees have been encouraged to restrict the number of standing committees to four or five (academic policy, finance, buildings and grounds, student and alumni affairs, and investments) and to observe careful procedure in the conduct of formal meetings and in the expression of a collective (not individual) judgment. A fairly standard concept of top-management organization has emerged in recent years, with presidents of universities urged to associate with themselves a vice-president for academic affairs, a vice-president for student affairs, a vice-president for development, a vice-president for administrative or financial affairs, and occasionally a vice-president for research or a vice-president for medical affairs (Nance & others, 1965; Williamson, 1961). Within the realm of administrative or financial affairs, a more or less standard organizational pattern recognizes such activities as campus planning, collection of accounts (bursar), disbursement, accounting, internal auditing, investment analysis, affairs of non-academic personnel, purchasing, buildings and grounds, security, operation of residence halls, operation of student centers, and the handling of central services (Burns, 1962).

The fault with all such organizational study has been the omission of the central problem, which is organization to accomplish the academic objectives of a college or university (Litchfield, 1959). The basic work unit of the academic structure is ordinarily an instructional department. The range of departmental activity is seldom fully defined in such terms as undergraduate and graduate instruction, research, public service, and related interests. In addition, there may be special research centers, special public service agencies, special instructional centers, and other special activities organized as basic work units of a university.

Instructional departments are sometimes grouped together for supervision of common interests into schools and colleges of a university. Sometimes the designation "faculty" may be employed to designate common departmental interests, such as a faculty of arts and sciences, a faculty of pure science, a faculty of social science, a faculty of humanities, a faculty of medicine, or a faculty of law.

Increasingly, the most complex issue of academic organization in the United States is that of appropriate handling of undergraduate and graduate instruction. There are two possibilities: to establish separate departments within an undergraduate college or to establish departments with both undergraduate and graduate instructional duties but subject to the separate supervision or coordination of these two different programs. Each arrangement is employed in various universities, but the actual structure is seldom clearly set forth and carefully directed.

There are other organizational interrelationships to resolve. How should the biological sciences be organized to meet the needs of both medical instruction and graduate study? How should the physical sciences and mathematics be organized to meet the needs of both their own students and engineering students? How should any department in a discipline be related to a corresponding department in an applied field of study? How should teacher education be organized to recognize both subject-matter content and pedagogical process? How should general education be organized in relation to the specialized education of individual disciplines? These and similar questions are the crucial issues of academic organization within a university, and these issues deserve more extensive discussion than they ordinarily receive.

FINANCING. Colleges and universities have three sources of income: charges to students, government appropriations (federal, state, and local), and philanthropy (in the form of either endowments or current giving from alumni, friends, private foundations, church bodies, and business corporations). Income must be utilized for current operations and capital accounts. In some circumstances capital improvement funds may be borrowed, with current debt service then defrayed from one of the three specified sources of income.

The income available to any particular college or university is utilized for one of five major purposes: instruction and general operation, research, public service, auxiliary services (student residence, student health, student activities, bookstore, and intercollegiate athletics), and student aid (scholarships, fellowships, loans, grants, etc.) (Moon, 1963a, 1963b; West, 1963).

The financing of colleges and universities is complicated by the diverse sponsorship and by the different levels of government interested in higher education. In the United States there are colleges and universities operating under private sponsorship and colleges and universities operating under public sponsorship. The privately sponsored colleges and universities may be nonsectarian with self-perpetuating boards of trustees, or they may be related to church bodies in some way. The publicly sponsored colleges and universities have been created for the most part by state government action, although the federal government has created military academies and one or two other units, and local governments have created a few universities and a number of community colleges.

Local and state government financial support has been directed mostly to the colleges and universities which they have created, although state governments have also established scholarship and other student aid funds and in a few instances have assisted privately sponsored colleges and universities in the construction of their instructional plants. One state has assisted privately sponsored institutions with operating grants.

Federal governmental programs of assistance to higher education generally do not differentiate between the public and private sponsorship of colleges and universities. But the federal government has also tended to avoid providing funds for the current support of instruction and general operation. Federal financial assistance has been largely directed to support of research, especially to research related to national defense, atomic energy, and space exploration. The federal government has also provided a number of student aid programs, has lent money for residence halls, has made grants for instructional facilities and equipment, and has encouraged continuing education activity in agriculture, urban affairs, teacher education, and technological development.

The role of philanthropy in support of higher education has not been carefully examined in recent years, although it is known to have increased substantially in the past ten years (Pollard, 1958). Endowment management has remained a matter of concern, and considerable emphasis has been given to diversity in types of investment and even to larger investment in common stocks (Halstead, 1965). No systematic study has been made since 1952 of the role of student charges in support of the various activities of higher education and in support of the various levels of instruction. There have been a number of useful general discussions of higher education finance (Chambers, 1963; Harris, 1962; Keezer, 1959).

STAFFING. The personnel requirements of higher education fall into three major categories: academic personnel (instructional and research), service personnel (stenographers, clerks, custodial and craft workers, food-service personnel, police, etc.), and management personnel (academic administrators, financial administrators, student personnel administrators, student health officers, public information officers, admissions officers, academic-records officers, purchasing officers, campus planners, space officers, etc.). Different personnel practices are usually followed in the recruitment and retention of the three different types of personnel.

The system of academic personnel has been described by Caplow and McGee (1958). Byse and Joughin (1959) have analyzed the practices of academic tenure. No general treatise has been prepared in recent years about personnel practices in handling service and management personnel.

The major personnel problems of higher education involve rates of compensation, tenure status, retirement benefits, so-called fringe benefits, and the available supply of needed manpower.

FACILITIES. As the various activities of higher education have expanded in the past ten years, a good deal of attention has been directed to utilization of space and to standards of space requirements, to college and university architecture, and to possible economies in facility construction. The whole subject of maintenance operations seems to have received much less concern, except as individual colleges and universities have utilized management consultants to examine maintenance practices or have otherwise sought to improve building maintenance.

The Educational Facilities Laboratories, a nonprofit corporation established by the Ford Foundation in 1958, has undertaken to assist American schools and higher education by encouraging research and experimentation in the design of buildings. In 1960 this organization published a study on planning for schools with television (*Planning for Schools with Television,* 1960). In 1961 it issued a helpful study on college housing (*College Students Live Here,* 1961). In 1964 it published a comprehensive report on college planning and design, with sections devoted to classrooms, laboratories, libraries, dormitories, campus planning, and building renovation (*Bricks and Mortarboards,* 1964). Another report dealt with four case studies of colleges which moved from old to new campuses (*New Campuses for Old,* 1962). All of this work has stimulated much greater interest in campus planning, space relationships and needs, and building design.

The whole subject of style in building design inevitably arouses considerable discussion, disagreement, and even acrimony on most college and university campuses. Many college and university campuses as built up in the nineteenth or early twentieth century tended to follow the Gothic style of Oxford and Cambridge or the colonial-Georgian style of Harvard and William and Mary. In some other instances a classical revival encouraged monumental design of columns and rotundas of Greek and Roman ancestry. Sometimes, as in the southwestern United States, there was an attempt at adapting a local, indigenous style of architecture.

In the period since World War I and especially since the end of World War II, a great deal of experimentation in structural design has been undertaken in western Europe and the United States. Although this style is usually labeled "contemporary," the designation embraces a wide variety of designs, appearance, and building materials. Individual colleges and universities have been persuaded to build in various contemporary forms, although often the symmetry of space relationships and the harmony of similar appearance and materials have been sacrificed. Some persons assert that a university campus should embody structures representative of the time and prevailing taste when built. Others maintain that a university campus should retain an essential symmetry of shape and harmony of style, even though some sameness or even monotony of appearance may result. This is a conflict of opinion and taste, with almost no objective standards available for guiding the process of decision making (Dober, 1964).

PROCUREMENT AND DISTRIBUTION. In 1961 the National Association of Educational Buyers arranged the publication of a handbook on college and university purchasing (Ritterskamp, 1961). This volume, in addition to sketching the place of purchasing within the business operation of a college or university, presents guide lines for determining supply and equipment needs, the placing of purchase orders, receiving procedure, payments on purchases, the operation of central stores, quality factors in procurement decisions, price factors in procurement decisions, quantitative and time factors in procurement decisions, and the legal problems of purchasing. This manual provides a ready reference work on college and university purchasing and storage.

CENTRAL SERVICES. The administration of a college or university involves a number of service operations, usually performed on a central basis for the enterprise as a whole. These may include the operation of a central heating plant, sometimes the operation of an electric generating plant or of a standby plant, arrangements for other utility services (electricity, water, sewage disposal, waste disposal), central telephone service, automotive transportation and maintenance, campus mail service, central reproduction and printing service, laundry service, and even, on occasion, air transportation service.

These services seem to attract little general concern and become annoying on an individual college or university campus only when a breakdown occurs in any particular service effort.

REVIEW OF ACCOMPLISHMENTS. The administration of colleges and universities in the United States has done very little in the field of assessing the results of its instructional, research, or public service activities or in endeavoring to maintain quality controls. Accreditation is supposed to guarantee a minimum standard of academic performance (Selden, 1960).

Qualitative judgments affecting higher education are continually made by students and parents in the selection of colleges and universities to attend, by faculty members in accepting appointment, by federal governmental agencies in making grants, by private foundations in making gifts, by corporations and wealthy citizens in making gifts, and by others. In the absence of any systematic practice of evaluation, these judgments necessarily reflect certain subjective beliefs or commonly accepted reputations.

Occasionally, surveys are made to ascertain student or faculty evaluation of the academic performance of colleges and universities. Faculty evaluation appears to be more meaningful because of the greater and more varied experience of faculty members. One such analysis of graduate programs in American universities, which may be mentioned as an example, is that by Cartter (1966).

The problem of evaluating instructional practice and accomplishment is complex, and yet administrators generally need to know something about the academic performance of their college or university in relation to other colleges or universities (*Proceedings, Invitational Conference on Testing Problems,* 1961). It is commonly recognized that an assessment of instructional accomplishment is necessarily related to instructional inputs, both the initial abilities of students admitted to a college or university and the instructional and scholarly abilities and techniques of faculty members. The measurement of these inputs is often difficult, even under carefully controlled circumstances. The measurement of output is equally complex. Standardized tests, the most reliable instruments for determining ability and accomplishment among a large number of students in various classes and in various colleges and universities, have their deficiencies (Brumbaugh, 1960; Dressel, 1961).

Research accomplishment is ordinarily evaluated in terms of contributions to knowledge or in terms of contributions to useful products and processes. Here again there is no readily accepted criterion for determining what results of research may actually constitute such a contribution. In many ways, however, the problem of the evaluation of research results is simpler than the evaluation of instructional results. Judgment in the latter case is usually made upon the basis of publications and their reception by other scholars or upon the basis of patents or other evidence of useful output.

Accomplishments in the rendering of public service are also difficult to determine, especially in the field of continuing education, which constitutes so large a part of public service endeavor. Since this whole area of higher education remains relatively small in contrast with those of instruction and research, the concern with evaluation is much less pressing than in the other two areas. It seems likely that the whole process of evaluation of instructional accomplishment by colleges and universities will receive increasing attention in the next few years (Lazarsfeld & Sieber, 1964).

Closely related to evaluation is the matter of cost effectiveness in undertaking the tasks of higher education. In higher education as in other enterprise, dollar costs provide the only common denominator for the many elements of input for the operation: elements of space, personnel, supplies and equipment, and technique. In higher education there is no ready unit of output to enumerate except the number of students instructed. Cost effectiveness in higher education can be determined only if there is a measurement of instruction accomplished in relation to dollars expended.

Administrative officials have experimented with the expenditure analysis of instructional programs and of general operations for a number of years. These efforts have endeavored to distinguish between undergraduate instruction in the arts and sciences, undergraduate instruction in such professional fields as teacher education and engineering, graduate instruction at the master's level, graduate instruction at the doctoral level, and graduate professional instruction in such fields as law, medicine, and dentistry. Various efforts at expenditure analysis have indicated substantial expenditure differences between programs of instruction and levels of instruction. Unfortunately, many comparisons of expenditure do not make clear distinctions among types and levels of instructional programs.

Although direct expenditures for instructional purposes are relatively simple to determine, complications begin when the allocation of "overhead" or of general operations must be made to various instructional programs. In addition to departmental instruction, a college or university has other expenses important to its general operation. These "other" expenses may often be 40 percent or more of the total expenditures for instruction and general operation, including such matters as operation of the library, the provision of student services including admissions and registration and placement, the operation of the physical plant, the general expense of public information and public ceremonies, and top management. The allocation of these expenditures must often be made upon the basis of some kind of formula.

A research study sponsored by the Office of Education and completed at the University of Michigan in

1966 explored the complexities of expenditure analysis for colleges and universities and set forth a recommended procedure for such analysis. This procedure appeared to be too complicated for more than a few large and well-staffed universities to undertake (Swanson & others, 1966).

REPORTING. Every college or university, whether functioning under private or under public sponsorship, serves a public purpose and is affected by a public interest. The availability of federal government funds for certain activities of privately sponsored colleges and universities testifies to their public responsibility.

Many publicly sponsored and privately sponsored colleges and universities publish annually or biennially a president's report and a treasurer's report. These would seem to be the minimum desirable components of public reporting. Needless to say, such reports should strive for accuracy, clarity, comprehensiveness, and timeliness.

The extent and content of public reporting by colleges and universities have not been studied carefully or fully in recent years. As agencies clothed with a public interest and utilizing public resources, proper public reporting is an essential ingredient of public responsibility and a pledge of continuing performance on behalf of the public welfare.

John D. Millett
Ohio Board of Regents

References

The Administration of Government Supported Research at Universities. Bureau of the Budget, 1966.
Babbidge, Homer D., Jr., and Rosenzweig, Robert M. *The Federal Interest in Higher Education.* McGraw-Hill, 1962.
Bell, Daniel. *The Reforming of General Education.* Columbia U Press, 1966.
Berelson, Bernard. *Graduate Education in the United States.* McGraw-Hill, 1960.
Bidwell, Percy W. *Undergraduate Education in Foreign Affairs.* King's Crown Press, 1962.
Bolman, Frederick deW. *How College Presidents Are Chosen.* ACE, 1965.
Bowles, Frank. *Access to Higher Education.* The United Nations Educational, Scientific and Cultural Organization and the International Association of Universities, 1963.
Bricks and Mortarboards. Educational Facilities Laboratories, 1964.
Brown, J. Douglas. "On Organization and Executive Leadership in a Liberal University." *AGB Reports* 8:12; 1966.
Brown, Nicholas C. (Ed.) *Higher Education: Incentives and Obstacles.* ACE, 1960.
Brumbaugh, A. J. *Research Designed to Improve Institutions of Higher Learning.* ACE, 1960.
Burch, Glen. *Challenge to the University.* Center for the Study of Liberal Education for Adults, 1961.
Burns, Gerald P. (Ed.) *Administrators in Higher Education.* Harper, 1962.
Burns, Gerald P. *Trustees in Higher Education.* Independent College Funds of America, 1966.
Byse, Clark, and Joughin, Louis. *Tenure in American Higher Education.* Cornell U Press, 1959.
Caldwell, Lynton K. "The Human Environment." *J H Ed* 37:149; 1966.
California State Department of Education. *A Master Plan for Higher Education in California, 1960–1975.* The Department, 1960. 230p.
Caplow, Theodore, and McGee, Reece J. *The Academic Marketplace.* Basic Books, 1958.
Carmichael, Oliver C. *Graduate Education.* Harper, 1961.
Cartter, Allan M. *An Assessment of Quality in Graduate Education.* ACE, 1966.
Chambers, M. M. *Financing Higher Education.* The Center for Applied Research in Education, 1963.
Chambers, M. M. *Freedom and Repression in Higher Education.* Bloomcraft Press, 1965.
Coggeshall, Lowell T. *Planning for Medical Progress Through Education.* Association of American Medical Colleges, 1965.
College Students Live Here. Educational Facilities Laboratories, 1961.
Conant, James B. *The Education of American Teachers.* McGraw-Hill, 1963.
Conant, James B. *Shaping Educational Policy.* McGraw-Hill, 1964.
Corson, John J. *Governance of Colleges and Universities.* McGraw-Hill, 1960.
Dober, Richard P. *Campus Planning.* Reinhold, 1964.
Dodds, Harold W. *The Academic President—Educator or Caretaker?* McGraw-Hill, 1962.
Dressel, Paul L., and others. *Evaluation in Higher Education.* Riverside, 1961.
Estrin, Herman. (Ed.) *Higher Education in Engineering and Science.* McGraw-Hill, 1963.
Federal Support of Basic Research in Institutions of Higher Learning. National Academy of Sciences and National Research Council, 1964.
Fletcher, F. Scott. (Ed.) *Education for Public Responsibility.* Norton, 1961.
Gardner, John W. *Excellence.* Harper, 1961.
Glenny, Lyman A. *Autonomy of Public Colleges.* McGraw-Hill, 1959.
Gordon, Robert Aaron, and Howell, James Edwin. *Higher Education for Business.* Columbia U Press, 1959.
Halstead, D. Kent. *College and University Endowment.* USOE Publication OE-53024, GPO, 1965.
Hanna, Paul R. (Ed.) *Education: An Instrument of National Goals.* McGraw-Hill, 1962.
Harbison, Frederick, and Myers, Charles A. *Education, Manpower, and Economic Growth.* McGraw-Hill, 1964.
Harris, Seymour E. *Higher Education: Resources and Finance.* McGraw-Hill, 1962.
Harris, Seymour E. (Ed.) *Higher Education in the United States.* Harvard U Press, 1960.

Harris, Seymour E. (Ed.) *Challenge and Change in American Education.* McCutchan Publishing Corporation, 1965(*a*).

Harris, Seymour E. (Ed.) *Education and Public Policy.* McCutchan Publishing Corporation, 1965(*b*).

Hawes, Gene R. "Civil Liberties for College Students." *Saturday R* June 18:61; 1966.

Henderson, Algo D. *Policies and Practices in Higher Education.* Harper, 1960.

Illinois Board of Higher Education. *A Master Plan for Higher Education in Illinois.* The Board, 1964. 72p.

Keenan, Boyd R. (Ed.) *Science and the University.* Columbia U Press, 1966.

Keezer, Dexter M. (Ed.) *Financing Higher Education, 1960–70.* McGraw-Hill, 1959.

Kellogg, Charles E., and Knapp, David C. *The College of Agriculture.* McGraw-Hill, 1966.

Kerr, Clark. *The Uses of the University.* Harvard U Press, 1963.

Lazarsfeld, Paul F., and Sieber, Sam D. *Organizing Educational Research.* Prentice-Hall, 1964.

Lazarsfeld, Paul F., and Thielens, Wagner, Jr. *The Academic Mind: Social Scientists in a Time of Crisis.* Free, 1958. 460p.

Litchfield, Edward H. "Organization in Large American Universities." *J H Ed* 30:353, 489; 1959.

Long, Durward. "Faculty Responsibility and the Executive Conquest of Academe." *Sch Soc* 94:89; 1966.

Machlup, Fritz. *The Production and Distribution of Knowledge in the United States.* Princeton U Press, 1962.

Manpower Report of the President, Transmitted to the Congress March 1966. GPO, 1966.

Martorana, S. V. *College Boards of Trustees.* Center for Applied Research in Education, 1963.

The Master Plan, Revised, 1964. State U New York, 1964.

McConnell, T. R. *A General Pattern for American Public Higher Education.* McGraw-Hill, 1962.

McGrath, Earl J. (Ed.) *Cooperative Long-range Planning in Liberal Arts Colleges.* Teachers College, Columbia U, 1964.

Medsker, Leland L. *The Junior College.* McGraw-Hill, 1960.

Millett, John D. *The Academic Community.* McGraw-Hill, 1962.

Moon, Rexford G., Jr. *Student Financial Aid and Institutional Purpose.* CEEB, 1963(*a*).

Moon, Rexford G., Jr. *Student Financial Aid in the United States.* CEEB, 1963(*b*).

Moos, Malcolm, and Rourke, Francis E. *The Campus and the State.* Johns Hopkins U Press, 1959.

Mushkin, Selma J. (Ed.) *Economics of Higher Education.* USOE Bulletin No. 5. GPO, 1962.

Nance, Paul K., and others. *Guide to College and University Business Management.* USOE Bulletin No. 30. GPO, 1965.

New Campuses for Old. Educational Facilities Laboratories, 1962.

Ohio Board of Regents. *Master Plan for State Policy in Higher Education.* The Board, 1966.

Order and Freedom on the Campus: Rights and Responsibilities of Faculty and Students. Papers for the Seventh Annual Institute for College and University Self-study, Western Interstate Commission for Higher Education, 1965.

Orlans, Harold. *The Effects of Federal Programs on Higher Education.* Brookings Institution, 1962.

Perkins, James A. *The University in Transition.* Princeton U Press, 1966.

Phenix, Philip H. *Education and the Common Good.* Harper, 1961.

Pierson, Frank C., and others. *The Education of American Business Men.* McGraw-Hill, 1959.

Planning for Schools with Television. Educational Facilities Laboratories, 1960.

Pollard, John A. *Fund-raising for Higher Education.* Harper, 1958.

President's Committee on Education Beyond the High School, Second Report to the President. GPO, 1957.

Proceedings, Invitational Conference on Testing Problems. ETS, 1961.

Rauh, Morton A. *College and University Trusteeship.* Antioch Press, 1959.

Ritterskamp, James J., Jr., and others. *Purchasing for Educational Institutions.* Teachers College, Columbia U, 1961.

Rivlin, Alice M. *The Role of the Federal Government in Financing Higher Education.* Brookings Institution, 1961.

Rourke, Francis E., and Brooks, Glen E. "The 'Managerial Revolution' in Higher Education." *Adm Sci Q* 9:154; 1964.

Rudy, Willis. *The Evolving Liberal Arts Curriculum.* Columbia U Press, 1960.

Sanford, Nevitt. (Ed.) *The American College.* Wiley, 1962.

Schultz, Theodore W. *The Economic Value of Education.* Columbia U Press, 1963.

Selden, William K. *Accreditation.* Harper, 1960.

Stoke, Harold W. *The American College President.* Harper, 1959.

"Student Discontent Today." *AGB Reports* 8; 1965.

The Student in Higher Education. American Council on Higher Education, 1965.

The Study of Academic Administration. Papers presented at the Fifth Annual Institute on College Self-study sponsored by Western Interstate Commission for Higher Education and The Center for the Study of Higher Education of the University of California (Berkeley), July 22–26, 1963. Western Interstate Commission for Higher Education, 1963.

Swanson, John E., and others. *Financial Analysis of Current Operations of Colleges and Universities.* Institute of Public Administration, U Michigan, 1966.

Technology and the American Economy. Report of the National Commission on Technology, Automation, and Economic Progress, February, 1966. GPO, 1966.

Thomas, Russell. *The Search for a Common Learning.* McGraw-Hill, 1962.

Tickton, Sidney G. *Needed: A Ten-year College Bud-*

get. Fund for the Advancement of Education, 1961.
University of the State of New York. The State Education Department. *The Regents Statewide Plan for the Expansion and Development of Higher Education*. U State of New York and the Department, 1965.
Vaizey, John. *The Economics of Education*. Faber and Faber, Ltd., 1962.
Weber, C. Edward, and others. "Academic Authority and the Administration of Research." Ed Rec 47: 218; 1966.
Weidner, Edward W. *The World Role of Universities*. McGraw-Hill, 1962.
West, Elmer D. *Financial Aid to the Undergraduate*. ACE, 1963.
Williams, Harry. *Planning for Effective Resource Allocation in Universities*. ACE, 1966.
Williams, Robert L. *The Administration of Academic Affairs in Higher Education*. U Michigan Press, 1965.
Williamson, E. G. *Student Personnel Services in Colleges and Universities*. McGraw-Hill, 1961.
Wilson, Logan. (Ed.) *Emerging Patterns in American Higher Education*. ACE, 1965.
Wolfle, Dael. (Ed.) *Symposium on Basic Research*. AAAS, 1959.
Woodring, Paul. *New Directions in Teacher Education*. Fund for the Advancement of Education, 1957.
Wriston, Henry M. *Academic Procession*. Columbia U Press, 1959.

COLLEGE ENVIRONMENTS

The college environment has become a special object of study and research within the past decade. Educators, and the lay public, have always known, indeed have taken for granted, that colleges differ from one another in various ways. The familiar classifications of institutions reflect this common knowledge: junior college, liberal arts college, university, teachers' college; public, private, Protestant, Catholic, coeducational, rural, urban, residential, commuter; and other distinctions in popular favor or official use. The research interest in the college environment, however, is directed not so much toward producing more refined classifications as toward exploring new ways of viewing and measuring the style of life and atmosphere, or general institutional context, within which learning, growth, and development take place.

This particular type of interest in the college environment appears to stem, consciously or unconsciously, from several prior and concurrent developments. For one, there has been the example of anthropologists characterizing primitive and contemporary cultures. Second, and somewhat more consciously influential, have been the numerous studies of change in college students' attitudes and values, with their efforts to identify, usually after the fact, which experience or conditions may have contributed to changing values and attitudes and their speculation that perhaps there was something about the total atmosphere of the college, or its programs, or about particular peer-group associations, that was significantly important (Dressel & Mayhew, 1954; Eddy, 1959; Jacob, 1956). Third, there has been a renewed awareness of the great diversity of abilities, backgrounds, and aspirations found among college students, with the consequent feeling that such differences in student bodies may explain the differences in atmosphere among colleges (Darley, 1962; McConnell & Heist, 1962). And fourth, the attention of social scientists from various disciplines has been turned to higher education as an object of research (Merton & others, 1957; Lazarsfeld & Thielens, 1958), thanks in part to activities of the Social Science Research Council and other agencies. In a first review of the literature on the college environment (Pace & McFee, 1960), about half of the citations were to individuals outside the field of educational psychology and measurement.

The perspective from which the college environment has been viewed, the measures used in viewing it, and the conclusions reached about it reflect these varied influences. Basically, the efforts of researchers to characterize the environment can be seen as related to the questions that have been asked. What image do people have of the environment? Who lives in the environment? What demographic features does the environment possess? How do people behave in the environment?

METHODS AND MEASURES. The first systematic and objective measuring instrument for characterizing college environments, the *College Characteristics Index*, or *CCI* (Pace & Stern, 1958), was stimulated by Henry Murray's need-press theory and by a practical interest in expanding the information which might usefully be considered in college admissions studies.

When students enroll in college they are presumably entering a new environment—presenting an assortment of expectations and activities, pressures and rewards, and facilities and people to which they must make adaptive responses. These characteristic demands and features as perceived by the students are called the environmental press. In Murray's theory, environmental presses are viewed as counterparts to personality needs, and performance in the environment is seen as a function of the congruence between need and press. The concept of environmental press determined the type of items composed for the *CCI*, items which could be regarded as environmental counterparts to a set of 30 personality needs included in the *Stern Activities Index, AI*. Although there was no comparable guide line for determining the content of items, an effort was made to include a great variety of events, conditions, and practices which might be found on different college campuses and which would have meaning and importance for students and educators.

The strategy followed by Stern (1960) in analyzing and interpreting the results obtained from the *CCI* has been to use the responses of individuals as the unit of analysis; that is, responses of students from different schools are put into a common matrix and are undifferentiated as to which school any given student's reply refers to. This produces a set of factors which characterize students' perceptions of environments in general. Among the labels given to these factors in a recent report (Stern, 1965) are vocational climate, intellectual climate, aspiration level, student dignity, self-expression, group life, and social form.

The combination of need and press, represented by the intended parallelism between the *AI* and *CCI* has not been empirically demonstrated as fully as had been hoped. Except for one large joint factor which concerns intellectual needs and the intellectuality of environments, each instrument produces its own unique set of factors (Saunders, 1962). In a further illustration of this (Stern, 1962), need-press scales classified under three major groupings—intellectual orientation, social relationships, and emotional expression—indicated that in the first group one-third of the scales were not parallel, and in the other two groups two-thirds of the scales were not parallel.

In Pace's strategy for analyzing the *CCI* (1960), which uses the institutional mean scores rather than the scores of individuals as the unit of analysis, and in the development of other instruments for describing the college environment using the collective perceptions of students as the basis for measurement, the need-press model has not been followed. For example, in the *College Characteristic Analysis* (Pace, 1964) items were written and selected to fit a specifically developed outline of educational content. There were three major categories: (1) administrative sources of press, referring to rules and regulations, general features, and facilities, (2) academic or faculty sources of press, referring to characteristics of faculty members, courses and curricula, and instructional practices and demands; and (3) student sources of press, referring to student characteristics, informal activities and interests, and extracurricular programs.

Another instrument, *College and University Environment Scales,* or *CUES* (Pace, 1963) is now being widely used. In its present form it consists of half of the *CCI* items, selected to measure most sharply the major dimensions along which a normative group of 50 college environments differed. The scoring and interpretation of *CUES* follow the rationale of public opinion polling. If students agree, by a consensus of 2 to 1 or greater, that a statement is true about their college, then that statement is scored or counted as characteristic of the college. The institutional score is determined by the number of statements that are characteristic of its environment. The scales are labeled scholarship, awareness, community, propriety, and practicality.

Other examples of the image or collective perception approach to describing environments are the college press scales developed by Thistlethwaite (1959). These scales are divided into two groups—faculty press scales and student press scales. Thistlethwaite's purpose was to identify items and item combinations which were related to a criterion index—namely, the institution's production of future doctorates in the natural sciences and in the arts, humanities, and social sciences. The type of item used was similar to those in the *CCI*. The purpose, however, was not to describe the general environment but rather to describe those aspects of the environment that are related to scholarly productivity. Scales similar to some of Thistlethwaite's were also used in a study of the environment at the Carnegie Institute of Technology (Kirk, 1965).

A different way of characterizing environments is to characterize the type of people who live in them. Striking differences between institutions in the mean scores of entering freshmen on the *American Council on Education Psychological Examination* were reported by Darley (1962). The Cornell values study (Goldsen & others, 1960) revealed large differences between the student bodies at 11 universities in educational values, with 80 percent of the students at one school indicating that vocational training was their main goal, compared with only 30 percent of the students at another school. Even within the restricted range of medical schools, Gee and Glaser (1958) found large differences not only in aptitude but also in value orientations as measured by the Allport-Vernon-Lindzey Study of Values. McConnell and Heist (1962) cited an example of two liberal arts colleges whose entering classes were alike in scholastic aptitude but distinctly different on many of the traits measured by the Omnibus Personality Inventory. The implication of these studies is that the atmosphere of a college may largely be determined by the types of students who enroll in it.

The *Environmental Assessment Technique,* or *EAT* (Astin & Holland, 1961), is based on this proposition. *EAT* assumes that the college environment or atmosphere is a product of its size, the average intelligence of students, and the personal characteristics of the students. Holland's *Vocational Preference Inventory* classified occupations into six categories related to personality characteristics: realistic, intellectual, social, conventional, enterprising, and artistic. A person's vocational choice is really a kind of personality test, since there are typical personality differences between occupational categories. Extending this empirically validated proposition to college students, who are not yet in occupations, requires only that one regard the student's major field of study as a forerunner of his later occupation. Then, by classifying major academic fields into the same six types into which occupations have been classified and noting what proportions of students at a given college are majoring in these subjects, one can characterize the environment as being predominantly enterprising, conventional, artistic, etc., as the case may be. The virtue of this approach is that one can get all the necessary information from public sources. Astin (1965a) demonstrated this by publishing standard scores on each of the eight *EAT* variables for all of the 1,000 or so accredited four-year colleges and universities.

Another approach based on the assumption that students make the college is the typology of student subcultures described by Trow (1960) and used by

Educational Testing Service in its *College Student Questionnaire* (Peterson, 1965).

Impressions gained by Clark and Trow from visiting several campuses and from observing and interviewing students led them to speculate that there were four main types of campus subcultures—vocational, collegiate, academic, and nonconformist. In the ETS questionnaire the characteristic values and orientations of each of these subcultures are presented to students in brief paragraph descriptions, and the student is asked to indicate which description comes closest to reflecting his values and interests, which comes next closest, etc. The institutional atmosphere can then be characterized by the proportion of students identifying themselves with each of these four value patterns.

A third question which has guided the study of college environments is: What demographic characteristics does the environment have? One of Astin's studies (1962a) illustrates this. He looked up 33 pieces of information about each college obtainable from directories or other public sources—such as size, form of control, proportions of men and women in the student body, number of fields in which degrees are offered, faculty-student ratio, percent of Ph.D.'s on the faculty, size of operating budget, and ratio of library size to enrollment. From a factor analysis of these data for about 300 schools, he identified five factors which he called affluence, size, masculinity, homogeneity of offerings, and technical emphasis. A similar study (Richards & others, 1965) of junior colleges identified a somewhat different set of factors —cultural affluence, technological specialization, size, age, transfer emphasis, and business orientation. There appears to be no particular theory which underlies this type of approach.

The fourth guiding question is: How do people behave in the environment? Becker and others (1961), through extended participant observation in the Kansas Medical School, viewed the student culture as illustrating a set of perspectives and responses to commonly perceived environmental pressures. In a subsequent study of general undergraduate life at the University of Kansas, Becker (1963) reported that prefreshmen had very hazy perspectives. As they moved through the freshman year, however, they came to define college as a place in which one demonstrated that he has become a mature adult. This is demonstrated by being successful, and success, in turn, is defined as earning acceptable grades, making friends, and participating in campus activities and organizations. How students behave on the campus is seen as a response to these perspectives about the institution.

As part of a larger study in which objectively observable behavior is the focus of inquiry, Astin (1965b) reported an analysis of classroom environments. He asked students to report about their own behavior and that of their instructors, using such items as the following: the instructor encouraged discussion; I was in the instructor's office one or more times; students had assigned seats; the instructor called students by their first names; and I took notes regularly; we sometimes had unannounced quizzes. The results showed that there were systematic differences in classroom environments among various fields of study.

Within certain limits, no one methodology or measuring device is logically or empirically superior to all others. Moreover, a comparison of existing devices with Barton's analysis of organizational measurement (1961), suggests that much more must be measured. Some current approaches, however, are broader or more direct than others. The factoring of an assortment of demographic characteristics is probably the farthest removed from being a direct measure of what impinges upon the life of the students. The approaches which emphasize student characteristics have the limiting assumption that the character of the environment is largely determined by the character of the people who inhabit it. This is partly true, but it is not the whole truth. The *EAT* assumes that the choice of a major field of study produces the same sort of personality differentiations as the choice of an occupation, an assumption which may be considerably less valid for many women liberal arts students than it is for vocationally oriented men. In another sense, *EAT* is based on the proposition that the character of the environment is largely determined by the breadth of curricular offerings in the college.

Measures based on the collective perception of students or on observable student behavior appear to be the most direct. These two direct approaches are also complementary. The work by Becker (1963) and his colleagues illustrates this interrelationship. His basic data are directly observed events and behavior, but these data are given meaning and significance by showing that much of the behavior is a response to collectively perceived environmental or institutional demands.

MAJOR DIMENSIONS OF ENVIRONMENT. Despite differences in approach, strategy, and assumptions, and despite differences in item content, there appear to be some general similarities in the results that have been obtained. These similarities can be regarded as major dimensions along which college environments differ. All of the investigations find some kind of an intellectual or scholarly dimension— indicated by perceived environmental press for academic achievement, or scholarship, intellectual orientation of students, academic selectivity of the institution, and the importance of getting acceptable grades. Many of the studies also find a variable which appears similar to the awareness scale in *CUES*, a variable which is also intellectual in its general character but which emphasizes humanistic and aesthetic matters—for example, self-expression, humanistic-intellectual press, and artistic orientation. Most of the investigations also find a vocational or pragmatic or instrumental variable—for example, vocational climate, faculty press for vocationalism and compliance, vocational student culture, and realistic emphasis. To some extent this appears to be an opposite of the scholarship dimension. But there is also associated with this variable in some of the studies a mixture of collegiate and bureaucratic elements—for example, play, student camaraderie, press for status, collegiate student culture, the importance of student activities, and the sheer size of the institution. Many of the studies also produce a dimension similar to the community scale in *CUES*—friendliness, faculty affiliation, social orientation, small size, and the importance of making friends. To some extent there appears to be a dimension similar to the propriety scale in *CUES*—suggested by such variables from other studies as social form, constraint, social conformity, age and tradition, and nonmasculinity.

In general, the degree of similarity of different measures within what appear to be major dimensions is expressed by correlations in the .40's to .60's. This magnitude is too small to argue that the various measures have produced nearly identical results but too large to argue against the existence of some underlying similarities.

What has been demonstrated up to this point is that college environments differ greatly from one another in many measurable characteristics. These differences in environments are at least as great as the differences between student bodies. Moreover, the accumulated results indicate clearly that the common classifications of institutions mask a great deal of diversity. For example, liberal arts colleges, as a class, run the gamut from top to bottom scores on all five of the dimensions measured by *CUES*.

ENVIRONMENTAL IMPACT. Given such large differences in environments, one would expect that what happens to students in college would depend on the particular character of their college environment. It does; but it is difficult to say how much can be attributed to the environment and how much is accountable for by other factors.

There is wide acknowledgement of the fact that students do change during the college years, not only with respect to knowledge and skills, but also with respect to personality, attitudes, interests, and aspirations. Much of the research on this point has been summarized by Webster and others (1962). At the same time, incoming freshmen at different colleges vary greatly with respect to these same attributes, so that the output may simply be a function of the initial input. Astin (1962*b*) has emphasized the need to control input variables before attributing output to environmental factors. Plant (1962) has shown that the scores of college-age youth on tests of ethnocentrism, dogmatism, and authoritarianism decrease significantly over periods of two and four years regardless of whether the students attended college for four years or two years or not at all. Nichols (1965) reported that college students generally become more aware of their shortcomings, more tolerant, and less dependent upon external standards and that their motives and interests become more specific; and he also concluded that the amount of the changes attributable to such gross characteristics of the colleges as are measured by the EAT and by Astin's factored dimensions of institutions was relatively small. Many personality traits may or may not be relevant to objectives of higher education, and the appropriateness of their use as criterion measures in studies of college impact is at least open to question.

Other studies have looked at college impact in relation to different criteria. Thistlethwaite (1962), in a statistically controlled study, demonstrated that many faculty and student press scales were highly related to changes in the level of aspiration of students who entered college with plans to seek something less than a Ph.D. degree. In a panel study of 2,000 students, tested at entrance and again two and four years later, Thistlethwaite (1965) found that students' dispositions to seek advanced training were positively related to such environmental factors as faculty and student press for intellectualism, teachers who provided positive evaluations of the student's ability, and honors programs and was negatively related to environments in which teachers demanded strict compliance with course or curricular requirements and in which there was high student press for social conformity, status, and play.

Further documentation of peer-group influences comes from two large-scale sociological studies. Davis (Davis & others, 1961), in a study of seniors from 135 colleges and universities, showed that about half of the students had changed their career plans between freshman and senior years and that there were distinct patterns of change at different schools. Wallace (1963), in a study of all freshmen at one liberal arts college, showed that the importance which students attached to getting high grades declined in the freshman year, primarily owing to the powerful normative influence of fraternity and sorority affiliation, whereas students who had a positive orientation to the faculty sustained or raised their evaluation of getting high grades. Newcomb (1962) has summarized a variety of peer-group studies and discussed the general problems of peer-group formation and influence.

In a study at the Carnegie Institute of Technology, Kirk (1965) found substantial differences in the environmental press of different departments and corresponding differences in the characteristics of students enrolled in those departments. The net effect of the environment was not to reduce these differences, but changes on the various scales—masculinity, conventionality, social maturity, and theoretical orientation—were more frequently attributable to the environment as a whole than to membership in a particular school or department.

Using students' self-ratings of progress toward the attainment of various objectives as the criterion measures, Pace (1964) found that attainment was somewhat more frequently consistent with congruent environmental press than with congruent personality characteristics. When the characteristics of students and of subcultures were both congruent with objectives, their combined association with attainment was substantially greater. He also found that the press of the total environment, rather than the press of particular academic subcultures, was more strongly associated with attainment of relevant objectives. These findings suggested a mass-action concept of educational impact: the more massive and more cumulative and more congruent the stimuli are, the greater is the impact they have upon the students.

C. Robert Pace
University of California

References

Astin, Alexander W. "An Empirical Characterization of Higher Educational Institutions." *J Ed Psychol* 53:224–35; 1962(*a*).

Astin, Alexander W. "Influences on Student's Motivation to Seek Advanced Training: Another Look." *J Ed Psychol* 53:303–9; 1962(*b*).

Astin, Alexander W. *Who Goes Where to College?* SRA, 1965(*a*). 125p.

Astin, Alexander W. "Classroom Environment in Different Fields of Study." *J Ed Psychol* 56:275–82; 1965(*b*).

Astin, Alexander W., and Holland, John L. "The Environmental Assessment Technique: A Way to Measure College Environments." *J Ed Psychol* 52:308–16; 1961.

Barton, Allen H. *Organizational Measurement and Its Bearing on the Study of College Environments.* CEEB, 1961. 82p.

Becker, Howard S. "Student Culture." In *The Study of Campus Cultures.* Western Interstate Compact for Higher Education, 1963. p. 11–25.

Becker, Howard S., and others. *Boys in White: Student Culture in Medical School.* U Chicago Press, 1961. 456p.

Darley, John G. *Promise and Performance: A Study of Ability and Achievement in Higher Education.* U California Press, 1962. 191p.

Davis, James A., and others. *Great Aspirations: Career Plans of America's June 1961 College Graduates.* NORC, U Chicago Press, 1961. 66p.+

Dressel, Paul L., and Mayhew, Lewis B. *General Education: Explorations in Evaluation.* ACE, 1954. 302p.

Eddy, Edward D., Jr. *The College Influence on Student Character.* ACE, 1959. 185p.

Gee, Helen, and Glaser, Robert J. *The Ecology of the Medical Student.* Association of American Medical Colleges, 1958. 262p.

Goldsen, Rose K., and others. *What College Students Think.* Van Nostrand, 1960. 240p.

Jacob, Philip E. *Changing Values in College.* Edward W. Hazen, 1956. 178p.

Kirk, Jerome. *Cultural Diversity and Character Change at Carnegie Tech.* Carnegie Press, Carnegie Institute of Technology, 1965. 150p.

Lazarsfeld, Paul F., and Thielens, Wagner, Jr. *The Academic Mind: Social Scientists in a Time of Crisis.* Free, 1958. 460p.

McConnell, Thomas R., and Heist, Paul. "The Diverse College Student Population." In *The American College.* Wiley, 1962. p. 225–52.

Merton, Robert K., and others. *The Student Physician: Introductory Studies in the Sociology of Medical Education.* Harvard U Press, 1957. 360p.

Newcomb, Theodore M. "Student Peer Group Influence." In *The American College.* Wiley, 1962. p. 469–88.

Nichols, Robert C. *Personality Change and the College.* NMSC, 1965. 27p.

Pace, C. Robert. "Five College Environments." *College Board R* 41:24–8; 1960.

Pace, C. Robert. *College and University Environment Scales: Technical Manual.* ETS, 1963. 81p.

Pace, C. Robert. *The Influence of Academic and Student Subcultures in College and University Environments.* USOE Cooperative Research Project 1083, U California, Los Angeles, 1964. 255p.

Pace, C. Robert, and McFee, Anne. "The College Environment." *R Ed Res* 30:311–20; 1960.

Pace, C. Robert, and Stern, George G. "An Approach to the Measurement of Psychological Characteristics of College Environments." *J Ed Psychol* 49:269–77; 1958.

Peterson, Richard E. *College Student Questionnaires and Technical Manual.* ETS, 1965. 60p.

Plant, Walter T. *Personality Changes Associated with a College Education.* USOE Cooperative Research Project 348, San Jose State Col, 1962. 83p.

Richards, James M., Jr., and others. *A Description of Junior Colleges.* ACT, 1965. 13p.+

Saunders, David R. *A Factor Analytic Study of the AI and the CCI.* ETS, 1962.

Stern, George G. "Student Values and Their Relationship to the College Environment." In *Research on College Students*, Western Interstate Compact for Higher Education, 1960. p. 67–104.

Stern, George G. "Characteristics of the Intellectual Climate in College Environments." *Harvard Ed R* 33:5–41; 1962.

Stern, George G. "Student Ecology and the College Environment." In *Research in Higher Education.* CEEB, 1965. p. 35–52.

Thistlethwaite, Donald L. "College Press and Student Achievement." *J Ed Psychol* 50:183–91; 1959.

Thistlethwaite, Donald L. "Rival Hypotheses for Explaining the Effects of Different Learning Environments." *J Ed Psychol* 53:310–5; 1962.

Thistlethwaite, Donald L. *Effects of College upon Student Aspirations.* USOE Cooperative Research Project D-098, Vanderbilt U, 1965. 188p.

Trow, Martin. "The Campus Viewed as a Culture." In *Research on College Students.* Western Interstate Compact for Higher Education, 1960. p. 105–23.

Wallace, Walter L. *Peer Groups and Student Achievement.* NORC, U Chicago Press, 1963. 306p.

Webster, Harold, and others. "Personality Changes in College Students." In *The American College.* Wiley, 1962. p. 811–46.

COMMUNITY COLLEGE EDUCATION

A notable educational development of the mid-twentieth century can be seen in the marked emphasis being placed on the role of the two-year college as the agent for accommodating the swiftly increasing number of young and older adults who will pursue education beyond high school. The numerous recommendations emanating from state and federal study commissions to the effect that education immediately beyond high school should become universal are also specifying that the institutions which should bear a large responsibility for making this possible are those variously known as junior colleges, community colleges, and technical institutes. The recommendations are no less noteworthy than the expansions which are taking place, for not only are these types of institutions growing in number with great rapidity, but in enrollments as well.

The *Junior College Directory* (American Association of Junior Colleges, 1966) lists 50 new junior colleges which first admitted students in 1965, and the overall enrollment was higher by 22 percent than the enrollment for the fall of 1964. Enrollments were significantly higher in almost every state, with the largest increase in California, where they were higher by more than 57,000 students. Junior colleges in New York gained over 25,000 students, Florida over 15,000, Texas over 13,000, both Michigan and Pennsylvania about 12,000, and Illinois over 11,000. Other states that showed gains of 6,000 to 8,000 were Oregon, Washington, North Carolina, and Ohio.

Most of this remarkable growth has taken place in those two-year institutions, generically junior colleges, which have come to be categorized as public community colleges because of the many services they render to their local communities. Private and independent junior colleges continue to render important services to their special constituents, although they have not increased materially in number or in enrollment and are neither normally perceived as agents of community college education nor referred to as "community colleges." The education provided by public two-year colleges or, in limited instances, by technical institutes includes (1) preparation for entry or reentry into the world of paid employment; (2) preparation for transfer to an institution offering a baccalaureate degree; (3) education for adults; and (4) various specialized educational services for the community in general.

HISTORY. Thornton (1960) distinguished three major stages in the historical development of the two-year college. During the 70 years from 1850 to 1920 the junior college was both conceptualized and realized. During this period junior colleges were developed as post-high school institutions or lower-division segments of universities or four-year colleges. By 1921 there were 207 junior colleges, 70 of which were public and 137 private. Of the 16,000 students enrolled in these junior colleges, 52 percent were in the public sector and the other 48 percent in private schools. With the organization of the American Association of Junior Colleges in 1920, terminal and technical as well as semiprofessional education began to gain acceptance.

In the second period, from 1920 to 1945, a variety of occupational programs were developed and expanded. An early influence on the rapid expansion of junior college occupational programs was the Smith-Hughes Act of 1917, which marked the beginning of federal legislation promoting vocational education below the four-year college level (Knight & others, 1960). The high rate of unemployment which began with the great depression of 1929 stimulated concern for occupational programs. Then, during the war years of 1940 to 1945, there was an increased need for trained personnel in industry, and returning veterans were provided with unprecedented educational opportunities under provisions of the 1944 Servicemen's Readjustment Act (Knight & others, 1960).

The third stage was characterized by the emergence of the community service concept, and with it the formation of the community college. The community services which had been offered as a temporary measure during World War II were not only continued after the war but further developed in response to their widespread acceptance by communities which had come to recognize their importance. The curriculum continued to include, in addition to the regular day programs, evening courses, specialized short courses for adults, and other activities to promote educational, vocational, recreational, and cultural opportunities for members of the community.

An early study of the development of the two-year-college idea (McDowell, 1919) throws additional light on the conditions which propelled the junior college into prominence. McDowell identified four main influences: (1) universities, burdened by classes growing in size, fostered the junior-college idea as a way of encouraging closer contact between faculty and student body; (2) small four-year colleges could not offer strong baccalaureate programs; (3) normal schools evolved into junior colleges out of a desire to offer college work in addition to their more pedagogically oriented curriculum; and (4) high schools in increasing numbers began to offer post-high school courses.

The first comprehensive study of the junior college, made by Koos (1925), reported that between 1900 and 1921, junior colleges grew in number from 8 to almost 200. Koos described three aspects of the junior college which seem increasingly to characterize it at mid-century: its democratizing effect (programs of different levels of difficulty were more readily available and accessible to young people); its conserving and socializing influences (more attention could be given individual students in the junior college, both in and out of class, than could be given in typical institutions of higher education); and its impact on the reorganization of higher education (the general acceptance of the junior college inevitably led to a clarification of the character and function of the four-year college).

CURRENT DEVELOPMENT. Koos (1925) predicted that the junior-college movement was destined, like the advent of the junior high school, to affect profoundly the organization of the American system of education. In 1965, forty years after Koos' publication, there were, according to the 1966 *Directory* of the American Association of Junior Colleges, 771 junior colleges in the United States, with a total enrollment of 1,292,753 students. Of these institutions, 268 were private and 503 public. Since the public institutions enroll 82 percent of the full-time students, it is clear that they are bearing the major burden for community-college education. One out of every four students entering college today enters a junior college, most of which would be classified as community colleges.

Factors underlying the current emphasis on community-college education are many and varied. They spring not alone from the sheer increase in the number of college-age students but also from other forces which constitute the social milieu in which community colleges operate. The rapid expansion in knowledge and the automation of production has brought about great changes in American society. Technological advances have improved men's lives, but they also have been responsible for creating new social problems, for with the automation of mass production has come the inevitable displacement of many workers (Blocker & others, 1965). It is predicted that by 1970 white collar workers will make up about 45 percent of the work force in the United States (Clark, 1962). In addition to the change in the composition of the work force, there has been a continuing trend for the population to become concentrated in urban areas. This has brought about a variety of economic, social, and political changes, among them a demand for new educational services beyond the high school. The institutions which evolved to meet this demand operate on an "open-door" policy: all high school graduates, as well as others who presumably can profit from instruction, are admitted. They are "comprehensive"; they serve many functions. And they are community-centered and adaptable (Medsker, 1960; Fields, 1962). No unit of American higher education is expected to serve such a diversity of purposes, to provide such a variety of programs, or to distribute students among so many different types of educational programs as the community college (Medsker, 1960).

LEGAL STATUS. The move toward either providing a legal basis for community colleges or strengthening such a basis in states where it has existed has progressed rapidly in recent years. At the close of the 1962 legislative year only 12 states remained without general enabling legislation for the establishment of public two-year colleges, and only 8 without such colleges could be identified (Martorana, 1963). Subsequently, legislation pertaining to public junior colleges, and enacted in the years 1962–1964, was reported by Martorana and McHugh (1966). The authors covered developments in 38 states, including 5 in which junior colleges were authorized for the first time. In other states, legislation materially revised and strengthened existing systems of public junior colleges. Some of the more recent legislative actions are dramatic. In Illinois, for example, the 1965 legislature enacted a new master plan for higher education in which was authorized a new state system of junior colleges under local control, but with a newly established state board to coordinate the system and serve the individual institutions.

In the majority of states the public two-year colleges are under some type of local control—either within local school systems, responsible also for elementary or secondary education or both or in separate districts established for junior-college purposes only. At the close of the legislative sessions in 1962, control through unified districts was provided for in 21 states, and separate districts had been authorized in 20 states. In a number of states it was possible for a junior college to be maintained by either type of district (Martorana, 1963). Since 1962 there has been a decided nationwide trend toward the establishment of separate districts. Among others, Henderson (1960) reported seeing the new trend in this direction.

In a few states, including Minnesota and Massachusetts, the public two-year institutions are not under complete state control. In certain other states, including Georgia and Oklahoma, the majority of these institutions are included in the state system of higher education and thus in effect are state institutions. Although the freshman-sophomore extension centers maintained by state universities in several states are not always considered to be typical community colleges, they do offer standard lower-division college work and may provide programs for occupational and adult education. They are found extensively in Wisconsin, Indiana, Ohio, Pennsylvania, and Kentucky.

The diversity of control of the public community colleges is still somewhat confusing despite certain fairly well defined trends in the direction of placing control under the jurisdiction of separate districts, with local governing boards and strong coordination at the state level (Hall, 1962). The question of coordination at the state level is receiving increasing attention. Medsker (1962, 1964) and Medsker and Clark (1966) have discussed the need for a state plan for junior colleges and some possible criteria for relationships between the state and the local districts.

Legislation in the various states provides for certain guide lines in the establishment of community colleges and for surveys to determine feasibility (Martorana, 1962). The Commission on Legislation of the American Association of Junior Colleges (American Association . . . , Commission on Legislation, 1962) has prepared a handbook which states seven principles as guides to legislative action for community junior colleges. The commission urged that state legislation should make legal provisions for state surveys, local surveys, a state agency with overall supervisory authority, a local board with responsibility only for the community college, continued financial support, a comprehensive educational program, and recognition of the institution's autonomy.

FINANCE. The means by which community-college education is financed is dependent in part on how the various types of public two-year colleges are organized and controlled (Medsker, 1960). Those maintained by some type of local district almost invariably get some of their support for operation from that taxing district and the remainder from the state. The proportions contributed by the local district and the state vary greatly among the states according to the legal provisions which have been made with respect to community-college financing. In some cases the state's contribution is a fixed portion of the unit cost of operation. In New York, for example, the state's share of operating costs is one-third. In accordance with the *Master Plan for Higher Education in Illinois* (Illinois State Department of Education, 1964), the state assumes approximately one-half of the operating costs. In Arizona the state pays $525 for each of the first 1,000 full-time-equivalent students and $350 for each full-time-equivalent student in excess of 1,000. In numerous other states a stipulated sum is paid by the state for each student in attendance. In a few states, among them Florida and California, state aid is based on an equalization formula which tends to guarantee a minimum level of support for each district and thus assures basic educational quality regardless of whether local districts can support an adequate program.

There is also great variation among the states in the extent to which community-college capital-outlay programs are supported. In the past there has been a tendency for the local community to bear most, if not all, of the costs of land and buildings. Now, with the great growth of community colleges and the general recognition of their role in meeting the state's needs in higher education, most states are contributing substantially to these costs.

In those states where community-college education wholly or principally takes place in state institutions, there is obviously no problem for the local and state governments over sharing of costs for either operation or capital outlay, since the state is primarily the responsible agent. Even under this arrangement, however, the state sometimes expects the local community to provide the campus site, particularly in states which rely on the major state university to provide local education through extension centers.

Student tuition charges are still another variable in community college support, regardless of the type of state system in effect. Philosophically, there is a general consensus that, concomitantly with the open-door policy of most community colleges, the tuition cost to the student should be sufficiently low to preclude the possibility of nonattendance because of any financial barrier set up by the school. The range in actual practice is from no tuition (for residents) in California, to as much as one-third of the annual cost of instruction, in New York. A variety of legal provisions is found in between. Some colleges make tuition optional with local districts; some set upper limits which are geared to other institutions in the same state; some set specific amounts.

THE STUDENTS. Questions have been raised repeatedly about whether there are important differences between community-college students and students who enroll in four-year colleges and universities. Empirical studies conducted by research agencies and the community colleges themselves are yielding a considerable number of findings concerning the nature of student bodies in these institutions.

General Characteristics. In general, the community colleges' lack of selectiveness, together with their appeal to low-socioeconomic-status groups, immediately suggest that their student bodies could be expected to differ in both socioeconomic background and aptitude from those in most other types of institutions of higher learning. This theory has been supported by the research. The more heterogeneous character of the junior-college students was well demonstrated by Clark (1960), who reported in his case study of San Jose Junior College that three-fourths of the students came from blue and white collar homes, the occupations of the students' fathers being closely representative of the range of occupational levels found in the city. Clark further reported that the median aptitude score of students was considerably below both the national average and the scores of students in other kinds of public colleges and universities in California. Medsker (1960) similarly indicated the differences in mean aptitude scores between students entering two-year and four-year colleges but in addition pointed out the great overlap in aptitude also found in the two types of schools.

Family Characteristics. There is remarkably close agreement among studies about the level of education attained by the parents of junior-college students. Each of several studies found that somewhat more than half of the fathers had had at least a high school education and that nearly 30 percent had attended college for some period (Florida State Junior College Advisory Board, 1963; Knoell & Medsker, 1964b; Medsker & Trent, 1965).

Although Medsker and Trent (1965) found that the overall distributions of occupations of the fathers of high school graduates and junior-college students closely resembled one another, the similarity between the distributions was less apparent in some states. In California and Florida, for instance, where junior colleges have been expanding rapidly and operate within a definite plan for higher education, there were somewhat larger percentages of fathers of junior-college students in the higher occupational groups (Florida State Junior College Advisory Board, 1963; Knoell & Medsker, 1964b). However, Tillery (1964) noted that the very brightest high school graduates with fathers in the highest occupational categories were not found in large numbers in California junior colleges.

Academic Characteristics. Project Talent (Flanagan & others, 1964), a study of a nationwide sample of students who were given the same aptitude tests at the same time and under approximately the same testing conditions, offers the most evidence to date about the academic ability of junior-college students. The conclusion drawn was that the academic aptitude of junior-college freshmen, as measured, was similar to that of high school seniors but considerably below the mean for students who entered four-year institutions. The junior colleges appeared to draw heavily, however, from the middle range of ability and less from the upper and lower extremes.

Project Talent placed the junior-college students slightly lower on the ability scale than did the studies by Darley (1962) and Medsker and Trent (1965). Darley concluded that junior college students were superior to 60 percent of high school graduates, while Medsker and Trent found that slightly higher percentages of junior-college students came from the upper two quintiles of ability than from the lower, although much less so than in the distribution found for students in other types of colleges. Findings of the Florida State Junior College Advisory Board (1963) also showed a tendency for junior-college students to come from the upper-ability quintiles. Based on norms developed for a statewide twelfth-grade testing program, it was shown that half of the Florida junior-college students came from the top two quintiles and only 8 percent from the bottom quintile. Furthermore, on the basis of their test scores, 74 percent of the Florida junior college students were eligible to enter the state universities. It is to be noted that the various studies reported on here were done during different years, which may account for the variability in findings, especially those on the ability level of entering students.

A study of high-ability students in California (Tillery, 1964) showed that 18 percent of the high school graduates who were eligible to enter the state university entered two-year colleges instead. It was estimated that this very-high-performance group constituted about 5 percent of the junior-college freshmen in 1961. Since only 26 percent of the university-eligible students registered at the several campuses of the University of California, the junior colleges evidently attracted a fair share of very good students.

Data on ability levels obtained in a study of transfer students (Knoell & Medsker, 1965) produced considerable evidence that the junior-college student who transferred to a four-year college or university was at a level of academic ability which was higher than the average high school graduate and probably higher than the average entering university freshman. However, an analysis of the ability of graduates from four-year colleges showed that students who had transferred from junior colleges tended to have somewhat less academic aptitude than the "native" students (Knoell & Medsker, 1964a).

Occupational Choice. The junior-college students' goal of financial stability and security was reflected in their occupational choices and the job satisfactions they expected to have (Berg, 1965; Florida State Junior College Advisory Board, 1963; Knoell & Medsker, 1964b; Medsker & Trent, 1965; Tillery, 1964). Men were attracted in large numbers to programs in business administration and engineering and women to teaching—except for the terminal group of women, the majority of which enrolled in secretarial and sales programs. In a study of college attendance Medsker and Trent (1965) found that about 80 percent of the junior-college students aspired to jobs classified as semiprofessional or higher, including 20 percent who expected to enter law, medicine, and other "higher" professions. Students in junior colleges were found to be less likely than those in four-year colleges to major in liberal arts and science, except in preparation for teaching in the public schools. And even among the lower-ability group studied (Berg, 1965), 50 percent of the students aspired to semiprofessional jobs or higher, 21 percent to white collar jobs, and only 7 percent to "skilled" occupations.

In separate studies, Berg (1965) and Tillery (1964) found that about 20 percent of their samples had expressed no occupational choice when they entered junior college. The fact that an occupational choice has been made does not, of course, obviate the need for occupational counseling in junior college. More than one-third of the transfer students reported that they had changed their minds about their chosen occupations at least once in junior college, and fewer than half were "very certain" about their choice by the spring semester after transfer (Knoell & Medsker, 1964b).

Financial Resources. The economic resources of junior-college students are likely to be an important determinant of whether they persist through junior college and also of the quality of their academic performances and participation in various phases of college life.

An examination of findings concerning family finances and employed students showed a disparity between the educational aspirations of junior-college students and their resources for financing their education beyond the two years. In each of several studies (Berg, 1965; Florida State Junior College Advisory Board, 1963; Knoell & Medsker, 1964b; Medsker & Trent, 1965; Tillery, 1964), more than half of the sample were engaged in some part-time work while attending junior college, and about one-fourth were working at least 20 hours per week.

Seventy-two percent of the Florida students (Florida State Junior College Advisory Board, 1963) said that their employment was unrelated to their major field of interest, and nearly two-thirds of them advised against outside employment while carrying a full college program. In a study of transfer students (Knoell & Medsker, 1964b), two-thirds of the sample reported earning some of their college expenses, and nearly 30 percent reported receiving no financial help from their parents.

Value Orientation. Too little is known about the interests, values, and other personality characteristics of the students who enter junior college or about the ways in which these variables relate to curriculum, instruction, and student personnel services. Many students enter with an attitude of seeking—to find out what the junior college can offer them, where their interests and capabilities lie, and how they might make their entrance into the adult world of employment. From a study of college attendance (Medsker & Trent, 1965) it was concluded that "academic concern" best distinguished between junior-college and university students; members of the former group tended more to postpone major decisions about college and career, received less encouragement from parents and teachers to attend college, and were less inclined to think that college was "extremely important" to them. A number of studies have found that about 40 percent of their samples of junior-college students would have preferred to enter another type of college (Knoell & Medsker, 1964b; Medsker & Trent, 1965; Tillery, 1964) but were probably kept from doing so by financial factors, late decisions about college, or both.

Five scales of the Omnibus Personality Inventory were administered to 10,000 high school seniors in 16 communities in a study of college attendance (Medsker & Trent, 1965). Analysis of scores for high school graduates who entered different types of two-year and four-year colleges showed that, with one exception, there were no significant differences for either men or women between those who entered junior colleges and those who entered public four-year colleges. On the other hand, significant differences were found, again with one exception, between students who entered junior colleges and those who entered public universities, the latter group having more desirable scores on all scales.

Two studies of subgroups of junior-college students suggest that students who enter these two-year institutions may have certain distinguishing characteristics which have implications for both counseling and instruction. The study of high-ability students in California (Tillery, 1964) showed that junior-college entrants had significantly lower scores than university enrollees on a "social maturity" measure and that junior-college women also had significantly lower scores on a measure of "intellectual disposition." Both junior-college men and women differed most from their university peers on a scale measuring autonomy; i.e., junior-college students were more conventional and less independent than entering university freshmen of comparable ability.

PROGRAMS. Many factors affect the nature of the educational program found in community colleges. The diverse characteristics of the student body necessitate a curriculum of sufficient breadth to accommodate students with varying levels of ability, interests, and backgrounds. In addition, the fact that the community college has a strong orientation to the local community and is generally expected to render a variety of services not commonly performed by the more conventional four-year institutions means that inevitably the program it develops will be diversified. It must serve the transfer student who plans to continue work toward a baccalaureate degree in a four-year college, the terminal student with no wish to transfer as well as the one unable to do so, the older student who returns to study for a variety of reasons and purposes, and the student entering directly from high school who needs remedial work before he can pursue a college program. Even this list of services does not, however, fully portray the complexity of community-college education. The community college is also generally expected to perform a variety of special educational services for the community, particularly those of a social and cultural nature, and to provide as much general education as possible for students who will not pursue education beyond what the junior college offers.

Blocker and his associates (1965) reported on a study of 663 two-year college administrators and faculty members which showed that the educational program is influenced by a variety of extrainstitutional, intrainstitutional, and administrative factors. In addition to the administration, faculty, and students, Blocker listed the following forces which operate to bring about changes in the curriculum: (1) accrediting agencies; (2) four-year colleges and universities and their faculties; (3) the state department of education; (4) the boards of control; (5) other two-year colleges and their faculties; (6) state and government agencies; and (7) advisory boards and committees.

The community college has become known as a multipurpose institution, with responsibilities to an exceedingly varied clientele. Its comprehensive nature was well identified in the *Fifty-fifth Yearbook* of the National Society for the Study of Education (National Society . . . , 1956), which listed the major purposes of the public junior college as preparation for advanced study, vocational education, general education, and community service. Although there is some speculation that occupational education at the post-high school level might be more effective in a specialized institution such as a technical institute, there are relatively few such schools under public control, hence the dominant pattern is for such education to be combined with other programs in comprehensive community colleges.

The Transfer Function. In many respects and for understandable reasons, the transfer program has been given special emphasis in most community colleges. Many critics believe it has been overemphasized. In a survey of 243 junior colleges it was found that over 90 percent offered a transfer program (Medsker, 1960). The fact that the original purpose of the junior college was to prepare students for upper-division work and that more prestige attaches to the academic than to the vocational program accounts in part for the concentration on the transfer function and curriculum. Medsker (1960) found that approximately two-thirds of all students who entered junior colleges in 70 institutions in 1956 stated their intention to transfer. In a later study of a large sample of community colleges, Medsker (1966) again found that two-thirds of the entering students declared their intention to transfer. The fact that only one-third of the students in each study did actually transfer constitutes one of the junior colleges' major problems—how to accommodate what Clark (1960) has called the "latent terminal" student.

In general, the community colleges appear to be performing the transfer function well. In a study of transfer practices, and of more than 4,000 junior-college transfer students in 43 four-year colleges in 10 states, Knoell and Medsker (1965) found that 62 percent of the transfers were granted their baccalaureate degrees within three years after transfer and that 9 percent were still enrolled at the beginning of the fourth year. By the beginning of the fourth year after transfer, 29 percent of the students had withdrawn, but only one-third of these dropouts had been dismissed because of unsatisfactory grades. The first-term differential was only −0.3 of a grade point for the entire group, although there were vast differences in the overall records of transfer students among types of institutions to which students transferred. Loss of credit in transfer was small. When compared with "native" students, the transfer group was found to have earned higher grades in lower-division work but somewhat lower grades in upper-division work, the latter finding attributable in part to the drop in grades often found in the first quarter or semester after transfer.

Articulation. Although planning a transfer program has been made somewhat easier by the trend away from specialization and toward a liberal arts base in the lower division, there are still problems of articulation between two-year and four-year colleges. One serious difficulty arises when four-year colleges adhere rigidly to specific course requirements without considering either the diversity of colleges to which students transfer or the effort on the part of many community colleges to provide courses of a general education nature.

An exception to this problem of articulation is found in Florida, where once a public community college has developed and published its general education program, other public institutions respect the integrity of the program and require no further lower-division general education courses of students who have been certified as having completed the program (Schultz, 1959).

Occupational Programs. The manner in which community colleges can best serve those students who are not to transfer is in many ways difficult to determine. That there will be an increased need for workers prepared for semiprofessional and technical jobs seems clear. After a comprehensive study of postsecondary vocational-technical education, Venn (1964) showed the extent of the need for such programs and predicted that our national economy and social structure would seriously suffer if greater numbers of semiprofessionals, technicians, and skilled workers were not trained.

Citing statistics of the National Science Foundation and the United States Department of Labor, Harris (1964) stated that the 630,000 technicians employed by industry in 1960 must be doubled by 1970. He estimated that 68,000 new technicians would have to be educated and trained each year merely to meet the industrial demand and concluded that junior colleges face a real challenge in the area of vocational-technical education for occupations related to engineering, business, and health services.

During the first half of the 1960's, when numerous programs of federal assistance to vocational education became law, the community college became eligible for additional funds to step up their occupational-training programs. The impetus given by such support to new and expanded occupational programs for nontransfer students is becoming apparent. The Manpower Development and Training Act of 1962, Public Law 87–415, authorized appropriations of $435,000,000 to be used over a three-year period to retrain men and women whose skills had been rendered obsolete by automation. Public community colleges are especially well suited to assume responsibilities for vocational training under the provisions of this Act (Vaccaro, 1963). Under the provisions of the Higher Education Facilities Act of 1963, $690,000,000 was authorized, on a matching basis, for construction, rehabilitation, or improvement of lower-division facilities, with 22 percent restricted for use by public community colleges and technical institutes. The Vocational Education Act of 1963 authorized appropriations of $450,000,000 over a four-year period to supplement aid for vocational training (*Junior College Journal*, 1964).

Community colleges face problems in implementing terminal programs. They must provide a sufficient variety not only to meet manpower requirements but also to accommodate varying skills and abilities. Many high-level technical programs, for instance, can be pursued only by very able students, and most authorities believe that community colleges must also offer occupational programs at a lower level—including courses in what are often called the trades. Another problem lies in the danger of overspecialization; in an era of expanding technology, workers may be trained in specific skills for which there will be, in time, no jobs. Related to this is the question of what proportion of a technical program should be devoted to general education.

General Education. But even if the question could be settled of the proportion of a technical program to devote to general education, there is still the problem of how general education is to be planned and administered, and on this there is no widespread agreement. Some think of general education as a common curriculum; others focus on the communication of major concepts, principles, and methodologies of major fields of knowledge (Medsker, 1960). After a survey of a sample of public community colleges, Thornton (1960) concluded that "only a minority of the public junior colleges have attempted to make certain that their students receive a comprehensive general education." In a study of general education in 243 junior colleges, Medsker (1960) came to the same conclusion, but at the same time commented as follows:

No one should be too quick to criticize junior college personnel for not having done more. There are major obstacles that hamper progress. The demands of vocational curricula make severe inroads on time for general education. The insistence on the part of senior colleges that junior college courses submitted for transfer credit be identical with their own is a real deterrent because, in meeting specific transfer requirements, the junior college is unable to set up its own general education program. Another difficulty is that of procuring teachers who understand general education and are committed to it—teachers who have the background for the kind of teaching general education requires.

INNOVATION. The current concern, in all segments of education, is for new developments and innovations, in both curriculum and instructional techniques. The community college should, of course, bear its fair share of this concern. In reporting on innovations in community colleges, Johnson (1964) concluded that, in general, junior colleges were not deeply involved with experimentation to determine how best to use faculty services. He suggested two reasons for the lack of experimentation in junior colleges—the relative ease with which junior-college faculty members are recruited in most areas and the rapid expansion which keeps administrators and faculty too busy to develop innovative practices.

However, from his survey of 95 junior colleges in 14 states, Johnson was able to identify a number of innovative practices used to improve teaching, accommodate larger numbers of students, and achieve financial economy. To improve teaching, some junior colleges have provided their faculties with consultants, teaching aides, and secretarial assistants; others have employed faculty members during their vacation periods to plan and develop new programs. To accommodate more students, several junior colleges have had special facilities constructed to teach large classes, utilizing television and other electronic devices. For more effective utilization of faculty services, some schools have developed plans for programmed learning, team teaching, work-study programs, and independent study.

Junior colleges also use a variety of community facilities. Many schools cooperate with local hospitals for the clinical instruction that is a part of the associate-degree program in nursing. Others make use of business and industrial facilities to teach courses "on location." To accelerate student progress and accommodate more students, some junior colleges are planning for year-round operation. A number of two-year colleges are permitting credit by examination and through agreement with the local high schools are permitting high school seniors to enroll in certain junior-college classes. To prevent duplication of expensive facilities and equipment, a few colleges are cooperating in the planning of courses and curricula, and some colleges share their staffs and facilities.

Tyler (1960) has stressed that the two-year college should examine its teaching methods carefully and reject those which are traditional but no longer appropriate and effective. He based his statement on the assessment that many students were neither motivated to engage in abstract intellectual activities nor had work habits and personal attitudes and values suited to the requirements of a conventional educational program.

STUDENT PERSONNEL SERVICES. An ardent claim made by and for the community college is that while it provides many special services to students, among its more important ones are counseling and guidance. Thornton (1960), Blocker and others (1965), and Medsker (1960) have examined this claim and the rationale behind it. They contend that both the diverse nature of the student body and the position of the community college as an intermediate unit of education between the high school and the four-year college or employment call for programs which offer students professional assistance in their personal development and in their decisions regarding work and education.

Many junior colleges do include, in their student personnel programs, health counseling, job placement services, provisions for financial aid, and opportunities for extracurricular activities. Some offer housing and food service.

However, a study of the National Committee for Appraisal and Development of Junior College Student Personnel Programs (Raines, 1966), which reported findings from an appraisal made of student personnel services in a stratified random sample of 123 junior colleges, concluded that three-fourths of the junior colleges have inadequate student personnel programs and that more than one-half of the colleges provide inadequate counseling and guidance.

Medsker (1960) also pointed to a number of grave deficiencies, but he, as well as the National Committee, found many instances of good programs and confirmed the fact that some counseling, guidance, and other student personnel services are found in all two-year colleges. The deficiencies reported pertained to the gap between what is and, on the basis of certain agreed-upon criteria, what should be.

After detailing the services needed for an adequate personnel program, McDaniel (1962) pointed out that with some exceptions, student personnel programs are understaffed and underfinanced. The problem of preparing and procuring staff for these services was also identified by the National Committee, and suggestions were made for a program to improve the situation.

Most authorities agree that the community college will be unable to discharge its obligations effectively unless it can organize and staff a student personnel program which includes essential services rendered in a professional and effective manner.

STAFF. The rapid growth of the community college poses many problems with respect to staff, both faculty and administrative. The *Directory* of the American Association of Junior Colleges (1966) showed that there were more than 50,000 faculty members in public junior colleges in 1965. There is serious concern about the availability of additional faculty for junior colleges in the years ahead. It has been estimated that in California alone, 840 new junior-college teachers will be needed each year between 1966 and 1970, and 980 each year from 1971 to 1975 (California State Department of Education, 1960). In a study of 566 institutions for the years 1963–64 and 1964–65, the National Education Association (NEA) reported 179 unfilled teaching positions and 67 unfilled administrative positions. A future shortage of qualified candidates was anticipated in 422 of the institutions in the study (National Education Association . . . , 1965).

Training and Recruitment. Questions arise about the source of future community-college teachers and the nature of their preparation. At present, the majority of faculty members in junior colleges hold a master's degree as their highest degree, and the probability is that there will be no major change in the general requirements. The competition among four-year institutions for people with doctorates makes it unlikely that very many with this degree will be recruited into community colleges (Caplow & McGee, 1961). It also seems unlikely that the community colleges will employ faculty without master's degrees to teach academic subjects. Reports from the NEA which covered the period from 1957 through 1965 showed that the number of new junior college teachers who hold the doctorate has remained at between 6 and 7 percent. In this same period the percentage of new teachers holding the master's degree increased so that by the 1964-65 school year, 72 percent had master's degrees and less than 22 percent had less than the master's.

In the past, community-college teachers have been recruited from secondary schools, hired immediately after completion of their graduate work, and enlisted from industry and the professions to teach vocational subjects. NEA reports (National Education Association . . . , 1965) showed that for the period from 1957 to 1965 about 30 percent of new junior-college teachers came from high schools, where they had taught the preceding year; about 23 percent came from graduate schools, with new master's degrees; about 17 percent came from four-year colleges and universities, where they had been teaching; and 11 percent came from business occupations. The remainder came from a number of sources, including homemaking, research institutions, and religious, government, and military services.

Certain foundations have recently shown interest in subsidizing various university training programs for community-college teachers. Consequently, it seems probable that in the future an increasing number of faculty will be employed directly out of graduate school.

Faculty Orientation. Concern is frequently expressed about the extent to which faculty members are in harmony with the purposes and philosophy of the community college. Medsker (1960) found great variation in this regard in his survey of more than 2,000 junior-college teachers in 15 states.

The preparation of students for transfer was rated as "important" or "very important" by 97 percent of the respondents, while 92 percent of them gave these ratings to vocational-technical programs. There was less agreement, however, about the junior college's other functions. The offering of remedial courses at the high school level for students ineligible to enter a regular college program directly was rated as "not important" by 28 percent of the respondents. Supplementary study opportunities for students with weaknesses in mathematics and English were opposed by 19 percent of the respondents. The vocational or in-service classes for adults were regarded as "not important" by 20 percent.

Differences in attitudes toward the role of the junior college were marked when respondents were grouped by teaching field. A higher percentage of teachers of applied than of academic subjects rated the remedial function as "very important." Teachers of academic subjects considered the vocational programs for adults to be not as important as the general education programs for adults, whereas the reverse was true for teachers of applied subjects.

Data from a current nationwide study of 59 public junior colleges (Medsker, 1966) show that about 8 percent of 4,098 responding instructors and administrators agreed with the statement that the main emphasis in the junior college should be on vocational education. About 91 percent of the respondents considered the two-year transfer program essential. The semiprofessional programs were considered essential by about 86 percent; the two-year semiskilled and remedial programs, by 51 percent; and the shorter-term apprentice and semiskilled programs, by 24 percent.

Perhaps some indication of staff attitudes toward an open-door policy is apparent in the responses to questions about admission and retention. While 89 percent agreed that junior colleges should admit non-high school graduates 18 years of age or older who, on the basis of tests and past performances, might reasonably be expected to succeed in the programs they chose, about 55 percent agreed that any high school graduate should be admitted. Also, approximately 55 percent agreed and 45 percent disagreed that a junior-college student whose grade average fell below C for two semesters should be dismissed.

That the junior college should sponsor community events such as forums and plays, and permit the use of college facilities by community groups, was considered essential by approximately 60 percent and 50 percent, respectively.

In a study that included 130 persons teaching in 11 junior colleges in Minnesota, Eckert and Stecklein (1959) found that teachers came into the junior college more by accident than through long-term design. It was found that junior-college teachers typically started out as high school teachers and moved on to the junior college after completing some graduate work on a part-time basis. Since these new teachers arrived without any orientation in the junior college, it became incumbent on the college to interpret its purposes and philosophy to them.

Academic Rank. Tillery (1963) saw the adoption of academic rank by junior colleges as a disjunctive force. He postulated that the system of professorial ranking would link the junior-college teacher to the purposes, philosophy, and academic orientation of the four-year college and might tend to undermine the comprehensive nature of the junior college.

Hendrix (1963) has also shown concern over faculty rank in junior colleges. In a study of faculty members of seven Texas public junior colleges he found that although some desirable characteristics in teachers were associated with academic-rank policies and procedures, a number of undesirable characteristics also arose which were cause for concern.

There are those, however, who believe that the creation of academic rank in junior college is imperative. Freiberger and Crawford (1962) have contended that the concern should be not about whether to adopt academic rank and title but rather about how to go about establishing them. In the middle 1960's the issue has not been decided, but the trend is in the direction of establishing faculty rank in more and more two-year colleges.

Administrators. The procurement of a sufficient number of well-trained administrators is also a major problem for the community colleges. Schultz (1965) has predicted that in the 15-year period from 1965 to 1980 there will be a need for more than 1,400 additional junior-college presidents, 1,500 additional chief academic deans, 900 chief student personnel administrators, and 1,000 chief business officers. About two-thirds of these administrators will be needed in public junior colleges and the other one-third in independent, Protestant, and Catholic two-year colleges.

The necessity for recruiting qualified administrative leaders in greater numbers has been recognized by the W. K. Kellogg Foundation, which has subsidized training programs in ten university centers toward the end of improving the preparation and quality of community-college administrators (Brick, 1964).

ACCREDITATION. The control of standards of community colleges in the United States is dispersed among various state agencies (state departments of education, state boards and commissions, and state colleges and universities), six regional accrediting associations, and about two dozen professional accrediting agencies.

It is the regional accrediting associations (Western, Northwest, North Central, Southern, Middle States, and New England) which evaluate the objectives of the college seeking accreditation, as well as its curriculum, instructional staff, facilities, student personnel services, administration, and financial support. Selden (1960) has identified the major purposes of accreditation by the regional associations: to control admissions and academic standards, stimulate self-evaluation, and serve as a bulwark against internal pressures that would change the "true goals" of the institution.

Of the 771 two-year institutions listed in the *Junior College Directory* (American Association of Junior Colleges, 1966), 59 percent are accredited by the regional accrediting associations, 39 percent by state associations, and 1 percent (composed mainly of technical institutes) by the Engineers' Council for Professional Development.

Although the scope of professional accrediting agencies in the United States is nationwide, their interest lies in particular fields of study or special programs. At the present time there is concern among community-college spokesmen about the necessity for specialized occupational programs to be accredited by professional agencies (Merson, 1965). As a case in point, Merson referred to the instance in which only 3 of the 119 community colleges which offered the associate degree in nursing were accredited by the National League for Nursing, the agency selected to accredit the nursing programs of schools before they could participate in the federal Nurse Training Act of 1964. Junior-college leaders contended that since their nursing programs had already been accredited by state boards of examiners, and since all nurses must pass a licensing examination, the accreditation by the National League involved unnecessary duplication.

Many states retain accrediting agencies primarily because of statutory requirements for accredited programs in teacher-training, nursing, and other programs that train for professions. Also, state accreditation is sometimes required if a college is to participate in certain government-sponsored programs, such as the Veterans Readjustment Assistance Act of 1952 (Gleazer, 1963).

PROBLEMS. The community college faces many problems as it strives to prepare itself to assume the obligation which society apparently will place upon it in the years ahead. It still is not fully understood either by the general public or by all of the education profession. And it still has not achieved a complete identity. McConnell (1962) referred to the ambiguity of the role of the unselective junior college and said that the institution "should be able to attain a better identity and a clearer status by articulating its multiple responsibilities for itself, its students, and its community."

The increasing tendency for the community college to be identified with higher education makes more difficult the fulfillment of its commitment to those purposes and functions not generally regarded as being related to college work. This emphasis on its academic function is being brought to bear at a time when, because of increasing college enrollments everywhere, many students headed for the bachelor's degree are being directed from overcrowded four-year colleges to community colleges. The danger lies in the possible overshadowing of those services for students not destined to transfer, who also will be enrolling in increasing numbers.

Clearly, the community college will have to serve the latter group more adequately in the future than it has in the past, or another type of post-high school institution will have to be established. The most appropriate way of serving the increasing number of young and older adults who will look to the community college for assistance will undoubtedly constitute a major problem in the future.

Aside from the matters of program, staffing, and the sharpening of purpose, the community college will continue to be faced with the inevitable problems pertaining to external organization, governance, and financial support. While it is unlikely that any one pattern for the maintenance of these institutions will emerge among the 50 states, the present trend toward increasing state involvement seems likely to continue.

However, the overriding problem which the junior college faces in the mid-1960's is the same one which has beset it throughout its history: the necessity for delineating and establishing a distinct identity. Many junior-college leaders agree with the executive director of the American Association of Junior Colleges, Edmund J. Gleazer, Jr., that the goal should be to conceive of the junior college neither as a post-high school nor as a precollege institution but as a new kind of college, integrated into the pattern of higher education, and offering broad programs, valuable in themselves.

Leland L. Medsker
University of California

References

American Association of Junior Colleges. *Junior College Directory*. AAJC, 1966. 89p.

American Association of Junior Colleges, Commission on Legislation. *Principles of Legislative Action for Community Junior Colleges*. AAJC, 1962. 18p.

Berg, Ernest H. "Factors Bearing on the Academic Performance and Persistence of Low Ability Students in Four California Junior Colleges." Doctoral dissertation. U California, Berkeley, 1965. 311p.

Blocker, Clyde E., and others. *The Two-year College: A Social Synthesis*. Prentice-Hall, 1965. 298p.

Brick, Michael. *Forum and Focus for the Junior College Movement*. Teachers College, Columbia U, 1964. 222p.

California State Department of Education. *A Master Plan for Higher Education in California, 1960–75*. The Department, 1960. 230p.

Caplow, Theodore, and McGee, Reece J. *The Academic Marketplace*. Basic Books, 1958. 262p.

Clark, Burton R. *The Open Door College: A Case Study*. McGraw-Hill, 1960. 207p.

Clark, Burton R. *Educating the Expert Society*. Chandler, 1962. 301p.

Darley, John G. *Promise and Performance: A Study of Ability and Achievement in Higher Education*. Center for the Study of Higher Education, U California Press, 1962. 191p.

Eckert, Ruth E., and Stecklein, John E. "Career Motivations and Satisfactions of Junior College Teachers." *Jun Col J* 30(2):83–9; 1959.

Fields, Ralph R. *The Community College Movement*. McGraw-Hill, 1962. 360p.

Flanagan, John C., and others. *The American High School Student*. Report of Project Talent. U Pittsburgh Press, 1964.

Florida State Junior College Advisory Board. *Florida's Community Junior Colleges: Their Contributions and Their Future*. State Department of Education, 1963. 166p.

Freiberger, Helenes T., and Crawford, W. H. "Junior College Academic Rank and Title." *Jun Col J* 33(2):89–92; 1962.

Gleazer, Edmund J. (Ed.) *American Junior Colleges*. ACE, 1963. 551p.

Hall, George L. "Confusion in the Control of the Junior College." *Jun Col J* 33(8):432–6; 1962.

Harris, Norman C. *Technical Education in the Junior College: New Programs for New Jobs*. AAJC, 1964. 102p.

Henderson, Algo. *Policies and Practices in Higher Education*. Harper, 1960. 338p.

Hendrix, Vernon L. "Academic Rank: Mostly Peril?" *Jun Col J* 34(4):28–30; 1963.

Illinois Board of Higher Education. *A Master Plan for Higher Education in Illinois*. The Board, 1964. 72p.

Johnson, B. Lamar. *Islands of Innovation*. UCLA, 1964. 80p.

Junior College Journal. "Two Legislative Landmarks in One Month!" *Jun Col J* 34(5):4–5; 1964.

Knight, Douglas M., and others. *The Federal Government and Higher Education*. Prentice-Hall, 1960. 205p.

Knoell, Dorothy M., and Medsker, Leland L. *Articulation Between Two-year and Four-year Colleges*. U California Press, 1964(a). 112p.

Knoell, Dorothy M., and Medsker, Leland L. *Factors Affecting Performance of Transfer Students from Two- to Four-year Colleges: With Implications for Coordination and Articulation*. Center for the Study of Higher Education, U California, Berkeley, 1964(b). 193p.

Knoell, Dorothy M., and Medsker, Leland L. *From Junior to Senior College: A National Study of the Transfer Student*. ACE, 1965. 102p.

Koos, Leonard V. *The Junior College Movement*. Ginn, 1925. 436p.

Martorana, S. V. "Surveys as Approaches to Establishing Legal Bases for Community Colleges." In *Establishing Legal Bases for Community Colleges*. AAJC, 1962. 43p.

Martorana, S. V. "The Legal Status of American Public Junior Colleges." In Gleazer, Edmund J. (Ed.) *American Junior Colleges*, 6th ed. ACE, 1963. p. 31–47.

Martorana, S. V., and McHugh, Robert F. "State Legislation: 1962–64." *Jun Col J* 36(6):27–36; 1966.

McConnell, T. R. *A General Pattern for American Public Higher Education*. McGraw-Hill, 1962. 198p.

McDaniel, J. W. *Essential Student Personnel Practices for Junior Colleges*. AAJC, 1962. 54p.

McDowell, F. M. *The Junior College*. U.S. Bureau of Education Bulletin No. 35. GPO, 1919. 139p.

Medsker, Leland L. *The Junior College: Progress and Prospect*. McGraw-Hill, 1960. 367p.

Medsker, Leland L. "Patterns for the Control of Community Colleges." In *Establishing Legal Bases for Community Colleges*. AAJC, 1962. p. 14–18.

Medsker, Leland L. "Governance of Junior Colleges." Paper prepared for the Seminar on Issues Affecting the Junior Colleges, California Coordinating Council for Higher Education, November, 1964.

Medsker, Leland L. Unpublished data from work in progress. Center for Research and Development in

Higher Education, U California, Berkeley, 1966.

Medsker, Leland L., and Clark, George W. *State Governance of California Junior Colleges*. A special study authorized by the California Coordinating Council for Higher Education. Center for Research and Development in Higher Education, U California, Berkeley, 1966. 101p.

Medsker, Leland L., and Trent, James W. *Factors Affecting College Attendance of High School Graduates from Varying Socio-economic and Ability Levels*. Center for the Study of Higher Education, U California, Berkeley, 1965. 110p.

Merson, Thomas B. "The Crisis in Accreditation." *Jun Col J* 35(5):6–8; 1965.

National Education Association, Research Division. *Teacher Supply and Demand in Universities, Colleges, and Junior Colleges, 1963–64 and 1964–65*. NEA, 1965. 92p.

National Society for the Study of Education. "The Role of the Public Junior College." In *The Public Junior College*, 55th Yearbook, Part I, NSSE, U Chicago Press, 1956. p. 64–74.

Raines, Max R. "The Student Personnel Situation." *Jun Col J* 36(5):6–8; 1966.

Schultz, Raymond E. *Administrators for America's Junior Colleges*. AAJC, 1965. 28p.

Schultz, Raymond E. (Ed.) *General Education in Community Junior Colleges*. Florida State Department of Education, 1959. 99p.

Selden, William K. *Accreditation: A Struggle over Standards in Higher Education*. Harper, 1960. 138p.

Stecklein, John E., and Eckert, Ruth E. *An Exploratory Study of Factors Influencing the Choice of College Teaching as a Career*. Cooperative Research Program, USOE, 1958. 46p.

Thornton, James W., Jr. *The Community Junior College*. Wiley, 1960. 300p.

Tillery, H. Dale. "Academic Rank: Promise or Peril?" *Jun Col J* 33(6):6–9; 1963.

Tillery, H. Dale. "Differential Characteristics of Entering Freshmen at the University of California and Their Peers at California Junior Colleges." Doctoral dissertation. U California, Berkeley, 1964. 254p.

Tyler, Ralph W. "The Teaching Obligation." *Jun Col J* 30(9):525–33; 1960.

Vaccaro, Louis C. "The Manpower Development and Training Act and the Community College." *Jun Col J* 34(3):21–3; 1963.

Venn, Grant. *Man, Education and Work: Post-secondary Vocational and Technical Education*. ACE, 1964. 184p.

COMPARATIVE EDUCATION

A brief working definition of comparative education is the careful analysis of educational systems, issues, and problems in two or more countries within the context of historical, socioeconomic, political, cultural, religious, and other influential factors. Basically, the study of comparative education involves the collection, authentication, and interpretation of data on the basis of direct observation, documentary analysis, person-to-person contacts, and reflection in as objective a manner as is possible. This means the application of disciplined judgment to a body of abundant and variegated data. A serious study in comparative education enables one to see a problem in regional or global perspective, as well as to comprehend the school system and issues in his own country in broad perspective.

Comparative education is an interdisciplinary field in that it draws upon educational history, philosophy, sociology, economics, and other areas of knowledge. Successful research in this field may also depend on a practical knowledge of reading, speaking, and understanding several foreign languages. Comparative education is essentially a scholarly study, but it may serve also as a basis for practical educational work, such as consultation, planning, and aid. Specialists in the field, as a rule, do not regard with favor the practice of wholesale borrowing by one country of another nation's school system, since it is not likely, in most instances, that the contexts are similar. Nor do they approve of the popular pastime of setting up a hierarchy of national educational systems. Rather, the task of the comparative educator, in the first instance, is full understanding and clear interpretation of the system or problem. Only then is there a firm foundation for the consideration of educational reform or change.

RECENT GROWTH OF THE FIELD. Throughout the first half of the present century, comparative education was promoted through research, publication, organizations, and instruction by such leaders as Sir Michael Sadler, I. L. Kandel, Friedrich Schneider, and Nicholas Hans. Since World War II, and more especially during the past decade, there has been a considerable growth of interest and activity in this field. To a significant extent, the recent development of comparative education may be traced to increased international cooperation in education through UNESCO and other agencies, the emergence of new and developing countries desiring a good educational system as soon as possible, the greater frequency of travel and conferences abroad, the rising awareness of the achievements (e.g., Sputnik) and difficulties of other countries, the rapidity of communication of information, and other factors. Symbolizing the growth of this area was the founding of the Comparative Education Society, in 1956, and that of the Comparative Education Society in Europe, in 1961, as well as the publication of such new journals as *Comparative Education Review* since 1957 and *Comparative Education*, since 1964. Another indicator is the recent report by UNESCO (1964*a*) on the growth of teaching and research in comparative education in universities all over the world. The proliferation of printed matter in numerous languages has made the process of selection difficult for a survey of the literature since 1957, the date of completion of the article by Kneller (1960) in the third edition of the *Encyclopedia of Educational Research*.

HISTORIOGRAPHY OF COMPARATIVE EDUCATION. As yet, there is no thoroughgoing account of the history of comparative educational literature and research. In recent years, however, there have appeared several research studies which have attempted to add to the historical knowledge of the subject. A French translation of the monograph by Goetz made available to a wider audience the painstaking German study (Goetz, 1954) of the life, work, and thought of Jullien, often considered the founding father of comparative education. Fraser (1964) issued an English translation of Jullien's classic work on comparative education together with a comprehensive historical analysis of its context, precedents, and influence. An analysis of a Russian educator's reports on education in Europe and America was made by Hans (1962), while Higginson (1961) indicated, but without specific citation of sources, the influence of Sadler on European and American workers in comparative education. Most recently, Brickman (1966) endeavored to trace the prehistory of the field from ancient times in Greece and Rome to late-eighteenth-century Europe.

THEORY AND METHODOLOGY. More and more attention has been paid during the past decade to questions of theory and methodology, generally intertwined, in comparative education. In one such analysis, Brickman (1956) pointed out the desirability of vertical, or historical, comparison and horizontal comparison. Horizontal comparison involves a synoptic study of education in two areas within a federated country, e.g., Quebec and Ontario in Canada. A very important compilation presented to Pedro Rosselló by Dottrens and others (1959) dealt with the historical, philosophical, sociological, statistical, global, and planning approaches. The essays in that book, which was a reprint of an entire issue of the *International Review of Education*, were written in English, French, German, and Spanish by such outstanding scholars as Kandel, Lauwerys, Hans, C. Arnold Anderson, and Idenburg. Rosselló (1960) explicated the method of analysis of "educational currents" used by the International Bureau of Education in Geneva, by which inferences may be drawn from facts and statistics supplied by various ministries of education. Such an approach, he shows, has yielded significant information about educational trends in comparable countries.

Critical thinking concerning methodology has been manifest in several essays. Kazamias (1961, 1963) evaluated critically the various approaches to comparative education and urged greater attention to historical and objective procedures. Recent comparative studies of school programs were criticized as lacking methodological rigor by Perkinson (1962), who also presented his concept of the applied dimension of comparative education, whereby education all over the world could be improved through testing and experimentation.

A magnum opus in methodology was provided by Bereday (1964) in a treatise which delineated the theory and specific application of methods. This work showed the dangers of cultural bias in writings and indicated the vast literary resources available for serious research in comparative education.

GENERAL WORKS AND TEXTBOOKS. One characteristic trend of the past decade has been the publication of general books and texts in a variety of languages and in countries in different parts of the world. A compilation of essays by an international authorship on the major aspects of comparative education was edited by Espe (1956). The third edition of the widely used text by Hans (1958) again highlights the role of various factors (e.g., race, religion, language) in education in international perspective. Samaan (1958) wrote a comprehensive work in Arabic with major emphasis on the theory and methods of Europe and America. Brief introductions to the field, with bibliographical and other research aids for Brazilian, Dutch, and Mexican students, were prepared, respectively, by Ribiero (1958), Idenburg (1959), and Villalpando (1961). The second edition of the text by Mallinson (1960) covered the characteristics and organization of education in seven West European nations, the U.S.S.R., and the United States. The Brazilian Lourenço Filho (1961) discussed the theoretical foundations of the field and offered descriptions and analyses of education in various countries, particularly in Latin America. Two German specialists, Schneider (1961) and Hilker (1962), presented substantial, documented studies of the history, theory, and methodology of comparative education.

The revised edition of the text by King (1963*b*) updated his analyses of education in Denmark, France, Great Britian, the United States, the U.S.S.R., and India. King (1962) also studied various problems, e.g., the social, technological, and other forces influencing education, in comparative perspective. Moehlman (1963) indicated briefly the interrelationship of cultural factors and education in various national school systems. A Norwegian specialist, Ruge (1964), analyzed twentieth-century educational thought and problems in international European context. A comparative approach to theoretical educational issues was delineated by Holmes (1965), who illustrated the principles in case studies of the United States, England, the U.S.S.R., and Japan. The second edition of the textbook by Cramer and Browne (1965) emphasized administration, control, and organization of school systems in Europe, the United States, Canada, Australia, and Asia. A documentary collection of statements by various specialists on aspects of education in international perspective was compiled by Adams (1966). Finally, illustrative of the growing interest in comparative education in new areas was the text by Chaube (1965), an Indian, chiefly a digest of facts on education in various countries in Asia and Europe and in the United States.

REFERENCE WORKS. A comprehensive series of detailed reference volumes was produced by

UNESCO (1955, 1958, 1962, 1966b). The first was an expansion and updating of the original *World Handbook of Educational Organization and Statistics*, published in 1952. The second was devoted to primary education, the third to secondary education, and the fourth to higher education in about 200 countries and territories all over the world. In addition to current developments and statistics, the research worker was provided with glossaries, diagrams, bibliographies, interpretative introductions, and comparative statistics.

The other reference works on higher education continued to appear in new editions. The 16th edition of *The World of Learning* (1965) presented current information on universities, libraries, research institutes, museums, and learned societies all over the world. The third edition of a compendium by Keyes (1965) contained uneven data on universities and other higher institutions of learning in all countries with the exception of the United States and the British Commonwealth of Nations. The 42nd edition of the comprehensive compilation by Foster and Craig (1966) was again exemplary in its thoroughness in the coverage of universities in the British Commonwealth.

In the field of comparative educational statistics, UNESCO (1961, 1966a) was a pioneer. One significant work (UNESCO, 1961) was a basic handbook on the international comparability of educational statistics, with illustrations from illiteracy, finance, and other aspects of education. UNESCO's latest statistical yearbook (1966a) contains recent data, as of about 1964, on population, education, libraries and museums, publications, film, radio, and television in countries all over the world. Liu (1966), formerly chief of statistics at UNESCO, prepared a manual indicating the procedures, with case studies, for determining the school enrollment projections in the developing nations of Asia and Africa.

Glossaries of educational terms were compiled for the aid of research workers in comparative education. The Italian ministry of public instruction (Ministero della Istruzione Pubblica, 1956, 1957, 1963) published translations in Italian of educational terminology in France, Great Britain, and Belgium. The second edition of the widely used educational dictionary edited by Good (1959) included a supplement with definitions of educational terms used in Canada, England, France, Germany, and Italy. Botiakova and others (1959) compiled an extensive Russian-English educational dictionary. Also noteworthy are the glossaries in the various editions of UNESCO's *World Survey of Education* (UNESCO, 1955, 1958, 1962, 1966b), already mentioned.

The area of bibliography received much attention during the decade. The *Review of Educational Research* published the comprehensive survey "Educational Research in Countries Other than the U.S.A." (No 11, 1957) covering studies in selected countries in northern and western Europe, Latin America, Asia, and English-speaking countries for the period 1950–1956. Rapacz and Kahn (1961) covered recent research in comparative education for the *Review of Educational Research*, while Brickman (1964) analyzed the literature for 1961–1964 in the same journal.

The report of a meeting of experts at the UNESCO Institute of Education in Hamburg contained a 50-page bibliography of selected references on comparative education, compiled by Bristow and Schlichter (1963).

A bibliography of great usefulness to researchers, especially to masters' and doctoral candidates, is the comprehensive listing by Eells (1959) of U.S. dissertations and theses on education in foreign countries and on the education of ethnic groups in the United States. This extensive work of 5,716 titles, which covered studies completed between 1884 to 1958, could well be updated at periodic intervals.

Another massive aid to bibliographic research in comparative education was the international guide by UNESCO (1963) to educational publications issued during 1955–1960 in 95 countries all over the globe. This volume presented annotations of reference works, legal and policy documentation, official reports, pedagogical literature, research studies, and other types of writings in the original languages. It is to be hoped that this valuable reference work will be issued, as planned, in subsequent five-year surveys of the literature.

The yearbook has been an important source of current and historical data and ideas in comparative education. The late I. L. Kandel's *Educational Yearbook*, which appeared during 1924–1944, is still of great value today to research workers. At the present time, those who desire to study year-by-year trends in most countries can refer to the *International Yearbook of Education: 1964* and its predecessors, published annually by the International Bureau of Education (1965) and UNESCO. More analytic studies centered on specific topics of significance are available in the yearbooks edited by Bereday and Lauwerys (1966). The latest volume, for 1966, offers 36 studies of various aspects of church-state-education relations in countries in Europe, Asia, Africa, and North and South America. Similar volumes in recent years have dealt with the educational explosion, international education, teacher training, the gifted child, concepts of excellence, communication media, higher education, the secondary school curriculum, and educational philosophy.

The series of annual proceedings of the New York University conferences on comparative education, begun in 1954, terminated with the sixth edition. The compilation, which concentrated on the background, methods, critiques, and improvement of research in comparative education, was edited by Brickman (1959).

The most recent yearbook, a promising international effort, was inaugurated by an editorial board under the chairmanship of the Dutch scholar Langeveld (1965). The initial edition of this reference work contained contributions on a variety of themes in English, French, and German. Of particular interest to specialists were the essay on the classification of European school types by Hilker and De Landsheere's plan for a dictionary of European educational terminology for use in comparative education research.

The field of comparative education is fortunate in that many pedagogical periodicals devote some attention to it and also because it possesses journals concentrating on research. By way of example, one finds both opinion and research articles on various aspects of comparative education in such American journals as *Teachers College Record, Educational Forum, Phi Delta Kappan, School and Society,* and *School Review,* as well as in those covering specialized subject matter. Moreover, foreign periodicals—e.g., *Bildung und Erziehung, Minerva, Sovetskaya pedagogika,* and *British Journal of Educational Studies*—offer articles of interest to comparative educators.

Of additional importance are other periodicals directly concerned with developments and issues in comparative and international education. Among these are *La educación, L'enfance dans le monde, L'actualité pédagogique à l'étranger, Oversea Education, Bulletin* of the International Association of Universities, *Foreign Educational Digest, Education Panorama, Rivista di legislazione scholastica comparata, International Journal of Adult and Youth Education,* and *Vergleichende Pädagogik.* Special attention may be directed to *Comparative Education Review,* published since 1957 by the Comparative Education Society under Bereday's editorship; the trilingual *International Journal of Education,* issued by the UNESCO Institute for Education in Hamburg; and the new British journal *Comparative Education,* edited at Oxford University since 1964. In the last-mentioned three there can be found numerous articles of theoretical and research significance.

One of the pressing needs of research workers is a well-classified index of articles, books, studies, reviews, documents, and other materials in comparative education. This applies to publications in English as well as to those in the most commonly used languages, at the very least. It has become increasingly difficult for students and even specialists to keep abreast of the vast amount of printed materials which shed light on the field.

STUDIES IN HISTORICAL-COMPARATIVE PERSPECTIVE. An increasingly important and interesting phase of research in comparative education has been the historical. A significant example of this type of literature was contributed by Robert Ulich (1961) in the form of a scholarly study of educational problems and issues from the medieval period to the present century, with particular stress upon England, France, Germany, Russia, and the United States. While his approach revealed that sociopolitical-cultural factors do produce educational change in nations, he showed that there was, nevertheless, a historical unity in certain regions. According to Ulich the historical-comparative analysis of education in a broad societal context yields a deeper understanding of the cultural problems of various nations plus "reliable criteria" enabling a country to rethink its own educational system and planning.

A competently documented study by Bidwell and Kazamias (1962) of the relations of church, politics, and publicly financed education in England and the United States since the nineteenth century revealed that different social developments led to varying solutions to this controversial issue. Such a study is illuminating up to a point, but it must be supplemented by inquiries within a broader international framework. A comparative analysis of educational legislation in France and England from 1789 onward, buttressed by a thoroughgoing bibliography of primary sources and secondary writings, was contributed by Hunkin (1962). A broader comparison, which included education and other aspects of French and British culture during 1850–1870 was made by Green (1965). Carr-Saunders (1961) also made effective use of documentary materials in historical-comparative perspective to analyze the development, since 1946, of universities in British overseas areas. Farrah (1964) presented a comparative study of educational reform in Geneva Canton, France, Yugoslavia, and Syria since 1945.

The textbook by Thut and Adams (1964) made use of the historical approach, describing patterns of educational development in several established European and Asiatic nations and in developing nations in Latin America, Asia, and Africa. Kazamias and Massialas (1965) analyzed several significant problems, such as equality of educational opportunity and curriculum, in historical-comparative perspectives for selected nations in different parts of the world. Ashby (1966) contributed a thoroughly documented study of the historical-sociological elements in British policy toward universities in India and Africa. Mary Ulich (1966) wrote a comparative history of adult education in England, Germany, and the United States. Finally, the second edition of the curriculum history from ancient times to the present era by Dolch (1966) furnished abundant, documented details enabling the student to determine criteria for comparative analysis. This study also included a comprehensive bibliography in several languages.

AREA STUDIES IN COMPARATIVE PERSPECTIVE. Because of the large number of one-country and even two-country comparative studies, it is not possible to discuss more than a sampling in a restricted space. Torborst and others (1962) compiled several documented essays on recent school reforms in such "capitalistic" countries as West Germany, France, England, Austria, and Sweden. Another analysis from the communist ideological viewpoint covered some educational systems of Western Europe, the United States, and Japan and indicated the superiority of the Soviet school system. This volume was produced in Moscow by the Vsesoyuznii Institut Nauchnoi i Tekhnicheskoi Informatsii (All-Union Institute of Scientific and Technical Information—1960). The third edition of a survey of the school systems of Scandinavia and other European countries, as well as of the United States, was presented by a team of Scandinavian educators under the editorship of Sjöstedt and Sjöstrand (1962). A comparative overview of education in the four Scandinavian countries was furnished by Ruge (1962). More comprehensive and analytical on this subject (minus Finland) is the study by Dixon (1965) of the interrelationship of school, society, and progress in Scandinavia.

Malkova (1961) edited a group of essays by communist educators on the educational problems in Czechoslovakia, East Germany, Bulgaria, China, Poland, the U.S.S.R., Albania, and Romania. A more detailed study of similar scope, but substituting Hungary for Albania and China, was produced by a team of east European educators under the editorship of Kienitz and others (1962). Another approach to education in communist countries, with special stress on the U.S.S.R., was a group of essays by English, Canadian, West Indian, and Polish educators, edited by King (1963a). In this compilation, particular attention was given to the influence of Marxist-Leninist ideology on the educational systems, and some note was taken of comparisons with noncommunist nations.

Among the other noteworthy works on areas were those by Hauch (1960) and Kitchen (1962). The former was largely concerned with changes in the Caribbean schools of the affiliated areas of Britain, the Netherlands, and France. The latter was a survey of educational development in the countries of Africa. Havighurst and his associates (1962) analyzed the social structure and social problems of Latin American education. Finally, because of the rarity of such publications, one should mention the compilation of descriptions of Arab national school systems issued by the Arab Information Center (1966).

TRENDS AND ISSUES IN COMPARATIVE PERSPECTIVE. Studies of various developments, problems, and issues in international perspective are available to the research worker and student. Whiting (1963) edited an encyclopedic book with essays by anthropologists reporting cross-cultural studies of the relation of child-rearing patterns to personality in India, Kenya, Mexico, Okinawa, the Philippines, and the United States. In the realm of primary and secondary education, works include an analysis of recent trends and common problems in some European nations by Thomas and Majault (1963), as well as a more specialized study of the teaching of civics in Europe by the Council of Europe (1963). Dottrens (1962) surveyed a variety of factors affecting the improvement of primary-school curricula around the world and indicated the role of research and comparative education in raising the standards of the elementary courses of study. Wall and others (1962), under the auspices of the UNESCO Institute for Education in Hamburg, studied the causes, outcomes, and remedies incident to pupil failure in different countries. Their eight-language bibliography of 375 titles is a useful research tool. Under the same sponsorship, Stern (1963) reported on experiences, experiments, and problems in teaching foreign or second languages in primary schools in Europe, Latin America, and the United States.

Several important problems and issues concerning Jewish education throughout the world, frequently in comparison with developments in Israel, were investigated in papers presented at international conferences in Israel under the sponsorship of the Jewish Agency (1958, 1961). An international authorship prepared essays, edited by Visalberghi (1964), on preadolescent education in ten European countries. Williams (1963) surveyed apprenticeship training in seven west European countries and drew lessons for Britain.

Majault (1965) outlined the provisions for teacher education in 18 European nations, while Male (1960) concentrated on such preparation in the Benelux countries. Mosson (1965) analyzed the institutions of four west European countries and of the United Kingdom which prepare individuals for management positions. The common problems of legal, medical, and engineering education in France, Great Britain, the U.S.S.R., and West Germany were pointed up by Brickman (1962) on the basis of original source materials, the historical contexts, and the current practices. While he found differences in detail in professional education among these countries, he also noted many similarities in aims, curricula, requirements, and length of preparation.

Studies of the higher-educational systems of Australia, Canada, France, West Germany, the Netherlands, New Zealand, Sweden, Switzerland, the United States, and the U.S.S.R. were made, after visiting, interviewing, and documentary research by the [Robbins] Committee on Higher Education (1964) in Britain. Carmichael (1959) made a comparative study of university and professional education in the United States, Great Britain, Australia, Canada, India, New Zealand, Pakistan, and South Africa. This volume was likewise derived from documents, interviews, and observations. A compilation by Shryock (1961) presented reports from 16 countries in various areas on the status of university faculty members. Schwarz (1962) presented an international compilation of essays on the aims and problems of higher education in Germany and in several other countries; of great value to the research worker is the comprehensive bibliography in 12 languages. Bowles (1963) analyzed the various aspects of accessibility to higher education. Another study, under the auspices of the International Study of University Admissions (1965) presented detailed statements of national practices of admission to higher education in 12 countries in different parts of the world.

There are some studies of interest on higher education in limited areas. Fischer (1964) investigated the possible utilization of the university as a unit for comparative analysis in developing countries in Southeast Asia—e.g., Ceylon, Indonesia, Burma, and Thailand. He visited the institutions and examined the relevant documents. A comparative study of higher education in the same area was made by Silcock (1964), with special stress on historical framework, values, finance, research, and instruction. Ashby (1964) showed the influence of European ideas, traditions, and values on west African universities, pointed up the problems of nationalism, and outlined the future role of universities in national, cultural and economic development.

Higher education in the Latin American republics and in the United States, with particular reference to historical development, aims, administration, instruction, statistics, and problems, was treated by Benjamin (1965) in an informative volume. Covering the same area is a collection of documented studies by Latin American and German specialists, edited by Steger (1965), emphasizing the historical, philosophical, economic, and sociological aspects. Of particular usefulness for research are the bibliographies. Danton (1963) contributed a documented, specialized, comparative study of selected university libraries in the United States with those of West Germany, taking special note of their book selection and collection policies and practices. Comparisons were made on the basis of observations, interviews, documents, correspondence, and current and historical statistical figures.

The subject of educational administration in international perspective was presented in a largely descriptive manner in a group of essays on 16 countries in Europe, Asia, and the United States, under the editorship of Reller and Morphet (1962). The volume contains much useful information but few comparisons other than what the editors have inferred from the data on recent issues and trends. Heath (1962) did a comparative analysis of official reports from many countries on the activities of their ministries of education. In addition to furnishing convenient information, otherwise generally unobtainable except in the original languages, these documents constitute in themselves primary educational source materials. Another unique volume in the literature on comparative education was a compilation of papers, edited by Lemberg (1963), on the administration and problems of educational research in West Germany, England and Wales, Sweden, and the U.S.S.R. These essays focused on the relationship of educational research to the needs of society in the various countries.

Also helpful to students of comparative education are texts of the provisions of European constitutions as collected and interpreted by Limiti (1960). Carelli (1963), an Argentinian, wrote a fully documented doctoral dissertation at the University of Hamburg in which he made a critical comparative analysis of the plans for the prolongation of compulsory education in England, France, Sweden, and the U.S.S.R.

Comparative studies also serve to shed some light on serious social problems and controversial issues in education. The United Nations (1958) issued an updated version of its five-volume *Comparative Study of Juvenile Delinquency* in all parts of the world. As might be inferred from the general title, these publications were mainly organized as compendiums of information and inner interpretation rather than as cross-cultural comparisons. Robison (1960) included a documented chapter on several foreign countries in her text on juvenile delinquency. In the field of race relations, Brickman (1960) placed school segregation in the perspective of policies and practices in the U.S.S.R., Japan, Brazil, and the South Pacific. Ammoun (1957) made a valuable contribution to the understanding of racial and other forms of discrimination in education through a careful analysis, under the auspices of the United Nations, of official documents of governments in all parts of the world.

The church-state-school issue has received some recent attention in international context. Benabarre (1958) surveyed the problem of the provision of public aid to private, church-related schools in 51 countries. The theory and practices of many governments in church-state questions in education were investigated by Dubay (1959). Brickman (1961) utilized source materials in 14 languages in his study of the educational interrelationship of church and state in historical perspective in numerous countries on six continents. He found few hard-and-fast solutions but rather "compromise and conciliation" in church-state-school relations throughout the world. A doctoral dissertation at the University of Hamburg by a Mexican, Latapí (1964), offered a documented comparative analysis of educational freedom with respect to the church-state-school controversy in Mexico, France, Belgium, and West Germany. Clayton (1965) made a comparative study of policies concerning the public support of church-oriented schools in England and Wales, Holland, and Sweden, with inferences drawn for the United States. Of paramount importance for the field is the latest yearbook edited by Bereday and Lauwerys (1966), which deals with historical backgrounds and contemporary developments in church-state-school relations in a large number of nations. It should also be borne in mind that this yearbook series also contains many articles on this theme scattered in recent and earlier editions.

Also of interest are several other studies written in less frequently cited languages. The well-known Italian scholar Volpicelli (1961) treated historically and contemporaneously the relation of the school to the state and church in various countries. In the Japanese language, Ishii (1962) made an analysis of the writings by English and German educators to determine the status of moral education in both countries, and Yoshida (1962) used sociological and anthropological works to establish the social framework of education in England and France.

A variety of other educational problems have been treated in comparative perspective during the past decade. In a global study by UNESCO (1957) of illiteracy, the statistics revealed a number of disturbing facts about the status of basic education in many regions all over the world. In another study, also sponsored by UNESCO, Cassirer (1960) made a detailed analysis of educational television in the United States and then presented briefer treatments of it for Canada, France, Italy, Japan, the U.S.S.R., and the United Kingdom. Cassirer's conclusion was that television is a promising form or tool of teaching in the modern world. A more recent survey covering some 30 countries, on the basis of documents, personal interviews, and correspondence with experts, was contributed by Dizard (1966). This up-to-date study was concerned with the educational and other aspects of television, with special note of the role of the United States in international television.

The historical development and current status of

adult education in Britain provide the backdrop for a presentation of adult education in the United States, West Germany, and underdeveloped countries by Peers (1958). A compact, but informative, monograph by Stern (1960), derived from works in several languages, discussed international developments and trends in the education of parents, with special reference to France, the United States, the United Kingdom, and West Germany. A unique bibliographical survey of references in a number of languages on the status of adult education in developing countries was prepared by Mezirow and Epley (1965).

Considerable data on the education and vocational training of the blind, the deaf, and the orthopedically handicapped in Europe outside the U.S.S.R. were offered in the survey by Taylor and Taylor (1960). This volume was based on ten months of field work in Europe, as well as on documents. Kammerer (1962) wrote an extensive, comprehensive, comparative analysis of the public administration of child-welfare programs and services, including juvenile delinquency, in the United States and Britain. The author made thorough use of official documents of various types, supplementing this procedure by interviewing responsible officials.

In recent years there has taken place a growth of activity in two-country comparisons, with one of them being the United States. Of particular interest is the fact that such writings have resulted from the inquiries made by laymen in addition to those by professional educators. Included among such studies is the comparison by Trace (1961) of selected textbooks used in the U.S.S.R. and in the United States in teaching humanistic and social studies in elementary and secondary education. While the theme is suitable for a thoroughgoing research study, Trace confined himself to citations from tables of contents, several textbook paragraphs, and a limited portion of a single course of study. With this sketchy foundation, Trace offered the conclusion that the U.S.S.R. textbooks and courses of study provide Soviet youth with more subject matter than the corresponding American teaching materials. Vice-admiral Rickover of the U.S. Navy, in his endeavor to prove the superiority of foreign school systems over those of the United States, presented his detailed survey of education in England (1962a) as an indictment of U.S. education. This report, published by the House of Representatives' Committee on Appropriation as unchallenged testimony at a committee hearing, contrasted mediocrity in America with the high scholastic quality in England. What is of interest to comparative educators in this subjective work is the lengthy appendix of sample tests, pupil compositions, and other materials of documentary value. Interestingly, Rickover's report was published the following year for a general audience under the main title *American Education: A National Failure*. In another work, Rickover again reprinted syllabi, examinations, and other useful documents pertaining to education in Switzerland (1962b). Once more he castigated the American school system and presented no critical analysis of Swiss education. While Rickover's aim of showing U.S. communities how to improve their schools was a commendable one, his subjective, unscholarly comparison made it difficult to use his book as a guide. Both Trace and Rickover, in sum, approached their theme with built-in biases, which were reflected in the selection of content and in the formulation of the conclusions. Research workers in comparative education, according to those who have labored long in the field, are required to make a serious effort to divest their inquiries and their writings of all kinds of preconceptions.

Covering a wider scope than Trace in less than a fourth of the space was the "comparative study" of arithmetic textbooks in the United States and Europe by Schutter and Spreckelmeyer (1959). This report compared "arithmetic programs" in the two areas on the basis of textbook content. The authors' conclusions, however interesting and useful they might prove to be, were derived from an analysis of 11 American texts published since 1946 and several earlier ones, as well as from textbooks published in 21 European countries. Some countries are represented by only one text or textbook series.

CROSS-NATIONAL EXPERIMENTAL STUDIES. One of the significant developments in research in comparative education has been the increase, over the years, in the studies using tests comparatively. With experience in international testing going back to the early 1950's, Preston (1957) tested grade 1 pupils in Munich and Philadelphia and concluded, contrary to the commonly held hypothesis, that the former made more reversal errors in reading and writing than the latter. After another experiment, involving grade 6 pupils in Hamburg, Philadelphia, and Baltimore, Preston (1956) expressed his skepticism of the broad generalization that American children are inferior in knowledge to German children. In still another study, of broader scope, Preston (1962) administered reading-comprehension tests to grade 4 and grade 6 pupils in Wiesbaden and Philadelphia. He found that the mean U.S. scores in three out of the four subgroups were higher than the corresponding scores of the German pupils. On the basis of the statistical treatment of the results, Preston concluded that the data in no way justified the customary, sweeping generalizations that German pupils are superior in reading to American pupils or that there is more reading retardation in the United States than in Germany. It is noteworthy that Preston's study was carried on in collaboration with a German specialist, Schultze, who reported similar results (1962) but who offered explanations which were contradicted by Preston (1963).

Mitsuhashi (1962) made a comparative study of conceptions and images of the geographic world held by "broadly comparable" grade 9 pupils in Tokyo and Chicago. The tests revealed that the Tokyo children possessed more precision and accuracy in the conceptualization of geography. The author attributed the greater aptitude shown by the Japanese to the possibility of better teaching, the location of Japan, and to the alertness to the influence of recent world developments on their nation.

Anderson and his colleagues (1964) compared the reading and spelling achievement and handwriting quality of English, Scottish, and American pupils, with the Americans scoring lowest. A study of spelling achievement of grades 2, 6, and 9 pupils in West Lothian County, Scotland, and in Jackson, Michigan, by Personke (1966) supported the conclusion that American children were inferior to the Scottish in spelling. The latter obtained an advantage, according to the experimenter, by an early start in school, and this was reinforced by much and high-quality instruction.

An important experimental study by an international team of specialists, consisting of Foshay and others (1962), under the auspices of the UNESCO Institute for Education in Hamburg, involved the testing of achievement in reading comprehension, mathematics, science, and geography in ten European countries, Israel, and the United States. Nearly 10,000 pupils took the tests in 1960 in their native languages. The results indicated that the various countries had strength in some subjects and weaknesses in others. French-speaking pupils were superior in mathematics, but English-speaking pupils were "consistently poor" in mathematics. In geography, Germany, Israel, and Poland were superior, while English-speaking children again did "notably poorly." American and German pupils were superior in science, whereas French and particularly Swiss pupils were the weakest in science. Yugoslav children achieved outstanding results on the reading-comprehension test, but Belgian and Polish pupils did "relatively poorly." No consistent pattern of superiority by any one nation emerged as a consequence of this study by U.S., French, German, and English specialists.

Another international study of significance, involving adolescents in Buenos Aires and Chicago, was reported by Havighurst and his colleagues (1965). This was an originally conceived research project in experimental comparative sociology, but it also had great value for comparative educators. The tests indicated that the Chicago adolescents were more self-assertive and autonomous, more resistive to authority, more instrumental in their approach to life, and more interested and active in heterosexual relations than those in Buenos Aires, but the latter were more expressive or appreciative in their orientation to the world.

The first major analysis of the intellectual and personal characteristics of prospective teachers in Britain and the United States was recently completed by Dickson and his associates (1965). On the basis of intelligence, achievement, attitude, and other tests, the team concluded that British preteaching students had higher general intelligence and verbal comprehension than their U.S. counterparts; that U.S. students were more learning-centered, while the British tended to be more child-centered and permissive; that the U.S. teacher education students judged school administrators more favorably than did those in Britain; that the British were better prepared in academic studies, except in science, in which U.S. elementary-education students had better preparation; that changes in academic competencies reflected the recency of study in the area examined and the sequences of courses, with British students improving and U.S. students dropping in academic performance during the three-year period tested; and that the Americans showed better results in the tests in professional education. The implications drawn from this study included the questioning of misconceptions about teacher education in the United States and Britain, the pointing up of the fact that there was as much diversity in the characteristics of the students within each nation as between them, and that the British teacher education programs apparently were more successful than American ones in integrating subject matter and professional education with respect to objectives, knowledge, and understanding.

DEVELOPMENT, ECONOMICS, PLANNING, AND SOCIOLOGY. The category of development, economics, planning, and sociology embraces works produced under various titles but basically dealing with one or more factors in educational, technical, and other types of development in both developed and developing countries. This form of literature has become increasingly popular since about 1960. First the collective works will be considered. Halsey and his associates (1961) edited a volume of essays by U.S. and foreign specialists on the various interrelationships of the school, society, and the economy. Among the topics discussed were the school and social mobility, selection for secondary school and university, the function of educational institutions in society, and the role of the teacher in several countries. Harris (1964) edited a compilation of papers which analyzed the economic problems of higher education, especially in relation to manpower needs in various countries. A group of essays issued by UNESCO (1964b) was devoted to different aspects of educational planning—e.g., human resources, economics, and social issues in a number of countries. The essays brought together by Piper and Cole (1964) concentrated on problems of economic and political development in secondary and higher education in the United States, Africa, and southeast Asia. Of special interest to comparative educators is the article by L. Gray Cowan which furnished a critical appraisal of the British and French school systems in Africa. Analyses of human-resource problems, the formation of human skills, the diffusion of schooling and educational opportunities, and the relation of time to socioeducational change in some countries were made by a group of scholars representing a variety of disciplines, under the editorship of Anderson and Bowman (1965). Harbison and Myers (1965) presented 11 studies by economists and other specialists on high-level manpower and education in relation to economic development in Latin America, Puerto Rico, Africa, and Asia. One of these essays is a detailed statistical comparison of education and manpower in Senegal, Guinea, and the Ivory Coast. Coleman (1965) brought together 17 documented studies of the types and problems of educational and political development in developing countries in Africa, Asia, and Latin America, as well as in developed countries; analyses of the education of modern elite groups in developing countries; and the problems and issues of educational planning in relation to political development. Research workers will no doubt appreciate the well-classified and partially annotated bibliographical guide to education and political socialization in different societies. The most recent compilation is an encyclopedic volume, edited by Robinson and Vaizey (1966), consisting of 24 papers delivered at a conference of the International Economic Association. The major themes treated by the international authorship were the comparison of national expenditures on education, the relation of education to economic progress in several countries, human-resource development, educational cost and financing, the balance between the different types and levels of education, and the problems of international aid in education.

Among the other substantial publications, one finds the seminal study by Harbison and Myers (1964) of the concepts, problems, issues, indicators, strategies, and planning of human-resource development on four levels: underdeveloped, partially developed, semiadvanced, and advanced countries. Cerych (1965) outlined the details enabling one to grasp the policy essentials of and conditions for an effective, internationally coordinated program of educational aid to developing nations. A detailed survey of technical aid to developing countries, with special stress on training programs by advanced countries to facilitate such aid, was provided by Vente (1961). Huq (1965) studied various aspects of education and development in India, Indonesia, Pakistan, and the Philippines, stressing the major aims and guiding ideas of their educational plans, the means utilized for putting them into operation, and the results achieved in these countries. Apart from supplying data and analysis, this volume was also intended as a guide for the other countries of South and Southeast Asia. Finally, of the many journal articles on this subject, space allows only a few to be mentioned. Among the instructive contributions in the category of education and economic growth are the essays by Vaizey (1961a, 1961b) and Edding (1965).

This brief survey of the literature on comparative education during the years 1957–1966 has presented a representative sampling of studies of various types and in several languages. It is clear that there is no dearth of published material in the field. It is equally evident that the writings, many of which could not be discussed in this article, are still subject to the traditional errors of ethnocentric bias, unscholarly and inadequate documentation, the lack of a historical and sociocultural framework, insufficient depth, and unilingualism. However, there is reason to believe that the standards of research are improving and that, in turn, this might have a positive effect on the general writing in comparative education.

There are topic areas in comparative education that call for more extensive and intensive research. One necessity would be thoroughgoing studies of educational problems and issues in international perspective which would yield rational explanations for variations among nations. Another need would be comprehensive studies of the various historical periods in the development of comparative education. Still other desirable areas of research will have become evident during the examination of the present article and of the literature cited herein.

William W. Brickman
University of Pennsylvania

References

Adams, Donald K. (Ed.) *Introduction to Education: A Comparative Analysis*. Wadsworth Publishing Co., Inc., 1966.

Ammoun, Charles D. *Study of Discrimination in Education*. United Nations, 1957.

Anderson, C. Arnold, and Bowman, Mary J. (Eds.) *Education and Economic Development*. Aldine Publishing Co., 1965.

Anderson, Irving, and others. *Comparisons of the Reading and Spelling Achievement and Quality of Handwriting of Groups of English, Scottish, and American Children*. U Michigan Press, 1964.

Arab Information Center. *Education in the Arab States*. The Center, 1966.

Ashby, Eric. *African Universities and the Western Tradition*. Harvard U Press, 1964.

Ashby, Eric. *Universities: British, Indian, African*. Harvard U Press, 1966.

Benabarre, Benigno, D.S.B. *Public Funds for Private Schools in a Democracy: Theory and Practice in Fifty-one Countries*. M.C.S. Enterprises (Manila), 1958.

Benjamin, Harold R. W. *Higher Education in the American Republics*. McGraw-Hill, 1965.

Bereday, George Z. F. *Comparative Method in Education*. Holt, 1964.

Bereday, George Z. F., and Lauwerys, Joseph A. (Eds.) *World Year Book of Education, 1966: Church and State in Education*. Evans, 1966.

Bidwell, Charles E., and Kazamias, Andreas M. "Religion, Politics, and Popular Education: An Historical Comparison of England and America." *Comp Ed R* 6:97–110; 1962.

Botiakova, V. V., and others. *Russko-angliiskii shkolno-pedagogicheskii slovar*. Yaroslavskoe Knizhnoe Izdatelstvo, 1959.

Bowles, Frank. *Access to Higher Education*, Vol. 1. UNESCO, 1963.

Brickman, William W. "The Theoretical Foundations of Comparative Education." *J Ed Sociol* 30:116–25; 1956.

Brickman, William W. *Research in Comparative Education*. New York U Press, 1959.

Brickman, William W. "Segregated Education in International Perspective." In Brickman, William W., and Lehrer, Stanley (Eds.) *The Countdown on*

Segregated Education. Society for the Advancement of Education, 1960. p. 95–103.

Brickman, William W. "Church, State, and School in International Perspective." In Brickman, William W., and Lehrer, Stanley (Eds.) *Religion, Government, and Education.* Society for the Advancement of Education, 1961. p. 144–247.

Brickman, William W. "Professional Education Outside the U.S.A." In Anderson, G. Lester (Ed.) *Education for the Professions.* U Chicago Press, 1962.

Brickman, William W. "Comparative Education." *R Ed Res* 34:44–61; 1964.

Brickman, William W. "Prehistory of Comparative Education to the End of the Eighteenth Century." *Compar Ed R* 10:30–47; 1966.

Bristow, Thelma, and Schlichter, Elly H. "Selected Bibliography on Comparative Education." In Holmes, B., and Robinson, S. B. *Relevant Data in Comparative Education.* UNESCO Institute for Education (Hamburg), 1963.

Carelli, M. Dino. *Was wird mit der Schulpflicht verlängerung beabsichtigt? Eine pädagogische Kritik der Schulpflichtverlängerungspläne in England, Frankreich, Schweden und der UdSSR.* Doctoral dissertation. Hamburg, 1963.

Carmichael, Oliver C. *Universities: Commonwealth and American.* Harper, 1959.

Carr-Saunders, A. M. *New Universities Overseas.* Allen, 1961.

Cassirer, Henry R. *Television Teaching Today.* UNESCO, 1960.

Cerych, Ladislav. *Problems of Aid to Education in Developing Countries.* Praeger, 1965.

Chaube, S. P. *Comparative Education.* Ram Prasad, 1965.

Clayton, A. Stafford. *Historical and Social Determinants of Public Education Policy in the United States and Europe.* Cooperative Research Project No. F-017. USOE, 1965.

Coleman, James S. (Ed.) *Education and Political Development.* Princeton U Press, 1965.

Committee on Higher Education. *Higher Education (Appendix Five): Higher Education in Other Countries.* H.M. Stationery Office, 1964.

Council of Europe. *Education in Europe: Civics and European Education at the Primary and Secondary Level.* Council of Europe, 1963.

Cramer, John F., and Browne, George S. *Contemporary Education: A Comparative Study of National Systems,* 2nd ed. Harcourt, 1965.

Danton, J. Periam. *Book Selection and Collections: A Comparison of German and American University Libraries.* Columbia U Press, 1963.

Dickson, George E., and others. *The Characteristics of Teacher Education Students in the British Isles and the United States.* U Toledo Press, 1965.

Dixon, Willis. *Society, Schools and Progress in Scandinavia.* Pergamon Press, 1965.

Dizard, Wilson P. *Television: A World View.* Syracuse U Press, 1966.

Dolch, Josef. *Lehrplan des Abendlandes,* 2nd ed. Henn, 1966.

Dottrens, Robert. *The Primary School Curriculum.* UNESCO, 1962.

Dottrens, Robert, and others. *Thoughts on Comparative Education: Festschrift für Pedro Rosselló.* Nijhoff, n.d. [1959].

Dubay, Thomas. *Philosophy of the State as Educator.* Bruce, 1959.

Edding, Friedrich. "The Use of Economics in Comparing Educational Systems." *Compar Ed R* 11:453–65; 1965.

Eells, Walter Cosby. *American Foreign Education.* NEA, 1959.

Espe, Hans. *Die Bedeutung der vergleichenden Erziehungswissenschaft für Lehrerschaft und Schule.* Orbis, 1956.

Farrah, Elias. *Le courant des réformes scolaires après la deuxième guerre mondiale.* Kundig, 1964.

Fischer, Joseph. *Universities in Southeast Asia.* Ohio State U Press, 1964.

Foshay, Arthur W., and others. *Educational Achievements of Thirteen-year-olds in Twelve Countries.* UNESCO Institute for Education (Hamburg), 1962.

Foster, J. F., and Craig, T. (Eds.) *Commonwealth Universities Yearbook: 1966.* Association of Commonwealth Universities, 1966.

Fraser, Stewart. *Jullien's Plan for Comparative Education, 1816–1817.* Teachers College, Columbia U, 1964.

Goetz, Helmut. *Marc-Antoine Jullien de Paris (1775–1848): Der geistige Werdegang eines Revolutionärs.* Mayer, 1954. Translated into French as *Marc-Antoine Jullien de Paris (1775–1848): L'Évolution spirituelle d'un révolutionnaire.* Institut Pédagogique National, 1962.

Good, Carter V. (Ed.) *Dictionary of Education,* 2nd ed. McGraw-Hill, 1959.

Green, F. C. *A Comparative View of French and British Civilization (1850–1870).* J. M. Dent & Sons, Ltd., 1965. Especially pp. 11–38.

Halsey, A. H., and others. (Eds.) *Education, Economy, and Society.* Free, 1961.

Hans, Nicholas. *Comparative Education.* Routledge & Kegan Paul, Ltd., 1958.

Hans, Nicholas. "K. D. Ushinsky—Russian Pioneer of Comparative Education." *Compar Ed R* 5:162–6; 1962.

Harbison, Frederick, and Myers, Charles A. (Eds.) *Education, Manpower, and Economic Growth.* McGraw-Hill, 1964.

Harbison, Frederick, and Myers, Charles A. (Eds.) *Manpower and Education: Country Studies in Economic Development.* McGraw-Hill, 1965.

Harris, Seymour E. (Ed.) *Economic Aspects of Higher Education.* Organization for Economic Cooperation and Development, 1964.

Hauch, Charles C. *Educational Trends in the Caribbean: European Affiliated Areas.* USOE, 1960.

Havighurst, Robert J., and others. *La sociedad y la educación en América Latina.* U Buenos Aires, 1962.

Havighurst, Robert J., and others. *A Cross-national*

Study of Buenos Aires and Chicago Adolescents. Karger, 1965.

Heath, Kathryn G. *Ministries of Education.* USOE, 1962.

Higginson, J. H. "The Centenary of an English Pioneer in Comparative Education: Sir Michael Sadler (1861–1943)." In *R Ed* 7:286–98; 1961.

Hilker, Franz. *Vergleichende Pädagogik.* Hueber, 1962.

Holmes, Brian. *Problems in Education: A Comparative Approach.* Routledge & Kegan Paul, Ltd., 1965.

Hunkin, Patience. *Enseignement et politique en France et en Angleterre.* Institut Pédagogique National, 1962.

Huq, Muhammad S. *Education and Development Strategy in South and Southeast Asia.* East-West Center, 1965.

Idenburg, Philip J. *Inleiding tot de vergelijkende Opvoedkunde.* Wolters, 1959.

International Bureau of Education. *International Yearbook of Education: 1964.* The Bureau, 1965.

International Study of University Admissions. *Access to Higher Education,* Vol. 2: *National Studies.* UNESCO, 1965.

Ishii, Jirō. ["Comparative Study on Moral Education: England and Germany"] In *Res Bul,* No. 10. Research Institute of Comparative Education and Culturé, Kyushu U, 1962. p. 1–46.

Jewish Agency. *Yesodot l'hinuch ha-ivri b'tfutzot ha-golah.* The Agency, 1958.

Jewish Agency. *Bayot ha-hinuch ha-ivri b'tfutzot ha-golah.* The Agency, 1961.

Kammerer, Gladys M. *British and American Child Welfare Services.* Wayne State U Press, 1962.

Kandel, Isaac Leon. *Educational Yearbook of the International Institute of Teachers College,* Columbia University. 21 Volumes, Macmillan, 1924–44.

Kazamias, Andreas M. "Some Old and New Approaches to Methodology in Comparative Education." *Comp Ed R* 5:90–6; 1961.

Kazamias, Andreas M. "History, Science and Comparative Education: A Study in Methodology." In *R Ed* 8:383–98; 1963.

Kazamias, Andreas M., and Massialas, Byron G. *Tradition and Change in Education: A Comparative Study.* Prentice-Hall, 1965.

Keyes, H. M. R. (Ed.) *International Handbook of Universities.* International Association of Universities, 1965.

Kienitz, Werner, and others. (Eds.) *Das Schulwesen sozialistischer Länder in Europa.* Volk und Wissen, 1962.

King, Edmund J. *World Perspectives in Education.* Bobbs-Merrill, 1962.

King, Edmund J. (Ed.) *Communist Education.* Bobbs-Merrill, 1963(*a*).

King, Edmund J. *Other Schools and Ours,* rev. ed. Holt, 1963(*b*).

Kitchen, Helen (Ed.) *The Educated African.* Praeger, 1962.

Kneller, George F. "Comparative Education." In Harris, Chester W. (Ed.) *Encyclopedia of Educational Research,* 3d ed. Macmillan, 1960. p. 316–22.

Langeveld, M. J., and others. (Eds.) *Paedagogica Europaea: 1965.* Elsevier Publishing Company, 1965.

Latapí, Pablo. *Die Unterrichtsfreiheit.* Doctoral dissertation. U Hamburg, 1964.

Lemberg, Eugen (Ed.) *Das Bildungswesen als Gegestand der Forschung.* Quelle & Meyer, 1963.

Limiti, Giuliana. *La scuola nelle Costituzioni europee.* Armando, 1960.

Liu, Bangnee A. *Estimating Future Enrolment in Developing Countries.* UNESCO, 1966.

Lourenço Filho, M. B. *Educação comparada.* Edições Melhoranmentos, 1961.

Majault, Joseph. *Education in Europe: Teacher Training.* Council of Europe, 1965.

Male, George A. *Teacher Education in the Netherlands, Belgium, Luxembourg.* USOE, 1960.

Malkova, Z. A. (Ed.) *O vospitanii uchashchikhsaya v stranakh sotsializma.* Uchpedgiz, 1961.

Mallinson, Vernon. *An Introduction to the Study of Comparative Education.* Macmillan, 1960.

Mezirow, Jack, and Epley, David. *Adult Education in Developing Countries: A Bibliography.* U Pittsburgh Press, 1965.

Ministero Della Istruzione Pubblica. *Dizionario di terminologia scolastica comparata (Francia).* The Ministry, 1956.

Ministero Della Istruzione Pubblica. *Dizionario di terminologia scolastica comparata (Gran Bretagna e Irlanda del Nord).* The Ministry, 1957.

Ministero Della Istruzione Pubblica. *Dizionario di terminologia scolastica comparata: Belgio.* The Ministry. 1963.

Mitsuhashi, Setsuko. "Conceptions and Images of the Physical World: A Comparison of Japanese and American Pupils." *Comp Ed R* 6:142–7; 1962.

Moehlman, Arthur H. *Comparative Educational Systems.* Center for Applied Research in Education 1963.

Mosson, T. M. *Management Education in Five European Countries.* Business Publications, 1965.

Noll, Victor H. (Ed.) "Educational Research in Countries Other than the U.S.A." *R Ed Res* 27:1–158; 1957.

Peers, Robert. *Adult Education: A Comparative Study.* Routledge & Kegan Paul, Ltd., 1958.

Perkinson, Henry J. "The Comparison of Educational Programs: A Methodological Proposal." *Sch R* 70:314–31; 1962.

Personke, Carl. "Spelling Achievement of Scottish and American Children." *El Sch J* 66:337–43; 1966.

Piper, Don C., and Cole, Taylor. (Eds.) *Postprimary Education and Political and Economic Development.* Duke U Press, 1964.

Preston, Ralph C. "A Comparison of Knowledge of Directions in German and in American Children." *El Sch J* 57:158–60; 1956.

Preston, Ralph C. "Reversals in Reading and Writing Among German and Among American Children." *El Sch J* 57:330–4; 1957.

Preston, Ralph C. "Reading Achievement of German and American Children." *Sch Soc* 90:350–4; 1962.

Preston, Ralph C. "Issues Raised by the Wiesbaden-Philadelphia Reading Study." *Compar Ed R* 7:61–5; 1963.

Rapacz, Richard V., and Kahn, Albert S. "Comparative Education." *R Ed Res* 31:57–69; 1961.

Reller, Theodore L., and Morphet, Edgar L. (Eds.) *Comparative Educational Administration.* Prentice-Hall, 1962.

Ribiero, José Querino. *Pequena introdução ao estudo da educação comparada.* U São Paulo, 1958.

Rickover, H. G. *Education for All Children: What We Can Learn from England.* GPO, 1962(a).

Rickover, H. G. *Swiss Schools and Ours: Why Theirs Are Better.* Little, 1962(b).

Robinson, E. A. G., and Vaizey, J. E. (Eds.) *The Economics of Education.* Macmillan, 1966.

Robison, Sophia M. "Juvenile Delinquency in Foreign Countries." In Robison, Sophia M. *Juvenile Delinquency.* Holt, 1960. p. 28–44.

Rosselló, Pedro. *La teoría de las corrientes educativas.* Centro Regional de la UNESCO (Havana), 1960.

Ruge, Herman. *Educational Systems in Scandinavia.* Norwegian Universities, 1962.

Ruge, Herman. *Skoletanker og skoleproblemer i det 20. århundre.* Cappelen, 1964.

Samaan, Wahib I. *Studies in Comparative Education* (in Arabic). Cairo, 1958.

Schneider, Friedrich. *Vergleichende Erziehungswissenschaft.* Quelle & Meyer, 1961.

Schultze, Walter. "Studie über das verständige Lesen amerikanischer und deutscher Kinder." *Westermanns Pädagogische Beiträge* 14:188–98; 1962.

Schutter, Charles H., and Spreckelmeyer, Richard L. *Teaching the Third R: A Comparative Study of American and European Textbooks in Arithmetic.* Council for Basic Education, 1959.

Schwarz, Richard (Ed.) *Universität und moderne Welt.* Walter de Gruyter & Co., 1962.

Shryock, Richard H. (Ed.) *The Status of University Teachers.* International Association of University Professors and Lecturers, 1961.

Silcock, T. H. *Southeast Asian University.* Duke U Press, 1964.

Sjöstedt, C. E., and Sjöstrand, W. (Eds.) *Skola och undervisning i Sverige och andra länder,* 3d ed. Natur och Kultur, 1962.

Steger, Hanns-Albert (Ed.) *Grundzüge des lateinamerikanischen Hochschulwesens.* Nomos, 1965.

Stern, H. H. *Foreign Languages in Primary Education.* UNESCO Institute for Education (Hamburg), 1963.

Stern, H. H. *Parent Education: An International Survey.* U Hull (England) and UNESCO, 1960.

Taylor, Wallace W., and Taylor, Isabelle W. *Special Education of Physically Handicapped Children in Western Europe.* International Society for the Welfare of Cripples, 1960.

Thomas, Jean, and Majault, Joseph. *Education in Europe: Primary and Secondary Education.* Council of Europe, 1963.

Thut, I. N., and Adams, Don. *Educational Patterns in Contemporary Society.* McGraw-Hill, 1964.

Torborst, Marie, and others. (Eds.) *Schulentwicklung und Schulreform in einigen kapitalistischen Ländern Europas.* Volk und Wissen, 1962.

Trace, Arthur S., Jr. *What Ivan Knows That Johnny Doesn't.* Random, 1961.

Ulich, Mary E. *Patterns of Adult Education.* Pageant, 1966.

Ulich, Robert. *The Education of Nations: A Comparison in Historical Perspective.* Harvard U Press, 1961.

United Nations. *Comparative Survey of Juvenile Delinquency.* 5 vols. United Nations, 1958.

UNESCO. *World Survey of Education.* UNESCO, 1955.

UNESCO. *World Illiteracy at Mid-century.* UNESCO, 1957.

UNESCO. *World Survey of Education.* Vol. 2: *Primary Education.* UNESCO, 1958.

UNESCO. *Manual of Educational Statistics.* UNESCO, 1961.

UNESCO. *World Survey of Education.* Vol. 3: *Secondary Education.* UNESCO, 1962.

UNESCO. *International Guide to Educational Documentation: 1955–1960.* UNESCO, 1963.

UNESCO. *Report on a Survey of Teaching and Research in Comparative Education, 1962–1963.* UNESCO, 1964(a).

UNESCO. *Economic and Social Aspects of Educational Planning.* UNESCO, 1964(b).

UNESCO. *Statistical Yearbook: Annuaire statistique, 1964.* UNESCO, 1966(a).

UNESCO. *World Survey of Education.* Vol. 4: *Higher Education.* UNESCO, 1966(b).

Vaizey, John. "Comparative Notes on Economic Growth and Social Change in Education." *Compar Ed R* 5:7–12; 1961(a).

Vaizey, John. "Education as Investment in Comparative Perspective." *Compar Ed R* 5:97–104; 1961(b).

Vente, Rolf E. *Die technische Hilfe für Entwicklungsländer.* Lutzeyer, 1961.

Villalpando, José M. *Líneas generales de pedagogiá comparada.* U Nacional Autónoma de México, 1961.

Visalberghi, Aldo. (Ed.) *La scuola del preadolescente in Europe.* La Nuova Italia, 1964.

Volpicelli, Luigi. *La scuola tra stato e Chiesa.* Rome, 1961.

Vsesoyuznii Institut Nauchnoi I Tekhnicheskoi Informatsii. *Sistema obrazovaniya v nekotorikh kapitalisticheskikh stranakh.* Vsesoyuznii Institut, 1960.

Wall, W. D., and others. *Failure in School: An International Study.* Unesco Institute for Education (Hamburg), 1962.

Whiting, Beatrice B. (Ed.) *Six Cultures: Studies of Child Rearing.* Wiley, 1963.

Williams, Gertrude. *Apprenticeship in Europe.* Chapman & Hall, Ltd., 1963.

The World of Learning, 16th ed. Europa, 1965.

Yoshida, Teigo. ["Social Background of Moral Education in Europe: England and France."] In *Res B,* No. 10. Research Institute for Comparative Education and Culture, Kyushu U, 1962. p. 47–105.

CONCEPT FORMATION

The acquisition of concepts concerns educators and psychologists alike. The responsibility of the curriculum specialist is to develop programs and courses of study to facilitate the learning of concepts, principles, and generalizations. The educational psychologist is more concerned with the conditions under which children learn effectively and economically, while the developmental psychologist is interested in determining the growth of conceptual learning from infancy through adulthood. All are concerned with developing explanatory theoretical structures to account for complex learning behavior.

It is easier to recognize misconceptions than it is to recognize that a concept has been learned. Parents are often aware of misconceptions (such as a child's calling a stranger "Daddy") before they realize that the child is in the process of learning a fairly complex concept.

Certainly one's culture and experience determine the meaning assigned to concepts and determine what concepts need to be learned. In cultures other than our own the concept of a camel may be so complex as to require subclassification in much the same way that "democracy" or "justice" needs to be analyzed before being properly understood.

No simple consensus of the meaning of *concept* exists, each investigator preferring one of a number of different definitions. In part this preference stems from one's theoretical orientation, and it is in part determined by personal preferences. Behaviorists generally have been concerned with discovering the historical antecedents of behavior while Gestaltists have been more concerned with contemporary causation (Anderson & Ausubel, 1965).

Even within a behavioristic orientation, however, differences exist in the meaning of a concept. In an early investigation, Hull (1920) required his subjects to identify common radicals (ideographs) hidden among complex Chinese characters. The task was to associate the radical with nonsense syllables and to disregard irrelevant cues. Osgood (1953) has questioned whether Hull was studying concept attainment or simple discrimination learning.

Nor is it necessary to argue (as did Smoke, 1932) that concept acquisition is dependent upon common perceptual relationships even when there are no clearly discernible identical elements. Objects A and B may both be classified as "males" although one is not identical with the other.

Osgood (1953) has proposed a mediation hypothesis to define and explain concept acquisition within a neobehavioristic framework. According to him, concept learning requires only that a common mediating response be given to a number of dissimilar stimuli. For example, umbrellas, raincoats, and galoshes evoke a common response or concept (rainwear). A concept is formed when stimuli evoke a common mediating or symbolic response, and there need be neither identical elements nor common perceptual relationships, although these features may assist in developing concepts.

The Kendlers (H. Kendler, 1964; H. Kendler & D'Amato, 1955; H. Kendler and T. Kendler, 1962; T. Kendler & H. Kendler, 1959; T. Kendler & H. Kendler, 1960) have been particularly interested in studying the mediational hypothesis by comparing the efficiency of learning reversal and nonreversal shifts. They hypothesized that a nonreversal shift should be easier to learn than a reversal shift, according to simple S-R theory. The mediation hypothesis, in contrast, suggests that a reversal shift would be easier to learn.

In a typical reversal-shift study, subjects may be presented with four objects that vary along two dimensions, color (black versus white) and size (large versus small). Symbolically, the four objects may be represented by B, W (large black, large white) and b, w (small black, small white). During an initial learning period, subjects are reinforced for responding to either B or W, the relevant dimension being size. In a second discrimination task, subjects are reinforced for responding within the same dimension (size) but now to b and w. In a nonreversal-shift experiment the initial task is the same, but the second discrimination task requires a change in the dimension from size to color, with B and b being reinforced.

The Kendlers found, as hypothesized, that college students learn reversal shifts more easily than nonreversal shifts and that rats find nonreversal shifts easier to learn than reversal shifts. They interpret these findings to mean that rats—and very young children—use simple associational techniques to learn concepts, whereas older persons use mediational responses. This conclusion has been challenged by Anderson and Ausubel (1965).

Cognitive theorists have proposed other definitions and classifications of concept learning. For Ausubel (1963) concept formation is an act of discovery in which the active role of the learner is emphasized. Bruner and others (1956) have distinguished between three types of concepts. A *conjunctive concept* is defined by the presence of two or more attributes such as the concept "green books." In a typical conjunctive-conceptualization task, subjects are required to identify the concept represented by a number of conjunctive attributes.

A *disjunctive concept* involves an *either-or* decision. It requires the use of attributes or examples of concepts that allow classification to proceed in one of a number of directions. Typically, subjects are asked to indicate whether one or more attributes constitute a given class or concept (a "strike" in baseball can be *either* a missed ball *or* a ball that was fairly pitched but not struck at).

A *relational concept* involves a specific relationship between attributes. A concept may be defined by the relationship of two or more conditions, events, stimuli, etc. Thus, income-tax brackets may be defined by the relationship of number of dependents to level of income.

Goss (1961) has presented an elaborate and complex model of concept learning which combines neobehavioristic and cognitive theories into a general paradigm. He identified three types of initiating stimuli: variations of stimuli along a single or multiple dimension having either physical or psychological characteristics in common, such as four squares which are red-small, red-large, blue-small, and blue-large; stimuli that can be subdivided into sets having some physical element or relationship in common, such as four stimuli two of which are similar in that they are S-shaped and two of which are sword-shaped; and sets of stimuli which evoke dissimilar responses between sets but similar ones within sets.

For Goss, a one-stage paradigm of concept learning involves only an initiating stimulus and a terminating response. A two-stage paradigm involves relationships between initiating stimuli, mediational stimuli and responses, and terminating responses. The advantage of using Goss's taxonomy is that it incorporates both neobehavioristic and cognitive principles. Goss has also been able to generate hypotheses needed to confirm expectations implied by the paradigm.

Concepts may also be defined within a systems-theory or information-theory framework (Hovland, 1952). Hunt and others (1966), for example, define concepts as decision rules which specify whether or not a name can be applied to an object. Using digital computers, they defined the concept of "legal driver" by a series of decisions: "Has [the applicant] passed the driver's examination? . . . Has he committed a felony?" If the answer to the first question is "no" and the second "yes," the person does not belong in the class known as a legal driver.

METHODS OF STUDYING CONCEPT FORMATION.
Methods of investigation are derived from one's definition of a concept. Three basic approaches have been used, although there are many more if one considers minor modifications.

Factor Analysis. Relatively little work on concept formation has used either Q-sort or other factor-analytic methods. It would be interesting to know, for example, if concepts could psychologically be classified as conjunctive, disjunctive, or relational or if concept attainment and concept identification represent different psychological dimensions. The lack of well-constructed and validated measures of concept attainment no doubt is at least one explanation for the failure to use multivariate techniques.

A number of models have been developed within a factor-analytic framework. Guilford (1959), for example, proposed a cubical model to represent intellect. The three dimensions of the cube were called *operations, products,* and *contents,* with each dimension capable of further analysis. Of greatest relevance to concept formation is Guilford's types of thinking: convergent (searching for a "correct" answer), divergent (searching for a novel response), and evaluation (determining goodness, correctness, etc.). A similar model has been proposed by Merrifield (1966), who has shown the relationship between factor-analytic studies of intellect and the types of learning suggested by Gagné (1965).

Another use of factor analysis is suggested by the work of Osgood and others (1957) on the semantic differential, a rating scale composed of bipolar traits used to measure the connotative meanings of concepts. Factor analyses of semantic-differential responses have led to the extraction of three factors: evaluative (good–bad), potency (strong–weak), and activity (fast–slow).

Case Studies. The case study has been used extensively by Piaget (1926, 1928) in studying developmental changes in concept formation. Although useful in developing hypotheses to be tested on larger numbers of subjects or in the preliminary stages of hypothesis testing, the case study does not readily allow generalizations to be made to larger numbers of subjects.

Experimental Approaches. The experimental approach has been used in a wide number and variety of concept-acquisition studies, some of which are now classic investigations (Hull, 1920; Smoke, 1933). The simpler (and older) approaches were to have subjects respond to a series of stimuli and then abstract a common element. In divergent thinking, however, it may be most difficult to discern what the common element is that the subject is responding to.

Experimental designs used by investigators studying concept acquisition are too diverse to be discussed here. However, there seem to be a number of different tasks which can be classified although they are not necessarily limited to experimental applications of concept formation.

Chinese Characters and Pictures. Chinese characters having common and irrelevant stimuli have been used by Hull (1920) and Sax (1960). Essentially, the task is to have subjects respond to Chinese symbols containing common radicals plus irrelevant cues by associating the radical with nonsense syllables.

Pictorial materials have also been used in a number of concept-acquisition studies. Johnson and O'Reilly (1964), for example, had subjects classify colored pictures of birds.

Words. According to Archer (1966), the distinctive aspect of concept learning is the ability of the subject to label or use words to identify concepts. Underwood (1966) has pointed out the relationship between verbal and concept learning. Concept learning is represented by an *A-B,C-B* paradigm (different stimuli but identical responses) whereas rote learning involves an *A-B,A-B* paradigm. Between these two paradigms are intermediate values (*A-B,A'-B*) where there is some similarity among stimuli but where responses are the same. Positive transfer occurs in rote learning using the *A-B,A'-B* paradigm. This same paradigm when applied to concept learning involves conjunctive and relational concepts. The *A-B,C-B* paradigm in rote learning produces negative transfer and represents disjunctive-concept formation.

Words can be used in concept-formation tasks in a variety of ways. One approach (Osgood & others, 1957) is to measure the connotative meanings of concepts through the semantic differential. Another

(Wallach & Kogan, 1965) is to have subjects tell stories about words such as *job, sky, sand,* and *people*. Gardner and Schoen (1962) had subjects provide a word (such as *animal*) that would subsume instances of animals. Where comparisons have been made between the learning of pictorial and verbal materials (Runquist & Hutt, 1961), words were found to be more easily learned.

Objects. The classification of objects (furniture, objects of clothing, kitchen utensils) may also be used to study concept acquisition (Kagan & others, 1963). Some concept-acquisition tests also make use of objects to be sorted (Goldstein & Scheerer, 1941).

Geometric Figures. Most concept-formation studies have used geometric figures of varying sizes and shapes. Typically, subjects are required to respond to one or more aspects (size, for example) of a concept (triangularity, circularity, etc.) and to disregard others (color).

VARIABLES RELATED TO CONCEPT ACQUISITION.

The learning of concepts depends upon conditions associated with the learner, the nature of the task, and methods used to analyze data.

Intelligence. Studies concerning the relationship between intelligence and concept acquisition have yielded contradictory results, probably because task and dependent variables are not comparable from study to study. One investigation has found an insignificant relationship between speed of conditioning in concept learning and Wechsler Adult Intelligence Scale (WAIS) scores (Mansfield, 1960). In contrast, Osler and Fivel (1961) found both Mental Age (MA) and IQ to correlate with errors. In another experiment, Osler and Trautman (1961) found that children of normal intelligence learn concepts through S-R associative learning, while brighter children use hypotheses to develop concepts.

Few studies of concept acquisition have used gifted or mentally subnormal children. In one investigation, Mannix (1960) found that subnormal children responded in the same way as average children did on concepts involving number and quantity. In an interesting study comparing classification behavior among literate and illiterate bush children, Price-Williams (1962) was able to find little difference between the two groups.

Sex. Differences in the ease of concept learning by males and females have been investigated by Mansfield (1960), who found differences insignificant for 11 variables under investigation. Elkind (1961) reported that a larger percentage of boys than of girls were able to attain an abstract concept of volume between 12 and 18 years of age. Learning of squares and parallelograms was easier for men than for women when form was relevant (Archer, 1962).

The most likely explanation of sex differences in concept acquisition involves differences in the specific nature of the task (Olson, 1963) and in the differential reinforcement of socially desirable responses for the two sexes. The second hypothesis receives some support from the work of King (1963) and of Olson (1963). In a developmental study of science concepts, King found sex differences at the high school level but not among ten-year-olds. Olson found differences in favor of males on a concept test concerning levers.

Motivation. Many of the studies relating concept acquisition to motivational states have used incidental learning tasks to measure motivation. Both Amster (1966) and Podell (1958) found intention to learn concepts to be more effective than having no intentional set. Amster demonstrated that older children did somewhat better than younger ones on incidental learning tasks.

French and Thomas (1958) reported that highly motivated subjects reach solutions in problem-solving tasks more often than less well motivated ones. Under extreme motivation (anxiety), subjects do not seem to perform less well than when they are in less anxious states (Wolfgang & others, 1962).

Reinforcement. Reinforcement is one of the conditions considered essential in learning among most behaviorists. In general, cognitive theorists have preferred to talk about "feedback" rather than reinforcement.

The extent to which reinforcement may be delayed and still be effective has been examined by a number of investigators interested in concept acquisition. Angell (1949), Meyer (1960), and Sax (1960) have found that immediate reinforcement facilitated concept attainment and that delays were detrimental.

The ratio of presentation of reinforcements to number of correct responses has also been investigated. Most studies (Bourne & Haygood, 1960; Bourne & Pendleton, 1958) have supported the position that the *acquisition* of concepts is facilitated by 100-percent reinforcement, although Sax (1960) found no significant differences either on acquisition or on retention trials between subjects exposed to 100-percent or 50-percent reinforcement.

Wittrock (1963) found it advantageous to provide rules for learning concepts to obtain the maximum amount of transfer and retention. Kittell (1957) found that where rules and answers were provided, subjects did not do as well as those who were given rules only. Evidently, transfer of concepts is enhanced if rules are provided and if subjects have to give their own responses.

Reinforcements can also vary along a dimension of strength. Wallace (1964) studied the effects of concept attainment under levels of responses varying from mild to strong using verbal comments and an auditory signal (a door bell) at different amplitude levels. Verbal comments were found to be more effective than the door bell. As feedback intensity increased, there was a corresponding decrease in the ratio of emitted hypotheses to number of instances (exemplars of a concept) selected. With strong feedback, low-dominance concepts were attained with fewer instances than high-dominance concepts. Wallace concluded that feedback not only provided information to respondents but also affected their motivation.

Suppes and Ginsberg (1962) found that if five- and six-year-olds were corrected when learning the binary system, they performed better than those who were not corrected. Byers (1965) obtained data to support his hypothesis that the invalidation of a subject's concept hypothesis had the effect of punishing subsequent hypothesis-offering behavior. This implies that teachers who punish children for failing to give "correct" solutions to problems are, in effect, teaching them to fail to respond to future problems of a similar type. The degree of teacher punitiveness evidently affects children's concepts of school misbehavior (Kounin & Gump, 1961). Children having punitive teachers had more-poorly developed concepts of misconduct than did those having nonpunitive teachers.

POSITIVE AND NEGATIVE INSTANCES. A positive instance of a concept may be defined as a stimulus which is a member of a given class composing a concept; a negative instance is not a member of that class. Thus, positive instances are examples of a concept and include its essential characteristics, while negative instances indicate to subjects what a concept is not. Circles of various sizes and colors may serve as positive instances of the concept "circle," whereas triangles, squares, and parallelograms are negative instances.

One of the earliest investigations to be concerned with the relative ease of learning concepts under differing presentations of positive and negative instances was by Smoke (1933). Using the paired-associates method, he prepared six nonsense syllables to be associated with different geometric designs. Eight positive and negative instances of each concept (nonsense syllable) were drawn on cards, and subjects were told whether each was a positive or a negative instance of the concept. Smoke found no statistically significant difference between the time required for learning concepts from a combination of positive and negative instances presented simultaneously and that required for the learning of positive instances alone. He stated, however, that there was less tendency to make errors if both positive and negative instances were presented than if subjects were given positive instances alone.

Hovland (1952), using an information-theory model within an S-R framework, was able to specify the potential advantages to be gained through the use of positive and negative instances. From this model one can determine the minimum number of positive and negative instances needed to communicate to subjects the characteristics of a concept to be learned. Hovland assumed that the subject is aware of the nature of the model and the number and types of dimensions that are involved. He demonstrated mathematically that the number of positive and negative instances required varies as a function of the number of instances that are relevant to the concept, the total number of values used for each dimension, and the number of correct values for the relevant dimensions. Hovland provided examples of conditions where only 2 positive but 625 negative instances would be required to define a concept and where 5 positive and 2 negative instances would be required.

In an empirical investigation Hovland and Weiss (1953) used exactly the number of predicted instances necessary to define a conjunctive concept to compare the effectiveness of different combinations of positive and negative instances. Problems were solved more easily when only positive instances were presented than when only negative instances were presented. The use of both positive and negative instances resulted in solutions that were of intermediate difficulty.

Bruner and others (1956), however, have argued that with disjunctive concepts the relative values of positive and negative instances would favor a larger proportion of negative over positive instances. In disjunctive-concept formation, a negative instance eliminates a larger number of possible concepts. Nonetheless, subjects tended, even when involved in a disjunctive-concept-formation task, to prefer (incorrectly) to use positive instances to form concepts.

In a later investigation Huttenlocher (1962) arranged experimental conditions to control for the amount of information presented to subjects per instance. She found that negative instances resulted in highly efficient learning with conjunctive concepts if there were equivalent amounts of information provided per instance.

Virtually all investigators have agreed that increasing the number of irrelevant cues has a detrimental effect on concept learning (Lordahl, 1961; Braley, 1962; Bourne & others, 1965; Bulgarella & Archer, 1962), with one exception (McKay, 1964). Still, a question may be raised concerning a possible interaction between the number of irrelevant stimuli presented and their obviousness. Archer (1962) found that concept learning was facilitated if relevant information was obvious. Shore and Sechrest (1961) concluded that repetition of instances was desirable if the concept was based on less-obvious characteristics of instances.

The sequencing of negative and positive instances has been shown to have an important effect on concept acquisition. Huttenlocher (1962) found significant differences in learning depending upon whether subjects are first presented with a negative or a positive instance. She found, in contrast to findings by Bruner and others (1956), on disjunctive-concept formation, that a negative-to-positive sequence was more efficient than a positive-to-negative sequence was; differences between a positive and negative sequence and two positives were not significant, and both were more significant than a series presenting two negative instances. Sechrest and Wallace (1962) found no significant difference between the performance of subjects asked to utilize information by a single positive instance and that of three other groups, of which one group received a positive instance with a list of remaining possible hypotheses on the nature of the concept, another received a positive instance and a list of hypotheses which included those eliminated by the first positive instance, and a third experienced a positive instance and the elimination of all instances negative to the concept.

The rate of forgetting was lower for instances

presented early in a sequence than for those presented later, according to Cahill and Hovland (1960). They found that subjects who had a greater number of memory errors than the average also had greater difficulty in acquiring the concept.

In teaching the concept "gross national product," Newton and Hickey (1965) found performance to be faster when the principle was given first and subconcepts (consumption and investment spending) were learned together rather than separately. Stern (1965) found that kindergarten children who rehearse concepts but not instance labels were superior in learning but not on transfer tests to those who did not rehearse; first-grade children did better in both a learning and a transfer task under concept-rehearsal conditions; it was easier for children to learn a relatively large number of concepts with few instances of each than it was to learn few concepts with larger numbers of instances.

The effects of allowing subjects to view instances of concepts while in the process of learning them was studied by Bourne and others (1964). By exposing different numbers of stimuli on each trial, they found that performance improved with increases in the number of instances made available. They concluded that the effect of stimulus availability is to reduce memory errors. In an earlier investigation, Cahill and Hovland (1960) found the simultaneous presentation of concepts to be more effective than the successive presentation of instances. Bourne and Parker (1964) provided empirical data to support their hypothesis that subjects will learn a concept more readily if information is embodied in a single, compact figure than if the same information is presented in a set of discrete units.

CONCEPT ATTAINMENT IN SCHOOL SUBJECTS. Since the publication of David Russell's entry CONCEPTS in the 1950 edition of this encyclopedia, much important research has been conducted on concept attainment in various school subjects. In *The Process of Education*, Bruner (1960) argued that "any subject can be taught effectively in some intellectually honest form to any child at any stage of development." Although that is perhaps an overgeneralization, Bruner was attempting to point out that the school curriculum should be organized by its logical and psychological structure. The child is ready to learn when the teacher is ready to teach.

Gagné (1965) has also argued that the curriculum should be based upon a mapping of the sequences of learning, beginning first with the objectives and working backward to determine prerequisites. Concept learning requires the prerequisite learnings of multiple discriminations, verbal associations, chaining, stimulus-response learning, and operant conditioning.

Developing Concepts in Mathematics. Before it is possible to study the development of mathematical concepts it is necessary to identify them. Lovell (1966) classified mathematical concepts as (1) pure concepts (numbers and their relationships); (2) notional concepts (methods of expressing numbers such as the use of zero as a "place holder"); and (3) concepts of length, weight, time, etc. According to Lovell, concepts of number and length are learned informally whereas notional concepts develop in an informal-formal sequence.

Suppes and McKnight (1961) and Suppes and Ginsberg (1962), however, have shown that the incidental learning of mathematical concepts is not effective and that the prior learning of one concept did not facilitate the acquisition of a related concept. For these investigators, mathematical-concept development is not a matter to be left to chance. Similarly, Pace (1961) found that systematic instruction in solving problems was more effective than was the provision of many examples of problems for pupils to solve.

Sax and Ottina (1958) found it advantageous to have the development of concepts precede the learning of computational skills. Tests of arithmetic concepts and skills were administered at the end of grades 3 through 8 to pupils from a "progressive" and a "conventional" school. Significant differences were found between the two groups on the concept test at the end of Grades 7 and 8, in favor of the progressive-school children even though they were not familiar with formal computational procedures until the fifth grade.

Based upon a factor-analytic study involving 389 children in a summer program for culturally deprived children, Caldwell and Soule (1965) were able to extract three factors: personal-social responsiveness, associative vocabulary, and concept activation. Concept activation was subdivided into numerical and sensory categories.

In an investigation using a scalogram technique, Wohlwill (1960) found three stages in the learning of number concepts: a stage where number is discriminated perceptually, a stage where mediating structures representing individual cardinal numbers are formed, and a stage where number is a superordinate concept embodying an awareness of relationships among integers and of more complex properties of this dimension. The ability to count by rote preceded the ability to count objects by pointing. Both Caldwell and Soule (1965) and Terman and Merrill (1960 found rote numerical skills to precede the ability to count objects.

Chase (1960) found that knowledge of concepts was necessary in learning problem-solving skills. He also found it necessary for children to learn computational skills and to learn to observe detail.

At the secondary level, Smith (1959) found chronological age to be unrelated to a test on limits although mental age correlated positively with the same criterion. Leake (1962) found that pupils in grades 7 to 9 had already acquired considerable knowledge of sample space, probability of a simple event, and probability of the union of two or more mutually exclusive events without formal instruction. These conclusions are, of course, dependent upon the degree of sophistication demanded by the tests. Some informal notions about probability exist in the young child who has learned the meaning of the term "sometimes," although the child may have only primitive concepts of the mathematics of probability.

The Development of Science Concepts. The development of science concepts has received less attention in the literature than that of mathematics concepts. Perhaps one reason is that concepts necessary in mathematics are more obvious than those necessary in science. The identification of science concepts is made even more complex when one considers the many meanings of concepts as used in the literature of science education. Novak (1966) has stated that a concept is often used in the literature with "conceptual scheme, theme, organizational thread, and major principle." What the National Science Teachers Association has called "conceptual schemes of science" (Novak, 1966) would be classified as principles by Gagné (1965). For example, the statement "All matter is composed of units called fundamental particles" is a chain of at least four concepts: matter, composed, units, and fundamental particles.

As with the development of mathematical concepts, science concepts at the elementary level have received greater emphasis than they have at the secondary level. Young (1958) found that at grade 3, boys scored significantly higher on a test measuring the understanding of science concepts than girls did but that differences were not to be found by grade 6. She also found that at least one-fourth of eight- and nine-year-olds were ready for advanced work in science, that misconceptions about atomic energy were prevalent, and that the impact of communications media on the science concepts of children was evident.

In a study concerned with the development of scientific concepts among gifted children, Garone (1960) kept logs of the children's reasoning processes. He found that appropriate problem-solving activities can improve children's science concepts.

Inbody (1963) analyzed the responses of 50 kindergarten children on a task designed to elicit scientific explanations of natural phenomena. He found that each child tended to use a particular style of explanation (causal, verbal without supporting examples, animistic, or descriptive) although more than one type of explanation might be given. King (1963) administered questionnaires to children from 5 to 12 years of age concerning such concepts as length, weight, time, direction, volume, mechanical principles, living things, and shadows. The relationship between volume and weight was not clearly grasped, but children did improve with age in estimating time and distance.

That children do not learn concepts when simply exposed to experiments without teachers' comments was found by Butts (1963). One of the most promising attempts at teaching scientific concepts was developed by Suchman (1961). By presenting his subjects with a puzzling or ambiguous situation (often a film), a state of dissonance was created. Subjects were then given training in asking relevant and meaningful questions to aid in developing concepts and understandings.

An interesting use of computers to help determine whether a given science concept can be understood by elementary-school children has been suggested by Smith (1962). By running an item analysis on a standardized test of science achievement and by comparing the results with national norms, a decision matrix was developed to accept or reject a given concept for inclusion in the curriculum.

Almost no empirical research has been published on the development of science concepts at the secondary-school level. Hurd and Rowe (1964), reviewing the literature in secondary-school science for the period 1961 to 1964, concluded that "there was no direct research on formation of scientific concepts or on ways in which a student learns science."

The Development of Concepts in Other Curriculum Areas. From the period 1960 to the present, there has been an almost complete lack of research interest in concept formation in areas other than mathematics and science, although Gagné (1965) has attempted to develop learning structures in foreign-language teaching and in English.

Generally, the published material on concept formation in the social studies, fine and industrial arts, and in foreign-language teaching has tended to be vague or weak in experimental design or has included suggestions for innovations without evidence to support them.

Nonetheless, there are published studies on concept formation which, although few in number, are scholarly in approach and execution. Wallach (1959), for example, has suggested five questions that, if put to the experimental test, should do much to improve the understanding of art concepts. Nelson (1965) has suggested a "concept unit" approach in the social studies curriculum. Instead of using chronological units (exploratory period, Reconstruction, New Deal) or topical units (modern man, Bill of Rights), the concept unit involves an interdisciplinary approach to such concepts as progress and freedom. In a very interesting empirical study, Gill (1964) investigated some common misconceptions of high school students about United States history. A range of 13,000 years (median of 470) was found in response to the question "How long ago did Christopher Columbus live?" Similar investigations are needed in all areas of the curriculum.

DEVELOPMENTAL INVESTIGATIONS OF CONCEPT ACQUISITION. Certainly the works of Jean Piaget, the Swiss psychologist, have stimulated a great number of investigations into the developmental sequences of concept acquisition. Because many of his earlier works (Piaget, 1926, 1928) were not well controlled and because the number of cases was either not mentioned or was extremely small, many of Piaget's early formulations have encouraged educators and psychologists to replicate his studies with more sophisticated controls, which have led to somewhat different conclusions (McCarthy, 1930; Oakes, 1947; Ezer, 1962).

Central to Piaget's theories is the notion of fixed developmental periods not to be confused with specific age ranges, although he does suggest limits. The first developmental period is called the period of sensory-motor intelligence and covers roughly the ages from birth to two years. In this period concepts at first appear as gross sensations later to become differentiated. The child is egocentric in the sense that the world is considered as an extension of the self. Late in this period he is able to separate common objects from himself when they are no longer in sight.

A second period (variously referred to as the period of preconceptual thought and as the period of representational thought) occurs between the ages of two and four years. It is in this period that the child learns symbolism and what Piaget calls preconcepts. These preconcepts are concrete, unstable, static, and irreversible.

The period of intuitive thought occurs betweeen the ages of four and seven. During this period the child is still unable to counterbalance the effects of his perceptions by means of logic and past experience. The child believes in the reality of the magician's tricks.

In a fourth developmental period (period of concrete operations—ages 7 to 11), the child is capable of using logical (operational) thoughts. These thoughts involve a series of operations such as addition, subtraction, multiplication, equality, and inequality. It is in this period that the child learns about relations, classes, identities, etc.

The final period is called the period of formal operations and occurs between the ages of 11 and 15. The child in this period is capable of using adult logic and symbolic processes.

Much of the work done on concept formation has been concerned with validating Piaget's developmental periods. Rather than refer to these studies in general, they will be reviewed here by topic: number and quantity, time, causality, length and size, and logic.

Number and Quantity. In *The Child's Conception of Number,* Piaget (1952) showed his subjects water poured into two differently shaped containers and asked them to estimate which contained the larger amount. In the first stage of concept development, the shape of the container markedly affected how subjects perceived quantity. In a second stage, some subjects were able at times to see that shape is irrelevant. In a final stage some subjects were able to use their past experience to form an adult concept of quantity.

In the same work Piaget dealt with the development of the number concept. Given a row of n objects, the subject is asked to construct a row containing the same number of objects. In the first stage, subjects make a row of the same *length* as the model but pay little attention to the number of objects. In the second stage of development, subjects can see a one-to-one correspondence between the number of objects in the model and the number to be placed next to each object. The third stage involves the actual counting of objects in the model.

In a replication study, Elkind (1964) found that Piaget's theories could be validated empirically. Regular increases in the child's ability to deal with numbers were noted. The findings of Lovell and Ogilvie (1961) also supported Piaget's main contentions concerning the development of volume concepts.

Time. One of the most interesting conclusions Piaget was able to draw concerned the development of time concepts (Piaget, 1955). Evidently, children confuse time with both speed and the movement of objects; they will not admit the simultaneity of both stopping and starting of two objects if, for example, the velocities of the two objects differ. Piaget also concluded that children estimate the ages of humans by their size. In a replication study, Lovell and Slater (1960) substantiated many of Piaget's conclusions.

Causality. In *The Child's Conception of Physical Causality,* Piaget (1930) identified five stages in the child's development of causal concepts. In explaining the movements of clouds, for example, the sequence proceeds as follows: a magical phase in which the child makes the clouds move by his walking; an animistic and artificial stage where God or man made the clouds move; a third stage where the clouds are able to move by themselves conditioned by moral and physical causes; a fourth stage in which the clouds are pushed by the wind although the wind is not a part of the clouds; and a fifth stage where a scientific explanation is provided.

In an excellent study, Ezer (1962) was, in general, unable to support many of these stages. Evidently, animistic and anthropomorphic explanations are a function of experience, with very religious children offering a significantly larger number of them than do those coming from less religious backgrounds.

Length and Size. In *The Child's Conception of Geometry,* Piaget and others (1960) identified five stages in learning to build a block tower from a model placed on a higher platform than the subject's. In the earliest stage the subject simply estimates the number of blocks needed. He fails to note that the platform the model is on is not of the same height as his work table. In a second stage the child uses himself as a measure of tower height. The third stage involves using measures other than himself (a stick) to estimate the height of the tower. In a fourth stage he is able to use a stick longer than the height of the model. In a fifth and final stage the subject can use a smaller stick than the model.

Results of research by Braine (1959) supported the developmental sequences described by Piaget. Subjects were asked to select a sequence of colored disks identical to that of a model. As Piaget predicted, subjects were unable to match long sequences before about the ages of six or seven. No child younger than four in the sample was able to perform the task.

Logic. Some of the most interesting of Piaget's works has been done on the development of logical reasoning (Piaget & Inhelder, 1959). Unlike some of Piaget and Inhelder's older investigations, the later ones were marked by larger numbers of cases and by greater sophistication in questioning subjects. Piaget and Inhelder indicated that logical classification systems develop in two stages: a figural collections stage where classifications are in a constant state of flux and where a figure is labeled only after it is constructed, and a nonfigural collections stage where subjects classify objects on the basis of similarities.

Few replication studies are available to either confirm or reject Piaget and Inhelder's double-stage theory. Lovell's study (1961), however, confirmed the general sequence.

It is not possible within space limitations to present more than a general introduction to Piaget's contributions to concept formation. For general references on Piaget and on replication studies, the reader is referred to Flavell's excellent treatment (1963).

Gilbert Sax
University of Washington

References

Amster, Harriett. "Effect of Instructional Set and Variety of Instances on Children's Learning." *J Ed Psychol* 57:74–85; 1966.

Anderson, Richard C., and Ausubel, David P. (Eds.) *Readings in the Psychology of Cognition*. Holt, 1965. p. 395–405.

Angell, George W. "The Effect of Immediate Knowledge of Results on Final Examination Scores in Freshman Chemistry." *J Ed Res* 42:391–4; 1949.

Archer, E. James. "Concept Identification as a Function of Obviousness of Relevant and Irrelevant Information." *J Exp Psychol* 63:616–20; 1962.

Archer, E. James. "The Psychological Nature of Concepts." In Klausmeier, Herbert J., and Harris, Chester W. (Eds.) *Analyses of Concept Learning*. Academic, 1966. p. 37–63.

Ausubel, David P. *The Psychology of Meaningful Verbal Learning*. Grune, 1963.

Bourne, Lyle E., Jr., and Haygood, Robert C. "Effects of Intermittent Reinforcement of an Irrelevant Dimension and Task Complexity upon Concept Identification." *J. Exp Psychol* 60:371–5; 1960.

Bourne, Lyle E., Jr., and Parker, B. Kent. "Differences Among Modes for Portraying Stimulus Information in Concept Identification." *Psychonomic Sci* 1:209–10; 1964.

Bourne, Lyle E., Jr., and Pendleton, R. Brian. "Concept Identification as a Function of Completeness and Probability of Information Feedback." *J Exp Psychol* 56:413–20; 1958.

Bourne, Lyle E., Jr., and others. "Concept Learning as a Function of Availability of Previously Presented Information." *J Exp Psychol* 67:439–48; 1964.

Bourne, Lyle E., Jr., and others. "Concept Identification: The Effects of Varying Length and Information Components of the Intertrial Interval." *J Exp Psychol* 69:624–9; 1965.

Braine, Martin S. "The Ontogeny of Certain Logical Operations: Piaget's Formulation Examined by Nonverbal Methods." *Psychol Monogr* 73:No. 5; 1959.

Braley, Loy S. "Some Conditions Influencing the Acquisition and Utilization of Cues." *J Exp Psychol* 64:62–6; 1962.

Bruner, Jerome S. *The Process of Education*. Harvard U Press, 1960.

Bruner, Jerome S., and others. *A Study of Thinking*. Science Editions, Inc., 1956. 330p.

Bulgarella, Rosaria G., and Archer, E. J. "Correct Identification of Auditory Stimuli as a Function of Amount of Relevant and Irrelevant Information." *J Exp Psychol* 63:254–7; 1962.

Butts, David P. "The Degree to Which Children Conceptualize from Science Experience." *Sci Teaching* 1:135–43; 1963.

Byers, Joe L. "Hypothesis Behavior in Concept Attainment." *J Ed Psychol* 56:337–42; 1965.

Cahill, Hugh E., and Hovland, Carl I. "The Role of Memory in the Acquisition of Concepts." *J Exp Psychol* 59:137–44; 1960.

Caldwell, Bettye M., and Soule, Donald S. *The Preschool Inventory*. State U New York, 1965. 22p.

Chase, Clinton I. "The Position of Certain Variables in the Prediction of Problem-solving in Arithmetic." *J Ed Res* 54:9–14; 1960.

Elkind, David. "Quantity Conceptions in Junior and Senior High School Students." *Child Develop* 32:551–60; 1961.

Elkind, David. "Discrimination, Seriation, and Numeration of Size and Dimensional Differences in Young Children: Piaget Replication Study VI." *J Genet Psychol* 104:275–96; 1964.

Ezer, Melvin. "The Effect of Religion upon Children's Responses to Questions Involving Physical Causality." In Rosenblith, Judy F., and Allensmith, Wesley. (Eds.) *The Causes of Behavior*. Allyn and Bacon, 1962. p. 481–7.

Flavell, John H. *The Developmental Psychology of Jean Piaget*. Van Nostrand, 1963. 472p.

French, Elizabeth G., and Thomas, Francis H. "The Relation of Achievement Motivation to Problem-Solving Affectiveness." *J Abn Social Psychol* 56:45–8; 1958.

Gagné, Robert M. *The Conditions of Learning*. Holt, 1965. 308p.

Gardner, Riley W., and Schoen, Robert A. "Differentiation and Abstraction in Concept Formation." *Psychol Monogr* 76:No. 41; 1962.

Garone, John Edward. "Acquiring Knowledge and Attaining Understanding of Children's Scientific Concept Development." *Sci Ed* 44:104–7; 1960.

Gill, Clark C. "Fractured Facts: How High School Students Interpret Indefinite Quantitative Concepts in United States History." *Clearing House* 39:35–9; 1964.

Goldstein, Kurt, and Scheerer, Martin. "Abstract and Concrete Behavior: An Experimental Study with Special Tests." *Psychol Monogr* 53:No. 2; 1941.

Goss, Albert E. "Verbal Mediating Response and Concept Formation." *Psychol R* 68:248–74; 1961.

Guilford, J. P. "Three Faces of Intellect." *Am Psychologist* 14:469–79; 1959.

Hovland, Carl I. "A Communication Analysis of Concept Learning." *Psychol R* 59:461–72; 1952.

Hovland, Carl I., and Weiss, Walter. "Transmission of Information Concerning Concepts Through Positive and Negative Instances." *J. Exp Psychol* 45:175–82; 1953.

Hull, Clark L. "Quantitative Aspects of the Evolution of Concepts." *Psychol Monogr* No. 123:1–86; 1920.

Hunt, Earl B., and others. *Experiments in Induction.* Academic, 1966. 247p.

Hurd, Paul De Hart, and Rowe, Mary Budd. "Science in the Secondary School." *R Ed Res* 34:293; 1964.

Huttenlocher, Janellen. "Some Effects of Negative Instances on the Formation of Simple Concepts." *Psychol Reports* 11:35–42; 1962.

Inbody, Donald. "Children's Understanding of Natural Phenomena." *Sci Ed* 47:270–8; 1963.

Johnson, Donald M., and O'Reilly, Charlene A. "Concept Attainment in Children: Classifying and Defining." *J Ed Psychol* 55:71–4; 1964.

Kagan, Jerome S., and others. "Psychological Significance of Styles of Conceptualization." *Monogr Social Res Child Develop* 28:73–112; 1963.

Kendler, Howard H. "The Concept of the Concept." In Melton, Arthur W. (Ed.) *Categories of Human Learning.* Academic, 1964. p. 211–36.

Kendler, Howard H., and D'Amato, May F. "A Comparison of Reversal Shifts and Nonreversal Shifts in Human Concept Behavior." *J Exp Psychol* 4:165–74; 1955.

Kendler, Howard H., and Kendler, Tracy S. "Vertical and Horizontal Processes in Problem-solving." *Psychol R* 69:1–16; 1962.

Kendler, Tracy S., and Kendler, Howard H. "Reversal and Nonreversal Shifts in Kindergarten Children." *J Exp Psychol* 58:56–60; 1959.

Kendler, Tracy S., and Kendler, Howard H. "Reversal and Nonreversal Shifts in Nursery School Children." *J Compar Physiol* 53:83–8; 1960.

King, W. H. "The Development of Scientific Concepts in Children. II." *Br J Ed Psychol* 33:240–52; 1963.

Kittell, Jack Edward. "An Experimental Study of the Effects of External Direction During Learning on Transfer and Retention of Principles." *J Ed Psychol* 48:391–405; 1957.

Kounin, Jacob S., and Gump, Paul V. "The Comparative Influence of Punitive and Nonpunitive Teachers upon Children's Concepts of School Misconduct." *J Ed Psychol* 52:44–9; 1961.

Leake, Lowell, Jr. "The Status of Three Concepts of Probability in Children of Seventh, Eighth, and Ninth Grades." Doctoral dissertation. U Wisconsin, 1962.

Lordahl, Daniel S. "Concept Identification Using Simultaneous Auditory and Visual Signals." *J Exp Psychol* 62:283–90; 1961.

Lovell, K. *The Growth of Basic Mathematical and Scientific Concepts in Children.* U London Press, 1961. 154p.

Lovell, K. "Concepts in Mathematics." In Klausmeier, Herbert J., and Harris, Chester W. (Eds.) *Analyses of Concept Learning.* Academic, 1966. p. 210.

Lovell, K., and Ogilvie, E. "The Growth of the Concept of Volume in Junior School Students." *J Child Psychol Psychiatry* 2:118–26; 1961.

Lovell, K., and Slater, A. "The Growth of the Concept of Time: A Comparative Study." *J Child Psychol Psychiatry* 1:179–90; 1960.

Mannix, J. B. "The Number Concepts of a Group of E. S. N. Children." *Br J Ed Psychol* 30:180–1; 1960.

Mansfield, Lucile D. H. "The Learning of Abstract, Function, and Concrete Relations Between Words." Doctoral dissertation. U Pittsburgh, 1960.

McCarthy, Dorothea. *The Language Development of the Preschool Child.* U Minnesota Press, 1930.

McKay, Charles E. "Concept Formation as a Function of Response Provoking Cues." *Psychol* 1:18–24; 1964.

Merrifield, Philip R. "An Analysis of Concepts from the Point of View of the Structure of Intellect." In Klausmeier, Herbert J., and Harris, Chester W. (Eds.) *Analyses of Concept Learning.* Academic, 1966. p. 19–33.

Meyer, Susan R. "A Test of the Principles of 'Activity,' 'Immediate Reinforcement,' and 'Guidance' as Instrumented by Skinner's Teaching Machine." Doctoral dissertation. U Buffalo, 1960.

Newton, John M., and Hickey, Albert E. "Sequence Effects in Programmed Learning of a Verbal Concept." *J Ed Psychol* 56:140–7; 1965.

Nelson, Jack L. "The Concept Unit in the Social Studies." *Social Stud* 56:46–8; 1965.

Novak, Joseph D. "The Role of Concepts in Science Teaching." In Klausmeier, Herbert J., and Harris, Chester W. (Eds.) *Analyses of Concept Learning.* Academic, 1966. p. 239–54.

Oakes, Mervin E. "Children's Explanations of Natural Phenomena." *Teach Col Contr Ed* No. 926; 1947.

Olson, Leroy A. "Concept Attainment of High School Sophomores." *J Ed Psychol* 54:213–6; 1963.

Osgood, Charles E. *Method and Theory of Experimental Psychology.* Oxford U Press, 1953.

Osgood, Charles E., and others. *The Measurement of Meaning.* U Illinois Press, 1957. 342p.

Osler, Sonia F., and Fivel, Myrna Weiss. "Concept Attainment. I: The Role of Age and Intelligence in Concept Attainment by Induction." *J Exp Psychol* 62:1–8; 1961.

Osler, Sonia F., and Trautman, Grace E. "Concept Attainment. II: Effect of Stimulus Complexity upon Concept Attainment at Two Levels of Intelligence." *J Exp Psychol* 62:9–13; 1961.

Pace, Angela. "Understanding and the Ability to Solve Problems." *Arithmetic Teach* 8:226–33; 1961.

Piaget, Jean. *The Language and Thought of the Child.* Harcourt, 1926. 246p.

Piaget, Jean. *Judgment and Reasoning in the Child.* Harcourt, 1928. 260p.

Piaget, Jean. *The Child's Conception of Physical Causality.* Harcourt, 1930. 309p.

Piaget, Jean. *The Child's Conception of Number.* Routledge, 1952. 248p.

Piaget, Jean. "The Development of Time Concepts

in the Child." In Hoch, P. H., and Zubin, Joseph (Eds.) *Psychopathology of Childhood.* Grune, 1955. p. 34–44.

Piaget, Jean, and Inhelder, Barbel. *La Genèse des structures logiques élementaires: Classifications et sériations.* Delachaux et Niestlé, 1959. 295p.

Piaget, Jean, and others. *The Child's Conception of Geometry.* Basic Books, 1960. p. 27–66.

Podell, Harriet Amster. "Two Processes of Concept Formation." *Psychol Monogr* 72:1–20; 1958.

Price-Williams, D. R. "Abstract and Concrete Modes of Classification in a Primitive Society." *Br J Ed Psychol* 32:50–61; 1962.

Runquist, Willard N., and Hutt, Valorie H. "Verbal Concept Learning in High School Students with Pictorial and Verbal Representation of Stimuli." *J Ed Psychol* 52:108–11; 1961.

Russell, David. "Concepts." In Monroe, Walter S. (Ed.) *Encyclopedia of Educational Research,* rev. ed. Macmillan, 1950. p. 323–33.

Sax, Gilbert. "Concept Acquisition as a Function of Differing Schedules and Delays of Reinforcement." *J Ed Psychol* 51:32–6; 1960.

Sax, Gilbert, and Ottina, John R. "The Arithmetic Achievement of Pupils Differing in Experience." *California J Ed Res* 9:15–9; 1958.

Sechrest, Lee, and Wallace, John. "Assimilation and Utilization of Information in Concept Attainment Under Varying Conditions of Information Presentation." *J Ed Psychol* 53:157–64; 1962.

Shore, Eugene, and Sechrest, Lee. "Concept Attainment as a Function of Number of Positive Instances Presented." *J Ed Psychol* 52:303–7; 1961.

Smith, Gary R. "Use of Probability Statements." *Sci Teach* 29:33–7; 1962.

Smith, Lihi Tingen. *The Role of Maturity in Acquiring a Concept of Limit in Mathematics.* Stanford U Press, 1959.

Smoke, K. L. "An Objective Study of Concept Formation." *Psychol Monogr* 42:No. 191; 1932.

Smoke, K. L. "Negative Instances in Concept Learning." *J Exp Psychol* 6:583–8; 1933.

Stern, Carolyn. "Labeling and Variety in Concept Identification With Young Children." *J Ed Psychol* 56:235–40; 1965.

Suchman, J. Richard. "Inquiry Training: Building Skills for Autonomous Discovery." *Merrill-Palmer Q Behavior Develop* 7:147–69; 1961.

Suppes, Patrick, and Ginsberg, Rose. "Experimental Studies of Mathematical Concept Formation in Young Children." *Sci Ed* 46:230–40; 1962.

Suppes, Patrick, and McKnight, Blair A. "Sets and Numbers in Grade One, 1959–60." *Arithmetic Teach* 9:96–7; 1961.

Terman, Louis M., and Merrill, Maud A. *Stanford-Binet Intelligence Scale.* 3rd. ed. Houghton, 1960. 363p.

Underwood, Benton J. "Some Relationships Between Concept Learning and Verbal Learning." In Klausmeier, Herbert J., and Harris, Chester W. (Eds.) *Analyses of Concept Learning.* Academic, 1966. p. 51–63.

Wallace, John. "Concept Dominance, Type of Feedback, and Intensity of Feedback as Related to Concept Attainment." *J Ed Psychol* 55:159–66; 1964.

Wallach, Michael A. "Art, Science, and Representation: Toward an Experimental Psychology of Aesthetics." *J Aesthetics Art Criticism* 18:159–73; 1959.

Wallach, Michael A., and Kogan, Nathan. *Modes of Thinking in Young Children.* Holt, 1965.

Wittrock, M. C. "Verbal Stimuli in Concept Formation: Learning by Discovery." *J Ed Psychol* 54:183–90; 1963.

Wohlwill, J. F. "A Study of the Development of the Number Concept by Scalogram Analysis." *J Genet Psychol* 97:345–77; 1960.

Wolfgang, A., and others. "Anxiety and Misinformation Feedback in Concept Identification." *Perceptual Motor Skills* 14:135–43; 1962.

Young, Doris. "Atomic Energy Concepts of Children in Third and Sixth Grade." *Sch Sci Math* 58:535–9; 1958.

COOPERATION, COORDINATION, AND CONTROL IN HIGHER EDUCATION

In the consideration of the general topic of cooperation, coordination, and control as it relates to the enterprise of higher education and to individual institutions and groups of institutions, it is useful to distinguish among those three terms. Points of misunderstanding and debate often arise from a misconception of the use of these terms or from their use as synonyms.

Glenny (1959) defined coordination as "the act of regulating and combining so as to give harmonious results." He then broadened this definition by suggesting that it implies some degree of integration, centralization, and force. Glenny differentiates among (1) the single-board type of coordination, which implies a governing agency, (2) boards which are empowered to coordinate and control selected activities of institutions but are restrained from general governance or administrative powers, and (3) those which are organized purely as voluntary systems with representatives from individual institutions meeting to coordinate activities of common concern.

Moos and Rourke (1959) identify five major means of coordination: (1) directly by legislatures or agencies, (2) by voluntary cooperation, (3) by consolidation, (4) by central governing boards with direct authority over day-to-day operations, and (5) by master boards with supervisory power over regular governing boards.

Although it might be well to retain simply the one term "coordination" to cover the broad spectrum that ranges from no relationships to voluntary cooperation to voluntarily or legally imposed coordination to the total control by a single board, nevertheless, the use of the three terms "cooperation," "coordination," and "control" to describe the variety of practices will probably facilitate general discussion of the issues.

Several authors who have presented historical analyses and summaries of the development of coordination and control suggest that whereas the early agencies tended to be of the central-governing type for statewide higher education, the trend since 1950 clearly appears to be toward the coordinating-agency approach, leaving the matter of internal control to individual boards of trustees of institutions (Chambers, 1965; Glenny, 1959; Klein, 1938).

Most analysts of the situation generally conclude that although coordination of institutional roles, functions, and future developments is necessary, great importance is attached to the retention of institutional autonomy (Glenny, 1959).

Between 1896 and 1948 at least ten states enacted legislative statutes abolishing institutional governing boards and creating one board to govern all. Since 1948 no state has abolished all institutional governing boards and set up a single board. In New York the 1960 Governor's Committee on Higher Education recommended that the local institutional boards be reconstituted and given substantial powers (Chambers, 1965). The 1965 Michigan constitution provides for individual boards for each institution and lodges coordination in the state board of education.

HISTORICAL PERSPECTIVE. Numerous reasons may be identified for the continued emphasis on the development of coordinating agencies. Glenny (1959) suggests that there are two—namely, the increasing complexity of higher education and the increasing size of state government. Moos and Rourke (1959) point out that the idea of coordination and unification goes back to the creation of the State Board of Regents in New York in 1784 and to the charter of the University of Georgia in 1785. They suggest that the trend toward centralization probably began in 1896 with the establishment in South Dakota of a single board of control over its institutions of higher education. By 1932, 12 states had adopted some system of unified supervision (Hill, 1934; Martorana & Hollis, 1960; Glenny, 1962; Stevens, 1926; Byrne, 1940; Hungate, 1964).

One of the very early attempts at a single system of education including higher education was the act proposing the establishment of the University of Michigania in 1817 (Hofstadter & Smith, 1961). Envisioned under this act was a total system of education from the early years through graduate and professional schools. This idea never came to complete fruition in Michigan.

Bibliographies and general references with respect to coordination and control of higher education are found in a number of sources, including the works by Henderson and Chambers (1960), Meeth (1965), Eells and Hollis (1960), Henderson (1960), Wilson (1965), McConnell (1962), and Brumbaugh (1961).

Statutory or voluntary coordination and control activities generally derive from either the legal act setting them up or a charter among the institutions. The 1960 Donahue Higher Education Act in California sets up the structure of California higher education, including the Coordinating Council for Higher Education, the junior-college system, the California state college system, and the University of California (*Donahue Higher Education Act as Amended*, 1960). Comprehensive and extensive summaries of statutory acts are to be found in Martorana and Hollis (1961). Glenny (1959) presented a careful analysis of some of the legal provisions establishing coordinating systems. The Coordinating Committee for Higher Education in Wisconsin (Wisconsin, State of, 1964) has a set of by-laws (Boles, 1956). Recently, changes have been made by the Wisconsin legislature in the composition of the coordination board. (Other useful statutory references are to be found in Blackwell, 1956, 1961; Chambers, 1964; Oregon State Board of Higher Education, 1956; and the U.S. Office of Education, 1964.)

An illustration of a statutory act by a legislature providing for participation in regional cooperation is that of the Oklahoma House of Representatives (1957), an act making appropriations for regional cooperation with other Southern states in the Southern Regional Education Board.

TYPES OF CONTROL, COORDINATION AND COOPERATION. Detailed analyses and summaries of the various types of arrangements with respect to cooperation, coordination, and control are given in a number of sources, including the works by Glenny (1959, 1962), Moos and Rourke (1959), Stevens (1926), Chambers (1961), The Ohio Legislative Service Commission (1963), Hungate (1964), and Martorana and Hollis (1960). Some of the major changes during the past five years in such states as Ohio, Michigan, and Florida suggest the rapidly changing character of the concept and idea of coordination and control.

Hungate (1964) presents a very detailed, statistical summary of the various organizational patterns and the extent of enrollment under each of these patterns throughout the country. In the discussion of these patterns Hungate concludes that in their zeal for centralization, states have given to centralized state agencies much authority over higher education that impedes its management and in some instances permits noneducational personnel to impose their judgment over that of designated educational personnel. He points out that the trend in management today in business and industry is toward decentralization of authority. Further, he suggests that in recent legislation of some states there is evidence of recognition of this trend in public higher education.

In general, the literature tends to categorize the various arrangements as follows:

1. A single board for all institutions in a given state.

2. Several boards, but each responsible for a number of institutions.

3. Individual boards of control but with one coordinating board.

4. Individual boards but with two or three co-

ordinating units for universities, colleges, and community colleges.

5. Individual boards with a voluntary coordinative unit.

6. Individual boards with no attempt being made to coordinate them.

Russell (1965, 1958) provides detailed analyses and descriptions of various types of arrangements in states as they fall into the above categories. Similar descriptions are given by Chambers (1965) and Glenny (1959).

The three major, statutory efforts in regional coordination are the Southern Regional Education Board, the Western Interstate Commission on Higher Education, and the New England Board of Higher Education. These legal compacts provide for a broad scope of cooperation among the higher-educational institutions of member states. A detailed description of the history and work of the Southern Regional Education Board is given by Sugg and Jones (1960). The Western Interstate Commission has been active in various aspects of higher-education cooperation (McNickle, 1965).

INTERINSTITUTIONAL COOPERATION. In the midst of a historical tradition of autonomy it is interesting to note an upsurge in the effort toward voluntary cooperation among numerous groups of colleges and universities, both public and private. These efforts are, in the main, extralegal in nature and are set up on a purely voluntary basis, although there are instances of public funds being made available for them.

There are several factors which have given rise to an increasing number of cooperative efforts among institutions of higher education (Henry, 1961). First, there are considerations of educational adequacy and effectiveness; second, there are considerations of economy; and, third, there is the desire to maximize use of the available resources. Finally, it is to be observed that the emphasis on research in all of higher education has contributed substantially to cooperative endeavors among colleges and universities.

The various interinstitutional cooperative efforts in research and instruction are described in a number of articles and books, including those by Baskin (1965), Ertell (1957), E. Johnson (1966), Bunn (1964), Donovan (1965), Stewart (1960), and Bailey (1961). Other sources of information are Jamrich (1964) and the Council of State Governments (1963). Useful summaries are also provided by Martorana and others (1961), Messersmith (1962), Cadbury (1966), Blocker (1966), Shirley (1966), Brickman (1966), and Frase (1966). The work of the Committee on Interinstitutional Cooperation of the Big Ten and the University of Chicago is presented by Keenan (1961) and the Committee on Institutional Cooperation (1965). Another type of interinstitutional cooperative effort is indicated in the work of the California and Western Conference cost and statistical study for 1954–55 (*California and Western Conference . . .*, 1956). A description of the work of the Associated Colleges of the Midwest is given by Stewart (1960). A more recent cooperative venture includes two Roman Catholic colleges and 12 other liberal arts colleges in the Midwest. The association perceives itself as a university of 12 liberal arts colleges and provides for a variety of cooperative efforts among them (*New York Times*, 1966).

Eldon L. Johnson (1966) examines the necessary conditions for interinstitutional cooperation. He suggests some imaginative experiments which might be attempted under interinstitutional cooperative efforts by colleges.

A somewhat different type of cooperative endeavor is represented by the opportunity for the development of educational regional laboratories under Title V of the Elementary and Secondary Education Act of 1965. Under this act it is possible to obtain federal funds for a voluntary coordinated effort among institutions of higher learning and public and private school systems in the total realm of education. It is anticipated that perhaps 15 or more of these regional laboratories will be established throughout the country and will be funded substantially so that research and dissemination of research may be accelerated.

Another and perhaps a more elaborate arrangement is exemplified by the Compact for Education recently established. Allen (1966) argues affirmatively for the compact, while Longenecker (1966) suggests some of the reservations which are expressed about it. The compact is described in greater detail in a publication from its office (Education Commission of the States, 1966).

AREAS AND PROCEDURES FOR COOPERATION, COORDINATION, AND CONTROL. In the existing arrangements for cooperation, coordination, and control of institutions of higher education either within individual states or on a regional basis there are a number of areas of responsibility. Glenny (1959), Moos and Rourke (1959), and Hungate (1964) identify the most general of these. They include the areas of finance and budgetary coordination; considerations of facilities needed to provide for enrollment increases, including the establishment of new colleges and the development of new academic programs in existing colleges; and the development of master plans and the carrying on of overall surveys. They include also the coordination of extension services, the coordination of research, and the coordination of overall services to the state. Cooperative planning for use of computers in higher education is discussed by Hamblen and Atchison (1966).

Millett (1966) describes the work of the Ohio Board of Regents and characterizes it as being not authoritatively based but a centralized effort which provides for planned enrollment growth and coordination of program developments.

The establishment of new institutions, including community colleges, sometimes poses problems of coordination. Wells (1966) takes a position in favor of the establishment and development of branches of existing institutions. In general, the literature seems to support a position against branches. Included in this literature are analyses by Russell (1958, 1965), Brumbaugh (1956, 1963), and most of the state surveys referred to in this article.

A general discussion of fiscal control over higher-educational institutions is given by McNeeley (1940). An analysis of some of the problems in fiscal coordination in the state of Michigan is provided by Lederle (1959).

Specific budgetary analysis procedures have been developed by a number of the state coordinating agencies. Russell (1953, 1956a) describes the procedures of the New Mexico Board of Educational Finance. The Texas Commission on Higher Education (1959) has operated under a formal procedure for a number of years. Miller (1962) attempted to analyze possible, uniform fiscal budgetary approaches in the state institutions of Michigan. The Kentucky Council on Public Higher Education (1957) has an agreed-upon procedure for the uniform classification of accounts among its colleges and universities.

Analysis and commentary on fiscal control of higher education are given by Clark (1947) and Christopherson (1955). Specific illustrations of budget analyses by state institutions are to be found in the Colorado Association of State Institutions of Higher Education (1961) and the Oklahoma State Regents for Higher Education (1963).

Either through independently set-up study commissions or through the state coordinating agencies, several states have given considerable attention to the provision of adequate physical plant to accommodate increasing enrollments. Such analyses have been made by Jamrich and Dahnke (1963), Russell (1958), and by the state coordinating agencies in California, Wisconsin, Illinois, and elsewhere.

The development of surveys and master plans for state institutions of higher education by state coordinating agencies is receiving increasing attention (Ohio Board of Regents, 1966). The California Coordinating Council for Higher Education reports on its master plan in an evaluative sense and presents indications of the extent to which it has been implemented in the past five years (California State Department of Education, 1960; Holy & Semans, 1955). In Ohio the Board of Regents received specific recommendations on the extension of programs at the doctoral level in education (Jamrich, 1965a). Brumbaugh (1963) presents an analysis of statewide planning and coordination in higher education with attention to the notion of role and function for institutions of higher education in a given state. Knorr (1965) presents a summary of various papers on long-range planning in higher education, including fiscal planning, and analysis of resources and needs.

Cooperative long-range planning in liberal arts colleges is discussed by McGrath (1964). Long-range physical-facilities needs for small colleges are analyzed by Jamrich (1961).

The issue of community-college and junior-college coordination within a state system is discussed in an HEW, U.S. Office report (1957), in a report of the California Coordinating Council for Higher Education (1965), by B. Lamar Johnson and others (1956), and by Medsker (1960).

The development and the component elements of a master plan have been the subject of discussion by Jamrich (1965b) and Russell (1958) and have been utilized in the specific master plans developed in Illinois, Ohio, and New York. Jamrich (1960) discusses procedures in statewide surveys.

STATE SURVEYS OF HIGHER EDUCATION.

Although the idea of a survey of education on a statewide basis may very well be traceable to Henry Barnard's study of 1844 in Rhode Island and to the first state survey of higher education, which was completed by the Virginia Education Commission in 1912, it is only in recent times that there have been significant numbers of studies of higher education on a statewide or regional basis.

The reasons for the relative recency of such activity are numerous. One reason is that colleges and universities have generally prided themselves on their uniqueness and have avoided rather than welcomed studies which might lead to interinstitutional comparisons. Mass data-collection and data-processing techniques are of relatively recent development. The lack of generally accepted definitions on even such a simple statistic as student enrollment raises doubt about the comparability of data and the fear that the data will be overinterpreted, misinterpreted, or otherwise misused.

Nevertheless, there has been, in the last decade or two, a growing demand for reliable information with respect to the enterprise of higher education. State legislatures, accrediting agencies, institutional administrative officers, and boards of control as well as faculties themselves have been seeking reliable information and data about the operation of their own units.

A survey of higher education is designed to provide data and information for judging the adequacy, effectiveness, and efficiency of some part or all of the operations of an institution or group of institutions and to furnish a basis for assessing future needs and sources of support.

In the last ten years, legislative study commissions have been authorized in more than 20 states. Some notion of the extent and recent development of the state survey movement in higher education can be obtained by noting that between 1956 and 1959 there were approximately 153 surveys completed, whereas between 1909 and 1955 there was a total of 132.

The financial support of statewide studies and surveys is a determining factor of the scope of these surveys. There is a wide variation in the funding of these surveys, as is indicated by the fact that of 55 studies completed or authorized between 1950 and 1959 the range in financial support was from $3,000 to $300,000 for the individual studies (Martorana & Messersmith, 1960).

A number of sources include data on state surveys making it possible to identify for each state the date of the survey, its scope, the sponsoring agency, the financing agency, the amount of funds available, and the areas reported as having been studied (Martorana & Messersmith, 1960; Layton, 1949; Council of State Governments, 1958).

Surveys of some type have been conducted in 43 out of the 50 states in the decade from 1950 to 1960. Since 1960 at least 20 extensive studies have been conducted. In about 30 states there have been 2 or more surveys made, although the scope of these studies has varied. In Illinois, Iowa, and Virginia 5 distinct surveys have been conducted. In California, Florida, Minnesota, and Ohio 4 surveys for each state have been conducted.

About one-half of the surveys might be regarded as "complete" in the sense that they include most of the following broad areas of investigation: (1) enrollment, (2) organization and administration, (3) finance, (4) physical plant, (5) programs, (6) faculty, (7) junior colleges, and (8) control and coordination (Dressel & others, 1961).

State surveys and reports worth noting include those conducted in Georgia (Strayer, 1949); Tennessee (Pierce, 1957); Minnesota (Minnesota Commission on Higher Education, 1950); West Virginia (1958); California (McConnell, 1955); Louisiana (Brumbaugh, 1956); Florida (Brumbaugh & Blee, 1956); Illinois (Russell, 1951; Henry, 1961; Steiner, 1961); Virginia (Martorana, 1959; Russell, 1965); New Jersey (Strayer & Kellogg, 1962); New York (State University of New York, 1965); Kansas (Zook & others, 1923; Keller, 1960; Kansas *Plans* . . ., 1962); Michigan (Russell, 1958); Indiana (Indiana Survey Commission . . ., 1926); and Ohio (Russell, 1956b; Ohio Board of Regents, 1966).

In the state of Illinois the survey idea goes back to 1943, when the General Assembly created the first of several study commissions for this purpose. Other studies were authorized in 1950, 1954, and in 1957. The General Assembly established the present Board of Higher Education as a permanent coordinating and planning agency in 1961. The staff report to the committee recommends a state plan for public higher education in Illinois (Steiner, 1961). This preliminary report suggested a number of areas in which the institutions should continue to work cooperatively, including such areas as off-campus extension work for credit, adult education courses, community services to local governments, presentation of budget materials to state agencies, and the development of a continuous state plan to be maintained by an official state agency.

In 1964 the Board of Higher Education in Illinois presented a master plan for higher education in the state of Illinois (Illinois Board of Higher Education, 1964). This master plan evolved out of depth studies by a number of committees working for the board and consisting of faculty and staff from the various institutions of higher education in Illinois. The plan includes the following:

1. The development of colleges to serve commuter students.

2. The inclusion of two-year colleges in the realm of higher education.

3. Emphasis on the expansion of technical and semitechnical education.

4. Provision for further development of graduate and research programs.

5. Provision for extension and adult education.

6. Emphasis on the need for additional qualified faculty.

7. Provision for a better balance of enrollments at the various state institutions.

8. Provision for rational priorities in capital outlay.

9. Provision for increased utilization of physical facilities.

10. Provision of authority for the Board of Higher Education for planning (but not for administration) of all public higher education in Illinois.

The Michigan Survey of Higher Education (Russell, 1958) provided, through one of the most extensive and intensive studies of higher education to date, detailed data on numerous facets of higher education in the state, both public and private. It presented a number of important recommendations, many of which have been adopted either by statute or in practice by the state or the institutions of higher education. The recommendations included emphasis on greater coordination in the extension services of the state-controlled institutions of Michigan, identification of urgent capital-outlay needs for the various institutions, emphasis on the need for a uniform system of financial accounting and reporting in the state institutions, emphasis on the need for a better balance in instructional programs at the community colleges of the state, a carefully worked out plan of additional community-college development throughout the state, the recommendation that board membership for state-controlled institutions be by appointment of the governor with advice and consent of the senate, the recommendation that each of the state-controlled institutions have its own individual board of control, and the recommendation that the state create and establish a board for the coordination of the state-controlled institutions of higher education in Michigan.

The report on higher education in Florida (Brumbaugh & Blee, 1956) includes recommendations which emphasize the need for developing diversified programs of education beyond the high school, the need for developing a system of public community colleges throughout the state, the need for establishing additional degree granting institutions in certain populous portions of the state, and the need for a statewide board of control for the coordinated supervision of state-controlled higher education in the state.

The Ohio master plan presents a number of specific proposals regarding undergraduate and professional programs, graduate study and research, and the missions and roles of the several institutions. Another study of doctoral degrees in education in the State of Ohio for the Board of Regents made certain specific recommendations (Jamrich, 1965a). The first recommendation was that the Board of Regents establish an advisory panel on advanced graduate study in education. The functions of this panel would be to provide the Board of Regents with continuing evaluative advice regarding the various program proposals which will be received and to consult with the several institutions on proposals which might be submitted. A second recommendation provided for specifics as to where doctoral-degree programs should be established at the present time in the various institutions of Ohio.

A study of the needs of California in higher education (McConnell, 1955) resulted in the development of a master plan for higher education in California. The master plan contained a number of broad recommendations. They included recommendations regarding the structure, function, and coordination of institutions, including the University of California, the state college system, and the junior-college system. It made recommendations regarding selection and retention of students, state scholarships and fellowships, institutional capacities and area needs, levels of utilization of physical plant, enrollment limitations and projected plant needs, faculty demand and supply, adult education, estimated costs of higher education, and student fees.

The statewide plan of the Regents of New York (State University of New York, 1965) was developed as a result of careful study of the state needs and the analysis of a number of preceding statewide studies. The statewide plan places emphasis upon ways and means of meeting the needs of individuals by providing adequate facilities to accommodate the growing enrollments, by providing additional community colleges throughout the state, by providing for the expansion of private four-year colleges to take additional students, and by providing adjustments in the Regents college scholarship and the scholar-incentive-program plans. Recommendations were made for meeting the needs of the economy and of society for specialized manpower. The plan makes recommendations regarding the strengthening of institutions with respect to faculty, facilities, budgets, and organization. It also provides for recommendations regarding the improvement of teaching and learning, libraries, museums, and other state services.

The scope of the higher-education enterprise at the present time—the magnitude of the financial investment, the increasing number and proportion of the population involved, the increasing interdependence between higher education and economic and social developments—these have been factors cited frequently in support of more and more centralized control and coordination of colleges and universities. In the most recent five-year period there has been developing a clear recognition that it is this very magnitude and diversity of the total higher-education enterprise which provides compelling reasons to retain the individuality and autonomy of these institutions. It is becoming apparent that the magnitude and diversity of higher education in states such as Wisconsin, Ohio, Illinois, Michigan, and perhaps even California are, in fact, the very reasons for retaining individual boards of control and to provide, at most, for a general coordinative agency for statewide higher education. Individuality, autonomy, and diversity are essential ingredients of higher education for the broadest service to our society.

John X. Jamrich
Michigan State University

References

Allen, James E. "The Compact—New Strength for the States." *Ed Rec* 47:79–121; 1966.

Bailey, Jackson H. "Non-Western Studies in a Small Liberal Arts College." *Liberal Ed* 47:405–11; 1961.

Baskin, Samuel. *Higher Education, Some Newer Developments.* McGraw-Hill, 1965.

Blackwell, Thomas E. "Legislative Control of Tax Supported Universities." *Col U Bus* 26:34–5; 1956.

Blackwell, Thomas E. *College Law.* ACE, 1961.

Blocker, Clyde E. "Cooperation Between Two-year and Four-year Colleges." *Sch Soc* 94:218–22; 1966.

Boles, Donald E. "The Administration of Higher Education in Wisconsin." *J H Ed* 27:427–39; 1956.

Brickman, William W. "Historical Background of International Cooperation Among Universities." *Sch Soc* 94:227–34; 1966.

Brumbaugh, A. J. "Coordinator of Studies." In *Higher Education in Louisiana: Report of the Louisiana Commission on Higher Education.* 1956.

Brumbaugh, A. J. "Proper Relationships Between State Government and State Supported Higher Institutions." *Ed Rec* 42:173–8; 1961.

Brumbaugh, A. J. *State-wide Planning and Coordination of Higher Education.* Southern Regional Education Board, 1963.

Brumbaugh, A. J., and Blee, Myron. *Higher Education and Florida's Future: Recommendations and General Staff Report.* U Florida Press, 1956.

Bunn, Edward J. "A Five Year Plan to Coordinate Graduate Study in Five Universities." *Nat Cath Ed Assn* 60:8–11; 1964.

Byrne, Charles D. *Coordinated Control of Higher Education in Oregon.* Stanford U Press, 1940.

Cadbury, William E., Jr. "Cooperative Relations Involving the Liberal Arts Colleges." *Sch Soc* 94:213–7; 1966.

California Coordinating Council for Higher Education. *A Consideration of Issues Affecting California Public Junior Colleges.* The Council, 1965.

California Coordinating Council for Higher Education. *The Master Plan Five Years Later.* The Council, 1966.

California State Department of Education. *A Master Plan for Higher Education in California, 1960–1975.* The Department, 1960.

California and Western Conference Cost and Statistical Study: 1954–1955. California Printing Department, 1956.

Chambers, M. M. *Voluntary State-wide Coordination in Public Higher Education.* U Michigan Press, 1961.

Chambers, M. M. *The Colleges and the Court Since 1950.* Interstate, 1964.

Chambers, M. M. *Freedom and Repression in Higher Education.* Bloomcraft Press, Inc., 1965.

Christopherson, Victor A. "Dilemmas of Administration in Higher Education." *J H Ed* 26:210–4; 1955.

Clark, F. B. "Disciplinary Action Controlling Agencies of Publicly Supported Educational Institutions." *Sch Soc* 66:433–7; 1947.

Colorado Association of State Institutions of Higher Education. *An Analysis of the Budgets of the Colorado State Supported Institutions of Higher Education.* The Association, 1961.

Committee on Institutional Cooperation. *Development of an Idea.* Purdue U Press, 1965.

Council of State Governments. *Reports on Higher Education: An Annotated Bibliography of Recent Reports of State Study Commissions and Other Official Agencies.* The Council, 1958.

Council of State Governments. *Inter-institutional Cooperative Arrangements and Agreements Across State Boundaries in the Mid-West.* The Council, 1963.

Donahue Higher Education Act of 1960 as Amended. Division 16.5 Higher Education, 1960. (California.)

Donovan, George F. *College and University Inter-institutional Cooperation.* Catholic Press, 1965.

Dressel, Paul, and others. *Evaluation in Higher Education.* Houghton, 1961.

Education Commission of the States. *The Compact for Education.* Duke U Press, 1966.

Eells and Hollis. *Administration of Higher Education: An Annotated Bibliography.* USOE Bulletin No. 7. GPO, 1960.

Ertell, Merton W. *Inter-institutional Cooperation in Higher Education.* U State New York, 1957.

Frase, Stewart E. "Some Aspects of University Cooperation in International Education." *Sch Soc* 94:234–44; 1966.

Glenny, Lyman A. *Autonomy of Public Colleges, the Challenge of Coordination.* McGraw-Hill, 1959.

Glenny, Lyman A. "State-wide Coordination of Higher Education: Plans, Surveys, and Progress to Date." In Smith, G. K. (Ed.) *Current Issues in Higher Education, 1962.* Association for Higher Education, 1962.

Hamblen, J. W., and Atchison, W. F. *Cooperative Planning for Computers and Computer Science Programs in Higher Education.* Southern Regional Education Board, 1966.

Henderson, Algo. *Policies and Practices in Higher Education.* Harper, 1960.

Henderson, Algo, and Chambers, M. M. "Government, Administration, Coordination, and Financing of Higher Education." *R Ed Res* 30:385–95; 1960.

Henry, David D. *What Priority for Education?* U Illinois Press, 1961.

Hill, David S. *Control of Tax Supported Higher Education in the United States.* Carnegie, 1934.

Hofstadter, Richard, and Smith, Wilson. *American Higher Education: A Documentary History.* U Chicago Press, 1961.

Holy, T. C., and Semans, Hubert H. "Coordination of Public Higher Education in California." *J H Ed* 26:141–7; 1955.

Hungate, Thad L. *Management in Higher Education.* Teachers College, Columbia U, 1964.

Illinois Board of Higher Education. *A Master Plan for Higher Education in Illinois.* The Board, 1964.

Illinois Looks to the Future in Higher Education. A Summary Report of the Higher Education Commission of the Governor and Legislature and the State of Illinois, 1957.

Indiana Survey Commission on State Supported Institutions of Higher Learning. *Report of a Survey of the State Institutions of Higher Learning in Indiana.* The Commission, 1926.

Jamrich, John X. "Research Techniques in State Surveys of Higher Education." *Col U* 35:195–203; 1960.

Jamrich, John X. *To Build or Not to Build.* Educational Facilities Laboratory, 1961.

Jamrich, John X. "Inter-institutional Cooperation in Research and Instruction." *Col U* Fall:25–34; 1964.

Jamrich, John X. *Doctorate Degrees in Education.* A report to the Ohio Board of Regents. 1965(a).

Jamrich, John X. "A Basic Plan Needed for Higher Education." *Michigan Ed J* 42:22–3; 1965(b).

Jamrich, John X., and Dahnke, Harold. *Ten Year Building Needs for Higher Education in Ohio; 1962–72.* Michigan State U Press, 1963.

Johnson, B. Lamar, and others. *The Public Junior College.* 55th Yearbook, NSSE, U Chicago Press, 1956.

Johnson, Eldon L. "Coordination: The Viewpoint of a Political Scientist." *Annals AAPSS* 302:136–42; 1955.

Johnson, Eldon L. "College Federations." *J H Ed* 37:1–9; 1966.

Kansas Plans for the Next Generation. A Report on Higher Education in Kansas to the Board of Regents by a Panel of Advisors. Board of Regents, 1962.

Keenan, Boyd R. "Big Ten Harmony: Academic Style." *J H Ed* 32:252–9; 1961.

Keller, Robert J. *Comprehensive Educational Survey of Kansas.* 1960

Kentucky Council on Public Higher Education. "Agreement on Uniform Classification of Accounts for Kentucky State Colleges." The Council, 1957. (Mimeographed.)

Klein, A. J. *Cooperation and Coordination in Higher Education.* ACE, 1938.

Knorr, Owen A. *Long-range Planning in Higher Education.* Western Interstate Commission on Higher Education, 1965.

Layton, Elizabeth N. *Surveys of Higher Education in the United States: 1937–1949.* USOE, 1949.

Lederle, John W. "The State and Higher Education: A Report from Michigan." In Moos, Malcolm, and Rourke, Francis. *The Campus and the State.* Johns Hopkins Press, 1959. Appendix A.

Longenecker, H. E. "Some Implications of the Education Compact Proposal for Higher Education." *Ed Rec* 47:106–12; 1966.

Martorana, S. V. *Survey and Report, Higher Educa-*

tion in the Tidewater Area of Virginia. Virginia State Council on Higher Education, 1959.

Martorana, S. V, and Hollis, E. V. *State Boards Responsible for Higher Education.* GPO, 1960.

Martorana, S. V., and Hollis, E. V. *State Legislation Affecting Higher Education.* GPO, 1961.

Martorana, S. V., and Messersmith, James C. *Advanced Planning to Meet Higher Education Needs: Recent State Surveys.* USOE, 1960.

Martorana, S. V., and others. *Cooperative Projects Among Colleges and Universities.* USOE, 1961.

McConnell, T. R. *A Restudy of the Needs of California in Higher Education.* McGraw-Hill, 1955.

McConnell, T. R. *A General Pattern for American Public Higher Education.* McGraw-Hill, 1962.

McGrath, Earl. *Cooperative Long-range Planning in Liberal Arts Colleges.* Institute for Higher Education, Columbia U, 1964.

McNeeley, John H. *Fiscal Control over State Higher Education.* USOE Bulletin No. 8. GPO, 1940.

McNickle, Roma K. (Ed.) *The Changing West—Implications for Higher Education.* Papers presented at a symposium held in Boulder, Colorado, August 7–9, 1964, Western Interstate Commission on Higher Education, 1965.

Medsker, Leland. *The Junior College.* McGraw-Hill, 1960.

Meeth, L. Richard. *Selected Issues in Higher Education, An Annotated Bibliography.* Teachers College, Columbia U, 1965.

Messersmith, James C. "Ideas and Patterns for Future Programs of Inter-institutional Cooperation." In Smith, G. K. (Ed.) *Current Issues in Higher Education: 1962.* Association for Higher Education, 1962. p. 150–3.

Miller, Jerry. *Inter-institutional Cost Study for Michigan: An Appraisal.* Michigan Council of State College Presidents, 1962.

Millett, John D. "State Planning for Higher Education." *North Central Assn Q* 40:299–301; 1966.

Minnesota Liaison Committee on Higher Education. *Minnesota Liaison Committee on Higher Education, Report for 1963–1965.* The Committee, 1965.

Minnesota Commission on Higher Education. *Higher Education in Minnesota.* U Minnesota Press, 1950.

Moos, Malcolm, and Rourke, Francis. *The Campus and the State.* Johns Hopkins Press, 1959.

New England Board of Higher Education. *Regional Cooperation in New England Higher Education. A Report to the People of New England on the First Years of the New England Board of Higher Education.* The Board, 1961.

New York State Education Department. *Meeting the Increasing Demand for Higher Education in New York State.* A Report to the Governor and the Board of Regents, 1960.

New York Times. "Catholics Enter Education Pact." February 27, 1966.

Ohio Board of Regents. *Master Plan for State Policy in Higher Education.* The Board, 1966.

Ohio Legislative Service Commission. *Coordination of Higher Education.* Staff Research Report No. 53. The Commission, 1963.

Oklahoma House of Representatives. *An Act Making Appropriations for Regional Cooperation With Other Southern States.* HB 672, 1957.

Oklahoma State Regents for Higher Education. *A 1950 Evaluation of the Oklahoma State System of Higher Education Inaugurated in 1941.* The Regents, 1950.

Oklahoma State Regents for Higher Education. *Financing Current Operating Costs of Higher Education in Oklahoma: Self Study of Higher Education in Oklahoma.* The Regents, 1963.

Oregon State Board of Higher Education. *Administrative Code.* The Board, 1956.

Pierce, Truman M. *Public Higher Education in Tennessee.* Digest of a Report to the Education Surveys Sub-committee of the Tennessee Legislative Council, 1957.

Russell, John Dale. "Control of State Tax Supported Higher Education in Illinois." *J H Ed* 7:145–7; 1951.

Russell, John Dale. "New Mexico Board of Educational Finance." *J H Ed* 9:97–9; 1953.

Russell, John Dale. "The Board of Educational Finance of the State of New Mexico," Santa Fe, New Mexico, 1956(a). (Mimeographed.)

Russell, John Dale. *Meeting Ohio's Needs in Higher Education.* Ohio College Association, 1956(b).

Russell, John Dale. *Higher Education in Michigan: Final Report.* State of Michigan, 1958.

Russell, John Dale. *Control and Coordination of Higher Education in Virginia.* Staff Study No. 11. Study of Higher Education in Virginia, 1965.

Russell, John Dale, and Judd, Charles H. *The American Education System.* Riverside, 1940.

Shirley, John W. "Problems Involved in Cooperation Between Universities and Government Agencies." *Sch Soc* 94:222–7; 1966.

Southern Regional Education Board. *Summary of State Legislation Affecting Higher Education in the South.* The Board, 1966.

State University of New York. *The Master Plan Revised, 1960.* The University, 1960.

State University of New York. *The Regent's Statewide Plan for the Expansion and Development of Higher Education, 1964–1965.* New York State Education Department, 1965.

Steiner, Gilbert. *Public Higher Education in Illinois—Its Scope and Function to 1975.* Illinois Joint Council on Higher Education, 1961.

Stevens, Edwin B. "Coordinating Boards of Higher Education." *Ed Rec* 7:280–8; 1926.

Stewart, W. Blair. "Cooperation Among Liberal Arts Colleges." *Liberal Ed* 46:66–71; 1960.

Stone, James C. *California's Commitment to Public Education.* Crowell, 1961.

Strayer, George D. *A Report of a Survey of the University System of Georgia.* Atlanta, Georgia, 1949.

Strayer, George, and Kellogg, Charles. *The Needs of New Jersey in Higher Education, 1962–1970.* New Jersey State Board of Education, 1962.

Sugg, Redding S., and Jones, George. *The Southern Regional Education Board, Ten Years of Regional*

Cooperation in Higher Education. Louisiana State U Press, 1960.

Texas Commission on Higher Education. "Materials Pertaining to Formulas for Appropriations, Purposes and Role and Scope of Institutions." The Commission, 1959. (Mimeographed.)

Texas Commission on Higher Education. *Report to the Honorable Alan Shivers, Governor of Texas, and the Legislature of the State of Texas.* The Commission, 1956.

U.S. Department of Health, Education, and Welfare. "Coordinating Two Year Colleges in State Education Systems." A report of a conference in Washington, D.C., May 16–17, 1957. USOE, GPO, 1957.

U.S. Office of Education. *Survey of State Legislation Relating to Higher Education.* GPO, 1964.

Utah Coordinating Board of Higher Education. *A Proposed Coordinating Council in Higher Education for Utah.* The Board, 1958.

Wells, Herman B. "Branches for Opportunity—Regional Campuses." *Am Ed* 2:5–8; 1966.

West Virginia, State of. *A Study of State Institutions of Higher Education in West Virginia.* Sub-committee on Higher Education of the Joint Committee on Government Finance, 1958.

Wilson, Logan. *Emerging Patterns in American Higher Education.* ACE, 1965.

Wisconsin, State of. *Higher Education, An Investment in People.* Semi-annual Report, The Coordinating Committee on Higher Education in Wisconsin, 1957.

Wisconsin, State of. *By-laws of the Coordinating Committee for Higher Education.* State of Wisconsin Information Item, Coordinating Committee on Higher Education in Wisconsin, No. 11. 1964.

Zook, George F., and others. *Report of a Survey of State Institutions of Higher Learning in Kansas.* GPO, 1923.

CORRESPONDENCE INSTRUCTION

Correspondence instruction serves the educational and training needs of millions of people throughout the world. Men and women, young and old, undereducated and well educated, study by correspondence. People from all walks of life study for academic advancement, for professional and vocational reasons, for cultural purposes, and for fun. They study with colleges and universities, private schools, associations, unions, government agencies, and military schools. They study individually at home or in groups at school, on the job, or elsewhere. They study art and business administration, carpentry and computer programming, music and mathematics, flower arranging and nuclear physics, or any of thousands of skills taught by correspondence courses available in virtually all areas of learning.

Correspondence instruction, also called home study and postal tuition, is growing at a faster rate today than at any time in recent history. It is also being combined with other educational techniques and being used in more different ways than ever before.

By its curricula, its student body, and its objectives, correspondence instruction is clearly part of adult and vocational education or, more generally, continuing education. Correspondence instruction is characterized by two features: it is carried on by mail, and it requires examinations and exchange between student and instructor. Use of the mails distinguishes correspondence instruction from other forms of continuing education, and exchange between student and instructor distinguishes it from all other forms of "self-study."

Villaume (1958) points out, however, that correspondence instruction is similar to all conventional educational techniques in that it employs the three principal ingredients of the typical learning situation: student, instructor, and educational materials. Correspondence instruction differs in that the student and teacher are physically separated and generally communicate in writing.

WORLDWIDE SCOPE OF CORRESPONDENCE INSTRUCTION. The National Home Study Council (1967b) surveyed the correspondence-education field and estimated that in 1966 there were 5,270,913 students enrolled in U.S. correspondence programs. The total number of Americans who have studied by correspondence instruction since the movement began in the late nineteenth century can be conservatively placed at over 75,000,000.

Today, well over 8,000,000 students throughout the world are studying by correspondence. The number and kinds of programs offered vary widely from country to country, depending on the educational tradition and needs of the country. In the U.S.S.R., for example, correspondence study already has become the main form of university study (Peters, 1965; DeWitt, 1961). By 1962 more Russian students were pursuing college and university courses by correspondence than were attending regular day classes. In Japan more than 70,000 students get part of their secondary education through correspondence programs. In Australia and New Zealand correspondence instruction has been used in the compulsory school system to teach children who have never been to a classroom (Holmberg, 1960). In developing nations such as Malawi, Tanzania, Zambia, and others in East Africa, correspondence instruction has been only recently introduced experimentally as part of the secondary and college education system (Dag Hammarskjold Foundation, 1966).

In the United States correspondence instruction plays only a limited role in the formal secondary-school systems and in colleges and universities. Yet correspondence instruction is more extensive in the United States than in any other country. As the National Home Study Council's *1966 Correspondence Education Survey* (1967b) shows, the largest single user of correspondence instruction is the U.S. federal government, especially the U.S. armed forces, which enroll more than 2,000,000 students annually. Another two million students are enrolled in approximately 500 private home-study schools.

In addition, the National University Extension Association (National University Extension Association and the Association of University Evening Colleges, 1966) reported that 189,282 students were enrolled in correspondence instruction programs with 69 of its member colleges and universities. Still others are studying with religious schools and through programs conducted by business and industrial firms, unions, and associations. Virtually all of those enrolled in the armed forces correspondence schools are taking courses related to their military-service jobs. Seventy-five percent of the students enrolled in private home-study schools are also taking job-related courses, according to the National Home Study Council (NHSC), with the balance of the students taking academic, cultural, or hobby courses. Most of those studying with colleges and universities are enrolled in academic courses. Wedemeyer and Childs (1961) reported that for 1958–59, 98,696 were enrolled in college-level courses, 55,461 in high-school-level courses and 6,631 in noncredit courses covering cultural or hobby and recreational courses.

HISTORY OF CORRESPONDENCE INSTRUCTION. The instructive letter is the forerunner of formal correspondence instruction and has a history probably as old as letter-writing itself. Graff (1967) recalls the instructive letters in the Old Testament and others in early Greek and Roman history. Instructive letters have played a significant role in the Roman Catholic Church continuously from the epistles of St. Paul to the present pope's encyclical letters. The humanists revived epistolography as an art, and instructive letters flourished during their era and again later, during the Age of Enlightenment, which was perhaps the most fertile period for instructive letters.

The modern history of correspondence instruction began in 1840, when Isaac Pitman in Bath, England, conducted his course in shorthand with distant students via the new penny post (Noffsinger, 1926). In 1856 a school for teaching modern languages by correspondence was founded in Berlin by Gustav Langenscheidt and Charles Toussaint. In the United States the first efforts to organize correspondence instruction came in 1873, when the Society to Encourage Studies at Home was formed, but the program soon collapsed when it failed to meet student needs. In 1874, Illinois Wesleyan University began offering various college-credit courses to adults off campus, and this program lasted until 1910. In 1883 another effort was made when a group of college and university instructors formed the Correspondence University at Ithaca, New York. Although widely acclaimed at the outset, this program was also short-lived.

Meanwhile, on Chautauqua Lake in New York state, another educational movement was being established which was to provide a firm basis for the growth of correspondence instruction. In 1874, under the auspices of the Methodist camp meeting, the first Sunday School Teachers' Assembly was held to provide daily study and recreation during the summer months. The program and curricula expanded quickly, and in 1879 the School of Languages was founded at Chautauqua by Dr. William Rainey Harper, a professor of Hebrew. At summer's end several students asked him to continue teaching them through the winter months, by mail. The system proved so successful that the correspondence method of instruction was adopted by the Chautauqua movement. When Dr. Harper later became president of the University of Chicago in 1892, he immediately established a correspondence division within the school's extension department.

The correspondence education movement closely paralleled the development of college and university extension programs. In Philadelphia the American Society for Extension of University Teaching was organized in 1890 and later became the present National University Extension Association (NUEA). Throughout their history, college and university correspondence programs have been integral parts of their schools' extension divisions. Today some seventy of the NUEA members offer correspondence programs (National University Extension Association, 1967).

The private home-study school movement in the United States had an entirely different beginning. Thomas J. Foster, editor of the *Mining Herald* in Shenandoah, Pa., ran a question-and-answer column on mining problems in his newspaper for miners and their superintendents, who often knew little of mining technology and safety. The popularity of the column encouraged Foster to develop a systematized method of teaching coal mining. In 1890 he founded International Correspondence Schools (ICS), the oldest private home-study school in the United States. The school was an almost immediate success and by 1900 had enrolled a total of over 250,000 students. The success of ICS led hundreds of other private home study schools into the field (Clark, 1965).

In the mid-1920's, John S. Noffsinger (1926) conducted a study of correspondence schools, lyceums, and chautauquas under a grant from the Carnegie Corporation. Out of this study grew the NHSC in 1926, a nonprofit educational association which established standards for private correspondence schools. Today, the NHSC Accrediting Commission is responsible for setting standards to maintain academic quality and sound, ethical business practices. The commission is approved by the U.S. Office of Education as a nationally recognized accrediting agency. Membership in the council requires accreditation, and today some 100 proprietary schools have met the standards and are members of the NHSC (National Home Study Council, 1967a).

In Europe, pioneering work was done in Germany and Sweden in the 1890's, probably under the influence of the earlier work of Toussaint and Langenscheidt. Rustinsches Fernlehrinstitut was founded in Berlin in 1894, and in Sweden Hans Hermod organized a correspondence school in 1898 (Holmberg, 1960). After the turn of the century, other correspondence-instruction schools sprang up throughout Europe.

Several organizations of correspondence schools

outside of the United States have been founded, including the Association of British Colleges, the European Council for Education by Correspondence, and the International Council on Correspondence Education. The International Council, organized in Victoria, Canada, in 1938, meets in different parts of the world every four years. More than 230 delegates from 30 countries met for the Stockholm meeting in 1965.

THE CORRESPONDENCE-INSTRUCTION METHOD. Andrew (1965), Holmberg (1960), Homer Kempfer (1959), and numerous others describe the correspondence-instruction process, which begins when the school sends the student his first package of educational materials. These consist of text material and how-to-study advice, plus any audiovisual or other instructional aids required. The student studies the prescribed materials and then completes an assignment or examination, which he sends to the school. The instructor corrects, evaluates, and grades the student's work, adding personal comments when appropriate. The corrected assignment is returned to the student, and the cycle is repeated until the course is completed.

Although this procedure is virtually universal, there are a variety of refinements. Practically all schools use instructors to handle student assignments, but Birtwistle (1966) reports that in the giant U.S. Air Force Correspondence Education Program the student service is automated and student examinations are corrected by machine. Some schools require students to construct electronic equipment, and others sometimes require that students submit drawings, tapes, records, or clothing instead of written tests. Sometimes the instructional material itself includes phonograph records, filmstrips, equipment kits, testing devices, etc. A number of schools offer (or even require) "terminal resident training," which consists of several weeks at the end of the course when the student completes his program on school premises.

CORRESPONDENCE MATERIALS AND INSTRUCTION. Correspondence-instruction materials differ significantly from regular textbooks because, as Andrew (1965) says, the correspondence-instruction texts must, in effect, provide the equivalent of textbook, lecture notes, blackboard reinforcement, practice work, and periodical written tests. As a result correspondence-instruction materials are specially developed to present the subject matter in short, easy-to-grasp steps, which progress logically to achieve educational objectives. When standard textbooks are used in correspondence courses, they are accompanied by custom-written study guides which show the student how to study the text and also amplify and clarify the text as necessary.

The instructor's role is also different in correspondence instruction, since he does not lecture or lead class discussion. His chief responsibility, as Knowles (1966) says, is to make careful evaluations of the student's written work, challenge his interest, encourage and counsel him, and share some of the instructor's own wisdom and enthusiasm for study and learning.

APPLICATIONS OF CORRESPONDENCE INSTRUCTION. Because of its versatility and flexibility correspondence instruction has found many applications, including use in public and private secondary schools and in training employees. Hundreds of secondary schools use correspondence instruction provided by colleges and universities and private schools. As Broady (1952) and others point out, correspondence instruction provides the school with means to enrich its curriculum, to help both the accelerated pupil and the student who has fallen behind, and to solve scheduling difficulties. In addition, students become familiar with an educational technique available to them throughout life.

Correspondence instruction is used even more extensively in business and industrial firms. In 1962 the Chamber of Commerce of the United States (1962) reported that more than 7,000 U.S. business firms were using correspondence instruction for employee training. The correspondence-instruction programs vary from simple tuition-reimbursement plans to elaborate company-controlled programs. Thompson (1963) describes several case histories, and Clark (1963) and Ward (1963) describe apprenticeship training by correspondence instruction. The proceedings of the 1963 Conference on the "role of correspondence education in the development of manpower in science and technology" (National Home Study Council, 1964) present many articles relating correspondence instruction to technical training for business firms and other organizations. White (1963) tells how the New Mexico State Highway Department uses correspondence instruction in its in-service training programs. Wright (1967) describes how his company uses correspondence instruction for customer training, and Ramsdell (1963) describes his company's use of correspondence instruction coupled with on-the-job training.

In other organizations correspondence instruction has served many ends. For example, Loftus (1966) describes how a warehousemen's association uses private correspondence schools to provide management training to members. Some associations, such as the American Hotel and Motel Association and the International City Managers' Association, have their own correspondence schools.

Byrne (1952) describes the use of correspondence instruction in the Nebraska State Penitentiary; Clarke (1952) shows the value of correspondence instruction in rehabilitating the mentally ill; and Lee (1952) explains other uses of correspondence instruction in rehabilitation work. In fact, one private school caters exclusively to the handicapped, offering only courses in braille for the blind (Langford, 1960).

SUPERVISED CORRESPONDENCE INSTRUCTION. In many of the preceding applications, correspondence instruction is used in group-training situations, and often the technique used is supervised correspondence study. Childs (1952) describes supervised correspondence study as the procedure in which the sponsoring organization (local school, business firm, etc.) secures the instructional materials, provides regular study periods, supervises the student's work, and returns student assignments to the correspondence school for suggestions, corrections, and criticisms.

Although the educational technique used is pure correspondence instruction, the program is enhanced by providing regular study periods and by the program's being controlled through the supervisor. The supervisor does not teach, but serves, as Mitchell (1965), Smith (1965), and others indicate, as the connecting link between the student and the correspondence school. He controls the distribution of the materials to students and forwards student assignments to the schools. He supervises tests, answers nontechnical student questions, and provides motivation by encouraging and stimulating students.

Childs (1963) reports that the first recorded use of supervised correspondence study was in Australia in 1914 and that programs were carried out in British Columbia in 1919 and in New Zealand in 1922. Mitchell (1962) reports that the first organized program of supervised correspondence study in the United States was established at Benton Harbor, Michigan, in 1923. By 1930 more than 100 public high schools had experimented with this technique. Kefauver and others (1932) described how 46 high schools used correspondence courses.

After that time a number of studies on supervised correspondence study were published, but few provided significant data on student achievement until 1949, when Childs (1949) compared the achievement of 1,200 high school pupils enrolled in supervised correspondence study in 14 different subjects with the achievement of 1,800 pupils taking similar courses in regular classrooms. He found that the correspondence pupils performed better than the control group on standardized achievement tests. Other studies of achievement, before and since, have been less extensive, but virtually all show similar results.

CORRESPONDENCE INSTRUCTION AND OTHER TECHNIQUES. Correspondence instruction is being increasingly combined with other teaching techniques. Leskinen (1967) describes a program in Finland which combines correspondence and oral methods for teaching secondary-school subjects. Secondary-school students study mostly by correspondence but also attend 14-day class periods four times per year. Many private home-study schools in the United States also offer a combination of correspondence study and resident, or "terminal," training. Usually the resident training, lasting two to six weeks, follows the correspondence training and permits practical experience with equipment. Vásquez (1966) reports a program in Venezuela which joins correspondence instruction and summer classroom sessions to provide in-service education for elementary-school teachers.

The romance between correspondence instruction and the broadcast media has existed for many decades but has become more intense in recent years. Wedemeyer and Childs (1961) point out that educators were experimenting with radio and correspondence instruction back in the 1920's and 1930's. Today the combination is used more extensively overseas, especially in developing countries, than in the United States. Homer Kempfer (1966) reports its use in Malawi and its planned use in Ethiopia, Tanzania, and Zambia. Wedemeyer (1966) reports that in Japan radio and correspondence instruction have been combined to provide a four-year science and mathematics course at the high school level.

Recent experiments combining television and correspondence instruction are even more extensive and widespread than correspondence instruction by radio. Perhaps the best-known program of this kind, the Continental Classroom series, was begun in 1959 with the correspondence course developed by the University of California accompanying the television physics broadcasts. Wedemeyer and Childs (1961) describe the Continental Classroom program and other programs by the University of Wisconsin and the University of North Carolina. Wilshire and Bayliss (1966) explain how correspondence instruction and television are being combined in a program in England. Wedemeyer (1966) reports similar uses in Italy and the Netherlands. In Japan, television in combination with correspondence instruction is used extensively in teaching secondary-school subjects.

Correspondence instruction has also been combined with the newest of educational techniques, programmed instruction. Walsh (1962, 1963) reported two experiments which combined programmed instruction with correspondence instruction. The first involved 1,500 correspondence students, and the second involved 5,000 students. In both cases student achievement was essentially the same regardless of whether programmed instruction was added to the correspondence-instruction program. However, the use of programmed instruction did significantly improve student motivation as measured by the number of assignments completed. Reports by Sjogren (1964) and Schoen (1964) considered more limited research but arrived at substantially the same conclusions that Walsh did. Helen Kempfer (1965) reported a survey of the use of programmed instruction in correspondence courses in 23 schools. In general, replies were favorable to the practice.

ADVANTAGES AND LIMITATIONS OF CORRESPONDENCE INSTRUCTION. Childs (1963) calls correspondence instruction a remarkable educational instrument, far and away the most flexible educational technique. He points out that correspondence instruction is not limited by time and place restrictions, that it can be used individually or in a group, that it can be used at any level from elementary school to graduate college, that it permits the student to progress at his own rate, and that it can be a separate educational program or part of a school program or can be used in combination with other educational techniques.

Another significant feature of correspondence instruction is economy. Hosmer (1959), for example, compared the costs and results of correspondence study and resident training and found that the cost of correspondence study is but a fraction of the cost of resident study although student achievement is the same for both techniques. He determined cost per student hour at $0.92 for correspondence and $5.21 for resident student work. Depending on the kind of program and number of students involved, correspondence instruction is often more efficient and economical than any other technique.

Correspondence instruction does have some obvious limitations. As Homer Kempfer (1959) says, a person ought not to learn to drive an automobile entirely by correspondence instruction. Skills which require formation of habits and the development of body coordination cannot be learned entirely by correspondence. Also, correspondence instruction cannot, as Kelly (1963) points out, further such legitimate goals of a high school education as social development. Homer Kempfer (1965) also notes that developing the skills of conversation, teamwork, group discussion, group leadership, and oral persuasion requires participation in a group. Only the theory can be learned by correspondence.

Because of its versatility, effectiveness, and economy, correspondence instruction has earned a firmly held position in the field of education. The growing student body demonstrates that correspondence instruction is meeting educational needs on a global scale. The many new uses of correspondence instruction reflect the increasing recognition of the value of correspondence instruction in serving a wide variety of educational and training situations. And the experiments combining correspondence instruction with other techniques are creating new roles for correspondence instruction in the educational world of tomorrow.

John R. Sivatko
National Home Study Council

References

Andrew, E. R. "The Arrangement of Teaching Matter." In the Yearbook of the European Council for Education by Correspondence, 1965. p. 45–53.

Birtwistle, Owen G. "U.S. Air Force Correspondence Education Program." *Home Study R* 7:2; 1966.

Broady, K. O. "What Purposes Does Supervised Correspondence Instruction Serve." In *Bulletin 190*, National Association of Secondary-School Principals, 1952. p. 47–54.

Byrne, Victor. "Correspondence Instruction in the Nebraska State Penitentiary." *Bulletin 190*, National Association of Secondary-School Principals, 1952. p. 141–2.

Chamber of Commerce of the United States. "Accredited Correspondence Education—An Answer to Training Needs of Business." In *Special Supplement of the Washington Report.* The Chamber, 1962. 4p.

Childs, Gayle B. *A Comparison of Correspondence and Classroom Pupils in Achievement in School Subjects.* Doctoral dissertation. Teachers College, U Nebraska, 1949.

Childs, Gayle B. "Can We Really Teach Well by Correspondence?" In *Bulletin 190*, National Association of Secondary-School Principals, 1952. p. 7–29.

Childs, Gayle B. "Supervised Correspondence Instruction." In *Brandenburg Memorial Essays On Correspondence Instruction*, Vol. 1. U Wisconsin Press, 1963. p. 22–33.

Clark, Ronald D. "Serving Business and Industry through New Applications of Correspondence Training." *Home Study R* 4:2; 1963.

Clark, Ronald D. "The I.C.S. Story: Seventy-five Years of Service to the Individual to Industry and to the Nation." *Home Study R* 6:4; 1965.

Clarke, Charles R. "Supervised Correspondence Study at the Institute of Living." In *Bulletin 190*, National Association of Secondary-School Principals, 1952. p. 133–4.

Dag Hammarskjold Foundation. *Correspondence Instruction in Ethiopia, Kenya, Tanzania, Malawi, Zambia, and Uganda.* The Foundation, 1966. 139p.

DeWitt, Nicholas. *Education and Professional Employment in the U.S.S.R.* National Research Council, 1961. 856p.

Graff, Kurt. "Correspondence Instruction in the History of the Western World." *Home Study R* 8:1; 1967.

Holmberg, Börje. *On the Methods of Teaching by Correspondence.* U Lund [Sweden] Press, 1960.

Hosmer, C. L. "Results vs. Costs of Correspondence Study." In *National University Extension Association Bulletin.* U Iowa, 1959.

Kefauver, G. N., and others. "How Forty-six High Schools Use Correspondence Courses." *Sch Life* 17:161–2; 1932.

Kelly, Hal V. "Supervised Correspondence Courses." *NEA J* 8:26–7; 1963.

Kempfer, Helen. "Programmed Instruction in Correspondence Courses; Report of a Survey." *Home Study R* 6:3; 1965.

Kempfer, Homer. *How to Choose a Correspondence School.* Belman, 1959. 35p.

Kempfer, Homer. "The Printed Word in the Education of Adults." In *The Use of Mass Media in the Education of Adults.* Evelyn Hone Col Further Education, Lusaka, Zambia, 1965. 135p.

Kempfer, Homer. "Correspondence Education in Developing Countries." In *Brandenburg Memorial Essays on Correspondence Instruction*, Vol. 2. U Wisconsin Press, 1966. p. 19–34.

Knowles, Margaret I. "The Role of the Instructor in Correspondence Study." In *Brandenburg Memorial Essays on Correspondence Instruction*, Vol. 2. U Wisconsin Press, 1966. p. 100–6.

Langford, Robert P. "New Horizons for the Blind via Home Study." *Home Study R* 1:3; 1960.

Lee, Berenice H. "Practical and Therapeutic Values of Correspondence Study." In *Bulletin 190*, National Association of Secondary-School Principals, 1952. p. 130-2.

Leskinen, Heikki. "Combining Correspondence and Oral Methods in Teaching Secondary School Subjects." *Home Study Review* 8:1; 1967.

Loftus, John T. "An Association Uses Tailor-made Correspondence Training—A Case History." *Home Study R* 7:4; 1966.

Mitchell, Sidney C. "Supervised Correspondence Study for High Schools and for Adults Taking High School Courses." *Home Study R* 3:1; 1962.

Mitchell, Sidney C. "Adult Education Centers Offering Supervised Correspondence Courses." *Home Study R* 6:2; 1965.

National Home Study Council. "Proceedings of Conference on The Role of Correspondence Education in the Development of Manpower in Science and Technology." *Home Study R* 4:4; 1964.

National Home Study Council. *Directory of Accredited Home Study Schools*. The Council, 1967(a).

National Home Study Council. *1966 Correspondence Education Survey*. The Council, 1967(b).

National University Extension Association. *Guide to Correspondence Study in Colleges and Universities*. The Association, 1967.

National University Extension Association and the Association of University Evening Colleges. *Programs and Registrations 1965-1966*. The Associations, 1966. 22p.

Noffsinger, John S. *Correspondence Schools, Lyceums, Chautauquas*. Macmillan, 1926. 95p.

Peters, Otto. "Correspondence Education in the Soviet Union." *Home Study R* 6:4; 1965.

Ramsdell, Alden J. "On-the-job Industry Training Via Supervised Correspondence Courses." *Home Study R* 3:4; 1963.

Schoen, James R. "Programmed Instruction in Military Home Study Courses." *Home Study R* 5:3; 1964.

Sjogren, Douglas D. "Programmed Materials in High School Correspondence Courses." *Home Study R* 5:3; 1964.

Smith, L. C. "Supervised Correspondence Programs." *Home Study R* 6:2; 1965.

Thompson, O. I. "Effective Industry Home Study Programs." *Home Study R* 4:2; 1963.

Vásquez, Pedro Tomás. "The Expansion of Educational Opportunity in Venezuela." In *Brandenburg Memorial Essays on Correspondence Instruction*, Vol. 2. U Wisconsin Press, 1966. p. 50-3.

Villaume, John C. *The Place of Correspondence Education*. International Correspondence Schools, 1958. 12p.

Walsh, John E. "PL-100: A Programmed Learner Experiment of Correspondence Students." *Home Study R* 3:1; 1962.

Walsh, John E. "Adjunct Programming: A Technique for Home Study Training." *Home Study R* 3:5; 1963.

Ward, C. A. "Apprenticeship Training by Correspondence Study." *Home Study R* 4:2; 1963.

Wedemeyer, Charles A. "World Trends in Correspondence Education." In *Brandenburg Memorial Essays on Correspondence Instruction*, Vol. 2. U Wisconsin Press, 1966. p. 2-17.

Wedemeyer, Charles A., and Childs, Gayle B. *New Perspectives in University Correspondence Study*. Center for the Study of Liberal Education for Adults, 1961. 74p.

White, T. B. "Correspondence Training: New Mexico State Highway Agency." *Home Study R* 4:3; 1963.

Wilshire, Harold, and Bayliss, Fred. "Teaching Through Television." In *Brandenburg Memorial Essays on Correspondence Instruction*, Vol. 2. U Wisconsin Press, 1966. p. 36-49.

Wright, Herbert L. "Home Study for Customer Training in Numerical Control." *Trained Men* 46:4; 1967.

COUNSELING— COLLEGE AND UNIVERSITY

Research and reports on college counseling are reviewed here to describe the present status of counseling, persistent concerns and issues in counseling, available counseling resources, and trends and problems in college counseling. First, the locus of counseling in higher education and educational and social developments influencing it are discussed. Next, the extent of counseling, counseling functions, and counselor characteristics are described. Issues and concerns of college counselors are then described—dropouts, achievement, student "unhappiness," vocational planning, evaluation, and the counseling process. Finally, counselor resources are reviewed—tests, occupational information, therapy, campus facilities, and professional organizations—and problems and trends are anticipated.

PRESENT STATUS. Overt interest in and commitment to counseling vary between and within schools, and different amounts and kinds of responsibilities for providing counseling are assumed by different institutions. If a college does little or nothing systematically to provide counseling, students will seek it from members of the faculty and the administration, fellow students, and others. Counseling will be done, but by whom, how, and with what effectiveness is determined largely by the school's investment in and commitment to its students' welfare.

Counseling in colleges can be described in terms of who does it, the focus of the conversation, and the methods or orientation employed. When counseling is provided by members of the faculty it is usually called faculty advising. Provided by psychologists, it is called psychological counseling; provided by psychiatrists, it is called psychiatric counseling. Vocational counseling focuses on topics of jobs and occupations, marriage counseling on marriage and the family, educational counseling on school decisions, progress, and problems, and personal counseling on more intimate topics of emotional and social reactions.

Methods used in college counseling are those

used in other types of counseling—advice, teaching, interpretation, clarification of thought and affect, exhortation, conditioning, sympathy, referral, consultation, case study, psychological testing, and group methods. Comprehensive descriptions of the roles and functions of the college counselor are given by Tyler (1961) and Williamson (1950).

The locus of the systematized counseling program in a college varies. Different responsibilities for counseling are assigned to faculty members, counseling psychologists, medical staff, administrators, such as college deans, registrars, and their assistants, and student personnel officers, such as deans of students and deans of men and women, housing directors and their staffs, financial-aid officers, admissions officers, student-union staffs, foreign-student advisers, and chaplains and pastors.

The administrative location of counseling also varies. Usually the college's chief student personnel officer—vice-president, dean, or director—is responsible for making the college aware of the counseling needs of students and of the extent to which these are met and responsible for providing coordination and direction for counseling efforts. Often this official has direct management responsibility for many or most counseling activities, and counselors and advisers will be on his staff. Frequently, some counseling personnel are administratively assigned to college, faculty, or, occasionally, departmental offices. In 1964 a group of such counselors employed in college offices established themselves as a separate commission of the American College Personnel Association. These persons often are responsible for faculty advising programs and identify instructors to serve as advisers, train and supervise them, and assign students to them.

On many campuses the most visible site of counseling is the counseling center, office, or bureau. Williamson (1961, 1965) discusses the educational and social antecedents of college counseling centers. He himself directed the first "autonomous" counseling office established at the University of Minnesota in 1932.

Counseling also is located in the college's several student personnel offices concerned with the housing, placement, employment, financial aid, recreation, health, and organization of students. Depending on the extent to which these services are conceived of in terms of the counseling needs of students, staff and resources are made available for counseling.

The development of college counseling is one expression of the application of psychology in higher education and parallels similar applications in industry, government, and elementary and secondary education. Social influences bearing on this development are discussed by Wrenn (1962), and the opinions and actions of many persons influencing it are described by Williamson (1965). Some of the social determinants of college counseling are suggested by the following points.

1. The increased knowledge of the psychology of personality, student characteristics, and student behavior (Dennis & Kauffman, 1966; Sanford, 1962).

2. The increasing number of social alternatives and continuing emphasis on educational and occupational diversity (Wrenn, 1962).

3. Social concern over manpower problems and utilization (Wolfle, 1954).

4. Community and scientific attention to problems, programs, and definitions of mental health (Jahoda, 1958).

5. Educational and political analyses of questions of human rights (Williamson & Cowan, 1966).

6. The increased diversity of college students in terms of ability, economic status, and minority-group membership (Astin, 1965b; Heist, 1960). The implications of the U.S. programs of Work-study, National Defense Education Act loans, Upward Bound, and direct federal grants to students are obvious, as are those of state scholarship programs and increasing numbers of junior and community colleges.

7. Philosophical developments related to increasing acceptance, particularly by students, of existential and phenomenological questions and answers (Shoben, 1966) and the use of the identity concept (Erickson, 1959).

THE EXTENT OF COUNSELING. No satisfactory figures are available concerning the number of persons or colleges providing college counseling, but some reasonable estimates can be made.

A U.S. Office of Education survey reported by Ayers and others (1966) was based on information received from 95 percent of a 50 percent sample of United States universities, liberal arts colleges, teachers colleges, and junior colleges. About 86 percent of these institutions identified an officer who was the chief student-services officer, half of whom had the title of Dean of Students, Dean of Student Affairs, or Dean of Student Services. Of these persons, one-half had professional preparation in education, including guidance, one-fifth in the social sciences, including psychology, and 31 percent had other training. Of the 723 reporting institutions, 355, or 49 percent, reported having a director of counseling. These positions appeared to be more firmly established in publicly supported universities, somewhat less so in private universities, and least firmly established in liberal arts, teachers, and junior colleges. Ninety-nine percent of all colleges, both public and private, reported that they provided counseling to students, and 55 percent allocated complete responsibility for counseling to the student-services administration; 40 percent had this responsibility shared; and only 5 percent did not include counseling as a part of student services. Large institutions tended to assign greater responsibility for counseling to student services than did small ones, although very small schools also relied more on student-service divisions for counseling.

Clark (1966) obtained information in 1965 from 50 of the 82 American universities with more than 10,000 students, and 42 reported counseling centers on the campus. The mean enrollment was 15,000, the mean number of students counseled per year was 1,800, the mean number of hours spent with students was 3.3, the mean budget was $97,000, and the mean number of hours of professional staff time in the center was 218. The overall ratio of students to counselors was 3,000 to 1. Principal functions described were vocational counseling, educational- and occupational-information counseling, and personal-adjustment counseling. Major problems of operating centers involved staff, salaries, space, and support.

In 1966, Eugene Oetting reported the results of a survey of all four-year U.S. institutions of higher learning. Oetting does not report, but the U.S. Office of Education does (*Education Directory . . .*, 1966), that at that time about 1,500 such institutions could be identified. Oetting obtained responses from 59 percent of schools with less than 1,000 students, 95 percent of those with from 1,000 to 5,000, 89 percent of those with from 5,000 to 10,000, and 96 percent of those with over 10,000 students. Of all these schools, 605 reported they had counseling services and provided names of persons directing them. In large colleges the modal ratio of counselors to students was 1 to 2,250, in medium-sized schools 1 to 1,750, and in small schools 1 to 1,250. The amount of the counselor's time assigned to counseling was not specified, and the conclusion is not warranted that small schools provide more counseling. One-quarter of the largest schools reported ratios of over 1 to 3,000. Oetting's figures suggest an approximate ratio in four-year institutions of 1 counselor per 2,000 students and, with five million students in four-year institutions, this suggests about 2,500 college counselors. Oetting concluded that two-thirds of colleges have counseling services, that larger colleges are more likely than smaller colleges to have such services, and that their distribution is not related to geography.

No professional association consists only of college counselors, and the proportion of such counselors who belong to any one or several associations is unknown. Relevant organizations include the Division of Counseling Psychology of the American Psychological Association, which has among its 1,500 members counselors of many kinds, and the American College Personnel Association (ACPA), whose membership of 5,000 in 1965 included about 1,200 persons who classified themselves by function as college counselors (Hoyt & Tripp, 1967). A study reported in 1966 (Pruitt) based on a sample of 216 members of the ACPA employed in four-year institutions found that 13 percent reported as their major activity counseling and related activities. The numbers of college counselors belonging to ACPA as reported by Hoyt and Tripp and by Pruitt do not agree, but the sampling methods, response rates, and, presumably, biases and research methods of the studies also differed. No solid basis can be found for estimating how many persons today are employed as college counselors, but one might estimate the figure to be about 3,000.

College counseling in countries outside of the United States has been described (Lloyd, 1953, 1956), but no survey can be found reporting the number or types of universities offering such services, the countries in which they are located, or the differences distinguishing college counseling in various countries. Arkoff and others (1966) compared attitudes of students from different countries toward mental health and counseling and reported that Asians perceived counseling as more authoritarian than did American students.

FUNCTIONS OF COUNSELING. Functions of the college counselor can be classified according to the problems with which he works, the persons he counsels, the process in which he engages, or his goals. Traditionally, counselors have attempted to aid students in making vocational and educational decisions. Oetting (1966) reported that about 90 percent of counseling directors mentioned this as a function of their centers. Developmental and remedial counseling to help students acquire appropriate academic skills, including reading, was reported as a function by about one-third of Oetting's respondents, but over 90 percent assumed responsibility for helping students develop study skills.

Almost all college counselors work with students who have personal problems, and many centers have on the staff or have close working relations with psychiatric and medical personnel to assist with persons who are psychotic, severely disturbed, or presenting symptoms suggesting a need for medical attention. Students' personal problems involve their relationships with parents, siblings, spouses, children, friends, and teachers as well as problems of establishing and understanding the values and attitudes held by themselves and of others.

Specialized college counseling staffs and services may be made available to various groups: foreign students (Williamson, 1961), disabled students (Condon, 1957), married students (Mueller, 1960), students living in residence halls (Riker, 1965), students in financial need (Williamson, 1961), and those belonging to minority racial, religious, or economic groups.

The survey by Oetting (1966) provided evidence supporting the generalization that increasingly college counselors have provided psychological consultation services not directly involving counseling to their institution, colleagues, and community. Oetting reported that counseling staffs often participate, both at a policy and at a service level, in matters of admissions, student activities and organization, discipline, academic probation, examinations (developing, administering, and scoring), faculty in-service training, student housing, scholarships and loans, placement, student orientation, recruiting, staff selection, and educational research involving instruction, student characteristics, and administration. The knowledge requisite for counseling of individual differences, measurement, research, statistics, personality and learning theory, and personnel methods has considerable relevance for many operations of the college.

Traditional college counseling has emphasized face-to-face relationships with students, and the counselor's purpose has been to help students increase their self-understanding, facilitate their decision making, and improve their problem solving. The expanding role of the college counselor suggests an increasing awareness that students' problems frequently have origins in the situations in which the students live, often the college, and that the effectiveness of students' decisions depends in large part on the alternatives available to them. Students fail academically not only because of inadequate ability or poor study habits but also because of deficiencies in the curriculum, instruction, and examinations. Many students in college have trouble because they should not be there but alternatives other than college are not easily available to them. The frustrations of counseling students such as these force many counselors to the realization that a student's situation can be improved only by affecting the collegiate organization and processes. The counselor's assumption of the role of consultant on the campus is a move in this direction.

CHARACTERISTICS OF COUNSELORS. As little is known about the characteristics of college counselors as is known about their numbers. Ayers and others (1966) have provided some information about directors of counseling services. Of the 287 men identified, 71 percent were between the ages of 30 and 49 years, with only 24 percent being over 50. The modal age was between 30 and 40. Of the 68 women, 62 percent were in their thirties and forties, and 32 percent were over 50. Approximately one-half of all these directors had doctorates, with almost all others having master's degrees. In universities, 88 percent had doctorates, in liberal arts colleges 54 percent, in teachers colleges 65 percent, and in junior colleges 15 percent. About 30 percent of all directors of counseling reported that they belonged to no professional organization, while one-half belonged to the American Personnel and Guidance Association, including 28 percent who were members of the ACPA. Membership in the American Psychological Association was reported by 38 percent. About 28 percent belonged to only one association; 20 percent belonged to two. The modal number of years of experience of directors in their present positions was from two to four years, and only 37 percent had been in their jobs for more than five years.

An informal survey of directors of counseling services in 54 American colleges and universities, mostly large ones, in 1964, identified 147 persons counseling full-time, 184 part-time. Of full-time counselors whose sole function was counseling, 45 percent had doctorates. In the mid-1960's, perhaps slightly fewer than one-half of all full-time professional college counselors had doctorates; the remainder had M.A.'s, with many of these trained beyond the M.A.

Inferences can be made about the interests and claimed competencies of college counselors by looking at the characteristics of students they counsel. Hagenah and others (1960) presented a model for conducting such surveys, a model which has been applied by the counseling center staff of the University of Maryland (1966). The same authors (Hagenah & others, 1960) reported that in 1957 counselors at the University of Minnesota Student Counseling Bureau were allocating their efforts, as shown by the types of major problems they identified in students, as follows: 44 percent to vocational counseling, 34 percent to educational counseling, and 19 percent to personal, social, family, and emotional counseling. A miscellaneous category included the remainder.

That the case load, student problems, and presumably the interests and competencies of counselors in a center can change over a decade was demonstrated by Thrush (1957), who reported a case study of the Ohio State University center, where the vocational-counseling orientation evolved into an orientation involving greater emphasis on a broader range of student problems.

Minge and Cass (1966) asked a sample of 140 students at Washington State University how they perceived the counseling center. Of these, 14 percent had been there; 14 percent had not heard of the center; 22 percent would not go there; 6 percent would not refer other students; and the remainder had other perceptions. The perceived functions of counselors were not elicited.

The characteristics of students requesting counseling also provide information about how counselors are perceived and how they function. Differences are found here among campuses. At Minnesota, students who sought counseling did not differ much from those who did not (Schneidler & Berdie, 1942; Campbell, 1965; Berdie & Stein, 1966). Berdie and Stein found, however, as did Collier and Nugent (1965), that students seeking certain kinds of counseling or coming for counseling because of some specified reasons differed from other students. Mendelsohn (1966) found at the University of California center that counselees differed from other students on the Myers-Briggs Indicator and that counselor-counselee similarity on this index was related to duration of counseling.

More is known about facilities now available for the professional preparation of college counselors than is known of the training of persons now serving in this capacity. The American Personnel and Guidance Association's policy on professional preparation (1964) applies to college counselors, as does the "Greystone report" of the American Psychological Association's Division of Counseling Psychology (Thompson & Super, 1964). The latter publication contains reprints of earlier documents of the American Psychological Association (APA) and other papers pertaining to professional preparation. The American Personnel and Guidance Association (APGA) policy places greater emphasis than does that of the APA on the counselor's preparation in education, whereas the APA's emphasis naturally is more on psychology than the APGA's is. The APGA envisages a two-year graduate program, the APA a doctoral program. Both emphasize, but to varying degrees, the need for courses and seminars related to psychological measurement, personality theory, research and statistics, the individual in his social environment, and supervised practicum and internship experiences.

The American College Student Personnel Association (D. Robinson, 1966) and the Council of Student Personnel Associations in Higher Education

(1964) also have prepared general policy statements pertaining to the professional preparation of student personnel workers which have relevance for college counseling.

In 1965, as a result of changes in federal legislation, summer institutes for the training of counselors in two- and four-year colleges were offered under provisions of the National Defense Education Act (NDEA). The ACPA has adopted a resolution suggesting that federal funds available for preparing college-student personnel workers be used for developing programs which are a more regular part of an institution's graduate program than are summer or full-year institutes. Some NDEA funds also have been made available for fellowships related to college counseling.

Matson (1965), in a study done for the National Committee for Appraisal and Development of Junior College Student Personnel Programs, found meager evidence that universities were systematically preparing counselors specifically trained for junior colleges. She questions the assumption that training appropriate for school or university counselors suffices for those planning to counsel in junior colleges.

It is reported that in 1965 24 universities offered doctoral programs in counseling psychology which had been approved by the APA (Ross, 1965).

In the mid-1960's, current issues concerning the preparation of college counselors included the extent to which counselors are educators, psychologists, or behavioral scientists; the relative responsibility of departments of psychology, schools of education, and others for training counselors; the level of training to be required (masters or doctoral); the differences in preparing counselors to work at varying educational levels; and the extent to which they are to be prepared as therapists, teachers, group workers, and vocational-educational counselors.

ORGANIZATION OF COUNSELING SERVICES AND PROGRAMS. The administrative organization of college counseling is influenced by the size of the institution, the resources it is willing to commit, and its perception of the role of the professionally trained counselor. Perhaps even more important are the personalities and "historical accidents" that determine institutional evolution. Practically no research bears directly on counseling administration, except for that of Reeves (1961), who applied methods of job analysis and accounting to a university counseling bureau mainly to explore the feasibility of the method, but also to provide data regarding the costs of various services provided by the department. College counseling directors have met informally annually since 1950, and the proceedings of these meetings, some of which have been published (Berdie, 1951, 1953, 1954), contain papers discussing counseling personnel, public and institutional relations, confidentiality and records, in-service training, functions, and evaluation.

The American Council on Education, in an attempt to further the development of college-student personnel work, established a committee which, in 1937, published a monograph, *The Student Personnel Point of View*. This was revised in 1949 (Williamson & others). The committee for several years conducted a consultation program which made experts available to advise colleges regarding their programs, and in 1952 the committee reported on the effectiveness of its consultations (Brumbaugh & Berdie). This evaluation revealed that persons most responsible for the development of student services were presidents, deans, and administrators, not faculties, students, or governing boards.

Colleges show no consistent organizational patterns for counseling, but different approaches can be identified. Some colleges, particularly small ones, designate an instructor of psychology or education to devote a share of his time to counseling. In this capacity he may serve in the office of the dean of students or the academic dean. Other colleges employ a professional counselor who may, at least during some part of the year, teach one or more courses related to counseling. These counselors are expected to maintain working relations with other college officials and local physicians, psychiatrists, and clinics, and frequently they are responsible for the institution's testing program.

Other institutions, usually larger ones, establish a counseling office with a full-time or nearly full-time professional counselor in charge and with a staff of full-time or part-time counselors working with him. Some universities employ only or mainly counselors who have completed their professional training; others use graduate students in psychology, education, or counseling and guidance. In the latter instance these counseling opportunities may provide an important part of the graduate education program, and the positions may be treated as internships or practicums which involve available professional staff in considerable supervision.

Many colleges, regardless of whether or not they have counseling centers, have organized faculty-advisory programs, and professional counselors may aid in the organization and supervision of these and provide consultation to and a source of referral for faculty advisors (Hardee, 1959; Koile, 1954). Larger universities may have professionally trained counselors in a variety of offices providing services to students. Thus, counselors may provide counseling regarding both budgets and nonfiscal matters to students applying for loans, or regarding both student organizations and personal matters to students coming to the office of the dean of men.

The emphasis of a college counseling center is revealed by the characteristics and expectations of students it serves and by those of its staff. Some centers are mainly psychotherapy services (Hanfmann, 1963; Grummon & Gordon, 1948), some vocational-guidance bureaus, and some extensions of the academic divisions of the college, such as the early program at Ohio State University or that in the General College of the University of Minnesota. Danskin (1965) describes the role he prefers for a college center and emphasizes its research function.

Limited counseling staffs, large enrollments, and administration, faculty, counselor, and student concern over behavior pathology engender a condition which almost inevitably results in a campus counseling center drifting in the direction of becoming a psychological clinic. Students with severe problems are referred with urgency, given priority for appointments, and seen more often and more regularly by counselors, with the result that students with less dramatic needs experience increasing difficulty in availing themselves of the service of the center. Thus, a counseling staff with much commitment to developmental counseling and to working with students already making satisfactory progress must make special provisions to resist this drift. The number of interviews per student may be limited, differential charges may be levied (although most centers do not charge fees to their own students), certain types of cases may not be accepted, or blocks of time may be reserved for counseling and related activities for less disturbed students. Relevant here is the research of Johnson (1965) reporting a relationship at the University of Missouri counseling center between number of interviews and success of counseling for emotional problems but no such relationship for vocational problems or those with combined diagnoses.

PERSISTENT CONCERNS IN COLLEGE COUNSELING. The *Journal of Counseling Psychology*, the *Personnel and Guidance Journal*, and the *Journal of Student Personnel* provide means for identifying issues and concerns in college counseling. The chapters on counseling in the *Annual Reviews of Psychology* aperiodically summarize this and other information (Berdie, 1950, 1959; Bordin, 1950; Pepinsky, 1951; Stuit, 1951; Gilbert, 1952; Williamson, 1953; Wrenn, 1954; Hobbs & Seeman, 1955; Shoben, 1956; Shaw, 1957; Tyler, 1958; Brayfield, 1963; Patterson, 1966). In 1965 the *Journal of Counseling Psychology* first published a review of research in counseling in 1963 (Schmidt & Pepinsky, 1965). Myers (1966) published a similar review of research in 1964. The *College Student Personnel Abstracts,* first published in 1965, also provides information concerning research and other publications pertaining to college counseling.

THE COUNSELING PROCESS. College counselors have shown persistent curiosity regarding what happens during their interviews. The most "microscopic" observations of the process have been those of Francis Robinson and his students (F. Robinson, 1950), who have studied sequential processes, the significance of pauses, and related behaviors. The Minnesota group (Berdie, 1958) devised a bidimensional system for categorizing counselor responses according to purpose and technique, and the analyses of interviews of four college counselors revealed differential patterns which were consistent from interview to interview.

Parker (1958) had professional college counselors observe and report on their own covert language processes at varying stages of counseling and concluded that the "richness" of the counselor's explanatory thinking had little relationship to information revealed during counseling. He found little evidence that diagnosis was continuing and "hierarchical."

Evaluation of Counseling Outcomes. College counselors, perhaps even more than other counselors, have wished to know the extent to which students are influenced by counseling and have made many attempts to assess its impact. Only a few such attempts can be mentioned here. Observed as outcomes of counseling have been changes in the nature, appropriateness, and certainty of vocational choices, college grades, and persistence, adjustment, self-references, reports of others, scores on personality inventories, later success in life, and more specific behavior changes. Volsky and others (1965) and Campbell (1965) have carefully analyzed the strategy of such research and described studies which provide models for experimental design. Few of the studies reported in the literature observe changes in more than one modality of behavior; some do not use control groups; and some using control groups fail to consider motivational differences between students who seek counseling and others. Only a few studies relate specific counseling processes to specified and relevant outcomes.

One of the first studies to incorporate a control group was that of Williamson and Bordin (1941), who compared about 400 college freshmen one year after they had been counseled with a similar group of freshmen who had not been counseled. The two groups were matched on relevant variables, such as college, age, and ability, and compared on the basis of college grades as shown by university records and "adjustment," mainly educational-vocational, as judged by interviewers. Twenty-five years later Campbell (1965) located 99 percent of these former students and induced 90 percent of those still living to participate in his follow-up study. The college records of the counseled group were superior to those of the noncounseled, as were other indexes of success in life, but the noncounseled group showed consistent evidence that its members, perhaps since college or before, were somewhat more satisfied with their lives.

Volsky and Hewer (1960) observed the impact of group and individual counseling on the appropriateness of vocational choices of students and found no differences. They reported the difficulty judges found in agreeing on such appropriateness, and Gonyea (1962) discussed in detail the adequacy of the appropriateness criterion.

Other counselors have used college success as a criterion with which to evaluate counseling. Morehead and Johnson (1964) compared 48 engineering freshmen who received special counseling from faculty advisors to a matched control group and found the counseled group earned higher grades and had lower dropout rates. Guthrie and others (1953) reported a somewhat similar attempt to assess the impact of dormitory counselors. He found that dormitory counseling had no effect on academic achievement. Chestnut (1965) compared changes in grade-point average of two experimental groups experiencing two kinds of group counseling and a matched control group and found differences between the two group-counseling samples and between these samples and the control group. His results suggested that both counselor-structured and group-structured group counseling influenced academic achievement and that perhaps counselor-structured groups had more influence. Shepherd (1965) found a difference in graduation rates between counseled and noncounseled students favoring the counseled group. Vosbeck, reporting in Volsky and others (1965), reported a Minnesota study utilizing experimental and control groups carefully matched on ability, attitude, and motivation. Of the counseled group, seven years after counseling 64 percent had their degrees or were making satisfactory progress, as compared to 45 percent of the control group. On the other hand, Hill and Grieneeks (1966) at the University of Texas found no differences in grades or graduation rates between students who were counseled and a noncounseled control group matched on sex and ability.

Changes in self-references, self-description, and personality-inventory responses and scores have been used as criteria to assess the impact of college counseling. Some examples include the early work of Raimy (1948), who judged the positive or negative tone of statements made by counselees in interviews and charted changes occurring systematically during counseling. Rogers and Dymond (1954) observed experimental groups who were counseled, delayed-control groups receiving counseling after pre- and postmeasures, and noncounseled control groups; used Q-sorts, other self-rating scales, and ratings by others; and reported the proportions of persons changing in each group. Their evidence quite consistently suggested criterion changes related to counseling. Ashby and others (1957) used self-reports and judgments of others in comparing changes in students experiencing two types of counseling, reflective and leading. In order to control counselor variability, each counselor was to provide the assigned type of counseling to specified students, but occasionally when they judged the alternative type of counseling to be more appropriate for a given student, the counselors departed from the experimental design. This defect in experimental procedure raises serious questions concerning Ashby's results, which showed little difference in the outcome of counseling between leading and reflective methods.

Nichols and Beck (1960) studied changes in California Personality Inventory scores of 75 undergraduates each having at least five interviews and also obtained ratings of change from counselors and counselees. In all, 30 change indexes were available, which reduced to six factors, four reflecting improvement. A control group showed change on only some of these factors.

Success in later life has seldom been used as a criterion of counseling. Campbell (1965) had judges make reliable ratings 25 years after counseling of the individual's "contribution to society," and although all of his differences favored the counseled group, none was statistically significant. Krumboltz (1966) and Tyler (1961) have been among those advocating

that specific behavior changes be designated as counseling objectives, and the early studies of Aldrich (1942, 1949) showed how counseling was related to the social behavior of college students. Whittmore and Heimann (1966) compared students counseled with and without operant conditioning to observe changes in originality of responses and found a few suggestive differences.

DIAGNOSIS. Counselors have paid considerable attention to the classification of students' needs and problems—that is, to diagnosis. Williamson (1965) has described some of the early antecedents to educational diagnosis in colleges and universities, citing publications of President Daniel J. Gilman of Johns Hopkins in 1897 and President William Rainey Harper of the University of Chicago in 1899. In 1937, Williamson and Darley presented a diagnostic system for the use of college counselors and proposed that useful problem category labels were "educational," "financial," "vocational," "health," "family," and "emotional-social." Following the suggestion of Bordin (1946) that problems be classified according to causes so that treatment could be assigned selectively, Pepinsky (1948) tentatively explored diagnostic categories labeled "lack of assurance," "lack of information," "lack of skill," "dependence," "cultural self-conflict," "interpersonal self-conflict," "intrapersonal self-conflict," and "choice-anxiety." He found evidence supporting the use of at least five of these categories.

For several years relatively little research was devoted to diagnosis, perhaps as a concomitant of Rogers' observation (1942) that in many instances counseling requires no initial diagnosis. By 1951 Rogers had, in a sense, combined diagnosis and therapy ("In a very meaningful and accurate sense, therapy *is* diagnosis." Rogers, 1951, p. 223), and college counselors showed less interest than before in problems of diagnosis. In the mid-1960's interest again was demonstrated in diagnosis, and Callis (1965) described diagnostic categories useful for research purposes, as demonstrated by Borresen (1965).

The research on diagnosis, process, and evaluation provides a basic research model in college counseling. The counselor's essential problem is what counseling method (process research) made available to which student (diagnostic research) will achieve what change (evaluation research). No research report has been identified which reflects this broad and necessary model.

COLLEGE SUCCESS AND PERSISTENCE. College counselors have been concerned with college success and persistence not only as criteria of counseling but also as student problems and have directed much research to a better understanding of these phenomena. The most complete information regarding persistence in college was reported by Iffert (1957), who provided estimates that about one-half of college freshmen graduate. Darley (1962) related measures of ability and achievement to persistence of college students in selected states where comprehensive data were on record. Thistlethwaite (1963) studied success and retention in a large group of superior students, drawn from 300,000 taking the National Merit Scholarship Test, and found that 25 percent withdrew within two years from the college they originally had entered. Rose (1965) identified students who appeared to be potential college dropouts and provided counseling to an experimental group, which then had significantly fewer casualties than its control group. These results tended to agree with those already described by Vosbeck, in Volsky and others (1965). Rose and Elton (1966) also compared personality characteristics of withdrawing and persisting students, and a discriminant analysis incorporating scores on the Omnibus Personality Inventory and Rotter Incomplete Sentences revealed significant differences. Watley (1965) compared end-of-year freshmen who persisted with those who did not persist, each group being divided into subgroups of academically successful and unsuccessful students. He reported that academically successful students who withdrew had scores on the Minnesota Counseling Inventory more indicative of personal problems than did other students. A theoretical analysis of conditions related to academic success and a comprehensive review of both psychometric and sociological research has been provided by Lavin (1965).

VOCATIONAL DECISIONS. Many authors agree with Tyler (1961) and Brayfield (1961) that counseling psychologists are most effective in aiding students with problems of vocational decisions, and considerable effort has been devoted to related research and theory. Project Talent (Flanagan, 1964) represents the most extensive of these efforts and describes the career decisions and concomitants of youth in high school and college. The volume edited for the National Vocational Guidance Association by Borow (1964) contains the essence of much of what has been done.

College counselors have become increasingly aware of career decisions that their students make as they approach graduation, particularly choices involving graduate work. A report of the educational plans of 33,982 college graduates of 1961 revealed that 75 percent planned on postgraduate training (Davis, 1964). An earlier report (Bureau of Social Science Research, Inc., 1963) provided a mass of relevant information and revealed that over one-third of graduates of 1958 had continued their formal education by 1960. Much information is available about the input and output of graduate and professional schools, but little study has been made of the counseling of college students considering advanced work.

The Unhappy Student. Counselors devote considerable time to discussions with college students of behaviors and attitudes related to conditions other than school and jobs—family, friends, feelings of self-confidence, life goals and values, and relationships with oneself and others. In these areas the work of the counselor and that of the psychotherapist are hard to distinguish from one another, and Rogers (1942) early attempted to equate counseling and psychotherapy. In response to this definitional problem, the Division of Counseling Psychology of the APA (American Psychological Association, 1956) adopted a report defining counseling psychology as a specialty with its roots in vocational guidance, psychological measurement, and personality development and emphasizing the need for counselors to attend more to personality development. Vance and Volsky (1962) attempted to resolve an apparent dilemma by viewing both psychotherapy and one type of counseling as "psychological discordance reduction." Counseling and psychotherapy are seen as two distinct but closely related processes having as their purpose adding new responses or perceptions to the person's repertoire which reduce future behavior discordance.

Persons in psychiatric or "mental health" units of universities, usually within medical settings, have produced a considerable volume of literature dealing with students' problems, although most of this is not based on systematic research. No satisfactory estimates are available concerning the prevalence in the American college-student population of things such as suicide, major and minor emotional disruptions, alcoholism, drug addiction, and sexual disturbances. Blaine and McArthur (1961) discuss emotional problems of students and the roles of college psychiatrists, psychologists, and faculty advisors in dealing with neuroses, study problems, character disorders and homosexuality, psychoses, suicide, and apathy. They also discuss problems of special groups of students—women, graduate students, and those in medical schools and schools of business administration. Farnsworth (1957) has presented a more general discussion of mental health programs in higher education, and Bradten (1965) discusses problems of suicide and lists books on mental health of interest to counselors with particular attention to the literature on suicide.

Resources in College Counseling. College counselors make use of tests, occupational and educational information (books, pamphlets, and films), campus and community facilities, and the various procedures of modifying behavior derived from psychoanalysis, nondirective counseling, conditioning and learning theory, and centuries of less theoretically oriented experience.

The American Council on Education (1959) has described the role of measurement in higher education and presented seven "case histories" showing testing programs in different colleges. Gilbert and Ewing (1965) have developed a "counseling program" devised to impart information about test scores to counselees. A similar, more specific program has been developed and evaluated by Forster (1966). The American College Testing Program, in its series of research reports initiated in 1965, provides much information about tests of use to college counselors. The new comprehensive college tests published by the Educational Testing Service provide a means for counselors and administrators to work more effectively with students regarding problems of advanced placement and educational evaluation. Many other tests and state and national testing programs provide information to college counselors.

Occupational information and literature is as relevant for college counselors as it is for secondary-school counselors, but relatively little research or few publications recognize this. Most college counseling centers maintain some occupational information, but few invest enough staff time, space, or money for materials to justify calling this an important counseling resource. The potential, however, is great. Colleges increasingly are making available to high school students information to help in decisions of college choice, but graduate and professional schools still have far to go in this direction.

College counselors make much use of the facilities on their campuses. College residence programs provide a means for extending educational and counseling services to many students not otherwise initiating counseling contacts, and counselors and residence hall staffs frequently can cooperatively effect environmental changes to supplement counseling interviews and classroom instruction (Williamson, 1961). The research of Aldrich (1942, 1949) illustrates one way for counselors to use as a counseling resource the activities and organizations program of a university.

The relationships between the university's orientation program for new students and its counseling program are nicely demonstrated by patterns established at Michigan State University, Pennsylvania State University, and the University of Minnesota. Counselors find the medical and psychiatric facilities on campus to be useful resources, and currently a joint committee of the ACPA and the American College Health Association is studying these relationships. Counselors also have as a valuable campus resource faculty advisory programs where cooperative efforts touch on course selection, study skills, and college attitudes, as well as on educational and vocational choices.

PROBLEMS AND TRENDS. The foregoing discussion suggests many of the problems and trends in college counseling. The number of college students has increased faster than the supply of counselors and the funds available to employ counselors. Graduate facilities for preparing college counselors are relatively limited, and the number of students selecting this field as a career is not great. At the same time, the increasing complexity of society, the growing pressures on students, and the expectation of students and their parents that they *will receive* individual and personal attention and benefit from new developments in the behavioral sciences all increase both the need and the demand for counseling.

Counselors continue to be disturbed by a sensed isolation from the rest of academe (Berdie, 1966), and, at the same time, they realize how students must perceive the counselor's relatively unusual role. They are aware of their responsibilities to the student and to the institution and sensitive to possible conflicts involving these dual responsibilities.

Increasingly counselors are concerned with "behavior change," not only with problems of methods, procedures, and effectiveness but also with problems of social and personal values, morals, and ethics. Problems of special groups are drawing increasing attention—women, minority racial groups, and the economically underprivileged. Finally, college counselors are showing increasing awareness of the counselor's responsibility not only to aid the student with a problem but also to discover origins of problems and effect social changes that will result in a better milieu for student development.

Ralph F. Berdie
University of Minnesota

References

Aldrich, Margaret G. "An Exploratory Study of Social Guidance at the College Level." *Ed Psychol Meas* 2:209–16; 1942.

Aldrich, Margaret G. "A Follow-up Study of Social Guidance at the College Level." *J Applied Psychol* 33:258–64; 1949.

American Council on Education. *College Testing: A Guide to Practices and Programs.* The Council, 1959. 187p.

American Personnel and Guidance Association, Professional Preparation and Standards Committee. "The Counselor: Professional Preparation and Role." A statement of policy. *Personnel Guid J* 42:536–41; 1964.

American Psychological Association, Division of Counseling Psychology, Committee on Definition. "Counseling Psychology as a Specialty." *Am Psychologist* 11:282–5; 1956.

Arkoff, Abe, and others. "Mental Health and Counseling Ideas of Asian and American Students." *J Counseling Psychol* 13:219–23; 1966.

Ashby, Jefferson D., and others. "Effects on Clients of a Reflective and a Leading Type of Psychotherapy." *Psychol Monogr* 7; 1957. 32p.

Astin, Alexander W. "Effects of Different College Environments on the Vocational Choices of High Aptitude Students." *J Counseling Psychol* 12:28–34; 1965(*a*).

Astin, Alexander W. *Who Goes Where to College.* SRA, 1965(*b*).

Ayers, Archie R., and others. *Student Services Administration in Higher Education.* HEW Bulletin, 1966. 229p.

Berdie, Ralph F. "Counseling—An Educational Technique." *Ed Psychol Meas* 9:89–94; 1949.

Berdie, Ralph F. "Counseling Methods." In *Annual Review of Psychology,* Vol. 1. Annual Reviews, Inc., 1950. p. 255–66.

Berdie, Ralph F. (Ed.) *Concepts and Programs of Counseling.* U Minnesota Press, 1951. 81p.

Berdie, Ralph F. (Ed.) *Roles and Relationships in Counseling.* U Minnesota Press, 1953.

Berdie, Ralph F. (Ed.) *Counseling and the College Program.* U Minnesota Press, 1954. 58p.

Berdie, Ralph F. "A Program of Counseling Interview Research." *Ed Psychol Meas* 18:255–74; 1958.

Berdie, Ralph F. "Counseling." In *Annual Review of Psychology,* Vol. 10. Annual Reviews, Inc., 1959. p. 345–70.

Berdie, Ralph F. "Student Personnel Work: Definition

and Redefinition." *J Col Student Personnel* 7:131–6; 1966.

Berdie, Ralph F., and Stein, June B. "A Comparison of New University Students Who Do and Do Not Seek Counseling." *J Counseling Psychol* 13:310–7; 1966.

Blaine, Graham B., Jr., and McArthur, Charles C. *Emotional Problems of the Student.* Appleton, 1961. 254p.

Bordin, Edward S. "Diagnosis in Counseling and Psychotherapy." *Ed Psychol Meas* 6:169–84; 1946.

Bordin, Edward S. "Counseling Methods: Therapy." In *Annual Review of Psychology*, Vol. 1. Annual Reviews, Inc., 1950. p. 267–76.

Borow, Henry. (Ed.) *Man in a World at Work.* Houghton, 1964. 606p.

Borresen, Ann M. "Counselor Influence on Diagnostic Classification of Client Problems." *J Counseling Psychol* 12:252–8; 1965.

Bradten, Leif J. "Suicidal Tendencies Among College Students." *J Nat Assn Student Personnel Adm* 2:35–7; 1965.

Brayfield, Arthur H. "Vocational Counseling Today." In Williamson, Edmund G. (Ed.) *Vocational Counseling, A Reappraisal in Honor of Donald G. Paterson.* U Minnesota Press, 1961.

Brayfield, Arthur H. "Counseling Psychology." In Farnsworth, Paul R., and others. (Eds.) *Annual Review of Psychology*, Vol. 14. Annual Reviews, Inc., 1963. p. 319–50.

Brumbaugh, Aaron J., and Berdie, Ralph F. *Student Personnel Work in Transition.* ACE, 1952. 44p.

Bureau of Social Science Research, Inc. *Two Years After the College Degree.* GPO, 1963. 335p.

Callis, Robert. "Diagnostic Classification as a Research Tool." *J Counseling Psychol* 12:238–48; 1965.

Campbell, David P. *The Results of Counseling: Twenty-five Years Later.* Saunders, 1965.

Chestnut, William J. "The Effects of Structured and Unstructured Group Counseling on Male College Students' Underachievement." *J Counseling Psychol* 12:388–94; 1965.

Clark, D. C. "Characteristics of Counseling Centers in Large Universities." *Personnel Guid J* 64:817–23; 1966.

College Student Personnel Institute. *College Student Personnel Abstracts.* The Institute. 1965 to date (quarterly).

Collier, Boy N., and Nugent, Frank A. "Characteristics of Self-referred, Staff-referred and Non-counseled College Students." *J Counseling Psychol* 12:208–12; 1965.

Condon, Margaret E. "A Survey of Special Facilities for the Physically Handicapped in the Colleges." *Personnel Guid J* 35:579–83; 1957.

Council of Student Personnel Associations in Higher Education, Commission on Professional Development. *A Proposal for Professional Preparation in College Student Personnel Work.* The Council, 1964. 8p.

Counseling Center Staff, University of Maryland. "Inter-judge Agreement on the Use of Counseling Categories." *J Col Student Personnel* 7:213–7; 1966.

Danskin, David G. "My Focus for a University Counseling Center." *J Col Student Personnel* 6:263–7; 1965.

Darley, John G. *Promise and Performance, A Study of Ability and Achievement in Higher Education.* U California Press, 1962.

Davis, James A. *Great Aspirations.* Aldine Publishing Co., 1964. 319p.

Dennis, Laurence E., and Kauffman, Joseph F. (Eds.) *The College and the Student.* ACE, 1966. 390p.

Education Directory, Part III, *Higher Education, 1964–65.* USOE, HEW, 1966.

Erikson, Erik H. "Identity and the Life Cycle." *Psychol Issues* 1:18–171; 1959.

Farnsworth, Dana L. *Mental Health in College and University.* Harvard U Press, 1957.

Flanagan, John C. *The American High School Student.* Project Talent Office, U Pittsburgh, 1964.

Forster, Jerald R. "An Investigation of the Effects of Two Feedback Methods When Communicating Psychological Information." Doctoral dissertation. U Minnesota, 1966.

Gilbert, William M. "Counseling Therapy and Diagnosis." In *Annual Review of Psychology*, Vol. 3. Annual Reviews, Inc., 1952. p. 351–80.

Gilbert, William M., and Ewing, Thomas N. *An Investigation of the Importance of the Personal Relationship and Associated Factors in Teaching Machine Procedures.* Final report to HEW. U Illinois Press, 1965.

Gonyea, George G. "Appropriateness-of-vocational-choice as a Criterion of Counseling Outcome." *J Counseling Psychol* 9:213–9; 1962.

Grummon, Donald L., and Gordon, Thomas. "The Counseling Center at the University of Chicago." *Am Psychologist* 3:166–71; 1948.

Guthrie, George M., and others. "Effects of Dormitory Counseling on Academic Achievement." *Personnel Guid J* 31:307–9; 1953.

Hagenah, Theda, and others. "A Counseling Case Load Survey Method." *J Col Student Personnel* 1:11–5; 1960.

Hanfmann, Eugenia. *Psychological Counseling in a Small College.* Schenkman Co., 1963. 131p.

Hardee, Melvene D. *The Faculty in College Counseling.* McGraw-Hill, 1959.

Heist, Paul. "Diversity in College Student Characteristics." *J Ed Sociol* 33:279–91; 1960.

Hill, Arthur H., and Grieneeks, Laurabeth. "Criteria in the Evaluation of Educational and Vocational Counseling in College." *J Counseling Psychol* 13:198–201; 1966.

Hobbs, Nicholas, and Seeman, Julius. "Counseling." In *Annual Review of Psychology*, Vol. 6. Annual Reviews, Inc., 1955. p. 379–404.

Hoyt, Donald, and Tripp, Philip A. "Characteristics of ACPA Members." *J Col Student Personnel* 8:32–9; 1967.

Iffert, Robert E. *Retention and Withdrawal of College Students.* HEW, 1957.

Jahoda, Marie. *Current Concepts of Positive Mental Health.* Basic Books, 1958.

Johnson, Ray W. "Number of Interviews, Diagnosis

and Success of Counseling." *J Counseling Psychol* 12:248–51; 1965.

Koile, Carl A. "Faculty Counseling in Colleges and Universities." *Teach Col Rec* 55:384–9; 1954.

Krumboltz, John D. "Behavioral Goals for Counseling." *J Counseling Psychol* 13:153–9; 1966.

Lavin, David E. *The Prediction of Academic Performance.* Russell Sage, 1965.

Lloyd, Wesley P. *Student Counseling in Japan.* U Minnesota Press, 1953. 204p.

Lloyd, Wesley P. "Student Personnel Services in Universities of the World." *Personnel Guid J* 34:351–2; 1956.

Matson, Jane E. "Appraisal of Existing and Potential Resources for the Preparation of Junior College Student Personnel Specialists." In National Committee for Appraisal and Development of Junior College Student Personnel Programs. *Junior College Student Personnel Programs: Appraisal and Development.* The Committee, 1965.

Mendelsohn, Gerald A. "Effects of Client Personality and Client-Counselor Similarity on the Duration of Counseling: A Replication and Extension." *J Counseling Psychol* 13:228–34; 1966.

Minge, M. Ronald, and Cass, William A. "Student Perceptions of a University Counseling Center." *J Col Student Personnel* 7:141–4; 1966.

Morehead, Charles C., and Johnson, J. Clyde. "Some Effects of a Faculty Advising Program." *Personnel Guid J;* 1964.

Mueller, Kate H. "The Married Student on Campus." *Col U* 35:155–63; 1960.

Myers, Roger A. "Research in Counseling Psychology —1964." *J Counseling Psychol* 13:371–9; 1966.

Nichols, Robert C., and Beck, Karl W. "Factors in Psychotherapy Change." *J Cons Psychol* 24:388–99; 1960.

Oetting, Eugene R. *Problems and Issues in the Administration of College and University Counseling Services.* USOE final report, Colorado State U Press, 1966.

Parker, Clyde A. "As a Clinician Thinks." *J Counseling Psychol* 5:253–61; 1958.

Patterson, Cecil H. "Counseling." In *Annual Review of Psychology,* Vol. 17. Annual Reviews, Inc., 1966. p. 79–110.

Pepinsky, Harold B. *The Selection and Use of Diagnostic Categories in Clinical Counseling.* Stanford U Press, 1948. Also published in *Applied Psychol Monogr* 15; 1948.

Pepinsky, Harold B. "Counseling Methods: Therapy." In *Annual Review of Psychology,* Vol. 2. Annual Reviews, Inc., 1951. p. 317–34.

Pruitt, Anne S. "Characteristics of College Student Personnel Workers." *J Col Student Personnel* 7: 159–66; 1966.

Raimy, Victor C. "Self-reference in Counseling Interviews." *J Cons Psychol* 12:153–63; 1948.

Reeves, James H. "Analyzing Student Counseling Service Costs." Doctoral dissertation. U California, 1961.

Riker, Harold C. *Housing as Learning Centers.* APGA, 1965.

Robinson, Donald W. "Analysis of Three Statements Relative to the Preparation of College Student Personnel Workers." *J Col Student Personnel* 7:254–6; 1966.

Robinson, Francis. *Principles and Procedures in Student Counseling.* Harper, 1950. 321p.

Rogers, Carl R. *Counseling and Psychotherapy.* Houghton, 1942. 450p.

Rogers, Carl R. *Client-centered Therapy.* Houghton, 1951. 560p.

Rogers, Carl R., and Dymond, Rosalind F. *Psychotherapy and Personality Change.* U Chicago Press, 1954.

Rose, Harriett A. "Prediction and Prevention of Freshman Attrition." *J Counseling Psychol* 12:399–403; 1965.

Rose, Harriett A., and Elton, Charles F. "Another Look at the College Dropout." *J Counseling Psychol* 13:242–5; 1966.

Ross, Sherman. "APA-approved Doctoral Programs in Clinical and in Counseling Psychology." *Am Psychologist* 20:794–5; 1965.

Sanford, Nevitt. (Ed.) *The American College.* Wiley, 1962.

Schmidt, Lyle D., and Pepinsky, Harold B. "Counseling Research in 1963." *J Counseling Psychol* 12: 418–27; 1965.

Schneidler, Gwendolen, and Berdie, Ralph F. "Representativeness of College Students Who Receive Counseling Services." *J Ed Psychol* 33:545–51; 1942.

Shaw, Franklin J. "Counseling." In *Annual Review of Psychology,* Vol. 8. Annual Reviews, Inc., 1957. p. 357–76.

Shepherd, Robert E. "The Relation of Counseling and Student Problems to Graduation." *J Counseling Psychol* 12:244–7; 1965.

Shoben, Edward Joseph, Jr. "Counseling." In *Annual Review of Psychology,* Vol. 7. Annual Reviews, Inc., 1956. p. 147–72.

Shoben, Edward Joseph, Jr. *Student Stress and the College Experience.* U.S. National Student Association, 1966. 32p.

Stuit, Dewey B. "Counseling Methods: Diagnosis." In *Annual Review of Psychology.* Vol. 2. Annual Reviews, Inc., 1951. p. 305–16.

Thistlethwaite, Donald L. *Recruitment and Retention of Talented College Students.* Cooperative Research Project. USOE, 1963. 294p.

Thompson, Albert S., and Super, Donald E. (Eds.) *The Professional Preparation of Counseling Psychologists.* Report of the 1964 Greystone Conference, Columbia U, 1964. 165p.

Thrush, Randolph S. "An Agency in Transition: The Case Study of a Counseling Center." *J Counseling Psychol* 4:210–46; 1957.

Tyler, Leona E. "Counseling." In *Annual Review of Psychology,* Vol. 9. Annual Reviews, Inc., 1958. p. 375–90.

Tyler, Leona E. *The Work of the Counselor,* 2nd ed. Appleton, 1961. 327p.

Vance, Forrest L., and Volsky, Theodore C. "Counseling and Psychotherapy: Split Personality or Sia-

mese Twins?" *Am Psychologist* 17:565–70; 1962.
Volsky, Theodore C., and Hewer, Vivian H. "A Program of Group Counseling." *J Counseling Psychol* 7:71–3; 1960.
Volsky, Theodore C., and others. *The Outcomes of Counseling and Psychotherapy: Theory and Research.* U Minnesota Press, 1965.
Watley, Donivan J. "The Minnesota Counseling Inventory and Persistence in an Institute of Technology." *J Counseling Psychol* 12:94–7; 1965.
Whittemore, R. G., and Heimann, R. A. "Modification of Originality Responses." *J Counseling Psychol* 13:213–18; 1966.
Williamson, Edmund G. *Counseling Adolescents.* McGraw-Hill, 1950. 548p.
Williamson, Edmund G. "Counseling: Therapy and Diagnosis." In *Annual Review of Psychology*, Vol. 4. Annual Reviews, Inc., 1953. p. 343–60.
Williamson, Edmund G. *Student Personnel Services in Colleges and Universities.* McGraw-Hill, 1961.
Williamson, Edmund G. *Vocational Counseling: Some Historical, Philosophical, and Theoretical Perspectives.* McGraw-Hill, 1965. 214p.
Williamson, Edmund G., and Bordin, Edward S. "A Statistical Evaluation of Clinical Counseling." *Ed Psychol Meas* 1:117–32; 1941.
Williamson, Edmund G., and Cowan, John L. *The American Student's Freedom of Expression: A Research Appraisal.* U Minnesota Press, 1966.
Williamson, Edmund G., and Darley, John G. *Student Personnel Work.* McGraw-Hill, 1937. 313p.
Williamson, Edmund G., and others. *Student Personnel Point of View.* ACE, 1937; rev. ed., 1949. 20p.
Wolfle, Dale. *America's Resources of Specialized Talent.* Harper, 1954.
Wrenn, C. Gilbert. "Counseling Methods." In *Annual Review of Psychology*, Vol. 5. Annual Reviews, Inc., 1954. p. 337–56.
Wrenn, C. Gilbert. *The Counselor in a Changing World.* APGA, 1962. 195p.

COUNSELING—ELEMENTARY SCHOOLS

Counseling in education, or the counseling function or process in the educational setting, has not yet been clearly identified in terms of theory derived directly from educational objectives or processes. At the moment, counseling in the elementary school is normally seen as part of guidance, which as a construct can also include school psychology and school social work (Kehas, 1966). Thus, in the discussion that follows, although the emphasis is upon the counseling process in particular, the broader focus cannot help but be upon the guidance function, of which counseling is one of several implementing approaches.

In reviewing developments in counseling at the elementary-school level, the following headings will be used: "nature and characteristics of counseling activities," "personnel responsible for counseling activities," "related personnel services and resources," "programming for elementary counseling activities," and "counseling activities in foreign countries."

The growth of elementary-school guidance and counseling in the past 15 years has been phenomenal. As recently as 1949, only one professional book on guidance at the elementary-school level had appeared. In the period since that time, much progress has been made, not only in the form of publications but also in terms of professional activities and in national concern for support of guidance and counseling at this level.

A number of textbooks have appeared during recent years. Among those which deal specifically with elementary-school guidance are the works by Bernard and others (1954), Cottingham (1956), Martinson and Smallenburg (1958), Knapp (1959), Lloyd-Jones and others (1958), Hatch and Costar (1961), H. Peters and others (1963), Detjen and Detjen (1963), and H. Peters and others (1965). Several authors have written books deliberately addressed to classroom teachers: Gordon (1956), Barr (1958), Johnston and others (1959), Dinkmeyer and Dreikurs (1963), Garry (1963), Crow and Crow (1963), Strang and Morris (1964), and Willey and Dunn (1964). In addition, special references in pamphlet form or references limited to certain aspects of elementary-school guidance have been written by Norris (1963), Smith and Eckerson (1963), Holt (1964), NEA (National Education Association, Department of Elementary School Principals, 1964), and Delacato (1965). Both Riccio (1963) and Cottingham (1965) reviewed the status of elementary guidance as of 1963.

Professional leadership in developing programs in elementary-school guidance and counseling has been shown by both the American School Counselor Association (ASCA) and its parent body, the American Personnel and Guidance Association (APGA). The former group, ASCA, began its study in 1957, and in conjunction with APGA issued a statement in 1966 reporting on the progress of a joint Committee on the Elementary School Counselor of the Association of Counselor Educators and Supervisors and the American School Counselor Association (1966). This joint committee report culminates a five-year study begun by APGA and financed by the American Child Guidance Foundation in 1961 to survey crucial issues and present practices in elementary-school guidance. Another related activity, supported by funds from the National Institute of Mental Health, in 1961, is the Interprofessional Research Commission on Pupil Personnel Services (IRCOPPS). This joint effort, involving 16 national associations interested in improving the quality of pupil personnel services as a part of the total learning experience, centers upon research at four regional universities (Texas, Michigan, Maryland, and California at Los Angeles) and deals with the effectiveness of child-behavior consultants, preventive mental health, and similar educational innovations. The U.S. Office of Education is also becoming more active in promoting elementary-school guidance through many state pilot programs under Title V-A of the National Defense Education Act (NDEA), through Counseling and Guidance Institutes, NDEA, Title V-B, for elementary-school counselors, and through the Elementary and Secondary Education Act of 1965.

The current status of guidance and counseling activities at the elementary-school level is encouraging. Although a firm figure is not available, Hitchcock (1965) estimates that there may be somewhere between 2,000 and 3,000 elementary counselors in the United States. These counselors are operating, it is hypothesized, with a ratio of 1:700 in schools having such counselors. If the ratio of 1:600, recommended by the 1960 White House Conference on Children and Youth and the U.S. Office of Education is adhered to, 53,875 counselors will be needed in 1969–70. As of 1964, three states, Missouri, Connecticut, and North Dakota, had adopted special certification requirements for elementary-school counselors, according to Peters and others (1965). Accreditation of elementary schools having guidance and counseling programs was found in 15 states by Hill (1963a). Only recently have programs in counselor education made any differentiation between the preparation for counseling in elementary school and that in other educational levels, according to Nitzschke and Hill (1964). Funds for counseling personnel in many public school systems are available on an experimental basis from NDEA Title V-A as a result of amendments approved in 1964.

NATURE AND CHARACTERISTICS OF COUNSELING ACTIVITIES. Conceptual Foundations. In spite of the many recent publications in the field of elementary guidance and counseling, few, if any, have devoted much discussion to the theoretical bases for either the guidance function or the counseling process in the elementary school. This situation is due to a number of factors, not the least of which is the lack until recently of solid, creative or empirical research leading to the nature of guidance theory, regardless of educational level. Only since 1957 has the *Review of Educational Research* included sections dealing with the theoretical foundations of guidance, personnel work, and counseling (Kehas, 1966). During that period a limited number of writers were struggling with the same problem: Wrenn (1959), C. Miller (1961), Tiedeman and Field (1962), Mathewson (1962), Shoben (1962), Beck (1963), Weitz (1964), and Tiedeman (1964). The current concern for developing acceptable theoretical formulations of purposes, functions, and practices characterizing the guidance process or function in education is predicated on the need for independent theories of guidance not immediately derived from other disciplines (Kehas, 1966).

Counseling in the elementary school must be seen in a contextual relationship with several larger elements, each of which warrants brief review at this point: the goals of education, the guidance function in education, the guidance function in the elementary school, implementation of the guidance function through the guidance process, and guidance and counseling outcomes. These same elements could be reclassified as (1) purposes and values, (2) functions, (3) processes, and (4) outcomes described by Cowley in his "Tentative Holistic Taxonomy Applied to Education" (1963). The goals of education from such a source as the White House Conference, described by R. Tyler (1960) and by Chandler (1961), must subsume goals that can be attained through guidance activities. The goals of education, whether they be societal in origin, as enunciated by Hutson (1958), or psychosocial in origin, as set forth by Mathewson (1957), are implemented by administrative, instructional, and guidance activities, according to Tiedeman and Field (1962). Within the broad goals of education, the guidance function, as distinct from instruction, emphasizes decisions, goals, plans, and value judgments, while instruction stresses the acquisition of knowledge, skills, concepts, and facts (Cottingham, 1962). The "guidance learnings" described by Hill (1966), which compose the guidance function in education, are identified by Tiedeman and Field (1962) with the construct of discontinuity but have not been entirely agreed upon by other guidance theorists. In addition to Tiedeman's definition of guidance (1964) as "the science of purposeful action," such authors as Mathewson (1962), Shoben (1962), Katz (1963), and Weitz (1964) have also attempted to define the construct of guidance; Katz refers to "the guidance intervention" and Shoben to "social reconstruction." Although no postulated theories of guidance applicable to the elementary school currently exist, Munson (1966) has written "A Rationale for Elementary School Guidance," which gives serious consideration to the social and psychological origins of guidance at this level, drawing upon Bloom's cognitive domain (1956), Krathwohl and others' affective domain (1964), and on Bruner's theories of instruction (1964). Grams (1966) proposed a "learner-centered competence-building theory" as a postulated base for elementary-school guidance.

Farwell and Peters (1957) proposed several differential factors characterizing elementary-school guidance. While not defining the precise nature of the guidance function in the elementary school, Hill (1963b), Meeks (1962b), the American School Counselor Association (1964), Patouillet (1964), and Cottingham (1966a) have outlined the nature and the purposes of guidance work in elementary schools. With few exceptions, the developmental character of educational experiences as outlined by Mussen (1963) is strongly affirmed by those concerned with the definition of the elementary-school guidance function.

In implementing the guidance function at the elementary-school level, many authorities agree that it is carried out both within and beyond instruction. This point is stressed by the ASCD yearbook (Association for Supervision and Curriculum Development, 1955), Cottingham (1962), Watson (1964), and Peters and others (1965). The guidance function is administratively placed among several pupil personnel services, as reported by the Council of Chief State School Officers (1960), Johnson and others (1961), and Kehas (1966). As a function, guidance can be subdivided into such areas as behavior assessment, counseling, consulting, and coordination, with a liaison role in the school and community being a pervasive element, according to Frank Miller (1961) and Wrenn (1962).

Assessing the outcomes of the guidance process calls for an examination of human behavior changes in terms of, first, the acquisition of skills, knowledge, and facts (societal expectations), as well as of, second, maturity as related to reality, others, self, and values and meaning (self needs). Such sources as the ASCD yearbook (Association for Supervision and Curriculum Development, 1955) and Weitz (1964) have identified societal expectations, while Raebeck (1959), Mathewson (1963), Kelley (1962), and Tiedeman (1964) have described personal meanings and behavior related to self needs.

As a subaspect of guidance, the core process of counseling has been currently described theoretically by both Stefflre (1965) and Blocher (1966), although no specific reference was made to elementary-school counseling by either author. Except for efforts by Dinkmeyer (1965) and Krumboltz and Hosford (1966), who have issued position papers on "developmental counseling" and "behavioral counseling," respectively, little has been written on counseling theories uniquely applicable to the elementary school. Dinkmeyer indicated that his position is modeled after Hummel's ego counseling (1962). Herman J. Peters (1959) examined differential factors between elementary-school and secondary-school counseling but offered no theoretical bases for the observed differences.

Several problem areas of theoretical formulation where further research is needed have been identified. Cottingham (1966b) called for a cooperative, national-level position paper which might clarify several significant issues, including counseling. Kehas (1966) stressed the need to develop theories of teaching, instruction, and guidance which might point up conceptual and process differences at all educational levels. Lacking at the moment, too, is any formulated theoretical base for elementary-school guidance, or counseling, as distinct from guidance theory applicable to other educational settings. Similarly, research leading to systematic conceptualizations of the nature and characteristics of the guidance function, including the counseling process at the elementary-school level, is needed. A further problem is the need for research efforts to identify the specific functions with which the classroom teacher needs assistance from such specialized personnel as counselors, psychologists, and social workers.

A study of recent journal literature does not reveal a heavy emphasis on topics related to the conceptual foundations of either guidance or counseling in the elementary school. Smith (1963) and Wilson (1964) stressed the need for guidance activities as preventive measures. The salient features of guidance programs for elementary schools were outlined by Cottingham (1959a), Meeks (1962b), and Hill (1963b). Support for the concept of developmental and preventive guidance is given in articles by Bosdell (1960), Farwell (1961a), H. Peters (1963), and Royster (1964). Harris (1959, 1960) has identified several principles from developmental psychology which presumably are applicable to the elementary school. The characteristics of Adlerian counseling in the elementary school were described by Dinkmeyer (1964). Some writers, such as Freer (1962), see the teacher as a counselor, while the majority view counseling as the responsibility of a separate, professionally trained person. The latter group includes Newman (1956), Harrison (1961), Cassel (1963), Meeker (1963), and Helpern (1964).

Pupil Appraisal and Assistance. Agreement on the fundamental need to (1) assess behavior of elementary pupils, (2) identify problems, and (3) offer assistance (counseling, treatment, and environmental information) can be found among most writers in the elementary guidance field. It is also apparent that behavior-assessment strategies in a particular situation are most effective if based on well-known principles and research in child development. Of the numerous textbooks in elementary guidance, many stress procedures and methods adapted from child psychology, mental hygiene, or child study research. Works by Barr (1958) and Garry (1963) are illustrative.

The use of research findings as a basis for individual systems of child study is reflected in such broadly designed studies as that by Gerald Kowitz and others (1965), which examined the guidance needs of 1,760 children in the primary grades of a Texas community. These researchers concluded that teachers could categorize pupil problems at the second-grade level as enrichment, personal-social, learning (educational), or average-normal (present conditions adequate). Another experimental program which sought to assess ways of pupil diagnosis and help was reported by Lafferty and others (1964). For some years the child-guidance conference and the child study program concept, as developed by Prescott at the University of Maryland (described by Richardson, 1958), have been used by elementary schools. The use of traditional sources and types of data for understanding pupils, such as cumulative records, interviews, observations, test results, anecdotal records, and sociometric information, are recommended by Willey (1960), DeHaan (1961), Hatch and Costar (1961), Ahmann and Glock (1963), and H. Peters and others (1963, 1965). Basic principles for studying children's behavior are reiterated by Moustakos (1957), Ausubel (1959), Dinkmeyer (1961), Slobin (1964), and Marshall (1964). Current trends in approaches to behavior assessment, according to Carnes and Doughtie (1966), reflect increasing concern for multiple causation, impinging cultural factors, and such noncognitive elements as creativity, anxiety, and stress.

Characteristics of counseling for elementary-school children have been reviewed by many writers, although the distinctive approaches most suitable for children at that educational level have not been clearly identified, according to Koeppe and Bancroft (1966). At this stage the elementary-school counseling process apparently must derive its methods and goals from general counseling theories, since only Dinkmeyer

(1965) and Krumboltz and Hosford (1966) have proposed any unique approaches (and with limited research). Counseling techniques useful for releasing emotional concerns have been described by Harper and Wright (1958), Smillie (1958), Gowan (1965), and Caldwell (1965), while Murphy (1960) and Nelson (1966) recommend play media and Cianciolo (1965) the use of bibliotherapy. Sonstegard (1964) proposes an interview pattern for parent conferences. The use of group process, psychodrama, or group psychotherapy is recommended by Wells (1961, 1962), Sperber (1962), Moreno (1963), Cohn and others (1963), Combs and others (1963), Boy and others (1963), and Ohlsen (1965a).

Play therapy as a counseling medium was stressed by H. Martin (1963) and Alexander (1964), while individual psychotherapy was urged by Koehler (1964). Louise Tyler (1964) concluded that the ideal teacher-student relationship is very similar to the ideal therapeutic relationship. On nonpersonal problems, such as vocational concepts and educational planning, Lifton (1959) and Leonard (1964) supported the use of occupational information and interpreted test data, respectively. Such writers as Kaback (1960), Grell (1960), and Arbuckle (1963) deplored the limited use of occupational information as an aid in counseling for value and concept formation in the elementary school.

Consulting Functions. There is wide agreement that one aspect of the elementary guidance program involves counselor consultation with parents, teachers, administrators, and other pupil personnel specialists. Peterson and others (1961), Wrenn (1962), Dinkmeyer (1962), and Nowlin (1964) have emphasized this need. The specific role of the consultant or specialist has been set forth by Dinkmeyer (1962), Smith and Eckerson (1963), and Helpern (1964). Almost unanimous agreement exists on the principle that a consultant must work with school and community personnel, as well as with parents. Crocker (1964) and Lowe (1964) feel that family counseling in some depth may also be advisable.

Research and Evaluation of Outcomes. Efforts to conduct research both on effectiveness of practices and on program outcomes in elementary counseling have been numerous and varied. Increasingly, research has been conducted by local school systems cooperating with universities, research organizations, or government agencies. The availability of grant monies and federal funds has obviously increased the quantity (and hopefully the quality) of research on elementary counseling activities. Several categories of research are found in the elementary guidance literature and used in this discussion: personal and social adjustment of pupils, guidance and counseling procedures and techniques, behavior-appraisal studies, roles and functions of guidance workers, services and program evaluation, and vocational-development studies.

Personality variables were studied by Feldhusen and Thurston (1964), who examined anxiety level and integration of self concept and found that low-anxiety-level children had higher mean scores than high-anxiety-level children on integration of self concept as rated by psychologists. Watson (1964) also reported on Operation Self Concept, a longitudinal study designed to help children with self-understanding and self-concept development. Lighthall (1963) studied children's responses to personality questionnaires. Peer studies are reported by Cassel and Martin (1964) and Spaulding (1964). The former compared peer status ratings of pupils with their guidance data and learning efficiency indexes, while the latter reviewed empirical research of peer and school influence on personality development. Child-behavior problems were examined by Peterson and others (1961), Mangan and Shafer (1962), and Rice (1963), who studied pupil problems as related to parental attitudes, children's attitudes toward behavior, and referral behavior problems, respectively. Chance (1961) reported that with first graders, the time of independence training by mothers was significant.

Various procedures and techniques related to elementary counseling have been the subject of research. Lister and Ohlsen (1965) examined the improvement in self-understanding through test interpretation, while Medinnus (1961) did research on the First Grade Adjustment Scale. Play-therapy techniques were the subject of research by Ginott and Lebo (1963), while Ohlsen and Gazda (1965) analyzed methods of group counseling with underachieving bright pupils. Kranzler and others (1966), using sociometric criteria, conducted an experimental counseling study with fourth graders.

In the area of pupil identification, two studies examined high learning ability in relation to 17 physical, social, and intellectual variables and types of problems reported by primary teachers. The authors of these studies were Klausmeier (1959) and G. Kowitz and others (1965). The latter study reported that 63.4 percent of the boys had personal-social problems, compared to 56.3 percent of the girls; similarly 56.3 percent of the boys had learning-educational problems, as compared to 43.7 percent of the girls. Radin (1963) categorized the behavioral concerns of elementary pupils as follows: academic, social, conflict with authority figures, and overt behavioral manifestations. The Higher Horizons Project of New York City, reported by Hillson and Myers (1963), illustrates a demonstration project which focused on helping culturally deprived youth reach new goals.

The roles and functions of elementary-school guidance personnel have been the subject of much discussion and considerable research. McDougall and Reitan (1963) and Shertzer and Lundy (1964) examined the image of the counselor as perceived by the school administrator. Foster (1965) made a study of counselor educators' perceptions of the role and function of the future elementary counselor. Bosdell (1958) explored role perceptions of teachers, counselors, principals, and school psychologists toward each other, while Gatchel (1958) obtained teachers' reactions to specific guidance services in a 1958 study. Muro (1965) studied perceptions of the elementary guidance specialist by teachers and principals. McCreary and Miller (1966) analyzed the qualifications and functions of elementary counselors in

California. Two counselor roles, consultant and psychotherapist, were compared through experimental and control groups by Oldridge (1964), while Jones (1966) evolved a competency pattern for elementary-school counselors from criteria reviewed by a jury of both state and national counselor educators.

Research on counseling activities and total guidance-program features has increased. Hart (1961) surveyed the need for a guidance counselor among St. Louis elementary teachers. Reactions to available or potential services were studied by Riccio and Wehmeyer (1961) and Parmer (1960), who examined, respectively, guidance services recommended by public and parochial teachers and the demand for psychological services in elementary schools. Wieland (1966) conducted a national survey of 220 school counselors, 84 school psychologists, and 49 school social workers in selected communities to determine duplication and uniqueness of duties. Illustrative of the recent research made possible by Title V-A of NDEA is a project report by Gerald Miller (1964), who described a series of studies dealing with dropouts, underachievers, articulation problems, and experimental counseling in California. In the narrower vein of evaluative research, outcomes of selected activities by counselors and teachers, respectively, were analyzed by Lynn Martin (1959) and Bancroft (1962). Also part of a national pattern are the IRCOPPS researches reported by Shaw (1965) and Byrne (1966). The former described a regional study at the University of California at Los Angeles based on the hypothesis that the guidance specialist's prime responsibility is assisting in the provision of an optimum climate for learning. Byrne's project, at another of the four IRCOPPS centers (Maryland), hypothesized that a new type of in-school pupil service worker could replace the more traditional counselor, psychologist, social worker, nurse, and similar personnel. Some of the theoretical as well as the practical difficulties in the evaluation process have been described by Mildred Peters (1964) and by Herman J. Peters and others (1965). Eddleman (n.d.), in a broader perspective, examined the research role of the elementary counselor.

Limited research in the area of vocational development is reported by O'Hara (1962), Diamond (1966), and Tennyson and Monnens (1963). O'Hara used Ginzberg's theory of vocational choice in a study with children in grades 5 and 6. Tennyson and Monnens explored the various ways the world of work is presented to elementary children through reading texts. Diamond, using pupils in the Skokie, Illinois, schools, examined occupational perceptions.

Issues and Trends. The pace of the elementary guidance movement has increased rapidly, and some rather controversial issues, as well as some obvious trends, have become apparent. Several authors have addressed themselves to the trends now evident in this field. They include Wrenn (1960), Meeks (1961), Riccio (1963), Stripling and Lane (1964), and Cottingham (1966a). Most of these writers agree on a number of characteristics of guidance activities in the elementary school: elementary guidance and counseling should be developmental; teachers, as well as counselors, are important guidance functionaries; assuming the availability of counseling services, referral resources (school psychologist, school social worker) will also be needed; the counselor is part of a personnel services team; counselor–pupil ratios should be 1:600, rather than the present disproportionate ratio (estimated at not less than 1:1,000 in some systems); and the counselor has a triple role as consultant, as coordinator or liaison with the school staff and community, and as counselor (group and individual) to pupils.

With respect to issues, few authorities agree upon more than the crucial ones. A review of the literature reveals several areas where lack of agreement or voids currently exist, among them the following:

1. Theoretical formulations of the nature of the guidance and counseling function in the elementary school (Cottingham, 1966b; Munson, 1966).

2. The unique characteristics of the elementary-school counseling process (Dinkmeyer, 1965; Krumboltz & Hosford, 1966).

3. Types of assistance desired by teachers in the areas of guidance learnings (Hill, 1966; Witmer, 1966).

4. Qualifications (preparation, counseling orientation, basic disciplines) of personnel responsible for the elementary guidance and counseling function (Nitzschke & Hill, 1964; Raines, 1964a).

5. Clarification of the teaching function as related to the guidance function; subsequent primary responsibility of teacher and counselor (Shertzer & Stone, 1966; Kehas, 1966).

6. Appropriate role and title for elementary guidance specialist—counselor, consultant, child-development specialist, guidance worker, or helping teacher (Patouillet, 1957; Smith, 1966).

7. Complementary functions of elementary guidance person in relation to other pupil personnel specialists (Meeks, 1962a).

8. A strategy for creating school philosophy and a climate for learning which recognizes and shows pupils that they are valued as individual, worthy persons (Association for Supervision and Curriculum Development, 1962; Ferguson, 1966).

9. The basic philosophy underlying the guidance and counseling relationship—conditioning or liberating (Tiedeman, 1962; Blocher, 1965).

PERSONNEL RESPONSIBLE FOR COUNSELING ACTIVITIES. Much has been written on the question of responsibility for counseling in the elementary school; most writers concur on the fact that the elementary counselor carries the primary responsibility, although others may assist. Such researchers as Hart (1961), McKellar (1963), Raines (1964b), and Nitzschke and Hill (1964) have examined the functions that are or should be provided by elementary counseling personnel. In addition, many discussion articles have expressed opinions on the role and function of the elementary counselor. Among those expressing themselves seriously on this subject are: Science Research Associates (1960), Farwell (1961b, 1963),

Harrison (1963), Meeks (1963b), Brison (1964), Kaczkowski (1964), Smallenburg (1964), H. Peters and Hansen (1964), Mahan (1965), Ohlsen (1965b), Reaves and Reaves (1965), and Zaccaria (1965). Purkey (1962) offered a narrative report of an elementary counselor's workday. Wrenn (1962) surveyed a national sample of elementary counselors and obtained their opinion regarding future functions. An outline of services which an elementary counselor might appropriately perform was suggested by Nelson (1962).

Most of these writers agree on a threefold function of the elementary counselor: counseling (individual and group), consulting (with parents, teachers, and other pupil personnel specialists, administrators), and coordination (liaison) with school staff and with community and school resources. These roles include making comprehensive studies of pupils, counseling, providing pupils with information (personal and environmental), and supplying pupil information to school and community personnel. The stress upon the elementary counselor's being a pupil personnel services team member is generally evident, although some writers use the term "guidance worker" in preference to "counselor." As to the actual job function of the counselor, McCreary and Miller (1966) found that in California counselors spent 50 percent of the time working with pupils, 17 percent with teachers, 10 percent with administration, 12 percent with parents, and 11 percent with probation, welfare, and other agency officials. Unusual roles for the counselor were described by Farwell (1963) and Mahan (1965). Farwell emphasized the counselor's responsibility for developmental counseling (as opposed to complete client-centeredness or mechanistic guidance services), while Mahan charged the counselor with changing "perceptual sets" of people, toward things, themselves, and others. He is also to assist in improving the quality of teacher-pupil interaction.

The concern for organizational attitudes toward the counselor's role is reflected in the work of the Association for Counselor Education and Supervision and the American School Counselor Association, both divisions of the American Personnel and Guidance Association. In a statement issued at the national convention in Minneapolis in 1965 and clarified in Washington, D.C., in 1966, the associations issued a joint committee report (Association of Counselor Educators and Supervisors and American School Counselor Association, 1966) which explicitly sets forth the professional identity, responsibilities, competencies, and preparation for counselors in elementary schools. The primary areas of responsibility as stated are as follows:

1. Participating in creating an environment conducive to learning and growth for all children.
2. Helping parents to understand the developmental needs of all children and working with parents to meet the needs of their own children.
3. Helping the individual child to grow in self-understanding and in positive, maximum use of his potential.
4. Participating in curriculum development and change; three processes, counseling, consultation, and coordination are seen as divisions of responsibility of the counselor.

The preparation of elementary-school counselors has been the subject of some research. Nitzschke and Hill (1964) examined some 45 graduate programs purporting to prepare elementary counselors, although relatively few programs were significantly different from secondary-school preparation programs. Faust (1966), on a descriptive level, developed a theoretical model for the preparation of elementary counselors.

Although there may be some controversy as to the need for specialized personnel for counseling in elementary schools, the evidence is overwhelming that with some exceptions, the public and educators in general have accepted the concept of assistance to teachers and pupils in the area of guidance and counseling. At the national level the 1960 White House Conference on Children and Youth, the National Defense Education Act as amended in 1964, and the Elementary and Secondary Education Act of 1965, all make strong recommendations regarding legal provision for counseling personnel in elementary schools. Furthermore, the concern of such organizations as the NEA, APGA, ASCD, and the National Association of Elementary School Principals is shown by their strong policy statements and official publications. Research evidence on the role of specialized personnel is indicated by a national survey of some 5,500 elementary-school principals by Smith and Eckerson (1966). They sought information on three types of child-development consultants (school counselor, school psychologist, and school social worker) who were available on an average of one day per week in individual schools having enrollments over 100. About one-fourth of the schools (1,300) had some type of child-development consultant in 1962–63. Three-fourths of the principals in schools without child-development consultants expressed a need for their services. In schools having such specialists, more services were provided for children than for teachers and parents. The median number of pupils per child-development consultant was 789 in schools having such personnel, although principals thought this ratio should be lowered. In view of the increase in counseling personnel, the federal funds available for services or training, and the national association support for improving guidance functions in schools, it would appear that the use of specialized personnel for assisting elementary pupils, teachers, and administrators is an accepted practice in American education.

RELATED PERSONNEL SERVICES AND RESOURCES. As supportive resources some attention is given in the literature to the counseling functions of the teacher, consultant, or other pupil personnel specialists. Eckerson and Smith (1962, 1963), in describing a general resource person, used the term "elementary guidance consultant" in 1962 but in 1965 seemed to prefer the expression "child development specialist" (Smith, 1966). A number of writers have expressed the opinion that the teacher also has a guidance function. Daubner (1964) feels that there may be conflict between a teacher's instructional and counseling roles, while Ferris (Ferris & Leiter, 1965) states flatly that a teacher can do the best job of guidance. Cottingham (1959b), Topetzes and Ivanoff (1963), and H. Peters and others (1965) all take the position that the classroom teacher has a guidance function although it is different from that of the elementary counselor.

The support of resource personnel such as the school psychologist, school social worker, and school administrator is important, according to the NEA (National Education Association . . ., 1965). Faust and Perkins (1964) and Scheibe (1965) delineated the contribution of the school psychologist to the elementary-school guidance program. The special services of the reading teacher were outlined by Kilanski (1966), of the school social worker by DeRoche (1964), and of the school nurse by Klein (1959). The need for coordination of all pupil personnel services and for the support of the principal was stressed by Mattick and Nickolas (1964). The value of a college guidance clinic as a resource for elementary schools was explained by Abbe (1961). The use of other personnel specialists to the exclusion of school counselors was supported by Waetjen (1965), who opposed "crisis" pupil contacts in favor of counselors working with parents and teachers as a resource person. Waetjen predicted that the majority of principals would oppose having counselors placed in their schools.

PROGRAMMING FOR ELEMENTARY COUNSELING ACTIVITIES. Unfortunately, not a great deal of emphasis has been given in the literature to either research or discussion approaches to planning for guidance and counseling activities in the elementary school. It is commonly agreed that counseling is part of guidance work, which in turn is one of several pupil personnel services, operational at all school levels. Johnson and others (1961) and Eckerson and Smith (1963) both offer descriptions of the component elements. The *Review of Educational Research* (1963), even though recognizing the pupil personnel services concept as an administrative device, reported that until recently most elementary guidance services outside the classroom were performed primarily by school psychologists.

A current overview of strategies for programming elementary counseling does not indicate much solid research. Two studies, one by Eckerson and Smith (1962) and one by McKellar (1963), are exceptions to this trend. Eckerson and Smith studied some 24 elementary guidance programs to determine underlying theories, functions performed, and organizational features. McKellar examined the administrative design in schools served by 182 counselors giving at least half-time service. She also obtained information on functions, attitudes toward certain issues, and philosophical positions in comparison with the literature. Numerous school administrators as well as guidance specialists have described their approach to the programming of elementary counseling activities. Frank Miller (1961) and Apostal (1962) outlined objectives, while Straight (1963) discussed the relationship between the educational philosophy of the school and the implementation of guidance functions. Gelatt (1963) stressed the need for early appropriate educational experiences for each child. According to Meeks (1963b), there are at least 30 comprehensive elementary guidance programs in 15 states. Program descriptions from some school systems have been made available by Powell (1964), Frost (1964), and Johnston (1966). Orgel (1960) offered a 13-point guidance program for elementary schools. In an effort to base organizational designs on teachers' expressed need for noninstructional help, J. Young (1962) ascertained that elementary teachers in Tucson, Arizona, could use outside professional help for 75 percent of the pupil problems which inhibited learning.

As to trends in organizational patterns, three types of designs have appeared: (1) teachers are given primary responsibility with no clearly coordinated leadership, (2) specialized personnel (counselors and others) are centrally located or placed in single units, or (3) shared services are available from a central system which supplies part-time pupil personnel consultants, including elementary counselors, with the principal having the significant role in the individual school (Munson, 1961). Herman Peters (1965) has proposed a "pupil behavioral system" as a restructuring of the pupil personnel service concept; the main thrust would be upon pupil self-viewing through a variety of interdisciplinary specialists functioning as an individual resource unit. Several organizational principles apparently undergird many current programming efforts: the program must be based on individual school needs and pupil characteristics; group involvement of teachers, specialists, and administration is necessary; services must be developmental in nature; acceptable philosophy must precede structure and function; use must be made of instructional and extrainstructional situations, and limitations should be placed on counselor function (counselors should have no administrative, clerical, or disciplinary responsibilities).

Suggestions for initiating or developing guidance functions are varied. Farwell and Riccio (1961) recommend the case study, Hollister (1960) a mental health program, and F. Young (1964) an experimental ungraded primary program of prevention. The availability of NDEA Title V-A funds for elementary guidance purposes has stimulated much activity and some state-certification controls. Missouri, for example, has developed several two-year pilot programs, according to Moore (1963). The concept of guidance through the curriculum as well as beyond (through specialists) is strongly endorsed by the ASCD (Association for Supervision and Curriculum Development, 1955, 1962) and by H. Peters and others (1965). Several persistent issues remain, however: the nature of the counseling function of the teacher (Ferris & Leiter, 1965), the primary responsibilities of the counselor—coordination, consulting, or counseling;

the need for teaching experience as a prerequisite for counseling; and the most effective approach to changing behavior of elementary school counselees (McKellar, 1963).

COUNSELING ACTIVITIES IN FOREIGN COUNTRIES. A careful search of textbook literature reveals a dearth of information descriptive of counseling activities in the elementary schools of foreign countries. Although foreign guidance programs have increased in number and presumably in quality, the general emphasis has been upon secondary-school services aimed primarily at vocational and educational processes, according to Humphries and others (1960). Their publication gives a brief history of the guidance movement in Australia, Canada, France, Germany, Great Britain, Japan, and the U.S.S.R. With the possible exception of Japan in the middle 1920's, those foreign countries have failed to develop counseling at the elementary school level.

A review of recent periodicals reveals a limited concern for procedures and methods designed to assist children in elementary schools. Graf (1959) reported on success with Moreno's impromptu therapy with floating populations of children in Leicester, England. The need for improved mental health services was voiced in the *Times Educational Supplement* (1964) in an article demanding greater coordination between medical services, psychological units, and child-guidance clinics. An emphasis on preventive approaches was clear. In New Zealand (and Minnesota) Flanders (1959) conducted a series of studies analyzing frequency and characteristics of teacher-pupil interactions in the classroom and compared social-educational with intellectual-content material. Hansen (1965), a Minnesota counselor, reviewed guidance progress in Norway, where the law now requires provision for counseling in the plans for the comprehensive nine-year school. Unfortunately, no Norwegian word equivalent to "counselor" was found. Two visitors to Poland, Malecki and Walker (1966), reported that vocational guidance in that country includes selection and placement for upper-grade children.

Burrell (1963) summarized guidance activities in Britain and western European countries. In England considerable use is made of child-guidance clinics at all grade levels, but particularly in primary schools. Their functions are to diagnose and recommend, with parental cooperation assumed. Burrell indicated that formal guidance programs do not appear to exist in the educational systems of Germany, Switzerland, or Italy; teachers and administrators assume responsibility.

Several writers have provided observations on guidance in the Soviet Union. Heisler (1959) confirmed the influence of party and state on guidance work in Russia. She found a philosophy of exploitation of human potentiality based on behavioristic psychology. The state works closely with parents and uses parent committees to help improve parent-child relationships in the community. Little attention is given to personal-social guidance, while preschool readiness is determined by informal testing. Gass (1959) outlined a brief history of guidance in the Soviet Union. School failure and other educational difficulties are seen as pedagogical problems rather than counseling concerns. Considerable use is made of group leaders who are sought for educational, vocational, or personal advice; these people make home visits, keep records, check on grades, and make class observations. Sievers (*Guidepost*, 1965) found no evidence of elementary counseling in the Soviet Union, except for health assistance. He reported the American concept of guidance to be in sharp contrast to the quota and incentive plans used by Russian educators.

Evidence of the growing international interest in guidance activities in elementary schools is indicated by two European professional meetings, one in July 1962 and another in May 1963, both sponsored by the International Association for Educational and Vocational Guidance (1963a). One of the several working groups examining "the adjustment of young people to a world in accelerated technical and economic revolution" discussed personality assessment, child "conversations," and group methods of vocational guidance, indicating that teachers and counselors were jointly responsible for this work. At an international seminar also sponsored by the association at Geneva in 1963 (International Association . . ., 1963b), one study group was devoted to vocational guidance in the elementary schools and another to collaboration between elementary schools and special (education) schools. The need for close cooperation between teachers and vocational consultants was stressed.

According to Bentley (1966), guidance services in schools and other institutions in Latin America are in their infancy. There is, however, great interest in developing guidance programs throughout Latin America, since educators and government officials see in a program of guidance an answer to several of the serious problems in Latin American education. At present, elementary-school guidance has not been separated, either conceptually or practically, from guidance services at the secondary level.

The education of counselors in Latin America appears to be influenced by two trends: the European philosophy of guidance, represented by France and most prominent in Brazil, and the American tradition, which predominates in Chile, Peru, Panama, and Venezuela. The European attitude, which emphasizes selection and classification, results in a focus upon vocational problems.

Venezuela has what is perhaps the most complete and well-staffed institute for the preparation of counselors in all of Latin America. Whether a graduate of the two-year course works in the elementary school or secondary school depends entirely upon the branch of the educational system which sent him to the institute. An important influence in the preparation of elementary counselors at all levels has been the ready acceptance of clinical psychology as one aspect of training (Bentley, 1966).

In summary, progress is apparent in the development of guidance and counseling in many foreign countries. At the moment, however, the emphasis is more upon vocational and to some extent educational assistance than on personal-social help. More functions are found at the secondary level in noneducational settings (private agencies, government centers) than at the primary levels or in institutions of higher learning. In spite of philosophies of education which are somewhat at variance with those in the United States, the need for counseling activities is becoming more obvious to many educators in foreign countries. There is increasing evidence too, of the impact of the American guidance movement on the educational program of some countries on almost every continent.

Harold F. Cottingham
The Florida State University

References

Abbe, A. E. "Consultation to a School Guidance Program." *El Sch J* 61:331–7; 1961.

Ahmann, J. Stanley, and Glock, Marvin D. *Evaluating Pupil Growth*, 2nd ed. Allyn and Bacon, 1963. 640p.

Alexander, Eugene D. "School Centered Play Therapy Program." *Personnel Guid J* 43:256–61; 1964.

American School Counselor Association. "Dimensions of Elementary School Guidance." The Association, October 1964. Committee report.

Apostal, Robert A. "Objectives of Elementary Guidance." *Sch Counselor* 10:23–6; 1962.

Arbuckle, Dugald S. "Occupational Information in the Elementary School." *Voc Guid Q* 12:77–84; 1963.

Association of Counselor Educators and Supervisors and American School Counselor Association. "Report of the ACES-ASCA Joint Committee on the Elementary School Counselor." APGA convention, Washington, D.C. APGA, April 1966.

Association for Supervision and Curriculum Development. *ASCD Yearbook: Guidance in the Curriculum.* NEA, 1955. 231p.

Association for Supervision and Curriculum Development. *Perceiving, Behaving, Becoming.* NEA, 1962. 256p.

Ausubel, David P. "Developmental Issues in Child Guidance: Plasticity, Direction, and Conformity." *J Nat Assn Women Deans and Counselors* 22:106–12; 1959.

Bancroft, J. F. "A Study of Teachers' Effectiveness in Performing Guidance Services in the Intermediate Grades of Public Elementary Schools." Doctoral dissertation, U Iowa, 1962.

Barr, John. *The Elementary Teacher and Guidance.* Holt, 1958. 435p.

Beck, Carlton E. *Philosophical Foundations of Guidance.* Prentice-Hall, 1963. 171p.

Bentley, Joseph C. "Elementary Guidance in Latin America." Personal communication, July 1966.

Bernard, Harold Wright, and others. *Guidance Services in Elementary School.* Chartwell House, 1954. 403p.

Blocher, Donald H. "Issues in Counseling: Elusive and Illusional." *Personnel Guid J* 43:796–800; 1965.

Blocher, Donald H. *Developmental Counseling.* Ronald, 1966. 205p.

Bloom, Benjamin S. (Ed.) *Taxonomy of Educational Objectives Handbook.* Vol. 1: *Cognitive Domain.* McKay, 1956. 207p.

Bosdell, Betty Jane. "Perceptions of Guidance Services as Related to Personality Needs and Job Title." Doctoral dissertation. U Illinois, 1958.

Bosdell, Betty Jane. "Guidance in the Elementary School." *U North Dakota Col Ed Rec* 65:88–92; 1960.

Boy, Angelo, and others. "Multiple Counseling: A Catalyst for Individual Counseling." *Sch Counselor* 11:8–11; 1963.

Brison, D. "The Role of the Elementary Guidance Counselor." *Nat El Sch Prin* 43(No. 5):41–47; 1964.

Bruner, Jerome S. "Some Theories on Instruction Illustrated with Reference to Mathematics." In *Theories of Learning and Instruction.* U Chicago Press, 1964. p. 306–7.

Burrell, Jessie. "Guidance Practices in British and Western European Schools." *Sch Soc* 49:10–1; 1963.

Byrne, Richard H. "The Problems and Design of a Research in Elementary School Counseling." Paper presented at the meeting of the APGA convention, Washington, D.C., April 1966.

Caldwell, Edson. "Guidance Competencies in the Classroom." *El Sch Guid Counseling* 1(No. 2):7–12; 1965.

Carnes, Earl F., and Doughtie, Eugene B. *Rev Ed Res* 36:288–97; 1966.

Cassel, Russell N. "Teacher and Counselor." *Ed* 83:259–62; 1963.

Cassel, Russell N., and Martin, Gilbert. "Comparing Peer Status Ratings of Elementary Pupils with Their Guidance Data and Learning Efficiency Indices." *J Genet Psychol* 105:39–42; 1964.

Chance, June. "Independence Training and First Graders' Achievement." *J Cons Psychol* 25:149–54; 1961.

Chandler, B. J. *Education and the Teacher.* Dodd, 1961. 403p.

Cianciolo, Patricia J. "Children's Literature Can Affect Coping Behavior." *Personnel Guid J* 43:897–903; 1965.

Cohn, Benjamin, and others. "Group Counseling: An Orientation." *Personnel Guid J* 43:355–8; 1963.

Combs, Charles, and others. "Group Counseling: Applying the Technique." *Sch Counselor* 11:12–8; 1963.

Cottingham, Harold F. *Guidance in Elementary Schools: Principles and Practices.* McKnight, 1956. 325p.

Cottingham, Harold F. "Guidance." *Grade Teach* 76:56; 1959(*a*).

Cottingham, Harold F. "Guidance and Instruction." *Grade Teach* 77(No. 2):50+; 1959(*b*).

Cottingham, Harold F. "Implementing Two Vital

Teacher Functions: Guidance and Instruction." *Counselor Ed Sup* 1:166–9; 1962.
Cottingham, Harold F. "The Status of Guidance in the Elementary School." In Adams, James. (Ed.) *Counseling and Guidance. A Summary View.* Macmillan, 1965. p. 340–9.
Cottingham, Harold F. "The Counselor's Role in Elementary School Guidance." *H Sch J* 49:204–8; 1966(*a*).
Cottingham, Harold F. "National-level Projection for Elementary School Guidance." *Personnel Guid J* 44:499–502; 1966(*b*).
Council of Chief State School Officers. *Responsibilities of State Departments of Education for Pupil Personnel Services.* The Council, 1960. A policy statement.
Cowley, W. H. "A Tentative Holistic Taxonomy Applied to Education." In Lloyd-Jones, Esther, and Westervelt, Esther. (Eds.) *Behavioral Science and Guidance.* Teachers Col, Columbia U, 1963. p. 37–54.
Crocker, E. C. "Depth Consultation with Parents." *Young Children* 20:91–9; 1964.
Crow, Lester, and Crow, Alice. (Eds.) *Mental Hygiene for Teachers: A Book of Readings.* Macmillan, 1963. 580p.
Daubner, Edward V. "Teacher as Counselor." *Cath Ed R* 62:91–9; 1964.
DeHann, R. F. "Using Test Results in Pupil Guidance." *Nat El Prin* 41(No. 2):23–6; 1961.
Delacato, Carl H. *The Elementary School of the Future: A Guide for Parents.* Thomas, 1965. 108p.
DeRoche, Edward F. "Responsibilities of the School Worker." *Nat El Prin* 43(No. 5): 50–2; 1964.
Detjen, Ervin, and Detjen, Mary Ford. *Elementary School Guidance,* 2nd ed. McGraw-Hill, 1963. 240p.
Diamond, Esther E. "Occupational Perception of Seventh and Eighth Grade Boys and Girls at the Lincoln School." Paper presented at the meeting of the APGA, Chicago, Illinois, April 1966.
Dinkmeyer, Don. "Understanding Children's Behavior." *El Sch J* 61:314–6; 1961.
Dinkmeyer, Don. "The Consultant in Elementary School Guidance." *Guid J* 1(No. 4):95–101; 1962.
Dinkmeyer, Don. "Conceptual Foundations of Counseling: Adlerian Theory and Practice." *Sch Counselor* 11:174–8; 1964.
Dinkmeyer, Don. "A Theory of Child Counseling at the Elementary School Level." Paper presented at the meeting of the APGA, Minneapolis, Minnesota, April 1965.
Dinkmeyer, Don, and Dreikurs, Rudolf. *Encouraging Children to Learn: The Encouragement Process.* Prentice-Hall, 1963. 162p.
Eckerson, Louise, and Smith, Hyrum. *Elementary School Guidance: The Consultant.* HEW, USOE, 1962.
Eckerson, Louise, and Smith, Hyrum. "Pupil Personnel Services." *Occupational Outlook Q* 7(No. 3):1–3; 1963.
Eddleman, Riley R. "The Research Role of the Elementary School Counselor." In *Research and the Counselor.* Guidance Services Section, Missouri State Department of Education, n.d. p. 34–41.
Farwell, Gail F. "Continuity in the Guidance Program." *Ed Leadership* 18:338–42; 1961(*a*).
Farwell, Gail F. "The Role of the School Counselor." *Counselor Ed Sup* 1:40–3; 1961(*b*).
Farwell, Gail F. "The Counselor's Role and Function: Conceptions and Conflicts." *Theory into Practice* 2:10–6; 1963.
Farwell, Gail F., and Peters, Herman J. "Guidance: A Longitudinal and Differential View." *El Sch J* 57:26–31; 1957.
Farwell, Gail F., and Riccio, Anthony C. "The Case Study—A Means of Introducing Guidance Services." *Nat El Prin* 40(No. 7):38–40; 1961.
Faust, Verne. "Theory in the Development of Elementary School Counselor Education Models." Paper presented at the meeting of the APGA, Washington, D.C., April 1966.
Faust, Verne, and Perkins, Keith J. "Dimensions of Guidance." Arizona State U, 1964. (Mimeographed.)
Feldhusen, John F., and Thurston, John R. "Personality and Adjustment of Low and High Anxious Children." *J Ed Res* 57:265–7; 1964.
Ferguson, Annabelle. "Issues and Problems in Elementary Guidance." Paper presented at an Elementary Guidance Workshop, U North Carolina, June 1966.
Ferris, Robert R., and Leiter, Sarah L. "Guidance in the Elementary School; Opinions Differ." *NEA J* 54(No. 6):48–9+; 1965.
Flanders, Ned A. "Teacher-Pupil Contacts and Mental Hygiene." *J Social Issues* 15(No. 1):30–9; 1959.
Foster, C. M. "Perceptions of the Role and Function of the Elementary School Counselor." Doctoral dissertation. Purdue U, 1965.
Freer, J. J. "The Teacher as Counselor." *Ed* 82:336–8; 1962.
Frost, Jim. *Elementary Guidance in Action.* Report presented at the Fourth Annual All Ohio Elementary School Guidance Conference, November, 1964.
Garry, Ralph. *Guidance Techniques for Elementary Teachers.* Charles E. Merrill, Inc., 1963. 539p.
Gass, Gertrude Zemon. "The Foreign Scene in Guidance. II: Guidance in Russia." *Personnel Guid J* 38:34–9; 1959.
Gatchel, Mary H. *The Elementary Classroom Teacher's Personal Opinion Concerning Several Aspects of an Organized Guidance Program at That Level.* Col Education, U Oklahoma, 1958.
Gelatt, H. B. "Early Guidance Essential." *Ed* 83:263–5; 1963.
Ginott, Haim G., and Lebo, Dell. "Most and Least Used Play Therapy Limits." *J Genet Psychol* 103: 153–9; 1963.
Gordon, Ira J. *The Teacher as a Guidance Worker.* Harper, 1956. 350p.
Gowan, J. C. "Changing Self-concept in Exceptional Children." *Ed* 85:374–5; 1965.
Graf, A. K. "Modified Children's Groups and Moreno's Impromptu Therapy." *Group Psychotherapy* 12: 322–6; 1959.
Grams, Armin. *Facilitating Learning and Individual*

Development. *Toward a Theory for Elementary Guidance.* Minnesota Department of Education, 1966. 224p.

Grell, Lewis A. "How Much Occupational Information in the Elementary School." *Voc Guid Q* 9:48–53; 1960.

Guidepost. "Guidance Around the World: U.S.S.R." 7:(No. 6):2–3+; 1965.

Hansen, L. S. "Norway Adapts Guidance into a New Educational Structure." *Personnel Guid J* 44:244–7; 1965.

Harper, Louis, and Wright, Benjamin. "Dealing with Emotional Problems in the Classroom." *El Sch J* 58:316–25; 1958.

Harris, Dale B. "What Child Development Has to Say to Guidance Workers." *J Nat Assn Women Deans and Counselors* 22:99–105; 1959.

Harris, Dale B. "Development of Potentiality." *Teach Col Rec* 61:423–8; 1960.

Harrison, Edna L. "The Counselor's Role in the Early Identification of Gifted Children." *Personnel Guid J* 39:735–7; 1961.

Harrison, Edna L. "The Elementary School Counselor's Unique Position." *Sch Counselor* 11:107–10; 1963.

Hart, Robert N. "An Analysis of the Position of the Elementary School Guidance Counselor." Doctoral dissertation. U Southern California, 1961.

Hatch, Raymond N., and Costar, James W. *Guidance Services in the Elementary School.* Brown, 1961. 194p.

Heisler, Florence. "The Foreign Scene in Guidance. I: Guidance Practices in the Soviet Union." *Personnel Guid J* 38:27–33; 1959.

Helpern, Joan M. "The Role of the Guidance Consultant at the Elementary School." *J Ed* 146(No. 3):16–34; 1964.

Hill, George E. "Elementary School Guidance: Criteria for Approval by State Departments of Education." *Counselor Ed Sup* 2:137–43; 1963(a).

Hill, George E. "Guidance in Elementary Schools." *Clearing House* 38:11–6; 1963(b).

Hill, George E. "Guidance for Children in Elementary Schools." Paper presented at the meeting of the APGA, Washington, D.C., April 1966.

Hillson, Henry T., and Myers, Florence C. *The Demonstration Guidance Project 1957–62.* New York [City] Board of Education, 1963.

Hitchcock, Arthur A. "Counselors: Supply, Demand, Need." In McGowan, John F. (Ed.) *Counselor Development in American Society.* Conference Recommendations from Invitational Conference on Government-University Relations in the Professional Preparation and Employment of Counselors, Washington, D.C., June 1965. p. 83–111.

Hollister, William G. "Child Guidance in Your School." *Nat Parent Teach* 55(No. 2):29–31; 1960.

Holt, John C. *How Children Fail.* Pitman, 1964. 181p.

Hummel, Raymond D. "Ego-counseling in Guidance: Concept and Method." *Harvard Ed R* 32:463–82; 1962.

Humphreys, J. Anthony, and others. *Guidance Services.* SRA, 1960. 414p.

Hutson, Percival W. *The Guidance Function in Education.* Appleton, 1958. 680p.

International Association for Educational and Vocational Guidance. *Bulletin* No. 9:15–6; 1963(a).

International Association for Educational and Vocational Guidance. *Bulletin* No. 10:36–40; 1963(b).

Johnson, Walter F., and others. *Pupil Personnel and Guidance Services.* McGraw-Hill, 1961. 407p.

Johnston, Edgar G. "Waterford Studies Elementary School Guidance." *El Sch Guid Counseling* 1(No. 3):23–6; 1966.

Johnston, Edgar G., and others. *The Role of the Teacher in Guidance.* Prentice-Hall, 1959. 276p.

Jones, Charles R. "A Competency Pattern for Elementary School Counselors." Doctoral dissertation. Texas Technological Col, 1966.

Kaback, Goldie R. "Occupational Information in Elementary Education." *Voc Guid Q* 9:55–9; 1960.

Kaczkowski, Henry R. "Role and Function of the Elementary School Counselor." U Illinois, 1964. (Mimeographed.)

Katz, Martin. *Decisions and Values: A Rationale for Secondary School Guidance.* CEEB, 1963. 67p.

Kehas, Chris D. "Theoretical Formulations and Related Research." *R Ed Res* 36:207–18; 1966.

Kelley, Earl C. *Another Look at Individualism.* Wayne State U Press, 1962.

Kilanski, Doris M. "Reading Teacher and an Elementary Guidance Program." *Reading Teach* 19:429–32; 1966.

Klausmeier, Herbert J. "Identifying Children Through Measurements." *Ed* 80:167–71; 1959.

Klein, Ruth A. "The School Nurse as a Guidance Functionary." *Personnel Guid J* 38:318–22; 1959.

Knapp, Robert H. *Guidance in the Elementary School.* Allyn and Bacon, 1959. 394p.

Koehler, Ruth I. "Relationships Between Techniques and Theories in Child Therapy." *J Marriage Family* 26:174–81; 1964.

Koeppe, Richard P., and Bancroft, John F. "Elementary and Secondary School Programs." *R Edu Res* 36:219–32; 1966.

Kowitz, Gerald T., and Kowitz, Norma G. *Guidance in the Elementary Classroom.* McGraw-Hill, 1959. 314p.

Kowitz, Gerald T., and others. *Guidance Needs in the Primary Grades.* Bureau of Educational Research and Services, U Houston. 1965. 49p.

Kranzler, Gerald D., and others. "Counseling with Elementary School Children: An Experimental Study." *Personnel Guid J* 44:944–9; 1966.

Krathwohl, David R., and others. *Taxonomy of Educational Objectives,* Handbook 2: *Affective Domain.* McKay, 1964. 196p.

Krumboltz, John D., and Hosford, Raymond E. "Behavioral Counseling in the Elementary School." *El Sch Guid Counseling* 1(No. 3):11–9; 1966.

Lafferty, J. Clayton, and others. "A Creative School Mental Health Program." *Nat El Prin* 43(No. 5):23–35; 1964.

Leonard, George. "Utilizing Test Results in the Elementary Classroom." *Sch Counselor* 12:3–5; 1964.

Lifton, Walter M. "The Elementary School's Responsibility for Today's Vocational Misfits." *SRA Guidance Newsletter* December 1959.

Lighthall, Frederick F. "Defensive and Nondefensive Change in Children's Responses to Personality Questionnaires." *Child Develop* 34:455–70; 1963.

Lister, J. L., and Ohlsen, M. M. "The Improvement of Self-understanding Through Test Interpretation." *Personnel Guid J* 43:804–10; 1965.

Lloyd-Jones, Esther, and others. *Guidance in Elementary Education: A Casebook.* Teachers Col, Columbia U 1958. 118p.

Lowe, R. N. "Family Counseling. An Aspect of the Elementary School Guidance Program." School of Education, U Oregon, 1964. (Mimeographed.)

Mahan, T. W., Jr. "Elementary School Counselor: Disturber of the Peace." *Nat El Prin* 44: (No. 4): 72–4; 1965.

Malecki, Henry R., and Walker, John L. "Vocational Guidance in Poland." *Voc Guid Q* 14:253–5; 1966.

Mangan, Thomas, and Shafer, David. "Behavior Problems of Children as Viewed by Children in the Fifth Through Eighth Grades." *J Ed Res* 56:104–6; 1962.

Marshall, Hermine. "Behavior Problems of Normal Children: A Comparison Between the Lay Literature and Developmental Research." *Child Develop* 35:469–78; 1964.

Martin, Helen F. "Counseling and Guidance Techniques with Young Children." *Sch Counselor* 10:178–82; 1963.

Martin, Lynn Wiseman. "A Study of the Effect of Selected Guidance Activities upon Elementary School Children." Doctoral dissertation. U Missouri, 1959.

Martinson, Ruth, and Smallenburg, Harry W. *Guidance in Elementary Schools.* Prentice-Hall, 1958. 322p.

Mathewson, Robert H. *A Strategy for American Education.* Harper, 1957. 296p.

Mathewson, Robert H. *Guidance Policy and Practice,* 3rd ed. Harper, 1962. 397p.

Mathewson, Robert H. "The Meaning in Maturity." Lecture in guidance and student personnel service. Center for Educational Research and Service, Col Education, Ohio U, 1963.

Mattick, William E., and Nickolas, N. A. "Team Approach in Guidance." *Personnel Guid J* 42:922–4; 1964.

McCreary, William, and Miller, Gerald. "Elementary School Counselors in California." *Personnel Guid J* 44:494–8; 1966.

McDougall, William P., and Reitan, Henry M. "The Elementary Counselor as Perceived by Elementary Principals." *Personnel Guid J* 42:348–54; 1963.

McKellar, Rebecca L. "A Study of Concepts, Functions and Organizational Characteristics of Guidance in Elementary Schools." Doctoral dissertation. Florida State U, 1963.

Medinnus, Gene R. "The Development of a First Grade Adjustment Scale." *J Exp Ed* 30:243–8; 1961.

Meeker, Alice M. *Teacher at Work in the Elementary School.* Bobbs-Merrill, 1963. 129p.

Meeks, Anna R. *Elementary Guidance in the Decade Ahead. SRA Special Guidance Report.* 1961.

Meeks, Anna R. "Elementary Guidance in the Decade Ahead—A Positive Function Rather Than a Corrective Force." *Sch Com* 48(No. 9):16–8; 1962(a).

Meeks, Anna R. "Guidance in the Elementary School." *NEA J* 51(No. 3):30–2; 1962(b).

Meeks, Anna R. "Elementary School Counseling." *Sch Counselor* 10:108–11; 1963(a).

Meeks, Anna R. "Comprehensive Programs in Elementary School Guidance." Paper presented at the meeting of the APGA, Boston, Massachusetts, April 1963(b).

Miller, Carroll H. *Foundations of Guidance.* Harper, 1961. 464p.

Miller, Frank W. *Guidance Principles and Services.* Merrill, 1961. 426p.

Miller, Gerald. "New Directions in Elementary School Guidance." *California Ed* 2(No. 1):5–6; 1964.

Moore, Lamire H. "Guidance Project at the Elementary Level." *Sch Com* 49(No. 9):15+; 1963.

Moreno, J. L. "The Actual Trends in Group Psychotherapy." *Group Psychotherapy* 16:117–31; 1963.

Moustakos, Clark. "Spoiled Behavior in the School-age Child." *Child Study* 35:16–21; 1957–58.

Munson, Harold L. *Better Elementary School Guidance.* Report of the 1961 Workshop, Col Education, U Rochester, 1961.

Munson, Harold L. "A Rationale for Elementary School Guidance." Col Education, U Rochester, 1966. (Mimeographed.)

Muro, James J. "The Elementary Guidance Specialist as Perceived by Elementary School Teachers and Elementary School Principals." Doctoral dissertation. U Georgia, 1965.

Murphy, George W. "Play as a Counseling Tool." *Sch Counselor* 8:53–8; 1960.

Mussen, Paul H. *The Psychological Development of the Child.* Prentice-Hall, 1963. 109p.

National Education Association, Department of Elementary School Principals. *Guidance 1964.* NEA, 1964.

National Education Association, Division of Research and Guidance. *Guidance in the Elementary School.* Los Angeles County, Superintendent of Schools Office, 1965.

Nelson, Richard C. "Counselors in Elementary Schools: Promise and Proposal." *Guid J* 2:47–57; 1962.

Nelson, Richard C. "Play Media and the Elementary School Counselor." *El Sch Guid Counseling* 1(No. 3):10; 1966.

Newman, William H. "A Full Time Counselor in an Elementary School." *El Sch J* 56:354–7; 1956.

Nitzschke, Dale F., and Hill, George E. *The Elementary School Counselor: Preparation and Functions.* Center for Educational Research and Services, Col Education, Ohio U, 1964. 23p.

Norris, Willa. *Occupational Information in the Elementary School.* SRA, 1963. 243p.

Nowlin, Louis G. *The Use of the Child Development Specialist: One Approach to Improving Counseling* and *Psychological Services in the Elementary School.* Palo Alto Unified School District, 1964.

O'Hara, Robert P. "The Roots of Careers." *El Sch J* 62:277–80; 1962.

Ohlsen, Merle M. "Counseling Children in Groups." U Illinois, 1965 (a). (Mimeographed.)

Ohlsen, Merle M. "The Elementary School Counselor." *South Carolina Guid News* 14(No. 3); 1965(b).

Ohlsen, Merle M., and Gazda, George M. "Counseling Underachieving Bright Pupils." *Ed* 86:78–81; 1965.

Oldridge, B. "Two Roles for Elementary School Guidance Personnel." *Personnel Guid J* 43:367–70; 1964.

Orgel, Rita G. "Contemporary Views of Elementary School Guidance." *Sch Counselor* 8:22–7; 1960.

Parmer, O. E. "Psychological Services in Twenty-eight Elementary Schools of Columbus, Ohio." *J Exp Ed* 29:119–31; 1960.

Patouillet, Raymond. "Organizing for Guidance in the Elementary School." *Teachers Col Rec* 58:431–8; 1957.

Patouillet, Raymond. "Elementary Guidance Process and Content." Report of the Fourth Annual All Ohio Elementary School Guidance Conference, November 1964. p. 23–29.

Peters, Herman J. "Differential Factors Between Elementary and Secondary School Counseling." *Sch Counselor* 7:3–11; 1959.

Peters, Herman J. "Fostering the Developmental Approach in Guidance." *Ed Forum* 28:87–93; 1963.

Peters, Herman J. "Pupil Behavioral System." *Theory into Practice* 4:146–68; 1965.

Peters, Herman J., and Hansen, James C. "The School Counselor as a Researcher." *Sch Counselor* 12:165–70; 1964.

Peters, Herman J., and others. (Eds.) *Guidance in the Elementary School: Selected Readings.* Macmillan, 1963. 329p.

Peters, Herman J., and others. *Guidance in Elementary Schools.* Rand McNally, 1965. 278p.

Peters, Mildred. "Evaluating the Guidance Program." *Nat El Prin* 43(No. 5):26–7; 1964.

Peterson, Donald, and others. "Child Behavior Problems and Parental Attitudes." *Child Develop* 32:151–62; 1961.

Powell, W. K. *An Elementary Principal Talks About His Guidance Program.* Report presented at Fourth Annual All Ohio Elementary School Guidance Conference, November 1964.

Purkey, Ernest. "Elementary School Counseling." *NEA J* 51(No. 9):18–20; 1962.

Radin, Sherwin S. "Mental Health Problems of School Children." *J Sch Health* 33:252;1963.

Raebeck, Charles. "Teacher Guidance—A Three Dimensional Teaching Experience." Paper presented at the meeting of the APGA, Cleveland, Ohio, April 1959.

Raines, Bill. "Approach to Practicum for the Elementary School Counselor." *Personnel Guid J* 43:57–9; 1964(a).

Raines, Bill. "The Role of the Counselor in the Elementary Schools of Ohio." Doctoral dissertation. Ohio U, 1964(b).

Reaves, Gayle C., and Reaves, Leonard E., III. "The Counselor and Preventive Psychiatry." *Personnel Guid J* 43:661–4; 1965.

Review of Educational Research 33:138–25; 1963.

Riccio, Anthony C. "Elementary School Guidance: Its Present Status." *Theory into Practice* 2:39–43; 1963.

Riccio, Anthony C., and Wehmeyer, Donald J. "Guidance Services Recommended by Public and Parochial Elementary School Teachers." *Ed Res B* 40:12–8; 1961.

Rice, Joseph, Jr. "Types of Problems Referred to a Central Guidance Agency at Different Grade Levels." *Personnel Guid J* 42:52–5; 1963.

Richardson, Sybil. "Techniques of Studying Children." *California J El Ed* 26:227–36; 1958.

Royster, W. "Guidance in the Elementary School." *Nat El Prin* 43(No. 5):6–10; 1964.

Scheibe, James H. "The School Psychologist: Clinician, Coordinator, Consultant." *Nat El Prin* 45:43–51; 1965.

Science Research Associates. "*Roles of Guidance Workers in the Elementary Schools.*" SRA Guidance Newsletter. November 1960.

Shaw, Merville C. "Testing a Model for the Provision of Guidance Services." *El Sch Guid Counseling* 1(No. 2):13–6; 1965.

Shertzer, Bruce, and Lundy, C. T. "Administrator's Image of an Elementary School Counselor." *Sch Counselor* 2:211–4; 1964.

Shertzer, Bruce, and Stone, Shelley C. *Fundamentals of Guidance.* Houghton, 1966. 526p.

Shoben, Edward Joseph, Jr. "Guidance: Remedial Function or Social Reconstruction?" *Harvard Ed R* 32:430–43; 1962.

Slobin, Dan I. "The Fruits of the First Season: A Discussion of the Role of Play in Childhood." *J Humanistic Psychol* 4(No. 1):59–79; 1964.

Smallenburg, Harry. "Studying the Elementary Guidance Program." *Nat El Prin* 43(No. 5):15–8; 1964.

Smillie, David. "Reality, Possibility, and Children." *ETC.* 15:163–8; 1958.

Smith, Hyrum. "Preventing Difficulties Through Guidance." *Ed* 83:266–9; 1963.

Smith, Hyrum. *Hearings Before the General Subcommittee on Education. October 19–20, 1965.* House of Representatives, Eighty-ninth Congress. GPO, 1966.

Smith, Hyrum, and Eckerson, Louise O. *Guidance for Children in Elementary Schools.* HEW, USOE Bulletin. GPO, 1963.

Smith, Hyrum, and Eckerson, Louise O. *Guidance Services in Elementary Schools. A National Survey.* USOE, HEW, 1966. 145p.

Sonstegard, Manford. "A Rationale for Interviewing Parents." *Sch Counselor* 12:72–6; 1964.

Spaulding, R. L. "Personality and Social Development: Peer and School Influences." *R Ed Res* 34:588–98; 1964.

Sperber, Mae. "Micki's World: A Continuing Experiment in Psychodrama." *Group Psychotherapy* 15: 326–33; 1962.

Stefflre, Buford. (Ed.) *Theories of Counseling.* McGraw-Hill, 1965. 298p.

Straight, Dana G. "Relating Guidance to the Philosophy of the School." *Clearing House* 37:271–5; 1963.

Strang, Ruth, and Morris, Glyn. *Guidance in the Classroom.* Macmillan, 1964. 118p.

Stripling, Robert O., and Lane, David. "Trends in Elementary School Guidance." *Nat El Prin* 43:(No. 5):11–4; 1964.

Tennyson, W. Wesley, and Monnens, Lawrence P. "The World of Work Through Elementary Readers." *Voc Guid Q* 12:85–9; 1963.

Tiedeman, David V. "Purposing Through Education: The Further Delineation of Goal and Program for Guidance." In Landy, Edward, and Perry, Paul A. (Eds.) *Guidance in American Education: Background and Prospects.* Harvard Graduate School of Education, 1964. p. 162–72.

Tiedeman, David V., and Field, Frank L. "Guidance: The Science of Purposeful Action Applied Through Education." *Harvard Ed R* 32:483–501; 1962.

Times Educational Supplement. "Mental Health in Primary Schools: Plowden Evidence." *London Times* 2585:1034; 1964.

Topetzes, Nick J., and Ivanoff, John M. "Classroom Teacher's Role in Group Guidance." *Cath Sch J* 63: 33–4; 1963.

Tyler, Louise L. "Concept of an Ideal Teacher-Student Relationship." *J Ed Res* 58:112–7; 1964.

Tyler, Ralph W. "Educational Objectives of American Democracy." In Ginzberg, Eli. (Ed.) *The Nation's Children*, Vol. 2. Columbia U Press. 1960. 242p.

Waetjen, Walter B. "Counseling Services for the Elementary School." *Nat El Prin* 44(No. 4):59–62; 1965.

Watson, D. "A Teacher Looks at Guidance." *Nat El Prin* 43(No. 5):37–40; 1964.

Weitz, Henry. *Behavior Change Through Guidance.* Wiley, 1964. 225p.

Wells, Cecelia G. "Psychodrama with Children in a Sociometrically Structural Setting." *Group Psychotherapy* 14:160–3; 1961.

Wells, Cecelia G. "Psychodrama and Creative Counseling in the Elementary School." *Group Psychotherapy* 15:244–52; 1962.

Wieland, Robert. "A Comparative Study of the Duties Performed Regularly by School Counselors, School Psychologists and School Social Workers Working Together in Selected School Systems." Doctoral dissertation. Florida State U, 1966.

Willey, Roy Deverl. *Guidance in Elementary Education.* Harper, 1960. 462p.

Willey, Roy Deverl, and Dunn, Melvin. *The Role of the Teacher in the Guidance Program.* McKnight, 1964. 487p.

Wilson, L. A. "Needs for Guidance in the Elementary School." *Peabody J Ed* 41:289–95; 1964.

Witmer, J. Melvin. "The Use, Value, and Improvement of Certain Guidance Principles and Practices as Perceived by Classroom Teachers in Selected Elementary Schools in Florida." Doctoral dissertation. Florida State U, 1966.

Wrenn, C. Gilbert. "Philosophical and Psychological Bases of Personnel Services in Education." In Henry, Nelson B. (Ed.) *Personnel Services in Education*, Part II, The 58th Yearbook of the NSSE. U Chicago Press, 1959. p. 41–81.

Wrenn, C. Gilbert. "Editorial Comment on School Counseling." *J Counseling Psychol* 7:162; 1960.

Wrenn, C. Gilbert. *The Counselor in a Changing World.* APGA, 1962. 195p.

Young, Joe Miller. "A Study of the Noninstructional Problems Which Inhibit Learning in the Elementary School and Their Implications for the Organization of Elementary Guidance Services." Doctoral dissertation. U Arizona, 1962.

Young, Frances. "Program for Preventing School Maladjustment." *Sch Com* 50:16–17+; 1964.

Zaccaria, Joseph S. "Varied Contributions of Guidance." *Ed* 86:75–7; 1965.

COUNSELING—SECONDARY SCHOOLS

Counseling in secondary schools is a major element in the guidance program, which in turn can be considered a distinctive component of pupil personnel work. The term "counseling" is often used loosely, however, to refer to the entire guidance program, and even to many other personnel services.

If counseling is what a secondary-school counselor does, it includes a host of activities besides counseling. That counselors are not entirely content with these conditions was documented by Wrenn (1962), who asked a sample of American School Counselor Association (ASCA) members which of their present activities did not belong in a guidance program. Half of them expressed a willingness to surrender clerical work, and considerably smaller proportions believed that supervision of study halls, disciplining of students, scoring tests, and other such duties were not appropriate for a counselor. Only 35 percent of the full-time counselors in this study devoted as much as half of their time to "counseling students." Nevertheless, they regarded counseling as their most basic and distinctive activity. When asked which of their present activities should be maintained during the next twenty years, virtually all hoped to continue counseling. Substantial numbers (but less than half) wanted to continue to hold conferences with parents and teachers, to administer and interpret standardized tests, and to carry on group guidance and orientation programs. Only small proportions of the counselors expected to engage in research, evaluation, and follow-up studies (16 percent), to refer students to community agencies and maintain contacts with such agencies (16 percent), to deal with vocational information and job placement (12 percent), or to be involved in curriculum development (8 percent).

Counseling itself—as distinct from these other activities—has been most frequently termed a process or a relationship. In its most specific and superficial manifestation, however, counseling appears to consist of talk between a counselor and a student. What do they talk about, and why?

PURPOSE AND CONTENT. Not only the activities but also the content and purposes associated with counseling have been diffuse. Current federal legislation, which has supplied financial aid to secondary-school counseling and guidance programs for specific aims, highlights this variety of expectations—and pressures. For example, the National Defense Education Act of 1958 sought to increase national resources of high-level talent by supporting the identification of able students in order that they might be encouraged to go on to higher education. The Vocational Education Act of 1963, as part of an attempt to prepare youth for the needs of the labor market, made funds available for secondary school counseling programs dealing with the choices of occupation and vocational education of students who were not headed for college. The Elementary and Secondary Education Act of 1965, concerned largely with compensatory education for youth who are economically disadvantaged, tended to emphasize counseling for motivational and remedial purposes. Other funds have been granted specifically for counseling to reduce the incidence of dropping out of school, underachievement, and delinquency. Indeed, "counseling" is often preceded by a modifier; among the adjectives most frequently encountered are "vocational," "educational," "academic," "developmental," "behavioral," "adjustment," "personal," "social," "ethical," and "financial"—each suggesting a somewhat different purpose or content. This diffusion of content and purpose can be traced back to the forces that presided at the birth of secondary-school counseling and shaped its early development.

Historical Origins. Brewer (1942) suggested that four conditions at the turn of the century led to the emergence of the vocational-guidance movement (from which secondary-school counseling and guidance grew). Two of these were economic—the increasing division of labor and the growth of technology. Because occupations had become more specialized and less visible, formal attention to individual differences and to ways of classifying and presenting occupational information seemed necessary as a basis for vocational choice. A third condition was ideological—interpretations of democracy that emphasized humanitarianism and reform. Rockwell and Rothney (1961) have pointed out that pioneers in vocational guidance and secondary-school counseling (Frank Parsons, Jesse Davis, Eli Weaver, Anna Reed, and David S. Hill) shared a strong belief in the improvability of man and of society: they had faith that man could control his own evolution. Their concern with uplift (which seemed to survive in counselors' attempts to develop students' potentialities, to "build character," to foster morality and acceptable behavior, to motivate for high achievement, and to prevent or remedy delinquency) was apparently mingled with what Weber (1930) has called the "Protestant ethic": the glorification of success in work as a means of salvation. Brewer's fourth condition—the extension of vocational education—was instrumental in placing guidance (which had started in a settlement house) in the transitional and early stages of secondary school and established firmer connections between educational and vocational decisions.

It should be added that developments in psychology (particularly in measurement, which grew up along with the guidance movement, but also in clinical work) had a strong impact on counseling.

Thus, it can be said that counseling was fathered by economics, mothered by ideologies, housed largely in secondary schools, and befriended by psychology. Its character at birth and during infancy was molded by all of these forces. But these shaping forces have not been static. As they have changed, their influences have changed; and as counseling has matured, it has tended toward a more purposeful control of its own destiny. Thus, data from surveys suggest that the educational setting may have become prepotent in determining the primary content and purposes of counseling. The counseling profession itself, however, has indicated some desire to redirect this trend.

Surveys and Expectations. According to Project Talent data (Goldberg, 1962) the two types of counseling mentioned most frequently as being performed regularly in a national sample of secondary schools both concerned educational decisions: choice of college (84 percent of the schools) and planning high school programs (80 percent of the schools). In the academic domain, counseling low achievers took place regularly in 63 percent of the schools, and counseling on subject-matter difficulties in 58 percent. Adjustment counseling was practiced regularly in a majority of the schools only insofar as it pertained to students' problems with teachers (thus perhaps overlapping the academic area); counseling on personal and family problems, or on relations with classmates, took place regularly in only about a third of the schools. Such general counseling aims as "helping students make the most of their potentialities" and "assisting students in making valid self-appraisals" were checked under "regularly" by 68 percent and 51 percent of the schools, respectively. Vocational counseling was practiced regularly in only 54 percent of the schools.

In general, students' perceptions of the counselor's role seem to coincide with this rank order of counseling functions. For example, Grant (1954) found that students frequently indicated that they would go to counselors about matters of educational planning and (to a lesser extent) vocational planning, but rarely about personal-emotional matters.

A number of surveys of what pupils, parents, teachers, administrators, counselor educators, educational statesmen, and others expect of counselors are summarized by Roeber (1963). While the findings of these studies vary in many ways (it is not clear to what extent these variations are attributable to differences in methodology), there seems to be universal agreement on the paramount importance of educational and vocational planning. That even these two functions may be viewed as quite distinct from each other appears in the evidence (Crary, 1966) that many school districts are naming counselors to specialized educational or vocational (as well as other) assignments.

Statement by Profession. In the face of many pressures and expectations, secondary-school counselors—perhaps beset by an "identity crisis"—have striven to reach a consensus on their role. Fitzgerald (1965) reported that over 90 percent of the total membership of the ASCA approved a statement of policy that defined counseling as "an accepting, non-evaluating relationship in which [a pupil] is helped to better understand himself, the environment he perceives, and the relationship between these" (Fitzgerald, 1965, Appendix C). This aim to effect tripartite improvement in the pupil's understanding—especially as spelled out in "Guidelines for Implementation of the ASCA Statement of Policy for Secondary School Counselors" (Fitzgerald, 1965)—echoes the famous triad formulated by Parsons (1909) as "[the main factors in the] wise choice of a vocation . . . : (1) a clear understanding of yourself, your aptitudes, abilities, interests, ambitions, resources, limitations and their causes; (2) a knowledge of the requirements and conditions of success, advantages, compensations, opportunities, and prospects in different lines of work; (3) true reasoning on the relations of these two groups of facts." Secondary-school counselors have not been untouched by developments during the half-century since Parsons' book was published. For example, the "Guidelines" incorporates a reference to the pupil's *acceptance* as well as understanding of self. The ASCA statement also implies that the counselor must not be content with purveying information about options but must deal explicitly with the student's *perceptions*. And Parsons' expression of the goal of vocational guidance—"the choice of a vocation, adequate preparation for it, and the attainment of efficiency and success"—seems somewhat less extensive than the ASCA statement of the purpose of counseling: "that most pupils will enhance and enrich their personal development and self-fulfillment by means of making more intelligent decisions." Nevertheless, the striking similarities between the two statements seem to suggest a considerable degree of continuity from the rationale developed for some of the earliest secondary-school counseling programs to the "official" rationale endorsed by current practitioners.

Both statements focus on the pupil's decisions, specifically occupational in one case, more general in the other. In keeping with this emphasis is another professional statement, by the Division of Counseling Psychology of the American Psychological Association (1961), that counseling psychology "focuses on *plans* individuals must make to play productive *roles* in their social environments." These recent statements are notable for their omissions of other counseling purposes.

Limits on Counseling. During the years following Parsons' pronouncement, secondary-school counseling quickly overflowed the channel marked by that statement and flooded the entire plain of educational purposes. The levees collapsed under the combined impetus of progressive education and the "mental hygiene movement" (Miller, 1961). Such functions of counseling as the recognition and measurement of individual differences, plus the efficacy of dealing with pupils on an individual basis, seemed admirably suited for instruction generally. Counseling was regarded as a way of reaching pupils who did not learn what was taught in the classroom. Counselors were also expected to supplement the teachers' efforts to attain instructional objectives for which there was no course name in the syllabus. It was expected that such diverse matters as reading, health, citizenship, morality, manners, and study habits could all be improved by counseling. This tendency reached the height of nondefinition with such statements as "Guidance is education, and education is guidance," or "All counselors are teachers, and all teachers are counselors." Thus Brewer, in a book entitled *Education as Guidance* (1932), included "anything that has to do with instruction or with learning" under the term "educational guidance."

Myers (1941) made a strong effort to stem this tide. He insisted that adapting teaching methods to individual needs was not guidance; it was just good teaching. He reserved the term "guidance" for helping the pupil to choose among possible courses of action open to him. Katz (1963) emphasized that there can be little serious talk of choosing and decision making if the culture has predetermined what the choices and decisions should be. American culture unequivocally favors good health, good study habits, and so on. These values are among what B. Othanel Smith and others (1957) called the "universals." Counselors often do attempt to supplement the functions of administrators and teachers in transmitting the culture, drawing on whatever special skills they have for remedial and adjustive work. Their distinctive concern is not with the universals, however, but with the alternatives, toward which the culture tends to be more nearly neutral: "If the role of education is to transmit the culture, the role of counseling is to help the individual come to terms with the culture—that is, to see himself in the culture. But first he must see the culture in himself. Thus, his first question should be, where have my values come from? His second, where are they taking me?" (Katz, 1963).

In a similar vein, Tiedeman and Field (1965) delineated distinctive but overlapping roles for teacher and counselor in developing students' "purposeful action," which they have stated to be the purpose of guidance. They listed three prerequisites for the development of goal-seeking behavior: the student must "1) know of goals and their bases as favored by others, 2) experience the expectation that he will learn how to evolve goal-directed activity of his own accord, and 3) continually subject his wishes and expected responsibilities for purposeful action to critical examination." They held that the teacher should work primarily in the realm of the first two of these conditions, and the counselor in the last two.

Thus, teaching and guidance complement each other in helping the student to cope with discontinuities in his career.

These formulations, like the ASCA statement, proposed to return counseling to its original stream bed, with a considerably deeper channel. While Parsons and many who followed him focused on the surface events of occupational choice and other vocationally oriented decisions, there has been more attention during the last two decades to probing into the deeper strata of the student's search for identity, the development of his self concept, his exploration and examination of values. In general, however, secondary-school counseling has tended to avoid the murkier depths of psychotherapy.

Discovery Versus Becoming. Until recent years, most secondary-school counseling that, in the tradition of Parsons, focused on vocational guidance tended to be obsessed with the goal of correct or appropriate choice. Counselors were judgmental and more or less subtly directive about the content of students' choices. If individual students' traits could be classified differentially in respect to occupational characteristics and requirements, it seemed logical that each pupil could be matched to the right occupation. The implicit—indeed, sometimes the explicit (Sears, 1925; Williamson, 1937)—purpose of this "trait-and-factor" theory (Super, 1954) was the avoidance of waste, of floundering, of trial and error. Beneath universal protestations on behalf of the pupil's freedom to choose (e.g., Jones, 1921; Koos & Kefauver, 1932) lay the conviction that the wise choice, the right choice, can be known to the expert counselor—but can be properly accepted and implemented only if freely reached by the pupil. This practical concession to individual freedom of decision was viewed more as a trick of the trade than as a basic goal of counseling. If, indeed, the pupil was keyed to one or a few correct occupational positions, counselors believed that his regular adult position could be known early and could—and should—determine all preliminary decisions (such as high school curriculum) leading up to it. Thus, the aim of pupil appraisal in counseling was the *discovery* of the key traits for predicting membership and success in an occupation. There was, of course, some dissatisfaction with the procedures available for appraisal and prediction. Counselors occasionally felt uneasy about the validity of their observations and interpretations. More scientific data would make them more persuasive. In short, counseling in the horse-and-buggy days of guidance was a set of practices in search of a technology.

A technology akin to putting the horses under the hood became available with rapid developments in psychometrics, statistical techniques, and computers. Still, Hull's prophecy (1928) that vocational decisions could be stamped out by a computer, although currently embraced by Project Talent (Cooley, 1966), was eventually rejected by counselors who insisted on maintaining a distinction between predictions and decisions. A somewhat phony conflict between "actuarial" and "clinical" predictions (Meehl, 1954) has been resolved by accepting the descriptive contributions of trait-and-factor theory but rejecting its imperative implications. For trait-and-factor theory, which started with the hypothesis that occupational choice *does* take place in a certain way (trait matching), had come to imply that it *should* take place in this way, only more so.

One reason for disillusionment with trait-and-factor theory was its essentially static nature. It did not incorporate sufficient provision for change or development on the part of the individual. Thus, it fell into the trap of premature concentration on the content of a pupil's occupational choice as he entered secondary school. This led to an approbation of consistency in the content of choice as verbalized by pupils. Repeated documentation of the inconstancy of choice—for example, only 16.8 percent of a national sample of males questioned in grade 9 and then again one year after high school graduation expressed similar career plans on both occasions (Flanagan, 1966)—was generally interpreted to mean that more or better guidance was needed.

A powerful influence in counselors' reaction against trait-and-factor theory was the inspirational eloquence of Carl Rogers (1942, 1951, 1961a), who converted many counselors to what he later regretted having called "nondirective" counseling. Out of a background of therapeutic work, Rogers stressed the capacity of individuals to change. He attributed maladjustments not to lack of knowledge or of intellectual understanding but to attitudinal and emotional blocks that prevented acceptance and implementation of rational solutions to problems. Thus, the client's increased acceptance of himself, particularly of his feelings, was regarded as an immediate aim of counseling. This was expected to lead to self-actualization and growth.

Recognition of pupils' capacity for change encouraged counselors to deprecate the value of predictive data and indeed to discard much pupil-appraisal and information-giving activity. Many counselors played for a while at the role of Rogerian psychotherapist. As Hummel (1962) has noted, however, the obstacles, both economic and theoretical, to the practice of psychotherapy by secondary-school guidance counselors are formidable. According to Perry (1955), Rogers' writings during the 1940's and 1950's showed a tendency to mention counseling less and psychotherapy more, with emphasis shifting from short-term to long-term treatment. Thus, by the 1960's, Brayfield's review (1963) noted a consensus that counselors work with normal people, emphasize the strengths and assets of counselees, and focus on cognitive activities, especially those involving choice and decision. Still, Rogers had focused attention on the counselee's capacity for change and had helped to put "becoming" into the counselor's vocabulary as a substitute for "discovery." This perhaps increased counselors' readiness to accept goals related to developmental concepts.

Self Concept, Career Development, and Decision Making. Counseling, which had been a set of practices in search of a technology, became during the 1950's and 1960's a technology in search of a new theory.

Developmental theory, such as Piaget had applied to learning, Erikson (1950, 1959) to psychosocial tasks, and Jersild (1946) to the school curriculum, proved attractive for guidance (Beilin, 1955; Borow, 1961). Helping to demolish the view of occupational choice as a single event occurring at one point in time, Ginzberg and others (1951) stressed developmental stages. They believed these stages to be genetically determined. However, Tiedeman and O'Hara (1963) have summarized evidence that career development is not isomorphically related to general developmental psychology; in fact, the ordering of stages can be affected by a guidance program (Gribbons, 1960; Shimberg & Katz, 1962).

Most influential in the shift from trait-and-factor theory to career development theory was Super (1953, 1954, 1957), who advanced the proposition that vocational development is essentially a process of developing and implementing a self concept. A crucial part of this process is role playing—the formulation and testing of hypotheses about self. He also proposed (Super, 1955) that vocational maturity be defined in terms of the stage in vocational development which a pupil had reached at a given age and in terms of the pupil's effectiveness in dealing with tasks appropriate for that stage (compared with others engaged in the same tasks). From data gathered in the Career Pattern Study (Super & Overstreet, 1960), he concluded that vocational maturity in grade 9 boys consists of preparation for vocational choice—achieving a planning orientation and taking responsibility for decisions—but does not require consistent or realistic vocational preferences. He implied, therefore, that the goal of guidance at this stage should be to foster the making of plans, concern with the need to choose, and awareness of factors to be considered in choice; to fix on a specific vocational choice would be premature.

Still, vocationally relevant decisions of a specific nature (e.g., about which high school courses to take) have to be made at a number of choice points in secondary school. As was indicated earlier, these decisions have been perceived as the immediate business of counseling in secondary schools. According to the rationale for secondary-school guidance as described by Katz (1963), these decisions are not only important in their own right but also can serve as paradigms to help initiate the pupil into career decision making and to help him acquire skills in the process. Indeed, a career can be represented as a sequence of choices. The concept of a sequence suggests that any single decision bears some relationship to antecedent and subsequent decisions. The nature of this relationship is, to borrow Tiedeman's phrase (1961), "means-ends chain." Since man both remembers and imagines, he can evaluate his past experience and anticipate his reactions to new conditions. That is, he can bring both the past and the future into the psychological present. These evaluations and anticipations represent self-appraisals that contribute to his self concept. Self concept is thus engaged reciprocally with decision making; the concept of self both shapes an individual's choices and is shaped by them. Actuarial data are not neglected. They interact with existing self concepts in the formulation of hypotheses about the self that are subject to reality testing within the school context. These hypotheses can then be confirmed or revised. Thus, experience effects a series of reintegrations of self concept. Events—the perceptions and interpretations of outcomes—maintain or upset the balance between self concept and reality. Counseling may then focus on helping the student to test and reinstate his "mobile equilibrium" at appropriate times in a rational way.

Crucial to this rational behavior in the face of uncertainty—which may be the nearest he can get to wisdom—is the student's exploration and examination of values. He can learn early that making a decision—that is, if the decision is truly *to be made* and is not a foregone conclusion—requires essentially a choice between competing values. To help each student reason about his salient values and develop an internally consistent value system is, then, one aim of counseling. To help him identify the options that promise gratifications relevant to his value system is a second. To help him interpret his probabilities of entry and success in each option is a third. The fourth, and final, aim is to help him master an effective strategy for processing these insights and data that will arm him for encounters with future discontinuities and choice points. With this assistance, the student can find order in the complexities of decision making, can enrich his experience by examining it, and can become the conscious artist of his own career.

PROCESS AND METHOD. Originally devised to implement counseling goals, processes and methods may eventually tend to mold them.

Clinical Method. The clinical method of counseling that prevailed during the dominance of trait-and-factor theory was summarized by Williamson (1939) as consisting of six steps: analysis (collecting all possible data and observations concerning the student); synthesis (summarizing the data via case-study technique and test profiles); diagnosis (comparing the student's profile with educational and occupational ability profiles and discovering causes of any problems); prognosis (judging probable consequences of problems and adjustments and indicating alternative actions for the student's consideration); counseling or treatment (discussing plans with the student or advising him what to do); and follow-up (repeating the previous steps as new problems arise and assisting the student to carry out his program of action).

A considerable body of materials and techniques for differential prediction lent support to the clinical method. During the post-World War II period, a number of multifactor aptitude-test batteries came into use in the schools (for example, the Differential Aptitude Tests, Multiple Aptitude Tests, Holzinger-Crowder Uni-Factor Tests, Flanagan Aptitude Classification Tests, and Guilford-Zimmerman Aptitude Survey). All reflected to some degree the work of Spearman, Thurston, and others on identification and measurement of cognitive factors; each included an array of tests whose norms were based on the same population; all aimed at improving differential prediction through various combinations of some of the most important factors. As Super (n.d.) repeatedly emphasized in his review of validity data for these batteries, their predictive value for secondary-school students does not seem to be commensurately different from that of single-score or two-score scholastic aptitude tests. Cronbach (1956) pointed out that differential predictions based on specific empirical validity studies of such tests are often difficult to justify on theoretical or logical grounds. McNemar (1964) has also been severely critical of the use of these batteries.

Sophisticated techniques in differential prediction have been developed and used by Horst (1955), who dealt with such methodological problems as selection of optimal sets of predictor variables and allowance for biased criterion samples; by Tiedeman (1966) and a number of his associates (e.g., Tiedeman & Sternberg, 1952), who applied the multiple discriminant function to the prediction of occupational or curricular *membership;* and by French (1964a, 1964b), who used a large number of pure-factor aptitude tests, interest and personality measures, and biographical data in longitudinal comparative prediction studies. Such technological refinements, however, seemed to produce disappointingly small increments in *differential* validities (Katz, 1963).

On the positive side, "hard" prediction data of a more traditional sort have been made more accessible to secondary-school students (e.g., Hills, 1963; Swanson & others, 1961; Educational Testing Service, 1965), in the form of expectancy tables from which they can ascertain their predicted grades at various colleges.

Nondirective and Behavioral Processes. Departing quite drastically from the "clinical" method and indeed from any concern with measurement and prediction have been the Rogerian counselors (e.g., Boy & Pine, 1963). Rogers (1962) deprecated method or technique and emphasized the importance of the quality of the personal relationship established between counselor and student. In this relationship the counselor must be genuine, feel empathy, and have warm, positive, unconditional regard for the student.

In apparent contrast with these qualities is the method of operant conditioning proposed by Skinner (1948, 1953, 1955-56) and elaborated by Michael and Meyerson (1962) as a behavioral approach to counseling. This involves a rather straightforward application of principles of reinforcement so that the pupil will learn and practice desirable behaviors. For example, Krumboltz and Thoresen (1964) demonstrated that some counselors can reinforce students' information-seeking behavior. Krumboltz and Varenhorst (1965) inferred from another study that some counselors were more influential (more potent reinforcers?) than the pupils' parents and peers. They did not suggest how the counselors achieved this status.

However, Truax (1966) found some evidence that therapists who are rated high in the qualities named by Rogers (genuineness, empathy, warmth) may serve as more potent reinforcers than therapists rated low in these qualities. Thus, Rogers' own effectiveness as a therapist might be attributable to his potency as a reinforcer. Rogers himself (1961b) shuddered away from the image of control associated with operant conditioning. But Krumboltz (1966) rejected any incompatibility between behavioral counseling and such Rogerian goals as self-understanding and self-acceptance. He urged, instead, that objective descriptions of behavior be substituted for these terms so that such behaviors can be specifically reinforced in counseling and their attainment evaluated. He held that the goals of counseling could be stated differently for each student (he seemed to use "goals" sometimes to denote desired outcomes and sometimes to denote instrumental activities) and that the counselor's job is to "help the client translate his problem into a behavioral goal." Neither the principles nor the practices of behavioral counseling are new, but its recent emergence as a school of thought promises to produce some noteworthy attempts to devise and conduct experiments specifically linked to theory.

Rational Decision Making. Attempts to apply decision theory to counseling tend to start with the student's explicit specification of his own values (e.g., Cronbach & Gleser, 1957; Blau & others, 1956). Hills (1964) suggested use of a simple scaling technique Metfessel, 1947) whereby high school students could specify the importance they attributed to various levels of college grades. Multiplying these scaled values by a decimal representing the probability for each student of obtaining each grade level at each college would produce an "expected value" for each option.

Katz (1966b) adapted the same constant sum procedure for scaling larger domains of values in a "universal" model of guidance for career decision making. This model combines three systems of data involved in any career decision: a value system, an information system, and a prediction system. The first step induces the student to take full cognizance of the range of values in the culture and to make explicit the relative importance of each value dimension to him, quite literally laying his values on the line. This exercise may serve as a useful reprise of the student's previous exploration of his values with the counselor or may serve to initiate such an exploration. Definition and discussion of the various dimensions of the values domain, the striking of trial balances, and the revision of allotments all contribute to a first-draft identification of the satisfactions he seeks. Thus, the examination of the student's values need not be merely maieutic, uncovering and eliciting what is already there. It can sometimes lead the student—perhaps playfully, at first—to "try on for size" values that have previously been unfamiliar. Then, from the information system, come data on instrumentality. What is the capacity of each option to furnish returns appropriate to each value? A rating of instrumentality for each option, derived from available sources (still woefully inadequate), is combined with the corresponding value. Finally, the sum of these products for each option, representing its weighted total instrumentality, can be combined with data from the prediction system, indicating each student's probability of entry or success, or his joint probability of entry and success, in each option. In short, this model leads the pupil in simple steps to a ranking of options that combines subjective utility with objective probability. This ranking need not be regarded as permanent. It reflects the student's reasoned state of mind, interacting with available information, at a given moment in time. At appropriate intervals, he can go back to the starting point and repeat the cycle. Much of the operation of this model can be computerized—e.g., the entire information and prediction systems.

Counseling by Computer. Interest has developed recently in the use of computers not only for information storage and retrieval but also for simulating the counselor's interview behavior (e.g., Cogswell & Estavan, 1965). Counseling by computer may be expected to undergo further development with improvements in the capability of computers to process and analyze verbal material (Helm, 1966).

Group Programs. A more traditional way of conserving the time of counselors has been to use group programs of various sorts. Much of the content of counseling—information, concepts, procedures—lends itself efficiently to group rather than dyadic consideration. For example, Hoppock (1963) described a number of group procedures for conveying occupational information. A work text designed for classroom use at the early secondary-school level (Katz, 1957) introduced pupils to career decision-making concepts and procedures, focusing most specifically on immediate curriculum decisions but extending also to tentative formulation of intermediate and long-range plans. Pupils' exploration and examination of values, as well as their use of test scores and school marks for prediction, received special emphasis. The Palo Alto, California, secondary schools developed a group guidance program featuring use of local experience tables to help students make educational decisions (Clarke & others, 1965). Allen (1933, 1934) used hypothetical problems and situations as topics for group discussion and problem solving. Krumboltz and Thoresen (1964) found that information seeking could be reinforced in group as well as in individual counseling. Caplan (1957) used group counseling to improve the adjustment of junior high school boys who were in conflict with school authorities. Boocock (1966) has demonstrated the use of a "career game" with groups to convey information and to develop decision-making skills.

While many of these instances capitalized on the dynamics of group work—discussed, in relation to guidance, by Glanz (1962)—most of them did not propose group guidance as a substitute for individual counseling. Notwithstanding developments in both group guidance and computer simulation, there is still much concern about the supply of counselors.

PERSONNEL AND PROFESSIONAL PREPARATION. Growth in the supply of counselors has been spectacular during the postwar years. Greenleaf (1942) reported that in 1938 only 6 percent of the 23,000 public secondary schools had one or more staff members assigned at least half-time to counseling duties. These 1,297 schools, which employed 2,286 counselors, enrolled about one-third of all public high school students in the nation and had an average counselor–pupil ratio of 1 to 900. Thus, two-thirds of the nation's secondary-school students were in schools that did not have even one half-time counselor.

Precise comparisons with these prewar figures would not be meaningful, especially since the current convention has been to reckon the number of counselors as full-time-equivalents (f-t-e). Nevertheless, the trend can be clearly discerned. By 1958, when the National Defense Education Act (NDEA) was passed, there were 12,000 f-t-e counselors in the public secondary schools (U.S. Office of Education, 1964). Although many schools, especially the smaller ones, had no counselors at all, this total represented an overall ratio of one counselor to every 960 public high school pupils in the nation. Two-thirds of the counselors failed to satisfy the minimum requirements for certification in their own states. More than half of them were clustered in only seven states, serving one-third of the total secondary-school population.

After five years of NDEA, which supported both the hiring and the training of guidance counselors, the number of f-t-e counselors had increased by 127 percent to 27,180, for a ratio of one counselor to every 530 students in the school year 1962–63 (*ibid.*). At that time, 75 percent of all secondary-school students were in schools that met the standards of their own state's plans for guidance and counseling. A total of 13,784 counselors had received training at NDEA-supported institutes during the five years.

The numbers have continued to grow. According to recent U.S. Office of Education estimates, during the academic year 1964–65 there were 31,000 f-t-e counselors (a total of 40,975 people), making the counselor–pupil ratio 1 to 507. This still falls short of the 1 to 300 ratio generally espoused as a goal (Conant, 1959; Wrenn, 1962). Meanwhile, the increasing demand for counselors in elementary schools, in junior colleges, in Office of Economic Opportunity programs, in the state employment services, and in other agencies seems likely to compete with secondary schools for new trainees, as well as for experienced staff members. Despite this prospect of a continuing shortage of counselors, much concern has been expressed over the quality of many present counselor-education programs. It seems likely that more stringent standards may be established.

The five-year Planning Cooperative Study of Counselor Education Standards, launched by the Association for Counselor Education and Supervision in 1960, involved not only counselor educators but also counselors, teachers, administrators, and others concerned with the preparation of secondary-school counselors—over 700 people on 150 committees in all 50 states (Stripling, 1965a). The final report of the national committee was presented in 1964 to be used primarily for institutional self-evaluation, on an experimental basis for three years. The issue of eventually applying these standards—or a revision of them—for accreditation of graduate programs has not yet been resolved.

The standards (*ibid.*, Appendix B) describe a minimum program of counselor education as requiring two years of full-time graduate study. The curriculum includes courses in foundations of human behavior and education, as well as in such specific topics as principles of guidance, individual appraisal, vocational-development theory, counseling theory, statistics and research methodology, group-guidance procedures, professional ethics, related laboratory experiences, and supervised practice. The practicum requires no less than 60 hours of actual counseling with secondary-school students. The standards deal also with numbers and qualifications of faculty, adequacy of facilities, selective admission and retention of candidates, placement, follow-up, and other relevant activities.

Existing conditions fall far short of these standards. Of the 261 institutions that purport to prepare secondary-school counselors, only about 45 are rated as capable of meeting the minimum requirements (Stripling, 1965b). For example, about 90 percent of the graduates preparing to be secondary-school counselors complete only one year of professional preparation (*ibid.*).

While some attention has been given to the possible use of subprofessional personnel to help compensate for the short supply of counselors, there is as yet no consensus on the tasks and preparation for such counseling aides.

EVALUATION. Triennial reviewers have consistently decried the scarcity and poor quality of evaluation studies (Jones, 1939; Patterson, 1963). The criterion problem has been particularly slippery. Like a fussy fisherman who can't eat what he can catch and can't catch what he could eat, the evaluator has generally found that angling for data on long-range outcomes overtaxes his patience and resources, while the short-term data that are more easily netted often lack nourishment or flavor and may as well be thrown back.

Longitudinal. In the most notable longitudinal evaluation study, Rothney (1958) assigned all the grade 10 students in four Wisconsin high schools to an experimental or a control group; he and two of his graduate students counseled the members of the experimental group. His follow-up achieved a 100-percent response of all the students who graduated from the high schools and were still alive five years later and almost as complete a response eight years (Merenda & Rothney, 1958) and ten years (Rothney, 1963) after graduation. Criteria included such variables as completion of or enrollment in post-high school training, performance in college, promotions in jobs, and satisfaction with current status and with intervening decisions and actions. In general, differences between the experimental and control groups were small and insignificant when considered separately but tended to be in the directions hypothesized.

Correlational. Runkel (1962) conducted a comprehensive and methodologically sophisticated investigation into relationships between guidance programs in an extensive sample of Illinois high schools and the following intermediate criteria: (1) students' knowledge of education required to enter chosen occupation; (2) proportion of high-aptitude students in college-preparatory courses; (3) appropriateness of occupational choice to ability test scores; (4) knowledge of duties in chosen occupation; (5) knowledge of abilities and skills needed in the occupation; (6) appropriateness of occupational choice to curriculum chosen. (Verbalized occupational preference at a given time was treated as an occupational choice. There was no follow-up dealing with which occupation was actually entered.) Criteria 4, 5, and 6 were not significantly related to the two major predictor variables, counselor–student ratio and visiting the counselor. Furthermore, relationships between these predictors and the first three criteria were not simple and direct but appeared only when other variables were used as moderators, such as sex, aptitude, curriculum, and information-seeking activity of *teachers*. The role of the faculty in general emerged as one of the most significant variables. Thus, the tenuous relationships found between the counselor–student ratio and the criteria could not be clearly attributed to the effectiveness of counseling per se. Schools with high counselor–student ratios differed systematically in other ways from schools with low ratios.

Specific. Other evaluation studies have dealt with more specifically defined treatments or materials rather than with total guidance and counseling programs. Cuony and Hoppock (1957) found that members of an experimental group who had taken a job-finding and orientation course while in high school were better off than a control group after graduation in job satisfaction, average number of weeks employed, and annual earnings. Caplan (1957) reported that junior high school boys who had been in conflict with school authorities and had then participated in group counseling showed a significant increase in the correlation between perceived self and ideal self and also in citizenship marks, in comparison with a control group.

Criterion Measures. Other studies over the last thirty years, evaluating somewhat broader treatments, have used such criteria as students' satisfaction with counseling, persistence in school, comparisons of students' self-ratings with test scores, judges' ratings of realism of preferred occupations named by students, the proportion of a class expressing an occupational choice, the constancy of an expressed occupational preference over a period of time, a comparison between the proportion of a class preferring each occupation and the proportion of the working force in that occupation in the community, and so on. Many of these were appropriate for a trait-and-factor theory of guidance, but several recent evaluators, committed to career development and decision theory, have sought other fish to fry.

Experimental groups in grades 8 and 7 using a work text oriented toward decision making (Katz, 1957) scored significantly higher than control groups on an objective test of functional knowledge and problem solving relevant to their stages of career development (Shimberg & Katz, 1962). Another sample of eighth graders using the same text significantly improved in their ability to apply these concepts and decision-making principles to their own planning and in their willingness to assume responsibility for educational-vocational decisions (Gribbons, 1960). Gribbons (1964) and Gribbons and Lohnes (1964a, 1964b, 1965) have followed up this sample of pupils and have reported further on the reliability and validity of an interview schedule, Readiness for Vocational Planning, developed by Gribbons to gauge vocational maturity as defined by Super and Overstreet (1960) in the Career Pattern Study.

Another highly promising criterion instrument has been developed by Crites (1965a, 1965b). Also derived from the Career Pattern Study, his Vocational Development Inventory includes an attitude scale that attempts to measure (1) involvement in the process of vocational choice, (2) orientation toward the problem of vocational choice, (3) independence in decision making, (4) preferences for factors in vocational choice, and (5) conceptions of vocational choice.

Finally, simulation and gaming techniques offer unique opportunities for *assessing* as well as developing students' information-seeking behavior and decision-making skills. Standardized situations can be devised to ascertain whether students know what information they need, can get what information they want, and can use what information they have (Katz, 1966a).

The further development, definition, and acceptance of standardized criterion instruments is a crucial need for the evaluation of counseling in secondary schools. Improved evaluation can serve eventually to link processes more clearly to purposes and to integrate both in a coherent theory.

Martin Katz
Educational Testing Service

References

Allen, Richard D. *Case-conference Problems in Group Guidance.* Inor, 1933. 115p.

Allen, Richard D. *Self-measurement Projects in Group Guidance.* Inor, 1934. 274p.

American Psychological Association, Division of Counseling Psychology, Special Committee. "The Current Status of Counseling Psychology." APA, 1961. (Multilithed.)

Beilin, Harry. "The Application of General Developmental Principles to the Vocational Area." *J Counseling Psychol* 2:53–7; 1955.

Blau, Peter M., and others. "Occupational Choice: A Conceptual Framework." *Ind Labor Relations R* 9:531–43; 1956.

Boocock, Sarane S. "Simulation Games for Vocational Counseling." In Martin, Ann M. (Ed.) "Occupational Information and Vocational Guidance for Noncollege Youth." U Pittsburgh, 1966. (Multilithed.) p. 143–53.

Borow, Henry. "Vocational Development Research: Some Problems of Logical and Experimental Form." *Personnel Guid J* 40:21–5; 1961.

Boy, Angelo V., and Pine, Gerald J. *Client-centered Counseling in the Secondary School.* Houghton, 1963. 289p.

Brayfield, Arthur H. "Counseling Psychology." In Farnsworth, Paul R., and others. (Eds.) *Annual Review of Psychology,* Vol. 14. Annual Reviews, Inc., 1963. p. 319–50.

Brewer, John M. *Education as Guidance.* Macmillan, 1932. 668p.

Brewer, John M. *History of Vocational Guidance: Origins and Early Development.* Harper, 1942. 352p.

Caplan, Stanley. "The Effect of Group Counseling on Junior High School Boys' Concepts of Themselves in School." *J Counseling Psychol* 4:124–8; 1957.

Clarke, Robert, and others. "A Decision-making Paradigm for Local Guidance Research." *Personnel Guid J* 44:40–51; 1965.

Cogswell, John F., and Estavan, Donald P. "Computer Simulation of a Counselor in Student Appraisal and in the Educational Planning Interview." System Development Corporation document SP-1994. March 10, 1965.

Conant, James B. *The American High School Today.* McGraw-Hill, 1959. 140p.

Cooley, William W. "Redefining Career Plan Groups." In Flanagan, John C., and Cooley, William W. *Project Talent One-Year Follow-Up Studies.* Cooperative Research Project No. 2333. U Pittsburgh Press, 1966. p. 205–24.

Crary, Robert W. "Specialized Counseling—A New Trend?" *Personnel Guid J* 44:1056–61; 1966.

Crites, John O. "Measurement of Vocational Maturity in Adolescence. I: Attitude Test of the Vocational Development Inventory." *Psychol Monogr,* No. 595; 1965(a). 36p.

Crites, John O. "The Vocational Development Project at the University of Iowa." *J Counseling Psychol* 12:81–6; 1965(b).

Cronbach, Lee J. "Assessment of Individual Differences." *Annual R Psychol* 7:173–96; 1956.

Cronbach, Lee J., and Gleser, Goldine C. *Psychological Tests and Personnel Decisions.* U Illinois Press, 1957. 165p.

Cuony, Edward R., and Hoppock, Robert. "Job Course Pays Off Again." *Personnel Guid J* 36:116–7; 1957.

Educational Testing Service. *Manual of Freshman Class Profiles for Indiana Colleges.* CEEB, 1965. 93p.

Erikson, Erik H. *Childhood and Society.* Norton, 1950. 397p.

Erikson, Erik H. "Identity and the Life Cycle." *Psychol Issues* 1:18–171; 1959.

Fitzgerald, Paul W. "The Professional Role of School Counselors." In Loughary, John W. (Ed.) *Counseling, A Growing Profession.* APGA, 1965. p. 31–41.

Flanagan, John C. "Stability of Career Plans." In

Flanagan, John C., and Cooley, William W. *Project Talent One-Year Follow-Up Studies.* Cooperative Research Project No. 2333. U Pittsburgh Press, 1966. p. 171–9.

French, John W. "Comparative Prediction of High-school Grades by Pure-factor Aptitude, Information, and Personality Measures." *Ed Psychol Meas* 24:321–9; 1964(a).

French, John W. *Manual for Experimental Comparative Prediction Batteries—High School and College Level.* ETS, 1964(b). 57p.

Ginzberg, Eli, and others. *Occupational Choice: An Approach to a General Theory.* Columbia U Press, 1951. 253p.

Glanz, Edward C. *Groups in Guidance.* Allyn and Bacon, 1962. 385p.

Goldberg, Isadore. "Guidance Resources and Counselors in Public Senior High Schools." In Flanagan, John C., and others. *Studies of the American High School.* Project Talent Monograph Series, Monograph No. 2. U Pittsburgh Press, 1962. Ch. 3.

Grant, Claude W. "How Students Perceive the Counselor's Role." *Personnel Guid J* 32:386–8; 1954.

Greenleaf, Walter J. "Educational and Vocational Information." *R Ed Res* 12:86–108; 1942.

Gribbons, Warren D. "Evaluation of an Eighth-grade Group Guidance Program." *Personnel Guid J* 38: 740–5; 1960.

Gribbons, Warren D. "Changes in Readiness for Vocational Planning from the 8th Grade to the 10th Grade." *Personnel Guid J* 42:908–13; 1964.

Gribbons, Warren D., and Lohnes, Paul R. "Relationships Among Measures of Readiness for Vocational Planning." *J Counseling Psychol* 11:13–9; 1964(a).

Gribbons, Warren D., and Lohnes, Paul R. "Validation of Vocational Planning Interview Scales." *J Counseling Psychol* 11:20–6; 1964(b).

Gribbons, Warren D., and Lohnes, Paul R. "Predicting Five Years of Development in Adolescents from Readiness for Vocational Planning Scales." *J Ed Psychol* 56:244–53; 1965.

Helm, Carl. "Computer Simulation Techniques for Research on Guidance Problems." *Res Memorandum 66-4.* ETS, 1966. 11p.

Hills, John R. "College Expectancy Tables for High School Counselors." *Personnel Guid J* 42:479–83; 1963.

Hills, John R. "Decision Theory and College Choice." *Personnel Guid J* 43:17–22; 1964.

Hoppock, Robert. *Occupational Information,* 2nd ed. McGraw-Hill, 1963. 546p.

Horst, Paul. "A Technique for the Development of a Multiple Absolute Prediction Battery." *Psychol Monogr,* No. 390; 1955. 22p.

Hull, Clark L. *Aptitude Testing.* World Bk, 1928. 535p.

Hummel, Raymond C. "Ego-counseling in Guidance: Concept and Method." *Harvard Ed R* 32:463–82; 1962.

Jersild, Arthur. *Child Development and the Curriculum.* Teachers Col, Columbia U, 1946. 274p.

Jones, Arthur J. "Vocational Guidance and Education." *Ed R* 62:20; 1921.

Jones, Arthur J. "Secondary Education." *R Ed Res* 9:185–7; 1939.

Katz, Martin. *You: Today and Tomorrow.* Cooperative Test Division, ETS, 1957. 93p.

Katz, Martin. *Decisions and Values: A Rationale for Secondary School Guidance.* CEEB, 1963. 67p.

Katz, Martin. "Criteria for Evaluation of Guidance." In Martin, Ann M. (Ed.) "Occupational Information and Vocational Guidance for Noncollege Youth." U Pittsburgh, 1966(a) p. 167–82. (Multilithed.)

Katz, Martin. "A Model of Guidance for Career Decision-making." *Voc Guid Q* 15:2–10; 1966(b).

Koos, Leonard V. and Kefauver, Grayson N. "The Concept of Guidance." *Sch R* 40:206; 1932.

Krumboltz, John D. "Behavioral Goals for Counseling." *J Counseling Psychol* 13:153–9; 1966.

Krumboltz, John D., and Thoresen, Carl E. "The Effect of Behavioral Counseling in Group and Individual Settings on Information-seeking Behavior." *J Counseling Psychol* 11:324–33; 1964.

Krumboltz, John D., and Varenhorst, Barbara. "Molders of Pupil Attitudes." *Personnel Guid J* 43:443–6; 1965.

McNemar, Quinn. "Lost: Our Intelligence? Why?" *Am Psychol* 19:871–82; 1964.

Meehl, Paul E. *Clinical Versus Statistical Prediction.* U Minnesota Press, 1954. 149p.

Merenda, Peter F., and Rothney, John W. M. "Evaluating the Effects of Counseling—Eight Years After." *J Counseling Psychol* 5:163–8; 1958.

Metfessel, Milton. "A Proposal for Quantitative Reporting of Comparative Judgments." *J Psychol* 24: 229–35; 1947.

Michael, Jack, and Meyerson, Lee. "A Behavioral Approach to Counseling and Guidance." *Harvard Ed R* 32:382–402; 1962.

Miller, Carroll H. *Foundations of Guidance.* Harper, 1961. 464p.

Myers, George E. *Principles and Techniques of Vocational Guidance.* McGraw-Hill, 1941. 377p.

Parsons, Frank. *Choosing a Vocation.* Houghton, 1909 (reprint, Agathon Press, Inc., 1967, 165p.).

Patterson, Cecil H. "Program Evaluation." *R Ed Res* 33:214–24; 1963.

Perry, William G., Jr. "On the Relation of Psychotherapy and Counseling." *Annals N.Y. Acad Sci* 63:396–407; 1955.

Rockwell, Perry J., and Rothney, John W. M. "Some Social Ideas of Pioneers in the Guidance Movement." *Personnel Guid J* 40:349–54; 1961.

Roeber, Edward C. *The School Counselor.* The Center for Applied Research in Education, 1963. 107p.

Rogers, Carl R. *Counseling and Psychotherapy.* Houghton, 1942. 450p.

Rogers, Carl R. *Client-centered Therapy.* Houghton, 1951. 560p.

Rogers, Carl R. *On Becoming a Person: A Therapist's View of Psychotherapy.* Houghton, 1961(a). 420p.

Rogers, Carl R. "The Place of the Person in the New World of the Behavioral Sciences." *Personnel Guid J* 39:442–51; 1961(b).

Rogers, Carl R. "The Interpersonal Relationship: The

Core of Guidance." *Harvard Ed R* 32:416–29; 1962.
Rothney, John W. M. *Guidance Practices and Results.* Harper, 1958. 542p.
Rothney, John W. M. *Educational, Vocational and Social Performances of Counseled and Uncounseled Youth Ten Years after High School* Cooperative Research Project No. SAE 9231. U Wisconsin Press, 1963. 59p.
Runkel, Philip J. "The Effectiveness of Guidance in Today's Schools: A Survey in Illinois." 1962. (Unpublished report.)
Sears, Jesse B. *The School Survey.* Houghton, 1925. 440p.
Shimberg, Benjamin, and Katz, Martin. "Evaluation of a Guidance Text." *Personnel Guid J* 41:126–32; 1962.
Skinner, B. F. *Walden Two.* Macmillan, 1948. 266p.
Skinner, B. F. *Science and Human Behavior.* Macmillan, 1953. 461p.
Skinner, B. F. "Freedom and the Control of Men." *Am Scholar* 25(No. 1):47–65; Winter 1955–56.
Smith, B. Othanel, and others. *Fundamentals of Curriculum Development,* rev. ed. Harcourt, 1957. 685p.
Stripling, Robert O. "Standards for the Education of Counselors." In Loughary, John W. (Ed.) *Counseling, A Growing Profession.* APGA, 1965(a). p. 19–30.
Stripling, Robert O. "Training Institutions: Standards and Resources." In McGowan, John F. (Ed.) *Counselor Development in American Society.* Conference Recommendations from Invitational Conference on Government-University Relations in the Professional Preparation and Employment of Counselors. Washington, D.C., June 2–3, 1965(b). p. 112–31.
Super, Donald E. "A Theory of Vocational Development." *Am Psychologist* 8:185–90; 1953.
Super, Donald E. "Career Patterns as a Basis for Vocational Counseling." *J Counseling Psychol* 1:12–20; 1954.
Super, Donald E. "Dimensions and Measurement of Vocational Maturity." *Teach Col Rec* 57:151–63; 1955.
Super, Donald E. *The Psychology of Careers.* Harper, 1957. 362p.
Super, Donald E. (Compiler.) "The Use of Multifactor Tests in Guidance." Reprint series from *Personnel Guid J.* APGA, n.d.
Super, Donald E., and Overstreet, Phoebe. *The Vocational Maturity of Ninth-grade Boys.* Teachers Col, Columbia U, 1960. 212p.
Swanson, Edward O., and others. *Minnesota-test-norms and Expectancy Tables,* Part II. St. Paul Minnesota, Department of Education, 1961.
Tiedeman, David V. "A Geometric Model for the Profile Problem." Paper presented at the 1953 Invitational Conference on Testing Problems. Printed In Anastasi, Anne. (Ed.) *Testing Problems in Perspective.* ACE, 1966. p. 331–54.
Tiedeman, David V. "Decision and Vocational Development: a Paradigm and Its Implications." *Personnel Guid J* 40:15–21; 1961.
Tiedeman, David V., and Field, Frank L. "From a Technology of Guidance in Schools to the Profession of Guidance-in-society: A Challenge to Democratic Government." In McGowan, John F. (Ed.) *Counselor Development in American Society.* Conference Recommendations from Invitational Conference on Government-University Relations in the Professional Preparation and Employment of Counselors. Washington, D.C., June 2–3, 1965. p. 249–75.
Tiedeman, David V., and O'Hara, Robert P. *Career Development: Choice and Adjustment.* CEEB, 1963. 115p.
Tiedeman, David V., and Sternberg, Jack J. "Information Appropriate for Curriculum Guidance." *Harvard Ed R* 22:257–74; 1952.
Traux, Charles B. "Some Implications of Behavior Therapy for Psychotherapy." *J Counseling Psychol* 13:160–70; 1966.
U.S. Office of Education. *Commitment to Youth,* GPO, 1964. 44p.
Weber, Max. *The Protestant Ethic and the Spirit of Capitalism.* Scribner, 1930. 292p.
Williamson, Edmund G. "To Avoid Waste." *J Higher Ed* 8:64–70; 1937.
Williamson, Edmund G. "The Clinical Method of Guidance." *R Ed Res* 9:214–7; 1939.
Wrenn, C. Gilbert. *The Counselor in a Changing World.* APGA, 1962. 195p.

COUNSELING THEORY

Counseling theories are systematic ways of viewing the counseling process in order to organize what is known about it in such a fashion as to furnish guides to the counselor's behavior, clues to client understanding, directions for reasonable evaluation, and suggestions regarding the most promising research dimensions of the counselor-client interaction. Although most counselors will have implicit rather than explicit theories of counseling, their counseling behavior is influenced by the frame of reference they use in viewing counseling. Their decisions whether to advise, support, reflect, or interpret are influenced by a theory—however poorly formulated or unconsciously held. The client's total interview behavior is viewed from a theoretical base that permits many acts to be ignored, others to assume attention-holding significance, and still others to move in and out of the counselor's awareness. When the student stumbles over his teacher's name, the mistake may be seen as meaningful or meaningless depending on the theory held by the counselor. Signs of success or failure are also dependent upon counseling theory. Although at the higher levels of abstraction most would agree that we desire reasonable individual freedom with reasonable attention to societal standards, there might be disagreement as to whether the client should express or suppress his anger, conform or revolt. The general purpose of counseling theory is to make sense of the many data provided in counseling by relating experience to a network of inference so as to provide a provisional systematization of events—that is, a possible world which can be checked against the real one.

A continuing problem in counseling today is the wisdom and substance of a distinction between counseling and psychotherapy. Counseling may be defined as a professional relationship between a counselor and a client in which the counselor helps the client to understand himself and his life space in order to make meaningful and informed choices consonant with his essential nature in those areas where choices are available to him. When a distinction is made between counseling and psychotherapy, it is usually based on the training of the professional worker (psychiatrist and clinical psychologist or counseling psychologist and counselor), the client (psychotic and severe neurotic or relatively undisturbed normal), the setting (hospitals and private clinics or schools), and purposes (personality reconstruction or aid in choosing and planning). There are those who believe strongly that the school counselor must not do therapy and others who believe that distinctions between counseling and psychotherapy are not in the best interests of the children being served. Although a strict distinction is not always possible this article attempts to make use of research in a way that implies belief in the usefulness of a distinction between counseling and psychotherapy. At the college level this distinction may be less clear largely because of the higher level of training of the counselor. At the precollege levels the counselor is more apt to observe a distinction between his function and that of a psychotherapist and therefore to confine his work to aid with developmental tasks particularly in educational and vocational areas, though not to the exclusion of personal-social concerns.

ELEMENTS OF COUNSELING THEORY. Theories regarding the purpose and process of counseling rest on conceptions of the nature of man, conceptions of what man should be, and conceptions of how man changes. Counseling theory, therefore, rests on philosophy, values, and learning theory. Although the importance of each of these three bases would be different for each theorist, all would seem to be present in every case.

Nature of Man. One of the more marked differences among theories is the optimistic view of man held by client-centered counselors and the relatively more pessimistic view held by analytic counselors (Arbuckle, 1958). This issue is explored by Eysenck (1957), who moves it out of the philosophical realm into the physical by stating his belief that under- or oversocialization is related to constitutional factors. A most systematic attempt to consider the relationship between theory and conceptions of man was made by McCully (1966), who believes that what counselors do must be based on an image of man and who therefore proposed that we need to examine the distinguishing characteristics of man. These distinguishing characteristics included such elements as the social origin of his mind, his surplus of energy to be used for thought, his ability to take account of the past and the future, and similar human behaviors. Although it may not always be plain or conscious, certainly the counselor who behaves in any meaningful way toward the client must have some model of what man in the generic sense is like. He is good or bad, rational or irrational, controlled by cognition or affect, aware of his impulses or unaware of them, driven by biological or social motivations.

Goals. The general goals of counseling are usually expressed at a rather high level of abstraction. When these high-level abstractions are traced to specific referents some contradictions and confusion may eventuate. That is, when we ask the question "How can we tell if the client is better off than he was?" we get less than unanimity in the answer. Behavioral manifestations of having been helped by counseling might include such diverse outcomes as educational and vocational achievement (measured by such criteria as grade-point average, attendance, staying in school, money earned, and promotions received); different and more pleasing behavior as viewed by friends, teachers, and employers; establishment of vocational goals seen as more suitable by judges; and absence of symptoms previously present. The difficulty with such criteria is that for any one individual any given criterion might be completely inappropriate and misleading. This criterion problem exemplifies the controversy in counseling over the extent to which counseling should be guided by individual as opposed to societal goals. Should the client be helped to do what is best for him or what is best for society? Are these two goals always compatible?

Change. Counseling theories have in common a view that intervention by the counselor into the life of the client is for the purpose of producing desirable changes. There are disagreements, however, about how these changes take place. Some believe that change results from cognitive reorganization and that therefore the counseling interview should concern itself with providing the client with information about himself and about the world—especially the world of work. Others believe that desirable changes are chiefly changes in feelings and attitudes and that these take place primarily as a result of an appropriate relationship between the counselor and the client and that consequently factual information is neither helpful nor necessary. Still another position maintains that it is the work of the counselor to systematically reinforce or extinguish specific behaviors in the client. It is because of these varying positions that, on the one hand, we may see a counselor using the interview to present psychometric and economic data which he believes the client will need in making decisions and carrying them out or, on the other hand, we may see him primarily furthering and reacting to feelings and attitudes of the client in the belief that it is the clarification and eventual acceptance of such feelings that will result in changed behavior in the client. Every counselor's behavior, then, is based, at least implicitly, on his view of what man is like, what he should be, and how he changes his behavior.

THEORETICAL ORIENTATIONS. While at one time counseling theory tended to focus on differences between directive and nondirective positions, it is now apparent that this one-dimensional model of the counseling process is inadequate to illustrate the various views held by counselors. What was formerly called directive counseling—diagnosis, the use of objective data, and activity on the part of the counselor to aid the client in problem solving—is now thought to be present to some degree in the work of all counselors. What was formerly called nondirective counseling—reflection of feeling, clarification of content, and relative passivity on the part of the counselor—has evolved into the client-centered position, but with changes that deemphasize technique and stress the counseling relationship. These techniques are also used on occasion by most counselors. Systematic treatments of several counseling theories are offered by Stefflre (1965) and Ford and Urban (1963).

Client-centered Counseling. The client-centered view of Rogers (1961) assumes the natural goodness of man. Man's nature affords him an innate basis for evaluating his experience (organismic valuing process) which, if unimpeded by inappropriate, learned values (conditions of worth), will guide his behavior toward personally and socially satisfying ends. The client's behavior is believed to be influenced far more by the manner in which he perceives external events than by any objective qualities that such events might possess. The counselor's concern is with the present dynamics of the client rather than with the historical base of the problem. Furthermore, he is concerned with the future—with helping the client to fulfill his potentialities. The purpose of counseling is to help the client make his own decisions on the basis of self-awareness and an understanding of the possibilities available to him in his environment.

Like Freud, Rogers assumes that the sole source of man's energy and action comes from within. But in describing this source the two differ. For Freud, energy is derived from the id, a repository of blind, impulsive, irrational, selfish drives (Freud, 1930). For Rogers (1961), energy is derived from the "Actualizing Tendency," a tendency toward growth, differentiation of organs and functions, autonomy, and maturity. As long as the actualizing tendency is unimpeded by inappropriate learnings, the person is most likely to engage in balanced, realistic, self-enhancing, other-enhancing behavior. This faith in the natural goodness of man, in man's capacity to make decisions both personally and socially satisfying, is the bedrock upon which Rogers' entire theory is built.

In a curious manner the need for positive regard from others is the root from which maladaptive behavior grows. In order to gain the approval of others the person will adopt values which may be alien to those which he experiences organismically. Such learned values may not always be best for him; they may indeed thwart the innate tendency to actualize his potentialities. The person may find himself behaving first according to one value system, then according to the other. Anxiety is a consequence of recognizing such discrepant behaviors. The integrity of the self-concept (an organized set of perceptions in regard to the self along with an evaluation of the self) is threatened by this discrepancy. Since the self concept reflects in large measure the values and opinions of significant others, the distintegration of the self concept threatens not only the client's self-regard but, he imagines, the positive regard of others as well.

Rogers' theory has undergone significant changes in the past few years. Gendlin (1962) identifies three major developments in client-centered therapy: (1) recognition that it is the counselor's attitude rather than his directive or nondirective approach which is related to success in therapy; (2) emphasis upon counselor genuineness or spontaneity rather than upon counselor techniques; and (3) emphasis upon experienced feelings of both counselor and client rather than upon insight, theoretical orientation of counselor, or techniques. Matarazzo (1965) observes that Rogers' present position with its strong proclivity toward existentialist ideas represents a long journey from his nondirective, technique-oriented position of the early 1940's.

The counselor creates a warm, permissive, non-threatening counseling atmosphere wherein the client is free to explore nonsymbolized aspects of his experiencing. The client's expression of attitudes and values incompatible with his self concept are reflected and accepted by the counselor. The counselor experiences unconditional positive regard for the client, and the client learns that in this setting it is unnecessary to adopt the attitudes, values, and interests of the counselor in order to be accepted. The client cautiously begins to rely upon the feedback of his organism to evaluate his experience. This procedure proves rewarding since it leads to behaviors more effective in meeting needs partly strangled by conditions of worth. This developing trust in the organismic valuing process is generalized to situations outside the counseling setting, and the person is again en route to becoming a spontaneous, self-actualizing, fully functioning human being.

The appropriateness of the client-centered approach for high school counseling has long been debated, and therefore the appearance of a description of a secondary-school counseling program based on this point of view elicited much interest (Boy & Pine, 1963).

Psychoanalytic Schools. From the pioneering work of Sigmund Freud have come the psychoanalytic, neoanalytic and ego-analytic schools. Freud saw man as an angry, sexual animal whose neurotic problems stem from his renunciation of basic impulses in the interest of civilization. While Freud did not recommend the behavior of the libertine, he did suggest that the progress of civilization in socializing its members and in demanding self-denial is purchased at the price of neurotic misery in many cases (1930).

The neoanalytic theorists lay great stress upon the cultural mold in which personality is formed. The effects of war, economic systems, child-rearing practices, class differences, interpersonal relationships, etc., are assessed for their impact upon personality. Ego analysts seem to hold an intermediate position between the biological emphasis of the Freudian position and the cultural emphasis of the neoanalysts. They stress the ego functions, the learned behaviors by which the individual controls his impulses and deals with his environment (Rapaport, 1958).

Freudian theory has undergone significant revisions, but certain recurrent themes have remained constant. Unconscious determinants of behavior, the crucial importance of early childhood experiences, and pan-sexualism appeared early and maintained their importance for Freud until his death. Certain psychosexual stages of development occasioned by the growing importance of a particular erogenous zone of the body (mouth, anus, or genitalia) were believed to be universal, and fixation at a given stage resulted in a predictable personality type.

Freud depended exclusively upon the clinical method as an approach to his data. He made extensive use of hypothetical constructs of a psychodynamic nature. Three of the more important of these are the id, the ego and the superego—constructs describing psychological processes operating within the individual. The id represents irrational, biological instincts; the ego the rational functions (thinking, remembering, perceiving, etc.) by which one deals effectively with reality; and the superego represents the person's moral and ethical sensitivity. When one's moral training has been overly restrictive, i.e., when the socialization process has been too successful, the superego is likely to reflect such training and make it exceedingly difficult for the individual to express his biological impulses. Inhibited impulses gather strength and threaten the organization of the personality with distintegration. The threat is experienced as anxiety, and anxiety is sometimes reduced by *repression*— a process wherein the person renders id impulses unconscious. Consequently, such persons become increasingly less aware of their basic needs and less effective in satisfying them.

The task of the psychoanalytic practitioner is clear. He must reverse the developing process referred to above by (1) helping the patient to recognize impulses inhibited by repression; (2) mitigating the severity of the superego to allow for reasonable expression of the impulse; and (3) helping the patient to discover socially acceptable behaviors which allow for the expression of the impulse. Free association (verbal disclosure of the patient's uninterrupted stream of consciousness), dream analysis, and interpretation are methods employed in rendering the patient's repressed impulses conscious. Transference (a phenomenon wherein the patient projects upon the analyst characteristics belonging to significant others in the life of the patient) is the chief tool used in restructuring the superego. The patient is helped to understand the inappropriate aspects of his interpersonal relationships and the irrational aspects of his superego.

Psychoanalytic techniques are probably not used by any counselors in elementary and secondary schools, although the personality theory on which the techniques are based may be helpful to them in understanding behavior. At the college level adaptations of this position may be suitable in some long-term cases, although it is unlikely that complete psychoanalysis is ever undertaken in an educational setting.

Behavioral Views. Counseling theorists have made greater use of the dynamic concepts of personality psychology than of the objective investigations of general psychology. Behavioral theorists represent an exception to this pattern. They share a concern for the application of learning theory to counseling (Wolpe, 1958; Eysenck, 1960; Eysenck & Rachman, 1965). Maladaptive behavior is believed to develop according to principles of learning either discovered or discoverable (Dollard & Miller, 1950). Consequently, learning theory should be employed in substituting adaptive behaviors for maladaptive ones. Emphasis has been focused more upon the *process* of learning than upon the *products* of learning. Because of the importance accorded environmental influences upon behavior, critics contend that behaviorists view man as an "empty organism"—neither intrinsically good nor intrinsically bad.

In spite of their common concern with learning theory, behavioral theorists differ markedly in other respects. The difference is most clearly seen in regard to the use of intervening variables (mediating responses).

Psychodynamically oriented behaviorists view nonintegrative behavior as symptomatic of basic *intra*personal conflict. Symptom removal is believed to be ineffective unless the intrapersonal conflict is resolved. The goal of counseling involves change in mediating responses and is variously described as bringing about personality change (Miller, 1964), restoring the "higher thought processes" (Dollard & Miller, 1950), and restructuring the socialization process so as to allow the client to generalize his learning (Shoben, 1953b).

Nonpsychodynamically oriented behaviorists protest the unparsimonious use of hypothetical constructs such as underlying, unconscious complexes. There is no neurosis underlying the symptom, there is only the symptom. Neurotic symptoms are simply learned habits. "Get rid of the symptom (skeletal and autonomic) and you have eliminated the neurosis" (Eysenck, 1960). The goal of counseling is described as altering the client's verbal or motor behavior (R. Watson, 1962) rather than as reconstructing his personality.

Further contrasts between these camps within behaviorism may be drawn. In each case the psychodynamically oriented exponents have aligned themselves with the classical counseling tradition. The nonpsychodynamically oriented members staunchly oppose the elaborate use of inner-self determining agents and other hypothetical constructs, whereas the psychodynamically oriented make use of them. The former group discounts the need for insight, whereas the latter group regards it as important. Definitions of neurosis for the former group are in terms of learned maladaptive behaviors, whereas the latter group offers definitions of the classical variety. The interest of the nonpsychodynamically oriented group in verbal interaction and other "relationship" variables is mild, while the psychodynamically oriented group has keen interest in such variables. And finally, the nonpsychodynamically oriented counselors make frequent use of physical types of reinforcement, while the psychodynamically oriented counselors limit themselves largely to social types of reinforcement (approval, empathy, respect, understanding, etc.).

Most psychodynamically oriented theorists have built upon a Freudian framework. Dollard and Miller (1950) attempted to blend Hullian learning theory and Freudian personality theory with the content of sociology and anthropology. Alexander (1963) shortly before his death abandoned the orthodox Freudian position for a modern learning-theory adaptation similar to that of Dollard and Miller.

Wolpe (1958) is in many respects typical of the nonpsychodynamically oriented theorists. His approach is called reciprocal inhibition—a process by which an unpleasant response (usually anxiety) is replaced by a pleasant one by the development of a strong association between the stimuli originally evoking the unpleasant response and rewarding consequences. His armamentarium includes the use of assertive responses by the client in real-life situations; desensitizing anxiety-arousing situations by arranging them in a hierarchy and presenting them sequentially while the client is experiencing muscular relaxation; the use of carbon dioxide therapy with clients suffering pervasive "free-floating" anxiety; and the use of the reinforcing qualities of the counseling relationship. Clearly, Wolpe is not limited to the typical verbal forms of psychotherapy. Similarities may be noted between the views of Wolpe and Eysenck, on the one hand, and the psychophysiology of the Soviet Union and East Germany, on the other hand (Razran, 1961; Mueller-Hegemann, 1963).

Because physical types of reinforcement are accorded primary importance and relationship variables are given only secondary importance, the nonpsychodynamic behaviorists have been criticized for employing manipulative techniques (Murray, 1963). Patterson (1963), however, suggests that the concept of manipulation represents a continuum and that everyone, including the client-centered counselor, manipulates the client. Verplanck (1955) demonstrated that a technique similar to Rogerian reflection could significantly control the incidence of certain kinds of client responses. Greenspoon (1955) found that simple counselor responses such as "good" and "mm-hm" served as reinforcers for classes of verbal responses from the client. Glad (Glad & others, 1959) and Krasner (1961) suggest that the counselor's theoretical background affects the kinds of material which the counselee discusses. Bandura (1961) contends that the counselor controls the client's responses by differential reinforcement, using interest and approval as reinforcers. Matarazzo (Matarazzo & others, 1963) offers evidence that the counselor controls the length of the client's responses by the length of his own responses. Hildum and Brown (1956) suggest that the counselor provides a value model toward which the client gravitates. Krasner (1963) concludes that psychotherapy (counseling) is but a special instance of a broader class of situations involving behavior control.

Behavior theory has enjoyed greater use in the clinic than in the schools, although Krumboltz and Thoresen (1964) demonstrated its use in encouraging information-seeking behavior and Weitz (1964) suggested its use for school guidance.

Trait-factor Theories. The trait-factor approach to counseling has been widely practiced by state-employment-service counselors, vocational rehabilitation counselors, and school counselors. It is chiefly concerned with vocational and educational problems and is sometimes difficult to distinguish from the broader practice of guidance. Williamson (1965*b*) suggests that it sometimes takes the form of classes on occupational counseling and information or of temporary groups organized preparatory to individual counseling. Chief proponents of this position are Brayfield (1963), Viteles (Viteles & others, 1961), and Lofquist (1957).

Trait-factor counseling has maintained a view of counseling in which the counselor diagnoses the client's interests and aptitudes, furnishes information concerning job opportunities and requirements, and relates the client's interests and aptitudes to job opportunities and requirements.

Current statements of trait-factor theory assume (1) that persons are capable of rational decisions, (2) that each person has a unique profile of interests and aptitudes, (3) that these can be accurately measured by objective tests, (4) that successful performance within a given occupation or curriculum requires certain identifiable aptitudes and interests, (5) that persons will make wiser vocational and educational decisions if they first engage in self-exploration and are helped to understand their interests and aptitudes as well as the requirements of certain occupations and curricula, and (6) that persons will be happier if they perform the tasks for which they are best fitted.

The counselor is quite active in administering and interpreting tests, furnishing occupational, social, and educational information, and in various ways expediting the client's self-exploration. Major emphasis is placed upon diagnosis of the client's aptitudes and interests. Such counseling, which has been much influenced by decision theorists, seems to be most appropriate for individuals who need information, understanding, emotional support, and acceptance in order to make proper decisions (McGowan & Porter, 1964).

Applicability. There are marked differences in the applicability of the four theoretical orientations to school counseling. The Freudian varieties and the existentialist and client-centered views should find their greatest use at the college level, where the length of contact with the client and the advanced training of the counselor may allow for a depth approach. King (1965) suggests that psychoanalytic theory has limited applicability to most institutional settings. Perhaps the greatest strength of the client-centered approach in working with students is its encouragement of the client's sense of independence and responsibility; however, it may tend to encourage the withholding of information needed by the student for decision making. To the extent to which the counselor is able to manipulate elements within the student's school and home environments so as to reinforce certain student behaviors and to extinguish others, the behavioral position, with its strong interest in environmental reinforcement, may enjoy increasing popularity among school counselors. Furthermore, social modeling would appear to hold great promise for school guidance programs. Trait-factor theory, with its emphasis upon decision making, diagnostics, information giving and other guidance concerns, is most readily adaptable to the school setting. It seems clear that this theory more than any of the others best describes what is most frequently practiced within the schools.

RESEARCH DIMENSIONS RELEVANT TO THEORY. Differences Related to Theoretical Positions of the Counselor. Fiedler's early studies (1950a, 1950b) indicated that theoretical orientation was not a determinant of counselor behavior. His research, however, was based on a description of the ideal therapeutic relationship and has been criticized for not making possible fine distinctions among positions. Some studies tend to support Fiedler's view that the theoretical orientation of the counselor is inconsequential and that experience is the major determinant of counselor behavior. Teachers have been found to describe the ideal therapeutic relationship in a manner very similar to the way Fiedler's group of therapists do (Soper & Combs, 1962). When psychiatrists were compared with clinical psychologists and social workers, no difference in the goals they set out for treatment were observed which were related to the discipline from which the therapist came (Michaux & Lorr, 1961). In studying the effect of the theoretical position of the counseling supervisor on the attitude of the counselor trainee, no significant differences were found which were related to the supervisor's orientation except that the trainees of client-centered supervisors were apt to do less probing and attempt more responses aimed at eliciting understanding (Demos & Zuwaylif, 1962). When time-limited therapy was compared with therapy without time limits (Shlein & others, 1962) for Adlerian and client-centered therapists, the effect of time limits overrode the theoretical orientation of the therapist. However, certain clusters of items relating to self concept and self-ideal differentiated the Adlerian from the client-centered client. In a straightforward attempt (Wrenn, 1960) to discover whether counseling theory or situational differences have greater influence on counselor behavior, counselors were asked to describe their theoretical orientation and then were classified as phenomenological, analytic, neobehavioral, or eclectic. The task involved their response to excerpts from interviews. There were essentially no differences attributable to theoretical orientations. The differences seemed to be accounted for by the situations in the interview. There was, however, a tendency for the client-centered and eclectic counselors to reflect feeling and for the analytic counselors to use a fuller range of response.

However, a new line of research begun by Sundland and Barker (1962) challenges Fiedler's results by showing that a general bipolar factor of analytic versus experiential accounts for much difference between therapists. Therapists at the analytic pole stress conceptualization, training, unconscious processes, and a proscription of spontaneity. Those at the experiential pole stress the personality of the therapist and an unplanned approach to therapy. A subsequent study (Wallach & Strupp, 1964) using psychotherapists from a variety of orientations found four factors explaining therapist behavior: maintaining personal distance, preference for intensive therapy, keeping verbal interventions at a minimum, and considering psychotherapy as an art. Orthodox Freudians were highest in maintaining personal distance, preferring intensive therapy, and keeping verbal interventions at a minimum and lowest in considering therapy as an artistic activity. The client-centered group was distinct in considering psychotherapy as an art and in their lack of preference for intensive therapy. The level of experience of the therapist seemed unrelated to reported therapy activity. Further confirmation for differences among therapists with different orientations resulted from a study (McNarr & Lorr, 1964) showing three dimensions associated with psychotherapeutic techniques: extent and utilization of psychoanalytic techniques, degree of control of the course of therapy, and degree to which personal-affective relationships are maintained. In general, psychiatrists were high on all three of these factors, but about one-third of psychologists were low on them. Again, the experience of the therapist did not relate to the use of various techniques. An especially provocative finding stemmed from a study (Strupp, 1958) in which analytically oriented and client-centered therapists were asked to respond as vicarious interviewers to a sound film of an unrehearsed initial interview. Rogerians were generally disinclined to plan for treatment or to set up therapeutic goals, and their prognostic estimates were more favorable. Furthermore, they rated their attitude toward the patient as being more positive than did the analytically oriented therapist.

In a memorable article, Kiesler (1966) states that none of the current counseling theories adequately deals with the myth of patient uniformity and the myth of therapist similarity. That is, they do not make explicit the independent and dependent variables stemming from the various counseling theories and their consequent problems of measurement. The Freudian therapist is at once neutral and ambiguous, and yet interpretive. But is insight the in-therapy goal, and if so, does it mean insight regarding childhood experiences or transference? Again, what is the extratherapy goal of the Freudian analyst? For the client-centered therapist, the independent variables would seem to be unconditional positive regard, empathic understanding, and congruence. However, we do not know at what level these conditions should be present, nor their interrelationship. Again we are asked, what is the relationship of in-therapy and extratherapy outcomes? The behavioral therapist operates with several kinds of practices, such as aversion, negative practice, desensitization, operant conditioning, and reinforcement. But what is the relationship of symptom removal to other criteria? And finally, does preparation for desensitization, which usually includes the arrangement of anxieties in a hierarchy, itself account for improvement in the patient because of stimulus discrimination?

The view that theoretical orientation really makes no difference in counseling does not seem as tenable as it once did. It now appears that the early studies by Fiedler resulted in a finding of no difference related to theoretical orientation because the items judged by the therapist were so clear that any experienced person would have agreed on their importance, while inexperienced workers might not have. Later studies suggest that the theoretical orientation of the counselor is a determiner in his treatment of his client.

Nature of the Volunteer. Evidence is accumulating that students who voluntarily seek counseling differ from those who do not. Such evidence calls into question counseling research in which volunteers for counseling are matched on demographic variables with controls who are not volunteers. By use of the Myers-Briggs Type Indicator college male volunteers for counseling have been shown to be concerned with perception more than with judgment and with intuition more than with sensation when compared with peers who do not seek counseling (Mendelsohn & Kirk, 1962). Female volunteers show these same differences and are also more concerned with feeling than thinking (Mendelsohn, 1966).

In junior high school the volunteer for counseling differs from the student referred for counseling by being more often a female than a male, by indicating more problems on the Mooney Problem Check List, by having a higher grade-point average, and by having more problems regarding "Relations with People in General." He differs from the student who has no contact with the counselor in the number and type of problems indicated on the Mooney list (Esper, 1963). Heilbrun and Sullivan (1962) developed a scale to measure readiness for counseling, and Heilbrun (1962) found that those who continued in counseling for at least five interviews were more apt to give evidence of "psychological-mindedness," responsibility, and attempts to create a good impression than were those who did not continue. In a study of marginally qualified applicants for university admission, Eells (1962) found that those who asked for and received counseling were three times as apt to decide not to attend college as those who did not ask for counseling but received it anyway. However, for those in both groups who did enter the university, there was no difference in the grades earned.

College students who sought counseling differed from those who did not in having poorer scores on a personality inventory, greater aspiration to expand their interests, a greater drop in aspiration over a one-year period, and, among males, more accurate knowledge of their measured interests, scholastic aptitude, and personality scores (Matteson, 1958). Although the differences were believed not to be of practical significance, David Campbell (1965) found that volunteers for counseling were less well-adjusted than those who did not seek counseling.

At this time the preponderance of evidence suggests that the voluntary client is different in important though not completely understood ways from other students. Results of tests of theory based on volunteers for counseling may not apply to other students, and it is hoped that research designs which do not take this conclusion into account will be found in the literature with less frequency.

Counselor Characteristics. Research findings have tended to buttress the common-sense observation that the personality of the counselor is influential in the counseling process. Counselors with high needs for nurturance and affiliation, when they were inexperienced, were found to like clients more than other counselors did, but this relationship did not hold for experienced counselors (Mills & Abeles, 1965). The therapist's characteristic way of dealing with hostility was found to influence his behavior in the interview and consequently his patient's reaction to hostility (Bandura & others, 1960). A usual relationship between counselor attitudes and client behavior was found to be reversed in a study which showed that the counselor's acceptance, interest, and forbearance in passing judgment were related to a failure on the part of the client to express his feelings. Counselors who were more inclined to pass judgment interacted with their clients in a way that resulted in greater expression of feeling (Waskow, 1963). A study of interview subrole behavior disclosed no relationship between personality-test scores and interview behavior. Differences were associated with the sex of the counselor and his vocational experience before coming into counseling (R. Campbell, 1962).

Although not specifically related to interview behavior, the results of a study of the occupational choice motives of counselors provide provocative data. In a study of graduate students in guidance, a number of factors were needed to account for the choice of counseling as a career. The most important of these factors were status and prestige, altruism, and the avoidance of physical labor (Shultz & Mazer, 1964). Bugental (1964) discusses the neurotic gratifications which the therapist may gain in the practice of psychotherapy. His argument is convincing that many counselors may be seeking satisfaction through their occupation at the expense of others. He also points out the healthy gratifications which the counselor can secure from his counseling activity. By classifying counselors on the two dimensions of experience and extent of dominance, it was found that the inexperienced counselor behaved more directively than the experienced counselor did but that dominance had no influence on extent of directiveness (Bohn, 1965).

The relationship of counselor personality to counseling behavior probably interacts with the relationship of the counselor's theoretical orientation to counseling behavior in subtle and complex ways not yet clear. Not the least important of such interactions may be the relationship between the counselor's personality and his acceptance of a particular counseling theory (Shoben, 1962). It seems likely that counselors who espouse a client-centered view of counseling have different needs from those who champion a behavioral counseling position. Training institutions which attempt to induct all their counselors-in-training into one theoretical camp may be doing great violence to the natural proclivities of the student. Exposure to a number of theories might result in the best fit between the demands of the theoretical view and the characteristics of the counselor.

Effects of Counselor-Client Similarity. Research indicates that both duration and success in counseling are curvilinearly related to counselor-client similarity of profiles on the Allport-Vernon-Lindzey Study of Values (Cook, 1966), on Minnesota Multiphasic Personality Inventory scores (Carson & Heine, 1962), and on scores on the Myers-Briggs Type Indicator (Mendelsohn & Geller, 1963; Mendelsohn, 1966; Mendelsohn & Geller, 1965) but unrelated to similarity on authoritarianism scores (Goldstein, 1966). Both very low and very high similarity contraindicate success, while moderate similarity is positively related to desired outcomes.

A sociometric study failed to show differences in similarity between pairs of counselors in training who chose each other as potential counselors for themselves, when compared with pairs who rejected each other when the dependent variables were selected demographic and personality measures (Stefflre & Leafgren, 1963). A review of numerous studies brought Gardner (1964) to the conclusion that while assumed similarity is related to liking (which in turn seems related to success [Stoler, 1963]), real similarity is related to liking when the variable studied is social class but is unrelated to empathy and curvilinearly related to success. Strategies for coping with the extent of similarity were discussed in an article suggesting that apparent similarities should be manipulated by the counselor in order to lessen or extend the counselor-client distance (Cartwright & Lerner, 1963).

Earlier studies seemed to show that counselor-client similarity increased as a result of successful therapy because the client changed to be more like the counselor (Pepinsky & Karst, 1964), but recent studies make this conclusion questionable. Clients have been found to improve without becoming more like their counselors, and, in fact, only the clients of less well-adjusted and less confident counselors converged toward their counselors (Farson, 1961). Lesser (1961) did research suggesting that similarity in self-perceptions between counselor and client was negatively related to success.

In an ingeniously designed study in which clients and counselors were able to indicate what constructs were important to them in describing a person, clients became more like the ideal therapist as described in the client's language but not more like him as described in the therapist's language, and dissonance between the client and therapist regarding the importance of various constructs in describing personality was unrelated to counseling outcome (Landfield & Nawas, 1964).

At present, it appears that assumed and actual similarity in certain dimensions is related to counseling outcome, but the belief that counseling success is necessarily accompanied by a change in the client so that he becomes more like the counselor is no longer tenable.

Client's View of the Counselor. Regardless of the theoretical orientation of the counselor, the client's expectations of him may influence his interview behavior. The client's view of the counselor thus becomes an important mediator of counseling behavior and a proper focus of counseling research. Junior high school students' views of the school counselor seem chiefly determined by actually talking with him, but other multiple and diverse sources also influence this perception (Brough, 1965). A field study in which the student's perception of the school counselor was measured before and after counselors were employed showed that the role expectation for the counselor changed with greater acquaintance with him. The direction of such change was determined by what the counselor actually did. In other words, "correct" behavior was followed by "correct" role expectation (Rippee & others, 1965).

Several studies were carried out to discover the relationship between meeting the client's expectation in the counseling interview and subsequent success. Meeting the client's expectation regarding empathy was related to satisfaction, but meeting expectations regarding degree of lead was not (Severinsen, 1966). In a more complex study (Pohlman, 1963) clients judged before counseling the extent to which they wanted certain counseling behavior to happen and later judged the extent to which such behavior had occurred. Counselors also judged the client's wishes and extent of fulfillment. Success was variously measured according to the client's judgment, the counselor's judgment, and the supervisor's judgment. All results were negative, and it was concluded that there was no relationship between fulfilling the expectations of the client and counseling success. In another study the expectations of clients with regard to counseling and counselors' behavior was shown to change as a result of counseling. At the end of counseling they wanted more active and directive behavior than they wanted at the beginning and than they received during counseling (Pohlman, 1961). Patterson (1958) and Goodstein and Grigg (1959) discussed the implications of studies which indicated that counselors who were not client-centered tended to be preferred by students. The question then becomes one of whether the student's desires should be met by more counselor directiveness. Is the client's request for more counselor direction evidence of neurotic dependency or a reasonable expectation of adult help and evidence of source credibility in the counselor?

In summary, the set that the client has toward the counselor and the role expectation that he holds for him has attracted considerable research interest. This set would seem to be a function of previous counselor behavior as observed by or reported to the student. Whether this role expectation is a major determinant in client satisfaction, counselor's adherence to or deviation from theory, or counseling success, is still an unanswered question.

Group Counseling. Research on group counseling has proliferated during the last decade; several reviews of the literature provide summaries (Kagan, 1966; Wright, 1963; Hoyt & Moore, 1960). Reviewers complain of inadequate research designs and particularly of problems of nomenclature that make it difficult to distinguish group counseling from group guidance and group therapy (Wright, 1959). Goldman (1962) proposed a two-dimensional model using content (usual school subject matter to nonschool topics) and process (leader structured and controlled to group structured and controlled) to define these three group procedures; that is, guidance, counseling, and therapy. Group guidance refers to a classroom-size group working with a teacher or a counselor serving as a teacher on problems of personal or vocational development not usually a part of the traditional curriculum. Group therapy is a form of psychotherapy in which several patients are treated simultaneously.

Group counseling permits clients within the normal range of adjustment to work with peers and with a professionally trained counselor to explore their concerns and feelings so that they are better able to deal with their developmental problems (Cohn & others, 1963). Groups are typically composed of six to ten members with a common concern. Characteristic criteria of improvement include grade-point average (Ofman, 1964) and improved adjustment (Ohlsen, 1960), although the logical relationship between the treatment and the expected outcomes are not always clear.

The relative value of group as compared with individual counseling has been investigated in various studies such as the one by Baymur and Patterson (1960), but for the most part differences in effectiveness tend not to be clear. A difficulty in such studies stems from the problem of whether the researcher should equate the time spent in counseling by the clients or the time devoted to counseling by the counselor. Some proponents of group counseling advance the saving of the counselor's time as an argument for the use of this procedure, but others believe that the group milieu itself is efficacious and therefore that the procedure is meritorious apart from reasons of economy. In contrast, some believe that the group-counseling experience will result in greater demand for individual counseling by the participants and therefore will ultimately increase the cost of counseling services. While group counseling may derive from any counseling theory, in practice it has probably had most impetus from the client-centered position with its emphasis on feelings and attitudes. Group counseling is being increasingly used in school and college settings with clients and in counselor education with counselor trainees while its value apparently is as difficult to demonstrate—but no more so—as that of individual counseling (Shaw & Wursten, 1965).

Vocational Counseling. The distinction between vocational counseling, educational counseling, and personal-social counseling is usually not maintained by counseling theorists, counselor educators, or counselors. Counseling that considers vocational problems must also deal with educational and personal-social matters, since the client himself is indivisible. There remain, however, interactions between counselors and clients which have as their prime focus vocational development and choice. Such counseling is frequently the special concern of school and college counselors.

Vocational counseling was once seen as primarily a matter of matching the traits of the client with the factors presumed to be important for success in the occupational area while keeping in mind predictions regarding future occupational needs and opportunities (Williamson, 1965a). While the theory was not well developed, it seemed to rest on the assumption that an act of vocational choice was possible and crucial in determining the vocational status of the client. A further assumption was that such a choice was made rationally and on the basis of facts which could be obtained through the services of a vocational counselor. These facts dealt with the characteristics of the client and the characteristics of suitable occupations. Little concern was shown for the affective elements of vocational satisfaction or for the series of vocational choices which would constitute the individual's career pattern. More recent theorists make it plain that they see vocational counseling as a much more complex process. These newer theories tend to discuss vocational development as opposed to occupational choice, to take more cognizance of affective elements in development than holders of the earlier position did, and to see vocational development theory as being based on theories of personality. In short, the more recent view of vocational counseling (Borow, 1964) is more complex and more sophisticated than was the earlier one.

The modern view of vocational development was stimulated by the publication of *Occupational Choice —An Approach to a General Theory* (Ginzberg & others, 1951) in which the stages of development were set forth as fantasy (up to age 11), tentative (11 to 19), and realistic (after 19) and occupational choice was viewed as a largely irreversible process characterized by compromise at each step.

Super (Super & others, 1963), perhaps the best-known and most prolific researcher of the current theorists, has applied self theory to vocational development. His general position is that the selection of an occupation constitutes an implementation of the self concept. He has done much to focus attention on careers as opposed to individual occupational choices and is engaged in a long-term longitudinal study of career development. In his view, the vocational counselor should help the client clarify his self concept and make plans for a vocational career congruent with his view of himself.

Roe (1956), after earlier studies of the vocational development of eminent scientists, concluded that vocational determinants were largely a function of parent-child interaction during the first few years of life. On the basis of such interaction the child seems to be directed either toward occupations which involve people toward those which involve things and ideas. Research has tended not to support her views, and modifications in her theoretical position are suggested by some of the findings (Roe & Siegelman, 1964).

Holland (1966) has built a theory of vocational development on the belief that a choice of a vocation is an expression of the individual's personality and that therefore members of a vocation have similar personalities and similar histories of personal development. The congruence between an individual's personality and of the environment in which he works then becomes a determiner of vocational satisfaction, stability, and achievement. The counselor's role would thus become one of helping an individual understand clearly the kind of person that he is and the kind of presses and expectations associated with a variety of work environments. Considerable research has been generated by Holland's theory, and results have tended to support his view that certain types of personalities select the types of jobs which would have been predicted for them on the basis of his theory.

While there is no one position advocated by sociologists in general, a number of sociological writers have emphasized the importance of such factors as sex, social class, ethnic background, and cultural press in determining vocational development (Caplow, 1954; Hughes, 1958). These sociologists look for an explanation of vocational development in the environment rather than in the individual. It is not always clear whether they believe the individual has a choice to make in the vocational sphere or whether environmental determinants do his choosing for him.

A number of writers are beginning to apply decision theory to the process of vocational counseling. Hilton (1962) advanced a theory of decision making as it applied to careers. Since then Hills (1964) and Hammond (1965), among others, have applied decision theory to elements of vocational development. This view of the counseling process would seem to hold much value for school counselors who are in the process of helping students make plans. Such matters as probability, utility, and values are of prime importance in such vocational counseling, and it would be the task of the counselor to provide probability statements and help the individual clarify the utility of certain outcomes for him.

A number of individuals have attempted to present a theory congruent with the psychoanalytic position which would apply to vocational development. The clearest statement of this position is found in the article by Bordin and others (1963). They attempt to account for work gratification on the basis of dimensions traceable to infantile physiological functions. They then describe occupations in terms of the relative strengths of these various dimensions and their relation to a series of modifying characteristics. Research, largely under the direction of Bordin, has supported their position.

Tiedeman, his colleagues, and his students at the Center for Research in Careers at Harvard University have done a good deal of research on vocational development, some of which unfortunately remains unpublished. Although their basic theoretical position is difficult to understand, they seem to focus particularly on the structure of the developmental processes which lead to vocational maturity (Tiedeman & O'Hara, 1963). Less complete statements of theory have been made by Stefflre (1966), Simons (1966), and Hadley and Levy (1962), among others.

The view of vocational counseling stemming from vocational-development theorists suggests that the vocational-counseling process must certainly involve the total individual with all of his characteristics, goals, and antecedents. The fact that we may be moving toward a world in which work will play a less essential part in man's life adds special importance to this newer view of vocational development as a part of total personality development.

EVIDENCE OF THE VALUE OF COUNSELING. Methodology. Evidence with regard to the value of counseling is highly conflicting. While certain researchers suggest that there is no evidence to support claims of its effectiveness, others contend that the evidence clearly justifies the activity. A significant amount of this difference may result from methodological deficiencies in research designs and the employment of different criterion measures.

Although some recent studies demonstrate sophistication in design, many continue to be plagued with glaring weaknesses which obfuscate results. A recurrent error is the failure to employ factorial designs comprehensive enough to account for the effects of otherwise confounding variables resident in the client, the counselor, or their environments. Adequate controls are still missing in a number of studies. And while the evidence clearly establishes important differences between motivated and nonmotivated clients, most studies continue to use nonmotivated persons as controls.

O'Dea and Seren (1953) conclude that the lack of a set of criteria appropriate for the evaluation of counseling in all situations constitutes the greatest single difficulty in measuring the outcomes of counseling. Since different criteria measure different aspects of the effects of counseling, they suggest that future studies use three or more criteria to get at the many aspects of counseling outcomes and to overcome the unreliability and biasing effects of a single criterion.

Criteria are frequently based upon the self-reports of clients, especially by theorists with a strong phenomenological bent. However, subjective factors, such as unconscious distortions and desires to please the counselor, render self-reports suspect as criteria of improvement. Zax and Klein (1960) caution that unless phenomenological changes (self-reports) and changes in verbal behavior in counseling are related to concomitant behavioral changes in the family and the community, the significance of such criteria remains clouded. They also write that the chief problem in using external measures as criteria is the development of criteria broad enough to represent a wide range of functioning and yet circumscribed enough to be measured with reliability.

Bordin (1965) and Zax and Klein (1960) suggest that the discovery of meaningful and reliable criteria appropriate to most counseling studies awaits future studies in personality. Bordin believes that evaluation of counseling will remain illusory until theoretical and empirical issues about personality and its relation to experiences motivating the client to seek counseling have been settled. Zax and Klein observe that what we now need is a series of broad normative studies of a personal–social–psychological nature. Bergin (1963) noted that the selection of criteria depends upon subjective value judgments and admonished psychologists to be more willing to make and acknowledge such judgments.

Research. For some of the reasons discussed above, research in regard to the worth of counseling has yielded confusing results. Eysenck (1952) directed a burning indictment against psychotherapeutic practitioners. His review of 24 reports involving 8,000 neurotic cases suggested that spontaneous remission accounted for a higher percentage of improved cases than did psychotherapeutic intervention. While Rosenzweig (1954) raised serious questions about the legitimacy of the studies upon which Eysenck leaned and discussed the problem of varying criterion measures, and Kiesler (1966) questioned the validity of the concept of spontaneous remission, Tyler (1961) concluded that no form of therapy has been clearly demonstrated to be more effective in curing neurosis than the miscellaneous processes of time and experience.

In a well-designed eight-year study of the effects of therapy with potential delinquents, Tuber and Powers (1951) report that the control group (the noncounseled group) displayed less delinquent behavior than the experimental group. Shelley and Johnson (1961), on the other hand, found that a group of youthful offenders assigned to a penal facility with an organized counseling program for six months obtained significantly lower antisocial scores on the Thematic Apperception Test than did a matched group assigned to a facility without a counseling program.

At the college level Williams (1962) found that counseling resulted in better adjustment scores obtained on Q-sorts. David Campbell (1965) followed up a sample of counseled students 25 years later. It had been found that the experimental group exceeded the control group in graduation rate, grade-point average, and participation in campus activities. Twenty-five years later Campbell found the counseled students still more successful but still, as they had been at the beginning of the study, more uncomfortable in their personal adjustment. Faries (1955) found that counseling significantly increased the graduation rate, and Ivey (1962) and R. Watson (1961) report that counseled students significantly surpassed noncounseled students in academic achievement.

Other studies at the college level were not so encouraging. Guthrie and O'Neill (1933) found that dormitory counseling had no effect upon academic achievement. Similarly, Scarborough and Wright (1957) concluded that a brief counseling-clinic experience had no effect on the academic achievement of entering students. Studies by Goodstein and Crites (1961) found no evidence that vocational-educational counseling improved the academic performance of low-ability college students. Similarly, Broedel and others (1960) report that while counseling improved the self-acceptance of underachievers, it did not help their grade-point averages. Ofman (1964), on the other hand, concluded that group counseling was an effective procedure for improving the scholastic performance of underachievers in college. In one of the best-designed and best-executed studies to date, Volsky and others (1965) found that only on 1 of 33 hypotheses tested did counseled students differ from noncounseled students: the *non*counseled students showed significantly greater improvement in problem-solving ability than the counseled students did. The authors suggest that the disappointing results of the study are probably in part attributable to the global nature of their criteria (anxiety, defensiveness, and problem solving). Follow-up studies on the same sample show that the counseled students did better than the controls in improving academic progress and grade-point average.

Kir-Stimon (1956) and Gellman and others (1956) found that counseling had improved the vocational adjustment of clients, and Jesness (1955) reports that counseling resulted in revised vocational planning and more-suitable vocational choices.

The most careful evaluative study of the effects of counseling at the high school level is that by Rothney (1958). In general, the findings support the view that counseled students are more successful and pleased with their lives than students who were not counseled. The differences, however, tend to be small, perhaps inconsequential, and often not statistically significant. Furthermore, the treatment effect is not directly comparable to that found in most high schools, for the counseling was done by graduate students in counseling supervised by a university staff, and the original sampling may involve factors that predispose toward the appearance of success.

Properly designed evaluative studies of school counseling are very difficult to do because of the problems of providing randomization of subjects, controlled treatment, protection from contamination, and suitable criteria.

Negative Consequences. Counselors and researchers of counseling have long accepted as an article of faith that although it may be difficult or impossible to establish the worth of counseling, it is, in any event, harmless. This comfortable position is now more difficult to maintain. An interesting line of research associated particularly with Traux and Carkhuff challenges this sanguine view. The absence of differences between the experimental and control groups in much research may be explained, not by assuming that the members of the experimental group have not changed, but rather by assuming that some have changed in a positive and some in a negative direction. In some studies the mean of the experimental group does not differ after treatment from that of the control group, but the changes within the experimental group are not random positive and negative changes but are systematically related to the client's relationship to the counselor. Some clients are helped because their relationship to the counselor was a good one and so their posttreatment scores show improvement; some are hurt because their relationship was poor and their scores show deterioration.

Present research would suggest that when the counselor exhibits active empathy, unconditional positive regard, and self-congruence the client gets better but that when these conditions are absent the client gets worse (Truax, 1963). These three crucial factors of empathy, warmth, and counselor integration seem to lead to an intense and intimate relationship which is correlated with counseling success, while their absence, or presence at a low degree, result in a damaging relationship (Truax & Carkhuff, 1964). Of the three necessary conditions for counseling success that of the genuineness of the counselor seems least crucial, and only when there is a gross absence of such genuineness does there appear to be a detriment to the self-exploration of the client and consequently damage to his adjustment (Truax & Carkhuff, 1965). These new findings would indicate that differential predictions regarding the success of counseling must be based upon the counselor-client relationship. They also serve as a challenge to the comfortable belief that counseling cannot hurt the client.

The following observations appear justified: (1) evidence that counseling is clearly superior to the unspecified happenstances of life in the treatment of complex personality problems remains to be demonstrated; (2) counseling appears to bring about changes in the self concept, as measured by Q-sorts, but accompanying behavioral changes have frequently not been shown; (3) counseling has sometimes proved valuable in promoting satisfactory occupational selection and adjustment, but it remains to be shown that it is valuable in improving academic achievement; (4) many studies have failed to obtain positive results either because their goals were too ambitious or because their treatments too brief; and (5) variation among rates of improvement claimed by different theoretical orientations is probably related to the kind of client problems characteristically dealt with by a given orientation and the degree of specificity employed by the orientation in the establishment of goals.

Past research has been characterized by far too much ambiguity in the specification of treatments and goals. Krumboltz (1965) pokes fun at the "here's the answer, what's the question" approach whereby it is assumed that one approach to counseling is applicable to every conceivable kind of human problem. Furthermore, the researcher often has not described the treatment beyond calling it "counseling." When several counselors are used in a study, it is highly likely that there may be significant differences among them, which differences may tend to attenuate outcomes. Future studies are needed which will ensure a great deal more consistency among treatments being administered. Finally, goals for counseling should be considerably more specific if adequate measurement of outcome is to be achieved.

RECOMMENDED SOURCES. The books and articles cited do not, of course, exhaust the literature on counseling theory. Unfortunately, much of the theoretically oriented literature deals with clearly psychotherapeutic counseling, and in most school guidance text books, although there is at least a chapter on counseling, technique often overshadows theory.

The Journal of Counseling Psychology continues to be the major source for articles about counseling research and theory, followed by *Personnel and Guidance Journal, Journal of Consulting Psychology,* and *Journal of Applied Psychology.* In the first of a contemplated series of annual reports on counseling psychology, Schmidt and Pepinsky (1965) considered the topics of counselors, clients, counseling process, counseling outcome, beliefs and attitudes toward counseling service, counseling as a group activity, and pastoral counseling.

The Review of Education Research has a policy of reviewing triennially the counseling literature; in the 1963 and 1966 reviews it took account of the movement to consider school counseling as one of the pupil personnel services.

The Annual Review of Psychology, which had a chapter on counseling in each issue from its inception in 1950 through 1959, reviewed the counseling literature in the 1963 and 1966 issues.

Buford Stefflre
Kenneth Matheny
Michigan State University
Georgia State College

References

Alexander, Franz. "The Dynamics of Psychotherapy in the Light of Learning Theory." *Am J Psychiatry* 120:440–8; 1963.

Arbuckle, Dugald S. "Five Philosophical Issues in

Counseling." *J Counseling Psychol* 4:211–5; 1958.

Bandura, Albert. "Psychotherapy as a Learning Process." *Psychol B* 58:142–59; 1961.

Bandura, Albert, and others. "Psychotherapists' Approach-avoidance Reactions to Patients' Expressions of Hostility." *J Consult Psychol* 24:1–8; 1960.

Baymur, Feriha B., and Patterson, Cecil H. "A Comparison of Three Methods of Assisting Under-Achieving High School Students." *J Counseling Psychol* 7:83–90; 1960.

Bergin, A. E. "The Effects of Psychotherapy: Negative Results Revisited." *J Counseling Psychol* 10:244–50; 1963.

Bohn, Martin J., Jr. "Counselor Behavior as a Function of Counselor Dominance, Counselor Experience and Client Type" *J Counseling Psychol* 12:346–52; 1965.

Bordin, Edward S. "A Simplification as a Strategy for Research in Psychotherapy." *J Consult Psychol* 29(No. 6):493–503; 1965.

Bordin, Edward S., and others. "An Articulated Framework for Vocational Development" *J Counseling Psychol* 10:107–17; 1963.

Borow, Henry. (Ed.) *Man in a World at Work.* Houghton, 1964. 585p.

Boy, Angelo V., and Pine, Gerald J. *Client-centered Counseling in the Secondary School.* Houghton, 1963. 289p.

Brayfield, Arthur H. "Counseling Psychology." In Farnsworth, Paul R. and others. (Eds.) *Annual Review of Psychology,* Vol. 14. Annual Reviews, Inc., 1963. p. 319–50.

Broedel, J., and others. "The Effects of Group Counseling on Gifted Adolescent Underachievers." *J Counseling Psychol* 7:163–70; 1960.

Brough, James R. "Sources of Student Perception of the Role of the Counselor." *Personnel Guid J* 43:597–99; 1965.

Bugental, James F. T. "The Person Who Is the Psychotherapist." *J Cons Psychol* 28:272–7; 1964.

Campbell, David P. *The Results of Counseling: Twenty-five Years Later.* Saunders, 1965. 205p.

Campbell, Robert E. "Counselor Personality and Background and His Interview Subrole Behavior." *J Counseling Psychol* 9:329–34; 1962.

Caplow, Thedore. *The Sociology of Work.* U Minnesota Press, 1954. 289p.

Carson, Robert C., and Heine, Ralph W. "Similarity and Success in Therapeutic Dyads." *J Cons Psychol* 26:38–43; 1962.

Cartwright, Rosalind Diamond, and Lerner, Barbara. "Empathy, Need to Change and Improvement with Psychotherapy." *J Counseling Psychol* 27:138–44; 1963.

Cohn, Benjamin, and others. "Group Counseling: An Orientation." *Personnel Guid J* 42:355–8; 1963.

Combs, Arthur W., and Soper, Daniel W. "The Perceptual Organization of Effective Counselors." *J Counseling Psychol* 10:222–6; 1963.

Cook, Thomas E. "The Influence of Client-Counselor Value Similarity on Change in Meaning During Brief Counseling." *J Counseling Psychol* 13:77–81; 1966.

Demos, George D., and Zuwaylif, Fadil H. "Characteristics of Effective Counselors." *Counselor Ed Sup* 5:163–5; 1962.

Dollard, John, and Miller, Neal E. *Personality and Psychotherapy.* McGraw-Hill, 1950. 488p.

Eells, Kenneth. "Voluntary Versus Compulsory Counseling With Regard to College Entrance Plans." *Personnel Guid J* 41:234–9; 1962.

Esper, George. "Characteristics of Junior High School Students Who Seek Counseling." *Personnel Guid J* 42:468–72; 1963.

Eysenck, Hans J. "The Effects of Psychotherapy: An Evaluation." *J Consult Psychol* 16:319–24; 1952.

Eysenck, Hans J. *The Dynamics of Anxiety and Hysteria.* Routledge, 1957. 311p.

Eysenck, Hans J. (Ed.) *Behavior Therapy and the Neuroses.* Pergamon, 1960. 479p.

Eysenck, Hans J., and Rachman, I. *The Causes and Cures of Neurosis.* Robert R. Knapp, 1965. 318p.

Faries, M. "Short-term Counseling at the College Level." *J Counseling Psychol* 2:182–4; 1955.

Farson, Richard E. "Introjection in the Psychotherapeutic Relationship." *J Counseling Psychol* 8:337–42; 1961.

Fiedler, Fred A. "The Concept of an Ideal Therapeutic Relationship." *J Cons Psychol* 14:239–45; 1950(a).

Fiedler, Fred A. "A Comparison of Therapeutic Relationships in Psychoanalytic, Non-directive and Adlerian Therapy." *J Cons Psychol* 14:436–5; 1950(b).

Ford, Donald H., and Urban, Hugh B. *Systems of Psychotherapy.* Wiley, 1963. 712p.

Freud, Sigmund. *Civilization and Its Discontents.* Hogarth Press, 1930. 144p.

Gardner, G. Gail. "The Psychotherapeutic Relationship." *Psychol B* 61:426–37; 1964.

Gellman, William, and others. *Adjusting People to Work.* Jewish Vocational Service and Employment Center, 1956. 139p.

Gendlin, Eugene T. "Client-centered Developments and Work with Schizophrenics." *J Counseling Psychol* 9:205–12; 1962.

Ginzberg, Eli, and others. *Occupational Choice—An Approach to a General Theory.* Columbia U Press, 1951. 253p.

Glad, Donald D., and others. *Operational Values in Psychotherapy.* Oxford U Press, 1959. 326p.

Goldman, Leo. "Group Guidance: Content and Process." *Personnel Guid J* 40:518–22; 1962.

Goldstein, Arnold P. "Psychotherapy Research by Extrapolation from Social Psychology." *J Counseling Psychol* 14:38–45; 1966.

Goodstein, Leonard D., and Crites, J. O. "Brief Counseling with Poor College Risks." *J Counseling Psychol* 8:318–21; 1961.

Goodstein, Leonard D., and Grigg, Austin E. "Client Satisfaction, Counselors, and the Counseling Process." *Personnel Guid J* 38:19–24; 1959.

Greenspoon, J. "The Reinforcing Effect of Two Spoken Sounds on the Frequency of Two Responses." *Am J Psychol* 68:409–16; 1955.

Guthrie, George M., and O'Neill, H. W. "Effects of

Dormitory Counseling on Academic Achievement." *Personnel Guid J* 31:307–9; 1953.

Hadley, Robert G., and Levy, William V. "Vocational Development and Reference Group." *J Counseling Psychol* 9:110–4; 1962.

Hammond, John S., III. "Bringing Order Into Selection of A College." *Personnel Guid J* 43:654–60; 1965.

Heilbrun, Alfred B., Jr. "Psychological Factors Related to Counseling Readiness and the Implications for Counseling Behavior." *J Counseling Psychol* 9:353–8; 1962.

Heilbrun, Alfred B., Jr., and Sullivan, Donald J. "The Prediction of Counseling Readiness." *Personnel Guid J* 41:112–7; 1962.

Hildum, D. C., and Brown, R. W. "Verbal Reinforcement and Interviewer Bias." *J Abn Social Psychol* 53:108–11; 1956.

Hills, John R. "Decision Theory and College Choice." *Personnel Guid J* 43:17–22; 1964.

Hilton, Thomas L. "Career Decision-making." *J Counseling Psychol* 9:291–8; 1962.

Holland, John L. *The Psychology of Vocational Choice.* Blaisdell Publishing Company, 1966. 96p.

Hoyt, Kenneth B., and Moore, Gilbert D. "Group Procedures in Guidance and Personnel Work." *R Ed Res* 30:158–67; 1960.

Hughes, Everett Cherrington. *Men and Their Work.* Free, 1958. 175p.

Ivey, A. E. "The Academic Performance of Students Counseled at a University Counseling Service." *J Counseling Psychol* 9:347–52; 1962.

Jesness, C. F. "The Effects of Counseling on the Self-perceptions of College Men." *Dissertation Abstr* 15:155; 1955.

Kagan, Norman. "Group Procedures." *R Ed Res* 36:274–87; 1966.

Kiesler, Donald J. "Some Myths of Psychotherapy Research and a Search for a Paradigm." *Psychol B* 65:110–36; 1966.

King, Paul. "Psychoanalytic Adaptations." In Stefflre, Buford. (Ed.) *Theories of Counseling.* McGraw-Hill, 1965. 298p.

Kir-Stimon, W. "A Follow-up Study of Counseling with Anxiety Neurotics." *Personnel Guid J* 34:474–80; 1956.

Krasner, Leonard. "The Therapist as a Social Reinforcement Machine." In Strupp, H. H. (Ed.) *Second Research Conference on Psychotherapy.* APA, 1961.

Krasner, Leonard. "Reinforcement, Verbal Behavior and Psychotherapy." *Am J Orthopsychiatry* 33:601–13; 1963.

Krumboltz, John D. "The Agenda for Counseling." *J Counseling Psychol* 12:226; 1965.

Krumboltz, John D., and Thoresen, Carl E. "The Effect of Behavioral Counseling in Group and Individual Settings on Information-seeking Behavior." *J Counseling Psychol* 11:325–333; 1964.

Landfield, A. W., and Nawas, M. M. "Psychotherapeutic Improvement as a Function of Communication and Adoption of Therapist's Values." *J Counseling Psychol* 11:336–41; 1964.

Lesser, W. M. "The Relationship Between Counseling Progress and Empathic Understanding." *J Counseling Psychol* 8:330–6; 1961.

Lofquist, Lloyd. *Vocational Counseling of the Physically Handicapped.* Appleton, 1957. 384p.

Matarazzo, Joseph D. "Psychotherapeutic Processes." In Farnsworth, Paul R., and others. (Eds.) *Annual Review of Psychology.* Annual Reviews, Inc., 1965.

Matarazzo, Joseph D., and others. "Interviewer Influence on Durations of Interviewee Speech." *J Verbal Learning Verbal Behavior* 1:451–8; 1963.

Matteson, Ross W. "Self-perception of Students Seeking Counseling." *Personnel Guid J* 36:545–8; 1958.

McCully, C. Harold. "Conceptions of Man and the Helping Professions." *Personnel Guid J* 44:911–8; 1966.

McGowan, John F., and Porter, Thomas L. *An Introduction to Employment Service Counseling.* Missouri Division of Employment Security, 1964. 197p.

McNarr, Douglas M., and Lorr, Maurice. "An Analysis of Professed Psychotherapeutic Techniques." *J Cons Psychol* 28:265–71; 1964.

Mendelsohn, Gerald A. "Effects of Client Personality and Client-Counselor Similarity on the Duration of Counseling: A Replication and Extension." *J Counseling Psychol* 13:228–34; 1966.

Mendelsohn, Gerald A., and Geller, Marvin H. "Effects of Counselor-Client Similarity on the Outcome of Counseling." *J Counseling Psychol* 10:71–7; 1963.

Mendelsohn, Gerald A., and Geller, Marvin H. "Structure of Client Attitudes Toward Counseling and the Relation to Client-Counselor Similarity." *J Cons Psychol* 29:63–72; 1965.

Mendelsohn, Gerald A., and Kirk, Barbara A. "Personality Differences Between Students Who Do and Do Not Use a Counseling Facility." *J Counseling Psychol* 9:341–6; 1962.

Michaux, William W., and Lorr, Maurice. "Psychotherapists' Treatment Goals." *J Counseling Psychol* 8:250–4; 1961.

Miller, Neal E. "Some Implications of Modern Behavior Theory for Personality Change and Psychotherapy." In Worchel, Philip and Bryne, Donn. (Eds.) *Personality Change.* Wiley, 1964. 616p.

Mills, David H., and Abeles, Norman. "Counselor Needs for Affiliation and Nurturance as Related to Liking for Clients and Counseling Process." *J Counseling Psychol* 12:353–8; 1965.

Mueller-Hegemann, D. "Methodologic Approaches in Psychotherapy: Current Concepts in East Germany." *Amer J Psychotherapy* 17:554–68; 1963.

Murray, E. J. "Learning Theory and Psychotherapy: Biotropic Versus Sociotropic Approaches." *J Counseling Psychol* 10:250–5; 1963.

O'Dea, J. D., and Seren, F. R. "Evaluating Effects of Counseling." *Personnel Guid J* 31:241–4; 1953.

Ofman, W. "Evaluation of a Group Counseling Procedure." *J Counseling Psychol* 11:152–9; 1964.

Ohlsen, Merle M. "Counseling Within a Group Setting." *J Nat Assn Woman Deans and Counselors* 23:104–9; 1960.

Patterson, Cecil H. "Client Expectations and Social

Conditioning." *Personnel Guid J* 37:136–8; 1958.

Patterson, Cecil H. "Control, Conditioning and Counseling." *Personnel Guid J* 41:680–6; 1963.

Pepinsky, Harold B., and Karst, Thomas O. "Convergence: A Phenomenon in Counseling and Psychotherapy." *Am Psychologist* 19:333–8; 1964.

Pohlman, Edward. "Changes in Client Preferences During Counseling." *Personnel Guid J* 40:340–3; 1961.

Pohlman, Edward. "Should Clients Tell Counselors What to Do?" *Personnel Guid J* 42:456–8; 1963.

Rapaport, David. "The Theory of Ego Autonomy: a Generalization." *B Menninger Clinic* 22:13–35; 1958.

Razran, Gregory. "Observable Unconscious and the Inferable Conscious in Current Soviet Psychophysiology: Interoceptive Conditioning, Semantic Conditioning, and the Orienting Reflex." *Psychol R* 68:81–147; 1961.

Rippee, Billy D., and others. "The Influence of Counseling on the Perception of Counselor Role." *Personnel Guid J* 43:696–701; 1965.

Roe, Anne. *The Psychology of Occupations.* Wiley, 1956.

Roe, Anne, and Siegelman, M. *The Origin of Interests.* APGA, 1964. 98p.

Rogers, Carl R. *On Becoming A Person: A Therapist's View of Psychotherapy.* Houghton, 1961. 420p.

Rosenzweig, Saul A. "A Transvaluation of Psychotherapy—A Reply to Hans Eysenck." *J Abn Social Psychol* 49:298–304; 1954.

Rothney, John W. *Guidance Practices and Results.* Harper, 1958. 542p.

Scarborough, V. B., and Wright, J. C. "The Assessment of an Educational Guidance Clinic." *J Counseling Psychol* 4:283–6; 1957.

Schmidt, Lyle D., and Pepinsky, Harold B. "Counseling Research in 1963." *J Counseling Psychol* 12:418–22; 1965.

Severinsen, K. Norman. "Client Expectation and Perception of the Counselor's Role and Their Relationship to Client Satisfaction." *J Counseling Psychol* 13:109–12; 1966.

Shaw, Merville C., and Wursten, Rosemary. "Research on Group Procedures in Schools: A Review of the Literature." *Personnel Guid J* 44:27–34; 1965.

Shelley, Ernest L., and Johnson, Walter S., Jr. "Evaluating an Organized Counseling Service for Youthful Offenders." *J Counseling Psychol* 8:351–4; 1961.

Shlein, John M., and others. "Effect of Time Limits: A Comparison of Two Psychotherapies." *J Counseling Psychol* 9:31–4; 1962.

Shoben, Edward Joseph, Jr. "The Counselor's Theory as a Personal Trait." *Personnel Guid J* 40:617–21; 1962.

Shoben, Edward Joseph, Jr. "A Theoretical Approach to Psychotherapy as Personality Modification." *Ed R* 23:128–42; 1953.

Shultz, Richard E., and Mazer, Gilbert E. "A Factor Analysis of the Occupational Choice Motives of Counselors." *J Counseling Psychol* 11:267–71; 1964.

Simons, Joseph. "An Existential View of Vocational Development." *Personnel Guid J* 44:604–10; 1966.

Soper, Daniel W., and Combs, Arthur W. "The Helping Relationship as Seen by Teachers and Therapists." *J Cons Psychol* 26:288; 1962.

Stefflre, Buford. (Ed.) *Theories of Counseling.* McGraw-Hill, 1965. 298p.

Stefflre, Buford. "Vocational Development: Ten Propositions in Search of a Theory." *Personnel Guid J* 44:611–6; 1966.

Stefflre, Buford, and Leafgren, Fred. "Mirror, Mirror on the Wall—A Study of Preferences for Counselors." *Personnel Guid J* 42:459–62; 1963.

Stoler, Norton. "Client-like Ability: A Variable in the Study of Psychotherapy." *J Cons Psychol* 27:175–8; 1963.

Strupp, Hans H. "The Performance of Psychoanalytic and Client-centered Therapists in an Initial Interview." *J Cons Psychol* 22:265–74; 1958.

Sundland, D. M., and Barker, E. N. "The Orientations of Psychotherapists." *J Cons Psychol* 26:201–12; 1962.

Super, Donald E., and others. *Career Development: Self-Theory.* CEEB, 1963. 94p.

Tiedeman, David V., and O'Hara, Robert P. *Career Development: Choice and Adjustment.* CEEB, 1963. 115p.

Truax, Charles B. "Effective Ingredients in Psychotherapy: An Approach to Unraveling the Patient-Therapist Interaction." *J Counseling Psychol* 10:256–63; 1963.

Truax, Charles B., and Carkhuff, Robert R. "The Old and the New: Theory and Research in Counseling and Psychotherapy." *Personnel Guid J* 32:860–6; 1964.

Truax, Charles B., and Carkhuff, Robert R. "Experimental Manipulation of Therapeutic Conditions." *J Cons Psychol* 29:119–24; 1965.

Tuber, H. L., and Powers, E. "Evaluating Therapy in a Delinquency Prevention Program." *Nerv Ment Dis* 31: 138–47; 1951.

Tyler, Leona E. *The Work of the Counselor,* 2nd ed. Appleton, 1961. 327p.

Verplanck, W. S. "The Control of the Content of Conversation: Reinforcement of Statements of Opinion." *J Abn Social Psychol* 51:668–76; 1955.

Viteles, Morris S., and others. *Vocational Counseling: A Reappraisal in Honor of Donald G. Patterson.* U Minnesota Press, 1961. 70p.

Volsky, Theodore, Jr., and others. *The Outcomes of Counseling and Psychotherapy: Theory and Research.* U Minnesota Press, 1965. 209p.

Wallach, Martin S., and Strupp, Hans H. "Dimensions of Psychotherapists' Activity." *J Cons Psychol* 28:120–5; 1964.

Waskow, Irene E. "Counselor Attitudes and Client Behavior." *J Cons Psychol* 27:405–12; 1963.

Watson, G. H. "An Evaluation of Counseling with College Students." *J Counseling Psychol* 8:99–104; 1961.

Watson, R. "The Experimental Tradition and Clinical Psychology." In Bachrach, Arthur. (Ed.) *Experimental Foundations of Clinical Psychology*. Basic Books, 1962. 641p.

Weitz, H. *Behavior Change Through Guidance*. Wiley, 1964. 225p.

Williams, J. E. "Changes in Self and Other Perceptions Following Brief Educational-Vocational Counseling." *J Cons Psychol* 9:18–28; 1962.

Williamson, Edmund G. *Vocational Counseling: Some Historical, Philosophical, and Theoretical Prospectives*. McGraw-Hill, 1965(a). 214p.

Williamson, Edmund G. "Vocational Counseling: Trait-factor Theory." In Stefflre, Buford. (Ed.) *Theories of Counseling*. McGraw-Hill, 1965(b). 298p.

Wolpe, Joseph. *Psychotherapy by Reciprocal Inhibition*. Stanford U Press, 1958. 239p.

Wrenn, Robert L. "Counselor Orientation: Theoretical or Situational." *J Counseling Psychol* 7:40–5; 1960.

Wright, E. Wayne. "Multiple Counseling: Why? When? How?" *Personnel Guid J* 37:551–7; 1959.

Wright, E. Wayne. "Group Procedures." *R Ed Res* 33:205–13; 1963.

Zax, Melvin, and Klein, Arman. "Measurement and Personality and Behavior Changes Following Psychotherapy." *Psychol B* 57:435–48; 1960.

CREATIVITY

Although creative thinking is considered the highest of mental functions and creative production the peak of human achievement, it is a peculiar fact that only within the past decade has creativity become a central concern in educational research. This increasing concern is clearly reflected in the successive editions of this encyclopedia. In 1941 no mention was made of the concept; in 1950 "creative" was added to the catalogue of higher mental processes but without further elaboration; in 1960 "creative thinking" appeared as a brief subsection of the article on higher mental processes; in the present edition the subject of creativity gained the status of an independent article. The transformation in the psychological literature is even more dramatic. In his presidential address to the American Psychological Association in 1950, Guilford (1950) observed that in the preceding two decades there had appeared only 186 books or articles on creativity. By 1965 the *Psychological Abstracts* listed 132 items in the one year.

DEFINITION. There is no universally agreed-upon definition of creativity, any more than there is of intelligence. In general, the most widely applied conceptions may be classified into three categories, depending on the relative emphasis given the product, the process, and the experience. Thus, some definitions are formulated in terms of a *manifest product*: it is novel and useful. MacKinnon (1962), for example, suggests that the criterion is a statistically infrequent response or idea that is adaptive and sustained to fruition. Other definitions are formulated in terms of an *underlying process*: it is divergent yet fruitful. Ghiselin (1952) speaks of creativity as a process of change and development in the psychic life of an individual leading to invention. Still other definitions are formulated in terms of a *subjective experience*: it is inspired and immanent. Maslow (1963), for one, insists on the importance of the flash of insight—the transcendent sensation itself—without reference to whether it will ever result in anything tangible. The salient issue is not the "inspired product" but the "inspired moment." Getzels (1964) has attempted to deal with creativity along somewhat different lines, giving primacy to the nature of the problem rather than to the solution. A distinction is made between presented and discovered problem situations, the former involving a problem that is already formulated, the latter a problem that still needs formulation. The significant element in creative performance is the envisagement of the creative problem; for it is the fruitful question to which the novel solution is the response (Getzels & Csikszentmihalyi, 1964).

None of the preceding conceptions of creativity is immune from the objection that each omits some characteristic vital to the others. Newell and others (1962) have presented an omnibus definition, which states that thinking may be called creative if (1) the product has novelty and value either for the thinker or the culture, (2) the thinking is unconventional, (3) it is highly motivated and persistent or of great intensity, and (4) the problem was initially vague and undefined so that part of the task was to formulate the problem itself. This statement has the advantage of inclusiveness but, like other omnibus conceptions, the disadvantage of being an inventory without a unifying rationale.

THEORY. Although there may be agreement on what constitutes an act of creative thinking, so that the formula $E = Mc^2$, the *Inferno*, and the *Eroica* are universally recognized as "creative," there is the greatest disagreement among theories attempting to account for the act. The more widely held conceptions derive from such diverse sources as logic or philosophy, learning theory, Gestalt principles, factor analysis, experimental psychology, and psychoanalysis.

Traditional logic held that thinking is concerned with truth, and being true or false is a quality of assertions and propositions. Certain combinations of propositions make possible *new* propositions, and reason establishes the correctness of the "creative" conclusion. Allied to this "rational-philosophical" approach is Dewey's famous conception (1910) of the five "logically distinct" steps in the "act of thought": a felt difficulty, its definition, suggestion toward a solution, reasoning of its bearing toward the solution, and observation and experiment leading to its acceptance or rejection. For theorists like E. L. Thorndike (1931), habit and past experience—association rather than reason—are the essential factor in thought. A novel solution is the outcome of conflicting action tendencies from previous associative learning which are tried out in the new situation. All thought, no matter how apparently "novel," "insightful," or "creative," rests ultimately on associative principles. For Wertheimer (1945), productive thinking does not proceed by either the piecemeal operations of logic or the piecemeal connections of associationism but through the cognitive reorganization of gestalten. The structural strains of a problem produce tensions yielding vectors in the direction of change and improvement; the problem situation, S_1, which is structurally incomplete, is transformed into a solution situation, S_2, which is structurally complete.

These formulations were concerned more with problem solving than with creativity as such and dealt primarily with problem situations of the form S_1-S_2. They did not take sufficient account of situations where the problem is not presented but is discovered, where the individual is motivated to seek out problems for solution through curiosity rather than necessity, or, as Wertheimer himself pointed out, where the individual begins with an S_2 that is to be created. Three disparate modes of inquiry are being applied to these issues. Factor analysis is dealing with the intellective elements in creativity, experimental psychology with motivational aspects like curiosity, and psychoanalysis with the subliminal or unconscious processes.

Although there have been many factor analyses of intellectual behavior (e.g., Thurstone & Thurstone, 1941), Guilford (1959) focused specifically on the problem of creativity. He distinguished between convergent and divergent processes, the former pertaining to new information that is maximally determined by the known information, the latter to new information that is minimally determined by the known information. It is divergent thinking that is the intellectual substratum of creative performance. Guilford himself and, later, others constructed divergent thinking tests which have since been widely used in the study of creativity.

Until a decade or two ago, the predominant assumption was that all human activity, including thinking, could be accounted for by the homeostatic model of self-maintenance and the drive-reduction theory of motivation (Hunt, 1960). Recent observations bring this assumption into serious question (e.g., White, 1959). As Berlyne (1966) points out, higher animals spend a substantial portion of their time and energy on activities which seem unrelated to drive reduction in the usual sense and to which only terms like "curiosity" and "play" seem applicable. A conspicuous part of human behavior is devoted to "entertainment," "recreation," "art," or "science," in all of which sense organs are brought to bear on biologically neutral stimuli. From the very beginning, the infant seems to strive not for the satisfaction of bodily wants alone but for satisfaction in discovery and exploration. The human being is not only a stimulus-reducing but also a stimulus-seeking organism. It is this that provides the motivational substratum for divergent thinking and creative behavior "for their own sake," so to speak.

Artists and scientists who have tried to account for their achievement have been led to credit not only "curiosity" but "subliminal" and "unconscious" forces (Ghiselin, 1952; Hadamard, 1954). Henri Poincaré, for example, spoke for many when he asserted, "The role of this unconscious work in mathematical invention appears to me incontrovertible" (Hadamard, 1954, p. 10). Preeminent among the formal theories of the role of the unconscious in creative work is psychoanalysis. The main cleavage in thought is said to be between unconscious or primary processes and ego-controlled or secondary processes, and the interaction between them is held to be conflictual, involving regression and defense. When "freely rising" primary process thought becomes ego-syntonic, the occasion exists for creativity (Freud, 1949). More recently, a greater role has been accorded the preconscious. Kris (1962) suggested that the ego may voluntarily gain access to primary process thought by way of the preconscious and that many creative products from wit to art derive from acts of regression in the service of the ego. Kubie (1958) goes further to argue that when conscious processes predominate thinking is rigid, since it is anchored in a preconceived reality, and when unconscious processes predominate thinking is even more rigid, since it is anchored in an immutable unreality. It is only when preconscious processes predominate that creativity is possible. Although the apparent convergence should not be pushed too far, it is of interest that the different modes of inquiry seem to be yielding related conceptions for further inquiry, viz., preconscious processes, stimulus-seeking motives, divergent thinking.

In view of the current volume of work and the limitations of space, it will not be possible to do more than touch on the significant empirical issues, and then only selectively for those most relevant to education. These issues have been the relation of creativity to each of the following: (1) intelligence, (2) school behavior, (3) individual development, (4) personal characteristics, and (5) educational facilitation.

INTELLIGENCE. That creativity and intelligence might not be perfectly related was suggested even before the standardized intelligence test was developed (Dearborn, 1898), and sporadically through the years there have been studies comparing performance on tests of intelligence and measures of imagination or originality (e.g., McCloy & Meier, 1939). But is was Guilford's address in 1950, calling attention to the concept of creativity, that gave impetus to the present volume of work in this domain. Of all his hypotheses, none provoked more controversy than his prediction that the relation between "intelligence" and "creativity" would be low.

There are two problems here, which regrettably are not always discriminated. One is the relation between intelligence and creativity represented by measures of recognized achievement; the other is the relation between intelligence and creativity represented by measures of divergent thinking. Although the terms "creativity" and "divergent thinking" have come to be used synonymously, the distinction as to what is actually being done in a particular study must be borne in mind. A number of studies have dealt with the relation between intelligence and recognized creative achievement (e.g., MacKinnon, 1962; Roe, 1953). There is no doubt that creative individuals perform better than the average on intelligence tests, but the correlation between their intelligence and their creativity tends to be low, MacKinnon (1962), for example, reporting a correlation of −.08 between the creative achievement of eminent architects and their performance on the Terman Concept Mastery Test.

The bulk of work—especially with children—has been on the relation between performance on intelligence tests and on divergent thinking or other types of so-called creativity tests. In an initial study, Getzels and Jackson (1959, 1962) found positive but low correlations (about .26) between measures of creativity (divergent thinking) and intelligence (IQ) for a sample of highly able children. Torrance (1962b) obtained similar data with his creativity instruments and a diversity of intelligence tests for a wider range of subjects. Hudson (1966) reported essentially the same results for samples of British children. A review of the literature (Taylor & Holland, 1962) concluded that the greater number of investigations report a positive but low correlation (.20–.40) for general populations and almost no correlation at the higher ability levels.

Critical questions about this line of research have been raised by Burt (1962) and by R. L. Thorndike (1963), especially with respect to the dimension underlying the various creativity measures. Burt argued that the general intelligence factor would account for the relations found by Getzels and Jackson, pointing out that although the correlations between the creativity and intelligence measures were low, the correlations among the creativity tests themselves were of the same magnitude. Thorndike reanalyzed the Getzels-Jackson data and some of the Guilford data and concluded that pooling measures of creativity into a single composite score was inadvisable since the intercorrelations were so low. But he also suggested that there might be a broad factor distinct from general intelligence to which the label creativity might be applied, although it is much more loosely formed than G.

The wide variety and rapid fluctuations of views regarding the relation between creativity and intelligence since the early work are illustrated by two successive studies by Yamamoto and a study by Wallach and Kogan, all published within about a year of each other. In a 1964 study, findings of Yamamoto (1964b) concurred with preceding results that the correlation between creativity and intelligence is *low*. In a 1965 study (1965a), he concluded that creativity tests do *not* form a factor independent of general intelligence. In the same year, Wallach and Kogan (1965) claimed that Guilford-type creativity measures do not constitute a domain independent of general intelligence, but their own creativity measures do. The net result of their efforts seems to be a reaffirmation of Guilford's original hypothesis, albeit with different instruments. The question has not, however, been settled. The variance due to trait and methods factors must be ascertained before a determination among the current views can be made with any certainty (Campbell & Fiske, 1959). And there are those who argue that the issue of dimensionality is not the crucial one in any case. Hudson (1966), for example, maintains that it is not; for him, the crucial issue is that a knowledge of IQ seems to be of little help if one is faced with a roomful of clever boys, for the one among them with the lowest IQ is almost as likely to be creative as the one with the highest.

SCHOOL BEHAVIOR. The unexpected observation by Getzels and Jackson (1959, 1962) that their high-creative group and their high-IQ group, despite a 23-point difference in mean IQ, performed equally well on standard measures of achievement launched a multitude of studies. The finding was soon duplicated in six of eight attempted replications by Torrance (1960, 1962b) as well as by others (e.g., Palm, 1959). But these early studies could be criticized on technical grounds, and the findings must be viewed with caution. More recently, Yamamoto (1964b) obtained the same results, which were confirmed in a searching reanalysis with more stringent technical assumptions (1965b). However, Flescher (1963) found no evidence for the phenomenon and questioned whether creativity should be related to scholastic achievement, which typically requires convergent rather than divergent thinking. Wallach and Kogan (1965) did not find any relationship between their measures of creativity and achievement. Ohnmacht (1966) found that although the creativity measures were related to achievement, the results were not independent of the communality with intelligence.

Torrance (1962b) offered two explanations for his "negative" and "positive" results—explanations which might be tested with other conflicting observations. The first explanation is situational. The two "negative" schools were a rural elementary school and an urban parochial school, both of which were characterized by more "rigid" learning conditions than were the "positive" schools. The second explanation was based on Anderson's ability gradient theory (1960) and suggested that intelligence exerted an effect on achievement up to a threshold level, beyond which increments in IQ do not make any difference but divergent thinking does. In the two negative instances the mean IQ of the high creatives was 100; in the six positive instances the mean IQ ranged from 112 to 127. He postulated a threshold point of about 120. The threshold hypothesis has itself become the subject of investigation. Roe (1953) and MacKinnon (1962) had both suggested such an effect in their studies of scientists and architects even before the hypothesis was proposed. Yamamoto (1964c) found some evidence for the hypothesis; Flescher (1963) did not; Cicirelli (1965) found a plateau in achievement at an IQ of 140 in three of nine analyses, and although he did observe a positive albeit weak relationship between creativity and achievement, he was unable to determine an IQ point at which creativity began to affect achievement differentially.

Two other school issues have been the subject of some inquiry. One is the relation of divergent thinking to different school subjects; the other is the differential relation of high-creative and high-IQ students to teachers. Torrance (1962b) noted a tendency for his high creatives to perform better in reading and language skills than in arithmetic and work studies, but Yamamoto (1964c) found exactly the opposite, and Feldhusen and others (1965) obtained significant and similar correlations for both reading and mathematics. In a British study, Hudson (1966) noted that most students specializing in the humanities were *relatively* weak in IQ tests and better in divergent thinking tests; most students specializing in the sciences were the reverse. Getzels and Jackson (1962) observed that despite the similar superior academic performance by their high-creative and high-IQ groups, teachers preferred the latter but not the former to the average group. Torrance (1962b) found that teachers preferred high-IQ over high-creative students, and Holland (1959) suggested that teacher performances correlate more highly with leadership and academic achievement than with creativity. However, Richards and others (1964) found that teacher ratings in originality did not favor the intelligent over the creative students, and Klausmeier and others (1962) obtained positive correlations between teacher ratings on creativity and performance on creativity tests.

INDIVIDUAL DEVELOPMENT. The source and development of creative ability is an intriguing question; attempts to answer it have a long history. Galton (1869) stressed the importance of heredity; J. Cattell (1915) insisted on the significance of the environment. But the source question in dichotomous heredity-environment terms seems a dead end at this time, here as in other areas of psychological functioning. A somewhat different question is the nature of the development of creativity with age, whatever the sources. Although his conclusions have been disputed (Dennis, 1956), Lehman's investigations (1953) show that adult creativity matures early, reaches its highest point in the thirties, and then gradually declines. Since no systematic criteria of creative output can be established for children, Torrance (1962a) examined changes in performance on divergent-thinking tests and found the following generalized curve: an increase in divergent-thinking abilities from ages 3 to 4½, a small drop upon entrance to kindergarten, a sharp decrement at about grade 4, and then, with variations by sex and certain subtests, except for a small decrement at grade 7, a steady growth through grade 11.

Noteworthy in this curve is that each decrement seems to occur at a period marking a transition from one to another of Sullivan's stages of interpersonal development (1953). To examine the possibility that distinctive American pressures may account for his data, Torrance (1962a) studied the developmental curves of children in grades 1–6 in Australia, Germany, India, and Samoa and those of segregated Negro children in the United States. Dissimilarities as well as similarities were found among the different cultures. The German and Australian curves were similar but leveled off earlier than in the United States. The pattern in India was much the same as the American pattern, although the level was lower. The curve for the American Negro children showed a continuity of development second only to that of the Samoan children, which had almost no breaks. Torrance suggested that the development of creativity may be related to continuities and discontinuities in the particular culture. But as elsewhere in this domain, there are opposing observations. Iscoe and Pierce-Jones (1964) did not find the indicated relation between ideational fluency and age for samples of lower-class Southern white and Negro children. Rather, fluency and originality scores seemed to be a function of specific test stimuli and the experiences of the respondents. Here again is the traits-methods problem mentioned earlier.

A number of studies have been directed toward the possible influence of early environmental factors on the development of creativity. Getzels and Jackson (1962) found that mothers of high-creative children less often than mothers of high-IQ children report worries about the dangers in the world, recollections of insecurity in their own childhood, admiration for conventional qualities in children, vigilance regarding their children's school performance, and restrictions on their children's independence. Drevdahl (1964), testing psychologists, and MacKinnon (1964), testing architects, also found that their more creative subjects were given more independence and responsibility during childhool than the average child. Drevdahl (1964), however, noted that the creative psychologists reported more than average family pressure for educational achievement.

PERSONAL CHARACTERISTICS. Comparisons of creative and noncreative individuals have produced both conflicting and highly consistent observations on a variety of affective and cognitive characteristics. Guilford and others (1957) found little relationship between performance on divergent thinking tests and personal interests or traits of temperament. But Torrance (1962b) surveyed a large number of studies and compiled 84 separate characteristics which discriminated between creative and noncreative subjects in one study or another. The separate items are often contradictory—e.g., "self-assertive," "timid and reserved"—and subsets of the list could describe almost any group.

More useful are *patterns* of characteristics which distinguish creative individuals with some consistency. Essentially the same pattern of values is reported for creative individuals in extremely diverse fields. Thus,

Taylor and Holland (1964) report that creative Air Force scientists placed a high value on thinking, manipulating ideas, and aesthetics. MacKinnon (1964) found that creative architects score high in theoretical and aesthetic values and low in economic values on the Study of Values; Getzels and Csikszentmihalyi (1964) found a similar pattern with the same instrument for art students. A number of studies converge also on a characteristic pattern of interpersonal relations. Drevdahl (1956, 1964) and R. B. Cattell (1963) found various creative groups low in extraversion, more concerned with ideas than with people, and rather uninterested in activities of a social nature; Taylor and Ellison (1964) report such related characteristics as self-sufficiency and low sociability for creative scientists; Getzels and Csikszentmihalyi (1964) provide similar data for art students. The portrait is not so much one of antipathy or even indifference to people but rather of greater interest in thought and beauty and of rejection of the pursuit of material goods and mere gregariousness or conventional sociability as barriers to self-expression, intimacy, and individuality.

Although terminologies of cognition are so varied that it is difficult to gauge the overlap in observations in different studies, a reasonably consistent pattern emerges here also. Barron (1963), for example, has repeatedly found that his creative subjects prefer complexity and some degree of apparent asymmetry in perceptual phenomena. Their judgment tends to be independent and highly resistant to group pressure. Torrance (1962b) found that children high in divergent thinking produce ideas that are "off the beaten track," and Getzels and Jackson (1962) found that such children tend to be "stimulus-free" rather than "stimulus-bound." Hudson (1966) reported that his "divergers" produced "rare themes" in drawings significantly more often than did "convergers." A striking and consistent finding in the three studies was the presence of *humor* in the associations and fantasy productions of the creative children, whether American or British. Perhaps as McClelland (1963) suggested, an important characteristic of the creative individual is a willingness to take risks. This seems to be manifested in freeing oneself from the given stimulus, juxtaposing irreconcilables to form surprising associations, seeing the wry and humorous aspects of what is real and earnest for others, and giving expression to ideas that are not consensual. Nonconformity may be a pervasive life style, for it appears not only in response to test items but also in such activities as the choice of a career (Getzels & Jackson, 1962). There has been a long and apparently irradicable tradition (e.g., Lombroso, 1891) that genius is "near to madness alike" and that the "quiz kid" is also a "queer kid." A number of studies with a variety of instruments and subjects show no relationship between measures of creativity and measures of anxiety or emotional disturbance (e.g., Feldhusen & others, 1965; Flescher, 1963; Ohnmacht, 1966).

EDUCATIONAL FACILITATION. Numerous strategies for teaching or at least liberating creative thinking have been proposed, usually, however, without accompanying evidence of effectiveness. Mearns (1958), for example, suggests that a teacher who would facilitate creativity not only must provide a permissive atmosphere and shun drill but also must manifestly reinforce original behavior at every opportunity. Osborn (1958) argues that his "brainstorming" strategy of requiring groups to produce large quantities of ideas under conditions which suspend criticism will develop creative thinking. Gordon (1961) proposes a strategy called synectics, which attempts to amalgamate disparate individual experiences in small groups to arrive at creative solutions through the use of metaphorical mechanisms. Soviet strategies (Danilov, 1962; Vorob'ev, 1963), though rather more convergent in character, attest to the widespread interest in developing creative abilities through training. But the question remains whether any of the proposals do in fact increase creativity.

The most widely studied of the strategies is brainstorming. Meadow and Parnes (1959) used creative problem-solving courses at the college level to show that experience in brainstorming generalizes to creative problem solving. Parnes and Meadow (1960, 1963) reported that subjects who had taken such a course produced significantly more good ideas than those who had not and that the effects of experience in brainstorming tended to persist. But these conclusions have not gone unchallenged. Taylor and others (1958) found that individuals working alone produced more and better ideas than those brainstorming in groups. Dunette and others (1963) obtained similar results but noted that group participation may be useful as a warm-up for individual brainstorming, a hypothesis confirmed by Lindgren and Lindgren (1965).

Maltzman (1960) is critical of brainstorming studies on methodological grounds; they do not control for the numerous variables which might account for the obtained effects. Accordingly, he and his colleagues carried out a series of carefully controlled laboratory experiments on the "training of originality." They found (Maltzman & others, 1958, 1960) that training in the production of responses low in an individual's response hierarchy increased originality of verbal associations and that the effect of such training tended to persist, at least under the given experimental conditions. But laboratory demonstrations are often not directly applicable to classroom practice, and research has increasingly turned to the school situation itself. Torrance (1961) found that pupils in the primary grades could be taught to use Osborn-type principles to enable them to produce more and better ideas. A surprising observation was that contrary to the experiments by Meadow and others (1959), instructions to produce a large number of ideas without regard to quality resulted in fewer responses than did instructions to produce interesting, clever, and unusual ideas. Thus, there seems to be no support for motivating pupils to produce a quantity of ideas without consideration of quality. Similarly, Guilford (1962) found that directions asking for "clever" titles decreased the number of low-quality but increased the number of high-quality responses over directions omitting the evaluative word *clever*. As Guilford points out, the effect of suspended judgment is not yet clear; immediate evaluation may be detrimental to creative production if there is any fear of being unconventional, but it may be beneficial if there is no such fear, and it encourages more efficient scanning of stored information.

An intriguing technique for stimulating originality in the classroom has been developed by Covington and Crutchfield (1965). They devised autoinstructional programs composed of detective- and mystery-story material, which they gave to fifth- and sixth-grade children. Subjects who used the programs markedly outperformed control subjects on criterion problem solving, creativity, and relevant attitude measures—findings which were replicated in a second study. Probably the most extensive work on classroom creativity may be found in the volume by Torrance (1965). Among the numerous observations is one that pupils permitted to practice without teacher evaluation were able to perform more creatively on subsequent occasions than were pupils who had practiced with teacher evaluation. However, although independent creative activities may at times lead to creative growth, the mere provision of such exercises does not guarantee such growth. The teacher's attitude toward spontaneity and originality has an important effect. Wodtke and Wallen (1965) report that a high degree of controlling behavior by teachers is detrimental to verbal creative performance.

CRITERIA AND MEASUREMENT. The critical issue underlying all work in the field of creativity is the criterion problem (Getzels & Csikszentmihalyi, 1964). What *is* an appropriate index of creativity? Among the most common criteria are the following:

 1. Achievement. An attempt is made to identify achievements which speak for themselves. At the adult level, for example, the Nobel prize or some other mark of outstanding accomplishment may be taken as an index that hardly anyone would dispute (e.g., Ghiselin, 1952).

 2. Ratings. It is assumed that a person who has had an opportunity to observe another person can provide a sound judgment of his inventiveness. Evaluation by peers, supervisors, and teachers has been used as a criterion (e.g., MacKinnon, 1964; Drevdahl, 1964).

 3. Intelligence. Performance on intelligence tests is the most widely used and best-validated index of mental functioning. Presumably creativity is a mental function, and a superior IQ may be used as a criterion (e.g., Terman, 1925).

 4. Personality. Characteristics of personality are evaluated in relation to an empirically derived or an a priori profile of the "creative personality," and the closeness of the fit is used as a criterion (e.g., R. Cattell & Drevdahl, 1955).

 5. Creativity-test scores. Although attempts to measure aspects of creativity through tests have a long history (see Taylor, 1964), the factor-analytical studies by Guilford inspired the great variety of so-called creativity tests not only in his terms but in related principles as well. Thus, among the many tests are Mednick's Remote Associates Test (Mednick & Mednick, 1964), built on associative theory; Flanagan's Ingenious Solutions to Problems Test (Flanagan, 1958), one of the few attempts at assessing creative thinking through multiple-choice items; and the AC Test of Creative Ability (Buhl, 1960), directed especially at problems of engineering. There are numerous other tests, including such older indexes as the interpretation of inkblots, block construction, and drawing tests. Perhaps the most extensive set of materials for use at all educational levels is the Minnesota Tests of Creative Thinking (Torrance, 1965), for which Yamamoto (1964a) has provided a scoring manual.

At the core of these as of most recent instruments is Guilford's conceptualization of creative thinking and his battery of tests, which include the following factors: sensitivity to problems, flexibility, fluency, originality, elaboration, and redefinition. Guilford's own instruments grew systematically from his structure-of-intellect model (1956), in which five operation categories intersect with four content categories, which in turn intersect with six product categories resulting in 120 intellectual-ability cells. The domain of divergent production contains those intellectual abilities considered most directly related to creativity, although cells in the other areas are also relevant. Of the 24 potential divergent-thinking cells, 16 have been demonstrated in adult and ninth-grade populations and 6 at the sixth-grade level; the others are still being investigated (Guilford, 1966). Among the more commonly used of the divergent-thinking measures are *ideational fluency,* stressing the quantity of ideas produced; *associational fluency,* requiring the production of synonyms for words; *expressional fluency,* asking for the construction of sentences using words beginning with given letters; *alternate uses,* measuring flexibility of thinking by requiring the transformation of concepts with respect to a given stimulus object; *consequences,* measuring originality by asking for possible consequences of new situations, "remote" responses providing a score in originality (Guilford & Merrifield, 1960).

Systematic educational research in creativity is a relatively new field of endeavor. The problems are as complex, the concepts as uncertain, and the results often as conflicting as the subject is enticing and vital. Whether it is about the relation between creativity and intelligence, about that between divergent thinking and creative achievement, about the threshold hypothesis, or about the possibility of facilitating creativity in the classroom, there seem to be almost as many points of view as there are studies. Among the many difficulties is the shifting nature of the criterion. Although IQ tests possess reasonable generality, measures of creativity as yet do not. Instruments, all labeled measures of creativity, are not interchangeable, and cutoff points even with single instruments are frequently referable only to the particular sample under study. Work on the facilitation of creativity through education is just now getting under way, and the criterion is often no more than pre- and postperformance on divergent-thinking tests. With rare exceptions, replications are nonexistent. But the complexity of the problem and the present uncertainty of concepts and conflict of results should occasion more rigorous and varied investigation rather than the foreclosing of inquiry through single-minded espousal of one's own view. What Allport (1955) said in another circumstance is eminently applicable to research in creativity: "Our [strongest] censure should be reserved for those who close all doors but one. The surest way to lose truth is to pretend that one already wholly possesses it."

Jack Getzels
The University of Chicago
George F. Madaus
The University of Chicago

References

Allport, Gordon. *Becoming.* Yale U Press, 1955. 106p.
Anderson, J. E. "The Nature of Abilities." In Torrance, E. P. (Ed.) *Education and Talent.* U Minnesota Press, 1960. p. 9–31.
Berlyne, D. E. "Curiosity and Exploration." *Sci* 153: 25–33; 1966.
Barron, Frank X. *Creativity and Psychological Health: Origins of Personal Vitality and Creative Freedom.* Van Nostrand, 1963. 292p.
Buhl, Harold R. *Creative Engineering Design.* Iowa State U Press, 1960. 195p.
Burt, C. "The Psychology of Creative Ability." *Br J Ed Psychol* 32:292–8; 1962.
Campbell, D. T., and Fiske, D. W. "Convergent and Discriminant Validation by the Multitrait-Multimethod Matrix." *Psychol B* 56:81–105; 1959.
Cattell, J. "Families of American Men of Science." *Popular Sci Mon* 86:504–15; 1915.
Cattell, R. B. "The Personality and Motivation of the Researcher from Measurements of Contemporaries and from Biography." In Taylor, C. W., and Barron, Frank X. (Eds.) *Scientific Creativity: Its Recognition and Development.* Wiley, 1963. p. 119–31.
Cattell, R. B., and Drevdahl, J. E. "A Comparison of the Personality Profile (16 P.F.) of Eminent Researchers with that of Eminent Teachers and Administrators, and of the General Population." *Br J Psychol* 46:248–61; 1955.
Cicirelli, V. G. "Form of the Relationship between Creativity, IQ, and Academic Achievement." *J Ed Psychol* 56:303–8; 1965.
Covington, M. V., and Crutchfield, R. S. "Facilitation of Creative Problem Solving." *Programed Instruction* 4:3–5, 10; 1965.
Danilov, M. A. "Cultivating Independence and Creative Activity in School Children." *Soviet Ed* 4:38–45; 1962.
Dearborn, G. V. "A Study of Imaginations." *Am J Psychol* 9:183–90; 1898.
Dennis, W. "Age and Achievement: A Critique." *J Geront* 11:331–3; 1956.
Dewey, John. *How We Think.* Heath, 1910. 224p.
Drevdahl, J. E. "Factors of Importance for Creativity." *J Clin Psychol* 12:21–6; 1956.
Drevdahl, J. E. "Some Developmental and Environmental Factors in Creativity." In Taylor, C. W. (Ed.) *Widening Horizons in Creativity.* Wiley, 1964. p. 170–85.
Dunnette, M. D., and others. "The Effect of Group Participation on Brainstorming Effectiveness for Two Industrial Samples." *J Applied Psychol* 47: 30–7; 1963.
Feldhusen, J. F., and others. "Anxiety, Divergent Thinking, and Achievement." *J Ed Psychol* 56: 40–5; 1965.
Flanagan, J. C. "Definition and Measurement of Ingenuity." In Taylor, C. W. (Ed.) *The Second (1957) University of Utah Research Conference on the Identification of Creative Scientific Talent.* U Utah Press, 1958. p. 109–18.
Flescher, I. "Anxiety and Achievement of Intellectually and Creatively Gifted Children." *J Psychol* 56:251–68; 1963.
Freud, Sigmund. "The Unconscious." In Jones, Ernest. (Ed.) *Collected Papers,* Vol. 4. Hogarth Press, 1949. p. 98–136.
Galton, Francis. *Hereditary Genius: An Inquiry into Its Laws and Consequences.* Macmillan, 1869. 390p.
Getzels, Jacob W. "Creative Thinking, Problem-solving, and Instruction." In Hilgard, E. R. (Ed.) *Theories of Learning and Instruction,* 63rd Yearbook, NSSE. U Chicago Press, 1964. p. 240–67.
Getzels, Jacob W., and Csikszentmihalyi, M. *Creative Thinking in Art Students: An Exploratory Study.* Cooperative Research Project No. E008. U Chicago, 1964. 202p.
Getzels, Jacob W., and Jackson, P. W. "The Creative Adolescent: A Summary of Some Research Findings." In Taylor, C. W. (Ed.) *The Third (1959) University of Utah Research Conference on the Identification of Creative Scientific Talent.* U Utah Press, 1959. p. 46–57.
Getzels, Jacob W., and Jackson, Philip W. *Creativity and Intelligence: Explorations with Gifted Students.* Wiley, 1962. 293p.
Ghiselin, Brewster. (Ed.) *The Creative Process.* New American Library, 1952. 293p.
Gordon, William J. J. *Synectics: The Development of Creative Capacity.* Harper, 1961. 180p.
Guilford, J. P. "Creativity." *Am Psychologist* 5:444–54; 1950.
Guilford, J. P. "Structure of Intellect." *Psychol B* 53:267–93; 1956.
Guilford, J. P. "Traits of Creativity." In Anderson, H. H. (Ed.) *Creativity and Its Cultivation: Interdisciplinary Symposia on Creativity.* Harper, 1959. p. 142–61.
Guilford, J. P. "Factors That Aid and Hinder Creativity." *Teach Col Rec* 63:380–92; 1962.
Guilford, J. P. "Intelligence: 1965 Model." *Am Psychologist* 21:20–6; 1966.
Guilford, J. P., and Merrifield, P. R. "The Structure of Intellect Model: Its Uses and Implications." In

Reports from the Psychological Laboratory, No. 24. U Southern California, 1960.

Guilford, J. P., and others. "The Relations of Creative-thinking Aptitudes to Non-aptitude Personality Traits." In *Reports from the Psychological Laboratory,* No. 20. U Southern California, 1957.

Hadamard, J. *An Essay on the Psychology of Invention in the Mathematical Field.* Dover, 1954. 145p.

Holland, J. L. "Some Limitations of Teachers Ratings as Predicators of Creativity." *J Ed Psychol* 50:219–23; 1959.

Hudson, Liam. *Contrary Imaginations: A Psychological Study of the English Schoolboy.* Methuen, 1966. 181p.

Hunt, J. "Experience and the Development of Motivation: Some Reinterpretations." *Child Develop* 31:489–504; 1960.

Iscoe, I., and Pierce-Jones, J. "Divergent Thinking, Age, and Intelligence in White and Negro Children." *Child Develop* 35:785–97; 1964.

Klausmeier, H. J., and others. "Relationships Between Divergent Thinking Abilities and Teacher Ratings of High School Students." *J Ed Psychol* 53:72–5; 1962.

Kris, Ernst. *Psychoanalytic Explorations in Art.* Int U, 1962. 358p.

Kubie, Lawrence S. *Neurotic Distortion of the Creative Process.* U Kansas Press, 1958. 151p.

Lehman, Harvey Christian. *Age and Achievement.* Princeton U Press, 1953. 358p.

Lindgren, H. C., and Lindgren, F. "Brainstorming and Orneriness as Facilitators of Creativity." *Psychol Reports* 16:577–83; 1965.

Lombroso, Cesare. *The Man of Genius.* William R. Scott, Inc., 1891.

MacKinnon, D. W. "The Nature and Nurture of Creative Talent." *Am Psychol* 17:484–95; 1962.

MacKinnon, D. W. "The Creativity of Architects." In Taylor, C. W. (Ed.) *Widening Horizons in Creativity.* Wiley, 1964. p. 359–78.

Maltzman, I. "On the Training of Originality." *Psychol R* 67:229–42; 1960.

Maltzman, I., and others. "A Procedure for Increasing Word Association Originality and Its Transfer Effects." *J Exp Psychol* 56:392–8; 1958.

Maltzman, I., and others. "Experimental Studies in the Training of Originality." *Psychol Monogr* 74:1–23; 1960.

Maslow, A. H. "The Creative Attitude." *The Structurist* 3:4–10; 1963.

McClelland, D. C. "The Calculated Risk: An Aspect of Scientific Performance." In Taylor, C. W. and Barron, Frank X. (Eds.) *Scientific Creativity: Its Recognition and Development.* Wiley, 1963. p. 184–92.

McCloy, W., and Meier, N. C. "Re-creative Imagination." *Psychol Monogr* 51:108–16; 1939.

Meadow, A., and Parnes, S. J. "Evaluation of Training in Creative Problem Solving." *J Applied Psychol* 43:189–94; 1959.

Meadow, A., and others. "Influence of Brainstorming Instructions and Problem Sequence on A Creative Problem Solving Test." *J Applied Psychol* 43:413–16; 1959.

Mearns, Hughes. *Creative Power: The Education of Youth in the Creative Arts,* 2nd rev. ed. Dover, 1958. 272p.

Mednick, S. A., and Mednick, M. T. "An Associative Interpretation of the Creative Process." In Taylor, C. W. (Ed.) *Widening Horizons in Creativity.* Wiley, 1964. p. 54–68.

Newell, A., and others. "The Process of Creative Thinking." In Gruber, H. E., and others. (Eds.) *Contemporary Approaches to Creative Thinking.* Atherton Press, 1962. p. 63–119.

Ohnmacht, F. W. "Achievement, Anxiety, and Creative Thinking." *Am Ed Res J* 3:131–8; 1966.

Osborn, Alexander F. *Applied Imagination: Principles and Procedures of Creative Thinking.* Scribner, 1958. 317p.

Palm, H. J. *An Analysis of Test-score Differences Between Highly Creative and High Miller Analogies Members of the Summer Guidance Institute.* Bureau of Educational Research, U Minnesota, 1959.

Parnes, S. J., and Meadow, A. "Evaluation of Persistence of Effects Produced by a Creative Problem Solving Course." *Psychol Reports* 7:357–61; 1960.

Parnes, S. J., and Meadow, A. "Development of Individual Creative Talent." In Taylor, C. W., and Barron, Frank X. (Eds.) *Scientific Creativity: Its Recognition and Development.* Wiley, 1963. p. 311–20.

Richards, J. M., Jr., and others. "Creativity Tests and Teacher and Self Judgments of Originality." *J Exp Ed* 32:281–5; 1964.

Roe, Anne. "A Psychological Study of Eminent Psychologists and Anthropologists and a Comparison with Biological and Physical Scientists." *Psychol Monogr* 67:1–55; 1953.

Sullivan, Harry Stack. *Interpersonal Theory of Psychiatry.* Norton, 1953. 393p.

Taylor, C. W. (Ed.) *Creativity: Progress and Potential.* McGraw-Hill, 1964. 241p.

Taylor, C. W., and Ellison, R. L. "Predicating Creative Performances from Multiple Measures." In Taylor, C. W. (Ed.) *Widening Horizons in Creativity.* Wiley, 1964. p. 227–60.

Taylor, C. W., and Holland, J. L. "Development and Application of Tests of Creativity." *R Ed Res* 32:91–102; 1962.

Taylor, C. W., and Holland, J. "Predicators of Creative Performance." In Taylor, C. W. (Ed.) *Creativity: Progress and Potential.* McGraw-Hill, 1964. p. 16–48.

Taylor, D. W., and others. "Does Group Participation when Using Brainstorming Facilitate or Inhibit Creative Thinking?" *Adm Sci Q* 3:23–47; 1958.

Terman, Lewis M. *Mental and Physical Traits of a Thousand Gifted Children.* Stanford U Press, 1925. 648p.

Thorndike, Edward L. *Human Learning.* Century, 1931. 206p.

Thorndike, R. L. "Some Methodological Issues in the Study of Creativity." In Gardner, E. F. (Ed.)

Proceedings of the 1962 Invitational Conference on Testing Problems. ETS, 1963. p. 40–54.

Thurstone, L. L., and Thurstone, T. G. *Factorial Studies of Intelligence.* U Chicago Press, 1941. 94p.

Torrance, E. P. *Educational Achievement of the Highly Intelligent and the Highly Creative: Eight Partial Replications of the Getzels-Jackson Study.* Bureau of Educational Research, U Minnesota, 1960.

Torrance, E. P. "Priming Creative Thinking in the Primary Grades." *El Sch J* 62:34–41; 1961.

Torrance, E. P. "Cultural Discontinuities and the Development of Originality of Thinking." *Excep Children* 29:2–13; 1962(*a*).

Torrance, E. P. *Guiding Creative Talent.* Prentice-Hall, 1962(*b*). 278p.

Torrance, E. P. *Rewarding Creative Behavior: Experiments in Classroom Creativity.* Prentice-Hall, 1965. 353p.

Vorob'ev, G. "Developing Independence and Creativity in Students." *Soviet Ed* 5:41–8; 1963.

Wallach, M., and Kogan, N. *Modes of Thinking in Young Children.* Holt, 1965. 357p.

Wertheimer, Max. *Productive Thinking.* Harper, 1945. 224p.

White, R. W. "Motivation Reconsidered: The Concept of Competence." *Psychol R* 66:297–333; 1959.

Wodtke, K. H., and Wallen, N. E. "The Effects of Teacher Control in the Classroom on Pupils' Creativity Test Gains." *Am Ed Res J* 2:75–82; 1965.

Yamamoto, K. *Experimental Scoring Manuals for Minnesota Tests of Creative Thinking and Writing.* Bureau of Educational Research, Kent State U, 1964(*a*).

Yamamoto, K. "Role of Creative Thinking and Intelligence in High School Achievement." *Psychol Reports* 14:783–9; 1964(*b*).

Yamamoto, K. "Threshold of Intelligence in Academic Achievement of Highly Creative Students." *J Exp Ed* 32:401–5; 1964(*c*).

Yamamoto, K. "Effects of Restriction of Range and Test Unreliability on Correlation Between Measures of Intelligence and Creative Thinking." *Br J Ed Psychol* 35:300–5; 1965(*a*).

Yamamoto, K. "Multiple Achievement Battery and Repeated Measurements: A Postscript to Three Studies on Creative Thinking." *Psychol Reports* 16:367–75; 1965(*b*).

CURRICULUM

The curriculum field came to life as a self-conscious area of speculation and inquiry early in the 1920's. It proceeded to evolve and subdivide itself in an orderly way, as earlier editions of this encyclopedia indicate, for forty years. By 1955 it seemed clear that the curriculum consisted of the experiences carried on in school under the guidance of the school officials, that the principal problems had to do with the statement of clear-cut, behavioral objectives, the integration of experience, and the question of social relevance and that the gap between the understandings and beliefs of the curriculum leaders and the practitioners was narrowing at a satisfactory rate.

None of this was true by the mid-1960's. After 1955 the entire field came under such fundamental questioning that the discourse became scattered, old questions were being asked as if they had not been thought of before, and the process of curriculum development had been largely restructured.

DEFINITION. The term "curriculum" had been defined as "all the experiences a learner has under the guidance of the school" since the late 1930's. It was so defined in the last edition of this encyclopedia (Kearney & Cook, 1960). This definition had stood unchallenged for a generation, but Scheffler (1960), representative of the postwar analytic philosophers, subjected it to an analysis that indicated its severe limitations. He pointed out that the definition of the curriculum as activities is "programmatic," intended to "extend the school's responsibility, hitherto limited to its so-called formal course of study, in such a way as to embrace the individual social and psychological development of its pupils" (p. 24). Programmatic definitions exhort. They are intended to prescribe and direct practice by emphasizing particular elements of the whole, in this case activities, needs, experiences. In other cases (e.g., "the curriculum is the program of school subjects") they emphasize subject matter, or disciplines. Such definitions tie the term to particular value referents which reflect, rather than state, the theoretical position taken by those offering them. While such statements have usefulness as exhortation to better practice, they are not useful for descriptive or explicative purposes. They do not invite inquiry; they may well block it. As Goodlad (1960) points out, they do not appear to have made a difference in the types of questions asked or the problems dealt with in the curriculum field. That is, the questions asked concerning the curriculum did not change in thrust or content after 1938.

The question of definition, once having been raised, continued to be examined. To be useful for explicative and descriptive purposes, a term must be defined operationally. Brodbeck (1963) discussed the properties of operational definitions. Such definitions usually contain nominal terms (words for observable characteristics) and dispositional concepts (conditions under which the characteristics occur). Such operational definitions can be accepted only after an adequate evaluation of the consequences of the relationships and conditions specified in the definitions. Komisar and McClellan (1961) pointed out that programmatic terms serve as "slogan systems," which are needed to facilitate educational discourse, especially between theoreticians and practitioners. Of course, slogans, even though useful in intent and origin, do run the risk of being taken literally by the practitioner, and even by some theorists and critics (Scheffler, 1960). Dewey's "learning through experience" was both vulgarized and popularized. Even when slogans have been taken from formal theoretical statements, they often divert attention from major curriculum problems, such as the interrelationship of knowledge and meaning, or the teaching problem of distinguishing between fact and value. They have, upon occasion, led to useless dichotomizing: "needs, not interests," "children, not subject matter," and the like (Caswell & Foshay, 1957, Ch. 1).

This discussion of the definition of the term served to signal a change in the kind of discourse characteristic of the field. In retrospect, it would appear that the old definition served the educational needs of the 1930's by calling attention to the responsibilities of the educators. However, it did not continue to serve the purposes of curriculum theory and design during the 1960's. As a definition, it is too gross for such purposes; the necessary specification of elements and relationships among elements is left to be done. Macdonald (1965) attempted to provide a framework for identifying elements of educational practice and a way of dealing with relationships among elements by applying systems analysis to the question. The curriculum is defined as the system of "planned actions for instruction," and instruction as "the system for putting the plan into action." He then named the components of each system. This separation of curriculum from instruction, and the emphasis on what is planned, makes distinctions not offered in the earlier statements. While Macdonald's definition is not operational, it seeks to avoid being programmatic in that it asserts no particular value. It is neutral. Moreover, it seeks to leave what is accidentally instructive about school—the "unintended curriculum," or what was called in the 1920's "concomitant learning"—to be dealt with in other terms.

CURRICULUM THEORY. Discussions of the definition of "curriculum," except for Scheffler's, have usually been undertaken in the context of attempts to build a theory of the curriculum. A renewed interest in curriculum theory grew out of the curriculum reforms and extension of research activity of the late 1950's (Taba, 1962; Macdonald, 1963; Bruner, 1963). Much of this literature, however, discusses what a theory would be about, rather than actually attempting to state comprehensive curriculum theories (Herrick & Tyler, 1950; Beauchamp, 1961; Maccia and others, 1963). This lack of actual theory construction has been attributed to a preoccupation with traditional orientations: means and ends; applications of theory from other fields; a concern with theory-making itself; and a preoccupation with language in the Oxford manner (Wann, 1966).

Theory Models. Several attempts at making theory models have been made. At this writing none of them had been tested empirically. The approach through models has been most actively advocated by Maccia and others (1963). The virtue of this approach, they say, is that it is "value-open," since models taken from scientific disciplines, rather than from philosophical positions, are necessarily free of prior values. This is true—or at least true enough—but it does not carry the discussion beyond Scheffler's opening point. To be useful, as both Maccia (1963) and Griffiths (1964) point out, a model must enable one to ask questions and offer clues as to how the questions may be answered. Just as Maccia borrowed models from mathematics (specifically, from graph theory, systems theory, and information theory), Griffiths borrowed from the model of a physical system.

Hughes (1962) attempted to apply decision theory to a curriculum plan by listing actions, outcomes for each action, the probability associated with each outcome, and the desirability of each outcome.

All of these attempts at model building take the same risks: (1) the original models are based on different sets of data—they do not deal with the domain of education, and in the application the goodness of fit may be imprecise; (2) the use of models powerful in one discipline, such as mathematics, may lead to a false assumption about their power in other fields; (3) a model frequently sets up a conceptual system that makes it difficult to entertain counterinstances. The model, being reified, can no longer be used as an analogical tool.

An attempt at building a model that does not suffer from these limitations has been made by Ginther (1965), who proposes a three-dimensional structure. The first dimension he calls programming, extending from errorless programs such as those in the earliest form of programmed instruction, to the "dialectical" pole, in which the student is to manifest ignorance, make errors, etc. The second dimension represents the various mental processes, from simple recall of information to the synthesizing of information to solve new problems, or the making of valid inferences from the material at hand. Ginther's third dimension represents the activity of the student, from covert to overt.

One of the difficulties with the attempts at model building so far is that while the models deal with instruction, they do not purport to deal with what shall be taught. When a comprehensive curriculum theory is built, it will have to take into account not only the learning methods and teaching methods ("strategies of instruction" and the like) but also the nature of the knowledge to be learned, the nature of the student who would learn it, and the nature of the societal responsibility shared by teacher and student. For if education is a moral affair before it is a technical affair, then the grounds for moral behavior have to be incorporated in one's theory of educational action.

A comprehensive theory may not be appropriate for some time. More productive directions may be found in devising quasi constructs and maintaining close contact with empirical work. Elliott and Foshay (1963) proposed that education be considered as still in the natural-history stage of its development as a field of knowledge. Beauchamp (1961) suggested that it is more appropriate now to construct subtheories, which can later be revised for the development of more comprehensive theories, than it is to attempt general theories. Tanner (1966) thinks that the curriculum field is too complex to permit one either to propose or to verify hypotheses.

Curriculum Design. Although "curriculum theory" and "curriculum design" are sometimes used interchangeably, the term "design" usually refers to the basic organization and plan for action for developing the scope and sequence of subject matter. Designs as proposed may reflect a theoretical position, but frequently they are based on a single unitary principle—e.g., the structure of the disciplines taken separately, or the nature of society, or the needs and interests of students, taken as clues to the various stages of human development, or the learning process itself. Despite repeated warnings against such single-focus designs, they continue to be offered. Taba (1962) pointed out once more that such designs tend to emphasize one element at the expense of others of equal importance.

The most recent single principle to be advocated as a basis for curriculum design is the "structure of the disciplines" (Bruner, 1966). Several statements calling for a discipline-centered curriculum have been made by others. Foshay (1962) wanted the disciplines, taken as modes of inquiry, to be central (though not alone) in the choice and treatment of subject matter. Phenix (1962) thought that subject matter outside of the framework of a discipline could not, in the last analysis, be either learned or taught in a way that yielded generative knowledge. Similar statements were made by the National Education Association (1963), Ford and Pugno (1964), and King and Brownell (1966), among others. None of these statements sets forth a comprehensive curriculum design, however. They call attention to the general usefulness of structure within a discipline as an organizing principle.

The emphasis on the disciplines is interpreted by a number of curriculum theorists as running counter to the requirement that any curriculum be considered as a whole. The "broad fields" approach of the 1930's has been revived and the discussion carried forward, notably by Bellack (1964), who considered that groupings of knowledge using similar modes of thought and language might offer a curriculum design. A similar approach is offered by Phenix (1964) and by Broudy and others (1964). The "unit of activity" or "unit of work" of the 1930's has been brought forward in new terms by Maccia (1964) and Goodlad (1964), among others; they consider this organizing idea helpful, if deepened by the application of Piaget's notions of intellectual development, which were revived and extended during the early 1960's.

Much of the curriculum reform during the 1950's and 1960's originated in college departments which sought to improve secondary-school offerings. This "top down" approach has been challenged by Taba (1962) and Goodlad (1964), among others, who would build the curriculum up from the elementary grades. They point out that every change at the secondary level presumes some state of affairs at the elementary level and that the hazard of discontinuity is always present. The problem of articulation among school levels, long recognized as the product of the gross organization of schools, could well be exacerbated by the current "top down" flow of curriculum innovation.

Procedures for Curriculum Change. It is necessary to distinguish between actual change in what is taught in school and proposals for change. Some proposals have resulted in substantial change; many have resulted only in discussion, not in change. The American educational climate is like many other aspects of the American mental climate in that it seems to value what is new because it is new; there are many examples of proposed changes in school systems intended primarily to attract a good press.

Historically, the most effective proposals for curriculum change have been made by national commissions. The best-remembered early commission was, of course, the Committee of Ten (National Education Association, 1893), a gathering of highly influential members of the intellectual elite of the time. The Commission on Economy of Time (National Society for the Study of Education, 1915) of the 1910's, together with the commission on secondary education (National Education Association, 1918) provoked the broadening of the secondary curriculum that, according to Cremin and Borrowman (1956), set the pattern for the principal educational debates ever since. The statements of the Educational Policies Commission (1937, 1944, 1948) on the elementary and secondary schools were highly influential. James B. Conant's books on the high school, the junior high school, and on teacher education in effect continue this tradition, since Conant's statements owe much of their influence to his peerless position in American life.

The response of the schools to highly placed authorities is in keeping with the basic organization of the school, as well as with its tradition. The schools are organized hierarchically; the basic point of entry for new ideas is the local school superintendent, who is more or less responsive to the local board of education. Since the local school system is a political unit, it is not surprising that the local superintendent uses overwhelming external authority to justify the introduction of new programs whenever he can. The alternative, for him, is to set in motion the exceedingly difficult process of local discussion, leading to local invention and consensus on what should be taught—a process as likely as not to lead to mistaken, overparochial decisions.

In any case, the function of the schools at the national level is to inculcate and deepen the ideals of American civilization; it is not surprising that local school officials turn to the most prominent exemplars of the tradition for authority. These exemplars have been, as often as not, members of the various national commissions.

The commissions have had yet another effect on the tradition of curriculum change strategies. Especially during the years after 1957, one manifesto or pronunciamento has followed another. These statements, usually shrill and tendentious, have effectively confused the process of change so that for a period of time—from 1958 until approximately 1963—much of it was random. The entry of the mass media into education effectively jarred the educational establishment, but the treatment of education on television and in the daily press was so reductionist and sensational that the effect was shock, and little more.

Several strategies for curriculum change have evolved since the formation of the commissions. During the 1920's massive curriculum development was undertaken within school systems by means of committees, which wrote courses of study, distributed them for criticism within the system, and adopted the revised versions that resulted. During the 1940's, it having been found that the courses of study had relatively little effect on teaching, a "democratic" approach was developed.

Between 1932 and 1940, during the Eight-year Study of the Progressive Education Association (1937), the workshop as a device for curriculum change had appeared. Being democratic was the watchword during that period, and an approach to curriculum development that involved the teachers directly in the change process matched the ideology of the times. The democratic approach has been described in a number of publications, several of them influential during the 1940's and 1950's (e.g., Miel, 1946; Wiles, 1950, 1956). The cooperative action research movement, which asked that teachers, with appropriate help, conduct small experiments and in other ways base their teaching decisions on data they themselves gathered, was an outgrowth of this same movement (Corey, 1953; Association for Supervision and Curriculum Development, 1957). Caswell, who had been a prime mover in the development of this approach, and who had himself seen the shortcomings of the approach through committees and commissions, collected a number of examples of the democratic approach in a book of the early 1950's (Caswell & others, 1950; McNally & others, 1960).

Another approach to bringing about change in schools may be called the "political" approach. It is described by Mackenzie in several places (see Miles, 1964, Ch. 17, for an example). It was strongly implied by Campbell and Ramseyer (1955), who describe how the prevailing opinion in a small community may be appraised through its emergent opinion makers. In general, the political approach considers a public school as a political entity and indicates the importance of assaying the political forces relevant to a proposed educational change in such a way as to make it likely that the change will be consonant with what is politically possible. Mackenzie points out that recent curriculum changes have tended to come from outside the educational system, rather than from within it, as was expected according to the democratic approach.

Since 1960 the question of procedures has begun to receive formal attention from social scientists. In a crucial book, Miles (1964) brings together a number of cases of educational change, several of them abortive, and indicates the state of theory in the field in chapters by himself, Griffiths, Fox and Lippitt, Eicholz and Rogers, Mort, Carlson, Kendall, and Barton and Wilder. Miles offers a way of thinking about curriculum change that is fresh to the literature. He considers a number of changes since the 1920's and theorizes that those that have caught on have been characterized by what he calls a "comprehensive strategy," by which he means a strategy that specifically includes provisions for careful design of the innovation, the development of local awareness and interest, local evaluation, and local trial. While the theory has not yet been tested empirically, it seems to offer some leads. The core curriculum, for example, was never widely used in the secondary schools, perhaps because it was not carefully designed, and provisions for local evaluation were inadequate, including the preparation of teachers for the program. The Physical Sciences Study Committee program in physics has been widely adopted, perhaps because it was designed with extraordinary care, local interest was aroused through the mass media, and provisions were made to train teachers and to assist somewhat with local trials. Where the program was abandoned, as it has been in some school systems, one may speculate that the program's failure to deal thoroughly with the problems of local evaluation may be at fault. The new mathematics programs are coming under increased criticism, perhaps for similar reasons. The Council for Basic Education publications, which have generally taken the form of scornful exposés of the inadequacies of the public schools, have produced very little actual change. Miles's theory would suggest that this arises from the council's concentration on the arousing of local awareness and interest, in the absence of clear designs or any of the other elements in his comprehensive strategy. Predictably, in the circumstances, much local anxiety would be created, and some heads would roll, but there would be no change, none having been proposed.

It is conceivable that procedures for curriculum change in the immediate future will take advantage of the attempts made during the past seventy years or more, though realism requires us to notice that they have not in the past and do not at present. National commissions continue to issue pronouncements. School-system curriculum committees continue to write courses of study, submit them for criticism, and adopt them. Workshops continue. Action research, never widely practiced in the United States, has nevertheless spread to India. The "democratic" approach is the most widespread approach to curriculum development at the local level. Since all of these approaches have demonstrated what they can do, it is possible that coupled with Miles's comprehensive strategy they can be employed in a less doctrinaire fashion than formerly, and curriculum development may yet become a rational affair.

The curriculum itself, which this article began by refusing to define, may perhaps be thought of in the light of this discussion as the operational statement of the school's goals. It is evident that it is the operational consequence of the school's goals, whatever they are and however clearly or inadequately they are expressed. Since the goals of a school system are themselves the consequence of the interaction of the cultural and political traditions in a given place, tempered by the educational and political beliefs and perceptions of the people, it should not be surprising that the operations of the school, and especially the offering of subject matter for learning, are responsive to gross social changes when they occur. During the nineteenth century, the subject matter was chauvinistic, the country being then in the process of discovering itself as a nation. With the expanding economy of the first thirty years of the present century, the curriculum became "useful." During the great depression, it became "socially conscious." During the 1950's it became an instrument of national defense. During the 1960's, when the United States is clearly a superpower, the curriculum responds through attempts to deepen and strengthen its intellectual, social, and moral meaningfulness.

At the same time, there is an obvious changing of the guard. It became evident to a number of educationists during the 1950's that the schools were still attempting to operate on the ideology of the 1930's, and the most influential educational leaders were those who had come to maturity during that period. During the 1960's a new group of younger people has appeared who feel no loyalty to the struggles of the 1930's who are willing to beg many of the questions of that period, and who sometimes angrily are taking control of the discussion. The 1960 edition of this encyclopedia reflects the thinking of the 1930's as it was being carried on during the 1950's. The present edition reflects the very rapid transition that is under way.

Arthur W. Foshay
Teachers College–Columbia University
Lois A. Beilin
Teachers College–Columbia University

References

Association for Supervision and Curriculum Development. *Research for Curriculum Improvement*. 1957 Yearbook. ASCD, 1957. 350p.

Beauchamp, George A. *Curriculum Theory*. Kagg Press, 1961. 149p.

Bellack, Arno. "Knowledge Structure and the Curriculum." In Elam, Stanley. (Ed.) *Education and the Structure of Knowledge*. Rand McNally, 1964. p. 263–7.

Brodbeck, May. "Logic and Scientific Method in Research on Teaching." In American Educational Research Association. *Handbook of Research on Teaching*. AERA, 1963. p. 44–93.

Broudy, Harry S., and others. *Democracy and Excellence in Secondary Education*. Rand McNally, 1964. 302p.

Bruner, Jerome S. "Needed: A Theory of Instruction." *Ed Leadership* 20:523–32; 1963.

Bruner, Jerome S. *Toward A Theory of Instruction*. Harvard U Press, 1966. 176p.

Campbell, Roald F. and Ramseyer, John A. *The Dynamics of School-Community Relationships*. Allyn and Bacon, 1955. 205p.

Caswell, Hollis L., and Foshay, A. W. *Education in the Elementary School*. American, 1957. 430p.

Caswell, Hollis L., and others. *Curriculum Improvement in Public School Systems*. Teachers Col, Columbia U, 1950. 462p.

Corey, Stephen. *Action Research to Improve School Practices*. Teachers Col, Columbia U, 1953. 161p.

Cremin, Lawrence A., and Borrowman, Merle L. *Public Schools in Our Democracy*. Macmillan, 1956. 226p.

Educational Policies Commission. *The Unique Function of Education in American Democracy*. NEA. 1937. 129p.

Educational Policies Commission. *Education for All American Youth*. NEA, 1944. 421p.

Educational Policies Commission. *Education for All American Children*. NEA, 1948. 292p.

Elliott, David, and Foshay, Arthur W. "Chart or Charter: Recent Developments in Educational Discourse." *R Ed Res* 33:223–4; 1963.

Ford, G. W., and Pugno, Lawrence. (Eds.) *The Structure of Knowledge and the Curriculum*. Rand McNally, 1964. 105p.

Foshay, Arthur W. "Discipline-centered Curriculum." In Passow, A. Harry (Ed.) *Curriculum Crossroads*. Teachers Col, Columbia U, 1962. p. 66–74.

Ginther, John R. "A Conceptual Model for Analyzing Instruction." In Lysaught, Jerome P. (Ed.) *Programmed Instruction in Medical Education*. U. Rochester Press, 1965. p. 43–54.

Goodlad, John. "Curriculum: The State of the Field." *R Ed Res* 30:185–98; 1960.

Goodlad, John. *School Curriculum Reform in the United States*. Fund for the Advancement of Education, 1964. 95p.

Griffiths, Daniel E. "Administrative Theory and Change in Organizations." In Miles, Matthew B. (Ed.) *Innovation in Education*. Teachers Col, Columbia U, 1964. p. 425–36.

Herrick, Virgil, and Tyler, Ralph. (Eds.) *Toward Improved Curriculum Theory*. U Chicago Press, 1950. 124p.

Hughes, P. "Decisions and Curriculum Design." *Ed Theory* 12:187–92; 1962.

Kearney, Nolan C., and Cook, Walter W. "Curriculum." In Harris, Chester W. (Ed.) *Encyclopedia of Educational Research*, 3d ed. Macmillan, 1960. p. 358–65.

King, Arthur R., and Brownell, John A. *The Curriculum and the Disciplines of Knowledge*. Wiley, 1966. 221p.

Komisar, B. Paul, and McClellan, James E. "The Logic of Slogans." In Smith, B. Othanel, and Ennis, Robert H. (Eds.) *Language and Concepts in Education*. Rand McNally, 1961. p. 195–214.

Maccia, E. S. "The Nature of a Discipline-centered Curricular Approach." Bureau of Educational Research Studies. Ohio State U, 1964. 12p. (Mimeographed.)

Maccia, E. S. "Curriculum Theory and Policy." Paper presented to the meeting of the AERA, Chicago, Illinois, February 1965. 11p. (Mimeographed.)

Maccia, E. S., and others. *Construction of Educational Theory Models*. Office of Ed. USOE Cooperative Research Project No. 1632. Ohio State U Research Foundation, 1963. 334p.

Macdonald, James B. "The Nature of Instruction: Needed Theory and Research." *Ed Leadership* 21: 5–7; 1963.

Macdonald, James B. "Educational Models for Instruction—Introduction." In *Theories of Instruction*. NEA, 1965. p. 1–7.

McNally, Harold J., and others. *Improving the Quality of Public School Programs*. Teachers Col, Columbia U, 1960. 331p.

Miel, Alice. *Changing the Curriculum*. Appleton, 1946. 242p.

Miles, Matthew B. (Ed.) *Innovation in Education*. Teachers Col, Columbia U, 1964. 689p.

National Education Association. *Report of Committee of Ten on Secondary Education*. NEA, 1893. 249p.

National Education Association. *Report of the Commission on the Reorganization of Secondary Education*. NEA, 1918. 32p.

National Education Association. *Education in a Changing Society*. NEA, 1963. 166p.

National Society for the Study of Education. *Report of the Committee on Economy of Time in Education*. 4 vols. NSSE, 1915.

Phenix, Philip H. "The Disciplines as Curriculum Content." In Passow, A. Harry (Ed.) *Curriculum Crossroads*. Teachers Col, Columbia U, 1962. p. 57–65.

Progressive Education Association. *Report of the Committee on Experimental Schools*. The Association, 1937. 64p.

Scheffler, Israel. *The Language of Education*. Thomas, 1960. 113p.

Taba, Hilda. *Curriculum Development: Theory and Practice*. Harcourt, 1962. 529p.

Tanner, Daniel. "Curriculum Theory: Knowledge and Content." *R Ed Res* 36:363–73; 1966.

Wann, Kenneth. "The Curriculum Field Today." In Robison, Helen. (Ed.) *Precedents and Promise*. Teachers Col, Columbia U, 1966. p. 12–26.

Wiles, Kimball. *Supervision for Better Schools*. Prentice-Hall, 1950. 330p.

Wiles, Kimball. *Supervision for Better Schools; The Role of the Official Leader in Program Development*. Prentice-Hall, 1955. 399p.

CURRICULUM EVALUATION

In many respects the systematic evaluation of curricula is only beginning to emerge as a recognizable field of educational research. Curriculum reform in recent years has grown out of attempts to (1) bring the modern conceptual and methodological status of subject-matter fields into the experience of students, (2) apply current pedagogical and psychological thinking to classroom instruction, and (3) use the educational process to achieve social-ideological goals. Typically, curriculum evaluation has followed, rather than inspired, these changes.

The lack of enthusiasm for rigorous curriculum evaluation has had several sources. The instruments employed have frequently been insensitive to the most important effects of instruction. Conventional tests, rating scales, and questionnaires have often been more convenient than relevant. Studies of curricular effects have answered questions of incidental interest, while issues of central concern have been left to informal, intuitive judgment. Though educators and parents are aware of socioeconomic, motivational, attitudinal, and emotional differences among students, these antecedent variables have been generally ignored in curriculum evaluation. Too often curricula have been defined in terms of texts, labels, and catchphrases rather than detailed objective descriptions of the educational treatment. Also, resistance to rigorous evaluation of instructional programs has come from criticism-sensitive educators and from curriculum innovators who have heavy personal and professional investments in their products. Finally, the agencies that sponsor nationwide curriculum developments have failed to support *impartial* evaluation of the programs they promote.

Nevertheless, the need for objective assessment of educational programs has become increasingly evident, and this need has been the subject of recent professional discussion (Cronbach, 1963; MacDonald & Raths, 1963; Hastings, 1964; Scriven, 1965; Abramson, 1966; Ausubel, 1966, Stake, 1966). In these discussions several functions of curriculum evaluation have been postulated.

(1) As an integral step in the development of a curriculum, evaluation can be used to identify specific strengths and weaknesses of trial versions. Thus, the development of an instructional program can be an iterative process of trial, evaluation, and redesign. In such a developmental process, the objectives, as well as the substance, of the curriculum will be clarified and refined.

(2) Evaluation of curricula may be geared to the needs of those who must select from among competing programs. The admonition to avoid comparing curricula with differing objectives is often heard. Yet this is precisely the comparison that the practicing educator must initially make. A meaningful and objective description of the content and typical effects of the curricula will probably be more helpful than "expert" opinion about the ultimate value of alternative programs.

(3) Without the testing of hypotheses, curriculum theory remains outside the field of educational research. And hypothesis testing requires evaluation. The principles that explain how curricula influence students are found through efforts to build internally consistent structures of verifiable knowledge. As a credible system of basic principles is developed, designing a curriculum can become something more than a crash program based on hasty generalizations.

ISSUES AND PROBLEMS. Whether as a developmental function, as an aid to the practicing educator, or as fundamental research, evaluation of the interaction between a curriculum and its environment seems essential. How is the program interpreted by different types of teachers? Are optimal sequencing and duration a function of circumstances? What happens to curricular effects when equipment and facilities vary? Do the region, neighborhood, and institution transform the curriculum? How does the program affect students with various intellectual, socioeconomic, and emotional characteristics?

Evaluation of curricula in a time context is another major issue. The need for documentation of the long-term direct and transfer effects of instructional programs is seldom satisfied. Changes in curricula have been proposed with little consideration of continuity through the academic years. Though these issues have been discussed frequently (Hastings, 1964; Heath, 1962; MacDonald & Raths, 1963; Stake, 1966; Woodring, 1964), it is extremely difficult to find corresponding substantive research.

A number of problems in curriculum evaluation involve questions about educational objectives. A measurement specialist is likely to ask the curriculum developer to explicate his instructional objectives in behavioral terms. Atkin (1963), Ausubel (1966), and others have noted that this is probably an unrealistic request. (For a contrary point of view see Walbesser, 1964.) The technical language of the behavioral scientist is of little interest and doubtful utility to most curriculum builders. Translating implicit goals into observable phenomena is perhaps the most crucial task of the evaluator. This task requires a thorough familiarity with both the content of the curriculum and the pedagogic rationale of the curriculum designers.

Ebel (1965) and Green (1964) have emphasized the distinction between, on the one hand, acquiring, through education, the *capacity* to perform in a given manner and, on the other hand, *using* this ability. Most evaluation procedures have been designed to assess *ability to perform*, while many curriculum designers speak in terms of influencing the *set* to use a skill or cognitive approach.

When a curriculum is designed to facilitate future learning, special evaluation problems are suggested. How long can, or should, one wait to test such long-range effects? How can the influences of intervening experiences be controlled or explained? How can data be maintained on large numbers of students, over long periods of time, in a mobile society? It would appear that practical strategies for evaluation of this type have not been developed. Similarly, important curricular objectives may refer to the transfer of learned skills to new problem situations. Even under highly controlled classroom conditions (Wittrock & Keislar, 1965) there are difficult problems in documenting transfer effects. The method of measurement is critical, the issue of similarities between training and criterion tasks is complex, and the degree of first-task learning is a complicating variable; the long history of experimental research on transfer is rich with experimental-design problems.

Sometimes a curriculum will place strong emphasis on *how* the student learns—by "discovery" or by using the "structure of the discipline" as a heuristic construct. Such terms are used, often ambiguously, to describe characteristics of an instructional program that are presumed to be important. The evaluator has the problem of finding operational definitions for the curricular method as well as that of assessing its effectiveness. How can it be demonstrated that one student "discovered" and that another did not? Is one "structure" more useful than another for instructional purposes? What are the relations between type of student, kind of content, and discovery learning? (For a more complete discussion see Cronbach, 1965.)

Another cluster of problems in curriculum evaluation is associated with methodology. Perhaps the most direct and obvious method of curricular evaluation is the comparative study. Typically such studies have been based on a comparison of criterion performance by students of "new" and "conventional" curricula, with scholastic ability used as a control variable. Several problems are associated with these studies: (1) It is difficult to find criteria that are relevant to the objectives of both curricula; (2) neither the experimental nor the control group is likely to represent a homogeneous population; (3) if analysis of covariance is used to test hypotheses, the necessary assumptions about regression effects are likely to be untenable; and (4) both students and teachers are likely to be selectively assigned to curricula. Potthoff (1963a, 1963b, 1963c) has developed statistical procedures that have applications to the use of analysis of covariance in curriculum evaluation.

Several research and evaluation strategies for curriculum analysis have been suggested. Cronbach (1963) proposed using *item data* rather than test scores for course evaluation. By assigning different questions to different students (as in Lord, 1962) a number of efficiencies may be achieved. These efficiencies can make essay tests, open-ended questions, and observations of laboratory and verbal performance practical tools of curriculum evaluation. In the same paper, Cronbach makes the point that evaluation for curriculum evaluation is based on *group data* rather than individual student scores. A technique for using group test-score data in curriculum analysis is discussed by Heath and others (1966).

In a proposal for a study to determine the need for a curriculum-specific College Board achievement test, Dyer (1964) designed an experiment that may be of interest to those engaged in more basic curriculum research. The proposed experiment, which uses controls for item difficulty and curricular orthodoxy, could be used to analyze qualitative differences between competing curricula.

The use of nontest criteria in curriculum evaluation is often neglected. As compensatory programs for disadvantaged students are subjected to systematic appraisal, the need for alternatives to the multiple-choice achievement test become increasingly evident. A series of behavioral signs to be observed in five- and six-year-olds has been developed in response to this need (Board of Education of the City of New York, 1965). The federal guide for evaluating Elementary and Secondary Education Act Title I programs (U.S. Office of Education, 1965) includes many sensible suggestions for designing studies of compensatory education programs.

MAJOR STUDIES. Several organizations have been formed for the purpose of conducting curriculum research and evaluation. The Center for Instructional Research and Curriculum Evaluation (CIRCE) of the University of Illinois was formally organized in 1964. The faculty and staff associated with CIRCE have conducted a series of curriculum studies and have prepared several theoretical papers.

Educational Testing Service has had an active role in developing tests for new curricula. Recently it formed a curriculum studies group with four stated purposes: (1) to survey instructional practices, (2) to perform research on definitions of curriculum objectives, (3.) to evaluate curricula, and (4) to develop and disseminate evaluation techniques.

The University of Minnesota has set up its Center for Curriculum Studies. Though too new to be appraised, the center represents a substantial commitment to curriculum research by a major university.

A series of evaluative studies of new science and mathematics curricula were reported as these courses were introduced on a national basis (Maier, 1962; Payette, 1961; Stickell, 1965; Heath & Stickell, 1963; Grobman, 1964; Rosenbloom, 1962; Shuff, 1962). These studies, for the most part, employed conventional achievement tests. Measures of cognitive preference or problem-solving style have been the object of later research (Heath, 1964b; Travers, 1965).

Two theoretical papers have recently appeared which seem likely to influence future research. Brownell (1966) mentions six difficulties in evaluative research and asks that the evaluator report and discuss the subjective judgments he must make in conducting quantitative research. Stake (1966) discusses a number of important issues and clarifies the functions and strategies of curriculum evaluation.

Robert W. Heath
Stanford University

References

Abramson, David A. "Curriculum Research and Evaluation." *R Ed Res* 36:388–95; 1966.
Atkin, J. Myron. "Some Evaluation Problems in a Course Content Improvement Project." *J Res Sci Ed* 1:129–32; 1963.
Ausubel, David P. *Crucial Psychological Issues in the Objectives, Organization, and Evaluation of Curriculum Reform Movements.* Bureau of Educational Research, U Illinois, 1966. 21p.
Board of Education of the City of New York. *Instructional and Assessment Materials for First Graders.* ETS, 1965. 27p.
Brownell, William A. "The Evaluation of Learning Under Dissimilar Systems of Instruction." *Calif J Ed Res* 32:80–90; 1966.
Cronbach, Lee J. "Evaluation for Course Improvement." *Teach Col R* 64:672–83; 1963.
Cronbach, Lee J. *The Logic of Experiments on Discovery.* Stanford U Press, 1965. 17p.
Dyer, Henry S. *Tentative Proposal for an Experiment to Assess the Need for a Special Test of BSCS Biology in the College Board Admissions Testing Program.* ETS, 1964. 12p.
Ebel, Robert L. *Measuring Educational Achievement.* Prentice-Hall, 1965. 481p.
Green, Thomas F. "Teaching, Acting, and Behaving." *Harvard Ed R* 34:507–24; 1964.
Grobman, Hulda. "Student Performance in New High School Biology Programs." *Sci* 143:265–6; 1964.
Hastings, J. Thomas. "Innovations in Evaluation for Innovations in Curriculum." In Steinberg, Erwin R. and others. *Curriculum Development and Evaluation in English and Social Studies.* Carnegie Institute of Technology, 1964. p. 140–7.
Heath, Robert W. "Pitfalls in the Evaluation of New Curricula." *Sci Ed* 46:216; 1962.
Heath, Robert W. "Comparison of Achievement in Two Physics Courses." *J Exp Ed* 32:347–54; 1964(a).
Heath, Robert W. "Curriculum, Cognition, and Educational Measurement." *Ed Psychol Meas* 24:239–53; 1964(b).
Heath, Robert W., and Stickell, David W. "CHEM and CBA Effects on Achievement in High School Chemistry." *Sci Teach* 30:45–6; 1963.
Heath, Robert W. and others. *The Use of Achievement and Ability Test Averages.* Research Memorandum 66–3. ETS, 1966. 10p.
Lord, Frederic M. "Estimating Norms by Item-sampling." *Ed Psychol Meas* 22:259–68; 1962.
MacDonald, James B. and Raths, James D. "Curriculum Research: Problems, Techniques, and Prospects." *R Ed Res* 33:322–9; 1963.
Maier, Milton S. *Evaluation of a New Mathematics Curriculum.* Research Memorandum 62–13. ETS, 1962. 8p.
Payette, Roland F. "Educational Testing Service Summary Report of the School Mathematics Study Group Curriculum Evaluation." In *Newsletter No. 10, Sch Math Study Group.* Stanford U, 1961. p. 5–11.
Potthoff, Richard F. *Some Scheffe-type Tests for Some Behrens-Fisher-type Regression Problems.* Research Bulletin 63–35. ETS, 1963(a). 31p.
Potthoff, Richard F. *Illustrations of Some Scheffe-type Tests for Some Behrens-Fisher-type Regression Problems.* Research Bulletin 63–36. ETS, 1963(b). 17p.
Potthoff, Richard F. *On the Johnson-Neyman Technique and Some Extensions Thereof.* Research Bulletin 63–4. ETS, 1963. 18p.
Rosenbloom, Paul C. *Effectiveness of the SMSG Material for Grades 7–12.* Publication No. 38-B-288. Minnesota State Department of Education, 1962. 7p.
Scriven, Michael. *The Methodology of Evaluation.* Indiana U Press, 1965. 58p.
Shuff, Robert V. "A Comparative Study of Achievement in Mathematics at the Seventh and Eighth Grade Levels Under Two Approaches, School Mathematics Study Group and Traditional." Doctoral dissertation. U Minnesota, 1962.

Stake, Robert E. *The Countenance of Educational Evaluation.* U Illinois Press, 1966. 26p.

Stickell, David W. *A Comparison of the Performance of BSCS and Non-BSCS Candidates on the CEEB Biology Achievement Test.* Test Development Report 65–1. ETS, 1965. 22p.

Travers, Kenneth J. "Forced-choice Preferences for Problem-solving Situations in Mathematics." Doctoral dissertation. U Illinois, 1965.

U.S. Office of Education. *Guidelines: Special Programs for Educationally Deprived Children, Section II Design and Evaluation of Projects.* OE-35079/Sec. II. GPO, 1965. p. 21–40.

Walbesser, Henry H. "The Measure of Behavioral Changes as the Measure of a Curriculum Evaluation." In Steinberg, Erwin R., and others. *Curriculum Development and Evaluation in English and Social Studies.* Carnegie Institute of Technology, 1964. p. 119–32.

Wittrock, M. C. and Keislar, Evan R. "Verbal Cues in the Transfer of Concepts." *J Ed Psychol* 56:16–21; 1965.

Woodring, Paul. "Introduction." In Heath, Robert W. (Ed.) *New Curricula.* Harper, 1964. p. 1–8.

DATA PROCESSING AND COMPUTING

The aspect of educational research which has probably undergone the most revolutionary changes in the last ten years is the processing of data. One way to see these changes dramatically is to study the entries in the *Education Index.* Prior to 1956 there were almost no entries under "Data Processing" or any closely related heading. Three years later the *Education Index* covering 1957–1959 had only 28 entries under "Calculating Machines," and there was no closely related topic. Most of those articles were concerned with the impact of computer developments on business education, appearing in such periodicals as the *Journal of Business Education.* Typical is the article by Salser (1957), who wondered what the electronic age can mean to business education.

In the 1959–1961 *Index* the new emphasis on statistical computing became evident. A good example is Kaiser (1959), who presented a computer program for Varimax rotation in factor analysis. About the same time we find such articles as Brisley's "When Should Schools Mechanize?" (1958). The trickle of articles on specific statistical programs and on school data processing that began in 1959–1961 became a flood by 1966. The 1966 *Index* had almost as many *pages* of entries for such topics as data processing, data transmission, computer programming, computers, and data processing service Centers as there were related entries in the 1957–1959 *Index.* Of course, this correlates very highly with the availability of the computer. In 1955 the computer industry sold $100-million worth of general-purpose digital computers for scientific and business applications. Ten years later they sold 22 times that amount (*Business Automation News,* January 1965). By February 1965 the number of computers installed in the United States included over 1,500 large-scale, 11,000 medium-sized, and 17,000 small computers, such as the IBM 1620 (*Business Automation News,* February 1965). There were fewer than 50 computers on college campuses in 1957 and more than 1,000 by 1967.

Three journals have stimulated articles on computer applications in education and psychology by having regular computer sections. The first was the computer section in *Behavioral Science* edited by Steven Vandenberg, which began in 1959. This was closely followed by William Michael's "Electronic Computer Programs and Accounting Machine Procedures" in *Educational and Psychological Measurement,* which first appeared in 1960. Focusing more on school data-processing applications, G. Ernest Anderson has been editing a computer section in the *Nation's Schools* since October 1963. A list of periodicals devoted exclusively to computers or computer applications in education follows the list of references at the end of this entry.

From a survey of the educational literature it is evident that there is some confusion regarding computer terminology. For example, one gets the impression that "data processing" and "computing" are synonymous. This is definitely not the case in the business and scientific fields. There are many computer applications which do not involve the processing of data, and there are many data-processing tasks which do not involve computing. Data processing, as the term is most generally used, involves the collection of data, the preparation of the collected data, and the organization of the data for easy retrieval for specific analyses. This is the sense in which "data processing" will be used in this discussion. Data processing will be considered as a tool in educational research and its products and procedures as the subject of educational research. In addition, statistical computing procedures will be reviewed because they are frequently classified under data processing and because there is no other entry in this encyclopedia which considers these related computer applications.

INTRODUCTIONS TO DATA PROCESSING AND COMPUTERS. The rapid increase in educational research has suddenly produced a very large number of people who want to know more about data processing and the use of the computer. The most efficient way to learn computer techniques is to attend a university which offers courses in computer science or computer applications in education. However, the many excellent textbooks now available also make it possible to design a program of self-study. A consideration of automatic data-processing systems with applications for business data processing is found in a recent textbook by Gregory and Van Horn (1965). This book does not require previous knowledge of electronic computing systems. A book on school data processing by Grossman and Howe (1965) considers such topics as report cards, test scoring, attendance accounting, student registration, scheduling, and cumulative records. Probably the most systematic treatment of data processing available is the book by Brooks and Iverson (1963) in which the topics range from manual sorting of papers into pigeonholes to the design of complex mechanized data-processing systems. All topics are considered in terms of a systematic notation and fundamental principles which are introduced in Chapter 1. This book is highly important for anyone who is about to institute new data-processing routines.

Manufacturers of computing equipment offer whole libraries of manuals to go with their machines. However, better teaching is sometimes found in works by independent authors. For example, we have Leeson and Dimitry (1962) on the IBM 1620 and McCracken (1962b) on the IBM 1401. An example of a textbook designed as an undergraduate introduction to computer science is the book by Arden (1963) in which he covers the computer in general abstract terms and also explains specific approaches to such problems as numerical integrations and simultaneous linear equations and such nonnumerical problems as searching and sorting. The most generally used computer language continues to be FORTRAN, and an excellent introduction to it is provided by McCracken (1961). He also wrote a guide to ALGOL programming (1962a), but ALGOL, while in many ways a superior language, is not as generally used in conjunction with computing installations as it is in the literature devoted to describing computer algorithms (unambiguous statements providing step-by-step solutions to mathematical problems. The very important field of computer software is well presented in a book by Flores (1965). "Software" refers to the more general programs which are needed to keep a computer running smoothly and efficiently, such as translators, supervisors, input-output control systems, monitors, and loaders. Without such software systems the computer cannot be approached at the level of symbolism convenient for the user but must be programmed in terms of its basic machine instructions, requiring detailed analysis of even such simple operations as reading a punched-card image from a tape. Consequently it is much more difficult and consuming of the programmer's time to use.

Once one gets involved in computer applications, he soon sees the need for some familiarity with various aspects of applied mathematics and the part they can play in computer applications. Books such as those by Faddeeva (1959) and Ralston and Wilf (1960) show how complicated problems in linear algebra can be solved by means of computing algorithms. Then, at the next level, there are books such as the one by Iverson (1962) which offers a special language for applied mathematics which is used to simplify the representation of algorithms. They, in turn, serve as the framework for building computer programs. After introducing this new language, Iverson illustrates its use in such areas as search techniques and sorting.

Of course, the great need is for more schools of education to provide their students an opportunity to study computer applications in educational research. As late as 1962 the number of institutions of higher learning offering such courses could be counted on one hand! Although at some universities it is possible to have education students take computer courses in engineering or, more recently, in computer-science departments, it is more frequently the case that these are inappropriate because of either the content of the courses themselves or the prerequisites required of the student. Baker (1962, 1963) and Borko (1962) both present their conceptions of the computer training needed for behavioral-science research. These seem to be the only published discussions on this very important topic.

Once in this fast-moving field of computer applications, a major task is to keep up with both hardware and software developments. One good way is to read one of the trade journals, such as *Datamation*, which is available free of charge to computer users (see the periodical list following the references). It is written at a level which is quite accessible to anyone who is familiar with the basic components of computers and who has had an introduction to programming. Probably the best recent survey of the whole computer field is a special issue of *Scientific American* (1966). Another activity useful in keeping track of the field is participation in computer-user associations, such as the SHARE group for the large IBM machines.

There is need for one final word before proceeding to specific topics within the areas of data processing and statistical computing—that word is *caution*. Educators are rushing into data processing and computer applications at full speed. They are often doing so with quite inadequate preparation and with the concepts "giant brain" and "automatic" blinding them to the pitfalls which lie ahead. Such terms do not convey the vast amount of planning and programming which are required to get the computer to do even a rather simple task such as getting out the school payroll. As one moves from paper-and-pencil methods, through desk calculators, to electronic digital computers, more and more planning and analysis of the task to be accomplished are necessary. As the direct, minute-by-minute involvement of the investigator in the processing becomes less and less, the planning required becomes greater and greater. Someone has estimated that approximately one-third of the computers installed in business in the early 1960's were initially complete failures because of inadequate planning and preparation. Computer applications in the schools have not been without their failures also. Anderson (1965), for example, was able to draw on the considerable experience of others in the field when he wrote "How to Make Educational Data Processing Fail."

The other reason for caution has to do with what Beaton (1961) has called the halo effect. The "gee-whiz" that has become associated with the computer has tended to sanctify results simply because they were computer output. All the fancy computer manipulations known to man will not produce meaningful results out of bad data. Research reports must devote more space to such problems as data collection and preparation if their results are to invoke confidence.

DATA COLLECTION. Unfortunately, too many investigators do not consider data processing until after data collection. This procedure generally results in large piles of data which the investigator then takes to some "computer expert" for advice on how to prepare the collected data for efficient analysis. Once that is done, he takes the punched cards to a "statistical expert" to see what sort of fancy manipulations might be done with these data. Whenever the late Professor Palmer O. Johnson was approached with a request to perform a postmortem on an ill-planned and ambiguously defined data collection, his usual response was, "Cremate the corpse."

The point is that no matter how small the research project might be, all aspects of data processing must be thoroughly planned in advance or troubles will certainly arise. In fact, in large projects the difficulties may be catastrophic if data processing is inadequately planned. As obvious as this point seems, it must be emphasized again and again, as the problem continually arises. With this in mind, let us turn to some specific aspects of data collection.

Tests. Probably the greatest strides in testing have been made by Lindquist and his Measurement Research Center (MRC). His test-scoring machine is a dramatic improvement over what was available only six years before. Today, for example, when it is necessary to administer a battery of tests with several answer sheets, the answer sheets can all be administered and scored together as a booklet, resulting in a single tape record written for each student directly on magnetic tape, ready for computer processing. This is in dramatic contrast with what MRC was able to do for Project Talent (Flanagan & others, 1962) in 1960, when that project tested 440,000 high school students, using five separate answer sheets. Although optical scanning was available at that time, it was not yet capable of reading answers directly onto magnetic tape, so that it was necessary to convert the data on each answer sheet into a set of IBM cards. The five answer sheets resulted in the equivalent of 17 IBM cards for each of the 440,000 students. Once these five answer sheets were converted to cards, Project Talent faced the task of organizing 7,480,000 card images on tape into 440,000 integrated tape records, one for each student. This sorting and merging task was further complicated by the fact that students were occasionally inconsistent in identifying themselves on these five answer sheets, resulting in many apparently incomplete records and the danger of mistakes in merging. Even with the high-speed electronic computers available in 1960, the completion of this task took four years. With today's technology the single tape record produced by the test-scoring machine itself would eliminate this big record-linkage problem. (See Flanagan, 1961, for an interesting contrast with studies preceding Project Talent, in which even fewer mechanical aids were available.) An example of current technological capabilities is provided by the American Council on Education's 1966 survey of more than 250,000 freshmen entering a representative sample of 307 colleges and universities. Tables of weighted national norms based on approximately 40 million questionnaire responses given by these students were published within about three months after the data had been collected (Astin & others, 1966, 1967). Such rapid processing of large quantities of educational-research data is possible when optical scanners are used and when the computer routines for editing and tabulating the data have been thoroughly "debugged" prior to the actual collection of data.

Where it is impossible to collect all of the data for a given student from a single booklet, such as in a longitudinal study, Lindquist has devised what he calls the "card pack system," which reduces the linkage problem by providing each student with a stencil with which he codes his identification number onto each answer card or answer sheet (described in Carroll & Ellis, 1965). It is also possible to have students use answer media such as mark-sense cards which have been previously identified from the data files, so that the identification number provided by the student will be the same number as that already in the file.

Questionnaires. The collecting of data using questionnaires should receive much more care and planning than it is generally given. Although an experienced test maker would never consider including an item which had not been thoroughly pretested and which was not designed for one particular measurement scale, the inveterate questionnaire writer too often asks whatever questions occur to him, even though he has no particular scaling or even data-analysis scheme in mind when he sends out the questionnaire. It is perhaps a generous estimate that only 10 percent of the data collected through questionnaires have been processed to the point of published conclusions. Probably the most important reason for this waste is that the investigator does not realize that the amount of data-processing effort required to process a returned questionnaire is inversely proportional to the amount of effort put into the design of the questionnaire in the first place. The use of precoded items is probably the biggest time-saver, and the only occasion when not using them may be excused is when the investigator is trying out an item and wants to know what type of natural response the population in question tends to give or when the known alternatives to the question are too many to allow the use of precoded options.

Another waste in questionnaire surveys is the duplication of effort, even within the same agency. For example, Hjelm (1961) has pointed out that in 1960 the U.S. Office of Education "used approximately 8,000 different queries in its questionnaires. Answers to almost all of the 8,000 questions could have been derived from responses to about 800 basic items."

Questionnaires also occasionally pose problems of record linkage if they are part of a longitudinal study. At Project Talent this problem is being handled by having the mailing label which is attached directly to the questionnaire contain the student's test number as well as his name and address, so that when the questionnaire is returned the test number is punched along with the precoded responses. The resulting card is then easily merged with previous data for the same respondent. Other data, such as sex and birth date, can serve as additional checks during the merge process.

Observations. Another popular data-collection scheme in educational research is to record observations of classroom behavior, small-group discussion, guidance interviews, etc. Again, these observational techniques are successful only insofar as they are designed in terms of the total data-processing and data-analysis tasks. Of course, there are many opportunities for technology to contribute here also. Such devices as mark-sense cards, Port-o-punches, and video tapes have been found useful.

Essays. Although the essay used to be a favorite data-collection device, it became quite unmanageable as educational research became more ambitious, tending to include larger samples and to be concerned with the problem of obtaining greater reliability. Today, however, the computer may make it possible for this very open response technique to come back into favor. Several workers have developed systems for processing natural language on the computer. One of the most significant developments for the behavioral scientist has been the General Inquirer, a system of computer programs for content analysis of English text developed at Harvard by Stone and others (1966). A general review of the area of natural language processing is provided by Garvin (1963). Page (1966) has been particularly active in devising schemes for scoring student essays. One big task in this field has been, of course, to get the essays onto tape in the first place. But new page readers such as the CDC 915, which can read typed copy directly and produce a tape record of the typed verbal text, may help solve this problem. Not too far over the horizon is machine reading of handwriting, which has been pioneered at MIT's Lincoln Laboratories by Selfridge and Niesse (1960) and others. Of course, the research going on in machine translation and emission of the spoken word may eventually eliminate the need for paper altogether!

Remote Terminals. A method of data collecting which is not so far in the future is the use by students or instructors of remote terminals which tie in directly to the computer. With the new on-line mass-storage devices such as data cells and batteries of disks, it is conceivable that test taking can be done at such terminals and the collected data added directly to the student's file. A more immediate possibility is a terminal in each school building which would accept data preprocessed by technicians at the school and sent out through this terminal by cards or tape to a central computer serving several school systems. It is quite possible that such devices could be in operation on an experimental basis before this encyclopedia goes to press.

In summary, data collection will be successful only if the steps involved are designed as a part of the total research or student accounting operation. This includes working out such details as the specific format to be used if the returned data are to be converted to punched cards. Inevitably, when this step is planned prior to data collection, modifications in the data-collecting instrument which facilitate processing will become obvious.

PREPARATION OF COLLECTED DATA. Although the care and efficiency used in preparing the collected data for analysis make up a very critical aspect of educational research, one does not get that impression from the educational-research literature. You have to look long and hard to find any discussion of that topic. There are so many pitfalls in moving from a pile of answer sheets or questionnaires to what may be considered data that are ready to analyze that more discussion on this topic is essential. About the only discussion which comes close to what I am talking about here is found in Traxler's chapter, "Administering and Scoring the Objective Test," in *Educational Measurement* (Lindquist, 1951), but portions of that discussion are out-of-date, and the chapter is restricted to a particular type of collected data. To supplement Traxler's discussion, which illustrates data-processing considerations in the area of objective testing, a brief discussion of questionnaire processing may be useful. Because other investigators tend not to discuss data-processing experiences in their report writing, I shall use familiar experiences at Project Talent for illustrations.

At Project Talent, questionnaire returns arrive from the post office in batches of 100. The first step in processing is to stamp the batch number on each questionnaire within the arriving batch. This batch number becomes a part of the eventual tape record, so that if it becomes necessary, a particular questionnaire can be located, since questionnaires are filed by batch. If the sample is small, the questionnaires can be resorted by individual identification numbers, but this is an unnecessary expense in large surveys (Project Talent processes about 100,000 questionnaires per year). A batch of 100 questionnaires is a convenient size for clerical handling. Batches are also convenient because records can be kept of the various processing steps through which each batch has progressed. By letting the post office do this batching, questionnaires which are being returned by the post office because of address problems are separated from those which represent respondent replies. This separation comes about because the two types of returns involve two separate postal rates. Those returned by the post office with address problems are of two types: those with forwarding addresses and those with the addresses unknown. In the former case, clerks add this new information to rosters, cards are punched from the rosters, and the cards are used to update the name-and-address file. When the address or addressee is unknown, we add to the name-and-address file the fact that the person cannot be located at that address. If a subsequent questionnaire is also returned as undeliverable, the individual becomes a "dead end" and no further steps are taken to locate him unless he is selected as one of the nonrespondents to be located in a special survey.

Questionnaires which are returned by repondents

are examined to make sure that each is complete and that the person responding to it is apparently the one to whom the questionnaire was sent. If follow-ups are planned for the people who have not yet responded to previous mailings, then a card is prepared which indicates that a completed questionnaire is available for the individual. In this way that subject is deleted from these future mailings.

So far these data-processing considerations have been aspects of the follow-up process itself. Once these tasks are completed, the clerks must turn their attention to the actual coding of the questionnaire. Each clerk has a manual which describes in detail all the operations to be performed on questionnaires. Usually a clerk operates on a particular batch, coding one item or a set of items. For example, one questionnaire item involves the description of current jobs held. It was designed as an open-ended question so that specific types of jobs could be studied without the thousands of possible jobs being listed in the questionnaire itself. Therefore, one coder task is to go through a batch and assign a four-digit code to the job description of the respondent.

After a batch of questionnaires is coded it is turned over to key-punch operators, who punch the information onto cards. Here, of course, the critical step is verification: once the cards have been punched a second operator goes through the same operations on a machine called a verifier, which flashes a red light if the information fed into the machine the second time is different from that previously punched onto the card. After the cards are punched and verified, the data on them are transferred to magnetic tape. Here the important step is editing: Before the new data are merged with previously collected data, we make sure there are no invalid or inconsistent responses. An example of an invalid response is one which is out of the range of possible responses. In this case the original questionnaire is pulled from the files for comparison purposes. If possible, a correct response is supplied. If not, the invalid, out-of-range response is converted to −0, which indicates "no response." Inconsistencies are such things as the respondent's indicating in one item that he had not gone to college and later in the questionnaire supplying the name of a college he had attended. In this case, too, the original questionnaire is pulled and appropriate changes made.

Lindquist's MRC operation can now greatly simplify the processing of questionnaire data also. The latest MRC optical scanning machine can operate directly on the questionnaire booklet, thus eliminating the need for separate answer sheets. The questionnaire booklet is fed automatically into the scanner, which slits off the stapled hinge, and then scans each page separately and records the integrated record for the entire questionnaire directly on magnetic tape, together with coded identifications of all omissions and inconsistencies in the data reported as well as clues to possible errors made by the respondent. All the coding of responses that is necessary for later computer processing is done at the time of scanning by the computer, which is on line with the scanner. This minimizes the errors in coding which characterized traditional procedures. A computer-controlled printer then prints out a list of the serial numbers of all suspect documents together with all suspect data for each suspect document. Clerical work is then limited to the editing operation, in which a clerk refers to each suspect original document and makes whatever corrections in the tape record are suggested by examination of the document itself.

ORGANIZATION OF THE DATA. Once the data are collected and prepared for processing, the next step is to organize the data for easy retrieval. With large files this is extremely important if retrieval costs are to be kept to a minimum. At Project Talent, for example, it costs about $1,000 to pass over the entire master file in order to retrieve selected cases for an analysis. Because a specific investigation generally requires dealing with only one sex (or, at least, data for the two sexes are analyzed separately), the search time can be cut in half by organizing separate files for the sexes. Since analyses also tend to be within grade, the Talent files are also organized by grade. By having these eight subfiles by grade and sex, the data for a study of ninth-grade male dropouts can be obtained by one pass over only one-eighth of the file instead of over the entire file.

In order to facilitate data retrieval for specific analyses, special programs are often necessary. For example, Project Talent has developed a program called GSCORE which performs a variety of selection, scoring, and recoding operations, producing up to six separate output files. This program also helps to cut down on retrieval expenses, since it is possible to produce a "work tape" of data on future doctors for a medical-school study and, at the same time, to prepare a work tape of high school graduates who went directly to work after graduation for a study of early work adjustment. Being able to recode and rescore original raw data within this retrieval program is also quite important, since we usually store data in terms of finer categories than are generally required for specific research studies. This principle is important, since different investigators commonly require different combinations of categories or test items or scores.

Hardware developments which should provide considerably greater flexibility for the investigator with a moderate-sized data file are the new on-line mass-storage devices and the remote terminals. These will make it possible for the investigator to be "closer to his data," thus answering a frequent complaint about using the computer. In the days before the computer, the investigator was in direct contact with his data, even to the point of doing hand tallies or watching cards fall into pockets, thus having a firsthand sense of what the data were "really like." With the emergence of the computer with its batch-processing mode, the investigator often feels too removed from the actual data analysis and therefore frequently feels frustrated by delays between getting ideas and seeing whether they are supported by the data. But with the remote terminal in his office which makes it possible to have all his data "on line" in a device such as the data cell, he can explore specific hypotheses with feedback that is even more immediate than was possible back in the hand-tally days. Of course, this increased flexibility will increase greatly the danger of the investigator capitalizing on the peculiarities of his particular set of numbers. But, although this danger must always be recognized, it should not prevent us from taking advantage of the heuristic value of the investigator's interacting with his data.

DATA BANKS. The increased capability to handle large data files and the significant increase in the amount of money available for educational research have resulted in the establishment of many very large data files which allow more research possibilities than any one investigator or research group is able to exhaust. This situation has led to the establishment of data banks which serve as resources for investigators not directly connected with the project for which the data were collected. Of course, scientists have always had informal ways of sharing data with other investigators, but such organized efforts of sharing are new in education. As a result, there have been special symposia at professional meetings and even special conferences devoted to this topic (Carroll & Ellis, 1965). Although the data-bank concept has been only grudgingly accepted by tough-minded experimenters, several achievements in the last few years have convinced most educational research workers of the value of data banks as they are evolving today (Astin & others, 1965).

Although the technical and financial aspects of data-bank operations have been solved, there is considerable concern today about problems involving the confidentiality and security of the information stored. If society is to be expected to support the existence and maintenance of large files of personal data for legitimate research purposes, it must also be assured that it is not possible for this kind of data to be used for illegitimate or unethical purposes. So far, the major safeguard seems to be that these data are in the hands of "honest, well-meaning people." That is not the sort of assurance that puts people at ease.

DATA ANALYSIS. In surveying the literature on data analysis one finds no dearth of articles and books. The range is also extremely great, from Meltzer's article (1961) telling us how to obtain accumulations on an accounting machine to monographs which describe entire computer systems for most types of univariate and multivariate analyses. The methods, however, have changed a great deal. For example, in Fattu's 1958 entry in the third edition of this encyclopedia, he was able to cite several reference works on paper-and-pencil shortcuts to statistical computing (Fattu, 1960). A search of the literature since then has revealed no similar articles. As pointed out earlier (Cooley, 1961), with the availability of the computer, methods of analysis which are feasible only with a computer are becoming more and more common.

Most of the articles which describe specific computing procedures are found in the computer sections of *Educational and Psychological Measurement* and *Behavioral Science*. Because these articles are well indexed within the two periodicals, there seems little point in reviewing them in detail. It should be pointed out, however, that the computer section in *Educational and Psychological Measurement* is quite varied in quality. The variation in part reflects the status of computing in educational research. At some universities, even at universities showing leadership in the establishment of general-purpose computer centers, the educational-research faculties have just recently acquired their first desk calculators, while at other institutions the education faculties were active in establishing computers on the campus.

Although the many articles which describe a very specific computing technique need not be summarized here, a few citations of more general efforts seem justifiable. Baker's proposed "library of statistical programs for the modern digital computer" (1961) was an early effort to outline the set of programs a computer center should have available for most educational-research needs.

A large and early library of statistical programs generally available was the BMD produced by the Division of Biostatistics at the University of California at Los Angeles (Dixon, 1962). The manual prepared by Hayward (1961) was also a very important document in helping other computer centers with large-scale equipment such as the IBM 7090 to make use of these programs.

An early book which offers a library of programs for computing multivariate statistics was written by Cooley and Lohnes (1962). In addition to listings of FORTRAN programs, the book has brief mathematical descriptions of each technique, computed examples from the behavioral sciences, and flow charts for those people who need or want to make extensive changes in the programs. Horst's new book (1965) on factor analysis is a more recent example of a work offering a whole set of computer programs. Experience in teaching computer programming has indicated that having the student examine a variety of programs involving simple statistical methods, such as those included in the books mentioned above, is an excellent way to have him learn statistical programming once he has mastered a few fundamentals of the computer language itself.

Very few articles have compared different computer approaches to the same problem, even though one may suspect that a good deal of this comparison is going on. Eyman and others (1962) present some comparisons of factor-analytic rotation programs, but they are more concerned with the nature of the solution than with the efficiency of the programs. Of course, their type of study should be encouraged even more than efficiency studies, since the computer's tremendous capability for allowing us to learn more about specific statistical methods should be utilized.

Before computers it was quite a chore just to complete one hand rotation, much less six for comparison purposes.

Another use of the computer in the study of statistical methods is the Monte Carlo approach. Using random-number generators such as those described by Green (1963), sampling distributions can now be studied in a way never before possible. The often-quoted Norton study summarized by Lindquist (1953) is something which can now be done simply and easily with the computer, varying population parameters and statistical techniques at will. A laboratory course offering such Monte Carlo experiences to the beginning student should greatly improve his conception of what it means for a difference to be statistically significant at the .05 level.

Once program libraries were fully established at major computer centers, the next search was for procedures to facilitate their use. One step was to chain the programs so that it would be possible to go from one computer program to the next without interruption. One of the first such chaining efforts seems to be that of Jones (1964), which was first described in the educational literature by Cooley and Jones (1964). Similar efforts have been reported by Buhler (1964) and by Beaton (1964).

The notion of linking previously existing programs together led to a rethinking of the units to be chained. Instead of a single core load being the entire analysis —for example, canonical correlation—chaining allows the programmer to break the analysis into a sequence of core loads, requiring much less of a program to be in memory at any one time. Thus, there is more space for larger matrices (i.e., more variables). Also, the separate core loads can be recombined to carry out other analyses. For example, the extraction of latent roots and vectors is a common technique. With this as a separate core load, we have a building block which is useful in a variety of chains. Of course, the same concept has been available in terms of subroutines, but with that approach all the subroutines must be available in memory at the time the main program is executed. Now, with large random-access devices such as the disk storage, this approach of using a sequence of core loads makes even more sense. Work in this area has been done at Project Talent under the direction of Wingersky. Beaton's new system seems to be very similar in approach in that one core load does not constitute a complete statistical analysis but is rather one step toward a particular statistical solution.

RESEARCH ON EDUCATIONAL DATA PROCESSING. The greatest need in education has been, and continues to be, the solution to the problem of individualizing instruction. Probably the greatest need in research on data processing is how to utilize the computer toward this end.

In the literature search conducted for the preparation of this entry such a promising title as "How Automation Facilitates the Individualization of Instruction" (Schwilck & Bagby, 1963) turned out to be a disappointing story about a high school's using an accounting machine to list all those students whose report card contained one or more F's.

In considering previous and current applications of computers in schools, two major areas are clearly discernible. The more typical area of computer application has been in the automation of previously existing data-processing tasks, such as scheduling classes, recording attendance, making up report cards, and other accounting needs of a school system. The second major area has been in the development of computer-assisted instruction (see, for example, Hartman, 1966). Here the student is in direct contact with the computer through a remote-terminal device, and, in the resulting interaction, the computer controls the minute-by-minute instruction of the student. Though this is useful both as an approach for studying the learning process and as an eventual approach to selected aspects of instruction, it is not likely that it will solve the massive problem of providing individualized instruction in the foreseeable future. The computer has its greatest aptitude in processing data, not conversing with students.

Now that the computer programs are capable of solving the class-scheduling program in a matter of minutes, in contrast to procedures which sometimes took the entire summer vacation, it is possible to develop a continuous scheduling process which allows students to be assigned to different educational experiences, not on a one-year course basis but on a week-to-week basis. In this approach the computer is primarily a device which processes the information needed by teachers and counselors for the week-to-week guidance of students in their individual, educational development. Although educators have felt the need for more individualized instruction for decades, it is only now possible for the new generation of computers to provide the information-processing power which is needed to plan individualized instruction.

For example, at least three research and development groups (the American Institutes for Research, the System Development Corporation, and the Learning Research and Development Center at the University of Pittsburgh) are developing new systems for education with the following very broad outlines. The key to this educational process is that the curriculum consists of modules of operationally defined teaching-learning units varying in length from one day's to about two week's work. The units may be either self-instructional or group instructed. A unit culminates in a feedback test designed to show the degree of success obtained. Another important aspect is that the students to be educated are identified in terms of age, aptitude, interest, learning style, and other variables that affect the students' educational goals and progress toward them.

A central computer will serve all participating school systems with at least one remote terminal in each school building. At first, technical assistants will operate these terminals. Eventually it may be possible for teachers to interact with the data base for their students.

When a new unit is to be assigned to a student,

several appropriate suggestions come from the computer to the remote terminal. After discussion with his educational counselor, a student selects his next unit from among those suggested and proceeds as the unit outline suggests. The schedule may involve going to a designated area either to receive the instructional materials needed for a particular self-instructing unit or to attend whatever group instructions may be designated or for some combination of the two. He completes the unit's work at his own pace and then goes to the testing center where he obtains the appropriate end-of-unit test. This test result is then fed through the terminal to the central computer where, with other information available for that student, it is used to determine the next suggested unit or units.

Such an individualized system of education assumes that the student has adequately defined short- and long-range goals. Guidance has an essential role in this system to ensure the validity of that assumption. Cooley and Lohnes (see, for example, Cooley & Jones, 1964) have been developing some basic principles for a computer-measurement system for guidance which could be integrated with a computer-measurement instructional system and would facilitate the definition of appropriate goals. Ingredients of this guidance system include the following.

1. The definition of a small number of orthogonal factors of both abilities and motives which allow an adequate description of student differences.

2. "Dynamic" norms based on longitudinal data which make it possible to relate student factor measures to questions about goals that are of current interest and concern to the *student.*

3. A career-development map which makes it possible for the student to see the probable future implications of educational decisions he is making today.

4. Instructional materials which help the student to see that his life is not predetermined by his studying the variety of things which students like him have found to be appropriate, satisfying activities.

A very important by-product of this shift in emphasis from year-long courses to one- or two-week learning modules in an information environment is the fact that this shift may greatly facilitate the solution of another very old problem in education, that of evaluation. One major difficulty with most previous efforts at evaluation has been the tendency to examine a semester- or year-long course of study in contrast with another, similar course of study. The results generally did not indicate how either of the contrasted courses of study might be improved. Also the results tended to be meaningless because the different approaches to, say, high school physics were based upon quite different educational objectives, making evaluative instruments inappropriate for at least one of the two approaches being compared. Finally, the results tended to be discounted because relevant differences among students and teachers were either ignored or inadequately taken into account.

The type of educational system which consists of small, interchangeable units geared to well-defined, measurable objectives is much more amenable to evaluation. The units will be used in an environment in which relevant information is readily available on the participating students and teachers. Information regarding the relative effectiveness of different units designed to meet the same objectives can be systematically collected so that decisions can be made regarding which units are more appropriate for which kinds of students at which points in their educational development. Weak units among those offered will be easily identified and removed from the system. Objectives for which no adequate units are now available can be detected and appropriate new units developed. This, in turn, will lead to a more potent system of education for each and every student.

A good survey of the computer's future in education is provided in a recent book edited by Loughary (1966). Although specifics differ, all the authors seem to agree that the computer makes it possible for educators to improve the teaching-learning process in a variety of dramatic new ways. Whether or not we realize this goal will depend to a large part on the extent to which educational-research workers will turn more attention to the study of data processing rather than simply accepting the developments which happen to come their way as by-products of other fields of endeavor. If this challenge is accepted, the next ten years will indeed be a very exciting decade in education.

William W. Cooley
University of Pittsburgh

References

Anderson, G. Ernest. "How to Make Educational Data Processing Fail." *Nation's Sch* 76:54; 1965.

Arden, Bruce W. *An Introduction to Digital Computing.* Addison, 1963. 389p.

Astin, Alexander W., and others. "Symposium: The Data Bank Concept." *J Ed Meas* 2:131–49; 1965.

Astin, Alexander W., and others. "A Program of Longitudinal Research on the Higher Educational System." *ACE Res Reports* 1(No. 1):42; 1966.

Astin, Alexander W., and others. "National Norms for Entering College Freshmen, Fall, 1966." *ACE Res Reports* 2(No. 1):52; 1967.

Baker, F. B. "Proposed Library of Statistical Programs for a Modern Digital Computer." *Ed Psychol Meas* 21:737–46; 1961.

Baker, F. B. "Computer Course for the Behavioral Scientist." *Ed Psychol Meas* 22:617–21; 1962.

Baker, F. B. "Use of Computers in Educational Research." *R Ed Res* 33:566–78; 1963.

Beaton, Albert E. "University Data Processing Centers." *Harvard Ed R* 31:244–9; 1961.

Beaton, Albert E. *The Use of Special Matrix Operators in Statistical Calculus.* ETS, 1964. 235p.

Borko, Harold. (Ed.) *Computer Applications in the Behavioral Sciences.* Prentice-Hall, 1962.

Brisley, E. C. "When Should Schools Mechanize?"

In *Assn Sch Bus Officials US Canada Proceedings.* The Association of School Business Officials, 1958. p. 203-7.

Brooks, Frederick P., and Iverson, Kenneth E. *Automatic Data Processing.* Wiley, 1963. 494p.

Buhler, Roald. *P-Stat: A System of Statistical Programs for the 7090/7094.* Princeton U Press, 1964. 79p.

Carroll, John B., and Ellis, Allan B. *Planning and Utilization of a Regional Data Bank for Educational Research Purposes.* Harvard U Press, 1965. 149p.

Cooley, William W. "Research Methodology and Modern Data Processing." *Harvard Ed R* 31:257-63; 1961.

Cooley, William W., and Jones, Kenneth J. "Computer Systems for Multivariate Analysis." *Ed Psychol Meas* 24:645-53; 1964.

Cooley, William W., and Lohnes, Paul R. *Multivariate Procedures for the Behavioral Sciences.* Wiley, 1962. 211p.

Dixon, W. J. "BIMED: A series of Statistical Programs for the IBM 709, Part 1." *Behavioral Sci* 7:264-7; 1962.

Eyman, R. F., and others. "Comparison of Some Computer Techniques for Factor Analytic Rotation." *Ed Psychol Meas* 22:201-14; 1962.

Faddeeva, V. N. *Computational Methods of Linear Algebra.* Dover, 1959. 252p.

Fattu, Nicholas, "Processing of Data." In Harris, Chester W. (Ed.) *Encyclopedia of Educational Research,* 3rd ed. Macmillan, 1960. p. 1047-56.

Flanagan, John C. "Data Processing in Large-scale Research Projects." *Harvard Ed R* 31:250-6; 1961.

Flanagan, John C., and others. *Design for a Study of American Youth.* Houghton, 1962.

Flores, Ivan. *Computer Software.* Prentice-Hall, 1965. 493p.

Garvin, Paul L. (Ed.) *Natural Language and the Computer.* McGraw-Hill, 1963. 398p.

Goodlad, John I., and others. *Computers and Information Systems in Education.* Harcourt, 1966. 152p.

Green, Bert F. *Digital Computers in Research.* McGraw-Hill, 1963. 333p.

Gregory, Robert H., and Van Horn, Richard L. *Automatic Data-processing Systems.* Wadsworth Publishing Co., Inc., 1965. 816p.

Grossman, Alvin, and Howe, Robert L. *Data Processing for Educators.* Educational Methods, 1965. 362p.

Hartman, T. F. "Computer Assisted Instruction, IBM Thomas J. Watson Research Center, Yorktown Heights, N. Y." *Audio Visual Instruction* 11:22-3; 1966.

Hayward, Lynn C. *BIMD Computer Programs.* School of Medicine, U California, Los Angeles, 1961. 300p.

Hjelm, Howard F. "Applications of Modern Data Processing at the Office of Education." *Harvard Ed R* 31:237-43; 1961.

Horst, Paul. *Factor Analysis of Data Matrices.* Holt, 1965. 730p.

Iverson, Kenneth E. *A Programming Language.* Wiley, 1962. 286p.

Jones, Kenneth J. "The Multivariate Statistical Analyzer." (Multilithed.) Harvard U, 1964. 180p.

Kaiser, H. F. "Computer Program for Varimax Rotation in Factor Analysis." *Ed Psychol Meas* 19:413-20; 1959.

Leeson, Daniel N., and Dimitry, Donald L. *Basic Programming Concepts and the IBM 1620 Computer.* Holt, 1962. 368p.

Lindquist, E. F. *Design and Analysis of Experiments in Psychology and Education.* Houghton, 1953. 393p.

Lindquist, E. F. (Ed.) *Educational Measurement.* ACE, 1951. 819p.

Loughary, John W. (Ed.) *Man-Machine Systems in Education.* Harper, 1966. 242p.

McCracken, Daniel D. *A Guide to FORTRAN Programming.* Wiley, 1961. 88p.

McCracken, Daniel D. *A Guide to ALGOL Programming.* Wiley, 1962(a). 106p.

McCracken, Daniel D. *A Guide to IBM 1401 Programming.* Wiley, 1962(b). 199p.

McCracken, Daniel E. *A Guide to FORTRAN IV Programming.* Wiley, 1965. 151p.

Meltzer, Leo. "Using the IBM Accounting Machine to Obtain Frequencies, Sums, and Sums of Squares, Ignoring Incomplete Data." *Ed Psychol Meas* 21:145-8; 1961.

Page, E. B. "Imminence of Grading Essays by Computer." *Phi Delta Kappan* 47:238-43; 1966.

Ralston, Anthony, and Wilf, Herbert S. (Eds.) *Mathematical Methods for Digital Computers.* Wiley, 1960. 293p.

Salser, C. W., Jr. "What the Electronic Age Can Mean to Business Education." *Nat Bus Ed Q* 26:45-51; 1957.

Schwilck, Gene L., and Bagby, Geraldine. "How Automation Facilitates the Individualization of Instruction." *Am Sch Bd J* 146:21-3; 1963.

Scientific American 3:64-260; 1966.

Selfridge, O. G., and Niesse, R. U. "Pattern Recognition by Machine." *Sci Am* 203:60-8; 1960.

Stone, Philip J. and others. *The General Inquirer: A Computer Approach to Content Analysis.* The M.I.T. Press, 1966. 651p.

Weinberg, Gerald M. *PL/I Programming Primer.* McGraw-Hill, 1966. 278p.

Wrigley, Charles. "Data Processing: Automation in Calculation." *R Ed Res* 27:528-43; 1957.

COMPUTER PERIODICALS

Datamation, F. D. Thompson Publications, Inc., 205 W. Wacker Drive, Chicago, Ill. 60606.

Data Processing for Education, American Data Processing, Book Building, Detroit, Mich.

Automated Education Handbook and Newsletter, Automated Education Center, Box 2658, Detroit, Mich. 48231.

Journal of Educational Data Processing, Educational Systems Corporation, Box 3711, Georgetown Station, Washington, D.C. 20007.

AEDS Monitor, Association for Educational Data Systems, 1201 16th Street NW, Washington, D.C.

Business Automation News, Business Publications, Inc., 288 Park Ave., West Elmhurst, Ill.

DISCIPLINE

The proper functioning of any social system requires some regulation of its members. This is no less true of a school system than it is of a society. For a school system to function properly the conduct of pupils must conform to conditions that are conducive to learning. Principals and teachers are by statutes and board regulations charged with the responsibility for maintaining such order in the school. In many cases this responsibility is extended to the conduct of pupils coming to and from school. The burden of maintaining order and dealing with the various forms of disorder that may occur in the school falls primarily upon the shoulders of classroom teachers, for they have a larger proportion of contact hours with pupils than do any other school personnel.

The procedures, including rules, by which order is maintained in a school are referred to as discipline. In general the system of discipline in a school will reflect the system found in the broader society. In the Western world the system of discipline characterizing society has been moving from force to persuasion and thence in the direction of self-control. The same development is occurring in the school system. In the early days order was secured by coercion, but persuasion and self-control are coming to be substituted for force. But, as in society generally, teachers and principals alike must resort to force when self-control and persuasion fail.

More specifically, the older form of school discipline maintained order by rules and regulations enforced by penalties. The severity of the penalty varied with the kind and degree of infringement. Among the penalties frequently employed were reprimands, detention, withdrawal of privileges, corporal punishment, and expulsion. While the use of such penalties has by no means been abandoned, they have been used less frequently in recent years. The tendency today is to seek proper conduct through learning rather than by arbitrary authority. The pupil is to be guided in the development of self-control and of a sense of responsibility to other pupils and the school. This view of discipline entails the organization and operation of the school in such a way that situations leading to disorder will be largely avoided, and at the same time a maximum amount of opportunity for the development of self-control is provided. Opportunities are created for pupils to participate in school management and in various types of classroom situations in which a sense of responsibility for proper behavior may be developed.

TYPES OF CONDUCT PROBLEMS. Problems of conduct have been classified by various authorities. In general, two criteria have been used most commonly: frequency of occurrence and seriousness.

When instances of misconduct are listed in terms of frequency it is found (Garrison, 1959; NEA, National Education Association, 1957) that in high school talking when silence is expected is the most common misconduct for which pupils are penalized. This is especially the case among girls, while among boys such behavior as inattention and class disturbance is the most frequently occurring form of misconduct. A study involving 225 high school principals (Henning, 1949) found that they rated the following as the most serious forms of misbehavior: lying, showing disrespect for faculty, petty thievery, and congregating in the halls and lavatories.

The perception of teachers of the seriousness of various types of misbehavior appears to be fairly constant. Although teachers tend to see behavior problems from a clinical standpoint more readily than they did three or four decades ago (Schrupp & Gjerde, 1953), little change has occurred in their ratings of problems. Using Wickman's study (1928) as a basis of comparison, Stouffer and Owens (1955) found that the chief problems identified by teachers 25 years later were about the same. Thirty-two percent of the teachers studied in 1927 thought undesirable personality traits constituted one of the most serious problems, and 31 percent of the teachers studied 25 years later held the same view. It is interesting to note also that during that time the following misbehaviors were practically unchanged in the percentage of teachers rating them as serious: violations of standards of morality and integrity, transgressions against authority, violations of general school regulations, violations of classroom rules, violations of schoolwork regulations, and difficulty with other children. Instances of misconduct among pupils in English schools have been classified in a similar manner. A survey of 27 types of behavior difficulties in English schools showed the highest frequencies occurred for (1) unsatisfactory attitudes toward school and schoolwork, (2) noise-producing and other distracting activities, and (3) uncooperative activities (National Foundation of Educational Research in England & Wales, 1952). The highest frequency of misbehavior occurred in boys' schools, the lowest in girls' schools.

Kinds of misbehavior among college students include such offenses as theft, gambling, violations of housing regulations, academic offenses, auto cases, and disorderly conduct (Prusok, 1961). These offenses may be contrasted with the more common public school problem of class disturbance, which is not an important problem in college. In a questionnaire covering 11 categories of offenses Prusok found that parents view civil offenses as more serious than campus offenses, while students hold the opposite opinion. Personnel workers expressed a more punitive attitude than either students or parents, although they were significantly less punitive than students with respect to offenses involving the use of alcoholic beverages.

Classification of cases of misbehavior by either the criterion of frequency of occurrence or teacher judgments of seriousness has yielded neither theoretical nor practical value. Yet some system of classification seems desirable. For if each case is a class in itself, logically there would be at least as many ways of handling behavior problems as there are cases. Recently efforts have been made to reduce the multiplicity of problems to a few basic categories by factor analysis. Using the data of Hayes's study (1943) of disturbances among eighth-grade boys and girls, Kooi and Schutz (1965) obtained five categories of problems which represent 72 percent of the variance. They are physical aggression, peer affinity, attention seeking, challenge of authority, and critical dissension. Although the data from Hayes's study are limited, the factorial approach to the classification of behavior problems in the classroom has considerable promise. But so long as the data used in the analysis yield descriptive rather than diagnostic categories the results will be disappointing. For no matter how neat the classes of misbehavior may be, they will be of little practical worth to the teacher. For he still will be unable either to make an adequate diagnosis of the misbehavior or to prescribe a way of dealing with it.

EXPLANATIONS OF MISBEHAVIOR. Current explanations of conduct problems lean heavily on the principles of mental hygiene. In the older view of human behavior it was generally believed that misconduct was due to deliberate intent on the part of the pupil at best and to the devil at worst. But with the growth of psychological knowledge has come a new set of concepts by which misbehavior is to be understood. It is now attributed to frustration, inhibition, broken homes, ill health, personal maladjustment, and the like. Sheviakov and Redl (1956) give six factors to which they attribute antisocial conduct of the pupil: dissatisfaction in schoolwork; emotional unrest in relationship to others; disturbances in the classroom climate; lack of harmony between classroom control and the need of a pupil for emancipation; emotional strains that accompany sudden changes from one activity to another; and composition of the classroom group. There is good reason to suppose that the home has a very strong impact upon the behavior of the child in school. Lying and stealing are more frequently observed in children of broken homes than in others, and extreme anger and disobedience are found more often in homes broken by divorce than by separation by death (Russell, 1957). A broken home resulting from death tends to be associated more with academic retardation. Impoverished backgrounds and low standards in values and ego ideals are associated with a lack of sensitivity to conventions and mores and a tendency toward defensive behavior (Jacques, 1958). These observations as to the sources of behavior problems are in keeping with conclusions reached by others (Bowman, 1959).

Some conduct problems arise also from dynamic relations among pupils (Foshay & others, 1954). On the basis of teacher approval, play skills, and physical appearance pupils tend to form opinions about one another and to express these opinions in terms of name calling, physical aggression, and snubbing. Furthermore, they tend to form some sort of pecking order with considerate behavior directed toward social equals and inconsiderate behavior directed downward toward those considered inferior. Misbehavior exhibited in the classroom may often consist of aggressions and counteraggressions arising out of these antagonistic feelings and reactions of pupils of which the teacher may be unaware.

The literature on discipline is replete with claims that a large proportion of the problems of conduct are rooted in academic failure. The theoretical support for this claim lies in the hypothesis that frustration very often leads to aggression and, in the case of the classroom, to misbehavior. It follows logically from this hypothesis that if a pupil is frustrated by failure in his schoolwork, he is more apt than the successful pupil to misbehave. Systematic empirical study of this explanation has not been made, and such studies as have been made are confounded by a number of uncontrolled variables.

Although teachers have become acquainted with the principles of personal and social adjustment, they still account for misbehavior in terms of ill-defined conditions. Among elementary teachers (Barnes, 1963), some of the most frequently mentioned causes of misbehavior are insufficient ability of teachers, differences in pupil interest, desire for attention on the part of pupils, differences in family values, insufficient parental interest, limited intelligence, and limited home backgrounds. When these explanations are grouped into categories they are found to comprise about four kinds of factors: those associated with the home environment, with the school, and with heredity, and those not associated with any of the foregoing three sets of factors.

Some of the conditions associated with college disciplinary cases are listed by Williamson (1956) as follows: repressive rules and mores of institutions; lack of proper institutional climate; transfer from parental restrictions to campus freedom; struggle for independence from parents transferred to college authorities; pathological character; and natural prankishness. Although these explanations of misconduct among college students were formulated over a decade ago, there is no reason to suppose them to be less valid today. Perhaps the emergence of militant ideologies among students should be added to the list. But even so, many recent disturbances appear to be rooted in dissatisfaction with institutional rules no less than in ideologies.

Another explanation of misconduct is that the school—its program of studies, rules, and operations, and indeed the staff itself—is weighted in the direction of the interests and values of the middle social class and hence discriminates against the lower classes (Hollingshead, 1949; Rich, 1960). In these circumstances, children of the lower classes do not respond to the incentives and motivations honored by the school and hence become more susceptible than the middle-class children to disciplinary action.

The claim that the school emphasizes middle-class values and to this extent biases the educational program against the possibilities of success of lower-class children has been questioned by some authorities. Havighurst (1966) points out that the values which the school attempts to emphasize are those which belong to an urban, industrial, democratic society. For example, punctuality, orderliness, and enjoyment of study are values of an industrialized, urban society rather than social-class values. It is claimed that the underprivileged home in central city subscribes to these values and attempts as well as it can to inculcate them in its young. If this view is correct, what is needed is a school that helps the parents as well as the children to find ways by which these values may be achieved.

It is claimed that the school is much more severe in its treatment of a lower-class child who has violated some important rule in the school than it is of a middle-class child who is guilty of the same violation. But empirical data in support of this claim are inadequate. There are, to be sure, many instances of such discrepancies in the administration of disciplinary measures, but the extent and degree of the differentiation is not known. A study by Hoehn (1954) of 19 third-grade teachers shows that middle-class pupils did not receive more attention from these teachers than lower-class pupils did. His findings are inconclusive on the question of whether the contacts of teachers with pupils were differentiated in such a way that the lower-class pupil received less integrative teacher behavior than those of higher status did. In addition, he points out that his findings are confounded because achievement was not controlled. When it is parceled out statistically, Hoehn hypothesizes that the differences in behavior of the teacher toward the children in the classroom is related to their achievement rather than to social-class status. But a study by Rich (1960) indicates that lower-class pupils who learn middle-class manners are rewarded more by teachers for this achievement than for academic achievement.

While the foregoing notions of why misbehavior occurs have opened up avenues of research that were not possible with the older conceptions, and while they have led to more considerate treatment of pupils, they are open to criticism on two counts. First, they do not supply the teacher with adequate criteria by which to decide in any given case that the behavior is due to frustration, broken homes, or whatnot. Second, they have led to few prescriptions for dealing with misconduct. If the teacher decides that the pupil's behavior is due to frustration, the teacher may find that he is no better off than he was before. In the absence of new prescriptions for dealing with the problem, he resorts all too often to the disciplinary techniques to which he is accustomed.

CONTROL TECHNIQUES. Few control techniques have been derived from the concepts of mental hygiene. In general, these concepts have been interpreted to mean that pupils strive for praise and approval, especially by individuals who are in positions of authority. Hence, the pupil will tend to act in ways that bring positive affective responses from his teachers rather than negative ones. Punishment or punitive behavior by the teacher may elicit aversive pupil behavior (Symonds, 1956) rather than lead him to engage in proper classroom conduct. The number of isolates is significantly lower when the ideology of the teacher is ingratiatory (Gold, 1962). It would appear that the classroom climate set by the teacher influences the interpersonal relations of pupils, especially those possessing less integrative patterns of behavior. According to this view, if the teacher does not dominate the classroom situation and if he understands the pupil's misbehavior and accepts it as a way of releasing his tensions or else takes steps to remove the cause of the behavior, the problems of discipline will tend to disappear.

Perhaps one of the most significant changes in the handling of conduct problems has come along with the development of guidance and counseling programs. Nowadays teachers who understand something of the psychology of personal adjustment are apt to be sensitive to the underlying factors of maladjustment and to refer difficult cases to counselors rather than trying to deal with them in the complicated conditions of the classroom.

The view is widely held that the response of emotionally disturbed pupils to techniques of classroom management is different from the response of nondisturbed pupils. More extensive studies of the question may show this to be the case, but recent investigations do not support this view. In a study of a number of parameters of teaching behavior (Kounin & others, 1966) it was found that the effects of these parameters were in the same direction for disturbed as for nondisturbed pupils. Apparently the techniques of teachers who are effective in managing groups of nondisturbed pupils are also effective with groups containing emotionally disturbed children.

DISCIPLINARY PRACTICES. Surveys of disciplinary practices are spotty and lend themselves to risky generalization. About all that can be done is to point to the findings of a few studies. If the findings of Barnes's study (1963) can be taken as typical, the techniques used by elementary teachers fall into four categories: nonaction—that is, ignoring the behavior; providing activities through special assistance, enrichment, and the like; reasoning with children; individualizing the work. Only 8 percent of the teachers relate misconduct to the needs of the children, and they tend to attribute discipline problems to single causes rather than to interrelated variables. The remedial measures are more often positive than negative. Among the positive actions, reasoning and discussion are resorted to less often than the removal of barriers to proper conduct. Punitive action is taken about 8 percent of the time. The most frequent types of negative measures found in high school (Garrison, 1959) appear to be reprimand before the class, followed by reprimand in private, detention, assignment to special tasks, sending the student from room, giving him a special seat, sending him to the principal, and reducing his grades.

Corporal punishment is prohibited by statute in New Jersey and the District of Columbia and probably in Rhode Island, where the law does not specifically mention such punishment but may be interpreted to forbid it (National Education Association, 1958). The laws of most states forbid cruel treatment of children, and in cases where corporal punishment is excessive, the teacher is subject to arrest.

In England, pupils for whom deterrents and incentives work as modes of control tend to be hypersensitive, introverted, and self-doubting (National Foundation of Educational Research in England & Wales, 1952). These types of control are much less successful with aggressive, extroverted, and distractible pupils. English teachers use corporal punishment most often to deter conduct in violation of regulations. But this sort of disciplinary measure is used only after other means have failed. The tendency in England is to lessen the degree of punitiveness, while in the United States the tendency is toward stricter measures (Eckstein, 1966).

Colleges and universities, unlike the lower schools, usually have committees and personnel officers to handle disciplinary cases. Many colleges have set up disciplinary committees to handle the cases of misconduct because of the increasing complexity of modern life. In discussing the disciplinary committee in the small college McKinney (1956) notes that there has been a decline in the hold which moral and religious principles have on society. Faculty as well as students are no longer always sure of what is right or wrong. While formerly violations of college regulations were dealt with positively and with dispatch, the erosion of standards and the development of psychology have resulted in a tendency to take more time in judging discipline cases and to be more lenient.

What the counselor's role should be in the disciplinary situation is a perennial problem. Even when it is resolved at a theoretical level, many cases arise in which the role of the counselor is not clear to everyone concerned. The tendency in most institutions is to separate counseling and disciplinary responsibilities and, at most, to make the counselor advisory to the committee on discipline. This separation does not mean that the counselor is to divorce himself from the student's task of adjusting to life on the college campus (Mueller, 1958). Rather, the counselor's task is to understand the various standards and values in the student population and to help the student to understand his problem in this context.

EXPERIMENTALLY TESTED TECHNIQUES. Despite developments in the psychology of personal adjustment and their influence on pedagogical thought neither the theory nor the technology of classroom management and control has been worked out. Partly as a result of the failure of psychological concepts to yield practical measures, research on discipline has shifted from mere theorizing about the handling of misbehavior by inferences from psychological concepts and principles to the empirical study of teacher behavior and its effects.

Empirical studies have revealed new dimensions of disciplinary behavior. Such behavior may exhibit different properties from moment to moment: firm, rough, clear, and so on. And the effects of these properties upon pupil behavior may vary from pupil to pupil, depending upon the pupil's maturity and his relation to the conduct toward which the control techniques are directed. Pupils may react to these qualities of teacher behavior in a number of ways. They may become worried and disruptive; they may conform by trying to "be good"; they may try their own brand of misbehavior; or they may vacillate between conforming and nonconforming. In their study of kindergarten children, Kounin and Gump (1958) found that clarity of control techniques (denoting the deviance and telling the child how to stop it) is apt to be successful in securing and maintaining appropriate behavior without noticeably affecting pupil worry or anxiety. Roughness does not tend to induce good behavior but does increase worries and anxieties as manifested in disruptive conduct. Techniques of control that exhibit a high degree of firmness lead to conformance on the part of on-looking pupils who are themselves inclined toward deviant behavior.

However, the foregoing conclusions should be qualified in the light of a later study (Kounin & others, 1966). In a study of teaching behavior involving grades 1–2 and 3–4 in regular classrooms, Kounin and others found that firmness, clarity, and punitiveness are not related to deviance. But this inconsistency with the earlier investigation (Kounin & Gump, 1958) may be explained by reference to other factors. First, the kindergarten groups, in the earlier study, were in the first four days of their school career, while the classroom groups, in the later study, were well-established, having been in school for about eight months. It is possible that the experience of these classroom groups with such variables as firmness, clarity, and roughness had tended to reduce their effects. Even in the kindergarten study it was observed that the effect of these variables was less after the first day. Second, there were few serious acts of misconduct, less than 1 percent, and the teachers resorted to no extreme punitive measures such as corporal punishment. While there is little knowledge of the conditions under which ways of handling discipline problems are effective, there is little reason to suppose that dimensions of teaching behavior as clarity and firmness are inconsequential.

Another dimension of teaching behavior, one that appears to be related to desirable classroom conduct, is what is called "with-it-ness" (Kounin & others, 1966). It is that quality of behavior that signals to pupils that the teacher is aware of what is going on. Pupils recognize when teachers do not have it. For example, if the teacher is not with-it, he attends to a minor deviance while a major one is going on, or else he attends too late to the major act of misbehavior. The greater the degree of with-it-ness, the lower is the rate of deviance and the higher the involvement of pupils in their work.

The way in which transition points in classroom work are handled may also affect the conduct of pupils. As the teacher guides a class through its daily program he shifts from one task to another—from arithmetic to spelling, from reading to art. The teacher may make these transitions skillfully or he may do it crudely. An example of unskilled management is afforded by the teacher who invites pupils to begin a new activity and then drops it or who gives confusing or conflicting directions about what to do.

Teachers who properly handle shifts from one activity to another have less misbehavior and more involvement of pupils in work than do teachers who fail to cope with these transitions (Kounin & others, 1966).

It has sometimes been claimed that the misbehavior of pupils is caused by teachers' demands for excessive attention to academic activities. But a limited study of the "attention span" (the length of time a pupil can engage in an activity without becoming restless) in relation to classroom conduct (Kounin & others, 1966) shows that such a claim is not necessarily valid when time alone is considered. On the other hand, a program designed to reduce satiation in learning activities is conducive to appropriate classroom behavior.

Individuals who work together will occasionally have conflicting desires. Some degree of frustration in such interpersonal relations is almost unavoidable. This is especially the case in a classroom group, where the goals of the teacher are often at odds with those of the pupils. In this circumstance some degree of hostility is almost certain to arise. The problem of handling such hostility is one which almost every teacher will face at one time or another. When the action of the teacher must go counter to the wishes of the pupil, the teacher will do well to avoid the appearance of being unfair and to help the pupil to perceive the teacher's actions as being legitimate (Horwitz, 1963). When the teacher is viewed by pupils as being the cause of their frustration rather than as the instrument of it, their hostility is apt to be heightened. It has been claimed, especially by those of a democratic persuasion, that such hostility is less apt to arise in democratically managed classrooms. But Horwitz's investigation of classroom management (1963) does not bear out this claim. To cite a single point, inconsistent behavior of an authoritarian teacher is less apt to arouse hostility than that of a democratic teacher. Hence the burden of consistency is greater for the latter than for the former. This is the case because an inconsistency of an authoritarian teacher will tend to show more regard for pupil desires and goals. On the other hand, a change in the direction of a democratic teacher's behavior is apt to be toward ignoring or repressing pupil desires and will in consequence evoke hostility.

How control techniques directed at a particular pupil affect others is a question of considerable importance in classroom management. This question has been studied by Kounin and Gump (1958). Their findings indicate that pupils who are not themselves targets of control techniques are nevertheless affected by these techniques. The effects of disciplinary action, under certain conditions, spread beyond the pupils toward whom the action is directed. The reactions of pupils who are watching the disciplinary situation tend to be related to the clarity, firmness, and roughness of the control techniques and to the degree of their orientation toward the behavior at the time. If the verbal commands of the teacher are clear, so that the pupil and his misbehavior are identified and he is directed toward a task rather than threatened, the witnessing pupils are less apt to misbehave. Similarly, increasing firmness in the teacher's behavior, provided it is not rough and overly threatening, tends to accentuate conformance of pupils who are interested in, and witnesses of, the misbehavior. Roughness tends, on the other hand, to increase worries and anxieties. On the whole, clear and firm behavior on the part of the teacher is conducive to acceptable pupil conduct, while rough and threatening behavior tends to lead to disruptive conduct.

The effects of control techniques on the overt behavior of pupils have been discussed in the foregoing paragraphs. It is now time to ask whether or not these techniques affect the way in which pupils perceive misbehavior, control techniques, and other factors in the behavioral situation. The effect of disciplinary techniques on children's attitudes toward misbehavior was studied by using three pairs of first-grade teachers, one of each pair rated as punitive, the other as nonpunitive (Kounin & Gump, 1961). The pupils were asked: "What is the worst thing a child can do at school?" and also "Why is that so bad?" Pupils of punitive teachers showed more concern with aggression and physical assault. In addition, punitive techniques tend to induce conflicts and uncertainty about misbehavior. Then, too, it was found that teachers' punitiveness distracts pupils from their concern with school work. Pupils with nonpunitive teachers talked more about learning, achievement losses, and violations of school values and rules as a result of misconduct than pupils whose teachers used punitive measures.

The question of what effect the prestige of a deviant and his reaction to a teacher's desist technique has upon onlooking pupils is of practical interest. A study made of four classes of fifth graders who were being shown a science film during the misbehavior (Gnagey, 1960) showed that pupils who saw the deviant submit to the teacher rated the desist technique as fairer and also recalled more facts from the film than pupils who saw the deviant defy the teacher. The magnitude of the difference in the reactions in the two cases was greater for pupils who were the audience to a high-influence deviant. This study, like that of Kounin and Gump (1958), shows that one reason why an onlooker is affected by a desist order directed at someone else is some sort of linkage with the deviant, in this case a sociometric linkage.

B. Othanel Smith
University of Illinois

References

Barnes, Donald L. "An Analysis of Remedial Activities Used by Elementary Teachers in Coping with Classroom Behavior Problems." *J Ed Res* 56:544–7; 1963.

Bowman, Herman J. "A Review of Discipline." *Nat Assn Sec Sch Prin B* 54:147–56; 1959.

Eckstein, M. A. "Ultimate Deterrents: Punishment and Control in English and American Schools." *Compar Ed R* 10:433–41; 1966.

Foshay, Arthur W., and others. *Children's Social Values.* Teachers Col, Columbia U, 1954. 323p.

Garrison, Karl C. "A Study of Student Disciplinarian Practices in Two Georgia High Schools." *J Ed Res* 53:153–6; 1959.

Gnagey, William J. "Effects on Classmates of a Deviant Student's Power and Response to a Teacher Exerted Control Technique." *J Ed Psychol* 51:1–9; 1960.

Gold, Hilary A. "The Classroom Isolate: An Additional Dimension for Consideration in the Evaluation of a Quality Education Program." *J Exp Ed* 31:77–80; 1962.

Havighurst, Robert J. "Overcoming Value Differences." In Strom, Robert D. (Ed.) *The Inner-city Classroom: Teacher Behaviors.* Charles E. Merrill Books, Inc., 1966. p. 41–56.

Hayes, Margaret Louise. *A Study of Classroom Disturbances of Eighth-grade Boys and Girls.* Contributions to Education No. 871. Teachers Col, Columbia U, 1943. 139p.

Henning, Carol J. "Discipline: Are School Practices Changing?" *Clearing House* 23:267–73; 1949.

Hoehn, Arthur J. "A Study of the Social Status Differentiation in the Classroom Behavior of Nineteen Third Grade Teachers." *J Social Psychol* 39:269–92; 1954.

Hollingshead, August B. *Elmtown's Youth: The Impact of Social Classes on Adolescents.* Wiley, 1949. 480p.

Horwitz, Murray. "Hostility and Its Management in Classroom Groups." In Charters, W. W., Jr., and Gage, N. L. (Eds.) *Readings in the Social Psychology of Education.* Allyn and Bacon, 1963. p. 196–212.

Jacques, Odilia Marie. "Predicting Juvenile Delinquency Proneness by Group Tests." *Personnel Guid J* 36:489–92; 1958.

Kooi, Beverly Y., and Schutz, Richard E. "A Factor Analysis of Classroom-disturbance Intercorrelations." *Am Ed Res J* 2:37–40; 1965.

Kounin, Jacob S., and Gump, Paul V. "The Ripple Effect in Discipline." *El Sch J* 62:158–62; 1958.

Kounin, Jacob S., and Gump, Paul V. "The Comparative Influence of Punitive and Non-punitive Teachers on Children's Concepts of School Misconduct." *J Ed Psychol* 52:44–9; 1961.

Kounin, Jacob S., and others. "Managing Emotionally Disturbed Children in Regular Classrooms." *J Ed Psychol* 57:1–13; 1966.

McKinney, Richard I. "Disciplinary Philosophy and Procedures in a Small College." *Assn Am Col B* 42:548–52; 1956.

Mueller, Kate Hevner. "Theory for Campus Discipline." *Personnel Guid J* 36:302–9; 1958.

National Education Association, Research Division. "Discipline in the Public Schools." *Res B* 35:152–5; 1957.

National Education Association, Research Division. "Corporal Punishment." *Res B* 36:88–9; 1958.

National Foundation of Educational Research in England and Wales. *A Survey of Rewards and Punishments in Schools Based on Researches Carried Out by M. E. Highfield and A. Pinsent.* Newnes, 1952. 432p.

Prusok, Ralph E. "Student, Student Personnel Worker, and Parent Attitudes Toward Student Discipline." *Personnel Guid J* 40:247–53; 1961.

Rich, John Martin. "How Social Class Values Affect Teacher-Pupil Relations." *J Ed Sociol* 33:355–9; 1960.

Russell, Ivan L. "Behavior Problems of Children from Broken and Intact Homes." *J Ed Sociol* 31:124–9; 1957.

Schrupp, Manfred H., and Gjerde, Clayton M. "Teacher Growth in Attitudes Toward Behavior Problems of Children." *J Ed Psychol* 44:203–14; 1953.

Sheviakov, George V., and Redl, Fritz. *Discipline for Today's Children and Youth.* Association for Supervision and Curriculum Development, NEA, 1956. 64p.

Stouffer, George A. W., Jr., and Owens, Jennie. "Behavior Problems of Children as Identified by Today's Teachers and Compared with Those Reported by E. K. Wickman." *J Ed Res* 48:321–31; 1955.

Symonds, Percival M. "What Education Has to Learn from Psychology." *Teach Col Rec* 57:449–62; 1956.

Wickman, E. Koster. *Children's Behavior and Teachers' Attitudes.* The Commonwealth Fund, 1928. 247p.

Williamson, E. G. "Preventive Aspects of Disciplinary Counseling." *Ed Psychol Monogr* 16:68–81; 1956.

DRAMATIC ARTS EDUCATION

From its ancient origins in fifth-century Athens to the present day, the theater and its drama have been related to education. The Greek term for a stage production was *didaskalia*, which also meant the teaching of a play to the chorus that performed it. Dramatic productions were both a religious and an educational responsibility of the state and hence were financed largely by the city-state, though a private citizen of means was given the civic responsibility of financing the employment and training of the chorus. Attendance at these performances was a major element in the adult education of the citizen. Tradition and the extant records indicate that literary drama and public productions in Rome were begun by a Romanized Greek schoolmaster, Livius Andronicus, who began by using Greek plays in translation with his students and who presented the first public performance in 240 B.C. Apparently from this time to the downfall of the Roman Empire the use of drama in the Roman schools as an instrument of instruction, especially in the Greek language, was general. It was perhaps this practice which influenced the later monastery schools of the Middle Ages in the utilization of Latin drama for similar instructional purposes (Arnott, 1959; Beare, 1951; Duckworth, 1952).

THEORIES OF DRAMA IN RELATION TO THE DIDACTIC. The Greeks. Before continuing the account of the historical development of the interrelations of theater arts and education, and more particularly of drama and instruction, a brief glance at that interrelationship as it appeared in theory and criticism may be illuminating. The interrelationship was a commonplace in Greek thought long before the dawn of criticism, for the Greeks considered the poet as the teacher of the people. A good part of ancient Greek education of youths centered on music and lyric poetry, on Homer and the Homeric hymns; indeed, the writings of the poets were the essential textbooks of that curriculum. Aristophanes in the *parabasis* of the *Acharnians,* as well as in that of other plays, stoutly asserts that he has taught and improved the citizens of Athens and thereby rendered service to the state. His great comedy *The Frogs* ends with a debate between Euripides and Aeschylus, a remarkable piece of extended literary criticism, in which it is repeatedly asserted that the ultimate criterion for judging the tragic poet and his tragedies is their moral instruction. It is not surprising therefore that Plato should insist upon and that Aristotle should recognize the instrumental function of poetry and drama. For Plato, however, almost the sole justification of poetry was its ability to instruct, and he clearly saw that poetry could teach vice as well as virtue. Moreover, in comparison with speculative philosophy it was "thrice removed from reality"; hence, for him, it was inferior to philosophy. Aristotle, though he recognized the instructive aspect of the arts and their potentials for either good or bad uses, especially in the *Politics,* held that art had its own justification as a made thing of beauty. This dual conception of the function of art gave rise to two modes or kinds of criticism that have persisted to this day, resulting from the two different, though not mutually exclusive, conceptions of the end or function of art (Crane, 1952).

Though Plato banned certain kinds of poetry from his ideal republic, he did, in the *Republic,* the *Protagoras,* and other dialogues, insist upon the educational values of poetry. He believed in the practical application of philosophy to personal, family, and social problems; hence he saw poetry and the other arts primarily as instruments of individual and social morality. Though Plato contributed other ideas to later criticism—poetry as imitation, poetry as inspiration, poetry as concealed symbolism—his most pervasive and persistent contribution is the didactic slant that he gave to the interpretation of all literature.

Aristotle borrowed the idea of art as imitation from Plato but improved upon that idea. Using a literal rather than an analogical method of reasoning, he subdivided knowledge into three kinds: theoretical knowledge, which has for its end simply to know (mathematics, physics, metaphysics); practical knowledge, which has for its end to do (politics, ethics, rhetoric); productive knowledge, which has for its end to make (medicine as the art of healing, architecture, poetics). Though the third category, productive knowledge, is only implicit in Aristotle's extant works, he makes it quite clear that each realm of knowledge has its own distinct principles and methods. The results of productive knowledge are made things, artificial objects brought into being through the artifice of a maker. There are two categories of such objects: those whose criterion is utility and those whose criterion is beauty—or, to use modern designations, the useful and the fine arts. Every art object that is brought into being through artifice has form and by virtue of its form (formulation) has powers or effects. These powers or effects are, in turn, determinants of the form (formulation) which the artist gives to the object. All fine arts are imitations, are mimetic, but in different modes and manners. As imitations they have three elements or principles: object of imitation, means (medium) of imitation, and manner of imitation. Differences in means result in difference in the kind of art object; differences in the object result in different forms; and differences in the manner result in different techniques. An art object must have wholeness or completeness if it is to fulfill its end; hence it must have unity. The origins of fine arts rests upon two fundamental aspects of human nature: man is by nature an imitative animal, and he takes delight (pleasure) in imitation. These are some of the fundamental considerations which form the basis of Aristotle's *Poetics,* the most influential piece of literary criticism ever written. It is not a treatise on aesthetics; it is a scientific (philosophic) treatise on the *poietes* making or constructing *poiesis.* That is, it is strictly concerned with the form and the structure of the theoretically best form of poetry, especially tragedy and epic (the sections or book on comedy have been lost). The *Poetics* is the foundation of all later formalistic criticism (Crane, 1952).

The Romans. Except for some traditions and a few scattered fragments of an early indigenous literature, Roman literature, theory, and criticisms are Hellenistic, resulting from the hellenizing of Roman culture after the First Punic War 264–241 B.C.). Rhetoric and oratory, rather than poetic and poetry, were primal concerns among the Romans. Even their concern with theory and criticism exhibits their bias toward the practical, patriotic, didactic, and utilitarian. Their great poet Vergil (Publius Vergilius Maro, 70–19 B.C.) is essentially a poet-propagandist. Horace (Quintus Horatius Flaccus, 65–8 B.C.) may, even more than Vergil, be so described. He left in his *Ars poetica* (*The Art of Poetry*), a versification of literary doctrine, the most influential Latin work of criticism. *The Art of Poetry* (perhaps written in 14 or 13 B.C.) had some currency in the Middle Ages and thus, as Weinberg says, "came to the humanistic period and the Renaissance as part of their immediate intellectual heritage" (Weinberg, Vol. I, 1961). In his concern for the audience Horace amalgamates rhetoric with poetic. For him the ends of poetry were to delight and to instruct (*utile et dulce*—useful and delightful), a conception reinforced for Renaissance critics by their heritage from medieval drama, discussed later, which was predominantly didactic in intent (Richardson, 1944).

The Renaissance. The efflorescence of interest in poetic theory and criticism which occurred in the Italian Renaissance is, as Bernard Weinberg has shown in his two-volume *History of Literary Criticism* *in the Italian Renaissance* (1961), a consistent attempt to relate the aims of poetry and drama to instruction. As he has further shown, the first flowerings of that extensive development stem from Horace's *Art of Poetry*, though later they centered chiefly on an interpretation of Aristotle's *Poetics*. Scores, even hundreds, of the treatises and discourses were written from the late fifteenth to the early seventeenth centuries, but perhaps the four that were most widely influential were the *Arte poetica* of Francesco Robertello, published in Florence in 1548; *L'arte poetica* by Antonio Minturno, published in Venice in 1564; *Poetica d'Aristotele vulgarizzata et sposta* by Lodovico Castelvetro, published in Basel in 1576; and *Poetices libri septem,* published in Lyon in 1561. Each of these is an explication of Aristotle's *Poetics* and an expansion of theory, amalgamating rhetoric and poetic in various ways. The consequences of this amalgamation and the ideas arising therefrom for both the theory and the practice of drama are far-reaching. The conception of the nature and function of drama was shifted away from the play itself as its own justification, having its full validity as a work of art, which focuses primary attention upon how a *poiesis* (mimetic work) is constructed by a *poeites* (mimetic poet). In the latter conception, form, structure, and principles of poetic composition are of primary importance in interpreting the dramatic poem. Instead of considering the poem (drama) as an art object in itself, these Renaissance critics, following Horace, thought of it as an effect upon a reader or audience, a kind of experience akin to that of an audience swayed by an orator. Emphasis, therefore, inevitably changes from the criterion of beauty as the end to the dual criteria of utility (instruction) and delight. Such a theory of the nature of drama makes it an obvious instrument of education, solidly grounding the argument that the theater is the school of morals and manners in the fundamental conception of the nature of drama. It was the general acceptance of this idea that supported the extensive uses of theater and drama in the Jesuit schools, to be noted later (Crane, 1952; Weinberg, 1961).

These Renaissance critical treatises, representing an amalgamation of Platonic, Aristotelian, and Horatian conceptions and principles, established that neoclassical theory of literature, and especially of drama, which became dominant in the latter part of the seventeenth century and through most of the eighteenth. French critics such as Nicolas Boileau (1636–1711), a strict adherent to theory and rules, and Saint-Évremond (Charles de Marguetel de Saint-Denis, seigneur de Saint-Évremond, 1610?–1703), a liberal in theory, built upon and codified the theories of the Italians. Their neoclassicism was grounded securely upon the twin bases of rationalism and authoritarianism. Thus, literature and art, in order that they might most effectively fulfill their twin functions of instruction and pleasure, were regularized and subjected to strict logical order, clarity, and symmetry. In Boileau's words the chief virtue of a poet was to *réduisit la muse aux règles du devoir* (to harness or subdue the muse with obligatory rules). A cardinal doctrine of neoclassicism, stemming in large part from the emphasis upon rationalism, was known as *vraisemblance*, verisimilitude, fidelity or truth to nature—in the seventeenth-century sense of nature as human nature generalized or typified, universal man as seen in all of the varied categories of human character and conduct. The ideal prototypes of these characters and patterns of conduct were to be seen in the great works of the ancients; hence, as Alexander Pope (1688–1744) said in *An Essay on Criticism* (1711): "Learn hence for ancient rules a just esteem; / To copy nature is to copy them" (West, 1908). Thus, rationalism leads to and supports authoritarianism.

Neoclassicism as a school of criticism and as an epoch in art and literature is far too complex, diverse, and extensive to be adequately summarized in any one article or monograph, but there is one further tenet of the school, among many, that is of special importance to didactic drama. That is the doctrine of poetic justice, the conception that poetry, especially drama, performs its instrumentalist function (pleasant teaching) best when, especially in its ending, it shows virtuous characters rewarded and vicious characters punished. Poetic justice, though not emphasized or insisted upon by all neoclassical critics, had important consequences in the eighteenth century in the development of sentimental comedy, *dramae* (bourgeois or middle-class tragedy), and later in the development of melodrama.

The scientific revolution, which may be said to have begun with Nicolaus Copernicus (1473–1543) and Galileo Galilei (1564–1642) and to have culminated with Sir Isaac Newton (1642–1727), exploded the ancient conception of an ordered and closed universe and destroyed the old ideas of the nature of man. The attempts to build a new metaphysics on the basis of the new science, notably the work of René Descartes (1596–1650) in France and John Locke (1632–1704) in England, shifted the emphasis of philosophy from a philosophy of being to a philosophy of knowing and culminated in a new conception of the nature of man. According to both, man is born into this world with a mental substance that has the capacity of consciousness and therefore can receive through sensory experience sense impressions which shape the kind of mind that each separate and unique individual will possess. Since no one can directly share the consciousness of another, all men, according to Locke, are born free and equal, for all mental substance is in its essential nature the same. The consequences of the Lockean conception are profound and operative down to the present in philosophy, politics, art, and literature. They are far too extensive and complex to be summarized here, but a few must be noted briefly (Northrop, 1947).

LOCKEAN MAN AND MODERN ART. By definition a man is an isolated and unique individual. His priceless heritage is complete individualistic freedom, a portion of which he gives up by consent to join with others in forming societies and governments. Hence all governments derive their just powers from the consent of the governed, and the best government is that which governs least—that is, that which places minimum restrictions on individual freedom. But government is a necessary evil in preserving the individual man's corporeal substance, his body, which houses his mental substance. Since the mind of man is shaped by experiences (sensations), environment and education assume paramount importance. The socially oriented literature and the realism of the nineteenth century are inevitable consequences of this conception of the nature of man. Thus, even before Henrik Ibsen (1828–1906) and his famous realistic social problem dramas the increasing concern of playwrights was with man as a social being, man in relation to the problems of his contemporary society. For these realistic writers of social problem plays, and even more for the later naturalistic writers, the test of drama was not beauty but truth—truth to the facts of life as these are observed and faithfully set down. Reality in this conception came to be more and more limited to sociological reality, and plays were judged in terms of the faithfulness with which they recorded and exposed social conditions. For many of the social realists drama was an instrument for the correction of social ills; thus, many of the realistic social problem plays are fully didactic in intent.

Certain of the trends, conceptions, and techniques apparent in nineteenth-century realistic drama were intensified in the theories and practices of the so-called naturalistic school. Naturalism accepted a complete determinism stemming from the Darwinian revolution in biological sciences and the application of scientific theories of heredity and environment to sociological phenomena. To the naturalists scientific truth as they saw it was the fundamental reality, indeed the whole of reality that was not mere illusion. Even more strongly than the realists, the naturalists insisted that the function of drama and literature in general was truth, not beauty. This insistence upon being true to observable fact interpreted in a rigorously deterministic manner further accentuated an ancient fallacy that had been strongly revived by romantic critics, the fallacy of confusing art and nature. To the naturalists man was wholly a conditioned animal, determined by heredity and environment, and a main objective of the dramatist was to reveal him as such. Thus they turned to the representation of the lowly and humble, the outcast and dissolute, the uncultivated and the primitive, among whom they assumed that primal human instinctual behavior, uninhibited by overlayers of cultural patterns, operated and could be observed. They sought the veritable language of such illiterate people, depicted their most depraved conduct, and denied the dramatist the right to organize the incidents of his play into a plot that would point a moral or draw a conclusion. By the last dictum they seemed to be denying didacticism in drama. In point of fact their dramas were usually rigorously didactic in that they insisted that they must reveal the basic conduct of man as a conditioned animal. Indeed, certain of the naturalistic playwrights turned to outright sociological thesis plays. They also brought into the modern drama the folk play and the drama of the proletariat. Since their underlying philosophy was similar to that upon which Karl Marx (1818–1883) based his theorizing, many of the plays of the naturalistic playwrights are Marxist in point of view. Though Ibsen was not a disciple of naturalism, some of his thoughts coincided with those of that school; hence Ibsen became a kind of standard bearer of naturalism in the Independent Theatre Movement, initiated by André Antoine (1858–1943) with the establishment of his Théâtre Libre in Paris in 1887 (Miller, 1951).

Didacticism of a more overt kind appears in the expressionistic drama written by the German dramatists, and others, especially between 1910 and about 1925. The basis of the theories of the German expressionists, stemming in large measure from the "dream plays" of August Strindberg (1849–1912), was their refusal to accept the conception of reality based upon scientific theory which the naturalists advocated. They held that naturalistic dramatists dealt only with the surface of life, not with its inner core and meaning. The central fact about man was not his appearance but his essence, his possession of a soul, and the spiritual world transcends the material. Thus, they accepted and attempted to represent the large element of irrationality in character and conduct, the meaningfulness of the dreamworld, and the importance of emotion heightened to ecstasy and visions. To represent these in drama and upon the stage they had to resort to a variety of devices, including the wide uses of signs and symbols, exaggeration and distortion, and characterization reduced to a bare element, an essential trait or characteristic. Therefore, their characters frequently appear without individualizing names, known merely as the son, the father, the millionaire, or—as in *The Adding Machine* (1923) by Elmer Rice (1892–1967)—as Mr. Zero. In such plays incidents often follow incidents without causal connection, much as they occur in dreams. Plot in the sense of a well-defined story with a clear beginning, middle, and end is often absent. The connection of the incidents into a complete whole is understandable only in terms of thought, the idea or ideas toward which all of the situations and unindividualized characters contribute. Thus, thought becomes the chief unifying element and didacticism the chief function of such plays. All of the resources of the theater—lights, sounds, motion pictures, machines effects, revolving platforms, music and choral elements, etc.—are utilized to convey some abstract idea, some mood or fancy of the playwright's own private vision. Almost all of the German expressionists were concerned with the regeneration of man and the new millennium that they hoped would follow the conclusion of World War I. The activists among the expressionists were usually propagandists for Marxism or communism, supporters of the Bolshevik revolution; others were concerned with antiwar statements, the freedom of man, and the ultimate coming of a brave new world that would usher in the brotherhood of man. The Locarno Pact of 1925 seemed to most of the expressionists in Germany to have destroyed these hopes and, some of the historians say, marked the end of expressionism. Actually the influences of that movement are widely apparent in theater arts to the present, and much of the so-called contemporary drama of the absurd is a continuation of aspects of expressionism (Samuel & Thomas, 1939; Esslin, 1961).

This cursory survey of certain aspects of theory and criticism of drama has served to show the persistence of two variously expressed ancient views of the nature and function of drama, the Platonic and the Aristotelian. It has revealed that through the ages theater and drama have in theoretical and critical writings been in one way or another related to instruction and hence to education in its broad sense. A survey of historical developments after the Greek and Roman ages will further reveal these connections.

THE CHRISTIAN TERENCE. The history of medieval school drama can be traced with some confidence from the tenth century onward. In that century the Benedictine abbess of Gandersheim in Saxony prepared prose versions of the six comedies of Terence (Publius Terentius Afer, 185–159 B.C.), an author greatly admired for his Latinity and elegance of style. The abbess wanted students and Christians to read Terence for his style but without the corrupting influence of his pagan subject matter and his sometimes racy vocabulary. On the model of Terence she wrote six plays whose subjects were drawn from Christian history and inculcated Christian morality. The publication of her plays at Nuremberg in 1501 initiated a movement in drama and in the schools known as the "Christian Terence." One of the early leaders in this movement was the famous German humanist Johann Reuchlin (1455–1522), whose comedies became widely known throughout Western Europe. His *Sergius* was written about 1496–97, and his *Henno* was first published in 1497. The latter is a medieval peasant farce modeled after Roman comedy. Another early leader in the movement whose Latin dialogues were widely influential was the French teacher Johannes Revisius Textor (c. 1476–1524).

One of the most prolific of the early writers, whose collected works gave the name to the movement, was the Haarlem schoolmaster Cornelius Schonaeus (1540–1611). As early as 1592 his collected plays were published under the title *Christian Terence or Sacred Comedies, Written in the Terentian style by Cornelius Schonaeus of Gouda*. Scores of other known humanist scholars and teachers utilized the classical drama in their instruction, especially in the teaching of ancient languages and in discussions of critical theories. One of the favorite subjects which these teachers amalgamated into the Christian Terence movement was that of the prodigal son. These prodigal-son plays are of considerable significance in the development of Renaissance comedy. Yet other favorite Biblical subjects similarly utilized were that of Susanna and the Elders, the story of Joseph, that of Judith and Holofernes, and Abraham's sacrifice of Isaac. This amalgamation of Scripture materials with classical structural devices, so characteristic of these academic plays, was a main source through which Renaissance tragicomedy evolved (Herrick, 1955; St. John, 1923).

RELIGIOUS AND MORAL INSTRUCTION IN MEDIEVAL DRAMA. The origins of medieval religious drama and its connection with instructional purposes are well known. The germ of that drama is to be found in the eighth- and ninth-century tropes, lyrical excrescences introduced into the liturgy of the Catholic church, and especially in the *Quem quaeritis* trope incorporated into the introit of the Easter Mass. From these and from the Christmas tropes there developed a series of Scripture plays based upon Biblical stories and performed in connection with and in explanation of various liturgical services. In the hands of priests and clerics this Biblical drama expanded, especially after it moved out of the church, to embrace the whole history of the created universe from the time of God's creation to the end of the world and the day of final judgment. Thus, for the church, almost the exclusive educational institution of the Middle Ages, these cycles of scripture plays, even when performed largely by lay societies and trade guilds, were a major means of educating the people in Christian doctrine and religious dogma. The vast series of separate plays or "pageants" which made up the cycles, though they included materials from the Old Testament, focused upon Christ's sacrifice and redemption of man. Mystery cycles or Scripture plays were performed throughout Western Europe from the early fourteenth to the end of the sixteenth centuries. In England four of the great cycles of plays, the Chester, the York, the Wakefield, and the Corpus Christi or Hegge cycles, have been preserved and many fragments or parts of other cycles are extant. After the close of World War II, the York plays were revived in performance and repeated in alternate summers (Chambers, 1903; Craig, 1955; Young, 1933).

Two other major types of medieval drama further exemplify the didactic nature of that drama and relate its construction to instructional ends. These are the miracle or saints' plays and the moralities. The greatest development of miracle plays occurred in France, though they became popular throughout western Europe. These plays are, as defined by John Matthews Manly (1927), "the dramatization of a legend setting forth the life or the martyrdom or the miracle of a saint." Among the earliest and most popular saints' legends that were dramatized was the story of St. Nicholas, who was the patron saint of schoolboys; hence St. Nicholas plays were from the twelfth century widely popular in the monastic schools. Perhaps an equally popular subject was the miracles of the Blessed Virgin. Extensive collections of these have been preserved in France. One of these ancient legends formed the basis of the spectacular piece, *The Miracle*, which Max Reinhardt first produced in London in 1911 and in an even more spectacular presentation in New York in the season of 1923–24. The legend of St. Catherine, who was the patron saint of schoolgirls, was likewise widely dramatized and apparently presented in the schools. Guilds and lay societies, too, had their patron saints, whose lives were presented in dramatic form. The richness and variety of human materials, the adventures which befell the various saints, and the triumph in the end of good over evil made these miracle plays highly popular. John Matthews Manly contended that it was these saints' plays which led to the development of Renaissance romantic drama. Cities and nations also had their patron saints, such as St. George of England. There are a number of St. George plays that still survive. Possibly the composition of such national saints' plays led to the dramatization of history (Coffman, 1911; Manly, 1927; Young, 1923).

The medieval morality play, even more obviously didactic in intent and structure than the miracle plays, originated at the end of the fourteenth or the beginning of the fifteenth century, probably in France, and flourished there, in the Low Countries, and in England. It may be defined as a play that is allegorical in structure, which has for its main objective the teaching of some lesson for the guidance of life and in which the principal characters are personified abstractions or highly universalized types. One of the earliest and one of the most often dramatized subjects was the Dance of Death, well represented in what may be the oldest of the extant English moralities, *The Pride of Life* (c. 1425), and also in what is often considered the best example of the type, *Everyman* (c. 1485 or 1500). In the former, Death summons the King of Life; in the latter, he calls Everyman to his final reckoning. Another early and favorite subject was the Parliament of Heaven or the Four Daughters of God, based on the Biblical verse "Mercy and Truth have met together, Righteousness and Peace have kissed." In almost all of these religious moralities there is a conflict of the virtues and the vices for the soul of man, though certain plays, such as *The Castle of Perseverance* (c. 1405), make that struggle a central motif. In these man's soul is often symbolized by a castle besieged by the vices and defended by the virtues. Moralities are divided by some scholars into full-scope and limited plays. A full-scope morality treats the whole of mankind's life from the cradle to the grave or the last judgment, whereas a limited morality explains a special part or aspect of human salvation. Dramatized allegory later served varied instructional functions. Even in the earlier plays devoted chiefly to moral and religious instruction the Devil and the Vice were made into comic characters, which, along with certain realistic depictions of ordinary life, must have aided in keeping these didactic pieces entertaining. Examples of the belated or late moralities include John Rastell's *The Four Elements* (c. 1517), devoted to the explanation of cosmography and geography, and John Redford's *Wit and Science* (1569-70), which relates the adventures and misfortunes of Wit, who sets out to woo and marry his natural complement, Science, daughter of Reason and Experience. Many of the early Tudor plays which purport to be histories, such as John Bale's *King John* (written before 1548) are essentially moralities. The influence of the moralities upon, and their contributions to, the development of later drama were varied and extensive (Brook, 1911; MacKenzie, 1904; Reed, 1926).

SCHOOL DRAMA IN THE RENAISSANCE AND LATER. Much of the great development of European Renaissance drama emanated from the schools, the universities, academies, and learned societies. The Jesuit order, from its foundation in 1540 to its temporary suppression in 1773, was a leader in this development, requiring priests and students to devote a large portion of their time and energy to every area related to the composition and production of plays. Many of the leading playwrights gained their first acquaintance with the stage and with playwriting in Jesuit schools and colleges. Among these were Molière, Pièrre and Thomas Corneille, Alain René Lesage, Denis Diderot, and Voltaire in France; Calderón de la Barca in Spain; Joost van den Vondel in Holland; and Andreas Gryphius in Germany. The Reformation, which entered England in the reign of Henry VIII (1509-1547), prevented the introduction of the Jesuit school drama there; nevertheless the English schools and universities were active contributors to Renaissance drama. Nicholas Udall's *Ralph Roister Doister*, probably written between 1534 and 1541 while Udall was a master at Eton school, was apparently performed by schoolboys, as was the anonymous *Jack Juggler*. The four Inns of Court (Lincoln's Inn, Inner Temple, Middle Temple, and Gray's Inn), the law schools of London which date from the thirteenth and fourteenth centuries, were especially active in the writing and production of plays. In 1566 George Gascoigne's *The Supposes* was performed at Gray's Inn, and the even more famous *Gammer Gurton's Needle* may have been given at Christ's College, Cambridge, probably between 1552 and 1563. William Stevenson, presumably the author, was a fellow of that College. These and other early Tudor comedies modeled upon Latin comedy, written and produced by students and teachers, established the foundations, the structure, and the technical devices which made possible the rich flowering of English Renaissance comedy. Similarly, *Gorboduc; Or, Forrex and Porrex*, another Inns-of-Court play, acted by the young gentlemen of the Inner Temple before Queen Elizabeth at the Christmas revels at Whitehall on January 18, 1561 or 1562, along with other academic imitations of Senecan tragedy, largely established the structure of tragedy.

England's first major professional playwrights, Christopher Marlowe, John Lyly, Robert Greene, and George Peele, known as the "University Wits," received their early training in playwriting and play production at Oxford and Cambridge universities, hospitable homes of the drama from the late Middle Ages. Records include a performance of a liturgical play at Magdalen College toward the close of the fifteenth century and performances of a number of plays in Latin in the following century. In 1566 Queen Elizabeth visited Oxford and was entertained by the performance of two plays in Christ Church Hall. The Children of the Chapel Royal and the Children of Paul's maintained companies growing out of their school productions that competed with London's major professional troupes. The annual Latin play presented at Westminster School, dating back at least to the age of Elizabeth, continues as a tradition in that school. Though the wide popularity of the school plays began to wane in the seventeenth century, academic productions in English schools and universities continued through the eighteenth century and gained new impetus in the nineteenth. The famous Oxford University Dramatic Society, known as O.U.D.S., where many of the present generation of British theater artists received their training, was founded in 1885. Even earlier, in 1855, the A.D.C. (Amateur Dramatic Club) was founded at Cambridge and since 1935 has occupied its own well-equipped theater. Another producing group at Cambridge, the Marlowe Society, was founded in 1908. These two last groups have likewise contributed notable theater artists to the British professional theater (Boas, 1914; Burnand, 1880; Churchill and Keller, 1898; Green, 1931; Mackinnon, 1910; Motter, 1929; Schnitzler, 1952; Smith, 1923).

Within the present century in Germany, partly as a consequence of the quickening interest engendered by student production groups and partly as a result of the new interests and ideas about theater arts promoted by such men as Richard Wagner, Adolphe Appia, and Max Reinhardt, there developed within a number of German universities a curricular program known as *Theaterwissenschaft*. This program of instruction was focused upon the study of and research in theater history and had little or no interest in the practice of theater arts or in the contemporary staging of plays in academic institutions. The development of academic theater throughout western Europe, especially after the close of World War II, was rapid and extensive. France, for example, reorganized its national theater in 1946, establishing in the Ministry of Education and within the Division of Beaux Arts a subdivision called La Direction des Spectacles et de la Musique in charge of the state support to the whole national theater, Parisian and regional. That bureau set up the Annual Competition of Young Companies in Paris, with some financial support, prizes, and awards, to encourage both the academic and the nonacademic producing groups. In 1953 in Italy the University of Parma, with full governmental and municipal support, organized the International Festival of University Theater, an annual week of performances by university theater groups from various nations. The first curricular instruction in theater in Europe was established within the Department of English at the University of Bristol, England, in 1947 with assistance from the Rockefeller Foundation. After the close of the war, under the leadership of Dr. Glynne Wickham, this curriculum was recognized as a separate degree-granting program and, with Dr. Wickham's promotion to professor, became the Department of Drama in 1962. For some years the program at the University of Bristol was the only curricular and degree-granting dramatic arts program in Great Britain. The universities of Manchester, Birmingham, Hull, Leeds, and Glasgow have followed the lead of Bristol. The course programs and focus of instruction differ in each of these institutions; thus, the curriculum organized at Manchester under the chairmanship of the distinguished director Hugh Hunt is oriented more toward the professional training of performers and theater artists than is the program at Bristol. The Department of Drama at Bristol has a close, though unofficial, alliance with the Bristol Old Vic School of the Theater, through which students may receive thorough professional training, leaving the departmental instruction opportunity to give emphasis to dramatic literature, analysis and theory, theater history, and research (Heffner, 1952).

ACADEMIC THEATER IN THE UNITED STATES. The first American school performance of record, a "pastoral colloquy" recited by the students of William and Mary College, occurred in 1702, long before there was a professional theater in the American colonies. On September 10, 1736, the "Young Gentlemen of the College" performed Joseph Addison's *Cato* in the theater in Williamsburg. Under the leadership of Francis Hopkinson, America's first poet-composer, the students of the College of Philadelphia staged *The Masque of Alfred* by James Thompson and David Mallet during the Christmas holidays of 1756–57. Hugh Henry Brackenridge and Philip Freneau wrote and staged at the college of New Jersey (later Princeton College) in 1771 a patriotic dialogue entitled *The Rising Glory of America*. Brackenridge, who after his graduation had become a teacher in the Maryland Academy, wrote two plays for production by the students, *The Battle of Bunker Hill* and *The Death of General Montgomery*, thus placing the school drama in the service of the American Revolution (Quinn, 1923). Though generally condemned by the Protestant divines who served as presidents of the early American colleges, dramatic performances were given with some regularity at Harvard, Yale, Princeton, and other institutions. At certain institutions of which Yale, Princeton, and Dartmouth are examples, the literary societies were instrumental in the production of plays, though the faculty in the various institutions exercised control, often rigid, over such activities until well into the nineteenth century. The development of instruction in oratory and elocution, especially through the nineteenth century, aided and supported dramatic ventures of various types. The organization of student clubs and societies, devoted in certain instances largely to dramatic performances, likewise characterize this era. The Hasty Pudding Club at Harvard, though founded in 1795, became prominent in college dramatics after 1844, presenting largely stock farces from the professional stage. After the Civil War such organizations multiplied. The Thalian Dramatic Association was founded at Brown University in 1866; Philaletheis, originally a literary society at Vassar College, became primarily a dramatic association in 1866; St. John's Dramatic Association was established at Williams College, and in that same year the Cornelian Minstrels was founded at Cornell. Tufts Dramatic Club was formed in 1876, and the Barrett Club at the University of Michigan was organized in 1880. Similar organizations appeared in most other colleges and universities, but two other famous societies should be mentioned: the Mask and Wig of the University of Pennsylvania, founded in 1892, and Princeton's Triangle Club, formed in 1893 (Clark, 1954). Yet another source of dramatic activity was found in the annual class play, which was often a production in the original language of a Latin or Greek drama. In 1876 Sanders Theater was completed in the Harvard memorial hall that had been erected to commemorate Harvard's Civil War dead. There in 1881 a lavish production of Sophocles' *Oedipus tyrannus* was given in the original Greek after six months of elaborate preparations and rehearsals. The change of attitude within academic institutions which presaged the developments in the twentieth century may be dated from the 1870's and 1880's and is marked, among other signs, by the appearances of professional theater artists as lecturers in college halls. In the 1870's Steele Mackaye, playwright, producer, and student of Delsarte, lectured at Princeton; Sir Henry Irving, the eminent British actor, spoke at Harvard during the academic year 1884–85; and Bronson Howard, the American playwright, gave his famous lecture "The Autobiography of a Play" there in 1886. In 1897 Joseph Jefferson, the distinguished American comedian, lectured at the University of Michigan on the actor and his art. In the light of the general puritanical opposition of most college administrators and many members of faculties, the persistence and even growth of theatrical activities in educational institutions in the United States during the nineteenth century are in retrospect a prophecy of the remarkable developments to occur in the twentieth.

The unique development of the American educational theater, unparalled in any other national educational system, though it has deep roots in the immediate and the ancient past, is in this century largely the results of the pioneering efforts of several eminent educators. The recognized dean of this group is George Pierce Baker (1866–1935). After graduation from Harvard University and some travel, he joined the faculty of the Department of English at Harvard in 1888, teaching courses in freshman rhetoric, argumentation, and eventually in dramatic literature. Even as an undergraduate his varied cultural interests had centered more and more upon theater and especially upon playwriting. By the turn of the century he had organized an informal group of students on an extracurricular basis who were interested in writing plays and who became known as Baker's Dozen. More and more he became the recognized leader in campus dramatic activities. Believing that the future of the American drama was linked with that of American universities, colleges, and schools, he organized at Radcliffe College in 1903 a course in playwriting, entitled "English 46: The Forms of Drama, Practice in Dramatic Composition." After considerable controversy, this course was incorporated in the curriculum of Harvard University as "English 47: English Composition—The Technique of the Drama." In 1915–16 he was allowed to add an advanced course, "English 47a: Technique of the Drama." By this time several of Baker's former students, such as Edward Sheldon, had won or were beginning to win professional reputations. Baker had, from the early days of his playwriting course, followed the practice of trying out in production some of the best plays written by his students, and increasingly he felt the need of a workshop in which this important educational experience could be systematized, controlled, and regularized. In 1913 he, his students, and supporters established the 47 Workshop as an extracurricular adjunct to English 47 and English 47a. Through the generosity of admirers, prizes had been established for the best plays written, including the John Craig Prize, the Oliver Morosco Prize, and the Richard Herndon Prize. Though Baker's personal interests were largely focused upon playwriting, he came more and more to the conviction that academic instruction must include all of the arts of the theater and that for this realization he must have an adequate theater plant as a laboratory. This theater he was never able to obtain at Harvard. In 1924 Yale University accepted an endowment from Edward S. Harkness that would provide a handsomely equipped theater plant and support for a department of drama. In 1925 Baker tore up his roots in Cambridge and moved to New Haven as the head of the Yale Department of Drama, now the School of Drama. *Theatre Arts Monthly* of July, 1933, was dedicated to George Pierce Baker and an assessment of his national influence. It included a map of the United States, showing where Baker students were active in various communities and institutions throughout the nation (Kinne, 1954).

Another distinguished pioneer educator was James Brander Matthews (1852–1929), a member of the faculty at Columbia University from 1900 to 1924 and the first individual in America to hold the title of professor of dramatic literature. He was himself a dramatist, novelist, and author of essays as well as influential works of scholarship. His main interest was in dramatic literature and especially in the development of structure and technique. Thus, like Baker, he was constantly counseling and encouraging students in their writing of plays. Though he established no workshop, he did much to promote student productions. His play *Peter Stuyvesant*, written in collaboration with Bronson Howard (1842–1908), then perhaps America's most distinguished professional playwright, was tried out in Providence, Rhode Island, and then presented at Wallack's Theater in New York City on October 2, 1899 (Quinn, 1937; Hughes 1951). He established in the Library at Columbia a collection and museum of drama and theater, named in his honor the Brander Matthews Museum. His extensive connections and friendships with professional theater artists and his urbane scholarship helped in the early pioneer days to bridge the chasm between the professional and the academic. Yet another distinguished pioneer scholar who almost alone made the study of the American drama and theater academically acceptable was Arthur Hobson Quinn (1875–1960) of the University of Pennsylvania. Though his main efforts were devoted to teaching and research, he was an unflagging supporter of student and community theaters, especially in and around Philadelphia. The distinguished dissertations of his former graduate students have enhanced our knowledge of American theater and drama, as have Quinn's own publications. Those former graduate students have been active in the development of instruction in American theater and drama throughout the United States (Quinn, 1923, 1937).

The department at Yale was not, however, the first department to be established in an American educational institution. That honor belongs to the Carnegie Institute of Technology, where the Department of Drama under the directorship of Thomas Wood Stevens was established in 1914.

In 1905 Frederick H. Koch became an instructor in the Department of English at the University of North Dakota and in his first year there became the director of dramatics on an extracurricular basis. He went to Harvard in 1909 to complete a master's degree under George Pierce Baker and then to the College of Oratory in Boston for additional training in oral interpretation and acting. Upon his return to North Dakota, after extended foreign travels and marriage, he continued the direction of plays and introduced a course in playwriting. Under his direction his students presented their first bill of original plays in 1916, leading to the organization of the Dakota Playmakers, which, in addition to regular campus productions, toured through the State. His success there led to his call to the University of North Carolina, whose faculty he joined in 1918. As a member of the Department of English, he offered courses in dramatic literature and especially in playwriting. Organizing the Carolina Playmakers, he staged the first bill of three original one-act plays written by his students in March 1919. In 1925 the Carolina Playmakers moved into a beautiful small theater, made through the reconstruction of Smith Hall, formerly the Library of the Law School. By this time their practice of touring their original folk plays throughout the State and through the South was well established. With the staging in 1936 of Paul Green's *The Lost Colony* on Roanoke Island the Playmakers entered upon an extensive new development, the writing and staging of historic pageant-dramas in outdoor theaters. Three series of *Carolina Folk Plays*, written by students, were published in 1922, 1924, and 1928. In the autumn of 1936 the curriculum in theater and drama was removed from the Department of English and established in the new Department of Dramatic Art. Upon the death of "Prof" Koch in 1944, Samuel Selden became the chairman of that department, continuing and expanding the program that Koch had so successfully established. Among Koch's most famous students are Paul Green and Thomas Wolfe (Selden & Sphangos, 1954).

At the University of Wisconsin Thomas H. Dickinson, who had given a course at Baylor University in 1901–02 devoted to the "staging" of plays, struggled valiantly between 1901 and 1916 to establish an academic curriculum in theater and drama. He was ably assisted by Gertrude Johnson and James M. O'Neill, who succeeded in establishing curricular instruction in theater and drama at Wisconsin after World War I. In 1921 Edward C. Mabie won similar recognition for such instruction at the State University of Iowa, and about the same time Alexander M. Drummond, after a long struggle, established a department at Cornell University. The theater programs at these three institutions, unlike those at Harvard and North Carolina, were allied with curricular instruction in speech. Between 1900 and 1921 similar developments were occurring in more than a score of other colleges and universities. As Clifford E. Hamar indicates in his article "College and University Theatre Instruction in the Early Twentieth Century" (1954), curricular instruction in these programs may be grouped in the following rough classifications: "(1) Dramatic interpretation (with two sub-divisions, Shakespearean and general); (2) Play presentation (with two sub-divisions, Shakespearean and general); (3) Acting; (4) Directing and 'Coaching'; (5) Play production; and (6) Theater history" (see also Coad & Mims, 1929; Hughes, 1951).

A stimulating and important influence upon the development of academic theater and community theater was the Drama League of America, founded in Evanston, Illinois, in 1910. Among its founders were idealistic professional theater artists, college professors, and clubwomen. One of the latter, Mrs. A. Starr Best, wife of a wealthy Chicago merchant, was the Drama League's first president and a constant supporter throughout its existence. The aim of the league was to establish a chapter in every town and city in the nation, and the officers and members almost succeeded in that aim. In February of 1911 they launched a quarterly review, entitled *The Drama*, which became a monthly publication in October of 1919. That journal published the text of many important European plays in translation, carried articles of a critical and informative nature, and chronicled the news of noteworthy events in the American theater and among the chapters of the league. The organization lent support to significant plays in production, encouraged ambitious actors and theater artists, and presented thousands of lecturers on theater and drama throughout the nation. It lent important encouragement and support to the establishment of hundreds of amateur and community theaters. Another of its major activities was the support of pageantry of all kinds and types. That movement expanded so widely, especially after the end of World War I, that a separate national organization, with a separate publication, was formed. In such a widespread organization as the Drama League and its offspring, the "little theater" movement, it is only natural that many of the activities were ludicrous. These George Kelly lampooned in his farce, *The Torch-bearers*, presented in New York in 1923. Nevertheless, the Drama League of America was a significant educator of the American public and should be given considerable credit for the revival which occurred in the American theater and its drama after World War I.

One of the consequences of the development of college and university theater and drama programs, which grew at an accelerated pace in the second and third decades of the twentieth century, was the incentive thereby given to the development of such programs in preparatory and high schools. From the nineteenth century on, these schools had presented annual class and commencement plays, usually coached by teachers without training on a strictly extracurricular basis as a mere student activity. Often the objective of these presentations was the raising of money in support of other school or student activities. By 1912, however, several teachers, such as Adela Cone of the Oxford (Ohio) High School and J. Milnor Dorey of the Trenton (New Jersey) High School, were urging the educational advantages of a dramatics program related directly to the curriculum, staffed by trained teachers, and scheduled on a regular basis. They, and others, pointed repeatedly to the advantages of instruction in music and art, already established within the curriculum. By 1913 Teachers College of Columbia University had introduced courses in the techniques of festivals, pageants, and dramatization, which developed in subsequent years into a full curriculum for the training of teachers in theater and drama. Other university programs in teacher education followed this lead. By 1925 well-trained teachers were in charge of scheduled programs of dramatics in many of the high schools in most of the states. A multiplicity of contests and festivals, often sponsored by the colleges and universities, with high school groups from throughout the state or region competing in the presentation of plays, were especially popular in the second and third decades of the twentieth century. These programs in high schools served to provide better-trained audiences for professional productions of drama and to awaken a professional interest within students, which they continued to develop in colleges and in the professional schools of theater, such as the American Academy of Dramatic Arts in New York. By the 1950's some high schools had staffs of well-trained theater artists and technicians, along with excellent physical facilities for the presentation of plays (Hamar, 1954).

Yet another rich educational reward accruing from the renaissance in academic theater was the development of children's theater and creative dramatics programs, especially valuable in the training of kindergarten and primary pupils. The pioneer leader in this development was Winifred Ward of Northwestern University. She and her students established extensive programs in the schools of Evanston, Illinois, and she developed a curriculum for the training of teachers in this area within the School of Speech at Northwestern. Many of her former students are now leaders in the children's theater programs operating throughout the United States. They are also leaders in the Children's Theatre Division of the American Educational Theatre Association (AETA). Other pioneer leaders in the movement include Mrs. Elizabeth Burger of Baltimore and Mrs. Hazel Robertson, formerly of the Palo Alto (California) Community Children's Theatre. The Division of Children's Theatre of AETA holds an annual Children's Theatre Conference, which includes a wide variety of workshops and other practical programs. The leaders in this movement were instigators of and chief participants in the Golden Anniversary White House Conference on Children and Youth, convened in Washington, D.C., in 1960, out of which evolved a number of significant programs, such as the Head Start Program for underprivileged children. Though perhaps a majority of children's theater programs in the United States are allied with school systems, others are sponsored independently as community enterprises, while still others are adjuncts of libraries and museums.

By the mid-twentieth century there were programs of curricular instruction in theater and drama in most colleges and universities. Some of these were organized as separate departments; many were divisions within departments of speech; others were allied with departments of English. The first edition of *The Directory of American College Theatre*, edited by Burnet M. Hobgood and published by the American Educational Theatre Association (Hobgood, 1960), presents data about programs, faculty, and curricula obtained from 1,278 accredited and 159 nonaccredited institutions in the 50 states. In addition to course offerings, most of these institutions maintain regular production programs as a laboratory training of students. Hobgood's *Directory* lists 172 colleges and universities offering graduate course instruction in theater and drama leading to M.A., M.F.A., or Ph.D. degrees. The number has grown steadily since 1960. In 1967 there were fifty or more universities offering doctoral programs. The faculties of these institutions have organized a number of national associations and societies. The major society is the American Educational Theatre Association, organized in 1936, which now has three subsidiary divisions, the Division of Children's Theatre, the Division of Community Theatre, and the Division of Secondary School Theatre. The oldest of the national associations is the National Theatre Conference, which evolved from a meeting of leaders in the field held at Carnegie Institute of Technology in the autumn of 1925. Other similar organizations include the National Catholic Theatre Conference, the National Thespian Society (for high schools), the National Association of Dramatic and Speech Arts (an interest group within the Speech Association of America), various regional and state associations, and various fraternal societies. The American National Theatre and Academy has from its organization cooperated with these national societies and participated in the annual convention of AETA and others (Halstead & Behringer, 1954; Heffner, 1964; Hobgood, 1960).

The courses of instruction offered in most of the degree-granting departments may for purposes of illustration be divided into two groups: (1) dramatic literature, playwriting, theory of drama, structure, analysis and interpretation, and theater history, and (2) theater arts, including acting, directing, scene design and construction, costume design and construction, stage production procedures and practices, stage lighting and sound, and theater management.

Many departments include one or more courses in children's theater and creative dramatics, and a number are allied with departments of music in the stage presentation of operas. Conversely, several departments and schools of music have independent programs of instruction and production in opera. The courses in group 1 above, especially those in dramatic literature and playwriting, are in many universities offered in the department of English or are joint offerings of that department and the department of theater and drama. In conjunction with instruction in group 2 all of the departments maintain programs of stage productions, including productions open to the general public and workshop productions for students only. Such productions serve as the laboratory in which the theoretical knowledge learned in courses is actualized and tested. This is one of the aspects of the academic theater programs that makes them effective educational means; they unite theory with practice, knowledge with skills. Another aspect is the highly motivated interest that the majority of students take in the subjects which they are studying and the work which they are doing. Two different, though not mutually exclusive, conceptions of the educational objective underlie the curricular organization and activities of these departments and are used to justify the extensive list of courses taught and the large number of students enrolled. These are (1) liberal education and (2) professional training. Many of the departments consider their undergraduate course programs one excellent means toward a liberal education. The graduate programs tend toward higher specialization and hence are more professionally oriented toward training talented students for careers in the professional theater or for academic careers. Almost all of the doctoral candidates and perhaps a large majority of the master's candidates are preparing for careers as teachers in high schools and colleges. For some years past these academic programs have been the chief training centers and recruiting grounds for the American professional theater; hence, many institutions, such as the University of Minnesota, Indiana University, Stanford University, Wayne State University, and others, have established professional companies on the campus or are allied with professional theaters in their community. Most of the best theaters and the best-equipped theater plants have, within the past three or four decades, been erected on college and university campuses. A trend which has grown rapidly since the end of World War II has been the establishment of highly professional training for talented students who seek careers on Broadway or in the many new regional theaters. In consequence of the growth of academic theater the professional and commercial theater in America year by year becomes more and more dominated by graduates from these schools and departments. Other graduates find careers in motion pictures, radio, and television. Until the recent establishment of such regional theatres as the Tyrone Guthrie Theatre in Minneapolis and such national festivals as the Connecticut Shakespeare Festival Theatre, the colleges and universities were almost the sole preservers of our Western dramatic heritage in live productions of classics from the past. They are still the chief centers in which Americans can come to know the great plays of the past and the present. Within the United States, despite the lack of a nationally endorsed theater such as that of France or that of Germany, and as amateurishly inadequate as many of their productions may be, college and university productions of the great plays make a significant contribution to the cultural education of students and to thousands of adult Americans (Heffner, 1964).

Hubert C. Heffner
Indiana University

References

Arnott, Peter D. *An Introduction to the Greek Theatre.* Macmillan (London), 1959.

Beare, W. *The Roman Stage.* Harvard U Press, 1951.

Boas, Frederick Samuel. *University Drama in the Tudor Age.* Oxford U Press, 1914.

Brook, C. F. Tucker. *The Tudor Drama.* Houghton, 1911.

Burnand, Frances Cowley. *The "A. D. C.," Being Personal Reminiscences of the University Club, Cambridge.* Chapman and Hall, 1880.

Chambers, E. K. *The Medieval Stage,* 2 vols. Oxford U Press, 1903.

Churchill, G. B., and Keller, W. "Die lateinischen Universitäts-Dramen Englands in der Zeit der Königin Elizabeth." *Shakespeare Jahrbuch* 34:221–4; 1898.

Clark, John L. "Educational Dramatics in Nineteenth-century Colleges." In Wallace, Karl. (Ed.) *History of Speech Education in America.* Appleton, 1954.

Coad, Oral Sumner, and Mims, Edwin, Jr. *The American Stage.* The Pageant of America, Vol. 14 Yale U Press, 1929.

Coffman, George Raleigh. *A New Theory of the Origin of the Miracle Play.* Minesha Press, 1911.

Craig, Hardin. *English Religious Drama of the Middle Ages.* Clarendon Press, 1955.

Crane, R. R. (Ed.) *Critics and Criticism, Ancient and Modern.* U Chicago Press, 1952.

Duckworth, George E. *The Nature of Roman Comedy.* Princeton U Press, 1952.

Esslin, Martin. *The Theatre of the Absurd.* Doubleday, 1961.

Green, Edwin Wigfall. *Inns of Court and Early English Drama.* Yale U Press, 1931.

Halstead, William P., and Behringer, Clara. "National Theatre Organizations and Theatre Education." In Wallace, Karl. (Ed.) *History of Speech Education in America.* Appleton, 1954.

Hamar, Clifford Eugene. "College and University Theatre Instruction in the Early Twentieth Century." In Wallace, Karl. (Ed.) *History of Speech Education in America.* Appleton, 1954.

Heffner, Hubert C. "Theatre and Drama in Liberal Education." *Teach Col Rec* 65:311–7; 1964. Re-

printed with additions by request in *Ed Theatre J* 16; 1964.
Heffner, Hubert C. "A Report on the National Theatre in France." *Ed Theatre J* 4:16–24; 1952.
Herrick, Marvin T. *Tragicomedy: Its Origin and Development in Italy, France and England.* U Illinois Press, 1955.
Hobgood, Burnet M. *Directory of American College Theatre.* American Educational Theatre Association, Inc., 1960.
Hughes, Glenn. *A History of the American Theatre, 1700–1950.* Samuel French, Inc., 1951.
James, D. G. (Ed.) *The University and the Theatre.* Allen, 1952.
Kinne, Winner Payne. *George Pierce Baker and the American Theatre.* Harvard U Press, 1954.
MacKenzie, W. R. *The English Moralities from the Point of View of Allegory.* Houghton, 1904.
Mackinnon, Alan. *The Oxford Amateurs: A Short History of Theatricals at the University.* Chapman and Hall, 1910.
Manly, John Matthews. "The Miracle Play in England." *Trans Roy Soc Literature* 7:133–53; 1927.
Miller, Anna Irene. *The Independent Theatre in Europe.* Ray Long and Richard R. Smith, Inc., 1951.
Motter, T. H. V. *The School Drama in England.* McKay, 1929.
Northrop, F. C. S. *The Meeting of East and West.* Macmillan, 1947.
Odell, George C. D. *Annals of the New York Stage,* 15 vols. Columbia U Press, 1927–1949.
Quinn, Arthur Hobson. *A History of the American Drama from the Beginnings to the Civil War.* Harper, 1923.
Quinn, Arthur Hobson. *A History of the American Drama from the Civil War to the Present Day,* rev. ed. Crofts, 1937.
Reed, A. W. *Early Tudor Drama.* Methuen, 1926.
Richardson, L. *Poetical Theory in Republican Rome.* Yale U Press, 1944.
Samuel, Richard, and Thomas, R. Hinton. *Expressionism in German Life, Literature and the Theatre, 1910–1924.* Heffer, 1939.
Schnitzler, Henry. "The Jesuit Contributions to the Theatre." *Ed Theatre J* 4:283–92; 1952.
Seilhamer, George O. *History of the American Theatre,* 3 vols. Globe Printing House, 1888–1891.
Selden, Samuel, and Sphangos, Mary Tom. *Frederick Henry Koch: Pioneer Playmaker.* U North Carolina Press, 1954.
Smith, C. G. Moore. *College Plays Performed in the University of Cambridge.* Cambridge U Press, 1923.
St. John, Christopher. (Trans.) *The Plays of Hrotswitha.* Chatto and Windus, 1923.
Weinberg, Bernard. *A History of Literary Criticism in the Italian Renaissance,* 2 vols. U Chicago Press, 1961.
West, A. W. *Pope's Essay on Criticism.* Cambridge U Press, 1908.
Wickham, Glynne. (Ed.) *The Relation Between the University and Film, Radio and Television.* Butterworth Scientific Publications, 1956.

Wickham, Glynne. *Drama in the World of Science and Three Other Lectures.* Routledge, 1962.
Young, Karl. "Concerning the Origin of the Miracle Play." In *Manly Anniversary Studies.* U Chicago Press, 1923.
Young, Karl. *The Drama of the Medieval Church,* 2 vols. Oxford U Press, 1933.

DROPOUT—CAUSES AND CONSEQUENCES

During the past sixty years the quality of public education in America has improved. The curriculum has been broadened and enriched to meet better the needs of all children. Teachers spend more years in preparation, and the quality of their preparation is better. The school year has been extended and the school day lengthened. More children and youth attend school and more graduate from high school and college. The median number of years of schooling completed by persons in the civilian labor force 18 years old and older exceeded 12 years—12.0 years for men and 12.2 years for women (U.S. Department of Labor, 1964a). No country in history can match this, or the huge sums spent in public education. Yet, despite all these gains, a constant and gnawing problem remains. For years educators tackled the problem and tried to resolve it, but instead of being solved it erupted violently and became, and still is, a national problem. It is the school dropout problem.

A NATIONAL PROBLEM. The dropout problem has reached such magnitude that two presidents of the United States found it necessary to focus public attention on it. President Kennedy, in his State of the Union Message to the Congress on January 14, 1963, said:

> The future of any country which is dependent on the will and wisdom of its citizens is damaged, and irreparably damaged, whenever any of its children is not educated to the fullest extent of his capacity. . . . Today an estimated four out of ten students in the fifth grade will not even finish high school—and *that is a waste we cannot afford.* (Kennedy, 1963)

Six months later, at a press conference, he pointedly referred to it as "a serious national problem" and then announced that he was going to allocate one-fourth of his special emergency funds of $1-million to school systems so that they could hire guidance counselors who would visit the homes of dropouts and get them to return to school.

Inroads were made; many youths returned to school, but the problem continued to grow. In his message on education to Congress on January 12, 1965, President Lyndon B. Johnson, after extolling America's concern with providing free education from elementary school through college for its children, had this to say:

There is a darker side to education in America. Almost a million young people will continue to quit school each year—if our schools fail to stimulate their desire to learn. In our 15 largest cities, 60 percent of the tenth grade students from poverty neighborhoods drop out before finishing high school. The cost of this neglect runs high—both for the youth and the nation. (Johnson, 1965)

Congress reacted positively to these presidential messages. Enabling legislation was passed which created the new and enlarged Vocational Education Act with a work-study provision, the Job Corps, the Manpower Defense and Training Act, the Elementary and Secondary Education Act, and the Higher Education Act. But the school dropout problem persists.

SOME DROPOUT STATISTICS. Today about four out of every six young people graduate from high school, and approximately half of them enter college; and of this group about half graduate (U.S. Department of Health, Education, and Welfare, 1962). To put this another way, perhaps negatively, we can say that for every six young people, five do not graduate from college: two of them left before graduating from high school, two graduated from high school but did not continue their education, and one dropped out of college.

By comparison, in 1900, of every 100 pupils in the fifth grade not more than 7 graduated from high school. In 1932, only 30 in 100 earned high school diplomas. And it was not until 1950 that, for the first time in U.S. history, more pupils graduated from high school than had dropped out—505 graduates for every 1,000 fifth graders. Since then this improvement in holding power has continued at a steady rate, so that today approximately 2 out of every 3 pupils graduate from high school (*ibid.*).

FACTORS EXTRINSIC TO THE SCHOOL. Paradoxically, the national concern with dropouts comes at a time when the dropout rate is the lowest. An examination of the paradox indicates that the dropout problem has been brought into focus by a multiplicity of factors, largely extrinsic to the school, and peculiar to our decade. Some of these are:
1. Continuing unemployment.
2. Migration from rural areas to urban centers.
3. The population explosion—a million more youth reached age 18 in 1965 than reached 18 in 1964.
4. The rise in delinquency and youth crime.
5. The rise in public-assistance payments.
6. The increased use of technology in farming.
7. The elimination of jobs through automation.

UNEMPLOYMENT. Prior to the escalation of the United States war effort in Vietnam, the national unemployment rate had not fallen below 5 percent during the previous five years. Two-thirds of the approximately 3½ million unemployed had less than a high school education. Many were "old" dropouts. Let us examine the plight of the "new" dropout.

Dropouts and Employment. Years ago, and even as recently as 1952, a boy could drop out of school and drop into a job. Today when a youth drops out of school and tries to enter the adult world, he finds, too often, that he is not wanted there. S. M. Miller found that the age of a dropout, usually 16, operates against him. Employers consider age more important than the actual grade completed (Miller, 1963).

A study done by the Bureau of the Census for the Department of Labor for the year 1961 showed unemployment among various age groups in the male labor force as follows (U.S. Department of Labor, 1962):

Age group	Percentage unemployed
16–17	21.5
18–19	15.2
20–21	10.6

Three years later, in 1964, the U.S. Department of Labor found that there was not much change in the unemployment rate of the 18–19 age group. For white men it was 11.4 percent, but for Negro men it was 20.2 percent (U.S. Department of Labor, 1964a).

Those with less education have always had more difficulty in finding jobs, even when the ratio of dropouts to high school graduates was more favorable to the dropout than it is today. In 1952 the number of years of schooling of unemployed males was 8.8 years, while the employed had a level of 10.4 years; in 1962 the levels were 10.0 years and 12.1 years, respectively (*ibid.*). The high school diploma has become the credential to employment, and personnel officers are using it as a screening device even where the job does not require it. In a national study (National Committee on Employment of Youth, 1964) it was found that there is a persistent tendency to oversimplify qualifications and that those who do not meet the requirement of high school graduation are suspect. One employer gave as his reasons for not hiring dropouts "We cannot use cowboys." A large group stressed social acceptability and good appearance.

The tendency of industry to raise its entrance requirements as the educational level of new workers rises, plus its real need for better-educated workers, will increase the desperate plight of the current and future school dropout.

Dropouts and Life Earnings. The correlation that exists between the number of years of schooling and unemployment also holds true between the number of years of schooling and lifetime income. In a fact sheet titled *Worth of Education, Youth Employment,* the U.S. Department of Labor (1964b) reported that the average lifetime earnings of males were $149,687 for elementary-school graduates, and $215,487 for high school graduates.

The difference of approximately $65,000 might conceivably represent the difference between owning one's home, renting a nice apartment, or living in a tenement. It might represent the difference between being able to feed and clothe one's children well or having them live largely on starches and wear second-hand clothing. More importantly, it might mean the difference between a person's feeling that he is a participating, contributing member of society rather than one who is alienated from it. Money does make a difference.

CHARACTERISTICS OF THE SCHOOL DROPOUT. It is apparent that the dropout problem is not the same everywhere in the country. Dropout rates vary considerably from state to state, from community to community, and even from school to school in the same district. Many kinds of studies have been made on the assumption that the number of dropouts could be reduced if we once learned why boys and girls quit school. These studies usually combine data from several of the following sources: (1) opinions of the dropouts themselves; (2) teachers' or counselors' opinion about dropouts; (3) comparisons of dropouts with pupils who graduate with respect to sex, age, intelligence, average marks, socioeconomic status of the family, number of years of schooling of parents, race, health, etc.; (4) examination of evidence in the cumulative record cards of dropouts; and (5) personal interviews with the dropouts and their families or answers to mailed questionnaires.

It is difficult to pinpoint the exact reasons for leaving school because quite often the reasons given by the pupil and by the school are contradictory. Also, youth who drop out of school do not readily supply information. On questionnaires where they are asked to check reasons for leaving school, the dropouts, like all individuals, tend to check those items which will show them in the best light.

Typically, the dropout is an adolescent, just past his sixteenth birthday, who has average or slightly below average intelligence; he is more likely to be a boy than a girl. He is not achieving according to his potential; he is not reading at grade level; and academically he is in the lowest quarter of his class. He is slightly overage for his grade placement, having been held back once in the elementary or junior high school grades. The *average* dropout has not been in trouble with the law, although he does take up an inordinate amount of the administrator's time because of discipline problems. He seldom participates in extracurricular activities, feels rejected by the school, and, in turn, rejects the school. His parents were school dropouts, as were his older brothers and sisters. His friendships are made with persons outside the school, usually older dropouts. He says that he is leaving school because of lack of interest but that he intends to get a high school diploma, in some manner or other, because without it he can't get a job. He knows the pitfalls that await him in the outside world, yet he believes that they can't be worse than those that confront him in school. To a great extent he is a fugitive from failure.

Age. The reason why the dropout is typically 16 years of age is that most state laws require school attendance to age 16. Psychologically and emotionally, the dropping out took place before then. For some, especially the minority-group child who migrated to an urban center, the fact of dropping out could be predicted by grade 3, at the latest.

A study done in Syracuse, New York (Miller, 1963), found that 45 percent of the dropouts were 17 years old or older; in Connecticut (Connecticut Commission on Civil Rights, 1959) 41 percent were 17 years old or older; in California (McCreary & Kitch, 1953) 26 percent were 17 years old or older. A recent study done in Modesto, California (Whitmore & Chapman, 1965), found that 52 percent of the dropouts were 17 or older, while in Louisiana (Jones, 1964) the percentage in that group was found to be 41. Interestingly, the percentages of white and Negro dropouts who were 17 or more years were almost identical—40 and 42 percent, respectively.

Although 16 is the modal age at which children can legally leave school, it is not unusual to find that many have dropped out before attaining that age. In Louisiana, 11 percent left at age 15; in Modesto, California, 8 percent; in Tacoma, Washington, 13 percent; and in California, 16 percent. The reason is not hard to find. The dropout becomes a truant, and because he will be 16 soon, the attendance officer usually does not bother to enforce the compulsory attendance law in his case. In effect, therefore, it is possible for youth to quit school at age 15 and a half.

Intelligence. Investigators are not in agreement concerning the importance of intelligence as a factor in dropping out of school. Some studies have found that intelligence is not particularly important, while others show that low scholastic aptitude is one of the characteristics of the potential dropout. Several studies are of particular interest on this point.

A U.S. Department of Labor study of dropouts in seven communities (U.S. Department of Labor, Bureau of Labor Statistics, 1960) found that three times as many dropouts as high-school graduates had I.Q.'s under 85 and that nearly three times as many graduates as dropouts had I.Q.'s of 110 and over.

Woollatt (1961) reported that in the New York State Holding Power Project 12.1 percent of the dropouts had I.Q.'s of 110 and above, and 30.4 percent had I.Q.'s below 90. Bowman and Matthews (1960) found a range of 60 to 115 in I.Q., with a mean of 83, and they found that 75 percent of the dropouts fell in the lower half of the distribution of intelligence scores.

The Los Angeles City School District (1965) found that whereas 34 percent of the graduates had I.Q.'s of 108 or above, only 10 percent of the dropouts were in this range. Yet 50.9 percent of the dropouts had I.Q.'s of 90 or above. Sixty percent of the dropouts in Orange County, California (McCreary & Kitch, 1963), and 69 percent of the dropouts in Modesto, California (Whitmore & Chapman, 1965), had I.Q.'s above 90. From this, we can safely conclude that at least one-half of all the dropouts have the intelligence to benefit from a high school education and to graduate from high school; and approximately 10 percent have enough intelligence to pursue a college education (Woollatt, 1961).

Grade at Dropout. Generally, about 25 to 40

percent of the dropouts quit school in grade 10. This, of course, because most of them reached age 16 in that grade, but it is also likely that many were in the stress of transition from junior high school to senior high school. In a Maryland study (Maryland State Department of Education, 1963), it was found that nearly 40 percent of the dropouts had never gotten out of junior high school and had dropped out in grades 8 and 9. In Louisiana (Jones, 1964) 1,436 left in grade 7, 1,897 left in grade 8, and 3,173 left in grade 9—a total of 6,506, or 40 percent, who dropped out of school to enter the world of work with less than 9 years of formal schooling.

At the same time, the U.S. Office of Education (1962) found that 13 percent of all dropouts left school in grade 12. In Orange County, California, the percentage was 24.9; in Louisiana, it was 9 percent. In the project "School Dropouts" (Schreiber, 1964), involving more than 500,000 high school pupils in 128 cities with populations over 90,000, it was found that 15.1 percent of the high school dropouts left school in grade 12.

A Bureau of the Census–Department of Agriculture study (1962) found relationships between color, sex, and residence and percent of high school seniors who do not graduate, as shown in the accompanying table.

TABLE 1

HIGH SCHOOL SENIORS IN OCTOBER 1959

Group	Percentage Who Graduated	Percentage Who Did Not Graduate
MALE	84.2	15.8
White	84.9	15.0
Nonwhite	76.0	24.0
FEMALE	91.2	8.8
White	91.9	8.1
Nonwhite	84.4	15.6
RESIDENCE		
Urban	85.9	14.1
Rural nonfarm	91.1	8.9
Rural farm	88.7	11.3

Source: Bureau of the Census and U.S. Department of Agriculture, 1962.

Grade Retention and School Achievement. The Maryland study (Maryland State Department of Education, 1963) found that more than one-half of the dropouts had been compelled to repeat a grade at least once in the elementary or junior high school. In Louisiana (Jones, 1964) only 20.3 percent were not academically retarded. In several other studies, as many as 70 percent had been retained at least once, and 40 percent twice or more.

The study of the Los Angeles City School District (1965) revealed that the subject marks of the dropouts during their last school year were substantially below those of the graduate. The dropout had a grade-point average of 1.19 (D); the graduate had a grade-point average of 2.63 (B−). Yet 30 percent of the dropouts were making C averages or better. Even at the junior high school level, grade 7, the differences in school marks were quite apparent. The future dropouts had C averages (passing), while the future graduates had B− averages.

Reading Failure. The dropout's level of reading achievement is significantly lower than that of the nondropout. For example, Bledsoe (1959) found that dropouts from the ninth and tenth grades had a mean reading-comprehension score of 7.9, and the rest of the ninth graders, a mean score of 8.9. Penty (1956) also found a relationship between reading ability and withdrawal from high school. Three times as many poor readers as good readers dropped out of school, and the likelihood of a poor reader's dropping out was greater when other factors pressuring a student toward withdrawal were present.

Nachman and others (1963) found that 75.4 percent of the dropouts for whom reading-test information was available scored below the median for their grade level; 53.4 percent were in the bottom quartile.

Whitmore and Chapman (1965) found that although 63 percent of the dropouts were retarded one year or more in reading, 19 percent were at grade level and 18 percent were reading one year or more above grade level.

Penningroth (1963) examined selected characteristics of disabled readers who dropped out of school and of those who remained to graduate. Both groups were matched in reading scores attained in grade 9, intelligence, school attendance, attitudes toward peers, parents, and teachers, etc. There were no significant differences between the two groups in reading ability or in intelligence. However, there was a marked difference in their primary-grade experience. The retarded junior high school readers who stayed on to graduate were significantly better readers in the primary grades than the dropouts. They had had, in effect, a successful school experience early in their school life, while the dropouts had encountered failure.

Extracurricular Activities. The dropout seldom participates in schoolwide activities. The Los Angeles City School District study (1965) found that only a small minority of dropouts had participated in such programs while in school. Eighty-three percent had records of little or no participation. The record was equally poor for both boys and girls.

A study in Dade County, Florida (Gillingham, 1964), showed that 91.9 percent of the dropouts were not participating in an extracurricular activity at the time of withdrawal and that 34.2 percent of the graduates were not participating in such an activity. The difference of 57.7 percent is statistically significant beyond the .01 level. The statistical results in the Maryland study (Maryland State Department of Education, 1963) and other studies are similar to these. Children who do not feel they belong are less apt to participate in the total life of the school. The dropouts, unfortunately, seem to feel this way.

School Discipline and Juvenile Delinquency. The Ohio study (Nachman & others, 1963) found that discipline was a frequent problem for 10 percent of the boys and 3 percent of the girls during their elementary-school years. At the secondary-school level discipline was reported as being a frequent problem for 27 percent of the boys and 11 percent of the girls—a threefold increase. For boys who dropped out of school at grade 9, 16.5 percent were in difficulty in the elementary grades, and 34.5 percent in the secondary grades. Yet, at the same time, slightly more than one-fourth of the boys and more than one-half of the girls were never reported as disciplinary problems during their secondary-school attendance.

The Los Angeles City School District study (1965), based on responses of vice-principals, found that one in five boys and one in ten girls had been in the custody of a law enforcement agency during the year preceding the dropping out. However, here again, for nearly three-fourths of all dropouts, there appeared to be no agency referral of any kind (see Table 2).

TABLE 2

LOS ANGELES CITY SCHOOLS, AGENCY REFERRAL FOR DROPOUTS

Agency	Percentage Boys	Girls	Total
Family service	1.7	3.6	2.4
Health agency	2.4	4.0	3.1
Law enforcement agency	19.9	10.1	15.4
Other agencies	8.8	8.5	8.6
None	70.3	75.4	72.7
Total[a]:	103.1	101.6	102.4

Source: Los Angeles City School District, 1965.
a. Total exceeds 100% because respondents were permitted to check more than one item.

The Maryland study (Maryland State Department of Education, 1963) reported that only one-quarter of the dropouts had previously been suspended from school and that one-fifth had been considered serious behavior problems by school authorities.

A recent study conducted in Hibbing, Minnesota, a city with a population of almost 18,000, in the northeastern part of the state, showed that 53 percent of the boy dropouts and 28 percent of the girl dropouts had five or more such notations on their records as truancy, class misconduct, and breaking of school rules. Yet only 17 percent of the boy dropouts and 4 percent of the girl dropouts, approximately one-fifth of all the dropouts, were forced to leave school as a result of disciplinary action (Kinney, 1962).

In Orange County, California, 18 percent of the dropouts were such serious discipline cases that the school initiated the process of early school leaving (McCreary & Kitch, 1953).

A follow-up study of potential dropouts in a single high school in Seattle, Washington, found that whereas the rate of delinquency, defined as involvement with a juvenile court, was 3 percent for the total youth population, it was 7 percent for those youngsters tentatively identified as dropouts but who did succeed in graduating, and 35 percent for those who, in fact, did drop out (Schneller, 1962). In Bridgeport, Connecticut, a study of court records revealed that 24 percent of the high school dropouts had personal court records. In addition, referrals for other members of the dropouts' families showed that one-third of the families of those youngsters had members with court records. Here, too, the area figure for juvenile offenses is approximately 3 percent of the total juveniles (Silverstone & Hoyt, 1963).

In both studies, the percentage of dropouts who became involved with the courts was extremely high, 35 and 24 percent, respectively. To put it another way, the delinquency rate among Seattle dropouts was 12 times that of the stay-ins, while in Bridgeport it was 8 times as great. Thus, while the majority of dropouts tend to be law-abiding, they are clearly more susceptible to delinquency and more often in trouble with law enforcement agencies than the average adolescent.

Pearl found that the pattern of delinquency was not limited to the dropout himself but appeared to be a constant of family behavior. He found that 43 percent of the families of dropouts had some involvement with crime or delinquency (Pearl, 1962).

Family Background. A child's attitude toward schooling is developed and nurtured first in the home and then in the community. How do parents of dropouts view education? The Los Angeles study (Los Angeles City School District, 1965) found that almost one-fourth of the parents of dropouts encouraged their children to drop out, and another one-fourth were indifferent; fewer than one-half of the parents of dropouts encouraged their children to stay in school.

The dropout problem, in its most important dimensions, is one area of the much larger problem of our so-called lower classes. However, dropping out is by no means strictly a lower-class problem; it can and does occur with great frequency anywhere along the socioeconomic scale. But it is predominantly a lower-class problem, so much so that while a middle-class child's dropping out of school will seem unexpected and somewhat incongruous, dropping out is rather endemic to the lower class. It is, in many instances, and for any number of reasons, a "norm" in lower class cultures.

The Maryland State Department of Education (1963) found that 52 percent of the parents of dropouts were either unskilled workers or unemployed. It can probably be safely assumed that a large proportion of the remainder were low-skilled or semiskilled workers. These are people, then, who generally occupy the lowest rungs of our social and economic ladder.

Hollingshead (1949), in his classic study, *Elmtown's Youth,* found that in the middle social class all boys and girls finished the eighth grade and 11 out of 12 of those who eventually dropped out had entered high school, but 75 percent of the children from the lowest social class had dropped out before they were 16 years of age.

In Rochester, New York (Pearl, 1962), a study revealed that one out of every three dropouts came from families on welfare.

In Los Angeles, a comparison of the occupational statuses of parents of dropouts and of graduates revealed that whereas almost one-half of the parents of dropouts were employed in unskilled, service, or semiskilled occupations, only one-sixth of the parents of graduates were so employed. Also, twice as many dropouts as graduates came from families in the lowest income brackets (35 percent and 15 percent), and twice as many graduates as dropouts came from families in the highest income brackets (23 percent and 12 percent).

Bowman and Matthews (1960) found in River City that 87.7 percent of the dropouts were in the lower class, and 1.4 percent were in the upper and upper-middle classes.

A study conducted in Tucson, Arizona (Young, 1954), showed that a majority of the dropouts there came from low-income families who lived in substandard housing and belonged to a racial minority. Children from such a background find it hard to feel that they "belong" in most schools or that what they learn in school will ever be of any use to them.

Greathouse (1964) found in a study done in nine Appalachia counties—three each in Kentucky, Tennessee, and West Virginia—that 30.9 percent of the fathers of dropouts were unskilled workers and 11.1 percent were unemployed, and more than one-half (51.8 percent) of the families had annual incomes of less than $3,000.

In a study of dropouts done in White Plains, New York, Graves (1964) found that 52 percent of the chief wage earners in families of dropouts were classified as unskilled.

In the Ohio study, Nachman and others (1963) found that 55 percent of the fathers of dropouts were classified as unskilled or semiskilled. However, according to the 1960 Ohio census, only about 30 percent of the employed males over 25 were in unskilled or semiskilled jobs. It was also found that fewer than 2 percent (1.7 percent) of the fathers of dropouts were classified as professionals, whereas the census data indicated that 10.9 percent of the employed males over 25 held professional positions. Also, the counselors indicated that 44 percent of the dropouts come from homes which were below the average economic level of their community, and only 2.7 percent came from homes which they rated as being above average.

Using a five-point social-class scale the Alabama State Education Department (1964) found that 78 percent of dropouts came from the two lowest classes and only 2 percent from the two highest classes.

It seems obvious that children whose parents are unemployed, or employed in unskilled or semi-skilled work, drop out of school in greater-than-average proportions, while children whose parents are employed in professional, managerial, clerical, or sales work drop out in less-than-average proportions.

Education of Parents. The educational level of parents has been found to be a significant factor, possibly the most significant factor, in dropping out. This is understandable in light of the parents' occupational, economic, and social level. Education does not have much relevance in their daily lives, except, of course, that they lack it, perhaps irreparably. It was found in the Maryland study (Maryland State Department of Education, 1963) that 78 percent of the mothers and 80 percent of the fathers of dropouts had themselves never finished high school. Also, 25 percent of the mothers and 30 percent of the fathers had never gotten beyond the sixth grade.

Nachman and others (1963) found that almost 70 percent of the mothers and fathers of dropouts were themselves dropouts, and the percentage rose to 80 in those cases where the pupils dropped out in grade 9. Also, more than one-third of the mothers and almost two-fifths of the fathers had completed fewer than nine years of education.

Fifield (1964), in Pocatello, Idaho, found that of 107 dropouts, only one had a parent who was a high school graduate whereas 70 percent of the stay-ins had parents who were high school graduates. Interestingly enough, 30 percent of the graduates came from homes where the parents had fewer than 12 years of education.

Bledsoe (1959) found an almost perfect inverse ratio between parents' educational level and percentage of dropouts. He found that those students whose parents had had some college education did not drop out; those whose parents had completed high school dropped out to the smallest extent; next ranked those with parents with one to three years of high school, then those with parents with eight years of school, and then those with parents with one to four years of school. Parents who had had five or six years of schooling had the largest proportion of dropouts among their children.

Gillingham (1964) found that among the dropouts in Dade County, 69 percent had parents who were dropouts, but that among the graduates only 37 percent of the parents had fewer than 12 years of schooling. To put the matter in a different way, 31 percent of the parents of dropouts had had 12 years or more of education, while 63 percent of the graduates had parents who had graduated. In Pocatello, Idaho (Fifield, 1964), there were 106 dropout parents for 107 dropout pupils. In the Appalachia study (Greathouse, 1964), 98 percent of the fathers and 96 percent of the mothers of dropouts had not graduated from high school. In Modesto, California, 90 percent of the parents of dropouts had had fewer than 12 years of education and 75 percent of them had fewer than 8 years (Whitmore & Chapman, 1965).

A breakdown of the Maryland study showed that in the rural schools 70 percent of the dropouts had quit before grade 10 and that 90 percent of the mothers and 93 percent of the fathers had never finished high school. And 70 percent of these parents were either unskilled workers or unemployed. In Alabama, 85 percent of the fathers and 84 percent of the mothers of dropouts were dropouts themselves; and even more revealing is the fact that almost one-half of the fathers (47 percent) and two-fifths of the mothers (40 percent) had never completed the seventh grade.

Self Concepts of the Dropout. Dropouts seem to be "loners." They are much more dissatisfied with their social relationships in school than are the stay-ins. They frequently consider themselves poorly treated or unesteemed by teachers and other pupils. They often feel that the teacher is not interested in them or their problems. Perhaps, more often than not, they are right in their perceptions. Too frequently, they permit these perceptions to downgrade an already deflated self-image, contributing to a vicious cycle of further failure, nonparticipation, and social withdrawal. Sometimes they engage in acts of rebellion in the form of remarks or other behavior. Girls are especially sensitive to snubs, to the lack of the "right clothes," and to rejection by established cliques.

The Modesto study (Whitmore & Chapman, 1965), which probed these relations, revealed that there were differences significant at the 1-percent level between self concepts of dropouts and of graduates (see Table 3).

Also, more than half of the dropouts said they did not like school, and almost two-thirds of them said they had trouble doing their assignments. The counselor, dubious about one boy's statement that he had had no trouble in doing his assignments, questioned him further; the boy replied, "I had no trouble. I didn't do them."

In the Ohio study (Nachman & others, 1963) counselors estimated that 44 percent of the boy dropouts and 36 percent of the girl dropouts were below average in emotional maturity and that 49 percent of the boy dropouts and 37 percent of the girl dropouts were below average in social maturity. As in the case of other characteristics studied, a higher percentage of the early dropouts than of those who dropped out in grades 10, 11, and 12 were rated below average in social and emotional maturity. For example, 63 percent of the ninth-grade boy dropouts were rated as below average in social maturity, whereas the percentage, though still high, fell to 38 percent for grade-12 boy dropouts.

The dropout tends to reject both school and self, is usually insecure in his school status, is less respected than other students by his teachers because of academic inadequacy, is usually hostile toward other persons, and has not established adequate goals.

TABLE 3

QUESTIONS ASKED OF STUDENTS AT MODESTO (CALIFORNIA) HIGH SCHOOL, CLASS OF 1963–64, IN A STUDY OF SELF CONCEPT

Item	Percentage Answering Affirmatively	
	Dropouts	Graduates
Do you feel spiteful toward other pupils?	62	11
Do you have many enemies in school?	31	7
Has a teacher ever rewarded or praised you?	39	88
Do you feel you are a slow learner?	62	18
Do you have any skills that will help you get a job?	41	90

Source: Whitmore & Chapman, 1965.

Guidance and the Dropout. The support and guidance a youngster receives in his home and in school help to determine his future. Many more dropouts than graduates come from broken homes, and evidence seems to indicate that a sizable portion of the physically intact homes of the dropouts are psychologically broken.

The Modesto study (Whitmore & Chapman, 1965) found that 64 percent of the girl dropouts and 48 percent of the boy dropouts came from broken homes, but only 12 percent of the girl graduates and 28 percent of the boy graduates came from such homes.

In Los Angeles it was found that 43 percent of the dropouts were not living with both natural parents, compared with 22 percent of the graduates (Los Angeles City School District, 1965), and in the Alabama study 42 percent of the dropouts were not living with both natural parents (Alabama State Department of Education, 1964). A comparison of the Alabama and Los Angeles dropouts reveals a marked similarity between the groups (see Table 4).

Unable in many cases to get proper guidance in his home, the potential dropout is forced to look to the school for such help. Yet in Louisiana fewer than 40 percent of the dropouts were counseled by licensed counselors. Swanstrom (1964) found that fewer than 25 percent of dropouts but more than one-half of graduates had received vocational counseling, either in school or at the employment service. Thirteen times as many graduates received guidance in school and from the employment service as did dropouts (see Table 5).

The Dropout and Work. Several studies have shown that at least 50 percent of the dropouts are, and remain, unemployed up to a year after leaving school. In Orange County, California, only 50 percent of the 427 dropouts were working, and many of these were working in part-time jobs, such as baby-sitting, lawn mowing, and car washing (McCreary & Kitch,

TABLE 4

COMPARISON OF LOS ANGELES AND ALABAMA DROPOUTS IN TERMS OF HOME LIFE

Lives With	Percentage of Dropouts Los Angeles	Alabama
Both natural parents	56.5	57.8
Parent and stepparent	15.0	7.1
One natural parent only	21.1	20.8
Another relative or parent substitute	7.4	14.3

Sources: Los Angeles City School District, 1965; Alabama State Department of Education, 1964.

1953). In Alabama, three-fourths of the more than 10,000 dropouts were unemployed (Alabama State Department of Education, 1964).

A follow-up study done in Tennessee in 1962 of the group who had dropped out in 1960–61 found that 49 percent were unemployed and that of those employed only 57 percent were employed in regular positions, with 82 percent employed as unskilled laborers (Tennessee State Department of Education, 1963).

TABLE 5

EMPLOYMENT GUIDANCE

	Percentage of Dropouts	Percentage of Graduates
Received guidance	22.4	56.1
School only	17.1	37.8
Employment service only	4.2	4.9
School and employment service	1.0	13.4
Did not receive guidance	77.6	43.9
Total:	100.0	100.0

Source: Swanstrom, 1964.

Although many dropouts indicate that they will return to school to graduate, few do so. In Tennessee, 9 percent returned to school. Swanstrom (1964) found that high school graduates were much more likely than dropouts to have entered training programs after leaving school—3 out of 10 graduates, compared to only 1 out of 10 dropouts.

These, then, are some of the characteristics of the dropout and some of the forces that have served to bring into sharper focus the long-standing but serious problems of the school dropout. In the past, there were alternative paths to growing up. A young person could quit school, find a job, discover what he was good at, and eventually become a successful, participating adult; or he could reach adulthood by remaining in school and graduating. Today, there seems to be only one way—the school way. The dropout, never really learning in school what he is good at, drifts into adulthood confused, bewildered, insecure, and unsure of himself, wondering whether he is good at—or, for that matter, good for—anything. For the overriding fact is simply that increasingly there is little place in our society for the dropout youngster and that increasingly the dropout has a poor future.

Daniel Schreiber
Brooklyn (New York) Board of Education

References

Alabama State Department of Education. "Facts and Figures on Dropouts in Alabama." The Department. 1964. (Mimeographed.)

Bledsoe, Joseph C. "An Investigation of Six Correlates of Student Withdrawal from High School." *J Ed Res* 53:3–6; 1959.

Bowman, Paul H., and Matthews, Charles V. *Motivations of Youth for Leaving School*. USOE Cooperative Research Project No. 200. U Chicago Press, 1960. 137p.

Connecticut Commission on Civil Rights. *Comparative Study of Negro and White Dropouts in Selected Connecticut High Schools*. The Committee, 1959.

Fifield, M. "Pocatello, Idaho, Dropout Study, 1963." Pocatello Board of Education, 1964. (Mimeographed.)

Gillingham, John. *A Study of Dropouts in Dade County, Florida, Public Schools. 1960–63*. Department of Research, Dade County, Florida, 1964. 124p.

Graves, M. F. "Dropout Study, White Plains, N.Y., Public Schools." White Plains Board of Education, 1964. (Mimeographed.)

Greathouse, L. M. "The Southern Appalachian Dropout Study 1962–63." Berea College, 1964. (Mimeographed.)

Hollingshead, August B. *Elmtown's Youth: The Impact of Social Classes on Adolescents*. Wiley, 1949. 480p.

Johnson, Lyndon B. "Message to Congress." *Washington Post*, January 13, 1965. p. 1.

Jones, Wallace. *The School Dropout in Louisiana, 1963–1964*. Bulletin 1026. Louisiana Department of Public Education, 1964.

Kennedy, John F. "Message to Congress." *Washington Post,* January 14, 1963. p. 1.

Kinney, Paul D. "Study of Hibbing, Minnesota, High School Dropouts, 1956–1961." Hibbing Board of Education, 1962. (Mimeographed.)

Los Angeles City School District. *Dropouts Vs. Graduates.* Report No. 266. The District, 1965.

Maryland State Department of Education. *Our Dropouts: What Can Schools Do?* The Department, 1963. 48p.

McCreary, W. H., and Kitch, D. E. *Now Hear Youth.* California State Department of Education, 1963.

Miller, S. M. *The Syracuse Dropout.* Syracuse Youth Development Center, 1963.

Nachman, Leonard R., and others. *Pilot Study of Ohio High School Dropouts, 1961–1962.* Ohio State Department of Education, 1963. 56p.

National Committee on Employment of Youth. "Getting Hired, Getting Trained." The Committee, 1964. (Mimeographed.)

Penningroth, M. P. "A Study of Selected Characteristics of Disabled Readers in the Ninth Grade of a Large Urban Population in Georgia." Doctoral dissertation. U Georgia, 1963.

Penty, Ruth C. *Reading Ability and High School Dropouts.* Teachers Col, Columbia U, 1956. 93p.

Pearl, Arthur. *The School Dropout Problem, Rochester,* Part I. New York State Division for Youth, 1962.

Schneller, Pete. "Unwilling Learner and Dropout Study 1958–1961." Ballard High School, Seattle, Washington, 1962. (Mimeographed.)

Schreiber, Daniel. "Juvenile Delinquency and The School Dropout Problem." Federal Probation September, 1963.

Schreiber, Daniel. *Holding Power/Large City School Systems.* NEA, 1964.

Silverstone, L., and Hoyt, C. G. *Bridgeport, Connecticut, School Dropout Study, A Preliminary Report.* Bridgeport Board of Education, 1963.

Swanstrom, T. E. *Out of School Youth—February 1963,* Part II. U.S. Department of Labor, 1964.

Tennessee State Department of Education. "Dropouts and Improved Census Enumeration." The Department, 1963. (Mimeographed.)

U.S. Department of Commerce. *Factors Related to College Attendance of Farm and Non-farm High School Graduates.* GPO, 1962. 18p.

U.S. Department of Health, Education, and Welfare. "Holding Power of U.S. School Rises." In *School Life.* USOE, 1962.

U.S. Department of Labor. *Counseling and Employment Service for Youth.* Bureau of Employment Security, 1962.

U.S. Department of Labor. *Summary of Current Economic Facts and Labor Force Data.* The Department, 1964(a).

U.S. Department of Labor. *Worth of Education, Youth Employment.* The Department, 1964(b).

U.S. Department of Labor, Bureau of Labor Statistics. *School and Early Employment of Youth.* Bulletin 1277. GPO, 1960. 89p.

Whitmore, P. M., and Chapman, P. W. "Dropout Incidence and Significance at Modesto High Schools 1964–1965." Modesto, California, 1965. (Mimeographed.)

Woollatt, Lorne H. "Why Capable Students Drop Out of High School." B Nat Assn Sec Sch Prin 45:1–8; 1961.

Young, Joe M. "Lost, Strayed or Stolen." *Clearing House* 29:82–92; 1954.

EARLY CHILDHOOD EDUCATION

In the context of formal education in the United States, the term "early childhood education" usually denotes the school experiences of young children in nursery school, kindergarten, and the primary grades. The current literature of child development and education reveals that few writers define early childhood in precise terms, employing instead such inclusive descriptions as "the first years of life" and "young children." Child psychologists usually distinguish between infancy, early childhood, and later childhood when discussing periods of growth and development, but they have apparently failed to establish standards for delineating exactly when the period of early childhood begins and ends. Some define early childhood in terms of chronological age: from one to six years (Olson, 1959), the years after two and through five years of age (R. Watson, 1960), or ages two or three through eight (E. Fuller, 1960); others by maturity indicators: childhood begins when walking alone is mastered or as soon as the rudiments of language are acquired and continues to the time of entering school, when the child can get on fairly well with his peers (McCandless, 1961). Erikson (1963) and Yarrow (1964) gauge the onset of each period of development by the depth and nature of the child's relationships—to his parents, to other adults and children, and to himself. Still other writers look at the qualitative changes which occur in the child's mental development (Gesell, 1940; Piaget, 1952). Educators, on the other hand, tend to refer to children by the grade level they have achieved in school. Adams (1965) feels that a more specific statement of the age group under discussion could remove the occasion for much theoretical warring about childhood and childhood education. He specifies three, four, and five years of age as early childhood.

The recent literature reveals considerable agreement as to the significance of early childhood and the importance of providing education for young children. During the past decade in the United States, an accumulation of scientific evidence has strengthened public conviction that the first years of a child's life are a crucial time for learning. Investigators from a majority of the social sciences looked to early childhood for solutions to persistent human problems and discovered that important learning occurs from the very beginning of life (Freud, 1960; Goldsmith, 1965). Evidence that early life experiences influence later development is now impressive. Research in infant behavior is increasing in quantity and quality with the growing awareness that the infant phase of development contributes significantly to the subsequent course of human development (Siegel, 1963, 1966). As the focus of interest has shifted from the physical well-being of the baby as a main concern to the psychological aspects of his birth and early weeks of life, increasing attention has been drawn to cognitive development in infancy and to the role of early stimulation in intellectual development (Stott & Ball, 1967). The competence of the growing infant to solve problems, to act on his environment, and to be acted on by it in turn, is intriguing contemporary psychologists (Wenar, 1964). This view of the infant as active and goal-seeking represents a change in viewpoint from the model of the child supported by earlier learning psychologists from Pavlov through Watson, which was that of a recipient organism—a reactive one (Kesson, 1963). It seems highly probable that certain environmental conditions in infancy have an important impact on later development and that adequate stimulation, even of a stressful nature, is essential to normal development (Levine, 1960). Kagan and Lewis (1965) find considerable theoretical importance in the manner in which the young infant distributes his attention to visual and auditory stimuli. They even go so far as to suggest a possible relationship between very early experiences that influence degrees of spontaneous motor activity in the one-year-old and individual differences in complex attentional phenomena in school-age children. Beginning very early, perceptual development takes place and the infant perceives his world through the sensory modalities of vision, hearing, touch, taste, and smell. According to Benjamin Bloom and others (1965), perceptual development is stimulated by environments rich in the range of experiences available, such as those provided by the typical middle-class home. By contrast, psychologically inadequate institutions, such as those described by Spitz (1945), Skeels (1966; Skeels & others, 1938), Goldfarb (1945), and Dennis (1964) and socially and culturally impoverished homes (R. Bloom & others, 1963) are, according to Casler (1961), characterized by the absence of tactile, vestibular, and other forms of stimulation and lack those forms of social stimulation necessary for proper language development. Their effect on infants reared in such environments often results in physical, emotional, and intellectual malfunctioning. Perceptual stimulation is extremely important for normal development. Yarrow (1964) points out, however, that the severity of personality disturbance and the degree of developmental retardation are in proportion to the degree of environmental deviation and deprivation.

The developmental approach stresses the importance of learning that is continuous and the consequent necessity for a smoothly integrated program which is personal and meaningful to the young child now and in the future (Fleiss, 1966). Education, to be effective at any level, must take into account what the learner has previously learned and experienced and must anticipate the next steps in his learning in the light of the expectations of his culture, the demands of the society in which he lives, and his own individual interests and readiness. When learning is piecemeal and lacking in continuity, failure and loss of self-esteem often result (Holt, 1964). In a very real sense the continuity of learning in early childhood is preserved and protected in the home. Because of his long period of helplessness the young child depends on his parents not only for physical survival but for emotional and intellectual development as well. This, Kardiner (1961) says, leads to idealization of the parent, and ultimately to the development of conscience, the ability to sympathize with and identify himself with others, to have a healthy self-esteem, and the ability to know what goes on in the minds of others. The development of these capacities results in powerful intellectual stimulation. As Chisholm (1957) puts it, the parent's role in the upbringing of a child is perhaps the most important thing that happens in our culture. How child-rearing practices affect learning in early childhood is summarized by Freeberg and Payne (1967) in an extensive review of the literature on parental influence on cognitive development. They found that although the most compelling lines of evidence point to a critical role for verbal patterns established by the parent, other consequences of parental practice are appearing, such as the development of cognitive skill in relation to pressures for achievement. They were also aware of a consistent indication from the studies reviewed that children of superior ability come from homes where parental interest in their intellectual development is evidenced by pressures to succeed and assistance in doing so, particularly in the development of verbal skills. It is the experience of the present writer that parents of some young children enrolled in nursery schools and kindergartens today not only apply pressure for achievement to their preschoolers but also challenge their teachers to keep ahead of parental teaching, which is often more stimulating to the child and more respected by him. Where such advantages are present, it is difficult to separate what the school does from what the home does.

Not all children share such advantages, however. According to Frost and Hawkes (1966) more than a million children starting school each fall in the United States are so disadvantaged that failure is a natural consequence. The educative process, according to a report of the Educational Policies Committee of the National Education Association (1962), is greatly complicated for the child whose home is characterized by poverty, disease, instability, or conflict. Such homes, the committee points out, tend to produce children who are tired, hungry, ill, and emotionally unstable. Silberman (1964), referring to Horace Mann's definition of education as "the great equalizer of the conditions of men—the balance wheel of the social machinery," insists that the wheel is out of balance in this nation. He demands, as one means of equalizing educational opportunities for children of the slums, that the schools reverse the effects of a starved environment and begin admitting children at age three or four instead of waiting until they are five or six, when culturally deprived children are already deadened by their environment and so far behind that even the best education will not be sufficient to let them catch up with middle-class children.

The word *early*, obviously, has taken on new significance in education. It is rare, as Gabbard (1959) has said, to find an educational organization today that is not pushing for a downward extension of the school system as public opinion seems to be gathering behind the idea that kindergarten and nursery school should be available to every child. This article, in keeping with the current trend apparent in the popular and professional literature, considers as early education that which takes place before the child enters the first grade of the elementary school, in what are commonly called nursery school and kindergarten. In doing so it recognizes that the kindergarten is an integral part of the elementary school in many states. It further recognizes that children in the primary grades are indeed young children with growth needs often identical to those of preschool children. However, education in the first and second grades will be dealt with elsewhere in the encyclopedia, in ELEMENTARY EDUCATION.

HISTORY. The young child holds an important place in the world today. His physical and psychological well-being are of unprecedented parental and community concern. The prediction (often attributed to Montessori) made some six decades ago that this century would be "the century of the child" seems more than a wish, for by comparison with earlier times in history, the past forty to fifty years have been a golden era for childhood. Childhood as a subject is a comparative newcomer to art, literature, and the social sciences (Mead, 1963). Artists of the tenth century were unable to depict a child except as a man on a smaller scale, according to Ariés (1962). It is probable, he concludes, that there was no place for childhood as we know it in the medieval world. This was not because children were rejected or neglected then but because medieval society was not aware of the particular nature of childhood which makes the child different from the adult. As soon as the infant could live without his mother or his nanny he joined the society of adults.

Kesson (1965), who selected readings from a vast range of writing about children that has appeared over the past two hundred years, tells us that it was only yesterday in human history that the majority of children could be expected to live beyond their fifth year. After gleaning the representative philosophical and educational ideas from publications about children since 1748, Kesson concluded that the history of child study is a history of modest advances toward truth. In the two centuries of writings he covered, Kesson traced the profound changes which have occurred in Western man's theory of the child. The child was the beneficiary of the physician's skill and the reformer's zeal and the object of speculation by philosophers and educators, who found him worthy of serious intellectual interest. Not until the turn of the century just past was *science* to claim the child in the research of biologists and psychologists. Robert Sears and others (1957), speculating about why science remained so long aloof from the study of child behavior, suggests that science was a male preoccupation and that even in the 1940's and 1950's those scientific and medical specialities which pertained to children attracted less than their share of men.

The history of early childhood education is a history of social change. As the political and economic conditions of human living are degraded by war, pestilence, and want or encouraged by intervals of peace, public health, and productive plenty, the conditions of childhood are also affected. In the course of two centuries, history reveals, the young child has been the victim of every social ill or the beneficiary of every social good, depending on the times in which he lived and the position to which he was born. Educational leaders stand out in the history of childhood because they advocated better infant care, exposed the evils of child labor, pleaded for the prevention of cruelty to children, and contributed to the discovery of the almost limitless mind of the child.

The kindergarten and the nursery school share a common background of educational theory at least since the time of Comenius. Hammond and others (1963) point out that many of the teachings proposed in the books Comenius wrote in the mid-seventeenth century are reminiscent of contemporary practice. His appreciation of the teaching function of parents, for example, is a basic assumption of the modern nursery-school movement.

Although some of John Locke's judgmental and punitive attitudes are unacceptably harsh, in 1693 he articulated many educational principles and practices which are valued today (Locke, 1892). His view of curiosity in children as a valuable appetite for knowledge and his awareness that spontaneous play and the delight in discovery are assets to learning have their parallels in contemporary educational theory. In the eighteenth century, the thinking of Rousseau (1911), radical for his day, gave new dignity and respect to childhood and to the very nature of the child, which was regarded by many at that time as inherently evil. In the late eighteenth and early nineteenth centuries Pestalozzi (1894) and Froebel (1887) brought the use of "the senses" and the "freedom to investigate" into a school dominated by rote memorization and harsh discipline. Indeed, the curriculum of compensatory education which is emphasized today as an antidote for cultural deprivation draws heavily from the thinking of Pestalozzi and Froebel, as well as from that of Montessori and McMillan, in this century. Braun (1966), writing about the current national interest in nursery education for deprived children, leads us back along the historical routes of the nursery-education movement to experiments carried on with the very children about whom we have been concerned. Froebel, he points out, conceived the kindergarten in Germany, and gave it the name it still goes by at the onset of the Industrial Revolution. His followers started kindergartens in the slums of Berlin and claimed success for them. Froebel advocated giving the child freedom of movement to explore the world and emphasized an ordered outer world which would in turn make for an ordered inner world. In addition, Braun tells us, Froebel's use of language during the child's exploring was aimed at making the impressions of the child conscious and unified. Agreeing with Froebel in allowing the child the freedom to explore and teach *himself,* Maria Montessori (1964) early in this century worked with slum children of Rome in their preschool years. She replaced Froebel's materials with her own, which were larger and therefore more manageable and easier for the child to control. Her total environment was more in tune with the child's size. The child in her preschool was left to pursue his own interests and free to solve problems without interference. In this way she was able to aid his personality development and foster a sense of competence. Montessori is best known for the design for sensory training and the utilization of synthetic intellectual functions. Margaret McMillan and her sister Rachel were influential in beginning the American nursery school, which, though it has typically served the middle-class child in this country, was patterned after the nursery schools she established in England, where her concern had originally been for children in the slum districts of London (McMillan, 1919). Her concept of the nursery school as making up for poverty, apathy, and neglect included provision for medical and dental care and for cognitive stimulation and work.

Until the middle of the nineteenth century the history of the concern for early childhood was a history of changing social attitudes toward children and learning, recorded by educational theorists and philosophers. Leaders in education were those who articulated a methodology or who pleaded for educational reform. With the publications of Charles Darwin (1897), however, the seeds of the child study movement were sown, and his concept of the hereditary determination of intelligence paved the way for the advance of modern child psychology. Hunt (1964) and Robert Watson (1960) attribute the influence of Darwinian theory on G. Stanley Hall to Hall's recognition of the importance of empirical study of the child, which in many respects made Hall's questionnaire approach the forerunner of modern psychological testing. Hall's students became leaders of the new psychology in America. One of them, Lewis Terman, was the author of the Stanford-Binet revision, the most widely known version of the Binet tests of intelligence in America. Terman and others, according to Hunt (1964), communicated their faith in "fixed intelligence" to those who spread the testing movement in America. This theory influenced teaching tremendously in the first half of this century and produced considerable controversy, according to Robert Watson (1960), when in 1940 child psychologists at the University of Iowa Child Welfare Station (Wellman, 1932; Crissey, 1937) claimed positive effects upon intellectual development from certain enriching experiences offered by the nursery school. Critics (Goodenough, 1940; McNemar, 1940) of these findings were so many and so authoritative, however, that the evidence from the Iowa studies lay dormant for almost two decades until recently rediscovered by the advocates of preschool enrichment for the educationally deprived.

John B. Watson, one of whose contributions to psychology was to make children legitimate subjects for psychological experiments, had an important influence on child-rearing practices of the 1920's and 1930's. Textbooks in early childhood education published before World War II reflect his behaviorist theories with respect to habit training, early socialization, and absence of affect in the teacher-child relationship. Watson's dogmatism (1928) was reflected for many years in the practices of parents and teachers of young children. Examples of this are evident in the widely distributed books on preschool education by Blatz and others (1935) and by Foster and Mattson (1929).

Arnold Gesell, whose writings actually date back to 1912 (Gesell & Gesell, 1912), took exception to the behaviorists' extreme environmental theories, which he saw as fraught with abnormal consequences for the young child. Gesell (1940) considered that the preschool period—the first six years of a child's life—exceeded all others in developmental importance. He was interested in the process of growth and in the inner drive of the organism for growth. Early childhood education was to him a cultural instrument for strengthening the normal functions of a normal home. His normative approach to development made him an authority figure for parents and teachers of young children.

Following World War II the influence of psychoanalytic theory began to be evident in preschool education. In the late 1940's an aritcle written several years earlier by Frank (1938) was reprinted and widely distributed. It drew attention to the young child's fundamental needs and suggested that the role of his teacher should be clinical as well as educational. Anna Freud and Dorothy Burlingham (1964) described the effects of separation anxiety on groups of young children and contributed insight into the salutory effects of grouping children in wider rather than in narrow homogeneous age groups in preschool. Spock (1946) advocated that the child be allowed to learn in his own way and time. In 1950 Erikson (1951), at the White House Conference on Children and Youth called by President Truman, introduced the concept of a healthy personality for every child.

Contributions from sociologists and cultural anthropologists in the years which followed the war have drawn attention to the effects of social position and color on young children and the variety of practices in the care and rearing of children exhibited by different social, economic, and educational classes and by different ethnic groups. An increase of experimental studies contributed to the knowledge of how early, how much, and in what ways children learn. The cognitive aspects of development inspired by the rediscovery of earlier writings of Piaget were dramatized by learning theorists and by the critics of the American system of public education. The question posed by Rudolph Flesch in 1955 in "Why Can't Johnny Read?," and the launching into orbit of Sputnik I, the world's first artificial satellite, by the U.S.S.R. in 1957, resulted in a frantic search for reasons why American children were behind the Russians in academic achievement. Doman (1964) and Pines (1963) suggested teaching babies as young as ten months and three years, respectively, to read. Talking typewriters (Moore & Anderson, 1960) and teaching machines (Suppes, 1967) were introduced as new teaching aids which could be developed, as research monies became available, for the maximal utilization of our intellectual resources. As Bronfenbrenner (1961) observed, achievement began to replace adjustment as the highest goal of the American way of life, and he predicted that the result might be children who are more aggressive, domineering, and cruel if education for excellence were pursued singlemindedly.

In the 1960's the direction of thought in early childhood education was toward rediscovering the mind of the child (Martin, 1960), stressing language development, fostering intellectual development in young children (Wann & others, 1962), and making available high-quality preschool programs for all children, especially for the economically disadvantaged.

The Nursery School. Although early childhood education can trace its beginnings far back in history, the nursery school as we know it today is a recent institution which developed in the twentieth century. The McMillan sisters had been working with preschool children in the slum districts of London, Braun (1966) tells us, for several years before the British Parliament passed the Education Act of 1918 to provide tax money for nursery services to children aged two to five years. Having demonstrated the possibility of reversing the effects of social deprivation by working with the young child and his mother in a nurturing and nurturant environment, the McMillans chose "nursery school" as an appropriate name for their new kind of early childhood education. These schools, according to Christianson and others (1961), attempted to meet the basic needs of young children which could not be provided by families living in crowded slum areas, and they assumed a responsibility to "educate every child as if he were [our] own." A few years later, in 1920, nursery schools patterned after the English model were introduced into the United States at Columbia University, at the Merrill-Palmer School in Detroit, and at Ruggles Street in Boston. Prior to that time there had, of course, been group day care for preschool children of employed mothers, which no doubt contributed in many positive ways to their growth and learning. Their primary purpose was, however, to provide custodial care.

According to Pauline Sears and Edith Dowley (1963) the first nursery schools in the United States were for the most part connected with universities and colleges and had as their purpose the discovery and demonstration of "better" ways of caring for young children. As laboratories and research centers, the functions of the early nursery schools varied one from another, in relation to the purposes of the department or college by which they were sponsored: home economics, education, psychology, or medicine. Some were used to prepare young women for motherhood. Some trained nursery school teachers, while a few were established for the opportunity they afforded for cross-sectional studies of child growth and development in a controllable setting and to maintain ongoing records of individual progress and change over an extended period of time. From these centers the basic principles and practices of early childhood education were carried to all parts of the country as nursery schools were established from coast to coast and from north to south. At the same time the nursery schools proved to be sources of discovery as laboratories for the study of human development. Longitudinal studies dating back before 1930 at Merrill-Palmer School and at the universities of Minnesota, Michigan, California, and Chicago, to name a few, have contributed imposing bodies of knowledge to physical anthropology, dentistry, and nutrition, as well as to the social sciences and medicine.

By an interesting coincidence, the nursery-school movement and scientific research in child development began about the same time and have contributed to each other in many ways ever since. This reciprocal arrangement has made the nursery school both a source of research knowledge and an implementer of research findings, which are often evident in the dynamic quality and broad diversity of preschool practice. Other phenomena have contributed to the flexibility and adaptibility of the nursery school which are associated with its twentieth-century beginnings. The nursery school was not bound by the traditions of education which often determine the direction of the elementary school. As a new social institution, it had freedom to work out its own philosophy and practice and to adapt and change in the light of contemporary knowledge. Its purposes were not limited to the first step on the ladder of education but could follow the path from the child's home as he began his search for wider horizons. The nursery school saw its role as an adjunct to the family, the community, and the culture in the education of the child.

The growth of the nursery-school movement has taken many directions. Its purposes have been varied, and this variety in many ways accounts for its growth. At the beginning of World War II, nursery schools as laboratories for the study of child development formed a part of the home economics division of each of the land-grant colleges and of departments of child development in each of the major women's colleges. During the depression years of the 1930's, federal legislation and support were instrumental in establishing nursery schools throughout the country under the Works Progress Administration (WPA) to give work to unemployed teachers, nurses, and helpers, as well as to provide nutrition, protection from disease, and an emotionally stable environment for 75,000 needy children two to five years of age. The supervision and training programs established for

WPA personnel were carefully planned and organized under professional leadership (Christianson & others, 1961).

The war years that followed brought more children into preschool programs, as the Lanham Act funds were made available for the group care of young children whose mothers worked in strategic war industries. Leading educators in colleges and universities joined hands with public school administrators and with industrial management to provide high-quality service to children and their parents. In California, for example, there were 338 nursery-school centers in the public schools. Two shipyards in Oregon built unique centers for the day or the night care of hundreds of young children whose parents were building warships on day, evening, or night shifts. These centers, which were an integral part of the war industry, were staffed by well-qualified nursery school teachers and specialists in child development and early childhood education. Not all of the children's centers were professionally staffed, however, nor were all the facilities which housed their programs of the quality desirable for little children, but the services they gave to children, parents, and indirectly to the industries employing mothers were extremely helpful and at times indispensable (Dowley, 1949). They had the further effect of introducing the group care and guidance of young children to a wider community, which resulted in increasing awareness by the general public of the value of nursery education.

Six months after the war ended, federal support for child-care centers was withdrawn on the assumption that women who had been brought into wartime employment would return to their full-time home responsibilities. This did not always prove to be the case, however, and a variety of ways and means were sought to keep the existing centers operating. In California (Smitter, 1949), for example, legislation was passed providing for continuing these services to children under the State Department of Education, on a year-to-year basis at first and later at two-year intervals, with certain limitations regarding income of families using them and fees to be paid by them. Permissive legislation existed in ten states and Hawaii in 1947 for the operation of nursery schools using state, local, or private funds (California Legislature, 1947). A Massachusetts legislative act provided for services to children 3 to 14 years old of mothers whose employment was determined to be "necessary for the welfare of their families"; this service was to be operated by school committees based on standards established by state departments of education and public health (Mitchell & Bill, 1962). However, limitation of finances and failure to provide for employees' retirement discouraged communities from taking advantage of this opportunity. The fact that good nursery-school education is not only valuable but, for some children, essential had not yet been accepted by the general public, who saw it merely as a solution to such emergencies as arise in times of national economic depression or war.

Parents of young children, however, were quick to see the values of planned group experiences for their preschool children and the parent cooperative nursery-school movement flourished in the postwar years. As a part of the State Adult Education program in California, where the rapid growth of nursery schools has been impressive, parent-child observation classes are in reality parent education classes with laboratory arrangements for mothers to observe their children one or more half days a week in supervised play and routine activities, which often include lunch and a nap (Christianson & others, 1961).

The withdrawal of public funds and the growing number of parent-operated nursery schools in the years 1948–1958 had an inevitable effect on the education and preparation of nursery-school teachers. Graduates of nursery-school training programs and child-development centers found that openings for teachers of three- and four-year-olds were few and widely scattered geographically and that salaries were unrealistically low in proportion to their professional preparation and to the demands of the job. Some of them found satisfaction in using their teaching skills at the kindergarten and primary levels of the elementary schools, where openings were many because of the increasing numbers of public school kindergartens and the high birthrate in the postwar years. Many, however, left the field for other sources of employment. Universities and colleges curtailed their programs of nursery-teacher training and either discontinued their laboratory nursery schools or used them for other puposes. When the demand for nursery schools began to grow at a rapid pace, there was a serious shortage of teachers and directors for early childhood education programs.

In the meantime a tremendous number of research studies from psychology, sociology and cultural anthropology dramatized the educability of the preschool child. A review of research on teaching in the nursery school by Pauline Sears and Edith Dowley (1963) for the *Handbook of Research on Teaching* (Gage, 1963) revealed a considerable body of knowledge in that area from 138 references. It also detected many gaps in knowledge and the absence of a clearly defined theory for the nursery-school teaching process. In 1964, Swift surveyed the literature on the effects of early group experience. From a vast number of sources she concluded that the effectiveness of a program will depend on its appropriateness to the child's developmental level and the providing of experiences which supplement, rather than merely duplicate, experiences he is receiving elsewhere (Swift, 1964). In 1965, Burgess carefully examined the literature of early childhood education for its values, and she concluded that never before has there been as much clear evidence pointing to the educational importance of the early years of childhood. She saw the goal of teaching nursery school as incorporating what is known about the nature of children and the process of their learning with the requirements of education for a changing society (Burgess, 1965).

New or changing conceptions of the nature of man and the responsibilities of society brought changes to the nursery school of the 1960's. The increasing recognition of the child's conscious awareness of his very early experiences, his dependence on sensory stimulation for cognitive development, and the dispelling of the notion that intelligence is fixed and genetically predetermined resulted in a tremendous emphasis on early learning. For the "disadvantaged child," whatever that term may denote with respect to his deficits —social, economical, educational, or emotional—the preschool years were viewed as crucial for removing the obstacles to his learning which deny him the equality of opportunity fundamental in the American tradition. Experiments by Deutsch (1964) indicated that preschool, kindergarten, or day-care experience or a combination of these are associated with higher scores on intelligence tests than are achieved by children without such experience. Regardless of social-class affiliation the advantage of preschool attendance is evident at first-grade level and even more at grade 5, he found. The decision to utilize preschool enrichment as an antidote to cultural deprivation (Hunt, 1964) culminated in federally funded preschool summer programs in 1965 known as Project Head Start. As a part of the antipoverty program of the Johnson administration, over half a million children who had never been to school before were enrolled in programs which provided medical, dental, and educational services of a highly personal but professional nature. The children were given a wide variety of small-group experiences by teachers oriented to their needs for growing and learning, and emphasis was placed on good language models and on the enhancement of the child's self-image as the result of his acceptance by his teachers and his increasing competence in coping with the school environment.

The demand for preschool teachers once again exceeded the supply, and short-term training programs in the form of workshops, summer courses, and night classes attempted to increase the supply of teachers for teaching not only the culturally deprived children but also the increasing numbers of middle-class children. The nursery school took on new stature and respectability with its growing literature of scientific studies. Evidence of this is that it has attracted more male teachers to the field and raised the standards for nursery-school teaching.

The Kindergarten. The roots of the kindergarten reach deeper into the history of early childhood education than those of the nursery school do. The kindergarten began to develop in Europe as the result of the thinking and writing of Comenius, Rousseau, Pestalozzi, and Herbart. But it was Friedrich Froebel who established the first kindergarten in 1837 in Blankenburg, Germany, and gave it the name it has been known by ever since.

Froebel (1887) saw educational opportunities in the earliest years of childhood and felt that in an enriched environment the child would develop worthwhile interests through experimentation and self-activity. Aborn (1937), on the hundredth anniversary of the kindergarten, described Froebel as a close observer of young children who saw value in their play, not only for physical but for all-around development, and who counseled teachers to lead children to think early in life. This he considered the foremost objective of child training. In Froebel's kindergartens the children spent much of their time out-of-doors, since he believed that each child should have a small garden of his own. Aborn, in describing these kindergartens, was confident that formality and regimentation had no place in Froebel's plan.

Mrs. Carl Schurz brought the first kindergarten to the United States in 1855. It was a Froebel school, developed for German-speaking children in Watertown, Wisconsin, and taught in the German language. The first kindergarten for American children was a private school started by Elizabeth Peabody of Boston, in 1860. It was in St. Louis, Missouri, in 1873, when William T. Harris invited Susan Blow to come and open one, that kindergartens were first introduced as part of the public school system. From that time on, kindergartens, with many modifications in practice and some changes in theory, were established in all parts of the country under a variety of auspices.

Headley (1966), in presenting the American kindergarten point of view, comments on the inadequacies of the first kindergartens in the United States and explains that a school planned for the children of an old country and steeped in German tradition would naturally fail to fulfill the requirements of a pioneering and predominantly practical land. She admits surprise, therefore, that so many of Froebel's original materials and methods clung to the transplanted school for so long. A second significant influence, again from Europe, affected the American kindergarten early in the twentieth century, however, when the practices of Dr. Maria Montessori in Italy became known and were absorbed with little difficulty into then existing programs.

Montessori became interested in insane and mentally deficient children when she was still a medical student in Rome. She followed the work of Jean Itard with great interest and utilized the methods of Édouard Seguin for educating mentally retarded children in the psychiatric clinic of the University of Rome. Out of this experience she devised materials and a methodology of her own for educating normal children in the slum tenements of Rome. She was so successful in her practice and so convincing in her writings that people from all over the world were impressed. Americans, Hunt (1964) says, were among the first to be interested, and her new ideas were given wide publicity in the United States. By 1916, Edmonson (1966) informs us, there were 189 authorized Montessori schools and over 2,000 schools using her name and probably parts of her methods without permission. Her views, however, ran contrary to the emerging psychology of education, and the American Montessori schools vanished almost as suddenly as they appeared.

As early as 1879, according to Hammond and others (1963), state legislators began to enact laws permitting the local establishment of kindergartens. The greatest demand for public schools for young children has arisen since 1940. In 1949 Smitter wrote that by 1945 32 states had authorized the use of state funds for kindergartens as many programs for young children started as emergency measures during the war were made a permanent part of the public school system (Smitter, 1949). Ten years later Gabbard (1959) reported that all but eight states had kindergartens in their public schools and that nearly half of America's 3.8 million five-year-olds were in kindergarten. With the rise in birthrate in the five years which followed the Gabbard report, however, the Bureau of the Census revealed that although more children in the United States were enrolled in kindergartens, the percentage had changed only slightly, with 2,176,000 of the 4,097,000 five-year-olds in kindergarten; and only 44.3 percent of this number were in public school kindergarten (Schloss, 1965). Peet (1965) asks, "Why don't all public schools have kindergartens?" in the United States today as they do in such countries as Switzerland and France? She feels that the answer is that there are many Americans who do not understand the value of kindergarten and do not even know what takes place in one. When we consider that kindergartens have been a part of the public schools in some parts of the United States for over a hundred years, this is difficult to understand.

The role of the kindergarten has changed in recent years. With the rapid growth of the nursery school throughout the country and the wider dissemination of information about young children to parents and to the public in general, children are entering kindergartens with more maturity in social and intellectual development than before. In addition, Maccoby (1964) reminds us that from the age of 3 to 16 the average American child watches television for one-sixth of his waking hours and that children who have grown up with television appear to come to school with about a one-year advantage in vocabulary. For reasons such as these some people expect that children entering kindergarten should begin immediately the formal learnings of the elementary school. Some people feel that because a child has had nursery-school experience he is prone to be bored in kindergarten, and still others would like children to begin kindergarten before they have reached the entrance age required by the school, especially if the child's birthday is within a month or two of the cutoff date. Olson (1959) reminds parents that the child who is younger than his peers remains younger throughout his school life and that by accelerating his formal learning he will lose out in some aspects of his growth and development, and if he is put ahead of his age mates in school, he does not close this age gap.

Headley (1966) challenges the suggestion that a child must be bored in kindergarten. She claims that such a condition would be the result either of a nursery-school experience that was too much like kindergarten or of a kindergarten program which fails to offer enough in the way of materials, experiences, subject matter, and problem-solving situations to stimulate the child. In the present author's experience children from nursery schools which afford not only a variety of stimulating experiences but also the opportunity to carry out their own exciting ideas and interests with help, when it is asked for, from the teacher find the larger numbers of children and the one-and-only teacher in most kindergartens today frustrating barriers to self-direction.

Although the kindergarten has a longer history and a more recognizable tradition than the nursery school, it has a less imposing body of references in contemporary educational literature. This is explainable in many ways. To begin with the nursery school is a more recent innovation, and its novelty has appeal. Then, too, close association with the family and with parent education is more typical of nursery-school than of kindergarten philosophy. From their beginnings, kindergartens have been affiliated almost exclusively with education, while the nursery school has been the concern of a wide variety of disciplines, and its programs take many forms and fulfill many purposes. Probably the most significant explanation, however, is that experimental research has found the nursery school a compatible place for gathering data because of the informality of its program and procedures, the availability of the children for observation and study, and the more natural behavior of the child under five years of age, with his briefer exposure to conventionalized ways of social living. The prevalent tendency to combine nursery school and kindergarten under the single umbrella of early childhood education gives emphasis to the former because it comes first and covers a wider age span than the kindergarten. Additionally, since more kindergartens are included in the public school system, they are considered a part of the elementary school which is variously referred to as kindergarten through sixth grade and as kindergarten through eighth grade (Headley, 1966).

NURSERY-SCHOOL PROGRAMS. In October 1964 the United States Bureau of the Census, for the first time in its history, collected data on the number of three- and four-year-old children in the population and on the number enrolled in school. Schloss (1965) reported the results of this survey, which found that of the 12,496,000 children aged three to five years, only about one-fourth, or 3,187,000, were enrolled in public and private nursery schools and kindergartens. Almost half a century after the first nursery schools were developed, three-fourths of the children under six years of age still did not have desirable educational opportunities because of the shortage of nursery schools and kindergartens in many parts of the United States. Heffernan (1964), in comparing early childhood education in this country with that provided in other countries, laments that the United States of America, a nation with about 7 percent of the world's population but with 55 percent of the world's wealth, lags behind France, England, and the U.S.S.R. in its provision for the education of young children.

Law (1963–1964) and Burgess (1965) attribute the lack of wide public support for nursery schools to confusion about nursery education. Although nursery schools have tended to take on similar characteristics and nursery-school teachers have learned to use similar language and terminology, nursery education does not have precisely the same meaning for all.

Read (1966) explains that the development of the

nursery school has been largely the result of meeting "emergencies," and it has been influenced by the events and forces of the times. Different types of nursery schools have been evolved to meet a diversity of needs, and Read views the contribution of nursery education to both the home and the school as an indication of progress.

Hymes (1967), who has been identified for many years with the nursery-school movement, expresses both optimism and uneasiness about patterns emerging in early childhood education. In spite of an insufficiency of preschool programs and of qualified teachers, there is an increasing demand for nursery schools and a reaffirmation of the soundness of nursery education. Although it is not a finished product with all of its problems solved, the background of experience accumulating since 1920 and the sound grounding in research in growth and development have provided a framework that seems adaptable to new children in new settings in new times.

In general the nursery school is an educational facility planned for the group experiences of three- and four-year-old children—and sometimes two-year-old children—under the supervision of a qualified teacher (Burgess, 1965). Good nursery teaching is usually described in such terms as "rooted in democratic theory"; "focusing on the child as a whole"; "respecting the individuality of every child"; "encouraging children to learn through exploration, experimentation and discovery"; and "providing a predominance of successful experiences for every child."

The nursery-school movement since 1920 has been characterized by variety. An interdisciplinary approach to early childhood education, the teamwork of educators, psychologists, psychiatrists, pediatricians, nurses, social workers, and nutritionists, has resulted in an awareness of the interrelatedness of development and the connection between intellectual growth, social, emotional, and physical health that Hymes (1967) sees as a valuable and important asset. Burgess (1965), however, viewed the four principal streams of influence contributing to the development of nursery education as not being in fruitful communication with each other. She felt that these four—psychiatry and mental health, behavioral psychology, social work, and education—had approached programs and influenced theory according to their own specific needs, with education exerting the least influence, although it should have been the logical discipline to bring all four influences together.

Various types of programs have developed since the first nursery schools. There are long-day and short-day programs and five-, three-, and two-day-a-week programs; groups have been segregated according to age, intelligence, handicap, social class, or color; there have also been groups integrated with respect to races, social classes, and broader age groups; there are groups which mix gifted, average, retarded, and emotionally disturbed children; and there are those that include blind, deaf, and crippled children in groups of sighted, hearing, and physically competent children.

Schools are sponsored by a variety of institutions. Some are private and operated either for profit or on a break-even basis. Some are sponsored by social welfare programs, some by public schools. Some are church affiliated, some are a service of industry to employees' children. Nursery schools are taught by a variety of methods, housed in a variety of facilities, and purport to serve a long list of objectives. The emphasis today on raising standards for teacher education and on preparation, program offerings, housing, equipment, size of groups, and the licensing of all nursery schools has helped to improve nursery education and reduce the differences which used to exist between day-care programs and nursery schools.

Although laboratory nursery schools represent only a small percentage of existing nursery schools, they have had continuing influence on nursery-school education. As demonstration centers, teacher training institutions, or laboratories for research they have contributed a body of theory and influenced philosophy and practice. Writings coming from laboratory schools often determine the direction of education as they set standards and add to the knowledge about young children. Books by Christianson and others (1961), Hammond and others (1963), and Read (1966) represent experience and knowledge gained through many years of teacher training in laboratory schools and are widely used by teachers of nursery education.

How research is carried on in a laboratory school operated by a department of psychology was described in a series of articles by Dowley and others (1960–1961).

The light of research knowledge today makes it possible for educators of young children to see some things more clearly than was possible in the past. It took a long time to gather convincing evidence that early childhood experiences make a difference in the lives of older children and adolescents, and longer still to measure the benefits of nursery-school attendance in later life. Research in many areas of development and behavior indicates that early experiences are highly relevant. White (1964) has concluded from the evidence of research that the sense of competence is the result of cumulative learning and is ever at work influencing the next thrust of behavior. Effectiveness in dealing with the environment is achieved largely through learning, and Hess (1966) points out that the behavior which leads to social, educational, and economic poverty is acquired in early childhood—that is, it is learned.

The nursery school has been guided into the area of compensatory education through programs funded by federal, state, and local legislation, where some observers think it should have been long ago. Through the thinking and research of Deutsch (1963), Hunt (1964), Reissman and Hannah (1966), Heffernan (1964), and others these programs have been established in areas of the country where poverty and its results have alarmed and shamed a nation dedicated to equal opportunity through free public education for all. Nursery schools for culturally deprived children are operating in public schools, colleges of education, and research centers where a variety of approaches to teaching and other enrichment are being attempted (Gray & Klaus, 1965; Hess & Shipman, 1965). It is still too early to evaluate the effectiveness of the many different approaches, but they are already influencing the direction of nursery-school teaching in the greater emphasis on intellectual stimulation, language development, and social reinforcement (Crandall, 1964; Wann & others, 1962; Bruner, 1961; Harris & others 1964).

Three concerns for nursery school teaching emerge as a result of research and practice: (1) to make the nursery school the best possible place for little children (2) to keep the educational practices of the nursery school constantly in line with the best available knowledge of child development, and (3) to foster and maintain among the teaching staff and students a genuine respect for the science of child study.

The nursery school, then, is an adjunct to family life in a rapidly changing society. It is a dynamic institution whose programs and practices reflect not only the social, economic, philosophical, and political climates in which they exist but also growth and change in the light of the enlarging body of child development research.

KINDERGARTEN PROGRAMS. The unit of the school which enrolls five-year-olds on a regular basis for a year prior to entrance to first grade is designated as a kindergarten, according to Hammond and others (1963). Mayer (1961) defines the essence of this level of education as orientation. In the kindergarten the child learns to sit still and listen; later, he learns to tell stories, to sing, and to listen when other children are speaking. He gradually gets used to going to school every day at the same time.

Many of the goals and objectives (Hoppock, 1960–1961) expressed by educators for kindergarten are very similar to those of the nursery school: building feelings of adequacy; giving the child opportunities to explore and understand his world; facilitating growth through providing the space, freedom, and equipment needed; protecting the child from hazards to health and safety; helping him to find a comfortable contributing place in his group; and encouraging him to grow in independence in managing himself and his activities.

Widmer (1967) sees the kindergarten year as a transition year between home and school and stresses the importance of readiness activities which will be helpful in first grade.

Much of the literature on kindergartens seems strangely out of touch with the child of today. To speak of his "beginning learning" in kindergarten ignores the tremendous influences on children which exist outside of the school. Unless the child has been isolated from the world completely, he has shared a wealth of experiences with his family and neighbors, including the tremendous impact of radio and television. Shaftel (1963), observing the revolutionary changes in the very nature of knowledge today, states that the kindergarten program also has to change. Kindergarten practices, she adds, which were really a great step forward for early childhood a few years ago, are now obsolete. She sees four major tasks for kindergarten teaching: helping the child develop feelings of competence and adequacy, fostering intellectual development (Wann & others, 1962), building feelings of mutual helpfulness and respect as functions of group living, and developing the skills for observation, communication, motor competency, and manipulation. Spodek (1965) describes contemporary social studies programs in the kindergarten as of three kinds: one that has as its goal creating greater awareness of the culture common to all; a second, which attempts to teach the techniques of living together more effectively through group membership and working together (this approach has more concern with process than with content); and a third, which he feels has more merit for today's children, that he calls the immediate environment approach. It has as its objective providing children with understanding that will increase their ability to cope with the present world. He advocates the utilization of play, which can be intellectually stimulating and emotionally satisfying.

The growth of the private kindergarten has reflected parental dissatisfaction in some areas of the country with public school kindergartens. Common criticisms are the inflexibility in the age of entrance to kindergarten programs, which some parents think is too late, and the short day—usually two hours—which is the consequence of double sessions. The unstimulating program and the discouragement of individual creative expression, which parents feel stresses conformity, is a third. Woodruff (1966) accounts for the obstacles to meeting parents' demands for kindergarten experiences by citing the following four factors: (1) the difficulty in finding teachers in early childhood education, (2) the inadequacy of facilities with respect to school plant and materials, (3) the sizes of kindergarten classes, and (4) the short time provided for kindergarten sessions.

Plans to attract more and better teachers to kindergarten teaching are constantly being discussed. The history of teacher training for early childhood education is one of too little and too late. Class size has been studied experimentally by Cannon (1966), who found that large groups in kindergarten (34–39 children) result in more-aggressive behavior, considerable waiting for use of equipment, and longer times awaiting turns for a favorite activity, which result in frustration and less teacher guidance. Keliher (1966) found that Head Start programs with a ratio of three adults to 15 children reported gains of 8 to 10 IQ points in six weeks. She emphasized the need for individual attention.

Kindergartens are also feeling the pressure of new emphasis on achievement by being asked to begin teaching reading and writing. Roeper (1966) feels that instruction in reading should definitely be included in the experience of gifted preschoolers, but only as one of many experiences. She feels that learning social skills, physical skills, communication skills, and developing along creative lines are of equal importance. Anastasiow (1964), using half of the kindergartens in Palo Alto, California, as an experimental group and the other half as a control, compared the progress of children given reading instruction in kindergarten with children who received no reading instruction. In general at the end of the second grade the group given reading instruction in kindergarten failed to show superiority over the control group; quite the reverse was true: the children whose kindergarten experiences followed along more child-development-oriented curriculum lines seemed to make higher scores in reading achievement two years later.

EARLY CHILDHOOD EDUCATION IN OTHER COUNTRIES. Articles about young children and childhood education in other parts of the world appear with greater frequency in American periodicals as nursery school and kindergarten educators around the globe find common areas of concern. Different, unfamiliar aspects of education in other countries often surprise us, but their many similar problems and practices are striking. Many countries are doing as much as, if not more than, we are doing in the United States to educate their youngest citizens.

Heffernan (1964) tells us that France has provided education for children two to six years of age since 1881. The école maternelle is an integral part of the general organization of French education. Attendance is optional; compulsory education begins at six. The teachers are paid by the state and have the same status as primary teachers. A similar situation exists in Belgium, where practically all children from three to six years of age attend the écoles maternelles or jardins d'enfants for one, two, or three years. Mayer (1961) observed that the écoles maternelles are relaxed and easygoing, in contrast to the rigid, severe, strict elementary schools of France and Belgium.

England's nursery schools are completing their first half century of service, and most people in England consider them educationally valuable (Preston, 1966). They are still very few in number, however, and all nursery schools in England have long waiting lists and are handicapped by a severe shortage of teachers. Their equipment is imaginative and improvised, with far less uniformity of ready-made apparatus and furniture than in American schools. Gardner and Cass (1965) agree that teachers have worked successfully in spite of conditions that are far from ideal because of their enthusiasm, initiative, and determination, but they feel that they should be encouraged by the promise of better buildings and equipment in the near future so they might fulfill their tasks with even greater facility.

There are not enough primary schools for the children in Uganda, according to Kibuka (1962), and competition for places is so great that parents pressure three- and four-year-olds to read, write, and recite psalms so they will be admitted to elementary schools. One of the primary objectives of nursery education, therefore, is to provide opportunity for young children to learn to play, since that is discouraged in most middle-class homes.

Bhoota (1962) describes an experiment in childhood education in Bombay, India, which attempts to introduce into the thinking of parents more scientific ideas of childhood education. There are many schools for children two years of age and older, and a school that promises to teach children reading, writing, and numbers without letting them "waste their time in play" gets filled up quickly and is sought after by parents. Only a few parents there are sympathetic to child-development approaches to nursery education.

Shuey (1962) says the people of Turkey in general feel that the child belongs at home. However, there is a growing awareness that preschool years are important, and a few private nursery schools are to be found in large cities. She found no facilities whatsoever for training nursery-school teachers, but plans were being made to start demonstration nursery schools and training courses for teachers under the Ministry of Education.

Japan has had a long history of institutional care for children in need (Kuroki, 1962), from the sixth century to the present time. Since 1948 many day nurseries have been established. They are usually open from 8:00 A.M. to 5:00 P.M. Teachers are professionally trained and must complete 14 years of education. There are at least two teachers to every group of 30 preschool children. Only mothers who work are permitted to enroll their children. Kindergartens are short-day schools, and parents pay tuition to have their children attend. Research studies on number concepts (Fujinaga & others, 1963) and on personality development and parent-child relationships (Tsumori & others, 1961) are carried on in kindergarten.

Jerome (1962) traveled through several countries of Europe to see nursery schools, and she found children everywhere relaxed and happy in their play outdoors. In both East and West Germany and in Austria, France, Poland, and the U.S.S.R. she observed children at play on soft, rolling, grassy areas with water in which to splash and play. Europeans for the most part believe children should grow up close to the earth.

The U.S.S.R. organizes its system of public education so that preprimary education constitutes the first stage (Heffernan, 1964). Usually there is a kindergarten in which pupils are divided into four age groups (three-, four-, five-, and six-year-olds). The basic plan is to provide good education for children in kindergarten while their mothers are working. The teaching of reading is not included in the kindergarten curriculum and does not begin until age seven. In the Soviet Union, education is the major instrument of national policy, and society has the right to judge what values the family teaches and how it brings up its younger generations. Jerome (1962) found that Russian nursery schools had plentiful supplies of toys, plants, pets, and picture books and that play outdoors is considered important.

Deprivation knows no national boundaries. In Israel the problem of cultural deprivation is similar to that in America today. But it is even more acute, since 60 percent of all the children there have come from 80 different countries which do not share a common language. Experiments have shown that the IQ's of preschool children who have previously experienced little or no failure, who are relatively confident, and predisposed to new experiences and are as yet relatively immune to the contagion of social prejudice can be raised by an average of 20 points (Smilansky, 1966). Israel therefore plans to begin work with two-year-olds because progress occurs with less effort in the preschool years than later. Beginning in 1966 the Ministry of Education put into operation a plan which within three years would provide free nursery-school education to every child of three or four years of age who comes from a culturally deprived background (Smilansky, 1966).

Hromadka (1964) visited and researched most of the countries in Europe with advanced child-care programs and studied their methods of training child-care workers. He found two ideas emphasized in most countries: (1) a child is a child regardless of his personal handicaps or living circumstances, and (2) basic training for workers in residential care and care outside the residence should encompass most of the same knowledge and skills. He believes workers should learn to regard child care not so much as a functional problem as an emotional and intellectual challenge and less as a form of corrective therapy than as a restoration and reeducation of children toward more healthful living.

PRESENT STATUS AND EVALUATION. Learning becomes important in infancy and early childhood, and adequate opportunities for full development in the first years of children's lives are extremely crucial for later periods (Olson, 1959). In the next decade, according to Buckminster Fuller (1966), society is going to be preoccupied with the child and the profound contributions he will make to the future of his society. Fuller assures us that given the right environment and thoughtful answers to his questions, the child from birth has everything he needs educationally. Certain directions seem to be clearly taking form in the teaching of young children. The child grows and learns as he moves about and explores the physical world around him, developing his "coping skills" by dealing with the stresses, challenges, and new opportunities which he encounters. Out of these experiences, he develops a feeling of confidence in himself and in his world (Murphy, 1962).

The environment for learning takes on new significance for education and becomes the primary source of learning in early childhood. Margolin (1965) tells us that the purpose of nursery school is to help the child become involved with his environment, not only with materials and objects, but also with other children. In order to learn and grow well, a young child needs to have confidence in his environment and security in his relationships. This confidence comes from living in a world that gives him some degree of order and predictability as well as flexibility and freedom to experiment, explore, and cope with new and unfamiliar situations. A dependable sequence of events and a comfortable orderliness in the arrangement of his materials and equipment permit the child to develop safely and to behave logically (R. Sears & others, 1965). A broader understanding of the learning potentialities of the environment must therefore be reflected in future educational planning for the young child (Shure, 1963).

Inadequate buildings and situations which are both hazardous and restrictive must be replaced in the near future with those which afford the child greater protection and contribute to the creative needs of developing human individuals. The need for better school buildings for early childhood is real. So too is the necessity for extending the reaches of his humanity by developing the love of beauty and the sense of wonder. These are associated with the earth, the sky, the sun, the wind, and the water, from which modern living has divorced the child of today, the limits of whose world are often determined by a network of concrete roads and skyscrapers. European schools for young children seem to have valued and preserved outdoor living more than American nursery schools and kindergartens have.

The second direction of thinking is that how the young child is taught and by whom are of tremendous importance to his later learnings. Swift (1964) speaks of the teacher as the most important single factor in determining the nature of the child's experience. It is not only the specific methods the teacher uses but also the degree of support she gives the child in the pursuit of his interests and in the goals and values stressed which are important. For as Buckminster Fuller (1966) points out, teaching is not done with a needle or a pump. It is, rather, best accomplished by individuals who are informed, self-disciplined and loving and who believe in the integrity of humanity and the educability of the child.

The teacher has many responsibilities to the young child. She preserves and maintains the continuity of his learning by working closely with his family and with his past and future teachers. Continuity is essential at all levels of education. As Hess and Shipman (1965) point out, it is not additional or more varied stimulation that is needed but experiences which give stimuli a pattern of sequential meaning.

The teacher also provides the very important respectability for childhood. She values the play and the player, respecting both the play which she plans for his learning and the child's spontaneous play (Almy, 1967) through which he discovers himself and his world. The teacher, finally, must be courageous in defense of childhood and recognize with Grams (1967) that it is good for children to be busy being children while they wait for the time when they will be adults.

Edith M. Dowley
Stanford University

References

Aborn, Caroline D. "Friedrich Froebel, Apostle of Childhood Education." *Child Ed* 13:211; 1937.

Adams, Paul L. "Children of Change." *Young Children* 20:203–8; 1965.

Almy, Milly. "Spontaneous Play: An Avenue for Intellectual Development." *Young Children* 22:265–80; 1967.

Anastasiow, Nicholas. *Evaluation of an Experimental Kindergarten Reading Program*. Palo Alto Unified School District, 1964. 12p.

Ariés, Philippe. *Centuries of Childhood: A Social History of Family Life*. (Translated by Robert Baldick). Knopf, 1962. 415p.

Bhoota, Kamala K. "Bal-Vikas: An Experiment in Childhood Education in Bombay, India." *J Nursery Ed* 17:161–5; 1962.

Blatz, William E., and others. *Nursery Education*. Morrow, 1935.

Bloom, Benjamin S., and others. *Compensatory Education for Cultural Deprivation*. Holt, 1965. 179p.

Bloom, R., and others. "Race and Social Class as Separate Factors Related to Social Environment." Paper presented at the meeting of the American Psychological Association, Philadelphia, Pennsylvania, September, 1963.

Braun, Samuel J. "Nursery Education for Disadvantaged Children: An Historical Review." In *Montessori in Perspective*. National Association for Education of Young Children, 1966. 77p.

Bronfenbrenner, Urie. "The Changing American Child: A Speculative Analysis." *Merrill-Palmer Q* 7:73–84; 1961.

Bruner, Jerome. *The Process of Education*. Harvard U Press, 1961.

Burgess, Evangeline. *Values in Early Childhood Education*. NEA, 1965.

California Legislature. *Technical Staff Report to the Joint Committee on Preschool and Primary Training*. The Legislature, 1947.

Cannon, Gwendolyn M. "Kindergarten Class Size: A Study." *Childh Ed* 43:9; 1966.

Casler, Lawrence. "Maternal Deprivation: A Critical Review of the Literature." *Soc Res Child Develop Monogr* 26; 1961. 64p.

Chisholm, Brock. *Prescription for Survival*. Columbia U Press, 1957. 26p.

Conner, Forrest E. "The Form and Substance of Tomorrow's School." *Am Sch U* 39:38–9; 1967.

Christianson, Helen M., and others. *The Nursery School: Adventure in Living and Learning*. Houghton, 1961. 302p.

Crandall, Virginia. "Achievement Behavior in Young Children." *Young Children* 20:77–88; 1964.

Crissey, O. L. "Mental Development as Related to Institutional Residence and Educational Achievement." *Iowa Stud Child Welf* 13; 1937.

Darwin, Charles. *The Descent of Man and Selection in Relation to Sex*. Appleton, 1897.

Dennis, Wayne. "Causes of Retardation Among Institutional Children: Iran." In Stendler, Celia B. (Ed.) *Readings in Child Behavior and Development*. Harcourt, 1964. p. 93–101.

Deutsch, Martin. "The Disadvantaged Child and the Learning Process." In Passow, A. H. (Ed.) *Education in Depressed Areas*. Teachers Col, Columbia U, 1963. p. 163–80.

Deutsch, Martin. "Facilitating Development in the Preschool Child: Social and Psychological Perspectives." *Merrill-Palmer Q* 10:249–64; 1964.

Doman, Glen. *How to Teach Your Baby to Read: The Gentle Revolution*. Random, 1964.

Dowley, Edith M. "The Role of the Nursery School in Community Education." *Am J Orthopsychiatry* 19:506–10; 1949.

Dowley, Edith M., and others. "Doing Research in a Nursery School." *J Nursery Ed* 16:2; 1960–1961.

Edmonson, Barbara. "Let's Do More Than Look, Let's Research Montessori." In *Montessori in Perspective*. National Association for Education of Young Children, 1966.

Erikson, Erik H. *A Healthy Personality for Every Child*. Report of Midcentury White House Conference on Children and Youth, 1951. p. 6–25.

Erikson, Erik H. *Childhood and Society*. Norton, 1963.

Fleiss, Bernice H. "The Continuity of Education from Prekindergarten to Primary." *Young Children* 22:78–82; 1966.

Flesch, Rudolph. *Why Can't Johnny Read?* Harper, 1955.

Foster, Josephine C., and Mattson, Marion L. *Nursery School Procedure*. Appleton, 1929.

Frank, L. K. "Fundamental Needs of the Child." *Mental Hygiene* 22:353–79; 1938.

Freeberg, Norman E., and Payne, Donald I. "Parental Influence on Cognitive Development in Early Childhood: A Review." *Child Develop* 38:65–88; 1967.

Freud, Anna. *Psychoanalysis for Teachers and Parents*. Beacon, 1960.

Freud, Anna, and Burlingham, Dorothy. *Infants Without Families*. Int U, 1964.

Froebel, Friedrich. *The Education of Man*. Appleton, 1887.

Frost, Joe L., and Hawkes, Glenn R. *The Disadvantaged Child*. Houghton, 1966. 426p.

Fujinaga, Tamotsu, and others. "The Developmental Study of the Number Concept by the Method of Experimental Education." *Japanese J Ed Psychol* 2:18–26; 1963.

Fuller, Buckminster. "How Little I Know." *Saturday R* 70; November 12, 1966.

Fuller, Elizabeth M. "Early Childhood Education." In Harris, Chester W. (Ed.) *Encyclopedia of Educational Research*, 3d ed. Macmillan, 1960.

Gabbard, Hazel F. "A Nation's Concern for Kindergartens." *Sch Life* 41:10–12; 1959.

Gage, N. L. (Ed.) *Handbook on Research in Teaching*. Rand McNally, 1963.

Gardner, Dorothy, and Cass, Joan E. *The Role of the Teacher in the Infant and Nursery School*. Pergamon, 1965.

Gesell, Arnold. *The First Five Years: A Guide to the Study of the Preschool Child*. Harper, 1940.

Gesell, Arnold, and Gesell, Beatrice C. *The Normal Child and Primary Education*. Ginn, 1912.

Gesell, Arnold, and Ilg, Frances L. *Infant and Child in the Culture of Today*. Harper, 1943.

Goldfarb, William. "The Effects of Early Institutional Care on Adolescent Personality." *J Exp Ed* 12: 106–29; 1943.

Goldfarb, William. "Psychological Privation in Infancy and Subsequent Adjustment." *Am J Orthopsychiatry* 15:247–55; 1945.

Goldsmith, Cornelia. "The Impact of a Growing NAEYC on Young Children." *Young Children* 20; 1965.

Goodenough, Florence L. "New Evidence on Environmental Influence on Intelligence." In the 39th Yearbook, NSSE. 1940. p. 307–65.

Grams, Armin. "In Defense of Childhood." *Merrill-Palmer News* 8:1; 1967.

Gray, Susan W., and Klaus, Rupert A. "An Experimental Preschool Program for Culturally Deprived Children." *Child Develop* 36:887–98; 1965.

Hammond, Sarah L., and others. *Good Schools for Young Children*. Macmillian, 1963.

Harris, Florence R., and others. "Effects of Adult Social Reinforcement on Child Behavior." *Young Children* 22:8–17; 1964.

Headley, Neith E. *Education in the Kindergarten*. American, 1966.

Heffernan, Helen. "A Challenge to the Profession of Early Childhood Education." *J Nursery Ed* 19: 237–41; 1964.

Heffernan, Helen. "Significance of Kindergarten Education." In Rasmussen, Margaret. (Ed.) *Readings from Childhood Education*. Association of Childhood Education International, 1966. p. 23–9.

Hess, Robert D. "Educability and Rehabilitation; The Future of the Welfare Class." In Frost, Joe L., and Hawkes, Glenn R. (Eds.) *The Disadvantaged Child*. Houghton, 1966. p. 406–18.

Hess, Robert D., and Shipman, Virginia. "Early Blocks to Children's Learning." *Children* 12: 194; 1965.

Holt, John. *How Children Fail*. Dell Publishing Co., Inc., 1964. 181p.

Hoppock, Anne. "What Are Kindergartens For?" Association of Childhood Education International, 1960–1961. (Mimeographed.)

Hromadka, Van G. "How Child Care Workers Are Trained in Europe." *Children* 11:6; 1964.

Hunt, J. McVicker. "The Psychological Basis for Using Preschool Enrichment as an Antidote for Cultural Deprivation." *Merrill-Palmer Q* 10:20–248; 1964.

Hymes, James L., Jr. "Emerging Patterns in Early Childhood Education." *Young Children* 22:158–63; 1967.

Jerome, Alice. "Children Need the Earth." *J Nursery Ed* 17:181–4; 1962.

Kagan, Jerome, and Lewis, Michael. "Studies of Attention in the Human Infant." *Merrill-Palmer Q* 11:128; 1965.

Kardiner, Abram. "When the State Brings Up the Child." *Saturday R* August 26:9; 1961.

Keliher, Alice V. "Effective Learning and Teacher-Pupil Ratio." *Childh Ed* 43:1; 1966.

Kesson, William. "Research in the Psychological Development of Infants." *Merrill-Palmer Q* April: 83–92; 1963.

Kesson, William. *The Child*. Wiley, 1965.

Kibuka, Katie. "Nursery Education in Uganda." *J Nursery Ed* 17:156–60; 1962.

Kuroki, Toshikatsu. "Day Nurseries in Japan." *J Nursery Ed* 17:171–2; 1962.

Law, Norma. *What Are Nursery Schools For?* Association of Childhood Education International Bulletin, 1963–1964.

Levine, Seymour. "Stimulation in Infancy." *Sci Am* 202:80–6; 1960.

Locke, John. *Some Thoughts Concerning Education*. Cambridge U Press, 1892.

Maccoby, Eleanor. "Effects of the Mass Media." In Hoffman, Martin, and Hoffman, Lois. (Eds.) *Child Development Research*. Russell Sage, 1964. p. 323–46.

Margolin, Edythe. "Variety, Vitality, and Response in Nursery School." *Young Children* 21:73–80; 1965.

Martin, William E. "Rediscovering the Mind of the Child: A Significant Trend in Research in Child Development." *Merrill-Palmer Q* 6:2; 1960.

Mayer, Martin. *The Schools*. Harper, 1961.

McCandless, Boyd R. *Children and Adolescents*. Holt, 1961.

McMillan, Margaret. *The Nursery School*. Dutton, 1919.

McNemar, Gwinn. "A Critical Examination of the University of Iowa Studies of Environmental Influences upon the I.Q." *Psychol B* 37:63–92, 1940.

Mead, Margaret. "Theoretical Setting—1954." In Mead, Margaret, and Wolfenstein, Martha. (Eds.) *Childhood in Contemporary Cultures*. U Chicago Press, 1963. p. 3–20.

Mitchell, Lucy M., and Bill, Audrey A. "Raising Day Care Standards in Massachusetts." *J Nursery Ed* 18:30–41; 1962.

Montessori, Maria. *The Montessori Method*. Schocken Books, Inc., 1964. 376p.

Moore, Omar K., and Anderson, A. R. *Early Reading and Writing*. Basic Ed, 1960. (Motion picture.)

Murphy, Lois B. *The Widening World of Childhood*. Basic Books, 1962.

National Education Association, Educational Policies Commission. *Education and the Disadvantaged American*. NEA, 1962. 39p.

Office of Economic Opportunity, Community Action Program. *Operation Head Start*. Office of Economic Opportunity, 1965.

Olson, Willard C. *Child Development*. Heath, 1959.

Peet, Anne. "Why Not Enough Public School Kindergartens?" *Young Children* 21:112–6; 1965.

Pestalozzi, J. H. *How Gertrude Teaches Her Children*. Bardeen, 1894.

Piaget, Jean. *The Origins of Intelligence in Children*. Int U, 1952.

Pines, Maya. "How Three Year Olds Teach Themselves to Read and Love It." *Harper's M* May: 58–64; 1963.

Preston, Laura A. "London Venture: A Look at England's Schools." *Young Children* 22:3–10; 1966.

Read, Katherine H. *The Nursery School.* Saunders, 1966. 371p.

Reissman, Frank, and Hannah, Arlene. "Teachers of the Poor." In Frost, Joe L., and Hawkes, Glenn R. (Eds.) *The Disadvantaged Child.* Houghton, 1966. p. 341–4.

Roeper, Annemarie. "Gifted Preschoolers and the Montessori Method." *Gifted Child Q* 10:2; 1966.

Rousseau, Jean-Jacques. *Émile; or, On Education.* Dent, 1911. 179p.

Schloss, Samuel. "Enrollment of 3-, 4-, and 5-year-olds in Nursery Schools and Kindergartens: October, 1964." USOE, 1965. 10p. (Mimeographed.)

Sears, Pauline S., and Dowley, Edith M. "Research on Teaching in the Nursery School." In Gage, N. L. (Ed.) *Handbook on Research in Teaching.* Rand McNally, 1963.

Sears, Robert R., and others. *Patterns of Child Rearing.* Harper, 1957.

Sears, Robert R., and others. *Identification and Child Rearing.* Stanford U Press, 1965. 262p.

Shaftel, Fannie. "Let's Look at the Kindergarten." Department of Education, Honolulu, 1963. (Mimeographed.)

Shuey, Rebekan. "Young Children in Turkey." *J Nursery Ed* 17:167–79; 1962.

Shure, Myrna B. "Psychological Ecology of a Nursery School." *Child Develop* 34:979–92; 1963.

Sigel, Irving·E. "Current Research in Infant Development." *Merrill-Palmer Q* 10:2; 1963.

Sigel, Irving E. "Introduction to the 1965 Infant Conference Papers." *Merrill-Palmer Q* 12:1; 1966.

Silberman, Charles E. "Give Slum Children a Chance, a Radical Proposal." *Harper's M* May:37–42; 1964.

Skeels, Harold M. "Adult Status of Children with Contrasting Early Life Experiences." *Soc Res Child Develop Monogr* 31:3; 1966.

Skeels, Harold M., and others. "A Study of Environmental Stimulation: An Orphanage Preschool Project." *U Iowa Stud Child Welf* 15:4; 1938.

Smilansky, Moshe. "Fighting Deprivation in the Promised Land." *Saturday R* 49:82–6; 1966.

Smitter, Faith. "A Study of Early Childhood Education in California." *California State Dept Ed B* 43; June 1949.

Spitz, R. A. "Hospitalism: An Inquiry into the Genesis of Psychiatric Conditions of Early Childhood." In Eissler, Ruth S., and others. (Eds.) *Psychoanalytical Studies of the Child,* Vol. 1. Int U Press, 1945.

Spock, Benjamin. *Common Sense Book of Baby and Child Care.* Duell, 1946.

Spodek, Bernard. "Social Studies Programs in Kindergarten." *Young Children* 20:285–9; 1965.

Spodek, Bernard. "Poverty, Education and the Young Child." In Frost, Joe L., and Hawkes, Glenn R. (Eds.) *The Disadvantaged Child.* Houghton, 1966. p. 183–8.

Stolz, Lois M. "Youth: The Gesell Institute and Its Latest Study." *Contemporary Psychol* 3:10–5; 1958.

Stott, Leland H., and Ball, Rachel S. "Infant and Preschool Mental Tests: Review and Evaluation." *Soc Res Child Develop Monogr* 30; 1967. 138p.

Suppes, Patrick. "The Computer and Excellence." *Saturday R* January 14, 1967.

Swift, Joan W. "Effects of Early Group Experience: The Nursery School and Day Nursery." In Hoffman, Martin L., and Hoffman, Lois W. (Eds.) *Review of Child Development Research* Russell Sage, 1964. p. 249–81.

Thompson, W. R., and Heron, W. L. "The Effects of Restricting Early Experience on the Problem-solving Capacity of Dogs." *Canadian J Psychol* 8:17–31; 1954.

Tsumori, Makota, and others. "Development of the Child's Personality and the Parent-Child Relationship." *Japanese J Ed Psychol* 9:129–45; 1961.

Wann, Kenneth D., and others. *Fostering Intellectual Development in Young Children.* Teachers Col, Columbia U, 1962.

Watson, John B. *Psychological Care of Infant and Child.* Norton, 1928.

Watson, Robert I. *Psychology of the Child.* Wiley, 1960.

Wellman, Beth L. "The Effects of Preschool Attendance upon the I.Q." *J Exp Ed* 1:48–9; 1932.

Wellman, Beth L. "Iowa Studies on the Effects of Schooling." In 39th Yearbook, NSSE, 1940. p. 377–99.

Wenar, Charles. "Competence at One." *Merrill-Palmer Q* 10:329–42; 1964.

White, Robert W. "Motivation Reconsidered: The Concept of Competence." In Stendler, Celia B. (Ed.) *Readings in Child Behavior and Development.* Harcourt, 1964. p. 164–94.

Widmer, E. L. "Why Kindergarten?" *Peabody J Ed* 44:210–15; 1967.

Woodruff, Myra. "The Administrator Looks at the Kindergarten." *Young Children* 21:212; 1966.

Yarrow, Leon J. "Separation from Parents During Early Childhood." In Hoffman, Martin L., and Hoffman, Lois W. (Eds.) *Review of Child Development Research.* Russell Sage, 1964.

ECONOMIC STATUS OF TEACHERS

Income, more than any other single factor, determines the relative strength or weakness of any occupational group to attract and to hold competent persons. The financial reward offered to members of the teaching profession thus becomes a matter of great importance in a discussion of the economic status of teachers. Fringe benefits, such as paid leave, health insurance, and the like, have also taken on new importance in recent years because of the increasing competition among the professions for well-trained capable personnel.

The bulk of the total income of teachers, in public elementary and secondary schools, and in institutions of higher education, as for most other professions, comes from salaries. Consequently, the types of salary schedules that are established both reflect and influence the economic status of the profession.

Studies of salaries *paid* as well as salaries *scheduled* have been, for the most part, concerned with public school personnel.

SALARY SCHEDULES FOR PUBLIC SCHOOL PERSONNEL. Payment of teachers according to a fixed salary schedule rather than on the basis of individual bargaining has long been recognized as important both to the security and to the dignity of the teaching profession. Salary schedules provide the basis for equality of opportunity for persons of equal training and ability. Most of the available research on salaries and salary scheduling is limited to studies of public schools.

The practice of paying teachers according to a fixed schedule was begun even before 1900. Dyke (1899) included in his study of teachers' salaries the basic provisions of 60 salary schedules. The National Education Association (1905), in a report of the Committee on Salaries, Tenure, and Pensions, included a detailed tabulation of schedules. Of 466 cities over 8,000 in population, 52 percent reported salary schedules. Many of them, however, were applicable only to teachers in elementary schools. There were no summary tables in the report. Inspection of the data supplied by reporting systems, however, indicated that higher salaries were scheduled for high school teachers than for teachers in elementary schools. Higher salaries were scheduled for men than for women, and there were very few increments between minimum and maximum. The study proposed no principles of structuring a salary schedule.

A landmark in the beginning of the study of salary schedules was the report prepared by Evenden (1919). This study was also done for a committee of the National Education Association. It showed that in 1919 about two-thirds of the 392 reporting cities used salary schedules for teachers in elementary schools, but less than half used them for high school teachers.

The NEA Research Division (National Education Association, Research Division, 1923) in its first salary-schedule study stated principles of scheduling under three objectives: (1) making teaching a profession, (2) securing and retaining competent and desirable people as teachers, and (3) assuring maximum service and professional growth from all teachers.

A broad view of the evolving principles of salary scheduling from 1890 through the 1930's was reported by Elsbree (1939).

Principles of Salary Scheduling. In recent years there has been considerable emphasis on the importance of structuring salary schedules to promote the general financial interest and professional development of the teaching profession. In a series of 12 *Guidelines for Effective Work To Improve Teachers Salary Programs* (National Education Association, Salary Consultant Service, 1965), the NEA Salary Consultant Service outlined the procedures and steps necessary for the development of a well-structured salary schedule. In addition to dollar amounts of scheduled salaries, consideration was given to numbers and amounts of increments between minimum and maximum, salary recognition for advanced preparation beyond the bachelor's degree, and the like.

The California Teachers Association, Southern Section, has issued a research monograph based on 10 tests for salary schedules (1966). First developed in 1962, these tests provided a formal evaluation of salary schedules for the school systems located in southern California. Scores were established for each test so that representatives of individual school districts could evaluate their own salary schedules in relation to what was considered the best practice for improving the quality of service and maintaining a high level of professional performance.

Salary schedules have been evaluated on a national basis by the NEA Research Division (National Education Association, Research Division, 1966*d*). The evaluation was made on the basis of 11 tests designed specifically to represent high goals of achievement in salary scheduling for classroom teachers both in salaries paid and in good salary-schedule structuring. These tests were so designed that interested individuals from various local school districts might evaluate their own schedules and determine where improvements needed to be made.

Issues in Salary Scheduling. The general principles of salary scheduling have evolved from a number of basic issues, among them (1) single-salary or preparation schedules, (2) minimum-salary laws, (3) merit rating as a factor in salary schedules, (4) extra pay for extra duties, (5) equal pay for men and women, (6) index salary schedules, and (7) salary schedules for administrative personnel.

With regard to (1), single-salary or preparation schedules, one of Evenden's conclusions (1919) was that teachers in elementary, intermediate, and high schools should be on the same salary schedule if they met the same standards of preparation. In 1919 he was unable to locate such a schedule. In the next few years, however, the single-salary policy was adopted frequently. The Utah Education Association (1961), in a two-volume study on salary scheduling, stated that the first single-salary schedules were adopted in 1921 by the Denver and Des Moines school systems. By 1946 more than 40 percent of all districts were using single-salary schedules; by 1950 about 97 percent of the school districts using salary schedules had adopted the single schedule with differentials based solely on levels of preparation, not on grades or subjects taught.

The Utah study credited much of the impetus for the general establishment of the single-salary schedule policy to the work of professional organizations. They favored this policy as a means of upgrading the entire teaching profession and alleviating cleavages between elementary- and secondary-school teachers by giving the same recognition to both groups on the basis of educational preparation and experience.

In the late 1950's, high school teachers in a few large school systems were still resisting the single-salary idea, but the handicap once faced by all elementary-school teachers was no longer a significant issue. In its annual analysis of salary schedules for teachers, the NEA (National Education Association, Research Division, 1966j) found no salary schedules which provided different classes for elementary- and secondary-school teachers.

As the Utah Education Association pointed out in the study mentioned above (1961), in the zealous effort to convert to the single-salary schedule frequently too little attention was given to the pattern of increments and to some of the more technical details associated with structuring a good salary schedule; many of these weaknesses are still prevalent.

With regard to (2), minimum salary laws, since 1946–47 minimum salary schedules for teachers guaranteed by state law have all been of the single-salary type. In 1966–67, teachers in 31 states had a legally guaranteed minimum salary (National Education Association, Research Division, 1966l). Ten years earlier, in 1956–57, minimum-salary laws were in effect in 21 states. In 1966 the statutes of 23 of the 31 states which provided minimum salaries also recognized both college training and years of service, providing for minimum and maximum salaries for both the bachelor's and master's degrees; 15 of the 31 also stipulated minimum and maximum salaries for teachers with preparation beyond the master's degree.

In all states where minimum-salary legislation had been enacted, local school systems were free to pay salaries higher than those required by law. No state schedule recognized superior-service or merit ratings.

With regard to (3), merit rating as a factor in salary schedules, as long ago as 1933, Young (1944), in a study of merit-type salary schedules in 59 cities, concluded that the methods of measuring teacher efficiency in use then were largely unreliable. A large committee worked for nearly 10 years (Tiedeman, 1956) on the study of teacher competence in relation to salaries for the New England School Development Council. It recommended a model schedule with four divisions to recognize progressively higher role fulfillment by teachers.

Beginning in the mid-1950's there was considerable interest in merit schedules. Many school-board members urged the adoption of such plans. The number of merit schedules actually adopted, however, continued to be relatively small. According to the NEA (National Education Association, Research Division, 1957) only 6.3 percent of all school systems in communities with populations of 30,000 or more authorized higher salaries for superior service in 1956–57. In 1966–67, only 5.0 percent of the salary schedules analyzed for districts with enrollments of 25,000 or more gave salary recognition for merit or superior service (National Education Association, Research Division, 1966j).

With regard to (4), extra pay for extra duties, salary differentials for time spent by teachers in directing extracurricular activities for pupils, such as sports, dramatics, musical activities, production of school newspapers, and the like, frequently are recognized in salary schedules. In 1965–66, almost one-half the salary schedules examined by the NEA (National Education Association, Research Division, 1966e) reported such differentials. The amounts of extra pay for such activities were relatively small; football coaches usually received the largest stipends above their regular teaching salaries.

The New Jersey Education Association (1965a) studied extra pay for extra duties in New Jersey school districts for the school year 1964–65 and found that teachers got extra pay for 93 percent of all extracurricular sports assignments, while only one-third of the nonathletic activities resulted in extra pay. A reduced work load in lieu of additional compensation was granted in 21 percent of the nonathletic assignments; only 1 percent of the athletic assignments were compensated for in this manner.

With regard to (5), equal pay for men and women, most salary schedules provide no monetary differentials on the basis of sex. This has not always been the case. Information derived from earlier studies was analyzed by Davis (1945) to show trends. In 1904–05 more than 85 percent of the cities reporting indicated salary differentials in favor of men teachers; only 22 percent of the same cities did so in 1944–45.

By 1966–67 only 1.3 percent of the schedules analyzed by the NEA for districts enrolling 25,000 or more students provided additional compensation for men teachers (National Education Association, Research Division, 1966j).

With regard to (6), index salary schedules, approximately 20 percent of the 1966–67 salary schedules analyzed by the NEA (ibid.) were constructed on an index or ratio basis. By this method every level on the salary schedule, both horizontally and vertically, is stated as a percentage of a given base, which usually is the beginning step of the scale for holders of the bachelor's degree. Thus, by establishing the dollar amount of the base, the other salaries on the entire schedule are computed easily, and increases are kept at a uniform rate throughout the schedule.

The Utah Education Association in a study of index salary schedules (1965) found that 95 percent of the districts included in their study which had adopted index salary schedules indicated an intention to continue this type of schedule. The major reasons given for retaining the index or ratio schedule were (a) the simplicity in administering and reviewing the schedule, (b) the more equitable distribution of funds available for salaries, (c) the good effect on the morale of most staff members, (d) the avoidance of blanket raises which distort relative positions of the staff on the schedule, and (e) the provision of a more objective basis for salary negotiations.

With regard to (7), salary schedules for administrative personnel, the practice of scheduling salaries for administrative and supervisory personnel is not universal; about 60 percent of the school systems which reported salary schedule information to the NEA in 1965–66 also furnished salary schedules for their administrative personnel (National Education Association, Research Division, 1966i). This same survey also showed that more than 60 percent of the administrative schedules furnished were related directly to those for classroom teachers either on a percentage or a ratio basis, or by the addition of varying dollar amounts for administrative responsibility. The latter amounts varied by the responsibility level of the various administrative positions within the school system. The base of reference to the schedule for teachers frequently was the maximum scheduled salary for teachers with master's degrees. However, it was found in some cases that salaries for administrators were derived by the application of varying ratios to the salary the administrator would have earned if placed on the teachers' schedule in accordance with his education and experience.

TRENDS AND COMPARISONS IN SALARIES PAID PUBLIC SCHOOL PERSONNEL. One of the first studies of trends in salaries *paid* public school personnel was made by Burgess (1920), who traced the changes in teachers' salaries back to 1841. Burgess concluded that city teachers had been paid more than teachers in rural areas, regardless of sex, and that men had enjoyed a status superior to that of women, although by 1920 the latter were gaining rapidly on men.

In 1927 a study made by the NEA Research Division showed that the average salary paid all gainfully employed persons in the United States was approximately $2,000, compared with an average of $1,300 paid classroom teachers (National Education Association, Research Division, 1927).

Salaries Paid from 1949–50 to 1966–67. Salaries paid the instructional staff in public elementary and secondary schools increased slowly in the postdepression years, and in 1949–50 the average salary was $3,010, according to the U.S. Office of Education (1963). By 1966–67 the average salary of the instructional staff was estimated to be $7,119 (National Education Association, Research Division, 1966c). In addition to classroom teachers, the instructional staff includes counselors, school librarians, school nurses, and all other professional and supervisory employees of individual school buildings but excludes all central-office employees.

By 1956–57 the average (mean) salary paid teachers was $4,571, but 25.6 percent of teachers were earning less than $3,500 (National Education Association, Research Division, 1966a). By 1966–67 the average salary paid classroom teachers was estimated to be $6,821 by the NEA Research Division, and only 0.3 percent of teachers were receiving less than $3,500 (National Education Association, Research Division, 1966c). At the other extreme, no teacher in 1956–57 was earning as much as $9,500; by 1966–67, 5.7 percent of all classroom teachers were earning $9,500 or more. This same survey also showed that the average salary of all classroom teachers increased 60.9 percent in the ten-year period from 1956–57 to 1966–67; the average salary of elementary-school teachers increased 63.4 percent, and that for secondary-school teachers 54.9 percent.

Comparison with Salaries in Other Professions. Comparisons of salaries paid classroom teachers with those paid other professional groups have always been very difficult, for two basic reasons. In the first place, a generally agreed-upon listing of the professions has never been established; in the second place, there have been no continuing series of figures over an extended period of time for the salaries of other professions which are comparable with the continuing series of data on teachers' salaries which have been available for many years.

The 1960 U.S. Census of Population (U.S. Department of Commerce, 1963) included a report on occupational characteristics. These data showed that of 18 selected professions the median income of $4,642 for teachers in 1959 was exceeded by that for all but 4 of the 17 other professions.

In fact, it was not until 1961 that the average salary of the instructional staff exceeded that for employees in manufacturing (National Education Association, Research Division, 1966a). Few of the latter group could be classified as professional workers, but prior to 1961 their annual earnings were higher than those of teachers. However, the average salary of the instructional staff increased 56.5 percent from 1955 to 1964, while the average earnings of all employees in manufacturing increased 40.2 percent during the same period.

In 1960, the U.S. Bureau of Labor Statistics began a series of studies on salaries paid certain professional, technical, and clerical occupations (U.S. Department of Labor, 1961). This series has been published annually since 1960 and provides data on average annual salaries for accountants, auditors, attorneys, chemists, and engineers.

Median annual salaries of scientists, according to their academic field of interest, have been published on an irregular basis by the National Science Foundation (1964).

The NEA Research Division for a number of years has been comparing beginning salaries for teachers with beginning salaries paid men graduates in engineering, accounting, sales, and general business. The latter data have been published by Endicott (1965). He reports on trends in salary offers to men graduates with bachelor's degrees made by corporations which regularly send recruiters to college campuses. Endicott has also included starting salaries for women graduates with the bachelor's degree for various professional and semiprofessional occupations.

Comparisons with Salaries of Other Professional Employees in Local School Systems. The NEA Research Division relates the median salaries paid classroom teachers to those paid various professional central office administrators and technical instructional personnel in individual school buildings within the same school system. Its two-volume biennial salary study for 1964–65 (National Education Association, Research Division, 1965) showed, among other things, that the median salary for superintendents in large local systems was 4.4 times the median for teachers for the same systems. The median salary of high school principals in 1964–65 in the same large systems was twice that of classroom teachers, while the median for elementary-school principals was 1.7 times that for teachers.

This study also pointed out that the ratio between salaries paid teachers and salaries paid supervisory and administrative personnel showed only slight variations by size of district.

SALARIES IN HIGHER EDUCATION. The increased need and support for higher education is contributing to enlarged enrollments and offerings at post-high school levels of education throughout the nation. Information on salaries paid and scheduled for the professional staffs of junior colleges and degree-granting institutions is important in a consideration of the economic status of school personnel.

Salaries Paid. Since 1953, the NEA Research Division has conducted biennial surveys of salaries paid faculty and administrators in four-year degree-granting institutions, both public and nonpublic, and in junior or community colleges. The seventh biennial survey, which reported salaries paid in 1965–66 (National Education Association, Research Division, 1966*h*), showed that the median salary of all full-time faculty personnel with teaching responsibilities was $9,081 for degree-granting institutions. As expected, the highest salaries for teaching personnel were reported for professors; the median for this group was $12,953. At the other extreme, the median salary of instructors in 1965–66 was $6,761.

The median salary for instructors in public junior colleges was $8,361 in 1965–66; for nonpublic junior colleges the median was $6,407.

Salaries Scheduled. In 1966 the NEA Research Division began to analyze salary schedules in higher education, starting first with those in junior colleges. The October 1966 *NEA Research Bulletin* (National Education Association, Research Division, 1966*k*) reported the preliminary results of the 1965–66 study. Approximately 80 percent of all public junior colleges reported having an officially adopted salary schedule. About two-thirds based their salary classes on academic preparation levels, and one-third were structured on the basis of professional ranks.

For a master's degree this study reported a mean minimum scheduled salary of $6,023 for junior-college instructors and a maximum of $8,971. With a doctor's degree the mean minimum scheduled salary was $7,246, and the maximum was $10,769.

The summary in the *NEA Research Bulletin* pointed out the difficulties of making valid comparisons between salary schedules based on academic preparation and those based on professorial ranks. The average minimum salary scheduled for professors in junior colleges in 1965–66 was $9,251, and the maximum was $12,667. For instructors, the average minimum scheduled salary was $5,928, and the maximum was $8,152.

NONTEACHING INCOME. From a study based on responses to questionnaires sent to a representative sample of teachers, the NEA (National Education Association, Research Division, 1967) found that 91.3 percent of the total income for all teachers in 1965–66 came from their salary as teachers: over 95 percent of the total income of women teachers, and 84.2 percent of the income for men teachers.

Almost 16 percent of the men teacher respondents said they had additional income; of these, 7.2 percent said it was derived from summer employment; 5.9 percent indicated extra earnings during the school year. Fewer than 2 percent of the women teachers who responded reported income from summer employment, and fewer than 1 percent had extra earnings during the school year.

On the other hand, the same survey showed that 32.1 percent of all teachers, and 58.1 percent of men teachers, did have summer employment, but earnings from such employment accounted for only a very small portion of their total annual income.

FRINGE BENEFITS. Supplementary non-"take-home" remuneration, usually called fringe benefits, has been adopted almost universally as an integral part of all employers' personnel and salary policies. These benefits increased sharply during World War II when wage stabilization made actual dollar salary increases impossible.

Prior to World War II the teaching profession enjoyed such things as retirement benefits, paid vacations, and leaves of absence to a greater extent than most other groups of workers. Often such benefits were used in an effort to offset the effect of low salaries paid the instructional staff. Since the late 1940's, however, fringe benefits available to employees in industry and government have outstripped those granted to most teachers. Accordingly, there has developed recently an increasing desire and effort to gain greater fringe benefits for more teachers.

The Chamber of Commerce of the United States (1966) reported that for 1,181 companies surveyed in 1965, fringe-benefit payments averaged 24.7 percent of the total payroll, or an average of $1,502 per year per employee.

Wilson (1964), in a study of the dollar value of fringe benefits in over 200 school systems in 1962–63, found that when retirement was excluded from the total cost of fringe benefits the cost of the remaining benefits was comparatively small. The mean expenditure was less than 2 percent of the average professional salary. Wilson concluded, among other things, that boards of education would do well to develop a fringe-benefit program jointly with school staffs, since any program is likely to be accepted more readily if the staff is committed to it.

Leaves of Absence. There are several types of leaves of absence frequently provided for teachers: (1) sick leave, (2) personal leave, and (3) maternity leave.

Type (1), sick leave, is the most prevalent type of leave granted by school boards. It should not be considered as additional income. As the New Jersey Education Association pointed out in a study of fringe benefits (1965*b*), sick leave should be treated as a positive method to improve instruction through increased teacher morale and efficiency.

The Educational Research Service (1966*c*) of the NEA, in a report on sick-leave provisions in large school systems, reported that 69 percent of the systems with enrollments of 25,000 or more provided 10 paid days of sick leave in 1965–66; 19 percent provided from 11 to 18 days; fewer than 1 percent provided no sick leave with pay.

The same study showed that 27.1 percent of the reporting systems permitted unlimited accumulation of earned sick leave; the median number of cumulative days was 129.4.

Type (2), personal leave, is often referred to as "short-term" leave. Many of the large school systems recognize the need for providing leave for brief absences with pay for emergencies not involving personal illness. The Educational Research Service (1966b) surveyed personal-leave practices among the large school systems in 1965–66. Absence for death in the family was the most frequent type of short-term leave; other types indicated were leaves for attendance at professional meetings, for illness in the immediate family, for religious holidays, for military reserve duty, and simply for "personal business."

With regard to (3), maternity leave, most of the large school systems have written maternity-leave policies, with considerable variation in the specific provisions. The Educational Research Service, in another study (1966a) reported that most of the large school systems specified a period of compulsory absence prior to the expected date of birth, with three, four, or five months being the most frequently specified length of time. Most systems also specified the earliest permissible time when a teacher might return to the classroom following the birth of a child.

Insurance. The basic types of insurance programs available to teachers are (1) group health insurance and (2) group life insurance. Some school systems make available other types of insurance, such as disability, occupational liability, fidelity, and auto insurance.

With respect to (1), group health insurance, Kleinmann (1962) pointed out that group health insurance was originated in 1931, not by an insurance company, but by a group of public school teachers in Dallas, Texas, who worked out a plan with the Baylor University hospital. Under that arrangement each contributing teacher could receive hospital care, subject to certain qualifications, for a payment of $6 annually.

Since that time group health insurance has experienced phenomenal growth. The NEA Research Division surveyed group insurance plans available to teachers in 1964–65 (National Education Association, Research Division, 1966b) and reported that group hospitalization insurance was available in 85 percent of all school systems with enrollments of 12,000 or more. The survey further showed that about one-third of these same school systems paid all or part of the cost of the health insurance programs made up of hospitalization, medical-surgical, or major medical coverage.

The NEA Research Division further pointed out that while the percentage of school systems paying part or all of the premium for employee health insurance had increased somewhat within recent years, the extent of employer cooperation was by no means as great as that found in private and government employment.

The U.S. Bureau of Labor Statistics made a survey in 1963 (U.S. Department of Labor, 1965) of approximately 690 companies and found that 97 percent of them cooperated in providing health insurance plans for their employees. Of these companies, 74 percent indicated that they paid all or part of the costs for these plans; 30 percent paid the entire cost.

Representative examples of group health insurance plans in effect in 1964–65 were reproduced in some detail in a report published by the NEA (National Education Association, Research Division, 1966f).

With respect to type (2), Group life insurance, life insurance programs available to teachers frequently are of the type which provide only for payment of the face value of the policy at the death of the insured; this usually is known as "term insurance." It cannot be converted to any other type of insurance should the teacher resign or retire. It was pointed out by the NEA (National Education Association, Research Division, 1966g) that the most frequent form of cooperation by school systems in the administration of group life insurance plans in 1964–65 was in making payroll deductions; 88.6 percent of the systems reporting were in this category. Almost half the systems signed the contract with the underwriter and thereby became sponsors of the plan. Almost 49 percent paid part or all of the insurance premiums.

Teacher Retirement Plans. By 1965 all states were providing some kind of retirement or pension system for public school teachers.

The NEA (National Education Association, Research Division, 1964) summarized retirement statutes through 1964 and reported that, with one exception, the retirement benefits in all statewide retirement systems to which teachers belong were financed jointly by members and by public contribution. In 1964–65 only Delaware had a pension plan which was financed entirely by the state.

The NEA Research Division also pointed out that the rates and amounts of salary on which teachers contribute toward retirement, exclusive of social security taxes, varied considerably from state to state. Requirements for retirement in terms of the number of years worked and mandatory retirement age also varied considerably.

INTERNATIONAL ASPECTS OF TEACHER STATUS. Information concerning the economic status of teachers in other countries, especially in the area of salaries paid and their relationship to the salaries of other professions, is not easily obtainable, nor is it directly comparable with data for schools in the United States.

International cooperation to improve the economic status of the teaching profession throughout the free world has frequently been the subject of attention by international organizations in recent years.

At a special intergovernmental conference on the status of teachers held in Paris in the fall of 1966, the unanimous adoption of the *International Recommendation Concerning the Status of Teachers* by delegates from 75 member states culminated a long international enterprise of UNESCO (UNESCO, 1966).

To this conference, status meant both the standing or regard accorded teachers "as evidenced by the level of appreciation of the importance of their function and their competence in performing it, and the working conditions, remuneration and other material benefits accorded them relative to other professional groups." It was further stated that among the various factors which affect the status of teachers, particular importance should be attached to salary, because under present world conditions, other factors, such as standing or regard accorded teachers, are largely dependent, as in other comparable professions, on the economic positions in which they are placed.

The conference further recommended that salaries of teachers should compare favorably with those paid in other occupations requiring similar or equivalent qualifications; teachers' salary scales should be established in agreement with teachers' organizations and should result in salaries sufficient to "provide teachers with the means to insure a reasonable standard of living for themselves and their families as well as to invest in further education or in the pursuit of cultural activities, thus enhancing their professional qualification."

In 1961 the first of three major surveys of the teaching profession was undertaken by the World Confederation of Organizations of the Teaching Profession (WCOTP). It included reports from 23 African countries. The report concluded that the status of the teaching profession in Africa was low; the teacher often did not receive a salary adequate to maintain a standard of life comparable with that of others having the same qualifications. The decline of the prestige of teachers has been relative, not absolute, because of the emergence of newer groups in African society.

WCOTP (World Confederation..., 1963) summarized the status of the teaching profession in 20 Asian countries The study considered both the academic and the economic aspects of teacher status in the member Asian countries. This study pointed out the widespread differences in the economic status of the teaching profession from country to country. It was found that, generally, teachers who come under a central government authority tended to fare better economically and socially than those who were employed by a regional or local authority.

It was also reported that many Asian countries were still scheduling higher salaries for teachers in the upper division of the school systems, where considerably greater amounts of preparation were required.

In 1964, WCOTP issued a report on the teaching profession in the Americas (World Confederation ..., 1964). This study encompassed the professional, economic, and social status of teachers in 23 countries on the American continent, including Canada and the United States. Each country was considered separately, but an appendix summarized data on the economic status of primary and secondary public school teachers, as far as possible on a comparable basis. This comparison included such things as the basis for establishing the salary scales, frequency of increments, provisions for adjustments to cost of living, and retirement allowances.

Gertrude N. Stieber
National Education Association

References

Burgess, Warren R. *Trends in School Costs.* Russell Sage, 1920. 142p.

California Teachers Association, Southern Section. *Ten Tests of Salary Schedules, 1966–67.* Research Monograph No. 51. The Association, 1966. 53p.

Chamber of Commerce of the United States. *Fringe Benefits—1963.* The Chamber, 1966. 35p.

Davis, Hazel. "Equal Pay for Men and Women Teachers." *Am Sch Bd J* 111:31–3; 1945.

Dyke, Charles B. *The Economic Aspect of Teachers' Salaries.* Macmillan, 1899. 84p.

Educational Research Service. *Maternity Leave Provisions for Classroom Teachers in Larger School Systems.* Circular No. 3. NEA, 1966(a). 24p.

Educational Research Service. *Short-term Leaves of Absence for Classroom Teachers in Larger School Systems.* Circular No. 4. NEA, 1966(b). 30p.

Educational Research Service. *Sick Leave Provisions for Classroom Teachers in Larger School Systems.* Circular No. 5. NEA, 1966(c). 26p.

Elsbree, Willard S. *The American Teacher.* American, 1939. 566p.

Endicott, Frank S. *Trends in Employment of College and University Graduates in Business and Industry.* Northwestern U, 1965. 10p.

Evenden, Edward S. *Teachers' Salaries and Salary Schedules in the United States, 1918–19.* NEA, 1919. 169p.

Kleinmann, Jack H. *Fringe Benefits for Public School Personnel.* Teachers Col, Columbia U, 1962. 164p.

National Education Association. *Report of the Committee on Salaries, Tenure, and Pensions of Public School Teachers in the United States.* NEA, 1905. 466p.

National Education Association, Research Division. "Salary Schedules and Public School Efficiency." *NEA Res B* 1:83–4; 1923.

National Education Association, Research Division. "The Scheduling of Teachers' Salaries." *NEA Res B* 5:135–90; 1927.

National Education Association, Research Division. *Superior-service Maximums in Teachers' Salary Schedules, 1956–57.* NEA, 1957. 23p.

National Education Association, Research Division. "Retirement Statistics, 1964." *NEA Res B* 44:99–107; 1964.

National Education Association, Research Division. *Twenty-second Biennial Salary Survey of Public-school Employees, 1964–65,* 2 vols. NEA, 1965.

National Education Association, Research Division. *Economic Status of Teachers in 1965–66.* NEA, 1966(a). 52p.

National Education Association, Research Division. *Employer Cooperation in Group Insurance Coverage for Public-school Personnel, 1964–65.* NEA, 1966(b). 191p.

National Education Association, Research Division. *Estimates of School Statistics, 1966–67.* NEA, 1966(c). 36p.

National Education Association, Research Division. *Evaluation of Salary Schedules for Classroom Teachers, 1966–67.* NEA, 1966(d). 71p.

National Education Association, Research Division. *Extra Pay for Extra Duties, 1965–66.* NEA, 1966(e). 30p.

National Education Association, Research Division. *Group Health Insurance Plans for Public-school Personnel, 1964–65.* NEA, 1966(f). 82p.

National Education Association, Research Division. *Group Life Insurance Programs for Public-school Personnel, 1964–65.* NEA, 1966(g). 60p.

National Education Association, Research Division. *Salaries in Higher Education, 1965–66.* NEA, 1966(h). 65p.

National Education Association, Research Division. *Salary Schedules for Administrative Personnel, 1965–66.* NEA, 1966(i). 137p.

National Education Association, Research Division. *Salary Schedules for Classroom Teachers, 1966–67.* NEA, 1966(j). 129p.

National Education Association, Research Division. "Salary Schedules in Public Junior Colleges." *NEA Res B* 44:67–71; 1966(k).

National Education Association, Research Division. *State Minimum-salary Laws and Goal Schedules for Teachers, 1966–67.* NEA, 1966(l). 51p.

National Education Association, Research Division. *The American Public-school Teacher, 1965–66.* NEA, 1967.

National Education Association, Salary Consultant Service. *Guidelines for Effective Work to Improve Teachers Salary Programs,* Nos. 1–12. NEA, 1965.

National Science Foundation. *Reviews of Data on Science Resources,* Vol. 1. GPO, 1964.

New Jersey Education Association. *Extra Pay for Extra Services, 1964–65.* The Association, 1965(a). 68p.

New Jersey Education Association. *Fringe Benefits.* The Association, 1965(b). 32p.

Tiedeman, David V. (Ed.) *Teacher Competence and Its Relation to Salary.* New England School Development Council, 1956. 110p.

UNESCO. Special Intergovernmental Conference of the Status of Teachers. *Records of the Conference.* UNESCO, 1966.

U.S. Department of Commerce, Bureau of the Census. *U.S. Census of Population 1960, Occupational Characteristics.* Final Report, Series PC (2) 7A. GPO, 1963. p. 377–95.

U.S. Department of Labor, Bureau of Labor Statistics. *National Survey of Professional, Administrative, Technical and Clerical Pay, Winter of 1960–61.* Bulletin No. 1310. GPO, 1961. Subsequent Bulletins Nos. 1346, 1387, 1422, 1469.

U.S. Department of Labor, Bureau of Labor Statistics. *Supplementary Compensation for Nonproduction Workers, 1963.* Bulletin No. 1470. GPO, 1965.

U.S. Office of Education. *Statistics of State School Systems, 1959–60.* Circular 691. GPO, 1963.

Utah Education Association. *A New Look at Salary Scheduling,* Parts I and II. The Association, 1961. Part I, 30p. Part II, 45p.

Utah Education Association. *Index Salary Schedules.* The Association, 1965. 8p.

Wilson, Leslie A. *The Dollar Value of Fringe Benefits.* Teachers Col, Columbia U, 1964. 65p.

World Confederation of Organizations of the Teaching Profession. *Survey of the Status of the Teaching Profession in Africa.* The Confederation, 1961. 148p.

World Confederation of Organizations of the Teaching Profession. *Survey of the Status of the Teaching Profession in Asia.* The Confederation, 1963. 149p.

World Confederation of Organizations of the Teaching Profession. *Survey of the Status of the Teaching Profession in the Americas.* The Confederation, 1964. 98p.

Young, Lloyd P. *The Administration of Merit-Type Teachers' Salary Schedules.* Teachers Col, Columbia U, 1944. 104p.

ECONOMICS OF EDUCATION

The past decade has produced an extraordinary growth of research on the economics of education. While economists and others have long maintained a keen interest in the interrelationships between economics and education, this sudden spurt of research comes as something of a surprise to many. Yet growing evidence on the role of education in contributing to economic growth, the impact of education on individual earning power, the links between formal schooling and on-the-job training, and the application of cost-benefit analysis to educational decision making —all of these have given the economics of education a new focus as well as an increased respectability. At the same time these developments have raised a wide variety of intriguing conceptual and empirical issues for research.

Few observers a decade or so ago would have forecast the emergence of this stream of research. Even as recently as five years ago this work was still viewed by many economists as something of a fad. But the sheer volume and diversity of the literature belies this, as revealed in the recent annotated bibliography by Blaug (1966a). Of the approximately 800 items listed, only 45 appeared prior to 1951. Another 53 appeared from 1951 through 1955. But in the next five-year period, 1956–1960, almost 200 items appeared. And for the period 1961 through 1966, almost 500 items are listed. Two recent mimeographed supplements (Blaug, 1966b, 1967) list over 220 additional items that appeared after the issuance of the bibliography itself. This pattern of extremely rapid growth clearly parallels that in many of the more publicized and rapidly expanding scientific fields, where discussion of the information "explosion" is rampant.

HUMAN-CAPITAL APPROACH. While there are a number of diverse strands to the research in the economics of education, the concepts of human investment and human capital provide the central focus for, and have shaped in an important way, the direction of much of the new work. By "human investment" or "human capital" we mean the flow of activities involving the diversion of resources from current consumption to those designed to augment the stock of human knowledge, skills, and capabilities embodied in people as a result of resource outlays for human investment. It is this *stock* of human capital which actually produces the stream of future output over its expected physical lifetime. The most sophisticated presentation of the theory of human capital is found in Becker's book (1964). Bowman (1962*a*) has set forth many of the concepts and discussed problems of their empirical measurement.

Through the human-capital approach it becomes possible to relate the future outputs of activities to the inputs required to perform these activities. This is most commonly done through comparisons between the value of the outputs and the value of the inputs. These comparisons require an allowance for the fact that at least some of the outputs or benefits are expected to materialize far in the future. Thus, the time stream of the benefits or returns must be "discounted" to yield the true magnitude of the payoff. Ordinarily, the resulting figure is expressed as the internal rate of return on investment or as the present value of the benefits, less costs. If the payoff is large relative to that available from other sectors of the economy, that fact is taken to suggest that additional resources might profitably be devoted to that activity; the converse is also true. The whole treatment is directly analogous to that accorded to investment in physical capital, such as plant, machinery, and the like.

The concept of human capital has a long history and has been applied to a wide variety of issues—among them health, migration, training, and education (Kiker, 1966). Marxists, and the classical economists, gave attention to the concept of human capital (Vaizey, 1962). For some unaccountable reason, however, this approach fell into disuse early in this century and has only recently been rehabilitated, largely by Schultz (1960, 1961, 1963).

The human-capital approach has recently been most successfully applied to the examination of education, and—to a lesser degree—of other forms of training and health (Schultz, 1962). For those scholars laboring in this area, important and challenging difficulties arise in defining, identifying, and measuring the inputs and by extension the costs; in defining, identifying, and measuring outputs or returns (benefits); and in comparing the costs and the returns so as to evaluate the private as well as the social returns to human-investment outlays. Consider each of these briefly, with respect to education.

First, "inputs" refers to the resources—teachers, buildings, books, and the time and effort of the students themselves—that go into producing education. "Outputs" refers to the results of the educational process, coming in the form of higher productivity, greater enlightenment, and so on. The technical or physical relationship between inputs and outputs can be referred to as a production function relationship; this describes how inputs are physically transformed into outputs (Burkhead & others, 1967).

The inputs to education can be specified and quantified without great difficulty. The various resources used to produce education are obvious and can be evaluated in dollar terms. These inputs or costs encompass the direct costs of schooling, plus the income which students forgo while acquiring (or "purchasing") their education. These costs, also called "opportunity" costs, are not insignificant—amounting to well over half of the private costs of college, as pointed out by Schultz (1960) and Bowman (1966). The bulk of these costs are paid by the individual, in the form of charges for books, tuition, and fees and through the earnings he forgoes during the period of school attendance; the remainder of the cost is paid by society. The most vexing issue on the input-cost side lies in the determination of what fraction of the costs should be viewed as "consumption" rather than "investment." Students clearly derive some pleasure from school attendance, but separating these two forms of costs presents serious difficulties.

The outputs of education present greater difficulties, both in concept and measurement, than the inputs. The nature of the outputs of the education process are not fully understood, since some are intangible; this has made it difficult to assign a value to education outputs. For lack of a better measure, economists have been forced to rely heavily on earnings as a measure of educational output. Accordingly, many of their analyses deal primarily with the financial returns as a result of education (Becker, 1964).

It is, nonetheless, recognized that there are other important, if less tangible, returns to individuals who receive education; some of these are investment-type returns, while others are consumption-type returns, to educational investment. Beyond this is a variety of tangible and intangible benefits which "spill over" to others, whether educated or not. These benefits—ordinarily called external or social benefits—accrue to others through, for example, raising the general level of literacy or causing people to be more responsible citizens (Weisbrod, 1962, 1964). Such benefits are difficult, if not impossible, for individuals or groups making educational investments in themselves to appropriate. In any case, to the extent that external benefits exist, there is a strong likelihood that the net benefits from educational expenditures are understated—at least when net returns are measured in increased individual earning power.

Comparing benefits and costs is not a simple matter of subtracting benefits from costs. Instead, a benefit-cost framework is required in which the present value of the net benefits of human investment or the internal rate of return on human investment is employed. Both procedures involve a discounting of future benefits to reflect the fact that far-distant benefits are valued less highly than are those near at hand. The purpose of these measures is to permit assessments of the payoffs of one form or type of human investment versus another, or of human investment versus nonhuman investment.

Having set forth the general framework currently employed in much of the research on the economics of education, we next survey the recent work. The major thrust of this work on the economics of education involves an estimation of the aggregate and the individual payoffs to various forms of education; this has led to extensive applications to underdeveloped areas, followed by an effort to understand the rapid expansion of education in the United States.

As an outgrowth of this general work, there have been a number of efforts to determine the nature of the production function for education as a part of the application of systems analysis to educational decision making. This in turn leads to issues of educational finance. Finally, a more explicit consideration of so-called equity versus efficiency considerations is beginning to take shape.

EDUCATION'S CONTRIBUTION TO GROWTH. The contribution of education to the well-being of society and more specifically to its gross national product (GNP) has long been recognized, but only recently have any reasonably precise empirical measures of this contribution become available. What provoked the effort to find such measures was the finding, about a decade ago, that the conventional inputs of labor (man-hours worked) and capital (dollar value of physical capital) left unexplained a large fraction of the twentieth-century growth in the U.S. economy. While GNP had increased by 3 percent per year, only about half of this growth could be explained (Fabricant, 1959). This set off a variety of efforts to explain the so-called residual—the unexplained portion of growth.

Initially, technological change was viewed as a prime and yet unexplored generator of economic growth, but it soon became apparent that the meaning of "technological change" was neither fully understood nor readily quantifiable (Solow, 1957). And so the search turned to the impact of qualitative change in the labor force.

The new research on investment in human beings, and of the growth of the stock of human capital resulting from investment in education, was launched by Schultz (1960). By viewing educational costs as investment outlays, he showed that human-capital formation was large and that it was growing rapidly —in contrast to the more conventional physical-capital formation. On the basis of these findings he demonstrated that under plausible assumptions increased educational investment accounted for approximately 20 percent of observed U.S. growth during the first half of the century. Shortly thereafter, in a more comprehensive effort to enumerate and measure all sources of economic growth, Denison (1962) concluded that the rise in educational attainment accounted for 23 percent of the increase in real GNP and for about 40 percent of the rise in real per-capita output from 1929 to 1957. Similar calculations have since been made for a number of countries, with the results varying, depending upon a wide variety of factors (Denison, 1966).

Since Denison's work, education as an input has received vastly more attention than ever before. It has been incorporated into a wide variety of economic growth studies, as well as in numerous production-function studies. Among the most successful of these latter ventures has been the work of Griliches (1963, 1964). Through the use of multiple regression analysis, such studies indicate the importance of education as well as other input variables in explaining output growth in a particular sector of the economy, such as agriculture or manufacturing.

IMPACT OF EDUCATION ON EARNINGS. Underlying the study of education's contribution to economic growth is the observed strong correlation between education and individual earnings; typically, college graduates earn several thousand dollars more per year than high school graduates do. This means that they have substantially greater lifetime earnings (Miller, 1960). But obtaining a college degree also involves a greater outlay of resources, in terms of both money and income forgone. To determine whether the monetary benefits exceed the costs, these two elements are combined and expressed as an internal rate of return on educational investment, i.e., the percentage return yielded by the investment.

Rates of return on investment in college for males were first calculated by Becker (1960) and have since been extended by him (1964) and others. In general, these calculations indicate that the private or individual before-tax rate of return to a college education, based on the private costs of education, was approximately 10 to 12 percent. After crude adjustments for ability differences, these rates of return were scaled downward by one or two percentage points. On an after-tax basis the rate of return was in the 8-to-10-percent range. Becker concluded from his analysis that private rates of return on educational investment were roughly equal to rates of return on physical investment (also about 8 percent), thereby indicating the absence of either over- or underinvestment in formal schooling.

Several investigators have extended Becker's results. Hansen (1963) calculated rates of return over the whole range of primary, secondary, and college education, showing that in 1949 the highest rate of return accrued to the completion of eighth grade, with a gradual decline thereafter. Both high school and college dropouts had much lower rates of return than those who completed their work. Hanoch (1967) has pointed up some of the regional variation in rates of return. Surprisingly, rates of return in 1960 tend to be somewhat higher in the South than in the North, as indicated by a 19-percent return on high school in the South versus 16 percent in the North. Hanoch attributes these results to a relative shortage of skills in the South and to the possibly lower costs of schooling in the South. He also finds that rates of return to nonwhites are well below those to whites. In general, however, the relationships between the rates of return by educational levels are substantially the same within each of these subpopulations.

Comparisons of rates of return and of present values of expected lifetime earnings patterns have also been employed in analyzing whether there are "excesses" or "surpluses" of various types of educated manpower (Blank & Stigler, 1957; Hansen, 1964; Bowman, 1963; Wilkinson, 1966). When rates of return are high we would expect more people to try to enter particular fields and vice versa. On the other hand, rates of return may be "high" because, for example, entry into some fields is restricted. The available results indicate substantial differences in the net payoffs to different occupational choices. They also provide some insight into methods for accelerating or decreasing the number of entrants into different fields, through varying the costs of entry by increasing or decreasing the amounts of student subsidy.

Virtually all of the rate-of-return studies are open to a number of criticisms, most of which are fully acknowledged by their authors (e.g., Becker, 1964). First, it is widely recognized that better-educated people are likely to have greater native talents, display stronger motivation, and possess more abundant financial resources; this is generally true of college graduates as contrasted to high school graduates. Thus far it has been impossible to isolate with any degree of precision the importance of these factors, all of which are likely to accentuate the apparent impact of education upon earnings. In several preliminary efforts, the impact of "ability" is thought to account for between 12 and 40 percent of the differences in earnings between high school and college graduates (Becker, 1964; Denison, 1964).

Second, efforts to separate out the impact of on-the-job training have not been entirely successful, though a noteworthy effort in that direction has been made by Mincer (1962). Such training is almost certain to raise earnings. But to the extent that the costs of securing such training are not taken into account, the observed differences in earnings commonly associated with education are likely to be greater than those reflecting additional education only. Presently, our knowledge of the amounts, costs, and benefits of on-the-job training and other informal postgraduate training is woefully inadequate.

Third, there is a question of whether earnings are an adequate reflection of the productivity of people with different amounts of education, given that labor markets may not be sufficiently responsive because of lack of competition, lack of information, and so on. In general, however, earnings are assumed to be reasonable proxies for productivity.

Finally, from society's point of view the external benefits of education should also be included in measures of the payoff of education. But, as noted earlier, it is difficult to assign a value to externalities, and it is even harder to specify what they are or to be certain whether they are positive or negative in their impact. Much more work is required in this area.

Rate-of-return estimates are now available for a number of countries, among them the United Kingdom, India, Mexico, Chile, and the Philippines (Hansen, 1967). While the results vary from country to country, there seems to be a rather surprising similarity in many of the results obtained.

HISTORICAL STUDIES. Probing the historical links between the payoff to education and the rapid rise in educational attainment has received only minor attention so far. Fishlow (1966a, 1966b) has established that levels of educational attainment have risen steadily in the United States since the early part of the nineteenth century; much of this early investment in education was no doubt motivated by a faith in its large external or social benefits. Bowman (1962b) has provided interesting insights into the early growth of the land-grant institutions. The rise of educational attainment in czarist Russia, as well as France, Japan, and several other nations is detailed by Anderson and Bowman (1965).

LINKS BETWEEN EDUCATION AND EARNINGS. The exact manner in which education serves to enhance productivity, and thereby earnings, remains unexplained. In the case of highly specialized, vocationally oriented training the link is rather obvious, but in the matter of more general training there is a notable lack of understanding of how education serves as input into the productive process and of how the schools produce educated labor by virtue of their activities. Several efforts have been directed at filling these gaps in our knowledge.

One such effort has sought to determine the extent to which education is a required input to the performance of various kinds of jobs. Given available information on the required educational component of job performance, Eckaus (1964) has indicated that jobholders increasingly possess more education than they really need. This excess of education may be indicative of the consumption aspect of educational investment. At the same time, however, manpower planners have been stressing the need for greater educational attainment in view of the projected course of technical change and the concomitant shifts in occupational structure (Parnes, 1962). But exactly what factors give rise to the market demand for more-educated persons remains unclear.

A second and major effort is now being launched to learn more about what the schools produce and how school inputs as well as personal and environmental forces affect school outputs. The work of Burkhead and others (1967) is an attempt to develop a production-function analysis of school systems so that the quantitative importance of different input mixes can be established. The work of Benson and others (1965) is similar. The effort on the largest scale is the recent study by Coleman and others (1966), which places great stress on nonschool variables. Though subject to some criticism, this report indicates that the link between school inputs and outputs may be much less critical than has been traditionally thought. These exploratory studies indicate some of the ways in which the research of educators and economists may fruitfully interact.

PROGRAM BUDGETING AND FINANCING OF EDUCATION. A topic of growing interest but on which little research has yet been done is program budgeting in education. The path-breaking approach sketched by Kershaw and McKean (1959) and elaborated upon by Hirsch (1965) James and others (1963), and Burkhead and others (1967) is now being developed in greater detail. One of the most noteworthy examples of this general kind of analysis is Weisbrod's study of programs to prevent high school dropouts (1965). His results indicated that in a number of dropout-prevention programs the benefits in greater incomes did not justify the costly outlays.

As the federal government as well as state and local governments accelerate their plans to apply program budgeting to an ever-wider range of activities (Novick, 1965), much additional research is needed to help give direction to their efforts. This is especially true in education.

The financing of education has received great attention for many years, and especially recently (Benson, 1961; Harris, 1960; Daniere, 1964; Organization for Economic Cooperation and Development, 1966), but no important new approaches have been developed. The extent to which the costs should be shared by students, parents, and taxpayers at various levels of government remains unclear (West, 1965). There is a real possibility, however, of merging the human-investment approach and issues of educational finance by viewing the extent to which recipients "repay," through taxes on their additional incomes, society's educational subsidies to them. Unfortunately, this work has not yet proceeded very far.

EFFICIENCY AND EQUALITY OF EDUCATIONAL OPPORTUNITY. While much of the research in the economics of education focuses on the efficiency of resource allocation, both within education and between other sectors of the economy, there is an increased awareness of the possible conflict in the goals of efficiency and equality of educational opportunity. Anderson (1965) notes some of the conflicts between efficiency and equity, and we see further evidence of this theme in the work of Benson and others (1965) and Burkhead and others (1967). As yet we can say little about the issues, in part because society's preferences are not clear and in part because we know so little about what education does in the way of altering people's potential performance. The continued concern with levels of school achievement rather than changes in levels of school achievement has also obscured these issues.

Much work remains to be done in developing and expanding our knowledge about the relationships between education and economic behavior and performance—at both the conceptual and the empirical levels. The nature of recent work in this field is, however, already showing itself in the discussion and implementation of policy and can be expected to do so increasingly in the future.

W. Lee Hansen
The University of Wisconsin

References

Anderson, C. Arnold. "Patterns and Variability in the Distribution and Diffusion of Schooling." In Anderson, C. Arnold, and Bowman, Mary Jean. (Eds.) *Education and Economic Development.* Aldine Publishing Co., 1965. p. 314–44.

Anderson, C. Arnold, and Bowman, Mary Jean. (Eds.) *Education and Economics Development.* Aldine, 1965. 436p.

Becker, Gary S. "Underinvestment in College Education?" *Am Econ R* 50:346–54; 1960.

Becker, Gary S. *Human Capital: A Theoretical and Empirical Analysis, with Special Reference to Education.* Columbia U Press, 1964. 187p.

Benson, Charles S. *The Economics of Public Education.* Houghton, 1961. 580p.

Benson, Charles S., and others. *State and Local Fiscal Relationships in Public Education in California.* Report. Senate of the State of California, 1965. 72p.

Blank, David M., and Stigler, George M. *The Demand and Supply of Scientific Personnel.* National Bureau of Economic Research, 1957. 200p.

Blaug, Mark. *Economics of Education: A Selected Annotated Bibliography.* Pergamon, 1966(a). 190p.

Blaug, Mark. *Economics of Education: A Selected Annotated Bibliography.* Addenda. 1966(b). (Mimeographed.)

Blaug, Mark. *Economics of Education: A Selected Annotated Bibliography.* 2nd Addendum. 1967. 33p. (Mimeographed.)

Bowman, Mary Jean. "Human Capital: Concepts and Measures." In Mushkin, Selma. (Ed.) *Economics of Higher Education.* USOE Bulletin No. 5. GPO, 1962(a). p. 69–92.

Bowman, Mary Jean. "The Land-grant Colleges and Universities in Human Resource-development." *J Econ History* 22:523–46; 1962(b).

Bowman, Mary Jean. "Educational Shortage and Excess." *Canadian J Econ and Political Sci* 29:446–52; 1963.

Bowman, Mary Jean. "The Costing of Human Resource Development." In Robinson, E. A. G., and Vaizey, John. (Eds.) *The Economics of Education.* St Martin's Press, Inc., 1966. p. 434–50.

Burkhead, Jesse, and others. *Input and Output in Large-city High Schools.* Syracuse U Press, 1967. 110p.

Coleman, James S., and others. *Equality of Educational Opportunity.* Nat Center for Ed Stat, USOE, GPO, 1966. 737p.

Danière, André. *Higher Education in the American Economy.* Random, 1964. 206p.

Denison, Edward F. *The Sources of Economic Growth in the United States and the Alternatives Before*

Us. Supplementary Paper No. 13. Committee for Economic Development, 1962. 297p.

Denison, Edward F. "Appendix to Edward F. Denison's Reply." In *The Residual Factor and Economic Growth.* Organization for Economic Co-operation and Development (Paris), 1964. p. 86–100.

Denison, Edward F. *Why Growth Rates Differ.* The Brookings Institution, 1966. 494p.

Eckaus, Richard S. "Economic Criteria for Education and Training." *R Econ Stat* 46:181–90; 1964.

Fabricant, Solomon. *Basic Facts on Productivity Change.* Occasional Paper 63. National Bureau of Economic Research, 1959. 57p.

Fishlow, Albert. "The Common School Revival: Fact or Fancy?" In Rosovsky, H. (Ed.) *Industrialization in Two Systems.* Wiley, 1966a. p. 40–67.

Fishlow, Albert. "Levels of Nineteenth Century American Investment in Education." *J Econ History* 26:418–36; 1966b.

Griliches, Zvi. "The Sources of Measured Productivity Growth: U.S. Agriculture, 1940–1960." *J Political Econ* 71:331–47; 1963.

Griliches, Zvi. "Research Expenditures, Education, and the Aggregate Agricultural Production Function." *Am Econ R* 54:961–75; 1964.

Hanoch, Giora. "An Economic Analysis of Earnings and Schooling." *J Hum Resources* 2:310–29; 1967.

Hansen, W. Lee. "Total and Private Rates of Return to Investment in Schooling." *J Political Econ* 71:128–41; 1963.

Hansen, W. Lee. "'Shortages' and Investment in Health Manpower." In Mushkin, Selma J. (Ed.) *The Economics of Health and Medical Care.* U Michigan Press, 1964. p. 75–92.

Hansen, W. Lee (Ed.) "Symposium on Rates of Return to Educational Investment." *J Hum Resources* 2:291–374; 1967.

Harris, Seymour E. *Economics of Higher Education.* Harper, 1960. 252p.

Hirsch, Werner Z. "Education in the Program Budget." In Novick, David. (Ed.) *Program Budgeting.* Harvard U Press, 1965. p. 178–207.

James, H. Thomas, and others. *Wealth, Expenditure and Decision-making for Education.* School of Education, Stanford U, 1963. 203p.

Kershaw, Joseph A., and McKean, Roland N. *Systems Analysis and Education.* Research Memorandum 2473-FF. The RAND Corporation, 1959. 64p.

Kiker, B. F. "The Historical Roots of the Concept of Human Capital." *J Political Econ* 74:481–500; 1966.

Miller, Herman P. "Annual and Lifetime Income in Relation to Education: 1939–59." *Am Econ R* 50:962–87; 1960.

Mincer, Jacob. "On-the-job Training: Costs, Returns, and Some Implications." *J Political Econ,* Suppl. 5, Part 2, 1962. p. 50–79.

Novick, David. (Ed.) *Program Budgeting: Program Analysis and the Federal Budget.* Harvard U Press, 1965. 382p.

Organization for Economic Co-operation and Development. *Financing of Education for Economic Growth.* The Organization (Paris), 1966. 285p.

Parnes, Herbert S. *Forecasting Educational Needs for Social and Economic Development.* Organization for Economic Co-operation and Development (Paris), 1962. 113p.

Schultz, Theodore W. "Capital Formation by Education." *J Political Econ* 68:571–84; 1960.

Schultz, Theodore W. "Investment in Human Capital." *Am Econ R* 51:1–17; 1961.

Schultz, Theodore W. *The Economic Value of Education.* Columbia U Press, 1963. 92p.

Schultz, Theodore W. (Ed.) *Investment in Human Beings. J Political Econ,* Suppl. 5, Part 2, 1962. 157p.

Solow, Robert M. "Technical Change and the Aggregate Production Function." *R Econ Stat* 39:312–23; 1957.

Vaizey, John. *The Economics of Education.* Faber & Faber, Ltd., 1962. 165p.

Weisbrod, Burton A. "Education and Investment in Human Capital." *J Political Econ,* Suppl. 5, Part 2, 1962. p. 106–23.

Weisbrod, Burton A. *External Benefits of Public Education.* Industrial Relations Section, Princeton U, 1964. 143p.

Weisbrod, Burton A. "Preventing High School Dropouts." In Dorfman, Robert. (Ed.) *Measuring Benefits of Government Investments.* The Brookings Institution, 1965. p. 117–49.

West, E. G. *Education and the State.* The Institute of Economic Affairs, 1965. 242p.

Wilkinson, Bruce W. "Present Values of Life-time Earnings for Different Occupations." *J Political Econ* 74:556–72; 1966.

EDUCATION IN DEVELOPING NATIONS

When we speak of education in developing nations we are referring to education in countries which contain over two-thirds of the world's population. The nations of Africa, tropical South America, Central America and the Caribbean, the Pacific islands, and Asia (except for Japan and the U.S.S.R.) constitute, by most definitions, the underdeveloped world. Although nations in this vast area are far from homogeneous, they reveal many common economic and social features and face common problems. Vaizey (1962) identifies as significant such common economic characteristics as low per-capita income, overpopulation in relation to employment opportunities, heavy reliance on agriculture carried on by backward techniques, and shortage of foreign exchange with which to acquire capital equipment. These economic characteristics are interwoven with social institutions, not the least of which is education. Thus, side by side with these economic characteristics Vaizey lists such educational features as low rates of literacy; expanding populations which contain unusually high proportions of school-age children; relatively few children in school, and these often attending for very few years; teachers in low supply and poorly trained;

schools frozen in traditional patterns unrelated to modern needs; and educational opportunities unequally distributed within nations. Political leaders of emergent nations have also come to view education and economic development as related. Intent upon accelerating economic growth, they see education as a vehicle at their disposal. Often, however, they fail to recognize the consequences to existing social and political systems which educational progress and economic growth will entail.

Many of the economic characteristics of underdevelopment can be quantified with relative ease. As indices they are invaluable to the economist interested in studying economic growth. They are likewise useful to the educator, for they both clarify the limits within which he is working and help him define intermediate goals for education. They are so often cited, however, that they can disguise the intricacy of the development process. The basic reason that the economies of these countries are underdeveloped, as Curle (1963) has shown, is that these are underdeveloped societies; that is, *societies which for a variety of reasons fail to make adequate use of their human resources.* Emergent nations appear caught in a vicious circle of poverty, disease, ignorance, and rigid social institutions and stratifications that kill initiative, banish hope, and stifle the urge to improve one's condition.

The problem of defining the process of *modernization* which eliminates these conditions has led to both analytical and field research. While readily quantifiable phenomena (such as illiteracy, overpopulation, or per-capita income) help identify underdeveloped societies, these are increasingly viewed as symptoms of underdevelopment rather than causes. O'Connell (1965) approached the problem of definition by trying to specify the elements in the modernizing outlook. He found the heart of modernization to lie in a point of view characterized by (1) a conviction that causes can be uncovered and that the search for knowledge will enable man to control his environment, (2) a willingness and ability to use the tools and techniques this conviction entails, and (3) a receptivity and capacity to accept change without losing a sense of identity. Although McClelland (1961), by amassing data on societies revealing rapid economic growth, has thrown some doubt on whether these are the particular qualities called for, his survey likewise reveals that it is attitudinal factors (specifically, *achievement motivation* and *other-directedness*) which produce economic growth. This latter quality is not unlike the quality of *empathy,* here defined as a high capacity for identification with new aspects of one's environment or the ability to view oneself in the situation of another, which Lerner (1958) found the indispensable element of the modernizing personality in his extensive study of modernization in the Middle East. Most authorities would also appear to agree with Hunter (1966b) that development involves not only change but continuity, cohesion, and a sense of shared values. McClelland (1961) has further shown that the basis of the social cohesion which characterizes development has shifted from impersonal tradition to an informed public opinion which sets new norms or values governing functional relationships between people.

An extensive literature relevant to ways in which education is or is not related to this process of modernization or development has appeared. Studies by scholars originally drawn from various disciplines and possessing extensive field experience such as those of Harbison (1962), Hunter (1963), Curle (1963), Harbison and Myers (1964) and Beeby (1966) constitute major strategy proposals.

ECONOMIC DEVELOPMENT IN EMERGENT NATIONS. When Margaret Read (1955) noted that Western educators in developing nations had found problems of teaching and the educational explosion so absorbing that they had been unable to consider the social and economic environment in which the school was set or the consequences of the education they were providing, she was pointing to a situation which was soon to change. Since then much attention has been paid to economic and social conditions and consequences, partly because attempts to transform traditional societies by pumping in physical capital have fallen short of expectations, partly in response to the educational aspirations of developing nations themselves, and partly due to untoward consequences of the education explosion. There has consequently been a convergence of the concerns of economists, political scientists, sociologists, and educators on examining the process of development and the role of education in that process.

The major scholarly impetus for this examination came from the economists. In his presidential address to the American Economics Association in 1960, Schultz propounded the thesis that hitherto "unexplainable" economic outputs could be accounted for by *investment in human capital,* presumably largely through education. This thesis was elaborated in his subsequent volume, *The Economic Value of Education* (1963). Although originally supporting his thesis largely with data from advanced economies, Schultz (1962) himself specifically extended it to low-income countries, concluding that with few exceptions they underinvested in human capital.

A number of comparative studies have been conducted to determine the extent and nature of the relationship between education and economic development. In these studies, some measure of either the "educational development" or "human resource development" of countries is correlated with a measure or measures of their economic development.

In one of the most extensive studies, Harbison and Myers (1964) examined the relation of high level manpower and GNP (Gross National Product) per capita in seventy-five representative countries. They found a high positive correlation (.888) between GNP per capita and a devised *composite index of human resource development* (simply the arithmetic total of enrollment at a second level of education as a percentage of the age group 15 to 19, adjusted for length of schooling, and enrollment at the third level of education as a percentage of age group, multiplied by five.) They further found high positive correlations between the enrollment ratios at all levels of education and GNP per capita, although the correlations between GNP per capita and secondary level enrollment ratios (.817) and first level ratios (.668) were lower than its correlation with their composite high-level manpower index. High positive correlations were also found to prevail between GNP per capita and such "stocks of high-level manpower" as teachers, physicians and dentists, engineers, and scientists. Using the percentage of the population engaged in agriculture as an indicator of *under*development, they further found a high negative correlation (−.814) between their composite human resource index and underdevelopment so measured.

Other comparative or ranking studies have employed different indices of development and produced dissimilar conclusions. Bowman and Anderson (1963) found the spread of primary education was a better predictor of the economic status of a nation than either the extent of its post-primary schooling or the percentage of adult literacy. Correlations between post-primary enrollments and incomes were found to be low in the countries they studied, particularly when they excluded from consideration countries in which literacy was widespread (presumably largely as a product of primary education). A study of 16 countries by Rado and Jolly (1965) revealed no simple relationship existing between manpower and Gross Domestic Product. The Economist Intelligence Unit (1962) reported a significant correlation between enrollment in primary and secondary schools and rate of growth of Gross Domestic Product. They also found a high correlation between literacy rate and per-capita income, but only when the wealthiest nations were eliminated from their sample. The complexity which Bowman and Anderson found in relationships between literacy and economic growth is significant. Thus, while their study revealed little economic development in countries with less than a 30 percent literacy rate, and a literacy rate of over 90 percent in countries in which per-capita income exceeded $500, they found that *within* the large middle range of countries (in terms of literacy) there was no significant correlation between literacy rate and per-capita income.

A further dimension of complexity is revealed by Curle (1964a). He found that the average investment in education in the 10 countries with the lowest rate of economic growth in his sample was actually higher than the investment of the 12 countries with the highest rate of growth. The *egalitarian-nonegalitarian* dimension of societies and political structures proved the decisive factor in determining relationships which did prevail, from which he concluded that egalitarianism rather than economic wealth is the important corollary of high per-capita expenditure on education. Although Harbison and Myers (1964) with extensive data available have found closer relationships prevailing between various indices of educational development and per-capita income than has been revealed by most other studies, the pattern in these relationships is still far from clear, and policy decisions to emphasize one rather than another level of education on their basis would be unwarranted.

There is also considerable dispute about the *interpretation* to be placed upon correlations which have been found between indices of educational development and indices of economic development, especially when these relate to emergent nations. Education as a consumer good can be expected to rise as per-capita income moves above the subsistence level. Thus, in studies of the role of education in expanding the exchange sector of the economy in Africa, both Blaug (1964), for former British Africa, and Khoi (1964), for former French Africa, concluded that thus far the impact of the growing modern sector of the economy on education had been greater than the impact of education on expanding that economy. Harbison and Myers (1964, 1965) have explicitly emphasized that the quantitative relationships they have found do not establish *causal* relationships. Rather, they conclude, the relationship is one of association, in which education both contributes to and profits from economic development.

Despite these cautions by scholars, policy makers in developing nations often appear to view the relationship as causal, anticipating that educational expansion will produce an economic leap forward. Scholars in various disciplines, such as the economists Balogh (1964), Cash (1965), and Rado (1966), the educator Curle (1964a), and the sociologist Anderson (1964), have all challenged conclusions that educational expansion in developing nations will produce such an economic leap. In addition to pointing out the danger arising from imputing causation to these correlations, Balogh argues that attempts to correlate rates of economic and educational development reveal methodological errors of inappropriate aggregation, falsely assumed homogeneity in education, and distortion arising from colonial salary structures (which fail to reflect economic contribution). Accepting the last of these, he further points out, can only perpetuate existing social and economic inequalities.

An important practical consequence of cross-national studies relating indices of educational development (or human-resource development) to economic growth is the support they do or do not provide for particular educational strategies and for the manpower-analysis approach to planning education. The high positive correlations which Harbison and Myers (1964) found between their human-resource index and per-capita income suggests that increases in high-level manpower play an important role in development. Using their composite index, they divide nations into four levels of human-resource development. These levels or stages are important in their target-setting approach to educational strategy, for they direct attention to the differences in high-level manpower associated with each movement toward economic development. Thus, by comparing a given nation with other slightly more advanced nations, and noting existing problems arising from shortages or surpluses of various levels of manpower in each nation, planners can set targets for the less-advanced nation on the basis of experience elsewhere.

The importance attached to manpower studies in determining educational objectives and assessing educational programs is revealed both by the number of national education reports and plans based upon such studies and by the growing volume of "country" studies of manpower development. Harbison and Myers (1965) reviewed a number of such studies by various scholars. These studies, while varying in research procedure and emphasis, are unified by their focus on the adequacy or inadequacy of educational programs and plans in meeting manpower needs. Most analyses reveal wide discrepancies between existing educational programs and estimated manpower requirements.

Manpower studies are not without difficulties and limitations, particularly when they deal with developing nations. On the basis of one such study in Iran, Baldwin (1965) found that the process had limited usefulness due to (1) uncertainties of demand estimates, (2) lack of dependence of many occupations upon specific amounts or kinds of education and training, (3) importance of decisions on how branches of the education system are articulated, (4) significant qualitative factors in education, and (5) the importance of policy decisions based on political pressure or social philosophy. Where it is yet too early to establish economic trends, where social and political stability are insecure, or where it is necessary to take account of major unemployment problems (conditions prevailing in many developing nations), further limitations arise. This type of analysis has, however, tended to reveal major educational lags in developing nations. Studies mentioned elsewhere such as those by Ruscoe (1963) on Jamaica, Lucas (1964) on Congo-Brazzaville, Donald Foster (1963) on Nationalist China, and White (1964) on Peru indicate that major segments of education in these countries are not being used effectively to promote economic development. In a study of Mexico, Myers (1965) reveals an additional problem in analysis; namely, that sharp regional differences within a country may be more significant than total country aggregates. Havighurst and Moreira (1965) also found wide regional disparities in both economic development and provision of education in Brazil. Disparities found in Mexico and Brazil appear to a greater or lesser extent in most developing nations.

Although the typology involving levels of human-resource development is best known, it is likewise possible to type educational development by other criteria. Where educational stages can be roughly equated with stages of economic development, educational strategies can be devised in terms of posited relationships between education and this development. Thus Laska (1964) has typed education in accordance with rates of completion of Grade 4, the last grade of primary school, and the general secondary course. By noting the historical development and present status of education in nations standing at different levels of economic development, one can suggest sequences and priorities for educational expansion in nations of each level. A second typology devised by Beeby (1966) has been derived not from quantitative considerations of educational expansion but from qualitative considerations related to the emphasis placed upon *meaning* in instruction, a measure which appears closely associated with the training and education possessed by teachers. His purpose is to point to resistances and sequences in development and to suggest the order and timing to be used in introducing educational innovations.

Only part of the contribution of education consists of directly preparing persons to carry on the jobs demanded by modern economies. More pervasive functions in changing motivations and creation of an environment in which change or innovation can occur, or in which they are actively prized, may prove to be even more crucial contributions. A cross-cultural study of relations between economic growth and motivational factors by McClelland (1961) found that with a single exception rapid economic growth occurred in countries where the achievement motive was high and where an other-directed orientation or public opinion had replaced tradition in defining specific functional relationships between individuals. The presence of these motivations or value orientations as revealed in children's literature proved to be a better predictor of later economic growth than did the economic factors usually presumed to be directly associated with the growth. McClelland found, however, on the basis of limited evidence from India and elsewhere, that schools and other isolated educational experiences failed to develop these motivations or orientations unless supported by ideological commitment in the larger society.

Whatever limitations education may be found to suffer in promoting economic development, however, the case for education in emerging nations does not rest there. Education serves many purposes beside the economic growth of nations or the economic well-being of individuals. Educational policy, therefore, cannot appropriately rest exclusively on economic grounds.

EDUCATION AND SOCIAL AND POLITICAL DEVELOPMENT. The concepts of *modernization* and *development* are not subsumed under economic growth. Emergent nations also seek social and political development. The concept of *social development* has proved, however, particularly elusive. Attempting to define social development for the ministers of education of the Latin American states, UNESCO and others (1962) pointed to two meanings attached to the term. First, social development refers to improvements in the standard of living of the people, often as a result of economic development. Second, the term refers to structural changes in society which either facilitate economic growth or, it is hoped, will accompany such growth. The heart of these structural changes is a shift from static two-class societies to patterns of life characterized by wide participation in national affairs, multiple or fluid social strata, and a general expectation of continuing change.

Relatively little empirical research has been done

on the relation between education (itself an important measure of social development) and other indices of general welfare. A basis for such research is developing, however. Russett and others (1964) have done much to operationalize the concept of social development by providing 75 indicators of the extent to which political rights, economic rights, and rights to information, health, education, religion, and respect or dignity are achieved. Such indicators, derived from goals enumerated in the Universal Declaration of Human Rights, may be considered measures of human welfare. As these indicators have likewise been chosen for their relation to theories of political and social change, they provide specific and potentially fruitful reference points for studies of the relation between education and other aspects of development. The authors have accumulated considerable comparative data from developing as well as developed nations, thus providing a basis for testing theories relating education to other factors in development. Summarizing the current state of empirical research on such relations, however, Adams (1965) points out that lack of theory relating educational and social development still raises problems of interpretation in statistical studies employing such indices. Having analyzed possible research approaches to relationships between variables, he concludes that the present state of our knowledge does not permit us to speak with assurance on the meaning of relationships which may be found to exist.

The relation between education and changes in social structure has been examined in rural contexts, where rigid class systems and inertia have proved barriers to education as well as to agricultural change. In the field this phase of social development is often intimately related with education. The Vicos action research project reported by Holmberg and Dobyns (1962) and by each of these scholars separately (Dobyns, 1965; Holmberg, 1965) is in many respects a study of the role of enlightenment in social development. In this project an attempt was made to transform a stagnant Peruvian *hacienda* inhabited by subsistence farmers into a modernizing community with institutions incorporating participant values. The goals enumerated by Holmberg (1965) included devolution of power to citizens, increased production, a more egalitarian sharing of economic returns, introduction of new schools, promotion of health, enlargement of role structures, a more open social system, and promotion of enlightenment. The study substantiated the hypothesis that when educational change is accompanied by change in related basic institutions the process is likely to prove most successful. Once freed from social restraints and provided encouragement and learning, the peasant population was able to transform itself into a productive citizenry. Education became enmeshed in wider social change as knowledge became the means to status and effective participation. The most modernized citizens in the emergent community were found to be the youngsters who had attended school.

Lerner's (1958) study of modernization in the Middle East likewise examined both faces of social development. The key to modernization was found to lie in the *participant* society; that is, one in which people go through school, read newspapers, are in the wage and market economy, participate politically through elections, and change opinions on matters of public business. Modernization developed sequentially through urbanization, literacy, and media participation to a stage in which individuals participated in all sectors of the social system. High multiple correlations were found between urbanization, literacy, media participation, and political participation, each correlated in turn with the other three. Literacy proved to be not only a key variable in moving from a traditional to a transitional society but also the pivotal agent in the transition to a fully participant society.

One facet of social development in new nations has commanded the particular attention of scholars: the extent to which Western education alienates its recipients from their traditional societies and the extent to which it enables them to create new social integrations around values more consonant with economic growth and political modernization. As Philip Foster (1963) points out in the case of Ghana, it was formal Western schooling that created a cultural environment in which innovation could take place, and it was the Western-educated elites, the most acculturated of Ghanaians, who not only achieved independence but developed the political culture to go with it. On the basis of his comprehensive study of the intellectual in India, Shils (1961) concludes that if there is to be any successful bridging of the gap between traditional and modern societies, it is the Western-educated intellectual who must perform the task.

The concept of *political development* possesses greater specificity than that of *social development*, although it lacks precise, agreed-upon statistical indices such as those often used to identify economic growth. Coleman (1965), in a major study of the role of education in political development, defines the latter as increased (1) *differentiation* of function, (2) attention to the claims of *equality*, and (3) adaptive and integrative *capacity* in the political system. It is thus a process of increasing participation and distributing the values of the polity in ways that meet the ethical claims of equality. The application of universalistic and achievement norms and relative freedom from ascriptive roles or rigidly fixed stations of life are notable characteristics of this process.

Political stability is one index of political capacity. Students of political development are not agreed that expansion of education will *automatically* produce such stability. Abernethy and Coombe (1965) point out that even though nationalist leaders have often looked to education to eradicate old divisions, where distribution of educational opportunities is uneven throughout a country old superiorities and rivalries may actually be reinforced. When this occurs, tribalism or regionalism may gain at the expense of national integration. Other studies support their conclusion. Noting that short-run regional inequalities in educational opportunity (which are almost inevitable during development) can exacerbate ethnic conflict, P. J. Foster (1962) found this to have proved the case temporarily in Ghana. This occurred *despite* expressed government policy in favor of equalizing educational opportunities throughout the country. We are now aware that in nations such as Nigeria, where regions and ethnic groups have responded quite differently to modern education, the resulting inequality in economic and political benefits derived from education has proved dangerously fissiparous.

Historical instances in which unequal provision of education or unequal response to education has contributed to creating apparently permanent political divisions are not lacking. For example, the unequal educational advance of India and Pakistan was found by Peshkin (1962) to have been a principal factor in convincing leaders of the Muslim League that political separation from India and the creation of a separate Pakistan were required. Caution must be exercised, however, in generalizing about the causes and effects of uneven distribution of education within countries. P. J. Foster (1962) has shown in his studies of Ghana that differences which might at first glance appear to be ethnically determined may prove on more careful scrutiny to be determined by economic and other social factors, and educational differences which develop between ethnic groups do not necessarily entail long-term barriers to national development.

It is not to be expected that the political impact of education will be the same in all types of societies. Curle (1964a) has studied the differing impacts of education in egalitarian and oligarchic societies. In the former, in which educational development tends to be both popular and fast, he found that although education can contribute to rapid political development, it may prove a threat to unity when educational expansion is more rapid than economic development. In oligarchic societies, in which the rate of educational expansion tends to be slow, he found education often leading to a struggle between traditional and educated elites.

Clearly the process of political development is dependent upon educated elites. Coleman (1965) lists political recruitment along with political socialization and political integration as major functions of education. As relatively easily identified groups, elites and potential elites (especially university students) in developing nations have been extensively studied. The indispensable role they play (and the role education plays in recruiting them) is reasonably clear. P. J. Foster (1963) has traced the process of national development in Ghana, finding that it was the elites, educated in Western schools, who became the nationalists and who provided the leadership to fashion an independent nation. Sutton (1965) in a more sweeping study concludes that the same has been true throughout Africa. Nonetheless, even in the formation of elites, education plays an ambiguous developmental role. Coleman's (1965) analysis of the developmental problems which may arise from education reveals this clearly. Among such problems he found: (1) a period of anti-intellectualism following independence, (2) tensions between incumbent political elites on the one hand, and civil servants and technical cadres with whom they must work, on the other, (3) frustration due to limited political mobility for second-generation elites, (4) the anomic potential present in reservoirs of unemployed school leavers, (5) accentuation of an elite–mass gap, and (6) perpetuation or intensification of ethnic, geographic, or parochial divisions. Failure to resolve any of these problems may retard development.

The threat which potential elites pose in underdeveloped countries is revealed in the study by Lipset (1964) of university students in developing nations. He reports their widespread alienation and disaffection with the status quo, particularly when they find themselves confronted (as they often do) with expanding university enrollments and declining prospects of access to elite positions. He finds that such students usually constitute a significant proportion of the rebellious or disruptive elements in their nations.

Clearly, education serves the cause of political development in many ways. It provides the skills required by modern political bureaucracies; in many emergent nations it has provided a common language; it helps recruit elites; and it has been a central force in independence movements.

Potentially it serves other purposes. It can provide the knowledge base for popular political participation; it can provide an alternative to ascriptive status; it can provide a common ideology and political culture. As Coleman's (1965) analysis and many of the studies he compiled indicate, however, it is often difficult to employ schools successfully for political purposes in times of rapid educational expansion and proliferation. There is, moreover, no reason to expect that various forms of development will necessarily contribute to each other. When educational expansion is out of line with economic growth, Coleman points out, it can prove politically destabilizing and thereby restrain rather than contribute to political development.

SALIENT EDUCATIONAL PROBLEMS. Although emergent nations are confronted with most or all of the educational problems faced by developed nations, certain problems assume saliency by reason of limited financial resources and social and cultural restraints on education. Study of some of these has already progressed.

Rural Education and Urban Drift. Most emergent nations rely largely upon agriculture for their income. In most developing nations rural people constitute 70 percent or more of the population. As rural populations are more dispersed than urban populations, the problems of providing educational opportunities for rural children and youth are increased. Moreover, the percentage of youth in rural populations is greater than that in urban populations, thus both increasing the potential clients and altering the ratio between those requiring schooling and those who are economically productive. The Latin American Demographic Centre (1962) found that the rural areas in Latin America had to carry the greatest educational burden, a situation probably common to much of the underdeveloped world. Carrying this burden becomes all the more difficult as per-capita income in the rural areas lags far behind income in urban areas, which enjoy wage economies. Attempts to protect central government funds for other development purposes by increasing the percentage of educational cost born locally thus bear heavily on rural people.

Although a UNESCO(1964a) survey found governments of most developing nations reporting that the number of children in school in rural areas was proportionate to the size of the rural population, most studies confirm Wharton's (1965) generalization that educational services in the rural areas of these nations lag far behind those provided cities. Both the Latin American Demographic Centre (1962) and Vera (1963), for example, found this to be the case in Latin America. This apparent conflict in data can be explained partially as the result of distortion of publicized statistics by some developing nations and partially by patterns of school attendance in rural areas. For example, the Food and Agriculture Organization (1962) found that the majority of school-age children who entered rural schools in Latin America dropped out after the second or third grade. Schools offering only a few grades, distances involved in attending school, inability to attract qualified teachers to rural areas, irrelevance of attending school to village life, and conflicts between school attendance and demands of agricultural production all result in irregular attendance and early attrition. Where populations are nomadic, problems of providing schooling become almost insurmountable.

Precise evidence on the role of education in the agricultural development of emergent nations is still minimal. Both Schultz (1964) and Wharton (1965) have argued that maintaining an optimum balance between inputs of human "capital" and inputs of physical capital is essential to agricultural growth and that the range of substitutability between the two types of inputs is very limited in early-stage agriculture. This can account for the fact that merely introducing new inputs of physical capital with subsistence farmers has rarely had the effect desired. The farmers acquiring the capital can seldom make sound decisions about its effective use, or they lack the skills required to employ new techniques or equipment. Arguing that the economic return on primary education of farmers can be very great in some circumstances, Schultz (1964) cites a study in Venezuela in which the incremental return on money invested in primary education was found to be 130 percent per annum when based on differences between the earnings of illiterate farmers and earnings of those who had completed primary school. Other studies referred to by Wharton (1965), however, have failed to reveal a clear-cut relation between the number of years spent in school and agricultural production in those countries characterized by few years of schooling. He attributes these results, however, largely to difficulties in finding significant measures of educational attainment and to difficulties in computing the agricultural returns which accumulate over a period of years.

Despite the paucity of precise empirical data, Bradfield (1964), Wharton (1965), and Mosher (1966) all agree with the Food and Agriculture Organization (1962) that education is an important or even indispensable condition for rapid agricultural development and that formal schooling is one important part of this education. As Bradfield points out, some formal education is a prerequisite for the effective use of conventional extension methods and it appears clear that literacy not only reduces the cost but increases the effectiveness of extension work. Some distinctions can be drawn, however. Citing illustrations from increases in sugar and rice production, Schultz (1964) concludes that where agricultural growth depends upon adopting and using a complex of several new production factors, schooling makes a difference; where use of one simple new factor is sufficient, however, rapid development may occur without schooling.

If education is an important factor in much agricultural growth, many nations may have underinvested in the education of farm people. This is frequently the result of social and political factors. Schultz (1964) finds that such underinvestment is accounted for largely by the interest of large landholders in maintaining the status quo, the decision of governments to concentrate upon industrial development as the road to modernity, and the elimination of private profit motives by political decisions. Of these, it is the relationship of landholding and land tenure to rural education which is most frequently noted. Barraclough (1962), for example, points out that the *latifundia–minifundia* complex in Latin America offers no incentive to provide rural education. The large estates do not rely on educated workers. An educated work force would, in fact, threaten the landholder system. At the same time, landless tenants or owners of minuscule holdings have little or no incentive to acquire education. Such situations support the frequent assertion that agricultural education unaccompanied by changes in rural social structure and land tenure is fruitless.

Some attempts to study the effect of altering the land tenure and social system have been made. The Vicos, Peru, action research project reported by Holmberg and Dobyns (1962) and Dobyns (1965) is the best known of these. They found that when the landholder system was broken and the economic returns of the hacienda were made available to the community, it was possible to develop a school so valued by the community that enrollments expanded rapidly, parents locked out teachers they felt were not providing good education, and schooled youngsters took over positions formerly associated with ascriptive status.

Despite its potential contribution to agricultural development, expansion of rural education has frequently had side effects detrimental to the rural area. These arise in part from what Capener (1964) refers to as the paradox of agricultural advance: Although education can ostensibly lead to agricultural development, virtually no farm boys receiving higher training return to their villages. Rather, they seek new jobs with salaries appropriate to their acquired status. This is illustrated in a study by Freeman (1964) who found that in Thailand an increasing number of Thai students in agricultural secondary schools viewed their education as preparation for further academic training rather than preparation for agricultural occupations.

Rural youth with no more than primary education also often migrate to cities. Here they join rising numbers of unemployed youth and constitute a threat to political stability and a drag on development. Margaret Read (1955) noted that anthropological studies in diverse cultural areas revealed that the schools lead to such a migration by opening up communication and increasing the mobility of peasant populations. Recent studies, including a UNESCO (1962) study of the economic implications of educational plans of Asian states, confirm this trend. Hunter (1966a) and Lucas (1964) found that the expansion of education in rural areas in Tanzania and Congo/Brazzaville respectively was accentuating the process of urban drift. This drift appears to substantiate the thesis propounded by both Ruscoe (1963) and Wharton (1965) that farm children in the developing nations look to education not as a means of improving rural life but as a means of escaping from it.

Empirical evidence remains scanty on whether this is a permanent or temporary phase in the life of the youth involved and also as to whether it is limited to nations in the first stages of development. Wharton (1965) and Hunter (1966a) believe that a majority of young rural migrants eventually return to the rural area when their hopes of entering the wage economy are frustrated. After examining the evidence in Tanzania, Skorov (1966) reaches the opposite conclusion. He believes that East African youth would rather remain unemployed in a city than return to farming.

As empirical studies of the post-school careers of rural youth are almost nonexistent, evidence on their whereabouts and attitudes remains impressionistic. A reasonable hypothesis would be that the response of youngsters to any anti-rural bias which may be implicit in school curricula or evidenced by some school teachers will vary widely depending upon the values, opportunities, and frustrations within the larger social groups of which they are members. Studies of the attitudes of primary school graduates in West Africa reported by Callaway (1962) and McQueen (1965) do not support the contention that rural primary schools reject agriculture *per se*, only that they reject traditional farming and the stagnation it represents.

Convinced of the urgency of rural development in providing a basis for raising the standard of living in most developing nations, the economists Balogh (1962) and Dumont (1964, 1966) have argued for altering the content and nature of education in these nations to give central emphasis to improving agriculture. Although present education does promote mobility and drain the countryside at least temporarily of youth, it is not clear that giving the school an agricultural bias would alter this. On the basis of Ghanaian and other data, P. J. Foster (1965) has argued that agricultural and vocational emphases in African schools did not produce the desired results in the past and should not be expected to do so in the future as such attempts ignore the social and economic reward system which is operating. Similarly Ruscoe (1963) has pointed out that as both parents and children in Jamaica see the function of schools as one of helping children secure the benefits of white collar employment, attempts to give rural schools an agricultural bias would surely lead to strong rural opposition. This may, however, depend upon the particular culture and the phase of development. In a study which followed up over 12,000 graduates of vocational agriculture schools in Taiwan, Meaders (1966) found that of those not in military service or further education, 53 percent were in farming or other agricultural occupations. Moreover, three-fourths of the graduates whose residences had been in rural areas when they initially enrolled in the agricultural schools were found to be in such occupations. Less fortunate from the standpoint of rural development, however, was his finding that those who had achieved best in school and those who had gone farthest in school were likely to leave agriculture and related occupations. As these results were based on those who had graduated as much as ten years prior to the study as well as recent graduates, they suggest that under certain circumstances youth receiving agricultural training will either remain in or later return to the rural sector.

Adult literacy programs are sometimes urged as alternatives to school expansion in rural areas. Illiteracy rates remain high in the underdeveloped world and especially in its rural areas. A UNESCO (1965) study found that in Asia and Oceania, illiteracy in 1962 was over 50 percent; in Africa and the Arab states it exceeded 75 percent. Furthermore, although the proportion of illiterates in adult populations was falling, the absolute number of illiterates was increasing due to the population explosion and low rates of school enrollment. In examining an international proposal for a world literacy program, Curle (1964b) pointed out that such a program would be enormously expensive and would pay uncertain dividends. He notes that adult literacy programs often prove ineffective unless instruction is tied to specific skills which can be demonstrably improved and which will yield tangible returns to the learner. These conditions are often not fulfilled in many parts of the developing world, particularly because of the lack of trained teachers. Literacy may provide one tool for altering rural life, or agricultural practices, but it cannot effect these changes alone.

Although evidence on the precise role education has played in agricultural growth is limited, it appears that it can be an important factor in much of agricultural development. It plays its role partly by disseminating specific agricultural knowledge and training people. Perhaps even more pervasively, it plays its role by creating an environment more receptive to innovation and by providing the basic skills whereby farmers can learn of new practices and make increasingly sound economic decisions.

Vocational and Technical Training. Much as in agricultural education, other types of vocational and technical training remain perplexing problems in developing nations. Studies of manpower and education, such as those compiled by Harbison and Myers (1965), quite consistently point to poor alignment between educational outputs and the demands of societies which are in the early stages of industrialization. Despite the need for technically trained manpower and especially for middle-level technicians, conventional academic education and higher education in the humanities have enjoyed prime favor. In formerly colonial areas this resulted from the requirements of the colonial power for personnel in administrative positions, from the attractiveness of the rewards which went with this administrative work, from emulation of colonial officials who had usually been so educated, and from resistance to vocational education which was often viewed as an attempt to keep the indigenous population in inferior positions.

The disfavor in which vocational education is held in most regions of the developing world is revealed by statistics Curle (1963) reports. He has shown that for Africa and Asia the percentage of secondary school population receiving vocational education varies with national per-capita income, falling to 3.5 percent and 2.4 percent respectively in African and Asian nations with annual per-capita incomes under $100. Latin America, interestingly, has much higher percentages of youth receiving secondary vocational education. Middle-level personnel (such as technicians, supervisors, and draftsmen) are in especially low supply in emerging nations, thus leading university graduates to fill positions which could more economically be filled by those with lower educational qualifications. A comparison of medical personnel in India and the United Kingdom reported by Curle revealed that while there were three nurses to every doctor in the United Kingdom, in India there were seven doctors to every nurse. However, such anomalies are often better accounted for by the status and reward systems operating in the economy than by inadequate provision of vocational schools. P. J. Foster (1965) has pointed out that in Africa rejection of vocational training by youth was a reasonable response to a situation in which the rewards continued to go to those with academic education.

Many independent nations, intent upon economic development, have given increased priority to expanding vocational and technical training. However, the need for skilled personnel does not necessarily imply the provision of vocational education through the formal school system. Harbison (1962), P. J. Foster (1965), and others agree that in low-income countries it is less expensive and more appropriate for most vocational training to occur outside the formal school system and partially under the auspices of employing concerns. Whether the training occurs inside or outside the formal school system, a crucial ingredient in its effectiveness would appear to be congruence between training offered and demands in employment. After studying vocational education in Brazil, Ghana, and the Philippines, the Economist Intelligence Unit (1959) found the major factor in effective vocational training to be close linkage of education with employing concerns. The most successful application of this principle was observed in the National Service of Industrial Apprenticeship (SENAI) in Brazil, to which all industrial and transport establishments must contribute.

It seems clear that the success of any vocational program designed to produce manpower for economic development is not a matter which rests exclusively with the school system. The Economist Intelligence Unit (1959), Harbison (1962), and P. J. Foster (1965) agree that a crucial variable in the success or lack of success of vocational-training programs is the system of rewards operating in the market. Studies such as those of Donald Foster (1963) in Nationalist China and White (1964) in Peru have confirmed that even those students who take vocational education often do not use the skills they have acquired. This phenomenon, which occurs in many emerging nations, appears to be the result of a complex set of factors including an inefficient labor market, an incentive system which does not reward technical skills, or a situation in which educational expansion has outpaced the generation of new jobs by the economy.

Education and Unemployment. Associated with problems of rural education and vocational training is the problem of unemployment. A major limitation on use of expanded education to promote economic development is the limited *absorptive capacity* of the modern sector of economies in emergent nations. Problems of politically destabilizing unemployment arise, Hoselitz (1965) notes, when mass education programs precede urbanization, industrialization, new agricultural enterprise, and changes in vocational values and beliefs. Furthermore, the first stages of industrialization create few new jobs. The capital intensive nature of most industrial development (e.g., a £4 million Nigerian cement factory which created only 300 jobs) is documented by Callaway (1962). It is also clear that a rise in per-capita national income does not assure a corresponding rise in employment opportunities. Skorov (1966) notes that recent increases in Gross Domestic Product in Tanzania (and in income from the modern sector) were accompanied by a decline in the absolute number as well as percentage of workers in the wage sector of the economy. Myers (1965) found that a rise of over seven percent in per-capita income in Mexico resulted in only a two-percent increase in jobs. The schools do not create unemployment, but they contribute to the complex situation which leads youth to leave the rural scene in search of jobs in cities which cannot cope with their numbers.

The seriousness of the unemployed-school-leaver problem is revealed by an analysis of unemployment in Tanzania, where the situation is not unlike that found in many developing nations. Here Hunter (1966a) found that for the 243,000 children who would become 16 during the single year 1969, only

23,000 new jobs would be created in the wage sector of the economy even if the national development plan proceeded on schedule. For these jobs, 40,000 primary school graduates would be competing with each other with the remainder of their age group who possessed less education, and with the large proportion of the school leavers of the preceding five years who were still out of employment. P. J. Foster (1964a) reports that between 1950 and 1960 school enrollment in Ghana (one of the most economically viable of African states) increased from 281,000 to 738,000. To serve this population not more than 25,000 jobs were being created annually in the modern sector of the economy. A similar problem in Nigeria was reported by Callaway (1962).

It is frequently alleged that unemployment is the result of a disdain for manual work on the part of the school graduates. Thus, studies by Maleche (1962) on Uganda, Van Der Kroef (1963) on South and East Asia, and Skorov (1966) on Tanzania all point to disdain for manual work or rejection of farming as factors which contribute to unemployment of school leavers. This is commonly believed true of West Africa as well. However, three studies in Nigeria and Ghana suggest that sweeping cross-cultural generalizations about the attitudes of school leavers are part of the folklore of development. Extensive interview and observation studies of school leavers in Nigeria by McQueen (1965) found not only that unemployed primary school leavers in Port Harcourt did not reject manual labor, but that the job of *factory worker* was ranked more highly than almost all "white collar" jobs including accountant, teacher, and clerk. It was selected as a preferred job almost as frequently as was *doctor*. The chief criticism primary-school leavers made of their government was that it was not creating factories fast enough. The occupation of modern farmer (as distinct from traditional farmer) was found to be almost as popular as that of factory worker. Studying school leavers in the same country, Callaway (1962) also found that they did not disdain manual work or modern farming and, in fact, readily accepted manual occupations or became apprentice artisans when the opportunity offered itself. A survey of the attitudes of Ghanaian secondary-school graduates conducted by P. J. Foster (1964a) revealed that whereas almost 22 percent favored technical jobs, only 7.5 percent of the boys favored clerical work and only 4.7 percent favored primary or middle school teaching. He found, however, that these students were realistic in their *expectations* (as distinct from *aspirations*), realizing that *the jobs actually open tended to be largely clerical or in schools*. All three researchers found the major factors which led young people into "clerical" type jobs were not disdain for manual work but the higher salaries these jobs commanded and the unavailability of other types of work in the modern sector of the economy.

It is the problem of the unemployed or lowly employed university graduate which poses the principal threat in other portions of the world. In Pakistan, Rashid (1966) found that unemployment of university graduates frequently existed side by side with demands for skilled persons. This resulted both from lack of balance between economic demand and courses being pursued and from the low *quality* of higher education provided. A similar situation was found by Kerr (1965) in Egypt, where a shortage of technical personnel exists side by side with a surplus of university graduates employed in positions which do not make productive use of their education. When universities place emphasis on the academic content of a degree without offering supplementary practical training and experience, Hunter (1966b) points out, this can lead to a situation where a surplus of degree-holders in agriculture or engineering exists side by side with a shortage of technicians, practical engineers, and agriculturalists.

The enormous expansion of higher education in the Philippines, Burma, Thailand, and Indonesia, as Hunter (1965) reveals elsewhere, has resulted in situations in which supplies of university graduates are unmatched by employment opportunities in the industrial sector, and yet there has been an inability to move graduates into rural sectors where they are badly needed. In Burma, where economic development has fallen far behind educational expansion, over 40 percent of the mechanical and electrical engineering graduates were still unemployed 18 months after graduation.

The unemployment problem does not always arise from the unavailability of jobs to be done or the type of education possessed. Lewis (1962) has pointed out that the chief employment problem with the university graduate is usually not one of balancing jobs and training but rather one of the abnormally high salaries graduates command relative to average per-capita output or the income of other producers. Thus while low-income countries frequently need many highly educated persons, they cannot afford to pay them and thus must leave them unemployed. This leads to a situation that is politically explosive but which is remediable only by altering the system of rewards in the larger economy or by awaiting the effects of the slow process in which the expectations of graduates become scaled down to levels which are realistic in terms of existing stages of economic development. As Coleman (1965) has indicated, this latter tends to be a very slow process indeed.

Educational Efficiency. Poor countries lack financial resources and must economize at all points in operating their schools. This need is strikingly revealed when one compares the cost of providing education with total national income. As Lewis (1962) points out, providing eight years of primary education to all children would cost about 0.8 percent of national income in the United States but would cost 1.7 percent of national income in Jamaica, 2.8 percent in Ghana, and 4.0 percent in Nigeria. Because a developing nation has many demands upon its limited capital resources, holding educational costs to the lowest possible level consistent with needed output is important if economic development is sought. Obviously serious inefficiency exists whenever school leavers cannot be absorbed by the economy or when they are employed in positions that fail to utilize their training, but internal inefficiencies in schools also represent great economic loss. A major factor in the high cost of education, as Lewis (1962) indicates, is the high salaries paid to teachers in comparison with per-capita national income. This is a cost difficult to reduce in the short term. Maintaining maximum efficiency in educational progress thus becomes doubly important in holding costs down.

One prevalent economic loss is occasioned by *attrition*. If it is assumed that the various terminal stages in the educational system constitute reasonable thresholds for differing levels of productive contribution to society, resources expended upon students who do not reach these thresholds must be considered largely wasted. For Latin America, Moreira (1963) noted that in 1950 the number of pupils taking the last grade of primary school ranged by country from 1.7 percent to 18.1 percent of the enrollments during the first year. By studying original groups of 100 pupils in the same region, the Latin American Demographic Centre (1962) reported that less than 10 reached the last grade of primary school in Honduras and Nicaragua and only 12 to 19 did so in a number of other Latin American countries. The greatest attrition occurred during the first year of school and probably represented complete loss.

Recent studies of education in individual Latin American states are numerous and amplify these data. Liu (1966) traced 1952 and 1956 beginning classes in Colombia schools. He found that only 13 percent of the 1952 class and only 16 percent of the 1956 class finished primary school. Attrition continued high during secondary school years and only 0.72 percent of 1952 school entrants were still attending after the eighth grade. Studying manpower shortages in Chile, Blitz (1965) found these to be the result of an educational pyramid in which the peak was too narrow. The pyramid appeared to be shaped by early school desertion and the related phenomenon of uneven income distribution in the society. Williams (1965), focusing directly on attrition in Guatemala, concluded that a large portion of the original entrants did not stay in school long enough to gain any significant benefit from the experience. He measured the inefficiency which attrition and grade repetition represent by computing the cost of producing one child who successfully completed primary school. In rural areas, where the problem was most extreme, he found that when total expenditures were divided by the number of those who completed school successfully the cost ran to 940.83 quetzals per graduate, although in the same area the *annual cost per enrolled pupil* was only 2.61 quetzals.

The results of studies on educational productivity in developing nations elsewhere are not dissimilar to those of studies on Latin America. Africa has provided many examples of low productivity. A UNESCO (1964b) study revealed that in one African country the cost of educating one primary school graduate was equal to 26 years of education. In urban Mali, Deblé (1964) found that only 15 of 100 entrants finished primary school. In rural Ivory Coast (one of the wealthier African nations) only 12 or 13 of an original 100 entrants did so. In Gabon, where almost all children start school, Proust (1964) reported that only 35 of 100 school entrants complete the 6-year program. Both the extent of attrition and its cost are revealed when one compares the number of years of attendance a government pays for with the number of children who complete primary school successfully. Khoi (1964) found that in Mali the government was paying for 20 school years to produce one child who completed primary school successfully. Similarly in Madagascar he found that the cost per primary school graduate was 3.5 times what it would be if attrition and retardation did not exist.

Most Asian nations are beset by the same problem. Summarizing evidence on the extent to which Asian nations were actually meeting educational goals they had set, Rahman (1963) found that the percentage of school entrants who completed primary school in emergent Asian nations varied from a low of 13.3 percent in Laos to over 85 percent in Korea. For India, Mukherjee (1965) reported that nearly two-thirds of the pupils who entered primary school dropped out along the way. Equally serious wastage rates among Arab countries of the Near East were reported earlier by Matthews and Matta (1949). They concluded that many of the children who left school early soon reverted to illiteracy.

Associated with the problem of attrition in reducing educational efficiency is *retardation*. The Latin American Demographic Centre (1962) found that in representative countries approximately one-fifth of the students were repeating the classes in which they were enrolled. Extensive retardation characterized nearly every country. Studying Colombia alone, Liu (1966) found more than a quarter of the students repeating the first grade and a similar percentage repeating second grade. The same pattern is often revealed in Africa and Asia. Proust (1964) reported that of the 35 percent of the pupils who did complete primary school in Gabon, only 5 percent did so without repeating a grade. In Senegal, Bowles (1965) found that it was almost certain that any child who secured his primary school certificate had been held back at least once and that at any given time at least 16 percent of the pupils were repeating a class. Reporting on still another part of the underdeveloped world, Mukherjee (1965) cites a study of "stagnation" in Bombay, where out of 10,000 first-grade pupils 4,542 passed the first year, 2,121 the second, 1,405 on their third or subsequent attempt. The remainder did not pass beyond grade 1.

Most authorities agree that unreasonable standards are often central to retardation. Many teachers consider holding students back evidence that they are maintaining standards. Bowles (1965) concluded that preoccupation with standards was so great in Senegal that it might be said that selection for the university began at the end of the first grade. Unfortunately repetition of classes not only augments school costs directly but also contributes to attrition and the further economic loss this entails.

The causes of attrition and the inefficiency it

represents are, however, clearly multiple. Many studies have tended to emphasize the role that poor instruction plays in this phenomenon. A UNESCO (1964b) study of African education, for example, found the shortage of teachers and their own poor education and training to be the major causes of the low productivity of education. Similarly Maleche (1962), Proust (1964), Williams (1965) and Mukherjee (1965) all conclude that the poor quality of instruction in the lower grades is a major cause of the high rates of attrition they found. Williams found attrition in rural schools in Guatemala to be so great when these schools were staffed by unqualified teachers that he proposed as a reasonable hypothesis that the funds expended on a school were almost entirely wasted from an economic standpoint unless at least one-third of the teachers in that school were qualified. Anyone familiar with the underdeveloped world, in parts of which primary teachers themselves may not have completed primary school, must recognize how central the teachers' own education and training are to most educational problems emerging nations confront.

Caution must be exercised in attributing wastage to factors internal to the school, however. Obviously, incomplete schools (schools lacking higher grades), distance from home to school, parental attitudes toward education (especially of girls), pregnancies, and marriage all contribute to dropping off the educational ladder. Less obvious but more important causes may be dysfunctions of the school in respect to the social structure and values of the surrounding community. P. J. Foster (1964b) attempted to get at causes of uneven patterns of schooling in Ghana by studying one Fanti village which represented an enclave of educational underdevelopment in an area otherwise characterized by a high degree of schooling. He found slow educational progress in this village to be a function of social and economic factors in the community, factors which in some instances appeared initially to have little to do with education but which actually determined its value and significance. In Vicos, Peru, Holmberg and Dobyns (1962) found that the rapid rise in school attendance and improved retention following the initiation of the Cornell Community Research Project in 1952 was associated with changing community values, new hope, new opportunities to display initiative, and the improved standard of living in a village previously stifled by an exploitative economic and social system. It appears likely that with further studies our understanding of low rates of educational productivity in developing nations will place greater emphasis on variables external to the school than has been customary in the past.

Teacher Qualification and Recruitment. If wastage is partly due to lack of qualified teachers, and educational quality to their presence, it is doubly important to attract, train, and retain able persons in teaching. Vaizey (1962) concludes that the supply and status of teachers is the central problem facing low-income nations in the development of their educational systems. Proposing basic strategies for human-resource development, Harbison (1962) similarly finds that the shortage of secondary school teachers is the "major bottleneck." This shortage was found to result largely from the fact that teachers leave the profession for more attractive jobs elsewhere. The mammoth proportions of the demand for teachers is revealed by Tinbergen and Bos (1962) who estimate that the developing world alone would require an *increase* of 730,000 secondary-school teachers between 1958 and 1970.

The ambitious educational plans which have been drawn up in many parts of the world may well be aborted by this shortage of teachers. The number of teachers who would be required to meet the target enrollment figures of the educational plans in Asia and Africa has been computed by Hansen (1965), who finds that these numbers far exceed the capacity of training facilities in the regions concerned. Consequently, the anticipated educational expansion could occur only by using large numbers of unqualified persons in the classroom.

By and large, sufficient quantities of able people are not being attracted into the teaching profession in developing nations. The situation in many countries does not show promise of improving soon, although in the long run lack of absorptive capacity elsewhere in national economies may lead more educated persons into the profession. Surveys conducted for the WCOTP by Jones (1963) in Africa and Franklin (1963) in Asia revealed a decline in teacher status and indicated that difficulty in making up shortages was being intensified by competition with more remunerative professions, by loss of respect for teaching, and by decreasing stability in the teaching profession itself. Despite general respect for teaching in South America, Davies' companion survey (1964) reported that economic rewards for teaching varied greatly from country to country. Wages for certain categories of teachers in some countries fell below those of unskilled laborers.

Major manpower strategies, such as those proposed by Harbison (1962), have emphasized the importance of adjusting salaries to meet development aims. Despite the emphasis that developing nations are according education, the size of the teaching profession (particularly as a proportionate group within the wage economy) makes it difficult to provide the remuneration to attract and hold well-qualified teachers. In most developing lands, incomes in the wage sector of the economy already greatly exceed national per-capita income. Thus, although teachers frequently complain of being underpaid as they compare themselves with other salaried workers, the salaries teachers command in many developing nations are higher, when compared with national per-capita income, than they are in developed nations. Lewis (1962) has calculated this cost for both primary and secondary school teachers. Secondary teachers on average receive 30 times annual per-capita income in Nigeria, 12 times annual per-capita income in Jamaica, but only twice annual per-capita income in the United States. The average salary paid a primary teacher is 3 times per-capita national income in

Jamaica, 7 times per-capita national income in Nigeria, but less than 1.5 times per-capita national income in the United States. Such figures suggest the high cost of educational expansion, especially in those countries that are striving to make primary education universal.

Even should the advent of new educational technologies ultimately increase the productivity of teachers, remedies for shortfalls in the supply of teachers are difficult to propose if anticipated rates of educational expansion occur. Loan of teachers from developed nations for secondary schools and universities is probably a short-term expedient. Other expedients are being tried. Harris (1963–4) has described one such expedient in Iran where teaching service is substituted for military service to provide teachers, albeit with little pre-service training. All university students in Ethiopia must meet a degree requirement of providing one year of service to rural areas, service which is often performed through teaching. The major solutions must be found in teacher training, however. As few developing nations have adequate pre-service or in-service training programs, it is difficult to see the problem of poor teaching righting itself in the near future. Heavy reliance on women teachers, and provision of teacher training in their regular school programs as practiced in Brazil, may help alleviate the situation.

If problems of teacher recruitment and status are difficult at best, they become even more severe in rural areas. Hey (1961) described the predicament and value conflicts confronting a rural teacher in one underdeveloped enclave, where the teacher was found to stand as an outsider and to espouse different values from those held around him. Similar problems confront the rural teacher in much of the underdeveloped world. Furthermore, the teacher in rural areas enjoys few of the rewards of modernization which appear first in cities. He may also at times be penalized in terms of salary; Davies' survey (1964) revealed differentials in salaries for rural and urban teachers in a number of Latin American countries. Thus the problems of rural education and teacher shortage tend to aggravate each other.

Population Pressure. One final social phenomenon also threatens to aggravate most other educational problems of the emerging nations, including the problem of providing qualified teachers. This is the population explosion. The sharp reduction of infant mortality in most emergent nations has led to a juvenescence of population which has changed the balance between economically productive adults and the school population. Vaizey (1962) points out that the ratio of children to economically productive members of society is 13 or 14 to 10 in developing nations compared to 6 or 7 to 10 in most advanced nations. He concludes that it will therefore be difficult to maintain even existing percentages of the school-age population in school. Tinbergen and Bos (1962) base their projection of manpower needs to staff schools on estimates that between 1958 and 1970 the total population in Africa will rise 24 percent, in Asia 28 percent, and in Latin America 36 percent.

Analyses of Latin American demography reveal additional factors that affect the provision of education. The Latin American Demographic Centre (1962) found that the number of children 5–14 years of age in that region could be expected to rise from 49.5 million in 1960 to 74 million in 1975. As this rate of increase exceeds that of the adult population, there will be yet more children of school age per productive worker than has been the case until now. Within countries, they found, the percentage of youth in the rural population, which is most impoverished, exceeds the percentage in the urban population. Furthermore, Vera (1963) found that it is the least economically and educationally developed countries that have the highest proportions of school-age population. Thus, not only is the economic burden of providing education greater in the developing than in the developed nations, but it is the poorest populations in the underdeveloped world which frequently must provide for the greatest numbers of youth.

EDUCATION AID, PLANNING, AND INNOVATION. Education Aid. Confronted by these problems and characterized by limited resources, emergent nations have not unsurprisingly relied on external aid to education. The need is great. Developing nations require personnel as well as financial assistance to maintain or improve educational systems. Tinbergen and Bos (1962) estimated the personnel requirements for the expansion of secondary and higher education if emergent nations were to achieve a reasonable increase in per-capita income during the decade preceding 1970. They concluded that between 1958 and 1970 the number of secondary students in the underdeveloped world should nearly double, the number of higher education students should double, and the number of the latter in science and technology should nearly treble. This would require an increase of 120,000 university teachers during the next decade, many inevitably coming from advanced countries. Moreover, advanced nations would have to provide between 8,000 and 10,000 "teachers of teachers" to meet needs generated by secondary-school expansion. The report of the Ashby Commission (1960) on Nigerian education reveals the need for teachers in a single country. The Commission found that if 25,000 "imported teacher years" were provided to Nigeria between 1960 and 1970 there would still be a gap before the supply of local graduates could meet the demand for teachers.

The way in which teachers are provided is also important. Vaizey (1962) concludes that sending isolated foreign teachers for short periods has usually proved ineffective and that more effective aid to developing nations is provided through "institution building," in which educational institutions in advanced nations assume responsibility both for training members of an institution in a developing country and for providing interim instructors. Some form of interinstitutional or intersystem relationship prevailed for most of the French and British colonies which have recently attained independence.

In one of the most comprehensive studies of the transplantation of educational institutions, Ashby and Anderson (1966) examined university development in India and Africa. They found that in India an attempt to build universities with a curriculum based on British arts and sciences and modeled after a nineteenth-century British university pattern (in which a central university administered degree examinations) failed to work when transplanted. The failure arose because the Indian examining authorities proved unable to maintain standards, because no provision was made by Britain to assure competent faculty or residential study in colleges, and because traditions of memoriter learning and low university entry points had already been established. The result was that the universities were not only alien to their own culture but unable to maintain academic standards or freedom from political interference. In the later development of higher education in tropical Africa, Britain profited from this earlier experience and employed a formula of *special relationship* between the University of London and residential colonial colleges, by which the parent institution assisted in procuring competent faculty and assured standards by visitations and examinations. The major limitations of this pattern arose from a degree structure too inflexible to meet emerging developmental needs and from failure to provide education in technical fields from the outset. A similar analysis of French educational strategies in Africa by Bolibaugh (1964) has revealed how institutions closely associated in content and organization with the French educational system have served to assimilate the African elite into French culture and progressively alienate it from its own cultural roots.

Recently American universities have provided considerable technical assistance to education in developing nations, often with the hope of introducing innovations. Surveying the technical assistance activities of American universities, Weidner (1962) found that about one-half of the programs undertaken have as one original goal the building of an institution, and that another one-quarter of the programs developed this objective later. These efforts were found to have met with varying success in creating institutions, and even where institutions have been created their recency precluded evaluation of their success in introducing lasting change. Obvious gaps in our knowledge of the factors involved has led to growing interest in studying the process of institution building. Esman and Blaise (1966) have developed a broad research model designed to build up a body of systematic knowledge on the process of developing innovative institutions. A number of studies employing this model are in progress.

In addition to establishing institutions, advanced nations have offered emergent countries new educational techniques. Unfortunately, almost no empirical research has been done on diffusion of educational innovations within developing nations and here experience from advanced nations may prove irrelevant. It was partly to codify experience and meet this problem that Beeby (1966) proposed his theory of stages through which all elementary education systems must pass, advancing the hypothesis that innovations derived from ends and technologies developed in countries at one stage of educational development are unlikely to be successfully transplanted to countries at other stages. As the general education and training of teachers appear the main factors in determining the stage of education in a given country, he suggests that new techniques which usually presuppose considerable education and training are unlikely to be adopted successfully in emergent countries.

Another form of assistance is provided when universities in advanced nations offer places to students from abroad. Qualitatively, as both Coleman (1965) and Smith (1964) have stressed, the growing eclecticism of this overseas experience provides returnees with alternative viewpoints which may prove developmental in that they make innovation more likely. Quantitatively the contribution of overseas education in many emergent countries is not great. Vaizey (1962) reported that only two percent of higher-education students of emergent nations were studying in European member states of the Organization for Economic Cooperation and Development. Smith (1964) has studied the extent and limitations of this form of assistance, especially as provided by the United States. He notes that although students from developing nations constitute an increasing proportion of foreign students in America and although their problems while here have been studied extensively, little evidence exists as to the transferability of their learning, their motivation to put learning into practice, or the extent to which they can in fact put it into practice at strategic points. He concludes, however, that it is obstacles to utilizing knowledge upon returning to the home country which chiefly limit the effectiveness of foreign study. The Useems (1955) found that less than ten percent of the Indian students returning to Bombay State from education overseas were able to put skills in their specialized field of training to work full time. They found a major limiting factor was that the job market was so inefficient it failed to allocate trained people already on hand to jobs crying for them. This problem is, of course, not limited to foreign-trained students. Fischer (1963) in a study of a single Indian university found that 85 percent of its graduates had entered government service, nearly half in fields in which they had not received training.

Educational Planning. Increasingly, external and international aid has been tied to educational planning, and one important form of external aid is that given in carrying out the planning process itself. The purpose of educational planning is to help a nation decide more rationally how it can employ available resources to provide education in the amount, type, and quality required to achieve national goals. Ministers of Education, meeting under the auspices of UNESCO at Karachi, Pakistan, stressed the need to establish planning units for education and to relate educational planning to overall plans for social and economic development.

Sound planning inevitably rests upon a solid knowledge base and such agendas for needed research as those of Bowman and Anderson (1962) and the International Institute for Educational Planning (1965) reveal the complexity of the problems involved. Units such as the International Institute for Educational Planning have been established to provide aid for planners, and documents such as *Educational Planning: a Bibliography* published by the Institute (1964) reveal a burgeoning literature of research, theory, and plans.

Despite the fact that educational planning in most developing countries is in its infancy, the International Institute for Educational Planning has supported a series of case studies that illuminate major problems confronting the planner and provisionally identify many of the factors which contribute to successful planning. The problems identified have included the integration of educational and economic planning, the financing of educational development, teacher supply and demand, effects of expansion on educational quality, the relation between planning and external aid, and the administration of planning. Studies by Skorov (1966), Hunter (1966a) and Chesswas (1966) cited in this article have emanated from this research effort. Such studies have cumulatively pointed to the importance of a central planning unit in which educational planning is directly related to broader planning for social and economic development, and especially to provision of needed manpower; the importance of basing planning on a fundamental government policy decision gearing education directly to development; the need for detailed statistical information; the importance of costing proposals when reaching policy decisions; and the desirability of entertaining a wide range of considerations, such as aspiration levels and problems of unemployment, within the scope of planning. Chesswas (1966) on the basis of an analysis of educational planning in Uganda concludes that the critical factors in the apparent success of planning in that country have been the basic decision to place control of all stages of planning and development in the hands of one unit, the close relations established between that unit and research organizations, and the availability to planners of relevant statistical data. It is, however, only with the passage of time that it will be possible to assess the long-range effectiveness of plans or determine more precisely under what circumstances plans are most likely to be translated from paper to program.

Major Educational Innovations. Since the formal education system in almost no developing country is indigenous but rather is borrowed from or remodeled to conform to that in the Western world, such systems represent one form of educational aid themselves. Although Western-type schools have proved to be one of the most easily exported and one of the most valuable of Western institutions to emerging nations, failure of these schools to achieve all the goals or to conform to strong ideological commitments of some developing nations has led to modifications or concurrent educational experiments departing markedly from Western patterns. Israel, faced with unusual problems, has provided some of the best illustrations of nonconventional types of education. Bentwich (1965) has described Kibbutzim schools which attempt to inculcate an entire way of life, including productive labor, through education. Rossillion (1966b) has studied the *Nahal*, the Israeli option of using economic and social work in lieu of defense service. In a situation in which the military service provided the essential organizational framework and in which organizational aims were tied closely to national goals, he found that it has been possible to train and settle permanently (as measured by three years continuous settlement) over 40 percent of the youth who entered the service after participating in previous youth movements. This service, which combines educational and production needs, has resulted in the founding of over 25 agricultural settlements.

Programs elsewhere in the developing nations, often undertaken with Israeli assistance, similarly attempt to combine production, national goals, and education. Most of these are of such recent origin that assessment of their results is impossible. Bourgoignie (1964) has examined a wide variety of comparable programs in Africa, each of which involves training and production. He concludes that some such formula offers the greatest hope for providing effective education at low cost to the nation. Similar projects have been studied descriptively with preliminary assessments of their usefulness by Mouly (1966) in the Central African Republic, Rossillion (1966a) in Mali, and Costa (1966) in Dahomey. Thus far it is clear that most such schemes, whether organized as "pioneer youth," "civic service," or "farm settlements," have proved too expensive to serve as prototypes for major new departures in education in less sophisticated or ideologically committed nations.

An even sharper break with the past has developed at a different educational level in Communist China. A study by Hsü (1965) of the rapid changes in higher education which accompanied the "great leap forward" shows this to have been an attempt to reshape a higher-education system so as to create industrialization rather than merely to meet needs growing out of industrialization. He reports evidence indicating that in keeping with this goal it has been possible to reverse a traditional bias for arts and the social sciences to the point where over 40 percent of university students are enrolled in engineering while enrollment in law and political science has fallen to less than 2 percent. Analysis of available data by Hsü (1965), Orleans (1961) and Hu (1964) all indicates that in this process a deliberate decision was made to abandon existing standards and concepts of university level education in order to achieve national goals. Hundreds of "Red and Expert" universities came into being, coupling education and production by requiring all university students to engage in productive enterprise. In many cases factories and colleges were merged, either by attaching "colleges" to factories or by creating production units at existing institutions of higher learning. Both Hu (1964) and Hsü (1965) report that following the extensive quantitative breakthrough in the early years, an attempt has been made to reintroduce qualitative standards through greater emphasis on expertness than upon political activity. This clearly represents the most extreme departure from Western educational patterns in the direction of combining education, production, and national service. In both Israel and Communist China such attempts have been possible largely because of a strong and well-developed ideological commitment, sustained in part by an effective organizational framework provided by state, community, or party. It is not clear that these preconditions exist in much of the developing world elsewhere.

FIELD CLARIFICATION. There remains the question as to whether or not education in the developing nations will define itself as a reasonably cohesive field of educational research. The developing nations are far from homogeneous: India is not Botswana; nor is Chile Algeria. Within Asia alone primary education in Nationalist China reaches more than 95 percent of the youngsters and in Afghanistan falls short of 10 percent; the divergencies are equally great in Africa. Despite such far-reaching differences, Peshkin (1964) has argued, educational development in these nations reveals four common dimensions: (1) an overriding desire for reform; (2) a commitment to *planning* as the means of achieving reform; (3) common problems (such as those described above) in carrying out reform; and (4) a reliance on foreign or international assistance. The summary of research above has perhaps suggested additional concerns or emphases which developing nations share and in terms of which experiences or research in one nation may be fruitfully applied elsewhere.

There is undoubtedly need for greater attention to micro-studies (which delimit educational problems and control the number of variables operating) if experience is to be transferable. Much current literature consists of sweeping generalizations and exhortations that lack universal validity even though they are based on field experience in one or more developing regions.

There is a sense in which the field is also subsumed under other research fields. Most or all educational problems which occur in advanced nations occur (often with increased severity) in poverty-stricken countries. It is clear also that the line between advanced and developing nations must be a shadow line, always on the move. The dearth of coherent and rigorous empirical studies is not solely the result of the difficulty of field research (where developing nations either do not have data, or alter data, or impose restrictions on their use), but is also the result of inadequate theory to guide research. Educational theories derived largely from manpower analysis such as that of Harbison (1962) have dominated the field during its early years. It remains to be seen whether more comprehensive theory, which takes greater account of other than purely economic factors in development, will refocus research. The selections compiled by Hanson and Brembeck (1966) and strategy proposals such as those of Curle (1963) and Beeby (1966) suggest that this may prove to be the case.

As the gap between advanced nations and most developing nations is increasing when measured by the usual standards of material well-being, it is likely that education in low-income countries will continue to fall short of expectations and that problems confronting their educational systems will increase commensurately. There is growing recognition that many educational models and generalizations based on experience or research within advanced nations are not directly applicable to problems arising in the social, economic, and educational settings which characterize emerging countries. As advanced nations are likely to continue assisting emerging countries in seeking solutions to the latter's educational problems, interest in and research on the unique dimensions of these problems can be expected to increase rather than diminish. The result should be a clearer definition of the field.

John W. Hanson
Michigan State University

References

Abernethy, David, and Coombe, Trevor. "Education and Politics in Developing Countries." *Harvard Ed R* 35:287–302; 1965.

Adams, Don. "The Study of Education and Social Development." *Compar Ed R* 9:258–81; 1965.

Anderson, C. Arnold. "Economic Development and Post-Primary Education." In Piper, Don C., and Cole, Taylor. (Eds.) *Post-primary Education and Political and Economic Development.* Duke U Press, 1964. p. 3–26.

Ashby, Eric, and Anderson, Mary. *Universities: British, Indian, and African.* Harvard U Press, 1966. 558p.

Ashby Commission (Commission on Post-school Certificate and Higher Education, Nigeria). *Investment in Education.* Lagos: Federal Ministry of Education, 1960. 140p.

Baldwin, George B. "Iran's Experience with Manpower Planning: Concepts, Techniques, and Lessons." In Harbison, Frederick H., and Myers, Charles A. (Eds.) *Manpower and Education.* McGraw-Hill, 1965. p. 140–72.

Balogh, Thomas. "The Problem of Education in Africa." *Centennial R* 6:526–52; 1962.

Balogh, Thomas. "The Economics of Educational Planning: Sense and Nonsense." *Compar Ed* (Oxford) 1:5–17; 1964.

Barraclough, Solon. *Agrarian Structure and Education in Latin America.* UNESCO, 1962.

Beeby, C. E. *The Quality of Education in Developing Countries.* Harvard U Press, 1966. 139p.

Bentwich, Joseph S. *Education in Israel.* Jewish Pub Soc of Am, 1965. 204p.

Blaug, M. *The Role of Education in Enlarging the Exchange Economy in Middle Africa: The English Speaking Countries.* UNESCO, 1964. 102p.

Blitz, Rudolph C. "The Role of High-level Manpower in the Economic Development of Chile." In Harbison, Frederick, and Myers, Charles A. (Eds.) *Manpower and Education: Country Studies in Economic Development.* McGraw-Hill, 1965. p. 73–107.

Bolibaugh, Jerry B. *French Educational Strategies for Sub-Saharan Africa: Their Intent, Derivation, and Development.* Stanford U Compar Ed Center, 1964. 111p.

Bourgoignie, Georges-Edouard. *Jeune Afrique Mobilisable.* Editions Universitaires, 1964. 213p.

Bowles, Frank. "Senegal." In Bowles, Frank. (Ed.) *Access to Higher Education.* Vol. 2. UNESCO, 1965. p. 337–47.

Bowman, Mary Jean, and Anderson, C. Arnold. "The Role of Education in Development." In *Development of the Emerging Countries: An Agenda for Research.* Brookings Institution, 1962. p. 153–80.

Bowman, Mary Jean, and Anderson, C. Arnold. "Concerning the Role of Education in Development." In Geertz, Clifford. (Ed.) *Old Societies and New States: The Quest for Modernity in Asia and Africa.* Free, 1963. p. 247–79.

Bradfield, Richard. "The Role of Educated People in Agricultural Development." In Moseman, Albert H. (Ed.) *Agricultural Sciences for the Developing Nations.* AAAS, 1964. p. 95–113.

Callaway, Archibald. "School Leavers and the Developing Economy of Nigeria." In Tilman, Robert O., and Cole, Taylor. (Eds.) *The Nigerian Political Scene.* Duke U Press, 1962. p. 220–38.

Capener, Harold R. "The Rural People in Developing Countries: Their Attitudes and Levels of Education." In Moseman, Albert H. (Ed.) *Agricultural Sciences for the Developing Nations.* AAAS, 1964. p. 115–22.

Cash, Webster C. "A Critique of Manpower Planning and Educational Change in Africa." *Econ Develop and Cultural Change* 14:33–47; 1965.

Chesswas, J. D. *Educational Planning and Development in Uganda.* UNESCO, 1966. 97p.

Coleman, James S. (Ed.) *Education and Political Development.* Princeton U Press, 1965. 620p.

Costa, E. "Back to the Land: The Campaign Against Unemployment in Dahomey." *Int Labour R* 93:29–49; 1966.

Curle, Adam. *Educational Strategy for Developing Societies.* Tavistock, 1963. 180p.

Curle, Adam. "Education, Politics, and Development." *Compar Ed R* 7:108–38; 1964(*a*).

Curle, Adam. *World Campaign for Universal Literacy: Comment and Proposal.* Harvard Graduate School of Education, 1964(*b*). 40p.

Davies, Margarita. *Survey of the Status of the Teaching Profession in the Americas.* World Confederation of Organizations of the Teaching Profession, 1964. 98p.

Deblé, Isabelle. "Les Rendements Scolaires dans les Pays d'Afrique d'Expression Française." In *Etudes Tiers Monde 1964.* Presses Universitaires de France, 1964. p. 53–103.

Dobyns, Henry F. "The Strategic Importance of Enlightenment and Skill for Power." *Am Behavioral Sci* 8:2–27; 1965.

Dumont, René. "Le Développement Agricole Specialement Tropical Exige un Enseignement Totalement Repensé." *Tiers-Monde* 5:13–38; 1964.

Dumont, René. *False Start in Africa.* Praeger, 1966. 320p.

Economist Intelligence Unit (London). *Secondary Technical and Vocational Education in Underdeveloped Countries.* UNESCO, 1959. 34p.

Economist Intelligence Unit (London). *Economic and Social Returns to be Derived from Investment in Education.* UNESCO, 1962.

Esman, Milton J., and Blaise, Hans C. *Institution Building Research: The Guiding Concepts.* U Pittsburgh, 1966. 19p.

Fischer, Joseph. "The University Student in South and South-East Asia." *Minerva* 2:39–53; 1963.

Food and Agriculture Organization. *Rural Education.* UNESCO, 1962.

Foster, Donald M. *Education as an Instrument of National Policy and Economic Development in the Republic of China.* Stanford U Comparative Education Center, 1963. 103p.

Foster, Philip J. "Ethnicity and the Schools in Ghana." *Compar Ed R* 6:127–35; 1962.

Foster, Philip J. *Education and Social Change in Ghana.* Routledge, 1963. 322p.

Foster, Philip J. "Secondary School Leavers in Ghana: Expectations and Reality." *Harvard Ed R* 34:537–58; 1964(*a*).

Foster, Philip J. "Status, Power and Education in a Traditional Community." *Sch R* 72:158–80; 1964(*b*).

Foster, Philip J. "The Vocational School Fallacy in Development Planning." In Anderson, C. Arnold, and Bowman, Mary Jean. (Eds.) *Education and Economic Development.* Aldine, 1965. p. 142–66.

Franklin, E. W. *Survey of the Status of the Teaching Profession in Asia.* World Confederation of Organizations of the Teaching Professions, 1963. 149p.

Freeman, Harold. *The Role of Agricultural Education in the Economic Development of Thailand.* Stanford U Comparative Education Center, 1964. 158p.

Hansen, W. Lee. "Human Capital Requirements for Educational Expansion: Teacher Shortages and Teacher Supply." In Anderson, C. Arnold, and Bowman, Mary Jean. (Eds.) *Education and Economic Development.* Aldine, 1965. p. 63–87.

Hanson, John W., and Brembeck, Cole S. (Eds.) *Education and the Development of Nations.* Holt, 1966. 529p.

Harbison, Frederick H. "The Strategy of Human Resource Development in Modernizing Economies." In *Policy Conference on Economic Growth and Investment in Education.* Vol. 3. Organization for Economic Co-operation and Development, 1962. p. 9–33.

Harbison, Frederick H., and Myers, Charles A. *Edu-*

cation, *Manpower and Economic Growth*. McGraw-Hill, 1964. 229p.

Harbison, Frederick H., and Myers, Charles A. (Eds.) *Manpower and Education: Country Studies in Economic Development*. McGraw-Hill, 1965. 343p.

Harris, Ben M. "Iran's Gamble to Conquer Illiteracy." *Int R Ed* 9:430; 1963–64.

Havighurst, Robert J., and Moreira, J. Roberto. *Society and Education in Brazil*. U Pittsburgh Press, 1965. 263p.

Hey, P. D. "The Rural Zulu Teacher in Natal." *Comp Ed R* 5:54–8; 1961.

Holmberg, Allan R. "The Changing Values and Institutions of Vicos in the Context of National Development." *Am Behavioral Sci* 8:3–8; 1965.

Holmberg, Allan R., and Dobyns, Henry F. "The Process of Accelerating Community Change." *Hum Organization* 21:107–9; 1962.

Hoselitz, Bert F. "Investment in Education and Its Political Impact." In Coleman, James S. (Ed.) *Education and Political Development*. Princeton U Press, 1965. p. 541–65.

Hsü, Immanuel C. Y. "The Impact of Industrialization on Higher Education in Communist China." In Harbison, Frederick H., and Myers, Charles A. (Eds.) *Manpower and Education*. McGraw-Hill, 1965. p. 202–31.

Hu, Chang-Tu. "Recent Trends in Chinese Education." *Int R Ed* 10:12–9; 1964.

Hunter, Guy M. *Education for a Developing Region: A Study in East Africa*. Allen and Unwin, 1963. 119p.

Hunter, Guy M. "Issues in Manpower Policy: Some Contrasts from East Africa and Southeast Asia." In Harbison, Frederick H., and Myers, Charles A. (Eds.) *Manpower and Education*. McGraw-Hill, 1965. p. 325–43.

Hunter, Guy M. *Manpower, Employment and Education in the Rural Economy of Tanzania*. UNESCO, 1966(*a*). 40p.

Hunter, Guy M. *South-East Asia: Race, Culture and Nation*. Oxford U Press, 1966(*b*). 190p.

International Institute for Educational Planning. *Educational Planning: A Bibliography*. The Institute, 1964. 131p.

International Institute for Educational Planning. *An Inventory of Major Research Needs*. The Institute, 1965. 53p.

Jones, S. H. M. *Survey of the Status of the Teaching Profession in Africa*. World Confederation of Organizations of the Teaching Profession, 1963. 148p.

Kerr, Malcolm H. "Egypt." In Coleman, James S. (Ed.) *Education and Political Development*. Princeton U Press, 1965. p. 169–94.

Khoi, Le Thanh. *Le Role de l'Education dans le Passage de l'Economie de Subsistance à l'Economie De Marché: l'Afrique Tropicale d'Expression Française*. Institut d'Etude du Développement Economique et Social, 1964. 102p.

Laska, John A. "The Stages of Educational Development," *Compar Ed R* 8:251–75; 1964.

Latin American Demographic Centre. *A Demographic Analysis of the Educational Situation in Latin America*. UNESCO, 1962.

Lerner, Daniel. *The Passing of Traditional Society: Modernizing the Middle East*. Free, 1958. 466p.

Lewis, W. Arthur. "Priorities For Educational Expansion." In *Policy Conference on Economic Growth and Investment in Education, Washington, October 16–20, 1961*. Vol. 3. Organisation for Economic Co-operation and Development, 1962. p. 35–49.

Lipset, Seymour Martin. "University Students and Politics in Underdeveloped Countries." *Minerva* 3:15–56; 1964.

Liu, Bangnee Alfred. *Estimating Future School Enrollments in Developing Countries: A Manual of Methodology*. UNESCO, 1966. 156p.

Lucas, Gerard. *Formal Education in the Congo-Brazzaville: A Study of Educational Policy and Practice*. Stanford U Comparative Education Center, 1964. 287p.

Maleche, A. J. "Wastage among School Leavers in West Nile, 1959 and 1960." In *Papers of the East African Institute of Social Research*. The Institute (Kampala), 1962. 12p.

Matthews, Roderic D., and Matta, Akrawi. *Education in the Arab Countries of the Near East*. ACE, 1949. 576p.

McClelland, David. *The Achieving Society*. Van Nostrand, 1961. 512p.

McQueen, Albert J. "Aspirations and Problems of Nigerian School Leavers." *Bul Inter-African Lab Institute* 12:35–51; 1965.

Meaders, O. Donald. *Educational and Occupational Attainments of Taiwan Vocational Agriculture Graduates*. Michigan State U Institute for International Studies, 1966. 114p.

Moreira, J. Roberto. "Education and Development in Latin America." In de Vries, Egbert, and Echavarria, Jose Medina. (Eds.) *Social Aspects of Economic Development in Latin America*. Vol 1. UNESCO, 1963. p. 304–44.

Mosher, Arthur T. *Getting Agriculture Moving*. Praeger, 1966. 190p.

Mouly, J. "The Young Pioneers Movement in the Central African Republic." *Int Labour R* 93:19–28; 1966.

Mukherjee, K. C. "Primary and Mass Education in India." In Bereday, George Z. F., and Lauwerys, Joseph A. (Eds.) *The Education Explosion: The World Yearbook of Education, 1965*. Harcourt, 1965. p. 175–85.

Myers, Charles Nash. *Education and National Development in Mexico*. Princeton U Press, 1965. 147p.

O'Connell, James. "The Concept of Modernization." *So. Atlantic Q* 64:549–64; 1965.

Orleans, Leo A. *Professional Manpower and Education in Communist China*. GPO, 1961. 260p.

Peshkin, Alan. "Education, the Muslim Elite, and the Creation of Pakistan." *Compar Ed R* 6:152–9; 1962.

Peshkin, Alan. "Education in the Developing Nations: Dimensions of Change." *Compar Ed R* 10:53–66; 1964.

Proust, Jacques. "Essai d'Analyse des Mouvements d'Effectifs dans l'Enseignement du Premier Degré au Gabon." In *Etudes Tiers Monde 1964*. Presses Universitaires de France, 1964. p. 107–62.

Rado, E. R. "Manpower, Education and Economic Growth." *J Mod African Stud* 4:83–93; 1966.

Rado, E. R., and Jolly, A. R. "The Demand for Manpower—an East African Case Study." *J Develop Stud* 1:226–50; 1965.

Rahman, A. F. M. K. "Educational Developments in Asia." *Int Ed* 8:257–75; 1963.

Rashid, M. "Absorption of the Educated." In Robinson, E.A.G., and Vaizey, J. E. (Eds.) *The Economics of Education: Proceedings of a Conference Held by the International Economic Association*. St. Martins Press, 1966. p. 261–75.

Read, Margaret. "The Contribution of Social Anthropologists to Educational Problems in Underdeveloped Countries." *Fundamental and Adult Ed* 7: 74–9, 98–103; 1955.

Rossillion, C. "Civic Service and Community Works in Mali." *Int Labour R* 93:50–65; 1966(a).

Rossillion, C. "Economic and Social Work for Young People During Defence Service: The Israeli Formula." *Int Labour R* 93:66–79; 1966(b).

Ruscoe, Gordon C. *Dysfunctionality in Jamaican Education*. U Michigan School of Education, 1963. 144p.

Russett, Bruce M., and others. *World Handbook of Political and Social Indicators*. Yale U Press, 1964. 373p.

Schultz, Theodore W. "Investment in Human Capital in Poor Countries." In Zook, Paul D. (Ed.) *Foreign Trade and Human Capital*. Southern Methodist U Press, 1962. p. 3–15.

Schultz, Theodore W. *The Economic Value of Education*. Columbia U Press, 1963. 92p.

Schultz, Theodore W. *Transforming Traditional Agriculture*. Yale U Press, 1964. 212p.

Shils, Edward. *The Intellectual between Tradition and Modernity: the Indian Situation*. Mouton, 1961. p. 9–120.

Skorov, George. *Integration of Educational and Economic Planning in Tanzania*. UNESCO, 1966. 78p.

Smith, M. Brewster. "Foreign vs. Indigenous Education." In Piper, Don C., and Cole, Taylor. (Eds.) *Post-primary Education and Political and Economic Development*. Duke U Press, 1964. p. 48–74.

Sutton, Francis X. "Education and the Making of Modern Nations." In Coleman, James S. (Ed.) *Education and Political Development*. Princeton U Press, 1965. p. 51–74.

Tinbergen, J., and Bos, H. C. "The Global Demand for Higher and Secondary Education in the Underdeveloped Countries in the Next Decade." In *Policy Conference on Economic Growth and Investment in Education, Washington 16th-20th October, 1961*. Vol. 3. Organisation for Economic Co-operation and Development, 1962. p. 71–80.

UNESCO. *The Economic Implications of the Plan of Educational Development in Asia*. UNESCO, 1962. 87p.

UNESCO. *Access of Girls and Women to Education in Rural Areas: A Comparative Study*. UNESCO, 1964(a). 62p.

UNESCO. *Evidence Emerging from the Implementation of the Addis Ababa Plan*. UNESCO, 1964(b). 22p.

UNESCO. *Statistics of Illiteracy*. UNESCO, 1965. 122p.

UNESCO and others. *The Demographic, Economic, Social and Educational Situation in Latin America*. UNESCO, 1962. 119p.

Useem, John, and Useem, Ruth H. *The Western Educated Man in India: A Study of His Social Roles and Influence*. Dryden, 1955. 237p.

Vaizey, John. "Some of the Main Issues in the Strategy of Educational Supply." In *Policy Conference on Economic Growth and Investment in Education, Washington 16th-20th October 1961*. Vol. 3. Organisation for Economic Co-operation and Development, 1962. p. 51–69.

Van der Kroef, Justus M. "Asian Education and Unemployment: The Continuing Crisis." *Compar Ed R* 7:173–80; 1963.

Vera, Oscar. "The Educational Situation and Requirements in Latin America." In de Vries, Egbert, and Echavarria, Jose Medina. (Eds.) *Social Aspects of Economic Development in Latin America*. Vol. 1. UNESCO, 1963. p. 279–307.

Weidner, Edward W. *The World Role of Universities*. McGraw-Hill, 1962. 366p.

Wharton, Clifton R., Jr. "Education and Agricultural Growth: The Role of Education in Early-Stage Agriculture." In Anderson, C. Arnold, and Bowman, Mary Jean. (Eds.) *Education and Economic Development*. Aldine, 1965. p. 202–28.

White, Harry Robert. *Possible Effects of Selected Educational Policies and Programs on Income Size and Distribution in the Industrial Sector of Peru*. Stanford U Press, 1964. 120p.

Williams, T. David. "Wastage Rates and Teacher Quality in Guatemalan Primary Schools." *Compar Ed R* 9:46–52; 1965.

EDUCATION OF WOMEN

In a preface to the proceedings of the third University of California symposium on man and civilization, Saunders (1963) recognized three advocates of the doctrine of feminism, i.e., the Mohammedan physician and philosopher Averroës (1126–1198), the publicist and reformer Petrus de Bosco (c. 1230–1341), and the Franciscan friar William of Ockham (died c. 1340). These and other learned men urged the emancipation of women, commending their aptitudes in war, their potential for governance of the state, and their competence as missionaries trained in the professions. Throughout the Middle Ages, there was correspondingly strong support of these views. Middle-class women with business acumen took an active part in the mercantile life of cities, and women of aristocratic birth were free to contribute to the literature of the time as well as to extend their patronage to the arts.

Then occurred a turn of events which changed the status of women. Inquisitors of the fifteenth and sixteenth centuries loosed a persecutory mania upon the Western world. Women were shackled by threat of pillory, burnings at the stake, and other recriminations for witchcraft. Suspicion outran scientific knowledge and fact, and physiological and psychological phenomena were displaced by superstition. In an era devoid of a holistic conception of human problems, woman fell from her pedestal. It was not until four centuries after the fall that she began her ascendancy, winning acceptance anew as a self-determined and independent individual.

WOMEN IN AMERICA. In America, perhaps the greatest impetus for viewing the role of woman in relation to her environment came from the work of the Commission on the Status of Women, established by President John F. Kennedy in 1961, and chaired by Mrs. Eleanor Roosevelt. Edited by Mead and Kaplan (1965), the Report of the Commission begins with an invitation to action, and thereafter calls attention to the education and counseling of women, home and community, employment, labor standards, employment security, and legal and political rights.

Although recognizing that more women are obtaining a better education in America today than at any other time or place in history, the Report points up the need for intensive and continuing work upon (1) motivating the culturally deprived, (2) providing counseling and guidance for girls and women of all ages and circumstances, and (3) encouraging part-time study arrangements.

The Commission's invitation to action received acceptance in some 39 states with the naming of Governors' Commissions on the Status of Women. Some citations of activities from the publication *Women's Education* show televised programs which feature suggestions for counseling women (Wisconsin), the distribution of summary reports of committees (Colorado), a conference for women in the professions (Florida), and legislative implementation of the commission's recommendations (Michigan).

As for wider regional activity, the Midwest Pilot Conference (1965) and the Middle Atlantic Pilot Conference (1965) reiterate problems encountered in counseling girls and women. Reports of both conferences point to an insufficiency of advisory personnel and a paucity of materials describing woman's status and her opportunities for education and employment. Counselors need education concerning the differences and similarities between the sexes in respect to life patterns, role expectations, native abilities, and interests. Overall, there is too little utilization of biographies, films, and interviews for effecting desirable role models.

Describing America as a society in transition, the Report of the Commission on the Status of Women (Mead & Kaplan, 1965) affirms the fact that the United States has had a last fling at high reproductivity and high employment. The issues to be faced are those of world stability, the so-called population explosion, and nuclear warfare. As American society moves from a traditional style of family life devoted to mating and breeding to other life patterns, the problems facing women will be as great as those experienced in the history of Europe. There is indisputable evidence that America needs skilled womanpower. In the social climate under construction, women must be given the choice of remaining in the home or of accepting responsibilities outside, thus ensuring that each life pattern be both feasible and dignified.

Major Issues. Assessing technological advances from the era of the steam engine to that of automation, Baker (1964) comments that the lives of women have been uprooted and redirected. Women, now constituting more than a third of the labor force, were accepted initially to reduce labor costs. The history of education for American women is a regrettable example of the weight of tradition and prejudice emphasizing differences in sex rather than experience, training, and ability. Despite advances in science and technology, the work of women is bound to be interrupted, with child-bearing remaining their lot. Written in advance of the rather widespread acceptance of oral contraception ("the pill"), this statement can be modified to account for "planned interruptions" of work.

A later seminar in the series devoted to man and civilization at the University of California directs attention to the population increase and the responsibility of women in the biological avalanche. Mueller (1966) adjudges the educational task as one of "massive attack" in effecting understandings about the role of well-educated women for America's life and culture. She recommends the naming of an expert on educational needs of women for each 1,000 women students on a campus. The major assignment of this specialist would be to induct teachers and administrators into the study of woman as an individual—her intellectual, physical, glandular, motivational, and sexual makeup. The massive attack is postulated upon the assumption—applauded but not adequately anticipated—that there will be growing numbers of women students in higher education.

WOMEN ENROLLED IN COLLEGE. Enrollment data compiled by Simon and Grant (1966) showed 2,151,722 women in institutions of higher learning in the Fall of 1965, in comparison with a figure of 3,374,603 men enrollees. The projected figure for Fall 1966 showed 200,000 additional women and approximately 300,000 additional men. The total number of bachelor's and first professional degrees granted to women rose from 36 percent of the total granted in 1955–56 to 41 percent in 1965–66. This figure is expected to increase to 44 percent in 1975–76.

At the graduate level, the proportion of master's degrees granted to women dropped from 34 percent of the total in 1955–56 to 32 percent in 1965–66 (Simon and Fullam, 1966). A further drop is expected in 1975–76 to bring the figure to 30 percent.

The proportion of doctoral degrees granted to women stood at 10 percent in 1955–56 and at 11 percent in 1965–66. This figure is expected to remain at about 11 percent to 1975–76.

Studies of Simon and Fullam (1966) show an increase in the percentage of women in first-time enrollment from 38 percent in 1955 to 43 percent in 1965, with an expected first-time degree-credit enrollment of 46 percent in 1975. Women represented 28 percent of all graduate enrollment in 1955, and 30 percent in 1965; 31 percent is projected for 1975.

Ward (1965) points to the female freshman enrollment figure as rising from 245,000 in 1954 to 520,000 in 1965, an increase of 110 percent, while the parallel figure for freshmen men was only 82 percent. In the opinion of some specialists these trends are likely to continue until the total number of women in college equals that of men, perhaps by 1980.

College enrollment figures must be viewed in reference to student retention as well as to non-college attendance. Heist (1962) states that less than 20 percent of women in the 18–24-year age group are enrolled in college. Of those who enter, between 30 and 50 percent have withdrawn by the end of the second year. College withdrawals come from all ability levels. With measured characteristics and values and attitudes of women supportive of their completion of undergraduate and professional education in the same ratio as men, the investigator questions the congeniality of the environment provided for college women. Regrettably, only a small fraction of the most intelligent women obtain the doctorate.

Flanagan and Cooley (1965), in a follow-up of 440,000 high school students tested in 1960, report that 23 percent of the students who entered college were no longer enrolled in 1962. The percentages of withdrawal for men and women were approximately even. The explanation most often given by men was "difficulties in financing education," while the most frequent reason of women was "marriage."

Matthews (1960) observes that from ages of about 11 through 14, girls demonstrate a pseudo-career drive, binding the fantasy wish for marriage and motherhood before its actualization in society. Thereafter, in the period from age 14 through 20, young women demonstrate their inclination to accept the marriage goal. The attractiveness of the goal of intellectual pursuit for the freshman woman in college is reduced by the anticipation of marriage. The investigator raises questions about the kind of education for women which will increase the holding power of college and university.

In an attempt to assess characteristics of women's college students, Rowe (1964) applied the Activities Index, College Characteristics Index, and the College and University Environment Scales. Findings for three women's colleges in the South indicated that there was little sign of a practical, vocational, or preprofessional orientation. Emphasis instead was placed upon achievement in the humanities, social sciences, and arts. Four women's colleges in the Northeast presented a different picture, stressing more intellectual-humanistic-aesthetic characteristics as well as greater interest in the natural sciences. The investigator recommends that a portion of the effort devoted to predicting performance of freshmen women from a combination of test scores and background characteristics be devoted to research on differing demands made upon students by the colleges, i.e., the climate or environment.

Academic personnel from a variety of disciplines have contributed other ideas concerning the congeniality of the campus to the needs of women. Newcomer (1959) comments that in coeducational institutions a great preponderance of men or women enrolled in a particular subject will keep members of the minority sex from electing subjects that genuinely interest them. The minority sex will be intimidated by the majority or will conclude that the studies popularly chosen by the majority are inappropriate to their sex. Heist (1962) observes that the young woman presents greater potential for gaining from liberal arts education than does the man because of her psychological orientation for constructive role-assumption in the community. Tiedeman (1959) believes that women's creative intellectual contributions may well be in the behavioral sciences rather than the physical sciences. Ward (1965) points out that women are less interested now than they were a few generations ago in preparing for traditionally feminine professions as is evidenced by the shortage of social workers and nurses. Irish (1962) writes of the important role assumed by women in the formulation of society's political and social attitudes and urges an education to assist women in sound decision making. In assessing professional womanpower as a resource Parrish (1961) states that college attendance has been too much based on individual need-fulfillment. Although recognition of the right of individuals to develop personally is important, other needs which involve the community must be recognized; i.e., economic growth which proceeds on the basis of innovation and discovery of creative minds, and national security which places value on talent and productivity of persons.

In a study of students at Sarah Lawrence College Murphy and Raushenbush (1960) call attention to the fact that education creates in women needs they would not evidence otherwise. Women's education, its utility and viability, has been given careful treatment in the writings of Mueller (1954), Kamarovsky (1953), and more recently in the compilation edited by Dennis (1962). Spirited debate continues to be waged on the question of coeducation for women or their separate education. The report of Merry (1965) covering developmental planning in nine women's colleges argues for their unique position in planning an educational program revelant to the needs of women. Freedom to innovate and experiment is believed to permit this education to direct itself to the realities of women's lives. From the time of its establishment, the curriculum of Stephens College has been based on the day-to-day activities of women as recorded by them in diaries. General education, individualized instruction, out-of-class activities, religious emphasis, advising, counseling, research and experimentation—

all these have characterized the Stephens College program (Mayhew, 1962) in its evolvement. Yet, as Raushenbush (1961) has pointed out, women's colleges were created "out of the rib of men's colleges" and the business of education for women remains, for the most part, unfinished.

Women and Role Relationships. Viewing the prospects that women face as they proceed into college and university work, Reisman (1965) finds a shift in American academic life toward a "male" mode of performance. The insistence of many leading institutions on college as preparation for graduate work, as opposed to pursuing studies for their personal enrichment or intellectual pleasure, is evident. Women students react by concluding they lack ability in certain fields. In actuality their shortcoming lies only in the manner in which they structure their thinking about the universe men have defined. Freedman (1965) has studied the attitudes of 49 Vassar seniors in progressive interviewing from their enrollment as freshmen. Careers, marriage, and the ideal position of women in society were discussed. College women may be preparing for a future in which conventional work assumes less importance than now, with leisure-time activities and relationships among people having increased importance. It does not appear that marked shifts in attitudes toward work and relationships between men and women are likely to occur in the immediate future.

Useem (1966) has emphasized the fact that we have not only changed the nature of work but have professionalized it, with the result that a profession becomes a way of life and not a time-contained job. The most crucial assignment in today's world lies in the field of man's relationships with men. There is need to consider sex roles in caring for both individuals and groups in the future of our society.

Erikson (1965), in studies extending over several decades, observed the different ways in which boys and girls use space in imaginative productions. For boys, exterior space and its traversion with speed and energy has a singular importance. In contrast, girls emphasize arrangements in which people and animals are contained in enclosures. Women may, he concludes, balance man's endeavor to stretch dominion over outer spaces in national and technical expansion by emphasizing the varieties of caring and caretaking necessary for each child born into a planned community.

Caring and caretaking, Seward (1964-1965) believes, can be best achieved when the college woman is directed toward vocational fields which themselves serve essentially nurturant goals, as in the case of the various healing arts and helping sciences. The Statement of the American Council on Education Commission on the Education of Women (1960) affirms, however, that the responsibility for directing young women in their educational and vocational planning has not been uniformly dispatched. Many parents and teachers do not give necessary guidance at essential times in the matter of continuance of study, early marriage, and career and job opportunities.

Counseling and Guidance of Women Students. Dolan (1963) asserted that the influence of professional counselors is important in all phases of women's education but is especially needed in the large institution where there is decentralization of programs and functions. Colleges and universities should seek to develop in the young woman a strong conviction of her own identity and individual integrity. Lloyd (1964) directed questions to college administrators concerning their responsibility for orienting young women to their future roles. Her findings show that while administrators in colleges for women acknowledge a responsibility, their efforts have been minimal. Neumann (1963) raised questions about the needs, attitudes, and capacities of women and how these can be realistically dealt with by a counselor. Douvan (1959) tested first-semester freshmen women at a Midwestern university to obtain answers to basic questions about their college goals, and found that a high percentage of women attempt to combine educational and marital goals. Hardee (1964) emphasized the importance of counseling women in the junior and community college in terms of their general education, technical and professional training, educational–vocational indecision, tentative choice of major, and their continuing education. In a study of career planning among senior women in 16 southern states, Grigg (1961) called attention to the low incidence of counselor–student contact in occupational decision making. Wagman (1966) compared the interests and values of career-oriented versus homemaking-oriented women, and found that the former rank relatively higher on the *theoretical* value scale of the Allport-Vernon-Lindzey Study of Values and on the physicians' and psychologists' scales of the Strong Vocational Interest Blank. Roe and Siegelman (1964), studying 142 male college seniors and 94 adults in subsamples of men and women engineers and men and women social workers, concluded that the choice of occupation of women engineers was in many instances related to identification with the father. The persistence of the woman in the science field may have resulted in part from a general resilience acquired in response to early-life difficulties and discontinuities. Women social workers apparently had more stress with parents than did the engineer group, with more personality problems resulting. The choice of occupation appears to have been based on a search for satisfying personal relationships. The conclusion points to the fact that the farther from the cultural sex stereotype the occupation is, the greater the chance that factors in early life have predisposed the choice. Tukey (1964) investigated differences between intellectually oriented and socially oriented women. Despite similarity in grades, the two groups were different in their fields of occupational choice. The intellectually oriented women pursued more demanding occupations, considered also to be less conventionally feminine. The intellectually oriented students showed greater need for autonomy, exhibition, and achievement, with the socially oriented women indicating greater need for deference. Zapoleon (1961), citing a study employing the Edwards Personal Preference Schedule, noted that women's stronger needs are to defer to others, to have close affiliation with others, to introspect their own personality and motives, to help others and accept help, and to be self-abasing. Freedman (1961) suggests the need for longitudinal studies to identify early determinants of choice of field, for studies measuring personality changes during college as a function of curriculum, and for studies of people who move out of one field into another. There is an accompanying need for studies of persons with similar personality profiles who pursue different fields and, conversely, of individuals in the same field who show differing personality profiles.

Graduate Education. In studies of women who enter graduate programs, some noteworthy beginnings have been made. Established in 1950 by General Dwight D. Eisenhower at Columbia University, the Conservation of Human Resources Project initiated research on talented persons. Ginzberg and associates (1966) studied some 300 women pursuing graduate education between the years 1945-1951. Employing a 40-item questionnaire, the investigators elicited four types of life style: Individualistic, Influential, Supportive, and Communal. Analysis of data points to some needed policy changes, including more educational and occupational guidance offered to freshmen and sophomore women, and an increased attempt to stimulate them to crystallize occupational plans within larger life plans. Added reforms in the way of campus housing, better scholarship and fellowship funds, and greater flexibility in admission, graduation, and certification for mature women students were suggested.

In a companion volume, Ginzberg and Yohalem (1966) presented the self-portraits of selected respondents together with information derived from the questionnaire referred to above. Twenty-six women graduates were selected from among the 300 respondents and thereafter categorized as Planners, Re-casters, Adapters, and Unsettled. Despite similar educational accomplishments, the women showed a wide difference in goals and values, life circumstances, and methods of coping with situations. Throughout, it is noted that the more education a woman has, the greater her attachment to work. The pattern of *innovating* women—those whose planning centers around continuous full-time careers—resembles most closely that of men.

Believing that the utilization of biographies to construct role models for contemporary women is important, Bernard (1964) has narrated the life histories of seven academic women of the nineteenth and early twentieth century. Her modal picture of the woman faculty member is of a bright individual, insofar as test-intelligence is concerned, one compliant rather than aggressive, who comes from an above-average social class and possesses a major interest in the humanities. There is no acknowledgment of alleged discrimination against women on college faculties in America, the investigator believing that what happens to women in academic settings is traceable to their own performance. That the academic woman may, at times, exhibit aggressive behavior is observed in the role she assumes in training graduate students, e.g., that of "fighter for truth." With the graduate student not yet having learned how to fight and with an absence of nurturing ingredients in the graduate-school environment, the woman teacher has an obligation to defend the student who must work in circumstances that are at times stressful. Tucker and others (1964) have described the ideal professor as one more interested in teaching than in conducting research, and one who treats students as members of a family, providing them with supervision, advice, and guidance on personal as well as academic matters. The responsibility clearly lies with the academic woman who must give encouragement to the intelligent and highly motivated young women who aspire to graduate and professional education and to careers in academic life.

Totaro (1963) has reported the proceedings from a symposium dealing with women in college and university teaching and the resistance frequently encountered by them in pursuing academic careers. It is predicted that equality for women will result from the encouragement given women to achieve maximum development; opening all institutions to both men and women; making educational programs equally available and appropriate to women students; removing prejudices against women in business, industry and the professions; and designing employment practices and work schedules that make greater use of the talents of women on a part-time basis.

Continuing Education of Women. Models for effecting the continuing education of women are to be seen in programs instituted at Sarah Lawrence College, the University of Minnesota, and Radcliffe. Raushenbush (1961), anticipating the need for educational innovation, established the Sarah Lawrence College Center for Continuing Education, which enables women who withdrew from college to complete their undergraduate work. It provides, in addition, assistance to college graduates planning appropriate advanced programs. Senders (1961) has referred to the Minnesota Plan for Women's Continuing Education as an attempt to return to the nation's manpower pool a group of intelligent educated women whose abilities would otherwise be poorly used in mid-life. Described as an all-university program building *into* existing agencies—i.e., student counseling, placement bureau, academic curriculum—the plan provides assistance to the mature woman who needs information or counseling or both. Bunting (1961) has characterized as a "luxurious ambiguity" in present-day education of women the fact that while women are as educable as men, their intellectual development and performance need not continue beyond the time of their marriage. The Radcliffe Institute for Independent Study, directing itself to constructive leisure, has moved to establish an experimental program upon a philosophy, applicable to both sexes, that no individual's talents should go unused for lack of opportunity to develop them. The program for the Institute scholar is directed primarily to the talented woman who, after marriage, finds it difficult to continue to be intellectually creative without assistance. It assumes educational guidance, conferences, opportunities for research as well as means of reciprocation, with the undergraduate program of the college gaining from the presence of such a scholar on campus. Stimulated by the success of the foregoing programs, other campuses have marshaled their resources to develop programs of continuing education for women. O'Neill (1965) has identified the collegiate institutions which offer such programs including short-term refresher activities and longer-term degree or certification pursuit combining evening, Saturday, and television credit courses. Commenting on programs of "sustained" education for women, Erickson (1966) has recommended that attention be given to the scheduling of special courses at convenient times for women enrollees, the adjustment of administrative procedures to facilitate the enrollment of mature women, and the establishment of a campus learning climate that is both encouraging and challenging.

THE INTERNATIONAL PICTURE. That doors for learning are opening for women at the collegiate level abroad is confirmed by Bowles (1963), who has observed that in colonial territories particularly, changes are taking place in the broad pattern of admissions. An early UNESCO publication (1952) showed relatively little discrimination against enrollment of women in institutions of higher education in countries such as Italy, Japan, the Netherlands, New Zealand, Switzerland, France, Belgium, and Sweden, with some acknowledged exclusion of women from institutes of engineering and military colleges. The picture, however, is different in the developing countries. The Committee on Educational Interchange Policy of the Institute of International Education (1963) polled women in Asia, Africa, and Latin America and scanned the literature relating to the role of women in the economic, political, and social life of developing areas. Admittedly, the economic impact of women is recognized when in a country such as Libya the labor supply is increased, greater specialization is predicted, and better quality of work output is anticipated. The major obstacle to mobility of women is the uneven educational opportunity afforded them. The Committee found that many developing countries have difficulty in providing adequate education for men, much less women. In Ceylon as late as 1963, only one university out of three admitted women; in Brazil, 19 percent of the university students were women; in India, 15 percent; in Nigeria, 7 percent.

A report of the U.S. Advisory Commission on International Education and Cultural Affairs (1963) recommended that the State Department provide more opportunities to bring women leaders to the United States from regions such as Africa and the Near and Far East. Representatives of different classes, age groups, organizations, and fields of interest visiting the United States may be helped to envision possibilities that exist in their own land for social, economic, and political activity. That this vision extends not only to women who must actively organize themselves but also to men with whom they will work is to be underscored. Not only must the principle of equality be voiced; it must be implemented by practical means. New methods of cooperative action between men and women's groups in the developing countries must be tried.

Noble (1956) has written of education as a process that encourages persons to enter into experiences that utilize and develop capacities for doing, thinking, feeling, and sharing with others. But the journey of man toward men on other continents and the journey of man into his own interior are pilgrimages of increasing proximity. In America, recriminations for witchcraft no longer exist. Feminists are remembered but fleetingly. Female crusaders and their crusades are subjects relegated to history books. Equality is no longer a banner word; freedom for women to learn has been won. Yet Erikson (1965) has reminded us that a historical lag will exist between any emancipation and the inner adjustment of the emancipated. It takes longer to emancipate what goes on inside—the prejudices and inequalities that have reinforced life and contributed to identity formation—than time has permitted.

The legislation which first gave women equal voting rights and more recently provided her equal employment opportunity will spur and speed the inner emancipation that must take place. What lies ahead is an immense and circuitous task: education must point women to the best possible uses of opportunities having transforming potential for them now and in the future. Thereafter, educated women must, in reciprocation, direct their learnings to the demands of a society in need of renewal.

Melvene Hardee
Florida State University

References

American Association of University Women Educational Foundation. *Women's Education.* The Association, 1966.

American Council on Education, Commission on the Education of Women. *The Span of a Woman's Life and Learning.* ACE, 1960. 4p.

Baker, Elizabeth Faulkner. *Technology and Woman's Work.* Columbia U Press, 1964. 460p.

Bernard, Jessie. *Academic Women.* Pennsylvania State U Press, 1964. 331p.

Bowles, Frank. *Access to Higher Education,* Vol. 1. Columbia U Press, 1963. 212p.

Bunting, Mary I. "The Radcliffe Institute for Independent Study." *Ed Rec* 42:279–84; 1961.

Dennis, Lawrence E. (Ed.) *Education and a Woman's Life.* ACE, 1962. 153p.

Dolan, Eleanor F. "Higher Education for Women: Time for Reappraisal." In *Higher Education.* USOE, 1963. p. 5–13.

Douvan, Elizabeth. "Adolescent Girls: Their Attitude Toward Education." In David, Opal D. *The Education of Women—Signs for the Future.* ACE, 1959. 153p.

Erickson, Mildred B. "Sustained Education for Women." *U Col Q* 12:25–8; 1966.

Erikson, Erik H. "Inner and Outer Space: Reflections on Womanhood." *Daedalus* 89:582–90; 1964.

Erikson, Erik H. *Women and the Scientific Professions*. Massachusetts Institute Technology Press, 1965. 250p.

Flanagan, John C., and Cooley, William W. *Project Talent: Report of the Eleventh Grade Follow-up Study*. U Pittsburgh, 1965.

Frankel, Charles. "The Era of Educational and Cultural Relations." *Dept State B Pub* 8093:1–9; 1966.

Freedman, Mervin B. *Measurement and Evaluation of Change in College Women*. Mary Conover Mellon Foundation, 1961. 62p.

Freedman, Mervin B. "The Role of the Educated Woman: An Empirical Study of the Attitudes of a Group of College Women." *Col Stud Personnel* 6:145–55; 1965.

Ginzberg, Eli, and others. *Life Styles of Educated Women*. Columbia U Press, 1966. 224p.

Ginzberg, Eli, and Yohalem, Alice M. *Educated American Women: Self-Portraits*. Columbia U Press, 1966. 198p.

Grigg, Charles M. *Career Plans of College Seniors*. Florida State U, 1961. 36p.

Hardee, Melvene Draheim. "Counseling Women Students." *Jun Col J* 34:16–20; 1964.

Heist, Paul. "A Commentary on the Motivation and Education of College Women." *J Nat Assn Women Deans Counselors* 25:51–9; 1962.

Institute of International Education, Committee on Educational Interchange Policy. *Women in Educational Exchange with the Developing Countries*. The Institute, 1963. 27p.

Irish, Lois. "Needed: Unique Patterns for Educating Women." *Col Bd R* 46:27–31; 1962.

Kamarovsky, Mirra. *Women in the Modern World: Their Education and Their Dilemmas*. Little, 1953. 319p.

Lloyd, Betty Jane. "The Need for New Counseling Programs at Women's Colleges." *J Nat Assn Women Deans Counselors* 27:190–3; 1964.

Matthews, Esther. *Marriage and Career Conflicts in Girls and Young Women*. Doctoral dissertation. Harvard U, 1960.

Mayhew, Lewis B. *Education: Conservative and Liberal, A Report of the Stephens College Self-study, 1959–1960*. Stephens Col, 1962. 31p.

Mead, Margaret, and Kaplan, Frances Balgley. (Eds.) *American Women*. Scribner, 1965. 274p.

Merry, Margaret Habein. *The Final Report of the Study of Development Planning in Women's Colleges*. Institute for College and University Administrators, 1965. 15p.

Middle Atlantic Regional Pilot Conference. *Counseling Girls Toward New Perspectives*. U.S. Department of Labor, 1965. 81p.

Midwest Regional Pilot Conference. *New Approaches to Counseling Girls in the 1960's*. U.S. Department of Labor, 1965. 82p.

Mueller, Kate H. *Educating Women for a Changing World*. U Minnesota Press, 1954. 302p.

Mueller, Kate H. "Education: The Realistic Approach." In Farber, Seymour, and Wilson, Roger H. L. *The Challenge to Women*. Basic Books, 1966. 176p.

Murphy, Lois B., and Raushenbush, Esther. *Achievement in the College Years*. Harper, 1960. 240p.

Neumann, Rebecca R. "When Will the Educational Needs of Women be Met? Some Questions for the Counselor." *J Counseling Psychol* 10:378–83; 1963.

Newcomer, Mabel. *A Century of Higher Education for American Women*. Harper, 1959. 266p.

Noble, Jeanne L. *The Negro Woman's College Education*. Teachers Col, Columbia U, 1956. 163p.

O'Neill, Barbara Powell. *Careers for Women After Marriage and Children*. Macmillan, 1965. 401p.

Parrish, John B. "Professional Womanpower as a National Resource." *Am R Econ Bus* 1:54–63; 1961.

Raushenbush, Esther. "Unfinished Business: Continuing Education for Women." *Ed Rec* 42:267–8; 1961.

Reisman, David. "Some Dilemmas of Women's Education." *Ed Rec* 46:424–34; 1965.

Roe, Anne, and Siegelman, Marvin. *The Origin of Interests*. APGA, 1964. 98p.

Rowe, Frederick B. *Characteristics of Women's College Students*. Monogr No. 8. Southern Regional Education Board, 1964. 55p.

Saunders, John B. deC. M. "Introduction." In Farber, Seymour M., and Wilson, Roger H. L. *The Potential of Women*. McGraw-Hill, 1963. 328p.

Senders, Virginia L. "The Minnesota Plan for Women's Continuing Education: A Progress Report." *Ed Rec* 42:270–8; 1961.

Seward, Georgene H. "Psychological Complications of Woman's Roles." *Int Understanding* 2:1–5; 1964–65.

Simon, Kenneth A., and Fullam, Marie G. *Projections of Educational Statistics to 1975–76*. USOE, 1966. 113p.

Simon, Kenneth A., and Grant, W. Vance. *Digest of Educational Statistics*. USOE, 1966. 124p.

Tiedeman, David V. "Career Development of Women: Some Propositions." In David, Opal D. *The Education of Women—Signs for the Future*. ACE, 1959. 153p.

Totaro, Joseph. (Ed.) *Women in College and University Teaching*. U Wisconsin, 1963. 54p.

Tucker, Allan, and others. *Attrition of Graduate Students*. Michigan State U, 1964. 296p.

Tukey, Ruth S. "Intellectually-Oriented and Socially-Oriented Superior College Girls." *J Nat Assn Women Deans Counselors* 27:120–7; 1964.

UNESCO. *Access of Women to Education*. International Bureau of Education, 1952. 207p.

U.S. Advisory Commission on International and Cultural Affairs. *A Report to Congress on the Effectiveness of the Educational and Cultural Exchange Program of the U.S. Department of State*. GPO, 1963. 27p.

Useem, Ruth Hill. "What Does Society Expect Higher Education to Do for Women: Who Knows and Who Cares?" In *Current Issues in Higher Education*. Association for Higher Education, 1966. 290p.

Wagman, Morton. "Interests and Values of Career and Homemaking Oriented Women." *Personnel Guid J* 44:794–801; 1966.

Ward, Paul L. "Women's Share in College Enrollments." In *Current Issues in Higher Education.* Association for Higher Education, 1965. 262p.

Zapoleon, Marguerite W. *Occupational Planning for Women.* Harper, 1961. 276p.

EDUCATIONAL COMMUNICATIONS MEDIA

With the advent of the atomic bomb and Sputnik it has become evident that the survival and progress of nations will increasingly depend upon the widespread utilization of technology. We have seen technology revolutionize our industries, entertainment, agriculture, and military. The application of technology to education has only begun; the potential for broader application is enormous. Education ranks as one of our largest businesses, accounting for a major part of local and state taxes. It is incumbent upon educational planners to apply technology to education wherever it can be utilized to improve quality and effect economies in this vast enterprise.

Educational communications media include the major technological means for the improvement of instruction. Through the use of media, instructional units can be created in a permanent form that can be studied in detail utilizing appropriate research techniques. Learning from these instructional sequences can then be increased to a maximum by progressive improvement of the instructional message and proper selection of the channels of communication. The resulting instructional material is generally superior to most instruction and potentially superior to the best instruction. Educators must put technology to work for the cause of education.

OBJECTIVES OF THE MEDIA PROGRAM. In 1962 the National Education Association's Division of Audiovisual Instructional Service convened a task force to develop a position paper on the function of media in the public schools. Morris (1963) cites the many forces in our society which mandate the application of technology to instruction. Two major functions of educational media are outlined. The first function of media is to supplement the teacher by increasing his effectiveness in the classroom. The second media function utilizes media alone for instruction. Media may thus be used to enrich existing instruction or to improve overall productivity through instructional media systems which do not depend upon the teacher for routine presentation of instructional material. By either method the material presented must be essential for achievement of the goals of education.

Thomas A. Edison commented that motion pictures could substitute for colorless, standardized lessons from textbooks. Commercial television is today teaching youngsters information that will help them understand our society. Entire courses of instruction are distributed by television networks and relayed from airplanes and satellites.

The Carnegie Commission on Educational Television (1967) described the role of television in providing general education to the public through a nationwide system of public television stations. This is a trend toward providing education whenever needed rather than confining it to our schools. For many years correspondence courses have provided instruction using books alone. Now courses of instruction are being taught by television, programmed texts, filmed courses, radio, tapes, records, teaching machines, electronic classrooms, computer-assisted instruction, and sound filmstrips. Educational media are often used alone to provide instruction which is at least as valuable as conventional instruction and is often better. However, the major use of communications media is to supplement the teacher by enhancing his effectiveness in the classroom.

The teacher today can call upon a myriad of instructional materials for assistance in the teaching or learning process. About 5,000 new films, filmstrips, tapes, recordings, models, and graphic materials become available each year. The Educational Media Index prepared under the direction of the Educational Media Council (1964) consists of 14 volumes and lists almost 30,000 items. With this wealth of material our instructional programs should be unequaled. The Council of Chief State School Officers (1964) described the role of the new educational media in the school program and identified responsibilities of state departments of education for extending and improving their use. The National Defense Education Act and the Elementary and Secondary Education Act have substantially increased the use of these materials. Although their use is increasing exponentially their total impact upon education reported by Morris (1963) amounts to only a small percentage of educational costs and classroom time. He reports that industry spends three times as much for its tools as it does for its buildings, while the educational investment for audiovisual equipment in 1958 amounted to six-tenths of one percent of capital outlay. The application of technology to education is still in its infancy.

In contrast, Brish (1964) reports on the extensive use of instructional television in Hagerstown, Maryland. With a budget of $280,000 a year elementary-school students were able to spend 10 percent of their classroom time utilizing television, while junior high school pupils spent almost one-third of their time in television classes. Pupil achievement improved significantly and it was possible to upgrade the curriculum and enrich the educational program more easily and economically.

Such programs require a major modification of the pattern of instruction. Through the use of media the teacher can reach 300 students at one time. The recorded presentations of the successful teacher who has been given time and assistance in the preparation of lessons can be studied by the beginning teacher as a means of improving his teaching. Computer technology permits retrieval of facts when needed more readily than relying on the individual's memory or upon information stored in books. Tyler (1962) describes the new role of the teacher as the manager of learning situations and the counselor of individual learners. In this capacity the teacher is more professional than he is when he acts as a purveyor of information. Acceptance of this new role by teachers should result in improved instruction and greater teacher satisfaction.

EDUCATIONAL COMMUNICATIONS PROFESSION. In this rapidly developing field a number of names have been accepted to describe the scope of media activities. A name has been relegated to a subordinate position when it becomes restrictive. Over a period of years the field has been known as visual aids, visual education, audiovisual education, instructional materials, learning resources, educational media, instructional technology, and educational communications. Anderson (1962) reviewed the development of educational technology from 1650 to 1900. Hoban and Van Ormer (1950) reviewed instructional film research from 1918 to 1950. Finn and others (1962) reported on the growth of audiovisual instrumentation for instruction from 1930 to 1960. In these reports the development of the profession can be traced from its beginnings. More recently Bern (1961) has presented a case for the title of audiovisual engineer and Finn (1965) has proposed the name of instructional technology for the field. Twyford (1965) justified educational communications as the name for the profession and showed its interrelationships with other terminology in a communications interrelations diagram. The term "technology" was not thought to cover verbal or printed communications. The term "media" included the channels of communication but lacked emphasis on input materials and effects upon the learners. The term "instructional materials" lacked emphasis upon equipment and upon the communications process. Ely (1963) clarified the terminology by compiling a glossary of terms associated with the field in general and with several of the areas of specialization.

The educational communications profession, like other professions, consists of subprofessions or specialties. Morris (1963) speaks of a media director having supervisory responsibility for systems design, television, library, programmed instruction, audiovisual equipment, and materials production. He also suggests that the media director might be responsible for textbooks, classroom supplies, graphics production, duplication, and electronic learning laboratories. The director is said to be a professionally qualified supervisor or administrator rather than a teacher or a specialist in a specific medium. A comparable array of specialists within a profession is found among engineers, psychologists, and doctors.

A further look at the scope of the profession may be obtained by consulting the *Quantitative Standards For Audiovisual Personnel, Equipment and Materials* prepared by Faris and Sherman (1966) and adopted by the Department of Audiovisual Instruction, NEA, and the Association of Chief State School Audiovisual Officers. This publication gives school standards for audiovisual personnel as well as for films, filmstrips, slides, study prints, maps, globes, dioramas, projection equipment, television receivers, record players, tape recorders, screens, radio receivers, video tape recorders, and closed-circuit television.

Educational communications personnel have been drawn into a consideration of the appropriate medium required to solve an instructional problem and have become concerned with message design to ensure the optimum transfer of information through each medium. The Department of Audiovisual Instruction, NEA, the National Association of Educational Broadcasters, and the National Society for Programed Instruction are the principal national organizations concerned with educational media. The Department of Audiovisual Instruction, NEA, is the organization most concerned with introducing all kinds of technological materials into education. The American Association of School Librarians of the American Library Association has recently become interested in the instructional-materials concept and is working with the Department of Audiovisual Instruction to further this program. Educational administrators searching for efficient management of these specialists have organized them under one head. In New York State a position of director of educational communications is certified at the administrative level in the state's schools. As the field develops, the next decade should see major growth of this profession.

APPLICATION OF MEDIA RESEARCH. Research on media for educational communications has been extensive. The potential of educational films, television, and programmed instruction has resulted in the funding of thousands of research studies. The Fund for the Advancement of Education of the Ford Foundation and Title VII of the National Defense Education Act have prompted extensive programs of research in support of technological innovations. The U.S. Department of Defense sponsored media research through the U.S. Naval Training Device Center, Human Resources Research Office, and the Human Resources Research Laboratories.

Personnel associated with these efforts were almost uniformly disappointed with the speed of research application to instructional uses. When media applications were successfully demonstrated there was little rush to acceptance within the operational units of the armed forces. This lack of ready acceptance of successful innovations prompted research personnel to begin exploring operations research and systems analysis as a means for obtaining a solution to the problem. This exploration revealed that the size of the task for gaining permanent acceptance of innovations has been underestimated.

Hoban (1956) spoke of user orientation of research and began to question the value of basic research alone. Too many variables occurred in a particular instructional situation to make very useful the application of basic research results.

OPERATIONS RESEARCH ON MEDIA. Research on media has generally been concerned with measures of effectiveness and occasionally with student and teacher acceptance. Rarely has it been concerned with cost factors or with sociological and psychological factors of acceptance of the innovation as a permanent part of educational practice. Research has shown that televised instruction can be effective and acceptable to students but administrators have often found the costs to be excessive and teachers unable to adjust to their new role. An outstanding series of research studies was conducted by Carpenter and Greenhill (1955) and by Carpenter and others (1958) in which the factors of effectiveness, acceptance, costs, and equipment variables were each considered in developing a program of television instruction for Pennsylvania State University. Research studies were undertaken on topics which would support televised instruction. In this regard the instructional-television operation was the consumer of the results of research. This program of research can be classified as operations research because it involved the disciplines of education, psychology, engineering, economics, and sociology. Models of proposed operations were constructed, tested, and finally incorporated into an efficient operation.

Operations research has had its greatest application in industry and is beginning to be applied to education and media. Twyford (1959) indicated how operations research could be applied to instructional films, giving consideration to media, production, utilization, and cost factors. In 1964 the Research Commission of the Department of Audiovisual Instruction, NEA, held a conference at Syracuse University to explore how operations research and systems analysis might be employed in research studies concerned with media. Oxhandler (1964) reviewed the potential for this approach to evaluation of innovations. Michigan State University has since adopted this approach in the study of some of its instructional programs. Operations research studies consider all factors involved in the introduction and operation of media in an instructional situation. They are also concerned with the size of the change required to affect significantly the total operation and the administrative changes required to carry out the new operation.

MEDIA SYSTEMS. Systems research and analysis may be applied to a particular course, unit, or lesson to integrate media into an effective instructional system. VanderMeer (1964) reported on this neglected field of study and foresaw applications resulting from the organization of instructional materials into curriculum units. The teaching of the laboratory section of an audiovisual course through the use of self-instruction materials is a typical media system. Popham and Sadnavitch (1960) demonstrated that filmed physics and chemistry courses can be used effectively for instruction. The filmed physics course was less effective than conventional instruction while the filmed chemistry course was superior. Popham (1960) also demonstrated that tape-recorded lectures at the graduate level were as effective and acceptable as the conventional lecture–discussion method.

An instructional-media system typically involves a number of instructional materials, often presented through several media and organized into an acceptable unified instructional unit. The systems analysis will consider factors of effectiveness, acceptability, economic feasibility, and administrative adaptability. In a closed-loop system, discrepancies from desired results are fed back into the system to correct for weaknesses and to obtain optimum results. The development of programmed instruction materials follows this pattern of improvement. Utilizing a classroom communicator, Twyford and others (1964) evaluated each lesson in a course in ninth-grade general science and utilized the daily results to determine what should be incorporated in succeeding lessons to produce maximum learning. Smith (1966) reported on the design of instructional systems and the manner in which instructional materials may be incorporated in them to maximum effect.

Computer-assisted instruction is one of the most recent methods of utilizing the technology of the computer to organize information and present it to the student. The computer may retrieve visual as well as printed material as required by the individual student. Gentile (1967) indicates that in addition to the costs of equipment and the need for programs to use with the equipment the role of the teacher in its use must be defined. It is clear that in this medium educational effectiveness, economic feasibility, and acceptability must be considered and provided for.

Systems analysis and operations research are relatively unexplored fields. Systems analysis is concerned with the various sources of learning, whether they be in the classroom, from the textbook, or from other sources. It is also concerned with retention as a practical limiting factor in any realistic feedback system. However, its greatest value is in determining exactly what behavioral objectives must be attained.

BEHAVIORAL OBJECTIVES. In the design of instructional films, programmed instruction, and other instructional materials it is essential to select the best content for inclusion in the final production. Once included in a film the message is presented to students repeatedly for years without change. To ensure inclusion of the essential information it is important to develop specific behavioral objectives. This can often be done by a task analysis, which reveals the information that an educated person needs to know about the subject. The Armed Forces have been foremost in the application of this technique. Haverland (1966) described how an analysis was made of the officer's role in operation of the Nike Hercules missile system. Programmed instruction material was prepared to teach this content. The test group using the programmed material scored significantly higher on nine specially prepared proficiency tests than the control group using conventional instruction. Twyford and others (1959) described a method for isolating factual and behavioral items in communications materials and for predicting their effectiveness.

EFFECTIVENESS OF EDUCATIONAL COMMUNICATIONS MEDIA. Educators who employ communications media and materials on a large scale feel an obligation to conduct research studies to demonstrate that the quality of instruction is equal to and probably superior to that which prevailed before its introduction. This need accounts for the large number of research studies in which instruction involving media is compared with instruction conducted in the conventional manner. These studies usually cover a semester or a year. From them we may conclude that instruction making extensive use of communications materials and media is at least as effective as conventional instruction.

Research on television instruction demonstrates most conclusively that it is effective. Holmes (1959) analyzed television research and found that in almost 90 percent of the comparisons there were no substantial differences in achievement or information gain over conventional instruction. Television was found to be better for teaching the sciences. Students learning from television at home usually obtained good scores on tests. Kumata (1956) summarized 74 television-research studies and concluded that television students usually do as well as other students and at times do better. He also reported on retention of learning, methods of teaching by television, value of feedback, attitudes toward television, amount of viewing, and use of color and visual materials. Twyford (1956) summarized Army and Navy research studies and listed findings in support of procedures employed in television instruction.

Carpenter and Greenhill (1955) and Carpenter and others (1958) described studies conducted to measure the effectiveness of televised college instruction. This program of television studies is the most exhaustive and insightful of the many carried out in this field and confirmed the conclusion that television instruction is generally effective. Erickson and Chausow (1960) studied open-circuit television for college use and concluded that learning was essentially equivalent for television and resident students. Davis and Johnson (1966) reported that classroom television at Michigan State University was as effective as regular classroom instruction. These television studies in support of programs of instruction clearly demonstrate that the quality of instruction does not suffer as television is normally applied to instructional applications. A similar number of controlled experimental studies have not been conducted at the elementary and secondary level. Brish (1964) reported that pupil achievement can improve significantly when television is used consistently throughout an instructional program.

The effectiveness of programmed instruction to teach entire courses or segments of courses is equally impressive. Schramm (1964) reviewed research on programmed instruction and provided an extensive bibliography. Fry (1960) summarized studies utilizing teaching machines. The 25 studies generally showed that teaching-machine programs provided superior instruction. Eigen and Komoski (1960) reported that learning from teaching machines and from programmed texts was substantially the same. Hughes (1961) found that students learning from programmed texts scored 10 percent higher than the conventional class on an achievement test and that instruction time was reduced 27 percent. Carpenter and Greenhill (1963) prepared special programmed courses in college algebra and English grammar for presentation in teaching machines, programmed texts, and filmstrips and by closed-circuit television. They found that each of the media could be employed for instruction without adversely affecting achievement. The study demonstrated that programmed material can be used for groups as well as for individuals.

Filmed courses have also been shown to be effective. The results are probably applicable to kinescope recordings of television programs. VanderMeer (1950) demonstrated that a semester course in general science could be taught effectively with 44 films alone. Wittich and others (1959) demonstrated that a filmed physics course was as effective as regular instruction.

Several methods employing audio materials have also been demonstrated to be effective. Popham (1960) found that tape-recorded lectures were as effective and as acceptable as the lecture–discussion method at the graduate level. Cook (1964) demonstrated that radio can be used effectively to teach Spanish, and Cutler and others (1958) found that instruction over the telephone was as effective as face-to-face instruction. Loubriel (1962) found that television could be used to advantage to broaden the in-service education of teachers. Galas (1961) utilized foreign-language records to permit teachers with inadequate knowledge of a language to teach the language. Lorge (1963) demonstrated that use of the language laboratory in teaching French pronunciation and comprehension resulted in greater learning than traditional methods. Dworkin and Holden (1959) found that sound filmstrips could be utilized as effectively as regular instruction in a college-level course. Newman and Highland (1956) demonstrated that tape recordings and a work book were as effective as an instructor who was rated as above average in instructional ability for teaching the unit of work.

PERFECTABILITY OF COMMUNICATIONS MATERIALS. Instructional materials may be thought of as frozen segments of instruction that can be tested and modified until their effectiveness reaches a maximum. Given the time and resources, it is possible to produce instructional materials of extraordinary effectiveness. The efforts of programmed-instruction specialists are directed toward this goal. Several studies have demonstrated this potential. Jaspen (1950) prepared 27 improved versions of an existing U.S. Navy film designed to teach recruits to assemble the breech block of the 40mm antiaircraft gun. Recruits seeing the best of these films required only one-sixth as much time to assemble the breach block as did those seeing the original films. The best film was capable of teaching the task to 98 percent of the recruits after one showing. Twyford and Carpenter

(1956) summarized the findings of 70 experimental studies into a series of statements designed to guide film planners and producers in producing films of greatest effectiveness.

In another approach Fletcher (1955) demonstrated that a specific film could be reduced in length by 24 percent without reducing effectiveness. He employed a profile technique for evaluating the effectiveness of each part of the film and removed those parts that were least effective. Increased learning could then be obtained if additional material known to be effective was added.

In view of the widespread use of currently available materials it would be educationally desirable to have materials tested and improved as much as possible. To do this requires a complete knowledge of what elements contribute to effective instructional materials. VanderMeer and others (1965) systematically modified two films and obtained a significant increase in learning by providing introductions, summaries, outlines, labels, and graphics and by modifying the commentary.

Improvement of learning from a course utilizing media is complicated by the various sources of learning that are measured by unit and course tests. The textbook is often a primary source of learning and this learning often occurs outside the classroom. Classroom instruction utilizing media often contributes to learning outcomes that are not covered by the textbook.

Several preliminary studies have indicated that a major portion of measured learning does not result from classroom activities. In this event media experiences may contribute little to learning or may not be measurable if test items on this material are not included in achievement tests. Marr and others (1960) demonstrated that the lecture did contribute significantly to learning psychology at the college level. However, it was apparent that students were also learning a large part of the content from the textbook alone. Smith and McAshan (1964) found that as much as 85 percent of course learning may result from sources other than the teacher and indicated that this fact has important implications for media research. It is important to know whether learning results more from out-of-class activities than from in-class activities because the contribution of media is usually limited to in-class activities. Miller and Brown (1964) developed a method for measuring sources of learning that may lead to substantial increases in learning through the use of media. Test items were based upon what was taught rather than upon course objectives. Using this method of measuring learning Church and others (1964a) obtained a learning gain score for a class utilizing media that was 67 percent greater than that obtained by the normal class.

RELATIVE EFFECTIVENESS STUDIES. On the basis of available research the effectiveness of a particular instructional material is more dependent upon the nature and quality of the message than upon the characteristics of the channel of communication. This assumption contrasts sharply with the common practice of improving communications by the addition of visuals. Klapper (1958) and Carpenter and others (1958) found that decreased learning may occur when televised courses are enriched through the addition of visual materials. Twyford and others (1964) demonstrated that some instruction utilizing visual materials can be five times as effective as other classroom activities. Sound films were found to be more than twice as effective as filmstrips in providing learning in a general science course. Those materials that proved to be effective incorporated much information in a concise form. Those instructional activities and instructional materials which resulted in minimum learning were those that contained little information to be learned, were not clearly stated, or were of an incidental nature. Church and others (1964b) obtained similar results in their study of algebra instruction. The relatively high learning obtained from instructional films and programmed instruction probably results from the well-planned and concise nature of the message they incorporate. These studies indicate that all media are not equally effective for a particular purpose and that the role of the educational-communications specialist is to select an effective medium and see that it is used to advantage.

Numerous studies reveal elements which do not contribute significantly to learning. Kanner and Rosenstein (1960) demonstrated that color television was no better than black-and-white television and thereby confirmed numerous earlier studies that reached similar conclusions on the value of color. These findings seem to have had no appreciable effect upon the purchase of color films, whose cost is twice black-and-white films. Twyford and Carpenter (1956) summarized several other characteristics of media that have little or no effect upon learning. Music, optical effects, stereoscopic projection, attention-gaining devices, dramatic sequences, motion, and realistic settings often result in little improvement in learning.

Lumsdaine and others (1951) found that simple animation techniques could be utilized to advantage to improve instruction. May (1965a) described and evaluated the current state of knowledge concerning those elements that motivate, reinforce, or identify and simplify communications. Silverman (1958) compared static transparencies with the more expensive animated transparencies and discovered no difference in effectiveness.

Each of these media characteristics can be important in specific cases but none appears to be crucial. In a study by the Instructional Film Research Program (1954) an expensively staged film in a realistic setting was no more effective than a filmograph utilizing still shots and inexpensive stock footage. Greenhill (1955a) demonstrated an inexpensive method of producing instructional films that retained the elements essential for a good film yet simplified production requirements. Barrow and Westley (1958) analyzed research studies to determine the various factors that might contribute to the effectiveness of television and studied theories of learning in their relation to these factors.

CHANNELS OF COMMUNICATION. During the past ten years there have been numerous research studies investigating the relative contribution to learning of the audio and visual channels of communication. This research has an economic importance because the visual channel of communication is more difficult to provide and is more expensive. Nelson and Moll (1950) tested two films in which the visual portion of the film was dominant and concluded that neither channel was better than the other and that the greatest learning occurred when both were used. Hartman (1961) reviewed the research on multiple-channel communication and proposed a model to describe the interaction of the channels and to determine whether interference exists between channels. Gropper (1963) made an analysis of the problem and questioned whether a picture was worth a thousand words. Travers and others (1964) concluded that considerable doubt had been thrown on the validity of many of the principles of design and utilization of audio-visual materials. He indicated that multi-sensory inputs to the learner are likely to be of value only when the flow of information is slow. It is possible that the contribution of the visual channel may operate to maximum effectiveness for purposes of identification during early periods of education and thereafter verbal communication may more efficiently call back these images in a modified form.

Several studies fail to show any great value in providing visual communications. Bourisseau and others (1965) concluded that pictures were not very effective in evoking correct responses. They concluded that the principle of a picture being worth a thousand words needed to be drastically revised. Spaulding (1956) concluded that an illustration has no educational value unless it is rooted in past experience. He recommended that items in a picture be kept to a minimum. He felt that captions on pictures are valuable in their ability to generalize, modify, relate, and extend the visualized concept. Saul (1956) reviewed the research pertinent to the design and use of effective graphic training aids and organized them for greater accessibility. May (1965b) gave basic consideration to the properties of words and pictures and analyzed the responses required for learning from them. Vernon (1953) concluded that children did not remember instructional content better from an illustrated text than from a text without illustrations. Although pictorial material did not seem generally to contribute greatly to learning, Butlar (1961) found that motion pictures sustained the attention of the rhesus monkey much better than did still pictures.

Pictorial material has been utilized in conjunction with language instruction in the language laboratory. Creore and Hanzeli (1960) found that utilizing visual materials for this purpose was superior for developing speaking skills but was inferior for learning to read and write a language. They concluded that the use of visuals was not recommended if the purpose was to teach all aspects of the language. Young and Choquette (1963) studied methods for utilizing the language laboratory and were unable to demonstrate value in providing activated headsets. Buch (n.d.) found audioactive record superior in pronunciation and audioactive listening superior for structural accuracy.

Multi-media presentations which present two or more pictures on several screens simultaneously with synchronized commentary have recently become popular. These impressive multisensory presentations may not be the reason for the increased learning that a few studies have demonstrated. The careful organization and presentation of instructional content may make the greatest contribution to increased learning.

COMMUNICATIONS EFFICIENCY. We have seen that instruction utilizing educational communications media and materials is generally effective and improvable. Such devices are capable of assuming a substantial portion of the task of providing information in the classroom, thereby permitting the teacher to become a supervisor of instruction and a counselor of students. Although media research has demonstrated the feasibility of this approach to providing education, there is still great need to study the problems that interfere with their adoption. Educators continue to speak of the promising innovations that are being studied in their schools but less often speak of those that have been permanently adopted.

To realize the advantages of media one must consider educational efficiency. Twyford and others (1964) pointed out that one cannot expect a significant improvement in course grades if highly efficient instruction is used only for a small fraction of the instructional time. Lorge (1963) concluded that language laboratories need to be employed for a substantial portion of course time if significant gains are to be expected. Fletcher (1955) demonstrated that not all parts of a film are of equal effectiveness and that a shortened film may provide as much learning. Chance (1960) utilized 200 transparencies and 800 overlays to teach engineering descriptive geometry. He saved 15 minutes in each 60-minute period by utilizing them instead of the blackboard. The students obtained better grades when taught in this manner. Increased instructional efficiency can be obtained if the time that is saved through use of media is used to teach additional material.

Efficiency usually refers to output in relation to the input to the system. An improved operation results if output can be increased and input reduced. The input consists of personnel, materials, buildings, and costs of providing education. The output is the change brought about in the individual which permits him to meet the challenges of society and make contributions to its betterment. These outputs are usually referred to as instructional or behavioral objectives and are commonly measured by tests and other evaluative measures.

Several studies have investigated the problem of costs and instructional efficiency. Carpenter and others

(1958) determined that instruction by television at the university level was more expensive than conventional instruction unless several hundred students were taught. Lepore and Wilson (1958) found that the break-even point for television at home or on campus was between 400 and 500 students. Seibert (1959) showed that if there were from 150 to 275 students taking a course it would be desirable to teach them by television. Erickson and Chausow (1960) found that the costs for broadcast television instruction were higher than for conventional instruction. Twyford and Doherty (1961) demonstrated that the costs of providing broadcast television instruction in New York City was one-ninth as expensive as providing the same instruction by supplementary teachers. They also developed cost comparisons for other examples of television instruction. Brish (1964) determined that the operational costs of television can be met without increasing the normal school budget.

Instructional media have found their greatest use in meeting the increasing demands for education. Trained teachers are not sufficiently available in many instructional subjects, such as elementary science and language instruction. Media can be employed to meet some of these expanding instructional needs. Very little research has been done to define the new role of the teacher when media are employed to simplify the instructional task and to increase the number of students that can be handled. At the college level, Carpenter and others (1958) demonstrated that large-group television instruction was practical and was often preferred by students.

MEDIA APPLICATIONS. Some of the most useful research has been that which is carried on in support of a practical application of media to education. Research has been carried out on instructional television because of its potential in education and specific sources of research funds. Reference has been made to studies by Brish (1964), Carpenter and Greenhill (1955), Carpenter and others (1958), Davis and Johnson (1966), Erickson and Chausow (1960), and others.

The more successful media applications are usually characterized by a firm administrative policy supporting the use of media backed up by an adequate supporting program of personnel, equipment, and materials. One cannot expect a sizable change in instructional methods without a comprehensive plan to bring about the change. Often initial costs may greatly exceed current operational costs.

Studies have been conducted to develop television plans for various regions. Starlin (1962) developed a plan for television in New York State; Tintera (1961) developed a similar plan for Michigan. Hill and others (1961) developed a plan for educational television in Hawaii. Many other state plans have been developed. Lenihan and others (1963) and Twyford and Doherty (1961) measured the size of the television audience in New York City. Langdale (1962) reported on the application of closed-circuit television in a public school and in a housing development. McKnight and Hunter (1966) found that a driver simulator could be used to teach driving safety. Pasewark (1956) found that typewriting could be taught effectively over television. Rugg (1960) gathered information on successful audiovisual programs and presented budgets for school districts of several sizes.

The Armed Forces have conducted numerous research studies on expensive flight simulators and trainers and have found that much of the training can be given on relatively simple and inexpensive devices. Dougherty and others (1957) found that an inexpensive photo mockup of a plane was in many respects as effective as a flight simulator. Swanson (1954) found no appreciable differences in the training effectiveness of mockups, cutaways, animated panels, charts, and symbolic diagrams. Torkelson (1954) found that there were no differences in the training effectiveness of cutaways, mockups, transparencies, and manual illustrations when used with a regular lecture, although the cost of providing them differed greatly. The report recommended that mockups and cutaways should be justified on grounds other than training effectiveness and that transparencies should be used more extensively. Similar studies have demonstrated the effectiveness of inexpensive television equipment.

There is reason to believe that knowledge of participation in a research project may distort the results obtained. To study this possibility VanderMeer (1953) showed two films on personal hygiene to military recruits. Objective measures of changes in behavior were obtained without the knowledge of the recruits. Neither film produced any significant change in behavior. Also Keating (1963) obtained scores for 5,000 students in language courses under relatively normal situations. Those utilizing language laboratories scored lower in most categories. In a more carefully controlled experimental study Lorge (1963) found that language laboratories were of value. Little research has been done to date to demonstrate the value of utilizing less expensive and simpler language equipment, although Galas (1961) demonstrated the effectiveness of records to assist inexperienced teachers of a foreign language. Hayes (1963) developed specifications applicable to language laboratories that have been widely accepted.

EVALUATION OF INSTRUCTIONAL MATERIALS. With 5,000 new instructional materials becoming available each year it is apparent that each cannot be adequately evaluated by every school district. A listing of titles and a brief description alone required 14 volumes of the *Educational Media Index* prepared by the Educational Media Council (1964). Booking records indicate that certain materials are more in demand than others and presumably these materials meet instructional needs to a greater degree. Film libraries containing often-used materials represent a better investment of media funds than a film library containing materials that are seldom used. Each school district with a film library conducts an informal evaluation of those materials that are purchased to ensure that they will receive adequate utilization after purchase and will relate to the curriculum. Teachers who may use the film are requested to view new films and complete a short questionnaire about each. A film that is inadequate for one purpose may effectively serve another. It may be too simple or too complex, be of the wrong grade level, cover little of the desired content, or may have technical flaws. Evaluations may include written comments or general ratings. An objective evaluation is difficult to obtain without a specific statement of instructional goals.

Several methods for evaluation of instructional materials have been developed by media-research personnel. Greenhill (1955b) developed a film evaluation form to be used by a panel of judges that had been trained to evaluate films. The panel learned about those characteristics that research had demonstrated to be effective. McCoy (1955) described how film-research findings should be applied to training-film production. Murnin and VanderMeer (1956) studied a method for determining which medium should be employed for a particular training task.

Evaluation of specific materials is often justified when costs are high. VanderMeer (1953) found that a dramatic film which cost ten times as much as a straightforward film was no more effective. This study was done to determine which type of film should be produced in the future. Many current films contain sequences such as those Fletcher (1955) found to contribute little to effectiveness. The usual subjective evaluations by teachers are unlikely to assess correctly the value of these films.

SYSTEMS ANALYSIS TECHNIQUES. While most evaluations of materials are made by teachers who estimate their value for students, there has been an increasing trend to have students participate in evaluation of materials as a part of the learning situation. Twyford (1951) found that students know when they are learning and can indicate their rate of learning during instruction. Students continuously turn a dial or depress a series of keys to indicate on a rating scale the rate of their learning at the moment. The ratings are usually summated with classroom communicator equipment and plotted as a profile indicating periods of maximum and minimum learning. Merrill (1959) employed electrically summated ratings of student learning as a means of training-aid selection. Fletcher (1955) used the technique to discover strong and weak sequences in a film commentary. Twyford and others (1964) evaluated a year course in general science utilizing this technique and were able to determine the relative effectiveness of various media and other classroom activities. Church and others (1964b) applied the technique to the evaluation of an algebra course. These research studies point to the conclusion that learning is greatest when factual information is concisely presented in sufficient quantity. Many classroom activities result in little learning because there is little being presented for learning. The research also implies that the value of efficient learning sequences should not be dissipated by their being followed with sequences providing little learning.

Classroom communicators involving electrical equipment to record and summate student responses have been used by other investigators to study classroom activities. Froelich (1963) reviewed several communicators and reported on applications made of them. Twyford (1954) listed audience-response recorders and analyzers and discussed their use. Twyford (1951) found that there was a negative correlation between liking and learning from sequences in an instructional film. This finding, which appeared to go counter to general assumptions in psychology, led Merrill (1956) to study a television program utilizing the learning profile technique. He found that learning from television sequences bore no relationship to students' liking of the same sequences. Becker (1964), utilizing similar techniques, concluded that the amount a student will learn has little to do with whether the student finds the materials he is viewing interesting or tension-arousing as measured by the galvanic skin response.

ACCEPTANCE OF MEDIA. The acceptance of instruction utilizing media is important because acceptance determines the extent to which the advantages of media may be realized. Acceptance is particularly critical when media contribute a major portion of the instructional content. Carpenter and Greenhill (1955), Carpenter and others (1958), and Macomber and Siegel (1960) studied student and teacher attitudes and their effect upon acceptance of television instruction. Holmes (1959) reviewed research on televised instruction and reported that students preferred conventional instruction. They preferred television in classrooms to television in a lecture hall. The instructor was found to be important in shaping students' opinions. Attitudes of students toward television were thought to be more accurately described as attitudes toward the instructor, situation, or content. Kumata (1956) reviewed research on attitudes toward learning by television from a number of studies. Popham and Sadnavitch (1960) found that the attitude of a group taking a filmed course was poorer than that of the group having an instructor. Popham (1960) found tape-recorded lectures at the graduate level as acceptable as conventional instruction.

The teacher's role, lack of interpersonal interactions, and the attitudes of students and teachers affect the acceptance of media. Fritz and Massialas (1964) studied the teacher's role in acceptance of televised instruction. Hoban (1965a) found that a major deterrent to enrollment in televised college courses was a lack of interpersonal interactions with instructor and classmates. Westley and Jacobson (1963) utilizing the semantic-differential technique studied the attitudes of students toward the television course, medium, and teacher. Tyler (1962) discussed the specific adjustments a teacher must make to utilize televised instruction. These adjustments involve interpersonal relationships with other teachers who are not using media on a large scale.

Acceptance is also conditioned by the characteristics of the media. Adkins (1959) found that the greatest obstacle to the use of radio was the inconvenience of the broadcast hours. Most teachers preferred tape recordings as a means of bringing radio into the classroom at the time required.

TECHNOLOGICAL INNOVATIONS. One of the largest sources of innovation within education involves media. Schools have often sought television, language laboratories, teaching machines, and computer-assisted instruction for their prestige value. Although this has facilitated change by introduction of innovations it has resulted also in some unwise expenditures. The director of educational communications can justify his position by careful analysis of innovations prior to their introduction.

Fry (1960) listed teaching-machine studies and the devices employed to present the programs. As an innovation the teaching machine captured the imagination of parents and teachers as well as students. Roe and others (1960) discovered that learning from a programmed lecture or programmed text was as effective as a program used in a teaching machine. Fisher and Malpass (1963) found that standard texts were as good as programmed texts. Although the question-and-answer format does provide reinforcement, Filip (1964) pointed out that reinforcement applicable to animals does not necessarily work with human training tasks. Hartman and others (1963) found no advantage in having students fill in blanks in a programmed text. The findings suggest that the improved learning is due to the program and not to the machine and to the selection, organization, and concise statement of content rather than to reinforcement features.

The visual channel is the basis for a number of innovative materials and the value of these materials is often attributed to the visual elements. Further research may show that a substantial portion of their increased effectiveness is due to the organization and presentation of content rather than the visual channel employed.

Two efforts of note have been made to facilitate the introduction of innovations. Meierhenry (1964) held a conference on media and innovation to explore ways in which improvements in education might be attained through the use of media. Brickell (1961) proposed an orderly method for bringing about educational change and prepared an inventory of current innovations in New York State.

Innovations in educational facilities to promote the use of media have received considerable attention from architects as well as from media-design personnel. Hauf and others (1961) prepared a publication which diagrammed new spaces for learning for the better utilization of media. Diamond and Lee (1965) described a storage and retrieval system for locating information on media, materials, and equipment. Information was made available on research studies, materials and equipment catalogs, programmed texts, and audiovisual books and texts.

Noel and others (1963) studied innovations in the practices of state departments of education in promoting the new educational media. They reported upon personnel, equipment, certification, facilities, publications, research, and materials-distribution activities.

COMMUNICATIONS THEORY. Educational-communications personnel have been eager to discover theoretical bases upon which to establish improved media practices. Norberg (1962) collected papers on theories of perception and their relationship to audiovisual education. Travers and others (1964) related research and theory to audiovisual information transmission. Other work has been done to relate theories of learning to media development. Models of the communications process have been frequently presented. Hoban (1965b) studied the problem of transforming theoretical constructs into practical policy decisions. He concluded that neither cognate theory nor media research is likely to contribute significantly to the improvement of instruction until theory and practice in education are more closely related.

EDUCATIONAL-COMMUNICATIONS PERSONNEL. Holtzman and VanderMeer (n.d.) studied graduate programs in educational communications. All programs covered theories and models of communication but none was designed specifically for educational-communications specialists. Martin and Stone (1965) studied media specialists, using functional job-analysis techniques. The basic personality traits for several specialist categories were obtained. Faris and Sherman (1966) established standards for media personnel in school systems. Administrators should be aware that media research should not be undertaken as a substitute for professional judgment and competent professional direction of a media program. Administrators often initiate media studies that duplicate studies done elsewhere on similar topics. Hundreds of television-effectiveness studies attest to this practice.

SOURCES OF MEDIA RESEARCH. The *Audiovisual Communications Review* published by the Department of Audiovisual Instruction, NEA, is the most readily available source of information on current research studies. Research abstracts in the journal give a concise description of the problem and the procedures employed to carry out the research as well as the principal findings.

The Institute for Communications Research at Stanford University has been designated as the Educational Research Information Centers (ERIC) clearinghouse for research on educational media and technology. A prototype media-research center was established by Barhydt and others (1965) at Western Reserve University and was described in a report by Barhydt (1965). The center contains about 4,500 documents and provides an information service to research personnel. Tauber and Lilley (1960) developed a list of subject headings that might be employed in locating media research.

Moldstad (1956, 1958, 1959, 1961) reported on doctoral dissertations concerned with media. Saul (1957) prepared a coordinate index of training-device literature in a publication that permitted rapid location of abstracts of media research through the use of key words. This work involved about 1,600 abstracts of research on the theory, design, and use of audiovisual materials. Also, Saul (1956) reviewed the literature pertinent to the design and use of effective graphic training aids.

Efforts have been made to coordinate media research for maximum application of research results. Hoban and Van Ormer (1950) reviewed most of the important film research from 1918 to 1950. Travers and others (1964) carried out an exhaustive evaluation of media research and related it to problems of information transmission. Kinder (1953) reported on many sources of audiovisual research in the literature. Twyford and Carpenter (1953, 1956) summarized film-research studies conducted by the Instructional Film Research Program at Pennsylvania State University.

Holmes (1959) summarized television-research studies in relation to the teaching and learning process. Kumata (1956) summarized television research as did Twyford (1956) for the U.S. Navy. Pflieger and Kelly (1961) reported on television studies conducted under a national program sponsored by the Fund for the Advancement of Education. Carpenter and Greenhill (1955) and Carpenter and others (1958) reported on a program of research studies in support of the use of television at the university level.

Smith (1967) prepared an annotated bibliography on the design of instructional systems, listing 449 studies. They were classified according to general systems studies, training systems, presentation of knowledge, practice of knowledge, practice of performance, and management of students.

Schramm (1964) prepared an annotated bibliography of research on programmed instruction. Duke (1963) reported on educational media research in the Far East.

Carpenter and others (1962) proposed plans for developing regional educational media research centers. As technology is applied increasingly to education the need for such centers is certain to become more urgent.

Loran C. Twyford, Jr.
The University of the State of New York

References

Adkins, Gale R. *A Study of Certain Factors That Influence the Use of Radio Broadcasts and Recordings in Public School Classrooms.* U Kansas, 1959. 33p.

Anderson, Charnel. *Technology in American Education 1650-1900.* HEW, 1962.

Barhydt, Gordon C. *An Operating Test of a Pilot Educational Media Research Information Center.* Western Reserve U, 1965. 55p.

Barhydt, Gordon C., and others. "An Educational Media Research Information Center (EMRIC): Progress Report." *Audiovisual Communications R* 13:296-302; 1965.

Barrow, Jr., Lionel C., and Westley, Bruce H. *Television Effects—A Summary of the Literature and Proposed General Theory.* U Wisconsin Television Laboratory, 1958. 184p.

Becker, Samuel L. "Interest, Tension, and Retention." *Audiovisual Communications R* 12:277-91; 1964.

Bern, Henry A. "Audiovisual 'Engineers'?" *Audiovisual Communications R* 9:186-94; 1961.

Bourisseau, Whitfield, and others. "Sense Impression Responses to Differing Pictorial and Verbal Stimuli." *Audiovisual Communications R* 13:249-58; 1965.

Brickell, Henry M. *Organizing New York State for Educational Change.* New York State Education Department, 1961. 106p.

Brish, William M. *Washington County Closed-Circuit Television Report.* Hagerstown, Maryland, 1964. 80p.

Buch, John N. *An Experimental Project to Measure Certain Facets of Language Growth for High School Students in Beginning French When Variations of Language Laboratory Equipment Are Utilized in the Instructional Process.* Easton, Pennsylvania Area School System, n.d. 35p.

Butlar, Robert A. "The Responsiveness of Rhesus Monkeys to Motion Pictures." *J Genet Psychol* 98:239-45; 1961.

Carnegie Commission on Educational Television. *Public Television, A Program for Action.* Bantam Books, 1967. 254p.

Carpenter, C. R., and Greenhill, L. P. *An Investigation of Closed-Circuit Television for Teaching University Courses.* Pennsylvania State U, 1955. 102p.

Carpenter, C. R., and Greenhill, L. P. *Comparative Research on Methods and Media for Presenting Programed Courses in Mathematics and English.* Pennsylvania State U, 1963. 74p.

Carpenter, C. R., and others. *An Investigation of Closed-Circuit Television for Teaching University Courses.* Pennsylvania State U, 1958. 110p.

Carpenter, C. R., and others *Operational Plans for Developing Regional Educational Media Research Centers.* Pennsylvania State U, 1962. 257p.

Chance, Clayton W. *Experimentation in the Adaptation of the Overhead Projector Utilizing 200 Transparencies and 800 Overlays in Teaching Engineering Descriptive Geometry Curricula.* U Texas, 1960. 49p.

Church, John G., and others. "Method for Increasing Learning Utilizing Learning Profile Findings." In Twyford, Loran C., and others. (Eds.) *New Media Studies for Improvement of Science and Mathematics Instruction.* New York State Education Department, 1964(a). 122p.

Church, John G., and others. *New Media for Improvement of Algebra Instruction.* New York State Education Department, 1964(b). 433p.

Cook, H. Robert. *The Effects on Learning of Structural Drills in Spanish Broadcasts Via High Frequency AM Radio.* Indiana U, 1964. 24p.

Council of Chief State School Officers. *State Department of Education Leadership in Developing the Use of New Educational Media.* CCSSO, 1964. 24p.

Creore, A. E., and Hanzeli, Victor E. *A Comparative Evaluation of Two Modern Methods for Teaching a Spoken Language.* U Washington, 1960. 77p.

Cutler, R. L., and others. "Teaching Psychology by Telephone." *Am Psychologist* 13:551–2; 1958.

Davis, Robert H., and Johnson, F. Craig. *Final Report: Evaluation of Regular Classroom Lectures Distributed by CCTV to Campus and Dormitory Classrooms.* Michigan State U, 1966. 50p.

Diamond, Robert M., and Lee, Berta Grattan. *A Storage and Retrieval System for Documents in Instructional Resources.* U Miami, 1965. 12p.

Dougherty, Dora J., and others. *Transfer of Training in Flight Procedures from Selected Ground Training Devices to the Aircraft.* U.S. Naval Training Device Center, 1957. 91p.

Duke Benjamin C. (Ed.) *Survey of Educational Media Research in the Far East.* HEW, 1963. 181p.

Dworkin, Solomon, and Holden, Alan. "An Experimental Evaluation of Sound Filmstrips Vs. Classroom Lectures." *J Soc Motion Picture and Television Engineers* 68:383–5; 1959.

Educational Media Council. *Educational Media Index.* 14 vol. McGraw-Hill, 1964.

Eigen, Lewis, D., and Komoski, Kenneth. *Automated Teaching Project.* Collegiate School, New York City, 1960. 27p.

Ely, Donald. (Ed.) "The Changing Role of the Audiovisual Process in Education: A Definition and a Glossary of Related Terms." *Audiovisual Communications R* 11:1–148; 1963.

Erickson, Clifford G., and Chausow, Hymen M. *Chicago's TV College—Final Report of a Three-Year Experiment.* Chicago City Junior Col, 1960. 98p.

Faris, Gene, and Sherman, Mendel. *Quantitative Standards for Audiovisual Personnel, Equipment And Materials.* NEA, 1966. 18p.

Filip, Robert T. "A View from the Terminal Frame." *Audiovisual Communications R* 12:205–9; 1964.

Finn, James. "Instructional Technology." *Audiovisual Instruction* 10:192–4; 1965.

Finn, James D., and others. *Studies in the Growth of Instructional Technology, I: Audiovisual Instrumentation for Instruction in the Public Schools, 1930–1960; A Basis for Take-Off.* U Southern California, 1962. 108p.

Fisher, Margaret B., and Malpass, Leslie F. *A Comparison of Programed and Standard Textbooks in College Instruction.* U South Florida, 1963. 109p.

Fletcher, Richard M. *Profile Analysis and Its Effect on Learning When Used to Shorten Recorded Film Commentaries.* U.S. Naval Training Device Center, 1955. 25p.

Fritz, John O., and Massialas, Byron G. "Instructional Television and the Classroom Teacher." *Audiovisual Communications R* 12:5–15; 1964.

Froehlich, Herbert. "What About Classroom Communicators?" *Audiovisual Communications R* 11:19–26; 1963.

Fry, Edward B. "Teaching Machines: An Annotated Bibliography." *Audiovisual Communications R* 8:1–80; 1960.

Galas, Evangeline M. *The Development and Evaluation of an Elementary School Foreign Language Teaching Technique for Use by Teachers with Inadequate Knowledge of the Language Taught.* HEW, 1961. 56p.

Gentile, J. Ronald. "The First Generation of Computer-assisted Instructional Systems: An Evaluative Review." *Audiovisual Communications R* 15:23–53; 1967.

Greenhill, L. P. *A Study of the Feasibility of Minimum Cost Motion Picture Films.* U.S. Naval Training Device Center, 1955(a). 43p.

Greenhill, L. P. *The Evaluation of Instructional Films by a Trained Panel Using a Film Analysis Form.* U.S. Naval Training Device Center, 1955(b). 68p.

Gropper, George L. "Why Is a Picture Worth a Thousand Words." *Audiovisual Communications R* 11:75–95; 1963.

Hartman, Frank R. "Single and Multiple Channel Communication: A Review of Research and a Proposed Model." *Audiovisual Communications R* 9:235–62; 1961.

Hartman, Thomas F., and others. "Active Responding in Programed Learning Materials." *J Applied Psychol* 47:343–7; 1963.

Hauf, Harold D., and others. *New Spaces for Learning: designing college facilities to utilize instructional aids and media.* Rensselaer Polytechnic Institute, 1961. 80p.

Haverland, Edgar M. *Development of Technical Training Materials for Nike Hercules Junior Officers.* George Washington U, 1966. 39p.

Hayes, Alfred S. *Language Laboratory Facilities: Technical Guide for the Selection, Purchase, Use and Maintenance.* GPO, 1963. 119p.

Hill, Kenneth, and others. *A Plan for Educational Television in Hawaii.* KQED, San Francisco, 1961. 72p.

Hoban, Charles F. "Research and Reality." *Audiovisual Communications R* 4:3–20; 1956.

Hoban, Charles F. *Determinants of Adult Enrollment in Televised College-Credit Courses, Part II: Motivation, Resistance, and Conclusions.* U Pennsylvania, 1965(a). 35p.

Hoban, Charles F. "From Theory to Policy Decisions." *Audiovisual Communications R* 13:121–39; 1965(b).

Hoban, Charles F. Jr., and Van Ormer, Edward B. *Instructional Film Research 1918–1950.* U.S. Naval Training Device Center, 1950. 179p.

Holmes, Presley D., Jr. *Television Research in the Teaching-Learning Process.* Wayne State U, Division of Broadcasting, 1959. 152p.

Holtzman, Paul D., and VanderMeer, A. W. *Interdisciplinary Graduate Programs in Communications:*

A Descriptive Study. Pennsylvania State U. 105p.

Hughes, J. L. *The Effectiveness of Programed Instruction: Experimental Findings for 7070 Training.* IBM, 1961. 26p.

Instructional Film Research Program. *Evaluation of the Film: Military Police Support in Emergencies (Riot Control) TF19-1701.* U.S. Naval Training Device Center, 1954. 37p.

Jaspen, Nathan. *Effects On Training of Experimental Film Variables.* U.S. Naval Training Device Center, 1950. 13p.

Kanner, Joseph H., and Rosenstein, Alvin J. "Television in Army Training: Color Vs Black and White." *Audiovisual Communications R* 8:243-52; 1960.

Keating, Raymond F. *A Study of the Effectiveness of Language Laboratories.* Teachers Coll, Columbia U, 1963. 61p.

Kinder, James S. "Audiovisual Research: Where To Find It." *Audiovisual Communications R* 1:234-41; 1953.

Klapper, Hope Lunin. *Closed-Circuit Television as a Medium of Instruction at New York University, 1956-1957.* New York U, 1958. 68p.

Kumata, Hideya. *An Inventory of Instructional Television Research.* Michigan State U, 1956. 155p.

Langdale, A. Barnett. (Ed.) *Closed-Circuit Television—A Report of the Chelsea Project.* New York City Board Education, 1962. 362p.

Lenihan, Kenneth J., and others. *Utilization of the Regents Educational Television Broadcast Programs.* New York State Education Dept, 1963. 228p.

Lepore, Albert R., and Wilson, Jack D. *An Experimental Study of College Instruction Using Broadcast Television.* San Francisco State College, 1958. 77p.

Lorge, Sarah W. *The Relative Effectiveness of Four Types of Language Laboratory Experiences.* New York City Board of Education, 1963. 48p.

Loubriel, Oscar. *A Project To Demonstrate the Effectiveness of the Use of Television as a Means To Broaden the Education of Teachers in Service in Puerto Rico.* U Puerto Rico, 1962. 100p.

Lumsdaine, A. A., and others. *The Influence of Simple Animation Techniques on the Value of a Training Film.* Human Resources Research Laboratories, 1951.

Macomber, F. Glenn, and Siegel, Laurence. *Experimental Study in Instructional Procedures.* Miami U, 1960. 96p.

Marr, John N., and others. "The Contribution of the Lecture to College Teaching." *J Ed Psychol* 51:277-84; 1960.

Martin, Ann M., and Stone, C. Walter. *A Study of Regional Instructional Media Resources: Phase I—Manpower.* U Pittsburgh, 1965. 172p.

May, Mark A. *Enchancements and Simplifications of Motivational and Stimulus Variables in Audiovisual Instructional Materials.* HEW, 1965(a). 109p.

May, Mark A. *Word-Picture Relationships in Audiovisual Presentations.* HEW, 1965(b). 115p.

McCoy, Edward. *An Application of Research Findings To Training Film Production.* U.S. Naval Training Device Center, 1955. 29p.

McKnight, James A., and Hunter, Harold G. *An Experimental Evaluation of a Driver Simulator for Safety Training.* George Washington U, 1966. 30p.

Meierhenry, W. C. (Ed.) *Media and Educational Innovation.* U Nebraska, 1964. 341p.

Merrill, Irving Rodgers. "Liking and Learning from Educational Television." *Audiovisual Communications R* 4:233-45; 1956.

Merrill, Irving Rodgers. *Application of Profile Techniques for Training Aid Evaluation.* U.S. Naval Training Device Center, 1959. 48p.

Miller, Sharon W., and Brown, Robert M. "Development of a Method for Measuring Sources of Learning." In Twyford, Loran C., and others. (Eds.) *New Media Studies for Improvement of Science and Mathematics Instruction.* New York State Education Department, 1964. 122p.

Moldstad, John. "Doctoral Dissertations in Audiovisual Education." *Audiovisual Communications R* 4:291-333; 1956.

Moldstad, John. "Doctoral Dissertations in Audiovisual Education: Supplement I." *Audiovisual Communications R* 6:33-48; 1958.

Moldstad, John. "Doctoral Dissertations In Audiovisual Education: Supplement II." *Audiovisual Communications R* 7:142-53; 1959.

Moldstad, John. "Doctoral Dissertations in Audiovisual Education: Supplement III." *Audiovisual Communications R* 9:220-9; 1961.

Morris, Barry. (Ed.) "The Function of Media in the Public Schools." *Audiovisual Instruction* 8:9-14; 1963.

Murnin, J. A., and VanderMeer, A. W. *A Methodological Study in the Development of a Training Aids Selection Form.* U.S. Naval Training Device Center, 1956. 42p.

Nelson, Harold E., and Moll, Karl R. *Comparison of the Audio and Video Elements of Instructional Films.* U.S. Naval Training Device Center, 1950. 16p.

Newman, Slater E., and Highland, Richard W. *The Effectiveness of Four Instructional Methods at Different Stages of a Course.* Lackland Air Force Base, 1956. 22p.

Noel, Francis W., and others. *Practices of State Departments of Education In New Educational Media/Audiovisual Education During 1960-61.* U Southern California, L.A., 1963. 543p.

Norberg, Kenneth. (Ed.) "Perception Theory and AV Education." *Audiovisual Communications R* 10:1-108; 1962.

Oxhandler, Eugene K. (Ed.) *Operation Research and Systems Analysis as Applied To Media: Report of a Conference.* Syracuse U, 1964. 102p.

Pasewark, William R. *Teaching Typewriting Through Television.* Michigan State U, 1956. 65p.

Pflieger, Elmer F., and Kelly, Fred C. *The National Program In The Use of Television In The Public Schools—A Report On The Third Year.* Ford Foundation, Fund for Advancement Education, 1961. 125p.

Popham, W. James. *Tape Recorded Lectures in the College Classroom: An Experimental Appraisal.* Kansas State Col of Pittsburg, 1960. 15p.

Popham, W. James, and Sadnavitch, Joseph M. *The Effectiveness of Filmed Science Courses in Public Secondary Schools.* Kansas State College of Pittsburg, 1960. 63p.

Roe, Arnold, and others. *Automated Teaching Methods Using Linear Programs.* U California, Los Angeles, 1960. 57p.

Rugg, K. C. *Improving Instruction—Budgeting Your Audio Visual Program.* Indiana U, 1960. 90p.

Saul, Ezra V. *A Review of the Literature Pertinent to the Design and Use of Effective Graphic Training Aids.* U.S. Naval Training Device Center, 1956. 216p.

Saul, Ezra V. *Coordinate Index and Abstracts of Training Device Literature.* U.S. Naval Training Device Center. 1957. 230p.

Schramm, Wilbur. *The Research on Programed Instruction: An Annotated Bibliography.* HEW, 1964. 114p.

Seibert, W. F. "Comparative Costs For Televised and Conventional Instruction." *Audiovisual Communications R* 7:254–63; 1959.

Silverman, R. E. *The Comparative Effectiveness of Animated and Static Transparencies.* U.S. Naval Training Device Center, 1958. 25p.

Smith, J. Robert. *The Design of Instructional Systems.* Human Resources Research Office, George Washington U, 1966. 85p.

Smith, J. Robert. *An Annotated Bibliography on the Design of Instructional Systems.* George Washington U, 1967. 136p.

Smith, Ralph, and McAshan, Hildreth H. "A Comparison of the Relative Effectiveness of Four Methods of Teaching Ninth Grade General Science." In Twyford, Loran C., and others. (Eds.) *New Media Studies for Improvement of Science and Mathematics Instruction.* New York State Education Department, 1964. 122p.

Spaulding, Seth. "Communication Potential of Pictorial Illustrations." *Audiovisual Communications R* 4:31–46; 1956.

Starlin, Glenn. *Television and Higher Education— A Plan for Statewide Development in New York.* New York State Education Department, 1962. 122p.

Swanson, Robert A. *The Relative Effectiveness of Training Aids Designed for Use in Mobile Training Detachments.* Lackland Air Force Base, 1954. 14p.

Tauber, Maurice F., and Lilley, Oliver L. *Feasibility Study Regarding the Establishment of an Educational Media Research Information Service.* Columbia U, 1960. 235p.

Tintera, James B. *Instructor in Michigan—A Report of the State of Michigan Educational Television Study, 1960–61.* Michigan State U, 1961. 54p.

Torkelson, G. M. *The Comparative Effectiveness of a Mockup, Cutaway and Projected Charts in Teaching Nomenclature and Function of the 40mm Antiaircraft Weapon and the Mark 13 Type Torpedo.* U.S. Naval Training Device Center, 1954. 21p.

Travers, Robert M. W., and others. *Research and Theory Related to Audiovisual Information Transmission.* U Utah, 1964. 503p.

Twyford, Loran C. *A Comparison of Methods For Measuring Profiles of Learning From Instructional Films.* Doctoral dissertation. Pennsylvania State U, 1951. 212p.

Twyford, Loran C. "Profile Techniques for Program Analysis." *Audiovisual Communications R* 2:243–62; 1954.

Twyford, Loran C. (Ed.) *Instructional Television Research Reports.* U.S. Naval Training Device Center, 1956. 372p.

Twyford, Loran C. "Operations Research On Instructional Films." *J Soc Motion Picture and Television Engineers* 68:375–7; 1959.

Twyford, Loran C. "Educational Communications." *Audiovisual Instruction* 3:194–5; 1965.

Twyford, Loran C., and Carpenter, C. R. (Eds.) *Instructional Film Research Reports.* U.S. Naval Training Device Center, 1953. 760p.

Twyford, Loran C., and Carpenter, C. R. (Eds.) *Instructional Film Research Reports—Volume II.* U.S. Naval Training Device Center, 1956. 924p.

Twyford, Loran C., and Doherty, Leo D. "Measurement of Television Utilization." *Audiovisual Communications R* 9:271–80; 1961.

Twyford, Loran C., and others. "Behavioral and Factual Analysis." *Audiovisual Communications R* 7:182–92; 1959.

Twyford, Loran C., and others. *New Media for Improvement of Science Instruction.* New York State Education Department, 1964. 526p.

Tyler, Keith I. "The Impact of Instructional Television On Teaching Roles and Functions." *Audiovisual Communications R* 10:51–7; 1962.

VanderMeer, A. W. *Relative Effectiveness of Instruction By: Films Exclusively, Films Plus Study Guides, and Standard Lecture Methods.* U.S. Naval Training Device Center, 1950. 51p.

VanderMeer, A. W. *Training Film Evaluation: Comparison Between Two Films On Personal Hygiene: TF 8–155 and TF 8–1665.* U.S. Naval Training Device Center, 1953. 27p.

VanderMeer, A. W. "Systems Analysis and Media—A Perspective." *Audiovisual Communications R* 12:292–301; 1964.

VanderMeer, A. W., and others. *An Investigation of Educational Motion Pictures and a Derivation of Principles Relating to the Effectiveness of These Media.* Pennsylvania State U, 1965. 93p.

Vernon, Magdalen D. "The Value of Pictorial Illustration." *Br J Ed Psychol* 23: Part 3; 1953.

Westley, Bruce H., and Jacobson, Harvey K. "Instructional Television and Student Attitudes Toward Teacher, Course, and Medium." *Audiovisual Communications R* 11:47–60; 1963.

Wittich, W. A., and others. *The Wisconsin Physics Film Evaluation Project.* U Wisconsin, 1959. 30p.

Young, Clarence W., and Choquette, Charles A. *An Experimental Study of the Relative Effective-*

ness of Four Systems of Language Laboratory Equipment in Teaching French Pronunciation. Colgate U, 1963. 110p.

EDUCATIONAL HANDICAPS

At the outset it may be worthwhile to speculate upon the types of problems and the types of youngsters who, in different periods of educational history, would be considered as being educationally handicapped but not mentally retarded or physically disabled. It is interesting that the 1960 edition of this *Encyclopedia* included a chapter on "Bilingualism" but none on either cultural deprivation or emotional handicaps.

Probably the earliest writings on difficulties regarded as handicapping in schools were those dealing with dyslexia. This was regarded as a disorder in its own right. Although for a number of years the term disappeared from American writings it continued to be used in Europe, and within recent years has come back into vogue in connection with the study of perceptual or neurological difficulties which could underlie some reading disabilities.

The 1940's and 1950's witnessed a tendency to regard the phenomena of poor learning on the part of children of adequate intelligence as being linked to emotional disturbances of various sorts. Many articles, books, papers, and talks reporting case study after case study reflected the hope that counseling, casework, or psychotherapy would prove the salvation of boys and girls who were hampered by emotional blocks to learning or who suffered from conflicts which found unconscious expression in poor learning. The 1960's saw a continuation of this line of research. If anything new was added, it took the form of interest on the part of psychologists in the self concept and, of psychoanalysts, in ego psychology.

What did appear as a major educational preoccupation of the 1960's was "cultural deprivation" as a handicapping condition. When the Elementary and Secondary Education Act of 1965 tied the bulk of federal grants for local school systems to programs for deprived children, there was so vast an outpouring of articles and books that by 1966 the Educational Research Information Center was able to publish a truly selective catalog of some 2,740 documents! Some cynics began to speak of a "poverty industry."

The sheer volume of material on all of the topics dealing with learning disabilities linked not only to cultural disadvantage but to bilingualism, emotional handicaps, neurological damage, and perceptual difficulties, makes it impossible to treat them comprehensively. This article presents comment on a few researches chosen as illustrative of trends in each area. The examples given were selected because of interest rather than because they are a representative sample.

With respect to the present surge of interest in cultural deprivation or differentness or handicap, it should be recognized that during the 1930's there was already concern with the fact that children who grow up in the slum areas of big cities tend to do poorly in schools. They arrived, and still arrive, on the average, with low IQ's and weak motivation. They fail; they drop out. In earlier periods of history, there was a tendency to consider their troubles as stemming from the effect of bilingualism. The reader will realize that the big-city slums and the rural slums of yesteryear were populated by families of immigrants who in total were a polyglot mélange. Although Mexican children in the American Southwest and Puerto Rican children on the Eastern seaboard today come from homes where Spanish is spoken, Negro children and white children from the Appalachian highlands, whose families have spoken English for generations, show the same type of performance in schools as their linguistically more varied peers. Although few authorities would deny that any child would have difficulty in a school which used an unfamiliar tongue, it has become apparent that the root cause of the most serious learning difficulties is related to growing up in an impoverished and impoverishing environment.

The rather sudden upsurge of interest in schooling designed to counteract "cultural deprivation" found the supporting sciences of education peculiarly unprepared to supply either a firm theoretic base or a tested technology. The very term "cultural deprivation" lacks precision. There is no consensus as to its specific meaning and even less as to the specific cause-and-effect chains by which it does its damage.

To an extent the scientific situation reflects the fact that the upsurge in interest arises from a major change in the nature of the American economy. As late as the 1930's, the economy needed a broad base of unskilled labor. If the son or daughter of an Italian or Polish family did poorly in school, there still was a job waiting for him; on the basis of his earnings he could move his family out of the slums; his children would speak standard English, finish high school or even college, and enter the middle classes. In a sense, the poor education of the first- and second-generation immigrants fitted neatly into the needs of the economy.

By the 1960's, however, the picture had changed. A highly automated economy has little use for the dropout; if now the Negro or Mexican or Puerto Rican boy or girl cannot negotiate the paths of academic education and leaves school, he may go without work for years. The epigram is, "They drop out at 16 and retire at 18." Recognizing the explosive potential in a hopeless and unemployed youth group, Conant (1961), in his now classic study, spoke of "social dynamite." And, in the years since, the demonstrations, school boycotts, and riots have shown that this was no figure of speech.

In a few short years, the educational problems encountered by children from the lower socioeconomic segments of the population have become the main business of the school systems in our major cities. The change in emphasis came with such rapidity that today we must confess that hundreds of millions of dollars are being poured into programs shaped more by good will and hopeful guesswork than by any knowledge tested in tough-minded research design.

There are two major questions to which research must quickly find precise answers: What are the specific effects of cultural deprivation? What educational strategies will counteract those effects? Here we shall deal principally with the first question.

Various writers come at it from quite different approaches. Some have taken the tack of looking for specific ways in which the intellectual functioning of the young people differs from that of middle-class children. There is a wealth of research indicating that children from the lower reaches of the socioeconomic scale not only earn low scores on mental tests but that their IQ's drop with age. The fact of this *cumulative deficit* has been established. It is the volume of the problem which becomes striking. In 1966, there were 10 elementary schools in Detroit where over 18 percent of the children in *regular* third-grade classes scored below the fourth percentile on national norms. The scores for the fifth graders, when compared with their scores in the third grade, saw no upward changes; all changes were downward.

In the 1950's there was a tendency to blame this type of finding on the tests. It had been argued, and with some surface validity, that the tests used to measure mental ability contained items and wording familiar to middle-class children but alien to lower-class children. However, when "culture fair" tests were constructed and utilized, lower-class children still showed gross disadvantage. Lesser and others (1963), for example, found that social class differences were associated with significant differences in verbal ability, reasoning, number facility, and space conceptualization; that ethnic-group membership (Chinese, Jewish, Negro, and Puerto Rican) also was associated with differences in the pattern of abilities.

Whiteman and others (1965) went directly to the question of deprivation by developing a Deprivation Index based on condition of housing, educational aspiration level of parent for child, number of children in the home, dinner conversation, cultural experiences, and attendance at kindergarten. The multiple correlation between these six factors and fifth-grade reading level was .49. They also found that not only was there a significant relationship between IQ and deprivation, but that intellectual deficits were linked to environmental factors associated with being Negro. In a sense, their findings would seem to indicate that many lower-class Negro children are victims of a one-two punch: early intellectual handicaps are related to socioeconomically linked deprivation; later educational deficits may be occasioned by disadvantaging factors associated with race.

One series of investigations has sought to tease out the precise nature of the learning disabilities linked either to class or race. The starting point is, as observed by Rapier (1962), that teachers observe wide differences in learning and inconsistencies in performance unsupported by anything measured in tests. As has been recognized for quite some time, intelligence tests measure what an individual has learned during his lifetime; the assumption is that all have had an equal opportunity to learn. A different measurement strategy, if we are interested in the ability to learn which can be brought to bear at any point in the lifetime, would be to compare performances on specific and unfamiliar tasks, from a zero point which would be the same for all subjects.

Using this strategy with respect to the learning of paired associates, Semler and Iscoe (1963) found no significant differences between a group of white children and a comparison group of Negro children in Austin, Texas, although the average IQ of the whites was 103 and that of Negroes, 95. At about the same time Jensen and Rohwer (1963) became interested in the extent to which verbal mediation affected both paired-associate and serial learning.

They found that among children of low learning ability from deprived backgrounds there were a number whose difficulties could be pinpointed as being linked to a failure on their part to engage in what the authors term "mnemonic elaboration." Middle-class children after reaching a correct answer tend to fix it in their memories by several devices, including that of verbalizing about the solution. When the conditions of a learning experiment were rigged to force such elaboration, a group of apparently mentally retarded, lower-class subjects showed a startling scatter; while some turned in a poor performance, a few proved equal to gifted middle-class children.

The significance of the program of research by Jensen and his coworkers lies in the demonstration that there may be specific and educationally correctable differences in sets or procedures which result from deprivations. From such a demonstration there are two lines of research programs which can follow. One is to attempt to devise and test learning exercises or experiences designed to teach the missing technique. As this is being written, a project with precisely this goal is under way. The second line of work would be to determine if there are additional and perhaps equally demonstrable lacks. In a later article, Jensen (1966) suggests that this may indeed be the case with respect to perceptual processes and learning to attend.

Using psychoanalytic schema, Bower (1966) lists five major dimensions of "ego processes," the lack of which can produce difficulties in learning how to use symbols, which he takes as the most significant aspect of human learning. These five dimensions are: differentiation vs. diffusion, fidelity vs. distortion, pacing vs. overloading or underloading, expansion vs. constriction, and integration vs. fragmentation. In each case the first term in the polar description represents the healthy state; the second, the handicapping condition.

Whether one follows the empirical isolation of handicaps in the mode of Jensen or the more theoretically based system of Bower, one must accord hope to the fact that efforts to locate the specific difficulties can in the long run result in the design of educational programs with much more definite rationale than is the case for many on which reliance is now being placed.

Interestingly, it is evident that not only socio-economically deprived children but many coming from middle-class or even upper-class homes may have educational handicaps. Although Jensen is concerned about the deprivation factor, Bower, as do many others with psychoanalytic orientation, does not concentrate upon social class associations. Rather, he ties the handicapping conditions to defects in mothering of early family experiences. These can and do occur at all socioeconomic levels, although they seem more likely to be epidemic where poverty adds its stresses to other conditions.

It is also interesting that much of the research in one way or another highlights the difficulties with verbalism of children from deprived backgrounds. This raises in somewhat different fashion the question of the effects of bilingualism and the question as to how much attributed in earlier research to bilingualism has a different origin. In one study conducted by the College of Education of Arizona State University (1960), an analysis was made of mental retardation and pseudo-mental retardation with relation to both bilingual and subcultural factors in a Spanish-speaking population in the American Southwest. It was quite apparent that the handicapping effect of bilingualism was linked to social class; there was less difference between bilingual and unilingual children at the upper than at the lower socioeconomic levels. Clear-cut bilingualism, in which the child spoke one language on some occasions and the second on others, was less handicapping than when the child spoke a mixture of the two in undifferentiated form. This suggests that, to the extent that they speak and understand non-standard English the so-called English-speaking "culturally deprived" children of today resemble the dialect-plagued third-generation immigrant children of previous generations.

One of the most clear-cut demonstrations of the relationship between social class and the effects of bilingualism comes out of Israel. Smilansky (1956) compared the ability to learn Hebrew of two groups of imigrants to that country—middle-class children from European backgrounds and lower-class children from Near Eastern or North African countries. In actuality the European tongues are more distant from Hebrew than the Arabic (which are in the Semitic family of languages) spoken in North Africa and Asia Minor. A difference of 16 IQ points, and concomitant difficulties in learning to read, were found in his samples of the two different groups.

Up to this point we have considered those lines of research which seem to link cultural deprivation either to specific learning disabilities or to linguistic difficulties. As is well known, there is a more sociologically inclined stream of research which takes the position that the directly causal factor is motivational in nature. Some research workers tend to view the damage as stemming from weak or negative self concepts on the part of learners; others look to weak motivation.

Wattenberg and Clifford (1962) obtained measures of self concept and of mental ability on children entering kindergarten both in a middle-class and in a working-class school in Detroit. Two and one-half years later they obtained test scores on reading. The measures of self concept proved somewhat more highly predictive of beginning achievement in reading than did the mental test scores. The relevance of this finding to the other issues we have been discussing is highlighted by papers delivered at the Conference on Relationship of Education to Self-Concept in Negro Children and Youth (1965).

A somewhat related line of research deals with the motivation to learn. Farquhar (1963) has compared underachievers with normal or overachieving students at the high school level. Using a varied battery of measures he found that the two groups tended to show distinctive patterns as to motivation. His interpretation of his results is given an intriguing twist in that he points out that much of schooling taps motivational patterns which are more typical of middle-class than of lower-class students. The implication is that if schools modified their procedures to build on the motivational characteristics of children from lower-class homes they could be more successful.

However, many writers dealing with emotional handicaps to learning are not so much interested in class-related phenomena or the direct or the indirect effects of cultural deprivations as they are in the general problem of how emotional blocks to learning arise. To be sure, psychological deprivations which can occur in homes at any cultural level may be included in the etiology of emotional conditions. In some instances, the outgrowth of the child's development may be an unconscious motivation to do poorly.

Much of the research along these lines consists of case studies reported usually by a single therapist. One of the more ambitious projects was a treatment study of 70 intellectually capable students considered actual or potential dropouts conducted by Lichter and others (1963).

One paragraph of the conclusions will be quoted here in full because it conveys the typical flavor of much work in its vein:

"School had an unconscious and specific psychodynamic meaning for quite a number of our students, mostly the boys. It had become involved in the dependency conflicts of some of the immature children who were afraid to grow up. Most of the more mature boys had a type of emotional disturbance that made them especially vulnerable to school problems: conflict around competitive aggression. The majority were inhibiting themselves in the face of social pressures toward aggressive masculine achievement. In high school, rivalry is intense for scholarship, sports awards, leadership, and social superiority. To the inhibited boys, seeking competence in any of these areas unconsciously represented becoming better than their fathers and carried the threat of castration. They were consciously afraid that they could not be successful and would get hurt in the process of trying to achieve. Much more security and safety lay in withdrawing from the competitive-aggressive struggle —in being nonachievers."

Radin and Masling (1963) reported on the results of three years of psychotherapy with a boy whose

Binet IQ's were, successively, 173 and 196! He had been referred to them because of impending school failure! Although the dynamics of this one case are too involved for summary the existence of it does underline the contention that emotional factors arising from family interactions can have amazing power to induce educational handicaps, even in the presence of great intellectual potential.

Since the processes which bring boys and girls to the attention of child guidance clinics and private therapists are more likely to be successfully negotiated by middle-class or upper-class parents, the case study literature tends to be heavily weighted with cases where the intellectual ability to learn has been counteracted by the emotional block or by disabling unconscious motivation. We can only surmise what happens in those cases where the negative motivation or the blockage coexists with low mental capacity. Cases of this latter type are most likely to come to attention if the compounding conditions also include delinquency. So to speak, the "good" child of below-average intelligence and working-class origin seldom gets treated for emotional problems; however, if he steals or assaults people, or if she gets pregnant, then there is a chance for study in depth. Almost always the reports mention the existence of educational handicaps of marked degree. Usually, however, the focus is on the misbehavior and the pathological processes which account for the delinquency. The personality problems which resulted in the behavior disorder are also implicated in the learning difficulties. And, as a corollary, when treatment produces a change in the delinquency, one symptom is that school work and conduct also improve. A good example of this is provided by Slavson's work (1965). In providing intensive group therapy to boys at the Children's Village in Dobbs Ferry, N.Y., he noted the presence in all of them of what he termed a "doom motif." They saw themselves as condemned to failure, and therefore as being unable to help themselves through their own efforts. As the group moved toward less damaging self concepts they began to think and, later, to act on the assumption that they could by their own efforts find better living. With almost monotonous regularity, the case reports include different attitudes toward school and the beginning of success in school.

As we review the literature dealing with educational handicaps we note in recent years a revival in new form of one of the oldest trends, work based on the thesis that there are defects in the central nervous system which account for the otherwise inexplicable fact that there are boys and girls who have adequate intelligence and yet who have problems with school learning which will not yield to any of the known programs of treatment. In some cases there is evidence of brain damage, of perceptual handicaps, and of neurological deficits. There has been a substantial increase in programs geared to the possibility that organic causes are at work. It is too early to provide a definitive evaluation of this renewed stream of research. It seems clear that there are young people whose handicaps reside in this domain. However, there also seems to be a propensity to lump all these possibilities together. For the hard-headed researcher, the vagueness in the classification system poses one problem; the lack of control groups poses another. With respect to brain damage, for example, one finds in the normal population a significant number of children who show unusual patterns on electro-encephalograms.

Despite the fact that there are difficulties with precision of diagnosis, we must report that there is evidence of cases in which medication has produced changes. For example, Nichamin and Comly (1964) have written about children whose learning in school was hampered by hyperactivity or by lethargy. In a study of one hundred such children they found that behavior in school and, with that, learning of academic work, improved after appropriate drugs were administered. With respect to learning disorders which have a neurological basis, considerable research has been conducted by Myklebust and Boshes (1960). Among the factors often implicated is "minimal brain damage." Some difficulties in interpretation of this line of research are presented by the fact that the reason for the qualifying adjective "minimal" is that the degree of damage is difficult to demonstrate; also, although symptoms can be detected in a number of children suffering from educational handicaps, there is some question as to how many children who have normal learning patterns also exhibit equal evidence of neurological dysfunction.

A parallel problem exists with respect to the linking of reading problems to "perceptual handicaps." Although perceptual functioning is measured by the well-known tests of Frostig, there is some question about the extent to which these tap but one facet of something which is primarily developmental or maturational.

The reason for the cautiousness with which this topic is being treated here is that, although there have been many programs advanced and although discussion of this topic in educational circles has risen to fadlike intensity, the number of basic studies reported in psychological journals is small. In the 1965 index issue of *Psychological Abstracts*, for example, there are only two citations relating to perceptual handicaps in children. One is to a doctoral dissertation dealing with the relative presence of sensori-motor handicaps in a group of poor learners and in a group of adequate learners. The other is an interesting discussion by Kephart (1964) of his ideas relative to the importance of perceptual-motor aspects of learning disability. When one realizes that for 1965, *Psychological Abstracts* published well over 10,000 citations to studies of all sorts, this paucity of scientific data is striking. With these facts in mind the present author feels he cannot say with any confidence either that study of perceptual and neurological disabilities is the wave of the future or that it is one of those weakly based enthusiasms which sweeps the educational scene from time to time. The only stance which can be recommended with integrity at the present time is an open-minded wait-and-see position.

The fact seems to be that many educational handicaps have a complex etiology. The extent to which this is the case is revealed in a study in which de Hirsch and her coworkers (1966) gave a series of 37 tests or other measures to 53 preschool children in New York and then waited until the children were near the close of the second grade, at which time their achievement in reading, writing, and spelling was tested. Nineteen of the tests were significantly co-related with later overall achievement in reading; 20 with spelling; and 16 with writing performance. Hyperactivity, distractability, uninhibited behavior, motor control, graphomotor abilities, ego strength, and work attitudes all proved to be substantially predictive. These could be taken to be indicative of neurological impairment, perceptual acuity, and emotional conditions, as well as other items linked to linguistic expressiveness. The mélange presented by the predictively efficient measures bespeaks the complexity of the situation. This argues against placing primary reliance on single-ingredient programs designed to correct only one disabling condition. It argues for the need to continue looking for better ways of describing with precision the particular pattern of difficulties found in each individual child and in looking for solutions through programs designed to bring to bear for each child the particular combination of ingredients needed to work with him.

William W. Wattenberg
Detroit Public Schools

References

Bower, Eli. "Personality and Individual Maladjustment." In *Social Deviancy Among Youth*, 65th Yearbook, NSSE. U Chicago Press, 1966.

College of Education, Arizona State University. *Investigation of Mental Retardation and Pseudo Mental Retardation in Relation to Bilingual and Subcultural Factors*. Arizona State U, 1960.

Conant, James B. *Slums and Suburbs*. McGraw-Hill, 1961.

Conference on Relationship of Education to Self-Concept in Negro Children and Youth. McGraw-Hill, 1965.

de Hirsch, Katrina, and others. *Predicting Reading Failure*. Harper, 1966.

Educational Research Information Center. *Catalogue of Selected Documents on the Disadvantaged*. HEW, 1966.

Farquhar, William W. *Motivational Factors Related to Academic Achievement*. Cooperative Research Project No. 846, Michigan State U, 1963.

Frostig, Marianne. *Developmental Test of Visual Perception*. Consulting Psychologists Press, 1961.

Jensen, Arthur R. "Social Class and Perceptual Learning." *Mental Hygiene* 50:226–39; 1966.

Jensen, Arthur R., and Rohwer, W. D., Jr. "Verbal Mediation in Paired-Associate and Serial Learning." *J Verbal Learning and Verbal Behavior*, 1:346–53; 1963.

Kephart, Newell C. "Perceptual-Motor Aspects of Learning Disabilities." *Excep Children*, 31:201–6; 1964.

Lesser, Gerald S., and others. *Mental Abilities of Children in Different Social and Cultural Groups*. Cooperative Research Project No. 1635, GPO, 1963.

Lichter, Solomon O., and others. *The Dropouts*. Free Press, 1963.

Myklebust, Helmer, and Boshes, Benjamin. "Psychoneurological Learning Disorders in Children." *Archives Pediatrics* 77:247–56; 1960.

Nichamin, Samuel J., and Comly, Hunter M. "The Hyperkinetic or Lethargic Child with Cerebral Dysfunction." *Michigan Medicine* 63:790–2; 1964.

Radin, Sherwin S., and Masling, Joseph. "Tom: A Gifted Under-Achieving Child." *J Child Psychol Psychiatry* 4:183–97; 1963.

Rapier, Jacqueline S. "Measured Intelligence and the Ability to Learn." *Acta Psychol, Amsterdam* 20:1–7; 1962.

Semler, Ira J., and Iscoe, Ira. "Comparative and Developmental Study of the Learning Abilities of Negro and White Children under Four Conditions." *J Ed Psychol* 54:38–44; 1963.

Slavson, S. R. *Reclaiming the Delinquent*. Free Press, 1965.

Smilansky, S. *Teaching Reading in a Second Language to Culturally Deprived Children*, Outline Presented at the First World Congress on Reading. Paris: UNESCO Palace, August 6, 1956. (Mimeographed.)

Wattenberg, William W., and Clifford, Clare. *Relationship of the Self-Concept to Beginning Achievement in Reading*. Cooperative Research Project No. 377, Wayne State U, 1962.

Whiteman, Martin, and others. "Some Effects of Social Class and Race and Children's Language and Intellectual Abilities." Paper presented to the Biennial Meeting of the Society for Research in Child Development, Minneapolis, March 1965.

EDUCATIONAL PROGRAMS—COLLEGE AND UNIVERSITY

Since 1957–58 the amount of literature about programs of higher education has increased to the point where only a selected sample can be reviewed. This is the period of growth for offices of institutional research, of the evolution of centers for the study of higher education, of expansion of research budgets of paraeducational institutions such as the College Entrance Examination Board and the Educational Testing Service, of a slight shift from disinterest to some concern for the study of higher education by people in academic disciplines, and, of course, of the radical expansion of funding for studies of higher education. It is also the period of elaborate state surveys of higher education and, one suspects, the period of increases in the number of conferences on higher education, each resulting in proceedings of varying degrees of sophistication. And this decade has been a time of experimentation with new forms, structures, and practices of higher education as the enterprise sought to cope with drastic increases in numbers of students, with the explosion of knowledge, and with the needs of a rapidly changing society. But perhaps a sample, if it be wisely chosen, will reflect the broad dimensions of higher education both within and without the United States.

In a way it is unfortunate that much research information is contained in omnibus compendia, books of readings, and conference reports, for specific items are likely to be lost under the overly generalized titles assigned. It is equally unfortunate that some of the more relevant research is still presented only in mimeographed form or is contained in speeches given by research workers. But this being the situation, a first source must be this fugitive literature.

Each spring the Association for Higher Education, an affiliate of the National Education Association, conducts an annual conference of higher education and publishes the texts of papers under the title *Current Issues in Higher Education*. Generally, these papers represent a range from quite platitudinous opinions to statements reflecting fresh and even ongoing research. But the conference theme each year provides some guidance. Thus, Guide Lines for the 60's, Goals for Higher Education in a Decade of Decision, Higher Education in an Age of Revolutions, Critical Decision in Higher Education, Undergraduate Education, and Pressures and Priorities in Higher Education, all suggest the dynamic quality of colleges and universities during this period of intense growth. At one time the American Council on Education presented the speeches from its annual meeting in issues of the *Educational Record*, but in 1964 it began commissioning background papers and publishing those, along with statements given at the conference, in book form. Wilson (L. Wilson, 1964) edited the 1964 effort to underscore the new ways of governance in higher education, and Dennis and Kaufman (1966) reported on the many forms a newly found concern for students took. Generally, the point of view in the latter study was ambivalent, not about the situation but about solutions. Some wanted full student participation in governance and some only enough student involvement to quiet demands.

The U.S. Office of Education, sensing the need for the practitioner of education to know of new developments and research results, initiated a pamphlet series under the title *New Dimensions in Higher Education*. In this series, Hatch and Bennet (1960a) indicate that class size or a specific ideal methodology are not nearly so important as the nature of teaching, particularly as it stresses problem solving and facilitates student learning. The same authors (1960b) show that allowing students to learn on their own is as effective as other, more orthodox devices and that there is a pronounced trend to make independent study available even in the freshman year. Duryea (1960) isn't able to report such substantive findings but does reveal a growing desire to find principles of administration and to apply them in practical situations. Freedman and Hatch (1960) summarize a number of studies to show that college does seem to make some difference. Compared with freshmen, seniors know more, are more tolerant, but are less stable. The student culture is the most potent force operating to change student behavior and it apparently persists from one student generation to the next. To summarize developments of a rapidly expanding approach, Radcliffe and Hatch (1961) indicate that over one-fourth (and the proportion has grown since) of all four-year colleges subscribe to the principles of the Advanced Placement Program, which enables superior students to receive appropriate placement and college credit for college-level work taken during high school. The program has generally succeeded in motivating superior students. A similar loosening of procedure is noted by Lewis (1961), who sees increased use of flexibility in class-hour arrangements, credit by examination, and comprehensive examinations as means of adapting to wide student differences with respect to abilities, experience, and changing institutional goals and objectives. And Cole and Lewis (1962) also discover emerging practices typically consisting of substitutions for specific course requirements, adapting courses to students, and making greater use of individual study.

The Center for the Study of Higher Education of the University of California at Berkeley and the Western Interstate Commission for Higher Education (WICHE) have since 1959 sponsored summer workshops, each of which has resulted in collections of published papers. Under the titles of *College Self Study* (WICHE, 1959), *Research on College Students* (WICHE, 1960), *Studies of College Faculty* (WICHE, 1961), *The Study of Campus Culture* (WICHE, 1962), *The Study of Academic Administration* (WICHE, 1963), *Long Range Planning in Higher Education* (WICHE, 1964), and *Order and Freedom on the Campus* (WICHE, 1965), this series has brought together perhaps the freshest research on each of those topics.

Of a somewhat different order but still presenting a number of topics developed by outstanding scholars are two books edited by Harris (1965, 1966). These volumes were based upon seminars in higher education held at Harvard. The first focuses on government and education, educational planning, and management of colleges and universities, and the second on political, qualitative, and economic issues in higher education. The papers generally establish that higher education has become an instrument of national and social policy and must be treated as such.

Another single-volume compilation is one which some wits have suggested will become the most widely quoted, least read book on higher education of this decade. In this compilation, Sanford (1962) obtained research or interpretative essays from scholars, chiefly in the behavioral sciences, and linked them together with his own insights. Generally, the book establishes that a unique age and stage exists for college undergraduates and stresses the influence of peer groups on student behavior, performance, and eventual change. For the less robust, the book has been edited into a shorter volume (1964). This presents findings but does not bother the reader with much methodology.

Daedalus, the Journal of the American Academy of Arts and Sciences, devoted its Fall 1964 issue to higher education (American Academy of Arts and Sciences, 1964). Estrin and Goode (1964) edited a number of articles appearing in *Improving College and University Teaching* and published them. And Cooper (1958) edited the papers of the Minnesota Centennial Conference on College Teaching. Each of these contains reports based upon research, but in such numbers that individual citations will not typically be made.

One should not overlook the several encyclopedias which contain important sections of relevance for colleges and universities. McKeachie (1963) summarizes many different studies which seem to show that a little, but not much, is readily known about how to engineer learning for college students. And Clark (1964) considers studies about education in society, the entire educational establishment, the internal life of educational institutions, and educational efforts being made outside of the established institutions. He points out that while social scientists have long ignored education as an object of study, they are now giving it considerable attention.

A last collection, specific parts of which will be cited later, is Baskin's collection of essays (1965) dealing with new colleges, the curriculum, students, new media, facilities, administration, and economics. Each chapter is written by an acknowledged scholar and represents in a way a summary of relevant research.

Purposes, objectives, or goals of higher education are essentially value statements; hence, research regarding their validity is in one sense impossible. But they are important in determining educational, social, and economic questions, and even at times have influenced teaching. Thus, a résumé of research about colleges and universities must give some attention to purposes, how they are arrived at, and, if possible, how well they have been achieved.

Purposes of higher education will usually be found someplace in a college catalog, in reports of regional and national committees, and in the statements of educational leaders and the pleas of lay leaders; and their existence may be inferred from observing what students do, what taxpayers will support, and how a college is organized. Perhaps no other aspect of collegiate education has attracted as much writing and oratory. And perhaps about no subject is genuine agreement less possible—even within a single institution or department.

National panels such as the Educational Policies Commission (1964, 1966) of the National Education Association have attempted to formulate the goals of education. In its 1964 statement the Commission affirmed that ". . . the nation's goal of universal educational opportunity must be expanded to include at least two further years of education, open to any high school graduates, and designed to move each student toward intellectual freedom." The 1966 statement affirms that this is the age of science and that science must pervade educational programs. Through historical inference, Brickman and Lehrer (1962) see that higher education has become one of the important keys to a better life and to survival on this planet. It has moved from a ". . . citadel of limited curricular offerings to a colossus of learning and expanding courses, expanding enrollments and expanding research facilities and new buildings." The various state surveys of higher education, of which over 40 were completed between 1958 and 1963 alone, have also tried to arrive at purposes and goals. Generally these purposes are accepted by the public and the profession in the abstract, as was true in New Jersey (1962). But whether or not they are put into effect through legislation depends on whether or not a state is wealthy or poor, growing or static in size, or rapidly or slowly becoming industrialized (Pollack, 1965).

Many of the attempts to state purposes for colleges or universities are the efforts of single writers, drawing upon years of experience in colleges and universities but making no pretense of having established their postulates on any sort of empirical base. Frankel (1959) sees that purposes and goals have not emerged out of deliberate decision or conscious adherence to a particular philosophy. Rather they have developed out of stubborn imperatives on the American scene. Hutchins (1964) holds that the purpose of education is to produce responsible citizens but that this purpose is jeopardized by the forces of industrialization, specialization, philosophical diversity, and social and political conformity. Adler and Mayer (1958) are much less sure, for they believe that the endowment of humans is such that the objectives of education can never be final. However, later they speak as though they know what those final objectives are. Gardner (1963–64) puts a different twist on the matter when he claims the purpose of education for renewal to be education for versatility. While recognizing the intense need for specialists, he believes that the greater need for much of college education is for it to be more general—general but, according to DeVane (1965), increasingly democratized, and, as a result, increasingly practical. Higher education has tried and continues to try to meet every demand—hence the variety of types of institutions. No one has made this same point with greater effect than Kerr (1963), who believes that ". . . the university is being called upon to produce knowledge as never before—for civic and regional purposes, for national purposes, and even for no purpose at all beyond the realization that most knowledge eventually comes to serve mankind."

Few individuals writing about purposes of higher education do so in the form of a systematic philosophy. One, however, who has attempted to do so is Brubacher (1965). By comparing the statements of many, he attempts by inference to establish what higher education seeks to do and to whom. What

Brubacher attempts as a philosopher, Rudy (1960) seeks to do as a historian. It is out of historical developments that higher education has created a workable compromise between the rival claims of liberal and specialized education.

Several other attempts to state purposes for higher education should be noted. The "Rockefeller Report" (1958), using a panel of experts, sees the end of education to be the development of each individual to the highest level of excellence his abilities and calling will allow. Also using a panel, supported by staff research, is the report of "Goals for Higher Education in the South" (Southern Regional Education Board, 1961). It points out that the South has lagged far behind the rest of the country in higher education and establishes goals and guide lines for their achievement. Perhaps no type of institution has been more self-conscious in its attempts to establish purposes and goals for itself than has the junior or community college. Medsker (1960), Thornton (1960), and Johnson (University of California, 1964) are just a few among many who through questionnaire, interview, and historical inference have sought to establish that the junior college offers transfer, general education, technical-vocational, and adult education curricula and serves as a community center as well. One study suggests that the junior college ought to be more parsimonious in its claims, even perhaps eliminating the transfer effort (Blocker, 1965). But the purposes of other types of higher education have also been studied. Berelson (1960) and Carmichael (1962) have each tried to determine from interviews, studies of catalogs, and conference reports what graduate education should attempt to do. And Cartter (1966) has attempted to rate graduate schools.

The purposes of another rapidly growing segment of higher education are presented by the Petersens (1960). Adult education is seen to serve remedial, vocational, cultural, and political needs of the community. And the purposes of the oldest type of collegiate institution, the liberal arts college, are shown by Wormald (1964) to be relevant and viable in the last half of the twentieth century. In general, the essays constituting this book are defenses against the judgment of Jacques Barzun (1964) that the liberal arts college is either dead or dying. The purposes of various professional forms of education have also been presented. Evans (1964), Hollinshead (1960), Perkins (1962), and Conant (1963) have respectively presented the goals of education in medicine, dentistry, history, and teaching. Medical education offered within the university has become more disease-oriented and less patient-oriented, thus producing doctors who don't appreciate the complex human roles they are expected to play. To meet even minimal needs for dental service, the output of dental schools should be doubled by 1975 and the public educated to use dental services more. Although American graduate departments of history have maintained rigorous standards of scholarship they have not been quite so successful at developing powers of teaching and it is high time they did. A review of requirements for teaching certification reveals a maze of ineffective and inappropriate courses. The power to certify should be given each college, which normally would then require only practice teaching and some work in psychology. The bulk of professional courses, as they are now taught, are judged not very good.

THE CURRICULUM. The bulk of the work published on the collegiate curriculum is descriptive, argumentative, or reflective and philosophical. Perhaps this must be so, although one could wish that research workers, especially those trained in psychology, might concentrate some effort on appraising the impact of various parts of the curriculum. Perhaps, although present performance does not make one sanguine, the growing number of offices of institutional research and centers for the improvement of instruction will remedy this situation before 1980.

General education still is the curricular subject attracting most study and receiving most treatment in writing. Mayhew (1960) attempts to describe general education and its administrative, curricular, teaching, staffing, and evaluational problems. Thomas (1962) traces the origin of the movement, as have others, and finds that ". . . most of the experiments have been honest efforts to correct weaknesses in our educational system." These two were the principal book-length studies of general education as a movement until Bell (1966) reported his analysis of the programs at three similar, yet dissimilar institutions—Columbia, Harvard, and Chicago. He seeks to answer the question of whether the general education of the present and future should be the same as that of the past 20 years. And generally he answers no. The changes in secondary schools and graduate schools have been too fundamental.

The literature is relatively full of descriptions of courses in general education. Under the general editorship of Earl J. McGrath, books descriptive of curriculum building, humanities, science, social science, communications, and personal development have been produced. Carlin (1960), Haun (1960), Fisher (1960), Mayhew (1962b), Morse and Dressel (1960), and Shoemaker and Forsdale (1960) have each edited collections of course descriptions and have made some attempt to evaluate the progress or changes made since an earlier and similar series was edited in the early 1950's. Generally, courses have maintained their interdisciplinary bias but typically reflect some movement toward the single-discipline position. The *Journal of Higher Education, Journal of General Education, Liberal Education,* and *School and Society* normally contain articles descriptive of individual courses in almost every issue. Illustrative of the genre is Hoffman's plea (1964) for a required philosophy course. The course should develop students' critical powers and should train them to think philosophically through being confronted with the best of philosophical thinking. Holton (1964), believing that science for the nonscientist should help orient people to external surroundings and to change them when necessary, would have such courses stress scientific and mathematical methodological rigor, the history of science, and the underlying structure of science. He would present these emphases in a two-year sequence, one in the physical and the other in the biological sciences. Jones (1966) argues that history, if taught in small segments with appreciation for detail, can and should show that men and women in other times led radically different lives than they do now. History need not be, indeed for general education should not be, panoramic.

Since World War II the United States and its people have been forced to discover the rest of the world, and to accommodate it in the curriculum. This accommodation has intensified with the advent of the jet airliner, which makes travel and study abroad well within the reach of many college students. Perhaps the most comprehensive survey of the actual achievements of American educational involvement with other nations was made by Weidner (1962). He finds that the better student-abroad programs have had impacts on substantial portions of students who participated in them. However, the majority have produced disappointing results thus far. The programs of some of the more deeply involved universities are described and assessed by Education and World Affairs (1966). This appraisal establishes the fact that university development is currently quite similar regardless of where it occurs. In the United States early experiments have now matured, and in the 1960's for the first time the entire university has come into focus as the major actor on the stage of international education. Universities currently are seeking to integrate internally their far-ranging international interests and are seeking new forms of interinstitutional cooperation in the international field. Bidwell (1962) is also critical as a result of his elaborate study of undergraduate courses in foreign affairs. He finds courses to be small and not particularly well taught. Basic courses such as those in American history tend to need reorganization so that international dimensions can be added. And the Morrill Commission (1960) also found much to be desired. The universities' response to the demand for greater international understanding has been to date largely sporadic and unplanned. But they and the colleges have enormous opportunities, which they can take advantage of if they will transcend their Western orientation, assign high priority to world affairs, cooperate to make better use of scarce resources, and devote more resources to the effort. As though to respond to such demands the Commission on International Understanding (1964) reports on what a number of colleges have done to overcome Western provincialism. After a long history of effort, non-Western language and area programs have finally been accepted as part of the collegiate curriculum. While the number of students is small, the outlook for growth is promising.

Since Jacob's report (1957), the place of moral and spiritual values in the collegiate curriculum has received more and more attention. Bushnell (1960), drawing on the Vassar Studies, seeks students still unaffected with respect to political, religious, or community concerns. Values, when they are changed, are modified more by the extracurricular than by the curricular efforts of the college. Raushenbush (1964), however, using visitation, interview, questionnaire, correspondence, and examination of records, sees collegiate education as making important value changes in students. Whether or not this happened, however, depended to a large extent upon whether or not the individual student and the selected institution meshed with each other. To present her findings she uses case studies of students selected from her sample. Her conclusions, like those of many others, stress the importance of small groups, peer groups, and close relations with a professor or adviser. This same feeling is reflected by Sanford and Katz (1966), who find that while many students do remain pretty much as they were, a fair number change significantly with respect to tolerance, openness, and concern for community. Pattillo and Mackenzie (Danforth Foundation, 1965) found in a major study of church-related colleges that student regard for courses in religion varied widely, as did knowledge of religious subjects, according to the institution. They found as particular items of weakness a lack of involvement in discussion of public issues and the fact that religion as a world view or explanation of existence is not really penetrating college education. As to what role religion should play in higher education, there are many statements but little systematic study. A good example is Gerstein's lectures (1964), which generally find that the study of religion is appropriate but question whether such study seeks to modify religious values.

Other elements of the curriculum have also been studied but the results do not by any means reveal a rounded picture of curricular concerns. Earl J. McGrath and his associates at the Institute of Higher Education have over the past several years studied and reported upon many parts of the liberal arts curriculum. Thus, Dressel and Lorimer (1960); Dressel, Mayhew, and McGrath (1959); McGrath (1958); and McGrath (1959) all provide questionnaire and interview data to support the belief that the liberal arts and sciences are indeed in danger of inundation by the influence of graduate and professional education. Anderson (1961) surveyed activities and opinions and reported on the state of the humanities. Dealing with course requirements, integrated courses, and teacher preparation of teachers, he seeks to provide an empirical base upon which curricular policy might be built. Burkett and Ruggiers (1965) describe how Oklahoma State has developed a bachelor's degree for working adults. Using short terms on campus and independent study, older students acquire a well-rounded liberal arts education.

Perhaps the most serious attempt to provide a research basis for the undergraduate curriculum stems from the ideas expressed by Ruml and Morrison (1958) and by McGrath (1961). Using 14 institutions McGrath established that the number of courses offered by individual departments bore no relationship to such things as students' satisfaction with their majors, students' subsequent success in graduate school, or administrative judgment of the worth of departments. He elaborated his study by adding 25 more institutions, with substantially the same findings

(McGrath, 1964a). This study provides an empirical base for Dressel's theory of curriculum (1963).

Colleges and universities and their programs seem always open to criticism and much of it comes from within. Indeed, there is almost a masochistic fervor with which spokesmen for higher education flay its imperfections. Sometimes barbs are thrown with a certain wry humor, as Boroff did when he etched profiles of college campuses (Boroff, 1961). He based his impressions on lengthy visits to a number of campuses and suggests his insights through chapter titles. Thus, he describes Imperial Harvard; Brooklyn College: Culture in Flatbush; and Smith: The College for All-around Girls. Or, the criticism may take the form of shrill diatribes, such as Freedman's alarm (1963) that the shadow of the major graduate institutions stunts the growth of genuine teaching institutions. He strikes out at the usual emphasis on the Ph.D. and on publication, and points up the dangers of dependency on the foundations. But he ends on a sanguine note that the best traditions of the university will enable American institutions to overcome present chaos. Many of the complaints about higher educational programs involve in one way or another judgments about the American graduate school. On the other hand, there are those of the Berelson (1960) persuasion who believe that generally the American graduate school and its Ph.D. are in sound shape and not particularly in need of major overhaul. This view is elaborated by Sawyer and others as they reflect on the state of graduate education (1961), while in the other camp, McGrath (1964b) sees the graduate school as contributing to the decline of liberal education and quite possibly to the loss of viability of undergraduate education generally. This is the thesis which Barzun (1964) argued in his Hofstra lecture when he suggested that the reform of secondary education and the specialism of graduate and professional education were responsible for the death of the undergraduate college. But other elements come in for licks as well. Since Sputnik, colleges and universities have been intensifying the rigor of their demands on students, and parents and students have become more and more concerned with obtaining a college degree from the right college. This has led to a variety of problems. Keats (1965) believes many students now attend college who would be much better off in some other kind of activity. Goodman (1962) feels the same way, and even for those who should be in college he feels that a new, smaller, less complex sort of institution would be appropriate. The Gordons (1963) add their voice to this chorus and see, stemming from current curricular pressures, a rising incidence of suicides, drug addiction, and nervous disorders.

Not all critiques are pessimistic. Frankel (1961) believes that the proper business of higher education is not to solve problems but to create them and that the American college is succeeding very well. And Wilson (L. Wilson, 1965) sees colleges and universities in the 1960's as being offered unprecedented opportunities and as being confronted with unparalleled responsibilities. Their biggest single task will be to refrain from attempting too much.

But the bulk of critical articles seems preoccupied with weaknesses as does the evaluative literature. Townsend (1956) found that college freshmen come to school with high expectations but that an appreciable number of them then experience dull and uninspiring teaching and courses which repeat work done in high school or which lack relevance for their lives as they see them. Davie (1958) also testifies to the significance of the freshman and sophomore years, for it is during this period that students are faced with the problems of understanding the curriculum and often experience disillusionment. By the junior and senior years things begin to look better. The curriculum conforms more to their needs and they have learned to make their own way about the institution. The pressures of these early years are involved in the high incidence of cheating which goes on on college campuses. While students believe cheating to be morally wrong, at least 50 percent of all students cheat sometime during their academic careers (Bowers, 1964). However, low incidence of cheating was found in selective, residential institutions having a low faculty–student ratio—the very same sort of institution which Stern (1963) found to be characterized by a high intellectual climate. His research seeks to identify the prevailing climate or press on each campus and to relate this to a similar typology of personality characteristics of individuals. In general, he finds that a college attracts the distinctive type of students who will conform well to that college's ethos. However, he implies that generally students, regardless of type, expect colleges to be the same. It is only after they experience an institution that they perceive marked differences. Much of the research concerning the outcomes of college refers to, and in one way or another is directed toward, that considered in Jacob's report (1957). Generally, Jacob found that students did not change much as a result of their college experience. Subsequent but more sophisticated analyses tend to support the main global features of the Jacob report but do find within any given campus a pattern of change which is related to each student's background, life style, interests, and the like (Newcomb, 1966). Typical of these newer, closer looks at the outcomes of college education is the work of Telford and Plant (1963). They find that ". . . many of the changes attributed to the collegiate experience by others may be no more than developmental changes under way in young persons like those who aspire to college whether or not they attend college."

One problem of collegiate education which has increased in importance has attracted considerable research effort. This is the matter of students who transfer from the growing number of junior colleges to four-year institutions. Knoell and Medsker (1964a, 1964b) have studied the matter more extensively than any other workers and present a rather consistent picture. Fewer junior-college students actually transfer than say they plan to do so. Those who do transfer, particularly if their high school records made them eligible for entry into a four-year college, perform about as well as do native students in the four-year institutions. However, junior-college transfer students do experience a transfer semester lag and they do drop out somewhat more frequently than do native students.

Perhaps the most comprehensive discussion of approaches used in evaluation of the outcomes of the collegiate experience is provided by Dressel and others (1961) at Michigan State University. They present a theory of evaluation, results of studies in a number of academic fields, studies of selection, and statewide studies of higher education.

In 1964 student activities at the University of California at Berkeley startled the entire educational world with the knowledge that students evaluated their educational experience as being considerably less effective than college catalogs suggested they would be. The events at Berkeley and at other institutions have spawned an entire genre of evaluative literature which must be noted and, hopefully, read and digested. Lipset and Wolin (1965), Draper (1965), and Miller and Gilmore (1965) all describe with varying degrees of objectivity the actual events at Berkeley. Mallery (1966), basing his judgments on field work, seeks to understand why the same phenomenon crops up all over the country. He, as do others, sees as one of the wellsprings the civil rights movement, in which many veterans returning to the campus are involved. They seek to bring reality to the campus and to their courses. A faculty committee at Berkeley (University of California, 1966) reached similar conclusions and recommended a variety of ways in which the curriculum could be made more relevant for students. These included new ad hoc courses which would be issue-oriented rather than discipline-oriented. Two works difficult to classify are included in this section because in a way they deal with inadequacies of college programs. The Committee on the College Student (1965) finds that students are searching for a new sexual morality and that colleges have vast, unfulfilled responsibilities to help them do so. Whittington (1963) sees this as one of the many problems toward the solution of which the campus psychiatrist can make a contribution, and he documents his claims through a series of case reports.

The Center for Applied Research in Education has attempted to produce a comprehensive list of titles that comprises the relevant research at all levels of education. The portion of the series dealing with higher education treats such topics as finance, administration, the presidency, and the like, as well as several clearly relevant to college programs. Mayhew (1962a) sees the smaller liberal arts college as a seventeenth- and eighteenth-century phenomenon struggling to adjust to the twentieth century and to compete with newer forms of higher education. And a companion piece on the church-related college shows the enormous contribution which religious denominations have made to American higher education. As to the future, the church-related college must remain true to its mission if it is to survive (Wiche, 1964). Although the liberal arts college has been one essential element of American higher education, another has been the pragmatic character of the entire effort. Types of institutions are included within the American university structure that would not be so located in other cultures. Typical is the gradual absorption of professional education, which seems to happen field by field whenever the time required to train a person draws equal to that needed to secure a bachelor's degree (McGlothlin, 1964). Similarly, the production of technical workers of below-professional qualifications is a growing responsibility of higher education. The technical institute is postsecondary, essentially terminal, related to the fields of science and technology, offers intensive instruction for relatively brief periods of time, and lays heavy emphasis upon application. It attracts students similar to those found in other college programs who are seeking to be trained for an important place in society. Offering similar work but perplexed by serious problems of support is the municipal university, which may very well surrender its function to community colleges (Carlson, 1962). These were institutions supported by city taxes that were designed to be of direct service to the people of the city. Only 12 remained in 1962 and a number of those have since been absorbed by states and converted into state colleges. However, the programs they offered, and still offer, show how American collegiate institutions respond to the needs of a wide range of students. And a similar demonstration is provided by state colleges and universities (Wahlquist & Thornton, 1964). Despite the growth of junior colleges, and the aspirations of those institutions to become the primary vehicle for lower-division undergraduate education, it appears likely that the state colleges and universities will be called upon to educate the bulk of the large increases in collegiate enrollments that are anticipated during the decades of the 1960's and 1970's. Many of these four-year state colleges and universities began as teacher-preparation institutions but have since developed their offerings to include business, engineering, nursing, and a wide range of other professional and subprofessional preparations.

Research on American higher education has typically been done in recent years by people in schools of education or in a number of paraeducational organizations. Gradually, however, some workers in a few of the traditional academic disciplines have turned their attention to areas of higher education as appropriate objects of study. Historians seem to be in the lead in this regard and have made several impressive contributions to an understanding of collegiate programs. The evolution of Princeton and Rutgers shows quite clearly how programs and institutional structure change in response to social demands and how these changes are affected by institutional tradition. Thus, two small Colonial colleges changed, one becoming a great private university and the other becoming the state university of New Jersey (Schmidt, 1964). In a sense, these two colleges reflected the transition that took place generally throughout the United States. The English-style college formed the base to which were added the elements of service to the people and the idea of a university as a research institution. Indeed, each age of American history seems to have created its own characteristic form of higher education (Rudolph, 1962). The American university, which flowered in the late years of the nineteenth century, owed much to the German university. The emphasis on research, the lecture and seminar systems, and the concentration on the production of Ph.D.'s were all transplants. But the canons of German scholarship in history and the social sciences did not take. The pragmatic character of the American mind developed its own, more relativistic orientation, with strong quantitative and behavioristic overtones (Herbst, 1965). The union of the concept of English college, emphasizing service to the state, which came ultimately to be called the Wisconsin Idea, and the concept of the German research university ended in two somewhat unique forms of the American university. One is the somewhat elitist form exemplified by Harvard, Chicago, and Stanford; the other is exemplified by the more pragmatic state universities and colleges. Veysey (1965) describes well the evolution of the first but does not attend to the equally dramatic growth of the other. However, his book is at this point the definitive work on the American university.

There are other strands of influence on American collegiate programs. From earliest times philanthropy has been significant in the support of higher education. In early years private giving did not seek to shape educational policy, but with the growth of large private fortunes and then with the conversion of some of these into large foundations, private philanthropy began to exert a real leadership. Such examples as the creation of Duke University to conform to ideas of the Duke family or the matching grants of the Ford Foundation to stimulate regional centers of excellence emphasize the point (Curti & Nash, 1965). Political statesmanship has also been influential, especially in leading higher education out of provincial concerns and points of view. In this regard the Fulbright Program has demonstrated at its best the cooperation of people in the university with people in government and the private foundations to ensure an enrichment of education and service to developing nations (Johnson & Colligan, 1965). These facets are all illustrated in varying degrees of fidelity by institutional histories. Two recent examples of the genre were prepared by Hug (1965) and McGrave (1963), describing New York University and the University of Cincinnati.

The 1950's and 1960's may ultimately be called the decades of innovation in college and university education. While many of the ideas attempted are not particularly new, their large-scale application is. This is the period of rapid creation of new colleges and the development of experimental colleges, many of which have attempted to offer a new and updated version of general education (Mayhew, 1965). Moreover, the experimental colleges have sought to create the spirit of small institutions on large campuses (Stickler, 1965). They have done so partly through cluster colleges and similar groupings and partly through emphasis on independent study, which allows students some one-to-one relationship with faculty. While this effort seems productive of educational values, it is a costly form of education, which some feel denies its use to all save the most affluent institutions (Bonthius & others, 1957). Independent study, which currently seems to have value for a wide segment of the academic aptitude–ability range, emerged as an essential part of programs designed for superior students. In the mid-1950's, alarm was expressed that college programs seemed best fitted for the middle-ability student. Remedial programs did provide for low achievers but the high-ability student or the gifted seemed to be the forgotten man. Colleges then began an intensive effort to create special courses, programs, and even degrees and, as is the American custom, those interested formed an association. Cohen (1966) describes these developments and points out that the weakest link so far is the lack of comparative evaluation studies.

One other important way of dealing with superior students is through assigning college credit or advanced standing to those who have had relevant prior experience or whose abilities allow acceleration. The idea of acceleration through a program of examinations has long been in the public domain. The comprehensive examination programs at the University of Chicago, Michigan State University, and the University of Florida are examples. However, nationwide respectability for the concept had to wait for the endorsement of several leading Eastern colleges and secondary schools. This endorsement came in the study *General Education in School and College* (1952), which later resulted in the formulation of the Advanced Placement Program of the College Entrance Examination Board (Dudley, 1959). This is a system which allows students to study college-level courses in high school, and upon completion of an examination, subject to college policy, to receive college credit. The idea seems well accepted by over half of the four-year institutions in the nation, although not all give actual academic credit.

Another cluster of innovations lies in the application of the new media to the problems of education. These involve radio, television, tape recordings, programmed instruction, overhead projectors, language laboratories, and the like. An early inquiry into feasibility developed the theme that ". . . American technology has produced a wide variety of devices which could be used in education" but that "Adaptation of new devices to the process of education requires adequate theory to undergird experimentation and a definite reconsideration of the role of the teacher" (Mayhew, 1959). Brown and Thornton (1963) surveyed the uses to which media were actually put and reached the conclusion that colleges experimenting with a variety of devices were able to achieve educational goals as well as, or better than, those using more orthodox techniques. Writing at about the same time, Carpenter and Greenhill (1965) suggest some of the necessary underlying theory.

Not only should on-campus activities be enriched but a variety of off-campus experiences should be provided. One major possibility here is to provide off-campus work experience articulated with academic effort. The inception of this notion began at the University of Cincinnati in 1906 and was made well known by Antioch College through its cooperative work program. Now more than 60 colleges have such programs and student testimony suggests that they do achieve the six or seven purposes postulated for them (Wilson & Lyons, 1961). Venn (1964) sees these programs as of considerable potential relevance for all post-secondary vocational and technical education.

Innovation also takes the form of questioning old practices. One of these which has elicited considerable emotion and provided some insight is the college grading system. It is well established that college grades are the most potent motivation to college achievement (McKeachie, 1963), but the side effects can be serious. Through cooperative efforts a number of colleges have now made provision for students to take some courses for which no grades are awarded. Early returns indicate student satisfaction with the experiments (*Journal of Higher Education,* 1964).

Since colleges stress book learning, it would seem appropriate that students read books. To stimulate this activity a number of colleges have started campus-wide reading programs, pre-freshman summer reading programs, and the like. Dartmouth, the University of South Florida, Franklin & Marshall, and Stephens College are examples of schools having such programs. The programs do seem to stimulate discussion, although the evaluation is rather sketchy (Ryf, 1962).

Although mention has already been made of international education, it should be cited here as one other innovative development in higher education. *The Journal of General Education* for January 1962 presents a reasonably accurate picture of the state of development of programs for study abroad.

Any topic as broad and amorphous as college and university programs does not lend itself to a complete taxonomy. Thus, a number of reports must be listed as individual entities, although each has clear relevance for the subject. One such is Bowles's analysis (1963) of national patterns of access to higher education. He finds that national concern with higher education almost follows laws of physics. If the capacity of lower levels of education is expanded, a demand is at once created for higher education. Of considerable interest is the similarity of patterns in the Soviet Union and the United States.

Other comparisons between national systems are made by Benjamin (1965) and Carmichael (1959). In Latin America there has been a steady growth of universities toward what might be called the American rather than the European pattern of university effort. Where several decades ago only law and medicine were taught in the universities, today there are faculties of nursing, economics, business, and other specialties. This seems to be a product of the level of national development and follows laws just as does the process of access to higher education. However, the Spanish-speaking countries do not emphasize general education as strongly as do the English-speaking lands.

Further, in British Commonwealth countries the university gradually is coming to be regarded as a proper home for schools for varied occupations. Law, medicine, agriculture, nursing, social work, and others are being drawn into the university orbit. As these have moved into universities the characters of both the professions and the university have changed. In a very real respect this development has been spurred by Soviet advances even as has scientific and technological training in the United States. Further similarities are also apparent. The status of women in higher education is now raised in Commonwealth nations just as it was at the turn of the century in the United States. And continuing education is also a growth industry.

The American College Testing Program has emerged as a major force operating on undergraduate colleges. Not only is its testing program serving as competition for older programs but also its research reports are calling into question older beliefs and myths. Thus, college grades are not seen as particularly good predictors of post-college achievement (Hoyt, 1965). Nor are high school grades good predictors of nonacademic success in college activities (Holland & Richards, 1965).

Creating tools for research on college programs, Krathwohl and others (1964), Dressel (1965), and Phenix (1964) have all made significant contributions.

Krathwohl and his colleagues continue work started earlier and show how concern for affective matters can be made explicit in planning an educational program. Dressel develops ten principles for curriculum construction, and Phenix shows how the areas of human concern can be so codified that a balanced curriculum could result, if professors were willing to use it.

Although in the past the academic calendar was like the weather, currently people are doing something about it. While there are three-three programs, four-one-four attempts, and revised quarter systems, the trimester has received the most support and research attention. Stickler and Carothers (1963) and Hungate and McGrath (1963) have each developed schemes together with rationales and some empirical data to support their belief in the trimester.

Since this essay reflects just a sample of relevant materials, some mention of further references should be made. Meeth (1965) has produced a reasonably complete bibliography of selected issues in higher education. The College Entrance Examination Board has developed bibliographies on transfer students, credit by examination, and the unaffiliated student (Flaugher, 1966). Mayhew (1964, 1965) has prepared two essays on the literature of higher education.

Lewis B. Mayhew
Stanford University

References

Adler, Mortimer J., and Mayer, Milton. *The Revolution in Education.* U Chicago Press, 1958.

American Academy of Arts and Sciences. "The Contemporary University: U.S.A." *Daedalus* 93:1027–1237; 1964.

Anderson, A. Edwin. *The Humanities in the Colleges and Universities of the South.* Southern Regional Education Board, 1961.

Barzun, Jacques. "College to University–and After." *Am Scholar* 33:212–19; 1964.

Baskin, Samuel. *Higher Education: Some Newer Developments.* McGraw-Hill, 1965.

Bell, Daniel. *The Reforming of General Education.* Columbia U Press, 1966.

Benjamin, Harold R. W. *Higher Education in the American Republics.* McGraw-Hill, 1965.

Berelson, Bernard. *Graduate Education in the United States.* McGraw-Hill, 1960.

Bidwell, Percy W. *Undergraduate Education in Foreign Affairs.* Columbia U Press, 1962.

Blocker, Clyde E., and others. *The Two-Year College: A Social Synthesis.* Prentice-Hall, 1965.

Bonthius, Robert H., and others. *The Independent Study Program in the United States.* Columbia U Press, 1957.

Boroff, David. *Campus USA.* Harper, 1961.

Bowers, William J. *Student Dishonesty and Its Control in College.* Columbia U Press, 1964.

Bowles, Frank. *Access to Higher Education.* Columbia U Press, 1963.

Brickman, William W., and Lehrer, Stanley. (Eds.) *A Century of Higher Education.* Society for the Advancement of Education, 1962.

Brown, James W., and Thornton, James W. *New Media in Higher Education.* Association for Higher Education, 1963.

Brubacher, John S. *Bases for Policy in Higher Education.* McGraw-Hill, 1965.

Burkett, J. E., and Ruggiers, Paul G. *Bachelor of Liberal Studies.* Center for the Study of Liberal Education for Adults, 1965.

Bushnell, John. "Student Values: A Summary of Research and Future Problems." In Carpenter, M. (Ed.) *The Larger Learning.* Brown, 1960.

Carlin, Edward. *Curriculum Building in General Education.* Brown, 1960.

Carlson, William S. *The Municipal University.* Center for Applied Research in Education, 1962.

Carmichael, Oliver C. *Universities: Commonwealth and American.* Harper, 1959.

Carmichael, Oliver C. *Graduate Education: A Program of Action.* Harper, 1962.

Carpenter, C. R., and Greenhill, L. P. "Providing the Conditions of Learning the New Media." In Baskin, Samuel. (Ed.) *Higher Education: Some Newer Developments.* McGraw-Hill, 1965.

Cartter, Allan M. *An Assessment of Quality in Graduate Education.* ACE, 1966.

Clark, Burton R. "Sociology of Education." In Faris, Robert L. (Ed.) *Handbook of Modern Sociology.* Rand McNally, 1964.

Cohen, Joseph W. *The Superior Student in American Higher Education.* McGraw-Hill, 1966.

Cole, Charles C., Jr., and Lewis, Lanora G. *Flexibility in the Undergraduate Curriculum.* USOE, 1962.

Commission on International Understanding. *Non-Western Studies in the Liberal Arts College.* Association of American Colleges, 1964.

Committee on the College Student. *Sex and the College Student.* Group for the Advancement of Psychiatry, 1965.

Conant, James B. *The Education of American Teachers.* McGraw-Hill, 1963.

Cooper, Russell M. *The Two Ends of the Log.* U Minnesota Press, 1958.

Curti, Merle, and Nash, Roderick. *Philanthropy in the Shaping of American Higher Education.* Rutgers U Press, 1965.

Danforth Foundation. *Eight Hundred Colleges Face the Future.* The Danforth Foundation, 1965.

Davie, James S. "Satisfaction and the College Experience." In Wedge, Bryant M. (Ed.) *Psychological Problems of College Men.* Yale U Press, 1958.

Dennis, Lawrence E., and Kaufman, Joseph F. *The College and the Student.* ACE, 1966.

DeVane, William Clyde. *Higher Education in Twentieth-Century America.* Harvard U Press, 1965.

Draper, Hal. *Berkeley: The New Student Revolt.* Grove Press, Inc., 1965.

Dressel, Paul L. *Undergraduate Curriculum in Higher Education.* Center for Applied Research, Inc., 1963.

Dressel, Paul L. "A Look at New Curriculum Models." *J H Ed* 36:89–96; 1965.

Dressel, Paul L., and Lorimer, Margaret F. *Attitudes of Liberal Arts Faculty Members Toward Liberal and Professional Education.* Teachers Coll, Columbia U, 1960.

Dressel, Paul L., and others. *The Liberal Arts as Viewed by Faculty Members in Professional Schools.* Columbia U Press, 1959.

Dressel, Paul L., and others. *Evaluation in Higher Education.* Houghton, 1961.

Dudley, David A. "The Advanced Placement Program." *Col and U* 34:171–79; 1959.

Duryea, E. D. *Management of Learning.* USOE, 1960.

Education and World Affairs. *The University Looks Abroad: Approaches to World Affairs at Six American Universities.* Walker and Company, 1966.

Educational Policies Commission. *Universal Opportunity for Education Beyond the High School.* NEA, 1964.

Educational Policies Commission. *Education and the Spirit of Science.* NEA, 1966.

Estrin, Herman A., and Goode, Delmar. *College and University Teaching.* Brown, 1964.

Evans, Lester J. *The Crisis in Medical Education.* U Michigan Press, 1964.

Fisher, James. *Humanities in General Education.* Brown, 1960.

Flaugher, Ronald L., and others. *Three Annotated Bibliographies.* ETS, 1966.

Frankel, Charles. *Issues in University Education.* Harper, 1959.

Frankel, Charles. "The Happy Crisis in Higher Education." In Smith, G. K. (Ed.) *Current Issues in Higher Education 1961.* Association for Higher Education, 1961.

Freedman, Mervin B., and Hatch, Winslow R. *Impact of College.* USOE, 1960.

Freedman, Morris. *Chaos in Our Colleges.* McKay, 1963.

Gardner, John W. *Self Renewal: The Individual and the Innovative Society.* Harper, 1963–64.

General Education in School and College. Harvard U Press, 1952.

Gerstein, Frank. *Religion and the University.* U Toronto Press, 1964.

Goodman, Paul. *A Community of Scholars.* Random, 1962.

Gordon, Richard E., and Gordon, Katherine K. *The Blight on the Ivy.* Prentice-Hall, 1963.

Harris, Seymour E. (Ed.) *Challenge and Change in American Education.* McCutchan Publishing Corporation, 1965.

Harris, Seymour E. (Ed.) *Education and Public Policy.* McCutchan Publishing Corporation, 1966.

Hatch, Winslow R., and Bennet, Ann. *Effectiveness in Teaching.* USOE, 1960(a).

Hatch, Winslow R., and Bennet, Ann. *Independent Study.* USOE, 1960(b).

Haun, Ray. *Science in General Education.* Brown, 1960.

Herbst, Jurgen. *The German Historical School in American Scholarship.* Cornell U Press, 1965.

Hoffman, Robert. "A Required Philosophy Course." *J H Ed* 35:247–51; 1964.

Holland, John L., and Richards, J. M. *Academic and Non-Academic Accomplishment: Correlated or Uncorrelated.* ACT, 1965.

Hollinshead, Byron S. *Dentistry in the United States.* ACE, 1960.

Holton, Gerald. "Science for Nonscientists: Criteria for College Programs." *J H Ed* 15:257–75; 1964.

Hoyt, Donald P. *The Relationship Between College Grades and Adult Achievement: A Review of the Literature.* ACT, 1965.

Hug, Elsie A. *Seventy-five Years in Education.* New York U Press, 1965.

Hungate, Thad L., and McGrath, Earl J. *A New Trimester Three Year Degree Program.* Teachers Coll, Columbia U, 1963.

Hutchins, Robert M. *The University of Utopia.* U Chicago Press, 1964.

Jacob, Philip. *Changing Values in College.* Harper, 1957.

Johnson, W. and Colligan, F. J. *The Fullbright Program.* U Chicago Press, 1965.

Jones, Howard Mumford. "Uses of the Past in General Education." *Harvard Ed R* 36:3–15; 1966.

Journal of Higher Education. "College Grading Systems: A Journal Symposium." *J H Ed* 35:89–103; 1964.

Keats, John. *The Sheepskin Psychosis.* Delta Books, 1965.

Kerr, Clark. *The Uses of the University.* Harvard U Press, 1963.

Knoell, D. M., and Medsker, L. L. *Articulation Between Two-Year and Four-Year Colleges.* U California Press, 1964(a).

Knoell, D. M., and Medsker, L. L. *Factors Affecting Performance of Transfer Students from Two to Four-Year Colleges.* Center for the Study of Higher Education, 1964(b).

Krathwohl, D., and others. *Taxonomy of Educational Objectives, Handbook II Affective Domain.* McKay, 1964.

Lewis, Lanora G. *The Credit System in Colleges and Universities.* USOE, 1961.

Lipset, S. M., and Wolin, S. S. *The Berkeley Student Revolt.* Doubleday, 1965.

Mallery, David. *Ferment on the Campus.* Harper, 1966.

Mayhew, Lewis B. *New Frontiers in Learning.* Stephens College Press, 1959.

Mayhew, Lewis B. (Ed.) *General Education: An Account and Appraisal.* Harper, 1960.

Mayhew, Lewis B. *The Smaller Liberal Arts College.* Center for Applied Research in Education, Inc., 1962(a).

Mayhew, Lewis B. *Social Science in General Education.* Brown, 1962(b).

Mayhew, Lewis B. "The Literature of Higher Education." *Ed Rec* 46:5–32; 1964.

Mayhew, Lewis B. "The Literature of Higher Education." *Ed Rec* 47:18–49; 1965.

Mayhew, Lewis B. "The New Colleges." In Baskin, Samuel. (Ed.) *Higher Education: Some Newer Developments.* McGraw-Hill, 1965.

McGlothlin, William J. *The Professional Schools.* Center for Applied Research in Education, 1964.

McGrath, Earl J. *Are Liberal Arts Colleges Becoming Professional Schools?* Teachers Coll, Columbia U, 1958.

McGrath, Earl J. *Liberal Education in the Professions.* Teachers Coll, Columbia U, 1959.

McGrath, Earl J. *Memo to a College Faculty.* Teachers Coll, Columbia U, 1961.

McGrath, Earl J. *Cooperative Long Range Planning in Liberal Arts Colleges.* Teachers Coll, Columbia U, 1964(a).

McGrath, Earl J. *The Graduate School and the Decline of Liberal Education.* Teachers Coll, Columbia U, 1964(b).

McGrave, Reginald C. *The University of Cincinnati.* Harper, 1963.

McKeachie, W. J. "Research on Teaching at the College and University Level." In Gage, N. L. (Ed.) *Handbook of Research on Teaching.* Rand McNally, 1963.

Medsker, Leland L. *The Junior College, Progress and Prospect.* McGraw-Hill, 1960.

Meeth, L. Richard. *Selected Issues in Higher Education, An Annotated Bibliography.* Teachers Coll, Columbia U, 1965.

Miller, M. V., and Gilmore, S. *Revolution at Berkeley.* Dell Publishing Company, 1965.

Morrill Commission. *The University and World Affairs.* Ford Foundation, 1960.

Morse, H. T., and Dressel, Paul L. *General Education for Personal Maturity.* Brown, 1960.

New Jersey Department of Education. *The Needs of New Jersey in Higher Education, 1962-70.* N.J. Department of Education, 1962.

Newcomb, Theodore M. "Research on Student Characteristics: Current Approaches." In Dennis, L. E., and Kaufman, J. F. (Eds.) *The College and the Student.* ACE, 1966.

Perkins, Dexter. *The Education of Historians in the United States.* McGraw-Hill, 1962.

Petersen, Renee, and Petersen, William. *University Adult Education: A Guide to Policy.* Harper, 1960.

Phenix, Philip H. *Realms of Meaning.* McGraw-Hill, 1964.

Pollock, Myron Frank. *State Surveys of Higher Education and Resultant Action: Discernible Patterns and Relationships.* Stanford U Press, 1965.

Radcliffe, Shirley A., and Hatch, Winslow R. *Advanced Standing.* USOE, 1961.

Raushenbush, Esther. *The Student and His Studies.* Wesleyan U Press, 1964.

Rockefeller Report. *The Pursuit of Excellence: Education and the Future of America.* Doubleday, 1958.

Rudolph, Frederick. *The American College and University.* Knopf, 1962.

Rudy, Willis. *The Evolving Liberal Arts Curriculum: An Historical Review of Basic Themes.* Teachers Coll, Columbia U, 1960.

Ruml, Beardsly, and Morrison, Donald. *Memo to a College Trustee.* McGraw-Hill, 1958.

Ryf, Robert S. "A Head Start in Self Education: The Occidental College Freshman Summer Reading List." *Liberal Ed* 48:405-07; 1962.

Sanford, Nevitt. (Ed.) *The American College.* Wiley, 1962.

Sanford, Nevitt. (Ed.) *College and Character.* Wiley, 1964.

Sanford, Nevitt, and Katz, Joseph. "17-22: The Turbulent Years." *Stanford Today* Winter:7-10; 1966.

Sawyer, Ralph, and others. "The State of Graduate Education." *Graduate J* 4:240-65; 1961.

Schmidt, George P. *Princeton and Rutgers—The Two Colonial Colleges of New Jersey.* Van Nostrand, 1964.

Shoemaker, Francis, and Forsdale, Louis. *Communication in General Education.* Brown, 1960.

Southern Regional Education Board. *Within Our Reach.* The Board, 1961.

Stern, George G. "New Research in Higher Education, Its Curricular, Instructional and Organizational Implications." In *New Frontiers in Higher Education.* Kellogg Junior College Leadership Program, 1963.

Stickler, W. Hugh. *The Experimental Colleges.* Florida State U Press, 1965.

Stickler, W. Hugh, and Carothers, Millan W. *The Year Round Calendar in Operation.* Southern Regional Education Board, 1963.

Telford, C. W., and Plant, W. T. *The Psychological Impact of the Public Two-Year College on Certain Non-Intellectual Functions.* San Jose State College Press, 1963.

Thomas, Russell. *The Search for a Common Learning: General Education, 1800-1860.* McGraw-Hill, 1962.

Thornton, James. *The Community Junior College.* Wiley, 1960.

Townsend, Agatha. *College Freshmen Speak Out.* Harper, 1956.

University of California. *Establishing Junior Colleges.* Junior College Leadership Program, Occasional Report No. 5, 1964.

University of California. *Education at Berkeley, Report of the Select Committee on Education.* Academic Senate, U California Press, 1966.

Venn, Grant. *Man, Education and Work.* ACE, 1964.

Veysey, L. R. *The Emergence of the American University.* Chicago Press, 1965.

Wahlquist, J. T., and Thornton, J. W. *State Colleges and Universities.* Center for Applied Research in Education, 1964.

Weidner, Edward W. *The World Role of Universities.* McGraw-Hill, 1962.

Western Interstate Commission on Higher Education (WICHE). *College Self Study.* The Commission, 1959.

WICHE. *Research on College Students.* The Commission, 1960.

WICHE. *Studies of College Faculty.* The Commission, 1961.

WICHE. *The Study of Campus Culture.* The Commission, 1962.

WICHE. *The Study of Academic Administration.* The Commission, 1963.

WICHE. *Long Range Planning in Higher Education.* The Commission, 1964.

WICHE. *Order and Freedom on the Campus.* The Commission, 1965.

Whittington, H. G. *Psychiatry on the College Campus.* Int U, 1963.

Wiche, Myron F. *The Church Related College.* Center for Applied Research in Education, Inc., 1964.

Wilson, James W., and Lyons, Edward H. *Work-Study College Programs.* Harper, 1961.

Wilson, Logan. (Ed.) *Emerging Patterns in American Higher Education.* ACE, 1964.

Wilson, Logan. "Selling Institutional Priorities." In Smith G. K. (Ed.) *Current Issues in Higher Education, 1965.* Association for Higher Education, 1965.

Wormald, F. L. (Ed.) *Reflections on the Role of Liberal Education.* Association of American Colleges, 1964.

EDUCATIONAL PROGRAMS— ELEMENTARY SCHOOLS

The term educational programs has not been defined as such in the literature. It has been viewed broadly as any practice in the schools involving

(a) organization of essential elements, principles, and facts; (b) learning opportunities planned for the learners; (c) methods of instruction; (d) actual instructional programs; (e) methods of organizing the teachers and/or learners for instruction; or (f) the materials used in instruction. In this article an educational program is defined as a program that is comprehensive in the sense that it considers objectives and the means of attaining them, creates and/or reorganizes a field of knowledge, develops material for teachers and learners, and has national acceptance in the field of education. Using this definition, one would include the School Mathematics Study Group, but not the Initial Teaching Alphabet. Unfortunately, these criteria embrace such a large number of projects that it has been necessary to select only a few for illustrative purposes in this article.

The article does not review all of the significant research in the area of educational programs. This task seems more appropriate for the *Review of Educational Research* or other such publications. Rather, we attempt to present a rationale for viewing educational programs that is intended to provide the reader with a basic framework in which to classify and better understand educational programs.

HISTORICAL PERSPECTIVE. The first and most fundamental question that should be asked in developing any curriculum and/or educational program is: What educational objectives should the school seek to attain? Historically, there has been little concern about objectives. Teachers taught what they had been taught by methods they had learned in teacher-preparation institutions. When objectives were developed, they were usually phrased in global, if not glorious, terms—such as how to prepare the learner to become a constructive, participating member of his society.

There was some limited concern about objectives, but on a societal rather than an instructional level. Several groups and commissions, composed of prestigious persons in education and representatives of other segments of society, prepared statements of objectives. One of the early statements concerning the qualities of the "educated adult" was the statement of the Commission of the Reorganization of Secondary Education in 1918, known as the Cardinal Principles of Secondary Education (National Education Association, 1918). The criticisms of this Commission led to the development of the Cardinal Objectives in Elementary Education in 1932 (University of the State of New York, 1932), a more appropriate statement of educational objectives for young children. In 1938, the Educational Policies Commission (1938) prepared a statement on the purposes of education in American democracy. The Mid-Century Committee on Outcomes in Elementary Education stated the general objectives of the elementary school in 1950 (Kearney, 1953).

Unfortunately, most elementary school teachers have great difficulty in translating global statements of objectives defined in terms of the qualities of the "educated adult," the "good democratic citizen," or "areas of competency," into specific learning opportunities for student. There is no logical way that one can be derived from the other. Thus, most schools have included such generalities in their statements of educational objectives but have continued to develop educational programs using the common subject-field definitions of the traditional elementary school curriculum (Herrick, 1960; Lindvall & Bolvin, 1966).

Tyler (1950) suggests that in formulating objectives three data sources should be used—subject specialists, the learners, and contemporary life. During the present century, all three data sources have been used; however, an imbalance has often been evident. An emphasis on one data source in one period of time generally led to a renewed emphasis upon a different data source for the next period of time.

During the first part of the century, subject matter was the principal, if not sole, data source for objectives. The subject matter not only was factual in character but also was atomistic and unintegrated. It is significant that Tyler suggested subject specialists as a data source rather than subject matter. By designating specialists or scholars, Tyler attempted to insure that subject matter or knowledge would be (1) relatively current with the most recent knowledge in the respective disciplines, and (2) determined by specialists in the disciplines rather than by practicing teachers, psychologists, or educators.

During the 1930's, the societal demand for universal education began to affect the quantity and quality of learners, and the demand of some professional educators for a more appropriate educational program for learners began to influence instructional practice. There was a gradual drift away from the almost exclusive use of subject matter as the determinant of objectives and a shift to the learner and his needs.

Dewey's (1916, 1938) ideas about learners and learning contributed to what is popularly known as the progressive education movement. It placed far more emphasis on the learner as a source of objectives. Dewey's philosophy, firmly based on pragmatism, formed the foundation which required that knowledge gained in school should have utility for the learner after he has left school; consequently, an understanding of contemporary life became much more important than it was previously. Dewey never supported the view that subject matter was undesirable or unnecessary. He simply placed subject matter in a new perspective, as a means to assist the learner seeking to accomplish his and society's goals. One result of the progressive education movement was that subject matter came to be viewed as one, rather than the sole, data source for determining objectives.

Using the factors of a maturing physiological organism, a demanding social environment, and an emerging purposive self, Havighurst (1949) and his associates at the University of Chicago utilized the term "developmental tasks" to be used as a basis for educational programs. The term describes the tasks the learner faces and must solve in some way as he matures. In this sense, these tasks serve as objectives the elementary school must consider in its effort to contribute to the learner's immediate and ultimate well-being. These tasks include learning physical skills necessary for ordinary games; building wholesome attitudes toward self as a growing organism; learning to get along with age mates; learning an appropriate sex role; developing fundamental skills in reading, writing and calculating; developing a conscience, morality, and a scale of values; and developing desirable attitudes toward social groups and institutions (Havighurst, 1949).

The effect that development tasks have had on educational thinking and planning has been slight. No significant efforts have been made to include these ideas in an organized educational program.

Maria Montessori (1959, 1964) advanced an educational program that supports using the learner as the data source for formulating objectives. The most important subjects in the curriculum, according to Montessori, include mastery of self and environment, including social competencies. She envisioned a unified ordered environment to match the needs of the learner from pre-school to postgraduate work. The number of Montessori schools remains small and their influence on conventional schools appears to be minimal.

The Summerhill School (Neill, 1960) in Leiston, Suffolk, England is perhaps the only school that has sought to develop a curriculum using the learner as the sole data source. The book describing this program has been read fairly widely in the United States, but the educational program at Summerhill has not had a measurable impact on the operation of schools in the United States.

Some programs have attempted to develop a curriculum with contemporary life as the major data source. These have included objectives determined through an analysis of "major functions of social life" (Marshall & Goetz, 1936), persistent problems of living (Caswell & Campbell, 1935), or "persistent life situations" (Stratemeyer & others, 1957). With this social-living orientation there was no conflict of individual and social needs, since they were not considered to be opposing or essentially conflicting demands. Instead, significant meaning could be given to democratic living as an essential part of all learning experiences the learner had in school. Subject matter and intellectual skills were considered sources to be utilized in the solution of important social problems, not as ends in themselves (Herrick, 1960). The Virginia State Board of Education (1943a, 1943b) program represents one of the earlier attempts to state the overall purpose of the elementary school in terms of 11 major functions of social life.

Stratemeyer and others (1957) identified three kinds of "persistent life situations" calling for (1) growth in health, intellectual power, moral choice, esthetic expression, and appreciation; (2) growth in social participation—person-to-person relationships, group membership, intergroup memberships; and (3) growth in ability to deal with environmental factors and forces—natural phenomena, technological resources, and economic-social-political structures and forces. These three kinds of persistent life situations appear in five major aspects of human life: (1) in the home—as a member of the family; (2) in the community—as a participant in civic and social activities; (3) in work—as a member of an occupational group; (4) in leisure time; and (5) in spiritual activities. These life situations have never been extensively translated into an educational program.

A review of the first part of this century reveals that no one data source for determining objectives has been used consistently. During the early part of the century, subject matter was virtually the sole data source for objectives. By the 1930's, progressive education ushered in an era when the learner became more prominent as a data source for objectives. After Sputnik was launched in 1957, subject matter again became the dominant data source for objectives. Throughout this period, there has been little use of contemporary life as a data source for the curriculum. Indirectly it has been the primary source, since the schools exist at the pleasure of society and must have objectives that are generally consistent with its desires. During the latter part of the century, responsible educators and citizens will be challenged to find ways to insure that the objectives for the schools take cognizance of all data sources.

Whatever the data sources used, it is clear that statements of objectives have had little impact upon the educational programs for learners in the elementary schools of America. Even the most thoroughly developed statements of objectives and even the most carefully planned theoretical bases for educational programs have rarely been adequately translated into practice. Historically, subject matter has been the dominant concern of most schools throughout the nation regardless of what objectives were stated. The most fundamental question in planning an educational program, that of determining objectives, has given little direction to the activities which occur in the classrooms throughout the nation.

THEORETICAL FOUNDATIONS. An examination of the research that provides a theoretical foundation for educational programs reveals that very little of a substantive nature has taken place during the last ten years. This is especially unfortunate since the major focus for change in educational practice during this period of time has been the curriculum, or more specifically, the national curriculum projects (Gagné, 1967). As Goodlad (1960) has stated, "Curriculum theorizing to date is best described as abstract speculation; curriculum research as 'dust bowl' empiricism; and curriculum practice as rule of thumb guesswork (often a wet thumb at that, held aloft to test the direction of the prevailing breeze)." Furthermore, theory has not played a decisive role in influencing curriculum change. The reasons have not been difficult to find. Curriculum specialists have found clues in other areas of educational research, but a comprehensive theoretical structure for curriculum has been conspicuously lacking (Shaw, 1966). Some persons have consistently stressed the importance of bringing increased rationality to the total process of curriculum and instruction. While the initial work of Ralph Tyler (1950) is more than 20 years old, it continues to provide the most rational foundation for answering the four fundamental questions in the field of curriculum: (1) What educational purposes should the school seek to attain? (2) What educational experiences can be provided that are likely to attain these purposes? (3) How can these educational experiences be effectively organized? (4) How can we determine whether these purposes are being attained?

It was mentioned earlier that Tyler believed objectives are obtained by studying three data sources —contemporary life, the learner, and the opinion of subject matter specialists. Others believe that contemporary life or "culture" is sufficient (Bellack, 1956). The objectives derived through Tyler's rationale would need to be screened through educational psychology to determine whether they can be taught, at what age they can most effectively be taught, and the length of time required to teach them. They would also need to be screened through educational philosophy to determine the value of learning them, and the internal consistency among them.

Tyler then saw a need for examining the structure of knowledge so that the essential elements (concepts, skills, and values) would be elaborated and arranged to have continuity, sequence, and integration. The notion of continuity and sequence has been explored considerably as a result of the emphasis on the structure of knowledge. Finally, learning experiences would be devised which would enable learners to make progress in developing the essential elements.

Goodlad uses the Tyler rationale as a theoretical framework in which to examine the essential questions in curriculum and instruction (Goodlad & Richter, 1966). He superimposes the rationale on Parson's (1959) levels of structural organization of a complex social system and creates a decision-making conceptual scheme for curriculum and instruction. The scheme suggests that decisions are at three levels of remoteness from the learner—the societal, the institutional, and the instructional. This conceptual scheme tends to complete the Tyler rationale in the sense that it takes cognizance of the critical fact that the aims of education in a republic are determined by a representative body at the societal level, and the means to attain these aims are determined by professional educators at the institutional and instructional level.

Herrick (1954) expanded the part of the Tyler rationale concerned with educational experiences. Using the term "organizing centers" instead of "educational experiences," he defines them as points in time and place through which the learner is guided toward the more fundamental organizing elements underlying the curriculum.

Goodlad (1959) has sought to clarify the criteria upon which organizing centers are based. The criteria he has suggested include (a) encourage learner practice of desired behavior, (b) economize by contributing simultaneously to the attainment of several objectives, (c) encompass the abilities of the group from the floor to the ceiling, (d) build on previous learning and prepare for future learning, (e) support and buttress learnings from other fields, (f) possess inherent educational significance, (g) include several ideas and catch-hold points for learners' differing interests, (h) combine learners, materials, and ideas in a meaningful way, and (i) possess capacity for movement—chronological, social, geographic, or intellectual.

The number of persons who have maintained an interest in conducting research in the total process of curriculum development has probably decreased. As a result, promising ways for inquiring about Tyler's four basic questions have not developed and do not appear likely to develop in the immediate future. The major research efforts that took place were in two areas: the structure of knowledge and the psychology of learning and instruction.

It has been mentioned that subject matter, the learner, and society were used at various times as data sources for formulating objectives. During the last decade the main data source for formulating the objectives of schools has been the opinions of subject-matter specialists. In this regard, considerable attention has been directed toward examining the structure of knowledge. Many who pursue this study believe that a discipline or disciplines can be conceived as a foundation for objectives. In fact, they would contend that it is the only sound foundation. Advocates of the structure of knowledge are not proposing a return to an emphasis upon traditional subject matter that dominated American education during the early part of the century, but a totally new concept of curriculum.

During the latter part of the 1950's there was an unprecedented change in the character of American education that resulted in a dramatic return to subject matter as the principal data source for objectives. The forces were both societal and intellectual. The societal change was precipitated by the launching of Sputnik in 1957. It was not surprising in a nation that had always considered its educational system superior to all others that Sputnik aroused the American people. It was also not surprising that the people would look to the schools—first as a scapegoat and finally as the principal instrument to solve the problem.

Another reason for the emphasis on the structure of knowledge was the tremendous increase of knowledge per se. One is reluctant to mention this factor because it has become almost platitudinous; however, the so-called "knowledge explosion" became dramatically apparent during the 1950's and 1960's and it is doubtful that a more intensive examination and organization of the disciplines could have been delayed much longer even if Sputnik had not occurred.

The intellectual rather than societal genesis of the movement would be difficult to trace; however, it is obvious that Bruner's *The Process of Education* (1962) was a timely effort because it focused attention on the concept of structure as it was related to learning. More specifically, it dealt with principles, structure, readiness for learning, and intuition.

Bruner, more than any other person, dominated the field in these areas and his work provided the starting point of most serious discussions concerning the structure of knowledge. His work cast an intellectual shadow on scholars engaged in research on learning at universities, on persons preparing national curriculum projects, and even on practitioners working in the schools. His popularity was so universal that it may have overshadowed the work of hundreds of researchers doing similar work.

Considerable work had been done before Bruner, but that work remained essentially obscure except for that of Piaget (1950, 1960, 1962). Bruner felt such a debt to Piaget's work that he dedicated his most recent book to him (Bruner & others, 1966). The earlier work in this area is obscure in part, of course, because Bruner failed to recognize its existence.

Bruner has been engaged in research on the structure of knowledge and learning throughout his career. His dramatic popularity, in part at least, is not so much *what* Bruner said, although he had many profound and penetrating statements; nor so much *how* Bruner said it, although his books are well written and even eloquent in parts; but more significantly *when* he said it. Judd (1915) had argued many of the issues presented by Bruner as early as 1926. More recently, Schwab and Brandenwein (1962) and Phenix (1956) have proposed the reorganization of the disciplines. But it was 1957 before Russia successfully launched a satellite. It was the mid-1950's before knowledge had accumulated to such proportions that the distance between what was being taught in the schools and the knowledge of scholars was viewed not as a gap but as a rapidly widening chasm.

During the 1950's and 1960's groups concerned with the disciplines began to meet. The Woods Hole Conference was held in September 1959 and involved 35 scientists, scholars, and educators (Bruner, 1962). It had representatives from virtually all of the major curriculum projects that were in operation at the time: the School Mathematics Study Group, the University of Illinois Arithmetic Project, the Minnesota School Mathematics Center, the Biological Sciences Curriculum Study, and the Physical Science Study Committee.

The movement to reorganize knowledge picked up considerable momentum in the late 1950's. Examples of its widespread influence can be found in the seminar conducted by the National Education Association, Center for the Study of Instruction, in 1962. The purpose of the disciplines seminar was to facilitate study and effect use of the disciplines by (a) focusing upon those fundamental ideas and methods of inquiry from selected fields of study which should be in the mainstream of the instructional program of the public school, and (b) exploring frontier thinking and research in the nature of knowledge and ways of knowing (National Education Association, 1962).

The principal goal of most persons who have been recently concerned with the structure of knowledge has been to present subject matter more effectively. If a learner grasps the structure of a subject, he understands it in a way that permits many other things to be related to it meaningfully. To learn structure is to learn how many things are related. Bruner (1962) used structure of a discipline to mean the interrelated ensemble of principles in a field of inquiry. The learner is to gain an understanding of the fundamental structure of whatever subject is being learned. The teaching and learning of structure, rather than simply the mastery of facts and techniques, are at the center of the problem of transfer (Schwab, 1962, 1964a).

There is virtually universal agreement that subject matter should be based upon a conceptual structure within the discipline—general, fundamental ideas that are placed into classes of phenomena and which show the relationships between phenomena. The popularization of the term "concept" has provided a theoretical base to support phrases such as Bruner's (1962) "spiral curriculum," which is built around the concepts that a society deems worthy of the continual concern of its members, presented, of course, in a way that is appropriate for the learner.

The conceptual structure of a discipline may be described as the organized ensemble of the discipline's underlying principles (Tagliacozzo, 1961); the scheme of categories by which the meaning in the disciplines is symbolized, making it possible to interpret the significance of the field within the total framework of meaning (Phenix, 1964); key concepts which summarize essential characteristics of a distinctive class of ideas in the various fields of knowledge (Phenix, 1956); the systematic body of interrelated propositions (Maccia, 1965a); and the fundamental ideas of a discipline (Bruner, 1962).

Conceptual structure is not just concepts. It involves rules, principles, hypotheses, theories, laws, and even models and paradigms. Using this frame of reference, concepts are not differentiated from values as in the work of Bloom and others (1964) and Krathwohl and others (1964) who have chosen to work within the theoretical framework advanced by Tyler, namely that the essential elements of a discipline may be organized into concepts, skills, or values.

Phenix supports Bruner's (1962) thesis that the structure of a subject should be determined by the most fundamental understanding of the underlying principles that can be achieved. The distinguishing mark of any discipline as far as education is concerned is that the knowledge which it comprises can be taught—that it is peculiarly suited for teaching and learning (Phenix, 1962). Phenix emphasizes that the nature of disciplines is of importance to the curriculum of the schools.

It should be mentioned, somewhat parenthetically, that the proposed close relationship between knowledge and learning has had immediate implications for the study of readiness. The understanding of readiness has been hampered because it has depended almost entirely upon the knowledge of the learner. Many persons now believe a learner's readiness is inextricably related to structure. This is what prompted

Bruner (1962) to hypothesize that "any subject can be taught effectively in some intellectually honest form to any child at any stage of development."

Many believe that one of the essential conditions of effective teaching is the practice of clearly charting a way through the subject of instruction so that the learners know how each topic as it comes along fits into the whole scheme of the course and of the discipline with which it is associated. The learner knows where he is in relation to what has gone before and to what is to be studied subsequently. The effect of such teaching is a growing appreciation of the inner logic of the subject, resulting at length in a grasp of its spirit and method which will be proof against the erosion of forgetting details (Phenix, 1960).

Schwab (1964b) believes that the structure of a discipline is important as a source for the organizing elements of a curriculum. He also maintains that each discipline has a particular syntactical structure or mode of inquiry, and that syntax effectively does away with the separation of method and content. Syntactical structure is concerned with concrete descriptions of the kinds of evidences required by the discipline, how far the kinds of data required are actually obtainable, what sorts of second-best substitutes may be employed, what problems of interpretation are posed, and how these problems are overcome (Schwab, 1964a). The rationale used is that a learner may be quite cognizant of the concepts, skills, and laws of a discipline and still be unable to conduct a simple experiment. Each discipline, according to Schwab, has a syntactical structure or mode of inquiry. Mathematics has a fairly mature syntactical structure while sociology and psychology do not. If this be true, the problems encountered in organizing a single discipline are simplified. The problems of building a curriculum from many disciplines, however, become enormously complex.

With these expectations concerning the structure of the disciplines, it is not surprising to find that many persons have devoted themselves to a more intensive understanding of this area. Regardless of the debate over the emphasis that should be given to knowledge in organizing a curriculum, and regardless of whether a mode of inquiry is inherent within each discipline, it is apparent that an analysis of the structure of knowledge has dominated the decade and has shed considerable light on an area of study that was sorely in need of an intensive examination. The knowledge gained helped to answer many significant questions. In doing so, it created a host of new questions; more accurately, it forced educators to ask anew the perennial questions that have confronted curriculum theorists and practitioners: (a) What knowledge shall be taught? (b) How is one segment of knowledge related to another segment of knowledge? (c) How shall the knowledge be organized into a total educational program? (d) To whom shall the knowledge be taught? (e) When shall the knowledge be taught? (f) How shall the knowledge be taught?

With the problem of the organization of the disciplines one must face some inevitable complexities of this terrain; for example, the fact that it does not and cannot supply a single, authoritative answer to the questions of what disciplines are, how many there are, and how they are related to one another (Schwab, 1964b).

While there was considerable research concerning the structure of knowledge, there was also a significant amount of work in a related area, the psychology of learning and instruction—the learning process. Research in this area led to auto-instruction and programmed instruction, or automated teaching. As the programs made use of computers, another term came into prominence—computer-assisted instruction.

The first deliberate investigations were in the area of teaching machines. Pressey's work (1926, 1927, 1932, 1950) began in 1915 and has spanned 50 years. His early devices were intended principally to supplement classroom instruction by providing the learner with rapid knowledge of results through the immediate scoring of his answers to specific questions.

Skinner (1938, 1953, 1954), normally credited with being the father of the teaching machine, is the leading exponent of linear, fixed sequence, or extrinsic programming. Linear programming arranges a series of minute steps by which the learner proceeds toward mastery of the prescribed material. Error avoidance is considered an integral part of the learning process.

Later efforts lead to what is referred to as non-linear, branching, or intrinsic programming. Crowder (1959) is the principal advocate of this type of programming. Non-linear programming commonly involves a choice, as contrasted with the construction of the response in the linear method. Depending upon the response made, new sequences can be presented. Such a method takes into account the learner's rate of work and the quality of his response.

Literally hundreds of programs and machines have been developed during the last ten years (Lumsdaine and Glaser, 1960). It would take several hundred pages to list them. The research is so current that a satisfactory manner of classification has not been found. Some system of classification, however, is needed. Stolurow's (1961) seems the most useful for our purposes. He uses minimally adaptive, partially adaptive, and maximally adaptive.

Minimally adaptive devices require a teacher or some auxiliary help to the learner for efficient instruction. Most of the devices developed during the early 1950's were minimally adaptive and tended to improve an already developed device. They included such devices as simple flashcards, memory drums, and automatic-loading 16-mm. film viewers.

Partially adaptive devices are less dependent on the teacher and learner. The most common characteristic is that they are paced by the learner. They include, essentially, teaching machines and printed devices. Programs for teaching machines have been developed in many content areas, although the humanities are treated very sparingly to date. Printed devices include programmed textbooks (linear), scrambled textbooks (non-linear), and assorted booklets.

Maximally adaptive devices make use of a computer. The computer was discovered late by the educational community, but it was almost immediately obvious that it was potentially capable of performing all the tasks of previous devices, more effectively and more efficiently.

The IBM teaching machine (Rath & others, 1959) was one of the first "complete" systems. Perhaps the most outstanding maximally adaptive devices were developed by Pask (1957, 1958). Pask has raised some of the most fundamental issues to date. The main concept of Pask's machines is that of organic control. The teaching machine seeks to work with the learner to find an optimum solution balancing several separate but interacting requirements. This is in opposition to the concept of automatic control, where the teaching machine tends to impose a behavior pattern upon the learner. Pask believes (1958) that the teaching machine must function as a learning machine; that it must obey and issue commands; that it not only has to improve the learner's rate of learning, but also must find out how the learner learns.

These initial explorations finally led to large-scale experiments with children in schools. The Project for Individually Prescribed Instruction (The Oakleaf Project) at the Learning Research and Development Center, University of Pittsburgh, is an effort to provide programmed instructional materials to learners from kindergarten to grade 6 in the areas of reading, mathematics, and science (Lindvall & Bolvin, 1966). Another notable project, under the direction of Patrick Suppes (1965), involves a computer-based laboratory for teaching and learning at Stanford University.

Some research efforts have been concerned not only with the structure of knowledge and the learning process, but also with curriculum; that is, they have investigated the relation of learning to the selection and organization of content. Does a particular item of content facilitate learning? Is one sequence or item better than another? Curriculum is most often defined by specialists as "planned learning experiences." Gagné (1965, 1967), however, defines curriculum as a sequence of content units arranged in such a way that the learning of each unit may be accomplished as a single act. This is under the condition that the capabilities described by specified previous units have already been mastered by the learner. Eisner (1965) is in essential agreement; he states that a teacher is active in curriculum development when he decides ". . . what to teach and how to order what he teaches."

Gagné (1967) believes that the content and sequence of a curriculum can be based upon a rational analysis; and further, that such a procedure can be used to build curricula that are satisfactory from the standpoint of their structural completeness. He is not alone in this belief. Glaser (1962), using essentially the same definition of curriculum advanced by Gagné (Gagné & others, 1962), has described several different approaches to the analysis of instructional objectives in an effort to define a learning structure. Several other persons have undertaken similar efforts. Hively (1963), Kersh (1965), and Schultz and others (1964) analyzed programmed instructional materials in elementary mathematical operations with sets. Gibson (1965) analyzed the stages of reading and clarified the behavioral meaning of the hierarchically ordered stages.

This view of curriculum is different from the more traditional position of Tyler (1950)—different not so much because it is in conflict with it, but because it is more limited in scope. Gagné and others with similar views do not believe that curriculum must answer such questions as: "What content should be included in the curriculum?" or "What data sources should be used in determining aims?" They do not maintain that these questions are irrelevant, only that they are not necessary to their definition of curriculum. One is inclined to ponder what area of educational research is going to seek to find answers to these questions.

The differences concerning the definition of curriculum are not of critical importance so long as the views do not become polarized. This does not appear likely. The leading exponent of the "narrower" definition of curriculum, Gagné (1967), recognizes the value of seeking answers to the types of questions raised by Tyler (1950). There is no doubt that a major activity of researchers during the next decade will be to build curricula from a sequence of content units that hopefully will be structurally complete.

There have been numerous efforts in the field of curriculum and instruction that were related to the structure of knowledge and the process of learning, but that did not have an immediate effect on the educational programs being developed during this period of time. It is safe to assume that some of these efforts will affect the educational programs that will be developed during the coming decades. In fact, these areas represent a natural outgrowth of the research on the structure of knowledge. Brief mention will be made of some of the research studies in these areas.

Several persons have come to view curriculum in terms of a "systems" model. Macdonald (1964) and Faix (1966), for example, have developed systems models for curriculum. In their systems, the elements are inputs, processes are the outputs and feedbacks. Macdonald (1964) has been concerned with the curriculum development process rather than curriculum per se; that is, he includes both content and process in his curriculum system. His system places people as its basic unit. The outputs of these units are transmitted to the instructional setting.

Maccia (1965a) contends that curriculum is a component of instruction. She defines instruction, for example, as "influence toward rule-governed behavior." Curriculum equals rules, a reason or criterion which leads to one behavior rather than another. Its function is to govern and regulate behavior, apparently the teachers' behavior.

Macdonald and Maccia, therefore, view curriculum and instruction in different ways. Macdonald sees them as separate concepts that overlap; Maccia (1963, 1965b) contends that curriculum is a component of instruction because it is a variable in teacher behavior.

A review of the theoretical foundations for educational programs reveals, therefore, that there has been little concern for most of the traditional questions raised by those who specialize in the total process of curriculum development. Rather, the research has been concentrated on the structure of knowledge and the psychology of learning and instruction. The research efforts admittedly have been far from definitive, but the field has been advanced considerably during the decade. The following section will show, however, that persons responsible for developing the educational programs did not, in general, utilize the knowledge that the research efforts made available.

ILLUSTRATIVE EDUCATIONAL PROGRAMS. The authors have chosen to delimit educational programs to those of national scope. The programs identified here have had a significant effect in schools during the past decade and probably will have for several years to come.

The educational programs of national scope, commonly referred to as national curriculum projects, were developed in the movement that has been described above. There were several factors that gave impetus and direction to the development of these projects. Two of these have already been mentioned: the Soviet Union's Sputnik program and the overwhelming increase of knowledge became overwhelming. A third factor was the great dissatisfaction voiced by scholars in colleges and universities in regard to precollegiate education in their fields. As a result of their dissatisfaction, they became actively involved in developing the national curriculum projects. The participation of university scholars and scientists, men distinguished at the frontier of their disciplines, was unprecedented. They came to effect needed change; they remained out of fascination with the complex problems of educating the young (Goodlad, 1966a). Fourth, relatively large amounts of money were made available by both private organizations and the federal government for the development of educational programs. The combinations of these factors were responsible for producing major revisions in many areas of the curriculum.

There are some characteristics which most of the projects have in common. Each project was developed by a group of persons who usually represented three different orientations. Scholars from colleges and universities assumed responsibility for the substantive part of the projects. Psychologists contributed their knowledge of learning. Teachers contributed their knowledge of pedagogy and tried out the new materials in their classrooms.

Each project attempted to develop important concepts from the disciplines. A few selected concepts replaced the coverage of many facts which were often not related in any meaningful way by the learner. The projects at the elementary level sometimes differed rather significantly from those at the high school level. The emphasis at the high school level has been upon the separate disciplines. Major concepts from a single discipline were identified by the scholars and these became the basis for organizing a new program for the curriculum. At the elementary level some projects identified significant concepts which several disciplines had in common or a single project combined ideas from several disciplines.

A new emphasis upon the kinds of behaviors demanded of learners also characterizes the projects. Learners are no longer expected to recall or recognize many facts. They are encouraged to observe and generalize from their observations; to discover principles for themselves and apply them in new situations; to hypothesize and develop procedures for testing hypotheses; to intuitively develop solutions to problems; to classify phenomena on the basis of several characteristics; and generally to engage in behavior which scientists in many fields utilize.

The projects are representative of only a segment of the curriculum. Mathematics and the physical and biological sciences have received by far the most attention. The social sciences and languages have received some attention. The arts and humanities have only recently begun to receive funds for curriculum projects. This has contributed to the creation of a very unfortunate imbalance in the curriculum.

All of the projects are concerned with the development of learning materials. A wide variety are produced. Textbooks for both teachers and learners, films, filmstrips, recordings, and original songs and poems help to develop the carefully selected concepts. Models and objects are included for learners to manipulate. Field trips are outlined for specific purposes.

Most projects are also concerned with teacher education. New behaviors and knowledge are required of teachers as well as of learners. A variety of ways is used to educate, and even to re-educate, teachers. Films demonstrate new procedures and ideas. Workshops, in-service courses, and university work are used. Often, the project staff sends consultants into districts interested in their materials. Newsletters keep teachers informed of new materials, new procedures, and new ideas. A few projects are included in the collegiate education of future teachers.

The projects vary widely in the adequacy in which the curricular questions of objectives, learning opportunities, and evaluation have been considered. Very few of the projects have objectives that are stated in terms of pupil behavior and content. Most have broad, elusive aims which are ill-defined for giving direction to instruction. The learning opportunities provide for the active involvement of the learner. Selected concepts usually form the basis of the learning opportunities and these concepts are presented in a spiraling fashion. The same concepts appear later to be reinforced and extended in their meanings. Evaluation is almost totally neglected in some projects and is well planned in others. Since objectives are not always carefully defined, the evaluative attempts do not always relate directly back to the objectives. The emphasis usually is on the concepts, and objective tests are generally used as instruments. Many of the evaluative efforts of the projects are devoted to comparing learner performance in the new projects on tests developed for traditional programs with learner performance in the traditional programs on tests developed for the traditional programs. The pitfalls in this approach have been stated by Ferris (1962). Far too few of the projects have given enough rigorous attention to evaluative instruments and procedures which would measure adequately the learner behaviors and development of concepts which were the central concern of the projects.

The following projects were selected to be included in this article because they represent varying emphases, and not necessarily because of their strengths or weaknesses. A brief description of the project is given and then the current views of authorities in the field of curriculum which were utilized are noted. Only those views which are obvious or seem to be uniquely used will be mentioned in the discussion of each project. A more extensive description and comprehensive analysis of these and other projects may be found in *The Changing School Curriculum* (Goodlad & others, 1960).

School Health Education Study. The School Health Education Study has followed the views of the authorities discussed in the previous section more extensively than has any other project at the elementary level. This program was planned in four levels for grades K–3, 4–6, 7–9, and 10–12. Three major concepts gave direction to the development of content: growth and development, decision-making, and interaction. These concepts were further elaborated into ten others which are called the major organizing elements. The physical, mental, and social aspects of each were stated. Behavioral objectives and learning materials were developed at the four levels and for the ten concepts. A well-developed packet of materials is available for teachers on each instructional level. The project gives attention to objectives for which content is defined at three levels of generality, and for which learner behaviors are stated in terms of knowledge, attitudes, and practices. Learning opportunities are suggested which presumably assist the learner in developing the content and the behaviors as stated by the project. The same concepts and behaviors reappear at different levels of the learner's development, but each time the learner is expected to deal with the concepts and behave in a more sophisticated, complex fashion.

Evaluation of student learning focuses on the desired behavioral outcome. The materials developed as teaching–learning guides include actual tests as well as suggestions for developing tests on designated topics.

Thus, the decision-making areas in curriculum of objectives, learning opportunities, and evaluation have received considerable attention by this project. This plan is largely in accord with the rationale for curriculum planning as proposed by Tyler (1950) and Goodlad and Richter (1966). Bruner's popular concept (1962) of the spiraling curriculum was also utilized in organizing the learning opportunities. Major concepts were selected which define the structure of the discipline. The concept of organizing elements as used by Tyler (1950) and by Goodlad (1963) was applied. The third level of content is called the focal organizing elements. These are combined with the desired behavioral outcomes to form the objectives of the project.

Elementary Science Study. The Elementary Science Study of Educational Services, Inc., is composed of self-contained units of work. These separate units do not form a curriculum, but are thought to form the threads of a curriculum which has yet to be developed. Five completed representative units are included in the sampler package. The number is to be expanded until 100 to 200 units are available.

The approach used in this project is to emphasize the common aspects of the sciences rather than to define the structure of a particular discipline within science. It uses a "predisciplinary" approach, and each unit presumably develops an important thread of science. This treatment of subject matter might be considered an attempt to loosely define the broad field of general science in the currently popular way of defining the structure of particular disciplines.

Learner inquiry would appear to be consistent with the process proposed by Schwab and Brandenwein (1962). Learners observe, investigate, record data, hypothesize and generalize. These behaviors receive prime emphasis in the learning opportunities provided.

It is possible to examine this project using the four major questions raised in the Tyler rationale (1950). Little attention is given to defining objectives in terms of learner behaviors. There are no carefully and precisely stated objectives giving direction to the development of learning opportunities; instead, the activities for learners follow a sequence of questions which learners might ask. These are evolved from the experimental work on the units in actual classrooms. The learning opportunities seem to meet many of the criteria for selections as suggested by Tyler (1950) and Goodlad (1959). The organization of the learning opportunities follows a logical sequence in the development of the content.

The lack of clearly stated objectives hampers the evaluative process of the Elementary Science Study. Only a few suggestions are included for the teacher. One apparent justification for this neglect seems to be that with the emphasis upon inquiry, if learners are inquiring and experimenting, the aims of the unit are being fulfilled. This loose approach to evaluation is not consistent insofar as evaluation is normally considered by authorities in the field of curriculum. The problem of evaluation in terms of learner behaviors is recognized, but not successfully resolved.

Elkhart Experiment in Economic Education. This is a project in economics education carried on in cooperation with the teachers of Elkhart, Indiana. It is planned to be a 12-year curriculum to make explicit the economic concepts which underlie many of the everyday activities in the lives of learners. Seven general economic principles give direction to the development of the program, and the ideas and activities are presented so that they reflect this structure of economics. The content of the program does not deal exclusively with economics, however; political science, sociology, anthropology, geography, and history are included.

This project can also be examined in terms of the Tyler (1950) rationale for curriculum planning. Objectives of the project are not defined in terms of pupil behaviors. They are often stated as broad statements of intent for teachers. The content section of these statements, however, is usually well defined and generally relates back to the seven major economic principles. The learning opportunities are extensively developed. A variety of activities ranging from discussion to dramatization are suggested in order to actively involve learners in the content. Many resources are included or suggested. Phonograph recordings introduce the major ideas of the lesson, and these are followed with many suggestions to reinforce the ideas. An extensive bibliography of materials is available for teachers to use, and original songs and poems were written and are included in the teacher guides. The lessons are designed to last from one to several weeks. The teacher's guide includes a wealth of materials and activities from which the teacher is encouraged to select those which would best fit the needs of his group. As well as meeting the criteria for selection of learning opportunities proposed by Tyler (1950), the activities are good examples of organizing centers as outlined by Goodlad (1959).

Evaluation is largely lacking in the design of the project. Some work has been done on developing tests for learners, but this is not included as a major part of the materials. Review activities are suggested, but they were not designed to assess where the learners are in the development of behaviors or ideas.

This project attempts to define the structure of economics and this is used to develop the learning opportunities. The ideas in the learning opportunities are organized in a spiraling fashion, as discussed by Bruner (1962), in which they reappear later to be dealt with in a more complex way and at a greater depth of understanding. This is an attempt to teach learners complex, abstract ideas from a discipline not normally included in a systematic fashion in the elementary school curriculum. The abstract ideas are presented to learners in a simple, sometimes concrete, way.

Although the project employs the term "discovery," it is not generally used in the activities as it was discussed in the preceding section. The suggested activities are directive and structured so that learners come to understand the basic generalizations. Learners are not encouraged to pursue any alternative path to achieve a solution or to resolve an answer to a problem.

The Madison Project. The Madison Project is concerned with the content of mathematics, but other concerns are also central. Teaching method, the involvement of learners, and a theory of instruction have received much attention. It is not considered to be a mathematics curriculum, but a supplement to the regular ongoing program in mathematics. The initial work of the project concentrated upon grades 2–8. Suggestions and recommendations are made regarding the "phasing in" of this work into the ongoing mathematics curriculum.

The most distinctive characteristic of this project is the emphasis upon discovery and intuition. The project disseminates many publications and films which explain and demonstrate how these behaviors are developed through the content of algebra, geometry, and arithmetic, which are taught simultaneously. Learners are very actively involved in problems and mathematical games.

Although the project is not considered to be a complete mathematical program for learners (except for a ninth-grade algebra course and the mathematics curriculum for the kindergarten) it is possible to examine it in terms of the rationale for curriculum planning proposed by Tyler (1950) and Goodlad and Richter (1966).

There are no specific objectives stated in terms of learner behavior. As the activities and materials are examined, however, it becomes clear that discovery by the learner is a prime focus. The process utilized would seem to be in agreement with that expounded by Schwab and Brandenwein (1962). The learner is encouraged to pursue the problem on his own initiative. The activities that are developed in this project meet five specific criteria very similar to those set forth by Tyler (1950) for learning opportunities and by Goodlad (1959) for organizing centers.

Some very abstract ideas and concepts are included in the project materials which have not been standard content for elementary school learners. The inclusion of these ideas and the successful learning of them lend additional support to Bruner's (1962) widely quoted proposition.

Methodology is also given considerable attention and emphasis. The active involvement of the learner, exploration and discovery, creative problem solving, and the role of the teacher as a guide rather than as an authority are successfully implemented in the "Madison approach."

Evaluation in terms of learner behavior in the traditional sense has been difficult. The emphasis upon divergent thinking rather defies assessment by the more formal, standardized methods. Attempts to evaluate learners' behavior as a result of participating in the project have been made, but evaluation as a formal traditional activity in curriculum development is not an essential part of the project.

Science Curriculum Improvement Study. The aim of the Science Curriculum Improvement Study is the development of scientific literacy. This is defined as a functional understanding of science concepts and an inquisitive intellectual attitude. It is thought that for learners to develop these, they need experiences with substances to be manipulated, instruments and devices which extend the range of the senses, unusual environmental conditions, and observations of living organisms. Materials are to be developed for grades K–6. Divergent thinking is encouraged and any honest answer from a learner is accepted. Learners are encouraged under the guidance, not the authority, of the teacher. Many concrete experiences are provided so that each learner can build a conceptual framework for dealing with later ideas.

The work of this project has utilized several of

the ideas included in the preceding section. The content of the program is based upon fundamental science concepts and the behaviors emphasized are observing, discovering, and experimenting. The concepts also reflect the structure of the particular discipline. The learner behaviors to be developed through the learning opportunities are those which scientists use. These concepts were originally drawn from the broad field of the physical sciences but have since been expanded to include the biological sciences.

Objectives as defined in the Tyler rationale (1950) are not consistently stated in the various units of SCIS. Although the content of the units receives considerable attention and is made explicit, the learner behaviors do not receive such careful attention nor are they usually explicitly stated. The learning opportunities involve the learner actively and are organized in a sequential fashion with an assumed increasing depth of understanding of the concepts. Evaluation receives limited attention in terms of the achievement of objectives, or learner behaviors and content, and of the aims of the project.

The process which learners are to follow would seem to be in close agreement to that outlined by Schwab and Brandenwein (1962). No preconceived "right" answers are waiting for learners after following a procedure "correctly." Rather, each learner is encouraged to pursue his own hypotheses to the formation of tentative conclusions.

The project makes explicit use of child-development principles as support for the approach taken. Piaget in particular is often quoted when discussing the theoretical positions of the project. This is a unique contribution of the project.

Greater Cleveland Mathematics Program. This project was developed under the auspices of the Educational Research Council of Cleveland, Ohio. This is a cooperative group of school districts in and around Cleveland which have banded together to solve pressing educational problems. Plans are to develop a mathematics curriculum for grades K–12. Work was developed initially for grades K–6.

The work in the project is typical of many and is somewhat traditional in some respects. The content of the program is drawn from the structure of mathematics as defined by this group. Emphasis is placed upon "the structural interrelationships of number" and upon computational skills. Learners are to deal with the content in a "guided discovery" approach. This does not seem to be in very close agreement with the concept of inquiry as discussed by Schwab and Brandenwein (1962), however. The work of GCMP would seem to be more directive and predetermined.

Objectives as defined by Tyler (1950) are given some attention. They are usually stated in terms of learner behaviors, but they are very broad and appear to give little direction to the development of learning opportunities. The content is well defined and is consistently reflected in the learning opportunities. The activities developed are quite traditional, as is grade placement of topics. The learning opportunities are organized in a spiraling sequential fashion in which topics continually reappear and increase in complexity. This would appear to be an organization of content similar to that proposed by Bruner (1962). Evaluation activities are suggested at the end of the units and these, too, are rather traditional in their approach. Quizzes and achievement tests constitute the major devices to assess learner behavior.

Special Programs. The preceding discussion has dealt with elementary educational programs of national scope which were developed for the "typical" school learner; that is, the programs were not developed specifically for certain populations such as gifted, culturally deprived, or slow learners. Although many of the projects have tried out their materials with such groups, the materials were not developed exclusively for use with any one such group. It would be possible to include in this article many additional types of programs developed exclusively for particular groups of learners such as the physically and mentally handicapped, the culturally deprived, and the academically able. It would also be possible to include examples of programs using different educational media ranging from programmed instruction and computers for individual use to the utilization of television for mass instruction. Many of these, however, will be included in other articles in this publication.

Perhaps they should not be singled out here for another reason. Historically, these have been viewed as completely separate programs which were developed to meet the needs of a specific, but limited, group of learners. These groups have often been isolated from the overall school population, both in terms of geographical location and programs. Each group pursued its own program with little or no contact with other groups. With the increasing emphasis upon individualization of instruction, it becomes feasible for a single school facility to provide for the atypical learner as well as the more typical learner. It may well become a common practice to have many special programs for all learners which are concerned more with diagnosis and prescription based on educational attainments and potentials of individuals rather than on group attributes of physical or mental handicaps.

IMPLICATIONS. It has been indicated that learners are expected to play a new role in the educational programs developed during the last decade. No longer is the learner expected to react quietly and passively; he is expected to react actively and at times aggressively. Not only do the educational programs have new expectations for learners, but they also have important implications for other facets of the school. Three such facets are school organization, teacher education, and facilities.

School Organization. Although this is a separate topic included in the *Encyclopedia*, it should be mentioned briefly here because of the effect that organization has upon the educational program. School organization is a structure or plan devised for assisting the faculty and learners in attaining the objectives of the school. It is a means to attain desired ends; it is not an end in itself.

Few of the new programs of national scope are

graded in the sense that textbooks traditionally are. Some programs have work recommended for use over a span of grades; virtually all recommend that the pacing of work be appropriate for each unique group rather than follow a rigid time schedule which calls for coverage of the materials. The development of important behaviors and concepts by individual learners, restricted only by unique capabilities and limitations, is the prime concern of all the programs.

There are two types of school organizational patterns which would seem to facilitate the concern for the individual's growth better than the traditional self-contained, graded structure does. These are nongraded and team teaching. In nongraded classes the grouping of learners is determined by many criteria rather than a few or, as has often been the case, by one criterion—age. The nongraded pattern of organization allows each learner to develop his capabilities as far as he can without being hampered by grade barriers. A concept or skill is no longer the possession of a designated grade or age level, but is appropriate content for any learner when he is at that level of development. Since the new curriculum projects have organized knowledge in a continuous and sequential manner, the continued use of grades with artificial barriers to progress in learning as a method of vertical organization becomes far less tenable. The characteristics of nongrading have been outlined and extensively discussed in the literature. One source, however, is generally recognized as the major work (Goodlad & Anderson, 1963).

Team teaching is a horizontal pattern of organization that allows for many alternatives in the daily work of the learner. The creative use of this pattern provides alternatives in using time, materials, and personnel. One of the most pertinent features of team teaching is the effective utilization of personnel. It is impossible for an elementary school teacher to be a specialist in every area of the curriculum for which he is responsible. Indeed, he cannot even be expected to have a broad foundation in each one. Yet, in these days of specialization, learners are expected to develop sophisticated behaviors and complex ideas in science, mathematics, social sciences, health education, arts, and the humanities. When several teachers combine their various competencies for a large group of learners, the curriculum is thought to be more likely to have adequate balance among the components. The literature on team teaching is becoming increasingly abundant. One source is particularly pertinent and comprehensive for understanding the concept and the implications for the new educational programs (Shaplin & Olds, 1964).

Teacher Education. The educational programs developed during the current period of curriculum reform place new demands upon the pre-service education of future teachers and upon the in-service education of present teachers. Goodlad and others (1960) have outlined some of the problems involved. As noted above, it is completely unrealistic to expect the teacher in the elementary school to be an expert in all the subjects for which he is responsible. The new projects with their emphasis upon the structure of the discipline and modes of inquiry require the teacher to have a substantial background in the subject field. Each new program requires considerable thought and study before it can be adequately implemented in the classroom. For most teachers, the implementation would probably require a completely new orientation to the subject field. This would not be a casual or easy process. It would require considerable re-education on the in-service level for any one program. For this reason, all projects have seen the need for and have given some thought to teacher education in the use of their materials. A few projects, but too few, have found their way into the pre-service education of teachers.

Each new program implemented would require a considerable amount of time, energy, and expense on the part of teachers, the school, and the school district. Additional or released time for teachers, purchases of new supplies and equipment, staff and/or materials to conduct the in-service work, and the amount of time required for study by teachers would represent a large investment. When more than one of the new programs is to be implemented, the re-education task becomes enormous. The in-service task should be greatly lessened as the new approaches to understanding the disciplines and the new school programs find their way into pre-service teacher education.

Not only do the projects require a new orientation to the subject matter field, but they also require new teaching behaviors. The traditional view of teaching has been that the teacher is an immutable authority who imparts his knowledge didactically, essentially by lecturing and then quizzing learners on how well they remembered it. None of the projects is designed to employ this mode of teaching. Rarely are the learners to be directly told any content. Rather, they are carefully guided to discover and explore pertinent data for themselves. Instead of an authority, the teacher is seen as a resource and a guide. Learners are expected to be actively, even noisily and "messily" involved in their learning; not sitting and passively listening to the teacher. They are expected to have the time and opportunity to explore blind alleys, erroneous ideas, and their own, perhaps inadequate, hypotheses. Learners are expected to learn much more than facts; they are expected to discover and apply principles, observe, analyze, and record data, and devise experiments to test hypotheses. The emphasis of all programs is upon the process of learning rather than upon teaching. This view of learning is quite different from what occurs in the typical classrooms found today throughout the nation.

Facilities. A thorough discussion of educational facilities is beyond the scope of this article. Yet, the implications of the new educational programs in regard to facilities need to be made explicit.

One of the most obvious requirements of the programs in terms of facilities is space. A desirable characteristic of space is flexibility. Learners need different types of space to be actively involved in various types of activities. One kind of space is needed for small-group work and another for total group instruction.

Still a different type and amount of space is required for the manipulation and storage of the learning materials required for the projects.

Space is not only needed by learners, but by teachers as well. The new educational programs and the new way of organizing the school into teams of teachers and learners require that teachers have a place where they can meet to plan and organize for instruction.

Facilities are also needed for a variety of types of instruction. Films and filmstrips are often used by projects. Records are used in some. Mathematics programs utilizing computers have been developed. It is reasonable to expect that an increasing emphasis upon electronic equipment for instruction will demand that facilities be available for all such types of instruction ranging from individualized programs on computers through mass media instruction with television. Facilities are needed to house a materials center which includes a much greater variety of learning materials than the books in a library.

Many new architectural designs are being tried throughout the nation. The typical egg-crate school construction is hardly adequate to meet the demands of the emerging educational programs described in the preceding section. Schools with individual learning carrels; schools with space unhampered by internal classroom walls; schools with movable partitions for walls; schools with airconditioning; schools with carpeting; schools with special acoustical materials; schools with all classrooms having immediate access to the centralized materials center—all are examples of new facilities designed to enhance the implementation of new visions of the educative process of the nation's future citizens (Educational Facilities Laboratories, 1960; Gores, 1966).

CRITIQUE. The authors have several concerns regarding educational programs which need to be discussed. First, it must be made explicit that, in most cases, the illustrative educational programs included in this article did not follow any particular rationale or theoretical framework in curriculum development. It would appear that few of the groups which developed the national curriculum projects were aware of the knowledge available in curriculum as a field of study. The authors have superimposed some external views and approaches from the curriculum field upon the selected programs to demonstrate particular ideas which are currently prevalent in the literature. It is unfortunate that more of the curriculum projects did not rationally and explicitly utilize the available knowledge in curriculum. Failure to use the available knowledge is another example of the all too familiar gap between theory and practice.

Many projects did not state any precise, explicit objectives with clearly defined learner behaviors and content. Those that did consider educational objectives usually stated broad, global behaviors which gave little direction to the planning of appropriate learning opportunities to develop the behaviors. All projects, however, had carefully defined content.

The learning opportunities in the projects were usually carefully devised, but often did not apply the criteria which are available in the literature (Goodlad, 1959; Goodlad & Richter, 1966; Tyler, 1950). The learning opportunities were usually organized in a spiraling, sequential pattern in order to logically develop the selected concepts of the discipline(s). Little or no attention has been given to the kind of psychological impact this organization has upon individual learners and their progress.

Evaluation in terms of learner progress has sometimes been limited or even overlooked. No easy ways exist to assess the newer behaviors and understandings presumably developed by the programs. Extensive work in this area is still needed in virtually all the programs. Many claims have been made—and will be made—but only when valid and reliable data are collected and interpreted can the true impact of these programs upon the learners of today and the citizens of tomorrow be known.

Second, the current emphasis upon the structure of subject matter was no doubt long overdue and sorely needed. Yet this emphasis has created an imbalance in the curriculum of schools as bad as that created by any other movement in the history of curriculum development. Subject matter was the prime data source for objectives, and very few of the projects gave even superficial consideration to the learner as a data source. Society as a data source was only indirectly considered. Tyler (1950) stated years ago that all three data sources should be considered in planning an adequate curriculum. The subject-matter curriculum will quite likely remain for many years. Already, however, predictions are being made regarding the type of curriculum which might eventually replace it. Goodlad has predicted first an emphasis on the total curriculum in which general education as breadth would be emphasized as opposed to the current emphasis on depth in the disciplines. Goodlad (1966b) then predicted a humanistic curriculum that would emphasize human values and interests.

Third, another type of imbalance in the curriculum has been created by the emphasis upon the sciences and mathematics. The many choices of programs which are now available to teachers in the sciences and mathematics need to be extended to include as many choices in the social sciences, the arts, and humanities. Only then will this type of curricular imbalance be corrected.

Fourth, it may be possible that, in simplifying the concepts and procedures of a discipline for young learners, the concepts and procedures may lose some of their integrity. They may be oversimplified to the extent that their meaning is distorted and perhaps even lost.

Fifth, even though some of the concepts can be adequately simplified for young learners, economy of instructional time should be considered. It may well be that some complex ideas from the disciplines can be learned if enough time is spent on them. It is also possible that too much time could be spent on learning complex abstractions which could create a curricular imbalance by neglecting other areas in the educational program of learners. The same complex ideas and procedures might require less time to be learned if they were postponed until a later time to be considered by older learners (Bloom & others, 1965). Unfortunately, this area has not been adequately pursued by researchers and, therefore, definitive answers to such concerns are lacking.

Sixth, a concern raised by Goodlad and others (1960) centers upon how the concepts in the various disciplines can be woven together to make an adequate educational program for young learners. Is the educational program to become a collection of the concepts which can be learned from all the disciplines represented? How is a meaningful program of ten to fifteen disciplines to be organized for young learners? Goodlad and others (1960) cite the need for valid bases of inclusion and exclusion of subject matter in the educational program.

Seventh, too many of the projects have sought to teach the learner to behave as the specialist in the discipline behaves. The implicit assumption seems to be that the learner will go on for more advanced work, culminating in a major specialization at the college or university level. It would be more appropriate if the programs sought to develop a course that would be useful for persons who are not going to be specialists in the field (Tyler, 1950).

The search for better educational programs for the future citizens of America continues. No one program appropriate for all learners will ever be developed. As a matter of fact, the number of programs is likely to increase considerably during the coming decade, creating alternatives that would have seemed impossible to educators as late as the end of World War II. The alternatives that the plethora of programs make available will not assure that wise choices will be made. Before wise choices can be made, the criteria upon which decisions are to be made will need to be developed. Wise decision-making based on valid, explicit criteria is mandatory. Unfortunately, no criteria exist at present.

Donald A. Myers
University of California
M. Frances Klein
University of California

References

Bellack, Arno. "Selection and Organization of Curriculum Content: An Analysis." In *What Shall the High School Teach*. ASCD, 1956.
Bloom, Benjamin S., and others. (Eds.) *Taxonomy of Educational Objectives: The Classification of Educational Goals, Handbook I: Cognitive Domain*. McKay, 1964.
Bloom, Benjamin S., and others. (Eds.) *Stability and Change in Human Characteristics*. Wiley, 1965.
Bruner, Jerome. *The Process of Education*. Harvard U Press, 1962.
Bruner, Jerome S., and others. *Studies in Cognitive Growth*. Wiley, 1966.
Caswell, Hollis L., and Campbell, Doak S. *Curriculum Development*. American, 1935.
Crowder, N. A. "Automatic Tutoring By Means of Intrinsic Programming." In Galanter E. H. (Ed.) *Automatic Teaching: The State of the Art*. Wiley, 1959. p. 109–16.
Dewey, John. *Democracy and Education*. Macmillan, 1916.
Dewey, John. *Experience and Education*. Macmillan, 1938.
Educational Facilities Laboratories. *Cost of the Schoolhouse*. Educational Facilities Laboratories, 1960.
Educational Policies Commission. *The Purposes of Education in American Democracy*. NEA, 1938.
Eisner, Elliot. "Levels of Curriculum and Curriculum Research." *El Sch J* 66:155–62; 1965.
Faix, Thomas L. "Structural-Functional Analysis as a Conceptual System for Curriculum Theory and Research: A Theoretical Study." Paper presented at AERA, February, 1966. (Mimeographed.)
Ferris, Frederick L., Jr. "Testing in the New Curriculum: Numerology, 'Tyranny,' or Common Sense?" *Sch R* 70:112–31; 1962.
Gagné, Robert M. *The Conditions of Learning*. Holt, 1965.
Gagné, Robert M. "Curriculum Research and the Promotion of Learning." In *Perspectives of Curriculum Evaluation*. Rand McNally, 1967.
Gagné, Robert, and others. "N.E. Factors in Acquiring Knowledge of Mathematical Tasks." *Psychol Monogr*, 1962.
Gibson, Eleanor J. "Learning to Read." *Science* 148: 1066–72; 1965.
Glaser, R. "Some Research Problems in Automated Instruction: Instructional Programming and Subject Matter Structure." In Coulson, J. E. (Ed.) *Programmed Learning and Computer-based Instruction*. Wiley, 1962. p. 67–85.
Goodlad, John I. "The Teacher Selects, Plans, Organizes." In *Learning and the Teacher*. NEA, 1959. p. 39–60.
Goodlad, John I. "Curriculum: The State of the Field." *R Ed Res* 30:185–98; 1960.
Goodlad, John I. *Planning and Organizing for Teaching*. NEA, 1963.
Goodlad, John I. "Curriculum." In Goodlad, John I. (Ed.) *The Changing American School*. NSSE, 1966(a).
Goodlad, John I. "Direction and Redirection for Curriculum Change." In *Curriculum Change: Direction and Progress*. ASCD, 1966(b).
Goodlad, John I., and Anderson, Robert H. *The Nongraded Elementary School*. Harcourt, 1963.
Goodlad, John I., and Richter, Maurice N., Jr. *The Development of a Conceptual System for Dealing With Problems of Curriculum and Instruction*. Cooperative Research Project, 1966.
Goodlad, John I., and others. *The Changing School Curriculum*. New York: The Fund for the Advancement of Education, 1960.
Gores, Harold B. "Schoolhouse in Transition." In

The Changing American School. U Chicago Press, 1966.
Havighurst, Robert J. *Developmental Tasks and Education.* McKay, 1949.
Herrick, Virgil. "Approaches to Helping Children Improve Their Instructional Practices." *Sch R* 52: 533–4; 1954.
Herrick, Virgil. "Elementary Education—Programs." In Harris, Chester W. (Ed.) *Encyclopedia of Educational Research.* Macmillan, 1960. p. 430–42.
Hively, W., II. *Defining Criterion Behavior for Programmed Instruction in Elementary Mathematics.* Harvard U Press, 1963.
Johnson, Mauritz, Jr. "Definitions and Models in Curriculum Theory." *Ed Theory* 17:127–40; 1967.
Judd, Charles Hubbard. *Psychology of High-School Subjects.* Ginn, 1915.
Kearney, Nolan C. "Elementary School Objectives." In *Report Prepared for the Mid-Century Committee on Outcomes in Elementary Education.* Russell Sage, 1953.
Kersh, B. Y. "Programming Classroom Instruction." In Glaser, R. (Ed.) *Teaching Machines and Programmed Learning, II: Data and Directions.* NEA, 1965. p. 321–68.
Krathwohl, David R., and others. *Taxonomy of Educational Objectives: The Classification of Educational Goals, Handbook II: Affective Domain.* McKay, 1964.
Lindvall, C. M. (Ed.) *Defining Educational Objectives.* U Pittsburgh Press, 1964.
Lindvall, C. Mauritz, and Bolvin, John. *The Project for Individually Prescribed Instruction (The Oakleaf Project).* U Pittsburgh Press, 1966.
Lumsdaine, A. M., and Glaser, R. (Eds.) *Teaching Machines and Programmed Learning: A Source Book.* NEA, 1960.
Maccia, Elizabeth S. "Science and Science in Education." In Kneller, George F. (Ed.) *Foundations of Education.* Wiley, 1963.
Maccia, Elizabeth S. "Instruction as Influence Toward Rule-Governed Behavior." Ohio State U, 1965(a). (Mimeographed.)
Maccia, Elizabeth S. "Curriculum Theory and Policy." Ohio State U, 1965(b). (Mimeographed.)
Macdonald, James B. "Curriculum Theory: Problems and a Prospectus." Paper presented at Prof of Curriculum Meeting. Miami Beach, April 3, 1964. (Mimeographed.)
Marshall, Leon C., and Goetz, Rachel M. *Curriculum Making in the Social Studies.* Scribner, 1936.
Montessori, Maria. *Education for a New World.* Theosophical Press, 1959.
Montessori, Maria. *Spontaneous Activity in Education: The Advanced Method.* Robert Bentley, Inc., 1964.
National Education Association. *The Scholars Look at the Schools: A Report of the Disciplines Seminar.* NEA, 1962.
National Education Association, Commission on Reorganization of Secondary Education. *Cardinal Principles of Secondary Education.* GPO, 1918.
Neill, A. S. *Summerhill.* Hart Publishing Company, 1960.
Parson, Talcott. "General Theory in Sociology." In Merton, Robert K., and others. (Eds.) *Sociology Today.* Basic Books, 1959. p. 12–16.
Pask, G. "Automatic Teaching Techniques." *Br Commonwealth and Electronics* 4:210–11; 1957.
Pask, G. "Electronic Keyboard Teaching Machines." *Ed and Commerce* 24:16–26; 1958.
Phenix, Philip H. "Key Concepts and the Crisis in Learning." *Teach Coll Rec* 58:137–43; 1956.
Phenix, Philip H. "The Topography of Higher Liberal Learning." *Phi Delta Kappan.* 61; 1960.
Phenix, Philip H. "The Use of the Disciplines as Curriculum Content." *Ed Forum* 26; 1962.
Phenix, Philip H. *Realms of Meaning.* McGraw-Hill, 1964.
Piaget, Jean. *The Psychology of Intelligence.* Harcourt, 1950.
Piaget, Jean. *The Child's Conception of the World.* Littlefield, Adams, and Company, 1960.
Piaget, Jean. "The States of the Intellectual Development of the Child." *B Menninger Clinic* 26:120–8; 1962.
Pressey, S. L. "A Simple Apparatus Which Gives Tests and Scores—and Teaches." *Sch and Soc* 23: 373–6; 1926.
Pressey, S. L. "A Machine for Automatic Teaching of Drill Material." *Sch and Soc* 25:549–52; 1927.
Pressey, S. L. "A Third and Fourth Contribution Toward the Coming 'Industrial Revolution' in Education." *Sch and Soc* 36:668–72; 1932.
Pressey, S. L. "Further Attempts to Develop a Mechanical Teacher." *Am Psychologist,* 1950.
Rath, G., and others. "The IBM Research Center Teaching Machine Project." In Galanter, E. (Ed.) *Automatic Teaching: The State of the Art.* Wiley, 1959. p. 117–30.
Schwab, Joseph J. "The Concept of the Structure of a Discipline," *Ed Rec* 62; 1962.
Schwab, Joseph J. "Problems, Topics, and Issues." In Elam, Stanley. (Ed.) *Education and the Structure of Knowledge.* Rand McNally, 1964(a).
Schwab, Joseph J. "Structure of the Disciplines: Meanings and Significances." *The Structure of Knowledge and the Curriculum.* 1964(b). p. 1–30
Schwab, Joseph J., and Brandenwein, Paul F. *The Teaching of Science.* Harvard U Press, 1962.
Schultz, R. E., and others. *Measurements Procedures in Programmed Instruction.* Arizona State U. 1964.
Shaplin, Judson T., and Olds, Henry F., Jr. *Team Teaching.* Harper, 1964.
Shaw, Frederick. "The Changing Curriculum." *R Ed Res* 26; 1966.
Skinner, B. F. *Behavior of Organisms.* Appleton, 1938.
Skinner, B. F. *Science and Human Behavior.* Macmillan, 1953.
Skinner, B. F. "Science of Learning and the Art of Teaching." *Harvard Ed R* 24:86–97; 1954.
Stolurow, Lawrence M. *Teaching by Machine.* HEW, 1961.
Stratemeyer, Florence B., and others. *Developing a*

Curriculum for Modern Living. Rev. ed. Teachers Coll, Columbia U, 1957.

Suppes, Patrick. "Computer-based Laboratory For Learning and Teaching." *Automated Ed Letter* 1:17–8; 1965.

Tagliacozzo, Giorgio. "The Literature of Integrated Knowledge." *Am Behavior Sci* 4; 1961.

Tyler, Ralph W. *Basic Principles of Curriculum and Instruction.* U Chicago Press, 1950.

University of the State of New York. "Committee for Elementary Education." In *Cardinal Objectives in Elementary Education—A Third Report.* U State New York, 1932.

Virginia State Board of Education. *Course of Study for Virginia Elementary Schools, Grades 1–7.* Virginia State Board Education, 1943(a).

Virginia State Board of Education. *Tentative Course of Study for Virginia Elementary Schools, Grades 1–8.* Virginia State Board Education, 1943(b).

EDUCATIONAL PROGRAMS— SECONDARY SCHOOLS

The educational program of a secondary school is a broad, complex entity. Its more important aspects involve: objectives and outcomes; curriculum; tool subjects; cultural subjects; vocational subjects; special education; intelligence and special aptitude tests; achievement tests; marks and marking systems; records and reports; counseling; discipline; student organizations and activities.

Also involved, though perhaps less extensively, are these matters: teaching methods; supervision; grouping; study; programmed instruction; educational communications media; libraries; textbooks; curriculum evaluation; improvement in educational practice; inservice education of teachers.

Articles dealing with each of these aspects of a secondary school's educational program appear elsewhere in this encyclopedia. Although these articles are not directed specifically nor limited entirely to educational programs at the secondary level, they contain much that is relevant, and their content will not be duplicated here. Rather, the present article will deal briefly with some general aspects of the topic under four headings:

1. School programs
2. Instructional programs
3. Differentiated programs
4. Criteria of excellence.

A review of recent research on these and other aspects of secondary school educational programs has been presented by R. S. Jones (1966).

SCHOOL PROGRAMS. The comprehensive high school, providing diverse programs to meet the diverse needs of all of its students, is commonly regarded as the ideal in American secondary education (Conant, 1959, 1967; Lupold, 1967). Despite conscientious efforts to achieve this ideal, however, many secondary schools are dissatisfied with their programs for the gifted, the disadvantaged, those not planning to attend college, and indeed those planning to attend college. Experimental programs, involving more or less radical innovations, appear frequently.

Whitmire (1965) has described the independent study program at the Melbourne, Florida, high school. A limited number of able students spend most of their school time working with the help of a faculty consultant, under the supervision of the independent-study coordinator, on diverse projects of interest to them. Extensive and varied educational resources—library, laboratory, shop, studio, etc.—are provided to support their efforts. The program appears to, and may in fact, lack structure. It is not well calculated to provide comprehensive general education. Failures of motivation and responsibility on the part of students do occur. But the concreteness, reality, and relevance of the educational experiences the program provides, and the challenge to initiative and self-realization it offers cannot be denied. Empey (1968) has provided a more general description of the purposes and nature of programs of independent study.

A somewhat different experimental program has been developed at Nova High in Broward County, Florida (Kaufman & Bethune, 1964). The program is based on a "hard-core" curriculum of conventional subjects supplemented by technical sciences such as electronics or special studies such as home nursing. The feature of the program is nongraded homogeneous grouping, for study of units (usually about three per trimester) of integrated subject matter. Extensive use is made of placement examinations, and of modern instructional media, financed by omission of such conventional school facilities as auditorium and cafeteria. R. V. Jones (1968) has presented another description of the use of instructional units to help individualize instruction.

An educational program outside of the "establishment" has been provided for young men and women in the Job Corps (Parker, 1968; Alden & Hodges, 1965). The aim of the program is to increase the employability of youth in the 16-to-22-year age range and to prepare them for the responsibilities of citizenship. It has achieved a considerable measure of success, but not without well-publicized incidents of trouble. Working with disaffected youth in an affluent economy, the Job Corps has a more difficult job to do than its conceptual precursor in the depression days of the 1930's, the Civilian Conservation Corps (Cohen, 1968). Like the CCC, the Job Corps will probably prove to be a temporary addition to the educational facilities of the nation. But its very existence serves to call attention to educational needs that more conventional school programs have not met, and perhaps cannot meet.

INSTRUCTIONAL PROGRAMS. Much of the instructional program of a secondary school is organized within, and limited by, a schedule of classes. In the typical secondary school of several decades ago the school day was divided into from five to eight periods of approximately equal duration. Each student was scheduled for either a class or a study hall in each of the periods. Typically, each class met every school day.

In recent years there has been a marked trend toward flexible scheduling. Many patterns of flexible scheduling are available, and many purposes are served (Davis & Bechard, 1968). Among the purposes are:

> To adapt instruction to differences in pupil interest and ability.
> To vary the size and composition of instructional groups and the length of the class period to suit the purposes of the lesson.
> To provide opportunities for independent study and self-expression in small groups.
> To make most efficient use of time, space, and materials.
> To increase the number of courses a student can take at the same time.

Simple patterns of flexible scheduling provide for partial attainment of some of these objectives. More complex patterns are required to attain them more fully.

In a simple block schedule, two teachers are given identical schedules. This permits team teaching, and various ad hoc arrangements for large group or small group instruction, and independent study. An extension of this arrangement, designated back-to-back scheduling, gives essentially parallel schedules to two pairs of teachers in different but related subject fields. This requires at least four class sections taking the course in each subject area. However, an interdisciplinary schedule, involving only one teacher in each discipline and two sections of pupils taking courses in both disciplines, permits some of the desired flexibility. Other patterns described by Davis and Bechard are school-wide block scheduling, rotating schedules, block-modular schedules, and flexible-modular schedules. But, as these authors are careful to point out, no schedule guarantees better education. The best it can do is to provide the opportunity for improvement. What is actually gained (or lost) as a result of flexible scheduling depends largely on the interest, the efforts, and the ingenuity of the teachers, and, particularly with respect to the success of the independent study aspects of flexible scheduling, on the interest and maturity of the pupils. Others who have contributed discussions of flexible scheduling include Trump (1963) and Sleight (1967).

The core curriculum has provided the structural framework of many secondary school educational programs for several decades (Phillips, 1964). Now interest in it appears to be waning (Overton, 1966). What a core curriculum is has never been entirely clear. In the minds of some it has been conceived as a means of breaking down subject barriers and of integrating learning experiences. This approach has sometimes been designated as the "broad-fields" curriculum, with subject matter fixed in advance, and emphasis on learning. An alternative conception of the core curriculum is sometimes designated as the "experience" curriculum, with subject matter not fixed in advance but evolving as the needs and interests of the students seem to direct, and with emphasis on direct experience rather than on second-hand knowledge. When the question "Can team teaching save the core curriculum?" is asked (Vars, 1966), the answer seems to be, "Possibly, if it is a broad-fields core, but probably not if it is an experience core." In general, however, interest in "saving" the core curriculum seems to be diminishing as emphasis has shifted to excellence, acceleration, automation, nongraded schools, and social rehabilitation.

Because of increasing concern for education of the disadvantaged, for reducing the rate of dropout, for increasing the supply of competent technicians, and for decreasing the number of unemployable adults in the population, there has been a resurgence of interest in vocational and technical education (Venn, 1964; Burkett, 1966; Benham, 1967), and in work-study programs (Burchill, 1962). But the issue of vocational versus general education is far from being resolved (Broudy & others, 1964). It is part of the larger controversy over whether schools should concern themselves primarily with teaching pupils to know and to do, or with teaching them how to learn and to adapt to what is seen to be a constantly changing environment (Baughman, 1968). Change is indeed a pervasive characteristic in the lives of individuals and of societies, but it is easy to exaggerate the pace of change. Most of what our grandparents knew about language, arithmetic, science, technology, business, medicine, law, literature, family living, social behavior, politics, and ethics is still useful for us to know, and what we have added to their knowledge, save in the realms of science, technology, and medicine, is not overwhelming. Human beings still need to know and to do. Perhaps the best way for us to learn how to learn is to seek knowledge and skill that is obviously useful in the foreseeable future. Vocational and technical training is not the whole of secondary education, but then neither is general education.

DIFFERENTIATED PROGRAMS. Should students of approximately the same age who are studying the same subject in a secondary school be grouped by level of ability? Logical arguments in favor of grouping, if the aim of instruction is to maximize achievement, seem almost unanswerable. But the research evidence on the question is decidedly equivocal (Shores, 1964). Clearly grouping per se does not improve instruction; it simply provides the opportunity to improve instruction. Unless the differences in background and ability among the groups are large, it is unlikely that radically different instructional procedures should be employed, or radically different amounts of achievement should be expected. In view of the fact that students learn not only by themselves or from the teacher but also from other students, French's finding (1960) that slow children do slightly better in high-ability classes may not be surprising.

No research calls into question the logical conclusion that gross differences in ability or educational background ought to be recognized in grouping for instruction. Our system of graded schools and of sequential courses is based on the obvious necessity of such grouping. That research fails to show significant gains from grouping where differences are not gross is easy to understand, especially in view of the usual limitations of our research designs, the imprecision of our measures of achievement, and our lack of knowledge of how to take full advantage of the instructional opportunities that grouping affords. The basis for opposition to grouping within subjects has been discussed by Tillman and Hull (1964), while the North Central Association of Colleges and Secondary Schools (1964) has outlined alternatives to grouping.

One differentiated program for the academically talented, with a longer history than is commonly recognized, is the Advanced Placement Program, now administered by the College Entrance Examination Board. It began with a program initiated by the University of Buffalo in the 1930's for the purpose of improving articulation between high school and college. Supported by studies made by Andover and Kenyon colleges in the 1950's, it was taken over by the College Entrance Examination Board in the late 1950's (Franklin, 1965). Since then it has prospered, though not without problems of evaluation of student achievement and policy in the award of credit or advanced standing. Bergeson (1967) reported that students awarded advanced standing did as well or better than their classmates in subsequent college work. Price (1966), however, argues that secondary schools can achieve substantially equivalent results without the extra costs, the specially qualified teachers, and the discrimination among students involved in advanced placement programs. On their face, these contentions seem difficult to accept.

The strong drive in the 1960's to establish civil rights for minority group members, coupled with growing recognition of social decay in the inner city, has led to the development of numerous Federal and local programs to improve the education of the disadvantaged. The Job Corps, mentioned earlier in this article, is one of these. Spiegler (1967) in a delightfully well-written discussion of provisions and programs for educationally disadvantaged youth in secondary schools, discusses the following as the principal elements of such programs: building a self-image; remedial reading; teaching of literature; supplementary reading; writing; speech-listening; science; mathematics; social studies; the world of work. That there is nothing radically new in this list of topics might persuade those who quest for dramatic breakthroughs that Spiegler has little to offer; that he is addicted to the same "middle-class values" and the same "outmoded" subjects that have failed to move and enlighten the disadvantaged in the past. He is, indeed. The thrust of his article is that these areas of subject matter are essential to education, and that if the teaching of them can be adapted to the backgrounds, the abilities, and the interests of disadvantaged youth, lamps of learning can be lit for almost all of them.

CRITERIA OF EXCELLENCE. One of the slogans of education in the 1960's has been the single word *excellence*. Most secondary schools have, within limitations imposed by their citizenry, their staffs, their students, and their educational philosophies, sought excellence in their programs. Some have sought it more diligently than others. Some few fortunate schools seem to have achieved it.

Cawelti (1966) has listed and discussed factors such as clarity of objectives, quality of staff and facilities, pupil guidance, program innovations, financial support, and effective administration that contribute to quality in a secondary school program. Harrell and Nelson (1967) stress innovation, and utilization of "the latest research, theory and practice" in education, perhaps not fully realizing how ephemeral the "latest" in education has often proved to be in the past; or perhaps feeling that change, even for the sake of change itself, is what keeps education interesting and alive for all concerned. Douglass (1967), reflecting on a wealth of experience, offers prescriptions for the quality secondary school of the future.

In the past, with preponderant local support and control of secondary education, few schools were much better educationally than were their communities, intellectually and socially. With increasing state support, and increasing Federal concern for the quality of education throughout the nation, there is reason to hope some of the poorer schools may improve rapidly.

Robert L. Ebel
Michigan State University

References

Alden, V. R., and Hodges, J. A. "When Classrooms Fail: The Federal Job Corps." *Teach Col Rec* 66: 305–9; 1965.

Baughman, Gerald D. "Education for a Continually Changing Environment." *J Sec Ed* 43:156–61; 1968.

Benham, L. G. "Vocational Challenge: A Comprehensive High School's Program." *Nat Assn Sec Sch Prin B* 51:15–23; 1967.

Bergeson, J. B. "Advanced Placement: A Report on Former Participants and Their Subsequent Academic Performance." *Clearing House* 41:365–7; 1967.

Broudy, Harry S., and others. *Democracy and Excellence in American Secondary Education.* Rand McNally, 1964. 302p.

Burchill, George W. *Work-Study Programs for Alienated Youth: A Casebook.* SRA, 1962. 265p.

Burkett, L. A. "National Program: Vocational Education." *Ed* 87:131–5; 1966.

Cawelti, G. "What Makes a High School Outstanding?" *Nations Sch* 77:72–4; 1966.

Cohen, Sol. "Remember the CCC?" *Phi Delta Kappan,* 49:369–372; 1968.

Conant, James B. *The American High School Today.* McGraw-Hill, 1959. 140p.

Conant, James B. "Comprehensive High School: A Further Look." *Ed Digest* 32:1–5; 1967.

Davis, Harold S. and Bechard, Joseph E. *Flexible Scheduling.* Educational Research Council of America, 1968. 26p.

Douglass, H. R. "Quality Secondary School of the Future." *Teach Col J* 39:75–80; 1967.

Empey, Donald W. "What is Independent Study All About?" *J Sec Ed* 43:104–8; 1968.

Franklin, M. P. "Advanced Placement: Past, Present and Future." *Ed Forum* 29:349–53; 1965.

French, John W. "Evidence From School Records on the Effectiveness of Ability Grouping." *J Ed Res* 54:83–91; 1960.

Harrell, R., and Nelson, G. "Criteria of a Model Secondary School." *Ed Leadership* 25:257+; 1967

Jones, R. S. "Instructional Problems and Issues." *R Ed Res* 36:414–23; 1966.

Jones, Richard V., Jr. "Learning Activity Packages: An Approach to Individualized Instruction." *J Sec Ed* 43:178–83; 1968.

Kaufman, Burt, and Bethune, Paul. "Nova High, Space-age High School." *Phi Delta Kappan* 46:9–11; 1964.

Lupold, H. F. "Education With Meaning; A Comprehensive High School in Action." *Clearing House* 41:440–1; 1967.

North Central Association of Colleges and Secondary Schools. *Problems, Practices, Procedures.* The Association, 1964. 99p.

Overton, H. "Rise and Fall of the Core Curriculum." *Clearing House* 40:532–7; 1966.

Parker, Franklin. "Salvaging School Failures: The Job Corps Acts." *Phi Delta Kappan* 49:362–9; 1968.

Phillips, J. E. "What's Good About the Core Curriculum." *Teach Col J* 36:29–30; 1964.

Price, J. "How a School System Can Avoid an Advanced Placement Program." *Clearing House* 41:25506; 1966.

Shores, J. Harlan. "What Does Research Say About Ability Grouping By Classes?" *Illinois Ed* 53:169–72; 1964.

Sleight, R. H. "Administrative Problems as a Result of Flexible Scheduling and Team Teaching." *J Sec Ed,* 42:358–62; 1967.

Spiegler, C. G. "Provisions and Programs for Educationally Disadvantaged Youth in Secondary Schools." In *The Educationally Retarded and Disadvantaged.* 66th Yearbook, Part I, NSSE. U Chicago Press, 1967. p. 184–210.

Tillman, Rodney, and Hull, J. H. "Is Ability Grouping Taking Schools in the Wrong Direction?" *Nations Sch* 73:70–1, 128–9; 1964.

Trump, J. Lloyd "Flexible Scheduling, Fad or Fundamental." *Phi Delta Kappan* 44:367–371; 1963.

Vars, Gordon F. "Can Team Teaching Save the Core Curriculum?" *Phi Delta Kappan,* 47:258–62; 1966.

Venn, Grant. *Men, Education and Work.* ACE, 1964. 184p.

Whitmire, Janet. "The Independent Study Program at Melbourne High." *Phi Delta Kappan* 47:43–6; 1965.

EDUCATIONAL PSYCHOLOGY

EDUCATIONAL PSYCHOLOGY AS SEEN IN TEXTBOOKS. The term "educational psychology" appeared as the title of a book by E. L. Thorndike (1903). While the term may have been used before that time, the book was probably the first to claim the existence of a body of knowledge bearing that name. The book itself can be considered an operational definition of educational psychology, for it defined the area as including those aspects of psychology which have application to problems of education. Thorndike's conception of what had application was broad, as is evident in the later three-volume edition (1913–1914) which virtually included all knowledge of psychology of the era which had any kind of quantitative basis.

Before the term "educational psychology" had become widely used, eminent psychologists, including Münsterberg (1909) and Morgan (1911), had written works entitled respectively *Psychology and the Teacher* and *Psychology for Teachers* without giving a name to this applied area. These texts were directed toward courses bearing a similar title in normal schools and teachers colleges—courses that had had a long history going back to the days of Johann Friedrich Herbart (1776–1841).

One way to provide a contemporary definition of educational psychology is to study the activities of persons who are in some way identified as educational psychologists. If membership in the Division of Educational Psychology of the American Psychological Association is the basis of identification, the group includes persons from every phase of psychology, including experimental, measurement, clinical, and social. The only characteristic shared by the members of the Division is that they are all concerned in some way with the applications of knowledge about psychology to educational problems. In other respects, members of departments of educational psychology have diverse interests and backgrounds. Some of these departments place an emphasis on measurement and psychometrics; some emphasize guidance and counseling; and one can find others that emphasize laboratory experimentation, or research on learning in schools, or research design, or numerous other specialties. The backgrounds of the faculty members of these departments are equally varied. It would not be uncommon to find within a single department of educational psychology one person trained in clinical psychology, another trained in psychometrics, and a third trained in child development. These individuals often receive their training outside a school of education—sometimes from departments of psychology, sometimes from departments of child development which are commonly subdivisions of home economics, and sometimes from other parts of the university. Persons who are identified as educational psychologists by one criterion or another appear to share only one common attribute; namely, that they are all concerned with applying knowledge derived from the behavioral sciences to the solution of educational problems.

One cannot clearly identify a body of knowledge as representing a discipline which can be appropriately named educational psychology. Thorndike's magnum opus on the subject (1913–1914) represents probably the broadest conception ever envisaged of what a discipline thus named might include. Indeed, the three volumes together summarize most of the empirical knowledge of psychology available at that time with the exception of the work of Titchener and his followers. Perhaps, even today, few psychologists would accept such a broad conception of educational psychology. While Thorndike's three-volume work was obviously written, in accordance with the customs of his era, as a comprehensive and all-inclusive work on the subject, works since that time bearing the same title have been much more limited in scope. Current textbooks on educational psychology are written for a first course taken typically by juniors enrolled in teacher-education programs. Such texts vary greatly in the quantity of research that is covered and also in the particular research articles to which attention is given. An examination of a collection of such contemporary texts reveals a state of great controversy in what should be taught to the prospective teacher and how much should be taught. While this is no place for reviewing textbooks on educational psychology a few comments on their differing emphases is appropriate.

During the mid-1950's the market in elementary textbooks in educational psychology was dominated by those of Cronbach (1954) and Lindgren (1956), though other books also had substantial sales. Both of these were theory-oriented. Cronbach emphasized a model of learning and, indeed, devoted most of the book to the elaboration of the model while placing much less emphasis on the description and documentation of research on which the model might be based. Lindgren, on the other hand, took off from a particular theoretical position, a phenomenological position, and developed the book in terms of that position. These books emerged from a period of psychology in which effort was devoted to the development of comprehensive learning models and global theories. In a sense they reflected both the age in which they were developed and also the views commonly held by those who taught the basic courses for which the texts were developed. There were other successful texts in the period which commanded a smaller fraction of the market, such as that by Stephens (1956), which this author judges to be a highly empirically oriented text and those by Frandsen (1957, 1961), which also showed a marked emphasis on bringing together the knowledge buried in related journal literature.

The early 1960's produced a flood of new texts as well as revisions of the old. Of interest is the change in Cronbach's second edition (1962), which placed substantial emphasis on the review of empirical research that had implications for the control of classroom phenomena, as opposed to the earlier edition's (1954) emphasis on a theoretical model. Psychology was moving out of an age which attempted to develop comprehensive theories and models and was emphasizing research and limited theoretical systems closely tied to laboratory data. New competitors appeared which were highly empirically oriented and which commanded a considerable share of the market. Among these were the new edition of Lindgren's book (1962), the text by McDonald (1959), and that by Klausmeier (1961, 1966). The latter provided a new orientation in that it emphasized individual differences and psychometric approaches to the prediction of learning outcomes. The fact that this widely used text has relatively little overlap with some other extensively used texts reflects the current lack of agreement concerning the outcomes of psychological research that have implications for teaching.

While some institutions continue to offer graduate courses called "Educational Psychology," no textbooks could be found specifically written for such courses. Undergraduate texts on educational psychology are widely used at the graduate level. There are also broad courses on the graduate level entitled "Psychological Foundations of Education," which attempt to cover the application of psychology to problems of education, but these also do not seem to have curricula sufficiently well recognized and standardized to provide a base for textbooks that would be acceptable to a substantial number of instructors. Whatever identity the literature of educational psychology may have at the undergraduate level seems to be lost in graduate schools. Publishers report that there is little uniformity in content in such courses. Some utilize undergraduate textbooks together with additional readings. Some have used the *Handbook of Research on Teaching* (Gage, 1963). Others have used everything from a group of selected paperbacks to textbooks from the areas of psychology of learning or personality.

In the last few years, another trend has become apparent in the literature available for use in educational psychology courses at the graduate level. This is the emergence of textbooks, firmly rooted in laboratory research on learning, that are, nevertheless, directed at teachers. Such books are exemplified by those of Bugelski (1964), Gagné (1965), and Travers (1963). Such an approach to the development of the academic knowledge of the practicing classroom teacher is to be contrasted with that of the Gage *Handbook* (1963) in that they emphasize data collected in laboratories rather than in the classroom. The differences in these two kinds of technical literature reflect the controversy taking place between those who believe that educational research should begin in the classroom and those who believe that a laboratory approach provides a more profitable start.

Educational psychology cannot be well identified in terms of a specific literature that covers a recognized body of knowledge. Perhaps this is as it should be. So long as psychologists concerned with problems of education are scanning psychology as a discipline for knowledge which may lead to educational change, there is some advantage in keeping an open mind concerning where to look for applicable material.

EDUCATIONAL PSYCHOLOGY AS VIEWED BY EDUCATIONAL PSYCHOLOGISTS. The need to provide a framework for the field of educational psychology has been expressed by many individuals and groups. In a recent report entitled *Handbook for Instructors of Educational Psychology* (1965), a committee, established by the Division of Educational Psychology of the American Psychological Association (Division 15), reviewed the many previous attempts to identify the content of educational psychology. One of the earliest of these was that of Blair (1941) who made an analysis of the technical vocabulary used in eight contemporary educational psychology texts. The lack of overlap of the vocabulary from text to text gives support to the commonly voiced opinion that there is little agreement on the areas of research in psychology that have maximum potential for educational application.

In 1946, both Division 15 and the National Society of Colleges of Teacher Education appointed committees to study the content of educational psychology and the role of educational psychologists. The latter committee became a prolific publisher of papers on the role of educational psychologists and the content of educational psychology. The *Handbook for Instructors of Educational Psychology* lists over 20 papers published by members of that committee on such topics. A review of these contributions simply adds to the impression that there is a vast amount of knowledge tucked away in psychology that has implications for education if only somebody will take a look at it.

The committee of Division 15, contemporary with the Committee of the National Society of Colleges of Teacher Education, called for a somewhat narrower content, limiting the field to applications from the areas of human growth and development, learning, personality and adjustment, measurement and evaluation, and techniques and special methods of educational psychology.

This committee also suggested that the educational psychologist should disseminate information and propose applications much as the systems engineer does today in his field.

The two committees whose work has been discussed here combined their efforts to produce a publication entitled *Educational Psychology in Teacher Education—A Guide for Instructors* (1953). At least one of the motives underlying the production of this publication was the hope that some action could be taken to improve the qualifications of those who taught educational psychology. The committees involved had both placed on record their concern for the fact that many who taught in the area had virtually no related qualifications.

The most recent committee of Division 15 in the area simply took the position that the subject matter to be included within educational psychology was so vast that there was little use in describing it. This committee, having disposed of this problem, then went on to discuss the methods that might be used for instruction. These methods are summarized in the *Handbook for Instructors of Educational Psychology* (1965).

ORGANIZATION OF EDUCATIONAL PSYCHOLOGISTS. The diverse identity of educational psychologists as a professional group is reflected in the fact that the third largest division of the American Psychological Association is Division 15, the Division of Educational Psychology. This division has shown extraordinary growth over the last decade, as is evident from an examination of the American Psychological Association directories (1956, 1966). While in January 1956, the Division had a total membership in all classes of 459, the total membership in January 1966 was 2,235. The growth in membership reflects the increase in the interest shown by psychologists of all kinds in problems of education.

Psychologists interested in the development of a technology of education and automated classrooms were at one time interested in the formation of their own division within the American Psychological Association, a move which indicates that they did not have an identification with other educational psychologists. However, in 1963 the Division of Educational Psychology indicated that this new group would be welcomed within the division and that its role in educational psychology would be given increased recognition. As a result of this and other moves, those psychologists interested in the technology of the classroom have come to play a significant role in the professional organization of educational psychologists. In recent years, the Division has presented the annual Thorndike Award for distinguished contributions by a psychologist to education. The first three awards went to S. L. Pressey, W. L. Brownell, and B. F. Skinner. The first two are closely identified with schools of education, but the third is clearly identified with experimental psychology and is a relative newcomer to the field of education. This group reflects the trend since mid-century of psychologists both inside and outside education devoting effort to the improvement of pedagogy.

While the main professional organization binding together educational psychologists is the Division of Educational Psychology of the American Psychological Association, there are other organizations in which educational psychologists play a key role. Notable among these is the American Educational Research Association, where the leadership role of educational psychologists is reflected in the fact that since 1955 seven of ten presidents have been educational psychologists and six of these at the time of their presidency were affiliated with colleges of education.

A printed newsletter entitled "Educational Psychologist" has been published by the Division of

Educational Psychology since 1964. In addition to the annual presidential address of the Division, the newsletter includes notes about members—particularly those members affiliated with schools of education—and brief discussions of professional issues related to the emerging role of these psychologists.

Educational psychologists are to be distinguished from school psychologists. Most members of Division 15 are not eligible to become members of the Division of School Psychology since the latter division requires that its members must have had a history of employment in schools. Very few of those who identify themselves as educational psychologists have ever had school employment.

The fact that educational psychologists have not generally had school employment gives them positions in schools of education different from those of most other faculty who have typically come through the teacher-certification mill. Indeed, they commonly represent the only professional specialist in teacher training programs who has not had classroom experience.

RESEARCH ACTIVITIES OF EDUCATIONAL PSYCHOLOGISTS. While the founders of educational psychology, such as Thorndike at Columbia and Judd at Chicago, emphasized a classical experimental approach, by mid-century this approach had almost vanished from graduate departments and schools of education. Experimentation of the kind that began to flourish in schools of education through the 1930's involved investigation of complex phenomena in school settings. Typical experimental studies were those that compared the effectiveness of one teaching method with another. They thrived in the 1930's, showed a decline in the 1940's, and virtually disappeared from the scene in the 1950's. The reason for the decline of such undertakings was reviewed by Wallen and Travers (1963), who pointed out that these studies were scientifically unsound. They required comparing the effect of one vague complex of variables with the effect of another vague complex. The typical result was that the teaching method designated as the new and experimental method was found to be slightly superior to the alternative method, which was typically dubbed the traditional method. One suspects that the rise of the popularity of such studies stemmed from the potential which they appeared to offer for justifying newer practices, and it is hardly surprising that studies thus conceived should have had little scientific merit. The decline of such studies can be attributed entirely to their futility and not to the emergence of any alternative approach of greater merit.

In the early 1960's a new trend became manifest. Classical laboratory experimentation, which had vanished from the educational scene almost thirty years before, began to undergo a revival. Laboratory experimental studies began to appear in the *American Educational Research Journal,* and each meeting of the American Educational Research Association began to show on the program whole sessions devoted to experimental studies. These studies did not generally show the use of equipment such as experimental psychologists now use. Indeed, the instrumentation tended to be typically crude, but it was a revival of classical laboratory experimentation within a setting of colleges of education.

Educational psychologists have not only undertaken extensive research on psychological problems related to education, but they have often moved out into the broader field of educational research within which psychological research constitutes a small compartment. Today, perhaps more than ever, educational research tends to be dominated by educational psychologists. This domination is very evident from even a cursory examination of the reputable publications devoted to the reporting of educational research contributions. This domination can be attributed largely to the training in research techniques which psychologists receive in comparison with persons who take their doctoral degrees in elementary and secondary education and educational administration. In the latter areas of specialization many candidates for a degree may never take a course even in simple statistics, and few will take courses in experimental design or measurement. Thus, the training of the doctoral candidate in schools of education in fields other than educational psychology hardly fits him to exercise leadership in matters of research.

In schools of education, educational psychologists typically function as advisers on matters of research design in the development of thesis and dissertation proposals. If any of the faculty engage in independent research then the probability is high that it will be the educational psychologists who are so engaged. The newly emerging research and development centers are manned and led, to a substantial extent, by persons who identify themselves as educational psychologists. Examples of notables playing such a role are N. L. Gage at Stanford, Robert Glaser at the University of Pittsburgh, and Herbert Klausmeier at the University of Wisconsin.

A review of research undertaken by educational psychologists or of research which can be classified as educational psychology is like an attempt to review the national affairs of a country which has no identifiable boundaries, but where the sovereignty flows into other sovereignties. This has been a persistent problem in the planning of the chapter on educational psychology in the *Annual Review of Psychology.* Since research undertaken by educational psychologists is commonly classified under other categories such as learning, guidance, or measurement, it tends to be covered in the chapters in the annual reviews that cover these latter topics. Stephens (1959) made this point well in introducing his annual review chapter on educational psychology. "No matter how the educational psychologist may define his subject," he said, "he will not be surprised to find his most useful materials, not in this chapter, but in the chapters headed Developmental Psychology, Learning, Theory and Technique of Assessment, Individual Differences, Personality, Social Psychology and Group Processes, Problem Solving and Thinking, or Counseling."

Research which can be classified only as educational psychology and in no other category represents a rather small area; for this reason the *Annual Review of Psychology* includes only an occasional chapter on educational psychology. The chapter by Smedlund (1964) covers topics such as the teacher, interest and set, reading, textbooks and curricula, automated teaching, concepts and complex knowledge, and a rather general discussion of the special statistical problems that educational psychologists encounter. That there is no consensus concerning what should be included in such a chapter is evident from the fact that the corresponding chapter two years earlier by Warburton (1962) used a very different system of categories, many of which do not even appear in Smedlund's review. Warburton classifies research in the area as follows:

The Educational System: Teaching method; Learning theory; Teaching machines; Teacher behavior; Visual aids; Practicing and coaching; Streaming of classes; Educational selection and guidance.

The Pupil: Ability; Handicapped children; Personality variables; Anxiety; Adjustment; Interests; Home environment; Cultural differences; Age; Heredity and environment.

Educational Performance: Logical judgment; Moral judgments; Academic attainment; Statistical method.

The conception of research in educational psychology presented by this array of topics is that it covers all educational research except possibly for educational administration. Warburton also reports in his chapter that an examination of the references cited in the annual reviews indicates a declining interest over the previous decade in studies involving abilities, selection, and guidance, and an increase in studies involving learning—particularly the input end of learning.

Research facilities available to educational psychologists working in colleges of education remain limited; for this reason, most research they conduct utilizes paper and pencil as equipment. The emphasis on paper-and-pencil techniques stems from the long association between educational psychologists and the testing movement. This limitation restricts the variables that can be introduced into an inquiry and limits the problems that can be investigated. The restricting effect that lack of facilities and equipment may have on the conduct of research has not been widely recognized by school of education officials, whose background is typically in educational administration—a field in which problems are dauntlessly attacked with paper-and-pencil weapons. Nevertheless, a change is in progress and one can point to a few institutions where well-equipped laboratories are emerging. Notable among these is the fine experimental laboratory in the John F. Kennedy Center for Research on Education and Human Development at George Peabody College for Teachers, the Conditioning Laboratory in the Department of Educational Psychology at Arizona State, and the Automated Teaching Laboratory in the Research and Development Research Center at the University of Pittsburgh. Particularly worthy of special note is the laboratory at George Peabody College for Teachers, which includes a primate colony and related experimental facilities. Only a few years ago such a venture would have been met with ridicule on the part of professionals in education. Today there are only doubt and mild skepticism. The trend toward the development of adequately equipped laboratories reflects the impact which experimental psychology is having on all applied fields, including the educational and the clinical, rather than any insight on the part of administrators into the nature of the tools of scientific advancement.

The growth of laboratories is making possible the development of a technology of education such as Pressey (1932) envisioned many decades ago. The development of equipment such as is represented by advanced types of teaching machines requires personnel with backgrounds in laboratory skills. That much research involving complex educational equipment is in progress is evident from a volume edited by Glaser (1965) on the topic of teaching machines and programmed learning. A point to note is that less than half of the work described in the volume is being undertaken in either school settings or in schools of education. Much of it is the work of persons attached to departments of psychology and industrial and research organizations. Research thrives where the soil is fertile and, in this case, where there are facilities for the development of equipment. Indeed, the author of this article was unable to locate a single facility located within a school of education which had any capacity at all for developing a technology of education.

Although educational psychologists are not readily identified as a group, they have long had an identifiable research literature. The *Journal of Educational Psychology* was founded in 1910. The first volume was introduced with an article by Edward L. Thorndike (1910) entitled "The Contribution of Psychology to Education," which proclaimed not only that the emerging science of psychology would produce radical changes in education but also that "the science of education can and will contribute to psychology." Whether history has validated the latter proposition is a matter for debate. The *Journal of Educational Research* was founded ten years later and immediately showed the impact of the work of psychologists with a heavy emphasis of articles on problems of measurement in education. The *American Educational Research Journal* was founded in 1964, and although this journal is intended to cover the entire area of educational research the majority of contributions at this time come from educational psychologists.

Another kind of technical literature has existed in the form of publications that attempt to present the implications of research for school practice. The National Society for the Study of Education emerged in 1902 as an organization with this kind of goal, and many of its yearbooks have concentrated on the interpretation of psychological research. For example, a recurring theme has been research on learning; it has formed the focus of three yearbooks

(National Society for the Study of Education, 1942, 1950, 1964). Other themes based on psychological literature that have less direct bearing on classroom procedures have been explored in other publications. The *Review of Educational Research* also performs the function of gathering together the findings reported in research literature that have implications for education, and periodic issues report on various aspects of the literature of psychological research.

EDUCATIONAL PSYCHOLOGISTS AND THEORY DEVELOPMENT. Although Thorndike developed educational psychology as a theoretically oriented area of scientific enquiry, with a strong emphasis on classical laboratory experimentation, it has not remained so in the hands of his successors. American educational psychologists are commonly criticized even by themselves as being empirically oriented and as having little interest in the development of theory. The tendency has been to conduct research on problems of immediate practical importance with little concern for building a science of behavior in educational situations. Just how educational psychologists should engage in theory construction, widely debated though the subject is, remains a matter on which no specific recommendations can be found. One approach to theory development is to take over and adapt conceptual systems outside the educational milieu. To some extent this latter approach is exemplified by the present enthusiasm for applying Skinner's ideas to the development of a technology of education. Skinner's approach to problems of learning has had substantial impact on educational thought, but whether it has influenced practice is still an open question. An earlier generation of persons in professional education attempted to assimilate the concepts of Kurt Lewin into educational thought. Although educational literature of the early post World War II period shows that the influence of Lewin was substantial, the impact of his thought can be found neither in contemporary educational research nor in contemporary classroom practice. Lewin's theoretical system appears to have been used *ex post facto* rather than predictively, but this may well be a result of the limitation of the system rather than a misuse of it by educators. The formal properties of psychological theories have tended to improve over the last few decades and, as a result, those that evolve in the near future may have much greater potential for having impact on education than those that have been developed in the past.

An alternative approach is for psychologists to develop theoretical systems within the context of educational problems. For example, a psychologist might attempt to develop a theory of how children learn to read. A survey of any of the well-known works on reading that are research oriented reveals that little has been done to develop a comprehensive theory in the area. The research tends to be empirically oriented and little has been done to integrate it. Perhaps one of the difficulties of developing theory in the area is that the evidence suggests that skill in reading may be acquired by many different paths which involve different processes. A person attempting to inject a theoretical note into the field might have to begin with the development of a theory of reading which pertains to only one of these paths. Another difficulty is that the form of the data found in an empirically developed field is often not the kind required for theoretical developments. Data pertaining to *what* techniques are effective may tell little about *why* particular techniques are effective. History would appear to show that laboratory data provide fertile soil for the development of psychological theory, but psychometric data of the kind found in research on reading have been sterile in this respect.

One suspects that the lack of work on theory development among educational psychologists stems partly from their training and partly from the tendency for empirically oriented psychologists to migrate toward an area of practical application. Added to this is the fact that schools of education have long showed little interest in problems of metatheory; that is to say, theory of theory. Problems of metatheory have been the focus of interest of philosophers of science, and although these have had substantial impact on the behavioral sciences, they have not influenced professional faculties of colleges of education.

The staffing of colleges of education with practitioners has also provided a poor milieu in which theory-oriented psychologists might operate. The situation would be different if schools of education were organized more like medical schools in which, for example, a laboratory biochemist can be appointed as, say, associate professor of psychiatry. Under the latter set of conditions, theory development can flourish. Until schools of education change their policies in this respect, theoretical developments are likely to come largely from the outside.

Not all would agree upon the names of those contemporary psychologists whose research and the ideas derived from it have had the greatest impact on educational thought. A brief survey of the index provided in each of a number of recent books on pedagogy turned up the names of H. F. Harlow, D. O. Hebb, J. Piaget, S. L. Pressey, and B. F. Skinner. Of interest is the fact that only one of these is a person who has had a life-long association with a college of education. The others represent experimental psychology in its classical laboratory forms. None except S. L. Pressey would refer to themselves as "educational psychologists," and yet all have played an important role in making the professional in education aware of the implications of psychological knowledge for the planning of education. The latter statement should not be taken to imply that the impact has been that of changing classroom practice, for the initial impact is rarely going to be of that character. A first impact is much more likely to be a change in the language used for describing and discussing educational phenomena. Indeed, an increase in the precision with which educational phenomena can be discussed would appear to be a prerequisite to educational reform. Much of the difficulty encountered in producing reform in the past has been the vague and ambiguous language available for discussing what needs to be done. When common language is used for the discussion of educational change, the discussion is likely to become a discussion of what is meant by the statements of proposed changes. The technical language provided by the developing behavioral sciences increases vastly the precision with which such discussions can be undertaken. This must be the first impact of the behavioral sciences. The impact will be on educational thought rather than on practice, but an improvement in thought almost has to precede an improvement in practice.

The names of a number of other psychologists also commonly appear in educational literature, not because they have conducted long-term research programs which have implications for educational practice, but because of their interest in educational reform. The names of J. S. Bruner and C. R. Rogers fall into this category. That they have had substantial impact cannot be denied, but the force of their impact does not derive from a program of research. The point to be made is that some psychologists share with other members of the community an enthusiasm for improving education, and their reforms generally derive color from the particular interests they happen to have as psychologists. Bruner's books on education (1960, 1966) represent contributions that derive from this kind of imaginative activity.

TRAINING PROVIDED BY DEPARTMENTS OF EDUCATIONAL PSYCHOLOGY. The training provided by departments thus designated in catalogues shows little uniformity from institution to institution. In some, the training of guidance workers is a major responsibility, but in others this function is undertaken by a separate department of counseling and guidance. In some, emphasis is placed on the training of educational research workers. In still others, the training of school psychologists is the central role. Despite the fact that educational psychologists and school psychologists participate in different professional groups, it is the educational psychologist who trains the school psychologist. Many departments of educational psychology have long emphasized training in psychometrics, a product of the fact that the early development of tests was closely associated with attempts to solve problems in schools.

Perhaps a main impact of psychology on the public schools has been through the distribution of objective tests and this, in turn, has made measurement a prime area in which schools of education have had to have strength. Indeed, there are institutions of higher education in which a doctoral degree in educational psychology is almost certainly a degree conferring expertness in problems of measurement. In addition, the fact that many agencies of both state and federal governments have numerous vacancies for evaluation and measurement psychologists has helped such doctoral programs to grow. Another source of employment which gives indirect support to doctoral programs in evaluation and measurement is the manufacturer of tests. Such manufacturers, both profit-making and non-profit-making, have become major employers of those educational psychologists trained in the field of measurement.

The variation in the functions served by departments of educational psychology probably stems from the variety of backgrounds that educational psychologists bring to their jobs. Departments tend to offer training in those areas in which their faculty have specialized knowledge.

A FINAL LOOK. Our review of the activities and role of contemporary educational psychologists indicates that the field of education can utilize and absorb psychologists with a great diversity of backgrounds and skills. The impact of psychology on education appears to be expanding. The kinds of services that educational psychologists can best offer cannot be defined at this time, for much of their activity is so new that insufficient time has elapsed to permit effective evaluation. One can say with some definiteness that psychologists are offering substantial leadership in the field of education and that this leadership is being encouraged by others engaged in the educational enterprise.

Robert M. W. Travers
Western Michigan University

References

American Psychological Association Directory, 1956. 808p.
American Psychological Association Directory, 1966. 1104p.
Blair, Glenn M. "The Vocabulary of Educational Psychology." *J Ed Psychol* 32:365–371; 1941.
Bruner, Jerome S. *Process of Education.* Harvard U Press, 1960. 97p.
Bruner, Jerome S. *Toward a Theory of Instruction.* Harvard U Press, 1966. 192p.
Bugelski, B. R. *Psychology of Learning Applied to Teaching.* Bobbs-Merrill, 1964. 278p.
Cronbach, Lee J. *Educational Psychology.* Harcourt, 1954. 628p.
Cronbach, Lee J. *Educational Psychology*, 2nd ed. Harcourt, 1962. 706p.
Educational Psychology in Teacher Education—A Guide for Instructors. Croft Press, 1953. 46p.
Frandsen, Arden N. *How Children Learn: On Educational Psychology.* McGraw-Hill, 1957. 546p.
Frandsen, Arden N. *Educational Psychology: The Principles of Learning in Teaching.* McGraw-Hill, 1961. 610p.
Gage, N. L. (Ed.) *Handbook of Research on Teaching.* Rand McNally, 1963. 1218p.
Gagné, Robert M. *Categories of Learning.* Holt, 1965. 308p.

Glaser, Robert. (Ed.) *Teaching Machines and Programmed Learning, II. Data and Directions.* NEA, 1965. 831p.

Handbook for Instructors of Educational Psychology. U Illinois, 1965. 51p.

Klausmeier, Herbert J. *Learning and Human Abilities: Educational Psychology.* Harper, 1961. 562p.

Klausmeier, Herbert J., and Goodwin, William. *Learning and Human Abilities,* 2nd ed. Harper, 1966. 720p.

Lindgren, Henry Clay. *Educational Psychology in the Classroom.* Wiley, 1956. 521p.

Lindgren, Henry Clay. *Educational Psychology in the Classroom,* 2nd ed. Wiley, 1962. 574p.

McDonald, Frederick J. *Educational Psychology.* Wadsworth, 1959. 748p.

Morgan, C. Lloyd. *Psychology for Teachers.* Scribner, 1911. 307p.

Münsterberg, H. *Psychology and the Teacher.* Appleton, 1909. 329p.

National Society of College Teachers of Education. *Educational Psychology in Teacher Education.* Monogr No. 3. Crofts, 1953. 48p.

National Society for the Study of Education. *Learning and Instruction.* 41st Yearbook, Part II. Bobbs-Merrill, 1942. 502p.

National Society for the Study of Education. *Learning and Instruction.* 49th Yearbook, Part I. U Chicago Press, 1950. 352p.

National Society for the Study of Education. *Theories of Learning and Instruction.* 63rd Yearbook, Part I. U Chicago Press, 1964. 430p.

Pressey, Sidney L. "A Third and Fourth Contribution Toward the Coming 'Industrial Revolution in Education'." *Sch and Soc* 36:668–672; 1932.

Smedlund, Jan. "Educational Psychology." *Annual R Psychol* 15:251–276; 1964.

Stephens, J. M. *Educational Psychology: A Study of Educational Growth,* rev. ed. Holt, 1956. 717p.

Stephens, J. M. "Educational Psychology." *Annual R Psychol* 10:104–130; 1959.

Thorndike, Edward L. *Educational Psychology.* Lemcke and Buechner, 1903. 177p.

Thorndike, Edward L. "The Contribution of Psychology to Education." *J Ed Psychol* 1:5–12; 1910.

Thorndike, Edward L. *Educational Psychology.* Vol. I: *The Original Nature of Man,* 327p; Vol 2: *The Psychology of Learning,* 452p. Teachers Col, Columbia U, 1913.

Thorndike, Edward L. *Educational Psychology.* Vol 3: *Work and Fatigue and Individual Differences.* Teachers Col, Columbia U, 1914. 408p.

Travers, R. M. W. *Essentials of Learning.* Macmillan, 1963. 544p.

Wallen, Norman E., and Travers, Robert M. W. "Analysis and Investigation of Teaching Methods." In Gage, N. L. (Ed.) *Handbook of Research on Teaching.* Rand McNally, 1963. p. 448–505.

Warburton, F. W. "Educational Psychology." *Annual R Psychol* 13:371–414; 1962.

ELEMENTARY EDUCATION

Public elementary education in the United States today stands as the realization of an educational idea which began to take form in this country as early as the mid-1600's. That idea was to develop a common school, free and tax-supported, that would provide education for all the children of all of the people (Cremin, 1951). From the first the concept "common" in the New World was turned toward the establishment of a school that would be open to all, no matter what their station in life, and attractive to all for the quality of the educational program it would offer. This stood in sharp contrast to the state of affairs in the Old World, from whence early immigrants to these shores had come. There, "common" was associated with pauperism, with charity schools, and with efforts to teach only the barest of literacy skills to the masses. That the idea of free and universal education for children has been largely realized can be seen in data on numbers of elementary schools and teachers and on school enrollment. In 1963–64 there were 75,538 public elementary schools operating in the United States, and now the number is even greater. It is reported that in 1965 there were some 30.526 million children enrolled in grades kindergarten through 8 in these public schools. At the same time there were 964,639 public elementary-school teachers providing instruction. Clearly this is a vast enterprise. Of course, there are still those who prefer to use nonpublic elementary schools, a choice made by parents who value a specific kind of private education or church-related education for their children. In 1965 it was estimated that there were 5.4 million enrolled in such schools, kindergarten through grade 8. Together these public and nonpublic data account for about 70 percent of 5-year-olds who could be enrolled in kindergartens and about 99 percent of 6-to-13-year-olds who could be enrolled in grades 1 through 8. By 1970, it is anticipated, these figures will have risen to 31.5 million and 5.6 million, respectively (National Education Association, Research Division, 1966; U.S. Department of Health, Education, and Welfare, 1965, 1966).

The purposes held for elementary education continue to be broad, and a dual responsibility for contributing to the development of the individual and to society is clearly discernible. As has been true for a long time, the elementary school accepts a major responsibility for helping children to develop competence in the English language and in mathematics. It also helps the child to comprehend in more explicit terms the social and natural environment in which he finds himself, through a program of instruction in the social studies and a recently strengthened program in science. Similarly there is some instruction in art and in music. Also, there is some instruction in health and physical education. However, instruction in these three areas is not universally as well developed as is instruction in the basics of language, mathematics, and social studies; instruction in science is also coming to be identified as basic. The most recent addition to this set of programs has been the inclusion in many elementary schools of instruction in a foreign language. To some extent, too, elementary schools that include grades 7 and 8 continue to provide instruction in homemaking and in industrial arts. Each of these in its own way embraces goals of understanding, attitude, and skill that the child can use satisfyingly in his personal life and usefully in the life of the larger group of which he is a part. Concurrently the elementary school gives attention to a broad range of goals that are more purely related to the socialization of the child, to assist in his general enculturation. These character- and personality-oriented goals tend to transcend subject areas and become a part of the total school experience. The most complete effort in recent years to state the objectives held for elementary education was the study published by the Russell Sage Foundation in 1953 (Kearney, 1953). Since that time most of the concerns over goals have dealt with priorities and emphases among them. In recent years a high priority has been placed on efforts to develop the child's rational powers, and to a degree cognitive goals have been stressed over affective goals in the conduct of elementary education (National Education Association, Educational Policies Commission, 1961). There has also been a concern with identifying the unique responsibilities of the elementary school in the totality of the child's education and a desire to coordinate whatever child-serving agencies may be present in a given community in such a way as to add strength to the whole effort. It is increasingly recognized, too, that a rightful set of priorities for the elementary school in one locale and with one group of pupils may not be so in another locale and with other pupils (National Education Association, Project on Instruction, 1963). In other words, there is reason to believe that elementary education as an instrumentality for the development of the child and the society may be used with greater precision in the next decade than it has been in the past several decades (Foshay, 1959; Levin & Meltzer, 1965).

Of course, the public elementary school as we know it today did not spring into being full-blown. Its beginnings were most inauspicious, and its struggle for survival and development has required the attention and consumed the energies of many educational leaders over the past 300 years. This history should be considered as a prelude to comprehending fully the current scene. That which follows has been developed from a number of historical materials published over the years (Cubberley, 1934; Reisner, 1935; Edwards & Richey, 1947; Butts & Cremin, 1953; Shane, 1953).

THE COLONIAL PERIOD. Most historians would agree that those who came early to these shores brought with them, among other things, ideas about education born of things experienced in the Old World and aspired to in the New. The fact that these early settlers came from several national groups and especially from more than one religious persuasion meant that there was variation in the value placed upon elementary education and in the form in which it was to be cast in the colonies. In New England, and more specifically in Massachusetts, legislation for the education of children was enacted early. In 1642, the government of the Massachusetts Colony passed a law requiring town officials to compel parents to provide elementary instruction for their children. While the law did not establish schools, or require the towns to do so, it did demand that parents provide instruction themselves or employ tutors and schoolmasters to instruct their children. The law even went so far as to stipulate the minimum instructional program: instruction was required in reading, in certain capital laws, and in catechism, and it was necessary for a child to be apprenticed in a trade. Five years later, in 1647, Massachusetts passed another law that required each town of 50 families to provide an elementary-school teacher and each town of 100 families to establish a Latin grammar school. Attendance at school was not compulsory, however, and parents still could choose to instruct their children themselves. These early laws seemed to be inspired by at least three motives. The first was clearly a religious one; children were to be taught to read so that they might understand and accept the religious base of the colony. A second motive was political and was related to needed knowledge and understanding of the capital laws of the colony. The third was economic; all children were to be taught vocations. This was, in part, an attempt to guard against the development of a large pauper class which would be a burden on society and in part a way of ensuring a supply of skilled workmen to meet a growing need in a developing colony. What has been described here for Massachusetts came to be the pattern in general for all of the New England colonies.

The schools themselves were referred to as "dame schools" and "writing schools," after an idea brought from England (Small, 1914). Essentially, one or more women in a community would bring several children into their homes for instruction. The program included reading, some spelling, certain moral and religious precepts, and, in some instances, writing and arithmetic. For most girls the completion of the dame school marked the end of formal education, and thus instruction in sewing and knitting might be added to their dame-school program. Boys, once they had achieved a beginning in reading, could go on to the *town school.* In the town school emphasis was on reading, writing, and usually arithmetic. It was at this very early date that the concept of a "three R's" curriculum for the elementary school began to take shape.

In the Southern colonies an aristocratic tendency in private life and the Angelican Church in religious life combined to support schooling as a private affair. Parents who could do so paid for education for their children. Free schools were seen as charity institutions for the poor only. Still, the aims of education and the content of the school program were much the same as in New England.

In the Middle colonies there was more diversification in the origins of the people and in their religious outlooks. This led to less of a unified demand for education, and each religious group tended to develop and operate its own parochial schools. The curriculum was much the same as in the other colonies.

From this sort of beginning the church continued to control and dominate education well into the 1700's. By mid-century, however, this domination had begun to be challenged somewhat. The right to vote had by now been separated from church membership, and there was accordingly wider involvement of people in the affairs of towns. Forces were slowly at work which seemed destined to move America toward democracy, and this, too, affected the church's control over education. The growing dispersion of population at this time also had its own effect on the development of the elementary school. As the population spread over the landscape, it became a potent force for individualism and localism in American life in general, and in elementary education specifically. Among "things of their own" which these small, dispersed communities began to want was a school. While the law in many instances required them to support a town school, it was often impossible for their own children to reach it. A first compromise was the development of a "moving" elementary school that would shift from one locale in the town to another over the year, staying a few weeks or months in each place. This did not prove to be satisfactory, however, and the people were able to exact recognition from their colonial governments for local school districts, which enabled them to keep their tax money in the locality and to operate their own schools. Again Massachusetts led the way with a 1789 law which legally recognized the local school district. Other colonies soon followed suit, and the supremacy of the colonial government over the local community in educational matters was altered significantly. Thus began the commitment to local control in education, symbolized in the small, one-room schools which the people established on the frontier and moved westward with them.

The curriculum continued to include the three R's, and the elementary school began to replace both the dame school and the writing school of an earlier day. These one-room schools were taught by one teacher, and the bulk of instruction was individual, with children of varying ages and in different years in school called up one by one for recitation. Class methods of instruction were not prevalent until the 1800's. The New England colonies continued to set the pace in educational development, and the schools in the Middle and Southern colonies remained much as they had been at an earlier time.

THE NATIONAL PERIOD. When the thirteen colonies became the United States of America at the close of the Revolutionary War, the need for access to education and schools inevitably captured the attention of many people. It was increasingly clear that the road to democracy, which the American people seemed bent on traveling, called for a literate populace. And the establishment of a viable nation-state called for unity among the people. Both of these goals seemed to demand a more extensive and more effective system of free education for all. Certain problems had to be overcome to attain this, of course. The domination of the schools by the church had to be lifted; the authority of the state over the locality in school affairs had to be restored; there had to be acceptance of general taxation to support the school for it to be free and therefore accessible to all. In the opening decades of the 1800's these problems were faced, and slowly but surely opposition was overcome. After 1850 most states passed laws requiring school attendance. Only the South lagged in this respect. The elementary school felt the full impact of the increasing use of the public schools which came in the wake of these developments. And as enrollment in the elementary school increased dramatically, its guiding purposes, its organization, and its program underwent reexamination and revision. As the century progressed, goals of citizenship education began to take their place alongside those of literacy and moral character. The three R's continued to dominate the program, but history and geography, and, somewhat later, government, began to be included in the curriculum. In fact, this citizenship concern was so strong that a number of state legislatures passed laws requiring the study of these areas in the elementary school. Some science, or nature study, began to find its way into the curriculum in the late 1800's, and some very limited attention was given to drawing, music, and physical education, though none of these were usual areas of curriculum even at the close of the nineteenth century.

The pressure of mounting enrollments led to two major developments in the organization and execution of elementary-school education. The one-room school gave way to a larger, graded school, with children of the same chronological age grouped together into a grade for instruction. And, group methods in instruction were developed which enabled a single teacher to work with a class group rather than with individual children. In the mid-1800's there were usually two elementary schools in a community—a primary school, comprising grades 1 through 5, and a grammar school, comprising grades 5 through 8. By the end of the 1800's this division had disappeared almost entirely, and the most common unit was an eight-year, graded, elementary school.

1900 TO 1950. Reform in Curriculum and Instruction. It was inevitable that a young nation with a commitment to a new concept of public education should eventually develop an educational philosophy and theory closely allied to that concept and indigenous to the developing American scene. The consistent movement in the early 1900's toward political, economic, and social reform prompted educational reform as well (Cremin, 1961). The shift of the economy from an agrarian base to an industrial one put new educational demands on the schools, and the increased national productivity made it possible to finance education more adequately than ever before. The future seemed almost assuredly to be different from the present; change was coming to be an expected and sought-after state of affairs.

This was a setting which invited fresh thinking about elementary education and it was not long in coming. G. Stanley Hall had already begun to investigate and write about the psychological aspects of the educative process and had tried to turn the attention of elementary educators from an almost single concern for subject matter to the need for careful study of child development. John Dewey enunciated a philosophy of education which took a forthright position on the use of the school as an instrument for self-realization and social progress. In 1904 he established a laboratory school at the University of Chicago in which he attempted to demonstrate what elementary education would be like were it consistent with his point of view on the role of the school in society and with his conception of the nature of childhood (Mayhew & Edwards, 1936). Thus began two major, successive movements to reform elementary education in America. The elementary school, as it had come to be, was criticized by many for being too machine-like in character. Some saw in the nature of the subject matter selected for study, the methods of teaching utilized, and the standards of behavior required an imposition of adult perceptions which placed the program beyond the experiences and the capacities of young children. They argued, also, that the enterprise was guided by a philosophy which assumed that the future would be much like the past, even though America was already a place where change was the rule and not the exception. Against such an approach a group of educational theorists began to offer a conception of education that put the experiences of learners, rather than organized subject matter, at the center of the educative process. They wrote of a child-centered school and of an approach to curriculum development that would identify and utilize the interests and concerns of pupils (Rugg & Shumaker, 1928). Thus was ushered in one of the most exciting and controversial periods in the history of elementary education, one that was to have a great effect on the elementary school. Supported by a young but developing psychology of education and by a social philosophy which valued the individual, these educators set about broadening purposes and revising procedures in elementary education. Children's interests and concerns, not subject matter, were allowed to dominate the school program. The latter was viewed as a resource to be used in the nurturance of the former. Purposes were broadened to include responsibility for social competence, emotional maturity, and physical well-being, as well as intellectual development. The individuality of each pupil was to be recognized and respected, and an especial effort was to be made to nurture whatever creative potential a child possessed. Teacher-pupil planning was seen as the key to an emergent school experience; a curriculum planned in advance was looked upon with skepticism. Projects or units of work, rather than lessons, would become a vehicle for sustaining learning experiences. Children were to be active participants and not passive listeners in the classroom. Evaluation of learning was to be concerned less with sheer memorization and more with pupil ability to use knowledge in solving problems. Implemented most completely in a group of private schools, this progressive movement became institutionalized in 1917 with the formation of the Progressive Education Association. From that date until about 1940 this set of ideas acted as a strong force for change in the practice of elementary education (Cremin, 1961).

The second effort to reform elementary education came on the heels of the first and in the main grew out of it. Those involved in stating this counterreform point of view accepted much of what the progressivists stood for. One of their major arguments against them centered on what they saw as an overcommitment to the concerns of the individual, to the neglect of the concerns of society. They urged a society-centered position to correct an imbalance that had developed toward child-centeredness as they perceived it. It was contended, too, that an emergent school curriculum resulted in an educational experience too highly influenced by chance, and it was argued that a general, overall design for the curriculum could be predetermined and still leave a sufficient place for teacher-pupil planning. They accepted the idea of using organized subject matter as a resource for problem solving. But they preferred to see areas of living or basic social processes (governing, protecting and conserving, etc.) used as the organizing centers for the scope of the curriculum instead of the interests and impulses of children. Attention in the school curriculum to the core values of society was deemed essential by these theorists, and for elementary education a high priority was placed on the pursuit of common learnings needed for survival of the culture. The great depression which was triggered in 1929–30 added support to the argument for attending to a sociology as well as a psychology of education in program planning, and the core curriculum, as it came to be called, commanded the attention of a great many elementary educators through the 1930's and into the World War II years. Projects in the State of Virginia and in Santa Barbara County, California, were pioneer efforts in this direction (Virginia, State Board of Education, 1934, 1943; Santa Barbara County, 1940).

Those still committed to the position that organized subject matter was the most defensible point of departure for developing the elementary-school program made adjustments in their thinking in the face of these two strong reform efforts. The major one was to reconsider the several separate subjects included in the curriculum and to recognize the natural relatedness among them. This was a move against the fragmented nature of the school curriculum as argued by critics and resulted in efforts to define and work with broad fields of subject matter in the school. The several separate parts of language training came together as the language arts; history, geography, and civics were seen as social studies; and as science developed it was a general science program. This extended the boundaries within which teachers were able to work while preserving a certain integrity for the organized nature of human knowledge. The classroom was still quite teacher-centered and teacher-controlled, though there was an effort to find ways to utilize child interest for motivational purposes and to provide a somewhat more active role for the pupil in the process.

By the end of World War II progressive education, as an organized movement, had run its course, but not without leaving an indisputable mark on elementary education. Interest in the core curriculum continued to attract attention and many elementary schools had adapted some of its features to their operation. The curriculum had come to be viewed primarily as a series of broad fields of subject matter to be dealt with. Seven fields had evolved that included language arts, arithmetic, social studies, science, art, music, and health and physical education. Theorists were still apt to debate the extent to which the enterprise should be child- or society-centered; the elementary-school program in operation in 1950 was primarily subject-matter-centered (Shores, 1949).

Problems of School Organization. Another set of problems for elementary education in the period 1900–1950 centered on plans of organization for the school. The great influx of students in the last half of the 1800's had stimulated the development of the graded school. In it, subject matter was subdivided through a largely logical process and assigned across the several grades, acceptable standards of pupil achievement for each grade level were rather arbitrarily agreed upon, and, year by year, children were either promoted to the next grade or retained another year in their present one in light of their performance measured against these set standards. This graded-school arrangement, however, ran head-on into the stubborn realities of individual differences in children and was a source of great concern almost from the beginning. One significant portion of the history of elementary education is the record of attempts made to invent a more flexible and useful way of organizing the elementary school (Otto, 1934). Basically this effort has been a search for a scheme that would recognize and respond to both intra- and interindividual differences in pupils. Many plans have been developed and demonstrated. For example, the Winnetka plan of the 1920's instituted an arrangement whereby a certain number of projects in each subject were assigned to each grade level, but a student was allowed to work his way through them at his own rate so long as he mastered the subject matter. The XYZ plan attempted to use intelligence tests to divide students into grade groups of similar aptitude and ability. Thus, the bright were not to be held back by the slow, the slow were not to be discouraged by the performance of the bright, and progress through the curriculum was differentiated accordingly for both. By the mid-1900's the most general solution to the problem of individual difference was for the classroom teacher to organize for instruction subgroups of children in reading, arithmetic, and perhaps spelling and to differentiate assignments for children in the other areas of the curriculum while instructing them as a total group. Thus, within any one grade group, pupils could be described as working at more than one grade level. Decisions on pupil promotion still had to be made, but they began to take into account a broader spectrum of information about any given child, and teachers came to expect differences in each new group of pupils assigned to them. This reduced considerably the arbitrariness of the graded-school concept and was the harbinger of arguments for the development of a nongraded elementary school.

Another organizational item of concern over the years has been the way in which teachers would be utilized in elementary schools. Basically the issue can be reduced to whether teachers should specialize in only a few areas of the curriculum and teach those areas to different groups of children during the day on a departmentalized basis or should be competent in all areas of the curriculum and teach the full program to one group of children during the day in a self-contained classroom. Both arrangements were used to some extent in the first half of the 1900's, but the trend was clearly to the self-contained classroom and away from departmentalized elementary schools. Broadened purposes for the elementary-school years seemed to demand a staffing arrangement that took into account goals beyond subject-matter learning. The developing literature in child growth and development was interpreted as supporting a plan whereby a child would not have to establish relationships with a great many different teachers and a teacher would have an opportunity to know his pupils intimately. It was often held that a teacher should be assigned to the same group of pupils for more than one year at a time to exploit even more the advantages attributed to self-containment. At the mid-point of the twentieth century this one-teacher-per-class arrangement was the most usual way for elementary-school education to be implemented, though there were those who had begun to argue that the concept of self-containment in these terms had outlived its usefulness.

ELEMENTARY EDUCATION SINCE 1950. The period 1950–1955 was a time of considerable debate over the future course of education in the United States. Critics stressed what they considered to be a tendency toward anti-intellectualism in the public schools. The titles of their writings are a clear indication of the nature of their criticism. For instance, Bestor wrote *Educational Wastelands* (1953); Lynd, *Quackery in the Public Schools* (1950); and Smith, *The Diminished Mind* (1954). Public school educators themselves were not unconcerned about improving the effectiveness of the schools. Statements were made fairly often to the effect that to the realization of quantity in public education (meaning the proportion of the child and youth population that was in school) must be added the realization of quality education for all. A broad set of forces was at work at home and abroad which made the realization of this goal absolutely essential. It was clear that the continued effectiveness of the elementary school, consistent with its earlier history, would be contingent on its ability to transform itself in the face of demands for increased extent and quality of services (National Education Association, Educational Policies Commission, 1960). Let us turn to selected aspects of elementary education as it is and as it is becoming in this time of transition.

CURRICULUM CHANGE IN THE ELEMENTARY SCHOOL. Since about 1955 there has been an increasingly comprehensive curriculum improvement effort underway in elementary education. Originally it centered in mathematics and science and included efforts to introduce instruction in foreign languages into the elementary-school program. It has since grown, however, to the point that there are now major projects underway in the language arts, social studies, art, music, and health and physical education, also (Association for Supervision and Curriculum Development, 1965). A curriculum-development team has come into being made up of scholars from the various academic disciplines, learning psychologists, and classroom teachers working together. Clearly this totality of activity is of such proportions as to be labeled a reform movement (Goodlad, 1964). Reference to the "new" curricula in all of these areas is common (Heath, 1964). The major thrust in these projects has been a search for a more appropriate basis for the selection of subject matter to be included in the curriculum and a more effective way to organize it for learning. Much attention has been given to the structure of the disciplines and to their unique processes for discovering and verifying knowledge as an approach to these curriculum problems (Bruner, 1960; Foshay, 1961; Association for Supervision and Curriculum Development, 1963). The movement has placed heavy stress on the intellectual development of children (Piaget, 1952; Hunt, 1961; Vinacke, 1957). Cognitive educational goals have received much more attention than have affective ones (Bloom, 1956; Krathwohl & others, 1964). That learning expectancies for children have been raised is clear, perhaps most obviously in the movement of subject matter "down" from the early secondary-school years to the elementary school. The feasibility of these increased expectancies is being tested in developmental and demonstration projects, large and small, across the country. The projects both include and serve to motivate efforts to improve teaching materials and equipment and to refine teaching methodology. Discovery-oriented learning and teaching has captured considerable attention. There is great concern with individualizing more of the elementary school experience for the pupil, and programmed approaches to instruction are being studied especially with this in mind (Schramm, 1962; Goodlad, 1964). There is an obvious effort, too, to harness technology to teaching; the most advanced expression of this is the attempt to utilize computers in computer-assisted instruction projects (Suppes, 1964; Atkinson & Hansen, 1966).

Most of the money for this improvement work comes from the federal government, through the National Science Foundation and the United States Office of Education. Long-held commitments to local, "grass roots" curriculum-development work are being challenged by conceptions of regional and national undertakings carried out in newly formed research and development organizations that strive to prepare total curriculum packages for the elementary school.

There are those who argue that this current reform effort may lead to a new kind of subject-centeredness in the elementary-school curriculum that would make severe inroads on many of the gains in practice of the past fifty years, and attempts are being made to guard against such a happening. Some are especially concerned that affective goals may be lost sight of in an overzealous pursuit of cognitive competence for children. Others state that the reform effort must begin to attend to the overall design of the elementary-school curriculum, not just to single components in it. Until this is done, they argue, the improvement enterprise is without the guidance of a unifying conception of the mission of elementary education to which new curricula can be seen as contributing. (For details see the sections of this encyclopedia which deal with general curriculum and with each of the special curriculum areas.)

ELEMENTARY EDUCATION SINCE 1950: SCHOOL ORGANIZATION AND ADMINISTRATION. Span of Years. Recent surveys indicate that considerably more than half of the elementary schools in the United States are organized to start with kindergarten; the remainder start with grade 1 (National Education Association, Department of Elementary School Principals, 1958; Dean, 1960; National Education Association, Project on Instruction, 1962). Approximately 70 percent of all such elementary schools terminate at the grade 6 level. About 25 percent of them continue to include grades 5 and 8 as a part of elementary education. The remaining 5 percent follow some other basic organizational arrangement.

Age of Admission Stipulations. Decisions are required about the age at which children will be eligible for initial enrollment in either kindergarten or grade 1. The optimum age for this is a matter of debate, and present policies undoubtedly reflect a combination of social custom and objective attempts to predict success for the child in that which the school will ask him to do. Doubt continues to be expressed over the confidence that can be placed in chronological age alone as a basis for admission, and some workable formula that takes into account other information about the young child has long been sought. Still, at the present time chronological age is the almost single criterion that is used. The most common requirement for admission to kindergarten is that the child must be four years, nine months old, and thus reach his fifth birthday by December 1 or January 1 of the kindergarten year. About one-fourth of all school systems that operate kindergartens will enroll children at four years, eight months; only a few regularly accept children younger than this. Some will make exceptions for transfer pupils or children with superior mental and social maturity. Approximately 70 percent of all school systems require for entrance to grade 1 that a child be six years old on or before December 1 or January 1 of the first-grade year. Again about one-fourth of these school systems will enroll a child in grade 1 who is one month younger than this (National Education Association, Research Division, 1963b). These data indicate a slight shift toward raising the minimum age requirement for admission over the five-year period from 1958 to 1963. There is no more-current evidence about whether or not this trend has continued.

Length of School Year. Children are most typically required to be in attendance in the elementary school for 180 days of the year. In practice the range is from 174 to 190 days. In spite of some arguments for a lengthened school year there has been little change in these requirements in recent years (National Education Association, Research Division, 1965a; Dean, 1960). Teachers are most often expected to be on the job for 185 days as their basic work year. The range in practice is from 175 to 204 days. These figures reflect the varied requirements of school systems for teachers to engage in certain activities in the fall before pupils are in attendance and to continue on the job in the spring after pupils have completed their attendance for the year.

Length of School Day. Elementary schools in the United States continue to be in session for five days a week. But the length of the school day varies with age and grade level. Younger children in the primary years (K–3) are in school most typically for 6 hours, 20 minutes, per day. Older children in the intermediate years (grades 4–6) are in school for 6 hours and 36 minutes per day. Young adolescents in the upper years (grades 7–8) are in school for 6 hours and 45 minutes. All of these figures include a noon lunch period and usual recess periods (Dean, 1960; National Education Association, Research Division, 1965b). Based on the 1965 data, approximately 75 percent of all school systems report no change in length of school day in the past five years; some 23 percent report a slightly longer day; about 2 percent report a shorter day.

Elementary-school teachers report their school working day to be about 7 hours and 30 minutes. This is exclusive of time spent in faculty meetings, parent conferences, sponsorship of extracurricular activities, and in-service training courses.

Use of School Time. A recent study of policies and practices in the use of time in the elementary schools of 64 metropolitan areas provides a further useful way to view the elementary-school program, especially as it reveals a certain sense of priority therein. Stated in terms of minutes per day, the predominant time allotments to subjects in 1963 in these school systems were as follows: reading, 60 minutes; arithmetic and social studies, 45 minutes each; English, 40 minutes; science, physical education, and music, 30 minutes each; spelling, 20 minutes; and opening exercises, 10 minutes. Handwriting, health, and Spanish were assigned two weekly 30-minute periods each. Normally, art had one 60-minute period each week (Jarvis, 1963). It remains to be seen what the full impact of the curriculum-improvement projects mentioned earlier may have on matters such as the use of time in the classroom.

Homework. There is always the possibility of increasing school time by assigning homework regularly to pupils. This has been a controversial way of extending the school day in elementary education for many years, and the use of homework varies from school system to school system. A recent study provides current data on the status of homework in one geographic area, the Hudson River Valley of New York State. This was a questionnaire study involving 372 elementary schools, 4,615 teachers, and 138,000 pupils. Forty-four percent of these schools reported an unwritten policy on homework; 27 percent a written policy; 29 percent no policy. Time called for varied from about 15 minutes a day in grade 1 to 120 minutes a day in grade 6. The most often reported reasons for using homework were to provide enrichment for pupils and to help them to develop research skills. The work usually involved social studies, mathematics, or science. Of the parents reporting, 45 percent felt that the school did not give enough homework; 17 percent felt that the school gave too much. It remains to be seen whether the emphasis on academic achievement will lead to the increased use of homework as a way of extending the school day (Bond & Smith, 1966).

Possible Changes. There is reason to believe that the next decade may see considerable change in these several aspects of the organization and administration of the elementary school. Two sets of forces are at work which may bring this about. The first centers on the growing body of evidence which suggests that children need the systematic stimulation which an organized school experience can provide at ages younger than five (Bloom, 1964). In support of this position the Educational Policies Commission has called for the extension of universal education to four-year-olds (National Education Association, Educational Policies Commission, 1966). Some argue for education for three-year-olds, especially for specific subpopulations of children born into an economically and socially depressed stratum of society (Hechinger, 1966). The second has to do with the demands on teacher competence, especially in grades 4, 5, and 6, which the newer elementary-school curricula make. There is a growing feeling that more special arrangements are going to have to be made for these intermediate school years. What may well develop is a division of the present elementary school into a lower and a middle school. The lower elementary school would enroll children from ages 3 or 4 through ages 8 or 9, encompassing what is now nursery school, kindergarten, and grades 1 through 3 or 4. The middle elementary school would enroll children aged 9 or 10 through about age 13, encompassing the present grades 4 or 5 through 8. The lower elementary school would probably continue to be a neighborhood one, because of the age of the children, and might well be operated much like the best of today's elementary schools. The middle school would draw its pupils from several lower schools, and thus from several neighborhoods, and special teachers and facilities would be utilized to a much greater extent than is currently the practice at those grade levels. Current head-start programs may well be a harbinger of the possible emergence of the lower school. Selected communities are organizing, for tryout purposes, prototypes of a new middle school.

Along with this may come more direct attention to a lengthened school year of some sort for children. An indirect extension of the school year has come about in the past decade through the operation of summer-school sessions, though less than 10 percent of the total elementary-school-age population is enrolled in them thus far. For those that do participate, the session extends most typically over six to eight weeks and for three to four hours per day. The program of such summer schools is usually oriented to some special problem, such as remediation for slow learners or enrichment for rapid learners. They are used sparingly to accelerate children through the elementary school (National Education Association, Research Division, 1963b). It remains to be seen whether society will decide that it is unwise to deprive children of access to elementary schools through the summer season. But there is some reason to believe that the increasing clustering of people into urban centers may constitute a persistent force for reexamining the practice of having long summer vacations in elementary education that was born of an earlier rural and agrarian United States (*Nation's Schools*, 1958). There is a great need to help children to occupy their time in enjoyable and constructive pursuits in the summer. To many it seems inefficient to close playgrounds, libraries, and classrooms to them as we generally do.

BRINGING PUPILS TOGETHER FOR INSTRUCTION. Size of Classes. A long-standing concern in elementary education has been to control class size in the belief that teachers can be more effective with small class groups than with large ones (Vandiver, 1957). The ratio that is most often cited as being desirable is one teacher to 25 pupils. Recent data show the following to be the case: A child is most likely to be enrolled in a class group that will range from 27 to 31 children. Almost 40 percent of all pupils in elementary schools are in classes that fall into this range. Approximately 14 percent would be in classes enrolling 35 or more pupils. Some 12 percent are in classes enrolling 25 or fewer pupils (National Education Association, Research Division, 1965c). Said differently, 83.9 percent of pupils are in classes of over 25; 48.3 percent are in classes of over 30; 13.1 percent are in classes of over 35; 3.2 percent are in classes of over 40. To the extent that small class size can be shown to relate significantly to pupil achievement these figures suggest a need for reduction in the number of pupils most commonly assigned to a teacher. This relationship has proved to be difficult to establish in any consistent way in research studies and most research on class size shows no differences in achievement, adjustment or other measurable outcome between large and small classes. Still, smaller class size continues to rank at the top of the list of those things which teachers feel would most improve their effectiveness with classes. There continues to be some evidence presented that calls attention to certain consequences of small class size, but it is debated more than it is studied. One effort to study it found that teachers of smaller classes showed more educational creativity, tried more new procedures, gave more individual attention to pupils, used a greater variety of methods, and kept more complete records on the children assigned to them than teachers of larger classes. (Vincent & others, 1960). These are all things which are attractive by their very nature to those who would improve the effectiveness of instruction. It may be that progress will be made most fruitfully in this area by continued investigation into the question of which learning experiences at school can most appropriately be undergone in large groups, in small groups, or individually. This variable approach to class size relates teacher–pupil ratio to the nature and demands of particular educational experiences, and perhaps this is where it really belongs. Some elementary schools across the country are testing this approach to class size, and it is to be hoped that they will begin to offer evidence as to its effectiveness in the years immediately ahead.

Composition of Classes. Not unrelated to the problem of the size of class groups in the elementary school is the long-standing argument over the internal composition of them. This argument has centered primarily on the extent to which class groups should be heterogeneously or homogeneously formed, and this has meant grouping over and above chronological age, for the elementary school has for a long time grouped children of the same age together. Advocates of heterogeneity in class groups argue that learning for all, considered in the light of the broad set of educational objectives held for elementary education, is actually helped by the very fact of pupil differences in the group and that teaching practices which include the use of small multiple subgroups within each class, in concert with whole-group experiences, make it feasible for the teacher to handle such an arrangement successfully. They argue, further, that homogeneity in class groups is impossible to achieve anyway in the light of the facts of intra- and interindividual differences in children. Proponents of homogeneous grouping argue that intellectual development can be achieved to the advantage of both student and teacher when the grouping criterion is tied to pupil ability or achievement or a combination of both. They argue further that this advantage is gained without negative consequences in the social and personal development of superior, average, and slow learners. Over the years the proponents of heterogeneous grouping have prevailed in elementary education. Data reported in 1960 indicated that in grades 1 through 6 this practice was followed in over 70 percent of elementary schools and, in about 60 percent of schools, at grades 7 and 8 as well. The remainder were using homogeneous grouping at all or some grade levels, with the largest use reported in grades 7 and 8. Where homogeneous grouping practices are being followed, the major data sources used for decisions about the placement of children are (1) the judgment of teachers, (2) scores on achievement tests, and (3) scores on intelligence tests—either singly or in combination. Social maturity and previous patterns of success and failure in certain school subjects are the next most likely factors to be utilized (Dean, 1960). At the same time there was a feeling reported by half of the respondents who furnished these data and by others in a later study that there would be an increase in the use of homogeneous grouping in the future (National Education Association, Project on Instruction, 1962).

The reasons for that feeling are difficult to explain. To some extent the use of nongraded arrangements as developed in some elementary schools can be viewed as a kind of homogeneous grouping by achievement and could account for this. Or it may be related to the growing realization that there are identifiable subgroups of pupils in the elementary school who may well demand experiences designed more precisely for them if they are to learn from the school to a degree commensurate with their potential for learning. Groups of so-called gifted pupils, slow-learning pupils, and, recently, educationally disadvantaged pupils, have been described, and plans have been developed to provide special school arrangements for them (National Education Association, Educational Policies Commission, 1962; Norris, 1958). (See articles in this encyclopedia on gifted children, slow learners, and compensatory education.) Thus, for at least a part of one's school experience a kind of homogeneity is sought in which one may undergo instruction. In the meantime there have been few new entries into the literature bearing on this grouping matter directly. There has been an analytical statement of the philosophical and historical considerations related to homogeneous grouping (Lawson, 1957). There was a study of first-grade achievement under different plans of grouping that came out favoring the flexibility that can be achieved in heterogeneous groups (Bremer, 1958). There was a favorable report on a curricular-enrichment program for mentally advanced students in a heterogeneous classroom group (Parker, 1956). Most of the studies identified later in this article in relation to nongraded organizational arrangements are in a sense related to this pupil-grouping problem quite directly, but they are cited there rather than here. There was one rather extensive grouping study completed recently that included a section on the effects on pupils of different grouping arrangements in the elementary school that deserves a more extended discussion.

A large group of pupils in two Utah school districts was studied over a four-year period. One district employed ability grouping and the other random or heterogeneous grouping. Data were collected and analyzed for three major types of differences: (1) those between comparable pupils in the two grouping situations, or between-treatment differences; (2) those between pupils of the same sex and in the same grouping treatment who differed in ability, or within-treatment differences; and (3) boys and girls in the same grouping treatment and with the same ability, or sex-related differences. The attempt was to collect data on the consequences of these two grouping patterns on pupil achievement, study methods, sociometric status, pupil attitudes, pupil problems, the self concept, and selected personality characteristics. The conclusions reached by Borg were, in general, the following: (1) Superior pupils achieved best in ability-grouped classes but developed better study methods in randomly grouped classes. Those in ability-grouped classes scored somewhat lower in sociometric status and in self concept than did their counterparts in randomly grouped classes, perhaps reflecting a somewhat more generally healthy attitude. The overall treatment effects during the intermediate grades of the elementary school favor the ability-grouping treatment slightly for superior pupils. (2) For average pupils there is nothing in terms of achievement that could serve as a basis for choosing between grouping treatments, though those in the randomly grouped classes did develop better study methods. Average pupils showed more favorable personality characteristics, higher self-concept scores, and fewer pupil problems in the randomly grouped situation. Only in sociometric status did the ability-grouped treatment favor the average pupil. The needs of the average pupil were better met in the heterogeneous classroom group. (3) The achievement gains and study methods of slow pupils were slightly but consistently higher in the randomly grouped situation. Slow pupils did, however, make tremendous gains in sociometric status, and their attitudes toward school and teacher were more favorable, in the ability-grouped treatment. Self-concept data and personality information tended to favor the randomly grouped situation, though much less than for superior or average pupils. The ability-grouping system, with the large gains in sociometric status, provided a more favorable environment for the slow pupil than did the random-grouping treatment (Borg, 1965).

Nongraded Organizational Arrangements. Increasing numbers of elementary schools report experiences with nongraded organizational plans. "Nongraded" is used to refer to an arrangement in which the usual school grade labels are discontinued and efforts are made to facilitate continuous progress for pupils over a period of two or more consecutive years. Nationally, in 1960, somewhat less than 20 percent of school systems were using nongraded sequences in their elementary schools in place of the usual age-grading practices. By 1965, 25–30 percent reported some use of nongraded arrangements. It is most common for the nongraded sequence to be used to replace the primary grades; only one in ten such arrangements is reported as extending through the intermediate years (Austin, 1957; Goodlad & Anderson, 1958; Dean, 1960; National Education Association, Project on Instruction, 1962; National Education Association, Research Division, 1965d). Various plans for achieving partial or complete nongradedness are described by its proponents, and obstacles to their realization are identified (Goodlad & Anderson, 1963; Lewin, 1966; Stoddard, 1961; Rhoades, 1966). Advantages cited for nongrading include (1) avoidance of promotion-retention decisions, since pupils begin each school year where they left off at the close of the preceding one, (2) reduced pressures on children, resulting in fewer emotional problems, (3) the possibility of differential rates of pupil progress through the curriculum, and (4) the requirement that the school accommodate itself to the pupil rather than the reverse. Obstacles to nongrading that have been cited include (1) problems encountered in conceptualizing the curriculum in nongraded terms, (2) difficulties in getting teachers to think in nongraded ways, (3) the demands of record keeping as required for each pupil's individual progress, and (4) developing parent understanding and support for the system.

Studies of the effects of nonpromotion on pupil achievement continue to report findings which support the desirability of attempts to implement continuous-progress plans (Coffield & Blommers, 1965; Willihan, 1956; Holmes & Finley, 1957; Hall & Demarest, 1958). It is rather consistently shown that in terms of educational achievement little is gained by the repetition of a grade. This sort of evidence adds support to the concept of nongraded elementary schools.

Elementary educators have been interested in the consequences of nongraded arrangements on pupil achievement, and to date the evidence is divided. Some of the studies reported show a slight advantage in achievement for pupils in so-called nongraded classes (Hamilton & Rehwoldt, 1957; Hart, 1962; Ingram, 1960; Siapski, 1960; Hillson & others, 1964). Other studies found the achievement of graded groups superior to nongraded ones or found no significant differences favoring either (Carbone, 1961; Hopkins & others, 1965; Kierstad, 1963). Clearly, continued study is called for, and care must be taken to be certain of what is truly being compared. Apart from general methodological problems, one cannot help but wonder if the ambiguity of findings may not be related in part to the fact that what is actually being compared is one approach to nongrading versus another. That is, many elementary schools have embraced intraclass nongradedness for a long time, and expectations for individual pupils have been held accordingly. Current nongraded schemes may not go far enough beyond this practice to show consistent and significant differences in results. The concept may need to be more completely developed before it can be more extensively tested. Efforts to apply it more in terms of curriculum and less in terms of administration would seem to be called for. More explicitly, nongraded sequences are needed in areas other than reading and arithmetic. And implementation must be extended beyond the primary years of the school into the intermediate years. The realities of individual differences support nongraded thinking. Certainly this set of ideas deserves continued and more exacting development and testing.

Even with this concern about continuous progress, many elementary schools continue to make pupil-promotion decisions each year. The usual differentiating feature in such practices is the extent to which academic achievement weighs in such decisions in relation to pupils' social, emotional, or physical development, here referred to as group progress. A national survey of promotion practices made in 1958–59 revealed that in 58.5 percent of the elementary schools reporting, academic achievement was the primary factor considered in promotion decisions; group progress in the above terms was a minor factor. Twelve-and-a-half percent used academic achievement exclusively. Group progress was used primarily and academic achievement secondarily in 10.8 percent of the reporting schools. Less than 1 percent used group progress exclusively. Eighty-five percent of the parents queried at the time endorsed and supported whatever the current policy was in their school system; only about 1 percent raised serious questions about it (Dean, 1960).

Reporting Systems. No matter how a school is organized, it is important and necessary for pupils and parents to be informed about the progress students are making toward the objectives held for elementary-school education. This necessitates some way of recording each pupil's progress which can be used as the basis for communication with students and parents alike. In fact, records have a major intraschool use, too, as a way of recording the development of a child from year to year.

The great majority of elementary schools and teachers, almost 90 percent in fact, reported a few years ago to be guided in this by a uniform school-system-wide policy for reporting on pupils' progress. Some kind of letter or word scale was used for the purpose of reporting in over 75 percent of all responding elementary schools. Over 30 percent used a letter scale exclusively; only about 4 percent used a word scale exclusively. Almost 40 percent combined a letter scale and personal conferences into a reporting system. Only about 2 percent reported exclusively through personal conferences. These data are not to be taken as suggesting a high level of satisfaction with whatever arrangement was being used, however. Almost 90 percent of the schools queried in this investigation reported revising the plan in the recent past, being involved in doing so at the moment, or planning to revise it in the immediate future (Dean, 1960). Thus, reporting systems have and continue to be difficult to develop and implement as well as the school would like. A recent review of research on reporting systems concluded that such practices would be improved (1) if a greater understanding was developed between the school and the parent and pupil as to the purposes of marking and reporting procedures, (2) if teachers would emphasize specific characteristics and behaviors when they describe skills, attitudes, and habits and try to avoid broad, ambiguous statements, and (3) if there was continual evaluation of the effectiveness of whatever reporting system was being used (Kingston, 1966).

STAFFING THE ELEMENTARY SCHOOL. The Utilization of Teachers. The most usual arrangement for utilizing teachers in grades 1 through 6 is to assign one teacher to each class group to operate what has come to be called a self-contained classroom program. Approximately 75 percent of these grades were using such a staffing pattern as recently as 1958; another 15 percent were using some kind of partial or complete departmentalized arrangement; the remaining 10 percent were using a variety of other arrangements. At the same time teachers in grades 7 and 8 were being used, proportionately, quite differently. About 40 percent of these grades were departmentalized, and teaching was specialized; another 33 percent were partially departmentalized. Only about 20 percent were organized as self-contained classrooms.

Of course, a great many elementary schools have not practiced self-containment in recent years quite as literally as the label may suggest. Many elementary educators have argued for assistance for the teacher because of the increasing demands of the job, assistance which would include (1) special consultant help for the teacher, (2) special teachers who would teach part of the curriculum for the regular teacher, and (3) teacher's aides who could assist with nonprofessional tasks in the classroom. Information reported in 1960 is of interest in relation to these points. Special subject assistance for elementary-school teachers was reported nationally as shown in the accompanying table.

TABLE 1
SPECIAL ASSISTANCE FOR ELEMENTARY-SCHOOL TEACHERS BY SUBJECT

Special Subject Area	Percentage of Teachers with Assistance
Music	89.3
Art	51.5
Physical education and health	52.4
Reading	22.8
Science	8.0
Library	32.7
Speech	39.1

About 30 percent reported access to help and assistance with audiovisual materials and procedures and to guidance services. Helping teachers were being used in some way in about 30 percent of the schools. Teacher's aides were utilized in about 20 percent of the schools (Dean, 1960).

Since 1958 there has been increasing conjecture that staffing plans in the elementary school would change, and there is some evidence that this is happening. One report found about one-third of all elementary schools, especially in grades 4 through 8, using some form of partial or complete departmentalization (National Education Association, Project on Instruction, 1962). Estimates were presented which suggested that fully half of the elementary schools in the country would have turned toward some arrangement other than the self-contained, one-teacher-per-class concept by 1966. This willingness to reconsider what had come to be established practice is motivated by several things. First, there is a growing feeling that no one teacher would be competent to handle the total elementary-school curriculum as it is coming to be. Second, there is an increasing belief that children can work with more than one teacher rather easily and, in fact, profit from it. Third, it is argued that teachers would be helped in their own continuing career development if they had increased contact with colleagues on the job, rather than working alone.

In the wake of growing reservations about the viability of the self-contained classroom for the future, interest has grown in staff-utilization plans that call for the teaming of teachers (Shaplin & Olds, 1960; Norwalk Board of Education, 1963). Most elementary educators continue to be reluctant to think in terms of departmentalization. They fear a lack of communication between teachers about both the school program and pupils. But the teaming concept is more attractive. Some 15 percent of elementary schools were using this arrangement in 1961, and it was estimated that this percentage would double by 1966 (National Education Association, Project on Instruction, 1962). The teaming concept calls for two or more teachers to be made responsible for providing instruction for approximately twice (or more than twice) the number of pupils that would normally be assigned to each of them singly. They are expected to plan together for instruction, to team up in the execution of plans, and to assess together the results of the instruction they provide. Some proponents of the team idea would organize teaching teams hierarchically, with a designated team leader, senior and junior teachers, interns, and paraprofessionals. Responsibilities and salary would be differentiated across the team accordingly, introducing formal career levels into teaching. Others would organize teams on a collegial basis, with leadership conceived as a functional and situational thing shifting with the nature of problems to be solved. Only the salary differential of teacher seniority and professional versus nonprofessional status would operate in such teams. There are strong supporters of both arrangements, and both are being used in elementary schools at the present time. In this respect, a review by Blake of small-group research and cooperative-teaching problems should be noted, for it is an attempt to call attention to a considerable body of evidence on the dynamics of small groups as it may bear on the organization of teaching teams and on the study of them (Blake, 1964).

To date, and though there has been considerable writing done about it, the research reported from projects using the teaming of teachers has not been extensive, and some that has been reported has suffered from inadequacies in design. It is to be hoped that both of these conditions will be corrected, for evidence on the consequences of teaming arrangements for both teacher and pupil is needed (Drummond, 1961; Heathers, 1965). A few reports of research can be cited, but their findings are limited. One study compared team-taught and self-contained fifth- and sixth-grade classrooms. Measures were taken of pupil performance, pupil social compatibility, and parent attitudes. Pupil achievement favored the team-taught class groups. There was a higher degree of pupil interest and motivation identified by parents of pupils in the team-taught groups. There appeared to be somewhat less social compatibility among the students in the team-taught classes. Teachers who received these pupils in the seventh grade reported greater success and more self-motivation for those who came from the team-taught classroom (Jackson, 1964). Another study was carried out in two elementary schools over a two-year period, with pupils randomly assigned to either a team or a self-contained organization. Pre- and postachievement tests were given to both the team groups and the self-contained groups, and the results showed a slight advantage for the team organizations. There was also evidence that pupil performance improved when pupils were taught by a team that had been working together for more than one year, suggesting a need to consider operational stability and maturity of teams as a variable related to their effectiveness (Lambert & others, 1965). One study pointed to findings of enhanced teacher prestige, higher morale, and greater adaptability as a consequence of varying the way in which teachers were utilized in the middle grades of an elementary school (Shoresman, 1963). Another study called attention to the differential effect of team-teaching settings on certain categories of teachers. Some reacted quite positively to being a member of a team; others reacted negatively to their role as a team member (Davis, 1963). There is little doubt that some teachers will take more readily to a team-work arrangement than will others, pointing up the need to consider personal as well as professional characteristics in forming such groups.

The Utilization of the Principal. Over the years it has become common practice to have a full-time, nonteaching principal to be responsible for the operation of one elementary school in the total system of schools of which it is a part. There are still some teaching principals, and there are still some principals responsible for more than one school, but both of these practices are decreasing (National Education Association, Department of Elementary School Principals, 1958). The position of principal has evolved from the very early days of the practice of designating a head teacher when the staff was made up of two or more teachers, through a period in which the job was predominantly clerical and managerial in nature, to its presently recognized position of responsibility for professional leadership (Frey, 1963). In the process the duties of the principal have increased many times over to the point that there are now demands for re-examination and redefinition of the role in order to increase its effectiveness (Ronniger, 1962). It would appear that efforts are beginning to be made to apply more directly the findings of behavioral scientists to an understanding of the potential in the elementary-school principalship, as has been done for the superintendency (Wayson, 1965; Erickson, 1965; Campbell, 1965). A few studies have been published recently which provide more evidence on the dynamics of the principal's role in an elementary school. Studies continue to be reported that attest to the increased readiness for and actual change in schools where the principal behaves in democratic rather than nondemocratic ways (Wiles & Grobman, 1958). A number of studies have been done which are concerned with the interactions which occur between principals and their staffs and with the extent to which differences in effectiveness occur in relation to the amount of congruity in role expectations that exist between the principal and his teaching staff, the parent group, and his superiors. These studies seem to suggest an increase in the rated effectiveness of the principal that is a function of congruence between his perception of the role and the perceptions of it as held by a specified reference group (Price, 1961; Brottman, 1963). Still, the evidence is not very extensive and the interpretations possible from it are necessarily limited. More such studies even more carefully formulated are needed (Lipham, 1965). The most extensive study reported recently that dealt with the leadership of the principal was conducted by Gross and Herriott (1965). They attempted to arrive at an "executive professional leadership" score for each of a large group of urban elementary-school principals and then to relate these assigned scores to such matters as morale of the teaching staff, professional behavior of the teaching staff, and even the achievement of pupils. They report statistically significant relationships between the so-called EPL scores attributed to a principal and those concerns: higher EPL is related to higher staff morale, to more-professional teacher behavior, and to pupil success in reading. Thus, they argue that the behavior of the principal can and does have an effect on the operation of the school. They note that more must be known about the personal and organizational factors that contribute to the development of the leadership style of a given principal. They call attention especially to the fact that the elementary-school principal looms as the executive officer of a professionally staffed organization and to the ramifications this has for acceptable and effective leader behavior (Gross & Herriott, 1965).

The breadth of responsibility which the principal is called upon to accept has led to some attention to the teaming of principals that is similar in intent to the concept applied to teachers. One such effort to team elementary principals has been described in a project report from a California school district (Anastasiow & Fischler, 1964). Another has been described that has been in operation for several years in an elementary-school district on Long Island in New York State (St. Mary, 1966). It may well be that we will see an extended tryout of such team arrangements as one way of solving some of the problems of expertise and competence that accompany administration and supervision in the elementary school.

ACCREDITATION OF ELEMENTARY SCHOOLS. In recent years there has been a growing interest in some workable procedures to ensure quality control in the conduct of elementary education. This had led to considerable discussion, pro and con, of the feasibility of an accreditation arrangement for elementary schools. Some have argued for such a system (Otto, 1964); others have cautioned against it (Pharis, 1964; Tyler, 1964). A recent national survey carried out by the U.S. Office of Education shed some additional light on the status of this matter in 1963–64. At that time, 7 states granted both public elementary-school approval and accreditation; 18 states granted only approval; 9 states granted only accreditation; and 16 states granted neither approval nor accreditation. Advantages cited most frequently for accreditation were (1) it served as an incentive for self-improvement, (2) it served as a way to raise the status of the elementary school in budgetary considerations and in community esteem, (3) it served as a way to assure uniformity and conformity with minimal standards, and (4) it served as encouragement for "quality education." Disadvantages cited were (1) lack of feasibility because of the size of the state, the number of schools, limitations of staff, and cost in time and money, (2) encouragement of rigid and inflexible standards which tend to become means rather than ends. Other common observations expressed by respondents were (1) accreditation should be a total K–12 concept, not applied to grade levels, (2) accreditation might assist in a needed reclarification of the purposes of the elementary school, and (3) accreditation has resulted in material gains for the elementary school and has thus emphasized the importance of its role in the total educational endeavor (Dean, 1964). A study was reported on the attitude of elementary-school teachers toward the accreditation of elementary schools. It showed teacher involvement in the accrediting process to be associated with a more positive attitude toward it. It also showed the career teacher to be more positively disposed toward accreditation than the noncareer teacher (Rubinowitz, 1966). At present only the Southern Association of Colleges and Schools among the six regional accrediting associations has an arrangement for accrediting elementary schools. It remains to be seen whether this practice will spread to other regions of the country.

ELEMENTARY EDUCATION IN OTHER COUNTRIES. The education of children in the age range of 4–5 years through 12–13 years is a concern of other countries of the world as well as of the United States. The developed nations have for many years operated systems of education for children. The developing nations are aware of the importance of formal education for children at these ages and are striving to extend the opportunity in a universal and compulsory way to ever greater numbers. All nations, developed and developing, seem to sense the extent to which the achievement of national goals and purposes in the modern world is tied to the excellence of education provided for children and youth. All over the world increasing importance is being attached to education. Change is being attempted on a scale and at a pace unknown at any earlier time. There is so much activity of one kind or another that the situation literally defies the drawing of any very general conclusions about what is happening. Clearly there is an intent to reach more children for longer periods of time in the elementary school (or primary school, as the case may be) and to provide for them an education consistent with the world as it is becoming. In that connection there are some basic source materials to which the elementary educator can turn for comparative purposes. UNESCO (1958) provided a world survey of primary education in a volume published about ten years ago. It is at one and the same time a world look at primary education and a country-by-country view as well. Two reviews of educational research in countries other than the United States were made available over the past several years (Noll, 1957; Hall, 1962). Each of these contains references to elementary or primary education or both. There are two different yearbook series published which contain references to developments in elementary education across the world. One of these, the *International Yearbook of Education*, reported in its last issue on educational developments in 93 countries of the world (UNESCO & International Bureau of Education, 1965). The other, *The World Yearbook of Education*, dealt with the "education explosion" and served to point up the extent to which all countries of the world were attempting to make improvements in their educational systems (Bereday & Lauwerys, 1965). The series being developed by the Division of International Education of the United States Office of Education, entitled "Studies in Comparative Education," continues to grow and provides the student of elementary education with another possibility for comparative and cross-national study of the education of children (U.S. Office of Education, 1954———). Most of the research noted in these various sources is descriptive in nature. The range of topics covered is suggestive of many of the problems faced by elementary school educators in the United States: infant schools for very young children, compensatory education for disadvantaged pupil populations, pupil placement and progress through the school, and the holding power of the primary schools. Undoubtedly the next ten years will see even more educational activity across the world, and the student of elementary education will find it useful and necessary to use this developing international literature as well as that from his own country.

G. Wesley Sowards
Stanford University

References

Anastasiow, Nicholas J., and Fischler, Abraham S. "A Proposal for Teaming Principals." *Nat El Prin* 44 (November): 59–64; 1964.

Association for Supervision and Curriculum Development. *New Insights and the Curriculum.* 1963 Yearbook. ASCD, 1963. 328p.

Association for Supervision and Curriculum Development. *New Curriculum Developments.* ASCD, 1965. 106p.

Atkinson, Richard C., and Hansen, Duncan N. "Computer Assisted Instruction in Initial Reading: The

Stanford Project." *Reading Res Q* 2 (Fall): 5–25; 1966.

Austin, Kent C. "The Ungraded Primary Unit in Public Schools of the United States." Doctoral dissertation. U Colorado, 1957.

Bereday, George Z. F., and Lauwerys, Joseph A. (Eds.) *The World Yearbook of Education: The Education Explosion.* Evans, 1965. 498p.

Bestor, Arthur E. *Educational Wastelands.* U Illinois Press, 1953. 226p.

Blake, Ray F. "Small Group Research and Cooperative Teaching Problems." *Nat El Prin* 43 (February): 31–6; 1964.

Bloom, Benjamin S. (Ed.) *Taxonomy of Educational Objectives,* Handbook I: *Cognitive Domain.* McKay, 1956. 207p.

Bloom, Benjamin S. *Stability and Change in Human Characteristics.* Wiley, 1964. 237p.

Bond, George W., and Smith, George J. "Homework in the Elementary School." *Nat El Prin* 45 (January): 46–9; 1966.

Borg, Walter R. "Ability Grouping in the Public Schools: A Field Study." *J Exp Ed* 34:1–97; 1965.

Bremer, Neville H. "First Grade Achievement Under Different Plans of Grouping." *El Engl* 35:324–6; 1958.

Brottman, Marvin A. "The Administrative Process and Elementary School Principals: An Empirical Test of a Concept." *Administrators Notebook* 11:1–4; 1963.

Bruner, Jerome. *The Process of Education.* Harvard U Press, 1960. 97p.

Butts, R. Freeman, and Cremin, Lawrence A. *A History of Education in American Culture.* Holt, 1953. 628p.

Campbell, Roald. "Application of Administrative Concepts to the Elementary Principalship." *Nat El Prin* 44 (April):21–6; 1965.

Carbone, R. F. "A Comparison of Graded and Nongraded Elementary Schools." *El Sch J* 62:82–8; 1961.

Coffield, William H., and Blommers, Paul. "Effects of Non-promotion on Educational Achievement in the Elementary School." *J Ed Psychol* 47:235–50; 1965.

Cremin, Lawrence A. *The American Common School.* Teachers Col, Columbia U, 1951. 248p.

Cremin, Lawrence A. *The Transformation of the School.* Knopf, 1961. 387p.

Cubberley, Elwood P. *Public Education in the United States,* rev. ed. Houghton, 1934. 782p.

Davis, Harold S. "The Effect of Team Teaching on Teachers." Doctoral dissertation. Wayne State U, 1963.

Dean, Stuart E. *Elementary School Administration and Organization: A National Survey of Practices and Policies.* HEW, 1960. 126p.

Dean, Stuart E. "The National Status of Public Elementary School Approval and Accreditation." *Nat El Prin* 43 (May):25–31; 1964.

Drummond, Harold D. "Team Teaching: An Assessment." *Ed Leadership* 19:160–5; 1961.

Edwards, Newton, and Richey, Herman. *The School in the American Social Order.* Houghton, 1947. 880p.

Erickson, Donald A. "Changes in the Principalship." *Nat El Prin* 44 (April):16–20; 1965.

Foshay, Arthur W. (Chairman) "The Educational Program: Early and Middle Childhood." *R Ed Res* 29:133–219; 1959.

Foshay, Arthur W. "A Modest Proposal." *Ed Leadership* 18:506–16, 528; 1961.

Frey, Barbara R. "An Analysis of the Functions of the Elementary School Principal 1921–1961." Doctoral dissertation. U Indiana, 1963.

Goodlad, John I. *School Curriculum Reform.* Fund for the Advancement of Education, 1964. 95p.

Goodlad, John I., and Anderson, Robert H. "The Nongraded Elementary School." *NEA J* 47:642–3; 1958.

Goodlad, John I., and Anderson, Robert H. *The Nongraded Elementary School,* rev. ed. Harcourt, 1963. 248p.

Gross, Neal, and Herriott, Robert. *Staff Leadership in Public Schools: A Sociological Inquiry.* Wiley, 1965. 247p.

Hall, Richard M. (Chairman) "Educational Research in Countries Other Than the United States." *R Ed Res* 32:213–362; 1962.

Hall, William F., and Demarest, Ruth. "Effect on Achievement Scores of a Change in Promotional Policy." *El Sch J* 58:204–7; 1958.

Halliwell, Joseph W. "A Comparison of Pupil Achievement in Graded and Non-graded Primary Classrooms." *J Exp Ed* 32:59–64; 1963.

Hamilton, Warren W., and Rehwoldt, Walter. "By Their Differences They Learn." *Nat El Prin* 37 (December):27–9; 1957.

Hart, R. H. "The Non-graded Primary School and Arithmetic." *Arithmetic Teach* 9:130–3; 1962.

Heath, Robert W. *New Curricula.* Harper, 1964. 292p.

Heathers, Glen. "Research on Implementing and Evaluating Cooperative Teaching." *Nat El Prin* 44 (January):27–33; 1965.

Hechinger, Fred C. (Ed.) *Pre-school Education Today: New Approaches to Teaching Three, Four, and Five-year-olds.* Doubleday, 1966. 150p.

Hillson, Maurie, and others. "A Controlled Experiment Evaluating the Effects of a Non-graded Organization on Pupil Achievement." *J Ed Res* 57:548–50; 1964.

Holmes, Jack A., and Finley, Carmen J. "Under- and Over-age Grade Placements and School Achievements." *J Ed Psychol* 48:447–56; 1957.

Hopkins, Kenneth D., and others. "An Empirical Comparison of Pupil Achievement and Other Variables in Graded and Ungraded Classes." *Am Ed Res J* 2:207–15; 1965.

Hunt, J. McVicker. *Intelligence and Experience.* Ronald, 1961. 416p.

Ingram, V. "Flint Evaluates its Primary Cycle." *El Sch J* 61:76–80; 1960.

Jackson, Joseph. "Analysis of a Team Teaching and of a Self-contained Homeroom Experiment in

Grades Five and Six." *J Exp Ed* 32:317–31; 1964.
Jarvis, Oscar T. "Time Allotments in Elementary Schools—Policies and Practices." *Nat El Prin* 43 (September):64–5; 1963.
Kearney, Nolan C. *Elementary School Objectives.* Russell Sage, 1953. 189p.
Kierstad, R. "A Comparison and Evaluation of Two Methods of Organization for the Teaching of Reading." *J Ed Res* 56:317–21; 1963.
Kingston, Albert J. "Research on Reporting Systems." *Nat El Prin* 45 (May):36–40; 1966.
Krathwohl, David, and others. *Taxonomy of Educational Objectives,* Handbook II: *Affective Domain.* McKay, 1964. 196p.
Lambert, Philip, and others. "A Comparison of Pupil Achievement in Team and Self-contained Organizations." *J Exp Ed* 33:217–4; 1965.
Lawson, Douglas E. "An Analysis of Historic and Philosophic Considerations for Homogenous Grouping." *Ed Adm Sup* 43:257–79; 1957.
Levin, Harry, and Meltzer, Nancy S. (Chairmen) "Educational Programs: Early and Middle Childhood." *R Ed Res* 35:103–64; 1965.
Lewin, David. "Go Slow on Non-grading." *El Sch J* 67:131–4; 1966.
Lipham, James M. "The Role of the Principal." *Nat El Prin* 44 (April):28–33; 1965.
Lynd, Albert. "Quackery in the Public Schools." *Atlantic Mon* 185:33–8; 1950.
Mayhew, Katherine, and Edwards, Anna. *The Dewey School.* Appleton, 1936. 489p.
McKenna, Bernard H., and Pugh, James B. "Performance of Pupils and Teachers in Small Classes Compared to Large." *Res B* 4:1–4; 1964.
National Education Association, Department of Elementary School Principals. "1958 Survey: Some Organizational Characteristics of Elementary Schools." *Nat El Prin* 38:52–62; 1958.
National Education Association, Educational Policies Commission. *Contemporary Issues in Elementary Education.* NEA, 1960. 27p.
National Education Association, Educational Policies Commission. *The Central Purpose of American Education.* NEA, 1961. 21p.
National Education Association, Educational Policies Commission. *Education and the Disadvantaged American.* NEA, 1962. 39p.
National Education Association, Educational Policies Commission. *Universal Opportunity for Early Childhood Education.* NEA, 1966. 12p.
National Education Association, Project on Instruction. *The Principals Look at the Schools: A Status Study of Selected Instructional Practices.* NEA, 1962. 75p.
National Education Association, Project on Instruction. *Deciding What to Teach.* NEA, 1963. p. 88–98.
National Education Association, Research Division. *Entrance-age Policies and Exceptions.* Educational Research Service Circular No. 3. NEA, 1963(a). 27p.
National Education Association, Research Division. *Summer School Programs: Opportunities and Trends.* Educational Research Service Circular No. 4. NEA, 1963(b). 46p.
National Education Association, Research Division. *Number of Days in Regular School Term 1964–65.* Educational Research Service Report. NEA, 1965(a). 26p.
National Education Association, Research Division. *Length of School Day for Teachers and Pupils 1964–65.* Educational Research Service Circular No. 6. NEA, 1965(b). 39p.
National Education Association, Research Division. *Class Size in Kindergarten and Elementary Schools.* Research Report 1965-R11. NEA, 1965(c). 27p.
National Education Association, Research Division. *Nongraded Schools.* Research Memorandum 1965-12, NEA, 1965(d). 20p.
National Education Association, Research Division. "Facts on American Education." *Res B* 44:35–40; 1966.
Nation's Schools. "Lengthening the School Year." 62:6–7; 1958.
Noll, Victor H. (Chairman) "Educational Research in Countries Other Than The U.S.A." *R Ed Res* 27:1–159; 1957.
Norris, Dorothy E. "Programs in the Elementary Schools." In NSSE, 57th Yearbook. U Chicago Press, 1958. p. 222–62.
Norwalk Board of Education. *The Norwalk Plan of Team Teaching, Fifth Report, 1962–63.* The Board, 1963. 50p.
Otto, Henry J. *Elementary School Organization and Administration.* Appleton, 1934. 652p.
Otto, Henry J. "Elementary School Accreditation: Yes!" *Nat El Prin* 43 (May):22–4; 1964.
Parker, Clyde. "Measured Experiment with Mentally Advanced Children." *Am Sch Bd J* 133:23–4; 1956.
Pharis, William L. "Sour Grapes and Gold Stars: The Case Against Accrediting Elementary Schools." *Nat El Prin* 43 (May):19–21; 1964.
Piaget, Jean. *The Origins of Intelligence in Children.* Int U, 1952. 419p.
Price, Alfred J. "A Study of the Interactions of Attitudes and Values of Elementary Principals and Their Staffs." Doctoral dissertation. Northwestern U, 1961.
Reisner, Edward H. *The Evolution of the Common School.* Macmillan, 1935. 590p.
Rhoades, Walter M. "Erasing Grade Lines." *El Sch J* 67:140–5; 1966.
Ronniger, Billy Jay. "A Summary Study of the Job Responsibilities of the Elementary School Principal." Doctoral dissertation. U Oregon, 1962.
Rubinowitz, Arthurea B. "An Investigation of the Attitudes of Elementary School Teachers Regarding the Accreditation of Elementary Schools." Doctoral dissertation. American U, 1966.
Rugg, Harold, and Shumaker, Ann. *The Child Centered School,* Harcourt, 1928. 359p.
Santa Barbara County. *Santa Barbara County Curriculum Guide for Teachers in Elementary Schools,* Vol. 2. The County, 1940.

Schramm, Wilbur. *Programmed Instruction—Today and Tomorrow.* Fund for the Advancement of Education, 1962.

Shane, Harold. (Ed.) *The American Elementary School.* Harper, 1953. 434p.

Shaplin, Judson T., and Olds, Henry F. (Eds.) *Team Teaching.* Harper, 1960. 430p.

Shores, J. Harlan. *A Critical Review of Research on Elementary School Curriculum Organization, 1890–1949.* Bureau of Research and Service, U Illinois, 1949. 29p.

Shoresman, Peter B. "A Comparative Study of the Effectiveness of Science Instruction in the Fifth and Sixth Grades Under Two Different Patterns of Teacher Utilization and Pupil Development." Doctoral dissertation. Harvard U, 1963.

Siapski, M. K. "Ungraded Primary Reading Program: An Objective Evaluation." *El Sch J* 61:41–5; 1960.

Small, W. H. *Early New England Schools.* Ginn, 1914. 401p.

Smith, Mortimer B. *The Diminished Mind: A Study of Planned Mediocrity in Our Public Schools.* Regnery, 1954. 150p.

St. Mary, Maurice E. "The Administrative Team in Supervision." *Nat El Prin* 45 (April):59–61; 1966.

Stoddard, George D. *The Dual Progress Plan.* Harper, 1961. 225p.

Suppes, Patrick. "Modern Learning Theory and the Elementary School Curriculum." *Am Ed Res J* 1:79–93; 1964.

Tyler, Ralph E. "Evaluating the Elementary School." *Nat El Prin* 43 (May):8–13; 1964.

UNESCO. *World Survey of Education: Primary Education.* UNESCO, 1958. 1387p.

UNESCO and International Bureau of Education. *International Yearbook of Education.* UNESCO, 1965. 453p.

U.S. Office of Education, Division of International Education. *Studies in Comparative Education.* USOE, 1954——.

U.S. Department of Health, Education, and Welfare. *Projections of Educational Statistics to 1974–75.* USOE, 1965.

U.S. Department of Health, Education, and Welfare. "Back to School Statistics." *Am Ed* 2:23; 1966.

Vandiver, Willis. *Class Enrollment and School Size: What Research and Opinions Say.* Education Brief No. 35. USOE, 1957. 7p.

Vinacke, William E. "Developmental Changes in Thinking." *Ed* 77:318–22; 1957.

Vincent, William S., and others. "The Question of Class Size." Teachers Col, Columbia U, *Res B* 1 (No. 1); 1960.

Virginia State Board of Education. *Tentative Course of Study for Virginia Elementary Schools, Grades I to VIII.* The Board, 1934. 613p.

Virginia State Board of Education. *Course of Study for Virginia Elementary Schools, Grades 1–7.* The Board, 1943. 553p.

Wayson, William W. "The Elementary Principalship—Will It Be a Part of the New Administration?" *Nat El Prin* 44 (April):10–5; 1965.

Wiles, Kimball, and Grobman, H. G. "The Role of the Principal in Curriculum Development." *Ed Adm Sup* 44:10–4; 1958.

Willihan, Robert S. "A Comparative Study of Retardation in the Primary Grades of the San Diego, California, City Schools." Doctoral dissertation. U Colorado, 1956.

ENGINEERING EDUCATION

Although many trace the history of engineering to ancient times (Finch, 1951; Granger, 1945), the first formal engineering school is generally believed to be the École Nationale des Ponts et Chaussée. It was founded in 1747 for designers of bridges and highways in the Corps des Ponts et Chaussée by the engineer to Louis XV of France, Jean Rodolphe Perronet (sometimes called the father of engineering education). The first military engineering courses were offered in the United States at the Military Academy at West Point, which was founded in 1802. Norwich University was established in 1819 and offered the first civil engineering courses. Rensselaer Polytechnic Institute (RPI) was founded in 1824 and is generally considered to be the first American engineering school; however, it did not grant its first engineering degree until 1835. Union College began offering engineering courses in 1845, Brown University in 1850, the University of Michigan in 1852, and New York University in 1854. Harvard, Dartmouth, and Yale created scientific schools between 1847 and 1854, but engineering curricula were not established until later.

European influences had an initial and sustaining influence on engineering education, but the pioneering spirit and practical bent of early America as well as the parallel development of agriculture and industry resulted in considerable unrest and finally revolt against the classical tradition in higher education. On July 2, 1862, the United States Congress passed and sent to President Lincoln the Land Grant Act authored by Vermont Representative Justin Smith Morrill, donating public lands to the several states and territories "for the foundation and maintenance of colleges where the leading object shall be, without excluding other scientific and classical studies including military tactics, to teach such branches of learning as are related to agriculture and mechanical arts . . . in order to promote the liberal and practical education of the industrial classes in the several professions in life" (Morrill, 1862). Although most of the colleges created under the Morrill Act became state-supported "A and M" (agriculture and mechanical arts) colleges and later state universities, a few became private institutions (notably Massachusetts Institute of Technology and Cornell University). As a result of the Land Grant Act and the increasing importance of engineering technology, the number of private and public institutions offering engineering programs between 1860 and 1890 increased from 6 to 110.

During the World's Columbian Exposition in Chicago in 1893, the World Engineering Congress held a divisional meeting (Section E) where the Society for the Promotion of Engineering Education (SPEE) was organized. Professor Ira O. Baker of the University of Illinois was elected SPEE's first president. The Society for the Promotion of Engineering Education had a significant impact on engineering education from its early beginning by joining with other engineering societies in the study of engineering education.

The first comprehensive national study of engineering education was initiated in 1907 with financial support from the Carnegie Foundation for the Advancement of Teaching. It was conducted by Charles R. Mann (1918), a University of Chicago physicist, and was released in 1918. It called attention to what has become a traditional issue in engineering education, namely, the proper balance between practice and theory, as well as other perennial problems such as selection and attrition, the importance of teaching versus research, etc. The second major investigation of engineering education was conducted by Dean William E. Wickenden and others (1930) between 1923 and 1929, and this study was also supported by the Carnegie Foundation. It was perhaps one of the most exhaustive studies ever conducted in engineering education, and Wickenden and his colleagues included detailed studies of curricula, institutions, teachers, the selection of students, industry requirements, graduate education, research, and technical institutes and a comparative study of engineering education in the United States and Europe. However, this report did not have the impact that the Flexner (1910) report had on medical education.

The growth of state engineering licensing laws, the concern for quality education, the need for cooperation among engineering societies, and the development of a professional consciousness resulted in the founding of the Engineers' Council for Professional Development (ECPD). In 1932, ECPD developed two major concerns which have had a marked influence on engineering education: recruitment of students and accreditation of curricula (Saville, 1952). With the assistance of the ECPD Committee on Student Selection and Guidance, extensive information on engineering careers was developed and supplied to secondary-school students, parents, and teachers. Considerable attention was also given to engineering aptitudes and interests. The parallel development of the educational-testing movement in America gave impetus to the legion of studies which have been conducted over the years by educators, psychologists, and others on the selection of engineering students and the prediction of engineering grades. Another major educational influence of ECPD was the inauguration of an extensive and comprehensive curricular and institution program of accreditation. Using the early efforts of the American Institute of Chemical Engineers as a basis for beginning, ECPD, under the chairmanship of President Karl Compton of Massachusetts Institute of Technology (MIT), made its initial studies, and the first list of accredited curricula was published in 1937 (Engineers' Council for Professional Development, 1937).

Other studies of engineering education were conducted prior to and during World War II by Dugland C. Jackson, professor emeritus of MIT (Jackson, 1939) and committees chaired by Dean Harry Hammond of Pennsylvania State in 1940 and 1944 (Hammond and others, 1940, 1944). The Hammond studies delineated in considerable detail the aims and scope of engineering curricula and gave strong support to what became known as the "humanistic-social" stem of engineering education.

When SPEE changed its name to The American Society for Engineering Education (ASEE) in 1946, the social impact of scientific, engineering, and technological developments was in considerable evidence. Illustrative of this post-World War II concern was the principal focus for a mid-century conference, the Social Impact of Science and Technology on Society, held at MIT (Burchard, 1949). The far-reaching social-economic implications of science and technology were coupled with the increasing support for basic and applied research and development in not only local, regional, and national affairs but also in international affairs as well. In 1952 ECPD requested ASEE to conduct another study of engineering education. Leading engineering educational administrators in their "Report on Evaluation of Engineering Education" (Grinter & others, 1955), under the chairmanship of Dean L. E. Grinter of the University of Florida, gave considerable support for a strong mathematics, science, and engineering-science base for undergraduate and graduate engineering education as well as an adequate undergraduate program in general education. Communications, the humanities, and the social sciences were given further support in the report of the Social-Humanistic Study Project which was based on the comprehensive field study of general education in engineering (Gullette & others, 1956).

In a comprehensive Ford Foundation-supported project under the chairmanship of Dean Harold Hazen of MIT graduate school, engineering educators turned their attention to faculty recruitment, development, and utilization (Foecke, 1960). Efforts to improve the pedagogical abilities of engineers bore fruit in the development of summer and in-service institutes for effective teaching (Lancaster, 1967; Kraybill, 1966).

Graduate work in engineering began in the latter part of the nineteenth century; the first doctorate in engineering in the United States was awarded in 1861 at Yale to Josiah Willard Gibbs, whose thesis title was "On the Form of Teeth in Spur Gearing" (Rukeyser, 1942) and the first master's degree in 1879 at Iowa State College (John & Hammond, 1936). However, the number and proportion of graduate students in engineering were quite small until 1960. In 1900 the ratio of B.S. degrees to graduate degrees was 100 : 1, in 1930 it was 20 : 1, in 1960 it was 4 : 1, and in 1967 it was 2 : 1 (National Center for Educational Statistics, 1967; American Society for Engineering Education, 1967).

The 1965 *Preliminary Report* of ASEE goals of engineering education, under the chairmanship of President Eric Walker of Pennsylvania State University, recommended (1) that the master's degree be "the first professional degree," (2) increased support for graduate education and research, and (3) institutional accreditation at the master's level rather than specific curricular accreditation at the B.S. level (American Society for Engineering Education, 1965). Although these recommendations were received with considerable controversy (Churchill, 1965; LeBold & others, 1967), the "Final Report" of the goals committee also stressed the importance of graduate work, stressing that basic engineering education should include at least one year of graduate education (American Society for Engineering Education, 1968).

The rapid changes in engineering methodology and science and the increasing demands of society have made engineers and engineering educators increasingly concerned about technical obsolescence. To meet this concern the various engineering societies prepared a comprehensive report outlining the role of professional societies, industry, government, and educational institutions in meeting the continuing educational needs of engineers (Weber, 1966).

TRENDS. The relative importance of science versus art, theory versus practice, and creativity versus reality have been perennial issues in engineering education. The long-range trends, however, have clearly indicated the increasing importance of advanced quantitative methods and basic science in engineering and a decline in empirical methods which have stressed the art and practice of engineering. This has been accelerated by the rapid changes in methodology, such as the development of computers, which have placed high premiums on a knowledge of higher mathematics and scientific theory. As a result there has been an increasing demand for greater competence in mathematics and science before completing a formal undergraduate or graduate program in engineering (Bode & others, 1961), during such education (Case Institute . . . , 1965; Mathematical Association of America, 1966) and after it (Engineering College Administrative Council–Relations with Industry Feedback Committee, 1965).

The increasing importance of the engineering graduate in the solution of the complex problems of society has also resulted in a demand for a broader education for engineers, especially in communications, humanities, and social science (Hollomon, 1967). To meet these demands for breadth, specialization at the undergraduate level has declined, especially in specialized options—e.g., communications and power in electrical engineering, and machine design and power plants in mechanical engineering. Some schools have provided a common core of unified programs at the undergraduate level and deferred specialization to the graduate years— e.g., the University of California at Los Angeles, the Case Institute of Technology, RPI (Rensselaer Polytechnic Institute, 1963), and Dartmouth College (Tribus, 1963). A parallel and somewhat contradictory trend has been the proliferation of specific degrees and specialties (Foecke & Tolliver, 1963). Eells and Haswell (1961) noted 348 different degrees conferred by recognized colleges and universities.

Since engineering does include a broad base of subject matter, including communications, humanities, and social science and a substantial amount of mathematics and natural science, some envision undergraduate engineering education as a form of liberal education for a technological-scientific society (Walker & Nead, 1966). There is some evidence to support such a view, especially since engineering graduates frequently are in demand as managers of industrial enterprises (Newcomer & Market Statistics, Incorporated, 1965) and as graduate students in business and science (Davis, 1963), although opinions have varied on this matter (*American Engineer*, 1967).

Another major trend in engineering education has been the adaptation and accommodation of engineering education to meet the demands of new technologies and missions of society; thus, the space age created the need for and implementation of graduate programs in aeronautics and astronautics (Dryden, 1965), and the development of atomic energy resulted in the development of nuclear-engineering curricula (American Nuclear Society, 1960–1962). Similar examples can be noted in such fields as bioengineering (Arthur, 1964), systems engineering, and environmental engineering (Fisher, 1967). Engineering and science, in administering to the needs of society, also create problems and issues of local, regional, national, and international concern; e.g., the development of the automobile has resulted in higher traffic-death rates, air pollution, etc. The identification of these needs (Engineers Joint Council, 1963) and problems (Engineers Joint Council, 1964) has become increasingly important in engineering educational planning. As a result of these trends, engineering education is witnessing two important changes: (1) an extension of the formal educational program downward to include two-, three-, and four-year engineering technician-technology programs (McGraw, 1962) and upward to include master's, doctoral, and postdoctoral programs (Pettit & Gere, 1963) and (2) a rapid increase in the continuing-education program in engineering schools (Ferdinand, 1966; Engineering College Administrative Council–Relations with Industry Feedback Committee, 1965).

PROBLEMS. The accelerating pace and role of science and technology in the United States and throughout the world has resulted in a rapid increase in the demand for professionally trained personnel, including engineers, scientists, and technicians. Engineering education has continually attempted to supply a wide spectrum of talented graduates, including those demanded by various industries (aerospace, chemical, electrical) and governmental agencies (federal and state) for various functions (research, development, design, production, etc.) and at various levels (associate, B.S., M.S., and Ph.D. degrees). In addition, with experience, engineering graduates frequently assume managerial responsibilities often only tangentially related to science, engineering, and technology. As a result, the ratio of engineers to the total work force has increased at a very rapid rate. In

1900, for example, there were almost 1,000 workers in the United States for each engineer; by 1940 there were 200 workers per engineer; and the 1960 census figures indicate that there are fewer than 100 workers in the United States work force per engineer and, in the male work force, about 50 workers per engineer (U.S. Bureau of the Census, 1961–1964). This demand for engineering personnel, coupled with the increasing competition for talented students, constitutes one of the major problems in engineering education.

Although entry into engineering positions is not limited to those graduating from engineering educational programs, this has increasingly become the common route. A related development influencing engineering education has been the increasing importance of precollege preparation in mathematics and science and the increasing difficulty of the academic program (Tribus, 1965). Hence, engineering education has found itself in a position where there are increasing quantitative demands for engineers in both number and proportion and at the same time an increasing demand for quality preparation before, during, and after college. To meet these needs, engineering educational institutions, technical institutes, and community colleges have developed a wide spectrum of programs to meet the demands of society for technicians, technologists, and engineers. In addition, other post–high school institutions have taken an increasingly important role in providing technical and scientific education for society; business schools provide programs in production control; liberal arts colleges offer mathematics and computer and applied science programs; and state colleges, technical institutes and community colleges provide applied science, technology, and technician programs. As a result, the need for engineering and engineering-related training and education is being met by a wide range of institutions, programs, and philosophies. The amorphous nature of scientific, engineering, and technological education has created internal and external pressures for quality and jurisdictional control which constitute one of the major problems in engineering education.

Engineering educators have faced the dual problem, not unlike that in other professions, of providing both breadth and depth within their programs. Unlike many other professions, such as law and medicine, engineering has chosen to integrate general education and professional or specialized education rather than to demand a preprofessional general education, e.g., premedicine and prelaw, to be followed by a formal education. However, the dual demand for breadth and depth has created many additional and perennial problems for engineering education. At every level, from freshman to doctoral, there is the problem of determining the proper balance between professional education and general education. As a result, a multiplicity of programs and philosophies have emerged which have created a form of diversity which is variously viewed with delight, indifference, and despair. Some institutions have continued to diversify or fragmentize by introducing new programs, such as nuclear engineering, bioengineering, engineering science, and aerospace engineering, while others have eliminated undergraduate options, such as communications and electronics. Still others have eliminated specialization by providing a unified core or a flexible elective type of engineering program (Boelter, 1962).

To provide for greater breadth and depth many institutions have substantially increased the nonengineering content of the undergraduate curriculum to include more mathematics and science as well as more courses in communications, humanities, and social science. In addition, the demands to reduce the baccalaureate load to more closely approximate the 120 semester-hour load required by other bachelor's-degree programs have further reduced the engineering and applied content of undergraduate engineering education. The fact of the declining applied content of engineering education has been faced with alarm, concern, indifference, and elation by the engineering profession and engineering education. At the graduate level the demands for more theory and depth have been met by the schools' demanding minors in mathematics and physical science and by incorporating these areas into graduate engineering courses; the demand for breadth has not generally been met by humanities, social science, or communications graduate-level course requirements but has more often manifested itself in the form of interdisciplinary studies and research projects, such as urban renewal, bioengineering linguistics–information theory, systems design, and international technical assistance programs. The dual demands for breadth and depth constitute another major problem facing engineering education, which runs the gamut of associate, bachelor, master, doctoral, and even postdoctoral programs.

The rapid increase in knowledge coupled with the declining period of time between discovery and its application have created an almost unprecedented demand for continuing education. Major conferences have been held on technical obsolescence. Credit and noncredit courses have been developed. On-campus and off-campus centers have been constructed, in-house training programs as well as special graduate curricula have been organized or expanded. This demand for contemporary knowledge of new discoveries, developments, and methodologies represents another major problem facing engineering education (Knowles, 1967).

Engineering education has tried, like many of the other scientifically related disciplines, to be a part of two somewhat different worlds, the professional or practitioners' world and the intellectual or academic world. Faculty members, administrators, and the students have many opportunities through consultations, professional meetings, and cooperative summer work programs to associate with engineers in private practice, industry, and government and at the same time have relatively close contact with their academic colleagues through faculty committees, graduate councils, joint-facility research centers, etc. As a result, engineering educators find themselves divided between the pragmatic and professional demands of industry and government, on the one hand, and the theoretical and academic demands of their colleagues in higher education, on the other hand. This represents another major problem for engineering education.

SELECTION OF STUDENTS. Many studies in engineering education and higher education have focused on the recruitment and career-selection process of engineering students. The primary reasons and influences cited by students for studying engineering include subjects taken in high school, especially mathematics and science, interest and aptitude tests, work experience, family (especially father), hobbies, vocational-educational literature, school counselors, and engineers (Case & others, 1967; LeBold & others, 1966; Perrucci & LeBold, 1967). Engineering is characterized by a wide spectrum of individuals including a relatively high proportion of high-ability first-generation college males whose fathers are skilled and semiskilled workers (Flanagan, 1964; Davis, 1963).

Supply and Demand. The critical role of engineering and scientific manpower in establishing and achieving national goals, such as space exploration, defense, and industrialization, has resulted in a general interest and concern regarding engineering enrollments, attrition, and graduation rates. The supply and demand for engineering manpower is studied on a continuing basis by the Engineering Manpower Commission (Alden, 1967) and periodically by the National Science Foundation (1963) and the Bureau of Labor Statistics. Enrollment and degree data in engineering are published annually in the *Journal of Engineering Education* and periodically by the U.S. Office of Education and the American Council on Education.

Several national studies have been conducted in regard to engineering enrollments (Griffin & others, 1965) and attrition (Bronwell, 1963). Engineering accounts for a substantial number and proportion of the male undergraduate and graduate students in the United States. In the fall of 1965, for example, engineering majors accounted for 79,872 new students, or 13 percent of the male freshmen; 253,412, or 9 percent, of the male undergraduate students; and 58,155, or 14 percent of the male graduate students in colleges and universities offering four or more years of college-level work. The number and proportion of college degrees awarded males in engineering has also been large. In 1964–65, 36,552, or 11 percent, of the bachelor's degrees; 11,889, or 16 percent, of the master's degrees; and 2,092, or 14 percent, of the doctor's degrees awarded in the United States were in engineering. On the other hand, engineering has attracted only a very small number and proportion of women; e.g., in 1964–65 there were only 2,147 women enrolled in engineering, or 0.1 percent of the total women in college (American Council on Education, 1967). The heavy academic loads (American Society for Engineering Education, 1967) and relatively high level of mathematics, science, and engineering content contribute to the relatively high rate of attrition in engineering. Although recent studies indicate that the rate of attrition in engineering is relatively high but comparable to that in mathematics, physical science, and premedicine (Nichols, 1964) this has not always been true. Iffert's studies of retention and withdrawal of college students (1958) indicated that 61 percent of the engineering students who entered college in 1950 had not changed their interests when queried four years later, compared to only 20 percent in mathematics and biology, 21 percent in chemistry, and 28 percent each in physics and prelaw. Davis (1963), in contrast, studying 1961 college seniors in a representative national study, found a net loss of 41 percent of those who as freshmen selected engineering, compared to a loss of 13 percent in physical science and 43 percent in medicine and net gains of 48 percent in business and 54 percent in social science.

Ability and Achievement. Engineering has generally attracted a large number and proportion of college males of above-average ability and achievement (Wolfle, 1954). Like most males, engineering students generally have higher abilities and achievements in the quantitative and physical-science areas than in the verbal areas and the humanities.

Project Talent (Flanagan, 1964) data indicated that 25 percent of the male high school seniors scoring in the upper 2 percent of the aptitude battery were enrolled the following year in engineering programs, compared to only 9 percent in the lowest 25 percent on the same battery. National Merit Scholarship data has also indicated that engineering has attracted between 15 and 30 percent of the male National Merit Scholars and semifinalists, yet only 10 percent of the entering male college students are enrolled in engineering, However, the National Merit Scholarship studies have also indicated that male National Merit scholars in engineering and physical science are more likely to transfer to other fields than are Merit scholars who begin in other fields (Nichols, 1964).

Johnson (1951), LeBold (1958), and McCampbell (1966) have reviewed academic-prediction studies in engineering which used cognitive and noncognitive data. Cognitive studies have generally resulted in individual correlations of about .3 to .5, and multiple correlations of .5 to .7 are fairly common, with high school rank being most frequently reported as the best single predictor and some combination of high school rank and verbal ability and quantitative and scientific achievements for prediction of academic performance after one year. However, after a semester or more in school, previous college achievement is perhaps the best predictor. Baker (1955) reported a correlation of .9 between first- and second-semester grades for Purdue University engineering freshmen.

Noncognitive Characteristics. Studies using noncognitive data have been generally less successful in predicting academic performance than those using cognitive data. Although modest positive and negative correlations of .2 to .4 have frequently been reported, demographic, interest, value and personality measures are usually correlated with other cognitive predictors and as a result do not make unique contributions. However, such studies have provided considerable information regarding engineering students. Lundy (1961) studied over 120 noncognitive variables including the Strong Vocational Interest Blank, the Edwards Personal Preference Schedule, the Stern Activities Index, the Inventory of Beliefs, the Allport-Vernon-Lindzey Study of Values, the Brown-Holtzman Survey of Study Habits and Attitudes, and Personal Values; the only variable correlating higher than .33 with achievement was the psychologist scale (.34) on the Strong.

Harrington (1965) and Salvo (1967) indicate positive changes in personality and interest during college, and Benjamin (1967) noted similar changes 30 years after college for engineering students. Davis (1963) and Rosenberg (1957) found that engineering students stress originality and tangible rewards and a preference for working with people rather than with things. Trent and Rayle (1965) and MacKinnon (1961), using largely noncognitive data—e.g., interests, values, and personality measures—questioned the intellectual and creative talents sometimes attributed to engineering students.

Bereiter and Freedman (Sanford, 1962), in their review of fields of study and the people in them, summarize the complexity of the problems as follows: "Liberalism is usually found to have a positive correlation with intelligence, but the ordering of groups on liberalism is clearly different from the ordering on general intelligence. Engineering is the most extreme case in point, regularly ranking among the first in intelligence and the last in liberalism."

ENGINEERING CURRICULA. Undergraduate engineering curricula have evolved to meet a variety of objectives including those of (1) providing a broad general education which includes mathematics, science, communications, humanities, and social science, (2) providing sufficient applied, practical, or professional content to enable the graduate to begin work immediately after graduation, (3) enabling students to continue their formal education in graduate or professional schools, (4) providing sufficient specialization to meet the diverse needs of various industries and forms of local, state, and national government, and (5) providing the student with information on current problems, methods, and developments which will enable him to accept responsibility and leadership in his postcollege activities. Engineering curricula began with a very practical job-related activity. Students spent a considerable amount of time in the late nineteenth century working on drawingboards, designing machines, structure processes, etc., and they frequently built these devices in laboratories or shops or on the job. This practical education was supplemented with classical or formal courses in rhetoric, mathematics, physics, chemistry, economics, and foreign languages. The academic loads were heavy, and the number of hours in class, in the laboratory, on the board, and in the shops were great. The rapid developments in the physical sciences and the pressures to meet the diverse needs of expanding industry and government services resulted in increased demands. As a result, engineering curricula became overloaded; loads of 170–200 semester hours were not uncommon in the 1920–1930 period for four-year bachelor's degrees. The growing importance of graduate education, on-the-job training, and continuing education caused engineering schools to reexamine their objectives and content. Less emphasis was placed on attempting to accomplish all things in a four-year period. Today, curricula are still designed to provide a broad general education and some applied professional education. Contemporary undergraduate engineering curricula are about equally divided between nonengineering and engineering content. The nonengineering content consists of about one course each semester in communications, social science, or humanities and, in addition, courses in mathematics, usually including the calculus, differential equations, and probability and statistics; courses in chemistry, including at least an introduction to physical chemistry; and courses in physics, including mechanics, heat, electricity and magnetism, and modern physics. The engineering content is about equally divided between engineering science and engineering analysis, synthesis, and design. Engineering science is concerned with the theoretical study of manmade systems. Engineering science includes the mechanics of solids, electric circuits and fields, thermodynamics, heat and mass transfer, information theory, fluid mechanics, and properties of materials. Engineering design and research are concerned with the developments of systematic techniques for optimally meeting the needs of society. Although the physical aspects are usually stressed in most engineering colleges, specialization is provided by combining the study in depth of the engineering science closely related to a field of application, e.g., electric circuits and fields in electrical engineering. Rosenstein (Kreith, 1964) and his colleagues developed a technique of curriculum synthesis as part of a national study of honor's programs in engineering and in conjunction with an educational-development program (Rosenstein, 1964). Design would seem to be the unique characteristic of engineering curricula (Everitt, 1951; Whinnery, 1965; Krick, 1965; Wilson, 1965).

Although there is some question about the extent to which engineers have a broad general education, there have been few comparative studies. Gatewood (1967), Dillenbeck (1961), and Downie (1950) compared undergraduate engineering students with social science and humanities majors, education students, and other college majors, respectively; general educational achievements of engineering students were found to be equal to or higher than those of students in other disciplines, but examination of subscore data indicated below-average achievement in the humanities and fine arts, average to above-average achievement in social science, and above-average performance in mathematics, physical science, and knowledge of current events.

COMPARATIVE ENGINEERING EDUCATION. As noted initially, undergraduate engineering education traces its historical roots to the system developed in Europe for training and educating engineers and artisans for military and civilian purposes. Wickenden and others (1930), in their investigation of engineering education in the late 1920's, devoted a major portion of their final report to describing the European system. Russia and the United States after World War II encouraged many refugee engineers and scientists to come to their respective countries to do research and development in rocketry, nuclear energy, and other disciplines. The United States and Russia sent exchange missions in 1955-56 to study engineering education (Tryten, 1955; Lindvall & others 1959). The United States and various western European countries sponsored a comparative study of their engineering education systems in 1948, 1953, 1957, and 1962 (Conference of Engineering Societies of Western Europe and the United States of America, 1960). The critical role of technological, scientific, and engineering education in underdeveloped and developing nations has also provided important information of a comparative nature. American engineering educational institutions have sponsored programs in South and Central America, Africa, and Asia designed to improve and enhance the engineering educational systems in these countries. Many of these countries send students and faculty to the United States for graduate study. In 1963, about 17 percent of the graduate students in engineering in the United States were foreign students (25 percent of the full-timers, but only 7 percent of the part-timers) (American Society for Engineering Education, 1968).

In 1964 the first World Congress on Engineering Education was held in Chicago; over 38 nations and 200 individuals from outside the United States participated (Morgen, 1966). It is anticipated that the international exchange of students, faculty, and engineers will continue to increase as communications, transportation, and world resources improve.

William K. LeBold
Purdue University

References

Alden, John D. *Demand for Engineers and Engineering Technicians.* Engineering Manpower Commission, Engineers Joint Council, 1967.
American Council on Education. *A Fact Book on Higher Education.* ACE, 1967.
American Engineer. "What Kind of Engineers Will Engineering Education Produce for the Year 2000?" 37:47-50; 1967.
American Nuclear Society. *Report on Objective Criteria in Nuclear Engineering Education.* American Society for Engineering Education, 1960-1962.
American Society for Engineering Education, Goals of Engineering Education Committee. *The Preliminary Report.* The Society, 1965.
American Society for Engineering Education, Goals of Engineering Education Committee. *Interim Report.* The Society, 1967. p. 30.
American Society for Engineering Education, Goals of Engineering Education Committee. "Final Report of the Committee on Goals of Engineering Education." *J Engineering Ed* 58:372-446; 1968.
Arthur, Robert M. "Bioengineering." *BioSci* 14:29-30; 1964.
Baker, Paul Cleo, II. "Experiments in Variable Selection for Prediction of Academic Achievement." Doctoral dissertation. Purdue U, 1955.
Benjamin, Darrell Raymond. "A Thirty-one-year Longitudinal Study of Engineering Students' Interest Profiles and Career Patterns." Doctoral dissertation. Purdue U, 1967.
Bode, H. W. "The Future of Engineering Mathematics." *J Engineering Ed* 52:189-99; 1961.
Boelter, L. M. K. *2nd Annual Report, 1961-62, of the Educational Development Committee.* U California, 1962.
Bronwell, A. B. (Chairman) *Engineering Student Attrition.* Engineers Joint Council, 1963.
Burchard, John Eli. *Mid-century.* M.I.T. Press, 1949.
Case, H. W., and others. *The California Bachelor of Science Engineering Graduate.* Educational Development Program Report No. 10-64. College of Engineering, U California, Los Angeles, 1967.
Case Institute of Technology, Stanford University, Purdue University, Committee on Survey. "Survey of Statistical Training for Engineering in 1963-64." The Committee, 1965.
Churchill, S. "Controversial American Society for Engineering Education Report Emerges Under Fire." *Chemical Engineering Progress* 61:40-3; 1965.
Conference of Engineering Societies of Western Europe and the United States of America. *Report on Education and Training of Professional Engineers,* Vols. 1-3. The Conference, 1960.
Davis, James A. *Great Aspirations.* NORC, 1963.
Dillenbeck, Harold Ladd. "Educational Administration." Masters thesis. Pennsylvania State U, 1961.
Downie, N. M. "The Knowledge of General Education of a Sample of Syracuse University Students as Revealed by the Cooperative General Culture Test and the *Time* Magazine Current Affairs Test." *Ed Psychol Meas* 10:294-306; 1950.
Dryden, Hugh L. "The University and the Exploration of Space." *Sci* 150:1129-33; 1965.
Eells, Walter Crosby, and Haswell, Harold A. *Academic Degrees.* GPO, 1961.
Engineering College Administrative Council-Relations with Industry Feedback Committee. *Education in Industry.* American Society for Engineering Education, 1965.
Engineers' Council for Professional Development. *Annual Report.* The Council, 1937.
Engineers Joint Council. *The Nation's Engineering Research Needs 1965-1985.* The Council, 1963.
Engineers Joint Council. *National Engineering Problems.* The Council, 1964.
Everitt, W. L. "Education for Action." *J Engineering Ed* 42:195-9; 1951.
Ferdinand, Theodore N. "On the Obsolescence of Scientists and Engineers." *Am Sci* 54:46-56; 1966.

Finch, James K. *Engineering and Western Civilization.* McGraw-Hill, 1951.

Fisher, Gordon P. "Systems Engineering and the Human Environment." *Engineering Cornell Q* 2: 30; 1967.

Flanagan, John C. *The American High School Student.* U Pittsburgh Press, 1964. p. 5–59.

Flexner, A. A. *Medical Education in America.* Carnegie, 1910.

Foecke, Harold A. "Engineering Faculty Development and Utilization." *J Engineering Ed* 50:757–828; 1960.

Foecke, Harold A., and Tolliver, Wayne E. "Engineering Enrollments and Degrees in Institutions with ECPD-accredited Curriculums." *J Engineering Ed* 53:354–77; 1963.

Gatewood, Robert Donn. "An Investigation of the General Academic Achievement of Engineering, Social Science, and Humanities Seniors at Purdue University." Masters thesis. Purdue U, 1967.

Granger, Frank. *Vitruvias on Architecture,* Vol. 1. Harvard U Press, 1945.

Griffin, Marvin A., and others. *Factors Influencing Engineering Enrollment.* American Society for Engineering Education, 1965.

Grinter, L. E., and others. "Report on Evaluation of Engineering Education (1952–55)." *J Engineering Ed* 46:25–63; 1955.

Gullette, Bardell, and others. "General Education in Engineering." *J Engineering Ed* 46:632–3; 1956.

Hammond, Harry, and others. "Report of the Committee on Aims and Goals of Engineering Curricula." *J Engineering Ed* 31:279–357; 1940.

Hammond, Harry, and others. "Engineering Education, After the War." *J Engineering Ed* 14:589–614; 1944.

Harrington, Thomas Francis, Jr. "The Interrelation of Personality Variables and College Experiences of Engineering Students over a Four Year Span." Doctoral dissertation, 1965.

Hollomon, Herbert. "Literate Engineering." *Saturday R* July 1:40–1; 1967.

Iffert, R. E. *Retension and Withdrawal of College Students.* USOE, 1958.

Jackson, Dugland C. *Present Status and Trends of Engineering Education in the United States.* Engineering Council for Professional Development, 1939.

John, W. C., and Hammond, H. P. *Graduate Work in Engineering in Universities and Colleges in the United States.* GPO, 1936. 1p.

Johnson, A. P. "Tests and Testing Programs of Interest to Engineering Educators." *J Engineering Ed* 41:277–83; 1951.

Knowles, Asa S. "Continuing Education: Fastest Growing Dimension in Higher Education." *J Engineering Ed* 57:555–7; 1967.

Kraybill, E. K. "Evaluative Study of Summer Institute on Effective Teaching for Engineering Teachers." Doctoral dissertation. U Michigan, 1966.

Kreith, Frank. *Honors Programs in Engineering.* Allyn and Bacon, 1964.

Krick, E. V. *An Introduction to Engineering and Engineering Design.* Wiley, 1965. 116p.

Lancaster, Otis E. "The ASEE–Penn. State Summer Institute on Effective Teaching for Engineering Teachers." *J Engineering Ed* 58:127–31; 1967.

LeBold, William K. "Intellectual and Nonintellectual Factors Involved in Predicting Engineering Success." *J Engineering Ed* 48:514–19; 1958.

LeBold, William K., and others. "The Engineer in Industry and Government." *J Engineering Ed* 56:237–74; 1966.

LeBold, William K., and others. "Reactions to the Preliminary Report of the Goals Study." *J Engineering Ed* 57:437–44; 1967.

Lindvall, F. C., and others. "Final Report of the ASEE Engineering Education Exchange Mission to the Soviet Union." *J Engineering Ed* 49:839–911; 1959.

Lundy, Robert Lee. "Intellectual and Non-intellectual Factors Involved in the College Performance of Engineering Students." Doctoral dissertation. Purdue U, 1961.

MacKinnon, Donald W. "Fostering Creativity in Students of Engineering." *J Engineering Ed* 52:129–.42; 1961.

Mann, Charles. *A Study of Engineering Education.* Carnegie, 1918.

Mathematical Association of America, Committee on the Undergraduate Program in Mathematics. *Mathematical Engineering—A Five Year Program.* The Association, 1966.

McCampbell, Molly Kelly. *Differentiation of Engineers' Interests.* U Kansas, 1966.

McGraw, J. L. *Characteristics of Excellence in Engineering Technology Education.* American Society for Engineering Education, 1962.

Morgan, Ralph A. "World Congress on Engineering Education." *J Engineering Ed* 57:99–100; 1966.

Morrill, Justin S. *The Land Grant Act.* U.S. Congress, 1862.

National Center for Educational Statistics. "Engineering Degrees 1965–66." *J Engineering Ed* 58:43–66; 1967.

National Science Foundation. *Scientists, Engineers and Technicians in the 1960's, Requirements and Supply.* NSF, 1963. p. 34–6.

Newcomer, Mabel, and Market Statistics, Incorporated. *The Big Business Executive/1964.* Scientific American, 1965.

Nichols, R. C. "Career Decisions of Very Able Students. *Sci* 144:1315–9; 1964.

Perrucci, C. C., and LeBold, W. K. *The Engineer and Scientist: Student, Professional, Citizen.* Purdue U, 1967.

Pettit, Joseph M., and Gere, James M. "Evolution of Graduate Education in Engineering." *J Engineering Ed* 54:57–62; 1963.

Rensselaer Polytechnic Institute. *Long Range Planning for Engineering Education.* The Institute, 1963.

Rosenberg, M. *Occupations and Values.* Free, 1957.

Rosenstein, Allen B. *Educational Development Committee Third Annual Report.* U California, 1964.

Rukeyser, M. *Willard Gibbs.* Doubleday, 1942. 136p.

Salvo, Vincent J. "Uniformity and Diversity Among

College Students: Subcultural Membership of Engineering Students. Master's thesis. Purdue U, 1967.
Sanford, Nevitt. *The American College*. Wiley, 1962.
Saville, Thorndike. "Achievements in Engineering Education." *J Engineering Ed* 43:231–3; 1952.
Trent, J. W., and Rayle, J. H. "Practicability and Creativity in Engineering and Liberal Arts." U California, 1965. (Unpublished paper.)
Tribus, Myron. *Secondary School Letter—The Unified Approach to Engineering Education*. Dartmouth Col, 1963.
Tribus, Myron. "The Next Steps in Engineering Education." *J Engineering Ed* 55:205–8; 1965.
Tryten, M. H. "Engineering Education in Russia." *J Engineering Ed* 45:389–95; 1955.
U.S. Bureau of the Census. *Census of Population*. GPO, 1961–1964.
Walker, Eric, and Nead, Benjamin. "An Interpretation by the Chairman, ASEE Goals Committee." *J Engineering Ed* 57:13–9; 1966.
Weber, E. *Continuing Engineering Studies*. Engineering Council for Professional Development, 1966. 112p.
Whinnery, John R. *The World of Engineering*. U California, 1965.
Wickenden, William E., and others. *Report of the Investigation of Engineering Education*. Society for the Promotion Engineering Education, 1930.
Wilson, W. E. *Concepts of Engineering Systems Design*. McGraw-Hill, 1965. 207p.
Wolfle, Dael. *America's Resources of Specialized Talent*. Harper, 1954.

ENGLISH COMPOSITION

SCOPE. Reflecting changes in curricula since the seventeenth century and disagreement over objectives in the first half of the twentieth century, the terminology of the field of English is confused. Some people still equate "English," "grammar," and "composition." Some distinguish between "creative writing" (meaning, for the most part, the writing of stories and poems) and "practical writing" (meaning the writing of reports, explanations, analyses, argument, letters, and the like), while others typically label as "creative writing" almost anything original which is longer than a sentence. "Grammar" has been used to refer to a stage in education ("the Latin grammar school"), to the study and writing of English compositions, to the parsing and diagramming of English sentences, and to the study (with or without application in original written composition) of syntax, usage, morphology, vocabulary, spelling, capitalization, punctuation, and even the handwriting or format of a written paper. The growing tendency, however, is to restrict the meaning of "grammar" to syntax and morphology, and that will be the meaning employed here, even if it is not the meaning used in all of the sources to which reference is made.

The teaching and learning of written composition, as distinct from speech, is the subject of this article. While they are obviously ingredients of written composition, handwriting and spelling seem to present unique problems in teaching and learning which merit their separate treatment. For convenience, vocabulary will receive consideration here to the extent that it is involved with writing, though vocabulary is also dealt with in discussions of reading. Grammar and usage will be treated only insofar as they become involved with the teaching and learning of written composition, even though English curricula increasingly are devoting attention to the history and nature of the English language as a liberal study in its own right. The teaching and learning of English as a second language (i.e., for people whose native language is one other than English) is considered in the article on modern languages.

This article, then, concerns the teaching and learning of written composition throughout the elementary, secondary, and college years. Rather than treating "creative writing" as something separate from other original writing, the article assumes that an element of creativity is involved in any writing which is not merely the copying of someone else's creation. While recognizing that in the last analysis clear distinctions cannot be made among the modes of discourse (exposition, argument, criticism, fiction, poetry, etc.), the article occasionally refers to one mode or another on the assumption that such distinctions are often useful in teaching and learning.

An understanding of English composition today depends upon an awareness of the many movements and conceptions of the past as well as of the research underlying present practice. Consequently, a large portion of this article is organized historically, but it refers to the documents—research or not—which have made the subject what it is today. After the historical sections, various aspects of English composition are discussed in the light of research and analysis particularly relevant today.

HISTORY TO 1900. In the early centuries, most young Americans who learned how to write English learned at home or were taught at neighborhood schools by people who had only a passing acquaintance with many areas of knowledge. During the latter half of the seventeenth century the "Latin grammar schools," the earliest institutions resembling our present secondary schools, offered Latin and Greek, not English, to boys who wished to prepare themselves for the early colleges, the curricula of which were entirely classical. But the spirit of the Reformation was strong in the new country, and editions of the Bible translated into English had become increasingly available. A preference for the English vernacular grew, perhaps being crystallized in England by the publication in 1693 of John Locke's *Some Thoughts Concerning Education* but certainly given most explicit form in the American colonies by Benjamin Franklin's "Proposals Relating to the Education of Youth in Philadelphia," which, in 1749, sponsored the development of a full vernacular program at the secondary level, including the teaching of English grammar and the cultivation of a clear and concise style:

> To form their Stile they should be put to writing Letters to each other, making Abstracts of what they read; or writing the same Things in their own Words: telling or writing Stories lately read, in their own Expressions. All to be revised and corrected by the Tutor, who should give his Reasons, and explain the Force and Import of Words, &c.

A number of private schools were teaching English by the middle 1750's, mostly in the middle colonies, following the lead of Franklin's Philadelphia Academy. The classics-bound New England private schools began adopting the innovation two decades later, after which the colleges and then the public schools followed Franklin's proposals, breaking the exclusive hold of the classics at the same time that the colonies were asserting their political independence (Lyman, 1922).

The teaching of English grew out of the teaching of Latin and was strongly influenced by the methods and rules used for instruction in Latin. Although grammar was often said at the time to be "the art of speaking and writing correctly," the pupils were to learn it by memorizing page after page of rules describing Latin grammar rather than English, by parsing sentences "according to strict Latin methods, and by correcting endless examples of false syntax." The most influential grammar textbooks of the day, using such methods and rules, were those of Lindley Murray, which sold more than a million copies in America during the first half of the nineteenth century and which were abridged or revised by others for perhaps another million copies. In the late 1830's and early 1840's, however, Henry Barnard and Horace Mann, leaders of the state school systems in Connecticut and Massachusetts, respectively, gave their strength to a reform movement which emphasized the importance of having pupils understand grammatical rules and apply them in sentence construction and composition, using oral instruction and blackboard work as well as textbook and pen (Lyman, 1922). Princeton had stipulated in 1819 that entering students be "well acquainted" with English grammar, and by 1870 most of the leading colleges had taken a similar stand. But the English grammar referred to in all these instances was Latin grammar superimposed on English, not a grammar developed from the description of English itself.

In 1869 Henry Barnard published a report which helps clarify the status of English at that time. Of the 30 leading city high school systems he surveyed throughout the nation, all reported some work in English: 28 offered rhetoric, 24 grammar, 24 composition, 21 English literature, 18 declamation, 8 etymology, and 5 English synonyms. These subjects were scattered through the high school years in an irregular manner, however; the same grammatical rules may have been memorized year after year, and in some schools rhetoric was little more than the memorizing of definitions of figures of speech, while composition and declamation achieved prominence mainly when the school had visitors (Hays, 1936).

Princeton again set a pattern in 1870 when it added to its grammar requirement the stipulation that candidates demonstrate their ability to write a "Short and Simple English Composition." In 1873 the University of Michigan instituted a requirement of familiarity with Hart's *Composition and Rhetoric.* But in 1874 Harvard College gave this trend a twist which had a sweeping influence on English instruction in the schools: it established the requirement that each candidate for admission "write a short English Composition, correct in spelling, punctuation, grammar, and expression, the subject to be taken from such works of standard authors as shall be announced from time to time" (Hays, 1936). The aim of the requirement may well have been to raise the level of secondary-school instruction in "correct" composition, but, though Harvard changed its list of standard works and authors from year to year, the college-preparatory schools and other secondary schools began to teach the literary works which tended to reappear on the lists issued by Harvard and the other colleges which adopted similar examinations. Ironically, the Harvard requirement seems to have been more instrumental in strengthening the teaching of literature in the secondary schools than in raising the level of instruction in composition. But the high school English teachers who wished their pupils to become familiar with the books listed were confronted with a welter of lists, each college having prepared its own. Groups of college and secondary-school representatives met to establish some uniformity in the book-list feature of the entrance examinations, and from a series of such meetings the National Conference on Uniform Entrance Requirements in English was founded in 1893, fulfilling its function on a national basis (Hays, 1936).

By 1900 most high schools had established some regular course of instruction in English, though, according to Hays (1936), it tended to be "unorganized, and sadly lacking in specific aims and methods."

> Literature was prescribed in order to provide a source for composition material . . . was dissected and analyzed, not for the sake of literature, but in the vain hope that the composition ability of pupils would somehow improve. The college entrance requirements stressed composition; but, strangely enough, the schools stressed literature and textbook rhetoric. . . . Composition underwent a change in subject matter from vague generalities or morals to artificial essays on literary topics.

In the colleges, on the other hand, the courses in freshman composition which had been established in recent years were, according to Kitzhaber (1953), losing their status because the college entrance examinations reduced rhetorical theory and practice to "little more than paragraph construction; . . . Unity, Coherence, and Emphasis; and the 'Four Forms of Discourse.'"

OBJECTIVES AND CURRICULUM: 1900–1935. Although the colleges may not have intended to dictate the nature of the secondary-school English curriculum, college entrance examinations had that effect. Reaction to the effect built up early in the twentieth century, spurred by the increasing proportion of adolescents attending the secondary school who were not going to enter college. The reaction played a strong part in the establishment of the National Council of Teachers of English (NCTE) in 1911. One of its founders, James F. Hosic, chaired a National Joint Committee on English (representing the NCTE and the National Education Association) which faced these two questions: "Do the college-entrance requirements in English, as at present administered, foster the best kind of English work in the high schools? If not, what changes should be made?" The answer of the Committee, published in 1917 as *Reorganization of English in Secondary Schools* (Hosic, 1917), established a new conception of English teaching, as the following quotations illustrate:

> 1. The college preparatory function of the high school is a minor one. Most of the graduates of the high school go, not into a higher institution, but into "life." Hence the course in English should be organized with reference to basic personal and social needs rather than with reference to college-entrance requirements . . . .
>
> 2. The chief problem of articulation is not how to connect the high school and the college but how to connect the high school with the elementary school. . . . [To this end, the committee included subcommittees on grades 7, 8, and 9 as well as subcommittees on grades 10, 11, and 12.]
>
> 5. It is a mistake to regard English as merely a formal subject. The implication of such a view is that skill is the sole end sought and that this may be attained by drills upon technique quite apart from an interesting or valuable content. . . . The content of both literature and composition is, first of all, the body of fact, interpretation, and imaginative conception to be expressed, and second, that small body of principles of technique the consciousness of which actually enables children and young people to improve their use of the vernacular.
>
> 6. Nor is English a subject that can be finished by dint of intense application on essentials in the early years of the high school, to be relegated thereafter to the place of an optional study. . . . the relation of language to the expanding life is so close and intimate that to drop the systematic practice of speaking, writing, and reading at any point in the school program would be like ceasing to exercise or to take food. English is unique in its relation to mental development and to the constant enlivening and reorganization of the pupil's whole life experience on ever-higher planes, with ever-widening horizons. Only so much technique should be taught at any one time as pupils can actually use or profit by.
>
> 7. English must be regarded as social in content and social in method of acquirement. The chief function of language is communication. Hence the activities of the English program must provide for actual communication. The pupil must speak or write to or for somebody, with a consciously conceived purpose to inform, convince, inspire, or entertain. . . .
>
> 8. . . . The English course should be so arranged as to couple speaking and writing for practical purposes with reading of the same character, and speaking and writing for pleasure and inspiration with the study of the novelists, the playwrights, and the poets.
>
> 9. Such a form of organization will make possible that cooperation of all teachers in establishing good habits of thought and of expression without which they are rarely attained . . . such observance of good usage, such thinking out of intellectual problems, such organizing of bodies of ideas, and such clothing of ideas in appropriate language as the instruction of the English teacher had made possible.

Hosic's statement further called for English classes that were reasonably limited both in size and in number per teacher, a library and reading room stocked generously with books "adapted to the needs of the pupils" and in the charge of a trained teacher-librarian, office equipment and visual aids, and professionally trained teachers rather than "the novice and the itinerant." (Hosic, 1917). Thus, the report viewed the objectives, content, methods, equipment, and teachers of English in a comprehensive, progressive manner. Subsequent developments in English may be seen, first, as results of the report and later, at least in part, as reactions to some of those results. One immediate result, even before final publication of the report, was that the National Conference on Uniform Entrance Requirements in English voted in 1911 to offer, alongside the existing "restricted" examination, a "comprehensive" examination which did not demand a familiarity with a prescribed list of literary works. (In 1931 the conference terminated itself, turning over its function to the College Entrance Examination Board [CEEB], which had existed since 1900.)

The suggestions of the Hosic report had their effect on the English classroom in an uneven manner. When Lyman (1929) summarized a number of recent investigations relating to the curriculum in language and composition, he found that the "criterion of 'social utility' for the various activities composing the English curriculum" was receiving more emphasis than it had but that the emphasis had been limited largely to matters of correctness. Grammar drill, he observed, was still the most common language work in the junior high school grades, though some of the emphasis was shifting from a classification to a functional approach toward grammar. Most damning was his conclusion that the aims of English instruction were "as yet vague, uncertain, and far from agreed upon."

Later in the year in which Lyman's summary

appeared, the NCTE created the Curriculum Commission under the chairmanship of W. Wilbur Hatfield to build an illustrative English course of study, to provide a pattern which local schools could use in building their own curricula. Published in 1935 as *An Experience Curriculum in English,* the Hatfield report went beyond the Hosic report in considering instruction in English from the kindergarten up. The Hatfield curriculum continued the Hosic emphasis on personal and social needs but more explicitly took its cue from the philosophy of John Dewey by dividing each major phase of English into "experience strands," each of which was "essentially a series of similar types of experience gradually increasing in scope and difficulty" and running vertically through the elementary or secondary level or both. Following the lead of the Hosic report, the *Experience Curriculum* separated its strands on "creative expression" from those on "communication." The strands of writing experiences from the communication sequence were as follows:

Kindergarten–Grade 6

Strand A. Social Letters
Strand B. Business Letters
Strand C. Blank Forms
Strand D. Labels, Titles, and Signs
Strand E. Announcements, Notices, and Advertisements
Strand F. Memoranda; Rules, Recipes, and Directions; Records, Notes, and Diaries
Strand G. Reports, Reviews, Summaries, and Outlines
Strand H. Bibliographies, Indexes, Tables of Contents, and Title Pages

Grades 7–12

Strand A. Social Letters
Strand B. Business Letters
Strand C. News Stories
Strand D. Reports
Strand E. Opinions

A third of the report consisted of suggested experiences, like the following, taken from the strand on written reports:

8. *Social Objective:* To answer a discussion question in a letter or in an examination.
Enabling Objectives: To state the theme or main point clearly and simply. To back this up by proof, by illustration, by quotation. To point out fallacies in arguments. To enumerate where that is effective. To mark suppositions and wishes by the use of subjunctive verb forms (I.G.U. 22, 23).

At the end of the suggested experiences for each strand, there was a summary of desirable techniques, both "social techniques" (e.g., "To detect fallacies and to evaluate opinions") and "language techniques" (e.g., "To employ, for conciseness, smoothness, clarity, and emphasis, the following structural devices: *a.* Participial and adjective prepositional phrases . . ." and "To employ, for ease, variety, economy, and emphasis, the following rhetorical devices: . . . *g.* Subjunctive verbs to mark suppositions, hopes, or wishes"). The "I.G.U." at the end of the suggested experience quoted above refers to a section of the report on "instrumental grammar units," one of those referred to above being quoted here from the material for grades 7–12:

23. *Primary Objective:* To reinforce the subjunctive implication of the conditional clause with a subjunctive in the conclusion.
Enabling Objectives: To see that *would have answered* in *If he had heard me, he would have answered* implies that he did not answer, and to apply the term subjunctive to it also. To see that the conclusions of contrary-to-fact present conditions usually have *would, could,* or *should* verb phrases and the conclusions of contrary-to-fact past conditions usually have *would have, could have,* or *should have* verbs.

Thus *An Experience Curriculum,* while containing much more material on grammar than had been in the Hosic report, tried to reduce the traditional emphasis on grammatical terminology and classification in favor of a "thought approach," evidence for the superiority of which was soon offered by Frogner (1939).

Furthermore, the Hatfield report continued the emphasis of the Hosic report on "functional grammar," attempting to include only those elements of grammar which posed difficulties in the language of pupils and adults. Studies like Stormzand and O'Shea's (1924) and Thorndike's (Thorndike & others, 1927) had counted the frequency with which certain grammatical problems appeared in contemporary writing. Others—many of which are listed in Lyman's bibliography (1929)—relied merely on surveys of opinion to determine which items to count as errors. Many used source material of various modes of written discourse, though Seegers (1933) has shown that sentence structure tends to vary among exposition, argument, narration, and description. And most of these investigators winnowed their items from the conventional Latinate grammar textbooks of their day, counting as errors such constructions as "I will see you later" and "It's me." But the Hatfield report declared its independence from "the tradition of authority, based upon the classics of literature and the rules of grammarians," and built upon the doctrine of usage enunciated by Hall (1917), Leonard (1929, 1932), and Pooley (1930, 1933), translated into practical methodology by Symonds (1931) and Cutright (1934), and developed into a curricular pattern by O'Rourke (1934). In a major section entitled "Corrective Teaching," the Hatfield curriculum included a chapter on usage which espoused a definition of good English, taken from Pooley (1933), as that which is "appropriate to the purpose of the speaker, true to the language as it is, and comfortable to speaker and listener. It is the product of custom neither cramped by rule nor freed from all restraint;

it is never fixed, but changes with the organic life of the language." While advising that teachers observe the speech and writing of their pupils to determine which pupils need drill on which errors, the report listed 45 forms to be mastered from kindergarten to grade 6 and 57 in grades 7–12.

The increased attention to grammar and usage in the Hatfield report undoubtedly reflected the situation rather than caused it, but surveys by Dora V. Smith (1938) and others showed that more time was being devoted to grammar and usage in American high schools than to any other phase of instruction. In view of the continued tendency to justify grammar teaching as an aid in improving composition, it is remarkable and ironic to see that, from the studies of Hoyt (1906) and Briggs (1913) through many others which preceded publication of the Hatfield report, almost no researcher has discovered any more correlation between knowledge of traditional grammar and quality of composition than would be found, for example, between grammar and geography. Summaries of such studies may be found in the works by Lyman (1929) and Meckel (1963).

INFLUENCES ON THE CURRICULUM: 1935–1965. Perhaps partly as a reaction to the previously described situation as well as to the struggle between ideologies which marked the depression years in America, several new emphases appeared, after publication of the Hatfield report, which had some effect on the composition and reading instruction of English teachers who rejected formal instruction in grammar. Working from the scholarly works of Ogden and Richards (1923) and Korzybski (1933), other authors brought out popular interpretations of general semantics which were read by many English teachers and applied in their classrooms. Chase (1938), Hayakawa (1941), and Lee (1941) were the most widely read, Hayakawa's in some high schools and more colleges through several editions, and Minteer's (1953) in junior and senior high schools. Related to the emphasis on general semantics was the interest which developed in propaganda analysis, seen more in reading instruction than in writing but useful as a basis for composition topics, especially as the subject developed in relation to the mass media of communication. Numerous studies of propaganda analysis had been published after the propaganda efforts of World War I had been exposed in the 1920's, but probably the first item to reach English teachers in any numbers was a brief article credited to the Institute for Propaganda Analysis (1937). Soon some were using Dale's text (1941) in their English or journalism classes or drawing ideas from collections of articles, like the one edited by Waples (1942).

The mass media and semantics each had a chapter of its own, while composition shared a chapter with speech in the first volume of the latest curriculum series published by the NCTE (National Council of Teachers of English, Commission on the English Curriculum, 1952, 1954, 1956, 1963; Gerber, 1965). The conception of composition in the first three volumes was not basically different from what it was in the Hatfield report. Influenced by such publications as those of Watts (1944) and Strickland (1947), the new curriculum series placed even more emphasis than the Hatfield report on the relationship of writing to the capacities and interests of growing children. Continuing a trend which had been noted twenty years earlier (D. Smith, 1933) and which had begun to develop a body of research (Artley, 1950), the new NCTE series struck out more boldly for interrelating the various aspects of "the language arts," which was now so key a phrase that it was made part of the titles of the first three volumes in the series. The emphasis on child development and individualization of instruction had made the idea of "minimum essentials" in achievement for each grade level even more unpopular than it had been in the 1930's, so the new series did not have the lists of assignments and "techniques" for the elementary and secondary levels which the Hatfield report had had. In short, the new series seemed more to present a discussion of the principles of a curriculum in composition than a blueprint for one.

The treatment of grammar and usage in the new series also reflected recent developments. Studies like Marckwardt and Walcott's *Facts about Current English Usage* (1938) and Pooley's *Teaching English Usage* (1946) had led to a strengthening of the position on usage and the enunciation in Volume 1 (National Council of Teachers of English, Commission on the English Curriculum, 1952) of "five basic concepts which are, or should be, the foundation of the current attitude toward any teaching of the English language today":

1. Language changes constantly.
2. Change is normal . . . not corruption but improvement.
3. Spoken language is the language.
4. Correctness rests upon usage.
5. All usage is relative.

The volume stated that the primary value of the study of grammar was "to help students so to analyze and understand parts of the English sentence that they can strive continuously for variety, interest, and exactness in sentence structure." Noting that individual differences make it impossible to assign specific aspects of grammar and usage to each grade, Volume 1 called for a program which "furnishes as broad and rich a field for communication in as real situations as possible, and then deals directly and specifically [often with the pupil individually] with whatever language problems arise." Volume 2, the elementary volume, devoted a total of some three pages to suggestions for helping pupils improve their grammar (National Council of Teachers of English, Commission on the English Curriculum, 1954). The secondary volume, Volume 3, in a 30-page section on grammar and usage, took a turn which cannot be observed in Volume 1, published only four years earlier. Volume 3 not only reaffirmed the position in favor of functional grammar and dealt with it in some detail but espoused "the importance of teaching the facts of American English" as a study interesting in and of itself. Six of the 30 pages called for teaching the pupil "to observe the way all of the people around him actually use the English language," "to understand that the language he uses is in process of change," and "to recognize the existence of many different 'levels' of usage" (National Council of Teachers of English, Commission on the English Curriculum, 1956).

Although English composition and grammar had long been a favorite subject of controversy among Americans, criticism of its teaching in the schools surged upward in the 1950's as an aftermath of World War II. The demands of military and defense activities upon high school teachers and parents during the war obviously disrupted the learning of children and adolescents attending school during the 1940's and meant that more of them than usual were inadequately prepared for college. The influx of veterans into the colleges under the provisions of the GI bill after the war, especially into colleges and state universities with an "open door" policy, added a flood of young men with mixed motives for attending college. The reaction of college professors and other English teachers to this situation became very important. The "communication" approach to freshman English which had become popular in the 1940's (McGrath, 1949) was being dropped at most universities, in part because it had become associated with the necessity of teaching grammatical and mechanical rudiments. Remedial freshman English was instituted in the late 1940's and dropped ten years later. The Advanced Placement Program (APP) was established in 1952 to assist "secondary school students who are capable of doing college-level work," including English, and "secondary schools which are interested in giving such students the chance to work up to capacity" (College Entrance Examination Board, 1964). The APP was soon instrumental in obtaining exemption from freshman English for thousands of high school graduates who had had APP English (Valley, 1959). The Council for Basic Education was founded in 1956 to promote "the maintenance of high academic standards" in the schools, with generous attention to English composition. In one of the later publications of the council, Lynch and Evans (1963) concluded from a study of 14 series of high school grammar and composition texts that the books were oppressively repetitious, included too much irrelevant "motivational" material, and strove too hard to devise "real" writing situations rather than to relate composition to literature and the classroom. College and university English departments, with or without the assistance of high school teachers, were publishing such statements as "Principles and Standards in Composition" (1956–1957) with grades assigned to illustrative compositions. English professors were arguing the relative merits of abolishing freshman English (Rice, 1960) or strengthening it (Kitzhaber, 1960), and Kitzhaber (1963) made what seems to be the most careful study to this date of the problems and some of the possibilities in teaching college writing.

An initial move to establish direction in the welter of controversy was taken when 28 English teachers— mostly professors, representing the American Studies Association, the College English Association, the Modern Language Association, and the NCTE—met a number of times during 1958 to clarify what was later published in the "Basic Issues in the Teaching of English" (1958). With a tone of urgency, the group called for "a thorough reexamination of the whole problem of the teaching of English, from the elementary grades through the graduate school," and identified 35 basic issues, ranging from "What is 'English'?" and "How should writing be taught?" to "What effect does class size have upon the quality of training in reading and writing?" As Stone (1965) showed, the Basic Issues conferences seemed to lead to many projects for the improvement of English. In 1959 the CEEB appointed the Commission on English (1960) and granted it a million dollars "to develop a three- to five-year program of analysis and recommendation" to seek solutions to the problems in English. Then, when there was much talk in the nation about federal support for education, the NCTE bid for federal funds for English by publishing *The National Interest and the Teaching of English* (National Council of Teachers of English Committee on the National Interest, 1961), a documented report of the "neglect of English" and the need for more and better teachers, better teaching conditions, and "better and more basic research in English." That year the United States Congress responded by allocating to the U.S. Office of Education (USOE), then under the direction of Commissioner McMurrin, the funds to establish "Project English" (1962), "designed to make a key contribution to raising the quality of English instruction" by financing research, surveys, and demonstrations and by establishing curriculum study centers to prepare new curricula in English, initially emphasizing "reading, composition, and related language skills." The new curricula, being published at the time this article is being written, are described in some detail by Shugrue (1966).

Meanwhile, the Commission on English, taking a cue from a similar foreign-language program, established a model by operating at 20 universities, during the summer of 1962, institutes to provide advanced training in composition, literature, and language (knowledge of the history and structure of the English language) for high school English teachers who had not had recent advanced study in those areas. An evaluation under the direction of Gerber (1963) gave a generally strong endorsement to the institutes, and the USOE, now no longer operating on the crash-program basis implied by "Project English" but having an appropriation of some $40-million to strengthen the English area, financed 105 institutes in English during the summer of 1965, most of them following the composition, language, and literature pattern of the Commission on English institutes and affording teacher-participants free tuition and a stipend of $75 per week for each dependent. These and the institutes held in 1966 have enabled thousands of English teachers, most of them from the secondary level, to take advanced study they otherwise would not have obtained. While perhaps 10 percent of the 90,000 high school English teachers in America (and a much smaller percentage of all the elementary teachers) had attended such institutes by the fall of 1966, it is too early to determine what the impact has been on the classroom. As of this writing the institutes were not open to participation by junior-college English teachers, whose needs and problems have been graphically demonstrated in a questionnaire study by Weingarten and Kroeger (1965).

Although their study was made of the English programs in 168 high schools "selected on the basis of their [high] state or national reputations," the report of Squire and Applebee (1966; also see Applebee, 1966, and Squire, 1966) gives the most complete and up-to-date picture of high school composition and grammar instruction available today. Based upon personal observation as well as questionnaires and checklists, the survey discovered that 15.7 percent of the classroom time observed was spent on composition and 13.5 percent on language, against 52.2 percent on literature. Noting that the teachers reported a median number of hours per week of 9–12 in correcting papers (against 17–20 in classroom teaching), the survey suggested that the English teachers in these superior schools "are not reneging on the task of teaching composition, but they have come to depend enormously on the process of teaching writing by correction—on instruction after the fact and after the act." The theme marking is additionally negative, the survey reports, "in that it is nearly always concerned with correcting errors of mechanics or expression and infrequently with errors in judgment." Some 20 percent of the schools were using lay readers. Noting that the 168 schools had not been stampeded into an exaggerated emphasis on exposition and analysis or on the relation of all composition to literature, the survey attributed part of the success of the English teachers to their use of a variety of writing assignments. Squire and Applebee suggested, however, "that more should be done to *teach* writing, or better to teach composing, rather than to provide writing activities alone and assume that students will necessarily learn from practice." The investigators also advised that "imaginative writing, especially the writing of poetry and fiction, can serve an important role," among other things to help give students "a unique understanding of literary forms and styles."

Squire and Applebee had "little good to say" about the programs in language at the selected schools. They found that many of the better schools, having abandoned formal study of English grammar, had little more than "a haphazard offering of sporadic usage drills determined solely by errors in students' speech or writing" and only here and there units on lexicography, semantics and symbolic logic, American dialects, or the history of the language. The survey also noted an expensive practice—"the tendency of many schools to impose strictures on the language program through large-scale, system-wide adoption of single textbooks and the tendency, where this is done, of teachers seldom or never to use these language books with their classes." That and similar practices relative to curriculum, employment and leadership of teachers, and use of instructional equipment and materials led the investigators to observe that "seldom indeed did we find the quality of instruction or the intellectual tone of a school in the multiple-school districts approaching the quality of the program of the single high school, no matter how large it may become." Squire (1966) concluded that the "greatest single strength—the most all-pervading characteristic—which any school can develop is its administration . . . the effectiveness which strong leadership of a department chairman and a building principal can bring to English teaching." He also found that administrators and English teachers alike are devoting little attention to students in the lower tracks. In their classrooms he noted "little attempt to introduce any intellectually stimulating learning . . . a much greater use of routine drill books, workbooks, and 'canned' dittoed lessons."

DIFFICULTIES IN RESEARCH. Anyone who has read a considerable portion of the research in the teaching and learning of English composition knows how much it leaves to be desired. In the first major summary and critical analysis of the research, Lyman (1929) wrote that "a complex phenomenon such as composition quality seems to defy careful analysis into constituent parts" and noted that the pioneer studies he reviewed "measure pupil products and assume that by so doing they are evaluating the manifold intangible processes of mind by which those products were attained." Over thirty years later, the NCTE Committee on the State of Knowledge About Composition published a second major summary and critique of the research in written composition (Braddock & others, 1963). The committee prefaced its chapter "Suggested Methods of Research" with the statement that "today's research in composition, taken as a whole, may be compared to chemical research as it emerged from the period of alchemy: some terms are being refined, but the field as a whole is laced with dreams, prejudices, and makeshift operations." Such opinions doubtless played a part in the decision of the USOE to finance a series of conferences during 1962 and 1963 on research in the teaching of composition and other aspects of English (Rosenblatt, 1963; Russell & others, 1964; Steinberg & others, 1963; Wasson, 1963). The papers published in the reports of these conferences suggest the difficulties of doing research in composition, language, and literature as well as proposing designs and problems for future studies. Criticizing the conferences for seeking authoritative solutions through the atomistic methods of an outdated science, Henry (1966) hypothesized that research in English teaching will have no real importance until a major unifying theory of the field is developed, within which varied research tasks in teaching may be conducted.

Rather than present here a detailed discussion of the difficulties and possibilities of research in English composition, this article refers the reader for general background to Gage's excellent *Handbook of Research on Teaching* (1963), for detailed suggestions concerning research in English composition to Chapter 2 in the report of the NCTE Committee on the State of Knowledge About Composition (Braddock & others, 1963), and for bibliographic suggestions to Chapter 5 in Gage's book and especially to the annual summaries of research which have been appearing in Spring issues of *Elementary English* (e.g., Petty & Burns, 1966) and the *English Journal* (e.g., Blount, 1966). In addition, the reader may refer to *Research in the Teaching of English*, a new periodical of the NCTE which will regularly feature an exhaustive bibliography of current research in the area and, in its first issue, Spring, 1967, will include a summary by Gunderson of Gerald H. Smith's helpful dissertation, "Inadequacies in a Selected Sample of Educational Research Proposals" (1964).

ENVIRONMENTAL FACTORS. Many of the studies on language development in children point to the educative influence of conversation with more-mature children and adults (McCarthy, 1954; Hill, 1967). The higher frequency with which socially disadvantaged children are raised in orphanages or, if in their own homes, in an atmosphere in which their conceptual and verbal skills are restricted by "emotional outbursts" doubtless explains why, on practically all aspects of language studied, such children are surpassed in achievement by children of higher socioeconomic levels (Raph, 1965). In a study of 200 compositions written by children in elementary schools representing three different grade levels, McClellan (1956) found that organization skill and length of sentences varied directly with socioeconomic level, although middle-class children wrote more words at all grade levels than children of other classes did. Bilingualism did not seem to have an adverse effect on the composition performance, however, of 96 children with bilingual backgrounds (56 Chinese and 42 Spanish) whose writing Lewis and Lewis (1965) compared with that of 114 children from monolingual backgrounds, all 212 children being in the sixth grade and of low socioeconomic status.

When Monk (1958) sought correlations between, on the one hand, the good writing and poor writing of 700 seventh graders in British Columbia and, on the other hand, their responses on a questionnaire, he found much the same results that the above investigators did. He also discovered that the good writers engaged in leisure-time reading more frequently than the poor writers (as did their parents) and tended to have homes well supplied with books, whereas the homes of poor writers tended to have more magazines and newspapers than books. Monk found little relation, however, between writing performance and the recreational or community activities of parents or between writing performance and physical handicaps, school attendance, or foreign-language background of the children. Similar investigations into the backgrounds of weak college freshman writers have been conducted by Culpepper-Hagen (1950), Baker (1954), Barch and Wright (1957), and Woodward and Phillips (1967). Although they did not all investigate the same characteristics, several of these studies were agreed that poor freshman writers tend to be male, to score lower than good writers in verbal and quantitative tests of ability, to be more concerned with grammatical and mechanical problems than with organization and content, and to select teachers of subjects other than English as their favorites.

Two pioneering studies on the primacy of a writer's own experiences may suggest something about sequence in composition instruction. An examination of the stories of 90 seventh graders led Edmund (1956) to conclude that their writing was better when they drew their ideas from such "derived" experiences as television programs and motion pictures. An analysis of 42 short stories written by freshmen in his college class convinced Anderson (1950), however, that his students wrote better when their settings and characters were based on "direct" experiences.

RHETORIC. "Rhetoric" has a range of definitions from "the art of persuasion" to, in outmoded practice if not in theory, "figures of speech and the mechanics of organization." In an article analyzing the state of rhetoric research, Steinmann (1966) submitted this definition:

> Rhetoric . . . is concerned with the effective choice of synonymous expressions; but, as the word "effective" suggests, it is concerned, not with utterances only, the mere forms, but with some of their relations to other things . . . : the speaker or writer, his utterance, his context (occasion or medium), his audience (listener or reader), his purpose (the effect that he intends his utterance to have upon his audience), and the effect of his utterance upon his audience.

Steinmann further defined five sorts of rhetorical research: *basic rhetorical research* (observing acts of speech or writing to develop rules or theories in "the knowing *how* sense" or "the knowing-*that* sense"), *metarhetorical research* (describing the properties of adequate theories), *pedagogical rhetoric research* (observing acts of teaching speech or writing to produce theories of teaching rhetorical ability), *rhetorical criticism* (analyzing the relationship of historically given utterances to exercise of rhetorical ability and to theories of rhetoric), and *historical or comparative rhetorical research* (investigating historically given theories of research and their historical or comparative relationships to each other). As Steinmann pointed out, what little basic research there is in rhetoric has occurred more or less in isolation among a half-dozen disciplines. Most of his examples refer to work in speech or to analyses of literary form and style. Some speech studies, like that of Knower (1936), reach interesting conclusions on the basis of comparisons of the relative effectiveness of reaching audiences through hearing speeches and reading the printed versions of the same speeches. Certainly many research projects in reading, like the one in which Parker (1962) found that a concluding summary seemed to aid comprehension more than a beginning summary, may add up to some practical guide lines for writing. It would be interesting for someone to do a critical synthesis, "What Research in Reading Suggests to Writers," which may get at the effect of rhetorical considerations on *various types of readers,* not merely on composition teachers or raters—the usual yardstick for this kind of research.

In recent years, investigators have been formulating hypotheses about the rhetoric of sentences and paragraphs. From his analysis of narrative and descriptive sentences, Christensen (1963) proposes that students be taught to improve their own sentences by adding to a main clause sets of parallel phrases and clauses at lower levels of generality. His article affords a way of describing and analyzing "cumulative" sentences, a way which may be useful in basic and pedagogical research. A useful supplement to Christensen's article is an analysis by Weathers (1966) of the rhetoric of the series. Christensen (1965) and Becker (1965) have formulated hypotheses attempting to explain the nature of paragraphs; Rodgers (1966) finds more promise in speaking of the nature of a "stadium of discourse," seeing paragraph indentations as too arbitrary to indicate the kinds of units referred to here. These three writers and others subsequently criticized the three articles in "Symposium on the Paragraph" (1966). But much more needs to be done here, if in fact it can be done, before one can say that the nature of units like the paragraph has been defined to the satisfaction of many.

Pedagogical research in rhetoric may have to await basic research before it can be helpful, but some pedagogical research may lead to basic research. An old interest has been revived in helping students prepare to write, the efficacy of which was attested to by Taylor (1962) at the junior high school level and explored by Rohman and Wiecke (1964) with college freshmen. A study by McColly and Remstad (1963) also involved what many have called "prewriting," though that factor was not isolated to determine its effects. Carlson (1960), studying the intermediate grades, used pictures, literature, and toys (not merely story titles) to stimulate children to write, then had three judges evaluate the compositions according to two scales she developed, a General Impression Scale and an Analytical Originality Scale. She found statistically significant differences favoring the experimental group in originality, versatility of vocabulary, and total number of words. Nelson (1965) has done some exploratory research on the influence of the topic on the length, content, and style of writing.

GRAMMAR. Several decades ago a number of pioneering scholars in English grammar challenged, in effect, the prescriptions of Latinate grammar, Curme (1931) and Jesperson (1924) working in the best traditions of nineteenth-century scholarship, and Sapir (1921) and Bloomfield (1933) building upon field studies conducted early in the twentieth century. A new dimension was added to such analyses by Fries, who based each of his major studies on a describable corpus, first of letters submitted to a government agency (1940) and then of recorded telephone calls (1952). Trager and Smith (1951), Fries (1952), and others, wishing to divest grammatical analysis of its notional features, adopted a structural approach, studying word order, inflections, and phonological characteristics of words, and pitch and stress patterns in sentences. A renewed interest in grammar was aroused among many English teachers, who saw in structural grammar an approach closer to the truth than anything they found in their textbooks. Roberts (1956) brought out the first high school text to apply "structural linguistics" in the teaching of grammar and composition.

Just as some schoolteachers thought they were becoming able to cope with "the new grammar" in their classrooms, another "new grammar" appeared— "generative grammar," as presented in Chomsky's *Syntactic Structures* (1957). According to Carroll (1964), Chomsky's book "struck at the roots of and . . . required a re-examination of nearly all previous linguistic theory." In Carroll's words, it postulated that:

[T]he grammatical and, for that matter, the actual phonological structure of speech output can be interpreted by assuming that the speaker of a language "generates" speech by the application of a certain series of rules specifying (a) the structure of basic phrases or "kernels," (b) the ways in which these kernels may be "transformed" to form new structures, and (c) the manner in which the resulting linguistic material is actualized in the spoken word. The three departments of generative linguistic theory are, correspondingly, phrase-structure grammar, transformation rules, and phonological rules.

Again, Roberts (1962) wrote a textbook applying the latest approach for the high school student and teacher, followed by a programmed introduction for mature students (Roberts, 1964). Meanwhile, English teachers with minds attuned more to notions than to structure were bandying about the term "psycholinguistics," though Carroll (1964) himself warned against it:

[M]ost of the work in the field centers around relatively simple laboratory forms of verbal learning, such as the learning of a list of items in order (serial learning) or a series of paired items (paired associates) . . . .
One may conclude that, despite the great scientific value of current work in verbal learning, it is not often likely to yield new propositions of immediate use in the classroom or even in that highly controlled type of teaching known as programmed instruction.

It is no wonder that English teachers have been confused (McDavid, 1965). They have been operating for the past fifteen years against a fast-moving background of linguistic research and scholarship.

Teachers have been shown in one experiment after another that the systematic study of traditional grammar has a "negligible or, because it usually displaces some instruction and practice in composition, even a harmful effect upon the improvement of writing" (Braddock & others, 1963). In his excellent summary of such research, Meckel (1963) came to much the same conclusion but qualified it by pointing out that the training periods in the studies have been comparatively short—a semester or less. But in a recent study not available to Meckel when he wrote his summary, Harris (1962) conducted a two-year experiment with 12- to 14-year-old children in London schools and came to the conclusion on which the wording of Braddock's statement is based. And Meade (1961) attested that pupils in the lower 50 percent in verbal intelligence did not even achieve success in the study of grammar itself.

As the "new grammars" became known, other experiments were undertaken to determine whether or not they could help pupils improve their writing any more than traditional grammar could. The evidence for structural grammar is mixed. Suggs (1961) found that structural grammar worked better with a group of eleventh-graders using Roberts' *Patterns of English* than traditional grammar did with another group. O'Donnell (1963) compared the results of two hundred college freshmen on the STEP Essay Test and on his Test of Recognition of Structural Relationships in English without discovering statistically significant correlation. White (1964) compared three groups of seventh graders: one studying the form classes of structural grammar, another studying the parts of speech of traditional grammar, and a third using the same time for free reading. He found that the structural-grammar group made significant improvement in writing whereas the other two groups did not. Klauser (1964), on the other hand, concluded from her comparison of structural- and traditional-grammar groups in three junior high school grades that the two groups had about the same success, though the seventh-grade traditional-grammar group made more significant gains in accuracy of writing and the ninth-grade structural-grammar group made more significant gains in understanding "effective writing." Recently, without having published any data on its effectiveness, Landry (1965) combined traditional and structural methods into one eclectic system correlating form and meaning.

Some teachers would maintain that the type of grammar used is not as important in improving sentence structure in pupils' writing as is the manner in which it is used, that pupils must learn how to form their own sentences, not merely analyze the sentences of others. Barnes (1964), for example, attested to the efficacy of having students form their own sentences in an experiment involving some ninety second graders. Half of these pupils used 60,000 small word cards and 100 grooved boards to assemble the cards into sentences. (He did not explain what the control group did while the experimental group did this for 45 minutes per week.) After a 16-week period, Barnes found that the experimental group wrote longer stories, used a wider variety of words, and exhibited greater imagination than the control group.

When generative grammar was developed, it seemed that teachers now had a grammar which, concerned as it was with synthesis as much as analysis, peculiarly lent itself to teaching the construction of sentences. In a two-year experiment directed by Bateman and Zidonis (1966), an experimental class studied phrase-structure rules in the ninth grade, transformational rules in the tenth. (Details were not given on what the control group studied during the corresponding portions of their English work.) The investigators collected six initial and six final compositions from all 50 of the experimental and control pupils and subjected their 1,731 sentences to transformational analysis. They concluded that the pupils in both groups increased the complexity of their sentences but that the experimental group increased the proportion of well-formed sentences significantly more than did the control group.

Research workers have long been studying the development of sentence structure in children. Many have used the sentence as a unit of measurement, usually assuming that longer sentences tend to be more complex sentences, reflecting more mature control of syntax; but that has not worked well because some immature writers are inclined to run independent clauses together without punctuation and with or without coordinating conjunctions. In a pioneering effort to develop a more exact unit, La Brant (1933) used the "subordination ratio," a ratio of what she called subordinate clauses to all clauses in a sample of writing. Recently Loban (1963, 1966) has used what he calls the "communication unit," Strickland (1962) the "phonological unit," and Hunt (1965) the "minimal terminable unit," or "T-unit." All of these terms are, for research purposes, more precise substitutes for "sentence." Because Loban and Strickland primarily studied speech, it seems pertinent here to focus on the work of Hunt (1965, 1966) and of a team of investigators (O'Donnell & others, 1967) who also used the T-unit. In essence, the analysis of writing samples from primary-grade children up through high school shows a more or less consistent increase in average number of words per T-unit. Hunt (1966) recently attributed much of this growth to increase in length of adjective clauses, rather than increase in length of adverb and noun clauses, and he said that "for the later grades and especially for superior students, clause length is indeed a better index than T-unit length." In a very recent study, Potter (1967) identified the 20 best and 20 worst of 100 high school sophomore compositions and applied various analyses to the papers to determine their usefulness in differentiating quality of writing. The subordination index proved to be of no use, sentence length and T-unit length (which had the same ratio to each other) of little use. On the other hand, Potter found that the best papers used fewer subject-verb-object sentences (35 percent, against 47 percent for the worst papers), more instances of the passive voice (twice as many), many fewer conditional clauses and transitional expressions, and more modifications of objects than the worst papers, about the same number of adjectival clauses, and more verbal structures of all types, twice as many in presubject positions as the worst papers. Although the corpus of data has been modest on which these studies of sentence development have been based, it is beginning to look as though quantity and quality of syntactical development are far from synonymous.

VOCABULARY. A report by Petty (1967) contains an evaluation and synthesis of vocabulary studies "concerned directly with pedagogical method, with the teaching of as opposed to the acquiring of vocabulary, and with teaching English vocabulary to native speakers of the language." As the report explains, vocabulary studies may be concerned with various degrees of understanding of words, from mere recognition of a word to a deep understanding of several meanings of it. Moreover, a given study may be concerned, as is this article, with a person's writing vocabulary, which is different in quantity and no doubt in other ways from his reading, speaking, or listening vocabulary.

From his analysis of many studies, Petty concludes that vocabulary can be taught but that there is no best way to teach it, that he could find no conclusive evidence "that a 'direct' method is better than an 'indirect' one, that teaching words in isolation is better than teaching them in context, that an inductive approach is better than a deductive one." He also criticized most of the studies for commonly evaluating vocabulary learning by performance on vocabulary tests, rarely by the effective use of words in writing or other application. Of the 14 studies reviewed in Petty's chapter on selected research, none was concerned with the use of vocabulary in writing. But the chapter "Research Design for Vocabulary Studies" would be of great use to anyone planning such an investigation.

A recent bibliography of vocabulary research, listing 3,125 titles, is that of Dale and Razik (1963), not available to the writer. The 1957 edition of Dale's bibliography (coauthored with Donald Reichert) listed 109 studies under the heading "Vocabulary in Use (Studies of Words Used in Writings and Conversations)," approximately three-fourths of which concerned words used in writing. But most of these studies seem to be counts of the frequency with which words occurred in the various types of writing (themes, letters, etc.) of children of various grade levels or of adults. No experiments in pedagogical method were identified. Investigators interested in consulting such frequency counts may refer to the Dale and Razik bibliography or to the word lists of Fitzgerald (1951), Horn (1926), Rinsland (1945), and Thorndike and Lorge (1944).

INSTRUCTION. This section of the article first considers three problems of particular interest to researchers and teachers—teaching load, different ways of marking papers, and writing frequency—and then treats other problems in methodology.

Teaching Load. After studying the various ways in which English teachers mark compositions, Dusel (1955a) concluded that a high school teacher needs 21.5 hours per week to mark adequately the 250-word compositions of 150 pupils and 7.0 hours per week to check their revisions of those papers. Adding to that the usual 25 hours per week spent in class and the time out of class needed to prepare his instruction, the conscientious English teacher has a workweek of well over 50 hours. In one way or another, investigators have sought ways to alleviate this problem. When the situation became especially acute with rising enrollments following World War II, the NCTE (National Council of Teachers of English, Committee on National Interest, 1961) at numerous annual business meetings officially endorsed a maximum English teacher load of four classes with no more than 25 pupils in each. This stand was taken despite the knowledge that an exceptionally able English teacher had demonstrated she could, with routine assistance, teach a large class of superior ninth graders as effectively as she could teach a small class of matched students (D. Smith, 1931). Furthermore, studies like Bittick's (1956) have shown that pupils from large high schools (where classes tend to be larger) do at least as well in English as pupils from small high schools (where classes tend to be smaller), although, of course, other factors besides class size are important in such studies.

The pressure of enrollment and teaching load led to a spate of experimentation for a solution in the late 1950's. Sherwood (1958) tried to increase the size of college freshman composition sections from 25 to 36 by using a "combination of tutoring in small groups and student criticism of papers." He found that the new system seemed to be about as effective as traditional procedures but that it did not seem to save any time and required "an abnormal expenditure of nervous energy" from instructors who found the succession of conferences exhausting. Diederich (1960), Ford (1961), and Sauer (1962) all reported experiments using "lay readers," usually college-educated and more or less trained housewives, to assist English teachers in marking compositions. Inasmuch as the success of such assistance depends greatly upon the quality and supervision of the lay readers and entails the costs of supervision and reader remuneration, that solution has not swept the nation even though many schools have been using it. Team teaching (Giltinan, 1963; V. Smith, 1960) has seemed to offer some relief in some schools, and the overhead projector (Bissex, 1961) has helped make the instruction of large classes effective, but the problem is still serious. Publication of "The Workload of a College English Teacher" (1966) indicated that college professors are becoming increasingly concerned about their teaching loads.

Marking Papers. Although the English teacher spends a considerable portion of his time marking compositions, not much research has been done on the relative instructional effectiveness of various methods of marking (annotating) and grading papers. Many articles have been published advocating the use of clear and precise annotations (Dusel, 1955b), student-group criticism, class discussion of themes displayed by the overhead or opaque projector, teacher comment via the tape recorder or dictating machine (Lumsden, 1961), and the like. N. Halvorson (1940), Wormsbecker (1955), and McMechan (1961) all have experimented with various methods of marking and grading, but their results have not been commanding. (The first chapter of McMechan's thesis has a useful review of such studies.) When G. Halvorsen (1960) compared the relative effects on the writing of sixth-grade children of an emphasis on stimulating interest or mechanical accuracy, she found the mechanics-emphasis group wrote shorter sentences and improved in spelling and in paragraph development, the stimulus group in plot development. Her conclusion seems plausible—that children tend to learn what they are taught. In perhaps the most carefully conducted research in this area to date, Buxton (1958) found that 85 college freshmen whose weekly writing was graded and thoroughly marked and criticized and who revised their papers in the light of these matters improved their titles, introductions, and the significance of their material significantly more than an equivalent group of 86 college freshmen whose weekly writing received a few general suggestions but no grades or intensive marking and who did not revise their papers. No statistically significant difference was observed, however, in such matters as critical thinking, originality, and paragraph organization. It cannot be determined from Buxton's experiment how much of the success could be attributed to intensive marking, how much to grading, and how much to student revision, but the three elements do constitute what many teachers consider to be one approach. Further experimentation would be necessary, of course, before one could assume that such an approach is justified with elementary-school pupils, with the kinds of high school pupils who do not go on to college, or with instruction in fiction writing instead of the expository writing used in Buxton's experiment.

Writing Frequency. Intertwined with teaching load and methods of marking papers is the problem of writing frequency. How often should pupils write? A number of recent investigations, by the following authors, have focused on this question: Burton and Arnold (1963), Christiansen (1964), Edmund (1963), McColly and Remstad (1963), Sutton and Allen (1964), and Wolf (1966). Their answers vary, depending somewhat on how the question is asked. It seems quite evident that *mere* frequency of writing, without motivation to write well or careful instruction in how to write well, produces no measurable results over a period as short as a semester. Edmund found, for example, that keeping "a well-summarized and well-organized" account of the day's activities each day for 12 weeks did not reveal any gains for his intermediate-grade pupils, even though a majority of the pupils seemed to enjoy keeping such diaries. Sutton and Allen discovered no significant differences between control groups of college freshmen who received no instruction or practice in writing and equivalent experimental groups who also had no instruction in the art of composition but who wrote weekly for 10 weeks, had their themes evaluated by a professor or a group of four other freshmen, and revised their papers. In some ways the Buxton experiment (1958), described above in the section "Marking Papers," is comparable to the Sutton and Allen study, yet contradictory. For Buxton's experiment included a control group which received no practice in composition. The Buxton experimental group whose weekly papers were marked intensively, graded, and revised improved significantly over the control group in such matters as title, introduction, variety, fluency, and diction. On the other hand, there is some indication—though it is not unanimous—that students do improve more when more frequent writing is accompanied by careful instruction. The clearest recent evidence is found in the McColly and Remstad study, which had two parts. In grades 8 and 9, they had an experimental and a control group at each level. Each group received the same amount of instructional time in composition each month, but the control group spent all the time in connection with a monthly theme and the experimental group divided the time into four equal portions, spending a portion in connection with each of four weekly themes a month. Thus, this part of the experiment tested the hypothesis that more writing, with instructional time held constant, yields better writing. Although the investigators did find significant differences between levels and between girls and boys, they found more between the mean final theme scores of the experimental and control groups.

In the second part of the McColly and Remstad study, there were two experimental classes and one control class at each of three levels, grades 10–12, all of which received an average of 2½ class periods of writing instruction for each composition written, but the two experimental groups wrote weekly and the control group monthly. Thus, the experimental groups in grades 10–12 received four times as much instruction as the control group. In addition, in one experimental group each student received help in about 27 tutoring sessions during the 30 weeks of the experiment, each session being held after an assignment was established but before the student had finished the writing. The other experimental group received no such tutoring. Although McColly and Remstad observed no significant differences among the groups (except by level) on three objective tests, they did find on the mean scores awarded to two final themes written by each student a difference between the untutored experimental group and the control group, significant at the .05 level of confidence, favoring the untutored experimental group. The tutored experimental groups mean theme score fell midway between the other two groups and was not significantly different from either. (The theme grading procedures were conducted with especial care and merit study by other investigators.)

McColly and Remstad concluded from their two-part investigation that "the act of writing in and of itself is fruitless," that English teachers "should not assign or elicit any writing for the purpose of developing composition ability unless this writing becomes the vehicle for functional instruction." They further inferred that, until more is known, high school English teachers should give a weekly writing assignment, about 300 words in length, accompanied by about 2½ class periods of practical analysis of the assignment; explanation and discussion of possible forms, techniques, and materials appropriate for the task; writing; editing; and, after the teacher has marked and graded the paper, rewriting. This conclusion becomes especially interesting in view of the observation by Applebee (1966) that the English teachers in 168 reputable high schools emphasized composition for only 15.7 percent of the 32,580 minutes of classroom time observed!

Other Problems. Despite the attempts of the various NCTE curriculum publications (reviewed above) to suggest a sequential program in composition, many teachers have expressed the need for a better order in the organization of instruction in writing through the grades (e.g., Hach, 1960). Although some surveys have been made, mostly in the 1930's and reviewed by Greene (1950), to establish the levels at which pupils make the highest frequency of certain grammatical and punctuation errors, new surveys are needed in the light of changes in school population, instructional emphases, and, especially, linguistic theory. Some studies have recently been made of punctuation (Odom, 1964) and syntactical complexity (Hunt, 1965, 1966; O'Donnell & others, 1967), but a sequential program in the rhetorical aspects of composition cannot be based on sound research until methods are developed to describe the rhetorical aspects in objective terms. Meanwhile, several of the curriculum-study centers financed by the USOE have begun publishing courses of study which include composition sequences (e.g., Steinberg & others, 1966), and others are applying to composition the format of the familiar "reading laboratory" boxes, with lessons in narration, description, and exposition arranged in an order of increasing difficulty which individual pupils in grades 5–8 can undertake at their own rates under the supervision of a teacher who has familiarized himself well with what is involved (Hoth & others, 1965; also, for junior and senior high school, Hook & Evans, 1964). To this date, evidence is divided on the effectiveness of programmed grammatical material (Gotkin, 1963; Edling & others, 1964).

The instructional effect of different types of writing assignments has been the object of much speculation but little research. After a study of 36 sixth-grade children, Clark (1954) concluded that they wrote better when they were expressing their own feelings. From her familiarity with many studies of writing assignments in elementary schools, Burrows (Burrows & others, 1952) suggested the use of a variety of procedures. When an official state survey asked each junior and senior high school English teacher of California to describe a successful writing assignment (Meckel & others, 1958), most teachers mentioned assignments developed from literature, personal experiences, classroom discussions, pictures, phonograph records, and films; few mentioned routine book reports. Meckel concluded "that these teachers' assignments, while designed to stimulate imaginative powers and certain types of verbal skills, did not appreciably require the thought processes, evaluative skills, or skills of organization necessary in writing an expository essay dealing with contemporary issues —the kind of writing typically required of freshmen for placement purposes by the colleges and universities of the state."

Two further studies in instruction bear mention. Jenkins (1952) studied the relative effectiveness of college instructors acting as resource persons in democratically structured classes in written and spoken English, finding them not significantly superior to instructors using more traditional methods. In a classic study, conducted in 1912, of the curriculum and methods of composition teaching in France, Brown (1963) pointed to the importance with which composition was viewed, the constant study of vocabulary and practice in dictation in the lower grades, the care with which material was analyzed and interest whetted in the upper grades, the emphasis placed on organization and general good form, and the constructiveness with which teachers offered their criticisms of compositions, leading pupils "to reflect upon the possibilities that the subject-matter possesses, rather than upon the magnitude of their own shortcomings."

EVALUATION. Elsewhere in this volume are discussions of the general objectives, procedures, and problems of evaluating pupils. The evaluation of pupil composition is complicated enough that this section will do little more than refer the interested reader to other comprehensive reviews. Strickland (1960) has reviewed principles important in evaluating the writing of elementary-school children—and in leading them to evaluate their own work, Meckel (Meckel & others, 1958) has performed much the same task for the secondary-school level. The chapter "Meeting College Entrance Requirements" in Volume 3 of the NCTE curriculum series (National Council of Teachers of English, Commission on the English Curriculum, 1956) has surveyed the nature of admissions examinations and placement tests. The treatment of evaluation by Searles and Carlsen (1960) in the third edition of this encyclopedia is still a helpful review for English teachers. Reviews of tests in English may be found by using two publications edited by Buros (1961, 1965).

From the standpoint of the researcher rather than the teacher, the evaluation of written composition has been an especially frustrating problem. It is common knowledge that the grading of compositions is notoriously unreliable. In the early decades of this century, an effort was made to improve the situation by establishing "composition scales," carefully selected compositions representing various degrees of excellence at various levels. A teacher or research worker was to compare a given composition to those on a scale and determine therefore more accurately the worth of the given composition. Lyman (1929) showed, in his thorough review of such scales, that they were not very helpful, that different aspects of writing tend to vary in quality more or less independently, making general worth difficult to determine through models. The development of objective tests (multiple-choice, interlinear, etc.) seemed to offer to some a promise of reliability in evaluation of writing, but most investigators whose speciality is English rather than tests and measurement seem to find that objective tests are useful for prediction (i.e., placement), not for evaluating achievement in writing. Pippert (1959) discovered, however, that tests in the mechanics of writing, administered immediately after graduation from high school, were not accurate predictors of mechanics scores five years later. A documented review of the controversy is offered in Chapter 3 of the report of the NCTE Committee on the State of Knowledge About Composition (Braddock & others, 1963), and a position paper is available in the terminal report of the Committee on Testing of the Conference on College Composition and Communication (Sherwood & others, 1966). Meanwhile, those on each side of the fence continue to attempt to perfect their methods. Chapter 2 of the State of Knowledge report brings together what is known about controlling the variables in the evaluation of actual writing for purposes of research. That chapter also reviews what was known at the time about measuring or describing composition by means of "frequency counts." Recent developments in the analysis of sentences, summarized above under "Grammar," seem to be carrying that knowledge further. Page (1966) and Daigon (1966) have achieved some initial success in grading compositions by computer. And Godshalk and others (1966) have described a "significant breakthrough" in the validation of the CEEB English Composition Test, although Steinmann's review (1967) of the description indicated that some of the knottiest problems of evaluating composition remain to be solved. Judging from the findings of French (1957), it would be difficult to convince English teachers that their composition instruction should be evaluated by objective tests administered to their pupils.

PREPARATION OF TEACHERS. An excellent continuing bibliography of published materials, most of them not research, on the preparation and certification of English teachers is Wiley's pamphlet (1957) and her annual supplements in *College English*. Most of the research relevant to the preparation of English teachers consists of surveys of their attitudes, of the preparation they have had in college, or of state certification standards. Two noteworthy exceptions, studies of classroom performance, are the comprehensive Squire and Applebee (1966) investigation, described earlier in this article, and the Scofield (1955) study. Scofield found that young language-arts teachers did not use many of the procedures espoused in English methods courses but tended to adopt routine procedures in conflict with the methodology they had been taught.

Surveys of teachers' attitudes and abilities present an uneven but generally an unflattering picture. Womack (1957), from a questionnaire survey of NCTE members which revealed a wide range of attitudes, concluded that "the tendency to accept items of debatable usage is directly related to linguistic sophistication." He noted that teachers holding the most prescriptive views tended to be high school teachers in small towns who had less teaching experience and not as much higher education as their colleagues. Parler (1952) gathered 300-word writing samples from 322 prospective high school English teachers from over 80 percent of the Negro colleges training teachers. She found that 92 percent of the essays had at least one error in sentence structure, 84 percent at least one in spelling, etc. (It would be interesting to see if the papers of white prospective English teachers were any better.) After reviewing pedagogical research on composition, grammar, usage, and spelling, Nordberg (1949) devised a test over the findings, administered it to student teachers, and concluded that they were relatively unfamiliar with the results of research. Perhaps it is no surprise that after Foff (1958) analyzed 62 novels in which teachers appear, he concluded that as a "citizen or as an individual aside from school, the teacher enjoys little esteem." On the other hand, from their analysis of scores on the National Teacher Examinations, Benson and Godshalk (1960) reported that the average total score of prospective English teachers on the Common Examinations (on professional education, general education, and nonverbal reasoning) ranked third in the list of 16 teaching fields, second on the English expression test (slightly lower than teachers of foreign languages), and first on the Social Studies, Literature, and Fine Arts test. The range of scores they reported was disconcerting, however; "about one-fourth of the English group scored lower on the English Expression test than did the average teacher of other subjects . . . ." The authors seemed to attribute the range of scores to the wide range of standards found among teacher education institutions. At least two methods have been proposed to force the raising of standards—increasing state certification requirements (Fisher, 1961) and administering qualifying examinations to prospective teachers (Slaughter, 1960). Volume 5 of the NCTE Curriculum Series (National Council of Teachers of English, Commission on the English Curriculum, 1963) includes much of the best thinking on how English teachers should be prepared for elementary, secondary, and college classrooms.

The most comprehensive documented picture of the preparation, certification, and needs of English teachers can be found in two companion publications of the National Council of Teachers of English, Committee on the National Interest, *The National Interest and the Teaching of English* (1961) and *The Continuing Education of Teachers of English* (1964). The first volume reported, among other things, that one-fourth of all elementary-school teachers had not graduated from college, that three-fifths of the institutions preparing elementary teachers did not require them to take a course in grammar and usage, and that four-fifths required no course in composition beyond freshman English. Of the institutions preparing secondary-school teachers, fewer than one-fifth required prospective English teachers to take a course in grammar and usage, but over one-fourth required a course in the history of the English language, and only two-fifths required a course in advanced composition. The second volume showed that English teachers have tended not to remedy the situation in the courses they take after certification. Of the 15.8 semester credits the average elementary teacher has taken since certification, 0.4 were in some aspect of the English language, 0.3 in composition. Although secondary-school English teachers have completed an average of 1.72 semester hours of college work per year since beginning teaching, more than 77 percent of this has been in literature, education, or subjects unrelated to English. "In more than nine years of experience, the average secondary teacher of English has completed only 0.4 semester hours in composition and 0.7 hours in language." Although the USOE-financed program of National Defense Education Act (NDEA) institutes (discussed earlier in this article) undoubtedly has made it possible for more English teachers to supplement their undergraduate preparation since these two volumes were published, probably the preparation of most English teachers to afford adequate instruction in composition still needs drastic improvement.

Richard Braddock
The University of Iowa

References

Anderson, Edward L. "A Study of Short Stories Written by Students in College Composition Classes to Determine Relationships Between Prior Experiences of the Students and Their Treatment of Setting and Character." Doctoral dissertation. New York U, 1950. 557p.

Applebee, Roger K. "National Study of High School English Programs: A Record of English Teaching Today." *Engl J* 55:273–81; 1966.

Artley, A. Sterl. "Research Concerning Interrelationships among the Language Arts." *El Engl R* 27:527–37; 1950.

Baker, William D. "An Investigation of Characteristics of Poor Writers." *Col Composition Communication* 5:23–7; 1954.

Barch, A. M., and Wright, R. L. "The Background and Self-picture of Good and Poor Writers." *J Communication* 7:192–3; 1957.

Barnes, Donald L. "An Experimental Study in Written Composition." *El Engl* 41:51–2; 1964.

Bateman, Donald R., and Zidonis, Frank J. *The Effect of a Study of Transformational Grammar on the Writing of Ninth and Tenth Graders.* Research Report No. 6. NCTE, 1966. 40p.

Becker, A. L. "A Tagmemic Approach to Paragraph Analysis." *Col Composition Communication* 16:237–42; 1965.

Benson, Arthur L., and Godshalk, Fred. " 'Bar Examinations' for NCTE Membership." *Col Engl* 22:133–5; 1960.

Bissex, Henry S. "Newton High School . . . Completes Four Years of Large-group Instruction." *B Nat Assn Sec Sch Prin* 45:101–13; 1961.

Bittick, Edsell F. "Differentials in College Success at the University of Texas of Graduates from Large and Small Texas High Schools." Doctoral dissertation. U Texas, 1956.

Bloomfield, Leonard. *Language.* Holt, 1933, 564p.

Blount, Nathan S. "Summary of Investigations Relating to the English Language Arts in Secondary Education: 1965." *Engl J* 55:591–608; 1966.

Braddock, Richard, and others. *Research in Written Composition.* NCTE, 1963. 142p.

Briggs, Thomas H. "Formal English Grammar as a Discipline." *Teach Col Rec* 14:251–343; 1913.

Brown, Rollo W. *How the French Boy Learns to Write.* NCTE, 1963. 258p.

Burke, Virginia M. *The Lay Reader Program: Backgrounds and Procedures.* Wisconsin Council of Teachers of English, 1961. 29p.

Buros, Oscar K. (Ed.) *Tests in Print.* Gryphon, 1961. 479p.

Buros, Oscar K. (Ed.) *The Sixth Mental Measurements Yearbook.* Gryphon, 1965. 1714p.

Burrows, Alvina T., and others. *They All Want to Write,* rev. ed. Prentice-Hall, 1952. 240p.

Burton, Dwight L., and Arnold, Lois V. *The Effects of Frequency of Writing and Intensity of Teacher Evaluation upon High School Students' Performance in Written Composition.* USOE Cooperative Research Project No. 1523, Florida State U, 1963. 99p.

Buxton, Earl W. "An Experiment to Test the Effects of Writing Frequency and Guided Practice upon Students' Skill in Written Expression." Doctoral dissertation. Stanford U, 1958. 135p. (Synopsis in Braddock & others, 1963.)

Carlson, Ruth K. "Stimulating Children in Grades Four, Five, and Six to Write Original Stories." Doctoral dissertation. U California, Berkeley, 1960. (Synopsis in *El Engl* 40:583–9; 1963.)

Carroll, John B. "Linguistics and the Psychology of Language." *R Ed Res* 34:119–26; 1964.

Chase, Stuart. *The Tyranny of Words.* Harcourt, 1938. 396p.

Chomsky, Noam. *Syntactic Structures.* Mouton & Co. 1957. 116p.

Christensen, Francis. "A Generative Rhetoric of the Sentence." *Col Composition Communication* 14:155–61; 1963.

Christensen, Francis. "A Generative Rhetoric of the Paragraph." *Col Composition Communication* 16:144–56; 1965.

Christiansen, Mark A. "The Relative Effectiveness of Two Methods of Teaching Composition in Freshman English at Metropolitan Junior College." Doctoral dissertation. U Kansas, 1964. 159p.

Clark, G. R. "Writing Situations to which Children Respond." *El Engl* 31:150–5; 1954.

College Entrance Examination Board. *Advanced Placement Program: Course Descriptions.* CEEB, 1964. 160p.

Commission on English. *Preparation in English for College-bound Students.* CEEB, 1960. 8p.

Culpepper-Hagen, Lessie. "An Investigation of General Factors Relating to the Writing Effectiveness of Freshmen at the University of Denver." Doctoral dissertation. U Denver, 1950. 154p.

Curme, George O. *Syntax.* Heath, 1931. 616p.

Cutright, Prudence. "A Comparison of Methods of Securing Correct Language Usage." *El Sch J* 34: 681–90; 1934.

Daigon, Arthur. "Computer Grading of English Composition." *Engl J* 55:46–52; 1966.

Dale, Edgar. *How to Read a Newspaper.* Scott, 1941. 178p.

Dale, Edgar, and Razik, Taher. *Bibliography of Vocabulary Studies,* 2nd rev. ed. Ohio State U, 1963. 257p.

Diederich, Paul B. "The Rutgers Plan for Cutting Class Size in Two." *Engl J* 49:229–36; 1960.

Dusel, William J. "Determining an Efficient Teaching Load in English." *Illinois Engl B* 43(October):1–19; 1955(*a*).

Dusel, William J. "Some Semantic Implications of Theme Correction." *Engl J* 44:390–7; 1955(*b*).

Edling, Jack V., and others. *Four Cases of Programmed Instruction.* Fund for the Advancement of Education, 1964.

Edmund, Neal R. "A Study of the Relationships Between Prior Experiences and the Quality of Creative Writing by Seventh Grade Pupils." Doctoral dissertation. Syracuse U, 1956. (Synopsis in *J Ed Res* 51:481–92; 1958.)

Edmund, Neal R. "Diaries for Better Writing?" *El Sch J* 63:270–2; 1963.

Fisher, John H. "1960 Certification Requirements." *Col Engl* 22:267–71; 1961.

Fitzgerald, James A. *A Basic Life Spelling Vocabulary.* Bruce, 1951. 161p.

Foff, Arthur. "Scholars and Scapegoats." *Engl J* 47:118–26; 1958.

Ford, Paul M. "Lay Readers in the High School Composition Program: Some Statistics." *Engl J* 50:522–8; 1961.

French, John W. "What English Teachers Think of Essay Testing." *Engl J* 46:196–201; 1957.

Fries, Charles C. *American English Grammar.* Appleton, 1940. 313p.

Fries, Charles C. *The Structure of English.* Harcourt, 1952. 304p.

Frogner, Ellen. "Grammar Approach *versus* Thought Approach in Teaching Sentence Structure." *Engl J* 28:518–26; 1939.

Gage, N. L. (Ed.) *Handbook of Research on Teaching.* Rand McNally, 1963. 1218p.

Gerber, John C. "The 1962 Summer Institutes of the Commission on English: Their Achievement and Promise." *Pub MLA* 78(September):9–25; 1963.

Gerber, John C. (Ed.) *The College Teaching of English.* NCTE Curriculum Series, Vol. 4. Appleton, 1963. 312p.

Giltinan, Betty. "We Solved the Problem of Size." *Engl J* 52:89–93; 1963.

Godshalk, Fred I., and others. *The Measurement of Writing Ability.* Research Monograph No. 6. CEEB, 1966. 84p.

Gotkin, Lassar G. "Experimentation with Programmed Instruction." In Fleischer, Erna. (Ed.) *Problems and Practices in New York City Schools,* Yearbook of the New York Society for the Experimental Study of Education, 1963. 212p.

Greene, Harry A. "English—Language, Grammar, and Composition." In Monroe, Walter S. (Ed.) *Encyclopedia of Educational Research,* rev. ed. Macmillan, 1950. p. 383–96.

Grommon, Alfred H. (Ed.) *The Education of Teachers of English.* NCTE Curriculum Series, Vol. 5. Appleton, 1963. 604p.

Hach, Clarence W. "Needed: A Sequential Program in Composition." *Engl J* 49:536–47; 1960.

Hall, J. Leslie. *English Usage.* Scott, 1917.

Halvorsen, Gladys C. "Some Effects of Emphasizing Mechanical Accuracy on Written Expression of Sixth Grade Children." Doctoral dissertation. U California, 1960. 159p.

Halvorson, Nelius O. "Two Methods of Indicating Errors in Themes." *Col Engl* 2:277–9; 1940.

Harris, Roland J. "An Experimental Inquiry into the Functions and Value of Formal Grammar in the Teaching of English, with Special Reference to the Teaching of Correct Written English to Children Aged Twelve to Fourteen." Doctoral dissertation. U London, 1962. 291p. (Synopsis in Braddock & others, 1963.)

Hatfield, W. Wilbur. *An Experience Curriculum in English.* A report of the Curriculum Commission, NCTE. Appleton, 1935. 323p.

Hayakawa, S. I. *Language in Action.* Harcourt, 1941. 243p.

Hays, Edna. *College Entrance Requirements in English: Their Effects on the High Schools.* Contributions to Education No. 675. Teachers Col, Columbia U, 1936. 141p.

Henry, George H. "English Teaching Encounters Science." *Col Engl* 28:220–35; 1966.

Hill, Jennie-Keith. "Recent Articles on Language Acquisition." *Int J Am Linguistics* 33:65–73; 1967.

Hook, J. N., and Evans, W. A. *Individualized English.* Follett, 1964.

Horn, Ernest. *A Basic Writing Vocabulary: 10,000 Words Most Commonly Used in Writing.* U Iowa, 1926. 225p.

Hosic, James F. *Reorganization of English in Secondary Schools.* U.S. Bureau of Education Bulletin No. 2. GPO, 1917. 181p.

Hoth, William E., and others. *Basic Composition Series: Writing Skills Laboratories.* SRA, 1965.

Hoyt, Franklin S. "The Place of Grammar in the Elementary Curriculum." *Teach Col Rec* 7:467–500; 1906.

Hunt, Kellogg W. *Grammatical Structures Written at Three Grade Levels.* Research Report No. 3. NCTE, 1965. 159p.

Hunt, Kellogg W. "A Review of T-unit Length Studies." Speech presented at the meeting of the NCTE, Houston, Texas, November 26, 1966. 16p.

Institute for Propaganda Analysis. "How to Detect

Propaganda." *Propaganda Analysis* 1:1–4; 1937.

Jenkins, Russell L. "The Relative Effectiveness of Two Methods of Teaching Written and Spoken English." Doctoral dissertation. Michigan State U, 1952. 209p.

Jesperson, Otto. *The Philosophy of Grammar.* Holt, 1924. 359p.

Kitzhaber, Albert R. *Rhetoric in American Colleges, 1850–1900.* Doctoral dissertation. U Washington, 1953. 382p.

Kitzhaber, Albert R. "Death—or Transfiguration?" *Col Engl* 21:367–73; 1960.

Kitzhaber, Albert R. *Themes, Theories, and Therapy: The Teaching of Writing in College.* McGraw-Hill, 1963. 175p.

Klauser, Eva L. "A Comparison of a Structural Approach and a Traditional Approach to the Teaching of Grammar in an Illinois Junior High School." Doctoral dissertation. U Colorado, 1964. 368p.

Knower, Franklin H. "Experimental Studies of Changes in Attitude. II: A Study of the Effect of Printed Argument on Changes of Attitude." *J Abn Social Psychol* 30:522–32; 1936.

Korzybski, Alfred. *Science and Sanity.* International Non-Aristotelian Library, 1933. 798p.

LaBrant, Lou L. "A Study of Certain Language Developments of Children in Grades Four to Twelve, Inclusive." *Genet Psychol Monogr* 14: 387–491; 1933.

Landry, Leonard P. *High School Grammar-Composition: Demonstrating a Correlation of the Traditional and Structural Methods of Language Analysis.* USOE Cooperative Research Project No. 1987. Colorado State Col, 1965.

Lee, Irving J. *Language Habits in Human Affairs.* Harper, 1941. 278p.

Leonard, Sterling A. *Doctrine of Correctness in English Usage.* U Wisconsin, 1929. 361p.

Leonard, Sterling A. *Current English Usage.* NCTE, 1932. 232p.

Lewis, Hilda P., and Lewis, Edward R. "Written Language Performance of Sixth Grade Children of Low Socio-economic Status from Bilingual and Monolingual Backgrounds." *J Exp Ed* 3:327–42; 1965.

Loban, Walter D. *The Language of Elementary School Children.* Research Report No. 1. NCTE, 1963. 92p.

Loban, Walter D. *Problems in Oral English.* Research Report No. 5. NCTE, 1966. 72p.

Lumsden, Robert. "Using Dictation Machines for Theme Correction." *Chicago Sch J* 43:17–9; 1961.

Lyman, Rollo L. *English Grammar in American Schools Before 1850.* GPO, 1922. 170p.

Lyman, Rollo L. *Summary of Investigations Relating to Grammar, Language, and Composition.* U Chicago, 1929. 302p.

Lynch, James J., and Evans, Bertrand. *High School English Textbooks: A Critical Examination.* Little, 1963. 526p.

Marckwardt, Albert H., and Walcott, Fred G. *Facts about Current English Usage.* NCTE English Monograph No. 7. Appleton, 1938. 144p.

McCarthy, Dorothea. "Language Development in Children." In Carmichael, Leonard (Ed.) *Manual of Child Psychology,* 2nd ed. Wiley, 1954. p. 492–630.

McClellan, Jack. "Creative Writing Characteristics of Children." Doctoral dissertation. U Southern California, 1956. 274p.

McColly, William, and Remstad, Robert. *Comparative Effectiveness of Composition Skills Learning Activities in the Secondary School.* USOE Cooperative Research Project No. 1528. U Wisconsin, 1963. 94p.

McDavid, Raven I. (Ed.) *An Examination of the Attitudes of the NCTE Toward Language.* Research Report No. 4. NCTE, 1965. 62p.

McGrath, Earl J. (Ed.) *Communication in General Education.* Brown, 1949. 244p.

McMechan, Melville Y. "The Relative Effectiveness of Four Procedures for Evaluating Students' Written Themes." Master's thesis. U British Columbia, 1961. 65p.

Meade, Richard A. "Who Can Learn Grammar?" *Engl J* 50:87–92; 1961.

Meckel, Henry C. "Research on Teaching Composition and Literature." In Gage, N. L. (Ed.) *Handbook of Research on Teaching.* Rand McNally, 1963. p. 966–1006.

Meckel, Henry C., and others. *Practices in the Teaching of Composition in California Public High Schools.* California State Department of Education Bulletin Vol. 27, No. 5, 1958.

Minteer, Catherine. *Words and What They Do to You.* Harper, 1953. 128p.

Modern Language Association. "The Basic Issues in the Teaching of English." *Pub MLA* 74:1–12; 1959.

Monk, Richard J. "A Study to Determine the Relationship Between Children's Home Environments and Their School Achievement in Written English." Doctoral dissertation. U Washington, 1958. 230p.

National Council of Teachers of English, Commission on the English Curriculum. *The English Language Arts.* NCTE Curriculum Series, Vol. 1. Appleton, 1952. 501p.

National Council of Teachers of English, Commission on the English Curriculum. *Language Arts for Today's Children.* NCTE Curriculum Series, Vol 2. Appleton, 1954. 431p.

National Council of Teachers of English, Commission on the English Curriculum. *The English Language Arts in the Secondary School.* NCTE Curriculum Series, Vol 3. Appleton, 1956. 488p.

National Council of Teachers of English, Committee on the National Interest. *The National Interest and the Teaching of English.* NCTE, 1961. 140p.

National Council of Teachers of English, Committee on the National Interest, *The Continuing Education of Teachers of English.* NCTE, 1964. 192p.

Nelson, Lois N. "Inquiry—Into the Influence of the Assigned Topic on Written Language." *California J Ed Res* 16:100–7; 1965.

Nordberg, H. O. "The Awareness Among Student Teachers Regarding Research in the Language Arts." Doctoral dissertation. U California, Berkeley, 1949.

Odom, Robert R. "Growth of a Language Skill: Punctuation." *California J of Ed Res* 15:12–7; 1964.

O'Donnell, Roy C. *The Correlation of Awareness of Structural Relationships in English and Ability in Written Composition.* USOE Cooperative Research Project No. 1524. Mount Olive Col, 1963. 45p.

O'Donnell, Roy C., and others. *A Transformational Analysis of the Language of Kindergarten and Elementary School Children.* Research Report No. 8. NCTE, 1967.

Ogden, Charles K., and Richards, Ivor A. *The Meaning of Meaning.* Harcourt, 1923. 544p.

O'Rourke, L. J. *Rebuilding the English-usage Curriculum to Insure Greater Mastery of Essentials.* Psychological Institute, 1934. 98p.

Page, Ellis B. "The Imminence of Grading Essays by Computer." *Phi Delta Kappan* 47:238–43; 1966.

Parker, John P. "Some Organizational Variables and Their Effect upon Comprehension." *J Communication* 12:27–32; 1962.

Parler, Nettie A. P. "Writing Skills of Prospective English Teachers." Doctoral dissertation. New York U, 1952. 140p.

Petty, Walter T. *Final Report, NCTE Committee on the State of Knowledge about the Teaching of Vocabulary.* NCTE, 1967.

Petty, Walter T., and Burns, Paul C. "A Summary of Investigations Relating to the English Language Arts in Elementary Education: 1965." *El Engl* 43: 252–77; 1966.

Pippert, Ralph R. "The Prediction of Correctness of Post-high School Written Language Performance." Doctoral dissertation. U Wisconsin, 1959. 119p.

Pooley, Robert C. *A Handbook of Current English Usage.* Bulletin, Series 30, No. 3. Colorado State Teach Col (Greeley), 1930. 52p.

Pooley, Robert C. *Grammar and Usage in Textbooks on English.* U Wisconsin, 1933. 172p.

Pooley, Robert C. *Teaching English Usage.* NCTE English Monograph No. 16. Appleton, 1946. 265p.

Potter, Robert R. "Sentence Structure and Prose Quality: An Exploratory Study." *Res in Teaching Engl* 1:17–28; 1967.

"Principles and Standards in Composition." *Kentucky Engl B* 6(Fall):3–72; 1956–1957.

"Project English." *Col Engl* 23:313–5; 1962.

Raph, Jane B. "Language Development in Socially Disadvantaged Children." *R Ed Res* 35:389–400; 1965.

Rice, Warner G. "A Proposal for the Abolition of Freshman English, As It Is Now Commonly Taught, from the College Curriculum." *Col Engl* 21:361–7; 1960.

Rinsland, Henry D. *A Basic Vocabulary of Elementary School Children.* Macmillan, 1945. 636p.

Roberts, Paul. *Patterns of English.* Harcourt, 1956. 314p.

Roberts, Paul. *English Sentences.* Harcourt, 1962. 294p.

Roberts, Paul. *English Syntax, A Programmed Introduction to Transformational Grammar.* Harcourt, 1964. 430p.

Rodgers, Paul C., Jr. "A Discourse-centered Rhetoric of the Paragraph." *Col Composition Communication* 17:2–11; 1966.

Rohman, D. Gordon, and Wiecke, Albert O. *Prewriting: The Construction and Application of Models for Concept Formation in Writing.* USOE Cooperative Research Project No. 2174. Michigan State U, 1964. 140p.

Rosenblatt, Louise M. *Research Development Seminar in the Teaching of English.* USOE Cooperative Research Project No. G-009. (N.p.), 1963. 79p.

Russell, David H., and others. *Research Design and the Teaching of English.* NCTE, 1964. 151p.

Sapir, Edward. *Language: An Introduction to the Study of Speech.* Harcourt, 1921. 258p.

Sauer, Edwin H. *Contract Correcting: The Use of Lay Readers in the High School Composition Program*, rev. ed. Harvard U, 1962. 59p.

Scofield, Alice F. G. "The Relationship of Teaching Methods in Language Arts Used in the Classroom to Those Advocated in Method Courses in Language Arts." Doctoral dissertation. Stanford U, 1955. 167p.

Searles, John R., and Carlsen, G. Robert. "English —Language, Grammar, and Composition." In Harris, Chester W. (Ed.) *Encyclopedia of Educational Research*, 3rd ed. Macmillan, 1960. p. 454–70.

Seegers, J. C. "Form of Discourse and Sentence Structure." *El Engl R* 10:51–4; 1933.

Sherwood, John C. "The Oregon Experiment: A Final Report." *Col Composition Communication* 9:5–9; 1958.

Sherwood, John C., and others. "Committee on Testing: Terminal Report." *Col Composition and Communication* 17:269–72; 1966.

Shugrue, Michael F. "New Materials for the Teaching of English: The English Program of the USOE." *Pub MLA* 41:1–36; 1966.

Slaughter, Eugene E. "The Use of Examinations for State Certification of Teachers." *J Teach Ed* 11: 231–8; 1960.

Smith, Dora V. *Class Size in High School English.* U Minnesota Press, 1931. 309p.

Smith, Dora V. *Instruction in English.* USOE Bulletin No. 17. GPO, 1933. 89p.

Smith, Dora V. "English Grammar Again." *Engl J* 27: 643–9; 1938.

Smith, Gerald H. "Inadequacies in a Selected Sample of Educational Research Proposals." Doctoral dissertation. Teachers Col, Columbia U, 1964.

Smith, Vernon H. "Team Teaching Has Advantages." *Engl J* 49:242–9; 1960.

Squire, James R. "National Study of High School English Programs: A School for All Seasons." *Engl J* 55:282–90; 1966.

Squire, James R., and Applebee, Roger K. *A Study of English Programs in Selected High Schools Which Consistently Educate Outstanding Students in English.* USOE Cooperative Research Project No. 1994. U Illinois, 1966. 601p. (For synopses, see Squire, 1966, and Applebee, 1966.)

Steinberg, Erwin R. *Needed Research in the Teach-*

ing of English. USOE Cooperative Research Monograph No. 11. GPO, 1963. 134p.

Steinberg, Erwin R., and others. *A Senior High School Curriculum in English for Able College-bound Students,* 5 vols. Curriculum Study Center in English, Carnegie Institute of Technology, 1966.

Steinmann, Martin, Jr. "Rhetorical Research." *Col Engl* 27:278–85; 1966.

Steinmann, Martin, Jr. "Review: The Measurement of Writing Ability." *Res Teaching Engl* 1:79–84; 1967.

Stone, George Winchester, Jr. "Five Years Since the Basic Issues Report." *Col Engl* 26:585–91; 1965.

Stormzand, Michael, and O'Shea, M. V. *How Much English Grammar?* Warwick, 1924. 224p.

Strickland, Ruth G. "The Language and Mental Development of Children." *B Sch Ed, Indiana U* 23:5–29; 1947.

Strickland, Ruth G. "Evaluating Children's Composition." *El Engl* 37:321–30; 1960.

Strickland, Ruth G. "The Language of Elementary School Children: Its Relationship to the Language of Reading Textbooks and the Quality of Reading of Selected Children." *B Sch Ed, Indiana U* 38:1–131; 1962.

Suggs, Lena R. "Structural Grammar Versus Traditional Grammar in Influencing Writing." *Engl J* 50:174–8; 1961.

Sutton, Joseph T., and Allen, Eliot D. *The Effect of Practice and Evaluation on Improvement in Written Composition.* USOE Cooperative Research Project No. 1993. Stetson U, 1964. 91p.

Symonds, Percival H. "Practice *versus* Grammar in the Learning of Correct English Usage." *J Ed Psychol* 22:81–96; 1931.

"Symposium on the Paragraph." *Col Composition Communication* 17:60–87; 1966.

Taylor, Philip H. "The English Composition in the Junior School: Prepared or Unprepared?" *Ed Res* (Britain) 5:57–62; 1962.

Thorndike, Edward L., and Lorge, Irving. *The Teacher's Word Book of 30,000 Words.* Teachers Col, Columbia U, 1944. 274p.

Thorndike, Edward L., and others. "An Inventory of English Constructions with Measures of Their Importance." *Teach Col Rec* 28:580–610; 1927.

Trager, George L., and Smith, Henry Lee, Jr. *An Outline of English Structure.* Battenburg, 1951. 92p.

Valley, John R. "College Actions on CEEB Advanced Placement English Examination Candidates." *Engl J* 48:398–401; 1959.

Waples, Douglas. (Ed.) *Print, Radio, and Film in a Democracy.* U Chicago Press, 1942. 197p.

Wasson, Richard. *Proceedings of the Allerton Park Conference on Research in the Teaching of English.* USOE Cooperative Research Project No. G-006. (N.p.), 1963. 126p.

Watts, A. F. *The Language and Mental Development of Children.* Heath, 1944. 354p.

Weathers, Winston. "The Rhetoric of the Series." *Col Composition Communication* 17:217–22; 1966.

Weingarten, Samuel, and Kroeger, Frederick P. *English in the Two-year College.* NCTE, 1965. 112p.

White, Robert H. "The Effect of Structural Linguistics on Improving English Composition Compared to That of Prescriptive Grammar or the Absence of Grammar Instruction. Doctoral dissertation. U Arizona, 1964. 197p.

Wiley, Autrey Nell. (Ed.) *The Preparation and Certification of Teachers of English: A Bibliography.* NCTE, 1957. 58p. (Supplements are published annually in *Col Engl.*)

Wolf, Melvin H. *Effect of Writing Frequency upon Proficiency in a College Freshman English Course.* Cooperative Research Project No. 2846. U Massachusetts, 1966. 52p.

Womack, William T. "A Study of Teachers' Attitudes Toward Debatable Items of English Usage." Doctoral dissertation. Teachers Col, Columbia U, 1957. 198p.

Woodward, John C., and Phillips, Arthur G. "Profile of the Poor Writer—The Relationship of Selected Characteristics to Poor Writing in College." *Res Teaching Engl* 1:41–53; 1967.

"The Workload of a College English Teacher." *Col Engl* 28:55–7; 1966.

Wormsbecker, John H. "A Comparative Study of Three Methods of Grading Compositions." Master's thesis. U British Columbia, 1955. 44p.

ENGLISH LITERATURE

The teaching of literature in the schools has been influenced less by educational research than by the recommendations of leading teachers, scholars, and curriculum specialists and by the trends in literary criticism and literary scholarship. Nevertheless, studies of response to literature, reading interest, and instructional method have yielded considerable data. The lack of valid and reliable instruments for assessing growth in literary appreciation has deterred researchers from studying the teaching of literature as extensively as other areas of the curriculum. Even so, the accumulation of knowledge presently available offers valuable insights to researchers and curriculum specialists.

HISTORY. The history of instruction in literature in this country has reflected the shifting relationships between the entrance requirements of the colleges and the curriculum of the schools. Mersand (1960) found that instruction in literature became important during the period from 1867 to 1889, an era characterized by three trends: the development of annotated textbooks for student study, an emphasis on selected reading, and the beginning of a movement for uniform college entrance requirements. This concern with the reading of college-bound youth, characteristic of all American education at the turn of the century, led to the prescription for the schools of a rigorous, highly disciplined curriculum in literature emphasizing a small number of texts, mostly British ones or classics in translation. The most influential list was prepared by the National Conference on Uniform Entrance Requirements in English (Butler, 1900) and suggested not only a common body of literary materials but common aims and standards.

A reaction against the college domination of the literature curriculum began early in the present century as educators developed greater concern for the education of all young people. In a classic statement for the joint committee of the Commission on Reorganization of Secondary Education of the National Education Association and the National Council of Teachers of English (NCTE), Hosic (1917) attempted to free the high school from prescribed lists and emphasized the function of literature to broaden and deepen imaginative life, to provide materials out of which may emerge worthy ideals, to enhance appreciation and enjoyment, and to stimulate sensitivity.

The effect of the Hosic report was a new freedom for school reading programs. During the next several decades prescribed reading lists gave way to suggested lists and intensive reading yielded to extensive reading. In a national status survey, Dora V. Smith (1933) reported that the purpose of literary instruction in a majority of schools was to extend the range of students' interests and understandings; that an increasing number of programs featured extensive, supplementary, and even "free" reading; and that the study of magazines and newspapers was replacing the study of some traditional literature.

Support for this new freedom came during the mid-1930's with the publication of two influential curriculum studies sponsored by the National Council of Teachers of English. Hatfield (1935), in *An Experience Curriculum in English,* emphasized the selection of stories within the emotional and intellectual range of pupils. Weeks (1936), in *A Correlated Curriculum in English,* suggested ways of relating literature to other school subjects. In addition to these, Rosenblatt, (1938) in *Literature as Exploration,* a study prepared for the Commission on Human Relations of the Progressive Education Association, reemphasized that a dynamic relationship exists between the book and reader, that reading provides intense human experience, and that the ways in which the sciences deal with human behavior can contribute much to the study of literature. Ideas presented in these three reports stimulated much curricular experimentation during the next two decades.

One of the major developments during this period was the widespread experimentation with thematic and topical units: large numbers of literary selections organized under topics or themes closely related to students' interests. In retrospect, this development seems to have been influenced not only by schools concerned with personal interests of pupils but also by literary scholars concerned with history of ideas and American studies, who emphasized the ideational content of literature. At this time a large body of modern literature was introduced into the curriculum, including literary works written expressly for children and adolescents. Here again school planners were encouraged by a growing scholarly attention to contemporary literature, especially modern American literature.

These changes occurred gradually over several decades. A study by Dora V. Smith (1941a) showed schools in New York state still clinging to traditional values, and a recent review of literature textbooks by Berberi (1964) indicated that during the 1935–1941 interlude, most literature anthologies prepared for the schools adhered to traditional views. Not until the 1950's were most school anthologies influenced by the newer trends.

Beginning with Dora V. Smith's report on instruction in New York state (1941a), concern has repeatedly been expressed with the quality and extent of literary experiences in the elementary program. Pooley and Williams (1948) and Farmer and Freeman (1952) reported that little organized attention was devoted to literature in the elementary school, the latter study suggesting that less than 4 percent of school time was devoted to literature in elementary schools in Georgia. Similar concern has been expressed recently by the NCTE Committee on the National Interest (National Council of Teachers of English, Committee on the National Interest, 1961, 1964).

A complete discussion of a program in literature reflecting and in some ways summarizing the attitudes which began with the Hosic report appeared in three volumes prepared by the NCTE Commission on the English Curriculum (National Council of Teachers of English, Commission on the English Curriculum, 1952, 1954, 1956). The first report of the commission, entitled *The English Language Arts,* outlined overall guide lines in all areas of English for the development of skills, interests, and attitudes from preschool through college education. *Language Arts for Today's Children* provided a detailed discussion of instruction at the elementary level; *The English Language Arts in the Secondary School* followed with guide lines for grades 7–12. All three reports stressed the importance of personal values in reading, the relationship of books to individual experience, the social uses of reading (including reading of the mass media), and the necessity of producing diversified reading for young people.

Toward the end of the 1950's the attitudes toward instruction in literature reflected in these reports were challenged by new formulations of purpose placing greater stress on the content and discipline of literary studies (see the section "Objectives," immediately following), placing a new emphasis on the intensive reading of a smaller number of texts, and encouraging a renewed interest on the part of college English departments in school programs. The substitution in college courses of analytical approaches to literature for historical, moral, sociological, and psychological approaches, marked by the widespread influence of *Understanding Poetry* by Brooks and Warren (1960) and *Theory of Literature* by Wellek and Warren (1956), was almost certain to have an impact on the attitudes of teachers educated by these modern intensive methods. Thus, the recent emphasis on a more narrow, selective literature program in high schools seems to have been an inevitable consequence of changes in college instruction.

Examining the recommendations since 1892 of various commissions and committees on the teaching of literature in the schools, Rosewell (1965) reported the following proposals to have been most pronounced: (1) literary content based on British literature in preference to American literature; (2) literary content organized chronologically; (3) literary content taught in connection with the authors themselves as craftsmen; (4) literary content composed of classics and major literary works taught in their entirety; (5) literature organized into a survey course covering a broad sampling of writers through excerpts of their writing; (6) literary content organized according to form or genre; (7) literary content based on pupil-interest or pupil-experience units; (8) literary content designed to prepare high school students for college; and (9) study of literature organized to follow logical sequence. In some ways, proposals have come full circle from an emphasis on rigorous, disciplined content, through the broader, general survey of classical and modern writing, and back to intensive programs emphasizing a narrow range of reading.

OBJECTIVES. A modern reassessment of the purposes of English instruction was heralded in 1958 by *The Basic Issues in the Teaching of English* prepared by a joint committee of NCTE, the Modern Language Association of America (MLA), the American Studies Association, and the College English Association (National Council of Teachers of English, 1959). By defining 35 basic problems confronting the profession, the statement generated discussion throughout American schools and colleges. The questions concerning the literature program focused new attention on perennial problems: Should certain literary works be required at various levels? What approaches to a literary work are possible and profitable at different levels? Is teaching the reading of factual prose as much of an obligation of the English teacher as training in the careful reading of literature? What is the relation between learning to write and the reading of imaginative literature?

Within a few years after publication of the Basic Issues report, the NCTE's Committee on the National Interest published two volumes calling for widespread changes in research, curriculum, and teacher education (National Council of Teachers of English, Committee on the National Interest, 1961, 1964). The College Entrance Examination Board (CEEB) appointed the Commission on English, whose creation of a tripartite division of high school English programs—language, literature, and composition—was to have an important influence (Commission on English, 1965). In 1961 the United States Office of Education launched Project English, a multimillion-dollar program of support for research, curriculum development, and ultimately for teacher institutes in English. Because pilot institutes sponsored by the CEEB commission had suggested the importance of teacher preparation in language, literature, and composition, many of the government-sponsored institutes followed the same pattern. This concern with a tripartite curriculum seemed to assure literature of greater attention in the national-institute program than it was receiving in many research and development programs which focused on language and composition. To redress the balance the NCTE appointed in 1964 the prestigious Commission on Literature, which three years later issued its first public statement (Stafford, 1967). The continuing discussion of aims is reflected also by Frazier's statement (1966) for the NCTE Commission on the Curriculum and two recent reports by Muller (1967) and Dixon (1967) of the Anglo-American Seminar on the teaching of English held at Dartmouth College in 1966.

The purposes of English instruction recommended by the CEEB Commission on English (1965) were fully developed in *Freedom and Discipline in English*. The commission saw the curriculum to be arrived at by a consensus of teachers in every school, with the timing and the sequence of study to vary with the competence and maturity of students. The purpose of instruction is to teach students to understand and to evaluate literature, a goal to be achieved by teaching students the art of criticism. Carefully planned, intensive study of selected major works, read in their entirety, was seen as the best way of achieving this goal, with the actual choice of books being made by teachers, who should balance the quality of each work against its suitability or unsuitability for particular groups of students. Clearly rejecting the concept of a prescribed reading list, the commission emphasized the reading of selected major works of continuing value and called for schools to encourage familiarity with legend and myth, the "literature beyond literature."

In a checklist for evaluating instruction developed after visits to 158 selected high school English programs, Squire (1966) suggested the need for balance between intensive and extensive reading.

Frazier (1966), in *Ends and Issues: 1965–1966*, writing for the NCTE Commission on the English Curriculum, identified the following major issues in curricular development, showing that some purposes of literary instruction remain unresolved: (1) the need for more attention to literature in elementary schools; (2) making use of student preferences in choosing literary selections; (3) determining the best way to organize programs: (4) the value of independent reading as a class activity; (5) the basis for sequence; and (6) the relationship of the humanities to the total program.

A similar concern for ends as well as means emerged at the Anglo-American Seminar on the teaching and learning of English, held at Dartmouth College in 1966, mentioned before. In separate reports, Muller (1967) and Dixon (1967) stressed the concern of conferees with the imaginative development of young people. Active, emotional engagement in the literary experience was seen as a major goal of instructional programs. Concern was expressed lest instruction in literary criticism and literary history inhibit the child's personal involvement.

The most complete contemporary statement of the objectives of literary study was written by Stafford (1967) for the NCTE Commission on Literature, reflecting the views of scholars, critics, writers, and teachers. The statement emphasized the significance of imaginative experiences for individuals in our society. Some acquaintance with the structure of literature, with literary history, and with literary biography was seen to contribute to the students' understanding and appreciation, but the ultimate test was held to be the power of the imaginative experience itself. Aware of the continuing blunting of student sensibilities in our culture through an overemphasis on the factual, the trite, and the trivial, the commission called for a reemphasis on the teaching of imaginative literature in the schools.

CURRICULUM. Recent widespread experimentation and change in the curriculum in literature was heralded by several status surveys. Jewett (1959) studied 256 local courses of study and found literature-centered units, thematically oriented, in three-fourths of all junior high school programs, with the percentage of thematically oriented units falling to 18 percent in grades 5 to 12, where the study of literary types predominates. Sherwin (1956) identified 2,300 assumptions concerning human behavior in a single curriculum, most of them related to the social and psychological behavior of man. He found that existing programs emphasized romantic views of life and the moral virtues of fidelity, chastity, and truthfulness.

Lynch and Evans (1963) examined 72 high school literature anthologies and found them critically wanting. Although praising the adequate treatment of vocabulary in context, the sufficient quantity of reading matter, and the physical format of the texts, they severely criticized the inadequacy of selections, the alteration of selections, the dominance of organization over content, the indiscriminate nature of questions and activities, the lack of clear purpose, the dismissal of the past, and the editorial tone of most texts. Perhaps because of such criticism, Berberi (1964) reported that literature textbooks published from 1960 to 1964 tend to be more traditional than those published during the 1950's.

Squire and Applebee (1966) examined the teaching of English in 158 outstanding high school English programs and reported that, on the average, 52.2 percent of classroom time was devoted to the teaching of literature. In grade 10 the proportion of time was 46 percent; in grade 12, 61.5 percent. Only 40.8 percent of the teaching time for terminal students was devoted to literature. The data from all the observations have been conveniently summarized by Applebee (1966).

Despite the analytical reading of selected major works, the long-time stress on individual reading and suggested reading continues to influence school planning. Rosewell (1965) found that of 934 titles proposed by the Committee of Ten in 1892, 123 appeared on school lists in 1935 and continued to be taught. Anderson (1964) conducted a survey of public, Catholic, and independent secondary schools and reported that 1,000 separate titles were being taught. Novels were more frequently taught than any other literary genre. Only three selections were taught by more than 75 percent of all schools reporting: *Macbeth, Julius Caesar,* and *Silas Marner.*

This variation in required reading tends to be supported by college English departments whose requirements were studied by Friedrich and Lander (1963). They found that most colleges do not prescribe any particular list of books but agree unanimously that students should study literature of real merit in unabridged form.

The reemphasis on the intensive reading of major or standard selections was partially offset by other developments. Changes in publishing reported by Squire (1960) made available a rich variety of books, often in inexpensive format. Lacampagne (1965 presented the recommendations of two national conferences of high school chairmen calling for classroom libraries of 500 separate titles, and the NCTE Committee on the National Interest (National Council of Teachers of English, Committee on the National Interest, 1961, 1964) emphasized the importance of good library collections to programs in literature.

With access to a greater variety of books and with contemporary literature receiving serious critical study, teachers of English and librarians became involved in widespread censorship incidents. A series of studies documented that outside efforts to control the books taught in English classrooms had affected a substantial number of teachers. In Wisconsin, Burress (1963) reported that 22 percent of all public school teachers had been involved in such disputes. Knudson (1967) found programs affected in 52 percent of California's public junior colleges. These findings were supported by Squire and Applebee (1966) and Farley (1964), who found voluntary censorship by teachers and librarians to be more frequent than involuntary censorship. To avoid controversies over books involving explicit treatment of sex, of racial or political problems, and often of sectarian issues, school personnel frequently removed titles from classroom and library shelves. In a national study, Ahrens (1965) reported that better-prepared teachers of English, those who have read widely and who encourage their students to read widely, are the teachers most likely to become involved in book-selection incidents. Although NCTE and other professional associations have strongly urged school systems to adopt standard policies of screening complaints about books read in schools, Ahrens found only 16 percent of English teachers reporting the adoption of such book-selection policies.

Concern has continued to be expressed over the need to strengthen the curriculum in literature in the elementary school. The Committee on the National Interest (National Council of Teachers of English, Committee on the National Interest, 1961) echoed earlier criticisms made by Pooley and Williams (1948) and by Farmer and Freeman (1952) that only a small percentage of time was devoted to literature in conventional elementary programs.

Durkin (1964) and Plessas and Oakes (1964) showed the important effects of preschool oral reading and literature experiences on the reading skill of children. Strickland (1964), reviewing the contributions of linguistics to children's language development, emphasized the significance of oral experiences in literature in expanding the linguistic repertoire of disadvantaged children. Cohen (1966) tested this hypothesis in slum-area schools of New York City and reported that daily oral reading by the teacher resulted in significant increases in vocabulary and reading comprehension.

An important development during the past decade has been the beginning of serious criticism of books written for children and adolescents. Studies of the quality of such writing will ultimately assist curriculum specialists in identifying those titles most appropriate for school reading. Dora V. Smith (1963) analyzed the books for children published during the preceding fifty years. Shepard (1962) and Stoer (1963), studying positive and negative portrayals of characters in children's books as determined by race, nationality, religion, socioeconomic status, and standards of conduct, differed on the extent to which most portrayals seemed to be idealized. Holmze (1966) found that fiction for children published from 1945 to 1960 depicted adult characters and urban settings more frequently than fiction published from 1920 to 1940. Burris (1966) evaluated the accuracy of treatment of Japanese customs and settings in children's books published between 1953 and 1964. Studies of this kind represent the beginning of serious critical evaluation.

"Junior" novels, fiction written especially for adolescents and often used as "transitional" literature suitable for young people not yet interested in mature adult reading, also have begun to receive serious critical study. Alm (1955) and Dunning (1959) analyzed assumptions in these books concerning human experience and the role of such books in the educative process. Although many junior novels tended to present unrealistic, didactic views of human behavior reflecting middle-class values, Dunning recommended their use as effective bridges to adult reading. Evans (1961), in a compared-group experiment, found *Swiftwater,* which he regarded as a superior junior novel, as effective as *Silas Marner* in preparing grade 10 students to read *The Pearl.* Magaliff (1964) provided the first full-length assessment of the genre. Blount (1963) compared students' concepts of the novel genre with the concepts held by selected experts. In a study of the reading of six grade 4 and 5 classes, he found that the study of three junior novels brought students' perceptions of the genre closer to the perceptions of specialists than did reading and discussion of three adult novels. Agee (1966) completed an archetypal analysis of the theme of initiation (into adult life) in the modern American novel about adolescents.

Without question the most influential developments in curriculum during recent years have been the work of the curriculum-study centers sponsored by the United States Office of Education (USOE). These centers, described by Bennett (1966) for the NCTE Commission on the English Curriculum and by Shugrue (1966), have developed and often tested in the schools pilot programs for teaching English at various instructional levels. Sample units of instruction, provided for study by participants at summer institutes on English, have served to spur local curriculum revision. As final reports of the work of these centers become published independently, schools will be provided with a variety of approaches for reorganizing programs in literature. Although varying in purpose, content, and approach, the programs provide rich resources for curriculum planning. Several seem likely to be especially influential in affecting future programs in literature. The center at Carnegie Institute of Technology has developed literature programs for both college-bound and general high school students organized on a thematic basis. At the University of Oregon center for grades 5–12, the literature program has stressed the sequential and cumulative study of concepts of literary form and craft. Influenced strongly by modern literary criticism, especially the insights of critic Northrop Frye, the K–12 program at the University of Nebraska has focused on the structure of literature and the reading of legends and folktales as "reservoir literature" needed to understand allusions. The state of Wisconsin's center, on the other hand, has adopted a more eclectic approach for grades K–12, reporting some of the most successful practices of teachers in that state. An "opus-centered" curriculum has been advanced by Purdue University's center, where the entire English program for grades 7–12 is organized around the study of such major works as *Treasure Island* and *A Midsummer Nights' Dream.* The project at Hunter College concentrated on developing literature-centered units for disadvantaged pupils in grades 7–12. At Florida State University three separate literature programs for the junior high school have been tested in the schools, one organized around themes and ideas, one around the "tripod" approach (separate units in language, composition, and literature), and an experimental literature program attempting to advance the cognitive processes described in the researches of Jerome Bruner and Jean Piaget. The new programs should generate a reconsideration of existing offerings as well as much activity in research.

In the college curriculum, the most significant publication has been *The College Teaching of English,* edited by Gerber and others (1965), which stressed the importance of sequential patterns in undergraduate programs. Rowland and associates (1966) summarized 180 articles on the college teaching of English published from 1957 to 1963, the great bulk of which reflected an increasing interest in American literature and the critical revolution that has directed attention to explication of text rather than to historical and biographical studies.

INSTRUCTION. Experimental studies of instructional procedures in teaching literature have been sporadic and disappointing, perhaps because researchers have lacked valid and reliable instruments for assessing the effectiveness of procedures. Until better instruments become available, studies with clear implications for teaching are not likely to emerge.

Several investigators attempted to identify the skills involved in comprehending literature. An early investigation by Irion (1925) identified four aspects of comprehension: broad reading, fact comprehension, word knowledge, and general comprehension. Hartley (1930) designed tests for four areas of comprehension of poetry: comprehension of figures or symbols, sense impressions, implications, and literal expressions. Analyses of the factors involved in comprehension reported by Davis (1944) and Harris (1948) suggested important avenues of exploration, but investigators have shown little interest in such problems during recent years. Harris found four operations involved in comprehending literature: translating the meaning from obscure passages, summarizing, combining details, and inferring the mood and intent of a selection. Such findings assist in identifying aspects of the process of reading literature which may require stress in the classroom.

Considerable recent interest has focused on the processes of classroom discussion of literature. Taba (1955) analyzed the responses of high school students in discussing literature and reported that factual restatement of ideas predominated. Only 12 percent of the students generalized concerning the meaning of the narrative. Taba noted, however, that group discussion tended to push the level of thinking beyond the levels which individuals reach on their own. Support for group discussion was also presented by Casper (1964), who found that adult-led junior Great Books discussions encouraged divergent thinking, the ability to form new ideas.

Wolfe and others (1967) found that the kinds of questions that elementary teachers ask children about literature influence the responses of children. Analytical questions tend to stimulate analytical thinking.

Levinson (1962) reported that the viewing of film versions of short stories, whether shown before or after reading, improved the response of both younger and older readers and of good and poor readers in the junior high school.

As a result of four years work in a center for curriculum development in English, Steinberg and others (1966) recommended inductive teaching of literature which encourages students to make their own discoveries in literature. LaRocque (1965), defining inductive teaching somewhat more rigorously, reported that a compared-group study in teaching figurative language to 211 high school subjects consistently showed deductive teaching to be less effective than inductive teaching.

Modification of the overall program in which literature is taught has been suggested by several recent studies. Walker (1964) reviewed modern criticism and the work of specialists in teaching literature and recommended that classroom study include a careful analysis of the work to see what structural relationships exist within the work. The study of structure, reported Walker, broadens the base of literary appreciation by enabling readers to respond not only to its meaning but to the craftsmanship involved in its creation. Fagan (1964) looked to field theory in the sciences as his model and suggested its extension to school literary programs. In an interesting pilot study, Henry and Brown (1966) suggested that teachers of English emulate strategies of thinking by explicitly teaching young people to understand and apply methods of mathematics, such as creating a structure of relations among ideas, abstracting, generalizing, and interpreting. A pilot analysis of two poems by four groups of students consciously employing such strategies yielded promising results.

A few recent studies advanced hypotheses for teaching and testing which require additional investigation. They demand attention less because of the conclusiveness of the findings than for their potential implications. Britton (1954) found that students' reactions to particular poems improve with planned rereading of the poems. Similar results were reported by Rees and Pederson (1965), who found positive evaluations of poetry associated with familiarity with the poetry, cooperative attitudes, and a factor called "sophistication." Glascow (1961) reported that two groups of college sophomore girls discriminated significantly between high-quality and low-quality oral presentation of literature. Prettyman (1965) contrasted a "lecture" method and an "activity" method of teaching literature to grade 12 students and reported that students receiving the lectures tended to outperform those in the "activity" classes.

Studies of the advantages of extensive and intensive reading have continued for 40 years, with virtually all studies indicating that extensive reading of literature results in the reading of more books, in the development of more favorable attitudes toward books, and in continued growth in reading skill. The classic study in this area by Coryell (1927) found no significant difference in the tested achievement in reading of students in intensive and extensive programs. LaBrant (1936, 1961) described the contributions of free reading to an expansion of the reading interest of young people, and in a follow-up study of subjects some 20 years later found that as adults the subjects who had completed a six-year free-reading program were doing significantly more reading than most other groups with which they were compared. Norvell (1941) matched 24 experimental and control classes and reported that pupils who completed programs of extensive reading made small but significantly greater gains in reading ability than did those in more restrictive programs. Superior pupils appeared to progress better in such programs than did average pupils.

Handlan (1946) found that extensive reading must be guided carefully by the teacher lest young people continue to read at their present level of quality and interest and not progress to more mature experiences.

Even in the elementary school, the effectiveness of extensive reading has been demonstrated. Sartain

(1961) found that self-selection of books encouraged wider reading among students. Lawson (1964) compared different proportions of extensive reading and systematic instruction in reading skills and reported that the most efficient practice was one combining 30 minutes of skill instruction with 15 minutes of free reading. Powell (1966) emphasized the importance of classroom libraries as a stimulus to recreational reading in the elementary school. Fink and Bogart (1965) placed paperback libraries in 50 schools (10 elementary and 40 secondary) for a year and reported that 62 percent of all students claimed the collections had increased their personal reading. A majority of teachers also felt that their methods of instruction had changed considerably (18.8 percent) or moderately (36.5 percent) as a result of the libraries.

READING INTERESTS. For four decades or longer the reading interests of children and adolescents have been surveyed in a series of studies which, if superficial in design and naïve in not recognizing the cause of reading interests, has nevertheless provided the schools with abundant evidence concerning the choices that children exercise in their reading. Reviewing the impact of such studies, Meckel (1963) observed that they have affected the supplementary reading programs in the junior and senior high schools.

By 1955 Robinson could point to more than 200 special studies of reading preferences; at a slightly decelerating rate, more have been reported each year. Among the more significant are those by Terman and Lima (1935), Thorndike (1941), and Wollnar (1949). The findings reveal broad agreement on the factors involved: intelligence, for example, is not a markedly significant factor affecting the reading preferences of a majority of readers; sex difference, on the other hand, is highly significant. The age of the child appears as a more significant factor during the elementary school years than later. Differences in socioeconomic backgrounds also appear to affect reading preferences. Specific elements of content in the reading material evoke markedly different response patterns. Scientific themes and such elements as humor, surprise, and a stirring plot appeal to most young readers. Boys respond well to sports, action, and adventure; girls to romance, fictional (as opposed to real) characters, and depictions of adolescent life. Using personal interviews with 153 boys in grades 4, 5, and 8, Stanchfield (1962) confirmed the general findings reported in earlier studies based on questionnaires, check lists, and similar devices.

Norvell (1950, 1958) reported the reactions of large numbers of children and young people to specific titles frequently included in school programs. His influential work has proven helpful in determining which standard works to require in the curriculum. Helpful suggestions are also provided by Whitman's report (1964) on the titles which superior college students recalled as their most memorable reading experiences in secondary school.

Only a few recent studies of reading interests have added to existing knowledge. Jungeblut and Coleman (1965) tested the reactions of 4,088 children to 32 selections and confirmed that reactions to style and content varied with age, although they found certain selections had general appeal. Squire and Applebee (1966) found 16,089 high school students in outstanding high school English programs reading an average of nine books a month and expressing a decided preference for the public library as the source of books for personal reading. The investigators attributed this preference to the inadequacy of school book collections.

Simpson and Soares (1965) asked 4,250 junior high school students to rate 862 short stories, then analyzed the 77 least-liked and best-liked selections. Among the factors of high appeal were physical action, conflict, suspense, a single unifying action, and concrete and clear language. Among the selections least-liked by the students were stories considered to be well-written by adult critics. Further evidence that children base their qualitative distinctions on criteria different from those used by adults emerged in studies by Peltola (1963, 1965). She found a significantly high number of "nonprize" picture books chosen over prize books by 192 grade 1 children. In a study of the favorite characters of 3,187 subjects, she discovered that grade 4 children named characters from significantly more recommended titles than did grade 6 children and that characters from realistic stories were preferred to those from fanciful writing. Peltola also found that children who tended to choose the nonrecommended-series books had a significantly higher reading achievement than others in the study.

Continuing research in this area appears to be important primarily for confirming that patterns of interest do not change markedly with each new generation of children.

RESPONSE TO LITERATURE. Comparatively little is known about the way in which readers respond to a literary work and about the reader's acquisition through reading of fresh insights into human behavior which affect his personal attitudes. Studies have continued to reveal that the nature of literary response is a highly personal phenomenon affected by emotional factors. Meckel (1946), Squire (1956), and Gray (1958) reported various case studies demonstrating that individual readers are affected by highly emotional reactions to the ideas in literary selections. Rogers (1965) studied individual differences in the responses of 14 high-level and 14 low-level readers and found the variation in individual responses (as distinct from attitudes toward reading) to be unrelated to reading ability. Whitehead (1956) found differences in sex, age, and school less important than the qualities of a novel in affecting the reader's ease of identification. Russell (1958) examined 73 studies on the impact of reading on the individual and identified four variables affecting responses: the form of the reading materials, the content and ideas, the reader himself, and the setting in which responses are made. Russell reported that investigators found it difficult to distinguish the influences of reading on other activities.

Several decades of study have only begun to develop understanding about the processes of response. In an early analysis, Downey (1929) related literary response to the psychological doctrine of identification. She presented a threefold classification of responses: the ecstatic, where the self-conscious reader is merged with the subject that he is enjoying; the participator, where the reader assumes one personality after another; and the spectator, who is detached from the action and evaluates as an observer. Downey hypothesized that the type and content of the literary selection affected the mode of response.

Richards (1929) analyzed the misinterpretations of selected college readers of 13 poems of unknown authorship and discovered not only stereotyped responses and difficulties in comprehension but also effects of general critical and technical prejudgments which the individual brings to his reading. Rosenblatt (1938) emphasized the interaction of the literary work and the reader, suggesting that individuals tend to read works that have possibilities for significant interaction.

Squire (1956) analyzed the responses of 50 adolescent readers to four short stories and reported covariation of literary judgments (dealing with formal qualities) and emotional self-involvement responses. Fewer literary judgments occur while adolescents read the central portion of a story than occurs before involvement or at the end of reading. Squire also identified six sources of misinterpretation in adolescent responses: failure to grasp the essential meaning; reliance upon patterns of stereotyped thinking; unwillingness to accept unpleasant facts in interpreting characters and their actions; critical predispositions; irrelevant associations; and unwillingness to suspend judgment until the story is completed. Wilson (1966), using a similar method for classifying responses of college students to novels, reported an increase in the proportion of interpretative responses over prescriptive judgments, suggesting that individuals may be better able to control their emotional reactions as they grow older. Wilson found that students begin involvement with literature in a comparatively groping and emotional fashion, with only their later responses formulated in logical ways. He suggested that teachers of literature should permit comparatively free responses to literary works before considering a close analysis.

The suggestion in Wilson's study that the more sophisticated reader is able to control his emotional reactions while reading and thus achieve a more objective reaction is supported by the theoretical views of Harding (1962), who believes that the mode of response of the mature reader of a novel can be regarded as an extension of the mode of response by an onlooker of actual events. The reader not only enters into the experience but also contemplates the experience; he knows that the characters in a literary selection are only part of a convention by which the author presents an evaluation of possible human experience. This view of the reader's response at the receiving end of a conventional mode of communication contrasts sharply with the conception of the process of response as one involving primarily identification and vicarious experience.

Early (1960) suggested that the maturity of the reader may affect the nature of his response and hypothesized that as readers grow older they pass through three stages of responses: from unconscious enjoyment to self-conscious appreciation to conscious delight.

A series of studies have identified some of the effects which reading can have on individuals. Waples and others (1940) reported that adult reading had five social effects: instrumental; acquisition of useful information; increased self-esteem and prestige; reinforcement of personal views; distraction from anxieties; and enriched aesthetic experience. Nila B. Smith (1948) found that 61 percent of elementary-school subjects reported changes in attitude as a result of reading. Loban (1953) reported significant differences in responses to reading between highly sensitive and less sensitive adolescent readers, particularly to stories intended to evoke human sympathy. Loban also reported a consistent tendency of subjects to identify with adolescents most closely resembling themselves.

Lodge (1956) showed that the reading of biography can influence the ideas held by some junior high school students. Blount (1963) found the reading of junior novels to influence adolescent concepts of the "ideal" novel; he also said that factors in the novel (e.g., form and content of ideas) are more important than factors in the reader (e.g., sex and scholastic ability) or the setting in which the novel is read. Tantara (1966) reported that the reading of four novels about scientists affected student attitudes about scientists, although not always in positive ways.

A number of studies thus suggest that reading can affect individuals in various ways, even though the nature of the interaction is highly individualistic. Russell and Shrodes (1950) and Herminghaus (1954) examined the possible uses of bibliotherapy and reported that the impact of literature on individuals cannot be predicted and cautioned against the indiscriminate use of books to promote change in attitudes and behavior.

A separate series of studies attempted to identify the factors involved in the appreciation of literature. Williams and others (1938) applied five tests of literary appreciation to more than 200 children and adolescents and found that a general factor of literary appreciation, correlated with intelligence, accounted for 50 percent of the variation in response, whereas a second bipolar factor, accounting for 20 percent of the variance, separated readers preferring the objective, form-conscious styles of the classicists from those preferring the subjective approaches of the romantic school of writers.

Gunn (1951) also identified a general factor associated with such factors as liking, emotional effect, mode of expression, and appeal of the subject, as well as a bipolar factor distinguishing readers concerned with rhyme, word music, and rhythm from those concerned with emotional effect, appeal of the subject, and mental imagery. The existence of a general appreciative factor was also reported by Forman (1951).

Carroll (1960) studied six dimensions of style: general stylistics evaluation, personal affect, ornamentation, abstractness, seriousness, and characterization versus narration. He attempted to quantify aspects of style by analyzing 150 passages of English prose in accordance with 29 adjectival scales covering major qualities and traits. He found a factor he called general stylistics evaluation indicating a positive or negative evaluation which seemed to support earlier findings on the existence of a general factor.

In a promising new approach, Peel (1964) reported using Osgood's semantic differential to analyze the preferences of readers in qualities of a work of art by applying a set of 20 scales including measures of vividness, depth, and clarity to selections from 12 major novelists. He noted that responses to paintings evoke more or less instantaneous attitudes, whereas responses to prose and poetry often require longer reflection on the part of the reader. His hypothesis seems to support Wilson's finding that initial responses to literature tend to be ambiguous and groping.

In studies of responses to literature, the method of analysis may be of as much importance to research as the reported findings. Investigators have relied on paper-and-pencil reactions, on case studies of readers, on written responses obtained after reading is completed, and on scales to indicate degree of identification. Forman (1951) found free responses more helpful than responses elicited by specific questions in attempting to measure appreciation. Squire (1956) recorded and analyzed oral responses to the reading of segments of short stories. Monson (1962) used three structured questions and one unstructured question in assessing the responses of grade 5 pupils and concluded that different methods of questioning result in different responses from children. Wolfe and others (1967) reported similar results in a study of classroom methodology.

An important new tool for assessing responses to literature is provided by Purves (1966, 1967), who examined the written responses and comments of 13 critics, 100 school and college teachers, and 200 children. He identified 70 separate elements involved in response to literature and classified them in four major categories: engagement (involvement), perception (understanding), interpretation, and evaluation. Using this method of analysis in a pilot study of reactions to literature, he found important differences in the reactions of 13-year-old American, British, German, and Belgian students, differences which he attributed to varying educational and cultural patterns.

EVALUATION. Research in the teaching of literature has been continually hampered by the lack of adequate instruments for measuring growth in literary appreciation. Until such instruments are available, investigators lack valid and reliable ways of assessing the impact of instructional practice, the adequacy of curricular programs, and the development of individual appreciation.

Attempts to devise appropriate methods of evaluation have been made periodically over the years. Loban (1948) suggested various paper-and-pencil devices for estimating student growth in ability to appreciate literature. Burton (1952) studied the reading of 190 grade 12 students and decided that although verbal intelligence and silent reading ability are important factors in appreciation, an additional appreciative factor exists independent of intelligence and reading. Squire (1956) also reported that the ability to appreciate seemed to operate independently of reading ability and intelligence. Burton suggested that one's socioeconomic background affects one's ability to appreciate, but unlike such researchers as Williams and others (1938) and Gunn (1951), he found that literary appreciation tends to be expressed in specific rather than general responses.

Forman (1951), experimenting with measurement of literary response, found that the degree of vividness of the reader's free recollections after reading offered a helpful index of appreciation.

Forehand (1966) constructed tests to measure understanding, interpretation, and evaluation of a single short story. Understanding was measured by factual multiple-choice items, interpretation by free-response items coded into ten categories, and attitude by use of semantic-differential scales applied to diverse concepts. Forehand also required readers to choose a "preferred" statement from several related to the short story. Purves (1966, 1967) developed a checklist of elements involved in writing about literature which was used as the basis for analyzing written responses of students.

Kuhn (1966) reviewed the research bearing on a proposed instrument to measure the literary appreciation of intermediate level children. In noticing that any valid instrument must consider what is known about reading preferences, comprehension, knowledge of literature, emotional response, apprehension of meanings, and judgment of literary quality, Kuhn reiterated the complex problems which continue to confront researchers in this area.

New approaches to evaluating instruction in literature may emerge from curriculum projects currently under way. As part of a project at Carnegie Institute of Technology, for example, Forehand (1965) developed a literary-discernment test and literary-preference test, the former to assess the student's ability to interpret, the latter the consistency of his interest in narrative, entertaining features, craft, or plot or theme.

As this article is being written, researchers on two large-scale projects for evaluating instruction in literature are at work. The National Assessment of Education in the United States includes literature as one of nine subject fields to be studied. The UNESCO Institute on Education at Hamburg is sponsoring an International Educational Achievement Study to include an assessment of instruction in literature. The new instruments designed for these studies may offer researchers important insights into the nature of evaluation.

TEACHER PREPARATION. The preparation of teachers in literature has been a major concern of educators during the past decade, with specific attention being paid to preservice teacher education and certification requirements and to the program of National Defense Education Act (NDEA) institutes for experienced teachers sponsored by the USOE.

The NCTE Committee on the National Interest summarized the status of teacher preparation (National Council of Teachers of English, Committee on the National Interest, 1961, 1964). More than 50 percent of all colleges require students majoring in secondary English to complete 12 to 18 semester hours in literature; two-thirds of the colleges require specific courses in English literature, American literature, and Shakespeare; one-third require work in world literature. Only a fifth require specific preparation in critical analysis, literary criticism, or contemporary literature. Only a few institutions impose a requirement to study literature written for adolescents. The majority of elementary teachers must complete a course in children's literature prior to certification; however, the number of semester hours available for the study of literature averages not more than six to eight hours, attesting to the fact that fewer than one-third of the institutions prescribe work for prospective elementary teachers in American literature, world literature, or English literature.

To recommend sound preparation for teachers at all levels, including the college level, Grommon (1963) edited for the Commission on the English Curriculum the volume *Education of Teachers of English*.

In 1965, three national associations, the NCTE, the MLA, and the National Association of State Directors of Teacher Education and Certification, launched a national series of conferences to secure a consensus on guide lines for preparing elementary and secondary teachers in English. Although unpublished at this writing, the guide lines, developed in cooperation with more than 1,000 professional leaders and scores of institutions, should prove influential during the coming decade.

The Illinois statewide curriculum-study center for the preparation of teachers of English, scheduled to complete five years of study in 1969, has involved 22 institutions of higher education in experimenting with new patterns of preparation.

The development of summer institute programs for teachers of English began in 1962 with 20 pilot programs sponsored by the CEEB. Three uniform components in each institute were courses in literature, language, and composition, with a workshop provided to assist teachers in integrating the course experiences. In an independent evaluation, Gerber (1963) found that 78 percent of the teacher participants responded favorably to the instruction in literature, the major purpose of which was to increase the teachers' knowledge of what was involved in close reading. The literature component included an examination of poetry, fiction, drama, with primary attention to genre, point of view, structure, meaning, and mode.

With the launching of the federal NDEA institute program in 1965, the pattern for institutes established by the CEEB was widely emulated. Squire and Gwynn (1965), concerned over the small number of institutes in English planned for elementary teachers, published a source book of ideas advanced by scholars and specialists on relating scholarship and pedagogy in offerings for the elementary teachers. More detailed recommendations for the preparation of elementary teachers in literature emerged from a conference of scholars and teachers at the University of Nebraska directed by Olson (1966).

Other dimensions of English education also received attention. Evans and Cardone (1964) studied the content of the methods course for secondary teachers. Meade (1964) described fifth-year and five-year programs of preparation for teachers of English. In 1966 the USOE launched an experienced-teacher fellowship program to provide year-long opportunities for selected elementary and secondary teachers of English and other subjects at selected universities.

Increasingly during recent years research and development in the teaching of literature have been influenced by the availability of grants to support large-scale programs. The involvement of large numbers of literary scholars and critics in pedagogically oriented projects has been an especially commendable development, and the funding of the National Endowment for the Arts and Humanities promises that current interest and activity will continue.

James R. Squire
University of Illinois

References

Agee, William Hugh. "The Initiation Theme in Selected Modern American Novels of Adolescence." Doctoral dissertation. Florida State U, 1966. 183p.

Ahrens, Nyla. "Censorship and the Teacher of English: A Questionnaire Survey of A Selected Sample of Secondary School Teachers of English." Doctoral dissertation. Teachers Col, Columbia U, 1965.

Alm, Richard S. "A Study of the Assumptions Concerning Human Experience Underlying Certain Works of Fiction Written for and about Adolescents." Doctoral dissertation. U Minnesota, 1955.

Anderson, Scarvia B. *Between the Grimms and "The Group": Literature in American High Schools*. ETS, 1964. 23p.

Applebee, Roger K. "National Study of High School English Programs: A Record of English Teaching Today." *Engl J* 55:273–81; 1966.

Bennett, Robert A. (Ed.) *Summary Progress Report of English Curriculum Study and Demonstration Centers*. NCTE, 1966. 44p.

Berberi, Edel Ann. "A Descriptive Analysis of Anthologies for the Tenth Grade as the Texts Are

Related to the Objectives for the Study of Literature as Expressed by National Professional Groups." Doctoral dissertation. Indiana U, 1964.

Blount, Nathan S. "The Effect of Selected Junior Novels and Selected Adult Novels on Student Attitudes Toward the 'Ideal' Novel." Doctoral dissertation. Florida State U, 1963.

Britton, J. N. "Evidence of Improvement in Poetic Judgment." *Br J Psychol* 45:196–208; 1954.

Brooks, Cleanth, and Warren, Robert Penn. *Understanding Poetry*. Holt, 1960. 584p.

Burress, Lee A. *How Censorship Affects the School*. Wisconsin Council of Teachers of English, 1963.

Burris, Miriam. "Japan in Children's Fiction." *El Eng* 43:29–38; 1966.

Burton, Dwight L. "The Relationship of Literary Appreciation to Certain Measurable Factors." *J Ed Psychol* 43:436–9; 1952.

Butler, N. M. "Unit Form College Entrance Requirements with a Common Board of Examiners." *Ed R* 19:68–74; 1900.

Carroll, John B. "Vectors of Prose Style." In Sebeok, Thomas. (Ed.) *Style in Language*. Wiley, 1960. p. 283–92.

Casper, Thomas P. "Effects of Junior Great Books Programs at the Fifth Grade Level on Four Intellectual Operations and Certain of Their Component Factors as Defined by J. P. Guilford." Doctoral dissertation. St. Louis U, 1964.

Cohen, Dorothy H. "The Effect of a Special Program in Literature on the Vocabulary and Reading Achievement of Second Grade Children in Special-service Schools." Doctoral dissertation. New York U, 1966.

Commission on English. *Freedom and Discipline in English*. CEEB, 1965. 178p.

Coryell, Nancy G. *An Evaluation of Extensive and Intensive Teaching of Literature: A Year's Experiment in the Eleventh Grade*. Contributions to Education No. 275. Teachers Col, Columbia U, 1927.

Davis, F. B. "Fundamental Factors of Comprehension in Reading." *Psychometrika* 9:186; 1944.

Dixon, John. *Growth through English*. National Association for the Teaching of English (United Kingdom), 1967.

Downey, June. *Creative Imagination: Studies in Psychology of Literature*. Routledge, 1929.

Dunning, Arthur S. "A Definition of the Role of the Junior Novel Based on Analyses of Thirty Selected Novels." Doctoral dissertation. Florida State U, 1959.

Durkin, Delores. "A Fifth-year Report on the Achievement of Early Readers." *El Sch J* 60:76–80; 1964.

Early, Margaret. "Stages of Growth in Literary Appreciation." *Engl J* 49:161–7; 1960.

Evans, William H. "A Comparison of the Effects of a Superior Junior Novel and *Silas Marner* on the Ability of Tenth Grade Students to Read the Novel." Doctoral dissertation. Florida State U, 1961. 195p.

Evans, William H., and Cardone, Michael J. *Specialized Courses in Methods in Teaching English*. NCTE, 1964. 32p.

Fagan, Edward R. *Field: A Process for Teaching Literature*. Pennsylvania State U Press, 1964. 216p.

Farley, John J. "Book Censorship in the Senior High School Libraries of Nassau County, New York." Doctoral dissertation. New York U, 1964.

Farmer, Paul, and Freeman, Bernice. *The Teaching of English in Georgia*. Georgia Council of Teachers of English, 1952.

Fink, Richard, and Bogart, Max. *Paperbound Books in New Jersey Public Schools*. New Jersey State Department of Education, 1965.

Forehand, Garlie A. "Summary and Conclusions from An Evaluative Study of a Senior High School Curriculum in English for Able College-bound Students." In Steinberg, Edwin, and Others. (Eds.) *A Senior High School Curriculum in English for Able College-bound Students—Summary Report*. USOE Cooperative Research Project H-015. Carnegie Institute of Technology, 1965. p. 77–102.

Forehand, C. A. "Problems of Measuring Response to Literature." *Clearing House* 40:369–75; 1966.

Forman, Earl. "An Instrument to Evaluate the Literary Appreciation of Adolescents." Doctoral dissertation. U Illinois, 1951.

Frazier, Alexander. (Ed.) *Ends and Issues: 1955–1966*. NCTE, 1966. 49p.

Friedrich, Gerhard, and Lander, Richard. (Eds.) *High School–College Articulation of English*. NCTE, 1963. 44p.

Gerber, John C. (Ed.) *An Independent Evaluation of the 1962 Summer Institute Program of the Commission on English of the College Entrance Examination Board, with Recommendations for Future Institutes*. USOE Cooperative Research Project G-004. U Iowa, 1963.

Gerber, John C., and others. (Eds.) *The College Teaching of English*. Appleton, 1965. 312p.

Glascow, George M. "The Effects of Manner of Speech on Appreciation of Spoken Literature." *J Ed Psychol* 52:322–9; 1961.

Gray, William S. "New Approaches to the Study of Interpretation in Reading." *J Ed Res* 52:65–7; 1958.

Grommon, Alfred H. (Ed.) *The Education of Teachers of English*. NCTE Curriculum Series, Vol. 5. Appleton, 1963. 604p.

Gunn, Douglas G. "Factors in the Appreciation of Poetry." *Br J Ed Psychol* 21:96–104; 1951.

Handlan, Bertha. "The Fallacy of Free Reading." *Engl J* 25:182–7; 1946.

Harding, D. W. "Psychological Processes in the Reading of Fiction." *Br J Aesthetics* 2:133–47; 1962.

Harris, Chester W. "Measurement of Comprehension of Literature." *Sch R* 56:280–9, 332–43; 1948.

Hartley, Helen W. *Tests of the Interpretative Reading of Poetry for Teachers of English*. Teachers Col, Columbia U, 1930.

Hatfield, W. Wilbur. *An Experience Curriculum in English*. Appleton, 1935. 323p.

Henry, George H., and Brown, John A. *An Inquiry into the Nature of Concept Development within the On-going Classroom Situation*. USOE Project D-067. U Delaware, 1966.

Herminghaus, E. G. "The Effect of Bibliotherapy on the Attitudes and Personal and Social Adjustment of a Group of Elementary Children." Doctoral dissertation. Washington U, 1954.

Holmze, Alma. "Interpersonal Relations in Children's Literature." *El Engl* 43:26–8, 52; 1966.

Hosic, James F. *Reorganization of English in Secondary Schools.* U.S. Bureau of Education Bulletin No. 2. GPO, 1917. 181p.

Irion, T. W. H. *Comprehension Difficulties of Ninth Grade Students in the Study of Literature.* Teachers Col, Columbia U, 1925.

Jewett, Arno. *English Language Arts in American High Schools.* USOE, 1959.

Jungeblut, Ann, and Coleman, John H. "Reading Content that Interests Seventh, Eighth, and Ninth Grade Students." *J Ed Res* 9:393–401; 1965.

Knudson, Rozanne. "Censorship in English Programs of California's Junior Colleges." Doctoral dissertation. Stanford U, 1967.

Kuhn, Doris Young. "Evaluation of Children's Responses to Literature." In Stryker, David. (Ed.) *New Trends in English Education.* NCTE, 1966. p. 69–76.

LaBrant, Lou L. *An Evaluation of the Free Reading in Grade Ten, Eleven, and Twelve.* Ohio State U Press, 1936.

LaBrant, Lou L. "The Use of Communication Media." In Willis, Margaret. (Ed.) *The Guinea Pigs After Twenty Years.* Ohio State U Press, 1961. p. 127–64.

Lacampagne, Robert. (Ed.) *High School Departments of English: Their Organization, Administration, and Supervision.* NCTE, 1965. 164p.

LaRocque, Geraldine. "The Effectiveness of the Inductive and Deductive Method of Teaching Figurative Language to 8th Grade Students." Doctoral dissertation. Stanford U, 1965.

Lawson, Hoyle D. "Effects of Free Reading on Reading Achievement of Sixth Grade Pupils." Doctoral dissertation. George Peabody Col, 1964.

Levinson, Elias. "Effects of Motion Pictures on the Response to Narrative, A Study of the Effects of Film Versions of Certain Short Stories on the Response of Junior High School Students." Doctoral dissertation. New York U, 1962.

Loban, Walter. "Evaluating Growth in the Study of Literature." *Engl J* 37:277–83; 1948.

Loban, Walter. "A Study of Social Sensitivity (Sympathy) Among Adolescents." *J Ed Psychol* 44:102–12; 1953.

Lodge, Helen C. "The Influence of the Study of Biography on the Moral Ideology of the Adolescent at the Eighth Grade Level." *J Ed Res* 50:241–55; 1956.

Lynch, James., and Evans, Bertrand. *High School English Textbooks: A Critical Examination.* Little, 1963. 526p.

Magaliff, Cecile. *The Junior Novel.* Kenicut Press, 1964.

Meade, Richard A. *Fifth-year and Five-year Programs for the Preservice Education of Teachers of English.* NCTE, 1964. 59p.

Meckel, Henry C. "An Exploratory Study of the Response of Adolescent Pupils to Situations in a Novel." Doctoral dissertation. U Chicago, 1946.

Meckel, Henry C. "Research on Teaching Composition and Literature." In Gage, N. L. (Ed.) *Handbook of Research on Teaching.* Rand McNally, 1963. p. 966–1006.

Mersand, Joseph. "The Teaching of Literature in American High Schools, 1865–1900." In Pooley, Robert C. (Ed.) *Perspectives on English.* Appleton, 1960. p. 269–302.

Monson, Dianne L. "Children's Responses to Humor in Literature." Doctoral dissertation. U Minnesota, 1962.

Muller, Herbert J. *The Uses of English.* Holt, 1967.

National Council of Teachers of English. *The Basic Issues in the Teaching of English.* NCTE, 1959. 16p.

National Council of Teachers of English, Commission on the English Curriculum. *The English Language Arts.* NCTE Curriculum Series, Vol. 1. Appleton, 1952. 501p.

National Council of Teachers of English, Commission on the English Curriculum. *Language Arts for Today's Children.* NCTE Curriculum Series, Vol. 2. Appleton, 1954. 431p.

National Council of Teachers of English, Commission on the English Curriculum. *The English Language Arts in the Secondary School.* NCTE Curriculum Series, Vol. 3. Appleton, 1956. 488p.

National Council of Teachers of English, Committee on the National Interest. *The National Interest and the Teaching of English.* NCTE Curriculum Series, 1961. 140p.

National Council of Teachers of English, Committee on the National Interest. *The National Interest and the Continuing Education of Teachers of English.* NCTE Curriculum Series, 1964. 192p.

Norvell, G. W. "Wide Individual Reading Compared with the Traditional Plan of Studying Literature." *Sch R* 49:603–13; 1941.

Norvell, G. W. *The Reading Interests of Young People.* Heath, 1950.

Norvell, G. W. *What Boys and Girls Like to Read.* Silver, 1958. 316p.

Olson, Paul A. (Ed.) *The Arts of Language.* U Nebraska Press, 1966. 224p.

Peel, E. A. "The Analysis of Preferences." In Russell, David H., and others. (Eds.) *Research Design and the Teaching of English.* NCTE, 1964.

Peltola, Bette J. "A Study of Children's Book Choices." *El Engl* 40:690–5, 702; 1963.

Peltola, Bette J. "A Study of the Indicated Literary Choices and Measured Literary Knowledge of Fourth and Sixth Grade Boys and Girls." Doctoral dissertation. U Minnesota, 1965.

Plessas, Gus P., and Oakes, Clifton R. "Prereading Experiences of Selected Early Readers." *Reading Teach* 17:241–5; 1964.

Pooley, Robert C., and Williams, R. D. *The Teaching of English in Wisconsin.* U Wisconsin Press, 1948.

Powell, William R. "Classroom Libraries: Their Frequency of Use." *El Engl* 43:395–7; 1966.

Prettyman, E. P. "Two Methods of Teaching English Literature and Student Attitudes toward these Methods." Doctoral dissertation. Pennsylvania State U, 1965.

Purves, Alan C. "An Examination of the Varieties of Criticism." *Col Composition Communication* 17:94–9; 1966.

Purves, Alan C. *The Elements of Writing About Literature.* NCTE, 1967.

Rees, Richard D., and Peterson, Darhl M. "A Factorial Determination of Points of View in Poetic Evaluation and Their Relation to Various Determinants." *Psychol Reports* 16:31–9; 1965.

Richards, I. A. *Practical Criticism: A Study in Literary Judgment.* Harcourt, 1929. 362p.

Robinson, Helen M. "What Research Says to the Teacher of Reading: Reading Interests." *Reading Teach* 8:173–7; 1955.

Rogers, Charlotte. "Individual Differences in Interpretive Responses to Reading Short Stories at the Eleventh Grade Level." Doctoral dissertation. U Arizona, 1965.

Rosenblatt, Louise M. *Literature as Exploration.* PEA, 1938.

Rosewell, Paul Truman. "A Historical Survey of Recommendations and Proposals for the Literature Curricula of American Secondary Schools Since 1892." Doctoral dissertation. U Nebraska, 1965. 416p.

Rowland, J. Carter, and others. *An Annotated Bibliography on the College Teaching of English, 1957–1963.* NCTE, 1966. 56p.

Russell, David H. "Some Research on the Impact of Reading." *Engl J* 47:398–413; 1958.

Russell, David H., and Shrodes, Caroline. "Contributions of Research in Bibliotherapy to the Language Arts Program." *Sch R* 58:334–42; 1950.

Sartain, Harry W. "Research on Individualized Reading." *Ed* 81:515–20; 1961.

Shepard, John P. "The Treatment of Characters in Popular Children's Fiction." *El Engl* 39:672–6; 1962.

Sherwin, J. Stephen. "Patterns of Assumptions in a High School Literature Curriculum." *J Ed Sociol* 29:321–9; 1956.

Shugrue, Michael F. "New Materials for the Teaching of English: The English Program of the USOE." *Pub MLA* 41:1–36; 1966.

Simpson, Roy H., and Soares, Anthony. "Best- and Least-liked Short Stories in Junior High School." *Engl J* 54:108–11; 1965.

Smith, Dora V. *Instruction in English.* USOE Bulletin No. 17. GPO, 1933.

Smith, Dora V. *Evaluating Instruction in English in the Elementary Schools of New York.* Scott, 1941(a).

Smith, Dora V. *Evaluating Instruction in Secondary School English.* Appleton, 1941(b).

Smith, Dora V. *Fifty Years of Children's Books, 1910–1960: Trends, Backgrounds, Influences.* NCTE, 1963.

Smith, Nila B. "Some Effects of Reading on Children." *El Eng* 25:271–8; 1948.

Squire, James R. "The Responses of Adolescents to Literature Involving Selected Experiences of Personal Development." Doctoral dissertation. U California, Berkeley, 1956.

Squire, James R. "Literacy and Literature." *Eng J* 44:154–60; 1960.

Squire, James R. *The Responses of Adolescents While Reading Four Short Stories.* NCTE, 1964.

Squire, James R. "Evaluating High School English Programs." *North Cen Assn Q* 40:247–54; 1966.

Squire, James R., and Applebee, Roger K. *A Study of English Programs in Selected High Schools Which Consistently Educate Outstanding Students in English.* USOE Cooperative Research Project No. 1994. U Illinois, 1966. 601p.

Squire, James R., and Gwynn, Frederick L. (Eds.) *Source Book on English Institutes for Elementary Teachers.* MLA, and NCTE, 1965.

Stafford, William. *Friends to This Ground.* NCTE, 1967.

Stanchfield, Jo M. "Reading Interests of Eighth Grade Boys." *Reading Teach* 16:41–4; 1962.

Steinberg, Erwin R., and others. "The Inductive Teaching of English." *Engl J* 55:139–57; 1966.

Stoer, Marion West. "A Second Look: The Treatment of Characters in Popular Fiction." *El Engl* 40:172–3; 1963.

Strickland, Ruth G. "The Contributions of Structural Linguistics to the Teaching of Reading, Writing, and Grammar in the Elementary School." *B Sch Ed Indiana U* 40:1–44; 1964.

Taba, Hilda. *With Perspective on Human Relations.* ACE, 1955.

Tantara, Walter T. "Effects of Novels on Ideas About the Scientist." *J Ed Res* 58:3–9; 1966.

Terman, Lewis M., and Lima, Margaret. *Children's Reading.* Appleton, 1935.

Thorndike, Robert L. *Children's Reading Interests.* Teachers Col, Columbia U, 1941.

Walker, Jerry L. "An Investigation into Individual Differences and the Structure of Literature." Doctoral dissertation. Wayne State U, 1964.

Waples, Douglas, and others. *What Reading Does to People.* U Chicago Press, 1940.

Weeks, Ruth Mary. (Ed.) *A Correlated Curriculum.* Appleton, 1936.

Wellek, René, and Warren, Austin. *Theory of Literature.* Harcourt, 1956. 375p.

Whitehead, Frank. "The Attitude of Grammar School Pupils Toward Some Novels Commonly Read in School." *Br J Ed Res* 26:104–11; 1956.

Whitman, Robert S. "Significant Reading Experiences of Superior English Students." *Illinois Engl B* 51:1–24; 1964.

Williams, E. D., and others. "Tests of Literary Appreciation." *Br J Ed Psychol* 8:265–84; 1938.

Wilson, James R. *Responses of College Freshmen to Three Novels.* NCTE, 1966.

Wolfe, Willavene, and others. *The Critical Reading of Elementary School Children.* USOE Cooperative Research Project No. 2612. Ohio State U, 1967.

Wollnar, Mary H. *Children's Voluntary Reading as an Expression of Individuality.* Teachers Col, Columbia U, 1949.

EXPERIMENTAL METHODS

The *Dictionary of Philosophy* (Runes, 1942) defines "experiment" as "Any situation which is deliberately set up by an investigator with a view to verifying a theory or hypothesis." The theory or hypothesis to be verified ("tested" would be more in accord with current usage) is generally an assertion of causal relations between phenomena. Guiding principles for the discovery of such causal relations were formulated by J. S. Mill (1848) in his time-honored Canons of Inductive Method: (1) The method of agreement; (2) The method of difference; (3) The joint method of agreement and difference; (4) The method of residues; (5) The method of concomitant variations. (For an exposition of these principles in a modern perspective, see Tiedeman, 1960.)

Mill's canons remain valid today, and they have an amazingly modern flavor despite being a century and a quarter old. For instance, his fifth canon says, "Whatever phenomenon varies in any manner whenever another phenomenon varies in some particular manner, is either a cause or an effect of the phenomenon, or is connected with it through some fact of causation." (Note especially the last clause, "or is connected . . . ," which many modern researchers would do well to heed.) Sound as they are, however, they are broad, general principles which do not offer concrete guides for putting those principles into practice. The science of experimental design (which is partly an art) picks up where Mill's canons leave off and seeks to give researchers concrete guides in the planning of experiments, collection of data, and their analysis. A large part of this science was developed by Fisher (1925, 1935) and his co-workers and followers of their tradition (e.g., Kempthorne, 1952) in the context of agricultural research. Adaptations to medical research have been made by Bliss (1951), and to psychology and education by Johnson (1949), Lindquist (1953), Winer (1962), and many others.

The methodology of experimental design is indeed elaborate and powerful in its applications to agricultural and "basic" (laboratory-conducted) medical and behavioral-science research. Nevertheless, voices of dissatisfaction are increasingly being raised against its "deliberately-set-up-by-an-investigator" requirement by those who would apply it to research on classroom teaching, to psychological research in the clinical setting, and the like—situations that are alike in that, by their nature, they preclude the investigator's having full control over the assignment of subjects to treatments. Campbell (1957), one of the foremost dissenters, has long been advocating the use of what he termed "quasi-experimental designs" for research conducted in natural social settings when "true" experiments are infeasible. More recently, Campbell (1963) and Campbell and Stanley (1963) have presented detailed expositions of the notion of quasi-experimental design, with numerous examples of actual applications cited from the literature.

It is impossible in this brief article to give a comprehensive coverage of all the technical details and intricacies of experimental design, let alone quasi-experimental design. For the latter, the reader should consult the articles by Campbell and by Campbell and Stanley, just cited, which are "musts" for any serious student of educational research. Also in the same category are two symposium volumes: one called *Problems in Measuring Change*, edited by Harris (1963), which contains the Campbell article, the other, *Improving Experimental Design and Statistical Analysis*, edited by Stanley (1967). As for traditional experimental design, numerous textbooks are available. Besides the ones already cited, those by Edwards (1960), Kerlinger (1964), and Ray (1965) are worthy of special mention.

What follows in the next two sections, then, is not a survey of various experimental designs, but rather an exposition of the rationale underlying the science and art of experimental design. As such, it occupies a position halfway between Mill's canons and a description of specific experimental designs; it is intended to help the reader in making an intelligent choice, for his particular research problem, from among various available designs—or in developing and critically evaluating a design of his own.

EXPERIMENTAL DESIGN. Imagine a simple physical experiment in which a compass needle (the "experimental group") is subjected to the *treatment* of having a wire carrying an electric current placed parallel to and above it. The compass needle will rotate to form an approximate right angle with the wire. This experiment may be schematically represented as follows:

(1) $\qquad (E) \quad T - O,$

where E stands for "experimental group," T for the treatment, and O for the observation (deflection of the needle).

If this experiment is repeated several times with the same result, almost everyone would accept the explanation that the proximal presence of an electric current and the deflection of the compass needle are *causally related* (more specifically, in view of the temporal sequence, that the former *causes* the latter). However, a skeptic (perhaps a five-year-old child in this instance) might claim that the current is irrelevant, and the sheer presence of a stretch of wire causes the deflection. To dissuade this skeptic of his alternative explanation, the experimenter may modify his experiment in either of two ways.

One way would be to first place the wire above the compass *without* the current, observe that no deflection occurs (O_1), then introduce the current (T), and observe the deflection (O_2). In this case he has conducted an experiment schematized as

(2) $\qquad (E) \quad O_1 - T - O_2.$

Alternatively, the experimenter could place two compasses some distance apart, bring a current-bearing wire (T) above one of them, and a current-free wire (NT, for "no treatment") above the other compass (C, the "control group"). He has then carried out the following experiment:

(3) $\quad\quad\quad (E) \quad T - O_e,$
$\quad\quad\quad\quad\quad (C) \quad NT - O_c.$

Simple-minded as the above illustration is, it serves to emphasize the basic purpose of using pre- and posttreatment measures or a control group. The *purpose* is not to observe the "pre-to-post difference" (often called "gain score") or the experimental- versus control-group difference. These are means to an end, the end being to *rule out alternative explanations*.

In the physical sciences, simple designs like 2 or 3, above, often suffice to establish the existence of a causal relation between T and a subsequent O (O_2 or O_e, above) as an empirical law. But in the biological, behavioral, and social sciences, such designs are usually unsatisfactory; and the degree of unsatisfactoriness generally increases from the first to the third discipline mentioned.

There are various reasons—some obvious, others subtle—why these designs are unacceptable for educational research, which involves, in varying degrees, all three of the above disciplines. One obvious reason is that our measuring devices are sometimes so imprecise (e.g., observer ratings) that it is hard to tell whether an effect has occurred or not; this would make design (3) unacceptable. Another is that vast individual differences usually exist among the subjects (e.g., pupils) in an educational experiment, leading to varying responsiveness to treatment T. A somewhat more subtle reason is that, in design 2 the very act of measurement O_1 may so affect the subjects that it becomes uncertain whether a change found in the posttreatment measurement O_2 is due to T or to the fact that O_1 was made (or both).

Diverse as the reasons are (depending on the particular research context) for rendering the foregoing designs unacceptable, they all have in common the ultimate effect of admitting explanations other than "T causes O" as plausible alternatives to account for the observed results. The fundamental rule in the art of designing an acceptable experiment, then, is to build into it enough checks and balances to rule out most (we can never say "all") plausible explanations other than the one asserted in the hypothesis being tested. To state it more dramatically, if colloquially: "Put yourself in the shoes of the guy who doesn't believe in what you're trying to 'prove'; anticipate his objections, and arrange to have an answer ready for each of his objections—an answer which you can support with data from your experiment."

Although no general rule can be given to prescribe just how to anticipate a skeptic's objections (for they will largely depend on the particular research problem), some guide lines will emerge from a consideration of the kinds of disturbing factors that tend to give rise to alternative explanations. We will here group these into three broad categories, namely, those related to (1) individual and subclass differences; (2) extraexperimental drift—i.e., conditions which may change during the course of the experiment, but outside of it; (3) intraexperimental drift—i.e., conditions which may change in the course of the experiment, *within* the experiment itself.

Besides the outright skeptic, the researcher will often encounter the critic who, while accepting his explanation, will question the scope of its generalizability. It behooves the researcher to be cognizant of the various factors that may militate to restrict the population to which his results may safely be generalized. These will be discussed after the three categories related to the fundamental rule.

Individual and Subclass Differences. In the category of individual and subclass differences are subsumed factors that offer grounds for a skeptic's objection that the observed effects may be results of the particular ways in which the experimental and control groups happened to be selected. His objection would be warranted if, as in the illustrative physical example, any conveniently available groups were used.

The trouble would be even more serious if, in design 2, a self-selection factor was involved in forming the experimental group. Consider an "experiment" in which the effectiveness of some counseling procedure for improving study habits among college freshmen is being investigated. If all freshmen who come to the counseling bureau because of failing grades (O_1) are used as subjects, we would have an extreme and atypical group. Not only does this atypicality delimit the scope of generalizability, but it also operates in a more subtle way to vitiate the results. This is the statistical effect of "regression toward the mean." Even without the treatment, we would expect the subsequent grades (O_2) to be less extremely poor for this group. (See Campbell & Stanley, 1963, for an elucidating discussion of this effect.)

The situation would improve a little if a control group comprising freshmen with grades just as poor but who did not come to the counseling bureau for help were also observed. For then the regression effect would operate equally in both groups and hence could not be responsible for any differences found. Even with this design, however, subclass differences between the two groups may contaminate the results: those who came for help are doubtless more concerned about their poor grades and more highly motivated to improve them than are their non-help-seeking counterparts.

The obvious remedy to this category of defects in design is to use randomization procedures. When this is done, designs 2 and 3 are modified to become

$(2=R) \quad\quad\quad R \longrightarrow (E) \quad O_1 - T - O_2$
and
$\quad\quad\quad\quad\quad\quad\quad\quad\quad (E) \quad T - O_e,$
$(3=R) \quad\quad\quad R$
$\quad\quad\quad\quad\quad\quad\quad\quad\quad (C) \quad NT - O_c.$

Subclass differences may sometimes operate in such a way as to "wash out" a genuine effect of T, rather than generating an effect which could be mistaken for a result of T. This would be the case, for instance, if the treatment has different effects for members of different subclasses (such as males and females; high-, medium-, and low-IQ pupils; etc.) and these are obliterated when observations are made on a heterogeneous group. When such a possibility can be anticipated, the researcher should employ stratified–random-sampling procedures in forming his groups. (See the section "Sampling," below.) Design 3-R would then be further modified to become:

$$(3=SR) \quad \begin{array}{l} R \diagdown \begin{array}{ll} (E_1) & T - O_{e1}, \\ (C_1) & NT - O_{c1}, \end{array} \\ R \diagdown \begin{array}{ll} (E_2) & T - O_{e2}, \\ (C_2) & NT - O_{c2}, \end{array} \end{array}$$

with more E and C pairs if more than two relevant subclasses (or strata) are identified.

Extraexperimental Drift. In the pre- and post-treatment design 2-R, especially when the two testing periods are far apart, intervening events other than the experimental treatment will often be responsible for part of the observed changes. A commonplace example is an experiment aimed at studying changes in attitude toward a minority group, produced by some antiprejudice indoctrination program. If, during the course of the experiment, an incident such as the murder of a civil rights worker takes place, any observed change in attitude may be attributable more to this event than to the experimental treatment. To preempt such an alternative explanation, a combination of designs 2-R and 3-R should be used:

$$(4=R) \quad R \diagdown \begin{array}{ll} (E) & O_{1e} - T - O_{2e}, \\ (C) & O_{1c} - NT - O_{2c}. \end{array}$$

Since both groups are exposed to the same extraexperimental influences, the difference between $(O_{2e} - O_{1e})$ and $(O_{2c} - O_{1c})$ cannot be attributed to such extraneous events.

It should be noted that normal changes with time taking place within the subjects, independent of unusual external events, are subsumed under the rubric of extraexperimental drift and are equally well controlled in design 4-R. Such changes include practice or fatigue effects (when the pre-to-posttest time lapse is short) as well as increased sophistication or decreased mental and physical agility (when the time lapse is extremely long).

Intraexperimental Drift. Changes less obvious than those noted above may occur within the experiment itself. For instance, if the measurements before and after treatment are dependent on human judgment (e.g., observer ratings), a shift in standards between the two occasions (either because different observers are making the ratings or because of the increased experience of the same observers) may take place. To minimize this disturbing factor, the observers should be thoroughly pretrained, the same observers should be used for rating both groups, and they should not know which group is the experimental one and which the control. If these precautions are taken, design 4-R should be adequate to control for this factor.

Similarly, the possible influence of the pretesting, mentioned earlier, is controlled in 4-R, because both experimental and control groups are affected by it. However, a more subtle perturbation related to pretesting may remain. This is the possible *interaction* between pretest and treatment. For instance, in a study investigating the effects of a movie on one's standpoint with regard to some social issue, the pretest may sensitize the experimental-group members on what to look for in the movie, thus making it easier for them to get the message than for an unpretested viewer to do so. In this situation, while the effect of pretesting per se is equated for both groups, the interaction effect can affect only the experimental group. Thus, the skeptic may rightly claim that whatever differences are found between the two groups are due to the joint effect of pretesting *and* the movie, rather than to the movie itself. To rule out this alternative explanation (if unfounded), a design more elaborate than 4-R is needed. A four-group design proposed by Solomon (1949) fills the bill. It is a combination of designs 3-R and 4-R, schematized as follows:

$$(5=R) \quad R \diagdown \begin{array}{lll} (E_1) & & T - O_e, \\ (C_1) & & NT - O_c, \\ (E_2) & O_{1e} - & T - O_{2e}, \\ (C_2) & O_{1c} - & NT - O_{2c}. \end{array}$$

If the $(O_e - O_c)$ difference is in the same direction as, and of similar magnitude to, the $(O_{2e} - O_{2c})$ difference, the skeptic's alternative explanation can be ruled out. If, however, $(O_{2e} - O_{2c})$ turns out to be substantially greater in magnitude than $(O_e - O_c)$, the researcher will have to concede that the pretest-treatment interaction effect is the more likely source of the experimental–control difference than is the treatment itself.

Another possible intraexperimental drift, and a most troublesome one, is that of attrition (dropouts) —or, more specifically, of *differential* attrition between experimental and control groups. When the experimental treatment is of such a nature (e.g., exposing subjects to frustrating experiences) as to cause greater attrition in the experimental group, there is really no effective way of *controlling* this. What the random assignment of subjects to experimental and control groups does is to provide a basis for determining whether or not different dropout rates actually occurred in the groups being compared.

Scope of Generalizability. A perennial question which remains (or should remain) after an experiment has been conducted and the results analyzed is this: "To what population may these findings be generalized?" Of course, the method of sampling employed (discussed in the section "Sampling," below) sets an upper bound to the scope of generalizability. Often, however, the conditions of the experiment itself impose further restrictions on the scope.

The example cited in connection with design 5-R illustrates the point. If the experimental–control difference is substantially greater for the pretested groups (E_2 and C_2) than it is for those not pretested (E_1 and C_1), then our generalization must be limited to a pretested population (people who answer the questionnaire before seeing the movie, in our example) instead of the original population sampled.

A more drastic curtailment of the scope of generalizability occurs when the well-known "Hawthorne effect" is permitted to operate. That is, if the pupils being used as subjects are aware that an experiment is going on, this awareness would no doubt create attitudes (such as curiosity, resentment, or a sense of importance) different from those toward the normal classroom situation. To generalize the results of the experiment to pupils in regular classes would then be quite hazardous. The solution, of course, is to keep the pupils unaware of the experiment, and in this respect a *well-planned* "quasi experiment" may have certain advantages over the "true" experiment.

QUASI–EXPERIMENTAL DESIGN. So great has been the impact of the Campbell-Stanley paper been in popularizing the idea of quasi experiments that a caveat may be in order. These authors themselves stated, clearly and repeatedly, that quasi experiments should be employed only "*where more efficient probes are unavailable*" (1963, p. 205). Stanley (1966) has further elaborated on the precautions to be observed in conducting quasi experiments and has warned us of the thin line between "quasi" and "pseudo" experiments.

After this reminder that quasi experiments by no means offer an easy road to valid knowledge, we outline their nature and examine a few of the more ingenious designs in this category. The reader has already been referred to two sources to be consulted for detailed expositions. Another good reference work is an article by Glass (1965) which does not span the field but deals in depth with one example (the "quasi" counterpart of design 2-R above), and suggests an appropriate statistical analysis of the results.

What Campbell (1957) signified by the qualifier "quasi" was that often, in natural social settings, the experimenter lacks full control over random assignment of subjects and the scheduling of experimental treatments but is nevertheless in a position to schedule the data-collection process in accordance with a prearranged design. It is important to note that unless the latter condition is satisfied, we do not have even a quasi experiment. The study must then be classified as a "pseudo experiment," or an associational study, and to draw a cause-and-effect conclusion from it would be quite unsound; the most we can hope for is to generate a causal hypothesis for subsequent experimental study.

The distinction between "true" and "quasi," as well as that between "quasi" and "pseudo," may be clarified by taking a close look at one of the most widely used designs in educational research: one which is superficially almost indistinguishable from design 4-R. This is the design in which two naturally existing groups (most often classrooms) that are "as similar as possible" are selected for study. One of the two is *randomly* assigned to the experimental condition and the other to the control. Thus, the design may be schematically represented as follows:

$$(6) \quad \begin{array}{c}(G_1) \\ \\ (G_2)\end{array} \searrow R \nearrow \begin{array}{l}(E) \quad O_{1e} - T - O_{2e} \\ \\ (C) \quad O_{1c} - NT - O_{2c}\end{array}.$$

It differs from design 4-R in that subjects are not drawn from a common population and assigned at random to the E and C groups. The decision as to which group, G_1 or G_2, will receive the experimental treatment must, however, be made at random. Failing this, we probably have a pseudo experiment of the ex post facto analysis variety. For it would probably mean that two classes were found which had been given a standardized aptitude or achievement test, and one of them had subsequently—either by self-selection or by administrative decree—undergone a special treatment (such as trying out a new teaching method) and the other had not. Under these circumstances, the investigator has absolutely no control over possible selection factors and Hawthorne effects. In short, he has nothing resembling an experiment, and any apparent effects he might observe must be regarded as only suggestive.

In contrast to the above widely used (and often misused) design is the time-series design, which has rarely been used but which can, under certain conditions (which are described by Campbell, 1963), be quite successfully employed. This design consists in having a series of observations on a single group and interpolating an experimental treatment between some two observations in the series, thus:

$$(7) \quad O_1 - O_2 - \cdots O_i - T - O_{i+1} - O_{i+2} - \cdots O_n.$$

Therefore, the time-series design may be regarded as an extended form of the single-group before-after design 2; but the extension of having more than one observation both before and after the treatment makes a big difference in the interpretability. This is true because, with a series of observations, a *trend* in time can be established, and detection of an experimental effect is based on a discontinuity in this trend (either in its slope or elevation) rather than on the single difference $O_i - O_{i+1}$. As regards the significance tests, it was pointed out by Gene Glass that those suggested by Campbell (1963) are "hypersensitive" to small changes in elevation and that a test proposed by Box and Tiao (1965) is more appropriate.

The acceptability of this design depends to a large extent on how the decision is made about when the treatment will be introduced. Ideally, this decision should be made at random, with the restriction that the interpolation occur somewhere near the middle of the series of observations. But often, especially if the treatment involves the adoption of new teaching materials or methods, the decision rests with the school administrator. If this is the case, it may happen that the timing coincides with some external event (e.g., Russia's launching of Sputnik I) which gives impetus to the change (e.g., adoption of modern math and science curricula) and may simultaneously cause a discontinuity in the trend of observations. Under these circumstances, the investigator may be forced to look for a similar group for whom a comparable series of observations was recorded but which did not have the new treatment introduced at the same time, and try to induce this group to undergo the treatment at a subsequent date.

Fraught with the foregoing difficulties as the time-series design is, it has the advantage that, if circumstances and the nature of the treatment are such as to permit introduction of the treatment at a randomly selected point in the series, it stands a greater chance of leaving the subjects unaware that an experiment is going on than does a "true" experiment of comparable intricacy. This would especially be the case if the series of observations take place as part of a periodic, routine testing program in the school.

An especially ingenious design is that which Campbell and Stanley call the "recurrent institutional cycle design." As the name implies, its applicability is limited to situations in which some institutional treatment is continually being given to new groups of subjects on a recurrent-cycle schedule. A repeatedly offered short-term training program in which a new crop of apprentices or inductees is "processed," say, every eight weeks, is the ideal situation for this design; but the ordinary school situation may (with some reservations owing to the length of the cycle) also be treated in this manner.

The essence of this design is that observations are made in many stages (following the institutional cycle), and the hindsight gained at each stage is utilized in adding a different type of control group (or groups) in the next cycle. As Campbell and Stanley say, the result may be "an inelegant accumulation of precautionary checks" (hence the characterization "patched-up design"). But alternative explanations of an observed effect, such as those offered by our hypothetical skeptic, often occur only as hindsights. It is far better, then, to incorporate this hindsight in the next stage of an ongoing experiment than to conduct a one-shot experiment yielding equivocal results.

The "patched-up" recurrent institutional cycle design, then, reflects a frank admission of our inability to foresee *all* possible alternative explanations and at the same time seeks to compensate for this limitation by using multistage observations on several waves of subjects. It is thus a highly realistic design and in a sense embraces (or potentially *may* embrace) all possible designs. Consequently, no general prescription can be given for this design; each problem will call for a different set of "subdesigns"—and even for the same problem, different workers may come up with a different set. The researcher here has fullest rein in exercising his ingenuity in the art of experimental design.

STATISTICAL ANALYSIS. Although we spoke of the "science and art" of experimental design, the reader may so far have gained the impression that it is all art and no science. In a sense, this is true. The actual *designing* of an experiment is largely if not wholly an art; the only guiding principles are such broad ones as were described under the somewhat grandiose title "fundamental rule," above. The science consists mainly in coordinating a particular design used with the appropriate method of statistical analysis.

Traditionally, experimental design has been closely linked with the statistical technique of analysis of variance. This and related methods are described in the article STATISTICAL METHODS. The reason for including this brief section on statistical analysis here is to alert the reader to the existence of other methods of analysis that do not seem to be quite as widely known to educational researchers. One of these is the approach of using several separate comparisons, or contrasts, among the various group means involved.

The term "contrast" is here used in a technical sense denoting a *linear combination* in which the coefficients (combining weights) sum to zero. For instance, the linear combination

$$2M_1 - M_2 + 2M_3 - 3M_4$$

is a contrast among the four means M_1, M_2, M_3, and M_4, because the sum of the coefficients (2, −1, 2, and −3) is equal to zero. In general, a linear combination of k means $M_1, M_2, \cdots, M_k$,

$$L = c_1 M_1 + c_2 M_2 + \cdots + c_k M_k$$

is called a contrast if $c_1 + c_2 + \cdots + c_k = 0$.

The importance of contrasts lies in the fact that any question about the existence of effects can be recast into a question of whether or not a certain contrast is significantly different from zero. As a simple example, consider a study comparing two methods *A* and *B* for teaching writing to first graders, some of whom are high, and some low, in their eye-hand coordination. A two-way analysis of variance would normally be carried out to test the significance of the *methods* and *coordination* main effects, and the interaction. But these tests are equivalent to testing the significance of the difference from zero of the following contrasts, respectively

$$M_{AH} + M_{AL} - M_{BH} - M_{BL}, \quad \text{(methods)}$$
$$M_{AH} - M_{AL} + M_{BH} - M_{BL}, \quad \text{(coordination)}$$
$$M_{AH} - M_{AL} - M_{BH} + M_{BL}. \quad \text{(interaction)}$$

(The meaning of the last contrast may be more easily grasped by rewriting it as the difference between two differences: $(M_{AH} - M_{AL}) - (M_{BH} - M_{BL})$.)

For an experimental design possessing an intrinsic symmetry, like the factorial design cited above, the use of separate contrasts provides at most a refinement of the information obtainable from the usual analysis of variance. In these cases the contrasts of interest have the further property of pairwise orthogonality. (See references listed below for definition of this property.) But in complex designs like 5-R or an intricate quasi-experimental design, the neat symmetry leading to orthogonal contrast is usually lacking. In such cases, significance testing using separate contrasts may be the only available method.

The main problem in utilizing contrasts is the determination of the appropriate standard error for use in significance tests. When the entire set of contrasts is planned ahead of data collection and the individual contrasts are pairwise mutually orthogonal, the standard error for each contrast is the square root of the error mean square that would be used if an analysis of variance were to be carried out. Then, for each contrast L, the ratio $L/\sqrt{\frac{MS_e}{n}}$ may be referred to the t-distribution with degrees of freedom equal to that for MS_e.

When the design is such that an analysis of variance would not apply, the determination of the standard error becomes much more difficult, and the advice of a professional statistician may be needed. If, furthermore, the contrasts of interest are not all mutually orthogonal (as will usually be the case with designs lacking symmetry), the t-test approach mentioned above cannot be used even after the appropriate standard error has been computed. One of the simplest methods for conducting significance tests in this situation is that developed by Scheffé (1959). A description of this method may be found in the books by Edwards (1960), Hays (1963), and Winer (1962)—the last-mentioned of which also describes a method developed by Tukey. Each of these books gives considerable attention to the whole problem of separate contrasts. A more extensive treatment of the subject is given by Miller (1966) in a book devoted entirely to multiple comparisons and related topics.

Another mode of statistical analysis which deserves greater attention from educational researchers than it has been getting is multivariate analysis (see STATISTICAL METHODS). Educational research often involves the use of more than one dependent variable —as when tests of concepts, computational skills, and applications are used for measuring arithmetic achievement. The usual practice in these situations has been to conduct a separate t-test or analysis of variance for each dependent variable. Sometimes it may be desirable or necessary to do so; but often it makes more sense to treat the entire set of dependent variables as a single whole. Significance tests in multidimensional space are then needed. Multivariate analysis offers these tests—and more. A concise description of the nature and scope of multivariate analysis is given by Tatsuoka and Tiedeman (1963); Cramer and Bock (1966) present a less technical review of the nature and applications of multivariate analysis. A comprehensive treatment of one particular application (personnel classification) is provided by Rulon and others (1967). Several illustrative examples of applications to educational research were presented by Bock (1966), and an extensive technical treatment of multivariate analysis in educational and psychological research is given by Tatsuoka (1968). Computer programs for most existing multivariate techniques are given by Cooley and Lohnes (1962).

SAMPLING. It is gratuitous, at this point, to state that "sampling" refers to any procedure by which a relatively small number of observational units is selected for study, with a view to generalizing the findings to the population from which these units were drawn. Obviously, sampling has a much broader scope of application than in experimentation. Opinion polling (see SURVEY RESEARCH METHODS), marketing research, and industrial quality control are but a few of the other fields in which sampling is employed. In fact, it was largely through the impetus of applications in these fields that sampling theory has developed into a fullfledged branch of applied statistics during the past few decades. (For a history of the early development of sampling theory, see Stephan, 1948.)

In this section we merely touch upon those aspects of sampling theory that have a direct bearing on experimental methods in educational research. Other aspects are discussed in the article SURVEY RESEARCH METHODS, and a concise but comprehensive exposition, with references to many standard sources, is given by Cornell (1960). Among the books on sampling theory that appeared since Cornell's article, those by Cochran (1963), Deming (1960), Kish (1965), and Yamane (1967) are worthy of special note.

Most of the available procedures for significance testing of experimental results are based on the assumption that the samples studied are *simple random samples* drawn from the relevant populations—by which is meant that each and every population element has an equal probability of being drawn into the sample, and, moreover, each is sampled independently of every other element. To draw a simple random sample it is necessary to have a complete list of the population, so that a mechanical device such as a table of random numbers can be used in selecting the elements to be included in the sample. In practice, however, the experimenter never has a complete list of the population. In fact, the population to which generalization is sought usually includes *future* cases (e.g., all seventh graders who *potentially* may be taught ratios and proportions by a given method), and hence a complete listing is impossible in principle.

How, then, can we justify the use of statistical methods based on random sampling when our samples are palpably not random samples from the total population of interest? The answer lies in distinguishing between the ultimate population (that to which we wish to generalize our findings) and the immediate population, or the *frame*, in the sampling theorist's terminology, from which random samples can and should be drawn, if our analysis is to be valid. Deming (1960) makes the point that statistical inference always goes from sample to frame, and never to the ultimate population, or the *universe*. The final step of generalizing from frame to universe can be justified only on the basis of "substantive judgment"—i.e., a judgment, based on knowledge of relevant variables in the particular field, of how representative the frame is of the universe. For instance, if the universe is "all seventh graders in the United States," the selection frame may be the totality of seventh graders in a certain school district; and a judgmental question remains of how "typical" these seventh graders are of all their counterparts in the country.

It should be pointed out that in survey studies, elaborate methods such as stratified, cluster, and multistage sampling (see Survey Research Methods) are used in order to have a reasonable assurance of determining a representative frame. This is necessary because precise, quantitative estimation of some population parameter (e.g., proportion favoring a certain bill) is the goal—and possible because the population is a specific, existing one (e.g., the totality of eligible voters in a given state).

In experimental studies, on the other hand, a conscientious selection of a "good" frame, followed by random sampling from the frame (and, of course, random assignment to different treatment groups) is about all that can be hoped for. And this is usually sufficient, for two reasons. First, the aim of an experimental study is to investigate the presence or absence of some lawful relation between two or more variables in a definable but hypothetical population; and the occurrence or nonoccurrence of such relationships should be less susceptible to sampling fluctuation than the precise numerical value of some statistic (such as the proportion, in a given sample, of people favoring a certain bill). Second, the existence of a causal relationship is almost never established by a single experiment. Other researchers will, using different frames and samples from them, seek to replicate the experiment (if it is of sufficient scientific import). If the collective judgment of competent researchers, each independently selecting a separate frame, cannot assure the adequacy of the frames, then probably nothing can.

Often a method akin to the stratified–random-sampling method of survey research is used in experimental studies. This is the method in which the population (or, in practice, the frame) is divided into several strata in terms of some relevant characteristic (e.g., IQ level or socioeconomic class) and random sampling procedures are applied separately to each stratum. However, the purpose for drawing a stratified-random sample generally differs between survey and experimental studies. In the former, the purpose is to increase the precision of the estimate of the parameter by decreasing the sampling variance of the statistic used, and this purpose is achieved only if each stratum is more homogeneous than the population at large in the characteristic to be studied. In experimental studies, on the other hand, stratification is used when it is suspected that the relation being investigated may be present in some strata but absent in others or that it may take different forms in different strata. For instance, if several methods for teaching proportions to seventh graders are to be compared and it is suspected that one method may be most effective for pupils with high general intelligence while another may be most effective for those with average or low intelligence, it would be desirable to divide the population into high-, medium-, and low-IQ strata, and to draw a random sample from each stratum.

A perennial problem in educational research is that the investigator often has no choice but to use entire classes as his samples. This corresponds to *cluster sampling* without a subsequent second-stage subsampling (random sampling of individuals from the clusters). Adequate analysis is possible only when the investigator is fortunate enough to be able to assign a substantial number of classes (say, ten or more) *at random* to each treatment condition. He may then use the class means as the basic observations and essentially follow the usual analysis-of-variance or multiple-comparison procedures. (See Lindquist, 1953, pp. 177–187.) If, however, resources or other circumstances permit the researcher to use only one or two classes for each treatment, he is in an awkward position. To use the foregoing method would diminish the power of his test drastically. An alternative would be to ascertain that the composition of the classes was based on more or less random, haphazard assignment of pupils and to use methods of analysis applicable to simple random samples. But in so doing, he would be stacking the cards in favor of observing a "significant" effect, for his estimate of error variance will generally be smaller than it should be—the degree of underestimation being dependent on how far from random assignment the actual composition of the classes had been. If the nonrandomness here is great—i.e., if any systematic selection (like homogeneous grouping) was used in forming the classes—he should not carry out the experiment at all. In any event, his findings would be only tentative, because the probability of error cannot be determined.

Another important problem of sampling is that of sample size. The uninitiated may not see this as a problem, thinking that (within budgetary limits) the larger the sample, the better. This would be true of survey studies, where precise estimation of a population parameter is the objective. But in experimental studies, where we are concerned with relationships among variables, using too large a sample can actually be deleterious. This is true because, given a large-enough sample, a relationship of the minutest degree may show up as "statistically significant" which is at best a nuisance and at worst can be actually misleading. It is therefore desirable to determine an appropriate sample size which is large enough to detect (with a preassigned probability) a relationship of practically important magnitude and is yet *small* enough to preclude from "significance" a relationship of trivial degree. The degree or strength of relationship can, in general, be measured in terms of the proportion of variance of one variable that is accounted for by the other variable(s); the familiar squared correlation coefficient is a special instance of this type of measure. Hay (1963) describes a general measure of this sort and shows how it can be utilized in determining optimum sample sizes.

Maurice M. Tatsuoka
University of Illinois

References

Bliss, C. I. "Statistical Methods in Vitamin Research." In Gyorgy, Paul. (Ed.) *Vitamin Methods*, Vol. 2. Academic, 1951. p. 448–610.

Bock, R. Darrell. "Contributions of Multivariate Experimental Designs to Educational Research." In Cattell, Raymond B. (Ed.) *Handbook of Multivariate Experimental Psychology*. Rand McNally, 1966. p. 820–40.

Box, G.E.P., and Tiao, George C. A. "A Change in Level of a Non-stationary Time Series." *Biometrika* 52:181–92; 1965.

Campbell, Donald T. "Factors Relevant to the Validity of Experiments in Social Settings." *Psychol B* 54:297–312; 1957.

Campbell, Donald T. "From Description to Experimentation: Interpreting Trends as Quasi-experiments." In Harris, Chester W. (Ed.) *Problems in Measuring Change*. Wisconsin Press, 1963. p. 212–42.

Campbell, Donald T., and Stanley, Julian C. "Experimental and Quasi-experimental Designs for Research on Teaching." In Gage, N. L. (Ed.) *Handbook of Research on Teaching*. Rand McNally, 1963. p. 171–246.

Cochran, William G. *Sampling Techniques*, rev. ed. Wiley, 1963. 413p.

Cooley, William W., and Lohnes, Paul R. *Multivariate Procedures for the Behavioral Sciences*. Wiley, 1962. 211p.

Cornell, Francis G. "Sampling Methods" In Harris, Chester W. (Ed.) *Encyclopedia of Educational Research*, 3rd ed. Macmillan, 1960. p. 1181–3.

Cramer, Elliot M., and Bock, R. Darrell, "Multivariate Analysis." *R Ed Res* 36:604–17; 1966.

Deming, William E. *Sample Design in Business Research*. Wiley, 1960. 517p.

Edwards, Allen L. *Experimental Design in Psychological Research*, rev. ed. Holt, 1960. 398p.

Fisher, Ronald A. *Statistical Methods for Research Workers*. Oliver & Boyd, Ltd., 1925. 239p.

Fisher, Ronald A. *The Design of Experiments*. Oliver & Boyd, Ltd., 1935. 252p.

Glass, Gene V. "Evaluating Testing, Maturation, and Treatment Effects in a Pretest-Posttest Quasi-experimental Design." *Am Ed Res J* 2:83–7; 1965.

Harris, Chester W. (Ed.) *Problems in Measuring Change*. U Wisconsin Press, 1963. 259p.

Hays, William L. *Statistics for Psychologists*. Holt, 1963. 719p.

Johnson, Palmer O. *Statistical Methods in Research*. Prentice-Hall, 1949. 377p.

Kempthorne, Oscar. *The Design and Analysis of Experiments*. Wiley, 1952. 631p.

Kerlinger, Fred N. *Foundations of Behavioral Research*. Holt, 1964. 739p.

Kish, Leslie. *Survey Sampling*. Wiley, 1965. 643p.

Lindquist, E. F. *Design and Analysis of Experiments in Psychology and Education*. Houghton, 1953. 393p.

Mill, John Stuart. *System of Logic*. Harper, 1848. 600p.

Miller, Rupert G. *Simultaneous Statistical Inference*. McGraw-Hill, 1966. 272p.

Ray, William S. *Introduction to Experimental Design*. Macmillan, 1965.

Rulon, Phillip J., and others. *Multivariate Statistics for Personnel Classification*. Wiley, 1967. 406p.

Runes, Dagobert D. *The Dictionary of Philosophy*. Philosophical Lib, 1942. 343p.

Scheffé, Henry. *The Analysis of Variance*. Wiley, 1959. 477p.

Solomon, R. L. "An Extension of Control Group Design." *Psychol B* 46:137–50; 1949.

Stanley, Julian C. "A Common Class of Pseudo-experiments." *Am Ed Res J* 3:79–87; 1966.

Stanley, Julian C. (Ed.) *Improving Experimental Design and Statistical Analysis: Seventh Annual Phi Delta Symposium on Educational Research*. Rand McNally, 1967.

Stephan, Frederick F. "History of the Uses of Modern Sampling Procedures." *J Am Stat Assn* 43:12–39; 1948.

Tatsuoka, Maurice M. *Multivariate Analysis in Educational and Psychological Research*. Wiley, 1968.

Tatsuoka, Maurice M., and Tiedeman, David V. "Statistics as an Aspect of Scientific Method in Research on Teaching." In Gage, N. L. (Ed.) *Handbook of Research on Teaching*. Rand McNally, 1963. p. 142–70.

Tiedeman, David V. "Experimental Method." In Harris, Chester W. (Ed.) *Encyclopedia of Educational Research*, 3rd ed. Macmillan, 1960. p. 486–90.

Winer, Benjamin J. *Statistical Principles in Experimental Design*. McGraw-Hill, 1962. 672p.

Yamane, Taro. *Elementary Sampling Theory*. Prentice-Hall, 1967.

EXTENSION EDUCATION

The term "extension education" refers to systematic and sustained educational programs primarily for adult part-time learners that are offered by any type of higher education institution. It constitutes the higher-education segment of adult and continuing education that is described in the article ADULT EDU-

CATION. Continuing-higher-education programs designed for adult part-time learners contrast with preparatory-education programs for preadult full-time resident students.

Continuing higher-education programs may involve evening or off-campus classes, correspondence or television courses, individual consultation or demonstration projects, or residential conferences and institutes or may be directly related to ongoing activity in an organization or a community. They may be for degree credit or especially for adults and may be scheduled for a few hours a week over several months or may meet full-time for several days or weeks. Most institutions of higher education assign primary responsibility for continuing education to a unit ordinarily termed a "division." Divisions may range in size from several hundred participants and a part-time administrator in a small liberal arts college to tens of thousands of participants and hundreds of administrators in a division of a large state university.

This article is based on an organizational analysis of continuing-higher-education divisions. The four major sections cover the establishment and assessment of outcomes, the acquisition of needed inputs, the processes of transforming inputs into outcomes, and trends in continuing higher education. Each section contains a general review of research on continuing higher education along with specific references to research on university extension, Cooperative Extension Service (including its connections with federal and county levels of government), and college extension (including the four-year liberal arts colleges and the two-year community junior colleges). This article is restricted to an analysis of educational activities in which the learners devote several sessions, at least, to the systematic study of a topic, although it is recognized that most divisions engage in other, related activities.

OUTCOMES. The intended outcome of most continuing-education programs is a gain in knowledge and skill by the adults who participate. Typical indexes of the extent to which participants gain or benefit from continuing education include the numbers and characteristics of the adults who are reached and their achievement and persistence. Johnstone and Rivera (1965) provide the most reliable estimate of number of participants, which was about 3½ million adults in 1962. It is estimated that almost 2 million of these adults participated in university extension educational programs during a 12-month period. The number of adults served by cooperative extension programs depends upon the definition of continuing higher education. The national survey of clientele by the Federal Extension Service (1965) estimated that 12½ million families were reached by county extension programs using all methods including home and office visits, group meetings, tours and fairs, and phone calls and direct mail. By contrast, Johnstone and Rivera (1965) estimated that the number of participants in sustained and systematic adult and continuing-education programs sponsored by Cooperative Extension Service (classified in the report as "government") was about 1 million adults. Their definition required that the adult recognize that he had received instruction on a topic for several sessions at least, a condition not met by many activities of the Cooperative Extension Service, which emphasizes a variety of informal methods for reaching predominantly rural adults. On the basis of his survey of more than 400 accredited, privately supported, predominantly undergraduate and nonprofessional, four-year liberal arts colleges, which were independent of any larger administrative complex such as a university, Crimi (1957) estimated that in 1953 about 45,000 adults were served by continuing-education programs of liberal arts colleges. Thornton (1966) reported that in 1964 about 500,000 adults were served by continuing-education programs sponsored by community junior colleges. The *Junior College Directory* for the subsequent year reported an additional 100,000 adult participants.

The range of acquired competencies in university extension is typically at least as broad as the range of preparatory-education subject-matter offerings, but with greater emphasis on professional fields such as business, teaching, and engineering. DeCrow (1959), after reviewing studies that analyzed the ability and achievement of participants in continuing-education credit courses, compared with preparatory-education students, concluded that the academic achievement of the two groups was equivalent. In a national study to identify correlates of achievement and persistence of university extension participants, Knox and Sjogren (1965) found that achievement was correlated with levels of verbal ability and education but not with age and that withdrawal during a course was relatively infrequent and largely unrelated to program and performance. These findings were supported by those of Wientge and DuBois (1964), who found that the best predictors of achievement of evening college students were tests of intellectual ability and ability-related biographical information. One constraint on efforts to assess the extent to which intended university extension outcomes have been achieved has been the lack of assessment instruments, especially for continuing-education objectives that have no parallel in preparatory education. A volume on evaluation procedures by Harry Miller and Christine McGuire (1961) provides both a rationale for instrument development and useful examples.

Few studies have explored the benefits of university extension programs beyond the increased competence of the individual participant, but one, a study of the role of continuing higher education in meeting the in-service education needs of school districts, conducted by Schulman (1964), found that expansion of services was limited by restrictive university policies and lack of visibility in the school districts.

The scope and responsibilities of the Cooperative Extension Service, as summarized by Paul Miller and others (1957), are production, marketing, resources, management, leadership, youth, family, community, and public affairs. The primary way in which the intended results of Cooperative Extension educational programs have been assessed has been by studies of the adoption of more-effective practices. Consequently, there are few studies of learning gain but many studies of adoption of improved practices and of increased productivity, such as those summarized by Rogers (1962), which documented the influence of cooperative extension on the adoption of improved practices. There are also a variety of studies designed to assess the perception of cooperative extension by such groups as meat packers, dairy-plant managers, and state legislators, to determine the image that selected public groups have of cooperative extension objectives and procedures. The major emphasis within the Cooperative Extension Service on achievement of objectives with and through other organizations was analyzed by Loomis and others (1953) and was further described by Sanders and others (1966). The continuing-education course offerings of the colleges tend to parallel the preparatory-education course offerings, but with greater emphasis on business administration, teacher education, humanities, and social sciences. Credit courses and occupationally oriented courses predominate. There have been no definitive studies regarding outcomes of continuing education in the colleges.

Although the primary emphasis regarding the results of continuing higher education has been on the benefits to the individual participant, there has been growing emphasis on the benefits to society in the form of the contribution of increased occupational productivity to economic growth and the contribution of increased knowledge and appreciation to the quality of community life. Also, limited research attention has been paid to the contribution of continuing-higher-education activities to the parent institution, to other types of continuing-education agencies, and to other community organizations. The benefits of the continuing-education division to the parent institution have included the improvement of community relations, the expansion of income, the increased use of facilities, and the provision of an organizational unit to achieve institutional objectives regarding the part-time student, community service, and institutional innovation. The primary benefit to other continuing-education agencies and community organizations has been the provision of program planners, resource persons, and learning materials to assist those in the agency or organization to develop more-effective educational programs for adults. There have been several major assessment studies of the results of continuing-higher-education programs, such as the assessment of an entire division by Roth (1964) and of a major program by Harry Miller (1966).

INPUTS. To achieve outcomes, continuing-higher-education programs must acquire from the institution and the community many types of inputs. The major input is the participants. According to Johnstone and Rivera (1965), 57 percent of the learners in college and university continuing-education programs were men, as were 53 percent of the participants in educational programs sponsored by the Cooperative Extension Service. Fifty-four percent of the participants in college and university programs were under 35 years of age, and only 7 percent were over 54. Seventy-five percent of college and university participants had completed some college, compared with 41 percent of cooperative extension participants. The size and characteristics of the clientele that a continuing-education division attracts depends in part upon the effectiveness of efforts by the division to interpret its program for its community. The review by Knox (1965a) of clientele analyses showed that university extension programs served a wide range of participants, most of whom had completed some college courses. The national clientele study by the Federal Extension Service (1965) showed that 45 percent of the adults served by cooperative extension live in communities with over 2,500 population and that the proportion of their clients who are Negro matches the proportion of Negroes in the general population. Some statewide studies have been conducted to ascertain the continuing-education needs of such occupational groups as lawyers, pharmacists, engineers, and hospital administrators.

A second input is the estimated 200,000 mentors in continuing-higher-education programs who, primarily on a part-time basis, serve as teachers, counselors, and writers in the planning and guidance of learning activities. Dekker (1965) has documented the commitment to continuing higher education by faculty in both liberal arts and professional schools of universities. A majority of the mentors are faculty members who teach in the continuing-education program in addition to their full-time work in research or preparatory-education programs. In the Cooperative Extension Service, however, and increasingly in the credit class programs of university extension, faculty members include continuing-education teaching as part of their regular load. Over the years, extension specialists have constituted full-time mentors with the Cooperative Extension Service, but in recent years the land-grant colleges of agriculture and home economics in some states have increased the proportion of joint appointments between extension and resident instruction. Many continuing-higher-education mentors, however, are not otherwise associated with the college or university but are associated with other educational institutions or are practitioners in fields related to the topic of the program. The study by Gowin (1961) makes a case for the use of practitioners as part-time college teachers and for procedures to increase their effectiveness as teachers. The Cooperative Extension Service has made extensive use of volunteers in leadership roles.

A third input is the subject-matter content of continuing-higher-education programs. The content of the continuing-education programs tends to parallel the full range of preparatory-education courses in the college or university. However, because community requests are a major influence on continuing-education offerings, there is greater emphasis on occupational programs. Also, some continuing-education programs do not have counterparts in the preparatory-education programs, as illustrated by the noncredit programs described by Glancy (1958). In general, continuing-education administrators seek to identify points at which community requests correspond with institutional subject-matter resources. Library resources constitute part of continuing-education materials, but in addition there are bulletins and home-study materials, materials prepared by mentors for specific programs, and, especially for community and group-oriented programs, there are documents made up of conclusions that result from analyses of aspects of the ongoing life experience with which the adult participants are associated. A major task of the mentor is guidance in the selection and organization of the program content. Burkett and Ruggiers (1965) have described this process in the evolution of a special degree program for adults.

A fourth input is the administrative staff, who have primary responsibility for continuing-education program development and supervision. Full-time staff at all levels of the Cooperative Extension Service total about 15,000, most of whom perform mentor roles, with an additional 2,000 in university extension. Reliable estimates of the number of college extension administrators are not available. These figures include the agency director and the program administrators, who have direct contact with learners and mentors. Continuing-higher-education administrators have available to them a growing body of professional knowledge regarding the development and administration of adult and continuing-education programs, and this body of professional knowledge benefits continuing-education programs primarily as it is utilized by administrators. The studies regarding needed competencies, such as that by Aker (1962), have concluded that in addition to specialized competencies directly related to extension education, important supporting knowledge is available from such fields as psychology, sociology, and administration. Relevant studies within the Cooperative Extension Service, such as those by Matthews (1950) and McCormick (1959), have focused upon county staff training needs.

A fifth input is the support staff, who along with the administrators and mentors do the work of the division. Included in this category are custodial, secretarial, and specialized personnel in such areas as accounting, purchasing, and public relations. Except in large continuing-education divisions, the services of many persons in support-staff positions are shared with other units of the institution. There are few research findings regarding continuing-education support staff.

A sixth input comprises the goals of the continuing-education division. The written and implicit goals of most divisions result from a network of demands and constraints emanating from various sources, including statutes, institutional regulations, community requests, and the commitments of division administrators and mentors. Requests from individual learners and community groups have a greater and more changeable influence on division goals than is the case for preparatory education. Continuing-education divisions often seek to discover the preferences of potential participants as part of the process of program determination (Matthews, 1952). With the exception of the Cooperative Extension Service, continuing-education divisions seldom have policy boards solely related to the division, and the policy boards for the total institution tend to be primarily oriented toward the preparatory-education programs. As a result, many continuing-education divisions have developed community advisory committees, with a major emphasis on need assessment and community relations. A comprehensive analysis of goals of continuing higher education was contained in the review by Houle (1959). The traditional and emerging goals of continuing education, as studied in evening colleges by Dyer (1956) and in other university extension programs by Morton (1953), have resulted from the interplay between institutional purposes and community requests. National guide lines for the Cooperative Extension Service were summarized by Paul Miller and others (1957). In the liberal arts colleges, continuing-education goals tended to be oriented toward either institution or community. Some community junior colleges have placed major emphasis on continuing education throughout the total institution.

A seventh input comprises facilities for group meetings and for staff offices. For most divisions, facilities are shared with other units of the college or university. Continuing-education facilities, especially for group meetings, are most often found in programs remote from the main campus, such as extension centers and county cooperative extension offices. In some divisions there is extensive shared use of facilities of other community organizations that may be program cosponsors, such as schools, churches, libraries, and businesses.

An eighth input, and one that is used to help acquire many of the other inputs, is finances. A major source of funds for most divisions is the tuition and fees paid by the participants. For some participants, a portion is subsequently reimbursed by employers. Other sources include tax funds designated for extension education, general tax funds for higher education, endowment and gifts, and income from the sale of materials. For the Cooperative Extension Service, almost all funds are from tax sources, with county, state, and federal government each paying about one-third. In addition, wide use of volunteer leadership constitutes a major resource. For university extension and college extension, there are great variations in the portion of the total costs that is paid by the participants. Typically, extension students pay a larger portion of the total costs than resident students do. Few major studies have been conducted regarding facilities or finances.

TRANSFORMATION. To produce outcomes, a continuing-higher-education division must transform or modify the acquired inputs. Learners, mentors, administrators, and support staff all contribute to this process, and the recurring patterns of interaction shape the structure of a specific continuing-education division. The predominant functional type of transformation within the continuing-education division is the teaching-learning transaction. The remaining functions, such as community relations, institutional relations, student personnel, research and development, and administration, each influence the extent to which the educational objectives are achieved.

The four basic settings within which systematic and sustained continuing education teaching-learning transactions occur are individual, group, organizational, and community settings. The individual setting includes both the interpersonal transaction with the counselor or tutor and the mediated transaction, such as correspondence (Wedemeyer & Childs, 1961) or television instruction (Erickson & others, 1964; Grinager, 1964). Participants in a temporary group setting typically have little contact with each other before or after the continuing-education program, whereas a continuing-education program in an organizational setting involves participants from many different organizations and concentrates on interrelationships between organizations within a specific neighborhood, community, or region.

The typical setting for the continuing-education program is the temporary group. Variations within the temporary group setting have been studied relatively frequently and have yielded such conclusions as the finding by Hill (1960) that lecture programs attract different types of adults from those attracted by discussion programs but that both types learn equally well with the method of their choice; and the finding by Solomon and others (1963) that various teaching styles are differentially effective in achieving selected learning outcomes.

The extent of and approach to adult learning in an individual setting has been studied by Wedemeyer and Childs (1961) in relation to correspondence study.

Many of the increasing number of short-term residential university extension programs (Glancy, 1958) typify the organizational setting, as do the leadership training programs of the Cooperative Extension Service that are developed within a community organization.

The community setting, long a major part of the Cooperative Extension Service and a minor part of University Extension, was succinctly reviewed by McClusky in the handbook by Knowles (1960). Bebout (1963) has described how community-development concepts, originally the result of projects in smaller towns, are currently being used in poor neighborhoods of large metropolitan areas.

A plurality of University Extension programs, including almost all of the evening and extension classes and a major portion of residential conferences and institutes, utilize the temporary group. Most other continuing-education methods are utilized to some extent. The Cooperative Extension Service has placed major emphasis on individual and community settings, with some emphasis on the temporary group setting, such as meetings and workshops. Typical individual methods include consultation and technical pamphlets. Demonstration projects and working with organizations have been characteristic approaches. Rural Area Development has been a typical program in a community setting. Boyle (1958) suggested principles of program development that applied in the variety of settings within the Cooperative Extension Service. The typical setting for College Extension has been the temporary group, primarily for evening credit courses, with very limited use of other settings.

It should be noted that a major portion of Cooperative Extension activities, and a growing portion of University Extension efforts to work with less-advantaged segments of the community, are not within the narrow definition of systematic and sustained teaching-learning transactions in continuing higher education. They include the many informal ways of providing encouragement, information, and support that bring otherwise reluctant adults into more systematic learning situations and encourage their followthrough to application.

The primary purpose of the community-relations function of continuing higher education is the establishment of linkage with potential participants or clients and the organizations with which they are associated. Loomis and others (1953) have analyzed this process in rural areas. Both Morton (1953) and Dyer (1956) have analyzed the ways in which the extension or evening division has interpreted its program to the adult community, and DeCrow (1962) has described typical procedures for doing so.

The institutional-relations function deals primarily with staffing continuing-higher-education programs with mentors. DeCrow (1962) has described typical practices in University Extension, and Boone (1959) has analyzed relationships between cooperative extension specialists and resident faculty. Daigneault (1963) analyzed the interrelated roles of the evening-college dean, the resident dean, and the department chairman in making staffing decisions.

There have been three or four major studies of continuing-higher-education student personnel services, such as the one by Simonaitis (1957). Extension Divisions usually offer few of the wide range of services that include registration advisement, educational counseling, referrals to other agencies, testing, and placement in jobs or other educational programs. The continuing-education research and development function is located in studies and training units in Cooperative Extension, and Knox (1963) has described the arrangements that occur in University Extension divisions.

The administrative function tends to facilitate and coordinate the other functions. Morton (1953) and Dyer (1956) have described typical patterns of administrative organization in University Extension, and Carey (1961b) has analyzed shifting patterns at various stages of institutional change. DeCrow (1962) has described typical administrative practices, and Deppe (1965) has analyzed the program-administrator role of the university conference coordinator. Regarding the Cooperative Extension Service, Creech (1957) has described the administrative organization in selected states, and Wilkening (1957) has analyzed the administrative role of the county agent.

TRENDS. Continuing-higher-education programs in the United States have emerged during the past century. The American Society for the Extension of University Teaching was founded in 1890, and by 1916, 30 universities had begun continuing-education activities (Grattan, 1955). During that same period the elaborate array of educational activities for farm families that had earlier been developed by agricultural societies and cooperative demonstration groups became part of the agricultural extension function of the land-grant colleges and universities. These extension activities were further coordinated through the passage in 1914 of the Smith-Lever Act (Grattan, 1955), which established the Cooperative Extension Service "to aid in the diffusion among the people of the United States useful and practical information on subjects relating to agriculture and home economics, and to encourage the application of the same." Similarities between the development of continuing higher education in the United States and in other industrialized countries were described by Grattan (1955), UNESCO (1952), and Kidd (1950).

In the early days of Cooperative Extension the primary focus was on the problems and interests of the clients, in contrast with University Extension and, more recently, College Extension, which has more frequently begun with faculty competence. During the past three or four decades, both types of Divisions have moved toward a similar approach in which the role of the Division is to facilitate a transaction between institution and community, from which a program appropriate to both will emerge.

Over the years, the Cooperative Extension Service has been financed almost exclusively from tax funds, with about 40 percent coming from the federal government. By contrast, financial support for the remainder of continuing higher education has come mainly from tuition and fees paid by the participants. Although this difference persists, some state Cooperative Extension programs are beginning to charge fees, and a small amount of federal funds are financing specific University Extension projects. The extent of federal participation in continuing education as it relates to higher education has been inventoried by Greenleigh Associates (1967). Also, Cooperative Extension is increasing its use of book-oriented methods for participants with higher levels of formal education and from urban areas, and University Extension is making greater use of non-book-oriented methods, especially in relation to reaching less-advantaged urban adults. Especially at the state universities, the Cooperative and University Extension divisions have been engaged in recent years in the establishment of closer working relationships, as their spheres of activity have become increasingly similar. Excellent analyses of these and other trends in continuing higher education have been prepared by Houle (1959), by DeCrow (1964), and by Liveright and Goldman (1965).

In addition to these studies of the field, two notable studies that have analyzed developmental phases for specific types of divisions, especially the evening college are those by McMahon (1960) and by Carey (1961a). Also, a slight increase in the quantity and quality of research related to continuing higher education can be discerned from the references to studies on continuing education in the research reviews of the past two decades. The most comprehensive summary of adult education research was compiled by Brunner and others (1959). Periodic reviews have been contained in the June issues of the *Review of Educational Research* for the years 1950, 1953, 1959, and 1965. The summer issues of the quarterly journal *Adult Education* contain summaries of adult education research recently completed or in process, and the Federal Extension Service prepares an annual *Review of Extension Research*. An analysis of current needs in adult education research was provided by Knox (1965b).

Alan B. Knox
Teachers College
Columbia University

References

Aker, George. "The Identification of Criteria for Evaluating Graduate Programs in Adult Education." Doctoral dissertation. U Wisconsin, 1962. 400p.

Bebout, John E. "Urban Extension." *Am Behavioral Scientist* 6:24–45; 1963.

Boone, Edgar J. "The Professional Status of Extension Specialists as Compared with Research-Resident Teaching Staffs of Selected Departments in Four Land-grant Institutions. Doctoral dissertation. U Wisconsin, 1959. 246p.

Boyle, Patrick S. "An Analysis of Selected Program Planning Principles of the Adult Programs of Vocational Agriculture and Cooperative Extension." Doctoral dissertation. U Wisconsin, 1958. 215p.

Brunner, Edmund deS., and others. *An Overview of Adult Education Research*. Adult Education Association of America, 1959. 275p.

Burkett, Jess E., and Ruggiers, Paul G. (Eds.) *Bachelor of Liberal Studies*. Center for the Study of Liberal Education for Adults, 1965. 107p.

Carey, James T. *The Development of the University Evening College as Observed in Ten Urban Universities*. Center for the Study of Liberal Education for Adults, 1961(a). 73p.

Carey, James T. *Forms and Forces in University Adult Education*. Center for the Study of Liberal Education for Adults, 1961(b). 229p.

Creech, Glenwood L. "Organization, Programming and Personnel Policies of the Cooperative Extension Service in Selected States." Doctoral dissertation. U Wisconsin, 1957, 208p.

Crimi, James E. *Adult Education in the Liberal Arts Colleges*. Center for the Study of Liberal Education for Adults, 1957. 38p.

Daigneault, George H. *Decision Making in the University Evening College: The Role of the Resident Department Chairman*. Center for the Study of Liberal Education for Adults, 1963. 62p.

DeCrow, Roger. *Ability and Achievement of Evening College and Extension Students.* Center for the Study of Liberal Education for Adults, 1959. 13p.

DeCrow, Roger. *Administrative Practices in University Evening Colleges.* Center for the Study of Liberal Education for Adults. 1962. 74p.

DeCrow, Roger. *Growing Time.* Center for the Study of Liberal Education for Adults, 1964. 82p.

Dekker, Tunis H. "Faculty Commitment to University Adult Education." Doctoral dissertation. U Chicago, 1965. 183p.

Deppe, Donald A. "The Conference Director as a Boundary Definer of the University." Doctoral dissertation. U Chicago, 1965. 128p.

Dyer, John P. *Ivory Towers in the Market Place: The Evening College in American Education.* Bobbs-Merrill, 1956. 205p.

Erickson, Clifford G., and others. *Eight Years of T.V. College.* Chicago Board of Education, 1964. 40p.

Federal Extension Service. *National Survey of the Clientele and Utilization of County Extension Staff Resources.* U.S. Department of Agriculture, 1965. 141p.

Glancy, Keith E. *Noncredit Adult Education at the University Level.* Purdue U, Division of Educational Reference, 1958. 23p.

Gowin, D. B. *The Part-time College Teacher.* Center for the Study of Liberal Education for Adults, 1961. 63p.

Grattan, C. Hartley. *In Quest of Knowledge.* Association Press, 1955. 337p.

Greenleigh Associates. *Inventory of Federally Supported Extension and Continuing Education Programs.* The Associates, 1967. 350p.

Grinager, Patricia. "Extension Education by Land-grant Colleges and Universities Through Television." Doctoral dissertation. Stanford U, 1964. 401p.

Hill, Richard J. *A Comparative Study of Lecture and Discussion Methods.* Fund for Adult Education, 1960. 153p.

Houle, Cyril O. *Major Trends in Higher Adult Education.* Center for the Study of Liberal Education for Adults, 1959. 47p.

Johnstone, John W. C., and Rivera, Ramon J. *Volunteers for Learning.* Aldine Publishing Co., 1965. 624p.

Kidd, J. R. *Adult Education in Canada.* Canadian Association for Adult Education, 1950. 249p.

Knowles, Malcolm S. *Handbook of Adult Education in the United States.* Adult Education Association of America, 1960. 624p.

Knox, Alan B. *Research Arrangements Within University Adult Education Divisions.* Center for the Study of Liberal Education for Adults, 1963. 38p.

Knox, Alan B. "Clientele Analysis." R Ed Res 35:231–9; 1965(*a*).

Knox, Alan B. "Current Needs in Adult Education Research." J Ed 147:21–31; 1965(*b*).

Knox, Alan B., and Sjogren, Douglas. "Achievement and Withdrawal in University Adult Education Classes." Adult Ed 15:74–88; 1965.

Liveright, A. A., and Goldman, Freda H. *Significant Developments in Continuing Higher Education.* Center for the Study of Liberal Education for Adults, 1965. 28p.

Loomis, Charles P., and others. *Rural Social Systems and Adult Education.* Michigan State U Press, 1953. 392p.

Matthews, J. L. *A Method for Determining the Training Needs of County Extension Workers as a Basis for Planning Training Programs.* U.S. Department of Agriculture, GPO, 1950. 13p.

Matthews, J. L. *National Inventory of Extension Methods of Program Determination.* U.S. Department of Agriculture, GPO, 1952. 13p.

McCormick, Robert W. "An Analysis of Training Needs of County Extension Agents in Ohio." Doctoral dissertation. U Wisconsin, 1959. 240p.

McMahon, Ernest E. *The Emerging Evening College.* Teachers Col, Columbia U, 1960. 163p.

Miller, Harry L. *Patterns of Educational Use of a Televised Public Affairs Program: A Study of Metropolis: Creator or Destroyer.* New York U Press, 1966. 189p.

Miller, Harry L., and McGuire, Christine H. *Evaluating Liberal Adult Education.* Center for the Study of Liberal Education for Adults, 1961. 184p.

Miller, Paul A., and others. *The Cooperative Extension Today—A Statement of Scope and Responsibility.* Michigan State U, 1957. 15p.

Morton, John R. *University Extension in the United States.* U Alabama Press, 1953. 144p.

Rogers, Everett M. *Diffusion of Innovations.* Free, 1962. 367p.

Roth, Robert M. *A Conspectus to the Self-study Project of University College, The University of Chicago.* Center for the Study of Liberal Education for Adults, 1964. 94p.

Sanders, H. C., and others. (Eds.) *The Cooperative Extension Service.* Prentice-Hall, 1966. 435p.

Schulman, Benson Richard. "The Role of University Extension in Meeting the In-service Education Needs of School Districts." Doctoral dissertation. U California, 1964.

Simonaitis, John. *An Investigation of the Status of the Student Personnel Program In Evening Colleges.* U Col, Syracuse U, 1957. 24p.

Solomon, Daniel, and others. *Teaching Styles and Learning.* Center for the Study of Liberal Education for Adults, 1963. 164p.

Thornton, James W., Jr. *The Community Junior College,* 2nd ed. Wiley, 1966. 300p.

UNESCO. *Universities in Adult Education.* UNESCO, 1952. 172p.

Wedemeyer, Charles A., and Childs, Gayle B. *New Perspectives in University Correspondence Study.* Center for the Study of Liberal Education for Adults, 1961. 74p.

Wientge, King M., and DuBois, Philip H. *Factors Associated with the Achievement of Adult Students.* U Col, Washington U, 1964. 68p.

Wilkening, Eugene A. *The County Extension Agent in Wisconsin.* Research Bulletin 203. U Wisconsin, 1957. 51p.

FACULTY CHARACTERISTICS—COLLEGE AND UNIVERSITY

The term "faculty" embraces a wide variety of professional people—chemists, historians, linguists, economists, and psychologists—who have but one readily identifiable common characteristic: they are employed part or full time by a college or university to engage in teaching, research, and public service or in administration of these functions. It should be noted that in the United States the term "faculty" usually means all those who serve in an institution rather than those who are organized into such subgroups as colleges or departments within the institution. Thus, a faculty may include a thousand or more people with diverse interests and backgrounds who are also affiliated with such a subgroup as a department of English or a college of engineering. In Europe a "faculty" refers more commonly to those in a discipline or broad area of knowledge. Thus, the members of a "faculty" of an institution in the United States usually have fewer common characteristics than do those in Europe. However, faculty members in the United States tend increasingly to identify first with their discipline or profession and only secondarily with their institutions (Clark, 1963).

Since most faculty members have advanced degrees which have focused on research and since they are affiliated with educational institutions, they do have some common interests and concerns. Furthermore, they operate in a culture with a pattern of behavior which in many respects is dissimilar to that of their counterparts employed in business or government or engaged in private practice.

DEFINITION. The problem of definition of the term "faculty" becomes evident when any institution attempts to answer the deceptively simple question of how many faculty members it employs. If faculty includes only those holding ranks under the usual tenure system—professors, associate professors, assistant professors, and instructors—it will include, on most campuses, a good many persons with miscellaneous administrative duties involving finance, students, student records, student activities, and university services which have only indirect relationships to teaching, research, and public service. This definition will also exclude many who, as assistant instructors, graduate assistants, lecturers, and readers, are heavily engaged in instruction but who, as temporary or part-time personnel, are excluded from tenure regulations. It also excludes research associates, research assistants, and other persons who may be extensively involved in research.

If "faculty" means only those who teach, it excludes administrators and many others who support the instructional program in vital ways, such as librarians, evaluation personnel, and academic counselors. In recent years faculty rank has also been attached to many staff positions in recognition of their importance to the institutional operation, rather than because such positions have much direct relevance to the instructional program or to research and service. Rank carries prestige, salary, fringe benefits, and tenure; thus, it has been demanded by and given to business managers, registrars, admissions counselors, placement office directors, campus architects, and the like. It is also often argued that because the functions of a university include not only teaching but research and public service as well, those persons who serve as extension specialists and those engaged in government research and research at experiment stations should also be regarded as faculty members.

Some large institutions have tried to clarify the definition and to simplify the counting process by designating "teaching" and "nonteaching" faculty or by designating "instructional," "research," and "administrative" faculty. But many faculty members divide their time among all these functions or divide their time between university duties and outside-sponsored research or other employment, as private practice. Thus, such designations are not accurate unless expressed in full-time equivalents. The question then arises whether a faculty member appointed for 9 or 10 months is a full-time equivalent, and, if so, how the increasing numbers of 12-month appointees are to be counted.

There is no simple definition of faculty and no simple way to count the number employed—as persons have learned who work on unified state budgeting or attempt to collect and report national data on faculty supply and demand or attempt to do meaningful research on faculty characteristics. Unless definitions are carefully controlled, no valid comparisons can be made between institutions, and no research on faculty characteristics can be very helpful in educational planning.

It has long been found useful to narrow the definition of "faculty" if an institution wants to make claim for the quality of its faculty, the attractiveness of the salaries it pays, and even in some cases for the size of the teaching loads; and equally useful to widen the definition if it wants to lower its faculty-student ratios, add attractiveness to a variety of positions related to the instructional function, or justify to boards of trustees or legislatures the size of the salary budget. Thus, the purpose for which data are gathered and the precise definitions used should always be ascertained before any use is made of them.

RESPONSIBILITIES OF A FACULTY. In any enterprise—business, governmental, or educational—the responsibility of *doing* is widely distributed among those who make up the enterprise, but only in educational institutions is final responsibility so widely diffused (Corson, 1960). Substantial independent authority is allocated not only to the president and to the deans but also to the faculty as a group and to the individual faculty members. Such diffusion results from (1) the nature of the student-teacher relationship, in which each teacher must motivate, guide, and support the learning process and finally take the responsibility for evaluating student achievement, and (2) the special competence of faculty members, in contrast to a lay board, to make educational policies.

Faculty rights and responsibilities as they are now understood evolve from a long history of struggle for academic freedom and the right to make educational policy. Hofstadter and Metzger (1955) in their analytical history of the development of academic freedom trace the evolution of the concept and point out that it is one of the remarkable achievements of man. They further point out "the slender thread by which it hangs and the yet wide discrepancies that exist among institutions with respect to its honoring and preservation."

Most institutions have accepted, at least perfunctorily, the principles set forth by the American Association of University Professors (AAUP) in 1940 regarding academic freedom—that is, freedom in the classroom to discuss relevant though controversial issues, full freedom in research and the publication of results, and freedom from institutional censorship and discipline consequent to actions taken as a citizen (American Association of University Professors, 1964). Along with these rights the statement charges faculty with the responsibility for adequate performance of assigned duties, for avoiding controversial matter unrelated to the subject, and for accuracy, appropriate restraint, and respect for other opinion.

The right to a voice in educational policy making is also almost universally claimed by faculty and in general is recognized by administrators and governing boards. It is defended on the grounds that subject-matter specialists and professional teachers are the most competent persons to formulate policy regarding subject matter and methods of instruction, to recommend facilities and support for research of faculty members and students, and to set standards for admission of students, for academic performance, and for degrees (Black & others, 1956).

Although the AAUP policy statement declares that "the faculty should have primary responsibility for determining the educational policies of the institution," it recognizes that the final decision must rest with the governing board (American Association of University Professors, 1965). Educational policies have financial implications, and the raising and spending of funds is the domain of the president and the board. Although the AAUP policy declares that funds "allocated to educational purposes should be budgeted and expended in accordance with educational policies which the faculty has determined within the areas for which it is primarily responsible," it calls for the faculty to be "informed" and "consulted" and "asked to express its view" rather than to participate actively in budget making (Brown, 1966).

The degree to which faculty members are accorded academic freedom and a voice in policy making is difficult to assess but surely varies among institutions from a strong influence to perfunctory approval of administrative decisions (Corson, 1960). No doubt in some institutions there is a deliberate if subtle curtailment of freedom and responsibility, but in many cases the increasing size of the institution and the changing role of the faculty member have generally diminished his autonomy and made impractical his direct participation in policy making.

In the classroom, teaching is becoming much more of a team enterprise, with master teachers taking responsibility for planning and perhaps doing the lecturing; with a variety of assistants leading smaller groups in discussion, supervising them in laboratories, and reading their written work; and with evaluation specialists measuring their academic achievement. Likewise, research efforts are beginning to depend heavily on teamwork, since research problems cross the boundary lines of many fields (Anderson, 1963).

In the area of policy making, institutions have become so large and complex and curricula so specialized that some faculty members have reason to question their own competence to decide curricular matters in areas outside their own. Furthermore, they concede that the only efficient and reasonable way to make important decisions is to delegate the responsibility to representatives and to give them time to do a competent job. Their interest and concern are therefore reduced to little more than the choice of good representatives. This is a welcome relief to many who now prefer, in this age of specialization, to devote their time to doing research and keeping up with the explosion of knowledge, and at best attending to decisions on the departmental or divisional level, but it is a source of irritation to some who consider their expertness in a very narrow field of specialization adequate qualification to make judicious decisions in all matters of educational policy, no matter how complex (Morrow, 1963).

It has been pointed out that the removal of most faculty members from the debate associated with decision making—debate on the purposes of an institution, the climate most conducive to achieving those purposes, ways of dealing with internal and external pressures, etc.—does cause a weakening of the faculty as a whole, and a strengthening of the faculty in its many parts (Clark, 1963; Mooney, 1963).

Faculty focus their interests on their disciplines and matters associated with the welfare of their own departments. The results are (1) less direct association between faculty and administrators and consequently a greater gap in understanding; (2) a decrease in the feeling of community among scholars in various areas; (3) the creation of a group of perennial committee members whom Clark (1963) calls the "faculty oligarchs" whose interest and growing experience perpetuate their appointment or election to faculty committees; and (4) a noticeable change in the characteristics of the faculty in general. They are further removed from institutional policy making, think less about the role of higher education, and find more time for research and professional activities. "Faculty authority becomes less a case of self-government by a total collegium, and more a case of authority exercised department by department, sub-college by subcollege" (Anderson, 1963).

The impact of the emerging organizational pattern of faculties on faculty characteristics has not been fully explored. Clark (1961) observes that a strong faculty has a strong self-replacing potential and that faculty are attracted to a college because of its combination of high status, distinctive name, strong faculty government, and related freedom from administrative and lay control. In a sense, he says, a faculty that captures control is also captured in return and committed to the college by involvement in policy making.

Lazarsfeld and Thielens (1958) found that the type of organization is related to the quality of the institution. The greater the voice of the faculty in matters of academic freedom and the more protective the administration of academic freedom, the higher the quality of the institution. However, Eckert (1959) reported that over a period of 13 years at the University of Minnesota, more than 80 percent of the eligible faculty members held no all-university committee appointments and that two-thirds of the appointments were held by administrators and department chairmen.

Others have warned of the danger of division of power and responsibility within the institution, which may either choke out effective leadership or so frustrate the leaders that progress is impossible (Dodds, 1962; Kerr, 1963; Mooney, 1963).

Henderson (1960) says there is a relationship between vigorous educational leadership and institutional vitality and excellence of achievement. McGrath (1961a), finding curricula of liberal arts colleges badly in need of review, challenged faculty to consider what proliferation of programs and courses was doing to the vitality of such colleges and to "willingly and objectively attempt to bring offerings within defensible bounds." Yet there are faculty members who insist that the curriculum exists to satisfy faculty rather than student demands, providing justification for Ruml and Morrison's contention (1959) that faculty members have performed so badly in their administrative functions that the trustees and president should take back the authority over design and administration of curriculum.

These observations suggest that faculty members are more jealous of their right to administer the academic program than they are willing to give thought and effort to the enterprise.

Corson (1960) suggests that what is needed in research in the area of faculty organization is not formulas and organizational charts but case studies that depict how administration and faculty work together or do not work together in policy making in those areas considered to be in the faculty domain.

The diverse responsibilities of teachers which range over governance, academic policy making, curriculum building, classroom teaching, student learning, research and scholarship, publication, and service to the public make any evaluation of the effectiveness of teachers extremely difficult. Although much has been written about the need for better teacher performance at the college level and a considerable amount of research has been aimed at identifying desirable characteristics of college teachers and superior methods of teaching, the results do more to point up the difficulty of the problem than to demonstrate effective methods of evaluation (McKeachie, 1963; McKeachie & others 1964). The difficulties lie in the lack of agreement on a definition of teaching; lack of agreement on the goals of higher education; too much focus, in research studies, on teacher behavior and too little on how and what and why students learn; and too much confusion among teachers about their roles. Institutions tend to expect good teaching but to reward those who engage in research and publish and those who are recognized by professional societies and organizations. The "flight from teaching" to research within the university, noted by the Carnegie Foundation report (1964), is accentuated by the reward system used in most institutions. This flight is also noted among graduate students who enter graduate study intending to teach but develop a strong desire to continue with research (Gottlieb, 1961).

The prestige associated with research and the availability of research grants, together with the relief from teaching large classes of undergraduates crowding today's colleges and universities, undoubtedly makes research and scholarship preferable to teaching. However, the trend in the four-year college and the university to much more-specialized training at the undergraduate as well as the graduate levels demands that faculty members be oriented toward research for teaching and engaged in research for directing graduate programs (Bell, 1966; Knapp, 1962; Walters, 1965).

CHARACTERISTICS OF FACULTY MEMBERS.
Not until recent years were data on faculty characteristics systematically gathered and organized. Personnel decisions were based on personal knowledge of faculty members and their performance. However, with the growth in size of institutions and their faculties, and with the impending shortage of college teachers, it became necessary for institutions to know more about the nature and utilization of their faculty resources and more about their chances for retaining good faculty members and attracting others (Dressel & Lorimer, 1961).

For the most part, data on faculty are gathered by institutions for their own use in decision making and lose much of their significance when removed from the context of given institutional objectives and organization. National statistics, gathered by such organizations as the National Education Association, the U.S. Office of Education, the National Academy of Sciences, and others (Baumol, 1965), on such things as average salaries and the supply of and demand for college teachers are useful in identifying problems in recruiting and maintaining faculties but offer limited help in identifying or solving local problems.

At best, data on faculty characteristics are descriptive of a faculty at a given point in time. Unless they are tested against some sound principles appropriate to the kind of educational program implied by an institution's objectives and purposes and observed over a period of time for trends, they serve little purpose.

Data on qualifications, as highest degree, source of all degrees, experience, and professional recognition through publications, honors, public service, etc., are useful not only in assessing the overall quality of the faculty but also, and more importantly, in determining the qualifications of those to be retained, promoted, and recruited for added strength. For example, it is usually desirable to maintain a rich mix of academic backgrounds. Data will reveal whether inbreeding exists because faculty have had too little teaching-research experience in other institutions or have taken degrees at the same institution. Data will also reveal whether faculty are qualified for the kind of task the institution has defined for itself. A predominantly undergraduate institution whose faculty is primarily interested in research and graduate teaching may be wasting talent and money. An institution aspiring to a strong graduate program will find data on present faculty valuable in planning faculty expansion.

Data on age, rank, and tenure have implications for cost, rate of turnover, attractiveness of open positions to candidates, and continuity of program. If a large percentage of the faculty is at the top rank or ranks, the salary budget will be high and younger or newer faculty will see little opportunity for advancement. If too many are in the upper age brackets, desirable continuity may be lost at their retirement. If a high percentage of faculty is on tenure, the institution may be granting tenure indiscriminately or possibly granting tenure in lieu of salary increases or promotions, thus stabilizing a faculty which should be able to change as the institution changes. Furthermore, the better faculty members on tenure can and do move, while the less able remain. Thus, a low salary schedule coupled with a high percentage of tenured faculty can be disastrous. The saving factor is that salary is not the sole motivation of faculty.

Data on satisfactions and dissatisfactions of faculty and on reasons why faculty remain or move when other job offers appear have become extremely important in the present tight academic market. A number of studies have identified those factors which make institutions desirable for faculty members. In general they show that while salary is the most important consideration, other factors are of major importance, such as the prestige of the institution and the department, the caliber of associates, and working conditions. Time for research, good lines of communication, participation in policy making, academic freedom, professional duties commensurate with rank and experience, and promotions based on merit generally bring satisfactions, while bad administration, internal tensions, unreasonable loads, and questionable standards and methods of evaluation are sources of dissatisfaction (Allen & Sutherland, 1963; Brown, 1965; Duxbury, 1963; Eckert & Stecklein, 1961; Marshall, 1964; Ness, 1957; Russell, 1962; Stecklein & Lathrop, 1960). Some studies have been designed to study specific sources of satisfaction or dissatisfaction as salaries (Ruml & Tickton, 1961), sabbatical leaves (Eells & Hollis, 1962), fringe benefits (Ingraham & King, 1965; Keane, 1961), research environment (Fincher, 1965), role conflicts (Allen & Sutherland, 1963), etc.

Data are being used increasingly for personnel decisions regarding retention, promotion, and salary increases. Relevant information is difficult to accumulate; questionnaires and forms tend to overemphasize quantifiable data and to underemphasize qualitative data. Teaching-load data and time-distribution charts do not adequately describe either the nature or the worth of a professor's activities. Consequently, data of these kinds must always be used as an aid to seasoned judgment and never fitted into a formula. They are most valuable when used by persons familiar with a wide variety and range of data who understand their limitations. Data should, of course, always be interpreted in the light of institutional objectives, departmental objectives, when applicable, and long-range plans (Doi, 1961).

Some institutions and some professional organizations have considered it advisable to launch major studies of problems and policies relating to faculty, which might serve as models for other studies (Shryock, 1959; National Science Foundation . . . ; Dressel & Lorimer, 1961). These studies are valuable if they lead immediately to establishment of policy or to needed change.

Many institutions now prefer regular data collection by some person or unit such as an office of institutional research. These offices make possible the observation of trends as well as current data. The reports are not normally published but are exchanged upon request with institutions of similar size and purpose. Actual data on one institution are usually of less interest to other institutions than the various methodologies and uses found for such data. However, data from a number of institutions on some matter such as the percentage of faculty on tenure may be useful in appraising the meaning of a percentage determined locally. Higher percentages noted elsewhere may allay some concern, but finding "good company" elsewhere should not remove the necessity for looking at the implications of local practice for the future aspirations of the institutions. If some definite plans result, continuing tabulation of data from year to year is necessary to show whether the plan is being followed and with what results.

A considerable body of sociological research on faculty exists which was intended to give insight into such matters as the type of persons motivated to teach (Corcoran, 1961; Gustad, 1960; Hartung, 1961; Kinnane, 1961; Stecklein & Eckert, 1958), their baccalaureate origins (Knapp & Greenbaum, 1953; Pfnister, 1961), their general attitudes (Caplow & McGee, 1958; Cranberg, 1965), and their concepts of the purposes of education (Dressel & others, 1959; Dressel & Lorimer, 1960). While these studies do provide some general characteristics of members of the profession, they must be regarded as historical studies which take on significance only as they suggest problem areas for study and as subsequent studies make trends visible.

Such sociological studies are quickly outdated. Just as colleges and universities undergo major structural and cultural transformations, so faculties undergo changes. Laumann (1966), who participated in a large-scale study of the academic profession, cited evidence of the emergence of "a new breed of faculty," which can be traced to massive changes in higher education, including the increasingly important role of specialized research and public service and the high mobility of faculty. Some results seem to be lack of interest in matters of institutional concern and general hostility toward administrative chores, low institutional loyalty and high willingness to make advantageous moves to other institutions, lack of communication between highly specialized faculty in various disciplines, greater intensity of interest in roles other than teaching, involvement in public service as extracurricular and extra-pay activity, and attention to those activities most visible in considerations of promotion, tenure, and compensation (Cranberg, 1965).

There appears to be very little variation in the characteristics of faculty sought by the great variety of institutions included in the American system of higher education. As one scans the descriptions of positions open at the various institutions, it seems that nearly every one prefers candidates with the doctorate, some professional recognition, and some creditable record of research or scholarship, either as graduate students or as professors in other institutions. However, community colleges, church-related colleges, liberal arts colleges, land-grant institutions, specialized institutes, and others do assemble faculties with quite different characteristics. Some of these differences can be attributed to the selection by the institutions on a variety of bases, but many must be attributed to the selection by the candidates themselves, who gravitate to those institutions whose characteristics interest them. In most cases, the mixture of backgrounds, personalities, interests, and philosophies of education guarantees healthy debate, ferment of ideas, and potential for change.

However, when institutions define characteristics desired in new faculty too carefully, the result may be a faculty too homogeneous for the good of the institution. Homogeneity may encourage narrowness of purpose, complacency, and stagnation. When institutions, in order to build prestige, emphasize certain characteristics, such as advanced degrees and research interests—qualifications for which they may have little use—rather than lesser qualifications which more nearly fit the needs of the institution, they risk not only faculty dissatisfaction but also the inability, on their own part, to reach institutional objectives. When institutions give too little attention to qualifications other than degrees, they may assemble faculty who have little interest in the institution except as it may further their own ambitions. Careful surveillance of overall faculty characteristics can point out some of these dangers in personnel selection.

Research on faculty characteristics, like research in many other areas, serves as a vital part of institutional self-study. It provides data necessary for assessment of institutional strength; it has implications for long range planning; and it contributes to intelligent personnel decisions.

Margaret F. Lorimer
Michigan State University
Paul L. Dressel
Michigan State University

References

Allen, Lucile A., and Sutherland, Robert L. *Role Conflicts and Congruences Experienced by New Faculty Members as They Enter the Culture of a College Community*. Hogg Foundation for Mental Health, 1963. 28p.

American Association of University Professors. "Academic Freedom and Tenure: 1940 Statement of Principles." *AAUP B* 50:251–2; 1964.

American Association of University Professors. "Report of the Self-survey Committee of the AAUP." *AAUP B* 51:169–70; 1965.

Anderson, G. Lester. "The Organizational Character of American Colleges and Universities." In Lunsford, Terry (Ed.) *The Study of Academic Administration*. Western Interstate Commission for Higher Education, 1963. p. 1–20.

Baumol, William J. (Chairman.) "Economic Status of the Profession." *AAUP B* 51:248–60; 1965.

Bell, Daniel. *The Reforming of General Education*. Columbia U Press, 1966. 320p.

Berelson, Bernard. *Graduate Education in the United States*. McGraw-Hill, 1960. 346p.

Black, Max, and others. "Faculty-trustee Relations." *AAUP B* 42:613–24; 1956.

Brown, David G. *The Market for College Teachers*. U North Carolina Press, 1965. 301p.

Brown, Ralph S. "Rights and Responsibilities of Faculty." *AAUP B* 52:131–40; 1966.

Caplow, Theodore, and McGee, Reece J. *The Academic Marketplace*. Basic Books, 1958. 262p.

Carnegie Foundation, *Flight from Teaching*. The Foundation, 1964. 14 p.

Clark, Burton R. "Faculty Authority." *AAUP B* 47:293–302; 1961(a).

Clark, Burton R. "The Role of Faculty in College Administration." In *Studies of Faculty*. Western Interstate Commission on Higher Education, 1961(b). p. 83–102.

Clark, Burton R. "Faculty Organization and Authority." In Lunsford, Terry. (Ed.) *The Study of Academic Administration*. Western Interstate Commission on Higher Education, 1963. p. 37–52.

Corcoran, Mary E. *Where Does College Teaching Stand in the Career Plans of Superior College Seniors?* Bureau of Institutional Research, U. Minnesota, 1961. 85p.

Corson, John J. *Governance of Colleges and Universities*. McGraw-Hill, 1960. 209p.

Cranberg, Lawrence. "Ethical Problems of Scientists." *Ed Rec* 46:282–96; 1965.

Dodds, Harold W. *The Academic President—Educator or Caretaker?* McGraw-Hill, 1962. 294p.

Doi, James. "The Proper Use of Faculty Load Studies." In *Studies of College Faculty*. Western Interstate Commission on Higher Education, 1961. p. 53–64.

Dressel, Paul L., and Lorimer, Margaret F. *Attitudes of Liberal Arts Faculty Members Toward Liberal and Professional Education*. Teachers Col, Columbia U, 1960. 55p.

Dressel, Paul L., and Lorimer, Margaret F. "Institutional Self-evaluation." In Dressel, Paul L., and others. *Evaluation in Higher Education*. Houghton, 1961. p. 393–432.

Dressel, Paul L., and others. *The Liberal Arts as Viewed by Faculty Members in Professional Schools*. Teachers Col, Columbia U, 1959. 68p.

Duxbury, David A. *Faculty Opinion Toward Salary, Fringe Benefits, and Working Conditions*. California State Coordinating Council for Higher Education, 1963. 55p.

Eckert, Ruth E. "The Share of the Teaching Faculty in University Policy Making." *AAUP B* 45:346–51; 1959.

Eckert, Ruth E., and Stecklein, John E. *Job Motivations and Satisfactions of College Teachers*. USOE, 1961. 96p.

Eells, Walter C., and Hollis, Ernest V. *Sabbatical Leave in American Higher Education*. USOE, 1962. 77p.

Fincher, Cameron. *Faculty Perceptions of the Research Environment*. Georgia Institute of Higher Education, 1965. 20p.

Gottlieb, David. "Teachers and Researchers in American Universities." *J H Ed* 32:452–4; 1961.

Gross, Neal. "Organizational Lag in American Universities." *Harvard Ed R* 33:58–73; 1963.

Gustad, John W. *Career Decision of College Teachers*. Southern Regional Education Board, 1960. 87p.

Hartung, Ernest W. *Some Factors in the Choice of a Career in College Teaching of Biology*. New England Board of Higher Education, 1961. 35p.

Henderson, Algo. *Policies and Practices in Higher Education*. Harper, 1960. 338p.

Hofstadter, Richard, and Metzger, Walter P. *The Development of Academic Freedom in the United States*. Columbia U Press, 1955. 527p.

Ingraham, Mark H., and King, Francis P. *The Outer Fringe*. U Wisconsin Press, 1965. 304p.

Keane, George F. "A Look at the Professor's Personal Finances." *Col U Bus* 30:42–3; 1961.

Kerr, Clark. *The Uses of the University*. Harvard U Press, 1963. 140p.

Kinnane, Mary. *Attitudes of Undergraduates Toward College Teaching as a Career*. New England Board of Higher Education, 1961. 35p.

Knapp, Robert H. "Changing Functions of the College Professor." In Sanford, Nevitt. (Ed.) *The American College*. Wiley, 1962. p. 290–311.

Knapp, Robert H., and Greenbaum, J. J. *The Scholar: His Collegiate Origins*. U Chicago Press, 1953. 122p.

Laumann, Edward O. "The New Breed of Faculty." In Smith, A. Kerry. (Ed.) *Current Issues*. Association for Higher Education, 1966. p. 198–202.

Lazarsfeld, Paul F., and Thielens, Wagner, Jr. *The Academic Mind*. Free, 1958. 460p.

Marshall, Howard D. *The Mobility of College Faculties*. Pageant Press, 1964. 152p.

McGrath, Earl J. *Memo to a College Faculty Member*. Teachers Col, Columbia U, 1961(a). 54p.

McGrath, Earl J. *The Quantity and Quality of College Teachers*. Teachers Col, Columbia U, 1961(b). 24p.

McKeachie, W. J. "Research on Teaching in Colleges and Universities." In Gage, N. L. (Ed.) *Handbook of Research on Teaching*. Rand McNally, 1963. p. 1118–72.

McKeachie, W. J., and others. *Research on the Characteristics of Effective College Teaching*. Cooperative Research Project No. 850, USOE, 1964. 156p.

Mooney, Ross L. "The Problem of Leadership in the University." *Harvard Ed R* 33:51–7; 1963.

Morrow, Glenn R. "The University of Pennsylvania Faculty Participation in University Government." *AAUP B* 49:114–23; 1963.

National Academy of Science. *Profiles of Ph.D.'s in the Sciences*. The Academy, 1965. 123p.

National Education Association. *Salaries in Higher Education, 1965–66*. Research Report 1966–R2. NEA, 1966. 65p.

National Education Association, Research Division, *Teacher Supply and Demand in Universities, Colleges and Junior Colleges, 1963–64 and 1964–65*. NEA 1965. 92p.

National Science Foundation and National Institutes of Health. "Project to Devise and Test Simplified Adequate Systems of Measuring and Reporting Financial, Manpower Facilities, Research, and Other Activities in Colleges and Universities." (In preparation.)

Ness, Frederic W. *The Role of the Colleges in Recruitment of Teachers*. Association of American Colleges, 1957. 83p.

Pfnister, Allan O. *A Report on the Baccalaureate Origins of College Faculties*. Association of American Colleges, 1961. 93p.

Ruml, Beardsley, and Morrison, Donald H. *Memo to a College Trustee: A Report on Financial and Structural Problems of the Liberal College*. McGraw-Hill, 1959. 94p.

Ruml, Beardsley, and Tickton, Sidney G. *Teaching Salaries, Then and Now*. Fund for the Advancement of Education, 1961. 93p.

Russell, John Dale. "Faculty Satisfactions and Dissatisfactions." *J Exp Ed* 31:135–9; 1962.

Shryock, Richard H. *The University of Pennsylvania Faculty: A Study of American Higher Education*. U Pennsylvania Press, 1959. 259p.

Stecklein, John E., and Eckert, Ruth E. *An Exploratory Study of Factors Influencing the Choice of College Teaching as a Career*. USOE Cooperative Research Project. USOE, 1958. 46p.

Stecklein, John E., and Lathrop, Robert L. *Faculty Attraction and Retention.* Bureau of Institutional Research, U Minnesota, 1960. 130p.

U.S. Office of Education. *Estimates of Demand for and Supply of Higher Education Staff, 1963-64 through 1973-74.* USOE, 1965. 9p.

Walters, Everett. (Ed.) *Graduate Education Today.* ACE, 1965. 246p.

FEDERAL PROGRAMS, RELATION AND INFLUENCE

There is no national system of higher education in the United States. Under the constitution of the United States the establishment and operation of schools and colleges have proceeded under the jurisdiction of state governments. The operation of schools has been conceived as a basic responsibility of the communities in which the children are taught, and the states have delegated large measures of responsibility to local boards of education elected by the communities which the schools serve. Thus, the United States has 50 independent state systems of public education, each operating without supervision or direction from any agency or authority in the federal government. In addition, there are hundreds of schools and colleges enrolling thousands of students that operate with state sanction under nonpublic auspices. The silence of the constitution, however, does not imply lack of federal interest in education. Over the years, education has been the subject of important action by all branches of the federal government—executive, legislative, and judicial.

The sweep of federal interest and action is traced in the following chronological list of significant federal actions.

1785—Land grants to territories for support of schools.

1787—Land grants for the endowment of public institutions of higher education.

1802—Establishment of the U.S. Military Academy, the first federal degree-granting institution.

1804—Provision for schools in the District of Columbia.

1819—The Dartmouth decision: Supreme Court rules that the charter granted to Dartmouth College constituted a contract not to be altered by the state without the concurrence of college authorities.

1845—Establishment of the U.S. Naval Academy.

1857—Establishment of Gallaudet College for the education of deaf persons.

1862—Land grants for the support of at least one college in each state to teach agriculture and mechanical arts (the Morrill Act).

1867—Establishment of the Federal Department of Education.

1870—Initiation of the principle of federal "matching grants" to states.

1879—Establishment of agricultural experiment stations at land-grant colleges.

1890—Authorization of continuing appropriations for instruction in specified subjects at land-grant colleges.

1910—Establishment of the U.S. Coast Guard Academy.

1917—National Vocational Education Act (Smith-Hughes). Provided federal appropriations for vocational training in schools offering below-college-level instruction.

1919—Initiation of the policy of making surplus federal property available to educational institutions.

1920—Initiation of the Reserve Officer Training Corps programs in educational institutions.

1931—Report of President Hoover's National Advisory Committee on Education.

1936—Initiation of international educational exchanges through promotion of Convention on Inter-American Cultural Relations.

1937—Initiation of policy of fellowship grants in connection with establishment of National Cancer Institute.

1941—Initiation of financial assistance to communities in which federal activities had created educational and tax burdens (the Lanham Act).

1942—Establishment of the U.S. Merchant Marine Academy.

1944—The Servicemen's Readjustment Act, popularly known as the G.I. Bill.

1948—Report of President Truman's Commission on Higher Education.

1950—Establishment of the National Science Foundation.

1950—Initiation of a program of low-interest loans to institutions of higher education for the construction of housing facilities.

1950—Supreme Court decision ruling that the University of Texas Law School is required to admit a qualified Negro.

1951—Initiation of contracts with educational institutions to provide technical and educational assistance to other countries.

1953—Establishment of the Department of Health, Education, and Welfare in the President's Cabinet.

1954—Supreme Court decision that compulsory segregation of students by race is a denial of equal protection of the laws at all levels of public education.

1954—Establishment of the U.S. Air Force Academy.

1958—The National Defense Education Act to strengthen American education at all levels in areas critical to national security and welfare.

1963—Higher Education Facilities Act: authorized grants to all colleges, public and private, for construction of buildings and improvement of facilities.

1963—Vocational Education Act of 1963: to strengthen vocational education.

1965—Elementary and Secondary Education Act: to improve educational quality and opportunities, with special attention to economically disadvantaged students.

1965—Establishment of the National Foundation for the Arts and Humanities to stimulate scholarly inquiry in the humanities and to develop creative and performing arts.

1966—International Education Act: to strengthen studies in non-Western cultures and programs of cultural exchange.

Federal legislation affecting education in the last 25 years exceeds both in volume and importance the legislative acts of the preceding 150 years (Tiedt, 1966).

Educational activities of the federal government involving schools and colleges now include (1) the direct operation of schools, academies, institutes, colleges, and universities and other educational programs for specific national purposes, or for specially defined groups; (2) land grants to states in support of the establishment of schools and colleges in the states and territories; (3) grants to states and territories in support of specified educational activities deemed to be in the national interest; (4) loans and grants for educational buildings and equipment, and donations of surplus property for school purposes; (5) financial assistance to students and scholars through loans, scholarships, fellowships, career professorships, and other types of subvention; (6) support of programs of research and scholarly inquiry in defined areas of knowledge, including training of research personnel; and (7) support of programs of educational assistance to other countries, including cultural exchange of teachers and students.

In addition, many activities of the Library of Congress, the Smithsonian Institution, the National Bureau of Standards, and other federal agencies have strong educational components but usually do not involve schools and colleges in formal programs. The in-service training of federal employees is another type of educational activity of most federal departments and agencies. (Quattlebam, 1960).

FEDERALLY-OPERATED INSTITUTIONS. The federal government operates a miscellany of schools, colleges, and educational programs. Undergraduate degree-granting institutions include the U.S. Military Academy, at West Point, New York; the U.S. Naval Academy, at Annapolis, Maryland; the U.S. Air Force Academy, at Colorado Springs, Colorado; the Merchant Marine Academy, at Kings Point, New York; and the Coast Guard Academy, at New London, Connecticut. The Naval Post-Graduate School, at Monterey, California, and the Air Force Institute of Technology, at Dayton, Ohio, award graduate degrees. Specialized advanced study is also provided in programs offered by the Judge Advocate General's School, the Foreign Service Institute, the Graduate School of Agriculture, the National Bureau of Standards, the National Institutes of Health, and the Atomic Energy Commission, but these units are not authorized to award academic degrees. In addition, the federal government makes appropriations for the support of Howard University, at Washington, D.C., a school established primarily for the education of Negroes; and Gallaudet College, at Washington, D.C., a school for the deaf.

At the elementary and secondary levels, federal agencies operate schools for the children of servicemen or federal employees who are stationed in areas where attendance at other schools is not feasible; schools for the education of American Indians; and schools for inmates of federal penitentiaries. In general, such special schools are administered by the federal agency which has primary responsibility for the special groups to be served. Congress also provides funds for the operation of the school system of the District of Columbia.

The U.S. Armed Forces Institute, at Madison, Wisconsin, offers an extensive program of correspondence study for the training and educational advancement of military personnel. Classroom programs are also organized when and where feasible. Quattlebam's comprehensive classification and analysis of federal programs in education is a mine of information about federal activities as of 1960 (Quattlebam, 1960).

THE EXECUTIVE BRANCH AND EDUCATION. The primary educational agency of the federal government is the Office of Education. This office began as the Department of Education in 1867, became a bureau in the Department of Interior in 1869, was shifted to the Federal Security Agency in 1939, and was made a unit of the new Department of Health, Education, and Welfare established in 1953. The office is headed by the United States Commissioner of Education, appointed by the president. Recently, the secretary of health, education, and welfare has included an assistant secretary for education in his secretariat.

For many years the function and status of the Office of Education reflected the weak role of the federal government in education. Its primary functions were advisory and informational. Since its establishment in the Department of Health, Education, and Welfare, and as a result of the growing federal involvement in education, the Office of Education has grown in responsibility and stature. The Office of Education now functions very largely as the administrative base for the operation of federally sponsored programs dealing substantially with education, as such (Campbell & others, 1965).

Major federal programs currently administered by the Office of Education include the Land-grant Act, School Assistance to Federally Affected Areas, the National Defense Education Act, vocational education acts, the Higher Education and Facilities Act of 1963, the Elementary and Secondary Act of 1963, and the Higher Education Facilities Act of 1965. Appropriations administered by the Office of Education have multiplied over sixfold in the last five years.

The chief executive of the United States wields important influence upon education through legislative proposals, appointments to office, public statements and other forms of leadership. Education has been the subject of special commissions or committees appointed by presidents Hoover, Truman, Eisenhower, and Kennedy. While specific outcomes of these studies are not many, the cumulative effect may have been considerable. The White House Conference on Education in the Eisenhower administration was followed by similar conferences in the states and invoked citizen appraisal of the educational needs of the nation. By 1960 scientists and educators, agitated by startling accomplishments in the U.S.S.R., were also issuing recommendations for strengthening the educational resources and scientific capabilities of the nation (President's Science Advisory Committee, 1960). President Johnson moved from sponsoring studies and conferences to proposing action on a broad front. Congress accepted his proposals for educational legislation with an alacrity not previously shown. In the Johnson administration, education became an object of federal interest in its own right. But Congress was still far from endorsing the idea of general federal aid to education. Education remains the last major governmental function assigned primarily to state and local governments (Munger & Fenno, 1962; Pierce, 1964; Campbell & others, 1965).

THE SUPREME COURT AND EDUCATION. Decisions of the Supreme Court have had important effects upon education in the United States. Cases affecting education have usually reached the Supreme Court on questions concerning the powers and jurisdictions of the states and the federal government or on questions concerning civil rights. The Dartmouth College Charter Case of 1816 was an early example. The Supreme Court's ruling that the charter granted to Dartmouth College was a contract with the State of New Hampshire prevented Dartmouth College's becoming a state-operated institution. This decision enhanced the security and early growth of private colleges in this country.

In 1925 the Supreme Court ruled that an Oregon law requiring children to attend public schools was void because it denied parents the right to educate their children for purposes other than those recognized by the state. This ruling protected the rights of parents to send children to nonpublic schools. In a succession of decisions upon issues about religion in education, the Supreme Court has consistently frowned upon any legislative enactment of school practice sanctioned by the state that abridges the right of an individual to freedom of religious choice or worship (Pierce, 1964).

In 1954 the Supreme Court ruled directly on the issue of racial segregation in schools. This historic decision declared that segregation by races in public schools violates constitutional rights that are guaranteed by the fourteenth amendment. This ruling reversed previous Supreme Court decisions that "separate but equal" schools were permissible (U.S. Supreme Court, 1954).

Wave effects of the 1954 decision have been felt with varying degrees of turbulence in many parts of the nation. Fifteen years after the decision, progress toward desegregation of schools remains slow. School attendance areas based upon residential patterns, new mixtures of populations in rapidly growing urban areas, migration of population within metropolitan areas, resistance to federal authority, and continuing hard cores of prejudice and emotional attitudes have complicated the enforcement of the decree. School systems and school authorities in urban areas with considerable mixture of races are in the vortex of the turbulence. On the principle of equal educational opportunity there is much agreement; on the method and manner of its accomplishment there is much disagreement. Attempts at enforcement by federal authorities have rekindled smoldering fires on the subject of federal control of education. A detailed account of the development and status of the federal government's efforts to provide equal protection under laws in public higher education is found in *Equal Protection of the Laws in Public Higher Education* (U.S. Commission on Civil Rights, 1960).

ELEMENTARY AND SECONDARY EDUCATION. With the exception of the field of vocational education, federal activity involving elementary or secondary education has lagged behind federal programs in higher education. Federal legislation for support of programs in elementary and secondary schools of the states, however, has a distinct pattern.

Appropriations are made to a duly constituted educational agency of the state, usually the state department of education. The legislation states the specific purposes for which the appropriations may be used, prescribes the formula by which federal funds will be allocated to the states, requires the states to submit plans for the use of the funds that meet the approval of a designated federal agency (usually the Office of Education), and frequently asks the state to match the federal appropriation on some prescribed ratio. The intention is to emphasize the specific national interest which prompts federal participation and to stimulate needed national action while leaving primary responsibility with the states. Many federal acts carry a specific provision that no federal agency or officer may exercise any control over the curriculum, administration, or personnel of any educational institution or school system. Examples of federal legislation of this type are the Vocational Education acts of 1917 and 1963, The National Defense Education Act, and the Elementary and Secondary Education Act of 1965. In some instances, however, the federal government has made payments directly to local educational authorities. The legislation providing financial assistance for construction and operation of schools in areas affected by federal activity is a prime example. Local school districts, however, apply for this assistance under plans approved by the designated educational agency of the state.

Provisions of federal legislation affect the range of education from preschool to adult education. They seek to improve the quality of elementary and secondary education for educationally deprived children of low-income families; to strengthen the occupational education of non-college-bound youth; to strengthen the curriculum and instruction in the sciences, languages, mathematics, and other areas; to improve counseling and guidance services; to increase library resources and instructional materials; and to expand research activities. A significant aspect of these measures has been the provision of financial assistance to state departments of education in order to strengthen their ability to direct and supervise the needed programs and to build greater capacity for research on educational problems. Despite the wide range of activity of the federal programs, their aims are usually to accomplish specific educational objectives or to meet needs of specially defined groups. But there is also evident a trend toward federal assistance to undergird the states' capacity to administer nationally needed programs (Pierce, 1964; Munger & Fenno, 1962; Barnard, 1962).

VOCATIONAL EDUCATION. Federal legislation for vocational education furnishes a useful case study of the evolution of federal activity in public education. In 1914 a commission on national aid to vocational education recommended federal grants to the states for occupational training in agriculture, home economics, and trade and industrial education. The successful federal-state partnership in vocational and technical training by land-grant colleges was cited as precedent for extending such programs to secondary schools. In 1917 the National Vocational Education Act (Smith-Hughes) was passed. This act set the pattern and precedent for federal-state relationships now used in most federal legislation affecting public education below the college level, as described in the previous section.

From 1917 to 1956, federally supported programs of vocational education continued in agriculture, home economics, trade and industrial, and distributive occupations. In 1956, fishing trades and occupations were added; and in 1958, the National Defense Education Act authorized the establishment of "area vocational schools" for the training of technicians necessary to the national defense.

In 1962 the Panel of Consultants on Vocational Education reported to the president that technical training at post-high school levels was a critical need and recommended that emphasis be placed upon occupational training for the following special groups: (1) high school youth who enter employment upon graduation; (2) youth with special needs; and (3) youth and adults who are not in high school but must prepare to enter the labor market. The panel recommended better occupational counseling, teachers with work experience, stronger basic education, expanded research activity, and training for any occupation for which there is demonstrated need.

Congress responded by enacting the Vocational Education Act of 1963—the first major revamping of vocational education since the original Vocational Education Act of 1917. The occupational fields supported now include new and emerging occupations. Funds for expanding teaching space, facilities, and staff are provided. Residential vocational schools may be constructed. A major investment in research and fact-finding in vocational education is authorized and, in total, federal funds for the support of vocational education were greatly increased. The federal government's tendency to emphasize specific outcomes of education, to maintain programs once established, and in recent years to expand them broadly, is well portrayed in its activities in vocational education (Hawkins & others, 1962).

No comprehensive appraisal of the impact on the labor force of the extensive programs of technical training in the armed services has been made. The President's Committee on Education Beyond the High School (1957) reported that 60 percent of the technical training provided by the military services has civilian application.

Other federal programs, such as the Area Redevelopment Act of 1961 and the Manpower Development and Training Act of 1962, provide for vocational training to relieve conditions caused by unemployment or underemployment in distressed areas and to upgrade skills of the labor force. The Department of Labor administers these programs, and vocational schools cooperate in the accomplishment of these objectives (Levitan, 1963).

HIGHER EDUCATION. Historically, federal interest in and support of programs in higher education have preceded federal activity in elementary and secondary education. Over a hundred years ago the federal government entered into partnership with the states in establishing and supporting colleges that emphasize agriculture and mechanical arts. Under the Morrill Act of 1862 the federal government made grants of land to enable each state to establish such colleges and, with later legislation, provided continuing appropriations for instruction in related subjects and for the establishment of experimental stations and cooperative extension services. The land-grant colleges, as they are now known, constitute a major national resource for research and educational services. In many states, the land-grant college is the state's strongest educational center (Kelly, 1952; Eddy, 1957).

Much of the present pattern of relationships between the federal government and higher education evolved from policies and practices developed during war emergencies, when federal agencies entered into contracts with or made grants to individual institutions for the training of military personnel, for the performance of defense-related research, for the use of campus facilities, or for other purposes. In concept, the federal government was purchasing services from educational institutions (Kidd, 1959).

Early examples of such programs are the Student Army Training Corps, established in 1918 to meet military needs for officer training and incidentally to prevent the closing of colleges because of their reduced enrollments, and a research contract with the Massachusetts Institute of Technology awarded by the National Advisory Committee for Aeronautics in 1915, cited as the first such contract awarded to an institution of higher education (Axt, 1952). These early ventures in cooperation between federal agencies and institutions of higher education during World War I, seemingly insignificant, actually foreshadowed a vast interconnection that developed during World War II.

The legislation most significant to the evolution of federal policy in higher education was the Servicemen's Readjustment Act of 1944, the "G.I. Bill" (Babbidge & Rosenzweig, 1962). This bill is important for its declaration of national interest in providing financial assistance to students who seek education beyond the high school. Originally designed as a program of educational benefits for disabled veterans, it was later amended to permit any veteran to pursue an educational program in an approved institution for a period equal to the period of his wartime service plus one year, with a limit of 48 calendar months. The act provided for direct payment to the institutions of the costs of tuition, books, and supplies. The veteran received a subsistence allowance varying according to the number of his dependents. Subsequent legislation has provided similar educational benefits to veterans of military operations in Korea and Vietnam. Under these acts, however, veterans receive a specified educational allowance but are responsible for payment of their own educational costs, including tuition, books, and subsistence.

The G.I. Bill furnished precedent and pattern for subsequent Federal programs of student financial assistance. In fact, financial aid to students has been the most popular and least controversial type of federal participation in higher education (Babbidge & Rosenzweig, 1962).

Since World War II, scientific advance, the demands of an expanding economy, and recurring international tensions have led to a growing interconnection between the wide-ranging commitments of the federal government and the nation's institutions of higher education. Activities of existing programs have multiplied, and new programs to meet new needs have appeared with each session of Congress. The establishment of the National Science Foundation, with the growth of its programs in basic research and education, is a significant example. The National Defense Education Act broadened such programs to include foreign languages, mathematics, and other subjects critical to national defense, and moved to strengthen the teaching staff and to modernize instructional procedures in the nation's schools. The Higher Education Facilities Act of 1963 provides grants and loans for the construction of academic facilities not only for graduate programs but also for undergraduate colleges, including two-year colleges and technical institutes.

Over the years, federal activity in colleges and universities has been directed toward the accomplishment of specific and national goals or missions. In the past decade the drive to increase the number and quality of the nation's scientific, professional, and technical personnel has been intense. The objectives have been to train military and defense personnel; to increase the capabilities of the nation for rapid scientific and technological advance; to conquer disease and promote health; to meet needs of a changing agricultural economy and rural life; to combat special problems arising from rapid urbanization; to bring needed assistance to handicapped persons and disadvantaged groups; and to provide technical assistance to other countries. In the accomplishment of such goals institutions of higher education are a key resource. They are the fountainhead of specially trained personnel; they provide a strong nucleus for the promotion of basic research; and they are an ever-present facility for specialized training during periods of national emergency.

In the use of colleges and universities to accomplish such missions, there was no intent to provide general financial assistance to institutions of higher education; nor was the pattern of federal-state partnership set in the Morrill Act followed. Rather, policies and procedures appropriate for purchasing such services evolved. There is no single, coordinated federal policy or procedure in these arrangements. Individual federal departments and agencies arrange contracts with, or provide grants to, selected institutions of higher education for purposes specific to the missions of the agencies. Although they grew out of experiences which related to national security and defense, the basic procedures for making grants and contracts with institutions of higher education have become standard practice among federal agencies that have research or educational missions. In a few instances, universities have been awarded contracts to operate government-owned research laboratories (Rivlin, 1961; Little, 1962).

SCIENCE AND EDUCATION. For more than a decade, federal investment in scientific research and development has had a pronounced effect on educational institutions, particularly colleges and universities. The establishment of the National Science Foundation in 1950 created a highly influential center of contact between the federal government and educational institutions. The programs of the National Science Foundation have had strong influence upon education from the elementary school through graduate school. Its programs include strengthening science curricula, improving the education of science teachers, stimulating interest in scientific careers, providing financial assistance for training scientists, improving science libraries, equipping science laboratories in educational institutions, providing grants for research projects, and facilitating exchange of scientific knowledge with scientists of other nations (Waterman, 1960).

The National Science Foundation has striven to develop relationships that would strengthen educational programs while safeguarding the independence of educational institutions. Its procedure has been to provide grants to individual faculty members whose research proposals have been evaluated by panels of experts in the field of the research proposed. The grants include payments for research assistants, clerical and computing services, special apparatus or equipment, and necessary travel. The grants also provide allowances to institutions for overhead costs of administrative services incident to research. The practice of purchasing research and other services from educational institutions for the accomplishment of specific federal missions had already been established, particularly by the Department of Defense. In such programs, however, the objectives are defined by the federal agency, and the educational institutions contract to perform the designated mission. The programs of the National Science Foundation allow much of the initiative for research and definition of research objectives to rest with the scientific community. Furthermore, the scientific community is directly involved in decisions about the research to be funded. While policies and programs of the National Science Foundation have been subject to criticism both within and outside the federal government, its practices in funding research have been adopted, with variations, by other federal agencies (National Science Foundation, 1958).

In time, The National Science Foundation broadened both its activities and policies to cover new fields of scientific research, to make institutional grants for construction of science facilities or other science-related purposes as determined by the institutions, and to enlist the scientific community in the improvement of science education at all levels of education.

The National Science Foundation seldom deals directly with elementary or secondary schools or with state systems of public education. Its programs are usually administered through colleges and universities which operate institutes and other special programs for selected groups of teachers or students. National Science Foundation programs in elementary and secondary education, therefore, emanate primarily from scholars in colleges and universities (Campbell & others, 1965).

The success and general acceptability of the idea and operations of the National Science Foundation are evidenced by the drive of other segments of the academic community to establish similar federally supported foundations. In 1965 the National Foundation for the Arts and Humanities was established. Agitation is growing for similar federal recognition in the social sciences (Tiedt, 1966). The establishment of separate foundations or agencies for separate areas of the educational curriculum thus continues to be preferred to plans that cover the educational program as a whole.

The history of the National Science Foundation illustrates how special national interests become intertwined with programs of educational establishments. For more than a decade, science and research have been favorite objects of federal activity. Measures supporting scientific activity are more exciting and politically palatable than measures to improve education generally. But it is doubtful that many in government or education foresaw the extent of federal involvement in education that was to arise from a proliferation of its mission-oriented programs. By 1965, however, Congress had found both the conviction and the courage to consider education as worthy of legislative action in its own right. Meanwhile, substantial improvements in education of some types and at many levels had been progressing under the cloak of accomplishing other federal purposes.

Despite its central role in the furtherance of basic scientific research, the National Science Foundation administers a relatively minor part of the research funds expended by federal agencies in educational institutions. By 1962, the National Institutes of Health were providing the largest amount of Federal funds for research in educational institutions, replacing the Department of Defense as the prime source (Green, 1963).

This shift in emphasis illustrates the growing tendency of the federal government to identify and support national goals other than those that are defense-related. Federal missions in public health are a prime example. Here the objective is not only to conquer man's most malignant and crippling diseases but also to strengthen and augment the nation's schools of medicine, nursing, and public health. Funds have been appropriated for the construction of hospitals, teaching facilities, health research centers, medical laboratories, and libraries; for career professorships to outstanding research specialists; and fellowships and training grants to students in many specialties. Probably every accredited medical school in the nation has shared in this panoply of federal programs (U.S. Senate, 1960). Congress has frequently increased appropriations for these programs beyond the levels recommended by the agencies administering the programs. The drive to strengthen the nation's medical and health resources illustrates how the federal government can provide broad support to a segment of an educational institution without consciously raising the policy questions that typically accompany proposals to support educational institutions as a whole (Little, 1962).

The Department of Defense continues to fund a large share of federal expenditures for research in colleges and universities. Other agencies expending major sums are the Atomic Energy Commission, the National Aeronautics and Space Administration, the Public Health Services, and the Department of Agriculture. Green's report (1963) details federal expenditures for all types of federal programs in 1962 and the number of persons affected by those programs.

Federal funds for research in education did not become available until the establishment of a cooperative research program to be administered by the Office of Education in 1954. Research funds for programs of the Office of Education, however, are a tiny fraction of the total amount expended in educational institutions by all federal agencies. In fact, the combined research funds of the Office of Education and the National Science Foundation—the two agencies with primary responsibilities in education—approximate 10 percent of funds disbursed by all federal agencies to educational institutions. Nevertheless, research has assumed new and large dimensions in the finance and function of the educational enterprise, in the careers of the instructional staffs, and in the training of the students.

INTERNATIONAL PROGRAMS. While advances in science and technology were expanding the role of research in education, the growing stature of the United States in the family of nations was adding new responsibilities in international affairs. In an effort to help other countries gain economic strength and political stature, the federal government turned to the colleges and universities for specialists to direct programs of technical assistance abroad. Faculty members began to serve as consultants, advisers, and members of technical teams that traveled to many continents and countries of the world. Cultural-exchange programs produced an influx of students and professors from other countries to study developments in American education, agriculture, business, and industry. Similarly, American students and professors were enabled to visit and make special studies of other areas of the world.

As a concomitant development, federally sponsored missions led to introduction of new "area studies" organized to prepare specialists in the cultures of specific regions of the world. Studies of Eastern civilizations and African nations were emphasized, but international programs included South America and Central America. International activities were sponsored primarily by agencies of the Department of State, such as the Agency for International Development, the U.S. Information Agency, the Peace Corps, and the Bureau of Cultural Affairs. The National Science Foundation, the Atomic Energy Commission, the National Institutes of Health, and the National Aeronautics and Space Administration also have substantial international programs. In 1966, Congress passed the International Education Act, which provides for the development of educational activities, directly. This measure is intended to strengthen the programs of intercultural education in colleges and universities. As a result, stronger resources are being built for the international missions of all federal agencies (Weidner, 1962; Ford Foundation, 1961; Bodenman, 1957).

ISSUES AND TRENDS. Federal activity in education has evoked much debate among educators, members of Congress, state and federal agencies, and citizens' groups. Conferences and committees have attempted to assess the impact of federal programs upon individual institutions, groups of institutions, and education as a whole. The reports voice apprehension about trends toward centralized control of education; they maintain that the primary responsibility for education must remain with the states, and they urge vigilance to safeguard the independence of educational institutions. But the consensus is that emerging needs of the nation strongly reaffirm the basic interdependence of government and education and that the magnitude of the nation's educational requirements necessitates support from all available resources, including the federal government. The issue is not whether the federal government should support education but what shall be the nature of federal support and the manner of its administration (Knight, 1960; Little 1962).

While the impact of the most recently enacted legislation, such as the Vocational Education Act and the Elementary and Secondary Act, is yet to be assessed, studies of earlier federal activities upon educational programs in elementary and secondary schools point to (1) the effects of National Science Foundation programs in strengthening curricula and instruction in mathematics and the sciences; (2) changes resulting from National Defense Education Act programs in counseling and guidance, language instruction, instructional equipment and facilities, and in-service programs for teachers; (3) improved facilities through remodeling and construction programs; (4) innovations in curriculum planning, and (5) research in many aspects of school organization and curriculum.

Federal programs are seen as one part of a trend toward nationalization of education shared by activities of foundations, national testing programs, national scholarship programs, and national accrediting associations. Trends include a shift in decision making from local and state levels to the national level, a shift in the center of power for policy making from public school officials toward university scholars and administrators; and an expanding federal role in educational programs directed at hard-core problems of American society—e.g., dealing with poverty-stricken areas and handicapped and underprivileged people, and developing new partnerships between local, state, and federal governments on many public problems. The studies echo a plaintive cry for greater coordination of the maze of federal activities in education. Moreover, there are strong crosscurrents of opinion about the growing federal involvement, particularly in states and cities which have felt the insistent hand of federal authority in the vexing problem of civil rights (Campbell & others, 1965; Sufrin, 1962).

Studies of the influence of federal activity on higher education include materials prepared for public discussions by civic leaders in many regions of the nation (Knight, 1960), government surveys of federal programs in higher education describing in detail the panorama of federal activities (Quattlebam, 1960; Little, 1962), self-studies by colleges and universities of their involvement in federal programs (Harvard University, 1961; Bowen, 1962; Little, 1960), studies of the effects of federal activities upon differing types of institutions (Orlans, 1962; Cagle, 1962), and reports of Congressional committees having responsibilities for educational legislation (Green, 1963).

A perceptive account of the interplay of forces, attitudes, and practices within higher education and government which operate for and against the goals of both is found in *The Federal Interest in Higher Education*, written by authors who have had important roles in both government and education (Babbidge & Rosenzweig, 1962).

The scientific community, which has had a

dominant role in the formulation of policy, practices, and procedures in federal research programs, has also concerned itself with assessing the impact of scientific research upon higher education as a whole (National Science Foundation, 1958; President's Science Advisory Committee, 1960).

Administrators of colleges and universities have made their viewpoints known in reports issued by their councils and associations (American Council on Education, 1954, 1961). While some fears of federal domination abated, new concerns arose about more-indirect influences of federally sponsored programs. Federal programs were found to be concentrated in relatively few institutions—the prestigious universities with strongly established graduate and professional schools. For example, studies showed that 68 percent of the funds for federally sponsored research in colleges and universities was expended in 25 institutions in 1960. Few strictly undergraduate colleges participated in federal programs, except those which provide financial assistance to students. Two-year colleges did not participate at all. Fears developed about the possible distortion of educational programs as a result of mission-oriented federal programs which provide much support to specified segments of an institution and little or none to others; administrators quarreled with federal agencies over the adequacy of their reimbursement for performance of federally sponsored projects and urged greater coordination of policy and practice among federal agencies.

Studies within colleges and universities indicate that federally sponsored programs have pervasive influence upon educational programs. The impact is strongest among institutions that are heavily involved in federal programs, but repercussions occur throughout the whole of higher education. Federal activities have tended to widen the gap between the very strong and the less-strong institutions, to emphasize graduate study at the expense of undergraduate instruction, to increase the prestige of research in comparison with teaching, and to lower the morale of faculty members in fields not supported by federal programs. Counterbalancing these criticisms are judgments that use of the strongest centers of research and graduate education was necessary to the accomplishment of the federal missions; that research has long been underfinanced in most institutions, and that research activity often benefits instruction. The issue of federal control seems to be debated more vehemently among citizens' groups than among educators. Educators tend to hold that there is greater danger from weak administrative policies and standards of educational institutions than from dictatorial tendencies of federal agencies.

Not everybody is happy, however. The misgivings of educational institutions that are minor participants in federally sponsored activities are strong. State educational authorities look askance at the shift in the power center toward Washington. With the broadening Congressional interest, however, it is likely that new educational legislation will bring an increasing number of colleges and universities within the scope of federally supported programs of many types.

Representatives of institutions of higher education, while favoring greater coordination of policy among federal agencies, do not favor centralized administration of federal programs. They prefer the choice and chance afforded by a diversity of fund-dispensing agencies and view with continued apprehension a centralized authority that is subject to political manipulation.

Federally sponsored activity and funds are becoming a built-in feature of the function and finance of educational programs at all levels of schooling. Areas of interdependence between the federal government and the nation's educational system have been steadily broadening.

The objectives of education and those of the federal government are not always congruent. Educational institutions strive for unity, balance, and excellence throughout their divisions and programs. Federal activities have tended to involve only segments of an institution, pieces of its programs, and parts of its purpose. Educators plead for programs which strengthen institutions and systems as a whole. Some federal agencies and programs have responded to these pleas by providing an increased number and type of institutional grants as well as appropriations for construction of libraries, laboratories, and classroom facilities of many types. Legislative proposals are now appearing which would return a part of federal income taxes to states for educational purposes, but Congressional approval of such a measure is far from imminent.

In its drive to increase the number of centers of excellence required in this age of science and space the federal government seems either to have forgotten, or to have discarded as inappropriate, its 100 years of experience with the type of federal-state partnership embodied in the land-grant college idea which was so successful in the development of centers of agricultural research and service in each of the 50 states.

Finally, neither the federal government nor education is identifiable as a single entity. Each is plural. No single voice speaks for either. The federal government strives to find ways to streamline its organization, to coordinate its activities, and to improve its information about the status and welfare of education in the nation. Educational forces strive to communicate with the decision-making forces in the federal government in a more coordinated fashion. Neither has succeeded. Both are preoccupied with problems of the climb toward the abiding national purpose of providing both quality and equality in education to all. Both are engaged in extending their values to peoples of other lands. The developing relationships between the federal government and the nation's educational establishment are providing a fascinating scene in the evolution of American education.

J. Kenneth Little
The University of Wisconsin

References

American Council on Education. *Sponsored Research Policy of Colleges and Universities.* ACE, 1954. 93p.

American Council on Education. *A Proposed Program of Federal Action to Strengthen Higher Education.* ACE, 1961. 11p.

Axt, Richard G. *The Federal Government and Financing Higher Education.* Columbia U Press, 1952. 295p.

Babbidge, Homer D., Jr., and Rosenzweig, Robert M. *The Federal Interest in Higher Education.* McGraw-Hill, 1962. 214p.

Barnard, Harry V. "An Historical Survey of Federal Aid to Elementary and Secondary Education." *H Sch J* 46:152–8; 1962.

Bodenman, Paul S. *American Cooperation With Higher Education Abroad.* GPO, 1957. 211p.

Bowen, William G. *The Federal Government and Princeton University.* Princeton U Press, 1962. 319p.

Cagle, Fred R. *Federal Research Policies and the Southern University.* Southern Regional Education Board, 1962. 146p.

Campbell, Roald F., and Bunnell, Robert A. *Nationalizing Influences on Secondary Education.* Chicago: Midwest Administration Center, U Chicago, 1963. 128p.

Campbell, Roald F., and others. *The Organization and Control of American Schools.* Merrill Books, Inc., 1965.

Chase, Francis S. "Educational Policy at the Federal Level." *Wisconsin J Ed* February:25–6; 1965.

Eddy, Edward Danforth, Jr. *Colleges for Our Land and Time.* Harper, 1957. 328p.

Ford Foundation. *The University and World Affairs.* The Foundation, 1961. 84p.

Green, Edith. *The Federal Government and Education.* GPO, 1963. 178p.

Harvard University. *Harvard and the Federal Government.* Harvard U Press, 1961. 36p.

Hawkins, Layton J., and others. *Development of Federal Legislation for Vocational Education.* The American Technical Society, 1962. 110p.

Kelly, Fred J. *Land-grant Colleges and Universities: A Federal-State Partnership.* GPO, 1952. 27p.

Kidd, Charles V. *American Universities and Federal Research.* Belknap Press, 1959. 272p.

Knight, Douglas M. (Ed.) *The Federal Government and Higher Education.* Prentice-Hall, 1960. 199p.

Levitan, Sara. *Vocational Education and Federal Policy.* W. E. Upjohn Institute, 1963. 30p.

Little, J. Kenneth. "Federal Programs in a State University." *H Ed* 17:3–6; 1960.

Little, J. Kenneth. "Higher Education and the National Purpose." *Ed Rec* 42:161–72; 1961.

Little, J. Kenneth. *A Survey of Federal Programs in Higher Education: Summary.* HEW, 1962. 56p.

Munger, Frank J., and Fenno, Richard F., Jr. *National Politics and Federal Aid to Education.* Syracuse U Press, 1962. 185p.

National Science Foundation. *Government-University Relationships in Federally-sponsored Scientific Research and Development.* GPO, 1958. 44p.

Orlans, Harold. *The Effects of Federal Programs on Higher Education: A Study of 36 Institutions.* The Brookings Institution, 1962. 361p.

Pierce, Truman M. *Federal, State and Local Government in Education.* Center for Applied Research in Education, 1964. 120p.

President's Committee on Education Beyond the High School. *Second Report to the President.* GPO, 1957. 108p.

President's Science Advisory Committee. *Scientific Progress, The Universities, and The Federal Government.* GPO, 1960. 33p.

Quattlebam, Charles A. *Federal Educational Policies, Programs and Proposals.* Part I: *Background: Relevant Considerations;* Part II: *Survey of Federal Activities;* Part III: *Analysis and Classification of Programs.* GPO, 1960. 798p.

Quattlebam, Charles A. *Federal Legislation Concerning Education and Training.* GPO, 1964. 156p.

Rivlin, Alice M. *The Role of the Federal Government in Financing Higher Education.* The Brookings Institution, 1961. 179p.

Sufrin, Sidney C. *Issues in Federal Aid to Education.* Syracuse U Press, 1962. 64p.

Tiedt, Sidney W. *The Role of the Federal Government in Education.* Oxford U Press, 1966. 243p.

U.S. Commission on Civil Rights. *Equal Protection of the Laws in Public Higher Education.* The Commission, 1960. 355p.

U.S. Department of Health, Education, and Welfare. *Vocational and Technical Education: A Review of Activities in Federally Aided Programs, 1953.* GPO, 1963. 68p.

U.S. House of Representatives. *The Federal Government and Education.* GPO, 1963. 176p.

U.S. House of Representatives. *Conflicts Between the Federal Research Programs and the Nation's Goals for Higher Education.* GPO, 1965. 74p.

U.S. Senate. *Federal Support of Medical Research.* GPO, 1960. 133p.

U.S. Supreme Court. *Segregation in the Public Schools.* GPO, 1954. 15p. Opinion.

Waterman, Alan T. "The Role of the National Science Foundation." *The Annals of the American Academy of Political and Social Science* 327:123–31; 1960.

Weidner, Edward W. *The World Role of the Universities.* McGraw-Hill, 1962. 366p.

White House. *The Administration of Government Supported Research at Universities.* Executive Office of the President, 1966.

FINANCE—COLLEGE AND UNIVERSITY

During the past decade, studies of college and university finance have been characterized by the application of new methods of analysis in two important areas: (1) the determination of the appropriate size of the system of higher education and (2) the efficiency of college and university operation.

Other topics on which significant work has been done are (3) faculty rewards and (4) sources of funds. Further, there is continuing concern (5) about the adequacy of data that are available for analysis in the field of higher education. The single volume that deals most broadly with all of these topics is that of Harris (1962).

THE DETERMINATION OF APPROPRIATE SIZE OF THE HIGHER EDUCATION SYSTEM.

What proportion of the college age group is to attend institutions of higher education in a given country? Simple demographic projections of past trends in enrollment, while useful as starting points of analysis, no longer appear satisfactory in answering this question, either in the United States or abroad. Yet the determination of the size of the educational enterprise has profound consequences for its structure and finance. McGrath (1965) has explored the implications of universal higher education, defined as the opportunity for higher schooling utilized by more than half of the 18-to-22-years age group. Since universal higher education is not yet within the grasp of the United States and is much further away in the case of countries that practice extremely selective recruitment of students (Europe and the white Commonwealth) or that are too poor to afford it (most of the rest of the world), the determination of the appropriate size of educational operation remains a subject for investigation. Bowles (1963) gives a quantitative appraisal of the world admissions scene; his volume serves well to raise the basic issues about size.

In the United States considerable efforts have been made to discover the determinants of educational aspiration (Brazer & David, 1962; Morgan & others, 1962). The most significant educational report of the mid-century in Great Britain suggested that the number of student places in universities and colleges be regulated in accord with the rising level of educational aspirations in that country (Robbins, 1963).

Similarly, there has developed considerable interest in regulating the size of higher education in terms of the requirements of national economic growth. The contribution of education to growth has been explored by Becker (1964), Denison (1962), and Schultz (1961). Critical appraisals of measurement techniques have been offered by Bowman (1964) and Eckaus (1962).

Assuming that a positive relation exists between higher-educational expenditures and national prosperity, a case for educational planning can be established in terms of social benefits. As shown by Weisbrod (1964), however, the range of social benefits provided by education is considerably broader than those related strictly to the productive efficiency of the private economy. The techniques of educational planning are well described by Parnes (1962), while a number of the practical difficulties are treated by Phillips (1962). The seminal work by Harbison and Myers (1964) develops the theme that the proper size of an educational system is functionally related to the stage of economic development in which a country finds itself.

Sophisticated methods of educational planning employ models of an econometric type. One of the earliest of these was developed by Tinbergen (1962), in which account was taken of the fact that education generates a demand for its own output, e.g., teachers. More refined models are described by Correa (1963) and Tinbergen and Bos (1965).

One aspect of education's contribution to national welfare involves the search for talent. This concept is discussed by Wolfle (1961). The screening function of education, once recognized, establishes concern about regional and class inequalities of provision for education (Reynolds, 1962). The most comprehensive study yet conducted of inequalities of provision for higher education with respect to social class is that of Coleman (1966). A briefer analysis for France was done by Ferrez (1961).

THE EFFICIENCY OF COLLEGE AND UNIVERSITY OPERATIONS.

A number of recent studies have dealt with factors that serve to determine college and university costs (Vaizey, 1958; Technical Committee on Costs of Higher Education in California, 1960; Machlup, 1962; Harris, 1964; Edding, 1962.) It is one thing, however, to search for forces responsible for change in costs per student and quite another to achieve worthwhile efficiencies in operation.

Proposals aimed at achieving efficiency appear to fall in three categories. The first of these categories is composed simply of pragmatic adjustments in the institutional structure of higher education. Heneman (1959) describes a number of these adjustments.

The second category is based on the use of "program budgeting" (Burkhead, 1956; Novick, 1965). Program budgeting is a refined system of functional or activity cost analysis; it allows comparisons from one point of time to another—and from one institution to another—in the cost per unit of performing some task, such as processing admissions papers or teaching language in a laboratory. Program budgeting is a guide to administrative decision making, but the technique, in and of itself, does not establish priorities for the allocation of resources in higher education. The present emphasis on program budgeting, nonetheless, is conceptually related to efforts to achieve long-term financial planning (Tickton, 1961; 1965).

The third category of techniques in the search for efficiency embraces more theoretical approaches. These represent the attempt to apply systems-analysis (or cost-benefit) tools in institutions of higher education. A pioneering presentation is that of Kershaw and McKean (1959). Very briefly, the process involves the following steps: the definition of a specific objective of the institution and of the units in which attainment of the objective is to be measured; the statement of various alternative means to attain the objective and of the units in which application of the alternative means is to be measured; the statement of the relation between the application of each alternative means and the rate of achievement of the objective; the pricing (per unit) of each alternative means; and, finally, the choice of the "best" means. As used here, the "best" device is the one which allows the institution to achieve the greatest proportion of the objective for any given volume of expenditure, or, alternatively, the one that allows any given degree of attainment of the objective to be obtained at lowest dollar cost. A particularly imaginative example of the application of cost-benefit analysis in higher education is given in Deitch (1960). On a broader scale, in the assessment of the net economic returns from the universal extension of junior-college education, Hirsch and Marcus (1966) make an exceptionally interesting test use of the cost-benefit methodology in the public sector.

FACULTY REWARDS. In the late 1950's and early 1960's there was considerable concern among economists that the level of faculty pay was grossly inadequate, with the projected result that the country would suffer a loss of social benefits through deterioration of the system of higher education. It was suggested that the level of faculty salaries should be approximately doubled (Harris, 1962). Data on recent levels of pay are given by D'Amico (1965) and the National Education Association (1964). The achievement of higher pay by the device of major shifts in faculty load is discussed by Ruml and Morrison (1959). A critical statement of the problem of salaries has been made by Caplow (1960), while a comparison of English and American practices in meeting specific shortages of faculty in particular subject fields is given by Bowen (1964). The role of the federal government in supplementing the pay of faculty members, especially through the devices of grants and contracts for summer work, is described by the U.S. Congress, House Committee on Education and Labor (1963).

SOURCES OF FUNDS. Two excellent general volumes on the sources of college and university revenue are those by Millett (1952) and Harris (1964). Higher education in the United States continues to rely on several major sources, but the one that has shown the most dramatic increase in recent years is the federal government.

Federal Support of Higher Education. Naturally enough, questions have been raised about the effects of federal contribution on institutions of higher education. In a major study undertaken for the Brookings Institution, Orlans (1962) reached the general conclusion that the effects have been quite favorable. Even those departments such as English and classics that receive little federal money directly appear to have been strengthened by a "spill over" of funds from the heavily subsidized departments, such as physics. It seems impossible to deny, however, that federal funds have abetted the devaluing of undergraduate instruction (Kidd, 1959).

Further, it is impossible to deny that there has been a concentration of federal funds in a small number of institutions. The implications of this fact for the deepening of regional disparities of educational provision is explored by Cagle (1962) and Engelbert (1963). One way to achieve a more even geographic distribution of federal funds would be for the government to make grants for educational purposes directly to institutions. Some of the difficulties with this approach are treated by Rivlin (1961).

Basically, there appears to be a need for the development of a new, more effective partnership between the federal government and higher education. Pressure toward this objective seems to be growing, as shown by a number of recent statements (Arnold, 1964; Harrington, 1963; Kerr, 1963; Little, 1963; Price, 1966; Wilson, 1963; U.S. Congress Committee on Government Operations, 1965). As background to this development, there were several major studies in depth at the federal–higher-education nexus, including those by Allen (1950) and Babbidge and Rosenzweig (1962). A succinct analysis of the range of financial devices that can be used to link the government to higher education is provided by Musgrave (1960).

Student Fees. Opinions about the degree of reliance that should be placed on student fees remains sharply divided. Danière (1964) has presented a brilliant theoretical argument in support of the position that the full cost of instructional programs should be met by fees. Vickrey (1962) has advanced an ingenious scheme under which students could meet such fees by loans, with repayment computed as a share of earnings, according to the ordinary concepts of income taxation. Assuming that fees are, indeed, to be relatively important, Eckstein (1960) has compared the differences in costs under prepayment and postpayment plans. Alternative patterns of student aid are discussed by Esty (1965) and Hill (1962), and evaluation of the effects of student aid programs is offered by Morse (1965). On the other hand, the damages of excessive reliance on student fees, notwithstanding the existence of student loans and other aids, are stressed by Millett (1959).

Other Sources for Expenditure Requirements. Projections of expenditure needs in higher education generally point to the likelihood of a relatively large rise in revenues of higher education (Carovano, 1966; Mushkin & McLoone, 1965; Simon & Fullam, 1965). Much has been accomplished in the past under diversified sources of finance, and one reason that this multifaceted revenue system makes sense is that higher education is so clearly a multiproduct "industry" (Kaysen, 1960). A case has been made on an abstract level in favor of maintaining a diversified revenue structure (Stubblebine, 1965). It is thus fortunate for public institutions that interest continues to be strong in the contributions that state governments can make to college and university support (Reeves, 1962; Sliger & Beard, 1963).

DATA FOR ANALYSIS. It is a common complaint that data for higher education appear with too great a publication lag, that they are incomplete with respect to coverage of institutions, and that they are insufficiently detailed on interesting questions. Rather than belabor these points it is perhaps more appropriate to note what some of the important sources are. The National Education Association

(1964, 1965) provides, among other types of figures, reasonably up-to-date material on faculty salaries and on faculty demand and supply. The U.S. Office of Education (1965a) provides figures state by state on various types of revenues and expenditures in institutions of higher education in the annual *Digest of Educational Statistics*. The most current national figures on revenue sources and major expenditure components (but without state-by-state detail) are provided in the annual *Preliminary Report of Financial Statistics of Institutions of Higher Education* (U.S. Office of Education, 1965b). Also, there is interesting material of fairly recent date in the *College and University Finance Series* (D'Amico, 1964). The U.S. Office of Education publications by Lind (1965) and Lindsay (1964) are perhaps the most sound and comprehensive data on higher-education finance, but the former is restricted to land-grant colleges and universities.

Data specifically on financial aid for students is given by McKee (1965). Some important but older information on federal grant programs (possibly useful as bench-mark data) is given by Jackson and Steinhilber (1962). Bokelman (1959) offers interesting material for planning and control in higher education, and the report by Colmey (1964) suggests that we may yet receive up-to-date, pertinent figures for the analysis of financial problems of our college and university system.

Charles S. Benson
University of California

References

Allen, Hollis P. *The Federal Government and Education.* McGraw-Hill, 1950, 333p.

Arnold, Christian K. "Federal Support of Basic Research in Institutions of Higher Learning: A Critique."*Ed Rec* 45:199–203; 1964.

Babbidge, Homer D., and Rosenzweig, Robert M. *The Federal Interest in Higher Education.* McGraw-Hill, 1962, 214p.

Becker, Gary S. *Human Capital: A Theoretical and Empirical Analysis, with Special Reference to Education.* Columbia U Press, 1964. 187p.

Bokelman, W. Robert. *Higher Education Planning and Management Data 1958–59: Salaries, Tuition and Fees, Room and Board.* USOE Circular No. 549. GPO, 1959. 126p.

Bowen, William G. *Economic Aspects of Education: Three Essays.* Industrial Relations Section, Princeton U, 1964. 127p.

Bowles, Frank. *Access to Higher Education.* UNESCO and the International Association of Universities, 1963. 212p.

Bowman, Mary Jean. "Schultz, Denison, and the Contribution of 'Eds' to National Income Growth." *J Political Econ* 72:450–64; 1964.

Brazer, Harvey E., and David, Martin. "Social and Economic Determinants of the Demand for Education." In Mushkin, Selma. (Ed.) *Economics of Higher Education.* USOE Bulletin No. 5. GPO, 1962. p. 21–42.

Burkhead, Jesse. *Government Budgeting.* Wiley, 1956. 498p.

Cagle, Fred. *Federal Research Projects and the Southern University.* Southern Regional Ed. Bd., 1962. 97p.

Caplow, Theodore. "Faculty Pay and Institutional Extravagance." *R Econ Stat* 42:122–4; 1960.

Carovano, J. Martin. "Financing Public Higher Education, 1969–70." *Nat Tax J* 19:125–37; 1966.

Coleman, James S., and others. *Equality of Educational Opportunity.* Nat Center for Ed Stat, USOE, GPO, 1966. 737p.

Colmey, James W. *Progress Report on the Development of a Data Collection System for Institutions of Higher Education.* USOE, GPO, 1964. 30p.

Correa, H. *The Economics of Human Resources.* North Holland Publishing Company, 1963. 262p.

D'Amico, Louis A. *Higher Education Salaries, 1963–64.* USOE Circular No. 759. GPO, 1965. 66p.

D'Amico, Louis A. "Financing Higher Education." *College and University Finance Series,* Division of Higher Education, USOE, 1964. 18p.

Danière, André. *Higher Education in the American Economy.* Random, 1964. 206p.

Deitch, Kenneth. "Some Observations on the Allocation of Resources in Higher Education." *R Econ Stat* 42:192–8; 1960.

Denison, Edward F. *The Sources of Economic Growth in the United States and the Alternatives Before Us.* Supplementary Paper No. 13. Committee for Economic Development, 1962. 297p.

Eckaus, Richard S. "Education and Economic Growth." In Mushkin, Selma. (Ed.) *Economics of Higher Education.* USOE Bulletin 1962, No. 5. GPO, 1962. p. 102–28.

Eckstein, Otto. "The Problem of Higher College Tuition." *R Econ Stat* 42:61–721; 1960.

Edding, Friedrich. "Estimating Costs of Educational Requirements." In Parnes, Herbert S. (Ed.) *Planning Education for Economic and Social Development.* Organization for Economic Co-operation and Development (Paris), 1962. p. 233–44.

Engelbert, Arthur F. "Short-term Grants and Long-range Goals: The Dilemma of Federal Policies." *Ed Rec* 44:161–4; 1963.

Esty, Hohn C., Jr. "Forms and Functions of Student Aid." In Harris, Seymour E., and Levensohn, Alan. (Eds.) *Education and Public Policy.* McCutchan Publishing Corporation, 1965. p. 253–62.

Ferrez, Jean. "Regional Inequalities in Educational Opportunity." In Halsey, A. H. (Ed.) *Ability and Educational Opportunity.* Organization for Economic Co-operation and Development (Paris), 1961. p. 69–87.

Harbison, Frederick, and Myers, Charles A. *Education, Manpower and Economic Growth.* McGraw-Hill, 1964. 229p.

Harrington, Fred Harvey. "The Federal Government and the Future of Higher Education." *Ed Rec* 44:155–60; 1963.

Harris, Seymour E. *Higher Education: Resources and Finance.* McGraw-Hill, 1962. 713p.

Harris, Seymour E. (Ed.) *Economic Aspects of Higher Education.* Organization for Economic Co-operation and Development (Paris), 1964. 252p.

Heneman, Harlow J. "Opportunities for Better Institutional Management." In Keezer, Dexter M. (Ed.) *Financing Higher Education 1960–70.* McGraw-Hill, 1959. p. 118–37.

Hill, W. W., Jr. "State Supported Student Loan Programs." In *Proceedings, 55th Annual Conference of the National Tax Association.* The Association, 1962. p. 493–501.

Hirsch, Werner Z., and Marcus, Morton J. "Some Benefit-cost Considerations of Universal Junior College Education." *Nat Tax J* 19:48–57; 1966.

Jackson, Penrose P., and Steinhilber, Delores A. *Federal Funds for Education: Fields, Levels, Recipients, 1959 and 1960.* USOE Circular No. 679; GPO, 1962. 82p.

Kaysen Carl. "Some General Observations on the Pricing of Higher Education." *R Econ Stat* 42:55–60; 1960.

Kerr, Clark. "The Realities of the Federal Grant University." *Ed Rec* 44:165–7; 1963.

Kershaw, Joseph A., and McKean, Roland N. *Systems Analysis and Education.* Research Memorandum 2473–FF. The RAND Corporation, 1959. 64p.

Kidd, Charles V. *American Universities and Federal Research.* Harvard U Press, 1959. 272p.

Lind, George. *Statistics of Land-grant Colleges and Universities: Year Ended June 30, 1963 (Final Report).* USOE Circular No. 763. GPO, 1965. 136p.

Lindsay, Felix H. I. *Financial Statistics of Institutions of Higher Education, 1959–60: Receipts, Expenditures, and Property.* USOE Circular No. 744. GPO, 1964. 191p.

Little, Kenneth J. "Higher Education and the Federal Government." *Higher Ed* 20:3–6; 1963.

Machlup, Fritz. *The Production and Distribution of Knowledge in the United States.* Princeton U Press, 1962. 416p.

McGrath, Earl J. *Universal Higher Education.* McGraw-Hill, 1965. 258p.

McKee, Richard C. *Financial Assistance for College Students: Undergraduate and First-professional.* USOE Circular No. 774. GPO, 1965. 91p.

Millett, John D. *Financing Higher Education in the United States.* Columbia U Press, 1952. 503p.

Millett, John D. "The Role of Student Charges." In Keezer, Dexter M. (Ed.) *Financing Higher Education 1960–70.* McGraw-Hill, 1959. p. 162–82.

Morgan, James N., and others. *Income and Welfare in the United States.* McGraw-Hill, 1962. 531p.

Morse, John F. "Academic Quality and Financial Aid." In Harris, Seymour E., and Deitch, Kenneth. (Eds.) *Challenge and Change in American Education.* McCutchan Publishing Corporation, 1965. p. 247–54.

Musgrave, Richard A. "Higher Education and the Federal Budget." *R Econ Stat* 42:96–101; 1960.

Mushkin, Selma, and McLoone, Eugene P. *Public Spending for Higher Education in 1970.* Council of State Governments, 1965. 68p.

National Education Association. *Salaries Paid and Salary Practices in Universities, Colleges, and Junior Colleges, 1963–64.* NEA, 1964. 59p.

National Education Association. *Teacher Supply and Demand in Universities, Colleges, and Junior Colleges, 1963–64 and 1964–65.* NEA, 1965. 92p.

Novick, David. (Ed.) *Program Budgeting: Program Analysis and the Federal Budget.* Harvard U Press, 1965. 382p.

Orlans, Harold. *The Effects of Federal Programs on Higher Education.* The Brookings Institution, 1962. 353p.

Parnes, Herbert S. *Forecasting Educational Needs for Economic and Social Development.* Organization for Economic Co-operation and Development (Paris), 1962. 113p.

Phillips, H. M. "Economic and Social Aspects of the Planning of Education." *Int Soc Sci J* 14:700 -18; 1962.

Price, Don K. "Federal Money and University Research." *Sci* 151:285–90; 1966.

Reeves, H. C. "Higher Education and State Tax Policy." *Nat Tax J* 15:291–6; 1962.

Reynolds, James W. "Higher Education." In *Educational Needs for Economic Development of the South.* Agriculture Policy Institute, School of Agriculture, North Carolina State Col, and Southern Regional Ed Bd, 1962. p. 91–6.

Rivlin, Alice M. *The Role of the Federal Government in Financing Higher Education.* The Brookings Institution, 1961. 179p.

Robbins, Lionel. *Higher Education: Report of the Committee under the Chairmanship of Lord Robbins 1961–63.* H.M. Stationery Office, 1963. 335p.

Ruml, Beardsley, and Morrison, Donald H. *Memo to a College Trustee: A Report on Financial and Structural Problems of the Liberal College.* McGraw-Hill, 1959. 94p.

Schultz, Theodore W. "Education and Economic Growth." In *Social Forces Influencing American Education,* 60th Yearbook, NSSE. U Chicago Press, 1961. p. 46–88.

Simons, Kenneth A., and Fullam, Marie G. *Projections of Educational Statistics to 1974–75.* (1965 edition.) USOE Circular No. 790. GPO, 1965. 68p.

Sliger, B. F., and Beard, Thomas R. "State Support of Public Higher Education." *Proceedings, 55th Annual Conference of the National Tax Association, 1962.* The Association, 1963. p. 464–76.

Stubblebine, William C. "Institutional Elements in the Financing of Education." *Southern Econ J* 32:15–34; 1965.

Technical Committee on Costs of Higher Education in California. *The Costs of Higher Education in California 1960–75.* U California Press, 1960. 124p.

Tickton, Sidney G. *Needed: A Ten-year College Budget.* Fund for the Advancement of Education, 1961. 40p.

Tickton, Sidney G. "Planning for Institutions of Higher Learning." In Harris, Seymour E., and

Levensohn, Alan. (Eds.) *Education and Public Policy.* McCutchan Publishing Corporation, 1965. p. 221–40.

Tinbergen, Jan. "Quantitative Adoption of Education to Accelerated Growth." In Parnes, Herbert S. (Ed.) *Planning Education for Economic and Social Development.* Organization for Economic Co-operation and Development (Paris), 1962. p. 159–65.

Tinbergen, Jan, and Bos, H. C. *Econometric Models of Education: Some Applications.* Organization for Economic and Social Development, 1965. 99p.

U.S. Congress, Committee on Government Operations. *Conflicts between the Federal Research Programs and the Nation's Goals for Higher Education.* 89th Congress, First Session, GPO, 1965. 114p.

U.S. Congress, House Committee on Education and Labor. *The Federal Government and Education.* House Document No. 159. GPO, 1963. 178p.

U.S. Office of Education. *Digest of Educational Statistics, 1965 Edition.* The Bulletin 1965, No. 4a. GPO, 1965(a), 182p.

U.S. Office of Education. *Preliminary Report of Financial Statistics of Institutions of Higher Education, Fiscal Year 1964, Based on a Sample of Institutions.* USOE, GPO, July, 1965(b). 6p.

Vaizey, John. *The Costs of Education.* Allen, 1958. 256p.

Vickrey, William. "A Proposal for Student Loans." In Mushkin, Selma S. (Ed.) *Economics of Higher Education.* USOE Bulletin 1962, No. 5. GPO, 1962. p. 268–80.

Weisbrod, Burton A. *External Benefits of Public Education: An Economic Analysis.* Princeton U Press, 1964. 143p.

Wilson, Logan. "A Better Partnership for the Federal Government and Higher Education." *Ed Rec* 44: 137–44; 1963.

Wolfle, Dale. "National Resources of Ability." In Halsey, A. H. (Ed.) *Ability and Educational Opportunity.* Organization for Economic Co-operation and Development (Paris), 1961. p. 49–65.

FINANCE—PUBLIC SCHOOLS

Public schools in the United States obtain almost all their financing (more than 99 percent) from revenues drawn from taxes levied by local, state, and federal governments. Consequently, most of the inquiries into financing of the public schools are concerned with (1) ability to pay taxes, (2) public expectations for school services as they affect willingness to pay taxes, and (3) the governmental arrangements for decision making about (a) how much to tax, (b) how tax funds and the services they buy are distributed, and (c) the benefits of those services. The most noteworthy feature of research in this field of study during the past decade was the extent to which the conceptual tools of economic analysis were brought to bear on these concerns, particularly with reference to cost-benefit relationships in education, and the several aspects of the economic value of education—value to the individual, to the community, and to the national economy. Certain subjects not directly related to the financing of the public schools will be found more fully discussed in other articles within this volume, such as SCHOOL-DISTRICT ORGANIZATION and STATE-SCHOOL SYSTEMS. While interactions of federal funds with state and local taxation will be noted here, the subject of federal support is treated more broadly in FEDERAL RELATIONS TO EDUCATION. The implications of educational spending at all levels upon the nation's economy are considered in NATIONAL ECONOMY AND EDUCATION. More specific matters, such as the techniques and trends of fiscal management, are reviewed in BUSINESS ADMINISTRATION—PUBLIC SCHOOLS. Other articles, such as PLANT AND EQUIPMENT, RURAL EDUCATION, STAFF—ECONOMIC STATUS, and TRANSPORTATION OF STUDENTS, deal with subjects that also have fiscal implications.

CONTRIBUTIONS TO THE LITERATURE. The third edition of the *Encyclopedia of Educational Research* gives a comprehensive coverage of research in school finance and its historical development in the first half of the twentieth century. In the last decade the changing economic, political, and social climate, and the growing concern of noneducators with problems of financing the schools changed the content of school finance. By comparing *The Theory and Practice of School Finance,* published by the National Conference of Professors of Educational Administration (1967), with the preceding volume, *Problems and Issues in Public School Finance* (Johns & Morphet, 1952), this change can be seen best. The coverage of school-finance research in the three-year cycle in *The Review of Educational Research* (James, 1958a, 1964; Johns & McLure, 1961) reflects the same shift in emphasis. No longer do questions of school finance relate primarily to the adequacy of resources for quality education or for the vastly increasing number of pupils. The questions of school finance center mainly on the distribution of resources within the educational enterprise for achieving specific goals and on the obtaining of resources for additional tasks of the schools. The proceedings of the Committee on Educational Finance of the National Education Association (National Conference on School Finance, 1959–1966) not only illumine these shifting concerns but also offer the most productive disseminator of current thinking about the fiscal relations of the schools.

Texts by Johns and Morphet (1960), Barr (1960), and Mort and others (1960) treated the problems of school finance in traditional terms familiar to the typical public school administrator.

Two general texts on public school finance that appeared during the past decade illustrate the interest of economists in education. Benson's *Economics of Public Education* (1961) was the first full-length text to treat school finance as a problem of public economics. Placing the school in the context of an economic system, he appraised the output of social benefits as a function of the institution's financing and considered its demands upon public funds from the point of view of marginal utility, thus treating the problem of allocation of funds to education in relation to satisfaction obtained from all services to be supported by taxation.

Burkhead, in *Public School Finance: Economics and Politics* (1964), reported the findings of a series of studies at Syracuse University. One of the conclusions of these studies was that while the resources necessary to satisfy an expanding demand for education are available, new organizational structures are needed to make the best possible allocations to education because optimum allocations are not made under the existing decentralized systems.

In an earlier era one could speak of the alternative sources of revenue: property taxes, local nonproperty taxes, and state grants usually provided from a broad-based tax levied by the state on sales or income. Federal funds were usually separately treated. The state-local partnership plan in school finance had four elements: (1) an amount per unit of need, (2) a measure of units of need, (3) a local contribution rate, and (4) a measure of local capacity or ability. Up to the late 1950's, research could be summarized in these terms. Some of the traditional research has continued during the 1960's, but the general emphasis has been on the accommodation of empirical insights to a developing conceptual framework. While the traditional notion of a fixed foundation program amount per child jointly financed by state and local taxes on the Strayer and Haig model (1923) continued to dominate state finance practice, attention moved toward the older concepts of Cubberley (1905) and Updegraff and King (1922). Research knowledge summarized below indicates important studies in the traditional framework, particularly on taxes and state financing but concentrates more on those research studies which go beyond the traditional framework, and particularly on those exemplifying the developing rationale for research and data collection on school finance.

The Property Tax. The *Census of Governments* for 1957 and 1962 (U.S. Bureau of the Census, 1957, 1962) with data on school expenditures and the first nationwide data on the property-tax base since 1922 gave a renewed emphasis to the study of the property tax. Bird (1960) analyzed the findings of the 1957 *Census of Governments* and concluded that property-tax administration could be vastly improved, bringing interarea inequalities in assessment into line with practices of the best jurisdictions. In a study also conducted by Bird, the Advisory Commission on Intergovernmental Relations, or ACIR (1961), gave detailed state-by-state recommendations for property-tax administrative reform. Netzer (1966) published a comprehensive economic analysis of the property tax. He compared lifetime property-tax payments and benefits and analyzed the effects on investment of using the property tax, which is based on physical capital, almost exclusively for education, which is viewed by the economist as investment in human capital. He drew the conclusions, contrary to conventional wisdom, that over an individual's lifetime, property-tax payments are neutral and that under present conditions property taxes do not provide a large boost for investment in human capital, since other taxes have offsetting effects. Netzer outlined the revenue programs necessary if the property tax were to be replaced and reluctantly concluded that the tax would continue because of the difficulties of readily providing replacement revenue. McLoone (1961) found that the elasticity of the property tax compared favorably with that of the sales tax. Burkhead (1963) found similar results for New York state and observed that the need for administrative reform remained but that the tools were at hand.

Other Taxes. The analysis of revenue sources for schools has not been limited to the property tax. The U.S. Office of Education (Alford, 1963) comprehensively reviewed nonproperty taxes on a local level and examined taxes on personal services, consumption, and income as potential sources. Findings of this study concurred with those of Burkhead (1963) that except for large cities or countrywide levies little use can be made of these sources. The National Committee for the Support of Public Schools (NCSPS), drawing on research findings, concluded in its fact sheet No. 8 (1966) that the likely trend for local sales and income taxes was "piggyback" taxes—that is, local supplemental rates on the state tax base administered by the state. The ACIR (1966) went a step further and suggested state legislation for a countywide levy in the foundation program—a step in the direction of local nonproperty taxes. McLoone (1962) suggested that uniform statewide property-tax rates be set at levels necessary to provide designated minimum programs, thus assuring that all property within the state would contribute to the basic educational program. Local communities with the capacity and the desire to spend more on their schools could levy nonproperty taxes, thus making available a complementary alternative to the property tax.

State Foundation Programs. The U.S. Office of Education continued traditional work in the inequality of school expenditures with *Profiles of School Support: A Decennial Overview* (Harrison & McLoone, 1965), and sporadically continued summaries of state finance programs with *Revenue Programs* (Munse, 1961), *State Programs* (Munse, 1965), and loose-leaf summaries (Munse & others, 1966). However, the last comprehensive state-by-state summaries on state-support plans are found in *Public School Finance Programs of the United States, 1957–58* (Munse & McLoone, 1960), and the only comprehensive study of state programs for capital outlays is *Financing Public School Facilities* (Hutchins & others, 1959). The historic index of ability to pay taxes is the valuation assigned to taxable property; other indexes have been devised, notably by Cornell (1936), but he concluded that these other methods are for temporary use only, until equity is achieved in assessments among school districts. Peterson (Peterson & others, 1963) claimed that while no single measure of wealth currently in use is adequate, income is preferable to property as a measure of the ability to pay taxes.

Davis (1963) found that when he held property values constant for counties in California, personal income tended to be higher in urban counties and lower in rural counties and higher in older communities and lower in new communities. Thus, he found that the standard foundation program using property valuation creates a disadvantage for rural areas and new suburban areas, since their taxpaying ability is overstated, thereby reducing state subsidies below the level they might have achieved. He further noted, however, that when income taxes constitute a significant factor in the accumulation of funds for state subsidies, this inequity is probably reduced. James and others (1966) noted that the relative ability of the great cities to produce tax revenue is declining whether measured in terms of property or income, despite the wealth of high-income groups found in the metropolis. Urban property is overburdened by other services of government, and the pupil population is rising even though total populations are declining, so that the ability of the cities to support education is declining as their needs increase.

Rossmiller (1965) provided evidence that assumptions implicit in the use of measures of need and ability now employed in most present-day support programs will not bear close scrutiny. Asserting that the quality of a school's program is better defined in terms of the program maintained rather than simply those of the level of expenditures, he concluded that fiscal capacity should be viewed in the context of total demand. At the state level of budgetary approval, Fox (1965) found that expressions of demand and uniqueness of programs under consideration are factors strongly supportive of the adoption of budget items.

James (1958b) called for measuring the amount of property tax collected by the local contribution rate in the foundation program, as he wished to call this amount a statewide property tax. Lindman (1964) suggested that at least the term "local contribution rate" should be changed to "property tax," so that the citizens would recognize it as such. Education, which always had a heavy reliance on the property tax, increased its reliance and became the main user of the property tax, with more than 50 percent of the proceeds of that tax being used for local schools. As the state governments almost universally abandoned direct property taxation and as more states relied upon both sales and income taxes and permitted local governments to use generally "piggyback" rates on these bases, the James and Lindman suggestions gained greater importance for equal treatment of schools and other governments in access to resources. As property-tax rates increase, resistance to the tax could restrict the access of schools to the state and community resources compared with the access of other governmental units.

Viewing the property-tax contribution in the foundation program as the state tax also could lead to simplification of the state foundation formula by replacing the complex equalization schemes with a foundation amount exclusively from state taxes. Harrison and McLoone (1965) indicated that such action by states would not differ too much from existing practice in 1959–60 after both general-purpose equalization and special-purpose grants were added together. A great deal of simplicity in the relations of the state to the local districts would ensue.

A number of other semantic or conceptual changes were suggested with far-reaching ramifications for researching and viewing the process of financing schools. James (1958b, 1961; James & Cronin, 1966, James & others, 1963) developed a new rationale for a view of state support of education that gave more attention to statewide decisions than the almost exclusively local view of Mort and his students. Johns and Morphet (1960) added the idea of a state salary schedule to specification of costs in the foundation program and urged a budget-item approach instead of a per-pupil amount in the foundation program. Lindman (1964) showed that the growing burden upon property tax necessitates a reexamination of the principle that every community should be expected to devote the same proportion of its property-tax base to support education. New York state enacted a partial provision of municipal overburden into law in 1964. Benson (1965), among others, called for a completely open-ended formula so that the state would guarantee the same amount per pupil for the same local tax effort in all parts of the state with local property-tax rates providing the only restriction. James (1960) and McLoone (1965) suggested that an open-ended formula required full state financing and that otherwise prorating the grant amounts among school districts negates much of the incentive to the less-wealthy school districts. Benson (1961) observed that the percentage from the state in the typical Strayer-Haig formula is determined solely by the variation in local ability among school districts.

Movement toward the open-end or shared-cost concept began with Wisconsin's enactment of a partially open-ended plan in 1949 and Rhode Island's adoption of an almost completely open-ended plan in 1961. California, Maine, New York, and Utah have adopted modified forms of these shared-cost plans. An open-ended grant is one in which there is no maximum amount set by the state toward which it will contribute a proportionate share.

The goal of such plans is to allow districts of varying wealth to let their educational preferences govern their tax rates, rather than having them depend on chance distribution of taxable resources. The Strayer-Haig foundation formula defines a state's minimum educational program in terms of a fixed-dollar amount; wealthier districts are able to finance a more substantial program at proportionally less cost than the cost of a modest educational offering in a poorer district. The legislated state-minimum program is thus a great burden upon poorer districts, whose efforts to rise above the minimum will continue to demand greater proportional sacrifice. As a means of reducing the variance in expenditures, the shared-cost plan guarantees a certain assessed valuation per pupil to every district. Districts below this level receive supplemental reimbursement from the state, while districts whose valuation exceeds that amount receive only the uniform grants.

In a successful attempt to bring to the thoughtful layman's attention the complexities of state educational finance programs, Benson (1965) commended this shared-cost approach. While Benson seems unduly critical of the regressive nature of the property tax, his point that the property tax is the ideal means of reconciling local demands with state minimum-level programs is well taken.

Attention centered on the open-end plan as the fixed foundation program amount in the Strayer-Haig formula rapidly became outdated with inflation, and on the rapid increase required in teachers' salaries if schools were to maintain their competitive recruitment position with the rest of the economy. The open-end plan was given extended consideration as more and more persons saw the least able school districts restricted the most by a fixed foundation amount, which became a smaller and smaller percentage of actual school expenditures per pupil.

McLoone (1965) demonstrated that the Johns variant of the Strayer-Haig foundation program approached the newer open-end foundation program of Wisconsin rather than the fixed-dollar-amount program. For that reason, he suggested the addition of the concept of "indirect" local contribution to the usual "direct" local contribution and showed that empirical results of the effects of the Johns variant for a single year could lead to false conclusions and that longitudinal studies of state support were required. Distributions of teachers by training and experience, and by wealth of school districts, were required before and after the adoption to evaluate the effects effectively.

Wisconsin's high assessment level, plus the guarantee that the state will bear all costs over the maximum allowable local levy, encourages local districts to improve on the state minimum-foundation program. Geiken (1965) found that in Wisconsin the variation in full-value total tax rates failed to account for variation in local expenditures per pupil. He suggests that people view school taxes in a frame of reference separate and distinct from that of other local taxes. Articles by Kahl and James in the book edited by Benson (1963) describe how the Wisconsin plan develops local initiative within the context of the shared-cost program. Vincent (1963) proposed that this feature be extended to the federal level. He projected the dollar amounts that would accrue to the states if a proportion of the total national educational expenditure were to be assumed by the federal government as a federal responsibility. Vincent's proposal provides to the states incentives to raise per-pupil expenditures in the same way that the shared-cost plan operates at the state-and-local level.

The growing interest in shared-cost methods of school support reveals a growing awareness of the advantages to a state of improving education. Since education is the function of the states, great variance in local educational expenditures implies malfunction; since many state constitutions, and the federal constitution, call for equal opportunity, pupils in low-expenditure districts are being deprived of their constitutional rights to an (equal) education. Using as analogies recent cases involving the rights of racial minorities and indigent criminals, Wise (1967) is exploring the legal implications of a hypothetical suit brought before the Supreme Court of the United States, claiming such educational deprivation. This investigation, when completed, is likely to be of interest to all serious students of state school support programs.

The states, confronted with variations among districts in ability and need, continue to search for ways to equalize the variations to some degree, or at least to maintain a "minimum" program. Thomson (1953) suggested using the economist's conceptual tool of marginal utility to determine foundation program levels. While it may be difficult to determine the point at which an additional dollar spent on education yields less benefit to the general welfare than it would if spent elsewhere, it is nevertheless an interesting question to consider.

New Directions in State Support. The considerations discussed above marked a break with the traditional concepts of school finance and called for a new look at effects of present methods of financing. The social, economic, and political context also gave rise to new insights. In a period in which state and federal funds were not used for property-tax relief but for joint sharing of the cost of education, or for the stimulation of new programs, attention was focused on the extent to which local school districts used funds from other government agencies as a substitute for local property-tax funds. Renshaw (1960) and Bishop (1964) found that local school districts tended to substitute state funds for local funds. James (1963) found that federal funds were likewise substituted for local funds and thus had a negligible influence on local expenditures. Renshaw (1960), Miner (1963), and Nygaard and Gregg (1958) found that state support tended to increase overall school expenditures. James (1961) showed that variations among school districts in per-pupil spending decrease as state aid increases per pupil and that the amounts of state aid per pupil are not correlated with expenditures per pupil. In general, these findings suggest that local tax burdens operate as a sufficient controlling device for open-ended grants.

The issue of the control of the decision-making powers of local school districts became more important as state and federal aid increased. Fowlkes and Watson (1954) surveyed the support patterns in 11 midwestern states and found no justification for the assertion that increases in the amount of state support resulted in increased state control over local districts. Munger and Fenno (1962) found similar results for federal funds, and Bailey and others (1963) supported the conclusions of both studies. A general impression from these studies is that the percentage of funds supplied by the state or federal government is not as important in determining the amount of control as is the type of support. Small amounts for special programs such as the National Defense Education Act and the Elementary and Secondary Act of 1965, and similar special state aids, appear to exert more control than general aids of much larger amounts. The extreme position in the control argument surrounding grants may be tested if the Heller-Pechman proposal for sharing with the states the automatic growth of federal income-tax revenue from a growing economy becomes a reality (W. Heller, 1964). The general aid argument moves from education to a consideration of educational aid as a specific function within the general functioning of state and local government.

PROJECTIONS OF SCHOOL COSTS. In the years since World War II, local school expenditures have been one of the fast-growing sectors of state and local governments, which themselves grew faster than the total economy. In 1965, one-third of all state and local government expenditures was devoted to educational services and facilities; members of school staffs constituted 48 percent of state and local employees; and the salaries of those staffs accounted for 52 percent of state and local payrolls. Of the total capital outlays undertaken by states and localities, over $5 billion, or 24 percent, went for school plants and related educational facilities. Because of their magnitude and rapid growth, the examination of the future direction of these trends becomes important.

Projection of school expenditures to 1970 and beyond is an important tool for decision making in school finance. The first major projection was done by the National Educational Association (Peterson & others, 1962). Textbooks by Barr (1960) and Johns and Morphet (1960) also contained projections, as did the report of the Committee for Economic Development (1959). Increasingly, attention was concentrated on this new aspect of school finance as school population continued to grow and school expenditures doubled in the short span of years from 1949–50 to 1955–56 and doubled again by 1963–64. A look ahead became important to foresee future conditions and to avoid, as much as possible, financing by crisis. Projections of school expenditures on a disaggregative basis, state by state, and for components of school expenditures as part of the total state and local government sector were carried out by Mushkin and McLoone (1965). These were done in the context of the economic models of the Federal Interagency Committee on Economic Growth for the Council of State Governments.

Data Needs. The limited availability of data restricted research on many questions or imposed restrictions on the general application of results. Benson (1963) called for a different classification in U.S. Office of Education publications concerned with state support. One problem noted time and again was the task of matching Census Tract data from the Census of Population with school districts' data (Miner, 1963; James & Cronin, 1966; Farner, 1966). Another was the need for ingenuity in using available data in place of desired data (James, 1958b, 1961; Thomas, 1963; Miner, 1963; Wilde, 1966; Burkhead, 1963; Fox, 1965). Often, this meant either the special collection of data for a study or the reconstruction of data collected by others to make possible the testing of hypotheses. One example of the problem is seen in the question of how much more secondary schools cost than elementary schools. Hogan (1966) showed that there is no easy answer to the question and that usual data of a limited nature may give an inaccurate basis for decision making.

The Office of Education continued to give statewide data on expenditures for even-numbered school years with its biennial publication. It also inaugurated a series on bond sales and elections (annually), and provided some budget estimates of expenditures in large cities. The most current data and the most consistent series on expenditures and related data were provided by Furno's *Cost of Education Index* (1965). His detailed annual data on the major budget categories of expenditures show great variations among districts, states, and regions. His data are based on budget estimates from a sample of school districts, not on complete records of school expenditures after the school year passes. Such tests as have been made of Furno's sample indicate a highly acceptable level of accuracy. These tests prove the worth of sampling for point and distribution estimates; however, they leave in question the use of the data for research studies. The budget estimates can be checked against *Census of Governments* data (e.g., U.S. Bureau of the Census, 1957, 1962), statewide estimates of the U.S. Office of Education, and individual state reports from state departments of education. There are sampling errors and, in addition, it appears that unexpected changes are not taken into consideration in budget estimates. Sometimes these factors affect the conclusion drawn from a study. The timeliness of the data make them useful to school administrators who cannot wait until actual data for the school year are reported. The Furno effort points up the needs for (1) faster data collection in a period of change and (2) data banks, so that research can probe further into questions of school expenditures without having to do the task of data collection as well as that of research.

TOWARD NEW CONCEPTS OF SCHOOL FINANCE. James, in a series of studies beginning with his doctoral dissertation (1958b), developed a more comprehensive rationale for examining school expenditures and the decision-making process connected with raising and spending funds for education. In his doctoral dissertation he factor analyzed commonly used descriptive data and concluded that a few carefully chosen variables reflecting ability to pay taxes, need for services, and a policy-making mechanism were the essential ingredients in the field of study. Subsequently, in a series of studies at Stanford University, he analyzed variables representing (1) the financial ability of local districts, (2) communities' shared expectations of educational services (James, 1961; James & others, 1963), and (3) governmental arrangements for decision making affecting school budgets (James & Cronin, 1966). The gradual refinement of the variables produced several models, one for predicting expenditures for education from socioeconomic data, another, refined and tested by J. Alan Thomas (1963), for predicting achievement scores by schools from socioeconomic data descriptive of neighborhoods, and a third, also developed by Thomas but not yet tested empirically, for predicting economic growth from school expenditures. Empirical work with the first two models produced very high multiple regression coefficients; for the postulated relationship of variables to educational expenditures an R of .897 was obtained, indicating that 80.5 percent of the variation in expenditures among districts had been explained.

McLure (1959) also departed from the Mort's traditional view of relating school expenditures to school processes in cost-quality studies and introduced school processes as an intervening variable between school expenditures and school outcomes. The McLure factor analysis produced a factor, beyond the traditional expenditure factor, dealing with school organizational climate. The Quality Measurement Project of New York State by Firman and others (1961) and the use of these data by Kiesling (1965) gave added emphasis to variables other than total current expenditures per pupil and especially the input of pupils to evaluate the output of schools. These changing facets of the rationale of school finance increased the importance of empirical studies, especially studies dealing with community expectations and underlying financial ability.

The Theory of Public Finance by Musgrave (1959) was directly applied to schools and their financing by Burkhead (1964). Musgrave (1961) extended this theoretical analysis to grants in aid. Several of his students, including Wilde (1966), applied the theoretical formulation to educational finance. Musgrave's theoretical framework again pointed up the need for a rationale in which school-finance research could be done and provided a better framework than strictly empirical data collection.

Community Expectations For Educational Services. The shared expectations a community has for educational services are a major factor in the dynamics of school finance. This is not an unmixed blessing, as Horace Mann noted over a century ago, because it leads the well-to-do, who know the value of education, to monopolize the best services and to withdraw their support from programs serving the apathetic and uncaring poor, who stand in greatest need of these services if they are to better their lot. The Negro civil rights movement has made a powerful impact upon many U.S. school systems in the past ten years. Hauser (1964) and Havighurst (1964) reported the intensification of demands placed upon the urban schools to redress social inequities. Particularly in the great cities, educational disadvantages of minorities, notably the Negroes, have been diagnosed, and the Economic Opportunity Act of 1964 represented massive federal treatment of that particular problem. Although debate continues as to the proper function of educative institutions with respect to social changes, it is clear that the schools must respond to local pressures under existing decentralized arrangements and that the aims of federal policy have been largely circumvented in many local districts.

Increased geographic and social mobility, along with the growing participation of low-income groups in policy matters, may bring some redefinitions in the task of the public schools. Sexton (1961) noted modifications of traditional power structures that were due to the increased effectiveness of low-income pressure groups and a heightened awareness of social responsibility by educators. Miner (1963) stated that in order for the schools to become a more effective agent in promoting social mobility and equality of economic opportunity, methods of financing educational services must be divorced from the individual household's capacity to pay and from the social position of the householder. Bloomberg and Sunshine (1963) placed heavy emphasis upon the schools' need to present their cases to their communities clearly and openly in order to create additional interest, thus modifying community attitudes. This appears to call for a more important voice for the professional in stating the aims of education.

That communities' expectations for school services vary systematically according to their religious composition was reported by Alkin (1964), who noted that the reason this phenomenon had not been clearly seen before his study was that the Protestant denominations were generally lumped together, whereas educational values are quite different among denominations; grouping them in three classes greatly increased the predictive power of this variable on school expenditures.

Farner (1966) found a high positive relationship between the percentage of males in the labor force and the level of educational expenditure.

The steady rise in the general level of expectations for educational services continues and is reflected in the extension of educational services to new age groups. While preschool programs for disadvantaged children reflect federal concern with the social conditions that inhibit learning, the revival of interest in beginning formal education at an earlier age is general and has brought about the reexamination of Montessori's methods, particularly by the more prosperous segments of the population. College enrollments continue to swell, and the junior-college movement demonstrates that provision of increased opportunities for higher education results in even greater demands for such services. While some junior colleges are financed as part of state systems of higher education, the more common practice is to form junior-college districts with their own taxing power. Voters apparently esteem the junior-college function sufficiently to finance it without decreasing support for other public schools. Urban areas were the first to generate powerful demands for the expansion of junior colleges; it will be necessary to study further their financial impact upon the support of schools because little attention has been paid to that question in the last decade.

Governmental Decision-making Arrangements. The decision-making processes controlling educational expenditures have received considerable study during the past decade. Thomas (1963) conceptualized budget decisions within the frames of reference of (1) efficiency of returns, (2) strategies for accomplishing goals, and (3) mobilization of support for programs competing for funds. One of the oldest arguments in the school finance literature involves vesting power over school decisions in the municipality or in the special district board—whether school districts should be fiscally dependent on the municipality or independent in making their budgetary decisions. Neither Miner (1963) nor James and others (1963), after reviewing the influence of the independent-dependent dichotomy on educational expenditures, was able to attach much significance to the variable. The extensive reliance upon set formulas to determine allocation of funds within the heavily bureaucratized large urban school systems leaves boards and municipalities little opportunity to obtain meaningful information on which to base budget decisions.

The great cities have become the subjects of considerable research regarding educational decision making, in large part because of the creation of the Research Council of the Great Cities School Improvement Program in 1959. McLure (1964) studied the distribution of funds within city school systems among educational programs and services; he used functional classifications to permit prorating of salaries, time of staff members, and costs of supportive services, in order to analyze inputs of funds in relation to outputs of achievement and services.

In one phase of the Metropolitan Studies Program at Syracuse University, Campbell and Sacks (1967) and Sacks and Ranney (1967) are dealing with socioeconomic variables, the relationship of suburban expenditures to central-city expenditures, fiscal dependence or independence, and the importance of noneducational expenditures.

Federal Funds for Education. The Committee for Economic Development (1959) considered the federal government's role in equalizing abilities among states. In calling for federal funding to support public schools in those states where income per public school child is substantially below the national average, it maintained that in more prosperous states the states themselves should assume a larger share of total school costs.

Sufrin (1963) analyzed the reactions of educational administrators to the National Defense Education Act of 1958 and found that categorical aid is considered less desirable than general aid. Meranto (1966) noted the long delay in federal aid to education, in contrast to aid for highways, housing, and other areas within the public sector. In an attempt to encourage local taxpayers to increase the amount of school support by increasing local property-tax rates, Robert Heller (1958) suggested that taxpayers receive more credit on their federal income tax for school taxes by being allowed to reduce their taxable income by the amount by which property taxes for education were increased.

ECONOMIC EFFECTS OF EDUCATION. The traditional study of school finance is an exercise in the effects of the economy upon schools. In recent years a new body of research on the obverse subject —the schools' effect upon the economy—has emerged, especially in relation to national development. It is noteworthy that economists as well as educators find this area deserving of their consideration.

This literature recently was comprehensively reviewed by Bowman (1966). The majority of studies on the subject have appeared since 1955; Bowman found that typically they were concerned with the allocation of educational resources (priority feasibility) or with the rate of return from education to nations as well as individuals.

Schultz and his students have provided impressive analyses of the effects of education on the rate of return on investment for the nation and for the individual. Noting that the economist can study the output benefits to the individual with greater precision than he can study benefits to society as a whole, Schultz (1961b) estimated that the rate of return on investment, including income forgone, in elementary education was 35 percent, in high school 10 percent, and in college 11 percent. Considering education's influence upon the national economy, based upon rates of return from 9 to 17.3 percent, he estimated that investment in education accounted for from 36 to 70 percent of the previously unexplained increase in national income (1961a). Denison (1962) estimated that between 1929 and 1957, 23 percent of the 2.93 percent annual growth rate of the GNP and 42 percent of the growth of per-capita income was a direct result of education. Considering the rate of return on investment in college education alone, Becker (1960) found that at 9 percent such investment was about in line with alternative investments. Schultz's expansion of his arguments (1963) to a costs-benefits framework clearly marks the transition from the consideration of education primarily as a consumer good to the consideration of education as a personal and national investment.

In responding to Schultz and Denison with respect to the part played by education in national income growth, Bowman (1964) developed the concepts of "Eds," defined as units of inputs of productive services derived from "embodied education." She cautioned that research may overestimate the influence of education upon economic growth and that other factors may have a much greater influence than education. The English economist Vaizey (1962) similarly considered education less a factor in economic growth than a function of social purpose. While education contributes to the economy by producing an integrated population capable of pursuing knowledge in a scientific and rational way, Vaizey regarded education's primary tasks as shifting consumer satisfactions and affecting the quality of life. Thus, economic growth is a product of consumed rather than invested education. Hirsch and Weisbrod

(1960), examining the relationship between tax payments for public education and benefits received in a case study of St. Louis County, Missouri, developed an analytic framework permitting the specification and the ultimate measurement of all benefits of public education to the community. Vaizey's approach suggests the extension of this study to a national scale. It is apparent that this area of inquiry will continue to be a profitable subject of study.

THE SCHOOLS AS AGENTS OF PRODUCTION. The convergence of economists' interest in schools and recent research on learning abilities has resulted in increased interest in the efficiency of schools as producers of a commodity—education. While schools will certainly continue to be criticized, this shift away from polemic toward analysis is a most promising and welcome change. The fundamental thesis of recent discussion has shifted from what *ought* to be taught to what *can* be taught, and *when*. Research on the early ages at which children can be taught differential calculus, reading, spelling, or typing has brought about far more constructive criticism of the schools than did all the disputes over progressivism.

Due (1959) called for study of the social effects of education using marginal analysis to determine whether there indeed were social effects of education. If these social effects diminish at a period prior to the end of our traditional 12 years of schooling, and if learning is at that point marginal, there is little reason to maintain the traditional structure. Machlup (1962) similarly drew attention to the value of the pupils' input (time) in relation to such matters as earnings forgone and optimum rates and periods of learning. A thorough economic analysis of the internal operation of schools and school systems will be the subject of Thomas' forthcoming book (1968).

Economy of scale, in school districts, continues to attract researchers at a time when interest in school district reorganization (unification) is at a peak. Clark (1963) called for an examination of the relative weight of quantitative factors that might improve the quality of education. Hanson's study (1963) of school-district size and unit costs showed that the unit-cost residuals declined with size of enrollment up to at least 20,000 pupils. The optimum plateau where unit costs were minimized was found to be around 50,000 pupils, with the difference in unit costs between districts of this size and those whose costs were highest being about $30 per pupil. Burkhead and others (1967) applied economic analysis to the evaluation of all the resources of a school system with less-than-satisfactory results for the economist. One would conclude from the study that educational decisions on alternatives will need to be made without rigorous economic analysis in the light of the present state of data.

PROGRAM BUDGETING. The adoption of a program-planning-budgeting system by selected agencies of the executive branch of the federal government, by executive order of President Johnson on August 25, 1965, will undoubtedly affect budgetary practices of state departments of education and public school districts. States and localities have moved independently in the same direction of applying these tools to their policy formulation. While a program-planning-budgeting system is not a completely new concept, its analytical approach—structuring objectives, ordering inputs, and analyzing outputs in terms of predetermined goals—is clearly adaptable to the functions of educational organizations. Burkhead (1956) regarded this method of ordering revenue and expenditure for decision making as a most important innovation in budgeting. Hirsch, in Novick's work on program budgeting in the federal government (1965), treated this aspect. Weisbrod (Dorfman, 1965) applied the test to problems of the dropout. Anderson's characterization of program budgeting (Association of School Business Officials . . ., 1963) in terms of school programs and activities rather than simply "things being bought" suggests benefits accruing from improved public relations as well as increased rationality in budget allocations. Such benefits are suggested by the findings of Thorson (1965). He noted that school-board members may be unwilling to authorize certain programs in spite of their own personal commitment to them, because they are sensitive to the expectations of others, who define the roles of board members as involving holding the line on expenditures. While program budgeting has yet to make an impact on any but the largest and the most innovative school districts, its influence will be pervasive in the future.

INTERNATIONAL CONTRIBUTIONS. The Organization for Economic Co-operation and Development, through its study group on the economics of education, has prepared cooperative studies of financing education in western European countries and the United States (1962a, 1962b, 1962c, 1964) and presented models of educational finance (1965). Denison (1966) extended his analysis of economic growth of the United States to western European countries.

Henry Thomas James
Stanford University

References

Advisory Commission on Intergovernmental Relations. *The Role of the States in Strengthening the Property Tax*, Vol. 1. GPO, 1961.

Advisory Commission on Intergovernmental Relations. *Measures of State and Local Fiscal Capacity and Tax Effort*. The Commission, 1962. 150p.

Advisory Commission on Intergovernmental Relations. *State Legislative Program of the Advisory Commission on Intergovernmental Relations, 1966*. The Commission, 1966. 481p.

Alford, Albert L. *Nonproperty Taxation for Schools; Possibilities for Local Application*. USOE, 1963. 144p.

Alkin, Marvin Carl. "Religious Correlates of School

Expenditures." Doctoral dissertation. Stanford U, 1964. 72p.
Association of School Business Officials of the United States and Canada. *Proceedings, 1962*, Vol. 48. The Association, 1963. 481p.
Bailey, Stephen K., and others. *Schoolmen and Politics; A Study of State Aid to Education in the Northeast.* Syracuse U Press, 1963. 111p.
Barr, W. William Montfort. *American Public School Finance.* American, 1960. 406p.
Becker, Gary. "Is There Underinvestment in College Education?" *Am Econ R* 50:346–54; 1960.
Benson, Charles S. *The Economics of Public Education.* Houghton, 1961. 580p.
Benson, Charles S. (Ed.) *Perspectives on the Economics of Education, Readings in School Finance and Business Management.* Houghton, 1963. 477p.
Benson, Charles S. *The Cheerful Prospect.* Houghton, 1965.
Bird, Frederick L. *The General Property Tax: Findings of the 1947 Census of Governments.* Public Administration Service, 1960. 77p.
Bird, Frederick L. *The Role of the States in Strengthening the Property Tax*, Vol. 2. GPO, 1963. 187p.
Bishop, George A. "Stimulative Versus Substitutive Effects of State School Aid in New England." *Nat Tax J* 17:133–43; 1964.
Bloomberg, Warner, Jr., and Sunshine, Morris. *Suburban Power Structures and Public Education: A Study of Values, Influence, and Tax Effort.* Syracuse U Press, 1963. 177p.
Bowman, Mary Jean. "Schultz, Denison, and the Contribution of 'Eds' to National Income Growth." *J Political Econ* 72:450–64; 1964.
Bowman, Mary Jean. "The Human Investment Revolution in Economic Thought." *Sociol Ed* 39:111–37; 1966.
Burkhead, Jesse. *Government Budgeting.* Wiley, 1956.
Burkhead, Jesse. *State and Local Taxes for Public Education.* Syracuse U Press, 1963. 110p.
Burkhead, Jesse. *Public School Finance: Economics and Politics.* Syracuse U Press, 1964. 394p.
Burkhead, Jesse, and others. *Input and Output in Large-City High Schools* Syracuse U Press, 1967. 110p.
Campbell, Alan K., and Sacks, Seymour. *Metropolitan America: Fiscal Patterns and Governmental Systems.* Free Press, 1967. 239p.
Clark, Harold F. *Cost and Quality in Public Education.* Syracuse U Press, 1963. 54p.
Committee for Economic Development. *Paying for Better Public Schools.* The Committee, 1959. 90p.
Cornell, Francis Griffith. *A Measure of Taxpaying Ability of Local School Administrative Units.* Teachers Col, Columbia U, 1936.
Cubberley, Ellwood Patterson. *School Funds and Their Apportionment.* Teachers Col, Columbia U, 1905. 255p.
Davis, Donald L. "Tax-paying Ability: A Study of the Relationship Between Wealth and Income in California Counties." Doctoral dissertation. Stanford U, 1963. 134p.
Denison, Edward F. *The Sources of Economic Growth in the United States and the Alternatives Before Us.* Supplementary Paper No. 13. Committee for Economic Development, 1962. 297p.
Denison, Edward F. *Why Growth Rates Differ; Postwar Experience in Nine Western Countries.* The Brookings Institution, 1966.
Dorfman, Robert. (Ed.) *Measuring Benefits of Governments' Investments.* The Brookings Institution, 1965. 429p.
Due, John F. *Government Finance*, rev. ed. Richard D. Irwin, Inc., 1959. 627p.
Farner, Frank. *Economic, Sociological, and Demographic Characteristics of Oregon School Districts and Their Relationship to District Financial Practices.* U Oregon Press, 1966. 164p.
Firman, William D., and others. *Procedures in School Quality Evaluation.* New York State Education Dept, 1961.
Fowlkes, John Guy, and Watson, George E. "A Report on State Financial Support and Local Educational Planning." U Chicago, 1954. (Mimeographed.)
Fox, Edward J., Jr. "Decision Criteria Applied to Innovative Educational Program Items in the Wisconsin State Budgetary Process." Doctoral dissertation. U Wisconsin, 1965. 278p.
Furno, Orlando F. *The Cost of Education Index, 1964–65.* Pitman, 1965. 72p.
Geiken, Lloyd A. "An Analysis of Selected Socioeconomic Factors Which Influence Expenditures for Education in One Hundred Wisconsin School Districts." Doctoral dissertation. U Wisconsin, 1965. 290p.
Hanson, Nels W. "Economy of Scale in Education: An Analysis of the Relationship Between District Size and Unit Costs in the Public Schools." Doctoral dissertation. Stanford U, 1963. 98p.
Harrison, Forrest W., and McLoone, Eugene P. *Profiles in School Support: A Decennial Overview.* USOE, 1965. 162p.
Hauser, Philip M. (Chairman) *Report to the Board of Education, City of Chicago.* Advisory Panel on Integration of the Public Schools (Chicago), 1964. 102p.
Havighurst, Robert J. *The Public Schools of Chicago: A Survey for the Board of Education of the City of Chicago.* Chicago Board of Education, 1964. 499p.
Heller, Robert. "A Proposal for Financing Tax Supported Education." *Harvard Ed R* 28:214–31; 1958.
Heller, Walter, quoted in Robert L. Heilbroner. "The Share the Tax Revenue Plan." *New York Times M* December 27:8; 1964.
Hirsch, Werner, and Weisbrod, Burton. *Spillover of Public Education Costs and Benefits.* USOE Cooperative Research Project No. 1045. Washington U, 1960. 465p.
Hogan, Lloyd D. *Variations in Public School Expenditures Associated with Changes in Elementary and Secondary Enrollments.* U State New York, 1966. 31p.
Hutchins, Clayton D., and others. *Financing Public School Facilities.* USOE, 1959. 214p.

James, H. Thomas. "Intergovernmental Relations in Education." *R Ed Res* 28:277–96; 1958(*a*).

James, H. Thomas. "Toward a Unified Concept of State School Finance Programs." Doctoral dissertation. U Chicago, 1958(*b*). 134p.

James, H. Thomas. "School Aid Apportionment: State Action Needed on the Property Tax." *State Government* 33:256–62; 1960.

James, H. Thomas. *School Revenue Systems in Five States.* USOE Cooperative Research Project No. 803. Stanford U, 1961. 143p.

James, H. Thomas. "Institutional Character of Education: Government and Politics." *R Ed Res* 34:405–23; 1964.

James, H. Thomas, and Cronin, Joseph M. "New Developments and Trends in School Finance: Projections and Observations." In Gauerke, Warren E., and Childress, Jack R. (Eds.) *Theory and Practice of School Finance.* Rand McNally, 1966. 876p.

James, H. Thomas, and others. *Wealth, Expenditures, and Decision-making for Education.* USOE Cooperative Research Project No. 1241. Stanford U, 1963. 203p.

James, H. Thomas, and others. *Determinants of Educational Expenditures in Large Cities of the United States.* USOE Cooperative Research Project No. 2389. Stanford U, 1966. 198p.

Johns, Roe L., and McLure, William P. "Economics and Finance of Education." *R Ed Res* 31:417–27; 1961.

Johns, Roe L., and Morphet, Edgar L. (Eds.) *Problems and Issues in Public School Finance.* Teachers Col, Columbia U, 1952.

Johns, Roe L., and Morphet, Edgar L. *Financing the Public Schools.* Prentice-Hall, 1960. 566p.

Kiesling, Herbert John. "Measuring a Local Government Service: A Study of Efficiency of School Districts in New York State." Doctoral dissertation. Harvard U, 1965.

Lindman, Erick L. *State School Support and Municipal Government Costs.* USOE Cooperative Research Project No. 2123. U California at Los Angeles, 1964. 130p.

Machlup, Fritz. *The Production and Distribution of Knowledge in the United States.* Princeton U Press, 1962. 416p.

McLoone, Eugene P. "Effects of Tax Elasticities on the Financial Support of Education." Doctoral dissertation. U Illinois, 1961. 161p.

McLoone, Eugene P. "Flexibility in Local Support of the Schools: A Proposal." *Sch Life* 44:5–7; 1962.

McLoone, Eugene P. "Evaluating the Weighting Factors in Use." In *Trends in Financing Public Education.* NEA, 1965. p. 63–79.

McLure, William P. "Using Factor Analysis in School Evaluation and Planning." *Phi Delta Kappan* 40:225–30; 1959.

McLure, William P. *The Structure of Educational Costs in the Great Cities.* Research Council of the Great Cities Program for School Improvement, 1964. 55p.

Meranto, Phillip. "The Politics of Federal Aid to Education in 1965: A Study in Political Innovation." Doctoral dissertation. Syracuse U, 1966.

Miner, Jerry. *Social and Economic Factors in Spending for Public Education.* Syracuse U Press, 1963. 159p.

Mort, Paul R., and others. *Public School Finance*, 3rd ed. McGraw-Hill, 1960. 512p.

Munger, Frank J., and Fenno, Richard F., Jr. *National Politics and Federal Aid to Education.* Syracuse U Press, 1962. 193p.

Munse, Albert R. (Ed.) *Revenue Programs for the Public Schools in the United States, 1959–60.* USOE, 1961. 79p.

Munse, Albert R. *State Programs for Public School Support.* USOE, 1965.

Munse, Albert R., and McLoone, Eugene P. (Eds.) *Public School Finance Programs of the United States, 1957–58.* USOE, 1960. 275p.

Munse, Albert R., and others. "Public School Finance Program, 1961–63: States." GPO, 1961–1963. 4p. (Loose leaf.)

Musgrave, Richard A. *The Theory of Public Finance: A Study in Public Economy.* McGraw-Hill, 1959. 628p.

Musgrave, Richard A. "Approaches to a Fiscal Theory of Political Federalism." In *Public Finances: Need, Sources, and Utilization.* Princeton U Press, 1961. p. 97–122.

Mushkin, Selma, and McLoone, Eugene P. *Local School Expenditures: 1970 Projections.* Council of State Governments, 1965. 84p.

National Committee for the Support of Public Schools. "Broadening the Base of State Support." In "Know Your Schools Fact Sheet," No. 8, October, 1966. (Unpublished.)

National Conference of Professors of Educational Administration. *The Theory and Practice of School Finance.* Rand McNally, 1967.

National Conference on School Finance. *Committee on Educational Finance, Proceedings.* NEA, 1959——. *Problems and Opportunities in Financing Education* (1959); *New Directions in Financing the Public Schools* (1960); *Financing Education for Our Changing Population* (1961); *Financing the Changing School Program* (1962); *Long-range Planning in School Finance* (1963); *A Financial Program for Today's Schools* (1964); *Trends in Financing Public Education* (1965); *Partnership in School Finance* (1966).

Netzer, Dick. *Economics of the Property Tax.* The Brookings Institution, 1966. 326p.

Novick, David. (Ed.) *Program Budgeting. Program Analysis and the Federal Budget.* Harvard U Press, 1965. 382p.

Nygaard, Joseph M., and Gregg, Russell T. "Shared Income Tax and School Support in Wisconsin." *J Ed Res* 52:142–4; 1958.

Organization for Economic Co-operation and Development. *Forecasting Educational Needs for Economic and Social Development.* The Organization (Paris), 1962(*a*). 113p.

Organization for Economic Co-operation and Development. *Planning Education for Economic and Social*

Development. The Organization (Paris), 1962(*b*). 270p.

Organization for Economic Co-operation and Development. *Policy Conference on Economic Growth and Investments in Education*. 5 vols. The Organization (Paris), 1962(*c*). 368p.

Organization for Economic Co-operation and Development. *The Residual Factor and Economic Growth*. The Organization (Paris), 1964. 279p.

Organization for Economic Co-operation and Development. *Econometric Models of Education*. The Organization (Paris), 1965. 99p.

Peterson, LeRoy J., and others. *Financing the Public Schools*. NEA, 1962. 152p.

Peterson, LeRoy J., and others. *Economic Impact of State Support Models on Educational Finance*. U Wisconsin Press, 1963. 311p.

Renshaw, E. F. "A Note on the Expenditure Effect of State Aid to Education." *J Political Econ* 68: 170–4; 1960.

Rossmiller, Richard A. "The Equalization Objective in State Support Programs: An Analysis of Measures Need and Ability." *Nat Tax J* 18:362–9; 1965.

Sacks, Seymour, and Ranney, David. *The Allocation of Fiscal Resources to Large City Education Systems*, 1967. (In press.)

Schultz, Theodore W. "Education and Economic Growth." In *Social Forces Influencing American Education*, 60th Yearbook, NSSE. U Chicago Press, 1961(*a*). p. 46–88.

Schultz, Theodore W. "Investment in Human Capital." *Am Econ R* 51:1–17; 1961(*b*).

Schultz, Theodore W. *The Economic Value of Education*. Columbia U Press, 1963. 92p.

Sexton, Patricia Cayo. *Education and Income: Inequalities of Opportunity in Our Public Schools*. Viking, 1961. 298p.

Strayer, George D., and Haig, Robert Murray. *The Financing of Education in the State of New York*. Macmillan, 1923. 205p.

Sufrin, Sidney C. *Administering the National Defense Education Act*. Syracuse U Press, 1963. 76p.

Thomas, J. Alan. "Educational Decision-making and the School Budget." In *Administrator's Notebook*, Vol. 12, No. 4. U Chicago Press, 1963.

Thomas, J. Alan. *The Productive School*. Wiley, 1968.

Thomson, Procter. "Notes on a Conceptual Framework for State Aid Programs in Public School Finance." U Chicago, 1953. (Mimeographed.)

Thorson, John R. "Expectations for the School Board Role as Related to Level of Local Financial Support and Allocation of Expenditures." Doctoral dissertation. U Wisconsin, 1965.

U.S. Bureau of the Census. *Census of Governments: 1957*, Vol. 5: *Taxable Property Values in the United States*. GPO, 1957.

U.S. Bureau of the Census. *Census of Governments: 1962*, Vol. 2: *Taxable Property Values*. GPO, 1962.

U.S. Office of Education. *Bond Sales for Public School Purposes*. GPO, annually.

Updegraff, Harlan, and King, Leroy A. *Survey of the Fiscal Policies of the State of Pennsylvania in the Field of Education*. Pennsylvania State Department of Education, 1922. 207p.

Vaizey, John. *The Economics of Education*. Free, 1962. 165p.

Vincent, William S. "The Shared Cost Plan as a Method of Federal Support for Education." *Institute of Adm Res B* 4:1–6; 1963.

Wilde, James A. "The Stimulating Effect of Grants in Aid." Doctoral dissertation. Princeton U, 1966.

Wise, Arthur E. *The Constitution and Equality: Wealth, Geography, and Educational Opportunity*. Doctoral Dissertation. U Chicago, 1967.

FOUNDATIONS

Foundations generally are nonprofit legal structures which channel private wealth into the service of the general public welfare. They may be called charitable, educational, community, eleemosynary, or benevolent; they may be titled foundation, fund, endowment, trust, or corporation. Regardless of the name they share the function of devoting the income from principal funds, portions of principal funds, or both, to the improving or uplifting of mankind.

While nonphilanthropic organizations sometimes use these titles and while organizations other than foundations engage in charitable activities, foundations probably must satisfy five criteria. They should (1) be nongovernmental, (2) be nonprofit, (3) have principal funds of their own, (4) be managed by their own governing boards, and (5) aid educational, religious, social, or other charitable activities in the common welfare (Andrews, 1964).

EARLY HISTORY. The establishment of funds for the aid of broadly defined but nonspecifically designated beneficiaries is probably as old as the concept of property. The structures and purposes of this philanthropy have changed in response to changing social organizations and cultural values.

Before the Christian era, in the Middle-Eastern progenitors of our present Western civilizations, religion and rule were both typically controlled by the same individual or by the same small group. Rights of property were reserved for the ruler. We have evidence that the pharaohs of Egypt established funds in perpetuity for religious purposes—perhaps the first evidence of philanthropy (Hollis, 1939). A clay tablet dating from somewhat later, about 1280 B.C., records the legal indenture of King Marouttach and gives evidence that the Chaldean civilization permitted royalty to form rudimentary philanthropic organizations (Hollis, 1960).

With the increasing interaction of the government with the governed in Greece, the Law of the Twelve Tables at the time of Solon, about 594 B.C., established the right of a private citizen to bequeath property. Even then, however, a living owner could not divert his property from his natural heirs without their consent.

Another five centuries were required before the concept of legal heirs being alternatives to natural heirs became accepted. In the early centuries of the Christian era in Rome various foundations were established for the support of educational institutions, hospitals, foundling and old people's homes, and poor relief. By A.D. 324, however, the assets of these groups had been confiscated (Hollis, 1960).

It was the emperor Constantine who recognized the social welfare obligations of the state. He designated the foundations of the Christian Church as the recipient of bequeathed endowments. He directed that these funds could not be used for other purposes, and, most significantly, he specified that they were not subject to taxation. The right of modern foundations to hold money and to be exempt from taxation rests on this social service principle of Constantine. The church thus became the distributor of all public funds for the underprivileged, and individuals were encouraged to donate to the church's charitable purposes (Fremont-Smith, 1965).

The revision of the Roman law in 550 more firmly established the legal bases of ecclesiastical foundations. The entire church hierarchy was given broad supervisory responsibility, a responsibility which even though presumably reviewable by the citizens gave the church great power throughout the Middle Ages (Hollis, 1939).

DEVELOPMENT IN ENGLAND. The Roman law and the concept of foundations eventually came to England. The Saxons added the word *corporation* and the concept behind it (Fremont-Smith, 1965).

After the Norman conquest in 1066, England developed a system of ecclesiastical courts. Although this system led to the power struggle between church and state which ultimately resulted in the end of charity holdings by the church, three qualities of philanthropy were established: (1) the privilege of indefinite existence; (2) the privilege of validity even if the gift is in general terms so long as its objective is exclusively charitable; and (3) the privilege of obtaining fresh objects if those laid down by the founder become incapable of execution, known today as the doctrine of cy pres (Fremont-Smith, 1965).

With the increasing size of the groups having rights of property, with the increasing power of the church, and with increasing encouragement to bequeath property to charitable purposes, the holdings of the church corporations by the time of Henry VIII were estimated to be between one-third and one-half of the entire wealth of England (Orton, 1931). It seems hardly surprising that the state continued to try to establish its right of control over charitable activities. A number of statutes were enacted, beginning with the Magna Charta in 1215, which limited gifts of land to charitable corporations. In 1391, Parliament enacted a statute which specifically prohibited the granting of the use of lands to religious corporations (Keeton, 1962). Nonmonastic charitable associations, such as the Oxford and Cambridge colleges, began to develop (Jordan, 1959; Davis, 1961).

The social changes of the sixteenth century led to the passage of the Statute of Charitable Uses in 1601 (Stat. 43, 1601), which has been described as "the starting point of the modern law of charities" (Keeton, 1962). This statute tried to correct the problems of poor charity administration and to encourage charitable gifts by listing a variety of charitable purposes (Committee on the Law and Practice Relating to Charitable Trusts, 1952). The law became very influential on both the structure and the purposes of charity in England and, subsequently, the United States.

DEVELOPMENT IN THE UNITED STATES. Charity and organizations for its administration came to colonial America under the English law. After the Revolution the legal structure of philanthropies in the United States became somewhat confused. Charitable *trusts* were held to be valid in some states—for example, Massachusetts—whose codification of laws repealed only those English laws in conflict with the concept of democracy. In other states, Virginia for instance, which had either specifically or by inference repealed all English law, charitable trusts were held to be invalid because the Statute of 1601 could not be taken as the legal precedent. Even though in 1844 in the case *Vidal v. Girard's Executors* (1844) the Supreme Court of the United States held that charitable trusts had their legal precedent in times and cultures preceding Elizabethan England and therefore were valid, many states held to the earlier, invalidating decisions (Miller, 1961). It was not until the start of the twentieth century that all states recognized the validity of charitable trusts.

Charitable *corporations* however, flourished early in the history of the United States because the states passed specific statutes enabling their establishment. In at least one case, New York, legislation enabling the establishment of corporations for charitable purposes preceded by more than 25 years the legislation enabling the establishment of business corporations (Fremont-Smith, 1965).

The distinction between charitable corporations and trusts is interesting because each is regulated by a separate body of law. Both foundation types are governed by bodies of men having similar responsibilities, but the laws governing the conduct of trustees are, perhaps, the more rigid. Trustees and directors are, similarly, required to be loyal to the conditions and laws under which the trust or corporation was established. This means simply that they cannot use the funds of the organizations in actions of self-interest. They are both required to keep and render accounts and to exercise reasonable care and skill. A trustee, further, has a duty not to delegate administration to others, while the very structure of the corporation almost demands that certain decisions be delegated. The responsibility of corporate directors is simply to retain overall supervisory control. Thus, the differing regulations for the operations of trusts and corporations result in the possibility that designated representatives of corporate directors may be able to exercise potentially greater decision-making authority than would be available to representatives of charitable trusts (Fremont-Smith, 1965).

CONTROL. Foundations are traditionally as free as possible of governmental control (Jenkins, 1950). However, with the establishment in the United States of the separation between federal and state powers and with the giving of the primary responsibility for the welfare of individuals to the several states, the chartering and the control of philanthropic foundations came to rest in the hands of the state governments. Indeed, until the period of growing nationalism and internationalism of the twentieth century there were, in the United States, no more than about 15 foundations which had more than a local interest (Andrews, 1964).

During the first decade of the twentieth century fewer than 20 new foundations were formed. In the second decade 76 new foundations were formed, including the Rockefeller Foundation, the Carnegie Corporation, and the Commonwealth Fund. In the 1920's over 169 foundations came into being, including 12 which had assets of over $10-million each. In the depression decade, the 1930's, about 330 foundations were established. Indeed, about 40 percent of all foundation assets today are held by organizations established during that period. During the 1940's as many as 2,500 foundations were created, including 272 which now have assets in excess of $1-million. The rate of growth of foundations, in numbers, has continued to increase. Between 1950 and 1959 approximately 4,000 foundations came into existence, and the rate of increase is currently estimated at about 1,200 per year. There are today perhaps 20,000 philanthropic foundations in the United States (Walton & Andrews, 1960; Walton & Lewis, 1964). The third edition of the *Foundation Directory* (in press) lists 6,803 relatively large and active foundations having combined assets of $19.9-billion and making grants during 1966 of $1.2-billion (Foundation Library Center, 1967).

It is extremely difficult to collect information on the number, assets, purposes, and functions of private foundations, for a number of reasons. They are, first, chartered under the laws of the several states. There is, also, a desire on the part of some donors for a certain anonymity. Even the increased federal control over foundations through the passage of the internal revenue acts has not totally solved this information-collection problem because many foundations listed by the Internal Revenue Service (IRS) refuse to participate in voluntary surveys of information. A further complicating fact is that all tax-exempt organizations file the same IRS report as foundations. In 1962 Congressman Wright Patman reported that there were an estimated 45,124 tax-exempt foundations, according to IRS records (U.S. Congress, 1962). These included, however, many charitable organizations not falling within the generally accepted definition of a foundation—such as hospitals, orphanages, and educational institutions having no student bodies.

The formation of the Foundation Library Center in 1956 has helped to bridge this information gap. The center attempts to compile and file comprehensive information on the activities of foundations. The center maintains a library, a branch, and seven regional collections; it publishes the *Foundation News;* and it has prepared the three editions of *The Foundation Directory*.

The public control of private, charitable foundations was established to be, and to remain, mainly in the laws and judicial decisions of the several states. Such laws differ somewhat from state to state, and it would only be by examining the codes and precedent-setting decisions of each of the states that the kind and extent of influence exercised over foundations could be determined. It is important to note, however, that it was the separate states which were designated to represent the general public as the unspecified beneficiaries of private charity.

While a foundation is still responsible to the laws of the state in which it is chartered, the federal government has had an increasing influence on the activities and structures of foundations. This has been reinforced by both the increasing concern of the federal government for the welfare of individual citizens and the widening of the scope of foundations' activities to national and even international concern.

FEDERAL CONGRESSIONAL INFLUENCE. The federal control over foundations rests primarily on the federal tax structure. The tax exemptions given to foundations from the outset of federal tax laws can be viewed as a reflection of an early governmental encouragement of private philanthropy. Within the last 25 years Congress moved to require such organizations to file federal income tax information returns. The increase in tax rates since World War II prompted an examination of the tax-exempt status of foundations as a possible mechanism for reducing the burden of personal and corporate income taxes. The Revenue Act of 1950 added a number of restrictions to the business activities of foundations wishing to maintain their tax-exempt status.

While the practice of asserting federal control over foundations by the manipulation of the tax laws has been debated, it must be noted that when the investigations of congressional committees have resulted in specific legislation influencing foundations the legislation has invariably been a modification of the federal tax acts.

A number of congressional committees have, through the years, been concerned with the organization and operations of foundations since the first such major investigation by the Senate Industrial Relations Committee in 1915.

The Committee on Interstate and Foreign Commerce (U.S. Congress, 1916) of the Senate conducted investigations in 1948 of the operations of an industrialist, Roy Little, who had been charged with using his tax-exempt foundation to finance several of his business ventures (U.S. Congress, Senate Committee on Interstate and Foreign Commerce, 1949). These investigations contributed substantially to the provisions of the Revenue Act of 1950, now the Internal Revenue Code of 1954.

In 1952 a select committee to investigate educational and philanthropic foundations and other comparable organizations which are exempt from federal taxation was formed (U.S. Congress, House of Representatives Select Committee to Investigate and Study Educational and Philanthropic Foundations . . . , 1953). Under E. E. Cox of Georgia and subsequently Brooks Hays of Arkansas, the committee used questionnaires, interviews, and public hearings to collect a substantial amount of information about the operation of foundations. Legislative recommendations coming from the committee were never enacted by the Congress.

In 1953 another committee under the chairmanship of Congressman B. Carroll Reece of Tennessee, was appointed to investigate tax-exempt foundations and comparable organizations with an eye to examining especially foundations' political purposes, propaganda, and attempts to influence legislation (U.S. Congress, House of Representatives Special Committee . . . , 1954). The committee's report, which was not signed by its entire membership, concluded that foundation activity was desirable in the natural sciences and when involving direct donations to religious, educational, scientific and other institutional recipients. However, foundation activities in the social sciences, because they were action-oriented rather than theoretical, tended to threaten the moral, religious, and governmental principles of the country. Indeed, foundations displayed, according to the committee's report, a distinct tendency to support "subversion."

While it is difficult to assess the impact of the congressional investigations of the early 1950's, it has been asserted that the investigations caused the larger foundations to be somewhat cautious in their programs. In 1961, Dean Rusk, who was then the president of the Rockefeller Foundation, argued, however, that foundations had not been intimidated by these congressional investigations (Rusk, 1961).

Largely under pressure from Wright Patman of Texas, in 1962 the House of Representatives' Select Committee on Small Business began an investigation of the impact of tax-exempt foundations on the American economy (U.S. Congress, House of Representatives Select Committee on Small Business, 1962). In the first report of this committee, the chairman called for an immediate moratorium on foundation tax exemptions.

While this interim report did not result in any specific federal legislation, its widespread national coverage prompted the president to announce the appointment of a White House task force to study whether tighter IRS administration or new legislation were needed. The IRS increased the number of scheduled audits for foundations from 2,000 to 10,000 per year. The service also established an exempt-organization council to aid the commissioner in dealing with tax-exempt organizations. Three other interim reports were released by the chairman (U.S. Congress, House of Representatives Select Committee on Small Business, 1963, 1964, 1967) which dealt primarily with anatomical investigations of several specific foundations. The findings contained in these reports have been widely discussed and argued and were probably responsible for some tightening of federal control over the tax status of foundations. It is generally agreed, however, that the Patman Committee simply reasserted the responsibility of a foundation to the public.

The Senate Finance Committee and the House Ways and Means Committee asked the Treasury Department in 1964 to examine the provisions in the 1950 amendment to the Internal Revenue Code relating to tax-exempt organizations. This report was submitted to Congress in February 1965, and it provides a fairly thorough description of the financial and management practices of foundations (U.S. Congress, Senate Committee on Finance, 1964).

Foundations have been subjected to four major criticisms: (1) they remove a substantial amount of taxable income from the federal tax base, (2) they serve as an intermediary between the donor and active charitable pursuits and thus cause delay in putting charitable funds to work, (3) they represent a disproportionately large section of the national economy, and (4) they represent a potentially dangerous concentration of economic and social power. All of these criticisms can be and have been at least partially refuted by a careful examination of foundation operations. They remain, however, the subject of much congressional concern.

ACTIVITIES. The interaction between foundations and governments has been much discussed but little studied (Caplin, 1963). It can be suggested, however, that until the past decade it was difficult to distinguish the role of the foundation from the role of the individual state. Within the past decade it has become increasingly difficult to differentiate the welfare role of the federal government from the charitable purposes of the foundations; this will probably continue to be true in the immediate future as well. It has been suggested that foundations are in a position intermediate between that of the individual members of the public and that of the federal government in both degree of power and ability to prescribe (Barbe & Hall, 1966). If this is the case and if the federal government continues to be increasingly concerned with public welfare, it would appear that the arena for foundations' operations is becoming somewhat diminished.

EDUCATION. Foundations, by definition, operate within all areas covered by the term "public welfare." Within this general heading it is difficult, if not impossible, to pick out those functions which might be called education. The remainder of this article, therefore, deals simply with the relation between foundations and the organizations and institutions of education.

Most foundation aid to the educational establishment continues to be in the form of direct support of research and programs designed to strengthen educational institutions. Such support is typically given by foundations in response to specific requests made by institutions. Usually the support is for a relatively short period of time, and the cost of the program, if it is to be on-going, must ultimately be borne by the institution from its normal financial sources (American Association of School Administrators, 1963). Typically, too, universities are the most frequent recipients of foundation support, although public elementary and secondary schools may be indirectly influenced (Eurich, 1963; Morison, 1964; Morrisett, 1965; Parker, 1964; Rioux, 1962; Woodring, 1960).

The role of the foundation in support of education is becoming increasingly complex. More and more, the foundations are finding federal governmental agencies engaging in programs in support of educational organizations and institutions. Increasingly the foundations' advisers on needed programs are becoming the same people who are advising government with regard to needed public programs. Educational administrators, faced with increasing educational costs, desire fewer restrictions on the purposes to which foundations' support can be put (American Association of School Administrators, 1963). And yet foundations feel the need to become increasingly prescriptive because their sphere of operation is being narrowed by the broadening of governmental programs. It would appear that more and more foundations are turning to the support of institutions and programs for international and intercultural education—areas in which the federal government cannot as yet operate very effectively. During the past decade the percentage of total foundation grants going to *education* has decreased from about 41 percent in 1957 (Walton & Andrews, 1960) to about 24 percent in 1966 (*Foundation News*, 1967). At the same time the percentage given to *international activities* has risen from 5 percent in 1957 (Walton & Andrews, 1960) to an estimated 21 percent in 1966 (*Foundation News*, 1967).

RESEARCH. In the past decade the studies of foundations which have been conducted have been largely given to the description of the histories of charitable organizations (Andrews, 1958; Curti & Nash, 1965; Fosdick, 1962; Marts, 1966). As more and better descriptive information becomes available, it would appear that two research areas are being opened: (1) the study of the growth and changes in the interrelation between foundations and other social welfare agencies, and (2) examining the present interaction between foundations and government seeking to redefine the role of foundations—perhaps as the agencies which can most flexibly and most powerfully be concerned with the noncollective welfare of individuals.

Richard H. Barbe
University of Delaware
Roy M. Hall
University of Delaware

References

American Association of School Administrators, Committee on Foundations. *Private Philanthropy and Public Purposes.* AASA, 1963. 43p.

Andrews, F. Emerson. *Legal Instruments of Foundations.* Russell Sage, 1958. 318p.

Andrews, F. Emerson. "Introduction." In Walton, Ann D., and Lewis, Marianna O. (Eds.) *The Foundation Directory,* 2nd ed. Russell Sage, 1964. p. i–lxiv.

Barbe, Richard H., and Hall, Roy M. "Effect of Planned Educational Change on National Agencies." *Theory into Practice* 5:54–7; 1966.

Caplin, Mortimer M. "Foundations and the Government: Some Observations on the Future." *Foundation News* 4:2–3; 1963.

Committee on the Law and Practice Relating to Charitable Trusts. *Report.* H.M. Stationery Office, 1952. 251p.

Curti, Merle, and Nash, Roderick. *Philanthropy in the Shaping of American Higher Education.* Rutgers U Press, 1965. 340p.

Davis, John P. *Corporations.* Capricorn Books, Putnam, 1961. 280p.

Eurich, Alvin C. "The Role of American Foundations in Future Teacher Training." In *Yearbook of Education.* Harcourt, 1963. p. 507–12.

Fosdick, Raymond B. *Adventures in Giving.* Harper, 1962. 369p.

Foundation Library Center. *Foundation Directory,* 3d ed. Russell Sage (in press).

Foundation News 8:2; 1967.

Fremont-Smith, Marion R. *Foundations and Government.* Russell Sage, 1965. 564p.

Hollis, Ernest V. "Evolution of the Philanthropic Foundation." *Ed Rec* 20:575–88; 1939.

Hollis, Ernest V. "Foundations." In Harris, Chester W. (Ed.) *Encyclopedia of Educational Research,* 3rd ed. Macmillan, 1960. p. 565–70.

Jenkins, Edward C. *Philanthropy in America.* Association Press, 1950. 183p.

Jordan, W. K. *Philanthropy in England, 1480–1660.* Russell Sage, 1959. 410p.

Keeton, George W. *The Modern Law of Charities.* Pitman, 1962. 345p.

Marts, Armand C. *The Generosity of Americans, Its Source, Its Achievements.* Prentice-Hall, 1966. 240p.

Miller, Howard S. *The Legal Foundations of American Philanthropy, 1776–1844.* State Historical Society of Wisconsin, 1961. 71p.

Morison, Robert S. "Foundations and Universities." *Daedalus* 93:1109–41; 1964.

Morrisett, Lloyd N. "Foundations' Influence on Education." *Phi Delta Kappan* 46:442–6; 1965.

Orton, William A. "Endowments and Foundations." In *Encyclopaedia of the Social Science,* Vol. 5. Macmillan, 1931. p. 531.

Parker, F. "Private Foundations Have Aided Public Educational Innovation." *Teach Col J* 36:13–4; 1964.

Rioux, J. William. "A New Dimension in the Improvement of Education; Financial Support of Teacher Research." *Nat Assn Sec Sch Prin B* 46:18–22; 1962.

Rusk, Dean. "Building a Professional Staff." In Sellin, Henry. (Ed.) *Proceedings of the New York University Fifth Biennial Conference on Charitable Foundations.* Bender, 1961. p. 178–9.

Stat. 43. Elizabeth I, c. 4, 1601.

U.S. Congress, House of Representatives Select Committee on Small Business. "Tax-exempt Foundations and Charitable Trusts: Their Impact on Our Economy." 87th Congress, Second Session. Committee Print, 1962.

U.S. Congress, House of Representatives Select Committee on Small Business. *Subcommittee Chairman's Report to Subcommittee No. 1.* 88th Congress, First Session. Committee Print, 1963.

U.S. Congress, House of Representatives Select Committee on Small Business. *Hearings.* "Tax-exempt Foundations: Their Impact on Small Business." 88th Congress, Second Session. Committee Print, 1964.

U.S. Congress, House of Representatives Select Committee on Small Business. *Report.* 90th Congress, First Session. GPO, 1967.

U.S. Congress, House of Representatives Select Committee to Investigate and Study Educational and Philanthropic Foundations and Other Comparable Organizations Which Are Exempt from Federal Income Taxation. *Final Report.* House Report 2514. 82nd Congress, Second Session. GPO, 1953.

U.S. Congress, House of Representatives Special Committee to Investigate Tax-exempt Foundations and Comparable Organizations. *Report.* House Report 2681. 83rd Congress, Second Session. GPO, 1954.

U.S. Congress, Senate Commission on Industrial Relations. *Report and Testimony,* Vol. 1. 64th Congress, First Session. GPO, 1916. 1024p.

U.S. Congress, Senate Committee on Finance. *Final Report, Revenue Act of 1964.* Senate Report 830. 88th Congress, Second Session. GPO, 1964.

U.S. Congress, Senate Committee on Interstate and Foreign Commerce. *Report.* Senate Report 101. 81st Congress, First Session. GPO, 1949.

Vidal v. Girard's Executors. 2 Howard 127, 11L. Ed. 205. U.S. 1844.

Walton, Ann D., and Andrews, F. Emerson. (Eds.) *The Foundation Directory.* Russell Sage, 1960. 817p.

Walton, Ann D., and Lewis, Marianna O. (Eds.) *The Foundation Directory,* 2nd ed. Russell Sage, 1964. 1000p.

Woodring, Paul. "Ford Foundation and Teacher Education." *Teach Col Rec* 62:224–31; 1960.

GENERAL EDUCATION

Much of the semantic confusion which surrounds efforts to define general education dissolves in the light of even a brief historical account of its origins and development. For example, in ancient Greece and Rome men who were free and enjoyed modest means neither studied for nor practiced a vocation. Slaves, aliens, and the poor performed life's menial tasks; for the free man, education meant physical exercise, music, grammar, rhetoric, arithmetic, and reading and writing. At higher levels, e.g., the "schools" of Plato and Aristotle, education embraced almost the entire range of philosophy known to us today. And the ultimate goals were beauty, truth, and goodness, rather than profit, wealth, and success stemming from technical excellence. Closest to the practical was instruction in military tactics, a necessity for survival and part of the traditional role of the free man.

In the medieval universities the student interested in the utilitarian could study for a doctorate in law, medicine, or theology. At the undergraduate level, however, which terminated with the master's degree, he studied the trivium (grammar, rhetoric, and logic) and the quadrivium (arithmetic, music, geometry, and astronomy). The feudal lords were gentlemen who, if educated, had studied the liberal arts; they hunted, fought, and engaged in sports and entertainments. The serfs were the workers. Down through the first part of the nineteenth century, at Oxford and Cambridge and on the Continent, the view prevailed that general education was for the aristocrat and technical training was for the lower classes (H. Good, 1960).

AMERICAN BACKGROUND. When the colonial colleges were established in America (beginning with Harvard in 1636), they followed the example of Oxford and Cambridge, especially the latter, in creating curricula for an elite: Greek, Latin, some Hebrew, logic, religion, philosophy, and mathematics. Utilitarian training was available through apprenticeship. Even frontier hardships and prejudices could not prevail against the age-old belief that true education was liberal and general, not vocational (Rudolph, 1962).

By the time of the Revolutionary War there were nine colonial colleges, all dedicated to general-liberal education. As men moved westward, so did new colleges, in time hundreds of them, mostly established and maintained by Protestant denominations committed to the traditions of both medieval and colonial education.

Proponents of the Practical. Only a few men raised their voices against the limited and impractical character of the curriculum—a curriculum that lacked academic departments, courses in depth, and opportunities for specialization. Benjamin Franklin, Thomas Jefferson, George Ticknor at Harvard, a faculty group at Amherst, President Holley at Transylvania, President Lindsley at Nashville, and President Nott at Union were among the more vociferous spokesmen for a "parallel" course—not a substitute for the classical program but an alternative that would permit the study of modern languages, more mathematics, English, and the sciences.

The Yale Report. Those efforts, and others like

them, would eventually enjoy a sweeping triumph, but for the moment they went down to defeat before the powerful thrust of the Yale Faculty Report of 1828 (Brubacher & Rudy, 1958). In this famous report, a Yale faculty committee declared that the college had neither the time nor the facilities to teach vocational subjects. The purpose of a college education, it added, was to provide the "furniture" (factual knowledge) and discipline (judgment, memory, imagination, and habits of thought) of the mind. Like a room, the mind had to be filled; like a muscle, it required exercise. In its undivided support of general education, the report asks: "Is a man to have no other object, than to obtain a *living* by professional pursuits? Has he not duties to perform to his family, to his fellow citizens, to his country; duties which require various and extensive intellectual furniture?" It proved to be an eloquent, influential, and in some ways a reactionary document (Hofstadter & Smith, Vol. 1, 1961). The statement was not wholly reactionary, for it did advocate retention in the curriculum of enduring general and liberal goals. On the other hand, American historians, almost all of whom do label it reactionary, are no doubt right in that the report was out of harmony with the needs of the day, the desires of most students and prospective students, and the requirements of a rapidly changing society.

TRIUMPH OF THE PRACTICAL. The election to the presidency of Andrew Jackson in 1828 was an ironic symbol of a new day. The nation was becoming more democratic in spirit, increasingly industrial, technological, practical, urban. A visitor to the United States in 1830, Alexis de Tocqueville (n.d.), commented on the pragmatic character of the American people and their equalitarian spirit. More and more students and their parents demanded an education which was in some large measure vocational. Employers insisted that the colleges serve the nation by providing practical training. The demands were irresistible.

As early as 1802, West Point came into being as a military school with strong engineering concerns. In 1824, Rensselaer Polytechnic Institute, the first school of engineering, was founded. Efforts to establish a "parallel" course have already been described. Finally, the Ivy League succumbed; Harvard opened its Lawrence Scientific School and Yale its Sheffield Scientific School, both in 1847. Dartmouth followed with its Chandler School in 1851. In the 1850's, Brooklyn Polytechnic Institute and Cooper Union opened. And in 1855, what are now Michigan State University and Pennsylvania State University were created to offer instruction in agricultural and "mechanical" subjects. The new railroads, canals, highways, and factories had created a need both for technicians and for technically trained managerial personnel. As the nineteenth century advanced, the number of students pursuing a technical education rose sharply. With the opening of the Massachusetts Institute of Technology in 1861 and the passage of the Morrill Act in 1862, undergraduate training in agriculture, technical fields, and preprofessional and professional subjects won a permanent victory in American higher education. Home economics in all its branches, police administration, business administration, hotel administration, radio, television, acting, teacher preparation, advertising, the most practical of technical courses and the most sophisticated of engineering courses, urban planning, nursing, and a host of similar offerings appeared in the college catalogs of the nation. Indeed, the day would come when university catalogs might include majors in a hundred or more fields and courses running literally into the thousands.

The Morrill Act (Land Grant Act), signed by President Lincoln in 1862, is the most dramatic event in this parade of historical changes in higher education from the general-liberal to the utilitarian-vocational (Ross, 1942; Eddy, 1957; Kuhn, 1955). The act provided money through the sale of federal lands for the establishment of at least one college in every state "where the leading object shall be, without excluding other scientific and classical studies, and including military tactics, to teach such branches of learning as are related to agriculture and the mechanic arts . . . in order to promote the liberal and practical education of the industrial classes . . ." (Hofstadter & Smith, Vol. 2, 1961; Nevins, 1962). The day would arrive in the 1960's when these land-grant institutions would enroll close to one-fourth of all the undergraduates in the country and would award about 40 percent of all the doctorates.

If the effect of the Morrill Act was to diminish the significance of general education in favor of teaching and research in the "practical arts," the influence of the German universities on American higher education in the decades after the Civil War threatened the total demise of general-liberal studies at the undergraduate level. Indeed, it jeopardized the very existence of undergraduate education.

With their strong emphasis on academic freedom (Hofstadter & Metzger, 1955), the German universities left the student pretty much to his own devices, with optional attendance at lectures, an elective system, and the absence of examinations until the student presented himself for a degree. The university assumed that the student was now, after graduation from the gymnasium, liberally educated and mature enough to look after himself with no trace of the spirit of *in loco parentis*. Most important of all, the university was regarded as an institution where men learned to be highly trained specialists who would later do some teaching to other prospective specialists but whose primary values were related to original research, the graduate seminar, the laboratory, the learned monograph, the journals, and the conventions of their disciplines. There was no place for the kind of undergraduate liberal education which continued to form part of the undergraduate curriculum in the United States.

More than 9,000 Americans studied at German universities in the nineteenth century. Some of these students were destined to become very influential in American higher education, and, perhaps inevitably, they sought to import the values of the German universities and impose them on American universities. Such men were Eliot at Harvard, Gilman at Johns Hopkins, White at Cornell, Angell at Michigan, Hall at Clark, Folwell at Minnesota, and Harper at Chicago—all university presidents. While these men were by no means unanimous in their views, several of them declared that the American university should close its dormitories and abandon the philosophy of *in loco parentis;* that the nation's colleges should become two-year institutions, offering general studies and not attempting advanced work in special fields; that the universities should abandon liberal education entirely and become wholly graduate institutions on the model of the German university. A few attempts of this kind were made, but they failed. The American university remained a unique blending of English undergraduate values, indigenous concern for specialized undergraduate training, and graduate schools modeled after the German pattern. Nevertheless, as with the Morrill Act, so with the influence of the German universities: specialism at the undergraduate level was strengthened, the prestige of research was enhanced, and the study of the liberal arts lost more of its status (Brubacher & Rudy, 1958).

Although President Eliot at Harvard spoke often and eloquently about the importance of "general education" (a term he preferred to "liberal education"), it was his advocacy of the elective system which still further undermined undergraduate general education (Thomas, 1962; Hofstadter & Smith, Vol. 2, 1961). Under the elective system, developed gradually during Eliot's long tenure (1869–1909), a student could literally take any courses he wanted to. This could mean courses that did not meet too early in the morning or courses known to require relatively little work, etc. But, in practice, it usually meant excessive or even total specialization at the undergraduate level. A student who wished to specialize in mathematics could, if he chose to do so, spend the entire four-year undergraduate period of study without taking a single course in any subject other than mathematics. The combination of the elective system and German university influence produced in American universities (and also in most colleges) academic departments offering courses in depth so that an undergraduate could emerge as a specialist who would go directly into some form of work or who would pursue his specialty still further in a graduate or professional school.

NEED FOR GENERAL EDUCATION. The growing technical needs of an increasingly complex society, the demand by students, parents, and employers for specialists, the Morrill Act, the influence of the German universities, and the elective system— all combined to create among thoughtful observers the fear that education in America's colleges and universities would produce highly specialized men who wholly lacked the characteristics of true humanity, the special province of general education. These fears were heightened by constantly mounting enrollments of students whose background and family life failed to provide some of the more liberal influences that presumably characterized the homes of the earlier generations of students from upper-class families.

In the twentieth century, a series of reforms, introduced by different men in different institutions and in different ways, reasserted the basic primacy of general education, an education that would enable a man to be truly human before he became a specialist. These reforms are collectively known as the "general education movement," and it is more important than any other development—with the possible exception of the rise of the community junior college —in higher education in this century.

DEFINITION AND OBJECTIVES. As early as 1837, in *The American Scholar,* Emerson had declared that a man must first of all be a Man before he could be a good farmer or tradesman or engineer. Similar sentiments appear in the writings of Cardinal Newman and John Stuart Mill and in the Yale Report. In his inaugural address at the University of St. Andrews, Scotland, on February 1, 1867, Mill said:

> Men are men before they are lawyers, or physicians, or merchants, or manufacturers; and if you make them capable and sensible men, they will make themselves capable and sensible lawyers or physicians. What professional men should carry away with them from a University is not professional knowledge, but that which should direct the use of professional knowledge, and bring the light of general culture to illuminate the technicalities of a special pursuit. Men may be competent lawyers without general education, but it depends on general education to make them philosophic lawyers.

In his inaugural address at Amherst in 1912, Alexander Meiklejohn was more specific: every student must have a general education which includes a study of the Western heritage, especially the moral, aesthetic, and religious; the social and natural sciences; history; and literature (Hamilton & Blackman, 1955). Years later, at the University of Wisconsin, Meiklejohn (1932) established an experimental college with these objectives. General-education programs appeared at Columbia after World War I, at Chicago in the 1920's, at the General College of the University of Minnesota in 1932, at Stephens College, and at Colgate, St. John's, Harvard, and Michigan State universities and many other places. Without doubt the major impetus in the rapid spread of general education after World War II was a book called *General Education in a Free Society: Report of the Harvard Committee,* which appeared in 1946 (Harvard Committee, 1946). This book, along with Volume 1 of *Higher Education for American Democracy* (President's Commission . . ., 1947), transformed the nature of the controversy about general education. Hitherto it had seemed adequate to talk about general education as being that portion of a student's undergraduate program which lay outside his area of specialization. Meiklejohn had referred to specific goals in terms of the kinds of courses to be included.

Now, however, general education (which, as the *Harvard Report* put it, was a more acceptable term than "liberal education" because the latter had an elitist connotation) began to acquire more useful definitions. Specific objectives were spelled out. Although not always identical, they did have substantial similarities, and the influence of World War II, recently ended, was everywhere apparent in the emphasis on democracy, responsible citizenship, the dignity of man, and similar values.

The objectives offered in *Higher Education for American Democracy* were as widely accepted and as representative as any:

> Present college programs are not contributing adequately to the quality of students' lives either as workers or as citizens. This is true in large part because the unity of liberal education has been splintered by over-specialization. . . . Today's college graduate may have gained technical or professional training in one field of work or another, but is only incidentally, if at all, made ready for performing his duties as a man, a parent, and a citizen. . . . A society whose members lack a body of common experience and common knowledge is a society without a fundamental culture; it tends to disintegrate into a mere aggregation of individuals. Some community of values, ideas, and attitudes is essential as a cohesive force in this age of minute division of labor and intense conflict of special interests. The crucial task of higher education today, therefore, is to provide a unified general education for American youth. . . . "General education" is the term that has come to be accepted for those phases of nonspecialized and nonvocational learning which should be the common experience of all educated men and women. General education should give to the student the values, attitudes, knowledge, and skills that will equip him to live rightly and well in a free society. (President's Commission . . ., 1947, pp. 47–9)

The statement adds that general education should provide an understanding of one's cultural heritage, ethical values, scientific generalizations, and aesthetic conceptions, as well as insight into our social institutions. General education, the document goes on to say, differs from liberal education only in that it has greater interest in the contemporary, the relevant, the world around us. It does not lack interest in the past, but it uses the past only to the extent that it enlarges our knowledge of the present. A list of specific objectives follows these more general statements.

The objectives include the following: to develop a personal ethical code which is consistent with the ideals of democracy; to participate actively in the affairs of society at all levels; to understand other cultures and try to foster international peace; to understand common phenomena in the physical environment and especially the methods of the scientist; to be able to communicate effectively; to attain satisfactory emotional adjustment; to maintain one's own health; to understand and enjoy aesthetic experiences and to share in some creative activity; to have a satisfying family life; to select an occupation realistically; and to think critically. In other sources one may find these and additional objectives: to achieve synthesis; to learn broad concepts, basic terminology, and methods of thought in various disciplines; to achieve integration of knowledge; to explore different areas of learning; and to nurture intellectual curiosity (McGrath & others, 1948; McGrath & Russell, 1958; Thomas, 1962; Harvard Committee, 1946; Storing, 1966; Reese, 1965; Creegan, 1960; Arnstine, 1966; Havighurst, 1952; Lehmann & Dressel, 1962; McGrath, 1959; Nowell-Smith, 1961; Rice, 1962; Dressel, 1960b; Mayhew, 1960b; Cowley, 1960; Husain, 1959; Wimpey, 1961; Havens, 1960; Morgan, 1961; Lehmann, 1966).

GENERAL AND PROFESSIONAL EDUCATION. A series of monographs published by the Bureau of Publications, Teachers College, Columbia University, discusses fully the relationship between certain professional fields and general education: music (Wager & McGrath, 1962); business (Kephart & others, 1963); home economics (Lee & Dressel, 1963); service academies (Simons, 1965); social work (Aldridge & McGrath, 1965); journalism (Dressel, 1960a); nursing (Russell, 1959); engineering (Holstein & McGrath, 1960); and pharmacy (Newcomer & others, 1961).

There exists substantial agreement that an undergraduate program should provide for a balance between specialization and liberal-general education. Often the warning is added that demands by the specialists for more of a student's time should be resisted. And such professional groups as the National Council for Accreditation of Teacher Education and the American Chemical Society are criticized for seeking to invade the general-education portion of the student's time. (Articles advancing arguments of this kind appear frequently, and a few references should suffice: Norris, 1963; Fen, 1961; Stokes, 1961; Kurth, 1963; Parker, 1962; Butterweck, 1961; Stull, 1962; Hutchins, 1964; Swelgart, 1964; Brubacher, 1959; Maruyama, 1965; Holstein & McGrath, 1960).

Although the desirability of a balance between general and specialized education is widely acclaimed, some writers do not agree. Richards (1960) wrote a vehement and distorted reply to McGrath. Some regard education outside the major as a waste of time, as, "an egghead stranglehold," as a repetition of work already done in high school, as contemptible "solids," as superficial and pretentious courses, and as too easy, promoting conformity, obsolete, precious, trivial, and impractical; their cry is "let's get back to the elective system" (Wanous, 1960; Tonne, 1960a, 1960b; Adams, 1963; Weisinger, 1963; Buckler, 1965; Jones, 1966; Feibleman, 1961).

More constructive, and yet essentially futile, are efforts to distinguish between general and liberal education. The words have been used interchangeably by too many people over too long a period of time to lend themselves to useful distinction. In the last twenty years, *liberal* has become a more respectable word than *general* and is used to suggest study in depth within the traditional disciplines of arts and sciences—in contrast to one of the major aims of general education, which is to offer courses intended not as stepping-stones to more advanced courses in the same area but rather as courses complete in themselves for the student not planning to major in the particular field (Allen & others, 1959; Weisinger, 1963; Dressel, 1960b; Morse, 1964). As often as not, articles which seek to clarify the distinction between *general* and *liberal* contribute to additional confusion.

TYPES OF GENERAL EDUCATION. Almost all colleges and universities in the United States require a student to satisfy general-education requirements by taking introductory courses in certain fields, usually English, one or more in each of the humanities, the social sciences, the natural sciences, and physical education. At some schools there are additional requirements in religion or Bible, a foreign language, and mathematics. Supporters of this so-called system of distribution (taking introductory courses which are the same for the student who will go on to major in the field and the student who is simply satisfying a general-education requirement) call attention to the rigor and discipline and factual content of such courses. Those who prefer the so-called integrated courses (where material from several related disciplines is taught in a unified manner designed to acquaint the student with essential matters in a broad area of learning rather than to prepare him for the next course in a sequence leading to a major) feel that the integrated course is more successful in guarding against narrow and specialized introductions to traditional disciplines (Blackman, 1963b). The number of schools offering wholly integrated approaches is small. At most schools the student can exercise some choices. Catholic institutions usually have a substantial number of required liberal courses. Michigan State has a required common core of general-education courses now in a state of transition to permit some choices by the student (Carlin & Blackman, 1960). The College of Basic Studies at Boston University is another example of the use of the common core, including also a system of team teaching and personal counseling (LaFanci & Richter, 1964). At St. John's, although the term "general education" is not employed, the curriculum consists of virtually a common core centering on the reading and discussion of "great books." The Integrated Liberal Studies program at Wisconsin is yet another example of a required core limited to 300 entering freshmen a year.

At a few colleges, such as Bard, Bennington, and Stephens, there is a major emphasis on individual self-development (R. Johnson, 1947).

To these several devices for providing general and liberal education, one must add those of church-related colleges, which display a special concern for character building, spiritual development, and values (Hong, 1956; Pattillo & Mackenzie, 1966). In a very real sense, however, all general education has at least some concern with individual self-development.

Because of the frequency of change in programs and courses, nobody can be sure that descriptions of various college requirements are currently accurate. Yet the matter is not of large significance, for the principles involved are the major concern. One can learn a great deal, though somewhat tediously, through a study of general requirements as listed in institutional catalogs. In *The Search for a Common Learning*, Russell Thomas (1962), in addition to providing excellent introductory and concluding chapters, describes the general requirements at Amherst, Antioch, Berea, Brooklyn, Goucher, Louisville, Macalester, Michigan State, Mills, Minnesota, Notre Dame, Oregon, Reed, St. John's (Annapolis), Saint Xavier, San Francisco State, Stanford, and Washington State.

Obviously there is great variety; and, since pluralism is the unique characteristic of higher education in the United States, this fact should occasion no surprise. Nevertheless, those who seek to learn what general education is are understandably bewildered by the many different kinds of programs and courses denoted by the same term. Fortunately, despite the apparent confusion, there do exist some common principles and goals which underlie almost all varieties of general education. And fortunately, too, there are books and articles which offer detailed descriptions of individual courses. The books that follow, each published by the Wm. C. Brown Company, describe individual courses in general-education programs offered at a number of different schools. The names given are those of the editors: *Communication in General Education,* 18 schools, 5 prefatory chapters on composition (Shoemaker & Forsdale, 1960); *Social Science in General Education,* 20 schools, introductory chapter (Mayhew, 1960c); *The Humanities in General Education,* 16 schools, introductory and concluding chapters (Fisher, 1960); *Science in General Education,* 21 colleges and one high school, introductory chapter (Haun, 1960); *General Education for Personal Maturity,* 16 schools, prefatory chapters on personal maturity, marriage, and vocational selection (Morse & Dressel, 1960); and *The Larger Learning* (teaching values), 5 schools (Carpenter, 1960).

INDIVIDUAL COURSES. The most universal and the most controversial course in any general-education program is likely to be English composition or some variant of it. It may or may not include speech; it may or may not review traditional grammar or the newer linguistic methods; it may or may not involve reading a great deal of literature (Pooley, 1962; Stewart, 1967; Blackman, 1959, 1964; Crockett, 1964; J. Miller, 1965).

Almost universal and sometimes controversial is physical education. The subject seems neglected in the literature, but the usual problems are: Should physical education be required for one year or for two? Should these courses carry academic credit or not?

Social science can be taught through having students read original sources or secondary texts; with emphasis on the contemporary or by the historical method; using a problems approach; with the use of geography as an integrating principle; by including law as the integrating principle (Dentler, 1959; Phalan, 1963; Fuson, 1961; Senn, 1961; Walker, 1963; P. Smith, 1959).

The Western heritage is frequently taught in courses with such names as "humanities" and "Western civilization." Whether to stress or deemphasize history is one kind of problem, usually settled by deemphasis. Such a course may use historical and cultural texts or may rely mainly on original sources. Frequent ingredients are music, art, literature, philosophy, and religion. While most courses of this kind follow a chronological approach, there is strong minority sentiment for courses which stress aesthetic appreciation and a smaller minority that seeks to encourage student creativity through actual performance or composition (Nowell-Smith, 1961; Crockett, 1962; Lister, 1963; Weigle, 1966; Verhage, 1959; Hubbard, 1966; L. Good & others, 1960).

General education in science creates a number of very difficult problems. What kinds of courses can be successfully offered to students with very uneven backgrounds in science and mathematics? How can the student of the humanities bridge the gulf to the sciences with a single course or two? Should there be two courses, one in biological science and one in physical science, or a single integrated natural-science course? Should the prospective science major enroll in general science courses? Should the general science student engage in laboratory exercises, or should demonstration exercises (live or on film) be substituted? However any individual institution may respond to these questions, the ultimate goal of the general science course cannot, in our time, involve a large component of factual content. It must use carefully selected content to demonstrate what science is, how the scientist works, science as a particular form of intellectual activity, science as a form of aesthetic behavior, principles of induction and deduction, evidence and hypotheses and conclusions and laws, and science as an example of a particular kind of objectivity and of cumulative knowledge which is, nevertheless, always subject to correction (Morris, 1960; Shannon, 1960; Lawson, 1962; Sleeman, 1961; Arnold, 1961; Wallace, 1962; Graubard, 1960; Pelham, 1966). Since the launching of Sputnik I, those who write on general science stress the need for scientific information among the citizens of a democratic society.

Religion has played so important a role in history and thought that a study of it must clearly be included in a general education. A large number of tax-supported colleges and universities offer courses in religion as such, but more commonly the subject is approached through history or humanities courses. In the more than 800 private, church-related colleges in the country, the approach to the study of religion can obviously be more extensive and even, on occasion, less objective. The general requirements are likely to include one or more of the following: the life of Christ, the Bible, the history of Christianity, and (more rarely) comparative religion. The quality of instruction in religion in these church-related schools is usually less than first-rate. Textbooks are sometimes obsolete or biased; facts are stressed to the exclusion of large and valuable concepts about religion as a special form of mental activity; dogmatic assertions too often replace honest inquiry; and today's student often questions the relevance of the entire subject. The place of instruction in religion, including what and how much, is surprisingly controversial within church-related schools (Pattillo & Mackenzie, 1966; Hong, 1956; Hutchison, 1961; Michaelsen, 1961, 1966; Nielsen, 1961; Harshbarger, 1961; E. Good, 1961; H. Smith, 1960).

Mathematics is rarely included in general-education programs because the problems of uneven preparation among the students seem insuperable. Yet a few schools do try, and the subject is of obvious importance in a scientific age (Carlin, 1964; Carceso, 1967).

Whether the study of a foreign language should be a required part of a general education is a question so widely and often and vigorously discussed that it will be omitted here—except to say that general-education faculties usually oppose it unless the particular language can be defended as a "tool" for the major (in which case it is really not part of general education).

The argument for general courses dealing with problems in personal adjustment was regularly made during and immediately after World War II. Persuasive presentations of the need for such courses have been made, but in practice courses of this kind have almost universally fallen into disfavor and disappeared.

The need no longer exists to argue the importance of including the study of non-Western cultures in general-education programs. Those who continue to do so beat a dead horse, for few new courses have spread so rapidly in American higher education. The preferred term now—and it is a better one—is "intercultural courses." The difficulties involve finding faculty, the wisdom of the year abroad, whether to have separate courses or include other cultures within courses in the Western heritage, and whether to engage in sweeping world-views or focus on a limited area in depth (the latter has become the more widely accepted approach). These courses do more than satisfy the faculty feeling that one "ought" to offer them; they effectively engage the interest of the students who take them. Further extension seems inevitable (Fairbank, 1959; Nason, 1963; Weaver, 1962; Caldwell, 1963; deBary, 1964; I. Johnson, 1960, 1967; Carlin, 1964; Forster, 1963; Reed, 1965).

Dramatic presentations (both tragedy and comedy) go back to the fifth century B.C. During long periods of history, political or religious pressures have curtailed public presentation of the drama. Today, reading drama, especially tragedy, is so much a part of several general-education courses that no one needs to rise to its defense. The articles that do appear on this matter argue for the presentation of live drama instead of, or in addition to, reading plays. The clash of wills and the conflict of values may be more vivid when seen on stage, but it is an open question whether the reading of a play is less valuable. There is even some plea for a general-education course in the cinema (Chu, 1961; Wills, 1964; Heffner, 1964; Loney, 1964; Stevens, 1965).

Perhaps the most interesting and exciting of all general courses is the senior capstone course, an integrated course often called "great issues." Taught by a team of faculty members, it can deal with several issues, either old and unresolved or contemporary and critical. Such a course not only attracts faculty from several disciplines but also brings together at the senior level students from a variety of majors. With but a few exceptions, such courses have been extraordinarily successful (Blackman, 1963a).

These, then, are the courses most frequently included in a general-education program. It is often argued that courses in specialized or practical fields may be of substantial value—or may be taught in such a way as to be of substantial value—to the general education of the student. Proponents of general education accept this point of view but feel that in practice general values do not derive from specialized courses. On the other hand, many opponents of general education have argued that general courses can be so taught, and often are so taught, that they are little different from technical or introductory disciplinary courses. Neither side is wholly right or wrong.

EVALUATION. In his evaluation of a professor wholly devoted to general education, an administrator is likely to give less weight to a man's research in his discipline than is usually the case and more weight to successful teaching, development of course materials, committee work, and research in teaching problems. Nevertheless, there is recent evidence to indicate that a general-education faculty can publish extensively, both on educational matters and within the traditional disciplines (Inge, 1966).

In evaluating student achievement in a general-education course, the test writer will try to test for the ability to see relationships, understand concepts, make significant comparisons, and perceive value implications—rather than to test exclusively for factual knowledge. Yet faculty often complain that tests measure factual content excessively and fail to evaluate the alleged outcomes of general education. While this may be true of final examinations, other testing techniques have been used with students who have completed a course or a program, with seniors, and with alumni.

Some interesting techniques by which a college and its "climate" may be evaluated have been developed by Astin (1965).

Studies have been made of personality changes (Plant, 1962); of critical thinking, attitudes, and values (Lehmann & Dressel, 1962; U.S. Department of Health, Education, and Welfare, 1961); of character changes (Sanford, 1964); of the general way of life of alumni (Pace, 1941; Havemann & West, 1952); of changing values (Dressel, 1965)—including a study of changing values measured by objective instrumentation which is statistically sound and which refutes much of the Jacob (1957) book (Lehmann, 1966); and of developing creativity (Anderson, 1964). Studies have also been done comparing the significance of changes stemming from class experiences with those resulting from the influence of peers, extracurricular activities, and the faculty culture (Keeton, 1961); determining objectively what subjects best contribute to critical thinking (Kazamias, 1960); evaluating the extent of achievement of general objectives through institutional examination (Blackman, 1964); and of evaluation in a total general-education program in one school (Dressel, 1958). The American Council on Education has sponsored a famous study of evaluation in general education (Dressel & Mayhew, 1954).

Few would now doubt that evaluation of programs and the extent to which students achieve objectives can be objectively measured. Students do move, from their freshman through their senior years, in desirable directions toward general-education goals. A major recent study confirms these findings (Nichols, 1967). But the distance traversed seems to some critics, mentioned earlier, to be tragically small. Anyone who studies the 11 "objectives of general education," as they appear in the 1947 *Report of the President's Commission,* together with the introductory paragraphs to Chapter 3 of that book (President's Commission . . ., 1947), must see that they are impossibly utopian and that they render general education open to the charge of failing to perform the impossible. No single set of courses can make a man ethical and democratic, informed and responsible, a seeker of international peace, a student of his physical environment, a master of effective communication, emotionally and socially adjusted, healthy himself and a contributor to the health of the community, a lover of the arts, a creator, a happy husband and father, cheerful in his vocation, and a critical and constructive thinker. These are lofty goals, and general courses do make some efforts in these directions with a modicum of success. But they can no more meet these utopian goals by a few courses than a Christian can achieve the ethical requirements of the Sermon on the Mount by studying its words carefully and passing an examination on them.

Thus, it is not unfair to say that general education has seriously damaged its own cause by making wholly unrealistic claims for itself, most of these claims growing out of the heightened enthusiasm felt after World War II.

JOURNALS. Almost all of the journals devoted to higher education carry occasional articles on general education. Two journals, however, are almost exclusively concerned with general education: the *University College Quarterly,* published at Michigan State University by the University College, and the *Journal of General Education,* the official journal of the Association for General and Liberal Studies, published at Pennsylvania State University.

SOCIETIES. Although several groups of educators give time in their meetings to discussions of general education, there are only two societies which are exclusively devoted to this purpose: the Association for General and Liberal Studies and the National Committee on General Education (whose name was recently changed to the Committee on Undergraduate Education) of the American Association for Higher Education.

ACCREDITATION. Accrediting agencies require that a school offer a general-education program before it can be accredited. The North Central Association, one of the six regional agencies, defines general education as signifying "acquaintance with the major areas of knowledge. . . ." It "implies possession of the facts in such areas and some proficiency in the modes of thought involved in understanding such facts. . . . It excludes definite vocational preparation." The agency does not say how these requirements are to be satisfied or how much time is to be devoted to them (Blackman, 1963a). A survey reveals that the total number of semester hours of general education required for the bachelor's degree varies from 35 to 67, with the average being 52 (Walker, 1961). As for the method of providing general education, by far the most common pattern is to ask the student to take one or more introductory courses in each of the three major areas of liberal education: the humanities, the social sciences, and the natural sciences. Since some faculties feel that a single course in, say, sociology does not provide adequate general education in the social sciences, they require a certain number of hours of sociology and psychology and economics—or some such combination—to provide the desired breadth. A few faculties, preferring to distinguish a general course for the nonmajor from the introductory course for the major, have created specially designed general courses, often integrated.

COMMUNITY JUNIOR COLLEGE. Administrators and faculties of community junior colleges are increasingly introducing and developing general education programs in their two-year institutions. The two major problems seem to be (1) what kind of general courses should be offered and (2) whether "transfer" students and "technical-terminal" students should be enrolled in the same general courses. One writer calls for courses which deal with the contemporary, are rigorous, but aim at self-development rather than factual content (Nall, 1962). Another recommends the same program for all students (Morse, 1965). The list of objectives developed by the California Study of General Education in the Junior College is held to be good but too long (B. Johnson, 1960); actually, it is the same long, impossible, utopian list referred to earlier. All community-college students should take general-education courses, but the humanities should not be excluded, as they almost universally are now (Zimmerman, 1966).

INSTRUCTIONAL PROBLEMS. General-education programs confront several instructional problems that the other departments do not have to contend with. For example, most young men with new Ph.D.'s prefer the seemingly greater rewards of advanced teaching and research to the extra work and lack of status in teaching a general-education course (McGrath, 1959). Yet, despite the almost complete absence of interdisciplinary Ph.D.'s, the specialist can learn to become a good generalist if he will (Bash & Sio, 1964). The "secret" of transforming the specialist into a good generalist lies in "in-service" activities in which men trained in different disciplines pool their knowledge and skills. Because general courses are often unconventional in their structure and use of materials, the use of commercial books on the market is sometimes impossible, and a department must prepare its own books and manuals (Mayhew, 1960b).

Because of the rapid growth of knowledge, changing world conditions, and a new student insistence on the current and the relevant, general courses often redefine their goals and revise their materials with unseemly frequency. While some may jest at this, the fact is that general education, by its nature, cannot do otherwise (Buckler, 1965; Carlin & Blackman, 1960).

In addition to problems of faculty recruitment, in-service training, preparation of new materials, and frequent revisions, there are added burdens of larger classes, lower status, unusually long hours of preparation, and the survival within general education of the belief, almost defunct elsewhere in the large university, that a professor should be available to students a reasonable number of hours each week.

IMPORTANT ISSUES. Most of the important issues have been debated endlessly for more than 20 years, yet a few new ones have appeared. Among the older ones are such questions as these: (1) Should general courses be integrated? The answer seems to be that they should, but the work involved is excessive and the results difficult to assess (Winthrop, 1963; DeVane, 1964; Carpenter, 1964). (2) Should a general-education program in a large university have its own dean, a separate faculty, a budget of its own, and a high degree of autonomy? While some universities have settled for compromise solutions of one kind or another, there is a recent development of "university colleges" to provide a central and separate administrative unit for the general-education offerings. The larger the institution is, the more appropriate this kind of arrangement becomes. On the other hand, some have argued bitterly that when a man joins a separate faculty of general education, he loses his ties to his discipline, fails to keep up with new developments in his field, abandons research, and pursues a second-rate academic career. (3) Should general education be limited to the first two years of college or spread out over the full four years? On this issue at least there is growing agreement: general education should be spread over the full four years, taking less of a student's time each succeeding year as he becomes more deeply involved in his major field (Thomas, 1963; Blackman, 1963a; Coles, 1963; Perkins, 1967). (4) Are general courses primarily ends in themselves or introductions to further work in a given field? The practical answer is that though they are intended to be ends in themselves, they do serve at most schools as introductory courses. (5) Should the student take a required core of general courses or be permitted to make some choices? The consensus, despite the cohesive values of the required core, is overwhelmingly on the side of student election.

A new issue has to do with the wisdom of establishing a degree in general education, without requirement of a major field, and making the degree available to adults. So far only a few schools have moved in this direction, but they may well establish a trend. The University of Oklahoma pioneered in 1951 in creating the degree of Bachelor of Liberal Studies for adults studying general courses, all integrated. A great deal of independent study is demanded, along with some very intensive on-campus study (Burkett, 1965; Burkett & Ruggiers, 1965). Although only some 1,000 adults are enrolled nationally, the demand is much greater than the willingness of the colleges and universities to respond to an important social need. The Goddard College program is similar to the one at Oklahoma, but probably less structured. Other programs, not all in general education but all for adults, are at Brooklyn and Queens colleges and Syracuse, New York, and Johns Hopkins universities (Liveright, 1964).

CURRENT TRENDS. The most important current trend, in progress now for several years, is toward a change in some basic assumptions about general education. To the extent that happy adjustment, satisfactory family life, wise vocational choice, active citizenship, and even critical thinking and creativity remain goals, they have become hoped-for results and byproducts of courses which, taken collectively, constitute a somewhat truncated and current version of the Yale Report of 1828. In short, general education has become, at almost all American colleges and universities, an intellectual experience, looking to a certain fundamental understanding and awareness in the major divisions of learning, especially for the nonmajor (Mayhew, 1960b). There are at least two reasons for this development. One is that the older objectives of general education, as indicated earlier, were impossible to achieve, in general courses or special courses, in formal or informal education, in the school, the home, the church, or wherever. No social process known to man, educational or otherwise, could produce such supermen. Since general education constitutes only a portion of a student's education in school, which in turn constitutes only a small portion of his total learning, it was extremely naïve to believe that it could really meet the goals assigned to it. The second reason for the change in general education from the primarily student-centered to the primarily content-centered course is that some of the old *liberal arts* disciplines have themselves become so highly specialized at the undergraduate level that they scarcely differ at all from the *professional* undergraduate majors and are not very hospitable to the enrollment of nonmajors. Only a very few schools still retain the older student-centered approach.

Another "current trend," developing gradually during the years following Sputnik I, is the alleged strengthening of the high school curriculum (Goodlad & others, 1966). I use the word "alleged" because, even though students now take more mathematics and science than before Sputnik I, and even though such new courses as psychology and economics have been introduced here and there, one may seriously question the value and rigor of these courses. Too many students who have studied a science in high school find that they cannot pass the next course in the sequence in college and must retreat to the first course. Too many students who have studied a foreign language in high school are unable to continue in college at the point where they presumably left off in high school. Courses in psychology, economics, and nonhistorical social sciences in high school are so elementary and superficial that the student who wishes to pursue the same field in college must usually begin with the most elementary college course instead of being able to build upon his high school learning.

Nevertheless, the belief (or myth) prevails in some quarters that high school students are now fairly well educated in general studies by the time they reach college. A few writers even suggest that they are so fully educated in general studies that they should spend the entire four-year undergraduate period in intensive specialization (Goodlad & others, 1966; Tonne, 1960a; Adams, 1963; Feibleman, 1961). It is true, of course, that in some universities a great many students enter with advanced-placement credits, often enough credits to make them sophomores on entrance (College Entrance Examination Board. 1956; Valley, 1964). In a famous observation, Barzun (1964) asserted that the demand for early and intensive specialization in the undergraduate years would eliminate general-liberal education.

Barzun went further, for he described not only the pressure from the high schools, which presumably completed a student's general education before he arrived at college, but also the downward pressure from the graduate schools, demanding ever more specialization among undergraduates (McGrath, 1959). Given this double threat—adequate general education in the high school and pressure from the graduate school for intensive specialization at the undergraduate level—the result could only be the demise of the liberal arts college. And it was precisely this which Barzun anticipated.

Although many authors stress the need for changes in general education, the overwhelming sentiment of those who write on the subject is that the pressure from the graduate school has been greatly exaggerated (grades are more important than the number of courses completed in a specialty) and that the improved high school curriculum—most writers do believe that it is improved—offers no threat to general education but rather a challenge to do better, more advanced, more exciting work (Shannon, 1960; Nowell-Smith, 1961; Horn, 1964; Carlin, 1964; Senkier, 1961; Newcomer, 1959; Sister Mary Sarah, 1960; Russell, 1959; Truman, 1964; DeVane, 1964).

Ironically, the next "current trend" concerns the

rise of general education in recent years in countries outside the United States. This trend, together with the previous one, suggests perhaps that higher education in the United States and that in other countries are moving toward, rather than away from, each other in their nonvocational goals. Studies were done on England (Nowell-Smith, 1961; *Times Educational Supplement*, 1961; Hallward, 1960; Loney, 1964; Kazamias, 1960); England, France, Italy, Germany, and Australia (Burn, 1964); Central America (Hatch, 1964); India (Webster, 1965); Nigeria (Zerby, 1965); Bombay (Patel, 1962); and England, France, Germany, the United States, and communist countries (Lauwerys & others, 1965).

A few other current trends have been discussed in detail earlier in this article and will be simply mentioned here: (1) the development of intercultural courses; (2) adult programs in general education leading to a degree; (3) the growth of general education in community junior colleges for both the student who plans subsequently to transfer to a four-year college and the student pursuing a two-year technical course which will be terminal; and (4) the slowly growing number of "university colleges," which assume the responsibility for instruction in general-education courses within large universities—a development which enables traditional colleges of arts and sciences to treat all their courses, including the introductory ones, as if they were designed for the prospective specialist.

The "New" Student. The final item is hardly a current trend, for it is still in the discussion stage among faculties and has been translated in only a few places into actual courses; yet there can be little doubt that in a very short time indeed, stimulated in part by the rise of the so-called free universities, this matter will become a current trend of considerable importance and unpredictable significance. The matter is that of student demands for courses which are contemporary, relevant, ungraded, or uninhibited. Open and candid discussion of such matters as sex, drugs, abortion, and the like will find their way into the general-education curriculum, not as credit courses, but within appropriate educational contexts. However, such matters as urban problems, civil rights, the war in Vietnam, and American obligations in remote corners of the world, the role of the police in a democracy, individual rights as defined by the Supreme Court, student rights within the college and university setting, the cult of youth (with its music, slang, values, and dress), the feeling of alienation from which many students say they suffer, the search for identity in which many students say they are engaged, the overriding faults of the "Establishment," which many students say they find intolerable, and the search for meaning in such activities as Vista and the Peace Corps and various poverty programs —these and many similar topics may well loom large in the regular curriculum, not necessarily treated as isolated problems but studied within some larger and perhaps more conventional framework. Curriculum planners in general education will avoid these demands at their own risk, a serious risk of loss of interest and boredom on the part of students, for the gulf that divides the faculty generation from the student generation is about the same as that which divides the generation of the parents from that of the students. And, for reasons we do not yet fully understand, that gulf is far wider than the one which normally separates one generation from another (Glazer, 1967; Gustad, 1966; Goldberg, 1967; Brammer, 1967; Weiss, 1967; Freedman, 1965; Williamson & Cowan, 1965; Ferdinand, 1965; Dennis & Kauffman, 1966; Muscatine & others, 1966). Some deplore student activism and favor a "hard" line (Brickman, 1967). Others would like to see a public relations policy that would "explain" some of the activism to an apprehensive generation of parents (Steinberg, 1966). Carl Davidson of Students for a Democratic Society would like to see a system of student syndicalism, something that comes close to control of the university by its students (1967). And many others have recently published articles on the "new student" (Cutler, 1966; Ratterman, 1966; Stanton, 1966; Tigar, 1966; Stern, 1966).

While nobody really knows what all this means, it is clear that general courses, because of their inherent nature and because they normally come early in the student's career, will be the first to feel the pressure for change—as, indeed, many already have. The pressure includes these items, some of them mentioned before and a few of them not specifically tied to general education: the virtual abandonment of parietal regulations; elimination or radical modification of grading systems; student rating of courses and instructors in published handbooks; student participation on almost all faculty committees; more-powerful student governments; the use of the sit-in and similar techniques to win one's goals; the politics of confrontation and ultimatum and deadline; and a substantial student voice in curriculum so that courses will be, as the students say, more relevant, more useful in the search for self-identity, and more helpful in resolving feelings of alienation. While many of these words and ideas have already, in a few short years, become platitudinous, they do portend large changes in institutional governance. And most of these factors will influence general education first of all—although no part of a college or university will be untouched by them. In general, so far at least, the larger the institution, the more insistent the pressures.

REASSESSMENTS. Because general education seems to some faculty to be new and unusual, it has always been subjected to a great deal of scrutiny and evaluation. And these frequent evaluations and reassessments have, in turn, produced frequent course revisions—all of which have been time-consuming but wholesome. Some reassessments are probably far less novel than their authors imagine (Hock, 1964; Winthrop, 1963a; Lonsway, 1967; Mayhew, 1960a, 1965a). Fresh reassessments are made by DeVane (1965), though his focus is limited to the Ivy League, and by Daniel Bell (1966). Although the Bell book is restricted in its scope to Columbia, Chicago, and

Harvard, especially the first of these, it makes valuable observations about all of general education, and it has stimulated considerable discussion among people occupied with general-education curricula. Bell, a sociologist, is a member of a Columbia University committee reexamining the place of general education in Columbia College. However, what appears in this book is not a committee report but the observations and reflections of one man, the author.

In what has been described as "the first comprehensive examination of general education in over twenty years," Bell rejects the Barzun thesis that the high schools are now teaching the general-education materials once part of the college curriculum or that the graduate schools are insisting on ever-narrower and earlier specialization, thus destroying, both from above and below, the old general-liberal arts we once knew. Before he embarks on new material, Bell reiterates the basic definitions of general education: ". . . the distinctive function of the college must be to teach modes of conceptualization, explanation, and verification of knowledge . . . not *what* one knows but *how* one knows. . . . The college can be the unique place where students acquire self-consciousness, historical consciousness, and methodological consciousness."

Bell reemphasizes what many students of higher education have previously observed: (1) the prestige of research has increased the power of the graduate school at the expense of the undergraduate college; (2) professors at major universities now play so many roles and are so busy that they have no time for general-education courses; (3) younger faculty are eager to become involved in their specialties and in research, for they know where the rewards are, and they regard instruction in a general-education course as unrewarding; (4) advanced-placement programs are successful in special high school environments for students who mostly go to elitist colleges; in any event, the results of advanced placement do not in any serious way affect the Columbia general-education program (Bell, 1966). There are two final critical points in connection with the high school: (5) a bright student can take an accelerated program in mathematics and science, but should he do so in Plato and Aeschylus? (6) An adolescent needs time to grow. Erode general education and you rob him of this precious time.

Bell's statement of the purposes of general education is limited to six items and is free of the utopian implications of other famous statements: (1) to overcome intellectual provincialism; (2) to appreciate the centrality of method (i.e., the role of conceptual innovation); (3) to gain an awareness of history; (4) to show how ideas relate to social structures; (5) to understand the way values infuse all inquiry; (6) to demonstrate the civilizing role of the humanities. Each of the six is discussed in some detail, in far too much detail for the needs of any intelligent reader, and the style is sufficiently ponderous to discourage even the eager. Somewhat novel is his rejection of the dichotomy between the general and the specialized. In both cases, the emphasis is on conceptual inquiry, and neither can do its proper job without the help of the other. The new use of multiple tracks for introductory courses taken by students with different motives will surely be imitated elsewhere.

Bell's own proposal for change includes "the first year as the acquisition of necessary historical and background knowledge, the second and third years as the training in a discipline . . . and the fourth year as a combination of seminar work in the discipline and participation in integrative courses"—courses which he labels "third tier" and which are offered in the sciences, the social sciences, and the humanities. Not all students would take the same third-tier courses; they would choose one of them on the basis of their major field. The third-tier courses appear to be a final philosophical analysis of the major, tying together the work of the whole four years to the extent that the work relates to the major in some way. There would be a fourfold offering of third-tier courses, one of which would emphasize non-Western cultures.

Proponents of general education will welcome this strong and informed voice in behalf of their ideals and the reaffirmation of the value of the integrative course in general education. However, the plan will be most useful in schools where the students are very bright, where the demands for undergraduate concentration are light, and where the distinction between liberal and general education is regarded as insignificant as long as the student achieves the goals of nonvocational learning.

BIBLIOGRAPHIES. In addition to the extensive bibliography which appears at the end of this article, there are several other places where the interested reader can find first-rate, long, detailed bibliographical lists. Among the most valuable are works by the following authors: Mayhew (1965b, 1966), Charles (1965), Cooper and others (1960), deBary (1964), Morehouse (1960), Brubacher (1959), Morse (1964), and Meeth (1965).

No danger exists that general education will be abandoned in the years ahead, for few colleges are likely to turn over their four undergraduate years to total specialization. Moreover, accrediting agencies would not permit that to happen. Nor would most students or parents or employers desire such a change. The American pattern seems overwhelmingly to be (1) a certain number of courses for a major, (2) a certain number of courses which are elective (but frequently prescribed or limited in some way), and (3) a certain number of general-education courses. The large disputes are likely to continue to center on such matters as how many general-education courses, how organized (distributive or integrative), how administered (separate faculty and dean or not), and how taught (who prepares the curriculum).

Prophecy may have scant value in an academic area as volatile as general education. But some things seem destined to happen. The church-related school, seeking to define or redefine its mission in terms of community spirit and common goals, is beginning to look more kindly than ever before at the required core for all students. And it is also, as resources shrink, contemplating large, integrated courses, especially at the freshman level, a move that the late Beardsley Ruml would have applauded.

Most faculty members know that a single introductory course in one broad area of learning is not general education—even though it may be a good way of keeping graduate students employed. That the common distributive pattern should ultimately give way to a series of integrated courses seems inevitable.

Finally, the explosion of knowledge and the rate at which knowledge becomes obsolete will compel professors, in specialized courses as well as in general courses, to be extremely selective in the choice of factual content and, instead of trying to convey an ever-larger body of encyclopedic information, to stress, in Bell's words (1966), "a more liberal conception of specialization itself, one that emphasizes not the specific subject, or the training for a concrete task, but the grasp of a discipline and the grounding in method." "Only in this fashion can a man relate the particular task to the general intellectual field and thus acquire sufficient agility of mind and mobility of skills to move from problem to problem in the unfolding development of knowledge itself. . . . In fact, I do not think that the distinction between general education and specialism really holds. The common bond of the two is the emphasis on conceptual inquiry" (Bell, 1966). Bell comes very close here to saying that undergraduate education, all of it, even that part of it which is somewhat specialized, is and must be general. These may be the most prophetic words of all.

Edward B. Blackman
Michigan State University

References

Adams, Mollie. "Liberal Studies in Technological Education." *U Q* 17:274–85; 1963.
Aldridge, Gordon J., and McGrath, Earl J. *Liberal Education and Social Work.* Teachers Col, Columbia U, 1965. 102p.
Allen, Lucille, and others. "Nature and Functions of Higher Education." *Col U* 1:29–32; 1959.
Anderson, Harold H. "Creativity and Education." In Rice, James G. (Ed.) *General Education: Current Ideas and Concerns.* Association for Higher Education and NEA, 1964. p. 86
Arnold, Luther A. "Some Phases of Research in the Development of a General Education College Chemistry Course." *Sci Ed* 45:443–9; 1961.
Arnstine, Donald. "The Aesthetic as a Context for General Education." *Stud Art Ed* 8:13–22; 1966.
Astin, Alexander W. *Who Goes Where to College?* SRA, 1965. 125p.
Barzun, Jacques. "College to University—and After." *Am Scholar* 30:212–20; 1964.
Bash, Wendell H., and Sio, Arnold A. "The Preparation of Teachers for General Education." *Col U B* 16:2,5–6; 1964.
Bell, Daniel. *The Reforming of General Education.* Columbia U Press, 1966. 312p.
Blackman, Edward B. "American Studies in the Freshman English Course." *Am Stud* 6:1–2; 1959.
Blackman, Edward B. "Accreditation and General Education." *North Cen Assn Q* 37:303–6; 1963(*a*).
Blackman, Edward B. "On Method: Sequence and Source in Curriculum." *U Col Q* 8:27–9; 1963(*b*).
Blackman, Edward B. "Lay Readers in 13th Grade English." *Improving Col U Teach* 12:243–5; 1964.
Brammer, Lawrence M. "The Student Rebel in the University." *J H Ed* 38:257–63; 1967.
Brickman, William W. "Activism Among College Students." *Sch Soc* 95:4; 1967.
Brubacher, John S. "Should Liberal Education Bake Bread?" *Liberal Ed* 45:532–47; 1959.
Brubacher, John S., and Rudy, Willis. *Higher Education in Transition, An American History: 1636–1956.* Harper, 1958. 390p.
Buckler, William E. "Challenge to Liberal Education." *U Col Q* 10:15–22; 1965.
Burkett, J. E. "Curriculum Leading to the Bachelor of Liberal Studies Degree." *Ed Rec* 46:195–203; 1965.
Burkett, J. E., and Ruggiers, Paul G. (Eds.) *Bachelor of Liberal Studies: Development of a Curriculum at the University of Oklahoma.* Center for the Study of Liberal Education for Adults, 1965. 107p.
Burn, Barbara B. "At What Level a General Education: A Comparative View." *Liberal Ed* 50:328–34; 1964.
Butterweck, Joseph S. "Post-baccalaureate Program in General Education." *Liberal Ed* 47:483–91; 1961.
Caldwell, Oliver J. "Liberal Arts in a Revolutionary World." *H Ed* 19:3–6; 1963.
Carceso, George E. "A Terminal Mathematics Course." *Improving Col U Teaching.* 15:88–91; 1967.
Carlin, Edward A. "General Education for the Future." In Rice, James G. (Ed.) *General Education: Current Ideas and Concerns.* Association for Higher Education and NEA, 1964. 86p.
Carlin, Edward A., and Blackman, Edward B. (Eds.) *Curriculum Building in General Education.* Brown, 1960. 133p.
Carpenter, Marjorie. (Ed.) *The Larger Learning: Teaching Values to College Students.* Brown, 1960. 788p.
Carpenter, Marjorie. "Depth: Third Dimension in Learning." In Rice, James G. (Ed.) *General Education: Current Ideas and Concerns.* Association for Higher Education and NEA, 1964. 86p.
Charles, Norman. "College Curriculum: An Annotated Bibliography of Recent Literature; General and Liberal Education." *Ed Rec* 46:447–51; 1965.
Chu, Yu-Kuang, "Liberal Education for Women in Our Times." *Liberal Ed* 47:497–509; 1961.
Coles, James S. "General Education for College Seniors." *Sch Soc* 91:302; 1963.

College Entrance Examination Board. *Advanced Placement Program.* CEEB, 1956. 135p.

Cooper, Russell M., and others. "Educational Program: General and Liberal Education." *R Ed Res* 30:334–6; 1960.

Cowley, W. H. "Three Curricular Conflicts." *Liberal Ed* 46:467–83; 1960.

Creegan, Robert F. "Decision Centered Education." *Sch Soc* 88:52–3; 1960.

Crockett, H. Kelly. "Use of the Novel for General Education." *J Gen Ed* 14: 56–68; 1962.

Crockett, H. Kelly. "Some Oil for Troubled Waters." *U Col Q* 9:24–9; 1964.

Cutler, Richard L. "The New Role of the Student in the Academic Society." In Smith, Kerry. (Ed.) *Current Trends in Higher Education.* Association for Higher Education, 1966. p. 154–7.

Davidson, Carl. "University Reform Revisited." *Ed Rec* 48:5–10; 1967.

deBary, William Theodore. "Education for a World Community." *Liberal Ed* 50:437–57; 1964.

Dennis, Lawrence E., and Kauffman, Joseph. (Eds.) *The College and the Student.* ACE, 1966. 390p.

Dentler, Robert A. "General Education in Social Science; A Small Liberal Arts College Program." *J Gen Ed* 12:113–8; 1959.

DeVane, William C. "Time and Place for Liberal Education." *Liberal Ed* 50:198–212; 1964.

DeVane, William C. *Higher Education in Twentieth Century America.* Harvard U Press, 1965. 181p.

Dressel, Paul L. (Ed.) *Evaluation in the Basic College at Michigan State.* Harper, 1958. 241p.

Dressel, Paul L. *Liberal Education and Journalism.* Teachers Col, Columbia U, 1960(a). 102p.

Dressel, Paul L. "What Should be the Content of the Liberal Arts Curriculum?" In *Current Issues in Higher Education.* National Conference on Higher Education, 1960(b). p. 62–6.

Dressel, Paul L. "Factors Involved in Changing the Values of College Students." *Ed Rec* 46:104–13; 1965.

Dressel, Paul L. "Content of the Liberal Arts." *U Col Q* 6:19–24; 1966.

Dressel, Paul, and Mayhew, Lewis B. *General Education: Explorations in Evaluation.* ACE, 1954. 302p.

Eddy, Edward. *Colleges for Our Land and Time.* Harper, 1957. 328p.

Fairbank, John K. "East Asia in General Education: Philosophy and Practice." *J Gen Ed* 12:100–3; 1959.

Feibleman, James K. "Well-rounded Graduate." *J Ed Sociol* 34:417–21; 1961.

Fen, Sing-Nan. "Vocational and Liberal Education: An Integrated Approach." *Sch R* 2:206–15; 1961.

Ferdinand, Theodore N. "The Academic Malaise." *J H Ed* 36:435–42; 1965.

Fisher, James. (Ed.) *The Humanities in General Education.* Brown, 1960. 258p.

Forster, Kent. "Pragmatic Program in General Education; The Penn State Course in International Understanding." *J H Ed* 34:371–8; 1963.

Freedman, Mervin B. "College Students Under Pressure." *J Gen Ed* 17:85–90; 1965.

Fuson, Robert H. "Geography and General Education." *J Geog* 60:422–7; 1961.

Glazer, Penina M. "The New Left." *J H Ed* 38:119–30; 1967.

Goldberg, Maxwell. "The Humanities and the Alienated Adolescent." *Sch Soc* 95:257–61; 1967.

Good, Edwin M. "Purpose of Religious Studies in General Education." *J Gen Ed* 13:180–93; 1961.

Good, H. E. *A History of Western Education.* Macmillan, 1960. 606p.

Good, Leonard, and others. "What Is General Education's Responsibility for Creativity in the Language Arts and the Humanities?" In *Current Issues in Higher Education.* National Conference on Higher Education, 1960. p. 103–14.

Goodlad, John J., and others. *The Changing School Curriculum.* Fund for the Advancement of Education, 1966. 114p.

Gordon, Robert A., and Howell, James E. *Higher Education for Business.* Ford Foundation Report. Columbia U Press, 1959. 474p.

Graubard, Mark. "Teaching of Science in a Liberal Arts Program." *Sci Ed* 44:187–94; 1960.

Gustad, John W. "Community, Consensus, and Conflict." *Ed Rec* 47:439–51; 1966.

Hallward, B. L. "General Degrees: Liberal Arts at Nottingham." *Times Ed Supplement* 2377:809; 1960.

Hamilton, Thomas, and Blackman, Edward. (Eds.) *The Basic College of Michigan State.* Michigan State U Press, 1955. 122p.

Harshbarger, Luther H. "Role of Religious Studies in General Education." *J Gen Ed* 13:169–79; 1961.

Harvard Committee. *General Education in a Free Society.* Harvard U Press, 1946. 267p.

Hatch, W. R. "General Education and University Reform." *Improving Col U Teach* 12:134–50; 1964.

Haun, Robert R. (Ed.) *Science in General Education.* Brown, 1960. 291p.

Havemann, Ernest, and West, Patricia S. *They Went to College.* Harcourt, 1952. 277p.

Havens, Joseph. "Counselor's View of Liberal Education." *Liberal Ed* 46:318–30; 1960.

Havighurst, Robert J. "Social Foundations of General Education." In *General Education,* 51st Yearbook, NSSE. U Chicago Press, 1952. p. 71–96.

Heffner, Hubert C. "Theatre and Drama in Liberal Education." *Teach Col Rec* 65:311–7; 1964.

Hock, Louise E. "New Conception of General Education." *Ed Leadership* 21:243–7; 1964.

Hofstadter, Richard, and Hardy, G. DeWitt. *The Development and Scope of Higher Education in the United States.* Columbia U Press, 1952. 239p.

Hofstadter, Richard, and Metzger, Walter P. *The Development of Academic Freedom in the United States.* Columbia U Press, 1955. 506p.

Hofstadter, Richard, and Smith, Wilson. (Eds.) *American Higher Education: A Documentary History.* 2 vols. U Chicago Press, 1961. Vol 1, 474p; Vol. 2, 1002p.

Holstein, Edwin J., and McGrath, Earl J. *Liberal Education and Engineering.* Teachers Col, Columbia U, 1960. 128p.

Hong, Howard. (Ed.) *Integration in the Christian Liberal Arts College.* Olaf Col Press, 1956. 252p.

Horn, Francis H. "Forces Shaping the College of Arts and Sciences." *Liberal Ed* 50:5–16; 1964.

Hubbard, Guy. "Art in General Education; An Historical Review With Contemporary Implications." *Art Ed* 19:10–3; 1966.

Husain, Abid. *What Is General Education?* Asia Publishing House, 1959. 82p.

Hutchins, Robert M. "The Time Is Now." *Liberal Ed* 50:249–62; 1964.

Hutchison, John A. "Four Questions on Religion and General Education." *J Gen Ed* 13:149–59; 1961.

Inge, M. Thomas. (Ed.) *Publications of the Faculty of the University College at Michigan State University: A Bibliography.* Michigan State U, 1966. 143p.

Jacob, Philip E. "Changing Values in College." Harper, 1957. 174p.

Johnson, B. Lamar. "Toward General Education in the Junior College." *Jun Col J* 30:517–24; 1960.

Johnson, Irmgard. "Oriental Literature in General Education." *J H Ed* 31:121–6; 1960.

Johnson, Irmgard. "The Non-specialist in Asian Studies." *J H Ed* 38:312–6; 1967.

Johnson, Roy I. (Ed.) *Explorations in General Education: The Experiences of Stephens College.* Harper, 1947. 262p.

Jones, Howard M. "Uses of the Past in General Education." *Harvard Ed R* 36:3–15; 1966.

Kazamias, Andreas M. "What Knowledge Is of Most Worth? An Historical Conception and a Modern Sequel." *Harvard Ed R* 30:307–30; 1960.

Keeton, Morris. "Routes to Effective General Education." *J H Ed* 32:329–35; 1961.

Keeton, Morris. "The Climate of Learning in College." In Rice, James G. (Ed.) *General Education: Current Ideas and Concerns.* Association for Higher Education and NEA, 1964. Ch. 3, p. 23–31.

Kephart, William J., and others. *Liberal Education and Business.* Teachers Col, Columbia U, 1963. 110p.

Kuhn, Madison. *Michigan State: The First Hundred Years.* Michigan State U Press, 1955. 476p.

Kurth, E. L. "Both Sides of the Coin." *Sch Shop* 22:2; 1963.

LaFanci, Horatio M., and Richter, Peyton E. "Unity and Variety in a General-education Program; A Multi-level Approach to Learning." *J H Ed* 36:379–84; 1964.

Lauwerys, Joseph A., and others. "General Education in a Changing World." *Int R Ed* 11:385–422; 1965.

Lawson, Chester A. "Platform for the Sixties: The Natural Sciences." *J Gen Ed* 14:169–74; 162.

Lee, Jeanette A., and Dressel, Paul L. *Liberal Education and Home Economics.* Teachers Col, Columbia U, 1963. 208p.

Lehmann, Irvin J. "Yardsticks for Gauging Values." *U Col Q* 2:21–7; 1966.

Lehmann, Irvin J., and Dressel, Paul L. *Critical Thinking, Attitudes, and Values in Higher Education.* HEW, 1962. 325p.

Lister, I. "Making History Interesting: Developments in General Studies." *Times Ed Supplement* 2527:587; 1963.

Liveright, A. A. "Special Degree Programs: Liberal Education for Adults." *Ed Rec* 45:419–26; 1964.

Loney, Glenn M. "Theatre and College: Adventure in Liberalization." *Teach Col Rec* 65:693–701; 1964.

Lonsway, Francis A. "Liberal Arts and the Changing Curriculum." *Cath Sch J* 67:75–6; 1967.

Maruyama, Magoroh. "General Education: A Realistic Perspective." *Col U* 40:145–52; 1965.

Mayhew, Lewis B. "The Future of General Education." *U Col Q* 6:8–19; 1960(a).

Mayhew, Lewis B. (Ed.) *General Education: An Account and Appraisal.* Harper, 1960(b). 205p.

Mayhew, Lewis B. (Ed.) *Social Science in General Education.* Brown, 1960(c). 269p.

Mayhew, Lewis B. "Liberal Arts and the Changing Structure of Higher Education." *Liberal Ed* 51:366–78; 1965(a).

Mayhew, Lewis B. "The Literature of Higher Education." *Ed Rec* 46:5–32; 1965(b). Special issue.

Mayhew, Lewis B. "The Literature of Higher Education, 1965." *Ed Rec* 47:18–49; 1966.

McGrath, Earl J. *Graduate School and the Decline of Liberal Education.* Teachers Col, Columbia U, 1959. 65p.

McGrath, Earl, and Russell, Charles H. *Are Liberal Arts Colleges Becoming Professional Schools?* Teachers Col, Columbia U, 1958. 26p.

McGrath, Earl, and others. *Toward General Education.* Macmillan, 1948. 224p.

Meeth, L. Richard. (Ed.) *Selected Issues in Higher Education. An Annotated Bibliography.* Teachers Col, Columbia U, 1965. 203p.

Meiklejohn, Alexander. *The Experimental College.* Harper, 1932. 421p.

Michaelsen, Robert. "Religion in General Education: An Example." *J Gen Ed* 13:194–200; 1961.

Michaelsen, Robert. "The Study of Religion." *J H Ed* 37:181–6; 1966.

Miller, Joseph M. "Public Address and Liberal Education." *Speech Teach* 14:207–10; 1965.

Miller, Starr. "Liberal Arts: Curriculum or Spirit?" *Clearing House* 40:226–7; 1965.

Morehouse, Ward. "Adding a New Dimension to Liberal Education." *Liberal Ed* 46:380–7; 1960.

Morgan, George W. "Liberal Education: An Assessment of Afflictions and Suggestions for Reform." *Liberal Ed* 47:376–95; 1961.

Morris, John G. "Arts and Sciences: Graduates' Knowledge Compared." *Times Ed Supplement* 2335:314–5; 1960.

Morse, Horace T. "Liberal and General Education: A Problem of Differentiation." In Rice, James G. (Ed.) *General Education: Current Ideas and Concerns.* Association for Higher Education and NEA, 1964. 86p.

Morse, Horace T. "Between the Ivory Tower and the Market Place." *Jun Col J* 35:16–20; 1965.

Morse, Horace T., and Dressel, Paul L. (Eds.) *General Education for Personal Maturity.* Brown, 1960. 246p.

Muscatine, Charles, and others. *Education at Berkeley: Report of the Select Committee on Education.* 1966. 228p.

Nall, Alfred W. "What About Terminal General Education in the Junior Colleges?" *Jun Col J* 33:20–4; 1962.

Nason, John W. "Credo of a College President." *Sch Soc* 91:214–6; 1963.

Nevins, Allan. *The State Universities and Democracy.* U Illinois Press, 1962. 140p.

Newcomer, James. "Liberal Arts in the Business Administration Curriculum." *Liberal Ed* 45:285–95; 1959.

Newcomer, James, and others. *Liberal Education and Pharmacy.* Teachers Col, Columbia U, 1961. 136p.

Nichols, Robert C. "Personality Change and the College." *Am Ed Res J* 4:173–90; 1967.

Nielsen, Niels C., Jr. "Relevance of Religion: A Point of View." *J Gen Ed* 13:201–14; 1961.

Norris, Louis W. "Breadth and Specialization in Undergraduate and Graduate Education." *Liberal Ed* 49:66–9; 1963.

Nowell-Smith, P. H. "Education in a University." *J Gen Ed* 13:71–87; 1961.

Pace, Robert. *They Went to College.* U Minnesota Press, 1941. 148p.

Parker, G. "General Studies; Possibilities for the Technician." *Times Ed Supplement* 2479:675; 1962.

Patel, L. J. "General Education in India." *U Col Q* 7:27–8; 1962.

Pattillo, Manning M., Jr., and Mackenzie, Donald M. *Church-sponsored Higher Education in the United States.* ACE, 1966. 277p.

Pelham, William F. "Analysis of Science Courses Designed for General Education." *Sci Ed* 50:337–45; 1966.

Perkins, James A. "Liberal Learning and the Learning Community." *Liberal Ed* 53:5–15; 1967.

Phalan, Reed T. "Basic Law Course for Undergraduates." *J Gen Ed* 14:248–56; 1963.

Pierson, Frank C., and others. *American Businessmen.* McGraw-Hill, 1959. 731p.

Plant, Walter T. *Personality Changes Associated with a College Education.* HEW, 1962. 831p.

Pooley, Robert C. "Platform for the Sixties: Language Arts in General Education." *J Gen Ed* 14: 159–68; 1962.

President's Commission on Higher Education. *Higher Education for American Democracy,* Vol. 1: *Establishing the Goals.* Harper, 1947. 428p.

Rattermann, P. H. "The New Breed of Student." In Smith, Kerry. (Ed.) *Current Trends in Higher Education.* Association for Higher Education and NEA, 1966. p. 158–63.

Reed, Howard A. "Intercultural Studies in General Education." *U Col Q* 10:27–33; 1965.

Reese, William L. "Education for Human Competence." *Ed Forum* 30:43–6; 1965.

Rice, James G. "General Education: Present Condition." *J Gen Ed* 14:77–92; 1962.

Rice, James G. (Ed.) *General Education: Current Ideas and Concerns.* Association for Higher Education and NEA, 1964. 86p.

Richards, Irving T. "General Education: A Delusion." *Liberal Ed* 46:241–4; 1960.

Ross, Earle D. *Democracy's College.* Iowa State U Press, 1942. 267p.

Rudolph, Frederick. *The American College and University: A History.* Knopf, 1962 496p.

Russell, Charles H. *Liberal Education and Nursing.* Teachers Col, Columbia U, 1959. 149p.

Sanford, Nevitt. (Ed.) *College and Character.* Wiley, 1964. 298p.

Senkier, Robert J. "Liberal Arts Preparation for Graduate Professional Education in Business." *Col U* 36:181–4; 1961.

Senn, Peter R. "New General Course in Social Science." *J Gen Ed* 13:53–66; 1961.

Shannon, James P. "Educated Man Is Creative, and Adds to the Culture." *Minnesota J Ed* 41:20–1; 1960.

Shoemaker, Francis, and Forsdale, Louis. (Eds.) *Communication in General Education: College Composition and Communication.* Brown, 1960. 208p.

Simons, William E. *Liberal Education in the Service Academies.* Teachers Col, Columbia U, 1965. 230p.

Sister Mary Sarah. "Liberal Arts vs. Specialized Education." *J Bus Ed* 35:350–1; 1960.

Sleeman, Richard A. "Proposed Science Program for General Education at Castleton Teachers College, Castleton, Vt." *Sci Ed* 45:353–7; 1961.

Smith, Huston. "Interdepartmental Approach to Religious Studies." *J H Ed* 31:61–8; 1960.

Smith, Paul A. "Social Science at Dickinson Four Years Later: A Communication." *J Gen Ed* 12:205–8; 1959.

Stanton, Charles M. "The Committed Student." In Smith, Kerry. (Ed.) *Current Themes in Higher Education.* Association for Higher Education, 1966. p. 166–8.

Steinberg, Charles S. "Public Relations on the Campus." *J H Ed* 37:129–36; 1966.

Stern, George G. "Of Bardot and the State of Our Colleges." In Smith, Kerry. (Ed.) *Current Trends in Higher Education.* Association for Higher Education and NEA, 1966. p. 180–5.

Stevens, George, Jr. "Mass Media in a Liberal Education." *Jun Ed Rec* 46:68–71; 1965.

Stewart, Daniel K. "The Communication Process and Its Contingencies." *U Col Q* 12:21–2; 1967.

Stokes, Joseph Morgan. "Liberal Arts and Adult Education." *Adult Leadership* 10:64–6; 1961.

Storing, James A. "Modern Design for General and Liberal Education on a College Campus." *J Gen Ed* 18:155–62; 1966.

Stull, Richard Allen. "Liberal Arts: Our Guardian." *J H Ed* 33:38–43; 1962.

Swelgart, John, "Interrelated Knowledge, In Absentia; The Development of Intellectual Perspective." *J H Ed* 35:256–63; 1964.

Thomas, Russell. *The Search for a Common Learning; General Education, 1800–1960.* McGraw-Hill, 1962. 302p.

Thomas, Russell. "General Education: Complementary or Preparatory?" *J Gen Ed* 15:33–45; 1963.
Tigar, Michael E. "Student Participation in Academic Governance." In Smith, Kerry. (Ed.) *Current Trends in Higher Education.* Association for Higher Education and NEA, 1966. p. 169–74.
Times Educational Supplement. "Liberal Education for All." 2397:839; 1961.
Tocqueville, Alexis de. *Democracy in America,* Vol. 1. Vintage Books, n.d. 450p.
Tonne, Herbert A. "How Liberal Are the Arts?" *J Bus Ed* 35:248–9; 1960(a).
Tonne, Herbert A. "How Liberal Is Liberal If You Can't Earn a Living?" *Balance Sheet* 42:173; 1960(b).
Truman, David B. "The Changing Character of Undergraduate Education." *Sch Soc* 92:380–3; 1964.
U.S. Department of Health, Education and Welfare. *The Impact of a Value-oriented University on Student Attitudes and Thinking.* HEW, GPO, 1961. 106p.
Valley, John R. "Advanced Placement Examinations." *U Col Q* 9:74–8; 1964.
Verhage, William. "History in General Education." *J H Ed* 30:383–90; 1959.
Wager, Willis J., and McGrath, Earl J. *Liberal Education and Music.* Teachers Col, Columbia U, 1962. 209p.
Walker, Kenneth R. "Problems in General Education in State-supported Colleges." *J Gen Ed* 13:128–44; 1961.
Walker, Kenneth R. "Trends in Social Science in General Education in College." *Peabody J Ed* 41:110–7; 1963.
Wallace, William A. "Place of Science in Liberal Arts Curriculum." *Cath Ed R* 60:361–76; 1962.
Wanous, S. J. "Let's Break the Egghead Stranglehold on Business Education." *Balance Sheet* 42:104–10; 1960.
Weaver, Paul. "Study Abroad and General Education." *J Gen Ed* 13:243–50; 1962.
Webster, J. C. "Experiment in General Education at Baring Union Christian College." *Christian Scholar* 48:125–30; 1965.
Weigle, Richard D. "Uses of the Past in General Education. A Reply to H. M. Jones." *Harvard Ed R* 36:326–8; 1966.
Weisinger, Herbert. "In Criticism of General Education." *J Gen Ed* 15:161–74; 1963.
Weiss, Donald. "Freedom of Association for Students." *J H Ed* 38:184–9; 1967.
Williamson, E. G., and Cowan, John L. "The Role of the President in the Desirable Enactment of Academic Freedom for Students." *Ed Rec* 46:351–72; 1965.
Wills, J. Robert, Jr. "Theatre Education in the Liberal Arts." *Liberal Ed* 50:375–9; 1964.
Wimpey, John A. "Value Perspectives in Liberal Education." *Peabody J Ed* 38:285–91; 1961.
Winthrop, Henry. "Must We Revise the Content of Liberal Education?" *Soc Ed* 27:305–9; 1963(a).
Winthrop, Henry. "What Can Be Done to Counteract Specialization?" *Peabody J Ed* 41:67–74; 1963(b).
Zerby, Lewis. "General Education for Nigeria." *U Col Q* 11:10–4; 1965.
Zimmerman, Paul A. "Impact of Technological Society on General Education in the Two-year Colleges." *North Cen Assn Q* 40:276–86; 1966.

GIFTED CHILDREN

The heady winds of change have been blowing through American education for the past decade driven by the twin stimuli of a threatening political force from outside the culture and the needs of a complex technology internally. No single group of students has been affected so thoroughly by these changes as the highly talented, who are seen as both the shield from the external force and the prime movers for the complex society of the future.

Consequently, there is a distinct change in the kinds of material covered here as opposed to that covered in past reviews. There is less concern for the nature of giftedness and more concern for the role of the gifted in the classroom; less concern for administrative adjustments and greater concern for the nature of the program given to gifted students; less interest in the high-achieving gifted and more concern for the talent loss represented by the chronic underachiever and the talented student with low socioeconomic status; a greater interest in the multidimensional nature of talent and less interest in a single dimension of giftedness represented by the IQ score.

CHARACTERISTICS OF THE GIFTED. Since both characteristics and identification depend on definition, they must be discussed in terms of a broader definition which includes the talent potential in the culturally disadvantaged and a new look at the "creative" student.

High-IQ Samples. The classic longitudinal studies by Terman and his associates established a consistent portrait of superiority for his large sample across most measurable dimensions. The last volume (Terman & Oden, 1959) continues and extends this favorable portrait. Since these results were obtained for a group that mainly had high socioeconomic standing, there has been some question whether the differences were due to intelligence or to the generally superior social advantages of this group. When socioeconomic differences were controlled for the differences along the dimensions of physical ability (Laycock & Caylor, 1964) and personality characteristics (Bonsall & Stefflre, 1955), the differences between gifted and nongifted samples were less marked.

When controls are established for social class, gifted children from advantaged circumstances are similar to the gifted from lower classes in physical or personality dimensions. Some differences were found in leisure-time preferences, with the advantaged gifted preferring reading while the disadvantaged gifted were more interested in games and competitive sports. Even so, the disadvantaged gifted seem to choose reading more often than the disadvantaged average student did (Frierson, 1964).

In the development of moral values, a comparison of gifted and nongifted from both middle- and lower-class groups produced predictable results (Boehm, 1962): academically gifted elementary students showed earlier maturation of moral judgment than nonacademically gifted ones. The distinction was not as great between gifted and average in working-class families.

The superiority of the gifted child in academic achievement, while long acknowledged, is not often reflected in an adjusted educational program. Those of high ability (IQ score) are often found four or five grades above their grade level in reading related subjects (Gallagher & Crowder, 1957). The massive Project Talent program indicated that 20 percent of ninth graders (Flanagan, 1964) had already attained a higher level of achievement than the twelfth-grade average. A lockstep educational program that keeps close to grade level must ignore these kinds of findings.

There has been growing evidence that gifted students not only have superior problem-solving abilities but also possess favorable personality characteristics and effective work habits that guarantee continued enhancement of that ability. The bright student is more independent of his school environment for self-esteem, gaining his rewards from his own performance, while the average student is more dependent upon the opinions of teachers and peers (Sears, 1963). The gifted student seems more independent than the student of average ability (Smith, 1962) and less swayed by the opinion of his peers in what he believes is the right decision (Lucito, 1964). All of these traits seem to form a productive working style for high academic achievement which, in fact, the gifted student has.

The social status of the gifted student seems to be partly a function of age. During the elementary years he seems to hold a superior social status in his peer group (Gallagher, 1958; Pielstick, 1963), but at the secondary-school level his social status suffers a reversal (Martyn, 1957). In a study giving some insight into the social problems of the gifted at the secondary-school level, the value preferences of the secondary student were found to reveal a negative attitude toward "brilliance" unless it was leavened by interest in athletics or by a nonstudious attitude (Tannenbaum, 1962).

The differential sex role of gifted boys and girls and its influence on the educational scene have received some much needed attention. As early as the fourth grade, gifted boys appear reluctant to write poems and plays or make up original dances, while girls avoided the planning of experiments, keeping weather records, or mixing colors (Torrance, 1965). Differential choices of occupations also reflected these distinctively perceived sex roles.

Gifted girls also seem to be less expressive than gifted boys in the public arena of classroom discussion but not in the more private area of written expression, suggesting some sex-role inhibition (Gallagher, 1965*a*). In a younger sample, gifted girls still showed participation in language arts but some avoidance classroom behavior during arithmetic (Perkins, 1965).

Very little of substance has been added to our knowledge of the student of extraordinarily high IQ first described by Hollingworth (1952) some decades ago. She, Terman, and Oden (1959) had suggested that the social acceptance of this high-ability child would not be as favorable as for the student in the 125–155 IQ range, and there has been some confirmation of this (Gallagher & Crowder, 1957).

Identification. Previous reviews indicated that teachers have a difficult time identifying students of superior intellectual ability. These results have been supported by more recent studies—a comprehensive one at the junior high school level (Pegnato & Birch, 1959) and at the kindergarten age level (Baldwin, 1962). When teacher judgment was combined with group-test data, it became an important part of the screening procedure (Martinson & Lessinger, 1960). Group tests themselves tend to overestimate the IQ's of children of above-average ability in comparison to the results achieved by those children on individual tests (Blosser, 1963).

Some studies stressed identification procedures for specific skills, such as scientific aptitude. Some indications are present that such specific aptitude skills can be identified even in primary-age children (Davis & others, 1960).

The Highly Creative Student. The great interest in creativity shown in the past decade can be traced to the realization that memorized knowledge alone is of little use in a rapidly changing culture. Mackworth (1965) presents an admirable argument for the need for "problem finders" rather than "problem solvers" in the computerized society of the future.

The theoretical underpinnings for this interest were provided mainly by Guilford (1959, 1966), who stressed the intellectual operation of divergent thinking as part of his model of the structure of the intellect and closely tied divergent thinking to the creative process. A key—although highly criticized—study by Getzels and Jackson (1962) opened a whole new area of research by identifying a subgroup of highly creative students who scored high on tests mainly measuring divergent thinking but not performing particularly high on IQ tests. They noted that such a "creative" student was characterized by more intellectual risk taking and less social conformity than the usual high-IQ student. He appeared to play the lively, if not too responsible, grasshopper to the more stodgy ant personality of the high-IQ student. The replication of these results by Torrance (1962*b*) played an important role in the acceptance of these concepts.

In other controlled studies (Yamamoto, 1964; Wallach & Kogan, 1965), more attention was given to those students who scored high on both IQ and creativity measures and who seemed to have the desirable combination of both control and freedom. The high-creativity student had a kind of rebellious approach to society, while the low-creativity but high-intelligence student was found to be a conformist who was addicted to school achievement.

Getzels and Jackson had suggested that teachers might prefer the more conformist high-IQ student to the high-creativity student, though their own data did not convincingly demonstrate the point. In one study this point was supported for boys but not for girls (Gallagher, 1965a). In another study it was not supported at all (Richards & others, 1964).

Some of the findings from the use of creativity-test batteries suggested interesting cross-cultural differences. There were very different developmental curves for intellectual fluency or originality in six different cultures (Torrance, 1962a). An unusual aspect of these developmental curves was their tendency to slump or dip at the fourth-grade level. While the usual explanation for this dip has been that the children at that age come face to face with an inflexible curriculum and a school program that places a premium upon conformity, it might also be due to the child's achieving a higher level of mental integration, which causes him to be more critical of his own performance and thus less willing to give silly answers.

After the initial enthusiasm for these new findings had cooled, a closer and more critical look was focused on those instruments purporting to measure the elusive thread of creativity. Earlier results which had obtained low correlations between IQ tests and creativity batteries (Holland, 1961; Torrance, 1962b) were noted to have highly restricted IQ ranges, and one study, using a wider range of ability, showed much higher correlations between the two sets of measures (Ripple & May, 1962). It was noted that most of these instruments had only face validity to support them and that few attempts had been made to substantiate these scores with accepted measures of creative production (Yamamoto, 1965).

Another approach to the investigation of creativity was to compare adults in various fields who had demonstrated creativity with adults in similar positions who had not manifested substantial originality or creativity. The results of such studies (MacKinnon, 1960; Barron, 1963) stressed the distinctive personality characteristics of the creative individual as opposed to his cognitive abilities. The creative person seemed to be more open to experience, not to be defensive, and to be able to use regression in the service of the ego. In short, by not having to use repression as a defense mechanism, he tended to maximize the usage of all of his experience and abilities. A fine review of this area has also become available (Stein & Heinze, 1960).

TALENT LOSS. The Underachiever. The characteristics of the chronic underachiever have received much attention during the past decade. The current interest in talent preservation has increased the urgency with which attempts are made to find the key variables in the etiology of this condition.

Although there has been some question whether the two different criteria for identifying the gifted underachiever—low grades and high aptitude or low achievement scores and high aptitude—really identify the same group of students (Pippert & Archer, 1963), there has been a certain consistency in the characteristics regardless of criteria used. Some studies had indicated a poor self concept for the underachiever, and this has been confirmed (Combs, 1964; Nason, 1958). Such findings still leave a chicken-and-egg problem, however. Do underachievers have poor self concepts because they underachieve, or do they underachieve because they have low self-esteem?

The student who underachieves in secondary school often has a long and chronic history of underachievement which could be identified as early as the third grade for boys and the sixth grade for girls (Shaw & McCuen, 1960).

In investigating family relationships, some studies have suggested that the male underachievers have particularly poor relationships with their fathers (Pierce, 1961). Others have found a more punitive home environment for the underachiever (McGillivray, 1964).

One attempt at summarizing the many areas of differences between achiever and underachiever focused on the reaction to stress. The underachiever was apparently unable to persist in a frustrating situation, sought thrills and excitement in his recreation, showed greater feelings of hostility (Shaw & Black, 1960), sought out peers with similar negative feelings for school (Morrow & Wilson, 1961), and spent more classroom time working in other than academic areas, with withdrawal a predominant symptom (Perkins, 1965).

In summary, the underachieving child from a middle-class background perceives the world as unfriendly and unsympathetic. The school is a threatening place which demands persistence in the face of frustration and is unrelated to the life he would like to lead. The family is unsupportive and often punitive.

The Disadvantaged Student. When the IQ was considered an indicator of genetic potential, it seemed almost un-American to suggest that there were differences between ethnic or racial groups. Now such differences are attributed to differential environmental opportunities, particularly since a low incidence of talent in a group always seems related to limited educational and occupational opportunities (Pettigrew, 1964). One indicator of differential opportunity is the percentage of a group going on to higher education. One study indicated that while roughly 25 percent of graduating high school students go to college, only 1 percent of American Indians and 2 percent of American Negroes attend interracial colleges. Another 10 percent of American Negroes attend Negro colleges in the South (Plaut, 1957).

There is some indication that talent loss is not confined to the lower class or to certain minority groups. Though some reports are optimistic, noting that only 4 percent of top-scoring students in the National Merit scholarship tests did not go on to college (Thistlethwaite, 1958), other research reviewing over 400,000 students (Flanagan & others, 1962) reported that 20 percent of the students in the top quarter of their graduating classes failed to enter college. Of course, equating talent salvage and college attendance is a procedure justified only by its convenience and objectivity. More-rigorous criteria are clearly needed.

Previous research indicated a high incidence of Jewish students and a low incidence of Negroes, Italians, and other minority group members in the gifted range of IQ scores. One plausible explanation of these differential proportions lies in the cultural values of the subgroups. In one such study (Strodtbeck, 1958), the Jewish philosophy of life seemed to involve (1) a belief that the world is orderly and amenable to rational mastery, (2) a willingness to leave home to make one's way in life, (3) a preference for individual credit for work done, and (4) the belief that man could improve himself through education and need not submit to fate. Such values seem to provide the basis for the substantial upward mobility found in the Jewish families. The Italian families in the study did not subscribe to these values and were not upwardly mobile.

PROGRAM ADJUSTMENTS. The High Performer. The threat of a hostile communism and the needs of a booming and complex technology forced an agonizing reappraisal of our educational system and its ability to prepare persons for social and intellectual leadership. The most influential of these appraisals was done by Conant (1959). His recommendations for the secondary schools have been widely followed, and many of these directly concern superior students. Among other things, he suggested a stronger program in the sciences and mathematics, grouping by ability and achievement in content areas, tutors to help challenge highly gifted students, and the use of acceleration as part of an advanced-placement program.

While his report and similar critiques tended to raise the general level of academic expectations for talented students in the secondary school, another major movement was changing the content of the academic program for many gifted students. From the 1920's to the mid-1950's, curriculum programming and development were mainly in the hands of educators rather than content-area specialists (Schwab, 1964). During the past decade there has been a substantial shift, particularly in regard to the physical sciences and mathematics, with the content-area specialists developing extensive and expensive curriculum programs which reflect a different educational philosophy (Goodlad, 1964). This philosophy has at its base three major goals:

1. To teach the basic conceptual structure of the content discipline.
2. To have the student approach the subject matter as the specialist would approach it.
3. To introduce important ideas in the program at as early an age as possible (Bruner, 1960).

The comparison of these new programs with those they replaced is not an easy matter, since they differ not only in method but in goals as well. Some favorable results have been reported in mathematics in attitude and performance (Passow & others, 1961; Tatsuoka & Easley, 1963), and some consistent evaluations of performance in BSCS biology (Wallace, 1962) suggest that superior students respond well to such a program. In a similar attempt to introduce mathematical logic to elementary-school students, the upper-quartile students responded well to the program (Suppes & Binford, 1964). Still, few of these major efforts in curriculum development have so far addressed themselves seriously to the question What do we want the learner to be able to do after instruction that he was unable to do before instruction?

Similar curriculum developments in the social sciences have been slower and less opulently organized but seem to be following similar patterns and goals. A special program to increase the self-actualization of intellectually superior ninth graders consisted of explorations into the natural, aesthetic, technological, and human worlds of mankind, accompanied by films of adult role models (Drews, 1965). Girls in the program showed significant increases in aestheticism and in critical thinking, while boys showed increase in the theoretical dimension of the Allport-Vernon-Lindzey Scale of Values and in critical thinking over a control sample.

In the flush of enthusiasm for the flexibility of IQ, it seemed to be forgotten that genetic influences still play a part. A study of over 1,500 sets of twins (Nichols, 1965) showed consistently higher correlations in achievement-test scores between monozygotic than between dizygotic twins, even when corrections were made for differential experiences of some of the twins.

The classroom has become a medium for investigation during the past decade and provides another dimension for looking at the gifted. One study indicated that teachers in classes of gifted students tended to ask predominantly cognitive memory questions, and in some class sessions no emphasis was found on questions in the evaluative or divergent dimensions. Furthermore, the cognitive expression of the students closely followed the patterns set by the teachers (Gallagher, 1965a).

One complicating factor in curriculum evaluation lies in the diversity of program application by the individual teacher of even well-established curriculum programs. An analysis of three consecutive days of classroom interaction with six biology teachers introducing the concept of photosynthesis to high-ability junior high school classes indicated significant teacher variation in levels of conceptualization, in skill training, and in emphasis on various biological concepts (Gallagher, 1966).

While "enrichment" was the banner under which most school systems said they were providing for gifted children, little research is available to evaluate the impact of such procedures. One study that compared the influence of enrichment programs for gifted at the primary and intermediate grade levels reported modest increase in achievement over control groups (Martinson, 1961). Another investigation which used case-study techniques to plan individualized programs for 54 students with Binet IQ's of 150 and over reported only modest change, because of limited knowledge of content and lack of time to apply the recommendations of the case-study team on the part of teachers (Gallagher & others, 1960). In both of the instances above, considerable additional personnel were added to the regular school complement, which created a more favorable environment than that obtaining in the school system attempting enrichment with no additional aids for the teacher.

The important question of the 1930's and 1940's in the education of the gifted was the influence of ability grouping. There is now some general recognition that the question has little meaning unless there is some specificity about the treatment variable or the program applied. If no difference in program is introduced, a mixed and varied set of results occurs that probably matches the variation of program within the various classrooms (Borg, 1964; Goldberg & others, 1965).

When specific program changes are made in addition to the ability grouping, it is possible to observe positive results in attitude and aptitude (Passow & others, 1961).

Some attempts have been made to aid gifted students in attaining a more useful intellectual style. A study along those lines, designed to improve the student's ability to inquire on a systematic basis (Suchman, 1962), showed some positive results, but changes were not consistent. Other studies have shown that changes in the teacher's structuring of the task—be neat or be original—significantly changes the students' performances (Torrance, 1965; Eberle, 1965).

Most of the studies done so far have been of a short-range variety in which the evaluation of the influence of the intervention technique was made immediately after the training or intervention. While there seems to be good reason to believe that temporary changes can be made in the student's style, there remains the important question whether they continue their influence or whether the student reverts back to previous patterns of performance when the experimental conditions are removed.

Acceleration. As the length of time required for advanced training and graduate education consistently increases, the practice of acceleration, or reducing the total amount of time spent in the educational program, for a superior student becomes more popular. Two methods seem to be in increasing use: early admission to school and advanced placement. A review of the research related to early admission (Reynolds & others, 1962) continues to be favorable, although there seems to be a limited selection of students for this procedure (Birch & others, 1964).

The report *New Dimensions in Higher Education* (U.S. Department of Health, Education, and Welfare, 1961) reveals that the number of colleges participating in advanced-placement programs has risen from 12 colleges and universities in 1955 to over 400 in 1960. While formal evaluation is lacking, the widespread acceptance of the procedure speaks well for its lack of harmful effects.

Several follow-up studies have been added to trace the long-range influence of acceleration (Adler & others, 1963; Mirman, 1962) and have found it to be benign. The use of summer sessions to remove a year of elementary schooling for bright students also indicated no ill effects (Klausmeier, 1963). Perhaps what is needed is some social psychologist to explore why this procedure is generally ignored in the face of such overwhelmingly favorable results.

Remediation for the Underachiever. Two different kinds of intervention strategies have been used to ameliorate underachievement. The first approach takes note of the poor self concept and negativistic feelings of the underachiever and applies various types of counseling. The application of group counseling to chronic underachievers has been marked with indifferent success (Baymur & Patterson, 1960; Broedel & others, 1960; Mink, 1964). Attempts to involve the families in the counseling either directly (Shaw, 1961) or in a supportive role (Shouksmith & Taylor, 1964) have shown somewhat better results. It is difficult to evaluate these findings. Is counseling really not called for or is the condition too much for the kind of short-term counseling used in these studies, which is often applied by persons of limited experience? One thing is certain; chronic underachievement is not easily remedied through short-term counseling.

The second strategy has been to modify the educational program to take into account the limited ego strength or limited aspirations of the underachiever. In one instance, placement of gifted underachievers in a classroom with a teacher who was warm, receptive, and flexible resulted in improved grades, but the gains were lost when a rigid teacher with high standards was introduced (Goldberg, 1959). In a similar attempt, two groups of underachievers were placed together in homeroom guidance classes for three years of senior high school. No substantial gains were noted in grades or aptitude scores (Passow & Goldberg, 1962).

In a unique attempt to modify the educational environment and level of aspiration of the elementary-level underachievers, small groups of underachievers were placed in classes with high-achieving gifted children. Significant gains were noted in school achievement and intellectual fluency (Karnes & others, 1961).

Both strategies of intervention seem to suggest that sustained efforts are needed to modify substantially the long-standing nonadaptive patterns of adjustment to school found in the chronic underachiever.

While intervention methods have been applied on a widespread basis for the culturally deprived, little specific attention has been given to reversing talent loss among the most talented of the deprived groups. The best-known project of that nature was the demonstration guidance project that late became the Higher Horizons project. In its initial pilot form, positive results were obtained in terms of fewer dropouts and better grades (Hillson & Myers, 1963).

Legislative Support. State planning for the gifted has developed at an accelerated rate since 1960. Currently 18 states have a state program or personnel specifically assigned to the education of the gifted. One such example was the establishment of an extensive program in the state of Illinois (Jackson & Rogge, 1963). A $7-million appropriation has allowed support for a five-pronged attack:

1. Reimbursement to schools for establishing a variety of special provisions for the gifted in local schools.

2. The establishment of demonstration centers to provide models of exemplary programs in ordinary school settings.

3. Support for research and development activities to advance knowledge that would enhance educational programming for gifted children.

4. Provision for support of a variety of summer training programs, in-service training programs, and year-round fellowships.

5. Establishment of administrative staff positions and field consultants on the gifted in the Office of the Superintendent of Public Instruction.

More-generalized support for program innovation for the gifted has been available, though not specifically earmarked, through the increasingly broad level of federal support of education.

James J. Gallagher
University of Illinois

References

Adler, Marilynne, and others. "A Study of the Effects of Acceleration Programme in Toronto Secondary Schools." *Ontario J Ed Res* 6:1–22; 1963.

Baldwin, J. W. "The Relationship Between Teacher-judged Giftedness, a Group Intelligence Test, and Kindergarten Pupils." *Gifted Child Q* 6:153–6; 1962.

Barron, F. *Creativity and Psychological Health*. Van Nostrand, 1963.

Baymur, Feriha, and Patterson, C. H. "Three Methods of Assisting Underachieving High School Students." *J Counseling Psychol* 7:83–90; 1960.

Birch, J. W., and others. "Early Admission of Able Children to School." *Sch Life* 46:7–9; 1964.

Blosser, G. H. "Group Intelligence Tests as Screening Devices in Locating Gifted and Superior Students in the Ninth Grade." *Excep Children* 29:282–6; 1963.

Boehm, Leonore. "The Development of Conscience: A Comparison of American Children of Different Mental and Socioeconomic Levels." *Child Develop* 33:575–90; 1962.

Bonsall, Marcella, and Stefflre, Buford. "The Temperament of Gifted Children." *California J Ed Res* 6:162–5; 1955.

Borg, W. R. *An Evaluation of Ability Grouping*. Cooperative Research Project No. 577. USOE, 1964.

Broedel, J., and others. "The Effects of Group Counseling on Gifted Underachieving Adolescents." *J Counseling Psychol* 7:103–7; 1960.

Bruner, J. S. *The Process of Education*. Harvard U Press, 1960.

Combs, C. F. "Perception of Self and Scholastic Underachievement in the Academically Capable." *Personnel Guid J* 43:47–51; 1964.

Conant, J. B. *The American High School Today*. McGraw-Hill, 1959.

Davis, F. B., and others. "Identification and Classroom Behavior of Gifted Elementary School Children." In *The Gifted Student*. GPO, 1960. p. 19–32.

Drews, Elizabeth. *The Creative Intellectual Style in Gifted Adolescents 1-11 Being and Becoming*. Aircraft Press, 1965.

Eberle, R. F. "An Experiment in the Teaching of the Creative Thinking Processes to a 'Broad Range Group' of Eighth Grade Pupils for the Purpose of Determining Teachability Aspects of Creative Thinking." Edwardsville Junior H School, 1965.

Flanagan, J. C. "Project Talent: Some Early Findings from a Nationwide Survey." *NEA J* 53:8–10; 1964.

Flanagan, J. C., and others. *Design for a Study of American Youth*. Houghton, 1962.

Frierson, E. C. "A Study of Selected Characteristics of Gifted Children from Upper and Lower Socioeconomic Backgrounds." Doctoral dissertation. Kent State U, 1964.

Gallagher, J. J. "Peer Acceptance of Highly Gifted Children in Elementary School." *El Sch J* 58:365–70; 1958.

Gallagher, J. J. "Expressive Thought by Gifted Children in the Classroom." *El Engl* 42:559–68; 1965(*a*).

Gallagher, J. J. *Productive Thinking of Gifted Children*. USOE Cooperative Research Project No. 965. U Illinois, 1965(*b*).

Gallagher, J. J. *Teacher Variation in Concept Presentation in BSCS Curriculum Program*. U Illinois Press, 1966.

Gallagher, J. J., and Crowder, Thora. "The Adjustment of Gifted Children in the Regular Classroom." *Excep Children* 23:306–12; 1957.

Gallagher, J. J., and others. "Individual Classroom Adjustments for Gifted Children in Elementary Schools." *Excep Children* 26:409–22; 1960.

Getzels, J. W., and Jackson, P. W. *Creativity and Intelligence*. Wiley, 1962.

Goldberg, Miriam. "A Three Year Experimental Program at DeWitt Clinton High School to Help Bright Underachievers." *High Points* 41:5–35; 1959.

Goldberg, Miriam, and others. *The Effects of Ability Grouping*. Teachers Col, Columbia U, 1965.

Goodlad, J. I. *School Curriculum Reform in the United States*. Fund for the Advancement of Education, 1964.

Guilford, J. P. "The Three Faces of Intellect." *Am Psychologist* 14:469–79; 1959.

Guilford, J. P. "Intelligence: 1965 Model." *Am Psychologist* 21:20–6; 1966.

Hillson, H. T., and Myers, Florence. *The Demonstration Guidance Project, 1957–62*. New York Board of Education, 1963.

Holland, J. L. "Creative and Academic Performance Among Talented Adolescents." *J Ed Psychol* 52:136–47; 1961.

Hollingworth, L. S. *Children Above 180 I.Q.* World Book, 1942.

Jackson, D., and Rogge, W. *Illinois Plan for Program Development for Gifted.* (Springfield, Illinois) Office of the Superintendent of Public Instruction, 1963.

Karnes, Merle, and others. *The Efficacy of Two Organizational Plans for Underachieving Intellectually Gifted Children.* Champaign (Illinois) Public Schools, 1961.

Klausmeier, H. J. "Effects of Accelerating Bright Older Elementary Pupils: A Follow-up." *J Ed Psychol* 54:165–71; 1963.

Laycock, F., and Caylor, J. S. "Physiques of Gifted Children and Their Less Gifted Siblings." *Child Develop* 35:63–74; 1964.

Lucito, L. "Independence-Conformity Behavior as a Function of Intellect: Bright and Dull Children." *Excep Children* 31:5–13; 1964.

MacKinnon, D. W. "The Highly Effective Individual." *Teach Col Rec* 61:367–78; 1960.

McGillivray, R. H. "Differences in Home Background Between High-achieving and Low-achieving Gifted Children: A Study of One Hundred Grade Eight Pupils in the City of Toronto Public Schools." *Ontario J Ed Res* 6:99–106; 1964.

Mackworth, N. H. "Originality." *Am Psychologist* 20:51–66; 1965.

Martinson, Ruth. *Educational Programs for Gifted Pupils.* California State Department of Education, 1961.

Martinson, Ruth, and Lessinger, L. "Problems in the Identification of Intellectually Gifted Children." *Excep Children* 26:227–31; 1960.

Martyn, K. A. "The Social Acceptance of Gifted Students." Doctoral dissertation. Stanford U, 1957.

Mink, O. G. "Multiple Counseling with Under-achieving Junior High School Pupils of Bright-Normal and Higher-Ability." *J Ed Res* 58:31–4; 1964.

Mirman, N. "Are Accelerated Students Socially Maladjusted?" *El Sch J* 62:273–6; 1962.

Morrow, W. R. and Wilson, R. C. "Family Relations of Bright High Achieving and Underachieving High School Boys." *Child Develop* 32:501–10; 1961.

Nason, Leslie J. "Academic Achievement of Gifted High School Students." *U Southern California Monogr Series* 17; 1958.

Nichols, R. C. *The Inheritance of General and Specific Ability.* NMSC, 1965.

Passow, A. H., and Goldberg, Miriam L. "The Talented Youth Project: A Progress Report, 1962." *Excep Children* 28:223–31; 1962.

Passow, A. H., and others. "Enriched Mathematics for Gifted Junior High School Students." *Ed Leadership* 18:442–8; 1961.

Pegnato, C. W., and Birch, J. W. "Locating Gifted Children in Junior High Schools: A Comparison of Methods." *Excep Children* 25:300–4; 1959.

Perkins, H. V. "Classroom Behavior and Underachievement." *Am Ed Res J* 2:1–12; 1965.

Pettigrew, T. "Negro American Intelligence: A New Look at an Old Controversy." *J Negro Ed* 33:6–25; 1964.

Pielstock, N. L. "Perception of Mentally Superior Children by Their Classmates." *Perceptual and Motor Skills* 17:47–53; 1963.

Pierce, J. V. "Personality and Achievement Among Able High School Boys. *J Individual Psychol* 17: 101–2; 1961.

Pippert, R., and Archer, N. S. "A Comparison of Two Methods for Classifying Underachievers with Respect to Selected Criteria." *Personnel Guid J* 41: 788–91; 1963.

Plaut, R. L. *Blueprint for Talent Searching.* National Scholarship Service and Fund for Negro Students, 1957.

Reynolds, M., and others. "Review of Research on Early Admission." In Reynolds, M. (Ed.) *Early School Admission for Mentally Advanced Children.* Council for Exceptional Children, 1962. p. 7–17.

Richards, J. M., and others. "Creativity Tests and Teacher and Self Judgments of Originality." *J Exp Ed* 32:281–5; 1964.

Ripple, R. E., and May, F. B. "Caution in Comparing Creativity and IQ." *Psychol Reports* 10:229–30; 1962.

Schwab, J. *Biology Teacher's Handbook.* Wiley, 1964.

Sears, Pauline S. "The Effect of Classroom Conditions on the Strength of Achievement Motive and Work Output of Elementary School Children." USOE Cooperative Research Project No. 873. Stanford U, 1963.

Shaw, M. C. "The Interrelationship of Selected Personality Factors in High Ability Under-Achieving School Children." Project 58-M-1. California State Department of Public Health, 1961.

Shaw, M. C., and Black, Doris. "The Reaction to Frustration of Bright High School Under-achievers." *California J Ed Res* 11:120–4; 1960.

Shaw, M. C., and McCuen, J. T. "The Onset of Academic Underachievement in Bright Children." *J Ed Psychol* 51:103–8; 1960.

Shouksmith, G., and Taylor, J. W. "The Effect of Counseling on the Achievement of High-ability Pupils." *Br J Ed Psychol* 34:51–7; 1964.

Smith, D. C. *Personal and Social Adjustment of Gifted Adolescents.* Research Monograph No. 4. Council for Exceptional Children, 1962.

Stein, M. I., and Heinze, Shirley J. *Creativity and the Individual.* Free, 1960.

Strodtbeck, F. "Family Interaction Values and Achievement." In McClelland, D. (Ed.) *Talent and Society.* Van Nostrand, 1958.

Suchman, J. R. *The Elementary School Training Program in Scientific Inquiry.* U Illinois Press, 1962.

Suppes, P., and Binford, F. "Experimental Teaching of Mathematical Logic in the Elementary School." USOE Cooperative Research Project No. D-005. Stanford U, 1964.

Tannenbaum, A. *Adolescent Attitudes Toward Academic Brilliance.* Teachers Col, Columbia U, 1962.

Tatsuoka, M. M., and Easley, J. A., Jr. *Comparison of VICSM* vs. *Traditional Algebra Test Scores.* Research Report No. 1. U Illinois Committee on School Mathematics, 1963.

Terman, L. M., and Oden, Melita. *Genetic Studies*

of *Genius*. Vol. 5: *The Gifted Group at Mid-life*. Stanford U Press, 1959.

Thistlethwaite, D. C. "The Conservation of Intellectual Talent." *Science* 128:822–6; 1958.

Torrance, E. P. "Cultural Discontinuities and the Development of Originality of Thinking." *Excep Children* 29:2–13; 1962(*a*).

Torrance, E. P. *Guiding Creative Talent*. Prentice-Hall, 1962(*b*).

Torrance, E. P. *Rewarding Creative Behavior*. Prentice-Hall, 1965.

U.S. Department of Health, Education, and Welfare. *New Dimensions in Higher Education*. HEW, 1961.

Wallace, W. L. "The BSCS 1961–62 Evaluation Program—A Statistical Report." *BSCS Newsletter* 19: 22–4; 1962.

Wallach, M. A., and Kogan, N. *Modes of Thinking in Young Children*. Holt, 1965.

Yamamoto, K. "Role of Creative Thinking and Intelligence in High School Achievement." *Psychol Reports* 14:783–9; 1964.

Yamamoto, K. "Validation of Tests of Creative Thinking: A Review of Some Studies." *Excep Children* 31:281–90; 1965.

GRADUATE EDUCATION

Graduate education in the United States is defined as that segment of higher education in the arts, letters, and sciences following upon the successful attainment of a baccalaureate degree in one of these fields. It leads to the academic degree of Master of Arts or Master of Science, and eventually to the Doctor of Philosophy, the highest degree in course awarded by American universities. Graduate education should be clearly differentiated from postbaccalaureate education in certain of the learned professions, such as law, theology, and medicine, leading to the so-called first professional degree (Bachelor of Laws, Bachelor of Divinity, or Doctor of Medicine). It is also not concerned with nondegree postbaccalaureate work that is offered by many universities and colleges to qualified adults for their professional advancement or personal satisfaction. Although there are some gray areas, as we shall see later, in the strictest sense the term "graduate education" is applied only to organized advanced study and research leading to a higher academic—not professional or quasi-professional—degree (Carmichael, 1961).

Graduate education is administered by a more or less well-defined academic unit variously known as a graduate school, a graduate college, and a graduate division. Its functions, differing from those of the undergraduate college, can be described as follows: (1) it not only preserves and disseminates advanced knowledge through teaching but also discovers and develops new knowledge through research and independent investigation on the part of both its faculty and students; (2) it educates and trains in depth in their specialties the vast numbers of scholars, scientists, and educators needed by our highly complex and rapidly changing society, economy, and technology; (3) in recent years, particularly, it has used its resources of specially skilled manpower and sophisticated research equipment for the investigation and solution of the problems of local, state, and federal governments as well as of industry. Through these activities the modern graduate school is not only the apex of the educational system but has also become a major national resource in the service of civilization.

THE BEGINNINGS. Formal graduate education in the United States is less than 90 years old, although the first earned Ph.D. degrees were awarded in 1861 by Yale University. Between that time and the establishment of the first graduate school in 1876 a total of 18 doctorates were conferred by Columbia, Harvard, Illinois Wesleyan, Michigan, New York, and Syracuse universities. Master's degrees were conferred much earlier, not in recognition of advanced studies, but rather as gratuitous marks of distinction by colleges to their bachelor's degree holders. The first of these were awarded by Harvard College in 1645, three years after graduation, to men who were engaged in literary or professional pursuits and who paid a required fee to the college (Berelson, 1960).

The history of undergraduate higher education in America began with the establishment of Harvard College in 1638. In the following 150 years a relatively small number of colleges were founded, most of them in New England. The College of William and Mary in Virginia, opened in 1694, is the oldest in the Southern states and second only to Harvard. The University of Georgia at Athens, chartered in 1785 and opened in 1801, was the first state university. Almost all of the early colleges were, at least originally, church-related and were patterned, as might be expected, upon the model of the English residential college. They were intended, as might be expected also, primarily for the training of the learned professions, particularly the ministry, but they also offered a "genteel" education, as a contemporary put it, "to the eldest sons of persons of quality who, being commonly brought up to no employment, have a great deal of time lying upon their hands." This aristocratic character and tradition of the liberal arts college continued through the nineteenth century and, indeed, persists to some extent to the present day.

As early as the beginning of the nineteenth century many American educators had become thoroughly dissatisfied with the limitations of the colleges and began to look to Europe for new models. A number of younger scholars from New England visited German universities and were amazed to find a measure of spiritual independence and academic freedom that was quite unknown in their colleges. The principle of free inquiry and independent research, rather than rote learning, particularly stimulated their imaginations. They returned, filled with ambition to reform their colleges on the German model. But in spite of the fact that several of these young scholars then and later occupied positions of prominence and influence in their colleges—two were successively presidents of Harvard College—they were unable to break down and change the established traditions. For one thing, they had failed to take into consideration the fact that the American system of lower education was not geared, like the German, to the training of students for advanced study. The result was that, from about 1820 to 1900, many hundreds of American scholars went to Europe, particularly Germany, for the advanced training they could not get in the United States. The faculty lists of American colleges in those decades were studded with doctorates from Heidelberg, Leipzig, Marburg, and Berlin. Physicians in the metropolitan centers were assured of a good practice and professional distinction only if their M.D. degrees were from Munich or Vienna (Walters, 1965).

This intolerable cultural and academic dependence upon Europe eventually prompted the modest beginnings of graduate study in the colleges. American professors, trained in Germany, gathered students about them and more or less privately introduced them to advanced studies and, above all, to scholarly research. These ultracurricular studies were perhaps tacitly sanctioned by the colleges but were certainly not officially recognized before 1861, when Yale awarded the first three Doctor of Philosophy degrees earned on the North American continent. The Ph.D. and other doctorates had previously been granted by many colleges *honoris causa* to scholars of distinction or to some of their own graduates who had maintained a good moral character and, of course, paid an appropriate fee to the college (Eells, 1960).

The first "aristocratic" phase of higher education came to an end with the Morrill Land-grant Act of 1862, "for the promotion of the general welfare through education, research, and service in the fields of agriculture and the mechanical arts." This enlightened and forward-looking legislation, introduced by Justin Smith Morrill, U.S. representative (later senator) from Vermont, provided for the granting of public lands for the establishment of educational institutions. This act represents the first unique contribution of America to the field of education. At the same time, although it was hardly the intention of its sponsors, the act provided the great and needed impetus for the development of graduate education. It may seem strange to us that the idea of higher education for practical purposes was a novel and controversial notion only a century ago. It was looked upon with doubt and concern by the liberal arts colleges, but it took hold rapidly in the public institutions, already devoted to the service of their agricultural, industrial, political, and professional constituencies. Eventually the conservative private institutions, too, bowed to the principle of applying learning to social needs. It is no exaggeration to say that the Morrill Act gave new meaning and direction to higher education.

THE FORMATIVE YEARS. The next thirty years, beginning roughly in 1870 and ending sharply in 1900, were years of revolutionary changes in higher education. They firmly established the Doctor of Philosophy degree as the highest accolade to be earned in the universities and also established the pattern of requirements for its attainment. They saw the beginnings of the evolution of the administrative structure that eventually became the modern graduate school. And they also witnessed several bold experiments that failed. In short, this period established graduate study and determined many of its enduring qualities.

Johns Hopkins is usually credited with the founding of the first graduate school, then as now called the Faculty of Philosophy. It opened in 1876 and granted its first two doctorates in 1878. It must be noted, however, that Harvard organized its Graduate Department under an academic council in 1872 and awarded its first degree in 1873. Columbia's first doctorate came in 1875, but its governing bodies were not established until some ten years later. Michigan and Syracuse joined the pioneers in 1876, to be followed by California in 1885, Pennsylvania in 1889, and Clark and Chicago in 1891. The real innovation at Johns Hopkins was the attempt to follow completely the pattern of the German university by offering only graduate work without a supporting undergraduate college. A few years later Clark and Chicago tried the same experiment. All three failed, and undergraduate colleges were added in a short time. It is interesting to note that in the succeeding 75 years only two attempts were made to found strictly graduate universities. Rockefeller University was so chartered in 1954 and continues its operation as such. The University of California at San Diego opened in 1961 as the Graduate School of Science and Engineering but within three years added several undergraduate colleges. One may surmise that in the American climate a graduate school is not likely to survive without the underpinning of a strong undergraduate college (Walters, 1965).

At the height of the formative period, about 1895, it appeared that the Big Five—Harvard, Columbia, Johns Hopkins, Chicago, and California—were firmly entrenched as the major purveyors of the doctorate. But by 1900 the scene had radically changed, and the period of monopoly was drawing to a close. In that year the presidents of the Big Five sent invitations to the slightly less prestigious Big Nine (Catholic University, Clark, Cornell, Michigan, Pennsylvania, Princeton, Stanford, Wisconsin, and Yale) to meet with them and to organize what they hoped would be a closed corporation for the protection of graduate work and especially of the Ph.D. degree. They also hoped to devise a method of accreditation of undergraduate colleges for admission purposes to the graduate schools. This was the birth of the Association of American Universities (AAU), whose 14 member institutions in 1900 awarded 90 percent of all doctorates. But 35 other universities had already committed themselves to doctoral study, and some 110 more were engaged in master's degree programs. Today the AAU has grown to 43 member universities (including two in Canada). It is still regarded as the elite organization, but today its members award only about 48 percent of all doctorates. This is an indication not of their decline but of the rapid rise of a very large number of universities of good quality which now compete successfully with the long-established prestige schools (Berelson, 1960).

THE YEARS OF TRANSITION. In 1900, when the AAU was organized, about 150 institutions were offering graduate work, but fewer than 50 of these were awarding the doctorate. In 1965 the number of institutions committed to graduate work had risen to 697, of which 227 offer the doctorate. The number of doctorates awarded in 1900 was only 250, in 1910 only 440, and in 1920 no more than 620. But educators were already shaking their heads at the "overproduction of doctorates" and feared a resulting decline of standards. As early as 1903, William James warned that the "Ph.D. Octopus" would crush the true spirit of learning. In 1909, the year he became president of Harvard, Abbott Lawrence Lowell spoke of the "monstrous numbers attending graduate schools." Arthur Lovejoy said that there were "far too many graduate schools" and that "20 to 25 real universities" would be plenty. In spite of these predictions of doom, graduate education grew at an accelerated pace, producing 2,300 doctorates in 1930, 3,290 in 1940, and passing the 8,000 mark in 1950. The year-by-year statistics for the past decade, shown in the table below, dramatically illustrate the recent phenomenal growth of graduate education (Simon & Fullam, 1965; Wright, 1966).

Year	Graduate enrollment	Master's degrees	Doctorates
1955–56	271,000	59,294	8,903
1956–57	288,000	61,955	8,756
1957–58	312,000	65,614	8,942
1958–59	331,000	69,584	9,360
1959–60	356,000	74,497	9,829
1960–61	387,000	78,286	10,575
1961–62	422,000	84,889	11,622
1962–63	464,000	91,418	12,822
1963–64	517,000	101,122	14,490
1964–65	590,000	111,000	16,467

Maintenance of Standards. In the course of this rapid expansion of graduate work and with the annual addition of five to ten institutions newly committed to it, the chief problem of universities has been the maintenance of a high standard of excellence. The administration and the faculty must understand the long tradition of excellence associated with graduate degrees and must be aware of the responsibilities inherent, particularly, in Ph.D. instruction. The university, as an institution, must therefore be dedicated to freedom of inquiry and expression. A tradition of scholarship and publication must be long established in the faculty and cannot be expected to burgeon suddenly with the initiation of new activities. Of highest importance is the existence of a core of at least four or five specialists in each field of graduate study and of a strong supporting faculty in related or complementary departments. Acceptable doctoral programs cannot be developed by one or two scholars in intellectual isolation, no matter how brilliant or distinguished they may individually be (Bent, 1965).

The university must be prepared to meet the needs of the graduate faculty in terms of salaries, moderate instructional load, research and laboratory facilities, office space, stenographic and technical assistance, and sabbatical or professional leave. There must, likewise, be adequate resources for the support of graduate students in the form of fellowships, assistantships, and loan funds. What has been said above of the critical size of the graduate faculty of a department is equally true of the graduate student body. It must be large enough to justify graduate courses and seminars and to ensure a stimulating association of students with each other. A doctoral program with two students in it is not viable. Nor does an adequate student body exist when students live and work off campus and enroll in late afternoon and evening classes on a part-time basis. The university must have adequate library facilities for independent study, laboratory facilities for research, and funds for equipment, supplies, and travel needed in research. It is self-evident that the initial investment in a graduate program is not the final one and that the university is committed to continuing and generally increasing support (McCarthy & others, 1965).

ORGANIZATION OF GRADUATE SCHOOLS. An appropriate organization within the university is essential for the development and coordination of policies and procedures for the graduate programs and especially for the maintenance of uniform standards for the admission of students and for the awarding of graduate degrees. Since the development of American graduate schools has been, as we have seen, quite haphazard and unplanned for almost a century, it is not surprising that there is an astonishing variety of organizational patterns, ranging from highly sophisticated and well articulated to informal, casual, and disjointed. There are, of course, good historical reasons for this diversity. Although the pattern of graduate work was imported originally from Germany, an American university is not a university in the German sense. It is an accretion of schools or colleges that have generally been attached to an older undergraduate college. These colleges and schools have evolved as more or less self-contained entities, each with an organization that requires thoughtful faculty planning. Each has a staff that has been recruited, a curriculum that was planned and put into operation, a budget that must be calculated, and funds that must be secured and spent. All these responsibilities require a sense of group identification and action, which these colleges in the university have had. But when a school at the graduate level is imposed upon the established academic units, without curriculum, budget, or direct recruiting responsibilities—sometimes even without a dean—the essential ingredients have been omitted and too little motivation is provided for carrying on a real group enterprise (Walters, 1965).

The most common pattern of graduate instruction in most American universities is based upon the existence of a graduate faculty and a graduate dean. The composition of this graduate faculty varies from place to place. It may include all members of the university faculty who are approved to give graduate courses and seminars and to supervise doctoral theses. In large universities, membership in the graduate faculty may be restricted to professors of tenure rank; in still others, members are elected by the general university faculty. In any event, the graduate faculty exercises legal authority over the development of general policies and procedures for graduate programs (Eshelman, 1966).

In order to facilitate and expedite its functions, the graduate faculty elects from its members a graduate council, to which it delegates some of its functions. This is a body of manageable size, ordinarily of not more than 18 to 20 members, which meets frequently to deal with current matters. The council, in turn, establishes standing or special committees, which act in an advisory capacity to the council. These typically include an administrative committee, a committee on curriculum, a committee on faculty, and a committee on fellowships. These committees submit their recommendations to the graduate council, which usually has final jurisdiction over procedural matters and over many policy matters.

Other patterns than this are in existence in a few universities, particularly those which have been engaged in graduate work since the nineteenth century.

The executive officer of the graduate school is the graduate dean. The responsibility and authority assigned to him in different institutions varies widely, and in many cases the extent of his authority is determined by his own personality. He rarely has any actual statutory power. On the other hand, he frequently is the most influential figure in the development and administration of graduate work and of the university as a whole. He is ex-officio chairman of the graduate council and of the graduate faculty. He is generally by statute a member of the university's budget committee, the library committee, the building and major-equipment committee, and in short, of all committees whose actions have a bearing on graduate work. Since he is primarily responsible for the development and supervision of graduate work, he plays an important role in the selection and promotion of the faculty who participate in it (Chase, 1966).

Since the conduct of research is one of the major activities of the graduate school, the graduate dean must have an intimate connection with the university's organized research effort. There is a growing tendency in many universities to strengthen his position by making him additionally vice-president or coordinator for research. In this capacity he administers the intramural research funds and exercises supervision over externally supported research to determine whether a proposed project is an appropriate one for the university. Finally, one of his important duties is the appointment of doctoral and master's thesis committees upon the nomination of department chairmen. In brief, the position of the graduate dean is one of the most important in the university, and the quality of graduate work in the institution is largely dependent upon the competence, imagination, and administrative ability of the dean.

NATIONAL COORDINATION OF GRADUATE WORK. The first attempt to bring about a form of organization or control for the protection of graduate standards took place in 1900 through the establishment of the AAU. The original membership of 14 universities was expanded very slowly over the following 50 years and reached only 43 by 1950. Until 1946 the chief activity of the AAU consisted of the establishment of standards for liberal arts colleges, from which the universities recruited their students. Beyond this the AAU did little for the coordination of the universities themselves. This is not surprising in view of the traditional independence and autonomy of American graduate schools. The maintenance of standards and the internal organization of graduate work were left to the universities themselves.

In 1948 the Association of Graduate Schools (AGS) in the AAU was formed. The new body included the graduate deans of the universities whose presidents represented the AAU. The AGS met annually in the same city and on the same days as the AAU meetings, and the activities of the two groups were more or less coordinated. It is only natural, however, that the interests of the graduate deans were confined largely to the concerns of their graduate schools, whereas the interests of the presidents extended to the entire university.

The rapid expansion of graduate work to a very large number of institutions not included in the AAU or AGS soon made it necessary to think of broadening the scope of the existing organization. The graduate deans annually urged the presidents to admit a number of qualified universities to membership in the AAU, but the presidents were reluctant to agree with these proposals. This difference of opinion within the two related groups eventually prompted the graduate deans to suggest other measures in order to provide for broader representation of universities committed to graduate work. Various proposals were made and rejected. The one which received the widest support suggested the establishment of a federation of the various regional organizations of graduate schools, some of which had existed for a number of years. The oldest of these was the Conference of Deans of Southern Graduate Schools; the largest was the Midwest Conference on Graduate Study; the newest was the Western Association of Graduate Schools. The federation of these regional associations with the AGS seemed to be a promising solution, but an appropriate organizational plan could not be worked out. In 1960 the AGS called a meeting of the representatives of the five regional organizations in order to devise a plan for the establishment of a comprehensive body representing the interests of graduate education in universities and colleges in all parts of the United States. As a result of this planning session, invitations were issued to 100 universities to send voting representatives to an organization meeting.

The 100 institutions were chosen on the criteria that they had awarded 50 or more doctorates during the period 1936 to 1956 and that they awarded five or more doctorates in 1958. The meeting took place in Chicago on March 22, 1961, and 96 of the 100 invited institutions sent delegates (Henle, 1962).

The new organization which was formed at that meeting was named the Council of Graduate Schools in the United States. A constitution was drafted and officers and an executive committee were elected. The criteria for membership beyond the original 100 charter members provided that universities and colleges were eligible if (1) the institution was accredited by the appropriate accrediting agency; (2) the institution had conferred at least 30 master's degrees or 10 doctorates within the three-year period preceding application; and (3) the degrees conferred fell within a spread of at least three fields which were commonly recognized to be distinct disciplines. It was estimated that approximately 225 to 250 universities and colleges in the United States were eligible under these criteria. In 1962 the Council of Graduate Schools established an office in Washington, D.C., with a permanent president and secretariat. The membership of the organization grew quite rapidly from the original 100 to 249 in 1966 (U.S. Office of Education, 1966).

The purpose of the Council of Graduate Schools, as stated in its constitution, is

> to provide graduate schools in the United States with a comprehensive and widely representative body through which to counsel and act together . . . to provide a forum for the consideration of problems and solutions, and in meetings, conferences, and publications define needs and seek means of satisfying them in the best interests of graduate education throughout the country. . . . In the analysis of graduate education, in the indication of desirable revision and further development, in the representation of needs, and in all other functions relating to effecting its purpose, the Council not only shall be free to act as an initiating body but it shall assume direct obligation for so doing (Henle, 1962)

Graduate Programs. The proliferation of fields in which degrees are offered has been as fantastic as the growth of graduate work itself. This is in part due to the discovery of new learning, such as electronics and endocrinology; in part to the fractionation of old disciplines into subdivisions, such as biology into various subfields; and in part to the combination of disciplines into new ones, such as biochemistry, biophysics, and bioradiology. In 1900 there were about 35 recognized disciplines, and no one of the 30 or 40 graduate schools offered work in more than 20 of them. By 1920 the number of major fields of learning had increased to about 45 plus about 100 somewhat questionable subfields. In that year Cornell offered the doctorate in 49 fields; Columbia in 38; Chicago in 31; California and Johns Hopkins in 43; Yale in 21; and Harvard in only 15 (Berelson, 1960).

In 1965 the doctorate was offered in an incredible 595 fields, subfields, and combinations of fields. This large number is to some extent the result of the use of different names for the same disciplines: "computer science" and "control science" are probably the same; "classics," "classical studies," "classical languages and literatures," and "classical philology" are certainly all different names for the same subject. California (Berkeley) offered the doctorate in the most fields, 90, followed by Cornell with 72, and Harvard with 68, Chicago with 65, and Yale with a modest 38 (Graham, 1965).

Among the new fields of graduate study are aerospace science, astrophysics, and astrogeophysics, astronautical engineering, logopedics, nuclear science, polymer science, and virology. Among some of the older ones that still maintain themselves are hotel administration, household economy and management, range management, household equipment, and marriage and family living.

The introduction into the graduate curriculum of a large number of programs that are definitely intended as preparation for professional careers has resulted in a somewhat anomalous situation. Dentistry, law, medicine, and theology have traditionally been regarded as learned professions and are therefore not included in graduate schools. There are, however, numerous other equally professional programs that lead a kind of borderline existence between the graduate and the professional school, such as architecture, business administration, criminology, education, engineering, journalism, and librarianship. The problem is compounded by the fact that many universities offer both academic degrees (M.A., M.S., and Ph.D.) and professional degrees in these programs (Master and Doctor of Education, Master and Doctor of Engineering, etc.). The administrative difficulty is only partially resolved in most universities by assigning control of the professional degree to the appropriate school or college and of the academic degree to the graduate school. Since, in general, the requirements for the academic degree are more rigorous than those for the corresponding professional degree, this results in an unfortunate duality of standards (McCarthy, 1966a).

REQUIREMENTS AND DEGREES. Admission. The one universal requirement for admission to a graduate school is the attainment of a bachelor's degree from an accredited undergraduate college. Beyond this, the admission standards and requirements vary widely. All of the graduate schools in prestige universities and most of the graduate schools of good quality require an undergraduate record of at least a B average. Some of the less demanding institutions will admit students with an average of slightly below B. Some state universities and state colleges are required by law to admit all graduates of accredited colleges in the state regardless of the student's academic record.

In addition to the general requirements for admission, most academic departments have standards of their own which are frequently considerably higher than those of the graduate school. They may, first of all, require a grade-point average of at least half a point higher than the graduate school requirements. They may also require that a student have followed an undergraduate curriculum which prepared him fully for the successful pursuit of graduate studies. Such additional requirements are particularly common in those fields which are in great demand, such as physics, chemistry, and psychology. One of the reasons for such additional requirements is the necessity of providing laboratory space for every accepted student, and a department must therefore limit its admission to the number of students that can be accommodated.

Retention of Students. Just as the admission requirements of graduate schools vary greatly, so the conditions of continuing eligibility vary also. Most of the better graduate schools require that a student maintain a B average in all his work. If he drops below that average in any one semester he is placed on probation, and if the deficiency is not remedied within the following semester, he is dismissed. There are, however, a good many graduate schools that are more lenient in their requirements for continuing eligibility. It should be added that public institutions that are required by law to accept all college graduates usually have a very high attrition rate at the end of the first and second semesters.

The Master's Degree. The master's degree is customarily awarded by a college or university to an aspirant who achieves a substantial level of academic accomplishment during a one- or two-year period of graduate study beyond the baccalaureate. The master's program usually consists of a coherent pattern of courses concluding with a comprehensive examination or a thesis or both.

Two types of master's programs can be identified. The first of these leads to the Master of Arts (M.A.) or the Master of Science (M.S.) degree and provides an introduction to scholarly activities and research and often serves as preparation for a career in junior-college or public school teaching. These two degrees made up about 56 percent of the total of 111,000 master's degrees awarded in 1965.

The second type of master's degree is a professional degree intended to provide an introduction to a profession and often to serve as preparation for a career in that field. The names used to designate the professional master's degrees are generally stated as Master of Business Administration, Master of Education, and so forth. In 1965 the Master of Education was the most frequently awarded degree of this type, amounting to about 15 percent of all master's degrees awarded. In order of frequency, the Master of Business Administration was awarded by 118 institutions; Master of Music by 82; Master of Fine Arts by 71; and Master of Music Education by 38.

The master's program, in general, consists of a coherent sequence of lectures, seminars, discussions, and independent studies or investigations designed to help the student acquire an introduction to the mastery of knowledge, creative scholarship, and research in his field. Although many institutions announce that the time requirement for the master's program is one year, it very commonly requires at least a year and a half and frequently two years (McCarthy, 1966b).

A master's thesis is required by approximately 60 percent of universities awarding this degree. It represents a modest contribution to knowledge, a review, a report, a synthesis, or a design in the student's field. It is seldom a very lengthy production, and it is rarely expected to be an original contribution to learning in the field.

A rigorous comprehensive examination over the field of study is usually a part of quality programs, particularly of those which do not require a thesis. In general, the comprehensive examination is both written and oral, but the oral part is frequently waived where a thesis has been a part of the requirements.

The Doctor of Philosophy. The Doctor of Philosophy degree has become the mark of highest achievement in preparation for creative scholarship and research. The program of study leading to it is designed to prepare a graduate student for a lifetime of creative activity and research, often in association with a career in teaching at a university or college. The doctoral program consists of lectures, seminars, discussions, independent study, and research designed to assist a student to acquire as well as to contribute to knowledge in his field. During his first year or two of study, the doctoral student may take a number of formal lecture courses and seminars to advance his knowledge of his field, of its scholarly tools, and of its relationship to other disciplines. Frequently, especially in the physical and biological sciences, he begins his research shortly after entering the program (Wilson, 1965).

At the end of this period of preparation the student is expected to pass one or more rather comprehensive examinations in his field in order to demonstrate that he is now qualified to enter upon independent study. He is generally required at this time also to demonstrate a reading knowledge of two foreign languages, usually French and German, although now Russian and several other languages may be substituted. In some institutions one of the language requirements may be satisfied by the passing of an examination in a tool subject, such as statistics or advanced mathematics. In many universities the written comprehensive examinations are supplemented by a rigorous oral examination before a committee of the student's department.

After satisfactory completion of this battery of examinations the student may be admitted or advanced to candidacy for the doctoral degree and may then devote nearly all his time to completion of his research. This research is conducted under the guidance and supervision of a member of the graduate faculty or of a committee. The results of the research are compiled and presented in a doctoral dissertation, which is generally expected to represent a contribution to knowledge in the student's field. In former years many universities required publication of the dissertation, but this requirement can no longer be imposed, because of the vast number of dissertations now being produced and the very high costs of publication. The dissertation is therefore presented in typed and bound form to the university library and is frequently microfilmed for distribution to scholars in the field.

When the dissertation is completed and has been accepted by the candidate's doctoral committee, he takes his final oral examination. In former days this took the form of a defense of the thesis against the critical comments of the entire graduate faculty. Today it has become more or less a formality, giving the candidate the opportunity to display his erudition before his committee and invited guests. In some cases, especially when the student has completed his dissertation in absentia, the final oral examination may even be waived. Since it has lost most of its meaning, it is quite likely that the requirement will eventually be dropped.

Intermediate Degree. Since the completion of the dissertation frequently takes a number of years, and since, in fact, a considerable number of candidates actually never finish and therefore earn no doctorate, some universities have recently begun to award an intermediate degree at the time of advancement to candidacy. This degree is variously called Master of Philosophy (M.Phil.), awarded by Yale, Toronto, and others, and Candidate in Philosophy (Cand. Phil.), awarded by Michigan and other Big Ten universities. It is too early to predict how common this practice will become, but it seems to be gaining support.

FINANCIAL AIDS. In times not so long past, graduate students paid the costs of their education from their own or borrowed funds. Only a few fortunate ones received some slight assistance in the form of ill-paid teaching or research assistantships or of tuition scholarships. This situation began to change radically at the end of World War II as the universities, state and federal governments, and private foundations began to recognize that graduate students represented a national resource and therefore needed to be encouraged and supported (Davis, 1962).

The first great step in that direction was the Veterans Benefits Act, commonly known as the G.I. Bill, that provided scholarships and fellowships for returning soldiers. Since that time, support programs have proliferated to the extent that in 1962, 71 percent of all graduate students had some sort of stipend (Davis, 1962). For the year 1967–68 a total of 76,648 fellowships and traineeships are available, exclusive of those offered by the universities themselves (Quick, 1966). These are, of course, nonservice stipends. The number of service awards—teaching and research assistantships—is much larger, estimated to be in the range of 100,000 and more. Fellowships in the natural sciences are most numerous, provided chiefly by federal agencies—the Atomic Energy Commission, the National Aeronautics and Space Administration, the National Institutes of Health, and the National Science Foundation. The U.S. Office of Education awards 6,000 three-year fellowships with no restrictions on fields of study. The Woodrow Wilson Foundation offers 1,000 fellowships for prospective college teachers, mainly in the humanities and social sciences. Most stipends range from $2,000 to $3,500 per year, and allowances for dependents of $400 to $600 each are usually added (Quick, 1966).

RESEARCH. Research in the graduate school serves two purposes: first, it is an integral part of the instructional program and, as such, is inseparable from the teaching function. The young graduate, no matter what his field of study, is therefore introduced as early as possible to the objectives, methods, and tools of research in order to develop his initiative for independent study. The sooner he can liberate himself from the tyranny of rote learning, lectures, and textbooks, the sooner he will become an adult member of the community of scholars—which the graduate school should be. For these reasons the recurring debates over the relative importance of teaching and research are both fruitless and fatuous; in the graduate school there can be no teaching without research and no research without teaching.

Second, research in the graduate school exists for its own sake in furtherance of the university's commitment to discovery and development of new knowledge. This commitment is as old as the university itself, but it has never been so universally recognized and so well supported as it is today. Until about 1940 research in the graduate school was financed almost exclusively by intramural funds. Research was done because the professor enjoyed doing it, not for utilitarian ends. Then the federal government's urgent need for both high-level and basic research and development suddenly changed the picture and with it the graduate school. Almost overnight university laboratories became exploring and testing grounds for hundreds of projects in chemistry, physics, biology, psychology, and dozens of more esoteric subjects. Federal funds poured into the graduate schools and research became Big Business.

In the post-war years the scholars and their students turned their efforts to the peacetime problems of the nation—not only in the natural sciences but also in the social sciences and humanities. Professors and students in graduate schools are working on the problems of air and water pollution, soil erosion, climate modification, and virus, bacteria, and pest control. They are also working on urban renewal, city and regional planning, and humanistic and artistic improvement of communities. For research and development in these and in hundreds of other fields, the federal government in 1963 expended $1.573-billions (U.S. Office of Education, 1963).

POSTDOCTORAL STUDY. A by-product of these research activities and of the expansion of the graduate school has been the development in recent years of the practice of postdoctoral study. Beginning in the mid-1950's young Ph.D.'s engrossed in a research problem elected to stay with their professors for a year or two to continue their studies. By 1960 the National Science Foundation and other agencies recognized the value of such study and offered fellowships in support of it. Today postdoctoral study is an accepted fact of academic life, particularly in the natural sciences. It is becoming almost standard practice for a young Ph.D. in chemistry, physics, or biology to apply at once for a postdoctoral fellowship and to spend another two or three years in student status before he begins his active professional career. As a result, a few of the best graduate schools now have almost as many postdoctoral scholars as predoctoral students. Many of our best universities will not consider the appointment of a young Ph.D. to their faculties without such a period of additional study. There are certainly many great advantages in such additional work, particularly when it is not recognized by another and higher degree. On the other hand, there can be little doubt that the practice of postdoctoral study contributes to the shortage of college teachers. It may well be that the prevalence of this practice presages the future of the graduate school. It has just about reached the limits of possible horizontal expansion. It is not unlikely that the future expansion of the graduate school will be upward. The vast increase in the store of human knowledge makes it literally impossible for a student to acquire breadth as well as the necessary depth in his field of specialization in the course of his three to five years of predoctoral study. The time may not be far off when the postdoctoral level of graduate study will become the real capstone of the American educational system (Kerr, 1963).

Gustave O. Arlt
The Council of Graduate Schools
in the United States

References

Bent, Henry E. *New Doctor of Philosophy Degree Programs.* Council of Graduate Schools in the United States, 1965.

Berelson, Bernard. *Graduate Education in the United States.* McGraw-Hill, 1960. 346p.

Carmichael, Oliver C. *Graduate Education.* Harper, 1961. 213p.

Chase, John L. (Ed.) *A Directory of Graduate Deans at United States Universities, 1872–1965.* USOE, 1966. 40p.

Davis, James A. *Stipends and Spouses.* U Chicago Press, 1962. 194p.

Eells, Walter Crosby. *Academic Degrees.* GPO, 1960. 324p.

Eshelman, James N. (Ed.) *Proceedings of the Fifth Annual Meeting.* Council of Graduate Schools in the United States, 1966. 176p.

Graham, Jane. (Ed.) *A Guide to Graduate Study.* ACE, 1965. 608p.

Henle, Robert, S.J. (Ed.) *The Council of Graduate Schools in the United States.* Council of Graduate Schools in the United States. 1962. 24p.

Kerr, Clark. *The Uses of the University.* Harvard U Press, 1963.

McCarthy, Joseph L. *The Doctor's Degree in Professional Fields.* Council of Graduate Schools in the United States, 1966(*a*). 12p.

McCarthy, Joseph L. *The Master's Degree.* Council of Graduate Schools in the United States, 1966(*b*). 20p.

McCarthy, Joseph L., and others. *The Doctor of Philosophy Degree.* Council of Graduate Schools in the United States, 1965. 16p.

Quick, Robert. (Ed.) *Fellowships in the Arts and Sciences, 1967–1968.* ACE, 1966. 93p.

Simon, Kenneth A., and Fullam, Marie G. (Eds.) *Projections of Educational Statistics to 1974–75.* GPO, 1965. 68p.

U.S. Office of Education. *Digest of Educational Statistics.* GPO, 1963. 144p.

U.S. Office of Education. *Education Directory, 1965–66;* Part III: *Higher Education.* GPO, 1966. 242p.

Walters, Everett. (Ed.) *Graduate Education Today.* ACE, 1965. 246p.

Wilson, Kenneth M. *Of Time and the Doctorate.* Southern Regional Education Board, 1965. 212p.

Wright, Patricia. (Ed.) *Earned Degrees Conferred, 1963–64.* GPO, 1966. 283p.

GROUP PROCESSES

Studies of group processes have burgeoned during the past 12 years. In 1955, Hare and others annotated a bibliography of 584 items on small groups. By 1959, Raven had collected 1,445 references related to group processes, and in 1962 Hare published a *Handbook* consisting of 1385 items; and in 1966 McGrath and Altman presented a bibliography of 2,699 items. During the same period, classical books on small groups were being brought up to date. The 1953 edition of Cartwright and Zander's book was revised in 1960 and is undergoing revision again. The book by Hare and others (1955) was considerably altered, with 20 articles being added, in 1965. Shorter analyses have been published indicating both the magnitude of and interest in group processes (Golembiewski, 1962; Luft, 1963; Olmstead, 1959; and Shepherd, 1964).

An equally significant trend has been the direct application of group research for societal improvement. A notable invention was the technique, utilized by the National Training Laboratories for educating adults, referred to as the training group (T-group). Important volumes relevant to the T-group are those by Bradford and others (1964) and by Schein and Bennis (1965). A number of contributions on organizational group processes that included many applied studies were also related to the development of T-group technology (Katz & Kahn, 1966; Likert, 1961; March & Simon, 1958).

There was also a vigorous emphasis on the application of group processes to educational settings. The 59th yearbook of the National Society for the Study of Education (Henry, 1960) provided social-psychological theory on classroom groups and proposed ways of using research findings to improve instruction. Subsequent books and articles reviewed empirical data on group processes in the classroom and school (Bany & Johnson, 1964; Glidewell & others, 1966; Lippitt & others, 1967), while some utilized data to make recommendations for improving teaching (Schmuck & others, 1966; Fox & others, 1966; Chesler & Fox, 1966; Amidon & Hunter, 1966). The rise in concern and work in public education was due in part to increased federal funds and foundation grants. From 1950 to 1960 federal funds available for educational research and development increased tenfold. Funds for educational researchers have continued to increase at an even more rapid rate since 1960. The basis for increased funds can be found in the complexity of educational institutions, which was brought on by expanding urban centers, widespread bureaucratization, and a growing awareness of the importance of highly skilled people for managing complex technology.

WAYS OF CATEGORIZING GROUPS. Groups may be considered from conceptual or methodological perspectives. From the conceptual view groups have been categorized according to goals, structure, or interaction modes; while groups studied with research methods in mind have been categorized as laboratory, field experimental, natural, and training.

Conceptual Categories. Groups are constituted of several potentially antagonistic pulls. They have work to accomplish but also must maintain cohesiveness and morale. Since groups are made up of persons there exist persistent pulls between group goals and individual motives. Group goals describe a preferred or desired state which guides behavior, provided the goals are clear and have some degree of consensus.

Various dimensions for analyzing group goals have been advanced; the task–social-emotional and group–individual dichotomies have been the most popular. Hare (1962) built four categories descriptive of groups using these two dimensions. Industrial work groups in which completion of tasks requires concerted effort and in which individuals are viewed as interchangeable are in the task, group category. Classroom groups have learning tasks to accomplish, but typically the focus is on individual students and therefore classes are in the task, individual category. Training groups or group dynamics seminars which concentrate on emotional processes are in the social-emotional, group category, while group therapy would be illustrative of the social-emotional, individual category.

Groups may be more effective if they fulfill more than one of these goal conditions. A project in which an industrial group analyzes its social-emotional processes can enable the group to produce higher economic gains (Kuriloff & Atkins, 1966). The school class which sets out to perform a group task may strengthen individual motivations to learn (Schmuck & others, 1966). T-groups have been strengthened by working on tasks, and therapy groups have found it beneficial to analyze both individual problems and group issues (Bradford & others, 1964).

Groups also have been categorized by structure. Miller and Swanson (1958) defined as bureaucratic those groups with three or more levels of supervision, contrasting them with less complex units in which interpersonal interaction would occur more frequently. Groups with at least three supervisory levels may be qualitatively different from less complex units, since members of lower echelons are less likely to hold an overview of the group's goals. Likert (1961) suggested a structural alternative to reduce problems created by such organizational complexity. His proposal, termed "link-pin structure," assumed that man-to-man conceptions of structure, functional in smaller groups, are ineffective in bureaucracies. Likert's proposal attempted to capitalize on the power of small face-to-face groups by calling for work groups to be organized across hierarchical levels with persons participating in decisions at levels above and below their own.

Formal aspects and informal aspects of groups have been major structural distinctions drawn by researchers (Stock & Thelen, 1958). Formal aspects are ways in which various members work toward carrying out the officially specified group goals. In an industrial group, for instance, the chart of organizational responsibility and the ways roles are defined or work is to be carried out are part of the formal structure. One formal feature of classroom groups is the way children are expected by adults to perform the role of student.

Informal aspects involve ways in which each member personally relates to others. The industrial group is characterized by an influence structure that often is not parallel with formal authority. An informal feature of classroom groups is the distribution of students' preferences for one another. These informal features have effects on the ways in which stated formal objectives are carried out—e.g., the extent to which members like one another or their willingness to support one another influences the way academic tasks are accomplished (Schmuck, 1963b).

Jensen (1957) described the school as being made up of six structures. Two of these structures, work and authority, are formal; power, prestige, and friendship cliques are informal; and the last structure, communication, can be either formal or informal. A more inclusive analysis would have an informal counterpart for every formal structural element. For example, groups have membership boundaries that are prescribed formally; they also have inclusion-exclusion structures. Groups have formal authority and informal power structures or formal communication networks and informal structures of intimacy.

Informal structures can be described by a group's sociometric patterning. The ways members distribute their preferences on such dimensions as friendship and influence are examples of informal structure. In studies of classrooms, Schmuck (1966) found that peer groups with a wide sociometric dispersion had more cohesiveness and supportive norms concerning educational goals than groups with greater concentrations of choices.

Closely related to the categorization of groups structurally is their description by interaction modes.

The most notable conceptualization on interaction was that of Parsons (1951), who viewed a group as a network of interactive relationships. Five interaction modes, called the pattern variables, were suggested as dimensions along which groups can be categorized: *affective-nonaffective,* which focuses on the emotion involved; *self-collective,* which describes whether the interaction is aimed at satisfying personal motives or group goals; *universalism-particularism,* which describes how consistently persons in similar roles are defined by one another in the interaction; *achievement-ascription,* which refers to whether individuals gain status by performance or by some inherent characteristics; and finally, *specificity-diffuseness,* which describes how focused the interaction is in a content domain.

Schutz (1958) described groups by interaction preferences and styles from a psychological point of view. His theory assumed that group activities are predictable from knowledge of the persons and the principles governing their interaction. He computed compatibility scores for pairs in terms of their needs for inclusion, control, and affection. Scores are based on the ways persons express these needs and how much of each kind of need they wish others to fulfill. Schutz (1961) suggested how need homogeneity or heterogeneity might function when composing productive groups—e.g., problem-solving groups in which a variety of skills are desirable might better be structured heterogeneously, while therapy groups in which it is desirable to explore a single psychological theme should be composed homogeneously.

Research Methods Categories. Groups in the laboratory typically are composed of naive subjects who participate in a contrived and controlled situation. Emphasis continues to be placed on face-to-face groups of from 4 to 15 persons; however, much concern also has been shown with 2- and 3-person groups. Research on balance or congruity theories (Zajonc, 1960) has focused either on twosomes or one person's thoughts concerning his relationship with another. Such theories assume that when behavioral systems are in states of imbalance forces arise to restore balance. Imbalance occurs between two people when they are attracted to each other but hold discrepant attitudes. Price (1961) showed that when two people like each other very much but hold different attitudes about others they feel uneasy and strive to reduce the discrepancy. Concerning threesomes, Mills (1953) supported Simmel's theory that three persons tend to segregate into a pair and one other.

Experimental studies of larger groups have increasingly tended to be done outside the laboratory. In one such field experiment Sherif and others (1961) divided boys who were spending three weeks in an isolated camp into two groups which competed in a tournament of games. While the two groups worked in competition toward goals not available to all, they developed hostile intergroup interaction. In an attempt to reduce conflict between the groups, Sherif arranged circumstances which forced the boys to work together cooperatively. He created urgent, challenging situations such as a breakdown in the water supply, a food truck which would not start, and the need for a decision by the boys on how to finance a movie at camp. After the boys cooperated in working toward these superordinate goals they developed friendlier relationships.

Flanders and Havumaki (1960) showed that classroom interaction involving teacher praise was likely to increase a student's sociometric status. In some experimental groups, teachers rewarded students seated in odd-numbered seats. In comparison groups, statements involving praise were directed to the group as a whole, and all students were allowed to participate equally. Students in odd-numbered seats in the former situation received significantly more peer choices than did students seated in the even-numbered seats. In the comparison classes differences among students were not significant, and the peer choices were spread around more evenly.

Groups studied as they exist with no attempt being made to influence them are termed "natural groups." Newcomb (1961) combined aspects of the field experiment with a natural group by structuring interpersonal relationships in a college residence. Twice, he offered free rent for a semester to 17 students who agreed to be observed or interviewed each week. The overall findings substantiated balance theory—i.e., those who agreed on a variety of attitudes were attracted to one another; such attraction became stronger as students learned of more similarities that they shared.

Most studies of schools and classrooms fall into the natural-groups category. Gross and Herriott (1965) explored the determinants and effects of principals' leadership in a national sample of elementary schools through questionnaires and interviews. They found that principals high in a style labeled "executive professional leadership," compared with those lower in that style, had staffs with higher morale, teachers with better professional performances, and students with higher achievement.

Lippitt and Gold (1959) studied group processes in elementary classrooms and found that students who were low in the sociometric structure also had negative self-esteem. Moreover, such students were observed to respond to others with more hostility, insensitivity, and defensiveness than their peers. Teachers were found to reinforce this unhealthy pattern by their lack of constructive behavior toward the low-status children.

A T-group usually is made up of about 12 participants and a trainer who together face the task of developing a miniature society in a short period of time. Member interaction provides the curriculum for learning about self, interpersonal relations, and group processes. The trainer encourages participants to discover ways of learning how to learn about their own interpersonal competence and how to become more effective participants. Peculiar to the T-group is the help members are given in developing a recognition of more choices about their own group behavior and the engendering in them of feelings of openness and confidence in relations with others.

Miles (1965) has indicated some significant effects

of T-groups in a study of elementary-school principals. He found significant changes in the principals' interpersonal skills and attitudes as a function of how active they were in the T-group and their reception of personal feedback from others. Schutz and Allen (1966) found that the T-group changed people selectively, e.g., overly dominant persons became less dominant, while overly affectionate persons became more discriminating. In a follow-up study they found changes in personal behavior and feelings toward others, and continuing change in a positive direction of behavior of others toward the participants.

LEADERSHIP. "Leadership" refers to behaviors that bring a group closer to achieving its goals and is defined as interpersonal influence central to group action. It is differentiated from the concept of leader; the term "leader" identifies the person who has been appointed or elected to be the "head man." Leader is a static concept, while leadership is dynamic.

Leadership continued to be the most researched topic on group processes during the past decade. Numerous books were prepared (Hollander, 1959; Petrullo & Bass, 1961; Stogdill, 1959; Tannenbaum & others, 1961). Over 17 percent of the references in Hare's *Handbook* (1962) were on leadership. Interest also rose in the related areas of authority (Friedrick, 1958), coercive persuasion (Schein, 1961), dominance (Schmuck, 1964) influence (Kelman, 1958); and power (Cartwright, 1959).

Bass (1960) contributed a broad framework for relating leadership and group processes. He analyzed leadership as being attempted, successful, or effective. Attempted leadership refers to motives and actions involved in trying to change some aspect of a group's actions. Successful leadership consists of influencing a group's actions, while effective leadership requires that influential behaviors move the group toward achieving some valued objective. Successful leadership is necessary for effectiveness, but some successful leadership behaviors may not lead to positive outcomes.

Attempted Leadership. Individuals attempt leadership because of personal, interpersonal, and situational bases. Atkinson's motivational theory (Atkinson & Feather, 1966) is helpful for organizing some personal factors involved in attempted leadership. Atkinson proposed that the tendency to act is determined by a motive force, an expectancy factor, and an incentive value of acting, all put together in a multiplicative relationship. Following this theory, the tendency to attempt leadership would be a function of a motive to lead multiplied by an expectation of success in leading multiplied by an incentive for accomplishment.

The motive force to lead is viewed as a drive for influencing others which stems from a relatively stable aspect of personality. It is related to such personality needs as power, achievement, and affiliation. Hemphill (1961) reviewed four studies that supported the expectancy-of-success and incentive-value parts of the theory. Expectancy involves the belief that one can be successful when attempting leadership. Hemphill showed that persons who previously had been successful subsequently attempted leadership more often than before and also that persons who viewed themselves as expert in the discussion attempted leadership more often than did those who saw themselves as less expert. Incentive value is a reward for actually being successful in leading. In another experiment, Hemphill (1961) varied the amounts of reward for completing a group task and found that members of groups with high incentive attempted more leadership than persons in low-incentive groups.

The tendency to attempt leadership also is influenced by interpersonal and situational factors. Hemphill showed that support and acceptance of a person's ideas encouraged that person to attempt leadership more often. Moreover, Hamblin (1958) found that situations in which all group members face a common crisis induce more leadership attempts. Groups that are developing or changing show higher incidences of attempted leadership than static groups.

Successful Leadership. Successful leadership involves influencing the direction of group action and may be either emergent or imposed. Emergent leadership occurs when the acceptance of influence is based on the consent of followers; imposed leadership is based on superior authority as defined by group structure.

Hollander (1961) described the essential bases of a person's emerging with successful leadership as adherence to group norms and being seen as competent and approachable. Developmentally, the person initially behaves in ways that confirm members' expectations about how members should behave. Next, the emerging leader accumulates "idiosyncrasy credits," defined as being perceived as contributing to the group's task while living up to expectations. The accumulation of credits requires that the person accurately estimate opinions of other members. Bugental and Lehner (1958) found that emergent leaders are superior to nonleaders in judging group opinions on familiar and relevant issues. Hamblin (1958) showed that persons who gain influence may lose it if they are unable to maintain some attractiveness for others and to continue to be seen as competent. Kirscht and others (1959) discovered that emergent leaders reinforce and maintain their positions by giving and asking for suggestions, as well as summing up and integrating comments of others.

Successful influence in elementary classes was studied by Gold (1958), who found that higher-power members possessed personal attributes highly valued by the peer group. Such powerful youngsters were more friendly, more likely to be helpful to their peers, and more outgoing in social relations. Their less powerful counterparts used more physical force to influence peers and manifested more emotional disturbances.

Imposed leaders wield influence successfully especially when they have empathic ability. Moreover, members view designated leaders as contributing more to group solutions, and this perception is related to the leaders' skills in winning attention and support from members. Imposed leaders influence successfully when they reward members actively (Spector & Suttell, 1957), when these rewards are given frequently (Bennis & others, 1958), and when they allow the members to participate actively (Hare, 1953). The participation of followers generally has positive effects on their attitudes and job performances; however, those with weak needs for independence are unaffected by opportunities to make decisions (Vroom, 1959). Berkowitz (1953) showed that some members did not object to a dominating supervisory leadership when they knew they could participate and take the initiative. Thibault and Riecken (1955) found that highly authoritarian persons were likely to accept a leader who was hostile and direct but usually rejected low-status persons with similar characteristics.

Effective Leadership. Effective leadership requires that interpersonal influence lead to some valued outcome. Cleven and Fiedler (1956) showed how a leader's ability to discriminate clearly among subordinates was related to effectiveness. They found that supervisors whose crews had high production discriminated more sharply between the most and the least liked co-workers than did those whose production was below average. Fiedler (1958) also found that effective leaders perceived most and least preferred co-workers in their group to be more dissimilar than less effective leaders did. The effective men also maintained more emotional distance from the followers and had more task interest.

Maier and Solem (1952) found that effective leaders encouraged minority opinions and conflict more than less-effective leaders. Torrance (1957) indicated that more-effective groups had leaders who allowed for greater participation, initially wider divergence of expressed judgments, and greater acceptance of diverse decisions than did leaders of less-effective groups. Schutz (1961) viewed effective leaders as carrying out functions that other members were not performing, referring to such leaders as completers; e.g., when the group lacks task direction, the leader encourages it by making suggestions, initiating new ideas, or asking for plans of action.

Indirect and participative methods often have been shown to be more effective leadership practices than direct methods. Amidon and Flanders (1961) found that dependency-prone students taught by indirect methods learned more geometry than such students taught by direct methods. Katz and Kahn (1960) found that effective industrial supervisors delegated authority more and did not supervise as closely and directly as less-effective leaders did. They also found that effective leaders spent a lot of time planning instead of demonstrating and were more employee-oriented than technically centered.

Shaw and Blum (1966), in contrast, found that direct leadership sometimes is effective. Direct leaders were more effective than their indirect counterparts when group tasks were well understood and favored by the members. By implication, less clear and more unfavorable tasks required more indirect leadership. Flanders (1960) showed that students learn more under indirect leadership than direct leadership when they are unclear about their goals and direction. Students appear to learn well under direct leadership when they are clear about and like their work.

Dubin (1965), in a review of studies of industrial supervision, found that leadership behavior positively affects the productivity of workers if it is appropriate to the technological setting. The more production resembles a unit or batch technology, the greater is the probability that worker autonomy and indirect leadership will be effective. Close and direct supervision is more appropriate when technology resembles a continuous-production system.

Gross and Herriott (1965) found indications that effective school principals combine both direct and indirect leadership behaviors. The effective principals allowed for teacher autonomy, treated teachers as professional workers, and took interest in teacher participation in staff meetings. At the same time, the effective principals attempted to influence teachers directly by bringing to their attention educational literature and techniques, and they also prodded teachers to upgrade their classroom performances.

It appears clear that there is no one best leadership style for all situations. Several leadership styles are effective, but only in relation to appropriate work settings and particular personality characteristics of members. Variety in leadership styles presents a challenge to understand the setting in which each works best.

DYNAMICS OF GROUPS. Topics such as cohesiveness, norms, structure, and decision making continued to be popular for research in the past decade, but they were not studied as frequently during that time as they had been during the preceding decade. Topics that were studied intensively were attraction and hostility, conformity, and communication.

Attraction and Hostility. Perhaps the most researched problem aside from leadership has been why persons like or feel hostile toward each other. A set of filtering factors appear to operate during the development of interpersonal attraction. The most basic aspect of this progression involves physical proximity. Hare (1962) indicated that persons who are near to each other in residence or on a job become friends more often than others. Similarly, an important initial aspect for the development of romantic love is physical attractiveness. Walster and others (1966) showed that the largest determinant of how much a college male liked his date, how much he wanted to date her again, was simply how attractive she was, as judged by disinterested observers.

The next aspect of the filtering process involves social-status variables—e.g., social class, religion, and prestige. Hollingshead (1949) found that nearly 70 percent of all cliques were composed of social-class equals. Goodnow and Taguiri (1952) studied the friendships of Protestants, Catholics, and Jews from upper-class backgrounds in a preparatory school and found that each religious group chose a larger percentage of its own members as friends than would be expected on the basis of chance.

Proximity, physical attractiveness, and similar social-status characteristics are relatively superficial aspects of friendship formation. Similar attitudes and values, along with complementary personality needs, play more basic roles and enter the filtering process later. Newcomb (1961) showed that persons with similar attitudes and values became attracted to each other. Conversely, persons who were initially attracted became even more friendly if they shared values and less attracted if they differed on important values. Griffitt (1966) found that attraction between two persons increased as the proportion of similar self-descriptions between them increased.

Winch and others (1955) discovered that marital partners often choose each other to satisfy complementary needs—e.g., assertive persons tended to marry receptive persons, and dominant individuals sought out submissive ones. Kerckhoff and Davis (1962) collected measures of both value consensus and need complementarity from couples considering marriage and studied their progress toward permanent relationships. Value consensus was significantly related to progress for short-term couples, while need complementarity was significant for long-term couples. These findings supported a theory of a series of filtering factors operative during the development of interpersonal attraction, with proximity, physical attraction, and social status operating early, consensus on values somewhat later, and need complementarity still later.

Hostility and rejection are related in part to similar factors. There is more dislike for persons who live far away and work at different places than for those who live nearby and work at the same place; more hostility toward those who are physically unattractive than toward those who are physically attractive; more antipathy for those who are of different social status or hold different values than for those of the same social status or holding the same values; and more rejection of those whose needs are in conflict with the needs of the other than of those whose needs complement his. Furthermore, when groups are in competition toward a goal which is not available to all, the members often develop hostile interpersonal interaction.

Hostile interpersonal reactions also emanate from frustrations over potential or actual losses of reward, status, or security. Pepitone (1964) found that hostility was based upon how much the person was threatened with a loss of status or security. Conversely, the greater was the reduction of threat or status loss which another person brought about, the more attractive this person became.

Studies of classroom groups also have focused on dynamic processes in tracing the bases of attraction and rejection. Bonney and Powell (1953) found that differences in the behavior of high- and low-sociometric choices were exhibited on the first day of first grade. The highly acceptable students were initially more conforming, smiling, cooperative, and less likely to play alone. Iscoe and Garden (1960) uncovered differences between attributes of sixth-grade boys and girls and their sociometric status. Sociometric status and field dependence were related positively for girls, while the results were just the opposite for boys, suggesting that attractive boys adopted an active, analytic, independent orientation. A positive association between anxiety and rejection was obtained for girls, indicating that popular girls had low levels of anxiety. Perhaps field dependence and low anxiety place girls in a better position than boys to be attractive to teachers. Schmuck and Van Egmond (1965) showed that girls had more-compatible relations with their teachers than boys did and that female teachers had more-compatible relationships with students than male teachers did.

Conformity. Conformity, or compliance to group norms and pressures, has primarily been studied from two points of view, that of the group processes and that of the individual characteristics that are associated with it. Norms are rules which are shared and accepted as legitimate by members of a group and which specify the behaviors that are expected. When a member deviates from norms, others communicate with him in an attempt to induce conformity.

A group condition which induces pressures to conform is member friendliness and attraction (Jackson & Saltzstein, 1958). Moreover, one is likely to conform when the majority holding a contrary position is large, when he must present his opinion publicly, when the group is composed of persons perceived as experts, and when a question is discussed until a group consensus is reached. When individuals persist in not conforming to group standards, attempts are made to persuade them, and if these fail, the group ostracizes and rejects the nonconformer (Israel, 1956). When the nonconformer has one or more supporters he is more likely to continue not to conform unless his supporters turn against him, in which case the nonconformer is more likely to conform.

Psychological dynamics also affect a person's tendency to conform. One is more likely to conform when he is unclear about what is being discussed by the group (Sherif & Harvey, 1952). Compared with persons sticking with an objectively valid response, those who gave in to group pressure were characterized by lower intelligence, less spontaneity, more repression, less self-confidence, less tolerance for ambiguity, and more anxiety (Krech & others, 1962). Schachter (1959) discovered that first-born youngsters were more likely to be influenced by the opinions of others and theorized that they have greater anxiety than later-born children about being ostracized and left out. Sampson (1962) showed that first-born boys but not girls were more susceptible to influence compared to later-born children, and Schmuck (1963a) indicated that the sex of siblings may be more significant than birth order as an antecedent condition for girls' conformity behavior. Girls with brothers were more susceptible to group influences than girls with sisters were.

Communication. Research continued on the effects of communication networks. Attention moved to exploring the relationships among individual characteristics, role expectations, and one's position in a network. Kelley (1954) discovered that, regardless of the communication network, persons who believe that their job status is low, compared with those who think it is high, are less satisfied with their work and communicate more fantasies about higher-status jobs. High-status persons showed constraint in communicating criticism and confusion about their jobs to low-status persons.

Strodtbeck and others (Strodtbeck & Mann, 1956; Strodtbeck & others, 1957) found, in studies of simulated jury deliberations, that members with higher socioeconomic status participated more, had more influence on others, and were perceived by fellow jurors as more competent than members with lower socioeconomic status. Sex differences affected the communications also; e.g., men initiated extended comments on problem solutions, while women tended to react more to male contributions.

Communication networks may, however, have more dominating effects on interaction than do role expectations or personality characteristics. Berkowitz (1956) showed that highly ascendent persons in peripheral positions became passive, while low ascendents in the center position behaved with more assertiveness. A study by Hearn (1957) showed that group members tended to communicate more to persons opposite them at a table than to those next to them.

Major interest in communication has also centered on how emotions affect the communication of content. Every person in communication with another is confronted with cognitive and affective dimensions. Feelings are an integral part of relationships and the attitudes that persons hold toward each other influence their communications about work. Moreover, task interest and emotional experiences should be integrated for the maintenance and growth of a relationship (Slater, 1955).

Affective aspects of communications in the classroom were studied intensively. Flanders (1959) observed that 60 percent of the time someone is talking in an elementary or secondary classroom, and approximately 70 percent of that talk comes from the teacher. He found that teachers used less than 3 percent of talking time for praising and encouraging students and less than 5 percent in reacting to and using student ideas. Comparing the incidences of various kinds of teacher communication, he found that 85 to 95 percent were devoted to intellectual aspects and only 5 to 15 percent to affective aspects of the classroom interactions.

Schmuck (1966) compared teachers with positive emotional classroom climates and those with less-supportive climates. The former teachers communicated with a greater variety of students, rewarded individuals for helpful behaviors with specific statements, and controlled behavioral disturbances by making general statements. The teachers with less-positive climates called on fewer students for classroom participation, neglected the slower, less-involved students, and tended to reward less and to punish individuals more for breaking classroom protocol. Kounin and others (1961) found that punitive teachers activated aggression and tension in the students, created conflict about misbehavior, and distracted the children's attention from academic achievement. McKeachie and others (1966) showed that male students high in the need for affiliation made relatively better grades in classes characterized by a high level of affiliation cues, whereas men with low need for affiliation did relatively better in classes with few affiliation cues.

Obviously research on group processes, and especially group aspects of public education, has multiplied greatly since the third edition of this encyclopedia. All current indications are that such research will increase at an even faster rate during the next decade.

Richard A. Schmuck
The University of Oregon

References

Amidon, Edmund, and Flanders, Ned. "The Effects of Direct and Indirect Teacher Influence on Dependent-prone Students Learning Geometry." *J Ed Psychol* 52:286–91; 1961.

Amidon, Edmund, and Hunter, Elizabeth. *Improving Teaching.* Holt, 1966. 221p.

Atkinson, John, and Feather, Norm. *A Theory of Achievement Motivation.* Wiley, 1966.

Bany, Mary, and Johnson, Lois. *Classroom Group Behavior.* Macmillan, 1964. 412p.

Bass, Bernard. *Leadership, Psychology, and Organizational Behavior.* Harper, 1960.

Bennis, Warren, and others. "Authority, Power, and the Ability to Influence." *Hum Relations* 11:143–5; 1958.

Berkowitz, Leonard. "Sharing Leadership in Small Decision-making Groups." *J Abn Social Psychol* 48:231–8; 1953.

Berkowitz, Leonard. "Personality and Group Position." *Sociometry* 19:210–22; 1956.

Bonney, M. E., and Powell, James. "Differences in Social Behavior Between Sociometrically High and Sociometrically Low Children." *J Ed Res* 46:481–95; 1953.

Bradford, Leland, and others. *T-group Theory and Laboratory Method.* Wiley, 1964. 498p.

Bugental, Daphne, and Lehner, George. "Accuracy of Self-perception and Group-perception as Related to Two Leadership Roles." *J Abn Social Psychol* 56:396–8; 1958.

Cartwright, Dorwin. *Studies in Social Power.* U Michigan Press, 1959. 225p.

Cartwright, Dorwin, and Zander, Alvin. *Group Dynamics.* 1st ed., Harper, 1953; 2nd ed., Harper, 1960.

Chesler, Mark, and Fox, Robert. *Role-playing Methods in the Classroom.* SRA, 1966. 86p.

Cleven, Walter, and Fiedler, Fred. "Interpersonal

Perceptions of Open Hearth Foremen and Steel Production." *J Applied Psychol* 40:312–4; 1956.

Dubin, Robert. "Supervision and Productivity: Empirical Findings and Theoretical Considerations." In Dubin, R. and others. (Eds.) *Leadership and Productivity*. Chandler Publishing Company, 1965. p. 1–50.

Fiedler, Fred. *Leader Attitudes and Group Effectiveness*. U Illinois Press, 1958.

Flanders, Ned. "Teacher-Pupil Contacts and Mental Hygiene." *J Social Issues* 15:30–9; 1959.

Flanders, Ned. *Teacher Influence, Pupil Attitudes, and Achievement*. Cooperative Research Project No. 397. USOE, 1960.

Flanders, Ned, and Havumaki, Sulo. "The Effect of Teacher-Pupil Contacts Involving Praise on the Sociometric Choices of Students." *J Ed Psychol* 51:65–8; 1960.

Fox, Robert, and others. *Diagnosing Classroom Learning Environments*. SRA, 1966. 131p.

Friedrick, C. J. (Ed.) *Authority*. Harvard U Press, 1958.

Glidewell, John, and others. "Socialization and Social Structure in the Classroom." In Hoffman, Lois, and Hoffman, Martin. (Eds.) *Child Development Research*. Russell Sage, 1966. p.221–56.

Gold, Martin, "Power in the Classroom." *Sociometry* 21:50–60; 1958.

Golembiewski, Robert. *The Small Group*. U Chicago Press, 1962.

Goodnow, Robert, and Tagiuri, Renato. "Religious Ethnocentrism and Its Recognition Among Adolescent Boys." *J Abn Social Psychol* 47:316–20; 1952.

Griffitt, William. "Interpersonal Attraction as a Function of Self-concept and Personality Similarity-Dissimilarity." *J Pers Social Psychol* 4:581–4; 1966.

Gross, Neal, and Herriott, Robert. *Staff Leadership in Public Schools*. Wiley, 1965.

Hamblin, Robert. "Leadership and Crises." *Sociometry* 21:322–35; 1958.

Hare, A. Paul. "Small Group Discussions with Participating and Supervisory Leadership." *J Abn Social Psychol* 48:273–5; 1953.

Hare, A. Paul. *Handbook of Small Group Research*. Free, 1962. 512p.

Hare, A. Paul, and others. (Eds.) *Small Groups: Studies in Social Interaction*. 1st ed., Knopf, 1955; 2nd ed., Knopf, 1965.

Hearn, Gordon. "Leadership and the Spatial Factor in Small Groups." *J Abn Social Psychol* 54:269–72; 1957.

Hemphill, John. "Why People Attempt to Lead." In Petrullo, Luigi, and Bass, Bernard. (Eds.) *Leadership and Interpersonal Behavior*. Holt, 1961. p. 201–15.

Henry, Nelson. (Ed.) *The Dynamics of Instructional Groups*. 59th Yearbook. Part II, NSSE U Chicago Press, 1960. 286p.

Hollander, E. P. *Emergent Leadership and Social Influence*. Social Science Institute, Washington U, 1959.

Hollander, E. P. "Some Effects of Perceived Status on Responses to Innovative Behavior." *J Abn Social Psychol* 63:247–50; 1961.

Hollingshead, August B. *Elmtown's Youth*. Wiley, 1949.

Iscoe, Ira, and Garden, J. A. "Field Dependence, Manifest Anxiety, and Sociometric Status in Children." U Texas, 1960. (Unpublished.)

Israel, J. *Self-evaluation and Rejection in Groups*. Almquist and Wiksell, 1956.

Jackson, Jay, and Saltzstein, Herbert. "The Effect of Person-Group Relationships on Conformity Processes." *J Abn Social Psychol* 57:17–24; 1958.

Jensen, Gale E. *Socio-psychological Analysis of Educational Problems*. Ann Arbor, 1957.

Katz, Daniel, and Kahn, Robert. "Leadership in Relation to Productivity and Morale." In Cartwright, Dorwin, and Zander, Alvin. (Eds.) *Group Dynamics*, 2nd ed. Harper, 1960. p. 554–71.

Katz, Daniel, and Kahn, Robert. *The Social Psychology of Organizations*. Wiley, 1966. 498p.

Kelley, Harold H. "Communication in Experimentally Created Hierarchies." *Hum Relations* 4:39–56; 1954.

Kelman, Herbert. "Compliance, Identification, and Internalization." *J Conflict Resolution* 2:51–60; 1958.

Kerckhoff, Alan, and Davis, Keith. "Value Consensus and Need Complementarity in Mate Selection." *Am Sociol R* 27:295–305; 1962.

Kirscht, J. P., and others. "Some Factors in the Selection of Leaders by Members of Small Groups." *J Abn Social Psychol* 58:406–8; 1959.

Kounin, Jacob, and others. "Explorations in Classroom Management." *J Teach Ed* 12:235–46; 1961.

Krech, David, and others. *Individual in Society*. McGraw-Hill, 1962. p. 505–30.

Kuriloff, Arthur, and Atkins, Stuart. "T-Group for a Work Team." *J Applied Behavioral Sci* 2:63–94; 1966.

Likert, Rensis. *New Patterns of Management*. McGraw-Hill, 1961. 279p.

Lippitt, Ronald, and Gold, Martin. "Classroom Social Structure as a Mental Health Problem." *J Social Issues* 15:40–58; 1959.

Lippitt, Ronald, and others. *Understanding Classroom Social Relations and Learning*. SRA, 1967.

Luft, Joseph. *Group Processes*. National Press, 1963. 57p.

Maier, Norman, and Solem, A. R. "The Contribution of a Discussion Leader to the Quality of Group Thinking: The Effective Use of Minority Opinions." *Hum Relations* 5:277–88; 1952.

March, James, and Simon, Herbert. *Organizations*. Wiley, 1958. 262p.

McGrath, Joseph, and Altman, Irwin. *Small Group Research*. Holt, 1966.

McKeachie, Wilbert, and others. "Student Affiliation Motives, Teacher Warmth, and Academic Achievement." *J Pers Social Psychol* 4:457–61; 1966.

Miles, Matthew. "Changes During and Following Laboratory Training: A Clinical-Experimental Study." *J Applied Behavioral Sci* 1:215–42; 1965.

Miller, Daniel, and Swanson, Guy E. *The Changing American Parent.* Wiley, 1958. 302p.

Mills, Theodore. "Power Relations in Three-person Groups." *Am Sociol R* 18:351-7; 1953.

Newcomb, Theodore. *The Acquaintance Process.* Holt, 1961. 303p.

Olmstead, Michael. *The Small Group.* Random, 1959.

Parsons, Talcott. *The Social System.* Free, 1951. 575p.

Pepitone, Albert. *Attraction and Hostility.* Prentice-Hall, 1964. 238p.

Petrullo, Luigi, and Bass, Bernard. (Eds.) *Leadership and Interpersonal Behavior.* Holt, 1961. 382p.

Price, Kendall. "Intensity of Attraction as a Condition in a Social Psychological Balance Theory." Doctoral dissertation. U Michigan, 1961.

Raven, Bertram. *Bibliography of Publications Relating to the Small Group.* Technical Report No. 1. Office of Naval Research, 1959.

Sampson, Edward. "Birth Order, Need Achievement and Conformity." *J Abn Social Psychol* 64:155-9; 1962.

Schachter, Stanley. *The Psychology of Affiliation.* Stanford U Press, 1959.

Schein, Edgar. *Coercive Persuasion.* Norton, 1961.

Schein, Edgar, and Bennis, Warren. *Personal and Organizational Change Through Group Methods.* Wiley, 1965. 376p.

Schmuck, Richard A. "Sex of Sibling, Birth Order Position, and Female Dispositions to Conform in Two Child Families." *Child Develop* 34:913-8; 1963(a).

Schmuck, Richard A. "Some Relationships of Peer Liking Relations in the Classroom to Pupil Attitudes and Achievement." *Sch R.* 71:337-59; 1963(b).

Schmuck, Richard A. *Strategies of Dominance and Social Power.* Office of Research Administration, U Michigan, 1964. 64p.

Schmuck, Richard A. "Some Aspects of Classroom Social Climate." *Psychol Sch* 3:59-65; 1966.

Schmuck, Richard A., and Van Egmond, Elmer. "Sex Differences in the Relationship of Interpersonal Perceptions to Academic Performance." *Psychol Sch* 2:32-40; 1965.

Schmuck, Richard A., and others. *Problem Solving to Improve Classroom Learning.* SRA, 1966. 88p.

Schutz, William. *FIRO: A Three-dimensional Theory of Interpersonal Behavior.* Holt, 1958.

Schutz, William. "The Ego, FIRO Theory, and the Leader as Completer." In Petrullo, Luigi, and Bass, Bernard. (Eds.) *Leadership and Interpersonal Behavior.* Holt, 1961. p. 48-65.

Schutz, William. "On Group Composition." *J Ab Social Psychol* 62:275-81; 1961.

Schutz, William, and Allen, Vernon. "The Effects of a T-group Laboratory on Interpersonal Behavior." *J Applied Behavioral Sci* 2:265-86; 1966.

Shaw, Marvin, and Blum, J. Michael. "Effects of Leadership Style Upon Group Performance as a Function of Task Structure." *J Pers Social Psychol* 3:238-42; 1966.

Shepherd, Clovis. *Small Groups.* Chandler Publishing Company, 1964. 130p.

Sherif, Muzafer, and Harvey, O. J. "A Study of Ego Functioning: Elimination of Stable Anchorages in Individual and Group Situations." *Sociometry* 15:272-305; 1952.

Sherif, Muzafer, and others. *Intergroup Conflict and Cooperation: The Robbers Cave Experiment.* Institute of Group Relations, U Oklahoma, 1961.

Slater, Philip. "Role Differentiation in Small Groups." *Am Sociol R* 20:300-10; 1955.

Spector, Paul, and Suttell, B. J. *An Experimental Comparison of the Effectiveness of Three Patterns Of Leadership Behavior.* American Institute for Research, 1957.

Stock, Dorothy, and Thelen, Herbert. *Emotional Dynamics and Group Culture: Experimental Studies of Individual and Group Behavior.* New York U Press, 1958.

Stogdill, Ralph. *Individual Behavior and Group Achievement.* Oxford U Press, 1959. 352p.

Strodtbeck, Fred, and Mann, R. D. "Sex Role Differentiation in Jury Deliberations." *Sociometry* 19:3-11; 1956.

Strodtbeck, Fred, and others. "Social Status in Jury Deliberations." *Am Sociol R* 22:713-9; 1957.

Tannenbaum, Robert, and others. *Leadership and Organization.* McGraw-Hill, 1961.

Thibault, James, and Riecken, Henry. "Authoritarianism, Status, and the Communication of Aggression." *Hum Relations* 8:95-120; 1955.

Torrance, E. Paul. "Group Decision Making and Disagreement." *Soc Forces* 35:314-8; 1957.

Vroom, Victor. "Some Personality Determinants of the Effects of Participation." *J Abn Social Psychol* 59:322-7; 1959.

Walster, Elaine, and others. "Importance of Physical Attractiveness in Dating Behavior." *J Pers Social Psychol* 4:508-16; 1966.

Winch, R. F., and others. "Empirical Elaboration of the Theory of Complementary Needs in Mate Selection." *J Abn Social Psychol* 51:508-13; 1955.

Zajonc, Robert. "The Concepts of Balance, Congruity, and Dissonance." *Public Opin Q* 24:280-96; 1960.

GROUPING

"Grouping" is a much-used term in the vocabulary of school organization because group teaching is the prevailing practice and because many varieties of grouping have been devised to make the teaching of groups more effective or more manageable. For over a century, group teaching of grade-level classes has dominated instruction in elementary and secondary schools. Both grade placement and group teaching tend to ignore differences among students. The grade system calls for presenting the same basic grade-level curriculum to all students having the same number of years of schooling. Group teaching has been mainly whole-class teaching in which the methods and pacing of instruction, as well as the lessons taught, are largely the same for all members of the class.

The large differences in intellectual abilities and

educational attainments among students of any age level have forced a continuing examination of grouping practices and of instructional methods. A result has been the invention and tryout of many ways of setting up instructional groups as well as various methods of instruction that are intended to take account of differences among the students in a group. These two approaches to dealing with individual differences usually have developed independently of each other. Innovators either have tried changing the composition or size of the group or have tried new methods for differentiating the instruction given group members, not both.

VARIETIES OF GROUPING. The most comprehensive review of grouping practices and research is the volume edited by Yates (1966). This report was sponsored by the UNESCO Institute for Education in Hamburg and deals with grouping in various countries including England, Italy, Sweden, the United States, and West Germany. A feature of the book is a 125-page section presenting abstracts of 50 selected research studies on grouping.

Shane (1960) offers a list of 32 grouping plans within the elementary school. Yates (1966) presents a list of 17 varieties of grouping in elementary and secondary schools. A partial list of major sorts of grouping includes grade-level grouping; tracking students into different curricular sequences; ability or achievement-level grouping within a grade; assigning students to special classes; multiage or multigrade grouping; differential grouping, subject to subject; flexible grouping according to students' capabilities with different learning activities; and numerous methods of intraclass grouping. Most grouping practices are intended to produce classes that are relatively homogeneous in one or more characteristics related to learning. Some practices, however, seek to make the group heterogeneous in abilities, achievement, age, personal-social characteristics, etc.

A valuable selection of articles reporting studies of grouping has been edited by Hillson (1965). Anderson (1962) offers a concise summary of grouping practices. An early review of grouping practices and research is Part I of the 35th yearbook of the National Society for the Study of Education, edited by Whipple (1936). A number of recent surveys or bibliographies are available, by the following authors: Franseth and Koury (1963, 1964), Goodlad (1960), Morganstern (1966), Otto and Sanders (1964), Wrightstone (1957), and Yates (1966).

INTERSCHOOL GROUPING. Yates (1966) presents a survey of the approaches used in various countries to allocate students to schools. In reviewing the sparse research on the effects of assigning students to selective rather than comprehensive schools, he concludes that virtually all the studies of interschool grouping at the secondary level have found that schools with heterogeneous populations maintain achievement at least as high as that in selective schools. The ablest students are not found to suffer losses in achievement in comprehensive schools. There is some evidence that less-able students do not learn as well when segregated into special schools as when left in comprehensive schools.

SCHOOL ORGANIZATION AND GROUPING. Grouping is an aspect of organization for instruction that has intimate relations with such other aspects as staff assignments, scheduling, uses of space and equipment, and intrastaff communications. Goodlad (1963) offers an important distinction between vertical and horizontal organization of instruction. The former concerns how students move upward along the curricular sequences from year to year. It covers graded, nongraded, and multigraded progression. Horizontal organization concerns the assignment of students to teachers and instructional groups. It includes the self-contained classroom and departmentalization, heterogeneous and homogeneous interclass grouping, patterns of flexible scheduling, and team organization. Summary descriptions and analyses of three major types of organizational plans are presented by Heathers (1966).

Self-contained Classroom. The commonest basis for organizing instruction in the elementary school is the so-called self-contained classroom, in which a general elementary teacher is assigned one grade-level class for the full day and is called upon to teach all curricular areas except as assisted or replaced by specialists in art, music, physical education, remedial reading and speech, library, or foreign language. This plan of organization contrasts with the departmentalized program based on specialist teaching that is usual in secondary schools.

Proponents of the self-contained classroom, as represented by the contributors to the volume edited by Snyder (1960), have claimed that the one-teacher plan should be used for young children in order to meet their emotional-social needs and to assure them of instruction in the several curricular areas that is properly correlated. They have sharply criticized departmentalization in the elementary school, claiming that it leads to subject-centered rather than child-centered teaching and that it destroys the unity of the child's instructional program. An example of this position is found in the article by Fleming and others (1960), who take issue with the semidepartmentalized dual-progress plan devised by Stoddard.

Opponents of the self-contained classroom, represented by Stoddard (1961), contend that the all-purpose teacher cannot offer knowledgeable and inspirational instruction in all of the major curricular areas. They also claim that the grade-level curriculum and grade-level grouping as usually found in the self-contained classroom fail to provide for individual differences among learners of a given age level.

Research on the self-contained classroom largely consists of studies conducted by proponents of other plans who have compared outcomes of departmentalization, team teaching, or nongrading with outcomes of instruction in the self-contained classroom.

Departmental Organization. Between 1900 and 1930 departmentalization became a common practice in America's elementary schools. Otto (1932) found that in 1929 some variety of departmental organization existed in 84 percent of eight-year elementary schools and in 37 percent of six-year elementary schools. The practice declined thereafter. According to Dean (1960), over 75 percent of elementary schools employed only the self-contained classroom at the time of his study, and less than 1 percent were fully departmentalized.

A trend began about 1955 toward the increased use of departmentalization in elementary schools, especially in the upper grades. This trend is shown in a national questionnaire survey of elementary-school principals conducted by the National Education Association (1962). In the survey, 20 percent of the respondents reported that there had been some departmentalization in their schools in 1956. In 1961, 36 percent of the principals reported some departmentalization, and 49 percent predicted that their schools would have some in 1966.

The usual reason for departmentalizing instruction in the elementary school is to provide for specialist teachers of the major curricular areas. In the 1950's demands arose for specialist teaching of science and mathematics because of concerns about improving instruction in these areas in the interest of national security. Also, the new curricula being developed in these areas called for subject-matter knowledge that most general elementary teachers did not possess. In a study of attitudes of elementary teachers in an eastern city of about 25,000, Ackerlund (1959) found that the majority of teachers in the upper grades would prefer teaching in a departmental program to teaching in the self-contained classroom. A majority of them did not feel adequately prepared, either in knowledge of subject matter or of teaching methods, to teach all of the major subjects.

Research on departmentalization is limited, much of it is of poor quality, and the reports of studies do not provide the data needed to identify the features of departmentalization that are responsible for the outcomes. In many departmental programs the only readily observable differences from the self-contained classroom involve moving from room to room and teacher to teacher; student grouping remains unchanged, and no major changes can be observed in the contents or methods of instruction. Rouse (1946) found few differences in classroom practices in an observational study of departmentalized and nondepartmentalized programs in the elementary school. There is little reason to expect such differences when one considers that the teachers in departmentalized programs usually have had training and experience only as general elementary teachers. Elementary teachers assigned as specialists in science, mathematics, English, or social studies often have had few more content or methods courses in their specialty than the average among general elementary teachers, as Gibb and Matala (1962) and Heathers (1967) have shown.

Studies of the effects of departmentalization on academic achievement and on students' personal-social adjustment have not yielded consistent findings. Spivak (1956) found that ninth-grade students who had been in self-contained classrooms in grades 7 and 8 achieved significantly more than students who had been in a departmentalized program during these grades. Gibb and Matala (1962) obtained some reliable differences favoring departmentalization, though most of the comparisons did not reliably favor either the departmental plan or the self-contained classroom.

Tulsa, Oklahoma, employed a semidepartmental plan in its elementary schools in which students received instruction in language arts, social studies, and mathematics under a homeroom teacher during one half-day, while they studied during the other half-day under different specialist teachers of art, music, physical education, speech, and library. Broadhead (1960) presents evidence that pupil adjustment as measured with the Science Research Associates Junior Inventory was higher with Tulsa fifth-graders than with a control group composed of pupils from other school systems who had studied in self-contained classrooms. However, the validity of the Junior Inventory as a measure of adjustment is doubtful, and Broadhead does not offer sufficient evidence that population characteristics of his comparison groups were controlled.

Another semidepartmental plan for the upper years of the elementary school is the dual-progress plan devised by Stoddard (1961). The plan, as employed in Grades 3–4 or 4–5, calls for full-time specialist teachers of English and social studies, mathematics, science, art, music, and physical education. Instruction in English, social studies, and physical education is on a grade-level basis and occupies one half-day. Instruction in mathematics, science, art, and music in the plan is organized on a nongraded basis with cross-graded, achievement-ability grouping of students for each subject separately.

The pilot test of the plan, reported by Heathers (1967), accomplished implementation of its major structural features. However, numerous requirements of the plan were not implemented in the conduct of instruction. Thus, a mastery criterion was not employed in determining whether a student had completed a learning task and was ready to proceed to the next task in the curriculum sequence. Also, teachers often did not advance students at different rates, as was called for in the nongraded curricular areas. Interpreting results of the dual-progress plan is difficult because the plan introduces at the same time a semidepartmental schedule, specialist teaching, ability grouping, differential grouping from subject to subject, and nongrading in some curricular areas. The major findings associated with this plan are referred to in the later section of this article on ability grouping, since that appeared to be the most influential feature of the dual-progress plan.

In the junior high school, core programs provide a compromise between the self-contained classroom and the fully-departmentalized programs of most secondary schools. In the core approach, as described by Wright (1958) and Della-Dora (1960), English and social studies are taught as one integrated curriculum, in one time block, and by one teacher. Similarly, in many core programs, mathematics and science are taught together by one teacher. Core programs are meant to offer a more secure emotional-social setting than regular departmental programs do and to correlate instruction in related subjects better. Research studies reviewed by Michelson (1957) have not demonstrated any major effects of core programs on students' achievements or their adjustment at school. In the pilot study of the dual-progress plan an attempt was made to implement the plan in grades 7 and 8 of the junior high school. This called for having one teacher conduct instruction in English and social studies according to the core approach. This feature of the plan had to be dropped because, as reported by Heathers (1967), teachers could not be found who were prepared and willing to teach both curricular areas.

Research on departmentalization in the elementary school does not provide evidence that the practice lessens the unity of the child's educational program or that it has negative effects on his personal-social growth. The studies reported by Gibb and Matala (1962) and Heathers (1967) found that the great majority of students preferred having different teachers and liked changing classes. Also, Heathers (1967) reports that about 75 percent of elementary teachers in the pilot test of the dual-progress plan expressed a preference for being assigned as specialists in one curricular area. In the same study, over 80 percent of parents who responded to an anonymous questionnaire expressed favorable attitudes toward the semidepartmental program.

Team Organization. Team teaching, also called cooperative teaching, occurs when two or more teachers share in planning and conducting instruction that is offered to the same group of students, whether at elementary, secondary, or college levels. Departmentalization, in contrast, occurs when two or more teachers divide the instruction offered to students without joint planning and correlated teaching. Elementary-school teams usually cover all or almost all areas of instruction with the students assigned to the team. Teams in secondary schools usually cover instruction in one curricular area or in two closely related areas. A team organization frequently has been employed in college, especially in education courses.

A detailed treatment of the theory and practice of team teaching is available in the volume edited by Shaplin and Olds (1964). Briefer general accounts of cooperative teaching can be found in Anderson's book (1966) and in a special issue of *The National Elementary Principal* (1965). The program at Lexington, Massachusetts, is described and evaluated in Bair and Woodward (1964). Extensive bibliographies on cooperative teaching are to be found in the works just cited, in that by Davis (1964), and in that by Lambert and others (1964).

A great variety of organizational patterns are included under the umbrella label of "team teaching." Teams vary in size from two elementary teachers who share the instruction offered 40 or 50 students to teams made up of as many as eight teachers and over 200 students. Some teams are organized on one grade level, while others contain students from two or three adjacent grade levels.

Teachers' assignments within teams represent a considerable number of roles and specializations. Team roles include those of team leader, master teacher, part-time teacher, intern teacher, teacher aide, and team clerk. Team members may specialize in teaching one curricular area, in teaching certain units within a curricular area, in teaching large or small groups, in teaching children with certain kinds of learning difficulties, in conducting instruction with the use of technological aids, or in supervising intern teachers.

The term "team teaching" is misleading, since it usually happens that only one teacher conducts the instruction offered a group at any given time. Woodring (1964) suggests that a better descriptive label would be "team organization and planning." However, in many teams, planning of instruction in a given area is done mainly by the one or two team members who specialize in teaching that area. It should be clear that there cannot be sufficient time in whole-team meetings to do the many hours of instructional planning required. Team planning tends to focus on making overall curriculum decisions, on scheduling, on discussing special problems of students, and on assessing and reporting students' progress. Grannis (1964) offers an exploration of team planning of a curriculum unit that elucidates both the potential of teamwork and the demands it places on team members.

Some educators prefer introducing specialist teaching in the elementary school within the context of cooperative teaching rather than departmentalization in order to ensure that the instruction the student receives in different subjects is properly correlated. Cooperative teaching, however, does not guarantee that instruction in different fields will be correlated adequately. Many times the members of a team lack the training required for planning effectively together, and usually a team lacks the time needed for cooperative planning of individual students' programs.

A central aspect of most team plans is flexible grouping. The plans call for varying group size from very large to very small, depending on the learning task and the abilities of students. A working assumption has been that some curricular areas—particularly social studies, science, and literature—are well-suited for large-group instruction. A bonus that can result from large-group teaching is that some members of the team are freed to work with small groups or with individual students, to plan other work, or to confer with other teachers or parents. Wallace (1965) explored the issue of whether large-group instruction can take account of individual differences among students. His answer was positive, but he recommended following large-group sessions with small-group activities that involved all members of the instructional team.

The theme of flexibility applies to virtually all aspects of team organization and functioning. In addition to the continual variation of group composition and size, flexibility also occurs in scheduling of time, space, and personnel. The plan for the secondary school described by Trump and Baynham (1961) places emphasis on flexibility. Bush and Allen (1964) offer a method for flexible scheduling in the high school that uses an electronic computer.

Research on cooperative teaching is generally of poor quality. Most of the studies have been descriptive rather than evaluative. In a review of the research conducted up to 1963, Heathers (1964) found no well-controlled studies that measured outcomes of team teaching. The results reported could not be interpreted because of a lack of data on the implementation of the plans being compared. Also, the reports did not provide a basis for determining separately the effects of different features of the team organization, such as flexible scheduling, flexible grouping, staff specializations, the use of teacher aides, or team planning. The reports available then did not indicate any substantial effects of the plans on student achievement. Generally, attitudes of students, parents, and teachers were favorable toward the team plans.

Bair and Woodward (1964) report favorable outcomes of the Lexington Plan with respect to student achievement and attitudes of participants. Their analysis on financing team teaching led to the conclusion that the Lexington Plan need not be more expensive than conventional plans. Lambert and others (1964), in a study comparing team teaching with the self-contained classroom, found significant differences between the two plans in classroom interaction patterns and in student achievement, but not in student adjustment. Interpreting their findings is made uncertain by the fact that they did not offer data on the conduct of instruction in the two plans. Also, they did not offer data on the comparability of the staffs serving the two plans.

Nongraded Organization. Nongrading, as the concept is presented by Goodlad and Anderson (1963), refers to any approach that breaks away from conventional grade-level instruction and enables students to advance in the curriculum at rates corresponding to their individual capabilities. While nongrading or "continuous progress" can be accomplished by differentiating instruction within any organizational pattern, many school systems with nongraded programs make use of multiage grouping to bring together students who are at about the same level of advancement in one or more subjects. Other schools set up within-grade achievement-level grouping to facilitate differential pacing. In elementary schools, nongraded programs are most numerous in the primary years though some school systems have introduced nongrading on a K–6 basis. Usually nongrading in the elementary school applies only to skill learnings in reading and mathematics. Some high schools have adopted nongraded programs, most frequently following the model developed by Brown (1963). In this plan, nongraded advancement applies to mathematics, science, English, and history.

The general assumptions underlying nongrading are that learning effectiveness, motivation to learn, and mental health all will be enhanced by gearing the student's advancement in the curriculum to his learning rate. With slow learners, the allowance of more time for studying a unit is intended to permit them to master each task before proceeding to the next. With rapid learners, nongrading is intended to permit faster progress and to reduce experiences of boredom and cheap success associated with a pace geared to slower-learning students.

The use of achievement-level grouping to foster nongraded advancement assumes that teachers will differentiate instruction in level and range from group to group and from individual to individual within a group. Unfortunately, research studies on nongrading usually have been silent on how, or to what extent, teachers actually adapted their instruction to promote nongraded advancement. The research reports ordinarily offer a description of the structural features of the new program without giving data on how instruction was adapted to suit the purposes of the program. Lacking data on actual implementation, the reader is unable to interpret outcomes of so-called nongraded programs. The seriousness of this matter is indicated by the fact that Goodlad and Anderson (1962), in a survey of nongraded programs at the elementary level, found many where the local school leadership had set up homogeneous groups but appeared not to practice nongrading.

Despite the fact that nongraded programs have been in operation in hundreds of elementary schools for a number of years, there is an extraordinary paucity of research studies of nongrading. As Goodlad and Anderson (1963) indicate, most of the studies that have been conducted are subject to one or more of these weaknesses: a failure to report instructional practices within the nongraded structure, confusing interclass grouping with vertical progression, and using improper bases for comparing progress with graded and nongraded instruction. These authors review several studies, as does Halliwell (1963). Hillson and others (1964) report a controlled study of nongraded reading in the primary school. The commonest finding is that nongraded programs at the elementary level result in gains in the skill subjects that are made the foci of the programs. The researchers report favorable reactions of students and teachers toward the nongraded programs. However, Hopkins and others (1965) report no reliable effects of nongrading on reading achievement, and Carbone (1961) reports that a graded program was superior to a nongraded program in terms of both achievement and mental health of students. Anderson and Goodlad (1962) criticize the Carbone study because the report indicates that there were no significant differences in instructional practices between the graded and nongraded programs. The assumption underlying nongrading is that it introduces differences in vertical progress in the curriculum. When no such differences are introduced, there is no reason to expect that a nongraded program will produce changes in instructional outcomes.

As of 1966, no research study of the effects of nongrading at the secondary level was found in the literature. Brown (1963) asserts that the program at

Melbourne High School, Melbourne, Florida led to a great decrease in the frequency of dropouts. However, he does not present the data needed to support this assertion. Brown also claims that the proportion of Melbourne graduates attending college increased to 70 percent from a base of 40 percent prior to the nongraded program.

Despite the emphasis its proponents have placed on using nongrading as a way of removing the stigma associated with being a slow learner, no research reports were found that offer objective data on this matter. Also, no research reports were located that dealt with the role of nongrading in eliminating remedial problems through ensuring that a slow learner masters each level of work before proceeding to the next level.

ABILITY GROUPING. The great bulk of research on grouping has dealt with attempts to measure the effects of dividing students of a given grade level in a school into classes of restricted range in ability or achievement. Ability grouping, as that term is conventionally used, includes achievement-level grouping of members of a grade level. Achievement-level grouping that brings together students from different grade levels is variously called nongraded, ungraded, multigrade, multiage, and interage grouping.

The term "ability grouping" covers a great array of methods for setting up instructional groups. In the elementary school a frequent practice has been to assign the students of a grade level to groups made relatively homogeneous in IQ, reading achievement, or the two criteria combined. In secondary schools, a frequent practice has been to assign students to one of three tracks representing high, medium, and low levels of intellectual performance. The criteria for assigning students to tracks may be IQ, general grade average, achievement-test scores in such subjects as reading and mathematics, and teachers' ratings. Because of the variety of methods included under the rubric of ability grouping, it is vital to specify the students, curricular areas, and criteria involved in any instance of ability grouping.

Ability grouping became common in the United States around 1920, closely following developments in testing that provided standardized group measures of intellectual performance. The rapidity of adoption of ability grouping is indicated by Otto and Sanders (1932), who report that, as of 1926, elementary pupils in at least some grades were grouped by ability in 36 out of 40 American cities with populations over 100,000. In the late 1930's and the 1940's there was a decline in ability grouping, related in good part to objections raised by proponents of progressive education who felt that the practice stigmatized slow learners and made snobs out of the ablest students.

Since 1955 there has been a marked resurgence of interest in ability grouping, stimulated by the increased concern about academic attainment, especially on the part of gifted students. In a survey by the National Education Association (1962) it was found that 52 percent of a national sample of principals of large elementary schools saw an increase in ability grouping in their schools between 1956 and 1961, while only 7 percent saw a decrease during that period. However, heterogeneous grouping through grade 8 remained the commonest practice in America's schools, according to a study by Dean (1960): In 1960 a national sample of school leaders reported ability grouping in grades 1–6 at only 17 percent of schools and in grades 7 and 8 at 34 percent of schools.

Research on ability grouping in the United States has been concentrated within two periods, 1920–1935 and since 1955. All but a few of the hundreds of studies are so poorly designed that little reliance can be placed on their findings. Billet (1932) judged that 104 out of 108 studies he reviewed were not adequately controlled. Cornell (1936) pointed out numerous methodological faults in the studies. Eckstrom (1959) reviewed studies of homogeneous grouping, finding just 33 that were designed well enough to justify reporting their findings. The years between 1959 and 1967 were a banner period for research on ability grouping, with more major controlled studies reported than during all the previous years taken together. Several recent publications by the following authors offer valuable reviews of research in the field: Borg (1966), Daniels (1961), Eash (1961), Eckstrom (1959), Gold (1965), Goldberg and others (1966), Svensson (1962), and Yates (1966).

The basic assumptions underlying ability grouping are that it materially reduces the range of learning-related differences within a group as compared with random grouping and that this reduction of range facilitates teaching and learning. There is no doubt that one can achieve the intended reduction of range in terms of any one grouping criterion or in terms of a set of closely correlated criterion variables. Thus, if 75 students are divided into three classes of 25 in terms of rank-order scores on an intelligence test, the mean range for the three classes will be one-third that of the total group. However, students' characteristics as learners are not adequately represented by their scores on a general intelligence test. A student's ease and rate of learning vary greatly from one learning task to another. Also, his level of achievement varies considerably from one curriculum area to another and from topic to topic or task to task within each area.

It is generally recognized that scores on intelligence tests and standardized tests of achievement are substantially correlated. However, when pupils are grouped on the basis of IQ alone it has been found that the range of scores on achievement tests is still great. Goodlad (1960) cites evidence to indicate that dividing students of a grade level into groups on the basis of a measure of general intellectual performance reduces variability in school achievement only about 7 percent for a two-group division and 17 percent for a three-group division. With larger numbers of groups, the reduction of range becomes greater. The most effective way to reduce the range of a class in achievement is to group differentially, subject by subject, and to base this grouping on separate measures of achievement for each area. However, within such groups there would remain large differences in ability and in many other variables that influence learning.

The theoretical bases for ability grouping ordinarily have been implied rather than stated in research reports. A common assumption is that a teacher can more readily adapt instruction to differences among students when the range of differences within a class is reduced. Why should this be so? The answer, seldom stated in reports of studies, is that group teaching becomes more manageable when the members of a group have more characteristics in common. In short, the chief working assumption underlying ability grouping is that it facilitates teaching the members of a group as though they did not differ from one another.

Usually, reports of studies of ability grouping are vague about the ways in which teachers are expected to differentiate the instruction they offer classes representing different ability levels. Most often, the reports infer that teachers will vary one or more of the following: learning tasks, including the use of enrichment activities or advanced materials with gifted students; instructional methods—drill with slow groups, projects with abler groups, etc.; and the pace of advancement, with slow groups normally being allowed more time for each unit of work.

Some assumptions about the effects of ability grouping concern students' reactions to their group assignments. It has been claimed often that the rapid learner should benefit from ability grouping through being freed from instruction geared to less-capable learners and through being challenged to keep up with his intellectual peers. The slow learner, it is claimed, should benefit from instruction geared to his capabilities and from experiencing success more often in the absence of the ablest students. Opponents of ability grouping have claimed that slow learners are stigmatized by being placed in low groups and that they are apt, as a result, to lose interest in studying.

A limitation in research on ability grouping is that virtually all of the studies, including the large-scale researches conducted most recently, have failed to measure ways in which the instruction given to ability group compared with that given to the relatively heterogeneous groups making up the control populations. As Passow (1962) has noted, some studies called for differentiating the instruction given to high- and low-ability groups, while others called for keeping course content and methods similar for all groups. Even when the study design called for differentiating instruction, objective data were usually not obtained on the manner and extent of such differentiation. Data on the independent variables in the study usually were restricted to details on how groups were set up and on how teachers were assigned to groups. In some studies, impressionistic data were obtained on how teachers conducted instruction with the experimental and control groups. Such data usually have consisted of teachers' reports.

The lack of objective measures of independent variables is not uncommon in educational field studies.

The explanation is not hard to find. Obtaining specific data on instructional practices in the classroom is enormously difficult and time-consuming. Valid and efficient ways to measure classroom practices are virtually lacking. Teachers are unprepared to provide reliable data on how they teach. Staffs of research projects are never large enough to gather the needed data from a large number of classrooms over a lengthy period of time.

What effects has ability grouping been found to have on students' achievements? No consistent effects have been found when mean scores of experimental and control populations representing the full range of abilities were compared. Thus, Eckstrom (1959) identified 13 studies with findings favoring ability grouping, 15 where no significant effects were found or where results with heterogeneous groups were superior, and 5 where results were partially favorable and partially unfavorable to ability grouping.

Major studies conducted since 1959 have found no clear and consistent effects of ability grouping on students' achievement when total student populations were used. This finding has been obtained in the studies by Goldberg and others (1966) and by Wilcox (1961), where no efforts were made to differentiate the instruction given to groups of different ability levels, and in the studies by Borg (1966) and Drews (1963), where such efforts were made. In some studies the results varied significantly with the learning tasks under consideration. Thus, Borg found that achievement in subject matter tended to be greater with ability grouping, while study methods tended to be superior with heterogeneous grouping.

In the study by Goldberg and others (1966) a broad range of ability within a group, as compared with a narrower range, was associated with somewhat greater gains in all subjects except reading. It is important to note that this study sought to measure the effects of ability grouping per se without making specific provisions for varying instruction according to ability level. As Borg (1966) notes, this sort of study tells us nothing about the effects of ability grouping when it is accompanied with appropriate differentiation of instructional contents and methods. However, Borg's study does not solve this difficulty, since it merely calls for using enrichment to differentiate the instruction given gifted students in the heterogeneous control classes, while using differences in the rate of advancement with ability-grouped classes in the experimental treatment. The report of the study does not offer measures of the actual differentiation of instruction along the lines called for in the study design.

There is mounting evidence that ability grouping is apt to have significant, and significantly different, effects on the achievement of students of high and low ability even when it does not significantly influence the achievement means of total student populations. The studies reported up to about 1955, as summarized by Goodlad (1960), tended to favor ability grouping for both rapid and slow learners, with the latter benefiting more from the practice. Recent studies have cast serious doubt on this conclusion from earlier studies. Daniels (1961) found ability grouping to produce losses with both high-ability and low-ability students, though the latter suffered the greater losses. Some investigators, notably Borg (1966) and Heathers (1967), have found ability grouping to be associated with gains for rapid learners that were offset by losses for slower learners. This is a case of the rich getting richer and the poor getting poorer. The fact that Daniels (1961) and Heathers (1967) have found ability grouping to be associated with an increase in the dispersion of students' scores on standardized tests of academic achievement is readily understood when one considers that the practice tends to widen the gap in attainments between educationally advantaged and disadvantaged students.

Recent studies have in some cases found ability grouping to be associated with increased attainments by high-ability students and in other cases with decreased attainment. The former relationship was found in studies by Borg (1966), Douglas (1964), and Heathers (1967), while the latter was found by Abrahamson (1959) and Goldberg and others (1966). Probably these opposite findings reflect differences in the adaptation of instruction to meet the capabilities of superior students.

Major studies reported in the 1960's lend strong support to the view that ability grouping is associated with detrimental effects on slow learners. Such learners have been found to receive lower scores on achievement tests when placed in low-ability groups than comparable students received when taught in heterogeneous groups. This finding has been reported by Borg (1966), Dockrell (1964), Douglas (1964), and Heathers (1967). Several explanations can be offered to account for this. One is that slow learners, in the absence of superior students, have fewer opportunities to learn vicariously through paying attention during classroom discussions. Other explanations fall under the heading of "self-fulfilling prophecies," namely, that teachers expect less from students who are assigned to low groups and teach them correspondingly less. Also, students who are assigned to such groups expect less of themselves and behave accordingly.

The most dramatic evidence for the self-fulfilling prophecy comes from a study by Rosenthal and Jacobson (1968). In this study randomly selected students from a class were identified to the teacher as "academic spurters." Over the next several months, these students showed reliable gains in IQ scores. This finding was equally true of students who were in fast, medium, and slow groups. Teachers rated students who were labeled academic spurters more favorably in a number of characteristics, provided that they were members of the high- or medium-ability groups. They did not extend these favorable attitudes toward members of the slow groups. Evidently, they had difficulty believing that students in slow groups had desirable characteristics even though they had reacted to "academic spurters" in these groups in ways that increased their scores on an intelligence test.

There is evidence from some studies that the quality of instruction offered low groups tends to be inferior to that offered groups made up of abler students. In the study reported by Heathers (1967), teachers indicated that they stressed basic skills and facts with slow learners and used drill a great deal with these students. On the other hand, they stressed conceptual learning with high-ability groups and encouraged students in these groups to conduct independent projects. Squire (1966) reports that a national study of the teaching of English in high school revealed that teachers tended to employ dull, unimaginative instructional approaches with slow-learning groups.

Ability grouping has been criticized as a form of segregation that has unfavorable emotional-social effects on children who are assigned to low groups. Such groups tend to be used as dumping grounds for students who, for a variety of reasons, perform poorly in their academic work. Low achievement in school subjects results sometimes from limited intellectual endowments, but it may result also from low motivation to study, from emotional difficulties, from poor health, and from environmental handicaps. It is commonly recognized that low-ability groups in elementary school have a disproportionate number of boys, of children from lower-class origins, and of children from minority groups. Ability grouping may thus be, in effect, an agency for maintaining and enhancing caste and class stratification in a society.

Studies have shown that children from the middle and upper classes are found mainly in the high-ability groups, while children from the lower classes are found in the low-ability groups. This finding appears in reports by Douglas (1964), Husen and Svensson (1960), and Willig (1963). Deutsch (1963) presents a strong case for heterogeneous grouping in integrated schools.

Daniels (1961) found that once a child is assigned to an ability level he is very likely to remain there. In his study, although teachers thought that about 17 percent of students were shifted from one level to another each year, actually only about 2 percent were shifted.

Research on the effects of ability grouping on noncognitive variables has been summarized by Borg (1966). In Borg's own study, high-ability students were found to lose sociometric status with ability grouping, while low-ability students gained. However, both categories of students showed a loss in self-esteem with ability grouping. In studies by Drews (1963), Goldberg and others (1966), and Wilcox (1961), slow learners had higher self-concept ratings with ability grouping. Evidence that students prefer membership in high-ability groups comes from the study by Luchins and Luchins (1948), in which bright students indicated they would not want to be transferred from the topmost ability group to the next lower group even though the teacher in the latter group was "better and kinder."

A pair of studies by Atkinson and O'Connor (1963) tested the prediction that the effects of ability grouping would vary according to the strength of the student's motivation to succeed compared to the strength of his anxiety about failing. A study with sixth graders found that ability grouping had positive effects on achievement for those students who had high motivation to succeed compared to the strength of their anxiety about failing. A study with ninth graders did not support this finding. These studies have added an important dimension to research on ability grouping by seeking to test whether students' personality characteristics are determinants of the effects of such grouping.

OTHER INTERCLASS GROUPING PATTERNS. The bases for setting up instructional groups most often have involved the issue of heterogeneous versus homogeneous grouping at grade level or that of graded versus nongraded grouping. Other bases that have been used in setting up classes are planned (rather than random) heterogeneous grouping and "teachability" grouping.

Planned Heterogeneous Grouping. School systems often have set up within-grade heterogeneous groups on some bases other than random assignment. Sometimes they have balanced groups in terms of IQ distribution. At other times they have tried to distribute leaders and troublemakers equitably among the groups at a grade level. No studies have been located that test outcomes of such grouping practices.

Recently, heterogeneous multiage grouping has been tried, notably in elementary schools at Torrance, California. In reporting on the program there, Hamilton and Rehwoldt (1957) contend that grouping should be on the basis of students' differences rather than similarities on the assumption that "by their differences they learn." They describe a controlled study in which the experimental subjects were in groups composed of students from grades 1–3 or 4–5. They found that the academic achievement of students in wide-range classes was superior to that of students in single-grade classes. Also, the authors report favorable effects of multigrade grouping on students' social adjustment and their personality development. Similar results are reported by Hull (1958). Hull interprets the results as being due to students' being stimulated by the wide range of differences, to older students teaching younger ones, and to teachers' acceptance of the challenge to adapt their instruction to the widely different needs and readiness of children in the group.

Teachability Grouping. Thelen (1963) has developed a method of setting up a so-called teachable class on the basis of the assignment to a given teacher of a group of students similar to those in former classes whom the teacher felt "got a lot out of class." From a controlled study of teachability grouping, Thelen concluded that the practice resulted in more-manageable classes, better attainment of the teacher's purposes, and a more satisfied teacher. However, Thelen did not conclude from his study either that students learned more in these groups or that they gained greater satisfaction from being members of such groups. The choice of teachers remained a critical consideration.

INTRACLASS GROUPING. Teachers often subdivide their classes to facilitate instruction. Subgrouping is more apt to occur in heterogeneous classes than in ability-grouped classes, since teachers employ it to accomplish within-class ability or achievement-level grouping. Such subgrouping is most common in elementary schools and is used most frequently with instruction in the skill areas of reading, spelling, and arithmetic. In a recent survey conducted by the National Education Association (1962), a sample of elementary-school principals reported intraclass grouping for reading in about four-fifths of large school districts and similar arrangements for arithmetic in about two-thirds of such districts. Subgrouping also occurs often in the conduct of project activities in science or social studies. Group projects and individual learning activities are more apt to involve abler students, since these students are more capable of directing their own learning than are less-able students.

Spence (1958) studied intraclass ability grouping in arithmetic in grades 4 to 6. Content and instructional methods were adapted to suit the three group levels. In each of grades 4 to 6, subgroup teaching produced significantly higher achievement scores than whole-class teaching. Jones (1948) found that subgroups using individualized, nongraded materials achieved significantly more in reading, spelling, and arithmetic than the control group that learned the usual grade-level materials with whole-class teaching. Dewar (1963) found subgrouping for arithmetic instruction in the sixth grade to produce reliable gains in achievement by the high and low subgroups but not by the middle subgroup.

Durrell and others (1959) tested a pupil-team learning plan in which the elementary teacher divided the class into groups of two to five students who studied arithmetic and spelling team-fashion. They worked with programmed materials and were required to pass the mastery test for a learning task before proceeding to the next task. Each student learned on a nongraded basis, advancing as rapidly as he could learn. In the study, pupil-team learning produced significant gains in students' achievement as compared with a control group, and the plan was well-liked by pupils, parents, and teachers. Zimmerman (1965) employed another sort of pupil teamwork for the study of English in grade 9. The ablest students in the class ran "mastery booths" where they helped less-able students to learn both skills and problem solving.

Thelen (1949) proposed that principles of group dynamics should be employed in setting up a social organization for learning in the class. He recommended using a principle of least group size where the subgroup would contain the smallest number of students who had among them the capabilities required to accomplish the learning task.

The mere handful of studies on intraclass provisions for meeting differences among learners contrasts sharply with the large volume of research on interclass grouping. Very likely the explanation is that reliance has usually been placed on structural approaches to meeting individual differences rather than on methods of adapting instructional approaches to meet such differences. In support of this interpretation is the fact that most research reports on interclass grouping have not presented data on how instruction differed from one type of group to another. In this connection, it is significant that the most-used way of measuring classroom teaching, the interaction analysis method designed by Flanders (1960), was devised to measure teacher-student interaction in group settings without making provisions for measuring how the teacher adapted instruction to individual differences.

It appears likely that the 1970's will see a great deal of research on intraclass differentiation of instruction that utilizes new approaches to individualizing instruction. A major influence in this direction should be the programs of individually prescribed instruction under development that have been described by Goodlad (1965) and by Lindvall and Bolvin (1967). Even more influential should be the emerging uses of electronic computers, both for individualized scheduling, as described by Bush and Allen (1964), and for individualized learning, as described by Silberman and Carter (1965) and by Suppes (1967).

CRITIQUE. Writing an epitaph for grouping may well be the task of the reviewer of research on grouping for the 1980 edition of this encyclopedia. Even today it appears that grouping as a central theme of organization for instruction has nearly run its course and is in the process of being replaced by a familiar theme—individualized instruction—that became a focus of educational reform in the mid-1960's.

The concept of individualization has acquired such potency that it is reducing to subordinate status even those grouping arrangements being promoted under the banners of nongrading and team teaching. A major factor in the increasing attention being given to individualization is the development of technological devices and learning programs suitable for independent study. Also, recent research has made important contributions to the growing disenchantment with grouping as a theme in organization for instruction.

It may also happen that the practice of designing, testing, and marketing new organizational plans will have gone out of fashion by 1980. Instead of adopting prepackaged organizational plans, school systems would then design their own plans to incorporate a number of organizational themes that might include individualized programming, flexible scheduling, specialist teaching of several types, team organization, the use of teacher aides, and nongraded progression.

The research that is done during the next decade on school organization and grouping should correct a number of major shortcomings that are present in the research studies conducted up to the present. One of these shortcomings is the failure to measure the implementation of the arrangements that are being tested. Oddly, behavioral scientists who would never neglect measuring the independent variables in laboratory studies routinely commit this error when they conduct educational field studies.

A second major fault with the research studies has been the failure to design the plan under test on the basis of an adequate theoretical model. Typically, the learning outcomes that the program is intended to foster are not specified. Likewise, the requirements for implementing the plan at the point of instruction are not spelled out in the study design. The criteria used for judging the success of the organizational or grouping plan usually have been crude and often have been inappropriate. At best, nationally normed achievement tests give rough indications of instructional outcomes. The group measures of attitudes, interests, and emotional-social factors that have been employed in the studies usually have not been validated.

The evaluation of new organizational or grouping patterns has in virtually every instance consisted of a comparison with outcomes of conventional practices. The purpose has not been to determine how well the new practices accomplish desired outcomes but rather to determine whether they do a better job than existing practices. Had the innovators employed the research and development approach they would have started by specifying the purposes the new organizational or grouping plan was intended to serve and then would have evaluated the plan in terms of its success in realizing these purposes.

A serious fault with all studies on grouping or school organization that have been conducted to date is that the study designs did not permit a determination of the contribution made to outcomes by each of the features of the plan under test. We need to develop designs for field tests that permit analysis of the factors, or combinations of factors, that are responsible for the results obtained. Computers can be programmed to facilitate this analysis once we have developed and put to use appropriate measures of input and output variables in the instructional program.

Glen Heathers
New York University

References

Abrahamson, David A. "The Effectiveness of Grouping for Students of High Ability." *Ed Res B* 38: 169–82; 1959.

Ackerlund, George. "Some Teacher Views on The Self-contained Classroom." *Phi Delta Kappan* 40: 283–5; 1959.

Anderson, Robert H. "Organizing Groups for Instruction." In *Individual Instruction*, 61st Yearbook, Part I, NSSE U Chicago Press, 1962. p. 239–64.

Anderson, Robert H. *Teaching in a World of Change.* Harcourt, 1966. 180p.

Anderson, Robert H., and Goodlad, John I. "Self-appraisal in Nongraded Schools: A Survey of Findings and Perceptions." *El Sch J* 63:261–9; 1962.

Atkinson, John W., and O'Connor, Patricia. *Effects of Ability Grouping in Schools Related to Individual Differences in Achievement-related Motivation.* Project No. 1283. USOE, 1963. 175p.

Bair, Medill, and Woodward, Richard G. *Team Teaching in Action.* Houghton, 1964. 229p.

Billet, Roy O. *The Administration and Supervision of Homogeneous Grouping.* Ohio State U Press, 1932. 159p.

Borg, Walter R. *Ability Grouping in the Public Schools,* 2nd ed. Dembar Educational Research Services, 1966. 98p.

Broadhead, Fred C. "Pupil-adjustment in the Semidepartmental Elementary School." *El Sch J* 60: 385-90; 1960.

Brown, B. Frank. *The Nongraded High School.* Prentice-Hall, 1963. 216p.

Bush, Robert N., and Allen, Dwight W. *A New Design for High School Education: Assuming a Flexible Schedule.* McGraw-Hill, 1964.

Carbone, Robert F. "A Comparison of Graded and Non-graded Elementary Schools." *El Sch J* 62:82-8; 1961.

Cornell, Ethel L. "Effects of Ability Grouping Determinable from Published Studies." In *The Grouping of Pupils,* 35th Yearbook, Part I, NSSE. Bobbs-Merrill, 1936. p. 289-304.

Daniels, John C. "Effects of Streaming in the Primary School. II: A Comparison of Streamed and Unstreamed Schools." *Brit J Ed Psychol* 31:119-27; 1961.

Davis, Harold S. *Team Teaching Bibliography.* Educational Research Council of Greater Cleveland, 1964. 95p.

Dean, Stuart A. *Elementary School Administration and Organization.* USOE Bulletin No. 11. HEW, 1960.

Della-Dora, Delmo. "The Self-contained Unit in Action in the Junior High School." In Snyder, Edith R. (Ed.) *The Self-Contained Classroom.* ASCD, 1960. p. 65-81.

Deutsch, Martin A. "Dimensions of the School's Role in Problems of Integration." In Klopf, Gordon J., and Laster, Israel A. (Eds.) *Integration in the Urban School.* Teachers Col, Columbia U, 1963. p. 29-44.

Dewar, John A. "Grouping for Arithmetic Instruction in Sixth Grade." *El Sch J* 63:266-9; 1963.

Dockrell, W. B. "Edmonton Junior High School Streaming Project." In *Studies in Grouping.* Alberta Teachers' Association, 1964.

Douglas, J. W. B. *The Home and The School: A Study of Ability and Attainment in the Primary School.* MacGibbon and Kee, 1964. 190p.

Drews, Elizabeth M. *Student Abilities, Grouping Patterns, and Classroom Interactions.* Michigan State U Press, 1963.

Durrell, Donald D., and others. "Adapting Instruction to the Learning Needs of Children in Intermediate Grades." *Boston U J Ed,* 142:1-78; 1959.

Eash, Maurice J. "Grouping: What Have We Learned?" *Ed Leadership* 18:429-34; 1961.

Eckstrom, Ruth B. "Experimental Studies of Homogeneous Grouping: A Critical Review." *Sch R* 69: 216-26; 1959.

Flanders, Ned A. *Teachers Influence, Pupil Attitudes, and Achievement.* USOE, Cooperative Research Project No. 397. U Minnesota, 1960.

Fleming, Robert S., and others. "Reactions to the Dual Progress Plan." *Ed Leadership* 18:92-5; 1960.

Franseth, Jane, and Koury, Rose. *Grouping Children in the Elementary School: Research and Implications.* USOE, 1963.

Franseth, Jane, and Koury, Rose. *A Guide to Research and Informed Judgment in Grouping Children.* USOE, 1964.

Gibb, E. Glenadine, and Matala, Dorothy L. "Study on the Use of Special Teachers of Science and Mathematics in Grades 5 and 6." *Sch Sci Math* 62:565-85; 1962.

Gold, Milton J. *Education of the Intellectually Gifted.* Merrill, 1965. 472p.

Goldberg, Miriam, and others. *The Effects of Ability Grouping.* Teachers Col, Columbia U, 1966. 254p.

Goodlad, John I. "Classroom Organization." In *Encyclopedia of Educational Research,* 3rd ed. Macmillan, 1960.

Goodlad, John I. *Planning and Organizing for Teaching.* NEA, 1963. 190p.

Goodlad, John I. "Meeting Children Where They Are." *Saturday R* March 20:57-9, 72-4; 1965.

Goodlad, John I., and Anderson, Robert H. "Educational Practices in Nongraded Schools: A Survey of Perceptions." *El Sch J* 63:33-40; 1962.

Goodlad, John I., and Anderson, Robert H. *The Nongraded Elementary School,* rev. ed. Harcourt, 1963. 248p.

Grannis, Joseph C. "Team Teaching and the Curriculum." In Shaplin, Judson T., and Olds, Henry F., Jr. (Eds.) *Team Teaching.* Harper, 1964. p. 123-69.

Halliwell, Joseph W. "A Comparison of Pupil Achievement in Graded and Nongraded Primary Classrooms." *J Exp Ed* 32:59-64; 1963.

Hamilton, Warren, and Rehwoldt, W. "By Their Differences They Learn." *Nat El Prin* 37:27-9; 1957.

Heathers, Glen. "Research on Team Teaching." In Shaplin, Judson T., and Olds, Henry F., Jr. (Eds.) *Team Teaching.* Harper, 1964. p. 306-44.

Heathers, Glen. "School Organization: Nongrading, Dual Progress and Team Teaching." In *The Changing American School,* 65th Yearbook, Part II, NSSE, U Chicago Press, 1966. p. 110-34.

Heathers, Glen. *Organizing Schools Through the Dual Progress Plan.* Interstate, 1967. 228p.

Hillson, Maurie. (Ed.) *Change and Innovation in Elementary School Organization.* Holt, 1965. 387p.

Hillson, Maurie, and others. "A Controlled Experiment Evaluating the Effects of a Non-graded Organization on Pupil Achievement." *J Ed Res* 57: 548-50; 1964.

Hopkins, Kenneth D., and others. "An Empirical Comparison of Pupil Achievement and Other Variables in Graded and Nongraded Classes." *Am Ed Res J* 2:207-15; 1965.

Hull, J. H. "Multi-grade Teaching." *Nations Sch* 52: 33–6; 1958.

Husen, Torsen, and Svensson, Nils-Eric. "Pedagogic Milieu and Development of Intellectual Skills." *Sch R* 68:36–51; 1960.

Jones, Daisy M. "An Experiment in Adaptation to Individual Differences." *J Ed Psychol* 39:257–72; 1948.

Lambert, Philip, and others. *Classroom Interaction, Pupil Achievement, and Adjustment in Team Teaching as Compared with the Self-contained Classroom.* U Wisconsin Press, 1964. 258p.

Lindvall, C. M., and Bolvin, John O. "Programed Instruction in the Schools: Individually Prescribed Instruction." In *Programed Instruction*. 66th Yearbook, Part II, NSSE. U Chicago Press, 1967.

Luchins, Abraham S., and Luchins, Edith H. "Children's Attitudes Toward Homogeneous Grouping." *J Genet Psychol* 72:3–9; 1948.

Michelson, John. "What Does Research Say About the Effectiveness of the Core Curriculum?" *Sch R* 65:144–60; 1957.

Morganstern, Anne. (Ed.) *Grouping in the Elementary School.* Pitman, 1966. 118p.

National Education Association. *The Principals Look at the Schools.* NEA, 1962. 75p.

National Elementary Principal. Cooperative Teaching. Special issue. January 1965.

Otto, Henry J. *Current Practices in the Organization of Elementary Schools.* Northwestern U Press, 1932.

Otto, Henry J., and Sanders, David C. *Elementary School Organization and Administration*, 4th ed. Appleton, 1964. 409p.

Passow, Harry A. "The Maze of Research on Ability Grouping." *Ed Forum* 26:281–8; 1962.

Rosenthal, Robert, and Jacobson, Lenore. *Pygmalion in the Classroom.* Holt, 1968.

Rouse, Margaret R. "A Comparative Study of Departmentalization." *El Sch J* 47:34–42; 1946.

Shane, Harold G. "Grouping in the Elementary School." *Phi Delta Kappan* 41:313–9; 1960.

Shaplin, Judson T., and Olds, Henry F., Jr. (Eds.) *Team Teaching.* Harper, 1964. 430p.

Silberman, Harry F., and Carter, Launor F. "The Systems Approach, Technology and the School." In *New Approaches to Individualizing Instruction.* ETS, 1965. p. 71–91.

Snyder, Edith R. (Ed.) *The Self-contained Classroom.* ASCD, 1960. 88p.

Spence, Eugene S. "Intraclass Grouping of Pupils for Instruction in Arithmetic in the Intermediate Grades of the Elementary School." Doctoral dissertation. U Pittsburgh, 1958. 163p.

Spivak, M. L. "Effectiveness of Departmental and Self-contained Seventh- and Eighth-grade Classrooms." *Sch R* 64:391–6; 1956.

Squire, James R. "National Study of High School English Programs: A School for All Seasons." *Engl J* 55:282–90; 1966.

Stoddard, George D. *The Dual Progress Plan.* Harper, 1961. 225p.

Suppes, Patrick. "The Computer and Excellence." *Saturday R* January 14:46–50; 1967.

Svensson, Nils-Eric. *Ability Grouping and Scholastic Achievement.* Almqvist and Wiksell, 1962. 236p.

Thelen, Herbert A. "Group Dynamics in Instruction: The Principle of Least Group Size." *Sch R* 57: 139–48; 1949.

Thelen, Herbert A. "Grouping for Teachability." *Theory Into Practice* 2:81–9; 1963.

Trump, J. Lloyd, and Baynham, Dorsey. *Focus on Change: A Guide to Better Schools.* Rand McNally, 1961. 147p.

Wallace, R. C., Jr. "Can Large Group Instruction Provide for Individual Differences?" *Nat El Prin* 44:66–70; 1965.

Whipple, Guy M. (Ed.) *The Grouping of Pupils.* 35th Yearbook, Part I, NSSE. Bobbs-Merrill, 1936. 319p.

Wilcox, John. "A Search for the Multiple Effects of Grouping upon the Growth and Behavior of Junior High School Pupils." Doctoral dissertation. Cornell U, 1961.

Willig, C. J. "Social Implications of Streaming in the Junior School." *Ed Res* 5:151–4; 1963.

Woodring, Paul. "Reform Movements from the Point of View of Psychological Theory." In *Theories of Learning and Instruction*, 63rd Yearbook, NSSE. U Chicago Press, 1964. p. 292.

Wright, Grace. *Block-time Classes and the Core Program in Junior High.* USOE, 1958.

Wrightstone, J. Wayne. *Class Organization for Instruction.* NEA, 1957. 33p.

Yates, Alfred. (Ed.) *Grouping in Education.* Wiley, 1966. 314p.

Zimmerman, Donald. "Teaching 30 Like Teaching One." *Ed* 85:364–70; 1965.

HANDWRITING

In the language arts, reading and listening constitute input, and speaking and handwriting are vehicles for output. Handwriting is the visible record, the residual of human thought. Because the tangible product has always been superseded by the content it conveys, and, more recently, because mechanical means for writing have been discovered, formal study of handwriting per se has often been bypassed. It is so common, so ordinary that the study of its history and development has been neglected. Yet the ability to write as well as read is seen as a basic aspect of literacy (Gray, 1956), the quantity of handwriting may be increasing despite automation (Freeman, 1941; Templin, 1959), and over the years a considerable body of handwriting literature has been created (Herrick, 1961a). And the fact is that since 1950 there has been increased interest in research in handwriting (Herrick & Okada, 1963).

Interest in handwriting seems to center on three general focal areas. First, a relatively small but enthusiastic group is interested in handwriting as an art form, or calligraphy, as opposed to informal handwriting. The argument is that formal calligraphy has aesthetic and historical value that transcends simple, efficient letter-form production (Child, 1963). Nevertheless, the trend at the present time, particularly in the United States, is toward conceptualizing handwriting primarily as a tool for personal communication (National Council of Teachers of English, 1952). The emphasis is upon methods and materials for teaching the skills needed to produce legible handwriting with reasonable efficiency rather than on the aesthetic appeal of the product. Finally, there is some interest in the handwriting product, both as an entity with certain quality characteristics and as an idiosyncratic creation of the writer (Fluckiger & others, 1961). In considering handwriting as a tool, an art form, and a personal product, the bulk of recent contributions have had to do with the tool aspect.

HISTORY AND PRESENT STATUS. The history of writing is traced in two recent books, *The Art of Writing* (UNESCO, 1965) and *Writing* (Diringer, 1962). The former publication includes an outline of the history of writing and an exhibition of 50 illustrative panels with narration. The latter is part of a series, Ancient Peoples and Places, and the presentation is at once chronological, ethnic, and by type. The general concern in both books is with writing broadly defined, but the emergence of letter forms used in present handwriting systems is, of course, traced and discussed.

Taken together, a number of interesting points are made in the books. All forms of graphic inscription doubtless spring from the human need to communicate and express ideas, but the time of transition from pictography to genuine writing cannot be very precisely fixed. In general terms, the history of true writing goes back to the fourth millennium B.C. Alphabetic writing came much later, probably in the last half of the second millennium B.C. It was the last major form of writing to appear, and it came at a time when man had become aware of the internal structure of speech and was able to speculate on its use for practical purposes. The alphabet is the most flexible and useful method of writing yet invented, and it is the basis for most of the scripts employed by civilized peoples. For centuries handwriting was literally the principal means by which ideas were transmitted and preserved, but with the discovery of mechanical printing, handwriting became primarily a form for personal communication. The extent to which telecommunication, the mechanical recording of speech, will ultimately displace handwriting in personal communication remains to be seen.

The UNESCO survey of handwriting practices in 48 countries (International Conference on Public Education . . . , 1948) and the subsequent formal report by Gray (1956), both of which were reviewed by Harris (1960), remain the most comprehensive and recent sources of information regarding the status of handwriting at the international level. The salient points are summarized here.

During the nineteenth and early twentieth centuries, form and quality were emphasized in handwriting, but since then the concern has shifted to the writer and the development of the skills he needs to record his thoughts with reasonable speed and legibility. Considerable attention is given to activities designed to develop perceptual-motor readiness for handwriting instruction, and in many countries simplified letter forms—variously called script, printscript and manuscript writing—are introduced first to help children overcome some of the difficulties inherent in beginning handwriting instruction. A trend to practice writing whole words rather than single letters, based on the assumption that perception of whole words is easier and more meaningful, is evident; and there is greater interest in diagnosing, through the use of evaluative scales, and remedying poor handwriting. On the other hand, there are areas of disagreement at the international level: the extent to which individuals should be allowed to vary their personal style, the use of vertical versus slanted writing, and conditions of practice. And finally, if literacy is defined as the ability to write as well as to read simple messages, then the data show that about half of the world's population is illiterate. Progress is being made, but still greater efforts are needed.

In keeping with the international trend toward more concern with the writer, a new simplified style of handwriting was introduced in Russia in 1964 (Times Education Supplement, 1965b; de Vette, 1966). All of the strokes in letter formation are of equal thickness, the number of different detailed forms of letters is reduced by one-third, upper-case letter forms are in most instances simply larger replicas of lower case forms, and digit forms are simplified. The purpose is to permit children to master handwriting more quickly. When the new style was tried out experimentally, the achievement of first-form pupils was accelerated in both reading and writing.

A study of the use of ballpoint pens was undertaken in the Republic of South Africa (*Bulletin of the International Bureau of Education*, 1963). The general conclusion seems to be that the use of such pens is timesaving but also conducive to deterioration of handwriting quality. In Sweden a number of tests were devised to examine factors related to handwriting performance—e.g. hand movement, word imagery, memory, laterality, and personality (Lindell, 1964). A tentative conclusion was that persons who cannot speak clearly also have reading and writing difficulties, the implication being that training in phonetics would be useful. Simon (1957) reviewed a number of studies in the area of teaching reading and writing in France. The studies ranged from an assessment of developmental stages of readiness for certain writing tasks, to a study of characteristics of the handwriting product for diagnostic purposes, to an examination of uses of graphology and rhythm exercises in the instructional program. Taken together, these studies demonstrate the variety of research interests being pursued at the international level.

In the United States, several surveys of instructional practices and the status of handwriting were reported in the past decade. A number of important earlier surveys are summarized in preceding editions of the *Encyclopedia of Educational Research.*

A survey of practices advocated by 19 commercial systems of handwriting instruction, which supply about 95 percent of the instructional materials currently in use in the United States, was reported in 1960 (University of Wisconsin, 1960). Instructional practices within the schools would, of course, be expected to parallel practices advocated by the commercial suppliers of instructional materials rather closely. The salient conclusions from the survey are as follows: (1) There is substantial agreement among the systems that legibility is the fundamental objective of handwriting instruction. In operational terms, handwriting that is easily read and easily written is legible. (2) Handwriting is generally regarded in a functional role, as a tool for communication. Attempts are made, therefore, to correlate handwriting instruction with work in the skill and content fields. In some systems, handwriting performance is evaluated in application rather than within the handwriting period. (3) There is some agreement on procedures for developing the motor skills required for handwriting. For example, arm rather than finger movements are advocated as conducive to rhythmic movements and fluent writing. (4) Systematic procedures for learning the letter forms are proposed by some systems—e.g. seeing the letter or word, hearing it, and tracing it in the air. (5) There is general agreement that practice is necessary and that it should be purposeful; but the purposes suggested range from pupil experiences (e.g. labeling and letter writing) to mastery of a particular stroke (e.g. drawing circles and making vertical and horizontal strokes). (6) Scales are introduced for use in comparing pupils' writing with standard norms, but greater emphasis is placed upon pupils' self-evaluation of their own writing. (7) There is no expectation of a uniform degree of skill in a classroom. The fact that pupils' abilities vary is recognized, and lessons are planned accordingly. (8) The fundamental principles of good writing are the same for all grades, but at the upper elementary level there is a tendency to use the instructional time for remedial work. Pupils are helped to become more proficient in identifying general and specific inaccuracies in letter forms, slant, size, spacing and alignment.

In another study (Herrick & Otto, 1961) the letter-form models advocated by the 19 commercial systems were compared. The letter forms—upper and lower case, manuscript and cursive—advocated by each system were photographed and all were reproduced in a common size. Comparisons show that although there are similarities, there is by no means an accepted standard alphabet form. Equally important, this precise reproduction of the various letter forms is a potential research tool for examining certain questions, such as what constitutes a significant difference between letter forms.

The proceedings of an Invitational Conference on Research in Handwriting held at the University of Wisconsin, *New Horizons for Research in Handwriting* (Herrick, 1963), were published in 1963. The conference and the book demonstrate the vigorous state of handwriting research in recent years. Several of the papers included are summarized in this article; one is particularly relevant here.

A survey of practices in the teaching of handwriting in the United States was reported by Herrick and Okada (1963). Six urban school districts were queried, the number from each state being determined by the ratio of the number of that state's school systems to the national total, and 22 percent responded. Conclusions regarding actual instructional practices in the schools were that 96 percent teach handwriting, 79 percent teach both manuscript and cursive styles, 14 percent teach cursive only, and 7 percent teach manuscript only; that instruction begins in first grade; that the transition from manuscript to cursive writing usually comes between the last half of second grade and the first half of third; that in grades 1 to 4 there are typically five instructional periods per week, and there are three in grades 5 to 8; that sessions are, on the average, 15 to 20 minutes long; that respondents generally favor a special class plus teaching in all subject areas; and that few report that they help their pupils to recognize their own errors or to develop a personal style. Regarding instructional techniques, the conclusions were as follows: six factors are emphasized—formation, size of letters, uniformity of letters, spacing of letters and words, alignment of words, and neatness; four factors are emphasized in the transition from manuscript to cursive writing—proper connections between letters, proper slant, letter forms and, when necessary, reading cursive writing. Only 7 percent of respondents claimed to have diagnostic or remedial programs, which is not in line with the expectation from the survey of commercial systems; body and paper position and provision for left-handed children are considered important.

Other surveys and descriptions of instructional practices at the city level (How, 1964; Scott, 1960), county level (Soltis, 1963), regional level (King, 1961) and, in England, national level (Piggot, 1958) were reported. King's survey of 680 school systems in four midwestern states (1961) showed that (1) 70 percent had formal handwriting programs; (2) 14 commercial handwriting systems were being used, but two publishers provided 89 percent of the instructional material; (3) 59 percent offered a minimum of 50 minutes per week of handwriting instruction; and (4) 9 percent required some kind of handwriting training for elementary teachers. Also pertinent to this review are two articles in which Enstrom reviews the history and present status of manuscript writing (Enstrom, 1964*a*) and speculates on causes for the supposed decline in handwriting quality (Enstrom, 1965). But contrary to Enstrom, Erlebacher and Herrick (1961) found no appreciable difference in the legibility of handwriting samples gathered in 1912 and 1959. A partial cause for the discrepancy may be the fact that there is no standard operational definition of legibility. Some writers are willing to accept "readability" as the sole criterion, whereas others look also for a pleasing general impression.

THE HANDWRITING ACT. A discussion of writing instruments and style of writing as well as of handwriting movement is included here.

Movement. Anderson (1966) concluded from a review of the literature that the dimensions of handwriting movement most often considered are hand movements, velocity and rhythm, and pressure phenomena.

Early work by Freeman (1918) and Judd (1911) showed that sustained writing with acceptable legibility can be carried on only when there is an appropriate combination of finger and arm movement rather than exclusive finger or arm control of the writing instrument. This combined arm-finger movement has been accepted as desirable, if not always practiced, ever since, and a particular grip-movement pattern (Freeman, 1954) has come to be accepted as standard and in which the hand is canted so that it rests on the third and fourth fingers. It is not planted firmly but slides across the writing surface as the letters are formed. The writing instrument rests between the thumb and index finger and is grasped lightly by the thumb and the middle and index fingers. The arm, hand and fingers have a share in forming the letters. The research-based rationale has been discussed by Harris (1960).

Recently, an alternative grip was suggested by Callewaert (1963), who feels that the traditional grip and writing movements tend to be constrictive. He suggests that the shaft of the writing instrument be placed between the middle and index fingers and gripped with those fingers and the thumb, with the hand and wrist canted more sharply to the side than in the traditional grip. Furthermore, a "round" system of letter forms—which he feels is physiologically more defensible, particularly with the modified grip—is suggested. Most of the work to date has been clinical, with cases of hyperkinesia (writer's cramp); but the speculation is that a reduction in muscular tension through the use of the modified grip would be beneficial in terms of ease and comfort in writing for sustained periods. A test of the latter notion (Otto & others, 1966) yielded no support for the speculation; yet the researchers reported that although the subjects had no previous experience with the modified grip, both speed of writing and legibility were at acceptable levels. Transfer to the modified grip apparently is uncomplicated.

With regard to movement and position, the left-handed writer has received considerable attention, but little research has been done. Enstrom (1964b) reviewed existing research and summarized the results of his dissertation study of left-handed writers. He reported that there are probably more left-handed pupils in the schools than current estimates indicate. He described an efficient writing position for left-handed pupils and concluded that the left-handers' "hooked" writing position is difficult, if not impossible, to change beyond grade 4. He suggested that older "hooked" writers be assisted in making minor adaptations that will permit them to write with reasonable ease and legibility. Groff (1964) compared handwriting samples of left- and right-handed pupils in grades 4 through 6 and found that Ayres-scale ratings differed only for sixth-grade girls, with the right-handers achieving higher scores. In another comparative study, Smith and Reed (1959) found no support for the notion that left-handers write more slowly than right-handers. They concluded instead that neither handedness nor sex affected the handwriting product as much as did the schools from which their subjects were drawn. The implication seems to be that with proper instruction left-handers can write legibly and efficiently. Williams (1964) and Otto and McMenemy (1966), among others, described procedures for teaching left-handed pupils to write.

Finally, Zaslow (1966) studied normal and cerebral-palsied children with reversal problems. He found that a crossover procedure, in which subjects were forced to write on the side of the body midline that was opposite from normal, led to a correction of reversals in 63 percent of the normal subjects and 79 percent of the brain-damaged subjects.

Regarding velocity and rhythm in handwriting, it seems clear that speed and rhythm no longer receive the emphases they once did in handwriting instruction (Herrick & Okada, 1963). Andersen (1966) reviewed the studies in which the notion of rhythm in handwriting was examined and concluded that because there is neither a common definition of rhythm in handwriting nor clear data regarding the role of rhythm, further clarification is needed.

Norms for speed in handwriting suggested by Freeman (1954) have been widely accepted. He reported, for example, a normal rate of 30 letters per minute in second grade and 80 letters per minute in eighth grade; legibility, of course, also increased over the grades. The speeds were derived from studies of children's normal rates of writing, but speed is flexible and can usually be increased from normal rates without legibility being sacrificed. Gates (1924) has suggested a method for considering both quality and speed in rating handwriting samples. Speed and quality must be considered together because to develop one without the other is pointless.

Groff (1961) recently suggested new norms for speed of handwriting. He argued that earlier norms had been developed with subjects who copied familiar sentences, whereas his subjects did not have a "set" for the sentences. Therefore he believes that the lesser number of words per minute reported in his norms is more realistic. Groff (1963) also attempted to determine whether boys or girls and left-handed or right-handed children write faster. His conclusions regarding pupils in grades 4 through 6 were that the girls wrote faster than the boys but that there was no difference attributable to handedness. Love (1965) studied the quality, speed, and use of handwriting among normal and mentally retarded 12- to 15-year-olds. He found that the mentally retarded scored higher on Ayres-scale ratings of legibility but that the normal children scored higher in speed of writing. Neither group reached the standard rating of 60 on the Ayres scale.

Work with pressure phenomena in handwriting has taken two directions. One, based upon the assumption that such data reflect certain psychological attributes of individuals, is in the general area of graphology, which is discussed elsewhere. The other seeks instructional implications from a better understanding of grip and pressure phenomena in the total handwriting act.

Harris and Rarick (1957, 1959; Rarick & Harris, 1963) have studied pressure exerted on the point of a writing instrument as it relates to speed and legibility in handwriting. The studies have methodological significance because the problems of quantifying pressure and measuring variability of pressure were carefully considered and solutions were suggested. These problems are the very ones that have been troublesome to all researchers in this area, and difficulties in solving them have undoubtedly stood in the way of much research activity. Harris and Rarick's results with adults producing cursive writing indicate a low relationship between average pressure and either speed or legibility; but pressure variability is moderately related to speed and to legibility. Their conclusion was that when speed is increased, pressure variability is increased, habitual motor set is disturbed, and legibility is adversely affected.

Herrick and Otto (1961) studied pressure exerted on both the point and the barrel of a writing instrument. Barrel pressure was quantified through the use of a specially constructed pressure transducer pen, which had strain gauges built into the shaft at the three points of pressure with the traditional grip, and a polygraph recorder. Subjects were from grades 4 and 6 and college. The data showed that, in general, high and low grip pressure goes with high and low point pressure, and the distribution of major pressure points—thumb, index finger, middle finger, and pen point—varies over all possible patterns with individuals. Again, the major contribution of the study was in terms of methodology and instrumentation. More-definitive studies are needed.

Handwriting Instruments. There is little research basis for the design of handwriting instruments, and since Herrick's studies (1954, 1961b) virtually nothing more has been reported. A salient generalization from Herrick's work is that children prefer adult-size writing instruments to the beginner's pencils that are sometimes used; furthermore, there is no objective evidence to support the use of beginner's pencils. Both adults and children preferred round writing instruments, and the preferred specifications were a diameter of slightly less than half an inch, a weight of 18.5 grams, a center of gravity 2 or 3 inches from the writing tip, and grip point about 1.2 inches from the writing point.

Recently a group of industrial-design students described writing instruments they had designed for use by persons unable to grip a conventional instrument ("Writing Device Project . . . ," 1964). In general, the proposed instruments provide support for the entire hand and only minimal grasping is required to control the instrument. Tests in a rehabilitation-department setting, particularly with arthritics, brought enthusiastic reception. Whether there are implications for the design of writing instruments to be used by normally mobile adults and children remains to be seen.

Style. Herrick and Okada's recent national survey of practices in handwriting (1963) showed that almost all children are first taught manuscript writing and then required to make a transition to cursive writing, typically at some time between the beginning of second and the end of third grade. The widespread use of manuscript writing in the schools dates back only to the 1920's, so this almost universal adoption came about in the relatively brief span of only about three decades. The question now is not whether manuscript writing should be taught, for it is in fact taught, but whether, and, if so, when, the transition to cursive writing should be made. After reviewing the existing research relating to the question of which style best meets present-day needs, both Harris (1960) and Andersen (1966) concluded that there may be little evidence to recommend a change from manuscript to cursive. The former seems to meet the writing needs of adults in terms of both speed and legibility and to be most defensible as a beginning style for children. The more recent research and arguments are reviewed here.

Foster (1957) compared intermediate-grade children's manuscript and cursive writing and concluded from his data that the manuscript writing was slightly more legible than the cursive and that children who wrote legibly with one style also wrote legibly with the other. Herrick (1960) suggested that the straight lines, circles, and spacing of manuscript writing are more in line with young children's motor and eye-hand-arm coordination than are the strokes and formations in cursive writing. Hildreth (1963a) pointed out the interrelationship of manuscript writing and early reading and suggested that the two areas ought to be mutually reinforcing. Byers (1963) had the pupils in 24 third-grade classrooms write a paragraph using either manuscript or cursive form and, after ten days, rewrite using the other style. She found similar totals of spelling errors but found that more letters and words were omitted and more substitutions were made with cursive style. Templin (1963) studied the legibility of adults' manuscript and cursive writing to determine which remained most legible ten years after high school graduation. Among her findings were the following: subjects' socioeconomic background, style of writing, and amount of writing were interdependent; subjects who wrote more tended to write better; males, once exposed to manuscript writing, tended to adopt that style regardless of early training; fewer females than males used manuscript writing; subjects of both sexes who were trained with manuscript style and continued to use it as adults wrote most legibly; despite the clichés about physicians' handwriting, physicians wrote twice as legibly as college professors.

Regarding the transition from manuscript to cursive writing, both Templin (1960) and Hildreth (1963b) have argued that the process is wasteful and unnecessary. Templin pointed out that in other skill areas, early learnings are broadened and reinforced, not replaced. Enstrom (1960) feels that the transition is confusing, but he concluded that both styles ought to be learned and used throughout life. Groff (1960) found, through a survey, that the time of transition is based on tradition rather than research findings and expressed his opinion that although there is evidence as to the advantage of manuscript writing it probably will not replace cursive in the intermediate grades because of the schools' sensitivity to public opinion. Templin and King (1964) discussed the merits of each style, with Templin arguing for consistent manuscript style and King arguing in favor of learning and using both styles.

No end to the manuscript-cursive transition discussion is in sight, but perhaps the scope of the discussion will be expanded. The Society for Italic Handwriting advocates the adoption of the italic style at all levels (*Times Education Supplement*, 1965a). Berry (1961) reported a study of pupils in grades 1 through 8 in which she found improvement in the legibility and appearance of pupils' papers when they used the italic style. Freeman (1960) warned, however, that adoption of the italic style should come only after careful analysis and experimentation.

Another interesting suggestion regarding style was made by Schell and Burns (1963). They studied the cursive letter forms produced by college students in order to note changes from the model letter forms they had learned as children. On the basis of their observations they proposed that certain letter forms be simplified from the way they are ordinarily taught and made to conform more closely to the forms actually used by adults in their everyday writing.

THE HANDWRITING PRODUCT. Handwriting is unique among the basic skills in that the act results directly in a tangible product. This product may be examined for the purpose of rating its quality or with a view toward learning about the writer. The handwriting product, then, is considered with regard to quality, scale development, and graphology.

Quality. The focus in assessing quality in handwriting has shifted in recent years from its aesthetic appeal to its readability. Yet, the shift does not seem to be complete. Judges are able to rank-order handwriting samples that are equally legible in terms of the speed and accuracy with which they can be read. The implication is that they look for something more than absolute readability when they consider the legibility of handwriting samples. Quality of handwriting, then, seems to be a global concept that cannot readily be described in concrete, quantifiable terms. Nevertheless, researchers have grappled with the problem for years, and the result has been a wide variety of handwriting scales.

Scales. Thorndike (1910) produced the first handwriting scale in America in 1910, and since then a number of other scales have been devised. The historical development has been adequately covered elsewhere (Harris, 1960; Andersen, 1966; Otto & McMenemy, 1966; and Herrick & Erlebacher, 1963), but the most recently developed scales are described here.

Bezzi (1962) devised a series of scales for rating manuscript writing at the first-, second-, and third-grade levels. A sample of 7,212 specimens was collected from 130 schools throughout the United States, and these specimens were analyzed and judged in the preparation of a five-step quality scale for each grade. The result is one of the few scales available for rating manuscript writing. Herrick and Erlebacher (1963) reasoned that scales with the typical five-to-seven levels of legibility are not adequate, particularly when samples with different size and slant characteristics are to be rated. With this in mind, they devised a scale for the middle elementary grades that permits much finer discrimination among children's handwriting samples than earlier scales. The scale composes a master continuum of rated samples that cover the wide range of quality in handwriting. From the master scale, any number of subscales with predetermined size, slant, and legibility characteristics can be drawn for research and evaluation purposes. The procedures established in devising the scale should be useful to other researchers as they create scales for use at other grade and age levels.

A basic question regarding the value of scales is whether their use enhances reliability in judging the quality of handwriting samples. Two attempts to answer this question were reported recently. Feldt (1962) examined between-judge reliability with a set of scales used in grades 1 and 2. He found that reliability can be raised by analyzing scores from several independent sessions and by providing additional training materials for the judges. Rondinella (1963) had groups of elementary teachers rate handwriting samples from 239 pupils in grades 4 through 6 and found that the teachers tended to rate the samples subjectively and that many were unaware of the criteria for judging suggested in scales. The judges mentioned 14 different characteristics as being responsible for their judgments; this is in contrast to the single notion of general readability or the 3 to 5 characteristics suggested by most scale developers.

A justifiable conclusion seems to be that with sufficient training the reliability of teachers' judgments regarding handwriting quality can be increased through the use of scales. Nevertheless, Herrick and Okada's national survey of practices (1963) revealed that only in about one-third of the responding schools was some use made of scales.

GRAPHOLOGY. Interest in learning about the writer through analysis of his handwriting has persisted for years, but, as Frederick (1965) points out, it is only in recent years that the cloak of mysticism has been lifted and handwriting analysis has acquired some status. In Europe a number of psychologists are using graphoanalysis in their work, and in this country Allport and Vernon's book on expressive movement (1933) has enhanced its respectability.

One of the most troublesome facts is that workers in graphology have not generally been successful in identifying the handwriting characteristics that are associated with specific traits. Therefore it is extremely difficult to formulate hypotheses or to assess the validity of certain assumptions in a scientific way. Attempts to demonstrate validity have generally been done with graphology conceived as an art in the hands of an expert. After reviewing the research in graphology, Fluckiger and others (1961) concluded that the handwriting features that are of primary interest to graphologists are hardest to measure and have received the least research attention.

Studies like those reported by Frederick (1965), Kimmel and Wertheimer (1966), and Leonard (1964), where the attempt has been to assess the value of graphology as a tool for clinical diagnosis, have not lent strong support to the technique. Yet the fact is that the criterion measures in such studies typically are clinical judgments based upon techniques that some would say are no more valid or reliable than graphological techniques. An attempt to specify a handwriting feature and to explore its personality correlates was reported by Linton and others (1961). Their study, which was designed to investigate personality and perceptual correlates of secondary beginning strokes—the initial upstroke in the letters u, v, w, and y—led them to conclude that "the use of secondary beginning strokes is . . . associated with relative inadequacy and lack of energy in intellectual functioning and other forms of coping with the environment, with a tendency to accept things as they are rather than actively trying to control them, and with constriction that applies particularly to emotional interaction." In a related study, Otto and Lasswell (1962) found that in a sample of seventh and eighth graders, poor readers used secondary beginning strokes more frequently than good readers. Studies of specific handwriting features are likely to contribute most heavily to the demonstration of validity, or lack of it, of graphoanalysis as a means for assessing personality traits.

LEARNING AND INSTRUCTION. The volume of contributions to the literature on the teaching and learning of handwriting has continued to be great, but many of the contributions are descriptive rather than research-oriented. The discussion here deals with the general areas of learning correlates, diagnostic and remedial work, and teaching procedures, and it is limited to prototypic studies and articles in each area.

Learning Correlates. A wide variety of correlates of handwriting performance—ranging from intelligence to sex and from gross physical anomalies to reactive inhibition—has been studied. The following serve to demonstrate this range.

Harris and Herrick (1963) studied children's perception of the handwriting task in order to determine whether bright, average, and dull children perceive the handwriting task the same way and to determine to what degree children are able to establish a normative perception of their own handwriting. The value of a normative model is that it provides a personal referent to which an individual can compare other samples of handwriting and from which he can proceed toward an "aspired to" model. The subjects, fifth and sixth graders, wrote under varying conditions, and they attempted to rank-order their own and scaled samples. Bright children were best able to order samples according to adult criteria, and the dull children were least able. Samples produced by the subjects differed in legibility on the basis of sex, intelligence, and writing conditions: girls were better writers than boys; bright and average subjects were better writers than dull subjects; and subjects wrote more legibly when instructed to write their best than when told to write their fastest. In general, the subjects were neither consistent nor proficient in ranking samples. The implication is that if children are to proceed from their present handwriting toward an "aspired to" model, they will need more help in developing their own normative models. In a related study of psychological and motor correlates of handwriting legibility, Rarick and Harris (1963) found that legibility was affected by the conditions under which the writing was produced and also by the subjects' sex. Subjects who produced the most legible writing had the best fine motor control.

Perron and Mignard (1965) studied the handwriting of 243 mental retardates and found that handwriting achievement tended to be a bit ahead of achievement in other areas; boys' scores showed greater dispersion than girls', and developmental stage was a critical factor. Nichols (1965) described a single child who, despite adequate intelligence and motor coordination, was unable to progress in handwriting because of an inability to concentrate on the task. Otto (1965) found that intermediate-grade children who were rated "poor" in handwriting tended to generate more reactive inhibition than good writers, the implication being that rapid accumulation of reactive inhibition may prevent the efficient acquisition of skill in handwriting.

Diagnostic and Remedial Work. There is some agreement that once children have mastered the basic letter forms and sequences of producing them the bulk of instructional time in handwriting should be devoted to helping them to diagnose and remedy their own errors (Otto & McMenemy, 1966). In aiding the expediting of such an approach, the information contained in a report by Quant (1946) is classic. His is one of the few studies in which an attempt is made to single out and evaluate the factors which contribute to illegibility in handwriting. Once the specific causes for illegibility are known, the matter of correcting them becomes a reasonably straightforward task. More recently, Lewis and Lewis (1965) extended Quant's analysis, which covered cursive forms only, by making an analysis of first graders' errors in the formation of manuscript letters.

Enstrom (1966b) and McElravy (1964) described instructional procedures for teaching handwriting to slow learners. They agree on the importance of readiness and adapted pacing, and both feel that slow learners should make the transition to cursive writing, because it will enhance their self perception.

TEACHING HANDWRITING. Descriptions of current practices in teaching handwriting are given elsewhere in this article in the reviews of Herrick and Okada's national survey (1963) and the survey of practices advocated by commercial handwriting systems (University of Wisconsin, 1960). Other recent contributions in the specific area of handwriting instruction are action- rather than research-oriented, although some of the writers draw upon existing research in developing rationales for the procedures and practices they suggest. A representative sample is given here to demonstrate the range and focus of recently published articles.

Page (1964) noted the need for specific activities in developing readiness for writing. She pointed out that handwriting is dependent upon neuromuscular development, eye-hand coordination, visual discrimination, and recognition of the usefulness of writing. Lewis and Lewis (1964), in an application-oriented article based on their study of errors in manuscript writing (1965), discussed the manuscript letters that are hardest for first graders to make. A number of writers discussed what they considered essentials of teaching-learning good handwriting. Ediger (1965) suggested differentiated instruction for pupils with different levels of ability in handwriting and stressed the importance of motivation. Sister Mary Lauriana (1964) listed ten commandments of good handwriting directed at improving teaching. A particularly noteworthy suggestion was that pupils be given timed exercises to train them for writing under pressure. Enstrom and Enstrom (1964) discussed means for improving cursive writing through improved teaching. Meeker (1964), too, was concerned about the teaching of cursive writing; she stressed the need for motivation and regular practice. Enstrom and Enstrom (1966) focused specifically on the need for making legible numbers and discussed ways to improve digit formation, and Enstrom (1966a) pointed out the need for special skills in handwriting at the secondary level. And, finally, Satlow (1965) discussed the need for good handwriting in bookkeeping classes and discussed means for improving handwriting in the high schools.

In the area of handwriting instruction there seems to be more interest in finding out what is being done and in telling people what they should be doing than in testing hypotheses or creating new ones.

Wayne Otto
The University of Wisconsin
Dan W. Andersen
The University of Wisconsin

References

Allport, G. W., and Vernon, P. E. *Studies in Expressive Movement*. Macmillan, 1933. 263p.

Andersen, Dan. "Handwriting Research: Movement and Quality." In Horn, Thomas A. (Ed.) *Research on Handwriting and Spelling*. National Council of Teachers of English, 1966. p. 9–17.

Berry, Winifred. "Italic Writing." *Ed Digest* 26:50–1; 1961.

Bezzi, R. "A Standardized Manuscript Scale for grades 1, 2, and 3." *J Ed Res* 55:339–40; 1962.

Bulletin of the International Bureau of Education (Geneva) 37 (2nd Quarter) No. 147; 1963. 84p.

Byers, L. "Relationship of Manuscript and Cursive Handwriting to Accuracy in Spelling." *J Ed Res* 57:87–9; 1963.

Callewaert, H. "For Easy and Legible Handwriting." In Herrick, Virgil E. (Ed.) *New Horizons for Research in Handwriting*. U Wisconsin Press, 1963. p. 39–54.

Child, Heather. *Calligraphy Today*. Longacre Press, 1963. 96p.

de Vette, Robert O. "Notes and News: Russian Penmanship Simplified." *Mod Lang J* 50:220; 1966.

Diringer, David. (Ed.) *Writing*. Thames and Hudson, 1962. 261p.

Ediger, Marlow. "Essentials in Teaching Handwriting." *Ed* 86:37–9; 1965.

Enstrom, Erick A. "After Manuscript Writing—When Shall We Begin Cursive?" *El Sch J* 61:24–7; 1960.

Enstrom, Erick A. "Print—Handwriting Today." *El Engl* 41:846–50; 1964(*a*).

Enstrom, Erick A. "Research in Teaching the Left-handed." *Instructor* 74:44–6+; 1964(*b*).

Enstrom, Erick A. "Teaching for Greater Legibility." *El Engl* 41:859–62; 1964(*c*).

Enstrom, Erick A. "Decline of Handwriting." *El Sch J* 66:22–7; 1965.

Enstrom, Erick A. "Handwriting: The Neglect of a Needed Skill." *Clearing House* 40:308–10; 1966(*a*).

Enstrom, Erick A. "Out of the Classroom; Handwriting for the Retarded." *Excep Child* 32:385–8; 1966(*b*).

Enstrom, Erick A., and Enstrom, Doris C. "Numerals Still Count." *Arithmetic Teach* 13:131–4; 1966.

Erlebacher, Adrienne, and Herrick, Virgil E. "Quality of Handwriting Today and Yesterday." *El Sch J* 62:89–93; 1961.

Feldt, Leonard S. "Reliability of Measures of Handwriting Quality." *J Ed Psychol* 53:288–92; 1962.

Fluckiger, Fritz A., and others. "A Review of Experimental Research in Graphology, 1933–1960." *Perceptual and Motor Skills* 12:67–90; 1961.

Foster, Emmet M. "A Comparison of Intermediate Grade Manuscript and Cursive Handwriting in Two Typical Elementary School Programs." Doctoral dissertation. State U Iowa, 1957.

Frederick, Calvin J. "Some Phenomena Affecting Handwriting Analysis." *Perceptual and Motor Skills* 20:211–8; 1965.

Freeman, Frank N. *The Handwriting Movement*. U Chicago Press, 1918. 169p.

Freeman, Frank N. "Handwriting." In Monroe, Walter S. (Ed.) *Encyclopedia of Educational Research*, rev. ed. Macmillan, 1941. p. 555–61.

Freeman, Frank N. "Teaching Handwriting." *What*

Research Says to the Teacher, No. 4. NEA, 1954. 33p.

Freeman, Frank N. "On Italic Handwriting." *El Sch J* 60:258–64; 1960.

Gates, Arthur I. "Relation of Quality and Speed of Performance: A Formula for Combining the Two in the Case of Handwriting." *J Ed Psychol* 15:129–44; 1924.

Gray, William S. *The Teaching of Reading and Writing: An International Survey.* Monograph on Fundamental Education No. 10. Columbia U, 1956. 281p.

Groff, Patrick J. "From Manuscript to Cursive—Why?" *El Sch J* 61:97–101; 1960.

Groff, Patrick J. "New Speeds of Handwriting." *El Engl* 38:564–5; 1961.

Groff, Patrick J. "Who Writes Faster?" *Ed* 83:367–9; 1963.

Groff, Patrick J. "Who Are the Better Writers: The Left-handed or the Right-handed?" *El Sch J* 65:92–6; 1964.

Harris, Theodore L. "Handwriting." In Harris, Chester W. (Ed.) *Encyclopedia of Educational Research*, rev. ed. Macmillan, 1960. p. 616–24.

Harris, Theodore L., and Herrick, Virgil E. "Children's Perception of the Handwriting Task." In Herrick, Virgil E. (Ed.) *New Horizons for Research in Handwriting.* U Wisconsin Press, 1963. p. 159–84.

Harris, Theodore L., and Rarick, G. Lawrence. "Problem of Pressure in Handwriting." *J Exp Ed* 26:151–78; 1957.

Harris, Theodore L., and Rarick, G. Lawrence. "Relationship Between Handwriting Pressure and Legibility of Handwriting in Children and Adolescents." *J Exp Ed* 28:65–84; 1959.

Herrick, Virgil E. "The Design of Handwriting Instruments." Unpublished research report. U Wisconsin, 1954. 165p.

Herrick, Virgil E. "Handwriting and Children's Writing." *El Engl* 37:248–58; 1960.

Herrick, Virgil E. *Handwriting and Related Factors 1890–1960.* Handwriting Foundation (Washington, D.C.), 1961(a).

Herrick, Virgil E. "Handwriting Tools for Children." *NEA J* 50:49–50; 1961(b).

Herrick, Virgil E. (Ed.) *New Horizons for Research in Handwriting.* U Wisconsin Press, 1963. 276p.

Herrick, Virgil E., and Erlebacher, Adrienne. "The Evaluation of Legibility in Handwriting." In Herrick, Virgil E. (Ed.) *New Horizons for Research in Handwriting.* U Wisconsin Press, 1963. p. 207–36.

Herrick, Virgil E., and Okada, Nora. "The Present Scene: Practices in the Teaching of Handwriting in the U.S.—1960." In Herrick, Virgil E. (Ed.) *New Horizons for Research in Handwriting.* U Wisconsin Press, 1963. p. 17–38.

Herrick, Virgil E., and Otto, Wayne. *Letter Form Models Advocated by Commercial Handwriting Systems.* U Wisconsin Press, 1961.

Herrick, Virgil E., and Otto, Wayne. "Pressure on Point and Barrel of a Writing Instrument." *J Exp Ed* 30:215–30; 1961.

Hildreth, G. "Early Writing as an Aid to Reading." *El Engl* 40:15–20; 1963(a).

Hildreth, G. "Simplified Handwriting for Today." *J Ed Res* 56:330–3; 1963(b).

How, Jessie K. "Handwriting Is Important; Seattle Prepares a K-Twelve Program." *El Engl* 41:951–53+; 1964.

International Conference on Public Education Convened by UNESCO and the International Bureau of Education. *The Teaching of Handwriting.* Publication No. 103. UNESCO, 1948. 125p.

Judd, C. H. *Genetic Psychology for Teachers.* Appleton, 1911. 329p.

Kimmel, Douglas, and Wertheimer, Michael. "Personality Ratings Based on Handwriting Analysis and Clinical Judgment: A Correlational Study." *J Projective Techniques Pers Assessment* 30:177–8; 1966.

King, Fred M. "Handwriting Practices in Our Schools Today." *El Engl* 38:483–6; 1961.

Leonard, K. "Zum Problem der Graphologie in der Personlichkeits-diagnostik." ("The Problem of Graphology in Personality Diagnosis.") *Psychiatrie, Neurologie und medizinische Psychologie* 16:217–23; 1964.

Lewis, Edward R., and Lewis, Hilda P. "Which Manuscript Letters Are Hard for First Graders?" *El Engl* 41:855–8; 1964.

Lewis, Edward R., and Lewis, Hilda P. "An Analysis of Errors in the Formation of Manuscript Letters by First-grade Children." *Am Ed Res J* 2:25–35; 1965.

Lindell, Ebbe. "The Swedish Handwriting Method." Ejnar Muksgaard (Copenhagen), 1964. 84p.

Linton, H., and others. "Personality and Perceptual Correlates of Secondary Beginning Strokes in Handwriting." *Perceptual and Motor Skills* 12:271–81; 1961.

Love, H. D. "Comparison of Quality, Speed and Use of Handwriting Among Special and Regular Classroom Children." *J Ed Res* 58:475–7; 1965.

Mary Lauriana, Sister. "Ten Commandments of Good Handwriting." *El Engl* 41:854+; 1964.

McElravy, Anna. "Handwriting and the Slow Learner." *El Engl* 41:865–8; 1964.

Meeker, Alice M. "Cursive Writing in the Middle Grades." *Instructor* 74:45+; 1964.

National Council of Teachers of English, Commission on the English Curriculum. *The English Language Arts.* Appleton, 1952. 501p.

Nichols, Lois K. "Recording for Concentration." *Instructor* 75:32; 1965.

Otto, Wayne. "Inhibitory Potential in Good and Poor Achievers." *J Ed Psychol* 56:200–7; 1965.

Otto, Wayne, and Lasswell, Anne. "Relationship of Secondary Beginning Strokes in Handwriting to Reading Ability." *Perceptual and Motor Skills* 14:530; 1962.

Otto, Wayne, and McMenemy, Richard A. *Corrective and Remedial Teaching.* Houghton, 1966. 377p.

Otto, Wayne, and others. "Evaluation of a Modified

Grip in Handwriting." *Perceptual and Motor Skills* 22:310; 1966.
Page, Sarah M. "What's Involved in Getting Ready to Write?" *Instructor* 74:44+; 1964.
Perron, Roger, and Mignard, Edith. "Développement graphique, motricité et intelligence: Contribution au problème par l'étude des débies mentaux." ("Graphic Development, Moticity, and Intelligence: Contribution to the Problem by the Study of Mental Retardates.") *Enfance* No. 5:532–52; 1965.
Piggot, Reginald. *Handwriting, A National Survey*. Allen, 1958. 188p.
Quant, Leslie. "Factors Affecting the Legibility of Handwriting." *J Exp Ed* 14:297–316; 1946.
Rarick, G. Lawrence, and Harris, Theodore L. "Physiological and Motor Correlates of Handwriting Legibility." In Herrick, Virgil E. (Ed.) *New Horizons for Research in Handwriting*. U Wisconsin Press, 1963. p. 55–94.
Rondinella, Oreste R. "An Evaluation of Subjectivity of Elementary School Teachers in Grading Handwriting." *El Engl* 40:531–2; 1963.
Satlow, I. David. "Let's Improve Student Handwriting in Bookkeeping Class." *Bus Ed World* 45:12–3+; 1965.
Schell, L. M., and Burns, P. C. "Retention and Changes by College Students of Certain Uppercase Letter Forms." *El Engl* 40:513–7; 1963.
Scott, W. E. "Handwriting in Philadelphia's Secondary Schools." *Ed* 80:993–5; 1960.
Simon, J. "French Research in the Teaching of Reading and Writing." *J Ed Res* 50:443–59; 1957.
Smith, A. C., and Reed, F. G. "An Experimental Investigation of the Relative Speeds of Left- and Right-handed Writers." *J Genet Psychol* 94:67–76; 1959.
Soltis, Rose Mary. "Handwriting—The Middle R." *El Engl* 40:605–7; 1963.
Templin, Elaine. "A Comparative Study of the Legibility of Handwriting of 454 Adults Trained in Three Handwriting Styles: All Cursive, All Manuscript, or Manuscript-cursive." Doctoral dissertation. New York U, 1959.
Templin, Elaine. "Research and Comment: Handwriting, the Neglected R." *El Engl* 37:386–9; 1960.
Templin, Elaine. "The Legibility of Adult Manuscript, Cursive, or Manuscript-cursive Handwriting Styles." In Herrick, Virgil E. (Ed.) *New Horizons for Research in Handwriting*. U Wisconsin Press, 1963. p. 185–206.
Templin, Elaine, and King, Fred M. "Manuscript and Cursive Writing: Opinions Differ." *NEA J* 53:26–8; 1964.
Thorndike, Edward L. "Handwriting." *Teach Col Rec* 11:83–175; 1910.
Times Education Supplement. "Good Handwriting." 2592:188; 1965(a).
Times Education Supplement. "New Handwriting; Russian Style." 2641:1391; 1965(b).
UNESCO. *The Art of Writing*. UNESCO, 1965.
University of Wisconsin, Committee for Research in Basic Skills. *Comparison of Practices in Handwriting Advocated by Nineteen Commercial Systems of Handwriting Instruction*. U Wisconsin Press, 1960. 111p.
Williams, W. Neil. "What Do You Know About 'Lefties'?" *Grade Teach* 81:44–5; 1964.
"Writing Device Project by Industrial Design Students at Syracuse University." *Ind Design* 11:66–7; 1964.
Zaslow, Robert W. "Reversals in Children as a Function of Midline Body Orientation." *J Ed Psychol* 57:133–9; 1966.

HEALTH EDUCATION

The third edition of the *Encyclopedia of Educational Research*, in its section on health education, contains the following two sentences: "Documentation of these advances [the shift away from inculcation of health habits toward the development of "thinking behavior" in health] is more evident in conference and committee reports, statements of interprofessional groups concerned with school health education, and the judgment of individual leaders in the field than in definitive research. However, research in the comparatively new area of school health education is beginning to accumulate, and there is certainly a strong trend toward investigation of current procedures, programs, and problems through appropriate research methods" (Hein, 1960). In the ten years since this statement appeared there has indeed been an increase in research in school health education. A preliminary survey of the literature in preparation for this review uncovered over 500 studies directly related to the subject at hand—that is, research in some aspect of school health education. These have been reduced, and the bibliography to this article contains, not necessarily the most significant pieces of research, but rather a sample representing all directions and trends which research has taken in the past decade. Also, the emphasis of this review is on research per se, and so little or no reference is made to significant conferences, joint meetings, workshops, national meetings, and other similar events, which certainly have influenced direction and purpose but which have not added to research knowledge. The article by Hein (1960), cited above, provides an excellent orientation to the field of school health education, and it is suggested that if the reader desires a historical overview before reading this article, that work should be consulted.

Two further delimitations must be pointed out. First, the paragraphs that follow deal only with the research in school health education that has been conducted during the years 1957–1967. To cite earlier material would be redundant (cf Hein, 1960) and would reduce the depth of this contribution. Second, the subject is exactly as indicated—that is, published research relative to *school* health education. This represents a decided restriction which eliminates exhaustive research related to health practice, attitude, and knowledge (Young & others, 1963; Young, 1967), but again is necessary. Happily, research in school health education has been significantly influenced in the past decade by the advances made in the behavioral and social sciences. Occasional reference will be made to some of this more generic research when it becomes obviously appropriate.

HEALTH AS A UNIFIED CONCEPT. A position paper (American Public Health Association, 1967) states that "a health educated person, attests the National Education Association–American Medical Association Joint Committee on Health Problems in Education, understands the basic facts concerning health and disease, protects his own health and that of his dependents, and works to improve the health of his community. Health, concurs the National Commission on Community Health Services, is a community affair, and the school as an ever-present social structure for clustering public activity provides a convenient central focus in community planning for health." Since 1911 the Joint Committee has guided and influenced policy in school health education, including significant research. More recently a more encompassing group (National Commission . . . , 1966) has considered all aspects of personal and community health and effected legislation, Public Law 89–749, that will have far-reaching results. While the Joint Committee and the National Committee differ to some degree in their identification of means, they agree as to ends; that is, health is not to be valued in and of itself but rather as it contributes to and makes possible the optimum social functioning of the individual.

INTERRELATIONSHIP OF HEALTH AND EDUCATION. Two well-structured longevity studies have contributed conclusive evidence to the contention that health status and academic achievement are inexorably entwined. In a ten-year study (Hopwood & Van Iden, 1965) of scholastic performance and physical growth of 134 boys who graduated from Shaker Heights High School in Cleveland, Ohio, in the class of 1962, it was shown that unacceptable forms of growth (as defined by the authors) were accompanied by academic underachievement which grew worse as the years of subpar growth continued to accumulate. Entry upon a period of subpar growth was followed, not merely by a simple, temporary drop or diversion in a student's marks, but by a downward deflection that persisted to the end of secondary schooling. The academic aftermath of unsatisfactory physical growth was, very plainly, subpar scholastic achievement, and conversely, a state of health fitness was shown to be an important prerequisite to good scholastic achievement.

The second study (Cobb, 1965), still in process, is the California Joint Study of Student Health Problems and School Performance. This research seeks to test the central hypothesis that there are health characteristics (or groups of them) that are definitely related to certain aspects (or groups of them) of school performance. It is expected that this study will demonstrate, with well-defined validity where others have been suggestive but imprecise (Hardy, 1966), the direct relationship between health and education.

HEALTH EDUCATION AS A RESPONSIBILITY OF SCHOOLS. Since research has shown a tendency for good health and good achievement in schoolwork to go together, it follows logically that individual performance and social functioning will be affected directly by one's health throughout life. Responsible school officials accept the thesis that the health of students must be protected so that learning will be maximal. Equally important and understood is the fact that students must come to understand and appreciate this relationship for themselves and be able to make meaningful health decisions for and about themselves throughout their lives. It is the role of school health education to improve the health attitudes and behavior of students. To do this successfully requires a thorough and careful analysis of the knowledge, attitudes, goals, perceptions, social strata, power structure, cultural traditions, and other aspects of the environment, both school and community, in which students live (Derryberry, 1960; Rosenstock, 1961).

HEALTH EDUCATION WITHIN THE SCHOOL HEALTH PROGRAM. The objectives of health education are achieved through the influence of a part-fictional, part-real organizational construct known as the school health program and its three subcomponents: health services, the healthful environment, and health instruction. Considerable research has been directed at entire school health programs with varying degrees of indicated relationship between services, environment and instruction as each of these in turn affects health education.

RELATIONSHIP TO HEALTH SERVICES AND HEALTHFUL ENVIRONMENT. A number of broad districtwide (Sellery & Bobbitt, 1960; Young, 1961; *American Journal of Public Health,* 1962; Johns, 1962) and statewide (R. Lawrence, 1959) studies of the school health program have been completed in recent years. A related concern has been shown (G. Anderson, 1961) for the coordination status of health programs in selected schools, and at least one state association has developed a self-study guide (Oregon American Association for Health, Physical Education, and Recreation . . . , 1959) which may be used to evaluate college health programs.

Pressure has been exerted to evaluate school health services, not only in a general sense (Schultz, 1963) but with specific elements within services, such as medical examinations (Osborn, 1960), case-finding methods (Yankauer & others, 1962), referral and follow-through (Gabrielson & others, 1967; Cauffman, 1967), and the program for the handicapped (Wallace & Starr, 1960). Another approach to the evaluation of services has involved reference to specific deviations or diseases in students. Among the many investigated have been organic heart disease (Corliss,

1965), hearing disorders (Cozad, 1966), dental caries (Creighton & others, 1964), vision disorders (Blum & others, 1959), immunization status (U. Anderson & Winkelstein, 1966), nutritional screening (Wetzel, 1966), tuberculin testing (Normore, 1962), obesity (Garell, 1966), menstrual functioning (Doster & others, 1961), streptococcal infections (Cornfeld & others, 1961), and respiratory infections (Randall, 1962).

A summary of research relating to the environmental factors that affect health in colleges and universities (Bond & others, 1961), particularly with reference to accidents, underscores the need to maintain concern for this important element of the school health program.

BEHAVIORAL CHANGE AS A GOAL. Ideally, all elements of the school health program contribute to health education and, more specifically, to positive health-behavior change. Tyler (1963) has summarized recent developments in the behavioral sciences and pointed up five concerns which those who wish to be agents of change in the educational setting should recognize: (1) the importance of values in directing behavior, (2) the importance of motivation in learning, (3) the importance of social groups in the development of children and youth, (4) the importance of perception in guiding behavior, and (5) the importance of having essential conditions for learning provided in an imaginative way. It is possible for these five points to be applied at all levels of the school health program and for behavior to be altered by their use. The full range of research with a behavior base includes dental care (Moen, 1958; Kegeles, 1961), behavior disturbances (Oppenheimer & Mandel, 1959), social class (McClendon, 1965), mental health services (Hollister, 1963; Brickman & Meeker, 1967), and health examinations (Borsky & Sagen, 1959).

HISTORICAL FRAMEWORK AND CURRENT TRENDS. A knowledge of the past weighed against the great diversity of events in the present should guide an astute observer toward wise decisions in planning for the future.

The Past. A number of excellent historical studies have placed the field of health education in quite clear focus. Means (1962) published a detailed analysis of health education in the United States, and Nolte (1963) conducted a study of the Joint Committee of the National Education Association and the American Medical Association as this body has influenced the field of health education since its inception in 1911. The development of health instruction received close scrutiny by 16 writers under the guidance of the School Health Education Study (1963). The synthesis of research published by the study contains more than 400 references in the area of instruction alone, a few of which will be identified in this review. This publication (School Health Education Study, 1963) is to school health *instruction* what the previously cited works by Young (Young & others, 1963; Young, 1967) are to the wider field of public health education. It is currently in the process of being revised. One analysis of historical trends in school health services is the excellent study by Neilson (1960). This research analyzed 1,071 replies to a questionnaire seeking information about school health practices and found considerable lack of coordination between health services and health instruction and an inadequate number of full- and part-time personnel to adequately carry out the existing health-service program.

The Present. This writer suggests that the cornerstone separating the past from the present (and "present" is here loosely defined as the larger portion of the years being reviewed) in the field of school health education may be found in two studies, that by Ellis (1963) and that by Carroll (1965). The most basic issue which has confronted health education since the beginning of the modern school health-education movement, 1915–1920, has been the selection of specific content for the achievement of broad objectives. Consequently, there has been confusion in determining just what knowledge and intellectual abilities and skills should characterize the general education of all individuals if the broader goals of health education are to be realized. In the professional literature the broadly stated goals are useful in suggesting general policy and direction but are of little value for curricular or evaluation purposes until they have been more adequately defined. Ellis (1963) and Carroll (1965) applied Bloom's taxonomy of educational objectives to the fields of nutrition and alcohol education, respectively, and in so doing have accomplished between them one of the "discipline's" most significant steps toward the identification of a central core of information peculiar to health education or, more specifically, to health-science instruction.

The second significant event which has paralleled the taxonomy studies just discussed and which will probably have more far-reaching effects, because of its magnitude, is the School Health Education Study. Since this study will be referred to shortly in greater detail it is simply identified here for its contribution to current trends. Three of the many articles concerned with its progress warrant mention; they are those by Smith (1964), Creswell and others (1966), and Sliepcevich (1966). Excellent studies have also been conducted in the areas of current methods in elementary health instruction (Humphrey, 1960) and current trends in school and college health programs (Beyrer, 1960).

Research in any field is subject to the ebb and flow of interests and needs over time. This is especially so in the health field, as seen in the categorical areas of fluoridation, immunization against polio, obesity and nutritional fads, and sex education. In recent years the medical literature has reflected an increasing statistical relationship between smoking and a wide variety of health ailments. On January 11, 1964, this research culminated in the Surgeon General's Report on Smoking and Health (Advisory Committee . . . , 1964). A consequence of these demonstrated statistical relationships has been a crescendo of research with behavioral overtones. Smoking per se is relatively free from moral, political, and legal (but not economic) contamination, and so the increasing knowledge of the behavioral and social sciences has been brought to bear on this single issue to an unprecedented degree. Students in the school setting have been a prime target group for research about smoking.

Swinehart (1966) has shown that the Surgeon General's report itself was soon forgotten and that smoking, which declined slightly immediately after the report was released, actually increased three months later. Studies with high school students as subjects have demonstrated a relationship between smoking and a number of variables, including social class as measured by father's occupation and smoking patterns of parents and friends (Salber & MacMahon, 1961; Bajda, 1964). The effect of antismoking campaigns was studied in a sample of 1,002 school-age children in Missoula, Montana (Lampert & others, 1966). This study demonstrated that nonsmokers generally scored higher on a moralistic criterion but showed no difference over smokers on a fact scale. Also, there were more smokers in the lower grades (sixth to eighth) among the lower social classes, but in the high school grades smoking was not related to social class. The trends in concepts about smoking contained in health textbooks (Haar & Bishop, 1962) and techniques for changing attitudes as well as behavior toward smoking (Horn & others, 1959) have also been researched. Schwartz and Dubitsky (1967) have shown that only a small number of adult smokers (usually the light smokers) are able to give up cigarettes permanently. They indicate, however, that the public attitude toward cigarettes appears to be less favorable than before and suggest that the challenge to education is to communicate this changing climate to youngsters. One approach, for example, might be to reduce the emphasis on lung cancer and instead present cigarettes as unappealing and unattractive (McKennell, 1964).

The multitude of studies on smoking behavior suggest that health education is being tested, and the final report on the profession's ability to influence practices and habits favorably in this important area has not yet been made.

HEALTH INSTRUCTION IN THE SCHOOL. Most school health education takes place in the classroom in the form of formal planned instruction. A grouping, though grossly oversimplified, of research work in this area may be made using four key words: status, problems, approaches, and motivation.

Status of Health Instruction in the Total Curriculum. The second step of the School Health Education Study, following development of the *Synthesis of Research in Selected Areas of Health Instruction* (School Health Instruction Study, 1963) was a study of the status of health instruction in the United States. Findings were based on a random, stratified sample of school districts throughout the country representing 1,101 elementary schools enrolling 529,656 students and 359 secondary schools enrolling 311,176 students. Following analysis of the data the study director was prompted to write that "health instructional programs in the United States are in need of critical review" (Sliepcevich, 1964). This critical appraisal of all aspects of health instruction throughout the nation led to the recommendation that the following facets of the program be examined by local school districts and improved or initiated: professional preparation and teaching effectiveness; nature and extent of extra responsibilities conducted by designated health instructors; in-service opportunities; scheduling practices and time allotment; organizational patterns and administrative factors; factors in the teaching-learning environment; teaching of controversial areas; teaching methodology; accuracy of subject matter; interpretation to school staff, parents, and community; and evaluation procedures.

Studies that are less extensive than but of proportionate significance to the School Health Education Study, have been accomplished which add to the question of status. These include the relationship of health to other areas of the curriculum (Sliepcevich & Carroll, 1958); a self-study of instructional patterns of health teaching in a large city school district (Metropolitan Detroit Bureau of School Studies, 1958–1959); the problems that occur in developing an adequate instructional program (Nichols, 1958); subcommittee reports on methods and procedures in health teaching (Harnett, 1960); patterns of health teaching in the village schools of a large state (Marcum, 1960); the contributions of physical activity to health (Hein & Ryan, 1960); the extent to which superior teachers integrate health into other curriculum areas (L. Barber, 1962); and a number of studies concerned with selected health-education implications. One of these (Dowell, 1966) concluded that health education curriculums should place major emphasis on alcohol, drugs, and tobacco, mental health, and sex education; that the discrepancy between knowledge and practice demands that more effective teaching methods be developed; and that in teaching certain health areas the sexes should be segregated since health interests and worries differ greatly between the sexes.

Problems of Health Instruction. Determination of status invariably leads to the identification of problems. While there are certainly many in health education, an order of priority would place the need for a structured curriculum encompassing grades 1–12 at the very top. Again, the School Health Education Study, in its third and final phase, is seeking a solution. Since 1964 a writing team of eight members, assisted by classroom teachers in a number of communities across the country, has been creating a 12-year curriculum based on a conceptual approach. The major framework has been developed, and in gross, unjust summary, consists of (1) the unified concept of health in its physical, mental, and social dimensions; (2) three key concepts that serve as the unifying threads of the curriculum—namely, growing and developing, interacting, and decision making; (3) ten concepts that represent the scope of the curriculum; and (4) 31 subconcepts that serve as guides in selecting and ordering the subject matter of health education (School Health Education Study, 1967). At this writing, instructional materials and built-in evaluation procedures at four levels of progression have been completed for three of the ten concepts. The full task is scheduled for completion in 1970.

The curriculum must remain flexible, and each school district must exercise conscientious, considered judgment in the selection of objectives, content, and method. No single curriculum will ever be the panacea for all situations. "Adapt, not adopt" is the approach which should be taken. Out of local need different but never completely new approaches will be developed (Cauffman, 1959), while already existing syllabi will provide valuable information (Linden & Macero, 1958). At a lesser level of concern than overall curriculum construction, the handling of controversial areas (Keller, 1959; Greenslade, 1961) has been the focal point of study for a number of researchers.

Approaches to Health Instruction. How a subject should be presented has long been a fertile area for investigation. The Socratic dialogue, the blackboard, and Hopkins and his log are classic approaches that we view with pride and sentiment now. The last ten years have witnessed the mechanization of method, and we are struggling to identify the most relevant and effective methods from among the wide variety now available. Significant methods studies in health instruction include studies of television (Cauffman, 1960; Kaplan, 1963), programmed instruction (Podshadley, 1965; Campbell & Glass, 1965), developmental tasks (Kime, 1965), and experimental demonstration (Tuck, 1965). An excellent discussion which places the full range of technological developments in perspective has been presented by Eric R. Barber (1965).

Motivation Through Health Instruction. The task of those who teach health is a challenging one because, although the student must be motivated to learn, increased knowledge is of secondary importance to its desired outcome, positive change in health behavior. The subject of motivation to change through health instruction was dealt with briefly in the previous discussion of the school health program but demands attention again with specific reference to health instruction.

In health education in the 1960's, the behavioral sciences' interest in human behavior change has been focused on Festinger's theory of cognitive dissonance (1957) and on the application of this theory to the health field by Hochbaum (1960) and Rosenstock (1960). The theory holds that under certain conditions when an individual takes an action that is in conflict with his preexisting beliefs and attitudes, the discrepancies between the original attitude and the subsequent action set up internal pressures to reduce the conflict, or dissonance. A method by which the individual may resolve this conflict is for him to revise his initial attitudes so as to conform to and justify his action. Conflict or dissonance will not be aroused and subsequent attitudes changed unless the conflicting action represents a nearly voluntary choice of the individual. This theory is interpreted by Rosenstock (1960), who succinctly states that "an individual will not decide to take health action unless health matters are salient to him; he believes he is susceptible to a given health condition and believes that its occurrence would have serious consequences for him or his family; and these beliefs are moderately, but not excessively, intense."

The Festinger theory has been examined in the public health setting (Rosenstock & others, 1959; Kegeles, 1963), but experimental application of it in the school setting is not known to this writer. A few researchers, however, have been nibbling at related aspects (Rich, 1960; Schaller, 1960; Johnson, 1964), and study in this important area will increase during the next decade.

PREPARATION OF PERSONNEL. Content and method, however well described, will never eliminate or even reduce the need for skilled teachers and specialists. It is well that the profession continues to examine itself in this regard.

Classroom Teacher. Motivation is as much a variable for the teacher as it is for the student. When elementary teachers must teach a number of subjects, with each becoming more and more technical, and the secondary health teacher must contend with a full range of problems such as poor scheduling patterns, inadequate facilities and materials, and a sophisticated, often unyielding, audience, the desire and ability to teach health is sometimes blunted. The several studies in this area include an analysis of (1) perceptions of the functions and competencies of secondary-school health educators (Cook, 1959); (2) perceptions of prospective elementary teachers regarding their preparation in health (Ives, 1962); and (3) health knowledge of prospective teachers (Haag, 1963).

Specialists. The school health program employs or supports a wide variety of specialists, and the role which each specialist plays is subject to almost continual scrutiny and occasional recommendation for redefinition. Particular roles examined recently have been those of the secondary-school health counselor (Whiteley, 1962), the school nurse (Eidens, 1963; Fricke, 1967), and the school physician (Young & Phillips, 1966). Health standards for the employment of school personnel (Boys & Ifram, 1965) and an analysis of doctoral programs in health education (Johns & LeMaistre, 1966) have been peripheral areas of concern.

EVALUATION IN HEALTH EDUCATION. Skinner, Crowder, and Mager had an impact on education during the 1960's that will influence the organization and evaluation of information and learning experiences for many years to come. First Skinner (1954) and then Crowder (1963) described similar yet different methods for presenting brief, ordered bits of knowledge in a "program" that accelerated and ensured learning. But it was Mager (1961) who first described objectives in language amenable to evaluation, not only for the benefit of programmers but also for those working with more traditional curricular approaches.

Emphasis on Specificity. Objectives, precisely delineated, are not new on the educational scene, yet it took the advent of programmed instruction to focus attention on their importance. It is by way of objectives that the programmer communicates the changes he wishes to effect in the student. Consequently, they must be stated in such a way that they mean the same thing to every individual for whom they are intended. The key to communicating objectives successfully is to state them in measurable terms; and the beginning point, perhaps, is to recognize that we are using the term "objective" rather than any other—for example, "subjective." As an adjective, "objective" means detached, impersonal, and unprejudiced; objectivity is achieved by stating the unit of measure that will be used as the criterion. In health education we are just beginning to do this.

Once the role of an objective unit of measure in assuring good communication is accepted, the hurdle of semantics must be overcome. Nearly all health curricula, local and state, have consistently described their objectives, even at the operational level, with words like *know, understand, appreciate, enjoy, believe,* and *like*. These are ambiguous, are open to misinterpretation, and should be avoided.

Again, the School Health Education Study has provided a guide. The writers accepted Mager's point of view, and their operational or behavioral objectives for each of the ten concepts are replete with such descriptive verbs as *names, analyzes, applies, identifies, cites,* and *examines*. A note of caution has been voiced by Creswell (1967). He suggests that in stating objectives that are both clear and precise, the curriculum writer may be successful in getting the student to learn many different behaviors and still fail to develop the central concept. In other words, in the effort to be specific the point of diminishing returns may be approached and the total configuration lost. The many learning steps may not add up to the principal learning tasks that have been described. It will be interesting to watch the course which curriculum construction *and evaluation* in health education take in the next few years.

Measuring Expected Outcomes. Evaluation has continued despite its unspecific nature. A plethora of studies about misconceptions in health are represented by two of recent vintage, by Dzenowagis (1963) and by Baker and others (1964). Research about misconceptions, commenced in an ordered fashion during the late 1940's and early 1950's, has aided health educators immeasurably in their organization of health content.

Health texts (McTaggart, 1964) have been scientifically examined for accuracy and readability.

The classic health-education outcomes—interests, practices, attitudes, and knowledge—have absorbed the attention of many researchers. Corliss (1962) and Garrett and Pangle (1966) conducted two excellent longevity studies on health interests. Health practices were investigated by Flanagan and others (1958), Macgregor (1961), Cauffman (1963), Veenker (1966), and Griffiths (1966). The two monographs by Young (Young & others, 1963; Young, 1967) must again be cited as constituting the most complete and up-to-date review and analysis of health-practice research available. Attitude research in school health education has been critically reviewed (Mayshark, 1958) and quantified (Richardson, 1960; Meise, 1962; T. Lawrence, 1966). Finally, the multitude of studies in and about health knowledge defies all but a passing nod within the space limitations and time dimensions of this review (Kilander, 1959; Augustin, 1959; Dearborn, 1963).

COMMUNITY RELATIONSHIPS AND COOPERATIVE EFFORTS. Several significant developments have been described in this research review. One more which must not be overlooked is the increased cooperation between schools and the communities in which they find themselves. Examples outside the realm of health education include the rapid rise in adult education sponsored by local school districts, community college development, Project Head Start, and others. In health, the Department of Health, Education, and Welfare underwent a reorganization under the leadership of Secretary Gardner designed to integrate more effectively the still separate and quite independent entities of health, education, and welfare. As a further example the Office of Economic Opportunity has stimulated the creation of neighborhood health centers which in most instances are in close cooperation with the local schools. In recent times, however, the most auspicious piece of action research to demonstrate the part schools play in the community health service and education complex has been that of the National Commission on Community Health Services (NCCHS—1966).

The NCCHS was a nonprofit, independently operated organization established for a temporary four-year period, 1962–1966, to collect and study facts about community health services, needs, and problems and to promote the translation of the resulting knowledge into effective community health services. It was sponsored by the American Public Health Association and the National Health Council and was financed by the Kellogg Foundation, the U.S. Public Health Service, and the McGregor Fund.

It was organized in response to the demand of health leaders throughout the country who felt that something should be done to correct the increasingly disorganized state of community health services. This leadership expressed itself through the two agencies that subsequently became the sponsors.

The commission approached its work through the organization and implementation of three major projects: (1) the National Task Forces Project; (2) the Community Action Studies Project; and (3) the Communications Project. One project focused attention on the national level, one focused attention on the community level, and the other project was concerned with promoting the translation of the resulting knowledge into effective community health services. While each of these three projects was singularly important, the Community Action Studies Project (CASP) deserves further discussion in the present review.

Through stimulation by and guidance from CASP, 21 communities in 19 states embarked upon and completed exhaustive self-appraisals of their health services needs. In nearly all of these community studies specific needs were identified that related to the local school health programs, with regard to both services and instruction. For example, 5 of the 65 recommendations made by the Burlington (Vermont) Area Community Health Study identified elements of the school health program that needed upgrading (DeTurk, 1964). Contained in the Idaho Falls, Idaho, final report to CASP is the conception that "there is a need to more fully integrate the public health and public school health programs. A set of policy statements, goals, and purposes needs to be established to guide this integrated proposal" (Idaho Falls Chamber of Commerce, 1964).

The final report of the National Commission on Community Health Services (1966) contains many recommendations which will be implemented by states and communities across the country in the immediate years ahead. One which needs to be brought to the attention of school officials is phrased as follows:

Health education must become a fundamental part of the basic balanced curriculum; it can be effectively taught in school, and no other agency today offers health instruction to children of school age. State Departments of Education and local school boards should assume greater responsibility for the development of health curriculums. In so doing, the schools should look to health departments and voluntary health agencies for assistance in providing continuity and resources. Such combinations of community health resources and professional experience can supplement the school's program and help provide a meaningful health learning experience for students and teachers." (National Commission . . ., p. 64)

Other excellent summaries of the NCCHS effort may be found in the literature (Mico, 1965; National Commission . . ., 1966).

A study, using some of the NCCHS methodology, was made of the administrative patterns operative in six school health programs (Mayshark, 1967). Two procedures were employed to collect data: a closed-end questionnaire which 217 respondents returned and personal interviews with 155 selected school and community persons. Analysis of the data by narrative description, statistical study of the questionnaire, and comparison of the six programs with emphasis on four major variables led to the following broad conclusions: that (1) the quality of the school health program is related to administrative organization and relationships and to the source and extent of fiscal support; (2) maintenance or improvement of student health is related to administrative organization and relationship; and (3) effective integration of the three phases of the school health program (instruction, services, and environment) is related to administrative organization and relationships.

Other significant research has been accomplished in the area of relationships. Veselak (1958) described the relationships between schools and community health agencies, and Larimore (1960) defined the elements of health education in good public health programs. His analysis revealed the important role of school health education. Alderman (1966) and Mattison (1967) both describe the problems of and prospects for comprehensive health planning in the future. More specific investigation has focused on the local health officer's relations to schools (Behbehanian, 1967), minimal professional time of medical personnel in schools (Wagner, 1966), parental resistance to remedial and preventive services (M. Hardy, 1956), and the professional affiliations of school health workers (Wilson, 1964).

ROLE OF RESEARCH AND FUTURE PROJECTIONS. It seems appropriate to draw this review to a close by citing what one writer has called the "bottlenecks in health education" (Hoyman, 1966). These are the need to (1) promote professional unity in health education, (2) stimulate the development of integrated community and school health education programs, (3) improve health teaching in schools and colleges, (4) recruit, prepare, and place more good health educators, (5) launch a well-organized public and school health education drive, and (6) develop modernized health-science spiral curricula in our schools. If these needs or bottlenecks sound strangely familiar, it is because the research in the field over the past decade has been concentrated, sometimes poorly, sometimes well, in each of the six areas. The cogent point which emerges is that most of the problems in health education are rather well-defined and research to discover solutions has been going on and will continue to go on. Startling revelations will be few, but progress will be made. This last point becomes brilliantly clear to anyone charged with summarizing ten years' research in the field.

A number of writers have made excellent observations about research in health education. These include an evaluation of progress (Knutson, 1957), gaps and potentials (Rosenstock, 1960), research needs (Committee on Research, 1960), a unique epidemiologic approach to health education (Cornfeld & others, 1961), an evaluation of evidence (Gavras, 1962), the methodology of research (Humphrey & Slusher, 1963), the profession's view on research design and techniques in school and college health education (Research Commission . . ., 1964), research needs for schoolchildren (Doyle, 1964), implications of research for teachers and administrators (Sheets, 1966), and methods for encouraging research in school health education (Harris, 1966).

This review commenced with a quote from the previous edition of this encyclopedia. It concludes with the considered observation that good research in school health education has multiplied at a rapid rate. If it continues to mount in quality and quantity over the next ten years, as it most surely will, the next reviewer's task will be even more awesome and revealing than this has been.

Cyrus Mayshark
University of Tennessee

References

Advisory Committee to the Surgeon General of the Public Health Service. *Smoking and Health.* HEW, 1964. 387p.

Alderman, Michael H. "White House Conference on Health, November 3–4, 1965." *Public Health Reports* 81:111–21; 1966.

American Journal of Public Health. "Austin (Minn.) School Health Study." 52:290–9; 1962.

American Journal of Public Health. "The National Commission Reports." 56:865–7; 1966.

American Public Health Association, Committee on Resolutions of School Health. "School Health Education: A Public Health Concern." Paper presented at the meeting of the APHA, October 1967.

Anderson, Gordon W. "On Evaluation of the Coordination Status of Health Programs in and Among Eight Selected Central Schools of Broome County, New York." Doctoral dissertation. New York U, 1961.

Anderson, Ursula W., and Winkelstein, Warren. "Immunization Status of School Children in Buffalo, N.Y." *Public Health Reports* 81:755–60; 1966.

Augustin, Wilbert R. "The Construction and Standardizations of Two Alternate Forms of a Health Knowledge Test for Senior High School Students." Doctoral dissertation. Temple U, 1959.

Bajda, Lillian. "A Survey of the Smoking Habits of Students of Newton High School—A Cooperative Project." *Am J Public Health* 54:441–6; 1964.

Baker, Barbara, and others. "A New Approach in Determining Health Misconceptions." *J Sch Health* 34:300–3; 1964.

Barber, Eric R. "Improving Health Education Through Modern Technics." *Am J Public Health* 55:404–8; 1965.

Barber, Lois S. "A Study of the Extent to Which Superior Teachers Accomplish the Integration of Health Education in Other Curriculum Areas." *J Sch Health* 32:292–4; 1962.

Behbehanian, G. Reya. "The Role of Local Health Officers in Schools Not Having a School Physician." *Am J Public Health* 57:74–9; 1967.

Beyrer, Mary K. "Significance of Current Trends in School and College Health Programs." *Am J Public Health* 50:1934–43; 1960.

Blum, Henrik L., and others. "Design and Evaluation of a Vision Screening Program for Elementary School Children." *Am J Public Health* 49:1670–80; 1959.

Bond, Richard G., and others. "Environmental Health Needs in Colleges and Universities." *Am J Public Health* 51:523–30; 1961.

Borsky, P. N., and Sagen, O. K. "Motivations Toward Health Examinations." *Am J Public Health* 49:514–26; 1959.

Boys, Floyd E., and Ifram, Adnan F. "Health Standards for the Employment of School Personnel—A National Study." *J Sch Health* 35:224–31; 1965.

Brickman, Harry R., and Meeker, Marchia. "Mental Health Consultation in Schools: Preliminary Appraisal of an Urban Program." *J Sch Health* 37:79–85; 1967.

Campbell, Charles E., and Glass, L. H. "Venereal Disease Education: A Comparison of Programmed and Conventional Instruction." *J Sch Health* 35:322–7; 1965.

Carroll, Charles R. "Application of the Taxonomy of Educational Objectives to Alcohol Education." Doctoral dissertation. Ohio State U, 1965.

Cauffman, Joy G. "The Construction of a Health Science Guide for Columbus Public Schools." Doctoral dissertation. Ohio State U, 1959.

Cauffman, Joy G. "Experimenting With the Direct Teaching of Health Education by Television in the Columbus Public Schools." *J Sch Health* 30:260–8; 1960.

Cauffman, Joy G. "Appraisal of the Health Behavior of Junior High School Students." *Res Q* 34:425–30; 1963.

Cauffman, Joy G. "Medical Care of School Children: Factors Influencing Outcome of Referral From a School Health Program." *Am J Public Health* 57:60–73; 1967.

Cobb, B. Otis. "The California Joint Study of Student Health Problems and School Performance—Objectives, Methodology and Progress." *J Sch Health* 35:410–5; 1965.

Committee on Research. "Research Needs in School Health." *Am J Public Health* 50:1792–806; 1960.

Cook, Claude J. "Perceptions of the Functions and Competencies of Secondary School Health Educators." *J Sch Health* 29:50–4; 1959.

Corliss, Leland M. "Report of the Denver Research Project on Health Interests of Children." *J Sch Health* 32:355–60; 1962.

Corliss, Leland M. "Analysis of Recorded Prevalence, Amount of Medical Care, and Follow-through on Organic Heart Disease in 95,000 Pupils." *J Sch Health* 35:1–5; 1965.

Cornfeld, David, and others. "Epidemiologic Studies of Streptococcal Infection in School Children." *Am J Public Health* 51:242–9; 1961.

Cozad, Robert L. "A Survey of Hearing Conservation Programs Conducted by Public Health and School Nurses." *J Sch Health* 36:454–61; 1966.

Creighton, W. E., and others. "Effect of Fluoridated Water in Schools upon Dental Caries Susceptibility." *Public Health Reports* 79:778–80; 1964.

Creswell, William H. "Evaluation and the School Health Education Study." Paper presented at U Tennessee, 1967.

Creswell, William H., and others. "Results of Experimental Testing of the School Health Education

Study Materials." *J Sch Health* 36:154–64; 1966.

Crowder, N. A. "On the Differences Between Linear and Intrinsic Programing." *Phi Delta Kappan* 44:250–4; 1963.

Dearborn, Terry H. "The Junior College Health Knowledge Study in California." *J Sch Health* 33:90–2; 1963.

Derryberry, Mayhew. "Health Education—Its Objectives and Methods." *Health Ed Monogr* 8:3–15; 1960.

DeTurk, D. A. *Burlington Area Community Health Study*. Report No. 3: Goals and Recommendations. Burlington Area Community Health Study, 1964. 24p.

Doster, Mildred E., and others. "A Survey of Menstrual Function Among 1,668 Secondary School Girls and 720 Women Employees of the Denver Public Schools." *Am J Public Health* 51:1841–6; 1961.

Dowell, Linus J. "A Study of Selected Health Education Implications." *Res Q* 37:23–31; 1966.

Doyle, Patrick J. "The Broad Spectrum of Research for School Children." *J Sch Health* 34:374–8; 1964.

Dzenowagis, Joseph G. "Safety Misconceptions Among a Group of Sixth Grade Children." *J Sch Health* 33:26–32; 1963.

Eidens, Clyde O. "The Work of the Secondary School Nurse Teacher as Perceived by Selected Public School Staff Personnel." *J Sch Health* 33:187–8; 1963.

Ellis, John. "The Application of Taxonomy of Educational Objectives to the Determination of Objectives for Health Teaching." Doctoral dissertation. U Michigan, 1963.

Festinger, Leon. *A Theory of Cognitive Dissonance*. Harper, 1957. 291p.

Flanagan, John C., and others. "New Tool for Measuring Children's Behavior." *El Sch J* 59:163–6; 1958.

Fricke, Irma B. "The Illinois Study of School Nurse Practice." *J Sch Health* 37:24–8; 1967.

Gabrielson, Ira W., and others. "Factors Affecting School Health Follow-up." *Am J Public Health* 57:48–59; 1967.

Garell, Dale C. "Obesity in Children and Adolescents: A Double Blind Study With Cross-over." *J Sch Health* 36:273–5; 1966.

Garrett, Leon, and Pangle, Roy. "Health Interests After Five Years." *J Sch Health* 36:42–3; 1966.

Gavras, Emma B. "Searching for the Truth: Evaluation of Evidence in Health Education." *J Sch Health* 32:108–14; 1962.

Greenslade, Margaret. "Textbook Content in Controversial Areas." *J Sch Health* 31:288–96; 1961.

Griffiths, William. "Achieving Change in Health Practice." *J Sch Health* 36:311–22; 1966.

Haag, Jessie H. "Health Knowledge of Prospective Teachers." *J Sch Health* 33:350–3; 1963.

Haar, F. B., and Bishop, W. R. "Analysis of the Trend in Concepts About Smoking in Health Textbooks." *Res Q* 33:486–7; 1962.

Hardy, Martha C. "Parent Resistance to the Need for Remedial and Preventive Services." *J Pediatrics* 48:104–14; 1956.

Hardy, Richard J. *Case Studies of Secondary School Dropouts With Reference to Organic Health Problems*. Doctoral dissertation. U Utah, 1966.

Harnett, Arthur L. "Reports of the Sub-committee on Methods and Procedures in Health Teaching in Secondary Schools." *J Sch Health* 30:152–4; 1960.

Harris, William H. "Some Suggested Methods of Encouraging Research in School Health Education." *J Sch Health* 36:123–7; 1966.

Hein, Fred V. "Health Education." In *Encyclopedia of Educational Research*, Rev ed. Macmillan, 1960. p. 624–36.

Hein, Fred V., and Ryan, Allan J. "The Contributions of Physical Activity to Physical Health." *Res Q* 31:263–85; 1960.

Hochbaum, Godfrey M. "Modern Theories of Communication. *Children* 7:13–8; 1960.

Hollister, William G. "Some Problems of Strategy in Providing School Mental Health Services." *Am J Public Health* 53:1447–51; 1963.

Hopwood, Howard H., and Van Iden, Starr S. "Scholastic Underachievement as Related to Subpar Physical Growth." *J Sch Health* 35:337–49; 1965.

Horn, Daniel, and others. "Cigarette Smoking Among High School Students." *Am J Public Health* 49:1497–511; 1959.

Hoyman, Howard S. "Bottlenecks in Health Education." *Am J Public Health* 56:957–61; 1966.

Humphrey, James H. "Recent Research in Methods of Teaching and Its Implications for Elementary School Health Education." *J Health Phys Ed Recreation* 31:79–80, 98; 1960.

Humphrey, James H., and Slusher, Howard S. "The Application of Current Research in Methodology." *J Sch Health* 33:103–11; 1963.

Idaho Falls Chamber of Commerce. *Community Health Study: A Summary of a Public Health Study of Idaho Falls*. The Chamber, 1964. 28p.

Ives, Charlotte Y. "Perceptions of Prospective Elementary Teachers Regarding Their Preparation in Health Education." *J Sch Health* 32:235–41; 1962.

Johns, Edward B. "The School Health Education Evaluative Study, Los Angeles Area: An Example of a Modern Evaluation Plan." *J Sch Health* 32:5–11; 1962.

Johns, Edward B., and LeMaistre, E. Harold. "Doctoral Programs in Health Education." *J Sch Health* 36:249–61; 1966.

Johnson, A. L. "An Emerging Theory to Explain Health Behavior Using a Reward-cost Analysis." Doctoral dissertation. U North Carolina, 1964.

Kaplan, Robert. "Effectiveness of Television and Problem Solving in Health Education." *J Sch Health* 33:179–85; 1963.

Kegeles, Steve S. "Why People Seek Dental Care: A Review of Present Knowledge." *Am J Public Health* 51:1306–11; 1961.

Kegeles, Steve S. "Why People Seek Dental Care: A Test of a Conceptual Formulation." *J Health Hum Behavior* 4:166–72; 1963.

Keller, Dolores E. "Personality Aspects Related to Misinformation About Sex Among College Students." Sci Ed 43:156–63; 1959.

Kilander, H. Frederick. "Knowledge About Tuberculosis Held by High School and College Students." J Sch Health 29:160–3; 1959.

Kime, Robert E. "Feasibility of Using Developmental Tasks as a Source of Health Interests." Res Q 36:38–45; 1965.

Knutson, Andie L. "Evaluating Progress in Health Education." J Health Phys Ed Recreation 28:21–2; 1957.

Lampert, Kenneth L., and others. "The Effectiveness of Anti-smoking Campaigns: Moralistic or Scientific Approach." J Sch Health 36:34–40; 1966.

Larimore, Granville W. "The Elements of Health Education in Good Public Health Programs." Public Health Reports 75:933–6; 1960.

Lawrence, Ruth A. "Experiences of New York State Four Year Evaluation Study." J Sch Health 29:378–87; 1959.

Lawrence, Trudys. "Appraisal of Emotional Health at the Secondary School Level." Res Q 37:252–67; 1966.

Leonard, Alvin R., and Arnold, Mary F. "The Epidemiologic Approach to Health Education." Am J Public Health 51:1555–60; 1961.

Linden, Arthur V., and Macero, Florence D. "An Analysis of Available Syllabi Used for Alcohol Education in the Public Schools of the United States." J Sch Health 28:166–71; 1958.

Macgregor, Gordon. "Social Determinants of Health Practices." Am J Public Health 51:1709–14; 1961.

Mager, Robert F. Preparing Objectives for Programmed Instruction. Fearon Publications Inc., 1961. 62p.

Marcum, Cloyce E. "Health Instruction in Ohio Exempted Village Schools." Doctoral dissertation. Indiana U, 1960.

Mattison, Berwyn F. "New Horizons—Comprehensive Planning for Health." Am J Public Health 57:392–400; 1967.

Mayshark, Cyrus. "A Critical Analysis of Attitude Measurement in Health Education 1927–57." Res Q 29:309–19; 1958.

Mayshark, Cyrus. A Descriptive and Comparative Study of the Administrative Patterns Operative in Six School Health Programs. USOE, 1967. 127p.

McClendon, E. J. A Study of Social Class as a Factor in the Health Learnings of High School Pupils. Doctoral dissertation. Wayne State U, 1965.

McKennell, A. C. Adult and Adolescent Smoking Survey. British Central Office of Information, Social Survey Division, 1964.

McTaggart, Aubrey C. "Measuring the Readability of High School Health Texts." J Sch Health 34:434–43; 1964.

Means, Richard K. A History of Health Education in the United States. Lea, 1962. 412p.

Meise, William C. "The Construction of a Scale for the Evaluation of Opinions Toward Healthful Living." Doctoral dissertation. Colorado State Col, 1962.

Metropolitan Detroit Bureau of School Studies. A Study on Patterns of Health Teaching. The Bureau, 1958–1959.

Mico, Paul R. "Design for Research in Community Health Behavior." J Sch Health 35:166–72; 1965.

Moen, B. Duane. "A Motivational Study of Dental Care." J Sch Health 28:324–9; 1958.

National Commission on Community Health Services. Health Is a Community Affair. Harvard U Press, 1966. 252p.

Neilson, Elizabeth A. "Analytical Study of School Health Service Practices in the United States." J Sch Health 30:353–9; 1960.

Nichols, Harold L. "Problems in Developing an Adequate Health Instruction Program." J Sch Health 28:212–5; 1958.

Nolte, Ann E. "An Historical Study of the Joint Committee on Health Problems in Education of the National Education Association and the American Medical Association." Doctoral dissertation. Ohio State U, 1963.

Normore, Pearl R. "Student Participation in a Tuberculin Testing Program in a Senior High School." J Sch Health 32:156–8; 1962.

Oppenheimer, E., and Mandel, M. R. "Behavior Disturbances of School Children in Relation to the Preschool Period." Am J Public Health 49:1537–42; 1959.

Oregon American Association for Health, Physical Education, and Recreation and Oregon Tuberculosis and Health Association. "A Self-study Guide for College Health Programs." J Sch Health 29:40–9; 1959.

Osborn, Barbara M. "A Comparison of Four Plans for Providing Medical Examinations in the Secondary Schools of Orange County, California." Doctoral dissertation. U California at Los Angeles, 1960.

Podshadley, Dale W. "Programed Instruction: Highlights of Its Use in Teaching Public Health." Am J Public Health 55:887–91; 1965.

Randall, Harriett B. "Respiratory Infections in Schools." J Sch Health 32: 195–7; 1962.

Research Commission, Health Education Division of the American Association of Health, Physical Education, and Recreation. "Report of the National Institute on Research Design and Techniques in School and College Health Education." J Health Phys Ed Recreation 35:8; 1964.

Rich, Ruth. "Health Education Needs of High School Students in a Large Diversified Metropolitan Area." Res Q 31:631–7; 1960.

Richardson, Charles E. "Thurstone Scale for Measuring Attitudes of College Students Toward Physical Fitness." Res Q 31:638–43; 1960.

Rosenstock, I. M. "Gaps and Potentials in Health Education Research." Health Ed Monogr 8:26–36; 1960.

Rosenstock, I. M. "Decision-making by Individuals." Health Ed Monogr 11:19–36; 1961.

Rosenstock, I. M., and others. "Why People Fail to Seek Poliomyelitis Vaccination." Public Health Report 74:98–103; 1959.

Salber, Eva J., and MacMahon, Brian. "Cigarette Smoking Among High School Students Related to Social Class and Parental Smoking Habits." *Am J Public Health* 51:1780–9; 1961.

Schaller, Warren E. "Health Needs and Interests as a Basis for Selecting Health Content in Secondary Schools." *Res Q* 31:512–22; 1960.

School Health Education Study. *Synthesis of Research in Selected Areas of Health Instruction.* The Study, 1963. 191p.

School Health Education Study. *Health Education: A Conceptual Approach to Curriculum Design.* 3M Ed Press, 1967. 141p.

Schwartz, Jerome L., and Dubitsky, Mildred. "Research in Student Smoking Habits and Smoking Control." *J Sch Health* 37:177–82; 1967.

Sellery, C. Morley, and Bobbitt, Blanche G. "Evaluation of Health Education and Health Services in the Los Angeles City Schools." *J Sch Health* 30: Part I, 81–5; and Part II, 113–8; 1960.

Sheets, Norman L. "Implications of Research in Health Education for Teachers, Administrators, and Research Specialists." *J Sch Health* 36:433–41; 1966.

Shultz, Carl S. "Trends in School Health Services." *Am J Public Health* 53:1284–8; 1963.

Skinner, B. F. "The Science of Learning and the Art of Teaching." *Harvard Ed R* 24:86–97; 1954.

Sliepcevich, Elena M. *Summary Report of a Nationwide Study of Health Instruction in the Public Schools.* School Health Education Study, 1964. 74p.

Sliepcevich, Elena M. "School Health Education Appraisal of a Conceptual Approach to Curriculum Development." *J Sch Health* 36:145–53; 1966.

Sliepcevich, Elena M., and Carroll, Charles R. "The Correlation of Health With Other Areas of the High School Curriculum." *J Sch Health* 28:283–92; 1958.

Smith, Sara L. "Implication of the Report of the N.E.A. Project on Instruction for Health Education." *J Sch Health* 34:432–4; 1964.

Swinehart, James W. "Change over Time in Student Reactions to the Surgeon General's Report on Smoking and Health." *Am J Public Health* 56:2023–7; 1966.

Tyler, Ralph W. "Implications of Behavioral Studies in Health Education." *J Sch Health* 33:9–15; 1963.

Tuck, Miriam L. "Experimental Demonstration as a Method of Stimulating Learning." *J Sch Health* 35:172–5; 1965.

Veenker, C. Harold. "Evaluating Health Practice and Understanding." *J Health Phys Ed Recreation* 37: 30–2; 1966.

Veselak, Kenneth E. "A Study of the Relationships Between Public Schools and Community Health Agencies in Selected Communities." Doctoral dissertation. Columbia U, 1958.

Wagner, Marsden G. "An Experimental School Health Program Using Minimal Professional Time." *J Sch Health* 36:193–7; 1966.

Wallace, Helen M., and Starr, Helen M. "School Services for Handicapped Children in Urban Areas." *Am J Public Health* 50:173–80; 1960.

Wetzel, Norman C. "New Dimensions in the Simultaneous Screening and Assessment of School Children." *J Health Phys Ed Recreation* 37:33–5; 1966.

Whiteley, William E. R. "Recommended Guidance Competencies for Secondary School Health Counselors." *J Sch Health* 32:171–6; 1962.

Wilson, Charles C. "School Health Workers and the American Public Health Association." *Am J Public Health* 54:1333–4; 1964.

Yankauer, Alfred, and others. "A Study of Case-finding Methods in Elementary Schools: I. Methodology and Initial Results." *Am J Public Health* 52: 656–62; 1962.

Young, Marjorie, A. C. "The Brookline School Health Study." *J Sch Health* 31:47–55; 1961.

Young, Marjorie A. C. "Review of Research and Studies Related to Health Education Practice (1961–1966): What People Know, Believe, and Do About Health." *Health Ed Monogr* No. 23; 1967. 76p.

Young, Marjorie A. C., and Phillips, Harry T. "Changing the Role of the School Physician—The Newton Study." *J Sch Health* 36:424–32; 1966.

Young, Marjorie A. C., and others. "Review of Research Related to Health Education Practice." *Health Ed Monogr*, Suppl. No. 1, 1963. 113p.

HEALTH SERVICES—
COLLEGE AND UNIVERSITY

Health services in United States colleges and universities have been developing slowly for more than a century. In the early stages they were meager and their goals were mainly limited to promoting health through encouraging vigorous exercise and physical training. As the medical sciences advanced, concepts of preventive medicine in the modern sense gradually developed, health education became more effective and sophisticated, mental health emerged as a special category of interest, and the treatment of illness became more effective. Slightly more than a half-century ago, "modern" college health services were organized in several of the larger colleges and universities. The American Student Health Association was established in 1920 because a number of active and progressive directors of college health services wanted a forum to exchange views and experiences. In 1948 this organization became the American College Health Association, reflecting the change from exclusive concern with the health of students to responsibility for everyone in the institutions. In 1967 it had 511 institutional members, 1,154 individual members, and a full-time executive director. Special sections have been organized for administration, athletic medicine, clinical medicine, environmental health and safety, health education, mental health, and nursing service. A dental health section is projected. The parent body has encouraged regional college health organizations (13 in all)—some of them nearly as large as the national association. Close liaison is maintained between the national and regional groups, though the latter are not chapters of the former.

STATUS. College and university health services exist to promote health and treat disease and its consequences. Those which function best have been organized as separate departments or divisions within the institution, with the director reporting to the president's office. In many colleges the health service is considered one of the student personnel services, parallel with counseling, guidance, financial aid, student-union activities, and all the other activities coming under the general supervision of the dean of students. While such an arrangement may appear theoretically justified, in practice it can result in a mediocre health service. The various members of the health professions have special responsibilities (e.g., problems of confidentiality) and usually require more training than do members of some of the other personnel services. The vital factor in an effective health program is its cooperation with all other divisions of the institution and the concomitant maintenance of a freedom of action that encourages the wisest type of recommendations and decisions. Physicians and other health professionals are in the college or university to help its members perform their academic functions with as little hindrance as possible from ill health or injury. A condition of good health contributes to the learning process; thus, the vested interest of college physicians is in the health of students, faculty, and employees, rather than in their diseases. Hence, they must of necessity think in terms of disease prevention and safety measures. To reduce a medical department to the position of a first-aid station is to ensure its failure to live up to its maximum potentialities. Independence of action is essential, but physicians should not infringe upon the administrative responsibility of department heads, deans, or higher officials, whose consultants they are and whom they help, when it is desirable and appropriate, in making decisions that have significant health components.

A college health service may be called upon for help in many ways other than treatment of disease or injury. Correspondence reaching the president from those who may be dissatisfied about health issues or from those who threaten his safety often requires prompt attention. Admissions committees encounter a wide variety of health problems whose management can be facilitated by expert consultation. The health director should be an active participant in the determination of admissions policies insofar as health issues are concerned. Deans and department chairmen are frequently presented with problems which require medical opinion for their resolution. Directors of libraries have an unusual number of problems in whose solution psychiatric knowledge may be helpful (Farnsworth, 1964).

OBJECTIVES. The primary objective of a college health service is to promote health in such a way as to enable each individual to pursue his academic or other pursuits effectively. Its efforts include minimizing loss of time because of illness and injury and devising methods of financial coverage which cushion the impact of costs of medical care.

Environmental health and safety, together with preventive-medicine measures, receive much attention from college health-staff members. Every needless illness or injury adds to the cost of a health program and requires the expenditure of time and energy by staff members; inculcation of attitudes favorable to prevention is very important.

If the health needs of college students could be met by the use of local community agencies, there would be no reason for the establishment of special health services. Unfortunately, the health facilities available to the general public are not adequately equipped or organized to meet the special and varied needs of a college population. One objective of a college health service oriented to disease prevention and health promotion, and to the social needs of its constituents, should be to demonstrate its value by caring for the students with the hope that when the students later become established in their own communities they will aid in improving health services for all.

SERVICES AND PROGRAMS. In the large health services (particularly in institutions of more than 10,000 students) the division of responsibilities in a comprehensive program is made according to general hospital practice. The usual services include medical, surgical, psychiatric, environmental health and safety, dental, and, in some universities, research. Supervision of the medical aspects of athletics is usually assumed by the surgical service. Laboratory services, radiology, and the various other subspecialties may be assigned to one of the major services or may occupy a semiautonomous position, their activities being regulated by the health-service director.

Medical Service. The medical service is the core of any health program, no matter what its size. In many small colleges the entire staff consists of a part-time physician, usually an internist or a general practitioner, and one or more nurses. This team attends to the needs of those who seek help, utilizing consultants in surgery or psychiatry from the neighboring community, cooperating with community public health agencies on matters of sanitation, epidemics, and immunization, and sending patients with serious illnesses to a nearby hospital. Since comprehensive medical service frequently is not possible in many of the communities surrounding small colleges, it is not expected. The quality of the service rendered is then judged on the basis of the skill of the physician and nurses, their knowledge of when to refer complicated or serious cases to other medical facilities, and their devotion to students and understanding of their needs. The care received by students in many of these small services is of exceptional quality because of the staff members' concern, kindness, and warmth, which compensate for the lack of diagnostic facilities that are available in large medical centers.

In large health services the medical service deals with the great majority of all persons who seek help or advice, at least at the first contact. A survey of 13,208 students of Harvard University who sought help in the general medical clinic during the academic year 1960–61 revealed the following distribution of disorders:

Respiratory-system disorders	4,030
Injuries	2,552
Skin	1,829
Digestive-system disorders	1,378
Nervous-system disorders	757
Infectious diseases	616
Disorders of bones and organs of movement	297
Allergies	257
Circulatory-system disorders	194
Genitourinary-system disorders	148
Disorders of the blood and blood-forming organs	9
Ill-defined conditions	886

While this distribution varies somewhat from year to year, the general profile is valid for most health services, except for the occurrence of epidemics (Farnsworth, 1964).

Surgical Service. Surgical consultation in small colleges is usually supplied by a surgeon practicing in the community who responds to requests as the need arises. This consultant often holds regular office hours at daily or twice-weekly intervals for conditions not urgently requiring treatment. In many large institutions surgeons are on duty throughout the day and on call for emergencies at night. In colleges, as in any concentrations of young people, the most common surgical conditions are appendicitis and other abdominal disorders and athletic and motor vehicle injuries. The supervision of athletic contests is usually a surgical function, although much help is needed from internists. In some large universities the team physician is not a part of the health service, a custom outmoded and highly inappropriate. Current practice is that all health-service functions be combined and coordinated in one department.

Psychiatric Service. In recent years, students' emotional problems have attracted much attention from both the public and college administrators. Psychiatric services have increased in number and effectiveness, although there have been no formal surveys made for several years. Earlier studies indicated that no more than 100 colleges had significant mental health programs and that only about 40 psychiatrists were engaged full-time in college psychiatry (Gundle & Kraft, 1956). Judging from informed sources of information (particularly the attendance and activities of the Mental Health Section of the American College Health Association), the number of services and of psychiatrists working in such services has more than doubled in the last 15 years. Growth would probably be even greater were it not for the shortage of psychiatrists who can be attracted to positions in colleges, particularly in institutions away from large psychiatric training centers.

The extent of the clinical problems among college students has been estimated by Farnsworth as follows: For every 10,000 students, 1,000 will have emotional conflicts of sufficient severity to warrant professional help, 300 to 400 will have feelings of depression severe enough to impair their efficiency, 100 to 200 will be apathetic and unable to organize their efforts—"I can't make myself want to work," 20 to 50 will be so adversely affected by past family experiences that they will be unable to control their impulses (character disorders), 5 to 20 will attempt suicide and 1 to 3 will succeed, and 15 to 25 will become ill enough to require treatment in a mental hospital (Farnsworth, 1966).

Most colleges with extensive mental health services find that all the available time of their psychiatrists, psychologists, and social workers is taken up by students seeking help. This suggests that a proper use of psychiatrists in college mental health programs should include consultation with other counselors, deans, academic advisers, faculty members, student leaders, and others who are cognizant of significant evidence of emotional conflict in those students for whom they have some responsibility.

Reviews of various aspects of college psychiatric services, by the following authors, have appeared in the past decade: Wedge (1958), Funkenstein (1959), Blaine and McArthur (1961), deSmit (1963), Whittington (1963), and Farnsworth (1957, 1964, 1965, 1966).

Dental Service. Of all forms of college health services, dental service is the least developed. In 1963 a study was made of dental services among the 361 institutional members of the American College Health Association (Dunning & others, 1963). Only 31 dental clinics could be located, and of these 7 offered only emergency and consultation service. No college or university gives complete dental care. Ordinarily, even the largest dental services offer only emergency service, case finding, diagnosis, consultation, preventive measures, and dental health education, and a limited amount of restorative dental treatment (usually for those without access to private dental care). Many institutions that do not have dental services arrange for mouth guards from local private dentists (44 percent in the survey) and offer accident insurance programs covering the restoration of injured teeth or oral surgical operations.

Dental disease is very common in the United States. Dental caries are particularly prevalent in the period from adolescent to early adulthood. Education about preventive measures to decrease the incidence of future dental disease is needed in this age group. Acute dental pain is a common occurrence among college students. For all these reasons, college dental health services should receive more attention and support than they have so far.

Environmental Health and Safety. Although only the large universities have formal environmental health and safety sections in their health services, all colleges have problems in this category. Often the need for such a service is not recognized until a potentially avoidable epidemic or a catastrophic event makes it manifest. But whether or not there is a special group actively and continuously concerned with such problems, they do exist, and they warrant advance planning and management.

A health service's duties which are designed to prevent disease or injury include the examination of food handlers, periodic bacteriological examination of food-preparation facilities, supervision of the use of toxic materials in laboratories, regulation of the use of radioactive sources of energy, and the development of safety programs. Special programs may include fitting safety glasses for those who are frequently exposed to flying objects, requiring safety hats and shoes for workers in special-risk areas, fitting contact lenses for those athletes participating in contact sports who have visual defects requiring correction, and making plastic mouth guards to prevent tooth injury in "collision" sports.

Many of the activities of an environmental health and safety division, whether formally organized or not, involve close collaboration among members of the health service and persons in other college departments with a wide variety of knowledge and skills. A clear duty of health officials is to encourage the development of proper attitudes toward accident prevention and safety in all persons in the institution. A basic concept guiding health workers is that almost any research or other necessary procedure can be done safely if proper precautions are observed. In other words, the safety and prevention program should be designed to permit such activities to be done well, rather than to keep them from being done. Accordingly, requests for consultation from laboratory directors are welcomed as a means of instituting truly cooperative safety programs.

RESEARCH. Up to the present, research programs in health services have been few in number and relatively small in scope. Some progress has been made in the treatment of infectious mononucleosis (Prout & Dalrymple, 1966), some injuries to athletes have probably been prevented (Quigley, 1966), and considerable information has been obtained regarding causes of students' leaving college (Pervin & others, 1966). In most health services research is carried on with little specific financial support; physicians and others utilize their spare time for investigation. A notable exception is a long-term longitudinal study sponsored by the National Institute of Mental Health at Harvard University. The Harvard Student Study was initiated in 1958, and its publications are now beginning to appear (Vreeland & Bidwell, 1965, 1966). In this project the progress through college of 500 students has been followed; use has been made of psychological, sociological, psychiatric, and statistical methods of observation.

PERSONNEL. Personnel shortages obtain in almost all health services in the United States. If no medical progress had occurred during the past two or three decades, perhaps the increase in medical personnel would have kept pace with increasing population and no unusual strains would have occurred. However, not only has there been a dramatic increase in demand for medical services, but the forms of treatment have proliferated and the costs have advanced faster than those for other services. In addition to these strains, new legislation designed to meet the health needs of those who cannot pay for what they need on a fee-for-service basis has produced still further shortages. On the average, there are now about 12 persons in the health professions and occupations assisting each physician. It is anticipated that this ratio of 1 : 12 will increase in the next few years to 1 : 20.

College health services have also been affected by these changes, but they are in an advantageous position to make constructive adjustments to new conditions. Because of their relatively small size they can retain a flexibility of operation not as easily achieved in large, and particularly urban, institutions. Physician consultants can be engaged on a part-time basis. Nurses who cannot work full-time may devote a few hours weekly, especially during epidemic seasons. The services of medical technologists are nearly always in great demand, but other workers can often be trained to do the relatively simple laboratory procedures.

The great emphasis on the development of community mental health centers and facilities resulting from the recommendations of the Joint Commission on Mental Illness and Health has contributed to the difficulty of obtaining psychiatrists for college health services. At the same time, the development of such centers in widely scattered parts of the country has made it possible for many colleges to obtain some psychiatric consultation services when otherwise they would have been able to obtain none.

FACILITIES. Many colleges and universities have built new health centers since World War II, most of them quite adequate for the functions assumed by the institution. The nature of the building depends largely on whether the health center is conceived of as a first-aid station or as an intricate, often informal, network of communication between members of the health professions and all others in the college community.

Whatever the functions to be carried out, it is desirable that a health center be situated as near as possible to the center of daytime activities of the institution. Other planning principles include collaboration with representatives of all types of persons who will use the facility and the selection of an architect who will carefully consider the special aspects of college health programs.

To aid small colleges contemplating building health centers the Educational Facilities Laboratories has made an architectural study of the functions to be performed in them and developed a plan that can be modified to suit particular needs, yet which combines the majority of the needed characteristics of any college health center (Educational Facilities Laboratories, 1962).

FINANCES. The single greatest obstacle to the development of college health services is lack of finances—or, at least, that is the reason most commonly given for not organizing one. Under changing conditions of health-care financing, this obstacle may not remain the decisive one. According to Lee (1966), about $33.488-billion was spent in 1965 in the United States for "currently consumed health services and supplies," or about $167 per person. In contrast are health fees, including insurance, of $50 to $115 per person, which are the usual current lower and upper limits charged by colleges and universities with reasonably adequate health programs. It is well known that health care for the college-age population is less expensive than that needed by children and the elderly. A survey of 1963 costs showed that the average cost of health services for persons aged 18 to 34 was about $130 (Health Information Foundation, 1965). Since college health fees are considerably lower than that amount (although they usually do not cover all portions of possible medical or health expenses), it can reasonably be argued that good health services are no more expensive than the absence of organized health services. If it is assumed that colleges should not be expected to pay for the health needs of their students but only to make it possible, via the institutions' administrative structure, for students to obtain good medical care on a prepaid basis, the financial barrier assumes a different aspect. Whether or not a college or university has a good health service depends upon the willingness of students, their parents, and the administration to organize one and pay for it. Current emphasis on developing adequate health plans for everyone, together with the desire to keep medical costs within reasonable bounds, may stimulate an increasingly rapid development of financially sound health and insurance plans for all college students.

Health fees commonly cover the costs of all services rendered in college facilities by members of the health services, whether these be rendered in the clinic, in the infirmary, or while carrying out preventive and safety measures. Insurance premiums usually cover the costs of treatment in hospitals or of treatment for injuries or illnesses acquired while away from the college. In some institutions (mainly private) the health fee and insurance premium are automatically included in tuition charges. In most public institutions such a procedure is seldom followed because of political and public-relations considerations. In recent years many institutions have established Blue Cross–Blue Shield plans which compete favorably with commercial insurance plans that formerly served most colleges and universities.

IN OTHER COUNTRIES. In other countries health services in institutions of higher learning have been developing at a rapid rate, but progress is quite uneven. Great Britain has made progress at a rate comparable to that of the United States. In most of the western European countries new services are being established although usually with less extensive programs than those offered in the United States. Canada, Australia, and New Zealand are developing new services which are for the most part modeled on those of Great Britain and the United States.

In 1966 the World Health Organization Expert Committee on Professional and Technical Education of Medical and Auxiliary Personnel devoted a weeklong session to the need for, and nature of, university health services. The committee pointed out the desirability of such services' setting a valuable example of the application of social and preventive medicine to the needs of a community (which should influence the attitudes of students); furthermore, the committee stated that illness among the young adolescents and young adults that make up college populations frequently presents problems that cannot be solved effectively by health agencies available to the general population. It observed that university medical services which maintain a preventive and promotive outlook and which are sensitive to the needs of the society they serve can do much to reduce waste and improve working efficiency. Without such services the opportunity to study the health problems of the adolescent and young adult and to develop skill in their management is lost. The committee recommended that all institutions of higher learning provide such services; the suggested scope was in general accord with the principles discussed in this article (World Health Organization, 1966).

Dana L. Farnsworth
Harvard University

References

Blaine, Graham B., Jr., and McArthur, Charles C. (Eds.) *Emotional Problems of the Student.* Appleton, 1961. 254p.

deSmit, Bart N. W. *From Person into Patient.* Mouton & Co., 1963. 99p.

Dunning, James M., and others. "Prevalence and Characteristics of College Dental Health Services." *J Am Col Health Assn* 11:189–96; 1963.

Educational Facilities Laboratories. *A College Health Center.* The Laboratories, 1962. 32p.

Farnsworth, Dana L. *Mental Health in College and University.* Harvard Press, 1957. 244p.

Farnsworth, Dana L. (Ed.) *College Health Administration.* Appleton, 1964. 250p.

Farnsworth, Dana L. *College Health Services in the United States.* Student Personnel Series No. 4. APGA, 1965. 28p.

Farnsworth, Dana L. *Psychiatry, Education, and the Young Adult.* Thomas, 1966. 268p.

Funkenstein, Daniel H. (Ed.) *The Student and Mental Health—An International View.* World Federation for Mental Health, 1959. 495p.

Gundle, Sigmund, and Kraft, Allan. "Mental Health Programs in American Colleges and Universities." *B Menninger Clinic* 20:63; 1956.

Health Information Foundation. *Progress in Health Services*, Vol. 14. U Chicago, 1965. 6p.

Lee, Philip R. "New Demands for Medical Manpower." *J AMA* 198:1091–903; 1966.

Pervin, Lawrence A., and others. *The College Dropout and the Utilization of Talent*. Princeton U Press, 1966. 260p.

Prout, Curtis, and Dalrymple, Willard. "A Doubleblind Study of Eighty-two Cases of Infectious Mononucleosis Treated with Corticosteroids." *J Am Col Health Assn* 15:63–6; 1966.

Quigley, Thomas B. "Contributions of Sports to Medicine." *J AMA* 197:883–4; 1966.

Vreeland, Rebecca, and Bidwell, Charles. "Organizational Effects on Student Attitudes: A Study of the Harvard Houses." *Sociol of Ed* 38:233–50; 1965.

Vreeland, Rebecca, and Bidwell, Charles. "Classifying University Departments: An Approach to the Analysis of Their Effects Upon Undergraduates' Values and Attitudes." *Sociol Ed* 39:237–54; 1966.

Wedge, Bryant M. (Ed.) *Psychosocial Problems of College Men*. Yale U Press, 1958. 291p.

Whittington, Horace G. *Psychiatry on the College Campus*. Int U, 1963. p.328.

World Health Organization. *University Health Services*. Technical Report Series No. 320. WHO, 1966. 24p.

HIGHER MENTAL PROCESSES

As in the case of many psychological concepts, theories of thinking first were considered by philosophers. For example, Aristotle regarded mind as a process in which a potential realizes or actualizes itself. Descartes gave modern psychology the dualism of mind and body, regarding the two as separate but interacting. Liebnitz contributed the concept of degrees from the conscious to the unconscious. These are examples of philosophers who espoused a pre-experimental associationism. The following material is quoted from Russell's article "Higher Mental Processes" in the third edition of this Encyclopedia.

Perhaps the first beginnings of the psychological approach to thinking were in the Wurzburg school in Germany with its debates on the topic of imageless thought beginning about 1900. Early experimental studies reported by Ach, Bühler, and others described thought processes in such terms as awareness of meaning and of relation and consciousness of rule and intention. Such beginnings represent combinations of philosophical and psychological approaches. These have been treated in some detail by Humphrey (1951).

A second theory of thinking which flourished in the nineteenth and early twentieth centuries was that of associationism. The British Associationist School included such men as Hobbes, Locke, Hume, and Bain. It is to John Locke that we owe the phrase "association of ideas." Alexander Bain is important to American psychology because of his influence on James and Thorndike. The term *association* became the term *conditioned reflex* with the early behaviorists and is a forerunner of connectionist theories of learning. Historical accounts of the changes in associationist theories of learning and thinking have been given by Humphrey (1951) and by Murphy (1949). Many of the classical theories of associationism have been criticized severely in experimental studies.

INTELLIGENCE TESTING. Certain theories of intelligence prominent after 1910 had implications for the meaning of thinking processes. Growing out of associationism, but fully critical of the associationists' views, is the work of Spearman (1931). He based his views of thinking on three principles: (a) apprehension of experience—sensation and perception exist as mental acts or states; (b) education of relations, as when "mercury-glass" might stimulate the response "thermometer"; and (c) education of correlates, as when "short-opposite" brings the response "tall." Spearman believed that these three terms are adequate to describe most mental behavior.

Thorndike (1927) opposed Spearman's definition of intelligence in terms of a g factor, or a general mental energy, and proposed instead that it was made up of many specific abilities or s's. Although Terman (1916) defined intelligence as the ability to do abstract thinking, he was influenced by Binet to include a wide range of materials and mental activities in his intelligence tests. (Russell, 1960)

Recent work in factor analysis has led to the postulation of a considerable number of mental abilities indicative of different intellectual activities. Thurstone (1938) identified six predominant factors: Verbal, Number, Spatial, Word fluency, Memory, and Reasoning. Burt (1949) believed he had evidence of a hierarchy of mental abilities ranging from general intelligence, through relations, to associations based on more specific perceptions "each more or less independent of the rest, yet all included within a single unified system." Guilford (1967) has created a model "Structure of Intellect" for which he has constructed an extensive battery of tests which have been tried out with different groups of subjects. Factor analytic procedures are used to determine the distinctiveness of the tests in the model. Guilford's model includes mental operations, types of content, and kinds of products. He distinguishes five types of mental operations: cognition—awareness or possession of information; memory—retention of information; convergent production—proceeding from information to the logical possibilities; divergent production—proceeding from information to a variety of adequate solutions; and evaluation—process of comparing and matching items of information with regard to different logical criteria and making decisions with regard to satisfaction of these criteria. Guilford distinguishes four kinds of content categories: figural (directly perceived objects, events, drawings); symbolic (letters, numbers, musical notations, etc.); semantic (verbal); and behavioral (human interactions). He also distinguishes six kinds of products: units, classes, relations, systems, transformations, and implications

In Guilford's system there may be 120 cells or combinations of operations–content–products. He and his colleagues have developed and demonstrated 82 factors or tests with others under investigation. These tests, and the structure of intellect model, have stimulated a great deal of research on creativity and other areas of higher mental processes, since they provide instruments which can be used in a great variety of research problems on human behavior and education.

SCHOOLS OF PSYCHOLOGY. Since the time the Wurzburg school flourished in Germany, the concept of simple associative thinking has been supplemented by ideas such as "set," "latency," and "reinforcement." Simple association and conditioning could not explain much thinking, but with such additions as mediating processes, facilitating, and goal-directed activity, the terms have considerable validity in accounting for relatively complex types of thinking. Pavlov's (1955) second-signal system stresses the mediating role of language in learning and thinking processes. Building on this more complex view of conditioning, Vygotsky (1962), Bernstein (1961), Brown (1956), and Staats and Staats (1964) have developed very systematic ways of accounting for thinking and problem solving in terms of the use of language and linguistic forms which enable individuals to organize and relate various phenomena in new ways.

Skinner (1966) has argued for an operant analysis of problem solving. Problem solving, as he views it, is concerned with the relations which prevail between a stimulus, a response, and a reinforcing consequence. A problem is defined when a reinforcing event is contingent upon something, either a property of the response or a property of the environment. Problem solving is the behavior that brings about the condition under which reinforcement will occur. Skinner shows how language, rules, and laws enter into contingency-specifying rather than contingency-shaping (direct experience) behavior for problem solving.

Thorndike's (1898) experiments with cats in puzzle cages appear to be one of the vital links between behaviorism and Gestalt approaches to problem solving. Thorndike observed his cats and the procedures they used to escape from the cage. He interpreted these procedures in terms of exploration activity and accidental success. The cats' performance improved with practice, because, as he saw it, the successful activities were rewarded. This trial-and-error learning was defined in terms of association between stimuli in the problem situation and overt responses.

Skinner (1966) criticizes this interpretation because the term "error" does not describe behavior, it passes judgment on it. He would account for the changes in Thorndike's curves for trial-and-error learning in terms of adaptation and extinction of emotional responses, the conditioning of reinforcers, and the extinction of unreinforced responses.

Köhler (1925) applied the Gestalt approach to the behavior of apes solving problems. His account of these experiments emphasized the perception of relationships and insight into the organization of the solution pattern rather than associative learning of new responses.

There is some agreement today (Hilgard & Bower, 1966) that trial-and-error behavior is likely to occur in puzzle situations where the organism does not understand the situation or cannot perceive the relationships in the problem situation, while insightful behavior may occur in situations which the subject can perceive in a meaningful way.

The work of Wertheimer (1959) on human thinking emphasizes the place of patterns and the restructuring of the problem as necessary for a meaningful solution. Dunker's (1945) work on problem solving places as central the subject's perception of the problem situation as a whole, containing a definite conflict. He emphasizes the importance of reorganization of the elements in the situation and the discovery of functional solutions. Several of Maier's (1931) problem-solving experiments, including his "string problem," where the subjects had to bring two hanging strings together by attaching a weight to one and making it a pendulum, require for solution that the subjects reorganize the problem and perceive new structural elements in it. Katona's (1940) study of problem solution by means of principles and rules is illustrative of some of the same Gestalt principles.

The Gestalt psychologists have emphasized organization and dynamic interrelationship of thought patterns. Their work has led to some major changes in the methods used to study problem solving and has opened the way again to the use of the subjects' perceptions and reports as a vital source of data in understanding the nature of a problem and its meaning for the subject.

The psychoanalytic point of view has influenced some scholars with regard to conceptions about thinking. It has had an effect on the methods of studying thinking and, more especially, creative activity. Several writers (Adorno & others, 1950; Erikson, 1963; Rapaport, 1951) have emphasized the dynamics of mental activity and have shown that thinking is not merely an intellectual process but is influenced by the emotional history of the individual, his felt needs, and his unconscious drives. Dollard and Miller (1950) have leaned heavily on psychoanalytic ideas in their attempt to consider some of the principles involved in thinking and psychotherapy.

In his early writing, Freud (1927) distinguished three levels of mental activity: the preconscious, the conscious, and the unconscious. Kris and Kubie have written extensively on the implications of these concepts and of psychoanalytic methods for the study of creativity. Kubie's (1958) thesis is that the preconscious system is essential for all creative activity and that unless these preconscious processes can operate freely there can be no true creativity. He sees the goal of education (and therapy) as freeing the preconscious processes from the distortions and obstructions interposed by unconscious processes. The unconscious can spur creative activity and the conscious can criticize, correct, and evaluate it, but creativity is a predominantly preconscious activity. On the basis of psychoanalytic observations of creative individuals, Kris (1953) describes inspiration as a state in which the barrier between the id and the ego has temporarily become permeable.

Rogers (1954) has identified three inner conditions which he regards as necessary for creativity: openness to experience, the acceptance of one's evaluations as part of one's self and independent of outside valuation, and the ability to "toy" with elements and concepts and to combine them in new ways. He believes that the potential for creativity exists in everyone and only awaits the proper conditions to be released and expressed.

However, creativity and psychological health are interrelated in very complex ways. This is stressed by Barron (1963) on the basis of the assessment research conducted by him and his colleagues over a decade and a half.

That the individual's personality characteristics affect his thinking and work is supported by the large number of studies of creative scientists in many fields by Roe (1952). Roe has studied the life history patterns, the types of imagery, the patterns of intellectual functioning, and the personality attributes of physical scientists, biologists, and social scientists. She finds striking differences in these respects both within and between the different groups of scientists and these differences appear to be related to the types of work and the contributions made by these scientists.

PROBLEM-SOLVING PROCESSES. Various attempts have been made to break down the processes as well as products of thinking. Dewey (1910), by various subjective and introspective observations, formulated his well-known five steps in the process of thinking: (1) a felt difficulty; (2) its location and definition; (3) suggestion of possible solution; (4) development by reasoning of the bearings of the suggestion; (5) further observation and experiment leading to its acceptance or rejection. Wallas (1926), using similar methods, has broken down the stages of forming a new thought as involving: (1) *preparation*—the stage during which the problem is investigated from all directions; (2) *incubation*—the stage during which the individual is not consciously thinking about the problem; (3) *illumination*—the stage during which the idea for solution occurs; and (4) *verification*—the stage in which the validity of the idea is tested and the ideas are reduced to exact form.

These two formulations have led to a great many research studies as well as practical attempts to provide for the improvement of thinking. It is clear that few scholars now accept these steps or stages as straightforward prescriptions of how to think. Formulation of such steps and stages is helpful as a basis for further analytic attempts. However, in any problem-solving or creative activity there is a dynamic interplay of thought processes and activities such that the steps or stages represent only a primitive and crude way of noting the presence or absence of parts in a process. Patrick (1955) has studied artists, poets, scientists, and other groups to determine whether or not Wallas' stages were present in the creative thinking of these groups. In her work she has made extensive use of subjective reports by the subjects, including methods of "thinking aloud."

Related efforts to study the problem-solving processes of students were reported by Bloom and Broder (1950), who attempted to analyze the difficulties students had with a variety of achievement- and intelligence-test problems, and by Buswell and Kersh (1956), who studied tests and protocols of students to analyze their thinking processes in a variety of problems. Buswell and Kersh conclude that there was great variety in the sequences of thinking among their subjects.

These analyses of thinking and problem solving have been used as bases for the development of teaching strategies and testing methods. The Watson–Glaser Tests of Critical Thinking (Watson & Glaser, 1942) included several subtests to get at different aspects of thinking. Smith and Tyler (1942) summarized a large-scale effort to define and test particular skills and abilities in critical thinking at the secondary-school level, while Dressell and Mayhew (1954) summarized an effort to do the same at the college level.

The *Taxonomy of Educational Objectives*, edited by Bloom (1956), has been built upon the product of curriculum workers and testers. It presents a classification scheme for the major categories of cognitive objectives in education from *knowledge* to very complex *syntheses*. Each category and subcategory is defined and illustrated with the achievement-testing techniques which have been used by examining groups in the United States. Gagné (1965) has proposed a system which includes eight types of learning, from relatively simple signal learning (type 1) to very complex problem solving (type 8).

These and related efforts to describe, define, and analyze the various stages and types of thinking and learning have been referred to frequently as curriculum makers develop more complex and up-to-date courses of study, as testers develop aptitude and achievement tests for use in education, and as educational researchers attempt to investigate particular aspects of thinking and problem solving as affected by educational effort.

The computer has led to renewed efforts to analyze the process of problem solving. Simon and Paige (1966) have developed computer programs which are capable of solving problems in algebra as well as in other fields. This work represents an attempt to explain and analyze human behavior in problem-solving situations through comparisons with computer processes which not only will solve particular problems but also will make some of the same errors as humans at various stages in the learning process.

DEVELOPMENT OF HIGHER MENTAL PROCESSES. The age-old problem of tracing the mental development of the individual from birth to adulthood has been given further momentum by the evidence from longitudinal research (Bloom, 1964) that intelligence-test performance and various aptitudes are to a significant extent determined by the age of 4 or 5. Furthermore, when this evidence is related to the nature of the environment in the first few years, it becomes evident that some of the characteristics which are vital to school achievement and intellectual development are present before the age of entrance into school. Thus a problem which was for a long time of theoretical interest has now become one which has great practical implications for child rearing and preschool education, as well as for all aspects of education.

Developmental Schedules. A considerable amount of evidence on the development of humans is available in the age norms for various tasks used in the tests of infant development as well as in the tests of intelligence used at older ages. The *Gesell Developmental Schedules* (Gesell & others, 1949) include behaviors in four areas: motor, adaptive, language, and personal–social. In these schedules the reactions of the child to each task are compared with the norms for his age. The *California First-Year Mental Scale* (Bayley, 1933a) includes a set of items for children from one month of age to 18 months. Some notion of development is indicated by the placement of several of the items in Bayley's (1933b) study.

0.6 months—Momentary regard of ring
2.9 months—Manipulates ring
6.0 months—Vocalizes displeasure
6.5 months—Vocalizes satisfaction
8.6 months—Says "da-da" or equivalent
21.2 months—Names three pictures
25.0 months—Understands two prepositions
35.6 months—Remembers one of four pictures

In these first three years there is evidence of movement from perceptual and motor responses to simple language and simple thought responses.

Further evidence of the increasing complexity of language and mental operations with age is apparent in the norms for various items in the *Stanford-Binet Intelligence Scale* (Terman & Merrill, 1960) and the *Wechsler Intelligence Scales* (Wechsler, 1949, 1955, 1967). These tests cover the preschool years to adulthood.

Intelligence testing is only one way of investigating the development of thinking ability. Such testing is concerned with the product or result rather than the process itself. The norms for tests provide an index of the level of difficulty of a test item and show the percentage of children who can give a correct answer at a particular age. Tests usually present few clues about the ways in which children arrive at the correct solution. In general, developmental tests indicate what to expect rather than how to expect it or how to analyze what the child is doing.

In contrast to the schedule of items of a test, data on the development of thinking abilities range much more widely. In order to arrive at a more adequate picture of the child's development of thinking abilities, the parent, teacher, or psychologist must search for clues in the child's motor responses, his play, his language, his behavior in free situations, his activities in social situations, and his response to problem situations. Such a diversity of sources makes it difficult to provide any clear and single summary of the development of thinking abilities.

Developmental Stages. Piaget (1950) distinguishes between what he calls conceptual and sensorimotor intelligence. He believes that the latter is concerned with coordinating successive perceptions and overt movements and deals only with real entities on a level of practical satisfaction. Piaget sees the period of conceptual intelligence as an entire rebuilding of the structures of thought. He divides the development of thinking processes into consecutive periods which he calls "stages in the construction of operations." These may be summarized as: (1) the sensorimotor period; (2) the period of symbolic and preconceptual thought, from about one and one-half to four years; (3) the development of intuitive thought leading to the threshold of the operation; (4) the development of the concrete operations of sensory-stimuli grouping; and (5) the refining of formal thought and its groupings which appear in adolescence.

Bruner (1964) has proposed an alternative set of stages: *enactive*, a mode of representing events through motoric response; *iconic*, through images of the perceptual field; and *symbolic*, through design features involving remoteness and arbitrariness. Bruner argues that language provides the means not only for representing experience but also for transforming it.

Vygotsky (1962), with his linguistic approach to thinking, has proposed still another set of stages for concept formation. He labeled the first stage *unorganized congeries*, by which is meant a vague grouping of individual objects. His second stage is *thinking in complexes*, where there is a factual connection between the elements included in a single complex. *Thinking in concepts* is Vygotsky's third stage, which depends on the ability to abstract and view the abstracted elements apart from the totality of the experience on which they are founded.

While development need not take the form of clearly marked steps or stages, much of the analysis of development has used the stage construct. Kessen (1962) has suggested that the stage construct is a useful theoretical tool because it yields a highly compressed description of an aspect of behavior at some point in time and it organizes the description in a sequential fashion. Workers such as Piaget (1950), Bruner (1964), and Vygotsky (1962) appear to think of the stages as dynamic structures in which certain activities, internal as well as external, produce mental structures or rules of logic by which the child solves problems.

Wallach (1963), summarizing the research on children's thinking during the past two decades, finds that the types of development and stages formulated by Piaget are generally supported by other workers.

This is in contrast to some of the studies reported earlier which found it difficult to replicate the findings of the Geneva school. His conclusion that the "human's basic cognitive categories for analyzing physical reality are a product of slow and laborious construction" makes it clear that development is not a purely internal process but does represent the individual's interaction over time with a very complex environment which includes objects, people, language, and ideas.

THE IMPROVEMENT OF THINKING ABILITIES. During the past two decades there has been an unusual amount of emphasis on education for the higher mental processes. Spurred on by international rivalry in such areas as armaments, atomic energy, and space exploration, there has been a great deal of emphasis on curriculum development which stresses problem solving and creativity.

Curriculum Development. In the United States (and increasingly so in other countries) recent curriculum development has taken the form of large projects in which subject specialists, selected teachers, psychologists, and producers of instructional materials collaborate in long-term efforts to produce a new organization of a school subject. In many of these curriculum projects the avowed goal is to deemphasize the treatment of a subject in terms of the facts to be remembered and, instead, to emphasize the treatment of the subject in terms of the modern ideas and research methods used by the research scholars in the subject field. That is, the methods of inquiry and the thinking processes utilized by scholars in the field are the key changes in many of the new curriculum projects (Goodlad & others, 1966).

One underlying reason for the emphasis on the processes of problem solving (rather than information learning) in the new curricula has been an increased awareness of the rapidity with which the knowledge of a subject field changes. Especially in such subject fields as the physical sciences, the biological sciences, the social sciences, and even mathematics, the research scholars are aware of the extent to which many of the "facts" of the subject undergo transformation or are superseded by new ideas over a relatively short period of time. If many of the facts of the subject taught to a 16-year-old student are likely to be incorrect or irrelevant by the time he is 25, then the learning of such facts has dubious value. Unfortunately, the unpredictable nature of research and scholarship makes it difficult to determine which facts are likely to be modified by the advances in the subject.

It is frequently assumed that the methods of inquiry in a subject field are likely to be more stable and transferrable than the knowledge of the subject field at any one point in time. It is reasoning of this type that has led to the emphasis in the new curricula on the methods of research, the thinking processes, and the nature of evidence and conclusions in the subject fields (Thelen, 1960; Schwab, 1963). As a consequence of this, more of the instructional material in the new curricula includes the thinking of scholars and the kinds of evidence used to come to particular conclusions. Increasingly, the instructional material includes excerpts from the papers and books of scholars.

Changing the instructional material is far easier than changing the instructional processes. If teachers are to help students engage in inquiry they must shift from didactic teaching methods to the more complex dialectic teaching processes (Ginther, 1965; Goodlad & others, 1966; Siegel, 1967). Some attempts to help teachers change their methods of teaching are apparent in the many institutes for teacher training sponsored by the National Science Foundation and the U.S. Office of Education. Little evidence is available as yet on the extent to which teachers who attend these institutes are able to change their methods of teaching.

That the process of engaging in inquiry types of thinking can be carried on in the early years of elementary education is supported by the curriculum work and the evaluation methods used by the elementary science project of the American Association for the Advancement of Science (1964), the Berkeley Science Curriculum Improvement Study (Karplus, 1965), and the newer approach to the use of set theory in mathematics in the Suppes Experimental Project in the Teaching of Elementary School Mathematics (Suppes, 1962).

Some suggestion that logical operations are possible even at the preschool level is evidenced by Bereiter and Engelmann (1966) who worked with culturally deprived children at the age of five. In their work, they attempted to get the children to ask as well as answer questions and they attempted to develop the children's ability to use affirmative and negative statements and to make if–then deductions. They present evidence that the children did actually progress in these types of thinking.

Dressel and Mayhew (1954) studying students in a number of colleges found that the largest gains on a test of critical thinking were consistently made in the freshman year. Little gain in critical thinking was found in students in the colleges which laid little emphasis on critical thinking or which had only a single course (i.e., logic) that stressed critical thinking. However, when most of the courses in the general education program of colleges emphasized critical thinking as the central objective, very large gains were shown over a two-year period. Chausow (1955) had each of six instructors in a college social science course teach one section by a formal lecture approach and another section in which the instructional materials and the instructional procedures emphasized problem solving. For each instructor, the gains on a test of critical thinking were greater for students in the experimental section than for those in the lecture section. These studies suggest the importance of the nature of learning experiences as a significant variable even when the instructor variable is held constant.

Discovery Instruction. Bruner (1961) has proposed a series of hypotheses about what has come to be known as "discovery" methods of instruction.

Bruner suggests that the experience of learning through discoveries which one makes for himself should make the learned information more readily viable in problem solving, it should lead to increased competence or mastery motivation for learning, it should lead to the development of styles of problem solving or inquiry that can be used in attacking a great variety of tasks and problems, and it should lead to improved organization of memory so as to make retrieval more effective. Suchman has spelled out in some detail what he believes to be required for teaching and learning by discovery:

> It is clear that such a program should offer large amounts of practice in exploring, manipulating and searching. The children should be given a maximum of opportunity to experience autonomous discovery. New goals must be set for the children. Instead of devoting their efforts to storing information and recalling it on demand, they would be developing the cognitive functions needed to seek out and organize information in a way that would be the most productive of new concepts. Both the teacher and the pupil would have to be cast in new roles. The pupil must become more active and aggressive in his learning role. Direction of the concept formation process should be his own, and he should come to regard his environment (including the teacher) as a potential source of information which can be obtained through his own acts of inquiry. The teacher must abandon his traditionally directive mode and structure an environment that is responsive to the child's quest for information. The teacher must see to it that the child's efforts at inquiry are rewarded by success, that the child is able to obtain the information he needs, and that he *does* discover new concepts on his own. The teacher can help the child by posing problems that are reasonably structured and will lead to exciting new discoveries. The teacher can also coach him in the techniques of data collection and organization that will lend power and control to his searching. The educator should be concerned above all with the child's process of thinking, trusting that the growth of knowledge will follow in the wake of inquiry. (Suchman, 1961.)

Bruner (1966) illustrates the use of discovery methods in elementary-school classes in the social sciences. Davis (1966) illustrates the use of discovery methods in the teaching of mathematics, and Suchman (1963) has developed a program of material and instructional procedures for inquiry training at the elementary-school level.

While there has been considerable interest in the development of learning by discovery, definitive research is not yet available on the effects of this approach. Suchman (1963) found that pupils trained for inquiry did ask more general questions as well as more analytic questions than did control subjects although the two groups did not differ significantly on a measure of conceptual growth in physics. Kersh (1958, 1962) found that discovery tasks seem to have some motivational effects although there was no clear superiority for the guided discovery group in retention and transfer.

Creativity. Getzels and Jackson (1962) spurred a renewed interest in the development of creativity as a result of a study in which they compared a *high-intelligence group* of students in grades 6 through 12 with a *high-creative group*. The high-intelligence group was in the top 20 percent of the sample on the intelligence test but below that level on a battery of creativity tests. The high-creative group was in the top 20 percent of the sample on the creativity tests but below that level on the intelligence tests.

Both groups were at about the same level on achievement tests, but they displayed very different characteristics in other areas. The high-creative group showed more humor and aggressiveness and appeared to take more intellectual risks than did the high-intelligence group. The parents of the high-creative group tended to stress openness to experience while the parents of the high-intelligence group tended to emphasize good manners, studiousness, and having friends. The authors concluded that the high-creative group had a pattern of intellectual risk and independence while the high-intelligence group had a pattern of adaptation to proper and conventional standards.

Although this study was criticized from many points of view, much of the criticism had to do with the sampling procedures. Torrance (1962) extended this type of investigation to eight different schools and generally confirmed Getzels and Jackson's findings with regard to achievement and cognitive style.

Getzels (1964) has speculated on the relation between creative thinking, problem solving, and instruction, while Torrance (1959) has developed materials and methods for instruction which emphasize creativity. Much research still needs to be done to determine the long-term effectiveness of various procedures for enhancing the creativity of students by instruction and other activities in the school. Generally, there is optimism that creativity can be developed by school practices, but the evidence is still not available.

Whether or not the schools can actually enhance creativity and originality, there is some reason to believe that the educational system can reduce originality and creativity. This negative effect on creativity is most marked when examinations, instructional materials, and instructional processes all emphasize learning by rote and when the goals of teachers, parents, and children are primarily centered on getting over one examination hurdle after another (Bloom, 1958).

CONCLUSION. During the decade since the previous edition of this Encyclopedia, a great deal of writing and research has been completed on higher mental processes. This field has grown rapidly and it presently commands the attention of philosophers, psychologists, and educators. However, it does not seem to hold the attention of scholars for very long. It is difficult to find more than a handful of research workers who have devoted a major portion of their career to the study of thinking, problem solving, or creativity. We can do no better than quote Johnson on this:

> ... the scientific investigation of thinking is unsystematic and, in general, unsatisfactory. Many psychologists express an interest in thinking, and some make raids on it. The field is littered with disabled wisdoms cast off by hit-and-run theorists." (Johnson, 1955.)

This is a difficult field to organize. The terms are different for various workers, the studies are rarely cumulative or even addressed to common problems, and only recently have workers in the field been meeting each other in face-to-face conferences. It is to be hoped that the reader of this article will discern a crude map of this "littered" field.

Theory and systematic research on thinking do lag—but efforts to improve the thinking of students do not. The higher mental processes are rapidly becoming the central objectives of instruction at all levels of education. Achievement tests and aptitude tests are constructed to measure thinking and problem solving. And, teachers everywhere are determined that their students will think.

People do think and schools do try to develop better capabilities of thinking in their students. No one seems to wait for theory and research to tell them what to do or how to do it. Perhaps it is fortunate, considering the state of theory and research in this field, that action is far ahead of thought.

Benjamin S. Bloom
University of Chicago
Ernest A. Rakow
University of Chicago

References

Adorno, T. W., and others. *The Authoritarian Personality.* Harper, 1950. 990p.

American Association for the Advancement of Science, Commission on Science Education. *Science—A Process Approach.* AAAS, 1964.

Barron, Frank. *Creativity and Psychological Health.* Van Nostrand, 1963. 292p.

Bayley, Nancy. *California First Year Mental Scale.* U California, 1933(a).

Bayley, Nancy. "Mental Growth During the First Three Years." *Genet Psychol Monogr* 14:1–92; 1933(b).

Bereiter, Carl, and Engelmann, Siegfried. *Teaching Disadvantaged Children in the Preschool.* Prentice-Hall, 1966. 312p.

Bernstein, B. "Social Class and Linguistic Development: A Theory of Social Learning." In Halsey, A. H., and others. (Eds.) *Education, Economy and Society.* Free, 1961. p. 288–314.

Bloom, Benjamin S. (Ed.) *Taxonomy of Educational Objectives: Handbook I: Cognitive Domain.* McKay, 1956. 207p.

Bloom, Benjamin S. "Some Effects of Cultural, Social, and Educational Conditions on Creativity." In Taylor, Calvin W. (Ed.) *The Second (1957) University of Utah Research Conference on the Identification of Creative Scientific Talent.* U Utah Press, 1958. p. 55–65.

Bloom, Benjamin S. *Stability and Change in Human Characteristics.* Wiley, 1964. 237p.

Bloom, Benjamin S., and Broder, Lois J. *Problem-Solving Processes of College Students.* U Chicago Press, 1950. 109p.

Brown, Roger W. "Language and Categories." In Bruner, Jerome S., and others. (Eds.) *A Study of Thinking.* Wiley, 1956. p. 247–312.

Bruner, Jerome S. "The Act of Discovery." *Harvard Ed R* 31:21–32; 1961.

Bruner, Jerome S. "The Course of Cognitive Growth." *Am Psychologist* 19:1–15; 1964.

Bruner, Jerome S. "Some Elements of Discovery." In Shulman, Lee S., and Keisler, Evan R. (Eds.) *Learning by Discovery: A Critical Appraisal.* Rand McNally, 1966. p. 101–13.

Burt, Cyril. "The Structure of the Mind: A Review of the Results of Factor Analysis." *Br J Ed Psychol* 19:176–99; 1949.

Buswell, Guy T., and Kersh, B. Y. "Patterns of Thinking in Solving Problems." *U California Pub Ed* 12:63–148; 1956.

Chausow, Hymen M. "The Organization of Learning Experiences to Achieve More Effectively the Objectives of Critical Thinking in the General Social Science Course at the Junior College Level." Doctoral dissertation. U Chicago, 1955.

Davis, Robert B. "Discovery in the Teaching of Mathematics." In Shulman, Lee S., and Keisler, Evan R. (Eds.) *Learning by Discovery: A Critical Appraisal.* Rand McNally, 1966. p. 115–28.

Dewey, John. *How We Think.* Heath, 1910. 224p.

Dollard, John, and Miller, Neal E. *Personality and Psychotherapy: An Analysis in Terms of Learning, Thinking and Culture.* McGraw-Hill, 1950. 488p.

Dressel, Paul L., and Mayhew, Lewis B. *General Education: Explorations in Evaluation.* ACE, 1954. 302p.

Dunker, Karl, "On Problem Solving." *Psychol Monogr* 58(5); 1945. 113p.

Erickson, Eric H. *Childhood and Society*, 2nd ed. Norton, 1963. 445p.

Freud, Sigmund. *The Ego and the Id.* Hogarth Press, 1927. 88p.

Gagné, Robert M. *The Conditions of Learning.* Holt, 1965. 308p.

Gesell, Arnold, and others. *Gesell Developmental Schedules.* Psychol Corp, 1949.

Getzels, Jacob W. "Creative Thinking, Problem-Solving, and Instruction." In *Theories of Learning and Instruction.* 63rd Yearbook, Part I, NSSE, U Chicago, 1964. p. 240–67.

Getzels, Jacob W., and Jackson, Philip W. *Creativity*

and Intelligence: Explorations with Gifted Students. Wiley, 1962. 293p.

Ginther, John R. "A Conceptual Model for Analyzing Instruction." In Lysaught, Jerome. (Ed.) *Programmed Instruction in Medical Education: Proceedings of the First Rochester Conference, June 25–27, 1964.* Lakeside Press, 1965. p. 43–54.

Goodlad, John I., and others. *The Changing School Curriculum.* Fund for the Advancement of Education, 1966. 122p.

Guilford, J. P. *The Nature of Intelligence.* McGraw-Hill, 1967. 538p.

Hilgard, Ernest R., and Bower, Gordon H. *Theories of Learning,* 3rd ed. Appleton, 1966. 661p.

Humphrey, George. *Thinking: An Introduction to Its Experimental Psychology.* Wiley, 1951. 331p.

Johnson, Donald M. *The Psychology of Thought and Judgment.* Harper, 1955. 515p.

Karplus, Robert. *Theoretical Background of the Science Curriculum Improvement Study.* Heath, 1965.

Katona, George. *Organizing and Memorizing.* Columbia U, 1940. 318p.

Kersh, B. Y. "The Adequacy of 'Meaning' as an Explanation for Superiority of Learning by Independent Discovery." *J Ed Psychol* 49:282–92; 1958.

Kersh, B. Y. "The Motivating Effect of Learning by Directed Discovery." *J Ed Psychol* 53:65–71; 1962.

Kessen, William. " 'Stage' and 'Structure' in the Study of Children." *Monogr Soc Res Child Develop* 27:65–82; 1962.

Köhler, W. *The Mentality of Apes.* Harcourt, 1925.

Kris, E. "Psychoanalysis and the Study of Creative Imagination." *B New York Acad Med* 29:334–51; 1953.

Kubie, L. S. *Neurotic Distortion of the Creative Process.* U Kansas Press, 1958. 151p.

Maier, Norman R. F. "Reasoning in Humans: II. The Solution of a Problem and Its Appearance in Consciousness." *J Comp Psychol* 12:181–94; 1931.

Murphy, Gardner. *An Historical Introduction to Modern Psychology,* 3rd ed. Harcourt, 1949. 466p.

Patrick, Catherine. *What Is Creative Thought?* Philosophical Lib, 1955. 210p.

Pavlov, I. P. *Selected Works.* Foreign Language Publishing House, 1955.

Piaget, Jean. *The Psychology of Intelligence.* Harcourt, 1950. 182p.

Rapaport, David. *Organization and Pathology of Thought.* Columbia U Press, 1951. 786p.

Roe, Anne. *The Making of a Scientist.* Dodd, 1952. 244p.

Rogers, Carl R. "Toward a Theory of Creativity." *ETC: R of Gen Semantics* 11:249–60; 1954.

Russell, David H. "Higher Mental Processes." In Harris, Chester W. (Ed.) *Encyclopedia of Educational Research.* 3rd ed. Macmillan, 1960. p. 645–61.

Schwab, Joseph J. "Invitations to Inquiry." In Schwab, Joseph J. *Biology Teacher's Handbook.* Wiley, 1963. p. 45–226.

Siegel, Laurence. (Ed.) *Instruction: Some Contemporary Viewpoints.* Chandler, 1967. 376p.

Simon, Herbert A., and Paige, Jeffery M. "Cognitive Processes in Solving Algebra Word Problems." In Kleinmuntz, Benjamin. (Ed.) *Problem Solving: Research, Method and Theory.* Wiley, 1966. p. 51–119.

Skinner, B. F. "An Operant Analysis of Problem Solving." In Kleinmuntz, Benjamin. (Ed.) *Problem Solving: Research, Method, and Theory.* Wiley, 1966. p. 225–57.

Smith, Eugene R., and Tyler, Ralph W. *Appraising and Recording Student Progress.* Harper, 1942. 550p.

Spearman, Charles E. *Creative Mind.* Appleton, 1931. 162p.

Staats, Arthur W., and Staats, Carolyn K. *Complex Human Behavior.* Holt. 546p.

Suchman, J. Richard. "Inquiry Training: Building Skills for Autonomous Discovery." *Merrill-Palmer Q Behavior Develop* 7:147–69; 1961.

Suchman, J. Richard. *The Elementary School Training Program in Scientific Inquiry.* U Illinois Press, 1963. 150p.

Suppes, Patrick. *Sets and Numbers.* Blaisdell, 1962.

Terman, Lewis M. *The Measurement of Intelligence.* Houghton, 1916. 362p.

Terman, Lewis M., and Merrill, Maud A. *Stanford-Binet Intelligence Scale.* Houghton, 1960. 363p.

Thelen, Herbert A. *Education and the Human Quest.* Harper, 1960. 224p.

Thorndike, Edward L. "Animal Intelligence." *Psychol R Monogr Supplements* 2:1–109; 1898.

Thorndike, Edward L., and others. *The Measurement of Intelligence.* Teachers Col, Columbia U, 1927. 613p.

Thurstone, Louis L. "Primary Mental Abilities." In *Psychometric Monogr* No. 1. U Chicago Press, 1938.

Torrance, E. Paul. *Rewarding Creative Thinking: A Manual for Elementary Teachers.* U Minnesota Press, 1959.

Torrance, E. Paul. *Guiding Creative Talent.* Prentice-Hall, 1962. 278p.

Vygotsky, Lev S. *Thought and Language.* Massachusetts Institute Technology Press, Wiley, 1962. 168p.

Wallas, Graham. *The Art of Thought.* Harcourt, 1926. 314p.

Wallach, Michael A. "Research on Children's Thinking." in *Child Psychology.* 62nd Yearbook, Part I, NSSE, U Chicago, 1963. p. 236–76.

Watson, Goodwin B., and Glaser, Edward M. *Watson-Glaser Tests of Critical Thinking.* World Book, 1942.

Wechsler, David. *Manual: Wechsler Intelligence Scale for Children.* Psychol Corp, 1949.

Wechsler, David. *Wechsler Adult Intelligence Scale; Manual.* Psychol Corp, 1955.

Wechsler, David. *Wechsler Preschool and Primary Scale of Intelligence; Manual.* Psychol Corp, 1967.

Wertheimer, Max. *Productive Thinking.* Harper, 1959. 302p.

HISTORY OF EDUCATION

As a scholarly discipline, history is somewhat of an anomaly. Unless those who pursue it are content merely to be chroniclers of events now completed and, as teachers, to be mere purveyors of information that is hopefully factual but often not, it is always treading on the toes of other disciplines. It seems to have no domain that is truly its own.

For example, until well into the twentieth century in the United States, elementary- and secondary-school history was devoted largely to wars and military campaigns, with governmental or political events receiving much of the remaining attention. Actual content was mostly names, dates, and places, which were to be memorized and, on demand, repeated verbatim. This was the "history" required of elementary pupils for promotion to a next grade, or of high school students for a "credit" toward graduation. Not, perhaps, until Harold Rugg's pioneering in "social studies" during the late 1920's and the 1930's were matters much changed, and the consequent shift from "history," "geography," and "civics" was and still is hotly decried by the so-called objective historians and by others whose minds run along the same line. A graduate student was once sternly admonished approximately as follows: "It is of no concern to a history teacher whether the actions of Rockefeller and Standard Oil were good for the country, or bad. A history teacher's business is merely to present the record of events. That is all!"

Such an attitude, it would seem, grows out of the historians' dilemma of trying, on the one hand, to have a uniquely significant field of study and instruction and, on the other, to avoid encroachment on the domains of other disciplines. And these "other disciplines" are by no means confined to the social studies. If instruction in history is to emancipate itself from the memory level of learning by rote and from the sole objective of producing what are often called "walking encyclopedias," it will have to become concerned with what Dewey called "the problems of men." It will have to deal with matters that perplex mankind—with issues—and promote reflective studies that lead toward widely transferable (hence useful) generalizations or principles. Otherwise, history teachers are more tellers of tales or pedantic purveyors of inert information, maybe usable at some later time but probably by then forgotten.

However, when an "issue"—a problem that now perplexes or has perplexed human minds—is studied, it tends to fall within the realm of some discipline other than "pure" history. Washington's exploits leading to the surrender of Cornwallis at Yorktown are interesting when well told. However, when not studied in the light of military strategy, they represented only inert information. But, when American educationists, prodded perhaps by Dewey's writings, became conscious of this, they felt that elementary and even secondary school was obviously no place to concentrate on teaching military strategy. Hence, attention veered to matters governmental or political. In higher education, Charles A. Beard and others developed the economic interpretation of history. In this way, history as a school subject could be studied reflectively; the objects and events of mankind's experience could be examined for the light they threw upon the efficacies of the various ideas that from time to time were being subjected to human scrutiny and test. Names, dates, and places would be studied, but primarily for the interpretations or "lessons" they could promote or provoke; so whether they were remembered or not became a distinctly secondary consideration, maybe not even an important one. Scholarliness was not demonstrated solely by the *amount* of knowledge carried about in one's head or "known by heart."

The further entailment of this move, however, was not unrecognized by the "objective historians." If politics or economics were to be taught reflectively —as reflective study of the political or economic problems of men—then the *history* of mankind's study of a given problem would be *necessitated,* so that the wisdom of past experience would not be lost. Thus, economic history would be essential to the study of economics, and a department of economics could legitimately protest (as encroachment upon its domain) an offering of *economic* history by a department of history. The same would be true of any other school subject—politics or government (political science), literature, art, science, mathematics, or woodwork, to name a few. The objective historians, seeing this, chose therefore to confine their instruction solely to the chronicling of events and leave interpretation to the other disciplines, even though it confined "history" essentially to memory-level instruction.

CONCEPTUAL RESEARCH. When one essays to write a report on research in the history of education, one is confronted by an aspect of this very problem. Just what constitutes such research? Brauner (1964) follows Cowley in distinguishing between factual and conceptual research and defines the former as "adding new facts to the store of knowledge" and the latter as that which "either organizes facts already on hand or critically appraises existing concepts." Employing this terminology, we can therefore say that the only kind of research found really acceptable by the "objective historians" is the factual. This they think of as "pure" research, unsullied by human speculation or opinion and untarnished by practicality; it is supposedly objective, not subjective.

That most of what normally passes for research in the history of education is of this kind will hardly be considered news. Conventional textbooks in the field, whether new or old, are essentially compendiums of research findings of this kind. Hence, a major part of the writing of such a text is merely the reporting of research, not research itself; and a sharp distinction between carrying on research, on the one hand, and writing (and teaching from) texts, on the other, is a natural outcome. For this reason, the only justification for inclusion of conventional textbooks (albeit new ones) in a report such as the present one is embodiment of new data—newly uncovered facts that have not been reported elsewhere. Our coverage therefore, includes few texts of this kind.

However, when one recognizes history as legitimately concerned with the problems of men, then historical research has to become conceptual *as well as* factual. Human speculation and opinion, and the instrumental (practical) value of discovered data, are legitimatized. This does not mean acceptance of empty speculation; it supports only speculation (creative thoughts) that may and will be subjected to scrutiny on the basis of whatever criteria may be deemed pertinent. On the other hand, neither does this entail derogation of "empty" speculation per se; if one desires and can afford to indulge in such, that should be considered his own affair. And who knows, anyway, what may come of it? History is replete with delayed discoveries of practical uses for previously useless ideas. What alone is precluded is that empty speculation should, per se, be accepted as research.

On the topic, and during the period, under focal consideration in this essay, 1957 to 1966, there has been much ferment. Conceptual research has come to the fore. And a number of textbooks published during the past ten years embody the results, both in content and in organization. These books are seemingly written on the assumption that human beings act purposively—in pursuit of ends more or less consciously envisioned—and that such actions are *designed* on the basis of the designers' insights into the way those ends may be attained under the circumstances that confront them and with the resources at their command. Thus, "history" is to be studied as a record of the problems with which mankind has wrestled, of what has been tried toward solution of these problems, and of what have been the outcomes of such trials. So viewed, history is, as James Harvey Robinson put it, a study of mankind's "mind in the making" and is not a discipline separate from (say) science. It is a necessary part of any investigation into the "problems of men," be it scientific or otherwise.

Needless to say, the writing of books such as these requires much original historical research by the authors themselves, as well as employment of whatever pertinent findings have been provided by the research of others. Such books, therefore, though possibly designed as textbooks, should not be overlooked when a history of educational research is being written. Moreover, the subject matter of research of this kind is education theory, which is largely not amenable to statistical treatment or tabular presentation. An interesting exception is a recent study by Bidwell (1966) in which, by perceptive statistical analysis, social cause-and-effect relationships are teased out of seemingly noncommittal data. Bidwell's treatment commends itself for wider use as a research tool in the history of education.

Thut (1957) presents the "story of education" as various assumptions regarding the way to obtain truth or value. In fact, his "story" tells little of institutions, events, and persons involved; it is largely devoted to the theoretical. Written for an unsophisticated audience, the book represents research, not so much in the production of new knowledge as in formulating (and incidentally testing) new ways of making extant knowledge available to a wide range of readers. Thut speaks of "departures from the treatment of these matters which philosophers, by long tradition, have given them when they communicated with their fellow philosophers."

Thayer (1965) addresses himself to "formative ideas in American education" but leaves a reader somewhat in the dark on the nature of these ideas because in seeking wide coverage he becomes more presentational than analytical, thereby losing the sharpness that ideas must have if they are to be clearly directive of human action. Brauner (1964) seeks to promote conceptual research as a necessary adjunct to factual research but may possibly be criticized for somewhat of a tendency to skew the various proposals so as to make them fit into his own classificational framework rather than having the proposers speak for themselves.

Frederick Mayer's recent books (1958, 1960, 1963, 1964) deal with an overpowering array of educational ideas. They are, however, disappointing for their dogmatic curtness, for frequent failure to supply the factual evidence needed to support sweeping assertions, as noted in a review by Primack (1966).

The Bayles and Hood work (1966) represents a more modest intent than do those by Mayer. It is written for college or university seniors or for students in early graduate study, who seek orientation in the growth of American educational thought and its seeming effects on practice. Hence, clear lines of logical connection are teased out, with identification of consistency or lack of consistency as each case study shows. The changes in practice, if any, are delineated in broad strokes.

Several anthologies of supplementary or supportive readings in the concept-research vein have been published. Gross and Chandler (1964) furnish a well-chosen set of original documents. Nash and others (1965) present a set of essays by contemporary writers on outstanding figures in educational pioneering, which was reviewed by Butts (1966). Broudy and Palmer (1965) select ten historically great teachers who had more or less consciously formulated and presented their ideas on teaching and devote a chapter to each. As is so common, the authors are not sufficiently explicit on the theory embodied in each case to show its logical working out in practice or to identify the spots of internal contradiction if these exist. For example, Comenius' endorsement both of tabula rasa, leading to *Orbis Pictus,* and of following the order of nature and aiding natural unfoldment, leading to his 37 teaching principles, the bases for both of which are laid in the fifth chapter of *The Great Didactic,* is neither presented nor even hinted. Also, Kilpatrick is made to represent Dewey and both to endorse E. L. Thorndike's principle of "learning by doing," which Kilpatrick did endorse but Dewey did not.

Houston Peterson (1946) is responsible for assembling and editing the volume *Great Teachers,* originally published in 1946 but recently reissued in paperback, in which former students describe their impressions of what made for greatness. Bode's *Modern Educational Theories* (1927), in which he analyzed then-current theories of curriculum construction, has recently been reissued in paperback. Much of what he had to say then is, in a general way, still cogent. Three volumes in the "Studies in Educational Theory" series of the John Dewey Society have been published: *Bertrand Russell on Education,* by Joe Park (1963); *Whitehead on Education,* by Harold B. Dunkel (1965); and *Boyd H. Bode's Philosophy of Education,* by J. J. Chambliss (1963). Two significant studies have recently come from the University of Washington Press: a study of Charles Sanders Peirce's relation to John Duns Scotus, by John F. Boler (1963) and one on Chauncey Wright's relations with Peirce, James, and Dewey in the formulation of modern pragmatic thought, by Edward H. Madden (1963).

Since 1957 the valuable series "Classics in Education" has been published by the Bureau of Publications of Teachers College, Columbia University, under the general editorship of Lawrence A. Cremin (1957———), a majority of which would probably be classifiable as conceptual research.

Maxine Greene's *The Public School and the Private Vision* (1965) is a delightful variation in the treatment of educational history, showing existentialist influence in going to the literature of Hawthorne, Thoreau, Melville, Whitman, Twain, and others. And Bernard Mehl's is a review worthy of the book (1966). Richard Mosier's *The American Temper* (1952) is an earlier book, which also deals with what Mehl refers to as the zeitgeist—with education in light of the overall "American temper." Wynne's *Theories of Education* (1963) represents careful, sympathetic presentation and analysis of educational theories, whether old or new, that currently impinge upon the thinking of American educational personnel. Arthur G. Wirth's study of the development of Dewey's thinking, and of his activities, up to 1904 is reported first in two preliminary articles (1964, 1965) and then in a book (1966). Ratner and others (1964) have compiled and made available the correspondence between Dewey and Bentley from 1932 to 1951 that eventuated in their collaboration on *Knowing and the Known* (Dewey & Bentley, 1949). This book includes, in addition to the correspondence, a highly valuable biographical essay on both men, written by Ratner. Archambault's volume (1964) assembles a number of Dewey's most significant articles on education.

If it is thought that in including the several foregoing books we have gotten away from history of education and into educational philosophy, our reply is that this highlights our original point of the dilemma of departments of history: once reflective study of the problems of men is adopted as the educational program, then history gets into all manner of difficulties in terms of trespass on the domains of other disciplines. Making educational history a matter of looking into the *ideas* that educators have proposed and employed, and noting how they have worked out in practice, pushes educational history into the domain of educational philosophy—perhaps accounting for the frequent combination of history and philosophy of education, a practice decried by Power (1962). It may partially account for Lottich's reproach of the Bayles and Hood textbook (1966) for employment of the good-bad/active-passive assumptions regarding human nature as a way of looking at various educational proposals, characterizing it as a "gimmick." Yet the most recent edition of the Wilds and Lottich's textbook (1961) is predicated on the assumption that it is "not merely another factual textbook in the history of education, but primarily a history of educational thought." Wrestling with this entire problem of overlapping, the present writer has chosen not to discuss what he considers important treatises on education, such as Price's *Education and Philosophic Thought* (1962), Brumbaugh and Lawrence's *Essays* (1963), Russell's *Change and Challenge* (1965), Kimball and McClellan's *Education and the New America* (1962) or Neill's *Summerhill* (1964).

The compendium by Ratner and others (1964) is included because of Dewey's place in the history of twentieth-century American education.

Another aspect of the overlap problem is just how recent a topic must be in order to qualify as history of education, rather than as administration, psychology, theory, or something else. Since this volume includes reports on research in the several areas other than history, this report does not include many treatises such as the various recent books by Conant.

From the foregoing, it appears that during the past decade there has been a considerable showing of conceptual research in the history of education. It is characterized, however, by hesitancy in singling out clear, simple ideas—ideas that enable users to proceed by logical deduction from the plane of high abstraction to that of down-to-earth practice. Indeed, there are those who argue that in education this is not possible; that to do so requires oversimplification. But the simplification necessary to obtain a workable and working principle is not to be confused with *oversimplification*. $E = mc^2$ is a simplification; one that, completely and in all details, describes no concrete case. But it has demonstrated its high value as a practical directive. When pertinent, it has proven to be an accurate (hence a scientifically true) directive; it is simple, but not overly so. Those who engage in conceptual research should surely recognize this principle and be forewarned of and forearmed against the likelihood of being accused of oversimplification.

Perhaps a case in point is Bernard Bailyn's complaint that "to these writers [of educational history] the past was simply the present writ small" (1960). He then goes on to demonstrate what writing the past *large* means to him. In so doing, he fills in a host of details on American education during the seventeenth and eighteenth centuries and presents an imposing and valuable bibliography. But one finds in Bailyn's account no evidence of basically serious inaccuracies in, say, Cubberley's account of more than 30 years before (1934), even with the benefit to Bailyn of three subsequent decades of further research. Moreover, as Brickman shows in an article that is required reading for those concerned with educational history (1964), even though Bailyn and others disparage the scholarliness of educational historians they depend upon them much more than such disparagement would seem to justify. In criticizing a given document one ought to take into account not only the stage of the culture during which it was produced but also the level of sophistication of the readers to whom it was or is addressed.

FACTUAL RESEARCH. In the more conventional field—of predominantly factual research—much has been done during the past decade. Cremin's study of twentieth-century education (1961) has been widely acclaimed, even though for him everything passes as progressive education. This causes the movement that generally goes under that name to lose its identity, as do other movements that have been active but are based on different thought patterns. When history is written in this way, how can study of the past provide any lessons that may serve, albeit tentatively, as guides toward a better future? Chambliss' review (1963) should be read for a penetrating analysis of this kind of historical writing.

Generally recognized as one of the outstanding texts in the field of educational history is that by Edwards and Richey, revised in 1963. As Gross's review (1963) points out, the revision updates and refines the original. Frost's book (1966), although proposing in the Preface to present "the ideas that have been dealt with by the best minds of western culture, and the major issues that have emerged and how they have been faced," seems to cover too much to enable ideas to emerge with the specificity necessary to disclose how they may have influenced subsequent events. For example, in the fifteenth chapter, Pestalozzi, Froebel, and Herbart are quite fully and freshly presented, though with little backward reference to Rousseau, Locke, and Comenius. Then the sixteenth chapter deals factually with nineteenth-century United States, but with almost no mention of any of these six persons. If the ideas of men are not to be followed into their workings out in institutions and practices, to see what comes of them, then why should either the ideas or the men be studied?

Good's revisions of two earlier books (1960, 1962) are further justification for his long-standing eminence in the field. Adolphe Meyer's recent volume (1965) is, as he suggests in the Preface, "an educational history of all the people and the world in which they live and struggle and die." He writes with a verve that was not as evident in his earlier book (1957). Its over-500 pages represent both factual and conceptual research, and wide coverage. A valuable, 9-page Bibliographical Note terminates the text proper. Brubacher has not only brought older works up to date, but also, in collaboration with Rudy, has brought out a definitive treatise on American higher education (1958), that should be ranked with the two-volume compendium of historical documents compiled by Hofstadter and Smith (1961). Rudolph's is also an excellent treatise on American higher education (1965).

Valuable reports on various aspects of American educational experience or practice are furnished by Duker (1966), Eells and Hollis (1961), Harris (1961), Johnson (1963), Krug (1964), Mayer (1961), Myers (1960), Nietz (1961), Power (1958), Raywid (1962), Scanlon (1960), Sizer (1964), Washburne and Marland (1963), Wesley (1957), and Woelfel (1933). An older, two-volume biography of Charles W. Eliot should not go without mention (James, 1930).

The impact of this report seems to be that the thinking expressed by major publications in the field has for the past decade been very much in line with the recommendations in the second and third parts of the *Report of the Committee on Historical Foundations of the National Society of College Teachers of Education,* written by Anderson (1956) and by Chiapetta (1956), respectively. In it, for example, Anderson wrote:

What makes a tremendous difference is the awareness. . . . that the History of Education must be so organized and so taught that it affects the action, that is, the behavior, of the professional students who study it. This is the crucial test for the History of Education. If it cannot pass this test, it cannot hope to survive. (p. 93)

This is not to say that the report *caused* whatever change has come, but its weight was certainly cast in that direction.

A publication, highly valuable for those doing research in educational history, has recently been brought out by Park (1965). He characterizes it as "an annotated bibliography of the most important books in the history of American education. . . ." It includes a 16-page "Guide to *Sources* in History and Education." Of this nature also is Brickman's earlier *Guide to Research in Educational History* (1949). Krug has assembled a handy reference volume, *Salient Dates in American Education* (1966).

When one turns from books to magazine articles, there is not much to do but refer to the various periodical indexes, a list of which appears in Park's book (1965). First to consult would, of course, be the *Readers' Guide to Periodical Literature* and the *Education Index.* However, any research in educational history deemed really important by its author or by the profession is almost sure to be reported in the *History of Education Quarterly* (1961———) or its predecessor, the *History of Education Journal* (1949–1960). Moreover, the book-review section is excellent, and might be considered the most valuable part of each issue. An annual index appears in the last issue of each volume of either *Journal* or *Quarterly.*

From the showing, factual research dominates over conceptual, with coverage running the gamut of the field but with major attention given to American education and a reasonable share to the twentieth century. The tendency to deal with the recent rather than the remote past and to note its impact upon the present is distinctly in evidence.

Ernest E. Bayles
University of Kansas

References

Anderson, Archibald W. "Bases of Proposals Concerning the History of Education." *History Ed J* 7:37–98; 1956.

Archambault, Reginald D. (Ed.) *John Dewey on Education: Selected Writings.* Random, 1964. 439p.

Bailyn, Bernard. *Education in the Forming of American Society.* Random, 1960. 147p.

Bayles, Ernest E., and Hood, Bruce L. *Growth of American Educational Thought and Practice.* Harper, 1966. 305p.

Bidwell, Charles E. "The Moral Significance of the Common School." *History Ed Q* 6:50–91; 1966.

Bode, Boyd H. *Modern Educational Theories.* Random, 1927.

Boler, John F. *Charles Peirce and Scholastic Realism: A Study of Peirce's Relation to John Duns Scotus.* U Washington Press, 1963. 177p.

Brauner, Charles J. *American Educational Theory.* Prentice-Hall, 1964. 341p.

Brickman, William W. *Guide to Research in Educational History.* New York U Press, 1949.

Brickman, William W. "Revisionism and the Study of History of Education." *History Ed Q* 4:209–23; 1964.

Broudy, Harry S., and Palmer, John R. *Exemplars of Teaching Method.* Rand, 1965. 172p.

Brubacher, John S. *Modern Philosophies of Education,* 3rd ed. McGraw-Hill, 1962. 373p.

Brubacher, John S., and Rudy, Willis. *Higher Education in Transition.* Harper, 1958. 494p.

Brumbaugh, Robert S., and Lawrence, N. M. *Six Essays on the Foundations of Western Thought.* Houghton, 1963. 311p.

Butts, R. Freeman. "Review of Nash and Others' *The Educated Man: Studies in the History of Educational Thought.*" *History Ed Q* 6:101–2; 1966.

Chambliss, J. J. *Boyd H. Bode's Philosophy of Education.* Ohio State U Press, 1963. 98p.

Chambliss, J. J. "Review of Cremin's *The Transformation of the School.*" *History Ed Q* 3:43–52; 1963.

Chiapetta, Michael. "Recommendations of the Committee." *History Ed J* 7:99–132; 1956.

Cremin, Lawrence A. (Ed.) "Classics in Education." Teachers Col, Columbia U, 1957——. A series of paperbacks.

Cremin, Lawrence A. *The Transformation of the School.* Knopf, 1961. 387p.

Cubberley, Ellwood P. *Public Education in the United States.* Houghton, 1934. 782p.

Dewey, John, and Bentley, Arthur F. *Knowing and the Known.* Beacon, 1949. 329p.

Duker, Sam. *The Public Schools and Religion: The Legal Context.* Harper, 1966. 238p.

Dunkel, Harold B. *Whitehead on Education.* Ohio State U Press, 1965. 182p.

Eby, Frederick, and Arrowood, Charles Flinn. *The Development of Modern Education.* Prentice-Hall, 1934. 922p.

Edwards, Newton, and Richey, Herman G. *The School and the American Social Order,* 2nd ed. Houghton, 1963. 694p.

Eells, Walter Crosby, and Hollis, Ernest V. *The College Presidency 1900–1960: An Annotated Bibliography,* USOE, 1961. 143p.

Frost, S. E., Jr. *Historical and Philosophical Foundations of Western Education.* Charles E. Merrill, Inc., 1966. 539p.

Good, H. G. *A History of Western Education,* 2nd ed. Macmillan, 1960. 620p.

Good, H. G. *A History of American Education,* 2nd ed. Macmillan, 1962. 610p.

Greene, Maxine. *The Public School and the Private Vision.* Random, 1965. 183p.

Gross, Carl H. "Review of Edwards-Richey's *The School in the American Social Order.*" *History Ed Q* 3:234–6; 1963. Review of the second edition.

Gross, Carl H., and Chandler, Charles C. *The History of American Education Through Readings.* Heath, 1964. 488p.

Harris, Raymond P. *American Education: Facts, Fancies, and Folklore.* Random, 1961. 302p.

History of Education Journal. 1949–1960. (Published by the History of Education Section of the National Society of College Teachers of Education, at Ann Arbor, Michigan; edited by Claude Eggertsen.)

History of Education Quarterly. 1961——. (Official organ of the History of Education Society, now published in cooperation with the School of Education, New York University.)

Hofstadter, Richard, and Smith, Wilson. *American Higher Education: A Documentary History,* 2 vols. U Chicago Press, 1961. 1016p.

James, Henry. *Charles W. Eliot,* 2 vols. Houghton, 1930. 775p.

Johnson, Clifton. *Old-time Schools and Schoolbooks.* Dover, 1963. 381p.

Kimball, Solon T., and McClellan, James E., Jr. *Education and the New America.* Random, 1962. 402p.

Krug, Edward A. *The Shaping of the American High School.* Harper, 1964. 466p.

Krug, Edward A. *Salient Dates in American Education: 1635–1964.* Harper, 1966. 159p.

Lottich, Kenneth V. "Review of Bayles-Hood's Growth of American Educational Thought and Practice." *History Ed Q* 6:106–7; 1966.

Madden, Edward H. *Chauncey Wright and the Foundations of Pragmatism.* U Washington Press, 1963. 203p.

Mayer, Frederick. *Philosophy of Education for Our Time.* Odyssey, 1958. 245p.

Mayer, Frederick. *A History of Educational Thought.* Merrill, 1960. 494p.

Mayer, Frederick. *Foundations of Education.* Merrill, 1963. 184p.

Mayer, Frederick. *American Ideas and Education.* Merrill, 1964. 638p.

Mayer, Martin. *The Schools.* Harper, 1961.

Mehl, Bernard. "Review of Greene's *The Public School and the Private Vision.*" History Ed Q 6:104–6; 1966.

Meyer, Adolphe E. *An Educational History of the American People.* McGraw-Hill, 1957. 444p.

Meyer, Adolphe E. *An Educational History of the Western World.* McGraw-Hill. 1965. 516p.

Mosier, Richard D. *The American Temper: Patterns of Our Intellectual Heritage.* U California Press, 1952. 306p.

Myers, Edward D. *Education in the Perspective of History.* Harper, 1960.

Nash, Paul, and others. *The Educated Man: Studies in the History of Educational Thought.* Wiley, 1965. 421p.

Neill, A. S. *Summerhill: A Radical Approach to Child Rearing.* Hart, 1964. 392p.

Nelson, Jack, and Roberts, Gene, Jr. *The Censors and the Schools.* Little, 1963. 208p.

Nietz, John. *Old Textbooks.* U Pittsburgh Press, 1961. 364p.

Park, Joe. *Bertrand Russell on Education.* Ohio State U Press, 1963. 139p.

Park, Joe. *The Rise of American Education: An Annotated Bibliography.* Northwestern U Press, 1965. 216p.

Peterson, Houston. (Ed.) *Great Teachers.* Random, 1946. 351p.

Power, Edward J. *A History of Catholic Education in the United States.* Bruce, 1958.

Power, Edward J. "Persistent Myths in the History of Education." History Ed Q 2:140–51; 1962.

Price, Kingsley. *Education and Philosophic Thought.* Allyn and Bacon, 1962. 511p.

Primack, Robert. "Review of Mayer's *American Ideas and Education.*" History Ed Q 6:86–8; 1966.

Ratner, Sidney, and others. *John Dewey and Arthur F. Bentley: A Philosophical Correspondence, 1932–1951.* Rutgers U Press, 1964. 737p.

Raywid, Mary Anne. *The Ax-grinders: Critics of Our Public Schools.* Macmillan, 1962. 260p.

Rudolph, Frederick. *The American College and University.* Random, 1965. 515p.

Russell, James E. *Change and Challenge in American Education.* Houghton, 1965. 115p.

Scanlon, David G. *International Education: A Documentary History.* Teachers Col, Columbia U, 1960.

Sizer, Theodore R. *Secondary Schools at the Turn of the Century.* Yale U Press, 1964. 294p.

Thayer, V. T. *Formative Ideas in American Education.* Dodd, 1965. 394p.

Thut, I. N. *The Story of Education.* McGraw-Hill, 1957. 410p.

Washburne, Carleton W., and Marland, Sidney P. *Winnetka: The History and Significance of an Educational Experiment.* Prentice-Hall, 1963. 402p.

Wesley, Edgar B. *N.E.A.: The First Hundred Years.* Harper, 1957.

Wilds, Elmer H., and Lottich, Kenneth V. *The Foundations of Modern Education,* 3rd ed. Holt, 1961. 491p.

Wirth, Arthur G. "John Dewey's Design for American Education: An Analysis of Aspects of His Work at the University of Chicago, 1894–1904." History Ed Q 4:85–105; 1964.

Wirth, Arthur G. "John Dewey in Transition from Religious Idealism to the Social Ethic of Democracy." History Ed Q 5:264–8; 1965.

Wirth, Arthur G. *John Dewey as Educator: His Design for Work in Education (1894–1904).* Wiley, 1966. 322p.

Woelfel, Norman. *Molders of the American Mind.* Columbia U Press, 1933. 304p.

Wynne, John P. *Theories of Education.* Harper, 1963. 521p.

HOME ECONOMICS

The concept of home economics as a branch of study focused on the well-being of individuals and families is one which has been accepted from the first definition of the field. Each redefinition reaffirms this as its central thesis. Home economics synthesizes knowledge drawn from its own research, from the physical, biological, and social sciences and from the arts and applies this knowledge to improving the lives of families and individuals. In *Home Economics —New Directions,* The American Home Economics Association (1959) outlined its concern for such aspects of family living as relationships and child development; consumption and other economic aspects; nutritional needs; food selection and preparation; the psychological and social significance of clothing and its design, selection, construction, and care; textiles; housing for the family and equipment and furnishings for the household; art; and management in the use of resources. At the secondary level, in addition to the traditional purpose of education for family life, home economics is concerned with the preparation of students for employment in occupations utilizing home economics knowledge and skills. At the college and university level home economics prepares men and women for the several professions through which they may help society meet needs related to human development and to the factors in the environment which influence the condition and quality of family life.

DEVELOPMENT OF HOME ECONOMICS. Although some instruction in needlework and cookery was given in American public schools during the nineteenth century, the chief development of home economics as a subject in the public school curriculum has taken place in the twentieth century. An important factor in broadening the concept of home life instruction from the simple skills of cooking and sewing was the influence of the group of leaders who in 1899 began the series of meetings known as the Lake

Placid Conferences. In the course of ten annual meetings the name "home economics" was suggested and defined. (The American Home Economics Association was formed as an outgrowth of these meetings.) These leaders' objectives outlined a field of instruction whose aim was to focus primarily on strengthening the home by developing in students the ability to live constructively at home and with the family. The home economics pioneers affirmed the importance of utilizing all resources of modern science to improve home life. By 1914 home economics programs were available in some schools in all states, though it was not until the 1920's that the broad program envisioned at the Lake Placid Conferences began to be implemented (Coon, 1964).

State and Federal Support. State legislation authorizing education for home living as a subject of secondary-school instruction and direct grants to schools for such study were important factors in the development of home economics in the early 1900's. Federal support, beginning in 1917 with the passage of the Smith-Hughes Vocational Education Act, has had a marked influence on the home economics program through subsidies to states for instruction below the college level and for preparation of teachers. At the college level the land-grant institutions of Illinois, Iowa, and Kansas (supported by federal legislation in the Morrill Act) introduced home economics between 1872 and 1874. By 1914 over 250 colleges and universities offered four-year courses in home economics to about 12,000 students. Further federal legislation, the Smith-Lever Act provided for expansion of programs for rural women carried on by the land-grant institutions. Funds have since been provided through a continuing series of supporting legislative acts (Coon, 1964). Among the extensive purposes of the Vocational Education Act of 1963 is that of directing home economics toward education for gainful employment that will qualify individuals to engage in occupations involving knowledge and skills in home economics subject-matter areas (including child development, clothing and textiles, foods and nutrition, home and institutional management, and home furnishings and equipment). Research and development and periodic evaluation of goals and programs in vocational education are emphasized in the provisions of the act (Amidon, 1965).

HOME ECONOMICS EDUCATION TODAY. The program in home economics, initially focused on the girl, has gradually turned increasingly to the individual and the family; it is provided through the formal school organization at all levels—elementary, secondary, postsecondary, college, and university.

Elementary Level. Family-life education at the elementary school-level is generally aimed at helping children improve their relationships with other members of their own families. To a limited extent sex education, at least insofar as it deals with menstruation, reproduction, and other biologically oriented subjects, is seen as part of elementary or junior high school offerings (Kerckhoff, 1964). Little research has been conducted in this area. Hawley (1962) described some of the ways home economics concepts enriched experiences in an elementary group at Ohio State University School. McMillan (1957) assembled widely accepted concepts of family-life education suitable for elementary classes; an evaluation of her pilot program suggested the need for their interpretation for teachers and parents and the necessity for blending family-life concepts into the established curriculum content rather than teaching them in a specialized class.

Secondary Level. Home economics is now part of the curriculum in nearly all high schools in the country. Preparation for homekeeping remains the major purpose, though with the Vocational Act of 1963 a second purpose has emerged: education for gainful employment. A third also is important to the field: to motivate and recruit college-bound students for professional careers in the field of home economics.

A nationwide survey of 3,796 schools conducted in 1959 by the Home Economics Education Branch of the Division of Vocational Education, Office of Education, revealed that home economics instruction was available in 95 percent of the schools studied (38 percent more than in 1939). Most of the courses offered were in grades 9 and 10 (Coon, 1962). Usually seventh- and eighth-grade courses were required, but those in grades 9 through 12 were largely elective. An estimated 2.35 million girls were enrolled in home economics in 1959 (doubled since 1939)—49 percent of all girls in public secondary schools. Slightly more than 1 percent of all boys were enrolled in home economics courses—about 63,000. Although home economics aims at teaching all phases of family life in its secondary-school program, results of the 1959 survey disappointingly showed that more than half of high school teaching time was spent in food and clothing classes. Relatively little time was devoted to housing, home furnishing, family relationships, child development, financial planning, or management of resources, except in the twelfth grade, where the time was more evenly divided among the areas of instruction (Coon, 1962). Henderson (1965) suggests that an examination of college transcripts of high school home economics teachers graduated in the past 25 years would show two-thirds to three-fourths of the home economics credits allocated to foods and clothing. In-service education as well as current emphases in professional-education programs are aimed at motivating and helping teachers and those preparing to be teachers to include more work on consumer education, housing, child development, family and social relationships, nutrition, money and time management, and personal development in high school home economics programs. An examination of several new or recently revised state curriculum guides (Alabama State Board of Education, 1964; University of the State of New York, 1965; Illinois Curriculum Program, 1966) reveals a shift from an overemphasis on the food-preparation and clothing-construction aspects of home economics to a more desirable balance among all areas of family living.

Occupational Home Economics. In a study at the University of Illinois, Dewar (1966) collected data on the number of schools offering occupational courses in home economics, though no figures were available on the numbers of students enrolled. The study revealed that 309 schools in 38 states had a total of 423 programs underway in 1965–66 or planned for introduction in 1966–67. Most of these were in cities with populations between 10,000 and 30,000 persons. An additional 23 programs were reported by supervisors to be operating in nine cities with populations over 500,000. Somewhat over a third of the programs were designed to prepare young people for occupations in the food industry. About a fifth focused on occupations requiring knowledge and skills in clothing, and nearly another fifth were concerned with preparing child-care workers. Home economics programs are among the offerings in area vocational schools and in postsecondary technical institutes. A review of state-by-state reports (U.S. Office of Education, 1965) shows rapid progress in expansion and improvement of both facilities and programs in vocational education.

Home Economics in Higher Education. At the college and university level home economics programs aim to provide a liberal education in the social and natural sciences, the humanities, and the arts and to provide specialized instruction, based on these disciplines, as preparation for professional careers in which the interests and well-being of the individual, the consumer and the family are paramount. Some of the professions, such as teaching or dietetics, are well-established, and their documented need for new workers each year runs into the thousands. Others, such as home-management specialist in a low-income urban housing development, created as a result of social legislation of the mid-1960's are too new to have acquired recognized titles. The specialized studies preparing students for the widely differing professions which have in common their concern for human well-being relate basic knowledge to an understanding of the needs of people with regard to food, shelter, clothing, management of resources, and interpersonal and family relationships. In addition, home economics has a contribution to make to the education for family living of all college students.

Home economics enrollment in 1963 in institutions granting the bachelor's or higher degrees totaled slightly over 96,000, an increase of 12 percent in undergraduate enrollment from the previous biennial survey and a 20 percent increase in advanced-degree programs. Foreign students made up about 1 percent of the total enrollment (V. Thomas, 1964). In 1964–65 colleges and universities conferred 11,091 degrees in home economics, nearly half of them in home economics education. Seventy-two doctorates and about a thousand master's degrees are included in the total. Home economics baccalaureate degrees are granted in somewhat over 400 institutions.

Preparation-for-marriage Programs. In addition to the interest of home economists in education for family living, other developments in education have focused on a part of such education seen as functional preparation for marriage, including facts, skills, and attitudes related to dating, marriage, and parenthood. The social-hygiene and sex-education movement after World War I contributed to the marriage-education movement which formally began at the college level with the work of Ernest Groves in 1924 (Kerkhoff, 1964). From this beginning, courses developed relatively independently at several universities. In the main they emphasized increasingly the personal, social, and cultural factors involved in successful marriage, with correspondingly less emphasis on such topics as budgeting and household management. College and university programs in marriage education have become large and widespread; a 1959 survey revealed over 1,000 offerings. In secondary schools, special courses in preparation for marriage and in family life are among home economics offerings, but units on the family are also incorporated into general home economics courses. Units are sometimes provided in social science, health, and other subjects. At the elementary-school level objectives related to the improvement of family attitudes and understandings may be incorporated as appropriate into various parts of the curriculum (Kerkhoff, 1964).

Continuing Home-and-family-life Education. There is increasing interest among adults in continuing their education in home and family life and such education is a part of many communitywide programs of adult education. Courses offered are based on the needs and resources of a community and of the particular group to be served. In organized programs of parent education schools offer classes on the needs of individuals from birth through adolescence and into the retirement years. Apart from school-based programs, more than 4,000 extension home economists work in about 3,000 counties in all of the states. Through these professional home economists more than ten million women a year learn to apply the latest research to become more efficient homemakers and consumers. Use is made of educational television and other mass media to extend home-and-family-life education into the community. From close association with agriculture, cooperative extension in home economics has a rural image, though home economists in some states have worked in urban areas over a long period of time, and in a few cities extension work dates back nearly 50 years. Weeks (1965) evaluated a program for disadvantaged families in Boston which showed significant gains in nutrition knowledge, improved food-buying and meal-planning practices, improved housekeeping skills and attitudes, and increased confidence of parents in their ability to guide the development of their children. A 1966 publication, *Extension Home Economics Focus* (American Association of Land-Grant Colleges and State Universities, 1966), describes an increasing outreach to a variety of groups other than homemakers, among them professional builders, sales personnel and department-store buyers of fabrics, school lunch personnel, and area food-service-association members.

American Home Economists Abroad. As home economics began to emerge as a profession there were niches to fill in mission-sponsored schools and colleges throughout the world. By 1915 the International Committee of the American Home Economics Association had been organized to encourage home economists to assist in developing programs in other countries. The first government-sponsored activities abroad took home economists to the Philippines and Puerto Rico after the Spanish-American War, but large-scale involvement of American home economists in overseas work did not begin until after World War II. From that time various commitments of the United States to bilateral programs of assistance and the development of United Nations agencies for social and economic progress contributed to the increasing involvement of home economists in work abroad (Hanson, 1965). American colleges of home economics participate in the development of home economics abroad by giving direction to programs of research and education in cooperating institutions and by training students (both foreign nationals and Americans) for leadership positions in foreign countries and international agencies. From 1930 to 1965, 185 American Home Economics Association International Scholarship holders have studied in colleges and universities in the United States. Proceedings of the Conference on World-wide Developments of Home Economics in Higher Education held at Iowa State University (Iowa State University, 1965) provide an overview of opportunities and roles for home economists in developing countries, cross-cultural understanding, barriers to communications, developing home economics programs abroad, and the internationalization of graduate education and research.

RESEARCH IN HOME ECONOMICS EDUCATION. Prior to 1940 little research was carried on in home economics education except by graduate students at the master's-degree level. Between then and 1963 some funds were made available at federal and state levels for research. Doctoral studies became more numerous. With the passage of the 1963 Vocational Education Act there is emerging an unprecedented interest in research and development programs in home economics education, as well as financial resources for quality research programs. Research and development was assigned an important place in the act. Ten percent of the total appropriation for vocational education each year is to be used for training programs and research, and in addition at least 3 percent of each state's allotment of federal funds for vocational education is to be used for services and activities leading to the development and improvement of programs and for program evaluation. The amount and quality of research in home economics education is growing.

The study reported by Alice Thomas (1965) exhibits a testing of theoretically derived hypotheses, a careful design, and sophisticated treatment of data. Thomas attempted to test the cumulative hypothesis of the Taxonomy of Educational Objectives (the first three levels of the cognitive domain) with approximately 100 Grade-7 pupils in a highly controlled teaching-testing situation. She succeeded in preparing test materials that were judged to tap understandings at the levels designated and then demonstrated that high-level items dealing with a particular concept were correctly answered mostly by students who also passed related items calling for lower levels of understanding. Employing Guttman's simplex analysis, correlation matrices of subtests of knowledge, comprehension, and application (with two areas of subject matter and a combination of the two) yielded the general pattern of a simplex, and the pattern of regression weights was also consistent with that expected for the simplex model. Tests which yield such data are thought to differ only in complexity; hence, the data support the cumulative hypothesis of the taxonomy.

A pilot study to provide clearer conceptualization of the chosen problem and a runthrough on procedures was used in the Johnson programmed-instruction project at the University of North Carolina at Greensboro. The pilot study produced a pretested unit of programmed instruction on the use of the sewing machine, designed to be the first in a series (C. Moore, 1963). A second pilot study (Shoffner, 1964) revised and field-tested the program and assessed pupil and teacher reaction to this instructional device. Work is currently in progress on the large subsequent study.

Investigations formulated in terms of naive practical issues are not unusual in home economics, but research formulated in terms of theoretically cogent approaches also exists. Loftis (1962) sought to develop a measure of commitment, a quality theorized by educators, philosophers, psychologists, and sociologists to be necessary for the highest fulfillment of the professional role. She succeeded in developing a measure of commitment to teaching which was shown to produce highly consistent results, to discriminate among public secondary-school teachers with varying degrees of rated devotion to their jobs, to be independent of the personal factors of sex, age, marital status, education, and experience of the teachers, and to relate positively to validating criteria.

Encouraging are accounts of research under way which approach problems to be solved in an imaginative way. East is directing such a project in teacher education at the Pennsylvania State University, testing the value of experience with the life and work of the disadvantaged as a requirement for all students expecting to become vocational home economics teachers. Included in the experimental plan is a period of time term in which the student lives in a lower-class community and works in a job typical of those held by young dropouts or high school graduates from lower-class families. Pre- and posttesting is directed toward revealing changes in attitudes toward people different from themselves, self-actualization, and openmindedness. The tests should make it possible to estimate the contribution the experience makes to the sensitivity and effectiveness of teachers in their work with disadvantaged youth.

The commitment of a researcher to a particular dimension of his field which provides continuity in research and tends to result in the emergence of more clearly conceptualized problems is demonstrated in the research done by Blackwell and her associates (Byrd, 1963; Roth, 1963; Jacklin, 1964; A. Thomas, 1965). This cluster of researches focuses on an exploration of the cumulative nature of understanding and examines the relationship between behavior at each of three designated levels to IQ, critical thinking ability, or both. The latest of the series capitalized on a knowledge of the difficulties experienced in the earlier attempts and seems to have demonstrated a set of methodologically feasible procedures to accomplish the purposes of the project. Such a broad program of research offers meaningful and stimulating opportunities for graduate students to examine the problems that interest them in relation to the larger problem and also offers an alternative to the bits-and-pieces approach of a self-supported master's or doctoral thesis.

Since staffs are limited in number and in time available for research in most home-economics-education departments, cooperative effort either within a university or among institutions offers a means of improving the amount and quality of research in home economics education. A study which capitalized on the possible enhancement of generalizability of findings through multi-institutional cooperation is described by Dirks and others (1967) in a report of four institutions' findings in a cooperative study of the contribution of the college home economics supervisor to the student-teaching situation. A cooperative research study is reported by Chadderdon and others (1966) in which each of several institutions investigated various characteristics thought to be particularly important for home economics teachers.

In an effort to further the research knowledge and competence of vocational educators, six research seminars enrolling a total of 260 participants (among them home economics teacher educators) were held in 1966, supported by funds provided under the 1963 Vocational Education Act. Centers for research and leadership training in vocational and technical education have been established at the Ohio State University and at the University of North Carolina. The Ohio center has initiated a storage and retrieval system for research in vocational and technical education and related disciplines.

CURRICULUM DEVELOPMENT. A large proportion of the research and study in home economics education has been concentrated on problems relating to the curriculum, particularly at the secondary-school level. Some of the significant findings are pertinent to all levels of instruction in home economics, particularly those related to the identification of conditions and changes in society that affect the lives of individuals in their homes and families and those related to the organization of knowledge. Since decisions affecting curriculum development involve a diversity of considerations, researchers have approached the problem from several angles: trends and conditions in society; organization of knowledge; beliefs of educators and lay persons; needs, attitudes, values, beliefs and interests of students; and occupational manpower needs. Many of these studies have been local in scope and therefore limited in generalizability.

Identified as important trends and conditions which have implications for home economics and for marriage and parent education at all curriculum levels are the increasing geographical and social mobility of families, increasing urbanization, changes in the structure of our society (e.g., there are more old and more young people), the decreasing age at marriage, one-parent families, the increasing numbers of unmarried mothers, the strong emphasis on personal satisfaction, women's employment outside the home, the confused power structure in the family, the availability to the family of more goods and services and of increased choice among them, the decreasing home production of goods, and the rapidity of change (Spafford, 1957; Frank, 1959; Burchinal, 1963; E. Simpson, 1965). Educational developments which have implications for family life include the expansion of fields of knowledge, the increased attention to the organization of subject matter, the increasing length of school day and year, the emphasis upon higher standards of education, and the emerging emphasis on vocational education.

The Structure of Knowledge. A 1961 conference of home economists called by the Home Economics Division of the American Association of Land-Grant Colleges and State Universities to consider the problem of articulation and differentiation of home economics subject matter at various teaching levels indicated that the first step in solving the problem would be to define the cognitive content of the field through identification of key concepts and principles pertinent and significant to each of the subject-matter segments of the field. Mallory (1963) reported the efforts sponsored by the U.S. Office of Education to examine basic content resulting from home economics research and other knowledge to get at fundamental concepts and generalizations in terms of widely held common objectives of secondary-school home economics programs. Human development and the family, home management and family economics, food and nutrition, housing, and textiles and clothing were studied and important concepts and generalizations outlined. The more recently developed secondary-school curriculum guides reflect this work in structuring the subject matter of home economics (University of the State of New York, 1965; Illinois Curriculum Program, 1966). Dalrymple (1965) described teacher educators' tentative identification of a basic framework of competences and concepts for home economics teacher education at the preservice level. Concepts important for the orientation of youth to the work were identified by home economists at the University of Oklahoma (Warren, 1965). Exploratory efforts to classify in taxonomic form educational objectives in the psychomotor domain, in part through laboratory analyses of tasks to discover the psychomotor activity involved, also provide a framework expected to be helpful in curriculum development (E. Simpson, 1966).

Beliefs of Educators and Lay Persons. The judgments of educators and lay persons have been sought at intervals in relation to home-and-family-life education programs. Christensen (1958) polled secondary and college family-life teachers concerning goals for preparation-for-marriage courses. He found that assisting students in developing an understanding of the relationships in modern marriage and helping them to understand themselves in relation to other members of their families was most frequently cited as the most important objective. Goldsmith (1960) investigated attitudes toward home economics held by superintendents, principals, and guidance counselors. Based on approximately 1,400 usable replies from a sample of 2,000 such individuals to whom questionnaires were mailed, data indicated basically a positive, favorable attitude toward home economics, particularly in relation to programs in which a broad range of subject matter is taught rather than a narrow program restricted largely to cooking and sewing. Vossbrink (1966) sampled Michigan schools offering home economics programs and found that superintendents and principals were in general agreement that homemaking education was desirable for all grades in high school, that it was particularly suitable for the ninth and twelfth grades, that it was valuable for potential dropouts, and that it could make a contribution to preparation for employment. There was considerably less agreement on the value of home economics courses for boys or of coeducational senior-year courses in family living. Whitmarsh (1966) investigated opinions of child-development specialists and social workers, mothers, and workers in day-care centers as to specific knowledges in child development and guidance that they felt were needed by employees at various levels of responsibility in child-care services and by mothers. She found differences in the opinions regarding amounts and kinds of knowledge needed by child-care workers and by mothers.

Needs of Learners. Studies designed to give evidence of the needs, interests, values, beliefs, and attitudes of learners on which to base curriculum decisions have been numerous. One of the most extensive of these is the Texas Cooperative Youth Study (B. Moore & Holtzman, 1965) in which questions related to family living were asked of a stratified representative sampling of nearly 13,000 students in grades 9 through 12 in Texas public schools. The students expressed interest in various aspects of their own development and family life as areas of study. Over three-fourths of them believed that high school girls should spend considerable time in school learning how to take care of the home and family. Seniors were most emphatic concerning the necessity for education in home and family living for both sexes. A ten-year follow-up study of 1,585 girls randomly selected from those who had been enrolled during 1954–64 in the tenth grade of Virginia high schools offered bases for curriculum decisions (Jordan & Loving, 1966). Characterized as a group by early marriages and early childbearing, by a high rate of marriage, by only moderate levels of income, by recurrent mobility of residence, and by great prevalence of paid employment, these young women identified problem areas of the first years of marriage as adjusting to new situations, managing the family income, home and family care, managing time, and interpersonal relations. They indicated very strongly that girls today need preparation for homemaking in addition to whatever preparation they may have acquired in their parental homes and were almost unanimous in feeling that girls today need preparation for employment in wage-earning occupations. Loftis (1966) surveyed attitudes of ninth- and twelfth-grade girls in South Carolina schools toward jobs requiring home economics knowledge and skills. Those which appeared to be most appealing to students were related to the care of children and to the health and medical services. Data from 1,640 former homemaking students in 82 Arkansas schools identified home economics knowledge and skills found useful in gainful occupations. About half reported acquiring useful competences in homemaking courses. Those cited as directly useful in gainful employment were technical skills involving cooking, sewing, health care, home management and child care, also noted were skills in grooming, personal relations, neatness, and etiquette that had been of assistance to them in securing and progressing in a job (Roberts, 1966). Other researchers have explored marriage-role expectations (Dunn, 1960), money management (Powell & Gover, 1962), adolescent roles (Roy, 1963), home responsibilities (Pope & Loften, 1960), and family-living expectations of boys (Duvall, 1961).

In relation to preparation for wage earning in secondary-school home economics, manpower needs, employment opportunities, and the vocational aspirations of youth have been investigated to a limited extent. Increasing employment possibilities are seen for service occupations utilizing home economics knowledges and skills. Several local investigations of employment opportunities for women have been carried out, as in the Fetterman study for Connecticut (1966). Her findings indicated that the number of occupations and the employment outlook justify development of work-oriented programs for home economics in Connecticut.

INSTRUCTION. Home economics teachers employ a large variety of teaching methods: discussions of all types, laboratory, lecture, demonstration, role playing, supervised study, learning experiences carried out in home and community, home visits, and club programs. Actual materials and audiovisual representations of all kinds are common in home economics classrooms. Some recent research on methods and materials has been reported. Effectiveness of procedures used in teaching a unit on child development was evaluated by R. Simpson and others (1965). Impact of teacher-chosen methods for helping ninth-grade pupils reach generalizations relating to child-development concepts were estimated by gains in attitudinal scores and by gains in knowledge about young children. The following hypotheses concerning teaching procedures were suggested: having a variety of learning experiences contributes to change in pupil behavior; the use of problem-solving techniques adds to the effectiveness of the teaching; lessons are more effective when planned to meet pupil needs, interests, and abilities. Peterson (1963) developed a ninth-grade unit around problem-solving experiences based on competences considered desirable for effective personal and family life as identified by the American Home Economics Association (1959). Evaluation was focused on the detection of growth in skill in critical thinking. Pre- and posttesting as well as classroom observation revealed an improved ability to recognize important aspects of problems. Kupsinel's survey of 45 secondary-school programs in food-service training in 21 states (1964) pointed to the necessity of developing methods and materials suitable for teaching marketable skills. In a project in progress at Iowa State University, Hill is developing materials for employment-oriented courses in home economics for the educable mentally retarded pupil. The study includes the evaluation of the effectiveness of selected teaching methods for use with the mentally retarded.

At the college level Trotter (1960) compared laboratory and lecture-demonstration methods in teaching food-preparation classes. She found no significant differences between mean achievement test scores on basic food-preparation principles, on knowledge of management of equipment, and on practical applications of food-preparation principles. Objectives related to the use of equipment and to gaining security and self-confidence with regard to food preparation were found to be reached to a greater extent with the laboratory approach. Lecture-demonstration was less expensive, and it permitted coverage of more course content in a given amount of time. Students and professors alike preferred a combination of laboratories and lecture-demonstrations to either alone.

Programmed instruction has received some attention from home-economics-education researchers. Preliminary reports (C. Moore, 1963; Shoffner, 1964) have described sections of a large research project involving programmed instruction in the area of clothing construction for junior high school pupils. Students taught by means of a self-instructional program and students taught by methods usual in the conventional classroom are being compared on the extent to which they can use thought processes higher in the hierarchy of educational behavior than knowledge and comprehension. Tests given at such a point in time that they measure retention and tests of ability to apply learnings in the performance of specified tasks have been used. Weber (1965) stated generalizations about nutrition at a level appropriate to junior high school pupils, identified the basic concepts within the generalizations, and assembled the information pertinent to the concepts into eight units of programmed instruction. The effectiveness of the programmed material was measured by performances on achievement tests given before and after the period of instruction. The experimental group was composed of 119 pupils representative of all ability levels; 81 similar pupils composed a control group. The experimental group made significant gains from pretest to posttest on knowledge of basic nutrition, ability to deal with comprehension-test items, and recognition of valid generalizations. There was no gain in knowledge or comprehension of nutrition between tests by the control group.

In a demonstration attempt to provide independent study in professional home economics education, Nelson (1966) developed units of programmed instruction for each of eight areas usually taught in home economics education and considered suitable to be programmed. The programs were field-tested in the home-economics-education departments of 20 institutions throughout the United States with numbers of students varying from 113 to 155, depending on the program. Each program was subjected to a minimum of three trials. In the final trial, pre- and postprogram criterion tests demonstrated that the students made significant gains as measured by tests of knowledge and comprehension of the programmed materials. Likert-type attitude inventories for both students and teacher educators were developed to measure reactions of participating students and teachers. Responses from 228 students and their teacher educators in twelve of the cooperating institutions in nine states showed neither students nor teacher educators to be extremely favorable, but they tended to be predominantly positive in their feelings toward programmed instruction as a means of teaching and learning. Attitude toward programmed instruction was shown to be unrelated to academic competence.

Facilities and Equipment. It is generally agreed that an understanding of the scope, the nature of the classroom activities, and the instructional methods of the home economics program is basic to the development of functional facilities for the department. Considered important in developing facilities are considerations of variety through the use of flexible space and mobile equipment, of an aesthetically pleasing physical environment, of safety and comfort, of the elimination of distracting influences, and of the needs of high school students and adults in both day and evening school (Taylor & Christian, 1965). Lee (1966) described minimum space requirements for a department planned mainly for occupational home economics. The plan for facilities focuses on preparation for employment at different levels of food service, child care, clothing services, and homemaker services. Lee's illustration depicts a child-care laboratory, a food-service training laboratory, and a large multipurpose room between the two.

MEASUREMENT AND EVALUATION. Home-economics-education research relating to evaluation has produced techniques and instruments useful in classroom instruction and for program evaluation. Heltzel (1963) studied the effect within the individual of the evaluation of his performance, finding that the high school student's self concept and an evaluation must agree if the score is to be acceptable to the student. Competence was found to be expected of a teacher evaluator though not of a peer evaluator; teacher evaluation was held by the student to be more meaningful in academic areas than peer evaluation. Several useful evaluation devices have been recently developed, some of which are described here. A battery of instruments consisting of two forms of a paper-and-pencil test on clothing construction, a finger-dexterity questionnaire, and a survey of object visualization were revised and validated by Frandolig (1962) to aid teachers in estimating the clothing-construction ability of junior and senior high school pupils. Jacklin's (1964) development of an instrument to test the hypothesis of cumulative levels of understanding of concepts relating to food and nutrition did not support the hypothesis but produced a valid and useful test of secondary-school pupils' knowledge and understanding. Byrd (1963) developed items to test the early adolescent's understanding of selected concepts in child development: heredity, environment, maturation, readiness, learning, growth patterns, basic needs, individual differences, normality, socialization, and personality. Analysis after administration to more than 300 pupils in grades 6 and 9 demonstrated the items' potential for reliable testing of more than the lower levels of understanding. Dunn (1960) formulated an instrument to measure marriage-role expectations of adolescents. Her inventory is designed to determine attitudes toward role expectations in the following areas: homemaking and employment, education, personal characteristics, social participation, care of children, and authority. For their study of Texas youth, B. Moore and Holtzmann (1965) constructed inventories to assess attitudes toward personal and family living, concerns and problems in personal and family living, and interests in family living. An instrument to test critical thinking in the area of family relationships devised by Spangler (1963) and a parallel test of knowledge developed by Roth (1963) were found to be satisfactory for group evaluation. Administered to a group of 100 high school juniors and seniors the test showed a moderately high correlation between critical thinking and knowledge in the area of family relationships. Keenan (1962) constructed an instrument making use of case problems to help students understand how various ways of spending money can reflect the values held by an individual or a family.

Instruments useful in teacher education programs have been devised and tested. Lehman (Chadderdon & others, 1966) developed the Just Suppose Inventory to measure the degree to which students or teachers accept families of different types, such as broken families, farm families, parents with little education, families from low or high socioeconomic levels, and those with different religious beliefs. Total scores varied significantly for juniors in home economics education, depending upon the kind of experiences with groups they themselves had had or on learning about groups in church or college (Chadderdon & others, 1966). An instrument to measure a teacher's concern for her students was devised by Nygren (1960) and revised and tested for its relationship to teacher effectiveness by Ray (1960). The Student Estimate of Teacher Concern was found to be a highly consistent measure able to discriminate among teachers with varying degrees of effectiveness. Gritzmacher (1967) constructed a descriptive rating scale for the evaluation of student teachers in home economics using the critical-incident technique. College supervisors, cooperating teachers, and student teachers supplied 550 reports of 958 critical behaviors; these formed the basis of a first-stage rating scale. The use of this scale with 399 raters and subsequent analysis produced a final version of a 35-cell scale that was found to be valid and reliable.

Program Evaluation. Research in the area of evaluation includes assessing present courses or programs as bases for future development and for determining effects of instruction. Evaluations of marriage-education courses, occupational home economics courses, college core curricula, and teacher preparation programs are among those receiving attention in the past few years. Duvall (1965) undertook to review reports of the effectiveness of more than 80 preparation-for-marriage courses at both secondary and college levels. Major types of evaluation studies included collecting student and alumni reactions to courses they had taken, testing knowledge and attitudes at the beginning and end of courses, and administering standardized instruments to marriage-course students and matched controls before and after a course. Among the findings that Duvall synthesized were that the subjective responses of students and graduates overwhelmingly support the value of the courses, that measured gains in knowledge and understanding of the learning in the courses are favorable, and that there are evidences of improved interpersonal relationships. In general, the marriage courses reviewed were found effective by all measures used to evaluate them. Wetzel (1965) studied a marriage course at the college level and found that participation in the course modified personality traits in a significantly positive direction.

There are few reports of program evaluation in occupational home economics. Jacoby (1966) reported the effectiveness of a pilot program in training students for entry-level jobs in food service. An index of student success was computed by ranking students according to their scores on five instruments developed for the investigation: Becoming Employable Scale, Waitress Scale, Caterer Scale, Attitudes Toward Work Scale, and an achievement test. Significant positive relationships were found between the index and IQ, academic rank in class, and total hours of work experience but not between the index and socioeconomic status or the total score on a motivation questionnaire. The 14 girls who completed the course were unanimous in their approval of the training as indicated by interview data. Mildred Johnson (1965) also evaluated an experimental class preparing high school girls for entry-level jobs in food service. During one semester 15 students were given classroom and work experiences. Pre- and posttest scores showed an increase in knowledge of employment practices, in problem-solving ability, and in the recognition of personal qualities important in food-service jobs. Employers indicated that the trainees had positive attitudes toward criticism and work, had acceptable personal qualities, and did their work satisfactorily.

Spencer (1960) undertook a survey of 17 colleges

and universities in southern and southwestern states to identify strengths and weaknesses of home-economics-education curricula in the opinions of home economics administrators and of alumnae. Administrators in general judged that (1) the increase of enrollment of undergraduates majoring in home economics education was satisfactory, (2) in some cases the faculty-student ratio was too small for efficiency, in others too large for effective work with students, (3) home economics curricula were well-balanced between home economics subject matter and the liberal arts, (4) low grade-point requirements in some institutions were conducive to raising the status of home economics, and (5) the status of home economics had decreased in today's reevaluation of education. Alumnae in general agreed that basic courses in clothing and foods had been the most valuable, that they had been well prepared for the jobs they took, and that cultural courses taken in college had not been as valuable as the more practical utilitarian courses. Shear (1964) evaluated the revision of a college core curriculum in order to ascertain (1) the extent of faculty utilization of curriculum theory in the revision process, (2) faculty recognition of dynamics of change, (3) the extent of changes evident in the curriculum, and (4) the impact of the new core curriculum on students. Faculty and administration were found to have used a theory of curriculum development and to have recognized dynamics of change; students were pleased with the lessened number of core requirements. Materials developed revealed deficiencies in statements of objectives, in selection of learning experiences, and in recognition given to learning theory. A committee evaluated the entire vocational education program in Michigan; some aspects were studied by means of questionnaires to teachers. Findings relevant to home economics education include those concerning teacher preparation programs. Of 113 recent graduates the 50 who responded thought that their college program had been "about right" with respect to the emphasis given to the physical, natural, and behavioral sciences, communication skills, and education. Some believed that too little emphasis was given philosophy and the arts. Responses from 472 experienced teachers and teacher educators revealed 86 percent felt too little emphasis had been given to sociological and psychological aspects of the teacher preparation program. Also, a considerable number believed too little emphasis had been placed on certain areas of home economics: family relations, marriage, child development, home management, consumer education, and family economics. More satisfaction was noted with emphasis placed on foods and nutrition, clothing and textiles housing, home furnishings, household equipment, and art and design (Michigan Vocational Education Project, 1963).

Cross (1960) questioned first- and second-year teachers about the programs that had prepared them to teach home economics. The majority believed that they had been adequately prepared for about two-thirds of their professional activities. The areas where they believed themselves to have been less well prepared included activities related to community relationships, working with boys and with Future Home makers of America groups, working with an advisory council, and participation in the total school program.

TEACHER PREPARATION. Few areas in home economics education have attracted more research than has that dealing with factors related to the effectiveness of teaching and the preparation of teachers. Personnel from three universities studied attitudes and interests of home economics students during college and in the first year of teaching (Chadderdon & others, 1966). Attitudes toward children, vocational interests, and attitudes toward families and other groups (attitudes toward other groups were described earlier) were investigated. Attitudes toward children were studied by means of the Minnesota Teacher Attitude Inventory administered to students in several institutions. Scores of students increased significantly over the years in college, but when seniors were retested after a half-year of teaching, it was found that their scores had decreased considerably. Those who had more credit hours in family-relationships courses had lower scores on the attitude test. Vocational interests were investigated by means of the Johnson Home Economics Interest Inventory administered to students in their freshman year and again in their senior year in home-economics-education departments of 17 colleges and universities and administered after the first year of teaching to graduates of eight universities. Interest-in-teaching scores increased slightly over the years in college. Scores of those tested after a year of teaching fell. Interest scores of students were not related to type of institution attended, amount of homemaking education, or amount of experience with children before college. Interest scores of first-year teachers were not found to be related either to teaching load or to department facilities.

Researchers seeking answers to questions concerning teacher effectiveness encountered difficulties but found few answers. Crabtree's (1965) investigation of factors which might predict successful teaching included a study of personal qualities, attitudes toward different groups, and grade-point averages. Composite prediction measures were correlated with composite measures of success (pupil gain in problem solving, teacher–pupil rapport, and adjustment to school and community as judged by an administrator); the best predictors yielded a correlation of .41. Scruggs (1959) attempted to find criterion measures for determining the effectiveness of teachers and to determine the extent to which each criterion discriminated among teachers. Criteria of successful teaching included pupil growth in achieving cognitive and effective objectives, attitudes of pupils toward the teacher, and behavior of pupils and teachers in the classroom. Measures were selected or devised for each. Data were collected in the classrooms of 26 teachers at the beginning and at the end of the academic year. No significant differences among teachers were found on measures of pupil growth toward objectives based on mean gains of classes and none on measures of attitudes of pupils toward teachers. Ford and Hoyt (1960), as one part of a larger study, investigated psychological characteristics of home economics teachers on the assumption that these are related to effective teaching. Using pupil-centered attitude inventories constructed for the study and the Minnesota Teacher Attitude Inventory, the authors found a low negative correlation between scores on the inventories and criteria of classroom effectiveness as judged by observers. They suggest that it is possible that attitudes other than pupil-centered ones bear more relationship to good classroom learning situations. One attempt to predict the success of home economics majors in their student teaching from grade-point averages, the Guilford-Zimmerman Temperament Survey, the Minnesota Teacher Attitude Inventory, and the Johnson Home Economics Interest Inventory (H. Johnson, 1950) found the highest correlation to be that between the quality of student-teaching performance and the grade-point average in home economics courses (Monts, 1963). Dotson (1963), in a similar type of study, found grade-point average the best indicator of success on the measures she investigated.

A considerable number of investigations have examined the student-teaching phase of teacher preparation. Two are reported here. To explore the contribution of the college supervisor to student teaching, investigators in four institutions used the critical incident technique to collect data from student teachers, supervising teachers, and college supervisors. College supervisors were found to function largely in roles described as giving information and judgment and stimulating growth. Their behaviors were perceived as equally important by student teachers and supervising teachers. Both student teachers and supervising teachers felt the contribution of the college supervisor to be unique and her action to be necessary in many student-teaching situations. College supervisors' behavior more frequently had an impact on the student teacher than on the supervising teacher, but in many cases an effect on the student teacher was accompanied by an effect on the supervising teacher. Problems giving rise to college supervisory action were most apt to occur in the areas of student-teacher self concept, lesson planning, program policies and requirements, and rapport with supervising teachers Dirks & others, 1967).

In another examination of roles involved in the student-teaching situation, Leonard (1965) found significant differences among principals, supervising teachers, and college supervisors in role expectations and perceptions. Areas of sharpest differences were found to be related to frequency of participation in evaluation, leadership, and program coordination.

Innovations in teacher preparation programs are represented by the Pennsylvania State University experimental program involving prospective teachers in the life and work of the disadvantaged (East study, described earlier). At the same institution Ray has an innovative study under way which is testing group counseling as a means of maximizing professional potential of home economics teachers. Purposes of the study include identification of stress and influence of group counseling on reducing anxiety, determination of conflict in relation to commitment to a professional role, and assessment of the effects of group counseling using measures of professional commitment, self-concept concern for students, and success in student teaching.

In-service Education. A study with implications for in-service education of home economics teachers was carried out by Scott (1960) in eight southern states. Eighty-five married teachers entering teaching or reentering it after an absence of five years or more and 94 married teachers who had been continuously teaching five years or more were questioned with regard to difficulties encountered in teaching. Problems in evaluating the effectiveness of the home economics program, directing Future Homemakers chapters, planning the home and community experience phase of the program, and making home visits were reported more often by newly entering teachers than by their counterparts. Both groups mentioned difficulties in planning adult programs, planning department budgets, working with pupils of different abilities in one class, and managing worthwhile learning experiences with inadequate equipment, funds, and library facilities. Suggestions for help with problems included supervisory visits early in the year, extension classes, summer classes of two or three weeks, local study groups, and sectional meetings at state conferences. In-service programs to help prepare teachers for teaching occupational home economics have been carried out with funds allocated under the Vocational Education Act of 1963. One of these was the 1965 workshop at the State University of Oklahoma for teachers and leaders of gainful employment training programs in home economics (Cozine, 1965).

ISSUES AND PROBLEMS. Traditionally, at the secondary level, home economics educators have interpreted the phrase "training of students for *useful* employment" from the Smith-Hughes legislation to mean preparation for useful employment as homemakers. The rules and regulations for the administration of the 1963 Vocational Education Act add to the maintenance, extension, and improvement of existing programs the concept of home economics education directed toward *gainful* employment in occupations involving home economics subject matter. An issue now confronting home economics educators is the acceptance and implementation of employment education as an objective of secondary programs and its integration with the traditional purpose of preparation for home and family life and the purpose of preprofessional education. Related to this issue is the need for the identification of the unique knowledges and abilities required for each of the three purposes, for recognition of the commonalities, and for programs planned to take these into account (E. Simpson, 1965).

Leadership for home economics education has been shifting its base from the U.S. Office of Education in the direction of professional organizations. In implementing the provisions of the Vocational Education Act of 1963, the division of vocational and technical education of the Office of Education has been restructured. There is no longer a home economics education branch. Regional conferences for home economics have been discontinued; instead all branches of vocational education meet and confer together. Two new means of providing leadership are being explored: a home economics education section of the American Home Economics Association has been organized at the request of a large number of potential members; and home economics educators in the American Vocational Association are working toward a more active role in that organization.

Accreditation is a current concern of home economics in higher education. In 1961 the American Home Economics Association appointed a committee to work on standards for accrediting colleges and universities with the basic assumption that home economics is a discipline and not just a collection of professional areas under an administrative organization entitled "home economics." Administrators of home economics in both large and small departments express concern that criteria for evaluating programs be flexible enough to allow for creative approaches and experimentation and that accreditation will actually help institutions achieve quality.

The question whether home economists should be prepared as specialists or generalists is increasingly an issue which demands resolution. Instructional programs must provide sufficient specialization to equip the student for a job. Yet the curriculum for secondary teaching certification, for example, requires that graduates be prepared to teach all areas of home economics. With almost half of the usual four-year program expected to be devoted to study in humanities and art, physical, biological and social sciences, and communications skills, the time remaining is becoming increasingly inadequate to encompass all areas of home economics.

To answer questions relating to changes in home economics curricula and identify trends in changes at the college level between 1957 and 1962 the American Home Economics Association conducted a survey of home economics degree-granting institutions (Horn, 1963). Findings from about half of the institutions indicated that the majority had made at least minor changes during the previous five years. Few sweeping changes had been made; one report of a major curriculum revision is in published form (Mentzer, 1962). As of 1962, the direction of change was not clear in regard to credit requirements for degree, requirements in home economics subjects and in courses outside home economics, elective credits allowed, prerequisites for home economics courses, and professional areas offered. For those institutions reporting major modifications, the most significant was change in course content or in emphasis of content. Here the major shifts most frequently mentioned were related to decreasing emphasis on laboratory and manipulative skills and increasing emphasis on consumer education, management, and specialization within home economics. Changes in overall objectives reflected a transition from homemaking to professional objectives. In some instances, colleges have dropped the words *home economics* from their names and chosen other names that they believed more adequately reflected the academic concerns of their faculty; others are contemplating such a move. Ferment for change is increasing. The presidents of the land-grant colleges and universities have requested that a national study be made by an employed agency to determine the appropriate purposes and functions of the field of home economics today; the study is now under way.

Helen Y. Nelson
New York State College of Home Economics

References

Alabama State Board of Education. *State Course of Study in Home Economics for Junior and Senior High Schools in Alabama*, Vol. 3. State Department of Education, 1964. 528p.

American Association of Land-Grant Colleges and State Universities. *Extension Home Economics Focus*. Home Economics Subcommittee of Extension Committee on Organization and Policy, 1966. 35p.

American Home Economics Association. *Home Economics—New Directions, A Statement of Philosophy and Objectives*. The Association, 1959.

Amidon, Edna P. "Home Economics in Vocational Education, 1965." *Am Voc J* 40:18–20; 1965.

Burchinal, Lee G. "Research on Young Marriage: Implications for Family Life Education." In Sussman, Marvin B. (Ed.) *Sourcebook in Marriage and the Family*. Houghton, 1963. p. 503–29.

Byrd, Flossie M. "An Exploratory Study of the Early Adolescent's Understanding of Certain Concepts in Child Development." Doctoral dissertation. Cornell U, 1963. 270p.

Chadderdon, Hester, and others. *Home Economics Teachers—Preservice and Inservice Levels, Their Interest in Teaching, Their Attitudes Toward Children and Families*. U Minnesota Press, 1966. 221p.

Christensen, G. A. "An Analysis of Selected Issues in Family Life Education." Doctoral dissertation. Michigan State U, 1958.

Coon, Beulah I. *Home Economics in Public Secondary Schools, A Report of a National Study*. USOE, 1962. 156p.

Coon, Beulah I. *Home Economics Instruction in the Secondary Schools*. Center for Applied Research in Education, 1964. 115p.

Cozine, June. *Training Program for Teachers and Leaders of Gainful Employment Training Programs in Home Economics*. Oklahoma State U, 1965. 148p.

Crabtree, Beverly. "Predicting and Determining Effectiveness of Homemaking Teachers." Doctoral dissertation. Iowa State U, 1965. 151p.

Cross, Aleene A. "On-the-job Activities and Feelings of Adequacy of Preparation of Homemaking Teachers and Home Agents." Doctoral dissertation. Columbia U, 1960. 257p.

Dalrymple, Julia I. "Concept Structuring of Home Economics Education Curriculum." *J Home Econ* 57:431; 1965.

Dewar, Margaret A. *Problems Unique to Implementing Home Economics Occupational Education Courses at the Secondary Level.* U Illinois, 1966. 70p.

Dirks, Marie, and others. "The Special Contribution of the Home Economics Education Supervisor to the Student Teaching Situation." In *Studies in Higher Education*, No. 94. Purdue U, 1967.

Dotson, Jacqueline R. "Selected Factors Related to Performance of Home Economics Majors in Student Teaching at West Virginia University." Master's thesis. West Virginia U, 1963. 42p.

Dunn, Marie S. "Marriage Role Expectations of Adolescents." *J Marriage and Family Living* 22:99–111; 1960.

Duvall, Evelyn Millis. "Research Finds: Teenage Boys and Family Living." *J Marriage Family Living* 23:49–50; 1961.

Duvall, Evelyn Millis. "How Effective Are Marriage Courses?" *J Marriage Family* 27:176–84; 1965.

Fetterman, Elsie. *The Development of a Work Orientation Program for Home Economics Related Occupations.* Connecticut State Department of Education, 1966. 38p.

Frandolig, Carol H. "Validation of Three Instruments to Predict Clothing Construction Ability at the High School Level." Master's thesis. Iowa State U, 1962. 80p.

Frank, Lawrence. "Challenge of Family Life Education." *Merrill Palmer Q* 5:67–79; 1959.

Ford, Roxanna R., and Hoyt, Cyril J. *The Identification and Measurement of Secondary School Homemaking Teachers Attitudes and Other Characteristics Associated with Their Ability to Maintain Desirable Learning Situations.* U Minnesota, 1960. 182p.

Goldsmith, Frances S. "Attitudes of Secondary School Superintendents, Principals and Guidance Counselors Toward Some Aspects of Home Economics." Doctoral dissertation. Purdue U, 1960. 195p.

Gritzmacher, Joan E. "Evaluation of Student Teaching in Home Economics." Doctoral dissertation. Cornell U, 1967. 181p.

Hanson, Doris E. "Pioneers in the Field of Home Economics Work Abroad." *J Home Econ* 57:255–9; 1965.

Hawley, Alice H. "Home Economics for the Elementary Level." *J Home Econ* 54:289; 1962.

Heltzel, Frances B. "A Level of Aspiration Approach to a Study of the Differential Effects of Evaluation." Doctoral dissertation. Cornell U, 1963. 126p.

Henderson, Grace M. "Issues Confronting Home Economics in Colleges and Universities." *J Home Econ* 57:759–64; 1965.

Horn, Marilyn J. "Curriculum Change—How Widespread?" *J Home Econ* 55:237–40; 1963.

Illinois Curriculum Program. *Home Economics Education: Homemaking Aspect Grades 7–12.* Office of the Superintendent of Public Instruction, 1966. 193p.

Iowa State University. *International Home Economics: Proceedings of a Conference on World-wide Development of Home Economics in Higher Education*, Iowa State U, 1965. 283p.

Jacklin, Roberta O. "An Exploratory Study of Secondary Pupils' Depth of Understanding of Selected Food and Nutrition Principles." Doctoral dissertation. Cornell U, 1964. 183p.

Jacoby, Gertrude P. "Evaluation of a Secondary School Pilot Program in Preparation for Home Related Occupations." Master's thesis. Cornell U, 1966. 146p.

Johnson, Hildegarde. "Technique for Determining the Professional Interests of Home Economists." Doctoral dissertation. Iowa State U, 1950. 212p.

Johnson, Mildred. "A Wage-earning Oriented Experimental Program in High School Home Economics." Doctoral dissertation. U Wisconsin, 1965. 203p.

Jordan, Beth C., and Loving, Rosa H. *Young Women in Virginia.* Division of Educational Research, Virginia State Department of Education, 1966. 37p.

Keenan, Dorothy M. "An Exploration of Value Patterns." Doctoral dissertation. U Illinois, 1962. 162p.

Kerckhoff, Richard K. "Family Life Education in America." In Christensen, Harold T. (Ed.) *Handbook of Marriage and the Family.* Rand McNally, 1964. p. 881–911.

Kupsinel, Penelope. "Instructional Materials for Vocational Food Service Courses at the Secondary Level." Doctoral dissertation. Southern Illinois U, 1964. 137p.

LaRowe, Annette W. "The Special Contribution of the College Home Economics Supervisor to the Student Teaching Situation." Master's thesis. Purdue U, 1965. 134p.

Lee, Ata. "Minimum Space . . . Maximum Use." *Am Voc J* 41:23–5; 1966.

Leonard, Thelma H. "Role Expectations and Perceptions for the Home Economics Supervising Teacher." Doctoral dissertation. Oklahoma State U, 1965. 147p.

Loftis, Helen A. "Identifying Professional Commitment and Measuring Its Extent Among Selected Members of the Teaching Profession." Doctoral dissertation. Pennsylvania State U, 1962. 29p.

Loftis, Helen A. *A Survey of the Attitudes Held by Certain South Carolina Ninth and Twelfth Grade Girls Toward Home Economics Related Jobs.* Winthrop Col, 1966. 65p.

Mallory, Bernice. "Home Economics Curriculum Study." *Am Voc J* 38:35; 1963.

McMillan, Marian. "An Experimental Program of Family Life Education For Elementary Schools." *J Home Econ* 49:224; 1957.

Mentzer, R. A. *Report of the Process Used in Revising Curriculum in the College of Home Economics.* Michigan State U, 1962.

Michigan Vocational Education Project. *Vocational Education in Michigan.* Michigan State U, 1963. 252p.

Monts, Elizabeth A. "The Value of Selected Instruments in the Prediction of Success in Student Teaching of Home Economics, Fresno State Col-

lege." Doctoral dissertation. Texas Woman's U, 1963. 107p.
Moore, Bernice Milburn, and Holtzman, Wayne H. *Tomorrow's Parent: A Study of Youth and Their Families.* U Texas Press, 1965. 371p.
Moore, Catherine P. "Development of a Self-instructional Program on the Sewing Machine." Master's thesis. U North Carolina, 1963. 98p.
Nelson, Helen Y. *Development of Programed Instruction for Home Economics Education and Study of Attitudes Toward Its Use at the Undergraduate Level.* New York State Col, 1966. 27p.
Nygren, Gertrude. "Teacher Concern and Its Measurement." *J Home Econ* 52:177–80; 1960.
Peterson, Bernadine H. "Problem Solving in Home Economics." *J Home Econ* 55:179–83; 1963.
Pope, M. E. W., and Loften, M. T. *Responsibilities in Home and Family Living of First Year Homemaking Students.* Mississippi State Board for Vocational Education, 1960. 150p.
Powell, Kathryn, and Gover, David A. *Money Management Habits and Interests of Adolescents in South Carolina.* South Carolina Ag Ex Station, 1962. 5p.
Ray, Elizabeth. "Teacher Concern Related to Teaching Effectiveness." *J Home Econ* 52:181–4; 1960.
Roberts, Roy W. *Determining Kinds of Gainful Employment in Which Former Homemaking Students from Arkansas Secondary Schools Engage and What Knowledge and Skills Homemaking Curriculums May Contribute to Their Gainful Occupations.* U Arkansas, 1966. 75p.
Roth, Mary Margaret. "The Relationship of a Critical Thinking and a Knowledge Test in Family Life Education." Master's thesis. Cornell U, 1963. 105p.
Roy, Prodipto. "Adolescent Roles: Rural Urban Differentials." In Nye, F. Ivan, and Hoffman, Lois W. (Ed.) *The Employed Mother in America.* Rand McNally, 1963. p. 165–81.
Scott, Mary J. "In-service Educational Needs of a Selected Group of Homemakers Who Entered or Re-entered the Teaching of Homemaking." Doctoral dissertation. U Tennessee, 1960. 228p.
Scruggs, Mary Marguerite. "Criteria for Determining Effectiveness of Homemaking Teachers." Doctoral dissertation. Iowa State U, 1959. 215p.
Shear, Twyla M. "An Evaluation of Core Curriculum in the College of Home Economics." Doctoral dissertation. Michigan State U, 1964. 211p.
Shoffner, Sarah M. "Revision and Field Test of a Self-instructional Program on the Sewing Machine." Master's thesis. U North Carolina, 1964. 140p.
Simpson, Elizabeth J. "Projections in Home Economics Education." *Am Voc J* 40:41–3; 1965.
Simpson, Elizabeth J. *The Classification of Educational Objectives, Psychomotor Domain.* U Illinois, 1966. 35p.
Simpson, Ruby, and others. *A Pilot Research Project of Techniques Used in Teaching a Unit on Child Development.* U Kentucky, 1965. 18p.
Spafford, Ivol. "Home Economics and Today's World." *J Home Econ* 49:411; 1957.
Spangler, Mariann. "Development of a Test for Critical Thinking in Family Relationships." Master's thesis. Cornell U, 1963. 73p.
Spencer, Ruth G. "An Analysis and Evaluation of Home Economics Education in Selected Colleges and Universities in Seventeen Southern and Southwestern States." Doctoral dissertation. Texas Woman's U, 1960.
Taylor, James L., and Christian, Johnie. *Planning Functional Facilities for Home Economics Education.* USOE, 1965. 48p.
Thomas, Alice M. "Levels of Cognitive Behavior Measured in a Controlled Teaching Situation." Master's thesis. Cornell U, 1965. 167p.
Thomas, Virginia F. *Home Economics in Institutions Granting Bachelor's or Higher Degrees, 1963–64.* USOE, 1964.
Trotter, Virginia Y. "A Comparison of the Laboratory and the Lecture—Demonstration Methods of Teaching Survey of Food Preparation for Freshman Home Economics Students at the University of Vermont." Doctoral dissertation. Ohio State U, 1960. 201p.
University of the State of New York, State Education Department. *Home Economics Education: Syllabus for a Comprehensive Program.* Bureau of Home Economics Education, 1965. 224p.
U.S. Office of Education. *Summary Report of Vocational-technical Program Development by States.* GPO, 1965. 50p.
Vossbrink, Meta. *Attitudes and Beliefs about Homemaking and/or Home Economics Education in Michigan Secondary Schools.* Educational Publications Services, Mich State U, 1966. 141p.
Warren, Mary A., and others. *Identification of Concepts Important for Youth Orientation to the World of Work.* U Oklahoma, 1965.
Weber, Shirley. "The Development and Evaluation of Eight Units of Programed Instruction Designed to Teach Basic Nutrition." Doctoral dissertation. Cornell U, 1965. 126p.
Weeks, Shirley S. "Home Economics in a Low-income Urban Housing Development." *J Home Econ* 57: 437–41; 1965.
Wetzel, Rita J. "The Effect of a Marriage Course on the Personality Characteristics of Students." *J Marriage and Family* 27:419–20; 1965.
Whitmarsh, Ruth E. *An Exploratory Study of Knowledges in Child Development and Guidance by Mothers and Workers in Occupations Related to Child Care.* U Illinois, 1966. 124p.

HONORS PROGRAMS

"Honors" as a generic term in the rhetoric of American higher education has undergone a significant expansion in both meaning and use during the past century. Furthermore, from its initial employment as a means of recognizing and rewarding high scholarly achievement in terms of grades by bestowing Latin praise at commencement (e.g., "summa cum laude"), honors has been a part of most major curricular and pedagogical innovations in undergraduate education. After World War I many institutions introduced the preparation of senior theses as a requirement for graduation, and soon after, performance on these research and writing projects, rather than high grade averages, became the basis for granting honors in specific disciplines.

With the introduction of senior theses a new dimension was added to departmental programs. Soon only able students were selected to participate in senior seminars, independent study, and reading for comprehensive examinations. Here we have the origin of concern for the development of talent through providing special activities for selected undergraduates. Much of the inspiration for these changes came from the example furnished by President Frank Aydelotte and the faculty of Swarthmore College. With great energy and insight, they projected not only a set of successful practices spanning both the junior and senior years but an image of quality as well. The introduction of divisional honors at Swarthmore, based as they were on modified British tutorial methods, represents the most significant influence the Oxford-Cambridge system has had on American institutions (Aydelotte, 1944; Swarthmore College Faculty, 1941).

While the Swarthmore example was producing changes in honors in the disciplines, Columbia University's imaginative interdisciplinary offerings were influencing some mild stirrings in general education. General honors programs, in a sense, have their roots in Columbia's Contemporary Civilization and Humanities courses, but there is not a straight historical line from developments on Morningside Heights to the four-year, general and departmental programs that characterize most honors efforts today. The University of Colorado was a pioneer among schools that projected four-year programs in the 1930's, but these developments were not widely known until the late 1950's. Through the leadership of Professor Joseph W. Cohen, Director of the program, the Inter-university Committee on the Superior Student (ICSS) was formed in 1957 (Cohen, 1966a, 1966b).

The impact of the ICSS was realized through the development and dissemination of a set of alternatives for comprehensive four-year programs based on the collective experiences of faculties and administrations across the country. That they had wide influence is attested to by the significant growth of honors efforts in many institutions during the past decade (Phillips, 1967). Let us examine in a general way operational structures in different settings to see how honors curricula, methods, and approaches are employed.

Seeking, motivating, and educating the bright, creative maverick is one objective of the honors program at Western Washington State College, at Bellingham. General education through tutorials and colloquiums is the core. Improvisation and freedom are combined with dialogue and discussion. But discipline is not neglected, for the goal is ultimate discipline for all honors students, including the "late bloomer," who often suffers even from the restrictions of a flexible honors program (Adams & Blood, 1965).

One-to-one and group tutorials, usually for two credits, are carried on throughout the four years. Freshmen are encouraged to read widely on subjects more or less of their own choosing, but as they progress in the college their reading takes on a structure, albeit a loose one. The only ground rules are that for the most part students explore subjects outside their fields of interest and that they do as much writing as possible. In an academic year, papers totalling 30,000 words might be written by a single student.

The colloquiums have been devised to present unique experiences for the students—forums where ideas might be tested before a group of perceptive, critical peers. In the Western Washington context, and in the context of many other honors programs, the word *colloquium* denotes a distinct teaching method. This method values discourse, dialogue, and the writing of critical essays rather than research and the preparation of scholarly papers. It differs from the seminar method in these respects. Moreover, as Morris put it, "*to cut through* the academic (and non-academic) *clutter,* a colloquium necessarily fixes attention on a few select questions. If, as is often possible, the students will themselves suggest a general theme to be pursued, they may soon find themselves hunted by that very theme. In consequence, they will set themselves determinedly to sift out the trivialities from the vitalities. Once a colloquium reaches this point, there will be some who find . . . new forms of intellectual strength (and humility) they never realized they had. A mind that *finds this* kind of *intellectual bearing* is a joy to itself. . . . No longer a whimperer in the crowd, this mind has found a voice" (Morris, 1961). Representative examples of recent colloquiums at Western Washington include "Darwin and the History of Ideas," "The Morality of Overkill," "The Comic Spirit," "The Business Corporation in American Life," and "The 'New Hero' in Modern Literature: Rebellion and Protest."

While this type of experience is pursued throughout the four years, emphasis shifts to the departments when the honors candidates become juniors. Tutorials are then devoted to satisfying the department requirements and preparing a senior thesis. Students can enter the program at the beginning of the junior year and still graduate with honors. Such recognition requires a recommendation from the Honors Board, honors work over six or more quarters, completion of at least 20 honors credits, and the preparation of a senior essay. All departments except mathematics have such a requirement.

Among small private institutions, Hiram College, in Hiram, Ohio, stands out not only for its curricular experimentation over the years but also for its comprehensive general honors program. The development of this program a few years ago coincided with the introduction of a three course–three quarter system. Each of its components is interrelated: colloquiums with honors courses, honors courses with research, and independent study (Rochford, 1964).

Issues and ideas from important books are studied in the freshman colloquium. This is not a "great books" course, however. One term is devoted to the philosophy of science, another to philosophy, religion, and literature, and the third to the social sciences. The issues come from ideas developed in honors courses in chemistry and intellectual history that are offered at the same time. Professors who give honors courses also direct the colloquiums.

The sophomore colloquium, though restricted to one quarter because of the content, parallels honors courses in the humanities. The objective is an understanding of the means by which man creates and develops knowledge through abstractions, symbols, and systems. Almost all honors sophomores take this colloquium during the first quarter and then begin independent research. This is not research in the accepted definition of the term, however. Students can, of course, prepare scholarly papers, but they are encouraged to engage in creative activity, such as writing a play, composing a piece of music, painting several pictures, or devising a laboratory experiment.

In the junior year, a single, ten-meeting colloquium on ethics, as well as social and political philosophy, is spread over two quarters. Insight into values is sought through the study of issues that divide men and require moral choices. This colloquium is interrelated with honors courses in religion, physical science, and international relations.

Every Hiram student is required to complete the Senior Liberal Studies seminar. Honors sections of this course are presented by faculty on the Honors Board. Topics range widely. The purpose is to make students aware of their liberal arts experience, establish links between the disciplines, and develop a conception of the universality of knowledge. To achieve either magna or summa cum laude, a student must participate in the general honors program and prepare a paper that earns praise from the Honors Board. Graduation with honors in major disciplines is reserved for those who complete departmental honors projects. Special topics courses are arranged so that seniors writing separate honors papers for both general and departmental honors need not be overburdened. The preparation of at least one of these papers can constitute one regular course.

Students are permitted to complete general honors without taking the core program, however. In order to attract verbally articulate but not vocal undergraduates, provision has been made to study the colloquium content independently. Students who participate in this manner meet with a faculty panel several times during a quarter and write a lengthy essay summarizing ideas and issues.

Honors are handled by large universities in various ways. Most programs are centered in liberal arts colleges and, through rigorous and often brilliant course offerings, radiate out from there. Some are guided by a central administration but are lodged in and administered by individual colleges, professional schools included. Others are universitywide in the sense that they serve as arenas where bright students from all colleges can mix intellectually. This type is founded on the conviction that an engineer or a pharmacist should be just as much an educated man as a historian or an English teacher and that an honors program should represent a community of scholars from all parts of the university (Wynn, 1966).

Of those honors programs centered in arts and sciences colleges, the University of Colorado's and the University of Michigan's stand out. At Colorado, honors students may stand for general or departmental honors or both. There is deliberate emphasis, however, on the general program that has provided such great vitality over more than 30 years' existence. Citations of Latin praise are bestowed by the Honors Council on the basis of grade-point averages, Graduate Record Examination scores, written evaluations of students by instructors in all courses, written and oral comprehensive examinations, and departmental essays (Weir, 1966).

The general program includes four colloquiums in the humanities and a large number of honors theme groups. The colloquiums are arranged historically but deal with important ideas. Freshmen begin with Greek civilization, move on to Roman in the sophomore year, and so on. The theme groups, as their name suggests, are devoted to exploring specific themes. Professors sometimes present topics outside their specialties. A sampling would show that a distinguished physicist regularly gives a theme group in Russian poetry. A brilliant classicist, known for her studies of existentialism, offers a course on that subject, while a renowned composer teaches liberal arts undergraduates to read the scores and in this way understand the music of Bach. Students are required to take theme groups outside their majors, but they are not limited in the number they can take during their four years.

Michigan's program, on the other hand, is distinguished for its imaginative interdisciplinary courses —not colloquiums—and its strong departmental programs. This program has more students (fewer dropouts) and offers more courses than any other (at least 200 a year). One of the most unusual offerings is a sequence of courses beginning in the freshman year for students with strong interests and abilities in mathematics and science; the Unified Science Program is designed to make maximum use of mathematical skills. In the first semester, participants take physics, concentrating on mechanics. In the second term they begin physical chemistry, specifically atomic theory and thermodynamics. Students study unknowns and write one long report on their research. The third semester is also devoted to chemistry. Here kinetics, the structure of atoms, and ionic reactions are studied. In the final semester they return to physics, studying light, electricity, and magnetism, as well as modern quantum mechanics. United with these courses are two different mathematics sequences.

All sophomores in this program are eligible for Unified Science Research. They interview faculty members whose research seems particularly interesting and work out arrangements. Some use these tutorials to gain an introduction to research in their field of concentration, while others use them to sample several research interests in order to make decisions on future goals. In either case, these sophomore research activities have provided the basis for lasting relationships with professors from which students have made significant contributions to knowledge through publications.

In the upper division, a series of courses prepared under the leadership of the College Honors Council provides a number of valuable and demanding experiences. "Nietzsche and Nietzscheans in Contemporary Literature" is available for students who have a sound reading knowledge of either German or French. Three different categories of works are studied: (1) original works of Nietzsche in translation, including *The Birth of Tragedy, Beyond Good and Evil,* and *Genealogy of Morals;* (2) works by modern writers influenced by Nietzsche—André Gide's *Les Caves du Vatican,* Eugene O'Neill's *Lazarus Laughed,* Thomas Mann's *Selected Stories,* and George Bernard Shaw's *Man and Superman;* and (3) articles prepared by writers like Camus, Mencken, Ortega y Gasset, and Santayana, who were either indebted to Nietzsche or critical of his ideas.

Every student is required to read the Nietzsche materials in translation as well as the books included in the second category. Of the latter, each is introduced to the class by a volunteer who assesses its literary merit and explains relationships to Nietzsche's own ideas. Various articles are assigned to individual students, who present short critical reports on them orally. These often become the basis for term papers (Seidler, 1963).

Another example is a course for nonscientists, "Revolutionary Ideas in Science," with evolutionary processes as its theme. It is taught by professors in physics, astronomy, geology, and zoology. The physicist begins with observations on motion and the concepts of mass and force in order to delineate the principles of physical behavior. The astronomer describes the origin and life cycle of the earth and sun, as well as the origin of the planetary system. His discussion of the earth as a protoplanet serves as a springboard for the geologist's presentation of the evolution and anatomy of the earth and the concept of geologic time. The zoologist, finally, emphasizes Darwinian theory as well as modern refinements in genetics and ecology. "The interdisciplinary character of the course was especially profitable to each staff member, for it enabled him to see familiar concepts applied by his colleagues in fields less familiar to him than his own. Moreover, the students profited by seeing a given concept applied to systems in different sciences. For example, the concept of entropy developed in physics reappeared with additional subtleties when applied to biological systems" (Howard & others, 1960).

Among departmental programs at Michigan, the history department's is comprehensive, rigorous, and effective. It consists of a series of four courses designed to give students a sense of participating in history as historians themselves participate. During the junior year a colloquium and a seminar on historical method are offered. The colloquium deals with a particular problem concerning an era, personality, or idea that has produced intense historical controversy (e.g., the Pirenne thesis). Conflicting interpretations are dissected and discussed in order to dissolve the idea that history is a fixed body of facts. In the methods course, students are introduced to research and writing. Subjects for honors theses are chosen and preliminary bibliographies prepared. Research is begun during the summer between the junior and senior years, and the theses are completed during the following fall semester. The course taken during the last senior term is a seminar entitled "Systems of Synthesis"—a high level survey of world history. Each week, students read and discuss works dealing with different time periods, ranging from prehistory to the modern era. Books are chosen from the classics of historical writing—Herodotus, Gibbon, Henry Adams, Burckhardt, Weber, Marx, Parrington—and offer a wide variety of important interpretations (Tonsor, 1962).

One final word concerning Michigan's program. Honors students in every large institution have discovered the difficulty of finding quiet places to study in fraternities, sororities, or those modern bedlams called dormitories. Michigan has successfully counteracted this by installing honors housing. Two houses have been set aside where honors students can continue educational processes begun in classrooms and also develop various cultural activities. Student response has been enthusiastic (Kaplan & others, 1964).

The University of Illinois typifies universitywide operations with a central administration and separate programs in liberal arts and sciences, engineering, agriculture, commerce and business administration, and other professional schools. No other university offers honors opportunities in as many professional colleges. Engineering honors is probably the most innovative and exciting program in the university (Johnson, 1961).

The University Honors Program administration is very active and also very efficient. It maintains a vigorous recruitment program, an excellent research and testing operation, a more than adequate counseling setup, and a center that effectively coordinates overseas work and off-campus awards. But owing to the atmosphere of almost complete decentralization among the colleges and the vocationalism in the university, this sound administration has been unsuccessful in stimulating the organization of an intellectually exciting curriculum. Most of Illinois' programs consist of special sections of required courses and departmental offerings. Only arts and sciences and engineering, moreover, have four-year programs. Agriculture and commerce have tried special courses, but, for the most part, these were not supported by faculty or students. A program in veterinary medical science, the only one of its kind, permits honors scholars in arts and sciences to move into the veterinary school at an accelerated pace and complete both V.M.D. and Ph.D. degrees.

Michigan State University and the University of Oregon have pioneered in establishing honors colleges as a means of creating universitywide communities of scholars. In the former, outstanding students are recognized at the end of their freshman year. When a sophomore is admitted to the Honors College, all requirements, except total hours for graduation, are waived. The outstanding characteristic of this program has been its almost completely individualized approach. Honors College students are assigned advisors, and together they plan courses of studies. These study plans must have the approval of the Honors Councils in the students' colleges, however. Every effort has been made to achieve balance and to consider the individual's general education and specialized training.

The Honors College program might include regular courses, individual study under faculty supervision, credit by examination, the waiving of prerequisites for advanced courses, and many other things. It could include, in other words, whatever seemed appropriate to the individual aims of the bright student. The one missing ingredient has been special honors courses for credit. This need has been recognized and efforts are under way to remedy the situation. This program has prospered in spite of its great dependence on competent advising (Wynn, 1966).

Where the Michigan State Honors College allows flexibility, Oregon's presents a coherent, integrated set of challenges. The Oregon faculty wanted to create a small, high-quality liberal arts institution within the university that could utilize the university's resources. To them, an honors college would provide a modus operandi for fostering a sense of community as well as a setting in which experimental approaches to instruction could be tried. Oregon's administration, on the other hand, seized the college concept as a means of budgeting honors effectively.

The Oregon Honors College has its own curriculum and its own faculty, who are, however, members of university departments. The curriculum consists of a selection of core courses during the first two years that are articulated with departmental programs that follow. In their first year, Honors College students take approximately 60 percent of their work in special experimental courses, and thereafter this percentage diminishes. In the lower division, they are required to demonstrate competence in six core areas—literature; history of Western civilization; social science (either an introduction to the social sciences or the principles of economics, logic, ethics, or the problems of philosophy); mathematics (introduction to college mathematics or analytical geometry and calculus); and science, including either biology, chemistry, physics, or a physical-science survey. Honors sections of other courses also are available. In addition to demonstrating competence in the core areas, students must also gain proficiency in a foreign language equivalent to a second-year course and take an honors sequence in English composition that includes a one-term course on expository writing and two terms of composition tutorials.

Students demonstrate competence in the core fields by passing comprehensive examinations, not by attaining certain grade-point averages. They may prepare for these comprehensives by taking all or part of the core courses or through independent reading. If a student does not take the course but passes the examination, he is given credit but no grade. Passing the comprehensives is the principal requirement for advancement into departmental honors and for graduation from the Honors College.

Departmental programs vary from field to field, but generally they include seminars, independent reading, conference sessions, research, and senior theses. All departments except mathematics require senior theses, and students are required to take comprehensives on these projects. The senior theses at Oregon differ from those required in most honors programs, however, in that there is deliberate interdisciplinary emphasis. Subjects are centered in a department, but efforts are made to design topics that will require the application of other disciplines as well. Interdisciplinary emphasis is also evident in the requirement that upperclassmen must participate in two terms of interdisciplinary colloquiums outside their major areas.

Much of the success of this program has resulted from administrative provisions. Few directors of honors programs have as much authority as the Director of the Oregon Honors College. Besides having a budget to pay departments for faculty, he also has a voice in faculty promotions. This responsibility has been given him so that effective and enlightened teaching, as well as research, will be rewarded (Ellis & Marquis, 1964; Clark, 1965).

This brief overview shows that honors methods and procedures include special sections of required courses, interdisciplinary offerings of various types, colloquiums, seminars, waivers of requirements, and independent study (both individual and group tutorials). Have these been successful? Though this is an unfair question, since success is hard to define and equally hard to measure, honors work has been judged successful by faculty members, students, and researchers in almost every on-going operation. Many professors have expressed satisfaction with their honors experiences. But such expressions are not completely reliable because faculty by and large are incapable of evaluating their own efforts. They rarely give a course with a clear understanding of what is expected of them, and, as a consequence, their appraisals are reminiscent of "And God saw everything that he had made, and behold, it was very good."

Honors students have testified to the success and value of their educations. Evaluation by student committees has been employed very successfully, especially when students have worked in cooperation with faculty members. The use of combined student-faculty groups appears to be the most effective means of boldly, critically, and continuously assessing programs (Cuzzort, 1964b). Finally, success has also been measured in terms of whether students learn more in honors courses than in regular courses. At the University of Michigan, for instance, independent researchers tried to evaluate student learning in terms of performance on the area tests of the Graduate Record Examination. They administered the tests to honors seniors and a control group of equally gifted (judged by grade-point average) students. The former scored well above the ninetieth percentile on all tests, while the latter fell below that point. This indicated that bright students who had had special treatment performed better than bright students who had not had special treatment (Graf, 1962).

Other honors research, while not dealing with "success" specifically, has presented a different picture. Almost all honors efforts have suffered from student attrition. Why do 30 to 40 percent of highly selected students in innovative programs fail to make the grade? In one burgeoning state university, with an excellent program (judged by faculty standards), freshman failures have exceeded 60 percent. Studies have been focused on selection procedures, and these have been blamed for failures. This means that programs have been right but that students selected have been wrong.

The University of Illinois has thoroughly documented this conclusion. There, students in good standing or those with at least B averages at the conclusion of the freshman year in both regular courses and special honors sections steadily declined from 61 percent in 1959 to 51 percent in 1963. These freshmen had mean high school ranks in the 94th percentile and mean verbal and mathematical test scores above the 90th percentile. In terms of high school performance and scores on standardized aptitude and achievement tests, such as the College Boards, American College Tests, and the National Merit Scholarship Qualifying Test, they were uniformly bright students—among the top 5 percent of students going to college (Damrin, 1964).

What was wrong with the selection procedure? Illinois discovered that high school records and rank in class as compared with national test scores were the least valid predictors of success. Many students testified that high school courses were not demanding and that they were often given high grades because they had gained reputations for being bright (Damrin, 1963). Scores on national tests, when considered singly, also showed low validity. When high school performance and test scores were combined, however, they identified potential for honors participation (Damrin, 1963). There were, in other words, many nonintellectual considerations that determined success. These might have been discovered through depth interviews or the use of personality instruments such as the Allport-Vernon-Lindzey Study of Values or the Omnibus Personality Inventory, to mention only two.

The University of Illinois' research proved that their honors freshmen were a heterogeneous rather than a homogeneous group with respect to ability. The university faculty had designed a program into which the students were fitted rather than one fitted to the students' talents. Among honors programs of recent origin, those with the fewest false starts have been in institutions where talent had been carefully assessed over a long period and where there was a clear and accurate picture of the nature of the institution's best students.

New curricula and methods, sprung on bright but unsophisticated undergraduates, can be a traumatic experience, but they need not be. The Honors Council of the University of Arkansas has wrestled with the question "What is an honors section?" throughout the ten-year history of the program (Hantz, 1965). Two types of courses have been identified, the novel course and the extended course.

The novel course represents a significant departure in purpose, content, and method from regular courses. Concepts are analyzed, evidence is examined critically, and a measure of "discovery" is introduced by allowing students to investigate in depth subjects of their own choosing. Developing inquiring minds is emphasized. Extended courses, by way of contrast, are simply extensions of regular offerings. Such courses are on a higher level because more work is required (Hantz, 1965).

The Arkansas Honors Council discovered that instructors who had prepared novel offerings were more satisfied with their own performance and less critical of the abilities of their students than other instructors were. The expectations of teachers and students seemed to mesh. Professors in extended courses, on the other hand, were critical of their students' competence. Their objective was to get deeper into the course work by providing more of the same thing. They had not discarded the conception that students are like vending machines: You put something in, and you get something out; if students are bright, the return should be greater.

What is the significance of such findings? The problems of honors programs are not different from the problems of undergraduate education generally. Research at Illinois, Arkansas, and elsewhere has presented in bold relief many of the inadequacies of undergraduate instruction. We cannot afford to regard our students as a uniform, homogeneous whole. More should be known about their abilities and aspirations. The content of higher education must be changed, and more flexibility and freedom must be introduced into the system so that individual aspirations might achieve some fulfillment. An honors program with a limited number of students, a limited number of courses, and a select group of dedicated faculty could serve as an ideal setting for experimentation. An honors program, in fact, should perform a dual function. It should provide for educating the talented, but, more important, it should be a laboratory where a critical assessment of undergraduate education could be carried on with a view to improving the whole enterprise.

Philip I. Mitterling
University of Colorado

References

Adams, Henry L., and Blood, Don F. "Creative Potential in Honors Students." *Sup Stud* 7:41–3; 1965.

Anderson, James R. "An Honors Student Assesses Graduate Education." *Sup Stud* 7:14–8; 1965.

Angell, Robert C. "Issues in Honors." *Sup Stud* 3:18–24; 1960.

Aydelotte, Frank. "Honors Courses in American Colleges and Universities." *B Nat Res Council* January; 1924.

Aydelotte, Frank. *Breaking the Academic Lockstep: The Development of Honors Work in American Colleges and Universities.* Harper, 1944. 183p.

Bryan, J. Ned. "Talent and Today's Schools." *Sup Stud* 6:3–9; 1963.

Cadbury, William E., Jr. "Challenging the Superior Student in the Small Private College." In Cohen, Joseph W. (Ed.) *The Superior Student in American Higher Education.* McGraw-Hill, 1966. p. 191–219.

Clark, Robert D. "Unsolved Problems in Honors." *Sup Stud* 7:5–11; 1964.

Clark, Robert D. "Organization of an Honors College." *J H Ed* 36:313–21; 1965.

Cohen, Joseph W. "Changing Attitudes of Students and Teachers Toward Scholarship." *Sup Stud* 5:8–15; 1962.

Cohen, Joseph W. "Development of the Honors Movement in the United States." In Cohen, Joseph W. (Ed.) *The Superior Student in American Higher Education.* McGraw-Hill, 1966(a). p. 9–25.

Cohen, Joseph W. "The First Coordinated Effort: The ICSS." In Cohen, Joseph W. (Ed.) *The Superior Student in American Higher Education.* McGraw-Hill, 1966(b). p. 25–50.

Copley, Frank O. *The American High School and the Talented Student.* U Michigan Press, 1961. 92p.

Cuzzort, Ray P. "Contrasting Commitments to Talent." *Sup Stud* 6:3–9; 1964(a).

Cuzzort, Ray P. "Evaluating Honors Programs." *Sup Stud* 6:3–8; 1964(b).

Cuzzort, Ray P. "The MA-3 in 1964." *Sup Stud* 6:3–10; 1964(c).

Cuzzort, Ray P. "The Superior Student in Graduate School." *Sup Stud* 7:3–13; 1965.

Damrin, Dora E. "College Honors Courses: Privilege or Penalty? A Comparative Study of Academic Grades." Research Report No. 5. U Illinois, 1962(a). (Mimeographed.)

Damrin, Dora E. "James Scholars' Opinions Regarding the Creation of an Honors Residence Hall." Research Report No. 6. U Illinois, 1962(b). (Mimeographed.)

Damrin, Dora E. "Student Attitudes Toward the Honors Program at the University of Illinois." *Sup Stud* 4:11–4; 1962(d).

Damrin, Dora E. "High School Students' Preparation for College Work." Research Report No. 8. U Illinois, 1963. (Mimeographed.)

Damrin, Dora E. "Selection of Edmund J. James Scholars at the University of Illinois, Urbana Campus." Research Report No. 9. U Illinois, 1964. (Mimeographed.)

Damrin, Dora E. "Selection of Honors Students at the University of Illinois." *Sup Stud* 7:23–8; 1965.

De Rocco, Andrew G., and Holland, Morris K. "Effectiveness of the NSF Undergraduate Science Program: An ICSS Survey." *Sup Stud* 5:3–14; 1963.

Ellis, Robert A., and Marquis, Lucian. "Evaluation of the University of Oregon's Honors College." *Sup Stud* 6:23–6; 1964.

Fenton, Edwin. "Honors Programs in the Secondary School." In Cohen, Joseph W. (Ed.) *The Superior Student in American Higher Education.* McGraw-Hill, 1966. p. 219–53.

Fricke, Benno G. "An Evaluation of Assessment Procedures." *Sup Stud* 7:3–9; 1965.

Graf, Otto G. "Does Honors Work? An Evaluation of the Honors Program at the University of Michigan." *Sup Stud* 4:8–10; 1962.

Hantz, Harold D. "A Decade of Honors." Arkansas, 1965. (Mimeographed.)

Hantz, Harold D., and Trapp, E. Philip. "Evaluation of Honors at the University of Arkansas." *Sup Stud* 6:27–9; 1964.

Heist, Paul, and Langland, Lois. "Evaluating Honors Programs: History, Problems, and Prospects." In Cohen, Joseph W. (Ed.) *The Superior Student in American Higher Education.* McGraw-Hill, 1966. p. 253–82.

Holton, Gerald, "Physics and Culture: Definition of Goals and Proposals for Science Instruction." *Sup Stud* 5: Insert 21 p.; 1963.

Howard, William F., and others. "An Experimental Interdisciplinary Course in Science for Gifted Nonscience Majors." *Sup Stud* 3:3–9; 1960.

Johnson, Robert E. "Programs and Problems: The University of Illinois All-university Honors Program." *Sup Stud* 4:2–5; 1961.

Kaplan, Stephen, and others. "Honors Housing Opportunity at the University of Michigan." *Sup Stud* 7:14–5; 1964.

Kreith, Frank, and Allen, J. M. (Eds.) *Honors Programs in Engineering.* Allyn and Bacon, 1964. 175p.

Langland, Lois. "Selection Procedures for Gifted and Honors Programs at UCLS." *Sup Stud* 7:29–33; 1965.

Lewis, Lanora G., and others. *Talent and Tomorrow's Teachers: The Honors Approach.* HEW, 1963. 83p.

Mitterling, Philip I. "A Plea for Teaching." *Sup Stud* 6:1–2; 1964(a).

Mitterling, Philip I. "The Honors Frontlash." *Sup Stud* 7:3–4; 1964(b).

Mitterling, Philip I. (Ed.) *Proceedings of the Conference on Talented Women and the American College: Needed Research on Able Women in Honors Programs, College and Society.* Cooperative Research Project No. F-028. USOE, HEW, 1964(c). 181p.

Mitterling, Philip I. "The Removal of Redundancy." *Sup Stud* 6:1–2; 1964d.

Mitterling, Philip I. "Selection of Talent: A Problem?" *Sup Stud* 7:1–2; 1965.

Morris, Bertram. "Colloquia at the University of Colorado: The Colloquium Is Not a Course." *Sup Stud* 4:20–1; 1961.

Phillips, M. Jean. (Compiler.) *Index of Honors Programs in Institutions of Higher Education.* Stipes, 1967.

Reithel, Francis J. "Honors and the Sciences." In Cohen, Joseph W. (Ed.) *The Superior Student in*

American Higher Education. McGraw-Hill, 1966. p. 166–91.

Rochford, Paul A. "Evaluating the Honors Program at Hiram College." *Sup Stud* 6:34–5; 1964.

Sanford, Nevitt. (Ed.) *The American College.* Wiley, 1962. 1084p.

Seidler, Ingo. "Honors Courses & Seminars: Nietzsche and Modern Literature, University of Michigan." *Sup Stud* 5:17–8; 1963.

Swarthmore College Faculty. *An Adventure in Education: Swarthmore College Under Frank Aydelotte.* Macmillan, 1941.

Tennille, Norton Fortune. "A Student View of Education for the Academically Talented." *Sup Stud* 2:3–4; 1960.

Tonsor, Stephen J. "Departmental Honors Programs: History, University of Michigan." *Sup Stud* 4:20–1; 1962.

Tyler, Ralph W. "Research on Honors: The Social Sciences and Honors Programs." *Sup Stud* 4:15–21; 1961.

Waggoner, George R. "Departmental Honors at the University of Kansas: A Case History." In Cohen, Joseph W. (Ed.) *The Superior Student in American Higher Education.* McGraw-Hill, 1966. p. 137–66.

Weir, Walter D. "Honors and the Liberal Arts Colleges." In Cohen, Joseph W. (Ed.) *The Superior Student in American Higher Education.* McGraw-Hill, 1966. p. 75–96.

Wynn, Dudley, "Honors and Creative Writing." *Sup Stud* 5:20–4; 1963.

Wynn, Dudley. "Honors and the University." In Cohen, Joseph W. (Ed.) *The Superior Student in American Higher Education.* McGraw-Hill, 1966. p. 96–137.

IMPROVEMENT OF EDUCATIONAL PRACTICE

The approach to the improvement of educational practice is dependent on how educational practice is viewed. One view of educational practice sees it as the maintaining of an educational system, or some part of that system, such as a curriculum design, evaluation instrumentation, a teacher role, or instructional materials. On the other hand, educational practice can be viewed as a series of related activities, each designed in relationship to the other, with the expectation of producing certain predetermined outcomes in students' behavior.

The first approach has the shortcoming of introducing educational practices that may or may not be relevant to desired outcomes. The possibilities for systematic evaluation are very few. The relevant judgments as to cause and effect are almost impossible to document.

The second approach allows the construction of a series of models based on the nature of the students and outcomes desired from educational operations. Taken as a whole, some of the elements of the model would appear to be the following:

1. Outcomes desired.
2. Characteristics and needs of students.
3. Hypotheses regarding means to produce outcomes.
4. Experiences deemed necessary to produce outcomes.
5. Characteristics of the learning environment required to provide experiences.
6. Tools and materials required to provide experiences.
7. Teacher roles in managing the learning environments.
8. Other human roles in operating the learning environment.
9. Evaluation systems to determine outcomes achieved.
10. Instrumentation to measure the relationship between outcome and means.
11. The systematic development of instrumentation to measure the effectiveness, efficiency, and costs of means in securing outcomes desired.

When one approaches the proposition of what is the "best" way of conducting an educational program, more often than not he deals primarily with one item or a few items of the model, without relating to the other units in some specified framework. Thus, prescriptions for changing curriculum, or for the use of a variety of types of instructional materials, or for different ways of managing the learning environment are proposed, but rarely is an analysis made of the relationships among the several elements of a model.

Defining terms is an arbitrary but necessary part of the verbal treatment of issues relevant to improvement of educational practice. "Change," "innovation," and "improvement" are three critical terms that, unfortunately, are sometimes used as if they were equivalent. "Change" is the most expansive of the three terms. "Innovation" and "improvement" are more restrained words, each in a different way. Any alteration of the status quo constitutes change, whether or not the alteration is innovative or is an improvement. Any alteration or change which brings an identifiably *new* element to the situation would be an innovation. In an objective analysis of a social change, "innovation" is a value-free term. It should not be used to connote a bettering or worsening of the situation. The term implies only a change which has some element of newness or novelty. Even to use "innovation" to denote an unproved alteration or an experimental change is confusing, since the simple word standing alone should not be given, by association, the negative tone of "unproved" or the positive tone of "experimental." The only element that "innovation" adds to "change" is the matter of newness. "Improvement" is the only strongly denotive term among the three. This word is strongly value-oriented. It would be easy enough to establish that a social situation has or has not changed and only slightly more difficult to establish that a change is or is not innovative, but to establish that a change, whether or not innovative, is an *improvement* is a much more complicated matter.

There is need to use these three terms with care and discrimination, because even in their casual uses, they reflect motives. Each of the terms, "change," "innovation," and "improvement," when contained in a statement of aspirations, reveals a different set of motives. The desire to change reflects a dissatisfaction with the status quo. It indicates little more than a willingness to exchange a present situation for another situation. It implies very little value orientation other than the devalued existing status quo.

The intention to innovate reflects a motivation to achieve distinctiveness through newness. It shows dissatisfaction with or rejection of the status quo in the more precise terms of predictions or judgments of its archaic character or its obsolescence. "Innovate" implies the sort of change that updates or brings uniqueness. It does not necessarily imply a call for prior experimentation, investigation, or evaluation with respect to any terms other than the criterion of newness.

The motives reflected in the correct use of the term "improvement" are essentially value-based. To want something to be improved reflects both negative and positive valuing. The status quo is perceived to have aspects of negative values. The needed change is given positive value. This value represents the anticipated gains in conformity to a "good" model of activity which they will help produce. Thus, there are at least three elements present in the correct use of the term "improvement": the *change* of the status quo, *direction* of the change toward a desired model, and *assessment* of the results of the change. It is difficult to imagine a bona fide improvement in an educational enterprise lacking any of these elements.

In summary, the terms have these meanings and reflect these motives:

change: alteration in order to make different
innovation: alteration in order to renew, make new, or add new elements
improvement: alteration in order to
(1) change an inadequate status quo,
(2) direct changes toward a projected model, and
(3) assess the outcome against the former status quo.

Improvement, then, is a value-based concept. Evaluation of alteration to establish whether or not improvement can be claimed demands separate assessment of goals, process (methods of arriving at change), and outcomes of the changed entity. With special reference to the field of education, defining "improvement" raises questions about the value and relevance of goals, and the efficiency and effectiveness of procedures which attempt to reach these goals.

VARIETIES OF OBSOLESCENCE. Educational institutions can be obsolete in many ways. Obsolescence of goals or functions, obsolescence of methods, and obsolescence of management are three problems confronted by the educational administrator in a changing society.

Whether or not the basic values of a society are changing, the functions of the institutions within the society are constantly in process of being reassigned among the institutions. The secondary school's responsibility for the function of vocational efficiency was commonly accepted earlier in the twentieth century—but before the century is out this function may shift away from the secondary school to some new vocational-training school for certain students and to the university for others. Administrators and teachers who continue to orient the institution toward functions that have or should have shifted to some other institution contribute to the obsolescence of the school.

Another aspect of obsolescence of functions is that of refusing to accept new or newly assigned functions for the institution. Whether or not the secondary school is the "right place" for driver education, the legislatures of many states have assigned the function of developing driver proficiency to the local high school; thus, while refusing to accept the responsibility might be academically defensible, the high school which lacks such a program will tend to be obsolete.

The functions of most educational institutions have not been adequately defined. Much might be gained from a thorough taxonomic analysis of each level and kind of school within the American society (Bloom, 1956; Krathwohl & others, 1964). The lack of clearly specified and commonly held functions and goals in education makes functional obsolescence difficult to diagnose.

Obsolescence of method gets much attention. The simplistic argument for employing new procedures seems to be very attractive: the new way should be employed because it is new; the old way should be abandoned because it is old. Motivation to adopt the "new" may be like the legendary motivation for mountain climbing ("because it is there"), or it may be a compulsion to identify with the new modes of culture. Regardless of motivation, the new methods are taking hold. In a technological age, classrooms are still largely manned by those who seem suspicious of technology. Yet the current changes in method are increasingly technological (Goodlad & others, 1966). Television has entered the classroom, a variety of optical projection devices are in common use, the tape recorder is running, the computer is on the threshold. It is tempting to think of the lecture and the blackboard as being obsolete. But the deeper issue of method obsolescence is elusive. The shifts in perceptual styles and learning processes which may be already upon us demand a reassessment of the instructional environment of today's schools (Culkin, 1967). The loss in effectiveness of the institution that has become methodologically obsolete can be serious.

The school is acquisitive and the classroom is absorptive. Problems are created when technological changes and new curricular units provide little demonstrable change in efficiency or effectiveness. Problems also arise when new curricula and techniques are added to the program of the school without any discarding of less effective ways. The institution which cannot effectively balance its input of the new with its discarding of the old is not likely to operate efficiently or economically. Finding ways to maintain fiscal integrity in the face of a potential overload of new functions and new methods is a compelling administrative problem (Norton, 1963).

Educational institutions must find efficient balances, must seek ways to compare the relative merits among alternative expenditures, and must determine what functions are to be reduced or eliminated in order to make room for the new. A management system incapable of dealing with these issues risks becoming seriously obsolete. Much innovation begins with some sort of a cost-effectiveness model in mind. Team teaching, instructional films, educational television, programmed instruction, individualized scheduling, and other innovations to come represent to teachers additional ways to add variety to the basic teaching procedures. To the efficiency-minded administrator they represent ways to supplant part of the present teaching procedure. Therein lies the conflict.

Many teachers seem overly ready to resist anything which either is difficult for them to understand or challenges their superiority or autonomy (Miller, 1967). Unless an innovative procedure or device is an "aid to the teacher" it is likely to be put on the closet shelf. Management which cannot overcome this human resistance to change is not likely to stimulate much improvement in educational practice.

But teacher resistance is not the only barrier to educational improvement. Another is the fault of management and is attributable to the incapacity of leadership to inject new ideas. The roots of this incapacity may lie in lack of imagination, lack of external viewpoints (becoming ingrown), or failure of the internal communication processes.

Change and potential change threaten people. Growth and development of an organization is easily stalemated when management stimulates beyond the tolerance of the subordinate staff. Impasse occurs when the worker interprets pressure for change as management's inability to appreciate the worth of his present contributions. The issues of improvement and leadership style are intertwined. Management which cannot effectively infuse new ideas is ineffective.

FORCES FOR CHANGE. Seeking progress and development through deliberate change and widespread applied experimentation with untried procedures can be interpreted as a reflection of the American historical tradition. If this be so, the tradition is becoming more a recognized attribute of institutionalized education. Feared and resisted for many years, expanded federal aid to education is now a reality and, ostensibly, is largely employed as an incentive and resource for change. The "traditionalist" finds it hard to adjust to the newly recognized thrust for innovation. The scholar who requires defensible evaluative evidence for assumptions about expected results of proposed change is similarly uncomfortable in the current situation (Harris, 1963).

The current topical emphasis on innovation can be taken both as a sign of vitality in the educational enterprise and as an evidence of a basic weakness in contemporary education: the incapacity to evaluate proposed change. This latter is reflected in the trends of research on innovation. At the heart of the current spate of studies of innovation is the concept of "change processes" (Brickell, 1961; Carlson, 1965; Kurland & Miller, 1966; Merz, 1967; Rogers, 1962). Many researchers are viewing innovation as a problem of process more than as a question of *substance*. Studies of change are commonly quantitative rather than qualitative.

The emotional impact of Russian space technology has energized the forces of change in American education. Since 1957 there has been an acceleration of major modifications in the educational system. Uneasiness about the soundness of the American educational establishment has made it increasingly unpopular to resist change. The ambivalence of the public toward the higher costs of education consequent on change has served as a major retarding force. And the style of inducements has changed: there seems to be less of the hostile postwar attack on teacher education and of the bitter vilifications of the McCarthy-era curriculum purges. In their place there are more "bandwagons" on which the change-minded members of the educational community take stimulating rides.

A drive toward a more technological and technology-utilizing curriculum has had wide public support. The curricular swing has been toward the technology-related subjects. Thus, the objectives of two educator factions have been served: those whose concern is for a more organized and more up-to-date approach to science and mathematics, and those who advocate a wider utilization of technological aids to instructional communication. A secondary effect has been the acceleration of experimentation with patterns of instructional organizations and management (College Entrance Examination Board, 1966; Heath, 1964).

The subject-matter competence demanded for effective teaching of the new curricular materials places the current general-purpose teacher in a difficult position. At the same time, increased use of nonhuman instructional mediation allows—perhaps demands—an alternative to the old concepts of teacher role, self-contained classrooms, and compartmentalized learning. Thus, the field of education is opened to the new approaches of human engineering and man-machine concepts of system analysis and system development (Egbert, 1964).

If processes of social change can ever be orderly, those observed in current educational innovation must be described as disorderly. Lacking adequate theory, such vital elements as instruction, educational-resource deployment, and the associated cost-effectiveness relationships are affected by unrelated changes. Evaluation is inadequate to describe the effects, to say nothing of predicting consequences.

In seeking ways to make the processes of educational change more orderly, a major handicap exists within the social structure of the school. Carlson (1965) finds that the social status of the chief decision makers functions as a barrier to their seeking advice. He further cites as major barriers to educational change the absence of a "change agent," the weak knowledge base in education, and the "domestication" of the public school as a noncompeting, passively accepting institution.

MOTIVATION FOR IMPROVEMENT. There are two fundamentally different concepts which may be at work in an educational organization that is concerned with improvement: the concept of perfectibility and the concept of dynamic equilibrium. These concepts are essentially descriptive tools for theoretical analysis of social institutions. The concept of perfectibility is essentially static, inasmuch as it assumes that a realizable ideal state exists, which, once achieved, would require no further change.

On the other hand, the concept of dynamic equilibrium sets up an expectation for continuous change. The institution is seen in a certain relationship, or set of relationships, to larger social entities, functions, and needs. In the introductory paragraphs of this paper the elements of a model were briefly outlined. These items illustrate the range of activities which must be kept in balance in an equilibrium model. As the social entities, functions, and needs change—and regardless of the forces which make them change—the educational institution is expected to respond with appropriate alteration to maintain its balanced role of interdependence within the social whole (Gardner, 1963).

In the practical sense, the equilibrium concept motivates people to alter the educational institution continuously so that it can contribute optimally toward meeting the ever-changing needs of the society. The concept is dynamic in that it assumes a constant state of change; it assumes a developing set of functions and needs in the social whole to which the institution must be constantly readjusting.

The fundamental difference in these two concepts of improvement leads to correspondingly different perceptions of what it means to "catch up" or, more precisely, to improve a social institution which is "behind the times." In the first concept, "catching up" is the temporary problem of overcoming a deficiency. In the second concept, the constant task of "catching up" is a permanent problem of staying in a proper relationship with the rest of a changing society.

It is not unusual to find educational leaders and segments of the public talking and acting as if the schools are perfectible (Keppel, 1966). But there are likely very few who would argue the hypothetical proposition that a "perfected" school in 1940 would still be adequate today. In fact, there may be a danger in a school's becoming too finely tuned to the needs of a given moment in history. When an educational institution becomes so thoroughly adjusted to a given time and place, it may become "stabilized." Rather than maintaining a *dynamic* equilibrium it can become rigid in a moment of static balance. Even as a biological organism rejects an alien organ, the educational institution can become so entrenched within a given set of functions that it rejects the incursions of the new elements that would give it renewed life for a new time.

The forces for improvement are people: people with ideas or with biases, people with hope or with fear, people who are selfish or altruistic. The mixture of these characteristics is usually very complex, and research on the forces and processes of change is a relatively new undertaking. But, clearly, the people forces are at work today. Some have stimulated far-reaching federal legislation and the needed funds to experiment on a broadly based front. Some declare that the nation's internal difficulties reflect basic weaknesses in its educational systems. Others see in education the only hope for healing the world's ideological schisms. Whether these people work together or neutralize one another in their disagreements, they all seem to recognize that education has a substantial contribution to make toward solving the problems of an obviously changing society. Thus, manifold stimuli for educational change have arisen. Some of the people forces are content with change. They contend that nothing can be worse than what we now have. Other forces demand innovation: it is not enough merely to change; there are so many new things we now know how to do and so much new information to teach. Still other people forces require some assurance that change is improvement: education, they claim, is too important to trust to the forces of haphazard change or unevaluated innovation.

AREAS OF INNOVATIVE CHANGE. Hardly an area of the educational establishment has been untouched by some sort of development, experiment, or arbitrary change since mid-century. Developmental activities include the use of educational television, ranging from single-school, closed-circuit operations to wide-area aircraft transmission and plans for statewide cable linkages. Massive efforts have been expended on curricular reorganization of the content in mathematics, biology, physics, and chemistry and, to a lesser extent, English and social studies. The use of programmed instruction has increased. The teaching of foreign languages has been deeply affected by audiolingual approaches made possible by tape recorders set up as "language laboratories" (Goodlad, 1966).

The utilization of teaching personnel has been changed in various patterns of "team teaching." Especially in the secondary school, there has been a shift of attention to the individual learner and a provision for more or less independent study situations ranging from a varied and daily modified "flexible schedule" to deliberate teaching of independent investigative strategies ("discovery methods").

To accommodate these new techniques and procedures, a somewhat different educational plant is needed. School plant planners have busily moved toward a more campus-like school layout, adding more leisure and independent-study facilities, clustering schools of all levels within "educational parks," and laying out classrooms in team-teaching clusters with screens and sliding walls for additional breaking down of space for small-group activities. The lecture-television hall idea has been borrowed from higher education to become a dominant feature of new senior and junior high schools. More "middle schools" are coming into existence, drawing fifth-, sixth-, and seventh-grade children (sometimes eighth-grade as well) into a separate organizational unit.

Audiovisual devices are being used increasingly. Their basic forms have been changed very little in the past decade, but their convenience in use and the increased availability of teaching materials for use in them has led to wider acceptance. It is widely speculated that computer-controlled devices will constitute the next large-scale innovation for the audiovisual field (Goodlad, 1966; Lumsdaine, 1964; Miles, 1964; Educational Testing Service, 1965).

EVALUATING CHANGE. The view of change, whether innovative or not, as being no improvement until proved to be improvement, places a high value on evaluative activity. If American education is to capitalize on the growing public consciousness of education's essential role in national survival, the next decades will be distinguished by refinements and increased capabilities of educational evaluation. Reliable and prompt feedback on the effects of changes is an essential element in an adaptive educational system.

Most important, of course, is the evaluation of any change in the educational system to determine its qualitative effects on learners and their learning. But there are other aspects of the matter of educational improvement which demand evaluation. First, there is the matter of evaluating costs in some sort of comparative terms; this evaluation can be seen as a part of the overall assessment of the "improvement" factor. Comparative study of the effects of curricular change on learning variables presents difficult problems for research design which are made even more complicated by adding the relation to cost variables.

The procedure used to induce change in the educational institution presents another problem for evaluation (Harris, 1963). Normative studies of the change process are now fairly common. Evaluative procedures may conceivably be forthcoming from this line of research; what is needed is a procedure, or procedures, which can assess the effectiveness of the management of institutional change. It is reasonable to assume that decisions about ways of injecting new ideas, soliciting suggestions about change from within the staff, and stimulating and rewarding innovative behavior are vital. Thus, if the basis on which these decisions are made can be assessed, the feedback of the assessment data could help to build a more reliable basis for the selection of change-inducing management procedures.

RESEARCH ON EDUCATIONAL CHANGE. Treating the diffusion of educational innovation as a researchable problem was itself an innovation of the 1930's. The work published by Mort and Cornell in 1938 reflected the empirical study of school systems as adaptive (innovative) social entities. A subsequent report (Mort & Cornell, 1941) provided data concerning the "rate of acceptance" curve, based upon a quantitative concept of adoption rate, changing over time as an evidence of the waxing or waning of an innovative idea's popularity. Factors which affect the rate of adoption have become the major concerns of research in educational innovation; presence or absence of these factors is thought to be an indication of a school's disposition toward or readiness for change.

Mort's early work was coincident with the landmark studies of adoption of agricultural innovations (Hoffer, 1942; Ryan & Gross, 1943). Study of the rate of adoption of technological innovations in agriculture, and the study of the rate of adoption of new educational practices, have been essentially simultaneous research developments. They spring from similar needs for data about means of interfering with the "natural" rate of change and the identification of optimal environments for introducing innovative practices (Trotter, 1934). These two fields of research have borrowed much from each other; researchers occasionally rediscover the similarities of the two problems.

Studies of the effects of particular innovative techniques have been increasing. Carlson (1965) examined the adoption of "modern math" programs and programmed instruction in terms of an assumed "natural history" of educational innovations in general. His emphases were upon the determinants of rate of adoption and rate of diffusion. His report underscores unpredicted consequences of adoption of the innovation. He observed that differences in the structure of "opinion leaders" in the two locales studied were related to the adoption patterns. He was also able to deduce a generalized description of the innovative person in the school setting.

Whether the findings of research in educational innovation (or in agricultural dissemination) can themselves be disseminated and adopted in the form of prescriptive plans and procedures for planning educational improvement is as yet uncertain.

The profession at large is becoming more aware of educational change, innovation, and improvement. The awareness is focusing on a series of adaptations of procedures, techniques, and equipment from other fields. Among these are two which promise a significant effect on the matter of educational change itself, making possible a more improvement-oriented change process (Borko, 1962).

The electronic computer is being employed as an information storage and retrieval medium. It is now feasible to design dissemination systems which are selectively focused on prime users of data about educational change. More information can be handled and handled faster than has been possible with topical journals and unclassified reports. A further advantage is the increased selectivity available to the information searcher (Kent, 1962). Computers can manage search problems which human efforts (and patience) would find unmanageable.

A companion trend-making development is the scientific study of information users. Communication research is contributing to thought about educational change and the decision-making functions basic to change. Investigation of the effects of information upon the roles and procedures in educational development can lead to more-informed, more-evaluable, and less-intuitive change procedures in education.

One of the basic differences between the testing of a changed procedure in education and a change in either agriculture or medicine is the place where experimentation takes place. In fields which have well-developed laboratories for evaluation of a technique or material before it reaches the dissemination phase, an ill-advised change is brought to an appropriate end before it has either large-scale public notice or widespread practitioner involvement. Lacking a highly organized evaluative laboratory, education often puts the dissemination step ahead of the testing. Thus, innovations can lead to widespread, undesirable outcomes before data about their consequences are available; perhaps the fear of this possibility is one of the more important roots for educators' resistance to change. It is widely hoped that the Regional Educational Laboratories program of the U.S. Office of Education will serve to relieve this problem (Keppel, 1966).

Lippitt (1965) cites other factors which distinguish change processes in education from those in other fields. He calls attention to the necessity of some degree of change in practitioner attitudes, skills, and values if a change is to be given a fair chance; the "invisible" quality of many important innovations; the lack of an organized engineering wing of the profession; the lack of agents of change; the social pressures which inhibit change; disarticulation from other behavioral fields; and the reluctance to alter a public system wherein the public is so quick, bold, and powerful in reacting. He further identifies these models of curriculum change: retrieving expert knowledge, identifying curricular innovations, collaborative action research, experimental feasibility testing, and employing deliberate diffusion strategies.

RESEARCH RELATING TO CHANGE. American education today is becoming more fluid. Social upheavals of the century have left their marks. Some even argue that producing change-oriented individuals is a requirement for the contemporary school—and in order to engage successfully in the production of this sort of output, the school itself must be constantly changing. Goslin (1965) relates this proposition to the observable social flux: (1) increased specialization and bureaucratization, (2) demographic changes, (3) urban-suburban dichotomization, (4) revolution in race relations, (5) increased government involvement and creation of interdependent functions and (6) cultural change springing from mass media.

The status and role of the teacher have changed dramatically in the twentieth century. Trends are growing toward making the teacher less an information dispenser and more a catalyst and facilitator of independent study. The teacher's role and status are a reflection of the forces which influence the nature of education (Lee, 1966). The teacher is what the educational system demands; thus, study of attributes and roles of the teacher is an appropriate method of inquiry into the nature of education. Current innovations are heavily oriented toward technological advances in communication media; schools are changing both in terms of added technical resources and in terms of the management aspects of scheduling and manpower deployment which the new resources demand for any sort of efficient utilization.

The changes brought about by instructional resources relate back to forces in the social environment. Contemporary education can be seen as being responsive to (1) mass production and automation, (2) job unpredictability and technological unemployment, (3) a belief in a "good future" and faith in changes being for the better, (4) demands for equalized quality of instruction, (5) federal investment in technical resources, (6) concern for those overlooked by previous educational systems, (7) the necessity of organizing and more carefully selecting subject matter, and (8) the shifting of educational responsibility from the teacher to the student (Dale, 1966).

In an early descriptive study, Ebey (1940) found the principal's opinion and the nature of the community to be the most important among eight selected factors related to a schools' capability of changing. Other factors concerned teacher opinion, age, and recency of training, parent participation, and other essentially demographic matters. Ebey also identified "adaptation patterns" through his efforts to relate evidences of change in the operations of a school to factors influencing adaptability. The six patterns described in his research differ in terms of the formality or informality of the change processes, and of internal or external forces promoting the particular element of change.

Ross (1955) views adaptability as a school's capacity to take on newer and more appropriate educational practices. He has discovered positive correlations between adaptability and per-pupil expenditures, wealth of school district, percentage of business and professional constituents in community, and the school staff's years of training, travel experience, salary, and possession of personal libraries. Unlike many studies of this sort, Ross attempts to treat the cost effectiveness of an innovative educational practice, not just its newness.

The findings which lead Ross to a generalization about the more experienced teachers being the more adaptable or innovative are not consistent with a number of other studies. For example, Willower (1963) reports a study conducted in a large junior high school which leads him to conclude that norms and standards maintained by the older teachers stressed firmness, social distance from the students, and preservation of the status quo. Further, he finds change resistance to be less characteristic of specialists and newer faculty, who would make small-scale changes related to improving the quality of their own work.

THE ROLE OF RESEARCH IN PLANNING EDUCATIONAL IMPROVEMENT. Pellegrin (1965) has attempted to explain the small influence of educational research on the planning of educational improvement. He criticizes the research for a failure to attack the problems which are seen by the practitioner as crucial. He further cites low quality and lack of sophistication in research design, and hence an output of research which cannot command the attention of the planner of change. In turn, he criticizes the planners' failure to distinguish empirical facts from values and his general ignorance of the worth of research.

Hope is frequently expressed that the impact of behavioral science research, in general, will have the effect of making educational planning more research-dependent. The sheer weight of data about human behavior will demand its own attention. Education will be permeated by the empirical facts about perception, personality, learning, social dynamics, leadership, and communication. Thus, research would have an indirect but definite bearing on the planning of improvement (Glaser, 1966).

Such indirect impact may be slow in coming. The requisite changes in knowledge and outlook of educational administration may be a generation away, because there is no particular reason to expect major change in the low rate at which innovations are adopted in the professional training institutions (Barrington, 1953).

Educational improvement continues to be a major challenge for educational research. In essence, innovation and other educational change has been a matter of treating symptoms rather than the basic mechanisms which produce the symptoms. The current state is largely one of emphasis upon the activities of teachers without adequate reference to the outcomes or effects of those practices. Change, particularly innovation, has been largely a concern for tools rather than for processes and functions. For example, the use of television is supposed to produce certain outcomes effectively or efficiently. Exactly what outcomes it is to produce is a matter often left untreated when reviewing television as an innovation. It is not enough to say that educational practice is improved because television is used—instead the focus should be upon *what* improvements in the teaching and learning processes television permits or provides. Instructional techniques can easily get out of touch with the learning phenomena they purport to mediate.

Educational practice can be viewed on the one hand as an instructional-technique problem or, on the other hand, as a behavioral-science problem which requires a whole system of functions in order to provide a basis for improvement. The concept of teaching as a professional practice with its basis in behavioral science owes much to educational research. The shift from "keeping school" to practicing education demands even more from its empirical data base. The practitioner of education functions as a clinical worker: he observes, diagnoses, prescribes, treats and evaluates. He cannot innovate or otherwise change his practice without anticipating consequent changes in the outcomes of his practice. Piecemeal innovation must give way to a broader concept of change which begins with a specification of desired outcomes, moves to analyze characteristics and needs of students, and then to hypothesize and test experiences, environments, materials, and roles in terms of the achievement of the desired outcomes.

Ted W. Ward
Michigan State University
John E. Ivey, Jr.
Michigan State University

References

Barrington, Thomas M. *The Introduction of Selected Educational Practices into Teachers Colleges and Their Laboratory Schools.* Teachers Col, Columbia U, 1953.

Bloom, Benjamin S. (Ed.) *Taxonomy of Educational Objectives,* Handbook I: *Cognitive Domain.* McKay, 1956.

Borko, Harold. *Computer Applications in the Behavioral Sciences.* Prentice-Hall, 1962.

Brickell, Henry M. *Organizing New York State for Educational Change.* New York State Department of Education, 1961.

Carlson, Richard O. *Adoption of Educational Innovations.* U Oregon Press, 1965.

College Entrance Examination Board. *The Challenge of Curricular Change.* CEEB, 1966.

Conant, James B. *Shaping Educational Policy.* McGraw-Hill, 1964.

Cremin, Lawrence A. *The Transformation of the Schools.* Knopf, 1961.

Culkin, John M. "A Schoolman's Guide to Marshall McLuhan." *Saturday R* Vol. II, March 18, 1967.

Dale, Edgar. "Instructional Resources." In *The Changing American School,* 65th Yearbook, NSSE. U Chicago Press, 1966. p. 84–109.

Ebey, George William. *Adaptability Among the Elementary Schools of An American City.* Teachers Col, Columbia U, 1940.

Educational Testing Service. *New Approaches to Individualizing Instruction.* ETS, 1965.

Egbert, R. L. "System Design for Schools." In Bushnell, Don D. (Ed.) *The Automation of School Information Systems* NEA, 1964. p. 128–31.

Gardner, John W. *Self-renewal: The Individual and the Innovative Society.* Harper, 1963.

Glaser, Robert. "The Design of Instruction." In *The Changing American School,* 65th Yearbook, NSSE. U Chicago Press, 1966. p. 215–42.

Goodlad, John I. *The Changing School Curriculum.* Fund for the Advancement of Education, 1966.

Goodlad, John I., and others. *Computers and Information Services in Education.* World Bk, 1966.

Goslin, David A. *The School in Contemporary Society.* Scott, 1965.

Harris, C. W. (Ed.) *Problems in Measuring Change.* U Wisconsin Press, 1963.

Heath, Robert W. (Ed.) *New Curricula.* Harper, 1964.

Hoffer, C. R. *Acceptance of Approved Farming Practices Among Farmers of Dutch Descent.* Michigan Agricultural Experiment Station, 1942.

Kent, Allen. "Problems in the Use of Electronic Data Processing for the Storage and Availability of Research Data." In *Dissemination and Implementation.* PDK, 1962. p. 1–47.

Keppel, Francis. *The Necessary Revolution in American Education.* Harper, 1966.

Krathwohl, David R., and others. *Educational Objectives,* Handbook II: *The Affective Domain.* McKay, 1964.

Kurland, Norman D., and Miller, Richard I. *Selected and Annotated Bibliography on the Processes of Change.* State of New York, 1966.

Lee, Gordon C. "The Changing Role of the Teacher." In *The Changing American School,* 65th Yearbook, NSSE. U Chicago Press, 1966. p. 9–31.

Lionberger, Herbert F. *Adoption of New Ideas and Practices.* Iowa State U Press, 1960.

Lippitt, Ronald. "Roles and Processes in Curriculum Development and Change." In *Strategy for Curriculum Change.* ASCD, 1965. p. 11–28.

Lumsdaine, A. A. "Educational Technology, Programmed Learning, and Instructional Science." In *Theories of Learning and Instruction,* 63rd Yearbook, NSSE. U Chicago Press, 1964. p. 371–401.

Merz, William R. "Education and the Process of Change." *Educational Leadership* 24:561–7; 1967.

Miles, Matthew B. (Ed.) *Innovations in Education.* Teachers Col, Columbia U, 1964.

Miller, Richard I. (Ed.) *Perspectives on Educational Change.* Appleton, 1967.

Mort, P. R., and Cornell, F. G. *Adaptability of Public School Systems.* Teachers Col, Columbia U, 1938.

Mort, P. R., and Cornell, F. G. *American Schools in Transition (How Our Schools Adapt Their Practices to Changing Needs—A Study of Pennsylvania).* Teachers Col, Columbia U, 1941.

National Society for the Study of Education. *The Changing American School.* 65th Yearbook. U Chicago Press, 1966.

Norton, John K. *Changing Demands on Education and Their Fiscal Implications.* National Committee for Support of Public Schools, 1963.

Pellegrin, Ronald J. "The Place of Research in Planned Change." In *Change Processes in the Public Schools.* U Oregon, 1965. p. 65–75.

Rogers, Everett M. *Diffusion of Innovations.* Free, 1962.

Ross, Donald H. *Measuring Institutional Quality of School Systems.* Teachers Col, Columbia U, 1955.

Ryan, B., and Gross, N. "The Diffusion of Hybrid Seed Corn in Two Iowa Communities." *Rural Sociol* 8:15–24; 1943.

Trotter, I. P. "The Effectiveness of Ten Years of Agronomic Extension Work in the Missouri Clover and Prosperity Program." *J Am Soc Agronomy* 26:561–9; 1934.

Willower, Donald J. "Barriers to Change in Educational Organizations." *Theory into Practice* 2:257–63; 1963.

INDEPENDENT SCHOOLS

Since the term "independent school" is relatively new, it will be well to start with an attempted definition. The term "nonpublic," used in government statistics, is not very useful, since it includes such a wide variety of schools. The classification of elementary and secondary schools as public, private, and parochial is also less than satisfactory. For one thing, although the "parochial" classification is usually taken to mean Roman Catholic schools, not all Catholic schools are parochial, and not all parish schools are Catholic. For another, the term "private" has connotations of exclusiveness, and the public often thinks of private schools as being privately owned, although the reverse is usually the case. The leaders in the realm of nonpublic, non-Catholic schools, over the past generation or so, have used the word "independent," and this is gradually becoming accepted.

What is an independent school? In contrast to the public school, it is supported chiefly by nonpublic funds, and it is controlled by a nonpublic body, usually a board of trustees. It is relatively independent of state control; conditions and regulations vary from state to state, but as a general rule it has considerable freedom to set its own standards and curriculum, admit and dismiss students, and hire and dismiss teachers, without state supervision or control. It is free, legally, to incorporate religious teaching in its curriculum, and free, practically, to encourage discussion of controversial topics. Of course, it must meet health, fire, and safety standards, and the state has ultimate control in the equivalency laws. The independent school is usually nonsectarian, but a moderate degree of church affiliation can be tolerated within the term "independent" if control by the church is minor or nonexistent and the school's board is essentially in control of its destinies and responsible for its management and support, as in the case of most Friends schools and Episcopal schools, for example. In these days almost all independent schools are incorporated not-for-profit, but there are still a few "proprietary" schools on the scene. It will be seen that the definition is not an exact one, but on the whole it is effective in differentiating the independent school not only from the public schools but also from schools which are part of a church school system, in which the individual school is under substantial control from a central church authority.

HISTORY. There were few private schools in the colonies in the seventeenth century (Morison, 1956). During the eighteenth century, when the Latin grammar schools offered a curriculum heavily weighted with classical studies, enterprising schoolmasters (Seybolt, 1925) came forward with private schools which performed a service by their flexible response to the needs of the time, providing instruction in practical subjects such as navigation, geography, and languages, as well as reading and writing; and private schools for girls were available too.

The academies, which flourished roughly from the Revolution to the Civil War, were legitimate predecessors of the modern independent school. Founded mostly by private initiative, though often having partial public support, these schools under relatively private control offered a curriculum of greater breadth than the narrow curriculum of the Latin school (Sizer, 1964). At one time, around 1850, there were more than 6,000 academies with over 250,000 pupils, but they faded away, or were converted to other uses, when the urban concentrations of population provided the tax base which could support a public high school.

At least four independent schools now operating date from the seventeenth century: Roxbury Latin School, founded in 1645; The Collegiate School in New York City, founded in 1638; the Hopkins Grammar School in New Haven, Connecticut, founded in 1660; and the William Penn Charter School in Philadelphia, founded in 1689. Since the Collegiate School was essentially a public school for a number of years, Roxbury Latin School, with its board of seven "feoffees" independent of the Town of Roxbury, can lay claim to being the oldest independent school in the country (Hale, 1946).

Governor Dummer Academy in Massachusetts, founded in 1763, is the oldest boys' boarding school still operating, and two of its early graduates shared in the founding in 1783 of Phillips Academy, Andover (Fuess, 1917, 1963), whose purpose was declared to be to instruct youth and "more especially to learn them the great end and real business of living." This academy was endowed, was incorporated not-for-profit and had a permanent board of trustees, the majority of whom were to be laymen and a majority nonresident. Thus, it is typical of many boarding schools of today.

Later years saw the appearance of military academies and especially of religious schools—Baptist, Catholic, Jewish, Lutheran, Presbyterian, Seventh Day Adventist, and others; and, principally in the Northeast, a great many boarding schools for boys (including a number with Episcopal Church affiliation) and for girls.

If any kind of independent school is "typical," it is probably the country day school. Although there were plenty of independent day schools in the nineteenth century, the country-day-school movement is generally considered to have begun with the foundation of the Gilman School in Baltimore in 1897. The emphasis of this type of school is on a location outside of the city (and many urban day schools, from choice or from force of circumstances, have moved to country locations), on an all-day program with athletics for all, and on sustained parent-teacher cooperation in the educational process.

TODAY'S SITUATION. In the 1960's there are about 4,000 nonpublic secondary schools and over 14,000 nonpublic elementary schools in the United States (Gertler, 1961, 1964), and in them are enrolled about 11 percent of all the students in secondary schools and about 15 percent of all the students in elementary schools, a total of about 6.7 million in nonpublic schools (Simon & Fullam, 1965). By far the largest part of these numbers are in Roman Catholic schools, which are the subject of a separate article elsewhere in this volume. The remainder comprises some 1,000 non-church-related and 2,900 church-related elementary schools with about 400,000 students, and in the secondary area about 1,500 schools (800 nonsectarian, 700 church-related) with nearly 200,000 students. According to our definition not all of these schools can be counted as truly independent schools, but certainly a large part of them can be. Over 90 percent are nonprofit schools.

When the totals are broken down state by state, and taking only the nonsectarian schools, we find that over one-third of them are in five states (New York, California, Pennsylvania, Illinois, Ohio), while six states have no nonsectarian independent schools at all. Analyzed by type of school, on the basis of the membership of the National Association of Independent Schools (1965, NAIS) they can be classified approximately as follows:

Girls' day	19.0 percent
Girls' boarding	6.2
Boys' day	15.5
Boys' boarding	19.6
Coeducational day	17.6
Coeducational day–elementary	16.1
Coeducational boarding	6.0
	100.0 percent

With regard to size, quite a few have less than 100 students; the majority have between 100 and 400. And with regard to their approach to education, there is much healthy diversity.

Teachers. The independent schools make a point of a low pupil–teacher ratio and of a correspondingly close teacher–pupil relationship, and this comes out strikingly in government statistics on nonpublic elementary schools (Gertler, 1964), where the pupil–teacher ratio for church-related schools is shown as 39.5 : 1, and for nonsectarian schools as 12.3 : 1. Figures compiled by NAIS from time to time show correspondingly low figures for secondary schools, often less than 10 : 1 for boarding schools and 12 : 1 for day schools.

Because of the insistence of the independent schools on pupil–teacher ratios of this order of magnitude, their problem of paying adequate salaries without raising tuition fees to astronomical heights has been accentuated, but they have not compromised on the basic principle. As a consequence, increases in independent-school salaries, though they have been substantial, have not on the whole kept pace with those in public school salaries.

With regard to the training of teachers, the administrators of independent schools have in the past looked somewhat suspiciously at the courses offered in schools of education and on the whole have preferred for the secondary schools teachers with thorough advanced knowledge of the subject to be taught and master's degrees, to those with a number of semester hours in "education" and a more modest contact with the subject. This point of view has resulted in some difficulties with certain regional accrediting agencies and with state education authorities in some areas. Indeed, in one part of the country many of the demonstrably best independent secondary schools have preferred to forgo formal accreditation rather than choose their teachers only from among those with the credentials in education specified as necessary by the regional accrediting agency.

However, this point of view has recently been modified, or at least less rigidly adhered to, as shown by a pamphlet prepared and widely circulated by NAIS (National Association of Independent Schools, 1958). The development of Master of Arts in Teaching programs has been well received by the independent secondary schools.

Program. There are, of course, independent schools for various special purposes, such as schools for the deaf, for the emotionally disturbed, for retarded children, and for children with severe reading or other disabilities; but basically the secondary independent school is a college-preparatory school, and the elementary independent-school program is designed for children who are expected to move eventually to a secondary college-preparatory school. The typical elementary school has a full program including the three R's, social studies, and science and good opportunities in art and music and handwork. One may well find a foreign language started on an oral-aural basis in the lower grades, and French, Latin or both seriously begun in the seventh or eighth grade, with first-year algebra covered in the eighth.

In a secondary school one may expect to find, in addition, of course, to four years of English, an offering of four or five years of mathematics, two or three languages, a year of each of three sciences with a second year of at least one, and several history courses. In a great many schools there are major courses in music and art available for those specially interested and minors in these subjects required of all. The larger schools, especially those with a selected student body of high academic potential, present many additional courses not found in the ordinary college-preparatory curriculum and offer advanced-placement courses in each of the sciences and in nearly every subject of the advanced-placement program.

Some figures collected by the U.S. Office of Education are pertinent and interesting (Gertler, 1965). The nonpublic secondary schools in 1961–62 devoted 14 percent of their offerings to foreign languages and 9 percent to music and art; the corresponding figures for the public schools in 1958 were 6 percent and 3 percent, respectively. Seventy-seven percent of all the students in nonpublic schools were studying foreign languages, compared with fewer than 30 percent in the public schools.

INDEPENDENT SCHOOLS AND THE STATE. There would be few, if any, in the school world, public or nonpublic, who would deny that the state has the right and the duty, in order to promote responsible citizenship, to pass compulsory attendance laws and, further, to require that nonpublic schools provide an education "equivalent" to that offered by the public schools. Some zealots would like to go further and outlaw the nonpublic school, but the legal right of these schools to exist has been affirmed by the U.S. Supreme Court in the Oregon case. The Oregon legislature in 1922 passed a law requiring all normal children between eight and sixteen who had not completed the eighth grade to attend public schools, beginning in September 1926. The law was challenged by a church school and a nonsectarian military academy, and the case eventually reached the Supreme Court, which in 1925 ruled, in *Pierce* v. *Society of Sisters* and *Pierce* v. *Hill Military Academy*, 268 U.S. 510 (1925), that the law was unconstitutional, using the following words:

> We think it entirely plain that the Act of 1922 unreasonably interferes with the liberty of parents and guardians to direct the up-bringing and education of children under their control. . . . The fundamental theory of liberty upon which all governments in this Union repose excludes any general power of the State to standardize its children by forcing them to accept instruction from public teachers only. The child is not the mere creature of the State; those who nurture him and direct his destiny have the right, coupled with the high duty, to recognize and prepare him for additional obligations.

State laws affecting independent schools are numerous and varied (Beach & Will, 1958). One authority asserts (Erickson, 1961) that 20 states have made no significant provision for regulation, another 20 have imposed controls that range from moderate to demanding, and in the remaining 10 one or another phase of school operation, such as curriculum, teaching methods and pupil–teacher ratios, is subject to state direction.

It is safe to say that most established independent schools would prefer a minimum of state regulation and particularly wish to avoid regulations which would limit their choice of the best teachers they can find. And they can point to their successful records and good standing as evidence that regulation is not needed; for, after all, if a school that charges tuition does not do a good job with its students, it will not long survive. They tend to view with alarm any proposal for licensing which would place unreasonable difficulties in the way of people wanting to start new schools and point to numerous examples of thriving and useful institutions which started on the proverbial shoestring.

On the other hand, the reputable established schools are sometimes plagued by the appearance on the scene of schools of questionable or definitely shoddy character, which tarnish the image of independent education and which a sensible regulatory policy would not have allowed to operate. So in some states the associations of responsible independent schools have joined forces with the state education authorities in a cooperative effort to assure respectable standards in nonpublic education in the state. But in no case yet, it may be said, has there been found a fully satisfactory answer to the problem of devising legislative and administrative methods by which the state can ensure the educational standards necessary for good citizenship without seriously damaging the diversity which it is one of the nonpublic school's functions to provide (Erickson, 1961).

State Aid. The issue of state and federal aid to nonpublic schools has generated much heat. Tax exemption is, of course, a form of aid; it is vital to the existence of the independent school, and so far no serious threat of removing the exemption, as applied to land and buildings used strictly for educational purposes, has developed. Direct aid to church-related schools is not possible under the constitution, but various forms of indirect aid are in force, justified on the ground that the aid is to the children or the teachers rather than the school.

Examples are the providing of textbooks and bus transportation, permitted by some states; eligibility (for schools incorporated not-for-profit, all but a small minority) for the special milk program, the distribution of surplus foods, the school lunch program, and the distribution of surplus property. Loans are available to nonprofit schools for buying equipment to improve education in various subjects of the curriculum. Nonprofit schools are exempt from manufacturers' and retail excise taxes. Public and independent schoolteachers alike are eligible for free tuition plus stipends for attending government-sponsored institutes for advanced study as well as for fellowships under the Higher Education Act of 1965, and are covered in the "forgiveness" feature of the National Defense Education Act (NDEA) loans to college students. Under the Elementary and Secondary Education Act of 1965 nonpublic schools can acquire library resources and textbooks and can take part in programs for increasing community educational resources; these provisions are sure to be challenged in the courts on the ground that they are, in fact, aid to the schools. (La Noue, 1966).

Administrators and trustees of independent schools fear that regulations and controls will inevitably accompany government aid and are accordingly wary of such aid, as shown by a poll of its members by NAIS showing 88 percent against federal grants to independent schools, 65 percent against loans to such schools (National Association of Independent Schools, 1961). There was a favorable vote (74 percent) on a proposal to provide tax relief for parents paying tuition fees, but this would be of only indirect aid to the schools. The funds available under the NDEA for loans for purchasing laboratory equipment were only partially used. On the whole it seems that whatever the problems, the majority of those responsible for the independent schools would rather *be* independent than depend on government aid.

THE INDEPENDENT SCHOOLS AND THE PUBLIC. The Oregon case guaranteed the right of the independent schools to exist. But should they? There have always been some who because of their dedication to public education or for some other reason have resented the existence of nonpublic schools. Two examples will suffice. In the Inglis Lecture at Harvard University in 1930 Briggs (1930) complained that the private schools were too independent of control and regulation, that they weakened or destroyed the interest of their patrons in public education, that an insignificant number did any useful pioneering, and that the 2,500 secondary schools did not contribute enough to justify their existence.

In an address before the American Association of School Administrators in 1952, Conant, then president of Harvard University, stated his conviction that independent schools were a divisive influence and that the more young people who attend such schools, the greater the threat to the country's democratic unity (Conant, 1952). It would be better, he said, if all young people attended comprehensive high schools together, and in his opinion the local control by school boards would assure the diversity that was desirable—an opinion that is at least debatable (Erickson, 1961).

Critics have emphasized the studies that show public school graduates outperforming the independent-school graduates in college (Seltzer, 1948; Koos, 1931; Educational Testing Service, 1954; Shuey, 1956). But Scholastic Aptitude Test scores, used to equate the academic ability of the two groups, reflect to some degree one's cultural and educational background. Even more important, undoubtedly, is the matter of motivation, and one factor affecting motivation is the economic. A Yale study (Crawford, 1929), examining students' records without reference to the type of secondary school attended, found that academic achievement had an inverse relationship to economic advantage: the higher the family income and students' annual expenses, the lower the academic grades. Interestingly enough, an excellent high school in a rich suburban area once found that the college records of its graduates fell disappointingly short of their academic potential. But all the published studies are ten years old or more, and an up-to-date study is needed, in view of new factors which have developed since the time they were conducted.

Innovation. For years the independent schools have insisted that their freedom to experiment is an important reason for their existence, and although by no means all have felt an urge to pioneer, a number of innovations, begun in independent schools, have been adopted in public education, as acknowledged by Inglis (1918): "practically every new movement in secondary education has begun in some private or semi-private institution and only gradually been adopted by the public high school."

Circumstances in recent years have, of course, brought on major experimentation in the public schools. Independent schools have, however, had an honorable share of the leadership in more than one important movement. One example is the progressive education movement, in which many independent schools and school people had a prominent part (Cremin, 1961), though by no means all independent schools enrolled under the banner of progressive education. Of the 30 schools in the Eight-Year Study, for instance, a program initiated to encourage experimentation in college preparation and to test the results on college admission and success in college (Aikin, 1942), 16 were independent schools.

Again, independent schools were among the leaders in furthering the advanced-placement program; they had a prominent part in two studies which started the movement which permits able students to study freshman courses while still in school and go on to more advanced work on entering college. The first was the work of three independent schools in collaboration with representatives of three liberal arts colleges (*General Education in School and College*, 1952) and contained "A Proposal for an Experiment in Advanced Placement." The second was known as the School and College Study of Admission with Advanced Standing, and in it 12 colleges and 27 schools, 10 of them independent, collaborated. Seven pilot studies were conducted, three of them in independent schools. The report of the study's Central Committee appeared in 1953 (Chalmers & Cornog, 1953), and the first examinations were given in 1954. In 1955, 38 schools presented 925 candidates; half the schools were independent schools, and they presented half the candidates. Now, of course, public school candidates are heavily in the majority, but the independent schools played an important part in getting this innovation started.

In other ways the independent schools have either led the way or shared the leadership. The first summer enrichment program for specially able boys was instituted by a New Hampshire independent school, not for its own students but for talented boys from schools in the state who could not find suitable advanced work in their own schools (Potter, 1966). Independent schools have taken a lively part in the movement to provide a variety of experiences for disadvantaged children (Yeomans, 1965). Independent boarding schools have joined together to help find and then help educate Negro boys and girls and other disadvantaged children whose home circumstances would give them little chance for an education suited to their needs and capacities (Potter, 1966). An independent school initiated a program involving several independent and public schools and colleges in providing instruction in the Chinese language (Potter, 1966). The name of the Emma Willard School, an independent school for girls, is a reminder that the independent schools played a pioneering part in fostering education for women. In 1961 NAIS published a booklet describing a number of curricular and other experiments in independent schools (Mallery, 1961)—none of them, perhaps, of vital significance to precollege education, but at least evidence that these schools are not standing still. And as this article is being written, the same national association is helping lead the way to better programs in sex education (Yeomans, 1966) and to more effective use of moving pictures in schools (Mallery, 1966).

Problems. As with any educational institution, the independent school has problems, and they are mostly financial. Contrary to the general impression, few schools have any substantial endowment, and with costs, especially salaries, constantly rising, balancing the budget becomes difficult. Schools try to keep tuition fees within reach of as many families as possible while providing the maximum amount of scholarship aid to help able children and make the student body as nearly as possible a cross-section of society. In 1965–66, 500 NAIS members awarded $12-million in scholarships to over 15,000 boys and girls (National Association of Independent Schools, 1965). For most schools the answer is annual giving by graduates, parents and friends; from this source came nearly $14-million in 1964–65 in support of about 500 schools. In this figure is included a small amount from corporations under matching-gifts programs which a number of businesses maintain for their employees.

A second concern of the schools is to correct a number of misconceptions held by the public. Many people cherish one or another (and some people all) of the following illusions: that independent schools are run for somebody's private gain, that they are all richly endowed, that they are "exclusive," that they are only for the rich and/or for disciplinary cases, that children from poor families cannot gain admission, that attendance at an independent school guarantees admission to highly selective colleges, that the New England boarding school is typical of all independent schools.

A third concern has already been mentioned, that of the shoddy or fly-by-night school which occasionally springs up and creates a damaging impression of the "private school." A somewhat similar concern is more recent, namely, the appearance in some Southern states of new "independent" schools formed only to help parents keep their children out of desegregated public schools. Responsible independent school people feel no kinship with such schools and give them no help. A study of its membership by NAIS in the fall of 1966 showed that about two-thirds of the approximately 700 member schools had a total of some 3,600 Negroes in their student bodies and that all but a small fraction of the schools have open-enrollment policies.

NAIS is the organization whose purpose is to represent the independent schools and help them. It has offices in Boston, 25 regional associations, and a membership of some 700 independent schools of all types, whose enrollments total about 220,000 students.

The association, besides representing the schools at the national level, keeps them informed on federal legislation, publishes (four times a year) the *Independent School Bulletin*, collects and publishes information about practices in the independent schools (including figures on gifts, scholarship programs, salaries, and the like); sponsored a book on independent school operation (Johnson, 1961); sponsors seminars for independent school administrators; and runs an annual conference which brings together several thousand teachers and administrators for three days of meetings and discussions. Some of its publications have already been mentioned.

THE FUTURE. Published figures point to an increase, not a decrease, in the number of independent schools and their enrollments. For example, 178 new nonsectarian independent elementary schools and an undetermined portion of 700 secondary schools were established between 1950 and 1961 (Gertler, 1963, 1964). Among nonsectarian schools only, the number of independent elementary schools nearly doubled from 1940 to 1961 (566 to 1,022). The enrollment in these schools increased 2½ times (42,154 to 106,825) in the same period (Gertler, 1964), and their share of the nonpublic school population showed a substantial gain. The government's published figures do not permit a similar comparison for secondary schools.

Despite such encouraging figures, those directing the destinies of the independent schools are conscious of the challenges of the future (Day, 1965). These schools, depending on private support, will find it hard to maintain themselves in an era of vastly improving public education supported with massive federal funds. Constantly rising salaries plus the cost of keeping up with technological advances increase the difficulties. The small, highly individualized operation is at a disadvantage in many ways in a mass-oriented culture. And ever-present is the problem of avoiding isolation from the main stream of education and society.

Philosophically the role of the independent school has been defined by detached commentators as being that of "saving" the public schools from the dangers of a monopolistic system of education (Hechinger, 1964) and of preserving the humane in education in the face of increasingly methodological and mechanistic perspectives in the public schools (Wheeler, 1966). More practically, the survival in strength of the independent school, in its particular aspect of free enterprise, will presumably depend on its offering something distinctive that cannot be found in public education and on there being enough people wanting that something, and able to support it with tuition and gifts.

Research about independent schools has been slight; more is much to be desired. A bibliography on the subject has been compiled (Anderson, 1959) but now needs to be up-dated. The library of the Harvard Graduate School of Education houses the NAIS respository of some of the literature, to which additions are constantly being made and which is available for scholars wishing to work in this field.

Francis Parkman
National Association of
Independent Schools

References

Aikin, W. M. *The Story of the Eight-year Study.* Harper, 1942. 157p.
Anderson, Pauline. *A Selected Bibliography of Literature on the Independent School.* National Association of Independent Schools, 1959. 120p.
Beach, Fred F., and Will, Robert F. *The State and Nonpublic Schools.* HEW, 1958. 152p.
Briggs, Thomas H. *The Great Investment.* Harvard U Press, 1930. 143p.
Chalmers, Gordon K., and Cornog, William H. *Reports of Committees, 1952–53.* The School and College Study of Admission with Advanced Standing (Philadelphia), 1953. 193p.
Conant, James B. "Unity and Diversity in Secondary Education." *Vital Speeches* 18:463–5; 1952.
Crawford, A. B. *Incentives to Study.* Yale U Press, 1929. 194p.
Cremin, Lawrence A. *The Transformation of the School. Progressivism in American Education, 1876–1957.* Random, 1961. 387p.
Day, Richard W. "The Independent School in 1975." *Independent Sch B* 24:15–8; 1965.
Educational Testing Service. *Academic Performance of Public and Private School Graduates at Princeton.* ETS, 1954.
Erickson, Donald. "On the Role of Nonpublic Schools." *Sch R* 69:338–53; 1961.
Fuess, Claude M. *An Old New England School; A History of Phillips Academy, Andover.* Houghton, 1917. 548p.
Fuess, Claude M. An unfinished typescript, cut short by the author's death in 1963, on the history of the independent school. (The writer of the article acknowledges with thanks the kindness of the author's son in making available the typescript.)
General Education in School and College. Harvard U Press, 1952. 142p. A Committee Report by Members of the Faculties of Andover, Exeter, Lawrenceville, Harvard, Princeton, and Yale.
Gertler, Diane B. *Nonpublic Secondary Schools, Directory 1960–61.* HEW, 1961. 106p.
Gertler, Diane B. *Statistics of Nonpublic Secondary Schools, 1960–61.* HEW, 1963. 53p.
Gertler, Diane B. *Statistics of Nonpublic Elementary Schools, 1961–62.* HEW, 1964. 48p.
Gertler, Diane B. *Subject Offerings and Enrollments, Grades 9–12, Nonpublic Secondary Schools, 1961–62.* HEW, 1965. 167p.
Hale, Richard W., Jr. "The First Independent School in America." *Pub Colonial Soc Massachusetts* 35: 225; 1946.
Hechinger, Fred M. "The Mission of the Independent School." *Andover B* (Phillips Academy, Andover) Winter: 2–5; 1964.
Inglis, Alexander J. *Principles of Secondary Education.* Houghton, 1918. 741p.
Johnson, William. (Ed.) *A Handbook for Independent School Operation.* Van Nostrand, 1961. 296p.
Koos, L. V. *Private and Public Secondary Education; A Comparative Study.* U Chicago Press, 1931. 228p.
La Noue, George R. "The Title II Trap." *Phi Delta Kappan* 47:558–63; 1966.
Mallery, David. *New Approaches in Education. A Study of Experimental Programs in Independent*

Schools. National Council of Independent Schools, 1961. 192p.

Mallery, David. *Beyond All Those Books.* National Association of Independent Schools, 1965. 56p.

Mallery, David. *The School and the Art of Motion Pictures,* rev. ed. National Association of Independent Schools, 1966.

Morison, Samuel E. *The Intellectual Life of Colonial New England.* New York U Press, 1956. 288p.

National Association of Independent Schools. *The Preparation of Teachers for Secondary Schools.* The Association, 1958. 52p.

National Association of Independent Schools. *Report No. 65:* The Association, 1961.

National Association of Independent Schools. *Report No. 15.* The Association, 1965.

Potter, Cary. "Cooperative Summer Enrichment Programs." B Nat Assn Sec Sch Prin 50:283–94; 1966.

Seltzer, Carl C. "Academic Success in College of Public and Private School Students: Freshman Year at Harvard." J Psychol 25:419–31; 1948.

Seybolt, Robert F. *Source Studies in American Colonial Education. The Private School.* U Illinois Press, 1925. 109p.

Seybolt, Robert F. *The Private Schools of Colonial Boston.* Harvard U Press, 1935. 106p.

Simon, K. A., and Fullam, M. G. *Projections of Educational Statistics to 1974–75.* HEW, 1965. 68p.

Sizer, Theodore R. *The Age of the Academies.* Teachers Col, Columbia U, 1964. 201p.

Shuey, Audrey M. "Academic Success of Public and Private School Students in Randolph-Macon Woman's College. I: The Freshman Year." J Ed Res 49:481; 1956.

Wheeler, James E. "The Distinctive Character of Independent Schools." Independent Sch B 26:9–13; 1966.

Yeomans, Edward. *And Gladly Learn. Summer Enrichment Programs for Urban Children.* National Association of Independent Schools, 1965. 50p.

Yeomans, Edward. *NAIS Institute on Sex Education.* National Association on Independent Schools, 1966. 24p.

INDIVIDUAL DIFFERENCES

THE PREVALENCE OF INDIVIDUALS. A teacher who deals with 300 students each year for forty years—a fairly long teaching career—will never encounter any two who are precisely alike. If he were able to teach twelve million or twelve billion human individuals instead of twelve thousand, the same statement would hold true. The uniqueness of the individual is a fundamental principle of life.

As Williams (1956) has demonstrated, human beings differ anatomically, physiologically, and biochemically from one another in every characteristic for which measurements have been made. Organs of the body, such as the heart and the stomach, differ markedly in size and shape. The chemical composition of body fluids, such as saliva and urine, shows considerable variation. Heart rate, respiration rate, and other such process variables show the same variability. Lacey (1950) has reported that individuals show their own characteristic patterns of response to stressful situations. In short, if we consider many characteristics simultaneously, there is no "normal" person who might serve as a medical standard against which others can be evaluated.

However, it is psychological individuality which is of the greatest importance to education. Each student in a classroom, no matter how carefully selected as a member of a "homogeneous" group, will of necessity react in his own unique way to the situation. There are differences in talents and aptitudes, in interests and motives, in habits and response styles, in emotional needs and vulnerabilities. In education as in medicine, there is really no "norm." When a teacher makes an assignment to a class of 30, it is actually 30 different assignments that are carried out.

It is evident that psychologists who wish to study human behavior and educators who wish to develop it in desirable directions need some way of organizing the enormous complexity of individual differences in order to develop general principles about human nature or strategies to carry out educational purposes. It has been a question of some interest to philosophically minded psychologists whether any classification system can be validly applied to the realm of human personality. Gordon Allport (1937) has been the most articulate American spokesman for the point of view that nomothetic research methods, such as rating all members of a group on the same rating scale, can never give us satisfactory answers to questions about individuality because they assume that individuals differ from one another only quantitatively, not qualitatively. To study these qualitative differences we must use *idiographic* techniques and observe characteristics peculiar to each individual we study, such as the quality of his voice that distinguishes it from all others. Controversy has revolved around the scientific status of idiographic research. Can a generalization made about one unique individual be considered a *scientific* statement? While this question has never been definitely answered, both nomothetic and idiographic approaches to understanding individuals have continued to be employed. Whether he is familiar with the terms or not, a successful teacher uses both sources of knowledge in his work.

In pursuing nomothetic knowledge, three systems of imposing structure upon human diversity have been devised. The first is to construct a typology and sort individuals into type categories. The oldest of these goes back to the dawn of human history; the latest to be widely used is Sheldon's threefold division into endomorphs, mesomorphs, and ectomorphs, with their accompanying viscerotonic, somatotonic, and cerebrotonic temperaments (Sheldon & others, 1940). The trouble with crude typologies is that individuals do not conform very closely to the type descriptions. In a system like Sheldon's this difficulty is obviated by a much finer differentiation into subtypes intermediate between the extreme type categories.

The second way of imposing structure on diversity is to sort people out into natural groups based on sex, race, or age. Schools have also found it convenient to consider the retarded and the gifted as groups of this kind, although they often find it difficult to draw exact boundaries to delineate such groups. Much of our accumulation of knowledge in the psychology of individual differences has come out of research in which this strategy has been used, and much of our organization for education is of this kind. While sex has not been generally used as a basis for classification of pupils in American public schools, it is a common one in many parts of the world. Until recently it has seemed natural in this country to draw sharp distinctions between Negroes and whites for educational purposes. Sorting according to age has been a prominent feature of our educational system. As a sole or principal means for dealing with human diversity, sorting into natural groups is far from satisfactory. There is too complex an assortment of differences within each group to warrant treating its members in the same way.

The third system devised for imposing order on the complex field of individual differences is to identify separate traits, work out techniques for measuring them, and evaluate individuals by assessing them with as many of these trait measurements as we wish. This is the dominant mental-testing approach to differential psychology, upon which large sections of applied psychology are based. There is some ambiguity in the concept of traits, and giving a trait a name can erroneously suggest a tangible existence for something that is really only an abstraction from behavior. The first trait to be intensively studied by psychologists, intelligence, has often been misinterpreted in this fashion. It is misleading to think of intelligence as something an individual "possesses" or "contains." It is simply a word we have chosen to use to refer to aspects of the behavior he exhibits in various specified situations. Any trait should perhaps be expressed as an adverb rather than a noun.

Partly because of this ambiguity, partly for mathematical reasons, psychologists specializing in the measurement of human characteristics have shifted to the more abstract concept of *dimension*. Any aspect of behavior to which numbers from low to high can meaningfully be attached can be considered a dimension. An individual's score or rating shows where one would locate him in some sort of hypothetical space. The relationships between dimensions can then be explored in order to permit us to make sounder statements about the nature of psychological differences. Factor analysis is the technique devised for this purpose. It has been an invaluable research tool in differential psychology, as the question "In what ways (along what dimensions) do individuals differ in their response to a given kind of stimulating situation?" is the first question to be answered before detailed research can proceed.

This way of imposing structure on differences is often called "trait and factor" theory to differentiate it from other approaches to the study of personality. It is really not a theory at all but simply a means of proceeding in research and practice. The investigator first singles out some aspect of behavior for consideration, then devises some way of measuring it in an appropriate group of subjects, and uses the average score of the group as a reference point for individual scores. Many systems of derived scores have been constructed, all having the same purpose—to indicate how far above or below the average of a defined group an individual is with respect to the characteristic measured.

PRINCIPAL TRAITS OR DIMENSIONS. The first characteristic to be singled out for research is intelligence. In the light of evidence produced during recent decades, it would be more accurate to speak of "intelligences" than simply "intelligence," but, singular or plural, this aspect of human functioning is of tremendous importance in human affairs and is closely tied in with a host of educational concerns.

The assumption of the early mental testers that an IQ obtained by a competent examiner using a reliable, well-standardized test would remain constant throughout the life of the person tested has turned out to be in need of modification. Longitudinal studies reported by Honzik and others (1948) and Sontag and others (1958), corroborated by less extensive studies in many parts of the country, have demonstrated that individual IQ's are not completely constant. Some children improve their relative positions; others show a decline. While most of them show changes of not more than 15 points during the school years, an occasional extreme shift of as much as 50 IQ points occurs. Whether a child increases or decreases in intellectual level is related first of all to the intellectual or educational level of his family (Bayley, 1954) and second to his own temperamental characteristics (Sontag & others, 1958). Boys are more likely than girls to show increases. Independent, aggressive, competitive boys increase more than those not showing these qualities. Children's IQ levels come to resemble those of their parents more closely as they mature, and even those who are reared by their true parents show a closer resemblance to them than to their adoptive parents (Honzik, 1957).

These deviations from complete IQ constancy should not cause one to lose sight of the fact that the correlations between scores on intelligence tests for successive years are positive and fairly high. Rising from practically zero for infant tests, through about .40 for preschool tests given between the ages of two and five, from about six on the correlations of early scores with scores at some later age are typically about .7 or .8 (Bradway & Thompson, 1962). Bright children tend to remain bright, dull children to remain dull.

Another major research effort, from Spearman's early work (1927) to the current large-scale, computer-based factor analyses, has been focused on the structure of mental abilities. The classic demonstration by Thurstone (1938) that correlations between scores on different varieties of intelligence tests lent support to a hypothesis that there are at least seven identifiable kinds of mental ability was followed by studies suggesting that even finer differentiations were possible. The most sophisticated and definitive research on this problem has been carried out by Guilford (1959.) In his system the abilities themselves are classified along three dimensions—contents, products, and operations. Empty cells in the three-dimensional cube Guilford uses to portray the system graphically suggest new kinds of intellectual ability not previously tested. One of the most valuable features of this theoretical formation is that it has led to renewed interest and research in creativity (Guilford, 1950) and in what was once labeled "social intelligence" (Guilford, 1966).

Next to intelligence, investigators of individual differences by psychometric means have devoted the largest amount of attention to the exploration of differences in school achievement. A large-scale study in Pennsylvania (Learned & Wood, 1938) demonstrated how extensive such differences are at the high school and college levels. For example, more than 10 percent of the 3,720 college seniors tested on a comprehensive general-culture examination scored below the 25th percentile for college sophomores. Almost all of the college seniors in the lowest 10th were below the median for high school seniors. At the other extreme, the top 10 percent of the high school seniors scored above the median for college seniors. Result from Project Talent, in which students from a carefully chosen sample of high schools throughout the United States were tested, provide more recent evidence for the same enormous variation in what different students at any one educational level actually know (Flanagan & others, 1964).

With the resurgence of public interest in education in the post-Sputnik years, more and more research effort has been focused on the low achiever. Achievement differences in the schoolroom are related to differences in intelligence, but the most carefully designed intelligence or scholastic aptitude test seldom correlates with school achievement to a greater extent than .6. It seems important to find out why students with the requisite brain power do not do well in school if the school is to carry out its mission successfully. Of the factors investigated, special abilities and disabilities do not seem to be an important source of variation, but motivational factors do (Tyler, 1965). However, the variables differentiating high achievers from low achievers are not those measured by most standardized personality tests. It is necessary to construct special scales in order to assess them. The significant characteristics are habits of work rather than drives, such positive qualities as interests, commitment, enthusiasm, and self-discipline rather than freedom from anxiety and neurotic traits. One significant study by Shaw and McCuen (1960) showed that underachievement begins in the first grade in the case of boys and in the sixth grade in the case of girls.

Since the 1920's vocational psychologists have been attempting to identify and measure the kinds of aptitudes and talents required for the many specialized kinds of work people do. It has become apparent here as in the case of intelligence tests (which can be considered aptitude tests for a special kind of work, namely, that required in school and college classrooms) that learning experiences as well as hereditary endowments play a part in the development of aptitudes. This being true, aptitude batteries for special purposes, such as selecting medical, legal, or engineering students, make use of materials much like those included in achievement tests—reading difficult passages, solving mathematical problems, and answering informational questions. An aptitude or talent is based on one's previous achievements. An aptitude test is usually distinguished from an achievement test by its purpose rather than by its content.

The purpose of aptitude testing is to predict occupational criteria. Research attempting to find out how well existing tests accomplish this purpose has come up with some discouraging results. Ghiselli (1955) showed that validity coefficients vary widely from one situation to another and that the predictive validity of a test for an occupational-training criterion is not indicative of its predictive validity for a proficiency criterion. Thorndike and Hagen, in a large-scale follow-up study of men who had taken the Air Force tests in 1943, found that degree of occupational success, as judged by seven different criteria, was not significantly related to any kind of test scores for any of their 124 occupational groups. While these findings must be interpreted with caution because they are based on a nonrepresentative sample of men and of tests, they certainly do not provide any positive basis for assuming long-range predictive validities for aptitude tests.

What the test scores did seem to relate to in the Thorndike and Hagen study, as in the earlier work at the Minnesota Employment Stabilization Research Institute (Dvorak, 1935), is the sorting-out process that differentiates the typical auto mechanic, for example, from the typical bank clerk. The average scores on many of the aptitude tests analyzed in both these research projects differed significantly from one occupation to another. What this finding suggests is that a certain level of a necessary aptitude may be necessary in order for a person to get a certain kind of job and hold it, even though correlational procedures do not show a relationship between aptitude and success rating.

The current need for many kinds of specialized workers makes it appear desirable that we develop aptitude tests with greater predictive validity than is shown by those now available. One of the promising new techniques for accomplishing this purpose is to discover and use a moderator variable to divide a group of persons to be tested into subgroups to be differently evaluated. Ghiselli (1956) has developed this procedure and tried it out in several industrial and educational situations.

Attempts to create a technology for the assessment of individual differences in personality and motivation have run into more obstacles and difficulties than were encountered in ability measurement.

While many approaches have been tried out, the one most frequently used has been the questionnaire. Various ways of scoring the subject's answers to questions about his own attitudes, feelings, and reactions to people and to situations have been devised, and a great many different traits or dimensions have been investigated. Attempts to create some order in this chaos of personality variables through factor-analytic procedures have produced diverse results. At the one extreme Eysenck (1953) finds it possible to account for all or most of his correlations between many tests on the basis of two personality variables, neuroticism and extraversion-introversion. At the other extreme, Cattell (1957) has presented factor-analytic evidence for at least 16 personality variables he considers to be well-enough defined to warrant releasing a standardized test for general use in clinics, industries, and schools. These formulations are not so different as they appear at first glance, however. Cattell's second-order factors (based on factor analysis of *factor* scores) look more like Eysenck's basic structure than the first-order factors do.

Probably the most widely used personality inventory of all is the Minnesota Multiphasic Personality Inventory(MMPI). It differed from most of its predecessors in that the scoring keys were devised by comparing actual responses of deviant groups with responses of equivalent normal groups. Factor analyses of correlations between these empirically derived scales have typically shown that two major factors account for most of the variance (Pederson, 1965; Block, 1964). There has been some difference of opinion about what these two factors should be named, but the pattern of factor loadings suggests that Eysenck's characterization of the two major personality dimensions—neuroticism and extraversion—would fit the factors fairly well.

A personality test more generally suitable for research on school populations is the California Psychological Inventory (CPI). Based on what Gough, the author, calls "folk concepts," it provides scores for variables like socialization, responsibility, tolerance, and achievement motivation. Gough has shown that combinations of these scores correlate significantly with a variety of educational criteria (Gough, 1964, 1966).

There is considerable question, however, whether any of these standardized personality inventories provide valid-enough data to be used in making educational decisions about individuals. The kinds of individual differences that enter into the relationships between teacher and pupil in the classroom are much more complex and subtle than those explored by the standardized methods. Furthermore, personality tests pose more serious hazards of misinterpretation and unethical utilization of recorded information than ability tests do.

Another kind of psychological characteristic, which could be classified under personality but is usually discussed separately, is measured by vocational-interest inventories. From the high school years on, these instruments provide useful indications of the directions in which individuals are motivated to move. For some, like the venerable Strong Vocational Interest Blank, recently revised by Strong and others (1966), and the recent Kuder Occupational Interest Survey (Kuder, 1966), the scoring scales indicate how closely the subject's interests correspond to those of successful workers in various occupations. For others, such as the widely used Kuder Preference Record—Vocational, the scores show how frequently the subject indicated preferences for activities of specified kinds—mechanical, social service, scientific, and the like. Research on interest tests has demonstrated that the traits they measure are remarkably stable from adolescence on, even over long periods of time (Strong, 1955) and that they predict with a fair degree of accuracy what occupation a person will enter and whether he will stay with it or shift out of it. Vocational counselors have found interest tests to be useful tools, although they do not cover by any means the full range of occupations in the modern world and although they are, like other nonability tests, subject to faking.

Less frequently used in educational institutions and less thoroughly studied by research workers are measures of attitudes and values. Properly designed, they should have some utility in school situations.

One relatively new line of research is opening up fresh possibilities for assessing characteristics that may be important for educators to understand. Witkin and others (1962) have been investigating cognitive styles. Their research has focused on differences in *psychological differentiation* and has shown that differences with respect to it are stable over several years and are related significantly to aspects of intelligence, self concept, and other important kinds of attitudes and behavior. Other sorts of cognitive styles in children are being studied by Kagan and others (1964), by Bruner and Oliver (1963), and by Gardner (1964).

ORIGINS OF INDIVIDUAL DIFFERENCES. For many years the nature-nurture controversy dominated all discussions of the origins of individual differences. Leading research workers and writers took strong positions on one side or the other, with liberals tending to prefer environmental explanations, conservatives opting for heredity (Pastore, 1949). As more and better research findings have become available, arguments have become much less frequent, and explanations in terms of interaction between hereditary and environmental influences have come to be preferred. Different assortments of genes provide individuals with different potentialities for development. In any given environmental situation some of these potential lines of development will be facilitated, others hindered. What a person is like at any point in time at which we study him depends upon what he was like at a previous stage of development, and no matter how far we push the question back in the individual's life history, both genetic and situational influences can be detected.

Research on the origins of individual differences has focused more and more on specific questions having to do with the relative "heritability" of various traits under relatively standard environmental conditions (Vandenberg, 1962) or the effects of particular kinds of environmental enrichment, such as preschool education for the mentally retarded (Kirk, 1958).

The most useful subjects for research on heredity and environment are monozygotic and dizygotic twins. Because the two members of a monozygotic pair have the same genetic makeup, differences between them at any stage of development can be attributed to environmental influences. Studies of pairs separated from one another early in life have demonstrated that environments differing in intellectual stimulation produce moderate IQ differences (Newman & others, 1937). Studies of resemblances between monozygotic, or identical, twins, on the one hand, and dizygotic, or fraternal, twins, on the other, have consistently shown substantially closer resemblances between the former than between the latter. These findings have been interpreted as showing the prepotency of hereditary over environment by those inclined to a hereditarian viewpoint. Several large-scale studies of twins are now in progress and should produce new information about the heritability of special abilities and personality characteristics.

In summary, each individual's genotype provides for him a *reaction range* with respect to each trait. Whether he ultimately functions at a level near the top of his range or at a level near the bottom of it depends upon the opportunities for learning he encounters in the situations in which development occurs. With respect to intelligence, for example, it cannot be anticipated that marked improvements in schools will wipe out all individual differences. What such improvement might accomplish is to enable each individual to develop to a higher level the potential he has.

Combining Dimensions in Describing Individuals. The major weakness of the trait or dimensional approach to individual differences is that it does not provide a very satisfactory means of actually describing individuals. Whether we think of an individual personality as the totality of all his traits or as a point in *n*-dimensional space, we seem to miss the essential quality of the person. Because we must deal with individuals in the classroom, counseling office, and work situation, as well as in research on personality, various ways of combining scores on several traits have been elaborated for different purposes.

In counseling situations, some sort of profile, or *psychograph*, that shows at a glance which of the subject's scores are high and which low, is the most commonly employed. It is essential, if such a graph is not to be misleading, that the derived scores to be compared are based on the same or comparable norm groups. It is obvious that the combination of a percentile rank of 90 on a mechanical aptitude test with a percentile of 65 on a clerical aptitude test does not indicate that the subject's mechanical ability is superior to his clerical ability if the higher figure compares him with the general run of high school boys while the lower compares him with employed clerical workers. For this reason, a "package" battery of aptitude or achievement tests, such as the General Aptitude Test Battery (GATB) used by the Employment Service, or the College Entrance Examination Board examination (Scholastic Aptitude Test, or SAT, plus achievement tests) is often more suitable for counseling purposes than a battery of tests assembled from different sources. It is also imperative that all tests to be employed in profile analysis of scores be highly reliable, so that perceived differences will represent something other than chance fluctuation.

In selection situations, the most common procedure for combining scores is to work out a regression equation to give each score its optimum weight for predicting the criterion variable. This procedure assumes that the weights are derived from an experimental group put through the whole procedure prior to the time when actual selection on the basis of scores is scheduled to begin, but various approximation procedures for using data obtained from subjects actually selected rather than from subjects tested without subsequent selection are available.

Either of these basic procedures or variations of them can be used for research purposes. Research workers are also making use of what is called Q-technique. After all of the measurements for individuals have been reduced to a common scale, correlations between individuals can be computed and subjected to different kinds of statistical treatment, such as multiple regression, cluster analysis, and factor analysis.

As indicated previously, none of these methods gives the satisfactory rendering of the uniqueness of the individual that is required for the empathetic understanding needed in the schoolroom and counseling office or for the exigencies of idiographic research. An emerging concept that seems promising is the concept of individual differences in *directions of development*. When we have the technology, mathematical and otherwise, to picture an individual at any one moment of time as a branching tree rather than a profile or a predicted score, we shall have the means of putting the new concept to work. Longitudinal studies, some of them covering several decades, are beginning to produce the kind of data that enable us to think developmentally about human individuality.

THE CHALLENGE TO EDUCATION. Educators need to consider individual differences for three main reasons. First and most important, the diversity within every classroom, at the elementary, secondary, or higher level, is always important to consider in connection with the curriculum. No matter what standards or objectives are set for a class, it is a fact of life that what is learned by each individual in the group will differ from these standards and from what is learned by other individuals. What we most frequently do—that is, reduce all of the variation to a single quantitative scale and assign grades to indicate how much each student has achieved—gives us a very inadequate expression of the complexity of individual differences in response to curricular requirements.

The second important implication of individual differences for educators, particularly at the elementary level, has to do with the concept of *readiness*. If, as now seems probable, there are critical developmental periods for the acquisition of particular kinds of knowledge and skill, teachers should become sensitive to individual differences in readiness within the classroom and individualize assignments accordingly. Besides waiting for readiness to develop, teachers should be equipped to provide for each child learning situations designed to accelerate such development.

The third implication of individual differences for educators is that they call for more clarity about the broad objectives of education than ordinarily exists. Should it be the aim of teaching to reduce the range of intellectual differences by bringing low individuals up to a predetermined standard and paying no special attention to those whose level of intelligence and achievement is already high? Most spokesmen for education would probably say that this is not their aim—that what is to be desired is achievement up to his own maximum for each individual, low or high. But actions often contradict words. To take seriously this purpose of facilitating the development of all students, different as they are, would require a degree of individualization of instruction as yet only rarely achieved in our classrooms.

Leona E. Tyler
University of Oregon

References

Allport, Gordon W. *Personality: a Psychological Interpretation.* Holt, 1937. 580p.

Bayley, Nancy. "Some Increasing Parent-child Similarities During the Growth of Children." *J Ed Psychol* 45:1–21; 1954.

Block, J. *The Challenge of Response Sets.* Appleton, 1964. 142p.

Bradway, K. P., and Thompson C. W. "Intelligence at Adulthood: A Twenty-five Year Follow-up." *J Ed Psychol* 53:1–14; 1962.

Bruner, J. S., and Oliver, R. R. "Development of Equivalence Transformations in Children." *Monogr Social Res Child Develop* 28:125–41; 1963.

Cattell, R. B. *Personality and Motivation Structure and Measurement.* Harcourt, 1957. 948p.

Dvorak, B. J. *Differential Occupational Ability Patterns.* U Minnesota Press, 1935. 46p.

Eysenck, H. J. *The Structure of Human Personality.* Methuen, 1953. 348p.

Flanagan, John C., and others. *The American High School Student.* Project Talent report. U Pittsburgh Press, 1964. 723p.

Gardner, R. W. "The Development of Cognitive Structures." In Sheerer C. (Ed.) *Cognition: Theory, Research, Promise.* Harper, 1964. p. 147–71.

Ghiselli, Edwin E. "The Measurement of Occupational Aptitude." *U California Pub in Psychol* 8:101–216; 1955.

Ghiselli, Edwin E. "Differentiation of Individuals in Terms of Their Predictability." *J Applied Psychol* 40:374–7; 1956.

Gough, H. G. "Academic Achievement in High School as Predicted from the California Psychological Inventory." *J Ed Psychol* 55:174–80; 1964.

Gough, H. G. "Graduation from High School as Predicted from the California Psychological Inventory." *Psychol Sch* 3:208–16; 1966.

Guilford, J. P. "Creativity." *Am Psychologist* 5:444–54; 1950.

Guilford, J. P. "Three Faces of Intellect." *Am Psychologist* 14:469–79; 1959.

Guilford, J. P. "Intelligence: 1965 Model." *Am Psychologist* 21:20–6; 1966.

Honzik, Marjorie P. "Developmental Studies of Parent-Child Resemblance in Intelligence." *Child Develop* 28:215–28; 1957.

Honzik, Marjorie P., and others. "The Stability of Mental Test Performance Between Two and Eighteen Years." *J Exp Ed* 17:309–24; 1948.

Kagan, Jerome, and others. "Information Processing in the Child: Significance of Analytic and Reflective Attitudes." *Psychol Monogr* 78; 1964.

Kallman, F. J. *Heredity in Health and Mental Disorder.* Norton, 1953. 315p.

Kirk, S. A. *Early Education of the Mentally Retarded.* U Illinois Press, 1958. 216p.

Kuder, G. Frederic. *Occupational Interest Survey.* SRA, 1966.

Lacey, J. I. "Individual Differences in Somatic Response Patterns." *J Comp Physiol Psychol* 43:338–50; 1950.

Learned, W. S., and Wood, B. D. *The Student and His Knowledge.* Carnegie, 1938. 406p.

Newman, H. H., and others. *Twins: A Study of Heredity and Environment.* U Chicago Press, 1937. 369p.

Pastore, N. *The Nature-Nurture Controversy.* King's, 1949. 213p.

Pederson, D. R. "Scope and Generality of Verbally Defined Personality Factors." *Psychol R* 72:48–59; 1965.

Shaw, M. C., and McCuen, J. T. "The Onset of Under-achievement in Bright Children." *J Ed Psychol* 51:103–9; 1960.

Sheldon, W. H., and others. *The Varieties of Human Physique.* Harper, 1940. 347p.

Sontag, L. W., and others. "Mental Growth and Personality Development: A Longitudinal Study." *Monogr Social Res Child Develop* 23:1–85; 1958.

Spearman, Charles E. *The Abilities of Man.* Macmillan, 1927. 43p.

Strong, Edward K., Jr. *Vocational Interests 18 Years After College.* U Minnesota Press, 1955. 207p.

Strong, Edward K., Jr., and others. *Strong Vocational Interest Blank for Men.* Stanford U Press, 1966.

Thorndike, Robert L., and Hagen, E. *10,000 Careers.* Wiley, 1959. 346p.

Thurstone, L. L. *Primary Mental Abilities.* U Chicago Press, 1938. 121p.
Tyler, Leona E. *The Psychology of Human Differences,* 3rd ed. Appleton, 1965. 572p.
Vandenberg, S. G. "The Hereditary Abilities Study: Hereditary Components in a Psychological Test Battery." *Am J Hum Genet* 14:220-37; 1962.
Williams, R. J. *Biochemical Individuality.* Wiley, 1956. 214p.
Witkin, H. A., and others. *Psychological Differentiation.* Wiley, 1962. 418p.

IN-SERVICE EDUCATION OF TEACHERS

The importance of in-service education for all educational personnel is recognized throughout the literature of the teaching profession: in popular articles, in textbooks, in special publications, and in research studies. This article is limited to an analysis of selected publications and research related to the work of the classroom teacher. The rapid expansion of knowledge, which has been reported extensively over the past several years, and its effect on changing methods and in developing technology utilized in the classroom are major factors in making the in-service education of this group necessary.

The need for programs to upgrade the performance of teachers has been stated throughout such works as Moffitt's (1963), where emphasis is placed on the continuing obsolescence of knowledge and methods of teaching. Without planned programs for upgrading their work, individuals who have not learned of the potentialities of, and issues regarding, team teaching, teaching machines, and programmed learning, as well as other developing techniques, will remain isolated on an educational island remote from innovative practices and new knowledge.

Any attempt to identify practices and activities in this important field will find it difficult to separate the importance of research in its true sense from the statements of principles and practices which grow from experience and observation. An effort is made here to blend aspects of each. Incorporated in the discussion is an identification of what in-service education is, of general activities associated with it, of programs in individual school districts, and of practices in special fields; the use of television, human-relations workshops, and other special activities in in-service education are also discussed.

NEED, DEFINITION, AND DESIGN. Stephen Corey (1957) has summarized the problems and issues in this field. He emphasized planned programs in contrast to independent attempts by teachers to improve themselves. He carefully stated, however, that wide reading, travel, attendance at conventions and at professional courses, and other activities conducive to professional growth are not meant to be undervalued by such emphasis. He clearly delineated the necessity for planned programs in in-service education for the improvement of school personnel and expressed the feeling that to depend entirely on preservice preparation and individual initiative is impracticable. He called for carefully planned, creative programs. A rapidly changing culture and its implications for curriculum change, continually increasing enrollments, the size of the teaching staff, the need for leadership in the schools, and the increase in our knowledge of pupils and the learning process make it necessary for teachers to strive continuously to keep abreast of what they must know and be prepared to do.

In an analysis of in-service education and continuing education for teachers, Childress (1965) emphasized that these terms are virtually synonymous. The in-service program was looked upon as a natural continuation of professional preservice education, as an obligation for teachers, and as a necessity for educational programming. Four major areas of concern stood out in this discussion:

1. The creation of a felt obligation on the part of teachers and professionals to undertake a planned and well-designed in-service or continuing education program.
2. The development of a set of guide lines for the "organization" or school district which will implement an appropriate and excellent in-service program.
3. Recognition by community and professional leaders that the rapid expansion of knowledge, both in the professional and in the content fields, will require full-time study and that this will necessitate resolution of issues of staffing and finance.
4. The need for schools of education and other divisions of universities and colleges to plan programs especially for individuals who will be continuing their education on a part-time or a full-time basis—often on a nondegree basis.

Smith and others (1961) emphasized that school districts should follow the lead of industry and request certain teachers to take special training. This concept is based on the experience of two California high schools in giving beginning teachers internship status for the first two years of their assignments. This program emphasized a lighter-than-normal load for the inexperienced teachers and the provision of experienced colleagues to work with these individuals so that their strengths and weaknesses could be observed. Dale (1964) posited that essential to an adequate program was a recognition on the part of those who work with the beginning teacher of the necessity of being sensitive to his needs.

Supervisors and administrators must reaffirm their commitment to practices that will recognize and foster individuality in teachers, develop self-understanding, allow for self-fulfillment, and provide for growth in the ability to live and to work harmoniously with oneself and with others (Openshaw, 1962). The in-service program which is well conceived will make the learning process the focus of organizational efforts, designed to serve the needs and purposes of individual teachers, and at the same time will take advantage of the particular characteristics of the situation in which the school operates. The greater the participation by the teacher, the better the learning which is likely to result.

Oviatt (1962) reacted against the fragmentation of the teaching profession and expressed the hope for an acceptance by all levels of teaching, primary through college, of a kinship rather than an isolationist philosophy regarding educational issues. Planned programs of interrelationships through an in-service educational scheme can bring about such a kinship. The need for this and similar planning is identified by Ogeltree and Edmonds (1964). A concept of an aggregate of incidental activities was rejected, and a planned program based upon three major principles was proposed. The principles are as follows:

1. In-service teacher education purposes are identified with a matrix of instructional-improvement activities and procedures.

2. In-service teacher education develops and utilizes adequate leadership.

3. In-service education is a curriculum within itself, conceptualized and treated as a total instructional program.

The need for large-scale programming was emphasized further by Stradley (1962).

Childress (1965) emphasized that the dramatic increase in technology and the inability of each individual to keep abreast in his field in any but a modest way combine to create a situation in which many things are taught which are no longer true. Education for children, youth, and adults in the United States can be meaningful only if the teaching staff is knowledgeable and professionally competent in modern technical information and research. Continuing education of the individual and of the profession is essential to maintain and to improve educational programs in classroom instruction. Failure to incorporate this concept into the activities of the entire profession will bring chaos and alteration of the prerogatives of the teacher.

STATUS AND SCOPE OF IN-SERVICE EDUCATION. Studies and analyses of various types of local, cooperative, statewide, and regional programs have shown widespread variations in success and programming. Although Whitmore (1960) reached the conclusion that few school districts with populations below 50,000 had organized in-service development programs, Taylor (1964) found indications that many school systems did have activities incorporated into the work of the teachers that suggest that such programs were being followed. Unfortunately, small high schools, those with enrollments under 600, were seen as doing less adequate programming than elementary schools, both large and small, and than larger high schools. This conclusion came from a study of 1,162 summer-school students at Indiana University. Of the study items identified as characteristic of in-service education, the small secondary schools had the lowest percentages of positive responses to virtually every one. Chi-square values, which compared the small elementary with the large elementary school and the small secondary with the large secondary school, were significant or highly significant in 14 of 18 comparisons. The larger schools were reported to be using a significantly greater number of the selected practices. When the size of the school was held constant, there were no significant differences between large elementary schools and large secondary schools. In 9 situations out of 18, the percentages favored the small elementary school over the small secondary school. The conclusion was reached that an in-service education program seemed to be neglected most often on the small secondary-school level (Taylor, 1964).

The positive results of cooperative planning were stressed and the necessity of in-service education being designed by teachers and administrators was noted in several studies. Hassel (1960) found that programs were planned and operated largely by administrators. Lewin (1963) ascertained through a sampling of 200 educators (deans, representatives of state departments of education, city school superintendents, and presidents of secondary-education associations) that these individuals believed in and recommended the cooperative, democratic approach in developing a philosophy of in-service education and in organizing and administering a program. The acceptance by teachers of these findings was confirmed by Gereheim (1959) and Cory (1959). The last two studies found that teachers accepted and valued in-service education programs which were planned carefully, locally, and cooperatively. Schwalenberg (1965) and Lucas (1963) concluded that the most successful orientation programs were those which derived their bases and objectives from teacher needs and which were based on knowledge of the background of teachers. Consideration of the needs, interests, and backgrounds of teachers is not always practiced. Schild (1964) attempted to determine the characteristics and the prevalence of four in-service practices in a selected group of medium-sized American public school systems. One facet of this attempt dealt with the planning and the coordinating of the program. The conclusion was that cooperative, long-range planning was rare. Sixty-three percent of the systems had no teachers participating in an advisory planning group. Recommendations which grew from this study included one that in-service programs should be cooperatively planned for a period of three to five years by a teacher-administrator advisory group. The emphasis on cooperative planning and individual needs, however, does not negate the need for administrative leadership. Studies by Harville (1960), Lewin (1963), Lucas (1963), and Schwalenberg (1965) all indicated that administrative responsibility had to be accepted within the school program. Lewin (1963) stated the principle that the assistant superintendent in charge of instruction is looked upon as the instructional leader of the district, while at the level of the individual school the principal is regarded as the instructional leader. The basic conclusion was that administrators should accept the responsibility for providing and organizing a program, whether of orientation or of in-service education.

Schild (1964) ascertained that there were single

in-service coordinators in 60 percent of the districts included in his study. Although only a small number of administrators and new teachers participated, McCreary (1960) reported that school superintendents and academic personnel in colleges did attempt to determine the individual needs of elementary teachers in order to individualize an orientation program. Schild (1964) included the provision of time for in-service education, the use of university consultants, and evaluation of the program among characteristics to be studied in determining practices in the schools. Responses to his study items by 73 school districts in 29 states were reported. The following conclusions were drawn:

1. The average system provided two formal in-service sessions per faculty member per month; the larger schools seemed to provide fewer opportunities. About one-half of the systems planned to expand their programs.

2. Released-time and in-service education was provided in 56 percent of the systems. Fewer than one-half provided for in-service education in an extended-year program; such a program affected fewer than 8 percent of the staff.

3. University consultants were provided in 81 percent of the systems.

4. All but nine districts used some evaluative procedure. Unfortunately, such procedures relied primarily on informal observations and administrative judgments. Many respondents voiced a need for more objective methods.

Studies of a more localized nature were conducted by Duncan (1964), Harville (1960), Hayes (1960), Johnson (1962), and the Wolfs (1961). Duncan (1964) attempted to identify some of the factors which have proved to be instrumental in the successful operation of programs in selected Alabama schools. Although each system used practices and techniques that varied according to local needs, certain recommendations seemed to be warranted. The existence and operation of in-service programs should be governed by policies adopted by the board of education. Local administrators and members of the instructional staff should identify their respective roles in an effective program. The organization of in-service programs should give adequate consideration to such factors as continuity, time of meeting, resources, and participation of the professional staff in program planning, operation, and evaluation. Careful consideration should be given to the relationship of in-service education efforts to the improvement of instruction.

Case studies of individual school systems were conducted by Harville (1960) and the Wolfs (1961). Harville's findings about the Knoxville, Tennessee, system indicated the existence of trends similar to those identified previously. Over a five-year period, the in-service program became more effectively organized. The Council for Curriculum Improvement coordinated the general program and provided direction for individual schools and city work groups. Opportunities for leadership by individual teachers were looked upon as a definite outgrowth of this endeavor and, when combined with problem solving and activities outside the classroom, seemed to improve the system's curriculum.

Johnson (1962) analyzed the Montgomery County, Maryland, coordinated program of staff development. Concern was expressed for improving instruction, as well as for fostering continuing personal and professional growth. Because curriculum and instructional improvement are dependent in part upon the rapid solution of personnel problems, Montgomery County placed a strong emphasis on systematic, cooperative efforts in conjunction with teacher education institutions. It was held that no better or more practical opportunity can be offered to the individual teacher in keeping abreast of the latest findings in the field and for examining his philosophy and practices than guiding and counseling an alert student teacher.

Singer (1963) further identified the need for teachers to remain up-to-date by raising the question of how the findings of educational research can be communicated to and tested by the practicing teacher. Through the Cooperative Center established for nine school districts, two considerations were stressed regarding curriculum research and development: the budgetary feasibility of educational innovations, and a means of providing teachers with research findings upon which to base their decisions. Teachers were given opportunities to view large-group instruction and to analyze this activity through large-group, small-group, and independent study. To promote in-service education and to maintain contact with teacher needs, a core of teacher communicators was organized to serve as liaison persons between the center and the participating schools. They were assigned to individual schools and were given the task of identifying problems for which this center or other groups could provide assistance. An effort was made to narrow the gap between research and practice.

The need for continuing study was further identified by an analysis made by Taylor (1961) of 218 new teachers. A questionnaire study was made of their plans for additional formal education, as well as of their needs for further preparation. Almost 75 percent of the group intended to do additional college work. More than 55 percent planned to complete a master's degree in the future.

The role of governmental agencies above the local school district was analyzed by Valsame (1963) and Black (1961). Valsame stressed that the federal government and in some cases the states have become directly involved in providing in-service education. The federal government has increased its activity through the efforts of the National Science Foundation and the enactment of the National Defense Education Act (NDEA). Several state departments of education have become more involved through the administration of scholarships, state-sponsored in-service programs, and implementation of the NDEA. Most of the state programs, as exemplified by North Carolina's, took on the character of leadership rather than regulatory programs. Black (1961) traced the history of the influence of Florida county boards on curriculum and on in-service education from 1885 to 1920. The conclusion was reached that the decisions of certain Florida county school boards about in-service education influenced the knowledge and skills of the teachers and hence indirectly influenced the curriculum. Rubin (1964) summarized the strategy for curricular change and in-service education. The principal components included the following:

1. Each teacher must be made to recognize that he plays a crucial role in curriculum development and that he has an obligation to assess the shortcomings of the existing program, to better it through experimentation, and to measure the value of suggestions put forth by the research of others.

2. Each teacher may have to have help in losing his sense of complacency and in drawing systematically upon the aggregate resources of the area to improve his performance.

3. Each teacher must have the time and materials required for him to be consistently well-informed about what is going on; each should be able to select intelligently from alternatives; and each must be challenged consistently about the appropriateness of his own purposes and methods.

4. Each teacher must have recourse to the kinds of technical assistance which he feels he needs. These may take the form of expert consultantships, cooperative planning endeavors, opportunities to gain and to master new skills, or provisions for theoretical study.

5. The leaders' task is to set forth what accomplishments are expected from in-service education, to provide the realistic wherewithal for their achievement, to provide opportunities for the release of individual teachers from those things which seem to restrict him or her, and to evaluate the end result of the programs.

PRACTICES AND PROCEDURES. Evaluations of certain practices and procedures in in-service education have been made by McCollister (1964), Boyd (1961), Karbal (1963), McDavid (1965), and others. McCollister's study involved a survey of the professional education courses offered by state colleges and universities in Louisiana in which practicing teachers were enrolled. Generally, the needs and desires of such teachers were being met satisfactorily by the services and facilities. Some of the teachers were only moderately satisfied, however, about the results.

Boyd (1961) attempted to evaluate several different methods of in-service education. He discussed the relative effectiveness of television, face-to-face lecture discussions, television supplemented by classroom consultant services, and face-to-face lecture discussions supplemented by classroom consultant services as methods of in-service education for elementary-school teachers of arithmetic. He concluded that there was no difference in effectiveness between television and face-to-face lecture-discussion methods of presentation. A difference was identified, however, in the extent to which the effectiveness of television and face-to-face lecture discussion methods was influenced by the type of consulting help offered.

Karbal (1963) undertook an evaluation of a workshop and its effects as a process in the in-service education of teachers by appraising the way which programs and schools were affected. Data were gathered from practicing teachers in one of the nine administrative districts of the Detroit public schools. Thirty-seven key teachers from 30 elementary schools made up the workshop. Their accomplishments were measured in several ways. Great gain was seen in the help given to inexperienced teachers, in human-relations activities, and in participation in school organizations, as well as in classroom management. Principals gave their evaluations of the outcomes of the workshop through questionnaires and interviews. After a year, 21 of the 25 principals were well satisfied with their choice of key teachers. They believed that positive behavioral changes in the teachers had made them more competent professionally because of the increased security and reinforcement which they had received. These individuals were more active and vocal in school committees and were better able than they had been to view the school as a totality. Many positive outcomes were identified in other phases of the study. Evaluations by co-workers indicated that the key teachers had grown as professional colleagues and had gained much from the experience; their colleagues also indicated that they were able now to exert a positive influence on the rest of the faculty.

McDavid (1965) investigated critical requirements for effective behavior on the part of department chairmen in orienting first-year high school teachers. Hurwitz (1966) emphasized the possibility of team teaching as a potential for in-service growth; he believed there to be virtue in having teachers watch others teach and in formulating evaluations of their work. Rosser (1963) emphasized the practicality of in-service education through the relationships between student teachers and classroom supervisors. The student teacher takes into the classroom fresh approaches to subject-matter content and the latest advances in methodology. If he is given some opportunity to experiment in teaching, he is able to give his cooperating teacher new ideas and insights both in content and in methods.

Special problems in in-service programs were analyzed by Doherty (1962) in his discussion of the tenured teacher, by Jones (1963) in a recommendation for in-service education for substitute teachers, and by Norris (1962) in raising the issue of credit for certain courses which are not normally listed among the academic offerings of colleges and universities. Hilarion (1963) moved in-service education out of the problem areas of supervision and inter-classroom visits. Group work meetings and demonstration classes were held very successfully in the dioceses in which she worked. Evaluations of the sessions indicated that teachers felt they were most appropriate and moving in the right direction. DeVita (1963) formalized a procedure which would allow teachers in a given school to observe other teachers. The respect and dignity of each individual teacher were emphasized. No judgments, no written reports, no names, and no signed observation forms were used. Each teacher was given an opportunity to observe other teachers, but no individual was required to participate. Although skeptical at the outset, many of the more experienced teachers were surprised and delighted to see many fine practices being followed by their colleagues. New teachers found the experience extremely stimulating and helpful. Harmonious reactions from the professional staff gave encouragement to further action research.

USE OF EDUCATIONAL TELEVISION. Educational television, both open- and closed-circuit, was studied as a usable means of in-service education for general activities (McKee, 1962; Cook, 1964), for the development of special lessons (Suchy, 1965), for methodology and orientation (Tarbet, 1963), and for work in special subject areas (Mayer, 1964; Winsor, 1961; Boyd, 1961; Kerns, 1962; Brandou, 1964; Adams, 1962).

In-service television programs of many types were offered in Atlanta, Georgia (McKee, 1962), including credit courses, new methodology, messages from the superintendent, analyses of the work of specialized personnel in the school from custodians to special teachers, and visits from outstanding consultants. The chief disadvantage of this plan was the lack of opportunity for questions and answers. This was offset by the advantages of telecasting to various segments of a large city and the stimulation which the teachers received.

Cook (1964) analyzed the use of television through a survey of 154 principals at various school levels. Clear recognition was given to the fact that teachers needed specific in-service aid if television was to be used successfully. In addition, the recommendation was made that teacher education programs should provide more adequate opportunities for the undergraduate prospective teacher to become acquainted with the theory and principles of the communication process and with the potential of the television medium as an asset in the learning process. Suchy (1965) found that it was possible for ten independent schools and school districts to develop cooperatively a ten-lesson educational television series, with each school working in isolation from the others except for cooperative meetings.

Through the educational-television station of the consolidated University of North Carolina a variety of in-service programs have been conducted. Tarbet (1963) discussed new teaching developments, including techniques, materials, and textbooks, all of which have been presented by experts. When new textbooks are adopted for statewide use, curriculum specialists present programs for their proper utilization. Audio-visual aids connected with the teaching of a particular field, such as history, science, or the language arts, have been used. In addition, programs for the orientation of teachers through a single administrative unit have been used in the Minneapolis, Minnesota, school system. Phonoscope for two-way communication has been utilized in Galveston, Texas. Tarbet's conclusion was that there is a need for the orientation of teachers to the use of television for educational purposes, because the technique is not a familiar one. Teachers need to be involved in planning sessions and to learn the proper use of television through in-service education.

Some evaluation has been made of the end results of programs conducted by this medium or through related activities. Rapp (1964) investigated the changes which occurred in the attitudes of regular classroom teachers after what was termed the "tele-lecture" method was used in teaching them about mental retardation. Definite progress was made between the pretest and the final test. Significant attitude changes were noted in comparable testing programs. Eighty percent of the respondents rated the course as good or excellent, and 94 percent indicated they would recommend the course to their friends. The conclusion was reached that as far as courses in mental retardation which are adaptable to the tele-lecture program are concerned, students taking the course by this means can achieve as much as students taking the course on campus. This was highly advantageous in the area served by this study, Nevada, Utah, and Colorado, where a group of 123 teachers and administrators who were widely separated geographically took the course.

Winsor (1961) and Boyd (1961) concluded that it was possible to provide adequate instruction in the area of arithmetic and mathematics through television. Students in television classes gained in understandings of arithmetic concepts and attitudes. Winsor's study combined television, seminars, and individual study, while Boyd's made use of consultants; the consultants seemed to aid in the development of better understanding.

The impact of television on in-service science education was examined by Brandou (1964) and Kerns (1962). Kerns concluded that, for the junior high school, in this particular area two functions were successfully combined: subject-matter instruction and in-service assistance. Kerns held that improved instruction by members of the viewing classes resulted from a replacement of obsolete instructional material. Although the program established wide contact with teachers, the teachers did not initiate adequate feedback into the program. The hypothesis that educational television alone could be an effective in-service educational instrument for teachers was concluded to be untenable. Although television had importance, its use had to be associated with other efforts. Teachers needed every resource available to improve their instruction. To restrict these resources to any one medium or facility is to restrict undesirably their growth and experience. Brandou's study (1964) indicated that it was feasible to use competent secondary-school teachers as in-service instructors for elementary classroom teachers. The contributions were related significantly to the amount of teaching experience and the number of years in the school system of the secondary science teachers. The contribution of the program to teachers of grades 3 through 6 was reported to be significantly greater than to teachers of grades kindergarten through 2. Adams (1962) found that identified needs in the teaching of reading could be met by an in-service television program. Twenty-eight aspects of the teaching of reading which needed better understanding were taught through this medium.

IN-SERVICE EDUCATION IN SPECIAL AREAS. Studies have been made of the effects of in-service education in specialized areas and academic fields. Studies have been made in skill areas such as mathematics and science and English and Spanish, as well as in the more general areas of guidance and pupil adjustment. Brown (1962), Frank Weaver (1962), and Stent (1965) conducted studies in the general area of guidance and child development. Stent's project was an attempt to identify ways of helping beginning teachers in day-care centers to improve their guidance of children through in-service courses. The focus of the study was on improvement of teaching skills, helping beginning teachers meet the unique problems of teaching in day-care centers, and attempting to make them alert to new developments and educational practices. Teachers who participated in the program improved their skills and were able to solve immediate problems more realistically.

Frank Weaver (1962) analyzed the effects on pupils of an in-service program for teachers. The teachers were involved in an intensive study of John C. Flanagan's Personal and Special Development Program. The students who were in the classes under these teachers made significantly greater gains in adjustment than students of teachers in the control group did. The experimental teachers seemed to have been stimulated by the in-service meetings to read more professional literature which related directly to their ultimate involvement with the individual student.

Brown (1962) analyzed in-service educational programs and college and university course offerings in guidance for teachers in Washington, Oregon, and California. Of 165 school districts in the study, 100 did not offer any in-service programs in guidance for their teachers or counselors, and 120 did indicate a need for such offerings. The conclusion was reached that since few teachers had done work in guidance in their preservice studies, such work was essential in an in-service program.

Several studies have been undertaken to determine the impact of various types of mathematical in-service education on teachers and teaching. Dossett (1964) found that workshops held under Title III of NDEA in Missouri contributed to the development of mathematical understandings and to a change in attitude toward arithmetic. All workshop participants made statistically significant gains between pretests and posttests on the mathematical understandings and on the arithmetic attitude inventory, with the exception of one group of primary teachers.

Dutton and Hammond (1966) also analyzed the workshop approach. They varied the activities between two comparable districts by using a formal workshop with a college professor of mathematics as an instructor in one and a district-planned in-service workshop using the district's own staff in the other. Although both school districts found that the in-service program helped elementary teachers make significant improvements in their understanding of mathematical concepts, the gains in the unstructured district-staff workshop were greater than in the more structured grouping. The district workshop provided many opportunities for individual teachers to work on specific difficulties rather than to repeat work that had been studied before.

An analysis of the learnings of teachers through institute study and their ultimate impact on the students under their jurisdiction was made by Selser (1962). Science and math teachers attained higher scores on specific tests given when they had attended the institute. In all cases the students in classes taught by the teachers from the institute made statistically higher scores on posttests than did students whose teachers had not attended the institute. Science groups scored significantly higher at the 1-percent level of confidence, and the means of all grade levels when pooled indicated that the pupils of participating teachers made gains which were significant at the 5-percent level of confidence. Todd (1965) evaluated a specific course in mathematics for teachers. The course resulted in significant improvement in understandings of arithmetic and attitudes toward arithmetic for those completing it, although many teachers were still inadequate and some planned to continue their course work. McLeod (1965) found similar results in a program conducted to remedy deficiencies in math.

J. Fred Weaver (1966b) studied a more specific area of mathematics by examining teacher understandings and learnings in nonmetric geometry. As a result of his analysis of a limited group of teachers, it appears logical to believe that some elementary-school teachers have a very low level of understanding of what may appear to be simple aspects of nonmetric geometry. These teachers seem also to have misunderstandings of some crucial facets of the content of this field. This may have implications for in-service as well as preservice programs. An analysis of individuals enrolled in in-service courses seems to indicate that those who did work in mathematics which was related to informal geometry scored higher on tests after such work than they had before. Through the use of a manual and a workshop Monk (1966) was able to improve the understandings of eleventh- and twelfth-grade math teachers in new concepts of mathematics.

Cooksey (1965) attempted to evaluate the effectiveness of an in-service education program for English teachers. The Teaching English Project consisted of 16 half-hour 16-mm. films combined with discussion and consultant visits. The changes in learning of students was a primary area of evaluation. There was a significant change in English achievement for all students when considered as one combined group. Classroom practices of the experimental group of teachers in teaching grammar, usage, and mechanics had a significantly greater rate of change than the classroom practices of the control group did; in some areas there were no gains. Overall results of the analysis show that the differential of change between the experimental group of students and the control group of students was not significant. A similar study was made to determine if teachers who participated in in-service education in the teaching of Spanish affected the scores made by their pupils on classroom tests (Lacayo, 1963). The type of in-service education conducted in this study had very little impact on the learning of children. Herman (1962) indicated that when there was a planned activity program, decided changes could occur in the teaching of grammar. Teachers became enthusiastic about making changes; they developed new grammar tests and appeared to improve in efficiency in the classroom (in contrast to their distinct expression of dissatisfaction with an unplanned program).

Positive results similar to those in mathematics and other skill areas were noted in in-service courses for teachers responsible for art and music instruction. Reed (1964) found that beginning teachers needed specific help in meeting problems identified as urgent: provisions for the talented student, evaluation, and classroom control or discipline. Beginning teachers made little provision for the talented students and seemed to have difficulty within the classroom because of an air of friction. The experienced teachers were observed to have developed procedures that made for effective teaching. In-service education aided in the development of skills to handle the problems of beginning teachers. Glasgow (1961) found that it was possible to improve a program in music through in-service education conducted by elementary teachers. Primarily by developing some basic skills he eliminated fear and stimulated interest. Teachers who have had improper or inadequate training in music can be helped to achieve competence through classes in applied music fundamentals.

HUMAN RELATIONS AND GROUP DYNAMICS IN IN-SERVICE EDUCATION. The works of Haan (1964), Flanders (1962, 1963), and Venditti (1966) have indicated the positive aspects that experience in group relations may have on teacher attitudes and activities and how new attitudes can be developed through in-service education. Haan (1964) reported specifically on a cooperative endeavor involving the faculty of a college of education, a psychoanalytic institute, and a group of teachers. Attempts were made to understand what an individual's behavior means to the individual himself and to understand the meaning of unconscious motivations, of the teacher's use of himself and the student's use of the teacher, of the role of personality development in learning, and the emotional involvement of cognitive processes. Through discussions, classroom demonstrations, observations, analyses, and further demonstrations, the group was able to learn to work without undue friction and to bring about an apparent increase in teaching skill. The self-improvement that characterizes a profession seemed to occur, such as the use of research data, a stirring of personal initiative for self-improvement, the employment of colleague cooperation as a means of professional improvement, a focus on the actual operation needing to be improved, the growth of personality, and a deepening understanding of human behavior.

Flanders (1962) investigated the use of interaction analysis in the in-service training of teachers. At the outset of the study involving 55 teachers who participated in a nine-week in-service training program, it was believed that too many teachers lacked a sense of experimentation with regard to their own behavior. Their skills for exploring different verbal patterns in the classroom were very limited. This was held to result from a lack of concepts that refer to behavior. They have too few tools for gathering information systematically. They lack time to develop, understand, and use these data-gathering tools. Teachers in this in-service program were provided with tools for studying classroom interaction, went through discussion periods with teacher teams, were introduced to concepts in theory that were related to the teacher's behavior and his control of classroom activities, and received several hours of observer training. Each teacher then observed, tabulated, and interpreted a matrix of factors relating to colleague's behavior in the classroom. Several assumptions were basic to the project. These included that only a teacher can change his own behavior; that changes can occur in teaching method; that no one pattern of teaching can be adopted universally by all teachers; and that the most effective environment for change allows for freedom of people to express their feelings and ideas, encourages self-direction, and is free of coercion. Not all of the 55 teachers became outstanding experimenters. However, they did show significant changes in their classroom behavior which were consistent with the intent of the training.

Similar positive results came from a cooperative plan for analyzing school integration reported by Venditti (1966). Eighty teachers who were working or would work in integrated or multicultural schools took part. Efforts were made to sensitize fully teachers and other professional staff members of the multicultural schools to the many problems of the culturally disadvantaged child, to focus attention upon specific educational problems that may confront school personnel in multicultural schools, and to provide them with incentive, knowledge, and skills that are requisite to a successful attack upon such problems. Lectures, small-group discussions, field trips, and other techniques were used in analyzing the problems. Because of a planned sequence of presentation of problems as general issues combined with movement toward the practical solution of them, no emotional trauma developed even though the program was integrated. Group discussions permitted the development of genuine rapport among participants. Although evaluation was just beginning when the report was made, definitive changes in attitude toward school integration were observed. Questionnaire responses provided positive reactions from the group about the utilization of information or ideas which were garnered from the material. Over 80 percent of the participants reported that the program had revealed fallacies in their previous beliefs about Negroes. As a result of sound planning and careful management, effective communication was attempted and was made to work. It was demonstrated that when the attempt is made in in-service education programs to present content meaningfully and systematically and to provide maximum opportunities for achieving genuine intergroup and interpersonal rapport, even the most difficult human problems can be made to yield.

A large-scale study of the process of change has been undertaken in five major metropolitan areas through a cooperative program funded by a U.S. Office of Education grant (Cooperative Project for Educational Development, 1966). Coordinated through a prime contract with the University of Michigan, six colleges and universities in the Chicago, Madison (Wisconsin), Detroit, New York, and Boston areas are collaborating on a project for the exploratory development of alternative models of planned change to improve educational systems. Efforts are directed toward contributing to organized knowledge about the processes of change in school systems through a joint university–school-system program in (1) conceptualizing and theorizing about the processes of change, (2) developing strategies for change, (3) trying out these strategies, (4) assessing the results, and (5) interpreting the results.

The Boston-area program is concentrating on three elements of in-service education which can have implications for specific situations:

1. A change-agent seminar designed to aid selected administrators and teachers in different school systems to identify the needs of their school districts and to plan and to implement programs of change.

2. A total faculty concentration on similar activities.

3. A total school-district concentration on districtwide planning in an attempt to move toward self-renewal—the "saturation" strategy.

This four-year program of process and in-service education has been designed to make evaluations of such activities. It may also provide direction for new utilization of group dynamics and human-relations procedures.

Jack R. Childress
Boston University

References

Adams, Mary Lourita. "Instructional Needs of Elementary Teachers in Teaching Reading with the Implications for Televised In-service Education." Doctoral dissertation. U Florida, 1962. 249p.

Black, Marian Watkins. "Florida County Boards and the Curriculum, 1885–1920." *Peabody J Ed* 38:225–33; 1961.

Boyd, Claude Collins. "A Study of the Relative Effectiveness of Selected Methods of In-service Education for Elementary School Teachers." Doctoral dissertation. U Texas, 1961. 166p.

Brandou, Julian Robert. "A Study of an Experimental Program for the In-service Science Education of Elementary School Teachers." Doctoral dissertation. Michigan State U, 1964. 219p.

Brown, Marjory Frances. "A Study of the Guidance In-service Training Programs and Courses Offered by Institutions of Higher Education in the Pacific Coast States." Doctoral dissertation. U Washington, 1962, 284p.

Childress, Jack R. "In-service or Continuing Education for Teachers." *J Ed* 146:36–45; 1965.

Cook, Thomas George. "A Study of In-service Education Programs for Classroom Teachers Utilizing Instructional Television in Selected Public Schools in Michigan." Doctoral dissertation. Michigan State U, 1964. 191p.

Cooksey, Henry Bennett. "Evaluation of an In-service Education Program for English Teachers." Doctoral dissertation. U Texas, 1965. 207p.

Cooperative Project for Educational Development. *An Inter-university Program for the Exploratory Development of Models of Planned Change to Improve Educational Systems.* USOE Project No. 251. U Michigan, 1966

Corey, Stephen. "Introduction." In *In-service Education,* 56th Yearbook, NSSE. U Chicago Press, 1957. p. 1.

Cory, Noel D. "Incentives Used in In-service Education for Teachers." Doctoral dissertation. Indiana U, 1959. 386p.

Dale, Joanne. "In-service Education and the Improvement of Instruction." *J Sec Ed* 39:299–302; 1964.

DeVita, Joseph. "A Stimulating Technique: Teachers Observe Other Teachers." *Clearing House* 37:549–50; 1963.

Doherty, Victor A. "A Solution to One Problem Created by Tenure." *Sch Bd J* 144:20; 1962.

Dossett, Mildred Jerline. "An Analysis of the Effectiveness of the Workshop as an In-service Means for Improving Mathematical Understandings of Elementary School Teachers." Doctoral dissertation. Michigan State U, 1964. 264p.

Duncan, Billy Milton. "A Study of Factors Associated with the Successful Operation of In-service Programs of Education in Selected Alabama Schools." Doctoral dissertation. U Alabama, 1964. 158p.

Dutton, Wilbur H., and Hammond, H. Reginald. "Two In-service Mathematics Programs for Elementary School Teachers." *California J Ed Res* 27:63–7; 1966.

Flanders, Ned A. "Using Interaction Analysis in the In-service Training of Teachers." *J Exp Ed* 30:313–6; 1962.

Flanders, Ned A. "Teacher Behavior and In-service Programs." *Ed Leadership* 21:25–9; 1963.

Fowler, H. Seymour. "Evaluation of an Institute for the Training of Elementary School Science Resource Teachers." *J Ed Res* 53:9; 1960.

Gerheim, Mearl F. "Teacher Evaluation of the Nature and Effectiveness of In-service Teacher Education in Selected School Districts." Doctoral dissertation. U Pittsburgh, 1959. 303p.

Glasgow, Robert Byron. "A Study and Evaluation of

an In-service Training Class in Music for Elementary Teachers." Doctoral dissertation. U Oregon, 1961. 145p.

Haan, Aubrey. "The Teaching Complex: Focus of an In-service Education." *Ed Leadership* 21:285–7; 1964.

Harville, Lacy Edward. "A Study of the In-service Education Program of the Knoxville City Schools." Doctoral dissertation. U Tennessee, 1960. 160p.

Hassel, Carl W. "A Study of Certain Factors to In-Service Education in Selected School Districts in New York State." Doctoral dissertation. Syracuse U, 1960. 366p.

Hayes, Robert Bruce. "A Study of Programs of Pre-service and In-service Education for Cooperating School Supervising Teachers Used by Selected Teacher Education Institutions." U Kansas, 1960. 169p.

Hilarion, Sister M., C.C.V.I. "Cooperation in Supervision." *Cath Sch J* 63:26–8; 1963.

Herman, Jerry J. "The Action Research Approach to In-service Education." *Clearing House* 36:479–80; 1962.

Hurwitz, Sidney N. "Master Teacher Supervision of Beginning Teachers." *Ed Forum* 30:295–301; 1966.

Johnson, Helen M. "Fostering Growth: Pre-service and In-service." *Ed Leadership* 20:97–100; 1962.

Jones, Annie Lee. "In-service Education of Substitute Teachers." *H Sch J* 47:102–7; 1963.

Karbal, Harold T. "The Effectiveness of a Workshop as a Means of In-service Education of Teachers." Doctoral dissertation. Wayne State U, 1963. 243p.

Kerns, Hanan Victor. "A Descriptive Study of the Development and Presentation of an In-school Television Program for the In-service Education of Junior High School Science Teachers." Doctoral dissertation. Auburn U, 1962. 160p.

Lacayo, Maria. "Effects of Spanish In-service Education Program for Teachers on Achievement of Pupils in Grades III Through VI." Doctoral dissertation. Florida State U, 1963. 90p.

Lewin, Charles Robert, Jr. "In-service Education in Relation to Curriculum Development Trends and Recommended Programs in Secondary Schools." Doctoral dissertation. U Southern California, 1963. 278p.

Lucas, John Arthur. *The Orientation of High School Teachers*. U Southern California, 1963. 310p.

Mayer, Frank C. "Closed Circuit Television for In-service Training." *Sch Bd J* 148:39; 1964.

McCollister, John Carl, Jr. "A Study of Courses in Education Offered by State Colleges and Universities in Louisiana in Which In-service Teachers Were Enrolled." Doctoral dissertation. Louisiana U, 1964. 251p.

McCreary, Anne Phillips. "Determining Individual Needs of Elementary Education Teachers as a Basis for an Orientation Program." *J Ed Res* 54:24; 1960.

McDavid, Fred Clyde. "The Critical Requirements of the Role of Department Chairmen in Orienting First-year Teachers in Selected High Schools in Illinois." Doctoral dissertation. Southern Illinois U, 1965. 137p.

McKee, Catherine. "Teachers Improve Their Skills Through On-the-job Training." *Clearing House* 36:259–63; 1962.

McLeod, Jeanne Annette. "In-service Training of Elementary School Teachers in Contemporary Concepts of Arithmetic." Doctoral dissertation. U Southern California, 1965. 296p.

Moffitt, John C. *In-Service Education for Teachers*. Center for Applied Research in Education, Inc., 1963. 107p.

Monk, Oliver Paul. "A Study of Topics in College Preparatory Mathematics with Evaluation of the Use of a Manual in Matrix Algebra for In-service Education." Doctoral dissertation. U Houston, 1966. 252p.

Norris, Robert B. "Credit for Non-credit Courses." *Sch Bd J* 145:7–8; 1962.

Ogeltree, James R., and Edmonds, Fred. "Programming for In-service Growth." *Ed Leadership* 21:288–91; 1964.

Openshaw, Karl. "Attitudes for Growth." *Ed Leadership* 20:90–2; 1962.

Oviatt, Delmar T. "Leaven Within the Loaf." *Ed Leadership* 19:323–7; 1962.

Rapp, William Edward. "Tele-lecture In-service Instruction: Teaching Regular Classroom Teachers About Mental Retardation Utilizing Tele-lecture Instruction." Doctoral dissertation. Colorado State Col, 1964. 95p.

Reed, Carleton Leonard. "Meeting the Urgent Problems of the Beginning Art Teacher in Classes I Through XII: The Teaching Problems of the Beginning Art Teacher, the Related Practices of Successful Art Teachers, and the Practices Recommended in the Art Education Literature." Doctoral dissertation. New York U, 1964. 203p.

Reynard, Harold E. "Pre-service and In-service Education of Teachers." *R Ed Res* 33:373–4; 1963.

Rosser, Neill A. "Student Teaching and In-service Education." *H Sch J* 47:108–11; 1963.

Rubin, Louis J. "A Strategy in Curricular Change." *Ed Leadership* 21:277–9; 1964.

Schild, Robert Joseph. "A Study of Certain Practices and Some Proposed Directions for In-service Education Programs in Selected Schools of the APSS." Doctoral dissertation. Columbia U, 1964. 140p.

Schwalenberg, Richard John. *Teacher Orientation Practices in Oregon Secondary Schools*. U Oregon Press, 1965. 210p.

Selser, Will Lindsay. "An Evaluation of an In-service Institute for Improving Science and Mathematics Instruction in the Hillsborough County Junior High Schools." Doctoral dissertation. U Florida, 1962. 120p.

Singer, Ira J. "Reducing the Research-to-practice Gap." *Audiovisual Instruction* 8:652–5; 1963.

Smith, Hamlin, and others. "The Schools and Teacher Training." *J Sec Ed* 36:224–30; 1961.

Stent, Madelon Delany. "An In-service Course for Beginning Teachers of Three-year Old, Four-year

Old, and Five-year Old Children in Selected Day Care Centers in New York City." Doctoral dissertation. Columbia U, 1965. 200p.

Stradley, William E. "The Perennial Student: Must a Teacher Go to College All His Life?" *Clearing House* 36:500–1; 1962.

Suchy, Robert R. "Co-op ITV for In-service Teacher Training." *Sch Bd J* 151:31; 1965.

Tarbet, Donald G. "Use of Television in In-service Education." *H Sch J* 47:112–7; 1963.

Taylor, Robert L. "In-service Education Needs of New Teachers." *California J Ed Res* 12:221–3; 1961.

Taylor, Robert L. "Are Small High Schools Doing an Adequate Job of In-service Education?" *H Sch J* 47:297–300; 1964.

Todd, Robert Marion. "A Course in Mathematics for In-service Teachers: Its Effect on Teacher Understandings and Attitudes." Doctoral dissertation. U Virginia, 1965, 217p.

Valsame, James. "The Role of the State Department of Public Instruction in In-service Education." *H Sch J* 47:118–22; 1963.

Venditti, Frederick P. "Cooperative Planning for School Integration." *Ed Forum* 30:152–8; 1966.

Weaver, Frank Byrd. "The Effect of a Teacher's In-service Program on Pupils' Adjustments." Doctoral dissertation. Pennsylvania State U, 1962. 83p.

Weaver, J. Fred. "Levels of Geometric Understanding: An Exploratory Investigation of Limited Scope." *Arithmetic Teach* 13:322–32; 1966(*a*).

Weaver, J. Fred. "Nonmetric Geometry and the Mathematical Preparation of Elementary School Teachers." *Am Math Mon* 73:1115–21; 1966(*b*).

Whitmore, Richard F. "Effective Methods for the Orientation and Administration of an In-service Education Program." Doctoral dissertation. U Nebraska, 1960. 158p.

Winsor, Donald L. "The Development of a Course for In-service Education Through Television." Doctoral dissertation. U Florida, 1961. 158p.

Wolf, Willavene, and Wolf, William. "Professional Teamwork Contributes to Professional Education." *Peabody J Ed* 39:43; 1961.

INTELLIGENCE

The nature and measurement of intelligence are of central concern to educators and psychologists. Yet the history of research on intelligence is confined almost entirely to the twentieth century. Prior to 1900 the word *intelligence* was usually a synonym for *knowledge* or *information,* as in the phrase "military intelligence." When used in a psychological sense, *intelligence* was interchangeable with *intellect,* an attribute which all men shared, not one in which they differed (Wechsler, 1958).

The connotations of the word changed radically after 1916, the year in which Lewis M. Terman published his famous *Stanford-Binet* intelligence test. In the half century since then, millions of Americans have taken intelligence tests. The construction and publication of the tests themselves has become big business. "IQ" has become a familiar, if often misunderstood, part of popular vocabulary.

There can be little doubt that intelligence tests have had more impact upon American society than any other invention of psychology, with the possible exception of Freudian psychoanalysis. However, the development of successful intelligence tests is a technological accomplishment. The scientific theory of intelligence has been less satisfactory. For fifty years psychologists have debated the real nature of intelligence and its relationship to scores on tests of intelligence.

Recently, the psychologists' debate has been overshadowed by vigorous public controversy. Ironically, it is the very growth of intelligence testing which is responsible. Decisions of fundamental importance to the individual—who goes to college, who gets the job, who gets drafted—are based in part on tests, and adverse decisions are blamed on tests. Society itself is concerned, for in our current racial difficulties both sides offer test findings to justify their views. How shall these findings be interpreted? Do tests prove the inferiority of minorities or simply reflect the effects of poverty? Are intelligence tests necessary for efficient teaching or simply devices for perpetuating segregation in the schools? Under what circumstances shall the use of tests for industrial hiring be allowed, in the light of court decisions that tests may be unfair to Negroes? (see Ash, 1966).

Clearly, social change is forcing a reexamination of the application of intelligence tests in contemporary society and of the theory of intelligence which underlies them. For an understanding of present-day controversies, we must consider their origins. This history is the substance of Peterson's valuable book (1925). Tuddenham (1962) offers a briefer account.

HISTORICAL DEVELOPMENTS IN INTELLIGENCE TESTING. The measurement of intelligence had its beginnings in the closing decades of the nineteenth century, when a few investigators undertook to quantify individual differences in various postulated mental faculties such as judgment, memory, and imagination. Typical of the approach was that of James McKeen Cattell, who in an 1890 paper first used the phrase "mental test." Testing of presumably separate mental faculties enjoyed a brief vogue. However, the studies of Sharp (1898–1899) and of Wissler (1901) failed to establish much relationship between test findings and academic performance. Interest in such tests waned rapidly, although Whipple's manuals (1914–1915) attest to the breadth of attack of the early investigators.

Binet's Contributions. A more fruitful approach was that of Alfred Binet, who in 1905 produced the first successful intelligence test of the modern type (Binet & Simon, 1905*a*, 1905*b*). Binet's purpose was a practical one—to locate retarded children in the Paris public schools, so that they could be given special education suited to their limited abilities.

Abandoning the faculty approach, Binet assembled a series of brief, varied tasks—defining words, repeating sentences and digit series, counting, copying simple figures, etc. These items were ordered by difficulty and chosen for simplicity of administration and scoring rather than because their content conformed to a priori definitions of particular faculties. A single, global score based on the number of items passed was taken as a loose measure of intelligence-in-general, though Binet did not conceptualize a unitary, linear dimension of general intelligence.

In 1908, Binet revised his scale, this time grouping together items of similar difficulty according to the average age level of the children who could pass them. This concept of mental age underwent further refinement in Binet's third and final revision of 1911, in which items were allocated months of mental-age credit. The number of items a child passed was transmuted into a "mental age" score, corresponding to the age of a theoretical "average child" who passed the same *number* of items.

The Stanford-Binet. Translations of Binet's work by Henry Goddard (1910) brought the new method to the United States. However, it was the publication of Lewis M. Terman's book *The Measurement of Intelligence* (1916) which introduced his American revision, the famous *Stanford-Binet* scale, and launched the testing movement in the United States. Adopting a proposal made by Stern (1914), Terman provided an index of brightness independent of age. This index, called an intelligence quotient, or IQ, was obtained by dividing a child's mental age score by his chronological age. The IQ was easily understood and easily calculated. It soon became the customary method for gauging intelligence. Not until later was it realized that the statistical properties of the mental-age scale are unsuited to the calculation of quotients.

The wide usefulness of the IQ for educational classification was demonstrated by a host of studies. Mental testing became a standard practice in America's schools. New intelligence tests were invented, many resembling the Stanford-Binet, and nearly all basing their claims to validity upon their correlation with it. Some were individual tests like the Stanford-Binet but intended for special groups—preschoolers, the deaf, the blind, the non-English speaking, etc. Some were group tests, designed to be given to many persons simultaneously. An early and influential test of this latter sort was *Army Alpha*, designed for testing large groups of World War I soldiers (Yerkes, 1921). Its companion test for the illiterate was designated *Army Beta*. Although statistically much refined, the *Army General Classification Test* (*AGCT*), administered to over four million soldiers in World War II, did not differ in fundamentals from the *Army Alpha* of a generation earlier (Staff, Personnel Research Section, AGO, 1945).

Age Scales Versus Point Scales. Many tests, both individual and group, adhered to the age-scale format of grouping items by age levels and yielded scores in units of mental age (MA) and of IQ. Other tests adopted the point-scale format, in which items ranging from easy to hard were grouped by content type, and points awarded for the number of items passed. Point totals could be converted to MA's, but in recent years they have been more often converted to standard scores. Such scores take advantage of the normal curve to describe an individual's rarity within his *own* age group, measured in standard deviation units above or below the group average.

The *Stanford-Binet* retained the age-scale format in its 1937 and 1960 revisions, though the IQ obtained on the latter is essentially a standard score. MA's and ratio IQ's based upon them involve statistical difficulties after the growth years of childhood and adolescence are past. Tests for adults, such as *AGCT*, ordinarily utilize the point-scale format and yield standard scores or percentile ranks. Recognition of the statistical complications inherent in the age scale led David Wechsler to adopt the point-scale format for his influential tests for various age groups (Wechsler, 1949, 1955, 1967). Although these tests yield "IQ's," the concept of mental age is wholly abandoned. IQ's on these tests are really standard scores.

Varieties of Tests. Present-day tests of intelligence vary from single-score instruments, e.g., the *Stanford-Binet*, for classifying subjects with respect to global ability, to elaborate batteries, e.g., the *Differential Aptitudes Test* (G. Bennett & others, 1952) yielding separate scores on half a dozen distinguishably different aspects of ability. Some, like the Wechsler tests, attempt to describe the individual's status both with respect to total ability and with respect to the separate components which constitute the whole. Depending upon one's purpose, one can find tests yielding scores at almost any level of generality.

Moreover, well-constructed and well-standardized intelligence tests provide norms for virtually the entire life span. Infant tests were included in Binet and Simon's original scale (1905b) and in Kuhlmann's second American version (1922). Gesell and his coworkers developed, as early as 1925, an extensive series of standardized materials which found their way into later infant and preschool tests such as the *California First Year Scale* (Bayley, 1933), the *Merrill Palmer* (Stutsman, 1931), the *Cattell Infant Scale* (P. Cattell, 1960), and the *Wechsler Preschool and Primary Scale of Intelligence* (Wechsler, 1967). Stott and Ball (1965) have recently provided a critical review and evaluation of infant and preschool tests.

Of individual tests for the school-age child or adolescent, the *Stanford-Binet* in its latest version (Terman & Merrill, 1960) and the *Wechsler Intelligence Scale for Children* (WISC; Wechsler, 1949), are much the most widely used. The former yields MA and IQ scores. The latter yields only "IQ's" but permits separate appraisal of verbal and nonverbal aspects of ability. It also offers for diagnostic use a profile of 12 part scores, though the subtests on which they are based are each too brief to be very reliable.

For adults, the most widely used test is the *Wechsler Adult Intelligence Scale* (*WAIS;* Wechsler, 1955) a revision of the *Wechsler-Bellevue* test.

WAIS closely resembles WISC in format. Guertin and others (1956, 1962, 1966) have provided comprehensive reviews of research involving the Wechsler intelligence scales for adults.

For an explanation of the construction, uses, and limitations of intelligence tests, the reader may consult standard textbooks on psychological testing, e.g., that of Cronbach (1960) or that of Anastasi (1961). Buros' monumental "Mental Measurements" yearbooks, now in their sixth edition (1965), offer detailed descriptions and critical evaluations not only of specific individual tests but also of a host of group tests for special purposes and for special categories of subjects.

Unfortunately, the development of intelligence tests that are statistically sophisticated and well standardized has not resolved controversy about the nature of intelligence itself.

THE THEORY OF INTELLIGENCE. Definitions and Assumptions; The Pragmatic View. It would be reasonable to begin with the definition of intelligence framed by Alfred Binet, the founder of the testing movement. However, nowhere in his voluminous writings did Binet adequately define intelligence as such. Although his later scales embodied all the essential features of modern tests of "general intelligence," they derived not from a formal theory of intelligence but from a lifetime of research devoted to discovering which types of items yield individual differences congruent with age and with judgments of ability. For Binet, intelligence was the resultant of all the higher mental processes in complex interaction. Hence, intelligence could be measured only by an extensive sampling of many kinds of test items.

Other test inventors have offered formal definitions of intelligence. Terman defined it as "the capacity to carry on abstract thinking" ("Intelligence and Its Measurement," 1921). Wechsler said it was "the aggregate or global capacity of the individual to act purposefully, to think rationally, and to deal effectively with his environment" (Wechsler, 1958). From neither definition would one be able to deduce the content of its author's test. As Garrett (1946) remarked, "Omnibus definitions are in general too broad to be wrong and too vague to be useful." Boring's operational definition that intelligence is what the tests measure ("Intelligence and Its Measurement," 1921) gives no guidance for the construction of the tests themselves and offers no resolution for discrepancies which arise between tests. However, it reminds us that the relationships which are asserted to have been discovered between intelligence and other variables such as education, race, and socioeconomic status, are in fact founded on empirical correlations between specific indexes of these variables and specific tests of intelligence.

Although early attempts at definition failed to resolve the nature of intelligence, pragmatic investigators developed a consensus of sorts as to the properties of intelligence. This consensus had wide currency for more than a generation after 1916, a period when the application of intelligence tests for educational and industrial classification went largely unchallenged. Three central assumptions were involved.

First, it was assumed that corresponding to the phrase "general intelligence" there exists a unitary human *trait* or attribute, analogous to stature or weight. This reification of the phrase represented a sharp turning away from Binet and an acceptance of the theoretical position of Charles Spearman (see below) who had provided in 1904 a theoretical rationale for Binet's practice of combining in one test a heterogeneous set of items.

Second, it was assumed that an individual's quantity of general intelligence grew during childhood and adolescence, like stature, along a fixed curve to a terminal maximum set by his heredity. Hence, one's brightness relative to others, expressed by the IQ, was expected to remain constant regardless of one's age.

Third, it was assumed that tests of "general intelligence" were direct measures of the postulated unitary trait. The biological potentialities of individuals and groups with respect to intelligence were considered to correspond to their scores on intelligence tests.

Factor Interpretations of Intelligence. While pragmatists based on the assumptions just mentioned a huge literature on relationships between "intelligence" and other variables, theoreticians continued to struggle with the problem of the ultimate nature of intelligence.

The first, and for many years the most influential, interpretation was that of Charles Spearman. Spearman (1904) assumed that tests were measures of underlying abilities in the persons tested. These abilities were of two kinds: first, specific factors, each to be found only in a single test and hence irrelevant to predicting any other variable; second, a general factor, denoted by "g," which was ubiquitous in *all* tests and in all criterion measures such as school or job success. Further, the general factor could be measured by simply averaging together a large set of heterogeneous test components. As Spearman explains in his autobiography, "In such a hotch-potch of multitudinous measurements, the specific factors must necessarily—since they vary randomly from one measurement to another—tend in the average or mean to neutralize one another. Whereas the general factor, being in every measurement just the same, must in the average more or less completely dominate. Accordingly the average . . . must approximate toward being a measure of the pure general factor. In such wise this principle of making a hotch-potch, which might seem to be the most arbitrary and meaningless procedure imaginable [has] really a profound theoretical basis and a supremely practical utility" (Spearman, 1930, p. 322–324).

Although neither Binet nor Terman was at first attracted by Spearman's theory, it soon dominated the field (Tuddenham 1962). The clear formulation of g, a measurable, unitary trait of *general intelligence*, seemed a major improvement upon Binet's vaguely described intelligence-in-general. To a generation of psychologists accustomed to explanations in terms of underlying faculties of the mind, it added the simplicity and elegance of a single cause. Further, it relieved psychologists of their embarrassing inability to formulate a definition of intelligence rigorous enough to permit one to deduce from it the form and content of an actual test of intelligence. Last, it explained and justified the empirical success of composite "hotchpotch" measures such as the Stanford-Binet.

With the additional doctrine that general intelligence or g is largely determined by heredity—a view sponsored by Henry Goddard, the enthusiastic eugenicist who had introduced Binet's work to the United States—we have the basis for assumptions about intelligence accepted both by educators and by laymen until rather recent times. Nevertheless, the failure of empirical test intercorrelations always to accord with Spearman's predictions made his two-factor view untenable as a rigorous theory of intelligence.

The solution proposed by L. L. Thurstone, called the multiple factor theory, retained Spearman's explanation in terms of underlying variables and retained the notion of specific factors. However, Thurstone proposed that g be replaced by several group factors of somewhat less generality, the actual number of such factors being kept to the minimum required mathematically to account for the intercorrelations observed among tests.

By studying the tests proving to be heavily saturated with a particular factor, the psychological nature of that factor might be deduced and the factor named. One famous factor analysis of intercorrelations of 56 intelligence tests led to the isolation of seven group factors (Thurstone, 1938). These were assigned the names verbal comprehension, word fluency, number ability, spatial visualization, associative memory, perceptual speed, and reasoning. The next task was to construct a new battery of tests, each one to measure a particular group factor, and as free as possible from contamination by the other factors. Thurstone's well-known *Tests of Primary Mental Abilities* (*PMA*) are the product of this approach.

In recent years there has been a general tendency to substitute for single-score "IQ" tests instruments yielding separate measures of several abilities. The variables to be measured by such tests are often chosen on the basis of factor analysis.

At the practical level, there is real advantage to a counselor in having a client's profile of scores across tests of different types, as compared with a single score on general intelligence. However, the factorial approach has not produced test batteries which are much superior for ordinary purposes to diagnostic batteries not based on factor analysis.

At the theoretical level, the replacement of Spearman's formulations by theories which, like Thurstone's, divide g into major components, has solved some problems only to create others. Additional factors have been discovered in such profusion as to destroy the hope that intelligence can be resolved into a handful of fundamental variables, though this was the basis for the doctrine of underlying factors in the first place. In a concise summary of the factor-analytic point of view, Cronbach (1960, p. 260) concedes that the number of factors is inexhaustible provided we are willing to let them be sufficiently trivial.

Guilford (1967) has attempted to bring order out of the welter of factors, with his theoretical "structure of the intellect." Guilford organizes the multiplicity of factors into three broad, abstract classes—*operations*, *products*, and *contents*. Content factors may be classified as figural, symbolic, semantic, or behavioral. Product factors may be grouped according to whether they involve units, classes, relations, systems, transformations, or implications. Operations factors are the most familiar—cognition, memory, divergent thinking, convergent thinking, and evaluation. The distinction between convergent thinking, skill with problems which have specific "right" answers, and divergent thinking, fertility of imagination in finding alternative solutions to nonspecific problems, is of particular interest. It provides a clear definition of and a logical place in the scheme for "creativity," a word whose loose and vague connotations have handicapped research on the subject.

An alternative resolution of the intricacies of mental organization from a factor point of view has been offered by Raymond B. Cattell and his co-workers (Horn & Cattell, 1966), who propose to classify mental factors into two broad groups, those which reflect biological endowment, collectively described as fluid intelligence, and those which reflect experiential-educative-acculturative influences, collectively described as crystallized intelligence.

In spite of, or perhaps because of, the proliferation of factors, Spearman's position has its contemporary advocates. Thus, McNemar, who helped to construct the 1937 and 1960 versions of the *Stanford-Binet*, devoted his 1964 presidential address before the American Psychological Association to a defense of general intelligence.

Some years ago, Thomson (1951) and Tryon (1935) proposed the "sampling theory" as an alternative to Spearman's doctrine of an underlying general factor of intelligence. This theory dispenses entirely with mathematical factors and substitutes the view that the mind contains an indefinitely large number of "bonds," interpretable as "connections" in E. L. Thorndike's sense (E. Thorndike & others, 1927), as synaptic junctions, or even as the "bits" of information theory. Each test calls upon a particular sample of bonds. The correlations between tests are to be explained by overlap in the particular bonds sampled. Men, too, can be thought of as samples of bonds, "each man possessing some, but not all, both of the inherited and acquired neural bonds which are the physical side of thought. Like the tests, some men are rich, others poor in these bonds. Some are richly endowed by heredity, some by opportunity and education; some by both, some by neither" (Thomson, 1951, p. 315).

The sampling theory accounts in simple and elegant fashion not only for the test intercorrelation patterns which Spearman's two-factor theory attempted to explain but also for the enormous proliferation of group factors since Thurstone's day, despite a theoretical commitment by factor analysts to parsimonious explanation.

The innumerable bonds of sampling theory interpreted as learned bits of information account well for the mental content which constitutes "crystallized intelligence" in Raymond B. Cattell's terminology. However, more dynamic variables are needed to account for the *process* of intelligent behavior. Psychological tests confound content and process since both are inextricably involved in thinking. Moreover, they tend to emphasize the content aspect, because they are concerned with estimating the total effectiveness of the person tested, not the plasticity of his nervous system at the time of testing. The work of Halstead (1947) is unusual in emphasizing the process aspect. Direct physiological, chemical, or electrical indexes of central-nervous-system efficiency are not in principle impossible, as Vogel and Broverman (1964) and Loranger and Misiak (1959) have demonstrated for electroencephalography and critical flicker frequency, respectively. Such measures would probably have great utility for diagnosing organic pathology, brain damage, and deteriorative states.

To sum up, alternative theories of the organization of intelligence range from Spearman's doctrine of a single general intelligence, through proposals for sets of multiple group factors of intermediate generality, to the sampling theory, which posits a large array of quite specific bonds and regards factors not as dimensions of the mind but as artifacts of the method. The multiple-group-factor conceptualization was intended to extricate Spearman's theory from its empirical difficulties while retaining his parsimonious description in terms of underlying variables. The proliferation of group factors, however, is forcing factor theorists rapidly toward a conceptualization requiring almost as many explanatory variables as the sampling theorists's. In this impasse, Guilford proposes to simplify the factorial interpretation by ordering the factors into a few broad classes, Cattell seeks theoretical coherence by a somewhat different ordering, and McNemar urges a neo-Spearmanian position.

Clearly, the theoretical nature and organization of intelligence remains controversial. Possibly the reification of the word *intelligence*—the assumption that to the word there must correspond a thing or entity within the person—has led all our thinking astray. As Chein has suggested, "No psychologist has ever observed *intelligence:* many have observed intelligent behavior. This observation should be the starting point of any theory of intelligence" (1945, p. 111). And again, "Intelligence is an attribute of behavior, not an attribute of a person" (ibid, p. 120).

Since we can offer no final resolution of the theory of intelligence, let us move on to a review of what empirical research has discovered about changes in intelligence within the individual.

INTELLECTUAL DEVELOPMENT AND THE LIFE SPAN. The intellectual transformation from infant to adult has been studied most extensively by Jean Piaget and his numerous disciples. This voluminous literature is treated elsewhere in the present volume and will be omitted here for that reason. Suffice it to note that it concerns the typical pattern, not the range of variation, and emphasizes qualitative stages in cognitive development rather than a continuous quantitative process.

Growth in Intelligence in Infancy and Childhood. The status of an individual of whatever age may be compared with the average by means of well-normed tests. Yet it is not possible to describe the shape of the typical growth curve with any precision. Unlike the measurement of stature, the measurement of intelligence is handicapped by the lack of a yardstick with a true zero point and with demonstrably equal units. The units of the mental-age scale almost certainly grow smaller from infancy to puberty, just as do the successive differences between the average one-year-old, two-year-old, three-year-old, etc., with respect to stature. The units of the standard-score scale are equal for a single age group but are measured not from a true zero but from the group average. One cannot splice together the standard-score scales of successive age groups without making dubious assumptions about their equality with respect to absolute variability. Hence, the shape of the typical curve of mental development is as much an artifact of the scale units in which it is plotted as of actual growth in the absolute sense. Nevertheless, it seems reasonable that intellectual development should follow the pattern of physical growth, with rapid gains in infancy, then a gradual deceleration to a stationary level at maturity, followed perhaps by a decline late in life.

Attempts to transcend the limitations of the data and derive an absolute growth curve have been made by Heinis (1926) for the Kuhlmann tests, by Edward L. Thorndike and others (1927) for the *CAVD* group test, and by L. L. Thurstone (1928). Most ingenious was Thurstone's attempt to locate an absolute zero of intelligence. He began by plotting against age the standard deviations of test scores of successive age groups. These standard deviations grew smaller, the younger was the group concerned. From this curve he located the zero point by extrapolation to the age at which variability vanished—a value which turned out to fall in prenatal life!

While these attempts at absolute scaling have been criticized on various grounds, they agree, in general if not in detail, on a negatively accelerated curve for intelligence not unlike that for height. On the basis of them, Bloom (1964) concludes that as much development takes place in the first 4 years of life as in the next 13. If one takes intelligence at 17 years as 100 percent, then 50 percent is achieved between conception and age 4, 30 percent between ages 4 and 8, and 20 percent after age 8.

Descriptions of childhood growth in intelligence are complicated not only by scaling problems but also by the changing nature of intelligence itself. Age changes in total score indicate a general curve of growth. Yet, as previous discussion has suggested, intelligence is a complex variable with many components, not a unitary trait that grows by simple accretion. These components have somewhat different growth curves. The curve of total score on any test is, hence, a sort of average of the curves for different functions.

As intelligence changes, so must the tests. In order to make their instruments maximally discriminating, test constructors choose for any given age level those items on which individual differences are largest. Such items usually involve the functions which are growing most rapidly at the age concerned. Moreover, tests are limited with respect to item content by the behavioral capacities of those for whom they are intended. For these reasons, infant tests typically emphasize sensory-motor skills and omit the reasoning items found at school age levels because infants lack the language skills which reasoning items demand. The *Stanford-Binet* preschool levels contain many motor-manipulative items, but the scale as a whole becomes progressively more verbal with age until little else is left at the adult levels. On the *WISC*, where items of a given content type are grouped from easy to hard in a single subtest, it proved impossible in some instances to preserve the standard item format over the needed range of difficulty. Verbal analogies and counting had to be substituted for similarities and arithmetic problems, respectively, for children younger than eight years old.

Within the limitations imposed by changes in the functions which can be tested at various ages, suggestive results have emerged on the growth of different components of intelligence. Hofstaetter (1954) applied factor analysis to correlations between age levels based on Bayley's longitudinal mental-testing program. He found three distinct factors, the first predominant up to age two, a second for the years two to four, and a third which accounts for nearly all the variance after age four. He named them respectively sensory-motor alertness, persistence, and manipulation of symbols. The last, which must await the acquisition of language, resembles Spearman's g. Smart's replication (1965) confirmed Hofstaetter's finding that the composition of intelligence changes markedly with age. Cronbach (1967) has demonstrated that factor analyses, such as Hofstaetter's, of interage correlations are likely to be antifactual, since arbitrary decisions regarding the beginning and ending of the series produce radical shifts in the ages where new factors become prominent. Nevertheless, the low correlations through time, and especially the progressive content changes in items suitable for preschool scales, demonstrate the sharp difference between functions measurable in infants and those measurable in school-age children.

Growth in Intelligence in Adolescence. In late adolescence, successive age groups cease to show marked increments in average test performance just as they cease to show gains in average stature. It is, hence, impossible to build age scales containing different item sets each appropriate to a specific age level. Instead, enough difficult items are included to preserve the symmetry of the score distributions for adolescent years. Such items do not correspond in difficulty to the average ability of any real age group. Hence, mental ages in late adolescence are in a sense fictitious.

Moreover, we continue to grow older when other growth has ceased. In order to prevent systematic decline in adult IQ's it is necessary to substitute for actual chronological age in the denominator of the IQ ratio an arbitrary chronological age (CA) set at the level beyond which ability ceases to increase. Each inventor of an age scale must choose which arbitrary CA to use for this purpose. If ability increases after the age chosen, the average IQ's of older subjects will rise above their theoretical mean value of 100.

Locating this terminal age level has been a persistent difficulty associated with age scales and a major reason to substitute for them the point-scale format. The 1916 *Stanford-Binet* chose age 16. The 1937 *Stanford-Binet* chose age 15. The 1960 Stanford-Binet Manual provides tabled IQ values to age 18 to allow for growth during late adolescence. However, Freeman and Flory (1937), Robert L. Thorndike (1948), and Bayley (1957) found small increments at least to age 21. The data for Wechsler-Bellevue–I located the maximum between 20 and 25, and the more-recent data for the *WAIS* placed it between 25 and 30 (Wechsler, 1958). Dearborn and Rothney (1941), extrapolating Harvard Growth Study data, concluded growth would continue to age 30, and Bayley and Oden (1955) suggest the possibility that small gains may persist as late as age 50 at least for the intellectually superior.

Different functions apparently grow for different lengths of time. Freeman and Flory (1937) found in repeated testings from 8 years to 17 years that their subjects' scores continued to increase on vocabulary and completion tests but leveled off on analogies and recognition of opposites. Thurstone (1955), using cross-sectional data based on his *Primary Mental Abilities* test, found that 80 percent of the adult standard was achieved on perceptual speed by age 12, on space and reasoning by age 14, on number and memory by age 16, on verbal comprehension by age 18, and on verbal fluency only by age 20.

Not only do different functions have different growth curves, but Garrett (1946) has offered evidence from a number of factor analyses that functions grow more differentiated and independent with increasing age. On the other hand, Meyers and others (1962) found that the differentiation of abilities isolated by factor analysis is already well advanced at age six. Normal children showed more differentiation than retarded ones, but a later study (Meyers & others, 1964) did not support the expectation that abilities would be increasingly differentiated with age. Data for two-, four-, and six-year-olds yielded roughly equal numbers of factors and data on the retarded as many as data on the normal.

Changes in Intelligence in Later Life. The direction and extent of changes in later maturity are as controversial as is the curve of growth in early adulthood. Although the Stanford-Binet rule for calculating adult IQ's with a fixed CA denominator implies that adult intelligence does not change, a pioneering study by Jones and Conrad (1933) cast doubt on the assumption. Administering *Army Alpha* to over 1,000 subjects living in rural New England, they found linear growth in point score up to age 16, slower growth to a peak around age 20, followed by a decline more gradual than the curve of growth, but one which by age 55 receded to the 14-year level. Decline in adulthood was sharpest on the analogies subtest, whereas vocabulary and information showed no decline at all.

The standardization data on the *Wechsler-Bellevue* (*WB*) and on the *WAIS* (Wechsler, 1958) concurred in showing a linear decline after the twenties in overall adult ability. This decline was gradual for three or four decades but speeded up after age 50 or 60. Wechsler regarded this decline as a biological phenomenon of aging and claimed as an advantage for *WB* and *WAIS* the fact that IQ tables for these tests make proper allowance for this downward trend in adult ability. However, Wechsler reported a later peak and a consistently smaller age decline on the more recent test.

Like Jones and Conrad, Wechsler (1958) found markedly different rates of decline on different subtests. Indeed, he proposed a method for evaluating mental deterioration greater than normal by comparing status on four subtests which show minimal age decline (including vocabulary and information) with status on the four most age-susceptible tests (including digit-symbol substitution and copying of block designs). Not surprisingly, the tests which hold up measure stored knowledge, whereas those which decline involve new learning and are scored for speed.

A major study of the *General Aptitude Test Battery* used by the U.S. Employment Service (Droege & others, 1963) found average declines, with education controlled, over the age range 18–70 on all scores except verbal aptitude. The largest drops were on form perception and dexterity. Sizable drops were obtained also on spatial aptitude, clerical perception, and motor coordination.

In contrast, Bayley and Oden (1955), reporting on two follow-ups of Terman and Oden's famous study (1947) of intellectually gifted children at the average ages of 29.5 and 41.5 years, found sharp gains on the second test as compared with the first and for spouses of study subjects as well as for the subjects themselves. The gains occurred at all age, educational, and occupational levels represented. The *Concept Mastery Test*, used by Bayley and Oden, is a high-level group test emphasizing breadth of vocabulary and of information. Speed is not involved in its scoring.

In close agreement with Bayley and Oden, Owens (1953) found gains of about one-half standard deviations in *Army Alpha* scores of men tested 31 years after initial testing as freshmen at Iowa State College. Owens' recent report (1966) on the same group reports a slight but nonsignificant drop from age 50 to age 60 but no increase in variability as a function of aging. Ghiselli (1957) reports similar results. Eisdorfer (1963) found little overall decline on the *WAIS* over a three-year period, even among volunteers aged 60–75 at initial testing.

Intellectual ability is maintained in adult life not only by those of initially superior intelligence. R. Thorndike and Gallup (1944) found that vocabulary level remained practically constant from age 20 to age 70 for a representative sample of American adults. An unpublished follow-up by the writer of career army men of average ability tested at retirement with the *AGCT* found stable scores on reading and vocabulary and on arithmetic, although small drops were found on a spatial-reasoning subtest. Baller and others (1967) found continuing gains in middle-life for subjects classified in childhood as mentally deficient and report that many are now indistinguishable in their communities from normals.

How may the divergent findings on intellectual change in later life be reconciled?

First, it should be noted that reports of gains usually involve tests of accumulated learning from the past—vocabulary, information, and the like. Declines are more often reported for tests which measure efficiency at handling novel tasks, especially where speed of response is a factor. As Raymond Cattell, Wechsler, and others have argued, older subjects may utilize accumulated wisdom, "crystallized intelligence," with little overall loss in effectiveness in dealing with problems which younger subjects solve by alertness and innovative facility.

Second, the declines have usually been found in cross-sectional studies of different subjects at each age. Reports of gains usually involve retests of the same individuals across appreciable intervals of time. A study comparing World War I and World War II soldiers on the same test (Tuddenham, 1948) suggests that older subjects, whose poor performance Wechsler took as evidence of biological decline with age, may never have scored much higher, even when they were young. Is there, then, a secular trend toward higher test intelligence in the population, perhaps in consequence of more and better education and more intellectual stimulation from television and other communication media? That seems likely. Bloom (1964, p. 89) remarks that "it is quite possible that the growth curve of intelligence after age 17 is more a function of the environment in which individuals live and work than it is a consequence of biological and maturational processes."

IQ Constancy: Predictability of the Individual. The Stanford-Iowa controversy of the 1930's over IQ constancy (R. Thorndike, 1940) concerned whether or not environmental enrichment can increase intelligence, an issue to which we shall return. However, the defenders of "IQ constancy" incorrectly inferred that IQ's of *individuals* were stable through time because retest reliability was high over intervals of a few days or weeks and because IQ means and standard deviations for *groups* were the same at successive age levels. It is now recognized that a properly constructed test such as the Stanford-Binet possesses the intrinsic property of yielding constant means and standard deviations of IQ's at successive age levels as a consequence of its structure. This fact is a necessary but not a sufficient condition for IQ constancy in individuals.

In the light of preceding paragraphs, it should be no surprise that IQ constancy, in the sense of temporal stability over appreciable intervals *within the same individual*, is rarely reported despite high retest reliabilities. In general, the agreement between two testings of the same person is the greater the older the child is when first tested and the shorter is the interval between tests. With respect to predictability of status from infant tests, Bayley (1955) found correlations averaging .82 between successive tests a month apart. However, correlations over intervals of a year or more were very low and were virtually zero between infancy and adulthood. She stated (1955, p. 806), "It is now well established that we cannot predict later intelligence from scores on tests made in infancy."

Attempts to improve prediction by constituting scales from items correlating with later status (e.g., Maurer, 1946) have been relatively unsuccessful even for predictions made as late as age two. Furthermore, items which have predictive value are often not the items that best characterize a child's current stage of development. The very nature of intelligence, a dynamic composite of many functions that wax and wane at different rates in the growing organism, severely limits prediction from mental-test scores among the very young.

There remains the possibility that other aspects of infant behavior may be predictive of intelligence in later years. Catalano and McCarthy (1954) reported a correlation of .45 between preverbal vocalizations recorded before eighteen months and IQ at three years. Recent work by Bayley and her colleagues pursuing this lead (Cameron & others, 1967) confirms a correlation of .4 to .5 between a composite vocalization score for the first year of life and IQ at age 26. However, the relationship appears to hold only for girls. The subject deserves much more investigation.

Growth slows during preschool years, and the developing behavior repertory, including language, makes it possible to measure functions more nearly like those tapped by adult tests. Correlations with adult status improve rapidly with age to around .6 or .7 for age 6 versus age 18. However, a part of this improvement is owing to the increasing proportion of variability assignable to overlap in content between tests. Even during "stable" school years between ages 6 and 18, Honzik and others (1948) found that 85 percent of the individuals in their sample showed a discrepancy of 10 or more IQ points between maximum and minimum scores, 58 percent showed discrepancies of 15 or more points, 9 percent of 30 or more points, and individual instances of IQ changes of 50 points were not unknown. Lest it be inferred that such instability characterizes only the brighter-than-average, one should note a study by Charles and James (1964), who found a range of IQ from 90 to 132 among 25 subjects retested at ages between 28 and 40, all of whom had had IQ's between 96 and 104 when tested initially at age 6.

While intelligence tests continue to serve a useful function for educational classification over short intervals, we can no longer regard the IQ as a fixed personal attribute like eye color. The implication is plain. Retests are required whenever major decisions are at stake, at least at intervals no greater than three or four years, until adult status is achieved.

GROUP DIFFERENCES IN INTELLIGENCE. An article of this length can barely touch on the vast literature of the last half century on sex, class, and race differences in intelligence. The topic is treated more adequately in standard texts on individual differences, e.g., those by Anastasi (1958) and Tyler (1965). Miner's comprehensive survey, *Intelligence in the United States* (1957), relates test scores to occupation, sex, marital status, age, race, religion, etc. Current work is periodically summarized in relevant chapters of the *Annual Review of Psychology*. Despite its complexities, the topic is too important to omit it altogether from this review.

Sex Differences. When the first modern intelligence tests were being developed in the years between 1910 and 1920, women's suffrage was an important social issue. At that time, the existence of sex differences in intelligence was very nearly as controversial a subject as is the existence of race differences in our day. Research during that period was largely devoted to refuting popular beliefs in female inferiority and tended to minimize the importance of sex differences.

Although Galton had concluded in the 1880's that men were superior to women in nearly all the simple functions he had measured (see Boring, 1929), Terman reported in 1916 that on tests of the Binet type sex differences were small in respect both to average and to variability. Indeed up to age 13, girls showed a negligible but fairly constant superiority. Thereafter, boys led but by a small margin.

Terman's finding offered test constructors the important advantage that it made unnecessary separate norms for boys and girls. While test material could have been assembled to favor either sex, such items were judged "unfair" to the other sex and eliminated. This is made quite explicit in McNemar's account (1942) of the development of the 1937 revision. The procedure was justified by his statement that "test batteries of extensive scope and varied content as a rule yield only small sex differences in total scores, and when individual test items do show large sex differences these can often be accounted for in terms of known differences in environment or training" (p. 43). Subsequent test constructors have followed the *Stanford-Binet* precedent. They have obviated the need for separate sex norms by selecting content to minimize sex differences; but such tests are hardly the instruments of choice for studying sex differences themselves!

After the battle for women's political rights was largely won, the defensive emphasis upon "equality" gave way to a renewed interest in sex differences.

These are, in fact, extremely common, though they can be averaged out of total test score by a judicious balancing of item content. For example, on the *Stanford-Binet*, girls succeed younger than boys at buttoning and at tying knots. Boys are rather consistently superior to girls at detecting picture absurdities and at certain reasoning items, especially those involving spatial considerations. On the *WAIS*, systematic but mostly negligible differences are reported in favor of men. Nevertheless, women do better than men on vocabulary, similarities, and digit-symbol items, leading Wechsler (1958) to conclude "what poets and novelists have often asserted and the average layman long believed, namely, that men not only behave but 'think' differently from women" (p. 148).

Recent investigators of the topic have placed the emphasis upon discovering the developmental *origins* of sex differences. For example, Honzik (1963) and Bayley and Schaefer (1964) have reported significant differences between boys and girls in the patterning of family variables associated with mental ability. Maccoby (1966) has devoted a book to the nature and development of sex differences in behavior of all kinds.

Class Differences. Test constructors have not ordinarily sought to eliminate class differences. It has been believed that except in a society of rigid castes which prevent mobility, differences in social class are at least as much consequences as causes of differences in intelligence. However, differences in test scores cannot be regarded as reflecting differences in ability unless those for whom the test is intended have had equal opportunity to acquire the experiential background and motivating attitudes presupposed by the test. Testers have attempted to eliminate content which is class-specific, but their success is a matter of keen controversy.

Most standard intelligence tests since the days of Binet have yielded substantial differences between members of different socioeconomic classes and between urban and rural children. Terman, in 1916, reported mean IQ's of 107, 100, and 93 for children classified as superior, average, and inferior in social status. On the 1937 Stanford-Binet, IQ means for children of professional families were 18 or 20 points higher than those of children of laborers, and only 10 percent of the latter exceeded the average IQ of the former (McNemar, 1942). Urban and suburban children resembled each other, but rural children averaged 5 to 10 points lower (*ibid.*).

A major finding from the military testing in World War I (Yerkes, 1921) was the existence of an ordering of occupations by Alpha score, a result which was amply confirmed by the Harrells (Harrell & Harrell, 1945) and by Stewart (1947) for World War II data. This ordering corresponds at least roughly to the ordering that would be obtained if social prestige or remuneration were the dimension instead of intelligence. In general, occupation, education, socioeconomic status, urbanization, and even geographic region of the United States have all been shown to be substantially correlated with average intelligence level (see Anastasi, 1958, or Tyler, 1965).

Some psychologists have contended that standard tests systematically favor the middle class (Eells & others, 1951) and have attempted to produce more nearly "culture fair" tests. The Davis-Eells Test (Davis & Eells, 1953) utilizes words and situations chosen to be equally familiar to middle- and lower-class children. Raymond B. Cattell's Culture Fair Test (1957) and Raven's Progressive Matrices (1958) utilize abstract problems, hopefully of equal novelty to both classes. The last two tests do not involve language and hence may be used with the non-English-speaking and with the deaf. However, average differences between social classes and between ethnic groups often remain conspicuous even on culture-fair measurements (Lesser & others, 1965). Further, if all class and cultural bias could be eliminated from tests, it is likely that much of their validity for predicting school success would be lost, since success in school, as on tests, depends upon possession not only of intellectual skills but also of values and attitudes which are themselves class- and culture-linked (see Noll, 1960).

Race Differences. In contemporary America few issues are as explosive as those involving race differences, specifically, white-Negro differences. There can be little argument over the brute fact that Negroes earn on the average lower scores on intelligence tests than do whites. This fact has been documented in scores of studies from 1918 (Yerkes, 1921) to the present time (e.g., Kennedy & others, 1963). However, the overlap between white and Negro distributions is often more conspicuous than the difference between means, and regional differences within a racial group can be as large as the racial difference itself (Alper & Boring, 1944).

Moreover, race is a biological concept. After more than three centuries of hybridization between African and European, the racial ancestry of the American Negro has a considerable white component. In this country race, so-called, is very much confounded with social class. The most convinced racist would be forced to concede that systematic discrimination against Negroes in education and employment has produced social inequities that make it impossible to attribute wholly to biological inferiority the score inferiority obtained on tests.

The crucial question is not whether differences in test intelligence exist. Rather, it is whether such differences are a consequence of ineradicable biological differences or a consequence of discrimination and hence within the power of our society to eliminate. The social importance of the issue and the emotional biases of investigators complicate what would at best be an extremely difficult question to resolve. Dreger and Miller's review (1960) of white-Negro studies offers criteria for evaluation which point up the inadequacy of nearly every investigation of the problem to date.

It is worth remembering that superiority and inferiority are not general attributes and can be measured only with respect to specific variables. When this is done, the mental superiority of whites to other races is not always found (Darsie, 1926; Dennis, 1942; Smith, 1942).

The study of race differences leads to a more general problem—the relative importance of heredity and environment as determiners of human variability in intelligence. A quarter of a century ago, the problem was to determine how much variance to assign to each factor. A variety of approaches were used, especially comparisons of fraternal and identical twins (Holzinger, 1929; Newman & others, 1937) and of biological and foster children (Burks, 1928; Leahy, 1935). Most of the careful investigations concurred in assigning roughly 80 percent of the variance in intelligence to hereditary factors. Able summaries of this extensive literature are to be found in Woodworth (1941) and in Jones (1954). Also, the National Society for the Study of Education devoted two of its influential yearbooks to the topic (1928, 1940).

In spite of careful observations and sophisticated analyses, the studies were not conclusive. With respect to environment, there was no suitable scale of measurement for evaluating similarity. With respect to heredity, it is impossible to specify precisely the genetic similarity of family members, except, of course, for identical twins. Further, assortative mating, policies of adoption agencies, and other complex factors tended to generate a correlation between the hereditary and environmental sources of variation which researchers were trying to disentangle.

Some investigators turned to animals, where better experimental control could be maintained. Selective breeding of rats (Tryon, 1942) demonstrated that genetic factors alone could produce wide variability in maze brightness when the environment was held rigorously constant.

However, the formulation of the problem of nature and nurture in terms of their relative importance led to an underemphasis of the interaction between the two. Recent studies have focused instead upon the amount of variability in one factor which obtains at various levels of the other. Thus, Cooper and Zubek (1958), replicating the Tryon study, found that both enriched and restricted living environments altered markedly the maze performance of selectively bred bright and dull strains of rats. Recent research (E. Bennett & others, 1964; Rosenzweig, 1966) has even demonstrated anatomical and physiological differences in the brains of rats reared in stimulating or impoverished environments.

Among human beings, Bloom (1964) estimates that impoverishment of the environment may depress IQ as much as 20 points. The effects of child-rearing practices upon the cognitive development of young children have been reviewed by Freeberg and Payne (1967).

Hunt (1961) has reinterpreted the earlier studies as implying that the crucial determiner of intelligence in human beings is not genetic endowment but environmental stimulation. Many of Hunt's premises are unquestionably correct. Intelligence as measured by tests is *not* a unitary, biological trait. It does not develop in an environmental vacuum, nor does it progress along an immutable course to a pre-destined end-point. Appropriate environmental intervention does seem to raise IQ, though the permanence of such improvement has not been established. Yet Hunt's implication that human differences derive mostly from differences in experiential opportunities is debatable. The counterevidence in relation to white-Negro differences is set forth in Shuey's recent volume (1966).

In any case, the evidence suggests that environmental interventions have greater influence, the younger the subject. Lee's study (1951) of Negro children in Philadelphia showed not only that migration to the more stimulating environment of a Northern city raised IQ, but also that migration was decreasingly effective, the older the child was when he moved North. It seems to follow that enrichment programs are more effective in ameliorating the consequences of slum living if they are undertaken as early as possible in the preschool years. However, gains are likely to be temporary unless the regular school curriculum is itself constructed to maintain the maximum stimulation and motivation of children who have had at best no more than a "head start."

For those who must evaluate the test performance of children ethnically unlike those for whom our tests were devised, Deutsch and others (1964) offer useful suggestions. However, Katz's review (1964) indicates that the consequences of desegregation for the intellectual performance of Negroes are complex. We do not yet have sufficient information in this area. Specific local circumstances have a major bearing upon whether desegregation assists or hinders the Negro pupil in achieving his own potentialities.

Intellectual Differences in a Democratic Society. *Intelligence* is a word whose connotations are obvious but whose precise, denotative meaning, after fifty years of intensive investigation, is still a matter for debate. If this discussion has seemed more concerned with intelligence tests than with intelligence, it is because our knowledge of intelligence does not transcend our measures of it and the assumptions, explicit and implicit, which underlie them. Further, the objective facts have a way of changing in parallel with the intellectual currents of society. Viewed in retrospect, facts are only interpretations, and often untenable ones at that!

Yet, for all its limitations, our understanding of the nature and conditions of intelligence is of the greatest social consequence. Increasing concern about and even hostility to intelligence tests (Brim, 1965; Brim & others 1965) on the part of important segments of the public are a consequence of the increasing part played by test results in educational and occupational decisions which affect the individual. A special issue of the *American Psychologist* (Vol. 20, No. 11, November 1965) wholly devoted to testing and public policy, and the rising frequency with which other articles on the subject are being published, are evidence that mental testers are increasingly aware of their responsibilities as de facto social engineers. However, their future activities are likely to be based as much upon their social philosophies as upon "facts" derived from research.

Research of the last 25 years has indicated that intelligence, far from being rigidly determined by the genes, is, like most complex human attributes, susceptible to considerable modification. Shall we use this knowledge to help each child achieve his own unique potentialities or to fit him more closely to some standard or norm? Shall we view human diversity as a resource of democratic society or as a threat to cherished values of political equality?

Gardner's thoughtful inquiry into excellence (1961) points out that society has alternatives in coping with human variability. It may attempt to institutionalize differences, real or imaginary, by a system of hereditary stratification; it may deny the existence of differences and attempt to iron them out; or it can capitalize on them by maximizing opportunity for each individual to achieve that position in which his social contribution and sense of self-fulfillment will be greatest. Tests, if well used, are a means to this end.

Aristocrats and equalitarians alike tend to be hostile to tests: the former because tests threaten to expose discrepancies between privilege and merit, the latter because tests refute the equalitarian dogma. Fifty years ago, agitation for overdue social reform created an atmosphere influencing even scientists to minimize sex differences in intellectual functions, though we are now finding them a fruitful field of inquiry. Today, impelled by the obvious and urgent need to secure justice for our racial and ethical minorities, a new generation of Procrusteans has arisen to assert that we are basically all just alike— and to work to make it true. Their humanitarian concerns lead them to attack intelligence tests not because they classify imperfectly but because they classify at all (see Gardner, 1961, p. 47–48).

Although stable societies tend toward class rigidities, mobility in our own is still possible. Mass education is one of the most powerful forces facilitating it, but it must not lose sight of differences among those it serves. We should all strive to increase equality of opportunity and to keep open the paths of mobility. It does not follow that we are or should be all alike. We should remember that although cultural deprivation is one causal factor in creating differences in intelligence, it does not follow that all differences are necessarily a consequence of cultural deprivation. In the long history of the species, variability of all sorts has had too much biological survival value ever to disappear while man himself endures.

Read D. Tuddenham
University of California

References

Alper, Thelma G., and Boring, Edwin G. "Intelligence-test Scores of Northern and Southern White and Negro Recruits in 1918." *J Abn Social Psychol* 39:471–4; 1944.

Anastasi, Anne. *Differential Psychology*, 3rd ed. Macmillan, 1958. 664p.

Anastasi, Anne. *Psychological Testing*, 2nd ed. Macmillan, 1961. 657p.

Ash, Philip. "The Implications of the Civil Rights Act of 1964 for Psychological Assessment in Industry." *Am Psychologist* 21:797–803; 1966.

Baller, Warren R., and others. "Mid-life Attainment of the Mentally Retarded." *Genet Psychol Monogr* 75:239–389; 1967.

Bayley, Nancy. *The California First-year Mental Scale*. U California, 1933. 24p.

Bayley, Nancy. "On the Growth of Intelligence." *Am Psychologist* 10:805–18; 1955.

Bayley, Nancy. "Data on the Growth of Intelligence Between 16 and 21 Years as Measured by the Wechsler-Bellevue Scale." *J Genet Psychol* 90:3–15; 1957.

Bayley, Nancy, and Oden, Melita H. "The Maintenance of Intellectual Ability in Gifted Adults." *J Geront* 10:91–107; 1955.

Bayley, Nancy, and Schaefer, Earl S. "Correlations of Maternal and Child Behaviors with the Development of Mental Abilities: Data from the Berkeley Growth Study." *Monogr Social Res Child Develop* 29 (No. 6); 1964. 80p.

Bennett, Edward L., and others. "Chemical and Anatomical Plasticity of the Brain." *Sci* 146:610–9; 1964.

Bennett, George K., and others. *Differential Aptitude Tests*, Manual. 2nd ed. Psych Corp, 1952. 77p.

Binet, Alfred. "Nouvelles Recherches sur la mesure du niveau intellectuel chez les enfants de l'école." *L'Année psychologique* 17:145–210; 1911.

Binet, Alfred, and Simon, T. "Méthodes nouvelles pour le diagnostic du niveau intellectuel des anormaux." *L'Année psychologique* 11:191–244; 1905(a).

Binet, Alfred, and Simon, T. "Application des méthodes nouvelles au diagnostic du niveau intellectuel chez des enfants normaux et anormaux d'hospice et d'école primaire." *L'Année psychologique* 11:245–336; 1905(b).

Binet, Alfred, and Simon, T. "Le Développement de l'intelligence chez les enfants." *L'Année psychologique* 14:1–94; 1908.

Bloom, Benjamin S. *Stability and Change in Human Characteristics*. Wiley, 1964. 237p.

Boring, Edwin G. *A History of Experimental Psychology*. Appleton, 1929. 699p.

Brim, Orville G., Jr. "American Attitudes Toward Intelligence Tests." *Am Psychologist* 20:125–30; 1965.

Brim, Orville G., Jr., and others. *Experiences and Attitudes of American Adults Concerning Standardized Intelligence Tests*. Technical Report No. 1 on the Social Consequences of Testing. Russell Sage, 1965. 194p.

Burks, Barbara S. "The Relative Influence of Nature and Nurture Upon Mental Development." In 27th Yearbook, NSSE, 1928. Part I, p. 219–316.

Buros, Oscar K. *The Sixth Mental Measurements Yearbook*. Gryphon, 1965. 1714p.

Cameron, James, and others. "Infant Vocalizations and their Relationship to Mature Intelligence." *Sci* 157:331–3; 1967.

Catalano, Frank L., and McCarthy, Dorothea. "Infant Speech as a Possible Predictor of Later Intelligence." *J Psychol* 38:203–9; 1954.

Cattell, James McKeen. "Mental Tests and Measurements." *Mind* 15:373–81; 1890.

Cattell, Psyche. *The Measurement of Intelligence of Infants and Young Children*, rev. ed. Psych Corp, 1960. 270p.

Cattell, Raymond B. *The IPAT Culture Fair Intelligence Scales*. Institute for Personality and Ability Testing, U Illinois, 1957. 54p.

Charles, Don C., and James, Suzanne T. "Stability of Average Intelligence." *J Genet Psychol* 105:105–11; 1964.

Chein, Isidor. "On the Nature of Intelligence." *J Gen Psychol* 32:111–26; 1945.

Cooper, R. M., and Zubek, John P. "Effects of Enriched and Restricted Early Environment on the Learning Ability of Bright and Dull Rats." *Canadian J Psychol* 12:159–64; 1958.

Cronbach, Lee J. *Essentials of Psychological Testing*, 2nd ed. Harper, 1960. 650p.

Cronbach, Lee J. "Year-to-year Correlations of Mental Tests: A Review of the Hoffstaetter Analysis." *Child Develop* 38:283–9; 1967.

Darsie, Marvin L. "Mental Capacity of American-born Japanese Children." *Compar Psychol Monogr* 3 (No. 15); 1926. 89p.

Davis, Allison, and Eells, Kenneth. *Davis-Eells Test of General Intelligence or Problem-solving Ability*, Manual. Harcourt, 1953. 72p.

Dearborn, Walter F., and Rothney, John W. M. *Predicting the Child's Development*, 2nd ed. Sci-Art, 1941. 368p.

Dennis, Wayne. "The Performance of Hopi Children on the Goodenough Draw-a-Man Test." *J Compar Psychol* 34:341–8; 1942.

Deutsch, Martin, and others. "Guidelines for Testing Minority Group Children." *J Social Issues* 22:129–45; 1964.

Dreger, R. M., and Miller, K. S. "Comparative Psychological Studies of Negroes and Whites in the United States." *Psychol B* 57:361–402; 1960.

Droege, Robert C., and others. "Relationship Between G.A.T.B. Aptitude Scores and Age for Adults." *Personnel Guid J* 41:502–8; 1963.

Eells, Kenneth, and others. *Intelligence and Cultural Differences*. U Chicago Press, 1951. 388p.

Eisdorfer, Carl. "The WAIS Performance of the Aged: A Retest Evaluation." *J Geront* 18: 169–72; 1963.

Freeberg, Norman E., and Payne, Donald T. "Parental Influence on Cognitive Development in Early Childhood: A Review." *Child Develop* 38:65–87; 1967.

Freeman, Frank N., and Flory, Charles D. "Growth in Intellectual Ability as Measured by Repeated Tests." *Monogr Social Res Child Develop* 2 (No. 2); 1937. 116p.

Gardner, John W. *Excellence: Can We Be Equal and Excellent Too?* Harper, 1961. 171p.

Garrett, Henry E. "A Developmental Theory of Intelligence." *Am Psychologist* 1:372–8; 1946.

Gesell, Arnold. *The Mental Growth of the Preschool Child*. Macmillan, 1925. 447p.

Ghiselli, Edwin E. "The Relationship Between Intelligence and Age Among Superior Adults." *J Genet Psychol* 90:131–42; 1957.

Goddard, Henry H. "A Measuring Scale for Intelligence." *Train Sch* 6:146–55; 1910.

Guertin, Wilson H., and others. "Research with the WB Intelligence Scale 1950–1955." *Psychol B* 53:235–57; 1956.

Guertin, Wilson H., and others. "Research with the Wechsler Intelligence Scales for Adults: 1955–1960." *Psychol B* 59:1–26; 1962.

Guertin, Wilson H., and others. "Research with the Wechsler Intelligence Scales for Adults: 1960–1965." *Psychol B* 66:385–409; 1966.

Guilford, J. P. *The Nature of Human Intelligence*. McGraw-Hill, 1967. 538p.

Halstead, Ward C. *Brain and Intelligence*. U Chicago Press, 1947. 206p.

Harrell, Thomas W., and Harrell, Margaret S. "Army General Classification Test Scores for Civilian Occupations." *Ed Psychol Meas* 5:299–39; 1945.

Heinis, H. "A Personal Constant." *J Ed Psychol* 17:163–86; 1926.

Hofstaetter, Peter R. "The Changing Composition of 'Intelligence': A Study in t-Technique." *J Genet Psychol* 85:159–64; 1954.

Holzinger, Karl J. "The Relative Effect of Nature and Nurture Influences on Twin Differences." *J Ed Psychol* 20:241–8; 1929.

Honzik, Marjorie P. "A Sex Difference in the Age of Onset of the Parent-Child Resemblance in Intelligence." *J Ed Psychol* 54:231–7; 1963.

Honzik, Marjorie P., and others. "The Stability of Mental Test Performance Between Two and Eighteen Years." *J Exp Ed* 17:309–24; 1948.

Horn, John L., and Cattell, Raymond B. "Refinement and Test of the Theory of Fluid and Crystallized General Intelligences." *J Ed Psychol* 57:253–70; 1966.

Hunt, Joseph McV. *Intelligence and Experience*. Ronald, 1961. 416p.

"Intelligence and Its Measurement." Symposium. *J Ed Psychol* 12:123–47, 195–216; 1921.

Jones, Harold E. "The Environment and Mental Development." In Carmichael, Leonard. (Ed.) *Manual of Child Psychology*, 2nd ed. Wiley, 1954. p. 631–96.

Jones, Harold E., and Conrad, Herbert S. "The Growth and Decline of Intelligence: A Study of a Homogeneous Group Between the Ages of Ten and Sixty." *Genet Psychol Monogr* 13:223–98; 1933.

Katz, Irwin. "Review of Evidence Relating to Effects of Desegregation on the Intellectual Performance of Negroes." *Am Psychologist* 19:381–99; 1964.

Kennedy, Wallace A., and others. "A Normative Sample of Intelligence and Achievement of Negro Elementary School Children in the Southeastern

United States." *Monogr Social Res Child Develop* 28 (No. 6); 1963. 112p.

Kuhlmann, Frederick. *A Handbook of Mental Tests.* Warwick, 1922. 208p.

Leahy, Alice M. "Nature-Nurture and Intelligence." *Genet Psychol Monogr* 17:235–308; 1935.

Lee, Everett S. "Negro Intelligence and Selective Migration: A Philadelphia Test of the Klineberg Hypothesis." *Am Sociol R* 16:227–33; 1951.

Lesser, Gerald S., and others. "Mental Abilities of Children from Different Social Class and Cultural Groups." *Monogr Social Res Child Develop* 30 (No. 4); 1965. 115p.

Loranger, Armand W., and Misiak, Henry K. "Critical Flicker Frequency and Some Intellectual Functions in Old Age." *J Geront* 14:323–7; 1959.

Maccoby, Eleanor E. (Ed.) *The Development of Sex Differences.* Stanford U Press, 1966. 351p.

Maurer, Katherine M. *Intellectual Status at Maturity as a Criterion for Selecting Items in Pre School Tests.* U Minnesota Press, 1946. 166p.

McNemar, Quinn. *The Revision of the Stanford-Binet Scale.* Houghton, 1942. 185p.

McNemar, Quinn. "Lost: Our Intelligence. Why?" *Am Psychologist* 19:871–82; 1964.

Meyers, C. E., and others. "Primary Abilities at Mental Age Six." *Monogr Social Res Child Develop* 27 (No. 1); 1962. 40p.

Meyers, C. E., and others. "Four Ability-factor Hypotheses at Three Preliterate Levels in Normal and Retarded Children." *Monogr Social Res Child Develop* 29 (No. 5); 1964. 80p.

Miner, John B. *Intelligence in the United States: A Survey, with Conclusions for Manpower Utilization in Education and Employment.* Springer-Verlag OHG, 1957. 180p.

National Society for the Study of Education. *Nature and Nurture: Their Influence upon Intelligence.* 27th Yearbook, Part I. Public-Sch, 1928. 465p.

National Society for the Study of Education. *Intelligence: Its Nature and Nurture.* 39th Yearbook, Parts I and II. Public-Sch, 1940. Part I, 471p.; Part II, 409p.

Newman, Horatio H., and others. *Twins: A Study of Heredity and Environment.* U Chicago Press, 1937. 369p.

Noll, Victor H. "Relation of Scores on Davis-Eells Games to Socio-economic Status, Intelligence Test Results, and School Achievement." *Ed Psychol Meas* 20:119–30; 1960.

Owens, William A. "Age and Mental Abilities: A Longitudinal Study." *Genet Psychol Monogr* 48:3–54; 1953.

Owens, William A. "Age and Mental Abilities: A Second Adult Follow-up." *J Ed Psychol* 57:311–25; 1966.

Peterson, Joseph. *Early Conceptions and Tests of Intelligence.* Harcourt, 1925. 320p.

Raven, John C. *Guide to the Standard Progressive Matrices: Sets A, B, C, D, and E.* Lewis, 1958.

Rosenzweig, Mark R. "Environmental Complexity, Cerebral Change, and Behavior." *Am Psychologist* 21:321–32; 1966.

Sharp, Stella. "Individual Psychology: A Study in Psychological Method." *Am J Psychol* 10:329–91; 1898–1899.

Shuey, Audrey M. *The Testing of Negro Intelligence*, 2nd ed. Social Science Press, 1966. 578p.

Smart, Russell C. "The Changing Composition of Intelligence: A Replication of a Factor Analysis." *J Genet Psychol* 107:111–6; 1965.

Smith, Stevenson. "Language and Non-verbal Test Performance of Racial Groups in Honolulu Before and After a 14-year Interval." *J Gen Psychol* 26:51–93; 1942.

Spearman, Charles E. "General Intelligence Objectively Determined and Measured." *Am J Psychol* 15:201–93; 1904.

Spearman, Charles E. "Autobiography." In Murchison, Carl. (Ed.) *A History of Psychology in Autobiography*, Vol. 1. Clark U Press, 1930. p. 299–333.

Staff, Personnel Research Section, AGO. "The Army General Classification Test." *Psychol B* 42:760–8; 1945.

Stern, William. *The Psychological Methods of Testing Intelligence.* Translated by Guy M. Whipple. Warwick, 1914. 160p.

Stewart, Naomi. "AGCT Scores of Army Personnel Grouped by Occupation." *Occupations* 26:5–41; 1947.

Stott, Leland H., and Ball, Rachel S. "Infant and Preschool Mental Tests: Review and Evaluation." *Monogr Social Res Child Develop* 30 (No. 3); 1965. 151p.

Stutsman, Rachel. *Mental Measurement of Preschool Children.* Harcourt, 1931. 368p.

Terman, Lewis M. *The Measurement of Intelligence.* Houghton, 1916. 362p.

Terman, Lewis M., and Merrill, Maud A. *Measuring Intelligence.* Houghton, 1937. 461p.

Terman, Lewis M., and Merrill, Maud A. *Stanford-Binet Intelligence Scale: Manual for the Third Revision, Form L-M.* Houghton, 1960. 363p.

Terman, Lewis M., and Oden, Melita H. *Genetic Studies of Genius. The Gifted Child Grows Up.* Vol. 4: Stanford U Press, 1947. 448p.

Thomson, Godfrey H. *The Factorial Analysis of Human Ability*, 5th ed. Houghton, 1951. 383p.

Thorndike, Edward L., and others. *The Measurement of Intelligence.* Teachers Col, Columbia U, 1927. 616p.

Thorndike, Robert L. "Constancy of the IQ." *Psychol B* 37:167–86; 1940.

Thorndike, Robert L. "Growth of Intelligence During Adolescence." *J Genet Psychol* 72:11–5; 1948.

Thorndike, Robert L., and Gallup, George A. "Verbal Intelligence of the American Adult." *J Gen Psychol* 30:75–85; 1944.

Thurstone, L. L. "The Absolute Zero in Intelligence Measurement." *Psychol R* 35:175–97; 1928.

Thurstone, L. L. *Primary Mental Abilities.* Psychometric Monographs, No. 1. U Chicago Press, 1938. 121p.

Thurstone, L. L. *The Differential Growth of Mental*

Abilities. Paper No. 14. Psychometric Laboratory, U North Carolina, 1955. 8p.

Tryon, Robert C. "A Theory of *Psychological* Components—An Alternative to 'Mathematical Factors.'" *Psychol R* 42:425–54; 1935.

Tryon, Robert C. "Individual Differences." In Moss, F. A. (Ed.) *Comparative Psychology.* Prentice-Hall, 1942. p. 409–48.

Tuddenham, Read D. "Soldier Intelligence in World Wars I and II." *Am Psychologist* 3:54–6; 1948.

Tuddenham, Read D. "The Nature and Measurement of Intelligence." In Postman, Leo. (Ed.) *Psychology in the Making.* Knopf, 1962. p. 469–525.

Tyler, Leona E. *The Psychology of Human Differences,* 3rd ed. Appleton, 1965. 572p.

Vogel, William, and Broverman, Donald M. "Relationship Between EEG and Test Intelligence: A Critical Review." *Psychol B* 62:132–44; 1964.

Wechsler, David. *Wechsler Intelligence Scale for Children,* Manual. Psych Corp, 1949. 113p.

Wechsler, David. *Wechsler Adult Intelligence Scale,* Manual. Psych Corp, 1955. 110p.

Wechsler, David. *The Measurement and Appraisal of Adult Intelligence,* 4th ed. Williams and Wilkins, 1958. 297p.

Wechsler, David. *Wechsler Preschool and Primary Scale of Intelligence,* Manual. Psych Corp, 1967. 129p.

Whipple, Guy M. *Manual of Mental and Physical Tests,* 2nd ed. Warwick, 1914–1915. Vol. 1, 365p.; Vol. 2, 336p.

Wissler, Clark. "The Correlation of Mental and Physical Tests." *Psychol R, Monogr Supplement* 3 (No. 6); 1901.

Woodworth, Robert S. *Heredity and Environment.* Bulletin 47. Social Science Research Council, 1941. 95p.

Yerkes, Robert M. (Ed.) *Psychological Examining in the United States Army.* Memoirs of the National Academy of Science, Vol. 15. GPO, 1921. 890p.

INTELLIGENCE AND SPECIAL APTITUDE TESTS

Interest in measuring intelligence goes back at least to 1838, when the French physician Esquirol attempted to assess different degrees of feeblemindedness, using a variety of procedures. His research caused him to conclude that the individual's use of language gave the best indication of his mental level, thus establishing the importance of verbal ability in the measurement of what we have come to designate as intelligence. His procedures enabled him to distinguish, to his own satisfaction, between two grades of imbecility and three grades of idiocy. He concluded, for example, that the higher-grade imbecile employs speech with some fluency whereas one of lower grade finds speech difficult and uses a limited vocabulary. He also indicated levels of idiocy by noting whether his subjects were able to use many or few words.

Those classified as higher-type idiots were able to use a few words and very short phrases, if any; the second group was capable of very few monosyllabic words; whereas the lowest class could manage no language at all (Anastasi, 1961a).

Before the end of the nineteenth century, several others had pioneered in the field of mental testing, notable among them being Francis Galton, whose approach to the problem was chiefly through tests of strength, speed of reaction, and sensory discrimination, which he believed would serve as indexes of intellect. One of the Americans to make significant contributions to the study of mental testing during this period was James McKeen Cattell. In his psychological studies he had worked with Wilhelm Wundt in the Leipzig laboratory. Despite Wundt's lack of interest in this type of investigation, Cattell chose to complete his doctoral dissertation on individual differences in reaction time. Later his contacts with Galton led to even greater interest in individual differences, which he continued to explore on his return to America. As a professor at the University of Pennsylvania, he sought to find a method of determining prospective students' abilities in order that he might advise them in advance on their chances for college success. It is interesting to note how very numerous have been later studies with the same objective, none of them meeting with complete success. The failure of Cattell's tests to show significant relationships between the scores on them and college grades may be attributed in large part to the nature of the tests, which were concerned with such matters as keenness of vision and hearing, color vision, sensitivity to pain, reaction time, rote memorization, and color preferences. Somewhat similar tests were tried by Jastrow and others, but none of them gave evidence of being very successful in predicting success in school or college (Guilford, 1959).

Some of the European psychologists were at that time working with tests of more complex functions. Among these workers were Oehrn, Emil Kraepelin, and Hermann Ebbinghaus in Germany and the Italian psychologist Ferrari. Alfred Binet in France had already shown an interest in measurement problems, and he and V. Henri in 1895 published an article critical of much of the work done up to that time as being too much devoted to tests of sensory functions and to tests of specialized abilities (Binet & Henri, 1895).

GENERAL INTELLIGENCE TESTS. Development of Individual Tests. It was the work of Binet which ultimately led to a better approach to mental measurement. When, in 1904, he became a member of a commission appointed by the French minister of public instruction to study procedures for the education of subnormal children in Paris and to devise means of identifying those who could not profit from the usual school procedures, he had already done much experimenting with various techniques. Also, he had come to the conclusion that the most rewarding procedure was to set up some tasks with which the intellect must cope and then to observe what happened. He was thus able, in collaboration with Simon, to publish in 1905 the first of the Binet-Simon scales. In common with other tests of this period, these scales included some sensory and perceptual tests, but the special emphasis was on reasoning, comprehension, and items requiring judgment. No systematic line of demarcation between the normal and the subnormal had as yet been developed; nor was there any precise method for obtaining a total score.

The second edition of these tests, published in 1908, was a decided improvement, with the number of tests increased, unsatisfactory items eliminated, and the tasks grouped for children of different ages from 3 to 13. For example, tests which normal 6-year-olds could pass but which proved troublesome for most 5-year-olds were placed at the sixth-year level. This procedure made it possible to express the child's level of intelligence in terms of "mental age," indicating that he was able to complete the tasks usually completed by children at a given chronological age level. Because the concept of mental age is so simple, it has been extensively used ever since. A third edition published in 1911, shortly before Binet's death, had minor revisions, more items at some levels, and an extension to the adult level; but the changes in fundamental procedure were minimal.

Problems of education in America being similar to those in Europe, the Binet-Simon tests were eagerly studied by psychologists and others in the United States. In 1910 Henry Goddard, director of the training school for retarded children in Vineland, New Jersey, made a translation with minor adaptations. Because of his enthusiasm for the tests, he gave encouragement to teachers and others with limited backgrounds in psychology to use them, with the result that they were often badly used, and their reputation suffered (Chauncey & Dobbin, 1963). Fred Kuhlmann also used a translated version with inmates of an institution for the feebleminded at Faribault, Minnesota, and later, in 1912, published an edition for American use which has been revised several times (Noll, 1965).

But it was the careful work of Lewis M. Terman which set in motion a large-scale movement of intelligence testing. Having done some work independently before the Binet-Simon scales appeared, he promptly set about making translations from the French and making adaptations that would make the items more suitable for American children. Some of Binet's items were eliminated and new ones added. Being a careful worker, he did not rush publication, and in 1916 there appeared the Stanford Revision of the Binet Scale which was to become the standard instrument for intelligence measurement in English-speaking countries for more than two decades. There were tests for each age from 3 to 10, inclusively, and also tests for ages 12 and 14. In addition, there were two more-difficult groups of tests, one designated as average adult, the other as superior adult (Terman, 1916).

Despite Terman's painstaking work, some weaknesses appeared as more and more studies with and of the Stanford-Binet were made. As a result, Terman and Maud R. Merrill (1937) developed a revision in 1937 which not only extended the scales downward to age two and provided for much more thorough testing at the adult level but also made improvements and additions throughout. Two forms, L and M, were provided, and standardization was made on a more normative population than that used in the 1916 edition. These two forms are still widely used, but in 1960 a third revision appeared, this time in a single form. Known as Form L-M, this revision contains those items of the two previous forms that had proven to be most valid and reliable (Terman & Merrill, 1960).

Aside from the Stanford-Binet, the most widely used individual tests of intelligence are those produced by David Wechsler. Partly because he found that the Stanford-Binet was limited in comprehensiveness and suitability for adult subjects, he published in 1939 the Wechsler-Bellevue Intelligence Scale. Probably because this scale, which was designed for and standardized for the most part on adults, came to be used with children, for whom there was somewhat inadequate material, there was published ten years later the Wechsler Intelligence Scale for Children (WISC). This scale, designed for children from ages 5 to 15, was extended in 1967 to provide also for 4-year-olds. In 1955 a revision of the Wechsler-Bellevue Scale, known as the Wechsler Adult Intelligence Scale (WAIS), also appeared. Each of these more recent editions consists of a verbal scale and a performance scale and provision is made for a verbal IQ, for a performance IQ, and for a full-scale IQ (Wechsler, 1949, 1958).

Development of Group Tests. Because individual tests of intelligence require so much time of competent and well-trained personnel for their administration—generally from 20 minutes to a full hour, or even more, per person—methods of testing groups were sought shortly after the intelligence-testing movement got under way. Binet had indicated an interest in the possibility of using such tests for the classification of army personnel (Peterson, 1925), but it was Arthur Otis who, by 1917, had made substantial progress in the development of group tests, working as a student under Terman. When the United States became involved in World War I, a committee of psychologists headed by Robert Yerkes was formed at the request of the War Department to devise a group test for use in classifying men entering the army. In part because it was permitted to draw heavily on the work of Otis, this committee was able to develop rather quickly a helpful test known as the Army Alpha. Administered to almost two million soldiers, the test required reading ability at about the sixth-grade level. However, some of the drafted men were unable to read at this level. Some were completely illiterate, and others, though literate, had little knowledge of English, so the Army Beta was later developed. It required no reading, and could be administered so as to be reasonably intelligible to those with language handicaps.

School personnel, seeing the possibility of testing

large numbers of students instead of the limited numbers possible with the Stanford-Binet, administered thousands of the Army Alpha and Army Beta tests, largely to high school and college students, when these tests were released for general use. Besides being of limited use in the elementary schools, these tests were found unsatisfactory for schools in other respects, but group tests especially designed for schools soon appeared. Among the earliest were the Otis Group Intelligence Scale, published in 1918, and the Terman Group Test of Mental Ability, which appeared in 1920. The use of intelligence tests increased rapidly, as did the number of different tests available. For many years several million group tests have been administered annually (Hawes, 1964). Most of the tests, with the exception of the performance scales, have a high verbal content, for it has been shown that verbal tests have a particularly high predictive value for success in most of the usual school subjects (McNemar, 1964). However, several of the tests include both verbal and nonverbal items, and many are so constructed as to give separate scores for ability in language and ability in mathematics, notably arithmetic.

Differences in format among the various tests are readily observable. For example, some of the tests are arranged with subtests, the scores on which are accumulated to determine equivalent mental age or IQ. The Kuhlmann-Anderson Test, in contrast, provides for converting the median score on the subtests to equivalent mental age. Other tests are arranged in what has been called the omnibus-cycle form, in which the subject is provided with, for example, first a verbal-recognition item, then an item on mathematics, and then an item on relationships. Authors favoring the subtest arrangement apparently feel that the subject reveals his abilities best when he can maintain a mental set for a given kind of task over a period of time. Those favoring the omnibus arrangement think of mental ability as including sufficient agility to turn quickly from one type of problem to another. There is no convincing evidence that one format yields better results than another, but the omnibus form is generally easier to administer and, because fewer time limits are involved, gives the subject an opportunity for uninterrupted application to the tasks presented.

CONTROVERSIAL MATTERS. A common characteristic of the tests of general intelligence, under which category the tests discussed above might be placed because they do not pretend to measure specific factors, is that they do provide for converting scores into mental ages or intelligence quotients (IQ's) or both. So common has the term "IQ," become that tests of intelligence are frequently known as IQ tests. Although the IQ, originally obtained by dividing the subject's mental age by his chronological age and multiplying by 100, was first used by Terman, credit for the idea is generally given to Wilhelm Stern (Chauncey & Dobbin, 1963). The concept is a useful one in that an IQ of a given magnitude is capable of the same interpretation, as far as ability is concerned, regardless of the subject's age. Its usefulness diminishes as the subject approaches what has been termed his "mental maturity." The particular chronological age at which mental maturity takes place has been variously estimated by test makers and others as occurring at ages ranging from 14 to 18. The idea that mental maturity is reached at about age 15 or 16 was earlier fairly well accepted, in large part because the average adult did not greatly improve his performance (at a more advanced age) on such tests as the early editions of the Stanford-Binet. Because of variations in mental maturity as in physical maturity, it may well be argued that the usefulness of the IQ concept diminishes in the later high school years. Percentile scores or standard scores are probably more useful and meaningful at ages above 14, or at least above 16. However, so thoroughly has the IQ nomenclature come to be used, and at least partially understood, that makers of tests for high school and even for colleges are besieged by requests for the IQ equivalents of scores if they fail at first to present them. With the 1960 edition of the Stanford-Binet it was recognized that improvement on the test continues to age 18 rather than to age 16, as had been assumed in the 1937 edition, and some researchers find improvements considerably later, at least in some instances. In at least one study (Bradway & others, 1958) there is an indication that in some cases the mental-growth ceiling had not been reached after 25 years following the first testing. The popular belief that general intelligence tends to decline after the period of early maturity is also questioned in another study (Corsini & Fassett, 1953). Instead, the authors conclude that ability varies downward if the subtests involve visual and motor factors but upward if the subtests contain material which depends on continued learning.

The extent to which the IQ remains constant through the years has been the cause of much controversy, speculation, and experimentation. Many of the early testers, imbued with the idea that what was called intelligence was strictly linked to inborn characteristics, felt that once a subject had made a score that gave him a particular IQ rating, there was no need to test him again. The IQ would remain the same, it it is assumed that the tests had been competently administered. As experimentation progressed, it became evident that while in most cases considerable stability was manifest, there were many instances of minor changes and a few cases in which changes were of major proportions. The most significant changes appear to be associated with marked variations in environmental conditions, changes in motivation, or emotional fluctuations. There is considerable evidence to indicate that the longer the interval between test and retest, the greater the likelihood of change (Honzik & others, 1949; Bayley, 1949). The IQ's found for very young children sometimes appear to have relatively little stability, whereas those determined by testing during the elementary-school years have much greater constancy, as shown by repeated tests after a three-or-four-year interval (Gehman & Matyas, 1956; Churchill & Smith, 1966).

Considerable evidence concerning the comparability of the numerous tests now on the market appears to be available (Lennon, 1953; Anastasi, 1961b; Rainey, 1965). Whether the differences are considered great is to some extent dependent on the judgment of the individual reviewer. Aside from the lack of complete reliability of the tests themselves, a statistical fact to be noted in all testing, differences may be attributed in part to differences in the population on which the tests were standardized, on the authors' concept of what the standard deviation should be, on the practice effect when one test has preceded the other, and perhaps on the nature of the content of the test. Tests using the ratio IQ described above were often found to furnish very similar IQ's in the middle range but varied more at the upper and lower ends of the range, at least partly because of differences in the standard deviations of the IQ's provided by different tests and particularly at different age levels. A modification of the method of determining IQ's used by Wechsler and in the 1960 revision of the Stanford-Binet has been adopted by most test makers. They are known as deviation IQ's and are standard scores with a mean of 100 and a standard deviation of 15 (Wechsler) or 16 (Stanford-Binet). Thus, a subject whose score falls one standard deviation below the mean on the Stanford-Binet is said to have an IQ of 84, whereas a subject with a score one standard deviation above the mean is assigned an IQ of 116 (Terman & Merrill, 1960). The general adoption of the deviation IQ should make for greater uniformity in IQ's derived from different tests and is advantageous in the statistical treatment of data. It has been argued that deviation IQ's tend to be more stable than conventional ratio IQ's (Pinneau, 1961). In some studies this contention seems to be borne out; in other studies the evidence is contradictory (Lindholm, 1965).

Some Additional Controversies. Whether so-called intelligence tests are properly named has resulted in much argument, and there has never been agreement on a definition of intelligence (Stanley, 1964). It should be noted, however, that the emphasis in intelligence testing has from the very beginning been on some way to determine success in school, and this is still the main concern despite the uses of these tests in industry and in assessing the competence of individuals for various occupations. It is conceivable, therefore that the tests might better be called tests of ability to do schoolwork or tests of scholastic aptitude. In any case, it is evident that these tests, though concerned with many aspects of intelligence, can hardly be said to be tests of global intelligence. They do provide fairly good prediction of success in school subjects which require considerable verbal facility but are much less successful in predicting success in such subjects as art, crafts, music, physical education, and other subjects requiring manual dexterity. Correlations with grades or achievement-test scores in the so-called academic subjects generally range from .5 to .7 or higher for elementary pupils and high school students. For college students, correlations of .4 to .5 are more common, at least in part because of the narrower range of ability represented (Guilford, 1959).

Both intelligence and achievement testing have come under heavy attack in recent literature (Black, 1963; Hoffman, 1962). Some of the criticisms of intelligence testing have come about because of abuses rather than because of flaws in the testing instruments. For example, much criticism has come about because of popular misconceptions concerning the IQ. A most prevalent idea has been that once a person's IQ has been determined, an index of ability has been established that will characterize his intellectual status for all time. Even Wilhelm Stern, the German psychologist who first suggested the IQ concept, after noting how much it had been misunderstood, asked one of his students who was coming to America to "kill the IQ" (Ebel, 1964). It now appears that it would be extremely difficult to arrange for its demise, so common has become its use. With the advent of the deviation-IQ concept, it may be more possible to create an understanding that the IQ is simply one form of standard score, lacking to some extent in stability but useful as an indication of academic success, at least for the near future.

Intelligence tests have also come under attack because they contain items that are not fair to those brought up in disadvantaged environments or in countries where the cultural pattern is different from that predominant in America or in the country in which the tests are produced. For that reason, attempts have been made to develop "culture-free" tests of various kinds. Even though some such tests minimize the use of language in favor of pictures or geometric forms, they do not necessarily eliminate the influence of cultural differences (Cronbach, 1960). There is some evidence that such tests do not predict achievement as well as other tests do (Noll, 1960; Ludlow, 1956; McDaniel & Carse, 1965). It has been suggested that improved conditions for the underprivileged are more important than attempts to make tests that are more fair to them (Rosinski, 1960). It is not clear either that so-called culture-free tests are "culture fair" for use in other cultures (Alzobaie, 1964).

Intelligence tests have sometimes been cited as being unfair to the physically handicapped, whose scores have been held down, not because of ignorance, but because the subject was unable to indicate understanding in the manner designated in the directions. Recently, heightened interest in such children has resulted in the development of tests especially designed for them (French, 1959). Most of such testing has been achieved by the development of methods by which the child can indicate his understanding of pictures or designs. For example, the Pictorial Test of Intelligence permits the child to indicate his understanding in any observable way (French, 1964). This test, like many others of this general character, is designed for young children (ages two to eight) inasmuch as most pictorial tests as well as formboards are too easy for persons of considerable ability.

Controversy concerning the relative influence of heredity and environment in the determination of the individual's intelligence has subsided greatly since the early days of intelligence testing. The belief that intelligence is completely dependent on genetic influences without appreciable change by environmental factors is now seldom held. The current tendency is to give both heredity and environment some of the credit for performance on intelligence tests, but agreement on their relative strengths is hard to find. It should be noted that when we speak of heredity and environment we are not speaking of entities but, in each case, of broad classes of factors.

Many arguments have resulted from the question whether it is desirable to inform children or their parents of scores made on intelligence tests. Many such questions might be resolved if there were better education of those dealing with the problems. As indicated, for example, in a survey of Nassau County on Long Island, too few courses concerned with test interpretation are available; inferior methods of reporting scores are common; and limited use of data for research purposes was evident (Elkin & others, 1964). Misunderstandings and abuses of test data appear to be responsible for a large share of the controversies and criticisms of the intelligence-testing movement.

Shortly after intelligence testing in the schools became common, the tests began to be used for the purpose of grouping pupils according to ability for instructional purposes. It was soon apparent that other items of information in addition to intelligence-test scores should be used in determining which pupils should be placed in the various sections (Lavin, 1965). The practice of homogeneous grouping has been the subject of many controversies, but it has become very common, with many variations in the grades in which it is used, in the instruments used in determining the individual pupil's placement, and in the extent to which different placement is provided in the various school subjects. Some of the advantages claimed for homogeneous grouping are that it tends to make for better progress of more pupils; that teachers generally react favorably to the practice (French, 1960); that the more rapid learners are not held back; and that the slow learners are not pushed beyond their abilities. Those who oppose the practice argue quite accurately that although groupings may reduce the range of abilities with which teachers must deal, by no means does it eliminate all differences (Pielstick, 1963). Obviously the practice is impractical in very small schools, and it is thought by some observers to produce serious personality problems. It is argued that pupils in the more rapidly moving sections become snobbish, whereas those in the lower groups suffer feelings of inferiority (Thomas & Thomas, 1965). Partly because of the variations in practice, the considerable research on the effects of homogeneous grouping has failed to produce conclusive evidence concerning its value (Passow, 1962). Early studies are reported in the Thirty-fifth yearbook, Part I, of the National Society for the Study of Education (Coxe, 1936). A review which includes more recent studies is presented by Ekstrom (1961).

FACTOR ANALYSIS. The tests discussed above are often called tests of general intelligence because they are not primarily concerned with the variation in abilities within the individual. It has long been recognized that such variations exist. For example, some persons whose scores are only average or even below-average on tests of intelligence are known to have unusual ability in such a field as music, mathematics, mechanics, or art. Similarly, persons with average or even superior intelligence-test scores sometimes show marked weaknesses in certain areas. Because the primary aim of the authors of intelligence tests was to provide materials that would predict success in school, these tests emphasize very heavily those verbal abilities which have been found to give the best prediction for success in the major portions of the school curricula. Authors who used the subtest format sometimes made relatively crude attempts to differentiate abilities, but the overriding emphasis was on the single index of ability, generally mental age or IQ. Differentiation between verbal and mathematical abilities often achieved some success, although portions designed to measure mathematical ability sometimes predicted success in mathematics less well than did the verbal portions of the test.

Many scholars have been interested in defining more carefully than Binet did the specific nature of intelligence. One of the earliest to advance what seemed to be a reasonable explanation was the noted English statistician Charles Spearman. His theory was that intelligence consists of a general factor, g, which is shared by all intellectual activities, and a considerable number of specific, or s, factors, each of which is involved in a single activity (Spearman and Jones, 1951). According to this theory, which has gained somewhat more general acceptance in England than in the United States, two functions which correlate highly would be said to contain large amounts of the g factor. For general tests of intelligence one would, therefore, measure the general factor, which permeates all mental activity. Later, Spearman conceded that there might also be group factors which differ from the general factor as well as from the specific factors inasmuch as they are common to a group of activities but not to all. In England the main idea that has since dominated factorial analysis is Spearman's two-factor theory (Thomson, 1951).

E. L. Thorndike's study of the problem convinced him that intelligence consists of a large number of specific functions or factors, probably without any general factor permeating them (E. Thorndike & others, 1927). The group-factor theory developed by Thurstone (1947) and others after elaborate statistical studies has probably had the greatest influence on the factor-testing movement in the United States. Although he was able to distinguish many relatively unrelated factors, Thurstone believed that intelligence could be fairly well tested by means of six factors which appeared to be dominant—namely, verbal, number, spatial, word fluency, memory, and reasoning. The tests, known as the Primary Mental Abilities Tests, have continued to arouse much interest as well as much controversy among factor analysts through the years. British workers who early made contributions to factorial analysis include Burt (1940), who originated factorial models which differed from those of both Spearman and Thurstone; Thomson (1951), who developed more fully some of Spearman's theories; and, more recently, Vernon (1961), who describes what is called the hierarchical theory of human abilities, also developed from the Spearman theories.

The main purpose of factor analysis is to determine which factors of intellect are relatively disparate. Analysts are also interested in trying to answer the question whether there is anything that might be called a general factor, something about which there has been little agreement. Though their purposes have been similar, there have been many different methods of factor analysis, which may account, at least in part, for the differences in findings reported. One of the most prolific writers in the field, Guilford (1959), has listed some 50 isolated factors and has proposed a theoretical model for the complete structure of intellect which yields 120 cells, each of which might correspond to a potential factor.

Tests based on factor analysis, or in part on such analysis, have begun to appear in some numbers, but many of them have been limited in usage and have as yet accumulated little evidence of usefulness. Two which have been well tested are the Differential Aptitude Tests, which have had wide usage in American high schools, and the General Aptitude Test Battery produced and used by the U.S. Employment Service throughout the country in an attempt to assess the potential of persons seeking work opportunities.

Factor analysis has also been used in an attempt to ascertain what factors are being tested by tests already well established. For example, a factor analysis of the Wechsler Bellevue Scales resulted in the conclusion that ten factors could be isolated (Davis, 1964). Such analysis has not always been fruitful, partly because the items designed for different age levels have not always been of the same type; as is the case, for example, in the Stanford-Binet tests.

Work during World War II, particularly in the testing of Air Force cadets, contributed much to the analysis of factors. Conclusions of one of the studies indicated the presence of no less than 29 factors, some of which may well have been subdivisions of the Thurstone factors (Davis, 1947). Because of the great amount of mathematical work involved in factorial analysis, regardless of which of several methods is employed, the availability of the computer has greatly accelerated the progress made in recent years. More tests of unquestioned merit should accordingly be forthcoming. It must be admitted that many questions remain to be answered. Not only must we know how many factors we need to isolate to get a reasonably accurate description of a person's intellect but also we must know how the information can be used to advantage. It is also important to know whether the factors remain stable for a given individual or change as a person matures. It would seem possible that when more is known about such matters, the use of factored tests will enable guidance counselors to make much more helpful suggestions to persons concerned about their future activities and to employers seeking a person with certain intellectual characteristics. As of the moment, studies fail to contribute much to such optimism. If, as some studies indicate, portions of factor tests fail to predict abilities in different areas better than do general tests of intelligence; and if the composite score on a factored test gives no better prediction than the shorter intelligence test, one may well question whether the time, expense, and effort involved in factor testing is really worthwhile (Lamke & Nelson, 1960). This certainly is not meant to belittle the efforts of the many workers in factor testing or to suggest a cessation of such efforts. Even if prediction should turn out to be disappointing, it would undoubtedly be useful as well as satisfying to the curious to know more about the composition of human intellect. The impact is as yet uncertain. One writer takes the position that tests of general intelligence that yield single scores have become obsolete (Davis, 1964). Another suggests that in deciding whether to use factored tests or single-score tests one needs to have in mind the purpose for which testing is to be done (Rosinski, 1960).

TESTING SPECIAL APTITUDES. We have already noted that intelligence tests are actually tests of aptitude, primarily aptitude for the more common curricular tasks in school. However, when one speaks of aptitude tests one normally thinks of tests which apply to a rather distinct type of ability, applied to a specific skill, subject, or enterprise. Because intelligence tests attempt to predict success in such a wide range of subjects or fields of endeavor, we tend to distinguish between them and the tests of more limited objectives. Thus, aptitude tests are thought of as being concerned with ability in mechanical pursuits, art, music, or other areas, for the prediction of which the intelligence-test data appear to be rather consistently inadequate.

Although special aptitudes are often considered as representing characteristics with which a given individual is born, it is obvious that most special aptitude tests measure much more than such attributes. One's score depends on such things as one's interest, the competence one has already acquired, and the stimulation one may have received in one's home and school environment, in addition to inborn characteristics one may possess (Michael, 1950).

It is noteworthy that tests of sensory capacities, which were used by the early researchers in the vain hope that scores on them would give reliable indexes of intellectual development, are now used very effectively in the schools to help determine the causes of unsatisfactory development. Cattell, Galton, and Jastrow, for example, all felt that visual acuity and ability to hear well would give one a clue to the individual's intellectual status (Anastasi, 1961). If this were true, one could secure very precise measurements, whereas more complex functions would be more difficult to measure, certainly with the same accuracy. Because measures of sensory discrimination were found wanting in differentiating persons of varying intellectual ability, they were somewhat neglected for a time. Later such tests were found to be helpful not only in schools but also in some industries where certain strengths are needed or where a worker needs particularly keen vision or hearing. New and sophisticated devices have been developed, particularly in testing vision and hearing, but some of the older devices, such as the Snellen Chart for testing visual acuity and the watch-tick auditory test, are still useful as screening devices. For some purposes, however, it is important to bear in mind that neither seeing nor hearing is a unitary capacity. For some tasks it may be of considerable importance to determine whether one's distance vision is adequate even though his perception of objects at close range is acceptable. In other instances it is by no means enough to distinguish an object; the object's color may be of prime importance. The ability to hear a sound may sometimes be of value only if one can detect differences in pitch or intensity as well.

Mechanical Aptitude. If mechanical aptitude is to be adequately tested, the tests must cover a variety of functions (Gendre, 1966), but some of the earlier developments were concerned with only one kind of activity. Stenquist, for example, who was one of the earliest workers in this field, developed a test that was devoted to the ability to assemble and put together common mechanical objects (Stenquist, 1923). Though no longer available in its original form, it was later revised and standardized as the Minnesota Mechanical Assembly Test. Although the standardization population involved other groups, too, the test is most often used with boys of high school age, for whom it seems especially suitable. Tests of this type do predict success in shop work reasonably well (Paterson and others, 1930), but they are somewhat difficult to administer, especially in large groups. A large number of tests in mechanical ability have been developed for use in the armed services, particularly in finding good prospects for pilot training and aviation mechanics. In schools, the MacQuarrie Test for Mechanical Ability has been standardized and fairly extensively used (MacQuarrie, 1927). It consists of seven subtests: Tracing, Tapping, Dotting, Copying, Location, Blocks, and Pursuit. Speed and accuracy of eye-hand coordination are measured by the first three subtests, while the remainder of the subtests were designed to measure spatial ability (MacQuarrie, 1925-1943). Though this particular test is no longer available, work in testing spatial ability has continued to be done, since it appears to be an important consideration in measuring mechanical ability. Such tests appear, for example, in the Differential Aptitude Tests, the Holzinger-Crowder Uni-factor Tests, and the General Aptitude Test Battery, all developed from factorial analysis studies. Although data concerning it are still quite limited, the Mellenbruch Mechanical Motivation Test, which is based on the assumption that individuals who are interested in tools and machinery are likely to be mechanically adept, appears to have excellent potential (Mellenbruch, 1956-1957). Perhaps the most widely used tests in this field for both civilian and military purposes are those developed by Bennett and others (1940-1954). Those in common use, in addition to the one which constitutes part of the Differential Aptitude Tests, are designed for boys in high school and trade schools, for unselected men, for certain industrial groups, for engineeering-school applicants, and for persons on especially high levels of mechanical ability. There is also a form for women.

Clerical Aptitude. Evidence concerning the predictive value of tests in clerical aptitudes has been somewhat limited and conflicting, probably partly because of the variety of clerical positions. In some clerical positions the ability to work rapidly is a major consideration; in others, speed is not of great consequence but accuracy is of utmost importance. The skills needed by workers in a bank are probably far different from those required in many more-general offices. Thus, the use of tests for clerical workers in bank positions may be very disappointing (H. Seashore, 1953), whereas the use of the same or similar tests may prove to be helpful in finding workers with the needed aptitudes for other positions. The Minnesota Clerical Test (Andrew and Paterson, 1933-1959) places great emphasis on perceptual speed. The two subtests involving number comparison and name comparison are separately timed and, because limited penalties are assessed for errors, give a distinct advantage to the rapid worker. Different tests might well be designed for typists, for shipping clerks, and for filing clerks; but even jobs with the same title may vary greatly with the size and nature of the company and the degree of specialization.

The Turse Clerical Aptitude Tests are devoted to verbal skills, number skills, following written directions, checking speed, classifying and sorting, and alphabetizing (Turse, 1953-1955). Two of the subtests of the Differential Aptitude Tests are especially useful in predicting success in many clerical positions. The first of these, known as the Clerical Speed and Accuracy Test, is designed to measure speed of response in a simple perceptual test, whereas the second, Spelling and Sentences, is involved with language usage. The combination of scores on these subtests, together with scores on other subtests in which intellectual ability is measured, seem to be of considerable value in predicting success in a variety of situations. In the General Aptitude Test Battery, provision is made for number- and word-checking tests similar to those in the Minnesota Clerical Test as well as for tests requiring one to distinguish similarities and differences in spatial items. Because of the diversity in clerical positions, it appears that a proper combination of subtest scores in the multifactor tests holds the greatest promise for predicting success in clerical pursuits.

Art Aptitude. It has appeared difficult to devise satisfactory tests that will predict success in drawing, painting, and design. At least to some extent, the difficulties stem from conflicting opinions of the experts concerning what is acceptable performance. Such differences exist, to be sure, in other fields as well, but probably not to the same extent. The common belief that intellectual ability is in no way related to abilities required for successful work in art appears unsound in view of findings that artistically gifted children reported in one study had IQ's ranging from 111 to 166 (Meier, 1942). Another study reports that successful artists had a mean IQ of 119 (Tiebout and Meier, 1936).

Not all tests known as aptitude tests in the artistic area are primarily concerned with performance. As an illustration, the McAdory Art Test, now primarily of historical interest because so many items have become obsolete, is concerned with taste in automobiles, clothing, household furniture, and appliances as well as with frankly artistic objects and paintings (McAdory, 1929–1933). Although Meier, and some others working with him conducted research over many years in an attempt to discover the various traits that comprise aptitude for art work, his tests are concerned with only one aspect—namely, art judgment, another test of appreciation (Meier, 1940–1942). Other important traits identified were manual skill, creative imagination, perceptual facility, aesthetic intelligence, and volitional perseveration. Meier's findings were not based on factor analysis, and it will be interesting to discover, when sufficient factorial analyses have been made, whether the same traits are identified. The Meier test appears to be well accepted, for it is the most widely used of the art appreciation instruments. It consists of 100 pairs of pictures, one of which is a reproduction of a work of art that is considered by experts in the field to have merit. The other represents the same picture altered in such a way as to violate one or more principles that are generally accepted. Reasonable correlations between scores on this test and grades assigned to art students have been reported (Kintner, 1933; Morrow, 1938). It is interesting to note that despite Meier's findings that persons of considerable artistic ability generally have high IQ's, scores on this instrument have shown almost no correlation with either individual or group tests of intelligence.

One of the problems encountered in tests of aptitudes, including those in art, is that they frequently contain items or exercises that are dependent on skills or knowledge already mastered instead of being concerned with the subject's inherent aptitude or promise of future success. Thus, the measures become tests of achievement or at least demonstrate both aptitude and the effects of previous learning. There has not been much recent activity in devising new tests to measure art aptitude. Two of the more recent are the Horn Art Aptitude Inventory and the Graves Design Judgment Test. The Graves test consists entirely of abstract designs. In each item one of the designs is aesthetically contrived, and there are either one or two other designs that violate one or more generally accepted principles included. The task is to indicate the preferred design in each item (Graves, 1948). The Horn Inventory, which appears to discriminate well among applicants to art schools, consists of three parts, the first of which requires the subject to make drawings of several simple objects. The second part requires the drawing of certain designated designs, and the third requires the completion of a drawing for which a few lines are supplied (Horn, 1951–1953; Buros, 1965).

Musical Aptitudes. The development of the first test of aptitude for music was one of the results of years of research by Carl E. Seashore during the early part of the present century. Limited modifications have been made, but the Seashore Tests of Musical Talents are very much like the original and are still the best-known tests in music. Reproduced on phonograph records, the tests are designed to measure pitch discrimination, loudness, rhythm, time, timbre, and tonal memory. The test for pitch discrimination requires the subject to indicate whether the second of two tones is higher or lower than the first, the test becoming increasingly difficult as differences in pitch are gradually reduced. For the loudness test the subject similarly indicates whether the two rhythmic patterns are the same or different in tonal quality. In the tonal-memory test the task is to indicate from a series of three to five tones which note has been changed in the second playing (Seashore, 1938). There is, of course, much in music that is not measured by these tests. It might be possible for one to do well on the tests and yet be unable to learn to perform well because of lack of motor abilities, including those involved in vocal production, or to compose good music or to serve as a director of a musical group or even to appreciate music. Some assert that "the tests have analyzed music down so far that very little music remains" (R. Thorndike & Hagen, 1955). While in some instances the test results have rather accurately predicted students' musical success, studies show conflicting results. Seashore came to the conclusion that one's pitch discrimination was almost entirely dependent on his biological inheritance and that it could be very little influenced by training, but others have insisted that it can be improved.

Another widely used test in this field is known as the Kwalwasser-Dykema Music Tests. They are designed to measure the same functions as the Seashore tests plus facility in reading musical notation and some aspects of musical appreciation. The authors give no data on reliability or validity of these measures, which are designed for grades 4 to 12, but norms are provided. Some investigators (Bienstock, 1942; Farnsworth, 1931) have found the scores on some of the subtests to be so unreliable, mainly because of the limited number of items, that their worth is questionable. Among more recent tests are the Drake Musical Aptitude Tests, which are confined to the measurement of musical memory and the ability to keep time. The manual indicates that both subtests have high reliabilities and that they do a good job of predicting achievement in the study of music (Martin, 1964).

Another recent test was developed in England and deals with several aspects of musical ability. Known as the Wing Standardised Tests of Musical Intelligence, they emphasize music appreciation as well as sensory discrimination of more difficulty than is typical of the Seashore and Kwalwasser-Dyekma tests.

The author justifies the nature of the tests by reference to factorial analysis studies which appear to indicate that there is a general factor of musical ability (Wing, 1958).

Miscellaneous Tests of Aptitudes. The aptitude tests discussed above are those with which test makers have been concerned for the greatest length of time. More recent years have witnessed developments in new fields, one of which is creativity. Growing out of his factor analysis studies, Guilford (1959) felt the need for measures of fluency in words, ideas, associations, and expression as well as tests of flexibility and originality. Other tests in this general area are the Minnesota Tests of Creative Thinking, which cover a wide range of situations (Torrance, 1962). Just how successful tests of this kind will be remains to be seen, for as yet such evidence as exists is conflicting (Skager and others, 1965; Cicirelli, 1965, 1966). One may well wonder whether tests which are valid for assessing creativity in the arts or literature, for example, will also be good predictors of creativity in the sciences. However, in view of the justifiable criticism of most tests—namely, that they emphasize convergent thinking only—it is encouraging that attempts to assess divergent thinking have emerged (MacKinnon, 1962; Getzels and Jackson, 1962; Clark and others, 1965).

Tests of listening, or auding, are of recent development and as yet are not numerous. As of this time they have not been proven to be effective, but few pertinent studies have been made. Among available tests are two forms developed by the Educational Testing Service as part of the Sequential Tests of Educational Progress and the Brown-Carlsen Listening Comprehension Test, published by Harcourt, Brace and World (Brown & Carlsen, 1952). There is still some question whether tests in this field will give significantly different results from those obtained from reading tests or tests of intelligence. Although we generally think of auding effectiveness as being related to the effectiveness of the speaker, at least one study indicates that whether the speaker is trained in speech makes little difference in scores on the tests (Haberland, 1958).

Many schools, colleges, and organizations have produced aptitude tests for their own specific purposes (Jones & Case, 1955). The Association of American Medical Colleges sponsored a test for use in selecting students for medical colleges (Moss, 1942) which has since been replaced by a test developed by the Educational Testing Service. A test for aptitude in law was developed at the State University of Iowa (Adams, 1943, 1944; Adams & Stuit, 1949). Several tests for engineering students, some of them applying to the physical sciences as well, have come into common use (Moore & others, 1951). In fact, most professional schools have come to use aptitude tests for their specific purposes, especially since the number of applications for admission have been so far in excess of the number that can be accommodated.

In general, aptitude tests have not been studied as carefully and revised as often as are the so-called tests of intelligence. With the current emphasis on factor analysis, it seems probable that many improvements will be forthcoming.

Martin J. Nelson
University of Northern Iowa

References

Adams, Michael. "Prediction of Scholastic Success in Colleges of Law." *Ed Psychol Meas* 3:291–305; 1943; 4:13–9; 1944.

Adams, Michael, and Stuit, Dewey B. "The Prediction of the 1946 Revision of the Iowa Legal Aptitude Test." *Ed Psychol Meas* 9:23–9; 1949.

Albright, Lewis E., and others. *The Use of Psychological Tests in Industry.* Allen, 1963. 196p.

Alzobaie, Abdul Jalil. "The Cattell Culture-free Test as Tried on Iraqui Students." *J Ed Res* 57:476–9; 1964.

Anastasi, Anne. *Psychological Testing*, 2nd ed. Macmillan, 1961(a). 664p.

Anastasi, Anne. "Psychological Tests, Uses and Abuses." *Teach Col Rec* 62:389–93; 1961(b).

Andrew, Dorothy M., and Paterson, Donald G. *Minnesota Clerical Test.* Psych Corp, 1933–1959.

Bayley, Nancy. "Consistency and Variability in the Growth of Intelligence from Birth to Eighteen Years." *J Genet Psychol* 75:165–96; 1949.

Bennett, George K., and others. *Test of Mechanical Comprehension.* Psych Corp, 1940–1954.

Bienstock, Sylvia F. "A Review of Recent Studies of Musical Aptitude." *J Ed Psychol* 33:427–42; 1942.

Binet, Alfred, and Henri, V. "La Psychologie individuelle." *Année psychologique* 2:411–63; 1895.

Black, Hillel. *They Shall Not Pass.* Morrow, 1963. 342p.

Bradway, Katherine P., and others. "Preschool IQs After Twenty-five Years." *J Ed Psychol* 49:278–81; 1958.

Brown, James I., and Carlsen, G. R. *Brown-Carlsen Listening Comprehension Test.* Harcourt, 1952.

Buros, Oscar K. (Ed.) *Sixth Mental Measurement Year Book.* Gryphon; 1965. 1714p.

Burt, Cyril L. *The Factors of the Mind: An Introduction to Factor Analysis in Psychology.* U London Press, 1940. 509p.

Chauncey, Henry, and Dobbin, John E. *Testing: Its Place in Education Today.* Harper, 1963. 223p.

Churchill, William D., and Smith, Stuart E. "The Relationship of the 1960 Revised Intelligence Achievement Test Scores over a Three-year Period." *Ed Psychol Meas* 26:1015–20; 1966.

Cicirelli, Victor G. "Form of the Relationship Between Creativity, IQ, and Academic Achievement." *J. Ed Psychol* 56:303–8; 1965.

Cicirelli, Victor G. "Vocational Aspirations and Creativity." *J Ed Res* 60:68–70; 1966.

Clark, Charles M., and others. "Convergent and Divergent Thinking Abilities of Talented Adolescents." *J Ed Psychol* 56:157–63; 1965.

Cooperative Test Division. *Sequential Tests of Educational Progress.* ETS, 1956–1958.

Corsini, Raymond J. and Fassett, Katherine K. "Intelligence and Aging." *J Genet Psychol* 83:249–64; 1953.

Coxe, W. W. (Chairman) *The Grouping of Pupils.* 35th Yearbook, Part I, NSSE, 1936.

Cronbach, Lee J. *Essentials of Psychological Testing,* 2nd ed. Harper, 1960. 650p.

Cronbach, Lee J., and Gleser, Goldine C. *Psychological Tests and Personnel Decisions,* 2nd ed. U Illinois Press, 1965. 347p.

Davis, Frederick B. *Educational Measurements and Their Interpretation.* Wadsworth Publishing Co., Inc., 1964. 422p.

Davis, Frederick B. *Utilizing Human Talent: Armed Services Selection and Classification Procedures.* ACE, 1947.

Drake, Raleigh M. *Drake Musical Aptitude Tests.* SRA, 1954–1957.

Ebel, Robert L. "The Social Consequences of Educational Testing." *Sch Soc* 92:331–4; 1964.

Ekstrom, Ruth B. "Experimental Studies of Homogeneous Grouping: A Critical Review." *Sch R* 69:216–226; 1961.

Elkin, Victor B., and others. "A Survey of Group IQ Practices." *J Ed Res* 57:526–9; 1964.

Farnsworth, P. R. "An Historical, Critical, and Experimental Study of the Seashore-Kwalwasser Test Battery." *Genet Psychol Monogr* 9:291–393; 1931.

France, Norman. "The Use of Group Tests of Ability and Attainment." *Br J Ed Psychol* 34:19–33; 1964.

French, John W. "What Is Factor Analysis"? *Col Bd R* 10:129–31; 1950.

French, John W. "Evidence from School Records on the Effectiveness of Ability Grouping." *J Ed Res* 54:83–91; 1960.

French, Joseph L. "Intellectual Appraisal of Physically Handicapped Children." *J Genet Psychol* 94:131–41; 1959.

French, Joseph L. *Manual, Pictorial Test of Intelligence.* Houghton, 1964.

Galton, Francis. *Hereditary Genius: An Inquiry into Its Laws and Consequences.* Macmillan, 1869. 390p.

Gardner, R. C., and Lambert, W. E. "Language Aptitude, Intelligence, and Second-language Achievement." *J Ed Psychol* 56:191–9; 1965.

Garrett, Henry E. *Testing for Teachers,* 2nd ed. American, 1965. 280p.

Gehman, Ila H., and Matyas, Rudolph P. "Stability of the WISC and Binet Tests." *J Cons Psychol* 20:150–2; 1956.

Gendre, F. "Tests psychometriques et formation dans la méchanique." *Psychologie* 25:236–57; 1966.

Getzels, Jacob, and Jackson, Philip W. *Creativity and Intelligence: Explorations with Gifted Children.* Wiley, 1962. 293p.

Ghiselli, Edwin E. *Theory of Psychological Measurement.* McGraw-Hill, 1964. 408p.

Glass, Gene V., and Maguire, Thomas O. "Abuses of Factor Scores." *Am Ed Res J* 3:297–304; 1966.

Graves, Maitland E. *Graves Design Judgment Test.* Psych Corp, 1948.

Grover, Burton L. "Prediction of Achievement in Divergent and Convergent Learning Situations." *J Ed Res* 59:402–5; 1966.

Guilford, J. P. *Personality.* McGraw-Hill, 1959. 562p.

Haberland, John A. "Speaker Effectiveness and the Brown-Carlson Listening Test." *Sch Soc* 86:198–9; 1958.

Hawes, Gene R. *Educational Testing for the Millions.* McGraw-Hill, 1964. 290p.

Helmstadter, G. C. *Principles of Psychological Measurement.* Appleton, 1964. 248p.

Hoffmann, Banesh. *The Tyranny of Testing.* Crowell, 1962. 223p.

Honzik, Marjorie P., and others. "The Stability of Mental Test Performance Between Two and Eighteen Years." *J Exp Ed* 17:309–24; 1948.

Horn, C. C. *Horn Art Aptitude Inventory.* Stoelting, 1951–1953.

Hughson, Arthur. "The Case for Intelligence Testing." *Phi Delta Kappan* 46:106–8; 1964.

Jaffee, Catherine A., and Clark, Vera M. "Creativity, Intelligence, and Values: A Study of Relationships." *Excep Child* 32:114–5; 1965.

Jones, Margaret H., and Case, Harry W. "The Validation of a New Aptitude Examination for Engineering Students." *Ed Psychol Meas* 15:502–8; 1955.

Kintner, Madeline. *The Measurement of Artistic Abilities.* Psych Corp, 1933.

Knief, Lotus M., and Stroud, James B. "Intercorrelations Among Various Intelligence, Achievement, and Social Class Scores." *J Ed Psychol* 50:117–20; 1959.

Lamke, Tom A., and Nelson, M. J. *Examiner's Manual, Henmon-Nelson Tests of Mental Ability, Grades 9 to 12.* Houghton, 1960.

Lavin, David E. *The Prediction of Academic Performance.* Russell Sage, 1965. 182p.

Lennon, Roger T. "A Comparison of Results of Three Intelligence Tests." *Test Service Notebook* 11:14–7; 1953.

Lindholm, Byron W. "A Longitudinal Study of Deviation IQs and Grades in School." *J Ed Meas* 2:123–8; 1965.

Lins, L. Joseph, and others. "Relative Usefulness in Predicting Academic Success of the ACT, the SAT, and Some Other Variables." *J Exp Ed* 35:1–29; 1966.

Ludlow, H. Glenn. "Some Recent Research on the Davis-Eells Games." *Sch Soc* 84:146–8; 1956.

MacArthur, R. S., and Elley, W. B. "The Reduction of Socioeconomic Bias in Intelligence Testing." *Br J Ed Psychol* 33:107–19; 1963.

MacKinnon, Donald "The Nature and Nurture of Creative Talent." *Am Psychol* 17:484–95; 1962.

MacQuarrie, T. W. *MacQuarrie Tests of Mechanical Ability.* California Test Bureau, 1925–1943.

MacQuarrie, T. W. "A Mechanical Ability Test." *J Personnel Res* 5:329–37; 1927.

Martin, James G. "Aptitude Test Score Changes Following Musical Training." *J Ed Res* 57:440–2; 1964.

McAdory, Margaret. *The McAdory Art Test.* Teachers Col, Columbia U, 1929–1933.

McDaniel, Ernest D., and Carse, William T. "Validation of the Kahn Intelligence Tests." *Ed Psychol Meas* 25:1153–6; 1965.

McNemar, Quinn. "Lost: Our Intelligence. Why?" *Am Psychologist* 19:871–82; 1964.

Meier, Norman C. *The Meier Art Tests. 1: Art Judgment.* U Iowa, 1940–1942.

Meier, Norman C. *Art in Human Affairs.* McGraw-Hill, 1942. 222p.

Mellenbruch, P. L. *Mellenbruch Mechanical Motivation Test.* Psychometric Affiliates, 1956–1957.

Michael, William B. "Aptitudes." In Monroe, Walter S. (Ed.) *Encyclopedia of Educational Research,* rev. ed. Macmillan, 1950. p. 59–63.

Moore, B. V., and others. *Engineering and Physical Sciences Aptitude Test.* Psych Corp, 1951.

Morrow, R. W. "An Analysis of the Relations Among Tests of Musical, Artistic, and Mechanical Abilities." *J Psychol* 5:253–63; 1938.

Moss, F. A. "Report of the Committee on Aptitude Tests for Medical Schools." *J Assn Am Med Col* 17:312–5; 1942.

Noll, Victor H. "Relation of Scores on Davis-Eells Games to Socio-economic Status, Intelligence Test Results, and School Achievement." *Ed Psychol Meas* 20:119–29; 1960.

Noll, Victor H. *Introduction to Educational Measurement,* 2nd ed. Houghton, 1965. 509p.

Owens, Thomas R., and Roaden, Arliss L. "Predicting Academic Success in Master's Degree Programs in Education." *J Ed Res* 60:124–6; 1966.

Passow, A. Harry. "The Maze of Research on Ability Grouping." *Ed Digest* 28:18–20; 1962.

Paterson, Donald G., and others. *Minnesota Mechanical Assembly Test.* Stoelting, 1930.

Payne, David A., and Tuttle, Cynthia E. "The Predictive Relationship of the Miller Analogies Test to Objective and Subjective Criteria of Success in a Graduate School of Education." *Ed Psychol Meas* 26:427–30; 1966.

Peterson, Joseph. *Early Conceptions and Tests of Intelligence.* Harcourt, 1925. 320p.

Pielstick, N. L. "Gifted Children and Learning Experiences." *J Ed Res* 57:125–30; 1963.

Pinneau, Samuel R. *Changes in Intelligence Quotient, Infancy to Maturity.* Houghton, 1961. 233p.

Rainey, Robert G. "Study of Four School-ability Tests." *J Exp Ed* 33:305–19; 1965.

Reynolds, Maynard C. "The Capacities of Children." *Excep Child* 31:337–42; 1965.

Rosinski, Edwin F. "Must All Tests be Multi-factor Batteries?" *J Exp Ed* 28:235–40; 1960.

Rushton, C. S., and Stockwin, A. E. "Changes in Terman-Merrill I.Q.'s of Educationally Sub-normal Boys." *Br J Ed Psychol* 33:132–42; 1963.

Schweiker, Robert F. "Factor Scores Aren't Sacred: Comments on 'Abuses of Factor Scores.'" *Am Ed Res J* 4:168–70; 1967.

Scott, Carrie M. "The Predictive Value of a Beginning First-grade Intelligence Examination." *Ed Psychol Meas* 25:613–8; 1965.

Seashore, Carl Emil. *Psychology of Music.* McGraw-Hill, 1938. 408p.

Seashore, Harold G. "Validation of Clerical Testing in Banks." *Personnel Psychol* 6:45–56; 1953.

Skager, Rodney W., and others. "Quality and Quantity of Accomplishments as Measures of Creativity." *J Ed Psychol* 56:31–9; 1965.

Spearman, Charles, and Jones, L. Wynn. *Human Ability.* Macmillan, 1951. 198p.

Stanley, Julian C. *Measurement in Today's Schools,* 4th ed. Prentice-Hall, 1964. 414p.

Stenquist, John L. *Measurement of Mechanical Ability.* Teachers Col, Columbia U, 1923. 101p.

Super, Donald E. "The Multifactor Tests: Summing Up." *Personnel Guid J* 36:88–91; 1957.

Terman, Lewis M. *The Measurement of Intelligence.* Houghton, 1916. 362p.

Terman, Lewis M., and Merrill, Maud A. *Measuring Intelligence.* Houghton, 1937. 461p.

Terman, Lewis M., and Merrill, Maud A. *Stanford-Binet Intelligence Scale: Manual for the Third Revision, Form L-M.* Houghton, 1960. 363p.

Thomas, R. Murray, and Thomas, Shirley M. *Individual Differences in the Classroom.* McKay, 1965. 567p.

Thomson, Godfrey H. *The Factorial Analysis of Human Ability,* 5th ed. Houghton, 1951. 383p.

Thorndike, Edward L., and others. *The Measurement of Intelligence.* Teachers Col, Columbia U, 1927. 616p.

Thorndike, Robert L. "Intellectual Status and Intellectual Growth." *J Ed Psychol* 57:121–7; 1966.

Thorndike, Robert L., and Hagen, Elizabeth. *Measurement and Evaluation in Psychology and Education.* Wiley, 1955. 575p.

Thurstone, L. L. *Multiple Factor Analysis.* U Chicago, 1947. 535p.

Thurstone, L. L. *The Vectors of Mind: Multiple-factor Analysis for the Isolation of Primary Traits.* U Chicago, 1935. 266p.

Tiebout, Carolyn, and Meier, Norman C. "Artistic Ability and General Intelligence." *Psychol Monogr* 48:95–125; 1936.

Torrance, E. Paul. *Guiding Creative Talent.* Prentice-Hall, 1962. 275p.

Turse, P. L. *Turse Clerical Aptitudes Test.* Harcourt, 1953–1955.

Vernon, Philip E. *The Structure of Human Abilities,* rev. ed. Wiley, 1961. 208p.

Wechsler, David. *Wechsler Intelligence Scale for Children.* Psych Corp, 1949.

Wechsler, David. *The Measurement and Appraisal of Adult Intelligence,* 4th ed. Williams and Wilkins, 1958. 297p.

Wing, Herbert Daniel. *Wing Standardized Tests of Musical Intelligence,* rev. ed. National Foundation for Educational Research, 1958.

Yourman, Julius. "The Case Against Group IQ Testing." *Phi Delta Kappan* 46:108–10; 1964.

INTERESTS

Informal observations of individual differences in interests rate back at least as early as Plato's comment in *The Republic* (Book II) that "No two persons are born exactly alike, but each differs from each in natural endowments, one being suited for one occupation and another for another." Formal scientific investigations of interests, however, were not initiated until well into the twentieth century. Strong (1955) has estimated the following percentages of articles and books on interests which were published between 1910 and 1949: 1 percent in 1910–1919, 9 percent in 1920–1929, 30 percent in 1930–1939, and 60 percent in 1940–1949. Only about 10 percent of the publications appeared in the decades between 1910 and 1929, yet it was during this period that the impetus was given to the study of interests which has made it one of the most thoroughly researched phenomena in vocational psychology. The pioneer work on the conceptualization and measurement of interests is usually attributed to Walter V. Bingham and his colleagues at Carnegie Institute of Technology, where Bingham established the Division of Applied Psychology in 1915. It was there that James Burt Miner developed a questionnaire to aid students in their vocational choices which included some of the first interest items ever devised; that Bruce V. Moore successfully differentiated the interests of design and sales engineers; and that C. S. Yoakim and his students experimented with interest measures in the selection and training of salesmen. And, probably most significant, it was also here that Edward K. Strong, Jr., launched a lifelong career of research on the measurement of interests. Pursuing the work of one of his students, Karl M. Cowdery, Strong published the first edition of his *Vocational Interest Blank* (*SVIB*) in 1927, after moving to Stanford University, and then reported more than 50 studies of it, and of the 1938 edition, over the next 36 years. Although many other measures of interests were constructed during this period, most of what is known about interests is based upon findings with the *SVIB*, and, to a lesser extent, the *Kuder Preference Record* (*KPR*), the first form of which was published in 1939. For comprehensive reviews of the literature on these and other instruments, as well as interests in general, see the works by Fryer (1931), Strong (1943, 1955), Berdie (1944), Carter (1944), Super (1949), Darley and Hagenah (1955), Layton (1960), and Super and Crites (1962).

DEFINITIONS OF INTERESTS. A phenomenon or variable is defined by specifying both what it is and what it is not (Cohen & Nagel, 1934). Definitions may be conceptual or literary (Underwood, 1957); they may be operational (Bergmann, 1957); or, ideally, they may be both. Interests have been distinguished from some variables but not others; their definitions have been more operational than conceptual, with only vaguely formulated relationships between the two. Strong (1955) discriminates between "interest" and "interests." He enumerates four criteria of interest, which he considers to be "an aspect of consciousness similar to feeling": persistent attention, feeling, activity, and direction. In addition to these attributes, interests are also characterized by intensity and duration. Hence, Strong defines interests as "activities for which we have liking or disliking and which we go toward or away from, or concerning which we at least continue or discontinue the status quo; furthermore, they may or may not be preferred to other interests and they may continue over varying intervals of time" (1955, p. 138). Interests have been designated operationally as vocational, educational, or some other kind, depending on the ways in which measures of them have been standardized—e.g., on occupational or curricular groups—but seldom have they been analyzed conceptually. In contrast, interests have been differentiated from abilities (aptitudes and achievement) and attitudes on both the operational and conceptual levels. Darley and Hagenah (1955) consider abilities, as measured by standardized tests, to be the "efficiency" variables by means of which goals or ends, as assessed by interest inventories, are reached. Strong (1943) states that both attitudes and interests involve "acceptance-rejection" of stimuli but along different dimensions: "agreement-disagreement" for attitudes, and "liking-disliking" for interests.

Conceptual definitions of interests have lagged considerably behind operational definitions and have not been necessarily (logically or theoretically) related to them, primarily because, from its beginning, the field of interest measurement has been dominated by the empirical model of test construction, as exemplified by the *SVIB*. No measure of interests, including the *KPR*, which was rationally derived, has as yet been constructed to define operationally the variables in an explicit theory of interests so that hypotheses deduced from it might be tested. On the contrary, interest inventories have been developed from a set of implicit assumptions about individual and group differences in specific likes and dislikes, which has seriously impeded the formulation of useful conceptual definitions. Either these definitions have been bound so closely to operational procedures that they have little theoretical relevance, or they have been given so much "surplus meaning" that they are extremely difficult to translate into empirical referents. Illustrative of the former is Super's (1947) fourfold classification of interests as expressions, manifestations, tests, and inventories, the definitional criterion being the observational mode or measurement method by which they are quantified. An example of the latter is Darley and Hagenah's (1955, p. 191) metaphorical statement that interests "reflect, in the vocabulary of the world of work, the value systems, the needs, and the motivations of individuals." One consequence of these definitional problems in conceptualizing interests has been the long-standing, and still unresolved, disjunction between theory and research in this area.

Definitions of interests, whether conceptual or operational, might be more theoretically articulated and scientifically sophisticated were it not for the indifferent intercourse of ideas which has traditionally existed between vocational and general psychology. Seldom has the literature on interests in one field been cited in the other. A major review article by Berlyne (1949), entitled "'Interest' as a Psychological Concept," for example, cannot be found in the references of the major works on interest measurement, nor does it list any of them, with the exception of Fryer's early work (1931). Yet the two fields of study might well complement each other. Conspicuous by its absence from Berlyne's discussion is any mention of how to measure interests; central to it, however, is a provocative summary of the meanings which have accrued to interests historically. These include meanings of interests referring to (1) some aspect of all forms of motivation; (2) special forms of motivation; and (3) the place of interests in personality and ego structure. Since the principal theories of interests in vocational psychology draw heavily upon motivational and personality constructs (see below), Berlyne's analysis is directly relevant, as is his subsequent book on arousal and curiosity (1960). His experimental investigations of these phenomena suggest that a wholly different and new approach to the study of interests, vocational as well as others, might be profitably undertaken in the more highly controlled conditions of the laboratory.

MEASURES OF INTERESTS. In the *Sixth Mental Measurements Yearbook,* Buros (1965) cites almost 50 different measures of interests. Most of these assess *vocational* interests, as contrasted with avocational, educational, and other kinds, and most of them have been constructed along the lines of either the *SVIB* or the *KPR*. None of them, however, has been nearly as extensively studied as either of these prototypic instruments. If there has been a trend in using one of them more than the other as a model for designing measures of interests, it has been toward the adoption of the general rationale and procedures by which the *SVIB* was developed. Not only has the *SVIB* been revised (*Manual for the Strong Vocational Interest Blank* [*Revised*], 1966) in the empirical tradition of which it was one of the first exemplars, but two recently published inventories have followed many of the same principles of item selection and scoring. Based upon more than 10 years of research on naval skilled and semiskilled specialties, the *Minnesota Vocational Interest Inventory* (*MVII*) (*Manual for the Minnesota Vocational Interest Inventory,* 1965) was devised by Clark (1961) to measure the interests of men in such nonprofessional civilian occupations as baker, electrician, plasterer, sheet-metal worker, and warehouseman. Although it employs a forced-choice response format like the *KPR*, the scoring keys were developed empirically, as in the *SVIB*, by differentiating the responses of an occupational group from those of tradesmen in general. Likewise, the scales of the KPR-*Occupational* (*Form D*) are based upon a comparison of specific occupations with a men-in-general reference group, and scores are expressed as differentiation ratios, which indicate similarity of interests much as letter ratings on the *SVIB*.

Despite their psychometric debt to the *SVIB*, however, these new instruments are not merely replicas of it. In their construction they have incorporated several modifications which have stemmed from a searching reexamination of some of the hitherto unquestioned methodological assumptions underlying the *SVIB*. One of these is the use of unit, rather than differential, weights in the *MVII*. Clark (1961, p. 28) observes: "The evidence on the comparative merits of multiple weights indicates clearly that superior separation of groups can be attained by use of unit weights." A persistent problem with the *SVIB* has been its differential weighting system, which has not only made it more costly to score but, more importantly, which has also confused the interpretation of scale intercorrelations, because of the confounding of weights and scores (Strong, 1955). Another change has been in the thinking about the relative value of homogeneous and heterogeneous interest keys. Again, Clark (1961, p. 54) comments: "Homogeneous scales allow, for persons with a clinical or counseling orientation, interpretation of a more complex order than do the heterogeneous collections of items resulting from the empirical approach to test construction. Homogeneous scales are more nearly pure measures of independent traits and by resembling other measures of the characteristics of individuals appear to be more meaningful psychologically than are the collections of items that are scored in empirical keys." If valid homogeneous scales can be constructed, they may eliminate some of the anomalies, such as the grouping of artist and architect with the biological science occupations, which have plagued users of the *SVIB* for years. Two other innovations, which have been proposed by Kuder (1950, 1957, 1963), are (1) the development of scales from a smaller but factorially more representative item pool and (2) the construction of an honesty scale to identify the faker on interest inventories. The *SVIB* has a large number of items and no verification key.

DIMENSIONS OF INTERESTS. All measures of interests have several scoring keys or scales, the empirically constructed inventories typically having many more than those developed rationally. The question naturally arises, therefore, of how many *independent* dimensions of interests there are. Does each scale represent a unique dimension, or are there fewer dimensions than scales? Factor analyses of the *SVIB*, in particular, but also other interest inventories, have confirmed that a reduced set of dimensions can represent most of the variance in the interrelationships of interest scales. In one of the first factorial studies of the *SVIB*, Thurstone (1931) extracted four factors, which he named science, people, language, and business. Strong (1943) obtained essentially the same factors, with the addition of a bipolar one, which he called "things vs. people," and a further breakdown of the business factor into system and contact. Using the group scales of the *SVIB*, Cottle (1950) conducted a factor analysis of it, the KPR, the *Bell Adjustment Inventory*, and the *Minnesota Multiphasic Personality Inventory*. He found that the factorial structure of the *SVIB* and *KPR* was much like that reported in previous studies and that there were no common interest and personality dimensions. Other analyses of the *KPR* and the Allport-Vernon *Study of Values* (Lurie, 1937; Brogden, 1952) are generally consistent with those of the *SVIB*, with the exception of the emergence of aesthetic factors (artistic and musical), which are not well represented in the latter. From a large-scale analysis of specially devised interest inventories, Guilford and others (1954) have concluded, however, that many more factors are needed to represent adequately the interest domain; but, in contrast to other investigations, they included measures of nonvocational, as well as vocational, interests in their study. The factors on which just the vocational variables loaded were similar to those found by other investigators. From the results of these various factor analyses, Super and Crites (1962) have extrapolated seven established dimensions of interests: scientific, social welfare, literary, material, systematic, contact, and aesthetic.

There have been no reported factor analyses of interest items, such as Comrey (1958) has done on the *MMPI*, although Campbell (as communicated through personal correspondence) has initiated this type of research at the University of Minnesota Center for Interest Measurement. His approach differs from Comrey's, however, in that he is factoring the total interitem correlational matrix for the *SVIB*, rather than the item matrices for each scale. What Campbell will obtain, therefore, will be factorially pure clusters of interest items, not the factorial composition of interest scales. Not only are studies of the latter needed, but, once they have been conducted, further research on the correlates of both item and scale factors should be carried out. Unless the significance or usefulness of these factors is established in terms of their relationships to other variables (Brodbeck, 1957), the large number of them which have been identified, particularly in studies like that of Guilford and others (1954), may well impede, rather than facilitate, the construction of a meaningful and parsimonious theory of interests. Crites (1963) has reported results, for example, which suggest that some of the factorial dimensions of the *SVIB* may be more theoretically salient than others. He correlated measures of vocational motivation with *SVIB* scales and found that they were associated most often with interests which were at one pole or the other of the "things vs. people" factor. He concluded that "this interest-motivation dimension may be the basic one along which occupations are differentiated" (Crites, 1963, p. 282). If other studies confirm and extend these findings, it may be possible to use a generalized factorial model—e.g., the hierarchical model for abilities (Vernon, 1950)—to conceptualize the dimensions of interests and their relationships to other variables.

DEVELOPMENT OF INTERESTS. Although there has been a considerable amount of research on the development of interests, there is at least an equal amount of controversy over whether interests change systematically with age or not. The issue has arisen because there is no general agreement upon what the criterion of stability or change in interests is. Some maintain that test-retest coefficients in the .70's and .80's over long periods of time (e.g., Strong, 1955) indicate very little change in interests, whereas others contend that even these reliabilities leave 40 to 50 percent of the variance in interests unaccounted for, most of which, it is argued, is probably attributable to change, as opposed to errors of measurement (e.g., Dressel, 1954). Bereiter (1963) has suggested that this dilemma might be avoided by estimating change directly through comparing item responses on different occasions, rather than indirectly through subtracting stable from total variance. Strong (1943) has reported data on changes in item responses for the *SVIB*, however, which indicate that, for an interest inventory of this type—i.e., an empirically constructed one with differential weights—there can be marked changes on the item level with no appreciable effect upon the stability of total scale scores, because increases and decreases in item weights are largely canceled out. Analysis of changes in item responses, therefore, not only does not circumvent the problem of what constitutes interest stability, but it compounds it with the additional problem of explaining why items change as they do.

Bloom (1964) has recently reviewed selected portions of the literature on interest development and has compared stability coefficients for certain scales of the SVIB and KPR with those which would be theoretically expected on the basis of an age curve of development. An age curve of development is simply a linear function of time over the period between two ages, but it may be as meaningful as any criterion for appraising change in interests. Bloom (1964, pp. 136–137) reasons:

> If a characteristic develops in equal amounts per unit of time, it would approximate an age curve of development. Although we have found that most stable characteristics do *not* develop in equal amounts per unit of time, we can use an age curve of development as one basis for determining whether a particular characteristic does indeed develop differentially over time. The contrast between the quantitative features of each characteristic's development and the age curve of development does offer one way of highlighting the developmental features of selected characteristics.

Accordingly, using the age curve, he computed the theoretical stability coefficients, based upon both perfect and actual test reliability, for the chemist, engineer, and lawyer scales of the *SVIB*, as well as the total interest profile, and for the artistic and mechanical keys of the *KPR*, males and females separately. He found that for the *SVIB* the test-retest r's for the period before entrance into college (18 years) were much below those which might be expected from an age curve of development, whereas after this point in time they were as high as or higher than the age-derived values. From these findings, Bloom (1964, p. 167) concluded: "Thus it is highly likely that vocational interests as measured by this instrument [the SVIB] are highly stabilized by the end of the college years and remain relatively constant thereafter." A series of recent studies by Campbell (1965, 1966a, 1966b) on the long-term stability of SVIB profiles further documents this conclusion. Similarly, the greatest changes on the KPR are before age 17, but there are sex differences on the artistic and mechanical scales, females being more stable on the former and males on the latter.

That sex-role typing may be a critical etiological factor in the development of interests has been hypothesized by Tyler (1951), who, in the first of several longitudinal studies of this phenomenon, found that, as early as the first grade (6 years of age), boys and girls differ in their preferences for outdoor play, indoor play, paper work, and helping activities. She also reported, however, that her boys and girls differed in the factorial structure of their primary mental abilities. Thus, it may have been these differences, either independently of or in combination with the sex differences, which produced the differences in interests. In a second study, Tyler (1955) attempted to measure the interests of her sample in the fourth grade (10 years of age) but discovered that, for both males and females, they had such a preponderance of "likes," and so few "dislikes," that it was very difficult to differentiate their preferences. Moreover, there appeared to be little or no relationship between "like" and "dislike" responses; e.g., a liking for professional occupations did not necessarily mean a disliking for unskilled occupations. She concluded from these and other results that "the matrix out of which patterned interests develop is not neutrality but rather a readiness to like everything . . . . The importance of dislike responses in this connection may be that they constitute the one way in our kind of society that a person can limit himself without criticism from others or without inferiority attitudes in himself" (Tyler, 1960, pp. 73–74). In her latest follow-up, which spanned the junior and senior high school years, Tyler (1964) gathered data with the SVIB, in order to "trace back" the antecedents of scientific interests in boys and career interests in girls. The number of subjects was so small for most of the analyses, however, that the study is better considered to be hypothesis-generating than hypothesis-testing. Several propositions suggested by Tyler are worthy of further research, the most provocative among them being the salience of early masculinity-femininity for later interest development. Such a dimension is similar to what Roe (1957) has termed "person-nonperson" orientation and which Roe and Siegelman (1964) have shown to be related to parental attitudes in childhood. But the relationships among these variables, and to interests as measured by the SVIB and KPR, are either quite low or nonsignificant (Brunkan, 1965).

CORRELATES OF INTERESTS. Research on the correlates of interests can be classified according to four types of variables: stimulus (S), organismic (O), response (R), and theoretical (T). An S variable is any physical incident, event, social circumstance, or condition which is related to a response (Brown, 1961; Underwood, 1966). An O variable is some characteristic, property, or state of an organism; examples are endocrine glands, physique, and heredity. An R variable is any observable change in the behavior of the organism, such as movement or speech. And T variables are one or the other of two kinds of abstractions: hypothetical constructs or intervening variables (MacCorquodale & Meehl, 1948). The former are exemplified by the phenomenological concept of self (Rogers, 1951) and the latter by the learning concept of drive (Hull, 1952).

Stimulus Variables. There is some evidence that socioeconomic status is a correlate of interests, but the relationship between the two variables is a complex one. Gustad (1954) was unable to establish a simple linear function between either actual or desired socioeconomic status, on the one hand, and level of occupational interests (SVIB OL scale), on the other. In a follow-up study of Harvard graduates, however, McArthur and Stevens (1955) have reported results which suggest that socioeconomic status may be a moderator variable (Saunders, 1956) for the relationship of interests to regular adult occupation. They found that the SVIB predicted this criterion better than expressed interests for middle-class subjects but that the reverse was true for upper-class subjects. Similarly, Hyman (1956) compared different socioeconomic and intelligence groups on the KPR but could not differentiate them until he classified subjects by levels on both variables: e.g., upper class, superior intelligence; middle class, normal intelligence; etc. These more homogeneous groupings yielded significant differences on six out of nine scales (the outdoor scale was not included). Thus, it may be that although socioeconomic status is not directly related to interests, it may moderate nonlinear relationships between them and other variables.

That the family exerts an influence upon the formation of interests is partially supported by the similarity of the interests of fathers and sons. In two studies, Strong (1943, 1957) correlated scores on the SVIB scales for groups of 110 and 100 father-son pairs and found that the r's ranged from .11 to .48 in the first, with a mean of .29, and from .30 to .35 in the second. The average intercorrelation for one sample of randomly matched fathers and sons was only .03. Other studies, either cited or conducted by Berdie (1943), have yielded comparable results. He reports that the sons of skilled tradesmen and businessmen have interests like those of their fathers but that this is not necessarily true in other fields. In two unpublished studies, Dvorak notes that the interests of physicians and their sons are similar, and Forster obtained r's ranging from .00 to .48, with an average of .33, for 125 pairs of fathers and sons on the SVIB. Although these findings are not conclusive, they indicate that, on the average, the interests of fathers and sons have a correlate of about .30 but that there are individual differences in this relationship. Some sons have interests more like those of their fathers than do other sons.

The effects of experience outside the home have been studied in several studies (Super & Crites, 1962), but the evidence is so equivocal that it is difficult, and probably unjustified, to draw conclusions from it. Not only is much of it indirect, being adduced from analyses of other problems (e.g., test-retest reliability studies of the *SVIB*), but the findings are largely specific to the instrument which was used to measure interests. In general, experience appears to have a negligible effect upon the *SVIB*, particularly after age 18, but does seem to influence the *KPR*. Findings with the KPR, however, are sometimes conflicting. Ewens (1956) and Matteson (1955a) obtained moderately high correlations between cognate experience and *KPR* scales, the r's ranging from .05 to .64, and Matteson (1955b) has reported that for college students retested after two years, their largest gains in experience and interests were in those experience-interest areas where the disparity was greatest at the beginning of college. Herzberg and Russell (1953) found, however, that the interests of new workers were more appropriate for their occupations —i.e., their scale scores were higher—than were those of experienced workers. A complicating factor in reconciling or rationalizing these apparently contradictory results is that none of the investigations of experience and interests has been properly controlled. Ideally, equivalent (matched or random) experimental and control groups would be compared for differences in interests after the experimental groups had been exposed to the effects of a presumably relevant experience. The only study of experience and interest which approximates this design is one by Bordin and Wilson (1953), in which they investigated the relationship between changes in the curricular choices of college freshmen and their *KPR* test-retest reliabilities. They constituted several groups of subjects, some of whom changed their curricula between test and retest and some of whom did not, but they failed to control variables other than the curriculum, such as course grades, which might have affected both choice and interests. Consequently, despite Bordin and Wilson's assertion (1953, p. 305) that "the results of this study provide unequivocal support for the assumption that inventoried interests are dynamic phenomena reflecting changes in the individual's perception of himself," the interpretation of their results is indeterminate because, since controls were inadequate, two equally plausible conclusions can be drawn: interests change as a function of curricular experience, *or* interests change as a function of course grades.

Organismic Variables. Super (1949, p. 404; Super & Crites, 1962, p. 410) has proposed that "interests are the product of interaction between inherited neural and endocrine factors, on the one hand, and opportunity and social evaluation on the other." The evidence upon which he postulates a relationship of interests to "inherited neural and endocrine factors" comes largely from two studies, however, neither of which is conclusive. To evaluate the influence of heredity upon the formation of interests Carter (1932) compared the pairwise correlations of 23 *SVIB* scales for three groups of twins: (1) 43 pairs of identical (monozygotic) twins; (2) 43 pairs of like-sex fraternal (dyzygotic) twins; and, (3) 34 pairs of opposite-sex twins. For the identical twins, the average r was .50; for the fraternal twins, it was .28; and, for the opposite-sex twins it was .30. As in most twin studies (Anastasi, 1958), the results were open to varying interpretations. Carter (1932, p. 653) concluded that "it seems probable that hereditary factors are more important in determining interests than are environmental factors," but then he added: "This conclusion can only be made tentatively, however, since a part of the greater similarity of identical twins must be attributed to greater similarity of environment." Super has questioned the latter assumption, because it would imply that the interests of fraternal twins, because of the greater similarity of their environment as well as heredity, would be more closely related than those of fathers and sons, but the correlations for these two groups are essentially the same, being .28 and approximately .30, respectively. Consequently, he argues that "the greater similarity of the interests of identical twins, as contrasted with those of fraternal twins, is not due to the potentially greater similarity of their environments, but rather to the *demonstrably* greater similarity of their heredities" (Super & Crites, 1962, p. 401). About the most that can justifiably be said, therefore, about the relationship between interests and heredity is that the available research on the problem is not definitive enough to draw an unequivocal conclusion.

The study which Super cites on the relationship of interests to endocrine factors was conducted by Sollenberger (1940), who investigated these variables in two groups ($Ns = 10$ and 23) of adolescent boys in the approximate age range of 13 to 17 years. The boys were inmates in a "cottage-type" reform school: none was considered to be psychologically abnormal (neurotic or psychotic), but all must be assumed to be delinquent by definition, because of their incarceration, and hence atypical in this respect. The endocrine factor which was analyzed was male hormone excretion, sexually mature boys being defined as those who had a high degree of androgenic activity over a 24-hour period. In the larger of the two groups, the sexually mature and immature boys were compared on their responses to items in the Furfey *Test of Developmental Age*, an inventory which covers such topics as "Things to Be When You Grow Up." The item analysis indicated that sexually mature boys preferred to be stock brokers, authors, jewelers, and builders rather than blacksmiths, postmen, scientists, and chauffeurs. They also wanted to be "kings" and "circus performers." These are the data which Sollenberger gathered on the relationship of interests to endocrine factors. Not only is it difficult to interpret them meaningfully, because of the phenotypic nature of the group differences, but they are based upon a small, nonrepresentative sample which was tested with an obscure instrument of unknown reliability and validity. Needless to say, little confidence can be had in either the verifiability of such findings or their value for theory construction.

One other organismic variable which has been investigated in relation to interests is body build, or physique. In an unpublished doctoral study, Fagin (1950) determined the somatotypes of 473 male college students and compared the different classifications on their *SVIB* scores. In addition, he rated the sample on gynandromorphy, which indicates the extent to which a person has the physical characteristics usually associated with the opposite sex, a high "*g*" index for males denoting such typically feminine attributes as a soft body, a broad pelvis, and wide hips. Analyses of variance for somatotype versus *SVIB* scales yielded only nine significant differences, but high and low *g* groups did differ significantly in the masculinity-femininity of their interests according to expectation—i.e., the low *g* group was more masculine. Only the latter finding seems to be of theoretical importance, not as an isolated relationship, but as another instance of the possible salience of the masculinity-femininity, person-nonperson dimension in the origin and development of interests.

Response Variables. Interests have been related to a variety of other response variables, including aptitudes, educational achievement, general intelligence, job success, occupation engaged in, personality characteristics, satisfaction, and vocational choice. The extensive literature on these correlates of interests has been reviewed and summarized in detail elsewhere (e.g., Darley & Hagenah, 1955; Super & Crites, 1962). Suffice it to point out here that most of the correlations are low, the major exceptions being vocational choice and occupation engaged in, for which they are in the .40's and .50's. Much has been made theoretically of the relationship of interests to ability and personality, but the evidence for any correlations there are among these variables is so spotty and of such borderline significance that it can be interpreted as either confirmatory or not. Further studies might yield more conclusive data one way or the other, but that is unlikely. It would appear that a more productive approach to take would be to initiate a new line of inquiry, such as Tyler (1964) has suggested. In speculating about the implications of her research on interest development, she comments that "more and more, the idea of considering interests to be personality *traits* of a particular sort gave way to another kind of formulation" (1964, p. 218). She proposes that interest research and theory be recentered to focus upon the problem of how individuals use their time. The central hypothesis would be that the allotment of time to some activities and not others and the relative amount of time spent in these activities would reveal the ways in which individuals organize their experience, the decisions they make, the strategies they follow, and the interests they develop.

Similarly, new ways of thinking about the relationship of interests to intellective variables—aptitudes, educational achievement, and general intelligence—might also be formulated. Strong's long-standing hypothesis (1943, p. 682) that "interests reflect inborn abilities" has been shown to be an oversimplification. It holds for some interests, e.g., scientific and linguistic, but not others. One reason may be that the studies which have been conducted on the problem have been based upon the untested assumption that the relationship between interests and abilities is linear, when, in fact, it may be nonlinear (Crites, 1957). It is plausible to predict, for example, that individuals of average ability may score highest on technical-interest scales, because skilled workers, on whom these scales are standardized, fall in the middle range of the intelligence continuum (Super & Crites, 1962). Another explanation may be that the relationship between interests and abilities is lower than expected because of the influence of other variables. Just as "third" variables have been postulated to account for the low correlation between job success and satisfaction (Brayfield & Crockett, 1955; Morse, 1953; Triandis, 1959), so it is reasonable to hypothesize that interests might be more highly related to abilities, were it not for the over-determining effects of some extraneous factor, e.g., parental or social disapproval of activities in which the use of abilities would lead to the development of interests. Still further analyses of the interest-ability relationship might be made in terms of moderator (Saunders, 1956) or geometric (Ferguson, 1960) models, both of which have promise as much-needed novel approaches to this old problem. Of course, it seems possible that interests and abilities may simply not be as highly related as many have assumed.

Theoretical Variables. Hypothetical constructs and intervening variables have not been rigorously formulated in conceptualizations of interest phenomena. With only one or two exceptions, they have been developed more or less expediently from counseling and other applied experiences. As a consequence, not only are they less useful, both conceptually and heuristically, than they might otherwise be, but they have confused rather than clarified certain theoretical issues. To illustrate, Darley (1941; Darley & Hagenah, 1955) has proposed that the occupational-level (OL) scale of the *SVIB* is a measure of drive. A number of studies have been conducted to test this hypothesis (Barnett & others, 1952; Kendall, 1947; Ostrom, 1949a; 1949b), but they have been open to contradictory interpretations, which cannot be resolved by resort to the data, for at least two reasons. First, Darley did not set the confirmability conditions for the hypothesis by specifying the criteria which had to be satisfied in order to define the OL scale as a measure of drive. Variables are usually considered to have drive properties, if they energize a wide variety of responses or facilitate the learning of new responses (Brown, 1961). And, second, Darley treated drive as a hypothetical construct, related only to responses, rather than as an intervening variable, linked to both stimuli and responses. As a consequence, an additional unknown was introduced into the problem: whether level of occupational interests is related to drive. Unless this relationship is assumed, it would not follow that the OL scale is a measure of drive. Thus, in order to test Darley's original hypothesis a new hypothesis has to be formulated and tested, a problem which frequently arises in the use of hypothetical constructs as theoretical variables because they subsume only *R-R* type relationships and consequently are nonexplanatory (Spence, 1944).

THEORIES OF INTERESTS. Theories of interests can be classified in two ways: by their substantive frames of reference and by their formal characteristics, i.e., the relationships which obtain between their conceptual (theory-language) and empirical (data-language) levels (Marx, 1963). Six fairly distinct approaches to the problem of explaining individual differences and developmental trends in interests can be identified and summarized by their central propositions: (1) interests are learned (Fryer, 1931; Strong, 1943); (2) interests are adjustment modes (Carter, 1940); (3) interests are an aspect of personality (Berdie, 1944; Darley, 1941; Darley & Hagenah, 1955); (4) interests are an expression of the self concept (Bordin, 1943; Carter, 1940; Super, 1949); (5) interests are motives (Darley & Hagenah, 1955; Strong, 1955); and (6) interests are multiply determined (Carter, 1940; Super & Crites, 1962). Difficult to categorize according to a specific orientation or hypothesis are the theories of Roe (1957; Roe & Siegelman, 1964) and Tyler (1951, 1960, 1964). Roe has emphasized the role of parental attitudes in the origin of interests but has broadly defined interests primarily in terms of an orientation toward persons or nonpersons, rather than measures of specific interests, such as the *SVIB* or *KPR*. And Tyler has continually revised her theory of interests, from one in which the core concept was "sex-role typing" to one in which the main construct is "programming experience." Both of these theories, however, can probably be broadly characterized as developmental.

With one possible exception, all of these theories of interests are what Marx (1963, p. 17) has defined as *inductive*: "This term is used to refer to the kind of theory which consists essentially of summary statements of empirical relationships and so contains a minimum of inferential commitment and deductive logic." The exception is Bordin's (1943) theory of "interests as dynamic phenomena," which would most likely be classified as *deductive*. That most of the theories of interests are of one type, and that none fits the other two modes of theory construction (model and functional) named by Marx, is indicative of the present scientific status of this field of inquiry. On the three dimensions of (1) control over observations, (2) operational specificity of constructs, and (3) testability of hypotheses, which Marx (1963) considers to be the basic elements of theory construction, the study of interest phenomena falls approximately midway between the realm of literature, art, and practical affairs at one extreme and the domain of science at the other. Observations are elicited in standardized and uniform ways by thoroughly researched interest inventories, but, with the exception of instructional sets to fake (Cross, 1950; Durnall, 1954; Longstaff, 1948), little control has been exerted over the stimulus conditions which produce interests. Constructs have been either so operationally specific that cognate scales on different interest inventories have been largely uncorrelated (Iscoe & Lucier, 1953; Triggs, 1943, 1944a, 1944b) or so conceptually broad that they cannot be measured. And, finally, hypotheses have been formulated more on an intuitive level than through rigorous logic, the consequence being that they have frequently been difficult to test empirically.

John O. Crites
University of Iowa

References

Anastasi, Anne. *Differential Psychology*, 3rd ed. Macmillan, 1958. 664p.

Barnett, Gordon J., and others. "The Occupational Level Scale as a Measure of Drive." *Psychol Monogr* 66 (No. 10); 1952.

Berdie, Ralph F. "Factors Associated with Vocational Interests." *J Ed Psychol* 34:257–77; 1943.

Berdie, Ralph F. "Factors Related to Vocational Interests." *Psychol B* 41:137–57; 1944.

Bereiter, Carl. "Some Persisting Dilemmas in the Measurement of Change." In Harris, Chester W. (Ed.) *Problems in Measuring Change*. U Wisconsin Press, 1963. p. 3–20.

Bergmann, Gustav. *Philosophy of Science*. U Wisconsin Press, 1957. 181p.

Berlyne, D. E. "'Interest' as a Psychological Concept." *Br J Psychol* 40:184–95; 1949.

Berlyne, D. E. *Conflict, Arousal, and Curiosity*. McGraw-Hill, 1960. 350p.

Bloom, Benjamin S. *Stability and Change in Human Characteristics*. Wiley, 1964. 237p.

Bordin, Edward S. "A Theory of Vocational Interests as Dynamic Phenomena." *Ed Psychol Meas* 3:49–66; 1943.

Bordin, Edward S., and Wilson, Earl H. "Change of Interest as a Function of Shift in Curricular Orientation." *Ed Psychol Meas* 13:297–307; 1953.

Brayfield, Arthur H., and Crockett, Walter H. "Employee Attitudes and Employee Performance." *Psychol* 52:396–424; 1955.

Brodbeck, May. "The Philosophy of Science and Educational Research." *R Ed Res* 27:427–40; 1957.

Brogden, Hubert E. "The Primary Personal Values Measured by the Allport-Vernon Test, 'A Study of Values.'" *Psychol Monogr* 66 (No. 16); 1952.

Brown, Judson S. *The Motivation of Behavior*. McGraw-Hill, 1961. 404p.

Brunkan, Richard. "Perceived Parental Attitudes and Parental Identification in Relation to Field of Vocational Choice." *J Counseling Psychol* 12:39–47; 1965.

Buros, Oscar K. *The Sixth Mental Measurements Yearbook*. Gryphon, 1965. 1714p.

Campbell, David P. "Vocational Interests of American

Psychological Association Presidents." *Am Psychologist* 20:636–44; 1965.
Campbell, David P. "Stability of Interests Within an Occupation Over 30 Years." *J Applied Psychol* 50: 51–6; 1966(a).
Campbell, David P. "Stability of Vocational Interests Within Occupations Over Long Time Spans." *Personnel Guid J* 44:1012–9; 1966(b).
Carter, Harold D. "Twin Similarities in Occupational Interests." *J Ed Psychol* 23:641–55; 1932.
Carter, Harold D. "The Development of Vocational Attitudes." *J Cons Psychol* 4:185–91; 1940.
Carter, Harold D. "Vocational Interests and Job Orientation." *Applied Psychol Monogr* 2:1944.
Clark, Kenneth E. *The Vocational Interests of Nonprofessional Men.* U Minnesota Press, 1961. 129p.
Cohen, Morris R., and Nagel, Ernest. *An Introduction to Logic and Scientific Method.* Harcourt, 1934. 467p.
Comrey, Andrew L. "A Factor Analysis of Items on the K Scale of the MMPI." *Ed Psychol Meas* 18: 633–9; 1958.
Cottle, William C. "A Factorial Study of the Multiphasic, Strong, Kuder, and Bell Inventories Using a Population of Adult Males." *Psychometrika* 15: 25–47; 1950.
Crites, John O. "Ability and Adjustment as Determinants of Vocational Interests Patterning in Late Adolescence." Doctoral dissertation. Columbia U, 1957.
Crites, John O. "Vocational Interest in Relation to Vocational Motivation." *J Ed Psychol* 54:277–85; 1963.
Cross, Orrin H. "A Study of Faking on the Kuder Preference Record." *Ed Psychol Meas* 10:271–7; 1950.
Darley, John G. *Clinical Aspects and Interpretation of the Strong Vocational Interest Blank.* Psych Corp, 1941. 72p.
Darley, John G., and Hagenah, Theda. *Vocational Interest Measurement: Theory and Practice.* U Minnesota Press, 1955. 279p.
Dressel, Paul L. "Interests—Stable or Unstable?" *J Ed Res* 48:95–102; 1954.
Durnall, Edward J., Jr. "Falsification of Interest Patterns on the Kuder Preference Record." *J Ed Psychol* 45:240–3; 1954.
Ewens, William P. "Experience Patterns as Related to Vocational Preference." *Ed Psychol Meas* 16: 223–31; 1956.
Fagin, William Barry. "Constitutional Factors in Vocational Interests." Doctoral dissertation. Columbia U, 1950.
Ferguson, Leonard W. "Ability, Interest, and Aptitude." *J Applied Psychol* 44:126–31; 1960.
Fryer, Douglas H. *The Measurement of Interests.* Holt, 1931. 488p.
Guilford, J. P., and others. "A Factor Analysis Study of Human Interests." *Psychol Monogr* 68 (No. 4); 1954.
Gustad, John W. "Vocational Interests and Socioeconomic Status." *J Applied Psychol* 38:336–8; 1954.

Herzberg, Frederick I., and Russell, Diana. "The Effects of Experience and Change of Job Interest on the Kuder Preference Record." *J Applied Psychol* 37:478–81; 1953.
Hull, Clark L. *A Behavior System.* Yale U Press, 1952. 422p.
Hyman, Bernard. "The Relationship of Social Status and Vocational Interests." *J Counseling Psychol* 3:12–6; 1956.
Iscoe, Ira, and Lucier, R. Omer. "A Comparison of the Revised Allport-Vernon Scale of Values (1951) and the Kuder Preference Record (Personal)." *J Applied Psychol* 37:195–6; 1953.
Kendall, William E. "The Occupational Level Scale of the Strong Vocational Interest Blank." *J Applied Psychol* 31:283–8; 1947.
Kuder, G. Frederic. "Identifying the Faker." *Personnel Psychol* 3:155–67; 1950.
Kuder, G. Frederic. "A Comparative Study of Some Methods of Developing Occupational Keys." *Ed Psychol Meas* 17:105–14; 1957.
Kuder, G. Frederic. "A Rationale for Evaluating Interests." *Ed Psychol Meas* 23:3–12; 1963.
Layton, Wilbur L. (Ed.) *The Strong Vocational Interest Blank: Research and Uses.* U Minnesota Press, 1960. 191p.
Longstaff, Howard P. "Fakability of the Strong Interest Blank and the Kuder Preference Record." *J Applied Psychol* 32:360–9; 1948.
Lurie, Walter A. "A Study of Spanger's Value-types by the Method of Factor Analysis." *J Social Psychol* 8:17–37; 1937.
MacCorquodale, Kenneth, and Meehl, Paul E. "On a Distinction Between Hypothetical Constructs and Intervening Variables." *Psychol R* 55:95–107; 1948.
Manual for the Minnesota Vocational Interest Inventory. Psych Corp, 1965. 31p.
Manual for the Strong Vocational Interest Blank (Revised). Stanford U Press, 1966. 4p.
Marx, Melvin H. (Ed.) *Theories in Contemporary Psychology.* Macmillan, 1963. 628p.
Matteson, Ross W. "Experience-interest Relationships as Measured by an Activity Check List." *J Counseling Psychol* 2:13–4; 1955(a).
Matteson, Ross W. "Experience-interest Changes in Students." *J Counseling Psychol* 2:113–21; 1955(b).
McArthur, Charles, and Stevens, Lucia B. "The Validation of Expressed Interests as Compared with Inventoried Interests: A Fourteen Year Follow-up." *J Applied Psychol* 39:184–9; 1955.
Morse, Nancy C. *Satisfactions in the White-collar Job.* Institute for Social Research, Survey Research Center, U Michigan, 1953. 235p.
Ostrom, Stanley R. "The OL Key of the Strong Vocational Interest Blank for Men and Scholastic Success at College Freshmen Level." *J Applied Psychol* 33:51–4; 1949(a).
Ostrom, Stanley R. "The OL Key of the Strong Test and Drive at the Twelfth Grade Level." *J Applied Psychol* 33:240–8; 1949(b).
Roe, Anne. "Early Determinants of Vocational

Choice." *J Counseling Psychol* 4:212–7; 1957.

Roe, Anne, and Siegelman, Marvin. *The Origin of Interests*. APGA, 1964. 98p.

Rogers, Carl R. *Client-centered Therapy*. Houghton, 1951. 560p.

Saunders, David R. "Moderator Variables in Prediction." *Ed Psychol Meas* 16:209–22; 1956.

Sollenberger, Richard T. "Some Relationships Between the Urinary Excretion of Male Hormone by Maturing Boys and Their Expressed Interests and Attitudes." *J Psychol* 9:179–89; 1940.

Spence, Kenneth W. "Types of Constructs in Psychology." *Psychol R* 51:47–68; 1944.

Strong, Edward K., Jr. *Vocational Interests of Men and Women*. Stanford U Press, 1943. 746p.

Strong, Edward K., Jr. *Vocational Interests 18 Years After College*. U Minnesota Press, 1955. 207p.

Strong, Edward K., Jr. "Interests of Fathers and Sons." *J Applied Psychol* 41:284–92; 1957.

Super, Donald E. "Vocational Interest and Vocational Choice." *Ed Psychol Meas* 7:375–84; 1947.

Super, Donald E. *Appraising Vocational Fitness*. Harper, 1949. 727p.

Super, Donald E., and Crites, John O. *Appraising Vocational Fitness*, rev. ed. Harper, 1962. 688p.

Thurstone, L. L. "A Multiple Factor Study of Vocational Interests." *Personnel J* 10:198–205; 1931.

Triandis, Harry C. "A Critique and Experimental Design for the Study of the Relationship between Productivity and Job Satisfaction." *Psychol B* 56:309–12; 1959.

Triggs, Frances O. "A Study of the Relation of Kuder Preference Record Scores to Various other Measures." *Ed Psychol Meas* 3:341–54; 1943.

Triggs, Frances O. "A Further Comparison of Interest Measurement by the Kuder Preference Record and the Strong Vocational Interest Blank for Men." *J Ed Res* 37:538–44; 1944(*a*).

Triggs, Frances O. "A Further Comparison of Interest Measurement by the Kuder Preference Record and the Strong Vocational Interest Blank for Women." *J Ed Res* 38:193–200; 1944(*b*).

Tyler, Leona E. "The Relationship of Interests to Abilities and Reputation among First-grade Children." *Ed Psychol Meas* 11:255–64; 1951.

Tyler, Leona E. "The Development of 'Vocational Interests.' I: The Organization of Likes and Dislikes in Ten-year-old Children." *J Genet Psychol* 86:33–44; 1955.

Tyler, Leona E. "The Development of Interests." In Layton, Wilbur L. (Ed.) *The Strong Vocational Interest Blank: Research and Uses*. U Minnesota Press, 1960. p. 62–75.

Tyler, Leona E. "The Antecedents of Two Varieties of Interest Pattern." *Genet Psychol Monogr* 70:177–227; 1964.

Underwood, Benton J. *Psychological Research*. Appleton, 1957. 298p.

Underwood, Benton J. *Experimental Psychology*, 2nd ed. Appleton, 1966. 678p.

Vernon, Philip E. *The Structure of Human Abilities*. Wiley, 1950. 160p.

LANGUAGE DEVELOPMENT

To all who contemplate human nature or human achievement, language must loom large as a key to that nature and as the basic instrument of that achievement. It is not surprising that man's consuming interest in himself has repeatedly focused on his attribute of language.

THE NATURE OF LANGUAGE. Men speak; their speech is patterned—a system inheres in it. This system is language. Language is thus an abstraction from behavior. It is a double system—a system of content or meanings and a system of expression or signs.

The study of language may have any one of several different emphases. The student may be primarily concerned with a language as a formal system; he may study the behavior—speech or responses to speech—that exemplifies language; he may be interested in language as an aspect of culture. The first of these concerns is the province of the linguist; the others are concerns of psychology, sociology, or anthropology.

Language as a Formal System. All natural languages appear to be hierarchically structured: a relatively small number of meaningless units (phonemes) are combined in different ways (though with some restrictions on permissible combinations) to form meaningful units (morphemes). Morphemes are further combined to form words or larger structures.

Phonemes are classes of sounds and are the smallest units that make a difference in the content of what is said. The difference between *sin* and *gin,* for example, is a difference in the initial phoneme in a series of three. Some phonemes are segmental (just illustrated), others are suprasegmental—stresses and pitches. A phoneme is a unit in the sound system of some particular language; the term has meaning only in reference to a particular language.

Languages differ in the degree to which the letter sequences of their written form correspond to the phoneme sequences of the spoken words, a fact that continues as the basis for a good deal of research in reading instruction.

The study or makeup of a language in terms of its phonemic structure is called phonology. The study or nature of a language in terms of the way morphemes are combined is called morphology. Many words are formed of a single morpheme (*teach*, for example); other words consist of more than one morpheme. (*Teachers* contains three morphemes: *teach,* plus both the agentive and plural). The manner in which morphemes and larger units are arranged in sentences is known as syntax.

In some ways languages are highly arbitrary. The number of distinguishable sounds that the human vocal apparatus can make is extremely large, yet relatively few of these (about 40 in English, depending on what is included) are the focuses of the phonemes of any one language. But the phonemes of one language may differ markedly from those of another. Thus, the sound system that one human infant must master may be quite different from that which another must learn.

Languages are also largely arbitrary in the aspects of the real world that they name and in the names that they assign, although they reflect environment and culture. For example, we tend to regard the division of the color spectrum into the six principal divisions that we call red, orange, yellow, green, blue, and violet as obvious, necessary, and natural. In Shona, however, the spectrum is divided into three divisions; one corresponding roughly to our orange, red, and purple; one to blue and blue-green; and one to green and yellow (Gleason, 1961). The child's acquisition of language is therefore truly, in some major respects, a learning task and cannot be simply the maturation of inherent capabilities.

Language is also impressively complete. One way of expressing this is to say that languages categorize a large part of the environment, that is, that they have names for most of the objects, actions, ideas, and attributes that are important to society. Another way of emphasizing the completeness of languages is to stress that they are used for general communication, that is, that with language one may say all things. Thus, the sheer quantity that the child must learn in learning language is enormous.

Finally, the grammar of language is complex, and although linguists have not yet been able to describe its full complexity, the child masters it. This is a prodigious accomplishment, although we should not underestimate the extensive opportunity that the child has for learning and for practicing (with knowledge of results available in many ways), nor should we forget the relative simplicity of the system that the young child has truly mastered or the obvious evidence of his ignorance of many details.

Language Behavior. A considerable range of opinion exists about the status that should be accorded language behavior—behavior that embodies the formal system of language. Skinner (1957) and many others believe that language behavior should not be regarded as different from other behavior in any fundamental way.

Chomsky (1959, 1965) disputes this view and contends that we should not neglect the possibility that the human infant is endowed with learning mechanisms especially suited for the learning of language. Lenneberg (1967) has assembled evidence relating to the possible biological propensities that man may have for language learning.

Another viewpoint, taken by Werner and Kaplan (1963), emphasizes the symbolic nature of language. Concern with language as a symbol system not only means concern for how such a system develops, what it is like, and how it works, but, perhaps more than other orientations, results in a concern for understanding the consequences of man's possession of language. Church (1961) argues that language transforms experience by providing new channels for the human environment to act on the child and by transforming the child himself so that he can do new things and do old things in new ways. Tikhomirov (1959) expresses a similar view, held by many Soviet psychologists, in saying that language in man is not just a new function but one that qualitatively transforms all other behavior.

The relationship between formal linguistic analysis and the analysis of behavior is one of interdependence. While the psychologist who studies language behavior has increasingly depended on the units and relationships identified by linguists, linguists in their turn have relied extensively on behavioral criteria—usually based on their own or informants' judgments—to analyze samples of behavior, i.e., samples of speech.

Language Description and the Study of Language Development. Important progress has been made in recent years in the validity and completeness of the descriptions of language that are available to the student of language development. As researchers have begun to use these more adequate descriptions of language, their work has begun to disclose more interesting and more basic characteristics of language development. It may be, however, that not all elements of a given language description correspond to response units or classes suitable for the study of language learning. Salzinger (1967) discusses this question.

The earlier studies of language development charted the growth of such language characteristics as vocabulary, parts of speech as classified by traditional school grammar, various ratios of different kinds of words, and measures of sentence complexity such as sentence length, number and type of clauses, and number of prepositional phrases.

The first major break in this tradition came with the adoption of Fries's (1952) form classes by many researchers for the classification of words on the basis of grammatical function. This classification is still often used, but it is apparent that an even more detailed functional classification is required, particularly for verbs. (See Allen, 1968, for an example of a more detailed system.)

Without question the linguistic theory and analysis that has had the greatest impact on research in language development has been the transformational grammar of Chomsky (1957, 1965). It is principally this work that has been seen as suggesting hypotheses concerning what it is that the child learns when learning language and concerning the sequence in which some of these learnings may occur.

Some fruitful recent studies of language development have been based on descriptions of language, such as Markov and simple constituent-structure models (G. Miller & Chomsky, 1963) that are known to be inadequate in some respect but that characterize language in such a way as to facilitate study of some of its properties.

Other important and fast-moving developments in language analysis are coming from those working in machine translation and other aspects of automatic analysis of language.

Contributions to language description from the field of language automation are doubly important to the language researcher, for they may eventually be accompanied by a workable program for computer processing of at least limited types of language samples. The idea of studying language development by collecting language samples and feeding them into a computer that will analyze their content and structure and then collate and organize the results is most appealing. But, aside from the limited nature of the current programs, a major obstacle is the nature of the spoken language itself. It is often fragmentary, run-on, full of partial repeats and corrections, and totally unready for analysis by a program designed for processing grammatically correct language. Nevertheless, collaboration between those studying language development and those working on language automation is needed and should be fruitful. The language researcher will need to keep abreast of developments reported in the publications of the Association for Machine Translation and Computational Linguistics.

FUNCTIONS OF LANGUAGE. In playing its casually vital role in men's lives, language functions in many ways. Perhaps the most obvious and, to the child, one of the most intriguing characteristics of language is the fact that it has a name (and often several) for practically everything. This referential function of language is at the core of much else that language is able to do.

Children may be unable to distinguish clearly between the name of a thing and the thing that is named or may regard the name as a property of the thing or in other ways imbue the word with power and substance. Church (1961) and Werner and Kaplan (1963) discuss this question and the general problem of the child's development of meanings. (See Ervin-Tripp & Slobin, 1966, for a concise review of psychological approaches to linguistic meaning.)

Man uses language both to communicate with others and to communicate with himself. Both of these functions are vital to the process of education. Language not only embodies the information that is transmitted to the student but furnishes the organizing patterns that permit him to remember what he experiences, the conceptual substance from which he can build new creations of thought, and the signals with which he can then direct himself.

The role of language in mental life and self-direction is less visible than its social functions, but research has demonstrated its importance and continues to reveal more about the ways in which this role is carried out. The degree to which lists of words conform to the syntactic patterns of the language strongly influences how well the lists are remembered (e.g., M. Brown, 1966). The ease with which items or associations are learned or remembered is influenced by the verbal structure and their position in it, in which they are presented to or placed by the learner (e.g., Glanzer, 1962). Shades of color that can be given names that effectively identify them are remembered better than other shades (Lantz & Stefflre, 1964). Young children and culturally disadvantaged youngsters who do not spontaneously use verbal mediational devices in learning paired associates sometimes learn much more rapidly after being shown how to use such devices (Jensen, 1968).

In the child's development of concepts, verbal labels are generally acknowledged to be important. The degree of, and basis for, this influence is difficult to determine. Carroll (1964b) gives a helpful background and relates work on concepts and word meanings to school instruction.

Verbal symbols are often essential features in human problem solving. This is perhaps obvious to anyone who has ever talked to himself or picked up a pencil while thinking through a problem of any sort. It is clear, for example, that explaining to oneself or others the processes, reasons, or assumptions underlying one's attempts to solve problems will often result in quicker solutions and in better transfer to new problems (e.g., Gagné & Smith, 1962). It is surmised that language habits and verbal associations may have a considerable influence on the nature of the solutions that are tried. To the extent that successful past experience with similar problems becomes mirrored in vocabulary and associations, this is probably true. It is known that degree of success in an academic subject-matter area is related to the verbal associations that the student forms (Johnson, 1965), and certainly verbal habits influence the solution to simple verbal problems (Beilin, 1967; Judson & Cofer, 1956). Judson and others (1956) have made an interesting and partially successful attempt to show the influence of verbal habits on more complex reasoning.

Through his use of language in problem solving, man uses language to give direction to his activities. He also uses language for self-direction in a more immediate way. Luria (1961) has provided some striking accounts of laboratory studies in which, as the child matures, his own instructions to himself gradually acquire influence as signals for simple movements. Gleitman and her co-workers (Gleitman, 1965) found that young children from 15 to 30 months old were most likely to respond to a simple command on those occasions when they had repeated it themselves, although such repetition was by no means a necessary condition for an appropriate response.

The fact that, in thinking, one may use the organization of the environment given by the concept labels of one's language and manipulate these within the framework of grammatical categories and relationships also given by the language has led many to ponder and some to proclaim the influence of language over thought.

If one's outlook, or even the ease of dealing with important classes of ideas, is significantly influenced by one's native language, the implications for children's intellectual development and for education are clearly profound. Bilingualism would assume far deeper meaning than is usually accorded to it.

The difficulties of investigating this hypothesis of linguistic relativity are very great. Two children who have learned different languages have invariably been subject to family and cultural influences that differ in many ways in addition to the language spoken. The same basic difficulty has plagued studies of billingualism. Thus far, although some differences in memory for specific colors and in the attributes of sounds and objects that are spontaneously noticed or used as a basis of classification have been found to be predictable from differences between languages, no major differences between languages have been demonstrated in their potential for general communication or in their influence on thought processes. Carroll (1963a) and Fishman (1960) have reviewed the work on this question. The work of Vygotsky, now available in English (Vygotsky, 1962), has had profound influence on the developmental study of the relationship between language and thought.

METHODS OF STUDYING LANGUAGE DEVELOPMENT. It is convenient to distinguish three general classes of method used in studies of language development: (1) observation, (2) testing, and (3) teaching (including conditioning). These categories are not formally adequate but help to clarify the trends and needs in research. Particularly for observation and testing, many studies have used unusually bright children as subjects. This tendency is unfortunate. While it may be that all children in their own time go through substantially the same stages of language development, if any children do telescope some of the stages or pass through them so quickly that they are not noted by an observer, it will be the linguistically precocious who do so.

Observation. The majority of the classic studies from which much of our knowledge of language development comes have been observational studies. Linguists, psychologists, and others have recorded the babblings of infants, their early words and developing vocabularies, their errors, their customary and their precocious sentences, and other features of their use and apprehension of speech. These studies have provided documentation of many of the general trends in language development and a few detailed case studies (e.g., Leopold, 1939–1949; Lewis, 1951). The data from detailed observations of language development are always voluminous and disorderly and are not very informative until they are skillfully organized and summarized in some way that clarifies the essential nature of trend and current status.

When students of language development turned to modern linguistics for guidance, they construed its methodology as involving first the collection of a large language corpus and then the unbiased analysis of this material to discover the units and structures of which it is composed. Indeed, this was the predominant message of the time. Much of the most interesting recent work in language development has therefore involved a renewed interest in careful observation and recording of children's speech, coupled with an analysis of the resulting corpus in its own right, as if it were a new, unknown language being described and analyzed.

Testing. Many things that one would like to know about language development are difficult to learn by observation. In the first place, if one wishes to know if a child is able to use a particular construction or if he knows the meaning of certain words, it may require an interminable period of observation before the occasion for their use arises. It is more efficient to provide the occasion. Also, even if the child does not employ a word or construction on an appropriate occasion, the investigator cannot be sure that the child is incapable of doing so. Finally, judging a child's comprehension of a given feature of speech on the basis of pure observation is hazardous. Careful testing is usually necessary to determine the nature of his understanding and on which aspects of the speech signal or other cues this understanding is based.

For these related reasons, the testing of children's understanding of language, and of their ability to use language, has played a prominent part in our growing knowledge of language development. The methods employed have ranged from simply asking a child if he knows what a word means to quite ingenious "games" that reveal his understandings.

The emphasis by Chomsky (1964, 1965) on the distinction between language performance and language competence, with his stress on the importance of the latter, will undoubtedly lead to increased emphasis on testing as opposed to observation in the study of language development. From the standpoint of the study of child development, however, what a child typically does do is still of interest in the study of any aspect of behavior, language included.

Teaching. Some investigators have studied language acquisition by observing and testing in conjunction with specific attempts to teach or to condition language behavior. There are relatively few teaching or conditioning studies directly relevant to language development, however, and in several of these the subjects have been adults or older children whose language development was essentially complete. Work with such older subjects will contribute to our eventual understanding of how, and how much, and when the nature of the language-learning process changes with age and experience, but at present the implications for initial language acquisition are hard to assess.

The difficulties of conducting definitive language-teaching experiments are similar to those that confront educational research in general: the period of learning is long, the number and frequency of influences are enormous, and if conditions are sufficiently controlled to provide definitive results, the relevance to real life becomes questionable. In particular, language stimuli are so numerous and so ubiquitous that it is most difficult to evaluate the subject's previous learning or to control exposure during the study.

In any study involving systematic testing or teaching of language ability, the investigator must select a sample of language to be tested or taught. In many cases the investigator will wish to generalize to a larger domain of language than was actually tested or taught, and, where this is so, the sample must be selected to represent that domain. The selection of this sample is often a weak point in such studies. Coleman (1964) has also pointed out that many language studies have used statistical tests that do not permit any generalization beyond the language sample used.

THE COURSE OF LANGUAGE DEVELOPMENT. Stimulated by the influence of linguistics and by the growing recognition of the importance of language for educational growth, a great upwelling of interest and research in language development has taken place since the early 1950's. Several excellent summaries of this work and of earlier work are available. Ervin-Tripp (1966) has provided a comprehensive account and intelligent interpretation of our present understanding of language development. Other important summaries of recent work are those by Ervin and Miller (1963), Roger Brown (1965), and Ervin-Tripp and Slobin (1966). A great wealth of earlier material is summarized by McCarthy (1954). Interpretations and abstracts of some of the extensive Russian work on language development have been prepared by Slobin (1966a, 1966b).

A sketch of some of the highlights in our current knowledge of English language development is given below. This sketch will illustrate the ways in which our knowledge of language development has been achieved, some of the important gaps in our understanding of language development, and some of the problems and considerations in the study of this familiar but complex phenomenon.

Preverbal Development and Initial Vocabulary. Actions may speak louder than words, but a young child's actions portend the weight that words will carry. By the time a child is four months old he attends to spoken words by turning his head, and he adjusts to simple commands before the end of the first year and before he uses any words of his own. His own vocalizations begin at birth, followed by cooing and babbling by the third month, by repetition of syllables by about the eighth month and by first words usually by the end of the first year (McCarthy, 1954). He spends, in a cumulative sense, months of solitary "practice" at producing vocal sounds in infancy (McCarthy, 1954), at producing appropriate phonemic and grammatical patterns in early childhood (Weir, 1962), and at social use of language in later childhood (Piaget, 1959). Many infants, at least after they have acquired a few words, "practice" rattling on, using appropriate stress and pitch patterns but without recognizable morphemic content (McCarthy, 1954).

Vocalizations during the first few months are relatively unsystematic and do not seem to be conditioned by the language the child will eventually speak. With increasing age, infant vocalization includes an ever-greater variety of speech sounds until, before the first words are spoken, speech sounds that resemble most of the phonemes of the adult language are included. (See Irwin, 1960b, for several references.) The relation of this preverbal growth to the phonological system of the adult language is not clear (Weir, 1966). It seems evident that the infant's later babbling is influenced by the language he hears, but to what extent and in what sense the preverbal development serves as preparation for later speech or later development of a phonological system remains unknown.

The later months of the preverbal period are characterized by a marked increase in the child's control of volume, pitch, and articulation as shown by his ability to sustain or repeat these features (Ervin & Miller, 1963). Weir (1966) noted evidence that learning of intonation patterns comes early, is often dominant in early comprehension of speech, and may play an important part in other aspects of language learning.

With the first few words used consistently and referentially, the child clearly begins the development of his phonological system. The "words" may not be the same as the adult forms, but the phonemic contrasts are consistent.

The ensuing stage of language development is described by Jakobson (Jakobson & Halle, 1956) as being characterized by the development of successive contrasts between features that form the significant dimensions of phonemes. Jakobson believes that the contrasts are learned in a developmental sequence that corresponds to the frequency with which these contrasts are found among the languages of the world.

Ervin and Miller (1963) note that studies of the speech development of individual children substantiate the general outlines of Jakobson's theory but point to the probable influence of visual cues and vocabulary on the order in which contrasts are learned. They list the following generalizations as being the most tenable current hypotheses: (1) The vowel-consonant contrast is one of the first to be learned. (2) A stop-continuant contrast is learned early. (3) If the child uses two consonants that differ in place of articulation but not in manner, the contrast will be labial versus dental (e.g., /p/ versus /t/). (4) Contrasts involving place of articulation are learned before contrasts in voicing. (5) Contrasts between high and low vowels (e.g., /i/ versus /a/) precede contrasts between front and back vowels (e.g., /i/ versus /u/). Ervin and Miller also include as tenable hypotheses that affricates (e.g., /ch/), liquids (e.g., /r/), and consonant clusters (e.g., /st/), are acquired relatively late, and they note general agreement that the use of initial consonants precedes in time the use of consonants in medial or final position and that ability to hear a contrast precedes its use.

As the child learns each consonant contrast, he could theoretically double the number of consonant phonemes in his system. (E.g., if a child possesses a labial stop and a dental stop, the new contrast voiced versus unvoiced would apply to both, yielding /b/ versus /p/ from the first and /d/ versus /t/ from the second.) Jakobson's theory thus predicts that children move toward the adult phonological system not gradually and steadily but by alternating periods of sudden development and consolidation, the former representing the acquisition of a new contrast splitting at least many of the existing phonemes into two. Some instances of such acquisition of contrasting features have been recorded.

Data on the proportion of children of different ages who can articulate the various phonemes of English correctly are given by Templin (1957). According to Templin, girls achieve mature articulation at about the age of seven, and boys about a year later.

After the child first begins to use words referentially, his vocabulary may then grow slowly for a time (at least in terms of numbers of words, though not so slowly, perhaps, in terms of proportional increase). Well before the end of the second year, however, a very rapid development of vocabulary has usually begun (McCarthy, 1954). The period of relatively slow vocabulary growth, approximately 12 to 18 or 20 months of age, is also the period of the one-word sentence, when single words used as whole sentences or phrases are common (Carroll, 1960). Such one-word sentences are typically used with a variety of meanings, a condition which McNeill (1966) sees as impelling the child to progress to a more complex language system.

Emergence of Grammatical Structure. The system that the child does then develop has been described in several careful studies (Braine, 1963b; R. Brown & Fraser, 1964; W. Miller & Ervin, 1964).

Once the child begins to use utterances of two or more words, the possibility of a rudimentary syntactic structure exists. The syntax that governs the two-word utterances of approximately the second half of the second year is based on two classes of words—a closed class of a relatively small number of what Braine (1963b) calls pivot words and a large open class. Each pivot word occupies a characteristic position. The word *off*, for example, was a second-position pivot word for one of the children studied by Braine, being used in such utterances as "shoe off," "light off," and "pants off." *More* was one of the first-position pivot words, being used in such utterances as "more toast," "more read," and "more hot."

The open class contains, as in several of the examples just given, many words that serve as nouns in adult speech but is by no means confined to them. The open-class words are frequently used alone; many of the pivot words seldom are. Braine observed that any new pivot word in the child's vocabulary was likely to be teamed quickly with a variety of open-class words.

A further development of two-word syntax occurs toward the end of the second year, when words of the large open class are paired. As with one-word sentences, these utterances may serve the purpose of more than one adult sentence. "Daddy car," for example, might substitute for "That's Daddy's car" or for "Daddy is in the car." Meanwhile, constructions involving three or more words have also appeared. Once this stage is reached, the number of possible different utterances that the child may use becomes extremely large. There are usually several alternative sets of rules that would account for much of the child's speech output, but all of them leave some utterances unaccounted for. Presumably children as well as adults use occasional deviant sentences, and it is not possible to ask a young child in so many words whether he regards a particular utterance as grammatical. Since the child eventually attains adult linguistic competence, there is temptation, and perhaps some grounds, for making choices that bias the set of rules ascribed to the child toward simplicity, comprehensiveness, and adult grammar. Those who have actually analyzed children's speech have, for the most part, been admirably cautious in this respect.

It is generally assumed that other grammatical classes develop by subdivision of the pivot and open classes. The manner in which this occurs is not precisely known. McNeill (1966) has reviewed the available data and offered some hypotheses.

Since small children are difficult subjects for tests and experiments, most research on very early language development has used observational techniques, Naturally enough, most observational studies are concerned with language production rather than language perception or comprehension, and our systematic data about very early language development are therefore largely about language production.

Language in Later Childhood: Grammar. Although the complexity of older children's language makes the complete linguistic analysis of speech samples very difficult, particular language subsystems have been followed through to later stages. Klima and Bellugi (1966), for example, have analyzed the development of negation and interrogatives in the speech of three children up to a stage where the average utterance length for each child was four words. Since older children are easier to test and can cooperate in experiments, there are many studies in which particular aspects of language have been tested in children of three years or more. There are also many studies that describe the language of older children in grosser terms or on the basis of comparison with adult forms. For the earlier work of this sort the reader is again referred to McCarthy's article (1954).

The exemplary studies by Roger Brown (1957) and by Berko (1958) initiated a surge of enthusiasm for and ingenuity in testing children's ability to understand and produce various features of the language system. The point of these studies and of much work that followed was an eduction of the grammatical rules that the children followed as distinct from specific utterances that embodied those rules. Berko studied children of ages four through seven years, and her study involved the morphological rather than the syntactic aspect of grammar. Nonsense words were used to assure that the child's performance was not rote repetition or recognition of words previously heard. To investigate the child's ability to form the plural, for example, she showed a child a drawing of a make-believe animal and said, "This is a *wug*." Then, showing a drawing of two of these animals, she said, "Now there is another. There are two of them. There are two _____." The children readily understood this task, and most of them responded with *wugs* as the completion. A similar procedure was used for several other morphological patterns, such as past tense, third person singular, and progressive.

Berko's general findings were that children learn to use many morphological rules productively at an early age. Not all the rules sampled, however, were well established. Relatively few of the younger children, for example, formed the plural properly when the syllabic form of the inflection was required, as in *gutch—gutches*. Wick Miller and Ervin (1964) found that the children were able to apply affixes correctly to familiar words before they generalized the patterns to nonsense words. The children also generalized the regular patterns to irregular forms (*go—goed*). Thus, the child soon grasps and uses the regularities of language, extending them even to inappropriate applications.

The regularities of language and the child's ready use of them undoubtedly facilitate language acquisition (R. Brown, 1958). In the language of nursery-school children, nouns are more likely to have referents with definite size and contour, and verbs are more likely to denote animal or human movement than are the nouns and verbs in adult writing (R. Brown, 1957). It is quite plausible that the "thing" and "action" denotations of children's nouns and verbs should help children learn the names of new things and actions. Brown illustrated this possibility with demonstrations like the following: A preschool child is first shown a picture of a pair of hands kneading a confetti-like substance in a bowl-like container and is told that it is a picture of *sibbing*. The child is then shown a panel of three pictures—one of which shows the hands making the kneading motion, one the confetti-like substance, and one the bowl—and is asked to point to the picture of *sibbing*. Most children in such circumstances choose the picture of the hands performing the kneading action. Other children, who are told that the original picture is a picture of *some sib* or *a sib*, point instead to the confetti-like substance or to the bowl, respectively, when asked to identify *some sib* or *a sib* in the panel of three pictures. In performing this task, the children apparently use regularities in the structure of language to help them identify the class to which the new word belongs and rely on the relative semantic consistency of the word class to identify the referent of the new word.

Cooper (1967) has tested second, fourth, and sixth graders with a simple written group test that extends the procedures of R. Brown (1957) and Berko (1958) to less common morphological rules. Although some of the less common rules are applied by children in the second grade, others are not productive for a large proportion of children even by the sixth grade. In general, derivations are used later than inflections.

The syntax that children use has not been so extensively studied by testing methods as has their morphology. Word-association tests have given some clues to the child's developing system of word classes. As the child grows older, a progressively larger proportion of his word-association responses fall in the same adult grammatical class as the stimulus word (e.g., R. Brown & Berko, 1960; Palermo, 1963). Count nouns and adjectives, which are the first word classes to be distinguished in this way, are also the classes that children employ most grammatically in new sentences after once hearing new (nonsense) words of those classes (R. Brown & Berko, 1960). There have been some attempts to show by experiment how word classes and their appropriate use might develop through the child's hearing or using different members of the class in the same position in the same sentences or phrases. McNeill (1963) used free association and usage tests to show that nonsense words learned in the same sentence frames acquire to some extent the same word-class membership. Braine (1963a) showed that, given some experience with an artificial language, nine- and ten-year-old children used nonsense words in appropriate locations in new "sentences."

Fraser and others (1963) included some syntactic contrasts in their comparison of the ability of three-year-olds to repeat, comprehend, and apply correctly various constructions. The children generally understood the contrasts between affirmative and negative, between subject and object in active voice, and between the present progressive and the future tense. The contrasts between subject and object in passive voice and between the indirect object and the direct object were much more difficult. Perhaps the difficulty of the passive is related to its auditory similarity to the present progressive, which is used and understood relatively early. Menyuk (1963) has extended to older children and to a more thorough inventory of structures the technique of asking children to repeat sentences.

One of the main characteristics of the speech of very young children is its telegraphic nature. Words are omitted—often the least essential words—while the order of the retained words is likely to be correct (R. Brown & Bellugi, 1964). When very young children imitate sentences, they also shorten them in much the same way (Ervin, 1964), suggesting that the memory or other processing limitations that are responsible for this may also be important in determining the form of their own spontaneous utterances.

R. Brown and Bellugi (1964) have noted the tendency of many parents to echo the child's utterances in an expanded, grammatically correct form and have suggested that this process may be important in the child's language learning. Certainly children do attend to some things that their parents say, allegations to the contrary notwithstanding. And novel things seem particularly to elicit this attention. The older children (about two years) in the group studied by Gleitman and her associates (Gleitman, 1965) had reached a stage where the tendency to repeat adult speech was much diminished. When novel (nonsense) words were introduced into the simple command spoken by the mother, the children were then more likely to repeat it.

Although tests of older children's mastery of syntax do not yet give a very complete picture, some additional evidence is available from records that have been made of the syntactic patterns that children use. Menyuk (1964) classified the speech patterns, recorded in a variety of situations, of an unusually bright group of young children according to the various transformations to which these patterns have surface resemblance. She found on this basis that most of the three-year-old children used the negative-question, inversion ("Sometimes I help my sister."), relative-question ("What's her name?"), separation ("He says, 'Take it off the grass.'"), got ("We've got a toy monkey."), auxiliary-*be* ("They might be fighting."), *do* ("It doesn't have wheels."), possessive, conjunction, pronoun, adjective ("That's a little bit."), and infinitive-complement ("They're going to fight.") transformations. Fewer than two-thirds of these children used the passive, pronominalization ("There was a big daddy dog."), auxiliary *have*, reflexive ("She feeds herself."), *if* ("We'll stay home if they don't have turtles.") *so* ("I pasted it so I get another one."), *because* ("You can't knock it down because it's going to be a big house for cars."), participial complement ("I like painting pictures."), iteration ("I'm trying to catch them to get them back to their cage."), and nominalization ("He gets a strapping.") transformations. Except for the passive, *because*, and reflexive transformations, these transformations were also used by fewer than two-thirds of the first graders during the observation period.

Menyuk also categorized the ungrammatical utterances of the children according to the particular transformations that she believes they failed to use correctly.

When the language of children is described through comparison with structures found in adult grammar, it must be remembered that a grammar is a unified account; a grammatical rule or operation must be compatible with the total structure of the grammar. Thus, the simple fact that a child uses a construction that is presumed to be generated, in adult language, by a certain grammatical rule does not mean that the child's grammar should be assumed to include the same rule. It may be undesirable to say, for example, that a child is using a given transformation simply because the appropriate surface structure appears in his speech or in a response to a test item. It is legitimate and important, however, to study in its own right the manifest progress of children's language toward the adult model. In describing language development for this purpose, it is convenient and clear if surface features of the child's language are labeled with terms from adult grammar as long as it is not implied without further evidence that these terms necessarily refer to the same grammatical units or operations in the child's language as in the adult model.

As children reach school age, their command of language becomes of great interest in relation to their school progress. In this setting, children's ability to comprehend speech of varying style and complexity from both visible and nonvisible speakers is obviously of great importance, but it has received too little attention. Research on the child's comprehension of discourse is sometimes found in educational literature under the rubric *auding*. Much of the literature in this field is listed in Duker's *Listening Bibliography* (1964).

Two extensive research studies in recent years, those by Loban (1963, 1966) and by Strickland (1962), have followed the language development of a large group of school-age children. These studies, particularly Loban's, provide the advantage of a good cross section of background and ability in the children studied, and they relate language development to school achievement. The analysis of language that was employed to organize the great volume of data in these studies does not, however, make particularly clear the growth of specific grammatical structures.

A striking indication of the influence that the situation can have on the findings of observational studies is provided through a comparison of Strickland's data with those from a study by Hocker (Strang & Hocker, 1965). Hocker used analytic procedures similar to those used by Strickland (1962), but, whereas in the Strickland study speech was encouraged in the presence of an adult, Hocker collected speech samples from children engaged in their own daily activities. The mean sentence length of first-grade children in Strickland's study was about 11 words, but in Hocker's samples of the spontaneous speech of first-grade children, the mean sentence length was only 5 words. The most common noun modifier in Hocker's sample was relatively infrequent in Strickland's sample. This word, predictable by hindsight, was *my*.

Language in Later Childhood: Vocabulary. Vocabulary development has been extensively studied from many standpoints—the kind of words used or known, the variety of meanings known for words with multiple meanings, the ability to use an appropriate word to give the right shade of meaning, and the richness and specificity of concepts (e.g., Russell & Saadeh, 1962).

Although vocabulary is the key variable in reading comprehension (Klare, 1963) and is a major feature of most tests of academic aptitude, emphasis in the study of language development is now on the acquisition of language as a system. Perhaps when the structure of semantics is better understood, vocabulary growth can be incorporated more fully into descriptions of the acquisition of the language system. In the meantime, vocabulary is somewhat outside current trends of study but in many practical respects remains an index of development outweighing all others.

By far the most extensive work in the study of vocabulary development has been done in the testing of vocabulary comprehension. The most comprehensive of such studies is a long-term effort with the ultimate aim of providing a catalog of difficulty for all words known by at least two-thirds of the children in even-numbered grades from grade 4 through grade 12 (Dale & Eicholz, 1960). The results are based on written, multiple-choice tests and hence depend on the particular selection of alternative answers provided.

Many attempts have been made, too, to assess the total vocabulary of individual children of different ages. This appears to be an interesting matter, but the double problem of defining what constitutes a distinct word and what constitutes knowing it infuses the answer with a great deal of arbitrariness. Estimates for older children and adults were at one time much too low, while later estimates have been too high. Lorge and Chall (1963) discuss many of the methodological problems. Dale and Razik (1963) have prepared an extensive bibliography of vocabulary studies.

The acquisition of meaning has been the focus of most of the efforts to use teaching or conditioning procedures to study language development. A number of experiments (e.g., Staats & Staats, 1963) show that at least some features of meaning can be conditioned through stimulus pairing. Most of this work has been done with older children and adults and has used the semantic differential as an index of meaning. Studies of children's developing affective meaning systems have been conducted by Di Vesta (1966) using the semantic differential with children in grades 2 through 7.

General Indexes of Language Maturity. For many kinds of studies of child development it is important to have some reasonably simple estimate of the general level of language maturity of the children being studied. As indicated earlier, performance on a suitable vocabulary test can often serve this purpose.

Where emphasis is more on the structural aspects of language, mean sentence length has often served quite well the purpose of a general index of language maturity. The value of this and other measures is discussed by McCarthy (1954). Mature language is often characterized by the use of transformations that recast the ideas of more than one simple sentence into a single clause. Also, young children often produce rather long sentences composed of simple coordinated clauses. These considerations suggest that some characteristic other than sentence length might provide a better index of language maturity. Hunt (1965) found that for written compositions, mean clause length and, particularly, mean T-unit length were indeed superior indexes. "T-unit" is the name given by Hunt to minimum terminable units composed of one independent clause and any associated dependent clauses. It is the same as the "communication unit" used by Loban (1963).

All measures such as sentence or clause length, however, are merely derivatives of the grammatical structures actually used by the child. Presumably a complete inventory of these structures could be summarized in some way that would provide a more sensitive index of language maturity. However, the complete grammatical analysis of the child's speech or writing in terms of various structures used is often prohibitively time-consuming. Serious attempts have been made to find indexes of word types or **structural features that characterize complexity or maturity** (McCarthy, 1954). It would be useful if particular structures or a small set of structures, perhaps differing at different age levels, could be located, the presence or prevalence of which would be highly correlated with a criterion of language maturity based on the total array of age-related changes in structural characteristics. Measures of structural difficulty such as mean word depth or the ratio of total nodes to terminal nodes in the phrase structure (G. Miller & Chomsky, 1963) might be good measures of structural maturity, but their computation involves the complete structural analysis of at least a reliable sample of the corpus.

There are, of course, many tests of reading comprehension and some of listening comprehension. These tests do not generally control in any specified way, however, the syntactic structures that are included, partly because vocabulary and subject content are such potent influences on comprehension. There are also many tests of specific language skills and a few batteries and developmental scales, used so far mainly in clinical settings (Irwin, 1960b).

The fact that word associations show age trends, such as the increasing number of responses in the same grammatical class as the stimulus word, suggests that they might be useful as indexes of language maturity. Word associations are so susceptible to the influence of set and other factors, however, that their usefulness as an index of maturity is restricted. Compared with hearing children, deaf children, whose language experience is relatively restricted and whose language development is delayed, may give as many or more responses in the same grammatical class as the stimulus word (Restaino, in press).

Language Behavior of Adults. The wealth of research on the nature and functions of adult language is important for the clues that it gives to the final state toward which child language evolves. The essential features of this material for the purpose of the present article were described in the earlier sections "The Nature of Language" and "Functions of Language." Much fuller accounts are given by Diebold (1965) and by Ervin-Tripp and Slobin (1966), who also give references to other summaries. An important new source of information on language research is *Language and Language Behavior Abstracts*. This journal abstracts current articles on language and language behavior that are of interest to those working in applied linguistics, developmental psychology, educational psychology, the psychology of learning, hearing pathology, speech pathology, and certain other fields relevant to education.

THEORIES OF LANGUAGE LEARNING. The major current issue in theories of language learning is the polarity between language behavior as conceptualized by learning theorists (e.g., Skinner, 1957; Mowrer, 1960; Osgood, 1963; Staats & Staats, 1963) and language competence as conceptualized by generative grammarians (e.g., Chomsky, 1964, 1965; Bever & others, 1965; Fodor & Garrett, 1966). Jenkins (1966) provides a clear statement of some of the considerations that lead to, and that arise from, these different points of view. He concludes that the outlook of the generative grammarian now dominates the study of language acquisition. This outlook focuses on the native speaker's ability to produce or understand the sentences of the language and asks what he must be like in order to do so. From this outlook, the important consideration is not the actual sentences that the speaker uses but the rules that he follows and, in general, his intuitive understanding of his language. This, roughly, is the distinction between performance and competence that is currently receiving emphasis. This distinction is not the same as the distinction between production and comprehension. Involving as it does the child's intuitions about the rules or patterns of language, the child's linguistic competence must be educed through the use of all available means, including observation and tests of both his comprehension and production of language.

Emphasis on linguistic competence directs attention to the linguist's description of the system that will generate the grammatical sentences of the language as an idealized description of the native speaker—as a theory about the speaker. Theories of language learning thus become more precisely conditioned by the description of the language system that is espoused by the theorist. As Fodor and Garrett (1966) point out, however, it is one thing to use a grammar as a formalization of the speaker's linguistic information and quite another, and a questionable, thing to assume that the grammar is a component of the system that produces speech.

The notion that the task of language-development research is to study the developing linguistic competence of the child has led to attempts to specify whether or not a child has "acquired" particular rules. It is difficult to say what an appropriate criterion of rule acquisition in this all-or-none sense would be. In the first place, such terminology usually ignores the point that a grammar is a unified account. Aside from this is the question of how consistent the child must be. Presumably a single sentence used or understood is not sufficient evidence that a child has acquired or incorporated a rule. On the other hand, adult native speakers make many conscious and unconscious departures from their intuitions about the rules of language, so one would not expect perfect performance, either, from the child who has acquired the rules. The child may well make additional departures, however, as a result of such factors as pronunciation difficulties and limited memory span. It may be, then, that evidence for the acquisition of rules should not only show that the child's behavior shows some conformity to an idealized description but should also demonstrate that major departures from this description are reasonably explicable as resulting from specific handicaps. This is a stringent, and perhaps an unrealistic, requirement, but if this terminology is to be used, some meaningful criterion is needed.

Sutherland (1966) distinguishes between studying competence and studying mechanism. Thus, a child may be competent in multiplication in the sense that he understands that "9 times 4," for example, means to add 9 4's, but this description does not specify how he adds such sums. He may break the 4's into units and add on his fingers, he may first generate a series of subtotals each less than 20, or he may use any of many other mechanisms. Sutherland maintains that it is important to know how the individual actually works—that the proper concern of psycholinguists is with mechanisms.

Sutherland suggests that linguistic performance may be controlled more by a system of analogies than by an application of linguistic axioms. Sturtevant (1947) discussed language learning under the topic of analogic creation. This conceptualization of language learning merits further analysis.

A natural outgrowth of emphasis on linguistic competence is an interest in the child's specific propensities and native capacities for acquiring a language system. This interest is evident in the term "language acquisition device" (e.g., Chomsky, 1965; McNeill, 1966). A child's linguistic competence results from the processing, by this theoretical device, of the language he hears. The child's own language has been studied intensively for clues to this device, but surprisingly little research has been devoted to the input.

LANGUAGE IN THE EDUCATIONAL PROCESS. Schooling is notoriously verbal. Although the highly verbal nature of education is frequently aspersed, competence in the modern world demands a high level of ability in language and similar symbolic skills. In large measure, the verbal nature of education simply reflects necessity.

Language and the School Subjects. It is instructive that tests of verbal ability are the prime predictors of academic achievement. Academic aptitude tests that are not obviously verbal usually involve considerable internal use of language. The dependence of school achievement on verbal ability not only substantiates the importance of language in school but makes clear the school's vital responsibility to foster the development of language skills. Two of these skills, reading and writing, are clearly recognized as primary responsibilities of the school. Speech, speech comprehension, and other symbolic manipulation are gradually receiving more attention.

The early mastery of reading is certainly crucial for success in school as schools now function. A child's reading-test score at the end of first or second grade (or even the level of basal reader that he has then reached) is highly correlated with both reading and arithmetic achievement three years later (Breen, 1965). Other language skills are in turn good predictors of initial reading achievement (Loban, 1963). See Carroll's article (1964a) for an analysis of reading instruction in terms of its basis in language.

One field where the school is traditionally concerned with the development of all language skills (not that all skills have always received appropriate emphasis) is second-language learning. Sound research in this field is surprisingly sparse, though much is now under way. (See Carroll, 1963b, for a review.)

Influences on Language Development. When children come to school, they come with vastly differing language abilities and backgrounds. Constitutional differences naturally influence language ability, but the child's environment also has an enormous effect on language skills and understandings, for these are complex and involve a long and intensive learning process. For some children, variations resulting from one or both of these sources become one of the recognized language handicaps.

Language handicaps affect a larger proportion of children entering school than is generally realized (Eisenson & Ogilvie, 1963). Since a handicap in language is a severe handicap in education, schools are showing an increasing concern for locating children with language handicaps promptly and providing special instruction that will help them to overcome their disability. Eisenson and Ogilvie (1963) give an introduction to problems of delayed speech development and other speech problems. Deafness dramatically illustrates the function of feedback in learning to speak. In the past, without special instruction and hearing aids, most deafs children did not learn to speak but remained "deaf and dumb." Even when special intensive instruction is provided, deafness generally results in retarded language development. Cooper and Rosenstein (1966) have reviewed the work on language development in the deaf. Many authorities recognize in children a constitutional condition similar in some respects to aphasia in adults, in which ability to speak or to understand words is curtailed (Hardy, 1965).

The home is obviously the prepotent source of environmental influence on language development. The extent and nature of language stimulation in the home reflects the play of many factors—the interest, affection, and ability of the mother, the presence of the father and other adults, the presence of siblings, and the nature of conversation and verbal planning in the family. The strength of such influences is made abundantly clear when one considers Hess and Shipman's (1965) striking examples of mother-child verbal interaction as being multiplied by days and years of more of the same. Obvious problems for school achievement come, of course, when the home teaches a different dialect or even a different language from that used at school. In such cases the language or dialect may be supported by peer-group or community values (Labov, 1964).

Problems of dialect and bilingualism are frequently associated with problems related to poverty and to social-class differences. Bernstein (1964) has proposed a theory relating the origin of the "restricted" language code of "lower working-class" children to the structure of social relations within their social groups. Labov (1965) and Loban (1966) describe educationally important language problems that are related to race, social class, and dialect.

How successful the school or other agencies can be in overcoming the language gap of the disadvantaged child remains to be seen. What the teacher does in school is obviously a primary factor in how well the child learns to read, and what the teacher does can influence some of the specific language skills that are related to initial reading success (e.g., Spache & others, 1966). What the teacher does might well be also a primary factor in the more direct development of language competence, but there is relatively little evidence on this point. The school's efforts to teach standard English in a way that will generalize to daily life or even to other school subjects have not traditionally been a resounding success (Searles & Carlsen, 1960). Some evidence (e.g., Irwin, 1960a) suggests that a program of language stimulation begun at an early age could be quite effective, but the age at which such a program must start, how long it should last, and what form it should take are not known. Several research programs now under way should supply some information on these points. What can be done for the deaf child, who must be taught language painstakingly, step by step, suggests that a great deal can be done for the disadvantaged child if his motivation can be maintained.

Walter M. MacGinitie
Teachers College,
Columbia University

References

Allen, Robert L. *The Structure of the English Sentence.* Noble and Noble, Publishers, Inc., 1968.

Beilin, Harry. "Developmental Determinants of Word and Nonsense Anagram Solution." *J Verbal Learning Verbal Behavior.* 6:523–7; 1967.

Berko, Jean. "The Child's Learning of English Morphology." *Word* 14:150–77; 1958.

Bernstein, Basil. "Elaborated and Restricted Codes: Their Social Origins and Some Consequences." *Am Anthropologist* 66(6), Part II:55–69; 1964.

Bever, T. G., and others. "On the Acquisition of Syntax: A Critique of 'Contextual Generalization.'" *Psychol R* 72:467–82; 1965.

Braine, Martin D. S. "On Learning the Grammatical Order of Words." *Psychol R* 70:323–48; 1963(a).

Braine, Martin D. S. "The Ontogeny of English Phrase Structure: The First Phase." *Lang* 39:1–13; 1963(b).

Breen, Joseph M. "Differential Prediction of Intermediate Grade Skills Achievement from Primary Grade Aptitude and Achievement Measures." Doctoral dissertation. U Connecticut, 1965.

Brown, Mari J. K. "Role of Single Word Variables in Recall of Statistical Approximations to English." *Psychol Reports* 19:627–34; 1966.

Brown, Roger. "Linguistic Determinism and the Part of Speech." *J Abn Soc Psychol* 55:1–5; 1957.

Brown, Roger. *Words and Things.* Free, 1958. 398p.

Brown, Roger. *Social Psychology.* Free, 1965. 785p.

Brown, Roger, and Bellugi, Ursula. "Three Processes in the Child's Acquisition of Syntax." *Harvard Ed R* 34:133–51; 1964.

Brown, Roger, and Berko, Jean. "Word Association and the Acquisition of Grammar." *Child Develop* 31:1–14; 1960.

Brown, Roger, and Fraser, Colin. "The Acquisition of Syntax." In Bellugi, Ursula, and Brown, Roger. (Eds.) "The Acquisition of Language." *Monogr*

Social Res Child Develop 29(1) (Serial No. 92): 43–79; 1964.

Carroll, John B. "Language Development." In Harris, Chester W. (Ed.) *Encyclopedia of Educational Research*, 3rd ed. Macmillan, 1960. p. 744–52.

Carroll, John B. "Linguistic Relativity, Contrastive Linguistics, and Language Learning." *Int R Applied Linguistics Lang Teaching* 1:1–20; 1963(a).

Carroll, John B. "Research on Teaching Foreign Languages." In Gage, N. L. (Ed.) *Handbook of Research on Teaching*. Rand McNally, 1963(b). p. 1060–1100.

Carroll, John B. "The Analysis of Reading Instruction: Perspectives from Psychology and Linguistics." In Hilgard, Ernest R. (Ed.) *Theories of Learning and Instruction*, 63rd Yearbook, Part I, NSSE. U Chicago Press, 1964(a). p. 336–53.

Carroll, John B. "Words, Meanings and Concepts." *Harvard Ed R* 34:178:202; 1964(b).

Chomsky, Noam. *Syntactic Structures*. Mouton & Co., 1957. 118p.

Chomsky, Noam. Review of B. F. Skinner's *Verbal Behavior*. *Lang* 35:26–58; 1959.

Chomsky, Noam. Discussion of Wick Miller and Susan Erwin's "The Development of Grammar in Childl Language." In Bellugi, Ursula, and Brown, Roger. (Eds.) "The Acquisition of Language." *Monogr. Social Res Child Develop* 29(1)(Serial No. 92): 35–39; 1964.

Chomsky, Noam. *Aspects of the Theory of Syntax*. M.I.T. Press, 1965, 251p.

Church, Joseph. *Language and the Discovery of Reality: A Developmental Psychology of Cognition*. Random. 1961. 245p.

Coleman, E. B. "Generalizing to a Language Population." *Psychol Reports* 14:219–26; 1964.

Cooper, Robert L. "The Ability of Deaf and Hearing Children to Apply Morphological Rules." *J Speech Hearing Res* 10:77–86; 1967.

Cooper, Robert L., and Rosenstein, Joseph. "Language Acquisition of Deaf Children." *Volta R* 68:58–67, 125; 1966.

Dale, Edgar, and Eichholz, Gerhard. *Children's Knowledge of Words*. Bureau of Education Research Service, Ohio State U, 1960. 188p.

Dale, Edgar, and Razik, Taher. *Bibliography of Vocabulary Studies*. 2nd, rev. ed. Bureau of Education Research Service Ohio State U, 1963. 257p.

Diebold, A. Richard, Jr. "A Survey of Psycholinguistic Research, 1954–1964." In Osgood, Charles E., and Sebeok, Thomas A. (Eds.) *Psycholinguistics: A Survey of Theory and Research Problems*. Indiana U Press, 1965. p. 205–91.

Di Vesta, Francis J. "A Developmental Study of the Semantic Structures of Children." *J Verbal Learning Verbal Behavior* 5:249–59; 1966.

Duker, Sam. *Listening Bibliography*. Scarecrow Press, 1964. 211p.

Eisenson, Jon, and Ogilvie, Mardel. *Speech Correction in the Schools*, 2nd ed. Macmillan, 1963. 399p.

Ervin, Susan M. "Imitation and Structural Change in Children's Language." In Lenneberg, Eric H. (Ed.) *New Directions in the Study of Language*. M.I.T. Press, 1964. p. 163–89.

Ervin, Susan M., and Miller, Wick R. "Language Development." In *Child Psychology*, 62nd Yearbook, Part I, NSSE. U Chicago Press, 1963. p. 108–43.

Ervin-Tripp, Susan M. "Language Development." In Hoffman, Lois Wladis, and Hoffman, Martin L. (Eds.) *Review of Child Development Research*, Vol 2. Russell Sage, 1966. p. 55–105.

Ervin-Tripp, Susan M., and Slobin, Dan I. "Psycholinguistics." *Annual R Psychol* 17:435–74; 1966.

Fishman, Joshua A. "A Systematization of the Whorfian Hypothesis." *Behavioral Sci* 5:323–39; 1960.

Fodor, J. A., and Garrett, M. "Some Reflections on Competence and Performance." In Lyons, J., and Wales, R. J. (Eds.) *Psycholinguistics Papers*. Edinburgh U Press, 1966. p. 135–54.

Fraser, Colin, and others. "Control of Grammar in Imitation, Comprehension, and Production." *J Verbal Learning Verbal Behavior* 2:121–35; 1963.

Fries, Charles C. *The Structure of English*. Harcourt, 1952. 304p.

Gagné, Robert M., and Smith, Ernest C. "A Study of the Effects of Verbalization on Problem Solving." *J Exp Psychol* 63:12–8; 1962.

Glanzer, Murray. "Grammatical Category: A Rote Learning and Word Association Analysis." *J Verbal Learning Verbal Behavior* 1:31–41; 1962.

Gleason, H. A., Jr. *An Introduction to Descriptive Linguistics*, rev. ed. Holt, 1961. 503p.

Gleitman, Lila R. "A Study of the Acquisition of Syntactic Structure." Paper printed at the Linguistic Circle of New York, New York, March 1965.

Hardy, William G. "On Language Disorders in Young Children: A Reorganization of Thinking." *J Speech Hearing Disorders* 30:3–16; 1965.

Hess, Robert D., and Shipman, Virginia. "Early Experience and the Socialization of Cognitive Modes in Children." *Child Develop* 36:869–86; 1965.

Hunt, Kellogg W. *Grammatical Structures Written at Three Grade Levels*. Research Report No. 3. NCTE, 1965. 159p.

Irwin, Orvis C. "Infant Speech: Effect of Systematic Reading of Stories." *J Speech Hearing Res* 3:187–90; 1960(a).

Irwin, Orvis C. "Language and Communication." In Mussen, Paul H. (Ed.) *Handbook of Research Methods in Child Development*. Wiley, 1960(b). p. 487–516.

Jakobson, Roman, and Halle, Morris. *Fundamentals of Language*. Mouton & Co., 1956. 87p.

Jenkins, James J. "Reflections on the Conference." In Smith, Frank, and Miller, George A. (Eds.) *The Genesis of Language: A Psycholinguistic Approach*. M.I.T. Press, 1966. p. 347–59.

Jensen, Arthur R. "Social Class and Verbal Learning." In Deutsch, Martin, and others. (Eds.) *Social-class, Race, and Psychological Development*. Holt, 1968.

Johnson, Paul E. "Word Relatedness and Problem Solving in High-school Physics." *J Ed Psychol* 56:217–24; 1965.

Judson, Abe J., and Cofer, Charles N. "Reasoning as

an Associative Process. I: 'Direction' in a Simple Verbal Problem." *Psychol Reports* 2:469–76; 1956.

Judson, Abe J., and others. "Reasoning as an Associative Process. II: 'Direction' in Problem Solving as a Function of Prior Reinforcement of Relevant Responses." *Psychol Reports* 2:501–7; 1956.

Klare, George R. *The Measurement of Readability.* Iowa State U Press, 1963. 328p.

Klima, E. S., and Bellugi, Ursula. "Syntactic Regularities in the Speech of Children." In Lyons, J., and Wales, R. J. (Eds.) *Psycholinguistics Papers.* Edinburgh U Press, 1966. p. 183–208.

Labov, William. "Stages in the Acquisition of Standard English." In Shuy, Roger. (Ed.) *Social Dialects and Language Learning.* NCTE, 1964. p. 77–103.

Labov, William. "Linguistic Research on the Nonstandard English of Negro Children." Paper presented at the New York Society for the Experimental Study of Education, 1965.

Lantz, DeLee, and Stefflre, Volney. "Language and Cognition Revisited." *J Abn Social Psychol* 69:472–81; 1964.

Lenneberg, Eric H. *The Biological Foundations of Language.* Wiley, 1967. 489p.

Leopold, Werner F. *Speech Development of a Bilingual Child: A Linguist's Record,* 4 vols. Northwestern U Press, Vol. 1, 1939, 188p.; Vol. 2, 1947, 295p.; Vol. 3, 1949, 200p.; Vol. 4, 1949, 176p.

Lewis, M. M. *Infant Speech: A Study of the Beginnings of Language,* 2nd ed. Humanities, 1951. 383p.

Loban, Walter. *The Language of Elementary School Children: A Study of the Use and Control of Language, Effectiveness in Communication, and the Relationships Among Speaking, Reading, Writing, and Listening.* Research Report No. 1. NCTE, 1963. 92p.

Loban, Walter. *Problems in Oral Language.* Research Report No. 5. NCTE, 1966. 72p.

Lorge, Irving, and Chall, Jeanne. "Estimating the Size of Vocabularies of Children and Adults: An Analysis of Methodological Issues." *J Exp Ed* 32:147–57; 1963.

Luria, A. R. *The Role of Speech in the Regulation of Normal and Abnormal Behavior.* Pergamon, 1961. 100p.

McCarthy, Dorothea. "Language Development in Children." In Carmichael, Leonard. (Ed.) *Manual of Child Psychology,* 2nd ed. Wiley, 1954. p. 492–630.

McNeill, David A. "The Origin of Associations Within the Same Grammatical Class." *J Verbal Learning Verbal Behavior* 2:250–62; 1963.

McNeill, David A. "Developmental Psycholinguistics." In Smith, Frank, and Miller, George A. (Eds.) *The Genesis of Language: A Psycholinguistic Approach.* M.I.T. Press, 1966. p. 15–84.

Menyuk, Paula. "A Preliminary Evaluation of Grammatical Capacity in Children." *J Verbal Learning Verbal Behavior,* 2:429–39; 1963.

Menyuk, Paula. "Syntactic Rules Used by Children from Preschool Through First Grade." *Child Develop* 35:533–46; 1964.

Miller, George A., and Chomsky, Noam. "Finitary Models of Language Users." In Luce, R. Duncan, and others. (Eds.) *Handbook of Mathematical Psychology,* Vol. 2. Wiley, 1963. p. 419–91.

Miller, Wick, and Ervin, Susan. "The Development of Grammar in Child Language." In Bellugi, Ursula, and Brown, Roger. (Eds.) "The Acquisition of Language." *Monogr Social Res Child Develop* 29(1)(Serial No. 92):9–34; 1964.

Mowrer, O. Hobart. *Learning Theory and the Symbolic Process.* Wiley, 1960. 473p.

Osgood, Charles E. "On Understanding and Creating Sentences." *Am Psychologist* 18:735–51; 1963.

Palermo, David S. "Word Associations and Children's Verbal Behavior." In Lipsett, Lewis P., and Spiker, Charles C. (Eds.) *Advances in Child Development and Behavior,* Vol. 1. Academic, 1963. p. 31–68.

Piaget, Jean. *The Language and Thought of the Child.* Humanities, 1959. 288p.

Restaino, Lillian C. R. "Word Associations of Deaf and Hearing Children." In Rosenstein, Joseph, and MacGinitie, Walter H. (Eds.) *Meaning and Association in the Language of Hearing-impaired Children.* Teachers College, Columbia U. (in press).

Russell, David H., and Saadeh, Ibrahim Q. "Qualitative Levels in Children's Vocabularies." *J Ed Psychol* 53:170–4; 1962.

Salzinger, Kurt. "The Problem of Response Class in Verbal Behavior." In Salzinger, Kurt, and Salzinger, Suzanne. (Eds.) *Research in Verbal Behavior and Some Neurophysiological Implications.* Academic, 1967. p. 35–55.

Searles, John R., and Carlsen, G. Robert. "Language, Grammar and Composition." In Harris, Chester W. (Ed.) *Encyclopedia of Educational Research,* 3rd ed. Macmillan, 1960, p. 455–70.

Skinner, B. F. *Verbal Behavior.* Appleton, 1957. 478p.

Slobin, Dan I. "Abstracts of Soviet Studies of Child Language." In Smith, Frank, and Miller, George A. (Eds.) *The Genesis of Language: A Psycholinguistic Approach.* M.I.T. Press, 1966(a). p. 363–86.

Slobin, Dan I. "The Acquisition of Russian as a Native Language" In Smith, Frank, and Miller, George A. (Eds.) *The Genesis of Language: A Psycholinguistic Approach.* M.I.T. Press, 1966(b). p. 129–48.

Spache, George D., and others "A Longitudinal First Grade Reading Readiness Program." *Reading Teach* 19:580–4; 1966.

Staats, Arthur W., and Staats, Caroline K. *Complex Human Behavior: A Systematic Extension of Learning Principles.* Holt, 1963.

Strang, Ruth G., and Hocker, Mary E. "First-grade Children's Language Patterns." *El Engl* 42:38–41; 1965.

Strickland, Ruth G. *The Language of Elementary School Children: Its Relation to Language of Reading Textbooks and the Quality of Reading of Selected Children.* Bulletin No. 38. School of Education, Indiana U, 1962. 131p.

Sturtevant, Edgar H. *An Introduction to Linguistic Science.* Yale U Press, 1947. 173p.

Sutherland, N. S. Discussion of "Some Reflections on Competence and Performance" by J. Fodor and M.

Garrett. In Lyons, J. and Wales, R. J. (Eds.) *Psycholinguistics Papers.* Edinburgh U Press, 1966. p. 154–63.

Templin, Mildred C. *Certain Language Skills in Children: Their Development and Interrelationships.* U Minnesota Press, 1957. 183p.

Tikhomirov, O. K. Review of *Verbal Behavior* by B. F. Skinner. *Word* 15:362–7; 1959.

Vygotsky, Lev S. *Thought and Language.* (Edited and translated by Eugenia Hanfmann and Gertrude Vakar.) M.I.T. Press, 1962. 168p.

Werner, Heinz, and Kaplan, Bernard. *Symbol Formation: An Organismic-developmental Approach to Language and the Expression of Thought.* Wiley, 1963. 530p.

Weir, Ruth H. *Language in the Crib.* Mouton & Co., 1962. 216p.

Weir, Ruth H. "Some Questions on the Child's Learning of Phonology." In Smith, Frank, and Miller, George A. (Eds.) *The Genesis of Language: A Psycholinguistic Approach.* M.I.T. Press, 1966. p. 153–68.

LEADERSHIP

Bennis (1959) has written of the concept "leadership" that it is one of the most hazy and perplexing notions in the behavioral sciences. Bennis argued that the complexity of research related to leadership theory is not without cause. Scholars interested in leadership have attempted to answer some of the most fundamental questions about human organizations: Why do people subordinate themselves to leaders? Why do leaders arise? What is the source of their influence and what is the process by which they exercise it? What difference does it make to an organization that leadership exists?

Leadership theory has been a subject which has enticed a large number of scholars into an even larger number of investigations. Such effort has resulted in the production of a great volume of research, a happy phenomenon in the behavioral sciences. However, a less happy phenomenon is that the research evidence is often contradictory and is always difficult to evaluate. For example, the argument that leaders possess personality or physical traits different from those of their followers has received some recent empirical support. So, too, has the counter argument that no such differences exist. Our ability to evaluate the results of research on leadership in viable organizations is made difficult by the types of samples used in the research. Because a great many of the research findings come from work with small *ad hoc* groups, such as college students, their applicability to actual organizations may be limited. With their histories, reward structures, battles with internal and external environments, and changing membership, ongoing production organizations may not be amenable to laboratory simulation (Lane & others, 1966).

It is clear that generalizations from small laboratory groups to organizations such as schools must be made with extreme care. However, schools do provide opportunities for the formation of innumerable small groups. To this extent they can be partially understood using research findings from small-group research.

A second difficulty in evaluating leadership research is the plethora of definitions of leadership. Further, the range of definitions is quite wide. Lipham (1964) has argued that leadership is behavior-oriented to initiating new organizational structure or to changing the goals of the organization. For him leadership and administration are incompatible since administration functions to maintain organizational equilibrium. Although equilibrium maintenance may require organizational change, Lipham's definition is analytically useful.

Katz and Kahn (1966) see no difference between leadership and administration. For them, leadership may take place at any point in the organizational hierarchy. However, leadership at different levels requires different personality traits and intellectual skills and demands different behaviors by the leader. At the highest level the leadership they describe is identical to Lipham's description. At lower levels of the organizational hierarchy, leadership is manifest in imaginative use of existing structure. According to Katz and Kahn, leadership consists of "all acts of influence which affect matters of organizational relevance," with special emphasis on an increment of influence which goes beyond that which formally accrues to a role incumbent. That is, a school principal who simply implemented a school policy would not be considered, normally, to be performing a leadership act. However, a principal who supplemented an existing policy or who imaginatively interpreted such a policy might be thought to be exercising leadership.

The obvious dilemma occasioned by the existence of many definitions of leadership is that a reader is never confident that research findings based on different definitions are comparable. A researcher limits the phenomena he will observe by defining them. The discussion, then, of research findings about leadership, as they appear in the literature, must be implicitly bound by the admission that the researchers may not have been examining the same phenomena.

In addition to difficulties arising from conceptual definitions of leadership, there are those which arise from methodological considerations. Perhaps the basic question to be raised is, "How does the researcher know he has observed leadership?" This question has been approached primarily by observing persons with formal or informal leadership status. In effect, the research worker defines leadership acts as behaviors of leaders, and defines leaders as those so designated by formal position or by status attribution. The work of Bass (1960) with initially leaderless small groups may provide clues to behavior associated with eventual leadership attribution by members. But even it provides little evidence of "leader" actions and their effects on changes in the group, presumably the critical measure of leadership. Without comparable data from large samples or data from well-controlled experiments, the methodological problems will continue large.

Still another difficulty in interpreting leadership is manifested in the intellectual history of such research. Although the history of the study of leadership is familiar enough to be almost dismissed from treatment in this entry (Trow, 1960), a reference to it is useful. The study of leadership has shifted from attempts to construct single variable explanations to those which account for leadership by positing multivariate relationships. This shift has increased the sophistication of the explanations, but it has also increased the intractability of the research problem and its results.

For example, Sanford (1952) has argued that leader behavior is a function of the leader, the group, the task, and outside pressures on the group, acting together in various undesignated combinations. Clearly he is correct. But to state the existence of all of these forces is not to explain them. Empirical substantiation of the existence of some combinations was provided by Harris and Fleishman (1961) and by Fleishman (1961). Managers, after training in human-relations techniques, were observed to return to their old leader patterns if their subordinates were not given concurrent training. Kahn and others (1964) have used the term "superordinate's role set" to describe the interaction network of a superordinate, subordinates, and the expectations for the superordinate held by the subordinates. This role set is believed to exert a powerful influence on the leader. Some researchers have argued that it is a powerful enough influence to alter leadership styles (Katz & others, 1957; Bridges, 1965).

The group task has also been observed to influence leader behavior. Burke (1965) found that if a leader with a task-oriented personality is given a structured task to lead, the group will perceive him as effective and will continue to do so in the next, unstructured, task. If the order of the tasks given to such a leader is reversed, he is not perceived as effective in either situation.

In addition to structural characteristics of the group, such as the degree of structure of the task and the power and authority given the leader by the situation, interpersonal factors are believed to affect leader behavior. Fiedler (1964) has argued that a leader's personal relations with group members is such a factor. Other interpersonal factors which are believed to affect leader behavior range from member need for dependence to member interest in the group task (Schmidt, 1962). The relationships among leader behavior and group member forces apparently hold irrespective of the level in the organizational hierarchy of the work group. Bowers (1963) found that the supportiveness of a foreman's supervisor was related to the foreman's behavior toward his subordinates. Perhaps the most candid summation of the relationships among such variables is that they exist in a form not yet fully understood.

But recognition of the complexity of the phenomenon of leadership is, in itself, a hopeful step. By accepting the probability that leadership is a complex phenomenon, research workers guard against oversimplification and too broad generalization. In turn, they may be led to nicer distinctions and, therefore, more meaningful explanation.

The focus on leadership in this entry can be expedited by asking three rather simple questions: What do leaders have that others do not? What do leaders do that others do not? What difference does leadership make? These questions represent a set of common-denominator problems with which researchers in leadership deal. As such they are useful vehicles for ordering the available research evidence.

The research findings which are reviewed in this entry come from behavioral sciences other than education, in addition to those from education. The addition of these findings is representative of a widespread recognition that research from a large number of disciplines increases our understanding of behavior in educational organizations. Research from other disciplines also provides a sounder basis for that theory generated by research workers interested primarily in education (Halpin, 1958).

WHAT LEADERS HAVE THAT OTHERS DO NOT. The traditional trait approach, in which leadership was explained by reference to personal characteristics of the leader, has been criticized as being an incomplete explanation of the phenomenon and as generating an almost infinite number of leader traits. However, the approach continues to be used, but in a somewhat different form. There has been a shift in identification of possibly relevant traits from physical attributes to those of personality. McGrath and Altman (1966), after factor analysis of 30 recent small-group studies, conclude that effective leadership seems to be a function of such attributes as intelligence, general ability, task ability, and level of formal education. Further, personality characteristics such as extroversion, assertiveness, and social maturity were found to be related to effective leader behavior.

A study of men at Antarctic scientific stations concluded that all leaders were high in self-confidence, alertness, job motivation, and aggressiveness. Moreover, well-liked, as opposed to less-liked, leaders were high in satisfaction, emotional control, and motivation to be part of a group (Nelson, 1964). In his study of educational administrators as leaders, White (1965) demonstrated that they tended to be practically oriented extroverts, and to be opposed to radical ideas.

In addition to possession of different personality characteristics, successful leaders appear to have a higher competence in group-related tasks. Hollander (1964) argues that it is not clear that task competence is a prerequisite for the assumption of a leadership role, but Barlund's data (1962) indicate that experimental groups change leaders as group tasks are radically altered. Perceived task competence of the leader is also related to group morale (Hamblin & others, 1961). The perception of a leader's competence, however, may be a function of needs of group members which are not related to the group's task. For example, Di Vesta and others (1964) indicate that experts who do their own research, who express certainty about their findings and who relay pleasant information to the group elicit more group confidence than do experts who only interpret already available research, are uncertain about the findings, and relay unpleasant information. To the extent, then, that the perception of a leader's competence rests on expertise which is based on his possession of information, it may be subject to dilution through the quality and source of the information.

In addition to its relationship to leadership, information is related to group effectiveness. As the total amount of task-relevant information available to all group members increases, so too does group effectiveness. It is possible that a crucial leadership responsibility is to assure the possession by group members of such information. However, as the amount of information available to any single member increases, group effectiveness does not necessarily increase correspondingly. The member in possession of the information must get it validated. If he cannot, the group may be confused (Shaw & Penrod, 1962). Whether this also applies to the leader is not known, although his position as leader may be sufficient basis for the validation of his information. Further, from Di Vesta we might hypothesize that success in validation is a function of the type of information.

This hypothesis raises a further point. Information flow in an organization is two-way. Successful leaders apparently need information about their impact on the group and use it to make adjustments in their own behavior in order to preserve their positions. However, Croft (1965) indicates that open-minded principals were no better at perceiving others' perceptions of their behavior than were closed-minded ones. He attributes the absence of difference to the possibility that open-minded principals saw teachers as a group holding many different perceptions of his behavior, thus reducing the possibility of accurate categorization of group perception. This finding would indicate that the task of perceiving one's impact on a group is a difficult one. Further, leaders who believe themselves more distant from their subordinates seem to have more effective work units than those who believe themselves to be closer. The resulting social barriers are thought to protect the leader from emotional involvement with followers (Fiedler, 1957). Given this apparently necessary social distance and the differing member perceptions of a leader's behavior, we can ask how a leader estimates his effect on the group.

A leader may attempt to establish organizational mechanisms by which he can gain such an estimation. However, Gouldner's (1954) work indicates that two of the major problems confronting a new leader is his lack of information about his group and his inability to penetrate the informal interaction network. His success as a leader may depend on his ability to gather and interpret clues about his impact. But a leader's choice of clues may be related to his self-confidence. Kipnis and Lane (1962) demonstrated that less self-confident leaders relied on rules and formal leader behavior and relayed administrative problems to superordinates for solutions more often than did self-confident leaders. Their actions symbolized an avoidance of the task of seeking clues through self-insulation in the formal structure.

Some research is available for speculation about the basis of leader self-confidence. From Blau (1964) we might speculate that one source of a leader's self-confidence is his ability to provide rewards to his group, thus increasing his power over them. Marak (1964) makes a similar point and Pelz (1952) argues that a first-line supervisor must be able to gain concessions for his men from his own superordinate if he is to be effective.

A possible measure of self-confidence is the extent to which a leader perceives new ideas as threatening. For instance, when foremen perceived subordinates as idea-men, as opposed to troublemakers, innovative solutions to problems, and group satisfaction with the solutions, increased, even though group members had had to change their original positions (Maier & Hoffman, 1965).

Thus, what a leader has that others do not, appears to be a combination of innate and achieved attributes. Achieved attributes in turn appear to be a function of the characteristics of the group members, the dynamics of the group, and the group's task.

WHAT LEADERS DO THAT OTHERS DO NOT. An attempt to discuss this question may be doomed from the start. Leaders do a great many things and the task of differentiating their critical behaviors may be unmanageable. Hemphill and others (1962) identify ten components of administrative performance. Gross (1961) argues that there are seven components of leadership, ranging from creation of goals to motivating members to act to achieve them. By abstracting 450 small-group studies, Heslin and Dunphy (1964) found three bases for member satisfaction and, by implication, leader behavior. Member satisfaction seems to rest on (1) high consensus over relative leadership status of all members, (2) perceived progress toward group goals, and (3) perceived freedom to participate.

Somewhat more analytic descriptions of leader behavior are also available. Cloyd (1964) argued that leading contributions at a given group meeting will be made by a different member for each of Parson's four functional categories. This indicates a relatively dispersed leadership. However, Williams (1965) discovered that in small rural communities, leadership acts in town meetings coalesced around only two of the functional categories: the instrumental and the expressive.

Bowers and Seashore (1966) have described eight major attempts since the Ohio State Studies of 1945 to categorize leadership behavior. These efforts have produced as few as two categories and as many as five. They propose a four-factor categorization which includes supportiveness, interaction facilitation, goal emphasis, and work facilitation. In an empirical test of the formulation they studied 40 life insurance agencies. Of 56 possible correlations between the 4 factors and 7 measures of performance for 2 groups, leaders and peers, 13 were statistically significant. The work facilitation category was the best single predictor of work performance, but even it was not powerful. As a result of their findings, they concluded that the phenomenon of leadership behavior is indeed complex.

Recent work by Katz and Kahn (1966) suggests that the task of categorizing leadership behavior in organizations is complicated by differential personality and behavior requirements for leadership at various hierarchical levels of the organization. Their reformulation of the research problem is partially supported by Wrapp (1967) in a discussion of critical activities of business leaders. The Katz and Kahn formulation points to the need for greater clarity and specificity by researchers with respect to structural variables as they affect leadership practices.

The Bowers and Seashore (1966) categories of leader behavior provide a convenient mechanism for ordering the available research evidence. Several studies seem to indicate the necessity for supportive behavior by the leader. Brown (1963) administered the LBDQ-12 to 1,551 teachers in 170 Canadian schools. A factor analysis of the findings indicated the existence of two crucial dimensions of leader behavior: behavior which responds to organizational needs, and behavior which responds to personal, idiosyncratic needs of members.

Knezevich (1962) argues that a principal's major function is to stimulate teachers and to provide, through the use of experts, the consultative services teachers need. Campbell (1965) views the principal as an influence agent responsible for obtaining resources for his school in his attempts to establish and maintain an environment conducive to major output by his staff.

Pelz (1952) shows, however, that attempted support behavior by the leader is not sufficient. He must be successful in obtaining resources from other parts of the system or in representing his subordinates to his superordinates. This finding was replicated by Hills (1963) in a study of 872 elementary teachers and 53 elementary principals. His tentative conclusion was that leadership must include the acts of successfully representing the group to higher organizational levels and to the school's clientele. Guest (1962) argues that the most effective leadership occurs when the leader simultaneously acts as the formal agent of higher management and as the informal representative of those at lower levels to higher management.

It is well accepted that leadership must provide mechanisms for interaction and communication among group members in order to promote group cohesion. Pelz and Andrews (1966) present findings about research scientists in organizations which indicate that interaction also enhances individual performances. They suggest that while contacts initiated by individuals were most useful, meetings originated by superordinates were helpful also. Interaction served to provide for error catching, coordination, support, and new ideas and intellectual stimulation, and, therefore, for increased group productivity.

Because it is human beings who are in interaction, increased productivity may result from several factors. One of these factors may be the personality composition of the group in interaction. Hoffman (1959) indicates that groups made up of persons with homogeneous personalities were less effective in finding creative solutions to problems than were heterogeneous groups. While data presented by Shaw (1960) cast some doubt on this finding, additional work by Hoffman and Maier (1961) provides support for Hoffman's earlier argument. They found that psychological heterogeneity resulted in a higher percentage of high-quality solutions, while group satisfaction with the solutions was similar for homogeneous and heterogeneous groups. In dyads, heterogeneity of personality and homogeneity of abilities seems to be a very effective combination (Triandis & others, 1965). Collins and Guetzkow (1964) conclude that where resources are needed, heterogeneity of group members is desirable, leading to increased creativity but to decreased solidarity. Thus psychological heterogeneity of group members is seen as a mixed blessing.

Much the same can be said for purely cooperative endeavors as opposed to intragroup competition. Julian and Perry (1967) conclude that a cooperative system of task performance produced less good-quality output than did competitive situations, but more favorable interpersonal relations. Faroqui (1958) indicates that competitive groups had cleavages and semiclosed subgroups. The problem faced by the leader is to provide mechanisms for interaction and some competition among members with diverse personalities and skills, but also to prevent cleavages from disrupting the common progress toward goal realization.

While the facilitation of interaction is thought to be necessary leader behavior during periods of relative peace for the organization, crisis presents special conditions. Hermann (1963) has hypothesized that in periods of organizational crisis the number and capacity of communication channels are reduced, authority contracts, standards are modified, and member withdrawal occurs. Marcus (1960) presents data which indicate that when facing a hostile environment groups cluster around a socio-emotional leader who becomes the hub of a wheel-like communication net, representing a reduction in communication channels among members.

In addition to providing for support and member interaction, leaders need to emphasize the attainment of organizational goals. Campbell (1965) and Knezevich (1962) both argue that a principal's role includes attention to the attainment of goals. In their content analysis of small-group research McGrath and Altman (1966) concluded that effective leaders tended to be characterized by a high frequency of problem proposing and information seeking. But a leader's ability to stimulate subordinates toward goal attainment is partially affected by the values of the subordinates with respect to the work task. For example, Cooper (1966) found that workers who valued work proficiency were affected by the work level of their leaders, while among those who did not, no relationship obtained. Patchen (1962) argues that worker productivity and supportiveness by leaders are related only if the leaders also encourage efficiency. Finally, in his criticism of the Hawthorne studies, Carey (1967) indicates that increased production may have been a result more of the high-production emphasis of one of the influential workers than of the psychological and social support given by the research team.

If he is to emphasize goal attainment, the leader must also provide for facilitation of the work through scheduling, planning, resource provision and other actions. The work of Gross and Herriott (1965), although it has received serious criticism (Erickson, 1965), indicates that such activities are part of executive professional leadership. The extent to which a school principal acts to facilitate work, however, may be related to the social-class composition of the school (Herriott & St. John, 1966). Brown's (1963) analysis indicates that effective leadership is related to the leader's response to organizational needs. Good leaders in research organizations were more often concerned with the coordination of activities and the provision for flexible operation than were poor leaders (Baumgartel, 1964). Much the same relationship seem to hold in voluntary associations (Smith & Tannenbaum, 1965). Lortie (forthcoming) reports that teachers demand of the principal that he provide an environment for teaching and take care of things that are not directly related to the teaching act. However, provision of an adequate environment, from a teacher's perspective, may present problems for the principal. Teachers seem to want the principal to treat arbitrarily pupils, parents, or custodians who are bothersome, but to treat teachers democratically (Sharp, 1962).

Supporting evidence for the work-facilitation role of leaders comes from research by Barlund (1962). He concludes that leaders are chosen by groups for their ability to help solve the group task. As tasks change radically, groups change their leaders, when offered the opportunity.

Part of the process of facilitating work is to clarify leadership expectations of subordinates (Smith, 1957). The existence of ambiguous role expectations reduces group productivity and satisfaction and increases defensiveness. Groups spend time and energy in their attempts to resolve issues of the proper function of various roles and the appropriate incumbents of those roles.

Finally, one of the crucial tasks of facilitating work may be the provision of time for group planning of work. In a small-group experiment, without the imposition of a temporal separation of planning time and working time, groups did not plan and were ultimately less efficient (Shure & others, 1962).

Having indicated that effective leadership seems to be related to all of these behaviors, three questions remain. The first is whether any individual, short of a mythical super leader, is capable of all of these actions. Clearly the answer must be no, but leadership, as a complex of roles rather than a single role within the organization, may be capable of meeting these demands. The second is whether all of these behaviors must be performed to an equal degree at any time. Research has not provided an answer. The third question concerns the resources available to a leader to validate his attempts to direct an organization. Blau (1964) argues that the major source of justification for leadership derives from a process of exchange, in which the potential leader can provide rewards for group members in exchange for their compliance with his commands. Marak (1964) concludes that the more valuable the reward provided, the more closely related are provision of reward and attainment of leadership. However, among nursing supervisors and school principals the provision of rewards is problematic due to the high degree of intrinsic rewards obtained from the performance of the tasks (Bennis & others, 1958; Lortie, forthcoming). Thus, although the ability to reward may be the most important leader resource, in schools there may be few rewards available to leaders to dispense.

WHAT DIFFERENCE LEADERSHIP MAKES. Although there is a great deal of research evidence concerning what leaders do or are expected to do, little evidence is available to appraise the difference leadership makes (McGrath & Altman, 1966). One of the more obvious consequences of effective leadership seems to be that it is followed by more of the same by the same individual. In an earlier study (Katz & others, 1957) leaders tended to persist over time and differing tasks unless they aroused antagonism in the group. In a later experimental situation (Pryer & others, 1962), groups which perceived themselves as effective and as gaining in effectiveness were much more consistent in leadership choice than those which were losing in effectiveness.

Effective leadership seems also to be related to group satisfaction and perhaps to group productivity. However, group satisfaction and productivity are not necessarily related to each other in a positive way. The relationships that do exist seem to be mitigated by leadership style and the nature of the group task. Research with experimental and natural groups seems to point to the conclusion that for simple tasks under static conditions a centralized or autocratic or nonparticipatory leadership structure is more efficient. For adaptability to changing conditions, acceptance of a new idea, and generally high morale and loyalty, a more egalitarian or decentralized leadership structure is better (Slater & Bennis, 1964). However, this generalization has not been fully accepted, nor do all studies support it. Anderson and Fiedler (1964) conclude that under a participatory structure there is more group output, but there is better output under a supervisory structure. They find no difference in member esteem for the leader or in satisfaction of group members. In abstracting 450 small-group studies, Heslin and Dunphy (1964) conclude that member satisfaction is related to perceived progress toward group goals and perceived freedom to participate. In a test of Gouldner's model where strategic leniency by the superior is thought to lead to reciprocal behavior by subordinates, Schwartz (1964) subjected experimental groups to four types of rule enforcement. Group productivity was highest under conditions of partial and constant enforcement and lowest under no enforcement and laissez-faire enforcement. The obvious question, then, is the extent to which member needs for participation in determining group functions and for achievement of group goals must both be fulfilled.

A corollary question concerns the extent to which group productivity and member participation are not complementary (Likert, 1961). From the study of two naval laboratories a conclusion was reached that there is little relationship between perceived productivity and employee morale under restrictive or permissive leadership styles (Tannenbaum & others, 1961). However, under permissive leadership there was greater group cohesion. Cornell (1954) found little relationship between classroom performance of teachers and the extent to which they participated in school decision-making. McGrath and Altman (1966) found no research data to indicate what effect the presence of a good leader had on the task performance of group members.

While the research evidence concerning the relationships among leadership style, group morale and group productivity is not conclusive, research relating leadership and organizational change is practically nonexistent. An early study by Wiles and Grobman (1958) showed a relationship between participation in decision-making by teachers and the incidence of curriculum change, although they had no measures of the quality of the changes or their effect on productivity. In a recent discussion by Carlson and others (1965) the state of the art, as it were, is portrayed as quite primitive. It appears that leaders can block organizational change, but their abilities to effect it are less well documented.

The evidence respecting leadership and change is a little stronger when changes in organizational policies are considered. Bailey and others (1962) have analyzed the impact of certain styles of leadership as they relate to educational policy making at the state level. Crain (1967) has presented research from several large cities on the role of the superintendent as an agent for change. Stout and Inger (1966) conclude that for policies affecting school desegregation, the school superintendent is the critical initiator of change. However, the question remains as to the degree of implementation of a changed educational policy. It would seem that the relationship between leadership and organizational change invites a great deal of high-quality research.

As must be obvious, the questions raised by Bennis (1959) have not been answered. However it may not be entirely premature to speculate about possible answers. The research evidence supports a tentative answer to why people subordinate themselves to leaders. In the process of subordination followers are able to gain satisfaction of needs they might not otherwise have been able to satisfy. Such needs include the achievement of group tasks, contribution to a worthwhile enterprise, and membership in an interaction network.

Correspondingly, the source of a leader's influence seems to derive from his ability to provide sufficient rewards and to facilitate the satisfaction of member needs. If Blau (1964) is correct, the exercise of influence is a cumulative process of exchange in which the provision of rewards serves to solidify a leader's possession of influence.

Whether or not leadership makes a difference to an organization is, perhaps, the hardest question to answer. The research evidence is far from unequivocal, specifying, as it does, a number of contingent questions. Perhaps by the time of issue of the next edition of this Encyclopedia the evidence will be stronger.

It is clear that the period of time since the last edition has produced a body of research which is somewhat more sophisticated in methodology and somewhat more limited in the scope of research problems. This is due to our increased awareness of the complexity of leadership. However, the research which has emanated from education does not fully share the gains made in other disciplines. Research in education is not yet capable of supporting an adequate treatment of leadership phenomena.

Robert Stout
Claremont Graduate School
Conrad Briner
Claremont Graduate School

References

Anderson, Lynn R., and Fiedler, Fred E. "The Effect of Participatory and Supervisory Leadership on Group Creativity." *J Applied Psychol* 48:227–36; 1964.

Bailey, Stephen K., and others. *Schoolmen and Politics*. Syracuse U Press, 1962.

Barlund, Dean C. "Consistency of Emergent Leadership in Groups with Changing Tasks and Members." *Speech Monogr* 29:45–52; 1962.

Bass, Bernard. *Leadership, Psychology, and Organizational Behavior*. Harper, 1960.

Baumgartel, Howard. "Leadership Style as a Variable in Research Administration." In Orth, C. D., and others. (Eds.) *Administering Research and Development*. Irwin and Dorsey, 1964. p. 86–98.

Bennis, Warren G. "Leadership Theory and Administrative Behavior: The Problem of Authority." *Administrative Sci Q* 4:259–301; 1959.

Bennis, Warren G., and others. "Authority, Power, and the Ability to Influence." *Hum Relations* 11:143–55; 1958.

Blau, Peter. *Exchange and Power in Social Life*. Wiley, 1964.

Bowers, David G. "Self-Esteem and the Diffusion of Leadership Style." *J Applied Psychol* 47:135–40; 1963.

Bowers, David G., and Seashore, Stanley E. "Predicting Organizational Effectiveness With a Four-Factor Theory of Leadership." *Administrative Sci Q* 11:283–93; 1966.

Bridges, Edwin M. "Bureaucratic Role and Socialization: The Influence of Experience on the Elementary Principal." *Ed Adm Q* 1:19–28; 1965.

Brown, Alan F. "Reactions to Leadership." *Ed Adm Q* 3:62–73; 1963.

Burke, W. Warner. "Leadership Behavior as a Function of the Leader, the Follower, and the Situation." *J Pers* 33:60–81; 1965.

Campbell, Roald F. "Application of Administrative Concepts to the Elementary Principalship." *Nat El Prin* 44:21–6; 1965.

Carey, Alex. "The Hawthorne Studies: A Radical Criticism." *Am Sociol R* 32:403–16; 1967.

Carlson, Richard O., and others. (Eds) *Change Processes in the Public Schools.* Center for the Advanced Study of Educational Administration, 1965.

Cloyd, Jerry S. "Functional Differentiation and the Structure of Informal Groups." *Sociol Q* 5:243–50; 1964.

Collins, Barry E., and Guetzkow, Harold. *A Social Psychology of Group Processes for Decision-making.* Wiley, 1964.

Cooper, Robert. "Leader's Task Relevance and Subordinate Behavior in Industrial Work Groups." *Hum Relations* 19:57–84; 1966.

Cornell, F. G. "Some Aspects of Teacher Participation in Administrative Decision-making. Unpublished report presented to AERA, 1954.

Crain, Robert L. *The Politics of School Desegregation.* Aldine, 1967.

Croft, John C. "Dogmatism and Perceptions of Leader Behavior." *Ed. Adm Q* 1:60–71; 1965.

Di Vesta, Francis J., and others. "Confidence in an Expert as a Function of His Judgements." *Hum Relations* 17:235–42; 1964.

Erickson, Donald A. "Essay Review: Some Misgivings Concerning a Study of Leadership." *Ed Adm Q* 1:52–9; 1965.

Faroqui, M. A. "Cooperation, Competition, and Group Structure." *J Psychol Res* 2:60–70; 1958.

Fiedler, Fred E. "A Note on Leadership Theory: The Effect of Social Barriers Between Leaders and Followers." *Sociometry* 20:87–94; 1957.

Fiedler, Fred E. "A Contingency Model of Leadership Effectiveness." In Berkowitz, L. (Ed.) *Advances in Experimental Social Psychology.* Academic, 1964. p. 149–90.

Fleishman, E. "Leadership Climate, Human Relations Training, and Supervisory Behavior." In Fleishman, E. (Ed.) *Studies in Personnel and Industrial Psychology.* Dorsey, 1961. p. 315–28.

Gouldner, Alvin. *Patterns of Industrial Bureaucracy.* Free, 1954.

Gross, Edward. "Dimensions of Leadership." *Personnel J* 40:213–8; 1961.

Gross, Neal, and Herriott, Robert E. *Staff Leadership in Public Schools: A Sociological Inquiry.* Wiley, 1965.

Guest, Robert H. *Organizational Change: The Effect of Successful Leadership.* Irwin Dorsey, 1962.

Halpin, Andrew. (Ed.) *Administrative Theory in Education.* Midwest Administration Center, 1958.

Hamblin, R. L., and others. "Group Morale and Competence of the Leader." *Sociometry* 24:295–311; 1961.

Harris, E. F., and Fleishman, E. "Human Relations Training and the Stability of Leadership Patterns." In Fleishman, E. (Ed.) *Studies in Personnel and Industrial Psychology.* Dorsey, 1961. p. 230–8.

Hemphill, John K., and others. *Administrative Performance and Personality: A Study of the Principal in a Simulated Elementary School.* Columbia U Press, 1962.

Hermann, Charles F. "Some Consequences of Crisis Which Limit the Viability of Organizations." *Administrative Sci Q* 8:61–82; 1963.

Herriott, Robert E., and St. John, Nancy Hoyt. *Social Class and the Urban School.* Wiley, 1966.

Heslin, Richard, and Dunphy, Dexter. "Three Dimensions of Member Satisfaction in Small Groups." *Hum Relations* 17:99–112; 1964.

Hills, R. Jean. "The Representative Function: Neglected Dimensions of Leadership Behavior." *Administrative Sci Q* 8:33–101; 1963.

Hoffman, L. Richard. "Homogeneity of Member Personality and Its Effect on Group Problem Solving." *J Abn Social Psychol* 58:27–32; 1959.

Hoffman, L. Richard, and Maier, Norman R. F. "Quality of Acceptance of Problem Solutions by Members of Homogeneous and Heterogeneous Groups." *J. Abn Social Psychol* 62:401–7; 1961.

Hollander, E. P. *Leaders, Groups, and Influence.* Oxford U Press, 1964.

Julian, James, James W., and Perry, Franklyn A. "Cooperation Contrasted with Intra-group Competition." *Sociometry* 30:79–90; 1967.

Kahn, Robert L., and others. *Organizational Stress: Studies in Role Conflict and Ambiguity.* Wiley, 1964.

Katz, Daniel, and Kahn, Robert L. *The Social Psychology of Organizations.* Wiley, 1966.

Katz, Elihu, and others. "Leadership Stability and Social Change: An Experiment with Small Groups." *Sociometry* 20:36–50; 1957.

Kipnis, David, and Lane, William P. "Self-Confidence and Leadership." *J Applied Psychol* 46:291–5; 1962.

Knezevich, Stephen. *Administration of Public Education.* Harper, 1962.

Lane, Willard R., and others. *Foundations of Educational Administration—A Behavioral Analysis.* Macmillan, 1966.

Likert, Rensis. *New Patterns of Management.* McGraw-Hill, 1961.

Lipham, James M. "Leadership and Administration." In *Behavioral Science and Educational Administration.* 63rd Yearbook, Part II, NSSE, U Chicago Press, 1964. p. 119–41.

Lortie, Dan C. "The Balance of Control and Autonomy in Elementary School Teaching." In Etzioni, Amitai. (Ed.) *Heteronomous Professions.* forthcoming.

Maier, Norman R. F., and Hoffman, L. Richard. "Acceptance and Quality of Solutions as Related to Leaders' Attitudes Toward Disagreement in

Group Problem Solving." *J Applied Behavioral Sci* 1:373–83; 1965.
Marak, George E., Jr. "The Evolution of Leadership Structure." *Sociometry* 27:174–82; 1964.
Marcus, Philip M. "Expressive and Instrumental Groups: Toward a Theory of Group Structure." *Am J Sociol* 66:54–9; 1960.
McGrath, Joseph E., and Altman, Irwin. *Small Group Research—A Synthesis and Critique of the Field.* Holt, 1966.
Merton, Robert K. "Bureaucratic Structure and Personality." *Social Forces* 17:560–8; 1940.
Nelson, Paul D. "Similarities and Differences Among Leaders and Followers." *J Social Psychol* 63:161–7; 1964.
Patchen, M. "Supervisory Methods and Group Performance Norms." *Administrative Sci Q* 7:275–94; 1962.
Pelz, Donald. "Influence: A Key to Effective Leadership in the First-line Supervisor." *Personnel* 29:209–17; 1952.
Pelz, Donald, and Andrews, Frank M. *Scientists in Organizations.* Wiley, 1966.
Pryer, Margaret W., and others. "Group Effectiveness and Consistency of Leadership." *Sociometry* 25:391–7; 1962.
Sanford, Frank H. "Research on Military Leadership." In *Current Trends, Psychology in the World Emergency.* U Pittsburgh Press, 1952. p. 17–74.
Schmidt, Warren H. "Executive Leadership in the Principal's Office." *Nat El Prin* 41:35–9; 1962.
Schwartz, M. "The Reciprocities Multiplier: An Empirical Evaluation." *Administrative Sci Q* 9:264–77; 1964.
Sharp, George. "The Principal as Professional Leader." *Nat El Prin* 42:61–3; 1962.
Shaw, Marvin E. "A Note Concerning Homogeneity of Membership and Group Problem Solving." *J Abn Social Psychol* 60:448–50; 1960.
Shaw, Marvin, and Penrod, William T., Jr. "Does More Information Available to a Group Always Improve Group Performance?" *Sociometry* 25:377–90; 1962.
Shure, Gerald H., and others. "Group Planning and Task Effectiveness." *Sociometry* 25:263–82; 1962.
Slater, Philip E., and Bennis, Warren G. "Democracy is Inevitable." *Harvard Bus R* 42:51–9; 1964.
Smith, Clagett G., and Tannenbaum, Arnold S. "Some Implications of Leadership and Control for Effectiveness in a Voluntary Association." *Hum Relations* 18:265–72; 1965.
Smith, Ewart E. "The Effects of Clear and Unclear Role Expectations on Group Productivity and Defensiveness." *J. Abn Social Psychol* 55:213–7; 1957.
Stout, Robert T., and Inger, Morton. *School Desegregation: Progress in Eight Cities.* Report to the U.S. Commission on Civil Rights, 1966.
Tannenbaum, Robert, and others. *Leadership and Organization: A Behavioral Science Approach.* McGraw-Hill, 1961.
Triandis, Harry C., and others. "Member Heterogeneity and Dyadic Creativity." *Hum Relations* 18:33–55; 1965.
Trow, William Clark. "Group Processes." In Harris, Chester. (Ed.) *Encyclopedia of Educational Research.* Macmillan, 1960. p. 602–11.
White, Kinnard. "Personality Characteristics of Educational Leaders: A Comparison of Administrators and Researchers." *Sch R* 73:292–300; 1965.
Wiles, Kimball, and Grobman, Hulda G. "The Role of the Principal in Curriculum Development." *Ed Adm Sup* 44:10–4; 1958.
Williams, Virgil. "Leadership Types, Role Differentiation, and System Problems." *Social Forces* 43:380–9; 1965.
Wrapp, H. Edward. "Good Managers Don't Make Policy Decisions." *U Chicago M* 60:12–7; 1967.

LEARNING*

SCIENCE AND APPLICATION. The processes by which learning occurs are the subject of scientific investigation, and it is to be expected that the study of learning should provide knowledge that educators can use in designing instructional environments and in carrying out the educational process. However, scientific findings and theories rarely are immediately available for practical use, and translation and development are required for their possible application. The assumption, too often made in the past, that the findings and theories of learning could be presented directly to educators for their use is not viable. While the analysis of learning is becoming increasingly relevant to educational problems, more needs to be understood about the relationships among basic science, applied science, and development and the process that leads to the methods and technology which can be used by the practicing educator. Five functions have been described as necessary for the successful relationship between research, development, and application, whether the outcome be a transistor or a new method of teaching arithmetic (Gilbert, 1965).

The first function, *exploratory research*, which the scientist calls theoretical, basic research, is characterized by questioning attitudes and relative independence of the application or further development of existing procedures or knowledge. In a coordinated research and development setting, the exploratory-research operation, which serves as a channel in contact with significant developments in science, may be the determining factor in whether exploratory scientists work on problems relevant to practical innovation.

A second research function, *fundamental development*, is the investigation of the many variables relevant to principles discovered in exploratory investigations. In transistor development, much experimental work was required to understand the characteristics of the materials and conditions that had some bear-

---

* The preparation of this review was supported by the Office of Education, U.S. Department of Health, Education, and Welfare, and by the Office of Naval Research (Personnel and Training Branch, Psychological Sciences Division).

ing on the construction of a transistor. In psychological research relevant to education, exploratory work has been undertaken on methods for measuring human attending behavior. However, more needs to be known about the variables that influence this behavior. Since the child learning arithmetic must learn, at the outset, certain kinds of "looking" behavior when regarding a field of numerals, the investigation of attending behavior has important implications for the training of early habits involved in number and word perception. When this work of fundamental development is carried out, engineered methods of teaching arithmetic and reading must then still proceed.

The third function, *specific development*, relates to the fact that after the theory of the transistor and its variables was discovered, the transistor had yet to be produced. Producing an efficient transistor required skills rather different from those involved in the more "basic" laboratory. Parts had to be acquired, investigated, and assembled with an eye toward use in the field. The production of an actual working transistor both serves as a test of the value of the preceding research and feeds back problems to the basic laboratory. Similarly, once the variables involved in learning number concepts have been investigated, the specific development program has still to produce an arithmetic-teaching program. The arithmetic-teaching items must be written and revised on the basis of testing done with small groups of children in the laboratory. When the program is actually taken into the classroom, the people concerned with development will continue to gather information and revise their material accordingly.

Design and proving is the fourth function. Once transistor or arithmetic programs are developed into functioning realities, they are not yet ready for introduction into field communication systems or into classrooms. The transistor developed in the laboratory may be one which would fail in the arctic cold, and the arithmetic program may fail with certain students. The product must undergo many detailed modifications before it can be a usable instrument in the school. Efficient and inexpensive machinery and procedures for its use must be designed, and changes in the work habits of the teacher and in the structure of the classroom may be required. Design-and-proving engineers are also charged with demonstrating product effectiveness under field conditions. What is important here is to test out the efficiency and economic value of variations in the conditions of use.

Finally, having researched and developed a new product, the research and development organization cannot detach itself from futher implications, and a fifth function, *training and follow-through*, is required. It is necessary to pass on the knowledge by providing a training program for certain key people in the schools. Furthermore, channels must be kept open for feedback about new problems or developments with the product or procedure.

The components outlined above seem to be necessary parts of the structure required for getting knowledge from the science of learning into practical educational efforts even though the regularity of the order of these components may be overemphasized. This review reports on basic research in learning, essentially representing the first two components just described.

THE PSYCHOLOGY OF LEARNING AND THE DESIGN OF INSTRUCTION. The employment of a psychological basis for the design of instructional procedures and materials suggests the following general requirements for this kind of development: (1) specification of the properties of the behavior or task to be learned; (2) specification of the characteristics of the learner; (3) specification of the conditions which permit the individual with the behavior specified in (2) to attain the behavior described in (1); and (4) specification of the conditions under which the learned behavior will be maintained and the individual will be motivated to use it (Glaser, 1965, 1966).

Analysis and Classification of the Behavior to Be Learned. An increasingly prominent feature of the psychology of learning and of attempts to apply it is the analysis and classification of the behavior to be learned (Melton, 1964; Gagné, 1965a; Glaser, 1962; Bruner, 1964; R. Miller, 1965). Two points are to be made in this regard.

The first is that the older, all-inclusive theories and schools are gone as major psychological forces and have been replaced by miniature systems which have resulted from the application of certain methods of behavioral analysis or of certain explanatory concepts and processes to describe a class of behavior. The working assumption at the present stage of learning theory is that the various classes of behaviors that human beings display differ in their stimulus and response characteristics and in the ways in which stimulus and response are related or structured. Depending upon these properties, the conditions for the learning of different categories of behavior have similarities and differences (Gagné, 1965b; Mechner, 1965, 1967). This fact has important consequences for the analysis of learning tasks relevant to classroom subject matters. School learning must be analyzed not only in terms of its knowledge content, e.g., vocabulary, grammatical structure, and scientific laws, but also in terms of the kind of behavioral repertoire that is being learned, e.g., a verbal association, discrimination learning, a behavioral chain, and concept formation. Categorizing learning tasks in this way permits specific investigation of the relevance of the variables that influence them and the design of effective conditions for the learning of these classes of behavior.

The second point is that the extrapolation of psychological findings to school learning requires that the scientific study of learning address itself to behavior at a level of complexity useful for describing educational problems. Until recently, psychology has been deeply involved in the analysis of simplified behaviors and processes (Hilgard & Bower, 1966). There are now apparently some trends toward synthesizing and reexamining the components of behavior studied in the laboratory as they are relevant to "real" behavioral complexity. This trend toward synthesis has been encouraged by the increasing movement of individuals between laboratory study and educational problems, as was done by Thorndike and more recently by Skinner. In the laboratory, a behavioral task performed by a subject has special properties for particular scientific interests; the task involved is so designed that its properties are clear enough for experimental investigation. In contrast, the behavior presented by school learning is not designed for the laboratory and must be analyzed so that it can be subjected to study. The necessity for this kind of "task analysis" adds a new requirement to the study of learning. Tasks cannot always be selected arbitrarily as they can be for laboratory study, but tasks appropriate to school learning must be analyzed into the kind of taxonomy and behavioral categories which learning theory is able to provide.

Specification of the Characteristics of the Learner. The specification of the characteristics of the learner raises the general problem of the interaction between individual differences and learning method. It is now well recognized that the fact of individual differences has been more honored in the breach than in the observance in educational procedures. In the study of learning there has been increasing concern about the lack of contact between test-and-measurement psychologists studying individual differences and the experimental psychologists studying learning (Cronbach, 1957; Gagné, 1967; Glaser, 1967). The investigation of individual differences in the study of learning and the incorporation of individual-difference parameters in learning theory are unavoidable assignments for increasing the relevance of such study to instructional practice.

Specification of the Conditions for Learning. Once the nature of the task to be learned and the entering characteristics of the learner are described, the conditions under which learning will occur can be specified. Instruction, or the educational process, is defined as the provision of the environmental conditions which allow the learner to proceed from a present "entering" behavioral repertoire to the educational goals described as the desired outcomes of instruction. Much of current psychological thinking (Underwood & Schulz, 1960; Skinner, 1957) divides learning into two aspects: (1) response learning, by which new forms of behavior are established —which refers to the fact that a significant component of learning is an increasing precision of the student's responses and that both learning experiments and classroom instruction set particular criteria for acceptable learner responses; and (2) environmental or stimulus control, by which learned responses are associated with or come under the guidance of certain stimulus contexts; effective learning is characterized by well-executed performance taking place in an appropriate situation. A wide variety of behaviors, from rote learning to problem solving, involve competent performance (that is, responses performed according to certain criteria defined as competence) which occurs in discriminated stimulus contexts. Awkward and imprecise responses and responses which are inappropriate to a particular situation are descriptive of poor performance and ineffective learning. Effective conditions for learning lead to response acquisition and the stimulus or context control of these responses. In addition, an adequately learned performance is characterized not only by the facility with which it occurs in different contexts but also in terms of its long-range properties—e.g., how well it is remembered, the degree to which it transfers to and facilitates new learning, the extent to which it continues to be engaged in for relatively long periods of time, and the extent to which it increasingly becomes independent from the supports required in earlier stages of competence. These long-term properties of learning are especially characteristic of school learning, and their investigation is a significant aspect of the scientific study of learning relevant to instruction.

It has been indicated that the fundamental processes of learning dictate the nature of the conditions for learning which must be implemented in educational design. The degree of relevance of these processes to how learning occurs is, to a large extent, a function of the kind of behavior involved. From this point of view, this review is presented in two main parts: *learning processes* and *categories of behavior*. In the ensuing paragraphs there is some sensitivity to the relationship between how behavior is learned and how it is taught.

PART I: LEARNING PROCESSES

The learner acts upon his instructional environment, changes it, and is changed in turn by the consequences of his actions. Certain processes alter behavior so that it achieves a useful interchange with a particular environment. When appropriate behavior has been learned, it sets up new consequences in the environment which work through similar processes to maintain this behavior and use it to develop more competent and subtle behavior. Relevant questions for a science of learning are, How is the behavior of the learner influenced and shaped by the environment or the people in it? How does the learner come to control his environment, and How, in turn, does this environment influence him? By arranging environmental consequences or contingencies, the probability of a behavior's occurring can be increased; by eliminating the consequences, the probability can be decreased. These are the processes of acquisition and extinction. The particular properties of the behavior acquired depend upon the details of the environmental contingencies. A complex repertoire can be taught by a series of environmental changes, each stage of which allows the learner to respond and also prepares him to respond at a later, more complex stage. Such an instructional sequence is carried out when the teacher devises environmental changes as the student goes through a curriculum; the instructional sequence also might be prescribed in advance, as in certain kinds of programmed instruction and other lesson materials. Certain behaviors require extensive instructional sequences; others, as a function of past learning, are acquired rapidly through such environmental events and procedures as verbal instruction and observation.

As responses and the integration of responses are learned, they are acquired in relation to particular events or stimuli so that the behavior performed occurs in relation to some context. Behavior is learned in the presence of contextual stimuli and is therefore likely to occur in the presence of this context. In a sense, stimuli come to control certain kinds of behavior so that, for example, competence in a subject matter is displayed when in the presence of certain subject-matter stimuli the student responds with appropriately skillful behavior. The more readily a stimulus context sets the occasion for the occurrence of certain behavior, the greater is the degree to which it can be said that the situation exerts stimulus control over the behavior. "Control" may be too awkward and dictatorial a word to use in the educational enterprise, but when one thinks of school learning, it is not too difficult to accept the statement that a competent performer is to some extent controlled by the rules and discipline of the subject matter. As competence grows, the student masters these controlling relationships and proceeds to manipulate them in creative ways. The topic of stimulus control is an old one in the psychology of learning and generally refers to the fact that an antecedent stimulus determines the probability of learned behavior. Work in classical and respondent conditioning is concerned with the establishment and strengthening of stimulus-response relationships. Classical conditioning has dealt primarily with reflex-type responses where an already strong response is brought under the control of some stimulus which did not originally evoke it. A transfer of stimulus control occurs from the original unconditioned stimulus to the new, or conditioned, stimulus (Grant, 1964). In instrumental or operant conditioning, the distinction between response learning and bringing the response under the control of an appropriate stimulus context can be seen clearly. In the classical experiments of Thorndike's cats in a puzzle box and Skinner's lever-pressing situations, the subject's behavior is influenced as a result of a response's being made and followed by a consequent environmental change—e.g., reinforcement or punishment. Concurrently, this response is differentially reinforced so that it occurs in the presence of particular stimuli. Stimulus control can be established with respect to a response that is available and well learned or with respect to behavior that is in the process of being learned (Terrace, 1966).

Two major phenomena in stimulus control are generalization and discrimination. These are processes describing the characteristics of a response as it becomes related to a stimulus. Generalization refers to the well-documented (Kimble, 1961, ch. 11) characteristic of behavior that when an individual learns to behave in a certain way in the presence of a particular stimulus, this behavior also occurs in the presence of stimuli having common properties with the stimulus or stimulus class used during the original learning. "Discrimination learning" is the name of the process by which stimuli came to acquire selective control over behavior. A learner is said to have learned to discriminate when he has learned to respond differentially in the presence of two stimuli and does so reliably. Basic to generalization and discrimination are the processes of reinforcement and extinction which refer to the ways in which behavior is strengthened and diminished.

REINFORCEMENT AND EXTINCTION. The law of reinforcement indicates how behavior can be shaped and learned through the use of reinforcers. A reinforcer is defined as an event, a stimulus, or a state of affairs which changes subsequent behavior when it follows the behavior in time. An event is identified as a positive reinforcer when its presentation, following (contingent upon) the occurrence of a response, increases the probability of occurrence of that class of responses. Responses are also strengthened by negative reinforcers; these consist of noxious or aversive events which are removed if the response occurs. Although there are various theoretical interpretations of the acquisition of behavior through reinforcement, in terms of drive reduction, the law of effect, and contiguity, the operations employed to manipulate responses in the course of learning are similar for the different types of explanatory theories. The operational statement is that behavior is acquired as a result of a contingent relationship between the response of an organism and a consequent event. There seems to be little doubt that a significant aspect of educational and instructional practice is the management of reinforcing operations. The term "reinforcement" is usually applied when an event (1) is response-contingent, (2) produces some relatively permanent behavioral changes (learning), and (3) is related to some relevant motivational state of the learner, e.g., conditions of deprivation and past training. Generally, the major classes of events which can produce reinforcing effects are categorized as (1) primary positive reinforcement—the presentation of events, such as food, water, and sexual contact, which are related to some organic need state; (2) primary negative reinforcement—the removal of aversive stimulation, such as electric shock, intense light, or loud sound; (3) secondary positive reinforcement—the presentation of a stimulus which has had prior association in the history of the learner with the condition in category (1) (these are conceived to be learned reinforcers such as money, praise, social approval, attention, or dominance); and (4) secondary negative reinforcement—the removal of a stimulus which has had prior association with the events in category (2) (Kimble, 1961; Wike, 1966).

Sensory Reinforcement. A recent, increasingly active area of study has demonstrated behavioral effects resulting from the response contingent presentation of stimuli which do not fall into these four categories but which conform to the three criteria for reinforcement presented above (Kish, 1966). This new category, referred to as "sensory reinforcement," seems quite relevant to educational matters. Sensory reinforcement appears to be a primary reinforcement process resulting from the presentation or removal of stimuli of moderate intensity. The phenomenon is observed in experiments with animals and children where visual stimulation, such as the onset of a light contingent upon a response, is found to act as a reinforcer; also, visual and auditory exploration contingent upon a response results in learning (Kish, 1966). In an analogous way, it is suggested that the manipulatory behavior in a puzzle problem is reinforced by the visual, auditory, kinesthetic, and tactile consequences of the manipulative behavior itself (Harlow, 1950; Harlow & others, 1956). It appears that stimulus change in many modalities may function in a reinforcing capacity. Apparently, reinforcing forms of stimulation events may be found in many sensory modalities, and a basic problem in understanding the process of sensory reinforcement is the specification of the properties of the reinforcing stimuli which distinguish these events from stimulation which is not reinforcing. It has been proposed that such reinforcing stimuli can be characterized as novel, complex, incongruous, etc., and as arousing or relieving of uncertainty or conflict (Berlyne, 1960). Experiments indicate that decreased novelty is associated with diminished reinforcement potential (satiation), and that nonexposure to the reinforcer may permit recovery of its reinforcing potential. Hence, the reinforcing effects of a novel stimulus can be manipulated by prior exposure of the subjects to similar or dissimilar stimuli. In general, the reinforcing properties of the stimulus are influenced by previous contact with it. Students subjected to different lengths of information deprivation show behavior positively related to the length of the deprivation period and to the amount of information in the reinforcing stimulus (Jones, 1961; Jones & others, 1961). Complexity is related to novelty in the sense that the more complex the stimulus is, the longer it takes for a stimulus pattern to become familiar and to satiate. The complexity of a stimulus pattern is related to its attention-holding value, its exploration-arousing value, and its sensory-reinforcing value; and the variables that contribute to the complexity of stimuli are a matter for study (Berlyne, 1960).

Exploratory Behavior and Curiosity. The properties of stimuli that act as sensory reinforcers also tend to elicit exploratory behavior and curiosity. Prior to 1950, research on this kind of behavior was absent except for a few isolated instances; in the past decade there has been increased interest (Fowler, 1965; Berlyne, 1960). Research has been aimed at the discovery and identification of variables which serve to elicit and maintain curiosity and exploratory behavior in the absence of conventional laboratory motives such as hunger or thirst or other conditions of deprivation. The specific responses which have been observed are such behaviors as orienting, approaching, investigating, and manipulating. Research has indicated that the strength of exploratory behavior which is elicited is positively related, within limits, to the degree of change in the stimulus situation provided by the novel, unfamiliar, or incongruous situations introduced into the environment. Too great or too abrupt a change, however, is disrupting and may preclude exploration. In complex situations, an individual encounters change by way of his interaction with or manipulation of the elements involved. Such interaction provides the stimulus change which can elicit curiosity and exploratory behavior.

Investigations also have demonstrated that behaviors are learned that lead to a change in the stimulus display. Thus, in addition to stimulus change eliciting exploratory behavior, experiments show that organisms will respond in order to secure novel, unfamiliar stimuli. In general, these findings demonstrate that stimulus change or sensory variation may be employed selectively to reinforce behaviors which result in stimulus change and that this variation in the stimulus situation will serve concomitantly to elicit exploratory behavior. When stimulus change is used as a reinforcing stimulus, it seems reasonable to hypothesize that learning variables which influence acquisition and extinction of other learned behavior will influence the acquisition and extinction of exploratory and curiosity behavior. This suggests that a student's curiosity and explorations may be both elicited and selectively maintained in an instructional environment which provides for appropriate variation and change in both the stimulus characteristics of the subject materials confronting the student and the responses required of him by these materials.

The Relativity of Reinforcement. The general conjecture for the kinds of reinforcing events that have been generally studied in the past and for the more recently investigated sensory reinforcements is that these kinds of stimuli act as reinforcers which have some drive-reduction function. A somewhat different approach to the notion of reinforcement has been introduced (Premack, 1959, 1965). Reinforcement has been formulated in terms of the preference values of certain activities or the probability of occurrence of these activities in a person's repertoire. A more preferred activity can be used to reinforce a less preferred activity. An activity will reinforce only activities of lower preference value or activities of lower probability of occurrence. Common-sense examples of this phenomenon are that parents permit their children to watch television only after they have eaten dinner and permit the eating of dessert only after other food has been eaten. This kind of hierarchical or relativistic nature of reinforcement has been demonstrated in a variety of experiments. The relative value of two events can be changed by the alteration of relevant conditions in an individual's history. Thus, the relative preference for eating versus sleeping can be manipulated by food or sleep deprivation. This relativistic notion of reinforcement points out that of any two responses the one that occurs more often when both are available can reinforce the one that occurs less often. For example, if, for a child, playing is a higher-strength behavior than eating, playing might be used as a reinforcing event for eating behavior; or if certain words occur with a higher probability than others, they might be used as reinforcing stimuli for words that have a lower probability of occurrence. Implicit in this kind of analysis of reinforcing events is that the particular event that constitutes a reinforcement is not necessarily a stimulus situation external to the learner so much as it is the behavior produced by the situation—under certain conditions it may not be the food but the eating that reinforces a hungry person. The reinforcing event may not be so much the achievement of the goal but the behavior produced by attaining the goal. Thus, reinforcers may be defined either in terms of external stimuli or in terms of behavior (which produce some sort of internal stimuli). Either definition may serve a particular purpose, and both seem to be useful ways of thinking about the operation of reinforcement.

Behavior Sequences. If carrying out a learned behavior can be reinforcing, then in a chain of activities which terminates in a reinforcing event each response can act as a reinforcer to a previous response if it has a higher probability of occurrence than the behavior it is reinforcing. The learning and maintenance of long, orderly sequences of behavior has been of interest to psychologists for a long time (Kelleher, 1966). Human behavior provides many examples—throwing a ball, playing the piano, solving a geometric proof, memorizing a poem, and driving a car. Early interests in this problem of behavioral sequences is exemplified by the classical double-alternation problem, where a rat in a maze learns that two right turns are followed by two left turns (Hunter, 1920). Double-alternation lever pressing has also been studied (Schlosberg & Katz, 1943). In these situations the experimenters were impressed by the fact that the behavior sequence becomes condensed in time and content, and stimuli and responses are fused into a continuous behavior pattern which is performed with relative ease. Such increasing precision and ease is characteristic of much of human behavior where a laborious sequence is eventually performed rapidly and smoothly, and intervening members of the chain apparently are dropped out or become covert. A prevalent hypothesis in the development of chains (Keller & Schoenfeld, 1950, ch. 7) is that in a behavioral sequence the stimulus first becomes a discriminative stimulus for some response; once so discriminated, it can become a reinforcing stimulus. In the chain, a response produces a stimulus, either exteroceptive or proprioceptive, and this stimulus serves as a reinforcer for the previous response and the discriminative stimulus for the next response. Response-produced stimuli are hypothesized to be an essential aspect of behavioral chains, and this notion has generated interesting research activity.

These notions of chaining have been extrapolated to instructional processes (Gilbert, 1962; Gagné, 1965b, ch. 4; Mechner, 1965, 1967). This extension represents an especially interesting way in which laboratory studies might influence instructional research. Once the members of a chain of behavior have been identified, an instructional sequence to teach the chain might proceed, with appropriate practice, as follows: in a chain consisting of four members, a, b, c, and d, the first response the student should learn is the last one in the chain, response d. Therefore, the first teaching step would be, given a–b–c, carry out d, and the correct response is d. Next, the student should learn to carry out the last two members of the chain; the teaching step would be, given a–b, complete the sequence, and the correct response would be c–d. Next, given a, perform b–c–d. Finally, the student would carry out the complete chain unassisted. This suggestion implies that operation d is learned first, then c–d, since d, as a higher-probability behavior, can reinforce the new response c and so on with operations a, b, c, d. The student always carries out the chain in a forward direction and does not perform the behavior backwards. What occurs backwards is the way in which the elements of the chain are added to the student's repertoire. Practical examples that have been suggested are the following. When teaching a child a manual skill, such as tying his shoelace, start by presenting him with the bow almost completely tied, but only loosely so, and allow him to tighten it. When he can do that, present him with the bow almost complete and allow him to complete it and make it tight. Continue this procedure, allowing the child to complete longer and longer segments of the chain until he can start with untied laces. When learning a proof in geometry, start by studying the proposition to be proved. Then look at the step in the proof which just precedes the final proposition until you understand the final step. Next, move to the preceding step, and so forth, until the starting axioms have been reached. In general, the procedure is reminiscent of the advice to start solving a problem by asking what the problem would look like when it is solved and then proceed to examine the kind of situations that lead up to the state of affairs defined as solution or terminal performance.

Reinforcement Schedules. Most often in practical affairs, reinforcing events follow behavior on an intermittent basis; it is the exception rather than the rule that an individual is regularly and continuously reinforced each time a behavior is performed. It has been shown that the schedule on which reinforcement occurs strongly influences behavior and is often much more important than the nature and quantity of the reinforcer. Schedules of reinforcement represent one of the most intensively studied influences on the generation and maintenance of operant behavior (Morse, 1966). A very wide range of behaviors has been produced in lower organisms by different schedules involving intricate relationships between responses and their contingent reinforcements. Schedules of reinforcement seem so powerful in producing patterns of responding that many investigators consider them a pervading influence in the psychology of learning (Skinner, 1966). In laboratory studies, a schedule of reinforcement is a prescription for initiating and terminating discriminative and reinforcing stimuli in time and in relation to some behavior. Schedules have been classified (Skinner, 1938; Ferster & Skinner, 1957) in terms of those that reinforce a response on the basis of time (interval schedules) and on the basis of response occurrence (ratio schedules). Interval schedules consider the time that has elapsed since some event, either a response or a reinforcement; ratio schedules make reinforcement contingent upon the number of emitted responses. Complex schedules are built up as variations or combinations of ratio and interval schedules. A notational and terminological system has been developed to describe systematically the different kinds of reinforcement schedules (Ferster & Skinner, 1957). When learning occurs under two different schedules, the differential effects are quite apparent. In animals under one condition of reinforcement (fixed-ratio reinforcement), the response being reinforced takes place to the exclusion of all other behavior, and the animal works at a great rate and seems "highly motivated, persistent and industrious." However, if another schedule is in effect (a variable-interval schedule with a low-rate contingency of reinforcement), responses occur at a much lower rate, and there are periods of "apparent lack of interest" in making a response. In general, the work on schedules in lower organisms has represented an active search for the relationship between the learning of complex patterns of behavior and the selective and strengthening effects of reinforcement.

Related to the notion of schedules of reinforcement is the long-standing evidence that delay of reinforcement influences learning (Hull, 1943, ch. 10; Spence, 1956, ch. 5). In general, responses temporally near reinforcement are learned more quickly than responses remote from reinforcement (Kimble, 1961, ch. 6). The shorter the delay of reinforcement, the steeper the slope of the learning curve. Much of the attention to programmed instruction and teaching machines is centered on the necessity for decreasing the delay of reinforcement in the instructional process. Nevertheless, the effect of reinforcement delay is far from clear-cut. It is apparent that individuals can learn to tolerate such delay and can learn to fill in delay intervals with symbolic reinforcers and verbal mechanisms (Deese & Hulse, 1967, ch. 2). A significant aspect of delay is that during the delay period other behaviors intervene which may be unrelated or detrimental to the ongoing learning. Such irrelevant behavior, if it is allowed to occur, may be strengthened by the onset of the reinforcer, and in this way such behaviors as inattention and distraction might be learned and maintained. The behavior that intervenes may be behavior which has been previously learned and, hence, is stronger than the newly learned behavior and requires less reinforcement for its acquisition.

In the light of these relationships of reinforcing conditions and operations to such behavior as curiosity, exploration, persistence, and inattention, there is a general growing doubt that the process of reinforcement can be legitimately separated, as it has been in the past, from the concept of motivation. Much of the literature that can be placed under the heading of reinforcement might also be classified under the heading of motivation. Indeed, the two are closely connected and may eventually become indistinguishable.

Extinction. The primary effect of reinforcement is to strengthen behavior. Once the behavior is acquired and reinforcement is terminated, the behavior persists for a while, becomes weaker, and gradually declines in frequency. "Extinction" refers to this subsequent decline after reinforcement has been discontinued. Relatively speaking, the acquisition of behavior occurs rapidly and extinction slowly. It has also been observed that when reinforcement is discontinued, behavior during extinction is intensified before it subsequently declines (Amsel, 1958, 1962; Morse, 1966). A frequently reported phenomenon about extinction is that there is increased resistance to extinction as a result of partial reinforcement during acquisition, as compared with continuous reinforcement. More generally, it has been pointed out that when learning occurs under relatively unfavorable conditions, such as a response's requiring much effort, punishment at the goal, delayed reward, or frequent extinction trials, a greater resistance to extinction is manifested (Festinger, 1961; Lawrence & Festinger, 1962).

These facts about extinction and the general observation that learned responses show little or no tendency to be forgotten with the mere passage of time lead to the notion that extinction is the result of some active process associated with nonreinforcement. This has led to theory and experimentation to explain the nature of extinction; in general, many of the investigations carried out have been designed to support or refute theoretical explanations of the extinction process. The hypotheses that have been advanced to explain extinction employ a wide variety of concepts—inhibition, response competition, discrimination, frustration and punishment, cognitive dissonance, and generalization decrement (Kimble, 1961, ch. 10). While certain facts about extinction may be evident, the variables controlling extinction seem even more complex than those controlling acquisition.

GENERALIZATION. When a learner has acquired a response to a particular stimulus it is evident that other, "similar" stimuli will also elicit the response that has been learned; once a response has been reinforced in one situation, the probability that the response will occur in other, similar situations is increased. The phenomenon that occurs when a stimulus situation, different from the one in which the learner has been trained is the occasion for the occurrence of the learned response is known as stimulus generalization. There is also a comparable phenomenon less well studied, known as response generalization or response induction. Early in its development, the concept of stimulus generalization was associated with neural mechanisms (Pavlov, 1927). The departure from this tradition is associated with Hull, Spence, and Skinner, who conceived of it as an empirical behavioral phenomenon and de-emphasized neural postulates. Generally speaking, "generalization" refers to making the same kinds of responses to different stimuli; as such, it involves learning common elements and disregarding differences, so that responses are made to new situations which are in some way similar to the situations in which previous learning occurred. Whether or not generalization is desirable or undesirable, appropriate or inappropriate, depends upon the particular task being taught.

The process of stimulus generalization has been widely studied and has been demonstrated in many species and in various learning situations to be a process characteristic of individual organisms (Guttman & Kalish, 1956; Kimble, 1961). The amount of stimulus generalization decreases with increasing differences between the originally learned stimulus and the newly presented stimuli; when response strength is plotted as a function of this difference, the result is a monotonic decreasing gradient between the original learning stimulus and the new stimuli. The process of generalization is influenced by a number of variables. The extent of a generalization gradient increases with the strength of the originally learned response so that the amount of stimulus generalization is increased as a response increases in strength. If a response is undergoing extinction, the range of generalization is restricted unless the original learning took place under conditions of intermittent reinforcement. Increased motivation during learning increases the range of generalization. Intermittent reinforcement results in wider generalization than continuous reinforcement. The intensity of stimuli influences generalization; new stimuli, stronger in intensity than the original stimulus, will increase the amount of generalization. The conditions of original learning influence generalization so that if the subject learns to discriminate stimuli along the dimension of generalization, the generalization gradient is steeper. Currently, active research is being carried out on the process of generalization (Mostofsky, 1965).

Since stimulus generalization occurs along a dimension of stimulus similarity, the question arises of the perception and properties of "similarity." Generalization occurs along many kinds of continua. Studies of "semantic generalization" show generalization gradients with respect to meaning and language habits and indicate that generalization occurs along dimensions of similar words and between a word and its object. Similarity along such dimensions is frequently explained in terms of mediation—i.e., the extent to which different stimuli elicit the same or similar mediated responses. The measurement of similarity is a problem requiring the development of quantitative measures. It has been pointed out (Shepard, 1965; Cross, 1965) that for the purpose of constructing gradients of generalization there does not appear to be any one measure of the similarity or dissimilarity between stimuli that has the kind of fundamental status that number of trials or number of reinforcements has for the construction of curves of acquisition. A problem under study is the determination of behavioral measures that can be used for a quantitative scaling procedure which specifies the underlying dimension of generalization.

Stimuli have various functions. They set the occasion for a response as elicitors or discriminative stimuli; they serve as reinforcers; and they also serve as inhibitors. Generalization effects refer to a variety of stimulus properties, although the properties have been less well studied in cases other than those in which stimuli serve as elicitors or discriminative stimuli. Generalization can occur with respect to a response which is inhibited in the presence of a stimulus, and gradients of inhibition have been empirically shown to exercise a range of inhibitory control (H. Jenkins & Harrison, 1962). Exposure to a punishing event which is consistently preceded by a neutral stimulus endows that stimulus with a capacity to inhibit or suppress behavior, and generalization occurs to stimuli which are similar to it so that these stimuli also exhibit this capacity (Estes & Skinner, 1941; Hoffman, 1965). Generalization gradients have also been studied for avoidance behavior, and the suggestion has been made that avoidance resulting from punishing stimuli can generalize very broadly; extremes of such kinds of stimulus generalization are found in neurotic and psychotic individuals (Hearst, 1965). Stimuli are not all equally effective in controlling behavior, and there might be postulated some kind of underlying attending hierarchy so that certain cues in a stimulus situation, e.g., color, size, or form, may be more effective in facilitating generalization or discrimination (Baron, 1965).

DISCRIMINATION. In a manner analogous to the contrast between acquisition and extinction, generalization and discrimination can be compared. Discrimination learning is a process by which stimuli come to acquire selective control over behavior; particular situations set the occasion for the occurrence of behavior in that situation. A learner is said to have learned to discriminate between stimuli when he responds differentially in different stimulus situations and does so reliably. In a simple two-choice discrimination problem the subject learns to make a response in one way if an instance of stimulus A occurs and to choose another response if stimulus B occurs. The simplest type of discrimination problem frequently used in the laboratory as a reference experiment for theoretical interpretation is where the learner is reinforced for responding in the presence of one stimulus, the $S+$, and not reinforced for responding in the presence of another stimulus, the $S-$. Traditionally, in such discrimination-learning problems both stimuli are presented to the learner, he initially responds to both, and eventually develops differential responses to each. The classical explanation of this kind of situation describes the learning that takes place in terms of reinforcement, extinction, and generalization (Spence, 1936; Hull, 1950; Keller & Schoenfeld, 1950). A response is acquired to the $S+$ through the cumulative effects of reinforcement. Extinction (or conditioned inhibition) occurs to the $S-$ The responses made to the $S+$ receive an increment in response strength, and depending upon the ismilarity of the stimuli, there is generalization to the $S-$ which receives a weaker increment in response strength. In a similar fashion, extinction or inhibition to the $S-$ generalizes to the $S+$. As this process is repeated, in conjunction with repetition of the $S+$ and $S-$, the strength of responding to the two discriminative stimuli draws apart and a discrimination is established. The net tendency to respond to any stimulus is then given by the interaction of the generalization of acquisition and the generalization of extinction. This formulation of the process of discrimination learning has provided the basis for many experiments and theoretical formulations.

One of the implications of the assumption of stimulus generalization in theories of discrimination learning is that responding in the presence of one stimulus is related to responding in the presence of another stimulus. In an experimental situation where reinforcement or extinction is manipulated for one stimulus and held constant for the other, the expectation is that responding to the fixed stimulus should increase or decrease as a function of the generalization between the two stimuli. In certain discrimination situations, however, an opposite result has been observed where response rates are negatively correlated; a reduction in reinforcement for one stimulus is accompanied by an increase in responding to the other stimulus. This effect has been called "behavioral contrast" and has been observed with animal subjects (Reynolds, 1961). This has generated some examination of the classical notions of discrimination learning.

Recently, to some extent growing out of work on teaching machines, a new procedure for discrimination learning has been investigated which has led to a new view of the process. An expressed principle in programmed instruction is that an optimal arrangement of a programmed sequence is one in which the student makes few or no errors in the course of learning. With this in mind, recent research has been carried out in which a discrimination is taught by a procedure in which the learner never responds or makes minimal responses to the S− throughout learning (Terrace, 1963). The procedure used to teach a discrimination is based on procedures previously shown to be effective in minimizing the occurrence of errors (Skinner, 1938; Schlosberg & Solomon, 1943); the critical variable in these early studies appeared to be the time and manner of the introduction of the S−. The procedure recently used involves introducing the S+ in its final form, but introducing the S− gradually (initially, for very brief durations and at very low intensities); over successive trials the intensity and duration of S− are gradually increased to their full value. In this way, a discrimination can be taught with minimal occurrence of "errors," i.e., nonreinforced responses to S−. This procedure was originally carried out in the animal laboratory, where it was compared with the classical discrimination-learning procedure. This comparison suggests that discrimination performance as a result of training by the errorless method was superior in two senses: (1) there were no responses to the incorrect S− stimulus; and (2) aversive or "emotional" behavior was not built up as a result of extinction to the S− stimulus. This study has been extended to the teaching of discriminations in young children and retardates (R. Moore & Goldiamond, 1964; Sidman & Stoddard, 1967).

Of special interest in discrimination learning is the question of what is the effective stimulus controlling the learner's performance. Generally, the effective stimulus that controls discriminative performance is a stimulus attribute or set of attributes present in the S+ and absent or different in the S−. The stimulus attributes become relevant because they correlate with the presence or absence of reinforcement. Relevant attributes can be complex aspects of a situation, including such relational features as "larger than," "different from," etc. This kind of relational discrimination learning has been studied in "transposition" experiments, which have a long history in psychology (Köhler, 1918; Spence, 1937; Zeiler, 1963). Complex discrimination learning has been studied in a variety of interesting ways: (1) The ability to transfer and reverse a learned discrimination along certain dimensions has been shown to be related to developmental stages in children and seems related to their increasing proficiency in verbalizing the discriminative features involved (Kendler & Kendler, 1962). (2) The facility to become increasingly proficient in learning to learn discriminations over a series of tasks has been studied in the work on learning sets (Harlow, 1949, 1959). (3) The way in which a previously learned discrimination can facilitate learning in a new situation has been examined in studies on the acquired distinctiveness of cues (Lawrence, 1949, 1950).

ATTENTION. Related to the control of behavior by selected aspects of a stimulus is the phenomenon of attention. The extent to which certain stimulus aspects of the situation fail to control or direct the learner's responses is often referred to as a failure of attention. Behavior labeled as "attention" has generally been conceived in terms of certain mediating responses that must occur before a stimulus element will reliably be associated with a response; such responses are considered preparatory responses which orient the learner to observe critical stimuli in a situation. These orienting responses (or receptor-exposure acts) are learned responses and as such are reinforced and extinguished (Spence, 1937, 1956; Skinner, 1953).

A response which causes an individual to pay attention to a particular attribute of a stimulus situation has been referred to as an observing response. These observing responses are reinforced because they produce or clarify a discriminative stimulus which then comes to control a response which is in its turn reinforced (Holland, 1958; Wyckoff, 1952; Atkinson, 1961). The observing response as it has been studied is primarily an overt act which produces, in some way, the stimulus involved in the ongoing learning. It also has been shown that learning can produce biases toward the use of a particular stimulus attribute (Berlyne, 1960). Previous reinforcement with respect to a particular stimulus element in one situation will transfer to other situations, and the learner's history can serve to make that aspect of the situation predominant or preferred as a cue for learning. When this learned cue is relevant, it can facilitate learning, and where it is irrelevant, it can inhibit learning.

Attention has been considered in terms of a coding response, where "coding" refers to a procedure for labeling and representing objects so as to provide a means for describing a complex stimulus by one or more of its properties (Lawrence, 1963). The "stimulus-as-coded" labels a particular stimulus as "blue," for example, which in turn serves to describe the stimulus as an entity to be responded to. If, in the course of learning, a stimulus pattern varies on many attributes, then during learning, different responses are tried out until the relevant attribute is settled on, and the subject learns to attend to that aspect of the stimulus as being relevant in this situation. In a variety of learning tasks, this sort of attribute learning (or learning what the functional stimulus is) occurs before learning, involving stimulus control over the response, takes place.

Attention has taken a key role in certain studies of discrimination learning with retardates and in comparing the nature of discrimination learning between brighter and duller individuals (Zeaman & House, 1963). In an elaboration of the observing response model, two responses are postulated: (1) an attention response to the relevant stimulus dimension and (2) the correct response to the positive cue of the relevant dimension. Experiments show that the differences between the brighter and duller subjects are not in the slopes of their learning curves but in the lengths of the initial plateau. This implies that it is not the rate of learning that distinguishes bright and dull but how long it takes the attentional response to discriminate out the relevant stimulus cue; after this occurs, improvement is uniformly fast for both groups. The general postulation is that there are two aspects of learning involved, one aspect controlling any individual differences in the rate of acquisition and extinction and the other controlling individual differences in the probabilities of paying attention to stimulus dimensions. A difficult discrimination task would be one in which the relevant dimensions involved have a low probability of being attended to; in an easy task, both bright and dull subjects have a high probability of paying attention. Retardate learners can be slow learners in the attentional phase, but once it occurs, they might learn in one or two trials. The initial probability of selecting a coding response, or discriminating out the positive stimulus, determines several aspects of discrimination learning: the length of the plateau prior to associative learning, the difficulty of the problem, and the "learning speed" of the subject.

A significant question in the study of attention is what variables influence stimulus selection during learning (Berlyne, 1960). The factors which determine initial attending hierarchies seem to be (1) innate factors, which are, perhaps, interspecies differences in the saliency or importance of particular stimulus properties; (2) stimulus aspects, which emphasize a particular cue or give a feature a distinctive tag, e.g., intensity, vividness, or size—these aspects are culturally learned or are features of the situation which arouse and reinforce exploratory and orienting behavior; and (3) specific past learning, in terms of training in looking for certain attributes or variations in the situation. In this regard it is also likely that facility in performing attention behavior involving the discovery of new features in a situation can be reinforced by the learner's being supplied with relevant coding operations. In general, as more knowledge is obtained about attending behavior and discrimination learning, it seems that there may be some success in extending the discriminative capacities of individuals. As this occurs, the ability to make fine discriminations in musical tones, for example, may be less accepted as innate musical talent and more of a behavior that can be taught.

Some investigation has been conducted on the kind of learning that takes place when a learner observes someone else performing a response and attempts to imitate it. The variables that influence this kind of learning have been described (Bandura, 1962, 1965), but more experiments are needed to analyze the mechanisms by which this kind of behavior takes place. A program of research has been carried out in an attempt to understand how humans learn from written material (Rothkopf, 1965). The activities that are involved in this behavior have been referred to as attention, concentration, orientation, and inspection behavior. In general, the experimental procedure that has been used employs questioning and testlike events which sample the knowledges that subjects acquire by reading. The attempt is made to find out how the quantity and variety of acquired knowledge is influenced by manipulations of the frequency, timing, and character of these tests in relation to the printed material. It has been found that these questioning and testlike procedures support the persistence of the kind of behavior that results in learning from reading. Factors contributing to the deterioration of activities which permit subjects to learn from reading text material are to some extent counteracted by the appropriate use of testlike events to which the student must respond in the course of reading. A salient fact is that the character of the questions in the test determines what knowledges are acquired and determines how students inspect, process, and think about the material. Students tend to process, organize, and remember material to meet the criteria posed by the test questions; hence, the nature of these testlike events in verbal material seems to go hand in hand with the kind of attention and complexity of the thought generated in the student.

PUNISHMENT. While few are likely to approach the topic of punishment in neutral terms, the effects of punishment upon learning can be studied with some degree of scientific neutrality. Work in this area has been carried out primarily with animals, but some work has been done with humans (E. Thorndike, 1932a, 1932b; Muenzinger, 1934; Estes, 1944; Weiner, 1962; Azrin & Holz, 1966; Fowler & Wischner, 1968). For scientific study, "punishment" has been defined operationally as the presentation of an aversive stimulus following a response—an aversive stimulus being defined as a stimulus that increases the probability of responses that terminate that stimulus. Punishment has also been defined in terms of its effects, i.e., the reduction of the future probability of a response as the result of the immediately consequent occurrence of a stimulus following the response. This definition is similar to the definition of a reinforcing stimulus, that is, a consequent event that results in a change in the future probability of behavior. Aversive stimuli that have punishing effects are (1) stimuli with primary aversive properties, such as direct assault and electric shock; (2) conditioned aversive stimuli, such as a frown or a shout—generally, a stimulus that has been associated with punishment; (3) a temporary or permanent discontinuation of positive reinforcement when a high level of reinforcement has been in effect; and (4) response cost, such as the subtraction of points or the loss of money as a consequence of a response. Punishment results in the reduction and suppression of behavior; they occur immediately if the punishment is effective. Their extent and duration is a function of the intensity of the punishment; intense punishment produces rather complete suppression, and mild punishment is followed by a characteristic recovery from punishment. This recovery is often accompanied by an increase in the behavior following the termination of the aversive stimulus. This has been labeled as a punishment contrast effect or designated as a making-up for the decrease of behavior produced by punishment. When punishment is administered on a continuous schedule after every response, the following recovery is immediate; punishment that is intermittently delivered is followed by gradual recovery. As is characteristic of behavior, the suppression of behavior generalizes so that after punishment, stimuli present during the period when reduction of behavior occurs may tend to elicit suppression for a period of time (Azrin & Holz, 1966).

While the suppressive effects of punishment have been the ones most commonly discussed, experiments have shown that punishment has nonsuppressive effects in that it can serve as a discriminative stimulus or cue to signal another event. It may signal another punishing stimulus, the absence of reinforcement, or the presence of reinforcement. In the last case, it may be a signal that a correct response has been made which will lead to reinforcement (Fowler & Wischner, 1968). The "nonsuppressive effects" of punishment generally refer to the fact that mild punishment for a correct response facilitates the learning of a discrimination by making the particular stimulus situation highly distinctive; this has been shown in animals treated with electric shock during discrimination learning. The general conclusion to be drawn is that the procedure and conditions of use of an aversive stimulus determine what effects it can have—either suppressive or facilitative as a distinctive cue. As a facilitator, the punishing shock can provide information about which responses will lead to reinforcement, and the fact that punishment signals a reinforcement deemphasizes its suppressive effects. Punishment also facilitates learning when an alternative response is available which will not be punished but will produce the same or greater reinforcement as the punished response. For example, punishment of criminal behavior can be expected to be more effective if non-criminal behavior is available which will result in the same advantages as the criminal behavior.

Although punishment has not been extensively studied, and therefore little is known about it, the general statement is that an aversive stimulus is indeed a stimulus and functions as such. Depending upon the conditions under which the aversive stimulus occurs, the different functions it serves can predominate: it can have rather dramatic effects in suppressing behavior; at the same time, it seems helpful in the learning process when used as a discriminative or information-carrying cue and when it is combined with reward for some other behavior which produces the same reinforcement as the punished response or greater reinforcement. While an aversive stimulus can act as a discriminative stimulus in facilitating learning, the elimination of a response by punishment does not, as such, result in an increase of unpunished, more-desirable responses unless these responses are concurrently being reinforced. When a subject is forced to choose between two responses, however, there may be an increase in the unpunished response without any obvious reinforcement for that response. Thus, it is inappropriate to consider punishment as a method for teaching new behavior; punishment is rather a method for suppressing behavior, and in this sense is an antithetical process to reinforcement.

Other procedures are also effective in suppressing behavior, such as extinction, satiation, and removal of a discriminative stimulus. Extinction could be a more effective procedure than punishment; however, under certain situations, it may be difficult to withhold reinforcement. Running or speeding in a car allows us to get where we are going quickly, and hence, running and speeding are inevitably reinforced in a situation where extinction, i.e., the withholding of reinforcement, may not be feasible (Azrin & Holz, 1966). In such situations, punishment probably serves to suppress behavior since it comes about "naturally" when the runner falls or the speeder has an accident. On the other hand, it is possible to eliminate punishment as an institutional procedure—procedures such as fines, imprisonment, dismissal from a job, withdrawal of privileges, etc. A frequent reason for wanting to eliminate punishment is that it produces disruptive and undesirable emotional states. This depends upon the conditions involved. The punishments which come about in the physical world, such as a child's being burned as a consequence of touching a hot stove, lower the likelihood of the child's touching the stove again but do not necessarily result in chronic emotional stress. It is when punishment is administered by one individual to another that the undesirable effects of punishment are particularly manifested (Azrin & Holz, 1966). When a teacher punishes a child for talking in class, the teacher desires to suppress the unauthorized talking and not to influence other behavior. However, when alternative behaviors are available, punishment tends to allow other behaviors, such as escaping from the situation, to be reinforced. In this case, punishment would result not only in the suppression of talking but also in an increase in likelihood of the child's leaving the punishing situation through tardiness, truancy, and dropping out of school. The social aspects of punishment are especially undesirable. When physical punishment is administered, the punished individual may eliminate the punishing contingency by aggressing against whoever or whatever is delivering the punishment in the effort to remove it. A related kind of aggression that has been intensively studied in animals occurs when a painful stimulus is delivered to an organism in the company of other organisms (Ulrich & Azrin, 1962). Even though the other organisms did not deliver the painful stimulus, reflexive fighting and social aggression occurs that appears to be a general response to the aversive stimulation.

PART II: CATEGORIES OF BEHAVIOR

As has been indicated earlier, the ways in which processes discussed above influence learning are a function of the kind of behavior being learned. Depending upon the kind of performance to be taught and the existing behavior of the learner, the various processes of learning come into play. Different classes of behavior require different conditions for learning. Major categories of behavior that have been and are being studied experimentally are rote verbal learning, psycholinguistics, memory, concept learning, problem solving and thinking, and perceptual and motor-skill learning.

ROTE VERBAL LEARNING. Three tasks, serial learning, paired-associate learning, and free recall have been most frequently used in rote verbal-learning studies. Characteristic of this area of study is that these tasks have been analyzed in detail and that the explanatory theories generated are highly specific to the kind of task involved. For example, the most documented and thoroughly studied characteristic of serial list learning is the "serial position effect." This term refers to the distribution of errors during learning, errors being most frequent in the middle of the list and progressively less frequent toward the ends of the list, with the peak of the error distribution displaced toward the end of the list. Attempts to explain this have a long history (Lepley, 1934; McGeoch & Irion, 1952; Hull & others, 1940; McCrary & Hunter, 1953; Deese & Kresse, 1952; Glanzer & Peters, 1962). In psychology in general, the way in which the subject perceives the stimulus has been of continued interest (Lawrence, 1963). This problem has been a particular focus in the study of verbal learning, where the distinction between the nominal and the functional stimulus—i.e., the stimulus as conceived by the experimenter and perceived by the learner—has been of interest (Underwood, 1963). In serial learning the serial list can be conceived of as a set of stimulus-response associations where each item in the list functions as both stimulus and response, so that the list of items a, b, c, d consists of links a–b, b–c, c–d, which are eventually integrated into the chain. The view held in this kind of analysis is labeled the "specificity" hypothesis; the stimulus for a given response is the specific prior item, and no distinction is made between the nominal and the functional stimulus. Alternately, however, the "ordinal position" hypothesis states that the functional stimulus is the item's ordinal position in the list, so that the functional stimulus for item c in the above list would be the learner's discrimination of c as the third item in the list (Ebenholtz, 1963; Young & others, 1963). A "cluster" hypothesis has also been advanced which suggests that the functional stimulus is not simply the preceding item but some group of items preceding the item to be anticipated (Horowitz & Izawa, 1963). The answer to the question of the functional stimulus, if indeed it is the correct question, is an open one (Jensen, 1962).

A two-stage analysis of acquisition in paired-associate learning dominates contemporary research on this task (Underwood & Schulz, 1960). The first stage is response learning, which consists of making the response available to the learner. For example, the difficulty of learning a verbal unit is related to its meaningfulness or familiarity; a response term which is a nonsense syllable requires more time for the subject to learn to recall it than a familiar word does. The second stage is the association stage in which responses are "hooked up with," or come under the control of, the appropriate stimuli so that each stimulus elicits an appropriate response. Much of the research in verbal learning is oriented toward the processes and variables that influence one or both of these stages of acquisition.

Conditions of Presentation. Paired-associate tasks are generally presented by the "anticipation method," where the subject anticipates the response coming up next when the stimulus is presented, or by the "recall method," in which a block of paired words is presented at one time followed by a test trial in which just the stimulus terms are presented. The anticipation method permits immediate feedback of response correctness. The recall method separates learning and test trials and delays any overt information feedback during the test trial until the following study trial. Comparisons of the relative efficiencies of these two methods do not show consistent advantages for one procedure over the other (Battig & Brackett, 1961; Battig & others, 1963). Studies of confirmation versus prompting procedures have been carried out. In the anticipation method a subject receives immediate confirmation of the correctness of his response, and early in learning he makes frequent errors. It is possible to prevent errors from occurring by prompting the subject as to what the correct response is on a trial. When confirmation and prompting are compared, the results obtained in different experiments are inconsistent (Cook & Spitzer, 1960; Hawker, 1964). Studies have also compared fixed versus random ordering of paired-associate lists and have continued to investigate the relative effectiveness of whole versus part learning (Kausler, 1966). In general, this kind of comparison studies of presentation conditions have been nondefinitive, and the variables that have been studied do not seem to represent particularly influential variables in the acquisition of rote verbal learning.

Temporal Factors. The amount of time that verbal materials are presented to the learner is an effective variable. Experiments show that not only is the amount of time per item (intratrial rate) important, but also the distribution of time between practice and rest, i.e., distributed practice, is important. With respect to intratrial rate, a significant generalization seems to be that presentation time multiplied by trials, i.e., the total time taken to reach criterion, is a constant. Total time in practice may be divided into many brief repetitions of the material or concentrated in a few repetitions with a longer time allowed for each repetition; either procedure with the total time constant appears to result in equal learning (Bugelski, 1962; Nodine, 1965; Keppel & Rehula, 1965).

With respect to the distribution of practice, a long-term systematic attack on the problem (Underwood, 1961b) complicates the earlier general conclusion that short periods of rest are beneficial to learning. The complicating factor is the nature of the task as a source of potential interference between items during the response stage of learning. If responses are highly similar to one another, e.g., nonsense syllables made up of only a few letters, distributed practice will improve performance (Keppel, 1964); but, in general, the greater the degree of meaningful internal organization within the material to be learned, the less the influence of distribution of practice (Deese & Hulse, 1967).

Instruction to Learn—Incidental and Intentional Learning. Incidental learning has a long research history in which differences between intentional and incidental learning have been explained in terms of the ambiguous concept of "set," or readiness to learn. Contemporary interpretations (Postman, 1964) view intent instructions as a stimulus for cue-producing responses which influence acquisition. These responses are a kind of orienting behavior which enables the subject to perceive or to discriminate certain features of the stimulus material. Instructions are effective to the extent that they elicit the cue-producing or orienting behavior necessary for a stimulus to be discriminated and related to a response. Incidental learning occurs to the degree that such orienting behavior is elicited by instructions or by the properties of the task materials involved (Rothkopf, 1965). The present literature leads to the conclusion that there is little reason to maintain a conceptual distinction between intentional and incidental learning. There is little experimental evidence demonstrating incidental learning in the traditional sense of a learning process which occurs when there is no motivation, self-instruction, or set to learn. What seems more relevant is to treat experimental instructions as a manipulable experimental variable and to investigate the properties of certain materials tending to elicit orienting responses (Postman, 1964).

Meaningfulness and Familiarity. The meaningfulness of rote material is positively related to its acquisition. It is generally assumed that differences in meaningfulness reflect variations in the frequency of prior experience—the greater the degree of prior experience, the higher the meaningfulness. As a result of this prior learning, more highly meaningful response units are emitted earlier in practice than are less meaningful components, and, hence, the more meaningful units are more readily available for the associative stage of acquisition (Underwood & Schulz, 1960). In this associative stage, the meaningfulness of both stimulus and response components is hypothesized to be an important factor because meaningfulness determines the number of associates that are accessible for mediational processes. "Familiarity" acts similarly to "meaningfulness," but an operational distinction is made between these two terms: familiarity is the consequence of frequency alone, whereas meaningfulness is the product of both frequency and multiple associations (Noble, 1963). A related variable is pronounceability: experiments show that the pronounceability of the response unit is a good predictor of paired-associate response learning (Underwood & Schulz, 1960; Martin & Schulz, 1963). There is little doubt that "meaningfulness" is an important variable influencing learning; the task of contemporary research is to analyze why this is so and to identify the process involved.

Similarity. Similarity can be "formal," i.e., similarity in terms of the commonality of the letter components of the verbal units, and also "semantic," i.e., similarity in terms of commonality of meaning. In general, similarity of either kind between the stimulus and response components in rote verbal learning tends to result in generalization gradients which produce intrusion errors that slow down acquisition. The study of the effects of similarity shows a long history of skillful experimentation to tease out empirical findings and to analyze theoretical explanations (Underwood, 1961a), but inconsistencies with respect to this variable abound.

Organizational Factors. In the free-recall task, because of its relatively unstructured nature, organizational processes have been more amenable to study than in more structured tasks (Tulving, 1962). Two representative and related processes are "coding" and "clustering." "Coding," as previously described, refers to the observation that people have a fixed memory capacity and appear to regroup or organize a stimulus sequence into manageable units. An encoding process is involved by which verbal strings are grouped and learned and remembered in terms of these groupings or "chunks" of information (G. Miller, 1956). For example, in learning a trigram such as GDO, the separate letter units may be coded into the meaningful sequences GOD and DOG—the encoded stimulus, being a meaningful word, now exists as a single unit, rather than as separate letters, and is easily acquired and stored for recall. In order to remember a sentence, we may need only to remember a few key words and its general structure. Mnemonic devices provide other means for introducing organization into material and serve to increase the number of words per chunk. Many facts about the learning and recall of verbal material fit into this view, and the particular ways in which the coding process operates is an important subject for study (Underwood & Keppel, 1962).

"Clustering" refers to the sequential organization during recall of items that are related to one another in some way, even though the items are exposed in a random order during study trials. Clustering is observed when related items follow one another when the subject recalls them. This grouping permits a list of *n* words to be encoded into fewer than *n* chunks. In general, acquisition measured in terms of the recall of items in a list is higher for lists which permit clustering than for those which do not. Clustering occurs in different ways. Taxonomic clustering occurs when a list contains items that are representative of distinguishable categories—e.g., animal, vegetable, and mineral. In this case, clustering is evident when the learner tends to recall items in groups according to such categories (Bousfield, 1953; Bousfield & others, 1958). Associative clustering occurs when a list contains words in which one word is a common response to another—e.g., chair as a response to table. In this case, clustering occurs as a function of the associative strength between the words (Cofer, 1965).

The influence of contextual organization on the basis of learned syntactic and semantic rules is being increasingly recognized in the study of organizational factors in rote verbal learning. Contextual organization, as an independent variable, has been studied in free recall and in the serial acquisition of strings of verbal material. Increasing approximations to continuous English text results in recall that increases as the material approaches English. Recall increases rapidly through the low orders of approximation to English with little change once a certain level of approximation is reached (G. Miller & Selfridge, 1950; Deese, 1961). Syntactic constraints by themselves have been studied through the retention of essentially the grammatical features of ordinary English, substituting nonsense material for nouns, verbs, etc. The syntactically structured strings are learned more rapidly than unstructured ones, even when both strings are semantically meaningless (Epstein, 1962). Both syntactic and semantic aspects of verbal material also facilitate their acquisition. Normal sentences, retaining either syntactic or semantic form, give higher recall scores than random word strings (Marks & Miller, 1964). As meaning and structure is introduced into verbal materials, many new variables interject themselves for study (G. Miller, 1962; Mandler, 1962).

Mediated Association. Mediation, defined as association learning between events where their contiguity is not evident, occurs through the common elements of organizational structuring that have been described above: clustering, contextual organization, etc. In the context of rote verbal learning, the principle of mediation asserts that associations sometimes come about between two elements *a* and *b* because they are both associated with a third element *c*. The third term serves to bridge the gap between two noncontiguous terms. Much effort has been made to analyze this hypothesized process and to describe the apparently noncontiguous associations which humans learn. Mediation behavior has been defined in a variety of experimental paradigms, and its occurrence or nonoccurrence under various conditions has been the subject of experimentation and theoretical explanation (Osgood, 1952; J. Jenkins, 1963). Verbal mediation also facilitates learning of nonverbal events; for example, it has been shown that words encode a visual display, so that the greater the difficulty in describing the pattern (or the greater the number of words needed to describe it) the less accurately it can be reproduced (Glanzer & Clark, 1963). Mediation, while generally thought of as a covert process, also appears to be a behavior which can be elicited, reinforced, and learned as readily as overt behaviors. Mediation is best thought of not as an automatic, unlearned process but as a behavioral act which depends upon the previous behavior of the learner and the conditions present in the immediate learning situation (J. Jenkins, 1963). In general, the behavior involved in mediation occurs through a chain of associative links or as a function of organizing concepts and rules which permit a variety of stimuli to be associated with a common concept or principle which enables a particular response to be generated (Deese & Hulse, 1967).

In recent years, the study of rote verbal-learning tasks has undergone some changes in perspective. A first point is that in the past, traditional association theory and the related laboratory techniques have been based upon two primary assumptions: (1) that a major element of learning is the paired contingency obviously apparent in list learning and (2) that it is necessary to keep at a minimum the possible influence of preexisting, preinstructional behavior. These two assumptions have dictated the emphasis on paired-associate and list learning tasks and on theory concerned with behavior in the learning of simple word pairs. Experimental evidence has shown that the behavior of the subject is less under the control of the experimental conditions than the experimenter has imagined. As a result, organizational factors or modes of response which result from the entering behavior of the subject and from the properties of a particular task have gained prominence as experimental variables.

A second point is that the associative laws in rote verbal learning are being restated in terms of the fundamental processes observed in other areas of human and infrahuman learning described earlier in this review. For example, data on the structure of associations among words are interpreted in terms of elements that are related because they are contrasted in some way (discrimination) and of elements which can be grouped because of common characteristics (generalization or acquired similarity) (Deese, 1965). The persistent and tightly planned research on contiguous paired learning may have obscured the relationship of rote verbal learning to other categories of behavior, and restricted the behavioral processes involved so that it has been difficult to devise experimental situations to bring them under appropriate control. During the past decade the area of verbal learning has grown at a very rapid rate, and much is changing in the field (Keppel, 1968).

PSYCHOLINGUISTICS. When human beings use language, they continuously produce utterances which may be quite new to the speaker or the listener but which, at the same time, are recognized by both as conforming to some rules which permit communication. Learning the structural rules or grammar of a language is a major task of the language learner, but until recently little psychological work has been concerned with it. Two reasons for this neglect are (1) the nature of the tasks generally used in the study of verbal learning and (2) the lack of adequate task analyses of language performance. At the present time, psychologists are involved in active study of the grammatical aspects of language, capitalizing on the systematic analyses provided by developments in linguistics (Lees, 1957; Ervin-Tripp & Slobin, 1966). The linguist has classified primarily two aspects of language: (1) the rules, structures, and transformations that make up the syntax of the language, and (2) the classes of units or parts of speech that the syntax orders. Within this context the psychologist is concerned with such questions as how the syntactic structure is learned and developed, what psychological processes influence these changes, what determines the use of particular syntactic forms under various conditions of performance in the adult, and how the speaker generates and the listener assigns parts of speech to appropriate categories.

For a number of years, psychologists working in this area have taken as their language model a finite-state grammar. Since the elements in English occur sequentially, the reasonable assumption is that each succeeding word should be probabilistically dependent on the preceding words. A Markov-type generating procedure seems useful for this model, since the probabilities at each transition point depend upon previous experience and learning, that experience providing both the lexicon and the rules of grammar involved in this transition (Osgood, 1963). Recently, it has been argued that such a finite-state generator could not produce the potentially infinite set of grammatical structures, including the novel ones that characterize any natural language (Chomsky, 1957). The Markov model also does not seem to be able to handle the deep embedding of qualifying clauses that characterize sentences in natural languages. To account for these difficulties, a phrase-structure grammar is employed which permits a sentence to be resolved into immediate constituents, such as a noun phrase plus a verb phrase, which are further broken down into their immediate constituents, which again may be further broken down. At each level "rewrite rules" prescribe the operation of going from one level of analysis to the next. When the structure of the sentence is laid out, words from a stored vocabulary (dictionary or lexicon) can be assigned to the elements of the sentence. This procedure defines a generative grammar in which certain rules of transformation are applied to basic, or kernel, sentences, and these sentences are rewritten according to these rules until the desired sentence is derived (G. Miller, 1962). Implicit in this analysis of grammatical structure provided by linguists is the assumption that the speaker of the language generates the grammatical structure of speech by applying these transformational rules. The rules specify the structure of basic word strings, or kernels, the ways in which these kernels may be transformed into new structures, and the ways the resulting structures incorporate a lexicon and are actualized in the spoken word. The model is presented, and it is assumed that it is related to the way individuals behave; it is this assumption about the behavior of individuals that provides a challenge to psychologists (Carroll, 1964a). Whether or not this model is useful as a theory of behavior, a central problem in psycholinguistics is to explain how humans acquire the kind of language competence described by linguists.

The impressive work of the linguists in analyzing language performance has had a significant influence on the study of verbal behavior. Syntactic categories, largely ignored in the traditional work in verbal learning, now appear as components of stimulus and response. The syntactic dimensions of word associations are being investigated (Deese, 1965). In paired-associate learning, the influence of syntactic categories has been shown by studying the different effects of content and function words (Glanzer, 1962). Systematic changes in word association have been shown to be correlated with increases in the ability to handle new words grammatically (Brown & Berko, 1960; Berko & Brown, 1960). The learning of syntactic and grammatical categories is being carefully investigated in young children. Theoretical learning models have been suggested for the process by which a child builds up the grammatical classes necessary for speech (J. Jenkins & Palermo, 1964). A generative grammar has been constructed on the basis of samples of the utterances of young children (Brown & Fraser, 1963). The learning of the grammatical order of words has been described in terms of "contextual generalization," which comes about when a child learns the position of a unit in a word sequence (Braine, 1963). These units are phrases within sentences, sequences of phrases, and morphemes within phrases. The learning of locations involves the process of learning the sounds of units in the temporal positions in which they recur. Thus, the child learns, one at a time, that each of a small number of words belongs in a particular position in an utterance; he learns to say *that doggy* but would never say or literally respond to *doggy that*. He learns, in the earliest phase of speech, that certain words act as pivots which occur in an initial position or in a final position and that these pivotal words are either preceded or followed by many of the words in his vocabulary. During this first phase, language grows structurally by the formation of new pivot words and by the child's learning the position of new words; the language grows in vocabulary as words are placed around these pivots, and in a sense, elementary syntax and a lexicon are built up. Linguists have made direct applications to the teaching of reading and spelling that have involved the detailed analysis of the relationship between the sounds of English and the orthography used to represent sounds (Fries, 1963).

Linguistic analysis has had a strong influence on

the restructuring of the work in verbal learning; however, much work still centers on the laboratory rote verbal-learning tasks, such as paired-associate and serial learning, previously described. While this work is of much scientific interest in verbal learning, it seems quite remote from language tasks in the classroom, since practically all the work has concerned itself with the learning of relationships between words and between nonsense syllables without regard to the influence of grammatical classes or the role of words in linguistic structures (Carroll, 1964a). While recent trends have emphasized syntactic behavior, "meaning" continues to be a problem needing a satisfactory method of experimental attack (Ervin-Tripp & Slobin, 1966). In this area, the work of psychologists has included the following: (1) associative meaning, involving various measures of similarity of meaning based on the overlap between associations to words (Marshall & Cofer, 1963; Underwood & Schulz, 1960; Deese, 1965); (2) the semantic differential, which appears to be a measure of metaphorical or affective connotation as distinguished from a measure of denotation (Osgood & others, 1957; Carroll, 1959); and (3) semantic generalization of conditioning indexes which involve the generalization of conditioned autonomic responses, e.g., galvanic skin response and heart rate, as measures of meaning similarity (Feather, 1965; Razran, 1961). Attempts have been made to consider linguistic notions in the area of semantics (Katz & Fodor, 1963). Further, the results obtained in many areas of learning through the manipulation of reinforcement variables are impressive enough so that such variables need to be included in studies of the learning of language. The literature on reinforcement variables in verbal behavior is sparse, but the number of studies is increasing (Holz & Azrin, 1966; Dulany, 1961). Another area in which an active trend seems to be continuing is that of the effect of language behavior on learning, involving such aspects as the effect of verbal instructions and labeling and the postulated effects of internal verbal mediation (or covert language control) on cognitive behavior and self-direction (Ervin-Tripp & Slobin, 1966).

MEMORY. Operationally speaking, "remembering" and "forgetting" refer to what takes place in the interval between the occurrence of learning and subsequent use of the learned behavior. The behavior referred to as "remembering" consists of such behaviors as reconstructing memories of the past or recalling some performance learned in the past, e.g., riding a bicycle, recognizing something that is familiar, or relearning a performance that has been to some extent forgotten. Traditional explanations of forgetting have included the following: (1) passive decay through disuse, as in Thorndike's law of disuse (E. Thorndike, 1913); (2) systematic distortion of memory, in which there are qualitative changes in what is remembered, such as have been shown in experiments on testimony; (3) interference effects, which suggest that forgetting is not so much passive decay over time but rather is determined by new learning or previous learning that interferes with memory; and (4) motivated forgetting, as exemplified by the principles of repression whereby memories become inaccessible because they relate to personal problems, or by the Zeigarnik effect, which hypothesizes that unfinished tasks are remembered more readily than finished tasks. In recent years, memory has been the center of increasing interdisciplinary interest, with studies being carried out in biochemistry, neurophysiology, and psychology. Within psychology, new experiments have changed the emphasis of what are significant variables for study, and there has been an increasingly strong theoretical interest in explaining the nature of the memory process (Melton, 1963; Adams, 1967; Keppel, 1968).

Work on the memory process has centered on three main issues. One is the dependence of memory retrieval on the reinstatement or similarity of stimulus conditions from trial to trial, the general principle being that remembering is a decreasing function of the amount of stimulus change from one trial to another (something like generalization decrement). Failure of memory in this case is a function of stimulus change. A second issue is the interaction of memory elements or traces. This is the focus of the interference theory of forgetting, which hypothesizes that memory retrieval is a function of the interactions between prior learning and new learning. From this point of view, failure of memory is the result of interference. When new learning interferes with old, the phenomenon is called retroactive inhibition. When prior learning interferes with the learning of new material, it is called proactive inhibition. A third issue is the relationship between repetition and memory. In recent developments, this issue has been reanalyzed into the examination of whether there is a fundamental discontinuity between memory established by a single repetition (short-term memory) and memory established by multiple repetitions or single repetitions with an opportunity for consolidation (long-term memory).

A significant development in interference theory has been the emphasis that a major mechanism influencing memory is long-term proactive inhibition as a result of prior language habits (Underwood, 1957; Underwood & Postman, 1960; Postman, 1961). A reanalysis of early experiments in combination with new experiments suggests the potentially greater importance of proactive inhibition (interference generated by previous learning) than of retroactive inhibition (interference generated by new learning) and suggests that proactive inhibition may be attributable to interference coming from outside the laboratory situation. This extraexperimental interference is more likely to be proactive than retroactive because the opportunity for acquiring competing verbal habits is greater prior to the experiment than during the relatively short time intervals used in laboratory investigations of retention. While losses in retention can result from interference by verbal behavior that occurs before or after a particular learning session, the new emphasis on proactive inhibition attributes forgetting primarily to interference from stable language habits with which the learner enters the learning situation. These notions have some important implications for the future direction of research on forgetting. Psychologists studying verbal learning are spending less time devising materials which strip away the influence of previously established verbal habits, as was Ebbinghaus' intention when he invented the nonsense syllable and as has been the intention of much of rote verbal-learning research. The strategy of the new type of studies, it has been suggested, will require the assessment of the staus of existing language habits in the subject prior to new learning, the definition of new learning tasks with explicit recognition of elements of the new task in relation to preexisting ones, and the measurement not only of the retention of new learning but of the recovery and memory of old learning which may interfere with it (Melton, 1961).

In recent years, duplex theories of memory have been proposed (Atkinson & Shiffrin, 1968; Broadbent, 1963; Waugh & Norman, 1965) which essentially postulate two components of the memory system: a short-erm memory store and a long-term memory store. The short-term store (STS) may be regarded as an individual's "working memory." The STS has a limited capacity, and information in it decays relatively rapidly over time; information in it can also be displaced by new incoming information. The long-term store (LTS) differs from the STS in that information stored in it is relatively permanent and does not decay and become lost. The LTS has a relatively unlimited capacity, although it may be modified or rendered temporarily irretrievable as a result of distortion or interference from incoming information. The LTS seems to involve the kind of decay and interference characteristics that have been investigated in the classical studies of memory. In the STS, in the LTS, and in the transfer between the two, it is postulated that the individual uses certain "control processes" to handle the memory task. These control processes involve storage, search, and retrieval strategies, and their particular mode of employment depends upon such factors as instructional set, the experimental task, and the past history of the subject. The main control mechanism for increasing storage in STS is a rehearsal process. Since the number of items of information that can be rehearsed is limited by the capacity of STS, information in STS in excess of the rehearsal capability decays at a rapid rate, and search must be performed efficiently. Transfer from short-term to long-term memory store involves coding processes. The information temporarily stored in STS is translated into "chunks" of information that can be readily stored in LTS. Coding processes involve the selective alteration of information so that it is more easily and more compactly stored by the individual. These coding changes can take a number of forms, such as the use of mnemonics, mediating categories, and organizational structures. The individual may organize information by grouping items of information into sets and memorizing the set as a whole rather than as the individual items, or he may break the information into chunks of a desired magnitude that facilitate remembering. Once information is transferred to the LTS, it is available for retrieval for subsequent remembering. In order to carry out a retrieval process, the individual can search the information according to certain organizational patterns, i.e., geographically, alphabetically, or temporally. It also seems reasonable to conjecture that cues or labels with which the individual enters LTS can determine the success or failure of the retrieval process. In contrast to these control processes which the individual implements, the processes of decay and interference are features which pertain to the underlying operation of memory. Within LTS, the work on interference theory would indicate that the effects of proactive and retroactive inhibition would cause confusion and competition between components that are similar and make search and retrieval difficult. At the present time, there are many experiments underway to investigate the speculations of duplex theories of forgetting, and particular features of the theories are being rejected and confirmed by experimental evidence (Atkinson & Shiffrin, 1968; Keppel, 1968).

CONCEPT LEARNING. The learning of concepts has been of sustained interest to psychologists and educators (Hull, 1920; Bruner & others, 1956; Bourne, 1966; Brownell & Hendrickson, 1950; Carroll, 1964b; Glaser, 1968). In general terms, concepts inject both a uniformity and adaptability into behavior; as concepts are learned, they establish what particular experiences have in common with other events and also indicate the extent to which they differ from each other. Concepts are learned by experience with appropriate and inappropriate instances or exemplars of a class; properties of these exemplars are abstracted and become the stimuli according to which an instance is classified as a member or a nonmember of a concept class. The formation of a concept and the process of abstraction are probably never complete; while simple concepts may become reasonably stable, subtle and complex ones constantly undergo emendation and revision as new instances occur. Operationally speaking, conceptual behavior involves the making of a common response to different stimuli; in contrast, in a paired-associate task, a different response is learned for each stimulus. In a concept task, the individual responds in one way to a *set* of stimuli and in another way to another *set*. In this sense, events are categorized by discriminating between instances and noninstances of a category or class, and, within a category, behavior is generalized so that a new instance with relevant properties is included in the concept class. When potential class instances are presented to the learner, they involve a number of attributes according to which they might be categorized. Some of these attributes are relevant to the concept being formed, and others are irrelevant to it. The concept-learning task usually involves the necessity for discriminating between irrelevant attributes and those attributes or combination of attributes which define the concept class.

In general, then, concept learning involves generalizing within classes and discriminating between classes. For example, given three sets of geometric figures—e.g., triangles, quadrilaterals, and circles—

the student learns these three concepts when he generalizes among the various kinds of triangles and categorizes them correctly as "triangles" and when he discriminates between the three classes of figures and labels them as belonging to different categories. Knowledge of whether concept learning has taken place is obtained when the learner makes these appropriate category responses and is able to apply the "classification rule" (verbalizable or not) to a new set of instances involving the concept attributes. The kind of rule by which attributes are combined to form a particular concept determines, to a large extent, the complexity and nature of the concept. When a rule is not too complex, it is possible that a student can memorize the instances that belong to that category without learning the rule; such a possibility leads to the concern in school learning about whether the student has "just memorized" or "really learned" the concept.

In studies of concept learning (Bourne, 1966; T. Kendler, 1961; H. Kendler, 1964) many different variables have been investigated: the effect of learning from positive and negative concept instances (Bruner & others, 1956; Hovland & Weiss, 1953); the number of relevant and irrelevant attributes involved (Shepard & others, 1961); the redundancy of concept instances (Bourne & Haygood, 1961); the order and sequence in which concept instances are presented to the learner (Hovland & Weiss, 1953; Detambel & Stolurow, 1956); the perceptual salience and dominance of concept attributes (Heidbreder, 1946a, 1946b; Grant & others, 1949; Wohlwill, 1957); the effects of prior verbal associations (Underwood & Richardson, 1956); reinforcement schedules (Green, 1955); and the amount and nature of information feedback (Buss & Buss, 1956; Suppes, 1965; Asuma & Crombach, 1966). A prominent experimental finding is that individuals do not learn efficiently from negative instances even when the informational content of these instances is equated to that of positive instances. It also appears that the difficulty of concept learning is related to the number of relevant attributes and that the addition of even a single irrelevant attribute adds considerably to the difficulty of the task. Task conditions have been analyzed to some extent in terms of the following: how the objective of the concept learning task is defined, the nature of the instances encountered, the opportunity for feedback and the validation of instances, the consequences of making correct or incorrect categorizations, and the nature of imposed procedural restrictions such as speed requirements and the opportunity for memory and record keeping (Bruner & others, 1956).

With some exceptions, the kind of concept rule that has been studied in the laboratory has been the conjunctive or disjunctive combination of attributes where the defining rule is their joint presence or absence. Recently, different types of concepts have begun to be investigated and logical operators other than conjunction and disjunction are being examined, e.g., exclusion, negation, and certain conditional rules (Haygood & Bourne, 1965). The empirical finding is that logical complexity is a factor contributing to the difficulty in concept learning. However, examination of the experimental literature makes it clear that the work on concept learning has been primarily performed with particular kinds of concept rules, and other types of concepts related to school subject learning need to be examined. Many school-learning concepts deal with relations among dimensions rather than their combined presence or absence; for example, such concepts as "many," "few," and "average" require the learner to think in terms of the relationships between a base quantity and a reference quantity. In addition, new concepts learned in school depend upon concept attributes which themselves represent concepts and depend upon a network of prerequisite concepts. This notion of the hierarchical structure of concept learning has been pointed out with respect to the teaching of mathematical concepts to children (Suppes, 1966). Research on the learning of concept hierarchies will undoubtedly emphasize the importance of measuring transfer effects as a way of assessing the effectiveness of instruction.

Other new looks at the study of concept formation are taking place. It has been pointed out (Bourne, 1966) that concept-learning problems in which the rule is neither familiar nor simple have not been studied very often. Typical concept-learning studies have emphasized the indentification of relevant attributes, and once the relevant attributes have been identified, the rule involving them is trivial or previously indicated to the learner in some way. Problems wherein the rule needs to be learned or discovered have been examined less often. Also, little research is available on concept learning in different sensory modalities, for example, auditory concept formation, which seems related to the teaching of music, and sensitivity to language tones. Language concepts and the influence of language on concept learning are essential aspects of school learning, and, although in the past most of the work in the learning laboratory has been on nonverbal concept attributes, such as geometric figures, work is increasing on language and language influences. The ability to use words appears to be an important factor in the speed of concept acquisition, and required verbalization may facilitate concept learning in very young children (Dietze, 1955; Jensen, 1966). However, the correlation between verbalization of a rule and correct responding is not clear, and verbalizations are not always a guarantee that categorizing behavior will be appropriate (Green, 1955). In addition, the fact that there is a difference between children and adults in performing solution shifts in concept problems suggests the influence of verbal mediation and of prior verbal habits (Kendler & Kendler, 1962).

Theories of concept learning have been interesting but have not contributed much to new information or to the search for it. Theoretical descriptions and formalism in this area have generally been used to flex the muscles of the theories themselves and examine how adequate they are to describe experimental data. Stochastic mathematical models (Bourne & Restle, 1959; Bower & Trabasso, 1964) have handled only the simplest situations; these models, however, have emphasized the issue of incremental versus one-trial learning, a question which may be significant for classroom learning (Suppes, 1965; Grier & Bornstein, 1966). Information-processing models (Simon & Kotovsky, 1963; Hunt, 1962; Reitman, 1965) are of interest in two ways: (1) they provide a description of the characteristics of skillful conceptual performance; and (2) they suggest a methodology of investigation which is sensitive to the individual differences among learners (Gregg, 1967). It would seem that concept learning, standing in a central position between basic and more complex behaviors, should be one of the main points of contact between various theories of behavior, as well as between behavior and its theoretical description. Finally, it is to be pointed out that present knowledge of concept learning has been quite directly applied to the teaching of the discriminations and generalizations required to produce conceptual behavior (Mechner, 1965).

PROBLEM SOLVING AND THINKING. Definition of problem solving and thinking and specification of the tasks and task environments that are identified as those in which problem solving and thinking take place have not constituted a very systematic endeavor in the psychology of learning. One thinks of the puzzles and problems used in psychological experiments such as the two-string problem, "twenty questions," the water-jar problem, Wertheimer's parallelogram, anagrams, trouble-shooting problems, and reversal-shift problems. Upon examination of such tasks, one is impressed with the diversity in the field and with the fact that many of the tasks employed are of a puzzle or game variety which are not especially designed to investigate problem situations relevant to various subject matters (Ray, 1955). It seems reasonable to include both problem solving and thinking in the same category; a recent detailed analysis and attempt at systematizing psychological work in this area employs the term "directed thinking" and defines it as thinking whose function it is to convey solutions to problems (Berlyne, 1965). Less experimental work is available on "autistic thinking," as exemplified by daydreaming or generalized free association.

In the studies that have been performed on problem solving, a major consideration that has been emphasized is that the identity or pattern of the stimuli (objects or events) in the situation changes in the course of problem solving. Objects take on different functions so that a solution can be achieved; as a consequence, stimuli are used or combined in a way that is different from the way in which they are presented or from the way in which they are most familiarly used. The responses of an individual achieving a solution are not tied to a particular physical configuration of the stimulus situation; rather, he imposes a reorganization upon these stimuli or sees in them a particular relationship which is generalizable to a similar class of problems, as is the case, for example, in transposition or oddity problems. Another aspect of problem solving is that an individual utilizes instructions which influence his behavior. Instructions serve such functions as "defining the problem," "providing an understanding of the goal," "establishing a set," and "introducing direction"; psychologists have been and are concerned with the analysis and investigation of such variables (Gagné, 1964; Duncan, 1959; Goldiamond, 1966). It has also been postulated that in the course of problem solving and thinking, an individual instructs himself through covert language and defines his strategy in that way (Skinner, 1957). It has been suggested (Gagné 1965*b*) that problem solving and thinking take place through the use of rules or principles which are built up from previously learned concepts. A rule specifies a relationship between concepts, and a higher-order rule is defined as a relationship between previously learned rules. In problem solving these rules are used to achieve some goal, and what emerges from problem solving is the combination of rules into a higher-order principle which the individual learns and generalizes to a variety of problems in a given class of situations. With respect to education, this implies that prerequisite concepts and rules must be taught to the learner in order for him to be successful in a problem-solving task. A successful course of instruction would ensure that necessary prior learning is in the student's repertoire because without this prior mastery, he would not have the concepts and rules of a particular subject matter available for use.

The study of higher-order cognitive behavior has been the focus of information-processing models of thinking (Reitman, 1965). These models assume that the human organism can be conceptualized as an information-processing system, and they attempt to examine thinking in terms of the processes and strategies by which an individual goes about thinking through a problem. The processes involved are set down precisely in terms of charts of information flow. These flow charts specifically define a program which attempts to simulate human cognitive activity. The first significant attempt to do this involved a description of a program called the Logic Theorist, which described an information-processing system that proved theorems in symbolic logic with which only humans had been able to deal previously (Newell & Simon, 1956; Newell & Shaw, 1957; Newell & others, 1958). The Logic Theorist did not try to solve problems by the brute-force technique of searching through all possible sequences of logical operations until one was found to yield a proof; rather, the approach taken was for the designers to incorporate in the program methods and rules of thumb (heuristics) of the type used by humans. Human thinking appears to involve such heuristic procedures as analyzing a problem to which the solution is already known in an effort to guide thinking in a present problem, working backwards in trying to solve a problem, and means–end procedures whereby a current state of affairs is compared with a solution to be obtained and the attempt is made to find an operation which reduces the difference between the two states (Polya, 1954, 1957). In chess playing, a heuristic might be such a rule as "Try to control the center of the board." The Logic Theorist made the assumption that programs could be written to solve problems as people do, and it was designed to solve a particular problem. A more significant approach was the development of the General Problem Solver (GPS) (Newell & others, 1960; Simon & Newell, 1964). The GPS represents an attempt to synthesize in a composite program a set of concepts and strategies assumed to underlie human problem solving quite generally, apart from the features that characterize activity in any particular subject area.

Different kinds of programs for concept learning, musical composition, and verbal learning have been presented (Reitman, 1965), and an interesting comparison has been made between the process incorporated in a computer program designed to solve algebra word problems and the behavior of high school and college students (Paige & Simon, 1966). The general method employed in this work is to simulate in detail the problem-solving behavior of human subjects. Data are obtained by asking humans to solve problems, "thinking aloud" as much as possible while they work. The GPS was constructed to describe as closely as possible the behavior of the subjects as revealed by their oral comments and in the steps they write down in working problems. The aim of this research is to understand the information processes that underlie human intellectual and adaptive ability and to construct computer programs that can solve problems requiring such intelligence and adaptation. Varieties of such programs are then matched to the data obtained on human problem solving. This procedure results in very complex and involved descriptions of performance, and the relationship between the kinds of behavior descriptions which result and the more usual methods for developing and verifying formal psychological theories is now being discussed.

PERCEPTUAL–MOTOR-SKILL LEARNING. Interest in on the part of psychologists in perceptual–motor-skill learning has fluctuated over the years and at present seems to be increasing because of man's interaction with complicated machines and because developments outside of psychology in communication models, control-system models, and adaptive systems seem relevant to the construction of explanatory models for perceptual-motor skill. Examples of this kind of behavior abound: behavior involving gross bodily activity, such as walking, jumping, swimming and balancing, and others involving less gross activity, such as manipulating tools and objects or controlling machines (writing, typing, playing a musical instrument, sewing, and driving a car). In general, these behaviors are characterized by a spatial-temporal patterning, the interplay of receptor-effector-feedback processes, and such characteristics as timing, anticipation, and fine adjustment of a response. The phases in skill learning that have generally been identified seem to be the following (Fitts, 1964, 1965): (1) An early cognitive phase, in which some sort of "intellectualization" occurs as the student attempts to understand instructions, to analyze the task, and to verbalize what he is learning. At this point in learning, verbal inputs and "talking through" the task appear to be useful. This phase may be similar to the response-learning stage discussed in rote learning, where coding or the integration of responses occurs. Also in this phase verbal instructions help shape behavior. (2) An intermediate or "automation" phase, which is not unlike the associative stage of rote learning. Stimulus control is established over a response so that responses take place in the presence of specific cues. This stage is characterized by a gradually increasing speed of performance either in terms of decreased time or decreased errors or both. The verbal support which was employed in the early stage of learning appears to drop out or be short-circuited during this second phase, but studies of skill learning in general have not been carried out to examine the detailed nature of this process. A second aspect of this intermediate phase, contributing to apparently increasing "automation," is that as learning continues there is a gradually increasing resistance to stress and to interference from other activities that may be performed concurrently. Neurological evidence suggests that there may be less and less involvement in cortical areas and increasing reliance on proprioceptive feedback and a shift to lower brain centers. Learning during these early and intermediate phases of skill learning might be conceived of as the acquisition of a number of semi-independent sequences (subroutines) which go on successively or concurrently. As learning progresses, these subroutines may be combined, and higher-order executive routines may become established; stimulus sampling and reference to external stimuli become less frequent; coding becomes more efficient; different aspects of the skill become integrated or coordinated; and strategies and decision processes become adapted to or match the probabilities associated with the occurrence of different stimulus sequences. (3) A late learning phase occurs about which there is relatively little experimental data available. Apparently even in quite simple tasks, such as telegraphy, typing, and industrial assembly work, performance continues to improve over millions of cycles of practice. In fact, there appears to be little evidence to contradict the conclusion (Keller, 1958) that a true plateau in skill learning has not been demonstrated and that when such effects are reported they are usually artifacts of measurement. Such very-long-term improvements with practice have been shown in industrial tasks and certainly appear to occur in the development of championship performance in athletics. The leveling off of performance may eventually be due as much to physiological effects, loss of motivation, or both as to the reaching of a true learning asymptote or limit in capacity for further improvement. In this respect skill learning may have a very special characteristic contrasted with other categories of behavior, although in neither case have there been enough studies on long-term learning for definite conclusions to be drawn.

An interesting line of research has been the correlational analysis of performance at different points in time in the course of skill learning (Fleishman, 1966, 1967). These studies reveal changes in the structure of ability at different stages of practice in the same task. The correlations between the kinds of abilities required in early trials and the abilities required in successively remote trials become progressively lower. For example, a particular ability—say, the ability to deal with spatial relations—may be relatively important early in practice because the first thing that the task requires is that the subject learn about certain directional aspects of the stimulus in relation to his response. Early in practice some learners may be better at this than others. Later in training, however, spatial relations may become a less significant aspect of the task, since all subjects learn this component and it no longer differentiates among them. At this time other aspects of performance contribute to the task performance and to subject differences in performance competence. In general, the factor structures of complex skills change with practice, indicating that ability requirements are different at different stages of learning. One implication of this is that aptitude tests which employ validation criteria at a particular stage of learning may give an erroneous picture of the prediction of learning success.

Many of the variables that have been studied in other kinds of behavior have been investigated in skill learning (Bilodeau, 1966). Particularly significant as it is in other areas of learning, information feedback in the form of knowledge of results and reinforcing stimuli also provides a significant influence in skill learning. The information feedback cycle in perceptual-motor performance seems especially prominent in the constant receptor-effector-feedback relationship that occurs in a task such as driving an automobile or playing tennis. There is increasing recognition that many of the processes involved in other forms of learning such as discrimination, short-term memory, and so forth, operate similarly in skill learning; and the identification of this category of behavior as a unique area for study is disappearing.

The work in skill learning has some special implications for instruction. The importance of continuing practice far beyond the point in time when some arbitrary criterion is reached needs to be emphasized. Individuals who have not had a great deal of practice beyond the early and intermediate stages of learning probably do not experience the beneficial increase in resistance to stress, fatigue, and interference that comes from extended overlearning. When the structure of a skill is appropriate, considerable gain may accrue from training on subroutines of a skill where it is difficult to provide "real life" training or the facilities for training on the total skill; subsequent "on-the-job" training can then be carried out on the total task. In a great many skills, subjects may cease to show improvement not because they are incapable of further learning but because some condition of the task environment restricts the opportunity for improvement; most frequently this restriction takes the form of the lack of appropriate performance feedback.

LEARNING AND INSTRUCTIONAL TECHNOLOGY. There is abundant evidence that the psychology of learning is entering a stage in which it can make increasing contact with techniques of instruction and the study of school learning. When the field of learning was reviewed 25 years ago (Melton, 1941; Estes, 1960) it appeared that impenetrable barriers of research tradition, special interest, and linguistic convention demarcated three principal areas: the laboratory study of animal learning, the laboratory study of human learning, and the study of school learning. It was pointed out almost a decade ago (Estes, 1960) that the striking development up to that time was the rapidly accelerated and obviously fruitful interchange of concepts and methods between the first two of these three areas. It was becoming possible to express the communalities and differences of the two areas in a common terminology and to interpret them in a common conceptual structure. (In contrast, it seems that today in some quarters, with the emphasis on complex cognitive, verbal-informational processes, the methods and concepts of the study of human learning vis-à-vis animal learning are drawing apart.) No such progress, it was said, could be reported toward bridging the gap between laboratory psychology and the study of school learning. The documentation for this was that, with rather few exceptions, reports of research on learning in the classroom carried no reference to the contemporary psychological literature and showed no signs of its influence.

At the present time, however, after another decade has gone by, there is evidence to report that this gap is narrowing. Experimental psychologists are turning their thinking and their enterprises to the analysis and investigation of the educational, instructional process (Skinner, 1958; Bruner, 1960; Holland, 1960; Lumsdaine & Glaser, 1960; Bugelski, 1964; Hilgard, 1964; Suppes, 1964; Gagné, 1965a; Gibson, 1965; Gilbert, 1965; Glaser, 1965; Groen & Atkinson, 1965; O. Moore & Anderson, in press). It was reported that the yearbook of the National Society for the Study of Education *Learning and Instruction* published in 1950 (Anderson, 1950) did not list Hull, Skinner, Spence, or Tolman in its index. The yearbook on the same topic in 1964 (Hilgard, 1964) lists them all in abundance, and the yearbook itself contains many chapters written by experimental psychologists. The Behavioral Sciences Subpanel of the President's Science Advisory Committee in 1962 specifically called for research in the behavioral sciences relevant to education. Of significance is the fact that research and development have been sponsored by the government to foster the interplay between behavioral science and the educational process. Centers have been established to develop mechanisms and agencies where the process of research, development, and application leading to the design of educational materials and procedures, as described earlier in this review, can be carried out.

There may be emerging an instructional technology based upon an underlying science of learning. Technology in this sense does not necessarily mean hardware and instrumentation, but it does mean technology in the sense of an applied discipline like engineering or medicine. The techniques and procedures which are used by the practitioners of these technological disciplines grow out of the findings in their underlying sciences and also grow by informing science of their needs. Instructional technology is taking a certain shape: (1) The analysis of tasks and task environments and the behavioral specification of educational objectives and subject-matter competence are becoming increasingly important endeavors (Lindvall, 1964). The question of what is being learned is being asked so that the study of how it can be learned can be examined with relevance to the subject matter. (2) Individual differences and the behavior with which an individual begins a learning experience are being increasingly taken into account in studies of learning and instruction. This is resulting in interaction between two rather independent traditions of psychology, individual-difference measurement and experimental psychology (Cronbach, 1957; Gagné, 1967). (3) The variables influencing the instructional process for tasks relevant to school learning are being examined in many quarters (Gagné, 1965b; Ausubel, 1967; Travers, 1964; Hilgard, 1964; Shulman & Keislar, 1966). (4) Questions are being raised about the appropriate methodology for the measurement and evaluation of the outcomes of learning (Glaser, 1963; Cronbach, 1963). These stirrings have significant implications for the future shape of learning theory and experimentation. Learning theories will take on different requirements. In all probability, in contrast to their present form, they will be more amenable to the social and developmental differences between individuals; they will take on more cognitive, subject-matter-like tasks; and they will pay attention to the design of experiments that optimize rather than only comparing conditions for learning.

Robert Glaser
University of Pittsburgh

References

Adams, Jack A. *Human Memory*. McGraw-Hill, 1967. 326p.

Amsel, Abram. "The Role of Frustrative Nonreward in Noncontinuous Reward Situations." *Psychol B* 55:102–19; 1958.

Amsel, Abram. "Frustrative Nonreward in Partial Reinforcement and Discrimination Learning." *Psychol R* 69:306–28; 1962.

Anderson, G. Lester. (Ed.) *Learning and Instruction*. 49th Yearbook, Part I, NSSE. U Chicago Press, 1950.

Atkinson, Richard C. "The Observing Response in Discrimination Learning." *J Exp Psychol* 62:253–62; 1961.

Atkinson, Richard C., and Shiffrin, R. M. "Human Memory: A Proposed System and Its Control Processes." In Spence, Kenneth W., and Spence, Janet T. (Eds.) *The Psychology of Learning and Motivation: Advances in Research and Theory*, Vol. 2. Academic, 1968.

Ausubel, David P. *Learning Theory and Classroom Practice*. Ontario Institute Studies in Education, 1967. 34p.

Azrin, N. H., and Holz, W. C. "Punishment." In Honig, Werner K. (Ed.) *Operant Behavior: Areas of Research and Application*. Appleton, 1966. p. 380–477.

Azuma, Hiroshi, and Cronbach, Lee J. "Concept Attainment with Probabilistic Feedback." In Hammond, H. K. (Ed.) *The Psychology of Egon Brunswick*. Holt, 1966. p. 258–76.

Bandura, Albert. "Social Learning Through Imitation." In Jones, Marshall R. (Ed.) *Nebraska Symposium on Motivation*. U Nebraska Press, 1962. p. 211–69.

Bandura, Albert. "Vicarious Processes: A Case of No-trial Learning." In Berkowitz, Leonard. (Ed.) *Advances in Experimental Social Psychology*, Vol. 2. Academic, 1965.

Baron, Martin R. "The Stimulus, Stimulus Control, and Stimulus Generalization." In Mostofsky, David I. (Ed.) *Stimulus Generalization*. Stanford U Press, 1965. p. 62–71.

Battig, William F., and Brackett, H. R. "Comparison of Anticipation and Recall Methods in Paired-associate Learning." *Psychol Reports* 9:59–65; 1961.

Battig, William F., and others. "Constant vs. Varied Serial Order in Paired-associate Learning." *Psychol Reports* 12:695–721; 1963.

Berko, Jean, and Brown, Roger. "Psycholinguistic Research Methods." In Mussen, Paul H. (Ed.) *Handbook of Research Methods in Child Development*. Wiley, 1960. p. 517–57.

Berlyne, D. E. *Conflict, Arousal, and Curiosity*. McGraw-Hill, 1960. 350p.

Berlyne, D. E. *Structure and Direction in Thinking*. Wiley, 1965. 378p.

Bilodeau, Edward A. (Ed.) *Acquisition of Skill*. Academic, 1966. 539p.

Bourne, Lyle E., Jr. *Human Conceptual Behavior*. Allyn and Bacon, 1966. 139p.

Bourne, Lyle E., Jr., and Haygood, Robert C. "Supplementary Report: Effect of Redundant Relevant Information upon the Identification of Concepts." *J Exp Psychol* 61:259–60; 1961.

Bourne, Lyle E., Jr., and Restle, Frank. "Mathematical Theory of Concept Identification." *Psychol R* 66:278–96; 1959.

Bousfield, Weston A. "The Occurrence of Clustering in the Recall of Randomly Arranged Associates." *J Gen Psychol* 49:229–40; 1953.

Bousfield, Weston A., and others. "Associative Clustering in the Recall of Words of Different Taxonomic Frequencies of Occurrence." *Psychol Reports* 4:39–44; 1958.

Bower, Gordon H., and Trabasso, Thomas R. "Concept Identification." In Atkinson, Richard C. (Ed.) *Studies in Mathematical Psychology*. Stanford U Press, 1964. p. 32–94.

Braine, Martin D. S. "On Learning the Grammatical Order of Words." *Psychol R* 70:323–48; 1963.

Broadbent, D. E. "Flow of Information Within the Organism." *J Verbal Learning Verbal Behavior* 2:34–40; 1963.

Brown, Roger, and Berko, Jean. "Word Association and the Acquisition of Grammar." *Child Develop* 31:1–14; 1960.

Brown, Roger, and Fraser, Colin. "The Acquisition of Syntax." In Bellugi, Ursala, and Brown, Roger. (Eds.) "The Aquisition of Language." *Monogr Social Res Child Develop* 29(1) (Serial No. 92): 43–79;

Brownell, William A., and Hendrickson, Gordon. "How Children Learn Information, Concepts, and Generalizations." In Anderson, G. Lester. (Ed.) *Learning and Instruction*, 49th Yearbook, Part I, NSSE. U Chicago Press, 1950. p. 92–128.

Bruner, Jerome S. *The Process of Education.* Harvard U Press, 1960. 97p.

Bruner, Jerome S. "Some Theorems on Instruction Illustrated with Reference to Mathematics." In *Theories of Learning and Instruction*, 63rd Yearbook, Part I, NSSE. U Chicago Press, 1964. p. 306–35.

Bruner, Jerome S., and others. *A Study of Thinking.* Wiley, 1956. 330p.

Bugelski, B. R. "Presentation Time, Total Time, and Mediation in Paired-associate Learning." *J Exp Psychol* 63:409–12; 1962.

Bugelski, B. R. *The Psychology of Learning Applied to Teaching.* Bobbs-Merrill, 1964. 278p.

Buss, Arnold H., and Buss, Edith H. "The Effect of Verbal Reinforcement Combinations on Conceptual Learning." *J Exp Psychol* 52:282–7; 1956.

Carroll, John B. Review of Osgood and others' *The Measurement of Meaning. Lang* 35:58–77; 1959.

Carroll, John B. "Linguistics and the Psychology of Language." *R Ed Res* 34:119–26; 1964(*a*).

Carroll, John B. "Words, Meanings and Concepts." *Harvard Ed R* 34:178–202; 1964(*b*).

Chomsky, Noam. *Syntactic Structures.* Mouton & Co., 1957. 118p.

Cofer, Charles N. "On Some Factors in the Organizational Characteristics of Free Recall." *Am Psychologist* 20:261–72; 1965.

Cook, John O., and Spitzer, Morton E. "Supplementary Report: Prompting Versus Confirmation in Paired-associate Learning." *J Exp Psychol* 59:272–6; 1960.

Cronbach, Lee J. "The Two Disciplines of Scientific Psychology." *Am Psychologist* 12:671–84; 1957.

Cronbach, Lee J. "Evaluation for Course Improvement." *Teach Col Rec* 64:672–83; 1963.

Cross, David V. "Metric Properties of Multidimensional Stimulus Generalization." In Mostofsky, David I. (Ed.) *Stimulus Generalization.* Stanford U Press, 1965. p. 72–93.

Deese, James. "From the Isolated Verbal Unit to Connected Discourse." In Cofer, Charles N. (Ed.) *Verbal Learning and Verbal Behavior.* McGraw-Hill, 1961. p. 11–31.

Deese, James. *The Structure of Associations in Language and Thought.* Johns Hopkins Press, 1965. 216p.

Deese, James, and Hulse, Stewart H. *The Psychology of Learning*, 3rd ed. McGraw-Hill, 1967. 514p.

Deese, James, and Kresse, Frederick H. "An Experimental Analysis of the Errors in Rote Serial Learning." *J Exp Psychol* 44:199–202; 1952.

Detambel, Marvin H., and Stolurow, Lawrence. "Stimulus Sequence and Concept Learning." *J Exp Psychol* 57:34–40; 1956.

Dietze, Doris. "The Facilitating Effect of Words on Discrimination and Generalization. *J Exp Psychol* 50:255–60; 1955.

Dulany, Don E., Jr. "Hypotheses and Habits in Verbal 'Operant Conditioning.'" *J Abn Social Psychol* 63:251–63; 1961.

Duncan, Carl P. "Recent Research on Human Problem Solving." *Psychol B* 56:397–429; 1959.

Ebenholtz, Sheldon M. "Serial Learning: Position Learning and Sequential Associations." *J Exp Psychol* 66:353–62; 1963.

Epstein, William A. "A Further Study of the Influence of Syntactical Structure on Learning." *Am J Psychol* 75:121–6; 1962.

Ervin-Tripp, Susan M., and Slobin, Dan I. "Psycholinguistics." *Annual R Psychol* 17:435–74; 1966.

Estes, William K. "An Experimental Study of Punishment." *Psychol Monogr* 57 (No. 263); 1944. 40p.

Estes, William K. "Learning." In Harris, Chester W. (Ed.) *Encyclopedia of Educational Research*, 3rd ed. Macmillan, 1960. p. 752–70.

Estes, William K., and Skinner, B. F. "Some Quantitative Properties of Anxiety." *J Exp Psychol* 29:390–400; 1941.

Feather, Ben W. "Semantic Generalization of Classically Conditioned Responses: A Review." *Psychol B* 63:425–41; 1965.

Ferster, Charles B., and Skinner, B. F. *Schedules of Reinforcement.* Appleton, 1957. 741p.

Festinger, Leon. "The Psychological Effects of Insufficient Rewards." *Am Psychologist* 16:1–11; 1961.

Fitts, Paul M. "Perceptual-Motor Skill Learning." In Melton, Arthur W. (Ed.) *Categories of Human Learning.* Academic, 1964. p. 243–85.

Fitts, Paul M. "Factors in Complex Skill Training." In Glaser, Robert. (Ed.) *Training Research and Education.* Wiley, 1965. p. 177–97.

Fleishman, Edwin A. "Comments on Professor Jones' Paper." In Bilodeau, Edward A. (Ed.) *Acquisition of Skill.* Academic, 1966. p. 147–67.

Fleishman, Edwin A. "Individual Differences and Motor Learning." In Gagné, Robert M. (Ed.) *Learning and Individual Differences.* Charles E. Merrill, Inc., 1967. p. 165–91.

Fowler, Harry. *Curiosity and Exploratory Behavior.* Macmillan, 1965. 216p.

Fowler, Harry, and Wischner, George J. "The Varied Functions of Punishment in Discrimination Learning." In Campbell, Byron, and Church, Russell. (Eds.) *Punishment and Aversive Behavior.* Appleton, 1968.

Fries, Charles C. *Linguistics and Reading*. Holt, 1963. 265p.

Gagné, Robert M. "Problem Solving." In Melton, Arthur W. (Ed.) *Categories of Human Learning*. Academic, 1964. p. 293–317.

Gagné, Robert M. "The Analysis of Instructional Objectives for the Design of Instruction." In Glaser, Robert. (Ed.) *Teaching Machines and Programed Learning*, Vol. 2: *Data and Directions*. NEA, 1965(a). p. 21–65.

Gagné, Robert M. *The Conditions of Learning*. Holt, 1965(b). 308p.

Gagné, Robert M. (Ed.) *Learning and Individual Differences*. Charles E. Merrill Books, Inc., 1967. 265p.

Gibson, Eleanor J. "Learning to Read." *Sci* 148:1066–72; 1965.

Gilbert, Thomas F. "Mathetics: The Technology of Education." *J Mathetics* 1:7–74; 1962.

Gilbert, Thomas F. "A Structure for a Coordinated Research and Development Laboratory." In Glaser, Robert. (Ed.) *Training Research and Education*. Wiley, 1965. p. 559–78.

Glanzer, Murray. "Grammatical Category: A Rote Learning and Word Association Analysis." *J Verbal Learning Verbal Behavior* 1:31–41; 1962.

Glanzer, Murray, and Clark, William H. "Accuracy of Perceptual Recall: An Analysis of Organization." *J Verbal Learning Verbal Behavior* 1:289–99; 1963.

Glanzer, Murray, and Peters, Stanley C. "Re-examination of the Serial Position Effect." *J Exp Psychol* 64:258–66; 1962.

Glaser, Robert. "Some Research Problems in Automated Instruction: Instructional Objectives and Subject-matter Structure." In Coulson, John E. (Ed.) *Programmed Learning and Computer-based Instruction*. Wiley, 1962. p. 67–85.

Glaser, Robert. "Instructional Technology and the Measurement of Learning Outcomes: Some Questions." *Am Psychologist* 18:519–21; 1963.

Glaser, Robert. (Ed.) *Teaching Machines and Programed Learning*. Vol. 2: *Data and Directions*. NEA, 1965. 831p.

Glaser, Robert. "The Design of Instruction." In *The Changing American School*, 65th Yearbook, Part II, NSSE. U Chicago Press, 1966. p. 215–42.

Glaser, Robert. "Some Implications of Previous Work on Learning and Individual Differences." In Gagné, Robert. (Ed.) *Learning and Individual Differences*. Charles E. Merrill Books, Inc., 1967. p. 1–18.

Glaser, Robert. "Concept Learning and Concept Teaching." In Gagné, Robert M. (Ed.) *Research Approaches to School-subject Learning*. F. E. Peacock, 1968.

Goldiamond, Israel. "Perception, Language, and Conceptualization Rules." In Kleinmuntz, Benjamin. (Ed.) *Problem Solving: Research, Method, and Theory*. Wiley, 1966. p. 183–224.

Grant, David A. "Classical and Operant Conditioning." In Melton, Arthur W. (Ed.) *Categories of Human Learning*. Academic, 1964. p. 1–31.

Grant, David A., and others. "The Relative Difficulty of the Number, Form, and Color Concepts of a Weigl-type Problem." *J Exp Psychol* 39:552–57; 1949.

Green, Edward J. "Concept Formation: A Problem in Human Operant Conditioning." *J Exp Psychol* 49:175–80; 1955.

Gregg, Lee W. "Internal Representations of Sequential Concepts." In Kleinmuntz, Benjamin. (Ed.) *Concepts and the Structure of Memory*. Wiley, 1967.

Grier, J. Brown, and Bornstein, Robert. "Probability Matching in Concept Identification." *J Exp Psychol* 71:339–42; 1966.

Groen, G. J., and Atkinson, R. C. "Models for Optimizing and Learning Process." *Psychol B* 66:309–20; 1966.

Guttman, Norman, and Kalish, H. I. Discriminability and Stimulus Generalization. *J Exp Psychol* 51:79–88; 1956.

Harlow, Harry F. "The Formation of Learning Sets." *Psychol R* 56:51–65; 1949.

Harlow, Harry F. "Learning and Satiation of Response in Intrinsically Motivated Complex Puzzle Performance by Monkeys." *J Compar Physiol Psychol* 43:289–94; 1950.

Harlow, Harry F. "Learning Set and Error Factor Theory." In Koch, Sigmund. (Ed.) *Psychology: A Study of a Science*, Vol 2. McGraw-Hill, 1959. p. 492–537.

Harlow, Harry, and others. "Manipulatory Motivation of Infant Rhesus Monkeys." *J Compar Physiol Psychol* 49:444–8; 1956.

Hawker, James A. "The Influence of Training Procedure and Other Task Variables in Paired-associate Learning." *J Verbal Learning Verbal Behavior* 3:70–6; 1964.

Haygood, Robert C., and Bourne, Lyle E., Jr. "Attribute- and Rule-Learning Aspects of Conceptual Behavior." *Psychol R* 72:175–95; 1965.

Hearst, Eliot. "Approach, Avoidance, and Stimulus Generalization." In Mostofsky, David I. (Ed.) *Stimulus Generalization*. Stanford U Press, 1965. p. 331–55.

Heidbreder, Edna. "The Attainment of Concepts. I: Terminology and Methodology." *J Gen Psychol* 35:173–89; 1946(a).

Heidbreder, Edna. "The Attainment of Concepts. II: The Problem." *J Gen Psychol* 35:191–223; 1946(b).

Hilgard, Ernest R. (Ed.) *Theories of Learning and Instruction*. 63rd Yearbook, Part I, NSSE. U Chicago Press, 1964. 430p.

Hilgard, Ernest R., and Bower, Gordon H. *Theories of Learning*, 3rd ed. Appleton, 1966. 661p.

Hoffman, Howard S. "The Stimulus Generalization of Conditioned Suppression." In Mostofsky, David I. (Ed.) *Stimulus Generalization*. Stanford U Press, 1965. p. 356–72.

Holland, James G. "Human Vigilance." *Sci* 128:61–7; 1958.

Holland, James G. "Teaching Machines: An Application of Principles from the Laboratory." In Lumsdaine, A. A., and Glaser, Robert. (Eds.) *Teaching*

Machines and Programmed Learning: A Source Book. NEA, 1960. p. 215–28.

Holz, W. C., and Azrin, N. H. "Conditioning Human Verbal Behavior." In Honig, Werner K. (Ed.) *Operant Behavior: Areas of Research and Application.* Appleton, 1966. p. 790–826.

Horowitz, Leonard M., and Izawa, Chizuko. "Comparison of Serial and Paired-associate Learning." *J Exp Psychol* 65:355–61; 1963.

Hovland, Carl I., and Weiss, Walter. "Transmission of Information Concerning Concepts through Positive and Negative Instances." *J Exp Psychol* 45:175–82; 1953.

Hull, Clark L. "Quantitative Aspects of the Evolution of Concepts." *Psychol Monogr* 28(No. 123); 1920. 86p.

Hull, Clark L. *Principles of Behavior: An Introduction to Behavior Theory.* Appleton, 1943. 422p.

Hull, Clark L. "Simple Qualitative Discrimination Learning." *Psychol R* 57:303–13; 1950.

Hull, Clark L., and others. *Mathematico-deductive Theory of Rote Learning.* Yale U Press, 1940.

Hunt, Earl B. *Concept Learning: An Information Processing Problem.* Wiley, 1962. 286p.

Hunter, W. S. "The Temporal Maze and Kinaesthetic Sensory Process in the White Rat." *Psychobiology* 2:1; 1920.

Jenkins, H. M., and Harrison, R. H. "Generalization Gradients of Inhibition Following Auditory Discrimination Learning." *J Exp Analysis Behavior* 5:435–41; 1962.

Jenkins, James J. "Mediated Associations: Paradigms and Situations." In Cofer, Charles N., and Musgrave, Barbara S. (Eds.) *Verbal Behavior and Learning: Problems and Processes.* McGraw-Hill, 1963. p. 210–45.

Jenkins, James J., and Palermo, David S. "Mediation Processes and the Acquisition of Linguistic Structure." In Bellugi, Ursula, and Brown, Roger. (Eds.) "The Acquisition of Language." *Monogr Social Res Child Develop* 29(1) (Serial No. 92):141–69; 1964.

Jensen, Arthur R. "Transfer between Paired-associate and Serial Learning." *J Verbal Learning Verbal Behavior* 1:269–80; 1962.

Jensen, Arthur R. "Verbal Mediation and Educational Potential." *Psychol Sch* 3:99–109; 1966.

Jones, Austin. "Supplementary Report: Information Deprivation and Irrelevant Drive as Determiners of an Instrumental Response." *J Exp Psychol* 62:310–1; 1961.

Jones, Austin, and others. "Information Deprivation as a Motivational Variable." *J Exp Psychol* 62:126–37; 1961.

Katz, Jerrold J., and Fodor, Jerry A. "The Structure of a Semantic Theory." *Lang* 39:170–210; 1963.

Kausler, Donald H. (Ed.) *Readings in Verbal Learning: Contemporary Theory and Research.* Wiley, 1966. 578p.

Kelleher, R. T. "Chaining and Conditioned Reinforcement." In Honig, Werner K. (Ed.) *Operant Behavior: Areas of Research and Application.* Appleton, 1966. p. 160–212.

Keller, Fred S. "The Phantom Plateau." *J Exp Analysis Behavior* 1:1–13; 1958.

Keller, Fred S. and Schoenfeld, William N. *Principles of Psychology.* Appleton, 1950. 431p.

Kendler, Howard H. "The Concept of a Concept." In Melton, Arthur W. (Ed.) *Categories of Human Learning.* Academic, 1964. p. 212–36.

Kendler, Howard H. and Kendler, Tracy S. "Vertical and Horizontal Processes in Problem Solving." *Psychol R* 69:1–16; 1962.

Kendler, Tracy S. "Concept Formation." *Annual R Psychol* 12:447–72; 1961.

Keppel, Geoffrey. "Facilitation in Short- and Long-term Retention of Paired Associates Following Distributed Practice in Learning." *J Verbal Learning Verbal Behavior* 3:91–111; 1964.

Keppel, Geoffrey. "Verbal Learning and Memory." *Annual R Psychol* 19: 1968.

Keppel, Geoffrey, and Rehula, Robert J. "Rate of Presentation in Serial Learning." *J Exp Psychol* 69:121–5; 1965.

Kimble, Gregory A. *Hilgard and Marquis' Conditioning and Learning.* Appleton, 1961. 590p.

Kish, G. B. "Studies of Sensory Reinforcement." in Honig, Werner K. (Ed.) *Operant Behavior: Areas of Research and Application.* Appleton, 1966. p. 109–59.

Köhler, Wolfgang. "Nachweis einfacher Strukturfunktionen beim Schimpansen und beim Haushuhn." *Abbd. d. königl Preuss* 2:1–101; 1918. (Translated and condensed as "Simple Structural Functions in the Chimpanzee and in the Chicken." In Ellis, W. D. *A Source Book in Gestalt Psychology.* Harcourt, 1938. p. 217–27.)

Lawrence, Douglas H. "Acquired Distinctiveness of Cues. I: Transfer Between Discriminations on the Basis of Familiarity with the Stimulus." *J Exp Psychol* 39:770–84; 1949.

Lawrence, Douglas H. "Acquired Distinctiveness of Cues. II: Selective Association in a Constant Stimulus Situation." *J Exp Psychol* 40:175–188; 1950.

Lawrence, Douglas H. "The Nature of a Stimulus: Some Relationships Between Learning and Perception." In Koch, Sigmund. (Ed.) *Psychology: A Study of a Science.* Vol. 5. McGraw-Hill, 1963. p. 179–212.

Lawrence, Douglas H., and Festinger, Leon. *Deterrents and Reinforcement: The Psychology of Insufficient Reward.* Stanford U Press, 1962.

Lees, R. B. Review of Chomsky's *Syntactic Structures. Lang* 33:375–412; 1957.

Lepley, William M. "Serial Reactions Considered as Conditioned Reactions." *Psychol Monogr* 46(No. 205); 1934.

Lindvall, C. M. (Ed.) *Defining Educational Objectives.* U Pittsburgh Press, 1964. 83p.

Lumsdaine, A. A., and Glaser, Robert. (Eds.) *Teaching Machines and Programmed Learning: A Source Book.* NEA, 1960. 724p.

Mandler, George. "From Association to Structure." *Psychol R* 69:415–27; 1962.

Marks, Lawrence E., and Miller, George A. "The Role of Semantic and Syntactic Constraints in the

Memorization of English Sentences." *J Verbal Learning Verbal Behavior* 3:1–5; 1964.

Marshall, George R., and Cofer, Charles N. "Associated Indices as Measures of Word Relatedness: A Summary and Comparison of Ten Methods." *J Verbal Learning Verbal Behavior* 1:408–21; 1963.

Martin, Edwin, and Schulz, Rudolph W. "Aural Paired-associate Learning: Pronunciability and the Intertrial Between Stimulus and Response." *J Verbal Learning Verbal Behavior* 1:389–41; 1963.

McCrary, John W., and Hunter, W. S. "Serial Position Curves in Verbal Learning." *Sci* 117:131–4; 1953.

McGeoch, John A., and Irion, Arthur L. *The Psychology of Human Learning*, 2nd ed. McKay, 1952. 596p.

Mechner, Francis. "Science Education and Behavioral Technology." In Glaser, Robert. (Ed.) *Teaching Machines and Programed Learning*, Vol. 2: *Data and Directions*. NEA, 1965. p. 441–507.

Mechner, Francis. "Behavioral Analysis and Instructional Sequencing." In *Programed Instruction*, 66th Yearbook, Part II, NSSE. U Chicago Press, 1967. p. 81–103.

Melton, Arthur W. "Learning." In Monroe, W. S. (Ed.) *Encyclopedia of Educational Research*. Macmillan, 1941. p. 667–86.

Melton, Arthur W. "Comments on Professor Postman's Paper." In Cofer, Charles N. (Ed.) *Verbal Learning and Verbal Behavior*. McGraw-Hill, 1961. p. 179–96.

Melton, Arthur W. "Implications of Short-term Memory for a General Theory of Memory." *J Verbal Learning Verbal Behavior* 2:1–21; 1963.

Melton, Arthur W. (Ed.) *Categories of Human Learning*. Academic, 1964. 356p.

Miller, George A. "The Magical Number Seven Plus or Minus Two: Some Limits on Our Capacity for Processing Information." *Psychol R* 63:81–97; 1956.

Miller, George A. "Some Psychological Studies of Grammar." *Am Psychologist* 17:748–62; 1962.

Miller, George A., and Selfridge, J. A. "Verbal Context and the Recall of Meaningful Material." *Am J Psychol* 63:176–85; 1950.

Miller, Robert B. "Analysis and Specification of Behavior for Training." In Glaser, Robert. (Ed.) *Training Research and Education*. Wiley, 1965. p. 31–62.

Moore, Omar K., and Anderson, Alan Ross. "The Responsive Environments Project." In Hess, R., and Bear, R. (Eds.) *The Challenge of Early Education* (in press).

Moore, R., and Goldiamond, Israel. "Errorless Establishment of Visual Discrimination Using Fading Procedures." *J Exp Analysis Behavior* 7:269–72; 1964.

Morse, W. H. "Intermittent Reinforcement." In Honig, Werner K. (Ed.) *Operant Behavior: Areas of Research and Application*. Appleton, 1966. p. 52–108.

Mostofsky, David I. (Ed.) *Stimulus Generalization*. Stanford U Press, 1965. 389p.

Muenzinger, K. F. "Motivation in Learning. I: Electric Shock for Correct Response in the Visual Discrimination Habit." *J Compar Psychol* 17: 439–48; 1934.

Newell, Allen, and Shaw, J. C. "Programming the Logic Theory Machine." In *Proceedings of the Western Joint Computer Conference*. Institute of Radio Engineers, 1957. p. 218–230.

Newell, Allen, and Simon, Herbert A. "The Logic Theory Machine: A Complex Information Processing System." *Transactions on Information Theory* IT2:61–79; 1956.

Newell, Allen, and others. "Elements of a Theory of Human Problem Solving." *Psychol R* 65:151–66; 1958.

Newell, Allen, and others. "Report on a General Problem-solving Program." In *Proceedings of the Internation Conference on Information Processing*. UNESCO, 1960. p. 256–64.

Noble, Clyde E. "Meaningfulness and Familiarity." In Cofer, Charles N., and Musgrave, Barbara S. (Eds.) *Verbal Behavior and Learning: Problems and Processes*. McGraw-Hill, 1963. p. 76–119.

Nodine, Calvin F. "Supplementary Report: Stimulus Durations and Total Learning Time in Paired-associate Learning." *J Exp Psychol* 69:534–6; 1965.

Osgood, Charles E. "The Nature and Measurement of Meaning." *Psychol B* 49:197–237; 1952.

Osgood, Charles E. "On Understanding and Creating Sentences." *Am Psychol* 18:735–51; 1963.

Osgood, Charles E., and others. *The Measurement of Meaning*. U Illinois Press, 1957. 342p.

Paige, Jeffrey, and Simon, Herbert A. "Cognitive Processes in Solving Algebra Word Problems." In Kleinmuntz, Benjamin. (Ed.) *Problem Solving: Research, Method, and Theory*. Wiley, 1966. p. 51–119.

Pavlov, Ivan P. *Conditioned Reflexes*. Translated by G. V. Anrep. Oxford U Press, 1927. 430p.

Polya, George. *Mathematics and Plausible Reasoning*, 2 vols. Princeton U Press, 1954.

Polya, George. *How to Solve It*, 2nd ed. Doubleday, 1957. 237p.

Postman, Leo. "The Present Status of Interference Theory." In Cofer, Charles N. (Ed.) *Verbal Learning and Verbal Behavior*. McGraw-Hill, 1961. p. 152–79.

Postman, Leo. "Short-term Memory and Incidental Learning." In Melton, Arthur W. (Ed.) *Categories of Human Learning*. Academic, 1964. p. 145–201.

Premack, David. "Toward Empirical Behavior Laws. I: Positive Reinforcement." *Psychol R* 66:219–33; 1959.

Premack, David. "Reinforcement Theory." In Levine, David. (Ed.) *Nebraska Symposium on Motivation*. U Nebraska Press, 1965. p. 123–80.

Ray, Wilbert S. "Complex Tasks for Use in Human Problem-solving Research." *Psychol B* 52:134–49; 1955.

Razran, Gregory. "The Observable Unconscious and the Inferable Conscious in Current Soviet Psychophysiology: Interoceptive Conditioning, Semantic Conditioning, and the Orienting Reflex." *Psychol R* 68:81–147; 1961.

Reitman, Walter R. *Cognition and Thought: An In-*

formation Processing Approach. Wiley, 1965. 312p.

Reynolds, George S. "Behavioral Contrast." *J Exp Analysis Behavior* 4:57–71; 1961.

Rothkopf, Ernst Z. "Some Theoretical and Experimental Approaches to Problems in Written Instruction." In Krumboltz, John D. (Ed.) *Learning and the Educational Process.* Rand McNally, 1965. p. 193–221.

Schlosberg, H., and Katz, A. "Double Alternation Lever-pressing in the White Rat." *Am J Psychol* 56:274–82; 1943.

Schlosberg, H., and Solomon, Richard L. "Latency of Response in a Choice Discrimination." *J Exp Psychol* 33:22–39; 1943.

Shepard, Roger N. "Approximation to Uniform Gradients of Generalization by Monotone Transformations of Scale." In Mostofsky, David I. (Ed.) *Stimulus Generalization.* Stanford U Press, 1965. p. 94–110.

Shepard, Roger N., and others. "Learning and Memorization of Classifications." *Psychol Monogr* 75 (No. 517); 1961. 42p.

Shulman, Lee S. and Keislar, Evan R. (Eds.) *Learning by Discovery: A Critical Appraisal.* Rand McNally, 1966. 224p.

Sidman, Murray, and Stoddard, Lawrence T. "The Effectiveness of Fading in Programming a Simultaneous Form Discrimination for Retarded Children." *J Exp Analysis Behavior* 10:3–15; 1967.

Simon, Herbert A., and Kotovsky, K. "Human Acquisition of Concepts for Sequential Patterns." *Psychol R* 70:534–46; 1963.

Simon, Herbert A., and Newell, Allen. "Information Processing in Computer and Man. *Am Scientist* 52:281–300; 1964.

Skinner, B. F. *The Behavior of Organisms: An Experimental Analysis.* Appleton, 1938. 457p.

Skinner, B. F. *Science and Human Behavior.* Macmillan, 1953. 461p.

Skinner, B. F. *Verbal Behavior.* Appleton, 1957. 478p.

Skinner, B. F. "Teaching Machines." *Sci* 128:969–77; 1958.

Skinner, B. F. "Operant Behavior." In Honig, Werner K. (Ed.) *Operant Behavior: Areas of Research and Application.* Appleton, 1966. p. 12–32.

Spence, Kenneth W. "The Nature of Discrimination Learning in Animals." *Psychol R* 43:427–49; 1936.

Spence, Kenneth W. "The Differential Response in Animals to Stimuli Varying Within a Single Dimension." *Psychol R* 44:430–44; 1937.

Spence, Kenneth W. *Behavior Theory and Conditioning.* Yale U Press, 1956. 262p.

Suppes, Patrick. "Modern Learning Theory and the Elementary School Curriculum." *Am Ed Res J* 1:79–93; 1964.

Suppes, Patrick. "On the Behavioral Foundations of Mathematical Concepts." *Monogr Social Res Child Develop* 30(No. 99); 60–95; 1965.

Suppes, Patrick. "Mathematical Concept Formation in Children." *Am Psychologist* 21:139–50; 1966.

Terrace, H. S. "Discrimination Learning With and Without Errors." *J Exp Analysis Behavior* 6:1–27; 1963.

Terrace, H. S. "Stimulus Control." In Honig, Werner K. (Ed.) *Operant Behavior: Areas of Research and Application.* Appleton, 1966. p. 271–344.

Thorndike, Edward L. *Educational Psychology,* Vol. 2: *The Psychology of Learning.* Teachers Col, Columbia U, 1913.

Thorndike, Edward L. *The Fundamentals of Learning.* Teachers Col, Columbia U, 1932(*a*). 638p.

Thorndike, Edward L. "Reward and Punishment in Animal Learning." *Compar Psychol Monogr* 8(No. 39); 1932(*b*).

Travers, Robert M. W. "The Transmission of Information to Human Receivers." *Audio-Visual Communication R* 12:373–85; 1964.

Tulving, Endel. "Subjective Organization in Free Recall of 'Unrelated' Words." *Psychol R* 69:344–54; 1962.

Ulrich, Roger E., and Azrin, N. H. "Reflexive Fighting in Response to Aversive Stimulation." *J Exp Analysis Behavior* 5:511–20; 1962.

Underwood, Benton J. "Interference and Forgetting." *Psychol R* 64:49–60; 1957.

Underwood, Benton J. "An Evaluation of the Gibson Theory of Verbal Learning," In Cofer, Charles N. (Ed.) *Verbal Learning and Verbal Behavior.* McGraw-Hill, 1961(*a*). p. 197–217.

Underwood, Benton J. "Ten Years of Massed Practice on Distributed Practice." *Psychol R* 68:229–47; 1961(*b*).

Underwood, Benton J. "Stimulus Selection in Verbal Learning." In Cofer, Charles N., and Musgrave, Barbara S. (Eds.) *Verbal Behavior and Learning: Problems and Processes.* McGraw-Hill, 1963. p. 33–48.

Underwood, Benton J., and Keppel, Geoffrey. "Coding Processes in Verbal Learning." *J Verbal Learning Verbal Behavior* 1:250–7; 1962.

Underwood, Benton J., and Postman, Leo, "Extra-experimental Sources of Interference in Forgetting." *Psychol R* 67:73–95; 1960.

Underwood, Benton J., and Richardson, Jack. "Some Verbal Materials for the Study of Concept Formation." *Psychol B* 53:84–95; 1956.

Underwood, Benton J., and Schulz, Rudolph W. *Meaningfulness and Verbal Learning.* Lippincott, 1960. 430p.

Waugh, Nancy C., and Norman, Donald A. "Primary Memory." *Psychol R* 72:89–104; 1965.

Weiner, Harold. "Some Effects of Response Cost upon Human Operant Behavior." *J Exp Analysis Behavior* 5:201–8; 1962.

Wike, Edward L. *Secondary Reinforcement: Selected Experiments.* Harper, 1966. 503p.

Wohlwill, Joachim F. "The Abstraction and Conceptualization of Form, Color and Number." *J Exp Psychol* 53:304–9; 1957.

Wyckoff, L. Benjamin, Jr. "The Role of Observing Responses in Discrimination Learning. Part I." *Psychol R* 59:431–42; 1952.

Young, Robert K., and others. "Backward Serial

Learning." *J Verbal Learning Verbal Behavior* 1:335–8; 1963.

Zeaman, David, and House, Betty J. "The Role of Attention in Retardate Discrimination Learning." In Ellis, Norman. (Ed.) *Handbook of Mental Deficiency.* McGraw-Hill, 1963. p. 159–223.

Zeiler, Michael D. "The Ratio of Intermediate Size Discrimination." *Psychol R* 70:516–33; 1963.

LEGAL EDUCATION IN THE UNITED STATES

HISTORY. Legal education in the United States has been influenced by both the English and the Continental methods of training lawyers. Early in American history, the preparation for the legal profession followed the English tradition of training the aspiring lawyer by a period of apprenticeship. Later, this method was replaced by a college or university experience very much in the tradition of the Continental countries. The transition presents an interesting picture of educational evolution.

In early America a person wishing to undertake a career in law had four ways to prepare himself for the profession. He might undertake a program of self-directed reading and study of the available legal information in his town or city; he could work in a clerk's office of some court of record; he could serve an apprenticeship in the law office of an attorney; or he could travel to England and undertake a program of training in one of the four Inns of Court in London and follow the traditional way of training English lawyers (Chroust, 1965). By far the most popular method of studying for the bar was to serve an apprenticeship in a lawyer's office and learn by actually observing and assisting the practicing attorney. For this privilege, the legal apprentice had to pay a fee to his mentor, and at best, the system was an informal one. The education of aspiring lawyers, especially at the time of the Revolution, was further complicated by the dearth of law books available for their use. The works of Lord Edward Coke and Sir William Blackstone were most readily available and most widely read. For instance, after finishing college, Daniel Webster entered the office of a lawyer and learned by watching and reading such books as *Coke on Littleton* and Blackstone's *Commentaries* (Maitland, 1963). These men had substantial influence on the young lawyer during this period.

Until the late eighteenth century, there was little or no influence by colleges and universities on the training of students for the legal profession. In 1779 a significant development took place under the leadership of Thomas Jefferson who established a chair of law at William and Mary College. Before long, other American universities adopted Jefferson's idea. Professorships were established at Harvard College in 1781, at The College of Philadelphia in 1790, at Transylvania University, Lexington, Kentucky in 1799, and at the University of Maryland in 1816 (Harno, 1953).

Simultaneously with the introduction of Jefferson's concept of establishing a chair of law, an independent law school was established in Litchfield, Connecticut, in 1784. The Litchfield School was to have a profound effect upon the formation of later law schools in the United States. It is estimated that over 1,000 individuals matriculated at Litchfield during its 50-year existence (Chroust, 1965). Its accomplishments during its short history have never been equaled and probably never will be. Of the approximately 1,000 men registered for courses at the school, 28 became U. S. Senators; 101, members of Congress; 34, state supreme court justices; 14, governors of states and 10, lieutenant governors; 3, vice presidents of the United States; 3, U. S. Supreme Court justices; and 6, members of the cabinet (Harno, 1953).

Accompanying these movements to formalize the training of lawyers was an awareness that regulations were necessary for controlling the admission of individuals to the legal profession. Several jurisdictions adopted requirements for bar admission by court rules, others by legislation, and some by action of the organized bar. At least ten of these jurisdictions adopted regulations in the period between 1770 and 1805 (Warren, 1966). Generally, these regulations dealt with a period of preparation and training for admission to practice in the courts of the jurisdiction.

The recognition that certain requirements had to be met for admission to the bar prompted universities and colleges to introduce a law curriculum. In 1826, Thomas Jefferson began The University of Virginia Law School. Yale Law School had its beginning in 1826, and by 1860 over a score of law schools with university affiliation were in operation (Harno, 1953).

Throughout these years of development, Harvard Law School under the guidance and direction of Judge Story was beginning to make its impact as a citadel for legal learning. By 1870 the 31 law schools existing in the United States were looking to Harvard as the pace-setter of American legal education. At this time, the scholarly Christopher Columbus Langdell of the Harvard faculty introduced a pedagogical device, the case study, which is still in use today in legal education (Currie, 1951). In 1871 Langdell published his first case book, *A Selection of Cases on the Law of Contracts* (Harno. 1953). Langdell regarded law as a science consisting of certain principles or doctrines. He felt that the lawyer should always go to the main source of the legal problem—the actual case—and that the pure lecture and text-reading system was a poor method of teaching the law. Today, Langdell's case-study system is still used in law schools and, although it has been modified, it is still the basis upon which our law students are educated.

Any consideration of the historical development of legal education must include the impact of professional organizations on the development and growth of the law school. In 1878, the American Bar Association was founded. At first, its function was primarily social. Special projects such as law libraries, standards for admission to the bar, and legal education were given some consideration, but by no means were they primary objectives of the ABA. In 1893 the Association took a significant step when it established a committee of the Association to be known as the Section of Legal Education. The work of this section was instrumental in coordinating the efforts of all law schools to conform to general standards with regard to legal education. It was highly instrumental in implementing a rule requiring the course of study in law school to extend over a three-year period. The section was also influential in providing a forum for the establishment of the Association of American Law Schools in 1900 (Harno, 1953). At the time, 35 law schools sent delegates to the first meeting of the newly formed association. Its growth and influence have contributed tremendously to the effectiveness of American legal education.

Although the Association of American Law Schools is an independent body, it does coordinate its efforts with the ABA Section on Legal Education to insure an effective program for the advancement of legal education by providing law school accreditation. Most law schools have the dual accreditation of the AALS and the ABA. There are 112 law schools accredited by the Association of American Law Schools, and 135 are approved by the American Bar Association (West Publishing Company, 1967).

THE STATUS OF LEGAL EDUCATION TODAY. The growth of legal education has not been in proportion to the increase in numbers of undergraduate students attending our colleges and universities. Since 1920 the enrollment in higher education has increased approximately 500 percent, while enrollment in law schools has increased less than 75 percent (Columbia Law Review, 1964). The small number of law schools and a desire by the profession to maintain an exclusivity for the number called to the Bar have been responsible for this lack of growth.

The primary purpose of legal education is to train individuals to be good lawyers. It might be said that legal education has two related objectives—the training of lawyers and the improvement of the law. More specifically, each law school should provide a program of education to train legal practitioners; to train its students in the work of solving problems not merely of individual clients, but of the society in which they live; and finally, to act as a center of research, criticism, and contribution to the better understanding of the laws by which societies are held together (Harno, 1953).

The functions and opportunities of any law school are controlled, in order of importance, by four elements: (1) the character of its students; (2) the adequacy of its faculty in relation to the basic educational job that has to be done; (3) the extent of its physical resources, particularly its law library; and (4) the closeness of the tie between the school as an institution and any single state or local Bar (Jones, 1958).

By no means can legal education be characterized as complacently satisfied with current teaching methods. The entire system is under examination, and it would appear that during the next decade change will be the rule rather than the exception. In contemplating the future, legal education will have to take into consideration the needs of our society, of the individual in that society, and the influence world events will have on our domestic and international staus as a nation.

PRE-LEGAL EDUCATION. Most law schools require four years of college and a baccalaureate degree for admission. There are a decreasing number that will accept students upon completion of their junior year of college (University of Notre Dame, 1965) under a three-three program. This procedure permits a student to begin his law study in what would be his senior year of undergraduate work. Upon the successful completion of his first year of law school, he receives his B.A. or B.S. degree, and two years later upon fulfilling his law school requirements he receives his first degree in law.

There is no single way for an undergraduate student to prepare himself for law school. In fact, there is no particular major or area of academic emphasis that a pre-law student must take in order to qualify for law school admission. Some universities or colleges will prescribe a course of study designated as pre-legal. Usually, one will find that such a program concentrates upon courses in history, political science, and economics, yet a student may major in any generally accepted discipline—from astronomy to zoology—and find that his college work is acceptable for admission to law school. The criterion is not one of area of concentration, but the caliber of the student's entire college record (Knickerbocker, 1960).

Legal educators do recognize that the success of law schools and of the profession rests on the use of certain abilities and developed talents. Students interested in law careers are encouraged to refine these abilities and talents. The first is the ability to read and write accurately. The lawyer spends most of his professional life reading and writing. For this reason, the pre-law student is encouraged to master the basic tools of the English language by taking an ample measure of work in English at the undergraduate level. Law school faculties consistently report the inability of their students to achieve a proficiency in the use of their native language which ultimately impedes or makes impossible a successful law school experience (Green, 1948).

It is also essential that the law student possess skill in expression and comprehension. These skills should be refined to the point where there is a sensitivity to the fluidity of language; that is, a comprehension and recognition of the varying meanings of words in different times and contexts, shades of meaning, and the hazards of the use of ambiguous terms. He must be attuned to the deceptiveness of language, such as the use of emotionally charged words, catch phrases, hidden meanings of words, and empty generalizations (Strong, 1955).

In addition, the law student preparing for law

school is encouraged to undertake courses in philosophy, mathematics, and other disciplines that will increase his powers to read, analyze, and synthesize. This training will provide an opportunity for the student to practice judgment in refining his ability to express abstractions and ideas which are so crucial in his professional life (Green, 1948).

In sum, a student contemplating a career in the law should work toward achieving a grasp or comprehension of the following: (1) the nature of man in the physical world of which he is a part; (2) the economic systems of societies; (3) the political organization of societies; and (4) the social structure and cultural heritage of societies. The student should develop the power to think clearly, carefully, and independently. His skills should be sharpened in the area of research, fact completeness, fact differentiation, fact marshaling, deductive and inductive reasoning, and reasoning by analogy (Strong, 1955).

THE LAW STUDENT. According to registration records, 67,802 students were enrolled in accredited law schools in September 1966 (Hervey, 1966). Law school admission is highly competitive today. It is not unusual for a law school to have two or three times the number of applicants for admission than it can actually accommodate, and competition for the prestigious law schools is even greater.

Generally each applicant for law school admission must submit a transcript of his college record and evidence that he has received his baccalaureate degree. He must take the six-hour Law School Admission Test (L.S.A.T.) which is administered by the Educational Testing Service of Princeton, New Jersey (Educational Testing Service, 1966). In addition to these requirements, the applicant's extracurricular activities, reasons for attending law school, and letters of recommendation are evaluated by each admissions committee. One will find a substantial portion of students entering law school who do not wish to undertake careers in law. A very important element in a student's decision to go to law school is that legal training will be useful to him regardless of the career he eventually chooses—politics, government service, business, or the legal profession itself. Of the students applying for law school, 57 percent majored in social science, history, or government; 23 percent majored in business or commerce; and the remaining 20 percent concentrated in the humanities, sciences, and engineering (Lunneborg & Lunneborg, 1966).

The usual period of study for the law degree is three years of full-time attendance. Part-time students are required to attend for a period of four to five years. Upon the successful completion of his academic requirements, the student is awarded the LL.B. or J.D. degree. Of the 135 approved law schools approved by the American Bar Association, 76 will award the Juris Doctorate (J.D.) degree as the first professional law degree in June 1967. This represents 43 percent of the total number of candidates receiving law degrees from ABA-accredited schools. Thirty-seven other approved law schools are giving serious consideration to the adoption of the J.D. degree in lieu of the traditional LL.B. degree. It is likely that within the next decade most, if not all, law schools will be awarding the Juris Doctorate as the first law degree (*Student Lawyer Journal,* 1967).

EXAMINATIONS. Law schools attempt to accomplish two primary objectives for their students: (1) to impart a knowledge of the basic principles of law and (2) to teach each student "to think like a lawyer." The term "to think like a lawyer" is an elusive one which defies precise definition. In general, it means the methods by which a lawyer dissects, studies, and analyzes the legal problems that he encounters. The student will never master the entire body of law. Throughout his career, it will be necessary for him to return to the law library to locate principles of law and keep abreast with current developments. This is kept in mind when testing the law student's academic progress.

Law schools use a variety of testing methods. Generally, the types of examinations used are essay (of the hypothetical problem type), true–false, multiple-choice, and short-answer questions (Association of American Law Schools, 1955). The essay-type question, usually consisting of a statement of a hypothetical case or set of facts, is by far the most popular and most prevalent method used to examine the student. The student is asked to react to the question by deciding the case and giving a judicial opinion. Despite the fact that the grading of such questions is tedious and requires a great deal of time, the extensive use of this method by law school faculties would seem to indicate that it is the best known testing technique for law students (Weihofer, 1950). In fact, student reaction to hypothetical-essay type questions is a favorable one. Students prefer to become involved with hypothetical legal problems on examinations for they closely approximate actual cases encountered in practice (Williams, 1950).

Generally, law school examinations last from three to four hours. In some cases, where schools favor a comprehensive type of examination, the test may extend for a period of five hours. Examinations are usually given at the end of each term. In some cases, an examination may be deferred until the work of a five- or six-hour course is completed (Amandes, 1959).

With few exceptions, law schools undertake a program, especially with first-year students, providing an opportunity for practice examinations usually midway through the first semester. The feeling is that a first-year law student finds law school an unfamiliar environment and needs some guidance with regard to the special demands that are made upon a student during law school examinations. Such testing is usually followed by a "post mortem," which helps to acquaint the freshman law student with the desired method of writing examinations, which many find different from college exams (Association of American Law Schools, 1961). In addition, the conferences following the practice examination give the student an insight into the objectives and the methods of the individual professor, and this has proved to be extremely helpful in facilitating the acclimation of the student to the law school environment.

CURRICULUM. Creating an ideal law school curriculum is a difficult if not impossible task. Faculty curriculum committees must react to at least three demands: First, they must guarantee the academic integrity of a course of study; second, they must prepare each student for the inevitable bar examination; and finally, they must be alert to the needs of our society for individuals who are trained in the law and are capable of understanding and dealing with the complexities of modern society. The situation is further complicated by the fact that laymen everywhere expect the young law graduate, as well as the veteran lawyer, to be an expert in every phase of human conduct.

Perhaps no area of legal education is currently under more severe scrutiny and examination than the law school curriculum. An increasing number of new areas or fields of law have emerged and entered into competition for recognition with the more-established courses that have traditionally been provided in the law school (Rohan, 1964). The problem has been compounded by a reluctance to extend the law course beyond a period of three years. Except for a few institutions, most of the law schools throughout the United States offer a curriculum that covers the following subjects: civil procedure, criminal law, contracts, personal and real property, trust, bills and notes, corporations, business organizations, family law, creditors rights, wills and administration, evidence, constitutional law, administrative law, taxation, and legal ethics (West Publishing Company, 1967). There appears to be a definite trend toward an expanded curriculum to encompass courses in labor law, international law, law and society, law and medicine, and law and poverty. In addition, there is some indication of a resurgence of courses in the foundations of law such as jurisprudence, legal history, and comparative law (Rohan, 1964). Emphasis on practical courses is also evident. Practice court, legal drafting, estate planning, and legal aid are courses finding their way into the law school curriculum (Association of American Law Schools, 1960).

Future changes in the law school curriculum must include consideration of the requirements established by state bar examining committees. Virtually every state in the union requires law graduates wishing to practice within its borders to sit for a bar examination upon the completion of law school. This represents a compelling reason for law schools to see that their program provides a sound grounding in those subjects that will be covered in the bar examination. Every law school must consider the success of its students on the bar examination and arrange its course of study accordingly.

Practicing attorneys and society as a whole often point an accusing finger at law schools, saying that they do not provide sufficient training in the practical aspects of the law for their students. Experience indicates that the young lawyer has a sound knowledge of the academic basis of the law, but is unable to cope with the practical problems encountered in practice. The law schools are giving greater attention to this matter, and there seems to be a clear indication that more emphasis will be placed upon those courses which prepare the student for the actual practice of law (Landman, 1961).

THE LAW TEACHER. The ideal law teacher is expected to be a teacher, a writer, and an expert counselor in the affairs of the times (Goodrich, 1952). This requires a selection process which must filter out a great number of people who would be inadequate to teach law. In contrast to many other areas of education, there is no designated program for training law teachers. Each school has its own methods for selecting its faculty, and there is wide variation. Recommendations for potential faculty members usually come from the present faculty of a law school, from experts who teach and do research in particular fields, and from law schools conducting graduate programs in law (Association of American Law Schools, 1961). In most cases, the final selection of a faculty member is the joint responsibility of the dean and the present faculty of the individual law school. They consider the academic record of the candidate, his published works, and references from those with whom the candidate has worked professionally.

The law teacher must bring to the classroom an ability to communicate with the student and to develop an appreciation of the principles and problems of the particular area of law being studied. Many of the nearly 2,000 full-time faculty members (American Bar Association, 1966) teaching at accredited law schools have had three to five years of legal practice (Prosser, 1951). Experience shows that a teacher with a number of years of practice has a better command of the subject matter and better appreciation of the practical problems involved than has one without such experience. It is also apparent that the law student respects the teacher who has worked with clients and appeared in the courtroom. It is reassuring to the student to know that his teacher can practice law as well as talk about it in a theoretical way. This is especially appealing to the modern student. Appointment to a law school faculty does not require an advanced degree, beyond the first degree in law—the LL.B. or J.D. In the past, most faculty members held the LL.B. or J.D. degrees, and their promotion depended upon their performance in the classroom, the contributions they made through writing, and their involvement in the legal affairs of their community. In recent years, there has been a trend for faculty members to complete an additional year of academic study for the LL.M. degree. Expanding facilities and opportunities for graduate law education and increasing demands for expertise and specialization in the law are reasons for this change.

Law schools have always drawn on the members of the bar as a source for part-time teachers. This practice is less common today because law school deans feel that a full-time faculty represents a more cohesive unit free from the distractions of the practice of law. Despite this trend, law schools will continue to be interested in appointing on a part-time basis lawyers who have shown a particular command of certain areas of the law. It is wise to call upon the training and experience of those who are willing to teach and have special expertise in a particular subject, for it adds an extra dimension to the law school curriculum. Consistent with this thought is the fact that the law is a profession and requires something more than merely an academic approach to the subject matter.

TEACHING TECHNIQUES. In the law school one will find the lecture, the seminar, the case method, and the problem method used as teaching techniques. Since 1870, when Langdell introduced the case method of study, it has been the generally accepted means of imparting law to students (Landman, 1961). The case method is primarily designed to teach the law student to "think like a lawyer" and secondarily, to impart principles of law. It increases the student's powers of analysis within the framework of a legal problem or situation. It utilizes a case book, which is a collection of cases dealing with a particular aspect of the law. The cases are taken from appellant decisions, which are rendered by judges, and serve as an explanation of the decision they have made in a case. Each case is studied by the student and discussed in the classroom with the instructor making certain observations about the court decision and eliciting the student's analysis of it. Generations of lawyers have been trained in this manner since 1870, and there is every indication that in the foreseeable future the case method will be continued.

Recently, there has been severe criticism of the case method because of the inefficiencies involved when using it, and there is a feeling that once the student is exposed during the first year to the proper methods of analyzing a case it becomes an exercise in drudgery and nonproductivity (Peairs, 1960).

Prior to the introduction of the case method, the text and lecture method was used at Harvard. The text and lecture method is still used at the law school level, but is often modified to complement the generally accepted case method. In the late 1920's, the problem method of studying law was introduced. With the problem method, students are directed to text decisions and other sources to aid them in arriving at a solution to a problem. In technical terms, the problem method takes on the form of classroom discussion of nonprescribed and prescribed problems. There is an increasing trend throughout the country to use the case method during a student's first year of study of law school and to introduce the problem method in the second and third years (Freeman, 1965). The acceptance of the problem method and its increasing popularity seem to indicate that it is more appropriate for the teaching of law in these times. The instructor is able to be more creative and free himself from the dictates of the particular case book that he has chosen, and the student is freed from the rather limited scope of a case book and is also free to react more creatively.

Despite recent developments and the overshadowing aspect of less emphasis on the case method, it is significant to note that more and more disciplines appear to be using the case method as a means of teaching. It does have its definite advantages in improving and refining the art of analyzing problems, whether they be in law, management, or some other academic discipline. Yet it must be recognized that the method is not the most efficient, and it would appear that the trend is toward the use of a combination of the case and problem methods in the law school curriculum.

Law teachers are finding that their students are demanding more emphasis on the practical aspects of law (Forer, 1961). Seminars are being offered where there can be a freer flow of ideas and concepts. Students are becoming more active in legal aid programs, which helps the student to get into the field and to relate his academic work to practical everyday problems. Legal internships are also being used to acquaint the students with the realities of the profession. Experience has shown that a combination of teaching methods is a more realistic, as well as a more effective, way of imparting legal knowledge to students. Of course, much depends on the personality of the teacher and the methods which he feels are best suited for his type of course. It is likely that the students, turning to teaching in the years ahead, will feel less affection for the case method and be more willing to experiment with a combination of methods to achieve desired results.

CO-CURRICULAR ACTIVITIES. Law Review. A unique feature of legal education in the United States is the participation of law school students in the work of a law review. Nowhere else in the world do law schools provide a similar opportunity for their students to contribute to and participate in the evolution and development of legal policy. In addition to textbooks, case books, and legal treatises, the law review is used as a means for imparting legal knowledge and providing an opportunity for students to express their legal scholarship in written form (Harno, 1953).

Students qualify for law review membership by achieving high scholarship. Usually the process is a highly competitive one and is coveted by those students who entertain ambitions of working for the more prestigious law firms. The administration and control of law review will vary from school to school. In some schools the student board has full responsibility for the publication; in others there is joint participation on the part of the faculty and students in preparing copy for publication. In all schools emphasis is placed on the educational value that students receive in preparing each edition of the law review. The nature of the work is to help the student develop proficiency in writing and research, which is a basic requirement for any attorney no matter what field he finally chooses to enter upon graduation.

The typical copy of a law review contains lead articles by authorities in particular fields. Feature articles are supplemented by research projects done by the students on the law review. Except for a few outstanding law reviews, their circulation is not large. Law school faculties and legal scholars are the most consistent and avid readers of these publications. Yet within the last decade, law review articles are finding their way more frequently into the opinions handed down by the courts. It is also clear that lawyers are more frequently turning to law reviews as a means to support their legal points in court and in cases on appeal (Traynor, 1962).

A justifiable criticism of law reviews is that they are too exclusive, providing an opportunity for no more than the top ten percent of a law school student body (Moreland, 1960). For much of the past 50 or 60 years, law reviews have represented practically the sole outlet of student scholarship. Because this outlet is confined to such a select few, law schools have begun to provide greater opportunities for more students to participate in law review activities. Intramural law reviews have been established and policies have been promulgated to encourage students who are not on the law review boards to contribute to the law review. This turn of events has encouraged the less talented student to write publishable material and to feel that the law review belongs to the entire student body rather than to the exclusive group serving on its editorial board.

There is no question that law review will continue to be an integral part of the law school program. In our modern age, legal problems are developing more rapidly than they can be solved, and experience has shown that the law review provides an opportunity, for both faculty and students, to contribute to the solution of important legal problems. One change that may be expected in the next decade is that law schools will see that more students will be given an opportunity to participate in this vehicle of legal scholarship.

Legal Aid–Public Defender. Among the most effective means available to a student in bridging the gap between law school and professional practice are the student legal aid and public defender programs. Of relatively recent vintage, they have served to introduce into the law school program an experience not unlike that of a doctor undergoing his medical internship. Known variously as legal aid, student public defenders, or legal clinics, the programs provide an opportunity for students to put their classroom learning to work in a meaningful way (Mancuso, 1966).

The student legal aid or public defender programs provide the student with experience in interviewing clients, evaluating the merits of actual cases, and researching legal problems related to actual clients. In addition, his duties may include drafting legal documents, engaging in some activity in a courtroom setting, and learning a law-office routine. Generally, students are allowed to assist the attorney and client up to the point when the case goes to court. In a few jurisdictions, Florida, for example (Florida Statutes, 1965), senior or third-year students are allowed to take selected cases before the courts. Of course, equally important is the legal assistance the student provides to the indigent who are unable to pay fees for legal representation (Allison, 1961).

The scope of each law school's legal aid program will vary. Some will encompass both civil and criminal matters. Others will concentrate their efforts in the area of criminal law. The programs emphasize careful supervision of the student's work, either by a faculty member or a practicing lawyer. At most schools, a student must achieve a minimum scholastic average to be eligible for legal aid work.

Today's court decisions recognize the need for providing better and more extensive legal services for the poor. This development will require greater participation by lawyers and law students alike. As a result, the law school and its students can look forward to a more active role in working with members of the bar who are providing legal aid and public defender assistance (Brown, 1965).

Moot Court. The oldest law school extracurricular activity is moot court. It was part of the program of the Litchfield Law School, whose existence extended from 1784 to 1833 (Harno, 1953).

Moot court provides an opportunity for students to experience the drama of the courtroom, as students compete against each other and reenact actual cases. The best students are chosen to represent their school in regional competitions. The regional finalists meet each year and argue cases to determine the best national moot court team. In addition to affording an opportunity for students to compete against each other, moot court also provides an opportunity for the student to expose himself to the problems the lawyer is confronted with in a courtroom situation. By researching his case, writing his brief and finally presenting it in a courtroom environment, the student gains invaluable experience.

During the course of moot court training, the student receives some sense of when to stand up, when to sit down, when to speak or when to remain silent in the courtroom. He gets the feeling of speaking extemporaneously, and he learns to think on his feet. Perhaps, most importantly, the student learns to respect, at least ostensibly, the rulings of the court (Richardson, 1952). It is a program that has helped train generations of lawyers in the proper procedures that should be used in trying or arguing a case before a judge.

GRADUATE LEGAL EDUCATION. In the United States today there are over 3,000 students studying for advanced degrees in law beyond the LL.B or J.D. degrees (Hervey, 1966). Of the 135 accredited law schools, only 38 offer advanced-degree programs. Seventeen of these institutions award the master's degree in law (LL.M.). The remaining 21 offer programs leading to the LL.M. and the J.S.D. degrees (O'Hara, 1967).

Most students taking advanced work beyond the first degree in law terminate their academic work after completing the requirements for the LL.M. degree. In order to qualify for a master's program, an applicant must have his first degree in law, and an academic record indicating an ability to perform at a level of superior quality. The course of study generally consists of 16 to 24 credit hours of classroom and seminar work. Before the degree is awarded, the student is required to complete a thesis, or a written project, which represents substantial research in a legal field. Work for the master's degree in law may be taken on a part-time basis, and at least half of the candidates for the degree do it in this manner. Part-time students usually complete their work within a two- or three-year period. A full-time student is able to complete the program in one year.

A select group of students will continue on for the doctor of science of law (J.S.D. or S.J.D.). In 1965 only 29 doctoral degrees in law were awarded in the United States (U.S. Department of Health, Education and Welfare, 1966). For the doctorate, the programs are aimed at requiring some course work, but the major emphasis is placed on intensive research, a thesis of distinguished excellence and an oral examination. The doctoral candidate is generally required to study in residence for at least one year (McDowell & Mewett, 1955).

The modern law school graduate, more than any other generation of lawyers, is deciding to undertake postgraduate work for an advanced degree in law. The primary reason for most graduates is specialization in one particular field of law for professional purposes. Others wish to prepare for a teaching career or become research specialists. It is likely that this trend will continue and a demand will be made for an expansion of current programs and an increase in their number. The results will be beneficial to the profession, for they will produce a better-informed lawyer who will be able to deal more effectively with today's legal problems.

CONTINUING LEGAL EDUCATION. The well-informed lawyer recognizes that his legal education does not stop when he graduates from law school. To keep abreast of the current changes and trends in the law, the lawyer often relies on programs of continuing legal education offered under law school auspices. The programs have three functions: to provide (1) post law school instruction for young lawyers, usually emphasizing the practical aspects of practice; (2) general courses for the practicing members of the bar; and (3) training for a specialty in a particular area of the law (Stumpf, 1963).

All three functions have to do largely with professional competence and are accomplished mainly by oral presentation, such as lectures, panels, and seminars. These are supplemented by printed and mimeographed materials. Experts in the field and members of the bar with special expertise and law school faculty conduct the courses.

A continuing legal education program may be offered in cooperation with a local bar association, or the law school may undertake it independently (American Bar Association Journal, 1964). Regardless of sponsorship, the program's main objective is to prepare practicing lawyers to provide improved legal services to a greater number of people. Herein lies the importance of the contribution of continuing legal education to the law profession today.

Legal education, as well as the legal profession, will have to plan for the evolution of new areas and fields of law which are in their infancy now or are even beyond the range of contemplation at this time. Scientific progress and discoveries constantly provide new areas for consideration. For instance, the law of atomic energy and space law are not now part of the standard law school curriculum, and the question becomes, should they be?

There are numerous other decisions that will have to be made to more clearly define the scope and direction of legal education and how it will prepare the modern lawyer in a highly complex society. A common complaint often lodged against law schools is that they do not provide sufficient practical education for the law student. Greater emphasis will have to be placed upon this area in an attempt to provide more extensive legal services for a growing population which is more aware than ever of remedies available under the law. The trend toward specialization in the law will continue and will require more individualized work of one sort or another for students in law school. As the university community becomes more involved in the work of our society, greater research activities and facilities will have to be provided by law schools to meet the demands of solving our social and legal problems. More efficient ways will have to be conceived and introduced to streamline the research of the law. The introduction of data processing as a tool of research seems to be inevitable. The law school will have to provide training so that the law student, when he becomes a lawyer, will be able to utilize to the fullest the modern means for rapid, efficient research (Griswold, 1953) and in this way, be able to contribute more effectively to his profession and the society it serves.

William T. O'Hara
The University of
Connecticut

References

Allison, Junius L. "A Survey Report on Legal Clinics." *Student Lawyer* 6:18–20; 1961.

Amandes, Richard B. "How We Examine." *J Legal Ed* 11:566–70, 1959.

American Bar Association. *Report of the Section of Legal Education and Admissions to the Bar.* The Association, 1966.

American Bar Association Journal. "Broadening of Continuing Legal Education Urged by Second Arden House Conference." *Am Bar Assn J* 50: 136–8; 1964.

Association of American Law Schools. *Report of the Committee on Teaching and Examination Methods.* The Association, 1955. p. 151–7.

Association of American Law Schools. *Report of the Curriculum Committee.* The Association, 1960. p. 167–82.

Association of American Law Schools. *Anatomy of Modern Legal Education.* West Publishing Company, 1961. 517p.

Brown, John R. "The Trumpet Sounds: Gideon—A

First Call to the Law School." *Texas Law R* 43: 312–8; 1965.
Chroust, Anton-Hermann. *The Rise of the Legal Profession in America.* U Oklahoma Press, 2:318; 1965.
Columbia Law Review. "Modern Trends in Legal Education." *Columbia Law R* 64:710–34; 1964.
Currie, B. "The Materials of Law Study." *J Legal Ed* 3:331–83; 1951.
Educational Testing Service. *Law School Admission Test, Bulletin of Information for Candidates 1966–67.* ETS, 1966. 70p.
Florida Statutes. "Florida Rules of Criminal Procedure, Rule No. 2." *Florida Statutes* 3:3935–6; 1965.
Forer, Lois G. "Training the Lawyer." *Am Bar Assn J* 47:354–8; 1961.
Freeman, Harrop. "Legal Education: Some Farther-Out Proposals." *J Legal Ed* 17:272–84; 1965.
Goodrich, Herbert F. "Law School and Law Teacher, 1952." *J Legal Ed* 5:7–17; 1952.
Green, Leon. "Basic Training for Law School." *J Legal Ed* 1:273–9; 1948.
Griswold, Erwin N. "The Future of Legal Education." *J Legal Ed* 5:439–49; 1953.
Harno, Albert G. *Legal Education in the United States.* Bancroft-Whitney, 1953. 211p.
Hervey, John G. "Law School Developments." *J Legal Ed* 19:200–16; 1966.
Jones, Harry W. "Local Law Schools vs. National Law Schools: A Comparison of Concepts, Functions, and Opportunities." *J Legal Ed* 10:281–93; 1958.
Knickerbocker, K. L. "Talents for the Study of Law." *J Legal Ed* 12:532–41; 1960.
Landman, J. Henry. "The Curriculum of the Law School." *Am Bar Assn J* 47:156–9; 1961.
Lunneborg, Clifford E., and Lunneborg, Patricia W. "Relations of Background Characteristics of Success in the First Year of Law School." *J Legal Ed* 18:425–36; 1966.
Maitland, F. W. *The Constitutional History of England.* U Press, 1963. 548p.
Mancuso, Edward T. "Law Students and Defender Offices." *Legal Aid Brief Case* 24:242–46; 1966.
McDowell, Banks, Jr., and Mewett, A. W. "What Are Teachers Made Of." *J Legal Ed* 8:79–88; 1955.
Moreland, Roy. "Unfair Domination of Law Reviews." *J Legal Ed* 12:424–5; 1960.
O'Hara, W. T. *The Directory of Graduate Law Study.* U Connecticut School Law, 1967. 41p.
Peairs, C. A. "Essays on the Teaching of Law." *J Legal Ed* 12:323–71; 1960.
Prosser, William L. "Advice to the Lovelorn." *J Legal Ed* 3:505–14; 1951.
Richardson, J. R. "Is There a Place for Moot Court in the Law School Curriculum." *J Legal Ed* 4:431–5; 1952.
Rohan, Patrick J. "Some Basic Assumptions and Limitations of Current Curriculum Planning." *J Legal Ed* 16:289–99; 1964.
Strong, Frank R. "Further Observations of Pre-Legal Education." *J Legal Ed* 7:540–51; 1955.
Student Lawyer Journal. p. 3; 1967.
Stumpf, Felix F. "Continuing Legal Education: Its Role in Tomorrow's Practice of the Law." *Am Bar Assn J* 49:248–50; 1963.
Traynor, Roger J. "To the Right Honorable Law Reviews." *U.C.L.A. Law R* 10:3–10; 1962.
U.S. Department of Health, Education and Welfare. *Digest of Educational Statistics.* USOE, 1966. 124p.
University of Notre Dame. *Law School Bulletin.* The University, 1965. 44p.
Warren, Charles. *A History of the American Bar.* Howard Fertig Inc., 1966. 586p.
Weihofen, Henry. "Types of Question." *Rocky Mountain Law R* 23:110–18; 1950.
West Publishing Company. *Directory of Law Teachers.* The Company, 1967. 317p.
Williams, Anthony W. "The Student View on What Examination Techniques Best Test Legal Capabilities." *Rocky Mountain Law R* 23:123–6; 1950.

LIBRARIES

For about 4,000 years, the task of librarians has been essentially unchanged. They try to select from the mass of material available that which will be useful to their particular clientele. They organize it in some fashion, usually involving a classification scheme to group like materials together and some type of index to the collection (in American libraries, usually a card catalog). Having arranged the material, they then attempt to help the user find those items most appropriate to his particular needs.

This task has always seemed a rather quiet and peaceful pursuit to the general public. Since World War II, however, whatever peace and quiet may have existed in libraries has been rudely dispersed by the intrusion of problems created by changes in the society surrounding libraries.

The unexpected growth of the American population, coupled with the much-noted increase in the volume of publication, has placed heavy burdens on a library system ill equipped to manage them. Librarians are increasingly concerned with finding new techniques for carrying out their traditional tasks as standard procedures creak and groan under present burdens. It is not necessary to review here in detail the growth and changes in the American population since the end of World War II. Demographers of the 1930's had predicted that the United States would reach a maximum population of 165 million by the year 2000, and that the population would thereafter decline. By September 1, 1966, the population had reached an estimated 197 million (*New York Times,* 1967), with predictions that it would surpass 220 million by 1975 (Day & Day, 1964). This greatly increased growth has created a need for vastly expanded physical facilities of all kinds to serve the increased population. In addition, the problems of social planners have been compounded by the skewing of the normal age distribution, with a relatively small working and tax-paying population supporting greatly increased populations of children and persons of retirement age. The older and younger age groups require expensive social service facilities, with the result that the tax resources of the states and local communities are nearly exhausted. Thus libraries (which have never held the highest priority in the allocation of public funds) must struggle for additional revenues at a time when funds are in short supply. The fact that an increasingly large percentage of persons of college age are enrolling in colleges creates even greater demands on library services. All studies of library users have shown a high degree of correlation between level of education and use of libraries: the more education, the greater the use of the library.

The population explosion has been paralleled by an explosion in publishing. A standard statistic, much repeated, asserts that 90 percent of all the scientists who ever lived are alive now—and they all seem to be publishing furiously. American book-trade publishing shows dramatic increases, in addition, in the number of ordinary trade books published. In 1950, the United States published 11,022 trade titles (*American Library Annual*, 1958). In 1966, the number had risen to 30,050 (*Bowker Annual . . .* , 1967).

In the field of journal publication, the increase has been even more startling. Chemists, who published about 1,000 articles monthly in 1950, published 13,000 per month in 1965 (*Time Magazine*, 1965). It has been estimated that the number of periodicals being published throughout the world now runs around 100,000 titles (Browne, 1962). Abstracting and indexing services have been unable to keep up with this increase, and the result has been a failure to achieve full bibliographic control of all the available material.

In addition to the journal publications, there is a vast tide of research-report literature, much of it uncontrolled by current systems, whether library-based, privately produced, or governmentally supported. It becomes increasingly difficult to determine if a given piece of information has been published, and some organizations have come to the conclusion that it is cheaper to repeat experiments than to attempt to discover if they have already been done.

FACILITIES. What are the resources with which the American library system must meet this growing pressure? A general statement can summarize quickly for all types of libraries: they are inadequate in collections, personnel, and budgets to cope with the demands being made upon them. Indeed, some extreme critics, unmindful of the chronic poverty of the American library system, have assured librarians that their institutions are obsolete. Having demonstrated to their own satisfaction that libraries are not able to meet current needs, they suggest a new type of institution (the computer-based information center) staffed with a new type of personnel (the information specialist or documentalist).

Academic Libraries. Samore (1965) outlines the factors that are expected to increase demand for college and library services. By 1975, it is estimated, 9 million persons—half the college-age population—will be enrolled in institutions of higher education. Furthermore, there is a significant increase in graduate study, and especially in programs leading to the doctorate. The annual rate of increase in doctoral programs has been about 7 percent since 1900—and, of course, doctoral candidates are the heaviest users of academic library resources. At the same time, universities are expanding their off-campus programs, with a concomitant need to build library resources in centers removed from the campus. Federal research programs have led to increased demands on libraries for materials to support this federally financed research. The growth of new programs in the curriculum places added pressures on budgets that are inadequate to support past programs. Tsien and Winger (1966) summarize the problems involved in the creation of the new area-studies programs in the universities.

After reviewing the adequacy of academic libraries to meet these demands, Samore (1965) concludes that American academic libraries are clearly understaffed, poorly housed, and inadequate in resources. A single set of figures may illustrate his point: 2 percent of American academic libraries own 39 percent of all volumes held, spend 36 percent of the total expenditures for library materials, and employ 35 percent of the total number of personnel. The other 98 percent, it may be suspected—which must divide the remaining money, staff, and books—do not have resources adequate to support significant programs of higher education.

If one measures academic libraries against the American Library Association's standards for such libraries, which were created by the Association of College and Research Libraries (1958), the results are disquieting: 73 percent are below standard in number of volumes; 72 percent are below standard in personnel; and 54 percent are below standard in expenditures. It should be noted that these standards are envisioned as minimum standards, not as criteria for resplendent excellence.

While the bulk of academic libraries are weak in resources, the largest libraries are faced with quite another problem, which hampers effective service. Two decades ago, Rider (1944) reported that the growth of the research library was not arithmetic, but exponential, and that the collections of research libraries had tended to double in size every 16 years since the year 1830. This initial study is supported by a more recent survey reported by Dunn and others (1965), which affirms that the exponential rate of growth still prevails, with no sign of slackening, although the holdings of the very largest libraries seem to be doubling every 18–20 years. The average rate, however, for the 54 libraries studied was 17 years, with annual acquisitions tending to double every 9–12 years.

These large libraries find it increasingly difficult to house their collections and almost impossible to keep cataloging current with acquisitions. They are discovering that access to such collections becomes increasingly difficult as the catalog becomes increasingly complex. In many of the libraries, as a result of overcrowding of the main building, it has been necessary to relocate volumes by the hundreds of thousands, without being able to alter all catalog records, so that the central catalog no longer is a reliable indicator of the actual physical location of the materials. This makes swift retrieval of the desired volume sometimes impossible.

Given this embarrassment of riches, however, the research collections are still unable to satisfy the demands of the university researcher. The large universities have been forced to admit that they are not able to buy all the materials they need for current research, and a variety of cooperative ventures have been embarked upon in the hope that they will satisfy the needs of the scholar, without committing the local institution to the hopeless task of trying to acquire everything that is being published or has ever been published. It must be admitted, however, that such devices also delay access to the material which a given scholar may want.

Public Libraries. The pattern in the public library field is strikingly similar to that in the academic libraries: a relatively few splendid collections, with the majority of public libraries inadequately staffed, supported, and supplied to meet the demands being placed upon them. Drennan (1965) reports that nearly 69 percent of public libraries in his study did not meet minimum standards in number of volumes, while 97 percent failed to meet the standard for general operating expenditures. These minimum standards were prepared by the Public Library Division of the American Library Association (1956), while another set of guidelines for small public libraries was issued by that same body later (1962). The American Library Association's new standards for public libraries were presented to the ALA Council in the summer of 1966 and met with considerable resistance from a minority because of the strict adherence to the systems concept.

Although many public libraries are short of staff and do not have adequate budgets, they are faced with increasing use, particularly by students at all levels of education. The problem is of such magnitude that in a recent annual conference, the American Library Association held a "conference within a conference" to discuss student use of libraries.

The general awareness of the inadequacy of the public library system has led to a variety of surveys aimed at finding solutions to this problem. The Martin and Bowler (1965) study of public library service in the state of California may be taken as a typical example. This study urges the development of systems of libraries to solve the problems of the inadequate small library, and it proposes that the state library take a role of leadership through the assumption of regulatory responsibilities. The Francis R. St. John Library Consultants (1965) survey of Ontario (Canada) libraries indicates that the same need is being felt in Canadian libraries. This firm surveyed all types of libraries, however, and urged that the various types join in cooperative efforts to overcome the weaknesses of libraries taken individually. Like American surveys, it criticizes the inefficiency of small units.

School Libraries. The American Association of School Libraries (1960) produced a set of standards for school library programs. Measurement of school libraries against these standards by Mahar (1965) revealed the same picture which obtains among the public and academic libraries: most schools did not meet minimum requirements. A most striking summary was given by President Johnson (1965), who reported to the Congress that almost 70 percent of public elementary schools lacked libraries, while 84 percent lacked librarians. He also noted that the majority of high school libraries did not meet minimum standards. The American Library Association (1965) reported that it would require $600 million to bring public school libraries up to a minimum standard of financial support.

Thus the public, school, and college/university library systems of this country face the greatly increased demands for service and the flood of new publications severely handicapped in their efforts to meet them. Confronted with a growing number of people, with a larger percentage of students going on to college, with changes in the curriculum at every level of education demanding expanded collections, with the growth of independent study by students, with new areas of knowledge to be represented in the collections (e.g., nuclear physics, lasers, masers, space technology), the library system of the country finds itself in difficulty. A variety of means have been proposed or adopted to aid in the solution of the library's problems.

INNOVATIONS. Federal Aid to Libraries. The first federal aid to libraries was accomplished by the passage of the Library Services Act in 1956. This legislation was intended to improve public library service to rural areas. The original five-year act was renewed in 1960, while in 1964 it was expanded under a new title, the Library Services and Construction Act (adding funds to support building programs).

In addition to this early aid to public libraries, more recent legislation has extended federal assistance to other types of libraries. The Elementary and Secondary Education Act includes a title supporting the purchase of school library materials. The 1967 appropriation for this purpose was $145 million, with an authorization for fiscal 1965 of $154.5 million. The impact of this legislation on school library collections was felt very soon, creating in its wake a pressure for additional staff to handle the new materials and accelerating the creation of new private or public organizations to process such materials centrally.

The Higher Education Facilities Act includes libraries among the buildings whose construction can be supported by federal funds. In 1967, $450 million was appropriated for undergraduate buildings and $60 million for graduate facilities. The combined authorizations for future years run to $848 million in fiscal 1968 and to $1.05 billion in 1969. In addition, the Higher Education Act appropriated $25 million for fiscal 1967 for college library resources; $3.75 million for training in librarianship, and $3.55 million for research in library problems.

The Medical Library Assistance Act for fiscal 1967 provides $7.5 million for construction; $1 million for training; $1.5 million for research; and $2.7 million for resources.

This developing federal interest in the library resources of the country was further indicated by President Johnson's creation on September 2, 1966, by Executive Order, of the National Advisory Commission on Libraries to "appraise the role of libraries as resources for scholarly pursuit, as centers for the dissemination of knowledge, and as components of the nation's rapidly evolving communications and information-exchange network" (*Federal Register*, 1966). The President charged the group with developing recommendations which would ensure an effective and efficient library system.

State Aid to Libraries. The federal program distributes its funds through the state library agencies. The first impact of the federal program has been to strengthen the several state libraries—and even to contribute to the establishment of such an agency when there was none. The sudden expansion of state library staffs to meet the increase in activity has not been without its problems. Long (1966) surveyed the 50 state libraries, discovering that the shortage of trained personnel to fill consultant positions was acute. Although such consultants are to aid libraries by giving them expert advice, Long discovered that 20 percent of the consultants had held no other library job. Some 31 percent had received their highest library science degree at least 20 years ago, while 65 percent received their formal training more than 10 years ago. Long's work suggests that the consultants, on the whole, are not as well prepared for their positions as would be desirable.

The matching nature of federal funds, however, has led to increased state appropriations for library service. It has also focused attention on the problems of libraries and has led to the development of state legislation aimed at encouraging library systems within the states. New York is perhaps the most advanced of the states in such legislation. Legislative enactments have so encouraged system planning that by 1966 the state had 22 library systems serving 98 percent of the population. In 1966, the legislature appropriated $700,000 for the development of a statewide information system and reference and research library program. Other states are moving in this direction. The state of Michigan authorized a study of library resources, done by the Nelson Associates (1966), which recommended the creation of regional reference centers and advocated the creation of a Coordination Council on Reference and Research Library Resources, which would report annually to the governor of the state. It further recommended that the libraries of the University of Michigan, Michigan State University, and Wayne State University—in addition to the Detroit Public Library and the State Library—be designated as statewide resource libraries, whose budgets would be augmented by state funds. Thus academic library resources would become available to the general public. The New Jersey Library Association Library Development Comitee has produced a plan calling for a network of area reference libraries, which was summarized by Gaver (1966).

Federal assistance, plus increased state concern for library problems, seems to be leading in the direction of systems of public libraries. In addition, however, there is a growing belief that libraries of all types should be joined in one interrelated library network, with the resources of any library at the disposal of all libraries.

Proposed National Systems. Kent (1965) presents the proposed National Science Library System conceived by Dr. Stafford Warren, Special Assistant to the President of the United States for Mental Retardation. Warren envisions a system of seven regional centers, holding the contents of the published scientific journals on tape or in some variety of microform, employing computer technology to analyze, store, search, and distribute those materials. Knox (1966) makes clear the reasons for the federal government's interest in such a system. He reported that federal expenditures on research and development in fiscal 1966 amounted to $15 billion. A 10 percent gain in R & D productivity by improved access to the literature would mean a savings of $1.5 billion released for other purposes. The federal government's Committee on Scientific and Technical Information has recommended that the federal government take an explicit responsibility for ensuring that a copy of all important scientific and technological literature be readily accessible to researchers anywhere in the United States. Following Warren's plan, it has been recommended that regional centers be established to receive copies in some form of all such literature.

Such a system has already been set up for part of the scientific literature—the Medical Literature and Analysis System (MEDLARS) of the National Library of Medicine. Regional centers have been selected to receive computer tapes of the medical materials which have been analyzed by the Library of Medicine. Subject searches for bibliographic citations are then possible at the regional centers.

Mohrhardt (Mohrhardt & Oliveri, 1967), Director of the National Agricultural Library, has proposed a national network of biological-agricultural libraries. He urges that such a system be computer-based and argues, therefore, that input must be made uniform to provide compatibility of information on which a computer system must depend. Programming and testing of a subject analysis system for the *Bibliography of Agriculture* is under way, which will provide monthly subject indexes for the first time. Automation of the citations themselves is scheduled for 1969. This will permit the preparation of periodic bibliographies on specialized subjects, selective dissemination of pertinent scientific information, and responses to demands for special searches. All of these proposed systems depend for their success, in the final analysis, on the perfection of the computer as a tool useful in information retrieval. Unless high-speed conversion of text to machine-readable form becomes possible, coupled with automatic subject analysis of computer-stored text, without human intervention, it is difficult to see how the proposed systems could contribute more than mere retrieval of bibliographic citations.

Information Retrieval and the Computer. A good summary of the hoped-for use of computers in information retrieval is given by Licklider (1965). He argues that we need to substitute for the book and journal some machine which will make it easy to transmit information without having to transport either the reader or the material. He also asserts that we need a device which will not only present information to people, but will have processed it for them beforehand—and automatically. The computer seems the likely candidate to satisfy these needs, in his view, although he is aware of the problems which must be solved before the ideal "pre-cognitive" system can be created.

Wasserman (1965) surveys the same general problem, introducing an examination of several systems which have been produced. He urges more studies of the users of libraries and the information system so that we will know what to build machine systems for. He argues that although it is clear libraries must adopt machines to do data processing, it is not yet clear that retrieval of information from large general collections can be done at a price which will be economically feasible.

A very ambitious experiment is underway at Massachusetts Institute of Technology, following a conference lasting five weeks and involving 35 people, assisted by more than 140 resource papers. Overhage and Harman (1965) summarize the recommendations of that conference. The basic objective of the Information Transfer Experiments (INTREX) which will be undertaken will be to demonstrate the feasibility of modernizing library procedures, using an on-line computer and looking forward to the integrating of a university library with a national library system. The experiments envisioned will alter a model library's services to test user reaction to the presentation or withdrawal of old services—or of new and previously unknown services and techniques. They will experiment with an "augmented" catalog (broader coverage and deeper subject indexing), with access to computer-stored text via telephone and remote consoles, with system integration with other libraries, and will also carry on various experiments in information retrieval. It is hoped that the results will provide a design for a system which can become operational in the 1970's.

Since most American libraries follow the cataloging of the Library of Congress, the decisions of that library in this area are of critical importance to any future network. The Council on Library Resources (1963) reported on the plans of the Library of Congress for automating its procedures. If the Library of Congress prepares machine-readable cataloging information, a massive base will have been prepared for a national computer-based system of retrieving information. In 1967, a selected group of libraries were receiving computer tapes containing the cataloging data on English-language monographs as an experimental undertaking. Buckland (1965) summarized the problem which would have to be met in preparing bibliographical data for machine use, and emphasized the importance of delineating each item clearly and coding it for future machine isolation.

In addition to the relatively simple matter of the bibliographic citation, there is the greater problem of automatic analysis of machine-stored text. Stevens (1965) prepared a state-of-the-art report which is optimistic, believing that such automatic indexing is possible and that eventually it will excel human indexing in speed and quality. At the moment, however, there are several problems which have not been conquered. The real villain of the piece is the "natural language," with its endless ambiguities and its fundamentally irrational procedures. A major difficulty in evaluating the success of information retrieval systems is the establishment of a meaningful measurement of relevancy of information retrieved—and then of comparing newer systems with the traditional ones in terms of the relevancy of information. She also points out that the problem of the cost of such systems is still an unsettled matter. Finally, she notes that some seem to suggest that subject indexes are not the most important source in literature searches—or even a major source—and therefore the extensive efforts to attempt to produce automatic subject analysis may be vain.

In reporting on an investigation into the automation of American libraries, Bryan (1967) was surprised at how little there actually is, considering the amount of literature on the topic. Of real information retrieval he could find no examples. He concluded that the most important part in setting up an automated system is the preliminary analysis and planning—as some failures have made lamentably clear. He urges librarians to do the requisite planning, rather than making a hasty commitment to the system (and then reflects that he suspects that there are many librarians who have very little intention of hastening into anything).

The caution of some librarians may be understood, although not documented at this moment, as a result of the experiences of some installations. At least one highly publicized automated library has fallen on evil days, if word-of-mouth reports are correct. But of printed evidence of disaster there is yet no sign. There seems to have been an occasional rush into a machine operation impelled more by a desire to be modern and up to date than by carefully researched preparation to accomplish a given job. But that American libraries must learn to use the computer effectively there can be no doubt: they will not have the manpower to handle increased demands by the old methods.

Standards and Measurements. The simple question "Will an automated system reduce costs?" has led librarians to an increasing concern with effective means of measuring the efficiency of specific services, in order that meaningful comparisons between the costs of current systems and of proposed automated systems can be made. In addition, there has been a growing awareness that the Congress which has given money to support service is eventually—in one form or another—going to ask for an accounting of those funds, and a demonstration that improvements have been made.

One of the first fruits of this concern is the statistical handbook prepared by the Statistics Coordinating Committee of the American Library Association (1966). It makes a first effort to achieve a set of definitions for use in reporting on library resources and services. The Committee is concerned with a national program of library statistics, and such a national reporting demands uniformity in terminology and analysis. One example of the differences which currently exist in reporting statistics may perhaps suffice to illustrate the whole range of library figures which need common definition. A frequently cited figure is the size of the library's book collection. There are two perfectly proper ways of counting books: one counts bibliographic units; the other counts physical volumes. In the first system, a periodical set which consists of 150 separately bound volumes is counted as one unit. In the second system, it would be counted as 150 units. Either is legitimate, but one can easily see that comparisons of two libraries of equal size, each reporting on a different basis, would make one look considerably smaller than the other.

There has also been introduced into library literature a type of material not unknown in other disciplines. Dougherty and Heinritz's (1966) presentation of the methods of analysis and measurement techniques used by business and industry may stand as an example of a growing body of material. The attempt is being made to introduce the procedures of management experts to library administrators. Thus there is a new concern with flow charting, operations analysis, and time-and-motion study. Although this field is not absolutely new in library literature, there is a growing emphasis upon it.

Following hard upon this emphasis is an increasing number of studies of costs, and especially of comparative costs as a basis for evaluating different systems of procedure. Once again, this is a field with many recent studies, but the report of Hendricks (1966) may serve as an example. He was concerned with comparing the costs of processing books in individual libraries with the costs of a processing center serving a group of libraries. One of the difficulties he encountered arose out of the fact that it was difficult to fix the role of such things as overhead costs in the individual libraries' expenditures. Many administrators who have shifted to automated procedures have been unable to make reliable comparisons of costs because of the lack of careful cost accounting under the older method. This will be an area of growing concern as library systems develop.

LIBRARY EDUCATION. This survey of the major issues facing American librarianship would not be complete without reference to the agencies training librarians for service at this vexing time. Library education has felt the direct impact of the changes in the library world, which have led to questions concerning current training and to proposals for its alteration to meet current needs more directly.

Current Pattern. As of July 1967, 42 master's degree programs had been accredited by the Committee on Accreditation of the American Library Association (*Library Journal,* 1967). These programs provide the professional credentials which many libraries require for new employees. There are a number of master's programs not accredited by ALA, and a larger number of schools offering a major or minor in librarianship at the undergraduate level. Most recently, two-year library-technician programs have been instituted in the community or junior colleges.

The master's programs are to train personnel for all types of jobs in all types of libraries. To accomplish this purpose, most schools have a core of required courses, taken by all students, regardless of the type of library in which they intend to work. This core is supposed to encompass the basis of professional library work. In addition, a relatively limited number of courses are taken as library science electives, giving the student some opportunity to specialize by type of library or type of work. In addition, some 11 schools offer the doctorate in library science. There has been a growing feeling that, in the face of the great shortage of librarians and the need for introducing the newer technology into library education, this system is no longer satisfactory. A number of proposals have been made suggesting alterations in the traditional pattern of library education.

Suggested Innovations. Unfortunately for the peace of mind of library-school administrators, the suggested changes divide into two quite different categories: (1) those aimed at producing more librarians by reducing the requirements for training, and (2) those asking for more training to meet the need for greater specialization. The year 1966 saw the following recommendations being made: (1) introduce a library aide program into the high school curriculum (Orne, 1966); (2) use graduates of the two-year community college programs as library technicians (Knapp, 1966); (3) accept an 18-hour minor taken in the undergraduate program (McDonough, 1966); (4) move the basic preparation to an undergraduate major (Franklin, 1966; R. Johnson, 1966; Mutschler, 1966; Nyren, 1966; Orne, 1966; Rees, 1966; Warncke, 1966); (5) accept the graduates of unaccredited programs (R. Johnson, 1966); (6) reduce the time required at the master's degree level to one semester (Powell, 1966).

All of these proposals suggest a reduction in training to produce more personnel for libraries. Concurrently, it is advocated that library positions be more carefully analyzed to separate out the clerical and paraprofessional aspects, with master's degree holders being assigned only to those positions which require additional training. Sudar (1966) advocates three distinct levels of training: (1) the graduate level for those who will be the leaders and researchers of the field; (2) a program at the bachelor's level for junior and senior professionals; (3) a two-year program to prepare library assistants to handle routines. He draws a parallel with other professions, which have created categories of technicians to free the professionals of lower echelon tasks.

At the same time, some librarians stress the need for more highly specialized training. Ellsworth (1966) admits that the large university library needs to utilize the time of its professionals to better advantage, but he believes that it would be a very serious error to lower the qualifications of librarians for university service. He feels that what is needed is people who know more, not less. At the Second Forum on Education for Special Librarianship (*Special Libraries,* 1967), there seemed to be agreement that more training, rather than less, is needed to meet the demands in the special library. Swank (1967), after summarizing the curricular alterations which documentation and information science appear to demand, noted that it may be necessary to extend the basic graduate program to two years, rather than reduce it.

These disparities of opinion may result from the fact that, generally speaking, public and school librarians face tasks different from those encountered by the librarians of large university or special libraries. If so, serious restudy of the core curriculum would seem in order. It may be that the amount of time devoted to this body of knowledge which all librarians should share can be drastically reduced. It may be feasible to introduce specialization into the master's program to a greater degree than has been heretofore held consistent with sound professional training. It seems clear, in any event, that a large-scale study of actual jobs performed in the various types and sizes of libraries, leading to a delineation of requisite skills and knowledges for each, is essential. These varying opinions need to be illuminated with a body of data concerning the realities of library work which is not presently available.

Wallace J. Bonk
University of Michigan

References

American Association of School Libraries. *Standards for School Library Programs.* ALA, 1960. 152p.
American Library Annual, 1958. Bowker, 1958.
American Library Association. *National Inventory of Library Needs.* ALA, 1965. 72p.
American Library Association. Public Library Division. *Interim Standards for Small Public Libraries: Guidelines Toward Achieving the Goals of Public Library Service.* ALA, 1956. 72p.
American Library Association. Public Library Division. *Public Library Service: A Guide to Evaluation with Minimum Standards.* ALA, 1962. 74p.
American Library Association. Statistics Coordinating Project. *Library Statistics: A Handbook of Concepts, Definitions, and Terminology.* ALA, 1966. 160p.
Association of College and Research Libraries. *College and University Library Accreditation Standards, 1957.* The Association, 1958. 46p.
Bourne, Charles P. "The World's Technical Journal Literature; An Estimate of Volume, Origin, Language, Field, Indexing, and Abstracting." *Am Documentation* 13:159–68; 1962.
Bowker Annual of Library and Book Trade Information, 1967. Bowker, 1967.
Bryan, Harrison. "American Automation in Action." *Lib J* 92:189–96; 1967.
Buckland, Lawrence F. *The Recording of Library of Congress Bibliographical Data in Machine Form.* Council on Library Resources, 1965. 54p.
Council on Library Resources, Inc. *Automation and the Library of Congress.* The Council, 1963. 88p.
Day, Lincoln H., and Day, Alice T. *Too Many Americans.* Houghton, 1964.
Dougherty, Richard M., and Heinritz, Fred J. *Scientific Management of Library Operations.* Scarecrow Press, 1966. 258p.
Drennan, Henry T. "The Public Library Service Gap." In *National Inventory of Library Needs.* ALA, 1965. p. 39–44.
Dunn, O. C., and others. *The Past and Likely Future of 58 Research Libraries, 1951–1980.* Purdue U Library and Audio Visual Center, 1965. 82p.
Ellsworth, Ralph. "Library Education and the Talent Shortage." *Lib J* 91:1765; 1966.
Federal Register 31:11709–10; 1966.
Francis St. John Library Consultants, Inc. *Ontario Libraries, a Province-Wide Survey and Plan.* Ontario Library Association, 1965. 182p.
Franklin, Robert. "Library Education and the Talent Shortage." *Lib J* 91:1762–3; 1966.
Gaver, Mary V. "The New Jersey Plan." *ALA B:* 60:1138–42; 1966.
Hendricks, Donald D. *Comparative Costs of Book Processing in a Processing Center and in Five Individual Libraries.* Illinois State Library, 1966. 89p.
Johnson, Lyndon B. "Full Educational Opportunity —Message from the President." *Congressional Rec* 111:499–502; 1965.
Johnson, Robert K. "Library Education and the Talent Shortage." *Lib J* 91:1768–9; 1966.
Kent, Allan. *Library Planning for Automation.* Spartan Books, 1965. 195p.
Knapp, Patricia. "Division of Responsibility." *Lib J* 91: 4889–91; 1966.
Knox, William T. "National Information Networks and Special Libraries." *Special Lib* 57:627–30; 1966.
Library Journal 92:2874; 1967.
Licklider, J. C. R. *Libraries of the Future.* Massachusetts Institute of Technology Press, 1965. 219p.
Long, Marie A. *The State Library Consultant at Work.* Illinois State Library, 1966. 103p.
Mahar, Mary H. "Inventory of Library Needs— School Libraries." In *National Inventory of Library Needs.* ALA, 1965. p. 23–7.
Martin, Lowell, and Bowler, Roberta. *Public Library Service Equal to the Challenge of California: A Report to the State Librarian.* California State Library, 1965. 132p.
McDonough, Roger. "Library Education and the Talent Shortage." *Lib J* 91:1764–5; 1966.

Mohrhardt, Foster E., and Oliveri, Blanche L. "A National Network of Biological-Agricultural Libraries." *Col and Res Lib* 27:9–16; 1967.

Mutschler, Herbert F. "Library Education and the Talent Shortage." *Lib J* 91:1772–3; 1966.

Nelson Associates, Inc. *Reference and Research Library Needs in Michigan; A Study of Resources, Needs and Patterns of Use, with Recommendations for Improvements in Service.* Nelson Associates, 1966. 184p.

New York Times. September 17, 1967. p. 11.

Nyren, Karl. "Library Education and the Talent Shortage." *Lib J* 91:1765–6; 1966.

Orne, Jerrold. "Library Education and the Talent Shortage." *Lib J* 91:1763–4; 1966.

Overhage, Carl F. J., and Harman, R. Joyce. *INTREX: Report of a Planning Conference on Information Transfer Experiments.* Massachusetts Institute of Technology Press, 1965. 276p.

Powell, Donald M. "Library Education and the Talent Shortage." *Lib J* 91:1768; 1966.

Rees, Louise. "The Practitioners are Right." *Lib J* 91:4885–6; 1966.

Rider, Fremont. *The Scholar and the Future of the Research Library.* Hadham Press, 1944. 236p.

Samore, Theodore. "Inventory of Academic Library Resources and Services: Needs and Prospects." In *National Inventory of Library Needs.* ALA, 1965. p. 45–63.

Special Libraries. "Second Annual Forum on Education for Special Libraries." *Special Lib* 58:21–40; 1967.

Stevens, Mary E. *Automatic Indexing: A State-of-the-Art Report.* GPO, 1965. 220p.

Sudar, Dan D. "Three Levels of Library Education." *Lib J* 91:4899–903; 1966.

Swank, Raynard C. "Documentation and Information Science in the Core Library School Curriculum." *Special Lib* 58:40–4; 1967.

Time Magazine. September 3, 1965. p. 52.

Tsien, Tsuen-Hsuin, and Winger, Howard. *Area Studies and the Library.* U Chicago Press, 1966. 184p.

Warncke, Ruth. "The Fifth-Year Halo." *Lib J* 91:4883–4; 1966.

Wasserman, Paul. *The Librarian and the Machine: Observations on the Applications of Machines in Administration of College and University Libraries.* Gale Research Co., 1965. 170p.

LISTENING

Listening, as a receptive communication skill, has a parallel relationship to reading and in its aural aspects is closely related to speech. Listening depends on hearing, but the two terms are not synonymous. Hearing involves the conversion of pressure waves into neural impulses which move to the brain for interpretation. Listening is the process of interpretation. A distinction is drawn by some authorities between listening to linguistic material and to other sounds. Brown (D. Brown, 1954) proposed the term "auding" for the former process, but this suggestion has not been widely accepted or adopted. A distinction must also be drawn between intelligibility and listening comprehension. Intelligibility is a function of both the original message and the signal by which the message is carried. If the signal can be heard, and can be converted into a message which can be interpreted in terms of his past experience by the person receiving it, then the signal and the message are said to be intelligible. When an intelligible message is related to his past experience by a listener, then listening comprehension occurs (Harwood, 1950). Extensive experiments on intelligibility have been reported by Broadbent (1958).

Just as the term readability is given to measures of reading ease, so the term listenability is given to measures of listening ease. Earlier investigations on ways of measuring listenability tended to the use of established readability formulas. This procedure did not yield satisfactory results. A measure based on the average length of "idea units" and the number of words used which were not on Dale's "Long List of Most Commonly Used Words" has been developed and validated by Rogers (1952).

SCOPE AND EXTENT OF LISTENING. Notwithstanding the fact that listening is least emphasized in a formal way in curricula at all levels, this skill is used to a greater extent than any of the other communication skills—reading, writing, and speaking. Rankin (1926) was the first to make this point. In a study based on diaries kept by a small sample of persons from various walks of life, he reported that the average person spends 68 percent of his waking time in one form or another of communication. Of this proportion of the day, 16 percent was spent in writing, 15 percent in reading, 32 percent in speaking, and 42 percent in listening. The correctness of this finding, insofar as listening is concerned, has been verified in a number of studies in which more adequate samples were employed.

Other studies have been concerned with the demands made on pupils to listen in the classroom. Wilt (1949) found from observations made in 18 classes that 568 elementary school pupils were actually required to spend substantially more of the school day in listening activities than teachers had estimated. Children in these classes spent 58 percent of the day listening, of which over one-half was spent in listening to the teacher. The median percentages of time spent in listening in Grades 1 through 7 were 84, 56, 61, 52, 59, and 62 percent respectively. While 61 percent of the teachers ranked reading as the language arts skill that it was most important to teach, only 16 percent ranked listening in this position.

Markgraf (1957) accompanied a number of high school students on their daily classroom rounds. He reports that during 6,211 minutes of observation, students were expected to listen during 46 percent of the time. When study hall time is left out of consideration, this increases to 53 percent. Of the time spent in listening, 66 percent was spent in listening to teachers.

Obviously, demands to listen also are made on children's time outside of school. For example, Witty (1966), in summarizing his research on children's use of the mass media, reports that his sample of elementary and secondary school pupils watched television on an average of 20 hours each week, and listened to radio for 7 hours a week while in elementary school, and for 13 hours while in secondary school. Even when account is taken of the visual component in television, it seems clear that well over half of the time that a child is awake is devoted to listening activities of one kind or another.

LITERATURE ON LISTENING. An annotated bibliography on listening by Duker (1964) lists 880 items on listening, and since its publication, well over 400 additional items have appeared in the literature.

A small number of books on listening, of which the one by Nichols and Stevens (1957) is best known, have been published. Almost all of these books are designed for use as textbooks either in college courses, in industrial and business training courses, or for other adult groups. The amount of space devoted to listening in high school textbooks in English and speech shows a steady increase from year to year. Books on methods of teaching speech, the language arts, and English are also showing a greater degree of attention to the topic of listening. Curriculum bulletins, of which Nashville Public School's (1951) is one of the earliest and best, are increasingly devoting more space to the teaching of listening at all school levels.

Most of the research concerning the various facets of listening has been reported in academic theses. At this time, there are more than 165 doctoral and more than 220 masters' theses that have been written on this topic.

Attempts in a popular vein have been made to call the attention of the public to the importance of listening. An article by Zelko (1957) is a typical and early example. Many more items appear in professional journals in the areas of education, speech, psychology, English, and sociology.

Periodical reviews of research on listening appear in the triennial Language Arts issue of the *Review of Educational Research*. Reviews of research done during the decade of the 1950's were prepared by Keller (1960) and Toussaint (1960). Taylor (1964) contributed a number on listening to the "What Research Says to the Teacher" series.

Russell (1964) describes research on listening as "sporadic, atomistic, and inconclusive." He cites a number of studies which "support the assumption that listening abilities improve with instruction" and that give "conclusive evidence of the existence of a listening ability, or abilities, related to, but separate from other verbal abilities." He lists as implications of past research findings: (1) A theory of listening is needed. "Research is required to explore further the nature and development of listening ability or abilities and to apply these findings to structure and sequence in the language arts"; (2) Analytical studies should be made of listening situations and ingenious tests should be devised to improve current scattered measures; (3) Teaching methods and materials should be developed; (4) The problem of interrelationships between listening and other verbal skills should be investigated further; (5) Early attention should be given to listening ability in the school; and (6) The findings of a number of research studies should be analyzed and collated in order to assemble useful ways of teaching and testing listening.

A very perceptive and thorough review of the literature on the nature of listening and the teaching of listening is to be found in Petrie (1961).

RELATIONSHIPS TO LISTENING. Investigations having to do with the interrelationship between listening and other factors rest upon the premise that there exists such a definable and measurable quality as listening. This has been questioned by Petrie (1961), but has been established conclusively by a number of factor analysis studies of which the one by Spearritt (1961) is the latest. If these findings are accepted, as they generally are (see, for example, Russell, 1964), then it becomes worthwhile to examine various interrelationships which may shed light on the nature of the listening factor.

Since reading and listening are both receptive communication skills, it is reasonable to expect that they would be based, in part at least, on common skills and therefore would be closely related. This expectation is verified by Vineyard and Bailey (1960) and Brown (C. Brown, 1965) who report the results of correlational studies which establish a meaningful relationship between reading and listening, even when other factors, such as intelligence and school achievement, are held constant.

It is often assumed that the teaching of reading skills tends to improve listening skills and that instruction in listening tends to improve reading. This assumption is based on sound principles of transfer of training and is supported by a number of studies, but its validity remains somewhat of an open question. Hollingsworth (1963), in a very carefully performed study, failed to find any improvement in children's reading performance after an intensive course of instruction in listening. It is possible that his finding may have been due to the particular materials and methods he used in the teaching of listening. However, Seymour (1965) found that college freshmen who were enrolled in a one-semester course in listening showed a significant increase in reading ability.

Armstrong (1953) investigated the auditory and visual vocabularies of children from 6 to 13 years of age and reports that up until the age of 10, the auditory vocabulary is substantially larger than the visual. After the age of 10, the auditory vocabulary remained the larger, but the size of the difference decreased rapidly. It is one thesis of this study that the size of a child's auditory vocabulary has value as a predictor of reading ability. Moe (1957) found that a listening test was a better predictor of reading capacity than was a reading readiness test. He reports that a combination of mental age and listening test results constitutes the best predictor of reading potential.

The answer concerning the relative effectiveness of reading and listening for learning purposes has been sought in many studies for almost a century. An excellent review of the earlier literature in this area, together with a report of his own investigation, is found in Carver (1934). Findings of these studies have been in sharp conflict due to a lack of consistency in the materials, the subjects, and the evaluative devices used. A number of generalizations are often made on the basis of these conflicting findings, such as one to the effect that difficult material is more effectively learned by reading, while easier material is more readily learned by listening. Just as Kibler (1962) has found this to be untrue, so many of the other generalizations that have been commonly accepted will not prevail in the light of recent studies. Jester (1966) has established the fact that some individuals are more adapted to the visual than to the auditory modality and vice versa. The fact that individuals from both these classes have been used as subjects accounts for the erroneous conclusion that the simultaneous presentation of visual and auditory modalities is the most effective. Since, in the case of such a joint presentation, each subject selects the modality that he finds most efficient, it is inevitable that the results of a joint presentation would yield higher comprehension scores than when only one modality was used. It is extremely unlikely, according to Broadbent (1958), that more than a single channel is employed under these circumstances.

Jacobson (1950) investigated the informational capacity of the eye and the ear. He concluded that the ear has a huge informational capacity which is, however, significantly smaller than that of the eye.

Intelligence and School Achievement. According to Vineyard and Bailey (1960) and Brown (C. Brown, 1965), the high correlations between listening and intelligence, and between reading and intelligence, are probably somewhat spurious due to the common factors found in tests of reading, listening, and intelligence. These writers do, however, show a significant relationship between listening and intelligence even after other factors are held constant.

The most thorough and painstaking study of the interrelationships between listening ability and other factors at the elementary school level is found in Hall (1954).

Nichols (1948) submitted the names of 20 very good listeners and of 20 very poor listeners to their college instructors who rated the good listeners as more conscientious in their general work habits, more attentive in class, and generally excellent in their attitude toward class work. They also predicted higher course grades for the good listeners. Other studies also show a generally strong positive relationship between listening ability and scholastic achievement. Seymour (1965) reports a number of significant correlations with listening at the college freshman level.

Cultural Status. A false assumption is frequently made concerning the teaching of disadvantaged children to the effect that their poor reading abilities can be offset by instruction of an aural nature. Smith (1956) reports findings that establish conclusively that the deficiency of these children is one of language rather than merely of reading. Thus, these children may possibly listen better than they read but, notwithstanding, they are not, therefore, necessarily efficient listeners.

Speech. Strangely enough, the manner in which a speech is organized, or the manner in which it is delivered, does not appear to have a material effect on the comprehension of that speech. Beighley (1952) found, for instance, that while an easy speech was comprehended better than a difficult one, the delivery and organization of the speech had no significant effect on the ability of a group of college students to comprehend the speech. These findings have been confirmed in a number of more recent studies.

Miscellaneous Relationships to Listening. The idea that learning might take place as a result of auditory material during sleep has long been an appealing one. Many studies have been reported in which it was found that such learning actually can take place under a variety of circumstances. It is notable that in none of the studies reporting such results was there an adequate measure of the subject's state of sleep. Whenever the electroencephalograph was properly used to measure the level of sleep, it was found that learning takes place only during the period when the subjects have been awakened from deep sleep (Emmons, 1954). It seems to have been determined definitely, then, that learning of auditory material cannot occur during sleep, although learning can, and does, take place during periods when the subject has been awakened. It is doubtful that this type of learning is very efficient.

Rosenberg and Cohen (1964) report that there is a link between free-word-association norms and the processes by which a speaker selects verbal cues in order to distinguish one word from another and by which a listener identifies the speaker's referent words. Brown (C. Brown, 1959) has previously reported that this relationship did not exist.

The question as to whether listening to verbal communication is related to listening to music was investigated by Wilson (1960). Wilson found two separate, but closely related, factors that are significantly and positively correlated.

TEACHING OF LISTENING. A large number of studies and expository articles (Duker, 1964) concern themselves with the teaching of listening at all levels, from preschool stages to adult education. There is general agreement that the teaching of listening skills is important to effective communication and that these skills can be taught and measured. Petrie (1961) and a few others contend that not enough is known about the nature of listening to teach it or to measure it.

There has been a constantly increasing amount of

attention given to the teaching of listening since 1950, evidenced in the space given this topic in curriculum bulletins, in methods textbooks, and in professional journals. In the elementary schools, listening is included in language-arts instruction; in high school and college, listening is usually taught in speech courses, while in industry, listening is included in communications and management courses.

Generally, the assumption once made that everybody knows how to listen has been repudiated. Bliesmer (1952) reported that a comparison of bright and dull children of the same mental ages revealed that the bright children excelled not only in reading, but in listening as well. Smith (1956) established that disadvantaged children were poor listeners as well as poor readers. Cohen and others (1956) found frequent lapses of attention during listening among groups of adults and of children.

The teaching of listening involves a number of factors of which the ability to give attention or to concentrate is basic. Attention forms the base on which the development of such skills as perception, judgment, reasoning, thinking, and imagining rest. These five skills enable a listener to make comparisons, note the sequence of details, draw inferences and conclusions, recognize relationships, form mental images, reorder material in terms of past experience, abstract main ideas, and classify.

Instruction in listening should begin in the home. Generally, it is agreed that parents who listen to their children tend to be the best teachers of good listening habits. Since most instruction in nursery school and kindergarten is at an aural level, stress should be laid on acquiring good listening habits at these levels.

More formal instruction is begun in the elementary school. Duker (1961) lists four principles that should govern listening instruction at this level: (1) Listening should be a pleasurable, rather than a threatening, experience. (2) Daily class activities should be so planned that the amount of listening required of the children is not overpoweringly great. (3) Listening in a classroom should not be confined to listening *by* the children *to* the teacher. (4) Classroom listening should be *for* rather than *at*. Goals for the teaching of listening at the elementary school level are listed as the development of a listener who not only knows how to listen, but actually does listen, and who is selective, skillful, critical, courteous, attentive, retentive, curious, reactive, and reflective.

Early (1954) gives specific and detailed suggestions about the materials and methods for teaching a number of listening skills but emphasizes her belief that all listening skills are interdependent and thus cannot be taught in isolation. Detailed lesson plans which were found to be effective in listening instruction are reported by Hollow (1955) and Pratt (1953). A detailed and complete plan for teaching critical listening skills to upper-grade elementary school pupils, which was found to be effective, is reported on by Lundsteen (1963). An annotated list of audio-visual materials available for the teaching of listening at the elementary as well as at other levels is given by Duker (1965).

Russell and Russell (1959) and Wagner and others (1962) make numerous suggestions concerning specific devices for the teaching of listening at the elementary level.

The literature on methods of teaching listening at the high school level is rather sparse and tends to be based on theoretical considerations rather than on empirical research findings. The college-level situation is much better. Seymour (1965) gives a detailed description, analysis, and evaluation of the procedure used to teach listening at the University of Minnesota. Markgraf (1960) made a survey of listening instruction in 411 American teacher-training institutions and reports on the status of listening instruction and, to some extent, on the teaching methodology employed.

Carter (1963) made a survey of 750 industrial and business firms and reported on the extent of, and practices employed in, the teaching of listening. Less than half of these firms reported an absence of listening instruction in their in-service training programs. The extent to which listening was taught varied widely in programs of the other firms. Listening is a frequent topic in many business and trade journals read by management and employees of such firms.

MEASUREMENT OF LISTENING SKILLS. There are three published tests of listening skills of which the one by Brown and Carlsen (1955) is the best known and the most widely used. It is designed to be used at the college and post-college levels but is used frequently at the high school level. The validity of this test rests on the fact that it was written to test those skills which a jury of experts deemed crucial in listening. Furthermore, it was determined that the test was not one of either reading or intelligence. The validity of the test has been called questionable by Petrie (1961) and by Kelly (1962) principally on the ground that not enough is known about the elements of listening to enable a valid measurement of this factor to be made. The problem of the validity of any test of a previously unmeasured skill is a sticky one at best and is very difficult to solve. The *Brown-Carlsen Test* has two forms, both of which have high reliability. Kelly (1962), in a study of a group of industrial foremen, found that high performance on the *Brown-Carlsen Test* did not indicate those who were regarded by their superiors and subordinates as the best listeners. While the wide and continued use of a test, even over a long period of time, certainly is not a technical way of establishing validity, it may well be that under the circumstances, it is at least somewhat persuasive evidence in favor of validity.

There are also a number of unpublished tests of listening which have been constructed as part of doctoral studies. The tests by Hollow (1955) and Pratt (1953) were very carefully designed and have been used as measurement instruments in a number of subsequent studies. Russell (1964) suggested that a superior listening test might be constructed by using various carefully refined subtests from the many unpublished listening tests now in existence. Lundsteen (1963) developed a test of critical listening abilities suitable for the upper elementary school grades.

Two areas have been touched on in research studies but have not been developed to any considerable extent yet. The first of these is the measurement of the effectiveness of oral administration of tests developed for visual presentation, for example, to the blind. Oral projective tests and their validation constitute another area of investigation. These tests usually consist of structured and unstructured human, mechanical, and other sounds concerning which the subject is asked to react. Such tests, if properly validated, could have many useful applications.

Rapid listening. There is little doubt about the fact that the human mind is capable of processing information at a more rapid rate than the human speech organs are capable of producing. This fact can be used to explain the "mind-wandering" phenomenon described by Cohen and others (1956) and constitutes one of the real difficulties in listening effectively and efficiently.

There are a number of ways in which the rate of speech, and thus of listening, can be increased. The speaker may speak more rapidly, but there are physiological limitations which prevent any major increase of speed in this manner. A second way to increase rate is to play recorded speech at a rate which is more rapid than the rate at which it was recorded. This introduces distortion which becomes intolerable when the discrepancy is more than a small amount. Surprisingly, some blind students have trained themselves to listen with good comprehension to material which to the untrained listener would sound like Donald Duck.

It has been established that speech can be interrupted and remain highly comprehensible, if the interruptions are of a sufficiently small length. The higher the frequency of the interruption, the less interference there is with the comprehensibility of the message. Interruptions at about 10,000 per second result in almost no interference with intelligibility, or with comprehensibility. This, of course, is the principle on which the possibility of sending two messages over a single telephone wire is based. At first, it was reasoned that it should be possible to cut small segments of a recording tape and splice the ends back together. While this was a laborious and time-consuming task because the segments had to be extremely small, it was found that words could be speeded to 2.5 times that of the original, with only a 20 percent loss in intelligibility.

There are now in existence mechanical means for accomplishing the same ends. The sampling interval of the most commonly used device is very small, about .03 second. The use of these devices has made possible extremely high rates. Even when the rate is so high that the comprehensibility of the material is adversely affected, it may still be more efficient than the original speech when the speeded speech can be presented two or more times during the same time span required for one presentation of the original message.

There are many practical applications for speeded listening to compressed speech. The Library of Congress's "Talking Books" for the blind have used compressed speech, with great success, on some recordings. Blocking a pretaped program into a set time slot on radio or television is another widely used application.

Orr and others (1965) report that subjects given practice in listening to compressed speech were able to score significantly higher on comprehension tests based on the content of very highly compressed speech, at a rate of over 450 words per minute, than were those who had not had this practice.

Jester (1966) found that there is very little loss of comprehension as the rate is increased from 200 to 300 words per minute but that there is a sharp decrease in comprehensibility as the rate of compressed speech is increased beyond that point.

It is also possible to expand speech to a lower rate. Very little research has been reported concerning this phase of rate control. It has been suggested that slower listening may be of benefit to the learning of the mentally retarded and to certain types of the auditorially handicapped.

Research on the possibilities of rapid listening to compressed speech is barely at the threshold. The possibilities inherent in the use of increased rates are tremendous, and the implications for the usefulness of listening are intriguing.

Sam Duker
Brooklyn College of
The City University of New York

References

Armstrong, Hubert C. "The Relationship of the Auditory and Visual Vocabularies of Children" Doctoral dissertation. Stanford U, 1953.

Beighley, Kenneth C. "An Experimental Study of the Effect of Four Speech Variables on Listener Comprehension." Doctoral dissertation. Ohio State U, 1952.

Bliesmer, Emery P. "A Comparison of Bright and Dull Children of Comparable Mental Ages with Respect to Various Reading Abilities." Doctoral dissertation. State U Iowa, 1952.

Broadbent, D. E. *Perception and Communication.* Pergamon Press, 1958. 338p.

Brown, Charles T. "Studies in Listening Comprehension." *Speech Monogr* 26:288–94; 1959.

Brown, Charles T. "Three Studies of the Listening of Children." *Speech Monogr* 32:129–38; 1965.

Brown, Donald P. "Auding as the Primary Language Ability." Doctoral dissertation. Stanford U, 1954.

Brown, James I., and Carlsen, G. Robert *Brown-Carlsen Listening Comprehension Test.* Harcourt, 1955.

Carter, Raymond E. "Listening Improvement Training Programs in Business and Industry in the United States." Master's thesis. U Kansas, 1963.

Carver, Merton E. "A Study of Conditions Influencing

the Relative Effectiveness of Visual and Auditory Presentation." Doctoral dissertation. Harvard U, 1934.

Cohen, John, and others. "Mind Wandering." *Br J Psychol* 47:61–2; 1956.

Duker, Sam. "Goals of Teaching Listening Skills in the Elementary School." *El Engl* 38:170–4; 1961.

Duker, Sam. *Listening Bibliography*. Scarecrow Press, 1964. 211p.

Duker, Sam. "An Annotated Guide to Audiovisual Aids Available for the Teaching of Listening." *Audiovisual Instruction* 10:320–2; 1965.

Early, Margaret J. "Suggestions for Teaching Listening." *J Ed* 137:17–20; 1954.

Emmons, William H., and Simon, Charles W. *The Non-recall of Material Presented During Sleep*. Rand Corporation, 1954. 11p.

Hall, Robert O. "An Exploratory Study of Listening of Fifth Grade Pupils." Doctoral dissertation. U Southern California, 1954.

Harwood, Kenneth A. "A Concept of Listenability." *Western Speech* 14:10–2; 1950.

Hollingsworth, Paul M. "A Study to Compare the Effects of Two Listening Programs on Reading Achievement and Listening Comprehension." Doctoral dissertation. U Arizona, 1963.

Hollow, Kevin, Sister M. "An Experimental Study of Listening Comprehension at the Intermediate Grade Level." Doctoral dissertation. Fordham U, 1955.

Jacobson, Homer. "The Informational Capacity of the Human Ear." *Sci* 112:143–4, 1950.

Jester, Robert E. "Comprehension of Connected Meaningful Discourse as a Function of Individual Differences and Rate of Modality of Presentation." Doctoral dissertation. U Utah, 1966.

Keller, Paul W. "Major Findings in Listening in the Past Ten Years." *J Communication* 10:29–38; 1960.

Kelly, Charles M. "Actual Listening Behavior of Industrial Supervisors, as Related to Listening Ability, General Mental Ability, Selected Personality Factors and Supervising Effectiveness." Doctoral dissertation. Purdue U, 1962.

Kibler, Robert J. II. "The Impact of Message Style and Channel in Communication." Doctoral dissertation. Ohio State U, 1962.

Lundsteen, Sara W. R. "Teaching Abilities in Critical Listening in the Fifth and Sixth Grades." Doctoral dissertation. Berkeley: U California, 1963.

Markgraf, Bruce R. *An Observational Study Determining the Amount of Time That Students in the Tenth and Twelfth Grades are Expected to Listen in the Classroom*. Master's thesis. U Wisconsin. 1957.

Markgraf, Bruce R. "A Survey of Listening Pedagogy in American Teacher-Training Institutions." Doctoral dissertation. U Wisconsin, 1960.

Moe, Iver. L. "Auding as a Predictive Measure of Reading Performance in Primary Grades." Doctoral dissertation. U Florida, 1957.

Nashville Public Schools. *Experiences in Listening*. Nashville, Tennessee, 1951. 30p.

Nichols, Ralph G. "Factors Accounting for Differences in Comprehension of Material Presented Orally in the Classroom." Doctoral dissertation. State U Iowa, 1948.

Nichols, Ralph G., and Stevens, Leonard A. *Are You Listening?* McGraw-Hill, 1957. 235p.

Orr, David B., and others. "Trainability of Listening Comprehension of Speeded Discourse." *J Ed Psychol* 56:148–56; 1965.

Petrie, Charles R., Jr. "An Experimental Evaluation of Two Methods for Improving Listening Comprehension Abilities." Doctoral dissertation. Purdue U, 1961.

Pratt, Lloyd E. "The Experimental Evaluation of a Program for the Improvement of Listening in the Elementary School." Doctoral dissertation. State U Iowa, 1953.

Rankin, Paul T. "The Measurement of the Ability to Understand Spoken Language." Doctoral dissertation. U Michigan, 1926.

Rogers, John R. "The Derivation of a Formula for Predicting the Comprehension Level of Material Presented Orally." Doctoral dissertation. U Texas, 1952.

Rosenberg, Seymour, and Cohen, Bertram D. "Speakers' and Listeners' Processes in a Word Communication Task." *Sci* 145:1201–3; 1964.

Russell, David H. "A Conspectus of Recent Research on Listening Abilities." *El Engl* 41:262–7; 1964.

Russell, David H., and Russell, Elizabeth F. *Listening Aids Through the Grades—One-Hundred-Ninety Listening Activities*. Teachers Col, Columbia U, 1959. 112p.

Seymour, Paul J. "A Study of the Relationship Between the Communication Skills and a Selected Set of Predictors and of the Relationship Among the Communication Skills." Doctoral dissertation. U Minnesota, 1965.

Smith, Thomas W. "Auding and Reading Skills as Sources of Cultural Bias in the Davis-Eells Games and California Test of Mental Maturity." Doctoral dissertation. U Southern California, 1956.

Spearritt, Donald. "A Factorial Analysis of Listening Comprehension." Doctoral dissertation. Harvard U, 1961. Reprinted: *Listening Comprehension, A Factorial Analysis*. Australian Council Educational Research, 1962. 149p.

Taylor, Stanford E. *Listening*. NEA, 1964, 33p.

Toussaint, Isabella H. "A Classified Summary of Listening—1950–1959." *J Communication* 10:125–34; 1960.

Vineyard, Edwin E., and Bailey, Robert B. "Interrelationships of Reading Ability, Listening Skill, Intelligence and Scholastic Achievement." *J Develop Reading* 3:174–8; 1960.

Wagner, Guy, and others. *Listening Games-Building Listening Skills with Instructional Games*. Teachers Publishing Corp., 1962. 132p.

Wilson, William C. "Some Interrelationships of Verbal and Musical Abilities in Elementary School Children." Doctoral dissertation. Berkeley: U California, 1960.

Wilt, Miriam E. "A Study of Teacher Awareness in Listening as a Factor in Elementary Education." Doctoral dissertation. Pennsylvania State Col, 1949.

Witty, Paul. "Studies of the Mass Media 1949–1965." *Sci Ed* 50:119–26; 1926.

Zelko, Harold P. "You Can Be a Good Listener." *Parade* 22:12–3; 1957.

LOCAL SCHOOL SYSTEMS

Research on the several kinds of local school districts, and on the boards of education which govern them, has at least a 50-year history (Dawson, 1941; Reller, 1941). The production of doctoral dissertations on district organization and boards of education is currently running at approximately 40 per year; and books and monographs on these topics also continue to appear frequently. The states that have many relatively small school districts seem most often to be the objects of investigation. In states where the counties and major cities constitute the nearest approach to "local" district organization, or in states such as Hawaii and Alaska, where the state itself largely governs the educational enterprise, fewer investigations have been made.

Observers of the various national systems of education throughout the world point to the decentralization of educational control, ultimately to a local district and a local school board in most states, as distinctive to the United States (Morphet & Reller, 1962). Created partly as a result of pioneer conditions during the formative years of the nation, and partly as a result of political theory (Russell & Judd, 1940), the nation's decentralized administration of education has been viewed by some as the finest flowering of democracy; by others as the greatest handicap to the achievement of universal quality in education.

THE SMALL LOCAL DISTRICT. The *principle* of local control of education has generally had support in the United States; but the extreme fragmentation of major areas of the nation into small local districts for basic schooling has been under continuous criticism from the days of Horace Mann in 1837 (Cubberley, 1927) to the present (C. Benson, 1965). In recent years several extremely influential research and committee reports have promoted district consolidation through appropriate state legislation and local referendum (Dawson, 1934; National Commission on School District Reorganization, 1948; National Education Association, 1948).

A national high in numbers of school districts may have been reached in the 1920's, with 189,227 one-room schools reported, most of them representing separate districts in rural communities (Dawson, 1941). By 1931-32, a total of 127,244 local districts of all types, from one-room schools to the largest of city school districts, was reported. This number has been steadily diminished, to 26,800 for 1956-66 (Morphet & others, 1967).

Research and other forces continue to press for fewer and larger local districts. A typical recent study found that 88 local districts in an area of southwestern Michigan could better be replaced by "12, 9, or even fewer" districts (Scarnato, 1967). A reduction from 264 to 30 or 40 local districts has been proposed following a study of the San Francisco Bay area (Reller, 1963). A saving of $120,000, over one-third of the current expenditure, for bus transportation alone, was forecast if the several school districts of a single county in Pennsylvania would combine into one; and a proportionate reduction in the hours of bus travel for the average pupil in the county was also calculated (Smith, 1964). In Mississippi, where accreditation was sought during the period 1950–1960 for 168 high schools having fewer than 30 seniors, 118 high schools were recommended in place of 336 studied (Coffman, 1964).

Standards of enrollment, tax base, travel distance, and the like are continually being applied to arrive at recommendations for district consolidation over entire states, including most recently Oklahoma (McCutchan, 1963); Oregon (Williams, 1965); Texas (Gilliam, 1961); and Utah, where counties are already established as the prevailing local unit (McHenry, 1965). For Iowa, the historical method of research has been used effectively to emphasize the need for continuing district consolidation, presenting median high school enrollments for the state of 75 in 1928, 79 in 1954, and 210 in 1964 (Truesdell, 1965). The figures suggest that Iowa must still have many school districts too small for efficient or effective education.

THE LARGE LOCAL DISTRICT. The extensive and continually growing body of research which presses toward ever fewer and larger local districts should not obscure another counter research movement, which is beginning to question the wisdom of largeness in school organization. There is evidence that in very large districts as well as in very small districts, conditions relating to school quality tend to become less favorable, with school systems in communities of 20,000 to 50,000 population at the optimum of size for school quality (Swanson, 1961).

The criteria established as tests of excellence are crucial in evaluations of optimum size. Many studies are available showing that large schools and large school districts excel in comparisons using such criteria as the range of course offerings, extent of student services, and specialization of administrative services (Kreiner, 1966). On the other hand, if high communication, identification, involvement, and participation by pupils, teachers, and citizens are accepted as criteria, disadvantages have been found to accrue very rapidly as size increases (Light, 1964). Theoretically it might be possible to secure all the management advantages of large districts along with all the personal advantages of relatively small individual schools. Unfortunately for this viewpoint, enlarged districts so often mean enlarged schools. School organization in the United States has not succeeded in following the pattern in Great Britain and other countries, where individual schools are in general small regardless of the size of the governing district, and where "houses" and "tutorial sets" have been perfected within individual schools to prevent the alienation of individual pupils and teachers (Baron, 1965). Research findings are not altogether consistent on factors associated with individual school size in the United States, but there is evidence that elementary schools ought not exceed two to four teachers per grade (Cole, 1965); and that secondary school enrollments ought not exceed 1,200 (Jackson, 1965; Ovaitt, 1966) to 2,000 (Monahan, 1965). If participation of pupils in extracurricular activities in the school is important, it seems clear that enrollments even as small as 300 to 400 have advantages (Kleinert, 1964).

THE SPECIALIZED LOCAL DISTRICT. In general, local school districts in the United States provide for education from kindergarten, or even nursery school, through grades 12 or 14. However, the separate elementary school district has been common, especially in the rural areas of a number of states. During the past few decades one-room elementary schools have been absorbed into districts providing both elementary and secondary education, but in 1962 there still remained more than 10,000 school districts responsible only for elementary instruction for fewer than 50 pupils on the average (American Association of School Administrators, 1964). California and Illinois, notably, have permitted the development of separate elementary districts, usually serving grades K–8, and of separate secondary districts, grades 9–12.

More recently, two additional types of specialized districts have been attracting attention—the specialized vocational–technical school district; and the junior or community college district. Objections have been voiced to this splintering of local educational control, but federal funds on the one hand and the great current demand for both vocational and higher education on the other have accelerated the formation of these specialized districts. Definitive research to decide between unified and separate districts for specialized functions has not been available. Two studies of the need for vocational districts indicate the dilemma, one finding a need for separate area vocational programs (McLure & others, 1960) and the other finding area vocational schools undesirable except temporarily (Guditus, 1965). With regard to college districts, a very large number of studies during the 1960's recommend separate junior or community college districts for various sections of the country, without confronting the issue of the college as part of an adequate unified local district.

COUNTY, INTERMEDIATE, COOPERATIVE, AND METROPOLITAN DISTRICTS. In some states, for example Florida, Utah, and West Virginia, the county has been designated the local school district. Local districts which are relatively large consequently prevail in these county-unit states. In most of the other states, where local districts are smaller, county school districts have historically been superimposed over the local districts to assist in local school administration. Evidence mounts that this type of district, which serves between local districts and the state, is an anachronism.

The intermediate district, which is the term for the superimposed county district that has been modified somewhat to meet contemporary needs, has not proved itself notably superior to the original county districts. Even though no longer tied strictly to county boundaries, sometimes now serving major portions of two or more counties, and with special tax levies and a new vision of services which could be provided to local school districts, the intermediate district remains relatively unimpressive. Designed primarily to aid one-room schools and other very small school districts, both the county district and its successor, the intermediate district, seem generally unable to do enough for the larger contemporary local districts that are emerging to warrant survival (McLure). Research data uncomplimentary to the two types of districts have come recently from California, where the progress of the intermediate district has often been proclaimed (Little, 1964); from Colorado (Mills, 1965); from Illinois (Otrich, 1965; Pringle, 1964); from Ohio (Rhinehart, 1957); and from Oregon (Sabin, 1965). Even from New York state, where a somewhat fresh approach has been tried during the past 15 years by the formation of "Boards of Cooperative Educational Services," dissatisfaction is apparent (Haweeli, 1964).

Several of the studies which have detailed the shortcomings of county or intermediate districts have pointed to regional intermediate districts as a possible improvement, apparently on the theory that increased size would yield increased strength for the intermediate unit. "Cooperative Regional Education Boards" serving districts of 125,000 population were recommended for New York (Haweeli, 1964); and 18 intermediate districts were proposed in place of the present 102 for Illinois (Pringle, 1964). However, no states has yet tried the large regional intermediate district—and its antecedents do not offer high promise for enlarged intermediate districts.

There is on the horizon a type of intermediate district with new antecedents: the metropolitan unit as created for the Toronto, Canada, metropolitan area. Results of investigations of the Toronto experience over the past decade have been highly favorable (Bollens & Schmandt, 1965; Larson, 1964; Smallwood, 1963). In Ohio, local school superintendents who had expressed little enthusiasm for county or traditional intermediate district services were intrigued by the possibilities of "a different approach" along metropolitan district lines (Heter, 1965). A study in Santa Clara County, California, has recommended that the present county department of education be replaced by a metropolitan district (Vance, 1966); and the Colorado study which recommended that the "county superintendent of schools should be abolished in most areas of the state" concluded that "some type of intermediate units" seemed necessary to serve the special needs of metropolitan areas of the state (Mills, 1965). The metropolitan district, capable of supplementing local district services, and indeed capable of coping with such issues as tax equalization and cooperative building and site development which have eluded traditional intermediate districts, yet tied more closely to the constituent local districts in a delicate balance of powers, appears to be a growing edge in the field of school-district evolution.

NEED FOR LOCAL DISTRICTS AND BOARDS. A half-century of investigation into the deficiencies of the several types of local districts, preceded by almost a century of discontent, has not seriously disturbed faith in decentralized school administration in the United States; but a few voices have been raised recently protesting the whole idea of local districts and local school boards. Not yet formulated as research, these protests may be only the normal extremes of expression typical of the times; but on the other hand they may be indicators of the thrust of future research. In view of trends toward larger local districts, larger intermediate districts, and greater state and federal participation in education, attention will likely be directed to such questions and statements as "Are local control and lay boards obsolete?" (Nugent, 1964); "the concept of local control . . . . is folklore and for some years has been outmoded" (Bailey, 1961); and "local control of education has clearly outlived its usefulness" (Lieberman, 1960).

Research has already provided some information on the extent to which local school boards are functional and operative. The data give little support to those who speak of the "folklore" of local control. Local control is apparently real, whether or not desirable. In Colorado a series of studies of various boards of education found them making "substantive and unrestricted" decisions on one-fourth to one-half of the issues before them (Park, 1966). A study of legislation and of local practices in California found no loss of local control by local boards of education from 1929 to 1963 (Chamberlain, 1966).

THE LOCUS OF POWER. Superficially, the local board of education appears to be a locus of power at the local level—a point at which decision-making responsibility is fixed within the limits set for local democratic government of the schools. However, upon careful investigation, the power over schools at the local level proves far more complex. No topic during the past decade has more fully engaged the attentions of researchers interested in school districts and school boards (Goldhammer, 1964). The sovereignty of the federal courts and laws over aspects of local control has been documented (Spurlock, 1955). Variations among states in the amount of power delegated to local boards of education have been displayed (Hall, 1959); and the political forces which establish state educational policies applicable to local districts have been described by several major studies (Kaufman, 1963). But the largest number of research studies in this area have explored power over school matters among the citizens of local school districts. Pre-empting the term "community power structure" as their field of endeavor, these researchers draw their methods of investigation notably from certain pioneer studies (Hollingshead, 1949; Hunter, 1953). Few research reports have been more widely read than Hollingshead's *Elmtown's Youth* (1949), reporting the major personalities and motivations influencing school decisions in a small Illinois city.

In general, there is much evidence to show that in any community a few individuals determine the main course of events for all agencies, including schools (Kimbrough, 1964). More often in the United States than in other countries, these "power figures" are business leaders in the community (Miller, 1958). Sometimes they are members of the board of education in a position to decide school matters directly, but when they are not they can still determine by subtle means the crucial decisions of the board of education (Vidich & Bensman, 1958). When "influentials" serve directly on school boards, the schools are likely to prosper (Maase, 1964). Only occasionally is the superintendent of schools one of the community influentials. Sometimes the superintendent, and even the board members themselves, are so removed from power that they are mere puppets in the hands of outside power figures (Dahl, 1961). Successful means open to the superintendent for gaining the support of influentials have been described (Easley, 1966). Different types of community structures have been identified, and the means of influence in each type have been clarified (Dilks, 1965). Altogether, research during the past two decades on the relationship of community power structure and school administration has mapped the sociological highways of community life, and has markedly clarified essential methods of achieving constructive decisions on school (or other) issues.

Exchanges of power or influence between the school board and other organizations in a community occur frequently. These exchanges may be somewhat informal (Dilks, 1965); or they may have legal force as when a city council has power to approve or veto the school board's budget. School officials have persistently protested "dependent" fiscal arrangements, with some justification in terms of research findings (Frasier, 1922; McGaughy, 1924); but schools have also been found to operate with reasonable success under a wide range of different local interagency arrangements (Henry & Kerwin, 1938). A new array of research has now explored these relationships, with equally ambiguous results regarding the merits of independent versus dependent fiscal status for school districts (James & others, 1963; Vincent & Bernardo, 1966).

In endeavors to cope with and perhaps to broaden the sources of power, two relatively new power structures have been created for many communities— the lay advisory committee, and the staff-negotiation team. Behind each of these bodies are their respective constituents—the general citizens and the employed staffs of the schools. Case studies of individual boards of education suggest that, in the absence of formalized lay-citizen committees, citizens or groups outside the schools involve themselves in fewer than ten percent of all school decisions (Smoley, 1965); but those community pressures which do develop are sometimes exceedingly disruptive (National Commission on Professional Rights and Responsibilities, 1967). Recommended procedures for lay advisory committees, to enhance their contributions without undue abrogation of board of education responsibility, have been provided by several studies (Peddicord, 1965).

Recommended procedures for the power struggle between teachers and boards of education have been harder to determine, at least in the present early years of active teacher contact negotiations and management. Studies of this relationship will undoubtedly reach flood proportions in the near future. Companion studies in Colorado clearly reveal the problem, showing the different expectations of board members, superintendents, NEA teachers, and AFT teachers (Chappell, 1966; Herbertson, 1966). The stereotype, that board members represent business interests and to a degree are incapable of understanding the teachers, has some validity according to several studies (Brandon, 1965; Holden, 1961).

BOARD OF EDUCATION DYNAMICS. Within the board of education, research has sought explanations for decision-making behavior by a variety of techniques, testing a number of different hypotheses. "Composition" studies, given visibility by Professor George Counts (Counts, 1927), have a long history, always finding that board members are likely to be (40 to 69 percent by various studies) male, white, affluent, well educated, Protestant, Republican parents, representative of the managerial, professional, or technical vocations (Proudfast, 1962). The implication that this background yields a bias to decision making has frequently been stated, and sometimes proved to a degree (Whitcomb, 1965). Some analysts, upon finding scant representation of special constituencies (e.g., only four percent of candidates over a period of time were from labor in one city), decry the backgrounds of school boards as undemocratic (Williams & Press, 1961). Others present data indicating that such characteristics as high education, affluence, managerial–technical–professional employment, and parenthood are precisely those most likely to produce good schools (Vincent & Bernardo, 1967). Generalized competency is not likely, however, to satisfy citizen groups desiring special legislation; hence, pressure will undoubtedly continue from civil rights groups, labor, teacher organizations, and other special constituencies for their own board representation (Havighurst, 1964).

Less well understood, and therefore more in need of further research, is the influence of personality and of small-group interaction on decision making within boards of education. Typical of the studies now available are investigations of the motivations which persuade citizens to become board of education members, and which presumably therefore also influence their decisions as board members (Beers, 1965); of the assumptions regarding behavior roles to adopt while serving on a board of education (Gross, 1958; G. Benson, 1965); of behaviors during board meetings which contribute to harmony or disharmony in arriving at decisions (Flewelling, 1964); of the attitudes toward power and consensus which prevail within the board (Sproule, 1966); and of the inputs, functions, and outputs (in political science terminology), managed by the board (Schribner, 1966). Perhaps the most practical report provided on school-board dynamics is one which concluded that each board member needs to be helped personally by administrative officers, in order to cope constructively with himself and his board colleagues operating under many pressures (Pintar, 1964). Quite probably, reciprocal personal help for administrative officers by board members is equally valuable for improved school service.

BOARD-SUPERINTENDENT RELATIONS. A persistent puzzle in the power matrix surrounding boards of education is the relationship which should exist between the board of education and the superintendent of schools. A long tradition of theory and research has sought to differentiate between boards and their superintendents by assigning policy making to boards and management within policy to superintendents; yet a recent survey of 1,543 school districts for the U.S. Office of Education showed nearly one-third of all districts having problems with school board policy, and another 20 percent having problems with board–superintendent relations (White, 1962). School boards cannot restrict their interest to policy. Over an eight-month period of typical board operation, 59 percent of board decisions were deemed by a recent investigator as administrative, 33 percent were housekeeping, and only 8 percent consisted of the establishment of policy (Cunningham, 1962). On the other hand, superintendents of schools cannot, and surely should not, restrict their interests to management without regard for policy. That they do not is indicated by responses from 38 school superintendents claiming "80 to 90 percent effective" influence on school-board policy in areas ranging from curriculum to finance (Skippen, 1964).

The importance of policy, for both boards of education and superintendents of schools, will no doubt continue to attract attention (White, 1959), but the study of relationships between boards and superintendents appears to have turned a corner. Attention is now being directed away from futile efforts at separating policy making and management, to more productive investigations of the roles of both board members and superintendents, in both policy determination and management. Typical recent investigations have explored the styles of association between boards and superintendents (Shock, 1960); the importance of mutual cooperation (Griffiths, 1956) and understanding (Olson, 1965); and the proper use of such methods of interaction as communication (Bennett, 1964) and socialization (Husebo, 1965).

Dan H. Cooper
The University of Michigan

References

American Association of School Administrators. *Management Surveys for Schools, Their Uses and Abuses*. AASA, 1964.

Bailey, Thomas D. "The Folklore of Local Control." NEA J 50:42–3; 1961.

Baron, G. *Society, Schools and Progress in England*. Pergamon, 1965. 228p.

Beers, Charles Meade. "An Analysis of the Community-Oriented and Self-Oriented Board Member." Doctoral dissertation. U Pittsburgh, 1965.

Bennett, Carl Eugene. "Communications Between Superintendents of Schools and Boards of Education." Doctoral dissertation. Ohio State U, 1964.

Benson, Charles S. *The Cheerful Prospect*. Houghton, 1965. 134p.

Benson, Gregory Michael. "A Comparison of Certain Behaviors of Board of Education Members from 'Above Average' and 'Below Average' Schools." Doctoral dissertation. Syracuse U, 1965.

Bollens, John C., and Schmandt, Henry J. *The Metropolis: Its People, Politics and Economic Life*. Harper, 1965. 643p.

Brandon, Warren Wayne. "Selected Personnel Policies and Practices Which Affect Faculty-School Board Relationships." Doctoral dissertation. U Pittsburgh, 1965.

Chamberlain, Robert Douglas. "Trends in the Status of Discretionary Powers of District Boards of Education in the Field of Personnel Administration." Doctoral dissertation. U California, Los Angeles, 1966.

Chappell, Harold Lloyd. "Teacher Negotiations as Perceived by School Board Members." Doctoral dissertation. Colorado State College, 1966.

Coffman, Charlie Quinn. "A Study to Determine the Extent to Which 100 Selected High Schools of Mississippi Met the 21 Recommendations of Conant and to Suggest General Locations for High Schools Large Enough to Meet His Criterion of Size." Doctoral dissertation. U Mississippi, 1964.

Cole, Blaine Leroy. "An Analysis of the Relationship of Selected Factors of Communication and Organizational Climate as They Relate to the Size of the Elementary School." Doctoral dissertation. U Missouri, 1965.

Counts, George S. *The Social Composition of Boards of Education*. Monogr No. 33. U Chicago Press, 1927. 100p.

Cubberley, Ellwood P. *State School Administration*. Houghton, 1927. 773p.

Cunningham, Luvern L. "Decision-making Behavior of School Boards." Am Sch Bd J 144:13–5; 1962.

Dahl, Robert A. *Who Governs?* Yale U Press, 1961. 355p.

Dawson, Howard A. *Satisfactory Local School Units*. George Peabody College for Teachers, 1934. 181p.

Dawson, Howard A. "Consolidation of Schools." In *Encyclopedia of Educational Research*. Macmillan, 1941. p. 362–7.

Dilks, Charles Raymond. "The Role of Selected Formal Organizations in the Decision-Making Process of Two Florida School Districts." Doctoral dissertation. U Florida, 1965.

Easley, John William. "Comparative Characteristics of the Power Structures of Three Selected Georgia School Districts." Doctoral dissertation. U Florida, 1966.

Flewelling, Robert Wealthy. "A Study of Some Critical Areas of the Discussion Process Which Influences School Board Unity." Doctoral dissertation. U California, Berkeley, 1964.

Frasier, G. W. "The Control of City School Finances." Bruce, 1922. 132p.

Gilliam, L. Camp. "Development and Validation of a Sound Plan of Reorganization of the Public School Districts in Texas." Doctoral dissertation. North Texas State College, 1961.

Goldhammer, Keith. *The School Board*. Center for Applied Research in Education, 1964. 114p.

Griffiths, Daniel E. *Human Relations in Administration*. Appleton, 1956. 458p.

Gross, Neal C. *Who Runs Our Schools?* Wiley, 1958. 195p.

Guditas, Charles William. "Guidelines for the Area Vocational (Technical) School in Pennsylvania." Doctoral dissertation. Lehigh U, 1965.

Hall, Donald Ellis. "Discretionary and Mandatory Provisions of State Education Law." Doctoral dissertation. U California, 1959.

Havighurst, Robert J. *The Public Schools of Chicago*. Board of Education of the City of Chicago, 1964. 499p.

Haweeli, Norman. "An Inquiry into the Function and Administration of Boards of Cooperative Educational Services in the State of New York with Proposals for their Improvement." Doctoral dissertation. Columbia U, 1964.

Henry, N. B., and Kerwin, J. G. *Schools and City Government* U Chicago Press, 1938. 104p.

Herbertson, Jack Ray. "Teacher Negotiations as Perceived by Representatives of Teacher Groups, Superintendents, and School Board Presidents." Doctoral dissertation. Colorado State College, 1966.

Heter, John Robert. The Small, Independent School District in Ohio and Current Proposals for District Reorganization. Doctoral dissertation. Western Reserve U, 1965.

Holden, Louis Edward. "Communication and Decision-Making in School Board-Superintendent Relations." Doctoral dissertation. U Oregon, 1961.

Hollingshead, August de Belmont. *Elmtown's Youth*. Wiley, 1949. 480p.

Hunter, Floyd. *Community Power Structure; A Study of Decision Makers*. U North Carolina Press, 1953. 297p.

Husebo, Raymond John. "The Relationship of Value-Orientations to Formal School Board-Superintendent Interaction Processes." Doctoral dissertation. U Wisconsin, 1965.

Jackson, Joe LeRoy. "School Size and Other Factors Affecting Program Adequacy in Southern High Schools." Doctoral dissertation. George Peabody College for Teachers, 1965.

James, H. Thomas and others. *Wealth, Expenditure*

and Decision-making for Education. Stanford U School of Education, 1963. 203p.

Kaufman, Herbert. *Politics and Policies in State and Local Governments.* Prentice-Hall, 1963. 120p.

Kimbrough, Ralph B. *Political Power and Educational Decision-making.* Rand McNally, 1964. 307p.

Kleinert, Erwin John, Jr. "Student Activity Participation and High School Size." Doctoral dissertation. U Michigan, 1964.

Kreiner, Leon Wallace. "Changes in Educational Programs in Selected Reorganized Nebraska School Districts." Doctoral dissertation. U Nebraska Teachers College, 1966.

Larson, Kenneth Louis. "Metropolitan School Government: Its Development and Operation in Toronto." Doctoral dissertation. U California, Berkeley, 1964.

Lieberman, Myron. *The Future of Public Education.* U Chicago Press, 1960. 294p.

Light, Kenneth Henry. "Community Power Structures and School District Reorganization." Doctoral dissertation. U Colorado, 1964.

Little, Arthur D. *The Emerging Requirements for Effective Leadership for California Education.* California State Board of Education, 1964. 49p.

Maase, Berard. "A Comparison of the Relationship of Influentials to Schools in High and Low Financial Support Communities." Doctoral dissertation. U Michigan, 1964.

McCutchan, George A. "School District Reorganization in Oklahoma." Doctoral dissertation. U Oklahoma, 1963.

McGaughy, J. R. *The Fiscal Administration of City School Systems.* Macmillan, 1924. 95p.

McHenry, Vere A. "School District Reorganization in Utah." Doctoral dissertation. U Utah, 1965.

McLure, William P. *The Intermediate Administrative School District in the United States.* U Illinois Press, 1956. 160p.

McLure, William P., and others. *Vocational and Technical Education in Illinois—Tomorrow's Challenge.* Bureau of Educational Research, U Illinois, 1960.

Miller, Delbert C. "Decision-Making Cliques in an American and an English City." *Am J Sociol* 64: 299–310; 1958.

Mills, Dale Herman. "A Study to Determine the Extent of Need for Services and Leadership of the Intermediate Unit in Colorado." Doctoral dissertation. Colorado State College, 1965.

Monahan, William Welsh, Jr. "Teacher's Knowledge of Students Related to Urban High School Size." Doctoral dissertation. U California, Berkeley, 1965.

Morphet, Edgar L., and Reller, Theodore L. (Eds.) *Comparative Educational Administration.* Prentice-Hall, 1962. 438p.

Morphet, Edgar L. and others. *Educational Organization and Administration.* Prentice-Hall, 1967. 569p.

National Commission on Professional Rights and Responsibilities, National Education Association. *Detroit: A Study of Barriers to Equal Opportunity in a Large City.* NEA, 1967. 111p.

National Commission on School District Reorganization. *Your School District.* NEA, 1948. 286p.

National Education Association, Research Division and Department of Rural Education. *A Model School District Reorganization Bill.* NEA, 1948. 16p.

Nugent, Donald. "Are Local Control and Lay Boards Obsolete?" *Ed Leadership* 22; 1964.

Olson, Richard Fischer. Factors Affecting Understanding Between Superintendents and School Boards. Doctoral dissertation. Stanford U, 1965.

Otrich, George H. "Extent of Agreement Among School Administrators Concerning Certain Services of the Intermediate Unit in Twenty-six Southeastern Illinois Counties." Doctoral dissertation. Southern Illinois U, 1965.

Ovaitt, Stanley Wixson. "A Study of the Optimum Size of the High School." Doctoral dissertation. Michigan State U, 1966.

Park, Don Larry. "Local Control of Education in Selected Large School Districts in the State of Colorado." Doctoral dissertation. Colorado State College, 1966.

Peddicord, Paul Wallace. "Citizens' Committees in the Public School Systems of North Carolina." Doctoral dissertation. Duke U, 1965.

Pintar, George Mathew. "Role Expectations and Perceptions of School Board Members as Viewed by Referent Groups." Doctoral dissertation. Southern Illinois U, 1964.

Pringle, Robert Andrew. "A Proposal for a New Intermediate Administrative Structure for Education in Illinois." Doctoral dissertation. U Illinois, 1964.

Proudfast, Alexander. "A Study of the Socioeconomic Status of Influential School Board Members in Alberta as Related to Their Attitudes Toward Certain Common Problems Confronting School Boards." Doctoral dissertation. U Oregon, 1962.

Reller, Theodore L. "Administration-City School." In *Encyclopedia of Educational Research.* Macmillan, 1941. p. 4–13.

Reller, Theodore L. *Problems of Public Education in the San Francisco Bay Area.* Institute of Government Studies, U California, 1963.

Rinehart, John S. "The Function, Organization, and Operation of the County School District in Ohio." Doctoral dissertation. Ohio State U, 1957.

Russell, John Dale, and Judd, Charles H. *The American Educational System.* Houghton, 1940. 554p.

Sabin, Robert Clarence. "A Survey of the Need for an Intermediate School District in Oregon with Implications for Its Future Development." Doctoral dissertation. U Oregon, 1965.

Scarnato, Samuel A. "A Study of School District Reorganization for Education in Southwestern Michigan." Doctoral dissertation. U Michigan, 1967.

Schribner, Jay Donald. "A Functional-Systems Analysis of School Board Performance." Doctoral dissertation. Stanford U, 1966.

Shock, Donald Paul. "Patterns in the Decision-Making Process of a School Board." Doctoral dissertation. Stanford U, 1960.

Skippen, Robert Errett. A Comparison of the Superintendent's Influence on School Board Policy as

Perceived by Superintendents of Schools and the School Board Chairman. Doctoral dissertation. U Oregon, 1964.

Smallwood, Frank. *Metro Toronto: A Decade Later.* Toronto Bureau of Municipal Research, 1963.

Smith, Curvin Carl. "The Reorganization of a Pupil Transportation Network in Conjunction with the Reorganization of School Districts." Doctoral dissertation. Pennsylvania State U, 1964.

Smoley, Eugene Ralph, Jr. "Community Participation in Urban School Government." Doctoral dissertation. Johns Hopkins U, 1965.

Sproule, Joseph Robert. "Decision Making Processes of Boards of Education." Doctoral dissertation. Cornell U, 1966.

Spurlock, Clark. *Education and the Supreme Court.* U Illinois Press, 1955. 252p.

Swanson, Arthur D. "Relations Between Community Size and School Quality." *IAR Res B* 2:1–3; 1961.

Truesdell, Wayne Palmer. "A History of School Organization and Superintendence in Iowa." Doctoral dissertation. U Iowa, 1965.

Vance, Glen Wesley. "School District Organization in the Metropolitan Area of Santa Clara County, California." Doctoral dissertation. U Arizona, 1966.

Vidich, Arthur J., and Bensman, Joseph. *Small Town in Mass Society.* Princeton U Press, 1958. 259p.

Vincent, William S., and Bernardo, Charles M. "Tax Limitation and Fiscal Responsibility of School Boards." *IAR Res B* 7:1–4; 1966.

Vincent, William S., and Bernardo, Charles M. "School Board Member Characteristics and Fiscal Responsibility." *IAR Res B* 7:6–11; 1967.

Whitcomb, Charles Lincoln. "The Influence of Certain Socioeconomic Attributes on the Acceptability to School Committee Members of Rhode Island of Certain Criteria Which Determine the Level of Teachers' Salaries." Doctoral dissertation. Boston U, 1965.

White, Alpheus L. "Local School Board Policy Manuals." *Sch Life* 42:23–5; 1959.

White, Alpheus L. *Local School Boards: Organization and Practices.* Bulletin No. 8. USOE, 1962. 81p.

Williams, Delos Dale. "Oregon School District Reorganization 1957–64 and Implications for Improvement." Doctoral dissertation. Oregon State U, 1965.

Williams, Oliver P., and Press, Charles. (Eds.) *Democracy in Urban America.* Rand McNally, 1961. 561p.

MARKS AND MARKING SYSTEMS

For the purposes of this article, a mark is defined as (1) a single summary symbol (2) covering achievement in some substantial segment of the educational enterprise, (3) given by an instructor (4) for purposes of record and report. It differs from other related phenomena that appear on the educational scene with respect to one or another of these four essential characteristics.

The first attribute serves to differentiate a mark from all types of evaluative or descriptive statements that are couched in running prose, i.e., such things as teacher comments, anecdotal records, and teacher letters to the home. A mark operates within a single, uniform, simple but highly abstract symbol system, whereas communications in continuous prose are almost infinitely variable in the specifics of their form and content.

A mark, as we use the term here, should be distinguished from a score on a specific test or exercise. The score expresses, with greater or less objectivity, performance on one defined and delimited task—a recitation, a paper, or an examination. A mark summarizes the evidence available on a student in a complete course, an aspect of a course, a temporal segment of a course, or the student's entire program. A mark is usually derived, at least in part, from evidence available in a set of scores. Sometimes scores are combined by a precisely stated set of arithmetical procedures, but the combination is often somewhat intuitive and tempered in greater or less degree by subjective considerations brought to bear by the instructor.

A mark is differentiated from a standardized test or external examination, which may also appraise achievement in a substantial segment of education, in that it is given by a teacher. It represents the teacher's perception of pupil achievement based on such combination of evidence as the teacher elects to use.

A mark also has the character of being a permanent record, made to be retained and to be reported to student, parent, later schools, and potential employers. In this respect, it differs both from the temporary notes or partial evaluations that may exist for a limited period in a pupil's file folder, and from the confidential information that a school may have upon a pupil but may feel it inappropriate to share with either parent or external agency.

The most common symbol system, especially in high school or above, appears to be the system based on A, B, C, D, and F, with or without the modifiers of + and − (Joint Committee . . . , 1962; Dolman & Michael, 1960; Downing, 1964). A good many schools continue to use a numerical symbol system, based on "percent." The notion that the numerals correspond in some meaningful way to "percent of perfect" or "percent of subject known" is, of course, naive and without substance, since scores on the tests or exercises in a course depend heavily upon the instructor's choice of questions to ask and his standards for evaluating the responses. Thus, a mark obtained by even the most rigid averaging of such scores is a relative appraisal, its numerical value depending upon the choice of tasks and standards for appraising responses.

Other symbol systems, usually using letters, occur less frequently. Many of these are systems with a reduced number of categories—e.g., S (superior), A (average), I (needs improvement). The use of these tends to occur in elementary schools, and often in connection with systems that break up a subject (such as reading) into a number of aspects with view to a more analytical appraisal. Mixed-symbol systems are not uncommon, a smaller number of categories being used in lower grades and in subjects of a less academic character (Chansky, 1963; Kingston & Wash, 1966).

OBJECTIONS TO MARKS. The most fundamental question that can be and is asked about marks, as defined above, is whether they should in fact be used at all (Goodlad & Anderson, 1963). Should a single summarizing symbol signifying the teacher's appraisal of the quality of a student's performance in a segment of the educational program be made a matter of lasting record and communicated to the student or his parents, and possibly to other agencies? Or should marks, as defined, be replaced by some radically different record and report system?

A number of reasons have been urged for the abolition of marking (Anderson, 1966), including at least the allegations listed and briefly discussed below.

1. Marks provide an inaccurate assessment of competence and are not used in a comparable way from school to school, department to department, or instructor to instructor.

The variations in scoring essay questions and the variability in standards of marking both within and between institutions have been repeatedly demonstrated. The variations have been shown to be systematically related to teacher attitudes, subject-centered secondary-school teachers failing more pupils than pupil-centered ones (Rocchio & Kearney, 1956). However, this variability is characteristic of all types of judgment, so there seems little likelihood that any assessment prepared by a teacher, in whatever terms it may be couched, will be free of it. Those who criticize marks rarely would propose the elimination of a teacher role in pupil assessment, so perhaps this facet of criticism points more to the need to supplement teacher appraisal with objective, externally anchored information than to the undesirability of marks as such.

2. Marks are little, if at all, related to achievement of the central and important objectives of the educational program, and focus attention upon false and inappropriate objectives.

This criticism has two aspects, one of philosophy and one of implementation. The philosophical issue concerns the extent to which the goals of education are to be seen in cognitive accomplishments having a degree of coherence and homogeneity, the achievement of which can be defined and observed by a teacher. If one or a few definable dimensions of accomplishment encompass a major part of one's educational goals, then one or a few symbols can conceivably summarize progress toward them. To the extent that goals are seen as multitudinous, unrelated, and diffuse, any system of summarizing symbols will be inadequate and perhaps meaningless.

From the implementation side, the criticism is a recognition that the assessment procedures actually used by teachers fail to cover fully and adequately the objectives that they would accept as representing the goals for their instructional program. That is, the criticism focuses not upon the act of marking but upon the evidence upon which marks are based. However, to the extent that the evidence is partial and unbalanced, this deficiency will affect any type of report that a teacher may undertake to make about a pupil. Thus, the remedy that is implied is not the elimination of formal reporting procedures, but rather the thoughtful and conscientious improvement of assessment techniques.

3. Marks fail to provide a constructive medium of communication between school and home.

This criticism can be subdivided into three. First, the information provided by a summarizing symbol is too general to provide the parent (or the pupil) any cues as to what can or should be done about it. Especially when the mark is poor, and where presumably some remedial action is indicated, the mark provides no guidance as to the nature of the difficulty or as to what can be done to overcome it.

Second, the mark is coldly impersonal and provides no basis for a positive and mutually accepting relationship between the school and the home. It tends to alienate where cooperative effort is most needed, and to foster rejection of school and child where support is most needed.

Third, the marking system is a one-directional communication, going only from school to home. It provides no basis for a much-needed flow of information from home to school or an interaction between these two agents responsible for the learner.

In view of this, especially at the elementary-school level, many (probably most) school systems recognize that a marking and reporting system provides no more than a part of the communication system between school, parent, and pupil. Various patterns, typically involving some form of parent-teacher conference, have been instituted to supplement and sometimes to replace the traditional pattern of marks and a report card.

4. Marks and report cards produce a variety of side effects detrimental to the welfare of the child.

At least four types of side effects have been of concern to critics: (a) the debilitating impact of chronic failure, in the case of those who are measured by a standard that they cannot meet; (b) cutthroat competitiveness and resulting anxiety in a society that allocates its rewards in part in terms of a successive screening on educational criteria; (c) widespread cheating and dishonesty, in an attempt to circumvent the competitive demands (Astin & others, 1967); and (d) distorted educational value patterns, which make the appearance rather than the substance of learning the important thing. All of these side effects would appear to have an element of reality. However, in some cases the indictment seems to be of the total social pattern in which the schools (and marks) are set, or of the way pupils are grouped and taught, or of the quality of assessment, rather than of marks and a marking system per se.

SUBSTITUTES FOR MARKS. In response to the criticisms cited, a number of alternate procedures have been proposed to replace or supplement marks as we have defined them (Wrinkle, 1947; Goodlad & Anderson, 1963). Most of these alternatives have been tried out, and have in turn presented problems that have limited their widespread acceptance and adoption. Three main categories are considered below.

Conferences. One proposal has been for periodic conferences between teacher and parent. (At the higher educational levels, this would presumably become teacher and student.) Advantages claimed for conferences are that they (1) are flexible and permit an adaptation of presentation, emphasis, and distribution of time to the needs of the specific case; (2) provide an opportunity to emphasize positive aspects of pupil performance and of parent–school relationships; (3) give an opportunity for two-way communication so that the teacher can obtain information about a pupil as well as give it; and (4) make it possible to focus on specific aspects of the pupil's school problems and specific ways in which the parent can cooperate in improving the situation. However, the initiation and maintenance of a system of teacher–parent conferences has been found to produce a variety of problems in implementation.

A first problem in a parent–teacher interview program is that of time—time to prepare adequately for a conference and time to conduct it. Writers supporting such a program emphasize the need for released time if the program is to be effective (Anderson, 1966). Problems of skill and personal security also arise, since not all teachers are equipped either by training or by temperament to carry on the semitherapeutic type of personal interaction that is involved in establishing effective communication with a possibly hostile and insecure parent. A third problem area is that of gaining parent cooperation in investing the time, year by year, in coming to school to meet with a teacher. Finally, of course, the fruitfulness of an interview is limited by the information available to the teacher. The teacher cannot share information that he does not have. Especially as school programs become departmentalized, a given teacher tends to interact with large numbers of pupils, and to interact with each only for a limited period during the day. Under these circumstances, the teacher's perception of many pupils may be largely limited to subject-matter achievement on the one hand and superficial personal impression on the other. The interaction in an interview can be no better than the understanding upon which it is based.

Letters. Letters from teacher to parent have been tried at times, but they do not seem to receive very widespread support in current writings. A letter possesses some of the flexibility and potential both to emphasize positive roles and to suggest constructive actions that a conference has, but it fails to provide the two-way communication that is seen as so important in the latter. Letters are also demanding upon the time and skill of the teacher, and consequently have been reported as likely to become stereotyped. Misunderstandings are reported to be likely, especially with less-educated parents, and since there is no possibility for the give-and-take that occurs in face-to-face contact, no way is provided to eliminate these misunderstandings.

Expanded Report Forms. The other main adaptation has been the use of expanded and elaborated forms reporting on many specific components within a subject area. The typical first step in preparing such a report form is to analyze the objectives in an area of instruction at a given level, such as reading in the primary grades, for example, into a number of specific skills. These, in turn, may be analyzed into even more specific components. Thus, one effort to develop report forms in reading for an ungraded primary program (Chadwick & others, 1966) made a first-level analysis into I—Auditory skills; II—Visual skills; III—Comprehension; IV—Silent and oral reading; V—Language (oral and written); and VI—Dictionary skills. Auditory skills were, in turn, subdivided into ten more specific components, and a similar division was made for each of the other categories.

Some selection of the specifics arrived at by an analysis such as the above is then organized into a report form. Typically the report form makes provision for use of two or three symbols representing broad categories for expressing progress with respect to each of the specifics.

The advantages claimed for such an expanded report form are that it is much more informative than a few summarizing symbols and that the strengths and weaknesses indicated in the pupil's profile can be used as a basis for constructive activity—presumably by parent and child as well as by teacher. However, for this to be possible, the specifics must be assessed sufficiently reliably so that the high and low points can be accepted and interpreted with some confidence. Information on the reliability of the appraisals that are represented in such an extended pupil analysis is not easy to come by. However, on a priori grounds, taking account of the number of judgments that a teacher is called upon to make and of the general experience with the halo and bias that frequently color subjective judgments, concern on this point seems warranted. There seems to be no question that schools that have tried such expanded systems have found the preparation of reports time-consuming and demanding.

The meaningfulness of the elaborated set of educational outcomes to a parent has also become a problem. The process of defining objectives and of trying to make explicit a pupil's progress toward them may be very instructive and rewarding for a teacher without being comprehensible to a parent, and parents have apparently often become confused by, and hostile to, highly elaborated report forms.

LIMITATIONS OF SUBSTITUTES. As one reviews the alternatives that have been proposed to replace marks, it seems clear that their usefulness varies with two aspects of the school situation. One is educational level and the other is school resources. Most of the modifications seem to be appropriate primarily for the elementary school. At this level there is usually, or at least often, some one teacher who has continuing and fairly intimate contact with each pupil, and she can take primary responsibility for interviews or reports concerning the limited number of pupils under her charge. At this level, it is usually easier to analyze instructional objectives into tangible and specific objectives. At this level, parent contact with the school is usually more intimate. In secondary school or college, instruction is departmentalized and a given instructor sees many students in only a single course. The instructor is more a specialist concerned with his area of knowledge and less a generalist concerned with students as persons. Course content has become complex and difficult to reduce to specific skills. The parent is now less protectively concerned about the welfare of his offspring. Under these circumstances a personalized or elaborated reporting system has seemed difficult to maintain.

Even at the elementary level, it seems clear that most of the substitutes for conventional marks and report cards make increased demands on teacher time and skill. Time is needed not only to produce the reports or carry out the conferences that are called for, but also to prepare for the job. Preparation involves indoctrination and training of the teachers in the procedures that they are to use. It also means making the observations and gathering the evidence that will permit the teacher to appraise the pupil accurately and analytically, and reviewing and organizing the various types of evidence so that they can be effectively communicated. Thus, many pleas for revised reporting procedures also include pleas for smaller classes and released time to make the system feasible (Anderson, 1966). It seems clear that such reporting procedures are most likely to survive in the educational setting that is sufficiently affluent to permit this type of support.

Up to the present time, and for schools as they are now constituted, no one pattern of reporting appears to have received general acceptance, or appears to be clearly and uniformly superior even at the elementary level. In view of this fact, and in view of the special difficulties of developing more informal and more analytic procedures of reporting in secondary and higher education, it seems clear that marks and the periodic reporting of them will continue to be a part of the educational scene for some time to come. The balance of this essay is therefore directed at a number of issues that have been raised with respect to marks and report cards of the conventional type, with a view to clarifying some of the problems that arise in their use and some of the proposals that have been offered for dealing with these problems.

WHAT SHOULD A MARK REPRESENT? The first and central question asks what, so far as possible, the single symbol that constitutes a mark should represent. The question has two sides. On the one hand, what aspects of student performance should the mark try to characterize? On the other, in relation to what reference group should the appraisal be expressed?

Turning to the aspect or aspects of student performance to be appraised, one again encounters a dual question. On the one hand, should a mark on a segment of the curriculum represent as unambiguously as possible competence in that segment of the curriculum? If so, on the other hand, how is competence to be defined and assessed?

It is clear that many of the primary troublesome issues about marks are issues of value and not issues of fact—of what should be, rather than of what is. Research may be helpful in assessing the realism of some of these "should be's"—in determining the extent that they are translatable into "can be's." But the existing confusion and conflict in the domain of values, sometimes implicit and poorly formulated, makes it difficult for a working consensus to be reached. The discussion that follows will attempt at least to make explicit some of the value conflicts.

One position would hold that a mark, as a single symbol, should represent as purely and clearly as possible competence in a segment of the curriculum. The rationale for this position is that the symbol is then more univocal, more understandable, and more universal as a unit of communication. The responsibility of the instructor is to define for himself and for students what constitutes competence (i.e., what the objectives of the course are), and then to develop and use evaluation techniques that are consistent with those objectives.

In practice, certainly many other considerations than that of pure competence *do* enter into marks. Such factors enter in as (1) industry and effort—i.e., completing all assigned work and even doing optional work for "extra credit" (a kind of educational bribe); (2) frequent and active participation in class discussion; (3) neatness in written work and mechanical correctness in such areas as spelling and grammar; and (4) personal agreeableness, attractiveness, cleanliness, and docility. To some extent and by some instructors, certain of these factors would be endorsed as legitimate influences on a mark. Others would more uniformly be accepted as extraneous influences, to be minimized so far as possible. To the extent that instructors in a given school differ in their practices with respect to these factors, marks will differ in their meaning. Thus, explicit consideration of what factors, if any, are to be considered in addition to competence, and an attempt to reach a consensus with respect to them, represent the first steps toward getting consistent meaning for marking symbols.

The defining and assessing of competence is coterminous with the whole process of educational evaluation. The issues in formulation of educational objectives and in development of assessment techniques are discussed in the article "Measurement in Education."

WHAT FRAME OF REFERENCE? If one assumes, as the author tends to, that the symbol used for a mark is most useful if the marker attempts to make it unequivocally an estimate of competence in the objectives set up for a unit of instruction, we then ask with respect to what frame of reference this competence is to be expressed. Should it be an absolute one or a relative one? If a relative one, relative to what? The individual's earlier level of competence? The individual's "potential," however that may be judged? Some type of reference group? If in relation to a reference group, then what type?

Mastery. There may be a few limited segments of the educational enterprise that can be divided into clear-cut learning units where the "mastery" of the unit can reasonably be assessed. Thus, there are 100 simple addition combinations, and it is possible that a pupil may respond correctly to all of them with high consistency—even when he is sleepy or distracted. He has mastered them. Or a typist may be able to produce straight copy at a rate of 40 wpm with no more than one error per 40 words. At a certain standard, she has mastered typing. But in relation to the objectives of most courses, the notion of complete mastery is an illusion. One does not master completely the concepts of geometry, the content of American history, or the skills of effective writing. Competence is a matter of degree, of more or less—and more or less must always be expressed in relation to something.

Performance Relative to Potential. One strongly expressed view is that performance evaluation should be relative to the individual himself—what he has done in the past, or what he should be expected to do. The advantage claimed for such a reference frame is that it approximately equates the possibility of "success" for all students, since each has an equal chance to improve or to do well in relation to his own potential. Limitations of this approach relate in part to the technical adequacy and in part to the social utility of marks reported in this frame.

From the point of technical feasibility, the fundamental question is whether teachers can (or will) make reliable judgments of growth, or reliable distinctions between potential and performance. Growth measures over a limited time span are notoriously unreliable even when based on standardized ability tests (Thorndike, 1966), and there is little basis for anticipating that they will be any better when based on subjective teacher judgments. And it has been reiterated for at least 40 years that the distinction between scholastic aptitude and measured achievement is a tenuous one, at least when achievement is represented by a paper-and-pencil test (Kelley, 1927). Thus, it seems unlikely that teachers can assess with any substantial reliability the gap between potential and competence. It is, of course, possible to get more reliable differences if and to the extent that teachers' marks represent dutiful industry, cheerful compliance, or some attributes other than sheer competence.

There has been little empirical study of teachers' behavior when they attempt to assess performance in relation to ability, but the contamination of marks on "achievement in relation to ability" (which should in theory show the same array of marks for each ability level) by ability level is shown by Halliwell (1960), who correlated these marks with scores on an aptitude test on the one hand and the deviation of achievement-test scores from what would have been predicted on the basis of aptitude on the other. The correlations were approximately .50 and .00. In theory, they should have been just the reverse. That is, since a good mark was supposed to show whether the pupil was doing well *in relation to his ability,* good marks should have been equally common at all aptitude levels and hence not correlated with aptitude. They should, however, have been related to the achievement–aptitude discrepancy, going more often to those who showed a positive discrepancy of achievement over aptitude. So far as this one study is concerned, marking achievement in relation to aptitude was an illusion.

Question has also been raised about the social utility of marks expressed in relation to a purely individual standard in any but the present and limited educational context. It is pointed out that decisions both by and for the student are often, perhaps usually, made in the light of his performance relative to others. To the extent that this is true, intraindividual marks will fail to provide usable information.

Performance Relative to Group. Once one accepts the position that a mark expresses performance in relation to some group, further issues revolve around definition of the desirable group and procedures to assure that marks do in fact relate in some consistent way to that group. Several alternative groups represent possibilities: (1) the national group of a given grade or age, (2) the total grade group in a smaller educational unit such as a community or more commonly a school, (3) the specific class in which the student finds himself, (4) the somewhat shadowy and ill-defined group that constitutes a particular teacher's concept of what is typical for a given age or grade.

National Group. The use of a total national population as a reference group provides the broadest possible base for purposes of prediction and decision. When such a national group is assessed on a common achievement test, the test results can serve directly to calibrate marks, as has been done in the schools of Sweden (Husen, 1963), for example. The number of marks at a given level (but not the pupils to receive them) can be specified from the scores on the anchor test. Or the nationwide test can provide a second variable that can be weighted in academic prediction and thus modulate between-school differences indirectly, as is done by College Entrance Examination Board (CEEB) and American College Testing Program (ACT) tests in the United States. That some of the same calibration can be achieved by cross-calibration of secondary-school and college marks is suggested by the studies of Bloom and Peters (1961), though Lindquist (1963) has failed to find support for the value of such a procedure. The universal use of a nationwide or statewide testing program to provide a national or regional anchor for local marking practices may be feasible within a highly centralized unit of the educational system. The local autonomy characteristic of American education limits such procedures to points such as the transition between school and college, where college entrance tests serve to calibrate school grades.

School Population. As one brings the problem of

the appropriate reference group down to the local level, one faces the problem of whether the reference group should be (and whether it can be) the total group at the given grade level in the given school. This problem arises in assigning grades in different sections of a single course or different courses within a department; it also arises in relation to comparability of grading as between departments and subject matters. The central problems here, as in much of the confusion on marking practices, are problems of philosophy and values, though psychometric problems of implementation do arise when and as a general agreement on values is reached (Anderhalter, 1962).

The basic value question is whether the same level of competence *should* receive the same mark wherever it is displayed. This problem becomes especially acute when some form of ability grouping is used, and different sections of a course are clearly unequal in talent. The situation may then often be further complicated by the fact that sections for different categories of pupils should and do have somewhat different instructional objectives and use different materials. Common evaluation instruments are then no longer appropriate, and direct comparison of performance may not be feasible.

But there is no real consensus on the basic issue. The position that a specific degree of competence need not receive the same grade in different contexts and that more lenient standards should be applied to less capable students, and vice versa, is fairly widely held and is supported on grounds of maintaining motivation and the opportunity for success for the less well endowed. On the other hand, however, concern is frequently expressed at penalizing honors groups by demanding higher accomplishment in them in order to earn the same mark, and this practice has been seen as potentially demoralizing to an honors program. Thus, in the absence of consensus on the desirable policy often little progress is made toward implementing any policy.

Various specific techniques have been suggested for maintaining the equity in grade assignment as between groups differing in ability. In general, these depend upon using, either explicitly or implicitly, some type of regression of marks upon a measure of aptitude or of achievement. Thus, Ebel (1965) gives a routine for modifying the distribution of college marks in the light of previous grade-point average (GPA) of the student group. Problems in using such procedures arise more from practical difficulties in record keeping and in getting faculty acceptance and compliance than from any basic problems of psychometric theory.

Problems that are more intractable in both the philosophical and practical sense arise when one aspires to maintain a common reference frame across different departments. Typically there are substantial interdepartmental differences in severity of marking (Aiken, 1964), and these have been found to show a degree of stability over time and from place to place. Thus, mathematics and physical science departments are rather generally found to be hard markers, in the sense that lower marks are given in relation to the aptitude level of the student group than in education, for instance, or music, or vocational agriculture. Should these differences exist? If not, what can be done to overcome them?

Again, the problem is partly the philosophical one of reaching agreement on the social values involved, and partly one of obtaining compliance from the faculty members who are affected; a reasonably satisfactory solution to the psychometric problems involved is not difficult to arrange. The basic value question can be phrased approximately as follows: Should a student of a given intellectual capability (estimated by test or by some composite of previous achievement) expect to receive the same mark, on the average, in any one subject as in any other? On grounds of general equity, one would tend to argue the affirmative; however, on grounds of the desirability of encouraging the student to continue to study and to seek employment in some field, one might argue the negative. Thus, certain fields of knowledge may be so demanding intellectually that it is poor social policy to encourage any but the most able to pursue them. Conceivably, a mathematician of less than a specified level of competence may be a liability both to himself and to the larger society. There is no easy solution to the value conflict. Nor is the practical problem of obtaining from those in the more highly selective fields acquiescence to a marking standard matching that in other areas, and guaranteeing that such acquiescence continue to function at the operating as well as at the verbal level, easily solved. One suspects that some centralized, computerized procedure for translating rank-in-class, adjusted for average ability level, into a mark is the only technique that would really do the job.

Class Group. The reference group that is often used as a frame for viewing the performance of an individual is the group meeting as an instructional unit. This may range from a small seminar group of eight or ten to the huge lecture class of hundreds or even thousands of students that is found in some American universities. The acceptability of the class group as a reference frame depends, of course, upon its size and representativeness. When the group is large and representative of other similar groups, it seems reasonable to apply rather rigidly a preestablished set of standard percentages in determining the number of pupils to receive each of the marking symbols. However, when the group is small, chance fluctuations in the distribution of student capability are likely and a rigid predetermination of the distribution of grades is unsatisfactory. The alternatives are two: (1) the small group may be anchored to a larger reference group by measures of aptitude or previous achievement or, where several sections exist, by a common examination, so as to use a larger group or the total class as a referent; or (2) the small group may be referenced to that vaguely defined standard that exists in the instructor's memories, the "typical class," and appropriate adjustments made in the assignment of grades. Such evidence as exists on variations of grading standards from instructor to instructor, and on insensitivity of grade distribution to changes in the intellectual quality of student input, suggests that the instructor's internal standard is a vague and vacillating one upon which to rely. Thus, Aiken (1963) found that despite a 50-point increase in average SAT Verbal score of entering freshmen in one college over a three-year period, and a corresponding increase in high school grades, there was no substantial change in freshman grade-point average. It is awareness of this fact that has sparked much of the literature of the past 50 years directed toward making more objective and uniform the standards of marking.

PROPORTION AWARDED EACH SYMBOL. Once one has decided upon the reference frame in terms of which marking symbols are to be assigned, the final problems center around the translation of the composite of scores that are available to the instructor into the symbols used for reporting quality of work. Problems are of two types: What weight should be given to each partial score in pooling them into a composite? What proportion of students should receive each of the symbols in the symbol set?

The determination of desired weights for specific scores—on recitations, homework exercises, papers, examinations, etc.—is a judgmental matter. It involves a judgment on how important the different course objectives are and how well the specific forms of evidence represent them. Achieving the desired weights then depends upon recognizing that the effective weight of a score is in proportion to its standard deviation and manipulating the standard deviations of the different scores either by modifying the length of the test, number of exercises, etc., or by applying an appropriate multiplying factor.

Determining the proportion of students to receive each symbol in the symbol set has been a matter of concern in a good deal of the literature on marks and marking (Smith & Dobbin, 1960). The concern to make marks, which are in their nature basically ordinal measures, represent steps that could be interpreted as representing an equal unit scale, has given rise to an extensive literature on "marking on the curve." The proposal has been that the percentage of pupils assigned each successive marking symbol should be such that each category would represent an equal distance on the baseline of the Gaussian "normal" curve. Thus, one proposed allocation of marks, 7–23–40–23–7 for the symbols A–B–C–D–F, would make each symbol cover one standard deviation of the range of performance and make C correspond to a segment exactly in the middle of the score scale.

This pattern has an appealing psychometric symmetry and elegance. It also has practical implications that bring it rather sharply in conflict with educational realities. The most immediate and obvious feature of the definition that centers C at the average of the group is that there must be as many D's and F's as B's and A's, which has dramatic social implications in terms of the proportion reported as failing a course. Less obvious is the fact that rigorous application of these standards throughout an educational institution has important implications with respect to the frequency distribution of grade-point averages. If the usual symbol equivalents are used of $A = 4$, $B = 3$, $C = 2$, $D = 1$, $F = 0$; then it follows automatically that the average grade-point average (GPA) will be 2.00. Furthermore, if we know the typical correlation among grades in different courses, we can immediately also estimate the spread of GPA's and the proportion of students who will fall below any given value. Thus, the proportion falling below a GPA of 1.50, given certain assumptions as to the average correlation between grades in different courses, is as follows:

Average Correlation	Percent Below 1.50
.50	25
.25	20
.00	13

The three values of intercorrelation that are shown probably cover the range that might reasonably be expected, so we have bracketed the range within which the percentage can be expected to lie. If, by administrative decision, it has been ruled that a GPA of 1.50 is required for a student to remain in good standing or to be eligible for intercollegiate athletics, our psychometric procedure (rigorously applied) will immediately have the effect of disqualifying 12 to 25 percent of the student body.

MARKS AND THE INSTITUTIONAL CULTURE PATTERN. Grading patterns are deeply embedded in a total institutional culture. The culture may be an imperfect and an irrational one, and the current grading behavior of faculty members may lack psychometric elegance and be in some respects erratic and even capricious. But a modus vivendi has typically been worked out between the traditions of marking and the rest of the institutional culture. Any substantial change in marking practices will almost certainly result in dislocations in other parts of that institutional culture. It is partly for this reason that faculty grading practices are so resistant to change. One who would reform the marking system of an educational institution needs first to acquire a profound understanding of the culture of that institution. He must become aware of the manifold ways in which marks affect the life of the institution. He must identify the range of actions that are taken and decisions that are made in which marks have a role to play, either by law or by custom. He must recognize that most of these decisions will have to be made on *some* basis—whether on the basis of recorded marks or some other. He must ask what impact any proposed changes in the marking symbols, the proportions awarded each, or the marking policies of specific departments will have on the total system that constitutes his local culture. Such a study of the educational culture seems potentially very rewarding. Like any other society, an educational institution has developed its culture through a host of unrelated and often unrealized changes. The present structure is often irrational, in some ways maladaptive and poorly understood. A more complete understanding of the culture and the full role that marks play in that culture provides the sound foundation for rational change. But cultures change slowly. And a change in a part will become effective only as it is consistent with the whole. One needs to see the marking system as an element in a larger system, and to see any change in the marking system in terms of its impact upon the equilibrium of the total institutional culture in which it is embedded.

In conclusion, much of the literature on marks and marking over the past 50 years seems to have missed the mark because it has operated in an unrealistic world. It has been unrealistic in two senses. It has been insensitive to the very real limits in time, precision of judgment, and skill in assessment within which the typical teacher operates. It has been largely unaware of the complex cultural pressures bearing upon instructors within the society of an educational institution and defining the bases and limits of their grading practices much more than does any psychometric theory. It is within these two limiting structures that any reform or improvement of grading practices must operate.

Robert L. Thorndike
Teachers College,
Columbia University

References

Aiken, Lewis R., Jr. "The Grading Behavior of a College Faculty." *Ed Psychol Meas* 23:319–22; 1963.

Aiken, Lewis R., Jr. "Interdepartmental Variability and Student Expectations of College Grades." *Ed Psychol Meas* 24:823–9; 1964.

Anderhalter, Oliver F. "Developing Uniform Departmental Grading Standards in a University." *J Exp Ed* 31:210–1; 1962.

Anderson, Robert H. "The Importance and Purposes of Reporting." *Nat El Sch Prin* 45:6–11; 1966.

Astin, Alexander W., and others. *National Norms for Entering College Freshmen—1966.* ACE, 1967. 25p.

Bloom, Benjamin S., and Peters, Frank R. *Academic Prediction Scales for Selecting and Counseling College Entrants.* Free, 1961. 145p.

Chadwick, Ruth E., and others. "The Report Card in a Non-Graded School." *Nat El Sch Prin* 45:22–8; 1966.

Chansky, Norman M. "Elementary School Teachers Rate Report Cards." *J Ed Res* 56:523–8; 1963.

Dolman, Howard, and Michael, K. E. "What are Some New Trends in Reporting Student Growth and Achievement to Parents?" *B Nat Assn Sec Sch Prin* 44:146–9; 1960.

Downing, Marjorie. "Variations in College Grading Systems: Symposium." *J H Ed* 35:89–103; 1964.

Ebel, Robert L. *Measuring Educational Achievement.* Prentice-Hall, 1965. 481p.

Goodlad, John I., and Anderson, Robert H. *The Nongraded Elementary School,* Rev. ed. Harcourt, 1963. 248p.

Halliwell, Joseph W. "The Relationship of Certain Factors to Marking Practices in Individualized Reporting Programs." *J Ed Res* 54:76–8; 1960.

Husen, Torsten. "Intra-pair Similarities in the School Achievement of Twins." *Scandinavin J Psychol* 4:108–14; 1963.

Joint Committee on School-College Relations. *Rank in Class.* National Association of Secondary School Principals, 1962.

Kelley, Truman L. *Interpretation of Educational Measurements.* Harcourt, 1927. 363p.

Kingston, Albert J., and Wash, J. A., Jr. "Research on Reporting Systems." *Nat El Sch Prin* 45:36–40; 1966.

Lindquist, E. F. "An Evaluation of a Technique for Scaling High School Grades to Improve Prediction of College Success." *Ed Psychol Meas* 23:623–46; 1963.

Rocchio, Patrick D., and Kearney, N.C. "Teacher-pupil Attitudes as Related to Non-promotion of Secondary School Pupils." *Ed Psychol Meas* 16:244–52; 1956.

Smith, Ann Z., and Dobbin, John E. "Marks and Marking Systems." In Harris, Chester W. (Ed.) *Encyclopedia of Educational Research.* 3rd ed. Macmillan, 1960. p. 783–91.

Thorndike, Robert L. "Intellectual Status and Intellectual Growth." *J Ed Psychol* 57: 121–7; 1966.

Wrinkle, William L. *Improving Marking and Reporting Practices in Elementary and Secondary Schools.* Holt, 1947. 120p.

MATHEMATICS

Activity in mathematics education during the past decade has far exceeded that of any other ten years in history. One would expect that in light of this activity, there would be a great deal of accompanying research; and, indeed, there have been many papers published that are classified as research in mathematics education. Weaver (1966a) has no trouble listing more than 100 research articles per year that pertain to elementary-school mathematics, and Brown and Abell's (1965) summary shows that there is as much or more research being done in secondary-school mathematics as in elementary-school mathematics.

In spite of all of this activity, the results of the research are somewhat disappointing. As Johnson (1965) suggests, there is little research evidence available to back up many of our most cherished beliefs. In fact, he points out, there may never be any such research evidence. Perhaps the most significant question that could be asked today about the school mathematics program is "Is the new mathematics better than the traditional mathematics?" Statistical research does not really supply a satisfactory answer to this question. There is much evidence that children exposed to a modern mathematics program do as well or better than those exposed to a traditional program on traditional tests. Summaries by Brown and Abell (1965, 1966a), Leiderman (1965), Lockard (1966), Payne (1965), and Whitman (1966) all support this thesis. However, much of the research they review is highly subjective, and the studies seldom have sufficient control to convince a reader that the Hawthorne Effect is not more important than the modern mathematics. This is not to say that there is any evidence that modern mathematics is not good—only that research that purports to answer the question, in general, does not. As Brownell (1966) suggests, value judgments are needed as well as objective data.

Popular reports of the international study directed by Husen (1967) provide an example of lack of judgment used in interpreting statistical data. Because of the populations involved and the natural limitations of the testing instruments, it is not legitimate to use the results as though they reported the results of an international race. However, this is just the way the results were reported in the popular press. What appears from a more careful examination of the study is that one of the best predictors of whether a child gets the correct answer to a problem is the teacher's estimate of the child's opportunity to have learned the subject matter involved. With this fact in mind, results which purport to show that a country's educational system is better than another's, or that "modern" mathematics is better than "traditional," can be discounted unless the pupils involved have been exposed to the same subject matter.

However, there are many questions pertaining to mathematics education for which research has, over the years, given partial answers. There is also evidence that interest in research is increasing. The National Council of Teachers of Mathematics, which has tended not to take an active role in research, has recently supported a conference on Needed Research in Mathematics Education jointly with the University of Georgia; has had sections on research at its national meetings; has published a collection of research papers, edited by Scandura (1967); and is considering publication of a journal on research in mathematics education.

HISTORY. The first revolution in the teaching of mathematics in this country began in 1821 with the publication of Warren Colburn's *Intellectual Arithmetic upon the Inductive Method of Instruction*. Glennon (1966) and Willoughby (1967) both discuss this early revolution, pointing out that prior to that time the teaching of mathematics consisted largely of the teacher's dictating rules to the children and then letting the children use the rules on a large number of exercises (also usually dictated by the teacher). Colburn, a follower of Pestalozzi, believed that the child would learn more by making his own rules and setting up his own generalizations. Colburn's books were widely used, and were still being revised and published as late as 1884.

Butler and Wren (1965), Willoughby (1967), and others describe the attempts to improve the teaching of mathematics through committee efforts in the latter part of the nineteenth century and during this century. Probably the most important efforts of that sort prior to 1950 were the Committee of Ten Report (1894) and the report of the National Committee on Mathematical Requirements (1923). Both of these reports favored the decompartmentalization of the teaching of mathematics and a reduction in exercise material designed for mental gymnastics.

Also, late in the nineteenth century, psychologists began producing research studies that had far-reaching effects on the teaching of mathematics. Rice (1902) found that there was a low correlation between scores on arithmetic tests and time spent studying arithmetic. The assumption that studying mathematics automatically makes one more logical was attacked by Thorndike, and his stimulus–response, or bond, approach to teaching arithmetic became the predominant method. Judd and others demonstrated that when a subject is taught for meaning, transfer may occur, but this evidence does not seem to have stemmed the tide of Thorndike's bond approach, as indicated by McLaughlin (1918) in her survey of textbooks, who says that most of the new arithmetics were following Thorndike's lead. Buswell and Judd (1925) summarize 307 of the early studies including those by Thorndike, Judd, and Rice; and Brownell (1930) gives an excellent analysis of 532 of the early published reports.

Smith and others (1912) deplored the state of mathematics education in this country, claiming that since there was no central control, experimentation was going on everywhere but no major nationwide improvements could occur. At that time, they said, fewer than half of the high schools in this country offered mathematics beyond three semesters of algebra and two semesters of geometry. Trigonometry and a fourth semester of algebra were generally college subjects. By 1955, the only major changes in content that Fehr (1955) noted during the first half of the century were the introduction of graphing into the algebra program and the pushing of some topics, such as trigonometry and part of analytic geometry and calculus, into lower grades. Fehr also mentions, somewhat prophetically, that the use of set language may be about to expand.

Clark (1965) and Rappaport (1965), in their histories of mathematics education during the first 65 years of this century, point out that the intellectual content was very heavy in 1900, but the psychologists took over after that and the content became weak, a stimulus–response approach was prevalent, and social utility was the main criterion for inclusion of a topic in the curriculum. The compulsory education laws and subsequent expansion of the school population also encouraged a watering down of the content. During this time, speed and accuracy of computation were important goals, and the stimulus–response approach seemed well suited to this purpose. During the late 1930's, mathematics educators began to emphasize meaning and understanding. Gestalt psychology played an important role in their arguments. Hartmann (1937), for example, attacks the connectionist theory, which he says was generally accepted at the time, and makes a plea for an emphasis on the whole situation rather than a concentration on isolated parts.

Clark and Rappaport both seem to feel that the situation since 1957 has been somewhat similar to that before 1900, with the mathematicians taking over leadership and the content becoming somewhat heavy again. Glennon (1966) agrees with this assessment, pointing out that before 1957 most research was on the learning process, and since that time effort has been concentrated on the structure of mathematics. He feels that the pendulum is beginning to swing back toward the needs of the child.

In 1957, when the entries on arithmetic and mathematics for the third edition of this Encyclopedia were written, Sputnik had just been launched, the Commission of the College Entrance Examination Board (CEEB) was meeting, and two or three other projects which seemed rather minor were under way. However, the entry on mathematics by Gibb and others (1960) devoted only one paragraph to these studies. At the time, the importance of mathematics to society was just beginning to be fully realized, and a major portion of the research reported by Buswell (1960) was designed to try to make children into faster and more accurate computers.

MODERN MATHEMATICS. The phrase "modern mathematics," if used prior to 1957, would ordinarily have meant "that mathematics which is modern." Most citizens would not have realized that the amount of mathematics produced in this century was substantially greater than that produced in all previous history. But they also would not have thought about little children when the phrase was used. Now, even mathematicians use such words as "the new mathematics" or "modern mathematics" to refer to curricular changes in the schools as well as to talk about mathematics that has been created recently.

The first of the projects that is clearly a modern mathematics project was the University of Illinois Committee on School Mathematics (UICSM), which began near the end of 1951. Beberman (1958) gives an early history of this project and discusses the program as it existed when other projects were just getting under way.

By 1955, the examiners of the CEEB had prevailed upon the board to set up a Commission on Mathematics to study the curriculum and make recommendations for future developments. Many teachers thought that the report of this commission would have relatively little effect on actual classroom practice, as had been the case with most previous reports of this sort. However, when the Commission on Mathematics of the CEEB (1959a, b) published its report, pressures for a change had become sufficiently great that publishing companies had already begun publishing textbooks on the new mathematics which purported to satisfy the commission's report.

Two other conferences, which produced reports somewhat similar to that of the CEEB's Commission on Mathematics, but on an international level, were held during the early 1960's. The Organization for European Economic Cooperation (1961a, b) sponsored several meetings. The report of the first meeting summarized practices in participating countries and cited the condemnation of these practices by the assembled mathematicians and educators. It also outlined programs that the conferees thought would be improvements. The second report spelled out many of the details of these programs. In 1962, a similar report on mathematical education in the Americas was produced under the editorship of Fehr (1962).

Meanwhile, curriculum projects in mathematics found ready support from government agencies and sprang up all over the country. Undoubtedly the most significant of these was the School Mathematics Study Group (SMSG), which has produced materials for all grades from kindergarten through grade 12, plus quantities of supplementary materials for teachers, bright pupils, and others. The work of the SMSG is reviewed in detail by Wooten (1965). Reviews, analyses, and summaries of the numerous projects can be found in studies by the National Council of Teachers of Mathematics (1961, 1963), Deans (1963), the American Association of School Administrators (1965), Butler and Wren (1965), and Willoughby (1967).

All available evidence seems to indicate that programs classified as modern are replacing traditional programs at a very rapid rate—in fact it is hard to find anybody at a meeting of mathematics teachers who does not believe that the program in his school system is at least semimodern. Alspaugh and Delon (1967) report statistical evidence that in at least one state, modern mathematics courses (as they define them) are replacing traditional courses very rapidly for college-preparatory courses but not for general courses. They conclude that about half of the algebra courses are modern, somewhat fewer geometry courses are modern, and the senior courses are beginning to incorporate more analysis. Solid geometry, as a separate course, has essentially disappeared from the curriculum.

In 1963, the Cambridge Conference on School Mathematics (1963) produced the recommendations of 29 mathematicians for future curricular reforms in mathematics. The views expressed were meant to cause discussion and thought for the future, and have done so. Perhaps the most talked-about reaction to the CCSM report was Stone's (1965) review, in which he accused the conference of being both unrealistic and unimaginative. Other reactions have been too numerous to list, but a generally favorable review was produced by Adler (1966a).

Although the modern mathematics programs had relatively clear sailing for many years, there were some mathematicians and educators who had reservations about the changes at a very early time. Kline was one of the earliest critics of "the new mathematics," and has continued to suggest that an intuitive, constructive, applied approach would be more appropriate than the highly theoretical approach he believes underlies most of the programs. In one of

his more recent expressions of his point of view, Kline (1966) outlines the kind of ninth-grade program he believes would be more appropriate than those produced by others. Kline has not been alone in his reservations about some aspects of the modern mathematics programs. Ahlfors and 64 other mathematicians (1962), including Kline, expressed their belief that many programs overemphasized deduction and words to the detriment of inductive processes and understandings. More recently, Mueller (1966) has traced the public image of school mathematics from 1956 to 1966 through articles in nonprofessional periodicals. He finds that in 1956 the public was appalled by the state of mathematics education but felt that the UICSM program seemed to offer hope for the future. After that, until 1966, articles generally expressed confidence in the new mathematics programs, but then a certain amount of disenchantment set in. The trend now seems to be more toward criticism.

OBJECTIVES. Mathematics was taught in the schools of this country both for vocational and for intellectual reasons from the earliest times. The early town schools taught both writing and arithmetic because their purpose was largely to teach clerks. Schools that were not in commercial towns tended to drop arithmetic from the curriculum and concentrated more heavily on reading and religion. In addition to the town schools, there were the colleges and the Latin grammar schools. Although these had as their primary purpose the training of ministers, they included subjects such as natural sciences, mathematics, and logic in their curricula, since Puritanism was an intellectual creed. As the academies, and later the high schools, arose, they tended to take over the practical, vocational aspects of the subject, while the grammar schools continued to concentrate more on the mental-discipline approach. But by the late 1800's most schools seemed to accept the mental-discipline theory.

After 1900, Thorndike's research and the expanding school population both encouraged a trend away from the mental-discipline approach and toward a social-utility approach. Since there was no exceptional amount of transfer of learning from mathematics to other subjects (a widely held interpretation of Thorndike's results) and since the vast majority of children were now in the schools, social utility became the primary criterion in determining whether a topic was to be taught, and how it would be taught. Typical of the large number of surveys that appeared at this time was Wilson's (1919) on the social and business usages of arithmetic. As more evidence began to accumulate showing that transfer did occur when mathematics was taught for understanding, and Gestalt theory began to have more influence in this country, there was again, in the 1930's and after, a tendency to teach mathematics for intellectual as well as social reasons.

During the past decade, educators and psychologists have been impressed with the accumulation of evidence that children can learn very difficult subject matter at very early ages. Bruner's (1960) remark to the effect that we can teach any subject to any child at any age in some form that is intellectually honest is simply one of the better-known overstatements of this position. Some of the curricular experiments seem to work from the assumption that if a very young child can learn something, then he ought to; however, as far as is known at this time, there have been no experiments with prenatal mathematics education.

An often-expressed objective in teaching mathematics is the improvement of the pupils' problem-solving ability. Buswell (1960) reported many experiments in which problem solving was an important aspect. The results seem to indicate that problem solving and reading are very closely associated. A recent report by Call and Wiggin (1966) suggests that an English teacher with very little background in mathematics may be able to do a better job of teaching problem solving than a mathematics teacher. Few of the experimenters have asked whether it is really the type of problem that is found in books that children should learn to solve, but Swenson (1965) makes a strong plea for more emphasis on solving real problems drawn from the actual experience of the children. Perhaps the reading difficulty in problem solving would be reduced substantially if the children could extract their information from reality rather than from a book. If this is the case, traditional problem solving might more suitably be taught in the English class than in the mathematics class.

CURRICULUM. In 1957, when the entries on arithmetic (Buswell, 1960) and mathematics (Gibb & others, 1960) for the third edition of this Encyclopedia were written, it seemed that the content of the curriculum for school mathematics was essentially constant. In the elementary schools, research centered around organization, readiness, and how to do better, which everybody agreed was necessary. Both the advocates of social utility and the advocates of a logical, intellectual organization seemed to agree that the content of elementary-school mathematics centered around the four basic operations with whole numbers and positive rational numbers, and with appropriate applications. In the secondary schools, there had been a few changes and several recommendations. Notably, arithmetic for grades 7 and 8 had become general mathematics; a general mathematics course for non-college-preparatory pupils had been introduced as an alternative to algebra in grade 9; graphing had become an important part of algebra; the number of theorems in plane geometry had been reduced; and recommendations for integrating plane and solid geometry had been made and ignored. There had also been some attempts to decompartmentalize the mathematics curricula by teaching algebra and geometry as parallel courses. However, in 1957, there was no indication that a major upheaval in the mathematics curriculum for elementary schools was about to get under way and only a slight indication of what was to come in the secondary schools.

The most obvious characteristics of the newer mathematics programs include the incorporation of new subject matter and deletion of some old subject matter, rearrangement of subject matter, acceleration, and new methods of teaching. All but the last of these will be considered in this section.

Subject Matter. The Commission on Mathematics of the College Entrance Examination Board was created in 1955 and produced several documents between that time and the time that it published its final report in 1959. Several of these were small pamphlets that warned of the direction mathematics education was going to take, and incorporated some of the recommendations of the final document. One was a textbook on probability and statistical inference for high school, published because there were no such books available at the time. The final report of the commission (Commission on Mathematics . . . , 1959a, b) included a general report and a set of appendixes in which details were spelled out. Because of the nature of its parent body, the recommendations of the commission were limited primarily to college-capable pupils. Some of its major recommendations were:

1. A graduating senior should be prepared (both in concepts and in skills) to begin a college-level calculus and analytic geometry course.

2. Deductive reasoning should be understood in connection with algebra as well as geometry.

3. Children should acquire a better appreciation of mathematical structure.

4. Such unifying ideas as sets, variables, functions, and relations should be used judiciously.

5. Inequalities should be treated along with equations.

6. Plane and solid geometry should be integrated.

7. Trigonometry, including coordinates, vectors, and complex numbers, should be introduced in grade 11.

8. Grade 12 should include an emphasis on elementary functions and also either units on probability with statistical applications or an introduction to modern algebra.

Also, at about this time (starting in 1954), the federal government began supporting National Science Foundation Institutes for teachers who wished to go back to school to update their education. This, added to the public demand for better mathematics teaching and the many other projects for improving curricula, resulted in the most substantial change in the mathematics curriculum of this country on record. Undoubtedly, the most influential of the curriculum projects has been the School Mathematics Study Group, which has produced sample text material for all school grades. Wooten (1965) has written a history of the SMSG.

Although it is hard to give simple objective evidence that the recommendations of the Commission on Mathematics have generally been accepted, there is a great deal of subjective evidence. Cahen (1965) and Goldberg (1966) both complain that it is hard to carry out a longitudinal study comparing traditional and new mathematics programs, because the school system using the traditional program will not continue to use it long enough. Alspaugh and Delon (1967) indicate that in at least one state there have been substantial changes in the curriculum and there is no reason to suppose that that state is unusually progressive in these matters. They also report, as do Brown and Abell (1966b), that solid geometry has almost disappeared as a course. Unfortunately, this does not necessarily mean that solid geometry has been integrated with plane geometry—if solid geometry has simply been eliminated, there is substantial doubt that this is an improvement. Schult (1966) reports that on the basis of her survey of 22 major cities, modern mathematics is being adopted rapidly.

To list all of the major programs for curriculum revision that have been carried on in this country and elsewhere would require too much space; however, good summaries or evaluations of many of these programs have appeared in studies by the American Association of School Administrators (1965), Deans (1963), the National Council of Teachers of Mathematics (1961, 1963), and the Society for Research in Child Development (1965).

Meanwhile, many other countries have begun to reform school mathematics programs. Fehr (1965) reports that the major impetus for this came from the U.S. sectional meeting on Mathematical Education at the International Congress of Mathematicians held at Edinburgh, Scotland, in 1958. Fehr continues in his article to review many of the other important international developments in mathematics education. Some of these include an approach to geometry that relies more heavily on vectors and introduction of probability and statistical inference into the mathematics curriculum. Athen (1966) also discusses a vector approach to geometry that has been used in Germany for some time. Fehr concludes that as of 1965, although most countries were taking steps to improve the mathematics curriculum for the schools, national or large-scale reforms have been limited to the United States and Scandinavia. Subsequent articles in the Department on International Mathematical Education of the *Mathematics Teacher* (edited by Fehr) have described continuing activities in other countries. One of these articles (Thwaites, 1966) has indicated that British schools have taken substantial steps forward, though they started later than U.S. schools and have been hampered by a countrywide testing program. Håstad (1966) discusses the elementary-school program in Sweden, pointing out that grades 4–6 use a School Mathematics Study Group translation. Vogeli (1967) discusses some remarkable innovations in the Soviet Union that hold promise of producing some truly outstanding mathematicians, though the experimental schools he describes are not yet widespread.

Several more recent conferences have made radical recommendations for future reform of the mathematics curriculum. Probably the most discussed of these has been the Cambridge Conference on School Mathematics (CCSM). The report of the conference (Cambridge Conference . . . , 1963) recommended that elementary-school pupils should study the real number line, including the negative portion, from a very early age; the order properties of the real num-

INDEX

A

Abilities: and aging, 59-60. *See also* Aptitude.
Ability grouping: *see* Grouping.
Absence: *see* Attendance.
Academic achievement: *see* Achievement; Pupil progress.
Academic freedom: conditions for, 2; and the courts, 5-6; and faculty, 489-90; history, 4-5; justification for, 1-2; meaning of, 1; official statements on, 6; and other freedoms, 3; protection of, 3-4; and purpose of education, 2-3.
Academic prediction systems: 33.
Accident research: 1162-63.
Accreditation: and admissions, college and university, 26-27; of community colleges, 182; in elementary education, 431-32; of general education, 529; of home economics, 617; and independent schools, 634-35; of professional education, 1005; of proprietary schools, 1024-25; and records and reports, 1107-1108; by the state, 1301-02; of student teaching, 1379-80.
Achievement: and athletics, 1371-72; and child development, 120-21; and individual differences, 641; and language development, 695; and listening, 749; and mental health, 821; and motivation, 120-21, 1333-34; and student activities, 1370-73; and student characteristics, college and university, 1318-1319, elementary and secondary, 1332-34. *See also* Pupil progress.
Achievement tests: choice, 11-12; construction of, 12-14; defined, 7-8; essay, 10-11; evaluation of, 14-15; history of, 8-9; and mentally retarded children, 831-32; and sex differences, 1218; special, 12; types of, 9-12. *See also* Education, measurement in.
Actualization and counseling: 245.
Administration: of admissions, college and university, 35-36; of agricultural education, 67-68; of attendance, 96-97; business school, *see below*; college and university, *see below*; of counseling, college and university, 222-23, elementary, 235; defined, 161; of elementary education, 425-27; of extension education, 484; of financing, 164-65; of graduate education, 546-47; of health services, school, 1181; of honors programs, 623; and leadership, 161-63, 699; of military education, 843-50; nature of, 994-995; organization of, 163-64; of physical education, 970; and planning, 163; programming, 163; professorship in, 1001-02; of proprietary schools, 1026-1027; public, 1006; recruitment for, 995-96; reports, 167; research on, 1000-01; school personnel, *see below*; and specialization, 1001; staffing, 165; by the state, 1301; of student activities, 1074, 1362-63; of student financial aid, 1354; of student teaching, 1379-80; study of, *see below*; and supervision, 1394-1400; by teachers, 157-59; of tests, 1462-64; theory, *see below*; of transportation for students, 1497; of vocational education research, 1519-20.
Administration, business school: certification, 1176; defined, 1175; and fiscal management, 1176-77; literature on, 1175-76; organization for, 1176; and purchasing management, 177-79; research, 1175.
Administration, college and university: of admissions, 35-36; authority of, 161-63; and central services, 165-166; of counseling, 222-23; defined, 161; evaluation, 166-67; facilities, 165; financing, 164-65; and leadership, 161-63; organization of, 163-64; planning, 163; programming, 163; reports, 167; staffing, 165.
Administration, public school: and behavioral sciences, 1045; future prospects, 1047; history of, 1039-1044; major concepts, 1044-47; principles of, 1041-1042; and staff participation, 1046; theory, 1041-42.
Administration, school personnel: defined, 1187; in elementary education, 1188-90; evolution of, 1187-1188; and higher education, 1188-90; national policy on, 1190-91; and secondary education, 1188-90; trends in, 1191.
Administration, study of: and administrative theory, 1001; evaluation of, 999-1000; history of, 994; inservice, 1002; instruction methods, 998-99; nature of, 997-98; postdoctoral, 1002; resident, 998; and social sciences, role of, 1000; and training programs, 996-1000.
Administration theory: and administrative training, 1001; and decision theory, 19-20; history of, 17; and leadership theory, 18-19; and organization theory, 20-21; and social systems theory, 18; status of, 21-22; research in, 21.
Administrators: preparation status of, 995; recruitment of, 995-96; tenure of, 1459-60.
Admissions: college and university, *see below*; elementary education, 425-26; graduate education, 26, 548-49; legal education, 734-35; medical education, 805-07; professional education, 26; for student teaching programs, 1379.
Admissions, college and university: and academic prediction systems, 33; accreditation, role of, 26-27; administrative organization of, 35-36; and college climate, measurement of, 33-34; decision process of, 36-38; demographic characteristics of, 28-30; educational associations, role of in, 26-27; financial aid, role of, 27-28; and graduate programs, interest in, 32; to graduate schools, 26, 548-49; international exchange and, 30; nature of process, 24-28; to professional schools, 26; research on, 27-28; secondary school, transition from, 25; and student flow through educational system, 28-30; students, institution's choice of, 34-40; student's choice of institution, 30-34; students' interest in, 30-32; and testing programs, 38-39; by transfer, 25-26.
Admissions tests: 38-39.
Adolescence: biological changes in, 45; defined, 44; developmental trends in, 44-45; and education, implications for, 48; intellectual abilities in, 45-46; and intelligence, 659; interests during, 45-46; peer relations in, 47-48; performance in, 45-46; and socio-

xxxiii

economic class, 47; and stage theory, 44-45; values in, 47.

Adult education: and aging, 62; comparative, 189-90; contemplative approach, 55; in developing nations, 349; eclectic approach, 55; growth of, 51; and home economics, 609; individual approach, 54-55; institutional approach, 52-53; instruction method, 52-55; legal, 739; literature of, 51-55; methodological approach, 55; social approach, 53-54; and speech education, 1274; and women, 364-65. *See also* Correspondence education; Extension education.

Adult life cycle: *see* Aging.

Adulthood and intelligence: 659-60.

Advisors: *see* Counselors.

Aesthetics in art: 83-84.

Aging: and abilities, 59-60; and adult education, 62; anatomical changes during, 57-58; and the church, 61; and competence, 60-61; and creativity, 270; developmental phases of, 62-63; and employment, 61; and the family, 61-62; and illness, 58-59; and learning capacity, 59-60; longitudinal studies of, 63-64; and motivation, 60; organizations studying, 65; and personality, 60, 64-65; self concept, effect on, 58-59; and sexual power, 59; and social environment, 62; and social role, 58; society, influence of, 61-62; stage theories of, 63; and the state, 61.

Agricultural education: administration of, 67-68; curriculum development, 69-71; in developing nations, 348-50; evaluation, 72-73; facilities for, 67; and higher education, 70; instruction methods, 70-71; management of, 67-68; and occupational structure, effect of changes in, 68-69; in other countries, 73-74; planning, 67-68; and postsecondary education, 67, 69-70; social variables and, 72; and socioeconomic class, 72; staff, 67; student teaching, effectiveness of, 71-72; teacher education, 71-72; teacher supply and demand, 71; and work experience programs, 70-71.

Aid: *see* Federal aid; Financial aid; State aid; etc.

American Federation of Teachers: 1014.

Aptitude: and student characteristics, college and university, 1318-19, elementary and secondary, 1332-34.

Aptitude tests: art, 673-74; clerical, 673; and individual differences, 641; mechanical, 673; modern language, 873; musical, 674-75, 896; miscellaneous, 675; special, 672-75. *See also* Intelligence tests.

Architecture: 1005.

Art: aptitude tests for, 673-74.

Art education: and aesthetic judgment, 83-84; assessment of, 79-80; and creative behavior, fostering, 81-83; and disadvantaged children, 79-80; history of, 77-78; philosophical research in, 84; research on, 80-81; scope, 76-77; theories of, 78-79.

Articulation of educational units: and colleges, 89-90; of community college education, 179; consequences of, 87-88; and curriculum, duplications in, 88; diversity in, 87; and elementary education, 88; horizontal, 87; improvement in, efforts at, 88; and junior college, 89; and junior high school, 88-89; preschool, 88; and secondary education, 88-89; vertical, 87.

Assignments and study: 1389-90.

Athletes and student financial aid: 1355.

Athletics and academic achievement: 1371.

Attendance: administration of, 96-97; behavior, nature of, 95-96; compulsory, 93-94; concept of, 90-91; and counseling, 224-25; and desegregation, 94; early development of, 92; and economic welfare, 94-95; and economic welfare, 92-93; and enrollment accounting, 96-97; history of, 91-95; and labor laws, 93-94; and nationalism, 92-93; and school census, 96-97; and social change, 94-95; and social perspective, 91-95; and state regulation, 1302; and student financial aid, 1346-49.

Attitude inventories and measurement theory: 793-96.

Attraction and group processes: 555-56.

Audiology: *see* Speech pathology and audiology.

Audiovisual aids: and military education, 854; and social science education, 1238; and student teaching, 1384. *See also* Communications media; Programmed instruction.

B

Behavior problems: causes, 100-01; and child guidance clinics, development of, 102-03; classified, 100, 292-93; comparative studies, 189; control of, 101-02, 294-96; defined, 89-100; and diagnostic facilities, 102-03; and dropouts, 312; incidence of, 100; prevention of, 101-03; research on, 295-96; sex differences in, 292; and special education, 259-60; theories about, 293-94.

Behavioral sciences and social studies education: 1233-34.

Binet, Alfred: 654-55.

Blindness: *see* Visual impairment.

Bookkeeping: 111-12.

Business education: administration of, *see* Administration, business school; basic, 112; and bookkeeping, 111-12; clerical, 112; in colleges, 105-06; and correspondence instruction, 215; and curriculum, college, 105-06, secondary, 107-10; defined, 105; distributive, 113; objectives, 105-06; and occupations, 107; in secondary education, 106-13; shorthand, 109-11; students, characteristics of, 106-07; teacher education, 106; typewriting, 107-09. *See also* Correspondence education; Proprietary schools.

C

Candidate in philosophy: *see* Intermediate degree.

Certification: by the state, 1302; of student teachers, 1379-80; of supervisors, 1398; of teachers, *see* Teacher certification.

Chief State School Officer: 1301.

Child development: and achievement motivation, 120-21; and child rearing methods, 119-20; cognition during, 121-22; defined, 116; and deprivation, 119-20; history of, 117; and infancy, 117-18; and intelligence, 658-59; and nursery schools, 320-22, 324-325; and separation from parent, 119-20; and social learning, 120. *See also* Social and emotional development.

Child rearing methods: and child development, 119-120; and comparative education, 188.

Church and aging: 61.

Church-state issue: 189.

Citizenship: *see* Politicization.

Civic education: in Soviet Union, 130-32, 138; in United States, 128-30, 138. *See also* Politicization.

Civil rights, influence on school systems: 511.

Class size: assessment criteria, 142-43; college, 144; elementary, 143-44, 427-29; and instruction method, 142; policy about, 144-45; secondary, 143-44; university, 144.

Classical languages: and computers, 149; contemporary trends, 146-51; and curriculum, 151; history, cultural, 150; instruction methods, 147-50; oral-aural practices, 147; professional activities, 151-52; and programmed learning, 149; status of, 151-52; structural approach to, 147-49; teacher education, 151; and tests, 150-51; textbooks, 150; translation, 149-50; word order, 147; writing, 150.

Cocurricular activities: *see* Student activities and organizations.

Cognition and child development: 121-22.
College: administration, 161-67; and articulation of educational units, 89-90; and business education, 105-06; and class size, 144; climate, measurement of, 33-34; comparative, 188-89; economics of, 502-07; educational programs, 384-92; environments, *see below*; federal, 495; and safety education, 1161; and student characteristics, 1318-29; and women, 361-365. *See also* Higher education.
College environments: demographic characteristics, 171; impact of, 172-73; measuring methods, 169-71; study of, 169.
College preparation and English composition: 445.
Commercial college education: *see* Business education; Proprietary schools; Vocational education.
Commissioner of Education: 1301.
Communications media: acceptance of, 368, 374-75; behavioral objectives, 369; effectiveness, 370-71; evaluation, 372-74; program objectives, 367-68; research on, 368-69, 375-76; systems, 369.
Community college education: accreditation, 182; articulation of educational units, 89, 179; current developments, 174-75; defined, 173-74; economics of, 175-76; and general education, 179-80, 529; history of, 174; innovation in, 180-81; legal status, 175; and local school districts, 754; and occupational choice, 177; and occupational programs, 179; problems with, 182-83; programs, 178-80; and socioeconomic class, 176; staff, 180-82; and student financial resources, 177; and student personnel services, 180; students, characteristics of, 176-78; transfer function of, 178-179. *See also* Higher education.
Community control: and community-school relations, 512, 1030; and local school districts, 753, 755-56; and state regulation of education, 1302-03.
Comparative education: area studies, 187-88; cross-national experimental studies, 190-91; defined, 184; economics, 191-92; growth of field, 184-85; historical studies, 187; historiography, 185; methodology, 185; and national development, 191-92; and planning, 191-92; reference works, 185-87; and sociology, 191-92; textbooks, 185; theory, 185; trends, 188-90.
Computers: and classical languages, 149; use in counseling, 248; use in curriculum design, 289-90; and data, collected, preparation of, 286-87; and data, organization of, 287-88; and data analysis, 288-89; and data banks, 288; and data collection, 285-86; and data processing, 283-90; and guidance, 290; and instruction method, 288-90; in libraries, 744; literature on, 283-84; use in military education, 853; and personality, 936-37; and questionnaires, 285-86; and records and reports, 1109; and research in education, 1139-40; and tests, 285; training in use of, 283-284.
Concept formation: of causality, 202; conjunctive, 196; in curriculum, 200-01; defined, 196-97; developmental investigations of, 201-03; disjunctive, 196; and intelligence, 198; and learning, 722-24; of length, 202; and logic, 202-03; and mathematics, 200-01; and motivation, 198; negative instances, 199-200; of number, 202; positive instances, 199-200; of quantity, 202; and reinforcement, 198-99; relational, 196; and science (subject), 201; and sex differences, 198; of size, 202; study, methods of, 197-98; of time, 202; variables relating to, 198-99.
Conduct problems: *see* Behavior problems.
Conformity: 556.
Conjunctive concept: 196.
Continuing education: legal, 739.
Cooperative teaching: *see* Team teaching.
Correspondence education: advantages and limitations, 216-17; applications of, 215; in business, 215; cross-national data on, 213-14; defined, 213; federal, 495; history of, 214-15; instruction methods, 215-16; and military education, 854; and programmed instruction, 216; scope of, 213-14; and secondary education, 215; and study, 1392; supervised, 215-16; teacher role in, 215; and television, 216.
Cost of education: 1346-49.
Counseling: and tests, 1465-66; and underachievement in gifted children, 541; of women students, 363-64.
Counseling, college and university: administration, 222-23; and attendance, 223-25; counselors, characteristics of, 221-22; diagnostic categories, 224; evaluation of, 223-24; extent of, 219-20; function, 220-221; issues in, 223; and personality inventory, 224; process, 223-24; research on, 224; resources of, 225-226; status of, 218-19; training for, 221-22; trends in, 226; and vocational choice, 223, 225-26.
Counseling, elementary education: conceptual foundation, 230-31; consulting functions in, 232, 234; diagnostic categories, 231-32; nature of, 230-33; in other countries, 236-37; personnel, role of, 232-34; programming for, 235-36; research on, 232-33; resources of, 234-35; status, 230; teacher, function of in, 234-35; textbooks, 229; training for, 234; trends in, 233.
Counseling, secondary education: and actualization, 215; behavioral, 247; clinical method, 246-47; by computer, 248; correlational studies, 249; as seen by counselors, 242-44; and decision theory, 247-48; defined, 242-44; and developmental theory, 245-46; expectations of, 243-44; evaluation of, 249-50; financial aid of, 243; function of, 243-46 *passim*; group programs, 248; historical origins, 243; limits of, 244-245; longitudinal study, 249; measurement criteria, 249-50; nondirective, 245, 247; processes of, 246-248; and self concept, 245-46; surveys of, 243-44; training for, 248-49; and trait-factor theory, 245-46.
Counseling theory: applicability, 256-57; behavioral, 255-56; and change, personal, 253; clients, nature of, 258; client centered, 254; client's view of counselor, 259-60; and counselor behavior, 257-58; and counselor characteristics, 258-59; and counselor-client similarity, effect of, 259; and decision theory, 261; defined, 252-53; ego-analytic, 254-55; elements of, 253; evaluation, 261-63; Freudian influence on, 254-255; and generic models of man, 253; goals of, 253; and group counseling, 260; negative consequences, 263; neoanalytic, 254-55; orientations of, 254-57; psychoanalytic, 254-55; and psychotherapy, 253; and research, 257-61; trait-factor, 256; and vocational counseling, 260-61.
Counselors: client's view of, 259-60; and counseling theory, 257-59.
Courts: and academic freedom, 5-6; and public education, 1300-01.
Creativity: in art, 81-83; and behavior in school, 269-270; criteria of, 272-73; defined, 267; and gifted children, 538-39; and higher mental processes, 595-96, 598-99; and individual development, 270; instruction methods for, 271-72; and intelligence, 268-69, 272; and personal characteristics, 270-71; and special education, 1257; theories about, 267-68.
Cross-cultural data: correspondence education, 213-214; counseling, 236-37; developing nations, 345; politicization, 130-34, 139-40; student characteristics, 1325-27. *See also* Comparative education.
Cross-national data: college enrollment, female, 365; developing nations, 342-57; early childhood education, 326-27; education, sociology of, 1241-52 *passim*; elementary education, 432; engineering education, 440-41; physical fitness, 966; rehabilitation, 1114; religion and education, 1120-21; safety education, 1164-65; science education, 1201-03; secondary education, 1216; student characteristics, 1325-1327; student financial aid, 1355-56; teacher role,

1439-40; teachers, economic status of, 335-36; textbooks, 1476-77; vocational education research, 1519.

Cultural deprivation: and educational programs, elementary education, 405. *See also* Disadvantaged students; Handicaps, educational.

Curriculum: agricultural education, 69-70; and articulation of educational units, 88; business education, college, 105-06; business education, secondary, 107-10; change, procedures for, 277-79; classical languages, 151; and computers, 289-90; and concept formation, 200-01; counselor education, 249; defined, 275-76, 278-79; design, 276-77; and education communications media systems, 369; and educational programs, college and university, 387-92, elementary, 402-05; elementary education, 422-25; engineering education, 440; English composition, 445-49; English literature, 464-65; evaluation, 280-282; extension education, 483-84; general education, 522-24, 531; health education, 582-83, 585; and higher mental processes, 598; home economics, 611-12; independent schools, 635; issues, 280-81; legal education, 736; mathematics, 769-71; medical education, 807-08; and mental health, 825-26; military education, 850-55; models of, 276; music education, 898-99; physical education, 969-70; politicization, influence of on, 128-33, 138; proprietary schools, 1026; and records and reports, 1107; secondary education, 1212-14; social studies education, 1235-37; speech, 1243-44; spelling, 1283-86; and state regulation, 1302; studies of, 282; teacher education, 71, 249; theory, 276-79. *See also* Educational objectives.

D

Data analysis: 288-89; and survey research method, 1402-05.

Data collection: 285-86, 1401-02.

Data processing: and computers, 283-90; and data analysis, 288-89; and data banks, 288; and data collection, 285-86; and data organization, 287-88; defined, 283; growth of, 283; and instruction method, 289-90; literature on, 283-84; and preparation of collected data, 286-87; and questionnaires, 285-86; research on, 289-90; and tests, 285; training in, 283-284. *See also* Statistical methods.

Data reduction and survey research method: 1402.

Deafness: *see* Hearing impairment.

Decision theory: in administration, 19-20; in counseling, 247-48; and vocational guidance, 261.

Degrees: Doctor of Philosophy, 549-50; intermediate, 550; Master's, 549; and military education, 849-50.

Dentistry: 1005.

Department of Defense and higher education: 497-99.

Departmentalization in elementary schools: 560-62.

Deprivation and child development: 119-20.

Desegregation and attendance: 94.

Developing nations: adult education in, 349; agricultural development, 348-50; characteristics of, 342-43; comparative studies, 343-44; economic development of, 343-45; economics of education in, 351-54; educational aid to, 355-56; educational efficiency of, 351-53; educational innovations in, 356-57; educational planning in, 355-56; educational problems of, 347-54; and exchange students, 355; field clarification, 357; and manpower studies, 343-45; modernization of, 343; political development of, 346-47; and population pressures, 354; retardation in, 353-54; rural education in, 347-50; social development in, 345-46; teacher qualification, 353-54; teacher shortage, 353-54; teacher training, 353-54; unemployment in, 350-51; and urban drift, 348-49; and vocational education, 350.

Development, emotional, social: *see* Social and emotional development.

Developmental psychology: *see* Child development.

Developmental studies of reading: 1080-81.

Developmental theory: and concept formation, 201-203; and counseling, 245-46; and early childhood education, 37; and higher mental processes, 597-98; and readiness, 1064-65; and sex differences, 1219-1220. *See also* Stage theory.

Dimensional approach to individual differences: 640, 643.

Disadvantaged children: and art education, 79-80; and behavior problem prevention, 103; and college admissions, 39-40; and financial aid, 1349-50; and intelligence tests, 670; and listening, 749; and social studies, 1235-36; and urban environment, 1502-03. *See also* Cultural deprivation; Handicaps, educational.

Discipline: defined, 292; and dropouts, 312; effect of, 295-96; methods of, 294-95; research on, 295-96.

Disjunctive concept: 196.

Distributive education: 113.

Divergent thinking: *see* Creativity.

Doctor of Philosophy: 549-50.

Dramatic arts education: criticisms of, 297-301; and general education, 527-28; history of, 301-06; theories about, 297-301; in the United States, 303-06.

Driver education: 1161.

Dropout: characteristics of, 310-15; and discipline, 312; and employment, 309, 315; and extracurricular activity, 311-12; guidance of, 314; income of, 309-310; as a national problem, 308-09; and socioeconomic class, 312-13; statistics on, 309; and student financial aid, 1353-54.

Durkheim, Emil: 1242-44, 1249.

E

Early childhood education: and child development research, 320-22, 324-25; defined, 316; and developmental theory, 317; history of, 318-23; importance of, 316-18; kindergarten, 318, 322-23, 325-26; nursery school, 318, 320-22, 323-25; other countries, 326-27; and socioeconomic class, 317-18; status of, 327; teacher training for, 325; theories about, 318-320.

Economic change and attendance: 94-95.

Economic development in emerging nations: 343-45.

Economic welfare and attendance: 92-95.

Economics (subject): and comparative education, 191-92; and educational programs, 403-04; and social studies education, 1233.

Economy, U.S.: and aging, 61; and education, 1246-1247; and public school financing, 513-14.

Education, American, comparative studies of: 190.

Education, economics of: in developing nations, 351-354; earnings, impact of education on, 339-41; and economic growth, 339; historical studies, 540; human capital approach, 338-39, 342-45; program budgeting, 341; research on, growth of, 337-38. *See also related entries.*

Education, history of: conceptual research, 602-05; factual research, 605-06; independent schools, role of in, 636-37.

Education, measurement in: attitudes towards, 780-781; history of, 778; literature, 778; purpose of, 780; subjects of, 779; technique for, 779-80. *See also* Marks; Measurement theory; Norms; Prediction; Scaling; Scores; Tests.

Education, objectives of: behavioral, 911-12; determination of, 909-11; expression of, 908-09; history of, 908; taxonomies of, 912; validation of, 911.

Education, philosophy of: generalizations, 949-50; key concepts, 949; methods, 947-49.

Education, research in: analytic tools of, 1138-39; and computers, 1139-40; design of, 1134-35; measurement of, 1137-38; methods, 1136-37; prospects for, 1140; and scientific approach, 1127-31; technical foundations of, 1131-39.

Education, research in, training for: future, 1481-82; institutional characterization of, 1478-79; program characterization of, 1479-80; student characteristics, 1479-80.

Education, sociology of: and developing studies, 1244-45; and the economy, 1246-47; and historical societies, 1244-45; history of, 1241-42; and politics, 1245-46; and school society, 1249-52; and society, types of, 1242-44; and stratification, 1247-49.

Education, state regulation of: and accreditation, 1301-02; and attendance, 1302; and certification, 1302; controls, 1301-04; and curriculum, 1302; and the federal government, 1304-05; financial, 1303; history of, 1299-1300; improvement of, 1304-05; legal basis for, 1300-01; and local school districts, 1302-03; and nonpublic schools, 1303-04; and state boards of education, 1301.

Educational aid to developing nations: 354-55.

Educational associations: admissions, college and university, role of in, 26-27; and grievances, 155.

Educational communications: *see* Communications media.

Educational efficiency in developing nations: 351-53.

Educational handicaps: *see* Cultural deprivation; Disadvantaged children; Handicaps, educational.

Educational media: *see* Communications media.

Educational practice, improvement of: areas for, 629-630; defined, 626-27; evaluation of, 630; forces for, 628-29; motivation for, 629; and obsolescence, varieties of, 627-28; research on, 630-32.

Educational problems, urban: *see* Urban educational problems.

Educational programs, college and university: 384-395; and curriculum, 387-92; literature on, 384-87.

Educational programs, elementary education: criticisms of, 407-08; defined, 395-96; examples of, 402-405; Greater Cleveland, 405; history of, 396-97; Madison project, 404; and school organization, 405-406; and teacher education, 406-07; theory, 397-402.

Educational programs, secondary education: criteria for, 412; differentiated, 411-12; instructional, 410-11.

Educational psychology: defined, 413-15; organization of, 415-16; psychologist's view of, 415; research on, 416-18; theory, 418-19; training provided by, 419.

Educational research: *see* Education, research in.

Educational television: 189.

Elementary education: accreditation, 431-32; administration of, 425-27; and articulation of educational units, 88; and class size, 143-44; during colonial period, 421-22; curriculum, 422-25, 1235; educational programs for, 395-410; federal, 495; and federal programs, 496-97; and grouping, 560-62; history of, 421-27; and home economics, 608; and local school districts, 754; during national period, 422-24; 1950 to present, 424-27; organization of, 424-27; in other countries, 432; and principal, role of, 431; purpose of, 420-21; and safety education, 1160-61; school personnel administration, 1188-90; and social studies education, 1235; student characteristics, 1330-39; and teachers, role of in, 429-31.

Emotional development: *see* Social and emotional development.

Emotionally disturbed children, special education for: 1259-60.

Employment of students: *see* Student financial aid.

Engineering education: curriculum, 440; history of, 435-37; in other countries, 440-41; problems in, 437-39; students, selection of for, 439-40; trends in, 437.

English composition: curriculum, 445-49; defined, 443; environment, influence of, 450; evaluation of, 455-56; and general education, 526; and grammar, 451-53; history to 1900, 443-44; instruction method for, 453-55; objectives of, 445-49; research on, 449-450; and rhetoric, 450-51; and spelling, 1291-92; and teacher education, 456-57, 650-51; and vocabulary, 453.

English literature: curriculum, 464-65; evaluation of, 469-70; history of, 461-63; instruction method for, 465-67; objectives of, 463-64; and reading, 467; and student response, 467-69; and teacher education, 470.

Ethnic groups and politicization: 135, 139.

Executive branch of government and education: 495-496.

Experimental methods: and experimental design, 474-77; and extra-experimental drift, 476; and generalizations, 476-77; and individual differences, 475-76; and interexperimental drift, 476; and quasi-experimental design, 477-78; and sampling, 479-81; and statistical analysis, 478-79; and subclass differences, 475-76.

Extension education: defined, 481-82; inputs, 483-84; purpose of, 482-83; research on, 386; and transformation, 384-85; trends in, 385-86. *See also* Adult education.

Extracurricular activity: and dropouts, 311-12; and politicization, influence on, 127-28, 138. *See also* Student activities and organizations.

F

Faculty, college and university: and academic freedom, 489-90; characteristics of, 489-92; defined, 488; and instruction methods, 489; and policy making, 489-90; responsibilities of, 488-90; salaries of, 504.

Family: and aging, 61-62; characteristics of student's, 176; politicization, role in, 126-27, 138.

Federal aid: to higher education, 504; to libraries, 742-43; and parochial schools, 928; and the physically handicapped, 974-75; to public schools, 513; to students, 1341-46; and teacher education, 1415-1416; and vocational education research, 1513-17.

Federal government and state regulation of education: 1304-05.

Federal programs: and the Department of Defense, 497-99; and elementary education, 496-97; and Executive branch, 495-96; and federally operated institutions, 495; and higher education, 497-98; history of, 494-95; international, 500; and science (subject), 498-500; and secondary education, 496-97; and student teaching, 1377; and the Supreme Court, 496; trends in, 500-01; and vocational education, 497.

Finance, college and university: cost per student, 503-04; and faculty rewards, 504; and federal support, 504; and program budgeting, 514; research on, 504-05; scope of, 503; sources of funds, 504; and student fees, 504. *See also* Education, economics of.

Finance, public school: and community expectations, 512; cost projections, 511; economic effects of, 513-514; and efficiency, 514; and federal funding, 513; and federal control, 513; new concepts of, 511-13; and property tax, 508; research on, 507-08; sources of, 507-11; and state programs, 508-11; and state regulation of education, 1303. *See also* Education, economics of.

Financial aid: and admissions, college, role in, 27-28; and counseling, 243; in developing nations, 354-55; student, *see* Student financial aid.

Foreign language: and general education, 527. *See also* Modern languages.

Foreign students, financial aid for: 1355.

Foundations: and congressional influence, 519-20; and education, 521-22; and government control, 519; history of, 517-19.

Free universities: general education, influence on, 531; and student rights movement, 1363.

Freudian theory in counseling: 254-55.

G

General education: and accreditation, 529; and community colleges, 529; and curriculum, 522-24; defined, 524-25; evaluation of, 528, 531-32; history of, 522-24; individual courses in, 526-27; need for, 524; objectives of, 524-25; and professional education, 525-26; staff problems, 529; trends in, 530-31; types of, 526.

Geography and social studies education: 1232.

Gifted children: characteristics of, 537-39; and creativity, 538-39; and educational programs, 405; program adjustments for, 540-42; and special education, 1255, 1257-58; and talent loss, 539-40.

Government (subject) and social studies education: 1234.

Government defense contracts and higher education: 497-99.

Graduate education: admissions, 26, 32; financial aids for, 550; history of, 544-46; legal, 738-39; national coordination in, 547-48; organization of, 546-547; and postdoctoral study, 550-51; requirements of, 548-50; research on, 550; and student financial aid, 1344; and women, 364.

Grammar: and English composition, 451-53; and language development, 691-93; and modern languages, 872.

Grants to students: *see* Student financial aid.

Great Issues (course): 528.

Greek: *see* Classical languages.

Group processes: categories, 552-53; dynamics of, 555-57; history of, 551-52; and leadership, 554-55.

Grouping: by ability, 564-67; criticisms of, 568; defined, 559-60; heterogeneous, 567; and intelligence tests, 671; interschool, 560; intraclass, 567-68; and school organization, 560-64; and special education, 1257; and teachability, 567; varieties of, 560.

Guidance: in agricultural education, 72; clinics, 102-103; and computer-run education, 290; and dropouts, 314; and records and reports, 1107.

H

Handicapped children: and health services, 1185-86; special education for, 1254-61.

Handicaps, educational: 380-84. *See also* Cultural deprivation; Disadvantaged children.

Handicaps, physical: brain injury, 979-80; classifications, 973-74; crippling, 978-79; defined, 973-74; and federal aid, 974-75; and health services, 1185-1186; hearing, 977-78; and intelligence tests, 670; international developments, 980; and reading, 1082-84; special education for, 1254-61; and state aid, 975; and teacher education, 975-76; visual, 976-77. *See also* Hearing impairment; Visual impairment.

Handicaps, speech, and special education: 1260-61.

Handwriting: act of, 573-75; and graphology, 575-76; history of, 571-73; product, 575; and spelling, 1290-1291; teaching of, 576-77.

Health education: and academic achievement, 580; and community relations, 484-85; curriculum, 582-583; and educational programs, 403; evaluation of, 583-84; history of, 581; research on, 581-82, 585-86; and school health programs, 1186; status of, 582.

Health services, college and university: finances of, 593; history of, 589-90; objectives of, 590; programs, 590-92; research on, 592; status of, 590.

Health services, school: administration of, 1181; and communicable diseases, 1184; and handicapped children, 1185-86; and health appraisal, 1183-84; and health education, 1186; legislation affecting, 1181; and major health problems, 1181; and nutrition, 1185; objectives of, 1181; personnel, 1182-83, 1186; and physical education, 1184; and safety education, 1184-85.

Hearing: instruction programs, 1278-79; and spelling, 1287. *See also* Listening.

Hearing impairment: and special education, 1258; and speech, 1270-71. *See also* Handicaps, physical; Speech pathology and audiology.

Heredity: and intelligence, 657, 670-71; and social and emotional development, 1221-22.

Higher education: and agricultural education, 70; coordination in, *see below*; and Department of Defense contracts, 497-99; and federal programs, 497-98; financing of, 502-07; and home economics, 609; salaries in, 334; and school personnel administration, 1188-90; and speech education, 1274; state surveys of, 208-10; and student characteristics, 1318-29; and student financial aid, 1339-56; and tenure, 1460. *See also specific entries, e.g.,* College; Correspondence education; Professional education.

Higher education, coordination in: areas for, 207-08; defined, 205-06; history of, 206; interinstitutional, 207; patterns of, 206-07; procedures for, 207-08; and state surveys of higher education, 208-10.

Higher mental processes: and curriculum development, 598; defined, 594-95; development of, 597-598; instruction methods for, 598-99; and problem solving, 596; and schools of psychology, 595-96.

History (subject) and social studies education: 1232.

History of education: *see* Education, history of.

Home economics: and accreditation, 617; and adult education, 609; curriculum development, 611-12; defined, 607; in elementary education, 608; evaluation of, 613-15; in higher education, 609; history of, 607-08; and instruction method, 612-13; issues in, 616-17; occupational, 609; in other countries, 609-10; research in, 610-11; in secondary education, 608; and teacher education, 615-16.

Home study: *see* Correspondence education.

Homework and study: 1389-90.

Honors programs: 619-24.

Hostility and group processes: 555-56.

Human-capital economics: 338-39, 343-45.

Humanities and general education: 527.

I

Independent schools: defined, 633; future of, 638; history of, 633-34; and the public, 636-37; and the state, 635-36; and state regulation of, 1303-04; status of, 634-35. *See also* Parochial schools.

Individual differences: categorization, 639-40; and education, 643-44; origins of, 642-43; prevalence of, 639-40; principal traits, 640-42.

Infancy: and child development, 117-18; and intelligence, 658-59; and language development, 690.

Inservice education of teachers: *see* Teacher education, inservice; Student teaching.

Instruction materials: in correspondence education, 215. *See also* Communications media; Textbooks.

Instruction method: in administrative education, 998-999; in adult education, 52-55; in agricultural education, 70-71; in business education, 107-13; in classical languages, 147-50; and classroom discourse, 1450-52; and class size, 142; college and university, 489; colloquium, 621; and computers, 289-90; in correspondence education, 215; and creativity, 271-72; and data processing, 289-90; defined, 1446-47; and dimensionalization, 1449-50; discovery, 1455-56; discussion, 1454-55; in elementary education, 422-24; for English composition, 453-55; for English literature, 465-67; and grouping, 560-68; for handwriting, 577; in health education, 583; heuristic, 1456; history of, 1447-49; for home economics, 612-13; in honors programs, 621; and learning, psychology of, 707-08, 726-27; lecture, 1452-54; in legal education, 737; for listening, 749-50; in mathematics, 771-73; in medical education, 809-10; in military education, 852-54; for modern languages, 869-73; in music education, 902-03; and the objectives-methods matrix, 1449; and politicization, 130-31, 138; programmed, 149, 216, 613, 772-73, 853-54, 1017-22, 1199, 1237-38, 1456, 1491; and pupil progress, 1057-58; for reading, 1084-93; in religious education, 1125-26; in safety education, 1164; in science (subject), 1195, 1197-1200; for spelling, 1286-89; for social studies, 1235-36; and student teachers, 1377, 1383-84; study courses, 1389; and teacher decisiveness, 155; team teaching, 562-63; for thinking, improvement of, 598-99.

Instructional technology: *see* Communications media.

Intelligence: and adolescence, 659; and adulthood, 659-60; and childhood, 658-59; and concept formation, 198; constancy of, 660-61, 669-70; and creativity, 268-69, 272; defined, 656; development of, 658-61; factor interpretation of, 656-58; group differences in, 661-64; history of, 654-56; and individual differences, 640-41; and infancy, 658-59; and listening, 749; and musical ability, 896; and politicization, 135, 139; and pupil progress, 1057; and race, 662-63; and reading, 1079; and sex differences, 661-62, 1218; and society, 663-64; and socioeconomic class, 662; testing, *see below*; theories about, 656-58.

Intelligence tests: age vs. point scale, 655; controversies about, 669-71; and factor analysis, 671-72; general, 667-69; group, 668-69; history of, 654-56; individual, 667-68; and mental retardation, 831; purpose of, 670; Stanford-Binet, 655; varieties of, 655-56. *See also* Education, measurement in.

Intercultural courses and general education: 527.

Interests: correlates of, 681-84; defined, 678-79; development of, 680-81; dimensions of, 679-80; and measurement theory, 793-96; measures of, 679; and reading, 1074-75; and sex differences, 1218-19; and student characteristics, college and university, 1321-22, elementary and secondary, 1135-37; theories about, 684.

Intermediate degree: 550.

Internship: *see* Student teaching.

IQ: *see* Intelligence tests.

J

Jewish education, comparative: 188.

Journalism: 1005.

Junior college: and articulation of educational units, 89; and local school districts, 754. *See also* Community college education.

Junior high school and articulation of educational units: 88-89.

Juvenile delinquency: *see* Behavior problems.

K

Kindergarten: and educational theory, 318; history of, 322-23; and local school districts, 754; programs, 325-26; and safety education, 1160-61. *See also* Early childhood education.

L

Language development: course of, 690-94; and the educational process, 695-96; functions of, 688-89; and modern languages, 867-68; nature of, 686-88; and psycholinguistics, 719-21; and speech, 1271, 1280-81; studying, methods of, 689-90; theories about, 694-95.

Latin: *see* Classical languages.

Law review: 737-38.

Leadership: behavioral differentiations, 701-03; characteristics, 700-01; consequences of, 703-04; defined, 699-700; and group processes, 554-55; and supervision, 1395-96; theory, 18-19.

Learning: and aging, 59-60; and articulation of educational units, 87-88; artistic, *see below*; and attention, 714-15; categories of, 717-27; and concept formation, 196-207, 722-24; and discrimination, 713-14; extinction of, 712; and generalization, 712-713; and instruction method, 726-27; and memory, 721-22; and mental health, 821; and motivation, 885; and motor abilities, 889, 893; and music education, 900-03; and perception, 932-33; and perceptual motor skill, 725-26; and problem solving, 724-725; processes, 708-17; psychology of, 707-08; and psycholinguistics, 719-21; and punishment, 715-17; and readiness, 1065; and reading, 1076-79; reinforcement of, 709-12; research, application of, 706-707; resources, *see* Communications media; rote verbal, 717-19; and social studies education, 1235-1236; and socioeconomic class, 1236; and thinking, 724-25; transfer, *see below*.

Learning artistic: assessment of, 79-80; research on, 80-81; theories about, 78-79.

Learning transfer: defined, 1484-85; determinants of, 1486-89; measurement of, 1485; positive, 1489-91; theory, 1485-86.

Legal education: admissions requirements, 734-35; continuing, 739; curriculum, 736; graduate, 738-39; history of, 733-34; and instruction method, 737; and law review, 737-38; and legal aid programs, 738; status today, 734; and teachers for, 736-37; and tests, 735-36.

Libraries: academic, 741-42; and computers, 744; education for, 745-46; evaluation of, 745; facilities of, 741-42; and federal aid, 742-43; history of, 740-741; innovations in, 742-45; military, 854; and national systems, proposed, 743-44; public, 742; school, 742; and state aid, 743; and study, 1391-92.

Listening: correlates of, 748-49; defined, 747; and instruction method, 749-50; and intelligence, 749; literature on, 748; measurement of, 750-51; scope of, 747-48.

Literature and speech: 1272.

Loans to students: *see* Student financial aid.

Local school districts: and administration, school, 1044; and community control, 753, 755-56; cooperative, 754-55; county, 754-55; and decision-making power, 510-11; intermediate, 754-55; large, 753-754; and local boards of education, 755-56; metropolitan, 754-55; need for, 755; small, 753; specialized, 754; and state aid, 509-11; and state regulation, 1302-03.

M

Maladjustment: *see* Behavior problems.

Marks: content of, 762; defined, 759-60; frame of reference for, 762-65; and institutional culture pattern, 765-66; objections to, 760; substitutes for, 761-62. *See also* Education, measurement in.

Mass media: and reading, 1072; and speech, 1272-73; and student teaching, 1383-84. *See also* Communications media.

Master's degree: 549.

Master of Philosophy: *see* Intermediate degree.

Mathematics: and concept formation, 200-01; and curriculum, 769-71; and educational programs, 404-405; and general education, 527; history of, 767-768; instruction method for, 771-73; modern, 768-769; objectives of, 769; and teacher education, 650, 773-75.

Maturation: 1062-64.

Measurement theory: and change, 802; derived, 787-788; fundamental, 787-88; and inventories, 793-96; and item analysis, 791-93; nature of, 785-87; pointer, 787-88; and scales, 785-87; and scaling, 1170-72; and standard error, 796-97; and strong true-score, 797-98; test reliability, 794-96; and test scores, 788-91; validity of, 798-802. *See also* Education, measurement in.

Medical education: admissions requirements, 805-807; curriculum, 807-08; evaluation of, 808-09; history of, 804-05; instruction method for, 809-10; trends in, 805.

Memory: and learning, 721-22; and motivation, 886.

Mental health: and achievement, 821; and children, 816-18, 821-25; concepts of, 814-16; and curriculum, 825-26; defined, 811-14; and general population, 818; history of, 818-21; models of, 816; and musical ability, 897; psychoeducational approach to, 823-826; psychotherapeutic approach to, 823-26; and student characteristics, 1322; and teachers, 826.

Mental retardation: characteristics, 832-35; classification, 829-30; defined, 829; in developing nations, 353-54; and educational programs, 405, 835-37; evaluation of, 832; identification of, 831-32; prevalence of, 830-31; and special education, 1256-57.

Military education: administration of, 843-50; curriculum, 850-55; history of, 839-43; and instruction method, 852-54; organization of, 843-50; and personnel, 855-58; and teacher education, 858-59; trends in, 859-60.

Minority groups: and politicization, 135, 139; textbook bias against, 132, 139.

Misbehavior: *see* Behavior problems.

Modern languages: achievement measurement, 873-874; and instruction method for, 869-73; and instruction problems in, 868-69; objectives of, 867; status of, 866-67; and teacher education, 874; theories about, 867-68.

Morphology: *see* Language development.

Morrill Act (Land Grant Act): 523, 545.

Motivation: and achievement, 1333-34; and aging, 60; and child development, 120-21; and concept formation, 198; and emotional development, 1222; and learning, 885; and memory, 886; and perception, 885; research on, 883-85; and sex differences, 1218-19, theories about, 878-83.

Motor abilities: analysis of, 891-93; and learning, 889, 893; *vs.* motor skills, 888-89; tests of, 889-91.

Musical ability, aptitude tests for: 674-75.

Music education: curriculum, 898-99; and instruction method, 902-03; and learning, 900-03; materials for, 899-900; and musical abilities, 895-97; and musical development, 897-98; research on, 895.

N

National development, comparative: 191-92.

National Education Association: 1012-14.

Nationalism: and attendance, 92-93; and politicization, 132-33, 138-39.

Negroes: politicization of, 129-30, 135, 138-39; textbook bias against, 132.

Nonclass activities: *see* Student activities and organizations.

Nongrading: 563-64.

Nonpublic schools: *see* Independent schools; Parochial schools.

Norms: test, 1467. *See also* Education, measurement in; Scores and norms.

Nursery schools: and child development research, 320-22, 324-25; and educational theory, 318; history of, 320-22; program, 323-25. *See also* Early childhood education.

Nursing: 1005-06.

Nutrition and health services: 1185.

O

Objectives, educational: *see* Education, objectives of.

Occupational placement: effectiveness of, 919-20; in European universities, 919; history of, 915-16; organizational structure of, 917; procedures for, 917-19; rationale for, 916-17.

Office of Education: 20-21.

Originality: *see* Creativity.

Outdoor education: 921-23.

P

Parochial schools, Roman Catholic: history of, 925-26; problems of, 927-29; rationale for, 926; status of, 927. *See also* Independent schools.

Peer relations: and adolescence, 47-48; politicization, influence of on, 127-28, 138.

Perception: connotations of, 931; defined, 929-30; and learning, 932-33; and motivation, 885; and problem solving, 932; and psychophysics, 931-32; *vs.* sensation, 930-31; theories of, 933-34.

Personality: and aging, 60, 64-65; and computers, 936-37; and counseling, 224-25; and creativity, 272; development of, 937-43; and individual differences, 642; and reading ability, 1079-80; research on, 943-44; and sex differences, 1218-19; and student characteristics, 1334-35; theory, 935-43.

Personality tests and measurement theory: 793-96.

Personnel, administration of: *see* Administration, school personnel.

Pharmacy: 1006.

Phonology: *see* Language development.

Physical development: anatomical, 952-54; defined, 951-52; height, 954-55; and puberty, 958-60; and tooth eruption, 657-58; weight, 955-57.

Physical education: administration of, 970; and curriculum, 969-70; and health services, 1184; history of, 963-64; and physical fitness, 964-67; and psychology, 968-69; and sports performance, 966-68; sociology of, 968-69; and teacher education, 970-71.

Physical handicaps: *see* Handicaps, physical.

Physical health and student characteristics: 1331-32.

Policy making, college and university: faculty, role of, 489-90; and student rights movement, 1363-64.

Political development in emergent nations: 346-47.

Politicization: attitude content, cross-national, 137-138, 140; attitude content, United States, 135-37, 140; and civic education, 128-32, 138; cross-cultural studies, 130-34, 139-40; curriculum influences on, 128-33, 138; defined, 125-26, 138; and ethnic groups, 135, 139; extracurricular influences on,

127-28, 138; family, role of in, 126-27, 138; and intelligence, 135, 139; mediators of, 135-36, 139; and minority groups, 135, 139; and nationalism, 132-33, 138-39; of Negroes, 129-30, 135, 138-39; peer group, influence of on, 127-28, 138; and race, 129-30, 135, 138-39; and school milieu, 133-34, 139; and secondary education, 128-34, 138-39; and sex differences, 134, 139; and socioeconomic class, 134-135, 139; in the Soviet Union, 130-32, 138; and teachers, 130, 138; and textbooks, influence of, 132-33, 139, theoretical framework of, 125-26, 138.

Politics and education: 1245-46.
Population pressure: 354.
Postal tuition: *see* Correspondence education.
Postdoctoral study: 550-51.
Postsecondary education, agricultural: 67, 69-70.
Prediction: and criterion analysis, 985-87; and cross validation, 987; defined, 983; and expectancy tables, 989; guiding principles for, 985; measures of, 985; and multiple criterion measures, 990-92; problems in, 984-85, 989; procedures for, 984; and scoring, 989-90; and single criterion, 987-88; and statistical methods, 988-89. *See also* Education, measurement in.
Preschool and articulation of educational units: 88.
Primary education, comparative: 188. *See also* Early childhood education.
Principalship: in elementary education, 431; history of, 1040-41; leadership function, 1042-43.
Private school: *see* Independent schools.
Professional education: accreditation of, 1005; in administration, public, 1006; admissions to, 26; in architecture, 1005; comparative, 188; in dentistry, 1005; and general education, 525-26; in journalism, 1005; in nursing, 1005-06; in pharmacy, 1006; in social work, 1006-07; in theology, 1007.
Professional education organizations: American, 1011-15; defined, 1008-11; history of, 1011-16; international, 1015-16; National Education Association, 1012-14.
Program budgeting: 341.
Programmed learning: and classical languages, 149; and correspondence education, 216; defined, 1017; *vs.* heuristic teaching, 1456; history of, 1018-19; and home economics, 613; and learning transfer, 1491; and mathematics, 772-73; and military education, 853-54; objectives of, 1019; and science education, 1199; and social studies education, 1237-1238; techniques of, 1019-20.
Proprietary schools: accreditation of, 1024-25; achievements of, 1027; administration of, 1026-27; associations, 1024; and curriculum, 1026; defined, 1022-23; history of, 1023-24; rationale for, 1023; status of, 1024; and teachers, 1025-26; types of, 1023. *See also* Business education.
Psychology and social studies education: 1233.
Psychophysics: 931-32.
Psychotherapy and counseling: 225.
Public relations: and behavioral science research, 1035-36; and communications media, 1032-33; and community control, 1030; defined, 1028-29; effect of, 1031-32; history of, 1029-30; and public support, 1034-35; research on, 1030-31.
Public schools: finance, 507-17; salary comparisons, 333-34; salary schedules, 331-33; salary trends, 333-34.
Punishment and learning: 715-17.
Pupil progress: history of, 1051-53; and human development, 1056-57; innovations in, 1054-55; and instruction method, 1057-58; and intelligence, 1057; and learning, 1057-58; and sex differences, 1058-59; status of, 1053-54; reporting on, 1059-60; research on, 1056-59; and teacher's attitudes, 1058.

R

Race: and intelligence, 662-63; and musical ability, 897; and physical development, 958-59; and politicization, 135, 139; and reading ability, 1071-72.
Readiness: and cognitive structure, 1065-66; and cognitive style, 1066-67; and knowledge structure, 1067-68; and learning theories, 1065; and maturation, 1062-64; and Piaget's theories, 1064-65; and reading, 1062, 1087-88.
Reading: adult, 1071; appraisal of, 1093; correlates of, 1079-82; development of, 1080-81; developmental, 1090-93; and English literature, 467; and environment, 1071-72; history of, 1069-70; hygiene of, 1081-82; and intelligence, 1079; and interest, 1074-1075; and learning, 1076-79; and listening, 748-49; materials, 1072-73; nature of process, 1075-76; and personality, 1079-80; physiological aspects, 1082-1084; psychological aspects, 1074-82; and readiness, 1062, 1087-88; remedial, 1093-96; and sex differences, 1079; as a social process, 1070-71; and social studies education, 1236; sociological aspects, 1070-75; and spelling, 1289-90; and student characteristics, 1330-31; teaching aspects, 1084-96.
Records and reports: anecdotal, 1108; cumulative, 1108; forms of, 1108-10; and parents, 1106-07; pupil case studies, 1108; research on, 1105; types of, 1108; use of, 1105-08.
Rehabilitation: defined, 1111-12; in other countries, 1114; need for, 1112; programs, 1112-13; research on, 1113-14.
Reinforcement: and concept formation, 198-99; and learning, 709-12.
Relational concept: 196.
Religion and education: and experimentation, 1119-1120; history of, 1115-18; philosophical considerations, 1117-18; and teaching, 1119; trends in, 1118-1119.
Religious education: and general education, 527; history of, 1123; instruction methods for, 1125-26; objectives of, 1124; programs of, 1124-25; scope of, 1123-24.
Reporting systems in elementary education: 429.
Reports: on pupil progress, 1059-60. *See also* Records and reports.
Research, educational, training for: *see* Educational research, training for.
Research methods: action, 1150; anecdotal, 1149; library, 1144-45; longitudinal, 1149-50; observational, 1145-47; and rating studies, 1147-48; sociometric, 1148-49.
Research organizations, history of: 1152-58.
Retarded, mentally: *see* Mental retardation.
Rural education in developing nations: 347-50.

S

Safety education: and accident research, 1162-63; defined, 1159-60; extensions in, 1163-64; future prospects for, 1165; and health services, 1184-85; history of, 1160; international, 1164-65; scope of, 1160-62.
Salary: comparisons, 333-34; in developing nations, 353-54; trends, public school, 333-34.
Salary schedules: in higher education, 334; issues in, 331-33; principles of, 331; for public schools, 331-333.
Sampling: and experimental methods, 479-81; and survey research method, 1401.
Scales: absolute, 787; interval, 787; nominal, 785-86; ordinal, 786-87; ratio, 787.
Scaling: and axiomatic systems, 1172-73; limens, de-

termination of, 1167-68; and measurement theory, 1170-72; models, through, 1166-67; multidimensional, 1169-70; *vs.* psychometrics, 1167; univariate methods, 1168-69. *See also* Education, measurement in.

Scholarships: *see* Student financial aid.

School boards and transportation of students: 1494-1495.

School business administration: *see* Administration, business.

School milieu and politicization: 133-34, 139.

School organization and educational programs, elementary: 405-06.

School personnel administration: *see* Administration, school personnel.

School society: 1249-52.

Science: and general education, 527; and research in education, 1127-30.

Science education: college and university, 1195-1201; and concept formation, 201; courses and programs in, 403-05, 1196-97; and federal programs, 498-500; history of, 1192-94; instruction methods for, 1197-1200; objectives of, 1195-96; in other countries, 1201-03; pre-college, 1192-95; and teacher attitudes, 1195; and teacher education, 1200-01.

Scores and norms: comparability, 1210; defined, 1206; and norms population, 1208-10; and norms sample, 1208-10; and statistical methods, 1308-1309; and tests, 1464-65; types of, 1206-08.

Secondary education: and admissions, college and university, 25; and agricultural education, 69-70; and articulation of educational units, 88-89; and business education, 106-113; and class size, 143-44; comparative, 188; and correspondence education, 215; and curriculum, 1213-14, 1235; federal, 495; and federal programs, 496-97; history of, 1212-13; and home economics, 608; and nationalism, 132-33, 138-39; organization of, 1215-16; in other countries, 1216; and politicization, 128-34, 138-39; problems in, 1216; and safety education, 1161; and school personnel administration, 1188-90; scope of, 1211-1212; and social studies education, 1235; and speech education, 1273-74; and student characteristics, 1330-39.

Self concept: and counseling, 245-46; and dropouts, 314.

Sex differences: in ability, 1218; in concept formation, 198; in conduct problems, 292; developmental concepts of, 1219-20; and English literature, 467; and gifted children, 538; historical trends, 1217-18; implications for education, 1220; and intelligence, 661-62, 1218; and interests, 681; and motivation, 1218-19; and music education, 900; and personality, 1218-19; in physical development, 958-60; and physical education, 969; in politicization, 134, 139; and pupil progress, 1058-59; in reading ability, 1079; and sex-role identification, 1224-25; and spelling, 1286; and student characteristics, 1333; and tests, 1218; and women, education of, 360-65.

Shorthand: curriculum, 109-10; instruction methods for, 110-11; testing, 111.

Social and emotional development: and aggression, 1223; and anxiety, 1222-23; and child development, 120; and cognitive style, 1226; defined, 1221-22; and education, 1228; and emotions, 1222-25; and fear, 1222-23; and intergroup relations, 1225; and love, 1223-24; and morals, 1225-26; and positive emotion, 1223-24; and self concept, 1227-28; and sex-role identification, 1224-25.

Social change: and attendance, 94-95; in developing nations, 345-46.

Social deviancy: *see* Behavior problems.

Social studies education: administration of, 1000; and audiovisual aids, 1238; and the behavioral sciences, 1233-34; content sources of, 1232-34; curriculum organization, 1235-37; and economics, 1233; evaluation of, 1238; and general education, 526-27; and geography, 1232; and government, 1234; and history (subject), 1232; history of, 1231; instruction methods for, 1235-36; materials for, 1237-38; objectives of, 1231-32; and programmed learning, 1237-38; and psychology, 1233; and reading, 1237; and sociology, 1233; teacher education for, 1238-39; and values, 1234.

Social systems theory: 18.

Social work: 1006-07.

Society and intelligence: 663-64.

Socioeconomic class: and accident research, 1162; and adolescence, 47; and agricultural education, 72; and child development, 120-21; and community college education, 176; in developing nations, 346; and dropouts, 312-13; and early childhood education, 317-18; and education, 1247-49; and group processes, 557; and handicaps, educational, 380-84; and intelligence, 662; and interest, 681; and medical education, 806; and motivation, 1333-34; and politicization, 134-35, 139; and social studies education, 1236; and student characteristics, college and university, 1319-21, elementary and secondary, 1330.

Sociology: comparative, 191-92; and social studies education, 1233.

Sociology of education: *see* Education, sociology of.

Special education: for emotionally disturbed children, 1259-60; for gifted children, 1257-58; and hearing impairment, 1258; history of, 1254; legislative provisions for, 1254-55; and mental retardation, 1256-57; for socially maladjusted children, 1259-60; and speech handicaps, 1260-61; trends in, 1255-56; and visual impairment, 1258.

Speech: and audience behavior, 1270; defined, 1263; and discussion, 1271-72; handicaps, 1260-61; and hearing impairment, 1270-71; history of, 1263-70; instruction programs for, 1278-79; and linguistics, 1271; and listening, 749; and mass media, 1272-73; and mentally retarded children, 835; and oral interpretation of literature, 1272; pathology, *see below*; and speaker's attitude, 1270; and spelling, 1291; teaching of, 1273-74; and voice research, 1271.

Speech pathology and audiology: history of, 1227; and instruction programs, 1278-79; and language, 1280-81; and psychoacoustics, 1279-80; research in, 1279.

Spelling: and composition, 1291-92; curriculum, 1283-86; evaluation of, 1292-93; and handwriting, 1290-91; history of, 1282-83; instruction methods for, 1286-89; and proofreading, 1291-92; and reading, 1289-90; reform, 1293; research, needed, 1294; and speech, 1291.

Sports and physical education: 966-68.

Stage theory: and adolescence, 44-45; and aging, 63; and artistic learning, 78; and early childhood education, 317; and higher mental processes, 597-98; and personality development, 938-39.

Stanford-Binet test: 653.

State aid: and independent schools, 636; to libraries, 743; to students, 1341-46.

State Boards of Education: 1301.

State programs: for gifted children, 541-42; and public schools, 508-11; and student teaching, 1377.

State regulation of education: *see* Education, state regulation of.

Statistical analysis and experimental methods: 478-479.

Statistical methods: and bivariate problems, 1314-16; criticisms of, 1313-15; descriptive, 1308-09; developments in, 1307-08; in experimental methods analysis, 478-79; and factor analysis, 1317-18;

inferential, 1309-13; and multivariate problems, 1313-16.
Stratification and education: 1247-49.
Student: activities, *see below*; characteristics, *see below*; college environment, impact of on, 172-73; choice of by institutions, 34-40; civil liberties of, 162-63; college interests of, 32; control, 1363-64; counseling, influence of on, 223-25; counseling, views on, 243; counselors, views on, 259-60; in developing nations, 347; engineering abilities of, 439-40; exchange, 30, 355; financial aid, *see below*; flow through educational system, 28-30; general education, influence on, 531; institutional choices of, 30-34; law, 735; literature, response to, 467-69; and mental health, 817-18; and modern languages, 873; organizations, *see below*; in proprietary schools, 1025; reading interests of, 467; rights movement, 1363-64; teaching, *see below*; transportation, *see* Transportation; and urban educational problems, 1502-03; women, 360-65.
Student activities and organizations: administration of, 1362-63; history of, 1361; patterns of, 1364-65; programs of, 1363-64; purposes of, 1361-62; research, related, 1365; scope of, 1359; and student rights movement, 1363-64.
Student activities and organizations, elementary and secondary: defined, 1368-69; evaluation of, 1370; history of, 1368-69; objectives of, 1369-70; problems of, 1374-75; research on, 1370-73; trends in, 1370-1374.
Student attitudes to study: 1387-88.
Student characteristics, college and university: academic interests, 1321-22; and achievement, 1318-19; and aptitude, 1318-19; of business students, 106-07; change in, 1323-25; of commercial college students, 176-77; of community college students, 176-78; of counseling clients, 221, 258; and creativity, 270-71; of educational research workers, 1480-81; nonintellective, 1322-23; in other countries, 1325-27; and socioeconomic class, 1319-21; and vocational interests, 1321-22.
Student characteristics, elementary and secondary: and achievement, 1332-34; activities, 1337-39; and aptitude, 1332-34; and health, 1331-32; and interests, 1335-37; and motivation, 1333-34; and personality, 1334-35; physical, 1331-32; and reading, 1330-31; and sex differences, 1333; and socioeconomic class, 1330, 1333-34; values of, 1337-39.
Student financial aid: administration of, 1354; and athletes, 1355; and attendance, 1346-49; bibliographies and directories, 1350; defined, 1340-41; and disadvantaged students, 1349-50; and dropouts, 1353-54; through employment, 1341-46, 1351-52; federal, 1341-46; and foreign students, 1355; through grants, 1341-46, 1350-51; history of, 1339-40; and intercollege cooperation, 1355; through loans, 1341-1346, 1352-53; miscellaneous sources, 1346; in other countries, 1555-56; scholarships, research on, 1350-51; state, 1341-46; total from all sources, 1344-1346; and transfer students, 1354.
Student personnel services in community college education: 180.
Student teaching: administration of, 1379-80; in agricultural education, 71-72; forces influencing, 1377; and internship, 1380-81; purposes of, 1378-79; status of, 1377; and supervision, 1381-83; and teacher education programs, 1417-18; technology of, 1383-84; terminology of, 1377-78; urban, 1384.
Study: attitudes about, 1387-88; correspondence, 1392; courses on, 1388-89; habits, 1387-88; and homework, 1389-90; independent, 1390-91; and libraries, 1391-92; manuals on, 1388-89; supervised, 1390.
Superintendent of Schools: 1301; history of office, 1040; leadership function, 1042-43; and relationship to school board, 1043.
Supervision: defined, 1394; evaluation of, 1396-97; and leadership, 1395-96; and morale, 1395; role of, 1397-98; of study, 1390; training for, 1398.
Supreme Court and education: 496.
Survey research method: and data analysis, 1402-05; and data collection, 1401-02; and data reduction, 1402; defined, 1400; examples of, 1405-08; instrumentation of, 1401-02; and reasoning, 1401; and sampling, 1401.

T

Teacher: administrative functions of, 1046; certification, *see below*; collective action by, 154-59; in correspondence education, 215; as counselor, 234-35; and early childhood education, 327; economic status of, *see below*; effectiveness, *see below*; in elementary education, 429-31; and English composition, 453-54; grievances, 155; and individual initiative, 154-56; insurance, 335; leaves of absence, 334-35; in legal education, 736-37; and mental health, 826; and parents, 1032; politicization, influence on, 130, 138; in proprietary schools, 1025-26; and reading, 1085; retirement plans, 335; roles, *see below*; and safety education, 1164; school management by, 157-59; shortage, 353-54; state regulation of, 1304; tenure, 1458-59; and urban educational problems, 1503-04; unionization, 157-59. *See also* Faculty.
Teacher, economic status of: in developing nations, 353-54; and fringe benefits, 334-35; and independent schools, 634; international aspects, 335-36; and nonteaching income, 334; salary, higher education, 333; salary comparisons, public school, 333-34; salary schedules, 331-33; salary trends, U.S., 333-34; salary trends, foreign, 353-54.
Teacher attitudes: about English composition, 456; to general education, 529; and pupil progress, 1058; to science education, 1195; and teacher education, 1430-31; and teacher effectiveness, 1429-34.
Teacher certification: defined, 1410; history of, 1410-1411; requirements, 1411-13; by the state, 1302; and student teaching, 1379-80; trends in, 1413.
Teacher education: agricultural, 71-72; business, 106; and classical languages, 151; comparative, 188; continuing, *see* Teacher education, inservice; and counseling, college and university, 221-22, elementary, 234, secondary, 248-49; and curriculum, 249; in developing nations, 353-54; for early childhood education, 325; and educational programs, 406-07; and English composition, 456-57; and English literature, 470; and home economics, 615-616; and independent schools, requirements of, 634-35; inservice, *see below*; institutions, number of for, 1412; for libraries, 745-46; and mathematics, 773-75; and military education, 858-59; and modern languages, 874; and physical education, 970-71; and physically handicapped children, 975-76; programs, *see below*; and science education, 1200-01; and social science education, 1238-39; and student teaching, 1376-87; and supervision, 1398; and teacher behavior, 1430-31.
Teacher education, inservice: defined, 645-46; and educational television, 649-50; group dynamics of, 651-52; procedures for, 648-49; status of, 646-48. *See also* Student teaching.
Teacher education programs: conceptualizations, 1414-15; evaluation of, 1418-19; and Master of Arts in teaching, 1416; preservice, 1416-19; research on, 1419-20; and student teaching, 1417-18; trends in, 1415-16.
Teacher effectiveness: and classroom process analy-

sis, 1425-26; other reviews, 1424-25; and pupil achievement, 1426-28; and pupil attitude, 1426-28; research trends, 1434; and teacher attitudes, 1429-1434.
Teacher qualification in developing nations: 353-54.
Teacher roles: changes in, 154-59; expectancy studies of, 1437-40; and performance studies, 1440-43.
Teaching machines: *see* Programmed learning.
Teaching methods: *see* Instruction methods.
Team teaching: 562-63.
Technical education: *see* Community college education; Proprietary schools; Vocational education.
Television: in correspondence education, 216; reading ability, effect on, 1072; and science education, 1199; and student teaching, 1383; and teacher education, 649-50, 1415. *See also* Communications media.
Tenure: 1458-60.
Tests: achievement, 7-15, 831-32, 1218; administration of, 1462-64; and admissions, college and university, 38-39; aptitude, 672-75; and classical languages, 150-51; and computers, 285; for creativity, 272; and data processing, 285; development of, 1462; intelligence, 654-56, 667-72; interpretation of, 1465-67; in legal education, 735-36; medical, 805; and mentally retarded children, 831-32; and motor ability, 889-91; musical, 896; norms, 1467; reliability, 794-96; scoring of, 789-91, 1464-65; and sex differences, 1218; and spelling, 1292; and statistical methods, 1308-09 *passim*; of statistical methods, 1311-13; and student characteristics, college and university, 1318-19; elementary and secondary, 1333; use of, 1461-62, 1465-67. *See also* Achievement tests; Admissions tests; Aptitude tests; Education, measurement in; Marks; Measurement theory; Prediction; Scales and Norms.
Textbook: adoption procedures, 1473-74; authors, 1474-75; bias, 132, 139; and classical languages, 150; on comparative education, 185; in correspondence education, 215; in counseling, 229; evolution, 1470-1471; functions of, 1471-72; history of the, 1470; influence of, 1472-73; in other countries, 1476-77; politicization, influence on, 132-33, 139; publishing, 1475-76; readability, 1474; selection, 1473-74; and social science education, 1237; state regulation of, 1303. *See also* Instruction materials.
Theology: 1007.
Thinking: *see* Higher mental processes.
Trade schools: *see* Proprietary schools.
Training: for educational research, *see* Educational research, training for; for teachers, *see* Teacher education.
Trait-factor theory: 640, 643; and counseling, 245-246, 256.
Transfer of learning: *see* Learning, transfer of.
Transfer students and financial aid: 1354.
Transportation: administration of, 1497; effects of, 1498; financing of, 1497-98; history of, 1493-94; and safety, 1495-96; and school board responsibility, 1494-95; and school buses, 1496-97; and state regulation, 1303.
Typewriting: curriculum, 107-08; instruction methods, 108; production, 109; skill, development of, 108-09; testing of, 109.

U

Underachievement: in gifted children, 539-41; and individual differences, 641.
Underdeveloped nations: *see* Developing nations.
Unemployment: 353.
University: administration, 161-67; and class size, 144; comparative, 188-89; and educational programs, 384-87; finance, 502-07; and student characteristics, 1318-29. *See also* Higher education.
Urban drift: 348-49.
Urban educational problems: and disadvantaged children, 1502-03; forces for change, 1504-05; history of, 1499-1500; organizational patterns, 1501-02; setting, 1500-01; with teachers, 1503-04.

V

Visual abilities and spelling: 1286-87.
Visual aids: *see* Communications media.
Visual impairment: 1258. *See also* Handicaps, physical.
Vocabulary: and English composition, 453; and language development, 693-94; and listening, 748-49; and modern languages, 872; and reading, 1079-81.
Vocational counseling: 223, 225-26, 260-61, 915-20.
Vocational education: in developing nations, 350; of the disabled, 190; and federal programs, 497; history of, 1507-08; and local school districts, 754; perspective on, 1506-07; research on, 1510-20; transfiguration of, 1508-10. *See also* Business education; Correspondence education; Proprietary schools.
Vocational interests: and individual differences, 642; of students, 1321-22.
Voice research: 1271.

W

Weber, Max: 242-44.
Women: and adult education, 364-65; in America, 361; and college, 361-65; counseling of, 363-64; and graduate education, 364; history of, 360-61; and role relationship, 363.
Work experience programs: 70-71.

bers, functions, elementary notions from set theory, logic, informal algebra with arithmetic, problem solving, elementary probability, and statistics; and the relation between the real world and mathematics. If a child completed the CCSM curriculum for grade 12, he would have completed the equivalent of three years of excellent college mathematics today. Rosenbloom has insisted that the Minnemast program, described by Rising (1965), incorporates most of the important points of the CCSM recommendations, and preceded it. Fehr (1966a) has also begun work on field-testing a program for grades 7–12 which has many aspects of the Cambridge report integrated with suggestions that have come out of the European conferences. The CCSM group itself has done a considerable amount of work on developing details of its program and trying these out on a short-term basis with considerable success, as indicated by Hilton (1966).

Acceleration. To separate acceleration from new content is not an easy process, since the two seem so closely associated. The CCSM report, for example, has introduced much new material, but the aspect that has caused the greatest reaction is the acceleration involved in the program rather than the new content. There is considerable evidence that children can learn more, earlier, as indicated by Brown and Abell's (1965) summary of research.

One of the major questions that has disturbed educators with regard to acceleration is the work done by Piaget and others which indicates that children go through various stages of concept development. Adler (1966b) gives a good summary of Piaget's findings and their implications for the teaching of mathematics, as does Skypek (1965). Although some people have suggested that Piaget's work should be interpreted to mean that these stages cannot be accelerated, Piaget does not say this, and there is evidence that significant gains in stage placement can be induced by instruction. Coxford (1964), for example, replicated and corroborated Piaget's findings on order of stages but found that instruction could advance stage placement. Overholt (1965) studied one of Piaget's stages as it relates to sex, IQ, and achievement in arithmetic. He found that about one-third of the nine-year-olds studied did not have the conservation concept yet and that girls were better on this concept and on IQ tests than boys, but the boys were better in arithmetic. These differences may support the contention of some people that segregation by sex is desirable in schools. Roskopf (in Fehr, 1966b) makes a strong plea for more Piaget-type experiments in this country with careful study of individuals rather than huge masses of statistical data. Of course, for purposes of communication and possible replication, statistical data ought to be kept and reported with such studies.

Evaluation. Although experimental programs in modern mathematics have been in progress in the schools since the early 1950's, there is still considerable doubt in many people's minds that the programs are an improvement. The masses of data mentioned in the first two paragraphs of this entry are, in general, either subjective, very short range, likely to be biased by the Hawthorne Effect, or not conclusive. In light of the questions that are being asked, this is not entirely surprising. How does one decide that one program is "better" than another? Some form of data has to be collected if the decision is to be statistical. But the instruments with which the data are collected, and the basic hypotheses assumed, are of great importance. If the goal is to turn out rapid, accurate computers, creating a testing instrument is relatively easy. As the goal becomes more complex, so must the decisions involved in choosing or creating a testing instrument. Brownell (1966) has pointed out the need for value judgments as well as objective data in evaluating programs, and mentioned some of the things that can go wrong if the data are collected without using good judgment. Glennon (1966) reiterates this with his reminder that statistical significance and educational importance are not the same thing.

One major problem with most of the statistical data that are available so far is that they apply to only a very short time span. It has been demonstrated that children can learn logic in the fifth grade, algebra in the fourth grade, set language in kindergarten, and so on. But very few long-term studies have been conducted to determine the cumulative effects of these programs on children. Goldberg and others (1966) reported the results of one three-year longitudinal study to compare acceleration with enrichment and modern with traditional programs. They concluded that for grades 7 through 9, acceleration was better than enrichment, and the modern program was better than the traditional program for learning how to solve problems, but the enriched traditional program resulted in the best attitudes on the part of the pupils.

Two major longitudinal studies are now under way, but results have not yet been reported. Cahen (1963, 1965) reports on the National Longitudinal Study of the School Mathematics Study Group, which is measuring attitudes, reasoning, and achievement. This study started with 110,000 pupils in 1962 but had lost almost 40,000 of them by 1964 through natural attrition of one sort or another. The results of this study should be available sometime during 1967, when the five-year period ends. Rising (1965) reports on the Minnesota National Laboratory study which is collecting data with which to compare various new mathematics programs with traditional programs. This program is also developing testing instruments that should be of considerable interest to experimenters and others interested in evaluation.

It is reported (in Husen, 1967) that pupils in modern programs do better than those in traditional programs, but the tests are clearly biased in favor of a modern program. The data from this program are available in data banks and may be used for future studies.

INSTRUCTION METHODS. As well as the changes in curriculum, an integral part of most of the new school mathematics programs has been a change in method. A major reason for organizing the curriculum in a logical way and emphasizing structure is that this makes it easier for the child to understand and "figure out." Although a tendency to emphasize pupil understanding was apparent before the advent of the new mathematics, it has been even more apparent in many of the newer programs.

Both Buswell (1960) and Gibb and others (1960) point out that transfer of training is possible but does not occur automatically. They point out that understanding and generalization are prerequisites to transfer and that these are therefore legitimate goals in teaching mathematics. Their findings are documented with a very substantial amount of research. Van Engen and Gibb (1956) consider arithmetic an organized system of general ideas, and show through research on division as successive subtractions how a child can learn with understanding. Throughout the yearbook edited by Fehr (1953), mathematics educators emphasize the idea that research in learning supports the belief that teachers should teach for understanding.

Discovery. The term that has most commonly been associated with methods of teaching the new mathematics is "discovery." The concept has many proponents, as for example, the Cambridge Conference on School Mathematics (1963); MacLean (1967), who emphasizes pupil activity; the U.S. Office of Education–National Council of Teachers of Mathematics Report (1964), which emphasizes pupil activity and receptiveness to questions; and Willoughby (1967). Unfortunately, it is not always clear what people mean when they talk about "discovery." Some are talking about a process of scientific induction; some refer to a Socratic approach, somewhat similar to that used by teaching machines; some mean a complete laissez-faire attitude on the part of the teacher; some are talking about a process in which teacher and pupils investigate a situation using the knowledge and logic of the pupils as much as possible with growing encouragement of pupil initiative and freedom; and some are thinking of some combination or variation of these.

As Ausubel (1961, 1964) points out, there is very little research evidence that supports discovery, and in fact, it may be a waste of time in some cases. However, the kind of objectives held by many proponents of discovery do not lend themselves to easy statistical analysis, and the statistical data gathered so far seem to be more inconclusive than negative.

Hendrix (1967) has long been a proponent of nonverbal awareness. She has written many articles suggesting that a child can discover and understand a fact without being able to verbalize it. She also contends that early verbalization may interfere with subsequent understanding.

A different sort of attempt to teach children mathematics is being carried on by Gagné and others at the University of Maryland. This project centers around the idea of task analysis. Task analysis depends upon describing an observable performance the learner is supposed to be able to exhibit. Then the experimenter must determine what subordinate behaviors are necessary in order to achieve the final performance. It turns out that some children can exhibit the final behavior without the subordinate behavior, most can exhibit the final behavior when they have learned all of the subordinate behaviors, and about five percent cannot exhibit the final behavior even though they have mastered all the subordinate behaviors. The Maryland group is now working on ways to help this latter group integrate learned behaviors so as to exhibit a new one. This program has been discussed by Walbesser (in Fehr, 1966b), Gagné (1963), and Mayor (1965).

Individualization. At this time, there is considerable interest in individualization of instruction. Research programs on individualization of instruction are being carried out in Wisconsin by DeVault, in California by Suppes, in Illinois by Kaufman, and elsewhere. These programs have different emphases, but each visualizes using a computer in some way to aid the teacher. Some make a careful distinction between computer-*assisted* instruction and computer-*controlled* instruction, believing that the latter is too stultifying. Unfortunately, there are not as yet any significant published findings on the projects.

In England, much of the research in elementary-school mathematics has been directed at the study of individual children, so that the teacher can be expected to direct the program to their individual interests. Readiness is stressed so as to avoid rote memorization by a pupil who cannot yet understand the concept being taught. This and other interesting innovations were discussed in broadcasts called "Q.E.D." heard over BBC (Land, 1963).

Gurau (1967a, b) reports on a successful attempt at individualization in which tests are used as diagnostic instruments, and programs, sets of exercises, and individual teacher help are used for remedial work. The fact that he worked with only 12 pupils in his class, however, indicates part of the reason other researchers are so anxious to find some form of help for the teacher, such as a computer, when individualization is tried.

Probably the most significant finding reported by Leiderman and others (1966) of the School Mathematics Study Group project for the culturally disadvantaged is the wide variability among children classified as disadvantaged.

As more information of this sort accumulates, it will probably support more efforts to individualize instruction, just as IQ tests in the early part of this century encouraged a beginning in that direction. Schult (1966) reports that there already is a significant move in this direction in the large cities of the country.

Programmed Instruction. Although Brown and Abell (1966a) report that programmed instruction has been reasonably successful with bright children, they and other researchers are not entirely satisfied with the present state of programmed instruction. Heimer (1966) contends that every part of the original Skinner paradigm for programs is either highly suspect or is clearly wrong in light of research. He suggests a much broader interpretation of programmed instruction, including films, filmstrips, text material, and television.

Chinn (1966) reports that the early field test of programmed material for SMSG led to boredom and frustration on the part of the pupils. This was remedied by creating a hybrid version of a program that included conventional text material, reviews, an index, and a mixture of Skinner- and Crowder-type programs. The results of this programmed version of the SMSG ninth-grade algebra course were quite promising.

May (1965, 1966) has studied programmed instruction in great detail and believes it may have a place in the education of the future, but he is sure it will not replace the teacher. He suggests that with computer assistance programs may be useful, but this process may prove to be prohibitively expensive for the good that is derived from it. The most promising use May sees for programs at present is to supplement the textbook. He also points out that their lack of index and table of contents, as well as their general format, make programs very hard to review. In spite of this, he has reviewed many and finds them generally of low quality, thin in content, and of very high cost.

Games and Physical Materials. Allen and others (1966) report that with a sample of 23 they were able to maintain great interest and raise the IQ of pupils taught through the use of educational games. Paschal (1966) also reports that games were of considerable value in working with the SMSG project for the culturally disadvantaged. This seems to be a promising field for further research if a sufficient number of appropriate games can be created and tested. Davis (1966) makes a plea for more use of physical materials in the classroom and more diversity of experience, as does the U.S. Office of Education–National Council of Teachers of Mathematics Report (1964) on low achievers.

The physical materials that have received the most attention by research workers recently are Cuisenaire Rods. Callahan and Jacobson (1967) report on a trial of Cuisenaire Rods with a special class and are enthusiastic about the results in terms of interest and achievement. Hollis (1965) also reports better results with the rods than with traditional methods, but Passy (1963) reports unfavorable results.

Written Work. Small (1967) has reported evidence suggesting that careful grading of student homework may be a waste of teacher time. His sample of 36 pupils is not sufficiently large to draw reliable conclusions, but it points to a field for further study.

Although it is not specifically oriented to mathematics, Bentley's (1966) article should be considered by teachers of mathematics. He has found evidence that academic examinations tend to favor memory and cognitive abilities while penalizing the highly creative student. Since it is well known that students often study more for an examination than for what a teacher says he is trying to teach, this evidence should encourage teachers to think carefully about their examinations. Is it desirable that schools discourage creativity?

TEACHER TRAINING. Complaints about the preparation of teachers are not new. Smith and others (1912) were upset that almost four-fifths of the elementary-school teachers of the time were women and didn't stay in teaching very long. Therefore, teacher education was a difficult problem. They also reported that the average newly appointed teacher of mathematics was a college graduate (though many were not) who had taken about one year's work in mathematics beyond the work of the school in which he taught. Usually he did not have any calculus, and also had no work in methods of teaching the subject.

Weak Mathematical Background. Brown and Abell (1965, 1966a) point out that research shows that elementary-school teachers have lower ability and less formal training than the rest of the college population. They also point out that these factors are directly related to attitude toward mathematics. Mayor (1966) reports that of 22 well-known people associated with mathematics education, 19 chose teacher training as being an important problem today —a far larger number than for any other problem. Young (1966) deplores the lack of well-trained teachers for elementary schools, and suggests a possible course of action. It may be small consolation to discover from Fehr (1962) that the background of teachers in most other American countries is even worse than in the United States, but Fehr (1965) also points out that in some European countries the training of teachers is much better than in the United States.

Carroll (1964) shows that although elementary-school teachers in general are badly trained (they score at about the eighth-grade level on standard tests), those who are graduating from predominantly Negro colleges are even worse. Thus, since segregation continues to be a fact of life in this country, Negro children are probably getting a worse education than others, and a vicious circle is established. Carroll recommends strong measures to correct this situation.

Grossnickle (1951) reported that 76 percent of the teachers colleges responding to his questionnaire did not require any high school mathematics for entrance and fewer than half provided background courses in mathematics for teachers of upper elementary-school grades. In his sample of 62 liberal arts colleges, only one provided a background course in mathematics for future elementary-school teachers. Gibb and others (1960) report research that indicates that students of teachers trained in teachers colleges were not as good as those of teachers trained in private colleges and universities. Husen (1967) supports this contention on an international level but produces evidence that the contrary is true in the United States.

Improvements. Beginning in 1954, the National Science Foundation has supported institutes for teachers of science and mathematics. Generally these institutes have concentrated primarily on improving and refreshing the teacher's background in his subject field. According to Lindquist (1965), by 1960 there were 365 National Science Foundation Institutes wholly or partly for mathematics teachers. These were attended by 11,875 mathematics teachers, which is about one-tenth of the total number of secondary-school mathematics teachers. Even assuming a substantial number of these teachers attend more than one institute, it is clear that a very substantial fraction of the mathematics teachers in this country have attended at least one institute.

The situation for elementary teachers, on the other hand, has not been so favorable. Since there are almost ten times as many elementary-school teachers as high school mathematics teachers, and because of the rapid turnover in elementary-school teachers, upgrading the subject-matter background of the elementary-school teacher has been a more formidable task. Furthermore, the elementary-school teacher is expected to teach all subjects, not just one specialty, and therefore should presumably continue to study all subjects. Recently the federal government has discontinued institutes for elementary-school teachers, which, even when they were being supported, reached only a small fraction of the teachers.

Several attempts to solve this problem have been made. The Committee on the Undergraduate Program in Mathematics (CUPM) of the Mathematical Association of America (1961) published a set of recommendations for the training of elementary-school teachers. They recommend four semesters of college mathematics with an entrance requirement of at least high school geometry. The CUPM has held conferences all over the country to try to encourage acceptance of their proposals, and has had substantial effect in getting them at least partially accepted. Information about the conferences and some of the changes made so far may be found in the report of the Committee on the Undergraduate Program in Mathematics (1966). Although very few colleges are actually requiring the full 12 credits recommended by CUPM, the majority are requiring 6 or more, and there are several that have begun to require 12. The specific courses recommended by CUPM are two semesters on the real number system and its subsystems, one semester of algebra, and one semester of informal geometry. The CUPM has also made recommendations for the training of teachers who teach in secondary schools and colleges. In general, the recommendations would require the teacher to have considerably more mathematical background than is now common.

Some people have suggested that recommendations such as those of the CUPM, and the somewhat stronger recommendations of the Cambridge Conference on School Mathematics (1967), are unrealistic in light of the shortage of teachers and of people trained in mathematics. Jewett (1966), however, has pointed out that if present trends continue, based on USOE and NEA figures, there will be no shortage of qualified teachers of mathematics to fill expected vacancies by 1969. Furthermore, by 1974 there should be one-third more qualified beginning mathematics teachers than vacancies. If these projections are correct, there is every reason to suppose that state and individual school systems can increase their requirements substantially without eliminating the source of supply.

Meanwhile, there have been other attempts at in-service improvement of teachers' mathematical background. Weaver (1965) reports on a reasonably successful attempt by Van Engen to teach a good modern mathematics program to children and their teachers at the same time via television. Both the teachers and the pupils seem to have learned a substantial amount from these programs.

One somewhat disturbing report by Huetting (Huetting & Newell, 1966) indicates that teachers with more experience tend to be more resistant to change. If this is true, it will, of course, make it more difficult to change the program in schools where teachers have been teaching for a long period of time, and it may be that schools with the most rapid turnover may find it easiest to change their programs.

Specialists. Elementary-school teachers must teach the language arts, natural science, social sciences, mathematics, music, physical education, and art. They also have to help children with snowsuits and other articles of clothing, wipe noses, collect milk money, help the children adjust to school, and generally act as a substitute mother in this home away from home. In short, the ideal elementary-school teacher would be a Nietzschean Superman who has the milk of human kindness flowing in his veins and loves little children. Even if this is not a contradiction in terms, it is certain that not very many people of this sort exist *and* want to teach school. In light of this consideration, the suggestion that specialists in the various subject-matter areas be used in the elementary schools has been made more than once, as, for example, by the Cambridge Conference on School Mathematics (1967), Fehr (1966b), and Weaver (1966b). However, the small amount of research that has been done on this subject indicates that children taught by specialists do not do better than those taught by generalists. Gibb and Matala (1962) found, instead, that pupils of good teachers did well and those of poor teachers did poorly, regardless of whether the teacher happened to be a specialist.

The Cambridge Conference on School Mathematics (1967) suggested many ways in which a specialist could be used other than to replace the regular teacher. For example, he could be used to help the regular teacher, he could be used as a supervisor, he could be used to give demonstration lessons and to help in planning, etc. Weaver (1966b) also suggests that, although research indicated that replacing a regular teacher by a specialist is not an improvement, "judicious" use of special teachers can probably improve the program. Schult (1966) points out that the number of supervisors in mathematics at both the state and local levels is increasing rapidly.

As one reviews the research on mathematics education, there are several factors that stand out. First, it is very difficult to locate and evaluate all of the research that has been done in this country and others. Weaver (1966a) and the conferees at the conference on Needed Research in Mathematical Education chaired by Fehr (1966b) agreed that some means of collecting, evaluating, and disseminating all such information quickly are needed. The Cambridge Conference on School Mathematics (1967) also made this point. It is important to note, however, that simply collecting and disseminating the material is not sufficient, since the quality of research varies greatly, and most potential consumers will have neither the time nor the background to evaluate all the research. More books and articles on what research says to the teacher, such as those by Fehr (1955) and Glennon (1958), might help to fill this gap if the writers had time and finances to do a truly excellent job.

A second major point is that research with human beings often does not tell us whether one program is better than another. Often statistical techniques developed for use in agriculture are applied to education as though the goals in education were as clear as those in agriculture, and as though the experimenter thought his presence would have as little effect on children as it does on corn.

Third, although the Hawthorne Effect may be the bane of the educational experimenter's existence, it can be used most effectively by the educator. Spitzer (1953), for example, reports on the great enthusiasm of a teacher for a new system of locating a decimal point in a division problem. The system is to subtract the number of decimal places in the divisor from the number in the dividend to find the number in the quotient. The fact that this process should give the wrong answer in approximately half the cases apparently did not disturb either the children or the teacher. Willoughby (1967) reports on a similar case in which a teacher found far more enthusiasm and understanding on the part of the children when he eliminated the use of the word *minus* and used only the "modern" word *negative*. Thus, "5 negative 3 is 2." Although it is not desirable to teach new methods that are wrong, it probably is desirable for teachers to change their methods every few years to increase their children's, and their own, enthusiasm. Thus, whether experimentation gives reliable results is probably not of as much importance as the fact that the experimentation is being carried on.

Davis (1966) points out that industries hire people whose only job is to improve the functioning of the industry, and that the industries would go bankrupt without such men. He suggests that schools also should hire people whose only job is innovation.

Stephen S. Willoughby
New York University

References

Adler, Irving. "The Cambridge Conference Report: Blueprint or Fantasy." *Math Teach* 59:210–7; 1966(a).

Adler, Irving. "Mental Growth and the Art of Teaching." *Math Teach* 59:706–15; 1966(b).

Ahlfors, Lars V., and others. "On the Mathematics Curriculum of the High School." *Math Teach* 55: 191–5; 1962.

Allen, Layman E., and others. "Programmed Games and the Learning of Problem-Solving Skills: The WFF 'N Proof Example." *J Ed Res* 60:22–6; 1966.

Alspaugh, John W., and Delon, Floyd G. "How Modern is Today's Secondary Mathematics Curriculum?" *Math Teach* 60:50–5; 1967.

American Association of School Administrators and others. *Administrative Responsibility for Improving Mathematics Programs.* AASA, 1965. 24p.

Athen, Herman. "The Teaching of Vectors in the German Gymnasium I and II." *Math Teach* 59: 382–93, 485–95; 1966.

Ausubel, David P. "Learning by Discovery: Rationale and Mystique." *B Nat Assn Sec Sch Prin* 45:18–58; 1961.

Ausubel, David P. "Some Psychological and Educational Limitations of Learning by Discovery." *Arithmetic Teach* 11:290–302; 1964.

Beberman, Max. *An Emerging Program of Secondary School Mathematics.* Harvard U, 1958. 44p.

Bentley, Joseph C. "Creativity and Academic Achievement." *J Ed Res* 59:269–72; 1966.

Brown, Kenneth E., and Abell, Theodore L. *Analysis of Research in the Teaching of Mathematics.* Bulletin No. 28. USOE, 1965. 99p.

Brown, Kenneth S., and Abell, Theodore L. "Research in the Teaching of High School Mathematics." *Math Teach* 59:53–7; 1966(a).

Brown, Kenneth E., and Abell, Theodore L. "Trends in Mathematics Offerings and Enrollments." *Math Teach* 59:652–5; 1966(b).

Brownell, William A. "The Techniques of Research Employed in Arithmetic." In *Report of the Society's Committee on Arithmetic.* 29th Yearbook, Part II. NSSE, 1930. p. 415–43.

Brownell, William A. "The Evaluation of Learning Under Dissimilar Systems of Instruction." *Arithmetic Teach* 13:267–74; 1966.

Bruner, Jerome. *The Process of Education.* Harvard U Press, 1960. 97p.

Buswell, Guy Thomas. "Arithmetic." In Harris, Chester. (Ed.) *Encyclopedia of Educational Research.* 3rd ed. Macmillan, 1960. p. 63–77.

Buswell, Guy Thomas, and Judd, Charles Hubbard. *Summary of Educational Investigations Relating to Arithmetic.* U. Chicago, 1925. 212p.

Butler, Charles H., and Wren, F. Lynwood. *The Teaching of Secondary Mathematics.* 4th. ed. McGraw-Hill, 1965. 613p.

Cahen, Leonard S. "The National Longitudinal Study of Mathematical Abilities." In *Sci Ed News.* AAAS, 1963. p. 5–6.

Cahen, Leonard S. "An Interim Report on the National Longitudinal Study of Mathematical Abilities." *Math Teach* 58:22–7; 1965.

Call, Russell J., and Wiggin, Neal A. "Reading and Mathematics." *Math Teach* 59:149–57; 1966.

Callahan, John J., and Jacobson, Ruth S. "An Experiment with Retarded Children and Cuisenaire Rods." *Arithmetic Teach* 14:10–3; 1967.

Cambridge Conference on School Mathematics. *Goals for School Mathematics.* Houghton, 1963. 102p.

Cambridge Conference on School Mathematics. *Goals for Mathematical Training of Elementary School Teachers.* Houghton, 1967. 169p.

Carroll, Edward Major. "Competencies in Mathematics of Certain Prospective Elementary School Teachers." Doctoral dissertation. Teachers Col, Columbia U, 1964.

Chinn, William G., and others. *The Programmed Learning Project.* School Mathematics Study Group, 1966. 93p.

Clark, John R. "Perspective in Programs of Instruction in Elementary Mathematics." *Arithmetic Teach* 12:604–11; 1965.

Commission on Mathematics of College Entrance Examination Board. *Program for College Preparatory Mathematics.* CEEB, 1959(a). 63p.

Commission on Mathematics of College Entrance Examination Board. *Program for College Preparatory Mathematics.* CEEB, 1959(b). 231p.

Committee of Ten. *Report of the Committee of Ten on Secondary School Subjects.* American, 1894. 249p.

Committee on the Undergraduate Program in Mathematics. *Recommendations of the Mathematical Association of America for the Training of Teachers of Mathematics.* Mathematical Association of America, 1961. 10p.

Committee on the Undergraduate Program in Mathematics. *Eleven Conferences on the Training of Teachers of Elementary School Mathematics.* Mathematical Association of America, 1966. 144p.

Coxford, Arthur F., Jr. "The Effects of Instruction on the Stage Placement of Children in Piaget's Seriation Experiments." *Arithmetic Teach* 11:4–9; 1964.

Davis, Robert B. "The Next Few Years." *Arithmetic Teach* 13:355–62; 1966.

Deans, Edwina. *Elementary School Mathematics: New Directions.* Bulletin No. 13. USOE, 1963. 116p.

Fehr, Howard F. (Ed.) *The Learning of Mathematics: Its Theory and Practice.* 21st Yearbook. National Council of Teachers of Mathematics, 1953. 355p.

Fehr, Howard F. *Teaching High School Mathematics.* NEA, 1955. 33p.

Fehr, Howard F. (Ed.) *Mathematical Education in the Americas.* Teachers Col, Columbia U, 1962. 180p.

Fehr, Howard F. "International Mathematical Education." *Math Teach* 58:37–44; 1965.

Fehr, Howard F. "A Unified Mathematics Program for Grades Seven through Twelve." *Math Teach* 59:463; 1966(a).

Fehr, Howard F. (Ed.) *Needed Research in Mathematical Education.* Teachers Col, Columbia U, 1966(b). 25p.

Gagné, Robert M. "Learning and Proficiency in Mathematics." *Math Teach* 56:620–6; 1963.

Gibb, E. Glenadine, and Matala, Dorothy C. "Study on the Use of Special Teachers of Science and Mathematics in Grades Five and Six: Final Report." *Sch Sci Math* 62:565–85; 1962.

Gibb, E. Glenadine, and others. "Mathematics." In Harris, Chester. (Ed.) *Encyclopedia of Educational Research.* 3rd ed. Macmillan, 1960. p. 796–807.

Glennon, Vincent J. *What Does Research Say About Arithmetic?* Rev. ed. ASCD, 1958. 77p.

Glennon, Vincent J. "Research Needs in Elementary School Mathematics Education." *Arithmetic Teach* 13:363–8; 1966.

Goldberg, Miriam L., and others. *A Comparison of Mathematics Programs for Able Junior High School Students.* 2 vols. USOE, 1966. 381p.

Grossnickle, Foster E. "The Training of Teachers in Arithmetic." In *The Teaching of Arithmetic.* 50th Yearbook, Part II, NSSE. U Chicago, 1951. p. 203–31.

Gurau, Peter K. "Individualizing Mathematics Instruction." *Sch Sci Math* 67:11–26; 1967(a).

Gurau, Peter K. "A Time for Testing." *Math Teach* 60:133–6; 1967(b).

Hartmann, George W. "Gestalt Psychology and Mathematical Insight." *Math Teach* 30:265–70; 1937.

Håstad, Matts. "An Experimental Course in Mathematics for Primary Schools in Sweden." *Arithmetic Teach* 13:392–6; 1966.

Heimer, Ralph T. "Designs for Future Explorations in Programmed Instruction." *Math Teach* 59:110–4; 1966.

Hendrix, Gertrude. "Learning by Discovery." *Math Teach* 54:290–9; 1967.

Hilton, Peter. "The Continuing Work of the Cambridge Conference on School Mathematics (CCSM)." *Arithmetic Teach* 13:145–9; 1966.

Hollis, Loye Y. "A Study to Compare the Effects of Teaching First and Second Grade Mathematics on the Cuisinaire (sic)-Gattegno Method with a Traditional Method." *Sch Sci Math* 65:683–7; 1965.

Huetting, Alice, and Newell, John M. "Attitudes Toward Introduction of Modern Mathematics Program by Teachers with Large and Small Number of Years Experience." *Arithmetic Teach* 13:125–30; 1966.

Hungerman, Ann D. "Achievement and Attitude of Sixth Grade Pupils in Conventional and Contemporary Mathematics Programs." *Arithmetic Teach* 14:30–9; 1967.

Husen, Torsten. (Ed.) *International Study of Achievement in Mathematics.* 2 vols. Wiley, 1967. 672p.

Jewett, John. "The Future Supply and Demand of Mathematics Teachers." Working paper for Conference Board of Mathematical Sciences, 1966.

Johnson, Donovan A. "A Pattern for Research in the Mathematics Classroom." *Math Teach* 59:418–25; 1965.

Kline, Morris. "A Proposal for the High School Mathematics Curriculum." *Math Teach* 59:322–30; 1966.

Land, F. W. (Ed.) *New Approaches to Mathematics Teaching.* Macmillan (London), 1963. 152p.

Leiderman, Gloria F. "Mathematics and Science Programs for the Elementary School Years." *R Ed Res* 35:154–62; 1965.

Leiderman, Gloria F., and others. *The Special Curriculum Project: Pilot Program on Mathematics Learning of Culturally Disadvantaged Primary*

School Children. School Mathematics Study Group, 1966. 131p.

Lindquist, Clarence B. *Mathematics in Colleges and Universities.* USOE, 1965. 104p.

Lockard, J. David. *Report of the International Clearinghouse on Science and Mathematics Curricular Developments.* AAAS, U Maryland, 1966. 291p.

MacLean, J. R. "The Quest for an Improved Curriculum." *Arithmetic Teach* 14:136–40; 1967.

May, Kenneth O. *Programmed Learning and Mathematical Education.* Mathematical Association of America, 1965. 24p.

May, Kenneth O. "Programming and Automation." *Math Teach* 59:444–54; 1966.

Mayor, J. R. "Issues and Directions." *Arithmetic Teach* 13:349–54; 1966.

Mayor, J. R., and others. "An Implication for Teacher Education of Recent Research in Mathematics Education." *J Teach Ed* 16:483–90; 1965.

McLaughlin, Katherine L. "Summary of Current Tendencies in Elementary School Mathematics as Shown by Recent Textbooks." *El Sch J* 18:543–51; 1918.

Meserve, Bruce E., and Sobel, Max A. *Mathematics for Secondary School Teachers.* Prentice-Hall, 1962. 367p.

Mueller, Francis J. "The Public Image of New Mathematics." *Math Teach* 59:618–23; 1966.

National Committee on Mathematical Requirements. *The Reorganization of Mathematics in Secondary Education.* Houghton, 1923. 652p.

National Council of Teachers of Mathematics. *The Revolution in School Mathematics.* The Council, 1961. 90p.

National Council of Teachers of Mathematics. *An Analysis of New Mathematics Programs.* The Council, 1963. 68p.

Organization for European Economic Cooperation. *New Thinking in School Mathematics.* The Organization, 1961(a). 246p.

Organization for European Economic Cooperation. *Synopses for Modern Secondary School Mathematics.* The Organization, 1961(b). 310p.

Overholt, Elbert D. "A Piagetian Conservation Concept." *Arithmetic Teach* 12:317–26; 1965.

Paschal, Billy J. "Teaching the Culturally Disadvantaged Child." *Arithmetic Teach* 13:369–74; 1966.

Passy, Robert A. "The Effect of Cuisenaire Materials on Reasoning and Computation." *Arithmetic Teach* 10:439–40; 1963.

Payne, Holland. "What About Modern Programs in Mathematics?" *Math Teach* 58:422–4; 1965.

Rappaport, David. "Historical Factors that Have Influenced the Mathematics Program for the Primary Grades." *Sch Sci Math* 65:25–33; 1965.

Rice, J. M. "Educational Research: A Test in Arithmetic." *Ed Forum* 34:281–97; 1902.

Rising, Gerald R. "Research and Development in Mathematics and Science Education at the Minnesota School Mathematics and Science Center and the Minnesota National Laboratory." *Sch Sci Math* 65:811–20; 1965.

Scandura, Joseph M. (Ed.) *Research in Mathematics Education.* National Council of Teachers of Mathematics, 1967. 125p.

Schult, Veryl. *Present Practices in Mathematics Instruction and Supervision.* USOE, 1966. 62p.

Skypek, Dora Helen. "Geometric Concepts in Grades 4–6." *Arithmetic Teach* 12:443–9; 1965.

Small, Dwain E., and others. "A Study of Two Methods of Checking Homework in a High School Geometry Class." *Math Teach* 60:149–52; 1967.

Smith, David Eugene, and others. *Report of the American Commissioners of the International Commission on the Teaching of Mathematics.* Bulletin No. 14. USOE, 1912. 84p.

Society for Research in Child Development. *Mathematical Learning,* Monograph No. 1. U Chicago, 1965. 150p.

Spitzer, Herbert F. *Teaching Arithmetic.* NEA, 1953. 33p.

Stone, Marshall H. "Review of Goals for School Mathematics." *Math Teach* 57:353–60; 1965.

Swenson, Ester J. "How Much Real Problem Solving?" *Arithmetic Teach* 12:426–30; 1965.

Thwaites, Byran. "Mathematical Reforms in English Secondary Schools." *Math Teach* 59:42–52; 1966.

U.S. Office of Education and National Council of Teachers of Mathematics. *Preliminary Report of the Conference on the Low Archiever in Mathematics.* USOE, 1964. 23p.

Van Engen, Henry, and Gibb, E. Glenadine. *General Mental Functions Associated with Division.* Iowa State U, 1956. 181p.

Vogeli, Bruce Ramon. *Soviet Secondary Schools for the Mathematically Talented.* National Council of Teachers of Mathematics, 1967.

Weaver, J. Fred. "Patterns in Arithmetic: A Three Year Report." *Arithmetic Teach* 12:291–3; 1965.

Weaver, J. Fred. "Research on Mathematics Education, Grades K-8, for 1965." *Arithmetic Teach* 13:414–27; 1966(a).

Weaver, J. Fred. "Differentiated Instruction and School-Class Organization for Mathematical Learning Within the Elementary Grades." *Arithmetic Teach* 13:495–506; 1966(b).

Whitman, Nancy C. "Project D: Program for Talented Students in Mathematics in Secondary Schools in Hawaii." *Math Teach* 59:564–71; 1966.

Willoughby, Stephen S. *Contemporary Teaching of Secondary School Mathematics.* Wiley, 1967. 430p.

Wilson, Guy M. *Survey of the Social and Business Usage of Arithmetic.* Teachers Col, Columbia U, 1919. 62p.

Wooten, William. *SMSG—The Making of a Curriculum.* Yale U, 1965. 182p.

Young, Gail S. "Problems in the Training of Elementary School Teachers." *Arithmetic Teach* 13:380–4; 1966.

MEASUREMENT IN EDUCATION

This article will undertake to provide a general survey of the role of measurement in education under the following headings:

History of Educational Measurement
Measurement Literature
What Is Measured
How It Is Measured
Why It Is Measured
Attitudes Toward Educational Measurement
Testing Programs and Services

Eight other articles in this encyclopedia deal with these other aspects of educational measurement:
ACHIEVEMENT TESTS
INTELLIGENCE AND SPECIAL APTITUDE TESTS
MEASUREMENT THEORY
TEST USE
NORMS
SCALING
PREDICTION
MARKS AND MARKING SYSTEMS

HISTORY OF EDUCATIONAL MEASUREMENT. Apparently no comprehensive, authoritative history of tests and measurements in education has yet been written. Brief surveys of their development in ancient or in modern times have been presented by Yates (1965), Lorge (1949), and Gerberich (1963). Textbooks on educational tests and measurement, such as those by Noll (1965), Stanley (1964), and R. Thorndike and Hagen (1961) present similar summary accounts. Those who undertake to trace the development of measurement in early history frequently mention the examinations used to select civil servants in ancient China (Kuo, 1915; Du Bois, 1965), and the examinations for professors and for students in European universities during the middle ages.

In the United States, pivotal figures in the development of educational measurement were Horace Mann, J. M. Rice, E. L. Thorndike, and Ben D. Wood. It was Mann (1845) who persuaded school committees in Massachusetts to shift from oral to written examinations. Joseph M. Rice (1891) campaigned for educational reform on the basis of data gathered by wide-scale objective tests. E. Thorndike (1918) developed the techniques of objective testing and popularized the use of such tests. Wood pioneered cooperative test development, statewide surveys of tested achievement, cooperative testing programs, and electrical test-scoring equipment (Downey, 1965).

No brief summary can do justice to all who have made notable contributions to the development of educational measurement techniques, to the trends and innovations that have shaped its present role, nor to the comparatively recent backlash of criticism and opposition that these developments have stimulated in some quarters. But whether they approve or disapprove, most observers agree that the present role of measurement in education is one of powerful influence.

MEASUREMENT LITERATURE. Previous editions of this encyclopedia have carried a number of articles on educational measurement. Articles on comparable measures, evaluation, examinations, intelligence and intelligence tests, marks and marking systems, norms, rating methods, reliability, and tests (achievement) appeared in both the first (1941) and second (1950) editions. The third edition (1960) also contained articles on evaluation, intelligence, marks and marking systems, norms, reliability, and tests and examinations; and it added articles on aptitudes, measurement, and scaling, prediction, and validity.

Research in educational measurement is summarized periodically in issues of the *Review of Educational Research* (American Educational Research Association, 1965). Since 1950 these have appeared every third year in February, most recently in February 1968. The title of these issues has been "Educational and Psychological Testing." Separate issues published prior to 1950 were "Educational Tests and Their Uses" and "Psychological Tests and Their Uses."

The nature and functions of tests in education have been dealt with in recent yearbooks of various professional organizations edited by Findley (1963b), Berg (1965), and Wilhelms (1967). Annual conferences on measurement problems sponsored by the Educational Testing Service are reported in published proceedings (Educational Testing Service, 1967b, 1963b). A selection of papers from 25 years of the Invitational Conferences (Anastasi, 1966) has been published by the American Council on Education. Special conferences on testing have been reported in various publications (National Education Association, 1962; Donahue & others, 1949; National Board of Medical Examiners, 1964; Educational Testing Service, 1959; Gray, 1936; Regents, 1965).

Periodicals including *School Life* (1959), *Education* (1960), *California Journal of Secondary Education* (1960) and the *Journal of Educational Research* (Woody and others, 1935) have devoted issues to the consideration of measurement problems. A handbook on college testing was published by the American Council on Education (1959). The American Psychological Association (1966), acting jointly with the American Educational Research Association and the National Council on Measurement in Education, has published a revised set of "Standards of Educational and Psychological Tests and Manuals."

Critical reviews of published tests are published periodically in the *Personnel and Guidance Journal* (Findley, 1966) and in the *Journal of Counseling Psychology* (Crites & Merwin, 1966). A comprehensive collection of critical test reviews is available in the *Mental Measurements Yearbooks* (Buros, 1965). Sources of standardized tests are listed in *Tests in Print* (Buros, 1961).

Chauncey and Dobbin (1963), G. Hawes (1966), and Karmel (1966) have written books presenting general discussions of measurement in education. Articles on the same subject have been prepared by Tyler (1961), Berdie (1964), R. Thorndike (1964), Turnbull (1963), Whitla (1960), Dyer (1960, 1962), and Fishman and Clifford (1964). A guide to references that will answer commonly asked questions about testing has been prepared by Katz and others (1961).

WHAT IS MEASURED. Measurement in education is concerned with achievement, intelligence, special aptitudes, personality, interests, attitudes, values, motor ability, and other human characteristics. Separate articles deal with these topics in this edition of the encyclopedia. But there is one aspect of the question of what to measure in education that may merit special attention here; namely, the question of the kind or kinds of achievement that ought to be measured.

The *Taxonomy of Educational Objectives* for the cognitive domain (Bloom & others, 1956) recognizes six general areas of achievement—knowledge, comprehension, application, analysis, synthesis, and evaluation—with many subdivisions. While the authors of the *Taxonomy* disclaim any evaluation of these different areas of objectives, they do arrange them from simple to complex. Many users have come to speak of "higher" and "lower" levels in the *Taxonomy*, with preference for instruction and testing directed toward the higher levels (McGuire, 1963).

The makers and users of objective tests have long resented accusations that their tests measured only superficial aspects of educational achievement such as rote memory or recall of isolated factual details. In response, they have tended more and more to emphasize items that would be classified at higher levels in the *Taxonomy*. The leaflet *Multiple Choice Questions: A Close Look* (Educational Testing Service, 1963a) illustrates this emphasis.

But items requiring application, analysis, or evaluation tend to be complex and wordy. They may reward general brightness and test-taking skill (Millman & others, 1965) more than specific achievements. And it is by no means clear that the subject-related achievements they do measure differ in any important respects from those that would be called knowledge or comprehension. E. Thorndike's spirited defense of facts in teaching and testing (1918) has lost little in relevance and nothing in cogency with the passage of time. The flight from "factual" items in testing may be due to be reversed.

HOW IT IS MEASURED. Measurement in education can be formal (i.e., derived from tests) or informal (i.e., based on incidental, opportunistic observations). The tests used can be written, oral, or performance tests. Most formal measurements involve the use of written tests, essay or objective.

Almost all wide-scale testing programs make use of objective tests, largely because of their convenience and economy in use, but also because it is easier for test specialists to prepare high-quality tests in objective form. Quality in this context refers to the precision and objectivity of the scores and to their relevance to the abilities the test is intended to measure. Many classroom tests, particularly those prepared by teachers who have had special training in testing, are objective in form also.

It is difficult, if not impossible, to find any specialist in testing who believes that essay tests are intrinsically superior, or superior in general, to objective tests, though most of them recognize special circumstances in which essay tests ought to be used. It is not difficult, however, to find teachers and professors (Di Leo, 1965; Hanchett, 1964; McCutcheon, 1952; Shideler, 1960; Salomon, 1953) who condemn the use of objective tests in fairly general terms. Others, such as Cooke (1965), recognize the value of objective tests, but regard them as more restricted in scope and utility than essay tests. Even at this late date in the development of educational measurement, little consensus exists among practicing teachers on the age-old issue of essay versus objective tests.

One persistent critic of the multiple-choice variety of objective tests is Hoffman (1961, 1962, 1967). The essence of his criticism is that in some multiple-choice test items the response considered correct is actually less correct than one of the foils (incorrect responses), and that the brightest students are most likely to see, and be victimized by, this deficiency. Some writers have endorsed and supported Hoffman's charges (Ballinger, 1963). Others have refuted them (De Pue, 1965; Noll, 1964).

The evidence Hoffman himself presents is none too substantial. If he were to claim that only occasional multiple-choice tests items exhibit the fault he criticizes, and that only occasionally are the brightest students particularly vulnerable to such faults, few test specialists would disagree. But they do not believe he has presented sufficient evidence to support his implication that mis-keying or indeterminacy are pervasive weaknesses of multiple-choice test items, or that bright students in general have more trouble with such items than those who are less bright.

In the early development of educational testing, true–false tests were widely used (Arnold, 1929). Currently, they have a bad name not only among the opponents, but even among the supporters of objective testing (Leviton, 1967). Storey (1964, 1966) has reported studies that seem to show that the item form is almost worthless. Another study, however, indicates that the form can be used quite effectively (Burmester & Olson, 1966). Though true–false items sometimes may be trivial, ambiguous, or both, they need not be. Further, if a true–false test is reasonably long, and reasonably fair, guessing is unlikely to impair seriously the reliability of the test scores. Thus, the ill-repute of true–false test items may be to some degree undeserved.

Standardized tests are widely used in education to measure intelligence, aptitudes, and general educational development, and to supplement teacher-made tests and other bases for evaluating achievement. Like other instruments used in education, they are not universally admired. They are criticized for imperfections such as poor item quality, unbalanced coverage of the subject, inadequate norms, and lack of evidence of validity. They are blamed for abuses such as inordinately influencing what is taught, misdirecting teaching to "pass the test," and encouraging inappropriate use of test scores in judging teacher competence. Some of these criticisms reflect common misconceptions (Traxler, 1967).

Despite their imperfections and the ways in which

they are sometimes misused, standardized tests are good enough and useful enough to remain popular. Ebel (1961b), Daniels (1964), and Rudman (1964) have discussed their uses and limitations. Pending availability of some superior alternative (which will probably simply consist of better tests, more wisely used), present tests will continue to serve the general good of education.

Most teachers, at all levels of education, have less competence in the use of educational measurements than they ought to have. Morris (1961) regards their deficiencies as serious enough to cast doubt on the value of the testing done under their direction. Both he and Moore and Feldt (1963) insist that education ought not to tolerate this kind of incompetence.

Despite the crucial role of measurement in the educational enterprise, few teachers have received substantial formal training in the construction and use of educational measuring instruments. Noll (1955) has outlined what teachers need to know about this subject, and has described (1961) how they might be taught it. Ebel (1961a) described an in-service program for improving the competence of teachers in educational measurement. In another article (1962b) he outlined ten basic principles of measurement with which teachers ought to be acquainted.

Since 1950, there has been increased concern with the education of atypical students, such as the gifted and the disadvantaged, of pre-school children and of adults who wish to continue their education. Chauncey and Hilton (1965) examined the validity of aptitude tests for the highly able and found it satisfactory. Negro students and other disadvantaged groups tend to do poorly on tests. Some of their difficulties may be ascribed to bias in the tests, but much more is an honest reflection of educational and motivational deficits (Jones, 1967). The problems of testing in cultural settings different from our own were discussed by Schwarz (1963).

In 1967, the Educational Testing Service announced a new series of ability tests for pre-school and primary-school children. Baker (1965) discussed the problems of evaluating adult achievement in general. The effectiveness of existing tests of basic education when applied to adults was examined by Whittemore and others (1966) and found to be satisfactory.

Wide-scale testing programs have been aided greatly by the development of high-speed scoring machines, some of which are adapted to the scoring of multi-test batteries (Finger, 1966; O'Malley & Stafford, 1966; Miller & others, 1967). The corresponding but even more spectacular development of computers has greatly facilitated the conversion of raw scores to standard scores, the analysis of test scores and item responses, and the rapid production of score reports (Cassel & De La Briandair, 1963). Computerized test production has been described by Tracey and Legere (1964) and Richards (1966). Page (1966) has developed procedures for machine grading of essays. Viens (1963) pointed out advantages of closed-circuit television in school-wide administration of a testing program. Thus, in many ways technology has contributed to measurement in education.

WHY IT IS MEASURED. Educational aptitudes are measured for selection and placement. Educational achievements are measured to help give purpose and direction to educational efforts, and to report the degree of success in learning. Packard and Floyd (1964) have offered a general defense of tests in education. Dressel (1965), F. Hawes (1967), Traxler (1960), and Walsh (1963) have described some of the educational contributions of tests. Moore and Feldt (1963) offered suggestions for the more effective use of tests to promote learning. The role of examinations in medical education was discussed in a conference sponsored by the National Board of Medical Examiners (1964).

Many institutions use comprehensive examinations regularly (Michigan State University, 1949) or in special studies (Ebel & Stuit, 1955). Apanasewicz and Rosen (1958) have described the comprehensive final examinations used in Russian schools. The disruption of educational programs by war and the increasing interest in continuing education have encouraged and supported a number of programs for credit by examination (Kurland, 1963; Dapper, 1963; Arbolino, 1965; Graff, 1965; New York State Education Department, 1965).

ATTITUDES TOWARD EDUCATIONAL MEASUREMENT. Public and professional attitudes toward measurement in education are divided. The widespread and growing use of tests in the schools would suggest that a majority of educators feel that they are necessary and useful. Wolfle (1963), Furst (1963), Barclay (1964), Forehand (1964), and Chauncey and Hilton (1965), among others, have spoken in defense of their educational value. A Gallup Poll (American Institute of Public Opinion, 1965) showed that 48 percent of the adults in the United States favored the use of a standard nationwide examination as the basis on which to issue high school diplomas.

Surveys of teacher attitudes toward testing by Sharp (1966) and Neulinger (1966) show general support, but with considerable opposition to certain testing practices. Extensive surveys of the use of tests in schools (Goslin & others, 1965; Brim & others, 1965), of adult attitudes toward intelligence tests (Brim & others, 1965), and of the social impact of testing (Goslin, 1966) have been made with support from the Russell Sage Foundation. Summaries of these surveys have been reported in the *Education Digest* (1966) and in articles by Goslin (1963, 1967). The social consequences of testing have been viewed with alarm by Hersey (1959), Grafton (1963), Young (1958), and Black (1963). Ebel (1964) and Dyer (1961, 1962) have recognized mistakes in testing that need to be corrected, but view its social consequences as generally beneficial. Cleary and Hilton (1966) reported an investigation of possible cultural bias in the Scholastic Aptitude Test.

Intelligence tests were a particular focus of controversy during the 1960's. Yourman (1964) and Hughson (1964) debated their value in the *Phi Delta Kappan.* Loretan (1965) and Gilbert (1966) discussed their value with particular reference to New York City schools. There is increasing tendency to regard a child's score on an intelligence test as a measure of developed ability. The extent to which genetic endowment facilitates or sets limits on that development is still a subject of controversy.

The shortcomings and misuses of educational tests were discussed in some detail by Trump (1963), Shideler (1960), and Macdonald and Clements (1966). Peters (1966) and Marshall (1967) deplore the overuse of tests in education. Weitz (1966) has described misuses, and Mehrens (1967) considered some consequences of misuse. Trow (1966) urged testers to develop more content or criterion-referenced meaning in test scores.

School administrators have studied the influence of external standardized tests on school programs, and have expressed concern over their possible harmful effects (American Association of School Administrators, 1962; Lake, 1962). One particular concern, the influence of external tests on the curriculum, has been articulated by Crosby (1966). Traxler (1958), however, pointed out that the danger can easily be exaggerated. Another particular concern, especially affecting personality inventories, is the invasion of privacy (Yamamoto 1966, U.S. Office of Science and Technology 1967). Unquestionably, some investigators have used the prestige of scientific research to justify offensive, and often unproductive, probing into highly personal and private affairs.

There is a sizable group of educators that deplores the use of tests to measure educational achievement, seeing it as a deterrent to effective learning (Thelen, 1960) and as a source of frustration and failure to substantial groups of students (Kelley, 1966). These critics tend to emphasize pretesting and diagnostic testing as aids to learning, and to prefer detailed reports on specific achievements and problems (Taba & Sawin, 1962; Morgan, 1959; Wilhelms, 1967). Using test information is a thoroughly commendable activity in education, but the use of tests to facilitate the process of education does not prevent their use to assess the product of education. Indeed, most teachers seem to agree that to do a good job in the process of education, one must carefully evaluate the product of education.

TESTING PROGRAMS AND SERVICES. Most school systems have established and used some kind of a local testing program. Most of them also participate, willingly or reluctantly, in statewide and nationwide testing programs. Bauernfeind (1963) has offered suggestions for building a local-school testing program. Criteria of an effective program were outlined by Lindquist (1951). Findley (1963a) described a complete testing program. A National Society for the Study of Education Yearbook (1963) discussed the impact and improvement of such programs. Large-scale testing programs for guidance were described and discussed by Educational Testing Service (1958). Womer (1961) pointed to some misconceptions surrounding testing programs, while Sabel (1962) and Snider (1963) discussed problems associated with them.

The external character of some testing programs—that is, the fact that they are established and operated by agencies outside of the local school—has been a source of some concern. The oldest, and probably the most successful of such programs recently celebrated its centenary (Regents, 1965). The much newer program mandated by the legislature of the state of California, has stimulated considerable discussion, and some expressions of anguish (Shellhamer, 1963; McCreary, 1964; Badal, 1966). The University of Kansas (1964) was host to a conference on external testing programs, and an issue of the *Journal of Secondary Education* (1963) carried a symposium on their influence. Dressel (1964) presented a balanced discussion of the role of such programs in education. A response to the criticisms of such programs was offered by Ebel (1962a).

One of the agencies most extensively involved in the operation of wide-scale testing programs is the Educational Testing Service. In addition to program development and operations which include test construction, administration, scoring, reporting, and analysis, ETS is involved in extensive research on testing and other educational problems. The scope and nature of its activities are described in annual reports of its president (Educational Testing Service, 1967a).

Two new nationwide programs involving the use of tests attracted wide attention in the decade of the 1960's. One was Project Talent, supported by the U.S. Office of Education and directed by Flanagan (Dailey & Shacoft, 1961). In addition to providing a survey of intellectual talents of students enrolled in school, this project undertook to establish basic standards with which a variety of other measures of educational attainment could be compared (Cooley & Miller, 1965). Follow-up studies of the educational and vocational careers of the students tested are being conducted (Flanagan & others, 1966).

The other program, still in development during 1967, is commonly referred to as National Assessment (Higgins & Merwin, 1967). Taking care to prevent unfair, and possibly embarrassing comparisons among students or among schools, the directors of the program seek to provide data on the educational attainments of groups from different regions, residential environments, economic levels, and age ranges. Opponents fear that the program may lead to Federal control of education, and to a national curriculum (Hand, 1965). Others object to the fact that the program was conceived and developed outside the "establishment" of educational administration. Its merits and dangers have been debated vigorously (National Education Association, 1966; Beymer, 1966).

CONCLUDING STATEMENT. Despite their limitations and imperfections, despite the occasional misuses, and despite the criticisms, reasonable and unreasonable, educational measurements have established themselves as versatile, indispensable tools of effective education. They are likely to be used more widely, and more wisely, in the future than they have been in the past.

Robert L. Ebel
Michigan State University

References

American Association of School Administrators. *Testing, Testing, Testing.* AASA, 1962. 32p.

American Council on Education. *College Testing: A Guide to Practices and Programs.* ACE, 1959. 189p.

American Educational Research Association. *Review of Educational Research.* AERA, 1965.

American Institute of Public Opinion. "Standard Nationwide Examination to Qualify for School Diploma?" In Gallup Poll Reports. The Institute, 1965.

American Psychological Association. *Standards for Educational and Psychological Tests and Manuals.* APA, 1966. 40p.

Anastasi, Anne. (Ed.) *Testing Problems in Perspective.* ACE, 1966. 671p.

Apanasewicz, Nellie, and Rosen, Seymour M. *Final Examinations in the Russian Ten-Year School.* HEW, 1958. 20p.

Arbolino, Jack N. *A Report to the Trustees of the College Entrance Examination Board: The Council on College-Level Examinations.* CEEB, 1965. 24p.

Arnold, H. L. "Defense of the True-false Test." *Col Q Sec Ed* 4:145–6; 1929.

Badal, A. W. "What Next for State Testing in California?" *California J Ed Res* 17:206–8; 1966.

Baker, J. F. "Evaluating Adult Achievement." *J Ed* 147:51–61; 1965.

Ballinger, S. E. "Of Testing and Its Tyranny." *Phi Delta Kappan* 44:176–80; 1963.

Barclay, J. R. "Attack on Testing and Counseling: an Examination and Reappraisal." *Personnel and Guid J* 43:6–16; 1964. Discussion 43:715–16; 1965.

Bauernfeind, Robert H. *Building A School Testing Program.* Houghton, 1963. 343p.

Berdie, R. F. "Measurement of Men." *Teach Col Rec* 66:113–22; 1964.

Berg, Harry D. (Ed.) *Evaluation in Social Studies.* 35th Yearbook. National Council for the Social Studies, 1965. 251p.

Beymer, L. "Pros and Cons of the National Assessment Project." *Clearing House* 40:540–3; 1966.

Black, Hillel. *They Shall Not Pass.* Morrow, 1963. 342p.

Bloom, Benjamin S., and others. *Taxonomy of Educational Objectives.* McKay, 1956. 207p.

Brim, Orville G., Jr., and others. *Experiences and Attitudes of American Adults Concerning Standardized Intelligence Tests.* Russell Sage, 1965.

Burmester M. A., and Olson, L. A. "Comparison of Item Statistics for Items in Multiple Choice and in Alternative Response Form." *Sci Ed* 50:467–70; 1966.

Buros, Oscar K. *Tests in Print.* Gryphon, 1961.

Buros, Oscar K. (Ed.) *Sixth Mental Measurements Yearbook.* Gryphon, 1965. 1714p.

California Journal of Secondary Education. "Place of Testing and Evaluation in Learning." *California J Sec Ed* 35:40–65; 1960.

Cassel, R. N., and De La Briandair, R. "Fast Processing of Psychological Tests using High Speed Computing Machines." *Ed and Psychol M* 23:461–6; 1963.

Chauncey, Henry, and Dobbin, John E. *Testing: Its Place In Education Today.* Harper, 1963. 223p.

Chauncey, Henry, and Hilton, Thomas L. "Are Aptitude Tests Valid for the Highly Able?" *Sci* 148:1297–304; 1965.

Cleary, T. Anne, and Hilton, Thomas L. *An Investigation of Item Bias* ETS, 1966. 20p.

Cooke, G. H. "Objective Tests." *Peabody J Ed* 43:145–51; 1965.

Cooley, W. W., and Miller, J. D. "Project Talent Tests as a National Standard." *Personnel and Guid J* 43:1038–44; 1965.

Crites, J. O., and Merwin, J. C. (Eds.) "Test Reviews." *J Counseling Psychol* 14:392–4; 1967.

Crosby, M. "Curriculum Control? We Can Get It for You Wholesale." *Ed Leadership* 24:119–23; 1966.

Dailey, John T., and Shaycoft, Marion F. *Types of Tests in Project Talent.* HEW, 1961. 62p.

Daniels, V. "Concerning the Validity of Standardized Tests." *Clearing House* 39:12–4; 1964.

Dapper, Gloria. "It's What's Up Top That Counts." *Saturday R* 48–9; 1963.

De Pue, P. "Multiple Choice and the Either-or Fallacy." *Sch and Soc* 93:154–6; 1965.

Di Leo, J. M. "Testing and Evaluation; A Critique of a Contemporary Theory." *New York State Ed* 52:18–9; 1965.

Donahue, Wilma T., and others. *The Measurement of Student Adjustment and Achievement.* U Michigan Press, 1949. 256p.

Downey, Matthew T. *Ben O. Wood Educational Reformer.* ETS, 1965. 106p.

Dressel, P. L. "Role of External Testing Programs in Education." *Ed Rec* 45:161–6; 1964.

Dressel, P. L. "Role of Evaluation in Teaching and Learning." *Nat Council Social Stud Yearbook* 35:1–20; 1965.

Du Bois, Philip. "A Test-Dominated Society: China 1115 B.C.–1905 A.D." In *Proceedings of the 1964 Invitational Conference on Testing Problems.* ETS, 1965. p. 3–11.

Dyer, H. S. "On the Assessment of Academic Achievement." *Teach Col Rec* 62:164–72; 1960.

Dyer, H. S. "Is Testing a Menace to Education?" *New York State Ed* 49:16–9; 1961.

Dyer, H. S. "Testing's Nine Major Pitfalls." *Senior Scholastic* 80:21T–3T; 1962.

Ebel, R. L. "Standardized Achievement Tests: Uses and Limitations." *Nat El Prin* 41:29–32; 1961(*b*).

Ebel, R. L. "Improving the Competence of Teachers in Educational Measurement." *Clearing House* 36:67–71; 1961(*a*).

Ebel, R. L. "External Testing: Response to Challenge." *Teach Col Rec* 64:190–8; 1962(a).

Ebel, R. L. "Measurement and the Teacher." *Ed Leadership* 20:20–4+; 1962(b).

Ebel, R. L. "Social Consequences of Educational Testing." *Sch and Soc* 92:331–4; 1964.

Ebel, Robert L., and Stuit, Dewey B. *A Study of the Relationship Between the Educational Backgrounds of Students and Their Performance in Comprehensive Examinations Designed to Measure Outcomes of General Education*. State U Iowa, 1955. 46p.

Education. "Eight Critical Questions About the Use of Tests." *Ed* 8:67–8; 1960.

Education Digest. "Ability Testing and the American Spirit." *Ed Digest* 32:18–21; 1966.

Educational Testing Service. *Large-Scale Programs of Testing for Guidance*. ETS, 1958.

Educational Testing Service. *Editors and Writers Conference on Testing*. ETS, 1959.

Educational Testing Service. *Multiple-Choice Questions: A Close Look*. ETS, 1963(a). 43p.

Educational Testing Service. *The Twelfth Annual Western Regional Conference on Testing Problems*. ETS, 1963(b). 42p.

Educational Testing Service. *Educational Testing Service: Annual Report 1965–1966*. ETS, 1967(a). 127p.

Educational Testing Service. *Proceedings of the 1966 Invitational Conference on Testing Problems*. ETS, 1967(b). 123p.

Findley, W. G. "Complete Testing Program." *Theory Into Practice* a:192–8; 1963(a).

Findley, W. G. (Ed.) *The Impact and Improvement of School Testing Programs*. 62nd Yearbook. Part II. U Chicago Press, 1963(b). 304p.

Findley, W. G. (Ed.) "Testing the Test." *Personnel and Guid J* 45:72–7; 1966.

Finger, J. A. "Machine Scoring Answer Sheet Form for the IBM 1231 Optical Scanner." *Ed Psychol M* 26:725–7; 1966.

Fishman, J. A., and Clifford, P. I. "What Can Mass Testing Programs Do for-and-to the Pursuit of Excellence in American Education?" *Harvard Ed R* 34:63–97; 1964.

Flanagan, John C., and others. *Project Talent: One-Year Follow-Up Studies*. U Pittsburgh, 1966. 250p.

Forehand, G. A. "Comments on Comments on Testing." *Ed Psychol Meas* 24:853–9; 1964.

Furst, E. J. "Question of Abuses in the Use of Aptitude and Achievements Tests." *Theory Into Practice* 2:199–204; 1963.

Gerberich, J. Raymond. "The Development of Educational Testing." *Theory Into Practice* 2:184–91; 1963.

Gilbert, H. B. "I.Q. Test Ban." *Ed Digest* 31:38–40; 1966.

Goslin, David A. "Social Impact of Standardized Testing." *NEA J* 52:20–2; 1963.

Goslin, David A. *The Search For Ability: Standardized Testing in Social Perspective*. Wiley, 1966. 204p.

Goslin, David A. "Social Impact of Testing." *Personnel and Guid J* 54:676–82; 1967.

Goslin, David A., and others. *The Use of Standardized Tests in Elementary Schools*. Russell Sage, 1965. 199p.

Graff, K. "High School Equivalency Program." *Voc Guid Q* 13:297–9; 1965.

Grafton, S. "Child Sorters." *McCalls* 90:98–101+; 1963.

Gray, William S. (Ed.) *Tests and Measurements in Higher Education*. U Chicago Press, 1936. 237p.

Hanchett, W. "Essay Examination." *J Higher Ed* 35:27–31; 1964.

Hand, H. C. "National Assessment Viewed as the Camel's Nose." *Phi Delta Kappan* 47:8–13, 1965.

Hawes, F. R. "Your Child and Testing." *NEA J* 56:37–52; 1967.

Hawes, Gene R. *How Testing Helps Your Child in School and College*. Association Press, 1966. 127p.

Hersey, John. *Intelligence, Choice, and Consent*. Woodrow Wilson Foundation, 1959. 28p.

Higgins M. J., and J. C. Merwin "Assessing the Progress of Education: A Second Report." *Phi Delta Kappan* 48:378–80; 1967.

Hoffman, B. "Tyranny of Multiple-Choice Tests." *Harper* 222: 37–44; 1961.

Hoffman, B. "Towards Less Emphasis on Multiple Choice Tests." *Teach Col Rec* 64:183–9; 1962.

Hoffman, B. "Psychometric Scientism." *Phi Delta Kappan* 48:381–6; 1967.

Hughson, A. "Case for Intelligence Testing." *Phi Delta Kappan* 46:106–8; 1964.

Jones, J. L. "Assessing the Academic Achievement of Negro Students." *Clearing House* 39:108–12; 1967.

Journal of Secondary Education. "State and National Curriculum and Testing Programs: Ally or Enemy of Expertness?" *J Sec Ed* 38:26–64; 1963.

Karmel, Louis J. *Testing in Our Schools*. Macmillan, 1966. 112p.

Katz, M., and others. "Testing, Testing." *Lib J* 86:838–44; 1961

Kelley, E. C. "News Approaches to Educational Outcomes." *Ed Leadership* 24:112–4; 1966.

Kuo, Ping Wen. *The Chinese System of Public Education*. Teachers Col, Columbia U, 1915. 209p.

Kurland, N. D. "College Proficiency Examinations and Honors Programs" *Sup Stud* 5:709; 1963.

Lake, E. G. "Case Against External Standardized Tests." *Nations Sch* 70:51–3; 1962.

Leviton, H. S. "Critical Analysis of Standardized Testing." *Clearing House*, 41:391–5; 1967.

Lindquist, E. F. "Some Criteria of an Effective High School Testing Program." In Traxter, A. (Ed.) *Measurement and Evaluation in the Improvement of Education*. ACE, 1951. p. 17–33.

Loretan, J. O. "Decline and Fall of Group Intelligence Testing." *Teach Col Rec* 67:10–7; 1965.

Lorge, Irving. "Trends in the Measurement of Achievement." In Donahue, Wilma T., and others. (Eds.) *The Measurement of Student Adjustment and Achievement*. U Michigan Press, 1949. p. 85–96.

Macdonald, V. B., and Clements, H. M. "Moral Concerns in Assessing Pupil Growth." *Nat El Prin* 45:29–33; 1966.

Mann, Horace. "Report of the Annual Examining Committees of the Boston Grammar and Writing Schools." *Common Sch J* 21:329–36; 1845.

Marshall, M. S. "Too Much Weighing." *Phi Delta Kappan* 48:281–4; 1967.

McCreary, W. H. "Policy Statement on the Use of Standardized Tests in California Schools." *California Ed* 2:8–10; 1964.

McCutcheon, Roger P. "The English Professor and His Natural Enemies." *AAUP B* 37:666–7; 1952.

McGuire, Christine. *Research in the Process Approach to the Construction and Analysis of Medical Examinations.* 20th Yearbook. NCME, 1963. p. 7–16.

Mehrens, William A. "The Consequences of Misusing Test Results." *Nat El Prin* 47:62–4; 1967.

Michigan State University. *Comprehensive Examinations in a Program of General Education.* Michigan State Col Press, 1949. 165p.

Miller, C. D., and others. "Scoring, Analyzing, and Reporting Classroom Tests Using an Optical Reader and 1401 Computer." *Ed and Psychol M* 27:159–64; 1967.

Millman, Jason, and others. "An Analysis of Test Wiseness." *Ed and Psychol Meas* 25:707–26; 1965.

Moore, G. D., and Feldt, L. "Positive Approach to the Use of Test Results." *Nat El Prin* 42:65–70; 1963.

Morgan, H. G. "What is Effective Evaluation." *Nat Ed Assn J* 48:15–7; 1959.

Morris, J. R. "To Test or Not to Test." *Nat Assn Sec Sch Prin B* 45:112–7; 1961.

National Board of Medical Examiners. *Examinations and their Role in Evaluation of Medical Education and Qualification for Practice.* The Board, 1964. 158p.

National Education Association. *Toward Better Evaluation of Learning.* NEA, 1962. 36p.

National Education Association. *National Educational Assessment: Pro and Con National Education Association and American Association of School Administrators.* NEA, 1966. 56p.

National Society for the Study of Education. *The Impact and Improvement of School Testing Programs.* 62nd Yearbook, NSSE. U Chicago Press, 1963. 304p.

Neulinger J. "Attitudes of American Secondary School Students Toward the Use of Intelligence Tests." *Personnel and Guid J* 45:337–41; 1966.

New York State Education Department. *The New York College Proficiency Examination Program.* The Department, 1965. 77p.

Noll, Victor H. "Requirements in Educational Measurement for Prospective Teachers." *Sch and Soc* 82:88–90; 1955.

Noll, Victor H. "Preservice Preparation of Teachers in Measurement." In *Measurement and Research in Today's Schools.* ACE, 1961. 65–75p.

Noll, Victor H. *Testing Under Fire.* Address given at invitational conference on testing problems, Dalhousie University, Halifax, Nova Scotia, May 25, 1964. (Available from Harcourt)

Noll, Victor H. *Introduction to Educational Measurement.* 2nd ed. Houghton, 1965. 509p.

O'Malley, J. M., and Stafford, C. "Scoring and Analyzing Teacher-made Tests with an IBM 1620." *Ed Psychol Meas* 26:715–7; 1966.

Packard, A. G., and Floyd, R. C. "Don't Throw Out Those Tests." *Ed Digest* 29:1–4; 1964.

Page, Ellis B. "Grading Essays by Computer." *Phi Delta Kappan* 47:238–43; 1966.

Peters, H. J. "Testing or Testomania." *Clearing House* 41:223–6; 1966.

Regents. *Proceedings Regents Symposium on Testing 1865–1965 Centennial of Regents Examinations.* U State of New York, State Education Department, 1965. 79p.

Review of Educational Research. "Educational and Psychological Testing." *R Ed Res* 35: 1–101; 1965.

Rice, Joseph M. "Need School Be a Blight to Child-Life." *Forum* 12:529–35; 1891.

Richards, James M., Jr. *Can Computers Write College Admissions Tests?* ACT, 1966. 11p.

Rudman, Herbert C. "How Good Are Standardized Achievement Tests." *Nat El Prin* 44:32–8; 1964.

Sabel, S. "Problems Presented by Large-Scale Testing." *H Points* 44:32–7; 1962.

Salomon, Louis B. "Punch-drunk with Punch Cards." *AAUP B* 39:441–51; 1953.

School Life "Testing Issue." *Sch Life* 42:3–25; 1959.

Schwarz, P. A. "Adapting Tests to the Cultural Setting." *Ed Psychol Meas* 23:673–86; 1963.

Sharp, E. W. "How Teachers See Testing." *Ed Leadership* 24:141–3; 1966.

Shellhamer, Thomas A. "Teaching and Statewide Testing." *J Sec Ed* 38:55–8; 1963.

Shideler, Emerson W. "What do Examinations Teach." *AAUP B* 46:277–80; 1960.

Snider, G. R. "Secondary School and Testing Programs." *Teach Col Rec* 65:57–67; 1963.

Stanley, Julian C. "Measurement in Today's Schools." 4th ed. Prentice-Hall, 1964. 414p.

Storey, A. G. "Achievement Testing and the True-false Item Case; a review of the evidence in the true-false item case." *Canadian Ed Res Digest* 4:261–7; 1964.

Storey, A. G. "Review of Evidence or the Case Against the True-false Item." *J Ed Res* 59:282–5; 1966.

Taba H., and Sawin, E. I. "Proposed Model in Evaluation." *Ed Leadership* 20:57–9; 1962.

Thelen, H. A. "Triumph of Achievement over Inquiry in Education." *Ed Sch J* 60:190–7; 1960.

Thorndike, E. L. "The Nature, Purposes, and General Methods of Measurements of Educational Products." *Yearbook* NSSE. 17:16–24; 1918.

Thorndike, E. L. "In Defense of Facts." *J Adult Ed* 7:381–8; 1935.

Thorndike R. L. "Educational Decisions and Human Assessment." *Teach Col Rec* 66:103–12; 1964.

Thorndike, R. L., and Hagen, Elizabeth. *Measurement and Evaluation in Psychology and Education.* 2nd ed. Wiley, 1961. 602p.

Tracey, W. R., and Legere, C. L. J. "Automated System of Test Production." *J Ed Res* 57:328–32; 1964.

Traxler, A. E. "Are the Professional Test-Makers

Determining What We Teach?" *Sch R* 66:144–51; 1958.
Traxler, A. E. "Educational Measurement: An Aid to School Administration." *Sch R* 68:196–209; 1960.
Traxler, A. E. "Some Misconceptions About Standardized Testing." *Ed* 87:407–10; 1967.
Trow, W. C. "On Marks, Norms, and Proficiency Scores." *Phi Delta Kappan* 48:171–3; 1966.
Trump, J. L. "What's Wrong with Testing." *Theory Into Practice* 2:235–42; 1963.
Turnbull, W. W. "Testing for Guidance and Selection." *Phi Delta Kappan* 44:372–8; 1963
Tyler, R. W. "Educational Measurement, A Broad Perspective." *Nat Ed Prin* 41:8–13; 1961.
U.S. Office of Science and Technology *Privacy and Behavioral Research.* GPO 1967. 130p.
University of Kansas. *University of Kansas Conference on External Testing Programs.* U Kansas Pub, 1964. 24p.
Viens, R. G. "Group Testing Via Closed-Circuit Television." *Voc Guid Q* 11:80–4; 1963.
Walsh, J. J. "Testing: a Catalyst for Education Innovations." *Theory Into Practice* 2:199–204; 1963.
Weitz, H. "There Ought not to be a Law Now! Misuse of Tests." *Ed Forum* 30:407–12; 1966.
Whitla, D. K. "Measurement for Educational Policy." *Ed Rec* 41:215–23; 1960.
Whittemore, R. G., and others. "Can We Use Existing Tests for Adult Basic Education." *Adult Ed* 17:19–29; 1966.
Wilhelms, Fred T. *Evaluation as Feedback and Guide.* ASCD, 1967. 283p.
Wolfle, D. "Educational Tests." *Sci* 142:1529; 1963. Discussion 143:997 145:533, 146:171, 598, 113 Mr 6 A 7 09, 30 N 27 1964.
Womer, F. B. "Testing Programs—Misconceptions, Misuses, Overuse." *Michigan J Sec Ed* 60:153–61; 1961.
Woody, Clifford, and others. "A Symposium on the Effects of Measurement on Instruction." *J Ed Res* 28:481–527; 1935.
Yamamoto, K. "Psychological Testing: Invasion of Privacy?" *Ed Leadership* 23:363–8; 1966.
Yates, Alfred. "Examinations." *Encyclopedia Brittanica* 8:931–8; 1965.
Young, Michael D. *The Rise of the Meritocracy.* Thames and Hudson, 1958. 160p.
Yourman, J. "Case Against Group I.Q. Testing." *Phi Delta Kappan* 46:108–10; 1964.

MEASUREMENT THEORY

NATURE OF MEASUREMENT. Measurement is any procedure whereby numbers are uniquely assigned to *entities*: persons, other organisms, objects, statements, events, etc. We first define a *domain* (finite or infinite) of entities, and an *attribute* of these entities, such as length, weight, beauty, aggressiveness, occupation, or hair color. The entities are to be measured with respect to the categories or magnitudes of the attribute, in such a way as to preserve certain defined empirical *relations* among these categories or magnitudes. The entities, the categories or magnitudes of the attribute, and the relations form an *empirical relational system*. We then specify a set of numbers (usually a subset of the real numbers), a set of relations among these numbers, and a set of axioms governing the relations; i.e., a *numerical relational system*. Each numerical relation must parallel exactly one empirical relation.

The first problem of measurement is to show that the empirical relations obey the axioms of the numerical system in such a manner that one entity can be assigned one and only one number. Such an assignment is termed *homomorphic*. If, in addition, a given number can be assigned to one and only one entity, the assignment is termed *isomorphic*.

Quite commonly, different sets of numbers (with the same relations and axioms) may be assigned to the entities; i.e., the *units of measurement* are arbitrary. The second problem of measurement is to define the class of admissible transformations from one set of numbers to another. The admissible transformations define the uniqueness of the scale types, and set limits on the allowable statistical operations.

Nominal Scales. Examples of an isomorphic nominal scale are the numbers assigned to football players, telephone numbers, or the serial numbers assigned to experimental subjects. The attribute is individual identity, any set of distinct numbers may be used, and any one-to-one transformation into another set of distinct numbers is admissible. The numbers are used merely for perceptual or mechanical convenience (e.g., for collating the answer sheets of examinees) or for preserving individual anonymity, and *no* statistical operations are allowable.

A homomorphic nominal scale is a *classification system* according to two or more categories of an attribute such as sex, occupation, national origin, style of architecture, area of residence, etc. The area codes preceding individual telephone numbers form a homomorphic nominal scale. In a classification system, all the entities of one category are considered *equivalent* with respect to the attribute. Equivalence is denoted by the symbol $=$. The axioms of an equivalence relation are that it be

1. Reflexive: $a = a$ (each entity is assigned to one and only one category);
2. Symmetric. if $a = b$, then $b = a$;
3. Transitive: if $a = b$ and $b = c$, then $a = c$.

Thus all entities in one category are assigned the same number, those in different categories are assigned different numbers, and every entity in the domain is assigned one and only one number. Any unique one-to-one transformation is admissible.

Allowable statistics relate to the frequencies (counts) of the entities in each category. We can compute the percentage or proportion of entities in each category, hypotheses about relative proportions can be tested by the Chi-square test, and if the entities are cross-classified according to two different attributes (e.g., occupation and national origin), the hypothesis of association can be measured on an ordinal scale by the contingency coefficient. These are merely examples; large portions of signal-detection theory and information theory deal essentially with nominal scaling procedures. Coombs (1953), Stevens (1959), and others have suggested that perception and concept formation are basically nominal scaling: recognition of equivalence classes and classification of stimuli. Other writers, e.g. Campbell (1928) and the British committee appointed to consider the possibility of quantitative estimates of sensory events (Campbell & others, 1940), would not term nominal or even ordinal scaling "measurement." For nominal scales, the admissible transformations include substitution of letters, words, or any other set of unique symbols for numbers.

Nominal scaling may be imposed arbitrarily on a continuous variable, even one which is continuous in more than one dimension. Hair color and eye color are examples. In such cases there will inevitably be imprecise boundaries between categories and disagreements among observers, resulting in errors of classification. These scales might be termed *quasi-nominal scales*. They have the same values and uses as any other nominal scales, subject to the limitation of unreliability in classification.

Ordinal Scales. In the isomorphic case there is an empirical asymmetric relation between every two entities of the empirical system, denoted by $>$. This symbol may mean "is older than," "is later than," "scratches," "pecks," "is more beautiful than," etc.; the corresponding attributes being age, time, hardness, aggression, beauty. In the numerical system, $>$ denotes "is greater than," and the following axioms define a *series*:

1. Connected: If $a \neq b$, then $a > b$ or $b > a$;
2. Asymmetric: If $a > b$, then $b \not> a$ and $a \neq b$;
3. Transitive: If $a > b$ and $b > c$, then $a > c$.

In the empirical system, $a \neq b$ implies merely that a and b are different entities. If the numbers are the positive integers, these axioms define the ordinal numerals.

If the entities are chicks and we define aggression as pecking, the existence of an isomorphic ordinal scale of aggression is demonstrated by observing that for every pair of chicks these axioms describe the behavior. If the entities are crystalline minerals and we define the harder of two minerals as the one which scratches the other, the existence of an isomorphic ordinal scale of hardness is demonstrated by showing that for every pair of minerals the axioms hold. For ordinal scales, then, the validity of the numerical assignment procedure is demonstrated by the method of paired comparisons.

Isomorphic ordinal scales are unique under any *monotonic* transformation. If a and b are any two original numbers, and a' and b' are the corresponding transformed numbers, the transformation is monotonic increasing if $(a > b)$ implies $(a' > b')$ for all pairs, and monotonic decreasing if $(a > b)$ implies $(a' < b')$ for all pairs. Thus the positive integers could be replaced by their squares, their positive square roots, their complements, their reciprocals, the even integers, or any arbitrary increasing or decreasing series. But if some of the original numbers were positive and some negative, their squares would not represent a monotonic transformation.

If we substitute $<$ for $>$ with the *same* empirical meaning and the same axioms (as in assigning rank 1 to the "highest" or "best" entity instead of the "lowest" or "poorest"), the result would still be an isomorphic ordinal scale.

In the homomorphic case we have a set of *ordered categories*, at least one of which includes two or more entities. The entities in each category are considered equivalent with respect to the attribute; they must obey the axioms of equivalence, and $a = b$ means that a and b are in the same category and are assigned the same number. Instead of a series, as in the isomorphic case, we have a *quasi-series*, and the axioms for $>$ are that it be

1. Irreflexive: If $a = b$, then $a \not> b$ and $b \not> a$;
2. Connected: If $a \neq b$, then $a > b$ or $b > a$;
3. Transitive: If $a > b$ and $b \geq c$, then $a > c$.

In the case of the chicks, two are in the same category (equally aggressive) if they do not peck each other. Similarly, two minerals are in the same category if neither scratches the other. But if two chicks peck each other or two minerals scratch each other, the irreflexive axiom is violated and we do not have an ordinal scale.

For a homomorphic ordinal scale, the admissible monotonic transformations are merely non-decreasing or non-increasing. We add $(a = b)$ implies $(a' = b')$ to the previous definitions of monotonicity.

A considerable variety of statistical procedures are allowable with ordinal scales. Medians, quartiles, and percentiles may be computed, but since they merely designate particular entities or categories they are seldom used. A single ordinal scale is not characterized by a measure of dispersion, but if the members of two groups are arranged in one series of quasi-series, the hypothesis of equal variability can be tested by the Siegel-Tukey (1960) procedure and other methods. Covariation can be measured on an ordinal scale by the Kendall and Spearman rank correlation coefficients (Kendall, 1962), and hypotheses of displacement (roughly equivalent to equality of medians) can be tested by the Wilcoxon-Mann-Whitney, Kruskal-Wallis, and allied procedures (Kruskal & Wallis, 1952).

Quasi-ordinal Scales. When the method of paired comparisons is used as a forced-choice method, the judgment "equal" not being allowed, we may obtain *circular triads*, such as $a > b$, $b > c$, but $c > a$, violating the transitivity axiom. If there are n entities and k circular triads, the *coefficient of consistency* (Kendall, 1962) is

$$C = 1 - \frac{24k}{n^3 - n}, \text{ if } n \text{ is odd;}$$

$$C = 1 - \frac{24k}{n^3 - 4n}, \text{ if } n \text{ is even.}$$

The value of C will be 1 if $k = 0$, and will tend to 0 if all decisions are random. If C is high, we can assign one point to each entity each time he (or it) is judged $>$ another entity, sum the points for each entity, and rank the sums to yield a quasi-ordinal scale. It will be an ordinal scale if and only if $k = 0$.

If several judges rank the same entities on the same attribute, with or without the types of errors represented by circular triads in the paired-comparison procedure, they may still disagree in their rankings. The amount of agreement (the inter-judge reliability) can be estimated by the coefficient of concordance or the average rank correlation (Kendall, 1962). If these coefficients are fairly high, Kendall shows that the best single ranking of the entities is obtained by summing the ranks of each entity and ranking the sums; "best" in the sense that the sum of squares of all the differences between the single ranks and the final ranks will be a minimum. For these operations, the numbers assigned must be the positive integers, and if the original rankings include ties, they must be resolved by the mean-rank procedure. The summing of ranks (and the summing of points in the previous paragraph) are not strictly ordinal procedures, and monotonic transformations are admissible only with the final quasi-ordinal scales.

Interval Scales. An interval scale is defined as one which has arbitrary but equal units of measurement and an arbitrary zero-point. The intuitive meaning of this statement is quite clear, but the axiomatic definition is complex and will not be attempted here. The admissible transformations are not only one-to-one and monotonic; they are also linear. If x represents a particular point on one interval scale, and y represents the same point on another interval scale measuring the same attribute, then

$$y = a + bx; \text{ and } x = y - \frac{1}{b}\frac{a}{b},$$

where a and b are constants. The classic illustrations of interval scales are the Fahrenheit and Centigrade scales of temperature. On the Centigrade scale 0 and 100 are, respectively, the freezing point and boiling point of water at sea-level pressure. The corresponding points on the Fahrenheit scale are 32 and 212, and the transformation equations are

$$F° = 32 + 1.8 \, C°, \text{ and } C° = .556 \, F° - 17.778.$$

Interval-scale units may be added and subtracted, but they may not be multiplied or divided. We can *not* say that Centigrade temperature 100° means twice as hot as Centigrade temperature 50°. On the other hand, there are only a few statistical procedures (e.g., the coefficient of variation, the geometric mean, and the harmonic mean) which require a true zero point. Almost all of the common statistical procedures are allowable with interval scales.

Quasi-interval Scales. A quasi-interval scale is one whose successive units vary *randomly* in magnitude. The standard deviation of the magnitudes of these units must be small in comparison to the standard deviation of the scores of any group of entities the scale is intended to measure if the scale is to have any useful reliability. Random variation of successive units implies that the magnitudes of the scale units and their scale locations will be statistically independent. Quasi-interval scales yield more or less unreliable measurements, but all ordinary statistical procedures are allowable with them.

Ratio Scales. A ratio scale is an interval scale having a true zero-point which denotes exactly none of the quantity measured. Length and weight are common examples. The numerical series consists usually of the positive real numbers or some subset thereof, and zero. The admissible transformations are multiplication by an arbitrary constant; i.e., the linear transformation $y = a + bx$ with $a = 0$. Thus if the length of an object is x inches, its length is also $2.54 \, x$ centimeters; and if its length is y centimeters, its length is also $1/2.54$ or $.3937 \, y$ inches.

Ratio scale units may be multiplied and divided as well as added and subtracted. If one person weighs 100 pounds and another weighs 200 pounds, the second *is* exactly twice as heavy as the first. All ordinary statistics are allowable with ratio scales, *including* the coefficient of variation, the geometric mean, the logarithmic standard deviation, the harmonic mean, the contraharmonic mean, etc.

Quasi-ratio Scales. Like quasi-interval scales, quasi-ratio scales have randomly variable units whose magnitudes are statistically independent of scale location, but they also have true zero-points. All of the statistics allowable with ratio scales are also allowable with quasi-ratio scales, with the reservation of reduced reliability.

Absolute Scales. An absolute scale is a ratio scale whose units of measurement are fixed, so that *no* transformation is admissible. The commonest examples are counts (e.g., number of persons per family).

FUNDAMENTAL, DERIVED, AND POINTER MEASUREMENT. In fundamental measurement, the direct empirical relations among the entities must parallel the relations of the numerical system and obey its axioms. The empirical relations thus yield an operational definition of the attribute measured. Clear examples are the pecking orders of chicks and the scratching orders of minerals. For a yardstick, equality of units is demonstrated by matching a physical object with each pair of adjacent marks, and showing that for every pair the two marks coincide with the ends of the object. A measurement of length is then defined by the operation of laying units end to end and counting the number of units necessary to reach from end to end of the object measured. To measure weight, we define a balance. We do *not* require length-type operations to determine that the arms are equal. Weights are defined as equal if on placing one in each pan the balance does not tip. The balance is defined as "true" if every pair of weights which balance with weight a in pan x and weight b in pan y balance also with weight a in pan y and weight b in pan x. The weight of an object (placed in one pan) is then defined as the number of unit weights (placed in the other pan) required to balance it.

Derived measures are defined in terms of relations among fundamental measures. Thus density is defined as mass/volume, IQ as 100 MA/CA, and linear correlation r as $\frac{\Sigma xy}{\sqrt{(\Sigma x^2)(\Sigma y^2)}}$, with x and y interval scales with zero-points at the means. Note that in this last case the formula relating r to x and y is nonlinear, and values of the correlation coefficient do not form an interval scale.

A pointer measurement results from the application of an empirical law or procedure to an attribute already defined by a fundamental measurement procedure. Thus a spring scale for measuring weight is a ratio scale only insofar as Hooke's law (equal increments of weight produce equal stretches of a spring) applies accurately to the particular spring in question. A thermometer is also a pointer instrument, depending upon the empirical validity of the law which states that the volume of a liquid is proportional to its temperature. Pointer instruments require *calibration*, the ultimate calibration being against a fundamental measuring procedure. Fundamental measurement of length and weight are straightforward, but fundamental measurement of temperature is extremely complex.

The behavioral sciences rest quite generally on types of measurement which cannot be reduced by any series of operations and/or relations to fundamental measurement of attributes defined operationally. Thus pecking behavior can demonstrate a pecking order, but "aggressiveness" is a much broader term. It is quite possible that behaviors of other types, even in chicks, might be considered symptomatic of aggression. In all such cases we are led into the pervasive problems of scale *validity*, to be discussed below.

This treatment has necessarily been sketchy and less than rigorous. The classic treatment is Campbell (1928). Hempel (1952), Stevens, (1951), Torgerson (1958), Luce (1956), Scott and Suppes (1958), and Coombs (1953, 1963) present more modern treatments, including scale types used more commonly in experimental and social psychology than in education. The most rigorous modern treatment appears to be Suppes and Zinnes (1963). Luce and Tukey (1964) discuss *simultaneous conjoint measurement* in axiomatic terms. Birnbaum (1957) and Rasch (1960) had previously discussed conjoint ordering of test scores and item difficulties on a single scale. Ross (1964), Eisler (1965), Brooks (1965), and others consider various aspects of this problem. A review is given by Keats (1967).

TEST SCORES AS SCALES OF MEASUREMENT. The first problem, generally neglected in the literature, arises from the fact that the attribute measured by a test must be defined as a function of the attributes measured by its items. Let Y be a measure of the attribute underlying the test scores, and let $Y_1, Y_2, \ldots, Y_n$ be measures of the attributes underlying the n item scores, all measured on hypothetical ratio scales having the same units. For simplicity, we assume that every examinee will attempt every item, so that Y is a function of *all* the Y_i. We must also consider a domain: the population of all entities (persons) for whom the test is to be considered suitable as a measure of the attribute, or some defined subgroup of this population. Then

$$Y = f(Y_1, Y_2, \ldots, Y_n),$$

and no one conversant with either psychology or neurophysiology would argue that f is a simple sum. But if we now expand this equation in multiple Taylor series, taking as constants the domain means, and drop all terms of the series except the first set of n, we obtain,

$$y = y_1 + y_2 + \ldots + y_n,$$

where $y = Y - \bar{Y}$, $y_1 = Y_1 - \bar{Y}_1$ etc. This procedure imposes several restrictions on f:

(1) f must be an analytic function over the range of values of Y and the Y_i in the domain. This restriction seems reasonable.

(2) f will clearly be a different function for every examinee, depending on his genetic constitution and environmental history. This is not a restriction in and of itself, but it implies that the actual restrictions apply to every examinee separately.

(3) The nature of f must be such that no one Y_i is of any considerable importance compared to all the rest combined, in determining the value of Y; and in particular, as n increases, the relative importance of every Y_i must decrease. As good tests are commonly written, with adequate numbers of items reasonably distinct from one another, and each of complexity considerably less than that of the test as a whole, this restriction seems also fairly reasonable. It is most likely to be violated "externally"; e.g., by examiners' instructions which are not so simple as to be clear to all examinees.

(4) The ratios $\dfrac{\sigma_{Y_1}}{\sigma_{\bar{Y}_1}}, \dfrac{\sigma_{Y_2}}{\sigma_{\bar{Y}_2}}$, etc., must all be quite small; i.e., for every Y_i, the domain standard deviation must be small in comparison with the mean level above the true zero-point. This is the crucial restriction; along with (3) it is the essential requirement for the sum of the later terms of the Taylor series to be small in comparison to the first n, and hence for the adequacy of the simple sum as an approximation to the complex function f. How well this restriction is met in practice must be determined ultimately by empirical investigation.

(5) The nature of f must be such that for any fixed value of Y, all Y_i must be statistically independent. This is the homogeneity requirement; without it the scale of y is not unidimensional. This requirement can only be approximated for any real test.

Since these restrictions can never be met exactly, the sum-measures y form at most a rough quasi-interval scale, or if restriction (4) is not well met, perhaps only a quasi-ordinal scale.

If two different tests (i.e., two forms of the same test) measure the same attribute, the test attribute is defined by all the item-attributes of both forms, and the two sets of y-scores must be equivalent within a linear transformation for a quasi-interval scale or within a monotonic transformation for a quasi-ordinal scale.

The second problem arises because test items are scored on arbitrary scales, usually 0 or 1. The standard deviations of the item-attribute scores determine the effective weights of the item-attributes in the test-attribute composite, and the item discriminations should be related to them, though the exact nature of this relation is so far unclear. The item standard deviations, on the other hand, are functions of the item difficulties ($\sigma_i = \sqrt{p_i q_i}$), and are essentially unrelated to the item-attribute standard deviations. In consequence, the cumulative test-score distribution can have almost any monotonic relation to the cumulative attribute-score distribution, this relation being a function of the item difficulties as well as the item discriminations. If we let X be a test score, and $X_1, X_2, \ldots, X_n$ the corresponding item scores, the test scores, defined by

$$X = X_1 + X_2 + \ldots + X_n,$$

can, in general, form at most a quasi-ordinal scale. Under exceptional conditions, however, they can form a quasi-interval scale or even a quasi-ratio scale.

The relation between test scores and attribute scores has been investigated extensively, most notably by Lord (1952a, 1953b). He starts with an assumption that the probability that an examinee will answer an item correctly is a normal-ogive function of his test-attribute score, implying that the attribute distribution is normal. He limits discussion to free-choice items scored 0 or 1 and to a population of examinees rather than a sample, and adds the equivalent of restriction 5 above, namely that for any fixed attribute score, the probabilities of answering any two items correctly are independent. He then deduces a number of important conclusions, among them:

1. The regression of test scores on attribute scores is curvilinear.

2. This regression will be *almost* rectilinear if the mean item difficulty is close to the mean attribute level (i.e., if an examinee at the mean attribute level has about a 50-50 chance of answering correctly an item of average difficulty) *and* (a) the item discriminations are *low* if the items are all equally difficult; *or* (b) the item-difficulty distribution is rectangular and of range greater than that of the attribute scores if the items have medium to high discriminations.

3. A test will have maximum discrimination at one particular level of the attribute score if all its items are of 50 percent difficulty for examinees at that attribute-score level. In this case, for a normal distribution of the attribute scores, the test scores will have a platykurtic distribution.

4. For maximum discrimination over a given range of attribute scores, the range of item difficulties should be appreciably less than the range of attribute scores.

5. For equal discrimination at all levels of the attribute score, the item-difficulty distribution should be rectangular, over a range greater than the attribute-score range, with item discriminations the same at all score levels. Note that by 2(b), above, this is also the condition for a rectilinear or almost-rectilinear regression of test scores on attribute scores. It would seem to follow, therefore, that this is the condition under which the distribution of test scores will most nearly approximate the distribution of attribute scores, and hence form a quasi-interval scale. On the other hand, considering 4 above, it will result in a test having low test discrimination (given the number of items and their item discriminations) at any one level of attribute scores. Over the mental-age range 5 to 14, the Stanford-Binet Scale comes close to meeting these requirements. Few, if any, other tests even approximate them.

With multiple-choice items, the conditions necessary for a quasi-interval scale have been only partially worked out. Note also that an *efficient* test, as described in conclusion 4, *cannot* yield a quasi-interval scale. Other aspects of the relations between item difficulties and discriminations and test scores, true scores, and attribute scores have been considered by Brogden (1946), Carroll (1945), Cronbach and Warrington (1952), Lord (1952b, 1953a), Tucker (1946), and various others.

TEST SCORING PROCEDURES. The standard formula for correcting true–false and multiple-choice tests for guessing and for failure of some examinees to reach the last item in the time limit is

$$K = R - \frac{W}{(a-1)}$$

where K is the corrected score, R the number of right answers, W the number of wrong answers, and a the number of alternatives per item. The general reasoning behind this formula is that for every a items the examinee guessed at, he got $a - 1$ wrong and one right, so we subtract from R one point for every $a - 1$ items wrong to obtain K, an estimate of the number of items whose answers he knew. If he did not finish, we must assume that he did not know the answers to any of the items he did not reach, and would have recorded only guesses had he attempted them. If he failed to reach items whose answers he knew, the formula would underestimate the value of K.

The assumptions underlying this formula are

(1) The all-or-none assumption: for every item, the examinee either knows the answer and marks it correctly or does not know it and either omits the item or guesses randomly among the a alternatives.

(2) The omission assumption: the examinee has zero knowledge of every item he does not mark.

(3) The inverse assumption. If we knew the number of items the examinee guessed at, say G, the expected number wrong would be $E(W) = (a-1)\frac{G}{a}$. But if we know only W, we cannot say that $E[(a-1)\frac{G}{a}] = W$, as we do in effect in the formula.

The effect of the inverse assumption was investigated by Calandra (1941). He found that the error inherent in it is in general not serious. Hamilton (1950) considered the inverse assumption an improper reversal of the regression of R on K to estimate the regression of K on R, and proposed modifications. Lyerly (1951) criticized this view, treated the problem as one in sampling rather than regression, and showed that the correction formula gives a value not more than one score-point different from the maximum-likelihood estimate of the true score, assuming binomial guessing.

A number of writers have criticized the all-or-none assumption, pointing out the reality of partial knowledge (hunches; knowledge that one or two wrong alternatives are wrong; etc.) and of negative knowledge or misinformation. Cureton (1966) allowed p, the probability that an examinee will mark the correct answer to an item, to take any value from 0 to 1, with $p_0 = \frac{1}{a}$ the chance probability, and defined k, the examinee's knowledge of the item, as 1 if $p=1$, and as 0 if $p=p_0$. Hence if $p<p_0$, k is negative. By the omission assumption $p=p_0$ and $k=0$ for every item omitted, and $E(R) = \Sigma p$ (summed over items). Then by the inverse assumption, $E(\Sigma p) = R$. Also $K = \Sigma k$, and $E(K) = E(\Sigma k)$. The final assumption, replacing the all-or-none assumption, is the *linear* assumption: k is related linearly to p. Since k is defined by p at two points, the equation is:

$$k = \frac{p-p_0}{1-p_0} = \frac{ap-1}{a-1}.$$

Straightforward algebra then leads directly to the original correction formula. Hence the linear assumption is in some sense equivalent to the all-or-none assumption.

Under the linear assumption, if $p=0$, $k = \frac{-1}{a-1}$, and the greatest negative value of k depends on the number of alternatives. It would seem logical to define $k = -1$ when $p=0$, for all values of a. This would suggest a curvilinear monotonic relation of k to p, but with only R and W given by the data, the problem of a correction formula based on such a relation has proved intractable.

Coombs and others (1955) propose that each examinee check all the alternatives to a multiple-choice question which he believes to be wrong, receiving one point for each one that *is* wrong, but $-(a-1)$ points if he checks the correct answer as wrong. Thus he receives partial credit for partial information (correctly checking some but not all of the wrong answers), and partial negative credit for partial misinformation (checking the correct alternative and also some but not all of the wrong alternatives). The authors present empirical evidence that use of this procedure increases the test reliability, especially for relatively hard tests.

Aiken (1965) derives the probability of chance success under zero knowledge for any number of stimulus options (problems or item stems) and response options (item alternatives), using a generalized matching model. De Finetti (1965) considers the assessment of several varieties of partial knowledge using a model under which the examinee indicates for each alternative the *probability* of its being correct. He also considers other marking procedures and models. Chernoff (1962) discusses a number of different cases using a minimum mean-square-error model. Davis and Fifer (1959) and Davis (1959) propose that tests be scored by assigning a weight (positive or negative) to each alternative proportional to its index of discrimination, and summing the weights. They give data indicating that this procedure increases the test reliability.

It has been shown repeatedly that use of the usual correction-for-guessing formula decreases test reliability but increases test validity (Ruch & Stoddard, 1925; Ruch & De Graff, 1926; Lord, 1963; Glass & Wiley, 1964; and various others). The decrease in reliability results from the removal from the corrected test scores of reliable guessing-tendency variance (Swineford 1938, 1941). The increase in validity comes about because the criterion measure does not include guessing-tendency.

If every examinee marks every item, no correction for guessing is necessary, since in this case the value of K given by the formula will correlate perfectly with R, the number of right answers. Even when the formula is used, examinees should be instructed to play all hunches, and whenever one or more alternatives can be recognized as wrong to guess among the remainder. Hunches are more often right than wrong, and if one or more alternatives can be eliminated, the odds under the formula are in favor of the examinee who guesses. The essential reason for this injunction has nothing to do with any effects on reliability or validity. It is the ethical principle that no examinee should be able to increase his **most** probable score by disobeying the examiner's instructions.

Despite its deficiencies, the correction formula should always be used unless every examinee is instructed to mark every item and given time to do so. If the test has a time limit, and especially if the hardest items come last, use of the formula will balance at least approximately the student who works carefully (but not *too* slowly) up to the time limit, but does not finish, with the one who uses the last minute or two to record random responses to all remaining items.

Raw, Normative, and Ipsative Scores. The raw score of an individual on a test is seldom directly interpretable, though there are a few exceptions. Thus on a test of the 100 basic combinations of the multiplication table, or of the 100 words most commonly misspelled in written communication, the raw scores might be interpreted directly. In each case the items cover a complete finite universe or subuniverse of subject matter, and the instructional objective is 100 percent permanent mastery.

Most aptitude and achievement test scores are interpreted in terms of the *distribution* of scores on the same test of a given group or sample: a single class, all classes in the same subject or in the same grade in a given school or school system, or a sample of all children in classes in the same grade or of the same age in the United States or in some defined region. This is normative measurement. If the raw scores are converted *via* a table of norms into percentile ranks, standard scores, grade-scores, age-scores, or any other type of scaled scores, these latter are normative scores.

Many interest and personality tests yield scores on several different traits. In some cases the items are arranged in *forced-choice* format, so that marking one alternative gives the examinee one or more points toward one trait-score but prevents him from gaining points toward other trait-scores represented by the other alternatives. Each of his final trait-scores is then interpreted as a deviation from *his own* average on all the traits. Scores of this type are termed ipsative scores. If, on a given instrument, the sum of all trait-scores is the same for every examinee, the scores are perfectly ipsative. Many widely used tests (e.g., the various forms of the Kuder Preference Record) are partially ipsative and partially normative. Ipsative scores, when treated normatively (i.e., by comparing one individual's ipsative scores with those of other individuals), have somewhat unusual statistical properties. The only comprehensive treatment of these properties is that of Clemans (1966), whose short bibliography includes most of the previous papers of any importance.

ITEM ANALYSIS. Item analysis consists of a set of procedures for determining the difficulties or popularities and the discriminations and/or validities of the items or alternatives of an experimental edition of a test. The objectives are to eliminate items having low discrimination or validity, to control the distribution of raw scores for some defined population of examinees by further item selection, and/or to construct two or more forms of the final test which are parallel or equivalent.

The experimental group should in most cases be reasonably representative of the population with which the final test is to be used, particularly as regards age, sex, school grade or grades, residence (urban-rural), and socioeconomic status. In some cases its range of ability should be greater than that of the target population. The highly exact representativeness required for a norms group, however, is not essential. In particular, an item-analysis sample may come entirely from one community if this community is near average for the target population.

If the final test is to be primarily a power test, with or without a time limit, the experimental item-analysis test should be administered without time limit (Wesman, 1949). The subgroup of examinees who reach the final items is never a representative sample of the whole group, and the correlation between ability or knowledge and speed of work, though low, is substantially greater than zero.

Indices of Difficulty. Ordinal indices of item difficulty are given quite simply by the percentages of correct answers in the experimental group. Quasi-interval indices are needed, however, when the item-difficulty distribution is to be controlled by item selection.

If the underlying distribution can be assumed to be normal, the difficulty of a free-answer item can be represented by the normal deviate x corresponding to the percent correct taken as a normal tail-area. The normal deviate $x = 0$ corresponds to 50 percent correct. But with recognition items, complications arise. Let p = proportion correct, and p_0 = chance proportion correct. Then $p_0 = \dfrac{1}{a}$ if the item has a alternatives. The scale-value $x = 0$ should correspond to the proportion half-way between p_0 and 1, and the distribution will be skewed with the longer tail at the bottom. The usual solution has been to treat the proportion above chance,

$$p'' = \frac{p - p_0}{1 - p_0},$$

as a normal tail-area. This puts the scale-value $x = 0$ where it belongs, but assigns the scale-value $x = \infty$ to $p = p_0$. Items as hard as or harder than chance cannot be scaled. Cureton (1967) has proposed as an alternative to take

$$p' = p^n$$

as a normal tail-area, with n so chosen that the scale-value $x = 0$ will correspond to the value of p' half-way between p_0 and 1. Scaling p' on the normal distribution is then equivalent to scaling p on a skew distribution, and items for which $p \leq p_0$ can still be scaled.

Some item-analysts prefer the arcsine transformation,

$$x = 2 \arcsin \sqrt{p} \ ,$$

where p may be either p or p'' or p'. This is a *variance-stabilizing* transformation: a given difference $x_1 - x_2$ has the same standard error at all scale levels except the extremes.

Quite commonly the value x, however obtained, is subjected to an arbitrary linear transformation in order to avoid negative numbers and decimals in the final index of difficulty.

Item Discrimination and Item Validity. The criterion against which passing or failing an item is compared is most commonly the total score on the experimental test itself. This is termed an *internal* criterion, or a criterion of internal consistency. It is used when the aim is to develop a homogeneous test (one whose items all measure the same attribute), and more generally whenever increased homogeneity is not too objectionable and the test is intended to serve a variety of purposes. The *index of discrimination* of an item is in general a measure of the item-criterion correlation (the extent to which high criterion scorers pass the item oftener than do low criterion scorers), or a test of the hypothesis that this correlation is not significantly greater than zero; and in particular it is such a measure or test of significance when the criterion is internal.

When a test is designed to serve only one purpose (e.g., prediction of success in college), and a criterion measure independent of the scores on the experimental test is available or can be constructed, items may be selected on the basis of their correlations with this *external* criterion (e.g., freshman grade-point average). A correlation between an item and an external criterion may be termed an *index of item validity*, but it may also be designated by the more general term *index of discrimination*.

In constructing a wide-range test, an external criterion may be one which is merely fairly highly related to, rather than being an actual measure of, the criterion attribute. For a school achievement test the criterion may be school grade; for a general intelligence test it may be age of children.

When a test is designed for a *very* specific purpose, such as prediction of success in a particular training course, *two-criterion* item analysis may be employed. The external criterion, success in the course, is usually heterogeneous, requiring several types of abilities and aptitudes not all of which correlate highly with one another. The items of the experimental test are heterogeneous also: some are designed to tap one relevant ability or aptitude and some another. Items are selected partly for high item validity (against the external criterion), and partly for *low* item discrimination (against the internal criterion). This procedure often yields higher test validity than does the use of the external criterion alone. Methods of two-criterion item analysis are discussed by Horst (1936) and by Gulliksen (1950).

Problems. In one-criterion discrimination (or validity) analysis, three problems can be recognized. (1) We may desire only a test of significance, in order to eliminate non-discriminating items. This is often the case in achievement-test construction, where further selection is based on balancing the items against a topic-by-function outline (see content validity, below), and perhaps to some extent on difficulty. (2) We may desire an ordinal index of difficulty in order to select, say, the best 100 items from an experimental test of 150. The test functions of the significance tests are used occasionally, but they are almost always correlated with difficulty, and it is often desirable to have indices of discrimination which are not necessarily correlated with the corresponding indices of difficulty. (3) If a test with particular properties is desired (e.g., an "efficient" test for a particular population or a test whose scores will form a quasi-interval scale), we may need quasi-interval indices of discrimination.

Experimental Designs. Three main experimental designs are in common use.

1. In the high-low group (HLG) design, the experimental sample is divided into three groups on the basis of the criterion scores, with 27 percent in the high group, 27 percent in the low group, and the remaining 46 percent in the middle group. The data for each item are the numbers or percents correct in the high and low groups; all other information provided by the criterion scores is ignored. It has been shown that for all sample sizes, the optimum size for the high and low groups is close to 27 percent, assuming that the score distribution is approximately normal (Kelley, 1939; Cureton, 1959; Ross & Weitzman, 1965). The HLG design is employed whenever it is less costly to obtain large samples than to perform complicated computations, and items of very high and very low difficulty are to be eliminated.

2. In the item-total-score (ITS) design, all information supplied by the criterion scores is used. With this design the basic data are the mean and standard deviation of the criterion scores, and for each item, the mean criterion score of those who give the right answer. The ITS design is used whenever the cost of a larger sample exceeds the cost of more complicated computations, and whenever it is desired to obtain accurate indices of discrimination for very hard and/or very easy items.

3. In the item-characteristic-curve (ICC) design, the criterion scores are grouped into five to ten levels, with mean level scores forming a quasi-interval scale. The highest and lowest levels should be above and below, respectively, the highest and lowest levels of the target population. Very large samples are required. The basic data are the proportions of correct answers to each item at each level, and the sample size at each level must be large enough to yield stable proportions. The item-characteristic-curve for each item is an ogive fitted to the five to ten proportions in the successive groups. The ICC design is used mainly in constructing wide-range tests. Extensive computations as well as large samples are required.

The HLG Design. The test of significance is the Chi-square test of association, with correction for continuity, against a one-sided alternative. Let H be the *number* of correct answers in the high group and L the number of correct answers in the low group. Let $D = H - L$, let $S = H + L$, and let $n(= .27N)$ be the number in each group. Since the numbers in the two groups are equal, the formula simplifies to

$$\text{Chi-square} = \frac{2n(D-1)^2}{S(2n-S)},$$

with one degree of freedom.

Let $p_H = \dfrac{H}{n}$, $p_L = \dfrac{L}{n}$, and $d = p_H - p_L$.

The index d itself orders the items according to the differences between the proportions of correct and incorrect classifications when we classify each examinee into group H if he gives the correct answer and into group L if he does not (Findley, 1956). This ordering, along with the (different) ordering given by the numerical values of Chi-square, is correlated with item difficulty. A few item-analysts use the fourfoldpoint correlation ϕ, or $\dfrac{\phi}{\phi\, max}$, as an ordinal index of discrimination, but most of them prefer the widespread-tails tetrachoric correlation, r_{tw}. Values of r_{tw} have been tabulated by Flanagan (1962) and by Fan (1952), with arguments p_H and p_L. Fan's table also gives estimates of the proportion correct in the total group (the ordinal index of difficulty) from p_H and p_L, and he has published the rationale behind the construction of this table (Fan, 1954).

There is neither a normalizing nor a variance-stabilizing transformation for r_{tw} (nor for d or ϕ or $\dfrac{\phi}{\phi\, max}$), but Fisher's z-transformation should tend *toward* both, since it replaces the limits ± 1 by $\pm \infty$. This is as close as we can come at present to an interval index of discrimination for the HLG design.

The ITS Design. The obvious test of significance here is the *t*-test of the hypothesis that the mean criterion scores of those who pass and fail the item do not differ significantly. For easy and hard items, however, the assumption of homogeneity of variance may be violated. A more conservative test, which does not require this assumption, is to consider the whole group a finite population rather than a sample, and those who pass the item a sample from this finite population. We can then test the hypothesis that the mean of the sample does not differ significantly from the mean of the population against the one-sided alternative that the mean of the sample is higher. The test statistic is

$$x = \sqrt{\frac{(m-M)^2 n(N-1)}{(N-n)\sigma^2}},$$

where m and M are the mean criterion scores for the sample and the population, n and N the numbers in the sample and the population, and σ^2 the population variance:

$$\sigma^2 = \frac{\sum_{1}^{N}(x-M)^2}{N}.$$

Then x may be taken as a normal deviate, and the significance probability against a one-sided alternative is the area beyond x in on tail of the normal distribution.

For an ordinal index of discrimination, the point-biserial correlation r_{pb} and the Pearson biserial correlation r_b have been used. r_{pb}, however, has limits less than ± 1, and if the criterion score distribution is not normal, r_b may exceed $+1$. The best index is probably the Brogden biserial correlation r_B (Brogden, 1949). It is derived on the assumption that the underlying item distribution is the same as that of the criterion rather than two-point or normal, its upper limit is always exactly $+1$, and it is more easily computed:

$$r_B = \frac{m - M}{m' - M},$$

where m' is the mean of the n highest scores in the criterion distribution.

No normalizing or variance-stabilizing transformation has been worked out for r_{pb}, r_b, or r_B under models appropriate to the item-analysis situation, though Das Gupta (1960) gives a variance-stabilizing transformation for r_{pb} under a model appropriate for the correlation between a continuous variable and a true dichotomous one. Use of Fisher's z-transformation, however, will again replace the limits ± 1 by $\pm \infty$, and hence should give at least a crude approximation to an interval index of discrimination.

The ICC Design. If the criterion consists of successive grade or age groups, the criterion scale will be a quasi-interval scale over the grade-range 1–8 or the age-range 6–13, since the mental growth curve and the educational growth curve are almost linear over this range. The sample then consists of sub-samples of equal or near-equal size from each grade or age group. If, on the other hand, the sample is from a high school or college population, or a single age or grade, or the adults employed in a particular occupation, and the criterion is either internal or some external variable such as school grades or job-proficiency ratings, the criterion distribution is likely to be roughly normal rather than roughly rectangular. In this case the subsamples must either be very unequal in size, or have mean locations at quite unequal intervals on the criterion scale.

The functions commonly used to represent item-characteristic curves are the normal ogive and the logistic. Fitting procedures are discussed by Baker (1965), who traces the history of the ICC design and provides an excellent bibliography. With this design, the index of difficulty is given in units of the criterion score scale. It is usually the score level at which 50 percent of the examinees pass the item, but it may also be the point of inflection of the fitted characteristic curve. The index of discrimination is usually the slope of the line tangent to the curve at the point of inflection.

The ICC design must be used whenever conjoint ordering or measurement of item difficulties and scores is attempted. Perfect conjoint ordering requires that the item characteristic curves do not intersect; perfect conjoint measurement imposes still more restrictive conditions (Keats, 1967).

PERSONALITY, INTEREST, AND ATTITUDE INVENTORIES. In an aptitude or achievement test, the items have predetermined right or best answers, and each examinee should try to make the highest score he can. In an inventory, by contrast, the items do *not* have correct or best answers, and each examinee should answer them as honestly and objectively as he can in terms of his *typical* (i.e., average) behavior, feelings, opinions, or preferences. The items are single words or short statements, and the examinee marks them as true or false in his opinion, true or false as applied to him, liked or disliked, or propositions with which he agrees or disagrees. The response scale may be trichotomous (Yes, ?, No), or it may have more than three points (agree strongly, agree, uncertain, disagree, disagree strongly). On multi-scale inventories, the items are often presented in pairs, triplets, or quadruplets, and the examinee marks for each set the one he likes most and the one he likes least, or the one which applies best to him and the one which applies most poorly, in which case the scores are usually partially or completely ipsative.

Criteria may be either internal-theoretical, internal-empirical, or external-empirical.

In internal-theoretical analysis, the items of each scale are written and allocated initially in terms of the theory. Then each item retained must not only correlate substantially with the scale to which it belongs; it must also correlate higher with that scale than with any other. Items which fail to meet either of these criteria are discarded.

In internal-empirical analysis, some loose theory still determines in general the type of items written, and in one procedure the items are allocated to preliminary scales by judgment. Each item is then correlated with each scale, and reallocated to the scale with which it correlates highest, with perhaps a residue of items which do not correlate significantly with any scale. The scales are then rescored, and the process is repeated until no further reallocation is needed. At the end, a score may be obtained on the items of the residue, and item-score correlations computed to see if some subset of these items forms an additional scale. In a second procedure, the inter-item correlations are subjected to a cluster analysis or a factor analysis to derive the scales.

In external-empirical analysis, there are a base group of examinees and several special groups; e.g., normal individuals and mental patients clearly diagnosed in several categories, or men-in-general and men in several specific occupations. Each item-*alternative* is scored positively (negatively) for a given scale if the proportion of members of the special group who mark it significantly exceeds (falls short of) the corresponding proportion of the base group. In some inventories, weights are assigned to the alternatives in accordance with some function of the magnitudes of, or the significances of the differences between, these proportions. With this procedure, the same item may be scored for more than one scale. In consequence the scoring keys for different scales will themselves be correlated, and the reliabilities of differences between scale scores will vary with the numbers of common items.

Response Sets. A response set is a tendency for an examinee to mark items in a certain manner regardless of their content. Thus a position response set is a systematic tendency for examinees to mark the first, the last, or some intermediate alternative of multiple-choice aptitude or achievement test items when they do not know the correct answer. Empirical evidence indicates that position response sets are slight, and have little effect on aptitude and achievement-test scores. The guessing or gambling response set exhibits much larger individual differences, with the effects noted previously in the discussion of the correction for guessing.

With interest, attitude, and personality inventories there is considerable controversy over the effects of response sets. Individual differences of considerable magnitude—so great as to vitiate interpretations of such inventories on the basis of their apparent contents—are claimed with respect to two major response sets. *Acquiescence* response set is a general tendency to agree with all sorts of statements, including admitting the presence in oneself of undesirable traits. *Social-desirability* response set is a tendency to mark the socially acceptable answers to inventory items, whether or not these answers are true of the examinee or represent his real opinions, attitudes, or interests. Jackson and Messick (1961) and Messick and Jackson (1961) present the case for acquiescence response set. Edwards (1957) stresses the importance of social-desirability response set. Block (1965) criticizes these authors and many others. He indicates that these response sets are less serious than the work of previous authors would suggest, and describes methods of inventory construction which he believes will almost eliminate their effects. His bibliography includes almost all of the previous studies of any importance.

RELIABILITY. Test reliability is the accuracy with which a test measures whatever function or combination of functions it does measure. If the test scores yield a quasi-ordinal or quasi-interval scale, it is a numerical index of the degree of approximation of the quasi-scale to a true ordinal or interval scale. The classical theory of reliability assumes quasi-interval scales, but considerable parts of it are still valid for quasi-ordinal scales if we merely substitute Spearman rank correlations for product-moment correlations in the formulas.

A raw score may be thought of as consisting of the sum of two parts: a *true score* and an *error of measurement*. The true scores are usually (though not necessarily) positive. They correlate perfectly with the attribute scores, but the correlation is in general curvilinear, approaching rectilinearity only in the special cases noted previously in the discussion of test scores as scales of measurement. The error scores are positive or negative, for different examinees, with equal probability.

True scores can be defined in a number of ways (e.g., Ghiselli, 1964), either as functions of attribute scores, as expected values of raw scores over an infinite number of duplicate forms of the test, or as whatever causes correlation among parallel forms. In all common cases, the same formulas are reached no matter which definition is taken as the starting point.

Basic Postulate. We are dealing here with what is termed *weak true-score theory,* which is the basis for all the usual formulas of reliability and validity. The basic postulate of weak true-score theory is as follows: *In a population of individuals, the errors of measurement in different tests and in different parallel forms of the same test are uncorrelated with one another, and are also uncorrelated with the true scores on all tests and on all forms of the same test.*

Coefficient and Index of Reliability. The *reliability coefficient* of a single test may be *defined* as the variance ratio of its true scores to its raw scores, or as the square of the correlation between its true scores and its raw scores (the coefficient of determination). But to *estimate* the reliability of one form, a second form is ordinarily required, and the computed estimate (from a sample of examinees who have taken both forms) is the correlation between the two forms. The *index of reliability* is the square root of the reliability coefficient. It is the ratio of the standard deviation of the true scores to the standard deviation of the raw scores, and it is the correlation between the true scores and the raw scores.

Parallel, Alternate, Equivalent, and Duplicate Forms. Two forms of a test may be defined as *parallel* if they measure the same function or combination of functions, apart from error, so that everything causing correlation between them is their common true scores, and everything causing unique variance in each of them is error of measurement. By "the same *combination* of functions," we mean that if two or more functions or attributes contribute to the true scores on one form, the same two or more functions or attributes and no others must contribute to the true scores on the other form, *and in the same proportions*. If two forms are parallel and also equally reliable we will term them *alternate*, and if in addition their raw scores have the same standard deviation we will term them *equivalent*. If their joint distributions of item difficulty, item discrimination, and functions measured are identical, which implies identical score distributions and hence equal means as well as equal variances and equal reliabilities, we will term them *duplicate forms*. For two or more duplicate forms, one table of norms is sufficient.

The correlation between two parallel forms is the geometric mean of their reliability coefficients. If the two forms are at least alternate (equally reliable), the correlation between them is the reliability coefficient of each of them.

The correlations referred to above are correlations in a *population* of examinees. When we estimate any such correlation by computing a product-moment correlation in a sample, the estimate is not unbiased, but the bias is usually small if the sample is fairly large.

Consistency, Stability, and Objectivity. Errors of measurement can be classified into three main types. *Inconsistency* errors arise because two or more finite sets of items (test forms) cannot be equally difficult for different examinees. The true score of an examinee would be his score on a test consisting of all possible items "such as" those of the actual test. But on a single form he will by chance know the answers to a greater or lesser proportion of the items than the proportion which represents his true score. If two forms are administered *simultaneously* (i.e., on the same identical occasion), as in the odd-even or split-half method, and are scored objectively, their correlation is the *consistency coefficient* of each form or half-test. In this case the true score of each examinee represents his working ability at the precise time he was tested.

Instability errors occur because the working ability of each examinee fluctuates around his average ability as a result of changes in physical condition, access to memory, motivation, inhibitory processes, cogency of reasoning, etc. These changes occur in irregular cycles that may last as little as a few seconds or as long as several months. When two forms of a test are given at different times, the true score of each examinee represents roughly his average ability over the time interval separating the two test sessions. The *stability coefficient* (Cureton, 1958) is given by

$$r_s = \frac{r_{1I}}{\sqrt{C_{11} C_{II}}},$$

where 1 and I refer to the two forms of the test (and the two test sessions), and C_{11} and C_{II} are the consistency coefficients of the two forms on the given occasions. Its value is independent of the lengths of the two forms, depending only on the nature of the attribute, the *types* of questions used to measure it, and the time separating the two test sessions.

When the same form is given on two different occasions, the test-retest correlation is *not* a stability coefficient, contrary to statements in several widely used elementary textbooks. It does depend on the length of the test. It is not wholly free from inconsistency: the same test booklet is not an identical stimulus on two different occasions. And perseveration effects, sometimes including memory on the second occasion of specific item responses made on the first occasion, may inflate or even in some cases attenuate the correlation. Hence test-retest correlations have no clear interpretation in terms of measurement theory, and should be avoided whenever possible.

The correlation between two forms given at different times contains both inconsistency errors and instability errors. The instability errors, moreover, are inflated by changes in the true abilities represented by learning, forgetting, mental growth, and mental decline if any. Every stability coefficient and every interform reliability coefficient, therefore, relates to the *particular* time interval between the two test sessions.

Subjectivity errors affect ratings and the grades assigned to answers given on essay tests. They arise because different judges evaluate the same answer or behavior differently, and because the same judge will evaluate the same answer or the same behavior differently on different occasions. The *objectivity* of an essay test or rating is the correlation between independent evaluations by two different judges of the same set of answers to the questions of an essay test or the same set of observed behaviors.

Spearman-Brown Formula. When the two halves of a test are administered simultaneously and scored separately, the correlation between them is the consistency coefficient of each of them. The consistency coefficient of the whole test is then given by

$$C_{11} = \frac{2C_{\frac{1}{2}\frac{1}{2}}}{1 + C_{\frac{1}{2}\frac{1}{2}}},$$

where $C_{\frac{1}{2}\frac{1}{2}}$ is the correlation between the two half-tests. The two half-tests are assumed equally consistent and equally variable; i.e., they are assumed to be *equivalent* forms, but these requirements are not very stringent, so that merely random division of the test into half-tests will almost always satisfy them to a sufficient degree of approximation. A special case arises when the test consists in whole or in part of super-items, such as paragraphs or tables or drawings each followed by several questions. In forming half-tests, each super-item as a whole must be allocated to one form. If this is not done, errors of comprehension of a paragraph or table or drawing as a whole will affect some questions in one form and some in the other, contrary to the basic postulate.

The Spearman-Brown formula can be generalized to

$$C_n = \frac{nC_{11}}{1 + (n-1) C_{11}}.$$

Here C_{11} is the consistency of one form (however computed), and C_n is an estimate of the consistency of a form n times as long, but equally reliable and equally variable per unit length. Solving for n,

$$n = \frac{C_n(1-C_{11})}{C_{11}(1-C_n)}.$$

If we know the consistency C_{11} of a given test, and wish to know how long a test would be required to attain the consistency C_n, the answer is given by this last formula, again under the assumption that both tests will be equally reliable and equally variable per unit length.

Since instability is not a function of test length, the Spearman-Brown formula does not apply to inter-form reliabilities when the two forms are not given simultaneously. The corresponding formulas for this case are as follows (Cureton, 1965):

$$r_{(1+I)(1+I)} = \frac{2r_{1I}}{1+\sqrt{C_{11}C_{II}}},$$

$$r_n = \frac{nr_{1I}}{1+(n-1)\sqrt{C_{11}C_{II}}},$$

$$n = \frac{r_n(1-\sqrt{C_{11}C_{II}})}{r_{1I}-r_n\sqrt{C_{11}C_{II}}}.$$

Note that in each formula both the inter-form reliability and the consistency coefficients are required. In the second formula above, let n approach infinity. Then r_n will equal $\frac{r_{1I}}{\sqrt{C_{11}C_{II}}}$, which is the stability coefficient.

Kuder-Richardson Formulas. A test may be defined as homogeneous if every item is a parallel form of every other item. For a homogeneous test of k items, an estimate of its consistency is given by

$$C_{11} = \frac{k}{k-1}\left(1 - \frac{\sum_{i}^{k} s_i^2}{s_t^2}\right),$$

where s_i^2 is an item variance and s_t^2 is the test variance. If the items are all scored 0 or 1, $s_i^2 = p_i q_i$, where p_i is the item difficulty—the proportion of examinees who give the right answers—and $q_i = 1 - p_i$. This is the Kuder-Richardson Formula 20 (KR-20). If item i is a super-item, s_i^2 must be computed directly, in the same way as is s_t^2. The original derivation (Kuder & Richardson, 1937) used unnecessarily restrictive assumptions based on a rational-equivalence model. Hoyt (1941) derived it from a variance-components model. Cronbach (1951) showed that it is the average of the split-half, Spearman-Brown coefficients for all possible splits, and that it is also the value of the split-half, Spearman-Brown coefficient for the one perfect split yielding exactly equal half-test reliabilities and variances. Guttman (1945) showed that in case of imperfect homogeneity, it is a lower bound of the true consistency.

A somewhat simpler formula is the Kuder-Richardson Formula 21 (KR-21):

$$C_{11} = \frac{ks_t^2 - \overline{X}(k-\overline{X})}{(k-1)s_t^2}.$$

In the original derivation it was assumed that all items are equally difficult, but Lord (1955) showed that it can be derived under less restrictive assumptions (see next section). It is at least necessary, however, that the item difficulty range be less than the score range, so that no item will have an index of difficulty (p_i) close to 0 or 1 (or below or close to p_0 in the case of recognition items).

In all of these formulas, as in the split-half, Spearman-Brown procedure, it is assumed that every examinee attempts every item. All formulas for consistency coefficients are inflated spuriously if some examinees do not finish, for in this case speed of work is identical on both forms.

STANDARD ERROR OF MEASUREMENT. If several duplicate forms of a test could be administered simultaneously to one examinee, the standard deviation of his several scores would be the standard error of measurement for him. He would have the same true score on all forms, and this standard deviation would in consequence be the standard deviation of the errors of measurement. Such a standard error of measurement would show only the dispersion of the inconsistency errors. The usual standard error of measurement is an average over all individuals tested:

$$SE_m = s_1\sqrt{1-C_{11}},$$

where s_1 is the standard deviation and C_{11} is the consistency coefficient of the test. It is also the standard deviation of the differences between the raw scores and the true scores of all the examinees.

Using this last definition, we can also estimate a standard error of measurement based on two *equivalent* forms administered at different times and hence including the instability error:

$$SE_m = s\sqrt{1-r_{1I}},$$

where s is the square root of a pooled estimate of variance:

$$s^2 = \frac{\sum^{N}(X_1-\overline{X}_1)^2 + \sum^{N}(X_I-\overline{X}_I)^2}{2(N-1)},$$

and r_{1I} is an inter-form reliability coefficient. Here SE_m is the standard error of measurement of one form (either one), over the given time interval.

For the consistency-only case, Lord has considered a model based on *randomly parallel* forms. Two or more forms are randomly parallel if each of them is an independent random sample of k items from the same item universe, or in the practical case if items from a finite pool are allocated randomly to forms without prestratification on difficulty or discrimination. Randomly parallel forms are also randomly alternate, randomly equivalent, and randomly duplicate.

Lord (1955) shows that under this model the standard error of measurement for one examinee (say examinee a) can be estimated from the binomial formula,

$$SE_m(a) = \sqrt{\frac{X_a(k-X_a)}{k-1}}$$

where X_a is the raw score of examinee a, and k is

the number of items. It is assumed that the examinee attempts every item. If we average the values given by this formula over all examinees, the result is KR-21. There is, however, a slight logical inconsistency (Lord, 1962): the s_t^2 of that formula *should* be computed by giving a different randomly parallel form to each examinee, but in practice the error resulting from giving all examinees the same form is quite small.

Reliability and Variability. The standard error of measurement expresses a test's reliability—either consistency or inter-form reliability—in terms of the score units of the test. Its average value is independent of the variability of the group tested, except insofar as this variability is affected by unequal units of measurement at different scale levels. The consistency coefficient and the inter-form reliability coefficient, on the other hand, are "pure numbers," with range 0 to 1 in all samples, but their values vary with the standard deviation of each particular sample. When a reliability coefficient is reported, therefore, the standard deviation (or with an inter-form reliability coefficient, the two standard deviations) should *always* be reported also, along with a description of the sample indicating the range of ability in practical terms.

The functional relation between reliability and variability is

$$r_{11} = 1 - \frac{s_1^2}{S_1^2}(1 - R_{11}),$$

where S_1^2 and R_{11} are the variance and the reliability in one sample, and s_1^2 is the variance in a second sample. The formula gives the estimate r_{11} of the reliability in the second sample. This formula is valid only insofar as the mean values of the units of measurement are the same in both samples. A reasonably safe rule of thumb might be to use it only when the score range in the sample of lesser variability is wholly or almost wholly within the score range of the sample of greater variability. If a test author reports R_{11} and S_1^2 for a large sample, the test user can estimate the reliability in his own group by computing only its variance, s_1^2, and substituting in this formula. For the test user to be able to apply the rule-of-thumb test of safety in the use of the formula, the test author must report the range (or better the entire distribution of scores) as well as the variance and the reliability coefficient.

Standard Error of Measurement at Different Score Levels. If the test-score units of measurement do not form a quasi-interval scale, the standard error of measurement will be different at different score levels. But since the standard error of measurement is not a function of the variability of the group, it can be computed for any segment of a total score distribution. If the scores of an examinee on the two half-tests or forms are X_1 and X_2, and his total score (on the two half-tests or on the two forms combined) is X, so that $X_1 + X_2 = X$, then (Rulon, 1939),

$$SE_m = \sqrt{\frac{\Sigma(X_1 - X_2)^2}{N} - (\overline{X}_1 - \overline{X}_2)^2}$$

and this formula applies even when all the N total scores X are identical.

In the half-test case we obtain an inconsistency-only standard error of measurement; in the two-form case the instability errors are included also.

STRONG TRUE-SCORE THEORY. In the present sketch we have omitted much of weak true-score theory which is primarily of theoretical rather than practical interest. Lord (1952a, 1953b, and later papers) derives a considerable number of results in addition to those mentioned in the section on Test Scores as Scales of Measurement, above. He and his associates are responsible also for the principal work in the development of strong true-score theory. The primary reference at the present time is Lord (1965a), but a forthcoming book on *Statistical Theory of Mental Test Scores* by Lord and Novick (1968) will deal with it much more fully, as well as presenting a rigorous treatment of weak true-score theory.

Strong true-score theory employs models containing explicit assumptions about the distribution of the errors of measurement and the shape of the true-score distribution. These assumptions can be contradicted by the data and must be tested, but when they are met stronger inferences can be drawn than are possible under the simpler assumptions of weak true-score theory, which are consistent with practically all data so long as improper experimental designs are not used.

In Lord (1965a), it is assumed that the errors of measurement follow a compound binomial distribution, and that the true-score distribution can be represented by a four-parameter incomplete-beta distribution. With rather complicated fitting procedures to estimate the population parameters from the sample data it is then possible to determine with considerable accuracy:

1. The true-score distribution.
2. The observed-score distribution that will result from lengthening the test.
3. Equivalent percentiles of the true-score distributions of two forms of the test.
4. The frequencies in the cells of the scatter-plot of two forms of the test, given only the marginal frequencies.
5. The frequency distribution of the scores on a long form, given only the frequency distribution on a short form, provided some other smaller group has been given both forms, thus permitting derivation of norms with only the short form given to the large representative sample.
6. The effects of selecting individuals on a fallible test.
7. The matching of groups on true scores when only fallible measurements have been made.
8. Whether or not two tests actually measure the same function when the relation between them is nonlinear.
9. Some of the properties, other than merely the reliability or consistency, of a specific test considered as a measuring instrument.

The price in practice of using strong true-score

theory in place of weak true-score theory is a very great increase in mathematical complexity. All of the above determinations will require the use of electronic computers.

Lord (1965b, 1965a) has also shown, both in theory and empirically, that the normal ogive and the logistic are not very good functions to represent item characteristic curves. In the empirical study, based on 103,275 examinees, he also showed that there are virtually no items which extremely high scorers (those above percentile 99.8) get right less often than those with slightly lower score (around percentiles 99.0 to 99.5). This finding would seem to contradict the claims of some recent critics of "external" testing programs.

VALIDITY. Validity encompasses at least three distinct problems:

A. What trait or combination of traits does a specific test measure?

B. How well does a given test or battery predict a given criterion measure?

C. How well does a particular test measure a trait-construct for which no single valid criterion measure exists, and what evidence is there that the trait-construct represents a real unitary or global trait on which substantial measurable individual differences exist?

Content Validity. This is the simplest case of validity of type A. In the case of an achievement test, there is usually no other criterion of students' knowledge which is as good as the test itself. In this case we must judge (we cannot measure) its content validity by the correspondence between the item coverage and the definition of the area to be covered. Content validity has two major aspects: topic validity and process validity.

Topic validity. The topic validity of a test is *defined* by a detailed outline of the topics and subtopics covered, and the particular item or items testing each subtopic. It is *demonstrated* by showing that these topics and subtopics correspond closely to the legitimate objectives of instruction in the unit, course, or subdiscipline which the test is intended to evaluate. Thus for a test of general literary knowledge, the outline might consist of a list of authors, for each author a sublist of his major works, and then finally under each author and work, a statement of the point or points to be tested. Demonstration of content validity would consist in showing that the authors and works included were those covered in leading anthologies and curriculum statements, that the number of questions per author correlated highly with the mean ratings of authors' importance by authorities on literature, and that the individual points tested were those commonly stressed by good teachers.

Process validity. This type of validity refers to the types of mental processes used in answering the test questions. The development of some of these processes is also a major objective of any educational effort. The most complete list of types of processes is probably the one given by Bloom and others (1956). They discuss the measurement of 24 different processes under the six major headings: knowledge, comprehension, application, analysis, synthesis, and evaluation. Examples of test items, most but not all of objectives types, are given under each of the 24 processes.

The actual outline for an achievement test should be, then, a topic-by-process grid, with item numbers entered in the cells. Sampling will in general be necessary: the number of cells is likely to exceed the number of test items. Not all processes will apply to a given test, and still fewer will be appropriate to a specific topic or subtopic. To buttress a claim of content validity, the test author should include in his manual the complete topic-by-process grid, and along with it an explicit statement on how it was derived.

Predictive Validity. This is validity of type B. It is also termed criterion validity and statistical validity. A test or battery can be used to predict performances of many types, and hence have many different predictive validities, some high, some moderate, and some low. To estimate predictive validity we require a *criterion measure:* an experimentally independent numerical assessment, for the members of a validation sample, of the trait or trait-complex to be predicted. We shall use "prediction" in a general sense to denote any use of a regression equation, an expectancy table, or a successive-hurdles procedure. The term "forecast" will be used whenever the criterion measure necessarily follows in time the administration of the predictor test or battery.

There are two fundamentally different types of criterion measures. The first may be termed a *sui generis* criterion. It exists independently of any validation study, and it is worth predicting. Examples are grade-point average, dollar volume of sales, units of production per hour or per day, graduation–nongraduation, retention–discharge, success or failure in a specific training course, etc. The second may be termed a *constructed criterion.* We start with a *trait-concept* such as academic achievement, sales ability, or work effectiveness, and construct the criterion measure in such a manner as to maximize its presumed content validity. The constructed criterion then serves as an operational definition of the trait-concept. It is accepted as such because it is clearly more content-valid than is the proposed predictor test or battery. We use the test or battery for operating prediction or measurement because the criterion measure may become available too late (as in student or employee selection), or because the criterion measure is too time-consuming or expensive (as in counseling based on tests rather than on job tryouts), or occasionally because the test is so much more reliable than the criterion measure that it is a better measure of the criterion true score than is the criterion raw score itself, despite the greater content validity of the latter. If the trait-concept is of such nature that no single constructed criterion measure can be accepted as an operational definition, the problem becomes that of construct validity (see below) rather than predictive validity.

Predictor selection and cross-validation. In most situations, empirical validation is concerned with predictor batteries rather than with single predictors. It is often combined with predictor selection. The experimental battery includes more predictors (and more kinds of predictors) than are to be included in the final battery. The best subset of predictors is selected, and the weights determined, by one of the procedures of stepwise multiple regression. If the battery is fixed at the outset, straightforward multiple regression gives the weights.

When the same criterion measure is used for item-validation of one or more of the predictors, a different sample is required for the determination of the weights. The error in attempting to use the same sample for both purposes is magnified when item selection for some predictors (such as biographical inventories or attitude tests) is based on the same criterion, while item selection for others (such as aptitude tests) is not.

In addition to direct predictors, predictor batteries sometimes include *suppressor* variables and *moderator* variables. A suppressor variable has a low or near-zero correlation with the criterion, and a higher correlation with one or more direct predictors. Its inclusion removes from these direct predictors some of their non-valid variance and hence effectively increases the validity of the battery. A moderator variable (which may be qualitative as well as quantitative), classifies examinees into subgroups on the basis of their *predictability,* or into subgroups within which different predictor batteries or different weights for the same predictors are required for the best prediction. Present evidence suggests that use of moderator variables holds more promise than does use of supressor variables for the improvement of prediction procedures. Dunnette (1967) gives illustrations of the use of moderator variables and his bibliography covers most of the important literature.

A sample different from both the item-validation sample and the predictor-selection and weight-determination sample is required to estimate the predictive validity of a test or battery. Error is especially marked when attempts are made to estimate the test validity from the item-validation sample (Cureton, 1950), but similar though not so large errors occur when the battery validity is estimated from the weight-determination sample, and these errors increase when the weight-determination sample is used also for predictor selection. The sample used to estimate predictive validity is called a cross-validation sample. In this sample, the weights used are those derived from the previous sample, and the aggregate correlation in the cross-validation sample is always less than the multiple correlation in that sample, and almost always less than the multiple correlation in the weight-determination sample. The only exceptions, in this last case, occur when the random sampling errors reduce the multiple correlation in the weight-determination sample and/or increase the aggregate correlation in the cross-validation sample, and these effects are larger than the systematic effect tending to lower the aggregate correlation.

The correlation or aggregate correlation between a test or battery and a criterion is commonly termed a validity coefficient, but should properly be called an *index* of validity, and its square the *coefficient* of validity. It is this squared correlation which is the coefficient of determination: the proportion of the criterion-measure variance accounted for (or predicted by) the predictor scores.

Some of the more complex statistical problems encountered in predictor selection and validation are discussed by Horst (1955).

Predictive validity can be classified in several ways. Perhaps the most fundamental, and certainly the least used so far, is a classification into raw validity, true validity, and intrinsic validity.

Raw validity. This is simply the correlation or aggregate correlation between the predictor test or battery and the criterion measure. Raw validity is the appropriate measure when we are predicting a *sui generis* criterion.

True validity. Prediction of the raw freshman-sophomore cumulative grade-point average may be important if a college or university has a rule that those whose grade-point averages are below some fixed value may not enter the upper division. Suppose, however, that we wish to measure *academic achievement*. This is a trait-concept. The best criterion would be some sort of an adjusted grade-point average, leaving out first-semester or first-quarter grades because they are too much a reflection of initial adjustment to college, grades in applied music and art, physical education, and other clearly nonacademic subjects, and grades of "incomplete," commonly recorded as F's until removed. In a criterion measure of *selling ability* we might include with appropriate subjective weights (positive and negative) not only dollar volume, but also number of sales, number of new customers added, number of old customers lost, and some estimate of the difficulty of each salesman's territory. Work effectiveness is quite commonly assessed by ratings or work-behavior checklists filled out by supervisors. There is a considerable literature on criterion construction, review of which is beyond the scope of this treatment.

Note again that a constructed criterion measure is to be taken as an acceptable operational definition of the trait-concept. The criterion error of measurement is no part of this operational definition. With a constructed criterion, in contrast to a *sui generis* criterion, we are interested in predicting the *true* criterion scores rather than the raw scores. The *index of true validity* is therefore the correlation between the test or battery raw scores and the true scores on the criterion measure, and the *coefficient of true validity* is its square. To estimate its value we require two parallel forms of the criterion measure. This complicates the job of criterion construction very considerably, and it is fortunate that the two forms need not have equal reliabilities, equal variances, or equal means. If the criterion measures are denoted y_2 and y_{II}, and the predictor x_1, the *coefficient* of true validity is

$$r_{1y}^2 = \frac{r_{12}\,r_{1II}}{r_{2II}},$$

and the *index* of true validity is the square root of this

expression. If there are several predictors, r_{12} and r_{1II} are aggregate correlations. The behavior samples on which y_2 and y_{II} are based may cover the same time period (e.g., odd and even days or weeks), or two different time periods, depending on how much criterion-behavior instability we wish to remove. If we wish to remove only the criterion inconsistency; i.e., to predict the true criterion behavior over only the time period during which it was observed, r_{2II} becomes a consistency coefficient, and the two sets of criterion observations must cover the same identical period of time. In constructing a grade-point-average criterion, course grades should be allocated to forms in such a manner that all the courses of a sequence taught by the same professor are assigned to one form of the criterion measure.

Correction for Attenuation and Intrinsic Validity. The stability coefficient is an inter-form correlation corrected for attenuation due to the inconsistencies of the two forms. The true validity coefficient is a test-criterion correlation corrected for attenuation due to criterion (but not test) unreliability. In complete correction for attenuation, we are estimating the correlation between two sets of true scores. Attenuation of the raw-score correlation due to both inconsistency and instability is to be removed. Instability errors are more troublesome, and experimental procedures are strictly limited. The general principle is that in a formula for correction for attenuation, the two variables entering into every correlation coefficient in the formula must be separated experimentally by the same identical time interval.

Suppose we have a vocabulary test with forms x_1 and x_I and true score x, and an arithmetic test with forms y_2 and y_{II} and true score y, and we wish to estimate r_{xy}, the correlation between the two sets of true scores; i.e., the intrinsic correlation between vocabulary and arithmetical ability, or the correlation we would obtain if we had two perfectly reliable tests. One procedure would be to print all four tests in a special booklet, with alternating vocabulary and arithmetic items. x_1 and x_I would be the odd and even vocabulary items, and y_2 and y_{II} the odd and even arithmetic items. With this procedure, all four tests would be administered over essentially the same identical time interval, and the corrected correlation would be

$$r_{xy} = \sqrt{\frac{r_{(1+I)(2+II)}}{\frac{2r_{1I}}{1+r_{1I}} \frac{2r_{2II}}{1+r_{2II}}}}.$$

Here x_1 and x_I, and also y_2 and y_{II}, must have reliabilities near enough to being equal to satisfy the requirements of the Spearman-Brown formula.

With only one form of each test, but with alternating items in the test booklet, the formula would be

$$r_{xy} = \frac{r_{12}}{\sqrt{C_{11} C_{22}}},$$

and C_{11} and C_{22} would be the KR-20 consistency coefficients.

For a second procedure, we could administer x_1 and y_2, one right after the other, at one session, and x_I and y_{II}, one right after the other, at a second session a week or more later. We could then compute

$$r_{xy} = \sqrt{\frac{r_{1II} \, r_{I2}}{r_{1I} \, r_{2II}}}.$$

Note that in this formula r_{12} and r_{1II}, the correlations between forms given at the same session do not appear: every correlation in the formula is a correlation between a form given at the first session and a form given at the second session. In this case the instability over a week or more would be affected only very slightly by the time differences introduced by serial rather than simultaneous administration of x_1 and y_2 and of x_I and y_{II}. For this design, neither x_1 and x_I nor y_2 and y_{II} need be equally reliable.

If y_2 and y_{II} are parallel criterion measures, this last formula becomes the *index of intrinsic validity*, and its square would be the *coefficient of intrinsic validity*. The two sets of criterion observations should cover two different time periods, and one form of the predictor test should be administered as nearly as possible at the exact middle of each of these periods. If the two sets of criterion observations cover the same period of time, the two forms of the predictor should be administered simultaneously at the middle of this period. In this case the first formula, above, is used, and the two criterion forms as well as the two test forms must be equally reliable or nearly so. Intrinsic validity is usually concurrent validity (see below). Occasionally, however, we might wish to try out two short forms of a new *type* of predictor, to see if longer forms would be worth constructing. In this case the predictor forms might logically be administered at one time and the criterion observations obtained at a later time.

Differential Validity. When we deal with problems of job classification and assignment, or with problems of educational and vocational guidance, we are interested not merely in how well the examinee would do on one criterion performance, but on which of two or more criterion measures he would do better, or best. The criteria are usually, but not necessarily, *sui generis*. These problems may be attacked by discriminant analysis, in which case the "criterion measure" is a nominal scale of group membership, or we may have actual measures of criterion proficiency. In this latter case there is usually available for each member of the experimental group a proficiency measure on only one criterion. The resulting statistical problems are discussed by Horst (1954).

Another classification of predictive validity is based on the time relations between the administration of the predictor test or battery and the occurrence of the behavior on which the criterion measure is based.

Forecast Validity. This is the case when the prediction, or some decision based on it, must necessarily be made before the criterion behavior occurs. The most common example is the selection situation. With a *sui generis* criterion we have forecast raw validity. With a constructed (two-form) criterion we have forecast true validity. In either case, the instability errors caused by the time lapse between the administration of the predictor(s) and the occurrence of the criterion behavior are intrinsic to the enterprise and cannot be corrected. Ideally all members of the experimental group should be selected and retained until the criterion behavior has occurred; when the same test or battery is used both for selection and for the validation of the predictor(s) the available correction procedures are unsatisfactory.

Concurrent Validity. Concurrent validity is a term commonly used in the sense in which we shall use "retroactive validity." It is used here in a special narrow sense. The enterprise itself is no longer prediction, but *substitute measurement*. This substitute measurement may be desired because the alternative content-valid criterion measure may be too cumbersome or costly for operational use, or because the substitute measure may be much more reliable and hence possibly a better measure of the criterion true score than is the criterion raw score. Concurrent validity is almost always either true validity or intrinsic validity. Concurrent raw validity would in general be meaningless. The substitute measure is applied at the middle of the criterion behavior period, or if the criterion behavior is reaction to training, immediately following this period. Two forms of the criterion measure are required, not necessarily of equal reliability, and for concurrent intrinsic validity, two forms of the predictor also.

Retroactive Validity. This is usually the case in which the interval over which the criterion observations are obtained precedes the administration of the predictor(s). More generally, however, it is *any* case in which, for reasons of expediency, the predictor-criterion time relations are not controlled by the logic of the question to be answered.

Factorial Validity. Here we are trying to answer question A (What trait or combination of traits does a specific test measure?), but the test is quasi-homogeneous (all items of the same general type), and is more likely to be an aptitude test than an achievement test. A crude answer is given by simply reporting several correlations between the given test and other more or less similar tests measuring fairly well-known traits or functions. A better answer is given by reporting the results of factor analyses including the new test and a number of other well-known tests. For aptitude tests, the Educational Testing Service has issued a set of recommended reference tests for such factor analyses (Franch & others, 1963).

Construct Validity. Here we come to question C. We start with a *trait-construct*: a hypothesis that a certain trait exists and can be measured. Then we build a test which we hope will measure this trait. The questions are then (a) Does the trait-construct actually represent a measurable trait? (b) Does the test measure that trait rather than some other trait?

The trait-construct is such that no single criterion measure can be constructed, and it names an aptitude or interest or attitude or personality trait of such a type that content validation is inapplicable. It implies, however, that correlations with some measurable traits should be fairly high, with others moderate, and with still others low or near-zero. If the test has high to moderate correlations where the hypothesis says it should, this result is termed *convergent validity* If it has low or near-zero correlations where the hypothesis says it should, this result is termed *discriminant validity* (Campbell & Fiske, 1959). Construct validity cannot be demonstrated conclusively. All we can do is to pile up evidence until the hypothesis reaches a state of high credibility and can be termed at least a useful theory. A single correlation, on the other hand, which differs radically from prediction, will demonstrate either that the hypothesis is untenable or in need of radical revision, or that the test is invalid as a measure of the trait-construct. Thus R. Thorndike (1936) factor-analyzed the subtest scores on a test of social intelligence and a test of mental alertness. The social intelligence subtests did not generate a substantial distinct factor, but loaded mainly on a verbal factor along with several of the mental alertness subtests. The social intelligence test was *too good* a verbal intelligence test to be measuring anything much different from verbal intelligence.

Consider the trait-construct "general intelligence," and the Stanford-Binet Scale.

(a) "General intelligence" increases during the period of growth. So do Stanford-Binet scores, but so also do height and weight. Clearly, increase of scores with age during the period of growth is only a partial criterion.

(b) Teachers have some ability to rate differences in "general intelligence" among children of the same age. Stanford-Binet scores correlate positively and substantially with such estimates, but not highly. Teachers may overrate docile children, and underrate class nuisances, so this also is only a partial criterion.

(c) Inmates of institutions for the mentally defective make quite low scores, as a rule, but a few do not. Procedures are such that some pre-psychotics, severe reading disability cases, children with intense negative attitudes toward school, and seriously maladjusted children are committed. Of these latter, some make very low scores but some do not.

(d) Eminent individuals should and do make high scores on the Stanford-Binet. Most but not all of them make *very* high scores. Eminence, however, commonly requires exceptional traits of character or personality, or special talents, as well as high "general intelligence." Outstanding scholars, great writers, scientists, musical composers, philosophers, etc., make higher scores than do equally great statesmen, business executives, military leaders, and musical performers. It is these latter for whom the requirements of exceptional non-intellectual traits are most apparent.

(e) Tests measuring diverse but clearly cognitive traits should all correlate positively and substantially. They do. Factor analyses of large batteries of such tests yield several first-order factors. These factors are all positively correlated and yield only one major second-order factor. "General intelligence" appears then to be a global trait rather than a primary trait. The items of the Stanford-Binet sample a variety of cognitive functions. Their inter-item correlations yield a large general factor and a number of relatively small group factors.

(f) Reliable homogeneous tests measuring different primary traits should have higher correlations with the Stanford-Binet than with one another. In general, they do.

(g) Reliable tests of clearly noncognitive traits, such as strength, agility, dexterity, reaction time, sensori-motor coordination, sensory discrimination, etc., should and do have low or near-zero correlations with the Stanford-Binet.

(h) Tests judged to be borderline-cognitive, such as rote memory, verbal fluency, mechanical knowledge, etc., should have intermediate-level correlations with the Stanford-Binet. They do.

Considering all of these predictions and results, along with others not cited above, the hypotheses that "general intelligence" is a measurable global trait and that the Stanford-Binet Scale is a good measure of that trait are supported.

The basic reference on construct validity is Cronbach and Meehl (1955). Loevenger (1957) discusses construct validity, among a number of other things, in a general treatment of the relations between testing procedures and psychological theories. Campbell and Fiske (1959) argue that a genuine trait must be demonstrable by different methods of measurement (e.g., tests and ratings), and propose the use of a multitrait–multimethod matrix to establish the validity of a trait-construct.

MEASUREMENT OF CHANGE. We can offer here little more than a sketch of this important and developing field. It was opened by E. Thorndike (1924), who pointed out that if x_1 is an initial score, y_2 an end score on a duplicate form, and $g_3 = y_2 - x_1$, then r_{13}, the correlation between initial scores and gains, will contain a spurious element because the end-score error of measurement enters positively into both y_2 and g_3. Thomson (1924, 1925) derived the correction for attenuation, r_{xy}, and showed that in some cases a positive uncorrected correlation can yield a negative corrected correlation. Cureton (1930) proposed a slight modification of Thomson's formula, described the experimental design to which it applied, and derived its standard error. Zieve (1940) derived an alternative form of this correction.

More recent writers have suggested that the gain score should be estimated by regression rather than simple subtraction. There are several ways to do this. Authors of some of the chapters in Harris (1963) discuss these methods, and the bibliography of this book is relatively complete through 1962.

Manning and Du Bois (1962) consider the correlation between an independent variable, say w_4, and a gain score. They are concerned mainly with the *prediction* of gains in a training course. They discuss two types of partial correlation, $r_{42.1}$ and $r_{4(2.1)}$, the correlation between the independent variable and the end score, with the effect of the initial score eliminated either from both or only from the end score.

The latest attack on this problem is reported by Tucker and others (1966). They distinguish between two independent parts of the true gain score, the part that is independent of the initial test and the part that is wholly dependent on the initial test, provide formulas for estimating these components of the true-gain variance, and compare their model with the earlier difference models and regression models.

Edward E. Cureton
University of Tennessee

References

Aiken, Lewis R., Jr. "The Probability of Chance Success on Objective Test Items." *Ed Psychol Meas* 25:127–34; 1965.

Baker, Frank B. "Origins of the Item Parameters X_{50} and β As a Modern Item Analysis Technique." *J Ed Meas* 2:167–80; 1965.

Birnbaum, Allan. *Efficient Design and Use of Tests of Mental Ability for Various Decision-making Problems.* School Aviation Medicine, United States Air Force, 1957.

Block, Jack. *The Challenge of Response Sets.* Appleton, 1965.

Bloom, Benjamin S., and others. *Taxonomy of Educational Objectives, Handbook 1, Cognitive Domain.* McKay, 1956. 207p.

Brogden, Hubert E. "Variation in test Validity with Variation in the Distribution of Item Difficulties, Number of Items, and Degree of Their Intercorrelation." *Psychometrika* 11:197–214; 1946.

Brogden, Hubert S. "A New Coefficient: Application to Biserial Correlation and to Estimation of Selective Efficiency." *Psychometrika* 14:169–82; 1949.

Brooks, R. D. *An Empirical Check on Rasch's Model for Item Difficulty Indices.* State U New York, 1965.

Calandra, Alexander. "Scoring Formulas and Probability Considerations." *Psychometrika* 6:1–9; 1941.

Campbell, Donald T., and Fiske, Donald W. "Convergent and Discriminant Validation by the Multitrait-multimethod Matrix." *Psychol B* 56:81–105; 1959.

Campbell, N. R. *An Account of the Principles of Measurement and Calculation.* McKay, 1928.

Campbell, N. R., and others. "Final Report." *Advancement Sci* 2:331–49; 1940.

Carroll, John B. "The Effect of Difficulty and Chance Success on Correlations Between Items or Between Tests." *Psychometrika* 10:1–19; 1945.

Chernoff, Herman. "The Scoring of Multiple Choice Questionnaires." *Annals Math Stat* 33:375–93; 1962.

Clemans, William V. *An Analytical and Empirical Examination of Some Properties of Ipsative Measures.* Psychometric Society, 1966.

Coombs, Clyde H. "Theory and Methods of Social Measurement." In Festinger, Leon, and Katz, Daniel. (Eds.) *Research Methods in the Behavioral Sciences.* Dryden, 1953. p. 471–535.

Coombs, Clyde H. *A Theory of Data.* Wiley, 1963.

Coombs, Clyde H., and others. "The Assessment of Partial Knowledge." *Ed Psychol Meas* 16:13–37; 1955.

Cronbach, Lee J. "Coefficient Alpha and the Internal Structure of Tests." *Psychometrika* 16:297–334; 1951.

Cronbach, Lee J., and Meehl, Paul E. "Construct Validity in Psychological Tests." *Psychol B* 52:281–302; 1955.

Cronbach, Lee J., and Warrington, Willard G. "Efficiency of Multiple-choice Tests as a Function of Spread of Item Difficulties." *Psychometrika* 17:127–47; 1952.

Cureton, Edward E. "A Modification of Thomson's Formula for the Correlation Between Initial Status and Gain, and its Standard Error." *J Exp Psychol* 13:358–64; 1930.

Cureton, Edward E. "Validity, Reliability, and Baloney." *Ed Psychol Meas* 18:715–38; 1958.

Cureton, Edward E. "The Upper and Lower 27% Rule." *Psychometrika* 14:169–82; 1959.

Cureton, Edward E. "Reliability and Validity: Basic Assumptions and Experimental Designs." *Ed Psychol Meas* 25:327–46; 1965.

Cureton, Edward E. "The Correction for Guessing." *J Exp Ed* 34:44–7; 1966.

Cureton, Edward E. "Difficulty Scaling of Recognition Items." *Psychometrika* 32:195–8; 1967.

Das Gupta, S. "Point Biserial Correlation Coefficient and its Generalization." *Psychometrika* 25:393–408; 1960.

Davis, Frederick B. "Estimation and Use of Scoring Weights for Each Choice in Multiple-choice Test Items." *Ed Psychol Meas* 19:291–8; 1959.

Davis, Frederick B., and Fifer, Gordon. "The Effect on Test Reliability and Validity of Scoring Aptitude and Achievement Tests with Weights for Every Choice." *Ed Psychol Meas* 19:159–69; 1959.

DeFinetti, B. "Methods for Discriminating Levels of Partial Knowledge Concerning a Test Item." *Br J Math Stat Psychol* 18:87–123; 1965.

Dunnette, Marvin D. "Development of Moderator Variables to Enhance the Prediction of Managerial Effectiveness." *J Applied Psychol* 18:87–123; 1967.

Edwards, Allen L. *The Social Desirability Variable in Personality Assessment and Research.* Dryden, 1957.

Eisler, H. "On Psychophysics in General and the General Psychophysical Differential Equation in Particular." *Scandinavian J Psychol* 6:85–102; 1965.

Fan, Chung-Teh. *Item-Analysis Table.* ETS, 1952.

Fan, Chung-Teh. "Note on the Construction of an Item Analysis Table for the High-low-27-per-cent Group Method." *Psychometrika* 19:231–7; 1954.

Findley, Warren G. "A Rationale for Evaluation of Item Discrimination Statistics." *Ed Psychol Meas* 16:175–80; 1956.

Flanagan, John C. *Calculating Correlation Coefficients.* American Institutes for Research, 1962.

French, John W., and others. *Kit of Reference Tests for Cognitive Factors.* ETS, 1963.

Ghiselli, Edwin E. *Theory of Psychological Measurement.* McGraw-Hill, 1964.

Glass, Gene V., and Wiley, David E. "Formula Scoring and Test Reliability." *J Ed Meas* 1:43–9; 1964.

Gulliksen, Harold E. *Theory of Mental Tests.* Wiley, 1950.

Guttman, Louis. "A Basis for Analyzing Test-retest Reliability." *Psychometrika* 10:255–82; 1945.

Hamilton, C. Horace. "Bias and Error in Multiple-choice Tests." *Psychometrika* 15:151–6; 1950.

Harris, Chester W. (Ed.). *Problems in Measuring Change.* U Wisconsin Press, 1963.

Hempel, C. G. "Fundamentals of Concept Formation in Empirical Science." In *International Encyclopedia of Unified Science.* U Chicago Press, 1952.

Horst, Paul. "Item Selection by Means of a Maximizing Function." *Psychometrika* 1:229–44; 1936.

Horst, Paul. "A Technique for the Development of a Differential Prediction Battery." *Psychol Monogr* No. 380, 1954.

Horst, Paul. "A Technique for the Development of a Multiple Absolute Prediction Battery." *Psychol Monogr* No. 390, 1955.

Hoyt, Cyril. "Test Reliability Estimated by Analysis of Variance." *Psychometrika* 6:153–60; 1941.

Jackson, Douglas H., and Messick, Samuel. "Acquiescence and Desirability as Response Determinants on the MMPI." *Ed Psychol Meas* 21:771–90; 1961.

Keats, J. A. "Test Theory." In Farnsworth, Paul R., and others. (Eds.) *Annual Review of Psychology.* Annual Reviews Incorporated, 1967. p. 217–38.

Kelley, Truman L. "The Selection of Upper and Lower Groups for the Validation of Test Items." *J Ed Psychol* 30:17–24; 1939.

Kendall, Maurice G. *Rank Correlation Methods.* 3rd ed. Hafner, 1962.

Kruskal, William S. and Wallis, W. Allen. "Use of Ranks in One-Criterion Variance Analysis." *J Am Stat Assn* 47:583–621, 1952.

Kuder, G. Frederick, and Richardson, Marion W. "The Theory of the Estimation of Test Reliability." *Psychometrika* 2:151–60; 1937.

Loevenger, Jane. "Objective Tests as Instruments of Psychological Theory." *Psychol Reports* 3:635–94; 1957. (Monograph Supplement No. 9.)

Lord, Frederick M. *A Theory of Test Scores.* Psychometric Monograph No. 7. Psychometric Corporation, 1952(a).

Lord, Frederick M. "The Relation of the Reliability of Multiple-choice Tests to the Distribution of Item Difficulties." *Psychometrika* 17:181–94; 1952(b).

Lord, Frederick M. "An Application of Confidence Intervals and of Maximum Likelihood to the Estimation of an Examinee's Ability." *Psychometrika* 18:57–75; 1953(a).

Lord, Frederick M. "The Relation of Test Score to the Trait Underlying the Test." *Ed Psychol Meas* 13:517–49; 1953(b).

Lord, Frederick M. "Estimating Test Reliability." *Ed Psychol Meas* 15:325–36; 1955.

Lord, Frederick M. "Test Reliability: A Correction." *Ed Psychol Meas* 22:511–2; 1962.

Lord, Frederick M. "Formula Scoring and Validity." *Ed Psychol Meas* 23:663–72; 1963.

Lord, Frederick M. "A Strong True-score Theory, With Applications." *Psychometrika* 30:239–70; 1965(*a*).

Lord, Frederick M. "An Empirical Study of Item-test Regression." *Psychometrika* 30:373–6; 1965(*b*).

Lord, Frederic M., and Novick, Melvin R. *Statistical Theories of Mental Test Scores*. Addison, 1968.

Luce, R. Duncan. "Semi-Orders and a Theory of Utility Discrimination." *Econometrika* 24:178–91; 1956.

Luce, R. Duncan, and Tukey, John W. "Simultaneous Conjoint Measurement: a New Type of Fundamental Measurement." *J Math Psychol* 1:1–27; 1964.

Lyerly, Samuel B. "A Note on Correcting for Chance Success in Objective Tests." *Psychometrika* 16:21–30; 1951.

Manning, W. H., and DuBois, P. H. "Correlational Methods in Research on Human Learning." *Perceptual and Motor Skills* 15:287–321; 1962.

Messick, Samuel, and Jackson, Douglas H. "Acquiescence and the Factorial Interpretation of the MMPI." *Psychol B* 58:299–304; 1961.

Rasch, G. *Probabilistic Models for Some Intelligence and Attainment Scales*. Danish Institutes for Educational Research, 1960.

Ross, John, and Weitzman, R. A. "The Twenty-seven Per Cent Rule." *Annals Math Stat* 34:214–21; 1965.

Ross, S. *Logical Foundations of Psychological Measurement: A Study in the Philosophy of Science*. Scandinavian U Books, 1964.

Ruch, Giles M., and De Graff, M. H. "Correction for Chance and 'Guess' Versus 'Do Not Guess' Instructions in Multiple-response Tests." *J Ed Psychol* 17:368–75; 1926.

Ruch, Giles M., and Stoddard, George D. "Comparative Reliabilities of Five Types of Objective Examinations." *J Ed Psychol* 16:89–103; 1925.

Rulon, Phillip J. "A Simplified Procedure for Determining the Reliability of a Test by Split-halves." *Harvard Ed R* 19:99–103; 1939.

Scott, D., and Suppes, Patrick. "Foundational Aspects of Theories of Measurement." *J Symbolic Logic* 23:113–28; 1958.

Siegel, Sidney, and Tukey, John W. "A Nonparametric Sum of Ranks Procedure for Relative Spread in Unpaired Samples." *J Am Stat Assn* 55:429–45; 1960.

Stevens, S. S. "Mathematics, Measurement and Psychophysics." In Stevens, S. S. (Ed.) *Handbook of Experimental Psychology*. Wiley, 1951. p. 1–49.

Stevens, S. S. "Measurement, Psychophysics, and Utility." In Churchman, C. West, and Ratoosh, Philburn. (Eds.) *Measurement: Definitions and Theories*. Wiley, 1959. p. 18–63.

Suppes, Patrick, and Zinnes, Joseph L. "Basic Measurement Theory." In Luce, R. Duncan, and others. (Eds.) *Handbook of Mathematical Psychology*. Vol. I. Wiley, 1963. p. 1–76.

Swineford, Frances. "The Measurement of a Personality Trait." *J Ed Psychol* 29:295–300; 1938.

Swineford, Frances. "Analysis of a Personality Trait." *J Ed Psychol* 32:438–44; 1941.

Thomson, Godfrey H. "A Formula to Correct for the Effect of Errors of Measurement on the Correlation of Initial Values with Gains." *J Exp Psychol* 7:321–4; 1924.

Thomson, Godfrey H. "An Alternative Formula for the True Correlation of Initial Values with Gains." *J Exp Psychol* 8:323–4; 1925.

Thorndike, Edward L. "The Influence of Chance Imperfections of Measures Upon the Relation of Initial Score to Gain or Loss." *J Exp Psychol* 7:225–32; 1924.

Thorndike, Robert L. "Factor Analysis of Social and Abstract Intelligence." *J Ed Psychol* 27:231–3; 1936.

Torgerson, Warren S. *Theory and Methods of Scaling*. Wiley, 1958. p. 1–60.

Tucker, Ledyard R. "Maximum Validity of a Test with Equivalent Items." *Psychometrika* 11:1–13; 1946.

Tucker, Ledyard R., and others. "A Base-free Measure of Change." *Psychometrika* 31:457–73; 1966.

Wesman, Alexander G. "Effect of Speed on Item-test Correlations." *Ed Psychol Meas* 9:51–7; 1949.

Zieve, L. "Note on the Correlation of Initial Scores with Gain." *J Ed Psychol* 31:391–4; 1940.

MEDICAL EDUCATION

The first American program of medical education was a formal series of lectures designed to supplement an apprenticeship. Today, two centuries later, most students enter their medical studies after graduating from college, spend four years in a medical school, move on to a hospital for one year of internship, follow this by one to five years of residency (specialty) training, and are then expected to engage in a program of continuing education for the rest of their professional lives. This evolution reflects not only an enormous growth in medical knowledge but also the changing values of the medical profession and the university community to which medicine is now firmly bound. Although educational empiricism has played a greater role than educational research in this slow evolutionary process (summarized by Norwood, 1965), the effect of one study carried out more than 50 years ago is still felt today.

Reviewing the history of medical education in North America, Abraham Flexner (1910) noted that between 1765 and 1910, 457 medical schools had been spawned. Flexner visited the 155 that were still functioning and found that most were frankly commercial ventures. Only 22 required as much as two years of college preparation for admission, 50 accepted students with a high school diploma "or equivalent" (very loosely interpreted); the remainder, including some that were nominally part of a university, made little pretense of academic prerequisites.

Instructional programs were generally a parody of sound education for a scientific profession. The facilities for teaching the basic medical sciences were often no more than a lecture room and a dirty laboratory with a few dreary anatomical specimens and broken or unused equipment of the most primitive kind. Clinical teaching was little better; in many schools, students gained no direct experience with patients beyond an occasional opportunity to watch their teachers at work in a dispensary or ward. The resulting report was so merciless that nearly half of these medical schools closed their doors, and a majority of the survivors rushed to find a university haven. Flexner was so successful in establishing the importance of a formal collegiate premedical course of study (to include physics, chemistry, and biology), two medical-school years of basic sciences (anatomy, biochemistry, physiology, pathology, pharmacology, and bacteriology) built upon direct laboratory experience, followed by two years of clinical experience with patients (in the major fields of medicine, surgery, obstetrics, and gynecology), that fifty years later this curricular format is still the standard.

TRENDS. Basic shifts in educational patterns and emphasis are now appearing. Some reflect the view that added strength will be gained by integrating the basic scientific disciplines, whose sharp borders have become blurred, with the clinical disciplines whose increasingly sophisticated techniques and methods of study more and more resemble those of the laboratory sciences. Others suggest that the infusion of physical and biological science required to strengthen medical schools in 1910 must now be complemented by a comparable infusion of social and behavioral sciences to make medical education more relevant to the social needs of 1970 (Evans, 1964).

The most widely known break with tradition has taken place at Western Reserve University (Ham, 1962), where the conventional departmental and subject-matter focus of instruction has shifted to a student and topic focus, where the provision of substantial amounts of free time has replaced the rigidly scheduled program, and where the usual emphasis upon simple acquisition of information has been modified by encouraging personal inquiry into problems. Instead of the conventional departmental offerings, instruction in the first two phases is provided by interdepartmental subject committees dealing with systems rather than disciplines. Patients are introduced at the outset through a family-care program to which each entering student is assigned. A long-term evaluation of the program is under way (Mawardi, 1965) through follow-up of graduates of the earlier educational system as well as of the new program. A description of the more immediate impact of the program upon 20 students has been accomplished through intensive interviews over four years and an accumulation of extensive background and medical-school performance data on this group (Horowitz, 1964).

Lee (1962) has included in a summary of other significant innovations of the last decade those that attempt to integrate medical-school and university education and those that focus upon teaching comprehensive patient care. Among the integrated programs, acceleration has been a major goal or an important by-product. At Northwestern and Boston universities, for example, specially selected students admitted directly from high school can gain their M.D. degrees in six rather than the usual eight years. In all integrated programs, special courses have been designed and a substantial amount of elective time is also provided. The comprehensive-care programs (e.g., those at Cornell, Colorado, and Temple) have made a special effort to incorporate into clinical teaching the disciplines of sociology and psychology and to highlight the critical importance of disease prevention as a balance to a common faculty preoccupation with diagnosis and treatment.

As specialty practice has displaced general practice as the modal career goal, internship and residency training have been subjected to increasing scrutiny. The Citizens' Commission (Millis, 1966) has proposed elimination of the traditional rotating internship in favor of immediate postgraduate specialty training, including the specialty of family practice devoted primarily to nonsurgical, continuous, comprehensive, and preventive patient care.

A final trend reflects recognition of the view that education is a complex and demanding professional task built upon a vast literature and a definable set of skills and acceptance of the thesis that the practice of medical education is likely to be improved if it is based upon research. To implement this conclusion, nine medical schools have established educational-research units since 1959, and others are in the planning stage (Miller, 1966).

STUDENT SELECTION. At the present time, only one of every two applicants to medical school gains admission. The primary criteria in the selection process are past achievement (chiefly premedical grade-point average), performance on the Medical College Admission Test (a standardized measure of verbal and quantitative aptitude and of achievement in selected premedical sciences and general information categories), recommendations from premedical advisors, and personal interviews. An extensive description of these and other procedures has been included in the report of the Fourth Teaching Institute of the Association of American Medical Colleges (Gee & Cowles, 1956).

The purpose of this selection process is to identify candidates who (1) can complete training, (2) do well in training programs, (3) possess the personal characteristics of professional persons, and (4) will perform creditably as practitioners.

It is widely agreed that the premedical grade-point average is the best and most consistent predictor of success in medical school (Gottheil & Michael, 1957; Gough & others, 1963; Johnson & Hutchins, 1966) when success is measured by grades. Tests of intelligence, achievement (other than in science), reading skill, interests, personality, and background variables generally have low correlations with academic performance in medical schools. The usefulness of the *Medical College Admission Test (MCAT)* has been widely debated (Gough & others, 1963). Sanazaro and Hutchins (1963) have reviewed the rationale of the *MCAT* and have attempted to separate the selection and prediction issues, noting the special problems of correlational studies when the performance criterion is often questionable (e.g., medical-school tests and faculty judgments of undetermined reliability).

The validity question is especially pressing since none of the selection measures presently employed assesses adequately the self-reliance and critical judgment required of the professional; all seem to stress convergent thinking or, at best, a very narrow range of forecasters.

Studies of academically successful and unsuccessful students have revealed, among other things, frequent manifestations of inhibition and rigidity in the *Rorschach Test* and more frequent evidence of abnormal adaptation to medical school among the low-success group than among the high-success group; a significantly greater intellectual curiosity in the high-success group; and a steadily declining identification with medicine in the low-success group (cause or effect of academic difficulty?). Intrinsic emotional problems appear only slightly more frequently in the low-success group, but these individuals seem far less able to deal with their own feelings than the high achievers, who often use their drive to succeed to augment their performance rather than allowing it to impede it (Lief & others, 1965).

Most medical educators are prepared to agree that medical schools attract a reasonable share of the most talented students, but some are concerned that the length and cost of medical education, the academic prerequisites, the nature of the medical-school program, or the criteria for selection eliminates candidates whose interests and values would make them especially desirable practitioners in a world of changing health needs and patttterns of medical care. In one study of undergraduates who abandoned their plans for medical careers (Funkenstein, 1961), none of the undergraduates cited the duration or the cost of medical education as a reason for the career shift, although one-quarter of the group was even then receiving financial aid. Among those with a "favorable" image of the physician (socially oriented, a healer), a majority withdrew because of low science grades. Among those with an "unfavorable" image of the physician, one group saw him as a kind of inferior scientist, while another saw him as a narrow, nonhumanitarian, coldly scientific practitioner.

Rosinski (1965) looked at another dimension of the selection problem. Categorizing students in four medical schools according to generally accepted criteria, he found that 50 percent fell into the upper- or upper-middle-class (against a national incidence of 14 percent), while only 13 percent were derived from upper-lower- or lower-lower-class families (against a national incidence of 54 percent). Whether this skewness represents a motivational problem, an economic issue, or a fault in the selection process, the implication that medicine draws its students from a very limited segment of the population deserves the most thoughtful attention.

Attrition. The problem of prediction of academic success is not limited to medicine, but the duration and cost of medical education are so great that neither individual students, the schools, nor society can afford a system that does not screen out most of those who are unable to survive. Following the process of more than 75,000 students admitted to 72 American medical schools between 1949 and 1958, Johnson and Hutchins (1966) found that 11,152 failed to graduate on time (i.e., four academic years after matriculation), and 6,556 failed to graduate at all. Since each of these failing students prevented another from being admitted, the actual loss of new physicians is substantially higher. The 9-percent annual loss from medical schools contrasts with 40 percent in law, 44 percent in nursing, 51 percent in engineering, and 20 percent in theology. After a steady decline from 25 percent in 1920 to 7 percent in 1950, the present rise is a matter of special concern, for the measured quality of applicants has not diminished during the 1950 to 1960 period. Approximately 5 percent of the attrition is attributed to academic and 4 percent to nonacademic causes. It is substantially higher for older students, for females (chiefly for nonacademic reasons), and for those with low *MCAT* scores and low grades in college. There is no perceptible difference in motivation (age of decision, intensity of interest, parental encouragement) between students who make regular progress and those who are delayed or dropped. Student factors are not the only identifiable variables. High-attrition schools are often characterized by great discrepencies between faculty and student perception of institutional purpose and procedure, by academic warfare among faculty groups, or by rigid departmental autonomy. High attrition is viewed as a symptom of an underlying institutional disease—a faulty interaction between students and school.

Career Choice. With the increasing variety of careers open to medical graduates, interest has grown in the identification of early predictors of career choice. Students with low *MCAT* scores are more likely than those with high scores to enter general practice (Schumacher, 1964b; Peterson & others, 1963). On the basis of data obtained when the students in one sample were medical-school applicants or freshmen, a set of distinguishing nonintellectual characteristics could also be identified (Schumacher, 1964b). For example, the theoretic-aesthetic combination (*Allport-Vernon-Lindzey Scale*) was high in the research group, low in the general-practice group, with a reverse pattern on the economic scale; the need for dominance (*Edwards Personal Preference Scale*) was the highest among those who chose surgical specialties, lowest among those who chose general practice. All groups, except those who chose research, were low on the social service scale (*Strong Vocational Inventory*). The choice of an academic career was far more likely among those who came from large cities or went to private medical schools. Nearly half of those selecting general practice, but fewer than 20 percent of those choosing other medical careers, were married when they entered medical school.

THE SETTING FOR LEARNING. Medical faculty members have strong feeling about the importance of institutional influence upon educational outcomes, but until the Association of American Medical Colleges turned its attention to the systematic study of these elements in the educational process, little solid information was available either to support or to deny the beliefs. Data now make clear the inaccuracy of a widespread assertion that a medical education of quality cannot be achieved in a school that admits more than an "optimal" 50 to 100 students per year. There is no perceptible relationship between class size and the quality of entering students, academic achievement, attrition rate, or career choice, although size may influence the way in which students perceive the environment (Hutchins, 1964; Sanazaro, 1966). Far more important influences upon educational outcome are such variables as the extent to which a school draws students from a national pool (i.e., percent of out-of-state students enrolled), expenditures for basic operations and sponsored research programs, and the faculty-student ratio (Sanazaro, 1965).

Curricular Influences. Despite the difficulty of identifying the ultimate effect of curricular form and instructional pattern upon the physician product, curricular changes continue and some have been analyzed with sufficient care to reveal the relative importance of multiple variables. A University of Colorado study (Hammond & Kern, 1959) attempted to separate the effects of an experimental program from those of individual student differences on the achievement of medical, psychological, and sociological knowledge, skills, and attitudes in the area of comprehensive medical care. The experimental program succeeded in preventing an increasingly negative view about comprehensive care that occurred among students in the conventional program, but positive achievement of the educational objectives was demonstrably more dependent on student differences than on program differences.

A program designed to encourage greater understanding of the multiple factors involved in health and illness and to encourage skill in working with other health workers and patients was no more successful than conventional instruction when standard methods of appraising student performance were utilized. Anecdotal records, however, suggested that many students exhibited the desired behavior when they were participants in the experimental program but found it unwise to continue when they moved to other clinical services where attention to such elements of professional behavior was not highly prized (Haggerty, 1962).

This may reflect a widespread faculty preoccupation with cognitive goals at the expense of psychomotor and affective objectives, and the apparent belief that the possession of information will lead to appropriate action. Since student acquisition of information ranks so high in the general faculty system of educational priorities, it is encouraging to note that even in medical school, students who are given assistance in defining objectives clearly, provided with a variety of learning resources, and offered periodic critiques of their performance will gain as much information by independent study as colleagues who are offered the facts in carefully prepared didactic form and will in addition develop important new skills and attitudes (Zimmerman & King, 1963).

This may not assuage faculty anxiety that students given such freedom will "waste" time, but the one solidly documented study of how medical students do use their time is reassuring. Although they made significant choices about the classes they would attend, the median student invested 65 hours per week in the task of learning. Further, there was no correlation between achievement, as conventionally judged by faculty measures, and the amount of time spent in formally scheduled activities (Fisher & Cotsonas, 1965).

Because the amount of medical knowledge has grown so large and continues to increase at a frightening rate, it is particularly important that faculties make judgments about the quantity and the purpose of what they expect students to learn. For example, a decision must soon be reached about whether it is really essential for medical students to become familiar with 13,000 new terms, of which 8,000 are in anatomy alone (Bridge, 1962); and if it is, whether the present random method of acquiring this vocabulary is sufficiently efficient. Most medical faculty members, however, know relatively little about the information taught, or the learning expected, outside their own narrow departmental area. A two-year effort to define and code the informational load at one medical school (Rosinski & Blanton, 1962) was both revealing and helpful in curricular reconstruction. An attempt to define cognitive goals and to design instructional and evaluation programs on an interinstitutional basis is also worthy of note (Ginther, 1963).

When physicians are asked what they identify as the greatest deficiency in their medical-school education, it is not information they cite but instruction in physician-patient relationships (Gee, 1960). This perception provides from the field some support for the current curricular changes that attempt to correct what many feel has been an unfortunate shift away from patient care as the central element in medical education.

Yet change in the structure of a curriculum will not necessarily alter the percieved educational purpose or the unwritten value system of a school. The sociological studies of medical education carried out over the past decade have provided persuasive evidence that the attitudes and expectations which students bring to medical school with them, the frequent conflicts between student and faculty goals that often convert an educational program into undeclared warfare, the internal forces that result from informal student groupings, the complex process of professsionalization, and the necessary adaptation to living with uncertainty that is part of the physician's life all contribute potential impediments to the achievement of desirable objectives. However, if they are understood, they may also be utilized to facilitate the learning process (Merton & others, 1957; Gee & Glaser, 1957; Becker & others, 1961; Bloom, 1965).

Most of these reports have dealt with medical-school programs. A study of 27 university-hospital internships reveals comparable problems at this level of training—lack of clarity about objectives, program planning dictated more by faculty interests or patient loads than by educational purposes, and instruction that often seems at odds with even ill-defined objectives (Saunders, 1961; Payson & others, 1961).

Such findings may arouse uneasiness or despair, but if examined in the perspective of the generally high quality of American physicians who have emerged from programs that could have been still better, they can be regarded as the documentary base from which program improvement can start and as a welcome replacement for the comfortable opinions on which so much of professional education has been built in the past.

EVALUATION. A significant aid to the growing concern for better appraisal of student progress has been the steadily increasing use of the technically excellent objective examinations prepared by slowly changing panels of distinguished faculty members working with the staff of the National Board of Medical Examiners. Part 1 of these National Board examinations tests knowledge of six basic medical sciences, Part 2 tests knowledge of six major clinical disciplines, and Part 3 probes clinical performance skills. Hubbard and Clemans (1960) have summarized the mean score and the percentages of honor and failure scores in each discipline, as well as in content categories of each discipline, for 30 medical schools in which all students take Parts 1 and 2. Such a national reference is very useful to an institution or to an individual student in delineating comparative academic strengths and weaknesses.

A factor analysis of 11 measures of performance (mean scores on the National Board Parts 1, 2, and 3; first-, second-, and third-year grade-point averages; and peer ratings on medical knowledge, diagnostic skill, and patient relationships) for 306 students in five medical schools revealed only two factors (Schumacher, 1964a). The first, accounting for 44 percent of variance and 83 percent of correlation in the original matrix, was best labeled general medical knowledge. Only one section of the Part 3 National Board examination (that requiring the taking of a history and the performance of a physical examination) and the peer rating on patient relationships failed to load heavily on this factor. Such a finding suggests either that this factor is very complex, with strong relationships among the various component parts, or that all the measures are assessing essentially the same thing.

In a systematic study of the intellectual process probed by written medical examinations (McGuire, 1963), subject-matter experts independently classified each item in four National Board examinations according to a taxonomy of intellectual processes ranging from recall of informational fragments to independent synthesis of ideas. Fewer than 8 percent of these items appeared to require interpretation or evaluation of data; the remainder assessed predominantly factual recall. In an observational study of 158 half-hour oral examinations carried out by eight trained observers using a standardized rating form, 70 percent of the interrogations appeared to require only simple recall of facts, 20 percent required interpretive skill (chiefly x-ray interpretation), and only 13 percent probed problem-solving ability (McGuire, 1966).

Development of methods to appraise the more complex cognitive, psychomotor, and affective educational objectives is being vigorously pursued. Hubbard and others (1965), reporting dissatisfaction with the Part 3 National Board examination, redefined, through a critical incident study, the clinical competence it was to assess. They then developed new test procedures using films, slides, and photographic reproductions to assess diagnostic recognition skills, and they programmed examinations to appraise sequential problem-solving ability. Other innovations have been reported by Rimoldi (1961), McGuire (1966), Barrows and Abrahamson (1964), and Cowles (1965).

The educational outcome of the internship year has never been satisfactorily documented. There is widespread debate about whether it is most profitably spent in a large or a small hospital, a community hospital or one affiliated with a university, a public institution or one privately controlled. Using National Board Part 2 and Part 3 scores as input and output measures of intern quality, Levit and others (1963) found that the university-affiliated hospitals attract significantly better interns than nonaffiliated institutions, that at the end of the internship a discernible, though barely significant, difference between interns is still evident, but that when the effect of input difference is eliminated, output difference vanishes. This suggests that the intern variable is more important than the program variable. Among university-affiliated hospitals, institutional size, public or private control, and size of stipend have no perceptible effect on either input or output.

Attention is also being directed to the ultimate outcome of medical education–clinical performance. Price and others (1964), using 200 elements presumably related to professional competence, found no significant relationship between medical-college achievement as measured by grade-point average and any of these variables. In an observational analysis of 94 general practitioners at work (Peterson & others, 1956), the quality of practice bore no significant relationship to the medical school from which the physician graduated, his medical-college admission-test score, his class rank (except for physicians under 35), the length of his graduate training, or the number of continuing-medical-education programs in which he participated. These findings have, in general, been confirmed by Clute (1963), using similar observational methods on another population, and by Williamson (1965), using simulated clinical problems as the test instrument.

Because of the extraordinary amount of time, effort, and money being invested in the continuing education of practitioners, program evaluation by some means more informative than an account of attendance or an impression of worth is imperative for feedback to program planners. A model study (McGuire & others, 1964) in which the staff of a community hospital requested, and a national organization provided, a superbly staffed, technically well-presented, and generally admired weekend course on cardiac auscultation revealed that participant skill in identifying a standardized set of unknown heart sounds showed a gratifying pretest to posttest increment which was not evident in a control group. The individual gain was not related to age, type of practice, previous education, or continuing education. However, on retesting six months later, the experimental group's mean score was not significantly different from the preinstruction level. A systematic review of hospital records showed no significant change in the recorded cardiac examination after instruction. Such discouraging documentation has succeeded in focusing attention more sharply upon the pressing educational questions of program cost effectiveness.

TEACHING. The concern for improving the structure of the medical curriculum has been accompanied by a growing recognition that the process of instruction and the qualities of instructors also deserve attention.

The Medical School Instructor Attitude Inventory, completed by 247 teachers in seven medical schools, has provided some insight into the nature of faculty positions on such scales as democratic versus autocratic stance toward teaching, critical versus complimentary view of medical education, liberal versus traditional view of education at large, and appreciative versus depreciative attitude toward students (Rosinski & Miller, 1962). Although the schools were selected to represent major institutional types (e.g., public support with largely full-time faculty, church supported, and school without university affiliation), the interinstitutional differences were generally smaller than the differences among faculty members in a single school. A significant exception was the school without university affiliation, whose faculty exhibited a consistent polar pattern: autocratic, traditional, depreciative, unfavorable to fulltime faculty. Within the total pool, clinicians and those with more than 15 years' teaching experience were significantly more democratic than basic scientists and than those who had taught for fewer than 15 years. Generally, basic scientists were more autocratic than clinicians, a finding that may be reflected in basic-science instructional programs, which are often more rigidly structured than clinical programs and appear to encourage less self-reliance and critical thinking.

Although students are the best potential source of information about teaching practices, faculties are often reluctant to accept their observations. Cotsonas and Kaiser (1963) developed a 35-item clinical-teacher-rating scale which, when subjected to factor analysis after wide student use, revealed (1) an attitude factor—the teacher's ability to promote warm relationships with patients and students; and (2) a teaching factor—the teacher's ability to promote critical thinking and independent study. When faculty ratings of the same teachers were added and the data analyzed once more, a third factor (identified as medical knowledge) made its appearance; 91 percent of the faculty ratings loaded here. When faculty were asked to rerank the same teachers on the basis of factors 1 and 2, the correlation coefficients approached unity, suggesting that these faculty members, at least, were unable to separate important components of teaching that students saw clearly.

The classroom behavior of 380 individual teachers in seven medical schools has been documented by a group of trained observers, using a standard rating scale designed to identify attitudes toward students, individual student differences, student needs, use of challenge, use of instructional materials and methods, and sensitivity to physical setting (Jason, 1962). A very wide range of practices was noted on each scale. Most striking was the infrequency with which students were challenged to analyze data, to interpret problems, or to think critically. The limited attention given to individual differences and the frequently primitive use of instructional materials and methods was also noteworthy. An unexpected finding was that teachers with more than 10 years' experience were significantly less sensitive to these elements of the teaching-learning exchange than the less experienced ones were.

Reichsman and others (1964), having observed 82 clinical teaching sessions in a distinguished medical school, noted particularly the frequency of instructional methods inappropriate to the achievement of the stated goals of clinical instruction; the lack of teachers' preparation for the task at hand; the failure to individualize instruction even in small groups; the preoccupation with disease and procedure at the expense of systematic attention to attitudinal goals; and the infrequency of explicit attention to clinical reasoning.

Such studies simply confirm what has long been suspected by some medical educators—that teacher training is imperative if the curricular opportunities in medicine are to be exploited fully and if the able students admitted to medical schools are to make the fullest use of their talents. The first sustained effort in this direction, a series of ten-day seminars on medical teaching, was included as a part of the University of Buffalo Project in Medical Education that initiated a continuing dialogue between professionals in medicine and those from education (Rosinski & Miller, 1962). The more elaborate training programs, including intensive faculty introductions to educational science, educational-research fellowships, and graduate-degree programs in medical education that have now been established (Miller, 1965, 1966), may prove to be the most significant of all the developments in medical education during the past decade.

George E. Miller
University of Illinois

References

Barrows, Howard S., and Abrahamson, Stephen. "The Programmed Patient: A Technique for Appraising Student Performance in Clinical Neurology." *J Med Ed* 39:802–5; 1964.

Becker, Howard S., and others. *Boys in White*. U Chicago Press, 1961. 456p.

Bloom, Samuel W. "The Sociology of Medical Education." *Milbank Memorial Fund Q* 43:143–84; 1965.

Bridge, Edward M. "The Language of Medicine: A Quantitative Study of Medical Vocabulary." *J Med Ed* 37:201–10; 1962.

Clute, K. F. *The General Practitioner*. U Toronto Press, 1963. 566p.

Cotsonas, Nicholas J., and Kaiser, Henry F. "Student Evaluation of Clinical Teaching." *J Med Ed* 38:742–5; 1963.

Cowles, John T. "A Critical Comments Approach to the Rating of Medical Students' Clinical Performance." *J Med Ed* 40:188–98; 1965.

Evans, Lester J. *The Crisis in Medical Education*. U Michigan Press, 1964. 101p.

Fisher, L. A., and Cotsonas, Nicholas J. "A Time Study of Student Activities." *J Med Ed* 40:125–31; 1965.

Flexner, Abraham. *Medical Education in the United States and Canada*. Carnegie, 1910. (Reprinted 1960.) 346p.

Funkenstein, Daniel. "A Study of College Seniors Who Abandoned Their Plans for a Medical Career." *J Med Ed* 36:924–33; 1961.

Gee, Helen Hofer. "Learning the Physician-Patient Relationship." *J AMA* 173:1301–4; 1960.

Gee, Helen Hofer, and Cowles, John T. (Eds.) *The Appraisal of Applicants to Medical Schools*. Association of American Medical Colleges, 1956. 228p.

Gee, Helen Hofer, and Glaser, Robert J. *The Ecology of the Medical Student*. Association of American Medical Colleges, 1958. 262p.

Ginther, John R. "Cooperative Research in Medical Education: An Example from Hematology." *J Med Ed* 38:716–24; 1963.

Gottheil, Edward, and Michael, C. M. "Predictor Variables Employed in Research on the Selection of Medical Students." *J Med Ed* 32:131–45; 1957.

Gough, H. G., and others. "Admission Procedures as Forecasters of Performance in Medical Training." *J Med Ed* 38:983–98; 1963.

Haggerty, Robert J. "Family Medicine: A Teaching Program for Medical Students and Pediatric House Offices." *J Med Ed* 37:531–80; 1962.

Ham, T. Hale. "Medical Education at Western Reserve University." *New England J Med* 267:868–74; 916–23; 1962.

Hammond, Kenneth R., and Kern, Fred, Jr. *Teaching Comprehensive Medical Care*. Harvard U Press, 1959. 642p.

Horowitz, M. J. *Educating Tomorrow's Doctors*. Appleton, 1964. 264p.

Hubbard, John P., and Clemans, William V. "A Comparative Evaluation of Medical Schools." *J Med Ed* 35:134–41; 1960.

Hubbard, John P., and others. "An Objective Evaluation of Clinical Competence." *New England J Med* 272:1321–8; 1965.

Hutchins, Edwin B. "The AAMC Longitudinal Study: Implications for Medical Education." *J Med Ed* 39:265–77; 1964.

Jason, H. "A Study of Medical Teaching Practices." *J Med Ed* 37:1258–84; 1962.

Johnson, Favis G., and Hutchins, Edwin B. "Doctor or Dropout: A Study of Medical Student Attrition." *J Med Ed* 41:1099–1269; 1966.

Lee, Peter V. *Medical Schools and the Changing Times*. Association of American Medical Colleges, 1962. 90p.

Levit, Edithe J., and others. "The Effect of Characteristics of Hospitals in Relation to the Caliber of Interns Obtained and the Competence of Interns After One Year of Training." *J Med Ed* 38:909–19; 1963.

Lief, V. F., and others. "Academic Success: Intelligence and Personality." *J Med Ed* 40:114–24; 1965.

Mawardi, Betty Hosmer. "A Career Study of Physicians." *J Med Ed* 40:658–66; 1965.

McGuire, Christine H. "A Process Approach to the Construction and Analysis of Medical Examinations." *J Med Ed* 38:556–63; 1963.

McGuire, Christine H. "The Oral Examination as a Measure of Professional Competence." *J Med Ed* 41:267–74; 1966.

McGuire, Christine H., and others. "Auscultatory Skill: Gain and Rentation After Intensive Instruction." *J Med Ed* 39:120–31; 1964.

Merton, Robert K., and others. *The Student Physician*. Harvard U Press, 1957. 351p.

Miller, George E. "On Training Medical Teachers." *Canadian Med Assn J* 92:708–11; 1965.

Miller, George E. "Medical Education Research and Development." *J AMA* 197:992–5; 1966.

Millis, John S. (Chairman.) *The Graduate Education of Physicians, The Report of the Citizens Commission*. AMA, 1966. 114p.

Norwood, William F. "The Mainstream of American Medical Education, 1765–1965." *Annals New York Acad Sci* 128:463–72; 1965.

Payson, H. E., and others. "Time Study of an Internship on a University Medical Service." *New England J Med* 264:439; 1961.

Peterson, O. L., and others. "An Analytical Study of North Carolina General Practice." *J Med Ed* (special suppl.) p. 165; December 1956.

Peterson, O. L., and others. "Appraisal of Medical Students' Abilities as Related to Training and

Careers After Graduation." *New England J Med* 269:1174–82; 1963.
Price, Philip B., and others. "Measurement of Physician Performance." *J Med Ed* 39:203–10; 1964.
Reichsman, Franz, and others. "Observations of Undergraduate Clinical Teaching in Action." *J Med Ed* 39:147–63; 1964.
Rimoldi, H. J. A. "The Test of Diagnostic Skills." *J Med Ed* 36:73–9; 1961.
Rosinski, Edwin F. "Social Class of Medical Students." *J AMA* 193:95–8; 1965.
Rosinski, Edwin F., and Blanton, Wyndham B., Jr. "A System of Cataloguing the Subject Matter Content of a Medical School Curriculum." *J Med Ed* 37:1092–100; 1962.
Rosinski, Edwin F., and Miller, George E. "A Study of Medical School Faculty Attitudes." *J Med Ed* 37:112–23; 1962.
Rosinski, Edwin F., and Miller, George E. "Seminars on Medical Teaching: A Recapitulation." *J Med Ed* 37:177–84; 1963.
Sanazaro, Paul J. "Research in Medical Education: Exploratory Analysis of a Blackbox." *Annals New York Acad Sci* 128:519–31; 1965.
Sanazaro, Paul J. "Class Size in Medical School." *J Med Ed* 41:1017–29; 1966.
Sanazaro, Paul J., and Hutchins, Edwin B. "The Origin and Rationale of the Medical College Admissions Test." *J Med Ed* 38:1044–50; 1963.
Saunders, Richard H. "The University Hospital Internship in 1960—A Study of the Program of 27 Major Teaching Hospitals." *J Med Ed* 36:561–676; 1961.
Schumacher, Charles F. "A Factor-analytic Study of Various Criteria of Medical Student Accomplishment." *J Med Ed* 39:192–5; 1964(*a*).
Schumacher, Charles F. "Personal Characteristics of Students Choosing Different Types of Medical Careers." *J Med Ed* 39:278–88; 1964(*b*).
Williamson, John W. "Assessing Clinical Judgment." *J Med Ed* 40:180–87; 1965.
Zimmerman, Jack M., and King, Thomas C. "Motivation and Learning in Medical School. III: Evaluation of Student-centered Group." *Surgery* 54:152–6; 1963.

MENTAL HEALTH

Past assaults on the concept of mental health are reminiscent of Robert Benchley's approach to the problem "Does the average man get enough sleep?" First, Benchley pointed out, one needs to ask what is meant by "enough sleep?" Then one needs to know what is meant by "average man," and finally one needs to agree on what is meant by "does." One approaches the concept of mental health with much the same respect for what is meant by "mental," by "health," and by "mental health." Undoubtedly, mental health has to do with being able to love, to work, to play, to have peace of mind, to be happy, to be secure, to be strong, and to be able to manage stress. Acknowledging the relevance of these competences to mental health, one still faces the task of defining each operationally. Nevertheless, to live in and with a group or a society one needs to feel a part of that group or society even if one desires to be alone in it, and one needs to be able to give some of oneself to others whether this is conceptualized as love, sympathy, or compassion. One also needs to be able to contribute one's skills and energies to the general welfare and receive reimbursement in some form, usually hard cash, so that one feels one's work is significant. Last, one needs to be able to find ways of escaping the realities of the real world in play. Based on the values of our culture and the prescribed channels for human functioning in it, it also appears that mental health has to do with man's ability to take the "thousand natural shocks that flesh is heir to" and as a result to be better able to take the next thousand. Is then mental health a kind of growing stronger as a result of the normal stress of living? Perhaps—but one is still left to founder on the shoals of what is meant by "normal stress."

Consequently, we ought to ask if mental health is such a difficult concept to define, why worry about it—why define it at all?

It is most probable that the need for a concept of mental health arose out of man's concern with the problem of mental illnesses. This affliction of mentality and health both puzzled and frightened men. These anxieties were accentuated by the discovery, by Freud and others, that many mental diseases were psychologically determined and that the mind of man is neither omnipotent nor free (Zilboorg & Henry, 1941). How does greater knowledge about the limitations and diseases of the mind help us build men with healthier minds? Is mental health the antithetical condition of mental illness?

Jahoda (1958) points out that there is hardly a term in current thought as difficult to define as the term "mental health." It certainly has the power to mean many things to many people. Nevertheless, despite its vagueness the concept is firmly established at the present in the matrix of our society. It is used by a great number of voluntary and government agencies and is presented as a primary goal by federal legislation (P.L. 88–164) and by many state programs. Funds are being raised by national organizations and by community organizations to promote better mental health. Campaigns are conducted to help people with their mental health. There is a growing number of practitioners in the behavioral sciences trying to help people maintain and promote good mental health. Mental health services aimed at helping people function more effectively are increasing in number and use. Finally, a great deal of research is going on in the behavioral sciences concerned with the development of mental health. While many of man's goals, such as maturity, development, education, and happiness, are vague and somewhat confusing, there is often a high degree of legitimacy and agreement on the direction one needs to go to seek such goals. Sanford (1967) has suggested ways of delineating and differentiating these concepts and utilizing them with some degree of consensual meaning.

One of the concepts about mental health which has emerged over the years is its relationship to emotional robustness, the ability to take the stresses of life without caving in or striking out violently against society. Bower (1961) has refined this notion to one of the degrees of freedom in which an individual has to think or act, or the number of behavioral alternatives available to deal with the stresses and strains of living. From this point of view one could think of mental health as the resilience or bounce of the individual's personality in managing his own physical, social, and psychological environment.

Another way to conceptualize mental health is to look for persons who are said to have or to show a high degree of mental health. One of the outstanding characteristics of such a person would be an aggressively constructive orientation to life—facing each day with a sense of courage and adventure, picking oneself up from the floor when one gets knocked down, and continuing on. Another characteristic of the mentally healthy person is that he makes choices, thereby making mistakes and thereby having the opportunity to learn or profit by one's mistakes. This is not to say that mentally healthy persons are error prone; they are, however, not deterred from action by the possibility of being wrong. The mentally healthy person has learned how to manage stress as a normal occurrence in life in such a way that he is able to handle additional stress. As a result he is able to see himself and others with a minimum of distortion. This suggests that mentally healthy persons have relatively accurate and open feedback mechanisms whereby information about the self and others is processed with fidelity and with a minimum of distortion.

If one were to look at the school and ask what mentally healthy children are like in this setting, what would one find? First, a mentally healthy child is one who is able to deal with and manage the symbols of his society. Such symbols include language symbols, mathematical symbols, sound symbols, as in music, and art symbols. Without such skill in managing symbols the child is virtually unable to function in the school society and, later on, in the adult society. Second, a mentally healthy child must be able to deal with rules, manage rapid and sometimes arbitrary changes in rules, and be able to accept penalties for breaking rules. It is highly significant that no society of adults or children can go on without goals, rules by which one reaches goals, and penalties for those who do not play by the rules. In the case of children who function in a play or child society, most of those who do not play by the rules are not permitted to play. Similarly, in society those who continually break the rules or who cannot be counted upon to act according to the rules are sent to institutions which prevent them from functioning in our society. A child has little alternative but to learn how to deal with such requirements. Third, as part of the skill of dealing with rules one must learn how to be an individual and yet function in groups and in peer societies. Associated with this trait, the mentally healthy child has learned how to deal with authority and with the wide variety of deference and controlling forces exercised by adults on children. Whether we like it or not, the mentally healthy child will develop his flexibilities and resilience to some degree in his interactions and mediations with such key adults as parents and teachers. Fourth, the mentally healthy child is able to control and manage his impulses. This does not mean that a child must give up his impulses or inner life in order to become a mentally healthy person. The ability to control one's impulses must also include the ability to loosen controls when such freedom is appropriate and desirable. It suggests freedom to be imaginative, to be spontaneous, or to be emotional when such behavior is enhancing and productive for the individual. Rational behavior can be just as irrational in some social and psychological contexts as impulsive behavior often seems to be. A mentally healthy child needs to have access to his impulse life and be able to utilize such access appropriately. Freud (1935) and other psychoanalysts conceived of rational thinking as the secondary thinking processes and of unconscious and nonrational thinking as the primary processes. Staying within this framework, one can say that mental health is a consequence of the kind of bridge a person builds between these two thinking processes and its accessibility to traffic between the emotional and rational modes of response and behavior within the individual.

One of the first tasks proposed by the Joint Commission on Mental Health and Illness in 1955 was the preparation of a monograph on concepts of positive mental health. In this monograph, prepared by Jahoda (1958), there is a courageous and productive attempt to clarify the value problems discussed previously, to summarize past efforts to define the nebulous concept of positive mental health and to delineate a variety of indicators for recognizing it. Jahoda discusses some unsuitable conceptualizations of positive mental health, such as the absence of mental disease and normality as a statistical frequency, of how people ought to function, and of the various notions about mental health which equate it with happiness, well-being, and contentment. She feels, for example, that it is necessary to differentiate between an unhappy disposition and unhappiness as a temporary or situational state of being. To be happy under some circumstances of living cannot be regarded as evidence of mental health. On the other hand, if a person is unhappy under certain circumstances, that may indicate that he is functioning optimally.

Jahoda singles out six specific dimensions which should be incorporated into a unified concept of mental health. These are the following. First is the attitude of the individual toward himself. This includes such attitudes as the bridge between a person's conscious and unconscious self—mentioned before as the link between the primary and secondary thought processes. Such self attitudes also include the correctness of one's perception of self, one's feelings about oneself, and one's sense of identity. The second set of criteria has to do with ones' efforts toward self-actualization or what a person does with himself over a period of time. Is one's time spent enhancing and expanding oneself, or is it spent in a more or less static, passive use of self? In Western culture man's health is enhanced through the unfolding of his specific potentialities, and for man it is through this process that he becomes most human. In other words, a mentally healthy individual is constantly moving toward new levels of development and growth. A third criterion of mental health mentioned by Jahoda is personality integration. This achievement is becoming a more difficult feat to accomplish for people as life becomes more and more segmentalized into sharply defined roles. Some mental illnesses can be conceived of as resulting from a compartmentalization of roles so that there is little bridge between one aspect of living, learning, and feeling and another. The achievement of personality-integrating mechanisms becomes more critical as life becomes more institutionalized and separated. "Integration" refers to a coherence in the personality, a unifying process which is able to connect thoughts, feelings, and actions to one another (Bower, 1966b). In clarifying the concept of integration, one needs to understand Hartmann's (1958) objection to Freud's thesis that "where id is, there shall ego be." Neither Freud nor Hartmann suggest that effective integrating mechanisms should result in complete rationality of behavior and thought. Hartmann's notion of a proper integrative balance in the personality suggests that the ego or self should be strong and flexible enough to accommodate unconscious or id forces in the personality and should not aim at eliminating or denying their demands. Thus, one hears of "regression in the service of the ego," that is, of being able to play or be childish as an integrating and personality-recharging mechanism for living more effectively in the real world. Integration, therefore, is regarded as a process of connecting the rational and irrational—not eliminating the irrational.

Jahoda's last three crtieria for mental health have to do with the individual's relation to the real world and his ability to "test" reality. The first of these is the degree of his independence from outside influences—his autonomy as a human being. Certainly the individual's ability to know what is in the external world and his own competences in dealing with these factors will make a significant impact on his emotional state. His ability to stand alone, his ability to take stress and come up smiling, and his skill in managing success and adversity are important considerations in the development of autonomy. It should be noted that there are vast differences in cultural values placed upon autonomy. For example, the Buddhist philosophy considers it a virtue to lose self in a universal self; in Western cultures it is considered of great value to gain self, to become somebody or someone and to develop a uniqueness as a separate human organism.

Another of the criteria mentioned by Jahoda has to do with the individual's perception of reality. It is notable that people with mental illnesses or disturbances do not seem to perceive correctly, i.e., their perception of the self and of others seems to be at some variance with a consensus of other perceptions. Such people can be said to be relatively inefficient persons, since they do not perceive the world as accurately or as efficiently as does a mentally healthy person. They are not only emotionally sick but cognitively wrong. The problem with defining objects, events, and feelings is one of determining whose perception is correct. One eventually returns to the notion suggested by Harry Stack Sullivan (1953) that consensual validation of perception is one of the cornerstones of good reality testing. One does not have to believe as others do, but one does need to understand, if one is at variance with others, how others perceive the situation.

The last criterion of mental health suggested by Jahoda is environmental mastery. In this are included the ability to love, the ability to work, to play, to have adequate interpersonal relations, to be efficient in meeting situational requirements, to be able to adapt and adjust, and to be effective in problem solving. Some investigators, such as Klein (1960) and M. Brewster Smith (1959) have attempted to make Jahoda's concepts of self, reality testing, and environmental mastery more operational. Klein asks, "Does a deficit in one of these competencies imply that an individual no longer enjoys good mental health or must all three be affected for ill health to ensue?" To answer his question Klein proposed mental health be conceptualized in terms of three interrelated concepts. The first of these is soundness, an enduring state of healthy personality functioning visible in such qualities as adaptability, social effectiveness, a high degree of initiative, autonomy, and a general air of modest optimism. Klein's other concepts are, second, well-being and, third, the immediate or current state of health or effectiveness in dealing with stress and emotional stability or the ability of an individual to cope with environmental stresses over a period of time while maintaining a state of emotional well-being.

Many behavioral scientists concerned with operational and measurable indexes of mental health have moved toward the general ability of the individual to develop coping mechanisms which build personality strength (Murphy, 1961). In this framework mentally healthy persons are those individuals who use stressful experiences to build within themselves the ability to cope with greater doses of stress. Consider sibling rivalry, which has often been regarded as a bête noir in the development of behavioral and emotional disorders in children; it can also be regarded as an opportunity for an immunity-producing experience that helps children manage the stress of competitive relationships (Frank, 1957). Under normal circumstances, there is no better place in which to learn to cope with stress than in a home in which there is reasonable and affectionate parental guidance. One cannot learn to cope or develop emotional robustness in a frictionless or nonstressful environment. Nor can such learning and developing take place if the friction or stress is too much for the child to manage. And in the long run what such coping with life ought to bring about are greater degrees of freedom to act, to think, and to connect acting and thinking.

Whether one behaves in a socially desirable or undesirable manner is a result of many factors; the mental health factors in such behavior are the number of alternatives or degrees of freedom the individual had to act.

To Kubie (1957), the essence of normal or mentally healthy behavior is revealed in one's flexibility in meeting different situations in different ways; in contrast, frozen or relatively unalterable behavior is characteristic of the neurotic or mentally unhealthy process, whether in impulses, purposes, acts, thoughts, or feelings.

Kubie holds that what is neurotic or unhealthy in the human personality are processes that predetermine automatic or repetitive behavior. Such automatic behavior is undoubtedly caused by unconscious forces in the personality which do not have relatively free access to levels of awareness in the personality.

There is very little question that behavior motivated primarily by unconscious personality processes will in fact become repetitive and fixed, and, since the goals of such behavior are rarely attainable, these processes will continue to influence the behavior of the individual. One might well question the assumption, as does Redlich (1957), that acts determined by conscious personality processes are healthier or freer than acts motivated by unconscious forces. He suggests that unconscious defense mechanisms are health-producing in their adaptive and self-protective goals and serve as a significant integrating mechanism in the human personality. One can argue, however, that the individual who is moved to a significant degree by such unconscious processes will in the long run use mechanisms of adjustment which tend to reduce the number of alternatives available to him for behaving.

There are other processes or deficits which limit an individual's freedom to act or think. Where knowing and feeling are separated, the storing of knowledge may go on without any effect on personality growth. On the other hand, one's mental health will rarely be developed without well-played cognitive "matches" between the child and his environment. Good emotional development could not by itself produce an effectively functioning or a free individual unless such development were linked to the learning of significant cognitive or developmental tasks. To be mentally healthy one must know as well as feel. To paraphrase Samuel Johnson, healthy emotions without knowledge are weak and empty, while knowledge without healthy emotions can be dangerous and ill-used. If one can conceptualize mental health as emotional robustness plus cognitive know-how, one can conceive, as did Meier (1959), of an index representing the varieties of constructive individual and social behaviors in a community or society as indicative of the mental health of that community or society. According to Meier time can have investment properties; education and the acquisition of cognitive-affective skills are examples of such investment in time. The payoff for such investment is not more time but increases in the range of choices in behavior, in employment, ideas, interests, and social activities.

PRESENT-DAY CONCEPTS OF MENTAL HEALTH. The major changes in the conceptual thinking about mental health today are (1) the notion of the contribution of cognitive competence to emotional development and its integration into the affective aspects of personality and (2) an emphasis on personality and ego competence to think and act rather than on freedom to think and act. To a large extent, these changes have resulted from increased interest in and development of programs dealing with what is called autonomous ego processes. Bower (1967) has attempted to define mental health in relation to the development of effective ego processes —i.e., personality processes which are able to take information from the environment, organize the information, and utilize it for the benefit of the individual. He describes ego processes as aspects of the personality which select, mediate, and symbolically bind inputs from the external or internal environment. The essence of such processing of information lies in the ability of the individual to mediate and bind experiences such as objects, events, and feelings. The concept of mediation implies active participation by the individual in interpreting the obect, event, or feeling and in working out the best response to it from all available alternatives. All information or inputs are mediated or polarized by ego processes in a variety of ways. For example, all inputs are differentiated—i.e., separated from other objects, events, and feelings in the environment. Ego-differentiation processes are also important in separating self from others, in learning a variety of symbols by which to "hold" onto objects, events, and feelings. Ego-differentiation processes are taught to children by adults who are good mediating persons in that they help others conceptualize objects, events, and feelings.

Another ego skill necessary to obtain effective information from the environment is ego fidelity. Ego-fidelity processes are necessary for tying symbols to objects, events, and feelings, for testing one's ideas and actions, and for creating and utilizing symbols for spontaneous and novel ideas and actions. The major goal of ego-fidelity processes is to gain as close a correspondence to the external object, event, or feeling as is possible, keeping in mind that complete correspondence with externality is philosophically and psychologically questionable.

A third kind of ego process necessary for good mental health is called ego pacing. Ego-pacing processes are used to regulate heavy emotional loads when they occur in the normal life of individuals as well as to manage a deficiency of stimuli. The metaphor of pacing is suggestive of being able to run a race so that sprinting and coasting can be utilized as needed. One should not run out of breath when one is required to sprint, nor should one become lethargic and depressed when one is required to coast. Ego pacing skills not only require that one be able to regulate overloads of inputs but also require techniques for unloading heavy emotional loads. Conversely, such skills require the maintenance of the relationship to the environment despite boredom or ennui.

The fourth ego skill required for mental health is called ego expansion and is related to Jahoda's notion of self-actualization. In ego expansion one seeks new bindings, new concepts by which one can better understand the world in which he lives. In addition one seeks and one learns to use a variety of new metaphors and new conceptual frameworks. Part of the task of ego-expansion processes is to enable the individual to live comfortably and productively with ambiguity and uncertainty in an ambiguous and uncertain world.

The fifth of the specific ego skills is ego integration. This includes taking in new information and connecting it with what is already in the personality, appropriately and effectively. Ego-integration processes attempt to establish communication between old information and new information, between past and present self, and to cultivate a wise passivity in encountering and assimilating the nonverbal, nonrational aspects of the natural and man-made environments in which we live (Huxley, 1962).

Effective ego processes are cognitive-affective skills for taking in data from the inner and outer environments. Each individual has developed a unique way or style of utilizing such ego processes. V. H. Rosen (1961) suggests that one's idiosyncratic responses to ambiguity or to problem situations where definitive answers are not available indicate the kinds of ego processes one has developed. This may be observed in one's artistic creations, one's use of fantasy, one's work, one's interpersonal relations, and other behavioral manifestations. It is also possible for one to change one's style of personality functioning as one does clothes. One needs to keep in mind that a variety of ego styles fall within the normal variations of personality functioning in a free society.

The use of ego concepts in defining mental health can often be as misty as the use of other concepts, since ego processes are inferential. They do, however, provide an operational base from which behavior can be observed and studied in relation to mental health. Ego processes are also the core or central area of concern of new concepts of research and development in mental health.

In the early history of the mental health movement most professional people drew their conceptual and operational tenets from Freud and from Freudian theories of personality functioning. Such theories began with a description of personality divided like Gaul into three inherently warring areas, the id, the ego, and the superego. The id represented the unconscious, biological nature of man. The ego represented the rational or civilized portion of man, and the superego represented the rules of society, the dos and mostly the don'ts which people build into their nature to guide them in their relationships with themselves and others. Most of the early theories of mental health focused on the severity of the war between these three contentious parts of the personality.

To fight, one needs energy; the source of such energy for the major and minor wars within the personality was seen as stemming from libidinal or sexually tinged wellsprings, usually in the id. An individual's personality could then be conceptualized as a motorcar plus driver with the id or motor providing four, six, or eight cylinders, depending on the nature of the individual, the ego at the wheel hoping to guide the vehicle in a safe and sane manner and to avoid being hit or running out of gas, and the superego or rules of the road tucked somewhere in the driving cap of the driver. Unfortunately, in the early days of psychoanalysis everyone was interested in lifting up the hood to see what the motor was like. Few, if any, were interested in the driver and his problems. To some extent the driver, as the ego or mediating mechanism, was seen as a block or obstruction in getting at the deeper problems in the motor, or id. Therefore, for many years mental health concepts and programs focused on finding out what was wrong with the motor as one way of getting the car to run effectively.

In a 1911 paper Freud (1959) proposed a new principle of mental functioning which he called the reality principle. In this paper Freud suggested that we treat ego processes with greater respect and consideration as mediators of conflict and as significant interpreters of conflict-free experiences. The significance of this paper was little recognized at the time. In addition to mediating inner conflict the ego or ego processes of the personality were seen as taking on the job of searching, receiving, assimilating, testing, and storing data from the environment which had survival value to the individual. The goal of this activity had to do with increasing the individual's competences with respect to the external world. In this development of the reality principle, expressed by George Bernard Shaw as one's being able to choose the line of greatest advantage instead of yielding in the direction of least resistance, it is necessary that ego processes find out how to control and express impulses and feelings and provide for easy access between the motor (id) and the driver (ego). The importance of this connection for mental functioning is suggested by Kris (1952) in his discussion of the idea of "regression in the service of the ego." This means that persons, like nations, preserve wilderness areas within themselves and provide access to them so that one can be primitive, spontaneous, and childlike and take vacations every once in a while from the rational ego processes.

In time some psychotherapists began to pay more attention to ego processes as the key to effective treatment of children with mental health problems, although the focus of most still remained on uncovering conflicts so that the war within the person could be reduced or even made to disappear. But absence of war does not make a nation or a person effective in the environment. One needs skills, knowledge, organization, goals, and rewards. In recent years it has become clear that especially for children attempts to cope or be successful in the environment can be crucial for mental health. Personality strengths are developed not only out of the resolution of inner conflict but also by how one can manage challenges in the external world. To do this one needs to use one's independent or conflict-free ego processes. Like Cinderella, these aspects of ego processes have always been around sitting unnoticed in the corner, lacking the glamour and visibility of the more attractive sisters. It is only within the past decade, as a result of the work of Hartmann (1958), Rapaport (1951), and White (1963), that this aspect of ego development has come into the light. Both Hartmann and White discuss ego processes in relation to one's effectiveness in the control of one's body, the use of one's muscles, sensory experiences in play and games, and other activities which are considered significant to the child in his attempt to find his way in his environment. As White points out, when most research on animals was being done on sexually aroused or frightened animals, play, curiosity, learning, and exploration behavior were seldom observed. Butler (1958), in his review of animal research up to 1958, concludes that learning does not require recourse to rewards such as water, food, sex, or escape from behavior but that perceptual consequences of behavior can and often do serve as the reward. One can be motivated to do things for the fun and zest of doing them and the challenge in learning to do better, as in a game.

It is clear that new federal programs, such as the Peace Corps, the Job Corps, the Economic Opportunity Act, Operation Head Start, and some of the new mental health programs are utilizing conceptually the notions of independent ego energies and social competence. For purposes of comparison and for highlighting the difference in mental health thinking two models are given below. Such differences are not discrete or exclusive but represent in a dichotomous, contrasting manner the emphases of mental health objectives in the social competence and the intrapsychic models (Bower 1966a).

Social-Competence Model

1. The aim is functioning effectiveness—anxiety is relevant only to the extent to which it reduces and interferes with or stimulates and enhances this goal.

2. The goal is to learn how to carry on those transactions with the environment which assist the individual in gaining individual and social competence.

3. Goals are measured by increased fitness or ability in functioning.

4. The program leverage is primarily task centered—the objective is learning new skills, including behavioral skills.

5. The model is conceptually allied to "conflict-free" spheres of ego processes.

6. The approach is primarily a direct, mediative one—ego building.

7. The focus is on increasing competence in present developmental tasks.

8. The model is based on the achievement of conscious satisfactions—pleasure felt in neuromuscular system.

9. Individual study leads to environmental and social-system manipulation.

10. Conceptualizes a continuum of social incompetences that are due to emotional problems ranging from mild to severe.

Intrapsychic Model

1. The aim is intrapsychic comfort—"peace of mind." Surplus anxiety is seen as major block to this goal.

2. The goal is mental health—emotional freedom to act, think, and feel with increasing levels of awareness.

3. Goals are measured by clinical or subjective judgment.

4. The program leverage is primarily affective and focused on self-understanding.

5. The model is conceptually allied to conflicts in ego-id-superego relations.

6. The approach is primarily an indirect, unmediative one—a peeling away of obsolescent ego defenses.

7. The focus is on intrapsychic blocks to functioning—freeing the individual to act or think.

8. The model is based on the achievement of internal symbolic satisfactions—finding suitable outlets for feelings and drives.

9. Individual study leads to individual "therapy."

10. The model conceptualizes a dichotomy between those who are sick and those who are not.

One must define what one means by mental health, in relation to schools and educational processes. When one proposes to promote mental health through educational processes, how exactly does one go about doing so? Part of the answer is that enhancement of mental health in children cannot be conceived of as a separate activity engaged in by the school but must be developed as part of the social, cognitive, and individual transactions between the child and his school environment. One cannot take a course in mental health, if such a course were indeed possible, to become mentally healthier. Educational and mental health processes are like the wool skeins in a sweater, inseparably interwoven. Mental health in today's world includes not only the emotional freedom to behave but also the necessary cognitive and social skills required to function in today's world.

MENTAL HEALTH PROBLEMS AMONG CHILDREN. Recent surveys by the Office of Biometry of the National Institute of Mental Health (n.d.) reveal that during 1963 about 4,000 Americans under 15 years of age and 27,000 between 15 and 24 were admitted to mental hospitals, both public and private. At the end of that year 5,000 children under 15 and 25,000 between 15 and 24 were living in these hospitals. Both the first-admission rates and the resident-population rates for children have increased at an accelerated pace during the last decade. This rise cannot be explained altogether by pointing to the relative increase in the number of children in the general population. For example, the number of boys between the ages of 10 and 14 has increased almost twofold since 1950, but their incidence of residence in a mental hospital has increased sixfold. This is occurring at a time when the resident-patient rate in the American mental hospital population as a whole is decreasing. Projections for the decade 1963–1973 by the National Institute of Mental Health (NIMH) show that one can expect an increase of 15 percent in the 10-to-14-year-olds in the country's population. However, for the same age group we can expect an increase of 116 percent in the mental hospital population. We can expect a 36-percent increase in the population as a whole between the ages of 15 and 24, compared to a 70-percent increase in their mental hospital population.

In public and private institutions for the mentally retarded 13,000 persons under 20 years were admitted for the first time in 1963, while 78,000 such persons were residents at the end of the year. Rates for this age group for both first admissions and resident patients have shown a gradual increase during the past decade. Of children outside the hospital with such mental disorders as psychoses, neuroses, and psychosomatic problems, it is estimated that at least 250,000 receive services each year at mental health clinics. More than 500,000 children are brought before the courts each year for the kinds of acts designated as juvenile delinquency. Many of these children are suffering from various mental health disorders. Many studies (e.g., Bower, 1960; Wall, 1955) have confirmed the fact that approximately 10 percent of our public school children are mental health problems and that about 2 to 3 percent of this group are in need of immediate psychiatric help. Using the approximate enrollment of 55 million children in the kindergarten through college age group, this means that there are approximately 5½ million children with moderate to serious degrees of emotional disturbance. In a mental health survey of Los Angeles County (California State Department of Mental Hygiene and Los Angeles County, 1960), teachers were asked to rate the degrees of disturbance among children in their classes from kindergarten through high school. From this study it was evident that young children are perceived as less seriously disturbed than older ones and that the peak of problems is reached somewhere in the middle grades, usually around the third or fourth grade, with a tapering off of problems, at least in part because students drop out, in high school. It is also interesting to note that special-education classes, especially those for retarded children, are seen as having a much higher percentage of disturbed children than regular classes.

Private and public facilities for children with mental health problems have always been in short supply and where available have been either inadequate or expensive. Private care in units of 20 to 60 children usually costs a minimum of $25 per day, or about $10,000 a year. The greatest shortage of professional people is found in the field of mental health workers for emotionally disturbed children. In 1965 there were approximately 300 members of the American Academy of Child Psychiatry, and fewer than 50 new workers were being trained each year. It is also interesting to note that the American Humane Society, a society set up to provide for the care and treatment of animals, was established in 1877 but that until approximately the middle of the twentieth century there were no societies or organizations interested in the care and treatment of emotionally disturbed children. In 1960 there were many states that did not have one hospital or school, public or private, where a child with a serious mental problem could get treatment and education. The old orphanages, which used to house many neglected and dependent children, have virtually disappeared. Institutions for homeless children are now often residences for emotionally disturbed children. Many such children are being cared for in such homes and go to public schools in the community. While it is difficult to ascertain the meaning of the increase in the percentage of emotionally disturbed children in our society, there is little doubt that children are finding it more difficult to take on the necessary cognitive and emotional skills to function well in it.

Attention must be paid to the mental health problems of adolescents, especially those enrolled in our colleges. In projections for the year 1975 (Pearlman, 1966) it is anticipated that the 18-to-21-year-old group will increase more than 30 percent, to nearly 16 million. Nearly 9 million of these young people will be enrolled or seeking enrollment in various institutions of higher learning. The health service at Harvard University (Farnsworth, 1965) noted that from 8 to 9 percent of the student body of about 14,000 sought psychiatric help each year. In addition, it was estimated that an unknown number of students, perhaps 3 percent, arranged for private psychiatric assistance on their own in the community. In a 10-year morbidity report (Evans & Warren, 1962) at the main branch of the University of Wisconsin, illnesses of students were grouped on the basis of frequency of occurrence. Illnesses with highest frequencies were respiratory infections, skin diseases, gastrointestinal upsets, and psychiatric problems. Using a small sample in a metropolitan church-affiliated liberal arts college one group of investigators (W. Smith & others, 1963) found that about 60 percent of the students were "normal" in that they had no clinical signs of pathology, about 30 percent showed some subclinical disturbance, and about 10 percent could be rated as clinically disturbed. Pearlman (1966) reports on a study of successive classes of entering freshmen at Dartmouth College in which it was found that about 12 percent of the students were significantly emotionally impaired in a clinical sense. What impressed the investigators most was the sharp increase in the incidence of such impairment over a six-year period, rising from 6.9 percent for the entering class in 1962 to 16 percent for the entering students in 1967.

Not all of the mental health problems at the college level are dealt with by the campus medical or health services. Many students get their mental health assistance through counseling by specialized counselors or faculty. Such services usually fall under the jurisdiction of a dean of students and are usually headed by counseling or clinical psychologists. At San Fernando State College in California, 15 percent of a student body of 9,000 students requested individual counseling or group therapy. The counseling services of Columbia College during 1962–63 served 331 students, or 12.7 percent of the student enrollment. Studies of college mental health services suggest that the larger the college or university, the more formally structured its mental health service. Moreover, the more organized the service, the smaller the percentage of the student body that is seen by it (Pearlman, 1966, p. 205).

With respect to mental health problems of differing age groups, the 10-to-19-year-old group is seen in outpatient psychiatric clinics more often than any other age group. Of the estimated 750,000 clinic patients served in 1962 approximately one-fourth, or 194,000, were adolescents (B. Rosen & others, 1965). This number represents about 62 patients per 1,000 adolescents in the population. It is interesting to note that the school was the predominant referral agent for both boys and girls from 10 through 15 years of age. A significant finding of this study was that 14-to-15-year-olds had the highest clinic utilization rate. This, however, may represent either a higher incidence of emotional disorders or simply increased anxiety on the part of significant adults and their inability to cope with this age group. There is also a significant drop in the rate of admissions to clinics for boys in the later teen years. This probably reflects not fewer problems but a decrease in the forces compelling a boy to stay in school and the chances of his being referred. After the age of 16 a school can use suspension and expulsion as a means of managing problems of children. On the other hand, the percentage of girls who use clinic help changes little during adolescence. During the later adolescent years, however, anxiety and depression reactions increase in girls.

Although there is a great deal of discussion about the problems children have in some families and the resulting impact on their mental health, there have been very few controlled, prospective studies of children who have come through broken or disturbed families. An interesting retrospective study of 400 eminent persons (Goertzel & Goertzel, 1962) found that almost three-quarters of this group came from troubled or broken families. The families of many of these children had to contend with poverty, and many of the children came from broken homes, had rejecting or overprotective parents, and had physical handicaps. Nearly half of the fathers were subjected to traumatic problems in their business or professional careers. Three-fifths of the 400 expressed dissatisfaction with school, and most were dissatisfied with their secondary schools.

MENTAL HEALTH PROBLEMS OF THE POPULATION AT LARGE. One of the most grotesque ironies of history is that wars, with their frightful carnage and lives lost and wrecked, often tend to give significant impetus to various health programs. Both World War I and World War II led to increased knowledge and understanding of the problem of mental and emotional disturbances. World War II especially accentuated the vulnerability of America's fighting forces to emotional disabilities; about 24 per 1,000 examinees were rejected for this reason in 1940 and 1941, 67 per 1,000 in 1942 and 1943, and 120 per 1,000 in 1944 (Plunkett & Gordon, 1960). At the present time it is estimated that 17.5 million Americans are suffering from mental illnesses severe enough to warrant treatment. Only about 10 percent of these, approximately 1,814,000, are treated during the course of the year. This is the number seen in hospitals or clinics or by private psychiatrists. It is estimated that nearly 90 percent of mental illnesses escape recognition and consequently any possibility of treatment, control, or prevention.

Plunkett and Gordon describe what has and has not been done in community surveys of mental illness from 1916 through 1958. They comment on the fact that the range of rates in studies of the prevalence of mental illness in our population is so great as to defy generalization. The problem is that recorded values are affected strongly by differences in study design, by study definitions, and by classification systems. The variables preclude projection of results to other similar populations or to the population at large. Nevertheless, they establish the fact that mental illness in the United States is a public health problem of alarming proportions, not only because there is something seriously wrong in the emotional and mental functioning of a significant number of Americans but because so little progress has been made toward understanding, defining, and treating this problem.

Mental and emotional disorders and illnesses are not the same as other health disabilities. They cannot be understood as other illnesses, because often the patient himself is not aware of what's wrong. While most mentally ill people are of immediate concern to themselves and their families, they represent long-term community problems and are often cared for by communities using public taxes over long periods of time. Occasionally mentally ill persons cause great traumatic events in our society, such as the assassination of presidents and senseless massacres of innocent children and adult. Fortunately such occurrences are rare, but when they do occur their morbid impact and aftermath linger on in the minds of men.

MAN'S PAST RELATIONSHIP WITH MENTAL HEALTH AND MENTAL ILLNESS. Man's interest in mental health originally stemmed from his concern for and problems with the mentally ill. The history of man's relationship to the mentally ill has not been resplendent with deeds of kindness, examples of humane treatment, or attempts to understand the true nature of the problem. In the past man appeared too frightened of his sick colleagues to face the problem, and only recently have a scientific acceptance and understanding of mental illnesses emerged. Zilboorg (Zilboorg & Henry, 1941) pointed out that we still admonish the neurotic or psychotic individual to pull himself together as if he were personally responsible for a kind of falling apart and could stop it, and in some cases we still tell persons to use their will power and give up the silly notions which afflict them. The record of what man has done about his fellow human beings afflicted with mental and emotional disorders includes many horrendous examples of man's inhumanity to man. A series of books capped by the famous and infamous *Malleus malificarum* (*The Witch's Hammer*, Summers, 1928) published at the end of the fifteenth century, provided guide lines and incentives for the identification and punishment of persons who were thought to be witches or possessed of the devil and who, therefore, were burned to death. The witch-hunters were excellent observers; they collected detailed behavioral information and wrote accurate clinical descriptions of the mentally ill persons whom they called witches. The hallucinatory and illusionary states that are characteristic of the serious mental illness known as schizophrenia were treated in this manner. Deutsch (1937) observes that between the middle of the fifteenth century and the end of the seventeenth century approximately 100,000 persons are estimated to have been executed as witches. The fate of mentally and emotionally disturbed individuals who managed to escape persecution or execution as witches was no better than those who were pronounced witches. Many of them lost all vestiges of human appearance and this condition only served to increase community anxiety and to widen the gap between the sick and the not sick. In the nineteenth century fear and neglect of mentally and emotionally sick individuals were gradually replaced by more humanitarian ideas, among which was the concept of asylum. In these places of "refuge" for the mentally ill, patients were usually shackled to floors and walls with irons. Attendants carried sticks and clubs and used them freely. Since insane persons were judged to be incurable, any attempt to administer treatment was considered itself an insane act. In 1792, Philippe Pinel, a Paris physician, appointed superintendent of the asylum at Salpetrière, proposed to unchain the "beasts" and to inaugurate a system of therapy. Almost at the same time in England, William Tuke presented, to a gathering of his Yorkshire friends, a proposal for a retreat—a place in which the unhappy might find a refuge, a family environment, employment, exercise conducive to mental health, and treatment as guests rather than as inmates. Institutions built on the Yorkshire retreat idea were later developed in New York by the Quaker Society.

The second quarter of the nineteenth century witnessed the beginning and rapid growth of state mental hospitals, efforts that were aided and abetted by such stalwart and energetic persons as Dorothea Lynde Dix. The moral reform which Miss Dix and the climate of opinion developed and supported in the early and middle years of the nineteenth century was not so much directed toward a search for scientific knowledge about mental illness and its cure as founded on an emotionalized, sentimental attitude toward mankind, tinged by religion and humanitarianism. In the end, much of the effort led to the idea of a large, relatively isolated institution, the mental hospital, where patients could be housed away from other people and where they might have a chance to find themselves. Built in isolation and left in isolation, such hospitals lacked help, direction, research, and overall professional development (Deutsch, 1937). Although many professional persons were openly against the large-hospital idea, the general public at that time seemed to find this an effective way of dealing with the problem, since many believed that mental and emotional illnesses were caused, in part, by immoral behavior and, therefore, that some distinct kind of punishment was necessary as part of the therapy.

By the late nineteenth century, the emphasis on moral causes of mental illnesses began to shift to the genetic, physiological, and psychological. In 1895, Freud and Breuer described a case of hysteria in which the cause appeared to be one of intrapsychic conflict (1959). A few years later, Clifford Beers (1921) published his experiences as a patient in a mental hospital in Connecticut in a book called *A Mind that Found Itself*. In this publication he outlined a plan for encouraging and carrying on research into the causes, nature, and treatment of mental disorders and for creating services directed toward the prevention of such disorders. Beers gathered a group of interested citizens together in New Haven in 1908 and formed the first mental health association, the Connecticut Society for Mental Hygiene. In 1909 Beers helped to create the National Committee for Mental Hygiene, which has since become the National Association for Mental Health.

In 1946 the United States Congress enacted the National Mental Health Act, and under one of its provisions, the National Institute of Mental Health was created as the core for a new federal program. From a modest beginning the program at NIMH has grown to a budget of $223-million in 1965, including $35-million for the construction of community mental health centers and for the support of research and training programs in public and private institutions. During the 1940's two important types of new facilities began to be established throughout the country. One was the outpatient clinic, which had its beginning in the nineteenth century but which accelerated markedly in the twentieth. Today there are approximately 2,000 clinics providing some degree of service to three-quarters of a million people a year. The other facility which was being developed at the same time was the psychiatric unit in a general hospital. The earliest was established in 1920. By 1939 there were still only 37. By 1964, about 400 public and voluntary general hospitals had psychiatric inpatient care units, most of them providing intensive treatment. In 1955 the U.S. Congress authorized the establishment of a nongovernmental, multidisciplinary, nonprofit organization, the Joint Commission on Mental Illness and Health, authorizing this body to conduct a study of the entire problem of mental illness and health in the United States. Under scrutiny at this time was the entire program of state mental hospitals and state institutions, mental health clinics, and other services for the mentally ill. The publication of this commission in 1961 of a report called *Action for Mental Health,* and the various monographs undertaken by designated persons authorized by the commission, make up the report and recommendations of this body. To a large degree the emphasis in the middle of the twentieth century has been on community efforts and community support for the mentally ill and especially for the prevention of mental and emotional disorders. On October 31, 1963, the 88th Congress enacted Public Law 88-164, the Mental Retardation Facilities and Community Mental Health Centers Construction Act of 1963, which authorized federal matching funds of $150-million over a three-year period for use by the states in constructing comprehensive community mental health centers. A community mental health center is perhaps best described in terms of its essential elements. Under the legislation signed by President Kennedy and the regulations issued in May 1964, a community mental health center must provide at least five essential elements. These are (1) inpatient services, (2) outpatient services, (3) hospitalization services, including at least day care, (4) emergency services, and (5) consultation and educational services to community agencies and professional personnel. In addition to these five services, five others were considered important enough to be mentioned: (1) diagnostic services, (2) rehabilitative services, including vocational and educational programs, (3) precare and aftercare services in the community, including placement in a foster home, (4) home visiting and halfway houses, both training services, and (5) research and evaluation. The idea of the community mental health center program is to establish a unified comprehensive service and one place that will provide whatever kind of treatment is needed at the time it is needed and in the community where the patient lives. A major purpose of the program is to prevent mental illnesses and to promote mental health in the community at large. M. Brewster Smith and Nicholas Hobbs (1966) have listed some of the prerequisites for an effective community mental health center. They suggest, for example, that for such a center to become an effective agency of the community, community control of central policy is essential. The more closely the proposed centers become integrated with the life of the community, the less the community can afford to turn over to mental health professionals its responsibility for the policies guiding the center's work. In addition, the community mental health center is comprehensive in the sense that it offers, probably not under one roof but under one management, a wide range of services. Some of these may include, in addition to the ones listed previously, special services for the aged, a camping program for emotionally disturbed children, and programs for people who do not respond to other services in the community. Effective community action for mental health requires continuity of concern for the troubled individual in his involvement with society. Despite the loosening of jurisdictional boundaries by agencies, institutions, and professions, no single program can encompass all the needs which mentally ill people require in the community. The center staff must engage in joint programming with the various other systems with whom patients and people are involved, such as the school, the welfare department, industry, justice, and public health. The community mental health center, however, must be a center for innovation and new ideas for such programs. One cannot lament the mental health manpower problem if one continues to try to solve the treatment needs of patients by individual psychotherapy. Current practices in prevention by the community mental health centers will require major emphasis on services for children (American Psychiatric Association, 1964). Such practices may get added impetus and support from the new Joint Commission instituted by Congress which is presently embarked on a study of the mental health of children in the United States. In part, this new commission will concentrate on what was lacking in the report of the 1955 Joint Commission. It is scheduled to report to Congress in 1968.

In fiscal year 1966 a total of $85-million was authorized by Congress for the construction of community mental health centers. As of November 1966, $42-million has been required for the construction of 91 centers. Community mental health centers represent partnerships of local initiative and federal money. The estimated operating cost for the first year of operation of a center is approximately $500,000. The figures are compatible with the figures for general hospitals, in which experience has shown that yearly operating costs are between 50 and 65 percent of the cost of construction. More than two-thirds of the centers already funded are planned as cooperative ventures involving two or more agencies, each of which contributes space and personnel. Examples of such cooperating agencies are nonprofit general hospitals providing inpatient service and county health departments providing outpatient service; private mental hospitals providing inpatient and partial hospitalization services; child-guidance clinics providing consultative services; and community clinics providing outpatient and inpatient service. One center has five member agencies providing one or more services.

One surprising finding in the early development of community mental health centers is that half of the centers funded are in cities of 66,000 people or fewer. More than 20 percent are in towns of 25,000 or fewer people, and only 13 centers are in cities of 500,000 or more. Thus, early experience with the centers suggests that they are being funded not in big cities, where there are concentrations of mental health manpower, but in some of the more rural and suburban areas. It also seems that the community mental health center idea is better geared to the needs of the middle-size and smaller communities than it is to the needs of the large metropolitan areas. In terms of staffing, the most striking fact is that the number of people proposed as needed staff is quite small. The median number of psychiatrists per center is only 2.2. Ten centers propose to employ eight or more psychiatrists. The centers will rely much more heavily on social workers than on any other professional group. There will be approximately as many of them working in centers as there will be psychiatrists and psychologists combined. As this national program goes into full gear, the first-year experience in funding community mental health centers suggests that the average center is costing about $1-million and is serving 160,000 people, is located in a city of 65,000, and is likely to be used by people in the outlying county as well as by the urban and suburban population. The major obstacle to the development of a good center program is the entrenched patterns of autonomy and isolation on the part of hospitals, clinics, and agencies with respect to each other—a condition which can produce segmentalization of patient care and other services (Knight & Davis, 1964).

ACHIEVEMENT, STRESS, AND MENTAL HEALTH. While it would be difficult to support the proposition that all children's learning difficulties are related to mental health problems, there are research studies which seem to indicate that there is a circular interaction between learning competence and mental health. For example, a compilation and analysis of a large body of research by the Educational Records Bureau confirms the high positive relationship between reading achievement and personal social adjustment (Traxler & Townsend, 1955). Yet from whatever etiologies or culmination of factors learning disabilities develop, there is little doubt about their impact on a child's feelings about himself and school. Competence in meeting the demands of school probably supersedes other factors affecting mental health. It has been found, for example, that in kindergarten, before academic goals are stressed, the child who achieves best is not perceived any differently from the nonachiever. However, in the first and subsequent grades those children who become successful achievers also become the most socially acceptable and seem to have good mental health (Buswell, 1953).

The relationship of anxiety to learning has been the subject of research by a number of investigators. Pickrel (1958) found that persons scoring high on a test of manifest anxiety were able to solve problems which contained only a few alternative solutions faster than a group scoring low on the same test. However, on problems that involve a greater number of alternatives or degrees of freedom low-anxiety students did better than high-anxiety students. McKeachie and others (1960) tested the hypothesis that the anxiety resulting from test items which were too difficult or ambiguous for students could be reduced if students were encouraged to write comments about the test items which "bugged" them. Such opportunities did indeed produce higher scores for those students who participated. Calvin and others (1957) confirmed McKeachie's findings and also reported that those subjects who made the most comments showed the greatest improvement.

Of all the metaphors that the human behavioral sciences have borrowed from their sister sciences and from literature, none has been more in need of habitation and name than the concept of stress. In the past it has been associated mostly with hardship, retardation, insult, and affliction, and it has been synonymous with noxiousness. Yet while some physicians, biologists, physicists, and engineers have equated stress with the more stormy battle conditions of living, no less an authority than Shakespeare spoke of stress as the "thousand natural shocks that flesh is heir to." If stress is a condition affecting elastic—i.e., living—material, its impact can be conceptualized as having two results: one leading to increased elasticity, the other to increased rigidity. The process of living itself can be regarded as stressful, whereas death can be considered as an absence of stress. Therefore, in relating the concept of stress to mental health or mental illness, one needs to differentiate degrees of stress, the quality of stress, and its idiosyncratic nature in human experience in that one man's meat can very easily be another man's poison. For example, Otto Fenichel (1945) found that compulsive personalities tend to develop acute anxiety symptoms as a result of severe environmental stress, whereas persons burdened by chronic latent guilt tend to react to misery by becoming less anxious than before. The successful management of stress is emphasized as one road to mental health and functional effectiveness. Life is made up of a series of stresses, such as birth, entering school, adolescence, vocational choice, and marriage, which are all fraught with danger. Why can't we ease the passage and safeguard the often bewildered and bedeviled organism to meet expected stress situations effectively? (Galdston, 1956).

One of the ways of dealing with stress and anxiety in any situation is to get out of the situation. Such action, however, is not possible for the underage child who is not doing too well in school and would like to leave. In 1960 the Department of Labor estimated that about 7.5 million youth dropped out of school before high school graduation. This was occurring during a decade in which the level of training for jobs was steadily rising. In the main, the largest proportion of dropouts come from low socioeconomic groups and have usually been classified as slow learners somewhere along the way. In an intensive study of 45 girls and 60 boys who were about to drop out, investigators found that the reason was not the result of any specific learning failure but a broad educational disability resulting in increased anxiety and stress. The dropping out to the child was a positive kind of action; to the school it was a turning away and an escape (Lichter & others, 1962).

PREVENTIVE APPROACHES TO CHILDREN'S MENTAL HEALTH PROBLEMS. One of the critical mental health tasks of the school is to identify, as early as possible, children who are beginning to have mental health problems and to assist them, their families, and their schools to take appropriate steps. The school is the single agency in our society which sees all children over a long period of time. Bower (1960) has defined five characteristics of children who are beginning to develop or who have developed mental health problems in the school. These are the following: (1) An inability to learn that cannot be explained by intellectual, sensory, or health factors. This characteristic is the most significant one in spotting children with mental health difficulties. (2) An inability to build or maintain satisfactory interpersonal relationships with peers and teachers. It isn't just getting along with others that is significant in this dimension; satisfactory interpersonal relations refers to the ability to demonstrate sympathy and warmth toward others, to stand alone when necessary, to have close friends, to be aggressively constructive, and to enjoy working and playing with others as well as enjoying by oneself. (3) An inability to act or feel appropriately under normal or stress conditions. Such a lack is often sensed by the teacher and especially by peer groups. "He acts funny," another child may say; or a teacher may find a child blowing up because of a simple command such as "Please take your seat." This is one dimension in which a teacher should trust her daily and long-term observation of children and her feeling that something is wrong without having to know exactly what it is. (4) An inability to shake the blues. Children who are unhappy most of the time may demonstrate such feelings in expressive play, artwork, written composition, or discussion periods. They seldom smile and usually lack any kind of joie de vivre in their schoolwork or social relationships. (5) A tendency to develop physical symptoms, pains, or fears associated with personal or school problems. This tendency is most often noticed by the school nurse or the parent. All of these characteristics can, of course, be said to be true of all children to some degree at different times. There seems to be no way of bypassing the question "How much is too much?" In any descriptive attempt to identify children who need special help early, it is important to trust the experience of professional people and to act on hunches where there is very little danger in learning more about a child but where great harm can be caused by overlooking a child who may need some help at a dangerous corner in his life.

Early Identification. Summaries of studies aimed at early identification of children with developing mental health problems are given by Bower (1960), Gildea and others (1958), and Ullman (1957). Bower pointed out the social and value conflicts inherent in such programs and the strategic position of the school in early identification of emotional problems in children. For example, one must question the assumption that detecting a problem early means that it can be managed more economically or effectively. Although this assumption seems logical, its psychological or scientific validity needs additional clarification. Some psychotherapists are reluctant to treat adolescents and feel that the results can be much more effective and lasting if treatment is started at a later time. A second assumption questioned by Bower is that personality disorders in adulthood are the result of progressively developing conditions visible in children's personalities and behaviors. Where normal behavior is equated with average behavior, it may be difficult to differentiate the child who is different from the child who is basically ill. Therefore, any appraisal of children with suspected mental health problems must differentiate between "sick" behavior and the wide range of normal behavior. Another related problem is the fact that the same behavior may be interpreted as having different meanings under different circumstances and at different times. For example, a boy who is hostile or rebellious toward his parents when he is 11 years old may be considered a problem. However, a couple of years later, when he is 13, hostility and rebellion against adults can be considered normal behavior.

In addition to the problem of determining what it is that is to be evaluated as good mental health or poor mental health, one needs to know how early is "early." Is early recognition often too late, too costly or too ineffective if it is made after the child has completed the fourth grade? Does the process of identification carry with it the seeds of help for those who have been identified? Can school systems and teachers realistically undertake a program designed for early identification and correction of mental health problems which are causing children some concern?

Summaries of recent research on early identification of children with mental health problems indicated the following: much information obtained by the teacher in her routine interaction with children can be used in predicting the future emotional status of children and adolescents; teacher and peer ratings are highly effective predictors of the emotional status of children; and few, if any, tests discriminate well enough to be used by themselves in assessing the mental health of children.

The California study (Bower, 1960) found that children's judgments of other children's behavior were surprisingly accurate and predictive; teachers' judgments of the emotional status of children were also accurate; teachers identified about the same number of children as being overly withdrawn that they identified as being overly aggressive; about three children in each classroom had moderate to serious emotional problems; and differences between children with mental health problems and their classmates increased in each succeeding grade.

Identification in the Preschool Period. The early recognition of children with developing mental health problems prior to school entrance is dependent on the accuracy and validity of recognizable signs of such disorders and the presence of some agency or professional person who can read the signs and can do something about them. For example, there are indications that prematurity and medical complications during the mother's pregnancy are associated with brain injury in children and in some cases with morbidity (Pasamanick, 1956). It is also true that complications in pregnancy and prematurity are associated strongly with socioeconomic level and are of highest incidence in lower-class groups. Further studies (Kawi & Pasamanick, 1959) indicate that the more abnormalities in pregnancy, the greater the reading disabilities of such children in school. Children born prematurely have been found to be children most susceptible to mental health problems, with brain injury designated as a general or chief cause of their problems. Yet as Schwartz (1956) has noted, it may be presumed that birth normally produces circulatory disturbances in the infant which are transmitted to deeper parts of the brain. In fact, Schwartz notes that almost every baby born normally suffers some disturbance of cerebral circulation as a result of the release effect. Silver and others (1958) suggest that the behavior of a child with brain damage not only is a function of the insult to the tissue itself but also is dependent upon the child's psychological defense pattern and on the environmental forces acting upon him. Eisenberg (1956) describes the effects of such damage as the result of three interacting factors: (1) the degree of altered neurophysiology in the brain, (2) the reaction of the child to the damage and to any loss in function, and (3) the reaction of the social environment. Maladaptive behavior or mental health problems in children can result from damage to the cortical analyzer that mediates between the child and his world. Effects are no less forceful in the opposite direction. Disorder in a social situation to which the child endeavors to adapt can be just as disabling as a neurophysiological injury.

There seems to be ample evidence to indicate that a "healthy" birth can be an important factor in the mental health of the child and that major prebirth and birth conditions can have significant effects on the emotional or behavioral problems in children.

Pediatricians as a Mental Health Resource. In any age of anxiety, especially anxiety surrounding the mystery of raising healthy, normal children, the pediatrician, or the baby doctor, is perceived as being Merlin the Magician by mothers and fathers; witness the magic of Dr. Spock (1957) in calming the fears of parents about the growth of young children. Pediatricians have become more interested, more concerned, and more verbal about the mental health of children and parents. In May 1954 an editorial in *Pediatrics* commented on the need for pediatricians to get more training in the area of mental health. Psychologists and pediatricians have long been aware of the effects of early parental separation on the child. Studies by Brody (1958) and Spitz (1954) have helped emphasize the fact that early separation or detachment of the child from the mother may have a marked effect on the infant's emotional and developmental balance. In addition, Brody found some mothers who showed a hyperresponsiveness to the child to such a degree that the mother interfered with the child's spontaneous reactions. Responses by mothers to children may also be too frequent or infrequent or markedly inconsistent, oscillating between indulgence and strictness. In all this the pediatrician's role is to help the mother perceive the imbalance or excesses in one direction or another and to help her correct them.

Pediatricians are aware that there is a reliable and positive relationship between the frequency, duration, and severity of symptoms as reported by mothers and the degree of mental health problems found in a child. Mothers' reports of problems can be used with more success than most medical screening techniques (Glidewell & others, 1959). In summary, the pediatrician represents a potential resource in the early identification of children with mental health problems. He is a specialist in individual development, an authority to whom parents will listen, and a liaison with other community agencies. His contribution to the prevention and treatment of mental health problems can be great. He is, however, a professional person who usually carries a high patient load and can see parents for only brief periods of time. In some cases pediatricians have asked social workers or psychologists to work with them. However, this practice is at present used in only a few settings.

Identification in the Preschool Period. With the initiation of Project Head Start and the increased interest in nursery-school programs many communities are attempting to introduce opportunities for screening children who need help at this point. For example, it was found (Oppenheimer & Mandel, 1959) that of 60 older children seen at a clinic, in 32 cases the problem had been first noted prior to school entrance. In 20 cases it had been first noted in the kindergarten and in 5 cases it had been noted in the first grade. Bolton (1955) studied the early history of 100 children of school age who had visited a child-guidance clinic. She found that 3 out of 4 had shown observable symptoms in the first five years of life.

Investigators have been interested in ways of assessing a child's mental health development in the nursery school. One study included a standardized clinical examination of the child, interviews with parents, systematized observation of the child, nursery-teacher ratings, and sociometric data. This study employed ratings of four variables observed in these settings. These were (1) ease with which the child separated from his mother, (2) extent to which the child controlled his emotions, (3) amount of unusual behavior, and (4) number of special demands made on the experimenter (Lindemann & Ross, 1955).

PSYCHOEDUCATIONAL AND PSYCHOTHERAPEUTIC APPROACHES. The road to mental disorder and mental illness is not a single track. It combines a multitude of psychic, constitutional, and physiological factors. Children in our society grow up in our primary or humanizing institutions. Such institutions are the family and the school. One approach to children with mental health problems is to help them to become more effective in their learning and living skills in order to improve their functioning in these primary institutions. In the past, children with mental health problems were dealt with through a variety of other ways, including an attempt to get at some of the underlying pathology or conflict via play therapy or through a program of psychotherapy which may or may not have included other members of the family. In some cases both psychotherapy and psychoeducational approaches have been used collaboratively.

The problem of educating children with mental health problems has produced a shotgun marriage between the mental health and education professions.

Hollister (1959) identified three general trends in mental health programming in the classroom. These were (1) increased confidence in the group as a basis for individual development or change, (2) increased use of mental health personnel as the help and support of educational practitioners, and (3) a greater and more imaginative use of psychoeducational classroom and diagnostic techniques, special education, and guidance programs. Bower (1967) has classified five groups, constituting five levels of functioning, of children with mental health problems and the school program most relevant and helpful to each group. Group 1 contains children with normal problems of everyday living for whom positive mental health programs can be instituted in the school. Group 2 contains children with beginning or minor learning and behavior problems which persist beyond normal expectations. Group 3 contains children with marked and recurrent learning and behavior problems. Group 4 contains children with severe learning and behavior problems. Group 5 contains children unable to function in school because of severe problems of mental illness or unsocialization. In planning educational programs for all such children, varieties of approaches will have to be used.

Group-5 children who are severely disturbed and sometimes unable to attend school can often be helped in a 24-hour residential program in a private or public facility. For others a day-treatment program may be better. Many states, such as California, provide assistance to school districts for home-instruction or individual-instruction programs. Such programs, however, should be thought of as transitional toward the goal of getting the child back and functioning in his peer group and in his primary humanizing institution. Hewett (1964) suggests a hierarchy of educational tasks through which severely mentally ill children can be helped to move as they become more effective in their psychoeducational functioning. Beginning with a child totally inaccessible to control or learning, some gratification mechanism may be introduced, such as candy, gum, money, or attention. This may lead to a level of functioning in which there is an acceptance of the teacher by the child that is still primarily on the child's terms. When this is mastered, the child can go to a level where tasks and routine learning can be introduced. This can then be followed by more exploratory tasks leading to learning content and some beginning intellectual achievement. In other words, where the goal of treatment and psychoeducational intervention is clear the child will move from a sick or ineffective relationship with the environment to a more effective, more salutary relationship. This movement, however, must be operationally planned and programmed.

Another new approach in the education of markedly disturbed children has been the use of "teacher-moms" (Donahue & Nichtern, 1965). A psychiatrist and a school superintendent working together contacted a number of mothers whom they felt had personal attributes which would make them effective "teaching moms" of disturbed children. The "moms" were asked to contribute two mornings each week to working with a child under the supervision of the educational staff and the psychiatric director. Twenty mothers were selected to work with 10 children, and after three years 21 children have been worked with in the project. Of these, 11 have returned to the regular classrooms, 1 has been hospitalized, 1 moved away, and the rest are still in the program. The program was housed in a community center containing six classrooms, and although there was much individual work, the children came together as a class for morning exercises, "show and tell," story time, snacks, and birthday parties. The total cost of the program to the district was $718.00 per pupil, or $38.00 above the average pupil cost for all children. Carl Fenichel (1966) has voiced doubts about the use of untrained volunteers with disturbed children. He also feels that clear distinctions should be made between the role of nonprofessional teachers' aides, as in the Elmont Project (Donahue & Nichtern, 1965), and professional personnel working with highly disturbed children.

In the category of Group 4 children, children with severe mental health problems but still able to function in a school setting, many large school systems have developed special classes with special teachers. In some large cities there are special schools and special classes for such children. Usually such classes are composed of small groups of from 8 to 20 children taught by a single teacher assisted at rare times by a matron and sometimes by mental health consultants or a ready supply of tranquilizers. The problem of grouping children in such classes is that it is a seemingly- hit- or-miss endeavor. A national study of public school classes for emotionally disturbed children (Morse & others, 1964) found a diversity and an ambiguity of goals and content. There are, however, some excellent special class programs taught by highly competent teachers assisted by administrative personnel, mental health consultants, and a variety of curriculum consultants. Placement of children with marked mental health problems in classroom groups seems to be best accomplished with the highest priority given to obtaining a workable and functional teacher-group interaction. Often such placement may have little to do with individual diagnostic labels, suspected or known neurological or psychiatric etiologies of the problem. The essential nature of the program in the special classes hinges on helping the teacher to use clinical information in planning educational experiences which will enhance the child's ego strength and functional effectiveness. The training of teachers for this job has received major impetus from federal legislation, P.L. 88–164, which provides help to colleges in the development and implementation of training programs for teachers of emotionally disturbed children. In addition, this program has received support from Title VI of The Morse-Carey Amendment to the Elementary and Secondary Education Act of 1965, P.L. 89–10. Under this title, states will submit plans showing how they intend to initiate, expand, and improve programs and projects for exceptional children, including children with serious emotional disturbances. State departments of education will receive additional money for such programs, and help will be provided to state institutions and day schools.

Despite new legislation, the development of some training programs, and a small increase of personnel in this field, the development of programs for disturbed children has been slow and difficult. The role of the teacher has moved away from therapy toward the concept of the master teacher with orientation in basic school content. Teachers in this field should know how to teach, what to teach, how to manage groups, how to make educational sense out of clinical material, how to use mental health consultation for program purposes, and how to use experts or to be expert in remedial techniques in basic school subjects.

Another program for Group 4 children is a dayschool type, such as the one developed at the George Peabody College for Teachers in cooperation with the states of Tennessee and North Carolina (Hobbs, 1967). This was begun in 1961 as a seven-year experimental program for the reeducation of emotionally disturbed children. The project was aimed at developing and evaluating the effectiveness, feasibility, and economy of a residential program staffed by teacher-counselors and backed by consultants from the mental health professions. Two schools are now (1967) in operation, one in Nashville, Tennessee, and the other in Durham, North Carolina. The program of Project Re-ed puts an emphasis on what the child can do rather than on what he cannot do; on learning rather than removing blocks to learning; on the mediation of new experiences rather than on the unmediation of old conflicts; on the present and future rather than on the past; on competence in peer groups and in the social system of the school; and on rapid return to home and school as soon as the odds for success seem to be weighted in favor of the child. Since both schools are situated in cities they can be used as boarding schools with a variety of plans for children, some staying on for a full seven days, some going home on weekends, some going home every day. Both schools have case workers and other personnel who function as liaison with the social agencies and the families.

Group 3 children are those with long-term mental health problems who have been permitted to develop a chronic or borderline style of adjustment. Many can just about make it through the school semester and are sent on to the next class by teachers with some misgivings but with a certain amount of relief. This kind of homeostatic relationship between the child and the school is often the result of a silent treaty: "If you don't bother me, I won't bother you." Since many of the children are behind in school skills, a great deal of effort goes into remedial sessions in reading and arithmetic. In some cases such remedial programs have been developed using student volunteers from adjacent high schools or junior high schools. In one study in which volunteer students were used the investigators felt that this method could be more effective than one in which adult professionals were used, since the volunteers were closer to the period of development of the younger boys they were helping (Bloomberg & Troupe, 1964). Programs of mental health consultation can be helpful to teachers with children in this group. In such programs consultants may be periodically available to teachers or may meet with them individually or in groups to discuss individual children. In such discussions there is a sharing of information and perceptions about the child's learning problem or his mental health difficulties as seen by the teacher. The consultant attempts to add his behavioral-science knowledge to the teacher's for the benefit of the student.

Group 2 children are those having initial learning or behavioral difficulties who can be identified early in this development. Screening programs, such as those carried out by the Wellesley Human Relations Service, the St. Louis County Health Department program, the California Study, and the Sumter, South Carolina, studies (Klein & Lindemann, 1964) can be of significant help in identifying and helping children who are temporarily in trouble. Such screening programs should produce the kind of help which immediately recognizes the problem and does something to alter the course. It also has been helpful to develop parent-counseling programs, especially in the primary grades, where mental health problems are not severe but can become worse if left alone. (Bower, 1960). In such programs it is important to keep the focus of the counseling school-centered. The sanction and purpose of the program is to help the parents assist their children to do better in school. It is also important to have sufficient school social workers and school nurses at this point to enable them to attend to early problems. Such personnel can be excellent screeners and help keep teachers and school administrators alert to the need for action when a child begins to show signs of difficulty.

What goes on in any school system with respect to the children with mental health problems has as its firm base the general curriculum. To the extent to which the school is effective enough to encompass ranges in the competences of children and in their values, there will be less need for putting children into various special programs. More importantly, educational experiences for all children must include qualities and varieties of learnings which help them to develop ego processes and ego strengths which mediate stress and build skills in the processing of data from the outer and inner environments. To do this, the school may find it necessary to introduce a greater variety of experiences, some more closely allied to understanding feelings, the self, or the interpersonal. Ojemann (Ojemann & Snider, 1964), in his work curriculum, has pointed out that children learning in the ordinary classroom tend to become arbitrary and noncausal in their approaches to human and social problems. His research has dealt with the inability of schools to develop children who can deal with problems on a multiple-causation basis instead of tending to seek arbitrary and simple solutions to complex problems. There is some evidence that education in the behavioral sciences can produce significant changes in the way a child learns to deal with daily personal situations in that he becomes less authoritarian and less anxiety ridden in his problem solving behavior. The organization and communication of behavioral-science information and principles for elementary-school children should be developed and evaluated. Basically, the child's ability to deal with symbols, his ability to read with enjoyment, to communicate in speech and writing, and to enjoy learning and working with others are the essential elements of a good mental health program in a school. Malamud and Machover (1964) and Spolin (1963) have proposed new approaches in education which can be helpful in improving the mental health of children. Spolin has developed a series of theater games which are intended to help a child develop spontaneity and opportunities for integrating his intellectual with his emotional self. Her emphasis is on helping students to communicate by nonverbal means, that is, to show, not to tell, to feel free to respond spontaneously to problems under certain circumstances, and to develop the sensory equipment of students. Malamud and his colleagues have developed a series of carefully planned experimental classroom situations in which students are given the opportunity to experience such concepts as that (1) all behavior is caused, (2) unconscious phenomena are real and meaningful, (3) childhood experiences have a crucial bearing on personality, (4) trivial things can be significant, (5) a coherent and understandable style of reacting may be discerned in one's life, and (6) the self is an active agent in one's development. One of their classroom exercises is the seat-changing experiment in which the leader instructs the students to shift their seats to places as different as possible from their present ones. The leader then asks questions such as "How radically different is your new seat from your old one?" "Who thought of sitting in the leader's chair?" "Who thought of sitting on the arm of the chair, or on the table or on the floor?" "Why didn't these seating places occur to you?" "If they had would you have sat in those places?" The leader then requests the members to return to their old seats and discuss their reactions to the change again. The requirements for these experiments, as listed by the investigators, are that they be simple enough so that all can participate, that they be sufficiently novel and disarming that stereotyped responses cannot be used, that they possess a surprise effect, and that they evoke a wide variety of individual responses and provoke students to wonder whether their reactions were as inevitable as they thought they were.

MENTAL HEALTH AND THE TEACHER. By and large what schools can do about mental health rests on what teachers can do. Mental health workers, such as psychiatrists, psychologists, and social workers, may often be shocked by the fact that schools and teachers have different priorities with respect to the mental health of children. Not only are there a multitude of other interests and activities with which the teacher must be concerned, but the mental health worker may find his concern for the mental health of the child not especially high in the school's set of priorities. To the teacher mental health is only one ring in a many-ringed circus. To the mental health worker it is the circus. Teachers often have difficulty sizing up exactly how the knowledge and know-how represented by the public health nurse, the psychiatrist, the social worker, or the psychologist can really help her teach better. As a result she may separate what she does in the classroom and what the mental health worker can do outside the classroom in such processes as play therapy, psychotherapy, testing, or family consultation. The mental health worker is in general much clearer about his role and his objectives, coming out of training programs and experiences for helping the relatively sick to become relatively well or to help the relatively rigid to become relatively flexible. The purposes of psychotherapy are specific and uncomplicated. On the other hand, the teacher is asked to be peer and surrogate, policeman, group worker, bookkeeper, specialist in environmental health, a clothes sorter, a parent confidant, a student counselor, a recreation specialist, a subject-matter specialist, and a child-development specialist. This role diffusion and confusion on the part of the teacher is often sensed by the mental health worker, with some empathy.

It is in the nature of public education that the school is unselective with regard to its clients. Also, the processes of education are primarily mediative ones and are planned in relation to content. Schools see their job with respect to students as adding, expanding, producing, and creating new ideas and concepts. Mental health workers see these functions less clearly, coming from a professional background of learning to deal with conflict, emotionality, infantile behavior, and mental illnesses. Working with mental health personnel, at least to some teachers, is perceived as loosening classroom controls, being more sympathetic, giving in to the child, or just giving up disciplining him. Teachers have had more experience than any other single professional workers in what "normal behavior" is like at various age levels. Most research confirms the fact that teachers can sense deviance and pathology in children and can recognize when something is awry. Teachers will often solicit help from mental health workers to refine, confirm, or reject their observations and judgments about children.

Mental health workers can find their most significant preventive impact in helping the teacher and administrator to become more effective in carrying out the school's goals. One must develop and promote a liaison between the behavioral sciences and the educator which fits the social system in which educational processes take place. Educators cannot expect the mental health workers to be curriculum supervisors or classroom-management magicians. Mental health services to schools will be effective and useful to the extent to which teachers are helped to learn how to use themselves professionally in the organization and communication of knowledge and how to teach and help children with mild, moderate, or severe learning and behavior problems.

Eli M. Bower
National Institute of Mental Health

References

American Psychiatric Association. *Planning Psychiatric Services for Children in the Community Mental Health Program.* APA, 1964. 47p.

Beers, Clifford. *A Mind That Found Itself.* Doubleday, 1921.

Bloomberg, Claire, and Troupe, Caroline. "Big Brothers to Troubled Children." *NEA J* 53:22–5; 1964.

Bolton, Anne. "A Prophylactic Approach to Child Psychiatry." *J Mental Sci* 101:696–703; 1955.

Bower, Eli M. *Early Identification of Emotionally Handicapped Children in School.* Thomas, 1960. 120p.

Bower, Eli M. "Primary Prevention in a School Setting." In Caplan, Gerald. (Ed.) *Prevention of Mental Disorders in Children.* Basic Books, 1961. p. 353–77.

Bower, Eli M. "The Achievement of Competency." In Waetjen, Walter, and Leeper, Robert. (Eds.) *Learning and Mental Health in the School.* ASCD, 1966(a). p. 23–48.

Bower, Eli M. "Personality and Individual Social Maladjustment." In *Social Deviancy Among Youth*, NSSE, U Chicago Press, 1966(b). p. 103–34.

Bower, Eli M. "A Conceptual Framework for the Development of Programs for Emotionally Disturbed Children." In Berkowitz, Pearl H., and Rothman, Esther P. (Eds.) *Public Education for Disturbed Children in New York City.* Thomas, 1967. p. 255–91.

Bower, Eli M., and Hollister, William G. (Eds.) *Behavioral Science Frontiers in Education.* Wiley, 1967. 512p.

Brody, Sylvia. "Signs of Disturbance in the First Year of Life." *Am J Orthopsychiatry* 28:362–72; 1958.

Buswell, Margaret. "The Relationship Between the Social Structure of the Classroom and the Academic Success of the Pupils." *J Exp Ed* 22:37–52; 1953.

Butler, R. A. "Exploratory and Related Behavior: A New Trend in Animal Research." *J Individual Psychol* 14:111–20; 1958.

California State Department of Mental Hygiene and Los Angeles County. *Mental Health Survey of Los Angeles County.* The State and County, 1960. 567p.

Calvin, Allen D., and others. "A Further Investigation of the Relationship Between Anxiety and Classroom Examination Performance." *J Ed Psychol* 48:240–4; 1957.

Deutsch, Albert. *The Mentally Ill in America.* Garden, 1937. 530p.

Donahue, George, and Nichtern, Sol. *Teaching the Troubled Child.* Free, 1965. 202p.

Eisenberg, Leon. "Dynamic Considerations Underlying the Management of the Brain Damaged Child." *GP* 14:101–6; 1956.

Evans, A. S., and Warren, J. "Patterns of Illness in University of Wisconsin Students." *Archives Environmental Health* 4:579–87; 1962.

Farnsworth, Dana. *College Health Services in the United States.* American College Personnel Association, 1965. 32p.

Fenichel, Carl. "Mama or M.A.? The 'Teacher-Mom' Program Evaluated." *J Special Ed* 1:45–51; 1966.

Fenichel, Otto. *The Psychoanalytic Theory of Neurosis.* Norton, 1945. 703p.

Frank, Jerome. "Are You a Guilty Parent?" *Harper's Magazine* April:56–9; 1957.

Freud, Sigmund. *A General Introduction to Psychoanalysis.* Liveright, 1935. 412p.

Freud, Sigmund. "Formulations Regarding the Two Principles in Mental Functioning (1911)." In *Collected Papers*, Vol. 4. Basic Books, 1959. p. 13–21.

Freud, Sigmund, and Breuer, Joseph. "On the Psychical Mechanism of Hysterical Phenomena (1893)" In *Collected Papers*, Vol. 1. Basic Books, 1959. p. 9–23.

Galdston, Iago. "The Trials of Normalcy." *Mental Hygiene* 40:78–84; 1956.

Gildea, Margaret C. L., and others. "Community Mental Health Research; Findings After Three Years." *Am J Psychiatry* 114:970–6; 1958.

Glidewell, John C., and others. "Behavior Symptoms in Children and Adjustment in Public School." *Hum Organization* 18:123–30; 1959.

Goertzel, Victor, and Goertzel, Mildred. *Cradles of Eminence.* Little, 1962. 362p.

Hartmann, Heinz. *Ego Psychology and the Problem of Adaptation.* International, 1958. 121p.

Hewett, F. "A Hierarchy of Educational Tasks for Children with Learning Disorders." *Excep Children* 31:207–16; 1964.

Hobbs, Nicholas. "The Re-education of Emotionally Disturbed Children." In Bower, Eli M., and Hollister, William G. (Eds.) *Behavioral Science Frontiers in Education.* Wiley, 1967. p. 336–54.

Hollister, William G. "Current Trends in Mental Health Programming in the Classroom." *J Social Issues* 15:50–8; 1959.

Huxley, Aldous. "Education on the Nonverbal Level." *Daedalus* 91:279–93; 1962.

Jahoda, Marie. *Current Concepts of Positive Mental Health.* Basic Books, 1958. 136p.

Kawi, A. A., and Pasamanick, Ben. "Prenatal and Perinatal Factors in the Development of Childhood Reading Disorders." *Monogr Soc Res Child Develop*, 1959. 80p.

Klein, Donald C. "Some Concepts Concerning the Mental Health of the Individual." *J Cons Psychol* 24:288–93; 1960.

Klein, Donald C., and Lindemann, Elizabeth. "Approaches to Pre-school Screening." *J Sch Health* 34:365–73; 1964.

Klein, Donald C., and Ross, Ann. "Kindergarten Entry: A Study of Role Transition." In Krugman, M. (Ed.) *Orthopsychiatry and the School.* American Orthopsychiatric Association, 1958. p. 60–9.

Knight, James A., and Davis, Winborn E. *Manual for the Comprehensive Community Mental Health Clinic.* Thomas, 1964. 184p.

Kris, Ernest. *Psychoanalytic Explorations in Art.* Int U, 1952. 369p.

Kubie, Lawrence S. "Social Forces and the Neurotic

Process." In Leighton, A., and others. (Eds.) *Explorations in Social Psychiatry*. Basic Books, 1957. p. 77–104.

Lichter, Solomon O., and others. *The Drop-outs*. Free, 1962. 302p.

Lindemann, Elizabeth, and Ross, Ann. "A Follow-up Study of a Predictive Test of Social Adaptation in Preschool Children." In Caplan, Gerald. (Ed.) *Emotional Problems of Early Childhood*. Basic Books, 1955. p. 79–93.

Malamud, D. I., and Machover, S. "The Workshop in Self-understanding: A New Approach to Mental Health Education." In Abt, Lawrence E., and Riess, Bernard F. (Eds.) *Progress in Clinical Psychology*. Grune, 1964. p. 200–8.

McKeachie, J. W., and others "Relieving Anxiety in Classroom Examinations." In Seidman, J. M. (Ed.) *The Adolescent: A Book of Readings*. Holt, 1960. p. 408–20.

Meier, Richard L. "Human Time Allocation: A Basis for Social Accounts." *J Am Institute Planners* 25: 27–33; 1959.

Morse, William C., and others. *Public School Classes for Emotionally Handicapped Pupils*. Council for Exceptional Children, 1964. 124p.

Murphy, Lois B. "Preventive Implications of Development in the Preschool Years." In Caplan, Gerald. (Ed.) *Prevention of Mental Disorders in Children*. Basic Books, 1961. p. 218–48.

National Institute of Mental Health. "Unpublished Surveys." Office of Biometry, The Institute, n.d.

Ojemann, R. H., and Snider, B. C. "The Effects of a Teaching Program in Behavioral Science on Changes in Causal Behavior Scores." *J Exp Ed* 57:256–60; 1964.

Oppenheimer, E., and Mandel, M. "Behavioral Disturbances of School Children in Relation to the Preschool Period." *Am J Public Health* 49:1537–42; 1959.

Pasamanick, Ben. "The Epidemiology of Behavior Disorders of Childhood." In McIntosh, Rustin, and Hare, Clarence C. (Eds.) *Neurology and Psychiatry in Childhood*. Williams and Wilkins, 1956. p. 397–403.

Pearlman, Samuel. "Mental Health in Higher Education." In Abt, Lawrence E., and Riess, Bernard F. (Eds.) *Progress in Clinical Psychology*. Grune, 1966. p. 191–208.

Pickrel, E. W. "The Differential Effect of Manifest Anxiety on Test Performance." *J Ed Psychol* 49: 43–5; 1958.

Plunkett, Richard J., and Gordon, John E. *Epidemiology and Mental Illness*. Basic Books, 1960. 125p.

Rapaport, David. (Ed.) *Organization and Pathology of Thought*. Columbia U Press, 1951. 786p.

Redlich, Fritz C. "The Concept of Health in Psychiatry." In Leighton, A., and others. (Eds.) *Explorations in Social Psychiatry*. Basic Books, 1957. p. 138–64.

Rosen, Beatrice, and others. "Adolescent Patients Served in Outpatient Psychiatric Clinics." *Am J Public Health* 55:1563–77; 1965.

Rosen, V. H. "The Relevance of Style to Certain Aspects of Defense and the Synthetic Function of the Ego." *Int J Psychoanal* 42:447–57; 1961.

Sanford, Nevitt. "The Development of Cognitive-Affective Processes Through Education." In Bower, Eli M., and Hollister, William G. (Eds.) *Behavioral Science Frontiers in Education*. Wiley, 1967. p. 52–64.

Schwartz, P. "Birth Injuries of the Newborn." *Archives Pediatrics* 73:429–50; 1956.

Silver, Archie. "Behavioral Syndrome Associated with Brain Damage in Children." In *Pediatric Clinics of North America: Symposium on Behavioral Disorders*. Saunders, 1958. p. 687–93.

Smith, M. Brewster. "Research Strategies Toward a Conception of Positive Mental Health." *Am Psychologist* 14:673–81; 1959.

Smith, M. Brewster, and Hobbs, Nicholas. *The Community and the Community Mental Health Center*. APA, 1966. 24p.

Smith, W. G., and others. "Psychiatric Disorder in a College Population." *Archives Gen Psychiatry* 9: 351–61; 1963.

Spitz, René. "Problems of Infantile Neurosis." *Psychoanal Study Child* 9:16–71; 1954.

Spock, Benjamin. *Baby and Child Care*. Duell, 1957. 627p.

Spolin, Viola. *Improvisation for the Theater*. Northwestern U Press, 1963. 399p.

Sullivan, Harry Stack. *The Interpersonal Theory of Psychiatry*. Norton, 1953.

Summers, Montagne. (Translator.) *The Witch's Hammer*. Limited Editions, 1928.

Traxler, Arthur E., and Townsend, Agatha. *Eight More Years of Research in Reading*. Educational Records Bureau, 1955. 283p.

Ullmann, Charles A. "Teachers, Peers and Tests as Predictors of Adjustment." *J Ed Psychol* 48:257–67; 1957.

Wall, W. D. *Education and Mental Health*. Columbia U Press, 1955. 347p.

White, R. W. *Ego and Reality in Psychoanalytic Theory*. International, 1963. 210p.

Zilboorg, Gregory, and Henry, George. *A History of Medical Psychology*. Norton, 1941. 606p.

MENTALLY RETARDED CHILDREN

The accelerated interest in the mentally retarded has resulted in an extensive literature. A significant recent addition to the resource literature is the quarterly *Mental Retardation Abstracts*, a publication of the National Institute of Mental Health. Started in 1964, this publication was by 1967 screening over 200 periodicals for articles on mental retardation and carrying over 2,000 abstracts annually. Broad reviews of the research on mental retardation appear every three years in the *Review of Educational Research*, and a restricted topic is reviewed in each issue of the *Mental Retardation Abstracts*.

This brief overview attempts to be representative

of the present state of theory, research, and practice in the broad area of mental retardation, with particular orientation toward the mentally retarded of school age. It is in no sense complete and of necessity has been selective.

DEFINITION. The term "mental retardation" has gradually received greater acceptance as the preferred term to replace the variety of descriptive terms, such as "mental deficiency" and "feeblemindedness," and of historical terms, such as "amentia" and "oligophrenia," and was adopted recently by the American Association on Mental Deficiency (AAMD) because it appeared to be the term most used by professional workers in the interested disciplines. The AAMD defined mental retardation as "subaverage general intellectual functioning which originates during the development period and is associated with impairment in adaptive behavior" (Heber, 1961, p. 499). Although a number of minor changes have been suggested (e.g., Kidd, 1964), the definition generally has been received favorably. Universal acceptance, however, of this or any other proposed definition within the next few years appears unlikely.

A number of earlier definitions, while differing somewhat in terminology or in inclusiveness, stressed, of course, the essential and common feature of mental retardation—subnormal mental development. They have differed primarily through their concepts of etiology, criteria, and prognosis. Doll (1941) proposed six criteria essential to an adequate definition: (1) social incompetence, which results from (2) mental subnormality, which has been (3) developmentally arrested, which (4) obtains at maturity, (5) is of constitutional origin, and (6) is essentially incurable. Tredgold (1937) stressed the inability of the mentally retarded person to adapt to a normal environment and his inability to maintain existence independently of supervision, control, or external support. A somewhat similar concept was expressed by Benda (1954), who defined the mentally deficient person as one who is incapable of managing himself or his affairs or being incapable of learning to do so and who requires supervision and control not only for his own welfare but for that of society as well. These three definitions, emphasizing social incompetence, are concerned primarily with adult behavior and offer limited direction or criteria for a diagnosis of mental retardation in children. The use of Doll's criteria (4) and (6) lead logically either to a tentative prediction or to a retrospective judgment and are typically rejected in more recent attempts to arrive at a satisfactory definition of mental retardation.

Mental retardation, like the related term "intelligence," may be defined satisfactorily through a number of somewhat different abstractions. Similarly, in the final analysis its meaning is linked realistically to the criteria and procedures used to assess its dimensions. In the United States through common practice if not formal definition, mental retardation has become a quantitative concept related to a specific standard or cutoff point on the continuum of mental ability as measured by a standardized individual intelligence test. The cutoff has varied from about 65 to 80, depending upon local custom, state law, the test, or the purpose of testing.

CLASSIFICATION. Although more than 200 pathological conditions may result in retardation, a positive and accurate identification of the cause or interrelated causes is possible through our present resources in only about 20 to 25 percent of all cases. Because of the great variability within and among mentally retarded individuals and because of the specialized interests of various professional groups, it is not surprising either that several subgroupings have been proposed or that no single classification scheme has yet proved satisfactory for multidisciplinary usage.

Classifications have typically been devised around (1) degree of mental deficit, (2) etiology, (3) clinical types, or (4) educational or behavioral level. A number of dichotomous classifications have usually been related primarily to causality, e.g., subcultural versus pathological, brain damaged versus familial, exogenous versus endogenous. A good discussion is given by Sarason (1959) of dualistic classifications and of the problems inherent in making a suitable distinction. The once-popular clinical classification by degree which used the terms "moron" (IQ 50–70), "imbecile" (IQ 25–49), and "idiot" (IQ 0–24) has generally been replaced by a classification using descriptive terms, such as "mild," "moderate," and "severe," and in educational settings particularly by terms such as "educable," "trainable," and "custodial." Unfortunately neither diagnosis nor prognosis is affected by a simple name substitution, and the limitations in such classifications have remained. Further, the same descriptive terms have been applied to different IQ levels, so "severe" may be used to designate IQ 50 and below in one system, IQ 25–49 in another, or IQ 25 and below in still another. The possibilities for even greater confusion in classification terminology exist for somewhat higher levels of ability. Gelof (1963) has prepared a table which provides direct comparisons of 23 systems of classification which related degree of retardation to measured intelligence.

The AAMD has suggested a five-level classification system based upon the corresponding deviation scores on a reliable intelligence test (Heber, 1961). On a test with a standard deviation of 15, the IQ scores would be as follows: borderline, 70–84; mild, 55–69; moderate, 40–54; severe, 25–39; and profound, below 25. The cutoff points between levels would, of course, vary somewhat according to the standard deviation of the test used. Its borderline classification is made up preponderantly of slow learners, not usually considered to be mentally retarded by other classification systems.

Although the AAMD classification appears to be gaining acceptance in residential schools, it has made limited headway in the public day schools. Here the terms "educable mentally retarded" (IQ 50–75) and "trainable mentally retarded" (IQ 25–50) are commonly used. In some communities a trend has been noted toward grouping children according to a somewhat higher IQ level, such as 55–80 or 35–60. In New York City the educable group has been divided into Track 1 (IQ 60–75) and Track 2 (50–60). Cassel (1961) proposed five separate classifications for those with IQ's between 50 and 80 and who are typically found in classes for the educable. The practicability of Cassel's fine distinctions is questionable at this time in terms of the accuracy of our instruments and the level of current clinical practice.

PREVALENCE. Accurate statistics on the extent of mental retardation are difficult to obtain. Pintner (1933) cited variations from 0.4 percent to 6.1 percent among 17 studies or estimates reported between 1908 and 1929. The World Health Organization (1954) has reported large differences in the estimates of the numbers of mentally retarded children in different countries and also within the same country. Among the factors known to affect the reported prevalence are the definition and criteria of mental retardation, the case-finding techniques, and the sample.

Probably the best known of the various epidemiologic surveys of mental retardation are those by Lewis (1929) of six communities in England and Wales, by Lemkau and others (1942) of the Eastern Health District (Baltimore), and by the New York State Department of Mental Hygiene (1955) of Onondaga County. Lewis reported 0.8 percent to be retarded; Lemkau, 1.2 percent; and the New York study, slightly over 1 percent but with another 3.5 percent "possibly" retarded. The census design and procedures used in these studies and in four recent but less extensive surveys were described by Gruenberg (1964), who pointed out that the results of no two of these seven studies were directly comparable, since the studies were concerned with different goals, different techniques, and different features of community diagnosis under different circumstances. A relatively larger incidence of mental retardation is reported for males than for females and for low socioeconomic groups than for high or average groups.

Using 3 percent as the estimate of retardation in the United States, the President's Panel on Mental Retardation (1962) has subdivided the total group into three levels as follows: mild, 2.6 percent; moderate, 0.3 percent; and severe, 0.1 percent. The U.S. Office of Education (Mackie & others, 1963) uses a figure of 2.3 percent—the percentage expected to have IQ's below 68—but indicates that this criterion results in a very conservative estimate for school-age children. The estimate of 2 to 3 percent for the general population is in line with that reflected by the new AAMD levels of impairment, provided the borderline category is excluded.

Occasionally efforts are made to infer prevalence through a direct study of the numbers of children in special classes for the retarded, of children and adults in residential schools for the retarded, or of young men who fail to pass admission tests for the armed forces. Although such information is obviously of interest and may serve certain purposes, it does not provide data for generalizing a suitable estimate of the prevalence rate. Statistics on special classes tell us more about school philosophy and practice than about the extent of mental retardation. Similarly, admission rates or census figures for residential institutions reflect primarily the extent of financial support and available facilities. Ginzberg and Bray (1953) reported that about 4 percent of all men examined for U.S. military service in World War II were rejected on the ground of "mental deficiency" and that the screening procedures assessed primarily the individual's educational background or literacy level. The required literacy level has risen from about a grade 4 or 5 level in the 1940's to around a grade 9 level in the 1960's (Ginzberg, 1965). Obviously, in these practical considerations "mental retardation" is a relative term, and its dimensions change as conditions and pressures in society change.

Most studies rather consistently show a markedly increasing prevalence during the school years which falls off in the late teens, stabilizes in adulthood, and decreases slightly after middle age. Presumably the reported discrepancies in prevalence by age reflect not a *real* difference but a *measured* difference and result from the use of different criteria and procedures in case-finding. The criteria tend to shift in emphasis from pathology (medical) in the preschool years to academic achievement (psychoeducational) in the school years to community adjustment (vocational-social) in the adult years. Since the great majority of the mentally retarded fall in the upper level of the educable category, are not characterized by organic pathology, and are typically capable of supporting themselves at the adult level, most mentally retarded persons are not likely to be referred for diagnosis except for academic difficulty. Follow-up studies by Charles (1953) and by other researchers have shown that many graduates of special classes leave both the stigma and the designation of being retarded upon leaving the academic pressures of the school. Contending that the true prevalence of mental retardation is much greater than that brought to the attention of the health authorities, Goodman and Tizard (1962) pointed out that even though mongolians tend to be identified and reported earlier than other retarded children of the same level (typically trainable), about 16 percent of all mongolians in their study were not reported until after age 10.

From data in the Colchester Survey reported in 1938 on institutionalized mentally retarded patients, Penrose (1963) showed that high-grade defect and low-grade defect are distributed differently according to the occupational grades of parents. The upper occupational levels contributed twice as many children to the two lower levels (idiot and imbecile) as they did to the upper level (moron). For the lower occupations, however, there was a reversed tendency. Kirk (1962) estimated that in a comparison between low-socioeconomic-level communities and high-socioeconomic-level communities, the rates for totally dependent and trainable children would be the same but that the rate for educable and slow-learning children would be five to six times as great in the lower community. Dingman and Tarjan (1960) and other researchers have reported that the actual prevalence of mental retardation at the lowest socioeconomic levels is much greater than would be expected on the basis of a theoretical normal distribution of intelligence, probably because of an excess number at these levels suffering from a variety of pathological conditions.

IDENTIFICATION. The two major approaches to the identification and classification of mentally retarded children—medical and psychoeducational—differ in orientation and in examination content. The physician or neurologist is concerned primarily with etiology, physical characteristics and development, and sensory and neurological deficits. His attention is directed toward possible causal agents, such as infections, injuries, malnutrition, and metabolic disorders, or toward developmental stigmata which might further support other indications of mental retardation. In contrast, the school psychologist is most interested in identifying the present level of behavioral functioning and in assessing learning potential in relationship to school situations. Most of the custodial and trainable children are identified early in life because of physical defects, multiple handicaps, motor incoordination, apathy, or general developmental lag. For many of the educable mentally retarded, however, difficulty or failure in school is often the first clear symptom of inadequate intellectual functioning.

The roles of the physician and the psychologist are complementary and in an ideal diagnostic procedure would represent part of the effort of a multidisciplinary team working in a clinic setting. Although only a limited number of children presently have access to a diagnostic clinic for mental retardation, the number of such multidisciplinary clinics is increasing, especially through the support of the U.S. Children's Bureau.

The school psychological examination should include measurements of intelligence, achievement, and adjustment, along with informal developmental material supplied by the parents and by teachers and other professional school personnel. The child should be screened for visual, hearing, speech, and motor limitations in order to assess their possible effects on school behavior and on psychological-test performance and to determine whether the child should be referred to another specialist for a more complete evaluation in any of these areas. On the basis of such screening and the child's performance on initial tests, the psychologist may need to modify his procedures and to make substitutions in the test battery.

The AAMD (Heber, 1961) specified that the psychological or behavioral classification of mental retardation should be based on the related dimensions of measured intelligence and adaptive behavior and, further, that deficiencies in both of these must be demonstrated in order to meet its criteria of mental retardation. The AAMD concept of adaptive behavior is somewhat restrictive and has most relevance to the out-of-school child or adult.

Intelligence. The most suitable intelligence test for use with the suspected mentally retarded during the school years is the third revision (1960) of the *Stanford-Binet Intelligence Scale*, designed for ages two years and over. The original Binet test, published in 1905 by Binet and Simon, was designed to identify the mentally retarded or those children who would have great difficulty in school. Most present-day intelligence tests continue to be validated upon some form of the Binet and on the school achievement criterion. The *Wechsler Intelligence Scale for Children (WISC)* is popular with clinicians and is a good test to use with borderline and mildly retarded children or older retarded children (Wechsler, 1949). Published in 1967, the *Wechsler Preschool and Primary Scale of Intelligence* may be used with the younger or more seriously retarded child (Wechsler, 1967). In an effort to reduce testing time, a number of clinicians have devised abbreviated forms of several tests. Although testing time is reduced, so also is the reliability and thus the usefulness of the test.

For mentally retarded children with sensorimotor, language, or hearing impairment, verbal tests such as the Binet or the *WISC* may be inappropriate. In such cases, performance tests making little demand in these areas may be utilized: e.g., *The Arthur Point Scale of Performance Tests, Bender-Gestalt Test, Columbia Mental Maturity Scale, Coloured Progressive Matrices, Harris-Goodenough Test of Psychological Maturity, Leiter International Performance Scale, Nebraska Test of Learning Aptitudes,* and, for younger or more seriously retarded children, the *Gesell Developmental Schedules* and the *Merrill-Palmer Scale*. Quick estimates of intellectual level may be obtained through the use of a number of picture vocabulary tests, such as the *Peabody Picture Vocabulary Scale,* the *Full Range Picture Vocabulary Test,* and the *Quick Test*. (See Buros, 1965, for descriptions of these and other appropriate tests.) Performance or picture vocabulary tests may in certain situations be necessary substitutes for the Binet or the *WISC*, but they are not necessarily equivalent or adequate replacements and should be interpreted both cautiously and in relationship to as many other supplementary or substitute tests as practicable.

Achievement. In the school situation, the individual intelligence test yields either a predictive measure of adaptive behavior or an "explanation" of the level of behavior. On the other hand, general academic performance is essentially a criterion or synonym for adaptive behavior. Since the majority of children referred to a school psychologist for intelligence testing are referred because of poor academic performance, an assessment of the school performance is at least as important as an assessment of intelligence.

Portions of standardized achievement-test batteries appropriate to the child's level are given to supplement informal test results and the teacher's observations. By far the most critical instructional area for the schools is the broad area of language arts. Many excellent tests sampling various skills are available (Buros, 1965). New tests in language and psycholinguistics have broadened the dimensions of clinical appraisal. The *Illinois Test of Psycholinguistic Ability (ITPA)*, although still in experimental form, has elicited a substantial number of studies which give information not only on related language processes but also on possible uses of the test itself in the diagnostic process with retarded children. Other language tests found to be useful with the retarded are Wepman's *Auditory Discrimination Test*, Mecham's *Verbal Language Development Scale*, and the *Parsons Language Sample*. Adler (1964) and others have suggested elaborate procedures for evaluating language abilities, including auditory perception, concept formation, body image, sensory modality acuity, visual-motor coordination, and other, related factors.

Adjustment. Screening for adjustment level and emotional problems should be a routine part of the psychological evaluation, since (1) mentally retarded children with behavior problems are much more likely to be referred for testing than are mentally retarded children with satisfactory adjustment and (2) emotionally disturbed children of average potential may actually function as if they were mentally retarded. Unfortunately, those personality tests which are easiest to administer are typically inappropriate, and the most complex projective techniques may make excessive demands on both examination time and clinical sophistication. Research on the suitability of projective techniques with the retarded is confusing and contradictory, but it does suggest that such techniques are promising in the hands of skilled and objective clinicians (Sarason, 1959). Tests most frequently used with retarded children include the *Rorschach, Blacky Pictures, Children's Apperception Test,* and various projective drawing tests.

Clinicians may obtain helpful information through teachers' comments, school records, and observation during the entire testing situation. For many years they have been urged to make qualitative and projective interpretations of intelligence tests, and a growing literature (e.g., Fromm, 1960) points out that the nonintellective factors which play a part in the obtained score may also be appraised if the examiner is sensitive to the subtleties of the child's specific responses and total behavior in the testing situation.

The child's social development and maturity may be appraised through the *Vineland Social Maturity Scale*, which yields a social age based upon a set of standardized questions to be answered by the parents or other responsible adults. Devised by Doll in 1935 for use with the retarded, the scale underwent slight changes and refinements in the fourth edition (Doll, 1965) but has not yet undergone major changes or a restandardization. It has sometimes been used in a nonschool situation as a substitute for a psychometric examination when such an examination was inadvisable or impracticable. Its major school use, however, is perhaps in parent interviewing to obtain information about the child's out-of-school behavior and his family relationships. For many years the Vineland was essentially the only scale of its type, but it has been joined recently by the *Cain-Levine Social Competency Scale* (Cain & Levine, 1963) designed for use with the trainable, and Gunzberg's (1963) *Progressive Assessment Charts,* which are probably most helpful at the youth and adult levels. Gunzberg (1963, 1964) has questioned the value of norms which are based upon "normal" expectancy and suggests that for actual teaching purposes, a more meaningful comparison could be made of the retarded person's performance with that of other retarded persons of comparable age and intellectual deficit.

Comparisons of social maturity with other developmental aspects may be made up to early school age through the *Preliminary Behavior Inventory* and other portions of the *Gesell Developmental Schedules* (Buros, 1965). The inventory uses an interview technique primarily but also provides for observation and testing. Based upon the Gesell approach, Blum and Fieldsteel's *Cumulative Record of Functional Behavior* and *Cumulative Record of Motor Behavior* are age charts of representative developmental activities (Buros, 1961).

EVALUATION. Administering and scoring standardized tests are relatively simple and straightforward tasks. The interpretation of such tests may be quite complex, however, especially with retarded children whose personal limitations and restricted experiences may raise serious questions about both the suitability of available tests and the significance or meaning of low or inconsistent scores (Newland, 1963). The psychologist needs to know intimately a large number of tests of various types and their relationships to each other in order to select appropriate tests, to confirm present data or hunches through new lines of inquiry, to assess the effect of sensory defects or cultural background on both test and school behavior, and perhaps to make differential diagnoses between mental retardation and a number of conditions frequently confused with it, such as deafness, autism, and aphasia (Gunzberg, 1965; Rappaport, 1965). As the expected usefulness of the distinction between brain-damaged and familial children (i.e., those at the lower end of the intelligence scale because of hereditary biological variation) has become increasingly more questionable, the psychologist has become less preoccupied with establishing etiology and more concerned with the diagnostic and prescriptive significance of different performance patterns (Benton, 1964).

CHARACTERISTICS. The mentally retarded make up a heterogeneous group who vary considerably among themselves in academic achievement, behavior, family background, emotional stability, physical and motor characteristics, personality, level of general development, and etiology. Even on the primary criterion of low intelligence they range mentally from a level so low that it cannot be measured meaningfully to a level approximating the normal and making any distinction between normality and retardation tenuous and arbitrary. Since the criteria for retardation vary qualitatively and quantitatively according to age level and to the agency responsible for referral and diagnosis, a person might be considered retarded at one time but not at another.

Marked variability may be observed within the same level of intelligence or within subgroups generally assumed to have the same etiology and characteristics. Mongolian children are among the earliest identified as being retarded because of a gross similarity in appearance recognizable even by nonprofessional workers. Of the more than 80 identified mongolian "signs," however, only a few may appear in some mongolians but half or more may appear in others, and some characteristics appear among average persons as well. In a study of 50 consecutive mongolian children seen at a medical facility, Levinson and Bigler (1960) reported a large number of individual developmental differences, of which these ranges are illustrative: ability to hold head up, 2 months to 2½ years; sitting unsupported, 6 months to 3 years; walking, 12 months to 4 years; first tooth, 5 months to 2 years; first words spoken, less than 1 year to over 6 years. Similar variability was found in the group with respect to the various physical symptoms associated with mongolism and also on intelligence and behavior. Even in this small sample of a so-called homogeneous group, the range in these developmental activities was from normal to marked delay and retardation.

Below an IQ level of 50 are found most of the special clinical types or those who have experienced neurobiological impairment because of injuries, infections, diseases, developmental anomalies, or inborn metabolic disorders. On the other hand, central-nervous-system damage is observed in only about 15 percent or so of those with IQ's between 50 and 75, leaving 85 percent of the educables or about 78 percent of all retarded below IQ 75 to be classed as familial, garden variety, or subcultural. Most of this group come from low-socioeconomic-level families in a culturally deprived, poverty-stricken environment which tends to be characterized by inadequate nutrition and medical care, interrupted schooling, limited intellectual stimulation, and poor adult supervision (Benda & others, 1963).

Child growth and development studies have rather consistently shown the tendency for (1) intercorrelations of various growth measures to be low but positive and (2) deviations on other traits to be toward the average for any group formed because of extreme low or high scores on any other measure. Both of these principles—correlation and regression—apply to the retarded, but observations and generalizations reported in the literature on the retarded suggest that the latter principle has more frequently been overlooked, perhaps because of the tendency to perpetuate generalizations from early studies made predominantly on institution populations. Studies on institutionalized subjects are not generalizable to the entire mentally retarded group, since considerations leading to institutionalization stress factors of severity of retardation, multiple physical and sensory defects, grossly inadequate home conditions, and behavior or conduct disorders. Fewer than 1 percent at the educable level (IQ 50–75) enter institutions, but this level accounts for about 92 percent of all the retarded below IQ 75. A similar claim could be made that even special class populations reflect a negative selection bias, since the majority of mentally retarded children in public or parochial schools are educated in the regular class even where special classes are available. In other words, the excessive negative and deviant traits which lead to admission to an institution or to the special class show up disproportionately, since most studies have been made on these two minority groups.

Physical. The mentally retarded as a group are slow in learning to walk and tend to show a general developmental retardation during the growing years. The median height, weight, and bodily dimensions are somewhat below the norm (Culley & others, 1963; Mosier & others, 1965). There is considerable overlap, however, and for the educable and borderline levels there is no appreciable difference from the normal (Francis & Rarick, 1959; Kugel & Mohr, 1963). The degree of physical retardation is related not only to the severity of the mental retardation but also to etiological classifications. Physical stigmata, although limited primarily to the lower levels of intelligence, appear to be more closely related to etiology of retardation than to degree of retardation. Direct comparisons of research findings are difficult, however, because of the great heterogeneity within present classification systems. Penrose (1963) has pointed out that in a number of clinical types, including mongolism, the physical peculiarities are attributable to a retardation of growth at an early critical period. Evidence is accumulating, at least on a limited front, that medical advances are changing some of the growth patterns previously thought to be irreversible. In a comparison between treated and untreated mongolians, for example, Benda (1965) reported that over 2½ times as many of the former as of the latter fell within the normal range of height and weight and hypothesized that through medical care the mongolian may lose so many of his physical signs that he is unrecognizable as a mongolian even to physicians.

The retarded tend also to be below the average in general physical performance as measured by tests of strength, balance, agility, and speed (Francis & Rarick, 1959; Heath, 1953; Malpass, 1960). On 11 tests of gross motor ability, Francis and Rarick found that the median performance of their public school sample was below the published norms at all ages and that the deviation from the average increased with age. By age 14 their group with an average IQ of about 68 was from one to five years behind the norm on specific tests. No comparative data were presented on local children of average mental ability.

The observed tendencies toward clumsy, awkward physical activity have been confirmed on the *Rail-walking Test* and the *Lincoln-Oseretsky Motor De-*

velopment Scale. Correlations between mental ability and various motor tests have been reported to be low or moderate but in general to be higher than corresponding correlations in a normal sample. Considerable variation in performance has been shown from test to test. Comparisons between institutionalized and noninstitutionalized mentally retarded and between pretraining and posttraining sessions in motor skills suggest that at least part of the lowered motor skill of the retarded is related to stimulation and training. Because of brain injury, individuals in the lower IQ ranges tend to show both more motor defects and more severe motor defects. The motor performance of most educable and borderline mentally retarded children will be about comparable to that of normal children.

Visual and hearing impairment are reported to be common among the mentally retarded. Prevalence figures for visual defects are almost nonexistent, however, and the generalization, if true, is probably applicable primarily to the lower IQ levels, which are characterized by a high prevalence of diseases which cause visual pathology as well as mental retardation. Studies and reviews of the prevalence of hearing loss among institutionalized mentally retarded children range from no loss to 50 percent (Kodman, 1958; Webb & others, 1966), with an average incidence of around 25 or 30 percent. Kodman estimated that the prevalence of loss among a residential group would be about three to four times as great as that for normal children. With institutionalized children there is apparently no relationship between degree of loss and level of IQ. Webb and others suggested that hearing loss is high not because of the retardation but because of preselection of persons for institutional placement because of such losses. An accurate estimate of hearing loss is difficult to obtain because (1) audiology has not been active with the mentally retarded until recently and (2) the limited number of studies have been inconsistent in their testing procedures and in their selection of criteria to designate a hearing loss. Auditory training prior to audiometric testing appears to reduce drastically the measured hearing loss among the institutionalized, suggesting further the importance of rapport and general test procedure (Lloyd & Frisina, 1965).

Personality. In spite of the extensive literature on the personality and adjustment of the mentally retarded, little is of value in understanding the nature or extent of the problem. Most of our empirical evidence is limited to the institutionalized mentally retarded, to adults who have been rejected by or discharged from the armed forces for psychiatric reasons, to clinical cases referred because of adjustment problems, to other special groups such as the delinquent or the dropout, to comparisons of mentally retarded in regular versus special classes, or to comparisons of brain-injured versus familial mentally retarded persons. None of these provide much information about the mentally retarded as a group (Best, 1965).

Evidence of a high proportion of mental disorders among institutionalized mentally retarded adults has been well documented. Among some of these patients, the decision whether the mental retardation or the emotional problem is primary may be difficult or impossible to make. Little information is available about mentally retarded school children, especially those in the regular grades.

Theoretical explanations for predicted behavior are rampant and stress the discrepancies between society's demands and the retarded's performance, with the expected frustration, feelings of inadequacy, lowered self concept, increased anxiety, and the gamut of defense mechanisms with the possible exception of sublimation. This common-sense approach is based not only upon his retardation but also upon his expected poor environment. It is thought that the mentally retarded child, because of a slower maturational development, is not only slower to develop appropriate concepts of right and wrong but also slower in developing self-control.

No simple clear personality or social pattern is characteristic of the mentally retarded as a group or at any level within the group. At the lower IQ levels, however, are found a relatively higher frequency and seriousness of behavior problems. For the most part, the personality variables are similar to those found among normal children. After a review of the research literature on the personality of the mentally retarded, Heber (1964) concluded that research data were not yet sufficient to support or to refute the textbook descriptions of the retarded as being anxious, passive, impulsive, rigid, suggestible, immature, withdrawn, or lacking in persistence or as having a low frustration tolerance and an unrealistic self concept and level of aspiration. Actually, most generalizations about the self concept had been that it was low, reflecting a low opinion of the individual's worth—an opinion gained by observing the reflected attitudes and behavior of other persons toward him. Since the publication of Heber's review, a limited number of studies have shown that the self concept is quite high and somewhat idealized (Eyman, 1964; McAfee & Cleland, 1965; Perron & Pecheux, 1964). One could question the validity of such unexpectedly high self concepts and theorize that such reports were merely further evidence of defense reactions to an awareness of unfavorable comparisons. On the other hand, a similar question could be raised toward most studies of the adjustment of the retarded, since these have not typically been characterized by procedural sophistication or restrained generalizations.

On the educable and borderline levels there are probably slightly more behavior problems and delinquency than among normal children (Beier, 1964). The etiology of such behavior appears to be rooted in the pressures and values of the society from which children come rather than in the factor of mental retardation itself. Similarly, studies suggest that when they are rejected or isolated by children in regular classes, the rejection comes not from their intellectual limitations so much as from their minority or low socioeconomic status or their compensatory behavior. Although research on social position is limited, most writers support the contention that the mentally retarded child tends to be isolated and rejected by his normal classmates in the regular class (Johnson, 1963; Jordan, 1966).

Language and Speech. Since the early work of Binet and Simon in the measurement of intelligence, the interrelationships among intelligence, language, and thought have been well documented. The size and complexity of vocabulary represent the best single indicator of intelligence as generally defined and measured. The level at which language functions, according to Terman and Merrill (1937), is one of the most important determinants of the level of the higher thought processes. Because of its intimate relationship to intelligence and the number of important communicative factors or behaviors which can be subsumed under the term "language" (e.g., reading, writing, thinking, speaking, and auding), it is not surprising that the mentally retarded show a variety of communicative deficits and retardation.

The delay in using or understanding speech is related generally to the degree of retardation. The dependent or custodial child may never be able to express himself orally in even simple sentences. The trainable retardate is likely to develop simple oral-communication skills but to be unable to read or write beyond a few simple words or phrases. The educable child, although probably slow in learning to talk and limited in vocabulary, typically develops satisfactory oral-communication and simple reading and writing skills.

In a survey of London children, Burt (1955) reported "severe defects" of speech in almost 11 percent of normal children and estimated that nearly one-fourth of the mentally retarded showed some defect of speech. Wallin (1949) found that 26 percent of mentally retarded children in special schools in St. Louis had defective speech, compared with 2.8 percent of children in regular elementary-school and high school classes. The percentage with speech defects in a group of 2,522 institutionalized persons was 31 for those with IQ's over 69, 47 for the moron group, and 74 for the imbecile group (Sirkin & Lyons, 1941). A survey by Mathews (1957) of the literature on incidence of speech defects for the retarded as a group showed a range of from 5 to 79 percent. The variance was probably due to rather widespread differences both in the criteria of what constitutes a speech defect and in the composition of the groups. Articulation problems account for the majority of speech defects among the retarded.

The language abilities of slightly more than 200 retarded children in Boston schools were studied by Speidel (1959). For the primary-grade children, listening comprehension was found to be 14 months higher than their mental age and 16 months higher than their reading age. In the intermediate grades, listening comprehension was 8 months higher than mental age and 23 months higher than reading age. The older children did not show as much advance in achievement as expected. Goda and Griffith (1962) reported that the expressive language of a group of high-grade adolescent retardates was comparable to that of normal children of seven years of age. They concluded, however, that there was no serious language retardation in the light of the limited changes in expressive language observed in normal children beyond age seven.

Milgram and Furth (1963) compared the performance of educable retarded children with normal matched mental age controls on a concept-attainment task. The retarded were superior on tasks in which language experience was not considered to be relevant but inferior on a concept task involving language; no difference was found between the performance of organic and familial retardates. A small number of studies have shown linguistic retardation (i.e., language age below mental age) among samples of retarded children (McCarthy, 1964).

The literature on speech and language of the retarded has increased rapidly, doubtlessly reflecting not only increased interest in the retarded but also a more positive attitude toward the efficacy of therapy. The development of a number of assessment techniques, such as the *Parsons Language Sample* and the ITPA, in turn have stimulated further research studies of both a survey and intervention nature. The literature—still primarily concerned with speech rather than with linguistic problems broadly—suggests that retarded children develop language skills in the same sequence as normal children do but at a lower rate of speed. Although there is a high incidence of speech and language defects among the retarded and the incidence is related to the severity of the retardation, mental retardation is not necessarily the cause of language and speech deficiency. Common etiological factors may be behind both conditions, and, further, the linguistic problem may be responsible at least in part for the retarded mental development.

EDUCATIONAL PROGRAMS. Residential institutions provided the first facilities for the care and education of the mentally retarded and in a number of countries continue to play the major role (Kanner, 1964; UNESCO, 1960; Wallin, 1955). In the United States and some other English-speaking countries particularly, special classes within the public schools enroll the majority of the mentally retarded receiving special education. The latest comprehensive figures for the United States are based on a biennial survey conducted by the U.S. Office of Education in February 1958 (Mackie & Robbins, 1961; Mackie & others, 1963).

By 1958 approximately 26 percent of the estimated mentally retarded children (IQ below 68) of school age were receiving special education, and of this group about 90 percent were enrolled in public day-school special classes. The other 10 percent were enrolled in about 200 public and private residential schools. The number of trainable children (IQ 25–50) in special-education programs was about equally divided between residential and public day-school classes. Between 1948 and 1958, the enrollment of mentally retarded children in public school special classes increased 157 percent, compared with a 40-percent increase in overall enrollment and a 31-percent increase in residential school enrollment. For public school enrollments only, the placement in 1958 for the educable and the trainable, respectively, was as follows: elementary-school building, 66 and 64 percent; secondary-school building, 25 and 2 percent; special school, 7 and 27 percent; other community building, 1 and 6 percent; and other types of programs, 1 and 1 percent.

Although professional opinion differs concerning the optimum administrative placement of the educable mentally retarded, the special class is generally well accepted. The question of the superiority, however, of the regular versus the special class cannot be answered empirically at this time. Limiting to a considerable extent the growth of the special classes have been lack of testing facilities, limited classroom space, and an inadequate supply of trained teachers. Through provisions and amendments of Public Law 85–926, the federal government has been stimulating teacher training programs. More than $24-million was allotted for the fiscal year 1967 for the training of teachers and paraprofessionals to work with handicapped pupils, with more than one-third of the total amount obligated to the training of workers with the mentally retarded (*American Education*, 1967).

The issue of public school versus institutional placement of the trainable (Goldberg & Cruickshank, 1958) has become less controversial as the public school continues to assume increased responsibility. Between 1953 and 1958 the enrollment of the trainable in special public school classes increased by 200 percent (Mackie & Robbins, 1961), and by 1961 state support for the trainable in the public schools had been provided by about three-fourths of the states.

A large number of curriculum guides, courses of study, and textbooks are available for the educable. They show a surprising commonality in terms of goals, organization, curriculum, and materials. In the larger schools the educable are typically grouped into these levels: the primary class (ages 6–9 or 6–10); intermediate (9–12); junior high (12–15); senior high (15–18). At the junior and senior high school levels, the retarded children may be assigned to a special class for part of the day, but most will usually go to one or more classes with other students. A number of systems have provided postschool programs, usually at night and stressing personal and vocational counseling as well as skills needed on the job. The broad objective of school programs is to develop independent living skills, and stress is placed upon the tool subject-matter skills, personal and social adequacy, and occupational competence.

The major objectives of the school program for the trainable are independence in self-care, social adjustment in the home and neighborhood, and economic usefulness at home or in a sheltered workshop. Since the trainable is expected to be dependent or semidependent all his life, the program objectives stress the development of minimal skills needed in a restricted and supervised environment. Major emphasis is given to oral communication, motor and sensory training, such self-care skills as dressing and grooming, such occupational skills as housework or yardwork and the use of tools, local travel, socialization, and health and safety.

Achievement. Mental age (MA) is used in estimating capacity and appraising achievement. For the retarded in school programs (IQ 25–75), the corresponding MA's at age 6 would range from 1-6 to 4-6; and by school-leaving age of 16 to 18, from 4 to 12, suggesting an expected achievement level of from below kindergarten to seventh grade. A child with an IQ of 50 would be 13 years old before reaching an MA of 6-6, a level frequently taken as a minimum for appreciable success at the beginning reading level.

Trainable Children. Short-term studies reveal that trainable children in special public school classes make some progress but that achievement appears to be related primarily to maturation and to IQ. For this reason, several investigators have recommended that the lower limit of eligibility for classes should be raised to around IQ 35. Slight gains have been noted for the trainable child in social and mental development, and secondary gains have been noted for the parents, who are provided some relief from constant care and supervision and who develop more objective and realistic goals for the child. By contrast, Cain and Levine (1963) did not find that the special class had the expected salutary effect on either parents or pupils. The relatively negative results from research on classroom training programs led Kirk (1964) to suggest that new program approaches may be necessary.

Adolescents and adults are likely to have developed functional oral-communication skills; to recognize common words, phrases, and signs; and to have some limited quantitative concepts. They do not typically learn to read even first- or second-grade materials or to use arithmetic beyond rote counting. A few are able to hold a simple job, and many receive some remuneration through a sheltered workshop or odd jobs in the community. The relatively high rate of institutionalization—up to 40 or 50 percent—at some time after leaving the class is not so much an indictment of the trainable as it is of the community, which fails to provide facilities for counseling and for supervised employment and recreation. The trainable seldom marry or become independent socially or economically and in the community usually continue to live with and to be supervised by relatives or friends.

Educable Children. By the end of his formal school program, the educable retarded child, depending upon his mental ability, may reach an academic level ranging from the second to the sixth or seventh grade. He is frequently reported to be an underachiever in terms of his capacity, perhaps because of motivational problems related to early failure and to the lag in experiencing an appropriate learning situation. His reading and arithmetic reasoning ages are likely to be somewhat below his MA, but his achievement in arithmetic computation tends to be appropriate to expected capacity. The few studies attempting to evaluate achievement in other subjects suggest that the level of performance, while frequently higher than in reading and arithmetic, is related to mental development.

Employability is probably much greater (Charles, 1953; Bobroff, 1956; Goldstein, 1964) than might be expected on the basis of reports from earlier studies and the decreasing proportion of the total labor force in those jobs traditionally held by the retarded. Older studies doubtlessly reflected not only inadequate training, placement, and counseling programs but unfavorable employer attitudes as well. Only a small percent of educable adults are unemployable, and, depending upon economic conditions, up to 85 percent or more are employed at any given time. Jobs held by the educable retarded are numerous and diverse, but most would be classified as semiskilled, service, or unskilled occupations (Strickland & Arrell, 1967). The large majority of the educable retarded make a satisfactory adjustment and become self-supporting citizens; in depressed economic conditions, however, they are more likely to become unemployed than are workers in general. For this group, employability appears to be related more to personal characteristics, interpersonal relations, and work habits than to degree of intelligence. The frequent job turnover reported for the educable retarded in their early work experience appears to be characteristic of persons in the labor force below the skilled category and has no particular relationship to mental ability.

The occupational outlook for the educable retarded is not clear. At the present time, however, the decrease in the number of available jobs traditionally associated with the retarded tends to be partially offset by the development of vocational rehabilitation training programs and by the policy of the federal government and certain industries to seek and train the retarded for selected occupations.

Jacob T. Hunt
University of Washington

References

Adler, Sol. *The Non-verbal Child*. Thomas, 1964. 163p.

American Education. "Education of the Handicapped." 3:30–1; 1967.

Beier, Delton C. "Behavioral Disturbances in the Mentally Retarded." In Stevens, Harvey A., and Heber, Rick. (Eds.) *Mental Retardation: A Review of the Research*. U Chicago Press, 1964. p. 453–87.

Benda, Clemens E. "Psychopathology of Childhood." In Carmichael, Leonard. (Ed.) *Manual of Child Psychology*, 2nd ed. Wiley, 1954. p. 1115–61.

Benda, Clemens E. "Mongolism." In Carter, Charles H. (Ed.) *Medical Aspects of Mental Retardation*. Thomas, 1965. p. 519–90.

Benda, Clemens E., and others. "Personality Factors in Mild Mental Retardation. I: Family Background and Sociocultural Patterns." *Am J Mental Deficiency* 68:24–40; 1963.

Benton, Arthur L. "Psychological Evaluation and Differential Diagnosis." In Stevens, Harvey A., and Heber, Rick. (Eds.) *Mental Retardation: A Review of the Research*. U Chicago Press, 1964. p. 16–56.

Best, Harry. *Public Provision for the Mentally Retarded in the United States*. Heffernan, 1965. 455p.

Bobroff, Allen. "Economic Adjustment of 121 Adults, Formerly Students in Classes for Mental Retardates." *Am J Mental Deficiency* 60:525–35; 1956.

Buros, Oscar K. (Ed.) *Tests in Print*. Gryphon, 1961. 479p.

Buros, Oscar K. *Sixth Mental Measurements Yearbook*. Gryphon, 1965. 1714p.

Burt, Cyril. *The Subnormal Mind*. Oxford U Press, 1955. 391p.

Cain, Leo F., and Levine, Samuel. *Effects of Community and Institutional School Programs on Trainable Mentally Retarded Children*. Research Monograph No. B-1. Council for Exceptional Children, 1963. 56p.

Cassel, Russell N. "Expected Educational, Occupational, and Personal Development for Five Discernible Groups of 'Educable but Mentally Handicapped' Students." *Am J Mental Deficiency* 65:801–4; 1961.

Charles, Don C. "Ability and Accomplishment of Persons Earlier Judged to be Mentally Defective." *Genet Psychol Monogr* 47:3–71; 1953.

Culley, William J., and others. "Heights and Weights of Mentally Retarded Children." *Am J Mental Deficiency* 68:203–10; 1963.

Dingman, Harvey F., and Tarjan, George. "Mental Retardation and the Normal Distribution Curve." *Am J Mental Deficiency* 64:991–4; 1960.

Doll, Edgar A. "The Essentials of an Inclusive Concept of Mental Deficiency." *Am J Mental Deficiency* 46:214–9; 1941.

Doll, Edgar A. *Vineland Social Maturity Scale: Condensed Manual of Directions*. American Guidance Service, 1965. 28p.

Eyman, Richard K. "Covariation of Level of Aspiration and Adaptation Level with Other Characteristics." *Am J Mental Deficiency* 68:741–50; 1964.

Francis, Robert J., and Rarick, G. Lawrence. "Motor Characteristics of the Mentally Retarded." *Am J Mental Deficiency* 63:792–811; 1959.

Fromm, Ericka. "Projective Aspects of Intelligence Testing." In Rabin, Albert I., and Haworth, Mary R. (Eds.) *Projective Techniques with Children*. Grune, 1960. p. 225–36.

Gelof, Malvin. "Comparison of Systems of Classification Relating Degree of Retardation to Measured Intelligence." *Am J Mental Deficiency* 68:297–317; 1963.

Ginzberg, Eli. "The Mentally Handicapped in a Technological Society." In Osler, Sonia F., and Osler, Robert E. (Eds.) *The Biosocial Basis of Mental Retardation*. Johns Hopkins Press, 1965. p. 1–15.

Ginzberg, Eli, and Bray, Douglas W. *The Uneducated*. Columbia U Press, 1953. 246p.

Goda, Sidney, and Griffith, Belver C. "Spoken Language of Adolescent Retardates and Its Relation to Intelligence, Age, and Anxiety." *Child Develop* 33:489–98; 1962.

Goldberg, I. Ignacy, and Cruickshank, William. "The Trainable but Noneducable: Whose Responsibility?" *NEA J* 47:622–3; 1958.

Goldstein, Herbert. "Social and Occupational Adjustment." In Stevens, Harvey A., and Heber, Rick. (Eds.) *Mental Retardation: A Review of the Research.* U Chicago Press, 1964. p. 214–58.

Goodman, N., and Tizard, J. "Prevalence of Imbecility and Idiocy Among Children." *Br Med J* 1:216–9; 1962.

Gruenberg, Ernest M. "Epidemiology." In Stevens, Harvey A., and Heber, Rick. (Eds.) *Mental Retardation: A Review of the Research.* U Chicago Press, 1964. p. 259–306.

Gunzberg, H. C. "Symposium in Problems of Social Education. I: Introduction: Identifying Weak Social Skills." *J Mental Subnormality* 9:3–7; 1963.

Gunzberg, H. C. "The Reliability of a Test of Psycholinguistic Abilities (ITPA) in a Population of Young Male Subnormals." *J Mental Subnormality* 10:101–12; 1964.

Gunzberg, H. C. "Psychological Assessment in Mental Deficiency." In Clarke, Ann M., and Clarke, A. D. B. (Eds.) *Mental Deficiency*, rev. ed. Free, 1965. p. 283–327.

Heath, S. Roy, Jr. "The Relation of Rail-walking and Other Motor Performances of Mental Defectives to Mental Age and Etiologic Type." *Train Sch B* 50:119–27; 1953.

Heber, Rick. *A Manual on Terminology and Classification in Mental Retardation.* Monograph Supplement to *Am J Mental Deficiency*, 2nd ed., 66; 1961. 109p.

Heber, Rick. "Personality." In Stevens, Harvey A., and Heber, Rick. (Eds.) *Mental Retardation: A Review of the Research.* U Chicago Press, 1964. p. 143–74.

Johnson, G. Orville. "Psychological Characteristics of the Mentally Retarded." In Cruickshank, William M., and Johnson, G. Orville. (Eds.) *Psychology of Exceptional Children and Youth.* Prentice-Hall, 1963. p. 448–83.

Jordan, Thomas E. *The Mentally Retarded*, 2nd ed. Merrill, 1966. 451p.

Kanner, Leo. *A History of the Care and Study of the Mentally Retarded.* Thomas, 1964. 150p.

Kidd, John W. "Toward a More Precise Definition of Mental Retardation." *Mental Retardation* 2:209–12; 1964.

Kirk, Samuel A. *Education Exceptional Children.* Houghton, 1962. 415p.

Kirk, Samuel A. "Research in Education." In Stevens, Harvey A., and Heber, Rick. (Eds.) *Mental Retardation: A Review of the Research.* U Chicago Press, 1964. p. 57–99.

Kodman, Frank, Jr. "The Incidence of Hearing Loss in Mentally Retarded Children." *Am J Mental Deficiency* 62:675–8; 1958.

Kugel, Robert B., and Mohr, John. "Mental Retardation and Physical Growth." *Am J Mental Deficiency* 68:41–8; 1963.

Lemkau, Paul, and others. "Mental-hygiene Problems in an Urban District." *Mental Hygiene* 26:275–88; 1942.

Levinson, Abraham, and Bigler, John A. *Mental Retardation in Infants and Children.* Yearbook, 1960. 308p.

Lewis, E. O. "Report on an Investigation into the Incidence of Mental Deficiency in Six Areas, 1925–1927." In *Report of the Mental Deficiency Committee*, Part IV. H.M. Stationery Office, 1929. 239p.

Lloyd, Lyle L., and Frisina, D. Robert. (Eds.) *The Audiologic Assessment of the Mentally Retarded: Proceedings of a National Conference.* Parsons State Hospital and Training Center, 1965. 314p.

Mackie, Romaine P., and Robbins, Patricia P. *Exceptional Children and Youth: A Chart Book of Special Education Enrollments in Public Day Schools of the United States.* USOE, 1961. 14p.

Mackie, Romaine P., and others. "Statistics of Special Education for Exceptional Children and Youth, 1957–58 Final Report." In *Biennial Survey of Education in the United States, 1956–58.* GPO, 1963. 120p.

Malpass, Leslie F. "Motor Proficiency in Institutionalized and Non-institutionalized Retarded Children and Normal Children." *Am J Mental Deficiency* 64:1012–5; 1960.

Mathews, Jack. "Speech Problems of the Mentally Retarded." In Travis, Lee E. (Ed.) *Handbook of Speech Pathology.* Appleton, 1957. p. 531–51.

McAfee, Ronald O., and Cleland, Charles C. "The Discrepancy Between Self-concept and Ideal-self as a Measure of Psychological Adjustment in Educable Mentally Retarded Males." *Am J Mental Deficiency* 70:63–8; 1965.

McCarthy, James J. "Research on the Linguistic Problems of the Mentally Retarded." *Mental Retardation Abstracts* 1:3–27; 1964.

Milgram, Norman A., and Furth, Hans G. "The Influence of Language on Concept Attainment in Educable Retarded Children." *Am J Mental Deficiency* 67:733–9; 1963.

Mosier, H. David, Jr., and others. "Physical Growth in Mental Defectives." *Pediatrics* 36:465–519; 1965.

Newland, T. Ernest. "Psychological Assessment of Exceptional Children and Youth." In Cruickshank, William M. (Ed.) *Psychology of Exceptional Children and Youth*, 2nd ed. Prentice-Hall, 1963. p. 53–117.

New York State Department of Mental Hygiene. *A Special Census of Suspected Referred Mental Retardation, Onondaga County, N.Y.* The Department, 1955. 84p.

Penrose, Lionel S. *The Biology of Mental Defect*, 3rd ed. Sidgwick & Jackson, Ltd., 1963. 374p.

Perron, Roger, and Pecheux, Marie-Germaine. "Do the Mentally Retarded Recognize Their Handicaps? Experimental Data on the Auto-estimation of Personal Equipment." In Øster, Jakob. (Ed.) *International Copenhagen Congress on the Scientific Study of Mental Retardation*, Vol. 2. Det Berlingske Bogrtykkeri, 1964. p. 620–2.

Pintner, Rudolf. "The Feebleminded Child." In

Murchison, Carl. (Ed.) *A Handbook of Child Psychology*, 2nd ed. Clark U Press, 1933. p. 802–41.

President's Panel on Mental Retardation. *A Proposed Program for National Action to Combat Mental Retardation.* GPO, 1962. 201p.

Rappaport, Sheldon R. (Ed.) *Childhood Aphasia and Brain Damage.* Vol. 2. *Differential Diagnosis.* Livingston Publishing Co., 1965. 164p.

Sarason, Seymour B. *Psychological Problems in Mental Deficiency.* Harper, 1959. 678p.

Sirkin, Jacob, and Lyons, William F. "A Study of Speech Defects in Mental Deficiency." *Am J Mental Deficiency* 46:74–80; 1941.

Speidel, Elizabeth B. "Language Achievements of Mentally Retarded Children." *Dissertation Abstracts* 19:3180–1; 1959.

Stricklan, Conwell G., and Arrell, Vernon M. "Employment of the Mentally Retarded." *Excep Children* 34:21–4; 1967.

Terman, Lewis M., and Merrill, Maud A. *Measuring Intelligence.* Houghton, 1937. 461p.

Terman, Lewis M., and Merrill, Maud A. *Stanford-Binet Intelligence Scale: Manual for the Third Revision, Form L-M.* Houghton, 1960. 363p.

Tredgold, Alfred R. *A Textbook of Mental Deficiency*, 6th ed. Williams and Wilkins, 1937. 556p.

UNESCO. *Statistics on Special Education.* UNESCO, 1960. 154p.

Wallin, J. E. Wallace. *Children with Mental and Physical Handicaps.* Prentice-Hall, 1949. 549p.

Wallin, J. E. Wallace. *Education of Mentally Handicapped Children.* Harper, 1955. 485p.

Webb, Clarence, and others. "Incidence of Hearing Loss in Institutionalized Mental Retardates." *Am J Mental Deficiency* 70:563–8; 1966.

Wechsler, David. *The Wechsler Intelligence Scale for Children.* Psych Corp, 1949. 114p.

Wechsler, David. *The Wechsler Preschool and Primary Scale of Intelligence.* Psych Corp, 1967. 129p.

World Health Organization. *The Mentally Subnormal Child.* WHO, 1954. 46p.

MILITARY EDUCATION

Much of the research concerned with military training and education appears in the literature available to civilian scholars and is reported in other sections of this encyclopedia. Therefore, in the main, this article concentrates on the more unique aspects of military training and education and does not repeat research findings reported elsewhere.

It will deal more with the training and education of officers than with enlisted personnel and, within that limitation, more with the professional military education of officers than with their specialized education or technical training. Throughout this section reference will be made to the work of various military boards and committees and to their conclusions and recommendations. These conclusions and recommendations are not necessarily reflected in current organization and practice. They are always received and considered. They are not necessarily always approved and implemented.

Beginnings to 1810 in Europe. A review of the historical influence of military education on the European secondary school curriculum (Hans, 1958) concludes that, because of the dual effects of added administrative duties and developments in weapon technology, the preparatory education of the warrior became more general and liberal and required, at the same time, the beginnings of a scientific background. As a result the European military schools were the first to introduce science, drawing, and life situations; they were the first to free the school from religious dogma; and they were among the first to use national languages rather than medieval Latin. They were, however, reactionary in that, unlike the clerical schools, which were international, they adopted national attitudes and promoted xenophobia. Vagts (1937, pp. 11, 53) describes the education of the feudal warrior. He distinguishes between *militarism and the military way*: "The military way is marked by a primary concentration of men and materials on winning specific objectives of power with utmost efficiency, that is, with the least expenditure of blood and treasure. It is limited in scope, confined to one function, and scientific in its essential qualities. Militarism, on the other hand, presents a vast array of customs, interests, prestige, actions and thought associated with armies and wars and yet transcending true military purposes. Indeed, militarism is so constituted that it may hamper and defeat the purposes of the military way."

The evolution of the military staff is traced from 2000 B.C. to modern times, and Gustavus Adolphus, a Swedish general who died in 1632, is credited (Hittle, 1961) with evolving a system that influenced the development of all European staffs.

The real beginning of professional military education is credited to the establishment, under Frederick the Great, of a school which was the forerunner of the famed Prussian War Academy. The academy, opened by Scharnhorst in Berlin on October 15, 1810 (Hittle, 1961), began to function on the same day as the University of Berlin. Karl von Clausewitz served as its director from 1818 to 1830 (Wilkinson, 1889; Hackett, 1963). The war academy educated general staff officers and future military commanders.

The basis of the German general staff corps was the German officer corps from which it was selected. Because of long tradition, the army in Germany enjoyed greater prestige than in most other countries, and the German officer corps had an exalted position within the army. The general staff was the cream of the officer corps, and the war academy was the school for the selection and training of this elite group. The effectiveness of the German general staff can be inferred by the fact that one of the provisions of the Versailles Treaty at the end of World War I was that it was to be abolished (Military Intelligence Division, 1946; Huntington, 1957).

European Developments to 1900. The influence of the German War Academy was reflected in the establishment of the French Staff School, École d'État Major, in 1818 and the École Militaire Supérieure in 1878 (Vagts, 1959; Huntington, 1957; Hackett, 1963; *Military Review*, 1956).

Historically, in Europe military officers formed an elite that was a social as well as a professional group. It tended to view itself as the preserver of the tradition of chivalry and exalted the virtues of personal honor, bravery, and good character (Barnett, 1967). But since the industrial revolution of the nineteenth century the waging of war has become increasingly complex, calling for a variety of technical and managerial skills. The history of a military education has been a contest between the conception of the man of arms as a fighter and ever-increasing demands for technical skills and military-management ability.

As was true in France, and later in England and in the United States, in Russia professional military education was directly influenced by the German pattern. Clausewitz, like many other German staff officers, was serving as a Russian staff officer when Napoleon invaded Russia in 1812 (Curtiss, 1965; Counts, 1957). Though an army college had been established in England in 1799, the development of an army general staff and of a program to prepare officers to serve on it occurred somewhat later in England than on the Continent (Wilkinson, 1889, 1916; Godwin-Austen, 1927; Hackett, 1963; Luvaas, 1964).

In most instances cadet schools in Europe predated the establishment of staff schools (U.S. Military Academy, 1943). As is frequently true of other social institutions, military schools in many instances reflected the influence of eminent persons who were either practitioners, theoreticians, or teachers. Prior to 1914, some of these men were Machiavelli, Vauban, Frederick the Great, Jomini, Clausewitz, Adam Smith, Engels, Marx, Moltke, and DuPicq (Earle, 1944).

Developments in America through World War II. Shaughnessy's study of the United States Military Academy concludes that perhaps the greatest single factor contributing to the establishment of national military education in America was the vision and active support of such men as Washington, Adams, Hamilton, Jefferson, and Madison. Congress, influenced by a highly vocal antimilitary bloc, took little interest in military education, and neither the press, the education profession, nor the general public knew or cared much about the academy. Connections with contemporary English and French systems of military education could be found; however, foreign influences were not of major importance in the development of the American system (Shaughnessy, 1956; Ekirch, 1956). In the United States, professional military education beyond that offered in the Military and Naval academies began to develop in the last half of the nineteenth century, and its development presents an interesting parallel to the rise of graduate education in our civilian universities (Shelburne & Groves, 1965).

Emory Upton, an American officer who studied foreign military developments for two years, reported in 1878 that the Military Academy at West Point was superior to any cadet school he had seen, but here military professional education ended. Except for the artillery school established in 1867, there was no provision in the American army for officers to study the higher duties of their profession. For this reason Upton recommended the establishment of postgraduate professional schools patterned on the German system (Upton, 1878). In a later report he recommended examinations as a condition for promotion, as well as the establishment of a general staff. All of Upton's recommendations were eventually accepted and implemented (Upton, 1917, Preface; Ambrose, 1964). Another American army officer, Ludlow, spent the summer of 1900 in Europe studying the war colleges of several countries. Ludlow also favored the German system. His report indicated that the military training and educational systems of England and the United States were the least progressive of all major countries he had studied (Ludlow Report, 1901).

The U.S. Naval Academy was not opened until 1845 (Crane & Kieley, 1945), though such an institution had been recommended as early as 1800 (American Guide Series, 1941). Military instruction in civilian colleges began as early as 1819, at Norwich University, later at the Virginia Military Institute and the Citadel, and in 1862 in land-grant colleges as a result of the Morrill Act (Reeves, 1914; Department of the Army, ROTC, 1959). In 1873 the Naval Institution was founded to advance professional and scientific knowledge (Masland & Radway, 1957). The training of American seamen, patterned after the English naval-apprentice method, was begun in 1875. The Naval War College, which was proposed by Luce, who in turn was influenced by Upton and by men in the Army Artillery School and the Army Cavalry School, was established in 1884 (Gleaves, 1925; Eure, 1959b; Luce, 1883). Largely through the influence of Sherman and Upton, the Infantry and Cavalry Schools, the forerunner of the Army Command and General Staff College, was established at Fort Leavenworth, Kansas, in 1881.

The capstone of the Army system of education, the Army War College, was established by Elihu Root, Secretary of War, in 1902 (Jessup, 1938). In his annual reports for 1889 and 1901, the secretary commented on the fact that since 1898, because of the Spanish-American War, practically all systematic education of officers had stopped and that almost two-thirds of the officers had been commissioned from the ranks or from civil life and therefore had not had the military education afforded by the Military Academy. Advances in military science, changes in tactics, and experiences gained in the recent war all pointed to the great importance of broad and thorough education for military officers. Therefore, Secretary Root directed that there were to be, besides the Military Academy at West Point, the following schools: at each military post an officer's school for elementary instruction in theory and practice; special service schools; the Artillery School, the Engineer School, the School of Submarine Defense, the School for Cavalry and Field Artillery, and the Army Medical School; the General Service and Staff College; and the War College for the most advanced instruction at Washington Barracks, in the District of Columbia. Root indicated that the advantages of the system of schools that was to be established would be (1) the bringing together of all the different branches of military education into one system under the direct supervision of officers whose special business it would be to make the system effective; (2) the establishment of a required curriculum in the officers' schools at military posts that would be the foundation of the whole system; (3) the establishment of the general service and staff school at Fort Leavenworth, so that officers with superior qualities would be instructed in every branch of military service; (4) the completion of the course of instruction by the War College, which would become a postgraduate course for the larger problems of military science and national defense (Turner, 1952).

The military school system established by Root in 1902 was, with one major exception, substantially the system in existence up to 1941, when America entered World War II. The exception was provided by the addition of the Army Air Corps Tactical School, established at Langley Field, Virginia, in 1920 (Finney, 1955).

As a part of a larger study of national mobilization, a plan was outlined in 1942 for training both enlisted men and officers (Harlow, 1942). By June 1943 approximately 475 American colleges and universities had been approved to receive training contracts for the army and the navy. The impact of these military wartime programs in civilian institutions is discussed under the headings off-duty education, general education offerings through the United States Armed Forces Institute, and acceptance of military experience toward college credit (Russell, 1943). In 1945 an agency was established by the American Council on Education to assist members of the armed forces to advance themselves educationally and vocationally through an evaluation of their service training and education (American Council on Education, 1962). British wartime experience in adult education for the armed forces was reported in the work of the Central Advisory Council for Adult Education in His Majesty's Forces (Wilson, 1950).

Developments Abroad Through World War II. In England Wilkinson's influence, to a degree, paralleled that of Root in the United States. Wilkinson wrote *The Brain of an Army* in 1890 to bring to the attention of British authorities the advantages of the German general staff system and of the Prussian war academy. A copy of this book reached Root through Ludlow. In 1919 Root wrote Wilkinson that his book had played a "great part" in preparing not only England but also the United States for World War I (Wilkinson, 1933). The formal beginnings of British Army education (A. White, 1963) date from the return from exile of Charles II in 1660. White traces the varied efforts to provide schoolmasters and other instructors for the children of army personnel and to provide other instructors in army schools from that date to the founding of the Corps of Army Schoolmasters (which was in existence from 1846 to 1920) and finally the Royal Army Education Corps in June 1920. He describes the use of these "educators in uniform" through World War II and the postwar period.

England was the first major power to establish an autonomous air force, and this was done in April 1918. The Royal Air Force Staff College was established in 1922, two years after the opening of the U.S. Army Air Corps Tactical School. By the beginning of World War II England had a well-developed system of professional military education, capped by the Imperial Defense College, established in 1927. During two world wars the United States and British air forces fought side by side. In the interim the two services exchanged students and data on school organization and course content (Shelburne, 1953).

In Germany, as a result of the Treaty of Versailles, military forces were sharply restricted, and Germany was not to have air forces, a general staff, or military staff training. There is ample evidence that Germany contravened these restrictions when it became apparent that the former Allied nations were not prepared to resort to force to stop Germany's efforts to rearm. Long before Hitler came to power in 1933 there was an illegal German general staff, and this staff created the nucleus of a forbidden air force. Flying training was made possible by what were ostensibly amateur sports clubs, by subsidized civil airlines, and by secret arrangements with foreign countries. Professional staff education was promoted by a functionally decentralized system until 1935, after which time the classic plan of German staff schools was reconstituted. Under the German plan education for staff duty was synonymous with preparations for command responsibility. Unlike in the United States and in Russia, in Germany it was the practice to select officers for staff and command potential early in their career. In Germany, attendance at a three-year staff school, interspersed with short tours of duty with troops of the various arms, constituted formal preparation for higher professional responsibility. From available evidence, the selection criteria used for officers in Germany were much more rigid and were more frequently applied than in other countries (Shelburne, 1953).

Beginning after the chaos of the Revolution of 1917 and with an almost wholly illiterate population, Russia succeeded by late 1939 in creating a military establishment that would soon be able to withstand the repeated attacks of Europe's most powerful military forces. Apart from great efforts in public education, technological development, and political indoctrination, the Soviet regime achieved success in creating a corps of professionally educated officers largely because the czarist command and staff officers were held over as instructors in the staff schools (Erickson, 1962), and officers of the German Reichswehr made tutorial contributions under agreements growing out of the Treaty of Rapallo (Shelburne, 1953; Berchin & Ben-Horin, 1942).

Italy was one of the first countries to have an autonomous air force. As was true in Russia and in Germany prior to World War II, in Italy, also, potential pilots learned to fly in government-sponsored clubs. The Royal Aeronautical Academy of Caserta, founded in 1923, trained officer pilots for the Italian air force. There was an air force staff school in Florence and, in addition to army and navy staff schools, there was in Rome a one-year advanced military school attended by officers from all services, as well as by civilians from the Italian diplomatic corps (Shelburne, 1953).

Japan has an old warrior tradition nurtured under the feudal system, which lasted until 1817. The Japanese officer corps has inherited the ethical code of the samurai, which is known as the Bushido, or the "Way of the Warrior." The samurai were a special military class which exercised a hereditary, and up until 1873, an exclusive military function (Lory, 1943). Until World War II Japan had never known defeat in a major war. Her forces had been victorious against China in 1895 and against Russia in 1905. Japan shared the Allied victory of 1918. By the beginning of World War II Japan had a well-developed system of service staff schools. There is no information available on a higher staff school in Japan or a war college for all services (Shelburne, 1953).

In China the founding of the Whampoa military academy in 1924 was reported as the first time in modern Chinese military history that a professional school was created for a revolutionary purpose. The influence of this institution and of foreign military and political advisors in the Chinese army is discussed in some detail by Liu (1956).

Comparable to the army cadet school at St. Cyr, the École de l'Air was established in Versailles in 1933. The École État Major (Staff School) served both the French army and the French air force. The highest military school in France prior to World War II was the National Defense College, the École Militaire Supérieur (Shelburne, 1953).

As World War II drew to a close there were many studies, reports, and investigations attempting to capitalize on lessons learned in wartime military training and education. These can be classified under two broad headings: implications for civilian schools and colleges and implications primarily for military or service training and education.

Implications of World War II for Civilian Education. Probably the most comprehensive series of studies that apply to civilian education were those sponsored by the American Council on Education with the assistance of the secretary of war and the secretary of the navy. In the series monographs were published covering such areas as selection and classification procedures, college programs, audiovisual aids, language and area studies, adult education, curriculum, and the training of women. Each of the studies contained conclusions and recommendations (Norton, 1960). The general conclusions of the studies were as follows: (1) The training programs were, in general, job training and orientation, all colored by specificity. Lessons in methodology were found, but few lessons for the future in intellectual freedom or contributing to a liberal education were noted. Of necessity these programs represented training for a specific operation, since modern war requires literally thousands of specialists. (2) Civilian educational agencies do not have the generous financial support from national sources that the armed services had in war. (3) Generally, unlimited wartime authority was exercised by the armed forces with a high degree of consideration for the human factor. (4) The services had to operate on a trial-and-error basis. If a program failed to produce, changes were ordered. The services were not hampered by tradition. (5) The distinctive methods used by the armed forces were not entirely new to civilian educators. The armed forces had utilized the services of many educators both in uniform and as civilian consultants. (6) The wartime experiences besides providing lessons for peacetime civilian education also should advance military training methods and contribute to the permanent task of national security (Grace & others, 1948). There were at least three major studies reporting on advances made in the various fields of psychology during World War II (Social Science Research Council, 1950; Bray, 1948; Flanagan, 1948).

Implications of World War II for Military Education. The prewar system of professional military training and education had made a major contribution to the success of American forces during the war. Efficient methods of training and education were needed to develop a trained cadre of about 452,000 men in uniform in 1940 that rapidly expanded to almost 13 million five years later (Dupuy & Dupuy, 1956).

Toward the end of the war military planners, as well as civilian agencies, began to evaluate lessons learned during World War II and their implications for future military education. They reexamined the military-schools system with which the services entered the war. Many people both in and out of uniform had become associated in various ways with the military and gave serious consideration to the responsibilities of officers and their professional education (Masland & Radway, 1957). The great technical and scientific advances in weapon systems culminating in the use of atomic weapons had their implications for training and education. A prominent scientist who served as the director of the Office of Scientific Research and Development during the war urged that men in uniform receive better and more fundamental scientific training (Bush, 1946). One of the most serious concerns, shared in varying degrees by both civilian and military educators, was the need for an improvement in the complex interrelationships between the military services, the civilian economy, science, and various agencies of the government.

Beginning as early as 1918, numerous bills which would either merge the War and Navy departments or create a separate air force had been introduced in Congress. Twenty-six departmental reorganizational studies were made before 1945, but none produced comprehensive results (Committee on Armed Services, 1950).

The need for joint education and training was expressed in these various studies, and limited attempts had been made to meet this need. Small numbers of officers from both the army and navy attended schools of the other service, and a few joint exercises were conducted. Only limited opportunity was provided, however, for senior officers and staffs of both services to develop a concept of joint operations. World War II forcefully demonstrated the need for mutual understanding and good will between the various military components. A cooperative attitude would be best developed by closer association and by joint planning, education, and training. Three basic requirements were proposed: (1) There must be an exchange of duties and joint training on levels designed to enable juniors to work together in the execution of joint plans. (2) Joint education must be provided at intermediate levels to develop officers capable of planning and participating in joint operations. (3) Joint education must be provided at high levels to develop officers capable of formulating strategic concepts and conducting large scale operations employing all the components (Joint Chiefs of Staff, Special Committee, 1945).

The requirements for joint action just outlined were considered by a civilian-led committee appointed by the secretary of the navy. Among others, the following recommendations were made for future military education and training: (1) A military education and training board was to be created to review the system of education and training of the several services. (2) Nine joint educational objectives were suggested. (3) Greater use should be made of selection, classification, and aptitude tests in choosing candidates for officer training and education. (4) Joint Reserve Officer Training Corps (ROTC) training should be established at civilian colleges. (5) Each academy would be a joint institution. (6) A system of joint postgraduate education was to be provided after about six years of service. (7) The greatest degree of attention should be given to the selection and training of instructors in all military schools (Eberstadt Report, 1945). A Congressional committee concluded that cross training was the ultimate solution to the problem of cultivating better interservice relations (Committee on Armed Services, 1950). On December 19, 1945, the president sent a special message to the Congress recommending the establishment of a department of national defense. Included in this special message was a recommendation that "we should establish the most advantageous framework for a unified system of training for combined operations of land, sea and air" (Truman, 1961). This message and previously cited studies, among others, were considered by the Congress and led to the adoption of the National Security Act of 1947 (Committee on Armed Services, 1950; McClendon, 1952). In the year before this act was passed, the Joint Chiefs of Staff had created three joint colleges: the National War College, the Industrial College of the Armed Forces, and the Armed Forces Staff College ("General Service Schools," 1963).

ORGANIZATION AND ADMINISTRATION.
Definitions. In studies of education and training programs in the U.S. armed forces, the terms "education" and "training" are frequently used interchangeably, or "training" is used all-inclusively. While there are no absolute distinctions between the two terms, it has been found to be useful to differentiate them. Training programs are those which develop specific skills, are job-oriented, or apply to a particular military specialty; they are likely to deal with large numbers of personnel and with expensive equipment and facilities. Education programs tend to be complex, implying instruction or individual study for the purpose of intellectual development and the cultivation of wisdom and judgment; these programs are usually smaller in volume and do not require extensive facilities beyond classrooms, libraries, and laboratories (Shelburne & Groves, 1965; Masland & Radway 1957).

Training and education programs in the services can be classified in a variety of ways and from many points of view, such as by service, by military or civil service personnel, by off-duty and on-duty programs, and by resident and nonresident programs. They can also be categorized under the following headings: (1) training and education of enlisted personnel, (2) officer training and specialized education, (3) professional military education, (4) unit training, and (5) off-duty education (Shelburne & Groves, 1965).

A civilian advisor to the Royal Canadian Air Force distinguished between skill training and professional military education and their resulting qualifications: An officer's basic trade is the work he is first employed or trained to do in the service. Flying is a trade, and Engineering and even medicine are trades in the military scheme of things even though they are valid professions in themselves. At the outset of his career an officer applies himself to the practice of his trade, without much concern about its relation to the air force as a whole. However, with time and promotion the officer uses his trade in this way less and less; instead he works at problems larger than his trade. He becomes a manager or an executive. To be effective in this role he needs more general knowledge about, among other things, the structure of his armed service and the other services, the nation's political and military aims, and the operation and doctrine of the combat aims of his service generally. The knowledge and skills he needs to manage and direct make up professional ability—schooling for this ability is professional military education (Jackson, 1957).

Scope, Complexity, and Cost. A study of programs in 1963 showed the Department of Defense to be more heavily involved in the educational process than any other department or agency of the government (Green, 1963). In 1966 there were over 4 million military and civilian personnel in the Department of Defense. Almost one out of every ten of these individuals was in a formal training program. The average duration of training was about three weeks, but the range was from one week, for short refresher courses and orientation instruction, to a full year or more, for certain technical subjects and advanced education. There was about one trainer or training-support person for every four people being trained, or a total of about 90,000 training-support personnel as of June 1966 (Morris, 1966). The magnitude of the technical training task in the Department of Defense can be gauged by the fact that each year more than 2,000 different courses are offered and more than 370,000 persons complete courses in one year. In 1963 the Department of Defense was judged to be the country's largest single training institution (Paul, 1964).

The increasing complexity of the military training task can be seen from the fact that, at the end of World War II, 6 out of each 100 enlisted jobs was related to electronics equipment. By the early 1950's this ratio had increased to about 10 per 100. In 1963 it was 14.4 per 100, and the proportion of enlisted jobs in electronics is still growing. Civilian industry turnover rates are typically highest among the unskilled and semiskilled occupations and lowest in the skilled, white collar, and professional groups. The enlisted-personnel turnover experience of the armed services, unfortunately, has been precisely the opposite (Paul, 1964). The skill structure of the military has become not only more complicated but also more readily transferable to civilian society. Military-type occupations for enlisted men accounted for 93.2 percent of the personnel in the Civil War; by 1954 only 28.8 percent of army enlisted personnel were engaged in purely military occupations (Janowitz, 1960). In 1963 the enlisted skill structure, in terms of the percentage distribution of a total of 2,030,000 jobs, excluding some 300,000 trainees, was reported to be as follows: ground combat, 14; electronics, 14; mechanics and repairmen, 25; administrative and clerical, 20; other technical, 8; crafts, 7; and services, 12 (Paul, 1964). There are twice as many mechanics as ground-combat specialists, and the number of electronics-equipment maintenance technicians exceeds the number of infantrymen (Wool, 1959).

Individual enlisted-men's training is essentially of two types: two months of basic combat training and training concerned with occupational skills. In occupational training about 12 percent of the enlisted men are trained in skills directly associated with firing a weapon of some sort, about 5 percent in medical and dental specialties, about 33 percent in supplying and administrative occupations, and the remaining 50 percent in other technical skills (Morris, 1966). To facilitate research analysis and program review, the various occupational-skill designations and nomenclatures that have developed independently in each service have been converted by the Department of Defense into a common occupational grouping and numerical coding system, one for enlisted personnel and one for officers (Office of the Assistant Secretary of Defense, 1966a, 1966b).

The intellectual content of the military profession requires the modern officer to spend about one-third of his professional life in formal schooling, probably a higher ratio of educational time to practice than in any other profession. The practice of his profession, which has been characterized as the management of violence, has become increasingly skilled, complex, and esoteric (Huntington, 1957; Haines Board, 1966). At least five factors have been advanced as influencing the organization and content of the officer's education: (1) changing organizational authority; there has been a shift from authoritarian domination to a greater reliance on manipulation, persuasion, and group consensus; (2) narrowing skill differential between military and civilian administrators; the new tasks of the professional military man require that he develop more and more of the skills common to the civilian administrator; (3) shift in officer recruitment; the base has shifted from a small group of relatively high social status to a broader group, one more representative of the population as a whole; (4) the significance of career patterns; a shift has occurred from technical and routine functions to careers with more decision-making aspects; (5) trends in political indoctrination: The military establishment is a vast managerial enterprise that has taken on increased political responsibilities and that has traditional military self-images and concepts of honor (Janowitz, 1960); within the past generation the more traditional functions of the military officer have greatly expanded in two ways: (a) officers have become increasingly concerned with the purposes for which, and the terms on which, forces are to be used and (b) functions of supply, finance, research and development, public relations, and manpower management have grown more numerous, difficult, and important; both tasks have complicated the task of military education (Masland & Radway, 1957).

The cost of military training and education for the fiscal year 1964 was reported to be approximately $3-billion. This amount was slightly more than 10 percent of the total annual expenditure for elementary, secondary, and higher education in the United States for that period. In 1960–61 the five federal academies produced about 2,000 graduates at an annual operating cost of approximately $91-million and a cost per student ranging from $3,224 to $12,382. The cost of conducting unit exercises and other maneuvers in the army in 1963 was reported to be approximately $100-million (Shelburne & Groves, 1965). More recent estimates of the annual cost of military training are reported to be $4-billion and of officer education approximately $400-million per year. The most time-consuming and costly training is that for pilots, with costs ranging from about $250,000 for a jet pilot, to $110,000 for a propeller-aircraft pilot, to $45,000 for a helicopter pilot. The annual cost of training military pilots is about $1-billion (Morris, 1966). The most recent comprehensive study of the cost of officer education reports total costs for two joint war colleges and three service war colleges to be $23,873,197, with a cost per student of $25,024 and a capital investment of $9,705,775. Comparable costs for one joint staff college and five service staff colleges were $43,156,889 as a total and $14,161,285 as capital investment. The cost per student was $9,567 for the 5-month course and $17,509 for a 10-month program (Office of the Assistant Secretary of Defense, 1966c). The costs of military training and education are difficult to compute and identify. In some instances funds expended and reported for a training activity are not separable from those expended for more general purposes in the organization of which the school is a part. Each service, within certain limitations, is free to determine what factors will be included in computing educational costs (Shelburne & Groves, 1965). The diversity of the programs and the fact that officer and enlisted training often utilize the same facilities compound the problem of cost determination (Office of the Assistant Secretary of Defense, 1966c). The resource management system of the Department of Defense, begun in August 1966, represents an attempt to make accounting and reporting procedures uniform and more meaningful.

Military periodical literature, consisting of 65 English language military and aeronautical periodicals, is replete with reports, studies, and articles treating schools, programs, or aspects of the training and educational system (*Air University Library Index to Military Periodicals*). Apart from the normal day-to-day staff supervision, the services employ a variety of methods in periodically assessing their training and educational programs and in projecting these programs, or segments of them, into the future.

Service Studies: Army. To evaluate its training and education programs, the army, in addition to using the judgment of individuals (Upton, 1878) or a group of outside consultants (Orleans, 1956) often follows the practice of convening a board of senior officers, sometimes assisted by civilian advisers or consultants. The members of the board are provided with meaningful data assembled by staff agencies, visit the training centers, and interview responsible school officials. Their reports and recommendations are advisory only. They require official approval, and they are sometimes amended before they are put into effect. These boards are frequently identified by the name of the chairman. The reports of the boards are not published, but they can generally be found either in the service headquarters or in a military library.

Some of the more important army boards convened to evaluate training were the Gerow Board, in 1946; the Eddy Board, in 1949; the Williams Board, in 1958; the Daly Board, in 1962; and the Haines Board, in 1966. While the reports of all these army boards were important, that of the Gerow Board, coming as it did just after the close of World War II, was of particular significance, since it had to deal with the controversial questions of whether there should be a single department of defense and an autonomous air force. Out of the recommendations of the Gerow Board came the three joint colleges—the National War College, the Industrial College of the Armed Forces, and the Armed Forces Staff College; the pattern for army schools; and the first plan for the education of army air force officers (Gerow Board, 1946). The report of the Haines Board (1966), the latest study of army schools and the most comprehensive one since that of the Gerow Board, reviewed the current system for the training and education of army officers, comparing it with that of the navy, the air force, industry, and foreign armies. The board made extensive recommendations on almost every aspect of the program and identified areas needing further study.

A comparison of the educational programs for U.S. army officers with those of the British, French, German, and Japanese systems concluded, in part, that advanced schooling for officers of the four foreign systems is sequential in nature and increasingly selective; that all four systems require extremely competitive examinations for attendance at the respective staff colleges; and that the total time spent by a successful officer in formal military schooling, not counting precommission and specialist training, was 2 to 3 years under the British system, 4½ years under the French system, and 5 years under the Japanese system (Haines Board, 1966).

The Chinese army and its political control have recently been studied. The army's program for professional military education is described, and 26 schools are listed (Joffe, 1965). The army staff colleges in England, India, France, Belgium, Brazil, Peru, Canada, and Australia are identified and described in an authoritative military journal (*Military Review*, 1956). Majumdar (1961) made contrasts between officer training in France, in the United States, and in India.

There is a natural interest on the part of professional military men in the Soviet army and its training and educational institutions, and, in spite of restrictions, some information is generally available. A U.S. army pamphlet describes Soviet manpower and conscription policies and officer and enlisted men's training (Department of the Army, 1958). Pruck (1964) describes the Soviet cadet schools, the academies, and the higher military schools and discusses some of their historical background. White (1944) describes the military reform that began in 1921 and discusses its influence. He informs us that by 1927 about 2,000 officers had graduated from the war college and other higher schools. D. Fetoff White traces the role of General Frunze in the reorganization and training of the Soviet army. Malinovsky (1966) and Atkinson (1950) describe the unique role of the political officer in the training and education of the Russian military officer.

Service Studies: Navy. The Cook Board of 1959 made one of the latest studies of naval education. On the basis of the study it made extensive recommendations concerning the number of officers who should attend the various courses at the naval Postgraduate School at Monterey, the prerequisites for naval courses in terms of years of service, selection procedures, reorientation of curricula to meet navy requirements, and expansion of the Navy Enlisted Scientific Education Program. It also summarized the work of the following navy training boards: the Knox-King-Pye Board of 1919, the Pye Board of 1944, the Holloway Board of 1945, the Will Board of 1948, and the Weakly-Daniel Board of 1956 (Cook Board, 1959). In addition to the statutory Board of Visitors to the Naval Academy authorized by Section 6968, Title X, U.S. Code, the navy uses a number of less formal boards usually designed to explore specific problems of most immediate interest.

Two of these boards are the Secretary of the Navy Advisory Board on Educational Requirements, whose purpose is to provide the secretary with policy guidance, and the Academic Advisory Committee to the Superintendent of the U.S. Naval Academy, accredited by both the Middle States Association of Colleges and Secondary Schools Evaluation Team and the 1966 Board of Visitors to the U.S. Naval Academy. In addition to the boards, the navy, in 1967, established advisory committees to the president of the Naval War College and to the superintendent of the U.S. Naval Postgraduate School.

Two recent articles compare the system for the education of Soviet naval officers with that of U.S. naval officers (Cockell, 1960; Valentine, 1959).

Service Studies: Air Force. The U.S. Air Force became an autonomous service in 1947. In anticipation of this action and because of recommendations made by the army Gerow Board in 1946, two army air forces educational conferences were held in February and in August of the same year at Maxwell Air Force Base, Alabama. On March 12 the Air University, the postgraduate center for the professional education of air force officers, was established at Maxwell (Shelburne, 1954). Growing out of extensive staff work begun in 1948 at Air University (Air Force Academy Planning Board, 1949) and the work of a board appointed by the secretary of defense (Service Academy Board, 1950), hearings were conducted (*United States Air Force Academy*, 1954), and legislation establishing the U.S. Air Force Academy was approved on April 1, 1954.

Like the army and the navy, the air force has found the judgment of boards of senior officers valuable in studying its programs of education. Some of the more significant boards that have reported on the total officer education program are the Fairchild Board, 1950; the Rawlings Board, 1956; and the Power Board, 1959. To make a continuing study of needs for officer education, the Air Force Educational Requirements Board was established at Air University in December 1958, and it functioned until July 1965, when its work was brought back under the air force personnel planning staff in Washington, D.C. The board, assisted by panels composed of officers representing major elements of the air force, developed statements of educational requirements for all officer specializations. In the area of professional military education, in place of the existing three-step system of air force professional military schools, consisting of a squadron officer school for officers with about five years service, a command and staff college at the ten-year level of experience, and a war college at the 18-to-20-year level, this board proposed a two-phase system. It would consist of an air force staff college at about the sixth year of experience and an air force war college for selected officers soon after their promotion to major, normally during the eleventh year of service. To supplement this recommended resident school plan there would be an extensive scheme of required correspondence programs to prepare officers for the resident schools or as a substitution for the residence school for those officers not selected to attend (Air Force Educational Requirements Board, 1963).

Like the other services, the air force also appoints committees from time to time to study a particular aspect of its education and training programs. In 1949 the Ridenour Committee studied the air force research and development program and made recommendations to improve the scientific education of officers (Ridenour Report, 1949). Recently the Morganti Committee reviewed the objectives of air force basic military training, determined the extent to which these objectives were being met, looked at training facilities, and made recommendations (Morganti & others, 1966). A study of the status of professional education in the air forces of Russia, Germany, Italy, Japan, England, and France through 1946 has been reported (Shelburne, 1953), and, more recently, a study has been made of the education of Soviet Air Force officers, with special reference to the sources from which they are recruited (Buchter, 1965).

Joint Studies. In the United States some comparative studies have been made of the military education and training programs of all the services and of joint programs. Toward the end of World War II the Joint Chiefs of Staff (1945) made an extensive study of the educational programs of the services with particular reference to joint education. Portions of this study were included in the report of the Eberstadt Committee appointed by the secretary of the navy (Eberstadt Report, 1945). In 1955 the U.S. Office of Education published for the first time a description of the educational programs of 34 professions, which included programs for the army, the navy, the marine corps, the coast guard, the air force, and the merchant marine (Blauch, 1955). In the 1962-63 edition of its *Education Directory*, the U.S. Office of Education (1963) added Part V, listing the names of professional persons in the Department of Defense and in other executive departments and agencies of the federal government who spend a major portion of their time in educational activity.

Included in the study of higher education published by the American Council on Education is a description of the structure of professional military education and some information concerning the use that the armed forces make of civilian colleges and universities in the education of their officers (Cartter, 1964). Two studies made of education and training in the defense establishment of the United States were designed primarily for the information of civilian educators. The first study (Clark & Sloan, 1964) describes the great variety of specialized curricula in the service school for both enlisted and commissioned personnel, as well as the instructor training programs and the innovations in teaching in armed forces programs.

The second study (Shelburne & Groves, 1965) describes the administrative organization for training and education in each service and in the Department of Defense. It categorizes the programs both for enlisted men and for officers, discusses the importance of professional military education, identifies seven levels at which this type of education takes place, and describes unit training—the kind of training that welds officers and men into an effective whole for a specific mission or for a series of missions or tasks.

The latest and most comprehensive study of officer education was made by a group of officers representing all services and appointed by the assistant secretary of defense (office of the Assistant Secretary of Defense, 1966c). Concerning the supervision of instruction, the study revealed that the army structure combined centralization and decentralization. Both military education and specialized training were conducted at the branch schools and, at any given time, a majority of the students were enlisted men. The navy structure generally separates training from education. Air University consolidates air force educational activities into a single organization, but some of the courses are of a specialized training nature. The marine corps structure places military education under one command at one installation but also teaches some specialist courses.

After comparing the program for professional military education of each service, the study reached the following conclusions: (1) Differing concepts of officer development contribute to basic differences among the services in the professional military education of officers but do not account for all the differences. (2) The army puts more emphasis on professional military education than the marine corps, the air force, and the navy, in that order. There is evidence that the air force is beginning to place more emphasis on this type of education. (3) The difference in emphasis placed on professional military education as defined by this study results in interservice differences in the number of courses, the purposes of the courses, the length of time they last, and the composition of the student body. (4) Although the percentage of officers educated at the senior level is roughly comparable for the services, there is a considerable variation in the percentage educated at the command and staff level. The navy and, to a lesser extent, the air force appear to be educating too few officers at this level. (5) Because of the emphasis placed on joint and combined operations at the command and staff colleges of all the services, the unique position of the Armed Forces Staff College is questioned. (6) Except in the navy, the majority of officers who are educated up to and including the command and staff level are educated by their parent service; at the senior-service level most officers attend schools conducted by other than their parent service; about 50 percent of the naval officers at each level attend schools other than those of the navy. (7) Quotas for the joint colleges appear to be based on the assumption that each service (army, navy, and air force) is entitled to one-third of the military spaces.

The study reached the following conclusions concerning postcommission academic education in such fields as engineering, physical sciences, and social sciences: (1) Each service sponsors a program for providing additional academic education for its officers. For this program the army relies on civilian institutions, but the other services use a combination of in-house facilities and civilian institutions. The navy and marine corps rely to the greatest extent upon in-house academic education. (2) Services select officers for advanced academic schooling on the basis of known requirements for such education. Although selection procedures differ among the services, they appear adequate. Selectees are universally volunteers, but they are sometimes invited to participate and sometimes may by mutual agreement be enrolled in a curriculum other than that given as their preference. The greatest requirement for officers with advanced degrees is in the warfare-support category. (3) At the present time the percentage of officers of all services enrolled in civilian schools falls far below any limits that may be set by law; the army and the air force are restricted to 8 percent of their officers at any one time. (4) The apparent reason for the continued existence of service in-house academic schools, such as the Air Force Institute of Technology and the Navy Post Graduate School, is that the programs they offer can be tailored to meet the specific requirements of the service. The study does not give objective data to justify the existence of these schools. All services have the policy that, in general, officers are selected for enrollment in advanced academic programs to acquire certain education, not necessarily to earn a degree. (5) Though the army and the marine corps continue to commission officers who do not have bachelor's degrees, neither of these services has a substantial program for upgrading young career officers in this group who show special promise. Both the navy and the air force have such programs. (6) In general, the academic qualifications of officers are high; 74 percent have at least a bachelor's degree. (7) The proportion of officers entering the service with a degree is high; the services tend, however, to retain a large proportion of those officers who do not have degrees, but advancement to the higher ranks appears to be definitely correlated with educational achievement. (8) The army has the largest educational and training system of all the services, and it is the program that is most decentralized. Confusion exists about the way the responsibilities for education and training are to be divided among the services, the Joint Chiefs of Staff, and the various elements of the office of the secretary of defense. These responsibilities need clarification (Office of the Assistant Secretary of Defense, 1966c).

A recent description of the Soviet armed forces system of education includes a discussion of its army and navy cadet schools that provide preliminary military training for boys 14 or 15 years of age, and the various higher specialist and command and staff schools. It lists 22 schools by name (Artemiev, 1966).

The Canadian military establishment began an experiment in joint education as early as 1948. All potential regular officers of the three services were brought together and educated on a triservice basis. After six years of operation the program was declared a success (Snider, 1956). More recently Canada has widened its concept of service unification to the point that it proposes to merge all the services into one organization to be known as the Canadian Armed Forces. The total system of military training and education is being affected (Gellner, 1967).

In 1962 a significant five-day conference was held in Paris to discuss the programs of professional military education in 13 of the 17 member nations of the North Atlantic Treaty Organization (NATO). The 85 military school officials attending the conference read papers and discussed such questions as the pattern of military education in their countries, the need for the joint and combined education of officers of member nations, and the need within the alliance for an agency whose primary concern would be military education (*Report on the NATO Military Education Conference . . .*, 1962). Following a recommendation of General Eisenhower, who was then supreme allied commander in Europe, the North Atlantic Council established the NATO Defense College, in Paris, on June 15, 1951. Radway (1962) discusses some of the difficulties encountered in the organization and administration of this international military institution.

Foot's excellent comparative study (1961) of the ways in which modern industrial societies man their forces and give basic military training concludes, in part, that ideally the manpower to be trained should be made up of volunteers. Conscription is used for obtaining military manpower in France, Turkey, Denmark, and the U.S.S.R.; citizen armies are used in Switzerland, Sweden, and Israel; volunteers are used in Canada and Australia; a mixed system with both conscription and voluntary choice is in use in Belgium, the United States, Germany, and the United Kingdom.

In a penetrating study, Masland and Radway (1957) point out that the senior-service war colleges have been successful in preparing officers to participate in policy making at the national level, and they conclude that the services can be justly proud of their accomplishments in professional military education. They point out, however, that this military education can and should be improved. Two of the principal limitations are identified as tendencies toward conformity and parochialism.

In January 1964 the secretary of defense established a single overseas military dependents' school system replacing the three separate and largely uncoordinated programs of the military services. The system included 291 schools in 28 countries, with an enrollment of some 155,000 pupils (Department of Defense, 1966; Shelburne & Groves, 1965).

ROTC Programs. One of the most complete studies, and a relatively recent one, of the place, purpose, and functioning of the ROTC programs in American colleges and universities (Lyons & Masland, 1959) drew the following conclusions, among others: (1) The objectives toward which the ROTC programs are directed need to be clarified now that more professionalization than formerly prevails in the armed forces. Circumstances now underscore the importance of having highly competent and effectively equipped professional military forces, and the role of the reserve forces has diminished in importance. (2) Evidence indicates that the ROTC produces an excellent officer, but too few of the officers educated under the program remain in the military. Resignations among graduates of the service academies are too numerous also. The principal reason for the resignations is that a military career is not made attractive enough, not that poorly qualified candidates are selected for the career. (3) The constantly more pressing needs of the nation for highly skilled talent in all professions and technical fields indicate that there should be a clearly defined national policy for education. (4) No matter how realistically men of intellect and liberal persuasion accept the necessity for strong defense forces, they continue to find it difficult to reconcile the authority and discipline of the military profession with the spirit of open inquiry so essential to a free educational system. Yet, the study concludes, ". . . it is this very reconciliation that is the key to the survival of democracy today" (Lyons & Masland, 1959, pp. 209–215).

Opponents of the ROTC program hold that it is antithetical to the high purposes of a free and inquiring mind (Brick, 1959) and that it injects militarism into education (Ekirch, 1956). An earlier study of the values of the ROTC program, based on replies to a questionnaire from more than 10,000 ROTC students who graduated from 1920 to 1930, mentioned the educational values of the program; indicated that the program brought to participants a definite and serious recognition of the more important duties and responsibilities of democratic citizenship; suggested that some colleges give more recognition to the program; indicated that better-trained instructors would improve the program; supported the view that graduates would "strongly oppose" abolition of the program; and indicated that over 90 percent of those responding attested that the program does not create a militaristic attitude (Bishop, 1932).

Academies. The Eberstadt Report (1945), prepared by a committee appointed by the secretary of the navy at the end of World War II and previously described, recommended that three or four national defense academies be established to replace service academies. The new academies were to offer specialization in land, sea, air, technical-service, and supply operations. Another study, looking to the establishment of an academy for the new U.S. Air Force, proposed a five-year plan for the basic education of officers; the instruction for the first two years was to be given in civilian colleges and for the last three years in an air force academy (Air Force Academy Planning Board, 1949, Vol. I, iii).

In March 1949 the secretary of defense appointed a board to recommend "the manner in which officer candidates should receive their basic education for a career in the armed services." The board, while critical of some aspects of the existing service academies, rejected all suggestions that the basic structure of the academies be changed, and it recommended that an air force academy be established to parallel the existing academies (Service Academy Board, 1950). It further recommended that in peacetime no fewer than 50 percent of the regular officers entering each branch of the armed services be academy graduates, but it proposed that the ROTC programs for the army, navy, and air force be continued and that a substantial portion of the officers entering a service each year come from civilian schools. The board further recommended that a new plan for the Congressional nomination of candidates for the academies be adopted. This plan, taken from the proposals of the Air Force Academy Planning Board, provided that for each vacancy, from the sources authorized by law, no fewer than four or more than ten candidates were to be nominated. Nominated candidates would take a mental examination administered by the academies. Candidates who passed the mental examination would report to academy selection boards for further examination. Final evaluations and selection would be made, and the highest-ranking qualified individual in each group would be selected for appointment. All other candidates would be placed in rank order as first alternate, second alternate, etc. Finally, the board proposed that a consulting board with rotating membership be established in the Department of Defense to report on the programs of the academies and to continue the study of the educational requirements the services have for commissioning officers.

Among the studies of the service academies appearing in periodicals, those of Boroff (1962, 1963a, 1963b) are of special interest. Boroff summarized his study of the academies by expressing his concern over the relative estrangement of the academies from civilian education and over civilian misconceptions concerning the academy graduate. He found that service-academy graduates do not control the military establishment: in the Army only 8 percent of the officers were academy graduates; in the navy, 14.3 percent; and in the air force, 9 percent; and these percentages were decreasing. Boroff held that American military history had been an honorable one and that our professional soldiers had always deferred to civilian leadership. He made four principal recommendations: (1) The academies should be upgraded academically and intellectually. Organized sports and peripheral military training should be given less emphasis. (2) Cadets should be allowed more time for independent study. (3) The intellectually elite group in the academies should be recognized and encouraged. (4) The present statutory boards of visitors should be changed to make them compare favorably with the best independent boards of ranking universities.

Following an incident at the Air Force Academy in which large-scale cheating on tests on the part of cadets was discovered, the secretary of the air force appointed a special advisory committee, in January 1965, to analyze the basic causes of the cheating in terms of an evaluation of the structure and functioning of the academy (Department of the Air Force, Special Advisory Committee on the United States Air Force Academy, 1965). The committee's report contained comments and suggestions concerning the academic program, the military training program, the physical education and athletic program, the cadet honor code, and the academy policies and goals. To give the Air Force Academy more definite goals and a greater sense of stability, the board proposed that the following steps be taken: (1) a permanent board be appointed to advise the secretary of the air force and the chief of staff on all major aspects of academy policy and operation; (2) highly qualified civilian educators, prominent businessmen, outstanding men from other professions, and active or retired general officers should be appointed to this advisory board; (3) the superintendent of the Air Force Academy and the commandant of cadets should serve for at least four years; and (4) better communication should be established to ensure that changes in policies and practices are made known to school officials and cadets alike.

Authority to Grant Degrees. A moot point in discussions both within the military establishment itself and between it and the U.S. Office of Education and educators in civilian colleges and universities is whether military schools should grant degrees. Beginning in 1933 the service academies, the Naval Postgraduate School, and later the Air Force Institute of Technology were given authority by Congress to grant degrees. Subsequently these institutions were accredited by regional and professional agencies. More recently proposals have been made, both in the United States and abroad, that the authority to grant degrees be extended to include the professional military schools or to equate graduation from certain of these schools with graduate degrees (Fursdon, 1964; Newman, 1961; Rao, 1965). The motivation for these proposals stems from the conviction that professional military education has scholarly content and that the civilian educational community should acknowledge this by recognizing academic degrees in military science.

In 1955, at the urging of the director of the Bureau of the Budget, the U.S. Office of Education documented authority for federal institutions to grant degrees, and, after noting the absence of any national policy by which an institution seeking such authority could be judged, convened a meeting of representative educators who were not connected with federal institutions. The consensus of this group was that before Congress granted federal institutions any additional authority to grant degrees, particularly at the graduate level, it should be evident that the need for granting such degrees could not be met by existing nonfederal institutions. Further, the need should be determined by an impartial group of representative educators. The secretary of the Department of Health, Education, and Welfare, and the director of the Bureau of the Budget approved these recommendations of the board. Therefore, at present it is national policy that if federal institutions are to be given any additional authority for granting degrees, the action must first be approved by a review committee appointed by the U.S. commissioner of education (Sanders, 1955).

In 1964, after noting that the granting of academic degrees by federal agencies had been a matter of concern to the American academic community for more than a decade, the National Commission on Accrediting and the American Council on Education (1964) each issued a policy statement concerning the nature and meaning of the academic degree which in effect supported the procedure and national policy noted above.

Since 1962 the commandants of the National War College, the Industrial College of the Armed Forces, the Armed Forces Staff College, and the three service war colleges have met annually as the Military Education Coordination Conference. The 1966 report of the conference to the Joint Chiefs of Staff contained a recommendation that each service, for the purposes of promotion and job assignment, equate completion of the courses in the five senior colleges with an advanced degree in a field appropriate to the course. The board thought that such action would increase the prestige of these colleges and the value of the courses. The Joint Chiefs of Staff rejected the proposal and stated (Joint Chiefs of Staff, 1966): "Such a policy would not add to the professional reputation of the individual graduate, would not enhance the prestige or the academic excellence of the college, would not decrease the desirability of obtaining an advanced academic degree in a specific discipline from an accredited university that would be recognized by both the academic community and by the services, and would not increase the assignment potential of the individual graduate to joint staffs or joint activities. The conclusion is that completion of the five Senior Colleges should continue to speak for itself and that additional policy was unnecessary."

CURRICULUM. Both the technique and the philosophy of instruction have been treated in the modernization programs of the armed services.

Effective use of closed-circuit television serves not only to increase the flexibility of classroom instruction in the armed forces but also to permit individual students to use videotapes for protracted review of materials. The use of both television instruction and programmed instruction has been thoroughly documented elsewhere in the academic press. These subjects are mentioned here only to point out that the armed services have done research and pioneered in these areas.

Similarly, the armed services have exerted extraordinary effort in attempting to define training and educational requirements; the fields in which education and training should be offered; and what factors related to successful vocational performance should be involved not only in education but also in selection and evaluation measures. Motivation to improve instruction in the services stems from pressure for success, resulting from almost-immediate feedback from field commands, and pressure for economy, resulting from competition for funds from the Department of Defense and aid from Congress.

Current philosophy in armed forces training programs, as contrasted with professional military education, is focused upon principles of teaching specific vocational knowledge and skills required in the subsequent assignment. Such knowledge and skills are taught in a framework of trainee-centered instruction. Curricula, study aids, and class organization are focused on having the student learn the necessary material at a pace geared to his abilities.

Requirements and Objectives. The requirements for and the objectives of instruction in service schools are largely derived from official statements of mission or purpose. These statements usually come from an authority superior to the school, and in the final analysis the success of the schools is judged by the extent to which they accomplish their assigned mission (Haines Board, 1966, pp. 167, 234, 299; and Department of the Air Force, 1966). The administrative organization within the military establishment that is responsible for training and education (Shelburne & Groves, 1965, pp. 9–16) is influenced by a variety of factors in arriving at statements of mission for its schools. Among these factors are recommendations of individuals in and out of the services (Bush, 1946, p. 91), Congressional acts, and, probably the most influential, the recommendations of appointed boards (Cook Board, 1959, p. 1). Beginning with a statement of mission, the school commandant and faculty usually develop written statements of the purpose and scope of a course and finally identify specific educational objectives or outcomes by which the educational experiences and the subject matter in the course are organized and the progress of students is judged.

A study of World War II military training and education concludes that the success of the armed services in determining and in attaining their specific objectives suggests the importance of clearly defining objectives for all elements of the curriculum in civilian colleges and schools (Goodman, 1947). Crawford (1962) stresses the primacy of a firm statement of objectives in curriculum construction, and the satisfaction of this requirement is in itself a significant contribution. Smith (1966a, 1966b) provides guidance in the area of training objectives in Army reports, emphasizing the critical need for objective data in developing job requirements. Tyler & others (1955) examined the programs of professional education in the air force and developed a rationale for arriving at statements of objectives, identified some sources from which suggestions for objectives could be derived, suggested the form in which objectives might be expressed to be most helpful in selecting learning experiences and in guiding teaching, and analyzed existing statements of objectives.

Ammerman (1966) reported that application of experimental procedures to a sample of junior army officers' jobs resulted in an inventory of 452 job tasks. From this number, 101 job tasks, or 22 percent, were selected as requiring some formal instruction. Identification of knowledge and skills to be taught for these 101 activities resulted in statements of 160 training objectives.

The objectives of the service war colleges have been the subject of several studies. Masland and Radway (1957) analyzed the curricula of these institutions in great detail and concluded, in part, that there is a great need for these colleges to provide more opportunity for examination of a few problems in greater depth and that the colleges should have more concern for intellectual discipline, for critical analyses of assumptions, for examinations of alternatives, and for testing of conclusions.

A former Department of Defense official who lectured at the war colleges contended that their missions were too static and that too much attention was being given to psychosocial and international questions and too little attention to the more purely military aspects of the curriculum (Katzenbach, 1965). Contrary views were advanced by two senior-service officers, who asserted that the war colleges are primarily concerned not with instilling professionalism in their students but rather with broadening the outlook and education of officers who have had years of professional experience. They also asserted that there is a difference between the mission of a college and its curriculum: the mission is concerned with the attainment of certain goals, and the curriculum is the method of achieving those goals; therefore, the mission may stay essentially the same, but the curriculum should be variable (Hitchcock, 1965, pp. 110–115).

The academies, at the other end of the spectrum of professional military education, have also had their purposes and objectives analyzed. A 1957 study, while noting that progress had been made in liberalizing academy curricula, identified the following obstacles to further evolution in that direction: (1) As weapons grow more complex, there is an increasing demand for a more technical curriculum. (2) Because the academies are national institutions, there is pressure to emphasize vocational subjects. (3) Academy applicants seem to have greater interest in and aptitude for technical and mechanical matters than liberal arts. (4) Academy commandants and their staffs exert pressure to relate the curriculum to the kinds of duties performed by junior officers and to combat skills. (5) The curriculum is prescribed, and it must be relevant to present service problems. (6) The purpose of the academies is clearly defined; the causes and consequences of such clarity may not be unmixed blessings. (7) The great responsibilities that academy officials have for preparing their graduates for modern war are not conducive to maintaining the same kind of inquiring attitude that is found in liberal education (Masland & Radway, 1957). A board appointed by the secretary of defense in 1949 to study precommissioning education recommended the following as educational goals for the academies: abilities in leadership and a basic knowledge of the techniques of modern warfare; knowledge and qualities necessary to provide wise, balanced, and experienced direction at all levels of military operations; a background of general knowledge comparable to that of graduates of leading universities; a firm grasp of the role that the military establishment should have within the framework of the American government and a democratic society; an awareness of the major problems of the nation and an understanding of the relationship between military preparedness and all other elements of national life; and an understanding of the concept of the Department of Defense as a single, integrated instrument and a sense of teamwork (Service Academy Board, 1950, pp. 1–2, 30, 43). A study of the curricula of the academies made in 1965 recommended greater permissiveness and diversity in academic requirements (Simons, 1965).

A current analysis of the British Army concludes that it is the most conservative of the three British military services in the way its members are trained and organized. Reform of its education is urgently needed if its commanders and staff officers are to be able to expound and defend a realistic strategy. An examination of officer training in the British Army indicates it is just that—training, not education. Staff-officer education is judged to be particularly unsatisfactory. This type of education in the British Army is contrasted with that in the German and French armies. The suggestion is made that the course at the British Army staff college be lengthened to three years (Verrier, 1966). The rudiments of military knowledge needed by the junior British Army officers are identified (Palit, 1950), and the importance of maintaining a proper balance between liberal studies and more professional studies in the education of British Army officers is stressed (Hackett, 1961).

The aims of Soviet officer education are discussed in three studies: The Zhukovssky Red Banner Air Force Academy is described by a U.S. Air Force cadet (Walen, 1959). Lemieux (1964) stresses the graduate technical training of Russian officers (Lemieux, 1964). In a review of the aims of the education of army officers, a marshal of the Russian Army points out that although an understanding of science and technology is important, an understanding of ideological and political matters is even more important (Malinovsky, 1966).

In 1962 a conference of senior military school officials from 13 of the countries making up NATO discussed the objectives of the military education of officers assigned to combined staffs. They found that these officers received alarmingly little joint education, and they concluded that, in order to fight together, these officers should have a common understanding of the economic, political, and military situation of the member nations. These subjects should be introduced early in an officer's education, and the emphasis placed on these subjects should be increased as the officer moves up in rank and responsibility. The importance of foreign-language training was also stressed (*Report on the NATO Military Education Conference* . . . , 1962).

Organization of Instruction. The proceedings of a conference held in June 1966 provide a description of the army, navy, air force, and marine training programs. The report gives good coverage of the history, scope, and future plans of the army, the navy, and the air force for using computer-based information and instruction systems and programmed instruction (Department of Defense & others, 1966). Clark and Sloan (1964) identify and classify the courses of instruction, including correspondence study for all the services except the U.S. Coast Guard.

The latest study by the Department of Defense of the programs of education for commissioned officers contains the following observations: (1) More-objective criteria are needed for determining the length of the professional military courses. (2) Present curricula at most of the professional military schools do not take into consideration the diverse experiences, educational background, intellectual capacity, and motivation of their students. There are some voluntary courses which are often remedial in nature and which are usually conducted after regular class hours, but the professional military schools, with the exception of the Industrial College of the Armed Forces, do not include true electives in their curricula. (3) The honors program of the army's Command and General Staff College requires considerably more administrative and faculty involvement than the number of participants would seem to warrant, particularly since no official army recognition is granted those officers who complete the program (Office of the Assistant Secretary of Defense, 1966c).

Each service has a basic reference manual or document that describes its training and education programs (Department of the Navy, 1964). Each service also maintains a formal schools catalog (Shelburne & Groves, 1965, p. 40) that gives complete data on each resident curriculum.

Rundquist (1966) outlines a systematic procedure for curriculum development, listing the following operational steps: (1) state mission, (2) identify tasks to be learned, (3) establish on-the-job standards, (4) group tasks, (5) derive knowledge and skills to be learned, (6) state the objectives, (7) develop lesson plans, (8) integrate lesson plans, and (9) evaluate course effectiveness.

Tyler and others (1955, pp. 146–184) discussed the place and importance of learning experiences in an effective curriculum and the characteristics of these experiences, and they made a critical analysis of learning experiences employed in certain schools of Air University. A 1966 article (Ortlieb, 1966) describes the Defense Systems Analysis Education Program, conducted by the Institute for Defense Analyses in cooperation with the University of Maryland, which leads to the degree of Master of Arts in Economics. The program is designed to provide career officers and civil servants with education in either systems analysis or cost effectiveness and analysis. The purpose of the program is to develop an understanding of the role, the basic techniques, and the limitations of systems analysis.

The curriculum of a junior professional military school was investigated (Connelly, 1950) in order to identify and describe provisions made for integration of all curriculum elements and to make recommendations for improvement; 57 elements were identified that could be used in organizing and integrating the curriculum for the students.

In 1956 the army's Command and General Staff College offered five courses. These courses were described, and the curriculum of the regular course was analyzed in some detail (Culp, 1956). The various changes in the length and content of the courses offered by the German war academy during World War II are described by former German general officers (Military Intelligence Division, 1946). The curriculum of the Royal Canadian Air Force Staff College in 1957 was reported to be organized into two areas: (1) staff training, composed of three phases: functional skills, functional knowledge, and personnel; and (2) air warfare, divided into two phases: supporting services and operations. The five phases were composed of 16 units of instruction (Jackson, 1957). A British military authority compared education in the profession of arms with that in medicine and law. In the military profession, the practitioner, instead of pursuing a long, single, concentrated period of instruction, as in medicine and law, goes back to school at various stages for specialist courses and for command and staff education. He spends no less than one-fifth of his professional life in school (Hackett, 1963). A U.S. Air Force officer, after describing in some detail the Soviet educational system, including the premilitary and paramilitary educational and training programs and the schools for the professional military education of air force officers, concludes that the system is comprehensive and serves the needs of the Soviet state and of its professional officers (Buchter, 1965). Some of the difficulties in developing a curriculum in an international military college composed of officers from over 13 nations are analyzed (Radway, 1962).

Methods and Materials. Goodman (1947) reported that during World War II the armed services succeeded to a remarkable degree in attaining realism in instruction. The development of realism in learning requires both a clear understanding of what one desires to teach and a great deal of planning and experimenting to create suitable exercises and to acquire the equipment and training aids needed to make the exercise effective. For civilian educators, then, the experiences that the armed services have had in training point up the importance of painstaking planning to achieve realistic learning situations, and they point to the desirability of pooling experience in the development of such situations.

In discussing the development of military science since the death of Stalin, a Russian Army general, Pokrovsky (1959), stressed three important principles in military training methods: (1) the conditions of training must simulate real combat as closely as possible; (2) training must be graphic; and (3) training must be based on a discovery and an analysis of the physical nature of the operation and on the use of the material studied.

A Department of Defense study (Office of the Assistant Secretary of Defense, 1966c) analyzed the methods of instruction used in the senior-service and at the command and staff schools and also analyzed the percentage of time devoted to each method. The following methods were identified: (1) formal presentations, consisting of lectures given by the resident faculty and those given by guest lecturers; (2) practical exercises made up principally of war gaming and simulation and map and field exercises; (3) other instructional exercises, including seminars, conferences, panel discussions, case studies, and committee work; (4) field trips; and (5) individual study and research.

In summarizing its analysis of these methods the study noted that, as might be expected, there were more formal presentations at the command and staff level than at the senior level. An exception was the National War College, where 29 percent of the instructional time was devoted to formal presentations and over one-fourth of the total time to guest lecturers. The same was true of the Armed Forces Staff College. The Industrial College of the Armed Forces devoted 17 percent of its time to formal presentations, while the service war colleges and command and staff colleges used this method considerably less. At the senior-service level the resident faculty gave comparatively few lectures. At the command and staff level the navy and air force relied more on individual study and research than did the others, which emphasized practical work.

As the result of an educational survey of the Army Command and General Staff College (Orleans, 1956), a member of the faculty discussed the advisability of shifting emphasis from teaching approved doctrine to teaching problem solving (Birrer, 1957). A recent study of Army education (Haines Board, 1966, pp. 73, 773–781) reviewed innovations in educational practices and techniques and found them generally to be "outstanding." It recommended that a biennial innovations seminar be conducted as a means of ensuring that knowledge of these new techniques would be diffused throughout the army school system.

Three studies employing the self-confrontation technique as a teaching method (the feedback of an individual's performance in a given situation through the use of videotape or sound motion picture film) have been reported in studies conducted by Haines and others (1965), by Eachus (1965), and by Eachus and others (1966). These three studies were concerned with the acquisition and retention of cross-cultural interaction skills, and one (Eachus, 1965) had as its purpose the teaching of complex skills through the use of this technique.

The economy to be achieved by reproducing the work environment in the training situation has resulted in the considerable use of mock-ups and simulators by all three services. Elaborate army studies (G. Brown & others, 1959; G. Brown & Vineburg, 1960) were concerned with the impact of specific performance aids and with the transfer of training that occurs when such aids were similar to actual equipment used in the field but not identical. Results similar to theirs were reported in the air force (Foley, 1964) and in the navy (Pickering & Anderson, 1966).

A summary of research for 1965 (Department of the Air Force, Office of Aerospace Research, 1965b) reports on the developments of an international-environment simulator, a project funded by the Office of Aerospace Research and initiated by Professor Harold Guetzkow of Northwestern University. It is a man-computer model of our international system. From five to nine hypothetical nations may be used for each run of the simulator. It can be used by policy makers, diplomats, and students and is considered to be a good training device for personnel in the military academies, in the staff colleges, and in the foreign service. It may also be used as a research device in the formulation of theories about international relations. Clark and Sloan (1964, pp. 88–91) have reported on the extensive work of the navy's Training Device Center in developing simulators for use in various training situations.

Eure (1959a) and McHugh (1967) trace the history of the use of war gaming as an instructional device at the Naval War College, beginning in 1887. It was proposed (Office of the Assistant Secretary of Defense, 1966c) that war gaming or simulation exercises be introduced in the programs of the National War College, the Air War College, and the Armed Forces Staff College. A report edited by Brossman (1965) mentions some 20 studies dealing with war gaming as a training and evaluation technique not only in logistics planning but also in a wide variety of training operations in all three services.

The first report, under navy contract, in a series of reports on the results of research on computer-assisted instruction appeared in January 1966 (Hickey & Newton, 1966). Subsequent reports are to be published at six-month intervals. The Air Force Office of Scientific Research has sponsored research and development of programmed instruction (Department of the Air Force, Office of Aerospace Research, 1965a). The report on the research includes an account of the Air Force Training Command's two-phase approach. Phase I covered the orientation of instructors and supervisors to the concepts of programmed instruction; the development of limited in-house capability of technical training centers; and the development of formal evaluation methods to determine the effectiveness, feasibility of expansion, means of exploitation, and problems associated with increased exploitation. Phase II includes plans and operations based upon an evaluation of Phase I. By the end of Phase I, 300 people were trained in techniques of programmed instruction, and 150 programmed packages had been produced. A preliminary analysis of the program made after one year indicated that test scores of 90 percent or above were achieved by the students and that training time had been reduced by 25 to 50 percent. As a direct result of this research, courses using programmed instruction were established in four other major commands of the air force, and plans are being developed to use this technique in on-the-job training throughout the air force. Air force members took a leading role in establishing the National Society for Programmed Instruction. A report on the status of training technology in the air force (Eckstrand, 1964) indicates that more attention was being given to the evaluation of training systems in terms of proficiency tests that were criterion-referenced and that the development of such tests involves problems in three areas: measurement, relevance, and sampling.

At a conference held in June 1966 the services

described their training and education programs to a large group of industrialists with extensive experience in applying systems analysis to the selection and design of weapon systems. The purpose of the conference was to report what the services were already doing in the area of programmed learning and other aspects of computer-assisted instruction and to discuss the implications of applying systems analysis to military training and education (Department of Defense & others, 1966). In contrast to developments in this country, there was little interest in programmed learning in the Soviet Union before 1960. Since that time the Soviets have been very active in this field, and they have developed more than 90 different models of teaching machines since 1961. Many of these have been developed by the military (Ratliff, 1966).

Harris (1956) reported on the growth of correspondence teaching by the Army Command and General Staff College from 1891, and Chapman (1964) discussed the heavy reliance on this method of education in the Soviet armed forces. The correspondence method of teaching offered by most of the U.S. military schools was reviewed and judged valuable and relatively inexpensive (Office of the Assistant Secretary of Defense, 1966c), and it was suggested that such courses might be introduced in the National War College, the Army War College, and the Armed Forces Staff College.

Three reports summarize the developments in audio-visual aids used by the services during World War II (Hovland & others, 1949; Miles & Spain, 1947; Svenson & Sheats, 1950). Extensive bibliographies reporting the results of research in the use of audio-visual aids have been published periodically by the Naval Training Device Center now located in Orlando, Florida. Typical of these reports is one on training films (Special Devices Center, 1950). More recently the results of research in audio-visual methods in the armed forces are reported in the indexes of the Technical Abstract Bulletin of the Defense Documentation Center.

The Officer Education Study (Office of the Assistant Secretary of Defense, 1966c, pp. 326–328) found that the curriculum content of the senior-service schools could be described under the following headings: fundamental military instruction; functions of command, staff, and management; tactics; military capabilities and strategy; counterinsurgency; joint, combined, and special operations; U.S. national security; international affairs; research and communicative skills; and other types of content.

Johnson (1957) conducted a study of 15 military libraries servicing 16 schools of the three major services and the joint schools. He found certain deficiencies in the place that these libraries have in the academic organizational structure, the size of the staffs, funding, physical facilities, procurement policies, and accountability controls. In a study reported five years later, Johnson (1962) pointed out that the distinction of important military libraries lies in their subject specialization more than in the number of items collected. A number of the military libraries have collections as unique as the curricula they reflect.

The latest study of army officer education (Haines Board, 1966) reported that the approximately 1,750 army libraries fall into three categories: (1) those supporting the education and training mission of the army; (2) those providing technical information and materials for specialized and research activities; and (3) those providing general informational, recreational, and educational materials to army personnel in the United States and overseas. The study found considerable variation among army school libraries and recommended that the following steps be taken: (1) to improve their professional competence, the librarians should pursue a program of graduate-level schooling; (2) professional librarians should be rotated throughout the library system, and they should participate more actively in professional conferences and workshops; (3) a centralized record facility should be established to ensure that research papers, student theses, committee studies, video tapes, and related material are more widely circulated throughout the school system.

After reviewing the military school libraries, the committee appointed by the secretary of defense (Office of the Assistant Secretary of Defense, 1966c) judged as excellent the Mahan Library at the Naval War College, the Air University Library, and the library of the Armed Forces Staff College. The libraries of the National War College and the Industrial College of the Armed Forces, located on the same installation, were also judged excellent. These two libraries are separate, but students and faculty of both colleges have access to them, as well as to the Defense Documentation Center and to the Clearing House for the Federal Scientific and Technological Information. Libraries in some of the service schools are housed in unsatisfactory temporary buildings. Others are badly located or poorly planned even when housed in permanent modern buildings. Most service-school libraries are comparable to departmental libraries of large universities rather than to the general libraries of colleges of similar size. The study of libraries concluded that there was a wide variation in the libraries and their staffs throughout the military school systems. Areas needing attention were the faculty status of the head librarian, the adequacy of staffs, physical facilities, and organization of collections. There appeared to be no problem in obtaining funds for most of the schools.

Some of the more important sources of instructional materials not referred to previously are the following: annual published abstracts of research reports and theses written by officers attending the senior-service schools, usually available in the school libraries; military periodicals (Marshall, 1953); and books (Cockle, 1957). Van Riper (1955) discusses some of the categories of materials relevant to the study of military management.

Evaluation. At the end of World War I it became the general practice of civilian institutions to give blanket credit, or advanced standing, for service experience, with no requirements that the candidate give evidence of competence. Recalling this procedure, a committee of educators recommended a more rational plan to the War Department (Tyler, 1943). The War Department then contracted with the University of Chicago Board of Examiners to prepare tests and examinations to be used by the United States Armed Forces Institute (USAFI) in evaluating service experience. A parallel development was the creation by the American Council on Education of an agency to evaluate whole military and education programs (Shelburne & Groves, 1965, p. 101) and to make recommendations to colleges and schools concerning credit to be allowed.

D. Fedotoff White (1944) discussed the role of increasingly severe entrance and end-of-course examinations in the Soviet staff colleges as a means of raising the level of military competence in the Soviet Army. After making an analysis of the curricula of certain schools in Air University, Tyler and others (1955, pp. 205–254) discussed the place of evaluation in measuring both student progress and instructional effectiveness.

The Graduation Order of Merit, which lists all cadets graduating from the Air Force Academy in order of rank, has been studied (Department of the Air Force, Special Advisory Committee . . . , 1965, pp. 26, 36), and the recommendation has been made that this practice be reexamined and that those courses be reviewed in which objective quizzes and examinations may be given with undue frequency.

A recent study of army schools made after a review of British, French, German, and Japanese staff colleges (Haines Board, 1966) noted that a significant feature of the four foreign systems was the "extremely competitive examination" required for admission. Concerning U.S. Army schools' evaluation practices, it recommended, first, that present methods of rating students in numerical order or in thirds of the class should be discontinued and that all schools should establish a commandant's list similar to the dean's list in civilian colleges; this list should include the names of the upper 10 to 20 percent of the class, and distinguished graduates and honor graduates should be designated on this list. Second, it recommended that narrative statements in the academic report, which become a part of the officer's record, be completed for graduates of the Army War College and for the graduates of the other schools at the discretion of the commandant.

PERSONNEL. Contributions to the Military. During the two world wars, but particularly during World War II, there was a close working relationship between the behavioral scientists in the civilian community and in the military forces. Many psychologists, sociologists, and educators have spent their entire careers with the armed forces either as professional civilians or as uniformed members. Others have served for shorter periods of time, more often than not to assist in an emergency or during wartime. Bray (1948) has prepared a survey history of the manner in which the state of the art in psychology was applied to the men and machines of World War II.

Another significant study provides a critical analysis of the selection, classification, and training procedures used by the armed forces during World War II and the period after the war to 1951 (Office of the Secretary of Defense, 1951).

Contributions of the Military. The contributions of the military services to education and training research have been extensive. In this respect, the military have played two significant roles: sponsoring research or conducting research. Glaser (1962) and Stolurow (1965) provide examples of research supported by the armed forces, and Flanagan and others (1948) give a comprehensive summary of the psychological and educational research conducted in and for the armed services during World War II.

The contributions of the armed forces to research in education and training have been brought about by the combination of a structured occupational environment and a firm requirement for economy of operation. These factors, coupled with the opportunity for systematic experimentation and collection of data, have provided a fertile laboratory for research in education and personnel management.

Each of the armed services has fostered research and development in training, education, and personnel management. The administrative modality for research has varied across the services, but uniformity of intent and of results has been obtained. In educational programs the military has, as indicated by the secretary of defense (McNamara, 1965), "pioneered some of the most advanced teaching techniques." "Indeed," he continues, "it has been in the vanguard of a whole series of innovations in educational technology. Its findings, and its philosophy, are making a significant contribution to the modernization that is sweeping throughout the entire American school system."

Organization of Research Activities. The organization of research in education, training, and personnel management in the U.S. Army, Navy, and Air Force follows systems based upon the traditional organization and operating principles of each of the three services.

In the Headquarters of the Army, personnel research is primarily focused in the deputy chief of staff for research and development and embodies both in-service and contract capabilities. The in-service capability is managed by the Army Personnel Research Office, which supervises the research operations of a number of laboratories housed in the Washington, D.C., area. The laboratories that were active in March 1967 included the Support Systems Research Laboratory, the Combat Systems Research Laboratory, the Statistical Research and Analysis Laboratory, the Military Selection Research Laboratory, and the Behavioral Evaluation Research Laboratory. It is noted that the Army Personnel Research Office is eclectic, having some units at work in functional areas and others in more generalized areas. There is also a small research and development group at Ft. Devens, Massachusetts, working under the Army Security Agency, in areas of job analysis and occupational structure.

The Army contract capability includes an on-going research arrangement with George Washington University, whose Human Resources Research Office ("HumRRO") exists to fulfill an army research contract. HumRRO operates seven research divisions throughout the army, including System Operations, Armor, Recruit Training, Infantry, Air Defense, Aviation, and Language and Area Training.

Additional development work in the army is accomplished under the deputy chief of staff for personnel, whose Office of Personnel Operations is supporting a contract program in occupational research and management modeling.

In the navy, personnel research is primarily centered in the Bureau of Naval Personnel. Although the navy supports research contracts from each of its inservice agencies, it has no unit resembling HumRRO in the army program. Control of navy personnel research is centered in the Personnel Research Division of the Bureau of Naval Personnel, which supervises a number of field activities. The Personnel Research Laboratory, in Washington, D.C., is primarily concerned with officer personnel in the context of billet analysis and evaluative criteria. The Navy Personnel Research Field Activity at Pensacola, Florida, is concerned with aircrew selection and evaluation; the Personnel Research Field Activity at San Diego, California, is involved in enlisted occupational analysis, personnel management modeling, and related fields. The Navy Training Device Center, at Orlando, Florida, as its name indicates, is concerned with research and development in aids to teaching. In 1966 the Office of Naval Research announced plans to establish a computer-assisted instruction center to accelerate research and to serve as a clearinghouse and information center within the navy for this aspect of training and education (Department of Defense & others, 1966).

In the air force, personnel research is placed under the deputy chief of staff for research and development, but the active research units are monitored by staff agencies of the deputy chief of staff for personnel. This arrangement separates the research agencies from the operating commands, but it leaves them responsive to action in the personnel channels within which research findings can be effectively applied, and research problems usually appear. In this area there are two primary operating agencies under the administrative control of the Air Force Systems Command, which are in the Aerospace Medical Division: the Behavioral Sciences Laboratory of the Aeromedical Research Laboratories at Wright-Patterson Air Force Base, Ohio, and the Personnel Research Laboratory at Lackland Air Force Base, Texas. The mission of the Behavioral Sciences Laboratory includes training research, as well as research in individual behavior associated with the operation of weapon systems and space vehicles. The Personnel Research Laboratory is concerned with research in selection, classification, utilization, and evaluation. It should be noted that the Air Training Command at Randolph Air Force Base, Texas, has worked closely with the Behavioral Sciences Laboratory in the establishment of training methods and methods of training evaluation.

The Office of Aerospace Research also sponsors or conducts related basic research under its program of study in the life sciences and in the behavioral and social sciences.

As a caution, it should be noted that the names of research agencies in the military services are subject to change without the agencies' necessarily undergoing a change in mission. For example, the navy's present Personnel Research Laboratory was formerly known as the Naval Personnel Research Field Activity. In the air force the organization now known as the Personnel Research Laboratory, Aerospace Medical Division, was called the Personnel Laboratory, Aeronautical Systems Division, in 1961. Similar changes have occurred in the army units, but as long as the laboratories have remained in the same place, it is probable that the basic organization involved has remained the same also.

The major bibliographical works that list completed research in armed services education and training are the monthly, quarterly, and annual Indexes of Technical Abstract Bulletins, published by the Defense Documentation Center, Alexandria, Virginia. In addition, each of the research laboratories and organizations publishes its own bibliographical reports.

Selection, Classification, and Performance. Probably the most significant areas of personnel research conducted for and by the military are those dealing with selection, classification, and performance. The effective use made by the armed services of aptitude tests for the selection of men and for vocational classification is well known and well documented by Chambers (1950) and Dailey (1953), for example. Ginsberg and others (1959) have provided a comprehensive survey of the screening and utilization during World War II of several million young men who had mental and emotional handicaps. They also reported case studies of soldiers who were ineffective as soldiers or as citizens following their service in the army. In addition to the individual's intellectual and other potentials, his acquired skills and competences, motivation, emotional stability, tolerance for stress, values, and social and physical environment are important. The authors concluded that governmental and army policies have a significant influence upon the performance of military personnel. Another study (Department of the Army, 1965) reviewed army experience from World War I through 1964 with men classified as marginal.

During World War II and more recently, through 1966, all selection and classification tests were validated in terms of their relationships to training success in various elements of the military services. Piecemeal attempts to use criteria of job success rarely worked out but rather demonstrated the high cost, low reliability, and administrative difficulties associated with either the collection of usable job-performance measures or the administration of performance tests. At the Aerospace Medical Division research laboratories, Foley (1963) summarized the status of performance testing and recommended a research program covering paper-and-pencil tests. The objectives of the program were to improve techniques in the construction and analysis of such tests in order to assure the relevance of the questions to the performance of interest and in order to investigate how well such tests could predict performance.

The army has undertaken a significant experiment in selection and classification, which includes the Differential Officer Battery (Willeman, 1964). The army work involves the collection of a wide variety of information on aptitude, biography, and attitude by the conventional techniques of paper-and-pencil tests, physical and perceptual tests, and peer evaluations. These data are related to performance scores collected 18 months later at the Officer Evaluation Center at Ft. McClellan under stringently controlled conditions to ensure reliability and accuracy. Final results of this work are not yet available.

The content of this army study reflects the common belief that job-performance measures must deal with noncognitive areas if they are to be successful. Air force research in this area, which covers a period starting in 1949, was beginning to reach fruition in 1966. The path taken assumes that personality characteristics based on descriptive trait ratings by peers would relate to successful performance as an officer. Tupes (1957) reported positive validity for peer ratings based upon descriptive traits which had been assembled and studied (Cattell, 1947; Fiske, 1949).

The stability and strength of relationships of peer ratings of men in officer candidate school with later effectiveness ratings in the field prompted Tupes and Christal (1961) to follow the trait-rating procedure into a number of different kinds of populations. They discovered a constant factor structure for the ratings as collected in samples as different as fraternity brothers and kindergarten students. In order to shorten the time required for collection of data and to avoid the peer-rating process, which is unpopular among cadet groups, an attempt is under way to capture the psychological variance of the trait ratings through a series of paper-and-pencil tests. Work in this direction has been initiated by the construction of tests by Norman, and his findings appear in three reports (Norman, 1961a, 1961b, 1962).

Noncognitive measures for use in the selection of navy enlisted personnel have been found to have significant relationships with supervisory ratings in the fleet (Glickman & Kipnis, 1960). These measures tend to have zero correlations with the aptitude measures predictive of training success in navy schools and therefore enlarge the pool necessary for the selection of sufficient students to fill school and fleet quotas. This problem is discussed at some length by Glickman and Kipnis, who invoke the principles of decision theory to arrive at sets of weights for tests to optimize the probability of both technical-school success and adequate job performance on the part of enlisted personnel.

A most significant step in the collection of objective information on job performance has been provided by Morsh (1965) and by Morsh and Christal (1966). The two reports provide some detail on the procedure developed by Christal in the air force to collect job information at the task level and render computer-prepared reports on job descriptions for workers in given career fields which are detailed, comprehensive, and objective. These data exceed those obtainable by conventional job-analysis procedures in that they are based upon samples of up to 2,000 workers in a field, thus avoiding the sample biases which cannot be avoided in worker samples small enough to be assessed by conventional techniques. Within the vocational structure of the military services these data are most useful. Civilian applications must await both computers of greater capacity and recognition by industry of the homogeneity of tasks across corporations; analyses of work in common vocations must have the support of those employing such workers.

Hahn (1956) has described the development and evaluation of a series of 18 situational performance problems which would be useful in assessing the human relations and leadership skills required of a junior navy officer. Overall results indicate that there is a statistically significant relationship between performance on the situational problems and performance as measured by performance records and by data from regular navy fitness reports. However, the correlation was considered to be only moderate for practical application of the tests in assessing training procedures and for selection purposes.

The army has conducted a considerable amount of research on performance in and after graduation from the U.S. Military Academy. One study provides a review of research on selecting cadets for the academy for the period 1942–1953 (Department of the Army, Personnel Research Branch, 1953). A series of academic selection examinations was developed which contributed to the effectiveness of academy selection procedures. This research also showed that the Aptitude for Service Rating, the academy measure of leadership potential, is a better predictor of the effectiveness of graduates than any other academy measure. Other nonacademic measures—for example, grades given for conduct and physical education—were more closely related to the subsequent success that the cadets had as officers than were measures of achievement in academic courses.

In spite of the considerable research on the prediction of military leadership, a highly valid method of selecting leaders continues to be elusive (Janowitz & Little, 1965). As Janowitz and Little report: "Much effort, both scientific and otherwise, has been invested in the attempt to select young men who will turn out to be good military leaders. It is fair to say that in contrast to the obvious success scored in recent years in the selection of people for various kinds of specific jobs, no one has yet devised a method of proven validity for selecting either military or non-military leaders."

Education and Career Progression. Almost every army, navy, and air force board mentioned above has considered the question of the appropriate time in an officer's career for him to attend a professional school. As indicated earlier, there are about seven levels of professional military education, with each level corresponding to an approximate career point. Thus, in the military profession education is spread throughout the career, whereas in most other professions the bulk of advanced education takes place at the beginning of the career (Shelburne & Groves, 1965, p. 91).

Of equal interest to the services is the relationship that attendance at professional military schools and rank in class has to success in the career. All of the services subscribe to the principle of sending the officers most qualified for promotion to school. However, there is considerable variation among and within the services in the extent to which the principle has been followed (Office of the Assistant Secretary of Defense, 1966c). Traditionally in the army, selection for professional military schooling has been considered mandatory for promotion. Until recently the air force and the navy placed less importance on professional military schooling as a factor in promotion. However, procedures for selecting all officers for attendance at schools have now become quite similar to those for selection for promotion. Consequently, it is quite likely that the correlation between school attendance and promotion will increase in the future for the armed forces as a whole (Office of the Assistant Secretary of Defense, 1966c).

The relationship between attendance at the U.S. Military and Naval academies and career success has been studied by Janowitz (1959), and his study has been backed by impressive statistics. He points out that "the most noteworthy result of the military education system has been, directly and indirectly, to reserve the preponderance of the highest military posts for the graduates of the military academies." Nevertheless, Boroff (1963b) reports that academy graduates do not control the military establishment. Janowitz' statement is based upon the large proportion of general officers who are graduates of academies. Boroff's conclusion is based upon the relatively small percentage of all officers on active duty who are graduates of the academies: in the navy 14 percent, in the army 8 percent, and in the air force 9 percent.

Nickolas (1952) studied the relationship between class standing in the U.S. Military Academy and achievement of the grade of major general or higher during the Civil War, World War I, and World War II. He found that the pattern for all three wars was the same, with the preponderance of officers with the grade of major general or higher having been in the upper levels of their graduating classes.

The Military Profession. Both within and without the armed forces there has been considerable discussion about the nature and status of the military profession. Probably the studies with the greatest depth and comprehension have been made by Huntington (1957, 1962) and Janowitz (1959, 1960). Huntington raises the question of the specialized skill that military officers possess that is not shared with civilian professions. Even though the officer corps contains a wide variety of specialists who have their counterparts in civilian life, and even though there is great variation in the duties and skills required of officers in land, sea, and air operations, there is a distinct sphere of military competence which is common to most officers and which distinguishes them from most professional civilians. This central skill, according to Huntington, is best summed up in Harold Lasswell's phrase "the management of violence." For Hackett (1961) the function of the profession of arms is "the ordered application of force."

Janowitz (1960) has pointed to the frequent reference of military officers to the linkage between their profession and the ministry. Service, dedication to a cause, and sense of mission appear to be the elements common to both professions. Carr-Saunders and Wilson (1933), on the other hand, in their comprehensive study of the professions omitted consideration of both the church and the army. Their reasoning was that many of the historical functions of the church had been taken over by other professions and that the service provided by the army was one which it was hoped would never have to be performed.

Coates and Pellegrin (1965) have discussed the meaning of professionalism and the origins and development of the military profession in the United States. Because of the concept of civilian control over the military and reliance upon the civilian soldier in the United States, the U.S. modern military profession is still faced with many problems of amateurism and semiprofessionalism. While other professions may have similar problems, the sheer magnitude of the military establishment makes the problem of military nonprofessionalism more apparent.

Freed (1966) has analyzed the professional reading and writing habits and attitudes of military officers and concluded that a high percentage of officers do not practice military scholarship to a significant degree; members of the military profession do not attend professional meetings to the extent that members of other professions do; the requirements imposed by service schools for reading and writing do not establish a firm foundation for scholarship in the military profession; and shortcomings in military scholarship militate against having officers participate in the formulation of national security policy. Freed recommended greater recognition of the officer who makes contributions to the professional literature, more stringent reading and writing requirements in the service schools, and the development of stronger faculties in the service schools.

FACULTY. Among the implications for civilian education that were derived from World War II training programs for women in the medical and nursing occupations were those concerned with instructor training (Schaffer, 1948, p. 218). Intensive programs for instructor training preceded the initial operation of a new training program. This aspect of the training program was closely related to its emergency character, but the methods used in instructing teachers in the uses of all available materials and teaching aids have significance for civilian teacher training schools. The services did more than provide the teachers with adequate materials and call them to their attention. They prepared preliminary courses of study during which the use of all training aids was demonstrated.

Masland and Radway (1957), in their analysis of service academies, war colleges, and joint schools, comment on the character of the instructional staff and conditions of service. They think that no answer will be found to the question whether teachers at the service academies should be officers or civilians; they suspect that both could do a fine or a poor job. Whether instructors are officers or civilians, they believe the more purely administrative duties performed by instructors should be greatly reduced and that they should have physical room in which to work.

Recommendations for selecting and maintaining the instructional staffs needed in wartime (Hammer, 1950, pp. 229–230) included (1) a survey of courses to determine the extent to which civilian instructors could be used; (2) a survey to determine the approximate number of instructors that would be needed, the rate at which they would be utilized, and the broad categories of assignments; (3) a national inventory of instructional manpower, which should be corrected annually; (4) a review by each service of policies concerning the use of instructors; (5) the establishment of a national voluntary instructional reserve; (6) the establishment of a reserve cadre of instructors in each service; (7) the creation of a joint army, navy, and air force office to monitor the national instructional reserve and the reserve cadre of each service; (8) the evaluation and coordination of the foregoing recommendations by the Manpower Division of the National Security Resources Board.

Air force policy stresses the responsibility that both the Air Staff and the major commands have to identify, develop, and assign competent officers as teachers (Department of the Air Force, 1966). It is also air force policy to select the faculty for the professional military schools from the best-educated officers and those of the highest caliber. The secretary of the air force has pointed out that advances made with new instructional devices have made it possible for the instructor to do more rather than forcing him to do less (H. Brown, 1966). In keeping with this point of view, the secretary cites three reasons why better instructors are needed: (1) the size and complexity of the training task, (2) the need for instructor participation in implementing new mechanical techniques, and (3) the importance of the personal influence of the instructor.

Janowitz (1960, p. 144, 1965, p. 234) found that of a sampling of military leadership made in 1950, "26 percent of Army generals had instructed at West Point, 32 percent of the admirals had instructed at Annapolis, and only 8 percent of Air Force generals had instructed at the military academy at West Point. Instruction at specialized service schools, at ROTC and Naval reserve units, at command and general staff school, and at war college, supply numerous additional teaching experiences. In all, it is a rare Army general, less than 5 percent, who has not been a teacher at some time in his career. In the Air Force more than 80 percent of the leadership samples have had some teaching experience; in the Navy almost half have had such assignments." Janowitz then discusses the nature of the instructional task in the professional military schools: "Teaching is designed to transmit not only skill but a professional orientation that involves a specialized style of life and a willingness to live with the uncertainties of military contingencies. Teaching is not merely instruction in a specific discipline or subject-matter but an indoctrination in the importance of making decisions."

A recent study of army educational programs made by the Haines Board (1966, pp. 69–72) gives careful attention to faculty selection, training, qualifications, and role. The board concluded that the faculties of the schools were competent, but commented as follows: (1) The military faculty, unlike its civilian counterpart, functions in an environment where career demands affect tenure. The officer's tour of duty on a faculty could be better stabilized if more officers with advanced degrees were used as instructors and civilian instructors were employed to teach nonmilitary subjects. (2) Teaching could be improved by making more effective use of the civilian educational advisor and by replacing a large number of second lieutenants who are instructors with officers of higher rank. (3) The schools should increase their contacts with civilian institutions and associations; and directors of instruction and educational advisors of army schools should meet annually with distinguished educators as guests, to study the military schools. (4) All army schools should have civilian educational advisors, and greater emphasis should be given to their career development.

In England, the army and the air force have a specialized corps of officers composed of schoolmen in uniform. A. C. T. White (1963) describes the instructor corps in the British Army, which was begun in 1943.

The navy stresses the importance of the role of its instructors, both enlisted and commissioned (Department of the Navy, 1964, pp. 140–144). Responsibility for instruction not only rests on personnel assigned to instructor duty but must be assumed by all commissioned and petty officers.

The military faculties of the senior-service schools and of the command and staff colleges do not have adequate academic qualifications, considering that these are graduate-level schools (Office of the Assistant Secretary of Defense, 1966c, pp. 86–87). At the level of the command and staff school particularly, there appeared to be too many faculty members who did not possess an undergraduate degree. The study of officer education cited agreed with the Haines Board that the educational adviser, as contrasted with the subject-matter specialist, had a contribution to make in the educational system of each service and that more consideration should be given to using such advisers and to their development, grade, progression in their careers, and tenure.

TRENDS AND PROBLEMS. Technical Change. In a survey of factors affecting service in the military structure in the last two decades, Sadler (1962) identified two as being the most important. The first was the increasing technical complexity of weapons and associated equipment, which implies that commanders will depend more and more for advice on subordinate specialists or on advisers outside the chain of command. Thus, technical specialization may become "one of the desirable military virtues." The second factor was the increased destructive power of weapons, which has two important effects: first, it heightens the complexity of planning and waging cold wars, and, second, it blurs the distinction between military and civilian roles because destruction threatens the civilian population as much as the armed services, and consequently the interchange of ideas between the military and the civilian community is increasing.

Increasing Educational Levels. The educational levels of the military have been increasing steadily since World War II. Masland and Radway (1957) have concluded that within a few years it is probable that officers assigned to policy-making assignments will have had more formal education and preparation for this role than civilians in comparable positions. Nearly all of the board reports have recommended increases in formal education levels of the officers either through selection for commissioning or through part-time and full-time assignments to school.

With respect to the enlisted grades, efforts are continuing to be made to increase their educational levels (Shelburne & Groves, 1965). However, a new development is taking place. The armed forces are being asked to accept large numbers of young men who heretofore were considered to be less than qualified (*U.S. News and World Report*, 1966).

The study of the education of army officers (Haines Board, 1966, pp. 101-102) concluded with the observation that most army schools are attended by both officers and enlisted men, and increasingly by civilians. Even though the ratio of enlisted students to officer students is four to one, the training of enlisted personnel has not received the amount of study that has been devoted to officers' education. A thorough study was proposed. Even though the training of army civilians is not the exclusive responsibility of the Department of the Army, the review and examination of the schooling of these civilians seem justified.

Educational Problems. The chairman of the group that conducted the latest analysis of service education (Office of the Assistant Secretary of Defense, 1966c) noted that while the service educational programs have become essential elements in the career development of the armed forces, there are areas in these educational programs needing further study, including the roles and interrelationships of the military colleges; a long-range look at officers' educational requirements for the mid-1980's; better ways of identifying, determining, and reviewing requirements for officers with advanced academic education and professional military education; developing more objective criteria for determining course lengths; improving faculties, including making greater use of civilian educational advisers; and introducing more elective courses into curricula to meet the individual needs of students. The apparent trend of centralization of authority (Shelburne & Groves, 1965, p. 107) in military training and education is also evident in programs of research and development in the Department of Defense. The disadvantages of too little replication and too little competition in innovational approaches to the solution of important problems are discussed by individuals who have been prominent in defense matters (Hitch & McKean, 1960).

Emphasis on Research. In a memorandum to the secretaries of the army, navy, and air force, the secretary of defense (McNamara, 1965) reported: "In reviewing last year's expenditure and the Five Year Force Structure and Financial Program for training and education, I have been impressed by the magnitude of the various programs and the relatively negligible funds being spent on innovation, including research and development and new methods and techniques . . . ." The secretary also asked the armed forces to examine these programs and to make recommendations for improving them.

Partly as a result of the secretary of defense's memorandum, the air force has developed Project Innovate, 1966, which includes eight major studies concerned with the application of recent advances in the areas of training and education to air force programs. This project is scheduled for completion in 1969.

Long before the secretary's memorandum, the army in 1964 began Project MINERVA, the objective of which was to develop a system which would enable a school to train more technicians better and faster with fewer resources. The results of this project should have a far-reaching impact on army training systems (Tracey, 1966).

An indication of a trend in navy education and training is the development of the Computer Assisted Instruction (CAI) research program. Regan (1966) states that within the next five years CAI capabilities will be developed in a wide variety of settings. It will be used, for example, for remedial electronics-technician training in a performance-assessment center. The navy also intends to use CAI in college-level engineering training to assist the student in the computational aspects of problem solving, as a tutor, and in providing sophisticated displays that can be manipulated by the instructor and the student. Part of the navy plan is the development of a support center to guide and assist those in the navy who wish to design computer-based instructional programs.

Janowitz (1964) reports a growing interest in research on the sociological aspects of the military profession. At present there is only a small group of specialists who have done work in this area, but their work is extensive. He comments, "There are now available more data and more analyses of the aspects of the military profession than on many other professional groups in the United States."

James C. Shelburne
Air University
Kenneth J. Groves
Air University
Leland D. Brokaw
Air Force Systems Command

References

Air Force Academy Planning Board. *Air Force Academy Planning Board Study.* 3 vols. Air U, 1949.

Air Force Educational Requirements Board. *Report on Professional Military Education.* Air U, 1963.

Air University Library Index to Military Periodicals. Published quarterly. Maxwell Air Force Base, Alabama, Air U.

Ambrose, Stephen E. *Upton and the Army.* Louisiana State U Press, 1964. 183p.

American Council on Education. *The Integrity of the Academic Degree.* ACE, 1964. 17p.

American Council on Education. *Commission on Accreditation of Service Experiences: Purposes, History, and Activity.* ACE, 1962. 11p.

American Guide Series. *A Guide to the United States Naval Academy.* Devin-Adair Company, Inc., 1941. 158p.

Ammerman, Harry L. *Development of Procedures for Deriving Training Objectives for Junior Officer Jobs.* Department of the Army, 1966. 84p.

Artemiev, V. P. "Soviet Military Educational Institutions." *Military R* 46:11–4; 1966.

Atkinson, Littleton B. *Dual Command in the Red Army 1918–1942.* Air U, 1950. 67p.

Barnett, Carelli. "The Education of Military Elites." *J Contemporary History* 2:15–35; 1967.

Berchin, Michel, and Ben-Horin, Eliahu. *The Red Army.* Norton, 1942. 277p.

Birrer, Ivan J. "Methods for Teaching Officers to Think." *Military R* 37:58–63; 1957.

Bishop, Ralph C. *A Study of the Educational Value of Military Instruction in Universities and Colleges.* U.S. Department of the Interior, USOE. GPO, 1932. 24p.

Blauch, Lloyd E. (Ed.) *Education for the Professional.* USOE, 1955. 317p.

Boroff, David. "West Point: Ancient Incubator for a New Breed." *Harpers M* 225:51–9; 1962.

Boroff, David. "Annapolis: Teaching Young Sea Dogs Old Tricks." *Harpers M* 226:46–52; 1963(a).

Boroff, David. "Air Force Academy: A Slight Gain in Altitude." *Harpers M* 226:86–98; 1963(b).

Bray, Charles W. *Psychology and Military Proficiency, A History of the Applied Psychology.* Panel of the National Defense Research Committee. Princeton U Press, 1948. 235p.

Brick, Allan. "Why Have ROTC on Campus?" *Am Assn U Prof B* 45:218–22; 1959.

Brossman, Martin W. (Ed.) *Proceedings Fourth Symposium on War Gaming.* AD 468994. Research Analysis Corporation (McLean, Virginia), 1965. 283p.

Brown, G. H., and Vineburg, R. *A Follow-up Study of Experimentally and Conventionally Trained Field Radio Repairmen.* Technical Report 65, AD-245 468. Human Resources Research Office, George Washington U, 1960.

Brown, G. H., and others. *Development and Evaluation of an Improved Field Radio Repair Course.* Technical Report 58, AD-227-173. Human Resources Research Office. George Washington U, 1959.

Brown, Harold. "Innovation and the Air Force Instructor." *USAF Instructors J* 4:6–8; Summer 1966.

Buchter, Richard F. *The Education of the Professional Soviet Air Force Officer.* Air U, 1965. 54p.

Bush, Vannevar. *Endless Horizons.* Public Affairs Press, 1946. 179p.

Carr-Saunders, A. M., and Wilson, D. A. *The Professions.* Clarendon, 1933. 536p.

Cartter, Allan M. (Ed.) *American Universities and Colleges,* 9th ed. ACE, 1964. 1339p.

Cattell, Raymond B. "Confirmation and Clarification of Primary Personality Factors." *Psychometrika* 12:197–220; 1947.

Chambers, M. M. "Armed Forces Educational Programs." In Monroe, Walter S. (Ed.) *Encyclopedia of Educational Research.* Rev. ed. Macmillan, 1950. p. 58–64.

Chapman, William C. "Soviet Military Correspondence and Evening Courses." *U.S. Naval Institute Proc* 90:140–2; 1964.

Clark, Harold F., and Sloan, Harold S. *Classrooms in the Military.* Teachers Col, Columbia U, 1964. 154p.

Coates, Charles H., and Pellegrin, Roland J. *Military Sociology.* Social Science Press, 1965. 424p.

Cockell, William A. "New Approaches to Officer Training in the U.S.S.R." *U.S. Naval Institute Proc* 86:138–41; 1960.

Cockle, Maurice J. D. *A Bibliography of Military Books up to 1642.* 2nd ed. Holland Press, 1957.

Committee on Armed Services. *Unification and Strategy.* GPO, 1950. 59p.

Connelly, Charles H. "Integration in the Air Tactical School Curriculum." Doctoral dissertation. U Chicago, 1950. 235p.

Cook Board. *Report by the Ad Hoc Committee to the Chief of Naval Personnel on Naval Officer Education* (Cook Report). Bureau of Naval Personnel, Department of the Navy, 1959.

Counts, George S. *The Challenge of Soviet Education.* McGraw-Hill, 1957. 330p.

Crane, John, and Kieley, James F. *United States Naval Academy.* McGraw-Hill, 1945. 53p.

Crawford, M. P. "Concepts of Training." In Gagné, Robert. (Ed.) *Psychological Principles in System Development.* Holt, 1962. p. 301–42.

Culp, W. W. "Resident Courses of Instruction." *Military R* 36:15–21; 1956.

Curtiss, John Shelton. *The Russian Army Under Nicholas I, 1825–1855.* Duke U Press, 1965. 386p.

Dailey, John T. "Development and Applications of Tests of Educational Achievement." *R Ed Res* 23:102–9; 1953.

Daly Board. *The Army School System, Report of Board of Officers.* Headquarters, U.S. Continental Army Command, Fort Monroe, Virginia, 1962.

Department of the Air Force. *United States Air Force Officer Professional Military Education System.* The Department, 1966. 25p.

Department of the Air Force. *Innovations in Training and Education.* The Department, 1967.

Department of the Air Force, Office of Aerospace Research. "Programmed Instruction." In *U.S. Air Force Achievements in Research*. The Department, 1965(a).

Department of the Air Force, Office of Aerospace Research. "Simulation of International Relations." In *U.S. Air Force Achievements in Research*. The Department, 1965(b). 156p.

Department of the Air Force, Special Advisory Committee on the United States Air Force Academy. *Report to the Secretary and Chief of Staff of the Air Force*. The Department, 1965. 94p.

Department of the Army, *Handbook on the Soviet Army*. GPO, 1958. 260p.

Department of the Army. *Marginal Man and Military Service: A Review*. The Department, 1965. 270p.

Department of the Army, Personnel Research Branch. *Personnel Research for the United States Military Academy, 1942–1953*. The Department, 1953.

Department of the Army, ROTC. *American Military History, 1607–1953*. GPO, 1959. 509p.

Department of Defense. *Annual Report, Department of Defense, for Fiscal Year 1964*. GPO, 1966. 432p.

Department of Defense and others. *Proceedings of the Engineering Systems for Education and Training Conference*. The Department, USOE, National Security Industrial Association, 1966. 166p.

Department of the Navy, Bureau of Naval Personnel. *Education and Training*. The Department, 1964.

Dupuy, R. Ernest, and Dupuy, Trevor W. *Military Heritage of America*. McGraw-Hill, 1956. 794p.

Eachus, Herbert T. "Self Confrontation for Complex Skill Training, Review and Analysis." AD 624-062. Aerospace Medical Research Laboratories, Wright-Patterson Air Force Base, 1965.

Eachus, Herbert T., and others. "Acquisition and Retention of Cross-cultural Interaction Skills Through Self-Confrontation." AD 637-719. Air Force Systems Command, Wright-Patterson Air Force Base. 1966.

Earle, Edward Mead. (Ed.) *Makers of Modern Strategy*. Princeton U Press, 1944. 553p.

Eberstadt Report. *Unification of the War and Navy Departments and Postwar Organization for National Security*. Report to Secretary of the Navy. GPO, 1945. 251p.

Eckstrand, G. A. *Current Status of the Technology of Training*. Aerospace Medical Research Laboratories, Wright-Patterson Air Force Base, 1964.

Eddy Board. *Report of the Department of the Army Board on the Educational System for Officers*. Department of the Army, Office of the Adjutant General, 1949.

Ekirch, Arthur A., Jr. *The Civilian and the Military*. Oxford U Press, 1956. 340p.

Erickson, John. *The Soviet High Command*. St Martin's Press, Inc., 1962. 889p.

Eure, Leroy T. "Development of War Gaming in the Naval War College: 1886–1958." Naval War Col, 1959(a). 6p. (Unpublished paper.)

Eure, Leroy T. *History of U.S. Military War Colleges*. Naval War Col, 1959(b). 14p.

Fairchild Board. *Report of the USAF Military Education Board on the Professional Education System for USAF Officers*. Maxwell Air Force Base, Air U, 1950.

Finney, Robert T. *History of the Air Corps School*. USAF Historical Studies No. 100. Research Studies Institute, Air U, Maxwell Air Force Base, 1955. 90p.

Fiske, D. W. "Consistency of the Factorial Structures of Personality Ratings from Different Sources." *J Abn Social Psychol* 44:329–44; 1949.

Flanagan, John C. (Ed.) *The Aviation Psychology Program in the Army Air Forces*. AAF Aviation Psychology Program Research Reports, No. 1. GPO, 1948. 316p.

Flanagan, John C., and others. "Psychological Research in the Armed Forces." *R Ed Res* 18:528–654; 1948.

Foley, J. P., Jr. *Performance Testing: Testing for What is Real*. AMRL Memorandum P-42. 6570th Aerospace Medical Research Laboratories, Wright-Patterson Air Force Base, 1963.

Foley, J. P., Jr. *Functional Fundamental Training for Electronic Maintenance Personnel*. AMRL Technical Report 85, AD-610 367. Behavioral Sciences Laboratory, Wright-Patterson Air Force Base, 1964.

Foot, M. D. R. *Men in Uniform*. Weidenfeld and Nicolson, 1961. 163p.

Freed, Debow. "The Sorry State of Military Scholarship." In *Air War College Supplement*. Vol. 5, No. 1. Air U, 1966.

Fursdon, F. W. E. "The Rationalization of Higher Officer Training in the British Army." *J Roy United Service Institutions* 109:131–5; 1964.

Gellner, John. "Service Unification in Canada." *Military R* 47:3–8; 1967.

"General Service Schools." In *Encyclopedia Americana*, Vol. 2. 1963. p. 300–1.

Gerow Board. *Report of the War Department Military Education Board on the Educational System for Officers of the Army*. U.S. Army Command and General Staff School, 1946. 90p.

Ginsberg, Eli, and others. *The Ineffective Soldier*. Vols. 1–3. Columbia U Press, 1959.

Glaser, Robert. (Ed.) *Training Research and Education*. U Pittsburgh Press, 1962. 596p.

Gleaves, Albert. *Life and Letters of Rear Admiral Stephen B. Luce*. Putnam, 1925. 381p.

Glickman, A. E., and Kipnis, D. *Theoretical Considerations in the Development and Use of a Noncognitive Battery*. Naval Personnel Research Field Activity, 1960.

Godwin-Austen, Alfred R. *The Staff and the Staff College*. Constable & Co., 1927. 319p.

Goodman, Samuel Myron. *Curriculum Implications of Armed Services Educational Programs*. Commission on Implications of Armed Services Educational Programs. ACE, 1947. 101p.

Grace, Alonzo G., and others. *Educational Lessons from Wartime Training*. The General Report of the Commission on Implications of Armed Services Educational Programs. ACE, 1948. 264p.

Green, Edith. *The Federal Government and Educa-*

tion. House Document No. 159. 88th Congress, 1st Session, 1963. 178p.

Hackett, John Winthrop, "The Education of the Officer." *J Roy United Service Institutions* 106:32–51; 1961.

Hackett, John Winthrop. *The Profession of Arms.* London Times, 1963. 68p.

Hahn, Clifford P. *The Development and Validation of Situational Problems for Training Effective Performance as a Junior Officer.* Office of Naval Research, 1956.

Haines, Donald B., and others. *A Preliminary Study of Acquiring Cross-cultural Instruction Skills Through Self-confrontation.* Aerospace Medical Research Laboratories, 1965.

Haines Board. *Report of the Development of the Army Board to Review Army Officer Schools.* 3 vols. Headquarters, Department of the Army, 1966. 840p.

Hammer, Wendell A. "Instructional Personnel in Wartime Schools of the Defense Establishment." Doctoral dissertation. U Southern California, 1950. 270p.

Hans, N. "Military Education." In *The Secondary School Curriculum.* World Bk, 1958. p. 412–20.

Harlow, B. N. "Training for Military Service." *Annals of the AAPSS* 220:29–49; 1942.

Harris, Benjamin T. "Nonresident Instruction." *Military R* 36:51–7; 1956.

Hickey, Albert E., and Newton, John M. "Computer-assisted Instruction: A Survey of the Literature." Office of Naval Research, 1966.

Hitch, Charles J., and McKean, Roland N. *The Economies of Defense in the Nuclear Age.* Harvard U Press, 1960. 422p.

Hitchcock, John H. "Comment and Discussion." *U.S. Naval Institute Proc* 91:12–5; 1965.

Hittle, J. D. *The Military Staff: Its History and Development,* Military Service Publishing Co., 1961. 326p.

Holloway Board. *Report on Naval Officer Education.* Bureau of Naval Personnel, Department of the Navy, 1945.

Hovland, Carl I., and others. *Experiments on Mass Communication,* Vol. 3. Princeton U Press, 1949. 345p.

Howland, John S. "Military and Academic Education of Armed Forces Officers." In *Self and Service Enrichment Through Federal Training.* GPO, 1967. p. 500–12.

Huntington, Samuel P. *The Soldier and the State.* Belknap Press, 1957. 534p.

Huntington, Samuel P. (Ed.) *Changing Patterns of Military Politics.* Free, 1962. 272p.

Jackson, J. I. "Professional Education in the R.C.A.F." *RCAF Staff Col J* p. 63–6; 1957.

Janowitz, Morris. *Sociology and the Military Establishment.* Russell Sage, 1959. 136p.

Janowitz, Morris. *The Professional Soldier.* Free, 1960. 464p.

Janowitz, Morris. (Ed.) *The New Military.* Russell Sage, 1964. 369p.

Janowitz, Morris, and Little, Roger. *Sociology and the Military Establishment.* Russell Sage, 1965. 136p.

Jessup, Philip C. *Elihu Root,* Vol. 1. Dodd, 1938. 563p.

Joffe, Ellis. *Party and Army: Professionalism and Control in the Chinese Officer Corps, 1949–1964.* East Asian Research Center, Harvard U, 1965. 198p.

Johnson, Robert K. "Characteristics of Libraries in Selected Higher Military Educational Institutions in the United States." Doctoral dissertation. U Illinois, 1957. 367p.

Johnson, Robert K. "Resources of Selected American Military Libraries." *Lib Q* 32:40–50; 1962.

Joint Chiefs of Staff. *General Plan for Postwar Joint Education of All Armed Forces.* JCS 962/2. Department of Defense, 1945.

Joint Chiefs of Staff. Memorandum to commandants of the five senior service colleges. Department of Defense, 1966.

Joint Chiefs of Staff, Special Committee. *Report of the Joint Chiefs of Staff Special Commander for Reorganization of National Defense.* Hearings Before the Senate Committee on Military Affairs on S. 84 and S. 1482. 79th Congress, 1st Session, 1945. p. 411–33.

Katzenbach, Edward L., Jr. "The Demotion of Professionalism at the War Colleges." *U.S. Naval Institute Proc* 91:34–41; 1965.

Knox-King-Pye Board. *Report on Naval Officer Education.* Bureau of Naval Personnel, Department of the Navy, 1919.

Lemieux, C. P. "Soviet Officer Training." *U.S. Naval Institute Proc* 90:137–9; 1964.

Liu, F. F. *A Military History of Modern China.* Princeton U Press, 1956. 312p.

Lory, Hillis. *Japan's Military Masters.* Viking, 1943. 256p.

Luce, Stephen B. "War Schools." *U.S. Naval Institute Proc* 9:633–57; 1883.

Ludlow Report. *Principles and Practical Methods Pursued by German and Other Armies of Europe.* Report submitted to the Adjutant General. Department of the Army, 1901.

Luvaas, Jay. *The Education of an Army: British Military Thought 1815–1940.* U Chicago Press, 1964. 454p.

Lyons, Gene M., and Masland, John W. *Education and Military Leadership: A Study of the ROTC.* Princeton U Press, 1959. 283p.

Majumdar, B. N. "The Selection and Training of Officers in a Modern Army." *Army Q* 83:81–9; 1961.

Malinovsky, R. Y. "Soviet Military Education." *Survival* 8:354–9; 1966.

Marshall, Max L. "A Survey of Military Periodicals." Doctoral dissertation. U Missouri, 1953. 356p.

Masland, John W., and Radway, L. I. *Soldiers and Scholars.* Princeton U Press, 1957. 530p.

McClendon, R. Earl. *Unification of the Armed Forces: Administration and Legislative Developments, 1945–1949.* Air U Research Studies Institute, Maxwell Air Force Base, 1952. 169p.

McHugh, Francis J. "War Gaming and the Navy Electronic Warfare Simulator." *Naval War Col R* 19:22–32; 1967.

McNamara, Robert S. *Innovation in Defense Training and Education.* Memorandum. Department of Defense, 1965.

Miles, John R., and Spain, Charles R. *Audio-visual Aids in the Armed Services.* ACE, 1947. 76p.

Military Intelligence Division. "Training of German General Staff Officers." War Department, 1946. 276p.

Military Review. "Other Staff Colleges." 36:77–112; 1956.

Morganti, Clyde J., and others. *Report of the Ad Hoc Committee for Review of Basic Military Training.* Department of the Air Force, 1966.

Morris, Thomas D. "Keynote Address." In *Proceedings of the Engineering Systems for Education and Training Conference.* Department of Defense, 1966. p. 7–13.

Morsh, J. E. *Identification of Job Types in the Personnel Career Field.* PRL-TR-65-9, AD-622 433. Personnel Research Laboratory, Aerospace Medical Division, Lackland Air Force Base, 1965.

Morsh, J. E., and Christal, R. E. "Impact of the Computer on Job Analysis in the United States Air Force." *Am Psychologist* 21:676–7; 1966.

Newman, Strode. "Academic Degrees in Military Colleges." *Army* 12:65–7; 1961.

Nickolas, Charles P. "Six Hundred and Eighteen Major Generals." *Assembly* (quarterly alumni magazine of the Association of Graduates, U.S. Military Academy) 10:10–1; January 1952.

Norman, W. T. *Development of Self-report Tests to Measure Personality Factors Identified from Peer Nominations.* ASD-TN-61-44, AD-267 779. Personnel Laboratory, Aeronautical Systems Division. 1961(a).

Norman, W. T. *Problems of Response Contamination in Personality Assessment.* Personnel Laboratory, Aeronautical Systems Division, 1961(b).

Norman, W. T. *Validation of Personality Tests as Measures of Trait Rating Factors.* Laboratory, Aerospace Medical Division, 1962.

Norton, John K. "Armed Forces Educational Programs." In Harris, Chester W. (Ed.) *Encyclopedia of Educational Research,* 3rd ed. Macmillan, 1960. p. 526–8.

Office of the Assistant Secretary of Defense. *Department of Defense, Occupational Conversion Table—Enlisted.* The Office, 1966(a).

Office of the Assistant Secretary of Defense. *Department of Defense, Occupational Conversion Table —Officers.* The Office, 1966(b).

Office of the Assistant Secretary of Defense. *Officer Education Study.* The Office, 1966(c). 592p.

Office of the Secretary of Defense. *Report of the Working Group on Human Behavior Under Conditions of Military Service.* The Office, 1951. 425p.

Orleans, Jacob S. *U.S. Army Command and General Staff College Educational Survey Commission Report.* Department of the Army, 1956. 131p.

Ortlieb. E. J. "Defense Systems Analysis Education Program." *United States Naval Institute Proc* 92: 148–50; 1966.

Palit, D. K. *The Essentials of Military Knowledge.* Gale & Polden, Ltd., 1950. 140p.

Paul, Norman S. *Nation's Manpower Resolution.* Part 8 of the hearings before the Subcommittee on Employment and Manpower. Senate Committee on Labor and Public Welfare, 88th Congress, 1st Session, 1964. 257p.

Pickering, E. J., and Anderson, A. V. *A Performance-oriented Electronics Technician Training Program,* 1. *Course Development and Implementation.* Department of the Navy, 1966.

Pokrovsky, G. I. *Science and Technology in Contemporary War.* Praeger, 1959. 180p.

Power Board. *Report of the USAF Educational Conference.* Air U, 1959. 91p.

Pruck, Erich F. "Officer Training in the Soviet Army." *Military R,* 44:61–6; 1964.

Pye Board. *Report on Naval Officers' Education.* Bureau of Naval Personnel, Department of the Navy, 1944.

Radway, L. I. "Military Behavior in International Organization: NATO's Defense College." In Huntington, Samuel P. (Ed.) *Changing Patterns of Military Politics.* Free, 1962. p. 101–20.

Rao, M. K. "Academic Recognition of Military Education." *United Service India J* April–June: 56–70; 1965.

Ratliff, Forrest R. "Soviet Developments in Programmed Learning and Teaching Machines." *USAF Instructors' J* 4:14–20; Summer 1966.

Rawlings Board. *Report of the USAF Educational Conference.* Maxwell Air Force Base, Air U, 1956. 106p.

Regan, James J. "Navy Plans for Computer Assisted Instruction (CAI)." In *Proceedings of the Engineering Systems for Education and Training Conference.* Department of Defense, 1966. p. 145–7.

Reeves, Ira Louis. *Military Education in the United States.* Free, 1914.

Report on the NATO Military Education Conference and Basic Planning Data. Supreme Headquarters, Allied Powers Europe, Paris, 1962. 121p.

Ridenour Report. *Research and Development in the United States Air Force.* Report of a special committee of the Scientific Advisory Board to the Chief of Staff. Department of the Air Force, 1949.

Rundquist, Edward A. "Course Design Manual for Job Training Courses" (preliminary ed.) Navy Training Research Laboratory Research Report SRR 66-17. Department of the Navy, 1966.

Russell, John Dale. (Ed.) *Higher Education Under War Conditions,* Vol. 15. Proceedings of the Institute for Administrative Officers of Higher Institutions, 1943. U Chicago Press, 1943. 159p.

Sadler, P. J. "Technical Change and Military Social Structure." In *Defense Psychology.* Pergamon, 1962. p. 312–6.

Sanders, Jennings B. "The Granting of Academic Degrees by Federal Institutions." *H Ed* 11:130–4; 1955.

Schaffer, Dorothy. *What Comes of Training Women*

for War? Commission on Implications of Armed Services Educational Programs. ACE, 1948. 223p.

Service Academy Board. *Report and Recommendation to the Secretary of Defense by the Service Academy Board.* Department of Defense, 1950. 82p.

Shaughnessy, Thomas E. "Beginnings of National Professional Military Education in America, 1775–1825." Doctoral dissertation. Johns Hopkins U, 1956. 222p.

Shelburne, James C. "Factors Leading to the Establishment of the Air University." Doctoral dissertation. U Chicago, 1953. 289p.

Shelburne, James C. "The Establishment of the Air University." *Sch Soc* 80:33–6; 1954.

Shelburne, James C., and Groves, Kenneth J. *Education in the Armed Forces.* Center for Applied Research in Education, 1965. 118p.

Simons, William E. *Liberal Education in the Service Academies.* Teachers Col, Columbia U, 1965. 230p.

Smith, R. G., Jr. *Controlling the Quality of Training.* Technical Report 65-6, AD-618 737. Human Resources Research Office, George Washington U, 1966(*a*).

Smith, R. G., Jr. *The Development of Training Objectives.* Research Bulletin 11, AD-448 364. Human Resources Research Office, George Washington U, 1966(*b*).

Snider, E. C. "Canada Leads the Way in Tri-service Education." *J Roy United Service Institution* 101:42–7; 1956.

Social Science Research Council. *Studies in Social Psychology in World War II,* 4 vols. Princeton U Press, 1950. 722p.

Special Devices Center. Instructional Film Research, 1918–1950. The Center, 1950.

Stolurow, Lawrence. "Model the Master Teacher or Master the Teaching." In Krumboltz, John O. (Ed.) *Learning and the Educational Process.* Rand McNally, 1965. p. 223–49.

Svenson, Elwin V., and Sheats, Paul H. "Audio-visual Aids in Adult Education." *R Ed Res* 20:216–23; 1950.

Tracey, William R. "Project MINERVA, A Systems Model for Military Instruction." In *Proceedings of the Engineering Systems for Education and Training Conference.* Department of Defense, 1966. p. 105–10.

Truman, Harry S. "Special Message to the Congress Recommending the Establishment of a Department of National Defense." In *Public Papers of the President of the United States, Harry S. Truman, 1945.* GPO, 1961. 668p.

Tupes, E. C. *Relationships Between Behavior Trait Ratings by Peers and Later Officer Performance of USAF Officer Candidate School Graduates.* AFPTRC-TN-57-125, AD-134 257. Air Force Personnel and Training Research Center, Lackland Air Force Base, 1957.

Tupes, E. C., and Christal, R. E. *Recurrent Personality Factors Based on Trait Ratings.* ASD-TR-61-97, AD-267 778. Personnel Laboratory, Aeronautical Systems Division, Lackland Air Force Base, 1961.

Turner, Gordon B. (Ed.) *A History of Military Affairs in Western Society Since the 18th Century.* Harcourt, 1952. 776p.

Tyler, Ralph W. "Acceptance of Military Experience Toward College Credit." In Russel, John Dale. (Ed.) *Higher Education Under War Conditions.* Vol. 15. Proceedings of the Institute for Administrative Officers of Higher Institutions. U. Chicago Press, 1943. p. 107–16.

Tyler, Ralph W., and others. *Analysis of the Purpose, Scope and Structure of the Officer Education Program of Air University.* Technical Memorandum OERL-TM-55-6. Officer Education Research Laboratory, Air Research and Develop Command, Maxwell Air Force Base, 1955. 260p.

United States Air Force Academy. Hearings before the Committee on Armed Services, U.S. Senate, 83rd Congress, 2nd Session, H.R. 5337; February 18 and 19, 1954. 72p.

U.S. Military Academy, Department of Economics, Government, and History. *United States Military Academy and Its Foreign Contemporaries.* The Department, 1943. 104p.

U.S. News and World Report. "McNamara's Plan for Rejectees." 61:26–7; 1966.

U.S. Office of Education. "Federal Government." In *Education Directory 1962–1963.* USOE, 1963.

Upton, Emory. *The Armies of Asia and Europe.* Appleton, 1878. 376p.

Upton, Emory. *The Military Policy of the United States.* GPO, 1917. 495p.

Vagts, Alfred. *A History of Militarism: Romance and Realities of a Profession.* Norton, 1937. 590p.

Vagts, Alfred. *A History of Militarism.* Meridian Books, Inc., 1959. 542p.

Valentine, Wilson. "Officers' Training in the Russian Navy." *U.S. Naval Institute Proc* 85:113–4; 1959.

Van Riper, Paul P. "A Survey of Materials for the Study of Military Management." *Am Political Sci R* 49:828–50; 1955.

Verrier, Anthony. *An Army for the Sixties.* Secker & Warburg, Ltd., 1966. 258p.

Walen, W. W. "The Russian Air Force Academy." *Talon* 4:8–10; 1959.

Weakley-Daniel Board. *Report on Naval Officer Education.* Department of the Navy, 1956.

White, A. C. T. *The Story of Army Education in 1943–1963.* Harrap, 1963. 286p.

White, D. Fedotoff. *The Growth of the Red Army* Princeton U Press, 1944. 486p.

Wilkinson, Spencer. *The Brain of an Army.* Macmillan, 1889. 115p.

Wilkinson, Spencer. *The Nation's Servants: Three Essays on Education of Officers.* Constable & Co., Ltd., 1916.

Wilkinson, Spencer. *Thirty-five Years: 1874–1909.* Constable & Co., Ltd., 1933. 319p.

Will Board. *Report on Naval Officer Education,* Department of the Navy, 1948.

Willeman, L. P. *Prediction of Officer Performance.* Technical Research Report 1134. Personnel Research Office, Department of the Army, 1964.

Williams Board. *Report of the Department of the*

Army Officer Education and Training Review Board. Department of the Army, 1958. 260p.

Wilson, N. Scarlyn. *Education in the Forces, 1939–1946*. Evans, 1950. 173p.

Wool, Harold. "The Armed Services as a Training Institution." In Ginzberg, Eli. (Ed.) *The Nation's Children*, Vol. 2. Columbia U Press, 1959. p. 158–85.

MODERN LANGUAGES

In the years since Birkmaier's (1960) comprehensive article that outlined the history, rationale, and present status of modern-language instruction and reviewed the major results of research, there has been a consolidation of the trends outlined by her. Because of plentiful support from the U.S. government and other sources, and because of increasing interest on the part of educators and the lay public, modern-language instruction has attained an even firmer place in the school curriculum at all levels. Americans have become more "foreign-language minded" and enrollments have continued to grow. More concern has been shown for better language-learning materials and better training of teachers. While many basic questions remain unanswered, there has also been a quickening of interest in research, and a number of valuable studies have been completed and reported. This article will limit itself to updating Birkmaier's review and tracing the recent accomplishments of educational research in the field of modern languages. Attention will also be paid to developments in the teaching of English as a second or foreign language.

BIBLIOGRAPHY. The single most useful source on research in language teaching, covering the years 1945–1964, is provided by Nostrand and others (1965). Walters (1965) has compiled references on psycholinguistics and the psychology of language teaching. Periodic abstract coverage was for some years provided by the publication *MLabstracts;* this service is now rendered by *Language and Language Behavior Abstracts*. In Britain this was done by *English Teaching Abstracts,* now succeeded by *Language Teaching Abstracts*. Annual selective bibliographies have appeared in *Publications of the Modern Language Association;* from 1967, topical bibliographies appear in each issue of *Foreign Language Annals,* a publication of the American Council on the Teaching of Foreign Languages. Two Educational Resources Information Centers (ERIC) have been established to serve the interests of teachers and researchers in modern languages. The Clearinghouse on the Teaching of Foreign Languages at the Modern Language Association in New York is concerned with general foreign-language-teaching methodology and methods and materials in the "commonly taught" languages—French, German, Italian, Russian, and Spanish. The Clearinghouse for Linguistics and Uncommonly Taught Languages at the Center for Applied Linguistics in Washington, D.C., deals with applied linguistics, methods, and materials in languages other than the five previously mentioned, and English as a second language. Large numbers of references are cited and analyzed in the summaries in the *Review of Educational Research* by Birkmaier (1958), Johnston (1961), Sawyer (1964), and Birkmaier and Lange (1967). Summaries of research have also been provided by Carroll (1963, 1966) and Ornstein and Lado (1967). Useful collections of articles on various problems of foreign-language teaching are those of Libbish (1964), Müller (1965), and Valdman (1966). Bibliographies of research and other materials relevant to the teaching of English as a second or foreign language have been compiled by Ohannessian and others (1964) and in the *Newsletter* of the Teachers of English to Speakers of Other Languages.

HISTORY. The history of foreign-language instruction in the United States for the period 1940–1960 was comprehensively treated by Moulton (1961). The MLA Foreign Language Program commissioned a series of histories of the teaching of specific languages: French (Watts, 1963), German (Zeydel, 1961), Italian (Fucilla, 1967), Russian (Parry, 1967), and Spanish (Leavitt, 1961). In every case it was shown that the teaching of these languages has roots that go back to the very early days of the country. Kendall (1961) summarized the history of foreign languages in the elementary schools from 1921 to 1950.

PRESENT STATUS. As of 1959-60 (the latest year for which detailed information is available), enrollments in foreign languages in elementary schools, grades K through 8, totaled 1,227,006, of which 61.5 percent were in Spanish, 34.2 percent in French, 2.1 percent in German, and the small remainder in such languages as Latin, Italian, Russian, and Japanese (Breunig, 1961). Typically these elementary-school programs start in grade 3 or 4, but some start as early as kindergarten. Enrollment statistics for secondary school have been published annually by the MLA. In 1964, 26.2 percent of all 11,075,343 high school students were enrolled in some foreign language (Dershem & others, 1966): 12.3 percent in Spanish, 10.8 percent in French, 2.6 percent in German, 0.2 percent in Italian, 0.2 percent in Russian, and a small remainder in other languages. These percentages are generally higher than they have ever been except (in the case of French and German, at least) in the early part of the century when high schools were more selective in their student bodies. The percentage enrolled in Latin was 5.3 percent in 1964 as compared to 7.8 percent in 1958, 16 percent in 1934, 37.3 percent in 1915, and 50.2 percent in 1905, but even the 1964 percentage represents an enrollment of some 600,000.

Despite increasing numbers of high school foreign-language students and increasing lengths of time that the typical student spends in foreign-language study, only about one-third of all liberal arts programs in colleges and universities have a foreign-language requirement for admission. This proportion seems, however, to be increasing slightly, from 28.5 percent in 1957 to 33.6 percent in 1966 (Lund & Herslow, 1966). The percentage of liberal arts institutions having a foreign-language requirement for graduation has remained high: in 1966 it was 88.9 percent as compared with 84.8 percent for 1957. In the academic year 1964-65 there were more than 12,000 students in colleges and universities "majoring" in a foreign language (Carroll & others, 1967), and that number had increased markedly over the preceding five years. All but 11 of the 208 universities surveyed by Lund and Herslow (1966) had a foreign-language requirement of some sort for the Ph.D. degree.

The Foreign Language Program initiated in 1953 with the support of the Rockefeller Foundation and conducted by the Modern Language Association continued to flourish. Many of the researches and publications to be mentioned later in this review stemmed from this program. In 1967 the Modern Language Association provided leadership in forming the American Council of Teachers of Foreign Languages (ACTFL), which sponsored a new publication in the foreign-language field, *Foreign Language Annals*. Established in 1959 with the support of funds from the Ford Foundation, the Center for Applied Linguistics facilitated cooperation among linguists, modern-language teachers, educational psychologists, government agencies, and others concerned with modern-language instruction. It publishes a newsletter, the *Linguistic Reporter*, and many books, pamphlets, and articles on modern-language instruction. It fostered the formation, in 1966, of an association of Teachers of English to Speakers of Other Languages.

The U.S. government continued to play a large role in the development of modern-language instruction, allocating funds chiefly through the National Defense Education Act of 1958 for numerous programs of teacher education, materials development, and research in modern-language instruction. Its achievements, summarized by Diekhoff (1965), were "some very significant changes in language education," including increased offerings and enrollments in modern languages at all levels, improvement of the quality of these programs, redefinition of objectives, support of advanced training for teachers, development of new texts and materials of instruction in a wide variety of languages, installation of language-laboratory facilities in thousands of schools, and stimulation of the study of unusual languages. Above all, according to Diekhoff, "the myth that Americans cannot be good linguists has been exploded."

Other branches of the government have become more interested in language teaching and research on language teaching—the Foreign Service Institute of the U.S. Department of State, the Peace Corps, various branches of the armed services, etc. Business and industry have recognized the value of language training for employees in overseas work, and for scientists and technicians who must keep abreast of scientific publications in foreign languages.

OBJECTIVES. Curricula at all levels are tuned to the "new key" in foreign-language teaching, which prescribes that the primary objectives of that teaching are an equal mastery of the four traditional skills: speaking, listening, reading, and writing, up to levels commensurate with the student's ability and the amount of time available in a foreign-language program. A typical syllabus for secondary school, for example, specifies "main linguistic objectives" as "to understand a native speaker speaking at normal tempo on a subject within the range of pupils' experiences, to speak sufficiently to make direct contact with a native . . . , to read with direct understanding material on a general subject and on a subject within pupils' experiences, to write without conscious reference to English, whatever pupils can say" (New York State Education Department, 1961). This syllabus points out that "it is felt that the audiolingual competencies should receive greater emphasis than in the past, while retaining the goals of competency in reading and writing skills, together with a familiarity with literature and aspects of culture and civilization," and that "these competencies cannot be achieved in the typical program of two to three years of a foreign language beginning in grades 9 or 10" (New York State Education Department, 1961). "Main cultural objectives," besides the furtherance of general education, are "a recognition of the universality of human experience, a knowledge of [the nations where the foreign language is spoken] in terms of their significant geographical, political and cultural features, their heritage, their unique contributions to Western civilization, an understanding of the relationships between [those nations] and our own, and of our mutual interdependence, a sympathetic understanding of the peoples of [those nations] through insights into their characteristics and behavior patterns, cultural and esthetic appreciations for individual growth, and an understanding of language in itself as a manifestation of culture." At the college and university level, knowledge and appreciation of literature are still stressed, but there has been an increasing acceptance of audiolingual objectives. Curricular change occurring on the elementary- and secondary-school levels has significantly affected curriculum and objectives at the college level, not only because of the increasing diffusion and acceptance of the audiolingual philosophy but also because students on reaching college are better prepared in foreign languages and make higher demands of their college foreign-language courses. The effect of this curricular change can be seen, for example, in higher score norms on speaking and listening tests for students who have taken courses with an audiolingual emphasis as opposed to a traditional emphasis (Educational Testing Service, 1965).

LINGUISTIC AND PSYCHOLOGICAL THEORY. There has been much attention given to the general ways in which linguistics and psychology might help in language teaching, but no great progress has been made in actually specifying principles and rules (Halliday & others, 1965; Rivers, 1964;

Belyayev, 1964; Lambert, 1963; Carroll, 1965). In discussing the field of applied linguistics, Ferguson (1966) suggests two major directions for research: (1) contrastive linguistics and (2) principles for ordering and grading foreign-language learning material with respect to difficulty. The contrastive study of the structures of two languages should be helpful in anticipating the kinds of problems the speaker of one language will have in learning the other. Already example, those of English and German by Moulton many contrastive studies have been published—for (1962) and Kufner (1962); a bibliography of contrastive studies was prepared by Hammer (1965). That a contrastive study will indeed predict at least some of the learning difficulties in phonology, grammar, or lexicon has been demonstrated by Theivananthampillai (1965) for Tamil speakers learning English, but there has still been no rigorous demonstration that the identifying of such difficulties actually aids at any point in the teaching and learning process. Many language courses appear to be successful even though little explicit reference is made to the contrasts between the target language and the learners' native language.

Transformational grammar as developed by Chomsky (1957, 1965) describes language structure in terms of three components: (1) a *phrase-structure grammar* that specifies basic structures such as noun phrases, verb phrases, and their collocations in simple declarative sentences; (2) a *transformational component* that specifies rules by which the basic structures may be transformed or combined into various more complicated structures (interrogative sentences, imperatives, negatives, sentences with "embedded" structures in the form of relative clauses, etc.); and (3) a *morphophonemic component* that specifies how deep, abstract structures are actualized in terms of sounds. Transformational grammar thus appears to offer principles for describing syntactic complexity, and it has been speculated that such principles may be of use in ordering language-learning materials—e.g., by first introducing simple phrase structures and then showing how more complicated structures can arise. Texts based on this idea have begun to appear. On the other hand, Saporta (1966) points out that a transformational grammar is not necessarily immediately convertible into a pedagogical grammar; as a practical matter, some higher-order rules (those of the phonology) would have to be taught before some lower-order rules. The major contribution of generative transformational grammar is to make explicit the nature of the competence that must be taught, not to specify how that competence should be taught.

The advent of transformational grammatical theory has aroused much controversy as to whether the accounts of language learning offered by behavioristic ("stimulus–response") psychologists (e.g., Skinner, 1957) are adequate (Chomsky, 1959, 1966). Chomsky's view is that language behavior is stimulus-free and innovative; it is based not on a habit structure but on a system of rules which the individual somehow acquires. The approach of the traditional grammarian was to try to specify these rules; in second-language learning this presents difficulties because actual linguistic behavior does not depend upon conscious application of rules. In contrast, the audiolingual method presents quantities of linguistic material for the individual to memorize and imitate; its relative success can apparently be attributed to the fact that the learner is somehow able to induce and internalize the rules of structure when he is presented with an adequate sample of linguistic material and when he is given an opportunity to practice applying these rules. Serious questions have been raised (Spolsky, 1966) as to whether it is possible, therefore, to "program" the acquisition of a second language by techniques involving small-step learning and reinforcement. There have been, of course, a number of demonstrations that it is possible to learn a second language by programmed instruction (see below); the theoretical question that is being raised is whether programmed instruction works in the way that its underlying theory says it does. While the arguments of the transformational grammarians have much merit, there is also merit in some of the principles that might be offered by a cognitively oriented stimulus–response psychology. For example, it would seem that in some sense a linguistic rule corresponds to a habit of behavior that would be subject to psychological laws. In transformational grammar we have a more explicit and accurate description of linguistic habits than has been previously available; programmed instruction and similar-principled approaches to second-language teaching conceivably might profit from such descriptions.

Lambert (1963) has reviewed the status of research regarding the theory that there are two forms of bilingualism: (1) a *compound bilingualism* that is exhibited by persons who have learned a second language in terms of translations and transformations from their native language, and (2) a *coordinate bilingualism* that is characteristic of individuals who have learned a second language with no reference to their native language. An experiment by Kolers (1963) shows that experiences can be tagged and stored separately in two languages. The distinction between these two forms of bilingualism is not clear-cut, however, and it is by no means evident that coordinate bilingualism should be a unique goal of foreign-language instruction, because translation and interlanguage interpretation, in which compound bilinguals tend to be more skilled, are also useful goals.

PROBLEMS OF INSTRUCTION. Foreign-language courses may be roughly classified into two types: *audiolingual* and *grammar–translation*. In audiolingual courses, speaking and listening are stressed as objectives and are introduced early; the teaching method makes much use of live foreign-language interaction between teacher and students along with practice and drill, often with auxiliary aids such as language laboratories. In grammar–translation courses, reading and writing are the main objectives, and the teaching method emphasizes the learning of rules and the conscious application of those rules in translating from one language to the other. Mackey (1965), however, lists as many as 15 different "methods" that can be distinguished, but goes on to point out that any method is actually a combination of a large number of specific practices and teaching procedures; he provides a detailed technique for identifying these practices and profiling them for a given language course in three separate but interrelated areas—the language, the text, and the teacher. Mackey comes to no definite conclusion as to what practices are optimal, but offers his technique of method analysis as a tool for research. A somewhat similar approach to the analysis of teaching method has been taken by Hayes and others (1967) in their list of points to look for in evaluating course design, program administration, and individual teaching performance. In using their checklist in a survey of 364 faculty members at NDEA institutes, they obtained a strong consensus in favor of practices that stem from the audiolingual method.

The "bible" for the audiolingual method has been Brooks's (1964) *Language and Language Learning*, which outlines its philosophy and rationale and gives general directions for conducting language instruction. He writes: "The comfortable grammar-translation days are over. The new challenge is to teach language as communication, face-to-face communication between speakers and writer-to-reader communication in books. The new technique is to model for the student, in speech and writing, all the new behavior patterns that he is to learn. Analogy, which plays so large a part in the learning of the mother tongue, now plays a key role along with analysis in learning a second language. A constant objective is to learn to do with the new language what is done with it by those who speak it natively" (Brooks, 1964). He recommends that the use of the mother tongue should be banished from the classroom as far as possible, and that spoken forms should be introduced before written forms. Somewhat similar recommendations are made in Lado's (1964) manual for language teachers; Lado is particularly concerned, however, with the problems the student has in acquiring patterns that are different from those of his native language.

Compilations of articles on teaching methods have been made by Donoghue (1967), for foeign-language teachers in general, and by H. Allen (1965), specifically for teachers of English as a foreign language. Methods especially appropriate for teachers at the elementary-school level are described by Finocchiaro (1964) and by various authors in a book of readings assembled by Levenson and Kendrick (1967).

Books on language-learning techniques that are addressed to the student have been written by Moulton (1966) and by Politzer (1965); both stress the nature of language and try to explain how the student can come to understand, from a linguistic point of view, the differences between his native language and the target language.

DESCRIPTIVE AND COMPARATIVE STUDIES OF METHOD. Ever since the Chicago Investigation of Second-Language Teaching (Agard & Dunkel, 1948), summarized in Birkmaier's (1960) article, there have been studies that attempt to show what kinds of student achievements can be expected from the audiolingual as compared with the grammar-translation approach. Although certain studies (e.g., Birkmaier, 1949; Hamilton & Haden, 1950) showed small but significant differences favoring audiolingual methods in oral and listening skills, the results have never been strikingly favorable to either method. Indeed, the average levels of achievement attained through regular high school and college courses in *any* of the skills, spoken or written, have been generally low. Apparently the amount of time devoted to foreign-language study is not usually sufficient to allow either method to show its superiority. It is only when students of relatively high aptitude are allowed to study a language for a lengthy period of time, or with an intensive scheduling of classes, that they can attain the degree of fluency in a foreign language that will enable them to communicate easily in that language or to read foreign literature with ease and profit. The virtue of the audiolingual method is chiefly that it stresses objectives having to do with the spoken language—objectives too frequently underplayed or lost sight of in more conventional courses.

An ambitious experiment on foreign-language-teaching methodology by Scherer and Wertheimer (1964) was another effort to compare audiolingual methods with traditional approaches. Controls were, if anything, more rigorous than any previously applied, and better criterion measures were used. The subjects were students in a two-year college German program. During the first year, these students took their training either in a set of audiolingual classes or in a set of grammar–translation classes. In the former the introduction of written materials in German was delayed for some weeks and students were taught spoken language skills through classroom and laboratory activities. In the grammar–translation sections reading, writing, and grammatical analysis were introduced from the start, although some attention was paid to pronouncing and speaking. At the end of this first year, listening and speaking skills were found to be far superior in the audiolingually trained group, while reading and writing skills were at least significantly better in the traditionally trained group. Administrative considerations made it necessary to merge the two groups during the second year in a common course of instruction that covered all four skills. At the end of the second year, the differences between the two groups in passive skills (listening and reading) had largely disappeared, but there were still significant differences in active skills: the audiolingually trained students were better in speaking fluency and the traditionally trained students better in writing, on the average. The conclusion that emerges from this experiment is that the differences between the audiolingual and traditional methods are primarily differences of objectives; not surprisingly, students learn whatever skills are emphasized in the instruction. This experiment provided little evidence that the early teaching of speaking and listening makes for superior reading skill at a later stage. Nevertheless, Scherer and Wertheimer (1964) concluded that "the audiolingual method, whether its results are measured objectively or estimated by the students themselves, appears to produce more desirable attitudes and better habituated direct association." Even in those cases where reading skill is the primary objective, then, that objective can be more comfortably attained by an audiolingual method that stresses all four skills. The great majority of students, however, seem to prefer an emphasis on spoken-language skills.

Other studies supporting the general conclusions reached by Scherer and Wertheimer are those by Dostal (1960), Jochmans (1963), Mueller (1962), and Valdman (1964). Because most teaching methods are rather eclectic, as Mackey (1967) has pointed out, it is unlikely that major differences in results are to be found in the comparison of methods.

Needed are careful descriptive surveys and "actuarial" checks on foreign-language achievements in various types of courses after given periods of study. Many local school systems, as well as colleges and universities, collect relevant data, but few reports are available in the literature. Normative data from such standardized tests as the MLA Cooperative Tests (Educational Testing Service, 1963–64*a*) for beginning and intermediate language classes and the MLA Foreign Language Proficiency Tests for Teachers and Advanced Students (Educational Testing Service, 1961) give some indication of skill levels typically reached after one, two, or more years of language instruction in secondary school or college.

Carroll and others (1967) used the latter series of tests in a comprehensive study of the foreign-language attainments of language majors graduating from U.S. colleges and universities; a summary of the investigation was published by Carroll (1967). Scores on the tests were equated to "absolute proficiency ratings" resulting from interview tests administered by the Foreign Service Institute of the U.S. Department of State (Rice, 1959); the major points on the FSI scales in speaking and reading are (1) elementary proficiency, (2) limited working proficiency, (3) minimum professional proficiency, (4) full professional proficiency, and (5) native or bilingual proficiency. In nearly all comparisons the language majors were relatively poorer in listening and speaking skills than they were in reading and writing skills. In the former the median performance was generally between the "2" and "3" levels on the FSI scale, while in the latter median performance was at or near the "3" level. Students of German approached the "3" level in spoken skills, but students of Russian were not much above the "2" level even in reading and writing. Nevertheless, there were wide individual differences in performance, some students performing at or near the upper limits of the test-score scales, while others had scores that corresponded to less than the "1" level on the FSI scale. Several variables were identified that might account for some of these differences.

First, strikingly significant variations in mean scores were found to be a function of whether the student had started his foreign-language study in elementary school, high school, or college; in general, the earlier study had started, the better the mean performance. This finding was interpreted not as proof that foreign-language study must necessarily start in elementary school, but as an indication that students who start at that stage and continue to the point of majoring in a foreign language have a distinct advantage. It is also a confirmation of the proposition that high success in foreign-language study requires a protracted period of study. A second variable, independent of the first, that accounted for much variance in scores was the amount of foreign travel and study in the student's background; those who had spent a year in a country where the language was spoken were dramatically superior to those who had had only a summer session or tour abroad, and, in turn, the latter were superior to those who had never been abroad. Foreign-language aptitude as measured concurrently by the *Modern Language Aptitude Test* (Carroll & Sapon, 1959) was another significant variable, as was also the student's exposure to use of the foreign language in the home. The better language students tended to be found in the larger college-level institutions and in private as opposed to publicly supported institutions. Age and sex were not significant variables in test performance, although it was noted that the majority of language majors were female. Those intending to teach at the college level made better scores, on the average, than those intending to teach at the high school level. Multiple and canonical regression analyses revealed that the several background variables (time of starting, travel abroad, specific kinds of language aptitude, etc.) had somewhat different effects on the patterns of scores attained on the MLA tests. The fact that typically students had had exposure to a wide variety of language-teaching methods and the fact that it was difficult to obtain reliable information on their experiences precluded the drawing of any definitive conclusions as to optimal teaching methods. A significant variable in test performance, however, was the amount of actual use of spoken foreign language the students reported from their classroom experiences. The amount of language-laboratory experience made no detectable difference in test performance; this finding should not be interpreted as evidence against language laboratories, because students who had not had language-laboratory experience could have made up for it in many ways—by being exposed to good classroom teaching, travel, etc.

Carroll and others (1966) reported a "parametric" study of an intensive course in Spanish given to trainees for service in the Peace Corps. It was designed "to be a prototype of a parametric study that would answer a question of the following type: Given a (a level of language aptitude), p (an amount of prior language training), and possibly other data on an individual, how much s (achievement) could one expect the student to attain after t (a specified number of hours of foreign language instruction or exposure to the foreign language milieu)?" At the end of the 12-week training program, comprising about 200 hours of audiolingual instruction in small classes sectioned by ability and prior training, it was found that only 24 percent of the cases attained a score level that had been objectively set as representing competence sufficient to cope with the demands of the Peace Corps field job situation, a level corresponding approximately to the "2" level on the FSI scale mentioned earlier. For persons who had had prior training in Spanish, the amount of competence demonstrated at the outset was the best predictor of eventual performance, while for those with no prior training in Spanish, language aptitude was the best predictor of progress. Prediction was significantly enhanced, also, by information on the individual's prior interest in foreign languages and his attitudes toward audiolingual objectives and training methods. The study also measured progress in language competence during field job experience and concluded that most students were able to attain sufficient competence in Spanish by the end of about a half year in the field.

There continues to be a scarcity of reports on progress made by children in FLES (Foreign Language in the Elementary School) programs. Dunkel and Pillet (1962), reporting on the teaching of French to children in a university laboratory school, felt the teaching was highly successful, if sufficiently prolonged, except with a small percentage of children with poor aptitude or motivation. The achievements of their students after four or five years compared favorably with those of much older university students who began their language work in college. Carroll (1960) reviewed research on teaching foreign languages to children and concluded that while there is reasonably good evidence that children acquire a good foreign-language pronunciation more readily than older people, in other respects they are slower learners in the classroom. The advantage of early language instruction inheres primarily in the fact that it gives the child an early start in what is inevitably a long process of second-language learning, and it may also help to develop desirable attitudes toward foreign-language study. Experiences and research problems concerning early foreign-language instruction from an international point of view were outlined in a publication edited by Stern (1963; see also Kloss, 1967).

Among reports of successful FLES teaching using television or film presentations were those of Schramm and others (1964), Garry and Mauriello (1961), and Johnson and others (1963a). These studies suggest, however, that languages cannot be optimally taught solely by audiovisual presentations; this instruction needs to be supplemented by work with adequately prepared teachers. There are several studies (Johnson & others, 1963b; Lopato, 1963; Gordon & others, 1963) which agree in finding that FLES study is not detrimental to achievement in other school subjects. Brega and Newell (1965) found evidence that students trained in FLES had an advantage in advanced French classes over students who started language study in high school.

There is little research on the common practice, in many countries, of using a foreign language as a medium of instruction in the primary school (Macnamara, 1967). Prator's (1950) report indicated that children in the Philippines attended school longer and were happier when their native language was used as the medium of instruction for the early years. Cooper (1962) was unsuccessful in sustaining his hypothesis that Guamanian children would benefit appreciably from a year of "conversational English" before being exposed to formal reading and writing in English. General experience would seem to indicate that, where possible, instruction should be given in the native language for at least two or three years in the primary school; a foreign language that is eventually to be used as the medium of instruction may be introduced as early as the first grade, but only for periods of instruction that are very short at first, gradually lengthening until they constitute the main bulk of instruction. It does not seem to make much difference in pupil progress whether reading and writing in a foreign language are introduced early as long as speaking and listening are also introduced.

SPECIAL METHODOLOGICAL PROBLEMS. In the past decade researchers have turned their attention to specific problems and strategies in foreign-language instruction. Asher (1965, 1966; Kunihira & Asher, 1965) showed that better learning, comprehension, and retention of words denoting physical objects and actions was attained when the learner was required to make a "total physical response," e.g., to respond physically to a sentence meaning *Walk to the desk and put down the pencil and the book*. Keislar and Mace (1965; Keislar & others, 1966) demonstrated experimentally that in young children learning French, a program in which speaking training was combined with listening training produced better results than one in which speaking training was given only after a period of discrimination listening practice. An opposite conclusion, however, was reached by Henning (1966), working with college-age subjects.

Pronunciation. Research has been particularly intensive in the area of teaching pronunciation. Sapon and Carroll (1958) found that the confusions experienced by native speakers of English, Japanese, and Spanish in discriminating phonemes of various European languages were largely predictable on the basis of contrastive linguistic theory. More detailed analyses of phoneme discrimination have disclosed, however, that the problem is very complicated. Lane (1964a, 1964b) indicated that success in discrimination may be dependent on the extent to which a particular contrast involves a discrimination already in the subject's repertoire, but according to Lane and also Brière (1966), the difficulty of a discrimination is not always easily predictable from contrastive phonological analysis; it must be determined through empirical study. Brière found that contrary to previous suppositions, competence in discrimination sometimes appears only after the individual attains the capability of differentiating the phonemes in *production*. Henning (1966) found that it is possible and desirable to train individuals in the ability to evaluate their own productions in order to prepare them to learn from self-instructional teaching devices. Crothers and Suppes (1967) did extensive experiments on phoneme production and discrimination in the learning of Russian, making predictions from mathematical learning theory. Clark (1967) developed methods for scaling the difficulties of foreign-language sounds in terms of their acceptability to native speakers at either the phonetic or the phonemic level. Lane and Schneider (1963) and Buiten and Lane (1965) have experimented with elaborate electromechanical devices for automatically "shaping," through the reinforcement of successive approximations, production of certain prosodic features of language such as intonation and tone (as in tone languages).

Research has continued to demonstrate that in most cases introduction of the written form of a language very early in instruction tends to have a negative effect on pronunciation (Muller, 1963; Lange, 1966). Nevertheless, as shown by research of Pimsleur and others (1964a) and Roland (1966), this effect depends upon the type of correspondence that exists between conventional orthography and the phonology. Sawyer and others (1963) showed that a phonemic transcription is advantageous in learning Japanese. Crothers and others (1964) found that speed of response to Cyrillic characters is a good measure of the learning of written Russian.

Grammar and Structure. A critical issue not yet well resolved by research is whether grammatical competence in a foreign language is attained by practice of patterns, conscious applications of learned rules, or some other process not yet well understood. Torrey's (1966) experiment seemed to support pattern practice, but it probably demonstrated that active practice in sentence construction was better than no practice of any kind (see Carroll, 1966). McKinnon's (1965) experiment showed that the superior method was one in which active practice in sentence construction was aided both by "referential support" in the form of pictures representing the meanings of the sentences and by grammatical explanations that allowed conscious applications of rules. Carton's (1966) studies suggested that there is also an advantage in training students to make inferences and draw analogies in grammatical learning. It would be of interest to determine whether students exposed to linguistic manuals such as those of Politzer (1965) and Moulton (1966) would prove to be better learners of grammar.

Vocabulary. Little attention has been paid to vocabulary learning in recent research. Fiks and Corbino (1967) found that the rate at which new vocabulary items are introduced is a good predictor of students' perceptions of the slow vs. fast pacing of an intensive language course. Higa (1965) reviewed factors making for the difficulty of vocabulary items. Carroll and Burke's (1965) laboratory experiment on the rate of learning paired associates suggested that a point of diminishing returns was quickly reached when large amounts of vocabulary were to be learned at a single sitting; these results argue for appropriate temporal spacing in vocabulary learning. Crothers and Suppes' (1967) elaborate experiments on block size in vocabulary learning tended to favor the smaller block sizes. Lado and others (1967) found that a simultaneous presentation of a foreign word and its referent was superior to any kind of sequential presentation.

Instructional Aids: Textbooks, Filmed Courses. Mackey (1967) commented that in the whole history of foreign-language-teaching research there has been little investigation of the relative effectiveness of different textbooks in introductory and intermediate courses. Yet, foreign-language teachers have definite opinions about the relative effectiveness of textbooks —which differ widely in implicit theory of instruction, in style and order of presentation, and in the types of students to whom they are addressed. Research on textbooks in modern languages has unfortunately been forbidden territory, as it has been in other areas of the curriculum. Evaluations of certain filmed courses have appeared (e.g., Borglum, 1964), however.

The Language Laboratory. Keating (1963) found that in a group of high schools near New York City students who used language laboratories did not achieve as well as students who had not used them. Although criticized for methodological flaws by Anderson (1964), Conwell (1964), and Porter and Porter (1964), this report is best interpreted as providing evidence that language laboratories have not in general been well or adequately utilized in high schools, partly because of student scheduling problems and partly because of deficiencies in teaching materials and procedures. In a survey of the use of language laboratories in a substantial sample of public secondary schools in the United States, Bumpass (1963) reported that laboratory directors saw certain positive advantages in them, particularly for the shy student, the slow-learning student, and the gifted student. One report of successful use at the high school level is by Lorge (1963); students had 60 minutes of laboratory work per week over a two-year period. Experiments favoring the use of language laboratories at the college or adult level are those of E. Allen (1960), Bauer (1964), and Banathy and Jordan (1964). Young and Choquette (1965), among others, found that effective teaching of French pronunciation can be done through language-laboratory equipment even without "activated headphones" that allow the student to hear his own pronunciations. Hayes (1963) and Locke (1965) have stressed the desirability of high fidelity in the electronic systems of language laboratories.

Programmed Instruction. As of 1966, Fiks (1967) was able to list 26 commercially available "programs" of the self-instructional type (exclusive of "nonprogrammed" courses such as have been available for years on phonograph records and tapes): 9 in Spanish, 8 in French, 4 in German, 2 in Russian, and one each in Modern Hebrew, Modern Greek, and Thai. They vary in objectives, length, price, and the educational levels for which they are designed. For most, the vehicle is a programmed text, which may be accompanied by tapes or phonograph records when the objectives include mastery of aspects of the spoken language. Many more programs are in preparation, including some for special teaching devices or for computer-aided instruction. Only a few reports on such programs have reached the literature (Saltzman, 1963; Mueller & Harris, 1966; Valdman, 1964; Garvey & others, 1967). There are reports on special-purpose programs for use primarily in the armed forces (Ferster & others, 1966; Fiks, 1966; Rocklyn, 1967).

Only fragmentary information is available as to how much use these programs receive in schools and colleges (Hanson & Komoski, 1965). One has the impression that in high schools they are most often used on an experimental basis with small groups of students that present special cases: slow learners, transfer students, and the like. There are apparently few high schools that have introduced self-instructional programs wholesale to replace classroom teaching. Use of self-instructional materials with high school students requires considerable detailed supervision of students' learning activities. McDonald and Bell (1963) reported success with programs in Spanish and Russian at the high school level, particularly with highly motivated, apt students. In colleges and universities the climate has been more favorable to experimentation; a number of institutions have conducted complete language courses using programmed materials, allowing students to proceed at their own rates.

According to the theory of programmed instruction, the evaluation of a program is inherent in the process of preparing it and successively revising it on the basis of field tryouts. Some of the reports cited above include information on the success of programs in certain defined situations. For example, Mueller and Harris (1966) reported that students trained with a programmed course in first-year college French were at least as well prepared for second-year French as students taught traditionally. Furthermore, language aptitude was uncorrelated with the success of students in the programmed course, while it was a highly relevant variable for the traditionally trained students; this implies that at least certain programmed courses permit the low-aptitude students to overcome their handicaps. As yet there is no publication that gives detailed evaluative information on programmed foreign-language courses.

STUDENT CHARACTERISTICS. Major investigations of the relevance of various student characteristics to foreign-language learning have been carried out by Carroll (1958, 1959, 1962) and Pimsleur (1963; Pimsleur & others, 1962a, 1962b, 1964b), and new tests of language aptitude have been published (Carroll & Sapon, 1959, 1967; Pimsleur, 1966a). These investigators agree that foreign-language aptitude is measurable and in many circumstances highly relevant to success in foreign-language learning. The aptitude tests appear to measure certain traits, cognitive abilities, and skills that are not well represented in the usual intelligence tests; among these are the ability to discriminate and remember sounds, the ability to perform grammatical analyses, the ability to memorize foreign-language vocabulary, and the ability to infer linguistic structure from given data. Carroll reports that general verbal intelligence as measured by native-language vocabulary tests is largely irrelevant to foreign-language learning in the introductory stages, but Pimsleur includes a vocabulary test as a part of his aptitude battery. Pimsleur also offers measures of interest and motivation in his battery, along with students' reports of general academic averages, which he finds valid in predicting foreign-language success. The test manuals report generally high-validity coefficients for these batteries. According to Carroll (1962), aptitude is a matter of rate of learning: the notion that low-aptitude students take longer to learn in a self-paced situation is supported by a number of studies, e.g., Fiks (1966). On the other hand, from the low-validity coefficients that are sometimes obtained for aptitude tests, it would appear that certain very-well-taught courses are equally successful with high- and low-aptitude students (Mueller & Harris, 1966).

Lenneberg (1967) has speculated that very young children exhibit a species-specific capacity to acquire their native language; this capacity may therefore extend to a second language if learned simultaneously with the first language. In foreign-language learning at school, however, this capacity probably exhibits itself only in increased ability to imitate foreign sounds and acquire a good foreign pronunciation, an ability that gradually decreases as puberty is approached. There may be a slight decline in foreign-language-learning ability over the adult years up to about 50, but adults even at that age have been known to learn a foreign language with reasonable success. The head start that girls apparently have in native-language development manifests itself in a slight but significant superiority in language aptitude throughout the years of schooling (Carroll & Sapon, 1959). Carroll and others (1967) found no significant sex differences in foreign-language achievement among college foreign-language majors, but it should be noted that this was a population of self-selected persons who had already demonstrated a considerable degree of interest and aptitude in foreign languages.

Little progress has been made toward solving the age-old question of whether study of one foreign language facilitates study of another. Milholland and Millman (1963) found a significant transfer effect between study of one language in high school and study of another in college.

MEASUREMENT OF ACHIEVEMENT AND PROFICIENCY. Useful general works on tests and measurements in the foreign-language field are by Lado (1961) and Valette (1967); Pimsleur (1966b) has written an interesting and comprehensive summary article. These publications emphasize problems of the construction of teacher-made tests. There is still need for a treatise that would adequately discuss the construction and use of standardized tests in this field.

A number of standardized tests in foreign languages are available (Buros, 1965). Of particular interest are the series of standardized tests in French, German, Italian, Russian, and Spanish sponsored by the Modern Language Association: the MLA-Cooperative Tests and the MLA Foreign Language Proficiency Tests for Teachers and Advanced Students (Educational Testing Service, 1961, 1963–64a). Constructed over a period of several years by committees of foreign-language teachers working with testing specialists, and adequately normed, these tests represent in many respects a considerable advance over previously available tests, especially in their success in measuring speaking proficiency. The MLA-Cooperative Tests are designed for beginning (Form L) and intermediate (Form M) language instruction in secondary schools and colleges; results are interpretable on a common score scale. The other series of tests are designed primarily for teacher evaluation and certification; besides the subtests for listening, speaking, reading, and writing, which are also found in the Cooperative series, they have additional sections on applied linguistics, culture and civilization, and professional preparation. Although the subtests of listening, speaking, reading, and writing purport to measure these four skills separately, they tend to be rather highly correlated, partly because, doubtless, all parts are substantially dependent on vocabulary knowledge. The tests do not, therefore, yield reliable diagnostic information concerning the examinee's competence in grammar apart from vocabulary; they measure, instead, his overall level of competence in the language.

The influence of audiolingual objectives on testing is seen in the widespread adoption of listening-comprehension tests as a part of the College Entrance Examination Board series (Scheider, 1962), and in the construction of a standardized listening-comprehension test for FLES students (Banathy & others, 1962). Lado (1965) has called attention to the possibility of using memory-span techniques in testing foreign-language competence. At the graduate-school level, standardized tests for appraising reading competence in French, German, or Russian for doctoral degree candidates are available (Educational Testing Service, 1963–64b).

Testing in English as a foreign language is less well developed. However, Ohannessian and others (1964) list 27 tests or test series suitable for various purposes, including the *Test of English as a Foreign Language* sponsored by the National Council on the Testing of English as a Foreign Language, primarily for foreign students desiring to study in English-speaking countries. This test is wisely subdivided into five diagnostic subtests: listening comprehension, structure, vocabulary, reading comprehension, and writing.

THE FOREIGN-LANGUAGE TEACHER. Although there has been much activity on the part of the Modern Language Association and its affiliates in establishing guide lines and goals for teacher preparation (Paquette, 1966) and in promoting ways of attaining these goals (Axelrod, 1966), there has been little research on characteristics and behaviors of foreign-language teachers as such. One of the purposes of the survey by Carroll and others (1967) was to describe the linguistic and professional qualifications of prospective teachers, but it shed no light on the actual relevance of these qualifications to teacher effectiveness. A superior degree of competence in the language to be taught may be taken as an obvious qualification, but there are doubtless many other factors that determine teacher success.

Some research has been done on specific methods of training teachers. Politzer (1966) has experimented with a "micro-teaching" procedure in which teachers are asked to demonstrate specific teaching skills in 10-15-minute performances that are videotaped and then played back to the teacher with comments and criticisms from supervisors. Moskowitz (1968) reported favorable results of programs in which preservice and in-service teachers of foreign languages were taught systems for describing pupil–teacher interactions. A self-instructional program for training teachers of English in developing countries was assembled by English Language Services, Inc. (1965), but there is as yet no report of successful use in the field under operational conditions.

John B. Carroll
Educational Testing Service

References

Agard, Frederick B., and Dunkel, Harold B. *An Investigation of Second-Language Teaching.* Ginn, 1948. 344p.

Allen, Edward D. "The Effects of the Language Laboratory on the Development of Skill in a Foreign Language." *Mod Lang J* 44:355–8; 1960.

Allen, Harold B. (Ed.) *Teaching English as a Second Language; A Book of Readings.* McGraw-Hill, 1965. 406p.

Anderson, Eugene W. "Review and Criticism (Keating Report)." *Mod Lang J* 48:197–207; 1964.

Asher, James J. "The Strategy of the Total Physical Response; An Application to Learning Russian." *Int R Applied Linguistics* 3:291–300; 1965.

Asher, James J. "The Learning Strategy of the Total Physical Response: A Review." *Mod Lang J* 50:79–84; 1966.

Axelrod, Joseph. *The Education of the Modern Foreign Language Teacher for American Schools.* MLA, 1966. 55p.

Banathy, Bela H., and Jordan, Boris. "A Test of Significance of the Class-laboratory." *J Sec Ed* 39:79–83; 1964.

Banathy, Bela H., and others. "The Common Concepts Foreign Language Test." *Mod Lang J* 46:363–5; 1962.

Bauer, Eric W. "A Study of the Effectiveness of Two Language Laboratory Conditions in the Teaching of Second Year German." *Int R Applied Linguistics* 2:99–112; 1964.

Belyayev, B. V. *The Psychology of Teaching Foreign Languages.* Macmillan, 1964. 230p.

Birkmaier, Emma M. "An Investigation of the Outcomes in the Eclectic, Reading and Modified Army Method Courses in the Teaching of a Second Language." Doctoral dissertation. U Minnesota, 1949.

Birkmaier, Emma M. "Foreign Languages." *R Ed Res* 28:127–39; 1958.

Birkmaier, Emma M. "Modern Languages." In Harris, Chester W. (Ed.) *Encyclopedia of Educational Research*, 3rd ed. Macmillan, 1960. p. 861–88.

Birkmaier, Emma M., and Lange, Dale. "Foreign Language Instruction." *R Ed Res* 37:186–99; 1967.

Borglum, George P. *Modern Language Audio-visual Research Project*. Wayne State U, 1964. 212p.

Brega, Evelyn, and Newell, John M. "Comparison of Performance by FLES Program Students and Regular French III Students on Modern Language Association Tests." *French R* 39:433–8; 1965.

Breunig, Marjorie. "Foreign Languages in the Elementary Schools of the United States, 1959–1960." In *Reports of Surveys and Studies in the Teaching of Modern Foreign Languages, 1959–61*. MLA, 1961. p. 1–14.

Brière, Eugène. "An Investigation of Phonological Interference." *Lang* 42:768–96; 1966.

Brooks, Nelson. *Language and Language Learning: Theory and Practice*, 2nd ed. Harcourt, 1964. 300p.

Buiten, Roger, and Lane, Harlan. "A Self-Instructional Device for Conditioning Accurate Prosody." *Int R Applied Linguistics* 3:205–19; 1965.

Bumpass, D. E. "An Appraisal of Language Laboratories in Public High Schools in the United States." Doctoral dissertation. Texas Technology Col, 1963.

Buros, Oscar K. (Ed.) *The Sixth Mental Measurements Yearbook*. Gryphon, 1965. 1714p.

Carroll, John B. "A Factor Analysis of Two Foreign Language Aptitude Batteries." *J Gen Psychol* 59:3–19; 1958.

Carroll, John B. "Use of the Modern Language Aptitude Test in Secondary Schools." *Yearbook, National Council Measurements Used in Education* 16:155–9; 1959.

Carroll, John B. "Foreign Languages for Children: What Research Says." *Nat El Prin* 39:12–5; 1960.

Carroll, John B. "The Prediction of Success in Intensive Foreign Language Training." In Glaser, Robert. (Ed.) *Training Research and Education*. U Pittsburgh, 1962; Wiley, 1965. p. 87–136.

Carroll, John B. "Research on Teaching Foreign Languages." In Gage, N. L. (Ed.) *Handbook of Research on Teaching*. Rand McNally, 1963. p. 1060–100.

Carroll, John B. "The Contributions of Psychological Theory and Educational Research to the Teaching of Foreign Languages." *Mod Lang J* 49:273–81; 1965.

Carroll, John B. "Research in Foreign Language Teaching: The Last Five Years." In Mead, Robert G., Jr. (Ed.) *Language Teaching: Broader Contexts*. MLA, 1966. p. 12–42.

Carroll, John B. "Foreign Language Proficiency Levels Attained by Language Majors Near Graduation from College." *Foreign Lang Annals* 1:131–51; 1967.

Carroll, John B., and Burke, Mary Long. "Parameters of Paired-associate Learning: Length of List, Meaningfulness, Rate of Presentation, and Ability. *J Exp Psychol* 69:543–53; 1965.

Carroll, John B., and Sapon, Stanley M. *Modern Language Aptitude Test: Manual*. Psychological Corp, 1959. 27p.

Carroll, John B., and Sapon, Stanley M. *Modern Language Aptitude Test—Elementary: Manual*. Psychological Corp, 1967. 12p.

Carroll, John B., and others. *A Parametric Study of Language Training in the Peace Corps*. Harvard U School Education, 1966. 146p.

Carroll, John B., and others. *The Foreign Language Attainments of Language Majors in the Senior Year*. Harvard U School Education, 1967. 256p.

Carton, Aaron S. *The "Method of Inference" in Foreign Language Study*. City U New York, 1966.

Chomsky, Noam. *Syntactic Structures*. Mouton, 1957. 116p.

Chomsky, Noam. "Review of B. F. Skinner's *Verbal Behavior*." *Lang* 35:26–58; 1959.

Chomsky, Noam. *Aspects of the Theory of Syntax*. Massachusetts Institute Technology Press, 1965. 251p.

Chomsky, Noam. "Linguistic Theory." In Mead, Robert G., Jr. (Ed.) *Language Teaching: Broader Contexts*. MLA, 1966. p. 43–9.

Clark, John L. D. "Empirical Studies Related to the Teaching of French Pronunciation to American Students." Doctoral dissertation. Harvard U School Education, 1967.

Conwell, Marilyn J. "An Evaluation of the Keating Report." *B Nat Assn Sec Sch Prin* 48:104–15; 1964.

Cooper, James G. *Conversational English for Non-English Speaking Children*. Col of Guam, 1962. 24p.

Crothers, Edward, and Suppes, Patrick. *Experiments in Second-language Learning*. Academic, 1967. 374p.

Crothers, Edward, and others. "Latency Phenomena in Prolonged Learning of Visual Representations of Russian Sounds." *Int R Applied Linguistics* 2:205–17; 1964.

Dershem, James F., and others. *Foreign-language Offerings and Enrollments in Secondary Schools. Fall, 1964*. MLA, 1966. 76p.

Diekhoff, John S. *NDEA and Modern Foreign Languages*. MLA, 1965. 148p.

Donoghue, Mildred R. (Ed.) *Foreign Languages and the Schools: A Book of Readings*. Brown, 1967. 462p.

Dostal, Naida M. "Audio-Visual Second-Language Learning: A Historical Review and Comparative Evaluation of the Use of Audio-Visual Instructional Materials and Teaching Techniques in First Year High School French." Doctoral dissertation. Wayne State U, 1960.

Dunkel, Harold B., and Pillet, Roger A. *French in the Elementary School: Five Years' Experience*. U Chicago Press, 1962. 150p.

Educational Testing Service. *MLA Foreign Language Proficiency Tests for Teachers and Advanced Stu-*

dents (French, German, Italian, Russian, Spanish). ETS, 1961.
Educational Testing Service. *MLA-Cooperative Foreign Language Tests (French, German, Italian, Russian, Spanish)*. ETS, 1963–64(*a*).
Educational Testing Service. *The Graduate School Foreign Language Testing Program (French, German, Russian)*. ETS, 1963–64(*b*).
Educational Testing Service. *Booklet of Norms, MLA-Cooperative Foreign Language Tests*. ETS, 1965. 83p.
English Language Services, Inc. *Teacher Education Program*. The Services, 1965. 97p.
Ferguson, Charles A. "Applied Linguistics." In Mead, Robert G., Jr. (Ed.) *Language Teaching: Broader Contexts*. MLA, 1966. p. 50–8.
Ferster, C. B., and others. *The Psychobiological Investigation of the Development of New Verbal Behavior*. Institute for Behavioral Research, Inc., 1966. 91p.
Fiks, Alfred I. "A Short Vietnamese Language Program: Training Course and Research Vehicle." *Int R Applied Linguistics* 4:235–54; 1966.
Fiks, Alfred I. "Foreign Language Programmed Materials: 1966." *Mod Lang J* 51:7–14; 1967.
Fiks, Alfred I., and Corbino, J. P. "Course Density and Student Perception." *Lang Learning* 17:3–8; 1967.
Finocchiaro, Mary. *Teaching Children Foreign Languages*. McGraw-Hill, 1964. 210p.
Fucilla, Joseph G. *The Teaching of Italian in the United States*. American Association Teachers Italian, 1967. 299p.
Garry, Ralph, and Mauriello, Edna. *Modern Language Project of the Massachusetts Council for Public Schools, Summary of Research on "Parlons Français," Year Two*. Massachusetts Council for Public Schools, 1961. 39p.
Garvey, Catherine J., and others. *A Report of the Developmental Testing of a Self-Instructional French Program*. Center for Applied Linguistics, 1967. 43p.
Gordon, Oakley J., and others. *Challenging the Superior Student by Making the Study of Russian Available in the Elementary School Curriculum Via Television*. U Utah, 1963. 72p.
Halliday, M. A. K., and others. *The Linguistic Sciences and Language Teaching*. Indiana U Press, 1965. 322p.
Hamilton, Daniel, and Haden, Ernest. "Three Years of Experimentation at the University of Texas." *Mod Lang J* 34:85–102; 1950.
Hammer, John H. *A Bibliography of Contrastive Linguistics*. Center for Applied Linguistics, 1965. 41p.
Hanson, Lincoln F., and Komoski, P. Kenneth. "School Use of Programed Instruction." In Glaser, Robert. (Ed.) *Teaching Machines and Programed Learning, II: Data and Directions*. NEA, 1965. p. 647–84.
Hayes, Alfred S. *Language Laboratory Facilities*. Bulletin No. 37, USOE, 1963. 119p.
Hayes, Alfred S., and others. "Evaluation of Foreign Language Teaching." *Foreign Lang Annals* 1:22–44; 1967.
Henning, William A. "Discrimination Training and Self-Evaluation in the Teaching of Pronunciation." *Int R Applied Linguistics* 4:7–17; 1966.
Higa, Masanori. "The Psycholinguistic Concept of 'Difficulty' and the Teaching of Foreign Language Vocabulary." *Lang Learning* 15:167–79; 1965.
Jochmans, Robert P. "A Statistical Analysis of Pupil Achievement in an Integrated Audio-visual French Course." Doctoral dissertation. Wayne State U, 1963.
Johnson, Charles E., and others. *The Development and Evaluation of Methods and Materials to Facilitate Foreign Language Instruction in Elementary Schools*. Foreign Language Instruction Project, Urbana, Ill., 1963(*a*). 265p.
Johnson, Charles E., and others. "The Effect of Foreign Language Instruction on Basic Learning in Elementary Schools; A Second Report." *Mod Lang J* 47:8–11; 1963(*b*).
Johnston, Marjorie C. "Foreign Language Instruction." *R Ed Res* 31:188–96; 1961.
Keating, Raymond F. *A Study of the Effectiveness of Language Laboratories*. Teachers Col, Columbia U, 1963. 61p.
Keislar, Evan R., and Mace, L. L. "Sequence of Listening and Speaking in Beginning French." In Krumboltz, John. (Ed.) *Learning and the Educational Process*. Rand McNally, 1965. p. 163–91.
Keislar, Evan R., and others. "Sequence of Speaking and Listening Training in Beginning French; A Replication Experiment." *Am Ed Res J* 3:169–78; 1966.
Kendall, W. L., II. "A Survey of Modern Languages in Elementary Schools from 1921 through 1950." Doctoral dissertation. U Maryland, 1961.
Kloss, Heinz. *Zum Problem des Fremdsprachenunterrichts an Grundschulen Amerikas und Europas*. Wissenschaftliches Archiv, 1967. 165p.
Kolers, Paul A. "Interlingual Word Association." *J Verbal Learning Verbal Behavior* 2:291–300; 1963.
Kufner, Herbert L. *The Grammatical Structures of English and German*. U Chicago Press, 1962. 95p.
Kunihira, Shirou, and Asher, James J. "The Strategy of the Total Physical Response: An Application to Learning Japanese." *Int R Applied Linguistics* 3:277–89; 1965.
Lado, Robert. *Language Testing*. McKay, 1961. 389p.
Lado, Robert. *Language Teaching, A Scientific Approach*. McGraw-Hill, 1964. 239p.
Lado, Robert. "Memory Span as a Factor in Second Language Learning." *Int R Applied Linguistics* 3:123–9; 1965.
Lado, Robert, and others. *Massive Vocabulary Expansion in a Foreign Language Beyond the Basic Course: The Effects of Stimuli, Timing, and Order of Presentation*. Georgetown U, 1967. 173p.
Lambert, Wallace E. "Psychological Approaches to the Study of Language. Part II: On Second-Language Learning and Bilingualism." *Mod Lang J* 47:114–21; 1963.
Lane, Harlan. "Acquisition and Transfer in Auditory

Discrimination." *Am J Psychol* 77:240–8; 1964(*a*).
Lane, Harlan. "Programmed Learning of a Second Language." *Int R Applied Linguistics* 2:249–301; 1964(*b*).
Lane, Harlan, and Schneider, Bruce. "Methods for Self-shaping Echoic Behavior." *Mod Lang J* 47: 154–60; 1963.
Lange, Dale L. "An Evaluation of Pre-reading Instruction in Beginning French in Secondary Schools." Doctoral dissertation. U Minnesota, 1966.
Leavitt, Sturgis E. "The Teaching of Spanish in the United States." In *Reports of Surveys and Studies in the Teaching of Modern Foreign Languages*. MLA, 1961. p. 309–26.
Lenneberg, Eric H. *Biological Foundations of Language*. Wiley, 1967. 489p.
Levenson, Stanley, and Kendrick, William. *Readings in Foreign Languages for the Elementary School*. Blaisdell, 1967. 555p.
Libbish, B. (Ed.) *Advances in the Teaching of Modern Languages*. Vol. I. Pergamon, 1964. 175p.
Locke, William N. "The Future of Language Laboratories." *Mod Lang J* 49:294–304; 1965.
Lopato, Esther W. "FLES and Academic Achievement." *French R* 36:499–507; 1963.
Lorge, Sarah W. "Foreign Language Laboratories in Secondary Schools." *A-V Learning* 7: Supplement No. 1, 1963. 4p.
Lund, Gladys A., and Herslow, Nina G. *Foreign Language Entrance and Degree Requirements in U.S. Colleges and Universities, Fall 1966*. MLA, 1966. 55p.
Mackey, William F. *Language Teaching Analysis*. McKay, 1965; Indiana U Press, 1967. 562p.
Macnamara, John. "The Effects of Instruction in a Weaker Language." *J Social Issues* 23:121–35; 1967.
McDonald, Pearl S., and Bell, Robert. *Experimental Use of Self-Instructional Courses in Russian and Spanish by Secondary School Students*. Arlington City, Virginia, Public Schools, 1963. 35p.
McKinnon, Kenneth R. "An Experimental Study of the Learning of Syntax in Second Language Learning." Doctoral dissertation. Harvard U School Education, 1965.
Milholland, John E., and Millman, Jason. "The Value of High School Foreign Language for the Study of College Introductory Foreign Language." *Mod Lang J* 47:235–8; 1963.
Moskowitz, Gertrude. "The Effects of Training Foreign Language Teachers in Interaction Analysis." *Foreign Lang Annals* 1:218–35; 1968.
Moulton, William G. "Linguistics and Language Teaching in the United States, 1940–1960." In Mohrmann, C., and others. (Eds.) *Trends in European and American Linguistics, 1930–1960*, Vol. 1. Spectrum, 1961. p. 82–109.
Moulton, William G. *The Sounds of English and German*. U Chicago Press, 1962. 145p.
Moulton, William G. *A Linguistic Guide to Language Learning*. MLA, 1966. 140p.
Mueller, Klaus A. "Experimentation and Research in the Development of Modern Foreign Language Materials and Teaching Methods." *Int J Am Linguistics* 28:92–104; 1962.
Mueller, Theodore, and Harris, Robert. "First Year College French Through an Audio-lingual Program." *Int R Applied Linguistics* 4:19–38; 1966.
Muller, Daniel H. "A Study of the Effects on Pronunciation and Intonation of Accompanying Audio-lingual Drill with Exposure to the Written Word." Doctoral dissertation. U California, 1963.
Müller, Gerhard. (Ed.) *International Conference on Modern Language Teaching, Berlin, 1964*. Franz Cornelsen Verlag, 1965. 483p.
New York State Education Department, Bureau of Secondary Curriculum Development. *Spanish for Secondary Schools*. The Department, 1961. 240p.
Nostrand, Howard Lee, and others. *Research on Language Teaching: An Annotated International Bibliography, 1945–64*. U Washington Press, 1965. 373p.
Ohannessian, Sirarpi, and others. *Reference List of Materials for English as a Second Language: Part I: Texts, Readers, Dictionaries, Tests*. Center for Applied Linguistics, 1964. 152p.
Ornstein, J., and Lado, R. "Research in Foreign Language Teaching Methodology." *Int R Applied Linguistics* 5:11–25; 1967.
Paquette, F. André. (Ed.) "Guidelines for Teacher Education Programs in Modern Foreign Languages —An Exposition." *Mod Lang J* 50:323–425; 1966.
Parry, Albert. *America Learns Russian*. Syracuse U Press, 1967. 205p.
Pimsleur, Paul. "Predicting Success in High School Foreign Language Courses." *Ed Psychol Meas* 23: 349–57; 1963.
Pimsleur, Paul. *The Pimsleur Language Aptitude Battery*. Harcourt, 1966(*a*).
Pimsleur, Paul. "Testing Foreign Language Learning." In Valdman, Albert. (Ed.) *Trends in Language Teaching*. McGraw-Hill, 1966(*b*). p. 175–214.
Pimsleur, Paul, and others. "Student Factors in Foreign Language Teaching." *Mod Lang J* 46:160–70; 1962(*a*).
Pimsleur, Paul, and others. "Foreign Language Learning Ability." *J Ed Psychol* 53:15–26; 1962(*b*).
Pimsleur, Paul, and others. "Further Study of the Transfer of Verbal Materials Across Sense Modalities." *J Ed Psychol* 55:96–102; 1964(*a*).
Pimsleur, Paul, and others. "Under-achievement in Foreign Language Learning." *Int R Applied Linguistics* 2:113–50; 1964(*b*).
Politzer, Robert L. *Foreign Language Learning: A Linguistic Introduction*. Prentice-Hall, 1965. 155p.
Politzer, Robert L. "Toward a Practice-centered Program for the Training and Evaluation of Foreign Language Teachers." *Mod Lang J* 50:251–5; 1966.
Porter, John J., and Porter, Sally F. "A Critique of the Keating Report." *Mod Lang J* 48:195–7; 1964.
Prator, Clifford H., Jr. *Language Teaching in the Philippines: A Report*. U.S. Ed Foundation in Philippines, 1950. 96p.
Rice, Frank A. "The Foreign Service Institute Tests Language Proficiency." *Linguistic Reporter* 1:2, 4; 1959.

Rivers, Wilga M. *The Psychologist and the Foreign-language Teacher.* U Chicago Press, 1964. 212p.

Rocklyn, Eugene H. "The Development and Test of a Special Purpose Foreign Language Training Concept." *Int R Applied Linguistics* 5:27–36; 1967.

Roland, Lyn. "An Experiment in a Pronunciation Problem." *Int R Applied Linguistics* 4:255–9; 1966.

Saltzman, Irving J. "Programmed Self-instruction and Second-language Learning." *Int R Applied Linguistics* 1:104–14; 1963.

Sapon, Stanley M., and Carroll, John B. "Discriminative Perception of Speech Sounds as a Function of Native Language." *Gen Linguistics* 3:62–72; 1958.

Saporta, Sol. "Applied Linguistics and Generative Grammar." In Valdman, Albert. (Ed.) *Trends in Language Teaching.* McGraw-Hill, 1966. p. 81–92.

Sawyer, Jesse O. "Foreign Language Instruction." *R Ed Res* 34:203–10; 1964.

Sawyer, Jesse O., and others. "The Utility of Translation and Written Symbols During the First Thirty Hours of Language Study." *Int R Applied Linguistics* 1:157–92; 1963.

Scheider, Rose M. "Evolution of the Listening Comprehension Test." *Col Bd R* 48:24–8; 1962.

Scherer, George A. C., and Wertheimer, Michael. *A Psycholinguistic Experiment in Foreign-language Teaching.* McGraw-Hill, 1964. 256p.

Schramm, Wilbur, and others. *The Context of Instructional Television: Summary Report of Research Findings, the Denver-Stanford Project.* Stanford U, 1964. 160p.

Skinner, B. F. *Verbal Behavior.* Appleton, 1957. 478p.

Spolsky, Bernard. "A Psycholinguistic Critique of Programmed Foreign Language Instruction." *Int R Applied Linguistics* 4:119–29; 1966.

Stern, H. H. (Ed.) *Foreign Languages in Primary Education: The Teaching of Foreign or Second Languages to Younger Children.* UNESCO, 1963. 103p.

Theivananthampillai, K. "An Empirical Test of Contrastive Linguistic Analysis as Applied to the Teaching of the English Auxiliary Verb System to Tamil Speakers." Doctoral dissertation. Harvard U School Education, 1965.

Torrey, Jane W. *The Learning of Grammar: An Experimental Study.* Connecticut Col, 1966. 67p.

Valdman, Albert. "Toward Self-instruction in Foreign Language Learning." *Int R Applied Linguistics* 2:1–36; 1964.

Valdman, Albert. (Ed.) *Trends in Language Teaching.* McGraw-Hill, 1966. 298p.

Valette, Rebecca M. *Modern Language Testing: A Handbook.* Harcourt, 1967. 200p.

Walters, Theodore W., S. J. *The Georgetown Bibliography of Studies Contributing to the Psycholinguistics of Language Learning.* Georgetown U Press, 1965. 125p.

Watts, George B. "The Teaching of French in the United States: A History." *French R* 37:1–165; 1963.

Young, Clarence W., and Choquette, Charles A. "An Experimental Study of the Relative Effectiveness of Four Systems of Equipment for Self-monitoring in Teaching French Pronunciation." *Int R Applied Linguistics* 3:13–49; 1965.

Zeydel, Edwin H. "The Teaching of German in the United States from Colonial Times to the Present." In *Reports of Surveys and Studies in the Teaching of Modern Foreign Languages, 1959–61.* MLA, 1961. p. 285–308.

MOTIVATION

The application of knowledge for socially useful ends often is preceded by the theoretical development of a science. In physics the theory of relativity gave rise to the use of nuclear power as a source of energy; in chemistry the table of atomic numbers resulted in the search for and discovery of new elements useful for industrial gains; and in psychology the amelioration of neurotic symptoms awaited Freud's theory of personality and behavior. These successes have led academic psychologists to search for the basic laws of learning and motivation before suggesting specific procedures which might enhance performance in the classroom. Indeed, psychologists have been more concerned with the theoretical "hows" of behavior than with the "whats" which might be of interest to educators: how people perceive and learn, rather than what is processed and stored; and how an organism is impelled to action, rather than what particular practice will motivate students, particularly dropouts and underachievers. The task which motivational theorists have set for themselves is to represent conceptually the determinants of behavior—that is, to specify mathematically the principles of performance. In this paper the historical evolution of the study of motivation and the conceptual advancements are presented. In addition, the potential relevance of this work to educators and findings in specific areas of research is discussed.

CONCEPTUAL SYSTEMS, SUPPORTING DATA, AND EDUCATIONAL IMPLICATIONS. In general, four theoretical positions have developed to explain the instigation, direction, magnitude, and persistence of a behavioral episode. Each theory is associated with particular reference experiments and research paradigms and is supported by a circumscribed body of empirical findings. Hence, the application of the theories to classroom behavior differs. However, the systems are somewhat overlapping, for identical explanatory constructs are at times employed in more than one theory. There are variants of each theoretical approach; the finer distinctions between theories ordinarily are neglected in this discussion.

Associative Theory. Perhaps the oldest principle of causation is association. It is suggested that if an event, *b*, frequently and contiguously follows event *a*, then on the reappearance of *a*, *b* will follow. Kurt Lewin labeled this the principle of adhesion: events are rigidly coupled by virtue of their temporal association (Lewin, 1935). Pavlovian classical conditioning is based on this principle. Some motivational theorists (e.g., Brown, 1961) believe this position to be nonmotivational, for dynamic (energy) constructs are not employed to explain the initiation of behavior. However, in the present context a pure associative approach is considered a motivational statement; one determinant is specified as the necessary and sufficient cause of behavior.

It is intuitively reasonable and within the functionalistic tradition to expect hungry rats to be motivated by a potential reward of food and to engage in behavior which is instrumental to the attainment of that goal. Animals deprived of a commodity necessary for survival have supplied the bulk of the data cited by motivational theorists. How might a pure associationist explain the behavior of a hungry or thirsty organism? Stimuli accompanying the deprivation state vary discriminately as a function of the type and degree of deprivation. Animals can differentiate hunger from thirst (Leeper, 1935) and are able to learn differential responses to different intensities of food deprivation (Jenkins & Hanratty, 1949). These internal stimuli persist until an instrumental response is made which leads to an appropriate goal object. The consummatory response then removes the stimuli maintaining the behavior (Guthrie, 1942). Upon recurrence of the deprivation state and the internal stimulation, the previous response tends to be repeated. Response strength (speed, probability, 1/latency) generally increases as a function of the time of deprivation. Associationists reason that the more severe the deprivation, the greater the quantity of deprivation cues, and the larger the proportion of the total stimulus situation which is conditioned to the instrumental response. The increased conditioning intensifies the strength of the observable response. (The reader is directed to Estes, 1958, for the most sophisticated extension of this position.)

While some associationists have argued that contiguity is a sufficient principle of causation, others reason that behavior also is determined by the hedonic consequences of the response. Thorndike (1911) conveyed this position in his law of effect, which states that when a stimulus-response bond is followed by a satisfying state of affairs, the strength of that bond increases. Thorndike's conception has been called a "hedonism of the past," for the consequences of an event strengthen a prior association. This view is closely linked with the current work in operant conditioning and with the research on reinforcement conducted by Skinner (1953) and his colleagues. Although a response followed by a reward increases in strength, stimuli are still considered the causal agents of behavior. If the stimuli associated with the rewarded response are removed, then the response sequence is not initiated.

The associative conception has led to a systematic search for the antecedent stimulus conditions, or the controlling stimuli, which determine a response. Watson's (1924) dictum—given the stimulus, predict the response; given the response, find the stimulus; given a change in response, find a change in the stimulus—has indeed been influential. This advice also has affected educational research. For example, Keislar (1960) presents four experiments which demonstrate the importance of stimulus control over problem-solving behavior. Keislar first paired a neutral stimulus with a reinforcer and then showed that the presence of that stimulus on a new task increases the amount of problem-solving activity. Further, he found that children learn more when the material is accompanied by a light which has been associated with prior reinforcement. That is, they can be taught when to learn. Keislar suggests that a child be reinforced for a variety of activities in the classroom; the cues in that setting can then be employed to elicit other (e.g., problem-solving) behavior.

Drive Theory. Prior to the 1920's, "instinct" was among the most cited determinants of behavior. Instinct is an extremely poor explanatory or descriptive construct. Holt (1931) poetically states why instinct is not acceptable as a scientific explanation of behavior:

> Man is impelled to action, it is said, by his instincts. If he goes with his fellows, it is the "herd instinct" which activates him; if he walks alone, it is the "anti-social instinct"; if he fights, it is the "pugnacity instinct"; if he defers to another, it is the instinct of "self-abasement"; if he twiddles his thumbs, it is the "thumb-twiddling instinct"; if he does not twiddle his thumbs, it is the "thumb-not-twiddling instinct." Thus everything is explained with the facility of magic—word magic.

The instinct doctrine waned in the 1920's and was replaced by the concept of drive (Woodworth, 1918). Drive, the psychological representation of a need, was assumed to result from a physiological deficit and instigated the organism to undertake behaviors which would result in the offset of the need. This is a homeostatic conception; behavior results from organic disequilibrium and ceases when the organism returns to a state of equilibrium. (Along with hedonism, homeostasis has been one of the guiding tenets of motivational theory. As we shall see later, this position no longer dominates psychological thought.)

Drive replaced the concept of instinct because needs could be experimentally manipulated and controlled in laboratory situations. During the years 1925–1940, various obstacle techniques and activity devices (see Marx, 1960) were used to assess the relative strength of needs and to determine the relation of the degree of deprivation to various indexes of response strength.

The concept of drive was formalized by Hull in 1943, in what proved to be one of the most dominant books in modern psychology. Hull conceived of drive as a nondirective energizer of behavior; drives supply the motor or energy for action. Drives activate habits, or stimulus-response units, and the habits determine the direction of behavior. Drives were assumed to pool into one unitary source of energy; it was postulated that there are many sources of drive (e.g., food deprivation or water deprivation), but all have an identical energizing function (Brown, 1961). Hull proposed that the relationship between drive (D) and habit (H) was multiplicative: Behavior = $f(D \times H)$. Given a drive level of zero, the organism was expected to remain at rest. Conversely, given some drive level, the organism would become active and hence more likely to discover an appropriate goal object in the environment which would decrease his drive. Originally Hull specified that the sources of drive were restricted to tissue deficits. He later modified that position because of the work of Miller and Mowrer (summarized in Miller, 1951, and Mowrer, 1960) demonstrating that fear also could initiate behavior. It was ultimately postulated that any stimulus of sufficient intensity could function as a drive.

Hull did not reject the associative view regarding the stimulus as a behavioral determinant. Rather, he supplemented that position by adding another component to the contemporary determinants of action. There are critical studies which appear to support the Hullian conception that drive (energy) affects behavior. Associationists specify that maximum response strength will be exhibited when conditions during training and testing are identical, that is, when the stimulus situation during learning is repeated during the subsequent test trials. However, it has been shown that animals trained when deprived of food for 3 hours perform better when tested after 22 hours of deprivation than when tested after 3 hours of deprivation (Loess, 1952). In addition, sources of drive combine to facilitate performance, although the stimuli associated with those drives would a priori be considered quite dissimilar. For example, food deprivation has been found to increase the intensity of a startle or learned fear response (Amsel, 1950). Given a pure associative position, the introduction of a drive not present during learning could facilitate later performance only if the stimuli associated with that drive were similar to the stimuli associated with the drive operative during learning.

There are a multitude of studies which support the drive-times-habit conception. In addition to the prototypical examples cited above, it has been found that performance curves diverge over reinforced trials for groups differing in drive level, that shock intensity is related to speed of escape and eyelid conditioning, and that consummatory behavior varies with time of deprivation (see Brown, 1961, for a review of these and other empirical investigations).

The most sophisticated extension of Hull's original ideas has been proposed by Spence (1956, 1960). Spence emphasizes the drive properties of incentives (K) and suggests that in instrumental learning situations drive and incentive are additive and combine to multiply habit strength: Behavior = $f[(D + K) \times (H)]$. (A number of theoretical derivations related to discrimination learning and data supporting these derivations are presented in Spence, 1958a.)

Spence also has expanded the application of the drive-times-habit conception to human learning. These extensions have important implications for classroom performance. Spence (1958b) reasons that in classical aversive conditioning the drive mechanism is a hypothetical internal emotional response (r_e). The magnitude of r_e varies as a function of the strength of the unconditioned aversive stimulus. Spence further reasons that individuals may differ in their tendencies to react emotionally. Given an aversive stimulus, some individuals act as if its intensity were higher than the actions of other individuals would indicate it to be. Since speed of conditioning is a function of drive level, these people would be expected to condition faster with an aversive unconditioned stimulus than individuals who exhibit less emotional reactivity. Spence (1958b) cites data which support this hypothesis.

The shift in focus to individual differences raised a number of problems for Spence and his colleagues. Among the difficulties was the development of a reliable and valid individual-difference measure of emotional reactivity. The measure, which was constructed by Taylor (1953), consists of items taken from the Minnesota Multiphasic Personality Inventory which clinical psychologists agree upon as reflecting overt manifestations of anxiety—e.g., "I cry easily" and "I work under a great deal of tension." The final scale, although entitled the Manifest Anxiety Scale (MAS), is conceived by Spence and Taylor to be a measure of drive. The instrument assesses the tendency to respond emotionally in aversive situations, rather than a chronic state which characterizes an individual's drive level in all settings.

The MAS has been employed in conjunction with the drive-times-habit conception in the study of human learning. The conditions most thoroughly investigated have been the learning of simple and complex lists of paired associates. Spence reasons that a simple task is one in which the correct response is dominant in the person's hierarchy. Given that response hierarchy and the postulated multiplicative relationship between drive and habit, an increase in the level of drive is expected to increase the absolute difference between the probabilities of responding with the correct or incorrect answer. Therefore, intensity of drive and level of performance should be positively related. A complex task is one in which the correct response is initially low in the person's response hierarchy. Further, a number of competing responses are aroused by the stimuli representing a complex task. Given that constellation of response tendencies, an increase in drive level is expected to decrease performance. Intensity of drive and level of performance are hypothesized to be inversely related. Spence (1958b) cites a number of studies which support the anticipated interaction between drive level and task difficulty. Individuals classified as high on the MAS perform better than low-MAS subjects at an easy paired-associates task, while the reverse is true when the list is difficult. The results appear to provide further evidence for the drive-times-habit conception and enhance the construct validity of the MAS as a measure of drive. (See Weiner, 1966c, for an alternative interpretation of these data.)

Some implications of these experiments for learning in the classroom are evident. Given a complex task, procedures which minimize anxiety should be employed. This will lower drive level and maximize performance. On the other hand, given an easy task, performance would be facilitated if the students' drive level were increased. In addition, the theory suggests that extra training is advisable for highly anxious individuals to ensure that correct responses are high in their hierarchy.

Cognitive Theory. Pure associative theory and the drive-times-habit approach provide mechanistic conceptions of behavior. The organism is propelled toward the goal by connections between incoming stimulation and motor responses. A number of more cognitively oriented psychologists, however, have argued that behavior is purposive—i.e., guided by an anticipation of ends. For example, Lewin states that the organism volitionally uses its motor apparatus as a tool to reach the goal, rather than responding automatically because of an association with a stimulus. Prior to Lewin, McDougall (1923) proposed that each instinct, or propensity, involves striving for a particular end state.

The theorists most closely identified with the cognitive approach to behavior are Edward Tolman and Kurt Lewin. Much of Tolman's research and that of his colleagues was designed to raise problems which associationists and drive theorists could not readily explain. For example, it was shown that animals learn where food is placed rather than learning a specific motor response leading to the food. Further, Tolman and his associates demonstrated that learning occurs without an apparent reward. Reward, they argue, only seemingly influences learning because knowledge remains latent without an available incentive or reason for action (Tolman, 1932).

Despite the differences between the cognitive and mechanistic positions, Tolman's conception of the principles of performance is very similar to that of Hull (1952) and Spence. Tolman (1955) states that approach behavior is a function of organismic demands (N), the expectancy that the response will lead to the goal stimulus (E), and the incentive value of the goal (I): Behavior $= f(N, E, I)$. Note that Tolman did not specify the mathematical relationship between the determinants of behavior. However, he did intimate that the relationship was likely to be multiplicative.

Lewin, unlike Tolman, was a product of the German school of Gestalt psychology. Lewin employed the Gestalt field-theoretical approach in the study of motivation and psychodynamics. He states that one must consider the totality of forces acting on the person at a moment in time when attempting to understand and predict behavior. A force acting on a person is created when an object in the environment acquires a positive or negative valence. For this to occur, a psychological need must exist. For example, if one is hungry, then food becomes attractive, and a force is applied on the individual in the direction of the food object. Lewin specifies that the strength of a force is a function of needs of the person (t), properties of the goal (G), and the psychological distance of the person from the goal (e): Behavior $= f(t, G, 1/e)$. Frequently, many forces are simultaneously acting on the individual, and he is pushed in different directions. Lewin delineates three types of such conflict situations: avoidance-avoidance, avoidance-approach, and approach-approach. Only the last type of conflict is unstable, or readily resolvable. Lewin suggests that in educational settings the forces acting on the student are often induced by an authority figure. These forces impel the student in one direction, while forces derived from his own needs frequently oppose the induced forces.

Lewin also contends that a psychological need (tension) persists if not satisfied. In a series of classic experiments, Lewin and his students demonstrated that there is a tendency to recall (the Zeigarnik effect) and resume incompleted activities. In addition, a persisting need may be satisfied by objects other than the original goal object. Goals have substitute value for one another. (The reader is directed to Cartwright, 1959; Heider, 1960; and Lewin, 1935, 1938, for a review of Lewin's conception and empirical evidence.)

The experimental studies initiated by Lewin most relevant to problems in educational institutions relate to level of aspiration. "Level of aspiration" refers to a standard of performance which one expects to attain at a task. Performance below that level generally is perceived as a failure, regardless of the objective performance attainment. Level of aspiration is affected by group and cultural norms, individual differences, objective task difficulty, defensive reactions to failure, and numerous other factors (Lewin & others, 1944).

The theoretical analysis of level of aspiration guided Atkinson's (1964) conception of motivation. Atkinson has concentrated primarily upon achievement-related behavior: behavior in which there is competition with a standard of excellence. This work is closely allied to issues in education.

Atkinson conceives achievement-oriented behavior to be a resultant of an approach-avoidance conflict. The relative dominance of the approach or the avoidance tendency is determined by individual differences in particular motive strengths. A motive is conceived of as a relatively enduring personality characteristic which determines the capacity to enjoy certain incentives and influences what environmental objects can serve as reinforcers. If the motive to approach success (M_S), known as the need for achievement, is greater than the motive to avoid failure (M_{AF}), then individuals are expected to approach achievement-related tasks. Conversely, avoidance behavior should be exhibtied when M_{AF} is greater than M_S. The motive strengths weight the anticipated affects of hope and fear when undertaking an achievement task.

The need for achievement generally is inferred from responses to a Thematic Apperception Test. The protocols are scored according to a reliable method of content analysis developed by McClelland and his colleagues (McClelland & others, 1953). A projective measure was selected to assess needs because it was believed that individuals often are not aware of or do not want to admit their desires. The motive to avoid failure generally is measured with a self-report questionnaire constructed by Mandler and Sarason (1952) which assesses the tendency to become anxious in a test situation.

It has been found that individuals relatively high in M_S perform with greater intensity at achievement tasks, learn faster, have lower perceptual thresholds for success-related words, and exhibit a greater Zeigarnik effect than individuals classified as low in M_S. In addition, when constrained in an achievement-related context, individuals in whom M_S is greater than M_{AF} prefer tasks of intermediate difficulty, while subjects in whom M_{AF} is greater than M_S tend to select tasks which are relatively easy or extremely difficult. The highly anxious subjects especially avoid tasks of intermediate difficulty (Atkinson, 1957, 1964). The differential task preference also has been exhibited in vocational aspiration. Individuals in whom M_{AF} is greater than M_S tend to choose occupations too easy or too difficult relative to their ability level, while those in whom M_S is greater than M_{AF} strive for success in occupations more congruent with their ability (Mahone, 1960). There also is evidence that the two motive groups exhibit differential reactions to success and failure experiences. Individuals in whom M_S is greater than M_{AF} tend to "relax" after success and exhibit immediate increments in performance following failure. On the other hand, subjects in whom M_{AF} is greater than M_S suffer performance decrements after a failure and are "encouraged" by a success (Weiner, 1965).

To capture conceptually the preference for tasks of intermediate difficulty among subjects high in M_S, Atkinson assumes that the expectancy of success (E) and the incentive value of success (I), or pride, are inversely related: $I = 1 - E$. That is, more pride is experienced following success at a difficult than at an easy task. In his model of achievement-oriented behavior, the approach tendency is a function of $M_S \times E \times I$. Because I and E are inversely related and multiplicative, the greatest approach tendency is derived for tasks of intermediate difficulty (E approaches .50). Further elaboration of this notion enables Atkinson to account for the avoidance of tasks of intermediate difficulty for subjects who are considered to be anxious about failure.

The findings of Atkinson and his colleagues suggest modifications in the classroom which might facilitate learning and performance (Weiner, 1967). Atkinson and O'Connor (1963) report that students in whom M_S is greater than M_{AF} perform better in a homogeneous ability-grouped classroom than in a heterogeneous one. Homogeneous ability-grouped classrooms mirror competitive situations in which the expectancy of doing well in comparison to others approximates an intermediate level. In addition, subjects in whom M_{AF} is greater than M_S indicate that they are less happy in a homogeneous than in a heterogeneous classroom. The experimental findings concerning the differential reactions to success and failure which the two motive groups exhibit suggest that they should be given differential feedback in school. Individuals in whom M_{AF} is greater than M_S should receive a great deal of positive feedback and encouragement, while those in whom M_S is greater than M_{AF} should experience challenges and occasional failures. Frequently, teachers assume that failing students on an initial exam will enhance subsequent performance. The data refute this notion and also deny the simple conception that positive feedback will increase the quality of future performance (Goldberg, 1965). Different experiences should be received by different students.

The most far-reaching consequences of the need for achievement have been explored by McClelland (1961) and his colleagues. McClelland relates the economic growth and decline of societies throughout history to the prior level of achievement motivation in the society. He argues that the rise of capitalism, which Weber postulated as caused by the Protestant Reformation, was mediated by an increase in the level of the need for achievement. Protestant mothers employ child-rearing practices, such as early independence training, which lead to high achievement-oriented children. McClelland and his associates have attempted to induce achievement striving in businessmen of underdeveloped nations and in students who are performing below their capabilities in school (McClelland, 1965).

Psychoanalytic Theory. Psychoanalytic theory often is considered the psychological theory of motivation. Indeed, analytic thought provided one of the earliest, most systematic, and most elaborate conceptions of motivation. The scope of the theory is so great that one cannot adequately discuss the conception in this context. Research generated by psychoanalytic theory invariably is relevant to a single concept within the theory; there are no crucial experiments which confirm or deny the entire conception.

The basic tenets of psychoanalytic thought include the assumption that all behavior is determined, a reliance upon concepts of energy and entropy to explain pleasure and pain, and a belief in a historical or genetic approach to the understanding of behavior. Instinctual drives provide the foundation of the theory. These drives, represented mentally as wishes, strive for expression. The wishes persist until the desired object or a derivative is attained. The ego, conceived of as a relatively enduring structure, regulates and delays drive expression. Its function is to maximize the amount of goal satisfaction while minimizing the punishment which might be imposed by society because of the attainment of taboo goals. This approach-avoidance conflict model is employed by Freud to explain slips of the tongue, dreams, and symptom formation (Rapaport, 1959). Freud vacillated in his taxonomy of instincts, ultimately postulating two basic instincts: life (Eros) and death (Thanatos). The goal of the life instinct is to preserve the self and perpetuate the species, while the death instinct is manifested in the desire to reduce all internal stimulation to zero. Freud explains aggressive behavior as the turning of the death instinct outward rather than inward (Freud, 1933; Rapaport, 1960).

Freud postulated that all psychological energy is derived from the id, which contains the instinctual drives. Current ego psychologists, however, assume that the ego has its own energy system. The conceptual change to a "conflict-free ego sphere" (Hartmann, 1958) enables those employing psychoanalytic theory to discuss higher mental processes, or ego functions, without relating these functions to basic urges. Hence, there is an increasing emphasis on self-actualization concepts, creativity, play, etc. (White, 1959). Freud's initial conception has undergone many other changes and elaborations which cannot be discussed here (see C. Hall & Lindzey, 1957; Munroe, 1955).

Most research relevant to psychoanalytic motivational theory has been concerned with ego functions. Defense mechanisms, such as repression and perceptual defense (MacKinnon & Dukes, 1962), and displacement (Miller, 1959) are prominent in the list. In addition, systematic studies have been undertaken to investigate individual differences in cognitive styles, such as the tendency to repress or sensitize threatening material (Byrne, 1964). There also are individual differences in the disposition to level or sharpen incoming percepts (Gardner & others, 1959). Levelers are believed to overassimilate incoming percepts with prior memories; they are less adept at making fine perceptual discriminations, and they forget incoming information more easily.

A number of other research areas in part owe their inception to psychoanalytic thought, although present investigations have carried them far from that position. There has been tremendous growth in the study of dreams (Kleitman, 1963). The discovery of objective indexes to detect dreams has led investigators to ask whether there is a "need to dream" comparable to other viscerogenic needs (Dement, 1960). Individuals do exhibit increased dreaming following dream deprivation. There also have been a number of studies demonstrating the importance of early experiences for later development. There are "critical periods"; the consequences of experiences (or lack of experiences) occurring during these periods are relatively irreversible. For example, restricted perceptual transactions early in life may permanently retard development (Riesen, 1950); stimulation in infancy enhances normal stress responses later in life (Levine, 1960); and the absence of adequate social relationships in infant monkeys retards later adjustment (Harlow & Harlow, 1962). It certainly behooves educators to be especially concerned about early learning experiences.

Current Trends. Despite the manifest differences between theories, some overall theoretical trends are visible. There is a growing realization that behavior is complex and determined by many factors; no single concept, such as instinct, need, or association, can adequately explain the diverse patterns of behavior. Further, there is a decrease in the reliance upon homeostasis as the basic principle of motivation. Behaviors which are ends in themselves (Koch, 1956) and which increase the amount of internal stimulation are being studied in more detail. This reflects a growing tendency to study approach, as well as avoidance, behavior. There also is an increasing concern with environmental determinants of behavior: incentives, ecological factors (Barker, 1965), and cultural and social variables. In addition, great stress is laid on the identification and measurement of individual differences to aid in the study of psychological processes, such as learning and motivation. Finally, organisms are no longer perceived at rest until goaded by some external stimulus. Organisms are being viewed as continually active and striving. The focus is on the direction of behavior rather than on its instigation.

SPECIFIC RESEARCH AREAS. Curiosity and Exploratory Behavior. It has been indicated that motivational psychologists are becoming more concerned with approach behavior and behaviors which increase the amount of internal stimulation. Foremost among these problem areas is the study of curiosity and exploratory behavior. Hebb (1949) and his colleagues (Bexton & others, 1954) dramatically demonstrated that external stimulation is necessary for normal functioning. They found that individuals placed in severely restricted sensory environments experience great discomfort, often hallucinate, and exhibit impaired intellectual performance. The apparent need for stimulation caused investigators to ask whether an increase in external stimulation can serve as a reinforcer. It is now evident that the probability of a response can be increased if that response is followed by an increment or a change in the pattern of external stimulation. Further, animals are less likely to repeat a previous response because of stimulus or perceptual satiation than because of response fatigue (Glanzer, 1953).

Berlyne (1960) has undertaken the most systematic study of the determinants of curiosity behavior. He finds that novelty, complexity, "surprisingness," and incongruity are included among the determinants of an orienting response, or attention. Although individuals attend to incongruous figures, they often rate them as unpleasant. Berlyne, following Hebb and others, suggests that there is an optimal stimulation level. If the amount of stimulation is below that level, organisms strive to increase environmental information; if the amount of stimulation is above the optimal level, the organism strives to decrease stimulation. This is a homeostatic conception; however, equilibrium is not at zero stimulation, as Freud and Hull suggested. For further discussion of this topic, the reader is directed to the works of Fiske and Maddi (1961), Fowler (1965), and Walker (1964).

Affiliative Behavior. The study of affiliative behavior, behavior which is instrumental to the initiation and maintenance of friendships, initially was guided by the work on achievement motivation discussed previously. The need for affiliation is assessed with thematic apperceptive protocols (Atkinson, 1958) and has been found to relate to the number of long-distance telephone calls made, volunteering for group experiments, increased performance in the classroom when the teacher is affiliative (McKeachie,

1961), and a higher probability of being rejected by fraternities.

Recent work on affiliation has had a different orientation. Schachter (1959), searching for the environmental determinants of affiliative behavior, found that in stressful situations individuals prefer to be together. That is, fear of potential pain arouses affiliative motivation. Schachter suggests that "misery loves company." The desire to be with others when fearful is especially pronounced among only and firstborn children. Firstborns also stay in psychotherapy longer, they are more likely to become chronic alcoholics, and fewer become fighter-pilot aces than later-born children. In addition, firstborn children have higher thematic affiliative scores than later-born children (Dember, 1964). It has been reasoned that parents are especially sensitive to the fears of first children, are more protective, and give more relief to those children than to later-born children. Because of this indulgence, firstborn children look toward others for comfort in times of stress or fear.

Imbalance. Heider (1958, 1960) submits that states of imbalance are motivational. For Heider, balance primarily concerns relations between people, such as liking or disliking, or unit relations of belonging. For example, if A likes B and O, but B does not like O, then a state of imbalance exists. Because balance is preferred to imbalance, motivation is aroused to resolve this situation. Equilibrium may be established by A's changing one of his cognitions. If A decides that he does not like B or O (but not both), then balance is restored.

Incongruity is a variant of an imbalanced structure. Incongruity may exist between a message and its source ("Hitler is for peace"), an object and an attribute ("a friendly truant officer") (Osgood & Tannenbaum, 1955), or two cognitions ("Smoking causes cancer"; "I smoke"). The last situation, formally analyzed by Festinger (1957), has generated a great variety of motivational research. Festinger postulates that when one statement follows from the obverse of another ("I do not smoke" should follow from the statement that smoking causes cancer), cognitive dissonance exists, and motivation is aroused to reduce this dissonance. One method to reduce dissonance is to gain additional social support for the espoused behavior or belief. Festinger and others (1956) found that a group predicting the world was coming to an end became active proselyters when their prophecy was not fulfilled. In a very different research setting, Festinger and Lawrence (1962) demonstrated that resistance to response extinction in rats is positively related to the effortfulness of the response, as well as to the delay and infrequency of the reward. They argue that when a difficult response is followed by an unequivalent reward, dissonance is aroused. To resolve this dissonance extra rewards are perceived in the situation. The psychology of insufficient rewards also has been studied extensively in humans. In one oft-cited study, Festinger and Carlsmith (1959) demonstrated that the perceived attractiveness of a boring task is negatively related to the monetary reward associated with that task. If only a small monetary reward is contingent upon doing the task, then it is dissonant to perceive the task as annoying. For further elaboration of balance theories, the reader is directed to the works by Brehm and Cohen (1962) and Zajonc (1960).

Frustration. "Frustration" has multiple meanings in motivational research (Lawson & Marx, 1958). It may refer to an experimental manipulation (independent variable) which prevents a response. "Frustration" also often denotes a dependent measure; one assesses whether individuals exhibit frustrated behavior following certain experiences. Finally, "frustration" can indicate an intervening construct or internal condition which is inferred from a variety of behaviors.

The establishment of frustration (intervening construct) requires that an ongoing behavioral sequence be blocked before the goal is attained. Many reactions to frustration have been observed in laboratory experiments—e.g., aggression, regression, apathy, lowered quality of performance, and fixation (Lawson, 1965). In studies relating frustration to fixation, animals are given an insoluble discrimination problem. In such situations, most of the animals fixate upon one particular response. Some of the animals do not alter this response when the situation changes and the problem becomes soluble. This aberrant behavior is exhibited even when the correct response is clearly indicated. Maier (1956) argues that fixated behavior is distinct from motivated behavior; it is not affected by rewards and is intensified by punishment. This position is not fully accepted by the majority of psychologists (Yates, 1962).

The most theoretical and systematic analysis of frustration has been advanced by Amsel (1958) and his colleagues (Amsel & Ward, 1965). Amsel incorporates frustrative behavior into the drive-times-habit conception. Amsel reasons that frustration functions as a drive. As is true of all drives, frustration has cue properties. In support of this position, Amsel demonstrates that animals exhibit increased response strength following nonattainment of an expected food reward. In addition, the reaction made in the absence of the expected food can function as a discriminative cue. Amsel also postulates that frustration generalizes from the place of the nonreward back into the start box of a runway apparatus. He employs this notion to explain extinction data generated in partial-reinforcement situations and discrimination learning. Birch (1961) employs this theory to account for the decreased resistance to extinction which appears following overlearning.

Aggression. The impetus for the extensive work on aggression has three sources. First, there is the evident social importance of understanding aggressive behavior. Second, Freud discussed aggression at length when developing his instinct theory. Finally, the work of Dollard and others (1939) made the experimental study of aggression feasible and helped bridge the gap between academic psychology and psychoanalysis.

Aggression is considered to be the purposeful causing of injury to some person or object. Freud postulated a constant source of energy pushing the organism to undertake behavior instrumental to self-destruction or destruction of another. Experiments on aggression, however, generally manipulate an antecedent condition which is believed to arouse aggression, such as failure at a task, insulting the subject, or thwarting attempts to reach a goal. Following these frustrating experiences, aggressive behavior ordinarily increases. A related question that is subject to much study is how to reduce the strength of the tendency to aggress. Direct expression toward the frustrator will fulfill this aim. However, indirect expression also has cathartic value. Further, action other than motor expression, such as changing cognitions, also may reduce overt aggression (Feshbach, 1964).

The effects of an aggressive action, whether directed toward the frustrator or directed toward a substitute object, are subject to debate. Some investigators (Bandura & Walters, 1963) believe that expression of or viewing successful aggressive responses will increase the subsequent probability of an aggressive act. However, it also has been demonstrated that both real and fantasized aggressive behavior can reduce the drive toward aggression and subsequent aggressive actions. One variable which apparently determines whether a successful aggressive act will increase or reduce subsequent aggressiveness is whether aggression is aroused prior to the act (Feshbach, 1964). The issues of substitution and catharsis raise a number of fundamental questions for motivational theorists. Does motivation persist, once aroused, as Freud, Lewin, and Atkinson (1964) postulate? If so, how can the persisting desires be reduced, and how can goal attainment be conceptualized within a motivational theory? (For further discussion, the reader is directed to Berkowitz, 1962, and Buss, 1961.)

RELATION TO OTHER PROCESS AREAS.
Learning. Two questions have been raised which relate learning and motivation. First, can motives (drives) be learned? And, second, does the level of motivation during learning influence the degree of learning?

The learning of drives has been clearly demonstrated by Miller and Mowrer. They paired a neutral cue with the onset of shock. Animals then were able to learn an escape response when the previously neutral cue was presented without the aversive stimulus. Miller (1951) reasons that the neutral cue aroused a learned drive of fear, and the escape response was maintained because of fear or anxiety reduction. Drive theorists, such as Brown, argue that learned anxiety may be the basis of many human actions. For example, individuals may work for money because the absence of money leads to anxiety. Similarly, needs such as affiliation also may be learned because of their association with a primary drive. During infancy hunger reduction occurs in the presence of another human. Motives, when defined as personality dispositions, also are learned behavioral tendencies. An important antecedent condition for the development of aggressive needs is a punitive mother; mothers of children with high need achievement encourage and reward achievement-related behavior; etc.

The relation of drive level during acquisition to the degree of learning is a controversial question. To study this problem, animals are induced to learn a response under a high or a low drive level. Then half the animals in each group are tested under high or low drive. This factorial design enables experimenters to assess the effects of drive on learning and performance. Thus far there is no conclusive evidence to support the intuitive notion that motivation enhances learning. The effects of drive during learning depend on the type of learning (classical conditioning, instrumental learning, or insight learning) and the type of task. There is suggestive evidence which indicates that drive level does affect learning in instrumental situations if the task is complex.

Heightened motivation also might retard learning. There is evidence that augmented motivation narrows the range of cues which the individual utilizes and hence interferes with learning. It has been postulated that there is a curvilinear relationship between learning and motivation, with maximum facilitation when motivation is at an intermediate level. The reader is directed to the works of Cofer and Appley (1964), Kimble (1961), and Rethlingshafer (1963) for a more detailed discussion of motivation and learning.

Perception. In the late 1940's an approach known as the "new look" in perception was initiated. This revolt was directed against the stimulus-bound methodology of the psychophysicists. Investigators associated with the "new look" movement were interested in the effects of the person on perception: how values, needs, and individual differences influence what is perceived. The experiments often used ambiguous pictures and affective words as stimuli; the object was to demonstrate that motivational factors induce nonveridical, yet adaptive, judgments.

The earliest studies in this series examined the number of food-related percepts which subjects deprived of food report to ambiguous pictures. It was established that food percepts are affected by prior deprivation. In subsequent investigations the effects of values on perception were examined. In one well-known study, Bruner and Goodman (1947) found that poor children overestimate the size of coins significantly more than rich children. Similarly, tokens associated with rewards are estimated as larger than tokens not exchangeable for a reward. It has been suggested that this "cookie effect" occurs because "large" and "valued" have been often associated in the person's history.

The most active research in the perception-motivation field investigates the effects of noxious stimuli on perception. It has been found that individuals display heightened perceptual thresholds for threatening words (perceptual defense) and exhibit greater emotional reactivity to stimuli associated with shock, although they cannot consciously identify the stimuli (subception). These findings have been criticized for methodological shortcomings (Eriksen, 1958), and definitive demonstrations of the phenomena remain to be devised. However, a great deal of interesting research has been generated in this area (Brown, 1961; Jenkin, 1957).

Memory. The study of motivation and memory initially was guided by Freud's conception of repression. It was suggested that individuals would remember pleasant rather than unpleasant events, because the latter were "dangerous" to the equilibrium of the individual (Rapaport, 1942). Experimentation, however, revealed that the intensity of affect is a more potent determinant of retention than its positive or negative quality. In addition, individuals high in achievement motivation recall more incomplete (failed) than completed tasks in achievement settings. The simple notion that "threatening" events will be poorly recalled has not been substantiated.

Recent investigations relating motivation and memory have advanced far beyond the early studies of repression (Weiner, 1966a). Walker (1958) has presented a general theory of behavior which interrelates the concepts of arousal, action decrement, and consolidation. Walker predicts, and finds, that heightened arousal (drive) during learning makes the trace of that event less available for immediate recall but results in greater permanent memory. Walker suggests a trace-consolidation phase during which the memory trace is being strengthened. Weiner (1966b) has demonstrated that memory is enhanced if retention is instrumental to the avoidance of a shock. In his studies motivation is enhancing if presented during the perception of the event or during the temporally subsequent phase of trace storage. Motivation aroused during the time of trace retrieval does not facilitate recall. Indeed, standing in the $64,000 booth does not aid recall.

More good studies have been conducted than could possibly be included in this review. Human motivation and molar behavior have been emphasized. Therefore, important areas such as hormonal and physiological factors influencing motivation and unlearned patterns of behavior have been completely neglected. For a more detailed discussion of motivation, the reader is directed to the works of Atkinson (1964), Brown (1961), Cofer and Appley (1964), and the Nebraska symposium on motivation series (1953–1967). Other books are those by Bindra (1958), Birch and Veroff (1966), Haber (1966), John F. Hall (1961), Murray (1964), Rethlingshafer (1963), and Teevan and Birney (1964a, 1964b).

Bernard Weiner
University of California

References

Amsel, Abraham. "The Combination of a Primary Appetitional Need with Primary and Secondary Emotionally Derived Needs." *J Exp Psychol* 40:1–14; 1950.

Amsel, Abraham. "The Role of Frustrative Nonreward in Noncontinuous Reward Situations." *Psychol B* 55:102–19; 1958.

Amsel, Abraham, and Ward, Joseph S. "Frustration and Persistence: Resistance to Discrimination Following Prior Experience with the Discriminanda." *Psychol Monogr* 79 (No. 4) (Whole No. 597); 1965.

Atkinson, John W. "Motivational Determinants of Risk-taking Behavior." *Psychol R* 64:359–72; 1957.

Atkinson, John W. *Motives in Fantasy, Action, and Society.* Van Nostrand, 1958.

Atkinson, John W. *An Introduction to Motivation.* Van Nostrand, 1964.

Atkinson, John W., and O'Connor, Patricia. *Effects of Ability Grouping in Schools Related to Individual Differences in Achievement-Related Motivation.* USOE Cooperative Research Project No. 1283. Michigan, 1963.

Bandura, Albert, and Walters, Richard H. "Aggression." In *Child Psychology*, 62nd Yearbook, NSSE, U Chicago Press, 1963. p. 364–415.

Barker, Roger G. "Explorations in Ecological Psychology." *Am Psychologist* 20:1–14; 1965.

Berkowitz, Leonard. *Aggression: A Social Psychological Analysis.* McGraw-Hill, 1962.

Berkowitz, Leonard. "Aggressive Cues in Aggressive Behavior and Hostility Catharsis." *Psychol R* 71:104–22; 1964.

Berlyne, Daniel E. *Conflict, Arousal, and Curiosity.* McGraw-Hill, 1960.

Bexton, William H., and others. "Effects of Decreased Variation in the Sensory Environment." *Canadian J Psychol* 8:70–6; 1954.

Bindra, Dalbir. *Motivation: A Systematic Reinterpretation.* Ronald, 1958.

Birch, David. "A Motivational Interpretation of Extinction." In Jones, Marshall R. (Ed.) *Nebraska Symposium on Motivation.* U Nebraska Press, 1961. p. 179–97.

Birch, David, and Veroff, Joseph. *Motivation: A Study of Action.* Brooks/Cole, 1966.

Brehm, Jack W., and Cohen, Arthur R. *Explorations in Cognitive Dissonance.* Wiley, 1962.

Brown, Judson S. *The Motivation of Behavior.* McGraw-Hill, 1961.

Bruner, Jerome S., and Goodman, Cecile C. "Value and Need as Organizing Factors in Perception." *J Abn Social Psychol* 42:33–44; 1967.

Buss, Arnold H. *The Psychology of Aggression.* Wiley, 1961.

Byrne, Donn. "Repression-sensitization as a Dimension of Personality." In Maher, Brendan. (Ed.) *Progress in Experimental Personality Research*, Vol. 1. Academic, 1964.

Cartwright, Dorwin. "Lewinian Theory as a Contemporary Systematic Framework." In Koch, Sigmund. (Ed.) *Psychology: A Study of a Science*, Vol 2. McGraw-Hill, 1959. p. 7–91.

Cofer, Charles N., and Appley, Mortimer H. *Motivation: Theory and Research.* Wiley, 1964.

Dember, William N. "Birth Order and Need Affiliation." *J Abn Social Psychol* 68:555–7; 1964.

Dement, William. "The Effect of Dream Deprivation." *Sci* 131:1705–7; 1960.

Dollard, John, and others. *Frustration and Aggression.* Yale U Press, 1939.

Eriksen, Charles W. "Unconscious Processes." In Jones, Marshall R. (Ed.) *Nebraska Symposium on Motivation.* U Nebraska Press, 1958. p. 169–226.

Estes, William K. "Stimulus-Response Theory of Drive." In Jones, Marshall R. (Ed.) *Nebraska Symposium on Motivation.* U Nebraska Press, 1958. p. 35–69.

Feshbach, Seymour. "The Function of Aggression and the Regulation of Aggressive Drive." *Psychol R* 71:257–72; 1964.

Festinger, Leon. *A Theory of Cognitive Dissonance.* Harper, 1957.

Festinger, Leon, and Carlsmith, James M. "Cognitive Consequences of Forced Compliance." *J Abn Social Psychol* 58:203–10; 1959.

Festinger, Leon, and Lawrence, Douglas H. *Deterrents and Reinforcement: The Psychology of Insufficient Reward.* Stanford U Press, 1962.

Festinger, Leon, and others. *When Prophecy Fails.* U Minnesota Press, 1956.

Fiske, Donald W., and Maddi, Salvatore R. *Functions of Varied Experience.* Dorsey Press, Inc., 1961.

Fowler, Harry. *Curiosity and Exploratory Behavior.* Macmillan, 1965.

Freud, Sigmund. *New Introductory Lectures on Psycho-analysis.* Norton, 1933.

Gardner, Riley W., and others. *Cognitive Control.* Int U, 1959.

Glanzer, Murray. "Stimulus Satiation: An Explanation of Spontaneous Alternation and Related Phenomena." *Psychol R* 60:257–68; 1953.

Goldberg, Lewis. "Grades as Motivants." *Psychol Sch* 2:17–24; 1965.

Guthrie, Edwin R. "Conditioning: A Theory of Learning in Terms of Stimulus, Response, and Association." In Henry, Nelson B. (Ed.) *The Psychology of Learning.* 41st Yearbook, NSSE. Bobbs-Merrill, 1942. p. 17–60.

Haber, Ralph N. *Current Research in Motivation.* Holt, 1966.

Hall, Calvin S., and Lindzey, Gardner. *Theories of Personality.* Wiley, 1957.

Hall, John F. *Psychology of Motivation.* Lippincott, 1961.

Harlow, Harry F., and Harlow, Margaret K. "Social Deprivation in Monkeys." *Sci Am* 207:136–46, No. 5, Nov. 1962.

Hartmann, Heinz. *Ego Psychology and the Problem of Adaptation.* Int U, 1958.

Hebb, Donald O. *The Organization of Behavior.* Wiley, 1949.

Heider, Fritz. *Psychology of Interpersonal Relations.* Wiley, 1958.

Heider, Fritz. "The Gestalt Theory of Motivation." In Jones, Marshall R. (Ed.) *Nebraska Symposium on Motivation.* U Nebraska Press, 1960. p. 145–72.

Holt, Edwin B. *Animal Drive and the Learning Process: An Essay Toward Radical Empiricism,* Vol. I. Holt, 1931.

Hull, Clark. *Principles of Behavior.* Appleton, 1943.

Hull, Clark. *A Behavior System.* Yale U Press, 1952.

Jenkin, Noel. "Affective Processes in Perception." *Psychol B* 54:100–27; 1957.

Jenkins, James J., and Hanratty, Jacqueline A. "Drive Intensity Discrimination in the Albino Rat." *J Compar Physiol Psychol* 42:228–32; 1949.

Keislar, Evan R. "A Descriptive Approach to Classroom Motivation." *J Teach Ed* 11:310–5; 1960.

Kimble, Gregory A. *Hilgard and Marquis' Conditioning and Learning.* Appleton, 1961.

Kleitman, Nathaniel. *Sleep and Wakefulness.* U Chicago Press, 1963.

Koch, Sigmund. "Behavior as 'Intrinsically' Regulated: Work Notes toward a Pretheory of Phenomena Called 'Motivational.'" In Jones, Marshall R. (Ed.) *Nebraska Symposium on Motivation.* U Nebraska Press, 1956. p. 42–86.

Lawson, Reed. *Frustration.* Macmillan, 1965.

Lawson, Reed, and Marx, Melvin H. "Frustration: Theory and Experiment." *Genet Psychol Monogr* 57:393–464; 1958.

Leeper, Robert W. "The Role of Motivation in Learning: A Study of Phenomenon of Differential Motivational Control and Utilization of Habits." *J Genet Psychol* 46:3–40; 1935.

Levine, Seymour. "Stimulation in Infancy." *Sci Am* 202:80–6; 1960.

Lewin, Kurt. *A Dynamic Theory of Personality.* McGraw-Hill, 1935.

Lewin, Kurt. *The Conceptual Representation and the Measurement of Psychological Forces.* Duke U Press, 1938.

Lewin, Kurt, and others. "Level of Aspiration." In Hunt, J. McV. (Ed.) *Personality and the Behavioral Disorders,* Vol 1. Ronald, 1944. p. 333–78.

Loess, Henry B. "The Effect of Variation of Motivational Level and Changes in Motivational Level on Performance in Learning." Doctoral dissertation. State U Iowa, 1952.

MacKinnon, Donald W., and Dukes, William F. "Repression." In Postman, Leo. (Ed.) *Psychology in the Making.* Knopf, 1962. p. 662–744.

Mahone, Charles H. "Fear of Failure and Unrealistic Vocational Aspiration." *J Abn Social Psychol* 60:253–61; 1960.

Maier, Norman R. F. "Frustration Theory: Restatement and Extension." *Psychol R* 63:370–88; 1956.

Mandler, George, and Sarason, Seymour B. "A Study of Anxiety and Learning." *J Abn Social Psychol* 47:166–73; 1952.

Marx, Melvin H. "Motivation." In Harris, Chester W. (Ed.) *Encyclopedia of Educational Research,* 3rd ed. Macmillan, 1960. p. 888–900.

McClelland, David. *The Achieving Society.* Van Nostrand, 1961.

McClelland, David. "Toward a Theory of Motive Acquisition." *Am Psychologist* 20:321–33; 1965.

McClelland, David, and others. *The Achievement Motive.* Appleton, 1953.

McDougall, William. *Outline of Psychology.* Scribner, 1923.

McKeachie, William J. "Motivation, Teaching Methods, and College Learning." In Jones, Marshall R. (Ed.) *Nebraska Symposium on Motivation.* U Nebraska Press, 1961. p. 111–41.

Miller, Neal E. "Learnable Drives and Rewards." In

Stevens, S. Smith. (Ed.) *Handbook of Experimental Psychology.* Wiley, 1951. p. 435–72.

Miller, Neal E. "Liberalization of Basic S-R Concepts: Extensions to Conflict, Behavior, Motivation, and Social Learning." In Koch, Sigmund. (Ed.) *Psychology: A Study of a Science,* Vol. 2. McGraw-Hill, 1959. p. 196–292.

Mowrer, O. Hobart. *Learning Theory and Behavior.* Wiley, 1960.

Munroe, Ruth. *Schools of Psychoanalytic Thought.* Holt, 1955.

Murray, Edward J. *Motivation and Emotion.* Prentice-Hall, 1964.

Osgood, Charles E., and Tannenbaum, Percy H. "The Principle of Congruity in the Prediction of Attitude Change." *Psychol R* 62:42–55; 1955.

Rapaport, David. *Emotions and Memory.* Williams and Wilkins, 1942.

Rapaport, David. "The Structure of Psychoanalytic Theory: A Systematizing Attempt." In Koch, Sigmund. (Ed.) *Psychology: A Study of a Science,* Vol. 3. McGraw-Hill, 1959. p. 55–183.

Rapaport, David. "On the Psychoanalytic Theory of Motivation." In Jones, Marshall R. (Ed.) *Nebraska Symposium on Motivation.* U Nebraska Press, 1960. p. 173–247.

Rethlingshafer, Dorothy. *Motivation as Related to Personality.* McGraw-Hill, 1963.

Riesen, Austin H. "Arrested Vision." *Sci Am* 183:16–9; 1950.

Schachter, Stanley. *The Psychology of Affiliation.* Stanford U Press, 1959.

Skinner, B. F. *Science and Human Behavior.* Macmillan, 1953.

Spence, Kenneth W. *Behavior Theory and Conditioning.* Yale U Press, 1956.

Spence, Kenneth W. "Behavior Theory and Selective Learning." In Jones, Marshall R. (Ed.) *Nebraska Symposium on Motivation.* U Nebraska Press, 1958(a). p. 73–107.

Spence, Kenneth W. "A Theory of Emotionally Based Drive (D) and Its Relation to Performance in Simple Learning Situations." *Am Psychologist* 13:131–41; 1958(b).

Spence, Kenneth W. *Behavior Theory and Learning.* Prentice-Hall, 1960.

Taylor, Janet A. "A Personality Scale of Manifest Anxiety." *J Abn Social Psychol* 48:285–90; 1953.

Teevan, Richard C., and Birney, Robert C. *Theories of Motivation in Learning.* Van Nostrand, 1964(a).

Teevan, Richard C., and Birney, Robert C. *Theories of Motivation in Personality and Social Psychology.* Van Nostrand, 1964(b).

Thorndike, Edward L. *Animal Intelligence.* Macmillan, 1911.

Tolman, Edward C. *Purposive Behavior in Animals and Men.* Appleton, 1932.

Tolman, Edward C. "Principles of Performance." *Psychol R* 62:315–26; 1955.

Walker, Edward L. "Action Decrement and Its Relation to Learning." *Psychol R* 65:129–42; 1958.

Walker Edward L. "Psychological Complexity as a Basis for a Theory of Motivation and Choice." In Levine, David. (Ed.) *Nebraska Symposium on Motivation.* U Nebraska Press, 1964. p. 57–95.

Watson, John B. *Behaviorism.* Norton, 1924.

Weiner, Bernard. "The Effects of Unsatisfied Achievement Motivation on Persistence and Subsequent Performance." *J Pers* 33:428–42; 1965.

Weiner, Bernard. "Effects of Motivation on the Availability and Retrieval of Memory Traces." *Psychol B* 65:24–37; 1966(a).

Weiner, Bernard. "Motivation and Memory." *Psychol Monogr* 80 (No. 18) (Whole No. 626); 1966(b).

Weiner, Bernard. "Role of Success and Failure in the Learning of Easy and Complete Tasks." *J Pers Social Psychol* 3:339–44; 1966(c).

Weiner, Bernard. "Current Conceptions of Achievement Motivation and Their Implications for Research and Performance in the Classroom." *Psychol Sch* 4:164–71; 1967.

White, Robert W. "Motivation Reconsidered: The Concept of Competence." *Psychol R* 66:297–333; 1959.

Woodworth, Robert S. *Dynamic Psychology.* Columbia U Press, 1918.

Yates, Aubrey J. *Frustration and Conflict.* Wiley, 1962.

Zajonc, Robert B. "The Concepts of Balance, Congruity, and Dissonance." *Public Opin Q* 24:280–96; 1960.

MOTOR ABILITIES

Motor skills involve movements of the body, limbs, or other body members (e.g., fingers) by action of the striated muscles. Most skills involve some (1) spatial-temporal patterning, (2) interaction of responses with sensory input and feedback from auditory, visual, muscular, and joint senses, and (3) learning. This article is concerned with the abilities (or aptitudes) which facilitate the learning of such motor skills. The article is not concerned with procedural or environmental factors influencing motor-skill learning (see the article on skills by Ammons and Ammons in the 1960 edition of this encyclopedia). The article presents a conceptual framework for thinking about motor abilities, describes tests which have been used to measure motor abilities, the varieties of motor abilities which have been identified, and the tests found most diagnostic of these different abilities. (The terms "motor," "sensory-motor," "psychomotor," and "perceptual-motor" are considered interchangeable.)

THE ABILITY-SKILL DISTINCTION. The term "ability" refers to a general trait of the individual which has been inferred from certain response consistencies (e.g., correlations) on certain kinds of tasks. These are fairly enduring traits, which in the adult are difficult to change. Many of these abilities are, of course, themselves a product of learning and develop at different rates, mainly during childhood and adolescence (Gagné & Fleishman, 1959). Some abilities depend more on genetic than on learning factors, but most abilities depend on both to some degree. At a given stage of life they represent traits or organismic factors which the individual brings with him when he begins to learn a new task. These abilities (e.g., manual dexterity) are related to performances in a variety of human tasks.

The term "skill" refers to the level of proficiency on a specific task or limited group of tasks. Examples of specific skills are proficiencies in flying an airplane, in operating a turret lathe, and in playing basketball. The assumption is that the skills involved in such complex activities can be described in terms of the more basic abilities. For example, the level of performance a man can attain on a turret lathe may depend on his motor abilities of manual dexterity and motor coordination. However, these same abilities may be important to proficiency in other skills as well. Thus, manual dexterity is needed in assembling electrical components and motor coordination is needed to fly an airplane.

ABILITIES AND SKILL LEARNING. Implicit in the previous analysis is the important relation between abilities and learning. Thus, individuals with high manual dexterity may more readily learn the specific skill of lathe operation. The mechanism of transfer of training probably operates here. Some abilities may transfer to the learning of a greater variety of specific tasks than others. The individual who has a great many highly developed basic abilities can become proficient at a great variety of specific tasks. (For a discussion of the development of abilities, their physiological bases, the role of learning, environmental and cultural factors, and evidence on the rate of ability development during the life span see Fleishman, 1964b, and Gagné & Fleishman, 1959.) Abilities appear to be relatively enduring traits of the individual. Unless he is subjected to marked environmental changes, a man's basic abilities are not likely to change much once he reaches adulthood. This probably results from the fact that they have been learned, relearned, and practiced many times during the individual's lifetime. The mechanism here is probably what we call "overlearning." Some decline with age often occurs, but this is true only of some abilities, not all. And the age at which decline begins and the rate of decline varies with the ability and the individual.

Human adults do show marked learning over time in practically any type of specific *skill*. However, the rate of learning and the final level achieved by particular individuals in certain skills are limited by the basic abilities of these individuals. The fact that these basic abilities are themselves fairly stable allows us to make useful predictions about subsequent performance on specific tasks. For example, knowledge about a person's manual dexterity helps us predict his probable success later on in assembly tasks. Knowledge about the relevant physical proficiencies should help us predict performance in complex athletic skills. Some abilities may be more important later in skills learning, while other abilities are critical earlier in learning (see, e.g., Fleishman & Hempel,

1954b, 1955; Fleishman, 1967). The idea that basic abilities place limits on later skill proficiency emphasizes the need to develop these abilities in preadult life.

MOTOR-ABILITY TESTS FOR CHILDREN. Early tests of mental functioning were largely sensorimotor in nature. Galton (1883) identified such performance with "intelligence." Similarly, Cattell (1890) constructed "mental tests" which included measures of grip strength, rate of arm movement, and reaction time, along with simple sensory and memory measures. It was actually Binet (Binet & Henri, 1895) who first concluded that tests of sensorimotor skills have little relation to "general mental functioning." Consequently, to Binet goes the credit for separating out at least two gross classes of human abilities (Fleishman, 1957a). Although the concept of "general intelligence" or "g" is still with us (less in the United States than in certain other countries), few today are willing to postulate a general ability embracing both psychomotor and intellectual classes of abilities.

Many "intelligence tests" for children, including the *Stanford-Binet Test*, contain tasks which involve motor components. In fact, many investigators view tests for young children not so much as evaluations of intelligence as evaluations of general developmental level. Because the most observable developments in young children are in motor facility, these tests have included many motor-skill types of items.

Thus, the *Gesell Development Schedule* (Gesell & others, 1940) includes among its tests at the 15-months age level turning book pages, putting a pellet in a bottle, climbing stairs, initiating a drawing stroke, and placing cubes in cups. Examples of items included in the 72-months-level test are jumping from a 12-inch height landing on toes, advanced throwing, standing on each foot alternately, and walking the length of a 4-inch board.

The *Merrill-Palmer Scale* (Stutsman, 1931) contains predominantly sensorimotor items. Examples are throwing a ball, pulling a string, and crossing the feet. The *California Scale* (Bayley, 1933), which tests children of 1 to 18 months, covers postural and motor development, manipulation of objects, perception, attention, and naming objects, the motor items being predominantly in the lower ages.

A test developed by Oseretsky in Russia in 1923 received attention in various countries. This test, known as the *Oseretsky Tests of Motor Proficiency*, was edited by Doll (1946) in the United States from a Portuguese adaptation. The tests were designed especially for use with feebleminded children and children with motor disorders. They covered "all major types of motor behavior from postural reactions and gross bodily movements to finger coordination and control of facial muscles." There were six tests for each age which served as indexes of "general coordination of hands," "motor speed," "simultaneous voluntary movement," and the "ability to perform without superfluous movements." Materials used included matchsticks, wooden spools, thread, paper, boxes, balls, and sieves. An example of a movement test is "walk a line two meters long (7 years)."

There are a number of other individual performance tests for children such as the *Pittner-Paterson, Cornell-Cox,* and the *Arthur Point* scales of performance. However, these performance tests are not tests of motor skill. They are essentially nonverbal scales of mental ability involving perceptual, spatial, or "insightful" behavior.

ADULT PSYCHOMOTOR TESTS. As indicated above, early tests of psychomotor skills were of the simplest kind. Between 1920 and 1940 most of the research on motor skills remained confined to such tests. Laboratory investigations were conducted on such problems as the specificity of simple motor abilities, with some small-scale attempts to identify factors underlying individual differences in these abilities. Thus, studies by Robert Seashore and his co-workers (R. Seashore, 1940, 1951; R. Seashore & others, 1941, 1942) and by Reymert (1923) and Campbell (1934) indicated that in fine motor skills the sense employed is of moderate significance, the musculature employed is of slight significance, and the pattern of movement involved is likely to be the most important factor. Moreover, the investigators largely concluded that motor-skill factors are relatively few and very narrow in scope (Buxton, 1938; Muscio, 1922; Perrin, 1929; R. Seashore, 1930, 1940; Seashore & others, 1941, 1949). In general, these early studies showed simple motor-skill tests to have low correlations with each other. We shall see later that this was largely a function of the choice of measures and the restricted range of skills investigated. It remained for subsequent research to exploit these relationships more thoroughly.

With the possible exception of certain dexterity tests, test batteries of special aptitudes during this era seldom included motor-skill measures. Robert Seashore pioneered an attempt to develop a more comprehensive motor-skills battery. This was called the *Stanford Motor Skills Unit* (R. Seashore, 1928), and it contained six tests of representative types of motor performances. It included (1) the *Koerth Pursuit Rotor,* to measure accuracy in following with a stylus a small target moving rapidly in a circle; (2) the *Miles Speed Rotor,* to measure speed of rotary arm, wrist, and finger movements in turning a small drill; (3) the *Brown Spool Packer,* to measure precision in reproducing rhythmic patterns on a telegraphic key; (4) the *Motor Rhythm Synchrometer,* to measure precision in reproducing rhythmic patterns on a telegraphic key; (5) the *Serial Discrimeter,* to measure speed in making discriminating reactions to signals which change as fast as they are reacted to correctly; and, finally (6), speed of tapping a telegraph key. These tests, described in 1928, were the forerunners of psychomotor tests dealing with more important types of psychomotor performances.

This era was characterized by an increasing number of validation studies of motor-ability tests in field settings. A large number of these studies indicated zero or low correlations between simple motor-ability tests and proficiency in more complex motor skills, such as typing (Walker & Adams, 1934), machine shopwork (R. Seashore, 1951), and winding-machine operation in knitting mills (S. Seashore, 1931). High validities were found in a number of studies for simple steadiness tests in predicting rifle marksmanship (R. Seashore & Adams, 1933; Humphreys & others, 1936; Spaeth & Dunham, 1921). Finger- and manual-dexterities tests were shown on occasion to have some validity for watchmaking, electrical fixture and radio assemblies, coil winding, packing and wrapping, and certain kinds of machine operation. The United States Employment Service is one agency which employs simple motor-ability tests in its comprehensive test batteries. Two of these, *Manual Dexterity* and *Finger Dexterity,* involve pegboards and assembly-type tasks. Two others, purporting to evaluate motor coordination and motor speed, are paper-and-pencil tests (e.g., tapping in circles). Actually recent research has shown that the latter tests measure neither "motor speed" nor "motor coordination" as such (Fleishman & Ellison, 1962).

The assumption underlying simple motor-ability testing was that it should be possible to develop a battery of simple motor tests which would indicate the likelihood of success in a more complex psychomotor skill. So strongly was this belief held that failures in prediction have often been attributed to faulty techniques, such as lack of reliability of the measures used. However, in most cases, the real cause was failure to sample the relevant psychomotor abilities.

World War II provided the impetus for developing more complex tests of psychomotor ability. The most extensive program of this type was conducted in the United States Air Force psychology research program (Melton, 1947). Some of the most critical jobs in the air force depended upon psychomotor skills of a complexity never before investigated. Outstanding examples were the tasks of pilot, gunner, and bombardier.

The tests employed apparatus that varied in complexity from simple pegboards to complicated mechanical and electronic devices. The complex-apparatus tests developed were shown to have substantial validity for predicting later proficiency in these jobs (Fleishman, 1956; Melton, 1947). For complete descriptions, with pictures, of these tests see the relevant works by Fleishman (1956) and Melton (1947).

The *Complex Coordination Test* is one example. The examinee must make appropriate control adjustments of stick and pedal controls in response to successively presented patterns of visual signals (Fig. 1). The task is to "match" the position of stimulus lights in each of three dimensions by coordinate movements of these controls. The score is the number of completed matchings in an eight-minute period. A validity coefficient of .45 was achieved for this test in predicting subsequent flying proficiency.

Another example is the *Rudder Control Test,* which also has been a consistent predictor of pilot success. The examinee sits in a mock cockpit arrange-

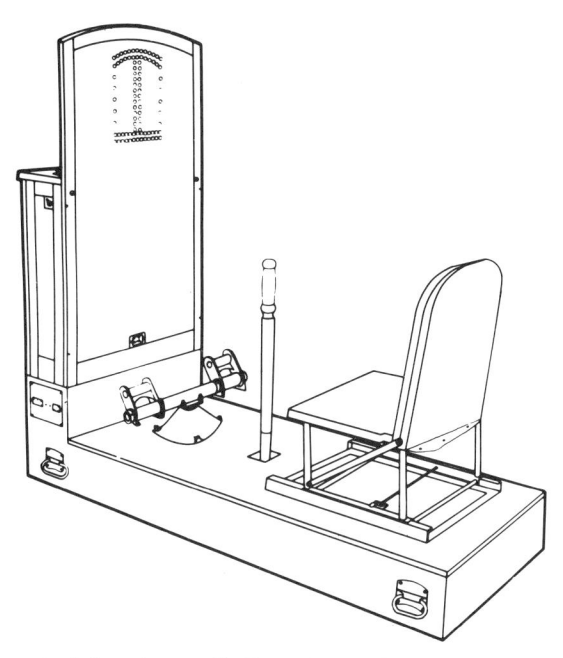

Fig. 1. Complex coordination test apparatus

ment. His own weight throws the seat off balance unless he applies correction by means of coordinated pedal adjustments. The score is the amount of time during which the apparatus is correctly aligned. The test takes 15 minutes to administer and has a validity of 40 for pilot selection.

The reader may infer that these tests are valid because they seem to represent a miniature job sample of certain aspects of the pilot's job. However, this is only a small part of the answer. Many tests thought to duplicate what seemed to be important aspects of the pilot's job failed to achieve any predictive value.

The reason the *Complex Coordination Test* and the *Rudder Control Test* are valid predictors is that between them they sample three of the underlying abilities which are crucial to pilot success (Fleishman, 1956). The resemblance of the task itself to the pilot's job is incidental to the fact that the *Complex Coordination Test* measures a spatial-orientation factor and two psychomotor factors, while the *Rudder Control Test* measures these same two psychomotor factors. These factors have been identified as control precision and multilimb coordination (defined below).

Now let us consider several other psychomotor tests found valid for pilots which do not resemble the pilot's job at all. These tests tap the human abilities measured by the *Rudder Control Test* and the *Complex Coordination Test*. An example is the *Rotary Pursuit Test*, which was used in the U.S. Air Force Battery for over 10 years (Fig. 2). This test resembles a phonograph turntable. The disk revolves at a speed of 60 rotations per minute. The subject's task is to keep a stylus in contact with a small target embedded near the edge of the disk. The score is the amount of time the stylus is on target in five 20-second periods. The *Rotary Pursuit Test* does

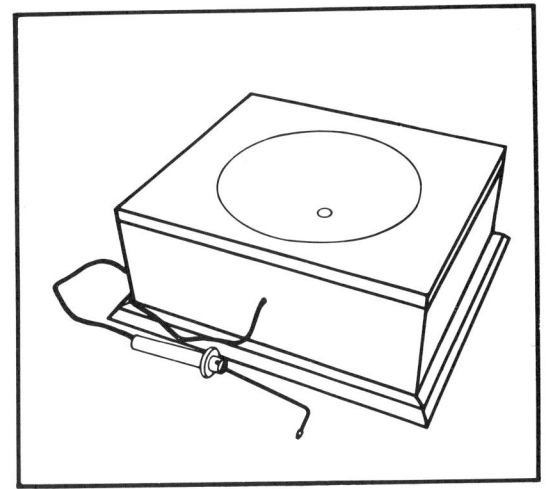

Fig. 2. Rotary pursuit test apparatus

not resemble the task of the aircraft pilot, but it does measure the control precision factor, which apparently accounts for its validity.

The *Two-Hand Coordination Test* is another example of a test which in no way resembles the pilot's task but which is valid nonetheless, because it measures relevant abilities. In this test, one lathe-type control handle moves a target follower to the right and left, while another control handle moves it to and from the subject. By proper coordinate movements of both hands, the subject can move the target follower in any direction. During the test he must keep the target follower on a visually perceived target as it moves along an irregular pathway. During World War II, scores on this test were found to be related to success in bombardier and flexible-gunnery training as well as to pilot proficiency (Melton, 1947).

ANALYSIS OF PSYCHOMOTOR ABILITIES. More recent research than that just described has investigated the *sources* of validity in such tests. A whole series of interlocking experimental-factor-analytic studies, attempting to isolate and identify the common variance in a wide range of psychomotor performances, has been carried out.

An early study in this series (Fleishman, 1953) reviewed previous factor analyses of motor skills and described the methodological issues. A second study (Fleishman, 1954b) was a large-scale attempt to put into a single study representative measures of all factors previously identified. Later studies have included analyses of fine manipulative performances, e.g., finger and manual dexterity (Fleishman & Hempel, 1954b; Fleishman & Ellison, 1962) and gross physical proficiency, e.g., push-ups and chins (Hempel & Fleishman, 1955; Nicks & Fleishman, 1961; Fleishman & others, 1961a, 1961b; Fleishman, 1962, 1964b). One study (Fleishman, 1958) focused on positioning movements (reaching, moving controls to specified positions, etc.) and "static reactions" (e.g., hand steadiness). Positioning movements are those in which the terminal accuracy of the response is critical, and static reactions involve primarily maintenance of limb positions (see Brown & Jenkins, 1947). Other studies (e.g., Fleishman, 1956, 1958; Parker & Fleishman, 1960) concerned "movement reactions," where the performance involves coordinated responses or smooth responses or precisely controlled movements or continuously adjustive reactions.

The psychomotor abilities thus far identified by factor analysis are discussed in the following sections.

Control Precision. Control precision is common to tasks which require fine, highly controlled, but not overcontrolled muscular adjustments, primarily where larger muscle groups are involved (Fleishman, 1958; Fleishman & Hempel, 1956; Parker & Fleishman, 1960). The ability extends to arm-hand as well as to leg movements. It is most critical where such adjustments must be rapid but precise.

Multilimb Coordination. Multilimb coordination is the ability to coordinate the movements of a number of limbs simultaneously, and it is best measured by devices involving multiple controls (Fleishman, 1958; Fleishman & Hempel, 1956; Parker & Fleishman, 1960). The factor has been found general to tasks requiring coordination of the two feet (e.g., *Rudder Control Test*), two hands (e.g., *Two-Hand Coordination Test*), and hands and feet (e.g., *Complex Coordination Test*).

Response Orientation. Response orientation is general to visual-discrimination-reaction psychomotor tasks involving rapid directional discrimination and orientation of movement patterns (Fleishman, 1957b, 1957c, 1958; Fleishman & Hempel, 1956; Parker & Fleishman, 1960). This ability appears to involve the ability to *select* the correct movement in relation to the correct stimulus, especially under highly speeded conditions.

Reaction Time. Reaction time represents simply the speed with which the individual is able to respond to a stimulus when it appears (Fleishman, 1954b, 1958; Fleishman & Hempel, 1955; Parker & Fleishman, 1960). There are consistent indications that individual differences in this ability are independent of whether the stimulus is auditory or visual and are also independent of the type of response which is required. However, once the stimulus situation or the response situation is complicated to involve alternate choices, reaction time is not the primary factor that is measured.

Speed of Arm Movement. Speed of arm movement represents simply the speed with which an individual can make a gross, discrete arm movement where accuracy is not the requirement (Fleishman, 1958; Fleishman & Hempel, 1954a, 1955; Parker & Fleishman, 1960). There is ample evidence that this factor is independent of the reaction-time factor.

Rate Control. Rate control involves the making of continuous anticipatory motor adjustments relative to changes in speed and direction of a continuously moving target or object (Fleishman, 1958; Fleishman & Hempel, 1955, 1956). This factor is general to tasks involving compensatory as well as following pursuit and extends to tasks involving responses to changes in rate. Research has shown that adequate measurement of this ability requires an actual response to the changing direction and speed of the stimulus object, not simply a judgment of the rate of the stimulus alone.

Manual Dexterity. Manual dexterity involves skillful, well-directed arm-hand movements in manipulating fairly large objects under speed conditions (Fleishman, 1953, 1954a; Fleishman & Ellison, 1962; Fleishman & Hempel, 1954b; Parker & Fleishman, 1960; Hempel & Fleishman, 1955).

Finger Dexterity. Finger dexterity is the ability to make skill-controlled manipulations of tiny objects involving, primarily, the fingers (Fleishman, 1953, 1954a; Fleishman & Ellison, 1962; Fleishman & Hempel, 1954b; Parker & Fleishman, 1960; Hempel & Fleishman, 1955).

Arm-Hand Steadiness. Arm-hand steadiness is the ability to make precise arm-hand positioning movements where strength and speed are minimized; the critical feature is the steadiness with which such movements can be made (Fleishman, 1953, 1954a, 1958; Fleishman & Hempel, 1955; Hempel & Fleishman, 1955; Parker & Fleishman, 1960).

Wrist and Finger Speed. Wrist and finger speed has been called "tapping" in many studies through the years (e.g., Greene, 1943; Fleishman, 1953). It has been used in a variety of different studies, primarily because they involved the use of printed tests, which are quick and easy to administer; the factor is best measured by printed tests requiring rapid tapping of the pencil in relatively large areas. However, research shows that this factor is highly restricted in scope and does not extend to many tasks in which apparatus is used (Fleishman, 1954a; Fleishman & Hempel, 1954b; Fleishman & Ellison, 1962).

Aiming. Aiming is measured by printed tests which provide the subject with a large number of very small circles to be dotted in (Fleishman, 1953, 1954a; Hempel & Fleishman, 1955; Fleishman & Ellison, 1962). The subject typically goes from circle to circle placing one dot in each circle as rapidly as possible.

Extent Flexibility. Extent flexibility is the ability to flex or stretch the trunk and back muscles *as far as possible* in either a forward, a lateral, or a backward direction (e.g., reaching tests). This factor and the following ones account for performance on tests of *physical fitness*, or physical proficiency, which constitutes another large area of motor performance. (For details of these factors and for the tests most diagnostic of each, see Fleishman, 1964b.) A battery of tests designed to measure these factors comprises the Fleishman Basic Fitness Tests (Fleishman, 1964a, 1964b). National norms and developmental curves for these tests, based on 20,000 males and females from 45 school systems, are available.

Dynamic Flexibility. Dynamic flexibility is the ability to make repeated, *rapid* flexing movements in which the resiliency of the muscles in *recovery* from strain or distortion is critical (e.g., twist and touch).

Static Strength. Static strength is the maximum force which a subject can exert, for a brief period, where the force is exerted continuously up to this maximum. In contrast to other strength factors, this is the force which can be exerted against external objects (e.g., lifting heavy weights or pulling against a dynamometer), rather than in supporting or propelling the body's own weight (e.g., hand grip).

Dynamic Strength. Dynamic strength is a measure of muscular endurance; it emphasizes the resistance of the muscles to fatigue. The common emphasis of tests measuring this factor is on the power of the muscles to propel, support, or move the body repeatedly or to support it for prolonged periods (e.g., pull-ups).

Trunk Strength. Trunk strength is a second, more limited, dynamic strength factor specific to the trunk muscles, particularly the abdominal muscles (e.g., leg lifts).

Explosive Strength. Explosive strength is the ability to expend a maximum of energy in one or a series of explosive acts. This factor is distinguished from other strength factors in requiring mobilization of energy for a burst of effort, rather than continuous strain, stress, or repeated exertion of muscles (e.g., shuttle run, softball throw).

Gross Body Coordination. Gross body coordination is the ability to coordinate the simultaneous actions of different parts of the body while making gross body movements (e.g., cable jump).

Gross Body Equilibrium. Gross body equilibrium is the ability of an individual to maintain his equilibrium, despite forces pulling him off balance, when he has to depend mainly on nonvisual (e.g., vestibular and kinesthetic) cues (e.g., balance board).

Stamina (Cardiovascular Endurance). Stamina is the capacity to continue maximum effort, requiring prolonged exertion over time (e.g., 600-yard run-walk).

ABILITIES AND SKILL ACQUISITION. Motor abilities have been found to be predictive of performance of different stages of learning complex perceptual-motor tasks. However, abilities predictive of performance at advanced stages of learning are different from those predictive of performance at early stages of learning. Thus, the particular combination of abilities contributing to performance on a task changes as practice on this task continues; these changes are progressive and systematic and eventually become stabilized (Fleishman & Hempel, 1954b, 1955; Fleishman, 1957a, 1960, 1966, 1967). The contribution of "nonmotor abilities" (e.g., verbal and spatial abilities), which may play a role early in perceptual-motor-task learning, decreases systematically with practice, relative to "motor abilities." There is also a decrease in the overall predictability of performance as practice continues; that is, the variance specific to the task itself, not definable by the subject's pretask abilities, increases from early to late stages of learning. An example is an experimental-correlational study of practice on a discrimination-reaction task. Early in learning, performance was a function of spatial and verbal abilities, but in later learning performance was more a function of the subject's speed of arm movement and reaction time as well as of a factor "specific to the task itself" (Fleishman & Hempel, 1955). Such findings have been confirmed for laboratory tasks as well as in training and operational settings (Parker & Fleishman, 1960; Fleishman & Fruchter, 1960).

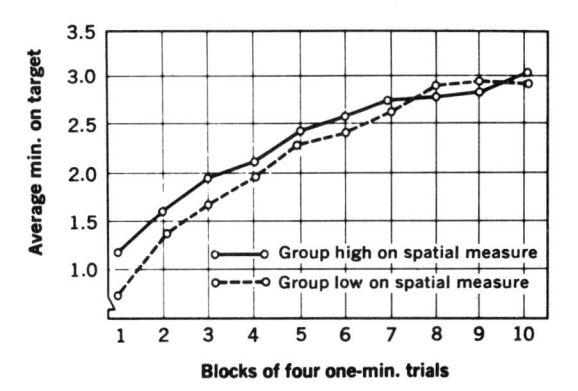

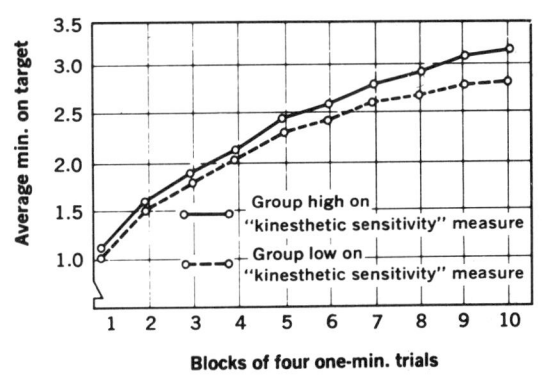

More recent research indicates the increasing importance of a person's "kinesthetic sensitivity" at advanced levels of motor learning, relative to the importance of nonmotor abilities (Fleishman & Rich, 1963). Figure 3 illustrates this for the learning of a two-hand coordination task.

There is also evidence that learning can be facilitated through training which makes use of knowledge of ability requirements at different stages of practice (Parker & Fleishman, 1961).

Edwin A. Fleishman
American Institutes for Research

References

Ammons, R. B., and Ammons, Carol. "Skills" In Harris, Chester W. (Ed.) *Encyclopedia of Educational Research*. 3d ed. Macmillan, 1960. 1283–6.

Bayley, Nancy. *The California First Year Mental Scale*. California Press, 1933.

Binet, A., and Henri, U. "La Psychologie individuelle." *Annual Psychol* 2:411–63; 1895.

Brown, J. S., and Jenkins, W. O. *An Analysis of Human Motor Abilities Related to the Design of*

Equipment and a Suggested Program of Research. GPO, 1947.

Buxton, C. E. "The Application of Factorial Methods to the Study of Motor Abilities." *Psychometrika* 3:85–93; 1938.

Campbell, M. "The 'Personal Equation' in Pursuit Performances." *J Applied Psychol* 18:785–92; 1934.

Cattell, James McKeen. "Mental Tests and Measurements." *Mind* 15:373–80; 1890.

Doll, Edgar A. (Ed.) *The Oseretsky Tests of Motor Proficiency.* Testing Bureau, 1946.

Fleishman, Edwin A. "Testing for Psychomotor Abilities by Means of Apparatus Tests." *Psychol* 50:241–62; 1953.

Fleishman, Edwin A. "Dimensional Analysis of Psychomotor Abilities." *J Exp Psychol* 48:437–54; 1954(a).

Fleishman, Edwin A. *Evaluation of Psychomotor Tests for Pilot Selection: The Direction Control and Compensatory Balance Tests.* Air Force Personnel and Training Research Center, 1954(b).

Fleishman, Edwin A. "Psychomotor Selection Tests: Research and Application in the U.S. Air Force." *Personnel Psychol* 9:449–67; 1956.

Fleishman, Edwin A. "Apports de Binet aux tests psycho-moteurs et développement ultérieur de ces techniques." *Revue de psychologie appliquée* 7:287–304; 1957(a).

Fleishman, Edwin A. "A Comparative Study of Aptitude Patterns in Unskilled and Skilled Psychomotor Performance." *J Applied Psychol* 41:263–72; 1957(b).

Fleishman, Edwin A. "Factor Structure in Relation to Task Difficulty in Psychomotor Performance." *Ed Psychol Meas* 17:522–32; 1957(c).

Fleishman, Edwin A. "Dimensional Analysis of Movement Reactions." *J Exp Psychol* 55:430–53; 1958.

Fleishman, Edwin A. "Psychomotor Tests in Drug Research." In Uhr, Leonard M., and Miller, James G. (Eds.) *Drugs and Behavior.* Wiley, 1960.

Fleishman, Edwin A. "The Description and Prediction of Perceptual-motor Skill Learning." In Glaser, Robert. (Ed.) *Training Research and Education.* U. Pittsburgh Press, 1962.

Fleishman, Edwin A. *Examiner's Manual for the Basic Fitness Tests.* Prentice-Hall, 1964(a).

Fleishman, Edwin A. *The Structure and Measurement of Physical Fitness.* Prentice-Hall, 1964(b).

Fleishman, Edwin A. "The Basic Fitness Tests." *J Int U Sports Federation* p. 125–30; 1966.

Fleishman, Edwin A. "Individual Differences and Motor Learning." In Gagné, Robert M. (Ed.) *Learning and Individual Differences.* Charles E. Merrill Books, Inc., 1967.

Fleishman, Edwin A., and Ellison, G. D. "A Factor Analysis of Fine Manipulative Performance." *J Applied Psychol* 46:96–105; 1962.

Fleishman, Edwin A., and Fruchter, B. "Factor Structure and Predictability of Successive Stages of Learning Morse Code." *J Applied Psyhcol* 44:97–101; 1960.

Fleishman, Edwin A., and Hempel, W. E. "Changes in Factor Structure of a Complex Psychomotor Test as a Function of Practice." *Psychometrika* 19:239–52; 1954(a).

Fleishman, Edwin A., and Hempel, W. E. "A Factor Analysis of Dexterity Tests." *Personnel Psychol* 7:15–32; 1954(b).

Fleishman, Edwin A., and Hempel, W. E. "The Relation Between Abilities and Improvement with Practice in a Visual Discrimination Reaction Task." *J Exp Psychol* 49:301–10; 1955.

Fleishman, Edwin A., and Hempel, W. E. "Factorial Analysis of Complex Psychomotor Performance and Related Skills." *J Applied Psychol* 40:96–104; 1956.

Fleishman, Edwin A., and Rich, S. "Role of Kinesthetic and Spatial-Visual Abilities in Perceptual-Motor Learning. *J Exp Psychol* 66:6–11; 1963.

Fleishman, Edwin A., and others. *The Dimensions of Physical Fitness—A Factor Analysis of Speed, Flexibility, Balance and Coordination Tests.* Yale U, 1961(a).

Fleishman, Edwin A., and others. *The Dimensions of Physical Fitness—A Factor Analysis of Strength Tests.* Yale U, 1961(b).

Gagné, Robert M., and Fleishman, Edwin A. *Psychology and Human Performance.* Holt, 1959.

Galton, Francis. *Inquiries in Human Faculty and Its Development.* Macmillan, 1883.

Gesell, Arnold, and others. *The First Five Years of Life.* Harper, 1940.

Greene, E. B. "An Analysis of Random and Systematic Changes with Practice. *Psychometrika* 8:37–52; 1943.

Hempel, W. E., and Fleishman, Edwin A. "Factor Analysis of Physical Proficiency and Manipulative Skill." *J Applied Psychol* 39:12–16; 1955.

Humphreys, L. G., and others. "Steadiness and Rifle Marksmanship." *J Applied Psychol* 20:680–8; 1936.

Melton, A. W. (Ed.) *Apparatus Test.* GPO, 1947.

Muscio, B. "Motor Capacity with Special Reference to Vocational Guidance." *Br J Psychol* 13:157–84; 1922.

Nicks, D. C., and Fleishman, Edwin A. *What Do Physical Fitness Tests Measure?—A Review of Factor-analytic Studies.* Yale U Press, 1961.

Parker, J. F., and Fleishman, Edwin A. "Ability Factors and Component Performance Measures as Predictors of Complex Tracking Behavior." *Psychol Monogr* 74; 1960.

Parker, J. F., and Fleishman, Edwin A. "Use of Analytical Information Concerning Task Requirements to Increase the Effectiveness of Skill Training." *J Applied Psychol* 45:295–302; 1961.

Perrin, F. A. "An Experimental Study of Motor Ability." *J Exp Psychol* 4:24–57; 1929.

Reymert, M. L. "The Personal Equation in Motor Capacities." *Scandinavian Sci R* 2:177–94; 1923.

Seashore, Robert H. "Stanford Motor Skills Unit." *Psychol Monogr* 39:51–66; 1928.

Seashore, Robert H. "Individual Differences in Motor Skills." *J Gen Psychol* 3:38–66; 1930.

Seashore, Robert H. "Experimental and Theoretical Analysis of Fine Motor Skills." *Am J Psychol* 53:86–98; 1940.

Seashore, Robert H. "Work and Motor Performance." In Stevens, S. S. (Ed.) *Handbook of Experimental Psychology.* Wiley, 1951.

Seashore, Robert H., and Adams, R. O. "The Measurement of Steadiness: A New Apparatus and Results in Marksmanship." *Sci* 78:235; 1933.

Seashore, Robert H., and others. "Group Factors in Simple and Discriminative Reaction Times." *J Exp Psychol* 29:346–9; 1941.

Seashore, Robert H., and others. "Multiple Factorial Analysis of Fine Motor Skills." *Am J Psychol* 53:251–9; 1942.

Seashore, Robert H., and others. "A Factorial Analysis of Arm-Hand Precision Tests." *J Applied Psychol* 33:579–84; 1949.

Seashore, S. H. "The Aptitude Hypothesis in Motor Skills." *J Exp Psychol* 14:555–61; 1931.

Spaeth, R. A., and Dunham, G. C. "The Correlation Between Motor Control and Rifle Shooting." *Am J Physiol* 56:249–56; 1921.

Stutsman, Rachel. *Mental Measurement of Pre-School Children.* World Bk, 1931.

Walker, R. Y., and Adams, R. D. "Motor Skills: The Validity of Serial Motor Tests for Predicting Typewriter Proficiency." *J Gen Psychol* 11:173–86; 1934.

MUSIC EDUCATION

Research in music education, with but few exceptions, has been in the form of theses and dissertations completed for advanced degrees. This body of literature, which has been developing since about 1930, has remained, for the most part, in unpublished form. Its existence has been made known to the profession through various publications of the Music Educators National Conference (MENC). The first listings of research studies, published under the sponsorship of the MENC Committee on Research and the MENC Research Council, respectively, were compiled by Small (1944) and Larson (1949). Additional compilations have been published by Larson (1957) and Roderick Gordon (1964) in the *Journal of Research in Music Education.* Since 1964, Gordon has published annual supplements to these lists in the Spring issues of this journal. These publications provide the primary sources for titles of completed graduate research in music education. Other sources of titles and abstracts of research relating to music education are found in *Psychological Abstracts, Sociological Abstracts,* and *Dissertation Abstracts.*

The *Journal of Research in Music Education,* which came into being in 1953, has been the primary dissemination source for reports of research in music education. In recent years, three other journals have been established for this purpose: the *Missouri Journal of Research in Music Education,* published, since 1961, by the Missouri State Department of Education; the *Bulletin of the Council for Research in Music Education,* published, since 1963, by the College of Education of the University of Illinois and the Office of the Superintendent of Public Instruction; and the *Colorado Journal of Research in Music Education,* published, since 1964, by the Colorado Music Educators Association and the Colorado State Department of Education. Other professional journals, particularly those in the fields of psychology, sociology, and education, continue to report research occasionally on problems related to music education.

The body of research literature in music education which developed from 1930 to 1966 has been reported by Schneider and Cady (1966) and by Cady (1967) to comprise approximately 9,500 titles. Descriptive studies (of the survey and status type) and historical studies constitute the majority of the reports in this literature. Experimental studies, while few in number, have increased considerably in recent years. The studies selected for review in this report were considered to provide basic knowledge of some practical and theoretical significance for the future development of music education.

BASIC ABILITIES IN MUSIC. Controversy exists among psychologists and music educators about the nature of musical aptitude or musical talent. Two distinct concepts have been advanced about the nature of this ability. One concept, the earliest in terms of development, places much emphasis on specific factors or traits and stresses the importance of sensory capacity. The other conceives of musical aptitude as more than the simple identification and measurement of sensory capacities. Advocates of this viewpoint seek a general factor and question the value of measures based on the isolation of the simplest elements of music outside the musical context.

The complex nature of musical aptitude and its measurement is seen in the lack of agreement among investigators of the traits which define this behavior. No agreement seems to exist on the relative number of musical traits to be considered or the relative importance of these traits. Early attempts at identification and measurement of musical aptitude, such as the work of Carl Seashore (1919) and Schoen (1940), were based on the conception that this ability consisted of a variety of traits. The traits most commonly proposed were identified by Whybrew (1962) as (1) perception of small differences in pitch, (2) recognition and retention of melodies and chords, (3) absolute pitch, (4) interval discrimination, (5) rhythmic sensitivity, (6) perception of specific pitches in chords, and (7) discrimination in degrees of consonance. Early musical aptitude tests contained sections for the measurement of several of these traits. None, however, included all the traits.

Factor analysis has been used to identify independent traits or factors in several measures of musical aptitude. Prominent among the investigators using this approach were Drake (1939), Karlin (1942), McLeish (1950), and Wing (1954). Among the factors identified were tonal sensitivity and tonal memory (memory for musical elements and form).

Gaston (1942), while not denying the importance of sensory capacities in the measurement of musical aptitude, gives greater import to perceptual ability in organizing sounds. Melodic apprehension and response are considered by Gaston to have high diagnostic value. Edwin Gordon (1965b) has listed musical expression, aural perception, and kinesthetic musical feeling as essential traits. Pitch discrimination along with musical and tonal memory are given by Rainbow (1965) as important facets of musical aptitude.

Of the musical aptitude tests currently available, some emphasize the importance of sensory capacities while others, particularly some of the more recent, give greater importance to perceptual responses. Most of these tests are designed for use with elementary, junior high, and senior high school students. Available tests include the *K-D Tests* developed by Kwalwasser and Dykema (1930), the *Seashore Measures of Musical Talents*, Series A, revised by Setveit and others (1940), Drake's *Musical Aptitude Tests* (1954), Whistler and Thorpe's *Musical Aptitude Test* (1950), the *Kwalwasser Music Talent Test* (Kwalwasser, 1953), Gaston's *Test of Musicality* (1957), the *Wing Standardized Tests of Musical Intelligence* (Wing, 1958), and Edwin Gordon's *Musical Aptitude Profile* (1965a). Detailed descriptions of and information about the development of these tests, with the exception of the Gordon *Musical Aptitude Profile*, can be found in the works of Whybrew (1962), Farnsworth (1958), and Lundin (1953). The mental measurement yearbooks edited by Buros (1959) also provide valuable information on these tests.

The major purpose of musical aptitude tests was initially conceived to be primarily to determine the degree of native musical ability present. Greater attention is being given currently, as indicated by Farnsworth (1961), to ascertaining which children will profit most from music study and what level of scores appear to be critical (empirically determined) in making such judgments. Scores earned on musical aptitude tests, as most authorities hold, should be considered as only one source of data for making predictions on possible success in music. Intelligence and extramusical factors, such as interest and motivation, parental encouragement, cultural background, and physical coordination, may be of equal importance in predicting success in musical endeavors.

Reliability and Validity of Tests. Musical aptitude tests generally have not achieved the standards of reliability and validity expected of comparable tests in other areas. This is particularly true of the earlier musical aptitude tests. Only a few studies have been conducted on most tests, and relatively small samples of subjects were used. This is particularly true for studies on validity. The criteria used in most validity studies are either music-class grades, teacher ratings of musicality, or ratings on musical performance.

Of the currently available musical aptitude tests, those reporting reliability coefficients generally in the .80's and low .90's, are the Drake *Musical Aptitude Test*, the Whistler-Thorpe *Musical Aptitude Test*, the Gaston *Test of Musicality*, the Wing *Standardized Tests of Musical Intelligence*, and the Gordon *Musical Aptitude Profile*. The reliability studies done by Bentley (1955) on the Gaston and Wing tests and by McLeish (1953) and Heller (1962) on the Wing test also reported coefficients of this order. The reliability coefficients of the *K-D Test* as summarized by Lundin (1953), of the revised *Seashore Measures of Musical Talents*, and of the Kwalwasser *Music Talent Test* as reported by Bentley (1955) and Farnsworth (1959), generally fall below this level of reliability.

The tests reporting validity coefficients generally in the high .40's, the .50's, and the low .60's are the Drake *Musical Aptitude Test*, the Whistler-Thorpe *Musical Aptitude Test*, and the Gordon *Musical Aptitude Profile*. Some validity coefficients are above and some below those given above for these tests, depending on the specific correlating criteria used. The validity of the Gaston *Test of Musicality* is expressed in the probability ratio (analysis of variance by ranks, chi-square r) of .05 for the total test. Bentley (1955) reported a validity coefficient of .52 for the Gaston test and of .481 for the Wing test. The validity studies done by Fosha (1964), Tarrell (1964), and Culver (1965) of the Gordon test reported coefficients of the kind indicated above. Validity coefficients for the revised Seashore *Measures of Musical Talents* and the *K-D Test* were reported by Lundin (1949, 1953) generally to be below the level of validity for the other tests.

Relation of Musical Ability to Other Traits. A positive relationship appears to exist between intelligence, musical aptitude, and musical achievement. Wenaas (1940), using students in grades 6 through 12, reported positive correlations ranging from .21 to 71 on the *K-D Music Tests* and the Otis and Kuhlman-Anderson Tests. Priestly (1942) found that students in grades 5 through 9 who scored high on the *Kwalwasser-Ruch Test* also ranked above the eightieth percentile on the *Otis Mental Ability Test*. Jenkins (1960) reported a positive correlation of .60 between scores made by high school music students on the *Drake Musical Memory Test* and the *California Test of Mental Maturity*. Outstanding high school music students as a group were found by Garder (1953) to be superior in intelligence to less able music students and to nonmusic students. Zack (1953) and Cramer (1958) noted the same relationships with high school instrumental music students. Intelligence was considered by Rhoades (1938) to be the most important single variable in predicting success in instrumental music.

The social adjustment of music students has not received extensive study. Only three studies relating to social adjustment or behaviors are found in the recent literature. Greenberg and MacGregor (1966) reported little or no relationship between elementary-school children's scores on the *Seashore Measures of Musical Talents* and ratings on the *Winnetka Scale of School Behavior and Attitudes*. Graves (1950) reported that adolescents taking private music lessons showed less emotional conflict and appeared to be better adjusted than adolescents of the same intelligence and socioeconomic status who were not involved in private study. Hughes (1955) has suggested that the social adjustment of music students appears to be closely related to the extent of participation in musical activities.

A difference in temperament and personality traits may exist between outstanding high school musicians and musicians of lesser talents. Garder (1955) has reported that outstanding high school musicians appear to be less stable emotionally, less objective, and less adept at personal relations than less able music students and nonmusic students. Kaplan (1961), however, has reported that outstanding high school musicians display a high degree of self-confidence, ambitiousness, and self-assertiveness. Comparative studies of emotional and personality traits of outstanding high school musicians and those of music teachers and professional musicians would probably provide data which would be useful, to some extent, in predicting success in musical endeavors.

Conflicting evidence exists about relationship of musical aptitude to national and racial origins. Investigators such as Gray and Bingham (1929), Streep (1931), and Van Alstyne and Osborne (1937) have presented some evidence that Negro children are somewhat superior to other children in some aspects of musicality as measured by musical aptitude tests. The investigation of Luke (1939), however, revealed that greater variability existed within each national or racial group than between groups. It would seem safe to assume, at least until further evidence is available, that musical ability is probably normally distributed throughout the population without respect to national and racial origins, geographical regions, or socioeconomic status.

MUSICAL DEVELOPMENT. The development of musical behaviors was studied extensively for many years by Gesell (1940) and Gesell and Ilg (1946) at the Yale University Clinic. The early literature on musical development has been summarized by Jersild (1939). Other reports, including some European studies, are given by Mursell (1937), Mursell and Glenn (1938), Schoen (1940), and Lundin (1953). The following paragraphs present a brief synthesis of developmental gradients or sequential stages in the growth of musical behaviors as presented in these works. The behaviors reported are to be interpreted as "on the average" and not as definite chronological occurrences in all children.

The one-year-old child appears to respond to music and likes simple repetitive rhythmical sounds. He tends to imitate sounds at approximately forty weeks. The two-year-old child listens and dances to music, repeats "singsong" sentences, and sings phrases of songs which are generally not on pitch. He uses his whole body in running, galloping, or swinging to music. First attempts at matching simple tones occur during the third year. A child at this age can recognize several melodies, and he may have definite favorites. He gallops, jumps, and runs in time to music. The four-year-old child likes to experiment at the piano. He may be able to sing some songs correctly and identify simple melodies. At five years of age he may be able to pick out tunes on the piano and learn to play a few familiar, simple melodies. He also may be able to sing accurately the tones from middle C to the second F above on the treble staff. It appears, however, that the preschool child apparently grasps tonal relationships as a general mass impression, and reproduction of melody, tone for tone, is most difficult for him.

When the child begins school at six, he likes radio programs accompanied by music, and he is able to keep better time to music when dancing. He appears to have no consistent preference for dissonant or consonant harmonies. At seven he may desire piano or dancing lessons and enjoys using various percussion (rhythm) instruments. As yet he has not developed a keen awareness for harmony and seemingly is not disturbed by dissonant sounds. The eight-year-old child has less desire to practice on the piano and he likes to change a passage to one of his own invention. He likes audiences and likes to play music with others. At nine years of age he begins to apply himself in practicing music. He enjoys executing legato or staccato notes and begins to become interested in composers. A definite preference for concords begins to appear at this age. It appears that improvement in pitch perception during these years is related to increase in attention span and improvement of memory function.

Developmental growth patterns in music have not been studied extensively in children over 10 years of age. The information available indicates that 10- and 11-year-old children find discords less pleasing, but at ages 12 and 13 interval preferences are similar to those of adults. Marked improvement in melodic memory seems to occur at ages 13 and 14. Children at these ages apparently conceive of melody and rhythm as a totality, not as separate elements.

Recent studies tend to reinforce and enhance the findings of earlier studies. Pflederer (1964) reported, for example, that third-grade children were better able to conserve (Piaget's concept) meter and tonal and rhythmic patterns than kindergarten children were. Petzold (1960, 1963) suggests that the development of musical perception (first six grades) is related to grade level and musical training and experience. In another report, Petzold (1966) concluded that a large majority of children learn to control their singing voices in the second grade and that because one has learned to imitate phrases does not mean that one has comprehended the relationships of the items within the phrase. Petzold (1966) also reported that all children (first six grades) have difficulty in maintaining a steady beat to a slow tempo.

Development of Singing and Rhythmic Response. Conflicting evidence exists on the value of preschool vocal training. Jersild (1939) reviewed some studies which showed marked gains in singing skills after individual preschool training. Other studies showed only limited gains. Boardman (1964) recently found no significant superiority in the singing accuracy of children participating in a preschool vocal-skill program. Primary-grade children appeared to perform with about equal facility and to make the same type of errors regardless of the presence or absence of preschool training in singing.

Relationships do seem to exist, however, between the home environment and the development of singing ability. Reynolds (1960) reported a direct relationship between accurate singing at the kindergarten level and singing and piano playing of the mother in the home, availability of children's records, and a home atmosphere encouraging musical expression. Strong relationships between singing ability and socioeconomic status of the home—culturally advantaged or culturally barren—also were reported by Kirkpatrick (1962). The development of singing ability seems to be an unfolding process rather than the result of a formalized training program. Critical periods of sensory stimulation during preschool years may exist for fostering the development of singing ability. This is a problem needing research attention.

Only children with superior ability in tonal apprehension and memory in the primary grades, according to Hartzell (1949), show regular growth of accuracy in singing. Growth in singing ability appears quite sporadic in other children.

The vocal range of young children (two to ten years in age) appears to be generally within the range from first-line E to fourth-space E of the treble staff. Jersild and Bienstock (1934) found this somewhat common range developing and concluded that a person realized a large portion of his potential pitch range while in the first three grades (six to nine years) of the elementary school. This would appear to be the time to emphasize singing and vocal development in the school music program.

Preschool training in rhythmic response, as with training in singing, apparently has little effect on later rhythmic development. The studies reported by Jersild and Bienstock (1934), and the study of Van Alstyne and Osborne (1937) support this fact. Children in the early grades of the elementary school find it easier to keep time to music played at fast tempos than to music played at slow tempos. Little difference seems to exist in the ability to beat time with the hands or to march in rhythm. Elementary-school children also appear to be quite consistent in their groupings of rhythmic patterns with accents. The grouping seems to be dependent on the configuration of the entire pattern and the relative positions of long and short notes. Information on these aspects of rhythmic development is provided in the work of Sievers (1932), Jersild and Bienstock (1934), and Van Alstyne and Osborne (1937) and by the recent work of Petzold (1966).

The pitch- and rhythmic-discrimination abilities of children of different age levels need restudy in the light of the increase in the amount of music and sound in the environment today. Children cannot escape the conditioning effects of the sound and music which saturate the environment through the mass means of communication. The effects of sensory deprivation on the development of musical perception, musical ability, interest, and motivation warrant serious study. Socioeconomic factors might, today, play a more important role in the development of musical abilities than they were assigned a few years ago.

Voice Change at Adolescence. A problem of major concern to music educators over the years has been that of the change in the boy's voice at the time of puberty. All sorts of descriptions and explanations of this phenomenon have been advanced. Few, however, were founded on adequate information.

The average boy's vocal range is greatest before he begins to lose the higher tones and smallest immediately after he loses the changed tones, according to Havlovic (1937). After the changing period the range develops to an average scope of an interval of an eleventh. The special characteristics of adolescent boys' voices before voice change (high versus low range, light or heavy quality, flexibility and agility, tessitura) are reported by Ekstrom (1959) to continue into the changed voice. Voice change generally occurs during the junior high school years, although some voices may change at earlier or later periods. Joseph (1959) reported that both before and after the onset of puberty, as range and overall size of body structure increases, the voice range lowers, and before 15 years and 4 months development patterns are less clearly discernible than from that time on.

Absolute Pitch. One ability in music which has been considered "basic" by most musicians is that known as "perfect" or "absolute" pitch. This ability, to name pitches without reference to other tones, has generally been considered an innate ability. Neu (1947), in his review of the literature, presented evidence that this ability was not a "gift" but rather a learned behavior. Lundin and Allen (1962), Lundin (1963), and Terman (1965) have recently presented objective evidence that this ability can be developed. The results of these studies seem to indicate that pitch discrimination and pitch naming can be improved and actually cultivated with certain kinds of training techniques. There seems to be some agreement, at least among psychologists, that "absolute pitch" is not an innate ability, but rather a highly refined degree of ability in pitch discrimination.

CURRICULUM AND MATERIALS. Little agreement appears to exist between persons holding different positions in education on the specific role and objectives of music education. For example, Jones (1961) and Kelley (1962) found little agreement on the importance and function of music in the schools among superintendents, principals, and music teachers. Noah (1953), somewhat earlier, reported little evidence of a "profound" statement of philosophy in the literature published by state departments of education. Freeman (1955) and Ernst (1955) found only a slight relationship between the program recommendations of the MENC and practices in the schools they studied. The data from reports such as these suggest that a common philosophy of music education does not as yet exist in the schools.

Curriculum. While little agreement seems to exist on the role and objectives of music education as practiced in the schools, survey studies of programs in the schools seem to indicate a quite common curriculum pattern. The studies of Kuhn (1953), Price (1950, 1953), Marvin G. Nelson (1955), Freeman (1955), and Uldrick (1961) provide excellent examples of this commonality. These reports have shown that (1) choral singing is the most prominent musical activity in the schools, (2) band is the most prominent instrumental activity, (3) general music is the most frequently scheduled musical activity in the junior high school, and (4) little time is given to music appreciation or academic-type music classes in the high school. Programs in the schools, in general, appear to be performance-oriented, with little specific attention given to the gaining of knowledge of and about music. The lack of content and curricular offerings in the more academic aspects of music has been recognized by the profession in recent years.

Various attempts have been made to determine the objectives, content, activities, and organizational plans of certain types of music classes. The purpose in most studies of this kind was to determine common elements and procedures. The general music class has received considerable attention in this regard. The term "general music" has been used with increasing frequency during the past twenty years. It refers to a type of music class, usually elective at the high school level and required or elective at the junior high school level, which is available to all students in a school. The purposes or objectives of these classes do not appear to have been standardized to any extent, and some confusion exists about the real objectives of the activities and learnings in such classes. Boyle (1960) has shown that specific objectives for such classes vary greatly, but an overall objective seems to be the promotion of a better understanding and appreciation of music. Keegan (1956) reported that music educators generally believe that this class should include, in addition to singing, listening activities, rhythmic and instrumental experience, music reading, and musical composition. Hollingsworth (1953), Mueller (1960), and Peterson (1962), however, have shown that the most frequent activities in the general music class are unison and part singing, listening, and study of music fundamentals. In terms of curricular organization, Swanson (1959) has reported that adolescent boys, during the changing-voice period, appear to gain more theoretical knowledge of music and to improve more in singing when placed in a general music class by themselves.

Other music classes of the nonperformance type in the high school, such as music history, music literature, and music appreciation, are found generally to be elective courses which consist chiefly of attending lectures, listening to recordings, and discussing textbook and reference book assignments. The musical compositions most often used in such courses are symphonies, operas and oratorios, and American folk music. Peterson's analysis (1962) showed this curricular pattern and content.

Some recent studies have dealt with innovative practices in music curriculum development. Thomas (1966) examined selected experimental music programs in schools throughout the country to compile information regarding content, procedures, and results. He reported that every program examined had a specific philosophical rationale underlying it, with clearly defined purposes and objectives. Campion (1966) investigated the feasibility of integrating the arts and humanities into existing curricula at the ninth-grade level without the necessity of great expenditures of time, energy, and money. Integration of the arts and humanities under these conditions was found to be possible. The systems approach appeared to be the most valid mechanism for achieving this goal.

Materials. The research literature in music education contains many studies on various types of literature and its possible uses in the educational setting. For the most part these studies are found in master's-degree theses, which regrettably are not available to the teacher in the schools. Bibliographies of available literature for different performance activities and instruments, analyses of classroom music materials, transcriptions of music, original materials in the form of music and class teaching materials, and evaluations of materials for specific educational purposes are found in this body of literature. Many studies of these types are listed in the bibliographies given in the introductory paragraphs of this report. A great need exists to evaluate these studies and to make the information available to the music education profession. The reviews which follow are examples of these types of studies.

The contents of frequently used fourth-grade music textbooks were analyzed by Smiley (1955) to determine the type, amount, and use of musical configurations. Blyler (1957) studied the preferred songs of elementary-school children and found that they contained strong melodic movement, well-defined cadences ending on the tonic major modes, primarily chordal backgrounds, and dynamic variations. Shull (1961) studied children's song literature written by distinguished nineteenth- and twentieth-century composers and found that most compositions were not considered appropriate because of pitch range requirements, extended periods in high or low tessituras, and the use of fragmentary melodies.

The appropriateness and the availability of various types of music for use in the schools have received attention by many investigators. Criteria for evaluating choral music for use in the schools were set forth by Christy (1947). Livingston (1957) studied English madrigals for the same purpose. Theno (1954) analyzed the choral works of Orlando di Lasso to ascertain which compositions would be most suitable for high school choral groups. Buebendorf (1947) established criteria for the selection of music to be used with school orchestras and adapted 25 symphonies of the classic period (1700–1800) for use in school groups. Wikstrom (1960) analyzed early string literature and selected materials which would be appropriate for use in heterogeneous string classes for the college music education major. Haderer (1961) obtained copies of unpublished symphonies of specific composers of the Mannheim school, selected appropriate works, and made them available in score form. Other examples of studies on appropriate literature are those on folk music by Knudsen (1946), on contemporary music by Philip Gordon (1949), and on Negro music by George (1953).

Analysis of the content of various types of music

and printed teaching methods has also received attention by many investigators. For example, Utgaard (1949) conducted an analysis of the teaching content (music) found in ensemble music for brass wind instruments, and Evans (1963) examined available method books for oboe from 1695 to about 1800 to determine the pedagogical principles and the type of music used in early oboe instruction. Similar studies are found in the research literature on most, if not all, of the musical instruments and ensembles used in the school music program.

These studies represent only an extremely small sample of the many studies conducted on various materials usable in the schools. A synthesis of the information in these studies, probably by performance areas and instruments, would be a worthy addition to the professional literature in music education.

LEARNING AND TEACHING MUSIC. Research pertaining to the learning and teaching of music generally is concerned with factors involved in various aspects of musical perception and with procedures and techniques utilized in the teaching-learning process in specific musical activities. Studies dealing with such problems have been conducted at all levels of education, from elementary school through college. Reviews of pertinent studies of these types are given below.

Basic Music Skills. There appears to be no significant difference in the musical perceptions of boys and girls of elementary-school age. Petzold (1960) reported that boys and girls in the first six grades perceive the general shape of the tonal configuration but that specific intervals within the pattern may not be correctly perceived. The development of music listening skills (aural perception and discrimination) appears to be enhanced when children are trained to master pitches given vocally or from the piano. Wolner and Pyle (1933) found this to be true even with so-called "pitch-deficient" children. The same results were reported by Wyatt (1945) with "pitch-deficient" adults. Petzold (1960) also indicated that skill in aural perception can be developed only if the child is able to "hear" the item before he sings it and that accurate reading is more likely to result when greater emphasis is placed upon understanding the significance of the notation rather than upon a mere "imitation" of musical sounds. The space-frame concept of having children match tones vocally while playing the same tones on the piano and observing the tonal relationships, as reported by Creitz (1943), appears to be an effective technique in developing aural discrimination and tonal memory.

Methods for the development of harmonic listening skills in high school students were studied by Lustre (1958). This work revealed that no significant differences existed between methods employing chords as separate units, those employing chords related to the composition being studied, and a combination of these methods in tests of immediate recall. Analysis of the delayed-recall data revealed, however, that the group which had received training in choral progressions out of context was significantly superior to the other groups.

The ability of high school students and nonmusic-major college students to recognize repeated and altered musical themes does not appear to be related to participation in music performance activities. Duerksen (1967) reported that recognition skills seem to be associated with listening experiences and that many years of participation in performance are necessary before any appreciable increase in recognition ability becomes evident.

The identification of intervals by college students was reported by Buttram (1967) to be related to such factors as interval quale, pitch distance, tonal context, and relative distinctiveness of the interval. Similar evidence was provided by Marquis (1963), who reported that the vocal performance of intervals by college freshmen was influenced by the contextual setting. Ability, or the lack of it, in the singing of isolated intervals apparently does not directly affect the correct singing of that interval in a melody.

Recent studies of programmed techniques indicate that the aural perception and discrimination of college students can be improved greatly through these types of learning techniques. Horacek (1963) and Spohn (1963, 1965) reported that interval discrimination, identification, and dictation skill, as well as other basic music skills taught in freshman music-theory courses, could be taught through various types of programmed instruction as effectively as, or more efficiently than, by the traditional teacher-classroom approach. Carlsen (1964) reported similar results in his study of programmed instruction in melodic dictation for college freshmen.

Teaching children to read musical notation has been, and continues to be, a major problem in music education. Elementary-school children, as the studies by Ernst (1955) and Petzold (1960) reveal, generally are not able to read the notation found in songbooks used at their particular grade levels. Many children, as indicated by Petzold (1960), experience considerable difficulty in reading even those tonal configurations commonly found in the songs they sing.

Studies of music reading have dealt, in the main, with the effectiveness of various teaching-learning methods, the use of tachistoscopic techniques, and the eye movements and characteristics of good music readers. The effectiveness of the solfège method of teaching music reading, which has been accepted and held in high esteem by many music educators over the years, has been questioned by some investigators; other methods seem to be as effective or even more effective. Evidence presented by Silvey (1937) and Gaston (1940) revealed that children and adults do not consider the solfège method as being primarily responsible for the development of music-reading skill. The use of this method, according to Gaston (1940), also seems to have a negative effect on the development of desirable positive attitudes toward music in the schools. The space-frame technique was reported by Creitz (1943) to be more effective in teaching music to elementary-school children than the solfège method. Hutton (1953) found that the use of special visual materials (flash cards, musical games, and slides) along with the more traditional techniques slightly improved music-reading ability. Evidence presented by Carl B. Nelson (1954, 1956) indicated that the use of instruments in the elementary-school classroom enhances achievement in music reading. The use of shaped notes in teaching music reading was shown by Kyme (1960) to be statistically superior to the solfège method. At the college level, Hargiss (1960, 1962) reported a significant improvement in the sight-singing ability of elementary-education majors who used the piano as an aid in developing music-reading skill.

These studies suggest alternate approaches, other than the solfège method, for practice and research in the teaching of music reading. Until more definite and conclusive evidence is presented, music teachers probably will continue to utilize a variety of techniques (verbal, visual, and aural), along with extensive experience in reading a variety of music, as the primary means of developing music-reading skills.

The results of studies utilizing tachistoscopic techniques in developing music-reading skills or sight-singing skills are inconclusive. The work of Stokes (1944) revealed that seventh- and eighth-grade children did improve their recognition of the musical patterns used but that no improvement occurred in general music-reading ability. Hammer (1961) found, however, that tachistoscopic training in melodic sight-singing appeared to be more effective than conventional techniques. Christ (1954) reported remarkable improvement by his subjects in rhythmic response (tapping) to appropriate symbols presented on a tachistoscopic device. Tachistoscopic training for the development of rhythmic sight-singing was reported by Wiley (1962), however, to be no more effective than traditional teaching techniques.

The eye movements of good music readers appear to be quite similar to those of good readers of the printed word. The studies of Jacobsen (1942), Van Nuys and Weaver (1943), and Weaver (1943) provide data which lead to this generalization. The work of Wheeler and Wheeler (1952) with fifth- and sixth-grade children, however, revealed only a slight positive relationship between music-reading and language-reading abilities. Eye movements of superior compared to average sight readers in music were reported by York (1952) to be characterized by a rapid reading rate, shorter fixational duration, fewer fixations, and a greater perceptual span. York also reported that more instrumentalists are superior sight readers than are vocalists.

Theoretical Knowledge. Very little attention has been devoted to the specific problem of the acquisition of theoretical knowledge of music by students in the public schools. Only two studies have dealt specifically with this problem. Each of these was concerned with the value of instrumental instruction in the achievement of theoretical knowledge and skill by elementary-school children. Carl B. Nelson (1954, 1956) reported that a combination of vocal and instrumental instruction produced significantly greater achievement in knowledge of musical notation and audiovisual discrimination than vocal instruction alone. The other study, conducted by the Pittsburgh Public Schools (1936), reported no significant differences in achievement between groups of elementary children receiving one-half instrumental instruction and one-half vocal instruction and groups receiving vocal instruction alone.

In the general music class at the junior high school level, Zima (1956) and Weigand (1962) have reported that the organization of activities and materials into broad units of instruction (resource units) produces a higher level of effective learning and teaching. Sources of motivation found to be most useful with below-average adolescents in these types of classes were reported by Gilfeather (1962) to be peer approval, interest, curiosity, working for tangible rewards, and competition.

In recent years, research attention has been given to this problem at the college level. Several studies have been concerned with the value of programmed instruction in teaching the fundamentals of music (the names of notes in different clefs, key signatures, scales, intervals, triads, etc.) to college students. In studies using elementary-education majors as subjects, Barnes (1964) and Cribb (1965) reported that programmed materials on the function and meaning of music symbols resulted in significantly more effective learning than the traditional lecture-demonstration approach. Wardian (1963) and Ashford (1966) used programmed materials on the fundamentals of music with college music students. They reported that the groups using the programmed materials performed significantly better and required less time in learning than the groups not receiving this instruction. Most investigators using programmed materials recommended that these materials be used jointly with the regular instruction or as ancillary study materials. The students in all studies reacted favorably to instruction of this type.

Music Appreciation. Studies of musical preferences and of the development of musical taste by Rogers (1956), Baumann (1958, 1960), and Burke and Grinder (1966) all lead to the conclusion that popular-commercial types of music are those generally preferred by all school children. The musical taste level of high school students, as reported by Rubin (1952), Rogers (1956), and Baumann (1958), does not seem to be affected by the amount and/or types of musical experiences in the schools. High school students as a group show a predominant interest and preference for the popular-commercial music currently in vogue. Socioeconomic status, age, and sex, as reported by Fisher (1951), Baumann (1958), do not appear to be significant variables in music preference or taste. Musical taste, as Farnsworth (1950) has suggested, appears to be a folkway which develops through social conditioning. Mass-communication techniques might be used advantageously in the schools in developing musical tastes and preferences. "Plugging" of certain types of compositions and repetition of certain compositions, through listening stations, or through the use of soft unobtrusive music in the library or study hall, might prove to be an effective means of bringing different types of music to the attention of students. This was a recommendation in the report of Palisca (1964) on the Yale seminar in music education.

Gernet (1939) reported that an inconsistent change toward preferences for classical types of music seems to occur at successive levels of maturity, particularly at the college level. It has been pointed out by Fisher (1951), however, that preferences for classical music are largely a function of the transmissions of specific judgments about specific compositions. Erneston (1961) reported that college students with more experience in music appear to have a higher level of acquired taste in music.

The possible relationships of emotional traits to preferences for certain types of music needs study in depth. Information relating to the factors operating in the general acceptance of popular-commercial music would be most useful to music teachers. What psychological processes are involved—attention, effects of rhythm, repetition, etc.? What sociological processes are in operation—group acceptance, status, etc.?

Very little is known about effective methods of presenting music literature or of teaching music appreciation to junior and senior high school students. The method of presentation of recorded music to junior high school students appears to have little effect on their enjoyment of music. Nash (1962) reported that the enjoyment of lively orchestral music in the classic tradition seems to increase with repetition of the same type of music, while enjoyment of slow orchestral music in the romantic tradition seems to decrease with repetition. Getz (1963) found that two or three repetitions of a composition were necessary after the introduction before familiarity and preference were affected. Bodie (1958) reported that the use of professional program notes did not enhance junior high school students' ability to recognize musical themes.

College students in music appreciation type classes were found by Yingling (1962) to be more interested in intellectual analyses of music than in the affective meanings conveyed by the music being studied. The value of notated examples of musical themes in college classes for purposes of differentiation among themes was shown by Smith (1953).

Studies are needed of the types of music literature seemingly most meaningful and appropriate to the various age and background levels of students and of the types of listening skills utilized by students. What elements in music appear to be most appealing to students? What types of listeners are various types of students—mood, ideational, cognitive? How does the type of listener relate to the age, sex, musical background, and social environment? What role does socialization play in the interest shown by adolescents in listening to musical recordings? The relationships of these variables to the objectives of various types of music-listening activities should also be determined. Investigation of the use and value of programmed listening and instruction is also needed. Models for teaching music appreciation should be developed and tested in the school situation.

Vocal Performance. Vocal performance in the schools has been studied in terms of the (1) singing problems and characteristics of elementary-school children, (2) the adolescent voice and singing characteristics, and (3) methods of teaching vocal music in the junior and senior high school.

Elementary-school children, as reported by Busse (1952), apparently learn songs in a rote fashion more quickly from recordings than from instruction by the classroom teacher. Children also seem to prefer the recorded voices of women and children. The learning of songs from recordings does not enhance the development of music-reading ability. Many classroom teachers, however, as Hansford (1962) reported, are able to provide musical experiences which develop the singing abilities of children. No significant differences in attitudes toward music were found by Broquist (1961) to exist between elementary-school children taught by the classroom teachers and those taught by a music specialist.

Singing during the period of voice change by the adolescent boy does not appear to be harmful but rather beneficial to the development of the voice. Ekstrom (1959) studied this problem quite extensively. Evidence was provided by Swanson (1959) which suggests that boys improve in musical ability, in attitude, and interest in music if segregated from girls (in a special class) during the period of the changing voice. The music usually selected for use in the schools after voice change is considered by Swanson (1959) to be generally unsuitable for a large percentage of boys because it exceeds their range capabilities.

Sims (1961) has reported that class voice instruction for beginning high school voice students is as effective as, or more effective than, the conventional private-lesson approach. The development of the minimal motor muscles to greater specificity, through the use of exercises based on a biological and phonetic knowledge of the human voice, appears to produce, as reported by Russel Nelson (1954), improved tone quality, more-normal vibrato, fuller resonation, and a higher degree of selectivity in articulation.

Instrumental Performance. A direct relationship appears to exist between physical maturation and musical progress in instrumental performance. The seventh or eighth grade, as reported by Pence (1942) and Cramer (1958), appears to be the time when optimum maturational conditions are present for beginning the purposeful study of instrumental music in the public schools. Martignetti (1965) has reported that students in elementary school indicate that they drop instrumental music because the instruments are too difficult. No evidence exists on the optimum time, psychologically, for beginning the study of an instrument in the schools. Other variables to be considered appear to be previous musical background and the influence of other interests and activities on perseverance in instrumental study. Instrumental-music teachers may be hindering their efforts by starting students on instruments at too early an age.

Pinkerton (1963) reported little agreement on the criteria used in selecting instrumental music students in the public schools. Rhoades (1938) reported that the level of intelligence was the best single predictor of achievement in instrumental music. Neither intelligence, musical aptitude, nor physical measurements, however, appears to be a valid predictor of the selection of a specific musical instrument. Achievement in simple-melody wind-instrument playing (tonette) does not seem adequate for determining instrumental aptitude. These were the conclusions reached by Lamp (1933) and by Lamp and Keys (1935) in their studies of this problem. Interest in playing an instrument has been revealed by Nagro (1954) to be related primarily to favorable influences existing in the home and the desire to play in the school orchestra or band.

Few studies have been concerned with problems in the teaching-learning process in instrumental music. In studies with beginning instrumental students, Tietze (1958) reported that a combination program of rhythmic training, melody wind-instrument instruction, and class instruction on band instruments was far superior in developing musical skills, instrumental skills, and musical knowledges to a program of instrumental instruction alone. Childs (1963) has shown that two 30-minute periods of instrumental class instruction per week can produce superior results with elementary-school students. Class instruction for beginning piano students in the age range six to nine years was shown by Hutcherson (1955) to be just as effective as individual private instruction.

Overlearning and negative practice (rehearsing errors) have been shown by Becker (1962) and Johnson (1962) to be of no value in preparation for instrumental performance by high school groups. Lester (1963) has reported that the specific use of aural and visual (stroboscopic) stimuli, as methods of improving intonation in the performance of high school instrumentalists, does not appear to be as effective as the conventional teacher-demonstration method. Silverman (1962) has demonstrated that high school instrumental-music students can learn improvisation through guided performance in small ensembles.

Erwin H. Schneider
The Ohio State University

References

Ashford, Theodore H. A. "An Investigation of Programmed Instruction in the Fundamentals of Music Theory." *J Res Music Ed* 14(3):171–77; 1966.

Barnes, Robert A. "Programmed Instruction in Music Fundamentals for Future Elementary Teachers." *J Res Music Ed* 12(3):187–98; 1964.

Baumann, Victor H. "Socio-economic Status and the Music Preferences of Teen-agers." Doctoral dissertation. U Southern California, 1958.

Baumann, Victor H. "Teen-age Music Preferences." *J Res Music Ed* 8(2):75–84; 1960.

Becker, William R. The Effects of Overlearning, Initial Learning Ability and Review upon the Memory of Junior High School Cornet and Trumpet Players." Doctoral dissertation. State U Iowa, 1962.

Bentley, R. R. "A Critical Comparison of Certain Music Aptitude Tests." Doctoral dissertation. U Southern California, 1955.

Blyler, Dorothea M. "The Song Choices of Children in the Elementary School." Doctoral dissertation. U Illinois, 1957.

Boardman, Eunice. "An Investigation of the Effect of Preschool Training on the Development of Vocal Accuracy in Young Children." Doctoral dissertation. U Illinois, 1964.

Bodie, Merry D. "A Study of Seventh Grade General Music Listening Experiences." Master's thesis. U Texas, 1958.

Boyle, John D. "A Study of Current Practices in General Music in the Senior High Schools of Kansas, Missouri, Nebraska, and Oklahoma." Master's thesis. U Kansas, 1960.

Broquist, Oliver H. "A Survey of the Attitudes of 2594 Wisconsin Elementary School Pupils Toward Their Learning Experiences in Music." Doctoral dissertation. U Wisconsin, 1961.

Buebendorf, Francis X. "A Study and Special Treatment of Classic Symphonies for the School Orchestra." Doctoral dissertation. Teachers College, Columbia U, 1947.

Burke, R. S., and Grinder, R. E. "Personality-oriented Themes and Listening Patterns in Teen-age Music and Their Relation to Certain Academic and Peer Variables." *Sch R* 74:196–211; 1966.

Buros, Oscar K. (Ed.) *The Fifth Mental Measurements Yearbook.* Gryphon, 1959. 1292p.

Busse, Bernard W. "An Experiment in the Use of Recordings in the Teaching of Elementary Grade Vocal Music." Doctoral dissertation. Northwestern U, 1952.

Buttram, Joe B. "The Influence of Selected Factors on Interval Identification." Doctoral dissertation. U Kansas, 1967.

Cady, Henry L. *A Conference on Research in Music Education.* USOE, HEW, 1967.

Campion, Lee E. *The CUE Report.* U State New York and State Education Department, 1966.

Carlsen, James C. "Programed Learning in Melodic Dictation." *J Res Music Ed* 12(2):139–48; 1964.

Childs, Carroll A. "A Comparison of Two Distributed Instructional Periods in the Training of Beginning Instrumental Students." Doctoral dissertation. Colorado State U, 1963.

Christ, William B. "The Reading of Rhythm Notation Approached Experimentally According to Techniques and Principles of Word Reading." Doctoral dissertation. Indiana U, 1954.

Christy, Van A. "Evaluation of Choral Music." Doctoral dissertation. Teachers Col, Columbia U, 1947.

Cramer, William F. "The Relation of Maturation and Other Factors to Achievement in Beginning Instrumental Performance at the Fourth Through Eighth Grade Levels." Doctoral dissertation. Florida State U, 1958.

Creitz, Dale P. "A Study of the Use of the Piano as

a Space-frame in Teaching Vocal Music to Children." Master's thesis. U Kansas, 1943.

Cribb, George R. "The Comparative Effectiveness of Conventional and Programmed Instructional Procedures in Teaching Fundamentals of Music." Doctoral dissertation. North Texas State U, 1965.

Culver, F. "A Study of the Musical Aptitude Profile." Master's thesis. State U Iowa, 1965.

Drake, Raleigh M. "Factorial Analysis of Music Tests by the Spearman Tetrad-Difference Technique." *J Musicology* 1:6–10; 1939.

Drake, Raleigh M. *Drake Musical Aptitude Tests.* SRA, 1954.

Duerksen, George L. "A Study of the Relationship Between the Perception of Musical Processes and the Enjoyment of Music." Doctoral dissertation. U Kansas, 1967.

Ekstrom, Robert C. "Comparison of the Male Voice Before, During, and After Mutation." Doctoral dissertation. U Southern California, 1959.

Erneston, Nicholas. "A Study to Determine the Effect of Musical Experiences and Mental Ability on the Formulation of Musical Taste." Doctoral dissertation. Florida State U, 1961.

Ernst, Karl D. "A Study of Certain Practices in Music Education in School Systems in Cities over 150,000 Population." Doctoral dissertation. U Oregon, 1955.

Evans, Kenneth Gene. "Instructional Materials for the Oboe, 1695–ca. 1800." Doctoral dissertation. State U Iowa, 1963.

Farnsworth, Paul R. *Musical Taste: Its Measurement and Cultural Nature.* Stanford U Press, 1950. 94p.

Farnsworth, Paul R. *The Social Psychology of Music.* Dryden, 1958. 304p.

Farnsworth, Paul R. "Fine Arts: Music." In Buros, Oscar K. (Ed.) *The Fifth Mental Measurements Yearbook.* Gryphon, 1959. p. 248–9.

Farnsworth, Paul R. "Testing for Music Talent." *Instrumentalist* 16(3):34–7; 1961.

Fisher, Rhoda L. "Preference of Different Age and Socio-economic Groups in Unstructured Musical Situations." *J Social Psychol* 33:147–52; 1951.

Fosha, L. "A Study of the Validity of the Musical Aptitude Profile." Doctoral dissertation. State U Iowa, 1964.

Freeman, Warren S. "A Study and Evaluation of the Current Status of Music Education Activities in the Public Schools of the United States." Doctoral dissertation. Boston U, 1955.

Garder, Clarence E. "A Study of Characteristics of Outstanding High School Musicians." Doctoral dissertation. U Kansas, 1953.

Garder, Clarence E. "Characteristics of Outstanding High School Musicians." *J Res Music Ed* 3:11–20; 1955.

Gaston, E. Thayer. "A Study of the Trends of Attitudes Toward Music in School Children with a Study of the Methods Used by High School Students in Sight-reading music." Doctoral dissertation. U Kansas, 1940.

Gaston, E. Thayer. *Test of Musicality.* Odell's Instrumental Service, 1st ed., 1942; 4th ed., 1957.

George, Zelma W. "A Guide to Negro Music." Doctoral dissertation. New York U, 1953.

Gernet, Sterling K. "Musical Discrimination at Various Age and Grade Levels." Doctoral dissertation. Temple U, 1939.

Gesell, Arnold. *The First Five Years of Life.* Harper, 1940. 393p.

Gesell, Arnold, and Ilg, Frances L. *The Child from Five to Ten.* Harper, 1946. 475p.

Getz, Russell P. "The Influence of Familiarity Through Determining Optimum Responses of Seventh-grade Children to Certain Types of Serious Music." Doctoral dissertation. Pennsylvania State U, 1963.

Gilfeather, Charlotte V. "Motivation of the Below Average Adolescent in Junior High School General Music Classes." Master's thesis. Texas Christian U, 1962.

Gordon, Edwin. *Musical Aptitude Profile.* Houghton, 1965(a).

Gordon, Edwin. "The Music Aptitude Profile: A New and Unique Musical Aptitude Test Battery." *Council Res Music Ed* 6:12–7; 1965(b).

Gordon, Philip. "The Availability of Contemporary American Music in High Schools and Colleges." Doctoral dissertation, Teachers Col, Columbia U, 1949.

Gordon, Roderick D. "Doctoral Dissertations in Music and Music Education, 1957–1963." *J Res Music Ed* 12:10–112; Spring 1964.

Graves, Winifred S. "Adolescents' Musical Training as a Function of Parent-Child Relationships and Associated Personality Variables." Doctoral dissertation. Columbia U, 1950.

Gray, C. T., and Bingham, C. W. "A Comparison of Certain Phases of Musical Ability of Colored and White Public-school Pupils." *J Ed Psychol* 20:501–6; 1929.

Greenberg, Marvin, and MacGregor, Beatrix. "Correlation of Musical Talents and Behavioral Traits." *Council Res Music Ed* 7:24–33; 1966.

Haderer, Walter L. "Selected Unpublished Symphonies of the Mannheim School for Use in Training School Orchestras." Doctoral dissertation. U Southern California, 1961.

Hammer, Harry. "An Experimental Study of the Use of the Tachistoscope in the Teaching of Melodic Sight-singing." Doctoral dissertation. U Colorado, 1961.

Hansford, Charles H. "An Appraisal of the Group Singing of Sixth Graders as Taught by Classroom Teachers in Twenty-five Elementary Schools in a Midwestern City of 100,000 Population." Doctoral dissertation. U Missouri, 1962.

Hargiss, Genevieve. "The Acquisition of Sight Singing Ability in Piano Classes." Doctoral dissertation. U Kansas, 1960.

Hargiss, Genevieve. "The Acquisition of Sight Singing Ability in Piano Classes for Students Preparing to be Elementary Teachers." *J Res Music Ed* 10:69–72; 1962.

Hartzell, Ralph E. "An Experimental Study of Tonality Apprehension and Tonal Memory in Young

Children." Doctoral dissertation. U Cincinnati, 1949.

Havlovic, Arthur J. "A Study of Boys' Voices and Song Material in the Senior High School." Doctoral dissertation. U Cincinnati, 1937.

Heller, Jack K. "The Effects of Formal Music Training on the Wing Musical Intelligence Scores." Doctoral dissertation. State U Iowa, 1962.

Hollingsworth, Beverly J. "A Survey of the Status of the General Music Program in the Junior High Schools of Texas." Master's thesis. U Texas, 1953.

Horacek, Leo. "Programmed Instruction in Music." R Psychol Music 1(2):1–6; 1963.

Hughes, JoAnn M. "Fifty-nine Case Studies on the Effect of Musical Participation on Social Development." Music Educators J 41:58–9; February 1955.

Hutcherson, Rita J. "Group Instruction in Piano: An Investigation of the Relative Effectiveness of Group and Individual Piano Instruction at Beginning Level." Doctoral dissertation. State U Iowa, 1955.

Hutton, Doris. "A Comparative Study of Two Methods of Teaching Sight Singing in the Fourth Grade." J Res Music Ed 1:119–26; 1953.

Jacobsen, O. Irving. "An Analytical Study of Eye-movements in Reading Vocal and Instrumental Music." J Musicology 3:197; 1942.

Jenkins, Thomas V. "A Study of the Relationship Between Music Aptitudes and Mental Ability, Science Aptitudes, and Mathematics Aptitudes Among Secondary School Pupils in Texas." Doctoral dissertation. U Texas, 1960.

Jersild, Arthur T. "Music." In Child Development and the Curriculum. 38th Yearbook, Part I, NSSE. 1939. p. 135–51.

Jersild, Arthur T., Bienstock, Sylvia F. "A Study of the Development of Children's Ability to Sing." J Ed Psychol 25:481–503; 1934.

Johnson, Gordon B. "Negative Practice on Band Instruments: An Exploratory Study." J Res Music Ed 10(3):100–4; 1962.

Jones, Donald W. "A Comparative Study of Selected Issues in Music Education as Represented in the Opinions of Principals, Music Teachers, and Professors of Music Education." Doctoral dissertation. Ohio State U, 1961.

Joseph, Warren A. "The Relationship Between Vocal Growth in the Human Adolescent and the Total Growth Process." Doctoral dissertation. Boston U, 1959.

Kaplan, Lionel. "The Relationship Between Certain Personality Characteristics and Achievement in Instrumental Music." Doctoral dissertation. New York U, 1961.

Karlin, J. E. "A Factorial Study of Auditory Function." Psychometrika 7:251–79; 1942.

Keegan, Arthur J. "A Study of Music in General Education and a Manual for Teaching General Music in the Lower Secondary Grades." Doctoral dissertation. New York U, 1956.

Kelley, William L. "Beliefs and Practices of Administrators and Musicians from Selected Midwestern Cities Concerning the Importance and Functions of Music in the Public Schools." Doctoral dissertation. U Kansas, 1962.

Kirkpatrick, William C. "Relationships Between the Singing Ability of Pre-kindergarten Children and Their Home Environment." Doctoral dissertation. U Southern California, 1962.

Knudsen, Emma R. "Folk Music as a Tool in Intercultural Education." Doctoral dissertation. Northwestern U, 1946.

Kuhn, Wolfgang. "A Study and Appraisal of Music Education in Selected Public Schools of Illinois." Doctoral dissertation. U Illinois, 1953.

Kwalwasser, Jacob. Kwalwasser Music Talent Test. Mills Music Inc., 1953.

Kwalwasser, Jacob, and Dykema, Peter W. K-D Music Tests. Carl Fischer, Inc., 1930.

Kyme, George H. "An Experiment in Teaching Children to Read Music with Shaped Notes." J Res Music Ed 8(1):3–8; 1960.

Lamp, Charles J. "The Determination of Aptitude for Specific Musical Instruments." Doctoral dissertation. U California, 1933.

Lamp, Charles J. and Keys, Noel. "Can Aptitude for Specific Musical Instruments Be Predicted?" J Ed Psychol 26(7):587–96; 1935.

Larson, William S. (Ed.) Bibliography of Research Studies in Music Education, 1932–1948. Music Educators National Conference, 1949. 119p.

Larson, William S. "Bibliography of Research Studies in Music Education, 1949–1956." J Res Music Ed 5:(2)64–225; 1957.

Lester, William. "A Comparison of Three Methods for Improving Intonation in the Performance of Instrumental Music." Doctoral dissertation. U Colorado, 1963.

Livingston, Jane C. "A Study of the English Madrigal and Its Use in the High School Vocal Program." Master's thesis. New England Conservatory, 1957.

Luke, Orral S. "Differences in Musical Aptitude in School Children of Different National and Racial Origin." Doctoral dissertation. U California, 1939.

Lundin, R. W. "Development and Validation of a Set of Musical Ability Tests." Psychol Monogr Vol. 63(No. 305); 1949. 20p.

Lundin, Robert W. An Objective Psychology of Music. Ronald, 1953. 303p.

Lundin, Robert W. "Can Perfect Pitch Be Learned?" Music Educators J 49:49–51; April–May 1963.

Lundin, Robert W., and Allen, J. "Techniques for Training Perfect Pitch." Psychol Rec 12:139–46; 1962.

Lustre, Warren W. "An Experiment Comparing Three Methods of Learning Selected Aural Harmonies." Doctoral dissertation. Peabody Col Teachers, 1958.

Marquis, James Henry. "A Study of Interval Problems in Sight-singing Performance with Consideration of the Effect of Context." Doctoral dissertation. State U Iowa, 1963.

Martignetti, Anthony J. "Causes of Elementary Instrumental Music Dropouts." J Res Music Ed 13(3):177–83; 1965.

McLeish, John. "The Validation of Seashore's Measures of Musical Talent by Factorial Methods." *Br J Psychol* 3:129–40; 1950.

McLeish, John. "Wing Standardized Tests of Music Intelligence." In Buros, Oscar K. (Ed.) *The Fourth Mental Measurements Yearbook*. Gryphon, 1953. p. 230–1.

Mueller, Paul R. "The Status of the Junior High General Music Class in California." Master's thesis. Fresno State Col, 1960.

Mirsell, James L. *The Psychology of Music*. Norton, 1937. 389p.

Mirsell, James L., and Glenn, Mabelle. *The Psychology of School Music Teaching*. Silver, 1938. 386p.

Nagro, Constantino F. "An Analysis of Certain Factors Relative to the Promotion of Interest in the Study of Musical Instruments." Doctoral dissertation. Chicago Musical Col, 1954.

Nash, Louis P. "The Enjoyment of Music by Junior High Students: Their Responses to Five Methods of Presenting Recorded Music." Doctoral dissertation. U California, 1962.

Nelson, Carl B. "An Experimental Evaluation of Two Methods of Teaching Music in the Fourth and Fifth Grades." Doctoral dissertation. U Minnesota, 1954.

Nelson, Carl B. "A Follow-up of an Experimental Teaching Method in Music at the Fourth and Fifth Grade Levels." *J Exp Ed* 34:283–9; June 1956.

Nelson, Marvin G. "A Comparative Study of Instrumental Music Programs in Selected Public School Systems in Four North Central States." Doctoral dissertation. Chicago Musical Col, 1955.

Nelson, Russell C. "A Physiological Study of the Utilization of the Vital Capacity in Phonation, Resonation, and Articulation, and Its Effect on Tone Quality in the Adolescent." Doctoral dissertation. U Michigan, 1954.

Neu, D. M. "A Critical Review of the Literature on Absolute Pitch." *Psychol B* 44:249–69; 1947.

Noah, Max S. "Promotion of Music Education by Southern State Departments of Education." Doctoral dissertation. Peabody Col for Teachers, 1953.

Palisca, Claude V. *Music in Our Schools: A Search for Improvement*. USOE Bulletin No. 28. HEW, 1964. 61p.

Pence, Don P. "A Study to Determine the Optimum Grade for Beginning Class Study of Wind Instruments." Master's thesis. U Kansas, 1942.

Peterson, Ruth D. "An Investigation of Academic Music Courses in the Public Secondary Schools of Missouri." Master's thesis. Northeast Missouri State, 1962.

Petzold, Robert G. "The Perception of Music Symbols in Music Reading by Normal Children and by Children Gifted Musically." *J Exp Ed* 28(4):271–319; 1960.

Petzold, Robert G. "The Development of Auditory Perception of Musical Sounds by Children in the First Six Grades." *J Res Music Ed* 11(1):21–43; 1963.

Petzold, Robert G. *Auditory Perceptions of Musical Sounds by Children in the First Six Grades*. Cooperative Research Project No. 1051. USOE, 1966. 120p.

Pflederer, Marilyn. "The Responses of Children to Musical Tasks Embodying Piaget's Principle of Conservation." *J Res Music Ed* II(4):–68; 1964.

Pinkerton, Frank W. "Talent Tests and Their Application to the Public School Instrumental Music Program." *J Res Music Ed* 11(1):75–80; 1968.

Pittsburgh Public Schools. "An Experimental Study of the Value of Instrumental Training in Public School Music." *Pittsburgh Sch* 11(2):49–58; 1936.

Price, David E. "An Analysis of Some of the Musical Experiences Provided the Students in the Tenth, Eleventh, and Twelfth Grades in the Public Secondary Schools Approved by the North Central Association. Doctoral dissertation. U Colorado, 1950.

Price, David E. "Music for Every Child (Except 53.3 Percent)." *Music Educators J* 39:45; June–July 1953.

Priestly, Ehud. "Pitch Discrimination and Certain Characteristics of Fifth, Seventh and Ninth Grade Children." Doctoral dissertation. New York U, 1942.

Rainbow, Edward L. "A Pilot Study to Investigate the Constructs of Musical Aptitude." *J Res Music Ed* 13(1):3–14; 1965.

Reynolds, George E. "Environmental Sources of Musical Awakening in Pre-school Children." Doctoral dissertation. U Illinois, 1960.

Rhoades, Fordyce L. "An Evaluation of Measures for the Prediction of Success in Instrumental Music Study." Master's thesis. U Washington, 1938.

Rogers, Vincent R. "Children's Expressed Musical Preferences at Selected Grade Levels." Doctoral dissertation. Syracuse U, 1956.

Rubin, Louis. "The Effects of Musical Experience on Musical Discrimination and Musical Preferences." Doctoral dissertation. U California, 1952.

Schneider, Erwin H., and Cady, Henry L. *Evaluation and Synthesis of Research Studies Relating to Music Education*. Cooperative Research Project No. E-016. USOE, 1966. 651p.

Schoen, Max. *The Psychology of Music*. Ronald, 1940. 258p.

Seashore, Carl E. *The Psychology of Musical Talent*. Silver, 1919. 288p.

Setveit, Joseph G., and others. *Revision of the Seashore Measures of Musical Talents*. Psych Corp, 1940.

Shull, Carl N. "A Study of Children's Vocal Literature Written by Selected Distinguished Composers." Doctoral dissertation. Florida State U, 1961.

Sievers, C. H. "The Measurement of Musical Development. II: A Study of Rhythmic Performance with Special Consideration of the Factors Involved in the Formation of a Scale for Measuring Rhythmic Ability." *U Iowa Stud Child Welf* 7(1):111–72; 1932.

Silverman, Marvin L. "Ensemble Improvisation as a Creative Technique in the Secondary Instrumental Music Program." Doctoral dissertation. Stanford U, 1962.

Silvey, Clel T. "A Study of Personal Reactions to the

Solmization Method of Teaching Music Reading." Doctoral dissertation. Peabody Col for Teachers, 1937.

Sims, Francis J. "An Experimental Investigation of the Relative Effectiveness of Group and Individual Voice Instruction at the Beginning Level to High School Students. Doctoral dissertation. U Oklahoma, 1961.

Small, Arnold M. (Ed.) *Bibliography of Research Studies in Music Education, 1932–1944.* Music Educators National Conference, 1944. 55p.

Smiley, Edna M. "A Study of the Musical Configurations, Symbols, Terms, and Words Found in Basic Music Texts at the Fourth Grade Level." Doctoral dissertation. Indiana U, 1955.

Smith, Edgar H. "The Value of Notated Examples in Learning to Recognize Musical Themes Aurally." *J Res Music Ed* 1:97–104; 1953.

Spohn, Charles L. "Programming the Basic Materials of Music for Self-instructional Development of Aural Skills." *J Res Music Ed* 11(2):91–8; 1963.

Spohn, Charles L. *A Comparison Between Different Stimuli: Combined with Two Methods for Providing Knowledge of Results in Music Instruction.* HEW, USOE, Title VII, Project No. 1088. 1965. 217p.

Stokes, Charles F. "An Experimental Study of Tachistoscopic Training in Reading Music." Doctoral dissertation. U Cincinnati, 1944.

Streep, Rosalind. "A Comparison of White and Negro Children in Rhythm and Consonance." *J Applied Psychol* 15:53–71; 1931.

Swanson, Frederick J. "Voice Mutation in the Adolescent Male: An Experiment in Guiding the Voice Development of Adolescent Boys in General Music Classes." Doctoral dissertation. U Wisconsin, 1959.

Tarrell, V. "An Investigation of the Validity of the Musical Aptitude Profile." Doctoral dissertation. State U Iowa, 1964.

Terman, Michael. "Improvement of Absolute Pitch Naming." *Psychonomic Sci* 3(6):243–4; 1965.

Theno, E. Charles. "A Study of Orlando di Lasso's Choral Works with Reference to School Performance." Doctoral dissertation. U Oregon, 1954.

Thomas, Ronald B. "A Study of New Concepts, Procedures, and Achievements in Music Learning as Developed in Selected Music Education Programs." HEW, USOE, 1966. 93p.

Tietze, William B. "The Effect of Pre-band Melody and Rhythm Instruments on the Musical Learning of Beginning Fourth Grade Instrumental Students." Doctoral dissertation. State U Iowa, 1958.

Uldrick, Johnnye M. "An Investigation of Curriculum Guides in Music in the Ffty States of the United States with Emphasis on the Guides for Senior High School Music." Master's thesis. Clemson Col, 1961.

Utgaard, Merton B. "Analysis of Teaching Content Found in Ensemble Music Written for Brass Wind Instruments." Doctoral dissertation. Colorado State Col of Education, 1949.

Van Alstyne, D., and Osborne, E. "Rhythmic Responses of Negro and White Children Two to Six." *Monogr Soc Res Child Develop* 2(No. 4):1–64; 1937.

Van Nuys, Kelvin, and Weaver, Homer E. "Memory Span and Visual Pauses in Reading Rhythms and Melodies." *Psychol Monogr* 55(No. 1):44–50; 1943.

Wardian, Jeanne Foster. "An Experiment Concerning the Effectiveness of Programmed Learning for Use in Teaching the Fundamentals of Music." Doctoral dissertation. Washington State U, 1963.

Weaver, Homer E. "A Survey of Visual Processes in Reading Differently Constructed Musical Selections." *Psychol Monogr* 55(No. 1); 1943. 30p.

Weigand, James J. "A Comparison of the Effectiveness of Two Methods of Teaching General Music in the Junior High School." *Emporia State Col Res Stud* 10(3):5–55; 1962.

Wenaas, Sigurd B. "A Study of the Relationship Between Musical Ability and Various Intelligence, Scholastic, and Personality Factors." Master's thesis. U Idaho, 1940.

Wheeler, Lester R., and Wheeler, Viola D. "The Relationship Between Music Reading and Language Reading Abilities." *J Ed Res* 45:439–50; 1952.

Whistler, Harvey S., and Thorpe, Lewis P. *Musical Aptitude Test.* California Test Bureau, 1950.

Whybrew, William E. *Measurement and Evaluation in Music.* Brown, 1962. 184p.

Wikstrom, Thomas N. "The Application of Early String Literature to Heterogeneous String Classes at the College Level." Doctoral dissertation." Florida State U, 1960.

Wiley, Charles A. "An Experimental Study of Tachistoscopic Techniques in Teaching Rhythmic Sight-reading in Music." Doctoral dissertation. U Colorado, 1962.

Wing, Herbert D. "Some Applications of Test Results to Education in Music." *Br J Ed Psychol* 24:161–70; 1954.

Wing, Herbert D. *Wing Standardized Tests of Musical Intelligence.* National Foundation for Educational Research, (London), 1958.

Wolner, M., and Pyle, W. H. "An Experiment in Individual Training of Pitch-deficient Children." *J Ed Psychol* 24:602–8; 1933.

Wyatt, Ruth F. "Improvability of Pitch Discrimination." *Psychol Monogr* Vol. 58(No. 2); 1945. 58p.

Yingling, Robert W. "Classification of Reaction Patterns in Listening to Music." *J Res Music Ed* 10(2):105–20; 1962.

York, Roy. "An Experimental Study of Vocal Music Reading of Public School High School Music Students Using Eye-movement Photography and Voice Recording." Doctoral dissertation. Syracuse U, 1952.

Zack, Melvin L. "A Study of the Influence of Selected Socio-cultural Characteristics on Participation in Instrumental Music." Doctoral dissertation. U Kansas, 1953.

Zima, Barbara H. "A Comparative Study of Two Approaches to the Teaching of Required Music Classes in the Junior High School." Master's thesis. Northwestern U, 1956.

OBJECTIVES AND OUTCOMES

Educational objectives have for centuries occupied the attention of educational specialists, of representatives of other areas of study, and of laymen. That they are matters of basic concern is attested to by the amount written about them; both educational and noneducational literature is replete with formal and informal statements of objectives of education and with descriptions of methods for determining what objectives should be.

Examination of research regarding educational objectives and outcomes reveals several important factors. First, the terms themselves have no universally accepted definition, so discourse about objectives occurs upon several levels of generality. Second, a statement of objectives or a recommended methodology for determining objectives is almost couched in value terms, which renders empirical research in the classical sense difficult. Third, the question of what objectives ought to be sought has a history which dates at least from Plato. Fourth, pronouncements about objectives are more or less explicitly analyzed and justified opinions. Fifth, studies of a largely empirical nature in relation to objectives are few compared to the number of statements of objectives based upon individual or group opinion.

HISTORICAL DEVELOPMENT. Generally, statements of objectives have come from three major sources: philosophers concerned with the totality of human experience who view education within this context; specialists in some measure responsible for the establishment, maintenance or both of some educational institution; and interested laymen. There appears to be a parallel between the development of educational institutions and the prevalent source of objectives. As education became a formal institution, the number of educational specialists and interested noneducators who attended to statements of objectives increased. While this is the case, it is also true that general philosophers have continued to enunciate statements of educational objectives. Illustrative of such statements are those of Plato (Davies & Vaughan, 1950), Mill (1957), Whitehead (1949), and O'Connor (1957).

Among the earliest statements of educational objectives from educators are the Yale report (Committee of the Corporation and the Academical Faculty, 1830), the report of the Committee of Ten (National Education Association, 1894), and the report of the Committee of Fifteen on Elementary Education (National Education Association, 1895). Later such statements came from the Commission on the Reorganization of Secondary Education (CRSE) (National Education Association, 1918), and the Educational Policies Commission (National Education Association, 1961).

Charters and Miller (1915) began to approach the question of objectives in what they saw as a different manner. They, and then Bobbitt, beginning in 1918, formulated a methodology for determining educational objectives. The hope was to make such determination scientific rather than a matter of personal opinion or whim. Others who worked to develop a methodology included Tyler (1950), French (1957), Kearney (1953) Goodlad and others (1966), and Ammons (1964).

Rarely has education been without its critics, and rarely has there been a period when interested individuals did not propose a set of objectives alternative to the ones supposedly underlying education. The reality of Sputnik apparently occasioned a renewed interest in the objectives of education in the United States. Among those who suggested a revision in purpose were Rickover (1963), Bestor (1953), Goodman (1964), and Bruner (1960).

A different and larger category of interested persons who are not specialists in education per se includes scholars in such disciplines as the sciences, mathematics, and foreign languages. While such groups do not always make educational objectives explicit, such objectives can often be inferred. One comprehensive examination of new programs and their objectives, either explicit or implicit, was done by Goodlad & Richter (1966). Although the parallel is not complete in any way, it is possible to compare the work of these latter groups to the work of the Committee of Ten. The likeness lies in the fact that purposes were developed by committees of scholars who were themselves educators but whose major fields of study were not that of education. Whether the influence of scholars who developed new programs for schools in the United States in the 1950's and 1960's will be as far-reaching as the proposals of the Committee of Ten cannot yet be determined.

Statements of objectives, then, have been for the most part reasoned reflections of individual or collective opinion, not results of empirical studies.

EXPRESSION. Objectives have not only mirrored the nature of social conditions at any given time but also have arisen from some concept of the nature of man. Thus, it is not possible to analyze any given historical period and discover a unique expression of objectives. For example, Krug (1964) states that the notion of mental training or disciplining through "properly selected studies" can be traced back at least as far as Plato. The Yale report (Committee of the Corporation and the Academical Faculty, 1830) was a later expression of this same idea, emphasizing the importance of exercising the important mental faculties. Among these faculties were "reasoning powers," "imagination and taste," and "memory." Others who adhered to this general purpose were the members of the Committee of Ten (National Education Association, 1894).

Another perspective on the expression of objectives is represented by Ragan (1960), who asserts that whatever the specific expression regarding educational objectives, such objectives have tended to reflect some identifiable "social reality" of a given time. Using elementary education to illustrate, he cites, for example, the religious climate of the New England colonies in 1647 and the resulting religious motive for education. Similarly, he describes the class structure of the Southern colonies, which was reflected in their tutorial and apprentice systems, each of which prepared an individual for his station in life. Ragan develops this idea for several other periods. In a somewhat different tone Wieman (1963) says that purposes must be acceptable to the community, which parallels Ragan's contention. That objectives tend to reflect social realities is supported by Krug (1964) in his description of the report of the Commission on the Reorganization of Secondary Education. This commission articulated the "seven cardinal principles of education": health, command of fundamental processes, worthy home membership, vocation, citizenship, worthy use of leisure, and ethical character.

Spencer (1880), with his plea for the complete life, gave rise to the concept of the major activities of life as a basis for objectives: those activities which directly minister to self-preservation; those activities which, by securing the necessities of life, indirectly minister to self-preservation; those activities which have for their end the rearing and disciplining of offspring; those activities which are involved in the maintenance of proper social and political relations; and those miscellaneous activities which fill up the leisure part of life—i.e., those devoted to the gratification of tastes and feelings.

Spencer, while exerting influence upon both the Committee of Ten and upon the CRSE, also had a marked effect upon those curriculum authorities who fell under the general rubric of education for social efficiency. Bobbitt (1918) serves as an explicit spokesman for this approach which included, among others, Charters (1923) and Draper (1936). Specifically, Bobbit held objectives to be the following: language activities, social intercommunication; health activities, citizenship activities, general social activities—meeting and mingling with others; spare-time activities, amusements, recreations; keeping oneself mentally fit; religious activity, parental activities; unspecialized or nonvocational practical activities; and the labor of one's calling. All these relate to his more general aim of education, which was to prepare the young to engage in adult activities.

Education for social efficiency had as its twin education for social control. Among those who argued for adherence to this latter view were, according to Krug (1964), Ross, Ward, Small, Snedden, Ellwood, and Groves. From such a viewpoint the individual was seen as subservient to society. Groves clearly came down on the side of social control in 1915, leaving the determination of purpose to sociology, such purpose being dependent upon society's needs for its own well-being.

Dewey (1915) sought to establish that growth and education are synonymous and relied heavily upon his theory of experience as the basis of educational objectives. He viewed the general purpose of education as social service and made a strong plea for classrooms which reflected the community.

Bruner (1960) saw as the objectives of education "schooling for better students" as well as "helping each student achieve his optimum intellectual development."

In its most recent statement, the Educational Policies Commission (National Educational Association, 1961) indicated as the central purpose of education the development of the ability to think. It supports this objective on the basis of man's rationality and a challenge that this particular objective will not be generally obtained unless the school focuses upon it.

DETERMINATION. As was stated above, it was not until 1918 that curriculum specialists attempted to make the determination of objectives a scientific endeavor. Although Charters and Miller (1915) had begun to use analysis of errors as the basis for establishing objectives, it was Bobbitt (1918) who published a formalized step-by-step procedure for arriving at objectives. Given his more general purpose of education—preparation for adult activities—he described in detail ways and means of examining adult activities to arrive at objectives. Activities were to be discovered through the examination of newspapers and through the analysis of social, civic, religious, health, and other activities as these were engaged in by social classes. He cites Charters' work in the analysis of grammatical errors as an example of analysis of shortcomings among students. He acknowledges the difficulty inherent in determining desirable activities in such fields as art and music and the necessity for agreement upon what ought to be in each of these areas.

Tyler (1950) proposed a broader attack on the problem of establishing objectives. He stated that objectives are the personal choice of those educators who write them but that such choice can be made more intelligently by the proper use of philosophy, psychology, and the special disciplines than is the case if these areas are ignored. He also advocated thorough examination of the "needs of society" and the "needs of learners," ultimately using philosophy and psychology as final screens for completed objectives.

Two other writers in the field of curriculum have proposed a somewhat different methodology from that of Tyler. Goodlad and others (1966) stipulates that objectives are drawn from a value position and that analysis of that position is basic to appropriate statements of objectives. He suggests that objectives can be judged according to criteria of validity, appropriateness, feasibility, precision, consistency, and comprehensiveness. Ammons (1964), using these criteria and defining them in operational terms, investigated what nine school systems had done to arrive at their objectives and then judged the quality of the objectives according to the criteria. She reports that although the data do not support the contention that process and product are related, there is a trend which suggests the need for further study before the process for determining objectives is discarded.

Jensen (1950) published a study designed to establish a methodology for validating aims in education. Although the emphasis was on validation, there was an explicit procedure for arriving at aims. This included the following steps: the identification of a value framework; the consideration of basic human needs, both organic and psychological; investigation of the field of human development; analysis of the "formal relations involved in validating aims"; attention to three given factors when a choice among or between aims must be made. The three given factors are (1) that American society is industrialized; (2) that the basic needs of people likely will not change; and (3) that the "democratic norms represent the social ideals to which the American people have clung tenaciously for over a hundred and fifty years."

Barton (1950) recommends a process involving interaction and clarification between philosophers of education and curriculum workers, for the purpose of establishing objectives.

Payne (1961) adapted the method recommended by Goodlad and applied it to the determination of objectives for dietetic internships.

The National Catholic Educational Association (1965) has established a somewhat different approach to the determination of objectives. They list questions to be asked in developing a statement of philosophy and list several questions which should influence objectives. They state that objectives should implement, in specific terms, the ideals set forth in the philosophy.

In a status study of selected instructional practices, members of a National Education Association (NEA) project (1962) discovered that "the textbook was the resource listed by both elementary and secondary principals as the one most useful for a teaching program (1960–61)." What the publishers printed for school use was indicated as a strong determinant of what the students had studied. It is possible to infer then that in this sample objectives will to some degree be determined by the materials published commercially.

Another category of determination of objectives is that of surveying something about peoples' perceptions of objectives. Slagle (1959), Seager (1959), and Downey (1959) administered a questionnaire, "The Task of Public Education," to a number of "publics" in the United States and Canada. In part, their findings revealed a general agreement among all publics on first and second priorities, "the skills for acquiring and communicating knowledge" and cultivation of a "love for knowledge," for elementary and secondary education.

Using the same instrument, Faber (1965) investigated the opinions of prospective teachers regarding the task of public education. His study revealed that prospective teachers rank the same on the first and second tasks as did the educators and noneducators in the study described above.

Doane (1942) surveyed a cross section of American high school youth using an indirect needs inventory. He concluded that secondary-school curriculum should be directed away from the adult concepts of the subject-matter needs of youth and should be directed toward needs recognized by students. These needs lie in the area of "themselves as individuals and as members of society, their problems of adjustment to their vocational future, to their fellow youth, and to their emerging adult status."

Nerbovig (1954) sought to discover something about teachers' perceptions of objectives, particularly as these relate to teachers' use of objectives. She discovered that intermediate-grade teachers with longer experience who participated in the formulation of the objectives use them more than do other teachers who have less experience, are primary teachers, and who did not participate in the formulation of objectives. Investigating these same factors, Ammons (1964) did not find that they were related to the use made of objectives by teachers in her sample.

Wright (1962) sought to discover the extent of agreement on general educational goals among new teachers, experienced teachers, and administrators in six public high schools. Using a Q-sort of general goals and objectives he found that there was more disagreement between administrators and experienced teachers than between administrators and new teachers or between experienced teachers and new beginning teachers. There was least disagreement between experienced and new teachers.

A study of the relation of certain sociological factors as these relate to the perception of goals for public elementary education was conducted by Sandmeier (1964). Judging results to a questionnaire administered randomly to the community she found that the more-educated Jewish professional women with a residency of 5–10 years were less traditional, according to a scale by Bereday, than other groups. Among the selected factors, age, sex, level of education, length of residency, and civic and professional-club affiliation were all significantly related to views of goals, while race, level of income, and patronage or nonpatronage of public schools were not significantly related.

Illustrative of a survey technique somewhat different from that employed by Slagle (1959) and others is the use of a jury. Studies by Hawse (1964) and Hanson (1965) submitted statements of objectives to panels to determine agreement regarding the objectives.

Still another survey technique was developed by Kearney (1953) and others. They identified specialists in fields considered to be relevant to education—e.g., human development and psychology—and invited representatives of each to state what they saw as important objectives for elementary education. A similar study was conducted by French (1957), in relation to objectives for secondary education.

Frazier's report for the Project on the Study of Instruction of the NEA synthesized factors influencing the decision of what to teach (National Education Association, 1963). Objectives should be in the framework of six basic values: "respect for the worth and dignity of every individual; encouragement of variability; equality of opportunity of all children; faith in man's ability to make rational decisions; share responsibility for the common good; and respect for moral and spiritual values and ethical standards of conduct."

Lyda (1960), using Goodlad's notion of a conceptual system, identifies the elements which he sees as necessary in such a system. These elements are establishing a need for curriculum improvement, developing a set of guiding principles, formulating questions to be answered, identifying sources of data to be investigated and the method of gathering data to be employed, organizing answers to questions, determining the structure and content of curriculum, and evaluating. Objectives are then determined when desired directions of growth are outlined.

Representative of two different schools of thought regarding the responsibility for determining goals are, for one view, Britton (1959) and Charters (1958), who feel that the lay public should be directly involved, and, for the other view, Vander Werf (1959) and Hanna (1960), who suggest that national groups of scholars bear primary responsibility for determining goals. Goodlad and others (1966) and Ammons (1964) specify a controlling agency as the body with the legal responsibility for determination of aims. In the case of public education in the United States, the controlling agency is the local board of education.

In general, methodology for the determination of objectives relies upon the consensus of some group or groups. The differences among approaches lie in the identification of the groups and the questions asked of the groups.

VALIDATION. The question of validation poses more problems than many of the others in relation to educational objectives. To a more obvious extent than questions having to do with surveys of opinion or examination of literature, validation rests upon a value base. Saylor (1959) pleads for goals valid on the basis of their importance to all other decisions made by educators. Tyler (1950), while not speaking of validity specifically, asserts that decisions about objectives are the most important because objectives serve as the criterion for all other decisions. Although Bobbitt (1918) does not use the term "validation," one can infer that his criterion for validity is the extent to which the objectives reflect adult activities.

Jensen (1950) was centrally concerned with this question in his own study. As stated above, he evolved a method for validating aims of education. Basic to his approach was the selection of dominant American values which served as the standard for judging aims. Other information was to come from psychology, human development, and societal conditions.

Goodlad and others (1966) and Ammons (1964) both propose validity as one criterion for judging objectives. Validity in this instance is defined as the extent to which objectives reflect the intent of the controlling agency with respect to the purpose of the educational institution. To determine such validity requires thorough analysis of the expressed intent of the agency and the translation of such statements into objectives. Objectives are then reviewed with the agency to determine the consistency between the intent and the objectives as formulated.

Replogle (1951) defined a valid curriculum as one which is derived and developed from the "interaction of three main curricular sources—social realities, needs, and values." His validation rests ultimately upon validated democratic ideals.

B. Othanel Smith and others (1957), using the approach developed by Jensen, suggest five criteria to be met by objectives if they are to be valid. In this system sound objectives must "(1) be conceived in terms of the demands of the social circumstances; (2) lead toward the fulfillment of basic human needs; (3) be consistent with democratic ideals; (4) be either consistent or noncontradictory in their relationships with one another; and (5) be capable of reduction to behavioristic terms."

Others identified by Smith and his colleagues who have given specific attention to the question of validation of aims or objectives of education include Brubacher (1939), Bode (1938), Havighurst (1948), Kilpatrick (1933), and Dewey (1939).

BEHAVIORAL OBJECTIVES. "Behavioral objectives" are typically defined as statements of purpose which describe desired student behavior and indicate the content through which the behavior is to be developed. While Eugene R. Smith and others (1942) were among the earliest to use the term as such, Bobbitt (1918) and Charters (1923) expressed objectives in this fashion. As stated above, B. Othanel Smith and others (1957) require that an objective be stated in behavioral terms. Taba (1962), Beauchamp (1961), Goodlad and Richter (1966), Hawthorne (1967), McClure (1965), Sand (1955), Krathwohl (1965), and Block (1965) are among those who have utilized the idea of behavioral objectives in conceptual research and as part of curriculum development. McNeil (1966) argues for behavioral objectives as the basis for supervision of instruction, suggesting that teacher and supervisor agree on specific objectives to be achieved by the students with subsequent evaluation of the instruction to be based upon the extent to which the teacher accomplished what she intended to accomplish.

Ammons (1964), in a survey of 300 school systems, found that there were no objectives of the kind described above. Where there were descriptions of behaviors they either were of teacher behaviors or were of such an ambiguous nature as to obscure for whom the behavior was described.

Mager (1962) presents perhaps the most explicit description of behavioral objectives and places two major qualifications on objectives not always expressed by other authors. These qualifications are that the behavior must be observable and that the behaviors are to be terminal. Ammons (1967) argues for consideration of behavior which is not observable but which can be inferred according to definitions agreed upon by those involved. She also sees objectives as descriptions of direction rather than as descriptions of terminal behaviors. Herrick (Anderson & others, 1965) also identifies objectives as setters of direction.

The authors cited in the foregoing paragraphs tend to make a distinction between objectives and other statements of goals, restricting the use of the term "objectives" to those statements which describe desired student behavior and appropriate content. Other kinds of statements of purpose may be called goals, aims, or purposes.

Among curriculum theorists, there are those who doubt the necessity of behavioral objectives. Eisner (1967) and Macdonald (1965) argue that formulation of objectives prior to instruction may not be possible. Eisner also questions the usefulness of objectives.

TAXONOMIES OF OBJECTIVES. Bloom (1956) and Krathwohl and others (1964) have published taxonomies of educational goals. Bloom's 1956 handbook was devoted to a classification of behaviors in the cognitive domain. Identified were six levels of cognitive behaviors: knowledge of specifics, comprehension, analysis, application, synthesis, and evaluation. The second taxonomy described five levels of behavior in the affective domain: receiving, responding, valuing, organizing, and characterization.

Studies and recommendations which use the taxonomies are increasing. Sanders (1966) developed a manual of questions designed to elicit the behaviors included in the cognitive domain.

Russell (1964), using the Bloom taxonomy to construct categories, classified and studied objectives in four adult educational agencies. He found that practical, applied, and skill objectives were more frequently reported to be in use than were academically, theoretically, and intellectually oriented objectives.

Harrison (1964) and Klein (1965) employed the cognitive taxonomy in two different studies, each of which was based upon the ability to describe and classify behaviors.

Guszak (1966), in part, based his analysis of teachers' questions during reading instruction on the Bloom taxonomy. He found that over 60 percent of the solicitations by teachers in second, fourth, and sixth grades were at the levels of recall and recognition.

Cox (1966) at the University of Pittsburgh has developed a cumulative record of studies which have employed one or more of the taxonomies. Other taxonomies are in the stage of development—e.g., Barrett's (1962) in relation to reading behaviors.

EDUCATIONAL OUTCOMES. The measurement of educational outcomes engages the attention of researchers in many fields. Following are examples of summaries in the fields of English language arts, reading, and mathematics.

Strom (1965) has published summaries of investigations relating to secondary-school English language arts. Petty and Burns (1966) have done the same with elementary-school English language arts.

In reading, Harris, and others (1966) presented an annual list of annotated studies, and, in mathematics, Weaver (1966) brought together such summaries.

In many studies, outcomes were developed by the researcher apart from the objectives sought by school people in any specific educational context. Thus, the results are variously useful to school people, depending upon whether the objectives of the researcher and of the school setting were identical or similar.

Tyler (1966) has stated that in terms of general educational outcomes throughout the entire United States information is limited. In order to obtain a more comprehensive picture of the results of education a program of national assessment was begun in 1963. Frymier (1967) describes the development and status of the program up to early 1967. The fall of 1967 is cited as the date of the beginning of the actual testing program. Such a program will produce many data not heretofore available and will give a different basis for discussing the outcomes of education in the United States.

Margaret Ammons
The University of Wisconsin

References

Ammons, Margaret. "An Empirical Study of Process and Product in Curriculum Development." *J Ed Res* 57:451–7; 1964.

Ammons, Margaret. "Evaluation: What Is It? Who Does It? When Should It Be Done?" In *Evaluation of Children's Reading Achievement*. Perspectives in Reading Monograph Series. IRA, 1967.

Anderson, Dan W., and others. (Compilers.) *Strategies of Curriculum Development; Works of Virgil Herrick*. Merrill, 1965. 196p.

Barrett, Thomas C. "Taxonomy of Cognitive and Affective Dimensions of Reading Comprehension." U Wisconsin, 1967. (Mimeographed.)

Barton, George E., Jr. "Educational Objectives—Improvement of Curricular Theory About Their Determination." In Herrick, V. E., and Tyler, R. W. (Eds.) *Toward Improved Curriculum Theory*. U Chicago Press, 1950. p. 26–35.

Beauchamp, George A. *Curriculum Theory*. Kagg, 1961. 149p.

Bestor, Arthur E. *Educational Wastelands: The Retreat From Learning in Our Public Schools*. U Illinois Press, 1953. 226p.

Block, Elaine C. "Sequence as a Factor in Classroom Instruction." Doctoral dissertation. U Wisconsin, 1965.

Bloom, Benjamin S. (Ed.) *Taxonomy of Educational Objectives: Cognitive Domain*. Longmans, 1956. 207p.

Bobbitt, Franklin. *The Curriculum*. Houghton, 1918. 295p.

Bode, Boyd H. *Progressive Education at the Crossroads*. Newson, 1938. 128p.

Britton, Ernest R. "Leadership in Defining Goals for Schools." *Ed Leader* 17:16–20; 1959.

Brubacher, John S. *Modern Philosophies of Education*. McGraw-Hill, 1939. 370p.

Bruner, Jerome S. *The Process of Education*. Harvard U Press, 1960. 97p.

Chambers, W. M. "Testing and Its Relationship to Educational Objectives." *J Gen Ed* 16:246–9; 1964.

Charters, W. W. *Curriculum Construction*. Macmillan, 1923. 352p.

Charters, W. W., Jr. "Dangerous Assumption." *Nation's Sch* 62:54; 1958.

Charters, W. W., and Miller, Edith. *A Course of Study in Grammar Based upon the Grammatical Errors of Children in Kansas City, Missouri*. Educational Bulletin No. 9. U Missouri, 1915.

Commager, Henry Steele. "A Historian Looks at the American High School." In Chase, Francis S. and Anderson, Harold A. (Eds.) *The High School in a New Era*. U Chicago Press, 1958. p. 3–19.

Committee of the Corporation and the Academical Faculty. *Reports on the Course of Instruction in Yale College*. Hezekiah Howe, 1830. 56p.

Cox, Richard C. "Addendum to Validation and Uses of the *Taxonomy of Educational Objectives: Cognitive Domain*; A Select and Annotated Bibliography," U Pittsburgh, 1966. (Mimeographed.)

Cox, Richard C. "An Overview of Studies Involving the *Taxonomy of Educational Objectives: Cognitive Domain* During Its First Decade." Paper presented at the meeting of the American Educational Research Association. Chicago, February 1966.

Cox, Richard C., and Gordon, John M. "Validation and Uses of the *Taxonomy of Educational Objectives: Cognitive Domain*; A Select and Annotated Bibliography." n.d. (Mimeographed.)

Davies, John L., and Vaughn, David J. *The Republic of Plato*, translated into English, with an analysis and notes. Macmillan, 1950. 370p.

Dewey, John. *The School and Society*, rev. ed. U Chicago Press, 1915. 164p.

Dewey, John. *Theory of Valuation*. U Chicago Press, 1939. 67p.

Doane, Donald C. *The Needs of Youth: An Evaluation for Curriculum Purposes*. Teachers Col, Columbia U, 1942.

Downey, Lawrence W. "The Task of the Public School as Perceived by Regional Sub-publics." Doctoral dissertation. U Chicago, 1959.

Draper, E. M. *Principles and Techniques of Curriculum Making*. Appleton, 1936. 875p.

Eisner, Elliot W. "Educational Objectives: Help or Hindrance." *Sch Rev* 75:250–60; 1967.

Ellis, John K. "The Application of the *Taxonomy of Educational Objectives* to the Determination of Objectives for Health Teaching." Doctoral dissertation. U Michigan, 1963.

Faber, Charles F. "The Task of Public Education as Viewed by Prospective Teachers." *J Teach Ed* 16:294–7; 1965.

French, Will. *Behavioral Goals of General Education in High Schools*. Russell Sage, 1957. 235p.

Frymier, Jack R. "National Assessment." In Wilhelms, Fred T. (Ed.) *Evaluation as Feedback and Guide*. ASCD and NEA, 1967. p. 249–59.

Gardner, John W. *Excellence: Can We Be Equal and Excellent Too?* Harper, 1961. 171p.

Goodlad, John I., and Richter, Maurice N., Jr. *The Development of a Conceptual System for Dealing with Problems of Curriculum and Instruction*. U California at Los Angeles and Institute for Development of Educational Activities, 1966. 69p.

Goodlad, John I., and others. *The Changing School Curriculum*. Fund for the Advancement of Education, 1966. 122p.

Goodman, Paul. *Compulsory Mis-education*. Horizon, 1964. 189p.

Grieder, Calvin. "Is It Possible to Word Educational Goals?" *Nation's Sch* 68:10+; 1961.

Guszak, Frank J. "A Study of Teacher Solicitation and Student Response Interaction About Reading Content in Selected Second, Fourth and Sixth Grades." Doctoral dissertation. U Wisconsin, 1966.

Hanna, Paul R. "National Curriculum Commission?" *NEA J* 49:25–7; 1960.

Hanson, Robert F. "Determination of Purposes and Objectives, Course Content, and Teaching Techniques for a College Undergraduate Course on the Youth Serving Agencies." Doctoral dissertation. Indiana U, 1965.

Harap, Henry. *The Technique of Curriculum Making*. Macmillan, 1928. 315p.

Harris, Theodore L. and others. "Summary and Review of Investigations Relating to Reading July 1, 1964, to June 30, 1965." *J Ed Res* 59:243–68; 1966.

Harrison, Joseph E. "Achievement of Selected Types of Educational Objectives Through Use of Programmed Materials and the Relationship Between the Achievement and Selected Aptitudes for Learning." Doctoral dissertation. U Pittsburgh, 1964.

Havighurst, Robert J. *Developmental Tasks and Education*. U Chicago, 1948. 86p.

Hawse, John E. "An Analysis of Industrial Arts Objectives as Determined by Opinions of Selected Population Groups." Doctoral dissertation. Colorado State Col, 1964.

Hawthorne, Richard D. "A Model for the Analysis of Team Teachers' Curricular Decisions and Verbal Instructional Interaction." Doctoral dissertation. U Wisconsin, 1967.

Jensen, Gale E. *The Validation of Aims for American Democratic Education*. Burgess, 1950. 124p.

Kearney, Nolan C. *Elementary School Objectives*. Russell Sage, 1953. 189p.

Kilpatrick, William H. (Ed.) *The Educational Frontier*. Century, 1933. 325p.

Klein, Frances. "Evaluation of Instruction: Measurement of Cognitive Behavior as Defined by the *Taxonomy of Educational Objectives*." Doctoral dissertation. U California, Los Angeles, 1965.

Krathwohl, David R. "Stating Objectives Appropriately for Program, for Curriculum, and for Instructional Material Development." *J Teach Ed* 16:83–92; 1965.

Krathwohl, David R., and others. *Taxonomy of Educational Objectives: Affective Domain*. McKay, 1964. 196p.

Krug, Edward A. *The Shaping of the American High School*. Harper, 1964. 486p.

Lyda, Wesley J. "A Suggested Conceptual System

for Decision-making in Curriculum Development." *Ed Rec* 41:74–83; 1960.

Macdonald, James B. "Myths About Instruction." *Ed Leadership* 22:571–6+; 1965.

Mager, Robert F. *Preparing Instructional Objectives.* Fearon, 1962. 62p.

McClure, Robert M. "Procedures, Processes, and Products in Curriculum Development." Doctoral dissertation. U California, Los Angeles, 1965.

McNeil, John D. "Antidote to a School Scandal." *Ed Forum* 31:69–77; 1966.

Mill, John S. *Utilitarianism.* Liberal Arts Press, Inc,, 1957. 79p.

National Catholic Educational Association. *Criteria for Evaluation of Catholic Elementary Schools.* Catholic U American Press, 1965. 246p.

National Education Association. *Report of the Committee of Ten on Secondary School Studies.* American, 1894. 249p.

National Education Association. *Report of the Committee of Fifteen on Elementary Education.* American, 1895. 235p.

National Education Association. *Cardinal Principles of Secondary Education. A Report of the Commission of the Reorganization of Secondary Education, Appointed by the National Education Association.* GPO, 1918. 32p.

National Education Association. *The Central Purpose of American Education.* NEA, 1961. 21p.

National Education Association. *The Principals Look at the Schools; A Status Study of Selected Instructional Practices.* NEA, 1962. 75p.

National Education Association. *Deciding What to Teach.* NEA, 1963. 264p.

Nerbovig, Marcella H. "Teachers' Perception of the Function of Objectives." Doctoral dissertation. U Wisconsin, 1954.

O'Connor, Daniel J. *An Introduction to the Philosophy of Education.* Routledge, 1957. 148p.

Palmer, R. Roderick. "Evaluating School Objectives." *Ed Res B* 37:60–6; 1958.

Payne, Arlene. *A Guide to Curriculum Planning in Dietetic Internships.* American Dietetic Association, 1961. 102p.

Petty, Walter T., and Burns, Paul C. "A Summary of Investigations Relating to the English Language Arts in Elementary Education: 1965." *El Engl* 43:252–77; 1966.

Ragan, Williams. *Modern Elementary Curriculum,* rev. ed. Holt, 1960 505p.

Replogle, Vernon Loyal. "The In-fold Approach to Elementary School Curriculum: An Examination of Major Curricular Approaches and a Proposal Based on Social Realities, Needs, and Values in Interaction." *Microfilm Abstracts* 11:941–2; 1951.

Rickover, Hyman G. *American Education, A National Failure; The Problem of Our Schools and What We Can Learn From England.* Dutton, 1963. 502p.

Rugg, Harold. *Foundations for American Education.* World, 1947. 826p.

Russell, George D. "The Development of a Classification of Educational Objectives to Study the Objectives of Four Community Adult Education Agencies." Doctoral dissertation. U Wisconsin, 1964.

Sand, Ole. *Curriculum Study in Basic Nursing Education.* Putnam, 1955. 225p.

Sanders, Norris M. *Classroom Questions: What Kinds?* Harper, 1966. 176p.

Sandmeier, Thelma L. "A Study of the Differences in Aims for Public Elementary Education as Related to Selected Sociological Factors." Doctoral dissertation. Rutgers State U, 1964.

Saylor, Galen. "Don't Just Do Something." *Ed Leader* 17:2–5; 1959.

Seager, Roger C. "The Task of the Public School as Perceived by Proximity Sub-publics." Doctoral dissertation. U Chicago, 1959.

Slagle, Allen T. "The Task of the Public School as Perceived by Occupation and Age Sub-publics." Doctoral dissertation. U Chicago, 1959.

Smith, B. Othanel, and others. *Fundamentals of Curriculum Development,* rev. Ed. World, 1957. 685p.

Smith, Eugene R., and others. *Appraising and Recording Student Progress.* Harper, 1942. 550p.

Spencer, Herbert. *Education: Intellectual, Moral, and Physical.* Appleton, 1880. 283p.

Strom, Ingrid M. "Summary of Investigations Relating to the English Language Arts in Secondary Education: 1963–64." *Engl J* 54:238–55; 1965.

Taba, Hilda. *Curriculum Development; Theory and Practice.* Harcourt, 1962. 529p.

Tyler, Ralph W. *Basic Principles of Curriculum and Instruction.* U Chicago, 1950. 83p.

Tyler, Ralph W. "The Objectives and Plans for a National Assessment of Educational Progress." *J Ed Meas* 3:1; 1966.

Vander Werf, Lester S. "National Boards for Curriculum Making." *Sch Soc* 87:98; 1959.

Weaver, J. Fred. (Ed.) "Focal Point, Research on Mathematics Education, Grades K–8, for 1965." *Arithmetic Teach* 13:414–27; 1966.

White, William H. *The Organization Man.* Simon, 1956. 429p.

Whitehead, Alfred N. *The Aims of Education, and Other Essays.* New American Library, 1949. 166p.

Wieman, Henry Nelson. "Purpose and Discipline in Education." *Ed Forum* 27:279–88; 1963.

Wright, William F. "A Study to Determine the Extent of Agreement on General Educational Goals, Objectives and in Attitudes Among the New and Beginning Teachers, the Experienced Teachers, and the Administrators in the Six Public High Schools in Albuquerque, New Mexico." Doctoral dissertation. Colorado State Col, 1962.

OCCUPATIONAL PLACEMENT

Broad changes have taken place in occupational placement in the more than two decades since the close of World War II. With the increasing effects of automation, professional and technical personnel dominate the labor scene, and shortages have developed in most areas, while there are surpluses in unskilled areas of work. The placement specialist of today must possess a dynamic drive for matching the occupational capabilities and desires of the jobseeker with job specifications set up by the employer. With major expansion in all areas of higher education, the college placement officer is hard pressed to fulfill the demands of colleges for competent teachers.

In times of labor surpluses or labor shortages, the job of the placement specialist becomes increasingly complex. When labor is plentiful, it is necessary to emphasize job development in placing workers in acceptable jobs. Conversely, when labor shortages exist, the placement specialist will be called upon to do intensive recruiting to serve the employer. In any case, the placement specialist may be called upon to negotiate with employers to revise unrealistic job specifications, or with jobseekers to change their requirements. In addition, the development of new tools and the improvement of existing tools, such as the third edition of the *Dictionary of Occupational Titles* (U.S. Employment Service, 1965), new testing procedures, computerized filing and matching, and many others combined with technological changes in industry all have affected the functions of occupational placement.

HISTORY. Early events in the development of placement services were discussed in doctoral theses by Geer (1955) and Gladfelter (1954). They described the firm establishment of commercial teachers' agencies during the first half of the nineteenth century, because, during that period, teacher training institutions would not be responsible for placement. The peak was reached between 1870 and 1890, when some 200 commercial teacher placement bureaus were in business. Early in the twentieth century the number had dropped to 150, and by 1948 to 80.

The decline in the number of commercial agencies coincided with an increase in the number of institutional teacher placement bureaus. The University of Nebraska, for instance, provided placement service whose responsibility rested with the chancellor from 1892 to 1898. From then until 1907 it was handled by a faculty committee headed by the secretary of the chancellor. In 1907 a teachers' college committee took control. Five years later a full-time director was appointed.

In the area of public placement, the establishment of the U.S. Employment Service took place in 1917, within six months of the declaration of World War I. Levine (1963) relates that some 400 local offices were established across the nation to recruit and place workers to continue the impetus of the war effort. Special activities were aimed at placing women, young people, and Negroes in war jobs, primarily at the unskilled levels. The U.S. Department of Labor's *Challenge and Change* (1963) describes the establishment of the U.S. Boys' Working Reserve by President Wilson for the placement of boys 16 years old and older in farm jobs. The Department of Labor also worked with the National League for Women's Services in recruiting women for war industries. In 1920 Congress continued the funding of the U.S. Employment Service, including its farm labor services, although, until the passage of the Wagner-Peyser Act (48 Stat. 113) in 1933, it served primarily as a clearinghouse for agricultural and unskilled workers.

With the coming of the depression of the 1930's and the unemployment of millions, drastic placement procedures were necessary. The placement of the unemployed into jobs under the various federal, state, and local agencies and the problem of placing workers into jobs in industry and on farms where no jobs really existed became a challenge. In 1933, to meet these needs, a federal-state employment system was instituted under the Wagner-Peyser Act (Levine, 1963).

It is of particular significance that of the 16 million placements made during the first three years of the fledgling Employment Service, about half were with private employers. While most of the placements were in unskilled, casual, and domestic work, they established beyond a doubt the need for a public nation-wide employment service to match workers and jobs, even in times of great labor surplus.

It was during this period, Levine points out, that the need for standardized placement procedures and tools became evident. Procedures for clearance and interarea recruitment were established by the middle 1930's, although the system was not put to a real test until labor shortages emerged, as a result of the defense buildup in 1940. Early local-office counseling programs were developed, primarily to assist inexperienced youth in their competition with experienced older workers for jobs. Aptitude-test experimentation also was getting under way. The gathering of occupational information began when simple counts of local-office workloads were made for administrative reports and planning. As early as 1934 an occupational research program was instituted to develop a rational basis for local-office reporting as well as to devise a scientific tool for applicant selection and referral. In fact, the history of labor-market research and information and the evolution of a broad national concern with the development and utilization of human resources coincide with the history of the federal-state public employment service. All are closely related and reflect the changing conditions and the needs of the times.

Adams (1933) found that by 1920 about 75 percent of teacher education institutions, and by 1931, 86 percent of all institutions of higher education, provided teacher placement bureaus. In support of this, Umstattd and others (1937) found that 90 percent of all teacher training institutions offered these services and that fewer than 5 percent of higher education institutions failed to recognize a need for placement service. Wrenn (1951) found that by 1951 the majority of American colleges and universities provided some type of placement service.

Two earlier works by Reed (1944, 1946) provide studies in depth concerning philanthropic, commercial, and public placement bureaus. In the 1944 work she reported a positive relationship between business cycles and interest in placement, comparing the wave crests in the rise and fall of public support of placement with those of successive business cycles accompanied by unemployment. By examining contemporary documents, she found varied opinions among educators and philanthropists concerning inclusion of placement as one of the secondary-school guidance services. Boards of education openly questioned expenditure of funds for placement, and some educators even condemned services that facilitate leaving school or place the attractions of school into unfavorable competition with those of the work world. In her 1946 work, she studied philanthropic, commercial, institutional, municipal, state, and federal employment services, including the Federal Bureau of Immigration, the Negro Division, Women in Industry, Handicap Division, Veterans, and Youth placement services.

Calvert (1952) examined the history and development of college placement services, beginning with the National Association of Appointment Secretaries in 1924. The association originally was concerned with teacher placement, but with the inclusion of business and industrial personnel, its direction has changed. Since reorganizing as the American College Personnel Association in the early 1930's, emphasis on placement has been only incidental.

In 1927 the Eastern College Personnel Officers organized and since then have concentrated on summer and part-time placements. Also, for some years they have been active in the field of senior placement. Since 1946 seven additional organizations of similar nature have entered the field throughout the United States and Canada. Their members include both college placement officers and industrial personnel officers. In 1940 the Pennsylvania Association of School and College Placement was founded and a year later was reorganized on a national basis as the Association of School and College Placement. The organization issued its first regular publication, *School and College Placement*, in October 1940 as a quarterly. Today the *Journal of College Placement* is published by a council of eight regional placement associations from the United States and Canada.

In the area of college teaching, although the individual college graduate, using informal methods, has generally found employment himself the activities of formal placement organizations have become increasingly significant. A survey by Brown (1965) of all college teachers placed in the 1964–65 academic year showed that 41 percent were placed through formal or institutional methods.

This seems to be evidence that the old idea held by many professionals, particularly in the field of teaching, that the use of agencies or of other means of direct action was undignified and unbecoming of a professional is gradually being broken down; on the other hand, the fact that 59 percent still use informal methods indicates that much remains to be done in selling these placement services. Another conclusion one might draw is that the professionals are realizing the magnitude and complexity of the current job market.

The figures for formal methods of college-teacher placement showed that the largest number, 19 percent, of persons were placed as a result of blind letters to various possible employers; 6 percent were placed by their graduate-department offices; 6 percent were placed through their college placement services; 2 percent each were placed by convention placement services, by answering a professional journal advertisement, by a professional-association placement service, and by commercial teachers' agencies; 1 percent were placed by church-related bureaus.

Fewer than 1 percent each found jobs by going to the state employment service or by placing an advertisement in a professional journal. It must be pointed out, however, that some of those placed through conventions may have been placed through the employment service, since, on request of the professional society, employment-service personnel provide convention placement services during many of the national, regional, and state professional conventions.

The remaining 59 percent of those placed found jobs by what Brown termed the "informal method." Nearly half of these, 26 percent, did nothing and were placed after being contacted by a recruiter; 18 percent were helped by a professorial acquaintance; 12 percent were helped by one of their graduate professors and 3 percent by an undergraduate professor; a final group, fewer than 1 percent, were recruited with the assistance of publishers' representatives.

RATIONALE. The techniques of placement vary with the economic conditions of the country and the local, state, and national job markets. Placement personnel involved in placing technical and professional workers, whether in a college placement office, a professional association, or a public or private agency, must relate to current conditions and vary their techniques accordingly. Their success will depend heavily upon tools developed by industrial, commercial, and governmental organizations. No longer is the placement office a mere clearinghouse for the listing of jobs and applicants. In this respect, the 59 percent of all colleges that used informal methods of placement will be affected by the job market in which they are participating. In times when there is a surplus of workers, the informal method of placement, particularly for those 26 percent who waited to be recruited, may prove inadequate—in fact, disastrous.

In the modern academic placement office, it is necessary to facilitate the flow of information in the vital labor market for academic personnel. Academic manpower is scarce today. An increase in college enrollment from a present 5 million to more than 8 million is projected by the United States Office of Education. The U.S. Department of Labor, Bureau of Labor Statistics (1966), predicts that the supply and quality of college teachers will be improved in years to come by federal legislation providing for fellowships to qualified graduate students and junior members of faculties who are interested in teaching in colleges and universities. Nevertheless, the Bureau of Labor Statistics predicts that the number of well-qualified persons available will be insufficient to meet the demands in many subject fields until the mid-

1970's. The cultural and economic welfare of the nation demands that this service be allocated properly and used wisely. With the continued expansion of higher education and increased specialization will come new problems that will demand new solutions. To be ready to make the proper decisions for the future, a full understanding must be gained of the present market structure and the role that intermediaries are currently playing (Brown, 1965). A comprehensive analysis of current conditions in the academic job market will be found in *Academic Labor Markets*, Vol. 1, of the preceding reference.

ORGANIZATIONAL STRUCTURE. Returns from a questionnaire sent to 638 state and private universities and colleges by Menke and Calvert (1967) indicate a considerable rise in the number of schools having centralized placement services since 1960 as reported in the third edition of this encyclopedia (Trump & Totaro, 1960). The returns showed that 65 percent had completely centralized placement services. Another 21 percent had centralized placement services except for teacher placements. Only 8 percent were decentralized. These figures are complete except for the 6 percent that failed to answer. Interpreting these figures, Menke and Calvert found that the tendency toward decentralization occurred mostly in large state universities where component colleges had their own placement services with authority delegated to the deans of the individual colleges.

Menke and Calvert (1967) also obtained data on the typical placement director in a college. He is about 45 years of age and has been on the job less than four years; he holds a master's degree and enjoys faculty rank but did not graduate from his employing school. Going further into staffing, they compared total staff of placement bureaus with numbers of degrees awarded annually. They found that in typical institutions awarding up to 1,000 degrees annually, the placement bureaus were staffed by one or two professionals aided by one or two clerical workers. For schools awarding more than 1,000 degrees annually, the picture is varied. Many schools still have only one or two professionals, while others have as many as eight or ten. The clerical staff seems to remain static at about 1.4 clerks to each professional. In peak periods, usually the spring months, part-time help, mostly clerical, is hired, usually from the student body. Some very small offices have only a director and a part-time secretary.

Eckberg (1967) surveyed placement in junior colleges and community colleges. Of the 136 replying to his questionnaire, 100 colleges had full-time placement services. The remaining 26.5 percent reported limited placement services, usually placing students in part-time jobs either on or off the campus. Of the colleges reporting full-time placement services, 90 percent were institutionally staffed and supported. The other 10 percent were staffed, financed, and supported by their state employment services. Eighty-three percent were under the direction of a single administrator, and of the remaining 17 percent, 12 percent had a decentralized setup coordinated by a single individual and 5 percent had two or more persons responsible for the operation but operating without particular coordination. Problems most frequently reported in the questionnaires were lack of funds, small staff, inadequate facilities, and lack of support from the faculty, top administrative officials, the community, and the employers.

Little can be said concerning the structure of either public or private employment offices. Both vary greatly in size as dictated by the needs of the communities they serve. Many private agencies serve only a single type of occupation, such as teaching. Personnel in the public employment offices are hired on the basis of criteria set up by state or federal civil service regulations.

Fees are charged by many agencies. The private agencies charge fees, sometimes set by law, payable by either the client or the employer, and usually amounting to about 5 percent of the annual wage for the first year of the job for professional-type jobs, for example. Most college placement offices charge no fees. Others charge fees ranging from as little as $5 to as much as $100. The public employment offices of the states affiliated with the U.S. Employment Service charge no fees for services.

PROCEDURES. The economic trend since World War II has considerably influenced procedures in the college placement office. There has been in most professional fields an excess of demand for qualified workers, which has resulted in little need or attempt by the placement office to do a selling or promotional job for individual jobseekers. Because of the nature of the typical jobseeker served by the college placement office—young, eager, trained in the latest methodology and theory, and holding a current or at least a recent college degree—the college placement office has had little to do other than bring the employer into touch with the jobseeker. In fact, many of the jobseekers are presented with a choice of employers.

In other types of placement offices, even professional placement offices, the trend has had varying but lesser degrees of impact. The jobseekers served by these offices are of varied backgrounds, and other factors, such as age, time since a college degree or refresher course was taken, job history, changing of field of endeavor, and many others, tend to make placement more difficult. It is particularly true the further one goes down the employment scale toward less-skilled jobs. Technological changes have made obsolete the skills of many workers, especially in the unskilled and semiskilled classes. When these hard-to-place workers become clients of public and private placement agencies they often require both personal and employment counseling, and the placement specialists often are required to do considerable job development in order to place them.

The element of race has become important in recent years in the placement of workers throughout the employment spectrum. A new organization, College Placement Services, Inc. (known as CPS), was started in 1964. Its purpose is to train and send visitation teams to underprivileged colleges, predominantly Negro, to install or improve placement systems. The organization includes leaders in placement from institutional, business, and public fields. Beaumont (1966), president of CPS, reports that by June 1966 the organization had trained 66 persons to work as members of visitation teams and that teams had visited 19 colleges. Most of the colleges that were visited planned to implement the work started by the teams, and seven had begun extensive reorganization of their placement services to meet the new standards.

The interview necessarily is a basic step in the placement process. Vesey (1954) recommended that the interview of candidates for teaching positions should take place at least a year ahead of graduation. Trump (1955) went further, suggesting that there is a need for greater counseling and information service, starting even in high school, and that continuing contacts should be made at least annually through college and until placement in a job is accomplished. Bernard (1955) discusses types of interviews useful in placement. Several interviews usually are necessary before placements are made. The initial interview makes possible the setting up of records for the registrant. The length of this interview can be kept to a minimum if initial registration forms are designed so as to provide comprehensive information about the registrant. A second interview is sometimes required to bring that data in the files up to date prior to presentation to a prospective employer. Interviews with prospective employers or their recruiters may take place either on campus or off. Usually, two or more are required before the applicant is hired. The first interview takes the form of a screening interview, and, if the applicant passes, subsequent interviews bring him closer to his new job.

A new development, in line with modern technology, is the use of the computer to match the qualifications of the applicant to the specifications of the job set up by the employer. Opponents fear and distrust the advent of the computer. They believe it will depersonalize the placement process, deprive all but the top applicants of opportunities to be interviewed, and possibly put the placement office as we know it today out of business. Proponents welcome the computer as an ally that will make recruiting more efficient, free the office staff for more counseling, and upgrade the role of the placement director. In this vein, Kauffman (1967) comments that the college placement office operations will be changed but that the placement office will not be supplanted. In his study he found that placements came from those passing the screening interviews anyway and that by using the computer for the screening process, the number of interviews was reduced by a little more than 50 percent. Unnecessary face-to-face screening interviews result in little gain and are a waste of time for both the applicant and the recruiter. Also, increasing enrollments in the colleges and universities will make it virtually impossible to rely on the interview as the sole tool of placement. The number of college placement offices using computers has become significant. Menke and Calvert (1967) in their survey of college placement offices found that 109 colleges—17 percent of the total—made at least some use of data processing. Utilization of the data-processing equipment varied widely. Some reported use of the computers to match applicants to jobs; others used them in the follow-up of registrants or alumni. Other uses included summarizing statistics for reports, maintaining current lists of candidates, codifying job interests of students, addressing labels, and recording student schedules. One college used resultant reports, indicating employer ratings, as a counseling tool. Menke and Calvert concluded that much more study must be done of the use of computers in placement.

Studies and projects are under way within the U.S. Employment Service and its component state employment services to develop procedures and techniques in the use of computers in placement and the use of interconnecting circuits between major offices to expedite clearance. Simplification of present reports and analysis procedures through the use of computers also is in the planning stage. The California State Employment Service has been most active in pioneering the use of computers for placement and clearance in a project known as LINCS (Bybee & Folkman, 1964).

Follow-up is a function which should be practiced in any complete placement office. Knox (1953), as reported in the 1960 edition of the *Encyclopedia of Educational Research,* evaluated the follow-up system at the University of Illinois. He queried teacher education graduates one year and three years after their graduation. Of those who did not respond, a sampling was taken, and the selected individuals were visited personally. By comparing the written set of answers with the oral set he found that the verbal answers were identical to those that would have been given had the first questionnaire been answered, showing that either method of follow-up produces valid results. Follow-ups are programmed to elicit specific information that may be of value in determining future placement techniques, as well as statistical data concerning the success of past operations.

Procedures within an individual college placement office necessarily must be tailored to meet the needs of the parent institution. Thomas (1966) gives a series of recommendations for basic procedural criteria within a college placement office. The mission, or objective, must be determined and clearly defined along with specific policies of operation. These must be written up in precise language, possibly in the form of a manual of operations, and be made easily accessible to all concerned. The relations to other on- and off-campus organizations should be spelled out. The placement office should be responsible for budgeting its own operation and for the employment of a qualified staff. Further, adequate office space must be provided for staff operations, interviewing, clerical operations and files, and an occupational-information section. Ideally, an additional area should be provided as a reception room. With respect to personnel, levels of responsibility and decision making should be assigned to each member of the staff.

A number of placement-related side services also

are provided by many college placement offices. Hoppock (1963) mentions, among others, making available results of periodic salary surveys of the College Placement Council, as they are published in the *College Placement Annual*. These and other types of occupational information are often available in the information room of the plaecment office. Shartle (1959) offers a discussion of occupational information in depth.

The U.S. Employment Service, in addition to sending personnel to augment college placement staffs or, as mentioned above, to provide placement services, also operates a statewide teachers placement service in 13 states through its professional office network. Nationally, the professional office network operates through more than 100 offices strategically placed in geographic areas having the most concentrated professional placement services. Each of these offices is connected to other nearby nonnetwork cities by a system of feeder offices.

The annual report of the U.S. Employment Service for the fiscal year 1967 (U.S. Department of Labor, Bureau of Employment Security, 1967), reveals that national occupational registries are maintained in Chicago and Washington. The Chicago Registry Center serves economists, librarians, and philosophers, and the District of Columbia Registry Center serves anthropologists and statisticians and serves as a repository of all orders and applications taken at national conventions through the Convention Placement Service. National conventions of 32 professional associations were served by the Convention Placement Service during fiscal year 1967. In addition, 37 nurses' registries are maintained by the various state agencies of the U.S. Employment Service.

PLACEMENT IN EUROPEAN UNIVERSITIES. Placement activities in European universities appear to be somewhat less intensive than in American universities. Dils (1967) reports that placement of university graduates on the Continent is largely carried out through correspondence and personal references. Some are placed through advertisements in professional journals and newspapers.

Dils found that the universities in England and Ireland have recognized the need for placement activities. Many universities have endorsed and set up appointment boards to provide placement services for the students. The efforts of the boards are hampered greatly, however, by personnel shortages. Because of a lack of help, employer information, job notices to candidates, and adequate records of student registration cannot be kept up to date, particularly during the peak load period each spring.

EFFECTIVENESS OF SERVICES. The effectiveness of any service can be measured in two ways. The first is on the basis of whether those who receive the services are satisfied with the results and the second is on the basis of whether the service reaches all for whom it is intended.

The answer to the first question was well expressed by Clifford (1956) and his findings, as reported in the third edition of the *Encyclopedia of Educational Research* are just as valid today. He found that placement and follow-up are inseparable in both theory and practice. Follow-up reports provide evaluations of placement services. Placement services may be evaluated as satisfactory when a graduate, in the case of a college placement office, or a client, in the case of agency-type organizations or public or private employment services, obtains placement in a job or profession which (1) is consonant with his interests, (2) is on a level with his mental abilities, (3) uses his achievements and skills; (4) makes no physical demands that cannot be satisfied—and this is of prime importance in placing the physically handicapped; (5) is personally satisfying and rewarding; and (6) makes a significant contribution to the person's economic or social improvement. Ideally, all six criteria should be fulfilled by each placement, and many times they are, but often outside factors, unforeseen at the time of placement, interfere.

As to the second question, whether the service reaches all it should, much work needs to be done in all areas of placement. The image of the placement office still suffers from several outdated ideas, such as that the placement office is merely a labor exchange that the use of a placement office is unprofessional, and that the only persons using such intermediary services are those who could not find jobs by "more professional" or other methods; in addition, many prospective clients do not know that the services are available at all.

In the professional placement area, Brown (1965) surveyed 7,500 newly appointed faculty members of four-year colleges and universities throughout the United States. He found that 26 percent did nothing and were hired, 32 percent used haphazard informal methods, 19 percent wrote numbers of blind letters of application, 2 percent answered advertisements, and fewer than 0.5 percent placed advertisements. The remaining 20 percent—or only one out of five—were placed through agencies or other placement services.

This could become very critical, because of the vast increase in the numbers of technical and professional positions being offered to the also increasing numbers of degree candidates each year. The informal placement procedure does not do an efficient job of placement either for the jobseeker or for the employer. The formal placement procedure, with its scientific screening technique, can do a more satisfactory job of matching the talents of the jobseeker with the job specifications of the employer, resulting in greater efficiency in placement plus greater satisfaction for both the candidate and the employer.

The problem to be met is, first, to provide adequately staffed placement agencies that operate in cooperation with each other and, second, to sell their services to degree candidates and other professionals who can be served by the agencies. To meet the needs of professional staffing of placement agencies, a number of universities now provide courses for training occupational counselors at the master's-degree level.

Techniques for placing the unskilled also are in

a state of flux. Here, an important problem is to make contact with the individual who needs the services. While many such persons do come to the public employment offices and to private service and labor agencies, there are many who do not. Perhaps they don't know of the services, perhaps they have given up hope of ever getting a job, perhaps handicaps prevent their taking advantage of the services; whatever the reasons, they must be sought out to be served. To meet this challenge, the appropriate offices of the federal-state employment service send teams of professionals into the slums and ghettos, sometimes from house to house, to seek out these disadvantaged workers. No longer is it just a matter of putting a person into a job. Because of technological advances, many of the jobs formerly held by many unskilled, some semiskilled, and even some skilled workers no longer exist. These workers must be shifted to other types of employment, and frequently this means that added training is required. It is the responsibility of the placement specialist to recognize such a need and to try to shift the worker into a line of work that can be depended upon for the future. Also, other disadvantages may have to be met, such as a lack of adequate education, physical defects, or difficult home situations. The placement specialist, whether in the office or in the neighborhoods, must be capable of recognizing these detrimental factors. While in most cases he can do nothing personally to overcome the difficulties, he must, through his broad knowledge of community resources, be able to refer the worker to the proper agency or to a counselor in his own office for the necessary specialized treatment. Once the worker's disadvantages have been overcome, the placement specialist can again work on finding an adequate job for the once-disadvantaged worker. This is known as "human-resources development," and it often is a process started by the placement specialist.

Charles E. Odell
United States Employment Service

References

Adams, Walter H. *The Placement of Students in Teaching Positions as Carried on by Higher Educational Institutions.* Abilene Christian Col, 1933. 131p.

Beaumont, André G. "A Fruitful Year for CPS." *J Col Placement* 26:54–61; November 1966.

Bernard, Lloyd B. "The Interview." In Woellner, Robert C. (Ed.) *The Dynamics of Teacher Placement.* U Oregon Press, 1955. p. 111–27.

Brown, David G. *Placement Services for College Teachers.* Office of Manpower, Automation, and Training, U.S. Department of Labor, 1965. 240p.

Bybee, Karl, and Folkman, Herb. "LINCS—Progress and Report." *Employment Service R* 1:30–5; 1964.

Calvert, Robert, Jr. "Placement Organizations—Past, Present and Future." *J Col Placement* 12:64–6; 1952.

Clifford, Paul I. "The Role of Evaluation in the Improvement of Placement and Follow-up in Institutions of Higher Learning." *J Exp Ed* 24:37–9; 1956.

Dils, Eugene. "Placement in Europe." *J Col Placement* 27:81–2; January 1967.

Eckberg, Arthur R. "Placement in Junior and Community Colleges." *J Col Placement* 27:103–6; March 1967.

Geer, Ralph H. "Teacher Placement Services in Ten Ohio Universities." Doctoral dissertation. Western Reserve U, 1955.

Gladfelter, Irl A. "A Critical Study of Institutional Teacher Placement Policies and Practices." Doctoral dissertation. U Denver, 1954.

Hoppock, Robert. *Occupational Information.* McGraw-Hill, 1963. 546p.

Kauffman, Warren E. "The Computer in Senior Placement." *J Col Placement* 27:42–9; May 1967.

Knox, Carl W. "An Investigation of the Job Satisfaction of Recent Graduates of the University of Illinois Now Engaged in School Teaching and Administration." Doctoral dissertation. U Illinois, 1953.

Levine, Louis. "An Employment Service Equal to the Times." *Employment Security R* 30:3–13; June 1963.

Menke, Robert, and Calvert, Robert. "Placement 1967." *J Col Placement* 27:30–1, 119–35; May 1967.

Reed, Anna Y. *Guidance and Personnel Services in Education.* Cornell U, 1944. 496p.

Reed, Anna Y. *Occupational Placement.* Cornell U, 1946. 350p.

Shartle, Carroll L. *Occupational Information, Its Development and Application.* Prentice-Hall, 1959. 384p.

Thomas, William G. "Placement's Role in the University." *J Col Placement* 26:87–92; May 1966.

Trump, J. Lloyd. "Counseling and Information Service to Registrants." In Woellner, Robert C. (Ed.) *The Dynamics of Teacher Placement.* U Oregon, 1955. p. 93–108.

Trump, J. Lloyd, and Totaro, Joseph V. "Occupational Placement." In Harris, Chester W. (Ed.) *Encyclopedia of Educational Research,* rev. ed. Macmillan, 1960. p. 933–8.

Umstattd, James G., and others. *Institutional Teacher Placement.* National Institutional Teacher Placement Association, 1937. 238p.

U.S. Department of Labor. *Challenge and Change.* GPO, 1963. 72p.

U.S. Department of Labor, Bureau of Employment Security. *Report of the United States Employment Service for the Fiscal Year 1967.* GPO, 1967.

U.S. Department of Labor, Bureau of Labor Statistics. *Occupational Outlook Handbook, 1966–67.* GPO, 1966. 862p.

U.S. Employment Service. *Dictionary of Occupational Titles,* 3rd ed., 2 vols. GPO, 1965. Vol. 1, 810p.; Vol. 2, 656p.

Vesey, Margaret A. "Initial Interview in a Teacher Placement Office." *Ed Res B* 33:94–100; 1954.

Wrenn, C. Gilbert. *Student Personnel Work in College.* Ronald, 1951. 589p.

OUTDOOR EDUCATION

Using the outdoor setting for educational experiences has been a practice that has existed for centuries in different forms and patterns. Man's close relationship with his environment has continually provided an incentive for him to learn to understand, use, and live comfortably within his surroundings, and educators have historically provided for this in developing school programs. Recognition of man's relationship to his environment has been expressed in the scope and sequence of curricula. Learning experiences have included field trips, study excursions, outings, and camping to provide a link between the classroom and the world outside. Outdoor areas have been used as laboratories for investigation, for developing skills and appreciations, and for collecting and interpreting learning materials. These laboratories have extended from the immediate school grounds to the resources of the community and beyond to as far as a forest wilderness. With respect to time, adventures into the outdoors have been as brief as five minutes for a particular observation to a week or more for an integrated experience at a resident facility.

The process of using the outdoors in the school program has come to be known as outdoor education. The outdoor-education concept is currently conceived of as a means of curriculum enrichment through the development of programs and practices which utilize the outdoor environment. Although expressed in a school frame of reference, such curriculum development may be considered as a broad educational effort that frequently includes programs provided by organizations and agencies that have a concern for the outdoors and man's use of it. Outdoor education then has meaning and a purpose for the total education activities of the community (American Association for Health, Physical Education, and Recreation, 1957).

The outdoor-education thesis has implications not only for applying methods appropriate for the outdoor setting but for accomplishing social and philosophical goals as well. Broadly, there are concerns for man's uses and misuses of natural resources and for man's physical and mental well-being in a rapidly changing world. Educators particularly are concerned with the necessity of direct experiences in the outdoors as fundamental in the teaching-learning process.

As an organized movement, outdoor education has existed for the past thirty years. Efforts in such areas as camping, nature study, natural sciences, recreation, health and welfare, and conservation, along with curriculum development in education, have been closely associated with this movement. An early expression of the concept of outdoor education grew out of the educational implications of summer camping during the 1930's and led to the development of many school camping programs (often termed "outdoor schools") around the United States in the decades that followed.

As with other phases of education, the direction taken by the outdoor-education movement has been in response to a recognition of broad social and cultural conditions and changes, a basic core of democratic goals for education, and current knowledge in child-development and learning theory. The expression of concern for the child and society in the late 1920's and the 1930's provided an impetus for early outdoor educators to examine relationships between the broadening aims of education and the potential contributions of camping and outdoor recreational activities. Encouraged by apparent successes in a few pioneering programs, school camping gained the attention of curriculum innovators in the 1940's and continued gradually to expand and to serve as the focal point of outdoor education in the decade that followed.

While school camping originally stood at the apex of a growing outdoor education movement, changes in the thinking of leaders brought about a shift of emphasis from outdoor education centered almost entirely in camps to outdoor education as an integral part of the curriculum, from kindergarten through high school and beyond to adult and community educational programs. And also there occurred a growing sense of the need to attend to the role of education in preparation for the wise use of leisure time and for more deliberate effort in teacher and leadership preparation. Throughout the periods of development and changes in outdoor education there has also been a focus on some of the problems growing out of the rapid shift from rural to urban living. This has served as a primary basis for devising appropriate educational experiences in the outdoors.

Outdoor education has continued to gain stature in educational thought and has recently been further stimulated through national interest as expressed in the Elementary and Secondary Education Act of 1965. Title I and Title III of that act have provided direction and funds for expanding outdoor-education activities in developing various kinds of outdoor laboratories, providing special outdoor programs during the summer months, aiding in the implementation of innovations in natural-science and conservation curricula, making possible a more meaningful experience base in cultural enrichment and community awareness, and furthering the opportunity for youth to participate in resident school camping programs (Wiener, 1967).

The great growth of public interest and participation in a wide variety of outdoor pursuits and the recent federal programs concerned with outdoor recreation have given greater dimension to outdoor education, particularly in the education of families for outdoor living (Stoddard, 1962). This is reflected in programs conducted by schools, colleges, recreation and camping agencies, and youth organizations in family camping and adult education. The lack of knowledge and skills related to outdoor living on the part of the increasing numbers of people who are turning to the outdoors for recreation, adventure, and escape from tensions is creating an urgent need for outdoor education. This situation is being reflected in the changing nature and greater scope of outdoor education.

RESEARCH STUDIES AND PROFESSIONAL LITERATURE. The inception and development of school camping programs beginning in the 1930's largely resulted from a recognition of camping's contribution to the goals of education as expressed by the Educational Policies Commission (National Education Association, Educational Policies Commission, 1938). Thus, some of the early studies from which present-day concepts of outdoor education were developed were concerned with the values of summer camping experiences. Sharp (1930) stressed the educational objectives of camping while providing leadership in the transformation of a welfare program from a fresh-air farm to a camp. He sought to apply progressive philosophy and to make recommendations for that program during a four-year experimental period. Sharp's study was particularly significant, and he continued to be a leader in outdoor education up to the time of his death in 1963.

Later, studies were devoted directly to school camping or camping education as more interest developed and the number of programs increased. One of the pioneering efforts in school camping was developed at the W. K. Kellogg Foundation Camp, at Clear Lake in Michigan. An experimental program in the early 1940's involved communities using the camp for an entire year as an outdoor school for two-week periods for grades 4 through 12 (J. Smith & others, 1963). Masters (1941) described the program of this community school camp, which served as an extension of the curriculum. Cross (1967) traced and analyzed the historical development of Clear Lake Camp, indicating its impact on outdoor education and implications for future outdoor-education programs. Clear Lake has served as a model for other resident outdoor-education programs up to the present time and has given impetus to many similar programs in Michigan and throughout the nation.

The experiments of Life Camps, Inc. (1948), with New York City children during a three-week period in June indicated that school objectives in some subject-matter areas could be effectively achieved in the camp setting. Other studies, usually in the form of theses and dissertations, were undertaken during the rapid period of growth of outdoor schools in the 1940's and 1950's. They formed a research background primarily concerned with administration, leadership, and evaluation of outcomes. Donald R. Hammerman (1967) listed 62 completed degree studies in school camping under the categories of (1) values of school camping, (2) administration and organization, (3) evaluative studies, (4) proposals for implementing outdoor education, (5) leadership training and teacher preparation, and (6) general studies.

Gilliland (1949) examined administrative factors in establishing a school camp program. Lenore C. Smith (1950) investigated personnel practices and program organization. Walton (1955) studied administrative practices used in operating a number of Michigan programs. Berger (1958) developed a plan for developing leadership competencies. Recently, Schafer (1965) produced an administrative guide for initiating resident outdoor education. Rupff (1956), Johnson (1957), Kranzer (1958), Beker (1960), and Stack (1960) each sought to evaluate aspects of the effectiveness of school camping programs. Although different outcomes were measured, there seemed to be agreement that the school camp environment has a positive influence on behavior, especially in social and personal development.

For a time, and to some degree at present, school camping and outdoor education were synonymous in the minds of some educators, particularly those who developed more extensive resident programs. Rogers (1955), defining outdoor education as a method or process, recognized its broader aspects but envisioned school camping as the ultimate experience. He identified principles and functions of outdoor education that might serve as a basis for camping and outdoor programs. Donald R. Hammerman (1967) traced the development of camping education and further refined the foundation of outdoor education.

Throughout the growth of the outdoor-education movement there have been efforts to examine and improve the leadership preparation programs, both preservice and in-service. Analysis of factors in the preparation of elementary teachers was the concern of William M. Hammerman (1957) and Cyphers (1961). Hug (1964) analyzed factors which influenced the use of outdoor activities by elementary teachers.

Along with an increasing number of studies reported over the past four decades, there has been a corresponding increase in pertinent outdoor-education literature in the form of textbooks, articles, pamphlets, and newsletters. Bibliographies of research and professional literature have been prepared from time to time to assist in searching out the background of outdoor education and determining its status (Donaldson & Donaldson, 1958; Wiener, 1962; American Camping Association, 1962; Rillo, 1966; D. Hammerman, 1967). During the early 1950's several descriptive books were published which described school camping programs in several parts of the country and which provided elements of a rationale for outdoor education (Irwin, 1950; Clarke, 1951; G. Donaldson, 1952; Manley & Drury, 1952). The American Association for Health, Physical Education, and Recreation (AAHPER—1957) appointed a committee under the chairmanship of Julian W. Smith to present a comprehensive picture of community-centered outdoor education.

The Outdoor Education Project of AAHPER, initiated in 1955, has had a significant impact on the nature and scope of outdoor education in the United States (J. Smith, 1966a). Serving as a spearhead within the educational family represented by the National Education Association, the project has interpreted outdoor education to include education in and for the outdoors. This broad concept embraces a wide variety of learning experiences, including the use of the outdoors as a laboratory for achieving classroom objectives and the learning of skills and appreciations that will help the individual to enjoy his outdoor heritage (Outdoor Recreation Resources

Review Commission, 1962; American Association for Health, Physical Education, and Recreation, 1963).

Wiener (1965) reviewed the historical development of the outdoor-education movement and traced the evolution of a basis for outdoor education through research studies and the careers and contributions of outstanding leaders. In developing a rationale for outdoor education, he linked process and content through the employment of curriculum-development principles. The study not only indicates a reasonable foundation for outdoor-education programs and practices but also suggests ways in which outdoor education can become a truly integral part of the curriculum through continuous study and improvement.

From 1961 to 1967 eight textbooks were published on outdoor education, dealing with broad interpretation, programming, administration, teaching techniques, and specific activities. Julian W. Smith and others (1963) and Freeberg and Taylor (1961, 1963) presented the most comprehensive treatment; Hammerman and Hammerman (1964), Hug and Wilson (1965) and Mand (1967) provided a wealth of ideas on activities and approaches to teaching. Gabrielsen and Holtzer (1965) and Garrison (1966) emphasized residency aspects in their interpretations of the nature of outdoor education.

In one sense, all of the studies and professional literature form a rich source of historical research data reflecting the growth of outdoor education and changes that have occurred. More important, they serve as the body of knowledge that supports and sustains the outdoor-education emphasis in education.

CURRENT DEVELOPMENTS. As mentioned earlier, outdoor education takes many forms and has significant impact on several areas of education. Ranging from simple laboratory experiences on the school site and in parks and other open spaces in the community to extended experiences in camp settings and through mobile classrooms, outdoor education enriches and expands many aspects of the curriculum. The use of the outdoors as a laboratory has had an influence on the size and development of school sites, so that more attention is now paid to preserving natural areas on school-owned lands. There is a trend toward the establishment of outdoor-education centers or complexes where experiences in farming, gardening, camping, and outdoor recreation can be provided which have implications for science, social studies, health and physical education, art, music, communication arts, crafts, and other curriculum areas (J. Smith, 1966b). There are also contributions to other educational areas such as conservation, safety, health, and citizenship.

Teacher and leadership preparation has done well in keeping pace with the program developments in outdoor education, particularly with respect to in-service education. Workshops and courses, many of them at the graduate level, are now offered by colleges and universities. Local school systems and professional-education agencies have conducted many in-service activities for administrators and teachers involved in the various aspects of outdoor education (J. Smith, 1962).

Outdoor education is multidisciplinary in character, and, significantly, many of the current programs of teacher and leadership preparation offered by colleges and universities are using the interdepartmental approach (J. Smith, 1964). While there is a need for more specialized preparation for supervisors and coordinators, the major emphasis in teacher preparation has been on training classroom teachers who can be effective in teaching outside the classroom in an outdoor setting.

Outdoor education, as it is today, is in harmony with good practices in curriculum and is consistent with modern learning theory. The present emphasis on education in and for the outdoors is timely in a day when a large segment of the population lives in cities, far removed from the close-to-the-land existence of our forebears.

Julian Smith
Michigan State University
Morris Wiener
Northern Illinois University

References

American Association for Health, Physical Education, and Recreation. *Outdoor Education for American Youth.* AAHPER, 1957. 150p.

American Association for Health, Physical Education, and Recreation. *Education in and for the Outdoors.* AAHPER, 1963. 96p.

American Camping Association. *Bibliography of School Camping and Outdoor Education.* The Association, 1962. 29p.

Beker, Jerome. "The Influence of School Camping on the Self-concepts and Social Relationships of Sixth Grade School Children." *J Ed Psychol* 51: 352–6; 1960.

Berger, Harriet J. "A Plan for Developing Competencies for Leadership in School Camping and Outdoor Education for Elementary Education Students." Doctoral dissertation. New York U, 1958. 417p.

Clarke, James M. *Public School Camping.* Stanford U Press, 1951. 184p.

Cross, Carole B. "A Study of the Development of Clear Lake Camp." Master's thesis. Northern Illinois U, 1967. 100p.

Cyphers, Vincent A. "A Study to Determine the Significant Outdoor Experiences for Elementary Teachers." Doctoral dissertation. Colorado State Col, 1961. 240p.

Donaldson, George W. *School Camping.* Association Press, 1952. 140p.

Donaldson, George W., and Donaldson, Louise E. "Outdoor Education—A Bibliography." Prepared for Outdoor Education Project, AAHPER, 1958. 13p.

Freeberg, William H., and Taylor, Loren E. *Philos-*

ophy of Outdoor Education. Burgess Publishing Company, 1961. 445p.

Freeberg, William H., and Taylor, Loren E. *Programs in Outdoor Education.* Burgess Publishing Company, 1963. 457p.

Gabrielsen, M. A., and Holtzer, Charles. *The Role of Outdoor Education.* Center for Applied Research in Education, 1965. 117p.

Garrison, Cecil. *Outdoor Education: Principles and Practices.* Thomas, 1966. 239p.

Gilliland, John. "A Study of Administrative Factors in Establishing a Program of School Camping." Doctoral dissertation. New York U, 1949. 190p.

Hammerman, Donald R. "A Historical Analysis of the Socio-cultural Factors That Influenced the Development of Camping Education." Doctoral dissertation. Pennsylvania State U, 1967. 210p.

Hammerman, Donald R. "A List of Doctoral Studies on Outdoor Education." Northern Illinois U, 1967. 4p.

Hammerman, Donald R., and Hammerman, William M. *Teaching in the Outdoors.* Burgess Publishing Company, 1964. 120p.

Hammerman, William M. "An Investigation of the Effect an Outdoor Education Experience Has upon Elementary Education Students' Understanding of How Learning is Facilitated." Doctoral dissertation. U Maryland, 1957. 144p.

Hug, John W. "Analysis of the Factors Which Influence Elementary Teachers in the Utilization of Outdoor Instructional Activities." Doctoral dissertation. Indiana U, 1964. 236p.

Hug, John W., and Wilson, Phyllis J. *Curriculum Enrichment Outdoors.* Harper, 1965. 214p.

Irwin, Frank L. *The Theory of Camping.* Barnes, 1950. 178p.

Johnson, T. M. "An Evaluation of a Semi-objective Method for Appraising Selected Educational Outcomes of School Camping." Doctoral dissertation. U Southern California, 1957. 172p.

Kranzer, Herman C. "Effects of School Camping on Selected Aspects of Pupil Behavior—An Experimental Study." Doctoral dissertation. U California, Los Angeles, 1958. 132p.

Life Camps, Inc. *Extending Education Through Camping.* Life Camps, Inc., 1948. 130p.

Mand, Charles L. *Outdoor Education.* J. Lowell Pratt, 1967. 180p.

Manley, Helen, and Drury, M. F. *Education Through School Camping.* Mosby, 1952. 348p.

Masters, Hugh B. "A Community School Camp." *El Sch J* 41:736–47; 1941.

National Education Association, Educational Policies Commission. *The Purposes of Education in American Democracy.* NEA, 1938.

National Education Association and Association for Supervision and Curriculum Development. *School Camping, A Frontier of Curriculum Improvement.* NEA, 1954. 58p.

Outdoor Recreation Resources Review Commission. *Outdoor Recreation for America.* GPO, 1962. 246p.

Rillo, Thomas J. "A Bibliography of Articles Pertaining to School Camping and Outdoor Education." Outdoor Education Center, Southern Illinois U, 1966. 28p.

Rogers, Martin H. "Principles and Functions of Outdoor Education." Doctoral dissertation. Syracuse U, 1955. 324p.

Rupff, Paul E. "A Comparison of Aspirations with Achievements in a Group of Selected Michigan Public School Camps." Doctoral dissertation. Michigan State U, 1956. 245p.

Schafer, Frank D. "An Administrative Guide for Initiating Resident Outdoor Education in the Public Schools." Doctoral dissertation. Teachers Col, Columbia U, 1965. 230p.

Sharp, Lloyd B. *Education and the Summer Camp, An Experiment.* Contributions to Education Series No. 390. Teachers Col, Columbia U, 1930.

Smith, Julian W. "Developments in the Field of Education Affecting Outdoor Recreation Resources." In Outdoor Recreation Resources Review Commission. *Trends in American Living and Outdoor Recreation.* Study Report 22. GPO, 1962. p. 133–55.

Smith, Julian W. "Leadership Preparation for Outdoor Recreation." In Bureau of Outdoor Recreation. *Proceedings of the National Conference on Professional Education for Outdoor Recreation.* The Bureau, 1964. p. 22–34.

Smith, Julian W. "A Decade of Progress in Outdoor Education." *J Outdoor Ed* 1:3–5; 1966(*a*).

Smith, Julian W. "Outdoor Education—A Development in Curriculum." *Michigan Sch Bd J* 13:21, 26–7; October 1966(*b*).

Smith, Julian W., and others. *Outdoor Education.* Prentice-Hall, 1963. 322p.

Smith, Lenore C. "An Investigation of Personnel Practices and Program Organization in Public School Camping and Outdoor Education." Doctoral dissertation. U Southern California, 1950. 179p.

Stack, Genevieve C. "An Evaluation of Attitudinal Outcomes of Fifth and Sixth Grade Students Following a Period of School Camping." Doctoral dissertation. U Oklahoma, 1960. 134p.

Stoddard, George D. "The Merging Pattern of Outdoor Recreation and Education—Problems, Trends, and Implications." In Outdoor Recreation Resources Review Commission. *Trends in American Living and Outdoor Recreation.* Study Report 22. GPO, 1962. p. 115–32.

Walton, Thomas W. "A Study of the Administrative Practices Used in the Operation of Thirty Selected Part-time School Camp Programs in Michigan." Doctoral dissertation. Michigan State U, 1955. 269p.

Wiener, Morris. "A Bibliography of Theses and Dissertations in Outdoor Education." Prepared for Outdoor Education Project, AAHPER, 1962. 9p.

Wiener, Morris. "Developing a Rationale for Outdoor Education." Doctoral dissertation. Michigan State U, 1965. 288p.

Wierner, Morris. "Outdoor Education Can Help Unlock the Schools." *Ed Leadership* 24:696–9; 1967.

PAROCHIAL SCHOOLS—ROMAN CATHOLIC

HISTORY. The first school in what is now the United States was established by Franciscan missionaries who accompanied the Spanish settlers of Florida. In 1606 they set up a short-lived classical school in St. Augustine. Catholic education, however, scarcely flourished during the colonial period. In the British colonies Catholics were regarded with suspicion and were the objects of repressive legislation restricting their freedom of worship, their right to participate in civic life, and their liberty to educate their children. Representative of this legislation, as McCluskey (1964) says, was "An Act to Prevent the Growth of Popery," enacted in Maryland in 1704. Among other things it forbade Catholics to keep school or instruct children and made any Catholic who did so liable to punishment by deportation.

Nevertheless, persistent efforts were made by Catholics to set up schools. Thus around 1640 Jesuits established a school in St. Mary's City, Md. Again, around 1673 they set up another such institution in Newton, Md. In 1684 Thomas Dongan, Catholic governor of New York, was instrumental in the establishment of a Catholic school at Broadway and Wall Street. But the pressures of penal legislation and anti-Catholic sentiment guaranteed that Catholic educational efforts throughout the colonial period and the early days of the republic would be sporadic and struggling.

Opinions differ as to where and when the parochial school system in the United States actually had its beginning. Some historians like Burns and Kohlbrenner (1937) credit this distinction to St. Mary's Church in Philadelphia. However, McCoy (1961) and others agree that the major impetus and model for the tuition-free parish school came from Mother Elizabeth Seton and her Sisters of Charity, who began their school at St. Joseph's Parish in Emmitsburg, Md., in 1810.

Growth of Parochial Schools. The growth of Catholic parochial schools corresponded to a growth in Catholic population in the United States. At the founding of the nation the number of Catholics was estimated at about 30,000; by 1820, as McCluskey (1962) reports, it was 195,000 and by 1850 it was 1,606,000. As large waves of Catholic immigrants crossed the Atlantic from Europe and landed in the new country, the necessity of providing for the education of their children grew. The alternatives were public schools or Catholic parochial schools, and more and more the preferred choice of Catholics was the parochial school. By 1840 there were 200 Catholic schools throughout the country, and the growth of the parochial school system from that point on was astronomical.

This growth cannot be understood apart from the history of public education in the United States. The common schools that emerged during the first half of the nineteenth century were strongly Protestant in tone and orientation. McCluskey (1958) shows that Horace Mann strongly favored the retention of religious instruction in the schools, and though the religion was to be "nonsectarian" its Protestant bias was apparent. The special cornerstone of the system was the reading of the King James Version of the Bible, a matter of both symbolic and substantive concern to Catholics. Spokesmen for the Catholics of New York, quoted by Conners (1951), stated the objection to the practice in these words:

> The Holy Scriptures are read every day, with the restriction that no specific tenets are to be inculcated. Here we find the great demarcating principle between the Catholic Church and the Sectaries introduced silently. The Catholic Church tells her children they must be taught by *authority*. The Sectaries say, read the Bible, judge for yourselves. The Protestant principle is therefore acted upon, slyly inculcated, and the schools are Sectarian.

At least some Protestants of the time did regard public schools as instruments for weaning Catholic children away from the religion of their parents. Gabel (1937) notes that one minister was said to have boasted that during 12 years Catholics had lost 1,900,000 children. Another spoke of the Bible and the common schools as "two stones of the mill that would grind Catholicity out of Catholics." In the circumstances the development of a Catholic school system was natural as a defensive measure, quite apart from considerations based on the intrinsic merit of such schools. A less conscious motive in the creation of the system perhaps, as Ryan (1964) says, was the instinctive desire to soften the shock of transition from the European culture to the American. Catholics did, of course, seek to de-Protestantize the public schools but their success was not immediately impressive. In 1854 the Maine Supreme Court (*Donahue* v. *Richards*) upheld compulsory reading of the King James Bible in public schools (McCluskey, 1962). Catholic students in Boston and New York were expelled from public schools for refusing to engage in the practice. It was not until 1890 that a Wisconsin court reversed the doctrine of the Donahue case on compulsory Bible reading.

The Councils of Baltimore. Major support for the creation of the parochial school system came from the four councils of Baltimore—one provincial and three plenary—held in 1829, 1852, 1866, and 1884, respectively, in which almost all of the American Catholic bishops of the time participated. The exhortations for the establishment of Catholic schools grew in intensity with each of these councils, culminating in the last and greatest, the Third Plenary Council of Baltimore in 1884. The council proclaimed the objective of multiplying Catholic schools "till every Catholic child in the land shall have within its reach the means of education." To this end it decreed "that near every church a parish school, where one does not yet exist, is to be built and maintained *in perpetum* within two years of the promulgation of this council, unless the bishop should decide that because of serious difficulties a delay may be granted."

The council also required all Catholic parents to send their children to such schools, "unless it is evident that a sufficient training in religion is given either in their own homes, or in other Catholic schools" or when for sufficient reason—approved by the local bishop—it was judged "licit to send them to other schools" (McCluskey, 1964).

Search for Public Aid. During the nineteenth century much controversy was engendered by Catholic efforts to secure a share of tax funds for the support of their schools. The Catholic contention was that, in the public schools of the time, they were obliged to pay for institutions to which they could not in conscience send their children and that they therefore had a right to look for tax aid for the schools which they could and did conscientiously support. As the New York Catholics put it in 1840, Catholics "bear, and are willing to bear, their portion of every common burden; and feel themselves entitled to a participation in every common benefit." This plea and others like it, however, met with no success. Indeed, such efforts may have contributed to the wave of anti-Catholic feeling, described by Billington (1938), that swept the country in mid-century. In some places efforts were made to effect a compromise in which public and Catholic education were combined in a single institution. The models for such programs, outlined by McCluskey (1962), were in Poughkeepsie, N.Y., and Faribault, Minn., where existing parochial schools were leased to the public school districts, which in turn operated them as public schools, with religious instruction and exercises conducted outside of regular school hours. Whatever the theoretical advantages of such plans, however, they met with no great support from either public or religious authorities and did not provide a lasting solution to the problem. Thus during the nineteenth century the parochial school became firmly entrenched as the typical expression of the American Catholic approach to education.

RATIONALE FOR PAROCHIAL SCHOOLS.

Since the initial Catholic objection to public schools was based on their Protestant orientation, it might be supposed that Catholic resistance to sending their children to these schools would have declined as the religious quotient in public education declined. That this did not happen is due to the rise of another factor in public education which, from the point of view of many Catholics, appeared at least as objectionable as sectarian bias. This was the growth of secular humanism—or simply secularism—as the guiding force in the ideological orientation of public education.

This development is closely linked with the name of John Dewey. In its most innocuous form it is reflected in the belief that schools exist to teach secular knowledge only and that the development of spiritual and religious values should be left to the home and the church. Underlying this more or less pragmatic approach, however, is a well-articulated philosophy of opposition between traditional religious values and the secularist understanding of values. As Dewey (1934) wrote: "The opposition between religious values as I conceive them and religions is not to be bridged. Just because the release of these values is so important, their identification with the creeds and cults of religions must be dissolved."

McCluskey (1962) observes that in the late nineteenth and early twentieth centuries the secularist philosophy became increasingly identified with public education, particularly through the influence of the Teachers College of Columbia University and such figures as Dewey. This in turn strengthened the Catholic objection to public education, for the secularist view was diametrically opposed to the Catholic view of the purpose of education. McCluskey (1962) has summed up the situation in these words: "Faced with the ultimate question of whether religion is the starting point and essence of true education, the public school has had to adopt a theoretical neutrality between those who believe in the God of the Western tradition and those who do not. Yet, the public school, in a Catholic analysis, is not really neutral, for it gives an equivalent denial to the questions by actually taking another starting point and aiming at another goal."

The Catholic philosophy of education is enunciated perhaps most notably in the 1929 encyclical of Pope Pius XI *Divini Illius Magistri*—commonly known by its English title, "On the Christian Education of Youth"—and in the Declaration on Christian Education of the Second Vatican Council, promulgated by Pope Paul VI on October 28, 1965. Defining a "true education," the latter document says it "aims at the formation of the human person in the pursuit of his ultimate end and of the good of the societies of which, as man, he is a member, and in whose obligations, as an adult, he will share" (Vatican Council II, 1966).

Catholic educational philosophy, as Redden and Ryan (1956) observe, traditionally points to three major agents in education: the family, the state, and the church. Of these, as the Declaration on Christian Education says, the parents are considered the primary and principal educators. The function of the state in education is said to consist in protecting the rights of parents and others in education, in carrying on its own educational activities in accordance with the wishes of parents, and in building schools and other institutions required by the common good. The right of the church to educate is said to arise both from its existence as a human society and from the teaching mandate bestowed on it by Christ.

The Catholic school is regarded as the special expression of the teaching function of the Church. "No less than other schools does the Catholic school pursue cultural goals and the human formation of youth," says the Declaration of Vatican II (1966), adding: "But its proper function is to create for the school community a special atmosphere animated by the Gospel spirit of freedom and charity, to help youth grow according to the new creatures they were made through baptism as they develop their own personalities, and finally to order the whole of human culture to the news of salvation so that the knowledge the students gradually acquire of the world, life and man is illumined by faith."

CURRENT STATUS OF PAROCHIAL SCHOOLS. For most of its history the U.S. parochial school system has, administratively speaking, been unusually decentralized (McCoy, 1961). Each parish school has been very much an entity unto itself. The office of diocesan school superintendent has existed and there have been diocesan boards of education. But, by comparison with the centralization of the public school system, these officials and agencies have exercised relatively little control over the policies and programs of individual schools. Authority for most decisions has rested instead with the local pastor and principal, as Fichter (1958) notes. More recently, however, McCoy (1961) observes, the increasing prestige and professionalism of diocesan superintendents' offices and school boards and the growth of parish and regional boards of education have tended to change this picture and foster greater centralization and standardization in parochial education.

Most parochial schools in the United States are elementary schools covering grades 1–8, although some also include kindergartens. Parochial secondary schools also exist in a number of places, although their number has declined, as Long says (1966), due to a trend toward consolidation of relatively small parish high schools into large central or interparochial high schools.

Long (1966) reports that U.S. Catholic elementary schools (most of them parochial schools) total nearly 11,000, with almost 110,000 classrooms and nearly 4,500,000 students. On the secondary level, where the proportion of parochial institutions is smaller, the number of schools is nearly 2,500 and the number of students about 1,100,000. The capital investment in Catholic elementary and secondary education in 1963 was $5 billion and the annual operating cost $850 million.

The growth in parochial school enrollment since the prewar years has been startling and dramatic. In 1940 the number of students in Catholic elementary and secondary schools was 2,396,000; in 1960, it was 5,253,791, an increase of 219 percent. By contrast, public elementary and secondary school enrollment in 1940 was 25,434,000; in 1960, it was 36,086,771, an increase of 142 percent. Even with this enormous growth, however, the goal of "every Catholic child in a Catholic school" remains far from realization and seems unlikely ever to be realized. In the school year 1962–63, for example, according to Neuwien (1966), only about 52 percent of the eligible Catholic children in the country were enrolled in Catholic elementary schools, while on the secondary level the percentage was about 32 percent. These figures did not represent lack of demand for admission to parochial schools; on the contrary, large numbers of applicants must regularly be turned away. Rather, they reflect a shortage of facilities to accommodate all those seeking entry to Catholic schools and a shortage of teachers to teach them.

The number of teachers in Catholic elementary schools (1965–66) is more than 121,000. Of this number about 44,000 are lay persons, 36 percent of the total. The rest are sisters, brothers, and priests, with the sisters by far the largest group. As the number of teachers and classrooms in the parochial school system has grown, the pupil–teacher ratio has dropped steadily. Long (1966) reports that it reached 36 pupils per teacher in 1965–66, compared with 38 per teacher in 1964–65, and 39 per teacher in 1963–64.

The growth in the number and proportion of lay teachers in the parochial schools has been a striking phenomenon. In 1946 there were only 2,768 lay teachers in Catholic parochial schools compared with the above-mentioned 44,000 in 1965–66. The obvious fact is that the enrollment in Catholic schools has grown faster than religious teachers could be found to meet the demand. At the same time, too, the Catholic Church has been engaged in a profound reassessment of the role of lay persons within the ecclesiastical structure. More responsibility and initiative are being entrusted to lay people, and one by-product of this is the growing reliance on and acceptance of lay teachers in parochial schools. Koob (1966) suggests that in years to come Catholic education may be primarily a work of the laity. Waters (1958) feels that religious teachers may specialize in and largely be restricted to the teaching of religion.

At the same time Catholic education has witnessed a striking and impressive new emphasis on the professional preparation of religious teachers. Neuwien (1966) sees as potent factors in this development the National Sister Formation movement and its organizational embodiment, the Sister Formation Conference, which came into existence in 1954. As of 1962, Neuwien (1966) reports, the median training level of the total Catholic elementary school teaching staff was the B.S. degree, with 49.8 percent of the teachers having less than a degree and 50.2 percent having a bachelor's degree or more. This picture is continuing to improve rapidly under the impact of Sister Formation and similar groups.

For a long time U.S. Catholic parochial schools were overdiscussed—both pro and con—and understudied. Recently, however, major sociological studies of the parochial system like those by Neuwien (1966) and Greeley and Rossi (1966) have begun to appear which at least partly right this imbalance. Much more needs to be known about both the history, the present status, and the future prospects of parochial schools, but the scholarly and educational communities now seem on their way to filling in these gaps in knowledge and understanding.

PROBLEMS OF PAROCHIAL SCHOOLS. Probably the main problem facing parochial schools in the United States is financial. Many of the other problems of parochial education could be resolved more or less easily if sufficient financial support could be guaranteed. This is true of the difficulty of obtaining an adequate supply of competent teachers. In the past this problem was not acute because parochial schools relied mainly on religious teachers who were willing and able to accept minimal salaries. During the 1960's, however, it became apparent that the number of religious teachers could not keep up with the rising enrollment in parochial schools and that necessity, if nothing else, would compel the hiring of a growing number of lay teachers. As the corps of lay teachers in parochial schools increases, Greeley and Rossi (1966) note, their salary demands will place an increasing strain on the financial resources of the system.

Financial pressures and the shortage of teachers have caused some Catholic educators to consider—and even act upon—proposals for cutting back parochial education by dropping one or more grades and relying on public schools to accommodate the children at these levels. Probably the best-publicized such case occurred in the archdiocese of Cincinnati, where beginning in the fall of 1964 the first grade was eliminated in all parochial schools. The action affected 10,000 children. Spokesmen for the archdiocese, Blum (1965) notes, attributed the decision to classroom overcrowding and the difficulty of obtaining lay teachers and paying them adequate salaries.

The growing financial squeeze on parochial schools has caused Catholic educators to cast about for other possible solutions besides grade dropping. One approach which has received widespread attention from both parochial and public educators is the "shared-time" plan under which students enrolled in parochial schools take some of their courses, such as shop, home economics, and physical education, in public schools, while receiving their instruction in academic courses and religion in parochial schools. Long (1966) says that as of the 1965–66 school year, 237 schools were reported to have such programs, involving 26,000 pupils. A number of educators, however, have questioned whether shared-time is either equitable or practical on a large scale. Blum (1965) and others argue that such programs undermine the rationale of church-related education and also require parochial pupils to go to public schools in order to obtain educational benefits which they have a right to receive in their own schools.

The Federal Aid Question. These considerations have sharpened the long-standing debate over whether or not parochial schools or their students are entitled to assistance from tax funds. The issue, as Blum (1965) notes, has been accentuated by the enactment of large new programs of federal aid to education and proposals for even more extensive federal activity in this field. Enactment of the Elementary and Secondary Education Act of 1965, which included some benefits for disadvantaged parochial pupils, seemed to represent a potentially viable compromise on this issue. But it also appeared likely that the question could not be settled without a definitive ruling by the U.S. Supreme Court. Marnell (1964) shows that in a 1947 decision (*Everson* v. *Board of Education*) the court made it clear that it was constitutional to provide parochial students with such incidental health and welfare benefits as tax-paid bus rides. In one of its much-discussed rulings on religion in public schools (*Schempp* v. *Abington School District*) the court in 1963 also set forth a formula which some felt could possibly resolve the issue of public assistance to church-related education: "What are the purpose and the primary effect of the enactment? If either is the advancement or inhibition of religion then the enactment exceeds the scope of legislative power as circumscribed by the Constitution. That is to say that to withstand the strictures of the establishment clause there must be a secular legislative purpose and a primary effect that neither advances nor inhibits religion" (Marnell, 1964). Many proponents of aid to parochial education, like Blum (1965), have based their case on the so-called "child benefit" theory, according to which aid could constitutionally be directed to the individual child, thereby bypassing possible constitutional difficulties over direct aid to institutions. It remains true, however, that these issues have not yet been finally settled by the Supreme Court.

The Quality of Parochial Education. Meanwhile, other problems besides financial and constitutional ones have arisen to confront parochial schools. In the late 1950's and early 1960's a number of critics suggested that the education provided in these schools was inferior to that given in public schools. Studies have not borne this out, however. On the contrary, as Neuwien (1966) shows, students in parochial schools consistently score higher on standard achievement tests than do students in public schools. Parochial school educators admit that such outcomes are not totally conclusive, since parochial schools are able to be relatively selective both as to the students they admit and those they retain. The findings do, however, indicate that parochial education is, on balance, not inferior to public education.

Another complaint frequently raised against parochial schools is that they foster divisiveness by segregating Catholic children from their contemporaries on religious grounds. Again, studies like those of Greeley and Rossi (1966) do not bear out this contention. So far as tolerant attitudes toward other groups are concerned, Catholics who have attended Catholic schools appear to be slightly—though not markedly—more tolerant than Catholics who have not attended these schools. They are also about as likely to be involved in community affairs and to have non-Catholic friends.

In some ways a more fundamental objection to parochial education, one which goes to the heart of its specifically religious objectives, is whether it provides a dynamic religious formation in line with the insights of Vatican Council II and contemporary Catholicism. Ryan (1964) suggests that parochial schools inculcate a relatively limited religious vision and that at the same time they require a disproportionate investment of time, energy, manpower, and money while large numbers of Catholic children unable to obtain admittance to such schools and Catholic adults are virtually neglected so far as religious formation is concerned. Thus it is said that Catholics would be well advised to abandon most of their educational system and concentrate instead on dynamic religious formation programs which would reach all Catholic children and adults. Debate on this issue continues strong in Catholic circles. Those who defend parochial schools note that no really effective alternate religious formation program has yet been developed as a substitute for that provided in parochial education. So far as the limited objectives of parochial school religious formation in the past are concerned, Greeley and Rossi (1966) point out that these goals generally coincided with the prevailing understanding of what religious formation could and should be and that it is unfair to criticize parochial schools for seeking the limited objectives of relatively minimal religious practice that were for a long time proposed and accepted by the American Catholic community at large.

Thus after more than a century and a half in existence parochial schools in the United States stand at a real crossroads. In sheer numbers of schools, students, and teachers they are stronger than ever before. One U.S. student in every nine is in a Catholic school. But at the same time parochial schools are facing unprecedented pressures and challenges both from within and from without. Should an all-out effort be made to expand the system in order to meet the rising demands of the immediate future, or should the system be held at its present level of size or even cut back, while efforts are concentrated instead on new educational and religious formation programs? If the decision is for expansion, where will the money to build the schools and pay the teachers come from? Will the American public, legislatures, and courts accept the argument of parochial school proponents that their institutions and/or students are constitutionally entitled to aid from tax funds, or will decisions of public policy or constitutional interpretation instead go against the interests of parochial education? Can parochial schools continue to meet the mounting demands for educational excellence? All these and other equally pressing questions must be answered before the future of parochial education can be considered certain.

C. Albert Koob, O. Praem.
National Catholic Education Association

References

Billington, Ray A. *The Protestant Crusade, 1800–1860.* Macmillan, 1938. 514p.
Blum, Virgil C., S.J. *Freedom in Education: Federal Aid for All Children.* Doubleday, 1965. 235p.
Burns, James A., C.S.C., and Kohlbrenner, Bernard. *A History of Catholic Education in the United States,* rev. ed. Benziger Brothers, 1937. 295p.
Connors, Edward M. *Church-State Relationships.* Catholic U America Press, 1951. 187p.
Dewey, John. *A Common Faith.* Yale U Press, 1934. 87p.
Fichter, Joseph H., S.J. *Parochial Schools: A Sociological Study.* U Notre Dame Press, 1958. 494p.
Gabel, Richard J. *Public Funds for Church and Private Schools.* Catholic U America Press, 1937. 858p.
Greeley, Andrew M., and Rossi, Peter H. *The Education of Catholic Americans.* Aldine Publishing Co., 1966. 368p.
Koob, C. Albert, O.Praem. (Ed.) *What is Happening to Catholic Education?* National Catholic Education Association, 1966. 211p.
Long, Winifred R. "An Up-to-Date Report on Catholic Education in the United States." *Nat Cath Ed Assn J* 62:32–6; 1966.
Marnell, William H. *The First Amendment.* Doubleday, 1964. 247p.
McCluskey, Neil G., S.J. *Public Schools and Moral Education.* Columbia U Press, 1958. 315p.
McCluskey, Neil G., S.J. *Catholic Viewpoint on Education,* rev. ed. Doubleday, Image Books, 1962. 189p.
McCluskey, Neil G., S.J. (Ed.) *Catholic Education in America: A Documentary History.* Bureau of Publications, Columbia U, 1964. 205p.
McCoy, Raymond F. *American School Administration, Public and Catholic.* McGraw-Hill, 1961. 484p.
Neuwien, Reginald A. (Ed.) *Catholic Schools in Action.* U Notre Dame Press, 1966. 328p.
Pius XI, Pope. "On the Christian Education of Youth." In *Papal Teachings: Education.* St. Paul Editions, 1960. 668p.
Redden, John D., and Ryan, Francis A. *A Catholic Philosophy of Education.* Bruce, 1956. 601p.
Ryan, Mary Perkins. *Are Parochial Schools the Answer?* Holt, 1964. 176p.
Vatican Council II. *Declaration on Christian Education.* Paulist Press, 1966. 158p.
Waters, Most Rev. Vincent S. "New Needs in the Church in the Days Ahead." In Rita Mary, Sister, C.H.M. (Ed.) *Planning for the Formation of Sisters.* Fordham U Press, 1958. p. 58–62.

PERCEPTION

DEFINITION OF PERCEPTION. "Perception," like many other terms, has a number of meanings and connotations. Some definitions are amazingly broad and general. This lack of restrictedness is to be found even in the usages given the term by those who study what they call perception. The gamut is partly to be accounted for by the evolution in the understanding of what psychologists study. In the early days of modern psychology, it was the study of mind or consciousness (James, 1900). Behavior expressed as motor phenomena was not a part of it. The advent of behaviorism (Watson, 1924) not only changed the understanding of psychology's subject matter but tended to change the concept of behavior. For many, the shift in the understanding of what is to be labeled as perception has not as yet fully extricated itself from mentalism. Many discussions of perception are still confined to experiential phenomena and thus, in effect, are still totally mentalistic in outlook.

One effective way of looking at perception is simply to regard it as the organism's immediate response to energistic impingements on sense organs (Bartley, 1958). This view thus regards motor phenomena, as well as experiential phenomena, as truly perceptual. According to this view, responses to be perceptual must be discriminatory—that is to say, the outcome of a configuration of factors. Such responses as are studied in simple actions and reactions in physical or chemical situations, of course, are not defined as discriminatory. That perceptual reactions are immediate, means that they are the direct outcome of the impingement (stimulus) input to sense organs. The study of perception, according to this view, is the tracing of the relations between energistic impingements on sense organs, the body processes that are set up, and the sensory end results that ensue. Sensory end results are not confined simply to sensations.

SENSATION AND PERCEPTION. From the very start, in modern psychology two terms have been in use, namely, "sensation" and "perception." It was supposed that sensation was the first result and perception was an elaboration beyond this first result (Titchener, 1909). Much effort at the turn of the century was expended in attempting to arrive at clear experimental demonstrations of this distinction between sensation and perception. After a time, it became apparent that the presupposed distinction was not being substantiated. In the 1920's, the beginning psychology student was being taught that perception was "sensation plus meaning."

Even with the failure to distinguish clearly between sensation and perception, the dichotomy has continued in various nebulous forms. It has seemed that many stimulus situations produce fairly predictable and stable sensory end results, and many others do not. Hence the results could be put into two categories. It was said that sensation was "stimulus bound" (Pratt, 1950), whereas perception was less rigidly determined by the stimulus. It appears now that the distinctions between the predictable and unpredictable in the stimulus-response situation are based on the degrees and kinds of controls that the experimenter is able to set up and utilize, rather than on some inherent difference ascribable to the mode of response.

It has become clearer and clearer that not all the conditions for producing sensory end results can be expected to lie external to the organism, i.e., in the stimulus (Bruner & Postman, 1948). In all cases, the outcome involves two sets of parameters, those lying outside the organism and those lying within it. It is the latter set of parameters that social psychologists have, in recent years, become concerned with. These parameters seem to be the ones that are subject to the kinds of change that we speak of as "learning."

One of the several implications, particularly in the earlier views of perception, was that sensations were among the building blocks of perception. Even in recent times, this idea has not been discarded completely. This attitude is manifested in the manner in which perception has been studied. There has been a continued search for sense modalities, identifiable body mechanisms, and correlated unique experiences. Criteria have been set up for the isolation of sense modalities, and the description of perceptual behavior categorized in accord with the number of modalities found. One of the criteria is the existence of a unique form of sensation or sensory experience. Thus, description of perceptual activity would include these experiences. Gibson (1966) recently has made it quite clear that sensation is by no means a way station to perception. Perception, according to him, is to be described as an active interrelation between organism and environment expressed as the obtaining of information. Information pick-up is the central theme in his view of perception.

One basis for this view of perception lies in the fact that those who have attempted to isolate sense modalities have never come to a firm agreement on how many sense modalities there are. Thus it is impossible to categorize and describe behavior in terms of this inherent indefiniteness.

Following the views of Pieron (1952) and then of Boring (1942), in which the classical five modes of interrelating with the environment had been retained, Gibson (1966) has enumerated five perceptual systems. They are based on the following: (1) general orientation; (2) listening; (3) touching; (4) smelling–tasting; and (5) looking. It should be noted that this list contains fewer items than the number of sense modalities generally enumerated. It should also be noted that these processes are regarded as *active* processes, rather than categories of *passive* reception. For instance, looking and listening are quite different from merely seeing and hearing. In accord with these active processes, Gibson listed five perceptual systems: (1) the basic orientation system, (2) the auditory system, (3) the haptic system, (4) the taste–smell system, and (5) the visual system. Much of this categorization would be merely a matter of words were it not for the fact that the activities that constitute expression of these systems do not follow the boundary lines of the conventional sense modalities. For example, the basic orientation system is all of the sense mechanisms and all the muscular mechanisms needed in orientation to gravity and to the ground on which the organism finds itself. Thus, this system's identity depends upon the activities involved and is not just a different name for something already labeled as a sense modality.

The auditory system does not merely permit hearing, i.e., provide auditory sensation. Its function is to pick up the *direction of an event*, provide *orientation* to it, discover the *nature* of the event, and to permit *identification* of it. Hearing is also proprioceptive in function. It registers and handles acoustic signals made by the organism itself. The hearing of these signals of vocalization permits setting up and controlling patterns, as in song and speech. Gibson points out that this forms a "social loop" through other organisms and thus is a prime factor in social interaction.

The haptic system is more than the sense of touch. It includes the whole body (most of its parts and all of its surface). Thus it includes the traditional muscle and joint senses. The body extremities are exploratory, and the system in general is performatory. The same tissues function as exploratory and as performatory organs. Thus a new application to the term "kinesthesis" is given.

As is well known, tasting and smelling have always been difficult to distinguish in everyday situations.

Only carefully controlled experimental conditions have permitted distinguishing between the two in many types of situations. Tasting involves mechanoreceptors and thermoreceptors as well as taste buds.

And, finally, vision is more than the use of the eyes, in the way usually implied. One of the situations that aptly brings this out is that of weightlessness. In this situation, top, bottom, up, down, etc., lose much if not all their visual meaning. So vision is to be regarded as a broader function than merely the use of the eyes. It is a form of perception that functions in a gravitational (force) field.

We can conclude, then, that perception is to be understood as more than a type of awareness which, by some, is equated with sensation, but is rather an expression of active relation to the environment. This expression can take on any of a number of forms, including mere motor reactions, just so long as these are elicited through the medium of sense mechanisms.

VARIOUS CONNOTATIONS OF PERCEPTION. When the strictly psychophysiological mode of dealing with human and animal behavior is not the basis for defining perception, the term takes on a wide variety of connotations and implications. We shall do no more than suggest several of the major ones here.

For example, the question of perception as a form of knowledge immediately arises (Blake & Ramsey, 1951). Is perceiving a form of knowing? Is perceiving to be regarded as veridical? In the more sophisticated modes of regarding perception, it is not taken for granted that perception is veridical. The meanings of "knowledge," "truth," and "understanding" are each quite varied and this is not the place to discuss them. Needless to say, however, the term "perception" has in some circles become so intertwined with these terms as to be partially synonymous. The dictionary reflects this in stating that there is *sense* perception and perception that is not directly connected with sensory processes.

A common example of the way in which perception and truth and knowledge are entangled is implied in the use of the term "illusion." An illusion is often defined as a mistaken perception (Stagner & Karwoski, 1952). This means, then, that a perception is not to be dealt with at face value. It is not seen as an example of natural cause and effect. Interest in it lies mainly in noting whether or not it tallies with certain other perceptions, or with the common expectations for it. When it doesn't, the perception is an illusion, and very often to explain it, the factors resorted to actually are various forms of perception which also are mistakes (when faced squarely). For instance, in a geometrical illusion in which some portion looks "larger than it is" or looks larger than some other part "when it oughtn't to," the fact is "accounted for" by saying that certain angles are overestimated and others are underestimated. This is explaining one "mistake" by asserting other "mistakes," and thus the problem of the occurrence of mistakes is never dealt with. If every perception has a basis for its existence, i.e., if one assumes a cause-and-effect universe, then the prime question is "What are the conditions that produce a given perception?" Mistakes have no place in a basic causal system. They involve getting something for nothing or getting nothing for something. The question of why various perceptions do not tally with each other should come in only secondarily.

When the class of cases generally called illusions is closely examined, the basis for the outcomes becomes more and more apparent, although no single general well-stated theory of illusions has appeared in the literature. Apparently, one of the bases for illusions is the fact that the organism can utilize various inputs to sense organs (information) in more than one way. Some situational (stimulus) configurations provide for little freedom; some, considerable freedom. The alternatives utilized depend upon the organism. Here purpose, set, habitual ways of doing things or regarding matters, are involved. Generally, the factors that lie within the organism are less accessible and more difficult to conceptualize and thus to subject to experimental manipulation. It has always been easier to talk about illusions and to see whether they can be accounted for in the stimulus.

The function of perception in behavior is partly described in Gibson's recent treatment of perception (Gibson, 1966). There it is spoken of as involving *information pick-up*. Perception is the entire immediate response which involves not only information pick-up but the expression of the organism's relation to the environment, whether this relation be an experience or a motor reaction. Gibson's view, in emphasizing the exploratory and the performatory nature of perception, implements this feature.

PERCEPTION AND PSYCHOPHYSICS. It was in the realm of sensory processes that the most precise study of human behavior was developed. Thus what we have defined as perception has been the object of study by the best-developed quantitative procedures. Such procedures are known as psychophysics. These involve quantification of the stimulus input and, likewise, a quantification of the perceptual end result. The use of psychophysical methods has not, in itself, assured appropriate results, however. In some cases, what was meant by perception was left quite nebulous or undefined. If, as we said, perceptual response is an immediate reaction, rather than performance or behavior that happens to follow the presentation of the stimulus after some indeterminate delay, with various other reactions intervening, then failing to confine attention to such responses adulterates the data with material that is not exclusively perceptual. Various studies labeled perceptual studies have not observed this necessary precaution. Hence what was being called perception might better have been called judgment or problem solving (Bartley, 1958). Perception, of course, was involved but the response unit was far more than perceptual. Variations (Allport, 1955; Klein & others, 1951; Levine & others, 1942) in response in such experiments were used as demonstrations of how perception was a product of one or the other of a number of factors not recognized by classical or the more conventional students of the sensory processes. This mode of experimentation served, among other things, to heighten the conflict between strict psychophysical investigators and those wishing to show the contribution of the organism in the perceptual outcome.

PERCEPTION AND PROBLEM SOLVING. Perception can, in a way, be viewed as a form of problem solving, but it is only one mode of such behavior. It is the kind that immediately solves a problem of the basic relation of the organism to some aspect of the environment. Nevertheless, in the course of categorizing the features of human behavior, perception is seldom, if ever, spoken of as problem solving or lumped with other more extended modes of problem solving. The view of Gibson that has been alluded to several times already would come close to categorizing it as problem solving, inasmuch as it describes perception as information pick-up and as having a performatory function.

PERCEPTION IN ADAPTATION AND LEARNING. One gains two different views of perception or perceptual achievement, depending upon whether one simply studies (1) thresholds of sensitivity or quantitative relations between input to sense organs and the sensory outcome in a fixed situation, or (2) what might be the adaptive process—namely, perception as it occurs in changing situations. Whereas earlier work was totally preoccupied with the former, more recent work has turned to the latter concern. While we can say that all studies of learning, such as conditioning in animals, dealt with perception whether wittingly or not, the question of the role of perception in learning and/or adaptation has come to be a matter of prime focus in more recent years. Here, learning curves are not the focus of attention. Rather, the mechanisms that subserve perception are the object of study.

There are at least nine fairly distinct lines of this work that deserve attention here. They are: (1) Senden's (1960) account of the findings in regard to the characteristics of vision in partially grown individuals who by removal of congenital cataract were able to see for the first time; (2) animal deprivation studies (Riesen, 1950) in which animals were reared in totally unilluminated environments or with blinders, and whose visual behavior was examined at various age levels; (3) studies of the blind (Revesz, 1950) to note the consequence of lack of vision in the performances tested; (4) the theorizing of such men as Hebb (1949) on the growth of perception from birth; (5) the studies of Birch and colleagues (Birch & Belmont, 1964, 1965; Birch & Lefford, 1963) on the interplay of the senses in the performance of children and the deficits involved in the brain-damaged, etc.; (6) the studies with a stimulus situation called "the visual cliff" (Gibson & Walk, 1960; Walk & Dodge, 1962; Walk & others, 1957; Walk & Trychin, 1964); (7) the determination of the nature of perceptual response and the effectiveness of various visual targets in the newborn and young infants (Bower, 1965, 1966; Fantz, 1956, 1958, 1959, 1963, 1964); (8) the study of the role of active muscular participation in visual response and its adaptation to various changes in the target situation (Held, 1965; Held & Freeman, 1963; Held & others, 1965); (9) studies with split-brain animals and humans (Gazzaniga & others, 1965; Sperry, 1964a, 1964b; Sperry & Gazzaniga, 1966).

Studies in (1) have shown that differences in object size could correctly be seen immediately after operation. Solid forms familiar to subjects tactually before operation generally could not be identified visually after operation. The same failure to recognize familiar persons by sight was found. In most cases, visual distinction between two- and three-dimensional items was not possible immediately after operation.

Studies in (2) were hampered because of some retinal deterioration produced by rearing the animals in the dark so that in many cases clear conclusions were not possible.

Studies in (3) are quite varied and difficult to summarize as to content. They have to do with the nature of tactual space. From these studies, Revesz (1950) formulated a set of principles which describe how the blind individual proceeds to acquaint himself with his surroundings. They indicate that he proceeds very differently from the sighted person, the main feature of which is sequential exploration of items bit-by-bit. No simultaneous impression of anything of extended dimensions can be obtained.

In category (4) Hebb proposed a neurological model whereby perceptions were built up by practice, starting with a primitive reaction to corners of a figure and eye movements that follow the components of the figure to the point at which the viewer is able to deal with the figure as a whole. The model suggested how changes and elaborations of the original response might come about.

In category (5) Birch and colleagues have devised ways to note the parallel development of the several sense modalities in children's dealing with objects. Part of this work consisted in presenting first a visual figure (line drawing) and then later determining whether the same object in the form of a three-dimensional solid could be recognized by touching it, handling it (haptic mode of presentation), or by tracing a representation of the visual figure in the form of grooves in a board (kinesthetic presentation). Birch's work also consisted in studying the developmental integration between the senses by noting the ability of children to see a pattern of dots and pick out identical patterns of clicks. This involves a transposition from the spatial to the temporal.

Studies in category (6) involve the use of a device called a visual cliff. It is a large horizontal sheet of plate glass on the underside of half of which is cemented a geometrical design such as a checkerboard. The glass is supported a foot or two above the floor. On the floor below the second half of the glass is the same checkerboard design. Across the middle of the glass along the division between the two halves is a board. On it either an infant or a small young animal can be placed. The fact that the subject cannot be coaxed to move onto the glass on the side on which the checkerboard design is on the floor is taken as an indication that the subject sees the situation as a cliff and resists falling over it. Use of various species at birth and shortly afterwards has enabled the collection of data bearing on the existence or advent of three-dimensional space perception.

Studies in category (7) are concerned with visual fixations in newborn and early infants when various visual patterns are presented to them in a well-controlled instrumental situation.

Studies in (8) have to do with discovering the resultant differences from viewing certain visual fields passively and actively. It has been found that adaptations to changes and anomalous conditions in stimulus situations are made possible when the initial exposures involve not only vision but muscular reactions. When only passive viewing was involved, adaptation was precluded. Here again not merely sensory input via the higher sense modalities (e.g., vision) but also the cooperation of the muscle and joint senses were necessary to accomplish the required responses as conditions changed.

In category (9) investigation of the roles played by the various sensory inputs was conducted in split-brain animals and humans. Split-brain subjects are those whose neural connections between the two cerebral hemispheres are severed. With such subjects various manipulations between hemispheres, one of which is receiving information and one of which is called upon to react can be made. While this is not particularly a developmental type of study, it goes along with such studies to produce a better understanding of the cooperation between the various parts of the organism in reacting to stimulus input.

THEORIES OF PERCEPTION. In recent years, a number of theories have emerged in connection with experimentation on perception. None of these theories are comprehensive formulations either as to what is involved in the perceptual outcome, or as to the body processes that give rise to them, or as to the essential mode of relating to externality. Thus, no theory attempts to explain all perceptual phenomena or the conditions for producing them. These theories are more appropriately to be called theories *about* perception rather than theories *of* perception. Some of the theories employ neurophysiological concepts; some, photochemical; some, purely formal, spatial or other concepts. The following are among those most frequently mentioned: (1) The core-context theory (Boring, 1942) which states that perceptions are functional groupings of sensations, images, etc. The cluster of sensations about a core gives meaning to the core, and it is this meaning that is the earmark of perception beyond sensation. This is one of the very early theories and is based on no solid experimental evidence. (2) The texture-gradient theory (Gibson, 1950), a theory regarding visual space perception which accounts for direction, size, location, distance, and other properties of items in the visual field by recognizing that the inhomogeneities of the visual field (hence, optical input) form a texture gradient in accord with whether the various surfaces are oriented obliquely or in the frontal plane with reference to the eye. The manner in which the item in question is located in the gradient or the way it participates in the gradient, determines its various spatial (three-dimensional) properties, location, etc. (3) The cybernetic theory (McCulloch & Pitts, 1948) is one in which the nervous system is supposed to possess the various properties now known for electronic systems such as computers. In accord with this basic presupposition, various processes are conceived to take place to produce the sensory end result. (4) The cell-assembly-phase-sequence theory (Hebb, 1949) is simply a conceptualization of how various portions of the central nervous system come to work together in patterns to give rise to over-all processes underlying perception. (5) The adaptation-level theory (Helson, 1951) is a formulation derived from psychophysical experimentation and findings. It points out that there is always a neutral range to which the organism is adapted. The theory predicts the nature of response to inputs falling above or below this range. (6) The motor adjustment theory (Freeman, 1948) is an energistic theory relating what is ordinarily called perception to motor behavior. The theory is a kind of application of the concept of homeostasis. (7) The sensory-tonic field theory (Werner & Wapner, 1952) is a tension theory, in which not only neural processes but muscular feedbacks are brought in to explain certain bilateral asymmetries in perceptual response. (8) The probabilistic-functional theory (Brunswick, 1940) focuses on the phenomenological facts of perception by the organism's use of "cues" whereby the organism makes a "reconstitution" of the object. This has a probabilistic chance of tallying with reality. (9) The transactional theory (Kilpatrick, 1952) is another theory that makes use of the probabilistic paradigm. Perception is taken to be a kind of transaction between the organism and its surrounds. Perception is only prognostic of the action which will be successful. Action is for the furtherance of individual purpose. (10) The directive-state theory (Bruner & Postman, 1948) is a formulation that recognizes that perception is the outcome of two sets of conditions—one, the structural which includes the stimulus and the anatomy of the organism; the other, the behavioral, which stems from higher level processes in the organism, and described by terms such as needs, value systems, biases, etc. This theory indicates that the very pattern of personality is represented in the individual's perceptual responses. (11) The hypothesis or expectancy theory (Bruner, 1951). This is a social theory of perception, and mainly refers to the supposition that perception does not arise from a neutral ground, but is the result of an antecedent. The pattern and role of these antecedents are such as to permit them to be called hypotheses. The stronger the hypothesis the more likely its activation in a given situation. In such cases, less input material will be needed for its activation. (12) The Gestalt theory (Allport, 1955) is one disavowing the atomistic concept that is expressed in such theories as the core-context theory. It is a doctrine which supposes the emergence of perception in line with field forces of "laws of Gestalten." These configurational laws have been various and many. Most of them have the status of pure hypotheses. These laws are said to pertain to physiological processes as well as to apply to the descriptions of the perceptions that result. The theory is a form of isomorphism between input, body processes and end result.

Among the best general discussions of perception theory are Allport (1955), Helson (1951, 1964), and Bartley (1958).

S. Howard Bartley
Michigan State University

References

Allport, F. *Theories of Perception and the Concept of Structure*. Wiley, 1955. 709p.

Bartley, S. Howard. *Principles of Perception*. Harper, 1958. 482p.

Birch, H. G., and Belmont, L. "Auditory-visual Integration in Normal and Retarded Readers." *Am J Orthopsychiatry* 34:853–61; 1964.

Birch, H. G., and Belmont, L. "Auditory and Visual Integration in Brain-damaged and Normal Children." *Develop Med Child Neurology* 7:135–44; 1965.

Birch, H. G., and Lefford, A. "Intersensory Development in Children." *Monogr Soc Res Child Develop* 28:1–28; 1963.

Blake, R. R., and Ramsey, G. V. *Perception: An Approach to Personality*. Ronald, 1951. 442p.

Boring, E. G. *Sensation and Perception in the History of Experimental Psychology*. Appleton, 1942. 644p.

Bower, T. G. R. "Stimulus Variables Determining Space Perception in Infants." *Sci* 149:88–9; 1965.

Bower, T. G. R. "Slant Perception and Shape Constancy in Infants." *Sci* 151:832–4; 1966.

Bruner, J. S. "Personality Dynamics and the Process of Perceiving." In Blake, R. R., and Ramsey, G. V. (Eds.) *Perception: An Approach to Personality*. Ronald, 1951. p. 121–47.

Bruner, J. S., and Postman, L. "Symbolic Value as an Organizing Factor in Perception." *J Social Psychol* 27:203–8; 1948.

Brunswik, E. "Thing Constancy as Measured by Correlation Coefficients." *Psychol R* 47:69–78; 1940.

Fantz, R. L. "A Method for Studying Early Visual Development." *Perceptual Motor Skills* 6:13–5; 1956.

Fantz, R. L. "Visual Discrimination in a Neonate Chimpanzee." *Perceptual Motor Skills* 8:59–66; 1958.

Fantz, R. L. "Response to Horizontality by Bantam Chicks in Level and Tilted Room." *Psychol Rec* 9:61–6; 1959.

Fantz, R. L. "Pattern Vision in Newborn Infants." *Sci* 140:296–7; 1963.

Fantz, R. L. "Visual Experience in Infants: Decreased Attention to Familiar Patterns Relative to Novel Ones." *Sci* 146:668–70; 1964.

Freeman, G. L. *The Energetics of Human Behavior*. Cornell U Press, 1948. 343p.

Gazzaniga, M. S., and others. "Observation on Visual Perception After Disconnexion of the Cerebral Hemispheres in Man." *Brain* 88:221–36; 1965.

Gibson, E. J., and Walk, R. D. "The Visual Cliff." *Sci Am* 202:62–71; 1960.

Gibson, J. J. *The Perception of the Visual World*. Houghton, 1950. 235p.

Gibson, J. J. *The Senses Considered as Perceptual Systems*. Houghton, 1966. 335p.

Hebb, D. O. *The Organization of Behavior: A Neuropsychological Theory*. Wiley, 1949. 335p.

Held, R. "Plasticity in Sensory-motor Systems." *Sci Am* 213:84–94; 1965.

Held, R., and Freedman, S. J. "Plasticity in Human Sensorimotor Control." *Sci* 142:455–62; 1963.

Held, R., and others. "Visual Accommodation in Human Infants." *Sci* 148:528–30; 1965.

Helson, H. "Perception." In Helson, H. (Ed.) *Theoretical Foundations of Psychology*. Van Nostrand, 1951. p. 348–89.

Helson, H. *Adaptation Level Theory*. Harper, 1964. 732p.

James, William. *Psychology*. Holt, 1900. 478p.

Kilpatrick, Franklin P. (Ed.) *Human Behavior from the Transactional Point of View*. Institute Associated Research with Office Naval Research, 1952. 259p.

Klein, G. S., and others. "The Effect of Personal Values on Perception: An Experimental Critique." *Psychol R* 58:96–112; 1951.

Levine, R., and others. "The Relation of Intensity of Need to the Amount of Perceptual Distortion." *J Psychol* 13:283–93; 1942.

McCulloch, W., and Pitts, W. "The Statistical Organization of Nervous Activity." *J Am Stat Assn* 4:91–9; 1948.

Pieron, H. *The Sensations*. Pirenne, M. H., and Abbot, B. C. (Translators). J. Gonet Miller, 1952. 468p.

Pratt, Carrol C. "The Role of Past Experience in Visual Perception." *J Psychol* 30:85–107; 1950.

Revesz, G. *Psychology and Art of the Blind*. McKay, 1950. 338p.

Riesen, A. H. "Arrested Vision." *Sci Am* 183:16–9; 1950.

Senden, von M. *Space and Sight*. Heath, P. (Translator). Free, 1960. 348p.

Sperry, R. W. "The Great Cerebral Commissure." *Sci Am* 210:45–52; 1964(*a*).

Sperry, R. W. "Problems Outstanding in the Evolution of Brain Function." *New York Am Museum Natural History*, 1964(*b*). p. 1–22.

Sperry, R. W., and Gazzaniga, M. S. "Simultaneous Double Discrimination Response Following Brain Bisection." *Psychonomic Sci* 4:261–2; 1966.

Stagner, R., and Karwoski, T. *Psychology*. McGraw-Hill, 1952. 582p.

Titchener, E. B. *A Textbook of Psychology*. Macmillan, 1909. 565p.

Walk, R. D., and Dodge, S. H. "Visual Depth Perception of a 10-month Old Monocular Human Infant." *Sci* 137:529–30; 1962.

Walk, R. D., and Trychin, S., Jr. "A Study of the Depth Perception of Monocular Hooded Rats on the Visual Cliff." *Psychonomic Sci* 1:53–4; 1964.

Walk, R. D., and others. "Behavior of Light- and Dark-reared Rats on a Visual Cliff." *Sci* 126:80–1; 1957.

Watson, J. B. *Psychology from the Standpoint of a Behaviorist.* Lippincott, 1924. 448p.

Werner, H., and Wapner, S. "Toward a General Theory of Perception." *Psychol R* 59:324–38; 1952.

PERSONALITY

The historical roots of the present scientific approaches to the study of personality are many and extend into other disciplines to which psychology is indebted. Indeed, personality was a concern of psychiatrists long before it became a problem in psychology. Freud and other early personality theorists and systematists were physicians, whose source of subjects were patients seeking relief from disturbing personal problems, and whose clinical methods and frame of reference for the domain of personality gave the field an orientation toward the abnormal from which it has not yet fully retreated. The influences of evolutionary biology, genetics, neurophysiology, anthropology and the cultural disciplines, mathematics, cybernetics, and the computer sciences are apparent in the developmental, cross-cultural, experimental, neurophysiological, information-processing, and multivariate statistical methods that characterize the developing thrust in this multifaceted area.

The interdependence of method and conceptualization, emphasized by Murphy (1966), is reflected in a shift in conceptual models of personality organization and function, paralleling the shift in methods, away from "schools," toward theoretical attempts to account for the development, organization, and functioning principles of self-regulative properties of man in interaction with his environment. Some methods have focused on various control systems from the vantage of genetics, neurophysiology, social learning theory, or social interaction, while others have attempted to represent them as patterns of traits. The result has been an informal division, often referred to as views related to processes and dynamics and views related to individual differences and structure of personality. However, most recent writers have concluded that this distinction is difficult to maintain and that it hinders discussion of the complexities of personality as well as generalizations that may be drawn about various aspects (Klein & others, 1967). Nevertheless these two views of personality, as processes by which the individual person maintains continuing transaction with his environment, and as traits or organization which define these processes uniquely and selectively for each individual, identify the topics to be covered in this discussion.

This approach is consistent with the work in this complex field and is necessary to a comprehensive treatment of personality (Klein & others, 1967; Sanford, 1963), but only the second view, expressed in Child's (1963) definition "as comprising consistencies of individual differences in behavior which are internally determined," truly identifies personality as an entity discrete from the general processes of behavior that constitute the universal problems of psychology.

CONTEMPORARY PERSONALITY THEORY. The aim of personality theory is to specify principles of self-regulation of individual behavior that achieve consistency of diverse functions in different situations. This assumes hierarchical organization in which higher-order integrative processes regulate behavior tendencies at lower levels to produce consistency in the face of varying stimulus conditions. Klein and others (1967) defined consistency in terms of "selection of situations responded to, guidance of responsiveness to situations, and the 'average expectable environment' for every consistency," and specified three hierarchically related classes of constancies that have been studied: *organismic states*, representing baselines or adaptation levels of the organism in the resting state; *situational reaction constants*, involving instrumental responses, insight into arousal situations and outcomes, operating at a higher level of integration; and *generic attitudes*, following Allport (1964), which include value orientations and broad cognitive schemata, such as orientation to authority and information acquisition, at a still higher level.

Viewing developments since 1937, Sanford (1963) has noted that nomothetic concepts of personality variables continue to be most popular; that emphasis on motivational components has decreased while that on cognitive variables has increased; that this salience of cognitive elements in personality is part of a larger current emphasis on higher mental processes and other distinctly human characteristics; that those who emphasize higher mental processes give a large place to the concepts of self; and that contemporary writing on self and ego reflects holistic and social trends.

The hierarchical network of relations, involving cognitive structures at the generic-attitude level and more specific constancies at the lower levels, is implied by such well-known work as that of Lacey and Lacey (1958), Witkin and others (1962), and Eysenck (1963). The impressive Lacey and Lacey research related basal autonomic responsiveness to higher-level cognitive organization. Witkin and others' developments on cognitive control, originally in terms of "field dependence and independence," and later, "psychological differentiation," have been related to physiological responsiveness, leveling and sharpening, and information processing, by other investigators inspired by their work. Eysenck has suggested that the trait of introversion-extroversion has roots in constitutional factors related to responsiveness of the nervous system. The higher-level cognitive structures have explanatory value with reference to the individual's selection of situations to which he will respond to a far greater extent than the lower-order constancies. However, the hierarchical model invites analysis of the linkages both to extend understanding and as measurement strategy. Conceptually, the type of organization discussed here fits Cattell's (1946) *dynamic lattice* precisely, and developments such as those cited present strong support for his theoretical structure.

The dominant types of conceptualization of central personality organization involve neurophysiological research, information processing, ego psychology in the psychoanalytic tradition, and self concept. The steps in development of personality dimensions from these sources have not been explicitly represented empirically, however, and here one can identify one of the major research tasks for personality research in coming years. Theoretical developments related to these core conceptions are discussed under six headings: neurophysiological, cybernetic, developmental, self and ego theory, cognitive control, and trait-factor analytic.

Neurophysiological Developments. Important new developments in neurophysiological research are believed by many writers to be converging on the brain as the locus of personality organization. Exciting Soviet research, interpreted by Diamond and others (1963) and Klein and others (1967), assumes that individuality depends on the nature of neural activity and must be studied in that frame of reference. Beginning with Pavlov's concepts of *strength, balance of arousal and inhibition,* and *mobility* of neural processes, this research is attempting to elucidate the basic characteristics of nervous system functioning and relations among patterns of these characteristics. Diamond and others (1963) examined the implications of organism-environment dependencies and analysis of the physiological state of the moment, namely "that each act must be considered in relation to the acts that have preceded it, and to the other acts that might have taken place in its stead." In this context, these authors stated, "It seems as if there is a principle underlying the organization of behavior which is very like Newton's third law of motion, that 'action and reaction are equal and opposite.' The mechanism of every act includes its behavioral counterpoise."

Pribram's (1960) review of theory in physiological psychology, though excluding the Russian literature and now somewhat dated, remains one of the finest overviews of this developing area. His concluding statements convey the breadth and excitement of the directions in which neuropsychology is moving:

> This view of an active organism gains support from the fact that the central nervous system, in conjunction with its receptors, is intrinsically and spontaneously active. Electrical activity is recorded in the total absence of environmental input. Even brief stimulation has long-lasting aftereffects that alter the intrinsic rhythms for hours and days and thus change the response of the organism to subsequent stimulation. Reinforcement by cognition, based on a mechanism of hierarchically organized representations; dispositions and drives regulated by multilinked and biased homeostats; representational organization by virtue of graded, as well as all-or-nothing, neural responses; spontaneously generated, long-lasting intrinsic neural rhythms: organisms thus conceived are actively engaged, not only in the manipulation of artifacts, but in the organization of their perceptions, satisfactions, and gratifications.

Despite progress and vistas of important developments that appear imminent, the reduction of personality to neurophysiological functioning is not the goal for contemporary personality theory. On the other hand, elucidation of significant correlations between physiological states and functions and more molar consistencies (at the generic-attitude level) in human behavior may have practical as well as theoretical implications. For example, Klein and others (1967) emphasize the implications of "idling properties" of the nervous system in relation to studies of training and work capacities, as well as "temperament"; the relation of high sensory sensitivity to a *weak* nervous system (in Pavlov's sense), and conversely, resistance to sensory stress at the expense of loss of sensitivity to lower levels of intensity, associated with a *strong* nervous system; and the fact that differences in nervous system sensitivity may account for learning differences, e.g., a "musical ear."

Cybernetic Concepts. The influence of cybernetics and computer concepts has inevitably inspired efforts to represent behavioral functions in information-processing terms (Blum, 1963; Borko, 1962; Feigenbaum & Feldman, 1963; Green, 1963; Hunt, 1961, 1963; Miller and others, 1960; Saunders, 1961; Simon, 1957; Tomkins & Messick, 1963). This approach has an affinity for cognitive structures and also for treatment of neural activities in input, memory storage, access and retrieval, channel capacity, central processor, output, and feedback loop terms and has many qualities of the *Zeitgeist* of the 1960's. It is not surprising, therefore, that the salience of cognitive elements in personality, noted by Sanford, should reflect a convergence of neurophysiological, cybernetic, and cognitive control formulations at this time.

This convergence was led by the work of Hebb (1949, 1959) and is seen in the formulation by Miller and others (1960) of the Test-Operate-Test-Exit (TOTE) sequence which they advocate in place of the static notion of reflex arc and which they conceived as adequate to perform the "similarity" or "matching" routines described by Newell and others (1960). It was expressed most elegantly by Hunt (1961) in his analysis of intelligence and experience, in which he drew heavily from the classic work of Piaget, which is also developmental, and again in his analysis of motivation inherent in information processing and action (1963).

An example of an effort to formulate personality characteristics in terms of interactions of computer components is seen in a paper by Saunders (1961) and is illustrated by his "portrait" of a psychopathic computer. He assumed a computer with the following profile of characteristics: B. *Speed of operation:* low in proportion to its *Memory Capacity* (A); C. *Input Buffer* (sensitivity of sensory system to the environment) and D. *Channel Capacity* (complexity of central processing unit): both average; E. *Memory Retrieval* from long-term memory storage: high capacity; F. *Output Buffer* (ability to translate computational results into overt behavior) and G. *Self Control* (ability of the system to modify its own internal programs and procedures on the basis of experience): both low in proportion to memory capacity. According to Saunders,

> The fact that this particular computer is below average with respect to both characteristics B and F means that it is both relatively stimulus-bound in its perceptions and relatively environment-oriented in its responses. That is to say, this computer is very closely tied to the real world in terms of both its input and its output. It has a lot of experience. At the same time, it shows a relative lack of ability to change its behavior on the basis of experience. And so we may infer that such experience as it engages in is going to tend to persist at a relatively primitive level of behavior. This approach to experience is further confirmed and intensified by the relatively high ability on characteristic E. That is, this particular mechanism is able to recall in an effective manner the temporal relationships of experiences in the past, and to use them as a basis for behavior in the present without further modification. This computer system is relatively very adept at recognizing and anticipating the sequence of behavior in which another computer or another person is engaged, and is prepared on the basis of its own long-term memory to play the role which is expected of it and which will bring to it the kinds of rewards in which it is most interested.

This is an example of a "simulation model" in which characteristics of persons are designed features of computer "hardware."

Loehlin's (1963) computer program for the Burroughs 205 computer, named Aldous, simulates a limited "person" with a repertoire of about 750 instructions and responds to "situations" coded as 7-digit numbers by printing out coded numbers as responses. Aldous has three subsystems that mediate his response to the environment: *Stimulus Recognition,* which retrieves instructions for responses from "memory," *Emotional Reaction,* with three modes: positive "attraction," anger, and fear, ranging in intensity from 0 (no action) through 3–5 (mild) and 6–8 (vigorous) to 9 (emotional paralysis), and *Action Preparation,* with three corresponding modes: approach positively, attack, or withdraw, each at two intensity levels: mild or vigorous. Aldous also has two memory systems: Immediate and Permanent, the latter coded to be modified by experience, and a subsystem providing capability of answering questions about his "feelings," as represented in internal programs, at any time. On the stimulus input side, Loehlin programmed "environmental press" in three dimensions, Satisfying, Frustrating, and Painful, and reported a number of ingenious experiments in which any given set of program characteristics could be tested under different environmental conditions, shifted from one type of "world" to another, and by changing program parameters, either personality "trait" characteristics, or environment, or both could be varied.

This type of simulation, as well as a different model for the simulation of a neurotic process, by Colby (1963), and the adaptation by Reitman (1963) of the earlier general problem solver of Newell and others (1960) to an approach to personality based on coalitions of problem-solving systems, has the advantage of greater flexibility than that implied in the Saunders model, above, because it is embodied in the "software" of programs rather than in the "hardware" of machines.

The problems of computer simulation of personality are well covered in a symposium chaired jointly by Tomkins and Messick (1963). Although computers may lack "flesh and bones and erogenous zones," as Messick stated, they are capable of significant contributions to the study of personality. Viewed as a means of *language translation* of process and action, the precise language of the computer forces precision of formulation and may stimulate needed empirical investigation to supply missing information to meet the requirements of rigorous specification of inputs, processes, and antecedent-consequent relationship patterns. However, as Messick and others have noted, the potential power of the computer for dealing with high orders of complexity can carry research far beyond that achievable simply by translation of ordinary research designs. This was demonstrated even by the comparatively simple simulations of Loehlin and of Reitman.

Computer simulation can be divided into two classes, conceptually described by *mathematical models,* which represent inputs and outputs related to theory or reality, but without attempting to imitate intervening processes, and *simulation models,* which aim to mimic reality through representation of intervening processes as well. Both have heuristic value, as Messick discussed, but serve different functions and should be evaluated by different criteria. The interplay of human research and computer simulation offers an exciting prospect of a significant accomplishment, as when simulation studies, which have the potential of enabling research in areas in which human research is constrained by funds or moral-ethical issues, can extend observations beyond customary limits. Studies by Jones (1963) and Johnson (1961) have demonstrated how computers can be programmed not only for general solutions, but also to accommodate to individual differences.

Personality Development. Contemporary personality theory views development as *hierarchically organized,* such that both in physical growth and in socialization, in moment-to-moment, short-term experience as well as in longer perspective, prior experience has a determining effect on later development. It is also *interactional,* regarding developed anatomical structures as well as behavior repertoires as cumulative outcomes of modes of adaptation to the experienced environment, well described by

Piaget's dual processes of *assimilation* (which includes conditioning, stimulus generalization, and response generalization) and *accommodation* (modification of response schemata through various means of coping with environmental variation) (Hunt, 1961). It gives broad recognition to *discontinuities* in hierarchical development, which are often associated with *critical periods* in development, such as optimal periods for learning, for infantile stimulation, and for the formulation of basic social relationships (Scott, 1962). Approaches in this frame of reference require concern with structure and function, recognition of the interplay of biological and psychological development, attention to specification of environmental variables, and focus on the development and continued modification of cognitive structures that moderate behavior.

Critical Periods of Development. The current interest in critical periods of development ties together a number of independent investigations from widely different sources. Some idea of the apparent generality of critical periods can be obtained from Scott's (1962) review, which reports animal and human instances that he claimed could be generalized to imply (1) that the important aspect of each developmental period is not time sequence but the fact that each represents a major developmental process, and (2) that the critical period for any specific sort of learning is that time when maximum capacities, sensory, motor, and motivational as well as psychological ones, are first present. One interesting outcome of the intensified interest in critical periods has been to revive attention to Freud's well-known observations that the influence of early experience in the origin of neuroses follows from the fact that certain periods in the life of an infant are times of particular sensitivity.

Developmental Milestones. Another influential developmental concept for personality theory is that of Loevinger (1965) who has emphasized the fact that while some functions may increase throughout life, others may be ascendant for a period and then wane. Loevinger used the term "developmental milestones" to describe these functions, which may vary in persistence and stability in a person's life. Erikson's (1963) conception of autonomous development or "identity" is similar. He believes that "milestone" solutions emerge from developmental crises during various critical periods of psychosocial development. Conflicts characteristic of each stage appear to be resolved on the basis of varying balances of strengths and weaknesses, which Erikson calls basic alternatives (trust versus mistrust). Thus initiative may emerge as a product of socialization in which competitive and assertive impulses must be controlled at the oedipal stage. Escalona's (1965) concept of "concrete experience," which shapes moment-to-moment behavior, is also related. Though behavior is influenced both by situational-environmental and constitutional factors, the critical intervening factor is their impact on concrete experience. In her studies of changes in infant states and behavior when approached and handled by their mothers, she noted significant differences in the reaction of *active* and *inactive* babies to similar maternal actions, thus demonstrating the interplay of maternal style and activity level in the developing experience of babies.

Perhaps the most influential theories of child development, which make profound inroads into personality theory, are those of Erik H. Erikson, Jean Piaget, and Robert R. Sears. Extended bibliographies of their works and critical summaries of their theoretical positions can be found in Maier's (1965) excellent comparative review. See also Hunt's (1961) fine review of Piaget.

Approaching development from a psychoanalytic viewpoint, Erikson's (1963) conception of ego development is concerned with the development of emotional maturity. He described eight epigenetic developmental stages, each conceived both as a *vertical crisis,* culminating in an individual psychosocial solution, and a *horizontal crisis,* calling for a personally and socially satisfactory solution to the problem of the conflicting motivational forces. The first five stages occur in infancy, childhood, and adolescence. They are (1) the sense of basic trust, (2) the sense of autonomy, (3) the sense of initiative, (4) the sense of industry, and (5) the sense of identity. The three adult stages are: (6) the sense of intimacy, (7) the sense of generativity, and (8) the sense of integrity. Erikson's use of the prefatory *sense of* at each stage reflects his recognition of the affective feeling of having achieved or failed to achieve the relationship characteristic of each succeeding stage as the most significant factor affecting development at succeeding stages. Although he acknowledges a deep obligation to Freud, Erikson's theory enlarges the function of the ego in relation to Freudian theory and focuses primarily on problems of socialization. Rapaport (1959) referred to Erikson's work as a "theory of reality relationships." Much similarity can be seen between this theory and the stages of ego development described by Loevinger, below.

Piaget's developmental theory (Piaget & Inhelder, 1958) focuses primarily on intellectual development, which is occupying an increasingly important role in personality theory. He divided the developmental continuum into three major phases: (1) the sensorimotor phase, through the first two years, (2) the period of preparation for conceptual thought, covering roughly the period from 2 to 11 or 12, and (3) the phase of cognitive thought, from 11 or 12 on. The six basic generalizations of his theory are discussed at length in his extensive work covering over 30 years of prolific output. First, he holds that there is an absolute continuity of all developmental processes. Second, development proceeds through a continuous process of generalization and differentiation. Third, this continuity is achieved by a continuous unfolding, whereby each succeeding level of development has roots in a preceding phase and also continues into a later phase. Fourth, each phase involves repetition of processes at an earlier level in a different schema or form of organization, as earlier behavior is perceived as inferior and becomes part of the new, superior level. Fifth, the differences in organizational pattern constitute a hierarchy of experience and actions. Finally, individuals achieve different levels within the hierarchy, although each individual is theoretically capable of achieving all levels. Throughout Piaget's voluminous writings, a number of related developmental sequences reappear and epitomize his conceptual framework. Thus, development always proceeds from simple to complex, from concrete to abstract, from experience with physical to social to ideational objects, from egocentric to objective to relative orientation, from activity without thought to thought with less activity, from conceptions of objects based on utility only to representative symbols and properties, and finally to relativity in space, time, and utility, from animistic to realistic concepts of causality, and from ethical-moral concepts anchored in authority to mutuality, to social reciprocity, and finally to social integrity. Although his primary data were necessarily based on very few subjects, in view of the fine-grained quality of his observations and experiments, Piaget's work has gained increased recognition and influence as that of one of the giants in psychology of all time.

In contrast to the emotional maturity emphasis of Erikson and the intellectual development emphasis of Piaget, Sears' work (1951, 1957) reflects major concern with learning (habit formation) and social interaction. His view of personality development involves a lifelong process of *dyadic action* which modifies the individual's potentiality for further action. Thus, human behavior reflects the interactive effects of all inherited and experienced influences through dyadic relationships, constantly modified by new dyadic experience. Dyadic relations, originally with the mother, expanding to other family members, and constantly broadening, provide the setting within which behavior develops. Behavior is both the cause and effect of other behavior; primary drives are instrumental only for the earliest behavior; environment shapes behavior as the individual develops; initially child-rearing practices are most conspicuous influences. Behavior is self-motivated by its tension-reduction effect. Every unit of behavior preceding a goal achieves a reinforcement potential, either by being repeated before the achievement or by the subsequent repetition of the behavior as a result of goal achievement. All reinforced behavior with drive-equivalent characteristics forms secondary motivational systems, which are the socially important motivators of behavior, comprising the culture-conforming, socially relevant behavior repertoire learned in social interaction. Frustration, aggression, identification, and social habits each have separate modes of development in social settings, involving the learning principles described. In addition to learning, Sears takes account of physical maturation. His theory places major emphasis on cultural conditioning and expectations of forthcoming behavior as conveyed by others.

The following table, based on Maier (1965), presents a comparison of the developmental phases of the theories of Erikson, Piaget, and Sears:

DEVELOPMENTAL PHASES OF PERSONALITY

Age (years)	Erikson	Piaget	Sears	Integration by Maier
0	Phase 1. Sense of basic trust	Sensori-motor phase	Phase of rudimentary behavior	I. Establishing primary dependency
1				
2			Phase of secondary motivational systems: family-centered learning	II. Establishing self-care
3	Phase 2. Sense of autonomy	Preconceptual phase		
4				
5	Phase 3. Sense of initiative	Phase of intuitive thought		III. Establishing meaningful secondary relationships
6				
7			Phase of secondary motivational systems: extrafamilial learning	
8				IV. Establishing secondary dependency
9	Phase 4. Sense of industry	Phase of concrete operations		
10				
11				
12				
13	Phase 5. Sense of identity	Phase of formal operations	Little research done by Sears thus far	V. Achieving balance between dependence and independence
14				
15				
16				
17				
18				
19				
20				
21 etc.	Phase 6. Sense of intimacy	Not yet investigated by Piaget		

This table, with a constructive integration by Maier, reflects much parallel conceptualization in these influential theories of development proceeding from psychoanalytic, cognitive, and learning theory orientations.

Self and Ego Theory. Self and ego concepts, dating from William James (1890, 1902) and Freud (1949), reflect concern with the individual as a whole and in a social context. The subjective and impalpable character and holistic nature of these concepts were rejected by the objective, reductionistic, behavioristic movements in psychology that flourished during the first half of the twentieth century, but gained support in the Gestalt movement (Koffka, 1935) which emphasized "membership character" of parts dependent on the nature of the whole and an approach to personality through "perceptual dynamics," which have a direct line to contemporary cognitive approaches and renewed interest in phenomenology. McDougall's (1933) *sentiment of self-regard*, broadly speaking including a class of attitudes variously described as self-respect, self-esteem, self-love, pride, and ambition, involves the qualities of self-enhancement and self-defense which Murphy (1947) considered common denominators of the psychoanalytic ego concepts. McDougall's *sentiments* were defined as "systems which give consistency, continuity, and order to our life of striving and emotion," and ones "in which a cognitive ability has become, through the individual's experience, functionally linked with one or more native propensities." He regarded each sentiment (which appears similar to generic attitude) as "a unique formation, a structural and functional unit of the total organization of the mind." Although for McDougall the self-regarding sentiment is one among a number of sentiment structures, it is described as pervasive and extending into most objects that "express one's personality or can in any way be regarded as parts of one's larger self." Cattell's (1957) more recent research on attitude structure produced a stable and very similarly described factor which he names "the Self-Sentiment" and which he related both to McDougall's self-regarding sentiment and Freud's ego and super-ego concepts.

Murphy (1966) described the problem of the self in terms of "the nature of that confrontation which each individual makes with his own individuality." In the literature there have been two distinct concepts, one, arising from William James, of self as perceived object, self-picture, endowed with various cherished characteristics and in a certain relation to others in the environment, and the other, developed by Freud, a system of dynamic operations by which the picture of the self is magnified, enhanced, and protected by socially active dynamic functions. The self is the preferred term for the former concept to distinguish it from the Freudian "ego" functions. As Murphy has noted, these two concepts are separate but related. However, some theorists emphasize attributes of the self while others focus on ego enhancing and defensive processes. In this context, McDougall's self-regarding sentiment is, as Cattell interpreted it, more closely allied to the ego.

Self Concept. Miller (1963), French and Sherwood (1963), Wylie (1961), Brownfain (1952), and numerous other contemporary psychologists have been interested in the self concept and in self-identity theory. In this frame of reference, emphasis is placed on the measurement and description of the total self-identity, through sub-identities or clusters of attributes subjectively perceived and generally favorably biased in relation to objective appraisal. Intelligence, honesty, strength, and body image are examples of self-attributes; father, doctor, sportsman, and scholar are examples of sub-identities corresponding to social roles with which attribute clusters are associated. Sub-identities and attribute clusters vary in centrality in relation to total self-identity and contribute differentially to self-esteem, which is the resultant of the individual's self-evaluation on scales of "goodness and badness" of his attributes and sub-identities. The accuracy and reality orientation of self-perception and self-evaluation in relation to objective assessment, the nature and relative weighting of sub-identities and total self-identity, and the degree of self-esteem, in relation to the individual's value system (conceived as his more or less enduring motives) are central factors in personality which affect the adjustment of the individual in his social roles and relations.

It is of particular interest that self-concept theorists, such as French and his colleagues (1963), have investigated relationships between self-concept variables, which may be considered at the level of generic attitudes, and organismic variables, such as blood pepsinogen level, a factor in peptic ulcer, which Mott and others (1965) found related to low self-esteem, and rheumatoid arthritis, which Cobb (1966), at the University of Michigan, recently found related to unmet needs for esteem in a sample of wives.

Ego Processes. Loevinger (1966), Rogers (1959), Erikson (1963), Hartmann (1964), and Fairbairn (Wisdom, 1963) are representative ego-process theorists.

In discussing her concept of *ego development*, which she considers related to maturity, Loevinger has argued that to understand ego development one must abandon the psychometrician's idea of development as proceeding in a straight line from more of something to less, or vice versa, and recognize that some of the most conspicuous phenomena turn up as midstages in a sequence, increasing up to a point and then decreasing. An example cited was *conformity* (favorable self-description) which is normal for small children but immature in adult life. For Loevinger, ego development is related to the "increasing capacity for interpersonal relationships" of Sullivan (1953) and Isaacs (1956), the growth in "capacity for moral judgment," as in Piaget (1932) and others, and growth in "conceptual complexity," of Harvey and others (1961). The following table, from her most recent paper (1966) summarizes the stages that she has identified in this "single sequence that is at once the capacity for interpersonal relations, the in-

MILESTONES OF EGO DEVELOPMENT, BASED ON LOEVINGER'S THEORY

Stage	Nature of impulse control and character development	Interpersonal style	Conscious preoccupation
Presocial		Autistic	Self vs. non-self
Symbiotic		Symbiotic	
Impulse-ridden	Impulse-ridden, fear of retaliation	Exploitive, dependent	Bodily feelings, esp. sexual, aggressive
Opportunistic	Expedient, fear of being caught	Exploitive, manipulative	Advantage, control
Conformist	Conformity to external rules, shame	Reciprocal, superficial	Things, appearance, reputation
Conscientious	Internalized rules, guilt	Intensive, responsible	Differentiated inner feelings, achievements, traits
Autonomous	Coping with conflicting inner needs, toleration	Intensive, concern for autonomy	Differentiated inner feelings, achievements, traits, conceptualization, and self-fulfillment
Integrated	Reconciling conflicting needs	Intensive, concern for autonomy, appreciation of individuality	Same as for autonomous level plus identity

creasing moralization of judgment, and increasing conceptual complexity." The similarity to Erikson is noteworthy.

Ego theorists, in common with those addressing the problem in terms of cognitive control systems, below, are deeply concerned, not only with the role of perception and cognition in personality, but also with the broader issues of the total self-regulative system. Approaches vary. Hartmann (1964), Rapaport (1959), and Erikson (1963) based their work on psychoanalytic assumptions. Hartmann conceptualized defenses and integrative controls that are conflict-free, autonomous, and utilize coping resources. Rapaport developed a theory of ego autonomy (1958), and his reformulation of psychoanalytic theory was a major clarification (1959). Erikson's concept of *identity* provides for self-feelings in their social and somatic contextual settings. Loevinger's developmental ego system, portraying development to maturity as a progressive change from impulsiveness and opportunism, through conformity, guilt-ridden conscientiousness, and autonomy, to full individuality and identity, and her ingenious use of the projective sentence-completion method to classify people according to these stages, reflects her broad academic as well as clinical background. Rogers (1963, 1964) has formulated the self concept as a developing matrix of motives which introduce selectivity in behavior in relation to the events, experiences, and situations that become important to the individual. Angyal (1965) recognized trends toward socialization (heteronomy) as well as autonomy in the development of the motive system.

Although the terms and concepts of ego psychology fit more readily into psychoanalytic theory and clinical communication than into the theories propounded by academic, scientific psychologists, the similarity of processes hypothesized is striking, and the prospects for rapprochement are encouraging.

Cognitive Control Conceptions. Without doubt, the cognitive control conceptions are the "new look" in personality theory of the 1960's. Most of the approaches, which differ in terminology and emphasis, can be linked in terms of basic assumptions and organization. The assumptions, sometimes implicit, often explicit, incorporate the self-regulating, "open system" conception favored by the *Zeitgeist*, with inputs, outputs, steady states, and individually differing central control "mechanisms," which "steer" by adaptive feedback. Organization, involving control mechanisms at several levels, is generally believed to be hierarchical, both in developmental aspects and in the dependence of lower on higher levels. Motivation, as expressed by Hunt (1963) and Cofer and Appley (1964), is conceived as implicit in the information-processing functions of the total system rather than as a special drive system.

Like the ego theories, cognitive control theories are essentially functional and conceptualize regulative constancies in terms such as "personal constructs" (Kelly, 1955), "field-articulating tendencies" (Witkin, 1964), and "adaptation level" principles (Helson, 1964; Goldstone & Goldfarb, 1964). Emphasis is on the regulative functions, with only secondary concern for organismic substrata, but the analogy with adaptively programmed "software" in computers is implied.

In Kelly's (1955) personal-construct theory, the basic personality functions are problem solving, learning, and coping with conflict. Behavior is assumed to be anticipatory rather than reactive, and regulation is implied in the selective guidance of anticipatory responses by a system of personal constructs. Witkin's (1964) earlier concept of field dependence and independence as basic modes of cognitive style has been reinterpreted within a longitudinal concept of "differentiation," in which the dichotomous modes are replaced by a number of articulating tendencies involving adaptation in a range of environmental situations. His appealing apparatus has been widely copied and his experimental methods and ideas have enjoyed increasing influence in personality research. Helson has proposed extension of his own adaptation-level theory to personality on the basis that personality is a hierarchical system of equilibrating principles. Goldstone and Goldfarb (1964) have gone further with this approach and formulated a conception of personality integration in terms of Helson's process of "pooling," in which focal stimuli and background in situations, interacting with organismic variables, attain levels of adaptation which regulate responses.

Whether the intense interest in cognitive controls and the extensive research attacking personality in terms of ways of perceiving and cognizing that has gained in popularity in recent years will result in new insights and understanding or turn out to be only a translation of ego concepts into the terminology of the times cannot yet be judged. The extensive range of the movement (see Klein & others, 1967), extending into developmental factors, psychopathology, psychophysiology, attention and consciousness, motivation, genetic and cultural factors, physical characteristics, personality correlates, and still other problem areas, suggests vitality and productivity.

Personality Trait Systems and Theory. A vast difference exists between the a priori personality questionnaire traits of the pre-World War II period and sophisticated personality factor systems of the 1950's and 1960's, illustrated by the work of Guilford (1959), Cattell (1957), and Eysenck (1957). These contemporary trait systems, although differing in technical respects, represent programmatic, multivariate research of major theoretical importance in defining the organization of stable, developed response patterns (common traits) of individuals on reliable measurement scales capable of reflecting variations among individuals, related to age, sex, background, culture, pathology, and other factors. Viewed in relation to other approaches to the conceptualization of significant functional constancies in the regulation of behavior, the multivariate psychologists have combined important skills and research strategies in the development of rating variables, questionnaire items, and objective tests representing well-defined universes of behaviors with large-scale sampling (frequently overlooked in other approaches) and powerful statistical analytic methods made possible by the availability of the new high-speed computers. While factor analysis is a method that has been grossly abused by a generation of publication-bent journeymen, in capable hands and coupled with experimental designs for replication, examination of correlates with external criteria, developmental traces, organismic states, and group differences, it is a powerful tool for achieving order among variables too extensive and complexly interrelated for rational classification. Whereas the other approaches have all tended to become preoccupied with selected strategic variables (e.g., field dependence–independence), the multivariate psychologists are virtually unique in approaching personality and other aspects of individual differences in the broad perspective necessary to grasp the totality of behaviors involved.

Guilford's (1959) encyclopedic mapping of the personality sphere has shown that in the past even the multivariate psychologists have explored only a fraction of the cognitive, motor, sensory, temperament, and attitudinal territory required to account for all of behavior. Guilford has a penchant for rational classification and systematization as well as empirical analysis. He grouped the 15 temperament factors derived from his empirical work into five dimensions—direction of attitude (approach vs. avoidance), responsiveness, activity level, degree of control, and amount of personal involvement—each having expression in three areas of behavior, as attitudes toward things in general, self, and the social environment. Guilford's factors are broad in scope, and since he prefers orthogonal factor structure, no higher-order relations among them exist mathematically, although his schematic organization may be intended for this purpose.

Cattell (1946, 1957; Cattell & others, 1965), whose total design is by far the most extensive and whose gifted and indefatigable efforts have advanced his work to prodigious lengths, has developed personality-factor systems in three media—ratings (life-record data), questionnaire (self-analysis), and objective test. Although his efforts to identify cross-media correspondences have been criticized, matching on some of the factors is undoubtedly encouraging. Since his factor rotation strategy is oblique, he has produced second-order factors, such as introversion-extroversion and neuroticism, from his 21 first-order factors, which are highly stable and correspond with those similarly named of Eysenck. Klein and others (1967) consider the results of higher-order factoring of major theoretical importance, as they lend themselves to conceptions of personality in terms of levels or hierarchies which have the capability of ordering variables from specific behaviors and instrument traits to broad regulatory principles. In this connection, it is of particular interest that Pawlik and Cattell (1964) derived third-order factors from seven second-order factors selected from three studies, which were interpreted as corresponding closely to the *id, ego,* and *superego* in Freudian terms.

Eysenck's factor-analytic work has produced only three factors—introversion–extroversion, neuroticism, and psychoticism. The first two correspond to second-order factors in Cattell's system as noted above. His most recent work has moved in the direction of developing and testing causal theories to link observations based on measures of his traits with responses at lower levels. For instance, he considers neuroticism as related to the lability or excitability of the autonomic nervous system and introversion–extroversion as related to the balance between cortical excitation–inhibition. His theories have generated extensive work and many confirmatory as well as contradictory findings. However, he, like Cattell, has tended to use contradictory results as a basis for clarification.

Although correspondences among higher-order traits exist, it is extremely difficult to compare the trait maps of different investigators, for example Guilford and Cattell, at the level of primary traits. Despite the tremendous amount of effort in this area, it appears that much further taxonomic research on personality trait structure is needed.

CURRENT RESEARCH AND ISSUES. The range and volume of significant contemporary research related to personality is too extensive to summarize in this condensed review. This section is restricted to the reporting of selected developments in a few areas. The extensive area of personality measurement, the somewhat disappointing experience with personality measures in prediction of academic performance and other criteria, the literature on manifest anxiety and on achievement motivation, all of which are currently popular, could not be included.

Peer Acceptance–Rejection as a Strategic Variable. A recently completed programmatic study directed by Sells and Roff (1966) investigated peer acceptance–rejection during the early school years as a strategic variable in personality development. Previously, Roff (1960, 1961) had demonstrated that peer rejection in this age range was a strong predictor of young-adult maladjustment. Beginning in 1962, Sells and Roff administered peer-choice questionnaires and obtained teacher ratings of peer status for 38,000 boys and girls in grades 3 through 6 in 19 north Texas school districts and two metropolitan Minnesota cities. The samples in five of the Texas districts and one of the Minnesota cities were reexamined annually for four years. The peer scores, in agreement with Roff's earlier findings, predicted early delinquency and early school dropout significantly.

In a series of studies of correlates of peer acceptance–rejection, family background and variables associated with family status, such as intelligence and socioeconomic level, were strongly related. Almost every index of family pathology in the areas of education, health, family tension, welfare status, delinquency, and crime was associated with low peer status of the child. In one critical study Cox (1966), using a sample of 100 families in one school district, further demonstrated the direct and indirect effects of parental education level, family income, family tension, parental child-rearing attitudes of loving versus rejecting and casual versus demanding, the child's health, self concept, and personality-trait patterns on peer acceptance–rejection. The effects of inheritance and early experience on personality development were explicated in terms of significant developmental processes. Sells and Roff concluded that peer status is not a reflection of the unique attractiveness of an individual, qua individual, but rather the lawful effect of measurable social influences in the developmental background of the child.

Primary Reaction Characteristics. An important study of organismic factors in development was the work of Birch and others (1962), who identified nine "primary reaction characteristics of children in the first two years of life." The importance of these lies in their significance in the developmental study of personality. They include *activity level, rhythmicity of functions, approach or withdrawal, adaptability, intensity of reaction, threshold of responsiveness, quality of mood, distractibility, attention span,* and *persistence.* Although some of them may be situationally modified by experience, even in infancy, these do appear to constitute a distinctive set of organismic variables dependent mainly on inner conditions of arousal and independent of situational specificity. Longitudinal studies observing the sequential incorporation of such characteristics into progressively more complex schemata are a potential source of extremely valuable information.

Cognitive Functions. Research, variously described under the terms "cognitive control" and "cognitive style," has appeared on such diverse topics as the behavioral and personality correlates of cognitive style, correlates of factor-analyzed measures of cognitive control, and the relation of various measures of cognitive control to development, psychopathology, physiological factors, attention and consciousness, motivation, genetic factors, culture, physique, and still others.

The increased popularity of Witkin's approach has been accompanied by simplified methods of testing field *dependence–independence,* such as individual and group forms of embedded-figures tests (Goodenough & Eagle, 1963; Jackson & others, 1964). Literature reviewed by Klein and others (1967) has shown that field-dependent subjects perform a number of cognitive and perceptual tasks more poorly than field-independent subjects, particularly under conditions of disapproval and when the stimuli are not socially relevant. The degree of physiological arousal, presumed to be an indicator of anxiety, has also been correlated with field dependence.

Another popular area involves *proneness to interference,* which has also been referred to as constricted versus flexible control and strong versus weak automatization. The most popular measure of individual differences on this dimension is the Stroop color-word test (Gardner & others, 1959). Interference proneness has been related to underachievement among teenagers, to lower occupational level, and to late maturing among male students. Jensen and Rohmer (1966) have cited over 60 studies using various procedures with the Stroop test, but standardization of forms and scoring formulas is needed to permit broader generalization of results.

Still another cognitive variable that has received much attention, variously called *conceptual differentiation, categorizing behavior,* and *cognitive complexity,* has been applied to styles of judgment of social and impersonal stimuli. Factored analytically, it is represented by object-sorting and behavior-sorting tests (Gardner & others, 1959). Another popular measure, also related to field dependence–independence, is Pettigrew's (1958) Category Width Scale. Category width has been found to be stable across a range of situations but appears dependent on the degree of personal involvement; the greater the personal involvement, the broader the categories used in judgment. High complexity, which corresponds to narrow band width in judgment, tends to be associated with greater certainty in judgments of incongruent, as compared with congruent, information, while the reverse pattern was found in subjects exhibiting low complexity (Bieri & others, 1966). Consistent individual differences have been found in extensiveness of *visual scanning* on size-estimation tasks.

Response Styles, Response Set, and Response Bias. The tendency to answer personality inventory questions according to cues from the situation, such as "to make a good impression," or according to some personal style of responding, such as a tendency to favor positively oriented questions ("tendency to agree"), rather than in response to the content and apparent intent of the question, has been the subject of extensive study and controversy about the interpretation of scales and factors derived from self-analysis questionnaires and inventories. The terms "social desirability" and "acquiescence" are commonly used to describe the two response sets mentioned above. Some authors of inventories have attempted to measure such factors and adjust scores for them; others have tried to eliminate them in test design; some have ignored them. Some have claimed that popular personality tests are so permeated with response bias that their substantive scales are worthless, while opponents have reported "evidence" contradicting the assertion. Finally, some authors have regarded them as meaningful personality variables and investigated their correlates. The literature in this area is extensive, and resolution of the issues is still in the future, as shown in reviews by Damarin and Messick (1965) and Messick (1966).

There is as yet inadequate specification of the processes underlying the various response sets and biases studied and the behavioral correlates hypothesized for them. The reviews suggest that ability and temperament, and possibly other factors, are involved in acquiescence, and that biases both in self-appraisal and in reporting, in relation to situational pressures, are involved in social desirability. Further research will undoubtedly explore these indications.

Research on personality appears to be at a peak of activity, with a number of interesting developments summarized in this presentation. It would appear that more convergence can be inferred by comparing the various conceptual formulations than would appear superficially in view of the diversity of terms, methods, and approaches reported. The increasing attention to cognitive structures as central functions in regulation of behavior is consistent with new conceptions of personality and motivation as inherent in the information-processing functions of the organism; it also reflects the computer influence of the *Zeitgeist*. Cognitive controls are compatible with self and ego theory and also with the more sophisticated multivariate-trait representations that have been developed. Since all of these depend on interactional transactions between individual and environment, it is probably not too optimistic to expect that a major new development, recommended by Barker (1965), Sells (1966), and others, will be programmatic efforts to dimensionalize the description of the environment. This is essential to enable personality research to realize its next major stride.

S. B. Sells
Texas Christian University

References

Allport, G. W. "Mental Health: A Generic Attitude." *J Relig Health* 4:7–21; 1964.

Angyal, A. *Neurosis and Treatment: A Holistic Theory*. Wiley, 1965. 328p.

Barker, R. G. "Explorations in Ecological Psychology." *Am Psychol* 20:1–14; 1965.

Bieri, J., and others. *Clinical and Social Judgment: The Discrimination of Behavioral Information*. Wiley, 1966. 271p.

Birch, H. G., and others. "Individuality in the Development of Children." *Develop Med Child Neurology* 4:370–9; 1962.

Blum, G. S. "Programming People to Simulate Machines." In Tomkins, S. S., and Messick, S. (Eds.) *Computer Simulation of Personality*. Wiley, 1963. p. 127–57.

Borko, Harold. (Ed.) *Computer Applications in the Behavioral Sciences*. Prentice-Hall, 1962. 633p.

Brownfain, J. J. "Stability of the Self-concept as a Dimension of Personality." *J Abn Social Psychol* 47:597–606; 1952.

Cattell, Raymond B. *Description and Measurement of Personality*. Harcourt, 1946. 602p.

Cattell, Raymond B. *Personality and Motivation Structure and Measurement*. Harcourt, 1957. 948p.

Cattell, Raymond B., and others. *Personality Factors in Objective Test Devices*. Knapp, 1965. 541p.

Child, Irvin L. "Problems of Personality and Some Relations to Anthropology and Sociology." In Koch, Sigmund. (Ed.) *Psychology: A Study of a Science*. Vol. 5. McGraw-Hill, 1963. p. 488–592.

Cobb, Stanley. Personal communication from U Michigan, 1966.

Cofer, C. U., and Appley, M. H. *Motivation: Theory and Research*. Wiley, 1964. 957p.

Colby, Kenneth Mark. "Computer Simulation of a Neurotic Process." In Tomkins, S. S., and Messick, S. (Eds.) *Computer Simulation of Personality*. Wiley, 1963. p. 165–80.

Cox, Samuel H. "Family Background Effects on Personality Development and Social Acceptance." Doctoral dissertation. Cooperative Research Contract No. OE 2-10-051, USOE, 1966. 239p.

Damarin, F., and Messick, S. *Response Styles as Personality Variables: A Theoretical Integration of Multivariate Research.* ETS, 1965.

Diamond, Solomon, and others. *Inhibition and Choice.* Harper, 1963. 456p.

Erikson, E. H. *Childhood and Society,* rev. ed. Norton, 1963. 445p.

Escalona, S. K. "Some Determinants of Individual Differences." *Trans New York Acad Sci* 27:802–16; 1965.

Eysenck, H. J. *The Dynamics of Anxiety and Hysteria.* Routledge, 1957. 311p.

Eysenck, H. J. "Biological Basis of Personality." *Nature* 199:1031–4; 1963.

Feigenbaum, Edward A., and Feldman, Julian. (Eds.) *Computers and Thought.* McGraw-Hill, 1963. 535p.

French, John R. P., and Sherwood, J. "Self-actualization and Self-identity Theory." In French, John R. P. (Ed.) *Self-actualization and the Utilization of Talent.* Cooperative Research Project No. E-006, U Michigan, 1963.

Freud, Sigmund. *An Outline of Psychoanalysis.* Norton, 1949. 124p.

Gardner, R. W., and others. "Cognitive Control: A Study of Individual Consistencies in Cognitive Behavior." *Psychol Issues* 4:1959.

Goldstone, S., and Goldfarb, J. L. "Adaptation Level, Personality Theory, and Psychopathology." *Psychol B* 61:176–87; 1964.

Goodenough, D. R., and Eagle, C. J. "A Modification of the Embedded-figures Test for Use with Young Children." *J Genet Psychol* 103:67–74; 1963.

Green, Bert F., Jr. *Digital Computers in Research.* McGraw-Hill, 1963. 333p.

Guilford, J. P. *Personality.* McGraw-Hill, 1959. 562p.

Hartmann, H. *Essays on Ego Psychology.* Int U, 1964. 492p.

Harvey, O. J., and others. *Conceptual Systems and Personality Organization.* Wiley, 1961. 375p.

Hebb, D. O. *The Organization of Behavior.* Wiley, 1949. 335p.

Hebb, Donald O. "A Neurophysiological Theory." In Koch, S. (Ed.) *Psychology, A Study of a Science. Vol. 1, Sensory, Perceptual, and Physiological Foundations.* McGraw-Hill, 1959. p. 622–43.

Helson, H. *Adaptation-level Theory: An Experimental and Systematic Approach to Behavior.* Harper, 1964. 732p.

Hunt, J. McV. *Intelligence and Experience.* Ronald, 1961. 416p.

Hunt, J. McV. "Motivation Inherent in Information Processing and Action." In Harvey, O. J. (Ed.) *Motivation and Social Interaction.* Ronald, 1963. p. 35–94.

Isaacs, K. S. "Relatability: A Proposed Construct and an Approach to its Validation." Doctoral dissertation. U Chicago, 1956.

Jackson, D. N., and others. "Evaluation of Group and Individual Forms of Embedded-figures Measures of Field-independence." *Ed Psychol Meas* 24:177–92; 1964.

James, William. *The Principles of Psychology.* 2 vols. Holt, 1890.

James, William. *The Varieties of Religious Experience.* McKay, 1902. 534p.

Jensen, A. R., and Rohmer, W. D., Jr. "The Stroop Color-Word Test; A Review." *Acta Psychol* 25:36–93; 1966.

Johnson, E. S. "The Simulation of Human Problem Solving from an Empirically Derived Model." Doctoral dissertation. U North Carolina, 1961.

Jones, Lyle V. "Beyond Babbage." *Psychometrika* 28:315–32; 1963.

Kelly, G. A. *The Psychology of Personal Constructs.* Norton, 1955. 1218p.

Klein, George S., and others. "Personality." In Farnsworth, Paul R., and others. (Eds.) *Annual Review of Psychology,* Vol. 18, 1967. p. 467–542.

Koffka, K. *Principles of Gestalt Psychology.* Harcourt, 1935. 395p.

Lacey, J., and Lacey, B. "The Relationship of Resting Autonomic Activity to Motor Impulsivity." In Williams and Wilkins. (Eds.) *The Brain and Human Behavior* 36: Proceedings Association for Research in Nervous and Mental Disease, 1958. p. 144–209.

Loehlin, John C. "A Computer Program That Simulates Personality." In Tomkins, Silvan S., and Messick, Samuel. (Eds.) *Computer Simulation of Personality.* Wiley, 1963. p. 165–80.

Loevinger, Jane. "Measurement in Clinical Research." In Wolman, B. B. (Ed.) *Handbook of Clinical Psychology.* McGraw-Hill, 1965. p. 78–94.

Loevinger, Jane. "The Meaning and Measurement of Ego Development. *Am Psychologist* 21:195–206; 1966.

Maier, Henry W. *Three Theories of Child Development.* Harper, 1965. 314p.

McDougall, William. *The Energies of Men.* Scribner, 1933. 395p.

Messick, Samuel. "Computer Models and Personality Theory." In Tomkins, S. S., and Messick, S. (Eds.) *Computer Simulation of Personality.* Wiley, 1963. p. 305–17.

Messick, S. *The Psychology of Acquiescence: An Interpretation of Research Evidence.* ETS, 1966.

Miller, D. R. "The Study of Social Relationships: Situation, Identity, and Social Interaction." In Koch, S. (Ed.) *Psychology: A Study of a Science.* Vol. 5. McGraw-Hill, 1963. p. 639–737.

Miller, D. R., and others. *Plans and the Structure of Behavior.* Holt, 1960. 226p.

Mott, P. E., and others. *Shiftwork: The Social, Psychological and Physical Consequences.* U Michigan, 1965. 351p.

Murphy, Gardner. *Personality.* Harper, 1947. 999p.

Murphy, Gardner. "Psychological Views of Personality and Contributions to Its Study." Paper presented at symposium, Rice U, 1966. 20p.

Newell, A., and others. "Report on a General Problem-solving Program." In *Proceedings International Conference Information Processing.* UNESCO, 1960. p. 256–64.

Pawlik, K., and Cattell, R. B. "Third-order Factors in Objective Personality Tests." *Br J Psychol* 55:1–18; 1964.

Pettigrew, T. F. "The Measurement and Correlates

of Category Width as a Cognitive Variable." *J Pers* 26:532–44; 1958.

Piaget, Jean. *The Moral Judgment of the Child.* Free, 1932. 418p.

Piaget, J., and Inhelder, B. *The Growth of Logical Thinking from Childhood to Adolescence.* Basic Books, 1958. 356p.

Piaget, Jean, and others. *The Child's Conception of Geometry.* Basic Books, 1960. 411p.

Pribram, Karl H. "A Review of Theory in Physiological Psychology." *Annual Review Psychology* 11, 1960. p. 1–40.

Rapaport, D. "The Theory of Ego Autonomy: A Generalization." *B Menninger Clinic* 22:13–35; 1958.

Rapaport, D. "The Structure of Psychoanalytic Theory: A Systematizing Attempt." In Koch, S. (Ed.) *Psychology: A Study of a Science.* Vol. 3. McGraw-Hill, 1959. p. 55–183.

Reitman, Walter R. "Personality as a Problem Solving Coalition." In Tomkins, S. S., and Messick, Samuel. *Computer Simulation of Personality.* Wiley, 1963. p. 69–100.

Reitman, Walter R. *Cognition and Thought.* Wiley, 1965. 312p.

Roff, Merrill. "Relations Between Certain Preservice Factors and Psychoneurosis During Military Duty." *Armed Forces Med J* 11:152–60; 1960.

Roff, Merrill. "Childhood Social Interactions and Young Adult Bad Conduct." *J Abn Social Psychol* 63:33–337; 1961.

Rogers, Carl R. "A Theory of Therapy, Personality, and Interpersonal Relationships, As Developed in the Client-centered Framework." In Koch, S. (Ed.) *Psychology, A Study of a Science.* Vol. 3, *Formulations of the Person and the Social Context.* McGraw-Hill, 1959. p. 184–256.

Rogers, C. R. "The Actualizing Tendency in Relation to 'Motives' and to Consciousness." In Jones, M. F. (Ed.) *Nebraska Symposium on Motivation.* U Nebraska, 1963. p. 1–24.

Rogers, C. R. "Toward a Science of the Person." In Wann, T. W. (Ed.) *Behaviorism and Phenomenology.* U Chicago, 1964. p. 109–40.

Sanford, N. "Personality: Its Place in Psychology." In Koch, S. (Ed.) *Psychology: A Study of a Science.* Vol. 5. McGraw-Hill, 1963. p. 488–592.

Saunders, D. R. "How to Tell Computers from People." *Ed Psychol Meas* 21:159–83; 1961.

Scott, J. P. "Critical Periods in Behavioral Development." *Sci* 138:949–57; 1962.

Sears, R. R. "Social Behavior and Personality Development." In Parsons, T., and Shils, E. A. (Eds.) *Toward a General Theory of Action.* Harvard U, 1951. p. 465–78.

Sears, R. R. "Identification as a Form of Behavior Development." In Harris, D. B. (Ed.) *The Concept of Development.* U Minnesota, 1957. p. 149–61.

Sells, S. B. "Ecology and the Science of Psychology." *Multivariate Behavioral Res* 1:131–44; 1966.

Sells, S. B., and Roff, Merrill. *Peer Acceptance-Rejection and Personality Development.* Cooperative Research Contract No. OE 2-10-05, USOE, 1966. 466p.

Simon, Herbert A. *Models of Man.* Wiley, 1957. 287p.

Sullivan, Harry Stack. *The Interpersonal Theory of Psychiatry.* Norton, 1953. 393p.

Tomkins, Silvan S., and Messick, Samuel. (Eds.) *Computer Simulation of Personality.* Wiley, 1963. 325p.

Wisdom, J. O. "Fairbairn's Contribution on Object Relationship, Splitting and Ego Structure." *Br J Med Psychol* 36:145–59; 1963.

Witkin, Herman A. "Origins of Cognitive Style." In Scheerer, C. (Ed.) *Cognition: Theory, Research, Promise.* Harper, 1964. p. 172–205.

Witkin, Herman A., and others. *Psychological Differentiation.* Wiley, 1962. 418p.

Wylie, Ruth C. *The Self Concept.* U Nebraska, 1961. 370p.

PHILOSOPHY OF EDUCATION

The structure of knowledge in a field of study may be characterized by its telling questions, its reliable and relevant methods, its key concepts, its substantive generalizations, and its values. We also need to know, in some fundamentally characteristic sense, what phenomena the field deals with, the occasions which give rise to the quest for knowledge, and the portion of human experience which is thereby illuminated by the knowledge produced by the field.

All philosophy is a philosophy of something (Ducasse, 1956). Logic is the philosophy of inference; ethics is the philosophy of guided choice and conduct; metaphysics is the philosophy of reality. Each branch of general philosophy has a characteristic set of questions and a domain within which answers are sought. General philosophy is only a name for all the many activities, and as a name it covers philosophy of education as well.

Inquiry in general philosophy arises when men reflect upon their experiences. Philosophy of education arises when men reflect upon the meanings and choices involved in understanding and controlling the educative experience. An educative experience may mean the activity of educating (teaching, schooling); the process of being educated (learning); or the outcome, intended or actual, of the two (Frankena, 1965). Man philosophizing looks for the meaning of some aspect of human experience as educative in order to make a choice, commit himself to action, and assess the consequences. All and any of these are legitimately occasions for educational philosophy.

A double-decker effect exists in both philosophy and philosophy of education (Hirst, 1963). Those studies which seek to describe and explain the nature of things, such as the various sciences and the humanities, may be said to be first-order (lower-deck) subjects. Philosophy can be said to be a second-order subject in that it seeks to describe and explain the way the first-order subjects work. The lower-deck concerns help us to understand ourselves and the world directly, while the upper-deck concerns help us to understand what goes on below. Philosophy of education should help us to understand the nature of knowledge, reality, value, and the nature of that personal educative experience which leads one to draw upon knowledge and value in leading one's life (Kaufman, 1966).

A sense of approach to this field of study is found in three of its telling questions. First, what philosophical concepts are embedded in actual statements of educational policy and practice? For example, what philosophical idea of freedom is found in the various statements of academic freedom? Second, how do differently defined philosophical concepts affect educational policies and practices? For example, the various philosophical conceptions of the nature of mind (Ryle, 1960) (as an immaterial substance or as a quality of behavior) may largely determine educational aims (training the mind) (Brauner & Burns, 1965) and procedures (testing for intelligence). In these two telling questions we are essentially beating a path back and forth between statements in philosophy and statements in education, simply starting from different points to reach the common ground.

A third telling question is this: What do we do when faced by the fact that education is a matter about which reasonable people disagree? What guidance does philosophy of education give? Philosophers recommend that the disagreement be clarified, that the range of possible choices be presented, and that the consequences of commitment to one or another course of action be anticipated. They also endorse a liberal intellectual outlook which inclines one toward being open-minded, receptive, and inquiring in matters of human dispute (Brown, 1966). Valuing the continual search for meaning and truth often means criticizing customs and conventions, making independent judgments, reconstructing beliefs no longer tenable, and avoiding the pressing demand for useful answers to all problems investigated. Formulating a telling question may be more illuminating than finding an expedient solution to a problem. To become open and honest about educational commitments is one thing; to do this well is also to know that other reasonable people will disagree. Philosophy of education helps by giving information about alternative defensible positions and competing frameworks of thought (Dupuis & Nordberg, 1964). The best arguments may not solve some educational problems. Perhaps there are no compelling solutions, and one reaches a point in philosophy where wisdom demands no more (Broudy, 1954).

We can identify two different impulses toward philosophizing in education. In one case we ask questions of this sort: What educational ideal is right? What education leads to the good life? What are the basic principles of right action which shape dispositions, intellectual and emotional? Is education itself one of the common rights and responsibilities of man? These questions are of the order: "What things are good?"

In the second impulse toward educational philosophizing we find questions of this sort: "What does 'good education' mean?" "What is an operational definition of 'mind'?" "On what reasonable grounds can we ask children to be responsible for their acts?" "What are the value claims, both instrumental and intrinsic, in the statement that education leads to the good life?" These first- and second-order questions, like the lower and upper decks, are related in important ways. That there is a basic philosophic difference between asking "What things are good?" and "What does 'good' mean?" does not entail necessary irrelevance of the one to the other (Aiken, 1962). Those critics (Hook, 1963) who claim that the problems of education are not being studied when only the language of education is being analyzed fail to accept the legitimate difference between these two modes of philosophizing. Problems of education are both more and less than philosophical: more, in that facts, customary practices, and relevant social sciences are included; less, in that much of philosophy is not relevant directly to these problems. What many people want, and what is often given, in a philosophy of education is an educational theory which guides practices in this lower-deck sense (Morris, 1961; Wingo, 1965; Thayer & Levit, 1966). To provide intelligent criticism of educational theories is to do the work of philosophy at the upper-deck level (Edel, 1956; Hardie, 1962).

METHODS. Research methods in philosophy of education are primarily conceptual, with ties to empirical methods of history and social science. These other fields, using different methods, contribute to the philosopher material he would not develop by his own methods, just as he contributes to other fields material worked out through his methods. In a manner of speaking, these other fields filter common experience and present the philosopher with refined experience which he further refines using his methods of work. He criticizes and clarifies the assumptions, research designs, problems, concepts of the sciences, returning to them useful refinements.

Historians foster philosophizing in at least three ways. Some study individual philosophers and seek to extract their ideas about education (McCaul, 1959; Dunkel, 1965; Frankena, 1965; Price, 1962; Brumbaugh & Lawrence, 1963). Others study educational ideas and practices as they exist across time in patterns revealing problems of interest to the philosopher (Brubacher, 1947; Brauner, 1964; Cremin, 1961; Callahan, 1962; Broudy & Palmer, 1965; Beck, 1965; Price, 1967; Edwards & Richey, 1963). Finally, as historians generalize about past events and ideas, they may generate new frameworks of thought, new conceptions through which issues in education may be better understood (Greene, 1965; Bailyn, 1960).

Because the data and methods of history expose issues which interest philosophers, these two fields have great affinity for each other. Philosophy fostered by scholarship in history is often based on the assumption that educational answers from an earlier time remain relevant. As a result of this affinity and this assumption, a large part of what is designated philosophy of education is in fact history. Neither philosophers nor historians seeking insight into education agree on the boundaries between the two disciplines.

Social sciences such as economics, psychology (McClellan, 1967), anthropology, and sociology stimulate philosophizing also. Some writers take the data, concepts and generalizations of a field and, using philosophical methods and concepts, develop meanings for education (Kneller, 1965; Brameld, 1965). Others in the course of their scientific work on education pause to philosophize over difficulties encountered (Bruner, 1962; Cronbach & Meehl, 1955). A third approach, small but rapidly growing, is the philosophy of educational research which analyzes and extends the concepts of science, such as operational definitions (Ennis, 1964), beyond their immediate scientific uses (Smith, 1938; Thomas, 1942). What scientists do in inquiry has been analyzed into a conceptual framework interesting to both scientists and philosophers (Schwab, 1960).

Several special problems beset this area. Since human values saturate educational phenomena, educational research should be framed in terms not systematically excluding these values (Kaplan, 1964). Further, the work of philosophy of science is not directly transferable to educational research for much the same reason (Gowin, 1963). Finally, it is important to note the assumption of many that social science alone can comprehend educational phenomena.

Several distinctively philosophical methods deserve attention (Passmore, 1961). The purpose of the method known as concept analysis is to clarify the meaning of an important concept, such as "teaching," so that good reasons can be given for stipulating the choice of one meaning over others examined (Green, 1964). Of two major moves the first is to isolate the conceptual questions and distinguish them from facts, values, and moral opinion. The second move is to supply the context. There are several ways to do this. Among the more promising is the search for the paradigm-case (Donnellan, 1967): Look for two or three clear instances of, say, teaching, and discover what is common among the instances. If one is unable to find a clear case of the concept in question, then it is possible that either the concept is faulty or the person using it does not have a sufficient understanding of the educational phenomena to which the concept refers. After a clear case is detailed, then one can search for contrary cases, counter-examples. Again, if no counter-examples are forthcoming, then what is being proposed may not be a real instance of anything. One counter-example falsifies any universal statement. The creation of imaginative cases, invented cases, supposititious cases, counter-factual instances are all ways of etching the boundaries of the concept under analysis and, by contrast, clarifying it.

Another useful technique for clarifying a concept is to ask how one would teach the meaning of the concept. If one is clear enough about what one would do in teaching another person, then one is clear enough about the meanings of the concept. For highly abstract philosophical concepts, such as probability, inference, and presupposition, this seemingly simple procedure is both difficult and useful.

Concept analysis is *per se* a way of teaching. One can teach student teachers how to analyze concepts and they in turn can teach the same thing to their pupils. This is an example where there is no problem of the relation of philosophy to educational practice. Another example of this point is the pedagogical criterion for a good definition as one both intelligible and effective in teaching its recipient the particular use intended (Black, 1952).

Language, according to many modern analysts, is always both misleading and illuminating. Thus, one way to begin analysis of the language of education is to discern in what ways the language is misleading and in what ways illuminating. The language of educational discourse often has an elastic quality, and the stretching of meanings (education is life, life is education) to cover every phenomenon can be disturbing. But it is also important to note (Wittgenstein, 1953) that one can get over a severe case of mental cramps by stretching language until it seems to break. The analysis of metaphors in which educational statements are presented is a creative way of seeing what is similar in widely dissimilar phenomena. Root metaphors, such as the organic, mechanistic, or cybernetic metaphors, may actually serve in education as preliminary organizations of intentions. The growth metaphor recommends itself insofar as a child may be considered a biological organism bound to develop through successive stages with development lush or sparse depending on outside nutrients. But this growth metaphor breaks down as soon as a cultural-social context is brought into the biological context. The growth metaphor implies one natural path of growth. Alternative paths are, however, possible. To what ends are the successive stages of the child's growth to be directed? If the child develops fully in any one area he is restricting his chances to develop in other areas: all the potentialities of every child cannot possibly be developed; choices must be made; to develop some aspects is to thwart others.

Every metaphor breaks down at some point, and the simple logical extension of similarities and differences helps to expose the breaking points. A metaphor, like all language, is a way of organizing experience. A metaphor that is apt and appealing in one context may be misleading in another, because distinctions essential to understanding in the new context may be the very ones blurred in the old context. Since education is a meeting ground for a variety of contexts, the fallacy of the misplaced context is common.

A method of philosophical study successfully used by John Dewey is the dialectic method. On any given issue look for opposing views, especially those views which seem to give rise to continued debate. The presumption is that both sides are making a common error which refuels the debate, since neither side can see it clearly enough to propose a genuine solution. Slogan analysis and formulation have produced some interesting studies (Scheffler, 1960). It is possible to think of philosophies of education as slogan systems (Komisar & McClellan, 1961). Since ideologies control more human behavior than sheer, clear rationality, so the argument goes, one need only invent appealing slogans to change educational practices.

A useful method for educational philosophy is theory construction (Maccia & Maccia, 1966). One may approach a field, such as vocational education, directly and, after identifying the relevant variables, propose a theory which relates the variables coherently. Sometimes it seems to help to approach this task indirectly through models. The method here is to analyze the structure of a theory in another field, to abstract it into a model composed of relations between various concepts, and then to carry the composed model over into educational discourse to see to what extent the concepts of education can be similarly ordered. In finding similarities in areas formerly thought diverse, model-making is like an extended analysis of metaphor.

It is often thought that philosophy is not as objective as empirical research. But if objectivity means what other persons can corroborate, then objectivity can result from philosophic discourse. Careful study of the many theses, rebuttals and rejoinders which appear in philosophical journals (*Studies in Philosophy and Education*, 1960 to present) substantiates the value of this intellectual means for obtaining objectivity.

KEY CONCEPTS. Most of the key concepts in philosophy of education are organized into three large categories: epistemology, axiology, and metaphysics. Epistemology, or the theory of knowledge, brings together concepts of definition, meaning, truth, logical validity of arguments (Kneller, 1966), and explanation. In discussing theories of knowledge (Scheffler, 1965) it is important to realize that modern philosophy has relinquished to modern science the task and role of telling us about matters of fact about the world, and assumes for itself problems of meaning.

Axiology, or the theory of value, brings together concepts of the content of values (desires, wants, interests), kinds of value (moral, intrinsic, instrumental, aesthetic, consummatory, utilitarian), the various intellectual standards for making value judgments between objects of value (degree of liking, conclusions of pure reason), and the various justifications for the intellectual standards themselves (the authority of radical subjectivity, custom, carefully criticized human experience). A major philosophical divide exists between those who argue that values and value judgments are founded on conditions within human experience (Dewey, 1916) and those who argue for highest ideals as somehow transcending human experience (Maritain, 1943).

Metaphysics, or the theory of reality, brings together concepts of the basic nature of the universe (as hostile, friendly, or neutral to man), freedom, chance, determinism (the regularity of nature, including human nature). Opinion is divided on the import of metaphysics. Some hold that metaphysics is an elephantine graveyard where old philosophies go to die. Others hold that all philosophies pose metaphysical problems because these are the problems that remain unsolved within any approach.

What are named here as key concepts of philosophy of education are actually a whole complex cluster of related ideas, each one requiring a large amount of detail and study. When these concepts are carefully tied together into philosophical arguments, something approaching substantive generalizations occurs.

GENERALIZATIONS. In epistemology there are questions of direct concern to the educational philosopher. What is the status of the object of knowledge? Is it a construct of methods of inquiry or is it somehow a real existent we only come to know through inquiry? What distinction is there between the percept of sense experience and the concept of intellectual cognition? Concepts present abstractions and meanings in a form that condenses the flux of immediate experience. These concepts might be more efficient in the processes of educating than random encounters with sense percepts.

Since science using scientific methods is often held to be the chief source of the best knowledge—that which we would have teachers teach—many topics in philosophy of science have relevance to philosophy of education. Of primary relevance is the claim that all of the special sciences actually hold in common a number of concepts, such as explanation, causality, definition, confirmation of a law, proof, probability, truth. When these concepts are analyzed philosophically (regardless of the special feature of the objects of knowledge in the various sciences), then the student has a powerful tool for integrating his knowledge (Pap, 1949, 1956). The so-called explosion of scientific knowledge need not seem to be so awesomely scattering in its effects if the small set of organizing concepts are seen as basically similar. Whether this claim is actually true is a problem for the philosopher of education, as is the fact that philosophers of science remain in disagreement about these concepts.

The structure of subject matter knowledge produces at least three problems deriving from the primary epistemological problem of the relation of knowledge to experience (Schwab, 1964; Ford & Pugno, 1964; Phenix, 1964). The substantive structure of a discipline consists in the related conceptions guiding the discovery, creation, and organization of knowledge. The syntactical structure of knowledge has to do with the pathway of inquiry, i.e., the orderly arrangement of moves from raw data to verification and interpretation. The curricular problem is to determine the significantly different disciplines and to identify their relations to each other. If the inquiries of different disciplines differ in context, form of problem, evidence, inference and interpretation, then the truths of subject matter knowledge also differ, an observation of great importance for educational practices.

In value theory, one of the important generalizations concerns the relation between fixed ends for education and indoctrination (Flew, 1966). When educational ends are thought of as fixed and final, and justifiably achieved by any means, then the charge of indoctrination is relevant. The military ends of Spartan education, the prescriptions of piety, and the racial superiority doctrine of the Nazis are educational ends which, under some circumstances, are achieved all too well. Criticism of fixed ends seems, however, to propound its own paradox: any end that replaces one of the objectionable ends will itself in turn become a fixed end. Critics of fixed ends seem to be forced to advocate no fixed end, hence aimlessness. The resultant baleful conclusion is that education must inevitably beget inefficiency, drift, and incoherence as the price to pay to avoid rigidity, narrow direction, and authoritarianism.

The philosophic question of the relation of the individual to the established order appears in instruction. Individual initiative and choice are pitted against the accumulated body of organized knowledge which forms the subject matter of teaching (Dewey, 1913). Granted that the teacher knows his material, does the pupil have any choice of material? If he has no choice, the charge of indoctrination may be made. If the individual cannot use his own initiative in pursuing his studies, then the charge of authoritarianism, lack of freedom, and lack of respect for the individual is possible. The doctrines of freedom of mind, intellectual honesty, experimental testing and proof of ideas, and tolerance in the face of ambiguities are values difficult to object to. For he who opposes such indoctrination will himself exemplify it (Perry, 1954). The influence of the teacher and his subject matter over the immature and unformed pupil is enormous, and improper influence should be restricted by the canons of scholarship and inquiry and not by ends external to the process of education.

Education, inevitably, involves deliberate influence. One must interfere with people to educate them. The moral and scientific dimensions of this fact are exceptionally important. Interference with the life of another person calls into play considerations of morality—of freedom, of equality, of choice, of respect for the individual, of authority (Peters, 1966a, 1966b). Successfully to influence another person involves considerations of science—of causality, of determinism, of uniform and universal consequences or effects. Both ethics and science are relevant to education, and they may conflict, thus providing an occasion for educational philosophizing. This fact of deliberate influence and these considerations of ethics and science create the context generating different major philosophies of education (National Society for the Study of Education, 1942, 1955).

D. B. Gowin
Cornell University

References

Aiken, H. D. *Reason and Conduct.* Knopf, 1962. 375p.

Bailyn, Bernard. *Education in the Forming of American Society.* Random, 1960. 147p.

Beck, Robert. *A Social History of Education.* Prentice-Hall, 1965. 149p.

Black, Max. *Critical Thinking,* 2nd ed. Prentice-Hall, 1952. 459p.

Brameld, Theodore. *The Use of Explosive Ideas in Education.* U Pittsburgh Press, 1965. 248p.

Brauner, Charles J. *American Educational Theory.* Prentice-Hall, 1964. 341p.

Brauner, Charles J., and Burns, Hobert W. *Problems in Education and Philosophy.* Prentice-Hall, 1965. 165p.

Broudy, Harry S. *Building a Philosophy of Education.* Prentice-Hall, 1954. 480p.

Broudy, Harry S., and Palmer, John R. *Exemplars of Teaching Method.* Rand McNally, 1965. 172p.

Brown, L. M. *General Philosophy in Education.* McGraw-Hill, 1966. 244p.

Brubacher, John S. *A History of the Problems of Education.* McGraw-Hill, 1947. 688p.

Brumbaugh, R. S., and Lawrence, Nathaniel M. *Philosophers on Education.* Houghton, 1963. 211p.

Bruner, Jerome. *On Knowing.* Harvard U Press, 1962. 165p.

Callahan, Raymond. *Education and the Cult of Efficiency.* U Chicago Press, 1962. 273p.

Cremin, Lawrence A. *The Transformation of the School.* Knopf, 1961. 387p.

Cronbach, Lee J., and Meehl, Paul E. "Construct Validity in Psychological Tests." *Psychol B* 52:281–302; 1955.

Dewey, John. "Philosophy of Education." In Monroe, Paul. (Ed.) *A Cyclopedia of Education.* Macmillan, 1913. p. 697–703.

Dewey, John. *Democracy and Education.* Macmillan, 1916. 434p.

Donnellan, Keith. "Paradigm-Case Argument." In Edwards, Paul. (Ed.) *The Encyclopedia of Philosophy.* Macmillan, Free, 1967. p. 39–44.

Ducasse, C. J. "On the Function and Nature of Philosophy of Education." *Harvard Ed R* 26:103–11; 1956.

Dunkel, Harold B. *Whitehead on Education.* Ohio State U Press, 1965. 182p.

Dupuis, Adrian M., and Nordberg, Robert. *Philosophy and Education.* Bruce, 1964. 334p.

Edel, Abraham. "What Should Be the Aims and Content of a Philosophy of Education?" *Harvard Ed R* 26:119–26; 1956.

Edwards, Newton, and Richey, Herman G. *The School in the American Social Order,* 2nd ed. Houghton, 1963. 694p.

Ennis, Robert H. "Operational Definitions." *Am Ed Res J* 3:183–201; 1964.

Flew, Anthony. "What Is Indoctrination?" *Stud Philos Ed* 4:281–306; 1966.

Ford, G. W., and Pugno, Lawrence. (Eds.) *The Structure of Knowledge and the Curriculum.* Rand McNally, 1964. 105p.

Frankena, William K. *Three Historical Philosophies of Education.* Scott, 1965. 216p.

Gowin, D. B. "Can Educational Theory Guide Practice?" *Ed Theory* 13:6–12; 1963.

Green, Thomas. "A Typology of the Teaching Concept." *Stud Philos Ed* 3:284–319; 1964.
Greene, Maxine. *The Public School and the Private Vision.* Random, 1965. 185p.
Hardie, Charles D. *Truth and Fallacy in Educational Theory.* Teachers Col, Columbia U, 1962. 156p.
Hirst, Paul. "Philosophy and Educational Theory." *Br J Ed Stud* 12:51–64; 1963.
Hook, Sidney. *Education for Modern Man.* Knopf, 1963. 235p.
Kaplan, Abraham. *The Conduct of Inquiry.* Chandler Publishing Co., 1964. 428p.
Kaufman, Walter. "Educational Development from the Point of View of a Normative Philosophy." *Harvard Ed R* 36:247–64; 1966.
Kneller, George F. *Educational Anthropology.* Wiley, 1965. 171p.
Kneller, George F. *Logic and Language of Education.* Wiley, 1966. 242p.
Komisar, B. Paul, and McClellan, James E., Jr. "The Logic of Slogans." In Smith, B. Othanel, and Ennis, Robert H. (Eds.) *Language and Concepts in Education.* Rand McNally, 1961. p.195–214.
Maccia, Elizabeth Steiner, and Maccia, George S. *Development of Educational Theory Derived from Three Educational Theory Models.* Ohio State U Press, 1966. 192p.
Maritain, Jacques. *Education at the Crossroads.* Yale U Press, 1943. 120p.
McCaul, Robert. "Dewey's Chicago." *Sch R* 67:258–80; 1959.
McClellan, James E., Jr. "Influence of Modern Psychology on Philosophy of Education." In Edwards, Paul. (Ed.) *The Encyclopedia of Philosophy.* Macmillan, Free, 1967. p. 243–7.
Morris, Van Cleve. *Philosophy and the American School.* Houghton, 1961. 492p.
National Society for the Study of Education. *Philosophies of Education,* 41st Yearbook. NSSE, 1942. 321p.
National Society for the Study of Education. *Modern Philosophies of Education,* 54th Yearbook. NSSE, 1955. 374p.
Pap, Arthur. *Elements of Analytic Philosophy.* Macmillan, 1949. 526p.
Pap, Arthur. "The Role of Analytic Philosophy in College Education." *Harvard Ed R* 26:114–8; 1956.
Passmore, John. *Philosophical Reasoning.* Scribner, 1961. 147p.
Perry, Ralph Barton. *Realms of Value.* Harvard U Press, 1954. 497p.
Peters, Richard S. *Authority, Responsibility and Education.* Atherton Press, 1966(a). 137p.
Peters, Richard S. *Ethics and Education.* Allen, 1966(b). 333p.
Phenix, Philip H. *Realms of Meaning.* McGraw-Hill, 1964. 391p.
Price, Kingsley. *Education and Philosophical Thought.* Allyn and Bacon, 1962. 511p.
Price, Kingsley. "History of Philosophy of Education." In Edwards, Paul. (Ed.) *The Encyclopedia of Philosophy,* Macmillan, Free, 1967. p.230–43.
Ryle, Gilbert. *The Concept of Mind,* 2nd ed. Barnes, 1960. 334p.
Scheffler, Israel. *The Language of Education.* Charles C. Thomas, 1960. 113p.
Scheffler, Israel. *Conditions of Knowledge.* Scott, 1965. 117p.
Schwab, Joseph J. "What Do Scientists Do?" *Behavioral Sci* 5:1–27; 1960.
Schwab, Joseph J. "Problems, Topics, and Issues." In Elam, Stanley. (Ed.) *Education and the Structure of Knowledge.* Rand McNally, 1964. p.4–42.
Smith, B. Othanel. *Logical Aspects of Measurement.* Columbia U Press, 1938. 182p.
Studies in Philosophy and Education. 1960 to present.
Thayer, V. T., and Levit, Martin. *The Role of the School in American Society.* Dodd, 1966. 589p.
Thomas, Lawrence G. "Mental Tests As Instruments of Science." *Psychol Monogr* 54:1–87; 1942.
Wingo, G. Max. *The Philosophy of American Education.* Heath, 1965. 438p.
Wittgenstein, Ludwig. *Philosophical Investigations.* Macmillan, 1953. 232p.

PHYSICAL DEVELOPMENT

SCOPE OF PHYSICAL DEVELOPMENT. Phylogeny and Ontogeny. Biological science includes two developmental facets termed "phylogeny" and "ontogeny." In the study of both facets attention centers on changes with time in the structure and function of organisms. Phylogeny traces, and seeks to explain, evolutionary modifications of organisms from generation to generation through the successive eons of geological time and centuries of historical time. Ontogeny traces, and endeavors to elucidate, the sequential modifications that organisms undergo during single life cycles. For instance, ontogeny is concerned with the discovery of laws for describing, controlling, and predicting varieties of change in human organisms between the beginning of prenatal life and the close of senility. This article is concerned almost entirely with ontogenetic development.

Anatomical and Physiological Ontogeny. Used in restricted reference to the individual life span of an organism, the term "physical development" encompasses both developmental anatomy and developmental physiology. The present article deals largely with the former. To forestall the erroneous inference that little information on the latter is available, the following items indicate the breadth and variety of human physiological changes known to occur from infancy through adolescence. Heart rate decreases rapidly during infancy and continues to decline at a slowing pace during childhood and adolescence. Heat production and loss are higher in infancy than in later childhood. Systolic blood pressure rises rapidly during infancy and at a slower rate throughout childhood and adolescence. The rate of respiration falls markedly, and also becomes more regular, during the first year after birth; in childhood and adolescence the declining trend continues at reduced rates. From early childhood through adolescence, there is a decrease in basal metabolism and an increase in strength and endurance (Smith, 1959; Shock, 1944).

Embryology, Pedology, and Gerontology. With advances in the study of human ontogeny, scholarly publications of individual scientists have tended to focus on different portions of the life cycle. The work of many present-day human embryologists is concentrated on somatic changes from germ cell to embryo to fetus and rarely extends to postnatal development (Arey, 1965). Again, many gerontologists largely confine their reports to organisms beyond adolescence, preferring to attain high competence and productivity with respect to knowledge of ontogenetic changes from early adulthood through middle age and senescence (Birren, 1959). Similarly, there are pedologists (child anatomists and physiologists; research pediatricians and pedodontists; and child psychologists, sociologists, and so forth) whose contributions to knowledge pertain almost exclusively to the segment of ontogeny between birth and late adolescence (Tanner, 1962; Watson & Lowrey, 1962). Except for sparse reference to gerontological findings and somewhat greater citation of embryological findings, this article treats human somatic changes during the periods of infancy, childhood, and youth.

HUMAN ANATOMICAL DEVELOPMENT. Human anatomical ontogenesis encompasses "all the changes in structure that take place during one life cycle" (Bonner, 1965). The gamut of known changes is vast; it includes replications and obliterations at the cell level, differentiations and resorptions at the tissue level, specializations and simplifications at the organ level, and ongoing series of volume, form, and compositional modifications at the organismic level. Exploration of structural changes is not completed; consequently, one cannot claim that all the varieties of change which occur have been discovered and studied. It is known at this time that during human ontogeny the body undergoes changes with respect to the kind, position, size, shape, number, and composition of its structural units.

Changes in Kind. The life span of a human individual commences with the merging of two kinds of parental haploid cells to constitute a new diploid cell or zygote. There follow many other changes in kind. Embryonic ectoderm tissue is replaced by nerve tissue, epidermis, the lens of the eye, and tooth enamel. Mesenchyme is replaced by muscle tissue, cartilage, bone, and tooth dentin. The face region acquires a nose and tongue, eyes and eyelids, lips and teeth, and eyebrows and eyelashes. The trunk region acquires heart and stomach, liver and lungs, shoulders and arms, and hips and legs.

Some kinds of structural units are found at most stages of ontogeny. Nerve cells are present from the first month of life, bone cells from the second month, and nail cells from the third month. The heart is present from the first month, limbs from the second month, and body hair from the fourth month.

Other kinds of structural units are transitory. The pronephros (forerunner of the kidney) is present for about two weeks, and the branchial, or gill, arches for no more than three weeks. Between the second and fourth months of life an external tail emerges and is submerged, and between the third and fifth months touch pads on the fingers are acquired and lost. In early infancy the umbilical cord is discarded, in childhood the primary dentition is shed, and in adolescence and early adulthood the cartilaginous metaphyses of the skeleton are obliterated.

Changes in Number. In its earliest ontogenetic state the human being is a unicellular organism; by early adulthood it has become an organism of more than 20 trillion cells.

Some cells are stable for long periods, others are labile. For nerve cells there is rapid increase in number during early prenatal life; little numerical change or replacement throughout childhood, adolescence, and early adulthood; and cellular decrease exceeding 20 percent during late adulthood and senility (Shock, 1962). The outer layer of human skin "renews itself completely about once a month" (Medawar, 1957). Similarly, for blood cells, from the first month of prenatal life until death, change in the absolute count is the product of ongoing cell production and dissolution, with a given red blood corpuscle living about four months. The pattern for striated muscle cells is a close variant of that for nerve cells, with no numerical change or replacement between infancy and middle adulthood.

During the middle third of the prenatal period taste receptors increase in number on the tongue, tonsils, palate, and parts of the esophagus. In late prenatal life and early childhood there is a decrease in the number of taste receptors to the extent that usually none remain except on the tongue. There is an increase in the number of developing teeth from the embryonic period into childhood; around five years of age the child has 48 to 52 teeth in varying stages of development A decade later the number has been reduced by at least 20, and with the passing years there may be further reduction. The number of bone masses does not progressively increase to some maximum; rather, there is staggered bone formation and coalescence which produces an overall increase for the period from the second prenatal month to puberty and a decrease thereafter. At puberty the numerical count of bone masses approximates 350; in early adulthood it is near 200. During the adult years there is a decrease in the number of kidney glomeruli to about two-thirds the number present in early adulthood.

Changes in Position. During ontogeny "cells and cell groups are frequently in motion, shifting positions or moving to new sites" (Moscona, 1961). At the cell level, examples are the essentially migratory blood cells and the nerve cells that extend out to the muscles and skin of the fingers and toes.

At the organ level there are movements in practically all directions. Initially the heart lies in the vicinity of the lower part of the face. Its positional changes include downward and backward migration, counterclockwise rotation, and oblique tilting from right to left. When the stomach first is identifiable, it is situated high in the trunk. Its repositionings include movement to a lower level, rotation clockwise, and oblique tipping from left to right. In early prenatal life the stomach has a vertical orientation, in early childhood it lies almost transversely, and in late childhood it returns to a predominantly vertical orientation (Arey, 1965).

The teeth first travel deeply into the jaws, then reverse themselves and erupt into the oral cavity. Combined with these vertical excursions there are tooth rotations, lateral movements, and migrations in oblique paths (Brodie, 1934). The ribs are formed in a nearly horizontal plane and tilt downward at the front. The ovaries move from their original vertical orientation into a transverse position; they also revolve about the uterine tubes and come to rest below them. The testes migrate from the abdomen through the pelvic cavity into the scrotum. In the neonate the intestines and bladder are located almost entirely within the abdomen; during early childhood they move down into the pelvis. There is a progressive shift in the positional relation of the vertebral column and larynx; the cricoid cartilage approximates the top of the fourth cervical vertebra in the newborn, the bottom of the fifth cervical vertebra in early adulthood, and the top of the seventh cervical vertebra in late adulthood.

Both pairs of limbs undergo prenatal torsion of 90 degrees; for the upper limbs turning at the shoulders occurs so that the elbows are rotated from an upward position to a posterior position, for the lower limbs turning at the hips occurs so that the knees are brought to the front. The feet first lie along the same axes as the shafts of the legs; during the last half of the second prenatal month they turn out of the leg planes and approach a right-angle relationship with the legs. When the great toes are individuated, each diverges from the four other toes and has its plantar surface turned toward them; gradually each moves to a position parallel with the other toes and rotates sufficiently to bring the plantar surface into the sole plane (Arey, 1965).

Changes in Size. During the first few days after formation of the zygote no change occurs in the size of the organism (Streeter, 1937); there is an increase in the number of cells without an increase in overall size. Then follow size changes that vary greatly in direction, rate, and duration.

Increases in size are too apparent to necessitate illustration. By contrast, decreases in size are sufficiently unfamiliar to warrant a listing of examples. The external tail becomes progressively smaller during the last half of the second prenatal month. A short time later there are decreases in the size of the müllerian ducts in boys and the mesonephric ducts in girls. During the last third of the prenatal period, Hunter's gubernacula shorten in boys by 75 percent, pulling the testes down into the scrotum. Body weight decreases by about 6 percent during the first few days after birth. There also are neonatal decreases in the size of the suprarenal glands, mammary glands, and female genitalia. The thickness of the subcutaneous adipose tissue on the thorax and calf decreases between the middle of the first postnatal year and the sixth year. Deciduous teeth undergo reduction in length for several months prior to being shed. There are decreases in the size of the thymus gland from late childhood to early adulthood and in the size of the pharyngeal tonsil in early adulthood. Later adulthood brings a shrinkage of cerebellar fibers and a reduced cross-sectional area of head hairs. In senility there are decreases in thickness of the skin, in the volume of the striated muscles, in the weight of the liver, and in the size of the corpus callosum (Scammon, 1930; Watson & Lowrey, 1962).

Some trends of change in size are complex. The size of the female mammary glands and uterus increases in the fetal period, decreases during the first month after birth, remains almost stationary throughout infancy and early childhood, increases in late childhood and adolescence, enters a fairly stable period except for fluctuations with pregnancies, and then enters a second period of slow decrease following the menopause. The alveolar processes increase in height preceding and during the eruption of primary teeth, remain at a fairly stationary height over the period they are supporting these teeth, show regional decreases as primary teeth are shed, increase again with permanent-tooth eruption, and decrease markedly with their loss.

Frequently when anatomical structures change in size there is an increase in one region and a decrease in another. The lower jaw changes in its breadth by deposition on the lateral surfaces and absorption along its mesial surfaces. For the thigh bone the interplay of increase at the periphery and decrease at the center is such that its inner cavity in adulthood is as large as the entire bone shaft at birth.

Changes in Shape. Two weeks after fertilization the human organism has the form of an ovoidal disk, the widest part being located toward one end. Approximately 65 percent of the disk represents the head region and 35 percent the trunk region. Three weeks later the organism has become cylindroid, with a large head flexed far forward and a thorax that is 50 percent greater in depth than in breadth. Aspects of body configuration at the end of the second prenatal month are larger breadth of head than breadth of shoulders, face and nose each broad and short, almost circular thorax, and limbs shorter than the length from shoulders to hips.

The length of the lower limbs increases from 37 percent of the trunk length at the end of the second prenatal month to 87 percent by the middle of the prenatal period. There is almost no change in that relation during the last half of the prenatal period, but during infancy and childhood the index rises again. In white children around the age of 12 years, the lower-limb length approaches 150 percent of the trunk length. Between this time and early adulthood the index declines to below 145 percent, i.e., the predominance of lower-limb length decreases (Meredith, 1939a).

During infancy the cervical and lumbar curvatures of the back become more pronounced, the hands and feet less stubby, and the nose more elongated and high-bridged. In childhood the abdomen attains a less protruding contour and the limbs become progressively more slender (Meredith & Sherbina, 1951). At adolescence the aperture of the male larynx becomes strongly elliptical, and the aperture of the female pelvis decreases in ellipticity (Greulich & Thoms, 1944).

Changes in shape or form are no less varied at the cell and organ levels. Cells elongate, flatten, invaginate, and branch; internal organs bulge, bend, loop, and convolute. The stomach, which undergoes a comparatively simple sequence of alterations in shape, begins as a swelling of one portion of the digestive tube, passes from this capsular form to a configuration resembling a cow's horn, and then changes to almost a J shape (Arey, 1965).

Changes in Composition. Many human tissues and organs exhibit ontogenetic change in texture, resilience, and color. These modifications usually register quantitative change in such variables as calcium, protein, water, and pigment.

The iris of the eye is blue or violet in the neonate and, as a result of increasing density of pigment, darkens during the childhood years. In senility there is decrease in the ratio of pigment-carrying cells to pigment-free cells, and eye color becomes lighter. During infancy and childhood there is darkening in skin color; this holds for Negroid as well as non-Negroid persons. Negro infants show a rapid increase in skin pigmentation during the first few months after birth and a slower increase over the childhood years. The hair of the head shows darkening over the childhood years, followed by graying in adulthood. During adulthood pigmentation occurs in the dentate nucleus of the cerebellum, and with advanced age the muscle fibers of the heart become densely pigmented.

Underlying the commonplace fact of the greater resistance to compression of subcutaneous adipose tissue in childhood than in infancy is the reduction in both extracellular water and the proportion of oleic acid. Compositional changes in striated muscle between birth and early adulthood include declines in water and chloride content and a rise in nitrogen content.

During the fetal and infancy periods the human body undergoes dehydration. This decline in total body water is from around 90 percent in the young fetus through about 73 percent at birth to 60 percent at the end of the first postnatal year. During the childhood and adolescent periods there is a moderate increase in total body calcium (Forbes, 1952).

The inorganic iron content of the liver rises during the fetal and neonatal periods, drops precipitously during the last half of the first postnatal year, remains fairly constant during the second year, and then gradually rises throughout childhood. During the adult years the kidneys show an increase in calcium and iron deposits. Changes with age in the composition of the skeleton include a decrease in water content, an increase in nitrogen content, and increases in calcium, phosphorus, and total ash. In old age the brittleness of many bones attests to a decrease in the ratio of organic components to inorganic components.

Compositional change is presently of great interest, with research activity ranging from the study of changes with age in bone, muscle, and fat components of the body during the childhood years (Maresh, 1961; Tanner, 1965) to the study of the lessening suppleness of the arteries and declining resiliency of the heart valves over the adult years (Birren, 1959).

The remainder of this article discusses three developmental topics selected as being of prime relevance for school personnel; height and weight of children and youth, tooth eruption and loss in childhood, and puberal changes of youth.

HEIGHT AND WEIGHT OF CHILDREN AND YOUTH. Average Height. Technically, "stature" is the general term for a measurement of the extended human body from the top of the head (vertex) to the soles of the feet. Many human biologists refer to stature in the erect position as standing height and stature in the recumbent position as vertex–soles length.

In the first month of prenatal life the human organism does not have lower limbs. During the early part of the second month the limbs develop rapidly, and by the close of this month the feet have formed and tilted to positions almost at right angles with the legs.

Average stature approximates 1.5 inches at the end of the second prenatal month, 9.5 inches at the middle of the prenatal period (4.5 months), and 19 to 20 inches at birth. Subgroup averages for vertex-soles length at birth are (1) somewhat lower on Chinese and Indian infants than on white infants of Europe and North America, (2) slightly higher on boys than on girls, and (3) a little less on firstborn infants than on infants of later birth orders (Ghosh & Beri, 1962; Millis, 1954; Meredith, 1943).

Today, the typical North American white boy is 20 inches tall at birth, 41 inches tall at age 4 years, 51 inches tall at age 8 years, 66 inches tall at age 15 years, and 69 inches tall at age 20 years. Eighty years ago the typical North American boy had a similar stature at birth but was shorter postnatally by more than two inches at age 4 years, by fully three inches at age 8 years, by fully five inches at age 15 years, and by less than two inches at age 20 years (Meredith, 1963).

At age 8 years, boys presently living in Scandinavia, Great Britain, Holland, Switzerland, Germany, Poland, and Czechoslovakia have average statures of 49 inches and 51 inches (Heimendinger, 1964), whereas averages between 46 inches and 48 inches are common for boys living in Japan, China, New Guinea, Guam, India, Kenya, and the Congo (Chang & others, 1963). Corresponding averages at age 15 years vary from 64 inches to 67 inches for boys residing in different parts of northern and central Europe (Sundal, 1957) and from 58 inches to 63 inches for boys indigenous to the African and Asiatic regions indicated (Inoue & Shimizu, 1965). North American

Negro children and adolescents are similar in height to those of white ancestry but taller than the American Japanese, Chinese, Navaho Indian, and Mexican ethnic groups (Altman & Dittmer, 1962).

Increase in stature takes place (1) at declining velocities throughout prenatal life, infancy, and childhood, (2) at rising velocities in early adolescence, and (3) at declining velocities in late adolescence. The first period of slowing growth rate is shown by the progressively longer times taken for stature to double itself; average stature doubles in the third month of prenatal life, in the last half of the prenatal period, and, for North American white children, in the period between birth and age 4 years. The crest of the adolescent acceleration is reached, on the average, near age 12 years for girls and fully two years later for boys (Meredith, 1939b). Average increase in stature approximates 50 percent from birth to age 1 year and 16 percent during the second year after birth. By late childhood the average annual increase has declined to less than 4 percent. In no year of adolescence does average increase reach 5 percent, and rarely does an individual boy or girl gain as much as 8 percent in any adolescent year. After ages 15 years (girls) and 17 years (boys), average yearly increases in stature fall below 1 percent.

Individual Differences in Height. Healthy newborn white infants vary in vertex–soles length from slightly less than 18 inches to approximately 22 inches. Individual variations in height among older North American white children and youth extend from 36 inches to 46 inches at age 4 years (both sexes), 47 inches to 59 inches at age 9 years (both sexes), 52 inches to 66 inches at age 12 years (girls), and 55 inches to 72 inches at age 14 years (boys). The distribution of human stature within groups homogeneous for age, race, generation, and sex closely approximates the Gaussian or normal frequency model. For present-day North American white persons of each sex, standard deviations for stature approximate 0.8 inch at birth, 1.3 inches at age 2 years, 2.2 inches at age 6 years, 3.0 inches at 12 years (girls), 3.4 inches at 14 years (boys) and, at age 20 years, 2.3 inches and 2.5 inches for women and men, respectively (Kasius & others, 1957; O'Brien & others, 1941).

Knowledge of a child's stature at birth is of little value for predicting either his stature at age 5 years or his stature in early adulthood. In both instances there is a low positive relationship near $r = 0.3$ (Meredith, 1965).

Changes in stature ranking are most marked in infancy and progressively stabilize in early childhood. In the period between middle and late childhood the stature ranks of individuals are highly stable (r's on each sex exceed 0.9 for height at ages 5 years and 9 years). During adolescence, as a consequence of individual differences in the timing and degree of accelerated growth, stature rankings change considerably. In practical terms, healthy children of average stature in middle childhood sometimes become tall or short as adolescents and, conversely, children tall or short in middle childhood sometimes shift ranks in the adolescence period to near-average (Meredith, 1939b). The adolescent spurt in stature may occur early or late, for both tall and short children in middle childhood; frequencies are slightly greater for tall children early and short children late. There is no association between the age at which the adolescent growth spurt occurs and height in adulthood (Meredith, 1965).

Components of Height. The distance from the vertex of the head to the soles of the feet can be regarded as a composite measurement including the length of the head and neck, the length of the trunk, and the length of the lower limbs. The growth rates differ for each of these subdivisions. This can be shown by an examination of the typical percentage contributions the segments makes to stature with increasing age.

At the end of the second prenatal month stature is about 45 percent head and neck length, 33 percent trunk length, and 22 percent lower-limb length. By the middle of the prenatal period, lower-limb length has become equal to head and neck length, each of these subdivisions constituting 32 percent of stature. At birth, stature is about 25 percent head and neck length, 39 percent trunk length, and 36 percent lower-limb length.

During childhood and adolescence, as in the last two-thirds of prenatal life, head and neck length increases less rapidly than either trunk or limb length. Its contribution to stature declines to slightly less than 19 percent by age 14 years, remaining practically constant thereafter. Lower-limb length increases to 48 percent of stature at age 12 years for white girls and 49 percent of stature at age 14 years for white boys. There follows a gradual decline, so that in early adulthood this component of stature approximates 47 percent and 48 percent for women and men, respectively. The decline reflects faster growth during late adolescence in trunk length than in lower-limb length (Meredith, 1939a).

The different components of stature are not highly correlated. One child may have short lower limbs and be average in lengths of head, neck, and trunk; a second may have long lower limbs and be short in lengths of head, neck, and trunk; a third may have a long trunk and be average in lengths of head, neck, and lower limbs; and a fourth may have a short trunk and long lower limbs and be average in head and neck length. Some children are long, average, or short in all segments. One way of summarizing the extent of variation is by correlation statistics; at every age during childhood and adolescence, r's approximate 0.3 for head and neck length with trunk length, 0.4 for head and neck length with lower-limb length, and 0.5 for trunk length with lower-limb length. These r's all imply poor levels of predictive efficiency (Meredith, 1939a).

Average Weight. Human body weight increases from less than one-thousandth of an ounce at the end of the first prenatal month to approximately one-fourteenth of an ounce at the end of the second prenatal month to about fourteen ounces at the middle of the prenatal period. Average weight at birth for full-term North American white infants is 7.5 pounds. Typically, newborn boys are nearly 5 ounces, or 4 percent, heavier than newborn girls (Meredith & Brown, 1939), and firstborn neonates are fully 10 ounces, or 9 percent, lighter than fifth-born neonates (Meredith, 1950).

Means for body weight on present-day North American white boys approximate 7.7 pounds at birth, 44 pounds at age 5 years, 75 pounds at age 10 years, 133 pounds at age 15 years, and 156 pounds at age 20 years. Eighty years ago the average North American white boy was lighter in weight by 5 pounds at age 5 years, 13 pounds at age 10 years, fully 30 pounds at age 15 years, and 15 pounds at age 20 years (Meredith, 1963). Findings on girls are similar, with the differences progressively increasing from infancy to age 13 years and becoming smaller at late adolescent and early adult ages.

At age 8 years, body-weight means for white boys presently living in Australia, Czechoslovakia, Germany, Holland, Norway, Switzerland, and the United States (also for American Negro boys) are between 55 pounds and 62 pounds. Comparable means for Guatemalan "mestizo" boys, for African Tutsi, Hutu, and Mandingo boys, for Jamaican Negro boys, and for boys indigenous to Japan, China New Guinea, Guam, and India fall between 43 pounds and 50 pounds (Heimendinger, 1964). Throughout the elementary- and secondary-school years, body-weight averages in the United States are (1) similar for American Negro and white children, and (2) two to four pounds higher for children whose fathers hold professional and managerial positions than those whose fathers are unskilled or semiskilled workmen (Meredith, 1951).

Recent studies of body weight for girls aged 13 years have obtained means below 80 pounds from Burmese, Chinese, and several African Negro samples and means above 100 pounds from British, Norwegian, Czechoslovakian, and American Negro samples (Foll, 1958; Lin, 1957; Sundal, 1957). Similarly, for boys aged 15 years, means below 100 pounds have been found on Indian, Mayan Amerindian, Bantu, and Egyptian samples, in contrast to means above 120 pounds on samples of white boys living in Australia, Sweden, and the United States (Méndez & Behrhorst, 1963; Meyers, 1956).

For North American Negro and white persons average body weight is about three times greater at age 1 year than at birth, ten times greater at age 10 years than at birth, and 18 times (girls) to 20 times (boys) greater at age 20 years than at birth. Increase in human body weight takes place at velocities that decline during infancy and early childhood, are fairly constant during middle childhood, rise during early adolescence, and decline again during late adolescence. In common with stature, the average age of the early adolescent spurt is later for boys than girls by a biennium (Tuddenham & Snyder, 1954).

Individual Differences in Weight. Normal full-term white infants vary in weight at birth from approximately 5 pounds to 11 pounds. At later ages, individual weight among normal United States Negro or white children varies from 30 pounds to 60 pounds at age 5 years and from 50 pounds to 105 pounds at age 10 years. As these figures denote, among healthy present-day elementary-school children of a given age, the body weight of some children may be twice that of others.

The typical body weight of today's United States white girls aged 13 years is near 105 pounds. The lightest 10 percent of these girls weigh less than 82 pounds and the heaviest 10 percent more than 132 pounds. Since the lightest one-tenth fall 24 pounds or more below the typical weight while the heaviest one-tenth fall 28 pounds or more above the typical weight, it follows that the weight distribution is "skewed positively." Distributions of human body weight for groups homogeneous for race, sex, and generation are skewed in the positive direction at all childhood ages, the asymmetry increasing from mild manifestation in early childhood to pronounced manifestation during adolescence (Keyfitz, 1942; Blommers & Lindquist, 1960).

During the period between birth and early adulthood there are appreciable shifts in individual rankings for body weight and weight-change velocity. Instances of low positive correlation (r's between 0.2 and 0.4) are as follows: weight at birth with weight at age 5 years, weight at birth with weight in early adulthood, gain in weight between ages 6 and 9 years with gain between ages 9 and 18 years, and weight at age 9 years with gain in weight between ages 9 and 18 years. Higher associations involving a quadrennium or longer include (1) r's between 0.5 and 0.7 for weight at age 5 years with gain in weight from this age to age 9 years, also weight at age 9 years with weight in early adulthood, and (2) r's approximating 0.8 for weight at age 6 years with weight at age 11 years, and weight at age 14 years with early adult weight (Meredith, 1965). Generalizing, one healthy child may increase in body weight during some years more rapidly than most of his peers and during succeeding years increase near the average for his peers; another healthy child may increase in body weight over a certain period more slowly than most of his peers and over a later period increase near the average for his peers; and so forth.

Height-Weight Interpretation Charts. Recently revised charts for interpreting height and weight records for United States Negro and white school pupils are available from the National Education Association and the American Medical Association. Sample copies can be secured from either source by requesting the "Height-Weight Interpretation Folder for Girls" and the "Height-Weight Interpretation Folder for Boys." The folders discuss how to measure height and weight, how to transfer records to the charts, and how the charts can be used in describing physical development and as an aid in health appraisal.

The chart for a given sex enables teachers, school nurses, or school physicians to determine, at ages from 4 years to 18 years, whether individual pupils are "short" (below the tenth percentile), "moderately short" (between percentiles 10 and 30), "average" (between percentiles 30 and 70), "moderately tall" (between percentiles 70 and 90), or "tall" above the ninetieth percentile). Using the same statistical procedure for weight, the chart allows pupils at any school age to be described as light, moderately light, average, moderately heavy, or heavy.

The charts are serviceable for both description and screening (Meredith, 1955). In addition to providing a graphic portrayal of height and weight status and progress, they can be used to select individuals considered to deviate in height-weight ranks, or growth rates, sufficiently to warrant special study. This second function recognizes the reciprocal roles of growth screening and medical exploration. The charts do not evaluate health; rather, they provide school health personnel with objective leads on *possible* departures from sound health. For example, screening identifies and selects a child of "average height" and "light weight" for intensive study. The school or family physician then determines whether this child is best appraised as a satisfactorily healthy individual of slender physique or as an "underweight" child in need of medical treatment, nutritional changes, or a modified activity program. Again, screening identifies and selects pupils whose progress records show small gain in height with loss in weight or below-average gain in height with large gain in weight. Responsibility for appraisal, and possible follow-up recommendations, passes to the physician and other therapists.

TOOTH ERUPTION AND LOSS IN CHILDHOOD. Eruption and Loss of Primary Teeth. The first set of teeth is designated the primary, or deciduous, dentition; typically this consists of 20 teeth. Moving from the center of each jaw outward and backward the primary teeth are named central incisor, lateral incisor, canine (cuspid), first molar, and second molar.

Eruption of the primary dentition into the mouth ordinarily occurs in the period between early infancy and three years of age. Typically, the first tooth emerges (pierces the gum tissue) approximately seven months after birth. In most children this first tooth erupts sometime between four months and one year after birth; in rare instances tooth emergence commences before birth or as late as 16 months following birth (Meredith, 1946; Lysell & others, 1962).

The characteristic eruption sequence for the primary dentition is as follows: lower central incisors, upper central and lateral incisors, lower lateral incisors, first molars, canines, and second molars. There are many individual variations in sequence (Meredith, 1946).

At age one year, (1) normal infants vary in tooth emergence from none to the full deciduous complement of 20, (2) 50 percent of infants have between four and eight erupted teeth, and (3) the average number of erupted teeth is six, usually the two lower central incisors and four upper incisors (Meredith, 1946; Falkner, 1957). Emergence of the deciduous dentition may be completed before one year or after three years; on the average it is completed by 2.5 years (Pyle & Drain, 1931; Haataja, 1963). In different individuals the 20 deciduous teeth erupt within periods varying from less than nine months to approximately three years (Meredith, 1946; Lysell & others, 1962). Deciduous incisors and canines typically erupt several months later in mongols than in normal children (Roche & Barkla, 1964).

In the period between ages four years and six years the roots of most primary teeth begin to show reduction in size. Usually three-fourths of a tooth's root is resorbed before the tooth is shed (Knott and O'Meara, 1967). Average ages of shedding approximate 6.5 years for lower central incisors, 7 to 8 years for other incisors, and 10 to 11 years for canines and deciduous molars (Hellman, 1923). Rarely is any deciduous tooth shed prior to age five years (Pyle & Drain, 1931).

Eruption of Permanent Teeth. Thirty-two teeth are the usual number composing the second, or permanent, dentition. The nomenclature is the same as for the primary dentition except that the five teeth in each jaw behind the canines are, successively, first and second premolars (bicuspids) and first to third molars.

Permanent teeth pierce the gum tissues at the following average ages: first molars and lower central incisors, between 6 years and 6.5 years; upper central and lower lateral incisors, between 7 years and 8 years; upper lateral incisors, between 8 years and 9 years; canines, premolars (the teeth that replace the deciduous molars), and second molars, between 10 years and 12.5 years; and third molars, approximately at age 20 years (Cattell, 1928; Knott & Meredith, 1966; Lee & others, 1965; Hellman, 1936; Fanning, 1962). There are marked individual variations (Haataja, 1963; Knott & Meredith, 1966; Fanning, 1962). At the age of six years, one child may have his full deciduous dentition, with no erupted permanent teeth; another child may have shed his deciduous incisors and erupted eight permanent incisors plus four permanent first molars. At the age of 12 years, one child may have 24 erupted teeth, 12 deciduous and 12 permanent; another child may have 28 erupted permanent teeth (Klein & Cody, 1939). Eruption of all permanent teeth except the third molars is found to occur sometimes by age 10 years and sometimes not until age 17 years (Shuttleworth, 1939).

Permanent-tooth eruption in the individual child commences with the first molars and central incisors; continues with the lateral incisors; shows high variation in sequence for the canines, premolars, and second molars; and terminates with the third molar. More than 20 different sequences occur, with no one being common to more than 30 percent of children. Two of the commonest sequences are (1) first molar, central incisor, lateral incisor, first premolar, canine, second premolar, second molar, third molar and (2) central incisor, first molar, lateral incisor, canine, first premolar, second premolar, second molar, and third molar (Knott & Meredith, 1966).

Despite the fact that there is no tendency for deciduous teeth in girls to erupt earlier than in boys (Meredith, 1946; Falkner, 1957; Lysell & others, 1962) this tendency is found for canine and premolar teeth of the permanent dentition (Cattell, 1928; Knott & Meredith, 1966). The permanent lower canine shows the greatest sex difference, the average girl erupting this tooth almost a year earlier than the average boy. Permanent incisor and canine teeth in the lower jaw tend to erupt earlier than corresponding teeth in the upper jaw (Hellman, 1923; Knott & Meredith, 1966).

Congenital Absence of Teeth. Although any tooth may not develop, agenesis (congenital absence) is commonest for the permanent third molars. Fully 20 percent of white persons lack at least one third molar, while in 3 to 4 percent all four of these teeth are missing (Hellman, 1936; Dahlberg, 1945). Frequencies of absence are higher for Eskimo than for white persons, lower for Negro than for white persons, and higher for females than for males. Agenesis in white persons occurs at frequencies between 1 and 3 percent for the permanent upper lateral incisors and the lower second premolars. There is a tendency for one or more of these teeth to be absent in association with missing third molars (Garn & Lewis, 1962).

PUBERAL CHANGES OF YOUTH. The termination of childhood is signified by an increase in the growth rates of breasts, ovaries, and the uterus in the girl; of testes, scrotum, and penis in the boy; and, in both sexes, of shoulders and hips, arms and legs, height, and total body mass. Other puberal changes include the beginning of menstruation in the girl, voice change and growth of facial hair in the boy, and development by both sexes of moderately coarse pigmented hair in the armpit and groin regions. On the average, those puberal changes common to both sexes occur fully two years earlier in girls than boys. For individuals of a given sex, any particular change may vary in its time of occurrence by more than five years; further, the different sorts of change do not occur in the same sequence for all individuals.

Size Changes and Hair Growth in Girls. The typical girl has an "adolescent spurt" in body height that begins shortly after age 10 years and reaches its crest approximately at age 12 years; there follows a sharp velocity decline, so that by age 14 years height is increasing much more slowly than in late childhood (Meredith, 1939b). Similarly timed "puberal velocity humps" characterize the average increase of trunk length, hip width, arm girth, leg girth, and body weight (Boynton, 1936; Shuttleworth, 1937). In individual girls these puberal changes commence, fairly simultaneously, at any age from 8 years to 13 years and, on rare occasions, either earlier or later (Meredith, 1939; Shuttleworth, 1939).

The average age of beginning breast enlargement in girls is approximately 10.5 years, individual girls commencing enlargement at all ages from 2.5 years earlier to 2.5 years later (Bryan & Greenberg, 1952; Lee & others, 1963). The length of time between beginning enlargement and full breast development is about three years (Reynolds & Wines, 1948; Nicolson & Hanley, 1953).

Changes in the size of anatomic structures during adolescence do not all fall in the categories of moderate acceleration (as do, e.g., changes in stature and hip width) or marked acceleration (as do, e.g., uterine and mammary growth). There are no puberal spurts in dimensions of the central nervous system, pineal body, or adenoid mass (Scammon, 1930; Todd, 1936). Although an increase of moderate velocity occurs in the external width of hips (Boynton, 1936), there is considerable resorption of bone at the rim of the pelvic inlet, with marked bone loss along both sides of this inner aperture in the vicinity of the acetabulum and more forward (Greulich & Thoms, 1944).

White girls typically show the first appearance of a few pigmented hairs in the pubic region near the age of 11 years (Nicolson & Hanley, 1953) and a few pigmented hairs in the axillary regions shortly after the age of 12 years (Hansman and Maresh, 1961). Individual variations normally extend below and above these averages approximately three years for the beginning of the growth of pubic hair and more than three years for the beginning of the growth of axillary hair. Instances are known of pubic- and axillary-hair development in early childhood (Montagu, 1946; Seckel & others, 1949). The time from first appearance of some pigmented pubic (or axillary) hair to attainment of a fairly full density is roughly three years (Reynolds & Wines, 1948). Compared with the average white girl, growth of pigmented pubic and axillary hair in the average Chinese girl commences somewhat later and is more sparse (Lee & others, 1963).

In relation to the first appearance of pigmented pubic hair, breast enlargement may begin two years earlier, simultaneously, or two years later (Reynolds & Wines, 1948). Beginning growth of pigmented axillary hair occasionally precedes beginning growth of pigmented pubic hair (Priesel & Wagner, 1931).

Menarche and Its Relationships. There have been many more investigations of the age at which menarche (beginning of first menstrual cycle) occurs than of puberal hair or breast development. A century ago the average age at which menarche occurred in white girls was 14.5 years or later (Bowditch, 1877; Montaque, 1946; Tanner, 1962). Recent studies of large samples of Australian, British, Hungarian, and Polish girls indicate that today the average age at which white girls reach menarche is approximately 13 years (Towns & others, 1966; Scott, 1961; Bottyán & others, 1963; Zukowski & others, 1964). Averages from large collections of menarche records obtained during the decade 1955–1965 for nonwhite girls are near age 13 years for Assamese, Burmese, Japanese, and Southern Chinese (Foll, 1961; Lee & others, 1963; Inoue & Shimizu, 1965), near age 14 years for Ibo girls in eastern Nigeria (Tanner & O'Keeffe, 1962), and near age 15 years for South African Bantu girls (Burrell & others, 1961; Oettle & Higginson, 1961).

Among present-day white girls, variations are about as follows: fully 50 percent reach menarche between the ages of 12 and 14 years, approximately 80 percent reach menarche between ages 11.5 and 14.5 years (Nicolson & Hanley, 1953; Scott, 1961), more than 95 percent reach menarche between ages 10 and 16 years (Bottyán & others, 1963), fewer than 2 percent reach menarche between ages 8 and 10 years (Seckel & others, 1949), and fewer than 2 percent reach menarche after age 16 years (Heimendinger, 1964). Menarche variations for American Negro girls are similar to those for white girls (Michelson, 1944). Instances are on record of menarche occurring before school age and later than age 20 years (Montague, 1946).

At the time menarche occurs a girl may be in any stage of puberal breast or hair development; i.e., breast variability at menarche extends from the infantile slight elevation of papilla to mature tissue enlargement with protruding nipple (Pryor, 1936), pubic and axillary variabilities extend from no evidence of pigmented hair to full density in each respect (Lee & others, 1963). In different individuals, breast and pubic-hair growth may commence any time from more than four years before to shortly after menarche; the velocity increase in height may reach its crest at varying times from more than three years before to one year after menarche; pigmented axillary hair may begin to appear any time from four years before to two years after menarche; pigmented pubic hair may start to grow at varying times from more than three years before to six months after the crest of velocity increase in height; and pigmented axillary hair may first appear any time from two years before to three years after the age of maximum puberal velocity increase in trunk and limb dimensions (Shuttleworth, 1937; Hansman & Maresh, 1961).

Several attempts have been made to discover ways of predicting menarche. Moderately strong associations (r's = .75 to .80) have been found for age at menarche with (1) age at beginning breast enlargement (Reynolds & Wines, 1948; Nicolson & Hanley, 1953) and (2) age at beginning ossification of a small sesamoid bone near the lower end of the thumb (Flory, 1935). Somewhat lower relationships (r's = .60 to .70) have been obtained between age of menarche and beginning of pigmented pubic hair, maximum puberal velocity in height increase, and height increase from age 10 years to age 11 years (Shuttleworth, 1937; Simmons & Greulich, 1943; Reynolds & Wines, 1948; Nicolson & Hanley, 1953). The last correlation denotes the tendency for a large increase in height between ages 10 and 11 years to be associated with early menarche and vice versa.

The typical amount of increase in height after menarche is 2.5 inches, with only one girl in seven growing four inches or more (Fried & Smith, 1962). Rarely does a girl have the ability to procreate at menarche; commonly there is a puberal sterility interval of three or more years between onset of menses and fertile ovulation (Mills & Ogle, 1936; Montaque, 1946).

Genital, Hair, and Other Changes in Boys. Usually the earliest externally observable indication of puberal change in boys is the increase in the size of the testes (Greulich & others, 1942; Stolz & Stolz, 1951). On the average, puberal enlargement of the male genitalia commences shortly before the age of 12 years for the testes and near the age of 12.5 years for the penis (Kubitschek, 1932; Stolz & Stolz, 1951). Individual differences in the age at the onset of these changes extend from 9.5 years to 14.5 years for the testes and from 10 years to 15 years for the penis (Schonfeld, 1943; Stolz & Stolz, 1951). The typical periods of time between the initial increase in velocity of growth and attainment of maximum size approximate five years for the penis and seven years for the testes; in most individuals puberal penis growth commences after the onset of testicle growth and ends before the termination of testicle growth (Stolz & Stolz, 1951). Quantitatively, the average length of the penis almost doubles between the ages of 12.5 years and 17 years and the average volume of the testes increases more than tenfold between the ages of 12 years and 19 years (Schonfeld, 1943).

The findings reported in the foregoing paragraph are for white boys. Findings on the penis for Chinese boys are as follows: the average age of beginning puberal increase is near 13 years, the time of beginning increase varies from 11 years to 16 years, and the average interval between puberal onset and full size is less than four years (Chang & others, 1966).

The puberal velocity increase for body height typically starts near the age of 12.5 years and reaches its peak shortly after the age of 14 years; rapid reduction in velocity ensues, and by age 16 years the average boy is increasing in height much more slowly than in late childhood. Individual boys vary from 10.5 years to 16 years of age at the onset of the height spurt and from under 12 years to nearly 17 years of age at the attainment of peak velocity (Meredith, 1939b; Shuttleworth, 1939; Stolz & Stolz, 1951). Maximum increase in the height of an individual boy during the year extending from six months before to six months after peak velocity approximates five inches, or 8 percent (Meredith, 1939b). This increase is large in comparison with the maximum gain for an individual during the year before puberal changes begin (roughly three inches, or 5.5 percent) and small in comparison with the average gain during the first year after birth (roughly 10 inches, or 50 percent). Among boys as among girls, except that for the former they occur two years later, "puberal velocity humps" are timed similarly for many measures of trunk size and limb size, average velocity crests occurring slightly earlier in leg length and hip width than in sitting height and body weight (Shuttleworth, 1939; Stolz & Stolz, 1951; Heimendinger, 1964).

The average age at which a few pigmented pubic hairs are first observable in white boys approximates 13 years (Dimock, 1937; Bryan & Greenberg, 1952). Individual white boys normally manifest the first pigmented hairs near the base of the penis sometime between ages 10 and 16 years, with 80 percent of boys showing this stage of development at ages from 11 to 15 years (Dimock, 1937; Schonfeld, 1943). Pigmented pubic hair is not seen in the typical Chinese boy before the age of 14 years, and some Chinese boys do not have any pigmented hair until after age 16 years (Chang & others, 1966). Instances are on record of pubic-hair growth, and also of accelerated growth of the external genitalia, in early childhood (Seckel & others, 1949). Pubic-hair growth is rapid in some boys, slow in others: one boy may remain at the stage of a few pigmented hairs for a period of two years, another may take less than six months in passing from the first appearance of any pigmented hair to a moderately dense growth (Stolz & Stolz, 1951). The average time from the beginning appearance of pigmented hairs to a dense growth is about three years.

A few boys exhibit sparse development of pigmented axillary hair by age 11 years, a few not until after age 17 years, and most between ages 12 and 16 years (Richey, 1937). Approximately 14 years is the average age of boys at first appearance of pigmented axillary hair (Kubitschek, 1932). This average age is similar to the average age of appearance of initial pigmented hairs near each end of the upper lip (Kubitschek, 1932; Schonfeld, 1943), puberal voice unevenness and huskiness (Kubitschek, 1932; Jerome, 1937; Chang & others, 1966), and the puberal velocity apex for body height (Nicolson & Hanley, 1953; Stolz & Stolz, 1951). The beginning of the growth of axillary hair typically precedes the modification of the contour of the hairline above the forehead and development of pigmented hair on the chest (Kubitschek, 1932; Greulich & others, 1942).

Puberal changes in boys include small to moderate amounts of breast enlargement. A node of firm tissue, sometimes exceeding one-half inch in diameter, develops under each nipple. Nodes are present in a few boys by age 11 years and in most boys at age 15 years (Jung & Shafton, 1935; Schonfeld, 1943; Stolz & Stolz, 1951). In late adolescence they frequently become too small to palpate.

In relation to onset of the puberal spurt in the size of testes, the spurt in penis size may commence soon after in one boy and fully two years after in another; in relation to the time at which the full size of testes is reached, the approximate full size of penis may have been attained two years earlier in one boy and only a few months earlier in another. Beginning development of pigmented pubic hair before noticeable increase in testicle size occurs in about 25 percent of boys (Stolz & Stolz, 1951). In rare instances, boys show some growth of pigmented axillary hair prior to any appearance of pigmented pubic hair (Priesel & Wagner, 1931; Greulich & others, 1942). At the time boys reach the apex of the puberal velocity hump in height, they vary in the amount of pigmented pubic hair present from a lack of any to practically a full density (Stolz & Stolz, 1951). Perceptible voice change sometimes occurs before penis acceleration or the presence of any pigmented pubic or axillary hair, and sometimes following full penis size, dense growth of pubic hair, and moderately dense growth of axillary hair (Greulich & others, 1942; Chang & others, 1966). At the time spermatazoa are first discharged in the urine, a boy may be in any stage of pubic- and axillary-hair development from the prepuberal condition to almost full density in each region (Baldwin, 1928).

Among boys 14 years of age, one may give no indication of puberal increase in penis size and another may show this organ to be near maximum size (Stolz & Stolz, 1951); again, one may give no indication of pigmented pubic or axillary hair and another may show a dense growth of pubic hair and some pigmented axillary hair (Kubitschek, 1932). During the year between 14 and 15 years of age, of three different boys one may increase in height four inches, one two inches, and one a half inch; the first boy is undergoing his puberal spurt, the second is either nearing his spurt or past it, and the third is close to his maximum adult height (Meredith, 1939b). The combination of fully developed testes, scrotum, penis, pubic hair, and axillary hair may be attained by age 15 years or may not be attained before age 20 years (Schonfeld, 1943).

Prediction of puberal changes has been investigated less extensively for boys than for girls. The early observation that boys tall in middle and late childhood tend to have their puberal spurt in height earlier than do the short boys (Baldwin, 1914) has been found to be too weak a tendency to have predictive usefulness. This is made explicit by noting that the correlation of height at age six years and age at maximum puberal velocity in height approximates $r = -.25$, yielding an index of forecasting efficiency below 4 percent (Meredith, 1965). Moderate positive association (r near .65) has been found between age at beginning enlargement of the testes and age at reaching maximum puberal velocity in height (Nicolson & Hanley, 1953).

There are other sorts of changes during adolescence than those directed toward accelerated growth of body organs and segments; cumulative increase of moderately coarse pigmented hairs on regions of the face, trunk, and limbs; or development of additional physiological functions. No puberal spurt occurs in volume of the brain, weight of the eyeballs, size of the bones of the inner ear, or number of erupting teeth (Scammon, 1930; Knott & Meredith, 1966). There is a gradual decrease in the weight of the cortex and medulla of the thymus (Boyd, 1936); loss of head hair, causing gradual indentation of the hairline on each side of the upper forehead superior to the eyebrows, also occurs (Schonfeld, 1943). The average thickness of adipose tissue between the skin and muscles of the arm and leg, although increasing to a plateau at age 15 years in girls, progressively decreases in boys throughout adolescence (Meredith, 1935; Boynton, 1936; Reynolds, 1950; Fry & others, 1965).

Howard V. Meredith
The University of Iowa

References

Altman, P. L., and Dittmer, D. S. (Eds.) *Growth, Including Reproduction and Morphological Development*. Federation of American Societies for Experimental Biology, 1962. p. 333–48.

Arey, L. B. *Developmental Anatomy*, 7th ed. Saunders, 1965.

Baldwin, B. T. *Physical Growth and School Progress.* U.S. Bureau of Education Bulletin No. 10 (Whole No. 581). GPO, 1914.

Baldwin, B. T. "The Determination of Sex Maturation in Boys by a Laboratory Method." *J Compar Psychol* 8:39–43; 1928.

Birren, J. E. (Ed.) *Handbook of Aging and the Individual.* U Chicago Press, 1959.

Blommers, P., and Lindquist, E. F. *Elementary Statistical Methods.* Houghton, 1960. p. 208–18.

Bonner, J. T. "Size and Cycle—An Essay on the Structure of Biology." *Am Scientist* 53:488–94; 1965.

Bottyán, O., and others. "Age of Menarche in Hungarian Girls." *Annales historico-naturales Musei Nationalis Hungarici pars anthropologica* 55:561–72; 1963.

Bowditch, H. P. "The Growth of Children." In Massachusetts State Board of Health, *Eighth Annual Report.* The Board, 1877. p. 273–324.

Boyd, E. "Weight of the Thymus and Its Component Parts and Number of Hassall Corpuscles in Health and in Disease." *Am J Diseases Children* 51:313–35; 1936.

Boynton, B. "The Physical Growth of Girls Between Birth and Eighteen Years." *U Iowa Stud Child Welf* 12(No. 4); 1936.

Brodie, A. G. "Present Status of Knowledge Concerning Movement of the Tooth Germ Through the Jaw." *J Am Dental Assn* 21:1830–8; 1934.

Bryan, A. H., and Greenberg, B. G. "Methodology in the Study of Physical Measurements of School Children." *Hum Biol* 24:117–44; 1952.

Burrell, R. J. W., and others. "Age at Menarche in South African Bantu Schoolgirls Living in the Transkei Reserve." *Hum Biol* 33:250–61; 1961.

Cattell, P. "Dentition as a Measure of Maturity." *Harvard Monogr Ed* No. 9, 1928.

Chang, K. S. F., and others. "Height and Weight of Southern Chinese Children." *Am J Phys Anthrop* 21:497–509; 1963.

Chang, K. S. F., and others. "Sexual Maturation of Chinese Boys in Hong Kong." *Pediatrics* 37:804; 1966.

Dahlberg, A. A. "The Changing Dentition of Man." *J Am Dental Assn* 32:676–90; 1945.

Dimock, H. S. *Rediscovering the Adolescent: A Study of Personality Development in Adolescent Boys.* Association Press, 1937.

Falkner, F. "Deciduous Tooth Eruption." *Archives Disease Childh* 32:386–91; 1957.

Fanning, E. A. "Third Molar Emergence in Bostonians." *Am J Phys Anthrop* 20:339–45; 1962.

Flory, C. D. "Predicting Puberty." *Child Develop* 6:1–6; 1935.

Foll, C. V. "Physical Development of Schoolgirls in Upper Burma." *Archives Disease Childh* 33:452–4; 1958.

Foll, C. V. "The Age at Menarche in Assam and Burma." *Archives Disease Childh* 36:302–4; 1961.

Forbes, G. B. "Chemical Growth in Infancy and Childhood." *J Pediatrics* 41:202–32; 1952.

Fried, R. I., and Smith, E. E. "Postmenarcheal Growth Patterns." *J Pediatrics* 61:562–5; 1962.

Fry, E. I., and others. "The Amount and Distribution of Subcutaneous Tissue in Southern Chinese Children from Hong Kong." *Amer J Phys Anthrop* 23:69–80; 1965.

Garn, S. M., and Lewis, A. B. "The Relationship Between Third Molar Agenesis and Reduction in Tooth Number." *Angle Orthodontist* 32:14–8; 1962.

Ghosh, S., and Beri, S. "Standard of Prematurity for North Indian Babies." *Indian J Child Health* 11:210–5; 1962.

Greulich, W. W., and Thoms, H. "The Growth and Development of the Pelvis of Individual Girls Before, During, and After Puberty." *Yale J Biol Med* 17:91–104; 1944.

Greulich, W. W., and others. "Somatic and Endocrine Studies of Puberal and Adolescent Boys." *Monogr Soc Res Child Develop* 7(No. 3); 1942.

Haataja, J. *Cephalic, Facial and Dental Growth in Finnish Children.* Helsinki Center for the Study of Child Growth and Development, 1963.

Hansman, C. F., and Maresh, M. M. "A Longitudinal Study of Skeletal Maturation." *Am J Diseases Children* 101:305–21; 1961.

Heimendinger, J. "Die Ergebnisse von Korpermessungen an 5000 Basler Kindern 2–18 Jahren." *Helvetica paediatrica acta* 19(Suppl. 13); 1964.

Hellman, M. "Nutrition, Growth and Education." *Dental Cosmos* 65:34–49; 1923.

Hellman, M. "Our Third Molar Teeth: Eruption, Presence and Absence." *Dental Cosmos* 78:750–62; 1936.

Inoue, T., and Shimizu, M. *Physical and Skeletal Growth and Development of Japanese Children.* Japanese Society for the Promotion of Science, 1965.

Jerome, E. K. "Change of Voice in Male Adolescents." *Q J Speech* 23:648–53; 1937.

Jung, F. T., and Shafton, A. L. "The Mammary Gland in the Normal Adolescent Male." *Proc Soc Exp Biol Med* 33:455–8; 1935.

Kasius, R. V., and others. "Maternal and Newborn Nutrition Studies at Philadelphia Lying-in Hospital. V: Size and Growth of Babies During the First Year of Life." *Milbank Memorial Fund Q* 35:323–72; 1957.

Keyfitz, N. *A Height and Weight Survey of Toronto Elementary School Children, 1939.* Department of Trade and Commerce, Dominion Bureau of Statistics, 1942.

Klein, H., and Cody, J. F. "Graphic Charts Which Depict the Variations in Numbers of Erupted Permanent Teeth in Grade School Children." *J Am Dental Assn* 26:609–11; 1939.

Knott, V. B., and Meredith, H. V. "Statistics on Eruption of the Permanent Dentition from Serial Data for North American White Children." *Angle Orthodontist* 37:212–22; 1967.

Knott, V. B., and O'Meara, W. F. "Serial Data on Primary Incisor Root Resorption and Gingival Emergence of Permanent Successors." *Angle Orthodontist,* 1967.

Kubitschek, P. E. "Sexual Development of Boys with Special Reference to the Appearance of Secondary Sex Characteristics and Their Relation to Structural and Personality Types." *J Nerv Ment Dis* 76:425–51; 1932.

Lee, M. C., and others. "Sexual Maturation of Chinese Girls in Hong Kong." *Pediatrics* 32:389–98; 1963.

Lee, M. C., and others. "Eruption of the Permanent Dentition of Southern Chinese Children in Hong Kong." *Archives Oral Biol* 10:849–61; 1965.

Lin, C. "Anthropometric Measurements of Shanghai Students and Preschool Children in 1954." *Chinese Med J* 75:1018–23; 1957.

Lysell, L., and others. "Time and Order of Eruption of the Primary Teeth." *Odontologisk revy* 13:217–234; 1962.

Maresh, M. M. "Bone, Muscle and Fat Measurements of the Extremities During the First Six Years of Life." *Pediatrics* 28:971–84; 1961.

Medawar, P. B. *The Uniqueness of the Individual.* Basic Books, 1957.

Méndez, J., and Behrhorst, C. "The Anthropometric Characteristics of Indian and Urban Guatemalans." *Hum Biol* 35:457–69; 1963.

Meredith, H. V. "The Rhythm of Physical Growth: A Study of Eighteen Measurements on Boys." *U Iowa Stud Child Welf* 11(No. 3); 1935.

Meredith, H. V. "Length of Head and Neck, Trunk, and Lower Extremities on Iowa City Children Aged Seven to Seventeen Years." *Child Develop* 10:129–44; 1939(a).

Meredith, H. V. "Stature of Massachusetts Children of North European and Italian Ancestry." *Am J Phys Anthrop* 24:301–46; 1939(b).

Meredith, H. V. "Physical Growth from Birth to Two Years. I: Stature." *U Iowa Stud Child Welf* 19:1–255; 1943.

Meredith, H. V. "Order and Age of Eruption for the Deciduous Dentition." *J Dental Res* 25:43–66; 1946. (See also Meredith, H. V. "A Chart on Eruption of the Deciduous Teeth for the Pediatrician's Office." *J Pediatrics* 38:482–3; 1951.)

Meredith, H. V. "Birth Order and Body Size. II: Neonatal and Childhood Materials." *Am J Phys Anthrop* 8:195–224; 1950.

Meredith, H. V. "Relation Between Socioeconomic Status and Body Size in Boys Seven to Ten Years of Age." *Am J Diseases Children* 82:702–709; 1951.

Meredith, H. V. "Measuring the Growth Characteristics of School Children." *J Sch Health* 25:267–73; 1955.

Meredith, H. V. "Change in the Stature and Body Weight of North American Boys During the Last 80 Years." In Lipsitt, L. P., and Spiker, C. C. (Eds.) *Advances in Child Development and Behavior,* Vol. 1. Academic, 1963. p. 69–114.

Meredith, H. V. "Selected Anatomic Variables Analyzed for Interage Relationships of the Size-Size, Size-Gain, and Gain-Gain Varieties." In Lipsitt, L. P., and Spiker, C. C. (Eds.) *Advances in Child Development and Behavior,* Vol. 2. Academic, 1965. p. 221–256.

Meredith, H. V., and Brown, A. W. "Growth in Body Weight During the First Ten Days of Postnatal Life." *Hum Biol* 11:24–77; 1939.

Meredith, H. V., and Sherbina, P. R. "Body Form in Childhood: Ratios Quantitatively Describing Three Slender-to-stocky Continua on Girls Four to Eight Years of Age." *Child Develop* 22:275–83; 1951.

Meyers, E. S. A. "Height-Weight Survey of New South Wales School Children." *Med J Australia* 1:435–53; 1956.

Michelson, N. "Studies in the Physical Development of Negroes. IV: Onset of Puberty." *Am J Phys Anthrop* 2:151–66; 1944.

Millis, J. "Gain in Weight and Length in the First Year of Life of Chinese Infants Born in Singapore in 1951." *Med J Australia* 1:283–5; 1954.

Mills, C. A., and Ogle, C. "Physiological Sterility of Adolescence." *Hum Biol* 8:607–15; 1936.

Montaque, M. F. A. *Adolescent Sterility.* Thomas, 1946.

Moscona, A. A. "Tissue Reconstruction from Dissociated Cells." In Zarrow, M. X. (Ed.) *Growth in Living Systems.* Basic Books, 1961. p. 197–220.

Nicolson, A. B., and Hanley, C. "Indices of Physiological Maturity: Derivation and Interrelationships." *Child Develop* 24:3–38; 1953.

O'Brien, R., and others. *Body Measurements of American Boys and Girls for Garment and Pattern Construction.* Miscellaneous Publication No. 366. U.S. Department of Agriculture, Bureau of Home Economics, 1941.

Oettle, A. G., and Higginson, J. "The Age of Menarche in South African Bantu (Negro) Girls." *Hum Biol* 33:181–90; 1961.

Priesel, R., and Wagner, R. "Gesetzmässigkeiten im Auftreten der extragenitalen sekundären Geschlechtsmerkmale bei Mädchen." *Zeitschrift für Konstitutionslehre* 15:333–52; 1931.

Pryor, H. B. "Certain Physical and Physiological Aspects of Adolescent Development in Girls." *J Pediatrics* 8:52–62; 1936.

Pyle, S. I., and Drain, C. L. "Some Conditions in the Dentition of Preschool Children." *Child Develop* 2:147–52; 1931.

Reynolds, E. L. "The Distribution of Subcutaneous Fat in Childhood and Adolescence." *Monogr Soc Res Child Develop* 15(No. 2); 1950.

Reynolds, E. L., and Wines, J. V. "Individual Differences in Physical Changes Associated with Adolescence in Girls." *Am J Diseases Children* 75:329–50; 1948.

Richey, H. G. "The Relation of Accelerated, Normal and Retarded Puberty to the Height and Weight of School Children." *Monog Soc Res Child Develop* 2(No. 1); 1937.

Roche, A. F., and Barkla, D. H. "The Eruption of Deciduous Teeth in Mongols." *J Mental Deficiency Res* 8:55–64; 1964.

Scammon, R. E. "The Measurement of the Body in Childhood." In Harris, J. A., and others. *The Measurement of Man.* U Minnesota Press, 1930. p. 173–215.

Schonfeld, W. A. "Primary and Secondary Sexual

Characteristics, Study of Their Development in Males from Birth Through Maturity, with Biometric Study of Penis and Testes." *Am J Diseases Children* 65:535–49; 1943.

Scott, J. A. *Report on the Heights and Weights (and Other Measurements) of School Pupils in the County of London in 1959.* No. 4086. London County Council, 1961.

Seckel, H. P. G., and others. "Six Examples of Precocious Sexual Development." *Am J Diseases Children* 78:484–515; 1949.

Shock, N. "Physiological Changes in Adolescence." In *Adolescence*, 43rd Yearbook, Part I, NSSE 1944. p. 56–79.

Shock, N. "The Physiology of Ageing." *Am Scientist* 206:100–10; 1962.

Shuttleworth, F. K. "Sexual Maturation and the Physical Growth of Girls Age Six to Nineteen." *Monog Soc Res Child Develop* 2(No. 5); 1937.

Shuttleworth, F. K. "The Physical and Mental Growth of Girls and Boys Age 6 to 19 in Relation to Age at Maximum Growth." *Monog Soc Res Child Develop* 4(No. 3); 1939.

Simmons, K., and Greulich, W. W. "Menarcheal Age and the Height, Weight, and Skeletal Age of Girls Age 7 to 17 Years." *J Pediatrics* 22:518–48; 1943.

Smith, C. A. *The Physiology of the Newborn Infant*, 3rd ed. Thomas, 1959.

Stolz, H. R., and Stolz, L. M. *Somatic Development of Adolescent Boys.* Macmillan, 1951.

Streeter, G. L. "Prenatal Growth of the Child." *Carnegie Institute Washington News Service B* 4:127–32; 1937.

Sundal, A. *The Norms for Height and Weight in Healthy Norwegian Children from Birth to 15 Years of Age.* Griegs Boytrykkeri, 1957.

Tanner, J. M. *Growth at Adolescence.* Blackwell Scientific Publications, Ltd., 1962.

Tanner, J. M. "Radiographic Studies of Body Composition in Children and Adults." In *Human Body Composition: Approaches and Applications.* Pergamon, 1965. p. 211–36.

Tanner, J. M., and O'Keeffe, B. "Age at Menarche in Nigerian School Girls, with a Note on Their Heights and Weights from Age 12 to 19." *Hum Biol* 34:187–196; 1962.

Todd, T. W. "Integral Growth of the Face. I: The Nasal Area." *Int J Orthodont Oral Surg* 22:321; 1936.

Towns, J., and others. "The Age of Menarche in Melbourne Schoolgirls." *Australian Paediatric J* 2:67–9; 1966.

Tuddenham, R. D., and Snyder, M. M. "Physical Growth of California Boys and Girls from Birth to Eighteen Years." *U California Pub Child Develop* 1:183–364; 1954.

Watson, E. H., and Lowrey, G. H. *Growth and Development of Children.* Year Book, 1962.

Zukowski, W., and others. "The Age of Menarche in Polish Girls." *Hum Biol* 36:233–4; 1964.

PHYSICAL EDUCATION

A department or school of health, physical education, and recreation at a university which trains teachers enjoys a unique position with regard to research. The investigative responsibilities include studies of methods of instruction and techniques of administration and a continual examination of its own philosophy. But, in addition to conducting studies which generally cross departmental lines with various departments in education, physical education has the responsibility of extending the limits of knowledge within the subject field itself.

Both types of research are indispensable in any college dedicated to the improvement of public and private programs of education. Furthermore, if experimental results are to be applied in the schools, the school setting must then be brought into focus. Much experimentation, however, is needed to provide a sound scientific basis before attempting application in the school setting. Departments of health, physical education, and recreation necessarily show a great diversity in research because of overlap with the fields of medicine, nutrition, psychology, sociology, etc., and because some of the professional students (generally not a large number) are not being trained for positions in the school.

HISTORY AND PHILOSOPHY. Physical education has had scant acquaintance with history and philosophy. Davis (1961) has outlined the philosophical process in physical education and has traced the historical influences and ideas that have shaped current philosophies. He notes that few, if any, authors in the history of physical education have written for the purpose of exemplifying philosophical writings. Cowell (1963) has composed a study of philosophical thought by leaders in physical education and has developed from this historical summary an objective view of the philosophical ideas of American physical educators.

An early effort to relate the philosophies of leaders in American physical education to systematic philosophies of education was made by Bair (1957). His ultimate purpose was to determine the philosophical directions which seem to be indicated for American physical education. A checklist was sent to a selected group of leaders in American physical education to obtain data for the study. He concluded that professional leaders are providing a predominantly naturalistic direction to physical education.

In recent years a growing interest has developed in defining the contributions which are unique to physical education. Snyder (1960) notes that the physical education profession is not in agreement in relation to its dominant purpose or to which elements make this discipline distinct from other disciplines. Henry (1964) has developed the concept of physical education as an academic discipline with a body of knowledge without any need to demonstrate practical application. Physical education has a scholarly body of knowledge drawn from anatomy, physics, physiology, cultural anthropology, history, sociology, and psychology.

Weston (1962) has written a concise history of American physical education. The history begins with the European background of American physical education and progresses through the development of colonial America to the early months of the Kennedy administration. Specific attention is given to the significant events that have altered the course of development of American physical education, such as the controversy concerning the various European systems of physical education, the effect of two world wars, and, finally, more recent developments resulting from the cold war and use of the Kraus-Weber physical fitness tests. In addition, the author has included many documents selected from the speeches and papers of outstanding leaders in physical education. This section concludes with a document by Charles H. McCloy entitled "What is Physical Fitness?" dealing with the subject that was the overriding concern of physical education in the 1950's and 1960's.

Eyler (1960) reviewed the nature of historical research in sports and physical education. He stated that the student of historical research might follow two paths. He might use documents to create a synthesis of what has actually happened, or he might try to explain the present status of sports and physical education in the light of historical events. Eyler included a large bibliography of historical work in the area of physical education but noted a decrease in the number of historical works in this field in recent years. Also included was a section on needed historical research in physical education.

PHYSICAL FITNESS. In recent years physical educators have become interested to a greater degree than ever before in the development and measurement of physical fitness. The body of knowledge in this area has increased considerably over the past decade. Many seminars have been held in order to analyze current ideas (Karpovich & others, 1960; Staley & others, 1960; Adams & others, 1963; Canadian Fitness Seminar, 1963).

Definition and Measurement. Consolazio and others (1963) stated that the quantitative measurement of physical fitness is one of the most complex and controversial problems in applied physiology. Linde (1963), in an appraisal of exercise fitness tests for children, reiterated the frequently expressed conclusion that no single test of physical fitness is completely satisfactory.

Consolazio and others (1963) included endurance, power, agility, strength, balance, and flexibility among the components of physical fitness. Endurance, considered one of the most important elements, is required for performing heavy work and is limited by strength, oxygen supply to the working muscles, an adequate source of energy, and motivation. Hence, at least one component of physical fitness is dependent on the high capacity of the respiratory and circulatory systems for supplying oxygen to the tissues (Dill, 1960).

Because the meaning of fitness embraces many different concepts, its various aspects can be measured and developed in different ways. The recently published survey of youth fitness by Hunsicker and Reiff (1965) attests to the multiplicity of the measurements needed to appraise this aspect of dynamic health. Thus, the 50-yard dash was selected as an indicator of speed, the 600-yard run was employed to measure endurance, and pull-ups (chins) were used to measure arm and shoulder strength. The tests used in this survey met certain practical criteria, i.e., the tests require little or no equipment and they are easily understood by children as young as 10 years of age.

In comparing the results for 1965 with those for 1958, the authors found that the physical fitness level of the public school children, grades 5–12, in 1965 was above that in 1958. The authors felt that the improvement in the level of fitness was due to two main factors: a greater familiarity of school pupils with the test battery and a greater interest of school personnel in physical fitness.

Strength. Muscular strength is important in the performance of many physical fitness test items. The 600-yard run, 50-yard dash, pull-ups, sit-ups, and standing broad jump are examples of test items in which muscular strength plays a significant role. The measurement of static muscular strength, defined as the amount of force exerted by a muscle, may be measured directly by the use of dynamometers and cable tensiometers. These methods have changed little since the dynamometer was developed in the eighteenth century. Various instruments used in the measurement of strength over the years are shown and described by Hunsicker and Donnelly (1955).

The physiology of muscle training has been discussed by Muller (1962). He points out that irrespective of the method used for training with isometric contractions, muscular strength increases at a continuously declining rate. Eventually a strength limit is reached. The time taken to reach this limit is dependent on the intensity of training. Muller found that when training with one daily maximum contraction of one second, the strength of the main muscles of the body ultimately increase about 1 percent before reaching a strength limit, whereas the rarely used muscles of the body might increase 63 percent in strength. The relationship of strength to age and sex and the effect of training on the histological and chemical changes in muscle have been described by Hettinger (1961).

Clarke (1960) has presented studies related to the muscular strength and endurance of man. His monograph includes references to many published and unpublished works on muscular strength. The studies presented are limited to those conducted by cable-tension testing methods.

The chemistry and physiology of strength were discussed in a recent symposium (Rodahl & Horvath, 1962). This is a detailed analysis of muscle function, structure, contraction, and performance. Such specific topics as skeletal-muscle performance, fatigue, tone and postural regulation, and cardiac-muscle performance are included in this collection of papers. The mechanism of muscular contraction has been described by Huxley (1965).

Flexibility. The relationship of bodily flexibility to physical fitness or health is not clear. DeVries (1963) found that flexibility did not determine speed or oxygen cost of a sprint run of 100 yards.

Massey and Chaudet (1956) studied the effects of continual heavy resistive exercise on the range of movement in certain joints. They observed that movements which receive emphasis in the training programs in which weights are used increased or showed less decrement in flexibility in the weight-training group compared with the control group. On the other hand, movements which were not emphasized in the weight-training program showed a greater decrease in flexibility in the weight-trainers than in the controls. The authors concluded that weight lifting increased the range of movement in joints which were exercised while it restricted movements in joints which were not exercised.

Broer and Galles (1958) found that the proportion of reach length to leg length is not an important factor in the performance of the toe-touch flexibility test for persons with average body builds. For those with extreme body builds, a longer trunk-plus-arm measurement in relation to shorter legs enhanced the performance on this test. These observations are confirmed by Mathews and others (1957) and Wear (1963). This has been a controversial question in recent years.

Reaction and Movement Time. Speed of reaction and movement are sometimes included as components of physical fitness. The effects of age and sex on this fitness parameter have been thoroughly studied in recent years (Pierson & Montoye, 1958; Pierson, 1959; Hodgkins, 1963). Movement and reaction time are slower at all ages in females. The shortest reaction and movement times occur at about age 20 in both sexes.

Kerr (1966) has summarized the differences of opinion with regard to the relationship between movement time and reaction time. Apparently, it is not clear as yet whether the two are significantly related. The effects of physical education or athletic conditioning on reaction time or movement time have not been studied sufficiently for conclusions to be drawn.

Work Capacity. Endurance, or the ability to continue strenuous exercise, involves three general factors. First, body build and technique are reflected in efficiency or energy cost. Second, motivation with related psychological characteristics and factors in part determine work performance. And, finally, the condition of the cardiovascular-respiratory system and other physiological systems influence the maximum rate of energy utilization and hence work capacity. This last factor—namely, physiological and biochemical considerations—is most closely related to physical fitness and probably is most sensitive to conditioning and physical education programs. Hence, most research efforts with regard to work capacity have been directed toward improvement via the physiological-biochemical state. Good discussions in this area may be found in the works of Chapman (1967), Chapman and Mitchell (1965), Brouha (1960), Dill (1960), Riley (1960), and Astrand (1952, 1965). The relationship of work capacity to age and sex is discussed, as well as mechanical efficiency, effects of training, and the importance of work capacity in sports, occupation, and leisure-time activities.

For a number of years, a measure of fitness of the physiological systems which are involved in physical working capacity has been sought. There is agreement among the authors cited above that one of the most important limiting factors in work performance is the ability of the individual to take in oxygen from the air and deliver it to the tissues. This can be measured with precision in the laboratory and is being so measured daily in many departments of physical education throughout the world. However, the techniques are much too complicated to use in school or other field testing. Hence, much research in recent years has been directed toward the development of a simple practical test of this aspect of physical fitness. Heart-rate response to a fairly strenuous standard exercise still offers most promise in this regard (Rodahl & Issekutz, 1960; Montoye & others, 1960). When feasible, a test of increasing intensity in which heart rate is determined at each new load level (a multistaged work test) has several advantages. This approach was used as early as 1941 (Lehmann & Michaelis, 1941), but recent modifications have added to its usefulness (Adams & others, 1961; Balke & others, 1953; Nagle & others, 1965). Good discussions of work capacity tests may be found in the symposium edited by Adams and others (1963).

Body-weight Control. It is clear that physical activity is a potent factor in weight control and the prevention of obesity. Largely through the efforts of Mayer and others (Mayer, 1955; Mayer & Bullen, 1960), data have been accumulated to refute two erroneous notions about exercise and fatness. The view is often expressed that exercise is ineffective in weight control because appetite is thought to increase in direct proportion to the physical exercise taken. However, this has been demonstrated to occur only when one engages in considerable exercise during the day. When human beings or animals become very sedentary, their food intake (hence also their body weight) actually increases above that when a moderate amount of exercise is taken. The other erroneous concept has to do with the belief that an enormous amount of physical activity is required to burn a pound of body fat and that it is useless to increase the physical activity in order to reduce or to maintain body weight. It is true that an appreciable amount of exercise is required to burn a pound of fat. However, it is not necessary to expend this energy at one session. All things being equal, a few extra minutes of daily exercise over a number of years can be the difference between accumulating or not accumulating considerable body fat. It is often not realized that the excess weight has usually been accumulated over a fairly long period of time. It is sometimes thought that if one has a predisposition to accumulate fat easily, it is useless to exercise in order to prevent this from happening. However, Mayer (Mayer & others, 1954) did some very interesting experiments with genetically obese mice. These animals normally get to be an enormous size and are extremely fat. There is another strain of mice which inherit an abnormal gene causing them to exercise by turning around almost continuously. They are called waltzing mice. By mating genetically obese mice with ones carrying the waltzing gene, Mayer was able to show that activity greatly reduced the fat accumulation in the otherwise very obese animals.

The important question whether instruction in physical education and participation in sports, dancing, and other physical activities change ones habits and attitudes with respect to maintaining body weight late in life has not as yet been answered.

A review of current knowledge regarding obesity, including the influence of exercise, may be found in a recent publication, *Obesity and Health*, of the U.S. Department of Health, Education, and Welfare (1966). This monograph also contains suggestions for future studies. A comprehensive review of methods of measuring fatness and the influence of various factors, including exercise in weight control, can be found in the proceedings of the conference on body composition (Brožek 1963).

Exercise and Health. An important research area in physical education during the past few years has been the investigation of the influence of physical activity on health. This is an extremely comprehensive and complex area involving questions of both positive and negative effects. Hence, only a few aspects can be touched upon here. In recent years much research effort has been expended in studying the role of physical activity in heart disease. A number of excellent conferences have been held on the topic and the papers presented at these meetings have been published (Karvonen & Barry, 1967; "Symposium on Work and the Heart," 1965; "International Symposium on Physical Activity and Cardiovascular Health," 1967). The evidence is quite conclusive that physical activity can be an important factor for some people in the prevention or delay of heart disease. Questions of how much activity, how strenuous the activity, and what kinds of people benefit from activity most have not been answered. Research is needed on related questions of (1) what motivates some people to maintain an exercise program and (2) what the influence of school programs in physical education is in this regard.

Longevity and causes of death of former college athletes apparently are little different from those among men who did not participate in interschool athletics (Montoye, 1960, 1967). Although the data are much less conclusive than they are for heart disease, there nevertheless is some evidence that regular exercise may have beneficial effects on the delay, control, or prevention of mental and emotional disorders, cancer, low-back pain, diabetes, hypertension, and problems associated with child-bearing and menstruation. A good review of research on the relationship of exercise to health is contained in a special issue of the *Research Quarterly* (Karpovich & others, 1960).

Comparative Studies. Campbell and Pohndorf (1961) compared the performance of children in England with children in the United States in the physical fitness tests described by Hunsicker (1958). In an entirely different battery of tests, American and European children were compared (Kraus & Raab, 1961). In these comparisons, American children were less fit than children in other countries. Contrary findings in a work-capacity test were reported by Rodahl and Issekutz (1960) in which no significant differences were found between samples of American, Swedish and German children. All of these studies can be questioned on the basis of comparability in sampling methods.

SPORTS PERFORMANCE. Training Techniques. Research in sports performance has developed along particular lines. The greatest advances have been made in the fields of exercise and environmental physiology, with efforts being directed at answering such questions as the following: What are the limiting physiological factors in maximum work performance? What physiological and anatomic changes take place as a result of strenuous athletic training? How can athletic performance be improved through changes in diet or training regimens? and What are the physiological mechanisms involved in adaptation to exercise and athletic performance at high altitudes, in the heat, or in the cold? The impressive increase in research studies by physical educators and others along lines that will give answers to these questions can be seen in the increase in percentage and total volume of articles in the *Journal of Applied Physiology*, in the establishment recently of two journals which contain articles on these topics (*Ergonomics* and *Journal of Sports Medicine and Physical Fitness*), and, finally, in the many symposia and conferences that have been held on these topics.

The physiological mechanisms involved in work and athletic performance are better understood now than ever before, but there have been few, if any, breakthroughs which can explain the new athletic records being registered. The improved performance must still be attributed not only to advances in scientific knowledge but also to the ferreting out of boys and girls with sports potential, an increase in population throughout the world, improved equipment, greater opportunity and time for sports participation, and improved coaching that includes the overcoming of psychological barriers. Recent knowledge of the physiological effects of training and the mechanisms involved have been summarized in a fairly recent book by W. R. Johnson (1960).

Training with weights has been added to conditioning programs for swimmers, shot-putters, football players, and athletes in many other sports and events. In the main, research has supported this approach, but there has been contradictory evidence as well. Interval training or modifications of it (for example, circuit training), are now in vogue for developing endurance. Recent evidence suggests that intensity of exercise is more important than duration in developing endurance or work capacity. This is in line with the trend for interval training. No impressive evidence for altering the diet of the athlete to improve performance has been reported in recent years (Van Itallie & others, 1960) with one exception. A recent report by Bergstrom and Hultman (1966) indicates that in preparing for an important endurance event, depletion of the carbohydrate stores four to five days before competition with a hard workout enhances the capacity of the body to store glycogen (carbohydrates). It is well known that during very strenuous exercise, the body preferentially burns carbohydrates. Hence, after a very hard workout with the body stores of carbohydrates depleted, the body seems to be somehow able to rebound and store during the next three or four days an extra supply of carbohydrates. If this can be confirmed, a change in the diet and training regimen during the week preceding an endurance event is indicated.

Environmental Influences. Research on sports and exercise at high altitudes has been stimulated by the fact that the 1968 Olympic games have been scheduled for Mexico City (which is at an altitude about 7,500 feet). Laboratory research and field studies indicate that the athletic events of short duration (for example, a 400-meter run or a 100-meter swim) will be affected very little by altitude. However, deterioration of performance can be expected to be quite dramatic in the endurance events. The physiological changes and mechanisms associated with altitude and altitude adaptation are still not completely understood. In general, it is thought that the higher the altitude at which performance is to occur, the longer the adaptation period required. A rule of thumb is one week for each 2,500 feet. However, there are some scientists who have proposed that performance deteriorates progressively at high altitudes for the first several weeks and that performance is, therefore, better soon after arrival at the high altitude than later (Dill & others, 1966). The effects of altitude on physical performance are summarized in the works of Balke (1960), Goddard (1967) and Dill (1964).

Exercise performance in the heat and cold has been summarized in a recent handbook edited by Dill (1964). Appreciably more is known about heat adaptation than cold adaptation insofar as exercise is concerned. However, many questions still remain unanswered.

Age and Maturation. Excellent reviews of the relationship of physical activity to growth and development are contained in the papers by Espenschade (1960) and Rarick (1960a).

It is clear that physical size and performance in sports and other physical tasks increase together in the growing child. This is true in both sexes even when the influence of age is eliminated. However girls' performance in most sports skills improves only until about the age of 13 or 14, whereas boys continue to show improvement throughout high school and even longer. In Olympic competition, champions in many sports are younger now than in previous years, especially among females. This may be a result of, among other things, earlier maturation and of exposure to training and competition at an earlier age. On the other hand, as summarized by Buskirk and Councilman (1960) numerous middle-aged men participate enthusiastically and profitably in professional sports, and many of the contestants in the Olympic games are middle-aged. The median ages of United States Olympic contestants from 1920 to 1936 in the Marathon, Bobsledding, and Equestrian events were over thirty. The span of ages of competitors in the 1952 Olympic games exceeded four decades.

Kinesiology. Kinesiological or biomechanical research in recent years has advanced very rapidly. To a considerable extent that is owing to a change in the approach to teaching in this area and also to the development of new equipment. In previous years, kinesiology was taught with the emphasis on anatomy, that is, on the origin, insertion, nerve innervation, and action of muscles. This has proved to be a sterile approach in many instances. More recently, the emphasis has been on the application of Newtonian laws of mechanics to human motion. This approach has offered more promise in creating a greater understanding of movement, particularly sports skills. This in turn should lead to improved teaching and coaching in the field of sports. In many instances, a seasoned coach with years of experience intuitively understands movement and sports performance, but he is unable to transmit this knowledge to students and beginning teachers and coaches. If this knowledge can be reduced to mechanical principles, the information can be assimilated much more readily by the neophyte.

Improvements in equipment for studying high-speed motion have contributed to the application of applied mechanics to physical activity. The development of the stroboscopic-light technique (Edgerton, 1958; Edgerton & Killian, 1954) and improvements in methods of timing used in high-speed photography have given impetus to this work. The strobe light provide an inexpensive method of analysis for classroom and laboratory use.

The more widespread use of electromyography and refinement in recording and analyzing techniques have contributed to our increasing knowledge of human movement. When a muscle contracts, tremendous increases in electrical activity may be recorded with electrodes in or on the muscles. When these electrical signals are properly amplified, they can be recorded. It is possible in this way to determine precisely when muscle groups contract or relax. So far, a good correlation between the quantification of the records and force of muscle contraction has not been demonstrated. However, this area has already added to our knowledge of exercise and sports, as shown by such reports as the one by Broer and Houtz (1967). The correlating of electromyography and energy-metabolism studies should produce interesting work in the future.

The technique employed by the late Dr. Dempster in refining and understanding forces and actions during sports performance is one of the most promising approaches. He used anatomical data from cadavers and living subjects to estimate quite precisely the masses and centers of gravity of various parts of the body in order to investigate the forces around joints. Plagenhoff (1966), one of Dempster's students, has been extending the work.

Until recently the measurement of angular motion about joints during rapid sports movements has been almost entirely limited to photographic measurements, generally two-dimensional photographs. With the development of an electronic goniometer it became possible to measure angular velocity and acceleration around joints in three-dimensional space. Karpovich and some of his students (for example, Klissouras & Karpovich, 1967) have already published a number of papers using this equipment. The development of a force platform (Brouha, 1960) has made available another approach to the study of kinesiology and energy metabolism. The principle of this equipment is based on the second law of motion, that every action will have an equal but opposite reaction. If a subject moves on a sensitive platform, this movement will be transmitted as forces in three planes. The resultant force should be a measure of energy cost.

Comparative Studies. There have been no comprehensive studies of sports participation and performance among various countries. Such data obviously are difficult to interpret because of the diversity of activities and cultures in various countries around the world. A comparison of Olympic participation and performance, because of the differences in selection and training and organization of teams, probably reflects little about the sports participation of the majority of people in a given country. A comparison of countries in terms of frequency and kinds of sports participation in various age groups is needed. It appears that in the United States sports participation is closely tied to school activities. Hence, there is an abrupt change in habits of living when school days are over. However, in many countries of the world the sports clubs are very prevalent. Young boys and girls frequently become members as a part of their families, and perhaps this practice has an influence on sports participation in later life.

Sports Tests. During the past 10 or 15 years there has been little activity in the development and validation of sports ability tests. Careful studies are needed in this field. A number of tests have been validated for a particular age group, but little is known about their usefulness at other age levels. There are few validated tests in any sports for the elementary or junior high school age group. The American Association for Health, Physical Education, and Recreation, through its research council, has been developing standard sports tests. Included with the standardized directions are performance norms. This project is directed by Dr. Frank Sills of the department of physical education at East Stroudsburg State University, Pennsylvania. So far, tests have been developed only in the following sports: softball (boys and girls), basketball (boys and girls), and football (boys). A review of other sports tests available may be found in one of the many published tests and measurements books (see for example, Clarke, 1959; Smithells & Cameron, 1962).

Sports Injuries. The medical profession during the past decade or two has shown an increased interest in the health implications and problems of exercise and athletics. The establishment of the American College of Sports Medicine brought physicians, physical educators, physiologists, and other scientists together for the cooperative study of problems related to sports and exercise. This organization, through its annual meetings and committees, has been studying problems on several fronts, including (1) the effects of exercise on health, (2) improvement of physical performance (including athletic performance) through scientific investigation, and (3) the prevention and treatment of athletic injuries. Through participation with other national sports-medicine organizations, an international journal, The *Journal of Sports Medicine and Physical Fitness*, publishes papers dealing with these topics.

Recent studies have produced careful epidemiologic surveys of sports injuries and have prompted the development of safer sports equipment, particularly ski equipment and headgear used in American football, baseball, and ice hockey. Deaths and disabilities due to participation in sports in the heat have received greater research emphasis in recent years than before and have increased our ability to prevent heat deaths in sports. Considerable work has been done on the use of drugs and their effect on sports performance. A number of national sports-medicine groups have organized to discourage the use of drugs for improving athletic performance.

SOCIOLOGY AND PSYCHOLOGY. Motor learning is of interest to both physical education and psychology. Davis and Lockhart (1960) have prepared a complete list of reference works on motor learning and performance. G. B. Johnson, Jr. (1960), has reviewed the literature in this area and has found a great overlap in the areas of interest of the two disciplines. Included is a discussion of current measurement techniques and the major problems that are inherent in these techniques. The effect of individual and group characteristics on motor learning are analyzed for age, sex, intelligence, and race. The merits of distributed and massed practice in learning motor skills are outlined with reference to the research in the area. A summary of the studies of motor learning concerned with the whole and part methods of presentation are also included. The author concludes that distributed practice has been found more effective than massed practice and, in general, that a combination of whole practice with repetition of difficult parts is the best method for efficient motor learning.

Harmon and Oxendine (1961) have found that different lengths of practice periods have different effects on the learning of a motor skill during the various periods in the learning process. Long practice periods were shown to be advantageous during the early stages of the learning process, whereas in the later stages shorter practice periods proved to work as well.

Richardson (1967) has reviewed the role of mental practice in the learning of a motor skill and concluded that the combination of mental and manual practice appeared to be more effective in changing human performance than was manual practice alone. Missiuro (1961) investigated the effect of external stimuli on man's performance of a motor task. Visual and acoustic stimuli are reported by the author to have a stimulating effect on performance. For example, the presence of onlookers brought about in the persons performing the task an increase in work capacity of 10 to 44 percent over the output during a period when no onlookers were present. Ikai and Steinhaus (1961) found that performance of a simple strength task could be improved by the firing of a shot behind the unwarned subject as the subject exerted his maximal strength. Hypnotic suggestions of strength increased the average pull by 18 pounds. The effect of group interactions upon improvement in performance have been studied by Cratty and Sage (1964). They observed that if the group interaction took place during the latter part of a learning task greater improvement was found in performance than if the group interactions took place in the initial stages of learning. Interaction of the subjects between trials produced a greater improvement than that shown by subjects who were isolated between trials.

The relationship between verbal and motor learning was explored by Cratty (1963). Two groups of 30 male students, equated on the basis of scores achieved when learning a series of nonsense syllables, were blindfolded and given 10 massed trials in two large maze tasks. No significant differences were found in performance on the motor tasks between those of high and low verbal ability, and no significant correlations were found between verbal and motor ability as measured by the experimental tasks.

In a survey of the literature Shaw and Cordts (1960) found that attempts to relate athletic participation to academic performance yield conflicting and inconclusive results. They also noted that almost no research has been conducted with regard to the possible relationship of physical fitness and academic performance.

Studies of the role of athletics and games in a social setting are difficult to find in the physical education literature. Exceptions are the studies by Stumpf and Cozens on the role of games and sports of the New Zealand Maoris (1947) and the Fijians (1949).

The reasons why people play and engage in sports have been reviewed by Cofer and Johnson (1960). Included in their report is a summary of the current literature on the personality traits of various athletes. The authors found very few articles on this subject and were unable to make any generalized statement with regard to specific identifying characteristics of athletic groups.

CURRICULUM IN PHYSICAL EDUCATION.
Maturation and Physical Education. Much is known about growth in children as related to performance in physical education activities. Reviews by Espenschade (1960) and Rarick (1960a) indicate that age, height, and weight are all related to performance and that body type and sexual development make additional independent contributions to sports and other physical performance. As children, especially boys, reach sexual maturity, there are substantial gains in strength and motor ability. Children whose sexual maturity occurs early in life are better performers after puberty. They have greater strength and are more skilled. In the case of boys, performance continues to improve during the growing years throughout high school. But in girls, particularly in endurance events and those activities requiring maximum effort, performance reaches a plateau at about age 13 or 14. In fact, performance may begin to deteriorate at this time. How much of the difference in performance in boys and girls is due to cultural and how much to biological influences is not known. It is well established, however, that the male hormone has marked muscle-strength-building effect. On the other hand, there is greater inhibition in girls for performing maximally in physical tests. This was brought out by the release of such inhibitions under the influence of hypnosis (Ikai & Steinhaus, 1961). The greater inhibition in girls probably has a cultural base to a large extent.

School Curriculum Development. In the previous edition of this encyclopedia, Rarick (1960b) indicated that there was little experimental data to implement the grade placement of physical activities in the school curriculum. Unfortunately this is still the state of affairs today, even though much is known about the interrelationship of physical skills and growth. Children are maturing earlier today, and this certainly has implications for curriculum planning. To what extent the young child can be pushed before harmful effects result is still not known, but it is becoming clearer that the healthy child can withstand greater physiological stress than was earlier thought to be the case. It is also obvious that greater attention must be given to individual differences in the school program. All evidence still points to the fact that basic physical skills can best be taught in the elementary and junior high schools, with emphasis on refinement and specialization at the high school level. In recent years more attention has been paid to motivation and teaching the "why" of exercise at the college level. This is exemplified in the publication by Van Huss and others (1969). This approach is probably more appropriate at the high school level because many of the children do not go on to college.

Adult Fitness and Physical Education. With an increase in coronary-artery disease in this country in recent years, and because of the evidence linking lack of physical activity to heart disease, there is an increase in enrollment in adult fitness classes and an increased interest in leisure-time exercise programs. It is anticipated that physical educators, both men and women, will be called upon more frequently in the future to provide leadership in such programs. A discussion of exercise problems and related research in middle and old age is presented by Norris and Shock (1960) and by Buskirk and Councilman (1960). The evidence strongly suggests that most exercise is well tolerated by middle-aged people who are free from serious medical disability, provided a judicious approach to the selection of and participation in physical activities is taken. The psychological and social benefits of leisure-time exercise may be as important as the physiological benefits. It would be helpful to know the energy cost of various activities as performed by middle-aged and older men and women. Unfortunately, data of this kind are meager. The best review and summary of energy costs of various activities has been written by Passmore and Durnin (1955). Tables 315 and 316 in the *Handbook of Biological Data* (Spector, 1956) are also helpful in this regard.

ORGANIZATION AND ADMINISTRATION. There have been few well-controlled investigations of administrative practices in physical education. The best thinking on the construction of facilities for high schools is contained in a publication by the Athletic Institute and the American Association for Health, Physical Education, and Recreation (1965).

Soon to be published by the Athletic Institute is a similar publication describing physical education facilities for colleges and universities. Included in this publication is a section devoted to research facilities.

Grading practices and determination of optimum class size for various activities, of the most appropriate grouping of children, and of the use of various kinds of equipment at different age levels are for the most part all still based on individual preferences and uncontrolled observations. Little research has been done on these problems.

The existing state school laws and regulations for health, physical education, safety education, driver education, and outdoor education are contained in a recent booklet published by the U.S. Office of Education (Maynard & Rinaldi, 1964). The state regulations requiring physical education in the elementary and secondary schools and the individual colleges or university's requirements are based in large measure upon the association of inactivity (that is, a sedentary existence) in later life with chronic disease and increased rate of aging. The critical question of how physical education in schools changes the attitudes of boys and girls insofar as the inclination to exercise in later life is concerned has not been tested through carefully designed research studies.

The place of interscholastic athletics at the high school, junior high school, and elementary-school levels also has not been subjected to rigorous research to the extent that clear-cut direction for conducting programs is provided. There are trends toward more competition at an earlier age and toward more interscholastic competition for girls. Research findings are not available to judge the wisdom of such trends. The publication *Desirable Athletic Competition for Children* (American Association for Health, Physical Education, and Recreation, 1952) is primarily a tabulation of opinions. Admittedly, the question of desirability of interschool competition is a difficult one to study and has many facets. There are obviously physiological, social, psychological, and emotional implications to athletic competition.

PROFESSIONAL PREPARATION. Status and Trends. In the area of professional preparation, also, there has been little carefully controlled research. A summary of opinions of many of the leaders in physical education is available in *Professional Preparation in Health Education, Physical Education, and Recreational Education* (American Association for Health, Physical Education, and Recreation, 1962). During the past decade there have been a few changes in patterns and programs in the professional training of teachers in physical education. Little change has occurred at the undergraduate level. Graduate programs have shown a greater emphasis on scientific courses, particularly those related to biology and health. This trend has been evidenced by the development of many exercise-physiology laboratories in departments of physical education around the country. During the past ten years the number of such laboratories has more than doubled. The development of laboratories has also taken place in Canada with the help of the funds from the Fitness and Amateur Sport Directorate. Almost no research has been done comparing the advantages of different kinds of professional training.

A report of the National Education Association (1963) indicated that male physical educators were in more definite oversupply than any other major group of teachers. A more recent publication of the association (1966) indicates that there was no change since 1963. There is still a marked shortage of women physical education teachers.

Comparative Studies. Almost no research has been done comparing the advantages of various professional training programs around the world. There are two good sources for locating descriptions of physical education as it exists in foreign countries, including physical education teacher training programs in these countries. One source is the section entitled "Elsewhere in the World" in the *Physical Educator*, published by Phi Epsilon Kappa Fraternity (4000 Meadows Drive, Suite L–24, Indianapolis, Indiana 46218). This organization has also published a separate booklet (W. Johnson, 1966) containing descriptions of physical education in Britain, Canada, Finland, Germany, Israel, Japan, New Zealand, Pakistan, Russia, and South Africa. Another excellent source for such descriptions is the international section of the *Journal of Health, Physical Education, and Recreation*.

It would appear that graduate programs in physical education in other countries are not as well-developed as they are in the United States. Little basic research is done in physical education by physical educators outside of the United States and Canada. However, the undergraduate training appears to be superior. Commonly, a physical education major must have another academic major as well. The status of the physical educator in the public schools appears to be more respected than in the United States. The physical education professional programs apparently require of applicants, in many instances, greater proficiencies in sports and physical fitness in order to be accepted in an institute training physical education teachers than is required in the United States. There is a greater emphasis on sports skills and experience in practice teaching in many of these institutes.

Henry J. Montoye
David A. Cunningham
The University of Michigan

References

Adams, F. H., and others. "The Physical Working Capacity of Normal School Children. I: California." *Pediatrics* 28:55–64; 1961.

Adams, F. H., and others. (Eds.) "Symposium on Exercise Fitness Tests: Their Physiological Basis and Clinical Application to Pediatrics." *Pediatrics* 32:653–789; 1963.

American Association for Health, Physical Education, and Recreation. *Desirable Athletic Competition for Children.* AAHPER, 1952. 46p.

American Association for Health, Physical Education, and Recreation. *Professional Preparation in Health, Physical Education, and Recreational Education.* AAHPER, 1962. 160p.

Astrand, P. O. *Experimental Studies of Working Capacity in Relation to Sex and Age.* Ejnar Munksgaard, 1952. 171p.

Astrand, P. O. "Human Physical Fitness with Special Reference to Sex and Age." *Physiol R* 36:307–35; 1956.

Athletic Institute and American Association for Health, Physical Education, and Recreation. *Planning Areas and Facilities for Health, Physical Education and Recreation,* rev. ed. The Institute and AAHPER, 1965. 272p.

Bair, D. E. "Identification of Some Philosophical Beliefs of Influential Leaders in American Physical Education." *Res Q* 28:315–20; 1957.

Balke, B. "Work Capacity at Altitude." In Johnson, W. R. (Ed.) *Science and Medicine of Exercise and Sports.* Harper, 1960. p. 339–47.

Balke, B., and others. "Gas Exchange and Cardiovascular Functions at Rest and in Exercise Under the Effects of Extoinoic and Intrinsic Fatigue Factors." School of Aviation Medicine Project No. 21–1201–0014, Report Number 1. Air U, 1953.

Bergstrom, J., and Hultman, E. "Muscle Glycogen Synthesis After Exercise: An Enhancing Factor Localized to the Muscle Cells in Man." *Nature* 210:309–10; 1966.

Broer, M. R., and Galles, N. R. G. "Importance of Relationship Between Various Body Measurements in Performance of the Toe-touch Test." *Res Q* 29:253–63; 1958.

Broer, M. R., and Houtz, S. J. *Patterns of Muscular Activity in Selected Sport Skills: An Electromyographic Study.* Thomas, 1967. p. 92.

Brouha, L. *Physiology in Industry.* Pergamon, 1960. 145p.

Brožek, J. (Ed.) "Body Composition." *Annals New York Acad Sci* 110:1–1018; 1963.

Buskirk, E. R., and Councilman, J. E. "Special Exercise Problems in Middle Age." In Johnson, W. R. (Ed.) *Science and Medicine of Exercise Sports.* Harper, 1960. p. 491–507.

Campbell, W. R., and Pohndorf, R. H. "Physical Fitness of British and United States Children." In *Health and Fitness in the Modern World.* Athletic Institute, 1961. p. 8–16.

Canadian Fitness Seminar. *Proceedings.* Physical Education, and Recreation, Canadian Association for Health, 1963. 160p.

Chapman, C. B. (Ed.) *Physiology of Muscular Exercise.* American Heart Association, 1967. 226p.

Chapman, C. B., and Mitchell, J. H. "The Physiology of Exercise." *Sci Am* 212:88–96; 1965.

Clarke, H. H. *Application of Measurement to Health and Physical Education,* 3rd ed. Prentice-Hall, 1959. 528p.

Clarke, H. H. *Muscular Strength and Endurance in Man.* Prentice-Hall, 1960. 211p.

Cofer, C. N., and Johnson, W. R. "Personality Dynamics in Relation to Exercise and Sports." In Johnson, W. R. (Ed.) *Science and Medicine of Exercise and Sports.* Harper, 1960. p. 525–59.

Consolazio, C. F., and others. *Physiological Measurements of Metabolic Functions in Man.* McGraw-Hill, 1963. 505p.

Cowell, C. C., and France, W. L. *Philosophy and Principles of Physical Education.* Prentice-Hall, 1963. 236p.

Cratty, B. J. "Comparison of Verbal Motor Performance and Learning in Serial Memory Tasks." *Res Q* 34:431–9; 1963.

Cratty, B. J., and Sage, J. N. "Effect of Primary and Secondary Group Interaction upon Improvement in a Complex Movement Task." *Res Q* 35:265–74; 1964.

Davis, E. C. *The Philosophic Process in Physical Education.* Lea, 1961. 301p.

Davis, E. C., and Lockhart, A. *References on Motor Learning and Motor Performance.* AAHPER, 1960. 64p.

deVries, H. A. "The 'Looseness' Factor in Speed and O_2 Consumption of an Anaerobic 100-yard Dash." *Res Q* 34:305–13; 1963.

Dill, D. B. "Fatigue and Physical Fitness." In Johnson, W. R. (Ed.) *Science and Medicine of Exercise and Sports.* Harper, 1960. p. 384–402.

Dill, D. B. (Ed.) *Handbook of Physiology,* Section 4: *Adaptation to the Environment.* American Physiological Society, 1964. 1056p.

Dill, D. B., and others. "Work Capacity in Acute Exposure to Altitude." *J Applied Physiol* 21:1168–76; 1966.

Edgerton, H. E. "Shock-wave Photography of Large Subjects in Daylight." R Sci Instruments 29:171–2; 1958.

Edgerton, H. E., and Killian, J. R. Flash! Seeing the Unseen by Ultra High Speed Photography, 2nd ed. Charles T. Branford Company, 1954. 215p.

Espenschade, A. "Motor Development." In Johnson, W. R. (Ed.) Science and Medicine of Exercise and Sports. Harper, 1960. p. 419–39.

Eyler, M. H. "The Nature and Status of Historical Research Pertaining to Sports and Physical Education." In Johnson, W. R. (Ed.) Science and Medicine of Exercise and Sports. Harper, 1960. p. 647–62.

Goddard, R. F. (Ed.) The Effects of Altitude on Physical Performance. Athletic Institute, 1967. p. 208.

Harmon, J. M., and Oxendine, J. B. "Effects of Different Lengths of Practice Periods on the Learning of a Motor Skill." Res Q 32:34–41; 1961.

Henry, F. M. "Physical Education: An Academic Discipline." AAHPER 35:32–6; 1964.

Hettinger, T. Physiology of Strength. Thomas, 1961. 84p.

Hodgkins, Jean. "Reaction Time and Speed of Movement in Males and Females of Various Ages. Res Q 34:335–43; 1963.

Hunsicker, P. A. Youth Fitness Test Manual. AAHPER, 1958.

Hunsicker, P. A., and Donnelly, R. J. "Instruments to Measure Strength." Res Q 26:408–20; 1955.

Hunsicker, P. A., and Reiff, G. G. A Survey and Comparison of Youth Fitness 1958–1965. U Michigan Press, 1965. 174p.

Huxley, H. E. "The Mechanism of Muscular Contraction." Sci Am 213:18–27; 1965.

Ikai, M., and Steinhaus, A. H. "Some Factors Modifying the Expression of Human Strength." In Health and Fitness in the Modern World. Athletic Institute, 1961. p. 148–61.

"International Symposium on Physical Activity and Cardiovascular Health." Canadian Med Assn J 96:695–917; 1967.

Johnson, G. B., Jr. "Motor Learning." In Johnson, W. R. (Ed.) Science and Medicine of Exercise and Sports. Harper, 1960. p. 600–19.

Johnson, W. (Ed.) Physical Education Around the World. Phi Epsilon Kappa Fraternity, 1966. 62p.

Johnson, W. R. (Ed.) Science and Medicine of Exercise and Sports. Harper, 1960. 740p.

Karpovich, P. V., and others. (Eds.) "The Contributions of Physical Activity to Human Well-being." Res Q 31:259–375; 1960.

Karvonen, M. J., and Barry, A. J. (Eds.) Physical Activity and the Heart. Thomas, 1967. 405p.

Kerr, B. A. "Relationship Between Speed of Reaction and Movement in a Knee Extension Movement." Res Q 37:55–60; 1966.

Klissouras, V., and Karpovich, P. V. "Electrogoniometric Study of Jumping Events." Res Q 38:41–8; 1967.

Kraus, H., and Raab, W. Hypokinetic Disease. Thomas, 1961. 193p.

Lehmann, G., and Michaelis, H. "Die Messung der korperlichen leistungs Fahigkeit." Arbeitsphysiologie 11:376–92; 1941.

Linde, L. M. "An Appraisal of Exercise Fitness Tests." Pediatrics 32:656–9; 1963.

Massey, B. H., and Chaudet, N. L. "Effects of Systematic, Heavy Resistive Exercise on Range of Joint Movement in Young Male Adults." Res Q 27:41–51; 1956.

Mathews, D. K., and others. "Hip Flexibility of College Women as Related to Length of Body Segments." Res Q 28:352–63; 1957.

Mayer, J. "The Role of Exercise and Activity in Weight Control." In Eppright, E. S., and others. (Eds.) Weight Control. Iowa State Col Press, 1955. 244p.

Mayer, J., and Bullen, B. "Nutrition and Athletic Performance." In Staley, S. C., and others. (Eds.) Exercise and Fitness. Athletic Institute, 1960. 248p.

Mayer, J., and others. "Exercise, Food Intake and Body Weight in Normal and Genetically Obese Adult Mice." Am J Physiol 177:544–8; 1954.

Maynard, Z., and Rinaldi, S. State School Laws and Regulations for Health, Safety, Driver, Outdoor and Physical Education. USOE, HEW, 1964.

Missiuro, W. "Emotions and Human Performance." In Health and Fitness in the Modern World. Athletic Institute, 1961. p. 199–206.

Montoye, H. J. "Sports and Length of Life." in Johnson, W. R. (Ed.) Science and Medicine of Exercise and Sports. Harper, 1960. p. 517–22.

Montoye, H. J. "Physical Activity and Cardiovascular Health: Participation in Athletics." Canadian Med Assn J 96:813–20; 1967.

Montoye, H. J., and others. "Effects of Conditioning on the Ballistocardiogram of College Basketball Players." J Applied Physiol 15:449–53; 1960.

Muller, E. A. "Physiology of Muscle Training." Revue Canadienne de biologie 21:303–13; 1962.

Nagle, F. J., and others. "Graduational Step Tests for Assessing Work Capacity." J Applied Physiol 20:745–8; 1965.

National Education Association. "Teacher Shortage Continues." NEA Res B 41:68–74; 1963.

National Education Association. "A New Look at Teacher Supply and Demand." NEA Res B 44:117–23; 1966.

Norris, A. H., and Shock, N. W. "Exercise in the Adult Years—With Special Reference to the Advanced Years." In Johnson, W. R. (Ed.) Science and Medicine of Exercise and Sports. Harper, 1960. p. 466–90.

Passmore, P., and Durnin, J. V. G. A. "Human Energy Expenditure." Physiol R 35:801–40; 1955.

Pierson, W. F., and Montoye, H. J. "Movement Time, Reaction Time and Age." J Geront 13:418–21; 1958.

Pierson, W. F. "The Relationship of Movement Time and Reaction Time from Childhood to Senility." Res Q 30:227–31; 1959.

Plagenhoff, S. C. "Methods for Obtaining Kinetic

Data to Analyze Human Motions." *Res Q* 37:103–12; 1966.

Rarick, G. L. "Exercise and Growth." In Johnson, W. R. (Ed.) *Science and Medicine of Exercise and Sports.* Harper, 1960(*a*). p. 440–65.

Rarick, G. L. "Physical Education." In Harris, Chester, W. (Ed.) *Encyclopedia of Educational Research,* 3rd ed. Macmillan, 1960(*b*). p. 973–95.

Richardson, A. "Mental Practice: A Review and Discussion." *Res Q* 38:95–107; 1967.

Riley, R. L. "Pulmonary Function in Relation to Exercise." In Johnson, W. R. (Ed.) *Science and Medicine of Exercise and Sports.* Harper, 1960. p. 162–77.

Rodahl, K, and Horvath, S. M. (Eds.) *Muscle as a Tissue.* McGraw-Hill, 1962. 331p.

Rodahl, K., and Issekutz, B. "Physical Performance Capacity of the Older Individual." In Johnson, W. R. (Ed.) *Science and Medicine of Exercise and Sports.* Harper, 1960. p. 272–301.

Shaw, J. H., and Cordts, H. J. "Athletic Participation and Academic Performance." In Johnson, W. R. (Ed.) *Science and Medicine of Exercise and Sports.* Harper, 1960. p. 620–30.

Smithells, P. A., and Cameron, P. E. *Principles of Evaluation in Physical Education.* Harper, 1962. 478p.

Snyder, R. A. "Images of the Future in Physical Education." In *Proceedings of the 64th Annual Meeting of the College Physical Education Association.* The Association, 1960.

Spector, W. S. (Ed.) *Handbook of Biological Data.* Saunders, 1956. p. 347–9.

Staley, S. C., and others. (Eds.) *Exercise and Fitness.* U Chicago Press and Athletic Institute, 1960. 248p.

Stumpf, F., and Cozens, F. W. "Some Aspects of the Role of Games, Sports, and Recreational Activities in the Culture of Modern Primitive Peoples. I: The New Zealand Maoris." *Res Q* 18:198–218; 1947.

Stumpf, F., and Cozens, F. W. "Some Aspects of the Role of Games, Sports and Recreations Activities in the Culture of Modern Primitive Peoples. II: The Fijians." *Res Q* 20:2–20; 1949.

"Symposium on Work and the Heart." *Am J Cardiology* 14:729–909; 1965.

U.S. Department of Health, Education, and Welfare. *Obesity and Health.* HEW, 1966. 77p.

Van Huss, W. D., and others. *Physical Activity in Modern Living.* Prentice-Hall, 1960. 122p.

Van Itallie, T. B., and others. "Nutrition and Athletic Performance." In Johnson, W. R. (Ed.) *Science and Medicine of Exercise and Sports.* Harper, 1960. p. 285–300.

Wear, C. L. "Relationship of Flexibility Measurements to Length of Body Segments." *Res Q* 34:234–8; 1963.

Weston, A. *The Making of American Physical Education.* Appleton, 1962. 319p.

PHYSICALLY HANDICAPPED CHILDREN

From 1960, when the third edition of the *Encyclopedia of Educational Research* was published, to the present time, there have been unprecedented advances in educational opportunities for physically handicapped children. Paralleling this, the amount of relevant literature has increased severalfold. It is not possible to report here on all of the important contributions, but efforts have been made to refer to publications which in turn will take the reader to still other literature.

The major special-education advances are in (1) concepts underlying the classification and description of children, (2) contributions of the federal government and national organizations and state education agencies, (3) increased enrollment of pupils in special education and extension of programs to more school systems, (4) improved opportunities for professional preparation, (5) increased knowledge about handicapped children's educational needs, and (6) international special education.

CLASSIFICATION AND DEFINITION. Fouracre (1960), who wrote the article on the physically handicapped in the third edition of the *Encyclopedia of Educational Research,* described the physically handicapped children as those "who suffer from a physical defect, either congenital or acquired, to an extent that their educational, social, or vocational pursuits are in some way impeded." He clarified the definition by saying that the "term physically handicapped includes the deaf, hard of hearing, blind, partially sighted, crippled, cerebral-palsied, and those with special health problems, such as cardiac, epileptic, allergic, and diabetic."

Fouracre commented further that in the area of the physically handicapped educational categories have been defined largely in medical terms which describe the medical limitations imposed by disability as related to actual functioning. The disability may be reduced to relative unimportance or magnified far beyond actuality by the afflicted individual's total reaction to it which must be measured and considered in helping him with educational, vocational, or other planning.

Within the past decade, movements at the local, state, federal, and international levels in behalf of the handicapped have been multiplied and strengthened. The fact that the education and welfare of handicapped individuals have become increasingly a concern of many social welfare agencies, as well as of the schools, is bringing favorable changes to children themselves as well as to programs for them. The fact that there are new community interactions in behalf of physically handicapped children further necessitates clarification of concepts and terminology in order to describe the children more accurately and to facilitate communications among those professional and lay groups involved in dealing with this problem. Some of the basic concepts underlying the traditional terminology are being questioned. The relative incidences of various handicapping conditions among children have changed, altering the nature of the assistance needed. To illustrate, there are very few children today who have crippling conditions resulting from poliomyelitis. At the same time there are many more children brought into schools crippled with cerebral palsy and other neurological conditions. Paradoxical trends seem to be in operation to refine classifications and at the same time to merge some of the categories. Educational programs for children with crippled and special health problems have often been merged for administrative purposes. The broad term "crippled" may be applied to children who are "motor-handicapped," "cerebral-palsied," and "aphasic" and also to children with "learning disabilities" or "cerebral dysfunction." These and other similar categories suggest the emergence of new concepts. In the literature one finds a new searching for a more refined terminology.

While one might even wish that the categories which are used in special education should be completely abolished, it is not practical to do so, since they are needed for purposes of communication, for law, budgeting, and program development. Willenberg (1967), past president of the Council for Exceptional Children, recently pointed to the necessity for categorical aid in maintaining special-education services.

CONTRIBUTIONS OF FEDERAL AND STATE GOVERNMENTS AND OF THE NATIONAL ORGANIZATIONS. It is impossible to report on the education of the physically handicapped during the past decade without reviewing some of the federal developments. As far back as 1937, there were extensive efforts to secure federal aid for education of certain handicapped groups. Early Congressional bills were designed to benefit children in such categories as the physically handicapped and the mentally retarded. Although handicapped pupils have always received some benefits under general federal laws, it was not until 1958 that categorical federal aid was available. The first special education act was P.L. 85–926 (U.S. Congress, 1958b), designed to encourage the expansion of programs for the preparation of teachers of mentally retarded children through grants to institutions of higher learning and to state educational agencies. This was soon followed by the passage of P.L. 87–276 (U.S. Congress, 1961) to make available to children who are handicapped by deafness the specially trained teachers of the deaf needed to develop their abilities, and to make available to individuals suffering speech and hearing impairments the specially trained speech pathologists and audiologists needed to help them overcome their handicaps. It is to be noted that both these laws were restricted to certain areas of special education. Forces were at work, however, to broaden the laws in order to include all major areas of the handicapped. In the fall of 1963, the Congress reached an important milestone for special education by passing P.L. 88–164 (U.S. Congress, 1963) to provide assistance in combating mental retardation through grants for construction of research centers and facilities for the mentally retarded and assistance in improving mental health through grants for construction of community mental health centers and for other purposes (U.S. Congress, 1958b, 1961, 1963).

In 1965 the Elementary and Secondary Education Act with its five titles was passed. Under this law, especially under Title I, for educationally disadvantaged children, the handicapped are receiving many benefits. Title I is designed to bring better educational opportunity to children in areas where there are concentrations of families with low incomes. Though the handicapped are not specifically mentioned in Title I of the act, legislative history indicates that they are included. Some of the ways school systems can serve handicapped children under this title are described in the conference report *Education of Handicapped Children and Youth: Title I, Elementary and Secondary Education Act of 1965* (U.S. Office of Education, 1965). In 1966 the act was amended by Title VI, which authorizes the creation of a bureau for the handicapped in the U.S. Office of Education (USOE) and authorizes certain other new benefits. These federal acts taken together have stimulated the nation's schools to extend and improve educational opportunities for handicapped children and youth. They have also altered considerably the role of the USOE in the field of special education. In addition to its former function as an information agency, it now has a number of grant programs designated for handicapped children (U.S. Congress, 1965a, 1966a).

Congressional Committees Provide Information. An enormous contribution to the literature on the physically handicapped has been made by Congressional committees. The material can be found mainly in committee reports on hearings which were held by members of Congress. In these documents, professional leaders and other citizens set forth problems, needs, and recommendations. Examples may be found in the report of the seven hearings held in various parts of the United States as a part of a study authorized by the late Congressman Graham A. Barden and directed by Dr. Merle E. Frampton. Beginning with Report No. 1, on the hearings held in New York City in October 1959, through the seventh report, on the hearings held in Portland, Oregon, in July 1960, one finds not only general statements on the handicapped but also highly specialized descriptions of the characteristics and needs of the blind, deaf, crippled, and cerebral-palsied and on those with multiple handicaps, muscular dystrophy, brain injuries, aphasia, and the perceptual handicaps (U.S. Congress . . . , Subcommittee on Education, 1959; U.S. Congress . . . , Subcommittee on Special Education, 1959, 1960a, 1960b, 1960c, 1960d, 1960e). In these statements by leaders, the problem and its magnitude are outlined and recommendations are made.

Hearings on special education and rehabilitation held during the 87th Congress by Edith Green, chairman of the Special Subcommittee on Education of the Committee of Education and Labor of the

House of Representatives (U.S. Congress..., Special Subcommittee on Education, 1961, 1962), were concerned especially with pending bills. These reports contain statements by congressmen and by professional and lay leaders and are especially significant for the inclusion of recommendations. Another recent contribution is the document issued by Hugh L. Carey, chairman of the Ad Hoc Subcommittee on Special Education (U.S. Congress..., Ad Hoc Subcommittee on the Handicapped, 1966). This document contains testimonies presented on hearings held in Washington during 1966. Comparison of the problems set forth in this report with those mentioned in the earlier reports shows that even though progress has been made, many handicapped children do not receive the special education they need.

State Legislation. A vital influence in the development and maintenance of special education for handicapped children is provided by state laws. Prior to 1900 almost all of these laws were concerned with residential facilities, but during the first half of the twentieth century many states passed laws to aid local school systems in developing and administering programs in special education. During the first half of the century the movement seemed to show more concern for the physically than for the mentally handicapped, especially for children who had been victims of poliomyelitis, tuberculosis, and so on. Within the past decade or so the stronger interest of the public has been the mentally handicapped, with the result that many of the recent state laws dealing with the handicapped have been slanted toward the mentally retarded. However, more attention is now being directed toward children with emotional disturbance. Some new categories are appearing, such as brain-injured children and children who are educationally disadvantaged because of some physical condition. Every state education agency now has at least one staff member, and some states have extensive staffs, concerned with the education of the handicapped. These agencies issue program descriptions, administrative and curricular guides, annual reports, directories, and newsletters (Hunter, 1963).

The United Cerebral Palsy Association (1963) has for a number of years assembled information on federal and state laws affecting the handicapped. It issued publications in 1960 and 1963 and is currently planning a similar study for the year 1967. The United Cerebral Palsy Association's main emphasis is on the cerebral-palsied, but the compilation of laws covers the range of the handicapped. As the report indicates, details in addition to those in the 1963 digest are available from the association in New York City.

WORKS DEALING WITH THE PHYSICALLY HANDICAPPED. A number of reports, studies, and textbooks have been written in the general field of special education which include significant contributions concerning the physically handicapped. Examples are given in the following sections.

Statistical Reports. Within the past decade the USOE has conducted two statistical surveys on certain aspects of special education. These include statistics on public school systems, public and private residential school enrollments of pupils, and number of teachers. These reports showed an unprecedented growth in special education (Mackie & Hunter, 1964; Mackie & others, 1958). By 1963, between 5,000 and 6,000 school systems had at least one special-education program for the handicapped. This represents a gain of about 4,000 school systems between 1948 and 1963. The number of pupils enrolled in special education has also advanced at an accelerated rate. On the basis of trend figures (statistics and estimates) more than 2 million handicapped children were in special-education programs in 1966. Thus, it can be seen that there has been a genuine narrowing of the gulf between the number of children requiring special education and the number receiving it. Statistics suggest a gap in special education for those with partial sight, for the crippled, for those who have hearing losses but are not profoundly deaf, and for other children sometimes classified as brain-damaged or neurologically impaired. There is an unmet need, but it is not statistically reported (Mackie, 1965).

Professional Preparation. Of all the conditions which stand in the way of providing quality education for all of the children in need of special education, none is so serious as the shortage of qualified special educators. On the basis of statistics and estimates, it is known that there are 85,000 to 90,000 special educators in the nation's schools; this is between one-third and one-fourth of the number needed. No amount of money, no amount of favorable public opinion, no array of legal provisions will enable the country to bring opportunities for quality education to handicapped children unless there are also available competent, specially prepared persons to instruct the children and to direct and supervise programs.

A nationwide study of the college and university programs offering preparation for such teachers was conducted in 1962 (Mackie & others, 1962). The report shows an increase of more than 100 percent in colleges and universities offering specialized preparation during the period from 1953 and 1962 (Mackie & Dunn, 1954). It also shows an increase in the number of students in special-education majors as well as an increase in college degrees granted.

During the years between the 1954 and 1962 studies there was a dramatic change in the geographical distribution of opportunities for preparation of teachers of the physically handicapped. As recently as 1954, opportunities for such training were found mainly in the eastern part of the United States. By 1962 they were fairly well distributed throughout the nation.

The 1962 report gave data not only for the overall field of special education but also for each of the areas. Opportunity was given for additional categories to be added. The only "write-in" addition by the colleges was the "neurologically handicapped."

There was also a shift toward dual preparation in some clearly related areas. A good example is in the visually handicapped. Under this terminology, colleges have moved in the direction of offering a sequence which prepares teachers for work with blind or partially seeing students or with both.

By 1962 about twice as many colleges reported at least the minimum sequence of preparation for teachers of the deaf. By this time programs were located in all the major regions of the United States. The study also shows a higher ratio of instructors to pupils than in any other area of special education. Closer observation of data, however, shows that most of these faculty members were not full-time but part-time. Therefore, it is not easy to determine the actual amount of time available to the greatly increased body of students in this field.

The USOE, recognizing the importance of professional preparation, conducted various activities to improve the teaching of handicapped children. One was a study of competences required by various types of special educators that resulted in many publications. These educators included teachers of the visually handicapped, of the crippled, and of the deaf. A summary report of this massive study is found in the bulletin *Professional Preparation for Teachers of Exceptional Children* (Mackie & others, 1960). The summary document views teacher competences from the standpoint of four groups of special educators. These are the teachers themselves, the supervisors in state education departments, the supervisors and directors of special education in local school systems, and college and university faculty members responsible for preparing teachers. Another study in improving professional standards was conducted by the Council for Exceptional Children of the National Education Association (Council for Exceptional Children, 1965). The final report set forth suggestions for professional standards in all the usual areas of exceptionality including that of the physically handicapped.

Textbooks and Research Findings. A number of books covering the general field of special education have been issued which also include extensive discussions of the physically handicapped. *Exceptional Children in the Schools,* edited by Lloyd M. Dunn (1963), includes information not only concerning the physically handicapped but also concerning the emotionally disturbed, the mentally retarded, and the gifted. The editor in his first chapter defines the field of special education and provides statistical information concerning the size of the national problem. He provides information on programs in various kinds of schools for the handicapped. He also presents data to reflect the gap between the provisions for exceptional children in the schools and their estimated number. Other chapters were prepared by specialists in their respective fields covering each of the areas included in the editor's introduction.

Another example of a textbook, a second edition, *Education of Exceptional Children and Youth* by Cruickshank and Johnson (1967), is a book covering all fields of exceptionality including the gifted and the handicapped. The introduction defines the problem of the exceptional child including not only the traditional areas but also some new emerging categories. The authors point to social attitudes as they affect the handicapped and refer to parent groups and to the increase in research in special education. Most of the other chapters in the book were contributed by specialists in the various fields of the education of the exceptional child.

A significant development within the past decade is the new knowledge about the handicapped resulting from many research studies and demonstrations. Both public and private funds have supported them. *Behavioral Research on Exceptional Children* (Kirk & Weiner, 1963) sets forth findings on many of them and throws light on the physically handicapped. Of specific interest are the chapters "Visually Impaired," by Nolan, "Children with Cerebral Dysfunction," by Reed, and "Children with Orthopedic Handicaps and Special Health Problems," by Jordan.

Relevant research supported by federal agencies is summarized in a number of grant reports which can be secured from the appropriate offices. An example of such a report is *Research and Demonstration Projects Supported by the Division of Research* (U.S. Office of Education, 1967).

Visually Handicapped. Visually handicapped persons are those whose sight is limited to such a degree that they need special consideration in their education and other life activities.

As Ashcroft (1963) says,

For educational purposes, the visually limited are distinguished from the normally seeing and within this group the partially seeing are differentiated from the blind primarily in terms of the degree of useful vision they retain, or in terms of the media in which they read and do school work. Blind children include those who have so little remaining useful vision that they must use braille as their reading medium. The traditional definition of the blind which has been accepted for economic and legal purposes and is often used for educational purposes is 20/200 or less in the better eye with the best possible correction or a restriction in field of vision to an angle subtending an arc of 20 degrees or less. The partially seeing are those children who retain a relatively low degree of vision and can read only enlarged print or those who have remaining vision making it possible for them to read limited amounts of regular print under very special conditions. The partially seeing are traditionally defined as those who have remaining visual acuity between 20/200 and 20/70 in the better eye with the best possible correction or who in the opinion of eye specialists can benefit from either temporary or permanent use of appropriate special educational facilities.

The visually handicapped constitute the numerically smallest area of exceptionality, but that area is made up of children with pronounced needs. It is estimated by the USOE (Jones & Collins, 1966) that 0.1 percent of school-age children need special education for blind or partially seeing conditions. Jones (1961) found that of 14,125 legally blind, 60 percent of those currently enrolled in special programs have some remaining vision, above light perception, and that fewer than 25 percent are actually totally blind. Awareness of remaining vision is important to the educator, for this vision is no longer being held in reserve but is being used to its fullest extent.

Causes of visual problems are continuously being explored. The rate of retrolental fibroplasia, at one time responsible for most of the blindness of preschool children, has dropped because of the closer control of oxygen use in incubators for premature babies (Patz, 1966). Rubella, or measles, is now a serious problem causing an increase in multihandicapped preschool children whose handicaps include severe eye disorders. An experimental measles vaccine has been made available, along with other proposed preventive measures. A promising light therapy, pleoptics, is being used to treat amblyopia. Early identification of visual defects helps in treating them and reducing educational and social problems. The National Society for the Prevention of Blindness (1966) estimates conservatively that one out of every four schoolchildren has need of eye care. Most schools (including many preschools), communities, and businesses use a screening procedure to identify those who need special consideration. Besides the Snellen test, classroom teachers are alerted to watch for indications of visual difficulties. Complaints of discomfort of the eyes, dizziness, nausea, and headaches should also be heeded.

Academic and social requirements of the visually handicapped are like those of any other student, but most of these children will need special help to meet their requirements. Kirk (1965) comments in her study of programs for the partially seeing in the Detroit Public Schools: "One of the most important findings was that children in classes for the partially seeing experienced a definite improvement in vision during the time they were in the program. Excluding those who moved from the city . . . more than 65 percent showed an improvement in vision. . . . The increase in visual efficiency was approximately 20 percent."

Braille and large-print books, typewriters, tape recorders, relief maps, and models facilitate learning for the sight impaired. The Detroit public school system has prepared, under the editorship of Kirk (1967), a typewriting manual entitled *Typewriting for Visually Handicapped Children* as a guide for teachers. She stresses the importance of typewriting as a common means of communication with the sighted. A good foundation in such skill enables the child to move into regular classrooms and later into vocational fields.

Ashcroft (1963) asks that visually limited students be thought of and treated as "valuable and important human individuals much more like other children than different from them." A visually handicapped child, like a sighted child, needs to explore and become familiar with his environment before he can travel and interact in his surroundings. Cruickshank and Trippe (1959) point out that 79.7 percent of the visually impaired children in New York state local schools are able to travel in familiar surroundings unaided, and 77.4 percent are able to do so at a reasonable rate.

Initiation into learning through special media and mobility-orientation methods demands a special program. After this is accomplished, emphasis is on education through regular classroom participation and in association with sighted children, hopefully with the result of better adjustment. A visually handicapped child is encouraged to remain in a regular class unless his needs are not being met. The itinerant (contact plan) and resource (resource-room plan) teachers provide services to both students and teachers in regular classes. Jones (1966) reports that these two are the most prevalent types of programs in local public schools. The itinerant teacher provides special materials to the student and provides aducational procedures, which also help the sighted children, to the classroom teacher. Special help and materials are provided by the resource teacher to the visually handicapped child in the regular class. Some programs use a cooperative plan where reading work is done in a special class and nonreading work is done along with seeing students in a regular class. Special classes, as such, are "self-contained," that is, all academic education is carried out in them. Students in these classes participate with their seeing peers in nonacademic activities. In recent years, residential schools which had been established solely for the blind have accepted some partially seeing children who can best benefit from this type of program.

Under the Federal Rehabilitation Program, rehabilitative centers for the blind provide counseling services, prevocational shops, mobility training, development of communicative skills and social competence, psychological testing and evaluation, and skills needed in daily living.

Research continues into all aspects of visual limitations and their implications. The American Printing House for the Blind (1966), which prepares literature and tangible aids for the visually handicapped, now has gone into what it calls "developmental work." Besides providing valuable information, the American Foundation for the Blind develops special aids and appliances and explores educational and rehabilitative techniques.

In the area of the visually handicapped, *Education and Health of the Partially Seeing Child* has been a standard textbook and reference work for teachers and others preparing to work with visually impaired pupils (Hathaway & others, 1959). The most recent edition was prepared by Foote, Bryan, and Gibbons, who worked closely with Hathaway during her lifetime. The book departs in some ways from earlier editions in that it suggests some of the newer methods of organizing educational programs for the partially seeing. Less emphasis is placed on self-contained classrooms and more on resource teachers. The text continues to present a wealth of information on health services, preparation of teachers, and relationships with professional personnel.

Education of Children with Impaired Hearing. In recent years there have been marked advances in the education of the deaf child. A new sense of experimentation seems to pervade the field, at least partially as the result of professional leadership and international exchanges of information. In the United States advances have no doubt been generated by resources made available as the result of several federal acts. In 1958, P.L. 85–505 (U.S. Congress, 1958a) was enacted to provide, in the Department of Health, Education, and Welfare, for a loan service of captioned films for the deaf; in 1961, P.L. 87–276 (U.S. Congress, 1961) authorized support for the training of teachers of the deaf; in 1965, P.L. 89–36 (U.S. Congress, 1965b) authorized the establishment of a national institute; and in 1966, P.L. 89–694 (U.S. Congress, 1966b) authorized a model secondary school in the field of the deaf.

In 1963 the Council on Education of the Deaf was host to the International Congress on the Education of the Deaf (1963). The Council is composed of representatives of the Alexander Graham Bell Association for the Deaf, the Conferences on the American School for the Deaf, and the Convention of American Instructors for the Deaf. The congress was convened at Gallaudet College in Washington, D.C., and was attended by more than 1,000 delegates from 50 countries. Papers were presented on topics of high interest such as assessment, learning, communication, curriculum, higher educational language development, guidance, religion, and multiple handicaps of the deaf.

In March 1964 the Secretary of Health, Education, and Welfare appointed an advisory committee to study the problems of the deaf. The full findings of this committee, which was conducted under the chairmanship of Homer D. Babbidge, are set forth in a document entitled *Education of the Deaf*. The report stated: "The American people have no reason to be satisfied with their limited success in educating deaf children and preparing them for full participation in our society" (U.S. Department of Health, Education, and Welfare, 1965). It summarizes the situations which need to be improved in order to bring the deaf to a suitable level of participation in society by recommending improvements in such matters as early attention to the deaf child, new research on how the deaf child learns, and demonstration programs at the postsecondary level to correct deficiencies.

In 1955 the USOE issued a report, based on the work of a committee and on teachers' opinion, entitled *Teachers of Children Who Are Deaf.* (Mackie & others, 1955). The data included in this study were assembled by a committee of experts and by questionnaires sent to a sample of superior teachers of the deaf. The information set forth in the report concerns itself with the knowledge, skills, and abilities needed by teachers for proficiency in educating the deaf.

In the spring of 1964 another conference was called by the USOE, the purpose of which was to outline the elements of professional preparation needed by teachers of the deaf and to publish the brochure *Preparation of Teachers of the Deaf* (Quigley, 1966). Experts worked together for several days in developing the material. The report is a broad guide to institutions preparing teachers, to agencies responsible for certification, and for the recruitment of appropriate persons to teach children with impaired hearing.

For technical information on the problem of hearing, the reader may turn to many sources. One is the revised edition of *Hearing and Deafness*, edited by Davis and Silverman (1964). Originally written for the layman with personal need for information, *Hearing and Deafness* has become a widely used introductory text for audiology students. With the contributions of a distinguished group of authors, the book is comprehensive in covering the medical, educational, social, psychological, economical, and rehabilitative aspects of hearing loss. The revised edition deletes little of the original and reflects the current advances in knowledge in this field.

To learn how deafness may affect an individual's personality, Levine's *Psychology of Deafness* (1960) affords a source. This book embraces the concept of the "whole man," combining discussion of psychological and rehabilitative aspects of deafness. The author makes the reader aware of the implications of hearing loss and points out areas for future research. Included are appendixes on explanations of hearing, on causes of handicaps, and on communication media used by the deaf, plus listings of selected psychological studies, test publishers and distributors, and nonmedical national organizations for the welfare of those with impaired hearing.

Children with Crippling and Special Health Conditions. Children with crippling and special health conditions form a heterogeneous group whose conditions result from such causes as disease, accidents, infection, birth injury, and congenital anomalies. The handicaps vary from very mild to very severe. The nature of this group of children has changed markedly over the half past century, largely because of advances in medical knowledge, health conditions, and general social welfare. To illustrate, the causes of crippling have altered since special education was first provided in local schools. Today one finds few children handicapped by poliomyelitis or tuberculosis. In contrast one finds many with cerebral palsy. The old "open air" classes have almost disappeared, and many children with histories of rheumatic fever attend regular classes.

There are miscellaneous health conditions which make special schooling necessary. Among these are chronic illness, cerebral palsy and perceptual and multiple handicaps. Schools make a variety of provisions for these children. Some attend special day schools; some are enrolled in special classes in regular schools. They may even receive their schooling in hospitals and institutions and, where no other plan is feasible, in their own homes (Mackie & Connor, 1960).

Wilson (1963) reports a trend toward different groupings of the physically handicapped. She indiactes that there is a new challenge because of multiple handicaps. Because of medical advances more children survive, including many of those born with severe congenital impairments. Wilson discusses prevalence rates, characteristics of such children, administrative provisions for education, and the nature of suitable instruction. Cerebral palsy is so prevalent a disability in this category that it calls for added attention. Wolfe and Reid (1958) conducted a survey in Austin, Texas, of cerebral palsy. On the basis of a sample of 5,901 pupils, 2,408 of which were studied comprehensively, they reported that the prevalence rate was 308 cases of cerebral-palsied persons of all ages per 100,000 of population.

In studying the problem, the Southern Regional Education Board (1960) conducted a study of cerebral palsy in the South. The report is significant in that it gives the status of the problem and sets forth the most urgent needs in the development of a program for cerebral-palsied children and youth.

Since 1945 California has had legislation authorizing the state department of education to set up two residential schools for cerebral-palsied children. These were originally designed to serve the cerebral-palsied, but they have changed somewhat in their scope because of changing conceptions of the children and because of their changing need. In 1965 the California State Department of Education issued a report which describes services to children who not only have motor handicaps but who also have such other conditions as nervous disorders (California State Department of Education, 1965). Under this broadened range, both state schools staffed with multiprofessional teams serve not only residential pupils but also several hundred others who receive their schooling in local communities but come to the institutions for extensive diagnosis, observation, and counseling. In addition to these schools the state has consultants who give much assistance to local communities. The need for improved instruction for cerebral-palsied children is set forth in the pamphlet *Teaching the Cerebral Palsied Child* (Gore & Stoddard, 1954). It is so full of practical aids and plans that it almost constitutes an in-service program for specialists or classroom teachers.

Brain Injuries and Other Emerging Categories. A review of literature on "brain-injured" children reflects the need for clarification of concepts and definitions. It appears thus far to be a category with somewhat undefined boundaries. The frequent use of this term and such others as "neurologically impaired" signals the existence of large numbers of handicapped children who need identification and a program within special education.

Lehman and Hall (1966), in discussing the problem of children in this category, ask "who is this child?" He is not mentally retarded; yet in certain skills he is retarded. He is not emotionally disturbed; yet he may have developed emotional problems as a result of his difficulties. What he is not is often more obvious than what he is. Parents are perplexed and bewildered and, accordingly, take their child to a doctor, psychologist, or child-guidance center for diagnosis. After tests and symptoms have been evaluated, the proper diagnosis will reveal that this child has learning disabilities resulting from what specialists call "minimal brain dysfunction." Lehman and Hall write:

This child has been labeled as brain damaged, brain injured, perceptually handicapped, the interjacent child, the reversal child, or simply as educationally handicapped.

These difficulties are attributed to damage to the parts of the brain which regulate the way an individual "sees" things after his senses have presented the facts to him and to damage to the parts which control his movements and his impulses. The damage may have occurred at any time—before birth, during birth, or after birth—and might have been caused by sustained high fever or a blow to the head."

Cruickshank and Johnson (1967) believe that a whole new field of special education has developed that is based on the concept of education for the brain-injured. They write:

[While] there is yet much to learn and much research to be accomplished, sufficient understanding of a group of children with brain injury is at hand to be able to plan adequately for them. This is not to say that all to be outlined in the pages which follow will meet the test of time. As more and more insight is obtained regarding brain-injured children, it is likely that much of our present thinking may need to be modified.

Irrespective of the terminology employed, the children dealt with in this chapter are essentially those who have experienced a disturbance of some sort in normal cephalocaudal neural maturation, prenatally, perinatally, or postnatally, which results in an inability to progress normally in learning situations related to the various sensory modalities. As a result, these children are characterized by visual-motor, audio-motor, and/or tactual-motor disturbances. If complete research were available, it might also be found that they are deficient in all sensory systems insofar as perception of reality is concerned; children included in this definition do not present gross motor handicaps as do the cerebral palsy children who also have central nervous system disorders.

Bower, however, appears to be not quite so sure of the category. He refers to the "magic phrase" to describe children with a wide array of problems. He says "the phrase I refer to is 'brain damaged' or 'minimally brain damaged' or 'neurologically impaired' or any of the other abracadabras used to explain learning or behavior disorders in children in one mystical phrase" (Mesinger, 1965).

The educational needs of the children, however, persist. A large amount of literature is accumulating. Recently the Woods School and Treatment Center (1964) issued an extensive reading list on the topic. In these selected readings one will find discussions of the various aspects of brain injury, including the problems of terminology.

As Wilson (1963) points out, many pupils in need

of special education have more than one handicap. They are referred to as children with multihandicaps. A careful look at handicapped children reveals that one may have one handicap, another two or three, and a third a whole array of handicaps. As early as 1959 the state of Illinois issued a report on the prevalence of multihandicaps among school-age children; by law, that state also provided a categorization of such children. Since that time a number of plans have developed within state and local special-education programs to aid those who have secondary handicaps, and it appears that increasing attention will be given to the diagnosis and education of such children. The first state to take action on this problem was Illinois (Illinois Board of Public Instruction, 1959).

International Developments. More than ever before, international forces in behalf of the handicapped have been at work. In response to requests from many leaders in the education of physically handicapped children, the International Society for Rehabilitation of the Disabled has sponsored three seminars on special education. The first of these, New Frontiers in Special Education, was held at West Point, New York, in 1960; the second in Denmark in 1963; and the most recent in Germany, in 1966 (International Society for the Rehabilitation of the Disabled, 1960, 1963, 1966). These have afforded an opportunity for the exchange of information among representatives of the different countries. A wide range of topics was covered in these seminars and included characteristics of pupils, philosophy of special education, standards for teachers, parent education, organization and administration of classes, and coordination of multiprofessional efforts. The International Society for Rehabilitation of the Disabled has also featured the education of the handicapped in its world congress programs and in regional conferences. The program of the Eighth World Congress of the organization, which took place in New York City, included a living demonstration of special education. The children who participated were enrolled in classes for the crippled, deaf, and blind in New York and New Jersey schools, both public and private (Taylor, 1960).

The international interest in educating the handicapped is reflected in the regional program of the 1965 Pan-Pacific Conference on Rehabilitation of Disabled. It included two full days of meetings for educators. They studied such topics as organization of schools, adapted curriculum, and the development of favorable attitudes toward the handicapped. The full report may be found in the conference proceedings (Japanese Society for Rehabilitation of the Disabled, 1965).

UNESCO, in cooperation with the International Bureau of Education, gave attention to special education at its 1960 conference on public education in Geneva. While the major emphasis on special education in the conference was on mental retardation, the representatives of public education from 78 countries made broad recommendations in behalf of all handicapped children. They passed a resolution to the effect that ministries of education have important functions to carry out in all areas of special education (International Bureau of Education, 1960). In 1960 UNESCO also published statistics on special education to reflect the enormous gap between educational provisions for the handicapped and those much needed (UNESCO, 1960). This report, *Statistics on Special Education*, is not simply an enumeration of statistics; it is prefaced by a philosophical discussion of special education. It also sets forth some of the problems in collecting statistics due to varying concepts and definition. The report states that even at the optimal point of agreement about vocabulary, education theory has not developed the same way in all countries, and there are differences with respect to which categories are educationally meaningful. A classification scheme is needed, therefore, that can be expanded as the field of special education grows and becomes more complex in each country (UNESCO, 1960).

The American Educational Research Association published two research monographs since the third edition of this encyclopedia was published. One of these (American Educational Research Association, 1959) included much material on the professional preparation of teachers of exceptional children. It summarized findings from the USOE's study of teacher competencies by Mackie and Williams. Its various sections also contain many reports by specialists on the teaching of various kinds of exceptional children.

The monograph on the education of special children (American Educational Research Association, 1966) includes a section by Burton Blatt on the preparation of special-education personnel. He points out some recent developments and adds culturally deprived children to the usual categories of children in need of special education.

Romaine P. Mackie
U.S. Office of Education

References

American Educational Research Association. *Review of Educational Research: Education of Exceptional Children*. AERA, 1959. 653p.

American Educational Research Association. *Review of Educational Research: Education of Exceptional Children*. AERA, 1966. 202p.

American Foundation for the Blind. *Services for Blind Persons in the United States*. The Foundation, 1960. 87p.

American Printing House for the Blind. *American Printing House for the Blind, Inc.: It's History, Purposes, and Policies*. The Printing House, 1966. 12p.

Ashcroft, Samuel C. "Blind and Partially Seeing Children." In Dunn, Lloyd M. (Ed.) *Exceptional Children in the Schools*. Holt, 1963. p. 413–62.

Beck, Harry S. "Detecting Psychological Symptoms of Brain Injury." *Excep Children* 28:57–62; 1961.

California State Department of Education. *California*

State Schools for Children with Cerebral Palsy and Similar Handicaps. California Office of State Printing, 1965. 28p.

Council for Exceptional Children. *Professional Standards for Personnel in the Education of Exceptional Children.* NEA, 1965. 87p.

Cruickshank, William M., and Johnson, G. Orville. (Eds.) *Education of Exceptional Children and Youth,* 2nd ed. Prentice-Hall, 1967. 230p.

Cruickshank, William M., and Trippe, Matthew J. *Services to Blind Children in New York State.* Syracuse U Press, 1959. 495p.

Davis, Hallowell, and Silverman, S. Richard. (Eds.) *Hearing and Deafness* rev. ed. Holt, 1964. 573p.

Dunn, Lloyd M. *Exceptional Children in the Schools.* Holt, 1963. 580p.

Fouracre, Maurice H. "Physically Handicapped Children." In Harris, Chester W. (Ed.) *Encyclopedia of Educational Research,* 3rd ed. Macmillan, 1960. p. 995–1008.

Gore, Beatrice S., and Stoddard, Jane. *Teaching the Cerebral Palsied Child.* Bulletin 4. California Department of Education. 1954. 82p.

Hathaway, Winifred, and others. *Education and Health of the Partially Seeing Child.* Columbia U Press, 1959. 201p.

Hunter, Patricia P. *State Education Agency Publications in the Education of Exceptional Children and Youth (1953–1963).* GPO, 1963. 18p.

Illinois Board of Public Instruction. *The Illinois Plan for Special Education of Exceptional Children: The Multiply Handicapped.* State of Illinois, 1959. 43p.

International Bureau of Education. *Recommendations of the 23rd International Conference on Public Education.* The Bureau, 1960.

International Congress on the Education of the Deaf. *Program.* The Congress, 1963.

International Society for Rehabilitation of the Disabled. *World Frontiers in Special Education: Proceedings of the International Seminar on Special Education.* The Society, 1960. 49p.

International Society for Rehabilitation of the Disabled. *Special Education International: Proceedings of the Second International Seminar on Special Education.* The Society, 1963. 93p.

International Society for Rehabilitation of the Disabled. *Proceedings of the Third International Seminar on Special Education.* The Society, 1966. 93p.

Japanese Society for Rehabilitation of the Disabled. *Practical Implementation of Rehabilitation: Proceedings of the Third Pan-Pacific Rehabilitation Conference.* The Society, 1965. 502p.

Jones, John Walker. *Blind Children: Degree of Vision, Mode of Reading.* GPO, 1961.

Jones, John Walker. *Educational Programs for Visually Handicapped Children.* GPO, 1966. 74p.

Jones, John Walker, and Collins, Anne P. *Education for Visually Handicapped Children.* GPO, 1966. 74p.

Kirk, Edith Cohoe. "The Detroit Program for Partially Seeing Children." *Sight-Saving R* 35:220–4; 1965.

Kirk, Edith Cohoe. (Ed.) *Typewriting for Visually Handicapped Children.* Board of Education of the City of Detroit, 1967. 111p.

Kirk, Samuel A., and Weiner, Bluma B. (Eds.) *Behavioral Research on Exceptional Children.* NEA, 1963. 369p.

Lehman, Eileen, and Hall, Robert E. "Who Is This Child?" *Am Ed* 2:10–2; 1966.

Levine, Edna Simon. *The Psychology of Deafness: Techniques of Appraisal for Rehabilitation.* Columbia U Press, 1960. 383p.

Mackie, Romaine P. "Spotlighting Advances in Special Education." *Excep Children* 32:77–81; 1965.

Mackie, Romaine P., and Connor, Frances P. *Teachers of Crippled Children and Teachers of Children with Special Health Problems.* GPO, 1960. 124p.

Mackie, Romaine P., and Dunn, Lloyd M. *College and University Programs for the Preparation of Teachers of Exceptional Children.* GPO, 1954. 91p.

Mackie, Romaine P., and Hunter, Patricia P. *Special Education Reaches Nearly Two Million Children: Education of Handicapped Children in Residential Schools.* GPO, 1964. 7p.

Mackie, Romaine P., and others. *Teachers of Children Who Are Deaf.* GPO, 1955. 87p.

Mackie, Romaine P., and others. *Statistics of Special Education for Exceptional Children and Youth 1957–58.* GPO, 1958. 120p.

Mackie, Romaine P., and others. *Professional Preparation for Teachers of Exceptional Children; An Overview.* GPO, 1960. 139p.

Mackie, Romaine P., and others. "College and University Programs for the Preparation of Teachers of Exceptional Children." USOE 1962. 138p. (Mineographed.)

Mesinger, John R. "Emotionally Disturbed and Brain Damaged Children—Should We Mix Them?"; and Bower, Eli M. "A Reaction." *Excep Children* 32:237–40; 1965.

National Society for the Prevention of Blindness. *Estimated Statistics on Blindness and Vision Problems.* The Society, 1966. 109p.

Patz, Arnall. "Present Status of Retrolental Fibroplasia." *Sight-saving R* 36:67–9; 1966.

Quigley, Stephen Patrick. (Ed.) *Preparation of Teachers of the Deaf: A Report of a National Conference, Virginia Beach, Virginia, March 15–19, 1964.* GPO, 1966.

Quigley, Stephen Patrick, and Frisinia, Robert. *Institutionalization and Psychological Education Development of Deaf Children.* NEA, 1961. 49p.

Southern Regional Education Board. *Education of the Cerebral Palsied in the South.* The Board, 1960. 74p.

Taylor, Eugene J. (Ed.) *Proceedings of the 8th World Congress of the International Society for the Welfare of Cripples.* Int So Rehabilitation Disabled, 1960. 433p.

Taylor, Wallace W., and Taylor, Isabelle Wagner. *Special Education of Physically Handicapped Children in Western Europe.* N. V. Lochemsche

Handels and Courantendrukkerij (Lochem), 1960. 497p.

United Cerebral Palsy Association, Legal and Legislative Department. *1963 Digest of State Laws and Regulations Affecting the Handicapped.* The Association, 1963. 57p.

UNESCO. *Statistics on Special Education.* UNESCO, 1960. 154p.

U.S. Congress. *Mental Retardation Facilities and Community Mental Health Centers Construction Act of 1963.* P.L. 88–164. 88th Congress. GPO, 1963. 18p.

U.S. Congress. *Elementary and Secondary Education Act of 1965.* P.L. 89–10. 89th Congress, GPO, 1965(a). 32p.

U.S. Congress. P.L. 89–36. 89th Congress, GPO, 1965(b).

U.S. Congress. P.L. 89–694. 89th Congress, GPO, 1966(b).

U.S. Congress. *Elementary and Secondary Education Amendments of 1966.* P.L. 89–750. 89th Congress. GPO, 1966. 32p.

U.S. Congress, House of Representatives, Committee on Education and Labor, Ad Hoc Subcommittee on the Handicapped. *Hearings: Investigation of the Adequacy of Federal and Other Resources for Education and Training of the Handicapped,* Part I. 89th Congress, 2nd Session. GPO, 1966. 611p.

U.S. Congress, House of Representatives, Committee on Education and Labor, Special Subcommittee on Education. *Hearings: Bills for Special Education and Rehabilitation of the Handicapped.* 87th Congress, 1st Session. GPO, 1961.

U.S. Congress, House of Representatives, Committee on Education and Labor, Special Subcommittee on Education. *Hearings: Bills for Special Education and Rehabilitation of the Handicapped.* 87th Congress 2nd Session. GPO, 1962. 179p.

U.S. Congress, House of Representatives, Committee on Education and Labor, Subcommittee on Education. *Hearings: Bills Regarding the Field of Special Education and Rehabilitation,* Part II. 86th Congress, 1st Session. GPO, 1959. p. 308–618.

U.S. Congress, House of Representatives, Committee on Education and Labor, Subcommittee on Special Education. *Hearings: Bills Regarding the Field of Special Education and Rehabilitation.* Part I. 86th Congress, 1st Session. GPO, 1959. 307p.

U.S. Congress, House of Representatives, Committee on Education and Labor, Subcommittee on Special Education. *Hearings: Bills Regarding the Field of Special Education and Rehabilitation.* Part III. 86th Congress, 2nd Session. GPO, 1960(a). p. 619–867.

U.S. Congress, House of Representatives, Committee on Education and Labor, Subcommittee on Special Education. *Hearings: Bills Regarding the Field of Special Education and Rehabilitation.* Part IV. 86th Congress, 2nd Session. GPO, 1960(b). p. 869–1192.

U.S. Congress, House of Representatives, Committee on Education and Labor, Subcommittee on Special Education. *Hearings: Bills Regarding the Field of Special Education and Rehabilitation,* Part V. 86th Congress, 2nd Session. GPO, 1960(c). p. 1193–522.

U.S. Congress, House of Representatives, Committee on Education and Labor, Subcommittee on Special Education. *Hearings: Bills Regarding the Field of Special Education and Rehabilitation,* Part VI. 86th Congress, 2nd Session. GPO, 1966(d). p. 1523–726.

U.S. Congress, House of Representatives, Committee on Education and Labor, Subcommittee on Special Education. *Hearings: Bills Regarding the Field of Special Education and Rehabilitation,* Part VII. 86th Congress, 2nd Session. GPO, 1966(e). p. 1727–2031.

U.S. Department of Health, Education, and Welfare. *Education of the Deaf: A Report to the Secretary of Health, Education, and Welfare by His Advisory Committee on the Education of the Deaf.* GPO, 1965. 103p.

U.S. Office of Education *Education of Handicapped Children and Youth: Title I, Elementary and Secondary Education Act of 1965.* GPO, 1965. 56p.

U.S. Office of Education. *Research and Demonstration Projects Supported by the Division of Research.* GPO, 1967.

Willenberg, Ernest P. "Critical Issues in Special Education: Categorical Aid." *Excep Children* 33:327–30; 1967.

Wilson, Marguerite. "Crippled and Neurologically Impaired Children." In Dunn, Lloyd M. (Ed.) *Exceptional Children in the Schools.* Holt, 1963. p. 463–520.

Wolfe, W. G., and Reid, L. L. *A Survey of Cerebral Palsy in Texas.* United Cerebral Palsy of Texas, 1958.

Woods School and Residential Treatment Center, "A Selective Bibliography on Brain-damaged Children." In Birch, Hubert G. (Ed.) *Brain Damage in Children—The Biological and Social Aspects.* The School and Center, 1964. 69p.

PREDICTION

Prediction represents an effort to describe what will be found concerning an event or outcome not yet observed on the basis of data or information considered to be relevant to this unobserved event. The physicist may wish to state what the volume of a gas will be when he alters its temperature or pressure; the engineer may need to estimate what the tensile strength of a metal is from measures of its hardness; the physician may want to prognosticate a patient's blood pressure one month hence after prescribed dosages of medication; a meteorologist on the basis of barometric and other related data available to him on a Friday night endeavors to forecast whether there will be rain at the doubleheader on Sunday; and in early fall the dean of college admissions may want to ascertain from indexes of high school achievement and aptitude-test scores what proportion of freshmen will still be in good standing nine months later.

In scientific work most predictions yield information about the unobserved event in numerical form with a margin of the error frequently specified. To minimize errors of observation the physical, biological, or behavioral scientist manipulates phenomena under controlled conditions, typically in a laboratory setting. With varying degrees of success, he determines the effects of his treatments on substances or organisms. If adequate control over the host of potentially contaminating influences can be achieved, he may be able to establish cause-and-effect relationships. He may try to test empirically the validity of hypotheses or predictions derived from theories, to modify existing theories in light of his findings, or to generate new ones. Gradually he may succeed in controlling new domains of the environment for man's own purposes.

Outside the laboratory the behavioral scientist—the educational researcher, psychologist, and sociologist—can carry out systematic observations as in surveys, field studies, and case histories that suggest useful hypotheses and bases for prediction, although the amount of error in predicting observable characteristics of human behavior is relatively large. Furthermore, predictions of such complex psychological characteristics as learning capacity, personal and social adjustment, and vocational success, which must necessarily be inferred from measures of questionable reliability and validity, pose serious methodological and philosophical problems in relation to their definition and interpretation.

SOME DEFINITIONS. In any formal discussion of prediction it is helpful for both clarity and ease of communication to describe certain frequently employed terms. An observed event that yields information for forecasting the unobserved event is often referred to as the "antecedent" or as the "independent variable." The outcome which could not be initially observed is often referred to as the "consequent" or the "dependent variable." If the dependent variable reflects important or socially desirable outcomes based on general purposes of the investigator, it is called in Astin's terminology (1964) a "conceptual criterion." Thus, teaching effectiveness, personal and social adjustment, and proficiency in typing constitute general statements, or concepts, of what are judged to be socially valued outcomes. A set of observable activities or behaviors that are relevant to the conceptual criterion and that potentially can provide measures may be termed the "criterion performance." The scores obtained on an instrument or scale representing the criterion variable such as an achievement test or rating form are termed "criterion measures." (There are many conflicting definitions concerning what is meant by criterion research. Some clarification in terminology has been achieved by Astin [1964].)

In laboratory studies and in theoretically oriented papers in psychology, the antecedent and consequent events are roughly equated, respectively, to the stimuli presented and to the responses observed. If an experiment has been carefully designed within a theoretical framework, inferences or interpretations may be made concerning the processes which intervene between the presentation of the stimuli (treatments) and the observations of the responses that usually furnish the data necessary for the evaluation of an experiment. Such inferences are frequently termed "constructs."

The term "variable," often designated by the letter x or y, is a symbol for an event to which two or more numerical values can be assigned customarily by the process of measurement. In the instance of a continuous variable individuals are placed in a rank order along a scale or on a continuum in terms of measures or scores obtained from an instrument such as a test or rating form that is judged to represent the characteristic under study. In the instance of a qualitative or discrete variable such as boy-girl, resident-nonresident, teacher-nonteacher, or promoted-nonpromoted pupil, values of 0 and 1 can be assigned—for example, 1 for boys and 0 for girls. In addition to such dichotomous variables, there may be discrete ones involving several steps, such as teacher-counselor-administrator or gifted, normal, or mentally retarded children. Some variables, such as those pertaining to sex or to marital, veteran, or resident status, are true dichotomies, whereas others, such as passing or failing a training program or owning three or more radios versus owning two or fewer radios, are artificial dichotomies. Certain arbitrary cutting points may be taken along a continuum of many values to form a convenient classification.

Among most workers who are involved in behavioral research on prediction there is a decided preference for operational definitions which represent exacting descriptions of the researcher's activities or procedures to measure constructs or to manipulate them in an experimental setting. Customarily expressed in quantitative or numerical language, operational definitions not only afford a relatively objective specification of activities which can be observed and repeated by others in their research but also tend to increase the degree of reliability (consistency and stability with which an instrument differentiates individuals along a scale) and the communicability of information obtained. Thus, the operational definition of a gifted child might be one who has earned an IQ score of 130 or higher on test X. A spelling list of 50 given words might be defined as learned when a child can go through it two consecutive times without making a single error. Similarly, a delinquent driver could be operationally described as one with three or more moving-traffic violations during a six-month period. In studies concerned with forecasting future academic and vocational success, operational definitions of independent variables (usually in terms of specific tests or scales employed) and criterion measures (readily described observable behaviors capable of objective quantification) can be expected to enhance the accuracy of the predictions made. Kerlinger (1964) presented a helpful explanation of operational definitions with numerous illustrations.

GENERAL CONCEPTUALIZATION OF PREDICTION PROCEDURES. Using the term "attributes" to stand for discrete or qualitative variables and "measurements" to describe a continuous variable on which scores are available, Guilford (1965) made four permutations of independent and dependent variables from which he postulated four cases of prediction: (1) attributes from attributes, as illustrated by the prediction of the presence or absence of delinquency from sex, race, or marital status; (2) attributes from measurements, as in, for example, the prediction of sex from weight or of promotion or nonpromotion from scores on an achievement test; (3) measurements from attributes, as when probable test scores are predicted from veteran status, a resident-nonresident classification, race, or religious creed; and (4) measurements from measurements, as in the case of predicting achievement-test scores from aptitude-test scores, job ratings from personality-test scores, or weight from height. Guilford also described statistical procedures for carrying out such predictions and for furnishing indications of the margin of error involved. In a related effort Guilford and Michael (1949) developed analytic methods for prediction of membership in categories from measurements (case 2, above) when the criterion variable is either a true or an artificial dichotomy. They also prepared a series of charts for use in problems involving personnel selection and clinical prognosis.

Embodying numerous implications for the conceptualization of the prediction process is Tatsuoka and Tiedeman's (1963) two-page table for classifying appropriate statistical techniques in terms of the number and scale type of independent and dependent variables. This comprehensive table makes reference both to the traditional techniques of regression analysis and to multivariate methods (procedures involving interrelationships among many variables) of factor analysis, discriminant analysis, canonical correlation, and analysis of variance that are useful in the study of prediction problems involving the simultaneous presence of one or several independent and of one or more dependent variables.

Comprehensive discussions of the statistical theory underlying and of the techniques for carrying out such multivariate analyses may be found in four books by Cattell (1966), DuBois (1957), Rao (1952), and Winer (1962). Two relatively elementary and lucid discussions concerning multivariate techniques are those by Pickrel (1958) and Regan (1965). Computer applications of multivariate analysis are described by Cooley and Jones (1964) and by Cooley and Lohnes (1962). A useful and detailed review of journal literature concerned with multivariate analysis is that by Cramer and Bock (1966). Two pertinent but highly mathematically oriented volumes concerned with certain topics in multivariate analysis are those by Harris (1963) and McKeon (1966). Somewhat more elementary in general level of mathematical sophistication than the four books cited at the beginning of this paragraph and seemingly more directly concerned with the conceptualization of problems of prediction in psychological measurement are the contributions of Ghiselli (1964), Guilford (1954), Gulliksen (1950), Hays (1963), Horst (1966, Horst & others, 1941), Kerlinger (1964), Lewis (1960), and Rozeboom (1966). Three highly technical and mathematically sophisticated volumes with implications for a theory of prediction in relation to the use of psychological tests are those by Burket (1964), Solomon (1961), and Tucker (1963).

REPRESENTATIVE TYPES OF PREDICTION PROBLEMS. In educational work, predictions are involved in making personnel decisions about such problems as grouping of students, employment of teachers or noncertificated personnel, admission of college applicants, formulation of vocational and educational choices, and retention or promotion of students. These problems may be placed into categories of *selection, classification,* and *guidance.*

In *selection* the objective is to choose a subgroup of applicants whose probability of success on the job or task involved is greater than that of the total group. Although certain individuals who are rejected would be successful and others who are selected are not successful, the use of valid tests (scores on which correlate significantly with criterion measures) will lead to a higher proportion of correct decisions than will failure to use any selection instrument. Additional information about personnel selection in relation to prediction methodology may be found in the works of Ghiselli (1964), Guilford (1954, 1965), Guilford and Michael (1949), Horst (1954b, 1955, 1960, 1966), Horst and others (1941), Michael (1957, 1966), and Thorndike (1949).

Whereas theoretically no special attention is given to the rejected applicant in the process of selection, in *classification* the goal is to place individuals in one of many possible categories (e.g., a job, training program, educational major, course of study, instructional method, or special class) such that he will have the highest chance of success, however it may be defined. Typically, public school personnel endeavor to place every student into some kind of program in which he can be expected to have a reasonable chance of success. Increments in accuracy of classification decisions depend on the ability of the investigator to predict the level of success for each person under all possible assignments. For a definitive and provocative treatment of the adaptation of decision theory to problems of personnel classification, see the book by Cronbach and Gleser (1965).

Although educational and vocational *guidance,* like classification, is concerned with predicting what will occur when individuals are exposed to different treatments, a key difference rests upon the fact that individuals (e.g., students) about whom the predictions are made—not the person making the prediction —actively take part in making the decision. The counselor may assist the counselee in building an understanding of his potentialities and motives, in furnishing information derived from tests and interviews about probabilities of success in different courses of study or vocations relative to other persons with similar aptitudes and interests, and in pointing out alternative courses of action. Eventually the counselee must weigh the relative advantages and disadvantages of each of several different courses of action by taking into account the amount of time and expense required in training, social status, aesthetic values, and service opportunities associated with a given vocation. Additional information concerning how measurement data may be used in decision-making activities of counseling and guidance was explicitly set forth by Adams and Torgerson (1964, p. 534–61).

TYPICAL MEASURES USED FOR PREDICTION. Many kinds of tests, scales, and indexes may be employed to make predictions. Thus, in attempting to foretell college or occupational success, high school marks (often converted to grade-point averages), teachers' ratings, achievement- and aptitude-test scores, biographical data, and information derived from interest and preference inventories as well as from personality scales involving both self-reporting and projective experiences are frequently used. In the elementary school, scores on tests of both reading comprehension and general mental ability have been helpful in forecasting a pupil's success. In vocational guidance as well as in academic advisement and grouping practices, high school and college counselors often make use of results of comprehensive series of aptitude tests. Frequently developed by factor-analytic approaches, such test batteries yield several relatively independent measures of different abilities that either are judged to be or have been shown empirically to be of importance to success in certain vocations or academic programs. Comprehensive and authoritative sources of information about published tests are contained in the volumes prepared by Buros (1961, 1965). Instructive discussions about the construction and use of tests were presented by Adams and Torgerson (1964), Cronbach (1960), and Thorndike and Hagen (1961).

GUIDING PRINCIPLES IN THE DEVELOPMENT OF PREDICTION DEVICES. Most scholastic aptitude tests involving language and mathematics abilities have been shown rather consistently to be related to success in academic programs. Ordinarily the complexity of academic and vocational behavior to be predicted is so great that several tests or scales must be employed. The variation in performance requirements from one school or college to another or in the same type of job from one social setting to another is so great that in each academic or vocational environment periodic empirical verification of the degree of relationship between each of several predictors and indexes of actual performance is necessary with groups of subjects who are judged to be a representative sample of the population for which a prediction is intended. Innovations in curriculum and technological changes in work requirements are taking place so rapidly that almost any summary of studies in academic and especially in vocational prediction is soon obsolete. Thus, keeping abreast of the current professional literature is more important today than ever before if a personnel worker is to gain ideas or leads regarding the predictors he might try to employ in his own particular set of circumstances.

CRITERION ANALYSIS AS AN AID TO THE SELECTION AND DEVELOPMENT OF PREDICTORS. The selection of existing measures or the development of new ones for the prediction of criterion performance can be facilitated by a detailed analysis of the skills, aptitudes, and personality characteristics involved in that performance. Such analyses yield hypotheses concerning what available or new predictor variables are likely to be efficacious in duplicating the psychological traits of the criterion. The complex nature of most criteria frequently necessitates the combination of several predictors which overlap as little as possible with one another in the information they furnish and which at the same time offer a broad coverage of the aptitudes, skills, and affective characteristics that seem necessary to the successful performance in the job behaviors being predicted. For example, in the prediction of scholastic performance in college, a battery (group) of tests (predictors) may involve scales devised to measure aptitudes, achievement in selected high school preparatory courses, academic interests, study attitudes and habits, and values.

The planning of a workable experimental battery depends upon an investigator's having adequate psychological background, familiarity with available tests and types of items, comprehensive and insightful understanding of the performance to be predicted, ingenuity in developing promising a priori hypotheses concerning which predictors are likely to be valid, skill in the design and preparation of tests necessary for specific purposes, and awareness of the social setting in which the criterion behaviors take place. With respect to this last cited social-psychological point, Astin (1964) emphasized, in carrying out criterion-centered research, the ecological nature of the criterion variable that involves a relationship between an individual and his environment. Thus, to be socially meaningful and relevant so-called "standards" of performance or "desirable" characteristics of behavior need to be defined in the social context in which they arise and in terms of relevant social goals which can be described in operational terms.

Three Common Approaches to Criterion Analysis. Highly useful in the description of the physical, psychological, and social factors of a work assignment is a *job analysis*. This method involves the logical formation of comprehensive, systematic, and relatively independent categories of observable behaviors that are psychologically interpretable and readily transformable into measurable operations or activities (Thorndike, 1949). Once the job analysis has been carried out aptitude measures (predictors) can be constructed to duplicate as closely as possible the psychological traits that are inferred on logical grounds to underlie the activities judged to be significant in the job. A second but somewhat limited approach to the development of predictors of work performance—especially in cases requiring psychomotor skills and mechanical information—is a *work-sample* test which is a replica or model of the job, as in the instance of a miniature lathe, a simulated set of automobile or airplane controls, or a trial sewing task. Although work-sample tests can afford considerable predictive power if they really resemble the job, they pose difficulties of being (1) time-consuming, (2) expensive to devise, maintain, and administer, and (3) limited in utility because of their customary specificity to one job. A third approach to the development of predictors that allows empirical verification of a priori hypotheses is that of *factor analysis* of intercorrelations among available as well as newly devised tests and criterion measures. In a carefully planned study such an analysis permits the determination of a minimum number of psychologically meaningful dimensions (factors) that represent relatively independent groupings or clusters of both predictor and criterion variables. From the content of the tasks involved and from examinees' introspective reports concerning thought processes used, inferences can be made concerning the nature of the psychological construct or function underlying each of the factors isolated. Once the factorial composition of the criterion has been mapped out, efforts can be made to build tests (each one frequently representing essentially one factor) to duplicate the psychological traits of the criterion. Such tests can be combined into a battery to predict a given criterion variable and can also be used to furnish profiles of one's relative strengths and weaknesses in a number of different aptitudes with respect to which normative data are available for successful individuals in numerous occupations. The utility of this factor analytic approach was noted by Guilford (1948) in his research on the selection of pilots in World War II.

Establishing Criterion Measures. Although it was written more than twenty years ago in reference to naval personnel research, Bechtoldt's (1947) discussion of how to establish criterion measures still remains one of the best guides for the necessary criterion analyses which ordinarily should precede selection of predictor variables. In Bechtoldt's view the criterion measures should meet the following requirements: (1) pertinence (relevance) and comprehensiveness in description of job activities, (2) discrimination (accurate differentiation of individuals along a scale) and reliability (consistency and stability of measures), (3) comparability in the meaning associated with the same value or score assigned to a criterion measure for different individuals, and (4) compatibility with an appropriate methodology when such measures are combined to reflect their intended contributions to a composite criterion. Among several potential sources of error found in the use of criterion data are (1) contamination of criterion measures assigned by a judge because of his knowledge of the rated individual's standing on predictor variables, (2) biases or misconceptions concerning the importance of particular characteristics of individuals such as age, experience, or social status that may lead to differences in assigned criterion scores or ratings even though the performance of two employees or students is actually the same, and (3) chance assignment factors leading to different opportunities either for the demonstration or development of specific skills and competencies or for the promotability of the individual.

The lack of reliability in criterion measures also poses a serious limitation in the extent to which a criterion variable is predictable, since a measure of criterion performance which is inconsistent and unstable (a measure which will not correlate with itself) cannot be expected to show a high relationship (correlation) with any other measure such as a predictor. A low degree of reliability or lack of agreement in criterion measures can be attributed to (1) errors or variations in measuring procedures, such as inadequate samplings of behaviors, ambiguities in directions, lack of uniformity in conditions of test administration, and differences in motivational levels of individuals; (2) errors or inconsistencies (low objectivity) in scoring procedures as found in different biases and varied interpretations of raters or of readers of examination papers; and (3) changes within the individual himself (low stability of individual behavior), such as short-term fluctuations in attention level, speed of work, metabolic function, and motivation.

The reliability of judgments may be increased by the extensive training of raters to help them to minimize personal biases, to attend to the evaluation of the same observed characteristics of behavior, and to weight in a comparable manner elements of the observed performance. Helpful discussions concerning both test and criterion reliability were presented by Bechtoldt (1947), Guilford (1954, 1965), Thorndike (1949), and Thorndike and Hagen (1961).

Construct Validation of Criterion and Test Measures. As initially described in an article by Cronbach and Meehl (1955) and subsequently elaborated upon by Clark (1959) and by the Joint Committee on Test Standards of the American Psychological Association, the American Educational Research Association, and the National Council on Measurement in Education (American Psychological Association & others, 1966), *construct validity* is concerned with the development of a theoretical framework or nomological network of concepts and experimental outcomes that serve to give some basic, real, and therefore valid meaning to psychological concepts (constructs). Although not equivalent to construct validity, factor analysis, if applied to appropriately designed studies, affords one methodology for obtaining evidence to validate constructs. Another useful methodology, which has been proposed by Campbell and Fiske (1959), is that of a multitrait-multimethod matrix that affords a systematic experimental design for assessing in effect two or more traits by two or more methods. Despite opposition from certain circles concerning the appropriateness of construct validity to a practical or logical theory of psychological measurement (Horst, 1966, p. 346), it may be contended that the development of a comprehensive theory of the nature of psychological behavior underlying both criterion and test measures could be expected to enhance the accuracy with which measures of criterion performance can be predicted.

Taking the position that a comprehensive theory of the teaching and learning process can lead to gains in the predictive validity of existing measures and to the development of even more promising ones, Michael (1961, 1964, 1965) urged that increased efforts be directed toward clarification of psychological constructs so that resulting refinements in both testing and criterion instruments may be realized. Essentially the thesis was that improved understanding of psychological constructs could lead to the development of new measures of these constructs and eventually to increased accuracy of prediction, since new sources of reliable score variance in factorially complex criterion measures could be accounted for and duplicated by the predictors.

CROSS-VALIDATION. Once an investigator has found that one or more predictor variables are related to the criterion measures he has employed, he is well advised to do additional research with new samples. In part, the initial promising relationship can result from chance factors, or sampling fluctuations, that yield an estimate of a test-criterion correlation for a sample considerably higher than that in the population from which the sample was chosen. Although there are statistical corrections for estimating how much shrinkage might be expected to occur in the correlations for new samples, it is preferable to determine the effectiveness of the one or more predictors involved on a new independent sample from the same population of persons on whom predictions will be attempted. This procedure, which has been termed "cross-validation," is commonly applied by personnel research workers, especially when samples are small and when several newly devised tests or scales are being subjected to validation procedures. One of the most helpful expositions concerning methods for carrying out cross-validation studies for realization of more effective prediction is that prepared by Mosier (1951).

PROCEDURES FOR PREDICTING A SINGLE CRITERION. One of the most common types of prediction problems is that of forecasting success on a continuous criterion measure from knowledge of scores on a single predictor variable which is also continuous. Even when several criterion variables exist, they are frequently combined by appropriate weights into a single criterion measure, as when grades in many courses are averaged to yield a single index of academic achievement.

One of the easiest and most direct ways of treating prediction data is to arrange scores on the predictor and criterion variables in the form of a chart called a scatter diagram or scatter plot, as illustrated in Table 1. From such a geometrical representation it is customarily possible to ascertain whether a relationship exists between the predictor and criterion variables and to ascertain the extent of this relationship. It is essential that there be sufficient range or variability in both sets of scores so that differentiation among the individuals on the predicted variable will be possible. Thus, if everyone earned approximately

TABLE 1

SCATTER DIAGRAM FOR COLLEGE-APTITUDE RATINGS AND FRESHMAN SCHOLARSHIP, 1923, 1924, 1925 (WOMEN).*

College aptitude ratings	Frequency of each grade average					
	F	D	C	B	A	Total
91–100		1	23	30	1	55
81–90		3	36	16		55
71–80	3	16	42	10		71
61–70	6	30	36	1		73
51–60	6	41	28			75
41–50	6	36	18	1		61
31–40	18	38	14			70
21–30	8	26	1			35
11–20	9	20				29
1–10	9	6				15
Total:	65	217	198	58	1	539

* Data from Johnston (1930).

the same score on the criterion measure there would be little point in making a prediction. However, when a fairly small range of criterion scores occurs for each predictor score, predictions can be carried out in a number of ways and with considerable accuracy.

When the criterion data are expressed in categories as shown in Table 1, it is possible to compute for an individual who falls within any test-score interval the probability of his obtaining any particular mark (or other desired measurable outcome) from the obtained frequencies, as indicated in Table 2. From that table

TABLE 2

EXPECTANCY TABLE OF FRESHMAN SCHOLARSHIP ACCORDING TO COLLEGE APTITUDE (WOMEN).

College aptitude ratings	Probability of grade attainments				
	F	D	C	B	A
91–100		.02	.42	.55	.02
81–90		.06	.65	.29	
71–80	.04	.23	.59	.14	
61–70	.08	.41	.49	.01	
51–60	.08	.55	.37		
41–50	.10	.59	.30	.02	
31–40	.26	.54	.20		
21–30	.23	.74	.03		
11–20	.31	.69			
1–10	.60	.40			

one can determine, for example, that women who scored from 81 to 90 on a test were most likely to earn C averages and that those scoring between 91 and 100 were most likely to earn B averages.

When the criterion data are continuous, it is feasible to compute the average criterion score at each level of the predictor measure, and the relationship between the two sets of scores may be shown by a curve drawn through these average values. Although this curve may be used directly for prediction, it is customary by mathematical means to find the equation of a straight line of best fit for the mean values. In mathematical terms, this regression line is one from which the sum of the squares of the deviations of observed values is a minimum. In conjunction with this method, one may compute a correlation coefficient, an index number ranging between 0 and 1 in value indicating the degree of relationship between the two variables (or between 0 and −1 in the instance of an inverse relationship). For additional information concerning the meaning of correlation and regression, see the works by Guilford (1965) and Michael (1966).

STATISTICAL METHODS. For the present illustration shown in Table 1, in which grades are assigned numerical values from 0 to 4, a product-moment coefficient of correlation of .67 is found. The regression equation for the line of best fit is given by $Y' = .023X + .15$, where Y' is the grade-point average and X is the aptitude-test score. This equation can be used to predict the expected grade for an individual with a known aptitude score in the population from which this sample was obtained.

The approach just illustrated is one of the most widely employed procedures for carrying out prediction studies involving educational and psychological tests. In the interpretation of the results of such investigations one needs to give attention to (1) sampling errors involved in the selection of individuals, (2) the degree of reliability in the criterion measures as well as in the predictor measures, and (3) any restriction (narrowing) of range in the abilities of the individuals which may arise because of prior selection or attrition. These three factors are often associated with the size of a correlation coefficient and with the accuracy of prediction.

There are some instances in which the relationship between a criterion variable and a predictor variable is not appropriately described by a straight line drawn through the means. The lack of what is known as a linear relationship necessitates considerable computational work. However, it is quite possible through techniques of curve fitting to find nonlinear regression equations, the simplest of which is the quadratic for describing the relationship between the two variables. Curvilinear relationships are often noted when physiological, motivational, and adjustment variables are correlated either with one another or with cognitive measures. For additional information concerning both linear and nonlinear regression as well as the indexes of correlation associated with these approaches, the reader is referred to the books by Ezekiel and Fox (1959), Guilford (1954, 1965), Hays (1963), Horst (1966), Lewis (1960), and Rozeboom (1966). For a comprehensive review of professional literature concerned with regression and correlation, one may consult the article by Moonan and Wolfe (1963).

Combining Many Predictor Variables. Frequently several predictor variables rather than a single one are examined in terms of their degree of relationship with the criterion variable, and from these variables a combination is chosen that will yield the most accurate possible prediction with the criterion measure.

By far the most commonly used procedure as well as the most elementary one in the prediction of a continuous criterion variable is that of the multiple linear regression model, a general description of which can be found in the books by Ghiselli (1964), Guilford (1954, 1965), Horst (1966), Rozeboom (1966), or Thorndike (1949). (See also STATISTICAL METHODS.) Weights known as regression coefficients are determined for each predictor variable, customarily by some variant of a least-squares procedure. The resulting sum of scores on the composite of these variables will show the highest possible relationship (multiple correlation) with the criterion variable for the sample of persons being studied. Little loss in the correlation will be realized if the weights are converted for convenience to integral values that maintain approximately the same ratios to one another as those of the weights in the initially derived set. This correlation tends to be maximized when each of the predictors is relatively unrelated to the others and when each predictor variable shows a substantial correlation with the criterion variable. Thus, tests that represent different constructs but duplicate individually one or more of the constructs represented by the criterion measure show promise for inclusion in a battery. Although several predictor variables may be significantly related to the criterion variable, it has been found that combining a great number of these variables usually contributes a relatively small increment to the accuracy of prediction over and above that realized by using only two or three of the most promising predictor variables. Thus, a verbal aptitude test might correlate .56 with a criterion of grade-point average; the addition of a quantitative-reasoning test might result in a multiple correlation of .63 for the composite of the two measures; and the addition of a third measure, such as an achievement test or a study-habits inventory, might raise the multiple correlation to a value of .65 or .66. The inclusion of three or four more tests would rarely increase the multiple correlation to a value much in excess of .70 or .71—a value which has been termed the "criterion barrier" (Michael, 1965).

It is important to realize that the multiple regression approach tends to capitalize on all chance relationships which may arise because of sampling perturbations. The resulting inflated value in the multiple correlation coefficient can be expected to drop when the observed criterion scores are correlated with the predicted criterion scores in a new sample. Therefore, large samples should be sought, especially when there are many predictor variables, since the amount of shrinkage in the correlation coefficient is a function of both the number of individuals and the number of predictor variables (or, in statistical terminology, of the number of degrees of freedom present).

Numerous computational procedures for multiple linear regression are available, and descriptions of them appear in the several sources just previously cited. Two commonly applied approaches now made feasible by electronic computers are those of accretion (adding predictor variables from a pool of potential ones until the multiple correlation coefficient seems to stabilize in value) and deletion (starting with a very large number of predictor variables and selectively eliminating them to the point at which any further reduction in the size of the multiple correlation coefficient would be judged unacceptable). In applying these procedures to problems of multiple absolute and multiple differential prediction (procedures to be explained in a subsequent section), Horst and MacEwan (1960) concluded that the deletion solution is superior to accretion, for at any stage it can utilize to a greater extent intercorrelations among the predictor variables. A detailed discussion of additional research efforts about these two approaches may be found in a review by Moonan and Wolfe (1963).

SOME SPECIAL PROBLEMS. Many special types of problems arise in the prediction of a criterion variable—for example, when grade-point averages in different high schools are involved in the prediction of grade-point averages of applicants to different colleges. To permit the prediction of scholastic performance at several different colleges when systematic differences exist in secondary-school grades and in college grading standards, Tucker (1963) proposed highly sophisticated canonical-correlation models of considerable promise that also allow the introduction of new predictor variables such as aptitude tests. In a similar vein, Lindquist (1963) made a logical analysis concerning how high school grades can be scaled or adjusted to permit them to be more predictive of college grades and more nearly comparable in meaning from school to school. He suggested and illustrated a promising and highly practical scaling method for centralized use simultaneously with large populations of secondary schools and colleges.

Another problem encountered in the prediction of a criterion variable from several tests has been that of the relatively small number of individuals who engage in a criterion activity long enough for reliable data to be obtained in comparison with the total number of potential applicants or individuals for whom comprehensive data are available on numerous predictor variables. To permit prediction of a criterion measure when only a small number of observations exists for the criterion variable, Burket (1964) developed analytic methods for increasing the accuracy of such predictions through the use of reduced-rank models.

EXPECTANCY TABLES. Expectancy tables may be constructed to demonstrate the probability of various levels of success on a criterion measure with respect to different combinations of scores earned on two or more predictor variables, which may be either continuous measures grouped into wide intervals or qualitative separations such as sex or residential status. In the instance of large samples these tables may be employed directly for prediction, or they may be studied to ascertain whether an analytic method, either linear or nonlinear, would be feasible for prediction.

Expectancy tables involving the use of three predictor variables of high school percentile rank, the

TABLE 3

PROBABILITY OF ATTAINING A GRADE OF C OR HIGHER FOR MALE AND FEMALE FRESHMEN.*

High school rank percentile	ACE percentile							
	0—24		25—49		50—74		75—100	
	M	F	M	F	M	F	M	F
75–100	.63	.68	.75	.80	.83	.90	.90	.94
50–74	.46	.40	.55	.52	.66	.65	.69	.72
25–49	.29	.44	.33	.50	.48	.29	.64	...
0–24	.17	.31	.30	.33	.47	.50	.42	...

* Data from Lins (1950).

American Council on Education (ACE) percentile standing, and sex for prediction of first-semester grade-point average at the University of Wisconsin were prepared by Lins (1950). An adaptation of one is reproduced in Table 3. Based on samples of 1,189 men and 600 women who entered the university during the fall of 1948, the table furnishes estimates of a male or a female student's probability of earning a grade-point average of C or higher with each possible combination of high-school percentile rank and ACE percentile standing. When data are presented in this form, it is relatively easy for both counselors and prospective students in a guidance program to grasp the significance of information furnished by predictor variables (Schrader, 1965).

PATTERN AND CONFIGURAL SCORING. Expectancy tables such as the ones prepared by Lins (1950) actually constitute a means for prediction of a criterion variable from a pattern or configuration of scores on several predictor variables. In pattern and configural analyses of scores, research efforts have proceeded along two principal avenues: (1) the employment of patterns of *test scores* to predict a criterion variable or to place individuals within categories and (2) use of patterns of *item responses* to generate a more valid scoring key for the prediction of an external criterion measure than that afforded by simple summation of scores on individual items. Underlying these two objectives is the basic rationale that although one predictor variable by itself may bear little relation to the criterion variable, in combination with one or more other predictor variables it will show a high predictive capability. This catalytic interaction, which represents a joint contribution, may be illustrated in terms of a situation in which the success of a student in a commercial or secretarial course could be more accurately predicted for those with high clerical-interest scores and high scores in a measure of compulsiveness than for those with high clerical-interest scores and low standing in compulsiveness.

For the case involving two continuous predictor variables (X_1, X_2), such as two tests, and a single predicted criterion score, Y', such as grade-point average, a general mathematical solution has been known for some time. The prediction equation as a general polynomial function assumes the form

$$Y' = A_1X_1 + A_2X_2 + A_3X_1^2 + A_4X_2^2 + A_5X_1X_2 + A_6,$$
where the A's are consonants. If A_3, A_4, and A_5 are equal to zero, the equation reduces to linear form (the equation represents a plane instead of a curved surface). The variables X_1^2, X_2^2, and X_1X_2 can be treated as separate independent variables, correlated with the criterion variable, and assigned weights by customary regression techniques (Ezekiel & Fox, 1959). It can also be determined whether the squared and product terms add significantly to the accuracy of prediction furnished by the linear composite.

Prediction of a Criterion Variable from Test-score Patterns. To take care of the prediction of a criterion variable when it is nonlinearly related to the two predictor variables or when interaction effects are suspected, Maxwell (1957) proposed an equation like the one just cited, described and illustrated a computational procedure involving use of analysis of covariance, and furnished a geometrical interpretation of the equation in terms of contour analysis. Saunders (1956), coining the term "moderator variable" to represent the product term X_1X_2 in the equation of the previous paragraph when this term is combined only with the two linear terms involving X_1 and X_2, cited several examples of moderated regression and reported results of a cross-validation analysis that revealed only slight differences in the correlations derived from the linear and moderated regression approaches. Customarily the use of moderator variables has not held up in cross-validation efforts, although in one empirical study involving the cross-validation of two moderator variables Hobert and Dunnette (1967) obtained confirming evidence of their usefulness. With reference to the linear composite Lubin (1957) described the rationale of a pattern-like function involving a suppressor variable (a predictor variable that has a correlation of nearly zero with the criterion variable but a modest or substantial one with another predictor variable) and furnished several formulas to assist the investigator in deciding whether to employ a suppressor variable.

Prediction of a Criterion Variable from Item-score Patterns. Since the appearance of Meehl's pioneering article on configural scoring of dichotomous items (1950), Horst (1954a, 1957) and Lubin and Osburn (1957, 1960) have demonstrated that Meehl's approach can be interpreted as a nonlinear composite of item scores that may be treated by the previously described polynomial function to predict a criterion variable. Upon cross-validation, one may expect considerable shrinkage in the predictive accuracy of such an equation, since it is inflated with sampling fluctuations to a much greater extent than is the linear equation. The influence of sampling error associated with individuals selected and the marked unreliability of scores on single items necessitate the use of large samples for accurate prediction. Although computer technology probably makes feasible the use of such equations, it is important to ascertain whether predictive accuracy afforded by a nonlinear composite is significantly larger than that already realized by linear multiple regression procedures. Additional contributions to the theory of pattern analysis are those of McQuitty (1956, 1957), who subsequently applied his pattern analytic methods to a study of typologies (McQuitty, 1967).

Strategies to Aid Selection Decisions. When selection decisions are made in terms of data furnished by predictions, a strategy of selection is advisably chosen. Customarily a point on the criterion scale is taken above which performance is judged satisfactory or successful and below which it is considered unsatisfactory or unsuccessful. With respect to each score or combination of scores on two or more independent variables, the probability of success on the criterion variable may be estimated.

In the instance of a single predictor a critical or cutting score on the independent variable is chosen in terms of the proportion of unsuccessful persons that the decision maker can accept among those selected and of the proportion of potentially successful individuals he can permit to be rejected. In part the decision with respect to the critical score depends upon the numbers of individuals to be chosen, the expense of training potentially unsuccessful individuals, the numerous consequences of unsatisfactory performance, and the quantity and quality of the applicant population. Cronbach and Gleser (1965), Guilford (1954, 1965), Guilford and Michael (1949), and Taylor and Russell (1939) elaborated upon the role of several key parameters involved in setting critical scores.

When two or more predictor variables are employed, decisions rest on how various characteristics measured by predictor variables are judged to contribute to successful performance. If these variables appear to be compensatory so that low standing on one can be offset by a high score on another, then a critical score can be found for the linear composite. On the other hand, if a minimal level in standing on one or more predictor variables (such as a minimum level of reading ability being required to succeed in a liberal arts college program) is judged to be necessary for success in the criterion variable, an individual may be rejected irrespective of how high his scores are on other predictor variables. This multiple cut-off procedure, which is paritcularly likely to be used when a curvilinear relationship exists between the criterion variable and one or more predictor variables, results in a somewhat different selection of individuals from that afforded by the multiple regression approach (i.e., a simple cutting score on the linear composite). A graphical explanation of this difference between the two approaches may be found in the book by Thorndike (1949) or that by Guilford (1965).

PROCEDURES FOR PREDICTION OF MULTIPLE CRITERION MEASURES. When decisions must be made concerning the classification of individuals into one of many criterion groups (categories), the prediction problem is considerably more complex than when one criterion variable is involved. In many jobs or courses of study similar aptitudes and skills are needed. However, considerable variation exists in their relative importance. One widely employed solution has been to use a single battery of predictors but to weight the composites differently for each classification or criterion measure corresponding to the class. Although this approach reveals the likelihood of a certain *absolute level* of success in each of several activities, it does not achieve an optimal prediction of the *differential level* of success in various pairs of criterion measures. In other words, it cannot be determined whether an individual will achieve at a higher level in one job or course (such as engineering or dentistry) than in another. Such *differential prediction*, which involves predicted difference scores on criterion measures, tends to be facilitated when the tests in the batteries show low positive, preferably zero, or even negative correlations with one another, for the higher the positive correlation between tests is, the lower is the reliability for the differences between scores.

Multiple Absolute and Differential Prediction. In two definitive monographs, Horst (1954b, 1955) rationalized the problem of prediction of multiple criterion variables from a composite of independent variables in terms of two approaches: (1) multiple absolute prediction and (2) differential prediction. *Multiple absolute prediction*, as developed by Horst (1955), is a technique for choosing from a battery of potential predictors (subtests) a weighted composite of subtests that will yield the *highest index of predictive efficiency on all criterion measures that are simultaneously being predicted*. In Horst's earlier formulation (1954b), *differential prediction* affords a means for selecting a set of tests from a battery that will furnish a *maximum amount of average variance in the predicted difference scores across all possible pairs of criterion measures*. Seeking a manageable solution to the differential classification problem, Horst (1960) introduced a quota system and noted that there should be at least as many predictor variables as criterion variables. He also suggested the desirability of finding a systematic procedure for merging criterion measures. For both multiple absolute prediction and differential prediction, Horst and MacEwan (1957) worked out a generalized solution to the optimal distribution of a newly specified overall testing time with respect to all predictors.

Clinical Prediction. In contrast to the previously cited prediction techniques involving the combination of scores in a predetermined mechanical manner for all persons, a clinical psychologist or counselor customarily bases his prediction of the behavior of an individual on the particular pattern of his scores on both structured and projective tests as well as on a qualitative judgment of the relative importance of numerous factors in his personal history that are derived from interviews and medical examinations. In stressing that the clinician makes use of whatever data are available to him to formulate a hypothesis about the dynamic interrelationships of needs, drives, and adaptive mechanisms of the individual, Meehl (1954) argued that the clinician makes his predictions in terms of propositions deduced from his hypothesis and in terms of his interpretation of a possible causal link between the person's psychological condition at the moment and the person's anticipated future behaviors. However, Sarbin (1944) expounded the view that when the clinician considers additional information in making his prediction he is in effect assigning the subject to a subgroup of individuals for whom an expected probability value exists that can be empirically verified. Thus, the clinician is in reality carrying out actuarial predictions involving subjectively determined expectancies. Hence, it can be argued that the clinician should explicitly state his hypotheses concerning which patterns are significant as well as subject them to empirical tests before trying to incorporate them into his predictions. Irrespective of the process employed by the clinician he not only can modify, as the need may arise, his predictions from feedback furnished by the subject but also can obtain both quantitative and qualitative information as required.

The accuracy of the clinician's prediction can be subjected to empirical test by comparing how closely behavioral outcomes correspond to prior predictions. In contrasting statistical with clinical prediction in relation to 16 to 20 articles (the number depends upon the criteria of admissibility), Meehl (1954) concluded that in all but one investigation statistically (actuarially) based predictions were, with respect to accuracy, either almost equal to or superior to those carried out by clinicians. Thus, it would appear that clinicians in comparable situations, given the same data as required by the multiple regression equation, are not likely to produce more accurate predictions than those afforded by statistical means. Moreover, the existence of giant electronic computers with substantial input and storage capabilities also makes feasible the use of intricate nonlinear mathematical equations for predictive purposes. The storage and operational capacities of sophisticated computer systems may well outstrip the clinician's intuitive capabilities and insights.

Stressing that in clinical versus statistical prediction attention must concomitantly be directed toward clinical versus mechanical *measurement*, Sawyer (1966) formed an eight-way table consisting of four modes of data collection—clinical, mechanical, both, and either or both—and two modes of data combination—clinical or mechanical—and evaluated 45 clinical-statistical prediction studies. Despite substantial uncontrolled difference in clinical training, the form in which data were reported, samples of subjects, statistical treatments, and criteria employed, he tentatively demonstrated a superiority of the mechanical approach with respect to both collection and combination of data over a clinical mode, suggested that the clinician's contribution is probably greater in observation than in integration activities, and pointed to the tremendous potential of the electronic computer in carrying out mechanical procedures involving patterned and nonlinear relations of predictor variables with criterion measures.

Perhaps the most comprehensive single source of information about clinical prediction, the validation of assessment techniques, and the comparison of clinical and statistical approaches to prediction is to be found in the collection of 58 recent research studies in clinical assessment that have been brought together from 20 American, Canadian, and British journals by Megargee (1966) into a single volume. From his overview in Chapter 12 of five studies of clinical assessment involving multiple sources of data, Megargee concluded that (1) sometimes under certain conditions clinicians could formulate inferences in excess of chance expectations, (2) psychological tests generally furnish somewhat more nearly correct inferences than minimal identifying information, though the increment is small, (3) case-history data appear considerably superior to test data, (4) projective tests offer somewhat less promise than structured tests, (5) clinical psychologists seemingly tend to judge a disproportionate number of members in so-called normal groups as being quite maladjusted, (6) the research need for appropriate weighting of signs of pathology is pressing, and (7) stable internal norms for personality patterns of well functioning individuals need to be established through additional clinical training.

William B. Michael
University of California

References

Adams, Georgia Sachs, and Torgerson, Theodore L. *Measurement and Evaluation in Education, Psychology, and Guidance.* Holt, 1964. 654p.

American Psychological Association and others. *Standards for Educational and Psychological Tests and Manuals.* APA, 1966. 40p.

Astin, Alexander W. "Criterion-centered Research." *Ed Psychol Meas* 24:807–22; 1964.

Bechtoldt, Harold P. "Problems in Establishing Criterion Measures." In Stuit, Dewey B. (Ed.) *Personnel Research and Test Development in the Bureau of Naval Personnel.* Princeton U Press, 1947. p. 357–79.

Burket, George R. "A Study of Reduced Rank Models for Multiple Prediction." *Psychometric Monogr* No. 12. Psychometric Society, 1964. 66p.

Buros, Oscar K. (Ed.) *Tests in Print.* Gryphon, 1961. 479p.

Buros, Oscar K. (Ed.) *The Sixth Mental Measurements Yearbook.* Gryphon, 1965. 1714p.

Campbell, Donald T., and Fiske, Donald W. "Convergent and Discriminant Validation by the Multitrait-multimethod Matrix." *Psychol B* 56:81–105; 1959.

Cattell, Raymond B. (Ed.) *Handbook of Multivariate Experimental Psychology.* Rand McNally, 1966. 959p.

Clark, Cherry Ann. "Developments and Applications in the Area of Construct Validity." *R Ed Res* 29: 84–105; 1959.

Cooley, William W., and Jones, Kenneth J. "Computer Systems for Multivariate Statistical Analysis." *Ed Psychol Meas* 24:645–53; 1964.

Cooley, William W., and Lohnes, Paul R. *Multivariate Procedures for the Behavioral Sciences.* Wiley, 1962. 211p.

Cramer, Elliot M., and Bock, R. Darrell. "Multivariate Analysis." *R Ed Res* 36:604–17; 1966.

Cronbach, Lee J. *Essentials of Psychological Testing,* 2nd ed. Harper, 1960. 650p.

Cronbach, Lee J., and Gleser, Goldine C. *Psychological Tests and Personnel Decisions,* 2nd ed. U Illinois Press, 1965. 347p.

Cronbach, Lee J., and Meehl, Paul E. "Construct Validity in Psychological Tests." *Psychol B* 52: 281–302; 1955.

DuBois, Philip H. *Multivariate Correlational Analysis.* Harper, 1957. 202p.

Ezekiel, Mordecai, and Fox, Karl A. *Methods of Correlation and Regression Analysis, Linear and Curvilinear,* 3rd ed. Wiley, 1959. 548p.

Ghiselli, Edwin E. *Theory of Psychological Measurement.* McGraw-Hill, 1964. 408p.

Guilford, J. P. "Factor Analysis in a Test-development Program." *Psychol R* 55:79–94; 1948.

Guilford, J. P. *Psychometric Methods,* 2nd ed. McGraw-Hill, 1954. 597p.

Guilford, J. P. *Fundamental Statistics in Psychology and Education,* 4th ed. McGraw-Hill, 1965. 605p.

Guilford, J. P., and Michael, William B. *The Prediction of Categories from Measurements.* Sheridan Supply, 1949. 55p.

Gulliksen, Harold. *Theory of Mental Tests.* Wiley, 1950. 486p.

Harris, Chester W. (Ed.) *Problems in Measuring Change.* U Wisconsin Press, 1963. 259p.

Hays, William L. *Statistics for Psychologists.* Holt, 1963. 719p.

Hobert, Robert, and Dunnette, Marvin D. "Development of Moderator Variables to Enhance the Prediction of Managerial Effectiveness." *J Applied Psych* 51:50–64; 1967.

Horst, Paul. "Pattern Analysis and Configural Scoring." *J Clin Psychol* 10:3–11; 1954(a).

Horst, Paul. "A Technique for the Development of a Differential Prediction Battery." *Psychol Monogr* No. 380; 1954(b). 31p.

Horst, Paul. "A Technique for the Development of a Multiple Absolute Prediction Battery." *Psychol Monogr* No. 390; 1955. 22p.

Horst, Paul. "The Uniqueness of Configural Test Item Scores." *J Clin Psychol* 13:107–14; 1957.

Horst, Paul. "Optimal Estimates of Multiple Criteria with Restrictions on the Covariance Matrix of Estimated Criteria." *Psychol Report* 6:427–44; 1960 (Monogr. Suppl. 6-V6).

Horst, Paul. *Psychological Measurement and Prediction.* Wadsworth 1966. 455p.

Horst, Paul, and MacEwan, Charlotte. "Optimal Test Length for Multiple Prediction: The General Case." *Psychometrika* 22:311–24; 1957.

Horst, Paul, and MacEwan, Charlotte. "Predictor Elimination Techniques for Determining Multiple Prediction Batteries." *Psychol Report* 7:19–50; 1960. (Monogr. Suppl. 1-V7).

Horst, Paul, and others. *The Prediction of Personal*

Adjustment. Social Science Research Council, 1941. 455p.
Johnston, John B. *The Liberal College in Changing Society.* Century, 1930. 326p.
Kerlinger, Fred N. *Foundations of Behavioral Research.* Holt, 1964. 739p.
Lewis, Don. *Quantitative Methods in Psychology.* McGraw-Hill, 1960. 558p.
Lindquist, E. F. "An Evaluation of a Technique for Scaling High School Grades to Improve Prediction of College Success." *Ed Psychol Meas* 23:623–46; 1963.
Lins, L. J. "Probability Approach to Forecasting University Success with Measured Grades as the Criterion." *Ed Psychol Meas* 10:386–91; 1950.
Lubin, Ardie. "Some Formulae for Use with Suppressor Variables." *Ed Psychol Meas* 17:286–96; 1957.
Lubin, Ardie, and Osburn, Hobart G. "A Theory of Pattern Analysis for the Prediction of a Quantitative Criterion." *Psychometrika* 22:63–73; 1957.
Lubin, Ardie, and Osburn, Hobart G. "The Use of Configural Analysis for the Prediction of a Qualitative Criterion." *Ed Psychol Meas* 20:275–82; 1960.
Maxwell, A. E. "Contour Analysis." *Ed Psychol Meas* 17:347–60; 1957.
McKeon, James J. "Canonical Analysis: Some Relations Between Canonical Correlation, Factor Analysis, Discriminant Function Analysis, and Scaling Theory." *Psychometric Monogr* No. 13. Psychometric Society, 1966. 43p.
McQuitty, Louis L. "Agreement Analysis: Classifying Persons by Predominant Patterns of Responses." *Br J Stat Psychol* 9:5–16; 1956.
McQuitty, Louis L. "Isolating Predictor Patterns Associated with Major Criterion Patterns." *Ed Psychol Meas* 17:3–42; 1957.
McQuitty, Louis L. "A Mutual Development of Some Typological Theories and Pattern-analytic Methods." *Ed Psychol Meas* 27:21–46; 1967.
Meehl, Paul E. "Configural Scoring." *J Cons Psychol* 14:165–71; 1950.
Meehl, Paul E. *Clinical Versus Statistical Prediction.* U Minnesota Press, 1954. 149p.
Megargee, Edwin I. (Ed.) *Research in Clinical Assessment.* Harper, 1966. 702p.
Michael, William B. "Differential Testing of High-level Personnel." *Ed Psychol Meas* 17:475–90; 1957.
Michael, William B. "Problems of Validity for Achievement Tests." In Huddleston, Edith M. (Ed.) *The Eighteenth Yearbook of the National Council on Measurement in Education.* NCME, 1961. p. 1–12.
Michael, William B. "The Realization of Reliable and Valid Criterion Measures for Special Undergraduate Programs and Courses Aimed at the Development and Expression of Creative Behavior." *J Ed Meas* 1:97–102; 1964.
Michael, William B. "Measurement and Prediction in the College Admissions Process: Some Possible Directions for Future Research." *Ed Psychol Meas* 25:55–72; 1965.
Michael, William B. "An Interpretation of the Coefficients of Predictive Validity and of Determination in Terms of the Proportions of Correct Inclusions or Exclusion in Cells of a Fourfold Table." *Ed Psychol Meas* 26:419–26; 1966.
Moonan, William J., and Wolfe, John H. "Regression and Correlation." *R Ed Res* 33:501–9; 1963.
Mosier, Charles I. "Problems and Designs of Cross-validation." *Ed Psychol Meas* 11:5–11; 1951.
Pickrel, E. W. "Classification Theory and Techniques." *Ed Psychol Meas* 18:37–46; 1958.
Rao, C. Radhakrishna. *Advanced Statistical Methods in Biometric Research.* Wiley, 1952. 390p.
Regan, Mary C. "Development and Classification of Models for Multivariate Analysis." *Ed Psychol Meas* 25:997–1010; 1965.
Rozeboom, William W. *Foundations of the Theory of Prediction.* Dorsey Press, Inc., 1966. 628p.
Sarbin, Theodore R. "The Logic of Prediction in Psychology." *Psychol R* 51:210–28; 1944.
Saunders, David R. "Moderator Variables in Prediction." *Ed Psychol Meas* 16:209–22; 1956.
Sawyer, Jack. "Measurement and Prediction, Clinical and Statistical." *Psychol B* 66:178–200; 1966.
Schrader, W. B. "A Taxonomy of Expectancy Tables." *J Ed Meas* 2:29–35; 1965.
Solomon, Herbert. (Ed.) *Studies in Item Analysis and Prediction.* Stanford U Press, 1961. 310p.
Tatsuoka, Maurice M., and Tiedeman, David V. "Statistics as an Aspect of Scientific Method in Research on Teaching." In Gage, N. L. (Ed.) *Handbook of Research on Teaching.* Rand McNally, 1963. p. 142–70.
Taylor, H. C., and Russell, J. T. "The Relationship of Validity Coefficients to the Practical Effectiveness of Tests in Selection: Discussion and Tables." *J Applied Psychol* 23:565–78; 1939.
Thorndike, Robert L. *Personnel Selection: Test and Measurement Techniques.* Wiley, 1949. 358p.
Thorndike, Robert L., and Hagen, Elizabeth. *Measurement and Evaluation in Psychology and Education,* 2nd ed. Wiley, 1961. 602p.
Tucker, Ledyard R. "Formal Models for a Central Prediction System." *Psychometric Monogr* No. 10. Psychometric Society, 1963. 61p.
Winer, B. J. *Statistical Principles in Experimental Design.* McGraw-Hill, 1962. 672p.

PREPARATION OF ADMINISTRATORS

Administration has been an activity of importance to society for many centuries. The administration of public (and private) schools in the United States dates back at least a couple of hundred years. Early schools were relatively simple institutions, and their administration was also simple. Under such circumstances, the administrator could learn his profession effectively on the job by trial-and-error processes. Little, if any, formal specialized preparation was needed, and none was provided. The minimal formal education which was designed for teachers was deemed sufficient for those who would become administrators. Similar conditions also prevailed in the field of business.

During the past several decades the complexity of society has increased at an amazingly rapid rate. Changes in science and technology, occupational structure, manpower needs, perceptions of human rights, governmental relations, and many other factors have contributed to the complexity of today's world. The little red schoolhouse of days past has been transformed into a comprehensive educational system to serve people from preschool age to after retirement. Education must deal with a great scope of needs of many kinds of people (Charters & others, 1965). Today it ranks as one of the largest activities of society and is considered by many people as the most important one. The future development of any significant aspect of society depends upon the availability of intelligent manpower developed through education. The more essential education becomes to society, the more important is its administration.

SOME HISTORICAL DEVELOPMENTS. As late as 1900 no college or university offered courses designed specifically to prepare administrators. Under the leadership of such men as Strayer on the east coast and Cubberley on the west, courses and programs were developed in the late 1910's and early 1920's. The nature of the job of the school administrator and, in turn, the kind of preparation for it has been described in terms of several stages by Callahan and Button (1964) and Gregg (1960). The major stages were (1) scientific management, which reflected society's concern for economic productivity and for rugged individualism, (2) human relations, reflecting a growing concern for people and their welfare in a democratic society, and (3) a theoretical and scientific stage, based upon a search for a more adequate cognitive understanding of effective administrative performance. Accordingly, during the past 40 to 50 years, preservice education for school executives has tended to stress first the technical and mechanical aspects of administration, then human relationships in cooperative educational activities, and, more recently, a theoretical-research approach to the study of administration. The American Association of School Administrators (AASA) declared that during the past century the school superintendent has gone through five roles: schoolmaster, scholar-statesman, manager-superintendent, technician, and professional superintendent (American Association of School Administrators, 1963).

The decade of the 1950's, particularly, was one of much ferment in the study of administration. This was true of the field of business administration as well as of that of educational administration. Business schools had not reached agreement on objectives and on how they could best be attained; consequently, two major surveys of collegiate business education were commissioned almost simultaneously, each by a separate foundation. Comprehensive reports of both surveys (Gordon & Howell, 1959; Pierson & others, 1959) were published. Both studies, and particularly that of Gordon and Howell, had considerable impact on programs for the preparation of business executives.

Through encouragement of the National Conference of Professors of Educational Administration (NCPEA), the AASA, and other groups and individuals, the Kellogg Foundation agreed to lend financial support to the comprehensive nationwide Cooperative Program in Educational Administration (CPEA). The five-year program got under way in 1950, and its activities were centered at eight universities known as regional CPEA centers (Kellogg Foundation, 1961). Moore (1957) published an annotated bibliography of more than 300 publications which were issued by the regional CPEA centers. Additional hundreds of studies and publications were directly or indirectly related to the CPEA. One significant publication, sponsored by the NCPEA, treated the topic of administrative behavior in education (Campbell & Gregg, 1957). There can be no definitive statement of the values accruing from the CPEA projects. Without question, however, the total program profoundly influenced the professional climate surrounding the study and practice of educational administration. One of the significant outcomes of the CPEA was the organization of the University Council for Educational Administration (UCEA). The UCEA has been a major instrument in the national effort to improve the study of educational administration and the preparation of school administrators.

NATURE OF ADMINISTRATION. There are many statements concerning the nature of the responsibilities of educational administrators (American Association of School Administrators, 1960; Leu & Rudman, 1963). Added together, they give an awesome picture of the tasks which the administrator faces. The complexities of modern society combine to fashion a new setting in which the schools must operate (Culbertson & Hencley, 1962). The administrator needs a high level of general knowledge, conceptual ability, leadership skills, and technical skills. Carlson (1963) stated that common functions of administration include definition of purposes, coordination of the organization's activities to achieve purposes, and management of the exchange system between the organization and its environment. According to Goldhammer (1963) the substantive concerns of the administrator include overseeing of the instructional program, dealing with personnel matters, handling business affairs and physical resources, administering auxiliary services, and managing a program of information both within the school system and between it and the public. In its 38th yearbook the AASA (American Association of School Administrators, 1960) emphasized that the school administrator's efforts should be focused on helping the board of education to select goals and policies that support and enhance teaching and learning, giving leadership to the professional staff in organizing and conducting the teaching and learning service, and managing the materials and personnel required to further the aims of this service. In addition to his substantive concerns, the administrator must attend to necessary administrative processes (Campbell & Gregg, 1957) and extraorganizational matters. The processes include decision making, planning, stimulating, coordinating and evaluating; the environmental matters include human needs, conditions, and wants as well as the unique requirements of the local community.

Culbertson (1962) maintained that administrators, particularly chief executives, should be "perceptive generalists." He described perceptive generalists as persons who are able to see the interrelationships of values represented in the different specializations in their respective organizations. Miller (1964) also emphasized the crucial need for perceptive generalists in school systems. The perceptive generalist is capable of blending diverse human talents and motivations into effective goal-achievement patterns. The larger the organization is, the more necessary it is to have decisions and actions based upon perceptive generalizations. The AASA (American Association of School Administrators, 1960) reported that the top qualification for the school superintendency, as perceived by superintendents, was the ability to see the whole picture, each problem in its broader context. The qualification which ranked second most important was an exceptional understanding of people; an unusual ability to live with high pressure was ranked third. Goldhammer (1963) indicated that the success with which an administrator can adapt the structure and functions of an organization to the changing needs of both the local and the broader society depends upon his knowledge of how society operates and of how men behave as they become involved in various social processes. Potential administrators should develop an understanding of the nature of the social, economic, and political environment in which organizations operate. They need an efficient method of collection and analysis of data required for decision making (Marker & others, 1966). Electronic digital computers are available for this purpose, but only a minority of school administrators understand their nature and capabilities, and a still smaller proportion know how to make use of them.

PREPARATION STATUS OF SCHOOL ADMINISTRATORS. The AASA reported a comprehensive study of the academic preparation of city school superintendents for the 1958–59 school year (American Association of School Administrators, 1960). Ninety-eight percent of the superintendents held a bachelor's degree of some type, and 96 percent held at least one advanced degree. About 75 percent of the superintendents held master's degrees as their highest degrees earned, although more than a fourth of these had done one year of graduate work beyond the master's degree. Slightly more than one-fifth had earned doctor's degrees. Similar surveys of the academic training of superintendents were reported in earlier yearbooks. The percentages of superintendents who held master's degrees as their highest degrees in 1921, 1931, and 1950 were 32, 57, and 79. Percentages holding doctor's degrees for the same years were 3, 3, and 14. Median years of college preparation for city superintendents in 1921 was 4.6 years; in 1931, 5.2 years; in 1950, 5.9 years. The above data indicate that substantial gains have been made with respect to the education of school superintendents. Similar evidence for the education of elementary- and secondary-school principals could be cited if space permitted.

The same study (American Association of School Administrators, 1960) revealed that the major fields of undergraduate study pursued by superintendents ranked in the following order: behavioral sciences, education, physical and biological sciences, and history and political science. Only 3 percent of the superintendents majored in health and physical education and 2 percent in industrial and vocational arts. Minor fields of undergraduate study ranked as follows: physical and biological sciences, English, behavioral sciences, and education. At the graduate level, about two-thirds of the superintendents majored in educational administration. Younger superintendents began their graduate work at an earlier age than did the older ones. Superintendents with 15 or fewer years of experience began their graduate study at an age that was two years and three months younger than that of superintendents with 40 or more years of experience.

RECRUITMENT AND SELECTION OF ADMINISTRATORS. The problems of recruitment and selection of administrators have received much attention during recent years. Hemphill and others (1962) published a selected bibliography of approximately 230 references covering the period from 1839 to 1958. In spite of the number of publications, only a few important research studies have been conducted. There have been doctoral studies, usually of a normative nature based upon responses to questionnaires, but ordinarily they have not made significant contributions to the basic problems of recruitment and selection.

As organizations become larger, more and more executive personnel are required and the competition for such talent becomes intense (University Council for Educational Administration, 1966b). Plans for recruiting educational leaders have not met the competition successfully. Education has not attracted its share of blue-ribbon talent. More than enough students are enrolled in preparation programs, but generally speaking their quality compares unfavorably with their counterparts in other fields. McIntyre (1965) reported that of 83 fields of study, including 18 in education, the field of educational administration and supervision ranked third from the bottom in the percentage of students with high academic competence. Only 2 percent of its students were in this superior group.

Culbertson (1962) urged that existing recruitment procedures be reexamined. He suggested that talented candidates be identified and recruited from such populations as high school seniors, college freshmen and sophomores, seniors completing teacher training programs, and even students who have completed their master's degrees in the behavioral sciences. As closer alliance is developed between preparation programs for administrators and the social science disciplines it is possible that increasing numbers of students may be attracted from those disciplines. Additional financial resources are needed to enable talented personnel to prepare for a career in administration.

In a national survey, conducted in 1962-63, the A.A.S.A. reported that the three admission requirements utilized most frequently by institutions preparing superintendents of schools were minimum grade-point average, teaching experience, and written examinations (American Association of School Administrators, Committee for the Advancement of School Administration, 1964). Tests were frequently used for screening purposes, greatest reliance being placed upon the Graduate Record Examination and the Miller Analogies Test. The survey revealed that there was no concerted national effort to admit only those persons who ranked in the upper quartile of learning ability. Admission procedures do not emphasize a high level of selection (American Association of School Administrators, 1960). McIntyre (1966) reported that the usual procedures used in selecting and admitting students are the unproductive ones of interviews, letters of recommendation, rating scales, and transcripts of college credits.

A significant research study which produced findings related to selection of prospective administrators was that by Hemphill and others (1962). The investigators attempted to determine criteria of success for elementary-school principals by providing them with a great variety of administrative tasks in a simulated school known as the Whitman School. Simulated experiences were provided by in-basket items, tape recordings, kinescopes, interaction problems, and a variety of printed materials. The subjects of the study were 232 elementary-school principals. Many items of the principals' personal characteristics were obtained. Subjective evaluations of the performance of the principals were made by their superiors, their teachers, the persons who scored the in-basket tests, and members of the research staff. The results of the study demonstrated the multidimensionality of administrative performance. Moreover, different reference groups, such as superiors and teachers, did not agree on what is good or successful administrative behavior. Mental ability, general education, and thorough professional knowledge appear to be useful criteria in selection. On the other hand, years of experience, amount of professional preparation, and sex are not valid criteria, regardless of their wide use.

Another important research study, by Gross and Herriott (1965), investigated the relationship of characteristics of elementary school principals to their executive professional leadership (EPL). EPL was defined as the efforts of an elementary-school principal to improve the quality of teacher performance. A large number of principals and teachers in about 40 cities participated. Lengthy interviews and questionnaires were utilized to obtain data. The investigators concluded that if EPL is the criterion, principals are often chosen on grounds that have little empirical justification. It was found that amount of teaching experience, experience as an assistant principal, number of courses in education, sex, and marital status did not discriminate among principals as to their EPL. The investigators suggested that a high level of academic performance in college, a high order of interpersonal skill, a motive of service, and relatively little seniority as a teacher deserve increased emphasis in selecting elementary-school principals.

Both research and expert opinion stress the importance of applying rigorous selection procedures in the administrative preparation program. No single device or a combination of devices will unerringly predict behavior (McIntyre, 1966). Traditional selection methods, such as the personal interview, the amount of teaching experience, and self-selection are certainly of dubious value. Also, in view of its difficulty, selection should continue into the preparation period. Until research produces more specific guide lines, the recommendation of the AASA that stress be put upon high intelligence, superior scholarship at the undergraduate level, emotional maturity and stability, and demonstrated leadership ability may well be heeded (American Association of School Administrators, 1963). It should be remembered, too, that situational factors, such as formal and informal organization and the nature of the community being served, may also be associated with the behavior of school administrators (McIntyre, 1966).

McIntyre (1965) investigated the selection procedures used by other professional groups which compete with educational administration for the same limited supply of talented manpower. After investigating the fields of business and industry, the military services, medicine, law, and a few other fields he concluded that these fields had little research findings on recruitment and selection to contribute. All fields apparently face the same problems in similar ineffective ways.

With reference to selection procedures, one may conclude that several relatively untried procedures, such as situational performance tests and sociometric approaches, may offer some promising leads; that certain test scores are useful for indicating a candidate's mental capacity; and that women should not be discriminated against as prospects for administrative training.

PREPARATION PROGRAMS FOR ADMINISTRATORS. The marked societal and technological changes which have taken place during the past two decades have been accompanied by developments, though at a slower rate, in programs for preparing school administrators. In the 1940's these programs were based primarily upon experiences of practicing administrators as they managed the various problem areas of school administration. Current preparation programs place more emphasis on concept development and research.

Reller (1962) discussed basic societal trends which have implications for educational administration. Among his predictions were that the mobility of the population will continue to increase, that citizens' involvement in policy formulation will be increasingly emphasized, that equality of educational opportunity will be redefined, that educational services will be more varied in nature, that there will be fewer school districts and consequently fewer chief educational administrators, that educational administration will be recognized as having much in common with other types of administration, and that central-office staffs will devote increased attention to research as a basis for policy decisions. Preparation programs for administrators have begun to respond to these societal changes. In addition to preparing administrators, these programs also have responsibility for educating future professors of educational administration and for discovering new knowledge through research.

Nature of Preparation Programs. The AASA indicated that a program of preparation for administrators should include a general core of introductory studies; advanced studies dealing with the content and processes of administration such as instruction, finance, administrator behavior, policy formulation, and community analysis; and on-the-job learning through various types of field experiences (American Association of School Administrators, 1960).

The selection of content to be taught is a task of real importance. As Miller (1964) has pointed out, factors complicating this task are the rapid growth of knowledge pertaining to administration, the many different jobs which are open to students after graduation, and the fact that schools are rapidly changing with respect to nature, size, and structure. One must attempt to distinguish between those knowledges and skills which are common to all educational administrators and those which are unique to particular positions (Leu & Rudman, 1963). The notion of an extended formal preparation program implies the existence of a systematized body of knowledge. As yet this body of knowledge has not been clearly defined. During recent years, however, efforts have been directed toward making observations of educational systems, ordering them, and theorizing about their relationships (Downey & Enns, 1963).

A number of recent doctoral studies have obtained and summarized opinions and suggestions from school administrators and from graduates concerning what the preparation program should be, but it is doubtful that these studies have fulfilled the expectations held for them. A few doctoral studies (e.g., Reeves, 1965) have attempted to get at the problem by the case analysis of problems encountered by administrators. The extensive research of Hemphill and others (1962) has produced a taxonomy of administrative performance which suggests experiences to be provided in preparation programs. Behaviors in this taxonomy include exchanging information, discussing with others before acting, analyzing the situation, maintaining organizational relationships, and directing the work of others.

The most recent comprehensive survey of preparation programs was published by the AASA (American Association of School Administrators, Committee for the Advancement of School Administration, 1964). It was conducted in 1962–63, and the results were compared with a similar survey made in 1958–59 (American Association of School Administrators, 1960). In the following four paragraphs major findings of the 1962–63 survey, together with comparisons with that of 1958–59, will be reported.

Two hundred and twelve institutions in the United States offered courses designed to prepare school administrators. Of these, 161 prepared principals and supervisors of instruction as well as superintendents of schools, and 131 institutions offered two-year graduate programs, doctoral programs, or both. About 90 percent of the full-time faculty members held earned doctor's degrees.

There is no general agreement among institutions on a specific set of courses which should compose a particular type of program. Courses frequently recommended or required at the master's and two-year levels are general ones in organization and administration, curriculum and supervision, educational foundations, and elementary research methods. At the advanced level, such courses as finance and business management, school law, administrative theory, and school-community relations, as well as internships, were offered. In general, courses were not offered that were unique to the preparation of the superintendent of schools. When the programs of 1962–63 were compared with those of 1958–59, a striking similarity in the courses recommended or required in administration during the two periods was noted. There were, however, two notable changes—a completely new emphasis on instruction in administrative theory and additional stress on student competence in research. At the doctoral level, the thesis and written and oral examinations were thought by the faculty to be important final experiences for students.

In 1962–63 there was more use of related disciplines than in 1958–59. A large majority of institutions recommended study in these disciplines, particularly economics, political science, and sociology, but such study was required by a considerably smaller number of institutions. About four times as many institutions offered internships in 1962–63 as in 1958–59; however, even during 1962–63 less than one-half of the institutions offered internships and only a very small percentage of students was involved. About one-half of the institutions utilized practicing school administrators for nominating potential students, serving as part-time faculty, and advising on the nature of preparation programs. The requirement of full-time resident study in advanced graduate programs of preparation was emphasized by a larger number of institutions in 1962–63 than in 1958–59.

According to faculty opinions, the major strengths of preparation programs for school administrators during 1962–63 were the quality of the faculty in educational administration, interdisciplinary arrangements with other departments, and internships and other field experiences. The faculty members believed that the major program changes during the preceding five years were increased emphasis on interdisciplinary approaches, improved internship programs, upgraded admission procedures, new methods of concept development, and establishment of a larger number of two-year graduate programs. Their judgments seemed to indicate that preparation programs should be characterized by high admission standards, a broad program of studies, and new methods and materials of instruction (American Association of School Administrators, 1963). The major deterrents to program improvements were inadequate funds, insufficient opportunities for research, shortage of facilities, and too small a number of highly qualified students.

Resident Study. There is evidence that most professors in the field of educational administration, and many school administrators, place much value upon full-time resident study in graduate preparation programs. If quality instruction and learning are to be achieved it appears necessary that able, career-committed students should have the opportunity to devote themselves to full-time study for a prolonged period of time. Neagley's survey (1967) of faculty and students in 36 member institutions of UCEA indicated the following advantages of full-time residence for the student: close association with professors and advanced graduate students, availability of major and minor professors, opportunity to participate in research, availability of university facilities and resources, and more time to make use of varied resources. Another study (American Association of School Administrators, Committee . . ., 1963) obtained the judgments of students and practicing school administrators concerning the values of full-time graduate study which they had experienced. The general consensus of the interviewees was that close relationship with professors and students, freedom from the distractions of day-to-day operational decisions, and opportunity to learn how social scientists view education all added up to greater intellectual challenge than was possible with part-time study. The practicing administrators were in agreement that rigorous, full-time graduate study was a prerequisite for a competently educated administrator.

Berelson reported (1960) that graduate students in education ranked practically at the bottom of the list of groups of graduate students with respect to the incidence of full-time study. Often the major professor in education is faced with the problem of supervising theses at long distances and in bits and pieces. Berelson also reported that for students in the field of education there was an average of seven years of employment between receipt of the bachelor's degree and commencement of doctoral study. The AASA survey of preparation programs in educational administration (American Association of School Administrators, Committee . . ., 1964) revealed that full-time resident study in advanced graduate programs was emphasized by a considerably larger number of institutions in 1962–63 than had been the case in 1958–59. In 1962–63, 90 of the 103 institutions offering doctoral programs in educational administration reported that a year of residence for the doctor's degree was required; however, the number of institutions that required a quarter or more of full-time residence for the two-year graduate program only slightly exceeded the number that required less than one quarter of residence. Much progress is yet to be made, however, since the 1962–63 survey indicated that there were 8,057 students enrolled part-time and only 1,465 enrolled full-time in educational administration at the graduate level.

Instructional Methods. The AASA was very critical of the methods employed in preparation programs for school administrators (American Association of School Administrators, 1960). The programs were described as being sterile, classroom bound, and relatively unaffected by newer techniques such as simulation and field studies. Similar findings were reported by Gordon and Howell (1959) for schools of business. For both types of preparation programs more emphasis on the reality of administration and on conceptual analysis of organizational problems was emphasized. The 1962–63 survey by the AASA of preparation programs for school administrators (American Association of School Administrators, Committee . . ., 1964) revealed that professors often indicated increased use of case studies, simulation materials, field experiences, and related disciplines, but the extent to which they are used is not known. Culbertson (1962) stressed that much attention may profitably be directed toward development and utilization of a variety of instructional methods. The potential values of newer instructional devices have been described by Thomas (1964).

Simulation has been emphasized in business and industry for a considerably longer time than in education. A publication of the American Management Association (1961) included a selected bibliography of more than 400 books, articles, and papers on simulation, gaming, and related topics. Culbertson and Coffield (1960) discussed the strength and weaknesses of simulation in administrator preparation programs. Simulations are lifelike and can make more probable the transfer of learning to real administrative situations; they give the student a better opportunity to develop understandings of relationships between concepts and facts; and they aid the student to gain insight about himself. Wynn (1964) pointed out that simulation permits the learner to profit from mistakes that might be quite disastrous on a real job. Simulation materials are often expensive to produce and may become outdated, and there is only a limited body of knowledge upon which the instructor can draw concerning their use. There is some reason to believe, however, that simulation models (Fattu & Elam, 1965) in the next few years will gain the attention in education that they have had in business during the recent past. Simulated situations give an opportunity to involve the student emotionally as well as intellectually and also help to bridge the gap between theory and practice.

The type of simulation which has been used most extensively in the education of school administrators is the in-basket method. The original in-basket materials were developed for a study of the principal of the simulated elementary school, the Whitman school (Hemphill & others, 1962). They have been used by about 90 universities (Wynn, 1964; University Council for Educational Administration, 1966a) in the United States, Canada, Australia, and England

(Taylor, 1966). Probably as many as 20,000 students and practicing administrators have had experience with in-basket materials. The UCEA has been engaged in developing new materials, not only for the elementary principalship, but also for the secondary principalship, the superintendency, and selected central-office positions (University Council for Educational Administration, 1966a). The new materials will provide for feedback to the student in an attempt to meet a criticism of the original in-basket technique. There remain, however, several criticisms of in-basket simulation, among them that nonverbal, covert aspects of administrator behavior are not measured (Erickson, 1964). The in-basket method appears to have proven effective in the training of executives for business (Roberts, 1965). Thomas (1964) indicated that in-basket simulation requires a substantial block of time available without interruption for its most successful utilization and consequently may offer less flexibility in its use than the case-study method.

During the past decade professors of educational administration have made frequent use of the case method of instruction (Sargent & Belisle, 1955). The UCEA has published a series of case studies, Case Series in Educational Administration, for use in administrator preparation programs. Evaluative studies (Hallsted, 1964) of the use of the case method indicate its potential effectiveness, but there is little evidence that there has been any marked increase in the use of the method during recent years. Thomas (1964) pointed out that cases seem to be useful strategies for introducing students to the reality of the work of administration.

Gaming has been used for the preparation of business leaders for many years (American Management Association, 1961) but has been relatively untouched in educational administration. A major motivational element of the game is competition, and this form of motivation is much less applicable in education than in business. Games combine aspects of the case method and of role playing; in addition, the players get feedback about the results of their decisions and may be forced to live with these decisions in later stages of the game. Dale and Klasson's study of business gaming (1964) revealed that two-thirds of the responding institutions reported using games to some extent and that nearly all respondents were convinced of the instructional value of gaming. The NCPEA directed attention to gaming as a simulation technique (Thomas, 1964), the UCEA has produced a game on the problem of professional negotiations in education (University Council for Educational Administration, 1966a) and efforts to conceptualize the technique have been made (Ohm, 1966).

Laboratory training in human relations has been given much notice for the past two decades (National Training Laboratory in Group Development, 1953). Recently there has been some emphasis on sensitivity training, which stresses group processes in situations where the usual group structures and restraints are removed. Sensitivity training aims to develop the trainee's insight into his own behavior and how that behavior affects others (Schein & Bennis, 1965). Only bare beginnings of this method, which puts emphasis on analysis of emotions rather than on intellectual logic, have been reported in the preparation of school administrators (Trusty & others, 1966).

Field Experiences. The literature of educational administration contains frequent mention of the values of field experiences in preparing school administrators. Such experiences include internships, apprenticeships, and field studies. Of these, the internship (Davies, 1962) offers the most value but its development and implementation in graduate programs has been slow (American Association of School Administrators, Committee . . ., 1964). Original emphasis on the utilization of the internship in educational administration was spurred by the Cooperative Program in Educational Administration (Moore, 1957). During the past decade there appears to have been a continuous, but unsuccessful, effort to define the internship. It has taken many different forms in various situations. Internships and other similar experiences have the potential for providing opportunity for the student to develop a realistic understanding of the stern realities of the field, the obstacles to professional leadership, and the strategies for dealing with these obstacles. Questions concerning the internship include those pertaining to a guiding conceptual framework, control of the intern's experiences, selection of interns and sponsors, the stage of preparation at which the internship should take place, finance, and evaluation (Hencley, 1963). An increasing number of school systems are developing apprenticeships and internships in relation to in-service administrator development programs. The perceived importance of the internship in the preparation of school administrators seems to be indicated by recent attempts to assess its strengths and weaknesses (Eden, 1965; Hartley & Holloway, 1966).

Evaluation of Preparation Programs. There has been very little concentrated effort to evaluate particular preparation programs over a period of time. A study by McIntyre (1957) is an exception. On the other hand, such organizations as the NCPEA and the UCEA have directed efforts for many years to the evaluation and improvement of university preparation programs. Nevertheless, relatively recent studies (American Association of School Administrators, 1960) have been very critical of most existing programs for administrator preparation. Gordon and Howell (1959) reported similarly for the field of business. Weaknesses in administrator preparation programs were reported to be a lack of conceptual and theoretical emphasis, too narrow specialization, neglect of social sciences, and too much "bookishness" with all too little emphasis on the realities of administration. In the present age of urbanization, preparation programs in education have not given sufficient emphasis to administration of schools in large cities (University Council for Educational Administration, 1966a). Preparation programs should be lengthened, broadened, and deepened (American Association of School Administrators, 1963).

Two major research studies, by Hemphill and others (1962) and by Gross and Herriott (1965), have revealed no significant positive relationships between amount of professional preparation and effectiveness of elementary-school principals. One explanation of this situation could be that principals of low quality tended to take more professional courses than those of high quality; another could be that the nature of the professional courses was such as to make little or no contribution to administrative competence. Some persons have questioned the appropriateness of prevailing organizational arrangements and faculty specializations for the preparation of administrators. Culbertson (1965) suggested an organization in which specialists in various branches of social science would teach courses related to the theory and content of administration qua administration in which students of education, government, business, and related fields would be enrolled. Such an experiment recently has been inaugurated at the new Irvine campus of the University of California. Departments of educational administration should make thorough appraisals of preparation programs. There should be critical review of objectives, inventory of problems and needs, critical appraisal of present activities, and utilization of all pertinent resources for program development.

SIGNIFICANT ISSUES. During the past decade a number of significant issues related to the preparation of educational administrators have received the attention of individuals and organizations. Five of these will be treated in succeeding sections but, because of limits of space, only brief discussions can be devoted to them.

Role of the Social Sciences. In the literature on educational administration the pertinence of the social and behavioral sciences to administration has been very strongly emphasized during the present decade (Charters & others, 1965; Culbertson & Hencley, 1962; Downey & Enns, 1963; Goldhammer, 1963). The administrator must relate his organization to society, and he must understand both individual and collective behavior. Administration is a social process and takes place in a vortex of social forces. Carrying on the process demands an understanding of leadership, decision making, bureaucracy, power structures, group processes, conflict resolution, change processes, and resource utilization (Goldhammer, 1963). The social and behavioral sciences deal with the goal setting, maintenance, integration, and attainments of social systems such as educational organizations. Charters and others (1965) assessed the actual and potential contributions of various disciplines to the advancement of educational administration. Cunningham and others (1963) stated five reasons why the social sciences should be incorporated into preparation programs for educational administrators: to provide a systematic way of looking at things, to contribute knowledge of the setting of administration, to indicate the significance of the phenomena of administration, to provide a basis for predicting consequences of decisions and actions, and to provide a basis for the selection of relevant data and also research techniques and instruments for analysis of data. Sociology, social psychology, anthropology, political science, and economics have important contributions for the school administrator (Charters & others, 1965; Downey & Enns, 1963). They provide sensitizing concepts which illuminate aspects of administrative phenomena which might otherwise be overlooked. They do, however, have certain limitations when related to the applied field of administration (Goldhammer, 1963).

A number of practices have been reported for utilizing the social sciences in preparation programs (DeLacy, 1966). The social scientist may offer courses for students in administration, professors of the social sciences and of educational administration may cooperatively offer courses, professors of educational administration may develop competence in a related discipline, and, in addition, a variety of informal arrangements may be developed.

In spite of all the emphases that have been put on the social sciences by leaders in educational administration, studies such as those by DeLacy (1966) and Stolworthy (1965) indicate that only slow progress has been made. Interdisciplinary emphasis in the preparation of administrators is apparently much more imagined than real. No general effort has been made by education specialists and social scientists to identify cooperatively the knowledges and skills which the social sicences should contribute to the education of administrators, nor has any general pattern of relationships between departments of educational administration and other departments been established. Some persons have been concerned over the possibility that the stress on social science in the literature has resulted in the relative exclusion of the humanities. Harlow (1962) maintained that the humanities deserved equal emphasis as compared with social sciences in the preparation of administrators.

Research in Educational Administration. The field of educational administration has not been distinguished by its research, whether done by students or by professors. Griffiths (1959b) was the first to highlight the need for more research and research of higher quality. A more recent paper by Griffiths (1965) indicated a continuing lack, as compared with other fields, of research of high quality. Recognizing the need for improving research, the UCEA (Culbertson & Hencley, 1963) sponsored three seminars in different parts of the nation for professors of educational administration.

Griffiths (1959b) pointed out that most research in educational administration was done by students. More recently, Hills (1965a) reported that the much-talked-about emphasis on research by professors of educational administration was more of a myth than a reality and that most research lacked theoretical or interdisciplinary emphases. Research is usually only descriptive of what is being done. It appears, however, that research in educational administration is beginning to take on a new character. Gregg (1961) reported that during the decade 1952–1961 there was a trend in the nature of research from overwhelming emphasis on description to some emphasis on empirical studies based on theoretical constructs. Briner (1964) reported that the principles and methods of scholarly inquiry in educational administration were being increasingly indicated in the research reviewed. There appears to be increasing emphasis on research to produce basically new knowledge; also, a trend can be discerned toward more collaborative research among professors and advanced graduate students (Culbertson & Hencley, 1963).

Theory and Educational Administration. During the past 15 years leading scholars have been decrying the lack of theoretical and scientific orientation in the field of educational administration (Griffiths, 1959a; Campbell & Lipham, 1960; National Society for the Study of Education, 1964). The first of a long series of seminars which have been sponsored by the UCEA for professors was devoted to the role of theory in research and administrator preparation (Halpin, 1958). Currently, it is recognized that educational administration lacks a systematic and coherent body of theory. This lack is the result of the scarcity of fundamental empirical research grounded upon adequate theoretical foundations (National Society for the Study of Education, 1964). Consequently, practice and instruction are more often based upon experience than upon proven principles and concepts. If a science of administration is to be evolved there must be concurrent emphasis on tying related theory and empirical studies one to the other (Goldhammer, 1963). A science of administration cannot exist without a theoretical foundation but it appears that this foundation will be composed of a number of theoretical constructs rather than a single, unified theory. In fact, Schwab (1964) stated that a sufficient theory of administration is a manifest impossibility in the foreseeable future. A recent promising research development in the direction of producing a more fruitful theoretical framework for educational administration is the Taxonomy of Organizational Behavior Project (University Council for Educational Administration, 1966a) completed in 1957. These and other scientific studies in educational administration may eventually suggest general understandings and implications for instruction and practice in educational administration.

Common and Specialized Learnings. In organizations there is need for overall administrative judgment and also for various types of specializations. During recent years considerable attention has been devoted to the problem of differentiating between desirable common and specialized learnings (Leu & Rudman, 1963; Miller, 1964) in the preparation of different types of school administrators. As Miller (1964) pointed out, this problem is highlighted by such factors as the explosion of knowledge, the increasingly specialized nature of many administrative assignments, and the mobility of administrators from one type of position to another.

Leu and Rudman (1963) emphasized that the problem of identifying common and unique elements in the preparation of administrators is an elusive one. Competence in the use of administrative processes such as decision making and communication is required in some degree of all administrators in leadership positions. Each should have an understanding of the tasks of education, the structure and controls of education, and of social processes. On the other hand, in complex organizations there are many highly specialized administrative functions which must be performed. The need for a superintendent of schools to be a perceptive generalist in order to meet effectively his responsibilities of policy development, coordination of the efforts of specialists, and the effective utilization of specialists' advice in decision making is obvious; yet the typical career path to the superintendency is from a principalship of a central-office specialist position.

Specialization in educational administration may be viewed in terms of administrative positions (e.g., principalship), administrative functions (e.g., school-plant planning), or disciplinary bases (e.g., politics of education). These different possibilities probably have militated against the development of specialized preparation programs. A decade ago Moore (1957) reported that there was no general agreement on differentiating the preparation of a principal from that of a superintendent. There is little or no evidence that there has been any marked change since (Pierce, 1966). Considerable expert speculation (Leu & Rudman, 1963) has been made, however, with respect to what should be the common and the specialized aspects of the preparation for different types of positions in school systems. The most common practice appears to be that of providing a large block of common learnings capped by intensive study of specialized areas. These areas are usually mapped out in terms of administrative positions or functions, but there is an increasing emphasis on specialization with respect to disciplinary bases such as the sociology, politics, or economics of education.

The Professorship in Educational Administration. The nature of the professorship obviously is an important factor in preparation programs for educational administrators. Its importance led the UCEA to arrange a seminar to give it special attention (Willower & Culbertson, 1964). Most professors of educational administration are generalists. The teaching of classes occupies the major portion of the professor's time; comparatively little time is devoted to research and scholarly production. Consequently, there have been instances where research requirements for advanced degrees have been downgraded. Recently, there has developed a new emphasis on differentiating the content of the field of educational administration. Hills (1965b) predicted that the process of differentiating among professorship roles would continue at an increasing rate and that the areas of specialization stressed most would be economics of education, organizational theory, and policies of education. Many leaders in educational administration believe that theory, research, and substantive specialization will characterize the professorship of the future (Willower & Culbertson, 1964). Professors will be qualitatively different in their roles and therefore will no longer be highly interchangeable. Experience in school administration will be of less significance in selection of professors (Pierce, 1966). These developments may suggest that there should be schools or departments of administration qua administration rather than departments of educational, business, or hospital administration.

In-service Education of Administrators. Most of the improvements to be made in the education of administrators during the next decade will result from the leadership of persons already prepared and employed in administrative positions. Several factors indicate the need for continuing in-service education of these persons (Lynch & Blackstone, 1966). Among them are the increasing complexities of educational administration and the explosion of educational and technical knowledge. As a result of these factors the preparation programs of leaders presently employed have reached, or are rapidly approaching, obsolescence. It is essential that administrators continue to develop professionally on the job by keeping abreast of research findings, technological developments, and cultural innovations. Appropriate in-service educational opportunities are now more essential than ever before.

Much thought is being given to the in-service education of school administrators of various types (American Association of School Administrators, Committee . . ., 1966; Cunningham, 1965; Holmes & Seawell, 1965). Different approaches, ranging from individual professional reading on the job to leaves of absence for full-time graduate study, are being utilized. Most emphasis is on conferences and workshops lasting from one to three days and devoted to problems of current interest. It has been traditional for school systems to offer orientation programs for teachers, but few have provided them for administrators; however, there seems to be increasing emphasis on such programs for administrators. In-service programs often are not, and should not be, burdened by irrelevant academic considerations such as credits and grades (Lynch & Blackstone, 1966).

Because of the importance and difficulties of in-service education, cooperative and coordinated efforts of universities, professional associations, state departments of education, and local school districts are necessary (American Association of School Administrators, Committee . . ., 1966). More adequate plans for the financing of in-service programs are needed. Available evidence indicates that in-service programs for administrators fall short of fulfilling the professional needs of practicing administrators. They are often sporadic and traditional in nature; moreover, there appears to have been very little improvement in these programs during recent years (American Association of School Administrators, Committee . . ., 1964). Cunningham (1965) has indicated the need for determining priority needs, utilizing improved instructional procedures, and obtaining increased financial support for in-service programs.

POSTDOCTORAL EDUCATION FOR ADMINISTRATORS. If, as seems probable, the field of educational administration continues to move toward greater differentiation and specialization in relation to appropriate basic disciplines, there will be increasing need for postdoctoral study. Berelson (1960) reported that there are few postdoctoral fellows in education compared with other disciplines; moreover, a much smaller percentage of faculty members in education believes that such programs are necessary than do faculty members in the physical sciences and the social sciences. Pierce (1966) maintained that postdoctoral programs should be developed for prospective professors of educational administration. Postdoctoral study could provide opportunity for scholars to develop specializations in the economics and politics of educational administration and in the sociology of educational organizations (University Council for Educational Administration, 1966a).

INTERNATIONAL INTEREST. There is increased concern in Australia, England, New Zealand, and Scotland for the education of school administrators. Through the efforts of the UCEA (University Council for Educational Administration, 1966a) and the Kellogg Foundation, representatives from these countries spent four weeks in the United States and Canada during the fall of 1966, attending seminars at the University of Michigan and the University of Alberta and visiting a number of universities in the United States for the purpose of observing administrator preparation programs. In the future, problems related to the preparation of educational administrators will be shared among the English-speaking countries.

Russell T. Gregg
University of Wisconsin

References

American Association of School Administrators. *Professional Administrators for America's Schools.* 38th Yearbook. AASA, 1960. 310p.

American Association of School Administrators. *The Education of a School Superintendent.* AASA, 1963. 33p.

American Association of School Administrators, Committee for the Advancement of School Administration. *The Case for On-campus Residence.* AASA, 1963. 27p.

American Association of School Administrators, Committee for the Advancement of School Administration. *The Professional Preparation of Superintendents of Schools.* AASA, 1964. 71p.

American Association of School Administrators, Committee for the Advancement of School Administration. *In-service Programs for School Administration.* AASA, 1966. 20p.

American Management Association. *Simulation and Gaming: A Symposium.* The Association, 1961. 135p.

Berelson, Bernard. *Graduate Education in the United States.* McGraw-Hill, 1960. 346p.

Briner, Conrad. "Foreword." R Ed Res 34:398; 1964.

Callahan, Raymond E., and Button, H. Warren. "Historical Change of the Role of the Man in the Organization: 1865–1950." In Griffiths, Daniel E. (Ed.). *Behavioral Science and Educational Admin-*

istration. 63rd Yearbook, Part II, NSSE. U Chicago Press, 1964. Ch. 4, p. 73–92.

Campbell, Roald F., and Gregg, Russell T. (Eds.) *Administrative Behavior in Education.* Harper, 1957. 547p.

Campbell, Roald F., and Lipham, James M. (Eds.) *Administrative Theory as a Guide to Action.* Midwest Administration Center, 1960. 201p.

Carlson, Richard O. "Common Learnings for all Administrators." In Leu, Donald J., and Rudman, Herbert C. (Eds.) *Preparation Programs for School Administrators.* Michigan State U, 1963. Ch. 2, p. 24–33.

Charters, W. W., Jr., and others. *Perspectives on Educational Administration and the Behavioral Sciences.* U Oregon, 1965. 120p.

Culbertson, Jack A. "New Perspectives: Implications for Program Change." In Culbertson, Jack A., and Hencley, Steven P. (Eds.) *Preparing Administrators: New Perspectives.* University Council for Educational Administration, 1962. p. 151–73.

Culbertson, Jack A. "Trends and Issues in the Development of a Science of Administration." In Charters, W. W., Jr., and others. (Eds.) *Perspectives on Educational Administration and the Behavioral Sciences.* U Oregon Press, 1965. p. 3–22.

Culbertson, Jack A., and Coffield, William. *Simulation in Administrative Training.* University Council for Educational Administration, 1960. 46p.

Culbertson, Jack A., and Hencley, Stephen P. *Preparing Administrators: New Perspectives.* University Council for Educational Administration. 1962. 173p.

Culbertson, Jack A., and Hencley, Stephen P. *Educational Research: New Perspectives.* Interstate, 1963. 374p.

Cunningham, Luvern L. "Continuing Professional Education for Elementary Principals." *Nat El Prin* 44:60–6; 1965.

Cunningham, Luvern L., and others. "Implications for Administrator Training Programs." In Downey, Lawrence W., and Enns, Frederick. (Eds.) *The Social Sciences and Educational Administration.* U Alberta, 1963. Part V, p. 97–109.

Dale, Alfred G., and Klasson, Charles R. *Business Gaming.* U Texas, 1964. 64p.

Davies, Daniel R. *The Internship in Educational Administration.* Center for Applied Research in Education, 1962. 117p.

DeLacy, Walter J. *The Social Sciences: An Aspect of School Administrator Preparation.* Pennsylvania State U, 1966. 23p.

Downey, Lawrence W., and Enns, Frederick. *The Social Sciences and Educational Administration.* U Alberta, 1963. 109p.

Eden, James E. *An Evaluation of the Internship in Educational Administration.* U Missouri, 1965. 244p.

Erickson, Donald A. "Dimensions of Administrative Performance That Hemphill Missed; Review of *Administrative Performance and Personality: A Study of the Principal in a Simulated Elementary School,* by J. K. Hemphill and Others." *Sch R* 72: 490–8; 1964.

Fattu, Nicholas A., and Elam, Stanley. (Eds.) *Simulation Models for Education.* Phi Delta Kappa, 1965. 172p.

Goldhammer, Keith. *Social Sciences and Preparation Of Educational Administrators.* U Alberta and University Council for Educational Administration, 1963. 45p.

Gordon, Robert A., and Howell, James E. *Higher Education for Business.* Columbia U Press, 1959. 491p.

Gregg, Russell T. "Administration." In Harris, Chester W. (Ed.) *Encyclopedia of Educational Research,* 3rd ed. Macmillan, 1960. p. 19–24.

Gregg, Russell T. "Foreword." *R Ed Res* 31:351; 1961.

Griffiths, Daniel E. *Administrative Theory.* Appleton, 1959(a). 123p.

Griffiths, Daniel E. *Research in Educational Administration: An Appraisal and a Plan.* Teachers Col, Columbia U, 1959(b). 59p.

Griffiths, Daniel E. "Research and Theory in Educational Administration." In Charters, W. W., Jr., and others. (Eds.) *Perspectives on Educational Administration and the Behavioral Sciences.* U Oregon, 1965. Ch. 2, p. 25–48.

Gross, Neal, and Herriott, Robert E. *Staff Leadership in Public Schools: A Sociological Inquiry.* Wiley, 1965. 247p.

Hallsted, Robert H. *Development and Use of a Set of Cases in Secondary School Administration.* Teachers Col, Columbia U, 1964. 284p.

Halpin, Andrew W. (Ed.) *Administrative Theory in Education.* Midwest Administration Center and U Chicago, 1958. 185p.

Harlow, James G. "Purpose-defining the Central Function of the School Administrator." In Culbertsen, Jack A., and Hencley, Steven P. (Eds.) *Preparing Administrators: New Perspectives.* University Council for Educational Administration, 1962. Ch. 4, p. 61–71.

Hartley, Harry J., and Holloway, George E., Jr. "Critique of the Internship in Educational Administration." *Peabody J Ed* 43:202–7; 1966.

Hemphill, John K., and others. *Administrative Performance and Personality: A Study of the Principal in a Simulated Elementary School.* Teachers Col, Columbia U, 1962. 432p.

Hencley, Stephen P. (Ed.) *The Internship in Administrative Preparation.* University Council on Educational Administration and AASA, 1963. 159p.

Hills, Jean. "Educational Administration: A Field in Transition." *Ed Adm Q* 1:58–66; 1965(a).

Hills, Jean. "Social Science, Ideology and the Professor of Educational Administration." *Ed Adm Q* 1:23–39; 1965(b).

Holmes, G. W., III, and Seawell, W. H. "Further Studies for Administrators and Supervisors: Purpose and Scope." *H Sch J* 48:242–9; 1965.

Kellogg Foundation. *Toward Improved School Administration.* Sequoia Press, 1961. 67p.

Leu, Donald J., and Rudman, Herbert C. *Preparation Programs for School Administrators: Common and Specialized Learnings.* Michigan State U, 1963. 269p.

Lynch, Patrick D., and Blackstone, Peggy, L. (Eds.) *Continuing Education of School Administrators.* U New Mexico and University Council for Educational Administration, 1966. 146p.

Marker, Robert W., and others. (Eds.) *Computer Concepts and Educational Administration.* State U Iowa, 1966. 144p.

McIntyre, Kenneth E. *Learning in a Block-of-Time Program.* U Texas Press, 1957. 94p.

McIntyre, Kenneth E. "Selection of Candidates for Professional Training in Fields Other Than Educational Administration." In *The Selection of Educational Administrators, Report of the U.C.E.A. Task Force.* U Utah, 1965. p. 34–52.

McIntyre, Kenneth E. *Selection of Educational Administrators.* University Council for Educational Administration, 1966. 19p.

Miller, Van. *Common and Specialized Learning for Educational Administrators.* University Council for Educational Administration, 1964. 13p.

Moore, Hollis A., Jr. *Studies in School Administration, A Report on the C.P.E.A.* AASA, 1957. 202p.

National Society for the Study of Education. *Behavioral Science and Educational Administration,* Daniel E. Griffiths (Ed.). 63rd Yearbook. Part II, NSSE. U Chicago, 1964. 360p.

National Training Laboratory in Group Development. *Explorations in Human Relations Training.* NEA, 1953. 87p.

Neagley, Ross L. *Program for Full-time Resident Students.* Temple U, 1967. 12p.

Ohm, Robert E. "Gamed Instructional Simulation: An Exploratory Model." *Ed Adm Q* 2:111–12; 1966.

Pierce, Douglas R. *Exchange Patterns of the Educational Administration Professorship.* University Council for Educational Administration, 1966. 43p.

Pierson, Frank, and others. *The Education of American Businessmen.* McGraw-Hill, 1959. 740p.

Reeves, Bill E. *The Improvement of College Preparation Programs at the Graduate Level for High School Principals Based upon Case Analysis of Problems Encountered by Principals in Selected Public High Schools.* Texas Technological Col, 1965. 606p.

Reller, Theodore L. "A Comprehensive Program for the Preparation of Administrators." In Culbertson, Jack A., and Hencley, Steven P. (Eds.) *Preparing Administrators: New Perspectives.* University Council for Educational Administration, 1962. Ch. 7, p. 103–19.

Roberts, Thomas S. "Training Managers to Make Decisions: The In-basket Method." *Personnel* 42: 58–66; 1965.

Sargent, Cyril G., and Belisle, Eugene L. *Educational Administration: Cases and Concepts.* Houghton, 1955. 474p.

Schein, Edgar H., and Bennis, Walter G. *Personal and Organizational Change Through Group Methods: The Laboratory Approach.* Wiley, 1965. 376p.

Schwab, Joseph J. "The Professorship in Educational Administration: Theory—Art—Practice." In Willower, Donald J., and Culbertson, Jack A. (Eds.) *The Professorship in Educational Administration.* University Council for Educational Administration, 1964. Ch. 4, p. 47–70.

Stolworthy, Reed L. "A Study of the Use of Academic Disciplines Outside the Department of Education in Doctoral Programs of Educational Administration." Doctoral dissertation. Brigham Young U, 1965. 211p.

Taylor, William T. "The Use of Simulations in the In-service Training of School Administrators in England." *J Ed Adm* 4:23–31; 1966.

Thomas, Michael P., Jr. *Strategies in the Preparation of School Administrators.* National Conference of Professors of Educational Administration, 1964. 51p.

Trusty, Francis, and others. "Preparation for the Administrative Intern." *Phi Delta Kappan* 47:454–5; 1966.

University Council for Educational Administration. *The Selection of Educational Administrators.* U Utah, 1965. 60p.

University Council for Educational Administration. *Annual Report, 1965–66.* The Council, 1966(*a*). 46p.

University Council for Educational Administration. *The Selective Recruitment of Educational Leaders.* The Council, 1966(*b*). 20p.

Willower, Donald J., and Culbertson, Jack A. (Eds.) *The Professorship in Educational Administration.* University Council for Educational Administration, 1964. 105p.

Wynn, Richard. "Simulation: Terrible Reality in the Preparation of School Administrators." *Phi Delta Kappan,* 46:170–3; 1964.

PROFESSIONAL EDUCATION

Professional education, under this heading, covers studies on the systematic preparation used to qualify students for entrance into and practice of the professions of architecture, dentistry, journalism, nursing, pharmacy, public administration, social work, and theology. Studies concerning other professions will be found under their individual headings in this edition.

Much too little has been done on studies of the professions and their educational programs in spite of their great and growing significance in contemporary life. In 1928, Carr-Saunders complained at Oxford that "The story of the evolution of the professions is . . . an unwritten chapter in the social history of the last two centuries" (Carr-Saunders, 1928). He shortly published the most extensive single study of the professions, describing and analyzing the activities of more than 25 groups. The volume considers the history and content of professional education in these fields, but restricts the study to England and Wales (Carr-Saunders & Wilson, 1933). No comparable study has yet appeared in the United States where the most famous and influential study of education for a profession is Abraham Flexner's 60-year-old study of medical education (Flexner, 1910).

Studies of education for the various professions as a group were stimulated by Blauch's compendium of brief accounts of 34 professional education programs. Each account was prepared by a knowledgeable person in the field according to a common outline. They provide almost a check list of characteristics of the educational programs (Blauch, 1955). Other efforts followed, some general, others more concerned with specific aspects. Of the general, McGlothlin (1960) compares the educational programs of ten professions from architecture to veterinary medicine in considerable detail, and later focuses more sharply on formulating principles for professional education derived from analyses of the various programs (McGlothlin, 1964). Anderson, with a distinguished company of authors (Anderson & others, 1962), treats professional education historically and prophetically. His volume includes Becker's brilliant analysis of the tension between the ideal and the reality of a profession, and Brickman's comparative account of professional education the world over. Lynn (1963) reports a symposium on the professions in 1963. It includes two papers on the sociology of professions and individual studies of nine professions including city planning and politics. Its comments on professional education are incidental to considerations of the professions themselves. Finally, Berelson's study (1960) of graduate education considers a number of programs for the professions, particularly for college teaching.

Studies of specific aspects of professional education are led by the series of pamphlets which the Institute for Higher Education at Teachers College, headed by McGrath, has issued. McGrath (1959) explores the curricula of professional programs, particularly undergraduate ones, to determine what impact liberal arts and professional studies have on each other. As time for professional subjects expands, the amount for liberal arts shrinks, he finds. Nevertheless, professional schools place great value on the liberal arts. Studies of specific professional fields made by McGrath and his colleagues will be mentioned later.

Accreditation is a troublesome aspect of education for professional fields. Again, Blauch (1959) compiled a handbook of accrediting practices. Selden's brief work (1960) analyzes how accrediting came to be and how it must be controlled. Both works include analyses of accrediting in the professional fields.

Architecture. The most substantial research on architectural education appears in Bannister (1954). Its treatment of architectural education is detailed and penetrating, filling 270 of its 513 pages. Kaye (1960) presents a sociological analysis of the growth of professionalism among British architects, and treats architectural training as a major part of that development. Data on the curricula of architectural schools throughout much of the world are charted by Muschenheim (1966). Pitcher and others (1962) report that the use of tests may increase accuracy of prediction of academic performance in architectural school.

Dentistry. The report of a national survey of dentistry (Hollinshead, 1961) supersedes previous studies of dentistry and dental education. It considers the dental profession as a whole, but treats dental education extensively, presenting data and analyses on students, faculties, curricula, libraries, financing, and licensure. Its bibliography contains only publications emerging from the survey. An earlier study by Horner (1947) includes brief descriptive sketches of the 40 dental schools in operation at that time. Gurley's book (1960) is a discursive history, largely of national organizations concerned with dental education. Its bibliography incorporates 755 references.

Dental education in Canada is described by Paynter (1965), and the World Health Organization has a brief report on dental education (1962) which makes proposals very similar to those in Hollinshead (1961), but with special emphasis on public health dentistry.

The concern of dental educators to expand attention to subjects of social import is evidenced in Blackerby (1960). *The Journal of Dental Education* is the major periodical on dental education.

Journalism. No major study of education for journalism in the United States has been made recently. O'Dell (1935) gives a concise account of the development of journalism education from the first courses at Washington and Lee in 1869, through the founding of the first school of journalism at the University of Missouri in 1908, to the opening of the first graduate school of journalism at Columbia University in 1935. Sutton (1945) covers much the same period. Dressel (1960) traces the development of journalism education, giving data on the proportion of liberal arts subjects required in the curriculum, and on attitudes of faculty and students toward the liberal arts. He concludes that journalism schools have not resolved the problem of liberal arts versus professional subjects.

UNESCO has been very active in producing studies of mass communication. Several of these consider education for journalism. One such study (UNESCO, 1958) discusses international collaboration in training of journalists and some training principles and methods. It then describes training facilities in the various countries, with comments on the state of journalism education as a whole. It lists journalism schools, country by country. The volume is supplemented by a later one (UNESCO, 1965) which summarizes much of the earlier study and adds a list of schools in the developing countries of the world.

Nursing. Over the past 20 years, research studies on education for nursing have rapidly increased in number. Only a few can be noted here. Brown (1948) reported an influential study from which many of the changes in nursing education have sprung. It proposed a basic reorganization of nursing and nursing education with emphasis on collegiate and university education for leaders in nursing. It was followed by that of Bridgman (1953), a careful and significant study of the practices of colleges and universities in conducting education for nurses. It places particular emphasis on organizational and curricular problems. Davis and others (1966) define some of the continuing problems of nursing education in the university, and Bergeron (1963) compares the status and functions of chairmen of nursing departments with chairmen of liberal arts departments in 19 private liberal arts colleges. Fivars and Gosnell (1966) outline ways of using the critical-incident technique in evaluating nursing education and nurses' performance.

Considerable study has been focused on curriculum and teaching method. Russell (1959) traces the growth of nursing education from apprenticeship to university status, showing that there has been a steadily increasing emphasis on liberal studies. He finds that nursing faculties place a higher value on liberal studies than do faculties of other professional schools. Pesznecker and Hewitt (1963) report on the process followed by the nursing faculty at the University of Washington in integrating psychiatric nursing concepts with the rest of the undergraduate nursing curriculum.

Programed instruction and television have been evaluated in research projects. Seedor (1963) reports on the experimental use of programed instruction in asepsis with 110 students in two community colleges in New York. She concludes that students learn as much from programed instruction as they do from conventional classroom instruction. For two years, Griffin and others (1965) studied the teaching of clinical nursing through television at Montefiore Hospital in New York, with experimental and control groups of students. They concluded that one instructor with television can teach 15 students as effectively as another instructor can teach 10 students by conventional methods.

Nursing Outlook publishes a considerable number of articles on nursing education.

Pharmacy. Much of the writing on pharmaceutical education appears in the *American Journal of Pharmaceutical Education,* first established in 1937 by the American Association of Colleges of Pharmacy, and now appearing five times a year.

A major study of pharmaceutical education was reported by Elliott (1950), giving the results of a national survey conducted between 1946 and 1949. It considers the status of pharmacy as a profession and in a detailed study of education for the field presents information on the educational system, student quality, curriculum and alumni, among other topics. Its publication was preceded by a preliminary document (Elliott, 1948) which gave a summary of findings and recommendations for discussion by the profession. Following publication of the major document special parts of the study were published separately. Blauch and Webster (1952) report a careful study of the curricula of the pharmacy schools. It gives information on content and organization of the curricula, and proposes that the curricula be lengthened and organized on a 2–4 plan instead of the four-year plan then current.

Deno and others (1966) present a textbook on the profession of pharmacy. It describes the elements of pharmaceutical education in brief fashion, and lists colleges of pharmacy as of July 1, 1965. Sonnedecker (1951) gives a historical account of the movement of pharmaceutical education toward and into the universities during the nineteenth century.

Public Administration. The literature on public administration is voluminous, and a good bit of it touches on educational problems, at least incidentally. Sweeney's study (1958) contains a series of papers on aspects of education for "administrative policy-making officers" in the public service. It includes discussions of organization, study and teaching, curricula and teaching methods, and analyses of the position and role of the administrative policy-making officer. The papers are written by well-known persons in the field, and reflect their experience as well as their study. Stewart (1961) gives a more factual account of public administration education in the United States. He presents general information on 145 graduate programs at 83 colleges and universities in the United States, giving the numbers of students and faculty members, the types of degrees awarded, and the distinctive programs conducted. He briefly describes every one of the programs at the 83 colleges and universities.

Wengert and others (1961) have a narrower focus in reporting a successful effort to construct an experimental course in administration which would be useful to graduate students in business, government, and education at the University of Oregon. Caldwell (1962) gives a rather generalized statement on the uses and methods of in-service training in public service, designed for use in countries throughout the world. What is already happening on the world scene is reported in Molitor (1959), whose volume is one of a series on teaching in the social sciences. It is a comprehensive and substantial survey, defining trends in the teaching of administrative sciences and outlining curricula in universities in 11 countries.

The Public Administration Review, as well as a number of other journals, contains articles on education for public administration.

Social Work. Social work education has been the subject of two extensive studies since 1950. Hollis and Taylor (1951) consider many of the issues of social work education in the postwar period, including the need for a single national organization concerned with social work education. Their recommendation that a Council on Social Work Education be established was followed in 1952. The study also pointed out the need for greatly increasing the education of social workers in order to come closer to meeting the needs of society.

The second major study (Boehm, 1959) is an exhaustive investigation of the curricular problems in social work education, covering 13 volumes of text and one of index. It considers undergraduate as well as graduate education but by far the greater emphasis is on graduate education. It is an essential reference on social work education.

Other more limited but substantial studies include one by the U.S. Department of Health, Education, and Welfare (1965) which reports a major survey of social work education and manpower, conducted over a 2½-year period. It defines a tremendous gap between the number of social workers the United States needs now and in the future and the number of social workers it can expect from the present schools. The study contains a great deal of statistical information and a useful bibliography. Towle (1954) reports a seminal study which delineates with great perception the ways in which professional education aids a student to become a professional person. It is composed of two sections: Part I, Learning Process and Educational Process, which considers general principles that have significance for professional education generally; and Part II, Application in Teaching Social Casework, which illustrates the impact of the principles in social work teaching. Pins (1963) analyzes the process by which students choose social work as a field of study. His work is based on questionnaires sent to each first-year student in social work schools in the United States and Canada in the fall of 1960. He provides an extensive bibliography. Meyer (1966) studies the in-service training of nonprofessional public welfare staff members, defining needs and proposing programs, as well as including a bibliography.

The fourth international survey of training for social work (United Nations, 1964) identifies trends in the education of social workers at all levels from 1954–1962. It focuses on objectives, administrative aspects, and curricula in the various countries, and includes suggestions for national and international action. Smith (1965) provides a brief history of social work education in Britain. First published in 1952, it shows that the concern for social work education in Britain goes back to the 1890's.

Aldridge and McGrath (1965) have compiled a survey of the attitudes of undergraduate and graduate faculty members in social work curricula toward the liberal arts (favorable) and the relationship of the type of undergraduate preparation of students to their later success in schools of social work (confused).

The Journal of Education for Social Work, a quarterly first issued in the spring of 1965, contains a variety of studies on social work education. Prior to its establishment, the *Social Work Journal* and the *Social Service Review* probably contained the most articles on social work education.

Theology. Niebuhr (1957) conducted the major study of Protestant theological education. It is the final report of an extensive study of graduate seminaries in the United States and Canada. After reviewing the situation and assessing trends, the study concludes that the most urgent needs in theological education are improvements in teaching methods and in faculty. The Directory of Theological Schools (American Association of Theological Schools, 1966) gives statistical summaries for Protestant theological schools in the United States and Canada, including sections on the distinctive characteristics of each. Allen (1960) lists and reviews the activities of theological schools and major seminaries in Africa, Asia, and Latin America which prepare ministers and priests for service in Protestant, Roman Catholic, and Eastern churches. Bier (1948) compares the performance of seminarians with medical, dental, law, and college students on personality tests, and finds that the seminarians are the most deviant group.

William J. McGlothlin
University of Louisville

References

Aldridge, Gordon J., and McGrath, Earl J. *Liberal Education and Social Work.* Teachers Col, Columbia U, 1965. 102p.

Allen, Yorke, Jr. *A Seminary Survey; a Listing and Review of the Activities of the Theological Schools and Major Seminaries Located in Africa, Asia, and Latin America.* Harper, 1960. 640p.

American Association of Theological Schools. *Directory of Theological Schools in the United States and Canada.* The Association, 1966. 131p.

Anderson, G. Lester, and others. *Education for the Professions.* NSSE, 1962. 312p.

Bannister, Turpin. (Ed.) *The Architect at Mid-Century: Evolution and Achievement.* Reinhold, 1954. 513p.

Berelson, Bernard. *Graduate Education in the United States.* McGraw-Hill, 1960. 346p.

Bergeron, Rita Marie. *The Nursing Departmental Chairman in the Liberal Arts College.* Catholic U America Press, 1963. 225p.

Bier, William C. *A Comparative Study of a Seminary Group and Four Other Groups on the Minnesota Multiphasic Personality Inventory.* Catholic U America Press, 1948. 105p.

Blackerby, Philip E. "Why not a Department of Social Dentistry?" *J Dental Ed* 24:197–200; 1960.

Blauch, Lloyd. (Ed.) *Education for the Professions.* GPO, 1955. 317p.

Blauch, Lloyd. (Ed.) *Accreditation in Higher Education.* GPO, 1959. 247p.

Blauch, Lloyd E., and Webster, George L. *The Pharmaceutical Curriculum.* ACE, 1952. 257p.

Boehm, Werner W. *The Social Work Curriculum Study.* 14 vols. Council on Social Work Education, 1959.

Bridgman, Margaret. *Collegiate Education for Nursing.* Russell Sage, 1953. 205p.

Brown, Esther Lucille. *Nursing for the Future.* Russell Sage, 1948. 198p.

Caldwell, Lynton K. *Improving the Public Service through Training.* Agency for International Development, 1962. 129p.

Carr-Saunders, A. M. *Professions; Their Organization and Place in Society. The Herbert Spencer Lecture.* Clarendon, 1928. 31p.

Carr-Saunders, A. M., and Wilson, P. A. *The Professions.* Clarendon, 1933. 566p.

Davis, Fred, and others. "Problems and Issues in Collegiate Nursing Education." In Davis, Fred. (Ed.) *The Nursing Profession.* Wiley, 1966. p. 138–75.

Deno, Richard A., and others. *The Profession of Pharmacy,* 2nd ed. Lippincott, 1966. 264p.

Dressel, Paul L. *Liberal Education and Journalism.* Teachers Col, Columbia U, 1960. 102p.

Elliott, Edward C. *Findings and Recommendations of the Pharmaceutical Survey.* ACE, 1948. 49p.

Elliott, Edward C. *The General Report of the Pharmaceutical Survey, 1946–1949.* ACE, 1950. 240p.

Fivars, Grace, and Gosnell, Doris. *Nursing Education: The Problem and the Process.* Macmillan, 1966. 228p.

Flexner, Abraham. *Medical Education in the United States and Canada.* Updyke, Merrymount Press, 1910. 346p.

Griffin, Gerald J., and others. *Clinical Nursing Instruction by Television.* Teachers Col, Columbia U, 1965. 79p.

Gurley, John E. *The Evolution of Dental Education.* American College of Dentists, 1960. 276p.

Hollinshead, Byron S. *The Survey of Dentistry. The Final Report, Commission on the Survey of Dentistry in the United States.* ACE, 1961. 603p.

Hollis, Ernest V., and Taylor, Alice L. *Social Work Education in the United States.* Columbia U Press, 1951. 422p.

Horner, Harlan Hoyt. *Dental Education Today.* U Chicago Press, 1947. 420p.

Kaye, Barrington. *The Development of the Architectural Profession in Britain.* Allen, 1960. 223p.

Lynn, Kenneth S. (Ed.) "The Professions." *Daedalus* 92:647–858; 1963.

McGlothlin, William J. *Patterns of Professional Education.* Putnam, 1960. 288p.

McGlothlin, William J. *The Professional Schools.* Center for Applied Research in Education, 1964. 118p.

McGrath, Earl J. *Liberal Education in the Professions.* Teachers Col, Columbia U, 1959. 63p.

Meyer, Carol H. *Staff Development in Public Welfare Agencies.* Columbia U Press, 1966. 230p.

Molitor, Andre. *Public Administration.* UNESCO, 1959. 192p.

Muschenheim, William. *Comparative Curricula at Architectural Schools in Europe, Africa, Near East, Orient, Mexico, Australia, and Canada.* Assn Col Schs of Architecture, 1966. 125p.

Niebuhr, H. Richard. *The Advancement of Theological Education.* Harper, 1957. 239p.

O'Dell, De Forest. *The History of Journalism Education in the United States.* Teachers Col, Columbia U, 1935. 116p.

Paynter, K. J. *Dental Education in Canada.* Royal Commission on Health Services, 1965. 109p.

Pesznecker, Betty L., and Hewitt, Helon E. *Psychiatric Content in the Nursing Curriculum.* U Washington Press, 1963. 134p.

Pins, Arnulf M. *Who Chooses Social Work, When and Why?* Council on Social Work Education, 1963. 212p.

Pitcher, Barbara, and others. *A Study of the Prediction of Academic Success in Architectural School.* ETS, 1962. 87p.

Russell, Charles H. *Liberal Education and Nursing.* Teachers Col, Columbia U, 1959. 152p.

Seedor, Marie M. *Programed Instruction for Nursing in the Community College.* Teachers Col, Columbia U, 1963. 117p.

Selden, William K. *Accreditation: A Struggle Over Standards in Higher Education.* Harper, 1960. 138p.

Smith, Marjorie. *Professional Education for Social Work in Britain.* Council on Social Work Education, 1965. 114p.

Sonnedecker, Glenn. *Science in American Pharmaceutical Education of the 19th Century.* American Institute of the History of Pharmacy, 1951. 32p.

Stewart, Ward. *Graduate Study in Public Administration.* GPO, 1961. 158p.

Sutton, Albert A. *Education for Journalism in the United States from its Beginning to 1940.* Northwestern U Press, 1945. 148p.

Sweeney, Stephen B. (Ed.) *Education for Administrative Careers in Government Service.* U Pennsylvania Press, 1958. 366p.

Towle, Charlotte. *The Learner in Education for the Professions.* U Chicago Press, 1954. 433p.

UNESCO. *The Training of Journalists: A World-Wide Survey on the Training of Personnel for the Mass Media.* UNESCO, 1958. 222p.

UNESCO. *Professional Training for Mass Communication.* Reports and Papers on Mass Communication, No. 45. UNESCO, 1965. 46p.

United Nations. *Training for Social Work.* United Nations, 1964. 120p.

U.S. Department of Health, Education, and Welfare. *Closing the Gap in Social Work Manpower.* GPO, 1965. 90p.

Wengert, E. S., and others. *The Study of Administration.* U Oregon Press, 1961. 149p.

World Health Organization. *Dental Education.* WHO, 1962. 32p.

PROFESSIONAL EDUCATIONAL ORGANIZATIONS

In 1966 there were 574 national and regional professional educational associations, 587 state associations (U.S. Office of Education, 1966) and over 8,000 local associations. This represented about a 25 percent increase in number in ten years (U.S. Office of Education, 1956). Most recently, voluntary associations have played a vital role in the major events in education by giving form to the trend toward teacher militancy and channeling much of the curriculum-reform movement. In spite of this involvement, and similar involvement for over a century, few aspects of education have been studied less (Groebli, 1959). What has been published in the educational literature consists mostly of discussions of issues related to specific controversies in which associations find themselves. Much more scholarly analyses of their professional organizations have been made by sociologists and political scientists. But even they have been hampered because they have not examined the full range of types of organizations across several fields and by the lack of agreement on basic definitions; the terms "education association," "professional association," and "scientific societies" are used loosely and often interchangeably.

The most frequently cited of the early studies of voluntary organizations for professionals was made by Carr-Saunders and Wilson (1933). They concentrated on describing the role of associations within professional fields and the differences in function between the professional association and the trade union. To them, the two basic purposes of associations are to help form a professional community and to help the professional interpret and apply pure science. In other words, professional associations are a way of welding knowledge to power. They discuss in some detail how associations respond to societal, economical and political forces.

Writing for an audience of engineers and scientists, Kornhauser (1962) uses a different set of terms. He sees three types of organizations: the learned or scientific society, the professional association, and the professional union. To Kornhauser, scientific societies are converted into professional associations when the branch of science is transformed from an avocation to a career. He lists seven functions of associations: advance and disseminate knowledge; set standards; improve training; regulate conduct; limit practice of unqualified; stimulate and support individuals; interact with the scientific community.

Kornhauser's unique contribution is his use of the term "professional union." He cites the conflicts that arise when scientists and engineers are placed in industrial settings and expected to perform in ways that they feel are inappropriate to the status for which they have been prepared. He also discusses their relatively unsatisfactory economic condition which leads them to seek redress through collective action. The result has been professional unions, exemplified by the Engineers and Scientists of America, which is devoted almost exclusively to the professional and economic welfare of its members.

Also writing about the same groups, Strauss (1963) lists seven categories of occupational organizations: learned societies; technical societies; professional organizations; "sounding boards"; certified unions; and two categories of trade unions. He sees them forming a continuum, but he cautions that many organizations most likely will exhibit the characteristics of two or more categories. Learned societies are those whose primary purpose is the advancement of knowledge; technical societies are established both to advance and apply knowledge and for the professional interests of their constituents. But professional organizations are created solely to advance professional interests.

Strauss's "sounding boards," the fourth category, although referred to by Kornhauser, were not listed by him as a separate category. Usually ad hoc committees of scientists or engineers, they meet with management to discuss professional matters and are important because, among some professional groups, they represent an innovation in coping with salary and welfare matters. Certified or "white collar" unions are Strauss's counterpart to Kornhauser's professional union. Since they still are in the formative stage, Strauss believes that unique techniques and organizational patterns will eventually emerge from them.

Merton (1958) concentrates on professional associations and sees six characteristics that they all share: membership is voluntary; they are organized for reasons other than the pecuniary benefit of individual members; they exercise control over the occupational performance of members; they support individuals in their occupational tasks and aid them to improve their competencies; they seek to advance knowledge of the field represented by their membership; they help the professionals relate to the larger society.

Kiger (1963) concentrates on examining learned societies but he does not include the academies that exist primarily to bestow honors. While he believes that such societies are specialized organizations created primarily for scholars and researchers, they are characteristically American in that they are open to wide audiences of interested persons who meet minimum qualifications. Their primary purpose is to provide a forum for the oral and written exchange of information and knowledge among experts, but because they are open, they also serve as a link to the professionals and practitioners. Professional associations, Kiger maintains, exist to assist those concerned with applying knowledge. He limits his study to 58 modern learned societies, including among the better known the American Statistical Association, Modern Language Association, American Historical Association, American Psychological Association, American Anthropological Association, American Political Science Association, and the American Sociological Association. He also examines two other types of organizations: the councils and the societal institutes. The four councils are the American Council on Education, the National Academy of Sciences–National Research Council, the American Council of Learned Societies, and the Social Science Research Council. Their common ground is representation from and close ties with learned societies and professional associations. For example, the American Council on Education has representation from two of the other councils as well as 140 other organizations including the National Education Association.

According to Kiger, the major purpose of these councils is to help scholars fill in or bridge gaps in knowledge created by the arbitrary demarcations of disciplines. To this purpose, the councils sponsor publications and study committees. The ACE differs from the other three in that it admits colleges and universities as members; in 1967 it had 1,261 institutional members. Consequently, ACE is most frequently thought of as an association of college presidents or other top administrators.

The five institutes studied by Kiger include the American Association for the Advancement of Science, the Federation of American Societies for Experimental Biology, the American Institute of Physics, the American Geological Institute, and the American Institute of Biological Sciences. Only two of these, the AAAS and the AIBS accept individual members; all are supported and controlled in varying degrees by constituent societies. The AAAS is the oldest, best known and most influential of the five. One of the 18 sections, "Q," is labeled "Education" and in 1966 had 1,400 of the total membership in the association of 110,000.

The institutes were organized for reasons similar to those that led to the creation of the councils: the need to bridge the gap among specialists and to coordinate the activities of many societies or associations in given disciplines. Of the institutes formed after World War I, the American Institute of Physics was formed by five organizations, the American Institute of Biological Sciences by 12, and the American Geological Institute by 11 American, one Canadian, and Section E of the AAAS.

Gilb (1966) concentrates on tracing the history of professional associations, but she includes in her definition several of the societies listed by Kiger and some of Strauss's scientific societies. She describes how associations respond to societal forces and conditions. The National Education Association is discussed in some detail. Her major thesis is that professional associations have moved through three distinct phases in the nineteenth century and into a fourth phase in this century. The first phase was shaped by the limitations of travel and communication so that local and regional associations predominated. Easing of travel difficulties encouraged the formation of national and state associations in the latter third of the nineteenth century. At this (second) stage, the organizations remained small, usually quite poor, elitist in structure and outlook, and dominated by administrative leaders, often in government.

The third phase occurred before the turn of the century and lasted through World War I. Professionals turned their attention to what Gilb calls "bread-and-butter" issues. Their associations expanded in size and in representation; they broke with the previous leadership and frequently assumed a contraposition to government agencies, even those that had fostered them.

The final phase has been marked by the formation of new groups for racial and religious minorities in the population, for specialists, and for different authority levels. Local groups have shown new vigor. National associations have had to reorganize and shift program priorities to accommodate these developments.

There are other dimensions in the evolution of associations, according to Brown (1946). Her concern was with their management, and she sees that association activities change as they pass through various levels of management sophistication. In the early stages, the president or secretary performs most of the tasks of the organization. Consequently, he is deferred to by other elected members and granted great power. In the second stage the association provides some staff, and the elected governing board or committee governs by a kind of round-table discussion method. It is not until the organization is large enough and sufficiently wealthy to employ a professional staff that it reaches the third stage. Brown calls for more scientific management and planning at that level.

These definitions of functions and role among types of organizations offer little information about their ecology; that is, how associations and societies influence the state of knowledge and competence of performance of any given field. The most promising leads for insights into these phenomena are coming not from students of associations, but from communications researchers who are examining the way scientists, teachers, and clinicians in the natural and behavioral sciences seek and use information. The study of information flow is many decades old, but only within the last 20 years has the emphasis shifted to an examination of the behavior of the scientist or scholar using information.

Most notable of the recent studies, according to Paisley (1965), is the study of the flow of information among biochemists, chemists, and zoologists by Menzell (1958) and the 15 studies published in two volumes that constitute the American Psychological Association's Project on Scientific Information Exchange in Psychology (1963, 1965). Methodological problems confronted all the investigations and Menzell operated from a small sample, so results must be transferred to other situations with caution. But some of the findings should cause associations to reexamine the type of publications and meetings they sponsor.

Those that have the most relevance can be summarized as follows:

1. The kind of oral or written source sought out for information will vary with the type of information to be received, the ease and expense of using face-to-face or printed sources, the availability of recognized expert assistance and the characteristics of the information seeker.

2. Informal communication plays a much larger role than may have been realized earlier. The most frequently used informal mechanisms are preprints, reprints, correspondence, and face-to-face exchanges. Use of these devices is due partly to the great lag, approximately 20 months, between the time a typical research project reaches the reportable stage and when it actually appears in print (Garvey & Griffith). The importance of paper sessions at annual meetings is reaffirmed by the fact that papers are read, typically, from 20 to 12 months earlier than they appear in print. The paper-reading sessions are not a satisfactory source of information for many scientists, however, who prefer to spend their time at symposia or in informal gatherings at conventions.

The importance of informal communication. has been explored in much greater depth by Derek Price (1963). In his chapter "Invisible Colleges and the Affluent Commuter," he develops the thesis that a typical scientist can monitor the productive output of preprints, reprints, and other written reports of about 100 of his colleagues. These 100 tend to form a network or an "invisible college" among whom there is frequent interaction and personal contacts. When any field of science expands so that the upper limit is appreciably exceeded, a new college materializes. Its "members" develop greater allegiances to the invisible college than to the institution at which they are employed. Price does not discuss the role of associations in detail but says he hopes that the invisible colleges will never be given formal recognition. His work should prod the student of associations to reexamine the fundamental purposes of literary societies and professional associations.

Another way of understanding the purposes of associations and societies is to examine their relationships to governments. Thackery (1965) discusses some of the current problems and tendencies of national associations. He points out that with the increase in federal support individual colleges and universities as well as associations seem to be rushing pell mell to open offices and establish secretariats in the nation's capital. He calls for more caution so that the lines of communication between the government and the educational community do not become hopelessly snarled. Fidler (1965) sees the need for a supra-association to accomplish the same purpose.

Don Price (1965) presents more fundamental problems. He carefully examines the impact that science has had on our society and particularly on the governing of our society since World War II. He concludes that scientists have become the fourth estate —the other three being Congressmen, administration officials, and professionals—that has developed a special and integral place in the operation of present-day government. He wants the roles of science and the scientists clarified, however, because scientific knowledge will become even more valuable for the operation of government in the future. The relationship, he feels, should be founded on the principle that the degree to which any part of the four estates is working to discover truth should also be the degree to which it is given freedom of self-government; to the degree that any part is working toward power, it should submit itself to the test of political responsibility.

Price makes only passing references to societies and associations, but many implications are quite clear. In his case histories he shows how administrative agencies and Congressional committees have from time to time used the services of the National Research Council. It seems quite plain to him that scientists must develop comprehensive organizations like the American Association for the Advancement of Science for dealing with the federal government; their present societies and the ones that will be formed by newly emerging specialists will be used primarily to help advance knowledge.

It is interesting that in his careful and enlightening treatment of the impact of science on government, Don Price does not see a more significant place for organizations established by scientists and educators. The reason may be, as Kiger (1963) points out, that, in general, government agencies and learned societies have not had much interaction; that relationship also has tended to be one-sided, with the societies benefiting from financial support. He sees the two moving closer together as the sciences play an ever increasing part in government.

HISTORY OF EDUCATIONAL ASSOCIATIONS BEFORE 1870. The earliest educational organizations in the United States were located in large cities. Fenner (1942) identifies the Society of the Associated Teachers founded in 1794 in New York City as one of the first, if not the first. The evolution from the local level to the creation of national associations took two parallel paths: through the organization of scholars and educational leaders in literary societies, and through the gradual organization of the profession itself, by state and by special interest groups.

Of the first type, three organizations deserve special attention: The American Institute of Instruction, founded in 1830; the Western Literary Institute and the College of Professional Teachers, founded in 1831; and the American Association for the Advancement of Education established in 1849. The AII had the longest life of the three but showed the most vigor in its first two decades when it attracted the support of men like Ralph Waldo Emerson, Theodore Parker, Henry Barnard, Horace Mann, and Samuel Howe (National Education Association, 1907). The Western Literary Institute and College of Professional Teachers was for the 15 years of its existence the western counterpart of the AII. It, too, attracted a large number of nationally known educators, scholars, and statesmen primarily from Ohio, Indiana, Illinois, and Kentucky. The American Association for the Advancement of Education was the most ambitious and auspicious of this kind of organization. Horace Mann, Henry Barnard, and Joseph Henry, Director of the Smithsonian Institution, are three of the better known of its presidents. The AAAE, like the AII and the WLI, provided channels through which educators and reformers could address national audiences and through which they could become acquainted with leaders and issues from related fields. None of the three organizations, however, ever won broad-based support from the profession or the lay public.

A parallel movement within the profession itself began in 1845 with the creation of state teachers associations in Rhode Island, New York, and Massachusetts. At first membership was limited to those engaged in teaching (Alexander, 1910). By 1857 there were 15 state associations, which should testify to their utility; most of them sponsored a magazine of some type and held annual meetings.

Interest in forming a national organization arose directly from the state associations (Fenner, 1942; Wesley, 1957). In 1857, 43 persons from ten states and the District of Columbia met in Philadelphia at the invitation of presidents of ten state associations to create the National Teachers' Association. Wesley points out that while William Russell contributed a paper for that meeting, all else was in the hands of the practicing teacher and those who were active in state associations.

The NTA did not burst upon the national educational scene as an instant success. Its beginnings were marked by wide swings of interest and support. No annual meetings were held in 1861 and 1862, for example, but by mid-nineteenth century standards the

1863 meeting was a rousing success; over 16,000 persons attended, 500 of whom were from New England. In these years, the sense of allegiance of the participants was low; business meetings were poorly attended, and the resolutions were far from controversial and passed without great enthusiasm. Yet in spite of the difficult days imposed by the Civil War, the Association made progress. Fenner credits it with being instrumental in creating, in 1867, the federal agency we now know as the Office of Education. Within ten years, it had attracted the support of many educational statesmen and all of the remaining state associations; this offset the fact that total membership never exceeded 200.

The NTA was not the only nationally based organization of educational practitioners, however. In 1858, the American Normal School Association was organized in Norwich, Connecticut. The National Association of School Superintendents was created in Harrisburg, Pa., in 1865 and met separately from the NTA the following year. The Central College Association was organized in 1869 as a federation of state organizations of college men. By that year it appeared that education was destined to be splintered into dozens of national groups organized by specialties.

AFTER 1870; THE NATIONAL EDUCATION ASSOCIATION. At the 1870 meeting of the National Teachers Association in Cleveland, president D. B. Hager asked for support for the recommendations of a year-old committee that would divide the association into four sections: the Department of Normal Schools; the Department of Elementary Education; the Department of School Superintendents; the Department of Higher Education. The recommendations were adopted and the NTA merged with the ANSA and the NASS to form the National Educational Association. ("Educational" was changed to "Education" some years later.)

The mergers did not have much immediate effect on the membership or on the program; the NTA could count 170 members in 1870 and the NEA's figures varied between 150 and 380 for the next 13 years. In 1884, due to the remarkable energy and promotional ability of Thomas Bicknell, the Madison, Wisconsin, convention had more than 5,000 visitors; the membership for that year jumped to 2,729. With only one lapse, the yearly figure never again dropped below 1,000.

Not only the size but the character of the Association tended to change slowly. The annual program of the convention in 1906 was remarkably similar, although larger, to that of the NTA's program in 1857. Throughout the first half of this century, the NEA continued to attract leading educational administrators, scholars, and statesmen to membership and service. But classroom teachers had little more influence in the organization just prior to World War I than they had had before the Civil War (Wesley, 1957). This is best illustrated by the little concern shown during the first 50 years about the economic conditions of teachers (Lieberman, 1960) even though many committees were appointed beginning in 1884, and in spite of several reports of which the most significant was the monumental statistical study of 1905.

Where the NEA did show its influence was in helping to shape educational trends. The establishment of high schools and normal schools and the remarkable expansion of higher education in our society were matters often debated on NEA platforms and studied by an almost endless line of committees and commissions. Wesley (1957) regards this function as being "the guardian of correct thinking." In 1880, the NEA established the National Council of Education as the "brain trust" for the profession; originally its membership was limited to 51 members. The council had four ways in which to influence thinking about education. It could influence the men within the Council itself, all of whom were opinion leaders; it could prepare or call for reports; it could direct research studies; or it could sponsor convention sessions. Its greatest influence was felt through the committees it created.

Two of the most noteworthy were the Committee of Ten on Secondary School Studies and the Committee of Twelve on Rural Schools. The Committee of Ten grew out of a council meeting at Saratoga Springs in 1892 and was chaired by Charles Eliot, president of Harvard. The reports of these and of many similar committees had great impact on schools (Butts & Cremin, 1953) during a highly formative period, but the council's effectiveness waned over the years. In 1908 its size was increased to 120, and in 1940 it was expanded to 178. In 1943 the council was abolished.

Only a small portion of the committees and commissions sponsored by the NEA were initiated by the council, however (Stinnett & Huggett, 1956). Some of the more influential have been the Committee of Fifteen, established by the Department of Superintendence in 1893, which dealt with the training of teachers, the program of studies and the administration of city schools; the Committee on College Entrance Requirements, which published a report in 1899; and the Committee on Normal Schools, which reported the same year. Other committees before 1910 dealt with the training of high school teachers, industrial education, contemporary education doctrine, libraries, and foreign languages. The Cardinal Principles of Secondary Education were created by an NEA commission.

In 1933, the NEA and the Department of Superintendence appointed an ad hoc commission to combat the ideological and financial attacks being made on the schools. The commission was composed of ten leading educators and 900 consultants and performed so satisfactorily that a five-year commission was established in 1935, called the Educational Policies Commission. The EPC differed only slightly from the National Council of Education which it eventually replaced. In 1947, the commission was reorganized to have more representation from departments. The reports from its many committees and commissions have been printed and distributed by the thousands, and provide standard reading materials in most teacher preparation courses.

After World War I, the character and style of operation of the NEA changed slowly but perceptibly so that the second 50 years are marked by greater attention to welfare issues, more interaction with the federal government, and less with the scholarly and academic community.

Soon after the turn of the century it was clear that the economy of the United States was entering a phase in which the relatively low economic position of the teacher became less tolerable. Formation of the first teachers union in the nation in 1902 in San Antonio, Texas, was an expression of this discontent. Fifteen years later, in Chicago, the American Federation of Teachers was affiliated under the AFL and enjoyed a startling initial success. Membership jumped from 2,403 in 1917 to 9,808 three years later (American Federation of Teachers, 1964). NEA membership was only 10,104 in 1918 and for the first time in decades, it was aware of competition for the allegiance of the classroom teacher.

A massive and successful membership campaign was launched. As a result, NEA membership increased to 52,850 in 1920, 87,414 in 1921 and 118,032 in 1922 (National Education Association, 1926). But the concerns of teachers then obviously had to be given higher priority and more visible expression (Stinnett & Huggett, 1956). The Department of Classroom Teachers had been organized in 1913 but not until 1922 did it receive its allocation of funds from the NEA. The 1920 reorganization which created the representative assembly was brought about partly by the demands of teachers for a greater voice in the management of the association. Wesley notes that after 1920, more speeches at annual meetings and articles in official journals were devoted to matters of teacher welfare and professional advancement.

It is not clear what effect these changes in the Association had on education. Ruml and Tickton (1955) claim that they have had very little, that the economic position of teachers did not improve between 1940 and 1954. It is not even clear whether the obviously increased concern for salary and welfare matters produced any significant changes in the operation of the association. An Educational Policies Commission report produced in the depth of the depression years (National Education Association, 1937) and based upon 572 returned questionnaires, showed that among 151 elected and appointed officers of the NEA and NEA-affiliated state and local associations, only three saw the primary purpose of national professional organizations to be welfare of teachers; one-third of the respondents even rejected the policy statement that would have given welfare matters equal attention with the improvement of education. In a similar report 20 years later, the basic posture of the association was unchanged (National Education Association, 1957).

In the 1960's, partly as a result of another challenge from the American Federation of Teachers, professional issues took on a greater sense of urgency. By 1964, the AFT had grown to over 100,000 members. While this was only a small fraction of the more-than-900,000 membership of NEA, 62,402 (out of a possible 69,858) of these had been gained by defeating the NEA in local exclusive bargaining rights referenda. The most astonishing of these victories had been in New York City in 1961. As a result, the NEA became more militant; the best illustration of its more forceful tone was the sanctions it imposed on the State of Utah in 1964 (National Education Association, 1967).

Increased interaction with the federal government is the second major change in the NEA since the turn of the century. Throughout its history, the association had maintained many close if informal ties with both the administrative and legislative branches of the government. It was chartered by Congress in 1906, but in 1920, in an effort to work more systematically with public officials, the Legislative Commission was created. The Commission began, and throughout the 1920's continued to seek (1) general federal aid for schools, (2) creation of the office of Secretary of Education, (3) increased funds to eliminate illiteracy and teach citizenship to immigrants, and (4) improved teacher training and better health services in the schools. The staff of the Commission produced thousands of booklets and made endless trips throughout the country to drum up support for specific bills.

In 1930, through a reorganization, the Commission shifted its focus to studying, interpreting, and advising the association at large on federal affairs. It established a legislative reference service, and published booklets on matters such as teachers' contracts and minimum-salary laws. The Commission has been credited with repeal of the 1935 federal law that required teachers to take an oath that they had not taught or advocated communism (Wesley, 1957) and with the modification of the Hatch Act so that teachers were not banned from political activity. After many years of frustration (Munger & Fenno, 1962), many of the Commission's objectives were reached with the passage of the National Defense Education Act of 1958 and the Elementary and Secondary Education Act of 1963.

The third major shift in NEA activities was its separation from the general scholarly community (Cremin, 1961; Conant, 1963). Alexander (1910) noted that the association was having difficulty in attracting leading scholars to its activities as early as 1909. Attendance at meetings of the Department of Higher Education declined so much that it was discontinued between 1924 and 1942. Many of the reasons for this change lay outside the NEA. The more specialized humanistic and social science societies began to claim more and more of the time and attention of the scholar. For example, of the 58 societies studied by Kiger (1963), 37 were organized after the turn of the century. Regardless of the cause, in the 1930's and 1940's the leadership of the NEA came almost exclusively from the schools of education and the educational practitioner.

By the 1950's, countermovements were evident. At first these took the form of attacks on education, educationists, and the NEA as their organization. But among other effects, the shock that emanated from the launching of Soviet Sputnik I produced among scholars and scientists a heightened sense of responsibility for improving the quality of the schools. The first organized effort actually antedated Sputnik by more than six years and was led by Max Bebberman, a professor of mathematics who developed a new high school mathematics course. Revisions to the physics curriculum followed in 1956. By 1966, reforms were underway in almost every area of the curriculum (Elam & Garvue, 1964). Major financing for these reforms was provided by the National Science Foundation and the U.S. Office of Education under provisions authorized in the National Defense Education Act (Goodlad & others, 1966).

The impact of these events on the NEA departments had not been realized as late as 1966, when the NEA engaged in a self-study. The conclusions and recommendations were directed almost entirely to problems raised by the increasing militancy of teachers. The study offered little overt evidence that the elected and appointed officers of the NEA were planning any major reorganization or refocus of activities to bring the educational community closer to the scholarly and scientific community.

National Society for the Study of Education. One of the direct, linear descendants of the literary societies of the nineteenth century, the National Society for the Study of Education originally was called the National Herbart Society when it was formed in 1895. Reorganized and renamed the National Society for the Scientific Study of Education in 1902, it was given its present name seven years later. In 1967 it continued to produce two volumes each year which dealt with current issues and problems in education of general interest.

American Association of University Professors. In the spring of 1913, a group of professors at Johns Hopkins University sent letters to professors at nine other institutions urging them to form a national association for professors. In January, two years later, 650 professors became the charter members of the AAUP. Metzger (1965) sees three purposes for its creation: to give professors more control of the quality of instruction, to aid them in gaining more representation in university affairs, and to offer protection against arbitrary behavior by administrators. Both Metzger (1965) and Lieberman (1960) point out that the AAUP was a very weak organization throughout its first 40 years.

The turning point came following the McCarthy era (Metzger, 1965). Stung by criticism that it had not protected the interests of professors or the cause of academic freedom, new officers began to rebuild program, image, and membership in the late 1950's. Since then membership has climbed from a low of 36,415 at the start of 1957 to 80,142 on January 1, 1967. The AAUP is working for better integration of faculty into university and college administration. The organization refuses to consider strikes and respects the right of each individual to decide for himself where he shall be employed and under what conditions. It will blacklist institutions that do not meet minimum requirements, but will not blacklist professors, or even members, who choose to teach there.

American Federation of Teachers. The first local teachers union was created in 1902 in San Antonio, Texas, and the second in Chicago later that same year. In 1916, nine locals met in Chicago to form the American Federation of Teachers.

After the initial burst in membership from 2,403 in 1917 to 9,808 three years later, the federation steadily declined throughout the early and middle 1920's. During the depression, membership again increased until it reached a peak of over 30,000 in 1939. This figure was later found to be slightly inflated during the struggle for control between the communists and noncommunists and was readjusted to 29,907 in 1940 after the communists had been expelled from the union. Following World War II, the membership continued to expand; the total for 1966 was 130,000 (American Federation of Teachers, 1964).

The AFT differs from the National Education Association in two basic ways: it refuses membership to those holding administrative positions; it will use the strike, although reluctantly, as a negotiating device. The NEA prefers to level sanctions against a district; that is, it will publicly attempt to deter teachers from seeking employment there. A third difference could be the most important if, as some authors have foreseen, the two organizations should ever consider merging (Lieberman, 1960). The American Federation of Teachers is an affiliate of the AFL–CIO, and therefore is influenced by trends and events in American unionism.

In 1967 a Council of AFL–CIO Unions for Professional, Scientific and Cultural Employees was formed. It included the AFT, the American Guild of Musical Artists, the Newspaper Guild, and the Association of Broadcast Employees and Technicians. If the creation of this council heralds greater prominence in the union movement for professionals, it appears that at all levels the educational community will continue to be divided by competing organizations for many years.

National Catholic Education Association. The National Catholic Education Association was organized in 1903 and held its first national convention a year later. Since 1897, there has been growing awareness of the need among the clergy for a voluntary association that would assist all parts of the growing Roman Catholic school system to communicate among each other. Also needed was an association that could represent the entire system with the church hierarchy, with the larger educational community, and with the federal government.

Over the years, the association has wrestled with the problems related to the constantly increasing professionalization of Catholic schools. One of the critical aspects of this issue occurred in the mid-1930's when, after prolonged debate and consideration, the NCEA voted to cooperate with the national and regional accrediting agencies (National Catholic Education Association, 1935). Helping Catholic schools meet accrediting requirements remains one of the more important services provided by the association; one full-time professional staff person was assigned to this task even in the 1960's.

Catholic education felt increased pressures for improved, more professional schools following World War II (McCluskey, 1966). As realization of the requirements for better education permeated American society, all sectarian and private schools were affected. Later, in the 1960's, parochial schools located in the inner urban centers felt pressures to assume tasks and services similar to those being adopted by the public schools. The NCEA has assisted its members with all these problems through the writing and distribution of booklets, newsletters, and journals, and through workshops and conferences.

Most of these activities are carried on by seven departments: elementary schools, secondary schools, major seminaries, minor seminaries, superintendents, special education, and colleges and universities. Each department is encouraged to be autonomous and has its own board and a full- or part-time staff. Membership in the NCEA is institutional and in 1967, 11,505 schools had joined; this represented close to 90 percent of all Catholic schools (National Catholic Education Association, 1967).

The National Catholic Education Association resembles the National Education Association in many ways; the major differences are of degree rather than kind. Both are facing very similar problems: centripetal forces of specialization; disparity of interests among the elementary, secondary and college levels; differences between administrators and teachers; and increased pressure from parents and society for improvements in the school program. The NCEA also feels pressure from the lay teachers for higher salaries and benefits; separate organizations of lay teachers existed in three cities in 1967 and more were expected in other cities. Unique to the NCEA, however, are the problems of Catholic education that arose from the ecumenical movement and the growing financial strain of trying to maintain a separate school system without tax support.

American Educational Research Association. In 1915, seven men, six of them directors of research in local school systems, formed the National Association of Directors of Educational Research (National Education Association, 1941). In the beginning, membership was purposely restricted to research producers; the executive committee reviewed and voted on each application. In 1930, AERA affiliated with the NEA. Membership requirements were relaxed considerably in the early 1950's and the Association began to grow; between 1964 and 1966 the membership rose from slightly over 3,000 to almost 6,000. While it remained one of the small research societies, AERA served a unique function as a bridge between education and several of the behavioral and social sciences.

Phi Delta Kappa. Phi Delta Kappa is known officially as a professional fraternity, but except for Greek letters and the method for selecting members, it differs little from most other educational associations (Lee, 1955). It was created in 1910 as an amalgam of three independently established fraternities. The first few years were taken up with organizational matters; there was little money for anything else. Nevertheless, at the end of its second decade, PDK could claim 55 chapters and over 11,000 members.

In the 1960's, Phi Delta Kappa had a membership of 67,000 in 280 locals and a central staff of eight (Phi Delta Kappa, 1966). The Phi Delta Kappa Educational Foundation, with an original capital of $500,000, was created in 1967 for educational research and dissemination (Phi Delta Kappa, 1967).

One of the youngest of all educational organizations, but in its conception alone one of the most significant, is the National Academy of Education. The idea of a separate association for scholars concerned with educational issues and problems had been discussed for many years. It finally was realized in 1964 when a committee consisting of James Conant, John Gardner, Clark Kerr, and Sterling McMurrin selected the first 8 members who endorsed the concept of an academy for education, and in turn, selected 13 additional members. In subsequent meetings the total membership was raised to 28 (National Academy of Education, 1965). The 28 members are divided into sections for the history and philosophy of education; politics, economics, sociology and anthropology of education; psychology of education; and the study of education practice.

Although the general purposes of the Academy were clear—that is, the promotion and maintenance of high standards of scholarship in education—its functions were the subject of intensive but cautious deliberation through 1967.

The first president of the Academy was Ralph Tyler; Lawrence Cremin was elected first vice-president; Gary Becker, second vice-president; and Stephen Bailey, secretary–treasurer.

International Educational Organizations. In the latter half of the twentieth century the United Nations Educational, Scientific and Cultural Organization emerged as the most significant international organization in education (Abraham, 1964). It has sponsored many activities of which the following are representative: (1) The exchange of scholars and researchers among several countries; (2) research into comparative achievement in mathematics among students in 12 countries, on attitudes of young people toward the race problem, and on value systems of young people in various cultures; (3) programs to eradicate illiteracy and promote adult education. It has sponsored an impressive array of seminars and conferences on almost every major aspect of education. One of its best-known programs has fostered experimental international education through the voluntary Associated Schools Project.

The best-known nongovernmental, international organization is the World Confederation of the Teaching Profession, which was created from a merger in 1952 of the International Federation of Teachers Association, the International Federation of Secondary School Teachers, and the World Organization of the Teaching Profession (Speeckaert & Tew, 1964). WCOTP had a membership in 1967 of 150 national associations from 97 countries (World Confederation of Organizations of the Teaching Profession, 1966a).

Associations which focus primarily on primary or secondary education affiliate directly with the IFTA or the IFSST and through them with the WCOTP. All affiliates are entitled to votes in the Assembly of Delegates which has met annually since 1953. The theme of the 1966 meeting in Seoul, Korea, was "The Role of Teachers' Organizations in Educational Planning" (World Confederation of Organizations of the Teaching Profession, 1966b). The WCOTP was established to improve education throughout the world by fostering the exchange of knowledge about international understanding and by improving the status of teachers. The organization works to increase the influence of the teaching profession in all international aspects of educational policy.

The WCOTP was shaken in 1967 by the revelation of secret funding by the Central Intelligence Agency of the United States. Leading officials were fearful at that time that the growing influence of the organization would be curtailed in many countries.

What value have educational associations had to society in general and education specifically? Absence of dependable data leaves each author to speculate for himself. Elam and Garvue (1964) points out that during the absence of strong central leadership from federal agencies, voluntary associations took up the slack. Lieberman (1961) claims that they have had no influence at all. Barber (1967) reminds us that they can impede as well as assist in new discoveries. Kiger (1963) and Gilb (1966) see societies and associations becoming more important; Gilb concludes that voluntary association will be as important in the near future to our society as guilds were in the medieval age. She reiterates what is almost a continuous refrain from students of associations that social scientists prepare for these changes by studying voluntary organizations more intensely and extensively.

Richard A. Dershimer
American Educational
Research Association

References

Abraham, Herbert J. "The Role of the United Nations Organizations in Education for International Understanding." In Bereday, G. Z. F., and Lauwerys, J. A. (Eds.) *Education and International Life.* Harcourt, 1964. p.365–79.

Alexander, Carter. *Some Present Aspects of the Work of Teachers' Voluntary Associations in the United States.* Teachers Col, Columbia U, 1910. 109p.

American Federation of Teachers. *Representing Today's Teachers, The Story of the American Federation of Teachers in 1963–1964.* The Federation, 1964. 112p.

American Psychological Association. *Project on Scientific Information Exchange in Psychology.* APA, 1963. 283p.

American Psychological Association. *Project on Scientific Information Exchange in Psychology.* APA, 1965. 292p.

Barber, Bernard. "Resistence to Scientific Discovery." In Barber, Bernard, and Hirsh, Walter (Eds.). *The Sociology of Science.* Free, 1967.

Brown, Esther L. *The Use of Research by Professional Associations in Determining Program and Policy.* Russell Sage, 1946. 39p.

Butts, R. Freeman, and Cremin, Lawrence A. *A History of Education in American Culture.* Holt, 1953. 628p.

Carr-Saunders, A. M., and Wilson, P.A. "The Rise and Aims of Professional Associations." In Carr-Saunders, A. M., and Wilson, P. A. (Eds.) *The Professions.* Clarendon, 1933. p. 298–304.

Conant, James Bryant. *The Education of American Teachers.* McGraw-Hill, 1963. 218p.

Cremin, Lawrence A. *The Transformation of the School.* Knopf, 1961. 353p.

Elam, Stanley, and Garvue, Robert. "Professional Organizations and Education." *R Ed Res* 34:101–11; 1964.

Fenner, Mildred S. "The National Education Association, 1892–1942." Doctoral dissertation. George Washington U, 1942.

Fidler, William P. "Problems of the Professional Associations and Learned Societies." In Wilson, Logan. (Ed.) *Emerging Patterns in American Higher Education.* ACE, 1965. p. 250–6.

Garvey, William D., and Griffith, Belver C. "Studies of Social Innovations in Scientific Communications in Psychology." *Am Psychol* 21:1019–36; 1966.

Gilb, Corinne Lathrop. *Hidden Hierarchies.* Harper, 1966. 254p.

Goodlad, John I., and others. *The Changing School Curriculum.* Fund for Advancement of Education, 1966. 122p.

Groebli, John M. *National Organizations in the Education Profession at Mid-Twentieth Century.* George Peabody Col for Teachers, 1959. 506p.

Kiger, Joseph C. *American Learned Societies.* Public Affairs Press, 1963. 291p.

Kornhauser, William. *Scientists in Industry.* U California, 1962. 230p.

Lee, J. W. "The First Fifty Years." *Phi Delta Kappan* 1937:3–44; 1955.

Lieberman, Myron. *The Future of Public Education.* U Chicago, 1960. 294p.

Lieberman, Myron. "The Influence of Teachers' Organizations Upon American Education." in Tyler, Ralph W. (chairman) *Social Forces Influencing American Education.* NSSE, 1961. p. 182–202.

McCluskey, Neil G. "Catholic Schools After Vatican II." In Koob, C. Albert. (Ed.) *What Is Happening to Catholic Education?* National Catholic Education Association, 1966. p. 1–12.

Menzel, Herbert. *The Flow of Information Among Scientists: Problems, Opportunities and Research Questions.* Columbia U, 1958.

Merton, Robert K. "The Function of the Professional Association." *Am J Nursing* 58: 50–4; 1958.

Metzger, Walter P. "Origins of the Association." *AAUP B* 51:229–37; 1965.

Munger, Frank J., and Fenno, Richard F., Jr. *Economics and Politics of Public Education.* Syracuse U, 1962. 185p.

National Academy of Education. *Background, Constitution, Founding Members.* The Academy, 1965.

National Catholic Education Association. *Quarterly B* 32:76–7; 1935. 19p.

National Catholic Education Association. *Quarterly B* 64: in press; 1967.

National Education Association. *Fiftieth Anniversary Volume, 1857–1906.* NEA, 1907. 949p.

National Education Association. *Change and Renewal.* NEA, 1967. 31p.

National Education Association, Division of Publications. *NEA Proceedings.* NEA, 1926. 208p.

National Education Association, Division of Publications. *NEA Proceedings.* NEA, 1941. 991p.

National Education Association, Educational Policies Commission. *A National Organization for Education.* NEA, 1937. 47p.

National Education Association, Educational Policies Commission. *Professional Organizations in American Education.* NEA, 1957. 65p.

Paisley, William J. *The Flow of (Behavioral) Science Information, A Review of the Research Literature.* Stanford U, 1965.

Phi Delta Kappa. *News, Notes, and Quotes.* PDK, 11:3; 1966.

Phi Delta Kappa. *News, Notes, and Quotes.* PDK, 11:1; 1967.

Price, Derek J. del Solla. *Little Science Big Science.* Columbia U Press, 1963. 115p.

Price, Don K. *The Scientific Estate.* Belknap Press, 1965. 278p.

Ruml, Beardsley, and Tickton, Sidney G. *Teaching Salaries Then and Now.* Fund for Advancement of Education, 1955. 93p.

Speeckaert, G. P., and Tew, E. S. "Non-Governmental Links Across National Frontiers." In *Education and International Life.* Harcourt, 1964. p. 385–404.

Stinnett, T. M., and Huggett, Albert J. *Professional Problems of Teachers.* Macmillan, 1956. 516p.

Strauss, George. "Professionalism and Occupational Associations." *Ind Relations* 2:7–31; 1963.

Thackery, Russell I. "National Organizations in Higher Education." In Wilson, Logan (Ed.) *Emerging Patterns in American Education.* ACE, 1965. p. 236–49.

U.S. Office of Education. *Education Directory, 1955–1956.* GPO, 1956. 78p.

U.S. Office of Education. *Education Directory, 1965–1966.* GPO, 1966. 134p.

Wesley, Edgar B. *NEA: The First Hundred Years.* Harper, 1957. 403p.

World Confederation of Organizations of the Teaching Profession. *Annual Report.* The Confederation, 1966(a). 59p.

World Confederation of Organizations of the Teaching Profession. *The Role of Teachers Organizations in Educational Planning.* The Confederation, 1966(b). 111p.

PROGRAMMED INSTRUCTION

Programmed instruction (PI) is not only a type of educational material called a self-instructional program; it is also a type of teaching technique. Whereas the first meaning refers to something tangible, used for instruction, several rather differently appearing materials are all properly called programs. Furthermore, they do not have to be verbal or printed but can be pictorial and conveyed by any medium. The second meaning refers to something abstract, one of several different types of instructional logic or strategy. These are ways of achieving instructional objectives. They determine the conditions, the organization as well as the presentation and response media used at different points in the program as it is presented to each student.

PI materials have four basic characteristics in common. First, they focus the student's attention on a limited amount of material at one time, which is usually called a frame or step. Second, they require a response (or answer) to each segment of material that is usually partially observable. Third, they give the student immediate knowledge of results (feedback) after every response. These three features, in sequence, constitute the learning cycle (Jacobs & others, 1966); it is used repeatedly throughout all programs. Fourth, they permit each student to respond at his own pace thereby providing for a degree of individualization of instruction.

PI is cybernetic when each response of the learner serves as an input (stimulus) to the teaching system and determines, at least in part, the next output of the system. The student–teacher (man–machine) interaction in PI is designed to produce convergence of student performance on a set of prestated goals, or behaviorally stated objectives.

Automated instruction and programmed learning are terms used synonomously, both with each other, and with programmed instruction. The common purpose of all PI is to guide the learner so that a particular set of desired changes occur in his performance.

Teachers and educational psychologists have long been aware that learning may be more efficient if conditions permit the student to rehearse or recite both actively and appropriately those responses needed for learning. Learning requires that some form of response be made; it can be covert or overt, simple or complex, unitary or integrated, concrete or symbolic, mediating or terminal. Various techniques of programming are deliberate attempts to require active responding, which is probably the most basic condition of PI. Programs guide the student's responses by the selective use of a variety of techniques. These techniques in different combinations constitute instructional strategy. They depend heavily for their effectiveness upon the effectiveness with which they handle stimulus materials (DeCecco, 1964; Taber & others, 1965).

The development of new discriminations, new cognitions, and new response capabilities are the three fundamental learning processes. All are involved and go on concurrently but at different rates depending upon the task to be learned and the learner's initial status. Each technique used to define the conditions of PI relates to one or more of these processes. Some PI techniques are used to teach the student to attend to particular things; others teach him to discriminate between similar objects (e.g., the letters d and b). Still others develop cognitions, such as concepts, meanings, and relationships. Some others "shape" behavior (eliminate irrelevant responses), "chain" responses (sequence them), or simply bring already well-defined responses under the control of a new stimulus.

Strictly speaking, teachers cannot manipulate responses as such. The only thing we can manipulate is the set of stimulus conditions that foster, or regulate, the occurrence of responses. Instructional guidance of learning reduces simply and completely to techniques that control the stimulus conditions for a learner.

What is now called PI had many precursors, quite independent of B. F. Skinner's work (see Lumsdaine & Glaser, 1960; Stolurow 1961; Dale, 1967). However, it was his now classic paper, "The Science of Learning and the Art of Teaching" (Skinner, 1954), that focused attention on what is known today as programmed instruction. While Skinner invented one type of PI, he did not create all of its elements. Also, other types have been described by Crowder (1959) as intrinsic programming and Stolurow (1965a, 1965b) as idiomorphic programming.

The appearance of PI in the 1950's was neither the direct result of a continuous evolutionary development in education, nor the sole product of psychology. Rather, a variety of related work, both past and present, seems to have been motivated by the same *Zeitgeist*. Several psychologists and educators wrote about elements of what today has become the set of ideas constituting PI. For example, both knowledge of results and reinforcement, each of which is contingent upon a response, were well established by Pavlov, Thorndike, and Hull, as important, if not necessary and sufficient, conditions of learning. For example, Thorndike (1912) wrote: "If by a miracle of ingenuity a book could be so arranged that only to him who had done what was directed on page 1 would page 2 become visible, and so on, much that now requires instruction could be managed in print." There was precedent for the use of sequential development of materials in Comenius, though not acknowledged by Thorndike or the current authors of PI. Skinner, beginning in the mid-thirties, developed operant conditioning with animals and later related his concepts to the problems of teaching people. Others developed detailed lessons, though seldom as detailed as a PI frame (the display unit of a program); for example, both teachers and students now and then reduced materials to flash cards. The catechetical form and Socratic dialogue have been used extensively, but not in conjunction with recognized contingent reinforcements and printed frames. The detailed specification of objectives, while early identified as an important factor, remained an art more often practiced in the breach than in the observance and seldom stated at the observable behavioral level.

The historical roots and the current view of the teaching machine overlap those of PI. They differ in the relative attention given to teaching functions and to the dynamics of the teaching process (Stolurow & Davis, 1965). Pressey (1926, 1927, 1932, 1958, 1959, 1960, 1963), beginning about 1915, first developed machines to automate testing and to some extent teaching. Pressey's devices were designed to supplement regular classroom instruction by self-paced multiple-choice testing. His devices provided the student with immediate knowledge of results and immediate scoring of test questions. His materials have been called adjunctive programs. Skinner (1954, 1961a, 1961b) developed other machines designed mainly to teach by making operant conditioning techniques explicit. Skinner stressed the concepts of stimulus control of response and shaping of behavior by reinforcement. He stressed the use of constructed response to insure that the desired response was actually under stimulus control. This led to some constraints on the learner so that the machine could compare the student's response with the one expected. With more complex verbal materials the student scored his own responses. The machine dropped out frames to which the student responded correctly, and retained for re-presentation the ones answered incorrectly. Skinner chose to delay the correction of the student's errors until the next pass through the program. He believed that wrong responses are to be avoided, and advocated programming and rewriting so as to minimize error rate. He justified his teaching machines and programming principles on theoretical grounds. However, empirical studies by Meyer (1959), Holland (1959), and Porter (1959) have clearly demonstrated that devices and linear programs can teach. The unsolved problems concern the techniques that work best. Prompting (the use of elicitors) and vanishing (their systematic withdrawal) were active topics of interest. Materials are introduced in a complete form in one frame (prompting) and gradually reduced so that the learner depends more and more upon memory to supply the entire response in later frames. This procedure insures that the stimulus that initially elicited the response (elicitor) is removed so that the response is transferred to a new stimulus which now "cues" it (Markle, 1964).

The linear or Skinnerian type of program has been presented in book form even more than in a mechanical device. Two formats, the "vertical" and "horizontal," have been used almost equally in printed linear programs. Each gets its name from the way sequences of frames are physically arranged—down the page or from page to page.

While the hardware–software distinction between teaching machines and PI is the most obvious one to invoke, the distinction is not very useful. A machine has to have a program in order to teach and a program has to have some functions performed on it to accomplish its objectives. Therefore, it seems useful to consider teaching as a requirement for a set of functions which can be accomplished by different means. Once computers are used for instruction, in what has become computer-aided instruction (CAI), the distinction between teaching machines and PI becomes even less clear than when books (either scrambled or linear) are used, or when mechanical or electromechanical teaching machines are used (Stolurow & Davis, 1965; Gerard, 1967). Not only are typewriters used as input-output (I/O) devices, but also film, slides, cathode-ray tubes (CRTs) can be controlled for display, and keyboards, light pens, and touch plates can be used for student response. The educational program and the media are controlled by the computer program. The computer provides a flexible logical capability, and a memory plus the ability to process student data.

Adaptations and extensions of Pressey's self-testing devices included the Tab Item (Glaser & others, 1954), the Punchboard-Tutor (Cantor & others, 1956), the Trainer-Tester (Dowell, 1955), the Subject-Matter Trainer (Bernard & others, 1955; Briggs, 1956; Irion & others, 1957) and the Multipurpose Instructional Problem Storage Device (MIPS) (Briggs, 1956). Ross and others (1962), Stolurow (1961), Kopstein and others (1961), Lumsdaine and Glaser (1963), and Smith and Smith (1966) describe many of the teaching machines that have been developed. The micro-objectives of today's PI must meet three substantive criteria (e.g., Mager, 1962; Gagné, 1965). Every unit of behavior has to be described. The conditions under which the behavior is to occur must be stated. The minimum acceptable level of performance must be specified. In addition, psychological criteria for judging the adequacy of the instruction must be described with respect to one or more of the following: rate of learning, degree of retention, and amount of transfer (e.g., understanding, use).

Every substantive objective in PI has to be stated explicitly. Each thing the learner must be able to do when he has completed the program is an objective. The operations that he must be able to perform, the words he must be able to pronounce or spell, the diagnostic problems he must be able to solve are all objectives. The statement of objectives of PI is a minimal list, but for even a short program, it is generally quite long. Each objective determines a set of frames and one or more test items used to determine learning.

Some distinguish the micro-objective, the lowest level, from the more common higher level, the macro-objective, e.g., to play a piano, fix a television set, or understand a poem. This higher level of objective has been systematized by Bloom and others (1956) for the cognitive domain and by Krathwohl and others (1964) for the affective domain, but the task has not been accomplished for motor skills.

Once objectives are formulated, the means to be used—machine or print—is one problem to be solved; another is the medium ot use. Then there are the problems of sampling and sequencing. The basic sampling principle is "teach the student only what he does not already know." The set of objectives for a program define what all learners should be able to do at the end of instruction. It is more inclusive than the subset which any one student needs to be taught. CAI permits the use of this principle by branching each student in terms of his performance on a pretest. Unless a means of selective sampling exists, all students will be given all frames.

Principles for sequencing are not well explicated. Basically, there are two sets: (a) those that relate frame sequence to learner characteristics and (b) those that relate the sequence to internal characteristics of the task. The use of the former, like the sampling principle, makes instruction more or less personalized or adaptive to individual learner requirements. The latter have been discussed by Thomas and others (1964) and Gagné (1965). The concepts and procedures of task analysis apply here.

Conditions used in administering a program can vary in many ways. The particular set of conditions used to teach a student is one of the sets of things defined by a teaching strategy. When operant programming is the strategy, all conditions are stated in advance and they are the same for all students. In intrinsic and in idiomorphic programming the particular set of conditions used with a student is not specifiable before the fact because a number of alternatives exist at each choice point; only after the response is made is the feedback known and the next frame of the student's program determined. To a greater or lesser extent the student determines his path through the material, and thereby generates his program, by the responses he makes.

Basic to these approaches to personalized or adaptive instruction is the concept of statistical interaction of the variables that comprise a teaching strategy with the characteristics of individuals. Whenever there is an interaction it means that it is necessary to be selective in using a strategy. One type of interaction that appears to have validity is that between the general intellectual ability level of the learner and the immediacy of knowledge of results (KR), or reinforcement (e.g., Little, 1934; Porter, 1961; Eigin, 1962). The lower the ability level the greater the need for immediate KR. Another interesting type of interaction is between aptitude and the sequence of frames (e.g., Cartwright, 1962; Smith, 1962; Stolurow & Davis, 1965). At this time, however, the data do not permit one to specify the best sequence from knowledge of the student's aptitude profile. A third type of interaction is between personality (in the sense of perceived needs) and the nature of the evaluative feedback (EFB) he gets when he makes right and wrong responses. A student's expectations can be considered as bases for the proper conditions for learning of which EFB is an example. Some data suggest that the student's expectations may determine what the most effective initial conditions of learning will be for him (e.g., Silberman, & others, 1962; Frase, 1963; Parisi, 1965). Regarding the use of either teachers alone or a teacher plus program, a study in the Denver Schools showed that with high-aptitude students, it is better to use the combination of a teacher who prefers innovative methods and a program. It also showed, however, that with low-aptitude students it is better to use only a teacher and one who prefers conventional methods (see Jacobs & others, 1966). More data need to be collected to identify interaction effects that could determine the bases for a decision-theoretic approach to adaptive instruction. These are only some of the possibilities suggested by current research.

The theory that defined the conditions employed in writing a program led not only to many polemics but also to research (e.g., Lumsdaine and Glaser, 1960; Glaser, 1965; Schramm, 1964). Peterson (1931) made the first research evaluation of Pressey's teaching machines. He found that the use of the chemical cards for self-scoring increased final test scores significantly. Little (1934) also evaluated a Pressey machine, as did Angell and others (1948), Jones and others (1949), Briggs (1947), Jensen (1949), Stephens (1960), and Severin (1955). Pressey's summary (1950) reported that immediate feedback was an efficient condition for learning. Also, repeated use of practice tests promoted learning whether or not the order of the test items was maintained. With more meaningful material, learning was more rapid and less affected by the changed order of the items. Students who used the punchboard machine also performed better on test items that were not a part of the practice set (transfer). Pressey's recent position is that machine testing is a useful adjunct to other teaching techniques.

Ten years after B. F. Skinner's paper, Schramm (1964) reported that there were ". . . approximately 190 reports of original research on programmed instruction. More than 165 of these have appeared since 1959." Therefore, more than three-fourths of all the research papers have appeared in the period 1960 to 1963. Unfortunately, there is no base rate from other areas of education with which to make a comparison of the proportion of studies revealing no significant difference between the conditions compared. For the reported studies, this is certainly the most common finding. A serious methodological question here is with the failure to include individual difference variables such as aptitude, personality, and interests in the design of the study so that they could be used as correlates of learning scores. Doing this would provide additional information that could reveal whether different individuals were benefiting from the different procedures, conditions, or techniques used, even though these variables did not have a significant effect on the mean performance of the groups.

Nearly half of the studies have dealt with presentation variables, e.g., prompting versus confirmation; linear versus branching, pacing, size of steps; machine versus text form and programmed television. Nearly 30 percent dealt with response mode, e.g., overt versus covert, multiple choice versus constructed. A large number of studies were designed to serve a particular applied purpose, namely, to compare the amount learned from a particular program with the amount learned from a particular example of conventional classroom teaching of the same subject. A small but increasing number of students have been concerned with special applications of programs—to slow learners, to students with language problems, to deaf children, to industrial trainees, to military groups, to volunteer individual users (e.g., state-fair visitors). A smaller number have used PI to implement approaches to improving retention, discovery learning, transfer of training.

Linear programs have been more widely used than branching, and printed verbal programs have been more typical than film, slides, television, or audio tapes. About 40 percent of the studies have used college students, 20 percent high school students, and the rest have been divided among adults in military or industrial employment, and primary or pre-school learners.

Research on PI leaves no doubt that students who use it learn. They learn from adunctive, linear, mathetic (Gilbert, 1962), branched, intrinsic, and idiomorphic programming. They learn when materials are in book and machine form. Many different kinds of learners have not only learned, but also liked programs. With PI, students have learned the gamut of school subjects from algebra to zoology plus a variety of college military and business courses and skills (Ofiesh & Meierhenry, 1964; Lysaught & Jason, 1967). The techniques work in the United States and in other countries such as England, Sweden, East and West Germany, France, Italy, Africa, India, Japan, Australia, New Zealand, and Russia. In fact, while PI began in the United States, it is probably enjoying a more flourishing development in other countries at the present time. They seem to have taken the results of early work more seriously than has the United States and have moved more rapidly toward the institutionalization of instructional technology within their educational and training establishments (e.g., Austwick, 1964; Unwin & Leedham, 1967).

Current trends suggest that linear teaching machines are out, branching machines are being used increasingly, and computer-based learning systems hold the promise of the future. Programmed texts are the mainstay and will continue to be used. The concepts originally systematized in the development of PI are beginning to influence the management of the classroom and the design and use of television and film. This trend, particularly in the use of feedback, will probably increase. The decision to use PI in and for education are not simple or easy, but any doubts about its permanence or effectiveness would have to stem from prejudice or ignorance. The only course of action for areas of application is how to use PI most effectively, and the only course for research is how to improve upon what little we now know so that we can begin to understand teaching and learning as they take place in schools, universities and training establishments.

Lawrence M. Stolurow
Harvard Computing Center

References

Angell, G. W., and others. "A New Self-scoring Device for Improving Instruction." *Sch and Soc* 67: 84–5; 1948.

Austwick, K. *Teaching Machines and Programming.* Permagon Press, 1964. 205p.

Bernard, and others. *Development of the Subject-matter Trainer.* AFPTRC Technical Memorandum ASPPLTM 55–7; March, 1955.

Bloom, B. S., and others. *Taxonomy of Educational Objectives. Handbook I: Cognitive Domain.* McKay, 1956.

Briggs, L. J. "Intensive Classes for Superior Students." *J Ed Psychol* 38:207–15; 1947.

Briggs, L. J. "A Trouble-Shooting Trainer for the E-4 Fire Control System." *United States Air Force Personnel Train Res Cent Develop Report* TN: 56–94; 1956.

Cantor, J. H., and others. *An Evaluation of the Trainer-Tester and Punchboard Tutor as Electronics Trouble Shooting Training Aids.* Office of Naval Reserve Technical Report NAVTRADEVCEN 1257-2-1, 1956.

Cartwright, G. P. "Two Types of Programmed Instruction for Mentally Retarded Adolescents." Master's thesis. Illinois, 1962.

Crowder, N. A. "Automatic Tutoring by Means of Intrinsic Programming." In Galanter, E. (Ed.) *Automatic Teaching: The State of the Art.* Wiley, 1959.

Dale, Edgar. "Historical Setting of Programmed Instruction." In Lange, Phil C. (Ed.) *Programmed Instruction.* 66th Yearbook, NSSE. U Chicago Press, 1967.

DeCecco, J. P. *Educational Technology.* Holt, 1964.

Dowell, E. C. *An Evaluation of Trainer Testers.* Keesler Air Force Base, Report No. 54–28, 1955.

Eigen, L. D. "A Comparison of Three Modes of Presenting a Programmed Instruction Sequence." *J Ed Res* 55:453–60; 1962.

Frase, Lawrence J. *The Effects of Social Reinforcement in a Programmed Learning Task.* 1963.

Gagné, Robert M. *The Conditions of Learning.* Holt, 1965.

Gerard, Ralph W. *Computers and Education.* McGraw-Hill, 1967. 303p.

Gilbert, T. F. "Mathetics: The Technology of Education." *J Mathetics* 1:7–73; 1962.

Glaser, Robert. *Teaching Machines and Programmed Learning II: Date and Directions.* NEA, 1965.

Glaser, Robert, and others. "The Tab Item: Technique for the Measurement of Proficiency in Diagnostic Problem Solving Tasks. *Ed Psychol Meas* 14:283–93; 1954.

Holland, J. G. "A Teaching Machine Program in Psychology." In Galanter, E. (Ed.) *Automatic Teaching: The State of the Art.* Wiley, 1959. p. 69–82.

Irion, A. A., and others. *Learning Task and Mode of Operation Variables in Use of Subject Matter Trainer.* Air Force Personnel and Train Res Center, 1957.

Jacobs, Paul I., and others. *A Guide to Evaluating Self-instruction,* Holt, 1966.

Jensen, B. T. "An Independent Study Laboratory Using Self-scoring Tests." *J Ed Res* 43:134–7; 1949.

Jones, H. L., and others. "A New Evaluation Instrument." *J Ed Res* 42:381–5; 1949.

Kopstein, F. F., and others. *A Survey of Auto-instructional Devices.* Behavioral Science Laboratory, Wright-Patterson Air Force Base, 1961.

Krathwohl, David R., and others. *Taxonomy of Educational Objectives. The Classification of Educational Goals. Handbook II: Affective Domain.* McKay, 1964.

Little, J. K. "Results of Use of Machines for Testing and for Drill Upon Learning in Educational Psychology." *J Exp Ed* 3:45–9; 1934.

Lumsdaine, A. A., and Glaser, R. (Eds.) *Teaching Machines and Programed Learning: A Source Book.* NEA, 1960.

Lumsdaine, A. A., and Glaser, R. "Instruments and Media of Instruction." In Gage, N. L. (Ed.) *Handbook of Research on Teaching.* Rand McNally, 1963. p. 583–682.

Lysaught, Jerome, and Jason, Hilliard. (Eds.) *Self-instruction in Medical Education.* Rochester Clearinghouse, 1967. 252p.

Mager, Robert F. *Preparing Instructional Objectives.* Fearon Publishers, Inc., 1962.

Markle, S. M. *Good Frames and Bad.* Wiley, 1964.

Meyer, Susan R. "A Program in Elementary Arithmetic: Present and Future." In Galanter, E. (Ed.) *Automatic Teaching: The State of the Art.* Wiley, 1959. p. 83–4.

Ofiesh, G. D., and Meierhenry, W. C. (Eds.) *Trends in Programed Instruction.* NEA, 1964.

Parisi, Dominico. *Social Reinforcement and Performance in Programed Learning in Italy.* U Illinois, 1965.

Peterson, J. C. *The Value of Guidance in Reading for Information.* Kansas Academy Science, 1931.

Porter, D. "Some Effects of Year-long Teaching Machine Instruction." In Galanter, E. (Ed.) *Automatic Teaching: The State of the Art.* Wiley, 1959. p. 85–90.

Porter, D. *An Application of Reinforcement Principles to Classroom Teaching.* Harvard 1961.

Pressey, S. L. "A Simple Apparatus Which Gives Tests and Scores and Teaches." *Sch and Soc* 23: 373–7; 1926.

Pressey, S. L. "A Machine for Automatic Teaching of Drill Material." *Sch and Soc* 25:549–52; 1927.

Pressey, S. L. "A Third and Fourth Contribution Toward the Coming 'Industrial Revolution' in Education." *Sch and Soc* 36:668–72; 1932.

Pressey, S. L. "Development and Appraisal of Devices Providing Immediate Automatic Scoring of Objective Tests and Concomitant Self-instruction." *J Psychol* 29:417–47; 1950.

Pressey, S. L. "Some Items for a History of Automation of Teaching: Self-instructional Devices." Paper presented at APA Convention, 1958.

Pressey, S. L. "Certain Major Psycho-educational Issues Appearing in the Conference on Teaching Machines." In Galanter, E. (Ed.) *Automatic Teaching: The State of the Art.* Wiley, 1959. p. 187–98.

Pressey, S. L. "Some Perspectives and Major Problems Regarding Teaching Machines." In Lumsdaine, A. A., and Glaser, R. (Eds.) *Teaching Machines and Programmed Learning. A Source Book.* 1960. p. 497–505.

Pressey, S. L. "Psycho-technology in Higher Education Vs. Psychologizing." *J Psychol* 55:101–8; 1963.

Ross, Wilbur L., and others. *Teaching Machines: Industry Survey and Buyer's Guide.* Center for Programmed Instruction, 1962. 154p.

Schramm, W. *The Research on Programed Instruction.* HEW, 1964. p. 282–96.

Severin, D. G. *Appraisal of Special Tests and Procedures Used with Self-scoring Instructional Testing Devices.* Ohio State U Press, 1955. p. 323–30.

Silberman, Harry, and others. *Development and Evaluation of Self-instructional Materials for Underachieving Students.* S. D. Corp., 1962.

Skinner, B. F. "Science of Learning and the Art of Teaching." *Harvard Ed R* 24:86–97; 1954.

Skinner, B. F. "Analysis of Behavioral Processes Involved in Self-instruction with Teaching Machines." In *New Educational Media News and Reports.* USOE, 1961(a).

Skinner, B. F. "Why We Need Teaching Machines." *Harvard Ed R* 31:377–98; 1961(b).

Smith, Karl U., and Smith, Margaret F. *Cybernetic Principles of Learning and Educational Design.* Holt, 1966. 529p.

Smith, L. M. *Programmed Learning in Elementary School: An Experimental Study of Relationships Between Mental Abilities and Performance.* Training Research Laboratory, U Illinois, 1962.

Stephens, Avery L. "Certain Special Factors Involved in the Law of Effect." In Lumsdaine, A. A., and Glaser, R. (Eds.) *Teaching Machines and Programmed Learning. A Source Book.* NEA, 1960. p. 89–93.

Stolurow, L. M. "Teaching by Machine." *Cooperative Res Monogr* 6:1961.

Stolurow, L. M. *SOCRATES: System for Organizing Content to Review and Teach Educational Subjects.* California, Berkeley, 1965(a).

Stolurow, L. M. "A Model and Cybernetic System for Research on the Teaching-Learning Process." *Programmed Learning* 2:138–57; 1965(b).

Stolurow, L. M., and Davis, D. "Teaching Machines and Computer-Based Systems." In Glaser, R. (Ed.) *Teaching Machines and Programmed Learning: Data and Directions.* NEA, 1965.

Taber, Julian I., and others. *Learning and Programmed Instruction.* Addison, 1965.

Thomas, C. A., and others. *Programmed Learning in Perspective: A Guide to Programmed Writing.* Educational Methods, Inc., 1964.

Thorndike, Edward L. *Educational Psychology.* Teachers Col, Columbia U, 1912.

Unwin, D., and Leedham, J. *Aspects of Educational Technology.* Methuen, 1967.

PROPRIETARY SCHOOLS

Standing quite apart from the conventional public and private educational institutions—elementary and secondary schools, colleges and universities—which are supported in whole or in large part by taxation and philanthropy is another group of institutions. They have been variously called proprietary, trade, and vocational schools, but no one of these terms covers the entire area. All of them, however, are concerned with preparing students for a particular business position or industry, skilled trade, semiprofession, personal service, recreational activity, or some other vocation or avocation. A recent study opines that this common characteristic suggests the utility of the generic term "specialty school" (Clark & Sloan, 1966).

Although there are more than 35,000 specialty schools in the United States, with a current enrollment surpassing 5,000,000, this discussion will be limited to vocational specialty schools only. In some cases the schools are the only source of training for certain vocations. Historically these institutions provided a functional type of education for a rapidly developing industrial civilization. Later they became largely post-high school institutions supplementing vocational education offered by the public high schools. Today they fill a large void in the conventional school system by doing on their own or under contract essentially what the federal government is encouraging in its training and retraining programs, and what so many outstanding authorities are urging upon the other schools of the nation (Clark & Sloan, 1966).

A comprehensive study of post-secondary education made in a northwestern state in 1966 defined proprietary schools as those "which are privately owned and managed, and which in addition to being service-oriented, are profit-motivated" (Oregon Post-High School Study Committee, 1966). Largely because of the profit motive, proprietary education has been viewed often as a hardy weed in the academic garden. Vestiges of this attitude may still be discerned, but to a growing extent academe and government have come to regard it as a respectable flower. A survey by the United Business Schools Association in 1966 found some 70 business schools which reported that their students have been able to transfer to baccalaureate-degree institutions with credit (Fulton, 1967). The teacher-certification program of the University of Buffalo in 1967 gave students observing classes in a local business school the same credit it gave fellow students observing in public schools (McConnell, 1967). But this does not necessarily indicate a consistent direction of flow. Conversely, an Oregon post-high school study committee (1966) reported that "there is not yet sufficiently ready communication between the proprietary schools and the community colleges," and that this has permitted distrust to weaken the educational potential within the state. Venn (1966) also notes a lack of articulation between proprietary schools and the "mainstream." On the whole, however, the idea that public education ought to have competition from other sectors has been expressed even in government quarters. Representative James H. Scheuer (1967) told an audience of educational supervisors that he would like labor unions, business organizations, and other public and private groups to establish elementary and secondary schools. Dr. J. Herbert Hollomon, when Assistant Secretary of Commerce, told *Fortune* magazine he "would like to see, for example, a profit-making organization running a chain of junior colleges under contracts with the communities in which they are located" (Ways, 1967). The private company, he went on, might develop a curriculum, pay what the market required to recruit teachers of quality, "and sell the package in competition with other junior college chains."

Professor Kenneth B. Hoyt (1967), director of the Specialty-Oriented Student Research Program at the University of Iowa, found that this new acceptance had arisen from the role the private schools perform in "fulfilling an important and unique function . . . which grows out of student needs and must continue to be performed."

RATIONALE. Many proprietary schools function in areas where instruction is available in free junior colleges or public evening adult-education programs. Why then, it has been asked, are people willing to invest hundreds of dollars for courses that are obtainable at low cost in publicly operated institutions (U.S. Office of Education, 1967)? Of the 3,316 students researched in Hoyt's (1967) SOS program, more than half gave as their reason for enrolling that "here we study only what we need to know." Students interviewed by the Stanford Research Institute (Podesta, 1966) gave three reasons: (1) *Time,* as expressed in (*a*) length of course, which is directly related to the subject matter and is therefore shorter than the more rounded programs in public schools; and (*b*) facility of enrollment, with frequent registration for classes scheduled to begin in one or two weeks, as against waiting for a new semester in a public institution. (2) *Course content,* directly contributing to the development of skills necessary to the chosen occupation; public school rules require subjects in nonvocational areas. (3) *Placement service,* under which private schools endeavor (apparently with considerable success) to obtain employment for their graduates, since the schools' continuation as commercial enterprises would depend on such successful placement.

TYPES OF SCHOOLS. In terms of educational objectives, proprietary schools may be classified as offering (1) preparation for employment, (2) instruction for a licensing examination, or (3) a combination of the two (Podesta, 1966). (It may seem odd that the three should sometimes be considered mutually exclusive.) Two major types of proprietary schools can be delineated by field of study: (1) business schools, which train specialists at every level from the beginning typist to the business-machine or computer operator and from programmer, accountant, medical, legal, or executive secretary, to business administrator; and (2) trade and technical schools, which run a broad range, including training of auto and airplane mechanics, pilots, cosmetologists, heavy-equipment operators, electronics specialists, printers, and draftsmen.

A survey undertaken for the Educational Coordinating Council of Oregon (Oregon Post-High School Study Committee, 1966) found that in 1965 the proprietary school field in Oregon was dominated by beauty and hairdressing schools, with business schools the second most numerous and aeronautics schools third. The Stanford study (Podesta, 1966) agreed that cosmetology came first and business education second, but found real estate schools the third most numerous in California.

HISTORY. Although texts on commercial practices and subjects were published on this continent as early as 1796, the first announcement of an actual school appeared in 1824, when James Gordon Bennett, later to found the New York *Herald,* published a notice about his "Permanent Commercial School." Reigner (1963) credits Benjamin Franklin Foster with establishing the first American proprietary school, *Foster's Commercial School,* in Boston in 1827. A printed announcement explained that "the Mercantile Education of young gentlemen is completed in superior and expeditious manner" through the teaching of "Penmanship, Arithmetic and Book-Keeping." In reserving "the hour from 11 to 12 A.M." for the "Ladies' Select Class" the circular concluded: "Those ladies who have long regarded an improvement in their chirography as impractical are assured that, by this system, they can attain a free, flowing hand." During the next 25 years, some 20 such schools were set up throughout the East and Middle West. Dr. John Robert Gregg, inventor of the shorthand he called "Light-Line Phonography," established Gregg Shorthand College in Chicago in 1895 (Miller, 1964).

The first practical typewriter, invented in 1868, spurred the entry of women into the business world on a larger, more serious scale. The usual three-month course in shorthand, available at business schools along with bookkeeping, penmanship and business arithmetic, was expanded to include typing. But while the nation was heading into the industrial century, opportunities were less than boundless for the nation's youth to train for careers in business and industry. In the 1897–98 academic year, only 5,800 students were enrolled in commercial courses in universities and colleges. Proprietary business schools had 71,000 students that year (James, 1900). President Garfield had said in 1881 that "the business colleges which this country has originated are a protest against that capital defect in our schools and colleges which consists in their refusal to give a training for business life" (Reigner, 1963). The years from 1890 to 1910 saw the educational world split apart by the issue of "vocationalism vs. traditional curriculum," and the growth of schools offering vocational programs took another spurt. Many of these were proprietary schools, teaching trade and technical courses in metalworking, home economics, and carpentry, in addition to the business schools whose rise has already been reviewed (Venn, 1966).

But the cycle since Garfield's day is almost complete! Many educators feel that colleges and universities ought to eliminate business skills and commercial subjects from their undergraduate curricula. At least two earlier studies leading to the conclusion that secretarial programs were not a legitimate part of college-degree education (Gordon & Howell, 1959; Pierson, 1959) received vigorous endorsement by William Benton (1961), founder of the Benton & Bowles advertising firm, later chairman of Encyclopaedia Britannica and U.S. ambassador to UNESCO. He wrote that he would like to see the complete elimination from the campus of undergraduate business schools and courses. As this vacuum occurred, the proprietary school would presumably once again respond to an unmet need.

ASSOCIATIONS. The National Union of Business Colleges was created in 1865, when fewer than 100 business schools existed in the United States. It had a short life, and was succeeded by the International Association of Business Colleges (IABC). The October 13, 1866, issue of *Harper's Weekly* published pen-and-ink sketches of all 50 members of the IABC who attended a convention in Cleveland, Ohio.

In 1912, the National Association of Accredited Commercial Schools was founded. The Association's "Statement on Standard's of Practice" exhibited good intentions, if not specificity, being "definitely committed to the general policy of effecting an immediate betterment of the individual schools . . . to the end that the whole system of private commercial education in the United States may be improved, and be placed in a more favorable light as a necessary part of the educational machinery of our country" (Miller, 1964). During the next 50 years, a number of constituent organizations of proprietary business schools were formed, enlarged, and merged. In 1949 the National Association of Accredited Commercial Schools merged with the National Council of Business Schools (formed in 1942) to set up the National Association and Council of Business Schools (Miller, 1964). In a separate operation, the American Association of Commercial Colleges, organized in 1931, merged with the Southern Accredited Business Colleges and the International Association of Vocational Colleges to become the American Association of Business Schools. Unification in the business school field was finally achieved in 1962 when the National Association and Council joined with the American Association of Business Schools to form the United Business Schools Association (UBSA). In 1967, the UBSA had a membership of 500 quality postsecondary independent business schools, junior and senior colleges of business. It is an affiliate of the American Council on Education. Some foreign schools are members of the association (Schever, 1967).

STATUS OF PROPRIETARY SCHOOLS. There are an estimated 5,000 nonpublic vocational schools on the postsecondary level in the United States, of which some 1,300 are independent business schools (Clark & Sloan, 1966). (Miller [1964] places the number at 1,500.) The numbers have remained fairly steady since 1960, but the impact of a host of newly formed schools of automation and data processing, now numbering in the hundreds, is still to be felt. It is estimated that half a million students (Miller, 1964; Fulton, 1967) are enrolled in independent business schools; by comparison, about 200,000 take business curricula in four-year colleges, and more than 50,000 in junior colleges.

In 1963, the UBSA conducted a member profile survey to determine the principal characteristics of the typical proprietary business school (Fulton, 1963). Replies from 156 independent schools indicate that the typical or "average" business school had 183 day students, of which 68 percent were women; six full-time instructors, most with baccalaureate degrees; a library, usually with a part-time librarian; 10 classrooms and 251 desks. It was organized as a business corporation; was accredited by the Accrediting Commission for Business Schools; taught Gregg Shorthand (although many schools taught more than one system, such as Speedwriting or Pitman); owned 69 typewriters, of which 25 percent were electric; had six adding machines, 10 calculators, and three duplicating machines. The length of the average secretarial course was 12 months. General education courses usually taught were economics, psychology, and English. A 1964 survey by the Accrediting Commission for Business Schools showed that the average tuition and fees for nine months was $700 (Sneden, 1964). U.S. Office of Education figures for the same year place the average tuition-and-fees figure at private nonprofit four-year degree institutions at $831 (Keppel, 1965).

ACCREDITATION. Licensing, certification, and accreditation are often unintentionally but erroneously considered as being synonymous (Selden, 1960) About a third of the states have laws for licensing or for certification of proprietary schools (Miller, 1964). The licensing power has had a stormy legal history since Massachussetts first proposed such a bill (it failed) in 1888. Later, state laws, generally unsuccessfully challenged in the courts, have clarified the rights of proprietors to operate schools as business enterprises (Hamilton, 1958) *Licensing* is nothing more than a permit to do business, having regard generally to safety and commercial standards. The Oregon Post-High School Study (1966) saw it as reflecting primarily the school's financial responsibility. *Certification,* on the other hand, is generally related to curriculum, instructional staff, facilities, etc., the responsibility as a rule of the state department of education, or a state board of examiners in a trade or vocation (Podesta, 1966). An eastern-state supervisor of private business schools wrote that in his state, approval implied scrutiny by the State Board of Education of curriculum, faculty, methods of instruction, facilities, enrollment, procedures, contracts, financial policies, advertising, and catalogs. Those that were approved filled an important place in the state's economy. Public secondary schools, he held, were unable to fully discharge the "responsibility to replenish the labor market with office workers and machine operators" (Thomas, 1966). A U.S. Assistant Commissioner of Education expressed the view to Congress regarding the public system of vocational education that "I think you could say safely that if we utilized every resource in the country to its maximum, we wouldn't meet the needs in all of these programs, and for all kinds of persons in the country, at different levels of schooling" (Arnold, 1966). The Oregon legislature in 1965 directed the State Superintendent of Public Instruction to create an advisory committee to, among other things, "develop recommended standards for vocational schools," and to issue certificates of compliance to schools which met the standards.

In 1912, accreditation made a beginning with the organization of the National Association of Accredited Commercial Schools (NAACS), which furnished a form of quasi- or self-accreditation to member schools. In 1949, Business Education Research Associates and the National Office Management Association formed the National Accreditation Authority for Private Business Schools; but for the sake of unity, it agreed to merge when the Accrediting Commission for Business Schools was officially created in 1952 by an enabling amendment to the bylaws of the National Association and Council of Business Schools (the predecessor of the UBSA). A host of federal education laws (Public Laws 82-550, 88-204, 89-287, and others) require that the U.S. Commissioner of Education publish a list of "nationally recognized accrediting agencies" which, by his determination, are "reliable authority as to the quality of training offered by an educational institution."

In 1956, the U.S. Office of Education added the Accrediting Commission for Business Schools (ACBS) to the list of "nationally recognized accrediting agencies" having responsibility for accrediting higher education (Accrediting Commission for Business Schools, 1967; Wilkins, 1960). Like recognition was later accorded the Accrediting Commission of the National Home Study Council, and in 1967 to the Accrediting Commission of the National Association of Trade and Technical Schools. The ACBS is sponsored by the United Business Schools Association, but has complete professional autonomy in its accrediting functions. It meets semiannually to evaluate schools in the four classifications: one-year business schools, two-year business schools, junior colleges of business, and senior colleges of business. In general, it requires reinspection and reevaluation every five years. As of November 1967, more than 315 schools, which train more than 100,000 students annually, were accredited by the Accrediting Commission for Business Schools (1967).

Prior to the 1965 federal program of insured student loans (which included accredited proprietary schools as "eligible institutions"), accreditation did not have the same financial significance for the proprietary schools that it did for public and nonprofit institutions, of which it is generally required to be eligible for federal aid for institutional support. Besides prestige, accreditation offers some very pragmatic advantages. Internally, it provides the school with an objective method of upgrading educational standards and practices, and externally it assists prospective students and practicing guidance counselors with a professional institutional evaluation. In a 1967 article, a Utah educator (Ivarie, 1967) advised counselors to provide themselves with a *Directory* of the Accrediting Commission for Business Schools (1967).

STUDENTS. Today's business school is a postsecondary institution whose students are either high school graduates or the mature equivalent. Approximately 50 percent have had some commercial courses in high school (including typewriting) (Fulton, 1963).

The University of Iowa's Specialty-Oriented Student Research Program (Hoyt, 1967), which interviewed 3,316 students in 11 private business schools, developed a general picture of the student body: more than 70 percent are between 18 and 21 years of age; nearly 8 in 10 of the business administration students are male; more than 90 percent of secretarial and clerical students are female. Almost all are high school graduates who ranked in the upper three-fourths of their graduating classes. They come from families of a lower-income socioeconomic background. Contrary to the popular assumption that proprietary business schools serve the commuter student, Hoyt found that 75 percent of trade–technical students come more than 100 miles to attend school and less than half of the business school students lived at home (Hoyt, 1965). About 70 percent completed their training programs; and more than 80 percent (including both graduates and dropouts) were employed in training-related jobs six months after leaving school. A two-year follow-up showed a significant increase in job success as measured by weekly earnings.

It is the predetermined objectives to be achieved in the minimum of time which best identify the students who include such diverse types as college graduates, junior college transfers, mature women returning to the work force, veterans in evening school, and Vocational Rehabilitation trainees.

TEACHERS. The Stanford Research Institute study (Podesta, 1966) found the quality of faculty in the business schools high, using educational background and related employment experience as criteria. Most teachers had college degrees at several levels, many had state teacher certification, and many had prior experience in teaching or as secretaries or bookkeepers. Instructors in machine-skill courses (keypunch, teletype, switchboard, etc.) who had less than a year of college usually had from six to ten years' experience in their instructional specialty and teaching experience in the proprietary school system. The 1963 UBSA survey (Fulton, 1963) found that of nearly 900 teachers reporting, 55 percent had baccalaureate and 23 percent advanced degrees. The Accrediting Commission for Business Schools (1967) requires that in junior colleges of business at least half the faculty teaching second-year work have master's, LL.B., C.P.A., or other professional equivalent degrees. In trade and technical schools it was found that the average teacher is male, between 36 and 55, and generally is recruited directly from the world of work. High school was completed by 99 percent, while 62 percent had one or more years of college of which 13 percent had had five to ten years of college background (Johnson 1967).

PROGRAM. The unusual flexibility of the private school enables it to render unique service to students and employers. When a new program is needed to meet an unexpected need in the changing community, or when an unprecedented number of applications are received for an ongoing course, it takes little more than the administrator's own decision to provide classroom, teacher, equipment, and materials in short order. There is no need to lobby a school board or persuade a bureaucracy. Every student can be given a program tailored to his individual need, whether his high school education was strong or weak. Streamlined adult and refresher courses are programmed and styled to allow students to progress as fast as their abilities allow (Fulton, 1967). Although the length of the study can vary from a few months to four years ending with a degree, the core curriculum still provides an educational program of from one to two years for secretaries, junior accountants, office managers, typists, stenographers, and data-processing personnel. Some schools may specialize in a single area such as the training of executive secretaries or court reporters; many offer varied curricula. Whatever the mix, offerings are closely related to job opportunities currently existing and as far into the future as the crystal ball can see.

INNOVATIONS IN PROGRAM. The impact of automatic data processing has been felt by business schools to no less a degree than by other sectors of the economy. Developments in programming have reduced the necessity for a high-level mathematics background; commercial program writing can now be done by people with a practical understanding of business operations, accounting, and computer concepts (Veigel, 1966). Field trips to automated offices are a common practice, presenting the student with a survey of equipment and procedures and acquainting him with job possibilities in this new field. Larger schools have highly developed computer-training programs for operators and technicians, and a broad range of equipment. The economics of computerization may lead to an additional role in the business community. Annual rental of computer equipment may run into six figures. To try to cover this entirely from student-derived income would make tuition prohibitively high. One school, at least, in addition to using the equipment for teaching and for record keeping, is therefore offering special computer time and services to local businesses and professionals. The additional effect is to keep the school staff in touch with developments in the world outside the classroom (Veigel, 1966).

In 1962, the chairman of the U.S. Civil Service Commission acknowledged "that the lack of credit in civil service examinations for business school training above the high school level has had two undesirable effects: It has discouraged the less talented and less ambitious students from taking such training since there was no apparent economic advantage to be gained, and it has influenced business school graduates to seek employment outside of Government where their additional training was recognized" (Dent, 1965). The commission now recognizes study in a business school. Describing a new Junior Federal Assistant Examination to be given in 1967, the commission wrote in its official announcement that applicants, in addition to passing a written test, must have successfully completed two academic years of post-high school study; it puts study at business schools on the same footing as study at four-year colleges or universities and junior or community colleges (U.S. Civil Service Commission, 1967).

ADMINISTRATION. As the name implies, most proprietary schools are organized as business enterprises in one of three ways: as sole proprietorships, as partnerships, or as business corporations. A significant number have become nonprofit corporations. Research studies made in 1939 and 1962 reveal the percentage of schools in each category and a marked tendency away from sole and toward corporate ownership. In Miller's 1939 survey of 576 business schools, 50 percent were sole proprietorships; 16 percent were partnerships; and 33 percent were corporations, of which 7 percent were nonprofit (Johnson, 1967). In Polishook's (1962) study of 64 accredited business schools, 16 percent were sole proprietorships; 16 percent were partnerships; and 66 percent were corporations, with 22 percent of those nonprofit. A new dimension may be on the horizon as large publicly held corporations are beginning to purchase business and technical schools which will be operated as subsidiaries. Examples are the Rochester Business Institute now owned by Lear-Siegler Corporation and De Vry Technical Institute owned by Bell & Howell Corporation. The Bank of America study (1965) indicates that a properly run proprietary school can be a sound investment.

One admittedly "slightly cynical analysis" of the entry of large corporations into the "knowledge industry" sounds the visceral alarm of the conventional academic community in a catechistic chain of dogmatic enthymemes. It finds that so far they have been most active in vocational training but that the trend is still in doubt (Harrington, 1967). In contrast, the author of the so-called Coleman Report (Coleman, 1966) urges the utilization of "entrepreneurs outside the school under contract" to create "open schools" for minority groups to help overcome "inequalities in the opportunity for educational achievement." Instead of assuming inherent conflict he proposes constructive cooperation. "The many post-high school business and technical schools that now exist would be potential contractors, *but always with the public school establishing the criteria for achievement, and testing the results* (emphasis added)" (Coleman, 1967).

ACHIEVEMENTS. The proprietary schools' precious heritage of educational independence has enabled them to anticipate, experiment, pioneer, and adapt quickly to the changing business climate. In addition to setting the pace for most specialized business education, introducing the typewriter, developing stenographic training, writing the first business textbooks, adopting office-machine training and more recently office automation, the independent business school really laid the groundwork for modern concepts of university business education. With its emphasis upon technical, management-oriented, and "professional" business education, it anticipated by many years the newer philosophy of collegiate business schools. Actually, the first authorizations to offer college-degree training were granted by state charter to Duff's Iron City College of Pittsburgh, an independent business school, in 1853, 40 years before the founding of the Wharton School of Finance and Commerce, usually considered the first college institution to offer business training (Miller, 1964). A 1964 report of the U.S. Senate Committee on Labor and Public Welfare said in part that "accredited business schools generally fulfill the major requirements of collegiate education by offering a post-high school program for high school graduates under quality standards of education. They provide terminal courses of study which produce qualified personnel available to industry and society. *Approximately 20 percent of the students in accredited business schools have enrolled after having one or more semesters of study in four-year colleges or universities*" (U.S. Senate, 1964).

While present public policy in federal legislation on education (as opposed to transportation and agriculture) limits grants and subsidies to public and nonprofit *institutions*, a détente appears to have been reached in the areas of *student aid* and under-contract training. Eight federal programs of financial grants, loans, and tax benefits include students enrolled in proprietary schools (Fulton, 1967). Obviously, it is the need of the student and the quality of the educational program (usually accredited) and not the corporate form of the institution which governs aid to the student.

Nine other U.S. government programs utilize proprietary schools for under-contract training (Fulton, 1967), in such areas as vocational rehabilitation (Switzer, 1964) and Manpower Development and Training Act programs (MDTA) (Rhude, 1966). The federal funds flow directly to the institution in the form of legal consideration under a contract for services performed (*quid pro quo*) and not as grants or subsidies (Fulton, 1965). Both the Secretary of Labor (Wirtz, 1966) and the former Secretary of Health, Education, and Welfare (Gardner, 1967) predict increased use of the schools under the MDTA. For 1966, HEW reports that 140 MDTA training projects in 28 states involved private schools at a cost of $6.8 million for some 7,858 trainees (Gardner, 1967). In 1967, the UBSA undertook an MDTA demonstration project for the departments of HEW and Labor to carry out training in eight states for nearly 500 persons in business schools and in a few trade and technical schools approved by the National Association of Trade and Technical Schools.

The indications are clear that proprietary schools and business corporations will play an increasing part in the federal design to broaden the nation's educational effort. This is justified by both social utility (Coleman, 1967) and economic efficiency (Burkett & Allen, 1967). Because these tax-supported programs must be based upon a profit-motivated economy, profit-motivated education no longer seems anomalous.

R. A. Fulton
United Business Schools Assn.

References

Accrediting Commission for Business Schools. *Official Directory of Accredited Institutions and Operating Criteria.* The Commission, 1967.

Arnold, Walter M. *Statement on Vocational Education Amendments to U.S. House of Representative General Subcommittee on Education.* USOE, 1966. 56p.

Bank of America. "Private Vocational Education." *Bank Am Small Bus Reporter* 6:11; 1965.

Benton, William. "The Failure of Business Schools." *Saturday Evening Post* 234:26; 1961.

Burkett, Lowell A., and Allen, Mary P. "Vocational Education." In *Curriculum Handbook for School Administrators.* AASA, 1967. p. 323.

Clark, Harold F., and Sloan, Harold S. *Classrooms on Mainstreet.* Teachers Col, Columbia U, 1966.

Coleman, James S. *Equality of Educational Opportunity.* USOE, 1966.

Coleman, James S. "Toward Open Schools." *Public Interest* 9:20–7; 1967.

Dent, John H. "New U.S. Civil Service Standards for Accounting Technicians," *Balance Sheet.* May, 1965.

Fulton, Richard A. *Unpublished Survey.* United Business School Association, 1963.

Fulton, Richard A. "Under Contract Training in State Federal Programs." *Balance Sheet* 56:349–51; 1965.

Fulton, Richard A. "Post-secondary Business Education . . . In the Independent Business School." *Bus Ed Forum* 21:13–14; 1967.

Gardner, John W. *1967 Education and Training,*

Fifth Annual Report of Secretary of HEW to Congress on MDTA. GPO, 1967.
Gordon, Robert A., and Howell, James E. *Higher Education for Business.* Columbia U Press, 1959.
Hamilton, William J. "The Regulation of Proprietary Schools in the United States," Doctoral dissertation. U Pennsylvania, 1958.
Harper's Weekly "The International Business College Association." *Harper's Weekly* October 13, 1866.
Harrington, Michael. "The Social-industrial Complex." *Harper's M* 235:55–60; 1967.
Hoyt, Kenneth B. *Statement on Higher Education Act of 1965 to U. S. Senate Subcommittee on Education.* GPO, 1965, p. 1082–7.
Hoyt, Kenneth B. "The Vanishing American." *Delta Pi Epsilon J* 9:1–8; 1967.
Ivarie, Ted. "Private Business Schools—Yes and No." *J Bus Ed* 42:138–9; 1967.
James, Edmund J. "Commercial Education." In Butler, Nicholas Murray (Ed.) *Monographs on Education in the United States.* No. 13. J. B. Lyon Co., 1900. p. 653–703.
Johnson, Elouise L. "A Descriptive Survey of Teachers of Private Trade and Technical Schools Associated with the National Association of Trade and Technical Schools." Doctoral dissertation, George Washington U, 1967.
Keppel, Francis. *Statement on Higher Education Act of 1965 to U. S. House of Representatives Special Subcommittee on Education.* GPO, 1965. p. 63–144.
McConnell, Earl L. "University Participation in the Business School." *Balance Sheet* 4:54–5; 1967.
Miller, Jay W. *The Independent Business School in American Education.* McGraw-Hill, 1964.
Oregon Legislature. *Oregon Laws.* Chapter 529, Section 7, 1965.
Oregon Post-High School Study Committee. *Education Beyond the High School—A Projection for Oregon.* Education Coordinating Council, 1966.
Pierson, Frank C. *A Study of University College Programs in Business Administration.* McGraw-Hill, 1959.
Podesta, Edward A. *Supply and Demand Factors Affecting Vocational Education Planning.* Stanford Research Institute, 1966.
Polishook, Morris M. Unpublished Survey. Business Education Research Associates, 1962.
Reigner, Charles G. *Beginnings of the Business School.* H. M. Rowe Co., 1963. 80p.
Rhude, A. Lauren. "Partnership in Training." *U. S. Employment Service R* 3:61; 1966
Scheuer, James H. Address at Eighth Conference for Supervisors of Elementary Education in Large Cities. Washington, D.C., November 13, 1967.
Selden, William K. *Accreditation, A Struggle over Standards in Higher Education.* Harper, 1960.
Sneden, Robert W. *Statement to U. S. Senate, Subcommittee on Education.* GPO, 1964. p. 510–16.
Switzer, Mary E. "Training Handicapped Students for Officer Careers." *Balance Sheet* 66:62–3; 1964.
Thomas, Ellis. "Private Business Schools." *New Jersey Ed Assn R* 40:14–15; 1966.
United Business Schools Association. *The 1967 UBSA Directory of Business Schools.* The Association, 1967.
U. S. Civil Service Commission. *Junior Federal Assistant.* Announcement No. 406. The Commission, 1967.
U. S. Office of Education. "The Job's the Thing." *Am Ed* 3: cover, No. 4; 1967.
U. S. Senate, 88th Congress, 2nd Session, Committee on Labor and Public Welfare. *Amendments to National Defense Education Act and Impacted Areas Legislation.* Report No. 1275. GPO, 1964.
Veigel, Robert E. "Three-way Use Helps to Justify Business School's Computer." *Bus Ed World* 47:12–13; 1966.
Venn, Grant. *Man, Education and Work.* ACE, 1966.
Ways, Max. "The Road to 1977." *Fortune* 75:93; 1967.
Wilkins, Theresa Birch. *Accredited Higher Institutions, 1960.* USOE, 1960. 120p.
Wirtz, Williard W. *1966 Report of the Secretary of Labor on Manpower Research and Training.* GPO, 1966.

PUBLIC RELATIONS

In its formal sense, "public relations" refers to those functions of an educational organization concerned with communicating to the public, or distinct segments of the public, regarding the organization's programs, policies, services, and the like, with the deliberate intent of creating or maintaining favorable public attitudes toward the organization. A second usage of the term denotes the actual state of public sentiment toward the organization—a state presumably eventuating from the organization's communication processes or lack thereof. Since a major problem for research lies in the causal connections between communications and the state of public sentiment, it is critical that the two meanings be kept distinct. We will maintain the distinction by using such phrases for the first meaning as public relations techniques, activities, programs, and so on.

Public relations arises as a problem for an organization when its survival or effective task accomplishment is dependent in some degree upon large, diffuse aggregates of people. In the case of American public education, under the structural arrangement of "local autonomy" that characterizes the system, it is the district residents who constitute the most significant aggregate for the school. The public school depends upon the "good will" of the local citizenry for the allocation of tax funds, for the validation of operational decisions reached by school officials, and for support in a number of ways in carrying out the technical task of instructing pupils. In private schools and in higher education, different publics, generally nonlocalized, are implicated in the organizations' well-being, as for example in financial support or in student recruitment.

This conception of public relations, and the accompanying definitions, assume affirmative answers to two questions of fundamental importance, one a question of empirical reality and the other a question of social philosophy. *Can* the school actively affect its conditions of existence within the community or is it simply a captive of the community's system of social and political control? *Should* the school strive to alter the interests and sentiments of the local citizenry with respect to education or should it attempt to determine community interests and adapt its educational program to serve them? Neither question is directly confronted in the public relations literature, and failure to debate the latter question has given rise to a second conception of public relations among persons inclined to answer it in the negative—a conception whose coexistence with the first gives the field a cast of ambivalence.

The prime impetus for developing the field of public relations has come from practicing administrators and others responsible for the operation of educational programs in schools. They take seriously the task of attempting to cultivate a promotive environment for the organization and, by assuming the responsibility, tacitly accept the proposition that it *is* possible to alter environmental conditions—in particular the sentiments and interests of the local citizenry. They believe it is incumbent on them to engage in the tactics of persuasion and influence (or "education" and "leadership") to protect the interests of the school and of education. The major purpose of public relations research from their perspective is to clarify how it can be done better.

Most of the research reviewed below has been conducted within this technical, or "practical," frame of reference. One must look outside the tradition of public relations research for investigations of the fundamental question itself, of the extent and nature of the community's control over the school. It is apparent that the social and political context of the public school severely conditions the technical task of public relations. Since several lines of contemporary research are examining this context, we shall call attention to them briefly after discussing the history of school public relations.

With respect to the philosophical question, a notable equivocation runs through the public relations literature. School administrators and other spokesmen *act* as though it is not only possible but right to influence public opinion and behavior in the interest of the school's purposes, but they often *talk and write* as though such actions were wrong. Indeed, one powerful philosophical position, which has all but dominated the school–community relations literature since the 1930's, holds that the school must actively shape its own policies and programs to the interests and needs of the local community. This philosophy has the effect, as Corwin pointed out (1965), of maximizing the community's potentiality for controlling the school. In the context of the so-called community school philosophy, public relations requires a definition different from that given above. "Public relations" refers to the efforts of school personnel to assess the interests and opinions among community members in order that organization policies can be made to reflect such expressed interests. Public relations research under this philosophy becomes a matter of systematic information gathering to serve particular and immediate organizational decisions, and it does not pretend to yield generalizable knowledge.

The strain between the "practical" conception of public relations and the "idealistic" position, rarely debated or even acknowledged, is apparent in both the discursive and research writings in the field and can readily be seen within a single paragraph of the same author.

HISTORY OF THE SCHOOL PUBLIC RELATIONS MOVEMENT. A broad-gauged social history covering the genesis and development of the school public relations movement has not yet been written, connecting it within education to such parallel developments as the rise of parent–teacher organizations and the school survey movement or outside of education to the growth and subsequent professionalization of commercial public relations, the development of public opinion polling, and other social, political as well as ideological forces in society. Historical treatments of business and industrial public relations can be found in Bernays (1952), Goldman (1948), and Gras (1945), while Davidson (1956) discussed college and university public relations and Bainbridge (1951) covered school public relations from 1920 to 1948. In a different vein, Magee (1938) explored the public relations-like problems of early American schools.

It is possible, nevertheless, to furnish a cursory account of the movement. Educational public relations apparently blossomed as a self-conscious movement virtually overnight at the close of World War I. A spate of textbooks, journal articles, and reports, as well as a few empirical studies, began to appear on the topic of educational publicity in 1920. Foremost among the writers in these years was Carter Alexander, whose *School Statistics and Publicity* appeared in 1919, followed quickly by a volume reporting publicity techniques employed in some 70 school election campaigns around the country (Alexander & Theisen, 1921). By 1924 a selective bibliography was published listing 116 books and articles on school publicity, only 20 of which had publication dates prior to 1920 (Vogelein, 1924).

Why the sudden interest in school publicity? Almost certainly it was related to the postwar shortage of classroom space to house the booming population of pupils, a situation nearing a national crisis. Schoolmen desperately sought ways of inducing the public to vote the funds required to replace and expand the nation's physical plant. The business community had found a bonanza in advertising during the previous decade, as the mass-circulated newspaper and popular journal came into their own, a fact that professional educators were quick to appreciate. They were further stimulated by enthusiastic commentaries, such as George Creel's *How We Advertised America* (1920), regarding the war-winning role played by publicity, propaganda, and the organized community drive. The direct influence of the business world can be observed in titles of school public relations articles such as "Ads for the Academic," "Selling Education," "Educational Advertising," and so on.

Underlying these momentary influences were certain profound changes that had occurred in the fabric of American society and the character of school systems to create conditions in which public relations was necessary. These included the transformation of the homogeneous community into an urban assemblage of anonymous, mobile individuals (Kimball & McClellan, 1962) and the emergence of educational bureaucracies whose very size made them more and more remote from their constituents. Still the system of local autonomy prevailed, making the schools all the more vulnerable to the whims of the district electorate (Callahan, 1962).

From the 1920's on, the flow of articles, reports, yearbooks, texts, and books of readings on public relations has continued unabated until the volume of writings has now assumed monumental proportions. *Education Index* since its inception in 1929 has covered the literature regularly under the entries of "Publicity," "Public Relations," and "School–Community Relations." Much of the literature consists of recommendations of practices, reports of "successful" techniques, instructions on such matters as preparing newspaper copy or conducting American Education Week, and general encouragements of school personnel to become "public relations-minded." Only a fractional part of the literature is devoted to reports of empirical research in even the loosest sense of the term.

SOCIAL CONTROL OF PUBLIC EDUCATION. Public relations deals with one side of the school–community relationship—the school's effort to influence the community. Such efforts must be carried on within the context of the social and political control exercised by the community and the society at large over the school, and to ignore this larger context is to render public relations an exercise in futility. The topic is a large one, beyond the scope of the present review, but several lines of contemporary research should be noted that have begun to clarify the dimensions of the problems and may eventually lead to a redefinition of the public relations task itself.

It is plain that the public schools in the United States are subject to many powerful influences emanating from beyond the boundaries of the local district (R. Campbell & others, 1965)—influences that may far outweigh those originating from within the immediate environmental setting. Schools are becoming *relatively* less dependent upon the "good will" of the local public. Even among the localized influences, a distinction must be drawn between those that reflect impersonal circumstances of the district, such as economic conditions and demographic forces, and hence incapable of alteration through communication and persuasion, and those that represent interests and attitudes of the local populace. Mort and his students, in studying the adaptability of school systems, separated a "public understanding" or "good will" factor from such factors as size and wealth of the district in an effort to estimate their independent contributions to district variance in adaptability (Ross, 1958). Pierce (1947) referred to the former as "controllable community characteristics," implying that they could be affected through public relations programs. Recent investigations, to be reviewed more fully later, raise doubts regarding the amenability of the attitudinal processes underlying "public understanding" to persuasion attempts. One remarkable study conducted in a Detroit suburb (Smith & others, 1964) suggests that the changes in citizen support for the schools resulting from public relations efforts ("contrived changes") were small in comparison with "natural changes" associated with the in-migration of new residents. Carter and Suttoff (1960) have argued that the issue is not one of the general public's "understanding" but rather the level of "understanding" among community leaders plus the existence of effective mediating agencies between leaders and the rank-and-file citizen.

James (1964) and Jenson and Staub (1961) review studies that center directly on the processes of political and social control over school policies. The research on community power structure (Bloomberg & Sunshine, 1963; Kimbrough, 1964) raises the question, but by no means settles it, regarding the conditions under which it is worthwhile at all for the school to deal with the general public as opposed to small coteries of local power wielders. The growing body of research on the political linkages of the school board (Cronin, 1966; Lutz, 1962; Minar, 1966), as well as on the internal dynamics of board decision making (Cunningham, 1959), raises the same question. The superintendents' role in mediating cross-pressures arising within the community (Gross, 1958; Gross & others, 1958) draws attention to other, potentially countervailing factors in the community's control of the school, including professional associations of teachers and of administrators and the bureaucratic character of the school organization itself (Corwin, 1965).

The principal lesson from the foregoing research is that we must not expect vast improvements in the school's environmental conditions to flow simply and directly from programs designed to influence the attitudes and interests of the general public.

NATURE OF THE EMPIRICAL RESEARCH. The school public relations movement has neither stimulated the production of empirical research, except among doctoral students, nor drawn on research in adjacent fields, although there are recent signs of change especially in this latter regard (Educational Policies Commission, 1958; Kindred, 1965). We will devote attention to some lines of relevant social science research at the end of the review. Experience and ideology have been the prime sources of inspiration for the discursive writings in the field. Textbooks, for example, rarely cite empirical studies in support of contentions and certainly do not cite investigations casting doubt on them.

Several bibliographies of public relations research are available in addition to the early ones of Alexander and his students (Alexander, 1928; Morris & others, 1928) and the regular surveys of the field in the *Review of Educational Research* from 1930 on, but they can be disregarded in favor of the detailed and comprehensive treatment of the research literature through the middle 1950's to be found in Pearson's dissertation (1956). His appendix contains 200 abstracts of studies, usually reported in sufficient detail to determine the procedures, populations, and central findings of the research.

As Pearson points out, the research mainly has been concerned with what was being done rather than the effectiveness of what was done in public relations. The studies that have examined the empirical link between techniques and the consequences intended for them in the public are sufficiently few that we have reported them in a separate section. The research has also been predominantly oriented to practices and techniques of public relations, and it is only since about 1960 that careful investigations have appeared concerning the targets of public relations efforts. The vast majority of studies over 50 years are of two kinds: *normative surveys*, or collections of professional opinion on the value of techniques and programs; and *status studies*, describing some set of circumstances related to public relations at a particular time and place. They deserve brief comment.

Normative Surveys. The most ubiquitous and in some ways the most curious research tradition in school public relations is one in which the investigator assembles a list of public relations techniques from the discursive literature and submits the list to some authoritative jury to rate with respect to their relative "effectiveness." When the returns are in, the investigator compiles the ratings statistically to rank-order the techniques according to their judged effectiveness and ineffectiveness. Miller's study (1943) was one of the more ambitious of this sort. The investigator, further, may list the techniques judged to be effective on a "score card" and administer it, perhaps in self-rating form, in a population of school systems, eliciting information on the presence or absence of the activities, and then evaluate the school systems in the effectiveness of their public relations programs.

The curiousness of the tradition resides in its practice of substituting consensus of opinion about cause–effect linkages for empirical demonstration of the linkages. It avoids testing whether or not, in fact, a given technique, X, leads to a definitive consequence, Y, in the attitudes or behavior of the public and rests its case on popular agreement that X does lead to Y. The ubiquity of this form of research has had an unfortunate result: there is no pressure on researchers to specify particular consequences in the public that they expect to ensue from the several public relations activities. It is left to the juries to invoke whatever implicit conceptions of "effectiveness" they choose. The entire literature on school public relations is devoid of concern for operational definitions of expected consequences, and authors' recommendations of activities and techniques or assertions regarding their worth are rarely phrased in a form amenable to empirical validation.

Status Studies. Descriptive studies have covered a bewildering array of matters related to school public relations, such as the communication media employed by schools, citizen opinions on particular school affairs, the organized groups with which the schools work, forms used to report pupil progress to parents, the distribution and readability of the superintendent's annual report, and the like, but their limited power to yield generalizable knowledge precludes their systematic review here. Pearson's dissertation (1956) provides satisfactory coverage. We will, nevertheless, refer to some of their more dependable findings in later sections.

Public Opinion Instruments. Considering the emphasis placed on the assessment of public opinion in the philosophy of school–community relations, it is surprising that so little research has been conducted on matters of methodology or so little sophistication has been imported from the social sciences. While the techniques of population sampling seem to be familiar to public relations researchers, the methodological developments in opinion and attitude measurement for the most part are not.

Some substantial efforts have been made to construct questionnaire instruments that have general applicability in measuring what people want from their schools and what they think they are getting (Hand, 1948), the level of "public understanding" of education (Ross, 1958), a variety of "school–community attitudes" (Bullock, 1959), views on the various "tasks of public education" (Downey, 1960), and "progressive–traditional attitudes" toward education (Kerlinger, 1958). These instruments, however, have not been subjected to the extensive and critical methodological analysis that are required to justify widespread use.

EFFECTS OF PUBLIC RELATIONS ACTIVITIES. The results of the handful of studies that have sought objective evidence regarding the effects of school public relations activities should make those who recommend the various techniques, activities, and practices less than sanguine. Simpson's study (1964) of the scope of public relations programs in 67 school systems in the Detroit area sets the tone. He found a *zero* correlation between program scope (measured by the presence or absence of 10 frequently recommended techniques) and an index of the number of school elections defeated. Considering the great variety of factors affecting the electorate's support of the schools and the crudity of his study, the finding is hardly surprising. He introduced only one control in his correlation, the density of population. Nevertheless, Simpson's results demonstrate the gratuitousness of expecting public relations activities of a few school personnel to be such a powerful source of influence on the public that all other influences pale in comparison.

The studies of effectiveness fall into three groups: (1) teacher relations with parents, (2) the transmission of information to citizens, and (3) citizen participation in school study committees.

Teacher Relations with Parents. Studies of teacher relations with parents deal with the effects of the kind of pupil reporting scheme used (Mann & others, 1966), kinds of parent conferences (Grant, 1962; Kitchens, 1961; Schiff, 1963), and home visits of teachers (McCutcheon, 1965). Most of these investigations are concerned as much with the effects on student achievement and behavior as on the attitudes and opinions of parents. *No* difference in effects on parent attitudes were found to be associated with an anecdotal vs. a regular pupil reporting scheme (Mann & others, 1966) or an intensive program of parent conferences vs. the usual school contacts (Schiff, 1963). Kitchens (1961) noted a *decline* in favorability associated with the simple presence as opposed to absence of parent conferences, and Grant reported a similar decline resulting from parent conferences in which teachers were instructed to furnish parents with global information about the school and its educational program. *Positive* consequences in parent attitudes were associated with two home visits by teachers vs. no home visits (McCutcheon, 1965) and with parent conferences in which teachers were trained in advance to interpret information about the child (Kitchens, 1961). Teacher participation in community organizations was no greater in Ohio school districts rated as "strong" in public acceptance of the educational program than in districts rated as "weak" in public acceptance (Armitage, 1960). Results from the above studies with regard to pupil achievement and behavior are equally as mixed.

Transmission of School Information to Citizens. Experimental studies of information transmission have tended to examine alternative techniques for communicating a single, pointed message to citizens, but one investigator studied the consequences of a school survey that had been vigorously publicized through a broad range of communications media over a nine-month period (Charters, 1954). No discernible changes could be found in a sample of community residents with respect to attitudes toward the schools, evaluations of the schools, criteria used for evaluation, or kinds of criticism leveled at the schools. In fact, one-half of the sample reported either that they had never heard of the school survey or that they had not followed it as it was being conducted. These pessimistic results duplicate findings on an unusually extensive publicity campaign to make Cincinnati "United Nations-conscious" (Star & Hughes, 1950) and are in keeping with the various sets of data outside of education reported by Hyman and Sheatsley (1957).

In a study of narrower scope, Hein (1947) reported changes in health practices among students that seemed to be associated with an intensive educational campaign directed to their parents. Sigband (1956) in a controlled experiment found some increases in citizen knowledge about a junior college that resulted from receipt of mailed bulletins but relatively small effects on their opinions about the college, and similarly Grout (1956) discovered changes in amount of knowledge about a school system's reading program as a consequence of four articles in a weekly newspaper, particularly when citizens received a letter from the superintendent commending the articles to them, but less impact on opinions about reading programs.

Both Pino (1965) and Zeller (1959) compared the efficiency of transmitting messages to parents orally (through children in Pino's case and directly to parents at PTA meetings in Zeller's case) with sending them home in written form with children. Slight superiority for written messages was found in parents' subsequent knowledge of message content. The most striking finding in the two studies was Zeller's discovery that "opinion leaders" among the parents were overwhelmingly more likely to have been exposed to the message and more effectively exposed, in the sense of being able to reproduce the message contents accurately, than non-leaders.

Citizen Participation in School Study Groups. In McLaughlin's study (1960) random samples of residents were no more favorable toward schools nor had higher levels of knowledge in two districts that had been through citizens' self-survey of the schools than in five districts without the self-surveys. Harris (1958) found little more opinion change on school issues among parents serving on elementary school committees than among nonparticipating parents from the same community, although there was some indication that greater change occurred among participants with no prior experience in school activities.

While it is generally true that these experimental studies of effectiveness are negative in their implications, it must also be noted that with one or two exceptions they do not exhibit the methodological sophistication to make them adequate tests of the hypotheses.

COMMUNICATION MEDIA AND PROCESSES. The oldest line of public relations research, albeit almost totally descriptive, has been on devices for communicating between school and home. Well before 1920 the superintendent's annual report was a topic of commentary and occasional study, but from 1920 on the attention of researchers has fastened on the public press. Pinnie's dissertation (1965) offers a useful summary of research both in and out of education on communication media relevant to school public relations. In recent years there has been a spread of research interest to the conditions under which community residents receive messages from the mass media and elsewhere, including informal sources.

School News and Parent Interests. Investigations of space devoted to education in the news and editorial columns of the public press are common in the literature, running from the early studies of Garlin and Pittenger (1921) and Reynolds (1922) up to the comprehensive, cross-cultural research of Gerbner (1964). One finding consistently emerges from the content studies: athletics and student activities dominate the space devoted to education, and such matters as curricular programs, teaching methods, school organization and finance, and educational goals are given short shrift (Pearson, 1956).

The import of the finding, in the view of educators, is that the press is devoting greatest attention to those topics least likely to promote a rounded public understanding of the schools. Local editors are inclined to reply that they are "giving the public what it wants." Farley (1929) approached this contention directly. He compared the order of interest in 13 items of school news among 5,000 parents with the order of space accorded them in the public press and observed an inverse relationship. The subject of extra-curricular affairs, for example, highest in the amount of news space, was lowest in parent interest. Thomas's (1944) replication of Farley's study confirmed the negative correlation. The question remains, of course, whether or not a redistribution of newspaper space would have an appreciable effect on public understanding.

A number of investigators have asked parents what they were interested in knowing about the schools, including Peters (1920) many years ago, but one of the most useful studies is that of Stout and Langdon (1957). They held unstructured interviews in some 900 homes on the single question, "What do you want to know about your child's school?" By eschewing statistical summaries in favor of topical discussion of their findings, they convey a realistic impression of the subjects about which parents are curious and thereby give the public relations practitioner food for thought.

Although not focused specifically on parent interest in schools, the Jenkins and Lippitt study (1951) of parent misperceptions of teachers and teacher misperceptions of parents should be noted here. The study has become something of a classic in the field, partly because it is the only one of its kind. Forbes (1955) missed an opportunity to check the replicability of their findings in his study of parent–teacher "empathy," despite the fact that he used methods similar to theirs. Jenkins and Lippitt disclosed a variety of erroneous impressions that parents and teachers held of one another and argued that misperceptions could be minimized by reducing barriers to communication between the parties. While the social-psychological basis for their argument is substantial (Newcomb, 1947), research has also shown that communication between people does not automatically reduce misperceptions or improve attitudes (Bruner & Tagiuri, 1954; Harding & others, 1954).

Power of the Press. An occasional attempt has been made to assess the impact of the public press on school issues within particular communities (Beck, 1954; Cohn, 1959; Shipton, 1956). (Also see the section above on the transmission of school information to citizens.) It is clear from social scientists' research on the mass media, however, that questions about the power of the press must be asked in far more differentiated form than they usually are. Except in the experimental laboratory, people are practically never exposed to just one source of persuasive influence, and it is a complicated affair to untangle the importance of one source from the multiplicity of others and to weigh their relative contributions to each of several different kinds of impact they might have (Katz & Lazarsfeld, 1955). In any event, students of mass communication suggest that the greatest persuasive effects are realized by supplementing the acknowledged efficiency of the press, or other mass media, in disseminating messages widely with the power of informal social contacts in getting messages noticed, accepted, and acted on (Klapper, 1960; Pool, 1965).

Sources of Information about Schools. A few investigators in the 1940's and early 1950's began asking parents and others directly about their usual sources of local school information. When the question is put to parents in a general way, such as "How do you find out what is going on in the schools?" without specifying any particular kind of information, one of the most frequently mentioned sources, if not *the* most frequent, is "the children" (Illini Survey Associates, 1948; Purdy, 1955; Van Winkle, 1956; Volgamore, 1943). This finding has lent support to the most prominent cliché in the public relations literature—that the student is the school's best public relations agent.

Subsequent investigation has indicated that the finding must be severely qualified. Different channels of communication are used depending upon the topic of school information. Dennis (1954) reported that citizens secured most of their information about a school-district-reorganization proposal from fellow citizens, not from students, and Carter's figures (1960) show that students rarely were involved in exchanges with adults regarding a pending school-bond election. Apparently parents take the question "How do you find out what is going on?" to mean "in the classroom." Under that inference they will respond, "through children." Carter's data (1960) show clearly the difference in sources of information elicited by questions specifying the topic of information and unspecified questions.

Another finding of Carter's, which is consonant with results outside of education, should make one wary of uncritical generalization from research. Different channels of communication are elicited from respondents when asked about their *actual* communication behavior ("Where *do* you get your information?") and when asked about *hypothetical* communication behavior ("Where *would* you go for information?"). Carter showed that 71 percent of his respondents *would* ask teachers and school officers for information they wanted about the schools, but only 8 percent *usually do* get information from these sources.

Informal Channels of Communication. As investigators have begun to attend directly to the communication behavior of citizens, their studies have pointed up the tremendous import of informal, person-to-person channels of information and influence as contrasted with the formal and impersonal channels, such as the mass media, school publications, conferences, speeches, open houses, and the like. Surprisingly, personal contacts and friendships between community citizens and school personnel have been little studied even at a purely descriptive level apart from the global reports of teachers concerning their participation in community affairs (Greenhoe, 1941; National Education Association, 1957, 1959). Correll's investigation (1963) of the frequency over a month's period of parent-initiated contacts with various categories of school personnel, from custodians to board members, stands virtually alone. He demonstrated a strong, positive relationship between frequency of contact and social-class level of parents but also a pervasive bias among parents toward contacting personnel at a level in the school hierarchy commensurate with their own social-class level. Thus, lower-class parents sought out custodians and cooks, while upper-class parents contacted board members. Foskett's (1955) study supports the positive relationship between social class and frequency of contact with school personnel.

In the Foskett studies (1955, 1956), as elsewhere (Carter, 1960; Dennis, 1954; Merrill, 1953), the prime sources of information and exchange with regard to school matters are the citizen's friends, relatives, and neighbors, typically overshadowing in frequency contacts with school personnel as well as with the more formal channels of communication. The importance of this observation (Charters, 1955; Merrill, 1955), heavily supported by substantial research in the social sciences (Katz & Lazarsfeld, 1955; Klapper, 1960; Schramm, 1954), has hardly begun to enter into thinking about the task of school public relations.

THE PUBLIC'S SUPPORT OF EDUCATION. If the goal of school public relations is to have an effect on attributes of the public—on knowledge, attitudes, or behavior—it is of more than passing interest to understand the conditions and forces that make these attributes what they are. In spite of the large number of public opinion and attitude surveys conducted in education over the years (e.g., National Education Association, 1958), greater illumination of the forces determining public inclinations appears to be emerging from the recent investigations of school elections and voter behavior.

A few investigators have examined factors contributing to the success or failure of school-bond and school-tax elections by means of aggregate statistics (Edmiston & Holcomb, 1942; Shannon, 1958; Smith, 1953), including the large-scale study of the influence of the size of voter turnout on election success (Carter & Savard, 1961). Data in the latter study showed an inverse (and slightly curvilinear) relationship between the probability of success and turnout size. This relationship suggested the hypothesis that a school district's electorate consists of a small group of confirmed supporters of the school, the first to be activated in an election, another small group of hard-core opponents, the second to be activated, and a large group of indifferent citizens who rarely or never vote. The hypothesis calls attention to the importance of understanding relatively stable and enduring orientations of citizens toward the schools rather than transient opinions or information about issues of the moment.

A number of interview studies in the last few years, examining citizen attitudes and behavior patterns toward schools, have begun to shed light on the social determinants of enduring orientations in the public (Agger, 1960; Busch & Deutschmann, 1955; Carter, 1960; Foskett, 1954, 1955; Foskett & Goldhammer, 1959; Giaudrone, 1955; Greenberg, 1965; Hyman, 1953; Litchfield, 1963; Shipton & Belisle, 1956; Smith & others, 1964; Suttoff, 1960). Results of these studies typically are reported in the form of zero-order relationships between attitudes, school participation, or voting behavior on the one hand and such population attributes as age, occupation, educational attainment, income, children in school, home ownership, religious affiliation, and length of community residence on the other hand. Rather than attempting to report the disparate and sometimes inconsistent relationships, we will draw out two strands that seem to integrate many of the findings, at least insofar as the correlational data permit such interpretation.

First, a citizen's orientation toward a strong local public school system is a function of his *vested interests* in (1) the financial costs of education, a negative factor, and (2) the economic and social benefits of the school system to himself and his family, a positive factor. His vested interests in turn are determined by his location within the economic and social structure of society. Location is not to be construed as socioeconomic level but rather in the Marxian sense of class and class interests (Mayer, 1953). Thus, opposition to the public schools is often found among middle-income landowners, urban or agrarian, whose children are out of school or whose children are in parochial schools—persons on whom the tax burden falls with little direct benefit to them. Support for the public schools, on the other hand, is consistently high in younger members of the professional and managerial classes, since entry of their children into such classes requires extensive higher education and, hence, solid public school preparation. Schools are also supported in certain lower-middle-income groups where education is seen as instrumental to the high mobility aspirations of their members (Rosen, 1959). While the data are absent on this, the same reasoning would lead us to expect strong support for schools in those particular sectors of industry and commerce whose economic well-being depends, for example, upon a school system capable of attracting technicians and professional-level employees; and opposition to the schools could be expected in sectors bearing a heavy local tax burden and requiring a source of cheap labor.

The second determinant of orientation to the local schools is the degree of the resident's *estrangement* from the social and political structure of the community. While estrangement, or alienation, is known to be inversely related to socioeconomic level, there is evidence indicating that it exerts an independent effect on degree of citizen support for the schools (Thompson & Horton, 1960). Shipton and Belisle

(1956), having constructed a scale of citizen agreement with stereotyped criticisms of education, found two measures of the respondent's relation to his social milieu to be powerful predictors of acceptance of the criticisms: a low sense of political efficacy and a high level of anomie. Knill (1960) virtually duplicated the findings in Oregon. The converse of estrangement is integration in the interaction and communication systems of the community, and several investigators have found high levels of community participation predictive of favorable attitudes and affirmative voting on school matters (Smith & others, 1964).

Some studies, however, warn against assuming too readily that citizen orientation is a unitary, internally consistent phenomenon. Haak (1956), for example, pointed out that a high level of information about schools does not necessarily go along with favorable opinions: nearly one-third of the Michigan citizens he studied held favorable opinions of the schools but were uninformed. Shipton and Belisle (1956) showed that a citizen's agreement with generalized criticisms of education was in no way predictive of his evaluation of the local schools. Smith and his colleagues urged that a distinction be drawn between latent and manifest support of the schools —between attitudes toward school issues and overt behavior, such as participating in school affairs or voting—on the grounds that the two are governed by different social forces and do not necessarily exist in a one-to-one relation. A community may have a high level of latent support among its residents but low manifest support. Just such a condition was detected through survey research techniques in sections of Birmingham, Michigan, before a millage election and was corrected by sharply pointed public relations efforts (Smith & others, 1964). A roughly parallel distinction was used in Busch and Deutschmann's (1955) investigation of California voters.

BEHAVIORAL SCIENCE RESEARCH. As practitioners of school public relations (and textbook authors and researchers as well) shift from a preoccupation with practices and techniques to a broader concern for the social and psychological circumstances of the people who are the targets of the efforts, they will encounter a vast array of relevant research in the behavioral sciences that has accumulated during half a century. Undoubtedly the principal contribution of this research, as matters now stand, is a negative one from the practitioner's standpoint. It demonstrates the complexity and strength of the various forces that govern human sentiments and behavior and points up the comparative feebleness of the tools with which the school must work. It would certainly controvert many of the implicit assumptions regarding the determinants of attitudes and behavior on which programs of public relations currently rest.

The most that can be done here in reviewing relevant behavioral science research is to note some contemporary areas of activity and to furnish references opening the door to further reading.

Mass Communication. Investigations in the mass media began before the turn of the century and by now have achieved an extremely broad range of research coverage (Hovland, 1954; Klapper, 1960; Larsen, 1964; Schramm, 1962, 1963). One finding relevant to the study of public relations that has emerged time and again from field studies is the high degree of self-selectivity in exposure of people to mass communication efforts. It is typically the case that the very persons who are the intended targets of change efforts are the least likely to expose themselves to the messages designed to influence them (Cartwright, 1949). Studies have elucidated, further, the extent to which people will go, when members of a captive audience, to shield themselves from the influence of messages contrary to their deeply held beliefs, even to the extent of misperceiving the point of the message and thinking it supports their beliefs.

Personal Influence. The work of Paul Lazarsfeld and his colleagues has emphasized the role of informal social relationships—the primary groups of friends and associates—in mediating mass communication effects on the individual (Katz & Lazersfeld, 1955). These investigators have advanced the "two-step flow of influence" hypothesis, which proposes that mass communication achieves its effects, when it has any, first by impinging upon one or more key individuals in the primary groups, the "opinion leaders," and then through them upon rank-and-file members of the groups (E. Katz, 1957; Lazarsfeld & Menzel, 1963). Or when messages impinge directly on the rank-and-file member, they require validation through group interaction in which opinion leaders play a central part.

The Lazersfeld group draws heavily on the social psychology of group processes and attitudes, aptly summarized through the middle 1950's in Part I of the Katz and Lazarsfeld volume (1955). The social-psychological research indicates that a person's attitudes are formed in the context of social groups and are often instrumental to him in maintaining valued social relationships; moreover, consensus in certain attitudes and opinions among group members is a matter of substantial import to the group itself. Thus, an individual's attitudes and opinions cannot be conceived as purely private phenomena.

The lesson research on personal influence holds for public relations practitioners is that efforts to change attitudes and behavior must contend with the powerful force of the social group in which attitudes and behavior are anchored. At the same time, the research point out the strategic importance of the opinion leader in the process of inducing change (Zeller, 1959).

Voting Behavior. While Lazarsfeld delved into voting behavior in his early studies of personal influence (Lazarsfeld & others, 1948; Berelson & others, 1954), political scientists, sociologists, and public opinion experts have been studying the behavioral processes in elections from a different standpoint. An important backlog of knowledge has accumulated concerning the determinants of voting in national and local elections largely through the application of survey research techniques and other analytical devices (Burdick & Brodbeck, 1959; A. Campbell & others, 1960).

Attitude and Attitude Change. The field of social psychology currently is investing much of its research energies in experimental studies of persuasion, conformity, social influence, and generally in attitude change. Two recent reviews give a picture of the extent of this activity and the kinds of theoretical issues under debate (McGuire, 1966; Muscovici, 1963), while Daniel Katz (1965) offers a modest report of some fruits of the research in the course of a school–community relations seminar. Some of the impetus for research grew out of the experimental studies of Carl Hovland during World War II and continued by Hovland at Yale University in subsequent years (Hovland, 1963). His early discovery that measurable changes in opinion could be produced in experimental settings by movies, lectures, pamphlets, and the like, enabled him and his co-workers to vary systematically a wide variety of experimental conditions in order to examine their relative effects.

Of especial importance to public relations practitioners are the studies that indicate the significance in persuasion of audience perceptions of the source of communication—perceptions of the communicator's credibility, trustworthiness, and impartiality. Hovland (1959) examined the question of disparity between results of laboratory studies of persuasion, where opinion change regularly was achieved, and findings of field studies, where change was rarely observed. He developed a theory of attitude change featuring, as a central component, the amount of discrepancy perceived by the audience member between his own attitudinal position and the position advocated by the communicator (Hovland & others, 1957; Sherif & Hovland, 1961).

Competing theories of attitude change have developed in association with such terms as balance theory, symmetry, cognitive dissonance, and so on, well summarized by Cohen (1964), which postulate change in attitude as one of several possible consequences ensuing from a psychological inconsistency between an attitude toward an object and information about it, behavior with respect to it, or attraction to other people who have opposite attitudes toward it. Some writers have marked these theoretical and experimental developments as the "breakthrough" of social psychology. One cardinal implication of the research is the contradiction of a standard dictum in educational circles: "In order to change a person's behavior, his attitudes must first be changed." Investigation shows, on the contrary, that attitude change will *follow* a change in behavior under appropriate conditions. Besides the references cited above, the reader can gain entrée to the area of attitude change through the Summer 1960 issue of the *Public Opinion Quarterly*, devoted exclusively to the topic (D. Katz, 1960).

Consumer Psychology. A final area of investigation to be noted, representing a relatively discrete tradition from the foregoing, is in advertising research and consumer psychology. The Lucas and Britt textbook (1950) compiles the older research, while Twedt's review (1965) indicates the lines of contemporary study.

W. W. Charters
University of Oregon

References

Agger, Robert E. "The Politics of Education: A Comparative Study in Community Decision Making." In Tope, Donald E. (Ed.) *A Forward Look —The Preparation of School Administrators, 1970.* Bureau Educational Research U Oregon, 1960. p. 131–72.

Alexander, Carter. *School Statistics and Publicity.* Silver, 1919. 332p.

Alexander, Carter. "Research in Educational Publicity." *Teach Col Rec* 29:479–87; 1928.

Alexander, Carter, and Theisen, W. W. *Publicity Campaigns for School Support.* Harcourt, 1921. 164p.

Armitage, Russell C. "A Study of the Community Participation of Teachers from Selected Schools in Ohio." Doctoral dissertation. Ohio State U, 1960.

Bainbridge, F. S., II. "The Growth and Development of Public Relations in Public Secondary Schools of the United States, 1920–1948." Doctoral dissertation. Indiana U, 1951. 298p.

Beck, John. "The Public Schools and the Chicago Newspapers: 1890–1920." Doctoral dissertation. U Chicago, 1954.

Berelson, Bernard R., and others. *Voting.* U Chicago Press, 1954. 395p.

Bernays, Edward L. *Public Relations.* U Chicago Press, 1952. 374p.

Bloomberg, Warner, Jr., and Sunshine, Morris. *Suburban Power Structures and Public Education.* Syracuse U Press, 1963. 177p.

Bruner, Jerome S., and Tagiuri, Renato. "The Perception of People." In Lindzey, Gardner. (Ed.) *Handbook of Social Psychology,* Vol. 2. Addison, 1954. p. 634–54.

Bullock, Robert P. *School-community Attitude Analysis for Educational Administrators.* School Community Development Study, Monogr No. 7, Ohio State U, 1959. 112p.

Burdick, Eugene, and Brodbeck, Arthur J. (Eds.) *American Voting Behavior.* Free, 1959.

Busch, Chilton R., and Deutschmann, Paul F. *The Inter-relationships of Attitudes toward Schools and Voting Behavior in a School Bond Election.* Department Commerce and Journalism, Stanford U, 1955.

Callahan, Raymond E. *Education and the Cult of Efficiency.* U Chicago Press, 1962. 273p.

Campbell, Angus, and others. *The American Voter.* Wiley, 1960.

Campbell, Roald F., and others. *The Organization and Control of American Schools.* Charles E. Merrill Books, 1965. 553p.

Carter, Richard F. *Voters and Their Schools.* Cooperative Research Project No. 308, USOE, 1960. 311p.

Carter, Richard F., and Savard, William G. *Influence of Voter Turnout on School Bond and Tax Elections.* Cooperative Research Monogr No. 5, USOE, 1961. 31p.

Carter, Richard F., and Suttoff, John. *Communities and Their Schools.* Cooperative Research Project No. 308, USOE, 1960. 228p.

Cartwright, Dorwin. "Some Principles of Mass Persuasion." *Hum Relations* 2:253–67; 1949.

Charters, W. W., Jr. "In a Public Relations Program Facts Are Never Enough." *Nation's Sch* 53, February: 56–8; 1954.

Charters, W. W., Jr. "Person-to-Person Influence." *Nation's Sch* 56, November: 49–52; 1955.

Cohen, Arthur R. *Attitude Change and Social Influence.* Basic Books, 1964. 156p.

Cohn, Adrian A. "The Relationship of a Community Newspaper to the Educational Problems of Its Community." Doctoral dissertation. U Wisconsin, 1959.

Correll, Nolan E. "*The Effect of Social Class on Communications with the Public School System.*" Doctoral dissertation. Washington U, 1963.

Corwin, Ronald G. *A Sociology of Education.* Appleton, 1965. 454p.

Creel, George W. *How We Advertised America.* Harper, 1920. 466p.

Cronin, Joseph M. "The Selection of School Board Members in 'Great Cities.'" *Adm Notebook* 14, February: 1–4; 1966.

Cunningham, Luverne L. "The Process of Educational Policy Development." *Adm Notebook* 7, January: 1–4; 1959.

Davidson, Robert C. "The Growth and Development of Public Relations Programs in American Colleges and Universities." Doctoral dissertation. U Southern California, 1956. 208p.

Dennis, David M. "Public Relations Programs in Local School District Reorganization." Doctoral dissertation. U Nebraska, 1954.

Downey, Lawrence W. *The Task of Public Education.* Midwest Administration Center, U Chicago, 1960. 88p.

Edmiston, Robert W., and Holcomb, James R. "Some Factors Favoring the Passage of School Bond Issues." *Am Sch Bd J* 104, January: 54; 1942.

Educational Policies Commission. *Mass Communication and Education.* NEA, AASA, 1958. 137p.

Farley, Belmont M. *What to Tell the People about Public Schools.* Teachers Col, Columbia U, 1929. 136p.

Forbes, Robert J. "Aspects of School-Community Tension." Doctoral dissertation. Claremont Graduate School, 1955. 311p.

Foskett, John M. "New Facts and Figures about Lay Participation." *Nations Sch* 54, August: 63–6; 1954.

Foskett, John M. "Who Discusses School Affairs?" *Sch Executive* 11, February: 79–81; 1955.

Foskett, John M. "Differential Discussion of School Affairs." *Phi Delta Kappan* 37:311–5; 1956.

Foskett, John M., and Goldhammer, Keith. "Characteristics of Voters and Nonvoters in School Elections." *Oregon Sch Stud Council B* 3(2); 1959. 21p.

Garlin, R. E., and Pittenger, B. F. "Educational Publicity in a Daily Newspaper." *Am Sch Bd J* 63, December:41–2; 1921.

Gerbner, George. *Mass Communications and Popular Conceptions of Education: A Cross-cultural Study.* Cooperative Research Project No. 876, USOE, 1964. 1964.

Giaudrone, Angelo. "Research into Social Relationships and 'Interest' in Schools." *Sch Executive* 74, March: 109–14; 1955.

Goldman, Eric F. *Two-way Street.* Billman Publishing Co., 1948. 23p.

Grant, Robert T. "The Effectiveness of Structured Parent-Teacher Conferences on Parental Attitudes toward Schools." Doctoral dissertation. Stanford U, 1962.

Gras, N. S. B. "Shifts in Public Relations." *B Bus Hist Soc* 19:3–49; 1945.

Greenberg, Bradley S. "Voting Intentions, Election Expectations and Exposure to Campaign Information." *J Communication* 15:149–60; 1965.

Greenhoe, Florence. *Community Contacts and Participation of Teachers.* American Council on Public Affairs, 1941.

Gross, Neal. *Who Runs Our Schools?* Wiley, 1958. 195p.

Gross, Neal, and others. *Explorations in Role Analysis: Studies of the School Superintendency Role.* Wiley, 1958. 379p.

Grout, W. Stuart. "Interpreting Education through the Local Newspaper." *Adm Notebook* 5, October: 1–4; 1956.

Haak, Leo A. "The General Public and the Public Schools." *Adm Notebook* 4, April: 1–4; 1956.

Hand, Harold. *What People Think about Their Schools.* Harcourt, 1948.

Harding, John, and others. "Prejudice and Ethnic Relations." In Lindzey, Gardner. (Ed.) *Handbook of Social Psychology,* Vol. 2. Addison, 1954. p. 1021–61.

Harris, Benjamin M. "Parental Committee Participation and Opinions about School Issues." Doctoral dissertation. U California, Berkeley, 1958.

Hein, Fred V. "A Study of Some Means of Presenting Information to Parents about the School Health Program." *J Exp Ed* 15:304–13; 1947.

Hovland, Carl I. "Effects of the Mass Media of Communication." In Lindzey, Gardner. (Ed.) *Handbook of Social Psychology,* Vol. 2. Addison, 1954. p. 1062–103.

Hovland, Carl I. "Reconciling Conflicting Results Derived from Experimental and Survey Studies of Attitude Change." *Am Psychologist* 14:8–17; 1959.

Hovland, Carl I. "Yale Studies of Communication and Persuasion." In Charters, W. W., Jr., and Gage, N. L. (Eds.) *Readings in the Social Psychology of Education.* Allyn and Bacon, 1963. p. 239–53.

Hovland, Carl I., and others. "Assimilation and Contrast Effects in Reactions to Communication and Attitude Change." *J Abn Soc Psychol* 55:244–52; 1957.

Hyman, Herbert H. "The Value Systems of Different Classes: A Social Psychological Contribution to the Analysis of Stratification." In Bendix, Reinhard, and Lipset, Seymour Martin. (Eds.) *Class, Status and Power*. Free, 1953. p. 426–42.

Hyman, Herbert H., and Sheatsley, Paul B. "Some Reasons Why Information Campaigns Fail." *Public Opin Q* 11:412–23; 1957.

Illini Survey Associates. *A Look at Springfield Schools*. Col Education, U Illinois, 1948. 247p.

James, H. Thomas. "Institutional Character of Education: Government and Politics." *R Ed Res* 34:405–23; 1964.

Jenkins, David H., and Lippitt, Ronald. *Interpersonal Perceptions of Teachers, Students, and Parents*. NEA, 1951. 119p.

Jenson, Theodore J., and Staub, W. Frederick. "School-Community Relations." *R Ed Res* 31:406–16; 1961.

Katz, Daniel. (Ed.) "Attitude Change." *Public Opin Q* 24:163–365; 1960.

Katz, Daniel. "Psychological Studies of Communication and Persuasion." In Kindred, Leslie W. (Ed.) *A Seminar on Communications Research Findings and Their Implications for School-Community Relations*. Temple U, 1965. p. 58–79.

Katz, Elihu. "The Two-step Flow of Communications: An Up-to-Date Report on an Hypothesis." *Public Opin Q* 21:61–78; 1957.

Katz, Elihu, and Lazarsfeld, Paul F. *Personal Influence*. Free, 1955. 396p.

Kerlinger, Fred N. "Progressivism and Traditionalism: Basic Factors of Educational Attitudes." *J Social Psychol* 48:111–35; 1958.

Kimball, Solon T., and McClellan, James E. *Education and the New America*. Random, 1962. 402p.

Kimbrough, Ralph B. *Political Power and Educational Decision-making*. Rand McNally, 1964. 307p.

Kindred, Leslie W. (Ed.) *A Seminar on Communications Research Findings and Their Implications for School-Community Relations*. Temple U, 1965. 238p.

Kitchens, Claud E. "The Parent-Teacher Conference as an Instrument for Changing Parent Perceptions of Attitudes toward Schools and Teachers." Doctoral dissertation. U South Carolina, 1961.

Klapper, Joseph T. *The Effects of Mass Communication*. Free, 1960. 302p.

Knill, William D. *An Analysis of Attitudes Toward the Public Schools*. Doctoral dissertation. U Oregon, 1960.

Larsen, Otto N. "Social Effects of Mass Communication." In Faris, Robert E. L. (Ed.) *Handbook of Modern Sociology*. Rand McNally, 1964. p. 349–81.

Lazarsfeld, Paul F., and Menzel, Herbert. "Mass Media and Personal Influence." In Schramm, Wilbur. (Ed.) *The Science of Human Communication*. Basic Books, 1963. p. 94–115.

Lazarsfeld, Paul F., and others. *The People's Choice*, 2nd ed. Columbia U Press, 1948. 178p.

Litchfield, Tickner B. "Interpretations of a Factor Analysis of Personal Attitudes of Lay Citizens toward Schools in Selected New York Central School Districts." Doctoral dissertation. Teachers Col, Columbia U. 1963.

Lucas, Darrell B., and Britt, Stewart H. *Advertising Psychology and Research*. McGraw-Hill, 1950.

Lutz, Frank. "Social Systems and School Districts." Doctoral dissertation. Washington U, 1962.

Magee, Carbus C. *Evidences of Community Interest in the Early Public School*. Doctoral dissertation. U Pittsburgh, 1938.

Mann, Lester, and others. "A Comparison of Formal and Informal Reporting Systems in First Grade Population." *J Ed Res* 60:75–9; 1966.

Mayer, Kurt. "The Theory of Social Classes." *Harvard Ed R* 23:149–67; 1953.

McCutcheon, David E. "An Investigation of the Effect of a Planned Program of Home Visitation By Teachers on Student Attitude, Attendance and Achievement of Selected Groups of Students in a School." Doctoral dissertation. U Kansas, 1965.

McGuire, William J. "Attitudes and Opinions." In Farnsworth, Paul R. (Ed.) *Annual Review of Psychology*, Vol. 17. Annual Reviews Inc., 1966. p. 475–514.

McLaughlin, Daniel R. "School-Community Studies and Socio-economic Classes of Seven Selected Michigan Communities." Doctoral dissertation. Michigan State U, 1960.

Merrill, Edward C., Jr. *Communication and Decision Making Related to the Administration of Education*. Doctoral dissertation. George Peabody Col for Teachers, 1953.

Merrill, Edward C., Jr. "How the Word Gets Around." *Am Sch Bd J* 130, February: 29–31; 1955.

Miller, Delmas F. *An Appraisal Technique for Programs of Public School Relations*. Doctoral Dissertation. U Pittsburgh, 1943.

Minar, David W. "The Community Basis of Conflict in School System Politics." *Am Sociol R* 31:822–35; 1966.

Morris, Lyle, and others. "An Annotated Bibliography of Researchers in Educational Publicity to June, 1927." *Teach Col Rec* 30:40–5; 1928.

Muscovici, Serge. "Attitudes and Opinions." In Farnsworth, Paul R. (Ed.) *Annual Review of Psychology*, Vol 14. Annual Reviews Inc., 1963. p. 321–60.

National Education Association. "The Status of the American Public-school Teacher." *NEA Res B* 35(1); 1957. 63p.

National Education Association. *Public Opinion Polls on American Education*. NEA, 1958. 20p.

National Education Association. "Teachers View Public Relations." *NEA Res B* 37:35–40; 1959.

Newcomb, Theodore M. "Autistic Hostility and Social Reality." *Hum Relations* 1:69–86; 1947.

Pearson, Robert J. "Public Relations Research Concerned with Public Elementary and Secondary Schools." Doctoral dissertation. George Peabody Col for Teachers, 1956.

Peters, A. J. "What the Parents Want to Know about the Schools." Master's thesis. George Peabody Col for Teachers, 1920.

Pierce, Truman M. *Controllable Community Characteristics Related to the Quality of Education.* Teachers Col, Columbia U, 1947.

Pinnie, Anthony F. "Reported Research Studies Dealing with Printed Mass Media of Communication, and the Implications of the Findings for School-Community Relations Programs." Doctoral dissertation. Temple U, 1965. 364p.

Pino, Edward C. "The Relative Effect of Structured Messages on the Attitudes of Parents toward Schools." Doctoral dissertation. Stanford U, 1965.

Pool, Ithiel de Sola. "Mass Communication and Political Science." In Kindred, Leslie W. (Ed.) *A Seminar on Communications Research Findings and Their Implications for School-Community Relations.* Temple U, 1965. p. 133–50.

Purdy, Ralph D. "Community Foundations for Educational Leadership." *Am Sch Bd J* 131, October: 50–2; 1955.

Reynolds, Rollo G. *Newspaper Publicity for the Public Schools.* Capital City Press, 1922.

Rosen, Bernard C. "Race, Ethnicity, and the Achievement Syndrome." *Am Sociol R* 24:47–60; 1959.

Ross, Donald H. (Ed.) *Administration for Adaptability.* Teacher Col, Columbia U, 1958.

Schiff, Herbert J. "The Effect of Personal Contactual Relationships on Parents' Attitudes toward and Participation in Local School Affairs." Doctoral dissertation. Northwestern U, 1963.

Schramm, Wilbur. "Procedures and Effects of Mass Communication." In *Mass Media and Education.* 53rd Yearbook, Part II, NSSE, U Chicago, 1954. p. 113–38.

Schramm, Wilbur. "Mass Communication." In Farnsworth, Paul R. (Ed.) *Annual Review of Psychology,* Vol. 13. Annual Reviews Inc., 1962. p. 251–84.

Schramm, Wilbur. (Ed.) *The Science of Human Communication.* Basic Books, 1963.

Shannon, Dan C. "Voting Records and the School Board." *Am Sch Bd J* 137, October: 33–5; 1958.

Sherif, Muzafer, and Hovland, Carl I. *Social Judgment.* Yale U Press, 1961. 218p.

Shipton, James M. *Politics, Prejudices, and Public Opinions about Schools.* New England School Development Council, 1956. 16p.

Shipton, James M., and Belisle, Eugene L. "Who Criticizes the Public Schools?" *Phi Delta Kappan* 37:303–7; 1956.

Sigband, Norman B. "The Effectiveness of School-Community Communications." *Ed Adm Sup* 42:78–86; 1956.

Simpson, Robert J. "Does PR Breed False Security?" *Michigan Ed J* 41, January: 5–8; 1964.

Smith, John A. *An Appraisal of School Bond Campaign Techniques.* U Southern California Press, 1953.

Smith, Ralph V., and others. *Community Organization and Support of the Schools.* Cooperative Research Project No. 1828, USOE, 1964. 131p.

Star, Shirley A., and Hughes, Helen M. "Report on an Educational Campaign: The Cincinnati Plan for the United Nations." *Am J Sociol* 55:389–400; 1950.

Stout, Irving W., and Langdon, Grace. "What Parents Want to Know about Their Child's School." *Nation's Sch* 60, August: 45–8; 1957

Suttoff, John "Local-Cosmopolitan Orientation and Participation in School Affairs." Doctoral dissertation. Stanford U, 1960.

Thomas, William J. "A Study of Interests of Readers of Public School Newspaper Publicity." Doctoral dissertation. U Pittsburgh, 1944.

Thompson, Wayne E., and Horton, John E. "Political Alienation as a Force in Political Action." *Social Forces* 38:190–5; 1960.

Twedt, Dick W. "Consumer Psychology." In Farnsworth, Paul R. (Ed.) *Annual Review of Psychology,* Vol. 16. Annual Review Inc., 1965. p. 265–94.

Van Winkle, Harold A. "A Study of School-Community Programs in Northwest Ohio." Doctoral dissertation. Indiana U, 1956.

Vogelein, L. Belle. "Selected Bibliography on School Publicity." *Ed Res B* 3:162–5; 1924.

Volgamore, V. H. "What the People Want to Know about Their Schools." *Colorado Sch J* 58, April: 6, 20; 1943.

Zeller, Robert H. "Diffusion and Recall Differences between Two Ways of School-to-Home Communications." Doctoral dissertation. Washington U, 1959.

PUBLIC SCHOOL ADMINISTRATION

Public school administration is an inclusive term which embraces, as Miller (1965) has suggested, the process of decision-making and action-taking in the conduct of public education from kindergarten through Grade 12. In some states and in some connections, junior or community colleges are regarded and legally provided for as part of the public school system, but the prevailing view is that they belong to the realm of higher education. While school administration cannot be satisfactorily discussed without reference to state and federal government relations to education, the center of interest in this article is the administration of local school systems.

The massive responsibilities carried by public school administrators are indicated by the magnitude of the U. S. educational enterprise and its projected growth, reported by Simon and Fullam (1966). About 85 percent of the age group 5 to 17 were enrolled in public schools in the fall of 1965. Enrollment in public schools (kindergarten through Grade 12) was 42.1 million; the number of teachers was 1.7 million; and total expenditures for 1965–66 were estimated as $26.3 billion. For 1970 and 1975 estimated figures are respectively 45.3 and 46.5 million pupils, and 2.0 and 2.1 million teachers; and total expenditures for 1970–71 and 1975–76 as $35.3 and $35.8 billion respectively.

THE ORIGINS OF SCHOOL ADMINISTRATION. Early in the colonial period of U.S. history, legislative authority and responsibility for education were expressed in the Massachusetts laws of 1642 and 1647. In the first law, parents and masters were required to instruct children in "the principles of religion & the capitall lawes of this country." Five years later, towns were required to set up schools or pay a fine for noncompliance (Cubberley, 1934). From these simple beginnings stemmed the exercise of state authority for providing and controlling public education, and eventually, 200 years later, the emergence of school administration as a profession.

Early Predominance of State Administration. Communities were allowed much latitude in education throughout the colonial and early national period, and the authority of colonial and state governments was largely overlooked. In New England, it became common for town councils to appoint some of their number as school committees for the supervision of schools. These antecedents of the modern board of education performed administrative duties, but as laymen, not as paid professionals. By the end of the colonial period, the school board and school district system had become firmly established.

However, it is at the state level that educational administration was first accorded official recognition. In 1812, 28 years after its creation, the Board of Regents of the University of the State of New York (equivalent to "state board of education") appointed the first state superintendent of public instruction. After nine years the office lapsed and was not filled again until 1854. In the meantime, 18 other states established the state superintendency. Among the appointees, John D. Pierce of Michigan and Horace Mann of Massachusetts served with such brilliant effectiveness that, as Thurston and Roe (1957) show, within less than three decades all the older states created the office, as did new states as they were admitted to the Union.

During the second quarter of the nineteenth century, it became standard practice for the states to provide for the office of county superintendent. Though often referred to in the literature of school administration as an intermediate office between the state government and the local school district, the county superintendent, as one can see from the NEA Department of Rural Education's survey (National Education Association, 1950), was engaged chiefly in the supervision of rural elementary schools.

School administration at both the state and county levels was embedded in the political structure in most states by either constitutional or statutory provisions. As late as 1965 nearly half of the 50 chief state education officers were elected by popular vote; most of the rest were appointed by state boards of education, a few by governors. The county superintendency typically has been an elective office. The criticism that chief state school officers who were successful at the polls were not necessarily well qualified professionally resulted, during the second and third quarters of the twentieth century, in a pronounced trend toward their appointment by state boards of education. The county superintendency was converted in some states to a district superintendency, the county becoming the basic administrative unit, e.g., in West Virginia, Florida, and Nevada. In other states the office was simply abolished because the number of school districts had been so drastically reduced that local district boards and superintendents had no need of an intermediate office between them and state authorities.

The Urban Origins of the District Superintendency. Gilland (1935) and Reller (1935) researched the origin and development of the position of superintendent of schools. The first city superintendents were appointed in 1837 in Buffalo, N. Y., and Louisville, Ky., but not until 1890 was the position generally found in large city school systems. Another quarter-century saw it adopted in small cities and even in villages. Superintendents were appointed because boards of education found that they could not cope with the multiplying problems of rapidly expanding educational services, and for many years the position, while not illegal, was extralegal. Hence the city superintendency was created to meet an immediate need, and took on executive and administrative powers and functions earlier than did either the state or county superintendency.

Typically, however, superintendents were distinctly limited in the scope of their duties and powers, expected only to supervise teachers. School boards reserved to themselves the management of school district business affairs. Superintendents themselves possessed a limited conception of their responsibilities, illustrated by the separation of supervision of instruction and business affairs reported in the NEA *Journal of Proceedings and Addresses* (National Education Association, 1895). City school boards were often quite large prior to 1900, ranging in membership from 20 to more than 100. They found it expeditious to operate through standing committees on finance, personnel, buildings and grounds, and other areas. Despite the development of educational administration as a field of advanced professional study, despite the radical reduction in size of school boards, and against the unanimous recommendation of respected leaders in administration, many school boards still utilize standing committees, although not so extensively as in earlier times.

Elementary and Secondary School Principalship. Schoolmastering was a well-known occupation, but only a few men, like Ezekiel Cheever and Elijah Corlett, attained renown in the early days, and they did so as teachers, not as administrators. Longstanding tradition in Europe exalted the schoolmaster as teacher, and this influenced American views. It is noteworthy that in such a definitive treatise as Brown's (1903) history of American secondary education, or for the early years in the study by Pierce (1934) of the origin of the principalship, it is difficult to find even oblique allusions to administration. Where more than three or four teachers constituted a school staff, one was ordinarily designated as head teacher. These conditions persisted until the last decade of the nineteenth century, secondary school heads first winning recognition as principals, and then elementary school heads. Undoubtedly the interest exhibited during the 1890's and early 1900's by institutions of higher education in high schools as college preparatory schools helped to raise their status to the relative disadvantage of elementary education.

THE ADOLESCENT PERIOD OF ADMINISTRATION. The period from the early years of the twentieth century, when Paul Hanus and E. P. Cubberley pioneered university teaching of educational administration, to midcentury saw great changes in public school administration. Before this, superintendents and principals acquired such knowledge as they got about administration from their own experiences and from practicing administrators to whom they looked for guidance. Interest in more nearly professional administration of education was probably accelerated by the dual cataclysms of depression and world war. Professional literature appeared in expanding volume, particularly reports of local practices. Scores of universities and colleges instituted programs of graduate study in educational administration and supervision. By 1950 there were approximately 90 universities offering doctoral work in the field, and several hundred institutions had programs leading to master's degrees.

Hundreds of surveys were made for school districts and state governments by experts brought in from outside or by staff committees, with a view to improving and rationalizing public education. This period witnessed also the proliferation of studies of educational problems employing newly developed statistical techniques. No facet of educational service was too small to be subjected to intensive study, in most instances by administrators and would-be administrators working for graduate degrees. The support of state and local teachers' associations and administrators' organizations had to be generated, and state school laws had to be amended or new ones enacted to give effect to the numerous changes advocated. Out of the welter of convention addresses and resolutions, survey reports, dissertations, books, monographs and articles, many improvements and changes in school administration did gradually issue, falling logically under two heads. One main current of improvement was in the organization and administration of education; the other led to the incipient formulation of principles of educational administration and administrative theory.

Changes in Organization and Practice of Administration. Some of the more significant outcomes illustrate the wide-ranging scope of activity in organization and administration, amounting to a virtual ferment. In addition, there was immense activity in other aspects of education, such as curriculum development, instructional methodology, teacher education and certification.

The size of school boards was reduced to a norm of seven to nine members. The number of boards was reduced from more than 130,000 in 1930 to about 83,000 in 1950, through reorganization of districts. Board members, formerly elected to represent wards, were in most districts elected at large. Standing committees were less frequently created, although many boards were unwilling to surrender them completely. The concept of "unit control" almost universally supplanted "dual" or "multiple control," as Knezevich and Fowlkes (1960) reported, thus centering in the superintendent of schools responsibility for all aspects of public school administration including business affairs. Standards for school sites and schoolhouse construction were elevated, and planning for the future became common practice. The financing of education was revolutionized during the first half of the twentieth century as states and school districts developed "foundation programs" supported by state and local taxes. School organization became diversified from the usual 8–4 plan, with eight years of elementary education and a four-year secondary school, to a variety of arrangements of which the 6–3–3 plan became the most favored. Kindergarten was added at the bottom, and the junior college at the top.

Early Attempts to Frame Principles of Administration and Formulate Administration Theory. During the first half of the century, educational administration as a process was strongly influenced by practices in business, industry, and the military. "Principles of line-and-staff organization" were developed; "flow of authority" and "span of control" were popular concepts. Charts showing relationships of "superiors" and "subordinates" in a hierarchical pattern were favored. The conception of that period, as summed up by Kefauver in the 45th Yearbook of the National Society for the Study of Education (Henry, 1946), tended to concentrate great authority in the superintendent. With the approval of the board of education, he largely determined policy and directed the work of the district's employees.

However, by the end of the period, the board of education had come to be quite generally viewed as the policy-making body at the local level, within the framework of state laws and regulations. The superintendent was regarded as the executive officer of the board whose duty it was to carry out the policies. This rather naïve view is at the date of this writing often supported by writers and practitioners, illustrated, for example, by Walton (1959), notwithstanding the severe erosion that has taken place in the demarcation between policy making and execution, as shown by Sears (1950), Grieder and others (1961), and Keppel (1966). The hardiness of this conception is probably rooted in the American conviction that public education is safeguarded from the vagaries of partisan political control by a lay board whose members are not associated with education in any professional capacity. That the distinction between policy making and execution could not be maintained was particularly well expounded by Sears. He demonstrated that there is a reciprocal relationship between policy making and execution, that board and administrator inform and influence each other, and need each other. Much emphasis on the administrator as a leader is found in publications that appeared between 1930 and 1950. The name of the 11th Yearbook, *Educational Leadership*, of the AASA (American Association of School Administrators, 1933) is indicative. The role of school principals as organizers and leaders of the personnel in their individual schools was also recognized in the yearbook. A few scholars were revealing a keen awareness of the importance of human relations in administration, notably Follett in her collected papers edited by Metcalf and Urwick (1942). This seminal book is the forerunner of the contributions of behavioral scientists whose insights have greatly colored the philosophy of administration since 1950.

By the mid-twentieth century, the conviction was widespread that school administration was too authoritarian; that it did not sufficiently draw on the disciplines of sociology, economics, psychology, political science, and anthropology; that it was resistant to change and innovation. These charges triggered a new era of inquiry into the nature and practice of public school administration, giving the two decades following 1950 a different character from preceding periods.

CARRY-OVER OF EARLIER PREOCCUPATIONS. It would be misleading, however, to convey the impression that at mid-century there were sweeping changes in public school administration, for several areas of earlier interest continued to command attention. Some researchers, among them Halpin (in Gregg & others, 1965) and Hills (1965), were critical of, and impatient with, what they considered the inordinately slow pace of change. Yet it may with propriety be observed that, while gradualism appears to be inharmonious with the temper and the tempo of the latter half of the twentieth century, it has been a dominant attribute of American education for three and a half centuries. When one reviews this history, he must be convinced that old and new practices, ideas, and theories are ever commingled. The old undergo constant change, often imperceptible at any given moment, as the new filter in. It is also true that terminology frequently retains its form but changes meaning, and this gives a mistaken impression of unshakable stability and reliance on tradition and convention.

Continued Emphasis on Leadership. Although it has been subject to an uncomfortably great variety of definitions, the leadership role of both superintendents and principals has received continued attention. Graff and others (1966) analyzed the applicability of various schools of philosophic belief to educational administration, giving considerable weight to leadership as synonymous with administration. Leadership, indeed, was found by Saunders and others (1966) to be a key concept in the role of administrators, and other investigators, including Gross and Herriott (1965), Riddle (1964), and Joel (1965), ascribe high importance to the leadership competence of superintendents at local and state levels. Statutory recognition of the position in 44 states was reported by Roesch (1960); the fact that in the remaining states the position also existed is a good example of how practice is often in advance of legal sanction.

The principalship at both elementary and secondary school levels has been invariably viewed by authors of research reports and administration textbooks as primarily a leadership position, with particular reference to the improvement and supervision of instruction. Idiculla (1965) reported above 90 percent agreement among high school principals, superintendents, and professors of educational administration on the importance of supervision and instructional improvement. Ovard (1966) discussed at length the leadership role of secondary school administrators, especially in the area of supervision and improvement of instruction. Shelton (1965) found in his research on elementary school principals in two midwestern states that in the 41 percent of their time that they spent on "communication," "instructional matters" outranked all other demands. However, Wallace (1965), in a study of the role of the elementary school principal, found less general agreement by principals on their instructional role, discovering variations related to principals' age, educational experience, opportunities for group interaction, and district policies. Gross and Trask (1964), in a study of elementary school principals in cities of over 50,000 population, found higher professional performance and pupil learning in schools with women principals. These investigators also reported that fewer women than men principals had aspirations for promotion, a finding corroborated by Burns (1964), who also found a marked decline in the proportion of women in administrative positions in the preceding decade. Two questions still waiting to be answered are why, if administration is a science as well as an art, more women do not aspire to it, and why a sharp drop occurred in recent years in the percentage of women principals.

A minority view, not so much on the importance of leadership as on the failure of administrators to exercise it, was trenchantly articulated by Keppel (1966) and Hauser (1966). The former, while Commissioner of Education, charged superintendents with overemphasis on managerial aspects of administration, school boards with being fearful of becoming really involved in the basic problems of education, and both with "evasion of leadership." Little notice was taken of the role of the states. Hauser described superintendents as "the most authoritarian group of people left in the U.S.," and as having failed "to rise to their mission." In addition to such unfavorable judgments, there were symptoms during the 1960's, especially at the federal level, of systematic attempts to denigrate professionalism in educational administration, in speeches and articles by high-ranking officials. The appointment to high position in the U.S. Office of Education and other agencies of persons without experience in, or professional connection with, public education exalted amateurism (after the British fashion). Having a somewhat contrary bearing on this matter, a study completed by Dolph (1964) found that criticism of schools was on the decrease nationally. And Johnston (1965), assuming that AASA resolutions reflect central concerns of the members, reported that the most dramatic increase for the period 1900–1965 was in attention given to professionalization and professional status of administration. Major concerns for the entire period were finance, international cooperation, philosophy and sociology of education, teacher education, certification and welfare, the U.S. Office of Education, and curriculum. If his assumption is valid, such findings do not reveal an evasion of leadership.

Superintendent–School Board Relationship. Of much influence on the leadership role of the school administrator, more specifically the superintendent of schools, is the character of his relationship to the board of education. This appears to be a subject of unflagging interest. A consensus is still lacking, however, on exactly what the superintendent's position is or should be. Superintendents in general feel, according to Edson's (1963) research, supported by many other inquiries, most adequate in administration of business affairs and least adequate in administration of the instructional program. The Regents Advisory Committee on Educational Leadership (1965) reported among the findings of a representative survey of districts in New York State that half the board members and three-fifths of the chief school officers were in disagreement over the respective roles of boards and administrators. Bowman (1962), in an extensive survey of Illinois, substantiated the suggestion by Houle (1960) that the relationship between superintendent and board was less that of professional administrator and lay governing board and more that of a partnership agreement with a wide range of appropriate behavior. He also found that the partners tended to become more impressed with their own importance to the organization and less in agreement on how they were to work together. Most typical preferred behavior of the superintendent, as expressed by superintendents, board members, and professors of educational administration, was the making of recommendations to the board, ranking ahead of "informing" the board and "determining" or decision making without board consultation.

A sharp contrast exists between the great attention focused on the position and responsibilities of chief education officers in local school districts in the United States and the mere nod given to them in all other countries. As Baron (1965) has pointed out, the role of educational administrators, including principals, is markedly different in Britain from what it is in the United States, being limited more to strictly instructional matters. Principals in the United States are regarded as representatives of the superintendent, while in other countries they are far more independent, and more closely associated with the teaching staff. This judgment is sustained by many other students of administration in Britain, e.g., by Dent (1963) and Pedley (1964). In other countries similar conclusions apply, as can be gathered from Fraser (1963) and Male (1963) writing on France; from Reeves and others (1962) for Canada; and from Walker (1964) for Australia. Grieder (1967) found extremely limited powers and duties conferred on local school officers in Germany, but great powers on the 11 state ministries of education, and in France no powers of more than the most minor significance assigned to either local or provincial administrators.

School administration is only beginning to gain recognition as a field of professional specialization and advanced university study outside the United States, and, as Reller and Morphet (1962) revealed, centralized control of education at either the national or provincial level of government is the general rule, in contradistinction to the U.S. pattern of state-and-local control.

Work Week and Allocation of Time. Actual and preferred allocations of principals' time have continued to be a topic of investigation. The average work week of elementary school principals was reported by the NEA Department of Elementary School Principals (National Education Association, 1958) as about 47 hours, with little change in the distribution of time since 1928. Administration claimed 30 percent in both 1928 and 1958; supervision and related activities 34 and 35 percent respectively; teaching duties 4 and 3 percent; clerical work 18 and 14 percent; and "other" responsibilities 14 and 18 percent. The principals recommended 49 percent for supervision and curriculum work, the increase to be gained from eliminating clerical work.

At the secondary school level, the median work week reported by Ovard (1966) and by Rock and Hemphill (1966) was 54 hours. The general criticism by Ovard and others had the same tenor as earlier studies: principals spend too much time on "managerial and routine duties and not enough time on curriculum improvement" and improvement of instruction. Austin and others (1966) devoted one-quarter of their high school administration textbooks to "The Principal and the Educational Program," a fair reflection of the importance that many writers attach to this aspect of secondary school administration. However, from a ten percent sampling of North Central Association high school principals, Salisbury (1963) concluded that no major change in business management functions and responsibilities had occurred in the preceding five years. Rock and Hemphill (1966) stated that junior high school principals conceived as the main task of their schools teaching pupils reading, writing, and arithmetic. McAbee (1958) in a study of time allocation of high school principals reported that only 12 percent was given to improvement of instruction and supervision, little more than half of the 22 percent recommended by the principals themselves, and substantially less than half the 31 percent recommended by "authorities" in secondary school administration.

Organization of Schools a Continuing Interest. The organization of schools for effective education was shown to be a subject of professional interest over a long period of time by Sadler (1966) in his treatise on Comenius and the concept of universal education. Comenius regarded school organization as highly important, and his 6–6–6–6 plan possesses merit even today. Textbooks and researches by Elsbree and McNally (1959), Griffiths and others (1962), Misner and others (1963), Otto and Sanders (1964), and Rushing (1966) indicates that problems of school organization remain very much alive. Emphases come and go and come again in a complicated pattern: the "common school" gives way to "graded schools," and they in turn are modified by the "nongraded" form of organization. At the secondary school level, the dominance of the 6–3–3 plan was challenged and in part yielded to a congeries of organizational plans, some involving "middle schools" for Grades 5–8, or whole schools populated by only one or two grades, as a "Seventh Grade Junior High School," or a "Two-Two Plan" for Grades 9–12.

One unexpected development in school organization in the years since 1950 was a serious attack on the time-honored concept of the neighborhood elementary school. Condemnation of the neighborhood school stemmed from the conviction of leaders of the civil rights movement that it resulted in "de facto segregation" of pupils on racial grounds. To school administrators this seemed to be an attack on the symptoms rather than the disease, which is racial discrimination and prejudice in patterns of residential housing. In a few cities, pupils were transported to effect a more nearly balanced mix of pupils of various racial origins; in some few others the development of "educational parks" for Grades K–12 was launched, serving either an entire school district or large subdistricts of metropolitan school systems.

School district organization has an important bearing on school organization, but a decline of interest in it occurred during the 1960's. In only seven midwestern states which had half of the 25,000 districts in 1967 was district reorganization of major importance from the standpoint of eliminating non-high school and all very small districts. The county superintendency began to fade, its anachronistic character becoming plain with the decline of rural elementary schools. In one state (Colorado), the office was abolished at the general election of 1966 in 34 of the state's 63 counties. Intermediate districts, advocated during the 1950's by McLure (1956) and others, fell far short of estimated numbers. Within ten years, Campbell and others (1965), reflecting the prevailing view, proposed that intermediate units should be converted into regional offices of state education departments or, preferably, abolished. A plan for a statewide system of 40 regional (intermediate) districts was, however, included in a major Illinois study prepared by a Task Force on Education (1966), to meet the needs of districts too small to provide all the services and programs needed for high-quality education. If local districts are large enough, it was conceded in the report, there is little reason for regional districts. A contributing factor to the abortion of intermediate district development was the rise of cooperative services financed and shared by two or more districts. The revitalization of this movement, which after a flurry of interest in the 1940's had lapsed into quiescence, is still in its infancy at this writing, but its facilitation by new statutory provisions in many states augurs its widespread acceptance. Incidentally, the minimum district enrollment suggested as essential for provision of all services steadily rose through the last two decades from 5,000 to widely accepted figures of 10,000 to 15,000, to the Illinois Task Force's figures of 25,000 to 30,000, and highest of all, Benson's (1965) 60,000 to 70,000.

MAJOR EMERGING CONCEPTS AND EMPHASES. Beginning in 1947 with the National Conference of Professors of Educational Administration (NCPEA), six major organized endeavors to conduct research on and improve the quality of public school administration have produced numerous conferences, reports of research, manifestos, and activities militating not only for modifications of practice but also for conceptual alterations and inventions. The NCPEA, which is still active, has directed its efforts chiefly to the improvement of the professional preparation of administrators. Between 1950 and 1956 the National Citizens Commission for the Public Schools, governed by a board of nationally known leaders of business and industry, generated a ground swell of civic interest in the financing and administration of public education. Approximately 15,000 local citizens' advisory committees were in existence at the high tide of this effort in the late 1950's. During the same period, the Cooperative Program in Educational Administration (CPEA), initiated by the AASA and funded to the extent of more than $10 million, largely by the W. K. Kellogg Foundation, operated through nine regional university centers in the United States and Canada. It stimulated many research projects, summarized by Moore (1957), for the improvement of the practice of school administration and the development of administrative theory. In 1955, near the end of the CPEA, the AASA created its Committee for the Advancement of School Administration to keep alive the interest sparked by the CPEA. However, the most impressive result issuing from the CPEA was the organization of the University Council for Educational Administration, which since 1958 has been the seedbed of research on administration and the professionalization of educational administration. The Council's membership consists of approximately 60 schools of education or departments of educational administration in major universities in the United States and Canada, and exerts a significant influence in the field of administration. Finally, in 1965, the Compact for Education was formulated as the instrument for an organization of political and educational leaders of the several states for action on problems of common interest. From the text of the Compact, and its explanation by Orentlicher (1965), it is apparent that the operating agency known as the Educational Commission of the States was conceived as a bulwark against the increased federal control of education which has tended to accompany expansion of federal aid. Within less than two years of its adoption by a small group of states, the Compact was subscribed to by 40 states. The Commission may prove to be the most potent agency yet underwritten to reassert the historic supremacy of the states in control of education, and to develop a tax-sharing plan for joint state and federal support of public education.

From these major efforts, as well as from others too numerous to mention or outside the scope of this account, have stemmed several recent developments in public school administration to which the remainder of this article is devoted. The day-to-day and year-to-year conduct of education continues much the same as always, with few surface intimations of change. Yet the decade of the 1960's brought more impetus for change (as well as considerable actual change) than had preceding generations. It is probably fair to say, as Keppel (1966) unequivocally stated, that in the United States the first struggle in education has been won—a chance for some sort of schooling for everyone. The second revolution was for equality of opportunity, the removal of social, economic, and other barriers to schooling. This battle, now well under way in the United States, has only lately been joined in Europe, which is entering a critical period documented by Poignant (1965) in his research on education in the Common Market nations, the U.S.S.R., the United Kingdom, and the United States, particular emphasis on access to secondary education, the crux of Europe's educational problem. The impending third and "necessary revolution" in the United States is that of quality, and this hangs on the development of higher conceptions of local and state educational administration, and its deep involvement in the formulation and execution of social, economic, and political policies. One of the largest studies ever made in education, however, with data on more than 600,000 children in Grades 1, 3, 6, 9, and 12 in 4,000 U.S. public schools, by Coleman and others (1966), revealed that the struggle for equality of educational opportunity was further from a favorable ending than Americans were prone to believe. This report showed also that improving the quality of schooling was very elusive, and it discounted the reported relationship of school and teacher quality to pupil achievement. The average socioeconomic level of pupils at a given individual school appeared to be the most important factor. Referring to this massive study, Nichols (1966) pointed out the need for additional and more carefully controlled research on the effects of differential schooling.

Broadened Scope of Educational Administration. There are almost as many different definitions of public school administration as there are persons who write or speak on the subject, and during the 1960's it took on more facets than ever. The central importance of decision making tended to receive increased attention. Representative investigations were those by Ziegler (1964) on the bases and process of decision making, and Fogarty (1964) on centralization and decentralization of decision making. Elaborating on his generalized definition referred to in the first sentence of this article, Miller (1965) stated that administration is "first and foremost communication . . . an interactive process . . . ," and this view was supported by many others. Campbell and others (1965) were inclined to regard administration from three angles: the job, the man, and the profession. They named the six major "task or operational areas" as school–community relationships, curriculum and instruction, pupil personnel, staff, physical facilities, and finance and business management. The University Council for Educational Administration (1966c) suggested that there are four ways of viewing specialization in administration. Two older ways are (1) from the perspective of administrative position, as elementary or secondary school principalship, superintendency, business managership; and (2) through administrative functions, as personnel administration, finance, curriculum development. Two newer ways are concerned with (1) the disciplines base of administration, e.g., economics, political science, social psychology, the sociology of organizations; and (2) the interdisciplinary or multidisciplinary base, for example organizational behavior, human relations, complex organizations, and change processes. It is plain that educational administration is a process and activity of utmost complexity, admirably expounded by Sears (1950, esp. ch. 9) as the bringing to bear harmoniously on the task of instruction of a large number of diverse elements: purpose, curriculum, personnel, housing, finance, public relations, government, research—in short, the marshaling of intellectual, physical, and human resources.

Perhaps the most striking manifestation of the rapidly expanding scope of educational administration is the endless stream of changes in social conditions and needs, and developments in technology, all of which are expected to be kept abreast of by administrators. During the years since 1950, much research has been done on compensatory education for culturally deprived children, for example by Bloom and others (1965); on the economics of education by Schultz (1963), Harbison and Myers (1964), and others; on political and economic issues facing education, as well as the critical question of what constitutes education of high quality and how to provide for it, by Harris (1965a, 1965b); and on the vast changes taking place in the relations of local and state educational authorities to the federal government by Tiedt (1966).

Growth of Interest in Behavioral Approach. Without doubt educational administration since 1950 has been most influenced by the behavioral sciences, with the appearance of *Administrative Behavior* by Simon (1945) serving as the point of departure. A continuous and enlarging application of behavioral science to administration is attested by such works, among many, as Griffiths' (1956) influential book on human relations; the compilation edited by Campbell and Gregg (1957); a casebook drawing on various disciplines to illustrate administrative behavior, by Culbertson and others (1960); the pioneering research by Hemphill and others (1962) on the relationship of personality to success in administration; Downey and Enns's (1963) work in which the social sciences are equated with the behavioral sciences; and Erickson's (1962) and Rielle's (1965) comparative studies of perceptions of superintendents' behavior by superintendents, principals, and teachers. The 63rd Yearbook of the National Society for the Study of Education, edited by Griffiths (1964), marked the end of isolationism in school administration, and its involvement with other disciplines, especially the behavioral sciences. In spite of its rather general title, Halpin's

(1966) critical exposition of theory and research in administration was largely devoted to their behavioral aspects. And to conclude this illustrative list, Sachs (1966), a psychologist, analyzed and tested behavioral concepts related to administration, and attempted to develop relevant social-psychological theory, to integrate behavioral science concepts with those of administration.

Expanded Participation in Administration by School Personnel. To school administrators, particularly those with more than 20 years' service, another volcanic change in administration was the movement for a broader base of participation in the formulation of policies and the making of decisions. In former times these were pretty much reserved to boards of education and superintendents. By the late 1960's, participation on a broad front was demanded by teachers, covering not only such commonplace items as salaries and class size, but also decisions on supervision, evaluation of teaching and pupil achievement, sharp definition of teaching duties, and curriculum development. In general, everything that related to the educational program and to professional welfare was subject, to a greater or lesser extent, to collective bargaining (the term favored by the American Federation of Teachers) or professional negotiations (favored by the National Education Association). Noncertificated personnel everywhere were rapidly becoming part of this movement which for this class of employees had been limited chiefly to large cities. The abolition of the school principalship was advocated not infrequently, in favor of administrative committees of teachers, especially at the high school level, as Rombouts (1959) reported. In this investigation of 25 Michigan school districts it was found, however, that support of the committee plan was inversely related to length of teaching experience. Teachers who participated in administration were found by Leiman (1961) to have higher morale than nonparticipants, more positive attitudes toward principals, colleagues and students, but also a conviction, held by a majority, that school boards make no effort to understand the classroom problems of teachers.

Perhaps the aspect of broad participation that agitated administrators most was their role in it, and on this there was a distinct cleavage of opinion. One school of thought, represented by Wildman (1965), held that the superintendent was the representative of management (the board of education). Lieberman and Moskow (1966) supported this view but with the reservation that the superintendent's role was not yet entirely clear. Sharply opposed to this position was that of the AASA (American Association of School Administrators, 1966), which regarded the superintendent as the professional adviser of the board and the professional leader of the entire school system personnel—a liaison or middleman serving both "management" and "labor." Ball (1967) and Washburne (1966) unequivocally endorsed this stand. The disagreement beclouding the problem led to proposals such as those by Fensch and Wilson (1964) that school administration be recognized as a team concept, the members of the team including the superintendent, deputy, associate and assistant superintendents, and principals. This conception would liberate the superintendent from an intolerable position as either the sole middleman in the negotiating process, or as the sole representative of either governing board or employee organizations.

Administration Looked to for Leadership in Change and Innovation. The gradualism that for centuries characterized change and innovation in education was questioned with increasing impatience after 1950, by educators, sociologists, philosophers, economists, and political leaders. Conant (1953) early posed the question of whether the schools should merely be improved or whether the pattern of schooling should be changed—a hint of things to come. Through the next decade or so a veritable rage for change and innovation occurred, whose scope was little more than adumbrated by Miles's (1964) weighty compilation and by Fallon's (1966) catalog of more than 600 innovations in every facet of schooling. Despite this showing, considerable impatience and disappointment with the slow pace of change were expressed, and superintendents were held chiefly responsible for it in a report by the AASA (American Association of School Administrators, 1960). Schafer (1963) also found inertia as the cause of slow acceptance by secondary school principals of recommendations made by Conant (1959). Validity was lent to these criticisms by Brickell (1961), whose penetrating research in New York State left no doubt about the key position of the administrator as a change agent, and by such reports as those issued by Hartley and Holloway (1965) and Carlson (1965).

Rapidly developing systems of educational data processing and instructional systems utilizing computers and other machines, described by Goodlad and others (1966) and Loughary and others (1966), created a new imperative in administration if its *raison d'être* was to continue as the facilitation of the many ramifications of educational services. An unremitting necessity for continually updating administrative competence was voiced by Douglass (1963) and many other scholars. Goldhammer (1966) effectively argued the case for continuous professional renewal by pointing out that during a career spanning 25 to 30 years, administrators will see major changes in the knowledge base, the practicing technology, and the basic practices of their field. For the first time, the lie was given to the assumption that each generation would live under substantially the same conditions as the preceding generation. The advanced state of U.S. culture itself undoubtedly contributed greatly to the predilection for change and innovation. When one reads about primitive societies as described by Benedict (1934), Mead (1961, 1962), and Moorehead (1966), one discerns that most of the time in tribal life is spent just on the means of existence itself. There is no margin for innovation or for changes by trial and error. This probably also is the reason why primitive peoples are ruled by elders, no matter how indulgent they may be with children. A primitive tribe must be conservative in the literal sense. U.S. society has such a large margin of time and effort not required for survival that it can afford change and innovation on a very large scale, even to the point of obsession.

Special Problems of School Administration in the Great Cities. More than half a century ago concern was evinced for the administration of city school systems by Chancellor (1908). The configuration of the subject was completely changed, however, by midcentury, when the largest cities were growing even larger, slums were becoming more noisome, patterns of housing more segregated, crime and delinquency more rampant, and the financing of public education (with a train of associated problems of staffing, schoolhousing, and the like) ever more inadequate. A spate of research reports and books on education in the great cities examined multifarious aspects of their problems, ranging from general surveys such as that by Chandler and others (1962), to specific inquiries on the board of education by Cronin (1965), the provision of schoolhouses by the Educational Facilities Laboratories (1966), and determinants of expenditures by James and others (1966). Havighurst (1966) dealt with the exceedingly complex and exacerbated problems of social and political relationships, conveying an unmistakable warning to school administrators and civic officials to cooperate or be prepared to see their cities disintegrate. An elementary school principal's successes liberally laced with frustration were portrayed in detail by Hentoff (1966), creating in the reader's mind, as indeed do all the works cited, an acute awareness that there were problems of school administration peculiar to the big cities. The Ford Foundation (1966) suggested an adaptation of rural extension services, which contributed much to the modernization of farm life, to the problems of city life. The impression was inescapable that it would be good if, in the next two or three decades, the great cities could be converted into city-states, which would free them from legal codes more nearly applicable to life in cities of small and medium size, villages and rural areas, and open up new avenues for the solution of their problems. Berlin, Hamburg, Bremen, and for all practical purposes London and Paris are examples of city-states, and Hawaii is an approximation.

GREATER CENTRALIZATION OF SCHOOL ADMINISTRATION IN PROSPECT. The environment of the 1980's and beyond is being shaped now. It will almost certainly exhibit three dominant aspects, as forecast by Morphet and Ryan (1966) in their report on prospective changes in society: world urbanization, industrial automation, and a revolution in information technology. Higher levels and far greater dissemination of cultural sophistication can be expected. A vast increase in leisure will enable people to do more of the things they want to do, and will reflect to a considerable extent their educational backgrounds. Thus new and larger responsibilities will be imposed on the educational systems of the world, and those charged with administering them hopefully will not only desire to learn all they can from each other but will also find it necessary to do so. International information and communication systems and travel will simplify the interchange of knowledge, ideas, and persons far beyond anything possible in 1970. In 1966 the University Council for Educational Administration (1966a, 1966b) (UCEA) gave concrete form to a burgeoning interest in worldwide approaches to school administration by sponsoring a four-week international intervisitation. Thirty professors of educational administration from Australia, New Zealand, Great Britain, and Canada met with their opposite numbers in U.S. universities, engaging in seminars for the first and fourth weeks at the University of Michigan and the University of Alberta, and in visits to major U.S. universities during the intervening fortnight. The values of such intercourse, summarized by Baron and others (1968), persuaded the UCEA to form a permanent committee, and to initiate plans for participation by more nations of the English-speaking community and later by others.

Although educational administration will, as indicated, become increasingly important, there are signs and portents that at the local or school district level it will decline. Clark (1965) concluded that decentralized control was coming under increasingly heavy pressure to accommodate modern social forces, especially concerns that are national in scope and defined by federal agencies and national private bodies. The locus of educational decision making tends to shift upward from local units to states, and from states to federal government. Self-constituted private organizations, usually funded by federal as well as foundation grants (e.g., the series of curriculum study groups of the 1960's) tend to bypass orthodox lines of decision making, thus weakening both state and local authority. In a major contribution on intergovernmental relations edited by Fesler (1967), the shifting relationships of the states and their local units of government were examined. From this and other works a clear trend can be deduced that public school administration will become more ministerial or mediative, carrying out state requirements and losing a great deal of its present discretionary power. How far the states will go in first recapturing their historic preeminence in educational control and administration, and then how far they will yield some of it to the federal government are still in the realm of speculation.

Calvin Grieder
University of Colorado

References

American Association of School Administrators. *Educational Leadership.* 11th Yearbook. AASA, 1933. 528p.

American Association of School Administrators. *Professional Administrators for American Schools.* 35th Yearbook. AASA, 1960. 310p.

American Association of School Administrators. *School Administrators View Professional Negotiations.* AASA, 1966. 58p.

Austin, David B., and others. *American High School Administration*, 3rd ed. Holt, 1966.

Ball, Lester B. "Collective Bargaining: a Primer for Superintendents." *Saturday R* 50, January 21:70–1, 80; 1967.

Baron, G. *Society, Schools and Progress in England*. Pergamon, 1965.

Baron, George, and others. *Educational Administration: International Perspectives*. Rand McNally, 1968. 350p.

Benedict, Ruth. *Patterns of Culture*. Houghton, 1934. 290p.

Benson, Charles S. *The Cheerful Prospect*. Houghton, 1965. 134p.

Bloom, Benjamin S., and others. *Compensatory Education for Culturally Deprived*. Holt, 1965. 179p.

Bowman, Thomas R. "The Participation of the Superintendent in School Board Decision Making." Doctoral dissertation. U Chicago, 1962.

Brickell, Henry M. *Organizing New York State for Educational Change*. New York State Education Department, 1961. 107p.

Brown, Elmer Ellsworth. *The Making of Our Middle Schools*. McKay, 1903. 547p.

Burns, Dorothy M. "Women in Educational Administration: A Study of Leadership in California Public Schools." Doctoral dissertation. U Oregon, 1964.

Campbell, Roald F., and Gregg, Russell T. (Eds.) *Administrative Behavior in Education*. Harper, 1957. 547p.

Campbell, Roald F., and others. *The Organization and Control of American Schools*. Charles E. Merrill Books, Inc., 1965. 553p.

Carlson, Richard O. *Adoption of Educational Innovations*. U Oregon, 1965. 84p.

Chancellor, William Estabrook. *Our City Schools: Their Direction and Management*. Heath, 1908. 338p.

Chandler, B. J., and others. (Eds.) *Education in Urban Society*. Dodd, 1962. 279p.

Clark, Burton R. "Interorganizational Patterns in Education." *Adm Sci Q* 10:224–37; 1965.

Coleman, James S., and others. *Equality of Educational Opportunity*. GPO, 1966. 743p.

Conant, James Bryant. *Education and Liberty*. Knopf, 1953. 169p.

Conant, James Bryant. *The American High School Today*. McGraw-Hill, 1959. 141p.

Cronin, Joseph M. "The Board of Education in the 'Great Cities,' 1890–1964." Doctoral dissertation. Stanford U, 1965.

Cubberly, Ellwood P. *Readings in Public Education in the United States*. Houghton, 1934. 534p.

Culbertson, Jack A., and others. *Administrative Relationships: a Casebook*. Prentice-Hall, 1960. 517p.

Dent, H. C. *The Educational System of England and Wales*, 2nd ed. U London, 1963. 224p.

Dolph, William Eugene. "Analysis of Pressures Affecting the Administration of Elementary Schools." Doctoral dissertation. U California, 1964.

Douglass, Harl R. *Modern Administration of Secondary Schools*, 2nd ed. Ginn, 1963. 636p.

Downey, Lawrence W., and Enns, Frederick. (Eds.) *The Social Sciences and Educational Administration*. U Alberta, 1963. 109p.

Edson, Gilmore Louis. "An Analysis of the Perceptions of Administrative Activity by Michigan School Superintendents and Professors of Educational Administration." Doctoral dissertation. Michigan State U, 1963.

Educational Facilities Laboratories, Inc. *The Schoolhouse in the City*. The Laboratories, 1966. 46p.

Elsbree, Willard S., and McNally, Harold J. *Elementary School Administration and Supervision*, 2nd ed. American, 1959. 551p.

Erickson, Eldridge Albert. "A Study of the Relationship Between Personality Structure and Perception." Doctoral dissertation. Colorado State Col, 1962.

Fallon, Berlie. (Ed.) *Educational Innovation in the United States*. PDK, 1966. 280p.

Fensch, Edwin A., and Wilson, Robert E. *The Superintendency Team*. Charles E. Merrill Books, Inc., 1964. 256p.

Fesler, James. (Ed.) *The Fifty States and Their Local Governments*. Knopf, 1967. 603p.

Fogarty, Bryce Martin. "Characteristics of Superintendents of Schools and Centralization-Decentralization of Decision-Making." Doctoral dissertation. U Wisconsin, 1964.

Ford Foundation. *Urban Extension*. The Foundation, 1966. 44p.

Fraser, W. R. *Education and Society in Modern France*. Routledge, 1963. 140p.

Gilland, Thomas M. *The Origin and Development of the Powers and Duties of the City-School Superintendent*. U Chicago, 1935. 279p.

Goldhammer, Keith. "The Problem of In-service Education." In Lynch, Patrick D., and Blackstone, Peggy L. (Eds.) *Institutional Roles for In-service Education of School Administrators*. U New Mexico, 1966. p. 31–45.

Goodlad, John I., and others. *Computers and Information Systems in Education*. Harcourt, 1966. 152p.

Graff, Orin B., and others. *Philosophic Theory and Practice in Educational Administration*. Wadsworth Publishing Co., Inc., 1966. 320p.

Gregg, Russell T., and others. "Behavioral Science and Administration." *Ed Adm Q* 1:42–57; 1965.

Grieder, Calvin. "Educational Revolution in Western Europe." *Colorado Q* 15, Winter:233–49; 1967.

Grieder, Calvin, and others. *Public School Administration*, 2nd ed. Ronald, 1961. 642p.

Griffiths, Daniel E. *Human Relations in School Administration*. Appleton, 1956. 458p.

Griffiths, Daniel E. (Ed.) *Behavioral Science and Educational Administration*. 63rd Yearbook, Part II. NSSE. U Chicago, 1964. 360p.

Griffiths, Daniel E., and others. *Organizing Schools for Effective Education*. Interstate, 1962. 338p.

Gross, Neal, and Herriott, Robert E. *Staff Leadership in Public Schools*. Wiley, 1965. 247p.

Gross, Neal, and Trask, Anne E. *Men and Women as Elementary School Principals*. Cooperative Research Project No. 853. Part 2. USOE and Harvard U, 1964.

Halpin, Andrew W. *Theory and Research in Administration.* Macmillan, 1966. 352p.

Harbison, Frederick H., and Myers, Charles A. *Education, Manpower, and Economic Growth.* McGraw-Hill, 1964. 229p.

Harris, Seymour E. (Ed.) *Challenge and Change in American Education.* McCutcheon, 1965(a). 346p.

Harris, Seymour E. (Ed.) *Education and Public Policy.* McCutcheon, 1965(b). 347p.

Hartley, Harry J., and Holloway, George E., Jr. (Eds.) *Focus on Change and the School Administrator.* U New York at Buffalo, 1965. 86p.

Hauser, Philip. *Education and Social Change.* Proceedings of the Fourth Annual Conference, National Committee for Support of the Public Schools. The Committee, 1966. 13–5.

Havighurst, Robert J. *Education in Metropolitan Areas.* Allyn and Bacon, 1966. 260p.

Hemphill, John K., and others. *Administrative Performance and Personality: a Study of the Principal in the Simulated School.* Teachers Col, Columbia U, 1962. 432p.

Henry, Nelson B. (Ed.) *Changing Conceptions in Educational Administration.* 45th Yearbook, Part II, N.S.S.E. U Chicago, 1946. 186p.

Hentoff, Nat. "The Principal." *New Yorker* 42, May 7:52–119; 1966.

Hills, Jean. "Educational Administration: a Field in Transition?" *Ed Adm Q* 1:58–66; 1965.

Houle, Cyril O. *The Effective Board.* Association Press, 1960. 174p.

Idiculla, Muttaniyil Eapen. "A Comparative Study of the Role Expectations of High School Principals in Selected Western States." Doctoral dissertation. Brigham Young U, 1965.

James, H. Thomas, and others. *Determinants of Educational Expenditures in Large Cities in the United States.* Stanford U, 1966. 198p.

Joel, Lewin George, Jr. "An Analysis of Leadership Characteristics in Relationship to the Tenure of Successful School Superintendents in Connecticut." Doctoral dissertation. U Connecticut, 1965.

Johnston, William Robert. "Trends in the Concerns of School Superintendents as Evidenced by a Review of the Resolutions Enacted by the American Association of School Administrators in the Twentieth Century." Doctoral dissertation. U Toledo, 1965.

Keppel, Francis. *The Necessary Revolution in American Education.* Harper, 1966. 201p.

King, Edmund J. *Other Schools and Ours,* rev. ed. Holt, 1963. 253p.

Knezevich, Stephen J., and Fowlkes, John Guy. *Business Management of Local School Systems.* Harper, 1960. 328p.

Leiman, Harold I. "A Study of Teacher Attitudes and Morale as Related to Participation in Administration." Doctoral dissertation. New York U, 1961.

Lieberman, Myron, and Moskow, Michael H. *Collective Negotiations for Teachers.* Rand McNally, 1966. 745p.

Loughary, John W., and others. *Man-Machine Systems in Education.* Harper, 1966. 242p.

Male, George A. *Education in France.* USOE, Bulletin 1963, No. 33. GPO, 1963. 205p.

McAbee, Harold V. "Time for the Job." *B Nat Assn Sec Sch Prin* 42, March:39–44; 1958.

McLure, William P. *The Intermediate Administrative School District in the United States.* Bureau Educational Research, U Illinois, 1956. 160p.

Mead, Margaret. (Ed.) *Cooperation and Competition Among Primitive Peoples.* McGraw-Hill, 1961. 544p.

Mead, Margaret. *Growing Up in New Guinea.* Morrow, 1962. 384p.

Metcalf, Henry C., and Urwick, L. (Eds.) *Dynamic Administration: The Collected Papers of Mary Parker Follett.* Harper, 1942. 320p.

Miles, Matthew B. (Ed.) *Innovation in Education.* Teachers Col, Columbia U, 1964. 689p.

Miller, Van. *The Public Administration of American School Systems.* Macmillan, 1965. 580p.

Misner, Jaul J., and others. *Elementary School Administration.* Charles E. Merrill Books, Inc., 1963. 422p.

Moore, Hollis A., Jr. *Studies in School Administration.* AASA, 1957. 202p.

Moorehead, Alan. *The Fatal Impact.* Harper, 1966. 230p.

Morphet, Edgar L., and Ryan, Charles O. (Eds.) *Prospective Changes in Society by 1980.* Designing Education for the Future (Denver), 1966. 268p.

National Education Association. *Journal of Proceedings and Addresses.* NEA, 1895. p. 375–397.

National Education Association, Department of Elementary School Principals. *The Elementary School Principalship—a Research Study.* 37th Yearbook. NEA, 1958. 259p.

National Education Association, Department of Rural Education. *The County Superintendent of Schools in the United States.* NEA, 1950. 188p.

Nichols, Robert C. "Schools and the Disadvantaged." *Science* 154:1312–4; 1966.

Orentlicher, Herman I. "The Compact for Education." *B Am Assn U Prof* 51:437–46; 1965.

Otto, Henry J., and Sanders, David C. *Elementary School Organization and Administration,* 4th ed. Appleton, 1964. 409p.

Ovard, Glen F. *Administration of the Changing Secondary School.* Macmillan, 1966. 531p.

Pedley, F. H. *The Educational System in England and Wales.* Pergamon, 1964. 249p.

Pierce, Paul R. *The Origin and Development of the Public School Principalship.* U Chicago, 1934. 223p.

Poignant, Raymond. *L'Enseignement dans les Pays du Marché Commun.* Institut Pédagogique National, 1965. 319p.

Reeves, A. W., and others. (Eds.) *The Canadian School Principal.* McClelland and Stewart, 1962. 311p.

Regents Advisory Committee on Educational Leadership. *School Boards and School Board Membership.* New York State Education Department, 1965. 68p.

Reller, Theodore L. *The Development of the City Superintendency of Schools in the United States.* The Author, 1935. 339p.

Reller, Theodore L., and Morphet, Edgar L. (Eds.) *Comparative Educational Administration.* Prentice-Hall, 1962. 438p.

Riddle, Bruce E. "An Analysis of State Departments of Education with Respect to Their Emerging Leadership Functions in Educational Improvement." Doctoral dissertation. U Oklahoma, 1964.

Rielle, Donald Francis. "Perceptions of Components and Administrative Behavior in the Process of Delegating." Doctoral dissertation. Ohio State U, 1965.

Rock, Donald A., and Hemphill, John K. *Report of the Junior High-School Principalship.* National Association of Secondary School Principals, 1966. 117p.

Roesch, Winston L. "Staffing for School Management—the Legal Factor." *Sch Life* 42:14–5; 1960.

Rombouts, Jack Robert. "The Role of the Committee Technique in School Administration as Expressed by Teachers in 25 High School Districts of the Upper Peninsula." Doctoral dissertation. Michigan State U, 1959.

Rushing, William A. "Organizational Rules and Surveillance: Propositions in Comparative Organizational Analysis." *Adm Sci Q* 10:423–43; 1966.

Sachs, Benjamin M. *Educational Administration: a Behavioral Approach.* Houghton, 1966. 412p.

Sadler, John Edward. *J. A. Comenius and the Concept of Universal Education.* Allen, 1966. 320p.

Salisbury, Arnold W. "A Study of the Business Management Functions and Responsibilities of the High School Principals in North Central Association High Schools." Doctoral dissertation. U Iowa, 1963.

Saunders, Robert L., and others. *A Theory of Educational Leadership.* Charles E. Merrill Books, Inc., 1966. 174p.

Schafer, Dan A. "Study of the Extent that James B. Conant's Recommendations for the American High School Have Been Implemented in Selected Indiana High Schools." Doctoral dissertation. Indiana U, 1963.

Schultz, Theodore W. *The Economic Value of Education.* Columbia U Press, 1963. 92p.

Sears, Jesse B. *The Nature of the Administrative Process.* McGraw-Hill, 1950. 623p.

Shelton, Raymond Orris. "An Analysis of Patterns of Communications of Certain Elementary School Principals in Selected School Systems in Iowa and Illinois." Doctoral dissertation. U Iowa, 1965.

Simon, Herbert A. *Administrative Behavior.* Macmillan, 1945; 2nd ed, 1957. 259p.

Simon, Kenneth A., and Fullam, Marie G. *Projections of Educational Statistics to 1975–76.* USOE, GPO, 1966. 113p.

Task Force on Education. *Education for the Future of Illinois.* State of Illinois, 1966. 220p.

Thurston, Lee M., and Roe, William H. *State School Administration.* Harper, 1957. 427p.

Tiedt, Sidney W. *The Role of the Federal Government in Education.* Oxford U Press, 1966. 243p.

University Council for Educational Administration. "The International Intervisitation Program." *UCEA Newsletter* 7; April:1–4; 1966(*a*); *UCEA Newsletter* 8; December:1–2; 1966(*b*).

University Council for Educational Administration. *UCEA Annual Report, 1965–66.* The Council, 1966(*c*). 46p.

Walker, W. G. "Educational Administration." In Cowan, R. W. T. (Ed.) *Education for Australians.* Cheshire, 1964. p. 193–217.

Wallace, Mildred Reed. "Concepts of Instructional Roles of Elementary School Administrators." Doctoral dissertation. U Southern California, 1965.

Walton, John. *Administration and Policy-making in Education.* Johns Hopkins Press, 1959. 207p.

Washburne, Carleton. "Whose Man Is the Superintendent?" *Com Sch and Its Adm* July, 1966.

Wildman, Wesley A. "Teacher Collective Action in the United States." In Ohm, Robert E., and Johns, O. D. (Eds.) *Negotiations in the Schools.* U Oklahoma, 1965. p. 25–6.

Ziegler, Walter John. "The Bases and Process for Decision-making by the Superintendent of Schools." Doctoral dissertation. U Southern California, 1964.

PUPIL PROGRESS

In the third edition of this encyclopedia, published in 1960, Henry J. Otto and Dwain M. Estes (1960) discussed the question of pupil progress under the heading "accelerated and retarded progress." Their article dealt largely with the administrative aspects of pupil progress. Research was reviewed on such matters as the age-grade status of pupils, promotion and nonpromotion practices, problems of the school dropout, and college acceleration practices. In general the studies reviewed assumed well-defined age norms and academic standards for each grade. They tended to be quantitative in nature and they relied heavily on city and state surveys and on other comparative statistical data.

In the 1960 discussion there were brief references to experimentation, particularly at the elementary-school level, in the direction of nongraded school arrangements and new approaches to the individualization of instruction. At the time the article was written, it now seems in retrospect, what later became known as a "revolution" in American education was then just in its infancy, and such concepts as nongraded school organization had not been subjected to very much discussion in the literature or to analysis through research.

After the passage of a decade, during which period there has been much research and development of topics related to pupil progress, it has become increasingly clear that the rates and patterns of pupil learning, and hence the many sorts of pupil environments and administrative mechanisms that are required to meet varying needs, are far more numerous than might have been imagined earlier. It has therefore seemed appropriate to employ the broader title "pupil progress" and to expand this discussion beyond the administrative realm to include research on human motivation, achievement, and related areas in the behavioral and social sciences in reviewing the factors that influence and facilitate the progress of children through the school system.

The literature produced over the past decade has shed further light on the historical trends that can be traced in school organization patterns over approximately a century. In particular, a better perspective has been obtained on the cycles through which graded school structure has passed since the early nineteenth century, although it must be admitted that the "nongraded" pattern, which promises eventually to replace gradedness, has been developing unevenly and largely on the basis of trial and error. American education is clearly going through a sometimes painful stage of transition, paradoxically clinging to certain outmoded forms and practices associated with graded structure and at the same time revealing a growing commitment to the less-well-defined but theoretically superior arrangements that are emerging and of which flexibility is a major characteristic.

A significant fact is that in a decade the educational profession has become far more aware of the individual differences that characterize the human population. In particular there is a heightened awareness of the poor fit between traditional mechanisms for regulating or influencing pupil progress and the many different kinds of children whose progress, for a great variety of reasons, has usually been unsatisfactory or disappointing. For the better part of a century the educational program and the administrative and pedagogical policies which have influenced and governed pupil progress were based largely upon certain assumptions concerning human educability and human motivation which now seem obviously false. The point of view that all children are innately capable of mastering grade-level-expectancy standards, given sufficient motivation and effort, has given way to the realization that many children are either temporarily or permanently unprepared for the types of school experiences which are offered. The nineteenth-century tendency to explain poor school performance in moralistic terms, linked to the evangelical concept of the sinfulness of man, has gradually eroded in the face of evidence concerning human variability and the impotence or irrelevance of typical classroom approaches for some children. Similarly, the objections of nineteenth-century educators to precocity in children, as revealed in their deliberate effort to prevent such children from advancing beyond their classmates in one or more aspects of the total program, have slowly given way to various provisions for accelerated programs or advanced programs. That most schools still do relatively little in recognition of the vast range of individual differences, however, seems a warranted though regrettable conclusion.

A HISTORICAL PERSPECTIVE. Acceleration and retardation were not major problems in the colonial and early national periods of American history, since most instruction was on an individualized basis and instructional procedures and materials were so primitive that no uniform policy with respect to pupil progress was possible. During the nineteenth century, however, both the growing size and the recognized national importance of the American educational enterprise led to several standardizing influences. One of these was the development of a textbook industry, which produced graded textbook series and which had an incalculable influence on both the instructional decisions of teachers and the curricula of the state-supported normal schools in which teachers were prepared. That strong school administrators emerged during this period, charged with the awesome responsibility for developing and managing complex school systems with a poorly trained staff, also explains why rigid, systematic procedures came into general use.

Cook and Clymer (1962), in a historical discussion of acceleration and retardation, indicate that by 1870 or so courses of study were so well organized and so tightly supervised that a superintendent could at a given moment predict exactly what problem or topic was being discussed or presented in all of the fourth-grade classes of the city. Likening this arrangement to an assembly line in an automobile plant, they deplore its essentially mechanical nature and its disregard for individual differences.

As Goodlad and Anderson (1963) point out, however, the development of the graded school between approximately 1848 and 1870 was a significant creative effort appropriate to the needs of its time. The orderly division of the curriculum into manageable segments, each at least plausibly related to the abilities of most children at the age level in question, made it possible to enroll and deal with the thousands of pupils who poured into the schools of a growing nation. The task of teacher training was simplified, and teachers were able to become reasonably familiar with the materials and the children of a given grade level. Granted that the system violated many of the principles of child development that were later recognized, it operated with amazing efficiency, and it enabled the United States to become the first nation to fulfill its commitment to free public education and thus to hasten its emergence as a world power.

Graded Education: A Closer Look. The graded school as defined by early advocates, such as Chicago's superintendent of schools, W. H. Wells (1867), was one in which the pupils are divided into classes "according to their attainments" and in which all of the pupils in each class "attend to the same branches of study at the same time." Wells stressed that children should not be allowed to advance in one branch before all other branches are brought up to the same standards, in part for the reason that a child could then easily move to another school and find a class equally advanced with himself in all studies. Of interest is that Wells described a system of ten grades, six of which were primary and four of which were associated with the grammar school. The tenth grade was for the youngest children, and first grade was the final year of grammar school. Classes were apparently organized according to ability since it was noted that "when practicable, all promotions from one grade to another should be made at the commencement of each month." Somewhat later, then, the system became more standardized along the lines deplored by Cook and Clymer.

In 1877 there appeared the first encyclopedia of education in the English language (Kiddle & Schem, 1877). Noting that the graded system prevailed mostly in the cities, and acknowledging the various advantages ascribed to the graded arrangement, the unidentified author of the article "Graded Schools" pointed out that a number of objections had already been raised against them, chief among them being that the interests of the individual pupil are often sacrificed to those of the many. The author then goes on to quote from an address presented before the National Educational Association in 1874 by E. E. White, who offered strong criticism of the graded system and the ways it forces uniformity on both teachers and pupils despite the fact that pupils differ markedly in ability.

While there were individuals such as White who recognized that uniformity should not and could not be forced, the prevailing counterassumption was that achievement is not based on interests, abilities and skills, but rather it follows from earnest effort, persistence and self-discipline. It was expected that children *should* be able to progress at an even rate through the grades and thereby acquire their education. According to this view, enunciated by Wells and others, precociousness in children was a hazard to be guarded against. The child who got ahead in his work was virtually considered a potential agent of the devil, intent on drawing himself and others into mischief. By the same token, the child who lagged behind was considered lazy, undisciplined, and sinful, and his failures were generally regarded as being of his own making. It was argued that the graded system served, among other purposes, to guard against the disruptive and destructive influences of both the slow and the precocious "problem students."

Implicit in the graded system was the idea that man's storehouse of information and knowledge could be organized into sequential units of "subject matter" ranging from easy to difficult. As graded textbooks and materials appeared on the market, each grade level came to signify definite levels of achievement. When a student did not achieve minimum grade standards, it became common practice simply to keep him at that grade level for another year or more. In time, it became apparent that large numbers of students were not meeting the required standards, that in some schools the failure rate was approaching 52 percent, with as many as 70 percent of the students being overage for the grades in which they were enrolled. Many statistics relating to pupils' failure rates were collected and discussed, by Maxwell (1904), Thorndike (1908), Leonard P. Ayers (1909), and others. By the early 1900's the "laggards in our schools," to use Ayers' phrase, had become a major educational problem.

Not until the depression of the 1930's, however, did it become vitally important to the public that the nation's schools increase their holding power. Then, as concern continued to mount over the growing failure rate, research studies were initiated to measure the effects of current nonpromotion practices on achievement. Saunders (1941) demonstrated that children, as a general rule, do not learn more by repeating grades. His conclusions were later substantiated by Coffield and Blommers (1956). Otto and Melby (1935) and others showed that pupils who are praised for their work make greater progress over a period of time than do pupils who have been reproofed and punished, that in fact the failing child frequently becomes discouraged and antagonistic. These conclusions have been further documented and reviewed by Sandin (1944), Goodlad (1952, 1954), Worth (1959), and others. Studies comparing achievement scores with age-grade data showed that grade levels are not indicative of definite stages of achievement: it was confirmed that not only do achievement-test results vary widely among children of the same age and grade but also the scores of any one child vary from test to test or from one section of a test to another. Burr (1931) concluded that homogeneous grouping reduced by only two or three the number of pupils in an ordinary class group who would require special assistance from the teacher. As was noted at the outset, Otto and Estes commented in detail on these and other related early research studies in their 1860 article.

Because of these early studies and because of mounting public concern, educators found themselves compelled to seek ways of varying instructional procedures in order to meet individual needs more adequately. In the late 1930's and early 1940's many accommodative remedies to the problems raised by graded education were devised, all of them fitting within the established framework of the graded structure. Ability grouping, or "tracking," within grades was adopted as one means for placing children according to their abilities. Children were assigned "remedial" or "enrichment" activities. Special curriculum plans were introduced in the secondary schools for terminal, vocational, and college-bound students. Specialists in reading, speech, and mathematics were assigned to schools, and special programs were offered to retarded, handicapped, or gifted children. The trend in promotion practices shifted away from promoting on the basis of achievement alone: age and maturity factors were increasingly taken into account as well, even to the extent that schools began to adopt "automatic promotion plans," "social promotion plans," and the like.

Clearly, such devices were merely facilitating measures, not basic solutions to the problems raised by the graded system. As efforts on the part of the schools to adapt to children's instructional needs, they were of relatively minor significance. By and large, most instruction in the schools continued to be conducted through group teaching on a grade-level basis, with limited provisions made for meeting individual learning needs. Well-defined standards for each grade continued to be the yardstick of pupil progress, and when grade standards were not met it was generally assumed that the child (rather than the teacher or the parent or the school system) was at fault.

Meeting Individual Needs (Before 1955). In 1862 pupils in St. Louis were organized in a plan that allowed for reclassification every six weeks. In this plan brighter students were placed in advanced sections. Several years later, at Batavia, New York, a plan was developed whereby two teachers used a single classroom (Goodlad & Anderson, 1963), and while one taught at grade level the other helped those students who had fallen behind in their work. A plan introduced in 1888 by Preston Search, superintendent of schools in Pueblo, California, emphasized individual work and individual progress, as opposed to group work and group progress (Search, 1894). The plan eliminated entirely the concept of nonpromotion. By 1890 there had appeared a number of other plans and systems intended to allow pupils to progress at their own rate. Homogeneous grouping became fairly common as an attempt to simplify the teacher's job in meeting the needs of children with varying abilities. A quarterly promotion plan, as reported by Fred C. Ayer (1923), gained favor in some of the large cities: students were advanced or were not promoted for one-fourth of a year rather than for the usual year.

At the turn of the century, such notables as President Charles W. Eliot of Harvard and President William Rainey Harper of the University of Chicago were calling for flexible school organization as a means of supporting unique abilities. Search had by this time published a most insightful book (Search, 1901) in which he spoke vigorously against graded education for not meeting the needs of the individual. He favored an ungraded plan that would develop differences and conserve individuality. Meanwhile, guided by John Dewey, teachers at the Laboratory School of the University of Chicago were encouraging the enrichment of "the whole child" by eliminating the arbitrary classification of grades, textbooks, and subject matter. Marks were never given. Activities were such that children could follow their own interests and judge for themselves their successes and failures. Although Dewey's work has been widely discussed and frequently misinterpreted, it has had a profound and salutary influence upon all subsequent studies of pupil progress, and scholars find much profit in examining such source materials as have been provided by Mayhew and Edwards (1936), two of Dewey's early colleagues.

In 1913 Frederic L. Burk at the training school of the San Francisco State Teachers College attempted to individualize instruction and create flexible, gradeless, continuous-progress schools. His work influenced Carleton W. Washburne, originator of the Winnetka Plan, and Helen Parkhurst, who established the Dalton Plan. These plans both sought to allow each child to master successive units of work at his own pace. The curriculum of the Winnetka Plan, about which Washburne and Marland (1963) have written a most useful report, was divided into "common essentials" and "group creative activities." It was assumed that all children needed mastery in the former but that the results achieved by children in the latter might legitimately differ. In the Dalton Plan children were free to set their own pace but were required to complete the corresponding (grade-level) units for each of the other subjects before proceeding to the next assignment in any given subject. These and other innovative experiments have been reviewed by Otto (1934), Goodlad and Anderson (1963), and Buffie (1967).

Although the early innovative experiments undoubtedly have had an effect on current educational trends and patterns, they were mostly demonstration models that did not win widespread acceptance. Perhaps because communications systems were insufficiently developed or because teachers were a fairly puritanical and unsophisticated lot, or perhaps because the experiments posed a threat to the prevailing values of the larger society, they had disappointingly little influence in their time on the prevailing educational practices of the nation's public schools.

THE PRESENT-DAY SETTING. The concept of educating individuals according to their unique needs and abilities is not new, but it has been only since the early 1950's, with modern advances in science and technology and with the incentive given in 1957 by Sputnik, that the actual meeting of these needs has become an attainable national goal. Sputnik and the outcry that followed awoke the nation to a new awareness of the need to educate each individual to his full potential. Also of great significance was the Supreme Court decision of 1954 condemning "separate but equal" education: it offered a powerful reminder that equal educational opportunity did not yet exist in this country. Since that time the public has been made more aware of the needs of "the other America," of the indignities and inequalities suffered by the poor and underprivileged, particularly the Negro minority. This new awareness and new concern for all the nation's subpopulations was behind President Johnson's 1964 speech declaring war on poverty and emphasizing the need to provide "every citizen with the opportunity to advance his welfare to the limits of his capabilities."

Education is conceived of as the means to achieving this goal. As a result, since 1960 federal funding for research and development has increased by 2,000 percent (Bloom, 1966). As specified in the Elementary and Secondary Education Act of 1965, federal funds are being used to strengthen elementary and secondary programs for educationally deprived children in the low-income areas; to provide additional school library resources, textbooks, and other instructional material; to finance supplementary-education centers and services; to broaden areas of cooperative research, and to strengthen state departments of education. Because the emphasis is on assisting educationally deprived children in all schools, public and private alike, for the first time in history federal funds are being spent for non-public school students below the college level.

Stimulated in large measure by massive injections of federal money, public education in the late 1960's mustered its energies toward the individualization of instruction and toward the development of flexible organization patterns to facilitate pupil progress, on a scale previously inconceivable. Progress reports such as that provided by Miller and others (1967), while acknowledging that an enormous task lies ahead, were nevertheless optimistic in tone.

Moreover, big business is involving itself in the educational market to such an extent that one cannot but speculate on the potential implications of automation and the technological revolution for education. Giant corporations entering the education market have the capability of developing vastly superior educational systems. Every important aspect of education—personnel, buildings, instructional materials, equipment—is being intensively researched for inclusion in the system. Indeed, education is coming to be thought of as the nation's most important industry.

Not surprisingly, therefore, educators are overcoming their traditional distaste for machines and are exploring the potential role of machines and electronic aids for the schools. They are becoming increasingly involved in industry's approach to management and organizational problems, and this has at least indirect implications for the individualization of instruction. A volume edited by Glaser (1962) shows how the approaches used in industry, government, and the military for conducting the innovative process can be employed in education. Volumes edited by Miles (1964) and Miller (1967) also deal with the problems and processes of conducting, evaluating, and disseminating educational innovations.

In the area of instruction two concomitant developments are taking place: a technology associated with mass instruction and techniques associated with individualized instruction are being united in all-encompassing instructional technology, one that meets group and individual needs alike. The New York University Language Laboratory, used by 2,000 pupils each semester, provides a case in point: each student there can hear himself as he practices the language he is learning; if he needs individual help he can signal the instructor by throwing a switch that turns on a light at the instructor's console; and he can profit from flexible group instruction by means of an elaborate intercom system. Bushnell and Allen (1967), Goodlad and others (1966), Suppes (1966), Finn (1963), Silberman (1966), and others have written with perception on the implications for the future of the new instructional technology and the uses of the computer in education.

It has been said that technology is more than an invention, more than a machine; it is a process and a way of thinking. As such it cannot help but force educators of today and tomorrow to evolve new patterns of staff deployment and new logistics of instruction. Hopefully, teachers and administrators of the future will be at home with the machine; they will learn to capitalize on technology's many time-saving devices.

EDUCATIONAL INNOVATION AND PUPIL PROGRESS. That educational technology can help to individualize instruction and increase the prospects of each child to discover an appropriate and rewarding means of learning is an apparently reasonable assumption. That technology alone can provide for the educational needs of a multivariate population, on the other hand, would seem to be a reckless expectation. Increasingly in the 1960's, it has become evident that educational reform and the attainment of educational excellence must involve a multidimensional program. Combinations of procedures and materials, rather than one or the other of these separately, will prove to be needed.

A case in point is the so-called nongraded school. A slow though firm national trend toward "nongrading" became noticeable in the mid 1950's, and by the late 1960's it had become a major movement, not without its difficulties, however. Though far more popular in elementary schools (Goodlad & Anderson, 1963), the idea has made a small but firm beginning in secondary schools as well (Brown, 1965). In current parlance the term "nongraded" refers to that pattern of vertical school organization which, in dramatic contrast to the rigid, lockstep pattern of graded schools, presumably permits the unhurried and uninterrupted progress of children through the school program each on a timetable uniquely suited to his own academic potentiality. While theoretically the ideal means of regulating pupil progress, the nongraded school in practice has rarely fulfilled its mission because its sponsors have usually relied on conventional curriculum guides and materials and on other conventional accouterments of the graded school they are trying to replace. Only where the initiation of nongraded structure has been accompanied and reinforced by other reforms, such as significant technological and curriculum changes or different ways of assigning teachers, has the inherent strength of the nongraded concept come fully into play.

In the 1960's it became common to refer to the numerous dimensions of educational change by terms such as "the revolution in education" or "the educational reform movement." An interesting fact is that although proponents of various specific reforms were prone to assign special virtue to them, nearly all were agreed that a multiplicity of reforms when in combination had far greater power than any of them individually—that, in fact, the whole is greater than the sum of its parts. Many were also agreed, however, that the introduction of numerous simultaneous reforms could prove to be a rather overwhelming experience for a school staff.

Given this caution, that changes designed to facilitate pupil progress and enhance the quality of programs must be introduced carefully and with due preparation, let us examine some of the reforms which have dominated professional thinking over the past decade. First and foremost has been the growing commitment of educators to the desirability and necessity of providing for individual needs in a variety of ways. Part and parcel of this commitment has been the effort to develop procedural alternatives: establishment of different learning goals for different students; allowing different students different lengths of time for a given learning unit; using different learning materials and devices with different students; and using different methods or techniques with different students.

Nongraded organization permits slower-learning pupils to spend more time at school tasks without suffering the penalties of nonpromotion. Similarly, it permits fast learners to advance to higher levels without the awkward problems of "skipping" grades through double promotion. A variety of devices which emerged in the 1950's for accelerating the progress of superior students was described and evaluated by De Haan (1963).

One manifestation of more flexible secondary-school organization was the development of "honors" classes and of advanced-placement programs in which college-level courses were offered to superior students. Such programs originated partly as a result of efforts to place ex-GI's in classes better suited to their age and experience after World War II. The success of these programs is reflected in the numbers of students applying for advanced standing through the Advanced Placement Program of the College Entrance Examination Board: in 1954, 532; in 1966–67, 42,338.

Whether fostered by these procedural arrangements or by other events, major curriculum improvements have been a second dimension of the reform movement. Prominent within this category has been the growing emphasis on process goals and other tool skills which equip children to learn, with a concomitant deemphasis on the conventional content goals. One result of this trend has been to raise many new questions about conventional approaches to the measurement and evaluation of pupil progress, and teachers have become increasingly aware of the diagnostic as well as the evaluative purposes that tests and other instruments can play in examining each child's school progress and needs.

Already mentioned above was a third dimension of reform—namely, the rapid development of technological devices for instruction and for various administrative and record-keeping tasks formerly done by hand. This, in turn, has stimulated interest in programmed instruction and other forms of self-directed learning, along with new patterns of small-group and large-group instruction.

One of the most interesting areas of current research and development is that of pupil grouping. Not only the optimum size of groups for this purpose or that but also the composition of the groups have been the object of many investigations. Thelen (1967b) recommends the matching of teachers and pupils, indicating that pupil reactions to the attitudes, enthusiasms, aversions, interests, and goals of a given teacher will largely determine the nature of his learning experience. However, the range and variety of pupil backgrounds and interests in a group or class, and thus the types of pupil-pupil interaction that are possible, are also seen as important determinants of the learning experience. The trend is to seek both variety and commonality in establishing classes or teams.

Anderson (1962, 1964, 1966b) examined the literature on grouping and concluded that heterogeneous, multiage classes or teams within which homogeneous subgroups can on occasion be created are superior to arrangements which limit the range of abilities and backgrounds with which a given pupil is likely to have continuing contact. Meltzer (1967) stated that the achievement levels of disadvantaged children are appreciably higher in educational settings heterogeneous with respect to social class, for example. Wolfson (1967) also supported the use of multiage classes in elementary schools, and Ridgway and Lawton (1965) described the advantageous use of such groupings in English infants' schools.

Jones (1966) reviewed the research on ability grouping with secondary-school pupils. Goldberg and others (1966) also examined the effects of such grouping and warn that it can lead teachers into mistaken complacency or wrong assessments of pupil capacities. Morgenstern (1966) has compiled journal articles dealing with various aspects of grouping. Johnston (1967) argued that intellectual segregation may be as damaging to personality as racial segregation or other kinds of segregation, and for many of the same reasons.

From available evidence it seems possible to make four observations about grouping. (1) Ability grouping is no longer viewed as a variable which independently affects achievement. (2) Grouping of whatever kind is primarily an administrative procedure and should be treated as such. (3) Despite the modern educator's commitment to new patterns of organization to facilitate the meeting of individual needs, research seems to indicate that teaching style and the individual pupil-teacher relationship are the most important variables in affecting change in learning. (4) To the extent that teaching styles and teacher-pupil relationships can be positively affected by one form of grouping over another, grouping can be most important. Beyond this, the content of the educational program becomes the important variable in influencing learning; accordingly, grouping must be planned with specific content and programs in mind to be most effective.

Although the problem of optimum pupil grouping has been studied for many years, almost all research and writing has been based on experience with pupils in self-contained classrooms under conditions which are now undergoing rapid change. With the emergence of alternatives such as team teaching, and as teachers experiment more extensively with grouping patterns, it is probably necessary either to discard much of the published research or to reconsider its findings in the light of options now available.

Another major dimension of educational reform has, in fact, been the growing interest in collegial patterns of teaching. In both secondary and elementary schools up to the late 1950's the prevailing pattern of staff organization was that described by the term "self-contained classroom." In elementary schools this meant that there was a nearly autonomous teacher responsible for teaching all subjects (except perhaps art, music, or physical education) to a stable group of some 25 or 30 children. In secondary schools it meant that there was an autonomous teacher dealing serially through the day with stable groups of some 25 or 30 students in one or more subject areas. This arrangement was warmly approved, for both theoretical and practical reasons nearly all of which now seem less valid. Anderson (1966b) discusses these at length and summarizes the arguments for team teaching as a more flexible and desirable staffing arrangement. Joyce (1967) confirms that team teaching has been a major development over some 15 years and reviews the research thus far completed. Shaplin and Olds (1964) provide what may be the authoritative discussion of team teaching as a major educational development.

Another important aspect of educational reform has been the emergence on a significant scale of various nonprofessional and paraprofessional roles in the schools. Almost 30 percent of American high schools and a smaller but growing percentage of elementary schools are reported to have added personnel to their staffs to fill such roles as clerical aide, teacher's aide, audiovisual technician, composition reader, materials assistant, and lunchroom-playground supervisor. The services of such people have made it possible not only to free teachers of numerous tasks which interfere with more important professional assignments but also to increase the attention that can be paid to each child in his progress through the school program.

Other reforms now under way, such as the reorganization of school units and architectural innovations and improvements, have important though less direct bearing on the school progress of children. Of special interest is an apparently strong trend to acknowledge the weaknesses of conventionally organized junior high schools and to adopt in its place the so-called middle school, which attempts to provide a more suitable and hygienic academic and social environment for the preadolescent and early-adolescent child. The desirability of this trend is revealed in data showing the extent of frustration and maladjustment among pupils in this particular age group, the typical junior high school being the first environment in which children are exposed to some of the pressures and conditions usually associated with secondary education.

In summary, the innovations under way in the 1960's included not only pedagogical and curriculum reforms but also various efforts to create a more flexible, efficient, and comfortable environment within which children can learn. Of these, the idea of nongraded schools came closest to representing a theoretical ideal, both philosophically and functionally, and all the other ideas were of interest largely because of their potential relationship to achieving that ideal. On the other hand, nongradedness has proved an elusive goal, especially where its proponents have failed to develop the curriculum guides and materials necessary to its operations. Moreover, continued loyalty to the self-contained classroom has diminished the effectiveness of nongraded organization by placing a heavy curriculum burden on each individual teacher and by limiting the pupil groupings and the patterns of staff utilization that can be used.

To many observers it has been encouraging to note that teachers working in teams have a far greater capability of adapting their programs to the needs of differing children, and in effect, teaching teams find it easier to ungrade their classes than do teachers working alone. Increasingly, as a result, it is argued that in order to accelerate the development of continuous-progress programs for children in the schools, patterns of cooperative teaching should be adopted as a strategic beginning.

RELATED RESEARCH AND IMPLICATIONS FOR SCHOOL PRACTICE. Interest in providing for individual pupil progress through such reforms as team teaching and continuous-progress programs can be traced at least in part to the laboratories of experimental psychologists and physiologists, to the work of cultural anthropologists and behavioral scientists, and to advances made in statistical analysis and standardized testing. A growing body of learning theory is discrediting long-accepted assumptions concerning human educability and motivation for learning, especially those on which grade-level-expectancy standards, promotion and nonpromotion practices, and competitive-comparative marking systems are based. Today there are on hand data which back up the insights of some of the early educational innovators. To be sure, much of the research is still in its infancy and is often inconclusive, but nonetheless it represents important steps forward.

Human Development and the Influence of Early Education. Longitudinal studies of human growth and development have contributed to an understanding and awareness not only of the predictable and orderly sequence of development that manifests itself from birth onward but also of the significant differences that exist in rates and patterns of growth. Researchers recognize the influence of the early years of childhood on later development and the fact that early stimulation—physical, social, and mental—is necessary for normal human growth. Data from about 1,000 longitudinal studies have been examined and interpreted by Bloom (1964), who observes that the most rapid growth of intelligence takes place before the age of four and that what a child learns in these years largely determines his future achievement. Hunt (1961) has estimated that the average IQ could probably be increased by 30 points, should formal education by age three be made available to all. Wilhelms (1967b) claims that not only can cognitive strength be increased by this means but so also can personal strength. He further maintains that educators have yet to appreciate the almost unlimited potential of young human beings. That greater optimism on the part of the teacher concerning a child's long-range capacities can have a salutary effect on actual

progress is argued by Wilhelms and supported by such studies as Rosenthal's (1968).

By the end of the 1960's there appeared to be a growing interest and optimism among developmental psychologists concerning the enhancement of intellectual development through preschool education. There has emerged over several decades of research a well-supported theory of interactionism, which holds that intellectual development results from a dynamic interaction between genetic and environmental variables. Manipulation and control of the environment, by means of such mechanisms as compensatory preschool education, has, according to this theory, the potentiality of offsetting the disadvantages suffered by those children who are reared in a relatively poor setting.

There are some indications that preschool programs modeled after the traditional middle-class kindergarten program with its emphasis on free play and group interaction is not appropriate for all children, that children from the poorer elements of our society in particular require a program with a special emphasis on cognitive, or intellectual, growth. Programs under the supervision of Carl Bereiter in Canton, Ohio, Glen Nimnicht in Greeley, Colorado, and Earl Schaefer in Washington, D.C., offer evidence that this approach is indeed rewarding. Most of the compensatory programs launched during the 1960's, however, seem either too traditional in character to be of significant value to those enrolled or are too new and too imperfectly developed to permit adequate assessment of results, and indeed the entire field of preschool education is too much in flux to warrant other than tentative predictions as to probable trends.

That remarkably greater emphasis will be placed upon early-childhood-education services, and upon supporting research, is a conclusion one can draw from the evidence now available. Another is that much of the educational effort at the preschool level will be directed toward parents in the realization that parents inevitably play important roles in the school success (or failure) of their children and that it is therefore desirable to equip the parent for his educative role in every way possible. Research in progress by Wolf (1965), Deutsch (1964), Bloom (1964), Strodbeck (1964), and others stresses the significance of parental expectations and aspirations. Hess (1965) and Lipchik (1964) have reported that mothers can be taught to develop cognitive facilities in their preschool-age children. Moreover, Bowman (1965) and Brookover and others (1964) report that, given proper supervision and training, parental influence on a child's mental health and self concept can be modified so as to make a marked difference on the child's performance in school.

Of interest is that Soviet educators have apparently come to some of these same conclusions. The Ministry of Education for the Russian Republic, whose educational policies frequently influence the other republics of the Soviet Union, announced in 1967 a program which encourages parents to give their preschool children a "head start" in reading, writing, and arithmetic. Help given at home, plus a growing willingness on the part of school officials to introduce formal instruction to pupils at the nursery and kindergarten levels, is expected to whet the intellectual appetites of youngsters and increase the prospects of satisfactory school progress.

Little agreement has been reached by American educators, and apparently in other countries as well, with respect to the content and the timing of preformal and formal instruction for young children. Investigations into the long-range values of kindergarten experience have on the whole been poorly designed, and until appropriate changes are made in curriculum and instructional practices in the early elementary program that follows kindergarten training its potential benefits may be canceled out.

Cognition, Learning, and Styles of Teaching. Research relating to cognition, or to the growth and development of the intellect per se, has received special attention in the past decade and has brought about a marked shift of emphasis from the identification of ability to its cultivation. Previously it was mistakenly assumed that intelligence is fixed once and for all by heredity and that nothing could be done to improve one's so-called native intelligence. Hunt (1966) has recently offered a comprehensive review of these earlier assumptions. Undue reliance was placed on measured intelligence and on the mastery by children of factual information at the sacrifice of deeper understanding, curiosity, creativity, and processes of reasoning. The more modern view is oriented toward nurturing intelligence rather than measuring it. As Ausubel (1965) notes, intelligence tests are now regarded as measures of developed ability or developed capacity rather than as measures of genetic potential or inherent capabilities.

Moreover, there are many facets of intelligence that have hitherto been unexplored. The model developed by Guilford (1959, 1965) of the structure of the intellect distinguishes among 50 different primary mental abilities. This presents a much larger picture of the range of human mental ability than the 4 or 5 abilities emphasized in most intelligence tests, and it invites teachers to experiment with greater ranges of inventiveness and competence. How various cognitive operations mature is the basic concern of a large group of researchers. One of Piaget's basic theses (1958) is that successive stages of growth are marked by increasing ability to perform abstract operations and to ignore the irrelevant aspects of a situation. His work in this area is recognized by curriculum reformers everywhere.

Teachers and researchers alike are investigating some of the possibilities suggested by the work of Guilford, Piaget, Bruner, and others. Crutchfield (1965), for example, reports significant results in the development of creative thinking through the use of automated instruction where creative feedback in addition to correct answers is given. Torrance (1965) reports that children who do the most manipulating of objects succeed in producing a larger number of ideas and a higher quality of original ideas. He further reports that boys receive more rewards from teachers for creative behavior than girls, whereas girls are rewarded more for conforming behavior.

Smith (1966) and Torrance (1965) have written extensively on setting conditions for creative teaching in the elementary classroom. Because of research of this sort, teachers and parents are becoming aware of the obstacles to learning which they have traditionally placed before children and they are beginning to overcome some basic long-standing assumptions. They are discovering that their role is not to *teach,* in the traditional sense of instilling knowledge and facts, but to remove obstacles, incite interests, encourage natural tendencies, make resources available, and so provide a nurturant setting in which the child is free to teach himself.

It is increasingly evident that the values held by teachers, as reflected in the decisions they make in curriculum and in classroom management, have great implications for the development of the success of children. The personality and the teaching style of the teacher, whether contrived or spontaneous, influence the environment to which the child is responding and adjusting. If the effect of that environment is to persuade the child that he is worthy and accepted, or that he is free to invent or discover or hypothesize, the child's growth and progress will obviously proceed in healthier ways than if the environment is unaccepting and critical of adventuresome behavior. This generalization is amply supported by extensive research in the self concept of children such as that done by Brookover and others (1964) and Bledsoe and Garrison (1962).

Waetjen (1966), working from the assumption that a positive self concept enhances a person's chances of learning and reduces the likelihood of failure, offers suggestions to teachers as to how pupils can be helped to develop better images of themselves as learners. He also advocates greater use of specialists to help teachers become better diagnosticians of pupils' strong and weak points, intellectual and nonintellectual factors alike, in order to help them best.

Kenneth Clark, in *Dark Ghetto* (1965), claims that teacher expectations can have a marked effect on the achievement levels of slum children. He claims that ghetto children will learn if those charged with teaching them believe they can learn and will help them to learn. Recent studies, not yet published, by sociologist Robert Rosenthal of Harvard University provide strong support for this argument. Indeed, it is becoming increasingly clear that teaching must be subordinate to learning: the teacher's role must be primarily that of facilitating learning by arousing the student's interest and curiosity and by helping him gain an increased sense of independence and self-confidence in his quest for knowledge.

Sex Differences and Learning. Just as basic research on man's cognitive development has applications in the school setting, so recent research on various physiological differences between the sexes has analogous applications. Work reported by Bentzen (1966) and others on bone development and on the growth of the reproductive system, for example, has well documented the fact that at the chronological age of six, girls are approximately 12 months ahead of boys in developmental age and that by the time they are nine years old this developmental difference has increased to 18 months. Traditionally, researchers have minimized these differences, even to the point of eliminating items on intelligence tests which would be less fair to one sex than the other. Bentzen reports that the higher incidence of language disorders, behavior disorders, general stress, blindness, and physical handicaps among boys correlates directly with the pressure put on young boys to compete with girls of the same age. Here, it would seem, is one type of persuasive evidence to support the current contention of educators that children do not necessarily profit most when they are grouped by age. By making use of such arrangements as team teaching, in which a fairly large number of children of both sexes can be included in the basic pupil family, it ought to be possible to experiment with sex-segregated subgroups for some purposes and to permit mixed-sex subgroups to exist for other purposes.

One of the better-known examples of experimentation on sex differences and learning that has been carried on within the schools is Kagan's study (1964) of second-grade children. When asked whether typical school objects such as blackboards, books, and desks are appropriate to males or females, both boys and girls perceived a significant number of these school-related objects as being feminine in character. Another well-known study, carried out by McNeil (1964), indicated that first-grade boys, especially the more aggressive ones, made more progress in learning to read under programmed instruction which reduced peer-group interaction but that girls did better in the usual reading groups under the teacher's direction. McNeil found that women teachers frequently fail to adjust their procedures to the needs of boys.

Preston (1962) compared reading-test scores of 1,035 fourth- and sixth-grade German pupils with scores of a corresponding group of 1,338 American pupils. His study suggests that differences in achievement performances of boys and girls may be culturally inspired. The mean scores for reading of American girls were significantly higher than those of American boys, with a greater incidence of retardation among boys than among girls. In the German sample the reverse proved true: **boys scored** significantly higher than girls, with the greater incidence of retardation occurring among girls. This may stem from the fact that teachers in German schools, even at the elementary level, tend to be men and that reading and learning are normally considered male activities. In the United States reading has a more feminine character assigned to it, and most primary teachers are female. In fact, fewer than 15 percent of all elementary teachers are males, and this may well be one of the greatest difficulties young children face in the schools.

As they learn more about the research being conducted on sex differences, educators are becoming seriously concerned about the feminization of American schools. Not only do boys suffer from it, but girls appear to suffer too in that they conform too readily to teacher expectations. Grambs and Waetjen (1966) suggest that more male research teachers and male coprincipals are needed, that older boys can help younger boys through tutoring, and that boys need more freedom and encouragement to enjoy the aesthetics of creativity and to develop sensitivity to human motivations and feelings. Girls, on the other hand, should be allowed to view boys as colleagues, not competitors, and ought to be given more access to problem-solving puzzles. They need the freedom to become more aggressive in their learning and intellectual development.

An authoritative book on this subject is Eleanor Maccoby's *Development of Sex Differences* (1966). This volume provides a thorough documentation of temperamental differences between boys and girls, differences which are associated with intellectual rather than with social or emotional performance. Maccoby theorizes that optimal intellectual performance comes about in children when boys are less bold and impulsive than the "real" boy and when girls are less timid and inhibited than the "real" girl.

It is difficult to assess at this time the implications for school practice of research on human development and cognition, including particularly the research on creativity and sex differences as they influence learning. Experimentation with different school practices, such as pupil grouping patterns and ways of rewarding pupil achievement, proceeds apace even as does research into the nature of learners. For the moment it seems safe to conclude that the academic progress and the ultimate maturity reached by each unique child are profoundly influenced by parents' and teachers' attitudes toward learning, by the teacher's responses to the fact of each child's sex, and by the teacher's tendency to be (or not to be) creative.

REPORTING ON PUPIL PROGRESS. In the foregoing sections we have reviewed many factors that influence pupil progress and some of the ways in which schools historically have attempted and currently are attempting to facilitate pupil achievement and growth. It now remains for us to examine briefly some problems and trends with respect to the reporting of pupil progress.

As an important aspect of individualized education and in recognition of the need for accurate and comprehensive data about each individual's school progress, reporting procedures have been a perennial topic of discussion among parents and teachers alike. No doubt intensified because of the scramble for admission to prestige colleges, the debate over traditional numerical or letter grades versus "pass-fail" or other mechanisms deemphasizing competitive-comparative rankings had by no means been resolved as of the late 1960's.

Despite the growing research evidence concerning the deleterious effects and the pedagogical inappropriateness of conventional marking and grading procedures, American schools have been slow to abandon them. Even the literature dealing with the reporting problem went through a sterile period of nearly a decade; and it was not until the Association for Supervision and Curriculum Development (ASCD) published its yearbook *Evaluation as Feedback and Guide* (Wilhelms, 1967a) that the important relationship of evaluation procedures to the fundamental needs of learners and teachers was again receiving national attention.

Of interest is that during this same period a number of colleges and universities began experimenting with ungraded classes (i.e., classes in which conventional grades are not given) and with pass-or-fail marking systems. Though in a few instances this was sparked by rebellion against the use of student grades in determining the students' military-draft status, in most it stemmed from a more fundamental disenchantment with the inadequate and distortive system of scaled grades.

The argument of the ASCD yearbook, in brief, is that evaluation must perform five tasks: facilitate self-evaluation, encompass all of the school's objectives, facilitate teaching and learning, generate useful records, and facilitate decision making on curriculum and educational policy. Feedback and guidance, the argument continues, are needed by a variety of persons—the pupil, his parents, and his teachers—and for a variety of purposes. They must take a variety of forms. No simplistic, cryptic, narrow system, such as most schools now have, can possibly accomplish these tasks.

That more adequate reporting procedures are not in common use is apparently owing in large measure to deficiencies in teacher training, both preservice and in-service, and to the lack of administrative and financial support. Most schools make little if any provision for extra clerical assistance, substitute budgetary provision for extra clerical assistance, substitute teachers, professional counselors, or other means of helping teachers to handle the special problems and the physical workload at reporting time. It is rare for a school system to free its teachers of regular duties, periodically, so that they can hold extended private conferences with pupils; and even the time provisions made for conferences with parents are usually only tokens. Neither the colleges that prepare new teachers nor the employer schools usually make much effort to train teachers in the diagnostic, interpretive, and communicative skills that good reporting requires.

Baker and Doyle (1959) have shown that teachers make more accurate assessments when they have learned to interpret pupil guidance data. Waetjen (1966) and Brandt (1966) note that specialists are needed to help teachers with the diagnosis of intellectual and nonintellectual strengths and weaknesses of children. Goodlad and Anderson (1963) discuss the ways school systems can train teachers in reporting techniques and enable them to carry out the reporting functions. Anderson (1966a) further proposes that reporting be done on a staggered schedule, as opposed to issuing all reports at the same time, partially to reduce the peak-load problem for teachers but also in the interest of reducing the artificial tension that report-card time creates.

Especially at the elementary level, it seems to be generally agreed that the face-to-face, parent-teacher conference is the best available means of conveying information on pupils' progress to parents (Goodlad & Anderson, 1963). There is also very strong support for the idea of emphasizing the child's own potential as the yardstick of progress and deemphasizing comparisons with other children. That parents (and the children) need to receive both kinds of information along the way is not denied, however. Rothney (1966) provides suggestions for improving reports to parents, and Kingston and Wash (1966) review the research on reporting systems.

As educational theorists generally argue that children must become more self-determining learners, it becomes more obviously important for teachers to include pupils in the total process of assessing learning goals and the child's progress toward them. It seems likely that in the decade ahead, more and more attention will be paid to the teacher-pupil conference and to devices for assisting pupils in self-evaluation.

Robert H. Anderson
Harvard University
Cynthia Ritsher
Harvard University

References

Anderson, Robert H. "Organizing Groups for Instruction." In Tyler, Frederick T. (Chairman.) *Individualizing Instruction*, 61st Yearbook, Part I, NSSE. U Chicago Press, 1962. p. 239–64.

Anderson, Robert H. "Organizational Character of Education: Staff Utilization and Deployment." *R Ed Res* 34:561–63; 1964.

Anderson, Robert H. "The Importance and Purposes of Reporting." *Nat El Prin* 45:6–11; 1966(a).

Anderson, Robert H. *Teaching in a World of Change*. Harcourt, 1966(b). 176p.

Ausubel, David P. "The Influence of Experience on the Development of the Intelligence." In Aschner, Mary Jane, and Bish, Charles E. (Eds.) *Productive Thinking in Education*. NEA, 1965. p. 45–62.

Ayer, Fred C. "The Present Status of Promotional Plans in City Schools." *Am Sch Bd J* 46:37–9; 1923.

Ayers, Leonard P. *Laggards in Our Schools*. Russell Sage, 1909. 236p.

Baker, Robert L., and Doyle, Roy P. "Teacher Knowledge of Pupil Data and Working Practices at the Elementary School Level." *Personnel Guid J* 37: 644–7; 1959.

Bentzen, Frances. "Sex Ratios in Learning and Behavior Disorders." *Nat El Prin* 46:13–7; 1966.

Bledsoe, S. C., and Garrison, K. C. *The Self-concepts of Elementary Children in Relation to Their Academic Achievement, Intelligence, Interests, and Manifest Anxiety*. Cooperative Research Project No. 1008. USOE, 1962.

Bloom, Benjamin S. *Stability and Change in Human Characteristics*. Wiley, 1964. 327p.

Bloom, Benjamin S. "Twenty-five Years of Educational Research." *Am Ed Res J* 3:211–21; 1966.

Bowman, Paul H. "Family Role in the Mental Health of School Children." In Torrance, E. Paul, and Strom, Robert D. (Eds.) *Mental Health and Achievement: Increasing Potential and Reducing School Dropout*. Wiley, 1965. p. 7–14.

Brandt, Richard M. "Needed: A Director of Pupil Assessment." *Ed Leadership* 24:243–6; 1966.

Brookover, W. B., and others. "Self-Concept of Ability and School Achievement." *Sociol Ed* 37:271–8; 1964.

Brown, B. Frank. *The Appropriate Placement School: A Sophisticated Nongraded Curriculum*. Parker, 1965. 198p.

Buffie, Edward G. "A Historical Perspective." In *Nongraded Schools in Action*. Indiana U Press, 1967. p. 3–27.

Burr, Marvin Y. *A Study of Homogeneous Grouping*. Teachers Col, Columbia U, 1931. 69p.

Bushnell, Donald D., and Allen, Dwight W. (Eds.) *The Computer in American Education*. Wiley, 1967. 294p.

Clark, Kenneth B. *Dark Ghetto: Dilemmas of Social Power*. Harper, 1965. 253p.

Coffield, William H., and Blommers, Paul. "Effects of Non-promotion on Educational Achievement in the Elementary School." *J Ed Psychol* 47:235–50; 1956.

Cook, Walter W., and Clymer, Theodore. "Acceleration and Retardation." In Tyler, Frederick T. (Chairman.) *Individualizing Instruction*, 61st Yearbook, Part I, NSSE. U Chicago Press, 1962. p. 179–208.

Crutchfield, Richard S. "Instructing the Individual in Creative Thinking." In *New Approaches to Individualizing Instruction*. ETS, 1965. p. 13–25.

De Haan, Robert F. *Accelerated Learning Programs*. Center for Applied Research in Education, 1963. 120p.

Deutsch, Martin. "Facilitating Development in the Pre-school Child: Social and Psychological Perspectives." *Merrill-Palmer Q* 10:249–64; 1964.

Finn, James D. "Instructional Technology." *B Nat Assn Sec Sch Prin* 47:11–119; 1963.

Glaser, Robert. (Ed.) *Training Research and Education*. U Pittsburgh 1962. 596p.

Goldberg, Miriam L., and others. *The Effects of Ability Grouping*. Teachers Col, Columbia U, 1966. 254p.

Goodlad, John I. "Research and Theory Regarding Promotion and Non-promotion. *El Sch J* 53:150–5; 1952.

Goodlad, John I. "Some Effects of Promotion and Non-promotion upon the Social and Personal Adjustment of Children." *J Exp Ed* 22:301–28; 1954.

Goodlad, John I., and Anderson, Robert H. *The Nongraded Elementary School*, rev. ed. Harcourt, 1963. 248p.

Goodlad, John I., and others. *Computers and Information Systems in Education.* Harcourt, 1966. 152p.

Grambs, Jean D., and Waetjen, Walter B. "Being Equally Different: A New Right for Boys and Girls." *Nat El Prin* 46:59–67; 1966.

Guilford, J. P. "Three Faces of Intellect." *Am Psychologist* 14:460–79; 1959.

Guilford, J. P. "Intellectual Factors in Productive Thinking." In Aschner, Mary Jane, and Bish, Charles E. (Eds.) *Productive Thinking in Education.* NEA, 1965. p. 5–20.

Hess, Robert D. "Maternal Teaching Styles and Educational Retardation." In Torrance, E. Paul, and Strom, Robert D. (Eds.) *Mental Health and Achievement: Increasing Potential and Reducing School Dropout.* Wiley, 1965. p. 15–23.

Hunt, J. McVicker. *Intelligence and Experience.* Ronald, 1961. 416p.

Hunt, J. McVicker. "The Psychological Basis for Using Pre-school Enrichment as an Antidote for Cultural Deprivation." In Hechinger, Fred M. (Ed.) *Pre-school Education Today: New Approaches to Teaching Three-, Four-, and Five-year Olds.* Doubleday, 1966. p. 25–73.

Jones, R. Stewart. "Instructional Problems and Issues." *R Ed Res* 36:414–23; 1966.

Johnston, A. Montgomery. "Intellectual Segregation." *El Sch J* 67:207–12; 1967.

Joyce, Bryce R. "Staff Utilization." *R Ed Res* 37:323–36; 1967.

Kagan, Jerome. "Children's Sex-role Classification of School Objects." *Child Develop* 35:1050–6; 1964.

Kiddle, Henry, and Schem, Alexander J. (Eds.) *The Cyclopaedia of Education: A Dictionary of Information for the Use of Teachers, School Officers, Parents, and Others.* Steiger, 1877. p. 375–77.

Kingston, Albert J., and Wash, James A., Jr. "Research on Reporting Systems." *Nat El Prin* 45:36–40; 1966.

Lipchik, Margaret. "A Saturday School for Mothers and Pre-schoolers." *Nat El Prin* 44:29–31; 1964.

Maccoby, Eleanor. *The Development of Sex Differences.* Stanford U Press, 1966. 203p.

Maxwell, William H. *Sixth Annual Report of the Superintendent of Schools.* New York City Board of Education, 1904. p. 42–9.

Mayhew, Katherine C., and Edwards, Anna C. *The Dewey School: The Laboratory School of the University of Chicago, 1896–1903.* Appleton, 1936. 489p. (Reissued by Atherton, 1966.)

McNeil, John D. "Programmed Instruction Versus Usual Classroom Procedures in Teaching Boys to Read." *Am Ed Res J* 1:113–20; 1964.

Meltzer, Jack. "Impact of Social Class." *Ed Leadership* 25:37–43; 1967.

Miles, Matthew B. (Ed.) *Innovation in Education.* Teachers Col, Columbia U, 1964. 689p.

Miller, Richard I. (Ed.) *Perspectives on Educational Change.* Appleton, 1967. 392p.

Miller, Richard I., and others. *Notes and Working Papers Concerning the Administration of Programs, Title III, The Elementary and Secondary Education Act of 1965.* GPO, 1967. 557p.

Morgenstern, Anne. (Ed.) *Grouping in the Elementary School.* Pitman, 1966. 118p.

Otto, Henry J. "Historical Sketches of Administrative Innovations." *Ed Adm Sup* 20:161–72; 1934.

Otto, Henry J., and Estes, Dwain M. "Accelerated and Retarded Progress." In Harris, Chester W. (Ed.) *Encyclopedia of Educational Research,* 3rd ed. Macmillan, 1960. p. 4–11.

Otto, Henry J., and Melby Ernest O. "An Attempt to Evaluate the Threat of Failure as a Factor in Achievement." *El Sch J* 35:588–96; 1935.

Piaget, Jean. *The Growth of Logical Thinking from Childhood to Adolescence.* Translated by Anne Parsons and Stanley Milgram. Basic Books, 1958. 356p.

Preston, Ralph C. "Reading Achievement of German and American Children." *Sch Soc* 90:350–4; 1962.

Ridgway, Lorna, and Lawton, Irene. *Family Grouping in the Infants' School.* London: Ward Lock Educational Co., 1965. 175p.

Rosenthal, Robert. *Pygmalion in the Classroom.* Holt, 1968. 256p.

Rothney, John W. M. "Improving Reporting to Parents." *Nat El Prin* 45:51–3; 1966.

Sandin, Adolph A. *Social and Emotional Adjustments of Regularly Promoted and Non-promoted Pupils.* Teachers Col, Columbia U, 1944. 142p.

Saunders, Carleton M. *Promotion or Failure for the Elementary School Pupil?* Teachers Col, Columbia U, 1941. 77p.

Search, Preston W. "Individual Teaching and the Pueblo Plan." *Ed R* 7:154–70; 1894.

Search, Preston W. *An Ideal School: Or, Looking Forward.* Appleton, 1901. 357p.

Shaplin, Judson T., and Olds, Henry F., Jr. (Eds.) *Team Teaching.* Harper, 1964. 430p.

Silberman, Charles E. "Technology Is Knocking at the Schoolhouse Door." *Fortune* 74:120–5, 198, 203–5; 1966.

Smith, James A. *Setting Conditions for Creative Teaching in the Elementary School.* Allyn and Bacon, 1966. 207p.

Strodbeck, Fred L. "The Hidden Curriculum of the Middle Class Home." In Hunnicut, C. W. (Ed.) *Urban Education and Cultural Deprivation.* Syracuse U Press, 1964. p. 15–31.

Suppes, Patrick. "The Uses of Computers in Education." *Sci Am* 215:207–20; 1966.

Thelen, Herbert A. *Classroom Grouping for Teachability.* Wiley, 1967(*a*). 274p.

Thelen, Herbert A. "Matching Teachers and Pupils." *NEA J* 56:18–20; 1967(*b*).

Thorndike, Edward L. *Elimination of Pupils from School.* U.S. Bureau of Education Bulletin No. 4. GPO, 1908. 63p.

Torrance, E. Paul. *Rewarding Creative Behavior: Experiments in Classroom Creativity.* Prentice-Hall, 1965. 324p.

Waetjen, Walter B. "The Prevention of Failure." *NEA J* 55:32–41; 1966.

Washburne, Carleton W., and Marland, Sidney P., Jr. *Winnetka: The History and Significance of an Educational Experiment.* Prentice-Hall, 1963. 402p.

Wells, W. H. *The Graded School: A Course of Instruction for Public Schools; With Copious Practical Directions to Teachers, and Observations on Primary Schools, School Discipline, School Records, etc.* Barnes, 1867. 200p.

Wilhelms, Fred T. (Ed.) *Evaluation as Feedback and Guide.* Yearbook. ASCD, 1967(*a*). p. 2–17.

Wilhelms, Fred T. "A New Progressive Education?" *Nat El Prin* 47:31–7; 1967(*b*).

Wolf, Richard M. "The Measurement of Environments." In *Proceedings of the 1964 Invitational Conference on Testing Problems.* ETS, 1965. p. 93–106.

Wolfson, Bernice J. "The Promise of Multi-age Grouping for Individualizing Instruction." *El Sch J* 67:354–62; 1967.

Worth, Walter W. "Promotion versus Non-promotion: The Earlier Evidence." *Alberta J Ed Res* 5:77–86; 1959.

READINESS

Naive, or common-sense, psychology includes notions about "when" learning can occur. That is, every society has beliefs and convictions about what behavior individuals should manifest at a given age and at what age they can be expected to establish a specific type of behavior. Children cannot be held responsible for their actions; they become responsible through maturation, which occurs automatically with age. Thus, parents judge when the child is "ready" to sit up without support, to own his own tricycle or racing car, and to smoke. Society relies upon maturation as a guide for controlling the behavior of "immature" individuals: "No one under 18 admitted to this movie"; individuals may vote when they become 21; children are required to go to school when they are six but may not enter before about 5 years, 9 months; adults are often admitted to university without formal requirements if they are "mature adults"—that is, have reached a chronological age "somewhat" in excess of the usual age of university entrance.

The idea of readiness has been and still is inherent in our thinking about education, although there is considerable diversity of opinion about both practice and theory.

Washburne (1936) wrote that teachers in the Winnetka schools kept a careful record of the date when a child became mentally 6½ in order to guard against any attempt to get the child to read before he reached that level of mental maturity. The name of Gates (1937) is often associated with this particular criterion of readiness, and yet he was careful to point out that the age at which a child can be successfully introduced to reading is related to the methods and materials of instruction.

More recently Heffernan (1960) claimed that there is a "mountain of evidence" that a normal child, IQ 100, cannot learn to read before about 6.5 years. However, Monroe and Rogers (1964) concluded that mental age (MA) alone is an unsatisfactory criterion of readiness. Blair and Jones (1960) propose (1) that the optimal-minimal MA for beginning reading is 6.5 years, but also (2) that the efficiency of instruction depends upon materials and methods. At the opposite extreme, Bruner (1960) maintained that any subject can be taught effectively in some intellectually honest form to any child at any stage of development.

What is being said about reading readiness at the kindergarten level? Todd and Heffernan, in *The Years Before School* (1964), dealt summarily with "reading readiness"; they did not even discuss reading at the preschool level. Hammond and others, in *Good Schools for Young Children* (1966), said little about teaching reading at ages three, four, and five years. Seemingly they accepted mental age as the criterion for readiness. However, they also recognized that the desirable level depends on the way in which beginning reading is taught. Dorothy Gardner and Joan Cass (1965) recorded very few instances in which teachers in infant schools (for ages 5 to 7+) heard children read during periods of "free activity." They added, however, that teachers did not deliberately avoid helping such children to acquire the skills of reading, writing, and arithmetic.

According to Durkin (1966), opinion among educators about the place of reading in the kindergarten varies widely. She points out that our beliefs about the learning potentials of preschool children have changed drastically in the last few years and proposes that teachers should provide help in reading to some five-year-olds.

Different theorists have different notions about the nature of child development. Some—for instance, Gesell (1954)—consider that it is a matter of maturation conceived as an unfolding of inherent structures and processes. Others, following Piaget (see Baldwin, 1967; Maier, 1965), include maturational forces, experiences, formal and informal teaching, and equilibration—i.e., the organization of knowledge occasioned by the appearance of contradictions in the child's system of beliefs. Still others, e.g., learning psychologists, regard it as a matter of accumulating new behavior through learning from experiences.

READINESS AND MATURATION. The term "maturation" has been, and continues to be, used in connection with educational theory and practice, along with such other expressions as "maturity," "inner maturation," "unfolding," "ripeness," and "readiness." The term has been used in discussions of intelligence as well as of neural systems and in considerations of mental, emotional, social, linguistic, physical, physiological, skeletal, and anatomic characteristics. The question of the significance of "maturity" was noted early by Woodworth (1921): What, he asked, does maturity mean other than that natural characteristics have attained their ultimate level of development? In his discussion he referred to the natural growth of neurones and the gradual unfolding of intelligence. Frank (1950) states that maturation does not represent a terminal state; rather, it is continuously at work. However, maturity is sometimes used to refer to the end of a process, e.g., maturity in height, and sometimes to the beginning of a process, e.g., physiological maturity and the onset of adolescence.

The major difficulty in dealing with questions about readiness arises from our use of words, and at present it is difficult to be consistent about such words as "growth," "development," and "maturation." The everyday significance of the words has not been translated into precise psychological terminology. In 1950 Krogman maintained that maturity and maturation are all things to all people (Krogman, 1950). The situation has not improved: Heath, in *Explorations of Maturity* (1965), after examining the conditions that have made research on maturity and mental health so unrewarding, concluded that research on maturity is bedeviled by problems of terminology. Research into the significance and measurement of maturity may help to clarify terminological issues.

Before considering Gesell's position, we may note that Werner's "nativistic" theory (1948) places more emphasis than does empiricism (the tabula rasa concept) upon the appearance of innate structures embedded in biological processes. Werner, relying upon analogy, maintains that psychological development follows those principles of biological development described by Coghill (1929) as a result of his studies of the behavioral embryology of the salamander. According to Coghill, development involves a change from undifferentiated to differentiated processes and the establishment of hierarchial organization. Furthermore, genic factors influence, if not determine, the time when we should expect children to learn specific behavior patterns, including those involved in classroom learning. (It may be noted that such concepts as differentiation, integration, and hierarchies are found in cognitive psychology, but the implications of a natural unfolding are less obvious, if not entirely absent.)

Gesell's position (1954) probably comes closer than any other to a pure maturation theory: Maturation is the product of certain internal forces which affect both structure and function rather than of environmental conditions. Environment, whether internal or external, is not a causal factor in development; environment, says Gesell, can support but cannot initiate the basic forms and sequences of individual growth.

From their co-twin control studies, Gesell and Thompson (1943) concluded that the maturity which comes from the passage of time is more important than early practice in the acquisition of skill in climbing stairs. Even though they warned that their recommendations were based on studies of gross motor skills, nonetheless many educators advocated the doctrine of postponement for educational practice in, for example, reading and arithmetic. Benezet (1935–1936) proposed that formal arithmetic be delayed until grade 6. Various writers believed children should not be introduced to reading until they have a mental age of 6.5 to 7.0 years or to phonics until their mental age is 7.0 years.

The results from research by Ilg and Ames (1950, 1951) on reading, arithmetic, and handwriting, based on Gesell's concepts of maturation, developmental gradients and trends, were taken to imply that there is a maturational, inner ripening, process that must be considered in curriculum planning.

On the other hand there are those who are and who have been concerned about undue delay in introducing certain materials into the school curriculum, especially if the reasons are given in maturational terms. Buswell (1938) expressed concern as early as 1938, as did Brownell (1938) at about the same time. Brownell (1960) made the same point more recently in connection with some of his observations on the teaching of arithmetic in British schools. Ausubel (1963) expressed concern about the dangers of thinking of readiness in maturational terms to the neglect of such environmental influences as the pupil's intellectual background, teaching methods, and instructional materials. In fact, Ausubel (1959), as late as 1959, believed it would take at least another generation of teachers before the more "fallacious and dangerous" overgeneralizations of developmental principles would be discarded.

There is an accumulating body of evidence about the learning potentialities of young children. For example, there is some evidence that the "talking typewriter" can be used to teach three-year-olds to read. Suppes (1966) is teaching geometrical constructions in grade 1 and introductory college logic to fifth graders and even to bright first-graders. Henkin (n.d.) has observed first graders learning the rules for adding and subtracting signed numbers.

Children can learn many skills and processes at an earlier age than has often been advocated. Nonetheless we can still ask whether we should expect them to learn certain things at these early ages (Brownell, 1960; Moskowitz, 1965). Is it desirable? Are they being subjected to undue pressure? Is it harmful? In fact, are there excessive demands at all levels of education which are affecting students' attitudes toward both school and society?

We turn to a related issue. In 1873, Spalding (Sluckin, 1965) described the results of systematic observations of approach and following behavior of newborn chicks. He concluded that chicks follow their "mother" provided the opportunity to do so comes at an "early" age and further that this behavior is observed only when the opportunity for it comes at a "critical" period in the bird's life. Spalding used the expression "the stamp of experience," while later, in the 1930's, Lorenz used the term *Prägung* to describe the phenomenon (see Sluckin, 1965). His word was translated as "imprinting," a term which is related to "stamping in." Since the behavior appears only during a brief "critical" period, it was judged that imprinting depends upon a rather specific physiological state. Consequently, imprinting seems to be related to biological maturity.

Attempts have been made to transfer the phenomenon to considerations of human behavior.

However, human attachments cannot be formed by "imprinting," since that process involves approach-and-following behavior. It has been suggested, although not clearly demonstrated, that human "imprinting" is produced by the smiling stimulus. Actually, we do not have definitive evidence about the impact of early "learning" as represented by imprinting. As late as 1965 Sluckin pointed to the need for an extensive series of longitudinal studies of imprinting before we can have valid evidence about its permanent effects. The evidence from many studies of the relationship between early-childhood experiences and later personality characteristics provides little reason for believing that there is a close relationship between them. Sluckin argues that the study of "imprinting-like early learning" requires a consideration of both biological and environmental conditions affecting the formation of personality traits.

Goodenough and Tyler (1959) pointed out that there seems to be a period of time during which the learner is "ripe" or ready for reading and proposed that the idea of the "psychological moment" has significance for the concept of development. The notions of biological and mental maturity have been associated with an "internal ripening," with biological unfolding, with neurophysiological-biochemical changes that occur as a "function of time" (McCandless, 1961). Here, too, we have the implication that readiness for learning is a matter of waiting for an appropriate moment.

Olson, in *Child Development* (1949), advocated a curricular sequence deriving from the concept of "critical periods." In his opinion, introduction to certain learning experiences, either prior to or following a critical period, can result only in failure. More recently, however, Heath (1965) pointed out that the fact of man's plasticity has been drawing attention away from biological to environmental factors, although there is continuing research on biological "readiness," such as the concepts of imprinting and critical periods.

Educators need to be cautious about using imprinting and its related concept of "critical period" as a justification for assessing "readiness" for learning.

READINESS AND PIAGET'S THEORIES. Biological maturation, as an internal unfolding leading to "ripeness," does not offer unambiguous help for the assessment of readiness for school learning. Piaget's theory (Baldwin, 1967; Maier, 1965), contrary to both strict maturational and learning theories, is possibly more helpful. Actually, Piaget, drawing parallels between biological and psychological processes, seems to include, as was mentioned earlier, both biological and environmental influences in his theory of development, although not all educators agree on the emphasis he gives to each (Baldwin, 1967). Maier (1965) believes that Piaget's is essentially a genetic theory which emphasizes internal forces more than those external stimulations stressed in learning theories. For Piaget, cognitive functioning represents an extension of native motor processes; the individual establishes new forms of behavior through applications of native reflexes.

Piaget, it sometimes appears, sees the establishment of cognitive structures as a sequential patterning of stages dependent upon both experience and the dynamics of the individual. On the other hand, his concept of hierarchical cognitive structures, apparently derived from biological considerations, seems to be rooted in internal changes rather than external stimulation. Early behavior patterns are regarded as "lower" although, as forerunners of later behavior, they subsequently become components of the "higher" structure. Development, thus, is a matter of progressing from lower to higher stages. The "sensorimotor stage" includes the first two years of life, the "preoperational stage" the next five, the "concrete operational stage" covers ages 7 to 11, and the stage of "formal operations" begins at age 11 (Baldwin, 1967). Some psychologists place considerable emphasis on the concept of stages, which are regarded as discontinuous, certain, unfolding, and hierarchical, although not bound to age. On the other hand, there are those who maintain that the reality of stages is immaterial, that the concept is used simply to indicate what forms of behavior appear early and what forms succeed one another (Berlyne, 1966). In any case, educational programs and curricula are being formulated in terms of cognitive sequences, even though there may not be agreement about whether the "hour" of cognitive growth is one of biological determination and universal sequence.

The Cambridge view of cognitive development, expressed in research from the Cognitive Center at Harvard, is that development is a matter of internalizing technologies from the culture, especially that of language. These writers contrast their views with those they believe to be held at the Jean Jacques Rousseau Institute in Geneva. In their opinion, the Geneva writers consider cognitive development to be a matter of maturation brought about by the internalizing of logical operations with but minor recognition of the role of environmental forces (Bruner & others, 1967). Possibly curriculum makers can utilize the concept of sequential development without, at this time, knowing whether the forces which produce empirically demonstrated sequences are biological or experiential.

The timing at which a specific stage is attained, organized, and succeeded by the next varies from one individual to another. Also, different cognitive structures are not equally advanced within a given individual. Such notions, of course, are reflections of other known facts about interindividual and intraindividual differences (Tyler, 1962) and again imply the need for diagnosis of cognitive structure for a given task.

Assessment, diagnosis, and instruction, then, are closely interrelated. This notion is inherent in the procedures adopted for the New York City Project (Loretan, 1965). The stages of cognitive development are described in behavioral terms and appropriate tests prepared. Instructional materials and methods may then be developed to nurture the desired behavior by starting at the level indicated by the diagnosis. This theory raises questions about the usefulness of much standardized testing for educational planning for individuals.

A hierarchical theory of cognitive organization seems especially useful for diagnosing readiness, especially if the stages are conceived in terms of intellectual structures built out of experiences. Such a concept of readiness, it may be noted, seems consistent with Pribram's suggestion (1964) that we can discover the boundaries of what a child knows simply by asking questions, and the boundaries provide evidence of readiness for moving from the familiar to the unfamiliar. Learning occurs when the learner perceives that a new experience resembles an old one.

In their consideration of readiness, Broudy and others (1964) propose two conditions affecting readiness, the subject matter and the logical operations required by the subject matter. For the former, which is similar to Pribram's suggestion, readiness can be cared for by taking account of vocabulary, sentence structure, and so on. For the latter, the solution is less apparent. Their position seems to be that ability in performing logical operations depends more upon the learner's level of "development" than upon the extent to which the operations can be simplified. They propose that we must allow development to catch up with the particular level of logical performance expected. Is this another form of the doctrine of postponement, of "letting" development appear?

READINESS AND LEARNING THEORIES. Presumably, readiness for learning can be discussed in terms of the theoretical considerations and empirical investigations of either S-R or cognitive psychologists. However, the former think of learning primarily in terms of contiguity and reinforcement, giving little or no attention to the individual's knowledge, as contrasted with unorganized "information" methods of approaching learning, or the organized aspect of knowledge, matters which have been investigated by cognitive psychologists.

There are several reasons why, in general, S-R psychology has had little to say about readiness. First, until recently, it has been assumed by verbal-learning theorists that functional and nominal stimuli are identical, an assumption which is coming under serious question (Underwood, 1963). If they are not the same, then the nominal stimulus has different perceptual and conceptual implications for different learners. The learning of each will be affected by what turns out to be his particular functional stimulus, which may be more appropriate for the expected learning outcomes of one individual than of another; that is, one learner has a greater degree of readiness. In his recent review of verbal learning, Keppel (1964) reported no studies concerning nominal and functional stimuli for which children were used as subjects. Second, verbal-learning theorists have excluded the concept of motivation from both their theoretical considerations and their empirical investigations. Yet it would appear logically that motivation, need achievement, and so on, affect the results from rote verbal-learning studies. Third, S-R psychologists investigating learning have sought to develop materials as devoid as possible of association value; in such a case, questions about readiness would be reduced to questions about learning sets, which topics have not been investigated by S-R psychologists. Fourth, the concept of "mediation" used in descriptions of rote verbal learning also implies some notion of readiness, because the learner's experiential background affects the mediators he employs.

There are certain indications that a rapprochement between S-R and cognitive psychology is developing. Ausubel (Anderson & Ausubel, 1965) points out that some neobehaviorists are interested in "higher mental processes" and that some cognitive psychologists are investigating certain "simpler" kinds of learning. Hilgard (1964) writes that disagreements among theorists may be about interpretations of facts rather than about the facts themselves. The differences, then, may be of minor concern to practitioners. Finally, while there are differences between the two broad theories there are also differences among the advocates of each theory.

"Readiness" may be discussed within a context that is somewhat consistent with certain aspects of cognitive psychology. Such eclecticism will be less than satisfying to some theorists, and the absence of definitive practical answers will be at least as unsatisfying to practitioners.

READINESS AND COGNITIVE STRUCTURE. The term "cognitive structure" is used to refer to a variety of psychological phenomena—concepts, habits, sentiments, motives (Sheerer, 1953). In this section, attention is directed toward the ideational components of cognitive structure—that is, the stability, clarity, and nature of organization of knowledge. As an example, consider the proposition by Bereiter and Engelmann (1966) that culturally deprived children have difficulty treating words as units and that this difficulty accounts for many of the problems they experience in other features of language development. The organization, stability, and clarity of their particular language patterns interfere with the formation of new patterns. They are not "ready" for the typical language work of formal schooling.

Readiness is a function of cognitive structure. As far as school learning is concerned, a pupil is ideationally or intellectually ready for something new in language or arithmetic when he has control and mastery over, and the ability to recall and use, the skills and information which underlie the behaviors to be learned. Some such notion as this was implied in the 29th yearbook of the National Society for the Study of Education (Washburne, 1930): The multiplication facts should not be taught to children who have not attained virtual mastery of the addition facts. Unfortunately, this emphasis upon the need for certain specifics in cognitive structure was undermined by an accompanying requirement that the multiplication facts should not be taught below a mental age of 8 years, 4 months, which is an index of a general level of mental maturity rather than of specific knowledge. Of course, the latter criterion would have been useful if it were highly correlated with the specific knowledge implied by "mastery of the addition facts," which it is not. As a result of introducing the concept of mental age for the learning of various arithmetical operations, the importance of cognitive structure was underestimated for many years, as was pointed out earlier, by certain educators.

More recently, Pooley (1961) suggested, rather conservatively, that reading readiness depends to a "considerable" degree upon familiarity with the content of the reading materials. Hence, to assess readiness we must determine the nature of the pupil's existing cognitive structure, i.e., discover what is known by the learner. Such information should enable the teacher to start his instruction at a point that is appropriate for the individual.

Brownell (1951) emphasized the importance of subskills for the acquisition of more complex skills in arithmetic. Recent investigations provide support for his position. An analysis of hierarchical learning sets (Gagné & others, 1962), using programmed materials for mathematical topics, reveals more clearly than was possible before the development of programmed instruction that mathematical learning proceeds in hierarchical fashion from "basic" abilities through a series of steps which follow one another in a definite sequence from the simplest activities to the final, complex task. Readiness is a matter of transfer from lower to higher levels of a structure (Tyler, 1964). Jensen (1967), too, discussing learning sets and mediational systems, believes that readiness may be thought of in terms of transfer.

A child's early experiences may provide, optimally or dismally, opportunities for him to establish those cognitive structures which contribute toward his readiness for the type of learning expected in the classroom. Covington (1962), for example, reported that training improved the ability of children from lower socioeconomic levels to discriminate visual stimuli. A relevant structure makes for readiness and hence for the possibility of transfer. A verbally enriched background makes success in a verbally oriented educational program more likely. Various emerging curricula. such as are found in Project Head Start (Dobbin, 1966) and the Illinois Project (Bereiter & Engelmann, 1966) for educationally disadvantaged children, are designed to enlarge and enrich the backgrounds of pupils—i.e., to form cognitive structures relevant to school learning. Readiness is being manipulated and established; it is not regarded as a state that will appear through the natural processes of an internal unfolding. If readiness is thought of as some condition other than some "maturational" state, then it becomes possible to propose instructional programs and materials and educational opportunities that will produce the appropriate cognitive structures or state of readiness.

Durkin's research (1966) supports the tendency, which is becoming more apparent in the past few years, to be less concerned about maturation, mental age, and reading-readiness tests and more concerned about materials and methods. She suggests that we need to reexamine some of the notions associated with the postponement of formal instruction in reading before the pupil enters the first grade and proposes that we may well provide help in reading to some five-year-olds.

READINESS AND COGNITIVE STYLE. The term "cognitive style" refers to the individual's characteristic, self-consistent ways of functioning in the cognitive, ideational, realm (Witkin, 1964). Such styles as those designated by the expressions "field independence" ("psychological differentiation"), "ability to resist distraction," and "leveling-sharpening" seem to have implications for the concept of readiness, even though much more research and thought must be given to questions about the origins, development, measurement, and correlates of cognitive styles.

Witkin (1964) has been especially interested in the cognitive style termed field dependence–independence. Individuals who are able to deal with a field analytically, as indicated by a ready ability to separate some specific item from its context, are "field independent"; those who are unable to break up an organized field, who are not analytical, are "field dependent." While his early studies dealt with perception, Wikin has now extended the concept to include ideational activities. Thus, field-independent individuals perform better on tasks which require them to isolate from the problem some specific element which must then be applied in a different relational setting. An example is the *Einstellung* problem, on which field-dependent and field-independent individuals show different types of behavior (for example, field-independent individuals are more capable of escaping the mental set). It has also been reported that while boys (aged 10 and 12 years) of the two types do not differ in general intelligence they do differ on those subtests of the Wechsler Intelligence Scale for Children which require analytical ability. Because the concept can be extended to both perceptual and cognitive functioning Witkin prefers the expression "analytic–global field approach." It may be noted that Witkin relates field-dependence to Guilford's adaptive-flexibility variable (1959).

From cross-sectional and longitudinal studies Witkin concluded that the developmental trend is from a relatively global to a relatively articulated way of experiencing and that even by age five there are definite individual differences in the global-articulated domain. There is still the question about the origins of this style. What are the roles of constitution and experience? Witkin approached the issue by postulating a relationship between the two. After recognizing that definitive answers are not yet available, he concluded that cognitive development is a function of a personal history. Such a conclusion about cognitive styles appears consistent with the experiential view of the formation of cognitive structures.

Readiness for different kinds of school learning is conceivably related to the extent to which the pupil experiences items apart from or tied to cognitive structure, i.e., organized content of knowledge. Analytic children may find it easier than the less analytic to make progress in a language other than that spoken in the home. A pupil whose "native" language does not include the *-ing* and *-ed* verb endings may have difficulties with English, more especially if his cognitive style is nonanalytical.

Kagan and others (1963) postulate that an analytic attitude is an aid in beginning reading. For instance, they point out that both differentiation and analysis of stimuli are necessary if the pupil is to discriminate between *cat* and *bat*. Studies of individual differences in analytic versus nonanalytic cognitive styles may provide information useful for instruction in reading and for the reduction of remedial work.

Grimes and Allinsmith (1961) taught reading by two different methods, one involving a carefully structured program of phonics and the other a less structured whole-word approach. Cognitive style, these authors suggest, is related to learning if compulsiveness and anxiety are thought of as components of cognitive style. They found a high degree of structuring to be especially useful for "defensive" pupils, pupils who are rated high for both compulsiveness and anxiety. If further research should support the hypothesis that defensive pupils learn best when they are given a good deal of support, then educational programs will need to take this relationship into account by planning to provide the support and yet, surely, also by planning to promote more independence (Cronbach, 1967).

Riley W. Gardner (1964) has for some time been interested in a variety of phenomena related to cognitive styles, including such concepts as categorization, leveling-sharpening, attention, cognitive controls. Now, "attention" is an important condition affecting learning and should be related to readiness for school learning. Gardner investigated three features of attention, including, for instance, two that appear to be independent of each other: selectiveness in attending to various stimuli and extensiveness in scanning stimuli. The place of such cognitive styles in school learning has not been explored in any definitive sense—yet they would appear to be cognitive phenomena of importance to success in the early stages of learning, especially if they are relatively stable characteristics with considerable generality and if they can be assessed. Gardner and others believe that cognitive controls are rather stable features of cognitive functions and that they affect behavior in relatively specific ways with particular stimuli.

Gardner is unable to propose a specific principle to account either for the development of the many aspects of cognitive style or for the hierarchies he obtained from his analyses of data from a group of children aged 9 to 13 years. He suggests that the nature of development varies from one component of cognitive style to another, and it is affected by genic and experiential forces, maturational conditions, and so on. He is particularly interested in more systematic studies of the role of genic conditions in the onset of specific cognitive styles.

"Readiness" for school learning probably depends as much upon cognitive style as upon cognitive structure. Little enough is known about cognitive factors and readiness, but even less is known about readiness and affective factors, sentiments, feelings, and emotions. What, for instance, can be said of emotional readiness, apart from cognitive factors, for a "successful" study of "Ode on a Grecian Urn" or "Ode to Immortality"?

One other example is suggested. A reasonable hypothesis states that "readiness" for learning includes a favorable attitude toward school. However, Jackson and Lahaderne (1967) report low correlation coefficients (.08 to .19) between satisfaction with school and scholastic success (grades and achievement-test scores) at the sixth-grade level. They suggest a number of reasons for their results, and further investigation is required before we can claim interest as a factor in readiness.

READINESS AND THE STRUCTURE OF KNOWLEDGE. In general, S-R learning theorists have been relatively uninterested in cognitive structure or the structure of either the materials or the psychological processes to be learned. In fact, as has been pointed out, rote verbal learning has been studied by the use of materials as distinct and separate from the learner's cognitive structure as possible and with no logical, internal relationship. Yet it seems reasonable to suppose, for example, that an individual with a well-developed spatial component will have a greater readiness for a spatially oriented curriculum than will a pupil deficient in this characteristic.

Readiness for the *Merrill Linguistic Readers* (Fries and others, 1966) involves numerous "facets that are well known to teachers," including two that are especially significant: (1) pupils must be able to identify all letters of the alphabet, both upper and lower case, and (2) pupils must recognize that words are separable units. These aspects of readiness are emphasized in the program developed for disadvantaged children at Illinois (Bereiter & Engelmann, 1966). Such pupils are lacking in readiness for the typical school because of the limited types of stimulation found in their homes. The Holt, Rinehart and Winston series—*Sounds of Home* (Martin, 1966)—stresses the inseparability of words as preparation for reading. Thus, the instructions to the teacher are that the title is "not to be taught as three separate words. It is a unified sound with its special meaning."

Each of the above materials has its own structure; one requires pupils to recognize words as separate units, the other expects the pupil to accept the inseparability of words. Readiness for one program is not necessarily the same as for the other.

In *The Process of Education*, Bruner (1960) emphasized the necessity for considering the "structure of knowledge" in curriculum planning and instructional procedures. Certain recent curricula, notably those in mathematics and the sciences, have made use of this concept, but is there a "structure" in the same sense in social studies or English literature? The amount of research relating readiness to structure is limited, and yet the concept seems useful. Bruner claims that teaching which emphasizes the structure is probably more necessary for the less than for the more able students. However, we need more research on this and related questions. He notes that the concept of structure is especially prominent in the learning of one's native language; once the child has learned the structure of a sentence he can produce other sentences from the original models.

This notion of structure is also found in Fries's proposition (1962) that the first phase of learning to read is a matter of transferring from auditory signs for language signals (which a pupil already knows) to visual signs for the same signals. Once this phase is complete the pupil moves on to later stages in the reading process. We see here a clear indication of the concept of readiness: the pupil must know auditory language signals before he can advance to visual signals. And many children do not have this readiness for that which is taught in the initial stages of learning to read. If children come from a background in which pronouns are not used or are underemphasized in speech or in which the tenses of verbs are different from that in traditional English speech, they do not have the auditory signals necessary for the visual signals they are expected to learn. It should be possible to diagnose language deficiencies and then propose instructional materials and methods which will lead to success in reading, that is, for transferring from auditory signals to their visual counterparts.

Structure of knowledge is related to readiness for learning. However, details about this relationship are far from adequate.

Readiness is a condition that affects teaching and learning for all educational goals, at all educational levels, and in all types of curricula. A specific curricular sequence, a prescribed instructional methodology, a fixed rate of presentation will fail to provide optimal learning opportunities for a given group of children. The range of individual differences is extensive, and the variability within an individual is almost as great, so that homogeneous grouping based on some measure of ability will not guarantee a homogeneous group for some other measure. Readiness can be assessed more reliably by specific diagnostic tests than by broad, general measures. Diagnoses will vary considerably from pupil to pupil; prescriptions will be equally variable. More attention needs to be directed toward the problems of individualizing instruction if each learner is to have an opportunity to reach toward his potential.

Frederick T. Tyler
University of Victoria, Canada

References

Anderson, Richard C., and Ausubel, David P. *Readings in the Psychology of Cognition.* Holt, 1965. 690p.

Ausubel, David P. "Viewpoints from Related Disciplines: Human Growth and Development." *Teach Col Rec* 60:245–54; 1959.

Ausubel, David P. *The Psychology of Meaningful Verbal Learning.* Grune, 1963. 255p.

Baldwin, Alfred L. *Theories of Child Development.* Wiley, 1967. 618p.

Benezet, L. P. "The Story of an Experiment." *NEA J* 24:241–4, 301–3; 1935; 25:7–8; 1936.

Bereiter, Carl, and Engelmann, Siegfried. *Teaching Disadvantaged Children in the Preschool.* Prentice-Hall, 1966. 312p.

Berlyne, Daniel E. "Discussion: The Delimitation of Cognitive Development." In Stevenson, Harold W. (Ed.) "Concept of Development." *Monogr Soc Res Child Develop* No. 31. U Chicago Press, 1966. p. 1–108.

Blair, Glenn M., and Jones, R. Stewart. "Readiness." In Harris, Chester W. (Ed.) *Encyclopedia of Educational Research,* 3d ed. Macmillan, 1960.

Broudy, Harry S., and others. *Democracy and Excellence in American Secondary Education.* Rand McNally, 1964. 302p.

Brownell, William A. "A Critique of the Committee of Seven's Investigations on the Grade-placement of Arithmetic Topics." *El Sch J* 38:495–508; 1938.

Brownell, William A. "Arithmetical Readiness as a Practical Classroom Concept." *El Sch J* 52:15–22; 1951.

Brownell, William A. "Observations of Instruction in Lower-grade Arithmetic in English and Scottish Schools." *Arithmetic Teach* 7:165–77; 1960.

Bruner, Jerome S. *The Process of Education.* Harvard U Press, 1960. 97p.

Bruner, Jerome S., and others. *Studies in Cognitive Growth.* Wiley, 1967. 343p.

Buswell, Guy T. "Deferred Arithmetic." *Math Teach* 31:195–200; 1938.

Coghill, George E. *Anatomy and the Problem of Behavior.* Macmillan, 1929. 113p.

Covington, Martin B. "Some Effects of Stimulus Familiarization on Discrimination." Doctoral dissertation. U California, Berkeley, 1962.

Cronbach, Lee J. "How Can Instruction be Adapted to Individual Differences?" In Gagné, Robert M. (Ed.) *Learning and Individual Differences.* Merrill, 1967.

Dobbin, John E. *Project Head Start at Work.* Institute for Educational Development, 1966.

Durkin, Dolores. *Children Who Read Early; Two Longitudinal Studies.* Teachers Col, Columbia U, 1966. 174p.

Frank, Lawrence K. "Introduction: The Concept of Maturity." *Child Develop* 21:21–4; 1950.

Fries, Charles C. *Linguistics and Reading.* Holt, 1962. 265p.

Fries, C., and others. *Merrill Linguistic Readers,* teach ed. Merrill, 1966. 79p.

Gagné, Robert M., and others. "Factors in Acquiring Knowledge of a Mathematical Task." *Psychol Monogr* 76; 1962. 21p.

Gardner, Dorothy E. M., and Cass, Joan E. *The Rôle of the Teacher in the Infant and Nursery School.* Pergamon, 1965. 175p.

Gardner, Riley W. "The Development of Cognitive

Structures." In Sheerer, Constance. (Ed.) *Cognition: Theory, Research, Practice.* Harper, 1964.

Gates, Arthur I. "The Necessary Mental Age for Beginning Reading." *El Sch J* 37:497–508; 1937.

Gesell, Arnold. "The Ontogenesis of Infant Behavior." In Carmichael, Leonard. (Ed.) *Manual of Child Psychology,* 2nd ed. Wiley, 1954.

Gesell, Arnold, and Thompson, Helen. "Learning and Maturation in Identical Infant Twins: An Experimental Analysis by the Method of Co-twin Control." In Barker, Roger G. (Ed.) *Child Behavior and Development.* McGraw-Hill, 1943.

Goodenough, Florence L., and Tyler, Leona E. *Developmental Psychology.* Appleton, 1959. 552p.

Grimes, Jesse W., and Allinsmith, Wesley. "Compulsivity, Anxiety, and School Achievement." *Merrill-Palmer Q* 7:247–71; 1961.

Guilford, J. P. *Personality.* McGraw-Hill, 1959. 562p.

Hammond, Sarah Lou, and others. *Good Schools for Young Children.* Macmillan, 1966. 397p.

Heath, Douglas H. *Explorations of Maturity.* Appleton, 1965. 423p.

Heffernan, Helen. "Significance of Kindergarten Education." *Childh Ed* 36:313–9; 1960.

Henkin, Leon. *An Experiment in the Berkeley Schools.* Department of Mathematics, U California, Berkeley. (Unpublished paper.)

Hilgard, Ernest R. "A Perspective on the Relationship between Learning Theory and Educational Practices." In Hilgard, Ernest R. (Ed.) *Theories of Learning and Instruction,* 63rd Yearbook, NSSE, Part I. U Chicago Press, 1964.

Ilg, Frances L., and Ames, Louise B. "Developmental Trends in Reading Behavior." *J Genet Psychol* 76:291–312; 1950.

Ilg, Frances L., and Ames, Louise B. "Developmental Trends in Arithmetic." *J Genet Psychol* 79:3–28; 1951.

Jackson, Philip W., and Lahaderne, Henriette M. "Scholastic Success and Attitude Toward School in a Population of Sixth-graders." *J Ed Psychol* 58:15–8; 1967.

Jensen, Arthur R. "Varieties of Individual Differences in Learning." In Gagné, Robert M. (Ed.) *Learning and Individual Differences.* Merrill, 1967.

Kagan, Jerome, and others. "Psychological Significance of Styles of Conceptualization." In Wright, John C., and Kagan, Jerome. (Eds.) "Basic Cognitive Processes in Children." *Monogr Soc Res Child Develop* No. 28. Child Development Publications, 1963. p. 1–196.

Keppel, Geoffrey. "Verbal Learning in Children." *Psychol B* 61:63–80; 1964.

Krogman, Wilton Marion. "The Concept of Maturity from a Morphological Viewpoint." *Child Develop* 21:25–32; 1950.

Loretan, Joseph O. *From Theory to the Classroom.* Board of Education of the City of New York, 1965. 29p.

Maier, Henry W. *Three Theories of Child Development.* Harper, 1965. 314p.

Martin, Bill, Jr. *Sounds of Home,* teacher's ed. Holt, 1966. 49p.

McCandless, Boyd R. *Children and Adolescents.* Holt, 1961. 521p.

Monroe, Marion, and Rogers, Bernice. *Foundations for Reading: Informal Pre-reading Procedures.* Scott, 1964. 208p.

Moskowitz, Sue. "Should We Teach Reading in the Kindergarten?" *El Eng* 42:798–804; 1965.

Olson, Willard C. *Child Development.* Heath, 1949. 417p.

Pooley, Robert C. "Reading and the Language Arts." In Witty, Paul A. (Chairman.) *Development in and Through Reading.* 60th Yearbook, Part I, NSSE. U Chicago Press, 1961.

Pribram, Karl H. "Neurological Notes on the Art of Educating." In Hilgard, Ernest R. (Ed.) *Theories of Learning and Instruction,* 63rd Yearbook, Part I, NSSE. U Chicago Press, 1964.

Sheerer, Martin. "Personality Functioning and Cognitive Psychology." *J Pers* 22:1–16; 1953.

Sluckin, W. *Imprinting and Early Learning.* Aldine Publishing Co., 1965. 147p.

Suppes, Patrick. "Tomorrow's Education? Computer-based Instruction in the Elementary School." *Ed Age* 2; 1966.

Todd, Vivian Edmiston, and Heffernan, Helen. *The Years Before School.* Macmillan, 1964. 658p.

Tyler, Frederick T. "Intraindividual Variability." In Tyler, Frederick T. (Chairman.) *Individualizing Instruction,* 61st Yearbook, Part I, NSSE. U Chicago Press, 1962.

Tyler, Frederick T, "Issues Related to Readiness to Learn." In Hilgard, Ernest R. (Ed.) *Theories of Learning and Instruction,* 63rd Yearbook, NSSE. U Chicago Press, 1964.

Underwood, Benton J. "Stimulus Selection in Verbal Learning." In Cofer, Charles N., and Musgrave, Barbara S. *Verbal Behavior and Learning: Problems and Processes.* McGraw-Hill, 1963.

Washburne, Carleton W. "The Grade Placement of Arithmetic Topics." In Knight, F. B. (Chairman.) *Research in Arithmetic,* 29th Yearbook, Part II, NSSE. Public-Sch, 1930.

Washburne, Carleton. "Ripeness." *Prog Ed* 13:125–30; 1936.

Werner, Heinz. *Comparative Psychology of Mental Development.* Follett, 1948. 564p.

Witkin, Herman A. "Origins of Cognitive Style." In Sheerer, Constance. (Ed.) *Cognition: Theory, Research, Promise.* Harper, 1964.

Woodworth, Robert S. *Psychology.* Holt, 1921. 580p.

READING

Reading, in its sociological, psychological, physiological, and pedagogical aspects, has for over a century been the most persistently investigated of the receptive processes of communication. The over 700 investigations in reading reported in print in American and British sources by Gray (1960) in 1957 have more than doubled in the past ten years.

The continued vitality of reading as a locus for investigation is at once a testimony to its educational significance, to the variety of conditions which influence its effective development and use, and to the host of unresolved questions which it still poses to the researcher. This article is addressed primarily though not exclusively to an assessment of the present status of reading research and of recent trends in relation to findings reviewed more extensively in previous editions of the encyclopedia.

Historically considered, the development of research in reading closely mirrors that of educational research in general and of educational psychology in particular. Interest in visual perception by European psychologists in the mid-nineteenth century was abetted, according to Gray (1925), by the development of short-exposure devices, and later, in about 1879, by Javal's recorded observation that eye movements in reading are discontinuous, a fortuitous discovery that ultimately led to the development of the eye-movement camera for objectively recording these phenomena. The study of word perception thus became the primary focus of reading research until about 1910, when two related concerns became evident on the American scene: that of the psychologist for individual differences and that of the schools for tests to measure the speed and comprehension of silent reading which the word-perception studies emphasized.

Although in the 1920's new research focuses appeared, notably the case-study approach to the disabled reader, the earlier research trends persisted. In the 1930's the evaluation movement under the leadership of Ralph Tyler began to make itself felt in attempts to define the objectives of reading instruction in behavioral terms. By the 1940's factorial analysis techniques were being used to describe more precisely the components of reading comprehension. More recently, at least two other important research trends may be noted: (1) significant advances in experimental design and technology which permit investigations in reading of increased power and scope, and (2) active work by scholars in other disciplines, notably in psychology, linguistics, sociology, and medicine, in bringing fresh conceptual and experimental tools to bear on reading phenomena.

Research workers in reading have indeed used virtually all the major tools and techniques of research. Yet the results of such research are largely fragmentary, and the hard core of research knowledge about reading is surprisingly small. Of the many possible reasons for this, four appear especially plausible. First, since reading is so public an educational concern, research questions asked in reading tend to change as educational concerns change. Second, such changing emphases have also fostered a predominantly descriptive, action type of "experimenting" rather than true experimental studies. Third, and closely related to the foregoing, is the relative paucity of long-term explorations of a major reading question or technique by the same experimenters, such work as that by Tinker on the legibility of print or by Buswell on eye-movement patterns being the exception, not the rule. Finally, the emphasis upon program research in many studies raises difficult problems in the adequate control of relevant variables. Hopefully, the more recent interest in reading by research workers in related disciplines and the greater accessibility of research expertise, conceptual and technical, will yield more fruitful ways of posing and answering questions of consequence about reading and its development.

SOCIOLOGICAL ASPECTS. The current worldwide availability of printed materials which, for example, have steadily outstripped population in rate of growth since 1880 in the United States, is unprecedented, as Gray has previously noted (Gray, 1960, pp. 1089–1090). Estimates of the world circulation of daily general-interest newspapers in the UNESCO *Statistical Yearbook* (UNESCO, 1965, p. 529) increased from 53,951,000 in 1952 to 63,831,000 in 1965, while the circulation of nondaily general-interest newspapers and other periodicals in 1963 reached 67,930,000 (*ibid.*, p. 536). World book production according to number of titles was also estimated in 1964 to be 408,000, of which 28,451 titles were produced in the United States (*ibid.*, p. 442). The 1954 estimate by Gray (1960, p. 1090) of over 1½ billion copies of newspapers, periodicals, books, and pamphlets published in the United States has undoubtedly been exceeded since that time, the publication of paperback trade books alone increasing from 188,329,000 in 1954 to 241,449,000 in 1963 according to the *Statistical Abstract* of the U.S. Bureau of the Census (1966, p. 524).

In the context of such heightened availability of the printed media, the question of how and to what effect people use the materials of reading becomes crucial. Research in the sociology of reading has in its short history been directed principally toward the examination of reading as a social process, the appraisal of the status of reading particularly among adults, environmental influences upon reading, the characteristics of reading materials, and the consideration of increasingly more specific effects of the interaction of people and print.

Reading as a Social Process. Reading is a learned act. Its major correlate, as Asheim (1956) has observed, is education. Waples and others (1940) early noted that adults read for different purposes, while Emans and Patyk (1967) recently reported that youth read chiefly for recreation and information but also for personal-social and aesthetic reasons. Literate man through the centuries has extended but not fundamentally altered the social interaction needs of preliterate man for communication: the endowment of meaning to symbols by communicant and recipient. While the written word has had to compete successively and cumulatively with the other powerful means of mass communication—the motion picture, the radio, and television—the act of reading remains highly valued as the cornerstone of fundamental education throughout the world. For those who learn to read, the printed word possesses unique characteristics as a vehicle of social transmission, sometimes mirroring, sometimes changing society (Winger, 1955). These characteristics, trenchantly noted by Waples and others (1940, pp. 4, 29), are still valid: "Print, to be sure, is not the only effective means of mass communication. It is probably not even the most important means of reaching the population directly. . . . But print still remains the only vehicle of communication which is not restricted to particular times and places, which can present all sorts of ideas to anyone who can read, and which can develop a subject to any desired fullness of detail. . . . Among the popular media . . . , reading alone proceeds at a rate of speed which the reader himself controls." These reciprocal powers of reader control and freedom constitute on the one hand the enduring power of reading as a social process and on the other its continuing demand for greater world literacy. For as Gray (1956b, p. 29) estimated from UNESCO figures in 1954, only one-half of the world's population has had sufficient schooling to be literate, and perhaps only a third could pass a test of functional literacy.

Status of Adult Reading. The reading abilities and propensities of an adult population freed from the constraints of formal schooling is a crucial test of how well a society educates to read. Five decades of inquiry into American adult reading habits, summarized in the National Society for the Study of Education's yearbook *Adult Reading* (1956), led to certain general conclusions which have not been appreciably altered by more recent research. (1) Most American adults read newspapers, about two-thirds read magazines, and about one-fourth read books with any regularity, according to periodic polls. Several other countries surpass the United States in extent of adult book reading. (2) The most important differentiating factor in group nonfiction reading interests was found by Waples and Tyler (1931) to be sex, and the most common interest factor to be reading about other people. (3) Individual differences in reading interests are great, desirable ones tending to crystallize between the ages of 12 and 16, according to research reported by Gray and Munroe (1929), while the reading purposes of mature readers studied in depth by Gray and Rogers (1956) are likewise varied. The latter study also revealed that relatively few superior readers consistently functioned at the higher levels of critical reading. (4) Gray (1956a, pp. 47–52) likewise concluded from data gathered in the mid-1940's that one-half of the American adult population could read at or above the ninth-grade level. Dale and Chall (1956), however, noted that in 1950 one-fifth of American whites and almost two-thirds of American nonwhites over 25 years of age had six years or fewer of schooling, with corresponding handicaps in reading ability and urgent needs for simpler reading materials. (5) Availability of reading material appears to be a more important determinant of what people actually read than are their avowed reading interests, according to Waples (1932) and Carnovsky (1934). (6) Studies of the reading habits and interests of the more literate American occupation groups presumed to be able and motivated to read show their reading to be largely instrumental, i.e., for immediate rewards and goals, and relatively meager in the extent of book reading, in the opinion of Asheim (1956).

The status of American adult reading habits revealed by such findings is far from reassuring. In the yearbook on adult reading, Schramm (1956) proposed a general model of reading choice to clarify why people read what they do in which the immediate decision to read or not read is governed by a "fraction of selection,"

$$\frac{\text{expectation of reward}}{\text{effort required}}.$$

Thus, an increase in expectation of reward (motivation) or a decrease in effort required (availability) enhances the probability that a given selection will be read. While such a model suggests a promising means of interpreting a specific reading choice, it is the view of Asheim (1956, pp. 27–28) that the failure of most American adults to engage in sustained reading of serious book content is a reflection of the prevailing commitment of a large segment of the American economy to a life of action rather than to one of reflection. The clear implication of this interpretation is that the broad social values of reading, the motivational component of the fraction, are not consistently sought by most adults. The further implication is that the future adults of American society need more rewarding experiences with the printed media to value their socializing functions wisely and to select materials for reading with discernment as adults. That cultural and educational expectations of a society may affect the nature and type of reading progress expected is an issue raised by Foster and Black (1965) in a comparative study of the reading development of New Zealand and Canadian children.

Environmental Influences upon Reading. Race, socioeconomic status, social mobility, home and parental influences, bilingualism, and mass media other than the printed word are among the environmental aspects which have been explored in relation to reading.

Research fails to support the conclusion that race is the primary or sole determinant of reading success. While Bernice Cooper (1964) has shown systematic differences favoring the reading achievement of white over Negro children in the United States, such differences appear to be a reflection of the total social environment, not of race alone. This view is supported especially by the work of Deutsch (1965) and his colleagues in studies of 34 language-related variables among middle- and lower-class Negro and white children in grades 1 and 5. It was found, for example, that all measures of a major correlate of reading, intelligence, including the *Wechsler Intelligence Scale for Children* (WISC) vocabulary score, were significantly related to socioeconomic status only in first grade but to both race and socioeconomic status in fifth grade and that scores on the Gates reading test in grade 5 were significantly correlated with socioeconomic status but not with race. The author interpreted these data as supporting a "cumulative deficit hypothesis" which suggests that lack of appropriate language stimulation in early home and school life makes success in school activities such as reading progressively more difficult with age. He stressed the need among disadvantaged children for intensive language saturation in preschool and early school programs and for devising functionally motivated learning strategies. Such concern has stimulated extensive new educational programs for such children and specific attention to this group, notably in headstart programs as well as in federally supported studies of first-grade reading programs reported in *The Reading Teacher* in 1966. One such study, by Spache and others (1966), revealed that when reading-readiness work was extended and intensified according to the needs of Negro and white children in first grade, Negro children appeared to profit more, somewhat in proportion to their level of reading readiness. Recent evidence, contrary to previously reported research, that social mobility as reflected in frequency of change in schools also adversely affects reading achievement among disadvantaged and lower-socio-economic-group elementary-school pupils has been reported by Justman (1965) in a study of over 900 children in New York City and also by Morris and others (1967).

There is considerable evidence that parental attitudes and the nature of the home environment are important determinants of a child's reading success. Of particular interest is the work of Durkin (1966), who has made longitudinal studies of children who learned to read before entering school. Among the home factors identified is evidence from the matched experimental-control portion of the study that in every case these children were read to by their parents, who for the most part believed they could help their children to learn to read. Other recent research suggests that such intrahome factors as parental child-rearing conflicts, studied by Kramer and Fleming (1966), and failure of children to establish sibling independence and identification with the same-sex parent, reported on by Mutimer and others (1966), may impede reading progress. A penetrating study by Clarke (1965) also offers evidence that parental socialization values and the nature of the child-parent relationship are important determinants of children's interest in serious newspaper content.

The problems of the bilingual in learning to read, complicated as they are by the factors just mentioned and by the many varieties and degrees of bilingualism, have been little researched and are poorly understood. Some evidence that the language medium in which reading is first taught is a relevant factor is suggested by recent research by Modiano (1966) among Mexican children. In this study, children first taught to read in their mother tongue were more successful in learning to read a second language than those not so taught. Kittell (1963) concluded from repeated testing in grades 3 and 5 of the mental and reading abilities of children of unilingual and bilingual backgrounds that the earlier testing did not reveal their true potential language and reading abilities as did later testing, which favored the bilingual children. The positive effect of degree of acculturation for the older bilingual is likewise emphasized by Snider's finding (1961) that twelfth-grade reading achievement by Nez Percé Indians and white children was not significantly different.

Evidence of the effects of other mass media, particularly radio and television, is mixed. As a new, powerful medium of communication is introduced to a culture, the use of more established media such as the printed word may at first be curtailed and then tend to be renewed as the new medium becomes culturally assimilated. In the United States this effect has been noted by Lazarsfeld (1940) for radio and by Bogart (1956) for television. A later study by Parker (1963) has shown more specifically that widespread television saturation in selected communities was associated with an early significant decrease in total library circulation and in fiction withdrawals and that subsequent increases in library circulation over a ten-year period were considerably greater among juvenile than among adult library users. That the amount of children's reading may be related to the degree of exposure to pictorial mass media is suggested by the finding by Bailyn (1959) that heavy exposure to pictorial media tended to affect adversely the amount of time fifth- and sixth-grade children spend in reading and listening to the radio. The amount of time spent watching television and the significance attached to it may be less, however, for senior high school students than for students at lower levels, according to Witty and Kinsella (1962).

Some evidence of the very real potentialities of television viewing for developing vocabulary and for stimulating reading is presented in a comprehensive survey of the viewing and reading habits of American and Canadian children by Schramm and others (1961). On the other hand, Bailyn's evidence (1959) that high exposure to pictorial media among fifth- and sixth-grade boys tended to produce in a reading task evidences of stereotyping of characters, passivity, and a reflection of persons seen in pictorial media in their projected self-images has disquieting implications. It is difficult to escape the fact that the combined weight of mass media in the United States— radio, motion pictures, recordings, and television— has for many individuals taken up much of the time and effort once available for reading. Even in the diffusion of major news, Deutschmann and Danielson (1960) found that the newspaper played a secondary and supplementary role to television and radio. Further assessment of qualitative interaction effects of the new "grammars" with the old at successive age levels is complex and difficult but greatly needed.

Characteristics of Reading Materials. The materials of reading have been examined chiefly for their content and readability. Among printed media, newspapers have been most widely subjected to analyses of their characteristics. A noticeable trend is that toward analyses of type of content, such as the press coverage of American political phenomena. For example, greater front-page newspaper attention to the role of the presidency than to that of the Congress has been noted since World War I by Cornwell (1959), while press anti-intellectualism was not found by Hage (1959) to be greater toward Stevenson in 1952 than toward Adams in 1828 in their presidential campaigns. Foreign press attitudes toward the United States have likewise been examined by Budd (1964), who found four New Zealand metropolitan newspapers more favorable than four Australian ones, and by Wolfe (1964), who found 20 Hispanic-American newspapers to present a range of favorable to unfavorable attitudes toward Americans. Other aspects of the newspapers, such as the characteristics and readership of the editorial page, have been examined by Baker and MacDonald (1961), changes in the content of American Sunday newspapers from 1939 to 1959 by Hachten (1961), and of the Sunday comics from 1900 to 1959 by Barcus (1961).

Socially related concerns are likewise reflected in analyses of magazine content. The attitudes expressed by Negro writers in *Ebony* magazine toward segregation and discrimination between 1948 and 1960 were shown by Rosen (1964) to change in ways directly related to the growing self-image of the American Negro. Preelection attitudes in 12 Southern Baptist state periodicals in opposition to a Catholic president were also found by Avery (1963) to shift in major emphasis from those based upon moral grounds toward Alfred E. Smith in 1928 to grounds of nationalism toward John F. Kennedy in 1960.

The content of children's major reading materials, their reading texts, has been most comprehensively analyzed by Nila B. Smith (1965). The early religious and moral emphasis, 1607–1776, became more nationalistic, 1776–1840, and then more realistic and informational, 1840–1890. In the succeeding two decades, 1890–1910, literary selections were paramount but soon gave way to factual and realistic narratives in 1910–1925. Since that time, 1925–1965, realistic narrative and informational materials have continued to dominate the content of children's readers, with a trend toward more established literature and poetry in recent years. A recent analysis by Tennyson and Monnens (1963–1964) of references to occupations in children's readers revealed that professional and managerial occupations on the one hand and service occupations on the other were most frequently mentioned, with less attention being given to skilled, clerical, and sales occupations. These findings were disproportionate to the actual distribution of occupations and were regarded by the authors as presenting an unrealistic picture of the world of work. Certain characteristics of multiethnic children's readers published between 1960 and 1965 have likewise been evaluated by Collier (1967), who also made specific recommendations for needed improvements if they were to be used more effectively by the disadvantaged.

With respect to readability, Gray and Leary (1935) estimated that as of 1930, one-half of published reading material in the United States was too difficult for one-half of the adult population to read. Dale and Chall (1956, p. 233) have also shown that the readership of five leading magazines is largely composed of persons with at least a high school education, a finding which implies that the level of readability of the magazines may be in part involved. The readability levels of a wide range of other materials—newspapers, elementary, high school and college textbooks, school resource materials, and children's magazines—have been actively studied in the past 30 years, principally by means of readability formulas. A salient finding of research in the past decade into the readability of school texts in various content fields is that they are frequently too difficult for the intended level of use. Belden (1961), for example, found that only one of five high school biology texts to which the Dale-Chall formula was applied was readable by over half of the students in the grade for which it was intended. K. Smith and Heddens (1964) also reported that certain new-mathematics curriculum materials for primary and intermediate use were similarly too difficult, though inconsistently so, according to the Dale-Chall and Spache readability formulas.

The development of readability formulas, beginning with the basic investigation of Gray and Leary (1935), arose in response to a need for greater precision, objectivity, and efficiency in assessing the reading difficulty of materials. The principal components of readability with which the readability formulas are concerned, as Dale and Chall (1956, p. 226), among others, have observed, are vocabulary, sentence structure, idea density, and human interest—i.e., aspects of readability which can be quantified and have been validated against independently established levels of reading ability among the population. The extensive technical data related to the construction, validation, and use of reading formulas have been comprehensively detailed recently by Chall (1957) and by Klare and Buck (1954). However, as many investigators have noted, other, more intangible factors which have tended to resist objective quantification affect readability: the conceptual difficulty of the materials, their organizational structure, the style and interest value of the content, and the format of the material. The clear implication is that these factors must also be considered in assessing readability, particularly of those materials dealing with highly abstract content yet written in a deceptively simple style.

A somewhat new and more direct approach to the measurement of the reading difficulty of materials is the use of the cloze technique, in which words are excised from the text and success in the restoration of the meaning of the passage is examined. This approach rests upon the assumption, derived from information theory, that written messages vary in redundancy and hence vary in the amount of material which may be omitted without their meaning being destroyed. MacGinitie (1961), using a Poe short story and a fairy tale as materials, studied the effect of frequency of omission of words singly, in pairs, and in groups of four upon restoration difficulty by 600 college students. He concluded that the influence of context upon word choice in English prose decreases rapidly with the distance of the context and that context more than about five words distant had relatively little effect upon restoration difficulty. More recently Bormuth (1964) has used the cloze technique to show that mean word depth, a device for measuring sentence complexity, is significantly related to comprehension difficulties among children at the intermediate level. In another article, Bormuth (1966) concluded from an extended series of readability studies with children in grades 4 through 8 that the further development of more sophisticated linguistics variables will improve the predictive power of readability formulas. To the extent that applications of the cloze technique yield further insight into the elusive qualities of style, that technique may prove useful in our understanding of and ability to predict the readability of materials.

Attempts to make materials more readable, principally through adjusting vocabulary and sentence length in connection with the use of readability formulas, have been vigorously pursued in textbook, newspaper, and magazine writing and have been extended into governmental publications, including the income-tax form. That readership of articles is increased as materials are written in a more readable style is the finding of a number of investigations, including one by Feld (1948). While the actual output of more readable materials has undoubtedly increased in the past quarter century, it is difficult to ascertain the extent of this trend because of the great increase in publication rate of all types of materials, including those of specialized and technical content.

Two recent studies relate to a different kind of control, that of qualitative characteristics of the reading diet of the American reading public. Evidence that real but capricious lay censorship of books and magazines considered objectionable by individuals or groups has extended into some public junior and senior high schools in Wisconsin, and in ways not recommended by the American Library Association, was reported by Burress (1963). Herbert A. Otto (1963), on the other hand, has reported the presence of a very substantial proportion of incidents of violence and sex in magazines, paperbacks, and newspapers easily accessible on newsstands. It is apparent from these and other data that the range in quality of available reading materials in the United States has become greater as a result of judicial decisions in the 1960's and that censorship purposes and activities are undergoing reexamination.

Readership Preferences and Effects. The broad social-psychological concern for reading motivation, be it called interest, habit, or attitude, is reflected in many specific studies of reading preferences. Prior to the 1960's approximately 300 investigations of reading interests, principally of books, selections, titles, and topics through questionnaire, interview, and library techniques were published, according to Gray (1960). Such studies permit several broad generalizations chiefly based upon American investigations but with some supporting data from other English-speaking countries. (1) Interest in book reading tends to increase with schooling, at least through early adolescence, and then either to stabilize or to decline; (2) interest in newspaper and magazine reading follows a similar pattern beyond the primary grades, the newspaper being read the more regularly and with greatest interest in the comics and sports; (3) fiction is preferred to factual exposition, and prose to poetry, in elementary and secondary schools; and (4) in general, specific reading interests vary widely according to age, sex, intellectual ability, social class, and reading ability. Norvell (1950, 1958) has provided the most comprehensive interest ratings of specific books and reading selections by over 24,000 boys and girls in grades 4 through 6 and over 50,000 in grades 7 through 12, while Humphreys (1941) and others have noted the importance of peer recommendations in influencing the book-reading choices of children and youth.

Recent research in reading preferences and habits has tended to become more particularized. For example, Peltola (1963) found little correspondence between 192 first-grade children's book choices and books judged aesthetically superior by adults. Although Macdonald and others (1966) found that first-grade children preferred reading to other school subjects in a series of forced-choice situations, other recent studies at higher levels suggest that there is less tendency currently for pupils to prefer reading as an activity. Greenberg and others (1965), indeed, secured evidence among disadvantaged fourth-grade Negro boys that the perceived value of reading is considerably higher than its perceived low potency or actual usefulness to them. In a study of choice of book content, Berninghausen and Faunce (1964) reported that when actual reading of books was verified, adolescent juvenile delinquents read more books with erotic content than did nondelinquents. The authors noted, however, that an analysis of book-reading-questionnaire answers alone did not reveal such a finding, which is an interesting commentary on the need for validating the questionnaire instruments so often used in studies of reading preferences and interests. A further study which supports the school use of contemporary literature relevant to the interests of youth is Blount's investigation (1965) of the attitudes of 159 students in grades 9 and 10 toward the novel. Experimental groups which read "junior" novels especially written for adolescents displayed attitudes toward the ideal novel closer to those of experts than did groups which read adult novels—i.e., classics commonly assigned for study in these grades.

Newspaper readership has received increased attention in the American and foreign press in recent years. McNelly (1962), for example, reported that among 104 high school and 126 college students meaning intensity in an unfamiliar foreign news article was enhanced by the reading of the article, as was subsequent expressed interest in the topic. Ray Carter and Peter Clarke (1962) noted the selective use made by city and suburban readers of daily and weekly newspapers for integrative or disruptive content. Among newspaper-readership studies in South America, Africa, and Asia, Kuroda (1965) secured evidence that Japanese newspaper readership was related to political involvement and occupation in a sample of 278 registered voters but also found age and sex differences contrary to those reported for newspaper readership in the United States.

Factors associated with resistance to persuasive arguments in print, particularly the effect of prior immunization to beliefs, have been intensively studied, principally at the college level, by McGuire and Papageorgis (1961) and by a number of other investigators. Reported evidence based upon experimental designs of considerable sophistication indicates that the appropriateness, strength, and time of introduction of counterarguments and other relevant information significantly affect the degree of reader resistance to persuasion. Semantic-differential techniques have likewise recently been employed to measure attitudinal changes in reading, especially by Greenberg and Tannenbaum (1961) in measuring the effect of by-line placement in newspaper copy and by Tannenbaum and Lynch (1962) to validate a sensationalism index, "Sendex," for news stories.

PSYCHOLOGICAL ASPECTS. A major goal of much research in reading is to gain greater understanding of the reading process and its crucial learning conditions as well as its major correlates, developmental trends, and desirable hygienic conditions.

Nature of the Reading Process. In spite of voluminous research, reading as a psychological process, either in its beginning or in its later, more refined stages, is still poorly understood in the sense that a common understanding of the reading process is accepted and translated into instructional practice. Three views of the reading process which differ more in emphasis than in the components involved are examined briefly here.

Reading may be viewed essentially as the visual perception of word forms and their meanings. Research into how words are perceived under short-exposure conditions, usually by adults trained in introspective techniques, has been most explicitly reviewed by Vernon (1937, Ch. 3). From such evidence Vernon concluded that there are four components of word perception: (1) a vaguely perceived form or contour, with (2) certain dominating or specific parts, which (3) stimulate auditory-kinesthetic imagery and which (4) arouse meaning. Vernon stresses that "some type of *auditory* or *vocal* process is always reported," which she attributes to the fact that "all words are primarily speech units." She also emphasizes that attaching meaning to the word symbol is essential to the perceptual act. While such research emphasizes perception in a static situation, the eye-movement camera records the perceptual-motor activity of the eyes in a dynamic one. Comprehensive reviews by Vernon (1931), and more recently by Gray (1960) and by Tinker (1965), detail the long history and findings of the many studies of this activity. Attention in such research has been primarily focused upon the number, placement, and duration of fixations during which perception takes place in relation to such factors as age and maturity, purpose of reading, and the nature of the content read. Thus, Buswell (1922) early described the changes from the immature to the mature reader in terms of more regular progress of fixations across the line of print, shorter fixation duration, fewer regressions, more accurate return sweeps to the next line, and a broader span of recognition. Judd and Buswell (1922) pioneered in studying the variable effects of different purposes of reading, and of content of different types and difficulty, upon eye-movement patterns. The results of the latter type of study have led many investigators to conclude that eye-movement patterns fundamentally reflect, not cause, the comprehension processes involved in reading. The view of the reading process stemming from the employment of the tachistoscopic and the ophthalmographic techniques of research thus acknowledges the role of comprehension in reading but tends to stress the efficiency of the visual-perceptual and related processes involved.

A second view of the reading process is that reading is essentially a process of meaning elaboration or thinking in relation to written symbols. This view, formulated by Thorndike (1917) in connection with a study of errors made by children in interpreting a paragraph, was later more specifically elaborated by Gray (1960, pp. 1101–1103). One type of inquiry, literary criticism, illustrated with particular relevance to the act of reading by I. A. Richards in his *Interpretation in Teaching* (1938) and *How to Read a Page* (1942), reveals something of the enormous complexities involved in exploring the meaning of meaning. Factor-analytic techniques have also been used to examine comprehension processes by a number of investigators. One of these, Chester W. Harris (1948), identified a general factor in comprehending literary materials plus the more specific operations of "translating," "summarizing," "inferring tone, mood, and intent," and "relating technique and meaning." Coincident with the appearance of Benjamin S. Bloom's *Taxonomy of Educational Objectives*, an attempt was made by Gray and Rogers (1956) to develop a scale to assess the maturity of reading processes in adults. They reported that mature readers to a much greater degree than immature readers engaged in processes of summarizing and organizing ideas in reading, of inferring meaning, conclusions, and generalizations, of making evaluative judgments about what was read, and of applying ideas so generated. The salient focus in such studies is clearly upon the cognitive processes that come into play above and beyond the basic perceptual processes in reading.

A third view of the reading processes with specific reference to beginning reading instruction has been described by Carroll (1964, Ch. 14) as the "perception and comprehension of written messages in a manner paralleling that of the corresponding spoken messages." This view, stressing the intimate relationship of the reading act to the expressive language processes studied by linguists, is essentially that presented earlier by Bloomfield (1942). One distinctive feature of such a conception is the position that reading be considered, according to Carroll, as two psychologically different processes: one a process of decoding from the written symbol, the grapheme, the appropriate phoneme or sound referent in the spoken language and the other a process of comprehending written messages so decoded. A second, related feature of this view is that priority be given to the discrimination of spelling-sound patterns, particularly the more regular ones identified through linguistic analyses, before specific attention is paid to the comprehension processes. In effect, learning to read is conceived of as a two-stage process, the implication being that one stage, discriminating grapheme–phoneme correspondences, precedes the other, the more complex comprehension processes, for more efficient learning. Such a view of the beginning-reading process is in sharp contrast to methodological practices derived from conceiving the beginning stages of reading essentially as a more generalized, visually oriented perceptual process of learning to recognize whole words and their meanings before or in conjunction with learning to differentiate their parts specifically. While each of these views of the reading process presented here has certain merits, the issue being vigorously explored in the 1960's is the optimal relevance of each, separately or in combination, to initial and later stages of that process in the reading curriculum.

Learning Processes and Conditions Affecting Reading. Research relating to basic learning processes and conditions involved in reading has been especially vigorous and productive in the past decade. Much of the research has been conducted by psychologists, with particular attention being paid to carefully designed and controlled experimental methodology.

Discrimination processes needed for efficient early progress in learning to read have been an important research focus. While Huey (1906, p. 116) over 60 years ago echoed Goldscheider and Müller's conclusion that even mature readers "read by phrases, words, or letters as we may serve our purpose best," the whole word as the basic unit of meaningful discrimination has dominated American beginning-reading practices during the first half of this century. Diack (1960), in reviewing the evidence for this in Gestalt theory, concluded that the evidence was inadequate and argued that letters have meaning. Recent experimentation with kindergarten and prereading first-grade children in the United States strongly suggests that word elements, not whole words, are the key discrimination units for efficiency in learning to read. Muehl (1960) reported that single letters or letter details appeared to be the basis of matching words learned in pretraining to the task of learning a vocabulary list by a paired-association anticipation method, according to pupil reports and to analyses of errors made by 37 kindergarten subjects. Later studies of kindergarten children by Muehl (1961) and by King (1964) reinforced this finding and led them to conclude that initial training in discriminating letter forms would enhance children's success in discriminating word forms. Marchbanks and Levin (1965), who studied the cues used by 50 kindergartners and 50 beginning first graders, reported from analyses of the children's performance on delayed-recognition tasks involving three- and five-letter nonsense words that specific letters were the most salient cues, the first letter being most often so used. Total shape was the least-used cue. That such findings may be related to the discriminability of the word lists used is suggested by Samuels and Jeffrey (1966), who found experimental support for the hypothesis that learning speed and the tendency to use letters as salient cues is significantly related to the discriminability of the word lists learned by a paired-associate method by 36 kindergarten children.

Evidence that children from four to eight years of age can make the fine discriminations necessary for letter forms has been supplied by Gibson and others (1962a). The 167 children of the study improved with age in matching 12 letter-like geometrical forms but had greater difficulty matching asymmetrical than symmetrical forms. Other evidence concerning the relative specific difficulty of letter-pair discrimination by kindergarten children was offered by Popp (1964), the most frequent greater-than-chance errors on 130 visual matching letter pairs being on the pairs $p-q$, $b-d$, $b-q$, and $d-p$. Graphemes that were difficult to recognize, from highest to lowest in number of errors, were u, q, d, h, p, v, b, e, f, i, and k. Reversals and rotations appeared to be the primary source of letter confusion. In a later study of 18 first graders with discrimination difficulties, Popp (1967) concluded that specific discrimination training was effective, as did Carolyn K. Staats and others (1962) for 36 kindergarten children. Further studies of discrimination processes related to reading have been conducted among older subjects. Bishop (1964), for example, compared the transfer value for reading of teaching the sounds of individual letters versus teaching whole words in an unfamiliar language, Arabic. The results consistently favored the letter-trained group among the 60 college subjects. The critical finding of the study was that although subjects learned to read by both approaches, those taught to associate letter and sound were significantly better in the transfer task of learning to attack new words. The essential methods and findings of this study were replicated by Jeffrey and Samuel (1967) among three groups each containing 20 kindergarten children. Gibson and others (1962b) concluded from tachistoscopic presentation to college students of lists of pronounceable pseudo words having a high spelling-to-sound correlation and lists of unpronounceable pseudo words lacking in such a correlation that "the proper unit for analyzing the process of reading (and writing) is not the alphabetical letter but the spelling pattern." Additional evidence of the positive influence of pronounceability and experience upon rapid and accurate perception of words by college subjects has been offered by Postman and Greenbloom (1967) and Postman and Rosenzweig (1957). Good readers in the elementary school were also found by Elkind and others (1965) to be significantly more successful in a perceptual-decentration task, a finding which the authors related to Piaget's perceptual-decentration theory with the recommendation that training in such tasks as early as the kindergarten level would help children master the sound-symbol relationships of English.

Several other aspects of discrimination training related to reading in young children have been studied. Hendrickson and Muehl (1962) reported that adding motor-response cuing to arrows used to aid the visual discrimination of the letters *b* and *d* did not facilitate transfer by 49 kindergarten children on a criterion learning task. King and Muehl (1965) likewise found that the type and combination of additional sensory cues needed by 210 kindergarten children to recognize similar words (*ball, bell*) was precisely the reverse of those needed for dissimilar words (*gate, drum*), the rank ordering of cue efficiency for similar words being (1) picture, (2) picture + auditory, (3) picture + auditory + echoic, (4) auditory + echoic, and (5) auditory. The fact that the five treatments each for similar and dissimilar words produced no significant differences in word recognition after 12 trials except for the poorer performance of the group receiving only auditory cuing with similar words supports the common intuitive judgment of teachers that the discrimination of similar words needs cuing in addition to that of the spoken word alone. Evidence is unclear, however, among studies of older readers as to the potency of any one or combination of perceptual modes utilized in reading. There are some indications, from paired associate discriminatory training experiments by Wayne Otto (1961) and by Cooper and Gaeth (1967), that the preferred mode may vary with age; that modality functioning among certain disadvantaged poor readers of low socioeconomic status may be unevenly developed and cross-modality shifting difficult, according to studies by Katz and Deutsch (1964, 1963); that difficulty in attaching relevant verbal labels to stimuli within a given modality may complicate effective cross-modal transfer in disabled readers, according to research by Blank and Bridger (1966); and that motivational and attentional factors may be important determinants in the effective use of a given modality, as is suggested by studies by Walters and Kosowski (1963) and by Birch (1967). Evidence that certain other stimulus characteristics affect discrimination has also been reported by Jones (1965) and by David R. Olson and A. S. Pau (1966). Jones found that the matching of black letters and black words by nursery-school children was at least three times as difficult as matching colored-letter stimuli when English words were presented in an unfamiliar script, while Olson and Pau secured significant differences favoring the learning of emotionally toned words such as *kiss* and *hate* over such neutrally toned words as *come* and *keep* among kindergarten children.

Considerable interest has also been generated by the work of Carolyn K. Staats and others (1962) and by that of Arthur W. Staats and others (1964) in the application of operant-learning techniques, with a planned-reinforcement schedule involving the use of extrinsic rewards in the form of tokens, to early reading-discrimination tasks. The conclusion of the authors to the effect that operant-learning techniques and token rewards can be successfully applied to early discrimination learning in reading, while based upon very few cases and lacking substantial replicative evidence, has nevertheless stimulated a flurry of applications to various reading- and language-disability cases, including the successful application of the technique by Arthur W. Staats and William H. Butterfield (1965) to a disadvantaged and disabled reader, a 14-year-old juvenile delinquent.

Still other aspects of learning processes and conditions related to reading have been recently studied experimentally. The finding by Wayne Otto and Robert C. Fredericks (1963) and by Birch (1967) that poor readers accumulate reactive inhibition more rapidly than good readers but dissipate it more during a rest period and thus perform better after rest illustrates one of the theoretical learning concepts investigated. Their results suggest that special attention be given to the frequent alternation of work and rest for poor readers. A second learning concept which has been recently explored and in which theoretical interest is high is that of cognitive style. The concept, which remains poorly defined and apparently has many dimensions, is derived from observations that learners often display characteristic modes of attack in learning which may be scaled or dichotomized for experimental purposes. Thus, Kagan (1965) reported that measures of the reflection-impulsivity dimension gathered in first grade enabled him to predict reading performance in second grade; specifically, that a greater number of errors in word recognition were made by the children characterized as impulsive than by those characterized as reflective. While the author recommends that training impulsive kindergarten children in reflection would aid their reading progress, the effectiveness of this recommendation was only partially supported by Rosenfield (1967). Nevertheless, as Santostephano and others (1965) have suggested, reading may be usefully conceptualized as a particularly appropriate example of perceptual-cognitive activity in which several dimensions of "cognitive style" relating to the selecting, organizing, assimilating, and processing of symbols may be studied.

The notion that acquisition and retention of specific facts through reading depends upon the extent to which the learner's cognitive field is structured to permit the appropriate categorization of the new material has been advanced as a theory of meaningful learning in several writings. Ausubel (1960), for example, reported experimental evidence of the effectiveness of an advanced organizer—material of a generalized nature which is topically but not specifically related to the learning task—on delayed retention for college subjects. However, Jerrolds (1967) found that with ninth-grade subjects, the introduction of neither advance organizers nor modified advance organizers, in the form of the main idea of the selection to be read, significantly increased retention in experimental subjects over their controls. Nevertheless, the plausibility of the concept, for which many approximations exist in those teaching practices designed to provide background information, suggests the need for further research, particularly with subjects of less intellectual maturity and experience than college students.

A number of studies of the relation of the nature and amount of context to meaning have likewise recently appeared. A series of studies by Tulvig and Gold (1963) among college subjects, for example, showed that the tachistoscopic recognition of certain target words was facilitated significantly more by congruous than by incongruous contexts and that less context was needed for such identification in congruous contexts. The cloze technique of omitting words has also been employed to study context effects. Thus, Shepard (1963) found that the amount of guessing or average rate of words misproduced by college students in attempts to restore missing words was directly related to the amount of context, in this case, 1, 2, 4, 6, 10, or 40 words.

The role of purpose in reading is a further topic of recent research activity. Comparisons of the extent to which 24 good and 24 poor fifth-grade readers could set and achieve purposes for reading led Edmund H. Henderson (1965) to conclude that good readers are more effective than poor readers in setting their own purposes for reading and that purpose setting is positively related to purpose attainment. Earlier, Torrance and Harmon (1961) had noted that college graduate students given successively different specific sets or purposes for reading (to remember, to evaluate, to apply creatively) for each week of assigned reading apparently maintained their reading sets for only about half of their reading time but that these sets nevertheless produced measurable effects on tests covering the reading assignments. Evidence was secured that sets had a differential effect upon the kinds of goals achieved, especially for creative thinking and evaluative thinking outcomes. While students found the memory set easiest to maintain, only in one of the three weeks did it produce superior results on a cognitive type of test. That reading purpose together with the nature of the material read should ideally determine one's reading speed is part of the concept of an efficient reader recognized many years ago by Judd and Buswell (1922) and more recently by Shores and Husbands (1950). Remarkably little evidence, however, supports the contention that students actually adjust their reading speeds to purposes and materials. Blommers (1944), who devised an experimental test to measure reading rate in terms only of the time spent in attaining comprehension of specific reading purposes among students in grades 11 and 12, found a correlation of approximately .30 between rate of reading comprehension and power of reading comprehension. Good comprehenders were more flexible in adjusting their reading rates to the difficulty of materials than were poor comprehenders. Further, when the experimental test was used as a criterion, the validities of several other well-known reading-rate tests were found to be very low. Shores (1960) likewise found that for such a purpose as reading for the sequence of ideas in science materials, the rate-power comprehension relationship was also low. Such evidence suggests that the frequently reported high correlation between rate and power of comprehension is an artifact of tests which do not control the purpose-comprehension relationship in measuring rate of comprehension. This relationship was controlled in further investigations of the development and transferability of flexibility in reading rate in two studies conducted in the intermediate grades by Theodore L. Harris and others (1965, 1966). Evidence was secured in the earlier study that when flexibility in reading rate was measured in terms of ratios of one reading speed to another, pupils at these grade levels initially read at different rates for such purposes as reading for specific facts, for the main idea, and for the sequence of ideas and could maintain such flexibility in the rate-purpose adjustment while greatly increasing their speed of reading through training. In the second study, in which flexibility in reading rate was defined as reading rate for one purpose in relation to the mean reading rate for all purposes, it was found that training in adjusting reading rate to such purposes on short, specific passages transferred positively to longer passages more characteristic of text materials when the training and test materials were expository but not narrative in nature. The general implication of the findings related to the role of purpose in reading is that purpose is an important and modifiable factor in efficient reading comprehension.

The substance of the extensive research into children's reading interests prior to the 1960's was briefly described in a prior section under readership preferences and effects. The fact that research in this topic has been conspicuous by its absence in psychologically based research, particularly in the past decade, suggests that much of the previous concern about reading interests has been curriculum-based, i.e., related to practical problems in the selection of appropriate materials for reading. A conspicuous exception to this is the careful methodological study of school-age children's reading interests in Finland by Lehtovaara and Saarinen (1964) in which questionnaire, book-list, text-sample, and paired-comparison methods were used and compared for subjects between 10 and 16 years of age. It would appear, also, that research contemplated by these authors into the interaction of psychological and sociological conditions which give rise to expressed interests would be especially fruitful in helping to understand the genesis of reading interests and to explore ways in which reading interests may be modified and extended. One recent study which methodologically moves in this direction is Byres's content analysis (1964) of the voluntary sharing periods of 1,860 first graders in 34 communities geographically representative of major regions of the United States. The author concluded that first graders were actively interested in their own environment, especially in living things.

A related question, children's preferences for illustrations accompanying their reading, has been explored to a limited extent, as has the contribution of pictorial material to improved comprehension of the accompanying text. The results of research on the latter topic have been particularly inconclusive not only because of certain limitations of pictorial representation applied to verbal content but also because of uncontrolled variables such as age, interests, and other experiential and attentional factors in the reader.

Correlates of Reading. Intellectual correlates of reading have been extensively studied over a period of years. Intelligence, reflecting as it does to a large measure the capacity to engage in symbolic language activity, is itself a major correlate of reading. Thus, among school populations, as Gray (1960) reported, correlations between intelligence and reading-achievement tests tend to cluster between .40 and .60. While this substantial positive relationship would be considerably higher if the full range of intelligence were sampled, the fact that it is not higher suggests that other factors than intelligence per se affect reading achievement, that specific aspects of intelligence may be more highly correlated with reading achievement than others, or both. Bond and Clymer (1955) investigated the possibility of the greater correlation between reading achievement and some specific aspects of intelligence than between it and others, showing that for a normal population verbal and reasoning subtest scores in the *Primary Mental Abilities* test were significantly related to reading achievement but that the space and number subtest scores were not. Harootunian (1966) found such intellectual variables as word fluency, ideational fluency, speed of closure, and flexibility of closure, which are often not identified in intelligence testing, to be associated with the reading achievement of 513 students in grades 7 and 8. Braun (1963) likewise showed that for boys in grades 3, 5, and 8 there was a high positive relationship between concept-formation ability and reading achievement when intelligence was either held constant or allowed to vary. Studies of the intellectual functioning of disabled readers, such as the extensive epidemiologic survey of Scottish boys by Belmont and Birch (1966), have shown, however, that verbal functioning on the WISC is inferior to performance functioning, while Sawyer's highly analytical study (1965) of 140 boys and 40 girls disabled in reading offers promise for the more precise identification of mildly and severely disabled readers on the basis of WISC subtest scores.

Several aspects of intellectual functioning relating to specific language abilities have been shown to be significantly related to reading performance. The most frequently identified factor is word knowledge, which Potts (1960), for example, identified as a significant aspect of a general mental ability which predisposes to reading success among English children as early as 72–78 months. Many years previously Hilliard (1924) had shown that intelligence and meaning vocabulary showed the highest positive relationship to reading comprehension among several factors studied. More recently in a study of 101 students in grade 12, O'Donnell (1962) secured only moderate correlations between level of comprehension and awareness of sentence structure (.44) and awareness of grammar (.46), but a high correlation between vocabulary and awareness of grammar (.90).

This author, as have others, inferred that good readers must possess some awareness of the basic structural relationship of words in sentences. The high positive relationship between reading success and spelling abilities has also been noted by many investigators in the United States as well as in Malmquist's study of reading disability in the first grade in Sweden (1958, Ch. 18) and in Ahlstrom's investigation of spelling among fourth-grade pupils in the same country (1964). The importance of visual memory for words among good readers who were also good spellers as contrasted to those who were poor spellers was observed by Plessas and Dison (1965). A further factor, listening ability, was found to be substantially correlated with reading achievement for 172 pupils in grades 4, 5, and 6 by Cleland and Touissant (1962) and for 216 students in grade 8 by Plessas (1963). Substantial correlations between reading and performance in other school subjects involving reading have been frequently reported. Such results might be expected, for example, from Fortna's representative finding (1963) of a high loading on the factor of verbal comprehension in the *Sequential Tests of Educational Progress (STEP)* tests of reading comprehension, writing and social studies, and from his observation in connection with other data presented in the study that "while STEP Mathematics and STEP Science are measuring a numerical facility factor, reading and verbal skills are nevertheless involved . . . ."

The chief nonintellectual correlates which have been studied in relation to reading achievement are sex and various aspects of personality. Although numerous studies have reported sex differences, usually favoring girls, in reading achievement, especially during the early years of reading instruction, it is by no means clear that such findings represent more than environmental differences. Gates thus (1961b) interpreted the sex differences revealed in the standardization of the *Revised Gates Reading Survey* in grades 2 to 8 for over 6,000 boys and girls each. Earlier, Prescott (1955) had observed in connection with the standardization of the *Metropolitan Reading Test* for grade 1 on over 15,000 pupils that there was nonetheless sufficient variability in the somewhat superior performance of girls as not to warrant the provision of separate sex norms. McNeil (1964) has indeed reported significant differences favoring boys in an autoinstructional reading program given to 132 kindergarten children. Further, Wozencraft (1963) noted for 364 pupils in grade 3 and for 603 pupils in grade 6 that although all sex differences significantly favored girls on the *Stanford Reading Test* in grade 3, this was not true in grade 6. These and other studies suggest that commonly reported early sex differences favoring girls in reading may indeed largely be due to environmental influences, including the instructional, and are not inherent.

The extent to which general personality factors likewise are significant correlates of reading achievement has not been entirely clarified by research. In general, results have been mixed and subject to sampling problems and to the uncertain validity of the methods of assessment used. These have varied from teacher ratings and group-personality inventories to the Rorschach and specialized anxiety scales. A. W. Anderson (1961), for example, reported moderate correlations between reading achievement and certain factors on the *Cattell 16 Personality Factor Questionnaire* among 415 entering university students in Australia, but Durr and Schmatz (1964), using the *California Test of Personality* and other group instruments, found no significant personality differences among 81 high-achieving and low-achieving gifted children in grades 4, 5, and 6. However, Ames and Walker (1964) concluded that certain parts of the *Rorschach* were of value in predicting less-than-normal progress in reading in grade 5 for 54 children tested in kindergarten. Degree of anxiety has also proved difficult to assess and relate to reading achievement. Sarason's *Test Anxiety Scale* (TASC) has been employed in a number of studies, including that by Neville and others (1967), who reported that reading-comprehension gains among 54 boys enrolled in a six-week summer program were greatest among the middle-anxiety-level group, high test anxiety appearing to have an inverse relationship to comprehension gains although not to vocabulary gains. Scarborough and others (1961) had previously noted a significant relationship among 162 pupils in grade 7 between three levels of anxiety on the *Castenada Anxiety Scale* and measures of reading and language achievement. They concluded that there was a significant relationship between anxiety level and reading and language performance "for some students, particularly those of average and high intellectual ability." That pupil anxiety as measured by the *Taylor Anxiety Scale* as well as pupil compulsiveness as determined by parental interviews are significantly related to school structuring of reading method (a "structured" phonic versus an "unstructured" whole-word recognition approach) was confirmed for 228 pupils in grade 3 by Grimes and Allinsmith (1961) to a highly significant degree. This study is of particular interest in that it showed the high achievement of highly anxious (and compulsive) children in a structured setting, their significantly lower relative achievement in an unstructured setting, and the resulting underachievement when their high anxiety was combined with low compulsivity in the latter setting. Such studies of anxiety, it should be noted, are clouded by questions of the definition of the level of anxiety in an absolute sense and frequently by questions of reliability of the instruments used. Other investigators have reported evidence, particularly in respect to poor readers, that peer status and the self concept may adversely affect reading progress. Much more extensive research, however, is needed to clarify the precise interaction of personality manifestations and the reading process to determine the extent to which intuitive clinical observations of their often intimate relationship may be extended to the general population.

Reading Development. Prior to World War II, considerable attention was directed toward describing the developmental progress of children in learning to read. Such evidence of typical progress was well reviewed by Gray (1939) to the effect that (1) progress in getting the meaning of simple passages is rapid in grade 1 and may be quite efficient in grade 3; (2) progress is also rapid in the understanding of more difficult passages and in reading for different purposes in the intermediate, upper, and high school levels; (3) the oral reading rate and accuracy improve rapidly in grades 1 to 3 but thereafter more slowly; (4) the rate of silent reading parallels that of oral reading in grades 1 and 2 but tends to exceed it in grade 3 and to become much greater thereafter; and (5) the span of recognition increases rapidly in grades 1 to 4 with steady but less rapid progress thereafter. Individual deviations from this general pattern were recognized. While such generalized trends were based upon the best available sources of that time, when there was greater consensus in methods and materials for teaching reading than today, it is not inconceivable that with continued experimentation and improvement in the teaching of reading, certain aspects of such trends may change.

Extended longitudinal studies of reading development are relatively rare. Because of time considerations and because of inadequate instruments to measure the complexities of the reading process, cross-sectional techniques across selected grade levels have been more typically used, as in Gray's summarized statements to assess change over time for rather specific aspects of reading. However, the impact upon reading philosophy and method of Willard C. Olson's early (1940) and subsequent longitudinal studies in connection with his organismic-age hypothesis, including as they did measures of reading growth, was very great. His view was that progress in reading is influenced more by the total growth pattern than by any one aspect of development, such as mental age, alone. In particular, the influence of this concept was felt in reaffirming the breadth and continuity of the concept of reading readiness and in making more explicit the areas and relationships which need study in cases of severe reading disability. The concept of organismic age has, however, been severely criticized, by John E. Anderson (1954) on methodological grounds and by Blommers and others (1955) on the grounds that the substantial correlation between reading age and mental age is not substantially improved by including the physiological measures which form so great a part of the organismic-age hypothesis.

The specific aspect of reading development other than children's reading interests which has received the greatest research attention is growth in word-meaning vocabulary. The salient finding is that vocabulary power increases with age. Williams (1961) found in a study of 216 children in England that vocabulary progress is rapid from ages 6 to 8 and becomes slower after 8½ years when the vocabulary scale is based upon a random sampling of the dictionary. A. W. Anderson (1961) also reported significant increases in vocabulary development with age but a decrease in reading speed and comprehension for 278 adults, aged 18–62 years, who were mostly from clerical and professional classes in western Australia. Changes in the qualitative aspects of word meaning have also been investigated. Russell (1954) explored the dimensions of depth, breadth, and number of word meanings known at upper-grade and high school levels, noting general progressive change though some fluctuations in raw scores between grades and among tests. Feifel and Lorge (1950) showed that between the ages of 6 and 14, children tend to shift from concrete, functional definitions of words to more abstract classifications of word meaning. Similar results supporting Kruglov's earlier study (1953) were reported by Russell and Saadeh (1962) for the level of meaning selected—concrete, functional or abstract—on a multiple-choice vocabulary test by 257 pupils in grades 3, 6, and 9. Osgood and others (1957), using a semantic-differential technique, also found that older children gave more denotative meanings while younger children used more repetition-illustration-inferior explanations in a study of word meaning in grades 3, 5, 7, and 8 and at the college level. Howards (1964) has likewise shown significant and progressive change for 526 pupils in grades 4, 5, and 6 in their ability to understand the multiple meanings of "easy" words, the idiomatic and figurative meanings of which proved to be a source of particular difficulty. Werner and Kaplan (1952) have also strikingly demonstrated that the ability to use the sentence context to determine the meaning of a given word improves with age. Somewhat in contrast to the preceding studies, Flavell and Stedman (1961) found an absence of developmental change in children's ability in grades 2–9 to make judgments of semantic similarity (synonyms, coordinates, contrasts, and whole parts); rather, between grades 3 and 5 an adult pattern emerged which suggested to the authors that children are able to make rather complex semantic judgments in categorizing words at a rather early age.

A developmental study of considerable import for reading is that of the nature and development of children's language patterns by Strickland (1962). A major purpose of the study was to seek implications for the improvement of reading textbooks. Linguistic techniques were designed to analyze the speech of 575 pupils in grades 1–6 into its phonological units. Many detailed developmental findings were reported in connection with the general conclusions that children learn the basic structure of their language at an early age and that their oral language is far more advanced and varied than is that of typical basal readers. Salzinger and others (1966) have in fact shown that children by the age of three are sensitive to the syntactical structure of sentences and can use it in ordering and encoding sequences while listening. The implication of Strickland's investigation appears to be that greater correspondence and consistency is needed in structuring the language of the materials for the teaching of reading to meet the language needs and abilities of children.

Hygiene of Reading. As usually considered, the "hygiene of reading" refers to the physical attributes and illumination of materials which contribute to ease of reading. Often not considered but equally important are the basic considerations particularly important for school children of good posture, proper distance from and angle with the eyes of the reading material, and the hygienic habit of frequently resting the eyes by closing them or by gazing at far point distances when engaged in extended reading tasks.

It has been shown by Carmichael and Dearborn (1947) and by others that the mature human eye is remarkably resistant to fatigue, the factor which would appear to be the most obvious and sensible criterion for assessing ease of seeing. In view of the fact that the mature eye does not tire easily, and since experimenters have usually worked with adults, it has been difficult to establish a satisfactory criterion of reading fatigue. Luckiesh and Moss (1942), for example, prefer the blink rate as the fatigue criterion, while Tinker (1946, 1950) prefers rate of comprehension as the more valid and realistic criterion. Tinker (1963a) has also used reader acceptance as an additional criterion. Since this issue has not been entirely resolved, it has often been difficult to make precise recommendations based upon firm evidence particularly for the hygienic requirements of school materials; instead, publishers often rely more upon tradition, common sense, and personal preference in deciding upon such matters as typeface and type size, line length and leading, and paper color, tint, and surface. The bulk of such research, including that on illumination, was conducted before 1960 and is briefly reviewed here with particular reference to the comprehensive work in Luckiesh and Moss's *Reading as a Visual Task* (1942) and Paterson and Tinker's *How to Make Type Readable* (1940). Tinker's more recent *Legibility of Print* (1963b) and portions of his *Bases for Effective Reading* (1965) are also valuable recent sources.

Research on paper color, tint, and surface indicates that black print on a white background is superior to other combinations, according to Cornelia D. Taylor (1934), Luckiesh and Moss (1942), and Paterson and Tinker (1940). Paterson and Tinker emphasize the importance of maintaining the brightness contrast thus secured in contrast to other combinations of ink and surface. Luckiesh and Moss likewise reported in the same source the reflectances of many paper surfaces, but experimental evidence that paper and surface tint affect legibility is negative, according to Webster and Tinker (1935). Nevertheless, Pyke's recommendation (1926) that paper surfaces be unglazed is commonly followed to reduce one contributing factor to eyestrain, glare.

Line length, type size, and leading are recognized as interrelated factors by Luckiesh and Moss, Paterson and Tinker, and Zachrisson (1957). The optimum combinations of these typographical factors remain, however, a matter of some dispute. Paterson and Tinker (1940) concluded that type sizes between 6 and 12 points, with 2-point leading, and line lengths between 14 and 28 picas, offer acceptable legibility. They reported that subjects preferred moderate line lengths in 10-point type. On the other hand, Luckiesh and Moss (1942) favor larger type size and shorter lines. They considered, for example, 12-point as the more optimum type size and reported that 10-point type with a 2-point leading was read less easily as line length increased from 13 to 21 picas (p. 203). Specific recommendations for type size for children, ranging from 24-point for children below 7 years of age to 11-point for those above 12 years, have been made by Burt and others (1955).

Research into the effect of size of type upon ease of reading as reflected in reading speed among children whose reading habits are not fully developed is conflicting and difficult to assess. Alderman (1938) found that in grades 1–6 smaller type was read more rapidly than larger type in a study using 8-, 10-, 12-, and 14-point type. However, McNamara and others (1953) reported no consistent relationship of reading speed to type size in grades 1–2 but faster reading of 10-, 12-, and 14-point type than either 8-, 18-, or 24-point type in a study of 3,000 children. While the smaller type size theoretically makes more print available per fixation and thus may enhance the span of recognition and reading speed, considerable caution is usually observed by publishers of children's reading materials in using type of sufficient size to avoid unnecessary eyestrain and perceptual-discrimination problems.

There is general agreement that many modern type faces are legible but could be improved by making them bolder. Burt and others (1955), whose work was conducted in England, also found that children under 12 years of age preferred older-style type faces to modern ones, the explanation offered by the investigators being that "older faces accentuate those parts that are different while the modern faces accentuate those that are similar" (p. 33). With respect to type form, Paterson and Tinker (1940) showed that copy set in lower-case letters was read faster and was preferred to that set in capitals and that boldface type was less preferred but was read as fast as regular type. Reading italics for 10 minutes or more decreases reading speed as compared to reading Roman type, according to Tinker (1955). The legibility of many special typographical arrangements, such as tables and formulas, has likewise been summarized by Tinker (1963b, 1965).

The critical illumination level for adults according to Luckiesh and Moss (1942) is 10–20 footcandles. Earlier, Tinker (1939) had found that 3–4 footcandles were adequate, though he recommended higher though conservative figures for schools. More recently Tinker (1965, pp. 233–234) has recommended considerably higher light intensities in relation to specific reading situations and different type sizes. Tinker has also noted (1954) that preference for illumination level is not necessarily related to efficiency but is related to degree of visual adaptation at the time. He also calls attention to the importance of controlling the distribution or diffusion of light as a factor in affecting the degree of permissible intensity of light and in preventing glare (1965, pp. 234–235).

It is important to recognize again the methodological problems and the highly specific nature of much of the research into legibility. William C. Howell and C. L. Kraft (1961), for example, are critical of much existing research upon legibility for what they regard as its failure to quantify such perceptual continua of letter recognition as image size, blur, and contrast, which their psychophysical experiments showed to be differentially related. Clearly, if further progress can be made in the determination of more acceptable criteria and methods of experimentation, greater resolution of certain technical problems and uncertainties in the hygiene of reading may be attained.

PHYSIOLOGICAL ASPECTS. Research interest in the physiological aspects of reading has been focused chiefly upon sensory-motor dysfunctions and upon neurophysiological functioning as related to reading disability. Such research was most prolific in the 1930's and 1940's but has since shown a sharp decline in most aspects except for a persistent interest in the neurophysiological, including studies related to laterality and reading. Occasional studies have likewise appeared having to do with the use of drugs in the treatment of reading disability and with physiological states, such as reading epilepsy, observed to be associated with the reading act.

Robinson's thorough review (1946) of the relationship between visual defects and reading efficiency points to its inconclusive nature, i.e., among unselected cases the correlation tends to be low, yet in selected cases the relationship may be a significant one. The author noted, for example, that certain visual defects are reported by eye specialists to be more frequently associated than others with reading disability in children: "hyperopia, hyperopic astigmatism, binocular incoordination, [restricted] visual fields, and aniseikonia" (1946, p. 29). In Robinson's own intensive study of 22 severely disabled readers, visual defects were considered contributing causes to reading disability in half of the cases, binocular incoordination and hyperopia being the most prominent defects. Aniseikonia, the relatively rare condition of unequal visual-image size or shape, was not part of this study. Eames (1948) later showed in a study of over 1,500 cases that farsightedness and near-point muscular imbalance of the eyes were associated with slower word-recognition habits, while Steinberg and Rosenberg (1956) found that abnormal lateral phorias (severe eye-muscle imbalance) retarded reading progress in a study of 1,000 children in grades 4–8. Eames (1957) also reported that restricted visual fields reduced speed of perception and, more recently (1964), that correction of unequal refractive eye conditions apparently markedly aided the reading progress of such children. A major problem to which several investigators allude is that of securing valid and reliable visual data, especially among children. Independent confirmation by a thorough ophthalmological examination of the presence or absence of visual defects is an important consideration in practice and in research which has been frequently violated.

Evidence regarding the precise relationship of auditory and speech defects to reading achievement in the general population other than the hard of hearing and the deaf also remains somewhat inconclusive. It would appear that auditory discrimination, for example, is a more demonstrable and positive factor in relation to reading success than is auditory acuity, as Ewers' study (1950) suggests, and as reviews by Robinson (1946) and others imply. While auditory acuity may set the limits within which auditory discrimination may operate, there is no evidence that presence of the former guarantees the latter. Nor is there evidence, as several investigators state or imply, from well-validated tests that auditory discrimination is an unlearned and hence causal factor in poor reading. On the contrary, the strength of many developmental reading programs appears to lie in their success in improving auditory discrimination of language sounds. Effective auditory function may, however, to a certain extent rest upon an adequate auditory memory span, Gray and others (1922, p. 14) having identified many years ago a short auditory-memory span as a possible cause of reading difficulty.

The relation of articulatory disorders and reading achievement is likewise not conclusive, according to the comprehensive review by Eames (1950). He concluded, as did Monroe (1932) many years earlier, that certain related speech and reading defects may stem from one or more underlying cause or causes in which defective auditory discrimination and memory may be implicated. Bond (1935) had previously found no difference in the number of speech defects in good and poor readers but did note that over one-third of the poor oral readers who were good silent readers had speech defects, while good oral readers who were poor silent readers revealed no speech defects. Although speech defects and reading difficulties may thus occur together, there is no substantial evidence that one causes the other.

Over a period of years there has been considerable theoretical and experimental interest in the specific question of the extent to which speech mechanisms are involved in and may hinder the rate of silent reading. The crucial experimental problem has been to isolate and measure accurately the activity of a speech muscle that is not simultaneously responsive to other peripheral muscle activity. The most conspicuously successful attempt to do this is the work of Edfeldt (1960). The experimenter worked with physicians to select such a muscle, the mylohyoid muscle at the base of the tongue. Electrodes were then carefully embedded in the muscle and electroencephalograph patterns under various reading conditions recorded for 84 college students divided into good, average, and poor readers. Edfeldt found that the good readers engaged in significantly less silent speech than did poor readers, that easy text materials were read with significantly less silent speech than difficult ones, and that the reading of clear text tended to produce less silent speech than did the reading of unclear text. Low reading scores were accompanied by high silent-speech scores, but even good readers showed increases in the amount of silent-speech activity when confronted with difficult text. The universal presence of "silent" speech as thus measured lends credence to the view that silent reading is indeed a motor-based speech activity. There is no valid experimental evidence, furthermore, that exceedingly high reading rates claimed for some readers are due to a complete short-circuiting of the motor-speech center; rather, the motor-speech center still appears to be involved, though to a minimal degree. There is evidence, however, from a study by Buswell (1945) that a reading program, the nonoral, explicitly designed to suppress vocalization during silent reading in the primary grades produced in later grades approximately as much lip-movement activity as in a control group.

Reading, in common with other advanced learned activities, rests upon an extremely complex neurophysiological structure, the basic integrity of which appears crucial to success in learning to read. If this structure is incompletely developed or damaged, the resulting neurological disorder is assumed to be a primary cause of reading disability. Such primary-reading-disability cases reflecting this assumption have received voluminous attention chiefly in the medical literature. One recent example of such a study conducted over a long period of time is that by Silver and Hagin (1964), who found the persistence of certain perceptual and neurological deficits in spite of remedial training in a clinical follow-up study of 24 young adults diagnosed as cases of specific reading disability 10 years earlier. A comprehensive review of the recent state of knowledge of the specific dyslexia type of reading disability is provided by Money (1962), in the Johns Hopkins symposium on reading disability, and in a brief but incisive paper by Eichenwald (1967). Both are concerned not with reading disability due to psychological causes or to specific sensory handicaps but with cases of "specific dyslexia" in which, in Eisenberg's words, "a child is unable to learn to read with proper facility despite normal intelligence, intact senses, proper instruction, and normal motivation" and in which the cause is unknown (Money, 1962, p. 5). The point that "dyslexia" is a purely descriptive term meaning "inability to read" and is thus not a causal explanation of such a condition is an extremely important one which is frequently overlooked. The authors cited in this symposium, furthermore, are careful to point out the fallacy of assuming a single cause for specific developmental dyslexia within the psychoneurological domain on the basis of present knowledge. Benton and Zangwill, for example, in assessing the extensive but conflicting research on directional confusion and laterality among normal and dyslexic populations are careful to note this principle in their discussion of the relation of dyslexia to cerebral dominance (Money, 1962, Chs. 6 and 7). In general, neurophysiologists are also extremely critical of remedial prescriptions which in effect violate the principle of multiple causation of severe reading disability. Eichenwald, for example, declares categorically that there is no medical evidence that endocrine imbalance due to faulty acetylcholine metabolism, as proposed by some, is related to specific dyslexia; that "current explanations of cerebral dominance are concepts not facts," the causal relationship assumed to exist in programs designed to strengthen cerebral dominance representing a nonscientific approach; that unfounded assumptions are often made about maturational relationships related to visual perception to promote questionable training programs in "visual motor and visual postural relatedness" for the treatment of specific dyslexia; and that misconceptions of the term "specific developmental dyslexia" and the inadequacy of available diagnostic tools and procedures yield frequent spuriously high estimates of its incidence, which he believes to be approximately 2 percent of the normal child population. Eichenwald regards specific developmental dyslexia as a type of receptive disorder in central cognitive integration, a view supported by Cohn's study (1961) of 46 clinical cases. He likewise recognizes the substantial evidence produced by Hallgren (1950) in Sweden that specific dyslexia may be hereditarily linked but has no necessary relationship to other frequently attributed disorders such as left-handedness and mental retardation. The clear implication of these observations, which correspond rather closely to the more extensive discussion by Money and his associates, is that great caution must be exercised equally by professional and lay persons in assuming a single neurological deficit to be causally related to more than the very few severe reading-disability cases in which organic neurological impairment may be demonstrated. The same investigators have, however, clearly identified research needs and have suggested types of research studies which may in time clarify the presently perplexing problem of specific developmental dyslexia.

TEACHING ASPECTS. Research in the teaching of reading, especially that done in recent years, exceeds by far research in other aspects of reading. Its scope is wide and includes research related to the aims and status of reading instruction, the role of the teacher, organization of reading instruction, reading readiness, developmental reading practices, reading appraisal, and diagnostic and remedial practices.

Investigations of the effectiveness of instruction in reading frequently reflect the curricular concerns for ascertaining the status of instruction and for judging its long-term effects as well as for appraising the more immediate question of instructional efficiency. Program research dealing with the latter question in the experimental or quasiexperimental sense has proved exceedingly difficult to conduct and evaluate in this teaching area, as in others. Such research is usually complicated by the need for extended program commitments and involves complex teaching procedures, diverse materials, and intricate teacher-pupil interactions. The effective control of such a matrix of variables challenges even the most sophisticated and advanced experimental designs. It is therefore seldom possible to place the same confidence in the results of much experimentation in the efficiency of the teaching of reading as one may place, for example, in the better examples of well-conceived and tightly designed psychological experiments in more specific aspects of reading instruction. Furthermore, extensive replication of studies of instructional effectiveness in the teaching of reading, so often needed, is frequently lacking. In other cases, changes in the value systems of experimenters and practitioners have been shown necessary to initiate change and indeed to accept a clearly demonstrated need for change in instructional practices in reading.

Aims and Status of Reading Instruction. Nila B. Smith (1965), as noted earlier, has shown how the aims of reading instruction in America have in the broad sense reflected and interacted with the changing values of the times. In recent years the ultimate objectives of reading instructors have moved far beyond purely utilitarian concerns to an emphasis on the importance of reading as a continuing source of personal valuing and social understanding. As the conception of desirable reading aims broadened in scope, this expanded view of reading objectives was likewise projected by national committees on reading, notably that of the National Society for the Study of Education (1948), into the high school and college years as a part of a projected instructional pattern needed for the refinement of reading skills and abilities and for the resulting worth to the individual. Consequently, the scope and complexity of the aims of reading instruction which are often elaborated into a dozen or more specific objectives make an adequate assessment of the status of the total instructional program precarious.

However, research into the more specific aspects of reading, measured by the administration of the survey type of reading-achievement test in the United States to the general school population by Worcester and Kline (1947) and by Gates (1961a), indicates that children as a whole read silently as well as if not somewhat better than their counterparts in the 1920's and 1930's. The former study is of particular significance because identical tests and norms were used to appraise performance in the two periods, a methodological factor not controlled in most comparisons of reading achievement over long periods of time. Similar confirmatory evidence among 11- and 15-year-old children in England and Wales was reported in the British study *Standards of Reading, 1948 to 1956* (British Ministry of Education, 1957). Gray and Iverson (1952) reached the same general conclusion from a comprehensive survey of available published evidence in the early 1950's but also noted that (1) average rate and accuracy in oral reading were apparently lower than before, (2) about the same proportion of children seemed to be engaged in personal reading, and (3) no reliable conclusions could be drawn about comparative quality of materials read in the two periods under comparison. Such comparisons nevertheless do not give evidence of change or lack thereof in more complex and mature reading abilities, since instruments to measure these were not available until relatively recently. However, the Harvard Report on reading, by Austin and Morrison (1963, pp. 39–43), reveals inadequate current instructional attention to the development of critical reading skills in elementary schools, as indicated by a nationwide questionnaire survey of 795 school systems. It may be presumed, furthermore, from the results of many studies at the high school level, and from those by, for example,

Homer Carter (1959) and Halfter and Douglass (1958) at the college level, that the more mature reading abilities, to say nothing of basic reading and study skills, are undeveloped in very substantial proportions of even selected reading populations in the United States today. Substantial evidence over a considerable period of time exists, moreover, that little if any progress has been made in reducing the number of significantly underachieving pupils in reading, estimated by Traxler (1949) from various studies to include from 10 to 25 percent of the school population by the end of grade 6. The recent rapid growth of special reading programs and remedial facilities, especially at the junior and senior high school and the college levels, indicates the persistent presence of a very substantial percentage of underachieving readers at the upper grade levels. These underachievers in reading, for reasons other than lack of capacity, have either (1) not learned to read well initially; (2) or, having learned to read well initially, have failed to develop the more advanced reading skills and abilities; (3) or, regardless of previous learning, have not retained and cannot transfer the necessary reading skills and abilities to the more complex reading tasks of later years. In assessments of the status of reading instruction in the United States, when the question of the extent to which the broad aims of reading instruction are being realized is extended to include the general school-age and adult population, the sociological, psychological, and pedagogical evidence strongly indicates the need for continued upgrading of the status of reading instruction to make it more congruent with and closer to the realization of the broad aims of reading instruction. More explicit attention in particular is needed to recognize and further the role and values of oral reading as a communication process in view of the predominant emphasis, both theoretical and practical, upon silent reading in American reading instruction.

The Teacher and Reading. The teacher is a crucial variable in reading instruction. Preservice programs for the preparation of teachers of elementary reading were generally characterized by Austin and others (1961) in a national survey in the United States as (1) attracting students of increasingly higher quality, though not so high as that of students entering secondary teaching and other academic fields, (2) not giving adequate professional course time to the teaching of reading, and (3) not providing fully adequate practice-teaching experience. College supervisors and cooperating teachers, for example, cited the most prominent of several deficiencies among practice teachers to be deficiencies in their understanding of phonetic principles, in their ability to group children for reading instruction, and in their ability to adapt to individual differences. As a result, the preservice preparation of teachers of elementary reading in the United States was judged to be inadequate in many respects. Consequently, 22 recommendations, largely administrative, were made for strengthening preservice preparation.

The instructional needs of practicing teachers with respect to reading have been explored in several studies. For example, Adams (1964), after a statewide random sample of 60 elementary teachers in Florida, reported that teachers expressed a need for greater understanding of most of the major aspects of reading instruction, with especially high consensus on the need for help in diagnosing and treating reading problems. Hutchinson (1961), in another state, showed the almost unanimous recognition of need by secondary English teachers, by their principals, and by their professors of the teaching of English for more adequate preparation in the teaching of reading at that level. A questionnaire study by Braam and Roehm (1964) among 70 high school teachers in several content fields further revealed marked discrepancies between these teachers and reading experts in their understanding of reading skills and the conflicting perceptions of these teachers with respect to student competence in reading, irrespective of the presence of a reading specialist or of reading programs in their schools and of their previous participation in in-service reading programs. It may be concluded from this and other evidence that more effective in-service programs and other means need to be sought to assist teachers in the field to meet effectively the reading instructional needs of their students.

Organization of Reading Instruction. Organizational considerations in reading are directed fundamentally toward creating appropriate learning conditions for the satisfactory progress of each pupil in all aspects of reading development. Research attention to such matters as needed instructional time for reading and class size is meager, but various ways of individualizing reading instruction have been explored.

It is difficult to determine precisely the time currently devoted to developmental reading instruction in the elementary school, since additional time beyond the basic instructional period may frequently be devoted to reading instruction in other, related activities such as language arts and in other content fields, and this time may or may not be reported. Early evidence cited by Gray (1960, p. 1119) showed remarkable stability in time allotments for reading instruction between 1919 and 1931, with probable increases in time so allotted by 1945 to reading instruction in the primary grades. More recently, Brekke (1963) has reported, in a nationwide study involving grades 1–8 in over 1,000 schools, that the amount of time spent in basal reading instruction, while progressively decreasing through the grades, accounted for slightly more than one-half of the total reading instructional time and was disproportionate to that spent in other reading activities, especially in the primary grades. Noting the discrepancies between these findings and the time allotments usually advocated, Brekke recommended spending less time in basal reading instruction and more in other reading activities in the primary grades, more time for both basal and supplementary reading instruction in the intermediate grades, and more time for other reading activities in grades 7 and 8. Jarvis (1965), noting that research had not clearly established optimum time allotments in relation to reading achievement, examined this relationship at the sixth-grade level. He found no significant differences in vocabulary and comprehension among those students who had received 60–78 versus 40–50 minutes of reading instruction in grades 4–6. He concluded that basic reading instructional time in excess of 50 minutes in the intermediate grades was unwarranted and also recommended more emphasis upon reading activities in other areas of the curriculum.

While Spitzer's earlier study (1954) of class size revealed no significant differences in reading achievement on the Iowa Test of Basic Skills for 50 third-grade classes averaging slightly more than 20 pupils and 55 sixth-grade classes averaging slightly more than 30 pupils, Frymier (1964) reported highly significant differences, favoring smaller classes, in first-grade reading achievement on the Williams Primary Reading Achievement Test among 9 classes enrolling fewer than 30 pupils and 6 classes enrolling more than 30 pupils. The prevailing disposition to favor small classes for instructional purposes, including reading in self-contained classes, obviously rests upon considerations other than reading achievement as measured by formal achievement tests. Further experimentation is clearly needed to establish critical limits of class size at various grade levels in relation to specific reading instructional purposes, different organizational programs designed to meet individual differences, and different reading outcomes, including the attitudinal.

The extent to which a reading program is individualized has been shown to be dependent upon several factors, such as the teachers' skill, the size and composition of the class, the materials for instruction and diagnosis, and the organization of the school program. Explicit suggestions for individualizing instruction in school subjects including reading were in fact the subject of a yearbook of the National Society for the Study of Education as early as 1925. Research has focused chiefly upon three problems: heterogeneous versus homogeneous in-class grouping according to pupil mental ability, interclass versus intraclass grouping according to reading ability, and highly individualized versus group procedures for reading instruction.

Russell's early study (1946) showed no significant differences in reading-achievement gains for intermediate pupils either for pupils at different ability levels or for entire experimental and control groups at three ability levels. A later study by Drews (1965) of three ability levels versus random grouping in ninth grade also revealed no significant differences in reading and other aspects of achievement measured. On the other hand, Borg's four-year study (1965) of the effects of heterogeneous versus homogeneous ability grouping in the intermediate, junior high school, and senior high school levels suggests that the general effects of a given type of grouping may vary with grade level and with the type of data, cognitive or noncognitive, considered. Division of the classroom into groups, usually three, chiefly on the basis of reading ability or on a combination of reading and intellectual ability has, however, for many years been considered superior to whole-group instruction in adjusting to individual differences in those American schools which follow basal reading practices. Such groups may differ in size, are relatively inflexible in composition, as Groff (1962) has shown, and may use the same or different text materials. The often artificial and inflexible nature of the typical three-group procedure, which may be used more as a small-group solution for classroom management considerations than as a means to individualize instruction within the subgroups, has been severely criticized on the grounds both that it does not necessarily reach the individual and that, as Mann (1960) and others have reported, it produced undesirable stereotyping of the pupil's self concept. However, one plan to reduce the size of the instructional group in reading to make provision for individual differences more feasible is the divided-day plan. Recent research by Warner (1967) and others has indicated that this plan results in generally superior reading performance. As reported, this plan does not abolish grouping practices but allows half of a reading class to meet earlier and separately for reading instruction.

Research evidence is conflicting about the effectiveness of other organizational plans to make reading instruction more diagnostic and more responsive to the needs of individuals, such as the nongraded plan of school organization, intraclass grouping, and "individualized reading." Carbone's careful study (1961) of the nongraded versus graded plans among 122 randomly selected pupils in each of grades 4, 5, and 6 revealed significant differences favoring the nongraded plan on all aspects of the Iowa Basic Skills Test, including reading, when the effects of intelligence were controlled by analysis of covariance. The nongraded groups also rated their teachers significantly more favorably on a semantic-differential scale of teacher characteristics and scored significantly higher in social participation, though not in other aspects of a mental health test. No evidence was found in this study, however, from a questionnaire that the nongraded plan of organization produced major changes in the instructional practices of teachers, a finding corroborated by Austin and Morrison (1963) in visits to five school systems using such a plan. Although other research evidence of its effectiveness is mixed, the long-range potentialities of this approach to the individualization of reading instruction appear promising, provided that teachers adapt their teaching practices accordingly.

Interclass grouping, in which pupils irrespective of grade level are grouped for reading instruction on the basis of reading ability, has not been shown by the majority of recent studies to produce significantly superior reading achievement in the intermediate grades to that in self-contained classrooms, according to such studies as those by Powell (1964), Moorhouse (1964), and Carson and Thompson (1964). An observation of particular interest is that by Moorhouse who, finding that the mean gains of experimental subjects was double that of his controls at the end of the first semester but only slightly different after three semesters, noted that significant differences occurred only when interclass grouping was novel and interesting to the pupils.

"Individualized reading" in its pure form, as advocated by Veatch (1959), is a radically different approach to the individualization of reading instruction. It ideally involves, among other things, the self-selection by pupils of either trade books or textbooks for instructional purposes, adjustment by the teacher to the reading needs of pupils as they attempt to read such materials, and the conduct of instruction on an individual conference basis. The concept of individualized reading is in essence a reaction to certain assumptions, materials, and practices exemplified in typical basal reading programs: the assumption that a sequence of skills appropriate for all children can be preplanned, the selection of reading materials primarily by adults rather than by children in accordance with their own individual needs and interests, and the inflexibility and undesirable personal-social consequences frequently attributed to the typical three-group classroom organization for reading instruction. The major differences between individualized reading and present basal reading approaches in their philosophy, materials, and procedures, plus the fact that in practice the ideal type of completely individualized instruction is often modified or combined with some systematic group instruction, make valid experimental comparisons between the two approaches virtually impossible. Such research as has been reported, illustrated by that of Sartain (1960), Rothrock (1961), Wilson and Harrison (1963) and Healy (1963), shows no significant differences in reading achievement between the two approaches. However, Sartain, Rothrock, and Healy have found motivational or attitudinal differences favoring the individualized reading approach, as have Macdonald and others (1966) in studying the merits of one feature only of this approach, the one-to-one instructional relationship in the first-grade use of basal reading instructional materials. The obvious desirability of the goal of individualized reading, to adapt reading instruction to pupil differences, has led Sartain and others to advocate the supplemental use of the self-selection of materials and the individual conference features of individualized reading with existing basal reading programs.

The organizational considerations reviewed thus far refer to developmental reading instruction for all children in the elementary schools which is still most typically conducted in self-contained classrooms. There is no substantial evidence, judging from that reviewed by Gray (1960, p. 1126) and that subsequently published, to indicate that the administrations and staffs of the high school and the college, or special field teachers in the elementary school, have caught the full implication of the developmental concept for the organization of reading instruction. This concept implies organizational provisions for the continued reading growth of all pupils commensurate with their ability and the acceptance of such responsibility by all teachers who use reading materials as a basis of instruction. This principle has been enunciated especially vigorously by Whipple (1949). The concept also implies that proper adaptation of the developmental reading program be made for slower-learning children and for faster-learning children, and that special remedial help be provided for pupils not achieving as expected according to the best estimates of their capacity to learn. The most typical organizational structure in the high school and college in the United States is the formation of special classes, often euphemistically called "reading improvement" or "developmental reading" classes but nevertheless created for remedial assistance. Some school systems have also organized remedial-reading clinics for the diagnosis and treatment of the most severely disabled readers. It is apparent, however, that the existing organizational policy of adding such classes to the existing structure at the high school level in particular is not designed to meet the developmental reading needs of its population and merely accentuates the problems faced by colleges in preparing students to cope with their reading demands. The organization of a high school developmental reading program for all students, with its implications for the preservice and inservice education of staff, thus merits the urgent attention of school administrators and staff alike.

Reading Readiness. "Reading readiness" is a descriptive term used to identify those characteristics in the pupil which apparently enable him to profit from reading instruction. As such, the concept was early applied to beginning reading but was later explicitly extended by Harrison (1939) and by others to all levels of the reading program. An often-unrecognized aspect of the concept of reading readiness, however, is that it has validity only in reference to the reading tasks which the pupil is expected to master; hence, it involves environmental considerations of home, community, and school. The bulk of research in reading readiness in the United States, for example, has until very recently been conducted among middle-class children using a well-established pattern of basal reading instruction. It is instructive to realize that assumptions often made about the mental and chronological age levels needed for success in beginning reading do not hold when reading tasks and expectancies are altered. Thus, Davidson (1931) demonstrated that bright three-year-olds could learn to read when reading materials and tasks were adapted to their needs. Evidence such as that provided by Christian D. Taylor (1950) attests to the fact that Scottish children with a mean IQ of 101 who entered school at age five and began to read shortly thereafter made significant early progress in reading on the *Metropolitan Reading Test* administered at the beginning of their second year, a finding which suggests that beginning-reading task expectancies may vary from culture to culture. Further evidence from kindergarten studies cited earlier of a psychological nature in the United States indicates that the definition of the reading task itself affects beginning-reading expectancies with respect to reading readiness.

Early research into reading readiness, as Gray (1960, pp. 1114–1117) has noted, was devoted largely to defining and exploring the dimensions of reading readiness in relation to reading success or failure. Gates and Bond (1936), for example, demonstrated the correspondence of the matrix of factors which may be used to describe a child's success in reading to that which needs to be investigated to infer probable causes of reading failure. The essence of the concept of reading readiness emerging from this and other studies is one involving the interaction of all major aspects of development—intellectual, physical, social, and emotional—and the environment. The concept also implies a necessary balance among these aspects such that a marked deficiency in one or more may seriously interfere with the adequate functioning of another, often in unique ways for particular children. Thus, the concept of reading readiness is more properly analogous to a generalized state of readiness across the several aspects of development for the instructional expectation of a culture than it is to some point in the development in the individual of a single aspect such as the intellectual. The implication of such an interpretation of reading readiness is clearly that the many aspects of developmental and environmental interaction must be considered and that the nature and timing of the reading instruction be adapted to the needs of individual children. The study by Spache and others (1966) referred to earlier illustrates one such adaptation.

Nevertheless, much research has been devoted to identifying specific instruments and techniques useful for predicting readiness for reading in terms of later reading success. It is, however, difficult to evaluate the research findings because of differences in the tests used, in the predictive interval employed, and in the experimental design employed. Intelligence and reading-readiness tests, separately or in combination, have been commonly used with varying degrees of success. Not unsurprisingly, the predictive value of such tests for first-grade reading success has in general been found to be only moderate and quite similar, as Senour's study (1937) illustrates. This finding led Senour to conclude that either type of test may be used, although others, such as Gates (1940), recommend the use of both. The long-range predictive value of the *Metropolitan Readiness Test* was studied more recently by Kingston (1962), who, using multiple regression analysis techniques, found it to be significantly correlated with reading achievement in grades 3 and 4 in reading programs tested but not high enough to predict individual success in reading at those levels. The positive predictive value of other more specific tests, such as the *Bender Gestalt*, has been reported by Koppitz and others (1961), but Arthur V. Olson (1966) reports the *Frostig Developmental Test of Visual Perception* to have little predictive value for reading achievement in grade 2. The results of more analytic reading-readiness studies based upon the development of multiple regression equations to predict for first-grade reading the usefulness of auditory-discrimination and of visual-discrimination measures for first-grade reading success have been reported by Dykstra (1966) and by Barrett (1965), respectively. Auditory-discrimination skills as a group were not found by Dykstra to be a significant predictor of reading success, although auditory discrimination of beginning sounds appeared to be the best of the auditory predictors. Barrett found that among visual-discrimination tasks, the best predictor was knowledge of the names of letters and numbers. This finding was confirmed by Bond and Dykstra (1967) from analyses of the results of the cooperative first-grade reading studies and had been reported to be a significant factor much earlier by Durrell (1958). When a prediction of reading success is applied to a reading program in which the early auditory and visual discrimination of letters is emphasized, however, intelligence and readiness tests have little predictive value for first-grade reading success as Henderson, quoted by Theodore L. Harris (1962, pp. 13–15), has reported. It would thus appear that as beginning-reading programs become more diversified in nature, the predictive value of existing measures may need to be reevaluated.

The very considerable recent interest in formal reading instruction as early as kindergarten reflects the emergence of a more dynamic conception of reading readiness than has prevailed for the greater part of this century. For various reasons, including social pressures as well as the results of recent psychological experimentation, the studies by Durkin and others of early readers, and the development of new procedures and materials for teaching reading, school systems are increasingly experimenting at the kindergarten level with readiness activities more specifically related to reading, if not engaging in formal instruction in reading. The most extensive and publicized of these studies is the Denver experiment which, as reported by Brzeinski (1964), has resulted in significantly superior reading performance at the end of first grade for the 61 experimental kindergarten classes given 20 minutes of instruction in reading a day over the same number of control classes. The original sample of this study included 4,000 kindergarten children. Particular progress was noted in the ability of the experimental subjects to recognize letter forms and to associate letter sounds and names. Brzeinski and others (1967) later reported that only the experimental subjects whose reading programs were adjusted thereafter through grade 5 made continued progress. No evidence was found that the early reading instruction of experimental subjects adversely affected their visual acuity or their attitudes toward school. Other positive evidence favoring early reading instruction includes studies by McManus (1964) on the television viewing aspect of the Denver study and those by Hillerich (1965) and Sutton (1964). Sutton's study reported the effectiveness of simply providing materials and informal opportunities for exploration in reading in the kindergarten classes. Professional opinion is mixed with respect to the wisdom of such an early emphasis upon formal reading instruction for most children, though there appears to be an increasing disposition for educators to concede its value for those children obviously more ready to read than others upon kindergarten entrance.

Beginning-Reading Method. Failure to identify the major components in beginning-reading methods and to specify clearly the referents of "phonic," "whole-word," "synthetic," "analytic," "eclectic," or "look-and-say" methods is a major source of confusion to reading professionals and to laymen alike. Theodore L. Harris (1962, pp. 6–8) suggested that beginning-reading methods be distinguished in terms of the relative emphasis first placed upon the meaning of whole words or upon the discrimination of word parts: a meaning-first emphasis, a discrimination-first emphasis, or a dual meaning-discrimination emphasis. More recently, Mitford Mathews (1966), a lexicographer and linguist, has presented an extended yet remarkably lucid exposition of reading method in his *Teaching to Read: Historically Considered*. He describes three basic methods which have evolved in the teaching of reading: (1) a purely synthetic, alphabetic "letters-to-words" method introduced by the Greeks, adapted by the Romans, and later used almost exclusively in German and English cultures until the eighteenth century; (2) a "words-to-letters" method developed largely by the Germans in the eighteenth century and later imported to the United States; and (3) a "words-to-reading" method developed in the United States in the nineteenth century which became the predominant "look-and-say" method in the first half of the twentieth century. Mathews makes a fundamental and illuminating distinction between the second and third methods. The "words-to-letters" method, while often called a "word" method, was in fact a modified synthetic, alphabetic method in which whole words were introduced not to build a meaningful sight vocabulary for immediate reading experiences but merely as vehicles for the direct analysis of letter forms and sounds. On the other hand, the analytic "words-to-reading" method, also often called a "word" method, was proposed to enable the pupil to move immediately from the whole word to its meaning in ideographic fashion ("as if the words were Chinese symbols," in the words of the early proponent, Dr. Keagy) and so repeat this "look-and-say" process until a substantial sight vocabulary is built and used for extensive reading experiences *before* attention is paid to letters. In this analysis of method, the essential distinction is the time at which the letters of our alphabetic language are taught. In synthetic programs letter discrimination is taught early; in analytic programs letter discrimination is delayed. The author marshals an impressive array of historical evidence to establish the validity of his contention that the essential thrust of a method, synthetic or analytic, be considered the basic criterion for considering the relative merits of beginning methods.

If such a methodological distinction is observed, it is apparent that comparisons of "methods" in many published studies of beginning reading and in many discussions have little validity and merely involve variations within an essentially analytic method, as in many "eclectic" approaches. Several lines of evidence, however, point to the highly probable superiority of beginning-reading programs in which an essentially synthetic method is used or is dominant in the early phases of instruction: (1) the results of recent psychological experimentation cited earlier which suggest that the letter is the key unit in word perception among beginning readers; (2) the finding that knowledge of letter names is the best single specific predictive factor in first-grade reading success in reading-readiness tests; (3) the results of 22 studies reviewed by Gurren and Hughes (1965) which indicated that explicit comparisons of the effects of intensive phonics (early synthetic letter-discrimination emphasis) and delayed phonics (early analytic emphasis) upon word recognition and comprehension significantly favored the early synthetic emphasis in 19 of the comparisons, only three studies showing no significant differences; (4) the conflict between analytic theory and teacher belief reported by Barton and Wilder (1962) from a random sample of schools in the United States: that while 90 percent of first-grade teachers use basal reading materials with an analytic orientation, 51 percent reported that they believed that "most children should be taught the sounds of letters and letter-combinations," either "before they start learning about words" or "at the same time as they learn their first words"; and (5) the growing disposition to experiment with newer reading programs, either in kindergarten or in first grade, which are essentially synthetic in their early methodological emphasis. It is clear that proponents of an analytic approach to the teaching of beginning reading are deeply concerned with the problem of meaning, a fundamental and proper objective of reading instruction. To Carroll (1964), an educational psychologist, and to Mathews and such other linguists as Bloomfield (1942) and Fries (1963), to place the prime instructional emphasis in beginning-reading instruction upon the direct translation of words into their meanings without attention to the intervening variables of their letters represents a fundamental misconception of the means and ends of initial instruction in learning to read an alphabetical, rather than an ideographic, language. In Mathews' words, ". . . no matter how a child is taught to read, he comes sooner or later to the strait gate and the narrow way: he has to learn the letters and the sounds. There is no evidence whatever that he will ultimately do this better from at first not doing it at all" (1966, p. 208). While Mathews' opinion may not be widely shared by reading educators, there appears to be no evidence that the analytic method in the many years of its ascendancy has succeeded in reducing the percentage of underachievers in reading in schools or that of functionally illiterate adults, two circumstances to which Mathews pointedly relates the question of method.

The results of many psychological and pedagogical investigations suggest the following current trends and conclusions concerning beginning-reading instruction: (1) While the relative merits of the analytic versus the synthetic method may never be completely resolved to the satisfaction of all through program research because of the difficulty in controlling all relevant variables and because of differing value systems among investigators, there is a growing disposition to introduce letter discrimination early. It is probable that existing as well as newer experimental programs will seek more adequate resolution of the meaning-discrimination dilemma in various ways but with increased emphasis upon early, specific discrimination skills. (2) There is substantial evidence that the synthetic method compares favorably with the analytic method on measures of word meaning and reading comprehension. Recent evidence includes that from the cooperative first-grade studies which revealed that programs in which the synthetic emphasis was prominent, including basal programs with supplemental phonics, were equal to analytic basal reading programs alone in developing reading comprehension and superior to them in developing word-recognition skills. This effect tended to hold true across intelligence levels. As Bond and Dykstra observe, "The relative success of the non-basal programs . . . indicates that reading instruction can be improved" (1967, p. 124). (3) Differential outcomes of different techniques for teaching reading must be recognized in an assessment of their total value. For example, individualized reading programs appear to have important attitudinal outcomes, while the strength of planned systematic programs appears to lie in the early development of maintenance of skills. Using a language-experience approach to reading and relating reading to other language arts appear to have value in reading programs, as many early investigators concluded and as further evidence from the cooperative first-grade studies indicates. (4) Insofar as reading programs can be defined, some children learn to read well and others not well in programs differing greatly in materials and techniques. When the generalization "There is no one best method of teaching reading" is made, the reference to method is unclear because the word may refer to any one of several combinations of reading techniques within the larger context of method. Greater uniformity is needed in defining the terms "method," "program," and "technique" in reading instruction if progress is to be made in ascertaining more precisely the effects of instructional adjustment within a given method to ensure the most satisfactory reading progress of each pupil. (5) The effectiveness of any reading method, program, or technique is directly related to the interaction of many factors inherent in the child, the teacher, and the total home and school environment. This interaction must be recognized in planning the nature, sequence, and scope of a beginning-reading program.

Developmental Reading Practices. Research interest in developmental reading practices has centered principally upon the improvement of word attack, vocabulary, comprehension, speed, interests and tastes, reading in the content fields, and teaching aids and media. Such research has in recent years dealt almost exclusively with investigations of silent-reading rather than oral-reading practices.

Word-attack skills, as broadly defined by Bedell and Nelson (1954), include the group of skills such as the contextual, the structural, the phonic, and the configurational which are used to identify the pronunciation and meaning of words. Research on all but the phonic aspect is very meager, although the recent work of Muehl (1961), King (1964), and Marchbanks and Levin (1965) suggests that the often-recommended use of word-configuration clues may have little value for beginning readers. Phonics, broadly defined as the linking of appropriate sound values to letters and letter combinations to permit the written message to be decoded into its spoken sound equivalent, has, on the other hand, received intensive research attention. The research into phonics, as summarized in 1957 by Gray (1960), clearly demonstrated the value of some type of phonic analysis, but such evidence in his opinion justified "caution against too vigorous emphasis on phonics early in the first grade" (1960, p. 1123). By the time that was written, however, more established and newer phonics programs were already being reevaluated, often in connection with established basal reading programs, as well as with other experimental programs. Types of programs regarded, for example, by Mathews as being promising from a linguistic point of view are those which incorporate scientific linguistic analyses to control the regularity of correspondence of letter-sound and sentence-patterns to oral language frequency, and those incorporating a modified orthography such as the i.t.a. (international teaching alphabet). The modified-orthography approach simplifies the initial learning of letter–sound correspondences regardless of other controls but requires a later transition to traditional orthography. Research into the i.t.a. medium has been especially vigorous in Britain under the direction of Downing (1967), who has reported favorable progress over a three-year period of beginning-reading instruction in this medium in comparison to traditional orthography. While the long-term effects of many of the newer phonic-oriented programs cannot yet be fully appraised or their comparative effectiveness adequately judged from research in the United States, the weight of the evidence, as noted earlier, indicates the greater effectiveness of earlier rather than later attention to some form of phonic analysis to teach letter–sound correspondences and thus help children acquire greater early independence in learning to read. Evidence especially pertinent to this interpretation includes that reviewed by Mathews (1966, Chs. 14, 15, 16) and by Diack (1965); the continuing studies of the effectiveness of an i.t.a. program by Downing and Jones (1966) and by Mazurkiewicz and his associates, such as that reported by Mazurkiewicz and Lamana (1966); and the relative merits of studies by Margaret Henderson (1955) and by Sparks and Fay (1957) of a phonics program emphasizing early letter discrimination and phonics generalizations, reviewed with special reference to the stability of Henderson's findings by Theodore L. Harris (1962, pp. 13–17). The utility of teaching phonics generalizations has been examined by Clymer (1963), who, examining some 45 generalizations derived from the teacher's manuals of four primary basal reading series, concluded that only 18 generalizations had utility values as high as 75 percent when their application to the vocabulary of these readers and to the Gates Primary Vocabulary was used as a criterion measure. Similar studies, using different validating criteria, have been made by Bailey (1967) for grades 1–6 and by Emans (1967) for grades 4–6, as well as by Burmeister (1966) for phonic and other word-analysis generalizations applying to words above the primary level based upon a 14-level random sampling of the Thorndike-Lorge *Teacher's Word Book of 30,000 Words*. Each of these investigators questioned the validity of many of the phonic generalizations taught but at the same time recognized that the acceptance of a given level of utility was a matter of judgment meriting further study. One consideration pertinent to such a judgment is the fact that their utility to the child is in part relative to when, how, and in relation to what materials a phonic generalization is taught in the instructional program. Since virtually all phonics generalizations admit to some exceptions because of the conglomerate nature of English, their teaching must have relevance to the instructional materials being used and their application must necessarily be tentative and be considered in relation to other word-attack clues. A further consideration is that the selection and definition of the phonic units to be analyzed in relation to a given generalization in such studies is a matter upon which there is considerable difference of opinion. Burmeister also found in an experimental comparison of inductive and deductive ways of teaching word-analysis skills generalizations to disabled readers in grades 8 and 9 that neither was significantly more effective than the other on delayed-oral-reading posttest performance. In another study, Winkly (1966) reported that 7 out of 18 accent generalizations sometimes taught were useful in significantly differentiating the performance of pupils at the end of grades 4 and 6 but not at the beginning of grade 4 or at the end of grade 8.

Research into ways of improving meaning vocabularies has been scant since the early work of Gray and Holmes (1938) in summarizing the apparent effectiveness of many specific techniques such as the use of context, word lists, and dictionaries and in demonstrating that the direct teaching of vocabulary in fourth-grade social studies material was superior in both silent- and oral-reading aspects of reading growth to incidental attention to vocabulary. Subsequent studies have confirmed the value of direct instruction at the high school and college levels. Serra's review of research (1953) emphasized such factors as the need for systematic attention to extending the breadth and precision of meaningful vocabulary through vicarious and direct experience with particular attention to multiple meanings and the differentiation of levels of verbal concepts. More recently, Eickholz and Barbe (1961) reported that self-instructional techniques were more effective than conventional techniques in improving vocabulary among seventh graders. Studies by Gates (1961c) indicated that second- and third-grade children could recognize the meanings of substantially the same number of new as well as old words at the following grade level, a finding which suggests that the common technique of introducing new words in basal readers in advance of reading may need reconsideration. A valuable source for studies relating to vocabulary, including the many studies of the frequency and difficulty of words and their meanings, is Dale and Razik's *Bibliography of Vocabulary Studies* (1963).

There is, in contrast, a dearth of research on techniques to improve the basic aspects of comprehension, such as a grasp of the main idea and its relevant supporting facts, and on ways to improve the more complex aspects of interpretation involving the inferential processes often associated with thinking. This is not surprising in view of the present state of knowledge regarding concept attainment and reasoning involving language activities. Early research, such as that by Alderman (1925) and by Holmes (1931), suggested the value, respectively, of learning to detect the organization of materials and of using questions to guide reading. A later study by Stordahl and Christensen (1956) of comparative organizational techniques for improving comprehension among air force trainees, however, revealed no significant differences among approaches emphasizing reading for understanding, outlining, summarizing, and merely reading. More recently, Bloomer and Heitzman (1965) have reported that the performance of eighth graders who took a comprehension pretest before reading the short McCall-Crabbs selections was not significantly differentiated from that of eighth graders who did not take a pretest. Other recent evidence of the effect of questions given prior or subsequent to reading on performance is supplied by Rothkopf (1966), who found that prior questions facilitated specific learning but not general learning of a relatively long passage in a study involving 159 college subjects. General learning, on the other hand, was facilitated by questions placed after the passage. The teaching of more-inferential aspects of interpretation has been studied by Nardelli (1957), who showed that sixth-grade pupils profited from a brief period of specific instruction in detecting and drawing inferences from propaganda, and by Covington (1967), who reported that emphasis upon certain aspects of critical reading in an experimental fifth-grade group yielded reading performances generally superior to those of their controls when judged in terms of their ability to make inferences, their sensitivity to discrepancies in fact, and their tendency to ask questions. It is clear, however, that much more is known about the characteristics of reading comprehension and interpretive processes than about their operation or about what may be done to improve them. Cultivation of the higher mental processes in the reading act will continue to be largely a pragmatic matter until much more extensive psychological research into the operational bases of such processes has been conducted.

Little is likewise known in a research sense about techniques for the improvement of reading tastes, of attitudes and appreciation toward reading, and of reading interests. If, as discussed earlier, the reading habits and preferences of American adults are accepted as criteria, there is little evidence that present techniques of teaching and of controlling the reading diet in American schools has positively influenced more than a small proportion of adult readers. There is, however, evidence of the immediate value of direct teaching of specific elements of appreciation for the literary appreciation of pupils in grades 4, 5, and 6, reported by Broening (1929), and of the value of the opportunity afforded in free reading periods for self-selection and appraisal in promoting more mature interests and tastes among pupils in grades 7–12, reported by LaBrant and Heller (1939). There is also the possibility, as yet unconfirmed, that reading programs emphasizing the self-selection principle, as individualized reading, and choice among a wider range of materials, may together with appropriate teacher guidance eventually enable individual pupils to develop more adequate self-standards for the selection of materials to meet their developmental needs. The practice of American schools to emphasize the use of the single text in reading instruction, which Herrick (1961, pp. 183–184) has noted is the general practice, may not foster the critical aspect of comparative reading of selections and may inhibit rather than facilitate the development of standards of judgment essential to the development of desirable tastes and interests in reading.

Research into techniques of improving the speed of reading is complicated by problems of defining, establishing criteria for, and reliably measuring reading speed, as Theodore L. Harris and others (1966) have noted. Reading-speed improvement in one sense refers to an increased efficiency in the basic processes of word, phrase, and sentence perception so that a maximum span of recognition for the individual is achieved. This sense has led to tachistoscopic and pacing techniques for improving visual-perception efficiency, and eye-movement photography is frequently used to measure such efficiency. In another sense it refers to the efficiency with which the broader aspects of comprehension take place. In the latter sense, reading speed is not absolute but relative to the comprehension task defined by the reader for himself, his purpose, and that inherent in the nature of the materials. As Blommers (1944) showed, appropriate speed variability is related to adequacy of comprehension. In this sense, flexibility in adapting reading speed to individual comprehension demands, not the development of a single reading speed, is the proper goal of instruction in efficient comprehension. In general, it is highly probable from informal evidence that the preoccupation of teachers of developmental reading and of the content fields with the more detailed aspects of reading comprehension tends to develop a set toward a relatively slow, inflexible reading speed. Such was the interpretation made by Buswell (1937) thirty years ago from evidence of the relatively slow reading speed of adults and of their marked improvement resulting from the paced reading of consecutive materials. The relatively recent concern for development of flexibility in reading speed, however, suggests that in the past that has not been a goal consciously implemented to a significant degree in the elementary school. Theodore L. Harris and others (1965, 1966), however, have shown the value of short, specific, self-instructional exercises in developing and in sensitizing pupils to the use of flexibility of reading speed in relation to different reading purposes and in securing its transference to longer selections. On the other hand, as Bormuth and Aker (1961) and others have shown, the transfer effects of specific tachistoscopic training to amount and speed of comprehension of materials are largely insignificant. Somewhat more favorable effects upon reading comprehension of extended training in recognizing continuous phrase segments by means of films was reported recently by Amble (1966) for experimental fifth- and sixth-grade subjects than for their controls. Improved speed of comprehension, as well as improved comprehension, has been consistently shown in controlled comparisons to be significantly related to the use of materials in the more normal consecutive reading contexts, through either timed reading exercises or mechanical pacing devices. The assumed value and necessary use of such pacing devices for effecting such improvement has been shown to be largely fictitious. The weight of the evidence, as illustrated by such controlled studies as those by Martens (1961) and McDowell (1964), indicates that the reading of the normal materials of instruction under timed conditions is as effective in improving reading comprehension and speed of comprehension as is the use of mechanical pacing devices. The chief value of pacing devices has repeatedly been shown to be their short-term motivational effect, which produces higher and relatively inflexible reading speeds under pacing conditions than the reader is able to transfer and sustain under self-timed conditions. For these reasons, greater emphasis upon flexible adaptation of reading speed to reading tasks under normal instructional conditions appears warranted; on the other hand, extensive investment by school systems in mechanical pacing devices and chief reliance upon their use to increase speed of comprehension appears unwarranted. Similar caution should be extended to uncritical acceptance of reported reading rates, including those derived from commonly used reading tests, unless the comprehension criterion is clearly specified and unless confirmatory evidence in normal reading situations with materials of reasonable length is supplied.

The improvement of reading in the content fields has long been an objective of developmental reading consistent with its broad conception of the scope and continuity of the reading program. It is also apparent, as Gray's summary of the evidence (1960, pp. 1126–1128) suggests, that there is not necessarily a transfer of reading skills from the basic instructional period to the specific problems of reading in the content fields without further teacher implementation therein at the elementary and higher school levels. The results of such specific implementation, however, are consistently favorable, though somewhat variable according to pupil ability levels. For example, Jacobson (1932) showed that training in work-type reading instruction involving locating, organizing, and comprehending science materials improved the knowledge of general science and the general scholastic achievement of ninth-grade students. In this experiment, the initially poor readers profited more than initially good readers. Hislop (1961) studied the effects upon high and low achievers in grades 4, 5, and 6 of four months of training on social studies problem-solving techniques. Only high achievers were found to be significantly superior to their controls on the *STEP* subtest in social studies reading and on the basis of their verbalized responses. While some studies have shown the positive influence of teaching specific study skills, as that by Wallace J. Howell (1950) in grades 4–8, and have explored the different values of intensive and extensive modes of study as in Good's early study (1927), the relative merits of several common format aids to reading and study in content fields do not appear to have been clearly established. Evidence presented by Christensen and Stordahl (1955) secured among air force trainees revealed no significant differences in the effectiveness of six organizational aids: a preliminary outline, a preliminary survey, a final summary, the underlining of main points, headings in statement form, and headings in question form. That finding strongly suggests that the critical organizational factors in reading and study lie in the mind of the reader. However, a number of studies, such as that by Mary E. Johnson (1952) and those summarized by Serra (1953, pp. 508–512), point to the need for specific instructional attention to the heavy concept burden incorporated in the material of different content fields especially at the intermediate and upper grade levels. More recently Stauffer (1966), finding little overlap between the vocabularies of primary basal readers and primary materials in health, arithmetic, and science, concluded that concept development in the content fields was essential to master the vocabulary of such materials at the primary levels. The development of meaning vocabularies has indeed been shown in a number of investigations to be the most common reading responsibility assumed by content-field teachers, who have generally been far less responsive to the application of techniques to develop other specific reading competences in the content fields such as those outlined by Leary (1948) in English, social studies, science, and mathematics at the high school level. The increasing number of content-field teachers at upper grade and high school levels who are seeking help to improve their teaching and are enrolling in developmental reading courses is an encouraging trend, however, as is the greater extent to which expository materials more representative of those found in the content fields are being incorporated into programs of basic reading instruction in elementary schools. Such interest coupled with further exploration of the more complex reading abilities may produce in the future more specific instructional techniques and evidence of their value in improving reading in the content fields.

The very considerable interest in newer media of instruction such as film and programmed formats has stimulated a number of recent studies. In general, controlled comparative studies of their relative effectiveness have produced negative results. Thus, Bradley (1960) found that the New Castle textfilms produced initially favorable results in grade 1, less favorable ones in grade 2, and no significant differences in grade 3 among experimental and control groups studied over a three-year period. More recently, studies at the college level have shown no significant differences when, for example, the media involves studying a branching programmed format, listening to lectures, or reading a mimeographed text, as in the study by McGrew and others (1966).

Appraisal of Reading. The many studies of reading appraisal have dealt mostly with standardized reading tests, certain aspects of which, such as studies of their correlation with other abilities and the predictive values of readiness tests, have been reported earlier. Several other aspects have also been examined. For example, the important curricular question of the applicability of a standardized reading test to the population of a local school system was investigated by Campbell and others (1964). The authors found that the national norms were not satisfactory and decided that local norms were necessary for adequate appraisal. This practice has been adopted by some larger school systems and has also led to the development of reading norms for special classes of pupils, such as the deaf by Wrightstone and others (1963). Some evidence to support the field observation that some reading tests rank pupils higher in reading achievement than others has been offered by Edward Taylor and James Crandall (1962) in an analysis of the norm equivalents of five commonly used elementary achievement tests.

There is also evidence of progress in test improvement since World War II. For example, Traxler (1953) has shown in a pilot study the steps taken to establish the validity of a vocabulary test for use by senior high school students and by college freshmen and to secure a sufficiently high reliability level, .90, to permit its use for individual as well as group purposes. The development of the *Cooperative Test of Reading Comprehension* and the *Davis Reading Test* has also significantly expanded the scope of measurable aspects of reading comprehension at the college and high school levels. Similarly, the development of such tests as the reading comprehension portion of the *Iowa Test of Basic Skills* has introduced children to more realistic reading-comprehension tasks involving longer selections, some of several paragraphs. Recent advancements in techniques of test construction and standardization have likewise contributed to the development of improved tests. There have also been recent attempts to examine the relationship of standardized test scores to more informal teacher estimates of reading performance. One illustrative study by McCracken (1961) at the sixth-grade level showed that while rather substantial correlations were obtained between standardized silent-reading-test scores and informal estimates of reading level, placement on the basis of test scores would place 63 percent of the pupils at their frustration level and 93 percent of them at a level too high for adequate reading performance. The implication of such a finding is clearly that for instructional purposes in reading, evidence in addition to that from standardized test scores should be considered.

Diagnostic and Remedial Practices. The research literature on reading disability is extensive, as summaries and studies by Robinson (1946), Vernon (1957), Malmquist (1958), Gray (1960, pp. 1128–1131), and Money (1962) show. Research findings relating to many of the concepts pertinent to specific aspects of reading disability have been introduced previously in the discussion of psychological aspects of reading, while research relating to the nature, diagnosis, and treatment of specific dyslexia has been considered under the section on physiological aspects of reading. The chief focus in this section will be upon research relating to the nature, diagnosis, and remediation of reading disability, in schools or school-related clinics, of pupils with nonneurological involvement.

Considerable confusion exists about the definition of reading disability. As Albert J. Harris (1961, pp. 16–18) has observed, since the term "retardation" commonly refers to retardation from grade level, the term "reading disability," which refers to the discrepancy between reading achievement and reading expectancy as defined by capacity to learn, regardless of grade placement, appears preferable. Failure to make such a distinction in school practice has resulted in the assignment of many pupils to remedial-reading classes who cannot profit from such instruction because of restricted learning abilities. Such pupils need an adaptive developmental reading program such as that described by Wayne Otto and Richard McMenemy (1966) in which reading instruction is conducted according to their learning rates and expectancies and not according to the unrealistic grade-level norms of reading achievement expectancy for more able pupils.

In this context, the determination of learning ability is of considerable consequence. For this purpose, mental age derived from standardized intelligence tests is the most generally accepted criterion in spite of evidence presented in the discussion of correlates of reading of other significant aspects of intellectual functioning not usually measured in intelligence tests. Further, the type of intelligence test used for determining learning potential has been shown to be important. Group intelligence tests have somewhat lower reliability than individual intelligence tests; hence, their error of measurement is greater and their value less in predicting individual intellectual capacity. If either group or individual tests contain subtests which require reading, this too may unfavorably affect the estimate of learning potential, as Nolan (1942) noted for group intelligence tests and Durrell (1927) for the Stanford-Binet. For these reasons, the use of intelligence tests which yield both verbal and nonverbal scores, such as the group Lorge-Thorndike test or the Wechsler scales for children and adults, has found increasing favor. The Wechsler type of scale has been especially studied for its possible diagnostic value in the more precise categorizing of intellectual functioning and in the determination of levels of reading disability, as the investigation by Sawyer (1965) illustrates. The determination of reading age, on the other hand, has in practice often involved any one of a great number of standardized reading tests, such as the *Stanford Reading Test*, the *Gates Reading Tests*, and the *Cooperative Reading Comprehension Test*.

Traxler (1952) has reported the great variation in actual practice in the application of the mental age–reading age discrepancy to form groups for remedial teaching. Pupils who are achieving approximately one year less than their expectancy in reading in the intermediate grades and above generally receive group corrective instruction, while those for whom the discrepancy is two or more years generally receive more individual and specialized help if such is available. The same investigator found, as others have, that four steps in corrective reading instruction were generally followed: identification of pupils through tests and teacher observation, diagnosis of specific reading difficulties and apparent causes, corrective training through a great variety of procedures, and appraisal of progress, most frequently by tests but sometimes by teacher and pupil reports and by changes in school grades.

With respect to the above steps, which differ more in degree than in kind from those taken in the diagnosis and remediation of more severe reading disability on an individual basis, research findings with respect to the relative merits of different instruments and techniques are less than satisfactory. In the identification of pupils for corrective and remedial work, for example, certain problems in ascertaining their mental capacity have been noted. Examination of critical reviews of reading tests in such a source as the *Sixth Mental Measurements Yearbook* edited by Buros (1966), and others in that series, reveals that standardized reading tests vary greatly in the scope of reading skills and abilities measured, in specific aspects of their construction and standardization related to their content validity and their reliability, and in the specific survey or diagnostic purposes for which they were designed. For these reasons the selection of reading tests for identification purposes is largely a matter of judgment, there being no research evidence of the universal superiority of any one reading test for either group screening or individual diagnosis. Some favorable evidence concerning a related question, the extent to which teachers make reliable judgments in selecting children for remedial instruction in English "adjustment centers" has been reported by Lytton (1961). The extent to which such judgments are generally reliable, however, is uncertain and may depend to a considerable degree upon the teacher's insight and experience in studying the abilities of children.

Diagnostic procedures involve the instructional diagnosis, assessing the specific reading difficulties, and the causal diagnosis, exploring and interpreting the probable causes of the reading difficulties. There is no direct evidence from the reading literature that those involved in remedial-reading theory or practice have shown the same concern as those in the medical profession for the importance of prognosis, the prediction of expected progress, to which—as Osborn (1966) discusses—diagnosis must be related for effective action. While the instructional diagnosis is based upon the pragmatic considerations of proceeding from the general to the specific by means of more diagnostic tests and other means of assessment, the basic principle of the multiple causation of reading disability in the causal diagnosis of reading disability is supported by a substantial body of research evidence which indicates that there is no single known cause to which severe reading disability may be attributed. The rationale and nature of supporting evidence for this concept, which was discussed thirty years ago by Witty and Kopel (1939, pp. 203–207), has led in severe cases to such diagnostic considerations as thoroughness in gathering relevant case-study data from the history of interaction of behavioral and environmental factors, the search for relationships among the data, and the tentativeness in the interpretation of data in a causal sense. It is axiomatic, however, that the depth of the causal diagnosis must be proportionally related to the severity of the reading problem. In corrective classes, remedial instruction may begin before the completion of the instructional diagnosis, and the causal diagnosis may be modified, abbreviated, or delayed if the pupil responds to instruction. In such cases it may be assumed that the chief source of the difficulty is educational in nature. Comprehensive discussions of diagnostic factors, principles, and procedures, in addition to previously cited sources, are found in the article by Albert J. Harris and Florence G. Roswell (1953), in Bond and Tinker's *Reading Difficulties: Their Diagnosis and Correction* (1957) and in Betts's *Foundations of Reading Instruction* (1957).

Corrective reading training and its appraisal ideally are specific to the diagnosis and highly individualized. Such training presumably proceeds on the assumptions that for the individual the effective learning process has broken down and that appropriate conditions of motivation must be established for the reconstruction of that process. There is substantial agreement, therefore, that the learning goals of remedial instruction must be specific, attainable, and immediate to foster a desirable level of aspiration in the pupil; and, further, that remedial work take place in a supportive atmosphere in which progress is known and confirmed to the pupil. Beyond these considerations of the importance of individualized work and a favorable motivational situation, the evidence reported by Traxler (1952) not unexpectedly indicates that many teaching procedures are employed in different sequences in many combinations, both group and individual, in corrective and remedial-reading instruction, including reading improvement classes in high school and college. Methods of appraisal are likewise diverse.

In general, the effectiveness of remediation has been shown to be positive, as Robinson and Smith (1962) concluded from follow-up interviews and questionnaire data on the subsequent progress and adjustment of 44 reading-clinic clients first seen ten years previously. Among more severely disabled readers, the relative effectiveness of group and individual procedures is somewhat conflicting, as studies in England by Lovell R. Johnson and D. Platts (1962) and by Keating (1962) illustrate. The former study reported no significant differences in gains according to treatment, whereas the latter reported that individual remediation was significantly more effective. A study by Roman (1957) comparing the effectiveness of three group approaches—usual remedial-reading procedures, tutorial therapy, and interview therapy—upon the oral-reading improvement and adjustment of delinquent boys revealed group-tutorial therapy to be the most effective of the three approaches. That study illustrates the growing awareness of the importance of psychological reorientation of pupils for effective reading development that is reflected in a number of recent studies of remediation in reading. That such a consideration may extend also to the parents is illustrated by a study by Studholme (1964), who reported evidence that group discussion with mothers who had hostile attitudes toward their sons who were disabled readers improved the mothers' attitudes and their sons' reading progress during the course of remedial instruction. The relative effectiveness of length and intensity of an eclectic pattern of treatment for subjects reading three years below expectancy has been studied by Balow (1965). Short-term, intensive treatment, with or without subsequent maintenance, and longer-term, less-intensive treatment were compared. Evidence was secured that the short-term, intensive treatment, while helpful, did not correct the reading disability but that the long-term and short-term treatment plus maintenance produced in a subsequent follow-up period rates of growth in reading which greatly exceeded that prior to clinic contact. Recent studies of specific techniques for the treatment of severe reading disability have been limited, although Ofman and Shaevitz (1963) have reported some experimental evidence of the value of kinesthetic reinforcement either by eye or by finger tracing among male disabled readers. In other studies, Arthur W. Staats and William H. Butterfield (1965) have reported the successful use of operant-conditioning techniques, and Downing (1963) has indicated the success of the i.t.a. medium of instruction with cases of severe reading disability. The growing interest in the last two approaches will doubtless spur further experimentation in their use with such cases.

Certain other questions relating to the effectiveness of group procedures in corrective and improvement programs have been examined in recent years at the college level, for which, as Deverell (1959) concluded and as the more recent controlled study by Arthur V. Olson and others (1964) indicates, there is apparently need and value. Typically, as in the latter investigation, studies of college reading-improvement programs report gains in one or more aspects of vocabulary, comprehension, and rate of comprehension. The usual method of reporting such gains has, however, been recently criticized by Rankin and Tracy (1965). These authors noted that crude gains ordinarily reported are based upon the difference between pretest and posttest scores, a type of calculation which prejudices the correct assessment of gain for superior or inferior improvers because of the regression to the mean effect involved in retesting. According to the criterion of a proposed residual-gain formula, 47 percent of crude gains were found to be in error and thus less preferable to the use of residual gains for the estimation of true gains. The problem of measuring and reporting gains for pupils in reading-clinic programs was also examined by Bliesmer (1962) in terms of the relative merits of average remedial gain, average yearly gains before remedial work, ratios of average remedial to average yearly gains before remedial work, ratios of average remedial to average yearly gains, and average potential–achievement-gap decreases. Studies at the college level which have attempted to examine different instructional emphases, usually a combination of procedures rather than a single technique, have rather uniformly failed to report significant differences in effectiveness. Thus, an illustrative study by Spache and others (1960) revealed no significant differences in effect between workbook, audiovisual, and individualized approaches upon reading rate, vocabulary, or comprehension, though more favorable student attitudes tended to accrue toward the individualized approach. Lafitte (1964) has also reported no significant differences in reading improvement attributable to emphasis on skimming, speed pacing, or a combination of these emphases. On the other hand, Rankin (1963) experimentally tested the order effects of emphasizing speed first and then comprehension against the opposite approach among 96 college students. At the end of a one-semester course, the speed-comprehension group was significantly faster in reading speed but not in vocabulary, comprehension, or total test results on the *Nelson-Denny Reading Test* and the *Barrett-Ryan-Schammel English Test*. The speed-comprehension group was also significantly happier with its progress. The authors, noting that the somewhat more favorable findings for the speed-comprehension approach are at variance with the usually recommended order of emphasis, speculated that the earlier speed emphasis may improve such factors in the reading act as concentration, speed of association, and awareness of structure of materials. Noall (1961), at the secondary level, has also reported favorably on the use of "massed differentiated skills instruction" designed for self-instruction. Other problems recently investigated in relation to group procedures include their effect upon academic aptitude as measured by the *Scholastic Aptitude Test* (*SAT*) and upon academic success, and reasons for attrition in such programs. While the reported evidence that reading improvement may improve academic aptitude scores is mixed, Whitla's finding (1962) that intensive tutoring at the secondary level did not significantly affect the performance of an experimental group on the verbal portion of the SAT is more in accord with other evidence of the negative effect of specific training on intelligence. Other studies, as that by Bloomer (1962), have reported a positive relationship between reading-improvement training and academic success, in this case in terms of predicted grade-point average. Several studies of attrition have also revealed that in voluntary college reading-improvement programs, attrition is positively related to personality variables affecting the individual's interpretation of the effectiveness of the situation for himself, as the study by Wright and Lazaraton (1963) illustrates.

Thus, while notable progress has been made since the 1920's in the identification, diagnosis, treatment, and appraisal of reading disability and in the extension of such efforts into the upper years of schooling and into adulthood, as Acker (1962) has indicated, many instructional problems remain. Among these are the need for more precise and reliable diagnostic instruments and procedures; more analytic studies of the effectiveness of specific remedial techniques, separately and in combination; further studies of ways of more effectively individualizing instruction within group corrective approaches; more adequately designed instructional materials, particularly for specific comprehension purposes; and more adequate instruments for the reliable assessment of specific dimensions of reading, within and across grade and age levels. Greater emphasis is likewise needed upon the earlier identification and treatment of reading disability, as DeHirsch and others (1966) stress and as Malmquist (1967) has recently shown to be feasible in Sweden. Such action in connection with improved developmental reading programs is the essence of prevention to reduce the present incidence of reading disability and the need for corrective and remedial reading at the upper elementary and higher school levels, including the college and adult population.

Theodore L. Harris
University of Wisconsin

References

Acker, Ralph S. "Reading Improvement in Government and Business." *Ed* 82:428–31; 1962.

Adams, Mary L. "Teachers' Instructional Needs in Teaching Reading." *Reading Teach* 17:260–4; 1964.

Ahlstrom, Karl-George. *Studies in Spelling*, Vol. 1: *Analysis of Three Different Aspects of Spelling Ability*. Institute of Education, Uppsala U, 1964. 46p.

Alderman, Everett. "The Effect of Size of Type on Speed of Reading and the Determination of Various Factors That May Influence the Results." *Pittsburgh Sch* 13:33–6; 1938.

Alderman, G. H. "Improving Comprehension Ability in Silent Reading." In *Eleventh Annual Conference on Educational Measurements*. Extension Division, U Indiana, 1925. p. 28–37.

Amble, Bruce R. "Phrase Reading Training and Reading Achievement of School Children." *Reading Teach* 20:210–8; 1966.

Ames, Louise B., and Walker, Richard N. "Prediction of Later Reading Ability from Kindergarten Rorschach and IQ Scores." *J Ed Psychol* 55:309–13; 1964.

Anderson, A. W. "Personality Traits in Reading Ability of Western Australian University Freshmen." *J Ed Res* 54:234–7; 1961.

Anderson, John E. "Methods in Child Psychology."

In Carmichael, Leonard. (Ed.) *Manual of Child Psychology*, 2nd ed. Wiley, 1954. p. 8.

Asheim, Lester. "What Do Adults Read?" In *Adult Reading*, 55th Yearbook, Part II, NSSE. U Chicago Press, 1956. p. 5–28.

Austin, Mary C. and Morrison, Coleman. *The First R: The Harvard Report on Reading in the Elementary Schools*. Macmillan, 1963. 269p.

Austin, Mary C., and others. *The Torch Lighters*. Harvard U, 1961. 196p.

Ausubel, David P. "The Use of Advance Organizers in the Learning and Retention of Meaningful Verbal Materials." *J Ed Psychol* 51:267–72; 1960.

Avery, Edward W. "Change in Attitudes Toward a Catholic for President." *Journalism Q* 40:98–100; 1963.

Bailey, Mildred Hart. "The Utility of Phonic Generalizations in Grades One Through Six." *Reading Teach* 20:413–8; 1967.

Bailyn, Lotte. "Mass Media and Children; A Study of Exposure Habits and Cognitive Effects." *Psych Monogr* 73:1–48; 1959.

Baker, Dean, and MacDonald, James. "Newspaper Editorial Readership and Length of Editorials." *Journalism Q* 38:473–9; 1961.

Balow, Bruce. "The Long-term Effect of Remedial Reading Instruction." *Reading Teach* 18:581–6; 1965.

Barcus, Francis E. "A Content Analysis of Trends in Sunday Comics, 1900–1959." *Journalism Q* 38:171–80; 1961.

Barrett, Thomas C. "Visual Discrimination Tasks as Predictors of First Grade Reading Achievement." *Reading Teach* 18:276–82; 1965.

Barton, Allen, and Wilder, David. "Columbia-Carnegie Study of Reading Research and Its Communication." Cited by Wilder in "Proceedings of the IRA." *Scholastic M* 7:172–4; 1962.

Bedell, Ralph, and Nelson, Eloise S. "Word Attack as a Factor in Reading Achievement in the Elementary School." *Ed Psychol Meas* 14:168–75; 1954.

Belden, Bernard R. "Readability of Biology Textbooks and the Reading Ability of Biology Students." *Sch Sci Math* 61:689–93; 1961.

Belmont, Lillian, and Birch, Herbert G. "The Intellectual Profile of Retarded Readers." *Perceptual Motor Skills* 22:787–816; 1966.

Berninghausen, David K., and Faunce, Richard W. "An Exploratory Study of Juvenile Delinquency and the Reading of Sensational Books." *J Exp Ed* 33:161–8; 1964.

Betts, Emmett A. *Foundations of Reading Instruction*. American, 1957. 757p.

Birch, Robert W. "Attention Span, Distractability and Inhibitory Potential of Good and Poor Readers." Doctoral dissertation. U Wisconsin, 1967. 59p.

Bishop, Carol H. "Transfer Effects of Word and Letter Training in Reading." *J Verbal Learning Verbal Behavior* 3:215–21; 1964.

Blank, Marion, and Bridger, Wagner H. "Deficiencies in Verbal Labeling in Retarded Readers." *Am J Orthopsychiatry* 36:840–7; 1966.

Bliesmer, Emery P. "Evaluating Progress in Remedial Reading Programs." *Reading Teach* 15:344–50; 1962.

Blommers, Paul J. "Rate of Comprehension of Reading: Its Measurement and Relation to Comprehension." *J Ed Psychol* 35:449–72; 1944.

Blommers, Paul J., and others. "The Organismic Age Concept." *J Ed Psychol* 46:142–50; 1955.

Bloomer, Richard H. "The Effects of a College Reading Program on a Random Sample of Education Freshmen." *J Develop Reading* 5:110–8; 1962.

Bloomer, Richard H., and Heitzman, Andrew J. "Pretesting and the Efficiency of Paragraph Reading." *J Reading* 8:219–23; 1965.

Bloomfield, Leonard. "Linguistics and Reading." *El Engl R* 19:125–30; 183–6; 1942.

Blount, Nathan S. "The Effect of Selected Junior Novels and Selected Adult Novels on Student Attitudes Toward the 'Ideal' Novel." *J Ed Res* 59:179–82; 1965.

Bogart, Leo. *The Age of Television*. Ungar, 1956. 348p.

Bond, Guy L. *The Auditory and Speech Characteristics of Poor Readers*. Teachers College, Columbia U, 1935. 48p.

Bond, Guy L., and Clymer, Theodore W. "Interrelationship of the SRA Primary Mental Abilities, Other Mental Characteristics, and Reading Ability." *J Ed Res* 49:131–6; 1955.

Bond, Guy L., and Dykstra, Robert. "The Cooperative Research Program in First-grade Reading Instruction." *Reading Res Q* 2:1–142; 1967.

Bond, Guy L., and Tinker, Miles A. *Reading Difficulties: Their Diagnosis and Correction*. Appleton, 1957. 564p.

Borg, Walter R. "Ability Grouping in the Public Schools: A Field Study." *J Exp Ed* 34:1–97; 1965.

Bormuth, John R. "Mean Word Depth as a Predictor of Comprehension Difficulty." *California J Ed Res* 15:226–31; 1964.

Bormuth, John R. "Readability: A New Approach." *Reading Res Q* 1:79–132; 1966.

Bormuth, John R., and Aker, C. "Is the Tachistoscope a Worthwhile Teaching Tool?" *Reading Teach* 14:172–6; 1961.

Braam, Leonard S., and Roehm, Marilyn A. "Subject-area Teachers' Familiarity with Reading Skills." *J Develop Reading* 7:188–96; 1964.

Bradley, Beatrice E. "Reading With a Dash of Showmanship." *El Sch J* 61:28–31; 1960.

Braun, Jean S. "Relation Between Concept Formation Ability and Reading Achievement at Three Developmental Levels." *Child Develop* 34:675–82; 1963.

Brekke, Gerald. "Actual and Recommended Allotments of Time for Reading." *Reading Teach* 16:234–7; 1963.

British Ministry of Education. *Standards of Reading, 1948–1956*. H.M. Stationery Office, London, 1957. 46p.

Broening, Angela M. *Developing Appreciation Through Teaching Literature*. Johns Hopkins U, 1929. 118p.

Brzeinski, Joseph E. "Beginning Reading in Denver." *Reading Teach* 18:16–21; 1964.

Brzeinski, Joseph E., and others. "Should Johnny Read in Kindergarten?" *NEA J* 56:23–5; 1967.

Budd, Richard W. "U.S. News in the Press Down Under." *Public Opin Q* 28:39–56; 1964.

Burmeister, Lou Ella. "An Evaluation of the Inductive and Deductive Group Approaches to Teaching Word Analysis Generalizations to Disabled Readers in Eighth and Ninth Grade." Doctoral dissertation. U Wisconsin, 1966. 187p.

Buros, Oscar K. (Ed.) *The Sixth Mental Measurements Yearbook*. Gryphon, 1966. 1714p.

Burress, Lee A., Jr., "The Presence of Censorship in Wisconsin Public Schools." *Wisconsin Engl J* 6:6–28; 1963.

Burt, Cyril, and others. "A Psychological Study of Typography." *Br J Stat Psychol* 8:29–57; 1955.

Buswell, Guy T. *Fundamental Reading Habits: A Study of Their Development*. U Chicago, 1922. 150p.

Buswell, Guy T. *How Adults Read*. U Chicago, 1937. 158p.

Buswell, Guy T. *Non-oral Reading: A Study of Its Use in the Chicago Public Schools*. U Chicago, 1945. 56p.

Byres, Loretta. "Pupils' Interests and the Content of Primary Reading Texts." *Reading Teach* 17:227–33; 1964.

Campbell, W., and others. "An Evaluation of the California Achievement Test, Elementary, Form W, Reading Comprehension." *J Ed Res* 58:75–7; 1964.

Carbone, Robert F. "A Comparison of Graded and Non-graded Elementary Schools." *El Sch J* 62:82–8; 1961.

Carmichael, Leonard, and Dearborn, W. F. *Reading and Visual Fatigue*. Houghton, 1947. 484p.

Carnovsky, Leon. "A Study of the Relationship Between Reading Interest and Actual Reading." *Lib Q* 4:76–100; 1934.

Carroll, John B. "The Analysis of Reading Instruction: Perspectives from Psychology and Linguistics." In Hilgard, Ernest R. (Ed.) *Theories of Learning and Instruction*, 63rd Yearbook, Part I, NSSE. U Chicago Press, 1964. p. 336–53.

Carson, Roy M., and Thompson, Jack M. "The Joplin Plan and Traditional Reading Groups." *El Sch J* 65:38–43; 1964.

Carter, Homer. "Effective Use of Textbooks in the Reading Program." In *Starting and Improving Reading Programs*. 8th Yearbook, National Reading Conference, 1959. p. 155–63.

Carter, Ray, and Clarke, Peter. "Why Suburban News Attracts Reader Interest." *Journalism Q* 39:522–5; 1962.

Chall, Jeanne S. *Readability: An Appraisal of Research and Application*. Bureau of Educational Research, Ohio State U, 1957. 202p.

Christensen, Clifford M., and Stordahl, K. E. "The Effect of Organizational Aids on Comprehension and Retention." *J Ed Psychol* 46:65–74; 1955.

Clarke, Peter. "Parental Socialization Values and Children's Newspaper Reading." *Journalism Q* 42:529–46; 1965.

Cleland, Donald T., and Toussaint, Isabella. "The Interrelationship of Reading, Listening, Arithmetic Computation, and Intelligence." *Reading Teach* 15:228–31; 1962.

Clymer, Theodore. "The Utility of Phonic Generalization in the Primary Grades." *Reading Teach* 16:252–60; 1963.

Cohn, R. "Delayed Acquisition of Reading and Writing Abilities in Children—A Neurological Study." *Archives Neurology* 4:153–64; 1961.

Collier, Marilyn. "An Evaluation of Multi-ethnic Basal Readers." *El Engl* 44:152–7; 1967.

Cooper, Bernice. "An Analysis of the Reading Achievement of White and Negro Pupils in Certain Public Schools of Georgia." *Sch R* 72:462–71; 1964.

Cooper, J. C., and Gaeth, J. H. "Interactions of Modality with Age and with Meaningfulness in Verbal Learning." *J Ed Psychol* 58:41–4; 1967.

Cornwell, Elmer J., Jr. "Presidential News: The Expanding Public Image." *Journalism Q* 36:275–83; 1959.

Covington, Martin V. "Some Experimental Evidence on Teaching for Creative Understanding." *Reading Teach* 20:390–6; 1967.

Dale, Edgar, and Chall, Jeanne S. "Developing Readable Materials." In *Adult Reading*, 55th Yearbook, Part II, NSSE. U Chicago, 1956. p. 218–50.

Dale, Edgar, and Razik, Taher. *Bibliography of Vocabulary Studies*, 2nd ed. Ohio State U, 1963. 257p.

Davidson, Helen P. "An Experimental Study of Bright, Average, and Dull Children at the Four-year Mental Level." *Genet Psychol Monogr* 9(Nos. 3 and 4); 1931. 166p.

DeHirsch, Katrina, and others. *Predicting Reading Failure*. Hayes, 1966. 144p.

Deutsch, Martin. "The Role of Social Class in Language Development and Cognition." *Am J Orthopsychiatry* 35:78–88; 1965.

Deutschmann, Paul J., and Danielson, W. A. "Diffusion of the Major News Story." *Journalism Q* 37:345–55; 1960.

Deverell, A. F. "Are Reading Improvement Courses at the University Level Justified?" In *Invitational Conference on Educational Research*. Canadian Education Association, 1959. p. 19–27.

Diack, Hunter. *Reading and the Psychology of Perception*. Philosophical Lib, 1960. 155p.

Diack, Hunter. *The Teaching of Reading: In Spite of the Alphabet*. Philosophical Lib, 1965. 191p.

Downing, John. "The Augmented Roman Alphabet for Learning to Read." *Reading Teach* 16:325–36; 1963.

Downing, John. *The i.t.a. Symposium: Research Reports on the British Experiment with i.t.a.* National Foundation for Education Research in England and Wales, 1967. 168p.

Downing, John, and Jones, Barbara. "Some Problems of Evaluating i.t.a.: A Second Experiment." *Ed Res* 8:100–14; 1966.

Drews, Elizabeth M. "The Effectiveness of Homogeneous and Heterogeneous Grouping in Ninth Grade English Classes with Slow, Average, and Superior Students." Cited in Borg, Walter R. "Ability Grouping in the Public Schools: A Field Study." *J Exp Ed* 34:1–97; 1965.

Durkin, Dolores. *Children Who Read Early.* Teachers Col, Columbia U, 1966. 192p.

Durr, William K., and Schmatz, Robert R. "Personality Differences Between High-achieving and Low-achieving Gifted Children." *Reading Teach* 17:251–4; 1964.

Durrell, Donald D. "The Effect of Special Disability in Reading in the Stanford Revision of the Binet-Simon Tests." Master's thesis. U Iowa, 1927.

Durrell, Donald D. "First Grade Reading Success: A Summary." *J Ed* 140:1–48; 1958.

Dykstra, Robert. "Auditory Discrimination Abilities and Beginning Reading Achievement." *Reading Res Q* 1:5–34; 1966.

Eames, Thomas H. "Comparison of Eye Conditions Among 1,000 Reading Failures, 500 Ophtalmic Patients, and 150 Unselected Children." *Am J Ophthalmology* 31:713–7; 1948.

Eames, Thomas H. "The Relationship of Reading and Speech Difficulties." *J Ed Psychol* 41:51–5; 1950.

Eames, Thomas H. "The Relationship of the Central Visual Field to the Speed of Visual Perception." *Am J Ophthalmology* 43:279–80; 1957.

Eames, Thomas H. "The Effect of Anisometropia on Reading Achievement. *Am J Optometry Archives Am Acad Optometry* 41:700–2; 1964.

Edfeldt, A. W. *Silent Speech and Silent Reading.* U Chicago, 1960. 164p.

Eichenwald, Heinz F. "The Pathology of Reading Disorders: Psychophysiological Factors." In Johnson, Marjorie S., and Kress, Roy A. (Eds.) *Corrective Reading in the Classroom.* International Reading Association, 1967. p. 31–43.

Eickholz G., and Barbe, R. "An Experiment in Vocabulary Development." *Ed Res B* 40:1–7, 28; 1961.

Elkind, David, and others. "Perceptual Decentration Learning and Performance in Slow and Average Readers." *J Ed Psychol* 56:50–6; 1965.

Emans, Robert. "The Usefulness of Phonic Generalizations Above the Primary Grades." *Reading Teach* 20:419–25; 1967.

Emans, Robert, and Patyk, Gloria. "Why Do High School Students Read?" *J Reading* 10:300–4; 1967.

Ewers, Dorothea W. F. "Relations Between Auditory Abilities and Reading Abilities: A Problem in Psychometrics." *J Exp Ed* 18:239–62; 1950.

Feifel, Herman, and Lorge, Irving. "Qualitative Differences in the Vocabulary Responses of Children." *J Ed Psychol* 41:1–18; 1950.

Feld, B. "Empirical Test Proves Clarity Adds Readers." *Editor Publisher* 24:81–8; 1948.

Flavell, J. H., and Stedman, D. J. "A Developmental Study of Judgments of Semantic Similarity." *J Genet Psychol* 98:279–93; 1961.

Fortna, Richard O. "A Factor-analytic Study of the Cooperative School and College Ability Tests and Sequential Tests of Educational Progress." *J Exp Ed* 32:187–90; 1963.

Foster, Marion E., and Black, Donald B. "A Comparison of Reading Achievement of Christchurch, New Zealand, and Edmonton, Alberta, Public School Students of the Same Age and Number of Years of Schooling." *Alberta J Ed Res* 11:21–31; 1965.

Fries, Charles C. *Linguistics and Reading.* Holt, 1963. 265p.

Frymier, Jack R. "The Effect of Class Size upon Reading Achievement in First Grade." *Reading Teach* 18:90–3; 1964.

Gates, Arthur I. "A Further Evaluation of Reading-readiness Tests." *El Sch J* 40:577–91; 1940.

Gates, Arthur I. *Reading Attainment in Elementary Schools: 1957 and 1937.* Teachers Col, Columbia U, 1961(a). 26p.

Gates, Arthur I. "Sex Differences in Reading Ability." *El Sch J* 51:431–4; 1961(b).

Gates, Arthur I. "Vocabulary Control in Basal Reading Material." *Reading Teach* 14:81–5; 1961(c).

Gates, Arthur I., and Bond, Guy L. "Reading Readiness: A Study of Factors Determining Success and Failure in Beginning Reading." *Teach Col Rec* 37:679; 1936.

Gibson, Eleanor J., and others. "A Developmental Study of the Discrimination of Letter-like Forms." *J Comp Physiol Psychol* 60:897–906; 1962(a).

Gibson, Eleanor J., and others. "The Role of Grapheme-Phoneme Correspondence in the Perception of Words." *Am J Psychol* 75:554–70; 1962(b).

Good, Carter V. *The Supplementary Reading Assignment: A Study of Extensive and Intensive Materials and Methods in Reading.* Warwick, 1927. 227p.

Gray, William S. *Summary of Investigations Relating to Reading.* U Chicago Press, 1925. 276p.

Gray, William S. "Reading." In *Child Development and the Curriculum,* 38th Yearbook, Part I, NSSE. Public-Sch, 1939. p. 185–209.

Gray, William S. "How Well Do Adults Read?" In *Adult Reading,* 55th Yearbook, Part II, NSSE. U Chicago, 1956(a). p. 29–56.

Gray, William S. *The Teaching of Reading and Writing: An International Survey.* UNESCO, 1956(b). 281p.

Gray, William S. "Reading." In Harris, Chester W. (Ed.) *Encyclopedia of Educational Research,* 3rd ed. Macmillan, 1960. p. 1086–135.

Gray, William S., and Holmes, Eleanor. *The Development of Meaning Vocabularies in Reading: An Experimental Study.* U Chicago, 1938. 140p.

Gray, William S., and Iverson, William J. "What Should Be the Profession's Attitude Toward Lay Criticism of the Schools?" *El Sch J* 53:1–44; 1952.

Gray, William S., and Leary, Bernice E. *What Makes a Book Readable?* U Chicago, 1935. 358p.

Gray, William S., and Munroe, Ruth. *The Reading Interests and Habits of Adults.* Macmillan, 1929. 305p.

Gray, William S., and Rogers, Bernice. *Maturity in Reading: Its Nature and Appraisal.* U Chicago, 1956. 273p.

Gray, William S., and others. *Remedial Cases in*

Reading: Their Diagnosis and Treatment. U Chicago, 1922. 208p.

Greenberg, Bradley, and Tannenbaum, Percy. "The Effects of Bylines on Attitude Change." *Journalism Q* 38:535–7; 1961.

Greenberg, Judith W., and others. "Attitudes of Children from a Deprived Environment Toward Achievement-related Concepts." *J Ed Res* 59:57–62; 1965.

Grimes, J. W., and Allinsmith, W. "Compulsivity, Anxiety, and School Achievement." *Merrill-Palmer Q* 7:248–71; 1961.

Groff, Patrick J. "A Survey of Basal Reading Group Practices." *Reading Teach* 15:232–5; 1962.

Gurren, Louise, and Hughes, Ann. "Intensive Phonics Versus Gradual Phonics in Beginning Reading: A Review." *J Ed Res* 58:339–47; 1965.

Hachten, William A. "The Changing U.S. Sunday Newspaper." *Journalism Q* 38:281–8; 1961.

Hage, George S. "Anti-intellectualism in Press Comment: 1828 and 1952." *Journalism Q* 36:439–46; 1959.

Halfter, Irma T., and Douglass, Frances M. "Inadequate College Readers." *J Develop Reading* 1:42; 1958.

Hallgren, B. "Specific Dyslexia." *Acta psychiatrica neurologica*, Scandinavia Suppl. 6, 5, 1950.

Harootunian, Berj. "Intellectual Abilities and Reading Achievement." *El Sch J* 67:386–92; 1966.

Harris, Albert J. *How to Increase Reading Ability*, 4th ed. Longmans, 1961. 624p.

Harris, Albert J., and Roswell, Florence G. "Clinical Diagnosis of Reading Disability." *J Psychol* 36:323–40; 1953.

Harris, Chester W. "Measurement of Comprehension of Literature." *Sch R* 31:280–9, 332–42; 1948.

Harris, Theodore L. "Some Issues in Beginning Reading Instruction." *J Ed Res* 56:5–19; 1962.

Harris, Theodore L., and others. *Experimental Development of Variability in Reading Rate in Grades 4, 5, and 6*. USOE Cooperative Research Project No. 1755. U Wisconsin, 1965. 236p.

Harris, Theodore L., and others. *Transfer Effects of Training Intermediate Grade Pupils to Adjust Reading Speed to Reading Purpose*. USOE Cooperative Research Project No. 3137. U Wisconsin, 1966. 84p.

Harrison, Martha L. *Reading Readiness*, rev. ed. Houghton, 1939. 255p.

Healy, Ann Kirtland. "Changing Children's Attitude Toward Reading." *El Engl* 40:255–7; 1963.

Henderson, Edmund H. "A Study of Individually Formulated Purposes for Reading." *J Ed Res* 58:438–41; 1965.

Henderson, Margaret. *Progress Report of Reading Study, 1952–55*. Champaign (Illinois) Board of Education, 1955. 57p.

Hendrickson, Lois, and Muehl, Siegmar. "The Effect of Attention and Motor Response on Learning to Discriminate B and D in Kindergarten Children." *J Ed Psychol* 53:236–41; 1962.

Herrick, Virgil E. "Basal Instructional Materials in Reading." In Paul A. Witty. (Chairman.) *Development in and Through Reading*, 60th Yearbook, Part I, NSSE. U Chicago, 1961. p. 165–88.

Hillerich, Robert L. "Pre-reading Skills in Kindergarten: A Second Report." *El Sch J* 65:312–7; 1965.

Hilliard, George H. *Probable Types of Difficulties Underlying Low Scores in Comprehension Tests*. State U Iowa, 1924. 60p.

Hislop, George R. "A Study of Division Two Social Studies Reading Skills." *Alberta J Ed Res* 7:28–38; 1961.

Holmes, Eleanor. "Reading Guided by Questions *versus* Reading and Re-reading Without Questions." *Sch R* 39:261–71; 1931.

Howards, Melvin. "How Easy Are 'Easy' Words?" *J Exp Ed* 32:377–82; 1964.

Howell, Wallace J. "Work Study Skills of Children in Grades IV to VIII." *El Sch J* 50:384–9; 1950.

Howell, William C., and Kraft, C. L. "The Judgment of Size, Contrast, and Sharpness of Letter Forms." *J Exp Psychol* 61:30–9; 1961.

Huey, Edmund Burke. *The Psychology and Pedagogy of Reading*. Macmillan, 1906. 469p.

Humphreys, Phila. "The Reading Interests and Habits of Six Hundred Children in the Intermediate Grades." In *Language Arts in the Elementary School*, Twentieth Century Yearbook of Dept of Elementary School Principals, Vol. 20, No. 6, 1941. p. 421–8.

Hutchinson, Earl J. "A Study of Reading Instruction in Wisconsin Public Schools in 1955 and 1960 with Special Reference to Teachers of English." Doctoral dissertation. U Wisconsin, 1961. 215p.

Jacobson, P. B. "The Effect of Work-type Reading Instruction Given in the Ninth Grade." *Sch R* 40:273–81; 1932.

Jarvis, Oscar T. "Time Allotment Relationships to Pupil Achievement." *El Engl* 42:201–4; 1965.

Jeffrey, W. E., and Samuels, S. J. "Effect of Method of Reading Training on Initial Learning and Transfer." *J Verbal Learning* 6:354–8; 1967.

Jerrolds, Bob W. "The Effects of Advance Organizers in Reading for the Retention of Specific Facts." Doctoral dissertation. U Wisconsin, 1967. 47p.

Johnson, Lovell R., and Platts, D. "A Summary of a Study of the Reading Ages of Children Who Had Been Given Remedial Teaching." *Br J Ed Psychol* 32:66–71; 1962.

Johnson, Mary E. "The Vocabulary Difficulty of Content Subjects in Grade Five." *El Engl* 29:277–80; 1952.

Jones, J. Kenneth. "Colour as an Aid to Visual Perception in Early Reading." *Br J Ed Psychol* 35:21–7; 1965.

Judd, Charles H., and Buswell, Guy T. *Silent Reading: A Study of the Various Types*. U Chicago, 1922. 160p.

Justman, Joseph. "Academic Aptitude and Reading Test Scores of Disadvantaged Children Showing Varying Degrees of Mobility." *J Ed Meas* 2:151–5; 1965.

Kagan, Jerome. "Reflection-Impulsivity and Reading Ability in Primary Grade Children." *Child Develop* 36:609–28; 1965.

Katz, Phyllis A., and Deutsch, Martin. "Relation of

Auditory-Visual Shifting to Reading Achievement." *Perceptual Motor Skills* 17:327–32; 1963.

Katz, Phyllis A., and Deutsch, Martin. "Modality of Stimulus Presentation in Serial Learning for Retarded and Normal Readers." *Perceptual Motor Skills* 19:627–33; 1964.

Keating, Leslie E. "A Pilot Experiment in Remedial Reading at the Hospital School, Lingfield, 1957–60." *Br J Ed Psychol* 32:62–5; 1962.

King, Ethel M. "Effects of Different Kinds of Visual Discrimination Training on Learning to Read Words." *J Ed Psychol* 55:325–33; 1964.

King, Ethel M., and Muehl, Siegmar. "Different Sensory Cues as Aids in Beginning Reading." *Reading Teach* 19:163–8; 1965.

Kingston, Albert H., Jr. "The Relationship of First Grade Readiness to Third and Fourth Grade Achievement." *J Ed Res* 56:61–7; 1962.

Kittell, Jack E. "Intelligence-test Performance of Children from Bilingual Environments." *El Sch J* 64:76–83; 1963.

Klare, George R., and Buck, Byron. *Know Your Reader.* Hermitage House, 1954. 192p.

Koppitz, Elizabeth M., and others. "A Note on Screening School Beginners with the Bender Gestalt Test." *J Ed Psychol* 52:80–1; 1961.

Kramer, David P., and Fleming, Elyse S. "Interparental Differences of Opinion and Children's Academic Achievement." *J Ed Res* 60:136–8; 1966.

Kruglov, Lorraine P. "Qualitative Differences in the Vocabulary Choices of Children as Revealed in a Multiple-choice Test." *J Ed Psychol* 44:229–43; 1953.

Kuroda, Yasumasa. "Newspaper Reading and Political Behavior in a Japanese Community." *J Communications* 15:171–81; 1965.

LaBrant, Lou L., and Heller, Frieda M. *An Evaluation of Free Reading in Grades Seven to Twelve, Inclusive.* Ohio State U, 1939. 158p.

Lafitte, Rondeau G., Jr. "Analysis of Increased Rate of Reading of College Students." *J Developmental Reading* 7:165–74; 1964.

Lazarsfeld, Paul F. *Radio and the Printed Page.* Duell, 1940. 354p.

Leary, Bernice E. "Meeting Specific Reading Problems in the Content Fields." In *Reading in the High School and College*, 47th Yearbook, Part II, NSSE. U Chicago Press, 1948. p. 136–79.

Lehtovaara, A., and Saarinen. P. *School-age Reading Interests.* Suomalainen Tiedeakatemia (Helsinki), 1964. 216p.

Luckiesh, Matthew, and Moss, Frank. *Reading as a Visual Task.* Van Nostrand, 1942. 428p.

Lytton, H. "An Experiment in Selection for Remedial Education." *Br J Ed Psychol* 31:79–94; 1961.

MacDonald, J. B., and others. "Individual Versus Group Instruction in First Grade Reading." *Reading Teach* 19:643–6, 652; 1966.

MacGinitie, Walter H. "Contextual Constraint in English Prose Passages." *J Psychol* 51:121–30; 1961.

Malmquist, Eve. *Factors Related to Reading Disabilities in the First Grade of the Elementary School.* Stockholm: Almquist & Wiksell, 1958. 428p.

Malmquist, Eve. "Studies on Reading Disabilities in the Elementary School." In Figural, J. Allen (Ed.) *Forging Ahead in Reading.* Proceedings of the International Reading Association, Vol. 12, Part I. Newark, Delaware, 1967. p. 504–13.

Mann, Maxine. "What Does Ability Grouping Do to the Self-concept?" *Child Ed* 36:357–60; 1960.

Marchbanks, Gabrielle, and Levin, Harry. "Cues by Which Children Recognize Words." *J Ed Psychol* 56:57–61; 1965.

Martens, Mary. "The Role of a Pacer in Improving Comprehension." *J Developmental Reading* 4:135–9; 1961.

Mathews, Mitford. *Teaching to Read: Historically Considered.* U Chicago, 1966. 218p.

Mazurkiewicz, Albert J., and Lamana, Peter A. "Spelling Achievement Following i.t.a. Instruction." *El Engl* 42:759–61; 1966.

McCracken, Robert A. "The Oral Reading Performance of a Second Grade Class Using an Informal Reading Test." *J Ed Res* 55:113–7; 1961.

McDowell, Neil A. "The Effectiveness of the Controlled Reader in Developing Reading Rate, Comprehension, and Vocabulary as Opposed to the Regular Method of Teaching Reading." *J Exp Ed* 32:363–9; 1964.

McGrew, J. M., and others. "Branching Program, Text and Lecture: A Comparative Investigation of Instructional Media." *J Applied Psychol* 50:505–8; 1966.

McGuire, William J., and Papageorgis, Demetrios. "The Relative Efficacy of Various Types of Prior Belief-defense in Producing Immunity Against Persuasion." *J Abn Social Psychol* 62:327–37; 1961.

McManus, Anastasia. "The Denver Pre-reading Project Conducted by WENH-TV." *Reading Teach* 18:22–6; 1964.

McNamara, Walter J., and others. "The Influence of Size of Type on Speed of Reading in the Primary Grades." *Sight Saving R* 23:28–33; 1953.

McNeil, John D. "Programmed Instruction Versus Usual Classroom Procedures in Teaching Boys to Read." *Am Ed Res J* 1:113–9; 1964.

McNelly, John T. "Meaning Intensity and Interest in Foreign News Topics." *Journalism Q* 39:161–8; 1962.

Modiano, Nancy. "Reading Comprehension in the National Language." Doctoral dissertation. New York U, 1966.

Money, John. (Ed.) *Reading Disability: Progress and Research Needs in Dyslexia.* Johns Hopkins Press, 1962. 222p.

Monroe, Marion. *Children Who Cannot Read.* U Chicago, 1932. 205p.

Moorhouse, William F. "Interclass Grouping for Reading Instruction." *El Sch J* 64:280–6; 1964.

Morris, John L., and others. "Mobility and Achievement." *J Exp Ed* 35:74–80; 1967.

Muehl, Siegmar. "The Effects of Visual Discrimination Pretraining on Learning to Read a Vocabulary List in Kindergarten Children." *J Ed Psychol* 51:217–21; 1960.

Muehl, Siegmar. "The Effects of Visual Discrimination Pretraining with Word and Letter Stimuli on Learning to Read a Word List in Kindergarten Children." *J Ed Psychol* 52:215–21; 1961.

Mutimer, Dorothy, and others. "Some Differences in the Family Relationships of Achieving and Underachieving Readers." *J Genet Psychol* 109:67–74; 1966.

Nardelli, Robert R. "Some Aspects of Creative Reading." *J Ed Res* 50:495–508; 1957.

National Society for the Study of Education. *Report of the National Committee on Reading.* 24th Yearbook, Part I. Public-Sch, 1925. 339p.

National Society for the Study of Education. *Reading in the High School and College.* 47th Yearbook, Part II. U Chicago Press, 1948. 318p.

National Society for the Study of Education. *Adult Reading.* 55th Yearbook, Part II. U Chicago Press, 1956. 279p.

Neville, Donald, and others. "The Relationship Between Test Anxiety and Silent Reading Gain." *Am Ed Res J* 4:45–50; 1967.

Noall, Mabel S. "Automatic Teaching of Reading Skills in High School." *J Ed* 143:1–73; 1961.

Nolan, Esther D. "Reading Difficulty Versus Low Mentality." *California J Ed Res* 17:34–9; 1942.

Norvell, George W. *The Reading Interests of Young People.* Heath, 1950. 262p.

Norvell, George W. *What Boys and Girls Like to Read.* Silver, 1958. 306p.

O'Donnell, Roy. "Awareness of Grammatical Structure and Reading Comprehension." *H Sch J* 45:184–8; 1962.

Ofman, William, and Shaevitz, Morton. "The Kinesthetic Method in Remedial Reading." *J Exp Ed* 31:317–20; 1963.

Olson, Arthur V. "The Frostig Developmental Test of Visual Perception as a Predictor of Specific Reading Abilities with Second Grade Children." *El Engl* 43:869–72; 1966.

Olson, Arthur V., and others. "Effectiveness of a Freshman Reading Program." *J Reading* 8:75–83; 1964.

Olson, David R., and Pau, A. S. "Emotionally Loaded Words and the Acquisition of a Sight Vocabulary." *J Ed Psychol* 57:174–8; 1966.

Olson, Willard C. "Reading as a Function of the Total Growth of the Child." In Gray, William S. (Ed.) *Reading and Pupil Development.* U Chicago, 1940. p. 233–7.

Osborn, Leslie A. *Prognosis: A Guide to the Study and Practice of Clinical Medicine.* Thomas, 1966. 286p.

Osgood, Charles E., and others. *The Measurement of Meaning.* U Illinois, 1957. 342p.

Otto, Herbert A. "Sex and Violence on the American Newsstand." *Journalism Q* 40:19–26; 1963.

Otto, Wayne. "The Acquisition and Retention of Paired-associates by Good, Average, and Poor Readers." *J Ed Psychol* 52:241–8; 1961.

Otto, Wayne, and Fredericks, Robert C. "Relationship of Reactive Inhibition to Reading Skill Attainment." *J Ed Psychol* 4:227–40; 1963.

Otto, Wayne, and McMenemy, Richard. *Corrective and Remedial Teaching.* Houghton, 1966. 377p.

Parker, Edwin B. "The Effects of Television on Public Library Circulation." *Public Opin Q* 27:578–89; 1963.

Paterson, Donald G., and Tinker, Miles A. *How to Make Type Readable.* Harper, 1940. 210p.

Peltola, Bette J. "A Study of Children's Book Choices." *El Engl* 40:690–5, 702; 1963.

Plessas, Gus P. "Reading Abilities of High and Low Auders." *El Sch J* 63:223–6; 1963.

Plessas, Gus P., and Dison, Peggy A. "Spelling Performances of Good Readers." *Calif J Ed Res* 16:14–22; 1965.

Popp, Helen M. "Visual Discrimination of Alphabet Letters." *Reading Teach* 17:221–5; 1964.

Popp, Helen M. "The Measurement and Training of Visual Discrimination Skills Prior to Reading Instruction." *J Exp Ed* 35:15–26; 1967.

Postman, Leo, and Greenbloom, Rose. "Conditions of Cue Selection in the Acquisition of Paired-associate Lists." *J Exp Psychol* 73:91–100; 1967.

Postman, Leo, and Rosenzweig, Mark R. "Perceptual Recognition of Words." *J Speech Hearing Disorders* 22:245–53; 1957.

Potts, Eric. "A Factorial Study of the Relationship Between the Child's Vocabulary and His Reading Progress at the Infants' Stage." *Br J Ed Psychol* 30:84–6; 1960.

Powell, William R. "The Joplin Plan: An Evaluation." *El Sch J* 64:387–92; 1964.

Prescott, George A. "Sex Differences in Metropolitan Readiness Test Results." *J Ed Res* 48:605–10; 1955.

Pyke, R. L. *Report on the Legibility of Print.* H.M. Stationery Office, 1926.

Rankin, Earl F., Jr. "Sequential Emphasis upon Speed and Comprehension in a College Reading Improvement Program." *J Developmental Reading* 7:46–54; 1963.

Rankin, Earl F., Jr., and Tracy, Robert J. "Residual Gain as a Measure of Individual Differences in Reading Improvement." *J Reading* 8:224–33; 1965.

Richards, Ivor A. *Interpretation in Teaching.* Harcourt, 1938. 420p.

Richards, Ivor A. *How to Read a Page.* Norton, 1942. 246p.

Robinson, Helen M. *Why Pupils Fail in Reading: A Study of Causes and Remedial Treatment.* U Chicago, 1946. 257p.

Robinson, Helen M. and Smith, Helen. "Reading Clinic Clients—Ten Years After." *El Sch J* 61:22–7; 1962.

Roman, Melvin. *Reaching Delinquents Through Reading.* Thomas, 1957. 125p.

Rosen, Bernard. "Attitude Change Within the Negro Press Toward Segregation and Discrimination." *J Social Psychol* 62:77–83; 1964.

Rosenfield, Sylvia S. "The Effect of Perceptual Style in Word Discrimination Ability of Kindergarten Children." Doctoral dissertation. U Wisconsin, 1967. 92p.

Rothkopf, Ernst Z. "Learning from Written Instructive Materials: An Exploration of the Control of Inspection Behavior by Test-like Events." *Am Ed Res J* 3:241–9; 1966.

Rothrock, Dayton C. "Heterogeneous, Homogeneous, or Individualized Approach to Reading?" *El Engl* 38:233–5; 1961.

Russell, David H. "Inter-class Grouping for Reading Instruction in the Intermediate Grades." *J Ed Res* 39:462–70; 1946.

Russell, David H. "The Dimensions of Children's Meaning Vocabularies in Grades Four Through Twelve." *U California Public Ed* 11(No. 5):315–414; 1954.

Russell, David H., and Saadeh, Ibrahim. "Qualitative Levels in Children's Vocabularies." *J Ed Psychol* 53:170–4; 1962.

Salzinger, Suzanne, and others. "Memory for Verbal Sequences as a Function of Their Syntactical Structure and the Age of the Recalling Child." *J Psychol* 64:79–90; 1966.

Samuels, S. J., and Jeffrey, W. E. "Discriminability of Words, and Letter Cues Used in Learning to Read." *J Ed Psychol* 57:337–40; 1966.

Santostefano, Sebastiano, and others. "Cognitive Styles and Reading Disability." *Psychol Sch* 2:57–62; 1965.

Sartain, Harry W. "The Roseville Experiment With Individualized Reading." *Reading Teach* 13:277–81; 1960.

Sawyer, Rita L. "Does the Wechsler Intelligence Scale for Children Discriminate Between Mildly Disabled and Severely Disabled Readers?" *El Sch J* 66:97–103; 1965.

Scarborough, Olive R., and others. "Anxiety Level and Performance in School Subjects." *Psychol Reports* 9:425–30; 1961.

Schramm, Wilbur. "Why Adults Read." In *Adult Reading*, 55th Yearbook, Part II. NSSE. U Chicago, 1956. p. 57–88.

Schramm, Wilbur, and others. *Television in the Lives of Our Children.* Stanford U Press, 1961. 334p.

Senour, Alfred C. "A Comparison of Two Instruments for Measuring Reading Readiness." In *The Role of Research in Educational Progress.* AERA, 1937. p. 178–83.

Serra, Mary C. "The Concept Burden of Instructional Materials." *El Sch J* 53:508–12; 1953.

Shepard, Roger. "Production of Constrained Associates and the Informational Uncertainty of the Constraint." *Am J Psychol* 76:218–28; 1963.

Shores, J. Harlan. "Reading Science Materials for Two Distinct Purposes." *El Engl* 37:546–52; 1960.

Shores, J. Harlan, and Husbands, Kenneth L. "Are Fast Readers the Best Readers?" *El Engl* 27:52–7; 1950.

Silver, Archie A., and Hagin, Rosa A. "Specific Reading Disability: Follow-up Studies." *Am J Orthopsychiatry* 39:95–102; 1964.

Smith, Kenneth J., and Heddens, James W. "The Readability of Experimental Mathematics Materials." *Arithmetic Teach* 11:391–2; 1964.

Smith, Nila B. *American Reading Instruction.* International Reading Association, 1965. 449p.

Snider, J. G. "Achievement Test Performance of Acculturated Indian Children." *Alberta J Ed Res* 7:39–41; 1961.

Spache, George D., and others. "Results of Three College Level Remedial Reading Procedures." *J Developmental Reading* 4:12–6; 1960.

Spache, George D., and others. "A Longitudinal First Grade Reading Readiness Program." *Reading Teach* 19:580–4; 1966.

Sparks, Paul E., and Fay, Leo C. "An Evaluation of Two Methods of Teaching Reading." *El Sch J* 57:386–90; 1957.

Spitzer, Herbert T. "Class Size and Pupil Achievement in Elementary Schools." *El Sch J* 55:82–6; 1954.

Staats, Arthur W., and Butterfield, William H. "Treatment of Nonreading in a Culturally Deprived Juvenile Delinquent: An Application of Reinforcement Principles." *Child Develop* 36:925–42; 1965.

Staats, Arthur W., and others. "A Reinforcer System and Experimental Procedure for the Laboratory Study of Reading Acquisition." *Child Develop* 35:209–31; 1964.

Statts, Carolyn K., and others. "The Effects of Discrimination Pretraining on Textual Behavior." *J Ed Psychol* 53:32–7; 1962.

Stauffer, Russell G. "A Vocabulary Study Comparing Reading, Arithmetic, Health and Science Texts." *Reading Teach* 20:141–7; 1966.

Steinberg, Philip M., and Rosenberg, Robert. "Relationship Between Reading and Various Aspects of Visual Anomalies." *J Am Optometric Assn* 26:444–6; 1956.

Stordahl, Kalmer E., and Christensen, Clifford M. "The Effect of Study Techniques on Comprehension and Retention." *J Ed Res* 49:561–70; 1956.

Strickland, Ruth. "The Language of Elementary School Children: Its Relationship to the Language of Reading Textbooks and the Quality of Reading of Selected Children." *B Sch Ed Indiana U*, 38 (No. 4); 1962. 131p.

Studholme, Janice M. "Group Guidance with Mothers of Retarded Readers." *Reading Teach* 17:528–30; 1964.

Sutton, Marjorie Hunt. "Readiness for Reading at the Kindergarten Level." *Reading Teach* 17:234–9; 1964.

Tannenbaum, Percy, and Lynch, Mervin. "Sensationalism: Some Objective Message Correlates." *Journalism Q* 39:317–23; 1962.

Taylor, Christian D. "The Effect of Training on Reading Readiness." In *Studies in Reading*, Vol. 2. U London, 1950. p. 64–80.

Taylor, Cornelia D. "The Relative Legibility of Black and White Print." *J Ed Psychol* 25:561–78; 1934.

Taylor, Edward, and Crandall, James. "A Study of the 'Norm-equivalence' of Certain Tests Approved for the California State Testing Program." *California J Ed Res* 13:186–92; 1962.

Tennyson, W. Wesley, and Monnens, Lawrence P. "The World of Work Through Elementary Readers." *Voc Guid Q* 12:85–8; 1963–1964.

Thorndike, Edward L. "Reading as Reasoning: A Study of Mistakes in Paragraph Reading." *J Ed Psychol* 8:323–32; 1917.

Tinker, Miles A. "Illumination Standards for Effective and Comfortable Vision." *J Cons Psychol* 3:11–20; 1939.

Tinker, Miles A. "Validity of Frequency of Blinking as a Criterion of Readability." *J Exp Psychol* 36:453–60; 1946.

Tinker, Miles A. "Reliability and Validity of Involuntary Blinking as a Measure of Ease of Seeing." *J Ed Psychol* 41:417–27; 1950.

Tinker, Miles A. "Light Intensities Preferred for Reading." *Am J Optometry Archives Am Acad Optometry* 31:55–6; 1954.

Tinker, Miles A. "Prolonged Reading Tasks in Visual Research." *J Applied Psychol* 39:444–6; 1955.

Tinker, Miles A. "Influence of Simultaneous Variation in Size of Type, Width of Line, and Leading for Newspaper Type." *J Applied Psychol* 47:380–2; 1963(a).

Tinker, Miles A. *Legibility of Print.* Iowa State U, 1963(b). 329p.

Tinker, Miles A. *Bases for Effective Reading.* U Minnesota, 1965. 322p.

Torrance, E. Paul, and Harmon, Judson. "Effects of Memory, Evaluative, and Creative Reading Sets on Test Performance." *J Ed Psychol* 52:207–14; 1961.

Traxler, Arthur E. "Research in Reading in the United States." *J Ed Res* 42:481–99; 1949.

Traxler, Arthur E. "Current Organization and Procedures in Remedial Teaching." *J Exp Ed* 20:305–12; 1952.

Traxler, Arthur E. "Development of a Vocabulary Test for High School Pupils and College Freshmen." *Ed Rec B* 83:67–73; 1963.

Tulvig, Endel, and Gold, Cecille. "Stimulus Information and Contextual Information as Determinants of Tachistoscopic Recognition of Words." *J Exp Psychol* 66:319–27; 1963.

UNESCO. *Statistical Yearbook.* UNESCO, 1965.

U.S. Bureau of the Census. *Statistical Abstract,* 87th ed. The Bureau, 1966.

Veatch, Jeanette. *Individualizing Your Reading Program.* Putnam, 1959. 242p.

Vernon, M. D. *The Experimental Study of Reading.* Cambridge U, 1931. 190p.

Vernon, M. D. *Visual Perception.* Cambridge U, 1937. 247p.

Vernon, M. D. *Backwardness in Reading.* Cambridge U, 1957. 228p.

Walters, Richard, and Kosowski, Irene. "Symbolic Learning and Reading Retardation." *J Cons Psychol* 27:75–82; 1963.

Waples, Douglas. "The Relation of Subject Interests to Actual Reading." *Lib Q* 2:42–70; 1932.

Waples, Douglas, and Tyler, Ralph W. *What People Want to Read About.* U Chicago, 1931. 312p.

Waples, Douglas, and others. *What Reading Does to People.* U Chicago, 1940. 222p.

Warner, Dolores. "The Divided Day Plan for Reading Organization." *Reading Teach* 20:397–9; 1967.

Webster, Helen A., and Tinker, Miles A. "The Influence of Paper Surface on the Perceptibility of Print." *J Applied Psychol* 19:145–7; 1935.

Werner, Heinz, and Kaplan, Edith. "The Acquisition of Word Meanings: A Developmental Study." *Monogr Soc Res Child Develop* 1; 1952. 120p.

Whipple, Gertrude. "Characteristics of a Sound Reading Program." In *Reading in the Elementary School,* 48th Yearbook, Part II, NSSE. U Chicago, 1949. p. 33–53.

Whitla, Dean K. "Effect of Tutoring on Scholastic Aptitude Test Scores." *Personnel Guid J* 41:32–7; 1962.

Williams, Phillip. "The Growth of Reading Vocabulary and Some of Its Implications." *Br J Ed Psychol* 31:104–5; 1961.

Wilson, Richard, and Harrison, Robert. "Skill Growth with Individualized Reading." *El Engl* 40:433–5; 1963.

Winger, Howard W. "Historical Perspectives on the Role of the Book in Society." *Lib Q* 25:295–305; 1955.

Winkly, Carol K. "Which Accent Generalizations Are Worth Teaching?" *Reading Teach* 20:219–24; 1966.

Witty, Paul, and Kinsella, Paul J. "A Report on Televiewing in 1961." *El Engl* 39:24–32; 1962.

Witty, Paul, and Kopel, David. *Reading and Educational Process.* Ginn, 1939. 374p.

Wolfe, Wayne. "Images of the United States in the Latin American Press." *Journalism Q* 41:79–86; 1964.

Worcester, D. A., and Kline, A. *Reading Achievement in Lincoln, Nebraska, Schools, 1921 and 1937.* U Nebraska Press, 1947.

Wozencraft, Marian. "Sex Comparisons of Certain Abilities." *J Ed Res* 57:21–7; 1963.

Wright, John C., and Lazaraton, Margaret L. "An Investigation of Attrition in a College Reading Class." *J Develop Reading* 7:40–4; 1963.

Wrightstone, J. Wayne, and others. "Developing Reading Test Norms for Deaf Children." *Am Annals Deaf* 108:311–5; 1963.

Zachrisson, B. *Studies in the Readability of Printed Text with Special Reference to Type Design and Type Sizes: A Survey and Some Contributions.* Graphic Institute, 1957. 179p.

RECORDS AND REPORTS

The widespread, systematic compilation of records about students by the staffs of American elementary and secondary schools is a phenomenon of the twentieth century. It is true that in the mid-1800's such educational leaders as Horace Mann in Massachusetts, Henry Barnard in Connecticut, and Samuel Lewis in Ohio instituted the keeping of registers in schools of their states (Heck, 1929). However, these men were ahead of most of their contemporaries, and it was not until after 1900 that the educational community paid serious, large-scale attention to matters of records and reports (Yeager, 1949).

The first study to exert nationwide influence in this field appeared in 1912. It was an investigation conducted by the Committee on Uniform Records and Reports of the National Education Association (1912). Since that time American education has witnessed periods of waxing and waning of research and development interest in gathering, recording, and storing information about students and in disseminating this information for a growing variety of uses.

From the standpoints of innovation and research activity, the decades from 1920 through the 1960's can be divided into three eras. During the first era, extending from about 1925 through the late 1930's, the child study and standardized-testing movements enjoyed their most active years for the creation and initial refinement of such information-gathering devices as standardized tests, anecdotal records, rating scales, and check lists. These years were also important for the development of cumulative-record forms, case studies, and newer approaches to reporting student progress to parents. The second era, encompassing the 1940's and early 1950's, saw the disseminating and refining of record systems and of reporting practices but relatively little innovation. The third era, from the mid-1950's through the 1960's, was a period of continued use and improvement of existing techniques, but its real distinction came from the introduction of record processing by machines, particularly by electronic computers. After investigations of computerized record systems made a modest beginning in the 1950's, activity in this field bounded ahead at an increasing pace in the 1960's.

NATURE OF THE RESEARCH. From the viewpoint of research design, the investigations in this field have been mainly of two types: case studies and surveys.

The case studies, which have been by far the more numerous of the two, have usually consisted of an investigator's introducing a new record or reporting practice into a school and then evaluating it through a comparison with the school's former practices. Conclusions about the success of the new practice typically have been based either on measures of convenience, speed, and accuracy in the recording and reporting procedures or on expressions of satisfaction or dissatisfaction by such users of the system as teachers, counselors, clerical workers, school administrators, parents, pupils, and employers.

To conduct surveys, most investigators have circulated questionnaires to schools to learn of current practices. Other surveys have consisted of a search of the professional literature to reveal trends in recording and reporting methods over a period of years.

Although the specific problems that have elicited the greatest amount of research interest have varied somewhat from decade to decade, the three basic questions encompassing all research problems in this field have remained the same: For what purposes do schools need records about students? What kinds of information should be recorded to serve these purposes? What are the most efficient ways of gathering, recording, storing, and disseminating these kinds of information? The following overview of answers that investigators have provided for these questions is organized under three headings: (1) uses and contents of records, (2) types of records, and (3) the form of records.

USES AND CONTENTS OF RECORDS. The uses which the school intends to make of student records determine what the contents of the records should be. Following are the principal ways records have been used in mid-twentieth-century American schools: (1) for diagnosing past and current strengths and weaknesses in the individual student's academic performance, in the condition of his health, and in his personality, (2) for reporting student progress to parents, to the student himself, to next year's teacher, to counselors, to schools to which the student transfers, and to potential employers, (3) for guiding the student's educational and vocational planning, (4) for helping determine how the school's curriculum or staff should be altered, (5) for reporting facts required by government agencies or by accrediting associations so that the school can qualify for financial support or for professional accreditation, and (6) for educational research.

In general, the trend over the years has been for schools to collect an increasingly great variety of information about the student so they can fulfill the foregoing roles more adequately. However, at any one time notable differences have existed between one school and another in the seriousness with which they gathered information and in the kinds of information they have considered worthwhile. The following list indicates the basic types of information recorded. The list begins with items collected by all schools. Items near the end of it have been collected by fewer schools. Kinds of data about students have included class attendance, program of study, marks reflecting academic success (i.e., grades given in each subject-matter area), health history, judgments of classroom citizenship, home and family identification, awards and honors earned, participation in school activities, more detailed information on home and family conditions, and personal-social adjustment or personality characteristics.

The amount of research devoted to functions of records has varied considerably from one type of use to another. More consideration has been given the use of records for diagnosing students' strengths and weaknesses, reporting to parents, and reporting to other schools than has been accorded to the function of records in curriculum and staff reorganization or in reporting to accrediting agencies.

The following discussion surveys common problems in this field and summarizes some of the more important findings.

Differentiating Learning Experiences. From the viewpoint of helping students learn more efficiently, the most important use of records has been for indicating learners' individual strengths and weaknesses so the school program could be fitted to their needs. Schools have adjusted to students' individual differences by administrative provisions (ability grouping, enrichment and remedial classes, acceleration or retardation of pupils, etc.) and by classroom teaching techniques (individualized assignments, programmed textbooks, reading groups, etc.). The following survey first treats the use of records for guiding administrative decisions, then for determining classroom procedures.

Most secondary and many elementary schools have assigned students to classrooms according to their apparent ability or performance levels in the various subject-matter areas. The kinds of records most often used for determining which ability group a student should enter have been (1) prior teachers' recommendations, (2) students' educational-vocational goals, (3) aptitude and achievement test scores, or (4) a combination of these (Thomas, 1966).

In large secondary schools the task of scheduling hundreds of students into the classes best suited to their individual goals and talents, at the same time maintaining optimum class sizes and satisfactory teacher assignments, has usually been so cumbersome that the welfare of a significant number of students has been sacrificed in the process. However, in the 1960's the capacity of electronic computers to manipulate a complex of information about large numbers of students and teachers and about factors in the school program has made flexible scheduling a reality. The kinds of record data most often utilized in the experimental computerized scheduling studies of the 1960's have been the school's course offerings, staffing and teaching assignments, facilities and room assignments, and students' course choices listed in the order of their importance to the student (Oakford & others, 1966).

Classroom teachers have found several common types of records useful.

Health reports have indicated ways the child's physical condition might affect his classroom behavior (Garber, 1963; Zolcznski, 1962). Test scores and marks in earlier grades have suggested the level of success that might be expected of the pupil in the various subject-matter areas (Thorndike & Hagen, 1961).

Anecdotal records and rating scales have indicated personality characteristics and attitudes that former teachers observed in the child (American Council on Education, 1945). Information about the family has often suggested the social and emotional climates in the child's home.

Teachers have used these data for estimating (1) at what level the pupil should begin working in the various subject-matter areas, (2) how rapidly the child is likely to progress, (3) probable causes for the student's behavior, and (4) special kinds of help he may require.

In the case of a pupil who has posed unusually serious and puzzling problems, school personnel have frequently collected a greater variety of data about his past and present personality characteristics, physical health, home environment, and academic abilities than have routinely been recorded about most pupils. By means of this more intense study, the school has tried to increase the chances of discovering the pattern of factors causing the student's difficulties. The data usually have been compiled by a team of specialists (social worker, teacher, school nurse, counselor, psychologist, physician) who, through the medium of periodic case conferences, have discussed the several facets of the child's life in order to arrive at an interpretation of his condition. Most research published about this use of records for the intensive study of problem children has appeared in the form of case studies (Millard & Rothney, 1957; Rothney, 1953).

Reporting to Parents. The chief questions about reports to parents that have demanded the attention of investigators have been In what manner should the report be made? What kinds of information should be reported? Against what standard should the student's performance be compared?

In answer to the first of these questions, schools have reported to parents in four ways: by report card, by teacher-parent conference, by letters from the teacher to the parents, or by a combination of these. At both elementary and secondary levels, report cards have been by far the most popular of these reporting media (Rothney, 1955; Thomas, 1960). To supplement report cards, teacher-parent conferences have long served schools as devices on emergency occasions for informing parents of their child's unusual behavior or his markedly unsatisfactory progress (Cutler, 1963). However, an increasing number of elementary schools have adopted teacher-parent conferences as the normal method for reporting the progress of all children, not just the deviants; in such schools conferences often have alternated throughout the year with report cards as the means of communicating with the home (DePencier, 1951; Gitelman, 1959). The use of the conference as the normal method of reporting to parents has been restricted almost entirely to elementary schools because (1) parents of young children have proved more willing to attend conferences than parents of adolescents, (2) high schools have found the task of scheduling a separate conference with each of the student's several teachers to be unduly complex, and (3) many teachers have considered report cards sufficient for their purposes.

Letters or notes to the home have been employed widely for informing an occasional parent of a special problem his child has posed for the school. However, the use of letters for regularly reporting each pupil's progress has been limited to a very small proportion of schools and chiefly to the elementary grades.

In deciding what kinds of information should be reported to the home, educators have universally agreed that parents should be told of their child's status in skills and subject-matter knowledge. Apparently most school personnel have approved of reporting behavior that composes school citizenship or study habits. But the issue of reporting test scores and certain personality characteristics to parents has been debated for half a century. Those educators who have advocated informing parents of aptitude-, intelligence-, or personality-test scores have contended that parents can set enlightened goals for their child only if they know everything possible about his current status and potential. In addition, these educators have claimed that parents have a legal right to all data collected about their children. In contrast, school personnel opposing the practice of telling the parents each child's test scores have claimed that since many parents do not understand how to interpret test results wisely, and frequently they themselves are part of the cause of personality problems, they distort the meaning of scores or personality evaluations and consequently develop unrealistic expectations for their children (Fischer, 1961; Tennyson, 1964).

The third main question which investigators have studied has been Against what standard should a pupil's performance be compared when his progress is reported to the home? More specifically, should the child be judged according to an ideal standard set by the teacher or school, should he be compared with his classmates, or should he be marked against a schoolwide or nationwide population? Most report cards, particularly at the secondary-school level, have compared students either with their classmates or with an ideal the teacher holds. However, in the past three decades more elementary schools have reported each pupil's performance in relation to his apparent individual abilities. Some reporting systems have furnished two comparisons, one describing the child in terms of his apparent potential and the other in terms of his classmates' performance (Chansky, 1963; Halliwell, 1963; Thomas, 1960).

The type of reporting system that is most suitable for a given school depends on such factors as (1) the kinds of information parents desire, (2) the amount of information teachers have about their pupils, (3) parents' interest in the child's school experiences, (4) the grade level, (5) the amount of teacher's time available, and (6) the goals of the school program (Austen, 1965; Chansky, 1964, 1965; Hammel, 1964).

Special types of report cards have been developed for such special kinds of pupils as the mentally retarded (Polansky & Barnett, 1965).

Reporting to Other Schools and to Employers. When a pupil has transferred from one school to another or has graduated to a higher institution, certain of his records usually have been sent with him. Most research about the transfer of records has been directed at high school reports (transcripts) required for college entrance. The kinds of information contained in these reports has been dictated chiefly by the kinds of data college officials have thought valuable for predicting students' college success. Such reports commonly have included high school marks, an overall grade-point average, the student's academic rank in his graduating class, aptitude-test scores, personality ratings, and data on the student's high school honors and activities. Of these kinds of information, academic grades have generally proved the most useful and personality ratings the least useful predictors of college success (Critchfield & Hutson, 1964). Regional school-accrediting associations and college admissions organizations have been unsuccessful in their attempts to convince all high schools to adopt one standard reporting form.

The kinds of information different employers seek from a high school about a former student depends somewhat on the kind of opening available in the organization. Marks or test scores earned in school subjects related to the type of work for which the student has applied usually have interested employers. The employer is also typically concerned about a student's character traits (initiative, diligence, reliability, etc.). Employers frequently have requested character reports either in the form of a letter of recommendation written by a member of the school's administrative or instructional staff or in the form of a personality rating sheet which the employer furnishes for the school to fill out. Information about the student's socioeconomic background and specific abilities also has been sought by many business organizations.

Guiding Educational and Vocational Planning. Guidance counselors and teachers who assist the secondary-school student in planning his educational and vocational future have used the following kinds of records as aids in estimating what courses of action will be most feasible for the student: (1) grades earned in previous classes, (2) former teachers' recommendations, (3) aptitude- and achievement-test scores, (4) vocational-interest-test scores, (5) information about aptitudes or interests reflected in the student's extracurricular pursuits, (6) the student's own ideas about what he would like, and feels he is able, to accomplish, and (7) data about his family's socioeconomic status and their hopes for his future.

Planning Curriculum and Staffing Needs. For each of the foregoing uses, the record of the individual student has been the focus of attention. However, when record information is utilized for forming curriculum and staffing plans, it must be reported as group data. For instance, the distribution of standardized mathematics-test scores for an entire school can aid the administration in deciding whether students should be divided into classes representing different ability levels. A distribution of all pupils' aptitude-test scores and marks from the previous year can suggest whether there are enough gifted pupils to warrant appointing a special teacher for them.

The types of student records which have usually been found of most value to school personnel charged with curriculum and staff planning include (1) aptitude- and intelligence-test scores, (2) achievement-test scores in the several subject-matter areas, (3) data on students' educational plans, (4) health information showing the numbers of pupils suffering various handicaps, and (5) marks earned in prior grades.

Reporting to Government Agencies and Accrediting Associations. Group data about pupils have been needed by schools to support their requests for funds from local, state, and federal agencies. To secure general-support funds that are computed on an average-daily-attendance basis, schools have had to report pupil attendance figures. Likewise, records of the numbers of pupils with physical, mental, or socioeconomic handicaps have been required from schools seeking government support for special-education programs.

Regional accrediting associations, in making their periodic appraisals of the quality of member schools, have required data about school attendance, the distribution of marks awarded by the teachers, amount of student participation in extraclass activities, the status of pupil health, and the nature of the pupil-personnel program (North Central Association, 1966).

TYPES OF RECORDS. Over the past half-century investigators have directed a significant amount of attention to four types of records: anecdotal, cumulative, case-study, and health or other special varieties.

Anecdotal Records. Anecdotal records are brief descriptions of pupil behavior which tell something particularly significant about the student's school progress, health condition, or personal-social adjustment. Most anecdotal records have been written by teachers; less often they have been contributed by a counselor, school nurse, social worker, or administrator. Anecdotes usually have not been recorded routinely for all pupils. Rather, they have been written to describe only behavior incidents involving an occasional student, in most cases a student who has faced unusually difficult problems of succeeding in school, either academically or socially.

Investigations have shown that anecdotes vary in the degree to which they represent objective descriptions of pupil behavior uncolored by the writer's personal opinions. Two common forms of opinion that teachers have inadvertently inserted into ostensibly objective records have been evaluative and interpretive comments. Evaluative comments are ones which attribute goodness or badness to the pupil's behavior. Interpretive comments propose a cause for the behavior. Not only have anecdotes varied in objectivity, but also they have varied in specificity. The specific anecdote is a report of a single incident. A more general anecdote summarizes a number of similar incidents (American Council on Education, 1945).

Cumulative Records. Cumulative records consist of year-by-year compilations of information about various facets of a pupil's life. Such records usually have been maintained for each student. They often have accompanied him from the elementary grades through high school. Schools have varied in the types of information included in cumulative records. In some districts a record has consisted of as few types of data as a report of the student's attendance, of his academic marks, and of his home address and the names of the members of his family. In other schools the cumulative-record folder has contained the pupil's history of school attendance, test scores (intelligence, aptitude, achievement, interest, and personal adjustment), prior school marks, honors and awards, behavior shown on anecdotal records, health history, social acceptance among peers, participation in school activities, hobbies, work experience, educational or vocational plans, family information (marital status of parents, siblings in home, socioeconomic level, health, parent-child relationships), and participation in community life (American Council on Education, 1947; Brewster, 1959; Johnson, 1961; National Association of Secondary School Principals, 1964).

Over the years, controversies about the following questions have regularly attracted the attention of those who have studied the use of cumulative records:

(1) In which of the following places is the cumulative record most appropriately located, from the viewpoints of usefulness to school personnel and of confidentiality of data: in the central office, in the counselor's file, or in the teacher's classroom file? (2) To what extent does a teacher develop an unfair bias toward a pupil if the teacher inspects the cumulative record before becoming personally acquainted with the pupil? (3) How much information in a record is truly useful for guiding school personnel in the wise treatment of pupils, and how much is more trouble to gather than it is worth? Universally satisfactory answers to these questions have yet to be found.

Pupil Case Studies. A pupil case study is an intensive investigation of the individual to determine the probable causes of some particularly troublesome aspect of his behavior. Unlike cumulative records, case studies have not been made routinely on all pupils but have been conducted on only those few whose problems have proven severe. Usually one member of the school staff has compiled the study by collecting data from other faculty members and from such outside agencies as welfare bureaus, church workers, physicians, and the pupil's family. A typical case study has consisted of the following sections: identification data, reason for the study, test data, educational history, physical health, environmental background, interests and attitudes, and summary and recommendations (Barbe, 1959).

Special Records. Of the several types of special records focusing on a single facet of a pupil's life (health, home environment, participation in school activities), the health record has received the greatest amount of study. The most common types of data accumulated about a student's health have been (1) teachers' observations of student's general health and behavior, eyes and sight, ears and hearing, and illnesses, (2) height and weight growth history, (3) immunization and test record, (4) sight and hearing screening records, (5) medical examinations, (6) dental examinations, (7) psychological examinations, (8) history of medical treatment, and (9) notes on health counseling and follow-up procedures (Irwin & others, 1962; Wilson, 1953).

THE FORM OF RECORDS. The most popular forms in which records have been used, stored, or both have been (1) in file folders (dimensions about 9 by 12 inches), (2) on large cards printed with special sections for writing each variety of data about a student, (3) in loose-leaf notebooks, and, most recently, (4) on cards (dimensions 7⅜ by 3¼ inches) containing patterns of punched holes that represent, in coded form, information about the student. A relatively small number of secondary schools have transferred records of former students to microfilm, so that data on thousands of graduates might be stored in a single file cabinet.

In deciding on the form in which different kinds of records should be kept, schools have sought to meet the criteria of ease and accuracy in the recording, storing, and retrieval of information. The retrieval aspect of the records process includes also the requirement that the information about students be available only to authorized school personnel. Each of the popular methods listed above meets these criteria to a different degree.

The file folder, which often has spaces printed on the outside for recording student identification data and test scores, has served as a useful container for such cumulative-record items as health-history cards, test papers, anecdotal notes, reports on interviews with parents, and a student autobiography. However, as folders have filled with data, they have posed storage problems, especially in large schools. Furthermore, they have not always been stored in the place most convenient to all potential users: administrative personnel, counselors, and teachers.

The large card, ranging in size from about 6 by 9 inches to 9 by 12 inches, typically is printed on both sides with lines and spaces designed for recording specified data. A card may focus on one aspect of a pupil's life, such as his health, or may provide for summarizing many aspects.

Loose-leaf notebooks have proved useful for storing listed data which school personnel frequently consult, such as alphabetized lists of students and their standardized test scores or lists of students ranked by grade-point average.

One disadvantage common to all of the foregoing forms is that the task of retrieving information from them must be accomplished by hand. To compile groups of pupils who share a common characteristic, like poor school attendance or honor-roll achievement, or to compute group statistics, like the average reading speed for a grade level, requires many hours of clerical work, and the process can result in errors.

Data cards, each consisting of 80 columns for storing punched information about a student, provide the advantages of conciseness, confidentiality, and machine-processing capability. Such cards and the electronic equipment which processes them have inaugurated the modern era of student record systems. Since the mid-1950's school districts, in cooperation with electronic-computer companies and universities, have been investigating ways of using electronic equipment for increasing the efficiency of recording, storing, retrieving, and reporting data about students. By the mid-1960's the amount of activity in this field had increased to a high level. However, only a small portion of the investigations conducted in the field had found their way into the traditional educational research journals. Instead, most development activities have been reported in school systems' data-processing handbooks (Rolens, 1961), in computer companies' case reports, in a few books treating educational uses of data processing (Bushnell, 1964; Goodlad & others, 1966; Grossman & Howe, 1965; Loughary, 1966), and in periodicals created in the mid-1960's for exchanging data processing information, principally the *Automated Education Handbook*, the *Journal of Educational Data Processing*, and *Monitor*.

The five chief advantages that electronic information processing has promised for the area of student records and reports have been speed, accuracy, conciseness of data storage, ability to combine a complex variety of data to produce an easily comprehended report, and savings of expensive human labor. The main problems encountered in applying computer technology have included those of discovering which record functions can most feasibly be performed by machines, of writing computer programs best suited to these functions, of educating administrative and teaching personnel in the use of the new technology, and of arranging for the use of computers at a cost reasonable enough for schools to afford.

The range of applications of computer technology has been very broad (Freeman, 1962; Grossman & Howe, 1964; Merz, 1966; Smith, 1962). One of the most fruitful areas of application has been that of registering students in secondary schools. One investigator estimated that the manual labor needed to cross check for students' course conflicts in a school system of 17,000 students required 1,000 hours, but when performed by machine it required only 6 hours (Kaimann & Ryan, 1964). Computers quickly identify and resolve schedule conflicts, print out individual students' schedules, and produce multiple copies of class lists, counseling lists, alphabetic lists, and master schedules.

In the field of pupil attendance, automation has simplified teachers' tasks of marking absences and has made possible the rapid production of accurate daily, monthly, and yearly attendance reports, dropout statistics, and information about how pupils with different types of attendance records tend to be alike or different from each other (Woodfin, 1963).

At marking periods, reports to parents have been speeded, the recording of student grades simplified, and lists have been provided showing honor students, failing students (with the reasons for the failures identified), boys eligible for interscholastic athletics, the range of grades given by different teachers and different departments, and the like.

Objective-test analysis and the recording of results have been performed with great speed and accuracy by machines. Furthermore, schools have been able to conduct correlational analyses on a variety of student-personnel problems which, in former years, most schools could attempt only by making questionable applications of the results of studies reported in the professional literature involving school populations often different from their own.

A variety of ways that machines can enhance the efficiency of the counseling and guidance functions of secondary schools have been studied. Thompson (1961) has developed a feasible way of analyzing guidance case studies using data processing procedures. Cooley (1963) has described the multivariate and longitudinal analyses made possible by modern computers. Ellis (1963) has shown how remote recording and dictation equipment attached to a central record room enable the counseling staff to improve services to students.

The feasibility of conducting effective follow-up studies of secondary-school graduates and dropouts has been increased by electronic data machines, and the preparation of transcripts for colleges has been made more efficient. Furthermore, computers have enabled the school to perform historical analyses of each student's program and of academic marks to provide semester-by-semester information concerning his eligibility for graduation and for college entrance.

The foregoing illustrations of machine data processing represent only a portion of the applications which have been made in recent years. Scores of others are currently under development. Clearly, the advent of electronics in the processing of student information has already had a major impact on practices in many schools. The ultimate possibilities for improving record and reporting practices through the aid of computer technology have barely been tapped.

R. Murray Thomas
University of California

References

American Council on Education. *Helping Teachers Understand Children.* ACE, 1945. 468p.

American Council on Education. *Manual for the American Council on Education: Cumulative Record Folders for Schools and Colleges.* ACE, 1947. 28p.

Austen, Mary C. "Report Cards and Parents." *Reading Teach* 18:660–3; 1965.

Barbe, Walter. "Preparation of Case Study Reports." *Ed* 79:570–4; 1959.

Brewster, Royce. "The Cumulative Record." *Sch Life* 42:16–7; 1959.

Bushnell, Don D. *The Automation of School Information Systems.* Department of Audio-visual Instruction, NEA, 1964. 134p.

Chansky, Norman. "Elementary School Teachers Rate Report Cards." *J Ed Res* 56:523–8; 1963.

Chansky, Norman. "Report Cards and Teacher Personality." *J Ed Res* 57:492–4; 1964.

Chansky, Norman. "Preferred Items on Pupils' Report Cards." *Ed* 86:169–73; 1965.

Cooley, William. "A Computer-needs System for Guidance." *Harvard Ed R* 41:724–6; 1963.

Critchfield, Jack B., and Hutson, Percival W. "Validity of the Personality Record." *Col U* 40–8; 1964.

Cutler, M. A. "Does Your Report Card Format Rate an A?" *Nation's Sch* 72:56–60; 1963.

DePencier, Ida B. "Trends in Reporting Progress in Elementary Grades, 1938–1949." *El Sch J* 51:519–23; 1951.

Ellis, Gordon. "A New Approach to Student Records." *Personnel Guid J* 41:724–6; 1963.

Fischer, J. H. "Should Student Records Be Made Available to Parents?" *Am Sch Bd J* 143:14–5; 1961.

Freeman, John P. "Starting a Program of Electronic Data Processing in a School System." *Proc Assn Sch Bus Officials United States Canada* 48:95–104; 1962.

Garber, A. T. "School Health Record Keeping." *J Sch Health* 33:125–7; 1963.

Gitelman, Robert E. "Two Report Cards Are Better Than One." *NEA J* 48:33–4; 1959.

Goodlad, John I., and others. *Computers and Information Systems in Education.* Harcourt, 1966. 152p.

Grossman, Alvin, and Howe, Robert L. "Human Economy and Data Processing." *Personnel and Guid J* 43:343–7; 1964.

Grossman, Alvin, and Howe, Robert L. *Data Processing for Educators.* Educational Methods, 1965. 362p.

Halliwell, James W. "Relationship Between Theory and Practice in a Dual Reporting Program." *J Ed Res* 57:137–41; 1963.

Hammel, J. A. "Report Cards: A Rationale." *Nat El Prin* 43:50–2; 1964.

Heck, Arch O. *Administration of Pupil Personnel.* Ginn, 1929. 479p.

Irwin, Leslie W., and others. *Health in Elementary Schools.* Mosby, 1962. 440p.

Johnson, Andrew. "An Addition for the Cumulative Records." *Jun Col J* 32:167–73; 1961.

Kaiman, Richard A., and Ryan, Leo V. "Efficient School Management Demands Data Processing." *Cath Sch J* 64:80–2; 1964.

Loughary, John W. *Man-Machine Systems in Education.* Harper, 1966. 242p.

Merz, A. F. "Use of Data Processing Equipment for Educational Records." *Nat Assn Sec Sch Prin B* 46:7–16; 1966.

Millard, Cecil V., and Rothney, John W. M. *The Elementary School Child: A Book of Cases.* Holt, 1957. 660p.

National Association of Secondary School Principals. "NASSP Offers Major Revision of Secondary School Record." *Nat Assn Sec Sch Prin B* 48:114–6; 1964.

National Education Association, Department of Superintendence. *Report of the Committee on Uniform Records and Reports.* U.S. Bureau of Education Bulletin No. 3. GPO, 1912. 46p.

North Central Association. "Policies and Criteria." *North Cen Assn Q* 41:147–62; 1966.

Oakford, R. V., and others. *Stanford School Scheduling System: School Manual.* School of Education, Stanford U, 1966. 91p.

Polansky, Frances M., and Barnett, Charles D. "Academic and Training Report Cards for the Mentally Retarded: An Institutional Approach." *Train Sch B* 61:173–7; 1965.

Rolens, Robert E. *Data Processing Handbook.* Ventura (California) High School District, 1961. 98p.

Rothney, John W. M. *The High School Student: A Book of Cases.* Holt, 1953. 271p.

Rothney, John W. M. *Evaluating and Reporting Pupil Progress.* NEA, 1955. 33p.

Smith, James T. "Personnel Records, Pupil and Staff and Electronic Data Processing." *Proc Assn Sch Bus Officials United States Canada* 48:105–11; 1962.

Tennyson, W. W. "Student Personnel Records: A Vital Tool but a Concern of the Public." *Personnel Guid J* 42:888–93; 1964.

Thomas, R. Murray. *Judging Student Progress.* McKay, 1960. 518p.

Thomas, R. Murray. "Grouping Practices in California

High Schools." Graduate School of Education, U California, Santa Barbara, 1966. 10p.

Thompson, Jack M. "The Analysis of Guidance Case Studies Using Data Processing Procedures." *California J Ed Res* 12:195–9; 1961.

Thorndike, Robert L., and Hagen, Elizabeth. *Measurement and Evaluation in Psychology and Education.* Wiley, 1961. 602p.

Wilson, Charles C. *School Health Services.* NEA, 1953. 486p.

Woodfin, Charles A. "Planning and Implementing New Data Processing Installations." *Proc Assn Sch Bus Officials United States Canada* 49:248–9; 1963.

Yeager, William A. *Administration and the Pupil.* Harper, 1949. 483p.

Zolcznski, Stephen. "Development of a Student Mental Health Record." *J Sch Health* 32:210–4; 1962.

REHABILITATION

Rehabilitation is a philosophy, a set of practices or services, and an area of research activity. In its most literal definition "rehabilitation" seeks to restore as full an existence as possible to individuals who have experienced ability loss as a consequence of disease, accident, or injury. It includes in its basic goals habilitation, or establishment of a fuller existence, for those individuals who, because of congenital or early ability deficiencies, have not known a normally productive life—e.g., the blind, the deaf, and the cerebral-palsied.

As a philosophy, present-day rehabilitation stands for such goals as human dignity, individual independence, social acceptance, economic contribution to society, and vocational and social opportunities equal to those of the rest of the population. As a set of practices and services, rehabilitation draws upon such professions as medicine, psychology, sociology, and social work. It also depends heavily for support and facilities on the community and on interested lay groups, such as organized labor. Research activity in rehabilitation is greatest in medicine, psychology, and sociology.

In early human societies an impaired person was viewed with fear and was avoided. If he could not be purged, charmed, or effectively prayed for, he was ostracized, set apart, or disposed of in some manner. Society accepted no real responsibility for those who experienced disabling conditions until the nineteenth century, when some attention was given to "cripples" and when mentally deviate individuals were viewed by some as being mentally ill. Impaired persons were viewed with pity and were given custodial "treatment." Only in the present century have organized efforts been effectively brought to bear on the problems of integrating physically, mentally, and emotionally disabled persons into societies as normal social and economic participants. As Allen (1958) indicated in his discussion of the concept and practices of rehabilitation, these developments have probably resulted from such forces as Christianity, democracy, the demands of population growth, and the need to rehabilitate veterans from the two world wars. Rehabilitation has grown rapidly in its short modern history, and the definition of the term has been broadened considerably. Obermann (1965), in a recent history, gave special attention to the development and rapid growth of the National Rehabilitation Association, the largest professional association of individuals interested in rehabilitation, an organization that cuts across academic disciplines and professions. The growth of this organization and the broadening of its interests over time reflect the growth of rehabilitation itself.

DEFINITIONS. A comprehension of both the diversity and the breadth of the rehabilitation concept in 1967 can be gained from a sampling of definitions of the term "rehabilitation." Such a set of definitions may provide a context for the viewing of the current research and training activity in rehabilitation.

The National Council on Rehabilitation (1944) defined "rehabilitation" as the "restoration of the handicapped to the fullest physical, mental, social, vocational, and economic usefulness of which they are capable." Hamilton (1950) interprets the term "rehabilitation" as a "realization by the disabled and handicapped individual of a life most useful socially and satisfying personally." He also sees rehabilitation as a creative process that aims at defining, developing, and utilizing an individual's assets. It seeks to restore ability to compete, to be independent, and to be self-determining. Kessler (1953) views rehabilitation as "an organized and systematic method by which the physical, mental, and vocational powers of an individual are improved to the point where he can compete with equal opportunity with the so-called nonhandicapped." White and others (1958) stress that rehabilitation should not be confined to economic and vocational goals but should strive also to maintain the individual's personal dignity and should aim at the expansion of capacity for living. Allen (1958) states that a proper definition of rehabilitation stresses making an individual aware of his potential and then providing a means for attaining that potential. Lofquist (1959) states that in defining rehabilitation we are essentially saying that we must help the individual to reintegrate with his society with optimum success. Frank (1959) stresses the planning of experiences that will build self-confidence, courage, and appropriate coping techniques, and helping an individual to develop a self-image as one who can rather than one who cannot. Rehabilitation has been viewed in the social-psychological sense (James, 1960) as a transformation from role deviance to role restoration. McGowan (1960) describes the process of vocational rehabilitation as one in which client-counselor interaction facilitates "improvement of client self-understanding and effective utilization of his positive vocational assets." Kliemke (1960), describing provisions of German law to an international meeting on rehabilitation, states that an individual's rehabilitation "shall not merely be restricted to his physical efficiency and his economic potential; it must extend to cover his value, temporal and supertemporal, as an entire personality within the active community of experience and creativeness of all men." A quite different approach is taken by Lofquist and others (1964) in a discussion of disability and work, where disability is defined literally as ability loss in a psychometric sense. Rehabilitation is viewed by this group as treatment and training which continues until the level and pattern of abilities and needs, in an individual who has experienced a disabling condition, do not change significantly. Obermann (1965) sees rehabilitation as the activity required to help an individual move from inadequacy to adequacy. Sussman (1965), recognizing the breadth of rehabilitation services, recalls Mayo's definition (1959), which emphasizes bringing to bear all pertinent knowledge and skills available on problems of illness and disablement and which stresses that rehabilitation belongs to many professions and to the entire community.

The present writer, in setting the stage for a research conference on rehabilitation (Lofquist, 1960), summed up the definitional question as follows:

> Whatever definition of rehabilitation is favored by a particular person or group, perhaps all would agree that: (a) rehabilitation is concerned with practical problems in the lives of individuals; (b) it is concerned with past, present, and future individual behavior and with assisting an individual to find an optimal balance of these which will permit living as well as possible within the handicaps imposed by disability and within the potential development described by the individual's particular balance sheet of plus and minus ability, aptitude, interest, and personality factors; and (c) it involves active interprofessional participation in planning with and for the individual. Most workers would also agree that rehabilitation could profit from more attention to the measurement of ways of changing the attitudes of the public and employers (and of professional workers and rehabilitation clients) toward the handicapped as a total group and toward specific disability classes.

NEED. Estimating the number of individuals who are disabled and who could profit from rehabilitation services poses many problems. Estimates vary with the focus of the survey and with methods used. It is not feasible to give medical examinations to survey samples and to extrapolate to the population. Even if this were done the presence of medically defined conditions cannot be equated to the existence of disability. When interviews or mail surveys are used one finds reluctance, varying with the disability condition, to disclose the presence of a personal or family member's disability condition. In determining need for rehabilitation, as indicated by the numbers of disabled persons, we are left, then, with only rough estimates.

In 1935–36 the U.S. Public Health Service (1938), sampling 83 representative cities by house-to-house canvass, estimated that 11.7 out of each 1,000 persons were unable to work, go to school, keep house, or do usual activities because of disease, accident, or physical or mental impairment. If one applies this finding to the nearest census year, 1940, approximately 1.6 million persons were affected. This would not have included the institutionalized population. In 1949 and 1950 the U.S. Bureau of the Census (Woolsey, 1952) estimated that 1.7 percent of the civilian, noninstitutionalized population between ages 14 and 64 had disabling conditions or illnesses which had incapacitated them for more than a year. Applied to the nearest census year, 1950, this would yield approximately 2.5 million disabled persons. In a carefully controlled study in the state of Minnesota (England & Lofquist, 1958), 10 percent of a statewide sample indicated they could not work or participate normally because of a disability. It is obvious that accurate and reliable figures are difficult to find. At the present time, rehabilitation workers appear to agree that there are probably about 3 million physically or emotionally disabled persons in the United States who could profit from traditional rehabilitation procedures. This estimate would, of course, be higher if one adds those who could profit from new approaches in rehabilitation that include working with such additional large client groups as the impoverished, the culturally disadvantaged, and the criminal offender.

PROGRAMS. Rehabilitation in this century is an active international enterprise. While it is by no means limited to activity in the United States, the sheer size of the program, in terms of both numbers served and funds expended, and the diversity of approaches dictate a primary focus on the description of rehabilitation in the United States.

In the United States, rehabilitation direct-service, training, and research activities are most strongly supported by the Vocational Rehabilitation Administration, the Veterans Administration, and the Public Health Service. The federal-state program administered by the Vocational Rehabilitation Administration is the largest service program for noninstitutionalized disabled persons. It embraces general agencies in the 50 states, the District of Columbia, Guam, Puerto Rico, and the Virgin Islands and separate agencies for the blind in 36 states, totaling 90 agencies. These agencies serve the handicapped population through approximately 800 local offices and support, in part, many community rehabilitation facilities. Information indicating the substantial growth of public rehabilitation services is given in two recent articles (Office of Vocational Rehabilitation, 1960; Vocational Rehabilitation Administration, 1964a). These articles describe the growth in the first 44 years of the federal-state rehabilitation program. For example, in 1921, the first year of operation of the program, 523 rehabilitations to gainful employment and a satisfying life were recorded. In 1961 the number had grown to 92,501. By 1963 over 110,000 disabled persons were reported as rehabilitated. The Vocational Rehabilitation Administration (1967) reported recently that, in the fiscal year ended June 30, 1966, 154,000 disabled persons were rehabilitated, a 14-percent increase over 1965. For 1967 the estimated, anticipated number of rehabilitations is 200,000.

In this same report by the Vocational Rehabilitation Administration progress in implementing a series of new grant programs, authorized in the 1965 amendments to the Vocational Rehabilitation Act, is indicated as follows: (1) 70 new grants, totaling $3,800,000 were made to voluntary and public agencies to facilitate expansion of services; (2) 28 grants, totaling $670,000 were made to state agencies to develop new ideas and services; (3) 36 grants were made, totaling $3,000,000, to support two-year programs of statewide planning in rehabilitation; (4) 35 new grants were made, totaling $254,492 to help support the construction of rehabilitation facilities and workshops; (5) 49 new grants, totaling $1,486,079 were made for state planning of rehabilitation workshops and facilities; and (6) 69 new grants, totaling $1,672,090, were made for improvement of workshops and facilities. In addition, the following organizations were set up to improve and coordinate rehabilitation activities: the National Citizens Advisory Committee on Vocational Rehabilitation, the National Policy and Performance Council, the National Commission on Architectural Barriers, and the National Advisory Council on Correctional Manpower and Training.

In order to make rehabilitation services possible and in order to raise the quality of services, the Vocational Rehabilitation Administration has supported education and training programs in universities and colleges throughout the country. Training has been supported in such areas as physical medicine, vocational rehabilitation counseling, social work, speech therapy, psychology, and occupational therapy. The graduates of these programs augment the personnel pool available to staff rehabilitation teams in the many operating agencies and centers. Some idea of the growth and contribution of these education programs can be seen from the experience in vocational rehabilitation counseling. The support program in rehabilitation counseling started in 1955 with four universities producing 12 graduates per year. In 1964 (Vocational Rehabilitation Administration, 1964b), this kind of training was supported in programs at 37 universities and colleges, and 1,750 graduates were reported to have completed their graduate training to the masters' degree level. About 60 percent of them were employed by agencies providing services to disabled individuals. In 1967 there were 63 such graduate training programs in universities and colleges.

A listing of some of the types of rehabilitation facilities in operation may provide some feeling for the variety of settings in which rehabilitation professionals work. An incomplete list would include state rehabilitation agency district office, state services for the blind, rehabilitation center, rehabilitation workshop, sheltered workshop, center for mentally retarded, state or federal hospital, jail or prison, institute for crippled and disabled, institute of physical medicine and rehabilitation, and regional center or workshop.

The personnel to be found in some combination on a rehabilitation team or staff might include specialists such as the following: physician, psychiatrist, physiatrist, clinical psychologist, counseling psychologist, rehabilitation counselor, social worker, psychiatric social worker, audiologist, speech therapist, physical therapist, occupational therapist, nurse, educational therapist, placement specialist, work evaluator, prosthetic-appliance specialist, prevocational training specialist, and manual arts therapist. This list does not include all of the individuals who are involved in rehabilitating people. Rehabilitation is broad, its services are diverse, it utilizes many specialized knowledges and skills, and it is growing rapidly.

RESEARCH. Obviously, in an area as broad as rehabilitation, one will find activity in the conceptualization of problems and in the carrying out of research reported for a large number of topics in a large number of professional journals and research monographs. Limiting a sampling of this literature to one year and to topics related mainly to work and to the psychological impacts of disability, one finds, in a by no means comprehensive sample, such topics as the following: the workshop as a clinical rehabilitation tool (Gellman & Friedman, 1965); predicting the success of schizophrenics in industrial therapy (Ritchey, 1965); the psychological impact of coronary-artery disease (Miller, 1965); rehabilitation with psychiatric clients (Hartlage, 1965); the employability of blind dictaphone operators (Abels & Cantoni, 1965); the measurement of needs of physically disabled college students (Stone, 1965); an inferential approach to occupational reinforcement (Weiss and others, 1965); and perceptions of the counselor role among a variety of rehabilitation counselor supervisors (Strong & Shepard, 1965).

Psychologists have been very active in research and rehabilitation. The report of the 1958 Princeton conference on psychology and rehabilitation (Wright, 1959) discusses the contribution psychology can make to rehabilitation research and lists a number of research areas. The Clark University conference (Frank, 1959) on the relationship between rehabilitation and psychology deals with conceptualization of the rehabilitation process and with research in rehabilitation. The Miami conference on psychological research and rehabilitation (Lofquist, 1960) illustrated how psychologists who were eminent in certain subareas (e.g., social, differential, and learning) approached rehabilitation research problems within their own conceptual-psychological frames of reference. Both the producers and the consumers (i.e., service personnel) of research appear to be most interested in research findings in such areas as client motivation, adjustment to work, vocational evaluation, social and psychological impacts of disability, the criterion problem with regard to evaluating techniques and outcomes of training and placement, and staff evaluation and turnover.

In the past seven years the Vocational Rehabilitation Administration has established a number of regional research institutes at selected universities.

Their general purposes include activity in core research areas, communication of research results to rehabilitation agencies and workers, consultation on agency research problems, and improved communication among researchers in the various institutes and on related research projects. The activities of these institutes have been described by Dawis and others (1964). The Vocational Rehabilitation Administration (1964a) described the core research areas of the first established university Regional Research Institutes as follows: Minnesota, methods of improving the work adjustment of disabled persons; Wisconsin, professional role of the rehabilitation counselor; Florida, motivational and personality factors in rehabilitation; Utah, interpersonal relations in rural rehabilitation; and Northeastern, motivation and dependency. The research activities of these universities are reported in a series of research monographs (e.g., Betz & others, 1966; Barry & Malinovsky, 1965; Goldin, 1965; Rushlau & Jorgensen, 1966). In the last year new institutes have been established so that one now exists in each of the nine regions of the Vocational Rehabilitation Administration. The Institute for Region VI that was centered at the University of Minnesota is now at the University of Missouri. The Minnesota project of research in work adjustment continues but not in the institute context.

To illustrate the level and scope of rehabilitation research being conducted by psychologists, the following illustrations are presented: Eber (1966) is utilizing advanced computer technology to predict rehabilitation-service outcomes; Muthard, at the University of Iowa, is completing a nationwide study of counselor roles and functions under the joint sponsorship of the Vocational Rehabilitation Administration and the American Rehabilitation Counseling Association; Truax (1966) won the annual research award of the American Rehabilitation Counseling Association in 1967 for his research on the process and outcome of counseling and psychotherapy; and the programmatic research in work adjustment (Betz & others, 1966) won the annual research award, in 1967, of the American Personnel and Guidance Association.

There is, obviously, a good deal of research activity. The reader will find it reported in many different journals. Hopefully, the references at the end of this article will provide the leads for more complete exploration.

In an article of this length it is not possible to cover the large amount of research carried out in medicine and other areas. The focus has been on psychology, because the writer is a psychologist. This brief overview of rehabilitation and its research activity cannot be concluded without at least brief mention of the extensive international activity in rehabilitation.

OTHER COUNTRIES. Allen (1958), discussing rehabilitation and the world community, points out that many countries have well-developed rehabilitation programs. Some were pioneers, and some have found greater social and political acceptance for programs than we have. The first institution entirely devoted to the crippled was established in Switzerland in 1780; the first known school for the blind was developed in France in 1786; and well-developed programs in the broad phases of rehabilitation exist in such countries as England, Germany, Canada, and the Scandinavian countries. International cooperation and communication have been facilitated by such organizations as the World Health Organization, the international labor organizations, and the International Society for the Welfare of Cripples. Some appreciation of international activity can be gained from articles such as those by Rusk (1956) and Wilson (1956).

Lloyd H. Lofquist
University of Minnesota

References

Abels, H. L., and Cantoni, L. J. "Employability of Blind Dictaphone Operators." *New Outlook Blind* 59:33–4; 1965.

Allen, W. S. *Rehabilitation: A Community Challenge.* Wiley, 1958.

Barry, J. R., and Malinovsky, M. R. Rehabilitation Research Monograph Series. U Florida, 1965.

Betz, Ellen, and others. *Minnesota Studies in Vocational Rehabilitation.* U Minnesota, 1966.

Dawis, R. V., and others. "Research Frontier: Regional Rehabilitation Research Institutes." *J Counseling Psychol* 11:185–9; 1964.

Eber, H. W. "Multivariate Analysis of a Vocational Rehabilitation System." In *Multivariate Behavioral Research Monograph.* Society for Multivariate Experimental Psychology, Incorporated, Texas Christian U Press, 1966.

England, G. W., and Lofquist, Lloyd H. *Minnesota Studies in Vocational Rehabilitation.* U Minnesota, 1958.

Frank, L. K. "Image of Self." In *The Relationship Between Rehabilitation and Psychology.* HEW, Office of Vocational Rehabilitation, 1959.

Gellman, W., and Friedman, S. B. "The Workshop as a Clinical Rehabilitation Tool." *Rehabilitation Literature* 26:34–8; 1965.

Goldin, G. J. *Northeastern Studies in Vocational Rehabilitation.* Northeastern U, 1965.

Hamilton, K. W. *Counseling the Handicapped in the Rehabilitation Process.* Ronald, 1950.

Hartlage, L. C. "Rehabilitation Counseling with Psychiatric Clients." *Rehabilitation Counseling B* 9:14–8; 1965.

James, F. *The Oregon Study of Rehabilitation of Mental Hospital Patients,* 2 vols. Oregon State Hospital, 1960.

Kessler, H. H. *Rehabilitation of the Physically Handicapped.* Columbia U Press, 1953.

Kliemke, E. "Rehabilitation and World Peace." In Taylor, E. J. (Ed.) *Proceedings of the 8th World Congress of the International Society for the Wel-*

fare of Cripples. International Society for the Rehabilitation of Disabled, 1960.
Lofquist, Lloyd H. "An Operational Definition of Rehabilitation Counseling." *J Rehabilitation* 25:7–9; 1959.
Lofquist, Lloyd H. (Ed.) *Psychological Research and Rehabilitation.* APA, 1960.
Lofquist, Lloyd H., and others. "Disability and Work." In *Minnesota Studies in Vocational Rehabilitation.* U Minnesota, 1964.
Mayo, L. *The Importance of Community Planning in the Development of Rehabilitation.* Conference on Rehabilitation Centers and Facilities, 1959.
McGowan, J. F. (Ed.) *An Introduction to the Vocational Rehabilitation Process.* HEW, Office of Vocational Rehabilitation, GPO, 1960.
Miller, C. K. "The Psychological Impact of Coronary Artery Disease." *Newsletter Res Psychol* 7:21–2; 1965.
National Council on Rehabilitation. *Symposium on the Process of Rehabilitation.* The Council, 1944.
Obermann, C. E. *A History of Vocational Rehabilitation in America.* Denson, 1965.
Office of Vocational Rehabilitation. "A Tide in the Affairs of Men." *Rehabilitation Rec* 1:3–12; 1960.
Ritchey, R. E. "Predicting Success of Schizophrenics in Industrial Therapy." *J Counseling Psychol* 12:68–73; 1965.
Rushlau, P. J., and Jorgensen, G. Q. *Utah Studies in Vocational Rehabilitation.* Utah, 1966.
Rusk, H. A. "Rehabilitation: An International Problem." *Archives Phys Med Rehabilitation* 37:136; 1956.
Stone, J. B. "The Edwards Personal Preference Schedule and Physically Disabled College Students." *Rehabilitation Counseling B* 9:11–3; 1965.
Strong, D. J., and Shepard, A. I. "Perceptions of Counselor Role Among a Variety of Rehabilitation Counselor Supervisors." *J Counseling Psychol* 12:141–7; 1965.
Sussman, M. B. (Ed.) *Sociology and Rehabilitation.* American Sociological Association, 1965.
Truax, Charles B. *Counseling and Psychotherapy: Process and Outcome.* U Arkansas, 1966.
U.S. Public Health Service. Sickness and Medical Care Series. Bibliography Series No. 5. GPO, 1938.
Vocational Rehabilitation Administration. "What State Programs Are Doing." *Rehabilitation Rec* 5:3–7; 1964(a).
Vocational Rehabilitation Administration. "V.R.A. Support of Professional Training." *Rehabilitation Rec* 5:28–32; 1964(b).
Vocational Rehabilitation Administration. *New Grant Programs in Vocational Rehabilitation.* GPO, 1967.
Weiss, D. J., and others. *Minnesota Studies in Vocational Rehabilitation.* U Minnesota, 1965.
White, P. D., and others. *Rehabilitation of the Cardiovascular Patient.* McGraw-Hill, 1958.
Wilson, D. V. "International Cooperation for the Handicapped." International Society for the Welfare of Cripples, 1956. Reprinted from *International Nursing Review.*
Woolsey, T. D. "Estimates of Disabling Illness Prevalence in the U.S." *Public Health Monograph* No. 4. GPO, 1952.
Wright, Beatrice A. (Ed.) *Psychology and Rehabilitation.* APA, 1959.

RELIGION AND EDUCATION

HISTORICAL PERSPECTIVE. The Ancient World. Church-state relations have ancient origins. Priest-king conflicts were evident in the Sumerian civilization. Hammurabi received his code of laws from the god Shamash (Wells, 1927). Moses received the Decalogue from God, and the Hebrews turned from the theocratic rule of the Judges to demand a king. Toynbee (1946, Vol. 2, p. 76–113) reports a church and a state in each of the 21 civilizations recorded in man's history and claims that the church is not the cancer which destroys the civilization but the chrysalis which provides continuity between the death of one civilization and the birth of the next. Indeed, he speculates that if the churches do not destroy themselves by schisms, human society may evolve toward a unified race which will find salvation in religious unity.

European Backgrounds. Exemplifying Toynbee's chrysalis theory, the early Christian church provided continuity between the dying Roman state and the birth of Western civilization, carrying forward the Judeo-Christian tradition (Kerwin, 1960). It should be noted further that the persistence of the Jews in maintaining their ethnic and religious identity has likewise contributed to this continuity.

The Renaissance and the Reformation cast direct shadows forward into the church-state milieu of the mid-twentieth century in America which so significantly enmeshes the educational system of the United States.

When Luther rebelled against the practices of the church (1517) he unwittingly crystalized the growing tension between the German princes of state and the Roman Catholic Church. This tension came to a head a century later in the Thirty Years' War, 1618–1648, settled by the Peace of Augsburg on the principle that the ruler determines the religion—*cuius regio eius religio* (Toynbee, 1946, Vol. 1, p. 482). This was the first break on the Continent in the theocratic position of the medieval church.

John Calvin, holding the conviction that church and state have separate functions but convinced of the supremacy of the church in spiritual matters (*Institutes* IV, 20, in McNeill, 1960), established a short-lived theocracy at Geneva (Hayes & others, 1950). His influence extended to England and was responsible for theocratic governments in Scotland and in Puritan New England (Miller, 1958). Indeed, Calvin's educational theories carried over to Massachusetts colonial schools, which were under the influence of the established Congregational Church (Cubberley, 1920). Churchill (1956), Hayes and others (1950), and Montgomery (1887) record how

Henry VIII, king of England from 1509 to 1547, broke with the pope and set the stage for the establishment of the Church of England under Elizabeth I. The excesses of the Church of England and the religious persecutions of the sixteenth and seventeenth centuries drove the Puritans and Separatists to New England.

France and Holland experienced the bitterness of the religious persecution of the Huguenots and the Massacre of St. Bartholomew's Day, assuaged by the Edict of Nantes; and Spain and the Low Countries were subjected to the Inquisition (Hayes & others, 1950).

These turmoils within the church and the spread of religious persecution, coinciding with the Renaissance, combined to fracture the West into religious pluralism and to create waves of anticlericalism on the Continent and, in notable instances, brought about the ascendancy of the state over the church.

Finally, there arose a school of thinkers who were secularists, deists, and the founders of the Enlightenment (Durant, 1927). The leaders of this movement included Voltaire, Rousseau, Hobbes, and Locke, who had profound influence on Jefferson and other founders of the American constitutional government (Stokes & Pfeffer, 1964; Padover, 1956).

Colonial Influence. The Puritan colonists in Massachusetts, having established a Congregational theocracy, were no more tolerant of dissenters than was the Church of England from which they fled. The Salem witch hunts, with the resulting persecutions and executions, were the epitome of religious intolerance in the colonial period (Beard & Beard, 1924; Miller, 1958). The banishment of Anne Hutchinson and Roger Williams was characteristic of the times. But as Stokes and Pfeffer (1964) note, the free spirit of Roger Williams reacted with his significant treatises on church and state, the "Bloudy Tenent of Persecution for Cause of Conscience" and the "ship letter." He founded Rhode Island as the first colony to grant religious freedom and to provide for the separation of church and state.

Two proprietary colonies, Pennsylvania and Maryland, though founded as havens for Quakers and Catholics, respectively, extended religious freedom to all Christian sects. Virginia "established" the Church of England, but, unlike the theocracy of Massachusetts, it took the form of a church dominated by a state.

It was in this atmosphere that Jefferson authored the Virginia Statute of Religious Freedom in 1786, which, according to his biographers (Arrowood, 1930; Padover, 1956; Cousins, 1958), he considered one of his major contributions. This statute was the immediate forerunner of the first amendment to the consitution, adopted in 1791.

The First Amendment. Like the confluence of several up-country streams forming a great river, numerous forces and movements converged in late-eighteenth-century America to give birth to the principles of religious freedom and separation of church and state. These streams were the ancient historical patterns of church and state; the nurture of the Judeo-Christian ethic by the medieval Christian church; the Reformation; the reaction against religious persecutions on the Continent and in colonial America; examples of separation set by Rhode Island, Pennsylvania, and Maryland; the Renaissance, out of which grew the Enlightenment; and the emergence of theories of government by the people resulting from the American Revolution.

The first amendment declares "Congress shall make no law respecting an establishment of religion, or prohibiting the free exercise thereof; or abridging freedom of speech, or of the press; or the right of the people peaceably to assemble, and to petition the Government for the redress of grievances."

Theories of Church and State Relationships. Four quite distinct theories have been distilled from history. Two of these theories, theocracy and the divine right of kings, have little direct bearing on the matter of religion in the schools of the United States in mid-twentieth century. A third theory, the Marxist conception of a godless dictatorship of the proletariat, though existent in significant parts of the world, does not contain any elements of a constructive resolution of the business of teaching America's youth. A fourth theory, "two there are" (*duo sunt*), provides the arena where constructive discussion and experimentation are now probing for solutions. Kerwin (1960) identifies the theory, stemming from Pope Gelasius, as the stance of the Roman Catholics, and Love (1965) interprets the Jesuit John Courtney Murray as leading a liberal group of Catholic scholars away from an extreme theocratic shading of the principle. Further, the theory has good Protestant heritage, for Calvin (*Institutes* IV, 20, in McNeill, 1960) found church and state not antithetical, and Luther took the same position in his correspondence with the German princes (Tappert, 1955, pp. 318–349; Gettell, 1924). Within this theory that the two have roles which complement each other, we shall see experimentation with mutually complementary programs and consider enlightened discussion of what can and should be done in the schools and in the churches.

The Emergence of the Public School. The forces leading to the adoption of the first amendment included no concept of a vast system of universal public education. New England colonial schools were under church control, and their purpose rested in the Calvinist theory that children should be taught to read the Scriptures. The Massachusetts theocracy enacted laws requiring parents to educate their children for this end in 1642. Then they brought to bear the power of government as a presumed agent of the church to provide public money so that children of the poor could be educated in order to fulfill their religious obligations (Drake, 1955; Cubberley, 1920). Thus began the precedent for public support of education. The history of the colonial schools affords no rebuttal to McCluskey's claim (1959) that they were church schools and that public funds were used to support them.

Historians tell us (Drake, 1955; Cubberley, 1920) that during the nineteenth century the public school system developed as a major institution of the United

States. Horace Mann in Massachusetts, Henry Barnard in Connecticut, and William T. Harris in the Middle West, were leaders in the movement which expanded the schools as instruments of the state divorced from church control. The first half of the century saw church control severed in Massachusetts, Virginia, and Maryland; the rise and fall of a Presbyterian system of parochial schools; and the rise of state systems in Pennsylvania, North Carolina, Illinois, Indiana, Ohio, and the pre-Civil War South.

Theory of Education for Civic Competence. Man's struggle for religious freedom in the sixteenth, seventeenth, and eighteenth centuries was paralleled by a struggle for political and civil freedom. This struggle was the motivating force of the American Revolution, and as the colonies emerged with a government resting on the will of the people a new reason for education—civic competence—was born.

Submerging the religious aims of education, the economic and political forces which supported the growth of public education were the industrial revolution, with its large numbers of immigrants requiring schooling in civic principles, the ascendancy of Jacksonian theories of mass education over the Jeffersonian theory of an educated elite, and the emergence of a theory that democracy requires an educated citizenry.

It was primarily the last idea evolving into the theory that the state has police power to protect itself from mass ignorance which gave judicial support to the extension of education for reasons of national security. "Without intelligence, properly cultivated and directed, good government would be almost impossible, especially where the particular form of state policy depends so largely on the will of the people" (*Collie* . . . , 1907). This principle was used to justify taxation for schools regardless of immediate benefit to the taxpayer (*Louisville* . . . , 1909; *King* . . . , 1889), and to justify encroachment by attendance laws on the parent's right to control his child (*Bailey* . . . , 1901).

Effect of the Principle of State Sovereignty. Since education was now resting on a political theory one must understand that the concept of the federal government was one of limited powers delegated by the sovereign states. Since education was not thus delegated, and since the limitations of the first amendment were placed upon Congress and not the states, the U.S. Supreme Court, theoretically, would not have jurisdiction over matters pertaining to religion in the state schools. This limitation has been overcome by the fourteenth amendment, adopted in 1868, which extended the protection of the first amendment to all who by this action had acquired citizenship in the United States (*Meyer* . . . , 1923; *Abington* . . . , 1963). A classic case, limiting the power of the state, granted an Oregon parent the right to send his child to a church school contrary to a statute requiring attendance at public school (*Pierce* . . . , 1925). It should be noted that the several states, have in their respective constitutions, established school systems and have prevented public support of church schools (Beach & Well, 1958, p. 152).

LAW: THE SERVANT, NOT THE MASTER. Since much of the current discussion about religion and the schools involves legal action, it is well to note the flexibility of the law to serve man's needs.

After noting several ends of law, and recognizing the existence of a form of supreme law originating in divinely ordained rules, Roscoe Pound (1922, p. 60) suggested that there was emerging a concept of law as affording an opportunity for the realization of the satisfaction of a maximum of human wants. The timing of this suggestion was significant in the light of subsequent social legislation of the decade of the 1930's and the expansion of judicial interpretation by the post-war Supreme Court.

Within this flexibility of the law the theory of education for national security is being probed for ways of providing some government assistance to church schools which, with programs and facilities not devoted to the teaching of religion, are presumed to contribute to national welfare (Higher Education Act, 1963).

Much testing has been applied to the interpretation of the "establishment clause" (Antieau & others, 1964; Kempner, 1958; *Abington* . . . , 1963).

Further, to the expanding purposes of education—spiritual growth and civic competence—there has now been added, by statute and judicial interpretation, the purpose of advancing the welfare of the child. This theory, which did not exist under the common law or under the theory of the police power of the state, has opened new areas for providing government assistance to parents who send their children to church schools.

The law in the United States in mid-twentieth century has a growing edge.

PHILOSOPHICAL CONSIDERATIONS. To understand fully the current discussion over religion and education one must inquire into the epistemological, ontological, and metaphysical positions of churchmen and twentieth-century educational philosophers.

The advocates of a religious dimension in education hold that there are absolutes which transcend man's experience; that truth and ultimate values are of divine origin; that knowledge is acquired not alone by sensory perception but through the functioning of the divinely endowed human intellect and through divine revelation; and that man's chief end is spiritual and eternal (Pius XI, 1929; Regis, 1945; McNeill, 1960; Burleigh, 1953).

The conflicting position advanced by the humanists and empiricists holds that there are no fixed absolutes; that values stem from human experience; that truth consists only of what can be demonstrated by empirical data; and that man's chief educational end is to acquire competence and knowledge which are useful, make him a good citizen, and are functional in his contemporary environment (Dewey, 1909, 1934; Kilpatrick, 1951; Geiger, 1955).

The aims of education set forth by the Educational Policies Commission (National Education Association, 1938) as a program of social action based on transitory value systems are not acceptable to McCluskey (1959) or to Kerwin (1960). The empiricist's position is at odds with the Thomist philosophy (Maritain, 1955), and Protestant voices are raised against it (Whittemore, 1960; Bennett, 1958, p. 238).

In large measure these basic philosophical differences constitute the crux of the conflict over religion and education, the outcome of which rests upon the influence of the current ecumenical movement and the voices of moderation among churchmen and educators.

MID-TWENTIETH-CENTURY PRACTICES.

There can be little denial of the charge that nineteenth-century America was dominated by Protestant influence. The principle of the Treaty of Augsburg that the ruler determines the religion is not applicable to the United States, where the ruler is vox populi and the constitutional amendments protect minorities. Nonetheless, it is evident that Protestant majorities in local communities demonstrated this dominance in religious practices in their local public schools (Gilbert, 1965).

Opening exercises with Bible reading, hymns, and prayer were common practice. Baccalaureate sermons were presented in the schools by Protestant clergy. Christmas and Easter were celebrated with Christian pageantry, music, and art. Textbooks and curricula generally reflected Protestant interpretations of history.

Tensions and Reaction. These practices have created tension in school and community. The American Association of School Administrators (1964) has acknowledged the tension and offered suggestions.

As minority groups have gained numerical strength, they have become more vocal. Jews have protested Christmas and Easter exercises, the failure of the schools to recognize the significance of Jewish holy days, and the intrusion on their Sabbath by weekend school activities. They have also protested the use of Christian hymns and have been quick to notice evidences of anti-Semitic bias on the part of teachers, textbooks, or curriculum. Roman Catholics have objected to the King James translation in Bible reading and to the Protestant version of the Lord's Prayer. They have been unhappy about sex instruction from a non-Catholic viewpoint by secular teachers. In Catholic-dominated communities Protestants have been equally disturbed about displays of religious figures and the wearing of religious garb by teachers.

In addition to tensions between Protestants, Catholics, and Jews, Jehovah's Witnesses have protested, on religious grounds, required flag salutes and oaths of allegiance; Christian Scientists have been disturbed about health instruction and administrative regulations with respect to the treatment of illness and injury contrary to their religious beliefs. Religious zealots have charged that the schools are godless, and the schools have been criticized for any and all semblances of religion by atheists and agnostics.

Distributive Justice. Approximately one-fourth of the country's population is committed to a conscientious Roman Catholic conviction that children must be educated by the church. Reports indicate that almost 12 percent of the total elementary- and secondary-school enrollment of the nation is in Catholic schools supported by fees paid by parents and the contributed services of religious orders (*World Almanac*, 1966, pp. 157, 757). With the increasing cost and complexity of education, it is little wonder that pressure has been exerted for public assistance under the theory of "distributive justice." The cry of double taxation is misleading, since it is the religious conviction, not the government, which levies for the cost of parochial schools. There is no question that the tax burden for public schools would be increased were it not for the education provided in nonpublic schools, but subsidy of religion is not the answer.

The plea for government assistance has taken several forms: (1) rationalization that the "establishment clause" does not preclude the distribution of public money equally among all religious groups (Antieau & others, 1964), a view appearing not to be acceptable to the courts; (2) argument that substantial parts of parochial school education are of a civic nature, serving the needs of the state, and in justice should be reimbursed; and (3) exploitation of the child-benefit theory to provide services for the child which do not directly contribute to his religious instruction but which relieve the parent's financial burden (LaNoue, 1965).

CURRENT TRENDS. Although the period following World War II has been one of ferment and strife there has been clearer definition of principles, the broad spectrum of a pluralistic society has been brought into better focus, and constructive answers have been sought. Action has taken place in the courts, in legislative halls, and in experimentation with new programs and formulas; and with this a new spirit of constructive conversation has appeared among some religious leaders and educators seeking mutually satisfactory solutions.

Action in the Courts. Prior to World War II a few landmark decisions had been rendered.

In 1905 the requirement of vaccination for school attendance was upheld on the theory that religious conviction does not supersede well-recognized requirements for public safety (Jacobson . . . , 1905).

It was held that public funds designated for the education of Indians could be paid to a Catholic mission chosen by the student, thus introducing the idea that funds intended for student benefit are not restricted to use in public schools (*Quick Bear . . .*, 1908).

A Nebraska statute prohibiting the teaching of German was held not to destroy the autonomy of a church school (Lutheran) to determine its curriculum (*Meyer . . .*, 1923).

In a classic decision it was held that although the state of Oregon could require the education of all children, it could not destroy the parent's prerogative of providing that education in a church school (*Pierce . . .*, 1925). This case protects the religious conscience of the individual, establishes the prerogatives of the parent in the nature of his child's education, and sets the United States apart from totalitarian philosophy.

Under the child welfare theory the use by a

parochial-school child of textbooks prescribed by the state and purchased with public funds was upheld (*Cochran* . . . , 1930).

Following World War II a plethora of cases greatly expanded the meaning of laws and, especially, has moved forward the meaning of the "free exercise" and the "establishment" phrases of the first amendment.

Reversing a 1940 decision (*Minersville* . . . , 1940) the Supreme Court denied the right of the public schools to require the flag salute of those objecting on religious grounds (*West Virginia State Board of Education* . . . , 1943). In classic language the Court upheld the right of freedom of belief and again set our government apart from totalitarianism. "If there is any fixed star in our constitutional constellation, it is that no official, high or petty, can prescribe what shall be orthodox in politics, nationalism, religion, or other matters of opinion, or force citizens to confess by word or act their faith therein."

In an interesting case involving Jehovah's Witnesses it was held that the parent's right to give religious instruction to his child does not supersede the rights of the child's protection by child labor laws (*Prince* . . . , 1944).

The establishment clause does not prevent the use of public funds to provide transportation to a parochial school in a bus traveling along established routes (*Everson* . . . , 1947), nor does it prevent the release of a child from public school time to receive religious instruction which does not use public property, funds, or personnel. (*Zorach* . . . , 1952).

However, the use of public property, funds, personnel, and administrative machinery was forbidden in a released-time program (*McCollum* . . . , 1948). Further, in the classic prayer and Bible decisions it was established that all forms of religious exercise in the public schools is forbidden as a protection of the individual from "established" religion. In the prayer case (*Engle* . . . , 1962) a prayer carefully intended to be nonsectarian was forbidden. The Bible case (*Abington* . . . , 1963) strictly proscribed the use of the Bible as a religious exercise but encouraged "study of comparative religion or the history of religion and its relationship to the advancement of civilization" and allowed "such study of the Bible or of religion, when presented objectively as parts of a secular process of education." The latter dicta have created prolific discussion ("Religion in the Public Schools," 1964) and some experimentation which is discussed later.

Legislative Action. Increasing pressures to relieve the tension over religion and public education, a clearer definition of legal metes and bounds, and an expanding governmental social policy have combined to produce significant legislation in the decade of the 1960.

The Elementary and Secondary Education Act of 1965 (P.L. 89–10) broke the half-century impasse in the struggle to obtain federal support for local education. For church-school supporters the law contained sufficient promise of assistance to low-income families and the inclusion of private schools in cooperative and experimental arrangements to abate the opposition which had been a major factor in preventing the passage of earlier proposals for federal aid. It should be noted that in Congressional hearings held before the passage of the bill, religious leaders gave important testimony which resulted in modifications such as those requiring that the title to all property should be vested in public bodies. (Kelley and LaNoue, 1965; Kelley, 1967). The child-benefit theory is the basis for extending aid to church schools.

On the theory of national welfare the Higher Education Act of 1963 (P.L. 88–204) provided direct grants to private colleges for part of the cost of construction and equipment of libraries and facilities for teaching science, mathematics, modern foreign languages, and engineering. Funds were available for all accredited private colleges, provided the facilities would not be used for sectarian instruction or as places of worship or for a program or department of divinity. The Higher Education Act of 1964 (P.L. 88–204) extended these provisions. It should be noted that the Maryland courts recently held that a similar state statute could not be applied to colleges which were owned by or under the major control of a religious body or used primarily for religious instruction. (*Horace Mann League*. . . , 1966).

The Higher Education Facilities Act of 1965 (P.L. 89–329) provided colleges with funds for community-service programs, library assistance, aid for developing institutions, and student assistance. The same provisions prohibiting sectarian instruction, worship, and divinity programs were included in this act.

Laws are now being made by state legislatures probing the limits of the child-benefit theory in such areas as transportation, textbooks and health and welfare programs. Some of these are good laws and will stand; others will be out of bounds and will be declared unconstitutional.

The expanding legal interpretations and new concepts in legislation have produced conservative action, and amendments altering the first amendment have been proposed. They have been opposed by considerable church leadership and have not been enacted.

EXPERIMENTATION. With continued pressure to resolve the problem of the religious instruction of youth in a heterogeneous nation and a clearer definition of principles, notable experimentation is under way.

Released Time. The program of released time has been in use for some time. It involves church-directed religious instruction in nonpublic buildings at times when children are released from school for the purpose of such instruction. If conducted within the limits set by the McCollum and Zorach cases it presents a live option for many churches. Stokes and Pfeffer (1964, pp. 364–367) report that estimates of the number of schools using some form of the plan run as high as 30 percent.

Out-of-school Classes. Late-afternoon classes and

weekend and summer programs are used by many groups. Protestant churches are generally expanding their religious education with double sessions on Sunday, weekend and summer retreats, camps, and conferences. Jewish congregations have traditionally operated Hebrew schools after school hours. Their success with this program contributes to their strict position of separation, their support of the public school, and their pressure to keep all semblance of religion out of the school.

The significance of this program is highlighted by a strong statement of the National Council of Churches (1963) supporting the public schools and their statement *Christian Responsibilities for Education Through the Week* (1965).

Shared Time (Dual Enrollment). A long-standing idea that public school services could be shared part-time by parochial school enrollees under conditions which would maintain separation of general education from religious instruction emerged in the 1960 decade with intensive discussion ("Shared Time," 1962). The idea has been widely discussed in the religious and secular press. The proposal was included in the 1965 Elementary and Secondary Education Act for experimental study. The plan has been generally accepted by Roman Catholics, and significant projects are in operation in the diocesan schools of Chicago and Pittsburgh involving sharing with their respective public school systems. The National Council of Churches (1964) has given sanction to the idea, with a vote of 103 to 2 in their General Board. The Lutheran Education Association (Zadeik, 1964) adopted a constructive but cautious attitude toward shared time. The American Jewish Congress is reported to be unfavorable (U.S. Congress, 1964). It was reported in the House hearings on shared time that in the school year 1963–64 280 school systems had reported programs in shared time and 111 systems were contemplating its use.

MORAL AND SPIRITUAL VALUES. The Educational Policies Commission published a statement on the teaching of moral and spiritual values that was designed as an answer to the criticism that the neutrality of the public schools leaves a religious gap in the education of youth. The document (National Education Association, 1951) purported to demonstrate that most of the ethic of the Judeo-Christian culture can be taught in the schools without violating religious neutrality. The statement is a good exposition of what can be done and is cited by many educators as a justification of the schools.

The acceptance of this proposal by churchmen as a solution to the moral education of youth has been something less than enthusiastic, because of the conviction that no instruction in values can be effective without reference to divine sources (McCluskey, 1959; Whittemore, 1960). Nevertheless, the schools can and must inculcate accepted moral principles, assuming that it is the role of the churches to provide youth with the understanding of the Author of the value system.

TEACHING ABOUT RELIGION. The dicta in the Bible case (*Abington . . .*, 1963) urging objective teaching about religion has stimulated much curriculum activity (University of the State of New York, 1965; Pittsburgh Public Schools, 1966; Pennsylvania Humanities Commission, 1965). In a significant manner such courses, presented objectively, may enable the schools to attain greater effectiveness than they were able to achieve through the cursory reading of the Scriptures and the mouthing of rote prayers.

Implicit and Explicit Teaching of Religion. Taking a lead from the proposal in the Bible case for objective teaching about religion, Phenix (1965) urges an implicit teaching which is "concerned about ultimate commitments" and "comprehensive life orientation" which do not have "conventional religious labels." Further, he declares that explicit teaching of religion can be done in the schools by teachers who exercise absolute objectivity without any proreligious or antireligious bias. Admitting that this may be difficult for some teachers who have biases against religion, he nonetheless relies on his faith in the objectivity of the "community of scholars" to provide implicit and explicit teaching, which he proposes as the best solution.

Role of the Churches. In commenting on the foregoing proposals it must be said that the public schools alone cannot complete the task of religious instruction of youth, nor should this expectation be laid upon them. With fuller understanding of the metes and bounds of public school performance, the churches themselves must revise existing programs and develop new ones to enable them to supply the religious dimension to the "objective teaching" of the schools.

PRACTICES IN FOREIGN COUNTRIES. Comparison with foreign countries must take into account the varying historical, political, religious, and social heritages of the respective peoples. Since there is no nation which offers a duplicate of the combined heritage of representative democracy, religious diversity, protection of religious freedom, and extensive free public education of the United States, it is improper to assume that practices of one nation could be transferred to this country with equal effect. Nonetheless, comparison helps to appraise current efforts to adjust to the changing milieu. The 1966 edition of the World Yearbook of Education is a valuable aid to such comparison (Bereday & Lauwerys, 1966).

England. With its tradition of "Established Church," England provides Anglican-oriented religious instruction in the state schools. Public support is given to religious schools operated by non-Anglican sects. The people seem to accept the arrangement, but there appears to be a significant lack of enthusiasm for the quality of religious instruction in the state schools, and it has been noted that widespread indifference to religion exists in the society as a whole (Bereday & Lauwerys, 1966, pp. 19–38).

France. There is a tradition of suspicion between church and state in France extending from Napoleon, in 1808, to De Gaulle, in 1960, leading to a strong tendency to centralized state control of education. Yet there is a strong popular Roman Catholic sentiment, activated by the principles of *Divini Illius Magistri* (Pius XI, 1929), which has resulted in Roman Catholic schools accounting for 15 percent of the primary enrollment and 30 percent of the secondary. There are a few other denominational and Jewish schools. A 1960 law extending public aid to the church schools exacted submission to considerable public control as a condition (Bereday & Lauwerys, 1966).

The Netherlands. Since the Reformation the prevailing emphasis in the Netherlands has been Calvinist, although an increasing Catholic population has resulted in a three-way cleavage—Calvinist, Catholic, and neutral. Each of these groups administers its own school system through denominational parents' associations. Approximately one-fourth of the student population are in public schools, one-fourth in Calvinist schools, slightly less than one-half in Roman Catholic schools, and a small percentage in nonsectarian private schools (Bereday & Lauwerys, 1966). Observation has been made that the arrangement results in a heightening of the religious cleavage in the population (Reller, 1963).

Canada. Despite Canada's long tradition of government support of church-controlled schools, a major revision is under way, the outcome of which appears to be centralized state control of all schools under a minister of education, counseled by a supreme council of education, itself advised by two confessional committees, Roman Catholic and Protestant (Bereday & Lauwerys, 1966).

Sweden. The practice of teaching the established Lutheran religion in Swedish state schools appears to be waning, leaving the churches to assume the task of instruction and to attempt to maintain a maximum of religious dialogue in the schools (Bereday & Lauwerys, 1966).

With evidences that non-Christian nations—for example, Turkey, Pakistan, and Ceylon—are tending toward government control and nationalization of religious schools, the total picture in foreign countries raises the suspicion of divisiveness, government control, and inefficiency resulting from state subsidy, with little to recommend it to the United States (Reller, 1963).

DIRECTION OF MOVEMENT. In mid-twentieth century the people of the United States are learning more fully for what their commitment to religious freedom means to their schools. With this learning a new atmosphere of mutual respect prevails among many liberal and considerate Catholic, Protestant, and Jewish churchmen and educators. Constructive progress is being made.

Unresolved is the question of the financial burden of parochial-school parents whose religious belief forces them to assume the cost of educating their children. Their pressure will continue for new formulas, such as shared time, and for any financial assistance that, within the law, can be made available. Pressure will also continue to maintain the strength of the wall of separation of church and state.

Finally, the unresolved problem which must burden all who believe that society must have a religious dimension stems from the large numbers of children not effectively exposed to any religious influence. Until the churches find better means of reaching unchurched youth, their contact with the values of society is achieved in the home, largely secular, through the commercial devices of communication, from the consensus of their peers, and from the public schools. Exposing these youth to moral and spiritual values and the "objective" teaching about religion will continue as a major contribution of the public schools to these youth and to the people of the United States.

Harry L. Stearns
United Presbyterian Church
of the United States of America

References

American Association of School Administrators. *Religion in the Public Schools.* 1964. 67p.

Abington School District v. *Schempp.* 83 Supreme Court 1560, 1963.

Antieau, Chester James, S.J.D., and others. *Freedom From Federal Establishment.* Bruce, 1964. 272p.

Arrowood, Charles Flinn. (Ed.) *Thomas Jefferson and Education in a Republic.* McGraw-Hill, 1930. 184p.

Bailey v. *State.* 157 Ind. 324; 61 N.E. 730. 1901.

Beach, Fred, and Well, Robert F. (Eds.) *The State and Non Public Schools.* USOE, 1958.

Beard, Charles A., and Beard, Mary R. *History of the United States.* Macmillan, 1924. 663p.

Bennett, John C. *Christians and the State.* Scribner, 1958. 302p.

Bereday, George Z. F., and Lauwerys, Joseph A. (Eds.) *Church and State in Education.* Harcourt, 1966. 386p.

Burleigh, John H. S. (Ed.) *Augustine: Earlier Writings.* Vol. 6. Westminster, 1953. 413p.

Churchill, Winston. *A History of the English Speaking Peoples,* Vol 2: *The New World.* Dodd, 1956. 433p.

Cochran v. *Louisiana State Board of Education.* 281 U.S. 370, 1930.

Collie v. *Commissioners of Franklin County.* 145 N.C. 170, 1907.

Cousins, Norman. *In God We Trust.* Harper, 1958. 464p.

Cubberley, Elwood T. *The History of Education.* Houghton, 1920. 849p.

Dewey, John. *Moral Principles in Education.* Houghton, 1909. 60p.

Dewey, John. *A Common Faith.* Yale U Press, 1934. 87p.

Drake, William E. *The American School in Transition.* Prentice-Hall, 1955. 624p.

Durant, Will. *The Story of Philosophy*. Garden, 1927. 592p.

Engle v. *Vitale*. 370 U.S. 421, 1962.

Everson v. *Board of Education*. 330 U.S. 1, 1947.

Geiger, George R. "An Experimentalist Approach to Education." In Henry, Nelson B. (Ed.) *Modern Philosophies and Education*, 54th Yearbook, NSSE. U Chicago Press, 1955. p. 137–74.

Gettell, Raymond G. *A History of Political Thought*. Century, 1924. 511p.

Gilbert, Arthur. "Major Problems Facing Schools in a Pluralistic Society." In *Theory Into Practice*. Ohio State U 1965. p. 23–8.

Hayes, Carlton J. H., and others. *World History*. Macmillan, 1950. 880p.

Horace Mann League v. *Board of Public Works of Maryland*. College and University Reports No. 50. Commerce Clearing House, Inc., 1966.

Jacobson v. *Massachusetts*. 197 U.S. 11, 1905.

Kelley, Dean M. "Elementary and Secondary Education Act (Analyzed)." *Wilson Lib B* p. 685–93; March 1967.

Kelley, Dean M., and LaNoue, George R. "Church-State Settlement in Federal Aid to Education Act, 1965." In *Religion and the Public Order*. U Chicago Press, 1965. p. 110–60.

Kempner, Maximilian W. "The Supreme Court and the Establishment and Free Exercise of Religion." In *Religion and the Free Society*. Fund for the Republic, 1958. p. 65–107.

Kerwin, Jerome G. *Catholic Viewpoint on Church and State*. Hanover House, 1960. 192p.

Kilpatrick, William Heard. *Philosophy of Education*. Macmillan, 1951. 463p.

King v. *Utah Central Railway Co*. 22 Pac. 158, 1889.

LaNoue, George R. "The Child Benefit Theory." *Theory into Practice* 4:15–8; 1965.

Louisville, City of, v. *Commonwealth*. 121 S.W. 411, 1909.

Love, Thomas T. *John Courtney Murray: Contemporary Church-State Theory*. Doubleday, 1965. 239p.

Maritain, Jacques. "Thomist Views on Education." In Henry, Nelson B. (Ed.) *Modern Philosophies and Education*, 54th Yearbook, NSSE. U Chicago Press, 1955. p. 57–90.

McCluskey, Neil G., S.J. *Catholic Viewpoint on Education*. Hanover House, 1959. 192p.

McCollum v. *Board of Education*. 333 U.S. 203, 1948.

McNeill, John T. (Ed.) *John Calvin: Institutes of the Christian Religion*, Vols. 20 and 21. Westminster, 1960. 1734p.

Meyer v. *Nebraska*. 262, U.S. 390, 1923.

Miller, William. *A New History of the United States*. George Braziller, Inc., 1958. 474p.

Minersville School District v. *Gobitis*. 310 U.S. 586, 1940.

Montgomery, D. H. *Leading Facts of English History*. Ginn, 1887. 420p.

National Council of Churches. *The Churches and the Public Schools*. The Council, 1963. 2p.

National Council of Churches. *A Protestant and Orthodox Statement Regarding Dual Enrollment*. The Council, 1964. 1p.

National Council of Churches. *Christian Responsibility for Education Through the Week*. The Council, 1965. 2p.

National Education Association, Educational Policies Commission. *The Purposes of Education in a Democracy*. NEA, 1938. 157p.

National Education Association, Educational Policies Commission. *Moral and Spiritual Values in the Public Schools*. NEA, 1951. 100p.

Padover, Saul K. *A Jefferson Profile*. Day, 1956. 359p.

Pennsylvania Humanities Commission. *Universal Values in Human Life*. Commonwealth of Pennsylvania, Department of Public Instruction, 1965. 156p.

Phenix, Philip H. "Religion in American Public Schools." In *Religion and the Public Order*. U Chicago Press, 1965. p. 82–109.

Pierce v. *Society of Sisters*. 45 Supreme Court 571; 266 U.S. 534, 1925.

Pittsburgh Public Schools, *Religion in the Social Studies*, Little, Lawrence C. (Ed.) Religious Freedom and Public Affairs Pamphlet. New York Conference of Christians and Jews, 1966. 122p.

Pius XI. "Christian Education of Youth." In *Five Great Encyclicals*. Paulist Press, 1929. p. 37–68. (Or see *Official and Complete Text of the Encyclical Letter of His Holiness Pope Pius XI*. National Catholic Welfare Council, 1930.)

Pound, Roscoe. *An Introduction to the Study of the Law*. Yale U Press, 1922. 318p.

Prince v. *Massachusetts*. 321 U.S. 158, 1944.

Quick Bear v. *Leupp*. 210 U.S. 50, 1908.

Regis, Anton. (Ed.) *Thomas Aquinas' Basic Writings: Summa Theologiae*. Random, 1945. 1177p.

"Religion in the Public Schools, A Symposium." *Religious Ed* p. 443–80; November 1964.

Reller, Theodore. "The Allocation of Funds for Education in Canada, England, and the Netherlands." Paper presented at the Institute on Religion and the Schools, Purdue U, October 6–9, 1963. 26p. (Mimeographed.)

"Shared Time; A Symposium on a Paper by Harry L. Stearns." *Religious Ed* 5–36; January 1962.

Stokes, Anson Phelps, and Pfeffer, Leo. *Church and State in the United States*. Harper, 1964. 660p.

Tappert, Theodore G. (Ed.) *Luther: Letters of Spiritual Council*. Westminster, 1955. 366p.

Toynbee, Arnold. *A Study of History*, 2 vols. Abridge by D. C. Somervill. Oxford U Press, 1946. Vol. I, 615p.; Vol. II, 414p.

University of the State of New York. *Social Studies: Tentative Syllabus*. State Education Department, 1965.

U.S. Congress, House of Representatives, Committee on Education and Labor. *Shared Time in Education*. 88th Congress, 2nd Session. GPO, 1964. 621p.

Wells, H. G. *The Outline of History*. Macmillan, 1927. 1190p.

West Virginia State Board of Education v. *Barnette*. 319 U.S. 624, 1943.

Whittemore, Lewis Bliss. *The Church and Secular Education*. Seabury, 1960. 130p.

World Almanac, A Book of Facts, 1967. Newspaper Enterprise Association, 1966. 912p.

Zadeik, Peter A. (Ed.) *Legal Aspects of Lutheran Parish Education.* Lutheran Educational Association, 1964. 82p.

Zorach v. Clausen. 343 U.S. 306, 1952.

RELIGIOUS EDUCATION

"Religious education," as used here, refers to those enterprises designed to induct each new generation into the attitudes, beliefs, and practices of a particular religion, thereby perpetuating the religion and at the same time providing for the individual a unifying center for his life. Forms of religious education are as diverse as the religions in which they are rooted and in fact can be fully understood only in relation to the total structure and history of those religions. Generalizations therefore tend to be misleading, and it is necessary to limit attention here to the three major faiths in the United States, Judaism, Roman Catholicism, and Protestantism, emerging historically in the order listed and resting on a common foundation in Judaism.

HISTORY. Early Jewish education during the Biblical period, before the exile, resulted from participation in a believing community (Schindler, 1966). Oral tradition, nurture in the home, undergirding and interpreting religious ritual, communal festivals and worship, all constituted ways by which natural expressions of faith became informal means for assimilation into faith. With the exile, more formal institutions, such as the synagogue, arose. Study of Torah emerged as the continuing emphasis pervading the various forms that developed. Education, built around a view of study as a religious mandate, has been crucial throughout Judaic history (Morris, 1964).

Primitive Christianity, adapting educational forms and processes of the parent religion, Judaism, consciously viewed teaching as a function essential to incorporating people into "the Way" (Muirhead, 1965). In the ancient church the catechumenate developed as a plan for preparing converts for baptism, and the catechetical school as a means for dealing with secular culture from a broadened educational base. Although medieval monasticism was rejected by the Protestant reformers, many Roman Catholic patterns continued to be basic to Protestant education—worship, pastoral teaching, home training, and guidance (Kennedy, 1966a). Only when Roman Catholics were in a minority position, faced with Protestant-dominated public schools, as in the United States, did they develop their extensive system of parochial schools, where religion could become the integrating perspective for all education (McCluskey, 1964).

Protestant education added its own new educational patterns—the centrality of the preached word in worship, public schools operated jointly by church and state, and, in the eighteenth century, the Sunday school. A worldwide institution, the lay-dominated Sunday school has been adapted by many faiths to their own purposes. For American Protestantism during the nineteenth century, it became the major instrument utilized alongside the public school in the development of an educational strategy (Kennedy, 1966b).

Religion and education, viewed historically, show themselves to be interdependent. Living religion is the source of vitality in religious education; it produces its own appropriate forms through which it influences and is influenced by ever-changing culture (Sherrill, 1944). What, then, may be said about the present situation?

At least three developments have profound implications for religious education. The United States is now consciously a pluralistic society (Littell, 1962). Ecumenism, as reflected in the Religious Education Association Convention of 1966 (Borowitz & others, 1966) is accompanied by a new openness on an interfaith level. Secularity, with its affirmation of the world and the meaning to be found there, and with its challenges to education, is viewed by some as destructive of religion; by others, as a rediscovery of a position fundamental to the three major historical religions in America. For Judaism these developments mean that Jewish education has shifted to become supplementary to general education as it seeks to prepare the Jew for Judaism as well as to pull him out of isolationism into appreciation for the societal context in which he exists (Cohen, 1964). For Roman Catholicism the church renewal attendant upon Vatican Council II in part encompasses these developments, in part goes beyond them in educational and liturgical innovations as well as in emphasis on the apostolate of the laity. For Protestantism the developments are congenial with new theological concerns (Hordern, 1966) displacing the neo-Reformation theology heralded at mid-century as a theological renaissance corrective of earlier weaknesses in Protestant curricula. A closer look at various aspects of contemporary religious education will reveal some of the implications of these developments, and others equally important, although it remains for the future to unveil full implications and to produce more stable patterns than exist currently.

SCOPE. Religious education focuses upon the Scriptures, tradition, and history of the faith to which witness is made. But it is not restricted to this narrow scope for either Jews or Christians. Whether religion is the integrative factor in all education, as is possible where school systems are under religious control, or whether curriculum must be structured so that other areas of knowledge and of ethical concern can be brought into dialogue with religious heritage, the scope broadens to include all life. The recent monumental cooperative effort in Protestant curriculum making (Cooperative Curriculum Project, 1965) illustrates attention to comprehensiveness and relevance. A similar concern for relevance is to be found in evaluative research in Jewish school curriculum

(Pilch, 1966) and in the Catholic view of the scope of modern catechetics (Sloyan, 1960).

OBJECTIVES. To the traditional Jewish view that study is required by faith and that all learning must serve the ends of faith, there is a more recently developed attempt to formulate specific goals relating to Jewish tradition. Articulated by reform Judaism through the Commission on Jewish Education, these goals are generally accepted by other branches of American Judaism. They call for knowledge about and appreciation of Jewish heritage, as well as participation in the faith and ethical standards of Jewish religion (Schindler, 1966). Roman Catholic educators likewise recognize the religious quality within all education, which aims at the formation of the human person. It is the special function of religious education to direct itself toward spiritual formation, a goal reaffirmed by Vatican II in its call for the church to engage in that kind of education which enables the entire lives of students to be penetrated by the spirit of Christ (Abbott, 1966). In their absorbing concern with curriculum development during recent years, Protestants have struggled with the formulation of objectives. Generally speaking, they have rejected objectives formed in terms of subject matter to be learned or character traits to be achieved. Instead, they have sought some unifying, global statement, as reflected in the interdenominational study recommending the supreme purpose of helping persons to become aware of and respond to God's seeking love in Jesus Christ (National Council of Churches, Commission on General Christian Education, 1958).

For all faiths, there are problems relating to general statements of objectives (Miller, 1966). How does one move to theologically valid, operational, specific goals and to the development of materials and activities consistent with the ultimate goal? How does one evaluate an intangible or religious objective?

AGENCIES AND PROGRAMS. There is a degree of similarity in the forms by which all faiths implement their stated goals and deal with the specified scope of studies. For example, Jews and Christians both affirm the decisive and primary responsibility of the family for religious nurture. All make some use of school systems, either those where religious education is integral to general education or institutions of higher education. All have numerous supplementary agencies related to the church or synagogue. More detailed attention to these three general categories will suggest possibilities and problems presently facing religious educators.

American culture today makes the viability of the family as an agency of religious education increasingly questionable (Russell, 1960). Both Jews and Catholics, however, seem to have a stronger, more unified base for education in the family than do Protestants, who often have difficulty knowing what kind of help or programs to plan for families (Fairchild & Wynn, 1961). Nevertheless, denominations are making important contributions in their ministry to families through such curriculum offerings as those illustrated by the Presbyterian Church, U.S., in its Covenant Life Curriculum (Fairchild, 1964). Aid in such denominational work comes from participation in cooperative efforts to survey the whole situation, sociologically as well as theologically, and to formulate policies that establish foundations for future directions in family education (Genné & Genné, 1961).

Schools controlled by religious bodies continue to be a major agency of religious education, particularly for Roman Catholics. Latest statistics show 13,475 diocesan, parochial, and private elementary and high schools, with an enrollment of almost six million. A total of 203,791 full-time teachers, 80,768 of them lay teachers, offer instruction (*Official Catholic Directory*, 1966). Figures indicate the importance attached to this agency and also point to the church-state problem in terms of philosophy and financial involvement when it is recognized that in several cities Roman Catholics account for more than 50 percent of the school-going population (McCluskey, 1964). A 1965 survey by the Lutheran Church, Missouri Synod, of Protestant church-related day schools shows a total of 4,117 elementary and high schools, with 436,193 students and 22,497 teachers (Hakes, 1966). Although the survey includes certain private schools, as well as those associated with nondenominational conservative groups such as the National Union of Christian Schools, so that it is difficult to ascertain denominational involvement, it does seem clear that there is an increasing number of Protestant day schools. Of approximately 600,000 children and youth enrolled in all types of Jewish schools, fewer than 10 percent attend full-time day schools (Schindler, 1966). But even in Jewish education, where there has been least emphasis on school systems, there seems to be a trend in the direction of adding Jewish high schools (Newman, 1964). Increased effort is made to accredit schools, to work toward certification and improved teacher preparation in a Jewish context, and to engage in curriculum and action-research programs. Meanwhile, both Protestants and Catholics continue to investigate the effectiveness of their parochial schools (Johnstone, 1966; Ryan, 1964; Neuwien, 1966). Evaluative efforts such as these are important and are increasingly a part of the religious-education enterprise.

The whole question of institutions of higher education and their purposes as related to religious education is also under consideration. Although Judaism does maintain colleges in addition to seminaries, it does not rely on them as agencies integral to a system of religious education in the way the Christian church has done, at least in its early history in America. Some denominations continue to maintain colleges as extensions of a parochial school system. Others are more concerned for achieving excellence in liberal education. There is a movement in the Roman Catholic church toward what is called "laicization" of their colleges, in terms of administrative and trustee personnel, in an effort to work toward a new pattern of relationships between church and college community (Greeley, 1967). Protestants, aware of the growth of departments of religion in state universities, are looking again at the distinctive function of church-related colleges (Patillo, 1966; Wicke, 1964). No consensus is apparent. The ministry carried out by campus chaplains, even though it continues to be utilized, in both cooperative and denominational patterns, also faces a somewhat uncertain future (Cantelon, 1964).

Whatever continuity exists in religious education eventually relates to ecclesiastical institutions and to professional theological education, which is therefore of basic importance. Extensive evaluations, analyses, and projections for the future are available for Protestant and Catholic seminary education (Feilding 1966; Wagoner, 1966).

Among the growing variety of supplementary agencies of religious education, the Sunday school and its adaptations continue to be the most prominent. Statistics are clearest for the Protestants, with the latest enrollment, reported as 41,539,495, a slight drop from the preceding year (National Council of Churches, Department of Research, 1967). Roman Catholics count 4,856,653 public school children receiving some form of religious instruction (*Official Catholic Directory*, 1966). Over one-half of the 600,000 Jewish students in various types of Jewish schools each receive approximately 2½ hours instruction on Sunday mornings, and 40 percent attend afternoon sessions once or twice a week (Schindler, 1966). Wherever there is a dependence on volunteer teachers, problems exist in terms of the quality of education. Nevertheless, extensive efforts are being made by all faith groups to provide more adequate leadership education. The professional church educator in Protestantism, the director of Christian education, centers most of his time in leadership development.

No period in the history of the Sunday school has seen more elaborate schemes or more carefully constructed curriculum materials than those available to contemporary Protestantism (Nelson, 1966). The pioneering work of the United Presbyterian Church, U.S.A., and the Protestant Episcopal Church in the 1940's and 1950's was followed by curriculum ventures among all major denominations. The Bible-centered Uniform Lessons, began in 1872, continue to be published, but the Cooperative Curriculum Project is more illustrative of current cooperative endeavors and of the ecumenical spirit. Denominational departments of research are approaching the task of evaluation with new seriousness, thus contributing to curriculum in all stages of its development, from field testing to revision.

Furthermore, flexibility of scheduling and variations of study patterns developing out of the Sunday school mean that adult classes, through-the-week youth groups, and other study groups have assumed a life of their own and have become effective agencies of religious education. Summer camps and conferences, the vacation church school and its outgrowths in youth weeks, family schools, and the like, continue to develop to meet particular purposes and are in use by all faiths. Lay schools of theology, both church-sponsored and independent, or offered by colleges for academic credit, are having their impact on the American scene. Retreats, specialized conferences, such as the liturgical conferences of the Roman Catholics, and vocational study groups are typical of the wide variety of agencies employed in religious education activities. The new ecumenism is demonstrated in planned lay conversations where matters of faith and practice are considered (Greenspun & Norgren, 1965). Programs and materials to supplement and interpret public school studies from a religious perspective, planned for a variety of settings, are being prepared (Eastman, 1966).

One of the most significant developments of recent years is what is called kerygmatic catechetics in the Roman Catholic church. Centering on the gospel message rather than on traditional catechetics, and involving laity in a new way in teaching, especially through the Confraternity of Christian Doctrine, the movement is worldwide. Evidently world leaders reached essential agreement on the future direction of catechetics in the International Study Week on Mission Apologetics held at Eichstätt, Germany, in 1960 (Hofinger, 1961). Men such as Gerard S. Sloyan (1958) have been instrumental in developing the work in America. Carefully structured leadership courses prepare lay catechists for their work and offer programs somewhat similar to some of the Protestant leader development patterns.

Agencies such as confirmation classes for Christians and the bar mitzvah for Jews continue to be used but also to be questioned in the light of the proliferation of other agencies of religious education and in view of the question of the proper age for a declaration of faith (Rosenberg & others, 1965). Progress has been made toward understanding and developing the various agencies within some unifying philosophy of religious education (Cully, 1965), but the situation is still too much marked by eclecticism for theoretical concerns and practical forms to always be consistently related. Some of the agencies have outlived their usefulness. Others, evaluated and adapted or arising new in response to a rapidly changing culture, give promise of the ability of religious groups to learn from the innovative inclinations of general education. The relating of theological norms to innovation activities, when theology itself is in a state of flux, is difficult but is considered necessary. Certainly disciplines other than theology are making a more decided impact on religious education than was the case in the second quarter of the twentieth century. A more critical approach to theoretical and institutional developments in Protestant education is evident (Chamberlin, 1965). And the reintegration of the Sunday school into the life and worship of the church, as church education, has brought back to Protestants a value never lost by Roman Catholics and Jews.

INSTRUCTION. Religious education, because of its nature, its concern with religious formation, and its relation to faith, necessitates, but is not limited to, instruction. Carefully controlled efforts to increase the effectiveness of instruction, buttressed by research and drawing on the methodologies of secular education, hold promise for the future. Mass media are increasingly utilized, but such developments as programmed instruction are only beginning to be explored for their usefulness (Nora, 1963). Peer group study follows the grading plan of public schools. Ungraded groupings and individualized instruction are in the experimental stage. Attempts to formulate learning theories appropriate to religious education, taking into account insights from secular disciplines and general education processes, but directed toward religious categories, are underway (Moran, 1966; Boehlke, 1962). An action-oriented approach to learning, moving from issues or responsibilities to resources of tradition, is proving its validity.

Even where instruction is placed in its most reputable setting, in schools under trained teachers, it is inadequate apart from the worship and fellowship of the religious community. Some theorists place such a thesis at the center of a philosophy of religious education (Miller, 1961). Research into knowledge and attitudes acquired, in countries such as England where religion is a required course of study in the school systems, indicates the inadequacies in the instructional focus (Dierenfield, 1967), as well as the need for a more effective approach to instruction itself (Goldman, 1964). Roman Catholic studies in the United States indicate the need for the reinforcement of formal religious instruction, even in parochial schools, by other institutions of socialization (Greeley & Rossi, 1966). Religious education, then, is facing the problem, as well as the promise, of finding its proper relation to both the religious and the educational community.

Sara Little
Presbyterian School of Christian Education

References

Abbott, Walter M. (Ed.) "Declaration on Christian Education." In *The Documents of Vatican II.* Guild Press, 1966. p. 637–51.

Boehlke, Robert R. *Theories of Learning in Christian Education.* Westminster, 1962. 221p.

Borowitz, Eugene B., and others. "The Ecumenical Revolution and Religious Education." *Relig Ed* 61: 336–95; 1966. Symposium.

Cantelon, John E. *A Protestant Approach to the Campus Ministry.* Westminster, 1964. 127p.

Chamberlin, J. Gordon. *Freedom and Faith.* Westminster, 1965. 156p.

Cohen, Jack J. *Jewish Education in Democratic Society.* Reconstructionist Press, 1964. 350p.

Cooperative Curriculum Project. *The Church's Educational Ministry.* Bethany Press, 1965. 848p.

Cully, Kendig Brubaker. *The Search for a Christian Education—Since 1940.* Westminster, 1965. 205p.

Dierenfield, R. B. "Religion for the County Secondary Schools of England." *Relig Ed* 62:38–45; 1967.

Eastman, Frances. "Christian Faith and Public School Learnings." *Int J Relig Ed* 42(No. 11):14–6, 37; 1966.

Fairchild, Roy W. *Christians in Families.* Covenant Life Curriculum Press, 1964. 262p.

Fairchild, Roy W., and Wynn, John Charles. *Families in the Church: A Protestant Survey.* Association Press, 1961. 302p.

Feilding, Charles R. *Education for Ministry.* American Association of Theological Schools, 1966. 258p.

Genné, Elizabeth Steel, and Genné, William Henry. (Eds.) *Foundations for Christian Family Policy.* National Council of Churches, 1961. 272p.

Goldman, Ronald. *Religious Thinking from Childhood to Adolescence.* Routledge, 1964. 276p.

Greeley, Andrew M. "'Laicization' of Catholic Colleges." *Christian Century* 84:372–5; 1967.

Greeley, Andrew M., and Rossi, Peter H. *The Education of Catholic Americans.* Aldine Publishing Co., 1966. 368p.

Greenspun, William B., and Norgren, William A. (Eds.) *Living Room Dialogues.* Paulist Press, 1965. 256p.

Hakes, J. Edward. "Evangelical Christian Education and the Protestant Day-school Movement." In Taylor, Marvin J. (Ed.) *An Introduction to Christian Education.* Abingdon, 1966. p. 316–28.

Hofinger, Johannes. *The Art of Teaching Christian Doctrine.* U Notre Dame, 1961. 290p.

Hordern, William. *New Directions in Theology Today,* Vol. 1: *Introduction.* Westminster, 1966. 170p.

Johnstone, Ronald L. *The Effectiveness of Lutheran Elementary and Secondary Schools as Agencies of Christian Education.* Concordia Seminary, 1966. 188p.

Kennedy, William Bean. "Christian Education Through History." In Taylor, Marvin J. (Ed.) *An Introduction to Christian Education.* Abingdon, 1966(a). p. 21–31.

Kennedy, William Bean. *The Shaping of Protestant Education.* Association Press, 1966(b). 93p.

Littell, Franklin Harmlin. *From State Church to Pluralism.* Doubleday, 1962. 174p.

McCluskey, Neil G. *Catholic Education in America.* Teachers Coll, Columbia U, 1964. 205p.

Miller, Randolph Crump. *Christian Nurture and the Church.* Scribner, 1961. 208p.

Miller, Randolph Crump. "The Objective of Christian Education." In Taylor, Marvin J. (Ed.) *An Introduction to Christian Education.* Abingdon, 1966. p. 94–104.

Moran, Gabriel. *Catechesis of Revelation.* Herder and Herder, 1966. 174p.

Morris, Nathan. *The Jewish School.* Jewish Education Committee Press, 1964. 266p.

Muirhead, Ian A. *Education in the New Testament.* Association Press, 1965. 94p.

National Council of Churches, Commission on General Christian Education. *The Objectives of Christian Education.* The Council, 1958. 22p.

National Council of Churches, Department of Research. *Yearbook of American Churches.* The Council, 1967. 197p.

Nelson, E. Ellis. "The Curriculum of Christian Education." In Taylor, Marvin J. (Ed.) *An Introduction to Christian Education.* Abingdon, 1966. p. 157–68.

Newman, Louis. "Jewish Education." In Fine, Morris, and Himmelfarb, Milton (Eds.) *American Jewish Yearbook 1964.* American Jewish Committee, 1964. p. 84–92.

Neuwien, Reginald. (Ed.) *Catholic Schools in Action.* U Notre Dame, 1966. 328p.

Nora, (Sister) Mary. "Programmed Instruction and Religious Education." *Relig Ed* 58:29–35; 1963.

Official Catholic Directory. P. J. Kenedy & Sons, 1966. 1424p.

Patillo, Manning M., Jr. "The Future of the Church College." *Relig Ed* 61:292–8; 1966.

Pilch, Judah. "Towards a Revised Jewish School Curriculum." *Relig Ed* 61:181–3; 1966.

Rosenberg, Stuart E., and others. "The Proper Age for a Declaration of Faith." *Relig Ed* 60:290–302, 313; 1965. Symposium.

Russell, Letty M. "The Family and Christian Education in Modern, Urban Society." *Union Sem Q R* 16:33–43; 1960.

Ryan, Mary Perkins. *Are Parochial Schools the Answer?* Holt, 1964. 176p.

Schindler, Alexander M. "Jewish Religious Education." In Taylor, Marvin J. (Ed.) *An Introduction to Christian Education.* Abingdon, 1966. p. 373–82.

Sherrill, Lewis J. *The Rise of Christian Education.* Macmillan, 1944. 349p.

Sloyan, Gerard S. (Ed.) *Shaping the Christian Message.* Macmillan, 1958. 327p.

Sloyan, Gerard S. (Ed.) *Modern Catechetics.* Macmillan, 1960. 381p.

Wagoner, Walter D. *The Seminary: Protestant and Catholic.* Sheed, 1966. 256p.

Wicke, Myron F. *The Church-related College.* Center for Applied Research in Education, 1964. 116p.

RESEARCH IN EDUCATION

Educational research is a complex activity whose conceptual foundations reach deeply into science and the philosophy of science. Its domain is human behavior related to educational processes and outcomes. It is, therefore, social scientific and behavioral research whose universe of discourse is all phenomena related to human behavior in educational processes. The general purpose of this article is to provide a conception of educational research that is rooted in contemporary scientific behavioral research notions. This general purpose is implemented by detailed discussions of the scientific, logical, conceptual, and technical foundations of educational research and by an assessment of its major problems and prospects.

THE SCIENTIFIC APPROACH AND EDUCATIONAL RESEARCH. Educational research is social scientific research applied to educational problems. While some educational research is not social scientific, it is, with the exception of historical research, not as important as social scientific research. It is social scientific research, especially psychological and sociological research, for a simple reason: an overwhelming majority of its variables are psychological, sociological, or social-psychological. Consider some of them: achievement, aptitude, motivation, intelligence, teacher characteristics, reinforcement, level of aspiration, class atmosphere, discipline, social class, race. All of these but the last two are psychological constructs. If the large proportion of the variables are psychological, sociological, or social-psychological, then the conceptual and methodological problems of educational research are very similar to the problems of psychological and sociological research.

The Aims and Functions of Science. *Science* is a misused and misunderstood word. It is not an activity whose purpose is to amass facts (Bronowski, 1965; Cohen, 1956; Poincaré, 1952). Nor does it have a primary concern for improving the world and mankind's lot, though it may often help to do this (Feigl, 1953). Its basic aim is to discover or invent general explanations of natural events (Braithwaite, 1953). In a word, its purpose is theory or explanation. And a *theory* is "a set of interrelated constructs (concepts), definitions, and propositions that presents a systematic view of phenomena by specifying relations among variables, with the purpose of explaining . . . phenomena" (Kerlinger, 1964, p. 11). It may clarify the scientist's purpose if we examine, briefly, the so-called nomothetic nature of science. *Nomothetic* means "law-making." A nomothetic science is one that seeks to establish laws or generalizations (Falk, 1956; Nagel, 1961, pp. 547–551). In contrast, what has been called idiographic science studies unique or singular events. *Idiographic* means "describing things," singular things. Physics is supposedly a nomothetic science, while history has been called an idiographic science. Hypotheses and propositions can also be called nomothetic and idiographic. To say "Achievement is a function of intelligence, of the need for achievement, and of the home background" is to talk nomothetically. To say, on the other hand, "This class's achievement is better than that of any other class I have had" is to talk idiographically.

Scientific research always is and has to be nomothetic. By its very nature it cannot be concerned with the individual or with the applications of its nomothetic laws and propositions to individuals. Many educators, in their legitimate concern for the individual child, deplore what they believe to be the irrelevance of much scientific educational research to this concern. They plead for research applied to individual educational problems (e.g., Briggs, 1964). Their demand is impossible to satisfy, however, since scientific research cannot be directed toward singular events.

Very bluntly put, there is no such thing as scientific research that is idiographic—by definition. And most educational research is and has to be scientific because we want the behavioral laws discovered to be applicable, ideally, to whole classes or sets of individuals and settings. This is not to say that idiographic methods have no use in scientific educational research; they do. But they do not lead to the general statements of regularity that are the essence of science (cf. Falk, 1956, for a somewhat different view).

Science is not technology, even though its findings often lead to technological innovations and improvements. The scientist is not an engineer, in other words. It is not his job, as a scientist, to construct bridges, to improve medical practice, to design curricula, or to improve learning and teaching. His job is to "explain" phenomena by specifying what other phenomena or conditions are related to the phenomena to be explained, and how and why they are so related.

It is safe to say that most educators and educational researchers have believed and still believe that educational research should be primarily, even exclusively, a practical enterprise (Ausubel, 1953; Briggs, 1964; Findley, 1960; Monroe & Engelhart, 1928; Silberman & others, 1966). To establish practicality as the sole criterion of research, however, is to restrict research unduly, to cut it off from its creative roots (Cronbach, 1966; Dubos, 1961; Hubbert, 1963; Kerlinger, 1959; Panel . . ., 1960; Waterman, 1966). While not denigrating practical and applied research, a number of thinkers have decried the lack of theory and theoretical development in education and educational research (e.g., Clark, 1963; Getzels & Jackson, 1963; Griffiths, 1959; Halpin, 1966; Ryans, 1957). These men, a relatively small minority among educators, believe that lack of theoretical orientation and overemphasis on practicality in educational research are serious weaknesses. Such views have become stronger in the last decade.

Concomitantly, the practicality view also seems to have become stronger. Probably the clearest sign of its strength, other than the articles cited above, is the policy, announced in 1966, of the Bureau of Research of the U.S. Office of Education (Cronbach, 1966; Welch, 1966; personal interview of author with Bureau of Research officials in 1966). The strong emphasis of the bureau on applied research and development has evidently had the effect of raising the practicality criterion to the most preeminent place it has ever had in American educational research.

Basic and Applied Research. Kidd (1959), in a definitive article on basic and applied research, points out that adequate definitions are difficult to come by. He says that there are two kinds of definitions: those that stress the motivation of the researcher and those that stress research outcomes. The investigator-centered definitions stress the interest of the problem and the curiosity of the investigator. The substance-centered definitions stress the breadth and significance of results and the impact on scientific thought and procedures. After reviewing a number of definitions, Kidd concludes that the two types are contradictory. He proposes, instead, a probabilistic view that uses criteria for doing basic research. Basic research, he thinks, can be stimulated by strengthening the social system, forces, and values that appear to increase the probability of basic findings. The requirements boil down to one basic requirement: freedom, which means broad definition of areas of research, ease and informality in the direction of research, stability of support, and freedom from onerous and unproductive reporting. In short, basic research requires few investigator restrictions.

Applied research is research aimed at solving specific problems. In contrast to basic research, which seeks broad generalizations to explain wide ranges of phenomena, applied research seeks answers to narrower practical questions. Basic-research questions in education might be: How do different types of reinforcement affect retention? How do stages of cognitive development affect children's learning of problem solving? Does problem solving by discovery of principles aid transfer more than direct instruction of principles does? Applied-research questions might be: Which method of teaching spelling (among, say, three methods) is most effective with which pupils? What instructional methods and procedures produce the greatest reading gains in underprivileged children? How do different modes of programmed instruction affect gains in retention of mathematical concepts?

Waterman (1966) holds that basic research contributes to the solution of practical problems by supplying clearer understanding of the phenomena underlying the practical problems. Thomson (1960) points out that the best way to make technological advances is to understand principles. It is not surprising that this notion is not well understood. It is a new discovery that has only recently been understood by scientists (Thomson, 1960). In 1960 a summary of ten years work of the National Science Foundation (Waterman, 1960) and a report of the Panel on Basic Research and Graduate Education of the President's Science Advisory Committee (1960) both stressed the importance of basic research. The former said, "It is only through comprehensive support of basic research . . . that one can discover the potentialities for application that are so important in the competitive technology of today" (Waterman, 1960, p. 1353). The latter said, "Nothing could be more unwise than an effort to assign priorities or judge results in basic research on any narrow basis of immediate gain" (Panel . . ., 1960, p. 1803).

As indicated earlier, however, many educators believe that educational research is and should be applied research. Ausubel (1953) makes a particularly strong case. He says that basic research's relevance is too remote and indirect, since it is not oriented toward solving educational problems, and much additional research is required to make it applicable. The resolution of the problem, of course, is that educational research has to be both basic and applied. Without basic research, applied research becomes superficial and empty. Without applied research, basic research tends to become remote from educational problems. (See also Brain, 1965; Dubos, 1961; Feigl, 1953; Pfaffman, 1965; Storer, 1963.)

Critical Inquiry and the Scientific Approach. Educational research has been severely criticized for its theoretical, conceptual, and methodological inadequacies (Coladarci, 1960; Jensen, 1962; Norton

& Lindquist, 1951; Stanley, 1957; Tiedeman & Cogan, 1958; Travers, 1958). To understand and judge the validity of the criticisms that have been made we must understand what will here be called critical inquiry and certain important aspects of the scientific approach.

Critical inquiry is the rational, objective, controlled, and, when possible, empirical investigation and analysis of problems. It is characterized by strong emphasis on obtaining objective evidence pertinent to problems, analyzing the evidence with probity and reliable methods, and arriving at carefully circumscribed conclusions from inferences drawn from the results of the analysis. Like scientific inquiry, critical inquiry is primarily concerned with the relations among phenomena. It is a general rubric that includes almost any kind of scholarly study and investigation. Scientific inquiry is one form of critical inquiry, its most powerful form. An educational investigation can be and should be critical inquiry, but it need not always be scientific inquiry. For example, the efficacy of a curriculum can always be studied by using critical inquiry when scientific inquiry might be impracticable, difficult, or impossible.

The scientific approach—there is no one scientific method—is much too complex to describe here. We must be content with mentioning and briefly describing three characteristics that distinguish scientific research from other types of inquiry: hypothesis formulation, systematic empirical testing, and systematic control.

All inquiry "tests" its notions. If nothing else, for example, an educator may "test" his preconceptions about curriculum matters by careful analysis and comparisons of different curricula. The scientist, on the other hand, insists upon systematic empirical testing—say, of the effects of different curricula on educational outcomes. He insists upon making actual observations of phenomena, and he uses systematic objective methods to make the observations. Since this feature of science is well known and rather well understood, it will not be pursued further here.

Hypotheses are conjectural statements of the relations among variables. Poincaré (1952) has said that any generalization is a hypothesis. Ideally, hypotheses are statements of the conditional type If p, then q, where p and q are variables. For example, we may say, "If positive incentive, then higher achievement" (Hurlock, 1925). Braithwaite (1953, p. 368) writes, "Man proposes a system of hypotheses: Nature disposes of its truth or falsity." He also says (p. 9) that the hypothetico-deductive method applied to empirical material is the essential feature of science. Properly understood, this is true. Another, somewhat narrower way to say this is that science is perhaps most characterized by its systematic formulation and testing of hypotheses. It is indeed true that the hypothesis (and its implied testing) is one of the most powerful intellectual tools of man.

There are three reasons why hypotheses are so important. First, they are the working instruments of theory. They may be deduced almost ad libitum from theory. They are thus, hopefully, more specific and testable expressions of aspects of the theory. Second, hypotheses can be tested and shown to be probably true or probably false. (They can never be "proved" or "disproved," as Braithwaite [1953, p. 14] has pointed out.) We test, in other words, an "If p, then q" statement by manipulating or observing variation in p and observing possible concomitant variation in q. Hypotheses are thus the critical intermediaries between general research questions—for example, How do incentives affect achievement?—and behavioral observations.

A third reason hypotheses are so important is that they enable investigators to get outside themselves, so to speak. That is, hypotheses can be tested apart from the investigator's values and beliefs. Though constructed by man and though perhaps reflecting his predilections, they exist and stand outside man and can be handled objectively (Polanyi, 1958). This is part of the famous self-correction feature of science that C. S. Peirce (Buchler, 1955) emphasized many years ago.

Finally, hypotheses direct investigation. They tell us what variables to manipulate or to measure, they tell us more or less what to look for, and they may even suggest how to make observations and how to analyze data. As Cohen (1956, p. 148) has put it so well: "Without some guiding idea we do not know what facts to gather. Without something to prove, we cannot determine what is relevant and what is irrelevant." Poincaré (1952) and Braithwaite (1953) have made much the same point.

One of the most important and yet most difficult concepts in science is control. A nonscientific investigator of course uses control. But the scientist carries control to an obsessive extreme. He controls everything he can control, and what he cannot control directly he tries to control indirectly.

All control in scientific research is control of variance: Different forms of control are similar in function and are really different expressions of the one underlying principle. The scientific investigator tries to so arrange matters that the only source of variation in his dependent variable or variables are his specified independent variables. He can do this by setting up restricted laboratory conditions and thus shutting out the perturbations of the outside world. He can also manipulate his independent variables. Experimental manipulation, in other words, is a form of control. He can match subjects and thus reduce the variance owing to the variable or variables used for matching to near zero. The investigator can also control variance by sampling. For example, he can use only boys or only girls. He is controlling sex.

The scientist controls variance with the very design of his research. For instance, he can include an independent variable, say social class, in his design. Or he can include "schools" as a variable. By so doing he can, in effect, extract the variances due to social-class differences and to the differences between schools. He can control variance statistically. A most useful technique for educational research analysis is analysis of covariance (see STATISTICAL METHODS), a statistical technique that accomplishes what matching accomplishes—without the headaches and drawbacks of matching (Stanley & Beeman, 1958). McNemar (1960) says that analysis of covariance can be a "real godsend" to educational research where intact groups must frequently be used. A more important and comprehensive method of variance analysis and control is multiple regression, a technique that nicely brings together correlation and regression methods, on the one hand, and analysis-of-variance methods, on the other hand (Bottenberg & Ward, 1963; Li, 1964; Ward, 1962). Excellent examples of its use occur in the massive study *Equality of Educational Opportunity* (Coleman & others, 1966) in which the effects of many variables on verbal achievement were exhaustively studied.

Randomization is the most interesting and potentially potent method of control of extraneous variance. Randomization means that members of a sample (that does not itself need to be a random sample) are assigned to experimental groups at random, usually by means of a table of random numbers. The idea behind randomization is this: Since every member of the sample has an equal chance of being assigned to any one of k experimental groups, members with certain distinguishing characteristics—extrovert-introvert, high and low intelligence, male-female, high and low anxiety, and so on—will, if assigned to a certain one of the k groups, in the long run probably be counterbalanced by the assignment of other members with the counterbalancing quantities or qualities of the characteristic. In other words, if one *assigns* subjects to experimental groups at random—and one does so thoroughly and adequately—then the groups can be considered to be statistically equal in all possible ways. This does not mean that the groups *are* equal; it means that the probability of their being equal is, with randomization, greater than the probability of their being equal if randomization had not been used. Random assignment, of course, is not limited to subject assignment. Experimental treatments can and should be assigned at random. Randomization is, theoretically and usually practically, the best possible method of control. It can be used only in experiments, however. Hence, it is unfortunately not a feasible method of control in much educational research, where the independent variables cannot be manipulated.

These, then, are the main characteristics of scientific research. It is clear that educational research must exhibit these characteristics if it is to be scientific. That it has not consistently exhibited them has been the source of most of the criticisms mentioned earlier. But it is evident, as we will see later, that educational-research studies are more and more satisfying scientific criteria.

Probabilistic Knowledge, Definitions, Variables, and Levels of Discourse. All knowledge of natural events is probabilistic in nature. Braithwaite even says that all general statements are in fact probability statements and that universal generalizations are special cases of probability statements since their probability is 1.00 (1953, p. 152). If it is possible to do so, we may say that generalizations in educational research are "more" probabilistic than generalizations in physical research because the evidence supporting the generalizations is weaker. What is so obvious as to be almost trite is that any statement made about any relation whatever must have, at least in the researcher's mind, a probability tag attached to it. This means that instead of saying—and believing—"if p, then q," we must say and think, "If p, then probably q," or "If p, then q, with such-and-such probability." In other words there are no scientific absolutes, and there are no educational absolutes. Indeed, in view of the great difficulty in controlling independent variables, the probabilistic nature of statements of relations, and the general flimsiness of human knowledge, especially in the social sciences and education, it is amazing that we have learned as much as we have about our social and educational worlds.

Psychologists use the word *construct* to express the idea that a concept has been deliberately adopted or created for special scientific purposes. Constructs are "type" or "class" words—for example, *achievement* expresses a class of behaviors associated with school work, *aggression* expresses a class that includes a number of particular behaviors that share the characteristic of hurting objects or people. A major difficulty of educational research is definition of its constructs. Educational constructs are often very broad and ambiguous. Learning, achievement, transfer of training, reinforcement, and so on must be defined in some functional way, or they cannot be handled in a scientific system. A necessary though not sufficient condition for scientific meaning is that the definitions of the constructs actually used in a research study must be operational.

An *operational definition* assigns meaning to constructs or variables by specifying the "operations" or activities necessary to manipulate or measure the constructs or variables. *Achievement*, for example, may be narrowed to "verbal achievement" and may be "defined" by scores on such-and-such a vocabulary test. Hurlock (1925) defined *incentives* by specifying experimentally different forms of reinforcing conditions: praising, reproving, ignoring. Although they yield only limited meanings of constructs, operational definitions are indispensable tools of educational research.

There is an inescapable dilemma here. The more interesting and significant constructs to the educator are those that are broad and ambiguous—school atmosphere, teacher morale, and achievement, for example. But in their broad and ambiguous form such constructs cannot be measured. To be amenable to scientific investigation, they must be made operational and thus measurable (or manipulable). They must, in short, be made narrow and specific. The narrower and more specific they are made, however, the less general interest they tend to have. The dilemma is partially resolved by realizing that the richness and interest of constructs like school atmosphere and achievement can be more and more approximated by different operational definitions used in different studies of different relations. Educational investigators have to some extent come to understand this dilemma, its resolution, and the necessity and virtue of operational definitions (see Langfeld, 1945; Margenau, 1950; Tate, 1950; Torgerson, 1958; Underwood, 1957).

When a construct is to be used in actual research, it is called a variable. A *variable*, loosely speaking, is a property that takes on different values: it is something that varies. More accurately, a variable is a symbol—say, x or y—to which numerals are assigned. Instead of this strict usage researchers usually say that "intelligence," "social class," "achievement," and so on, are variables. These words, however, serve the same function as x and y: they are symbols to which, ultimately at least, numerals are assigned.

Some writers make a distinction between quantitative and qualitative variables. This distinction does not seem to be useful or necessary. All variables are potentially quantitative by definition. So-called qualitative variables are really dichotomous variables to which the numerals 1 and 0, indicating presence or absence of some characteristic, can be assigned. The variable "sex," for instance, can be so quantified: say 1 for male and 0 for female.

Among the several ways that variables can be classified, perhaps the most useful is as independent and dependent. An *independent variable* is the *presumed* cause, or antecedent, of the *dependent* variable, the *presumed* effect, or consequent. In the conditional proposition "If p, then q," p is the independent variable and q the dependent variable. In educational research we often try to explain "achievement," a dependent variable, by relating to it a variety of independent variables—intelligence, aptitude, methods of teaching, level of aspiration, and others. Provided we do not assume causal relations, this independent–dependent-variable usage is flexible as well as useful, since we can keep the functional identity of our variables quite clear and since we can even change the function of a variable from independent to dependent, and vice versa. For example, it is possible to treat a variable like "anxiety" as an independent variable in one study and as a depenent variable in another study—or even in the same study.

A particularly difficult problem in education and educational research is knowing what we are talking about. This is what may be called the problem of relevance, or the problem of universes of discourse. If, for instance, we talk about the problem of studying empirically the determinants of achievement and then talk about the moral aspects of segregation, we have changed our universe of discourse. We have, in short, brought in irrelevant matters that, if not recognized as irrelevant, can obfuscate the discourse.

In scientific discourse the universe of discourse must be defined. Universes of discourse must not be mixed, unless we do so consciously and deliberately (in which case we would be relating them and not mixing them). As an example of what is meant, let U_1 be the presumed empirical determinants of school achievement—aptitude, home background, segregated schools, teaching methods, attitudes, and so on. To be relevant any "object" or element brought into the discourse must be a member of the set U_1. If, now, we bring in, say, the moral aspects of segregation, we have "slipped" our universe of discourse since U_1 includes only possible empirical determinants of achievement. It is, of course, not sinful to talk about the moral aspects of segregation. Strictly speaking, however, these aspects are irrelevant to the discourse: they belong to another universe of discourse—say, U_2. In other words, to talk relevantly to an issue we must ask the question Does this object, or matter, I am now bringing in belong to the defined universe of discourse? If not, it is irrelevant. It can only be made relevant by redefining the universe of discourse.

Ordinary discourse is full of irrelevancies. Indeed, many serious misunderstandings stem from "slippage" of universes of discourse. In research such slippage is disastrous. It effectively removes the empirical solution of research problems from our grasp. A wellknown case is, in talking about learning theory and education, to condemn learning theory because most learning research has been done with animals. It is said that the findings of such research are inapplicable to children. The universe of discourse here contains the results of animal learning research. No competent learning theorist would apply the generalizations obtained from animal research to children. He might say, of course, that such-and-such *may* be the case with children, but he would insist upon an empirical test of such extrapolation. In the latter case, the universe of discourse naturally changes.

In short, the investigator must ask himself: Do the objects I am now discussing or working with all belong to the set or sets of objects previously defined. In order to do this, the universe objects must be defined by a clear rule that tells us when an object is or is not a member of U. It is of course possible to work with subsets of U and with more than one U. The main thing is that U, or maybe U_1 and U_2, subsets of U, are clearly defined and that we are quite aware of what we are doing. To mix universes of discourse unknowingly can lead to conceptual disaster.

As a footnote to our discussion of the foundations of scientific research in education, we ask an important question: Is there a "science of education"? (Smith, 1950). The answer must be a clear no. The scientific approach can and should be applied to educational problems, but there is no science of education. To say there is, is as erroneous and confusing as saying that teaching is an art. Science is quite general: it is applicable to any discipline or field that has observable phenomena which can be put into relational juxtaposition in such a manner that hypotheses about the presumed relations can be systematically, objectively, and empirically tested. Education is such a discipline or field. But it is not itself a science.

TECHNICAL FOUNDATIONS OF RESEARCH. A crucial activity of scientific inquiry is the systematic testing of hypotheses. To understand scientific educational research, the conceptual and technical means or methods of testing hypotheses must be understood. This requires understanding what hypotheses are, the nature of relations in general, the logic of scientific inquiry, the design of research, measurement theory and practice, methods of observation and data collection, and methods of analysis. We now examine each of these topics in the context of scientific educational research. In doing so, we must see that all these aspects of inquiry are parts of a whole that should be viewed as a whole.

Relations and Hypotheses. Hypotheses were earlier said to be conjectural statements of the relations among variables. They are, then, relational propositions: they relate variables to variables, generally and specifically. We say p is related to q, or, if we know enough, p is related to q under conditions, r, s, and t. In actual research we may have several p's and even several q's, several independent variables and several dependent variables.

Science deals only with relations among classes or sets of "objects." When we say, for instance, that frustration produces aggression, we mean that a set of frustrated "objects" is connected in a "produce" relation to a set of aggressive "objects" and that the members of these sets are linked in what is called an ordered-pair way. A *relation*, then, is a set of ordered pairs (Kershner & Wilcox, 1950). The meaning and application of this definition are simple yet powerful.

Take the relation between two variables, verbal aptitude (VA) and reading achievement (RA). The set of VA objects consists of the VA test scores of a sample, say, of fourth-grade children, and the set of RA objects consists of the same children's RA scores. An "ordered pair" is the pair of test scores, VA and RA, of any child, always taking the VA score first and the RA score second. The whole set of pairs taken in this ordered way *is* the relation between VA and RA. The method is quite general: it applies to any relation and to any sets of objects and relations. Take another relation: between reading achievement and sex. We take the same RA scores and pair with each of them the child's sex. For quantitative purposes, we assign 1 to male and 0 to female. The set of ordered pairs of RA scores and sex scores (1 and 0) is the relation between reading achievement and sex. Of course, some index of the magnitude of the relation can and usually should be calculated.

While not as apparent as the above examples, any experiment can be viewed as a set of ordered pairs. Suppose five-year-old children are randomly assigned to two experimental conditions: a preschool reading-enrichment program and the usual kindergarten program. After a year the children's reading readiness is measured. We assign 1 to the reading enrichment program and 0 to the usual kindergarten program. The set of ordered pairs, each pair consisting of a reading readiness score and a 1 or a 0 depending on whether the child did or did not experience the enrichment program, is the relation between the experimental program and reading readiness. With more than two experimental groups, and even with factorial designs, the same reasoning applies.

Hypotheses are usually directional propositions of relations. While a pure relation may say nothing about direction and magnitude, hypotheses usually state the former and sometimes the latter. To say, for instance, frustration produces aggression, is to say that the correlation between frustration and aggression is positive. To say that anxiety lowers test performance is to imply a negative correlation between the two variables. Scientifically, directional hypotheses are usually stronger than statements of relations because they predict outcomes based on explicit or implicit theoretical notions. They are, therefore, the working instruments of theory, the essential tools of the hypothetico-deductive method. Without directional hypotheses, we cannot know whether or not observed data fit our theory (Cohen, 1956).

Logic and Scientific Inquiry. The skeleton of logical inference in science is fairly simple; p and q are propositions, or more simply, statements of some kind: the children were frustrated, the children exhibited aggressive behavior. Three logical connectives, *and*, *or*, and *if–then*, are needed. We write these as follows: "$\wedge$" for *and*, "$\vee$" for *or*, and "$\rightarrow$" for *if–then*. For example, $p \wedge q$ means "p and q," or "p and q are both true." This is logical multiplication. $p \vee q$ means "p or q," or "Either p is true, or q is true, or both are true." This is logical summation. $p \rightarrow q$ means "If p, then q." It is called a conditional statement.

The simplest form of scientific experiment requires that an independent variable be manipulated such that one group (experimental) receives a certain treatment and another group (control) does not. The many variations of this experimental design do not change its basic logical nature. Let p represent the statement "The children were frustrated." This statement is true of the experimental group: we "make it true" by frustrating the children in the experimental group in some way. Let $\sim p$, or "not-p," mean "The children were not frustrated." Let q mean "The children displayed aggressive behavior"; $\sim q$, of course, means that they did not exhibit aggressive behavior. Our hypothesis, deduced from theory (Dollard & others, 1939), says, in brief, "If frustration, then aggression," or "If p, then q." We seek to test the *empirical* validity of this hypothesis by means of our experiment. We want to know, however, what the underlying logic behind our experiment is and whether it is *logically* valid.

We somehow frustrate the experimental-group children. This establishes the "truth" of p, or "p is true." We do not frustrate the control-group children. This is $\sim p$, or "p is not true." We then observe the behavior of the children to see whether it is aggressive. We expect the experimental-group children but not the control-group children to exhibit such behavior. Let q mean "The children exhibited aggressive behavior." The meaning of $\sim q$ is obvious.

The symbols p and $\sim p$ represent, then, the experimental manipulation; q and $\sim q$ represent the observations of the dependent variable. Suppose the experiment "worked." Can we logically infer the truth of the hypothesis "If p, then q," "If frustration, then aggression"? Or even if the experiment did not "work," is our basic reasoning valid? It can be proved that the basic logical argument is valid (see Kemeny & others, 1956).

The experimental part of the argument is $(p \wedge q) \to (p \to q)$, which says "If p and q, then If p, then q." In the language of our experimental example, we can say, If the children were frustrated (p) *and* they exhibited aggressive behavior (q), then we can logically (validly) say "If frustration, then aggression." The symbolic representation of the control-group part of the argument is $(\sim p \wedge \sim q) \to (p \to q)$. It means "If 'not-$p$ and not-q,' then 'If p, then q.'" The reader can translate this into the material language of the experiment. This argument can also be shown to be valid.

The two arguments can be put together and proved to be valid when together. The symbolic representation of the joint argument is:

$$[(p \wedge q) \quad (\sim p \wedge \sim q)] \to (p \to q).$$

Remembering that "$\vee$" (*or*) means "both" (inclusive disjunction), we interpret the whole statement: "If p and q are 'true' [experimentally], or [and] $\sim p$ and $\sim q$ are 'true' [experimentally], then If p, then q." That is, if the children who were frustrated exhibited aggressive behavior, and the children who were not frustrated did not exhibit aggressive behavior, then we can validly infer "If frustration, then aggression."

This is a purely logical argument. It says nothing whatsoever about the worth of the experiment or the adequacy of the results. The important thing here is that arguments must be logically valid before they are anything else. Without logical validity the whole conceptual framework topples. It is quite possible in research to use invalid arguments. With the above hypothesis, for instance, we might have observed aggressive behavior in children and then in some way found that the children had been frustrated. While this procedure is not illegitimate, as we will see later, it would be a mistake if we reasoned "If aggressive behavior, then frustration; therefore, frustration produces aggression." This is the famous affirmation-of-the-consequent argument; it is not valid.

A useful by-product of studying the logic of scientific inquiry is an understanding of necessary and sufficient conditions (Kemeny & others, 1956, p. 40). To say "If q then p" is not the same as to say "If p, then q." We may be able to say, "If early deprivation, then children will be poor readers," but this does not mean that we can also say, "If poor readers, then early deprivation." This is the distinction between sufficient and necessary conditions. If we say that if p occurs, then q also occurs, or "If p, then q," we are stating that p is a *sufficient condition* for q. If, on the other hand, we say that if q occurs, then p also occurs, or "If q, then p," we are stating that p is a *necessary condition* for q.

To say that p is a *sufficient* condition for q means that whenever p occurs q also occurs. But q can, perhaps, occur without p. There are determinants of poor reading other than early deprivation, for example. When we say that p is a *necessary* condition for q, we mean "q only if p," or "Poor reading only if deprivation." Deprivation is now a necessary condition for poor reading. The statement "q only if p" is equivalent to "If q, then p," or, in the words of the example, "If poor reading, then early deprivation." In short, a necessary condition is the converse of a sufficient condition.

If we can say that p is a sufficient and necessary condition of q, we can say, "If p occurs, then q occurs, and q occurs only if p occurs," or "If early deprivation, then poor reading [sufficient condition], and poor reading only if early deprivation [necessary condition]." The difference between the two kinds of statements may perhaps be clarified by studying logical equivalents of a necessary condition. "If q, then p" is logically equivalent to "If not-p, then not-q." This means that when p is a necessary condition for q we can say "If p does not occur, then q will not occur." If early deprivation is a necessary condition for poor reading, we mean that if there were no early deprivation then there would not be poor reading. It should be clear that causal relations are not simple matters.

Scientists would like to be able to make statements of sufficient and necessary conditions. The harsh reality, however, is that they usually cannot—especially in the social sciences. Most, perhaps all, phenomena of psychological, sociological, and educational interest are determined by multiple and complex causes. Although the educational researcher often can say that p is a sufficient condition for q (though always with reservations), he can rarely or never say that p is a necessary condition for q. In other words, the educational researcher, like all other researchers, for the most part has to content himself with sufficient conditions (see Cohen & Nagel, 1934, p. 271). Indeed, he is lucky if he succeeds in establishing sufficient conditions. If the reader will reflect on the deprivation example given above, he may see what is meant.

The logic behind the testing of alternative or multiple hypotheses is an important part of the logic of scientific inquiry (Chamberlin, 1965; Cohen & Nagel, 1934, pp. 265–267). Platt (1964) has called the whole procedure and its logic strong inference. He goes so far as to say that any conclusion that is not an exclusion is insecure. The rule is simple: Test hypotheses other than the theoretically deduced, or basic, hypothesis, alternative hypotheses that are plausible and that, if substantiated, cast doubt on the basic hypothesis.

Actually, the procedure amounts to testing the relations between alternative independent variables, p_1, p_2, and p_3, say, and a dependent variable, q, the phenomenon to be explained. (In most research the phenomenon of major interest, the thing to be explained, is the dependent variable. For example, so-called underachievement is "explained" by its being related to a variety of independent variables; teacher success is "explained" by its being related to teacher characteristics, teacher training, intelligence, and so on.) Assume that $p_1 \to q$ is the basic hypothesis. Also assume that p_1, p_2, and p_3 exhaust the possibilities. Suppose that the researcher shows that $p_2 \to q$ is not true and that $p_3 \to q$ is not true. He also shows that

$p_1 \to q$ seems to be true. For example, r_{p_2q} might be .03 and r_{p_3q} might be −.01, whereas r_{p_1q} might be .48. The basic hypothesis, $p_1 \to q$, seems to be supported and the alternative hypotheses not supported.

Although testing alternative hypotheses is particularly important in education where plausible explanations are manufactured rather freely, we find few systematic examples in the literature. An instructive and important example, however, can be found in the large study of educational equality cited earlier (Coleman & others, 1966). In that study it was important to ascertain, among other things, whether home background (p_1) or school environment (p_2) was the major source of variance in verbal achievement (q). Study of the alternative relations seemed to show that home background was a more important source of achievement variance than school environment and education. (It should be noted that the alternatives here and in most behavioral research can never be exclusive. One shows, as best one can, that one source of variance is more important than other sources of variance.)

Logic is not a method of discovery, nor is it a method of ascertaining empirical truth. It is simply a method of testing the logical validity of arguments. It performs the valuable function of telling us the minimum essentials of inquiry. It should also be pointed out that no one can *prove* anything empirically. About the best any one can do is to use valid arguments and to combine confirmation and disconfirmation of hypotheses to build up evidence for or against theories. The reason we cannot prove anything empirically is that, although we know, and can prove, that the argument $(p \wedge q) \to (p \to q)$ is valid, we cannot ever be sure of the truth of $p \wedge q$. All we can say is that $p \wedge q$ is *probably* true. If we can say this with some confidence, however, we can validly reason to $p \to q$, though always probabilistically. As Russell has said so well, ". . . all human knowledge is uncertain, inexact, and partial" (1964, p. 507).

The Design of Research. A tremendous revolution in social scientific research has taken place in the last thirty years. The revolution, while manifested mostly in technical innovations, is actually a profound change in research outlook and thinking. We now approach the more technical aspects of the revolution by examining, if briefly, the areas of greatest impact: research design, methods of observation and data collection, measurement theory and practice, and statistics and data analysis.

Design is data discipline. Research design guides and imposes controlled restrictions on observations of phenomena. The design of research, broadly speaking, is its plan and structure; both are directed toward obtaining empirical answers to research questions in a systematically controlled manner. And all control is control of variance. The basic purposes of design, then, are to help provide answers to research questions and to control variance. Design provides the framework for adequate tests of the relations among the research variables. In short, a research design, once laid out, "tells" us what observations to make, how to make them, and how to analyze the data obtained from the observations.

One can see design's purpose of variance control nicely by examining the simplest form of so-called factorial design. A tripartite variance principle of the researcher is Maximize systematic variance (experimental, or independent variable, variance), control extraneous systematic variance (unwanted variance caused by independent variables not part of the research problem), and minimize error variance (variance of a random nature). A simple factorial design can be applied to a fairly common problem in educational research: the study of effects of different teaching methods (A) at various levels of intelligence (B) on some form of school learning—say, spelling (Y). Take two methods, A_1 and A_2, and two levels of intelligence, B_1 and B_2. *Methods* (A) is a systematic variable, of course. *Intelligence* (B) can be viewed, in this case, as a systematic extraneous variable whose variance we wish to control. (There is a better way to do this. The present case is only illustrative.) If we assign subjects at random within the two B levels to A_1 and A_2, we control all other possible sources of variance, except error variance.

It is now possible to study the variance due to methods, that due to intelligence, and, very important, that due to the interaction between methods and intelligence. That is, in addition to the possibility of studying the relations between each of two or more variables and a dependent variable, a factorial design adds an exceedingly important dimension to the classical experimental-group–control-group design. The investigator can incorporate a source of variation right into his design and can ultimately ask the data whether one variable, in this case methods, is differentially effective at different levels of another variable. Add to this that any number of experimental groups and any number of levels can be used, and we have a sharp and radical departure from the classical one-independent-variable-at-a-time approach. The studies done by the following workers are a small but particularly interesting sample that illustrate the power, richness, and elegance of modern research design applied to important educational problems: Amster (1966—specifically tested a theoretically deduced interaction hypothesis about concept learning), Marr and others (1960—studied effects of three independent variables in college teaching), McGuire (1961—dealt with four independent variables in a nonexperimental study), Overing and Travers (1966—studied transfer with three independent variables), and Wittrock (1963—dealt with three independent variables in a study of learning by discovery).

These design notions of Ronald Fisher's (1935, 1950), together with the invention of the form of statistical analysis known as analysis of variance, has revolutionized modern social scientific and educational research (Hotelling, 1951; Stanley, 1966; Yates, 1951). One might say that factor analysis and multivariate analysis, on the one hand, and analysis of variance and related notions, on the other hand, are two of the truly great inventions of our time. Together they are almost completely transforming behavioral and educational research (Walker, 1956).

Research design is of course much more than the analysis of variance. One uses principles of design, for example, to plan and execute nonexperimental, so-called ex post facto, studies. One may wish to study, as Gross and his colleagues did (1958), the different effects of different educational roles on perceptions of the school superintendent. One cannot manipulate the independent variable, role. Nevertheless, one must still design the research so that systematic controlled observations can be made and the resulting data analyzed in a manner that yields answers to the research questions. The analysis, for instance, may require the counting and comparing of different kinds of responses. No randomization may be possible. The overall research design is still data discipline and requires structure. The basic principles of maximizing or controlling independent-variable variance and minimizing error variance still apply.

An important general distinction that helps to clear up certain misunderstandings about research and research design is that between external validity and internal validity (Campbell, 1957; Campbell & Stanley, 1963). The *internal validity* of a study depends on the answer to the question Are x and y, the independent and dependent variables, really related as indicated by the data and its analysis? What this question boils down to is variance control. If observations have been made in a more or less uncontrolled manner, internal validity will be low. If, on the other hand, the design is adequate to the problem, randomization has been carried out, and care has been taken to exclude the effect of extraneous variables, then internal validity should be high. In other words, internal validity, when satisfactory, assures us that our x *is* the independent variable under study and that the discovered relation between x and y *is* the relation under study. If, for example, we have manipulated two teaching methods and found that a certain kind of achievement increases more with one method than with the other, we want to be assured that the increase in achievement is really a result of the method and not, say, of certain personality characteristics of the teachers who used the method.

External validity is the *representativeness* or *generalizability* of a study. The key question is, Do the findings of this study apply to other samples, to other situations? Strictly speaking, positive answers to this question depend upon random sampling of subjects—and even situations. Needless to say, seldom can successful answers be given in educational research. National and state random samples are rare because they are difficult and expensive to obtain. Still, we must ask external-validity questions. And it is often possible to sample randomly within a school district, within a school, or even within a county or other local geographical subdivision. An effort should always be made to obtain some kind of random sample, especially when external validity is an important consideration. (One must remember, however, that much research is not too much concerned with external validity. Investigators testing the predicted relations of a theory, for instance, are usually interested mainly in internal validity.)

Even if random samples cannot be obtained, studies *can* and should be replicated with different subjects from different places. Unfortunately, most studies in education (and psychology and sociology) are not replicated. Results obtained with one sample are reported, and the results frequently cited, more or less authoritatively. A good precept of educational research might be: Replicate every study with different samples in different places. Even different measuring instruments, different experimental manipulations, and different variables should be used. When a relation is found to be the same in different settings with different subjects, even with different kinds of subjects, the external validity of a study is greatly increased. The reader may find interesting the often imaginative replications done in the varied studies by the following people: Cooper (1959—replicated with different subjects and different procedures), Harlow (1949—done with monkeys and with children), Horowitz (1936—replicated in different regions of the country), Staats and Staats (1958—replicated with different stimuli); Stevenson and Zigler (1958—replications of experiment with normal children and with feebleminded children), Thorndike (1924—massive replication), Winter and others (1963—repeated at widely different times), and Yum (1931—same experiment with words and with visual patterns).

As Campbell and Stanley (1963) point out, internal validity is the sine qua non of research design. To be of any scientific worth at all, a study must have internal validity. It is desirable, but not absolutely essential, that it also have external validity. In other words, internal validity is a necessary condition of good research; external validity is a desirable but not a necessary condition (unless generalization is imperative, as in certain sample surveys).

Experimental and Ex Post Facto Studies. There are two general approaches to research: experimental and ex post facto. Both approaches study relations of the if p, then q kind. The experimental approach, however, has two inestimable advantages that the ex post facto approach does not have: the independent variables can be manipulated, and randomization can be used. In ex post facto research the independent variables have already "occurred." The investigator starts with observations of a dependent variable and then studies the independent variables retrospectively, so to speak, for their relations with the dependent variable. The independent variables are, strictly speaking, beyond the active manipulative control of the investigator. Randomization is also not possible.

The essential distinction between experimental and ex post facto approaches, then, is lack of direct control of independent variables. The investigator who wishes to study the effect of early deprivation on later school achievement, for example, cannot assign children to groups at random and then, say, systematically impoverish the background of one group of children, enrich the background of another group, and give another group a more or less normal background. What he must do is study the relation by comparing the school achievement of children whose backgrounds show differential deprivation. This is tantamount to observing y, school achievement, and then also observing a plausible x, deprivation, to see if the two vary together. If they do, he assumes that the proposition "If x, then y," "If deprivation, then poor school achievement," is established. But this assumption is comparatively weak because he has not controlled x directly.

The difference between the two approaches is profound. It may be believed that the investigator can strengthen his case by learning which children among large numbers of children live in deprived environments and then studying the school achievement of these children for some years. This belief is misguided. The case remains the same: direct control of the independent variable is not possible. Consequently, conclusions derived from ex post facto research are, other things being equal, weaker than conclusions derived from experimental research. Alternative conclusions are always possible and plausible, relatively more possible and plausible than with well-designed and controlled experimental research.

Although we cannot here discuss the ex post facto problem in the detail it deserves, we must look at two of its important features: self-selection and alternative independent variables. Actually, these are two sides of the same coin and will be discussed as such. *Self-selection* is the case where members of the groups being studied are in the groups, in part, because they differentially possess characteristics extraneous to the research problem. They "select" themselves into the deprived and nondeprived groups, for instance, because they are Negro and white. The correlation between deprivation and race, in other words, is substantial: Negroes tend to grow up in deprived environments, while the environments of whites tend not to be deprived. Let us say that the "real" determinant of low school achievement is not deprivation but rather the value-attitude system associated with being a Negro in American society. And in this case values and attitudes are, if we are saying "If deprivation, then poor school achievement," extraneous to the research problem (though not irrelevant to it). Similarly, deprivation might be extraneous if we were saying "If values and attitudes, then such-and-such school achievement."

The point is not that one or the other situation is "true" or "not true." The point is that in ex post facto research, where the direct controls of manipulation and randomization are not possible, self-selection and alternative independent variables are ever-present possibilities and either or both cases may be "true" or "not true." When Sears and others (1957) skillfully studied certain effects of certain child-rearing practices, for example, it is remarkable that they coped with the plethora of explanations of child behavior as well as they did in view of the variety and complexity of the variables involved.

For better or for worse, most educational research has to be ex post facto in nature simply because many variables are beyond direct control: all so-called sociological variables, such as race, social class, and environment, and many psychological variables—general anxiety, growth stages, creativity, parental upbringing, school atmosphere, teacher personality, and so on. It is important, then, to understand that many, or even most, educational research problems of large scientific and practical educational importance are ex post facto in nature but that there are ways to cope with such problems scientifically, even if these ways are essentially more difficult to handle and less sure in outcome than experimental ways. While it can be said that the experiment is the ideal of scientific investigation—indeed, the most powerful device man has invented to advance knowledge—it can also be said that nonexperimental research, while basically deficient in control, can be and must be done to yield scientific answers to many educational problems (see Nagel, 1961, Ch. 13). In the last analysis, of course, educational research must and should use both approaches to reliable knowledge of educational phenomena (Stanley, 1961).

Methods in Educational Research. A *method* is a systematic and standardized procedure for accomplishing some specific purpose: making observations, measuring variables, analyzing data. The purpose of methods of observation is to enable the researcher to so observe that symbols or numerals can be assigned to the sets of objects under study. An observation method, then, enables the researcher to obtain measures of variables in order to bring empirical evidence to bear on research questions.

There is always mutual dependence between problem and method. To a large extent problems dictate methods. If child-rearing practices are being explored to obtain measures of parental control, interviews are appropriate (see, for example, Sears & others, 1957). One might, of course, also observe parental behavior directly. Or one might set up parent-child interaction role-playing situations and observe the interactions directly. It is hardly likely that one would use an objective test or scale, since the focus of interest is in what parents do or have done or say they have done.

It would be foolish and unrealistic to deny that methods influence problems, both what problems are studied and how they are studied. Because reliable and valid methods to obtain measures of the kind of repression Freud talked about are at present rare, if not nonexistent, repression rarely enters research problems. Only recently has the meaning of concepts been used in research problems because methods of studying meaning were quite imperfect or nonexistent (Osgood & others, 1957). Important research problems involving choice, dominance, influence, and communication have only recently been opened up by the invention of sociometric methods (Lindzey & Borgatta, 1954).

Methods of observation and data collection are discussed elsewhere in this volume (see RESEARCH METHODS) and need not be discussed further here except to say that they must always spring from the demands of problems, even to the extent of being invented to fit the problems. We all have a tendency to feel warm toward certain methods and cold toward others. While it may do no great harm to indulge these feelings a little, blindly following them, or using methods through ignorance of the demands of problems or through lack of knowledge of the methods available, can and probably will be disastrous. For more complete discussions of these and other points and technical aspects of methods of observation see the works by the following workers: Festinger and Katz (1953, Chs. 6-9); Jahoda and others (1951, Vol. 2); Kerlinger (1964, Chs. 26-33); Lindzey (1954, Chs. 10-13); Mussen (1960); Stephenson (1953); Travers (1958, Chs. 6, 8, 9); and Walker (1956).

Measurement. Truly remarkable advances have been made in the last forty years in measurement theory and practice. The definition of measurement is well understood and generally accepted. The nature of reliability has been rather thoroughly and deeply explored. The nature of validity is better understood than it was twenty years ago. Scientific knowledge of intelligence, aptitudes, attitudes, and personality traits, while still meager compared to what remains to be known, is far greater than anyone could have foreseen in, say, 1910. A great deal is also known about the construction of tests, scales, and instruments to measure psychological and sociological variables.

Measurement is the assignment of numerals to objects and events according to rules (Stevens, 1951). The implications of this important definition have been penetratingly explored by Guilford (1954), Torgerson (1958), and Stevens (1951). The definition means that a set of numerals—$\{0, 1\}$, $\{0, 1, 2, 3, \cdots\}$, $\{I, II, III, \cdots\}$, or $\{.00, .01, -.01, .02, -.02, \cdots\}$, for example—can be mapped onto a set of objects according to some rule of correspondence: 1 if male object, 0 if female object; 5 if approve strongly, 4 if approve, and so on to 1 if disapprove strongly; rank 1 if highest, rank 2 if next highest, and so on. The rule, in other words, tells us which numerals with what meaning to assign to what objects, and how to make the assignment.

Kerlinger (1964, p. 414) has suggested that the definition of measurement may be summarized in one functional equation:

$$f = \{(x, y); x = \text{any object, and } y = \text{any numeral}\}.$$

This is interpreted as follows: f is a rule of correspondence that is defined as a set of ordered pairs, (x, y), such that x is some object and y is some numeral assigned to x. The definition tells us nothing about the quality of a measurement instrument; the rules can be "good" or "bad." It tells us, however, that anything is potentially measurable and that educational researchers indeed have a wide range of possibilities. Unfortunately, this has not been well understood. It has also not been too well understood that measurement is measurement, no matter what the field or the sets of objects. It makes no theoretical difference whatsoever whether we measure aggressiveness, anxiety, intelligence, group cohesiveness, racial prejudice, authoritarianism, school atmosphere, or human values: the same definition applies. Only the numerals, their meaning, and the rules change.

Two basic questions (among other questions) must be asked of any measurement procedure: Are we measuring what we think we are measuring? and How accurate are our measurements? These are questions of validity and reliability. Both validity and reliability have several types or aspects that have been well and thoroughly discussed in the literature (American Psychological Association, 1966; Campbell, 1960; Cronbach & Meehl, 1955; Guilford, 1954, Chs. 13 and 14; Gulliksen, 1950; Loevinger, 1957; Tryon, 1957). Among the newer contributions to measurement theory, one of the most significant for psychological and educational research is the development of the notion of construct validity. It is suggested that educational researchers will profit greatly from careful study of this notion and its implications because it forges a strong link between measurement procedures and scientific inquiry (Cronbach & Meehl, 1955). There is, however, dissent about the value of construct validity, and the student can of course profit from study of contrary opinion (Bechtoldt, 1959; Ebel, 1961).

Theory has been one of the most important and salutary, though infrequent, influences on the construction of measurement instruments. Most tests and scales have been constructed on an a priori basis. A researcher interested in the relation between, say, social conservatism and board-of-education budget decisions may write a number of items that seem to him to measure conservatism. The items may or may not be analyzed statistically. The interest in the conservatism measure is pragmatic; no real interest is taken in the dimensions of conservatism, and there is little explicit concern for relevant theory. Although this approach is still apparent in psychological and educational research, there are clear signs of change. Measurement instruments constructed on theoretical bases and with systematic concern for the factors underlying the items have been and are being constructed and used to good effect (e.g., Adorno & others, 1950; Cattell, 1957; Edwards, 1954; Getzels & Jackson, 1962; Guilford, 1959; McClelland & others, 1953; Morris & Jones, 1955; Rokeach, 1960; Ryans, 1960; Sarason & others, 1960; Sorenson & others, 1963; Stephenson, 1953; Stern & others, 1960). The sophistication of much contemporary measurement is in sharp contrast to the bulk of such activity in the past (with certain significant exceptions—for example, Allport & others, 1951; Hartshorne & May, 1928; Thurstone, 1944; Thurstone & Thurstone, 1941).

Unfortunately, the crucial importance of the measurement aspects of research, particularly validity, is not well recognized, even though its importance *is* well recognized in the construction of tests for large-scale use. That is, while hundreds of hours will be spent in the construction of an intelligence or aptitude test, and great pains taken to improve its reliability and validity, comparatively little effort is given to the construction of measures to be used in a research project. An educational investigator, for instance, may want to study attitudes toward education and the role perceptions of teachers. Assuming that measures of one or both these variables are not available, the investigator has to construct them. He must realize that both variables are complex. The construction of a scale to measure role perceptions, for example, is difficult and laborious (see Sorenson & others, 1963).

It is not enough to write or collect a set of items that one *thinks* reflect teacher role perceptions. One must demonstrate that the items actually do reliably and validly measure the role perceptions. There is no reasonable alternative. If reliability is low, correlations between variables will be low, perhaps considerably lower than they should be. Similarly, differences between means of experimental groups may not be statistically significant because of the low reliability of a dependent-variable measure. More important, however, substantial correlations and significant differences between means are quite misleading if one or more measures used have doubtful validity. Of what use is a study of creativity if the measures of creativity are not really measures of creativity?

Analytic Tools of Research. There can be little doubt that the greatest technical progress in research procedures has been in analysis of data, especially in statistics. This progress can be illustrated by the competent, even imaginative, use of analytic techniques that have appeared in the recent literature (e.g., Amster, 1966; Anderson, 1965; Astin, 1962; Coleman & others, 1966; Doris, 1959; McGuire, 1961; Page, 1958; Wallach & Kogan, 1965; Wittrock, 1963). The two most important sets of statistical methods are analysis of variance and multivariate analysis (including factor analysis). Analysis of variance, in addition to having strong analytic power and elegance, has had a most important influence on conceptualization of research problems and the design of research to solve the problems, as was shown earlier. Because its use and purpose are rather well known, and because it was discussed and illustrated earlier in this essay, we now concentrate on factor analysis and multivariate analysis, after briefly examining the purpose of analytic tools.

The purpose of analysis is to break down, order, summarize, and test data so that answers to research questions can be obtained. The analyzed data are then interpreted, which means that they are related to the research questions and hypotheses and to other data. A primary purpose of statistics, for example, is to summarize numerical data and to compare obtained results with chance expectations. If the chance expectations are exceeded at some accepted probability level, the hypothesized relations are said to be "significant" in a statistical sense. Perhaps more important, measures of the magnitude of relations can be and should be calculated in experimental as well as in nonexperimental studies (Haggard, 1958; Hays, 1963). Such analyses form the major portion of the analyses of published studies. They emphasize the summary and test functions of analysis and are most obviously connected to experimental studies.

So-called correlational methods exemplify the breakdown, order, and summary functions of analysis. The most powerful and impressive of these methods are factor analysis and multivariate analysis (which, if loosely interpreted, can include factor analysis). These are exceedingly important techniques that have grown vigorously in the last decade (though they are not new), that are profoundly influencing behavioral research, and that will influence it much more in the 1970's.

"Multivariate analysis" is a term used to describe a variety of statistical procedures whose purpose is to analyze multiple measures of N individuals (Cattell, 1966; Cooley & Lohnes, 1962; Kendall, 1957; see also STATISTICAL METHODS). Their practicability and fairly ready access are adding new dimensions to educational research. A number of educational-research problems that were either inconceivable or computationally intractable are now readily approached with multivariate techniques and the modern computer.

For example, take canonical correlation and the familiar academic prediction problem. The usual multiple regression approach is restricted to one dependent variable, some measure of academic achievement. But just as there are multiple determinants of achievement and thus multiple independent variables, there are multiple dimensions of achievement and thus need for simultaneous analysis, so to speak, of more than one measure of achievement. Canonical-correlation analysis is a multiple regression and correlation technique extended to k-dimensional dependent-variable space. It handles several independent variables and several dependent variables at a time and, among other things, calculates canonical-correlation coefficients between related subsets of independent and dependent variables. A canonical-correlation coefficient expresses the maximum correlation between the two sets of variables. Multiple regression is actually a special case of the more general canonical correlation. Although it has not been used very much, canonical correlation is indeed a powerful analytic instrument (Maxwell, 1961; Mukherjee, 1966).

Suppose we want to study the relation between a combination of verbal aptitude, numerical aptitude, and need for achievement, on the one hand, and verbal achievement, on the other hand. We can, of course, use multiple correlation and regression (see Coleman & others, 1966). Would it not be better, however, if we used other measures of achievement, too? For example, a combination of verbal achievement, mathematical achievement, and social studies achievement? Canonical correlation allows us to do this by providing us with a method that analyzes the relations between the two *sets* of variables. Its applicability to many educational-research problems should be evident.

Other methods of multivariate analysis are multivariate analysis of variance, multiple discriminant analysis, and certain miscellaneous procedures (Cattell, 1966; Cooley & Lohnes, 1962; Kendall, 1957). Within five or ten years these techniques will probably be commonly accepted ways of analyzing educational-research data. It will be understood, no doubt, that certain aspects of analysis of variance can be subsumed under and perhaps better accomplished with multiple regression and correlation (Bottenberg & Ward, 1963; Li, 1964; Williams, 1959).

Through analyzing the relations among a number

of measures obtained from a large number of individuals (or objects), factor analysis helps to determine the dimensions or factors underlying the measures. It has won a firm place for itself in psychological and educational research because it is a general and powerful method for determining the underlying dimensions of variable domains, for studying the substantive nature of these dimensions, and for testing hypotheses. While conceived primarily as an exploratory technique (Guilford, 1954, p. 522; Thurstone, 1947, p. 56), there is no substantial reason why it cannot be used for testing hypotheses, even in experimental investigations. Cattell (1952, Ch. 20) makes some interesting suggestions. So does Guilford (1961). Fruchter (1966) discusses possibilities and techniques in considerable depth. Thurstone himself, who evidently conceived of factor analysis as basically exploratory, with its "principal usefulness at the border line of science" (Thurstone, 1947, p. 56), actually tested hypotheses about the relations between tests of mental abilities and the structure of intelligence (Thurstone & Thurstone, 1941). Guilford's thinking and work are saturated with what might be called factor hypotheses (Guilford, 1950, 1956, 1959).

Factor analysis has been used primarily to determine the factors behind tests. French (1951) has exhaustively summarized earlier studies of this kind mainly by providing actual data. One should be aware, however, that factor analysis can be and has been used to study the factors behind various kinds of measures. Astin (1962), for example, has explored the qualities of higher-educational institutions. Hemphill and others (1962) have measured and analyzed administrative performance. Pruzek and Coffman (1966) uncovered the factors behind the mathematics sections of the Scholastic Aptitude Test in a significant item factor analysis. Ryans (1960) factor-analyzed observational ratings of teacher behaviors. Sears and others (1957) extracted and interpreted the factors behind a set of child-rearing measures obtained from mothers by interviews. Even the relations among concepts (Osgood & others, 1957) and among persons (Stephenson, 1953) have been factor-analyzed with fruitful results.

THE ELECTRONIC COMPUTER AND EDUCATIONAL RESEARCH. The extremely rapid and remarkable development in the past ten or fifteen years of the electronic digital computer has been the single most important technological factor in changing educational research. The heart of its influence has been in data analysis and in the development of data-analysis techniques. Before the computer, analytic methods requiring innumerable calculations could be applied only to a limited extent. Today, almost all known methods of analysis can be readily and repeatedly done with relative ease, given adequate knowledge of analysis and computer possibilities and limitations—and, of course, a computer.

That lengthy and complex analyses can be done is not the key point, however. The very nature of research problems has changed and will continue to change. This is what is important. Earlier we saw that by using canonical correlation the relations between several independent and several dependent variables could be studied. We also saw that this changes the kinds of problems that can be attacked. While adequate methods of factor analysis were rather well known, problems that required lengthy calculations were hard to conceive, let alone to do. For example, it has been known for some time that item factor analysis might be a powerful approach to the validity of attitude, personality, and other scales and tests (Cattell, 1952, pp. 388–389; Guilford, 1954, p. 433). But it occurred to very few researchers even to attempt it because of the forbidding calculations involved. Now quite feasible, its use should profoundly influence psychological theory and test and scale construction. Canonical analysis, too, was so forbidding computationally that hardly anyone tried to think canonically, so to speak, and to implement the thinking. To this day, therefore, adequate conceptualization and investigation of the academic prediction problem still lag.

The computer brings with it a number of side effects that are strongly influencing educational research. For one thing, the computer is a teacher: it forces the researcher to learn his methods in depth. To make a computer do something requires detailed operational instructions. Such instructions ordinarily require rather complete functional understanding of the methods used. A second side effect is that researchers must understand computer usage and programming. It is commonly believed that the practicing researcher need not know much about the computer and programming—all he needs are packaged programs or a programmer who will tell the machine what he wants it to do. Such a belief is dangerous. Package programs are sometimes inadequate. The methods they use are often not congruent with the analytic demands of research problems. Many professional programmers, unfortunately, do not understand the demands of analysis and inference. Hence, the researcher, even to communicate with a programmer, must have computer and programming know-how. Without it he risks the dangers of uninspired, mindless, and trivial data collection, the magnification of errors, and the abuse of a powerful tool for meaningless purpose (cf. Cattell, 1966, p. 7). Moreover, he is at the mercy of inadequate programs and programmers who may not really understand the needs of the researcher. To expect programmers to understand behavioral-research methodology is to expect too much. Instead, researchers must understand the computer and know how to use it.

Another side effect is educationally interesting: the computer is forcing curriculum changes in schools of education, particularly in graduate programs. In the next five years, learning computer usage and some machine language will probably become a required part of the graduate curricula of many schools. The substitution of a computer language for one of the usual natural languages required for the Ph.D. degree is probably not far off. Schools-of-education faculties will also have to consider how their students will learn the mathematics and statistics necessary for computer usage. At least the basic elements of matrix algebra, for instance, have to be known for an intelligent use of the computer for data analysis.

While data analysis is and will remain the main use of the computer in educational research, other uses will become increasingly important. Computer-assisted instruction, computer simulation of cognitive processes, artificial intelligence, information processing, and other areas of computer use are still in their infancy. However, they are growing rapidly, and some of them can be expected to influence education and educational research. How their influence will be felt and how much it will be felt is hard to say. Too little is now known about their potentiality and practical applicability. The interested reader will find informative discussions of these newer areas of computer work in the works of Borko (1962), Green (1963), Hilgard and Bower (1966, Chs. 12 and 16), Hovland (1960), and in the special issue of *Scientific American* (1966).

PROBLEMS AND PROSPECTS. As indicated in the beginning of this article, educational research has been severely criticized for its inadequacies. Coladarci (1960) and Travers (1958) attributed some of these inadequacies to educators' indifference to research, particularly in schools of education. In a survey of institutions that give the doctorate in education, Fattu (1960) found that only 10 of 94 institutions were making serious efforts to encourage research. Like other critics, Fattu observed that indifference to research is related in part to practitioner domination of the institutions. Foshay (1965) has also pointed out that the practical orientations of teaching and service have helped to impede research. Ryans (1957) even found that educational-research offices did not really do research. Instead, they did mostly administrative accounting and public relations.

Tate (1950) remarked that there was a "painful disproportion" between the amount of educational research done and the scientific value of the results. He said that most research results were unreliable and trivial, not deserving serious consideration. Stanley (1954, 1957) deplored the lack of experimental finesse of educational psychologists and the generally poor quality of research in education. He also pointed out that professors in schools of education do very little research. Norton and Lindquist (1951), in an instructive critical analysis of actual research studies, expressed their dissatisfaction with the general quality of contemporary educational research and especially with design and statistical analysis. Another source of educational-research inadequacy seems to be student quality. In a study of doctoral productivity, Harmon (1961) found the mean IQ of the holders of 1958 education doctorates to be considerably lower than the mean of all the groups of holders of 1958 doctorates (123.8 versus 130.8). Jensen (1962) said that graduate students of education lack scholastic drive and aptitude, work sporadically and half-heartedly, are too practical-problem-oriented, are intolerant of the abstract and the theoretical, and are even antipathetic to the objective, quantitative, and experimental study of behavior!

Schools of education have evidently provided atmospheres and conditions uncongenial to scientific research (Halpin, 1966, Ch. 8). Comprehension of scientific theory and research and understanding of their importance and potential value to education have been lacking. The most important causes of this situation seem to have been the very strong emphasis on practicality in schools of education, a general lack of research tradition in education, and questionable attitudes of professors and students toward research.

On the hopeful side, Bloom (1966), in his short history of recent educational research, said that significant methodological contributions have been made in statistics, computer technology, the mapping of human characteristics, testing, and instructional procedures. He has also said that educational research has contributed significantly to conceptions of individual development, effects of the environment on development, the predictability and modifiability of human characteristics (Bloom, 1964), individual differences of learners, principles of learning, and teaching methods and instructional strategies.

Perhaps the fairest statement that can be made about the status of educational research is that much of it has unquestionably been poor in quality and wanting in significance but that it has in general accomplished most of the things Bloom says it has, and it has improved markedly in recent years. But how can educational research be poor in quality and still have accomplished the things Bloom says it has? The answer is that the negative judgment is general: it applies to most of the studies done. The solid accomplishments come from relatively few investigators.

There *are* signs of improvement, however. The best of these signs are perhaps the clear indications in the literature of increased sophistication in the use of theory, hypotheses and alternative hypotheses, research design, operational thinking and definitions, and analytic tools. While it would be naïve to say that educational institutions have drastically altered their atmospheres and orientations and that all, or even most, professors and graduate students of education understand and appreciate research, there is considerable hope that school-of-education atmospheres will become more congenial to research, that understanding of research will grow, that research training will improve, and that better educational research will be done.

Educational research is entering an exciting decade. After twenty or more years of doldrums, it has finally emerged into a research world that has changed drastically in breadth and depth. Abundant resources of conceptual and technical knowledge are available. Financial support is available. More young talent is entering the field. Behavioral scientists are taking much more interest in education and are contributing substantially to educational research. The research literature of the 1960's clearly shows the effects of these resources.

Educational researchers are not magicians, however, and educational research can perform no miraculous cures of educational ills. Educational research brings into being no brave new world of education. But properly nurtured it can go a long way toward helping us to understand principles of learning and growth, methods of instruction, curriculum problems, and values and attitudes that influence learning processes and educational environments—in a few words, the fundamental principles that underlie educational processes.

Fred N. Kerlinger
New York University

References

Adorno, T. W., and others. *The Authoritarian Personality.* Harper, 1950. 990p.
Allport, Gordon W., and others. *Study of Values.* Houghton, 1951; 2nd ed., 1951. 12p.
American Psychological Association. *Standards for Educational and Psychological Tests and Manuals.* APA, 1966. 40p.
Amster, Harriett. "Effect of Instructional Set and Variety of Instances on Children's Learning." *J Ed Psychol* 57:74–85; 1966.
Anderson, Richard C. "Can First Graders Learn an Advanced Problem-solving Skill?" *J Ed Psychol* 56:283–94; 1965.
Astin, Alexander W. "An Empirical Characterization of Higher Educational Institutions." *J Ed Psychol* 53:224–35; 1962.
Ausubel, David P. "The Nature of Educational Research." *Ed Theory* 3:314–20; 1953.
Bechtoldt, Harold P. "Construct Validity: A Critique." *Am Psychologist* 14:619–29; 1959.
Bloom, Benjamin S. *Stability and Change in Human Characteristics.* Wiley, 1964. 237p.
Bloom, Benjamin S. "Twenty-five Years of Educational Research." *Am Ed Res J* 3:211–21; 1966.
Borko, Harold. (Ed.) *Computer Applications in the Behavioral Sciences.* Prentice-Hall, 1962. 333p.
Bottenberg, Robert A., and Ward, Joe H., Jr. *Applied Multiple Linear Regression.* 6570th Personnel Research Laboratory, Air Force Systems Command, 1963. 139p.
Brain, Walter Russell. "Science and Antiscience." *Sci* 148:192–8; 1965.
Braithwaite, Richard B. *Scientific Explanation.* Cambridge U Press, 1953. 376p.
Briggs, Thomas H. "Research in Education." *Phi Delta Kappan* 46:99–103; 1964.
Bronowski, Jacob. *Science and Human Values,* rev. ed. Harper, 1965. 119p.
Buchler, Justus. (Ed.) *Philosophical Writings of Peirce.* Dover, 1955. 386p.
Campbell, Donald T. "Factors Relevant to the Validity of Experiments in Social Settings." *Psychol B* 54:297–312; 1957.
Campbell, Donald T. "Recommendations for APA Test Standards Regarding Construct, Trait, or Discriminant Validity." *Am Psychologist* 15:546–53; 1960.
Campbell, Donald T., and Stanley, Julian C. "Experimental and Quasi-experimental Designs for Research on Teaching." In Gage, N. L. (Ed.) *Handbook of Research on Teaching.* Rand McNally, 1963. p. 171–246.
Cattell, Raymond B. *Factor Analysis.* Harper, 1952. 462p.
Cattell, Raymond B. *Personality and Motivation Structure and Measurement.* Harcourt, 1957. 948p.
Cattell, Raymond B. (Ed.) *Handbook of Multivariate Experimental Psychology.* Rand McNally, 1966. 959p.
Chamberlin, T. C. "The Method of Multiple Working Hypotheses." *Sci* 148:754–9; 1965.
Clark, David L. "Educational Research: A National Perspective." In Culbertson, Jack A., and Hencley, Stephen P. (Eds.) *Educational Research: New Perspectives.* Interstate, 1963. p. 7–18.
Cohen, Morris R. *A Preface to Logic.* Meridian, 1956. 224p.
Cohen, Morris R., and Nagel, Ernest. *An Introduction to Logic and Scientific Method.* Harcourt, 1934. 467p.
Coladarci, Arthur P. "Towards More Rigorous Educational Research." *Harvard Ed R* 30:3–11; 1960.
Coleman, James S., and others. *Equality of Educational Opportunity.* HEW, USOE, GPO, 1966. 737p.
Cooley, William W., and Lohnes, Paul R. *Multivariate Procedures for the Behavioral Sciences.* Wiley, 1962. 211p.
Cooper, Joseph B. "Emotion in Prejudice." *Sci* 130: 314–8; 1959.
Cronbach, Lee J. "The Role of the University in Improving Education." *Phi Delta Kappan* 17:539–45; 1966.
Cronbach, Lee J., and Meehl, Paul E. "Construct Validity in Psychological Tests." *Psychol B* 52: 281–302; 1955.
Dollard, John, and others. *Frustration and Aggression.* Yale U, 1939. 209p.
Doris, John. "Test-anxiety and Blame-assignment in Grade School Children." *J Abn Social Psychol* 58: 181–90; 1959.
Dubos, René. "Scientist and Public." *Sci* 133:1207–11; 1961.
Ebel, Robert L. "Must All Tests Be Valid?" *Am Psychologist* 16:640–7; 1961.
Edwards, Allen L. *Personal Preference Schedule: Manual.* Psych Corp, 1954. 18p.
Falk, John L. "Issues Distinguishing Idiographic from Nomothetic Approaches to Personality Theory." *Psychol R* 63:53–62; 1956.
Fattu, Nicholas A. "A Survey of Educational Research at Selected Universities." In Banghart, Frank W. (Ed.) *First Annual Phi Delta Kappa Symposium on Educational Research.* PDK, 1960. p. 1–21.
Feigl, Herbert. "The Scientific Outlook: Naturalism and Humanism." In Feigl, Herbert, and Brodbeck, May. (Eds.) *Readings in the Philosophy of Science.* Appleton, 1953. p. 8–18.
Festinger, Leon, and Katz, Daniel. (Eds.) *Research*

Methods in the Behavioral Sciences. Holt, 1953. 660p.

Findley, Warren G. "The Impact of Applied Problems on Educational Research." In Banghart, Frank W. (Ed.) *First Annual Phi Delta Kappa Symposium on Educational Research.* PDK, 1960. p. 43–53.

Fisher, Ronald A. *The Design of Experiments.* Hafner, 1935. 244p.

Fisher, Ronald A. *Statistical Methods for Research Workers,* 11th ed. Hafner, 1950. 354p.

Foshay, Arthur W. "Issues and Dilemmas in Nurturing the Educational Researcher in an Organizational Setting." In Guba, Egon, and Elam, Stanley. (Eds.) *The Training and Nurture of Educational Researchers.* PDK, 1965. p. 163–79.

French, J. *The Description of Aptitude and Achievement Tests in Terms of Rotated Factors.* Psychometric Monograph No. 5, U Chicago Press, 1951. 278p.

Fruchter, Benjamin. "Manipulative and Hypothesis-testing Factor-analytic Experimental Designs." In Cattell, Raymond B. (Ed.) *Handbook of Multivariate Experimental Psychology.* Rand McNally, 1966. p. 330–54.

Getzels, Jacob W., and Jackson, Philip W. *Creativity and Intelligence.* Wiley, 1962. 293p.

Getzels, Jacob W., and Jackson, Philip W. "The Teacher's Personality and Characteristics." In Gage, N. L. (Ed.) *Handbook of Research on Teaching.* Rand McNally, 1963. p. 506–82.

Green, Bert F., Jr. *Digital Computers in Research.* McGraw-Hill, 1963. 333p.

Griffiths, Daniel E. *Research in Educational Administration: An Appraisal and a Plan.* Teachers Col, Columbia U, 1959. 59p.

Gross, Neal, and others. *Explorations in Role Analysis: Studies of the School Superintendency Role.* Wiley, 1958. 379p.

Guilford, J. P. "Creativity." *Am Psychologist* 5:444–54; 1950.

Guilford, J. P. *Psychometric Methods,* 2nd ed. McGraw-Hill, 1954. 597p.

Guilford, J. P. "The Structure of Intellect." *Psychol B* 53:267–93; 1956.

Guilford, J. P. "Three Faces of Intellect." *Am Psychologist* 14:469–79; 1959.

Guilford, J. P. "Factorial Angles to Psychology." *Psychol R* 68:1–20; 1961.

Gulliksen, Harold. *Theory of Mental Tests.* Wiley, 1950. 486p.

Haggard, Ernest A. *Intraclass Correlation and the Analysis of Variance.* Holt, 1958. 171p.

Halpin, Andrew W. *Theory and Research in Administration.* Macmillan, 1966. 352p.

Harlow, Harry F. "The Formation of Learning Sets." *Psychol R* 56:51–65; 1949.

Harmon, Lindsey R. "High School Backgrounds of Science Doctorates." *Sci* 133:679–88; 1961.

Hartshorne, Hugh, and May, Mark A. *Studies in Deceit.* Macmillan, 1928. 306p.

Hays, William L. *Statistics for Psychologists.* Holt, 1963. 719p.

Hemphill, John K., and others. *Administrative Performance and Personality.* Teachers Col, Columbia U, 1962. 432p.

Hilgard, Ernest R., and Bower, Gordon H. *Theories of Learning,* 3rd ed. Appleton, 1966. 661p.

Horowitz, Eugene L. "Development of Attitude Toward Negroes." In *Archives of Psychology,* 1936.

Hotelling, Harold. "The Impact of R. A. Fisher on Statistics." *J Am Stat Assn* 46:35–46; 1951.

Hovland, Carl I. "Computer Simulation of Thinking." *Am Psychologist* 15:687–93; 1960.

Hubbert, M. King. "Are We Retrogressing in Science?" *Sci* 139:884–90; 1963.

Hurlock, Elizabeth. "An Evaluation of Certain Incentives Used in Schoolwork." *J Ed Psychol* 16:145–59; 1925.

Jahoda, Marie, and others. *Research Methods in Social Relations.* Holt, 1951. 759p.

Jensen, Arthur R. "The Improvement of Educational Research." *Teach Col Rec* 64:20–7; 1962.

Kemeny, John G., and others. *Introduction to Finite Mathematics.* Prentice-Hall, 1956. 372p.

Kendall, Maurice G. *A Course in Multivariate Analysis.* Hafner, 1957. 185p.

Kerlinger, Fred N. "Practicality and Educational Research." *Sch R* 67:281–91; 1959.

Kerlinger, Fred N. *Foundations of Behavioral Research: Educational and Psychological Inquiry.* Holt, 1964. 730p.

Kershner, R. B., and Wilcox, L. R. *The Anatomy of Mathematics.* Ronald, 1950. 416p.

Kidd, Charles V. "Basic Research—Description Versus Definition." *Sci* 129:368–71; 1959.

Langfeld, Herbert S. (Ed.) "Symposium on Operationism." *Psychol R* 52:241–94; 1945.

Li, Jerome C. R. *Statistical Inference,* Vol. 2: *The Multiple Regression and Its Ramifications.* Edwards, 1964. 575p.

Lindzey, Gardner. (Ed.) *Handbook of Social Psychology.* Addison, 1954. 1226p.

Lindzey, Gardner, and Borgatta, Edgar F. "Sociometric Measurement." In Lindzey, Gardner. (Ed.) *Handbook of Social Psychology,* Vol. 1. Addison, 1954. Ch. 11.

Loevinger, Jane. "Objective Tests as Instruments of Psychological Theory." *Psychol Reports* (Monogr. Suppl. 9) 3:635–94; 1957.

Margenau, Henry. *The Nature of Physical Reality.* McGraw-Hill, 1950. 479p.

Marr, John N., and others. "The Contribution of the Lecture to College Teaching." *J Ed Psychol* 51:277–84; 1960.

Maxwell, A. E. "Canonical Variate Analysis When the Variables Are Dichotomous." *Ed Psychol Meas* 21:259–71; 1961.

McClelland, David C., and others. *The Achievement Motive.* Appleton, 1953. 384p.

McGuire, Carson. "Sex Role and Community Variability in Test Performances." *J Ed Psychol* 52:61–73; 1961.

McNemar, Quinn. "At Random: Sense and Nonsense." *Am Psychologist* 15:295–300; 1960.

Monroe, Walter S., and Engelhart, Max D. *The Tech-*

niques of Educational Research. U Illinois Press, 1928. 84p.

Morris, Charles, and Jones, Lyle V. "Value Scales and Dimensions." *J Abn Social Psychol* 51:523–35; 1955.

Mukherjee, Bishwa Nath. "Application of Canonical Correlational Analysis to Learning Data." *Psychol B* 66:9–21; 1966.

Mussen, Paul H. (Ed.) *Handbook of Research Methods in Child Study.* Wiley, 1960. 1061p.

Nagel, Ernest. *The Structure of Science.* Harcourt, 1961. 618p.

Norton, Dee W., and Lindquist, Everet F. "Applications of Experimental Design and Analysis." *R Ed Res* 21:350–67; 1951.

Osgood, Charles E., and others. *The Measurement of Meaning.* U Illinois Press, 1957. 342p.

Overing, Robert L. R., and Travers, Robert M. W. "Effect upon Transfer of Variations in Training Conditions." *J Ed Psychol* 57:179–88; 1966.

Page, Ellis B. "Teacher Comments and Student Performance: A Seventy-four Classroom Experiment in School Motivation." *J Ed Psychol* 49:173–81; 1958.

Panel on Basic Research and Graduate Education of the President's Science Advisory Committee. "Scientific Progress and the Federal Government." *Sci* 132:1802–15; 1960.

Pfaffmann, Carl. "Behavioral Sciences." *Am Psychologist* 20:667–86; 1965.

Platt, John R. "Strong Inference." *Sci* 146: 347–53; 1964.

Poincaré, Henri. *Science and Hypothesis.* Dover, 1952. 244p.

Polanyi, Michael. *Personal Knowledge.* U Chicago Press, 1958. 428p.

Pruzek, Robert M., and Coffman, William E. *A Factor Analysis of the Mathematical Sections of the Scholastic Aptitude Test.* ETS, 1966. 20p.

Rokeach, Milton. *The Open and Closed Mind.* Basic Books, 1960. 447p.

Russell, Bertrand. *The Principles of Mathematics.* Norton, 1964. 534p.

Ryans, David G. "Are Educational Research Offices Conducting Research?" *J Ed Res* 51:173–83; November 1957.

Ryans, David G. *Characteristics of Teachers.* ACE, 1960. 416p.

Sarason, Seymour B., and others. *Anxiety in Elementary School Children.* Wiley, 1960. 351p.

Scientific American, Vol. 215(No. 3); 1966. (Complete issue).

Sears, Robert R., and others. *Patterns of Child Rearing.* Harper, 1957. 533p.

Silberman, Harry F., and others. "Discussion: The Effect of Educational Research on Classroom Instruction." *Harvard Ed R* 36:295–317; 1966.

Smith, B. Othanel. "Science of Education." In Monroe, Walter S. (Ed.) *Encyclopedia of Educational Research,* 2nd ed. Macmillan, 1950. p. 1145–52.

Sorenson, A. Garth, and others. "Divergent Concepts of Teacher Role: An Approach to the Measurement of Teacher Effectiveness." *J Ed Psychol* 54:287–94; 1963.

Staats, Arthur W., and Staats, Carolyn K. "Attitudes Established by Classical Conditioning." *J Abn Social Psychol* 57:37–40; 1958.

Stanley, Julian C. "Classroom Learning—An Educational Animal." *Sch Soc* 80:49–53; 1954.

Stanley, Julian C. "Controlled Experimentation in the Classroom." *J Exp Ed* 25:195–201; 1957.

Stanley, Julian C. "Studying Status vs. Manipulating Variables." In Collier, Raymond O., Jr., and Elam, Stanley M. (Eds.) *Research Design and Analysis.* PDK, 1961. p. 173–92.

Stanley, Julian C. "The Influence of Fisher's 'The Design of Experiments' on Educational Research Thirty Years Later." *Am Ed Res J* 3:223–9; 1966.

Stanley, Julian C., and Beeman, Ellen Y. "Restricted Generalization, Bias, and Loss of Power That Result from Matching Groups." *Psychol Newsletter,* New York U, 9:88–102; 1958.

Stephenson, William. *The Study of Behavior.* U Chicago Press, 1953. 376p.

Stern, George G., and others. "Two Scales for the Assessment of Unconscious Motivations for Teaching." *Ed Psychol Meas* 20:9–29; 1960.

Stevens, S. S. "Mathematics, Measurement, and Psychophysics." In Stevens, S. S. (Ed.) *Handbook of Experimental Psychology.* Wiley, 1951. p. 1–49.

Stevenson, Harold W., and Zigler, Edward F. "Probability Learning in Children." *J Exp Psychol* 56: 185–92; 1958.

Stone, Philip J., and others. *The General Inquirer.* M.I.T. Press, 1966. 651p.

Storer, Norman W. "The Coming Changes in American Science." *Sci* 142:464–7; 1963.

Tate, Merle W. "Operationism, Research, and a Science of Education." *Harvard Ed R* 20:11–27; 1950.

Thomson, George. "The Two Aspects of Science." *Sci* 132:996–1000; 1960.

Thorndike, Edward L. "Mental Discipline in High School Studies." *J Ed Psychol* 15:1–22, 83–98; 1924.

Thurstone, L. L. *A Factorial Study of Perception.* U Chicago Press, 1944. 148p.

Thurstone, L. L. *Multiple-factor Analysis.* U Chicago Press, 1947. 535p.

Thurstone, L. L., and Thurstone, Thelma Gwinn. *Factorial Studies of Intelligence.* U Chicago Press, 1941. 94p.

Tiedeman, David V., and Cogan, Morris L. "New Horizons in Educational Research." *Phi Delta Kappan* 39:286–91; 1958.

Torgerson, Warren S. *Theory and Methods of Scaling.* Wiley, 1958. 460p.

Travers, Robert M. W. *An Introduction to Educational Research.* Macmillan, 1958. 466p.

Tryon, Robert C. "Reliability and Behavior Domain Validity: Reformulation and Historical Critique." *Psychol B* 54:229–49; 1957.

Underwood, Benton J. *Psychological Research.* Appleton, 1957. 297p.

Walker, Helen M. "Methods of Research." *R Ed Res* 26:323–43; 1956.

Wallach, Michael A., and Kogan, Nathan. *Modes of Thinking in Young Children.* Holt, 1965. 357p.

Ward, Joe H., Jr. "Multiple Linear Regression Models." In Borko, Harold. (Ed.) *Computer Applications in the Behavioral Sciences.* Prentice-Hall, 1962. p. 204–37.

Waterman, Alan T. "National Science Foundation: A Ten-year Resumé." *Sci* 131:1341–54; 1960.

Waterman, Alan T. "Federal Support of Science." *Sci* 153:1359–61; 1966.

Welch, Jim. "D.C. Perspectives." *Ed Researcher* 17: 1–2; 1966.

Williams, E. J. *Regression Analysis.* Wiley, 1959. 214p.

Winter, David G., and others. "The Classic Personal Style." *J Abn Social Psychol* 67:254–65; 1963.

Wittrock, M. C. "Verbal Stimuli in Concept Formation: Learning by Discovery." *J Ed Psychol* 54: 183–90; 1963.

Yates, F. "The Influence of *Statistical Methods for Research Workers* on the Development of the Science of Statistics." *J Am Stat Assn* 46:19–34; 1951.

Yum, K. S. "An Experimental Test of the Law of Assimilation." *J Exp Psychol* 14:68–82; 1931.

RESEARCH METHODS

LIBRARY REFERENCES. Proficiency in the use of the library, always a prerequisite to successful research operation, is becoming progressively more important with the current geometric increase in the volume of new publications. More specifically, the researcher needs to be familiar with the basic library sources mentioned in such references as Burke and Burke's *Documentation in Education* (1967) and Winchell's *Guide to Reference Books* (1951, 4th suppl. 1963). *The Cumulative Book Index* (1898——) lists all books published in the English language, while the *Education Index* (1929——) was until 1961 clearly the most adequate index of published materials in education. In 1961 its coverage was drastically curtailed to the point that it is now largely a subject index of the periodical literature. Among the major references in the area of educational research, in addition to the *Encyclopedia of Educational Research,* Macmillan (1960) and the *Review of Educational Research* (1931——), are *Dissertation Abstracts* (1955——), *Master's Theses in Education* (Lamke & Silvey, 1952–1958; Silvey, 1959——), and *Research Studies in Education* (Brown & others, 1941–1951, 1952——). Another important source of educational data is the *Digest of Educational Statistics* (1962——; formerly *Biennial Survey of Education,* 1917–1961). Somewhat more general are the reports of the Bureau of the Census and *Statistical Abstracts of the United States,* U.S. Department of Commerce (1897——).

The major guide to the literature in psychology, *Psychological Abstracts* (1927——) provides both an indexing and an abstracting service. Similar abstracts in related fields include *Sociological Abstracts* (1952——) and *Child Development Abstracts and Bibliography,* National Research Council (1927——). A recent addition is *Educational Administration Abstracts* (1966——). The *Annual Review of Psychology* (1950——) offers a systematic evaluation of the psychological literature. A particularly comprehensive contribution to the psychological literature is the Koch series *Psychology: A Study of a Science* (1959–1967).

Of major interest are a number of handbooks covering special areas; the recent *Handbook of Research on Teaching* (Gage, 1963), for example, is undoubtedly the most comprehensive and authoritative source of the literature on the various aspects of teaching. The *Handbook of Research Methods in Child Development* (Mussen, 1960) and the *Handbook of Multivariate Experimental Psychology* (Cattell, 1966) are likewise major contributions to the research literature. The *Manual of Child Psychology* (Carmichael, 1954) is another important publication of earlier date. Berelson and Steiner, in *Human Behavior; An Inventory of Scientific Findings* (1964), provide a particularly good synthesis of the highlights of research on human behavior. Also of major interest are the various yearbooks of the National Society for the Study of Education, begun in 1901, of the Association for Supervision and Curriculum Development, begun in 1944, and of a number of societies in different subject-matter areas. More general references include Buros' "mental measurements" yearbooks (6th ed., 1965) and the *Dictionary of Education* (Good, 1959). At the international level are the many publications of UNESCO, most of which are listed in *Education Abstracts,* UNESCO (1949——).

A particularly fascinating publication is the American Library Association's *Library and Information Networks of the Future* (1963), describing the various aspects of modern library technology as displayed in the Library-21 exhibit at the Seattle World's Fair and projecting a national network of automated regional information centers. The report concludes with a section on current or near-current facilities ranging from office duplicating machines and computer indexing and abstracting to book-charging machines, home video displays, and electronic contact printers.

Undoubtedly the most significant development in this area is the use of electronic data storage and retrieval as a means of coping with the overwhelming volume of new research materials. The newly instituted Educational Research Information Center (ERIC) of the U.S. Office of Education constitutes a system through which all worthwhile educational research studies throughout the United States can be made available to the educational community (Burchinal & Haswell, 1966). Created in 1964 to "facilitate and coordinate information storage and retrieval efforts in all areas of educational research," ERIC was delegated through the Elementary and Secondary School Act of 1965 the responsibility of improving the availability of educational information.

As a first step, a number of clearinghouses, each specializing in one area of research, peruse documents for possible inclusion in the ERIC-central system. Those judged suitable are carefully abstracted in 200-word summaries and indexed with full bibliographic citation on an ERIC resume form which is then placed on *microfiche*, the heart of the dissemination system.

The key to efficient storage and retrieval is a thesaurus of educational terms. The documents in the ERIC-central collection are published in two companion volumes, one listing documents by document number with complete bibliographic citation and alphabetical listing of authors and the other a cross-reference or word list of index terms that would allow anyone looking for information on a given topic to identify readily all documents dealing with the subject. Present plans call for monthly publication of all new additions to the ERIC-central collection. Requests for information can be met either by typed message or by the display of an abstract on a cathode-ray screen. The full text of a given document can be provided at nominal cost by the ERIC Document Reproduction Service in either *microfiche* or hard copy. Eventually the entire ERIC index will be transferred to magnetic tape and made available to organizations wanting to develop their own search and retrieval facilities.

OBSERVATIONAL TECHNIQUES. For purposes of the present article, "observational techniques" may be defined as any direct method of collecting research data. The discussion, therefore, covers rating studies as well as the more informal anecdotal and sociometric research. The discussion also includes longitudinal and action research, both of which also tend to rely heavily on observation. Because of their similarity from the standpoint of nature and purpose, these methods tend to have in common essentially the same problems, primary among which is bias with regard to both sampling, on the one hand, and perception and/or interpretation, on the other. The latter can generally be minimized by the development of organizational perspective (i.e., the clear-cut definition of the phenomenon to be observed), the development of a schedule to guide the observation and to facilitate recording, and the pooling of the observations of different observers.

OBSERVATIONAL STUDIES. Observation is undoubtedly the most fundamental procedure of science inasmuch as all scientific data must originate in some form of observation. Many variables can be investigated in no other way. It plays an especially crucial role in studies of child development and animal behavior in which the human observer must, of necessity, emerge as the measuring instrument.

Observation is at once the most primitive and the most refined of modern research techniques, having a range from the most casual and uncontrolled observations to the most "scientific" and precise. In general, it is so loose and yet involves variables so complex that it is one of the most difficult techniques to harness in the service of science. It attempts to derive data directly rather than relying on the report of the subject, as is done in the case of the interview, and may, consequently, be more dependable. On the other hand, it is subject to a number of errors, and if it is to provide valid results, it must be systematic rather than haphazard or opportunistic. In dealing with the sampling problem, for example, Withall (1949) relied on a time-lapse camera taking pictures every 15 seconds. Kowatrakul (1959) used a "point-time" sampling schedule in which he observed a subject long enough to record one behavior, then immediately passed on to the next subject, whose behavior had to be independent of that of the first subject. The procedure was continued until one behavior point had been recorded for each subject, and then a new round of observations was begun.

As a research technique, observation must meet the usual criteria of reliability and, especially, validity that are required of all scientific data-gathering techniques. For it to do so, the field generally must be structured so as to permit the precise observation of each specific component of the total phenomenon deemed to be significant for the purposes of the study. The assumption is inherent that focusing on individual aspects leads to greater dependability of observation but, of course, one runs the risk of overlooking significant dimensions of the situation outside the framework of the observer's mental set.

A major determinant of the validity of observation is the competence of the observer. Scientific observation is a highly skilled technique requiring, among other things, insight into the overall situation so as to permit the recognition of the significance of what is observed to the problem under investigation and its interpretation within this overall context. The task is complicated, in the case of humans, at least, by the fact that the meaningful aspects of behavior are often the subtle ones; a person's annoyance may have to be detected through slight facial signs showing through a cloak of forbearance and composure.

Structured and Unstructured Observation. In the early stages of the investigation of a given phenomenon it is generally desirable to allow considerable flexibility of observation so as to promote the broadest view. Premature attempts to restrict the observation to areas considered significant on an a priori basis entail the risk of overlooking some of the more crucial aspects, particularly from the standpoint of interaction (Cattell & Digman, 1964). Later, as the investigation proceeds and the phenomenon is seen in clearer perspective, the investigator can attempt to develop a framework of anticipated events so as to orient his observation toward the more precise investigation of restricted aspects of the situation.

A major task in observational research is to develop the observational system in which the various dimensions of the phenomenon under study can be categorized. Jensen (1955), for example, presented a seven-faceted conceptual framework for observing the social structure and the interaction within a classroom group: (1) problem solving, (2) authority and leadership, (3) power, (4) friendship, (5) personal prestige, (6) sex, and (7) privileges. Bales's well-known observational system (1950) comprises six problem areas from orientation of the members to tension management and integration of the group. Steinzor (1949), in contrast, presents a social-interaction category system revolving about the group's motivational structure.

Recording of Observation. Recording is often a problem in observational studies; not only can it interfere with the observational process but, in the case of human subjects, it may actually inhibit or otherwise distort the behavior under study. Evaluation of what is observed presents another major problem. Interpretation has to be done by someone somewhere along the line of investigation: it can be done directly by the investigator at the time of observation, or, alternatively, the observation can be simply recorded as an observation to be interpreted subsequently, perhaps by the chief investigator. Both approaches have their strengths and their drawbacks (Cattell & Digman, 1964; Longabaugh, 1963; Thelen, 1959). The subsequent interpretation of the observations by an expert may provide greater equivalence in judgment, but it is obviously difficult for someone to evaluate an event he did not witness, particularly with respect to the more subtle aspects of human interaction or even events whose meaning depends critically on intangible aspects of the setting in which they occur. Such evaluation would be impossible in certain cases. A child may be observed seeking information from the teacher; perhaps more fundamentally he is seeking attention.

Classroom Observation. The classroom presents an endless variety of situations of major observational interest to educational researchers—e.g., the child showing hostility, dependence, or leadership. Historically, early research on classroom observation consisted primarily of listing teacher traits as observed, say, by a supervisor. Then came research into various teacher behaviors having a bearing on the quality of the pupils' learning, and a number of studies were conducted comparing teaching methods in relation to resulting changes in pupil behavior. A parallel series of studies was concerned with child growth and development. It is only recently that the classroom itself, and particularly the important pupil-teacher and pupil-pupil interactions, has become the subject of investigation. And, in a sense, this is precisely what might have been expected considering the expense in time, money, and professional skill, the disruption of classroom operation, and, perhaps above all, the relative unproductiveness of early attempts in this direction.

Observational techniques have featured prominently in the study of teacher effectiveness; Barr's series of investigations of the characteristics distinguishing efficient from inefficient teachers was undertaken in the 1920's (Barr, 1929). A major problem here is the choice of the criterion: in the final analysis, teacher effectiveness must be defined in terms of its effects on pupils, i.e., in terms of changes in pupil behavior. Unfortunately, research to date has failed to identify any significant relationship between teacher behavior patterns and pupil growth. As a result, research has concerned itself more with identifying "approved" patterns of teacher behavior, presumably on the assumption that the ultimate goal of a change in pupil behavior can be achieved only through the intermediate goal of a change in teacher behavior. Barr, for example, found good teachers to emphasize the interest appeal of the subject matter more frequently than poor teachers did. Unfortunately, this often leads to considerable circularity in that the extent to which a given teacher's behavior coincides with such "approved" patterns is the basis for both his selection and his confirmation as a good or a poor teacher.

Another aspect of the classroom that lends itself to observational research is its emotional climate. Anderson and Brewer (1946), for example, found that teacher domination tended to incite pupil resistance. An important early study of social-emotional climate in relation to teacher-centeredness and learner-centeredness is that of Withall (1949). On the premise that classroom climate could be appraised in terms of teacher behavior alone, Withall devised a scale providing for the categorization of teacher statements on a continuum from "learner supportive" to "reproving," with an additional category, "teacher self-supporting." Probably the most sophisticated technique for the appraisal of classroom climate to date is that of Flanders (1960), who rates the communication behavior of the classroom for each three-second interval into one of ten categories and records the ratings sequentially so as to provide a picture of the sequence of the communication pattern.

Observation Schedules. The major task in classroom observation consists of identifying the relevant dimensions of classroom operation and providing the means for their valid and reliable appraisal. Operationally, this implies focusing on certain categories of teacher or pupil behavior or both and organizing them into an observation schedule with the categories so clearly defined as to make coding easy and essentially foolproof. Ryans (1960), in his teacher characteristic study, for example, structured classroom operation along three continua of teacher behavior patterns: X_0, friendly versus aloof; Y_0, responsible versus slipshod; and Z_0, stimulating versus dull. Listed are 22 bipolarities (e.g., apathetic versus alert, uncertain versus constant), 18 referring to teacher behavior and 4 to pupil behavior, each to be appraised on a seven-point scale. Cornell and others (1953) likewise developed a classroom-observation-code digest designed to focus on eight dimensions of the classroom, with particular reference to teacher-pupil interaction.

Probably the best known and most adequate classroom observation schedule is the Observation Schedule and Record (OScAR) developed by Medley and Mitzel (1955, 1958, 1959) out of the earlier schedules by Withall (1949) and Cornell and others (1953) to quantify the behavior of beginning teachers. It has also been used in a number of subsequent studies attempting to relate various measures of teacher effectiveness to certain teacher behavior variables, as reported by Medley and Mitzel (1963) in their comprehensive article in the *Handbook of Research on Teaching*. OScAR gives dependable information about three rather discrete dimensions of classroom behavior: the social-emotional climate, the relative emphasis on verbal learning, and the degree to which the social structure centers on the teacher. Although it is in need of further refinement, particularly with respect to its ability to relate classroom behavior to pupil achievement in the cognitive domain, its approach offers considerable promise for research. An important consideration is that it provides data amenable to processing by fairly adequate statistical procedures; Bowers and Soar (1961), for example, used the Johnson-Neyman technique in their investigation of teachers with and without laboratory experiences in human relations.

Another aspect of research dealing with classroom observation is the development of theoretical perspective as the basis for item selection in the formulation of an observational schedule. The details of such an approach, along with statistical procedures for the analysis of reliability, etc., are presented by Medley and Mitzel (1963) in the *Handbook*. That the problem is of major complexity is best documented by the concluding statement of the Medley-Mitzel article: "Research in classroom behavior is not a pastime for amateurs; it is a full-time occupation for technically competent professionals."

Processing Observational Data. Observational data can be treated either qualitatively or quantitatively, depending on whether numerical units can be established—e.g., the frequency of the occurrence of the phenomenon under study. A common error here is to assume bipolarity when variables actually exist on a continuum. It should also be noted that frequently what is measured most precisely are the more trivial aspects of the situation, such as the number of words spoken; by contrast, subtle differences in intensity, while often most meaningful, are generally more difficult to appraise.

Evaluation of Observational Research. Observational studies are obviously time-consuming—as well as prone to certain types of error. To make matters worse, most of the data they provide are not amenable to precise statistical treatment so that a good part of the information they contain may be wasted. Their quality from the standpoint of reliability and validity varies with such factors as the nature of the problem and the setting in which it is investigated, and perhaps especially with the competence of the observer. Early studies were particularly concerned with reliability as measured by interobserver agreement, with the result that observational categories became more and more removed from any theoretical foundation. The trend in recent years has been to move away from exhaustive survey of all occurring behaviors toward the selection of particular aspects in order to answer specific questions incorporated in a particular observational system designed to fit the investigator's purpose and the framework he is using. Studies of classroom interaction based on observational systems as previously discussed have produced interobserver agreement of .70 and higher. It would seem that better use of observer time and effort can be made by increasing the number of single-observer observations than by having two or more observers view the same event (Medley & Mitzel, 1963).

Militating against the objectivity, and hence the validity, of observation is the fact that observers are essentially self-selected and therefore likely to harbor built-in biases. Not only has psychology emphasized the selectivity of perception, but it has also shown a considerable distortion of perception in the direction of one's motivation (e.g., Ashley & others, 1951); an observer with a high level of repressed hostility may not be able to maintain the necessary impartiality and objectivity to obtain valid observations of teacher punishment of pupil misbehavior, for example. Unfortunately, rarely are such problems given adequate consideration in published reports. The fact that training may sensitize the observers in the direction of the investigator's biases is also rarely mentioned. Yet because of this selectivity and distortion of perception, two observers looking at a given situation may be actually seeing very different things. It is also possible for the observer to structure a very different phenomenon from that which the subject is actually experiencing.

It is also necessary to recognize that the very act of observing may itself distort the phenomenon under study. One-way screens are often used to minimize this difficulty; Asano and Barrett (1964) report the use of a periscope for the same purpose. Recently, audio and video tapes have been found useful in the study of classroom interaction (Schueler & Gold, 1964; Stroller & others, 1964). Tapes present certain advantages over direct observation, particularly in providing a permanent record and thus a means for determining reliability and validity. Ideally they can increase validity by allowing for on-the-spot interpretation of the dynamics underlying the phenomena observed as well as their more subtle dimensions, such as the intensity of behavior as conveyed by tone of voice, gesture, etc.—crucial factors which are often hard to grasp in an ongoing situation.

RATING STUDIES. Research in the behavioral sciences is often concerned with phenomena that can only be categorized. At one extreme, these categories are merely qualitatively different dimensions—e.g., discipline can be classified as supportive, restrictive, punitive, etc. More commonly, these categories constitute steps of a continuous category system having a quantifiable relationship to one another. The task is to assign ratings to the phenomenon under study in terms of these steps identified either verbally, numerically, or graphically from, say, excellent to poor or democratic to autocratic. At a more sophisticated level, the separate ratings of the individual components of a given phenomenon are combined into a scale to provide an index of the individual's overall status on the variable in question. In a sense then, a rating scale is an instrument for the quantification of observations through the assignment of numerical values to ratings of the separate components of the phenomenon and the summation of these ratings into a composite score. Actually, however, there is no agreement on the meaning of "rating scale." As Remmers (1963) points out "The term *scale* is conceptually and operationally ill-defined when used with the adjective *rating*." While he discusses "cumulated point" rating scales which provide an overall score on the basis of the summation of scoring weights of 0, 1, 2, ···, for each item, he also lists graphic scales on which each item is basically separate and independent. Kerlinger (1964), on the other hand, lists three major types of rating scales: (1) the summated (Likert) scale, (2) the equal-appearing interval (Thurstone) scale, and (3) the cumulated (Guttman) scale, all of which are designed to give an overall index of the rated individual status. The topic is obviously of such complexity that a more comprehensive source than this should be consulted (e.g., Torgerson, 1958). A good overview of scaling theory is given by Schiffman and Messick (1963).

As in the case of observational studies, it must be recognized that the rater—whether the observer himself or another person—brings to the investigation personal biases which are likely to distort his perceptions and interpretations. An individual is not a particularly good judge of his own characteristics or of the dynamics underlying his behavior; the prejudiced person does not always see himself as prejudiced. Emotional involvement may likewise make it impossible for an individual to rate close relatives. A common error to which peer ratings are subject is that known as the *halo effect*, a general tendency for the rater to rate each of the individual's specific traits on the basis of a general overall impression rather than on the basis of the traits as they appear independently. This is sometimes combined with the *error of central tendency*, in which the rater, when he is not sure of his ratings, simply rates the subject close to the average. Frequently this stems from the *logical error*, which involves lack of clarity about the trait being rated or the status of the individual on this trait and a consequent tendency to play it safe. Another common error is the *generosity* or *leniency error*, in which a rater rates almost everyone above (or perhaps below) the average. This creates a problem when multiple raters are used in that their ratings may not be calibrated to a common point and therefore not comparable. It is essential for the raters to know the point of reference which is to act as a benchmark in their ratings; asking children to rate their teacher on a scale from "excellent" to "poor" presupposes that they know what constitutes an excellent, an average, and a poor teacher. Practice sessions in which a group of raters attempt to reconcile the differences in their ratings of a given phenomenon are effective in calibrating the rating to a common point of reference, in pointing out personal biases, and in clarifying the nature of the variable in question.

It is also essential for the rater to know specifically what is incorporated in the variable he is rating. The continuum "democratic–autocratic" with respect to teacher behavior, for example, may represent very different things to different raters. An important development in this area is the critical-incident technique developed by Flanagan (1952) on the premise that the validity with which a given continuum can be appraised can be increased by identifying typical incidents that characterize the possession or lack of possession of the trait in question. Ryans (1960), for instance, illustrates "apathetic versus alert" in terms of such descriptions as "Pupils were inattentive; showed evidence of wandering attention; indifferent to teacher" against "Pupils responded eagerly; appeared anxious to recite and participate." Another important development with respect to ratings is the Q-technique, developed by Stephenson (1953) for the analysis of such data. (See Mowrer, 1953, and Kerlinger, 1964, for a critical evaluation.)

SOCIOMETRIC TECHNIQUES. Sociometric techniques attempt to determine group structure as revealed through responses of intermember acceptance. Credit for their development goes to Moreno, who is generally considered the father of sociometry and whose book *Who Shall Survive?* (1953) presents the basic concepts and defines the terms peculiar to the field. While perhaps primarily of interest to sociologists, sociometric techniques—or, more narrowly, sociometric *measures*, a term used in order to exclude such approaches as role playing where the emphasis is therapeutic—are also of significance to educational research in that they permit the study of the child in the miniature social environment of the classroom. They are based on the assumption that within a group in which considerable interaction is allowed, there emerges a sort of informal group organization based on varying degrees of positive and negative interpersonal feelings among the members. Operationally, they assess the attractions-repulsions within a given group by asking each member to specify the other members of the group with whom he would like to engage in each of a number of specified activities (and possibly those with whom he would not like to engage in these activities). Sociometric studies are essentially rating studies in that the basic data consist of member ratings of positive-negative relations existing within the group. They differ from conventional ratings in that sociometric choices are based on general impressions—or perhaps irrational idiosyncrasies—and require no special training on the part of the rater. Nor do they require impartiality; on the contrary, interaction between the rater and the rated is intended to play a significant part in the ratings.

An important consideration is that of the analysis of sociometric data. A common approach at the descriptive level is to present the data graphically in the form of a sociogram in which each individual is represented by a triangle, a circle, or a square with connecting lines to represent each choice of one member by another. Sociometric status is sometimes shown on what is known as a target diagram, consisting of concentric circles in which the degree of acceptance of any member of the group is shown by the position he occupies marked off in distance from the center of maximum attraction (Northway, 1946). A number of authors have suggested converting sociometric scores into some form of index of acceptance-rejection status (see Proctor & Loomis, 1951). Another possibility of representing sociometric data is through matrix algebra (Forsyth & Katz, 1946); however, the method is rather laborious and usually requires the use of a computer. An interesting approach in this connection is that of Gardner and Thompson (1956), who developed five social-relation scales from which they derived eight indexes of the individual's social-relations status in the group and nine indexes of social-group structure.

The evaluation of sociometric techniques from the standpoint of the conventional notions of reliability and validity presents definite problems. With respect to test-retest reliability, for example, if the time interval is too short, the factor of memory will have undue influence. On the other hand, to the extent that changes in social structure are bound to occur, a high reliability over a long interval would imply insensitivity of the technique. From the standpoint of validity, a sociometric choice is actually a direct measure of the behavior under study so that the predictor is really the same as the criterion. Perhaps the best criterion of validity is the extent to which the choice is made honestly, which, in turn, is a function of the rapport between the experimenter and the subjects.

At the empirical level, studies like those of Mouton and others (1955a, 1955b) and Gronlund (1959) have shown sociometric ratings to have relatively high internal consistency and stability over time and to show a substantial relationship to such criteria as pupils' behavior outside the sociometric testing situation and teachers' judgments of pupils' choice status. All in all, it is perhaps best to think of sociometric techniques in relation to guidance or classroom management—or perhaps even action research—rather than in relation to rigorous research methodology. Even in a guidance or classroom context, they should generally be used in connection with supportive data from other sources (Ausubel, 1958). On the other hand, sociometric studies have yielded interesting data concerning the characteristics of accepted and unaccepted group members. Gronlund and Anderson (1957), for example, identified three major categories of pupil acceptance among seventh and eighth graders: the socially accepted, the socially rejected, and a third group who received neither positive nor negative mention. In that category were those with neutral personalities lacking in stimulus value who were overlooked rather than actively liked or disliked.

ANECDOTAL RECORDS. With respect to guidance, anecdotal records are simply notes concerning the behavior of a child in a concrete situation. Although they sometimes contain a sufficient variety of evidence to yield a reasonably adequate picture of a child's overall behavior pattern, they are generally less thorough and less extensive than a case study. Ideally, an anecdotal note should consist of a simple statement of an incident deemed by the observer to be significant with respect to a given child, together with a statement of the situation in which it occurred. Probably the most serious limitation of anecdotal records as a source of scientific evidence is that of the bias that is likely to result from inadequacies in sampling. It would seem that, as they are usually collected, they are perhaps of greater guidance than of research value; to develop them into a rigorous scientific technique, while not impossible, would require considerable structuring.

LONGITUDINAL STUDIES. Genetic or developmental research, although not strictly educational, is of prime interest to anyone concerned with child growth and development as it relates to the total process of education. It has provided some of our most conclusive research findings. On the other hand, genetic research is more a combination of research techniques than a research method in itself. Like historical research, it is concerned with the child's past. At times, it utilizes the experimental approach, as in the study of the development of identical twins compared under different conditions of environmental stimulation (e.g., Gesell & Thompson, 1929). It relies heavily on survey methods ranging from the measurement of physical characteristics and intellectual status to observation, rating, and interview and questionnaire techniques. It differs from these in that it is interested not so much in the present status of the child's development or in its historical background as in the pattern of this development as it emerges over a period of time. Genetic research employs a number of techniques even within the same study; in the study of infants and preschool children, for example, it is generally necessary to rely in observation and direct measurements where, for older children, interviews or pencil-and-paper tests might be used.

Genetic studies can be either longitudinal or cross-sectional, longitudinal studies being based on continuous measurements of the same group of children over a relatively long period of time and cross-sectional studies being based on measurements of random samples of children at successive ages. The longitudinal approach is ideally more rigorous but it raises a particular problem with respect to the selective attrition of the sample over the years. As a consequence, longitudinal studies have tended toward samples of superior and middle class socio-economic status where stability of residence is more likely to be found.

The number of significant studies of this type is far too extensive to permit more than a brief reference here; a more comprehensive report is provided by Kagan and Moss (1962). One of the earlier studies, mostly of physical growth, is that of Baldwin (1921) at the Iowa Child Welfare Research Station. In 1925, Gesell published his first account of a long series of studies of the behavioral development of infants and young children (Gesell & others, 1939). In the same year, Terman published the first report of his genetic studies of genius (Terman & others, 1925–1959). In 1922, Dearborn began the Harvard Growth Study involving annual measurements of both mental and physical traits of children from the first grade through high school (Dearborn & Rothney, 1941). A number of studies in the 1920's and 1930's dealt with the constancy of the IQ (National Society for the Study of Education, 1928, 1940). A particularly comprehensive longitudinal study currently in progress is Project Talent (Flanagan, 1962), begun in 1960 with the testing of nearly a half-million high school students with plans for follow-up 5, 10, and 20 years after graduation. A major objective of the study is to contribute to the improvement of the whole process of identifying, developing, and utilizing the talents of the nation's young people.

Genetic research has yielded a number of significant findings in all aspects of growth and development. Typical of these are (1) growth is sequential; however, the rate varies from child to child; (2) growth takes place in spurts; the prepubescent spurt in physical growth is especially evident; and (3) various aspects of growth are interrelated and interdependent. Probably most obvious is the wide range of individual differences which exist in any and all aspects of development, both throughout the period of growth and in the final status attained. Perhaps more fundamental is the basic concept of the developing organism as an open system changing with time toward greater complexity in organization as a result of both internal and external stimulation and yet maintaining some degree of stability and self-regulation. Longitudinal studies have shown considerable consistency in morphological characteristics and even in behavior patterns, thus providing a basis for predictability (Neilon, 1948; Kagan & Moss, 1962; Stone & Onque, 1959). An important corollary of the interdependence of the various aspects of growth is the fact that it feeds upon itself; higher levels of competence become possible as a result of potentialities which emerge from previous development.

Of particular significance for the structuring of current research efforts is the recent reorientation of psychology toward the crucial role played by experience—particularly early experience—in the development of the organism. As a result of evidence converging from various sources—e.g., the McGill studies of sensory deprivation (Thompson & Heron, 1954), Harlow's concept of learning sets (Harlow, 1949), and Skinner's success in training animals (Skinner, 1958)—as well as the rather convincing theoretical position taken by Hebb (1959), Hunt (1961), and others, psychology has made a rather complete about-face as to the development of the organism. An important consequence has been a major reconsideration of what constitutes the limits of both human and animal potential, as psychologists lean more and more toward capacity defined primarily as a function of previous learnings rather than as a matter of inheritance. Applied at the human level—and without discounting the role of heredity—research in this area suggests as a distinct possibility that the culturally disadvantaged child, for example, is more clearly the victim of early sensory deprivation than of inherited limitations.

To the extent that developmental studies involve a composite of research methods, they can be evaluated only in terms of the specific methods used. Controlled experimentation involving identical twins (Gesell & Thompson, 1929) or even the development of physical growth norms (Baldwin, 1921) involves a level of scientific precision not attainable in the interviewing of the mothers of five-year-olds about child-rearing practices or the rating of the children's later personality pattern (Sears & others, 1957). However, the more noteworthy feature of research in this area is the development of a meaningful theoretical position as background for putting into focus empirical findings and serving as a foundation for educational practice in such programs as Project Head Start.

ACTION RESEARCH. "Action research" refers primarily to on-the-spot research aimed at the solution of an immediate problem arising as part of the operation of the school. In contrast to "fundamental research," which is concerned with the derivation of generalizations of wide applicability, action research is undertaken to act as a guide in the solution of an immediate practical problem. It is willing to forgo scientific rigor in its primary concern for a usable answer to a problem existing here and now; making a contribution to the development of education as a science is generally a minor consideration. From the standpoint of methodology, it can take any form from survey to experimentation; it frequently develops along the lines of a case study.

Action research enables teachers to participate in the solution of their own problems as they actually experience them. As emphasized by its chief sponsor, Stephen M. Corey (1953), any change in teacher behavior must be preceded by a corresponding change in teacher attitude, a change which is more likely to take place as a result of research which the teacher actually helped plan, conduct, and evaluate than as a result of reading a study on the subject reported in a journal. Action research makes its greatest contribution in the area of the in-service education of teachers; among many other benefits, the participation of teachers as a group in the solution of their own problems is likely to lead to increased research conscientiousness and faculty morale and to promote a problem-solving approach to teaching. On the other hand, action research has a number of limitations ranging from poor quality (resulting from lack of competence in research) to the inability to generalize results beyond the specific situation under investigation. If teachers engaging in action research are to be successful, they should have ready access to adequate consulting services for the purpose of clarifying the problem enough for it to be researched and of developing and implementing the necessary research and statistical design.

George J. Mouly
University of Miami

References

American Library Association. *The Library and Information Networks of the Future.* ALA, 1963. 43p.

Anderson, H. H., and Brewer, J. E. "Studies of Teachers' Classroom Personalities. II: Effects of Teachers' Dominative and Integrative Behavior on Children's Classroom Behavior." *Applied Psychol Monogr* No. 8; 1946. 128p.

Annual Review of Psychology. Annual Reviews, 1950——.

Asano, S., and Barrett, B. H. "A Periscope for Behavior Observation." *J Exp Analysis Behavior* 7:430; 1964.

Ashley, W. R., and others. "The Perceived Size of Coins in Normal and Hypnotically Induced Economic States." *Am J Psychol* 64:564–72; 1951.

Ausubel, David P. *Theories and Problems of Child Development.* Grune, 1958. 650p.

Baldwin, B. T. "The Physical Growth of Children from Birth to Maturity." *U Iowa Stud Child Welf* 1 (No. 1); 1921. 411p.

Bales, Robert F. *Interaction Process Analysis.* Addison, 1950. 203p.

Barr, A. S. *Characteristic Differences in the Teaching Performance of Good and Poor Teachers of the Social Studies.* Bobbs-Merrill, 1929. 626p.

Berelson, Bernard, and Steiner, G. A. *Human Behavior; An Inventory of Scientific Findings.* Harcourt, 1964. 712p.

Bowers, N. D., and Soar, R. S. *Studies of Human Relations in the Teaching Learning Process,* Vol. 5: *Final Report: Evaluation of Laboratory Human Relations Training for Classroom Teachers.* Cooperative Research Project No. 469. USOE, 1961.

Brown, Stanley B., and others. *Research Studies in Education: A Subject Index of Doctoral Dissertations, Reports, and Field Studies.* PDK, 1941–1951; 1952——.

Burchinal, Lee G., and Haswell, Harold A. "The Story of ERIC." *Am Ed* 11:23–5; 1966.

Burke, Arvid J., and Burke, Mary A. *Documentation in Education.* Teachers Col, Columbia U, 1967. 413p.

Buros, Oscar K. *The Sixth Mental Measurements Yearbook.* Gryphon, 1965. 1714p.

Carmichael, Leonard, *Manual of Child Psychology,* rev. ed. Wiley, 1954. 1205p.

Cattell, Raymond B. (Ed.) *Handbook of Multivariate Experimental Psychology.* Rand McNally, 1966. 959p.

Cattell, Raymond B., and Digman, John. "A Theory of the Structure of Perturbations in Observer Ratings and Questionnaire Data in Personality Research." *Behavior Sci* 9:341–58; 1964.

Corey, Stephen M. *Action Research to Improve School Practices.* Teachers Col, Columbia U, 1953. 145p.

Cornell, Francis G., and others. *An Exploratory Measurement of Individualities of Schools and Classrooms.* Bulletin 50, No. 75. U Illinois, Bureau of Educational Research, 1953. 71p.

Cumulative Book Index. Wilson, 1898——.

Dearborn, W. F., and Rothney, J. W. M. *Predicting the Child's Development.* Sci-Art, 1941. 360p.

Digest of Educational Statistics. USOE, 1962——. (Formerly *Biennial Survey of Education,* 1917–1961.)

Dissertation Abstracts (originally *Microfilm Abstracts*). University Microfilms, 1938——.

Educational Administration Abstracts. University Council for Educational Administration, 1966——.

Education Index. Wilson, 1929——.

Flanagan, John C. *The Critical Incident Technique in the Study of Individuals.* ACE, 1952.

Flanagan, John C. *Design for a Study of American Youth.* Houghton, 1962. 240p.

Flanders, Ned A. *Interaction Analysis in the Classroom.* U Minnesota Press, 1960. 35p.

Forsyth, E., and Katz, L. "A Matrix Approach to the Analysis of Sociometric Data." *Sociometry* 9:340–7; 1946.

Gage, N. L. (Ed.) *Handbook of Research on Teaching.* Rand McNally, 1963. 1218p.

Gardner, Eric F., and Thompson, George G. *Social Relations and Morale in Small Groups.* Appleton, 1956. 312p.

Gesell, Arnold, and Thompson, H. "Learning and Growth in Identical Infant Twins." *Genet Psychol Monogr* 6:5–120; 1929.

Gesell, Arnold, and others. *Biographies of Child Development.* Harper, 1939. 328p.

Good, C. V. *Dictionary of Education.* McGraw-Hill, 1959.

Gronlund, Norman E. *Sociometry in the Classroom.* Harper, 1959. 340p.

Gronlund, Norman E., and Anderson, L. "Personality Characteristics of Socially Accepted, Socially Neglected, and Socially Rejected High School Pupils." *Ed Adm Sup* 43:329–38; 1957.

Guttman, Louis. "A Basis for Scaling Qualitative Data." *Am Sociol R* 9:139–50; 1944.

Harlow, Harry F. "The Formation of Learning Sets." *Psychol R* 56:51–65; 1949.

Hebb, Donald O. "Neuro-psychological Theory." In Koch, S. (Ed.) *Psychology: A Study of a Science,* Vol. 2. McGraw-Hill, 1959. p. 622–43.

Hunt, J. McV. *Intelligence and Experience.* Ronald, 1961. 416p.

Jensen, Gale E. "Social Structure of the Classroom Group; An Observational Framework." *J Ed Psychol* 46:362–74; 1955.

Kagan, Jerome, and Moss, Howard A. *Birth to Maturity: A Study in Psychological Development.* Wiley, 1962. 381p.

Kerlinger, Fred N. *Foundations of Behavioral Research: Educational and Psychological Inquiry.* Holt, 1964. 739p.

Koch, Sigmund. (Ed.) *Psychology: A Study of a Science.* Vols. 1–7. McGraw-Hill, 1959–1967.

Kowatrakul, S. "Some Behaviors of Elementary School Children Related to Classroom Activities and Subject Areas." *J Ed Psychol* 50:121–8; 1959.

Lamke, T. A., and Silvey, H. M. (Eds.) *Master's*

Theses in Education. Research Publications, 1952–1958.

Likert, R. "A Technique for the Measurement of Attitudes." *Archives Psychol* No. 140; 1932.

Longabaugh, Richard. "A Category System for Coding Interpersonal Behavior as Social Exchange." *Sociometry* 26:319–44; 1963.

Medley, Donald M., and Mitzel, Harold E. *Studies of Teacher Behavior: Refinement of Two Techniques for Assessing Teachers' Classroom Behaviors.* Research Series No. 28. Board of Higher Education, New York City, 1955.

Medley, Donald M., and Mitzel, Harold E. "A Technique for Measuring Classroom Behavior." *J Ed Psychol* 49:86–92; 1958.

Medley, Donald M., and Metzel, Harold E. "Some Behavior Correlates of Teacher Effectiveness." *J Ed Psychol* 50:230–46; 1959.

Medley, Donald M., and Mitzel, Harold E. "Measuring Classroom Behavior by Systematic Observation." In Gage, N. L. (Ed.) *Handbook of Research on Teaching.* Rand McNally, 1963. p. 247–328.

Moreno, J. L. *Who Shall Survive?* Beacon House, 1934, rev. ed., 1953. 763p.

Mouton, Jane, and others. "The Reliability of Sociometric Measures." *Sociometry* 18:7–48; 1955(a).

Mouton, Jane, and others. "The Validity of Sociometric Responses." *Sociometry* 18:181–206; 1955(b).

Mowrer, O. H. "Q-Technique—Description, History, and Critique." In Mowrer, O. H. (Ed.) *Psychotherapy: Theory and Research.* Ronald, 1953. p. 316–75.

Mussen, Paul. (Ed.) *Handbook of Research Methods in Child Development.* Wiley, 1960. 1061p.

National Society for the Study of Education. *Nature and Nurture.* 27th Yearbook. Part I: *Their Influence upon Intelligence.* Part II: *Their Influence upon Achievement.* Public-Sch, 1928.

National Society for the Study of Education. *Intelligence: Its Nature and Nurture.* 39th Yearbook. Part I: *Comparative and Critical Exposition.* Part II: *Original Studies and Experiments.* Public-Sch, 1940. Part I, 471p.; Part II, 409p.

Neilon, P. "Shirley's Babies After Fifteen Years: A Personality Study." *J Genet Psychol* 73:175–86; 1948.

Northway, Mary L. "A Method for Depicting Social Relationships Obtained by Sociometric Testing." *Sociometry* 3:144–50; 1946.

Proctor, C., and Loomis, C. "Analysis of Sociometric Data." In Jahoda, M., and others. (Eds.) *Research Methods in Social Relations*, Part II. Holt, 1951. p. 561–85.

Psychological Abstracts. APA, 1927——.

Remmers, H. H. "Rating Methods in Research on Teaching." In Gage, N. L. (Ed.) *Handbook of Research on Teaching.* Rand McNally, 1963. p. 329–78.

Review of Educational Research. AERA, 1931——.

Ryans, David G. *Characteristics of Teachers.* ACE, 1960. 416p.

Schiffman, Harold, and Messick, Samuel. "Scaling and Measurement Theory." *R Ed Res* 33:533–42; 1963.

Schueler, Herbert P., and Gold, Milton J. "Video Recordings of Student Teachers: A Report of the Hunter College Research Project Evaluating the Use of Kineoscopes in Preparing Student Teachers." *J Teach Ed* 15:358–64; 1964.

Sears, Robert R., and others. *Patterns of Child Rearing.* Harper, 1957. 549p.

Silvey, H. M. (Ed.) *Master's Theses in Education.* Research Publications, 1959——.

Skinner, B. F. "Reinforcement Today." *Am Psychol* 13:94–9; 1958.

Sociological Abstracts. Sociological Abstracts, Inc., 1952——.

Steinzor, B. "The Development and Evaluation of a Measure of Social Interaction." *Hum Relations* 2:103–22; 1949.

Stephenson, William. *The Study of Behavior.* U Chicago Press, 1953. 376p.

Stone, Alan A., and Onque, Gloria C. *Longitudinal Studies of Child Personality: Abstracts with Index.* Harvard U Press, 1959. 314p.

Stroller, Nathan, and others. "A Comparison of Methods of Observation in Preservice Teacher Training." *AV Communications R* 12:177–97; 1964.

Terman, Lewis M., and others. *Genetic Studies of Genius.* Stanford U Press, 1925–1959. (Vol. 1: *Mental and Physical Traits of a Thousand Gifted Children,* 1925. Vol. 2: *The Early Mental Traits of Three Hundred Geniuses,* 1926. Vol. 3: *The Promise of Youth: Follow-up Studies of a Thousand Gifted Children,* 1930. Vol. 4: *The Gifted Child Grows Up: Twenty-five Years' Follow-up of a Superior Group,* 1947. Vol. 5: *The Gifted Group at Midlife,* 1959.)

Thelen, Herbert A. "Work-Emotionality Theory in the Group as Organism." In Koch, Sigmund. (Ed.) *Psychology: A Study of a Science,* Vol. 3. McGraw-Hill, 1959. p. 544–611.

Thompson, W. R., and Heron, W. "The Effects of Restricting Early Experiences on the Problem-solving Capacity of Dogs." *Canadian J Psychol* 8:17–31; 1954.

Thurstone, L. L., and Chave, E. *The Measurement of Attitudes.* U Chicago Press, 1929. 96p.

Torgerson, Warren S. *Theory and Methods of Scaling.* Wiley, 1958. 460p.

Withall, John. "The Development of a Technique for the Measurement of Social-Emotional Climate in Classrooms." *J Exp Ed* 17:347–61; 1949.

Winchell, Constance M. *Guide to Reference Books,* 7th ed. ALA, 1951. 645p. (4th suppl., 1963).

RESEARCH ORGANIZATIONS

Edison's greatest invention probably was that of the industrial research laboratory which turned out inventions as a business. Large corporations quickly saw its advantages and soon followed his example at considerable profit to themselves. Invention has now largely come to mean not a sudden flash of insight by a lone worker, but the result of a careful comprehensive search by a team of competent scientists. Research organizations survived and proliferated because they were more productive than individuals working alone. To the extent that achievement is dependent on the successful solution of problems, it is important that resources be organized. It is not a question of whether there should be planning in research. Planning and research are inseparable. It is in defining the proper extent of planning that differences may arise. "Planning" may refer to a broad outline on a large scale at high administrative levels, or it may refer to exceedingly detailed procedures and operations at the opposite end of the spectrum. Ubiquitousness of research organizations may be noted from a variety of bibliographies. The Armed Services Technical Information Agency (1962) bibliography covers the literature of the Defense Department from 1953 to 1962 under the headings of cost administration, evaluations, and planning of research programs, selection and training of personnel, and economic considerations of research and development. Folger and Gordon (1962) reviewed the literature relating the social organization and scientific accomplishment. Goldberg (1963) summarized sociological and psychological studies for the Institute of Electrical and Electronic Engineers and indicated advances made in the areas of creativity, leadership, occupational values, and organizational structure. Goslin (1966) annotated approximately 1,000 references dealing with allocation of resources, budgeting, communication, control, decision making, creativity, evaluation of results, motivation, objectives, planning, responsibility, system, and theory. McClure (1964) presented a bibliography taken from periodicals only, relating project and research management. Marcson (1960), by means of extensive footnotes, presented a substantial bibliography of organizational determinants in manpower utilization of scientists in American industry. Rank (1963) published a bibliography of almost 900 articles from the open literature of 1959–1962 on research and development management. Rubenstein (1964) published a directory of research on research. The study of research organizations and the factors in their performance is a well-established part of academic sociology, psychology, and business and government research-laboratory management.

In contrast, the study of research organizations in education is conspicuously limited. This may be partly because of (1) a lack of clear definition of "educational research organization" (institute, center, bureau, agency), (2) a lack of clearly defined objectives (research, field service, etc., (3) a pervading lack of interest in research on the part of professional educators, (4) the intellectual climate of schools of education, (5) priorities established by professional educators, and (6) the small amount of funds allocated in the past to educational research by decision makers. This may be largely owing to the constantly shifting demands made on allocation. This phenomenon is well illustrated by the frequent reorganizations of the U.S. Office of Education (USOE).

Educational-research organizations are not a new phenomenon. The main ideas were developed by Joseph M. Rice prior to 1902, who suggested (1903) a national bureau of educational research. Up to that time, he said, "the science of pedagogy was based on a foundation of opinions. . . . Now that we have a ready means of learning with what success each teacher is meeting, and therefore a basis for studying why certain schools are successful and others are not, there ought to be no delay in taking advantage of it." Rice established a department of educational research sponsored by *Forum* magazine, but the unit was short-lived, as were most of the educational-research groups founded subsequently. Rice later founded the *Society of Educational Research* (Sieber and Lazarsfeld, 1965). His advocacy of a national research agency independent of the universities, which he regarded as hostile to the plan, was ahead of its time. In fact more than 60 years later, the closest approach to a national assessment of educational achievement has been Project Talent and the Coleman Report. The Exploratory Committee on Assessing the Progress of Education supported by the Carnegie Corporation seems to have suspended its efforts in 1967.

Although Rice was not successful in developing a national research unit, his advocacy of school surveys for appraising pupils' progress may have triggered the development of city and university testing bureaus, the directors of which met in 1915 to found the Association of Directors of Educational Research, now the American Educational Research Association.

Sieber (1965) computed the founding and mortality rates of research units by comparing results of surveys conducted from time to time since 1923—for example, those of the USOE (U.S. Office of Education, 1923, 1932) Eckert (1949), Chapman (1927), and Rosengarten (1963). Earliest and latest periods established the most units—19 percent per year from 1923 to 1932 and 21 percent per year from 1949 to 1964. Mortality rate was greatest, 15 percent per year, during the depression years, 1932 to 1936. In 1923 there were 16 research units; in 1964 there were estimated to be 70. Between 1932 and 1936 the number of bureaus decreased from 37 to 17. Lack of funds was only one of the reasons for the decline. Even in the nondepression years the mortality rate was about 3 percent per year.

Between 1923 and 1932 the increase in the number of research units was about the same as the rate of increase in doctoral programs. In the past 15 years the number of bureaus has almost tripled, but doctoral programs increased by about two-thirds. The ratio of research units to doctoral programs was 0.61 in 1923, 0.27 in 1949, and 0.64 in 1964. Sieber (1965) adds, "After more than thirty years, however, organizational development still has not regained the 1932 level." Sieber's data suggest that educational research units were constantly troubled by marginality —high mortality and little organizational effectiveness. In fact, the organizational regression of the 1930's and 1940's has been eliminated only over the past ten years—the years of federal support.

It does not seem possible at the present time to establish accurately the number of educational research organizations. A comprehensive list, but one that is far from complete, is the general directory published by Gale Research Company (1964). Among the 1,230 organizations listed, only 80 were involved in educational research. Young's directories (1957, 1959, 1962) were focused directly on educational-research units but still were incomplete. Both the research company and Young relied on voluntary compliance with a written request and were incomplete largely because of nonreturns. Sieber and Lazarsfeld (1966), in what is easily the most thorough and comprehensive study of educational-research organizations available to date, obtained information not only by a variety of mailed questionnaires to deans, directors, and coordinators but also by interviews and observations by their own field representatives. Catalogs of universities, publications, and USOE proposals of various research units were analyzed. In all they queried 133 directors and 38 coordinators of research, identified from responses of deans of the 107 schools that granted a doctorate in education at the time. This list does not include private, public school, and state educational-research units. Perhaps a more comprehensive list was developed from the National Roster of Educational Researchers maintained by Phi Delta Kappa. A tabulation prepared by their research director identified 355 possible research units. The mailing list of individuals who currently hold Title IV grants and who appear to be associated with research units indicates a possible 149 units. About all that one can safely say at the present time is that the total number of educational-research units is probably somewhere between 200 and 400.

Several studies of educational-research units provided descriptive information. McArthur (1958) gave an expository summary of interviews and observations made during his visits to several midwestern universities under a grant designed to provide information leading to the organization of a research bureau at the University of Alberta. Miller's study (1958) was designed to yield information that would help the Stanford University education faculty reach a decision about setting up a research bureau. Miller's provided an extensive description organized under seven categories: structure (internal organization of the unit), purposes, functions (characteristic activities), personnel, clientele, patrons, and controls. Material from university catalogs, reports of organizations, publications, and personal interviews provided the data. Historical background of units was reported at length. Unfortunately, descriptive reports provide little evaluative guidance relative to performance of the organizations. Typical of studies that attempt to examine activities of educational research organizations are those of Ryans (1957) and Phillips (1957). Ryans found that the most common activities were services and accounting, supervisory activities, conduct of public relations, demonstrations, action research, and school surveys. Only rarely did such organizations perform applied research in curriculum and instruction. Only about one-third of the organizations required directors to have had any previous experience in either experimental or descriptive research.

The conflict between service and research in education has been constant and pervasive and has usually been resolved in favor of service. Most of the activity of research units in education still appears to be oriented toward ad hoc data collection rather than toward the understanding of education. Greatest efforts seem to be exerted for specific local clients rather than in the interests of education at large. Parenthetically, early research units took their assignments almost exclusively from local schools in identifying problems for study. This was indicated by the popularity of surveys asking about problems for research prior to World War II. A questionnaire was sent to school officials asking them to list problems which they wished studied. In fact, prior to the advent of federal funding most research units were seen as service institutes for public school systems. Little effort was made to identify research questions based on professional expertise or theoretical concerns. Some bureaus attempted to carry on both field services and research, but, as one director indicated, "when services get under the same tent with research, research is crowded out." University administrators now seem to be more aware of the advantages of separating research and service, since some more recently created research units appear to be devoted only to research. Sieber and Lazarsfeld (1966) indicate that this separation appears to result from administrative rather than faculty initiative.

In large part the failure to institutionalize research in education can be attributed to lack of agreement on what distinguishes scientific from nonscientific work. In education the pressure for service work has been so dominant that the definition of educational research is still unclear. Despite the claim of some directors of combined service and research units that field service work actually contributed to research capability, the evidence of Sieber and Lazarsfeld (1966) on research climate suggests otherwise. Combined units showed fewer contacts with behavioral-science departments outside of education, research funds were less often supplied from federal sources, and research productivity was much lower than that of research-oriented bureaus.

Given our present structure of education, services for school systems are likely to continue to be a significant part of professional expertise. This fact is reinforced by the applied research and development funding by the USOE. These new USOE programs appear to indicate that it is possible to combine research and action so that both functions can be strengthened. However, this will not occur through provision of routine services for their own sake to certain schools on an ad hoc basis.

Federal funds have provided a means for decreasing marginality of research units by decreasing dependence on support from various schools for services and by increasing affiliation with a university teaching area. The likelihood that such a unit will increase the chance of obtaining outside research support has been attractive to schools desiring to do more research. Newer bureaus, growing out of needs of the university rather than needs of school systems, appear to be freer to do research, than having to do field service, than the older bureaus. Also, the traditional service-oriented bureaus now have giant competitors in federal aid to schools and to state departments of education and in the federally supported regional research laboratories. State departments and local schools are increasingly assuming responsibility for ad hoc research and social bookkeeping activities. But, the picture is not entirely clear. Federal funds for basic research have not increased substantially in recent years—most of the increase has been in the area of applied research and development. In this applied work, if the standards of intellectual competence and performance of basic research obtain, there is likely to be substantial progress. But if the standards of "action research" or service-oriented research are applied, there is likely to be substantial disillusionment. Sieber and Lazarsfeld (1966) indicated that team effort (about 2½ professionals per team) was more likely to occur in research units. Single-investigator and team projects were about equally divided in research units. The ratio of teams to single investigators was 0.7 within research units and about 0.3 outside of research units. Investigations in research units were more likely to be methodologically innovative and related to social sciences.

When Wilder (1966) asked a population of reading experts whether they preferred to work in teams or independently, the preferences were about equal. A majority of reading experts who had done some research beyond their doctorate preferred to collaborate. Lazarsfeld and Sieber's survey (1964) of authors of empirical research published in education periodicals during 1964 found that 65 percent of authors in education tended to publish alone, compared to 49 percent of those from liberal arts and sciences. They suggest that this is largely because of marginality of research in education. Because of other activities that have a prior claim on a person's time—teaching, service, administration, workshops, and advising—it may be hard to find people who are free to take part in a joint research effort. Departmentalization may also reduce collaborative effort, since there are often too few researchers in any one department to permit teams to develop within a department.

Bargar's study (1965) noted that a low level of preparation characterized educational researches. Only 3 percent of personnel doing research "oriented toward the concerns of professional education" were spending full time on research. About half of the group devoted less than one-fifth of their time to research.

Relatively few schools treated the preparation of researchers as a major goal. Half of the schools did not have training programs for researchers. It was claimed that even when the best students were in graduate school, the requirement of professional experience meant that many students had already chosen a nonresearch career before they took up graduate work. Also, a good many years of their possible scientific lives had already been spent elsewhere.

According to Sieber and Lazarsfeld (1966) availability of research courses in schools of education was not related to production of researchers. The amount of course work outside of education was slightly related. Apprenticeship alone did not seem sufficient to prepare or motivate students toward research careers. Selection was most important. Selectivity was related to productivity regardless of the research climate or formal provision made for training researchers. Selectivity produced larger differences than research climate and was a better predictor of research output. Research productivity increased with better research climate only among highly selective schools.

Wilder's study of reading experts (1966) indicated that Ph.D.'s who studied in a school that also offered the Ed.D. were less well trained for empirical research (had fewer courses in statistics and measurement, had less often been research assistants, and were more critical of the quality of their research training) than Ph.D.'s who studied in schools that did not offer the Ed.D. Conditions of the Ed.D. programs appeared to dilute the requirements and training for scholarly Ph.D. training.

Sieber (1965) indicated that the role of directors was critical to the development of their units. Directors had to carry on important administrative duties to keep their organizations functioning, and they had to give considerable attention to developing and sustaining the intellectual life of the units. It was the combination of roles that produced effective leadership. Directors said that intellectual activities were performed more often than administrative ones. Almost half of the directors indicated that their duties interfered with their own research. Directors who shared a topic of discourse with their staff were more likely to receive stimulation for their own work.

Size of staff seemed to be a factor (Sieber 1965). Directors of small units (1–5 members) and of larger units (11 or more members) seemed to be helped, directors of units of 6–10 members more often felt hindered in their own research by interaction.

All of the directors who said the position helped their research were doing research. Even among those who complained that the duties hindered their research, 80 percent were engaged in research.

The importance of interaction with staff is well documented by Pelz and Andrews (1966). Having people around with similar interests created an intellectual climate that made the work easier. Continual interaction with others appeared to be a fruitful source of ideas for all participants. But if staff members were poorly prepared for research, interactions become exploitative instead of rewarding.

An interesting typology of styles of leadership based on administrative and intellectual dimensions was developed by Sieber and Lazarsfeld (1966). For those interested in studying organizational performance in relation to leadership styles this study can be a fruitful source. Sieber (1965) also compared the roles of faculty research coordinator and research director. It was found that directors more often performed supportive and supervisory roles, while coordinators were more often concerned with stimulating research. Coordinators were more often located in schools which did not emphasize research, while research-oriented bureaus appeared to be more characteristic of the better research schools. This suggested that a faculty's lack of competence in and resistance to research work first had to be overcome before the advantages of working in a research organization could be fully put to use. Apparently, the quality-control activity of a director can be carried out only where research is under way.

The norm of intellectual autonomy did not seem to be violated inside research organizations any more than outside. On a measure of formal authority it was observed that certain organizational characteristics determined the amount of power which directors had. Directors who founded their units had less formal authority than did those who inherited their units. Since it was the highly productive who most often had established their own organization, the chief motive for founding a research bureau seemed to be to increase one's opportunity for serious scholarship.

For the remainder of the discussion it may be well to turn to certain organizational features in relation to research productivity. Pelz and Andrews (1966) spent the period 1956–1960 collecting data on the performance of more than 1,300 scientists in university, government, and industrial research organizations and five more years analyzing their data. They describe conditions, as perceived by the researchers, that were related to level of performance. They also describe characteristics of organizations that can be changed to more favorable forms. It is possible for an individual to alter his working relations with associates, to assume (or refuse) certain responsibilities, and to receive more stimulation from his environment. A director can similarly change his unit to improve its achievement.

Two types of data were collected by Pelz and Andrews: information about the members and conditions in the research unit and information about the members' performance.

Much of the information of the first type was collected by questionnaire. Information about the scientist's performance was based on judgments of each man's work made by senior people in both supervisory and nonsupervisory positions who were in the same unit, who knew the man's work, and who felt qualified to compare it with the work of others in that unit. Each judge indicated two different rankings of people he felt qualified to make—one according to their contribution to knowledge in the field within the past five years and another according to their overall usefulness to the organization.

Additional and more objective performance data were the number of various scientific products the person had produced in the past five years—papers, publications, patents or patent applications, and unpublished technical reports or manuscripts. Before making analyses, adjustments were made to remove the effects of certain factors that accounted for some of the differences in performance but which were extraneous to the study.

For example, Pelz and Andrews expected to find performance related to experience. If younger scientists were energetic and anxious to get ahead and older ones calm, and if younger ones had achieved less because of their youth, using raw data one might obtain the surprising finding that being energetic inhibited performance. Data on time elapsed since the doctorate was obtained did show that performance was low for people who had recently obtained their degrees, increased steadily for 15–20 years, and then dropped. Effects of this and similar factors were reduced by adjustments to equate average performance for scientists who differed in experience. The intent was a set of performance data which showed how a scientist was performing relative to his peers of the same level of education and the same amount of experience and located in similar units.

Some of the general findings are summarized below. In effective older groups, members interacted vigorously and preferred each other as collaborators, yet they felt free to disagree on technical strategy. Effective scientists valued freedom and were directed by their own ideas. At the same time, they interacted vigorously with colleagues and considered their comments in shaping their directions.

Pelz and Andrews' data indicate that a combination of freedom and coordination was helpful—e.g., the scientist involves several other people in shaping his assignments but keeps substantial control over the decision process. Interacting was more effective than being told; the man who was told what to do by his chief, with little voice himself, was not effective. Interaction appears to provide a testing ground, a means of sharpening ideas, provided that the discussants do not hold veto power. Also, interaction brings recognition for a job well done. Contact with different people brings a variety of views, and diversity seems to be a stimulus to achievement. Apparently, when direction in a research unit came only from the supervisor, the result was harmful.

Two paths to effective interaction were found: spending much time on communication or spending little time in each session but contacting many people frequently. The situation of spending little time on few contacts with few colleagues was to be avoided. Interactions were just as useful to highly motivated scientists as to less highly motivated ones. There was a positive relation between contact and performance even for people who were not especially interested in working with others and for people who indicated strong inner motivation. Colleagues probably aided performance by providing new ideas or getting a man out of his old ways of thinking. They provided information, and a peer might catch an error which was overlooked. Contacts provided friendly but real competition that helped keep a person alert. Contacts seemed to be most useful when originated by the persons concerned. Directors could ensure that men working in related areas were aware of each other's activities. Then the men themselves could initiate the contacts that appeared to be most useful. The productive goal was good communication among the group members, not just a set of meetings.

Diversity was essential to performance. Scientists who were highly specialized were less effective than those with several interests. Full-time researchers published less than those spending three-fourths time, and this held true in each academic rank. In industrial laboratories performance was lower for those spending full time on research than for those spending three-fourths time. When less than three-fourths time was spent in research, productivity was very low, but output of reports was high. When Ph.D.'s in research units who spent their nonresearch time mainly in teaching were compared with those who spent it on administration, the part-time administrators were judged to be the better scientists. In the laboratories administration was not a paper-shuffling exercise but apparently a channel to influence technical goals and decision making; hence, it seemed to expose a man to fruitful ideas outside of his immediate problem area. Parallel results were found for development and technical-services activities. The more effective scientists did not concentrate exclusively on research, or development, or technical services. For all three some diversity was better than none. It is quite possible that a scientist may benefit from mild exposure to administrative tasks that deal with the well-being of the organization—e.g., review conferences where each person outlines his future directions. If this responsibility were shared by the professional staff, it could add to the research climate.

It appeared better to encourage persons and groups to tackle both basic and applied problems. Assigning one group exclusively to research and another exclusively to development was not as productive as variety.

Dedication appeared to be a question of motivation—the will to succeed; it was not sustained by contentment. Satisfaction may drop as motivation rises. The extent to which different people were interested in or casual about their jobs did not depend on satisfaction or enjoyment. The better work was done by the better motivated.

Measures of involvement in work suggested the following: People who were thoroughly involved in their work, who took it home and slept on it, were consistently better performers than those who were less involved. But longest hours did not necessarily go with the highest performance. The highly involved person worked an hour or two longer each day, but he also took time out for other things. Consistently associated with high involvement was the ability to influence other people who had substantial influence over one's technical goals. It appeared that scientists who really share in the decision-making and policy progress and are not merely left alone to pursue whatever they like become more involved in and commited to the goals selected.

Among the various motives characteristic of high performers, self-reliance was outstanding. Effective scientists reported stimulation from several sources—from practical problems or technical literature, from professional colleagues or from self-study. The critical element was not the type of source but an underlying confidence in one's ideas, or intellectual self-reliance. Those who relied on supervisors for motivation performed below average. The measure of science orientation used by the National Institutes of Health had three components: desire to use one's skills, interest in scientific contribution, and need for freedom to follow own ideas; the first component did not show up in the Pelz and Andrews study, the second showed up as of mild importance, and the last (self-reliance) seemed to be the essential core.

Effective scientists reported good opportunities for professional growth and higher status but were not necessarily satisfied. Satisfaction was defined as the extent to which job factors desired by the individual were actually provided. Scientists whose personal interests were congruent with those perceived for the organization wrote many reports, but work of better scientific value and utility was done by those who disagreed moderately with the organization. Satisfaction was broken down into two parts—strength of desire for something (aspiration and expectation had an equivalent effect), and degree to which the desired factor was actually present. The congruence between these two indicated the feeling of satisfaction. Ambition for status was a poor basis for developing achievement among the staff, but the provision of status rewards was significantly associated with achievement. Intrinsic reward was even more clearly associated with achievement. Apparently extrinsic reward cannot be relied on to produce achievement, but when achievement occurs the extrinsic rewards should occur—their provision seems to stimulate further achievement.

Data were collected on the degree of congruence between activities which the individual personally valued and those he thought would help him to advance in the organization. The most productive scientists saw only moderate congruence between their personal interests and those of the organization. Perhaps a research unit remains vigorous when it encourages a certain amount of tension between what the members want and what they think the organization wants. Some dissatisfaction, based upon eager impatience, appeared desirable in a healthy research atmosphere.

In the matter of mixtures of people to encourage innovation, it was found that similarity to colleagues was related to performance in a complex way—the relationship depended on the frequency of contact with colleagues. Senior scientists who had daily contact with their major colleagues and who were dissimilar to them in career orientation and past experience had higher performance than others. For those who contacted colleagues weekly, the relationship was the opposite—better performance if the colleagues were similar. Similarity was measured relative to technical strategy, style of approach to problems, career orientations, and sources of motivation. The measure was based on personal perception. Scientists who performed better named as colleagues persons from whom they differed in strategy for tackling problems and in style of approach to their work. Results suggested that scientists benefited most from colleagues with whom they were personally compatible but intellectually competitive.

Pelz and Andrews' (1966) graphs relating age to

achievement were typically saddle-shaped. Mean scores for scientific contributions (over the previous five years) reached a peak when the individual was in his late forties, then dropped in the early fifties and recovered in the late fifties. This recovery phase stood in direct contrast to the pattern shown in a variety of earlier studies, including Lehman's (1953). That recovery was not simply a halo effect for past achievement was shown by the parallel rise in published papers and unpublished reports. Similar saddle-shaped curves were found earlier in a nationwide study on the performance of physiologists. Pelz and Andrews' hypothesis was that the earlier peak represented work of a more divergent or innovative type, and the later represented more convergent or integrative work. The data did not support the hypothesis that decrease in productivity was due to a decline in intellectual powers, but decline seemed to occur because individuals' motivation decreases. Strongly motivated persons (those with high self-reliance) resisted decrease in achievement with age. The hypothesis that capable men were burdened with administration and drawn away from creative work did not seem to be supported. Systematic attention to renewing or broadening one's technical skill appeared to be a useful way of prolonging the productive years.

As age increased performance was sustained by periodic change in project, self-confidence, breadth, and depth of interest.

Results suggest that the level of scientific performance of an individual varied with the kind of research climate. Older scientists, 50 and over, were more productive when they retained an interest in pioneering. Younger scientists gained more by prolonged exposure to a given project than did older. Especially after age 40, continued achievement depended on self-confidence, as seen by the person's willingness to take risks and rely on his own judgment.

The more loosely coordinated a situation, the more essential it was for the individual to remain strongly motivated if he were to achieve. A fairly high level of autonomy was effective mainly in the middle range of coordination. In loose coordination, where members had considerable freedom, the most autonomous scientists were below average in performance. It was suggested that in loose settings the most autonomous scientists tended to withdraw from outer stimulation, thus weakening opportunity to improve their performance. In rigid situations, autonomous persons were inhibited. In middle-range situations high autonomy was accompanied by several strong motivations and stimulations, and the setting appeared to improve performance. In the loosest settings full autonomy seemed to encourage complacency rather than motivation and narrow specialization rather than breadth. Isolation was not a good climate for achievement.

The study of educational research organizations has scarcely been touched upon. Both the strategies used by the students of industrial and other research organizations and the results have applications that could improve inquiry in educational organizations in general.

Nicholas A. Fattu
Indiana University

References

American Management Association. *The Management of Scientific Manpower*. Report No. 22. Research and Development Division, The Association, 1958.

Armed Services Technical Information Agency. *Management of Scientific Research: A Report Bibliography*. The Agency, 1962.

Bargar, R. R. "Who Is the Educational Researcher?" In Guba, Egon. (Ed.) *The Training and Nurture of Educational Researchers*. Sixth Annual Phi Delta Kappa Symposium on Educational Research. PDK, 1965.

Bell, G. D. (Ed.) *Organizations and Human Behavior*. Prentice-Hall, 1967.

Best, R. D. "Scientific Mind vs. the Management Mind." *Manag R* 52:23–6; November 1963.

Boehm, G. A. W. "Research Management: The New Executive Job." *Fortune* 56:164–70; October 1957.

Burns, T., and Stalker, G. M. *The Management of Innovation*. Quadrangle Books, 1961.

Bureau of Educational Research, Ohio State University. *National Register of Educational Researchers*. PDK, 1966.

Chapman, H. B. "Organized Research in Education." *Bureau of Educational Research Monographs*. No. 7. Ohio State University Studies, 1927.

Churchman, C. W., and Scheinblatt, A. H. "The Researcher and the Manager: A Dialectic of Implementation." *Manag Sci* 11:369–87; 1965.

Drucker, P. F. "Twelve Fables of Research Management." *Harvard Bus R* 41:03–8; January–February 1963.

Eckert, R. E. "Report on the Organization and Services of Bureaus of Educational Research in Leading American Universities." Office of Educational Research, U Minnesota, 1949. (Mimeographed.)

Evan, W. M. "Superior-Subordinate Conflict in Research Organizations." *Adm Sci Q* 10:52–64; June 1965.

Fiedler, F. F. *Leader Attitudes and Group Effectiveness*. U Illinois, 1958.

Folger, A. P., and Gordon, G. "Scientific Accomplishment and Social Organization: A View of the Literature." *Am Behavioral Scientist* 6:51–8; December 1962.

Froehlich, G. "Research Bureaus." In Harris, Chester W. (Ed.) *Encyclopedia of Educational Research*, 3rd ed. Macmillan, 1960. p. 1155–60.

Gale Research Company. *Encyclopedia of Associations*, 4th ed. Vol. 1: *National Organizations of the United States*. The Company, 1964.

Goldberg, L. C. "A Selected Annotated Bibliography of Empirical Investigation of Research Personnel."

IEEE Trans Engineering Manag EM-10:31-7; March 1963.
Gordon, G. "The Problem of Assessing Scientific Accomplishment: A Patented Solution." *IEEE Trans Engineering Manag* EM-10:192-6; December 1963.
Goslin, L. N. *A Selected Annotated Bibliography on R & D Management*. Bureau of Business Research, Indiana U, 1966.
Haire, M. *Modern Organization Theory*. Wiley, 1959.
Hirsch, I., and others. "Increasing the Productivity of Scientists." *Harvard Bus R* 36:66-76; March-April 1958.
Howton, W. F. "Work Assignment and Interpersonal Relations in a Research Organization." *Adm Sci Q* 7:502-20; March 1963.
Katz, D., and Kahn, R. L. *The Social Psychology of Organizations*. Wiley, 1966.
Lazarsfeld, Paul F., and Sieber, S. D. *Organizing Educational Research*. Prentice-Hall, 1964.
Lehman, Harvey C. *Age and Achievement*. Princeton U Press, 1953. 358p.
Machlup, Fritz. *The Production and Distribution of Knowledge in the United States*. Princeton U Press, 1962.
March, J. G., and Simon, Herbert A. *Organizations*. Wiley, 1958.
Marcson, S. *The Scientist in American Industry: Some Organizational Determinants in Manpower Utilization*. Industrial Relations Section, Princeton U, 1960.
McArthur, R. S. "Organization for Educational Research in Universities of Midwestern United States." *Alberta J Ed Res* 4:131-41; September 1958.
McClure, L. *Research Management—A Selected Bibliography*. Defense Documentation Center, 1964.
Meltzer, L., and Salter, J. "Organizational Structure and Performance and Job Satisfaction of Scientists." *Am Sociol R* 27:351-62; 1962.
Miller, H. K., Jr. "A Study of the Field Service and Research Units of Ten Schools of Education." Doctoral dissertation. Stanford U, 1958.
Noltingk, B. E. *The Human Element in Research Management*. Elsevier, 1959.
Parsons, Talcott. "Suggestions for a Sociological Approach to the Theory of Organizations." *Adm Sci Q* 1:237; September 1956.
Pelz, D. C., and Andrews, F. M. *Scientists in Organizations*. Wiley, 1966.
Phillips, B. N. "Survey of Research Personnel, Facilities, and Activities in State Department of Education." *J Ed Res* 51:43-5; September 1957.
Rank, C. S. *R & D Management—Bibliography Report*. AD 400-611. Armed Services Technical Information Agency, 1963.
Raudsepp, E. *Managing Creative Scientists and Engineers*. Macmillan, 1963.
Rice, Joseph M. "Educational Research." *Forum* 35:124; July 1902.
Rice, Joseph M. "The Society of Educational Research." *Forum* 35:119; July 1903.
Roberts, E. B. *The Dynamics of Research and Development*. Harper, 1964.
Rosengarten, W. "Organization and Administration of Educational Research in Departments, Schools and Colleges of Education in Universities." *Rho Monogr Ed* No. 1; September 1963.
Rubenstein, A. H. *A Directory of Research on Research*. Institute of Management Sciences, Northwestern U, 1964.
Ryans, David G. "Are Educational Research Offices Conducting Research?" *J Ed Res* 51:173-83; November 1957.
Schein, E. H., and others. "Career Orientations and Perceptions of Rewarded Activity in a Research Organization." *Adm Sci Q* 9:333-49; March 1965.
Shepard, H. A. "Nine Dilemmas in Industrial Research." *Adm Sci Q* 1:295-309; December 1956.
Sieber, S. D. "Existing Organizational Patterns in Educational Research." Guba, Egon. (Ed.) *The Training and Nurture of Educational Researchers*. Sixth Annual Phi Delta Kappa Symposium in Educational Research, PDK 1965. Ch. 7.
Sieber, S. D., and Lazarsfeld, Paul F. *The Organization of Educational Research*. USOE Cooperative Research Project No. 1974. Bureau of Applied Research. Columbia U, 1966.
Tannenbaum, A. D. "Control in Organizations: Industrial Adjustment and Organizational Performance." *Adm Sci Q* 7:236-57; 1962.
Tarkawski, Z. M. T., and Turnbull, A. V. "Scientists vs. Administrators: An Approach Towards Achieving Greater Understanding." *Public Adm* 27:213-56; August 1959.
U.S. Office of Education. *Educational Directories*. GPO, 1923, 1932.
Villers, R. *Research and Development: Planning and Control*. Rautenstranch & Villers, 1964.
Wilder, D. E. "The Reading Experts: A Case Study of the Failure to Institutionalize an Applied Science of Education." Doctoral dissertation. Columbia U, 1966.
Young, R. J. *A Directory of Educational Research Agencies and Studies*. PDK, 1957, rev. ed., 1959, 2nd ed., 1962.

SAFETY EDUCATION

Safety education involves a concern about the thousands of lives lost annually and millions of injuries resulting from accidents. Such chance occurrences are not restricted to any single walk of life. They are too numerous on farms, in homes, in business and industry, on streets and highways, in recreation, and in governmental occupations.

DEFINITION AND ROLE. Safety education utilizes administration, instruction, and protection in a comprehensive program for the conservation of human and material resources.

To conserve these resources, carefully planned on-going activities must be carried out as follows:

(1) In the area of *administration,* leadership is concerned with budgeting, program organization, and assignment of personnel to assure adequate safety education services. (2) The goal of the *instruction* is development of human values and patterns for safe living. The instruction extends from kindergarten to high school and into college—and it includes programs for adults. (3) School responsibility for *protection* includes the maintenance of an optimum level of safety in the school environment. Important parts of the environment are those relating to design and maintenance of buildings; student movement, including transportation; inspection of facilities; and appropriate direction of personnel to assure safe conditions (National Education Association, 1966).

PIONEERING PROGRAMS AND ACTIVITIES. In the United States formal safety lessons were taught as early as 1845. The safety concepts were integrated with other subject matter, particularly in connection with the development of skills in reading and writing (McGuffey, 1879). For the most part, the emphasis in the early materials was remedial rather than preventive instruction—what to do in case of an accident rather than how to prevent one.

A few pioneering school systems are known. In 1919 the Detroit schools appointed a full-time supervising instructor of safety education, and with this leadership a comprehensive program was developed. The public schools of Kansas City, Missouri, began an organized program in 1922. Student safety organizations were formed, including one of the early school safety-patrol projects.

Perhaps the most sophisticated early publication on safety education was the 25th yearbook of the National Society for the Study of Education. It included outlines for elementary and secondary instruction as well as a review of the status of safety education in teacher education institutions. This recognition by the society attracted widespread public attention (National Society for the Study of Education, 1926).

Safety-education research began to develop in the 1920's. Among the early studies was one on secondary-school safety which outlined a course of study, including materials on automobile-accident prevention (Stack, 1929).

A later nationwide survey of 100,000 teachers brought 14,000 replies. The returns revealed that, for those reporting, safety education was being taught by 82 percent of the elementary-school teachers, 41 percent of junior high school teachers, and 20 percent of senior high school teachers. While it is not suggested that these figures represented the extent of safety instruction in the nation as a whole, they do indicate a significant beginning. The approaches to teaching safety, as indicated by the survey, included appropriate use of classroom equipment items, motion pictures, class forums and general discussions of safety problems, student organizations and pupil patrols, and safety lectures by nonschool people. It was shown that 23 state departments of education provided courses of study in general safety and 24 in highway traffic safety (National Education Association, 1938).

The safety-education breakthrough in school administration came in 1940 with the publication of the yearbook *Safety Education* of the American Association of School Administrators (1940).

The period of World War II saw only limited advances, though many teachers did maintain their active role of safety instruction and protection. Major accident-prevention efforts were directed toward wartime training. Such essential safety instruction included preinduction driver education in schools and colleges, training for wartime motor vehicle fleet operation, and wartime training of school transportation supervisors and bus drivers (U.S. Office of Education, 1945).

Many invaluable contributions have been made to the field by numerous nonschool safety agencies, particularly during the years immediately following World War II. For a time, staff specialists of some of these organizations provided workshops and short courses for teachers and college professors, primarily in driver and traffic-safety education. Then, as the leadership in educational institutions accepted the responsibility, the role of the support groups became more frequently that of providing advice or consultation service upon request from colleges or school systems.

SCOPE AND STATUS. Authorities have long been in substantial agreement on the principle that the best framework for learning safe behavior is provided by the school. The school accepts the responsibility for teaching people to survive and to live effectively. Safety education involves specialists who are assigned responsibilities for leadership. It is not the exclusive responsibility of these specialists, however. It is a concern of all educators—and indeed a problem of all society (Brody, 1959).

With the assistance of safety specialists, the entire school population is responsible for maintaining awareness of the need for safety and incorporating the elements of learning and practicing safe behavior in their day-to-day activities.

Since 1920 the recognition of the need for safety education has spread rapidly. Schools and colleges have developed courses of study and curriculum guides for the conduct of comprehensive safety-education programs. The necessity for administrative and protective measures is today widely recognized in every state and in practically every community— in the schools, in business, in civic oragnizations, and through media of all types (Stratemeyer, 1964).

The Expanding Program. When the kindergarten child or first grader enters school for the first time, he finds himself in a new world in which many new experiences confront him. Learning depends on the physical and mental well-being of the learner, and safety education helps to instill the feeling of security that is so necessary to the child's well-being.

In the early school experience of the child, emphasis is placed on protection. As he gains insight and maturity the emphasis gradually shifts from protection to instruction which guides him toward self-reliant, safe behavior (Zirbes, 1953).

The instruction often starts with pedestrian and play safety and continues with instruction on safety in the home and in other areas of the child's daily activities, such as bicycle riding. In the junior high school it usually involves water safety, fire safety, and first aid. Later, in senior high school, experiences lead into lifesaving, firearm safety, civil defense, and traffic safety. A full semester of driver and traffic-safety education is often included at grade levels at which students reach legal driving age. In some high schools separate courses in general safety education, aviation safety, civil defense, and firearm safety are offered.

The instruction in elementary schools is an integral part of each basic area of learning. By incorporating the elements of education for safe living, teachers are able to relate the work of the schools more directly to life processes and situations (Key, 1967).

Recognizing that the benefits of safety education on a nationwide basis would depend upon programs, policies, and standards developed by the profession itself, educators began to conduct national conferences with the purpose of such development.

School Transportation. National conferences on school transportation have been held from time to time. Their primary purpose was to develop vehicle and operational standards for the safety of the thousands of children transported. The benefits of research and experience, both in industry and in school systems, are reflected in the standards developed by these conferences. The standards guide state and local school systems in the safe and efficient operation of school transportation service (National Education Association, National Commission . . ., 1964). The well-known color, national school bus chrome, resulted from the careful development of colorimetric specifications by the U.S. Bureau of Standards especially to provide a distinctive identification for school buses. This is illustrative of the effective collaboration by representatives of government, business and industry, safety organizations, and state school systems in the interest of safety in this important school activity.

Driver and Traffic Safety. National conferences on driver and traffic-safety education have served to extend and strengthen programs. A number of studies have reflected the influence of these conferences upon the growth of programs. One study, for example, showed that by far the majority of high schools met or exceeded the 30 hours of classroom instruction for each student, as well as the 6 hours of laboratory (or practice driving) instruction, as recommended by the conferences (Key, 1960). Also, a project on teacher preparation and certification has influenced the scope and quality of college offerings. This involved a special study of the status of teacher preparation followed by a national conference of leaders in teacher education institutions and state and local school systems. Finally, a series of six regional workshops helped to guide college and school system leaders in extending preservice and in-service preparation in this field (National Education Association, National Commission . . ., 1965).

Evaluative Criteria. Since the 1960 edition of *Evaluative Criteria* (National Study of Secondary School Evaluation, 1960) the major elements of safety education have been included in that overall guide for evaluating secondary schools. The instrument contains a section on driver education, with the elements of safety administration, instruction, and protection incorporated where relevant in other sections of the document. This helps to assure appropriate consideration of the secondary school's responsibility in this field when its program is being evaluated by professional teams representing the associations of colleges and secondary schools. A separate, new edition (National Study of Secondary School Evaluation, 1963) designed for the evaluation of junior high schools also incorporates safety education.

College Programs. Safety education in colleges and universities has been stimulated and guided by such national-level activities as the following: (1) The National Conference on Safety Education by Colleges and Universities outlined the program and identified the body of knowledge as integral parts of agricultural education, engineering education, liberal arts education, teacher education, university extension services, and safety in the college community (National Education Association, 1951). (2) A survey of college and university course offerings, jointly conducted by the U.S. Office of Education and the NEA National Commission on Safety Education (U.S. Office of Education & NEA, 1958), revealed that 328 institutions (at least one in every state) offered a variety of courses for the preparation of people in traffic-safety and driver education, traffic engineering, police traffic supervision, and related safety fields. (3) A case-study approach was used to examine in depth the types of services provided through transportation and accident prevention centers at nine different institutions of higher education. Following the analysis of information gathered by questionnaires and by site visits, guide lines were developed for use by institutions of higher education in establishing and operating such accident prevention centers (Association of State Universities and Land-Grant Colleges, 1962).

Elementary Safety. A stimulus for the extension and enrichment of safety-education programs was provided through the national conference on safety education in elementary schools (National Education Association, 1953). Subsequent national projects have included the development of safety instructional units, guides for planning and conducting safety activities, and the creation of safety-education motion pictures and filmstrips. In state and local school systems, safety content is frequently programmed for multimedia transmission to the students.

Professional Associations. The professional goals of driver-education and safety-education teachers reflect a development of their field of interest. The formation of state associations of driver and safety education began in 1949. Today there are 44 state associations. Some are associations of safety educators which include persons in the field of driver and traffic-safety education. Others concern themselves entirely with driver and traffic-safety education. Many of these organizations are affiliated with their respective state education associations. In 1956 a national professional association was organized as the American Driver and Safety Education Association. In 1960 it became a department of the National Education Association and subsequently changed its name to the American Driver and Traffic Safety Education Association.

THE SHIFTING EMPHASIS OF ACCIDENT RESEARCH. In the early history of accident-prevention research, particularly as it related to school safety instruction, efforts were directed primarily toward assembling and analyzing accident data for use in developing courses of study. It was assumed that if the masses could be exposed to enough information about accidents and their destructive nature, a significant reduction in accidents would result. There was little recognition of the importance of a behavioral approach to the study of accidents and accident prevention (McGuire, 1956). Then there was an overemphasis on attitude per se, as the focus of research shifted toward consideration of the role of human behavior in accidents (Mahony, 1957). Attempts have been made to design instruments which would measure attitude and even identify people who would be subject to accidents. To date, such instruments have not accomplished those objectives.

Employment of a three-way taxonomy with data on accidents of school-age children has shown the importance, in accident-causation research, of being able to classify accidents in terms of responsibility (Was the person being studied responsible for the accident?), social nature (Was the person alone or with others at the time of the accident?), and activity situation (In what activity and within what situation was the person engaged when the accident occurred?) (McGlade & Abercrombie, 1965).

Behavioral Approach to Accident Research. Accidents, like any single item of behavior, must be viewed in the context of the larger culture, if programs are to be designed to keep accident occurrence at some reasonable minimum. Through the process of enculturation each society introduces to the child certain demands, barriers, and controls. It is increasingly evident that accidents have a significance beyond themselves. Studies on relationship of socioeconomic class and mental illness have revealed a disproportionate concentration of mental illness in the lowest 20 percent of the population—lowest in terms of where they live, the kinds of work they do, and how much education they have acquired. Some studies suggest that there may be similar, disproportionately high accident frequencies among low socioeconomic groups (MacIver, 1961).

Some earlier studies indicated that certain people had characteristic, relatively stable traits which made them particularly susceptible to accidents. This concept came to be known as "accident proneness." Current evidence is rather conclusive that this is, for the most part, a misconception (Rosenblatt, 1955). At some time or other accidents are experienced by everyone to some degree. Everyone undergoes stress at times, and such experience requires adjustment. Fortunately—and this suggests the importance of safety education—the state of susceptibility need not lead to an accident. The individual may just as well be aware of potential hazard, with respect both to his own physical and emotional condition and to the environment in which he finds himself. Thus, it is suggested that the concept of accident proneness has been inaccurately employed in attempts to explain the problems of accident behavior. To designate one person as more accident prone than another it would be necessary to analyze scientifically all the confounding influences of differential exposure to hazards, differential rates of accidents of different types at each level, and differential distribution of protection of individuals so identified.

Host-Agent-Environment Concept of Accidents. Accidents are not diseases. Accidents are not passed along from one person to another in the same way that, for example, measles are transmitted from one child to another. Yet, there are some remarkable similarities in terms of causal relationships and in terms of the preventive aspects of the problem (Fox, 1961). Safety-education specialists and accident researchers have been aware that the cause of an accident is usually a combination of three forces—the host, most often man; the agent, an errant object or some other specific cause of injury; and the environment in which the host and agent are operating. Research is inadequate, however, if it is concerned only with itemizing the factors involved within these three areas or with counting the different types of accidents. Studies so limited have accumulated large amounts of statistical data which, alone, are not sufficiently revealing of the real nature of accidents. Interrelationships between and among the factors involved are too often missing. The significance of such interrelationships in both the design and execution of accident research is being recognized. This involves control for both time and place of environmental exposure, the examination of relationships of cases studied, and controls in terms, of age, sex, occupation, blood-alcohol concentration, family relationships, and other factors (Haddon, 1964). Inevitably, findings from investigations concerned with a greater variety of variables which bear upon accidents will produce more realistic substance for teaching safe behavior and for accident prevention in general. In safety instruction as well as in education generally, we need to know more about the physiological and psychological elements that increase the probability of accidents in maladjusted persons. Evidence points to the significant relationship of accidents to anxiety, fear, worry, guilt, early exposure to aggression, overauthoritative parents or parent figures, and fatigue (Schulzinger, 1956).

There is a need for the study of the use of alcohol and accidents in terms of medical, societal, cultural, and psychological perspectives. In the first place, drinking plays an increasingly important part in our social relationships. Many cultural patterns are related to the use of alcohol. It is known that alcohol plays a major role in the occurrence of accidents in traffic as well as in boating and other activities around water. Among workers in occupations where the consumption of alcohol usually is prohibited, its association with accidents is substantially lower than the average. Studies also indicate that even a very low level of alcohol concentration in the blood of a human will adversely affect performance (U.S. Department of Health, Education, and Welfare, 1966). Too many people assume that only "the drunk" is a menace to the safety of himself and others. A relatively small proportion of the population realizes that even light social drinking impairs the individual's critical judgment and all too often figures prominently in accidents.

Task Analysis and Safety. Consideration of task analysis in the study of accidents and safety education is a rather new approach. Yet the process is dramatically demonstrated in successful space exploration. Without it, not only would attempts at space flights have failed, but human and material losses would have been prohibitive. Task analysis involves the factors of foresight, planning, and recognition of hazards in a situation no matter how complex or how simple it may be. The process involves (1) learning a series of coordinated subtasks for hands, feet, eyes, and ears, and developing them to a semiautomatic state; (2) learning to make judgments of changing space-time relationships; and (3) learning to anticipate situations and conditions and reacting correctly, often in brief time intervals. Teaching for conscious application of the analytical approach and the choice of low-risk action will enable citizens to participate in a wider variety of activities with reasonable safety. To implement this more effective teaching, research is needed in many areas of accident prevention. For example, a job analysis of the driving task is urgently needed in order to determine (1) the requirements of the driver, (2) the specific skills needed to meet those demands, and (3) the appropriate, sequential presentation of content needed for safe and efficient performance in traffic (Freeman & others, 1960).

Testing for Safe Behavior. Safety is concerned with risk behavior. Though the objective of safety education is not to eliminate all of the risk in life, it does enable the individual to assess the amount of risk or threat in a given situation and to act in an efficient and safe manner. Generalizing about the safe behavior of an individual is impossible without knowing something of his personal condition, the nature of the activity in which he is involved, and the characteristics of the situation itself. Testing in this field has been quite limited; it has not advanced much beyond checking the individual's knowledge of safety (Ojemann, 1959). The "semantic differential," a tool for measuring meaning, could perhaps be applied in the scientific development of an instrument to assess the safety value concepts of individuals (National Education Association, 1963). (The term "safety value concept" is used here to describe a configuration of somewhat subjective traits, including attitude, which can be observed by the teacher over a period of time and scored as a composite representing a student's personal commitment to safe behavior.) Such an instrument, when used with appropriate tests of safety knowledge and safety performance, would more adequately serve in assessing the learner's development of safe behavior during and subsequent to instruction.

EXTENSION AND IMPROVEMENT OF SCHOOL PROGRAMS. Education for safe living is being extended and improved, as evidenced by the following developments. (1) An important goal of school safety is protection of children and youth, and an important part of the school's protection program is that of civil defense. The dangers of nature—fire, tornado, hurricane, flood, tidal wave, and earthquake—have long been well known. More recently civil-defense education and protection, substantially supported by the federal government, have become widespread as a part of the school's overall program. Leaders in American education have developed comprehensive guides for the administration of civil defense in schools, and federal civil-defense authorities have implemented extensive programs of research and development as means of advancing efforts in this field (Department of Defense, 1966). (2) Numerous studies of general safety education have had improvement as their major purpose. Criteria for evaluating safety instruction have been developed, and laws and regulations affecting administration, instruction, and protection for accident prevention have been analyzed. There is evidence of the need for further research to improve the articulation of safety content for the different grade levels and throughout the school program (Marshall, 1961). Further research is needed for guidance in what to teach about hazards and risks, as well as with respect to the optimum ages for acquiring different kinds of knowledge and the best organization and teaching strategy at different age and grade levels. (3) The professional school staff is as likely to fall victim to accidents as students are. The most common accident in the professional staff is a fall. Women are particularly susceptible to slips and falls, as Shaw has shown (1961). This study, though limited in scope and depth, suggests the need for special and continuing attention to the responsibility for adequate programs which directly involve professional staff. (4) A pressing need of our society is a comprehensive and effective program of accident prevention for adults and out-of-school youth. Senior citizens have demonstrated their interest in learning how to avoid accidents. In education there is a growing concern for the safety of adults, and out-of-school youth, including specialized training for driving vocations; community survival; safety for senior citizens; and safety in connection with new employment, particularly for adults who have been displaced by automation (Key, 1964). (5) The critical-incident technique employed in other areas (education and psychology) has been applied in research for the improvement of safety instruction (Tarrants, 1963). Such studies should enhance the current emphasis on the behavioral aspects of accident research and the effective teaching and learning of safe behavior. (6) Driver- and traffic-safety education activities, including research, receive substantially more attention than other areas of safety. Technology which is being utilized in education generally is finding its place in this field. Team teaching is common practice, and multimedia are being used more and more widely to extend and improve instruction. A four-phased program consisting of classroom instruction combined in various ways with practice on driving simulators, in automobiles on a driving range, and driving experience in real traffic situations seems to reduce the cost without lowering the effectiveness (Seals, 1966). (7) Recently, materials have been developed for teaching driver and traffic safety to poor readers—some of them virtually nonreaders. Adapted from basic text materials, they reduce to a minimum the demands upon the learner to communicate through reading and writing. Special pictures and diagrams, magnetic boards to illustrate traffic situations, guides for student discussion and student listening, and exercises for verbal means of assessing the learner's growth have been developed. Removal of emphasis on reading for reading's sake motivates the learner not only to become a competent traffic citizen but also ultimately to learn how to read better (Bonner & others, 1966).

For more effective instruction, research of a new kind is needed to improve the structure and organization of learning activities and to determine the most appropriate distribution of student experiences between the driving range and on-street traffic. Through research, criteria could be developed for the selection or development of simulation and range facilities which would contribute most effectively to teaching and learning at minimum cost. Research-developed instruments for assessing the growth of learners in terms of traffic-safety knowledge, personal growth in traffic-safety value concepts, and safe and effective traffic performance are much needed.

Improving Teaching and Teacher Education. Though technology has challenged the traditional role of the teacher, it may still be said that he is the key to all learning, including learning for safe behavior. The teacher may at any time be faced with the problem of what to do in case of a fire or tornado or other emergency. Since the teacher's insights and skills are cultivated in both preservice and in-service programs, all teachers should be exposed to appropriate elements of safety education as an essential part of their preparation. Learning theory suggests that teachers first study the nature of the child for underlying causes of high-risk behavior as a basis for guiding him in understanding his own behavior and thus for redirecting his action toward avoiding unduly great risks. Certainly safety education must not be too restrictive. The teacher must help the learner to assess the degree of risk in a situation and to adjust his conduct accordingly. Research-based instruments for assessing the individual's judgment of impending hazards in given situations may provide invaluable information for use by teachers in helping the learner to adjust to changing conditions. Also, research-developed safety communication models may lead to more effective strategy for influencing the behavior of persons for greater safety (Columbia University, 1966).

Federal and State Legislation. The importance of providing support for safety education has been recognized by legislators at federal and state levels. Two types of financial support are developing: 35 states provide special financial support for driver and traffic-safety education and for leadership at local and state levels. At the federal level, funds are available for safety education through the Elementary and Secondary Education Act of 1965. There are examples of safety education programs financed through all five titles of this act (Maul, 1966). The Federal Highway Safety Act of 1966 provides funds for traffic-safety education at all school levels as well as for research directed toward the improvement of highway traffic safety. Legislation requiring eye protection in specified school programs has been enacted in 19 states.

The history of safety legislation reveals that costly safety devices or regulations can be swiftly and effectively forced upon the public, the schools, or industry following a specific disaster such as the suffocation of children in a discarded refrigerator or tragedy resulting from a school fire. Ill-advised, restrictive legislation runs counter to the purpose of safety education and often fails to cover some conditions equally as hazardous as those which are the object of particular laws.

INTERNATIONAL CONCERN FOR ACCIDENT PREVENTION. Safety education as an integral part of the public school's program is virtually nonexistent in other countries. Many visitors from abroad have been amazed by the extent of driver and safety education in the public schools of the United States. A number of them have made special studies of the accident-prevention effort in the United States, particularly with reference to traffic accidents. Interestingly, visitors from other countries who have shown special interest in safety education have been, for the most part, representatives of government, police, or other nonschool organizations. The thousands of educators visiting the United States have seldom exhibited interest in safety education. This is consistent with the fact that accident prevention in other countries is exercised by officials of government, physicians, and engineers rather than by leaders in public education. Driver education, for example, is known to be offered in some areas of Canada, Australia, and in the Soviet Union, but neither in the public schools nor on as comprehensive a basis as in the United States. Traffic safety education was an area of concern at meetings of the Technical Committee on Traffic and Safety of the Pan American Highway Congresses in Mexico City, 1966, and in Montevideo, Uruguay, 1967.

There is growing concern in other countries, particularly in Europe, about the problem of the relation between use of alcohol and accidents. At an international conference on alcohol and traffic safety, which included many representatives of the medical profession, concern was expressed about the failure of schools to teach about the relationship of use of alcohol and drugs to driving (Indiana University Foundation, 1967).

Statistical information reported to the United Nations indicates that the human accident toll of the world exceeds three-quarters of a million deaths per year. As a result of a study of accidental losses, the World Safety Research Institute, Inc., was formed in 1966. The study showed a rising rate in accidental deaths in most of the European countries over the past ten years. On the basis of increased industrialization, population growth, and a rising living standard, increased human exposure to hazards and an accompanying increase in accidents are anticipated.

A LOOK AHEAD. Schools will continue to provide leadership in safety education. School leaders will look to colleges and universities for competent personnel to meet the growing demand for effective work in this field. Future occupations and free-time activities will require the broadest possible endowment of safety skills for every individual. Technological advance, the obsolescence of old skills, and the creation of completely new fields indicate the potential advantage of safety education. It will be increasingly important that individuals first acquire basic concepts for safe behavior. Then orientation to specific job or free-time activity will be needed as changes for the individual develop.

Despite numerous obstacles, a considerable amount of accident research has been carried out. New concepts in safety education, in medicine, and in the behavioral sciences are providing impetus for this important work. Computers are making accident data more readily available. Such new developments as systems analysis for accident prevention are contributing to greater research insight. The need for a more effective interdisciplinary approach to the study of accidents and accident prevention is recognized. A glaring weakness in much past research has been the lack of competence on the part of researchers themselves. Too often the investigator has been an inspired safety specialist who lacked the skills of research or, on the other hand, a research specialist who lacked substantial knowledge of the field studied. As the skills of researchers are combined with the knowledge of specialists in safety and accident prevention, more meaningful and more useful results will appear. As more accidents affect more of the population, there inevitably will be more public concern, more public support, and more and better research.

Norman Key
National Education Association

References

American Association of School Administrators. *Safety Education.* AASA, 1940. 544p.

Association of State Universities and Land-Grant Colleges. *University Transportation and Accident Prevention Centers.* NEA, National Commission on Safety Education, 1962. 43p.

Bonner, J., and others. *Basic Driver Education.* Special Education Publications, 1966. 174p.

Brody, Leon. "Accidents and 'Attitudes.'" In *Basic Aspects and Applications of the Psychology of Safety.* New York U 1959. p. 6–24.

Columbia University, Teachers College, Safety Research and Education Project. "Progress Report." Teachers Col, Columbia U, 1966. 4p.

Department of Defense, Office of Civil Defense. *Schools Built with Fallout Shelter.* TR–33. GPO, 1966. 55p.

Fox, Bernard H. "Discussion." In *Behavioral Approaches to Accident Research.* Association for the Aid of Crippled Children, 1961. p. 48–55.

Freeman, Frank, and others. *The Role of Human Factors in Accident Prevention.* HEW, 1960. 105p.

Haddon, William, Jr. "The Interrelationships of Host, Agent, and Environmental Variables." In *Accident Research: Methods and Approaches.* Harper, 1964. p. 231–2.

Indiana University Foundation. *Proceedings,* 4th International Conference on Alcohol and Traffic Safety. The Foundation, 1967.

Key, Norman. *Status of Driver Education in the United States.* NEA, National Commission on Safety Education, 1960. 76p.

Key, Norman. "Adult Safety Education—An Unmet Need." In *National Symposium on the Senior Driver and Pedestrian.* HEW, 1964. p. 11.

Key, Norman. "Safety Education." In *Handbook for School Administrators.* AASA, 1967.

MacIver, John. "Safety and Human Behavior." In *Behavioral Approaches to Accident Research.* Association for the Aid of Crippled Children, 1961. p. 59–76.

Mahony, Arthur L. "Teaching for Attitude Conducive to Safe Driving." Doctoral dissertation. New York U, 1957. 220p.

Marshall, Robert L. "An Analysis of Safety Education Programs in Selected Public Schools of the U.S." Doctoral dissertation. U Kansas, 1961. 261p.

Maul, Ray C. "Let's Get Help from P.L. 89–10." *Safety* 2:8–11; 1966.

McGlade, Francis S., and Abercrombie, S. A. "Accident Classification for Research Purposes." *Traffic Q* 19:481–503; 1965.

McGuffey, William H. *McGuffey's First Eclectic Reader,* rev. ed. American, 1879. 96p.

McGuire, Frederick L. "An Outline for a New Approach to the Problem of Highway Accidents." *US Armed Forces Med J* 7:1157–66; 1956.

National Education Association. "Safety Education thru Schools." *NEA Res B* 16:239–98; 1938.

National Education Association. *Safety Education by Colleges and Universities.* NEA, 1951. 44p.

National Education Association. *They Found a Way.* NEA, 1953. 32p.

National Education Association. *Pilot Study of School-age Accidents and Education.* NEA, 1963. 128p.

National Education Association. *A School Safety Education Program.* NEA, 1966. 16p.

National Education Association, National Commission on Safety Education. *Minimum Standards for School Buses.* NEA, 1964. 100p.

National Education Association, National Commission on Safety Education. *Policies and Guidelines for Teacher Preparation and Certification in Driver and Traffic Safety Education.* NEA, 1965. 62p.

National Society for the Study of Education. *The Present Status of Safety Education.* 25th Yearbook. Bobbs-Merrill, 1926. 410p.

National Study of Secondary School Evaluation. *Evaluative Criteria.* The Study, 1960. 376p.

National Study of Secondary School Evaluation. *Evaluative Criteria for Junior High Schools.* The Study, 1963. 330p.

Ojemann, Ralph H. *Tests and Evaluation Methods Used in Driver and Safety Education.* NEA, National Commission on Safety Education, 1959. 48p.

Rosenblatt, Gerald. "A Critical Examination of the Accident Proneness Concept." Master's thesis. Yale U, 1955.

Schulzinger, Morris S. *The Accident Syndrome.* Thomas, 1956. 234p.

Seals, Thomas A. "An Evaluation of Selected Driver and Traffic Safety Education Courses." Doctoral dissertation. Florida State U, 1966. 121p.

Shaw, Frederick. "A Study of Teacher Accidents." In *Bridge from Research to Safety Instruction.* No. 1. NEA, National Commission on Safety Education, 1961. 4p.

Stack, Herbert J. *Safety Education in the Secondary Schools.* American Insurance Association, 1929.

Stratemeyer, Clara G. *Accident Research for Better Safety Teaching.* NEA, National Commission on Safety Education, 1964. 32p.

Tarrants, William E. "An Evaluation of the Critical Incident Technique as a Method for Identifying Industrial Accident Causal Factors." Doctoral dissertation. New York U, 1963.

U.S. Department of Health, Education, and Welfare. *Alcohol and Accidental Injury.* Conference Proceedings. GPO, 1966. 43p.

U.S. Office of Education. *Training School Bus Drivers.* GPO, 1945. 162p.

U.S. Office of Education and National Education Association. *Courses in Highway Safety and Highway Traffic.* NEA, National Commission on Safety Education 1958. 99p.

Zirbes, Laura. "What Is Valid in Safety Education?" In *They Found A Way.* NEA, National Commission on Safety Education, 1953. p. 4–6.

SCALING

DELIMITATION FROM OTHER AREAS OF PSYCHOMETRICS. This article is designed to present the modern view of psychological scaling. As presented here, scaling concentrates upon the attaching of numbers to stimuli, objects, situations, and the like. There is little concern with attaching numbers to persons as subjects; this is deemed to be the province of test theory. Scaling of people as objects is touched upon where appropriate. Nor do we discuss object scales defined using interpersonal differences as a unit of measurement in any other than a general way; this is the goal of factor analysis. Statistics of the hypothesis-testing or estimation variety are also not focused upon except where it is explicitly used in testing a scaling model. Mathematical models, though, play a considerable part in our discussion, since they are tightly bound up with scaling as currently viewed. General treatment of scaling and measurement is provided by Guilford (1954), Torgerson (1958), and Coombs (1964). A recent literature review was conducted by Ekman and Sjöberg (1965).

MEASUREMENT THROUGH MODELS. Psychological scaling, in the form of psychophysics, is perhaps psychology's oldest scientific enterprise, dating back to the middle of the nineteenth century. In its earliest form it was considered to be the study of the relation between "psychic" quantities and physical ones, and it relied upon the subject's explicit observations of his internal states—i.e., introspection. The behavioristic view dominant during the present century found this objectionable, so the conceptualization of scaling changed to one in which it became the study of the relation between overt responses and objectively definable stimuli. Scaling was an attempt to quantify the typical organism's response to stimuli which could be specified in terms of their physical characteristics; the names of political parties or soap brands and the performances of students or employees could be studied, since they are about as objectively definable as the wavelength of a colored light. This is also the primary purpose to which scaling is currently put. It should be noted, however, that the conceptual view of scaling has recently been broadened in two main directions.

First, scaling has been placed more explicitly in the context of psychological modeling. For example, given stimuli $A, B, C, \cdots$ we can attempt to assign scale values $x(A), x(B), x(C), \cdots$ to them by presenting them in pairs and applying the Bradley-Terry-Luce theory [Luce, 1959(a); Bradley & Terry, 1952] to the resulting data. The theory states that $Pr(AB)$, the probability that A is preferred to B

(or judged larger than B, etc.), is given by the formula

(1) $$Pr(AB) = \frac{x(A)}{x(A) + x(B)},$$

which, given several stimuli, can be solved for the x's. Thus, the stimuli become scaled. However, this equation is not merely a formula for scaling the stimuli; it is also a straightforward theory of choice behavior which can be tested by an examination of the various observed proportions for certain kinds of consistencies implied by the theory.

The reconceptualization has two sides. Not only are scaling methods behavioral models, but many behavioral models can, and perhaps should, be used for scaling, even though they were not explicitly designed for that purpose. Stochastic learning models can be cited as one example (see Atkinson & others, 1965, p. 363). Equation 2 gives the probability of making a response G in a certain situation when it has been reinforced with probability p for n trials:

(2) $$Pr(G_n) = p - [p - Pr(G_1)][1 - \theta]^{n-1}.$$

The parameter θ is a "learnability" parameter which may be a constant; on the other hand, it may be variable from situation to situation in which the model is found to be applicable, in which case it can be used to scale the situations. Applications of this reverse type are rare, but a serious approach to scaling and models is likely to increase their frequency of occurrence in the future.

Scaling thus involves the application of a specific model to the analysis of data in order to arrive at numbers to attach to the stimuli, stimuli which may be taken either as entities or simply as labels that stand for mental states. In order for the models to be applicable, certain relationships must exist in the data. More than one model and therefore more than one scale may be consistent with a given set of data, at least approximately. The basic paradigm of scaling is then from data relationships through a model into scales.

The foregoing may seem to be an excessively general statement, especially in its inclusion of all types of models, but it seems desirable to make this generality clear at the outset, despite the fact that almost all applications of scaling and almost all scaling models use verbal or numerical *judgments* supplied by cooperative human subjects for the purpose of attaching numerical labels to stimuli.

The other, somewhat related broadening of the approach to scaling is a change in how scales are viewed once they are derived. The strict view, behavioristically influenced, that a scale value is *the* location of a stimulus on a particular continuum (or at least an estimate of it) is giving way to one in which the scale value has more of a mediational role. It is some representation of an internal state of the organism, which may even be transitory. While the view is highly consistent with the modeling aspect of scaling, it is made particularly necessary by multidimensional scaling, in which a complex stimulus map which may have no obvious physical referent is invoked, in conjunction with a particular model, as an explanation for relations among a large number of responses by the subject. It is perhaps not completely new, as witness the fact that Guilford (1954) distinguished between the R (internal) and J (overt) continua, but it does represent a change in emphasis. These newer developments, the broadening of scaling into the general field of models and its recasting as a method of finding out how people look at things, should increase the relevance of scaling to educational research in the immediate future.

METHODS FOR DETERMINING SENSITIVITY. There is still considerable effort devoted to the oldest problems in psychological scaling: the determination of absolute and difference limens, AL and DL. For DL determination, the methods employ numerous presentations of a standard stimulus and a comparison stimulus; the subject indicates whether or not the two stimuli appear equal on a given trial, and the data are treated statistically to yield the DL, basically defined by the proportion of times each variable was judged equal to a given standard. For AL determination, the experimental and statistical treatments are similar, but the judgment is of whether or not the stimulus is present.

The scaling model employed was Fechner's law:

(3) $$\psi = k \log \phi,$$

which states that the psychological magnitude is proportional to the logarithm of the stimulus magnitude. It was derived from two principal axioms: Weber's law, that the DL is proportional to stimulus magnitude, and the Fechnerian axiom, that DL's are equal at all parts of the scale. The latter was taken to mean that DL's can be mathematically integrated, Weber's law specifying the differential equation (Torgerson, 1958).

Luce and Edwards (1958) point out that it is not legitimate to integrate DL's to arrive at Fechner's law. Even when the mathematical difficulties are patched up (Eisler, 1963), the model has come under heavy conceptual and empirical criticism (see Stevens, 1961). This will be touched upon later. Of more immediate concern is the fact that there has come to be considerable dissatisfaction with the psychophysical methods as means of accomplishing the purpose for which they were designed: the measurement of limens. It is difficult to separate the influences of the subject's sensitivity from his criticism for reporting. How certain does the subject have to be that he heard the tone before he reports that he heard it? To what degree do apparent AL differences represent criterion differences rather than sensitivity differences? The classical methods were much less than completely satisfactory in separating these two influences, although Treisman (1964) has suggested they could be adapted to separate them.

The dominant approach to the problem is currently that of signal-detection theory (TSD), even though alternatives have been offered (see Luce, 1963). Green and Swets's book (1966) is a good text and source book. This approach has the advantage of providing a fairly clear separation between the influence of the subject's sensitivity to the signal and that of his criterion for reporting it. TSD was first developed in the context of electronics engineering (Peterson & others, 1954) but found ready adaptation to problems in psychophysics and sensory functioning (Tanner & Swets, 1954; Swets and others, 1961; Green, 1960).

In a typical TSD experiment involving the determination of sensitivity (corresponding to the classical determination of AL), stimuli (signals) of various intensities may be presented during test intervals, and the subject reports whether or not he perceives the signal; some intervals contain no signal (catch trials). For a given trial there are now four possibilities: stimulus (signal) and positive response (yes) $(Y|S)$, signal and negative response $(\overline{Y}|S)$, no stimulus ("noise only") and yes $(Y|N)$, noise and negative response $(\overline{Y}|N)$. The basic concept is that the probability of yes given signal, $p(Y|S)$, depends on the signal-to-noise ratio, the utilities attached to the four outcomes, and the probability of the stimulus' occurring. For a given stimulus intensity, the subject's behavior, according to the model, is then determined by two parameters. One, d', relates to the hypothetical normalized difference between signal and noise density functions, and the other to "bias," the subject's criterion for saying "yes," presumably dependent upon the probability of the signal and the payoff or utility structure. In the analysis of TSD data, the two parameters are estimated from the relation between two response measures, $p(Y|S)$ and $p(Y|N)$, in contrast to classical psychophysics, which depended on the relation between two physical quantities.

TSD analysis serves quite well in the function for which it was developed, the determination of sensitivity independently of response bias. It also serves as a model for responding under uncertainty, different experimental methods yielding quite similar values for the parameters (Swets, 1961; Markowitz & Swets, 1967).

The d' values for different signals can also be used as a psychophysical scale. The fact that responses are considered not to depend simply on the stimuli but also to be a function of the subject's expectations and goals has meant that TSD has been important in the change from the naïve view of the stimulus toward scaling as an attempt to reveal internal states of the organism.

UNIVARIATE JUDGMENT METHODS. The most common applications of scaling involve the univariate judgment methods in which the subject orders stimuli or assigns numbers to them with reference to some single attribute. Included here are the method of paired comparisons and its generalizations, the ubiquitous rating-scale methods, the ratio judgment methods, and the models that are associated with each.

Paired Comparisons. Because of its apparent simplicity, the method of paired comparisons has engendered more theoretical interest than perhaps any other. In it the subject is presented with stimuli in pairs and is asked which member of the pair is louder, smellier, more valuable, etc. The resulting judgment is an ordering or dominance relation on the pair, for which we will use the symbol "$\succeq$." When this is done for all $\tfrac{1}{2}n(n-1)$ pairs of n stimuli, it is an interesting empirical fact that a good deal of *transitivity* is observed. If $A \succeq B$ and $B \succeq C$, then usually $A \succeq C$. However, if the judgments are replicated, it is found that they are stochastic rather than deterministic. This leads to the hypothesis that $Pr(AB)$, the probability of $A \succeq B$, depends on some psychological scale values of A and B, and various models have been proposed to describe the nature of the dependence.

The two principal ones are those of Bradley, Terry, and Luce (Bradley & Terry, 1952; Luce, 1959a), briefly mentioned earlier, and of Thurstone (1959), the latter principally in its "case V" form. This states that

$$(4) \qquad z_{AB} = \frac{S(A) - S(B)}{C},$$

where z_{AB} is the normal deviate corresponding to $Pr(AB)$, $S(A)$ and $S(B)$ are scale values of A and B, and C is a constant (see Torgerson, 1958, pp. 155–204). In practice, with both models, the data usually consist of judgments from a number of subjects rather than repeated judgments of the same pairs from single subjects.

Both models usually account for a given set of data quite well, although not within statistically allowable limits. They are very difficult to distinguish empirically, making highly similar predictions about the relations among the sets of proportions (Morrison, 1963). Studies evaluating their relative merits have been inconclusive (Burke & Zinnes, 1965; Sutcliffe & Bristow, 1966; Hohle, 1966) but tend to favor Luce.

A drawback of the method of paired comparisons is its inefficiency as a data-gathering device where all pairs are called for. Coombs (1964) has presented a variety of generalizations of it, pointing out, for example, that the subject could pick the three most valuable of successive sets of ten objects rather than one out of sets of two. One type of such a generalization is a frequently used method of getting evaluations of individuals (Wherry & Fryer, 1949) where it is known as the nomination or "guess who" technique. While it is not generally applied, Luce's model would be applicable here as well, but Thurstone's would not.

Numerical Judgments. In most applications of scaling, as distinguished from studies evaluating models, the subject is required to give numerical judgments. The judgments are replicated either within or between subjects, and the scale values are some measure of central tendency of the numbers assigned. The scaling methods differ primarily in how the subject assigns the numbers and in the processing of the numbers after assignment.

Numerical scaling methods must be divided into two classes, depending on whether the numerical scale is bounded or unbounded. Bounded-scale methods include the familiar rating-scale and category methods, in which the response scale is limited, and the unbounded are the ratio methods and their relatives, in which there are no limits at the upper end of the response scale.

The rating methods are relatively simple for the subject and efficient for data gathering. They have been found, however, to be subject to context and order effects (Helson, 1964), and different subjects tend to use the scale differently. These defects may be minimized by the use of anchor stimuli to define the categories. Also, the scale values themselves are not given any of the support that is provided by a model prescribing relationships that should exist in the data. The principal exception is provided by the method of successive intervals (Torgerson, 1958). Bechtel (1967a, 1967b) discusses analysis of paired-comparison data in which the subject gives a numerical rather than an ordinary judgment.

The ratio methods (ratio estimation, magnitude estimation, and constant sum) have enjoyed wide popularity since the publication of numerous studies using them (Stevens, 1957, 1958, 1959a, 1959b; Stevens & Galanter, 1957) in the late 1950's. In them, subjects furnish numbers corresponding to the psychological magnitude of the stimuli, sometimes with a standard stimulus as a modulus, and these numbers are interpreted directly as representing points on a ratio scale. For sensory continua, such scales yield "power law" psychophysics, where

$$(5) \qquad \psi = c\phi^a,$$

in which ψ represents psychological magnitude and ϕ physical magnitude. The exponent is supposed to be a parameter characteristic of the particular continuum.

Validation of the ratio methods has taken place by means of examining scales constructed with different moduli, where they are used (Torgerson, 1958), and by "cross-modality matching" (e.g., Stevens, 1959a). It has been found that the resulting scales are somewhat sensitive to the choice of modulus (Engen & Levy, 1955) and to the range of stimuli. The exponent in 5 is apparently sensitive to the range of stimuli included, and subjects appear to differ in the number ranges they prefer to use (Künnapas, 1960; Ekman & Sjöberg, 1965).

The Psychophysical Laws. The systematic differences in the form of the relation between "subjective" and physical continua when the scales are constructed by the discrimination methods of classical psychophysics or of Thurstone and those constructed with ratio have led to a "two psychophysical laws" controversy. In a number of instances (e.g., Ekman & Künnapas, 1962; Galanter & Messick, 1961) a logarithmic relation has been found between scales constructed by Thurstonian and ratio methods. Ekman (1964) presents an interesting hypothesis to account for this relation, pointing out that the continuum of number itself obeys something like Weber's law and suggesting that the subject may be using a sort of equiprecision rule when he makes judgments following the power law. The issue of the relation between the two types of scales becomes clouded, however, when it is noted (Eisler, 1965) that in almost all published data using discrimination methods, intraindividual and interindividual variability have been confounded in defining the discrimination scales, and group averages have been used for the ratio scales (N.B. Künnapas, 1967) whereas any psychophysical law must apply to the individual. Thus, the relation between the two types of scales is not yet validly defined. Both sets of scaling methods, however, appear to yield scales that are useful for a wide variety of purposes.

MULTIDIMENSIONAL SCALING. All the methods discussed so far have centered on dominance, the observation or fairly direct inference of order relations between members of any given pair of stimuli. The methods and studies we will discuss next revolve around a fundamentally different observation, that of distance or difference or their complements proximity, similarity, or nearness. This distinction, between dominance and proximity, is one of the three fundamental ones emphasized by Coombs (1964). Formally, the proximity relation differs from dominance or order in being symmetric rather than antisymmetric and in not being transitive, although it can be made more numerical in such a way as to develop an analogue to transitivity, the triangle inequality.

Multidimensional scaling begins as a procedure for analyzing the distances among a set of points in order to find coordinates for the points on several underlying dimensions. Procedures for doing this were first described in the psychological literature by G. Young and A. S. Householder (1938) and Richardson (1938). These methods of analyzing distances follow from the fact that in euclidean space the squared distance between two points i and j is given by the following formula:

$$(6) \qquad d_{ij}^2 = \sum_m x_{im}^2 + \sum_m x_{jm}^2 - 2\sum_m x_{im}x_{jm}.$$

Here x_{im} and x_{jm} are the coordinates of stimuli i and j, respectively, on dimension m. The last term of the expression is a sum of products just like the fundamental equation of factor analysis, allowing for the application of factor-analytic methods to adjusted matrices of distances among points. These methods were improved by Torgerson (1952) and generalized by Ross and Cliff (1964). A crucial point here is that if one has a set of behaviorally obtained distances that are analyzed by these methods and that give a good fit, one is justified in concluding that the objects or stimuli are behaving as points in a euclidean space. In this sense multidimensional scaling provides a substantive model that may be applied to explain behavioral data.

The next aspect of the method is how one arrives at the distances that are analyzed. Most commonly these are derived from judgments of similarity or difference, such as in the method of triads (Torgerson, 1952), or from numerical judgments of the similarity of pairs, by either a rating-scale method or a ratio method. Other behavioral measures of difference can be used. Shepard (1958) employed the proportion of times that one response is substituted for another as an intrusion error in paired-associates learning. He suggests several other possibilities (Shepard, 1960).

As originally used, multidimensional scaling analysis (MDA) required that the distances between the points be on a ratio scale. The distances used in the first applications, determined by either triads (Richardson, 1938; Torgerson, 1952) or successive intervals (Messick, 1956) were only on an interval scale. Definition of a zero point for the distance scale was accomplished either by common-sense means, such as taking the distance between two virtually indistinguishable stimuli as a zero point, or by an analytical method (Torgerson, 1958; Messick & Abelson, 1956) to give an "additive constant" to be added to all the observed distances. In the analytical methods an interval scale of distance was transformed into a ratio scale by means of an appeal to maximum parsimony in the Iuclidean model.

Helm (1960) went one step further in using the power of the Iuclidean model to define the distance scale. He performed an exponential transformation of an obtained distance scale and found that the transformed distances required many fewer stimulus dimensions. Another aspect of his study provides one of the strongest pieces of evidence for ratio scaling methods; distances obtained by a ratio estimation procedure were found to give a two-dimensional solution immediately, thus indicating that the ratio judgments were highly consistent in a strongly quantitative way.

Thus we see that the Iuclidean model was used first to define a zero point for an interval scale of distance (Messick & Abelson, 1956) and then to suggest and validate (Helm, 1960) a monotonic transformation of the original distance scale. It remained for Shepard (1962) to see the complete generality of the process. This was to let the behavioral data (judgments or other responses) define the distances only ordinally and then to use the Iuclidean model to define the specific case of the ordinal scale which was most consistent with a space with a given number of dimensions. Thus a model is used to transform ordinal information into a higher-order scale, just as Luce's and Thurstone's do to preference data. The methods are extended and elaborated by Kruskal (1964a, 1964b).

There has been recent interest in the degree to which results of multidimensional scaling analyses have application to other behavior. Carroll and Chang (1967) and also Doelert and Hoerl (1967) have found that degrees of liking for particular products are relatable to their positions in MDA spaces. Cliff (e.g., 1966) found that a variety of univariate judgments could be related to the positions of the stimuli in multidimensional scaling spaces. There is also evidence that these spaces change in meaningful ways as a result of experience with the situations scaled.

There has also been concern with the true degree of Iuclideanness of the psychological spaces analyzed by MDA. An important property of Iuclidean space is that distance can be measured in any direction. This is in contrast to a "city-block" space (Attneave, 1950), in which distance must be measured "down streets and across avenues." Shepard (1964) found that for those with obvious and distinct dimensions the Iuclidean model had to be rejected. Torgerson (1965) comes to similar conclusions. Hyman and Well (1967) concluded that any of a whole gamut of spatial models may be appropriate, depending not only on the nature of the stimuli but also on the individual doing the judging. In order to handle these results MDA may develop in a looser, more topological as opposed to geometric direction if the relevant theory can be developed.

Limitations of space have precluded the discussion of certain methods such as Ekman's (1954, 1963). Also omitted from our discussion of multidimensional scaling are those procedures such as the semantic differential (Osgood and others, 1957) which are really ratings on a number of single scales. The reader is referred to recent developments in "three-mode factor analysis" (Tucker, 1966) for discussion of an important aspect of these multiple-rating-scale methods.

MEASUREMENT THEORY. According to Stevens (1959b, p. 19) measurement is "the assignment of numerals to objects or events according to rule—any rule." Most measurement theorists would agree with this definition or a paraphrase of it. As it stands, it has been criticized (Ellis, 1966) as being too inclusive, but doubtless all such theorists, including Stevens, would agree that not all of the procedures that fit the definition are *desirable* methods of measurement. Scaling is perhaps best described as the choosing of the best rule for a given set of observations. Measurement theory may be said to concern itself with the properties of different classes of rules, including the definition of the classes, their utility, and the implications of their properties for other aspects of research.

Measurement theorists usually have concentrated on the measurement properties of scales once they have already been defined, but Ellis (1966) justifiably places the emphasis on defining the scales.

According to Ellis a scale is defined by the relations it enters into, and those scales are used which enter into the widest variety and simplest forms of relationships. According to this view, even such a familiar scale as that of length (or, more properly, distance) is defined not so much by the existence of such things as rulers that may be put end to end as by the fact that distance, so measured, enters in quite a simple fashion into innumerable relations with other quantities. Moreover, this familiar scale of distance is *abandoned* when a different highly correlated scale, space-time, is found to simplify relationships between variables in some situations. The absolute (Kelvin) scale of temperature provides another example. It among all the possible temperature scales yields the simplest relations with other variables. Cliff (1959) made a parallel analysis of a semantic-meaning scale to arrive at a rational zero for it. Empirical relations are thus seen to determine what observables to use as variables, as in the case of the space-time scale, but also which of several alternative scales of the same variable to use, as in the case of the absolute temperature scale.

According to this view, the evidence in favor of magnitude scaling leading to ratio scales derives not from the fact that the subject is providing subjectively equal ratios but rather from data such as is provided by cross-modality matching (Stevens, 1959a) and Helm's multidimensional scaling study (Helm, 1964).

The dominant view of measurement theory in psychology, at least until recently, has been that formulated by Stevens (1951). Here, the important characteristic that distinguishes different kinds of scales is what kind of arbitrary transformations can be made of them without disturbing the empirical relations. Originally Stevens distinguished four types: nominal, ordinal, interval, and ratio. In the first, any one-to-one transformation of the scale is possible. In the second, any strictly monotonic transformation is legitimate. The third allows for only $ax + b$ (affine) transformations, and the last only for multiplication by a positive constant. This classification was expanded slightly by Stevens (1957) and Torgerson (1958) and appreciably by Coombs (1952).

Consideration of the scale-type problem and the questions of the relations among scales received considerable impetus with the publication of Luce's startling paper (1959b) which appeared to show that if there were a psychophysical law relating a psychological ratio scale to a physical ratio scale, the form of the law *must be* a power function (equation 5). The necessity for this arises from the seemingly innocuous requirement for such a function that legitimate transformations of one of the scales lead, without change in the form of the function, to legitimate transformations of the other. The only function that has this property for ratio scales is the power function. In view of this seeming mathematical confirmation of the power law in psychophysics, it is ironic to note that the most general form of it,

(5a) $$\psi = k(\phi - \phi_0)^n,$$

(Stevens, 1961, p. 44), amounts to employing an illegitimate transformation of the physical scale, a translation of the origin as if *it* were an interval rather than a ratio scale. Rozeboom (1962) shows how the seeming restriction can be circumvented by reducing laws to "dimensionless" form although such circumvention will lead to some loss of elegance and does not occur in the most coherent areas of physical-science theory (Luce, 1962). Ellis (1966, Ch. 9) has a rather extensive discussion of this and related problems.

Considerations of the scale type of a given set of data have influenced research workers' views of statistics. Most of the data from psychological and educational research cannot be very wholeheartedly defended as being on interval scales, but the interval property is an assumption underlying parametric statistics. The argument is often stated that it is objectionable to use, on a given set of data, a statistical operation that is not invariant under a legitimate transformation of the scale. Suppose, for example, that a research proposition is stated as "As a result of a certain treatment, A's change more with respect to a certain variable x than B's do." In a typical educational-research context this would be translated into a statistical problem revolving around whether the difference in pretest and posttest means was greater for A's than for B's. But suppose x is an ordinal scale and also that the pretest means for A and B differ. Now the statistical analysis may have widely different results depending on which of the equally acceptable versions of the x scale are used in the calculations, since we can stretch and squeeze the scale in different regions and differentially affect different score differences.

Adams and others (1965) clarified this issue by emphasizing that it is the calling into question of the statements made on the basis of statistics, not the questioning of the statistics themselves, that is at issue. They point out, for example, that statements that a certain mean lies in a given interval simply have no meaning when applied to ordinal data. In view of the doubtful status of the interval property of most empirical scales, complete acceptance of this point of view would imply the rejection of the bulk of current research, and one is naturally reluctant to do this. The resolution may lie in the following directions.

First, in the case of most data we work with, while we would not claim complete interval status for it, we would be equally reluctant to allow complete freedom of ordinal transformation. For example, if for some data on a scale x, we observe $x = 1, 2, 3, \cdots$, we might not accept $x' = 10^{2x-1}$ as a legitimate transformation, for the differences at the upper end of the x' scale would be astronomical compared to those at the lower, and we strongly believe that this is not the case. Apparently (Abelson & Tukey, 1959), some rather mild restrictions on the size of the tolerable interval changes exert quite strong stabilizing effects upon the range over which statistics can vary under these somewhat restricted scale transformations.

The second consideration arises out of the fact that inferential statistical analysis is performed for the purpose of attaching probabilities to statements. Fuzziness in scale properties leads to attenuation in the accuracy of the probabilities attached to statements. While this is highly undesirable, there is always a certain amount of it anyway, and it is a matter of judgment how much is introduced by the scale's failure to have completely interval properties. With assumptions, as with maidens, it is well to be able to discriminate violation from a little jostling in the subway.

Finally, one prefers to maintain at least quasi-interval properties for one's scales, even in the absence of confirmation, because any other course may vastly complicate the description of the relations in the data.

These considerations suggest that conclusions drawn from parametric statistical analysis of quasi-interval data are likely to be valid unless the scale used in the analysis is a wildly inaccurate transformation of the true scale. Against this may be set the consideration that ordinal statistics are nearly as powerful as parametric ones and may be more so if the assumptions involved in the latter are departed from.

AXIOMATIC SYSTEMS. In scaling, as in other areas of psychological model building, the rigorous, formal axiomatic approach is of growing importance. The most important aspect of this development has been the demonstration that the existence of certain data relations which are not too restrictive can be made to imply the existence of scales with very strong characteristics. We have already encountered this in one form, multiple order relations among distances being used to define scales in MDA (e.g., Shepard, 1962), but the developments with the most far-reaching implications have arisen out of conjoint measurement (Luce & Tukey, 1964). It represents a departure from the Stevens tradition, in which scales were defined by the transformations they permitted, into a broader context in which they are defined by the axioms the data satisfy.

This development is of special importance because it shows a way around the difficulty imposed by the fact that additivity (or concatenation) of the literal kind possible with physical measurements seems impossible for psychological ones. The following is a somewhat concretized description of their results.

A dependent variable y is observable under all possible combinations of conditions defined by two independent variables a and b. Let y_{ij} be the value of y observed at level i of a and level j of b. Then the axioms specify that the y_{ij} must satisfy certain rather mild-appearing restrictions, of which we will note the most important. First, y constitutes a weak ordering, i.e., it is an ordinal scale demonstrating transitivity, etc., and different a, b combinations can have equal y's. Second, for any given combination of levels i and j on a and b and a different specified level k on a, it is possible to find a level p on b such that $y_{ij} = y_{kp}$, and similarly if the level on b is specified. That is, a change in the effect of a can be compensated by a change in the effect of b.

The third pivotal axiom is called the cancellation axiom. It imposes an important consistency restriction on the order relations observed. Given any three levels on the two independent variables, say g, h, i on a and j, k, l on b, whenever $y_{gk} \leq y_{hj}$ and $y_{hl} \leq y_{ik}$, then $y_{gl} \leq y_{ij}$. The axiom is reasonable. It merely states, in effect, that if a pint of sand weighs more than a quart of water and if a quart of mercury weighs more than a gallon of sand, then it cannot be that a gallon of water weighs more than a pint of mercury. That is, the steps on the density scale have a consistently bigger effect than the steps on the volume scale.

In conjoint measurement, the independent variables, a priori, defined only on nominal scales, the combination of the last two axioms being sufficient to define an ordering of them. In place of concatenating levels on one variable, as in physics, we concatenate a level on one variable with a level on another. Moreover, it is fairly simple to introduce the notion of a zero point, thus making the scales ratio scales.

Space does not permit the tracing out of the antecedents of conjoint measurement theory, but important additional developments in conjoint measurement theory have been contributed by Krantz (1964), Roskies (1965), and Tversky (1967).

The axiomatic view was voiced by Weitzenhoffer (1951) and repeated by others since then (e.g., Cliff, 1959). These authors, however, represented a somewhat naïve view in which "the" axioms of the number system were to be listed and those which seemed to be satisfied by the data picked out. Conjoint measurement theorists have made use of the fact that the set of *possible* axioms is large, and quite different subsets evolve systems that have many of the same consequences (see especially Krantz, 1964), including many very powerful properties of the number system. In any event, defining scales in terms of the axioms they satisfy provides a more powerful and general system than defining them by the transformations they allow.

All of the most recent developments in scaling suggest that it is evolving away from a concern with attaching numbers to stimuli through analysis of human judgments. To some degree this is the result of a recognition of the generality of some of the procedures and concepts that have been developed. It is also a consequence of some empirical phenomena that have frequently intruded on attempts to determine scale values for stimuli. The many studies of the effect of context upon judgments, even simple ones (Sutcliffe & Bristow, 1966) make the position that a stimulus has a scale value difficult to use as a foundation of a field. Almost equally troublesome is the existence of individual differences as parameters of individuals' judgments. These limit the usefulness of any empirically determined scale values except as, say, estimates of means of *populations* of scale values.

The existence of individual differences tends to force one to study the individual's responses, attempting to fit them into an appropriate model. Procedures now exist, though, for determining subgroups of subjects whose responses are more or less homogeneous (Tucker & Messick, 1963; F. Young & Pennell,

1967) and using weighted averages of the responses of these subgroups rather than either the overall mean or the responses of single individuals. These weighted averages are then processed by whatever model is deemed appropriate, such as MDA. Thus a middle course between single individual and group average is followed.

As we have seen, the consideration of scales as variables in models, models from a variety of contexts, is providing the current framework for psychological scaling. Important here is the development of methods for building mathematically strong structures from a large number of weak observed relations, such as ordinal and proximity relations. These structures may then provide verification of the models employed or may provide useful "maps" of how the subject views the stimuli, and these are the most interesting current uses of scaling and measurement theory.

Norman Cliff
University of Southern California

References

Abelson, R. P., and Tukey, J. W. "Efficient Conversion of Nonmetric Information into Metric Information." In *Proceedings of the Social Statistics Section*, American Statistical Association, 1959. p. 226–30.

Adams, E. W., and others. "A Theory of Appropriate Statistics." *Psychometrika* 30:99–127; 1965.

Atkinson, R. C., and others. *An Introduction to Mathematical Learning Theory.* Wiley, 1965. 429p.

Attneave, F. "Dimensions of Similarity." *Am J Psychol* 63:516–56; 1950.

Bechtel, G. G. "The Analysis of Variance and Pairwise Scaling." *Psychometrika* 32:47–65; 1967(a).

Bechtel, G. G. "F Tests for the Absolute Invariance of Dominance and Composition Scales." *Psychometrika* 32:157–82; 1967(b).

Bradley, R. A., and Terry, M. E. "Rank Analysis of Incomplete Block Designs. I: The Method of Paired Comparisons." *Biometrika* 39:324–45; 1952.

Burke, C. J., and Zinnes, J. L. "A Paired Comparison of Pair Comparisons." *J Math Psychol* 2:53–76; 1965.

Carroll, J. D., and Chang, Jih-Jie. "Relating Preference Data to Multidimensional Scaling Solutions via a Generalization of Coombs' Unfolding Model." Paper presented at the meeting of the Psychometric Society, Madison, Wisconsin, 1967.

Cliff, Norman. "Adverbs as Multipliers." *Psychol R* 66:27–44; 1959.

Cliff, Norman. "Multidimensional Scaling and Cognition. II: The Relation of Evaluation to Multidimensional Meaning Spaces." Report No. 2. U Southern California, 1966. 19p. (Multilithed.)

Coombs, Clyde H. *A Theory of Psychological Scaling.* Bulletin No. 34. Engineering Research Institute, U Michigan, 1952. 94p.

Coombs, Clyde H. *A Theory of Data.* Wiley, 1964. 585p.

Doelert, D. H., and Hoerl, A. E. "Finding the Preferred Regions in a Multidimensional Space." Paper presented at the meeting of the Psychometric Society, Madison, Wisconsin, 1967.

Eisler, H. "Magnitude Scales, Category Scales, and Fechnerian Integration." *Psychol R* 70:243–53; 1963.

Eisler, H. "The Connection Between Magnitude and Discrimination Scales and Direct and Indirect Scaling Methods." *Psychometrika* 30:271–89; 1965.

Ekman, G. "Dimensions of Color Vision." *J Psychol* 38:467–74; 1954.

Ekman, G. "A Direct Method for Multidimensional Ratio Scaling." *Psychometrika* 28:33–41; 1963.

Ekman, G. "Is the Power Law a Special Case of Fechner's Law?" *Perceptual Motor Skills* 19:730; 1964.

Ekman, G., and Künnapas, T. "Scales of Aesthetic Value." *Perceptual Motor Skills* 14:19–26; 1962.

Ekman, G., and Sjöberg, L. "Scaling." *Annual R Psychol* 16:451–74; 1965.

Ellis, B. *Basic Concepts of Measurement.* Cambridge U Press, 1966. 219p.

Engen, T., and Levy, N. "The Influence of Standards on Psychophysical Judgment." *Perceptual Motor Skills* 5:193–7; 1955.

Galanter, E. H., and Messick, S. "The Relation Between Category and Magnitude Scales of Loudness." *Psychol R* 68:363–72; 1961.

Green, D. M. "Psychoacoustics and Detection Theory." *J Acoustical Soc Am* 32:1189–203; 1960.

Green, D. M., and Swets, J. A. *Signal Detection Theory and Psychophysics.* Wiley, 1966. 467p.

Guilford, J. P. *Psychometric Methods.* McGraw-Hill, 1954. 597p.

Helm, C. E. "A Successive Intervals Analysis of Color Differences." ETS, 1960. 89p. (Multilithed.)

Helm, C. E. "Multidimensional Ratio Scaling Analysis of Perceived Color Relations." *J Optical Soc Am* 54:256–62; 1964.

Helson, H. *Adaptation-level Theory.* Harper, 1964. 732p.

Hohle, R. H. "An Empirical Evaluation and Comparison of Two Models for Discriminability Scales." *J Math Psychol* 3:174–83; 1966.

Hyman, R., and Well, A. "Judgments of Similarity and Spatial Models." *Perception Psychophysics* 2:233–48; 1967.

Krantz, D. H. "Conjoint Measurement: The Luce-Tukey Axiomatization and Some Extensions." *J Math Psychol* 1:248–77; 1964.

Kruskal, J. B. "Multidimensional Scaling by Optimizing Goodness of Fit to a Nonmetric Hypothesis." *Psychometrika* 29:1–27; 1964(a).

Kruskal, J. B. "Nonmetric Multidimensional Scaling: A Numerical Method." *Psychometrika* 29:115–29; 1964(b).

Künnapas, T. "Scales for Subjective Distance." *Scandinavian J Psychol* 1:187–92; 1960.

Künnapas, T. "Note on Ratio Estimation." *Scandinavian J Psychol* 8:77–80; 1967.

Luce, R. Duncan. *Individual Choice Behavior.* Wiley, 1959(*a*). 153p.

Luce, R. Duncan. "On the Possible Psychophysical Laws." *Psychol R* 66:81–95; 1959(*b*).

Luce, R. Duncan. "Comments on Rozeboom's Criticism of 'On the Possible Psychophysical Laws.'" *Psychol R* 69:548–51; 1962.

Luce, R. Duncan. "Detection and Recognition." In Luce, R. Duncan, and others. (Eds.) *Handbook of Mathematical Psychology.* Wiley, 1963. p. 103–91.

Luce, R. Duncan, and Edwards, W. "The Derivation of Subjective Scales from Just Noticeable Differences." *Psychol R* 65:222–37; 1958.

Luce, R. Duncan, and Tukey, J. W. "Simultaneous Conjoint Measurement: A New Type of Fundamental Measurement." *J Math Psychol* 1:1–27; 1964.

Markowitz, J., and Swets, J. A. "Factors Affecting the Slope of Empirical ROC Curves: Comparison of Binary and Rating Responses." *Perception Psychophysics* 2:91–7; 1967.

Messick, S. "An Empirical Evaluation of Multidimensional Successive Intervals." *Psychometrika* 21:367–76; 1956.

Messick, S., and Abelson, R. P. "The Additive Constant Problem in Multidimensional Scaling." *Psychometrika* 21:1–17; 1956.

Morrison, H. W. "Testable Conditions for Triads of Paired Comparisons Choices." *Psychometrika* 28:369–90; 1963.

Osgood, Charles E., and others. *The Measurement of Meaning.* U Illinois Press, 1957. 342p.

Peterson, W. W., and others. "The Theory of Signal Detectability." *Trans Professional Group Information Theory* (Institute of Radio Engineers) 4:171–212; 1954.

Richardson, M. W. "Multidimensional Psychophysics." *Psychol B* 35:650–60; 1938.

Roskies, R. "A Measurement Axiomatization for an Essentially Multiplicative Representation of Two Factors." *J Math Psychol* 2:266–76; 1965.

Ross, J., and Cliff, Norman. "A Generalization of the Interpoint Distance Model." *Psychometrika* 29:167–76; 1964.

Rozeboom, W. W. "The Untenability of Luce's Principle." *Psychol R* 69:542–7; 1962.

Shepard, R. N. "Stimulus and Response Generalization: Tests of a Model Relating Generalization to Distance in Psychological Space." *J Exp Psychol* 55:509–23; 1958.

Shepard, R. N. "Similarity of Stimuli and Metric Properties of Behavioral Data." In Gulliksen, H., and Messick, S. (Eds.) *Psychological Scaling: Theory and Methods.* Wiley, 1960. p. 33–43.

Shepard, R. N. "The Analysis of Proximities: Multidimensional Scaling with an Unknown Distance Function." I and II. *Psychometrika* 27:125–40, 219–46; 1962.

Shepard, R. N. "Attention and the Metric Structure of the Stimulus Space." *J Math Psychol* 1:54–87; 1964.

Stevens, S. S. "Mathematics, Measurement, and Psychophysics." In Stevens, S. S. (Ed.) *Handbook of Experimental Psychology.* Wiley, 1951. p. 1–49.

Stevens, S. S. "On the Psychophysical Law." *Psychol R* 64: 153–81; 1957.

Stevens, S. S. "Problems and Methods of Psychophysics." *Psychol B* 54:177–96; 1958.

Stevens, S. S. "Cross-modality Validation of Subjective Scales for Loudness, Vibration, and Electric Shock." *J Exp Psychol* 57:201–9; 1959(*a*).

Stevens, S. S. "Measurement, Psychophysics, and Utility." In Churchman, C. W., and Ratoosh, P. (Eds.) *Measurement: Definition and Theories.* Wiley, 1959(*b*). p. 18–63.

Stevens, S. S. "Toward a Resolution of the Fechner-Thurstone Legacy." *Psychometrika* 26:35–48; 1961.

Stevens, S. S., and Galanter, E. H. "Ratio Scales and Category Scales for a Dozen Perceptual Continua." *J Exp Psychol* 54:377–411; 1957.

Sutcliffe, J. P., and Bristow, Rosemary A. "Do Rank Order and Scale Properties Remain Invariant Under Changes in the Set of Scaled Stimuli?" *Australian J Psychol* 18:26–40; 1966.

Swets, J. A. "Detection Theory and Psychophysics: A Review." *Psychometrika* 26:49–63; 1961.

Swets, J. A., and others. "Decision Processes in Perception." *Psychol R* 68:301–40; 1961.

Tanner, W. P., Jr., and Swets, J. A. "A Decision Making Theory of Visual Detection." *Psychol R* 61:401–9; 1954.

Thurstone, L. L. *The Measurement of Values.* U Chicago Press, 1959. 322p.

Torgerson, Warren S. "Multidimensional Scaling. I: Theory and Method." *Psychometrika* 17:401–19; 1952.

Torgerson, Warren S. *Theory and Methods of Scaling.* Wiley, 1958. 460p.

Torgerson, Warren S. "Multidimensional Scaling of Similarity." *Psychometrika* 30:379–94; 1965.

Treisman, M. "Noise and Weber's Law: The Discrimination of Brightness and Other Dimensions." *Psychol R* 71:314–30; 1964.

Tucker, L. R. "Some Mathematical Notes on Three-mode Factor Analysis." *Psychometrika* 31:279–311; 1966.

Tucker, L. R., and Messick, S. "An Individual Differences Model for Multidimensional Scaling." *Psychometrika* 28:333–67; 1963.

Tversky, A. "A General Theory of Polynomial Conjoint Measurement." *J Math Psychol* 4:1–20; 1967.

Weitzenhoffer, A. M. "Mathematical Structures and Psychological Measurements." *Psychometrika* 16:387–406; 1951.

Wherry, R. J., and Fryer, D. H. "Buddy Ratings, Popularity Contest or Leadership Criteria." *Personnel Psychol* 2:147–59; 1949.

Young, F. W., and Pennell, Roger J. "An IBM System/360 Program for Points of View Analysis." *Behavioral Sci* 12:166; 1967.

Young, G., and Householder, A. S. "Discussion of a Set of Points in Terms of Their Mutual Distances." *Psychometrika* 3:19–22; 1938.

SCHOOL BUSINESS ADMINISTRATION

Rather than being viewed as an independent entity, business administration in education can best be described as a service and support arm of the broad field of school administration. In this context school business administration is operationally effective to the degree that predetermined goods and services are made available to pupils and staff members. The precise nature of the responsibilities will vary because of different patterns of administrative organization in local school districts; however, school business administration normally encompasses financial management and planning; school facility planning, maintenance, and operation; service activities; and related activities.

Financial responsibilities would include supervision of the receipt and disbursement of all school funds, active participation in the development of the school budget, and involvement in the development of the long-term plans for the school district. School facility responsibilities normally encompass an interpretative and liaison role in the planning of facilities and direct responsibility for maintaining and keeping in good order all school facilities. An additional charge in this area is to operate the facilities as efficiently and economically as possible so that maximum utilization can be made of available financial resources. The area of school insurance constitutes an additional aspect of the facilities responsibilities assigned to school business administration. Basic policy decisions will have been made by the school board, but responsibility for administration of the program falls within the broad realm of school business administration.

Different types of service and support activities have been assigned to the business office because that office has the resources to perform the activity and constitutes the most logical alternative. The three most frequent areas are purchasing and supply management, food services, and transportation. If the local district has an electronic data processing installation, results of a survey conducted by the Educational Research Service (1966) indicated, the school business office will often be charged with the responsibility of overseeing this operation even though the principal users may be personnel not directly associated with the school business administration area. Related activities which are normally included in the broad area of school business administration include recruitment, orientation, and in-service programs for office personnel in the individual buildings in the school district. These programs are in addition to the personnel services provided for the employees included in the various service functions which are performed under the direct supervision of the business office.

As an integral facet of the broad area of school administration, school business administration should be responsive to the changing needs of school personnel, for the educational enterprise has become so complex that the success of the instructional process depends to great measure upon the availability of the human and material support services provided through the office of the school business administrator. Rather than consisting of a group of highly standardized activities, school business administration is concerned with the changing nature of the educational program and must shift its services as the total program changes direction. Hill (1960) has presented a concise summary statement of the role and responsibilities of the school business administrator.

Research Reports. From 1932 through 1950 on a triennial basis each April issue of the *Review of Educational Research* contained a summary of research which had been conducted in the areas of school finance and business administration. After the 1950 issue the space previously allocated to school business administration was substantially reduced and the research in this area was incorporated into the review concerned with the broad area of school administration and organization. Since 1950 Bates (1964), Conrad and Griffith (1964), Cooper and Pound (1962, 1963, 1964, 1965) Knezevich (1961), and Yankow (1966) have reported on the research findings in school business administration. The most comprehensive effort was made by Bates (1964) when he developed a serial catalog of 721 doctoral studies in the area of school business affairs which had been completed in American colleges and universities during the decade 1950–1960.

The recurring problem relative to the adequacy and sophistication of research in school business administration was emphasized once again when Conrad and Griffith (1964) stressed the need for significant research on the effects which various alternative school plant and business procedures have on the teaching and learning process. Knezevich and DeKock (1960) had earlier stated that the bulk of the material in the area of school business administration consisted of status reports and suggestions for improving existing practices. As is the case in other areas of school administration the need exists for research conducted under conditions which conform to rigid research criteria with special attention being devoted to the systematic gathering and interpretation of information while the project is under way.

Publications. During the past decade a large amount of material has been published in the area of school business administration. The three principal sources of pamphlets and related publications are American Association of School Administrators (AASA), Association of School Business Officials, and U.S. Office of Education (USOE). The AASA has published several short bulletins dealing with specific problem areas. To date the Association of School Business Officials has published 28 bulletins and other additional pamphlets which have been designed to be of practical benefit for the in-service or pre-service school business administrator. The Association of School Business Officials also publishes a monthly bulletin entitled *School Business Affairs* and distributes the proceedings of its annual meetings. Another source of information is *School Management*, a specialized monthly periodical which devotes its attention to reporting approaches which have been found successful in resolving school management problems.

The USOE has also published a variety of handbooks for local school officials who are concerned with the operation of various business administration programs. In addition to these sources state departments of education have prepared a variety of handbooks and guides for use by local administrators. These have normally been oriented toward the pattern of organization in each particular state; however, the state of New York has published several pamphlets which have been found useful on a national basis.

The most comprehensive treatment of the broad area of school business administration was written by Englehardt and Englehardt (1927) and still serves as a valuable basic reference. Other early texts were written by Moehlmann (1927), Morrison (1932), Reeder (1929), Smith (1929), and Womrath (1932). In addition various texts in the general field of school administration and school finance have devoted sections to school business administration. Starting with the book written by Linn and others (1956) texts were published within the next few years by Casey (1964), Hill and Colmey (1964), Knezevich and Fowlkes (1960), Roe (1961), and Yeager (1959). In addition to the classic by DeYoung (1936), Ovsiew and Castetter (1960) have also published a specialized text on budgeting. Other speciality areas include books on insurance by Linn and Joyner (1952) and Allen (1965). George and Heckler (1960) and Cronan (1962) have written texts concerned with the area of food services. Featherstone and Culp (1965) authored a rather exhaustive treatment of the area of school transportation programs. The most comprehensive treatment of the legal concepts relating to school business administration was edited by Garber (1957).

Professionalization. Professionalization and certification are often used as synonymous terms in discussions relating to the school business administrator. Endicott (1966) reported that specific state certification patterns for school business administrators were not in existence before 1960; however, by 1966 six states had developed certification standards for the position. During the same period Foster (1964b) reported that the Association for School Business Officials had developed professionalization standards and had begun issuing certificates for "Registered School Business Officials" and "Registered School Business Administrators." In each instance both at the state level and at the national level through the Association of School Business Officials, the emphasis has been placed on advanced preparation beyond the bachelor's degree, and the areas of specialization in school business administration include many of the rather common course offerings in school administration.

ORGANIZATION FOR SCHOOL BUSINESS ADMINISTRATION. Organization for school business administration can be viewed in two different dimensions. The first is related to the type of administrative structure used in the local school district, and the second refers to the degree to which the local school district is fiscally independent of other governmental agencies. In the latter instance state laws will determine the pattern for school districts in the state; however, in the former, local board practices and policies will determine whether the local administrative organization can be categorized as a unit, dual, or multiple pattern of organization.

Unit and Multiple Control. Under the unit pattern of organization a single administrator reports directly to the school board, and any additional administrators and other employees are subordinate to him and report to the board only through him. When the board chooses to assign specific administrative responsibilities to more than one executive officer, this pattern is referred to as the multiple type of organization with more than one administrator reporting directly to the school board. Knezevich and DeKock (1960) contended that studies and experience over an extended period of years indicated that the unit pattern of organization was superior to other patterns and lessened the possibility of internal conflict among the responsible school administrators. The general acceptance of the unit control concept was supported in a national study reported by the Educational Research Service (1966) which found that less than five percent of the responding school districts were operating under a multiple-type administrative organization.

Fiscal Controls. Fiscal dependence and fiscal independence should be considered as relative terms, for state laws vary among the several states with very few districts being easily classifiable at either end of the continuum. In some cases the school board may be the sole agency with authority to establish the budget and could thus be classified as fiscally independent, but it may lack authority to set the tax rate through which the necessary funds will be obtained and would therefore be fiscally dependent. Discussions of the merits of both positions and also of the existing patterns at that time have been presented by the National Education Association (1950) and Reuter (1960); however, a dearth of research which furnishes conclusive evidence to support either extreme was reported by Knezevich and DeKock (1960). Some support for fiscal dependence can be generated in view of the interdependence among different arms of government which are attempting to resolve social problems.

In addition to the controls on local districts imposed through fiscal dependence, states also limit local school tax rates through such devices as maximum tax rates and requirements that tax levies secure voter approval. After completing a national study of state limitations on local school districts Huls (1958) concluded that state legislatures should reexamine the legal limitations which have been placed on school expenditures.

FISCAL MANAGEMENT. Fiscal management constitutes the major area of responsibility in school business administration. This area includes budget preparation; collection, custody, and disbursement of funds; and preparation of reports concerning school expenditures.

Varying approaches have been used in defining the term, budget; a generally acceptable definition is that the budget is the planned pattern of expenditures used to achieve the educational goals over a given period of time. The period of time is normally one year, either a calendar or fiscal year as determined by state or federal legislation. Even though the budget may be prepared on an annual basis, sound educational planning will reflect both immediate and long-term program developments so that educational goals can be achieved in a systematic fashion. To accomplish this aim fiscal planning must extend over a period of time greater than one year even though the formal budget document may reflect only the expenditure plan for one year. Past patterns of receipts and expenditures should be studied and reviewed, but overreliance on these data will retard the continued growth of the educational program.

Traditional views of school budgeting and accounting have been exemplified in DeYoung's (1936) exhaustive treatment of the subject, followed later by Ovsiew and Castetter's text (1960). Tidwell (1960) has also prepared a comprehensive treatment of the area of public school fund accounting. Possibly the most important recent work has been the USOE publication by Reason and White (1957); with slight modifications in some instances, the accounting system outlined in this handbook has been adopted in virtually all states. As an additional aid to assist practitioners in the understanding of accounting in the schools Lanham (1964) has prepared a programmed textbook to assist in the evaluation of financial data.

Two additional aids are found in a school accounting manual and the discussion of school budget policies and finances for the small district which have been prepared by Mitchell (1961, 1962). A very practical aid has been prepared by Baum (1962) who has developed a checklist of 100 criteria to be observed in preparing and evaluating a budget. Federal funds used for educational programs must be handled in accordance with the accounting program as outlined by Reason and White (1957), but Pateros (1962) has provided additional assistance by summarizing the basic principles for management of federal funds involved in a state-directed activity.

Many local school districts invest their idle funds in various types of securities, and Schaerer (1965) found that investment yields can be increased through the application of the "cash flow" principle for scheduling the purchase and sale of investments.

Knezevich and DeKock (1960) indicated that studies of fiscal management have devoted their primary attention to reporting existing practices. Somewhat typical of a large number of status studies is Bowermaster's (1959) review of budget practices in Illinois which provided additional data to support the contention that there is a general lack of uniformity in the practices used in preparing local school budgets.

Through recent refinements in information systems as a result of advancements in data processing techniques, local school districts have acquired tools which permit a rather complex and detailed analysis of the local district expenditures. Cloyd (1964), Foster (1964a) and Reason and White (1957) have developed suggested approaches to serve as guides for local school districts which seek to utilize cost accounting techniques. Undoubtedly the greatest recent impact has been made by Furno's *The Cost of Education Index* (1966) which has become available on an annual basis since 1960. This new source of information permits the local school administrator to make total and internal breakdown comparisons of the local district's budget with a selected sample on both an expenditure and a staffing basis.

Computer technology and procedures used in developing the budget for the federal government have begun to have their effects on the practices used in formulating local school budgets. The concept of "program budgeting" as outlined by Novick (1965) may provide an impetus for the development of more refined techniques which can be used in developing local school budgets. In this approach primary attention is devoted to goals and output, and subsequent attempts are made to isolate the alternative choices through which the desired goals and output levels can be attained.

Rather than relying upon tradition and intuition, decisions are made from available data and possible alterations can be considered without jeopardizing the basic intent of the program. The need for additional work in the broad area of cost analysis was emphasized by Wasserman (1963) and Cloyd (1964) when they both pleaded for more investigation and the development of techniques through which quality variations can be isolated. Problems relating to compatible data among states will be minimized as accounting systems become more standardized and as continuing studies such as Furno's (1966) become more refined and generally accepted.

PURCHASING AND SUPPLY MANAGEMENT. As the process of education has become more complex, increased attention has been given to the important role that educational tools and products play in the schools. The magnitude of the purchasing operation will vary among school districts because of variations in total enrollment and in the amount of materials made available to individual teachers; however, Burns (1962), Jordan and Brock (1964), and Bloom (1965) have contended that certain basic principles should serve as guidelines regardless of local conditions.

A most comprehensive treatment of the practical aspects of purchasing has been prepared by Burns (1962). Kastman (1965) and Shaw (1961) have also stressed the importance of adequate specifications to combat price-fixing and foster open competition in bidding. Another valuable source of information in this area is available from the General Services Administration (1963).

Brock (1964), Burns (1962), and Roe (1961) have supported the "user's right of choice" in the selection of school supplies and equipment and have also recognized the importance of specifications and standardized items if efficient use is to be made of the educational dollar. Even though teachers and other school personnel have come to recognize the importance of adequate educational tools and supplies, Denton and Prien (1963) found that personnel in purchasing departments may not be viewed as contributing significantly to this aim. Further research is needed to isolate the problem areas and to determine if teachers do view the purchasing department as being in a supportive role.

Legal controls over purchasing will vary among the several states, but basic guidelines have been identified for local school administrators. Singer and Micken (1964) have prepared an exhaustive treatment of the various legal concepts which relate to purchasing in the public schools.

Supply management and property accounting are becoming increasingly important as more funds are devoted to the purchase of educational tools and equipment and to the construction of facilities. Historically, local school officials have failed to devote much attention to maintaining adequate records. Interested persons can now obtain assistance from a USOE publication prepared by Reason and Tankard (1959).

Authorities are in general agreement that a requisition and purchase order system should be used and that the purchasing responsibilities for the local school district should be centralized. Burns (1962), Linn and others (1956), and Roe (1961) have contended that the advisability of central warehousing will depend upon the size of the school district and also upon such factors as available facilities in centralized or decentralized locations. Caswell (1961) has prepared valuable data on warehouse usage and has also developed a cost analysis guide for use by local school administrators.

Insurance. Local school district insurance programs are normally classified into four broad categories: insurance through commercial stock or mutual companies, state insurance programs, self insurance, or no insurance. Johnson (1965) and Schaerer (1963) reported that various types of policies were available through commercial companies and that recently available special policies with a wide range of alternates for public institutions had resulted in considerable premium reductions with increased coverages. Edwards (1965) reported that the advantages of the newly developed policies included the requirements that property values be kept current and that annual inventories be conducted. Much of the moving force behind the development of the public and institutional property and multi-peril forms of insurance policies can possibly be attributed to the earlier research as summarized by Knezevich and DeKock (1960) which revealed that the fire-loss ratio for schools was rather low and that a revision of rates was in order since experience had proved that schools were preferred risks.

The earlier work on insurance by Linn and Joyner (1952) has recently been supplemented by Allen (1965). Finchum (1964, 1965) has authored several publications and has also collaborated with Viles (Finchum & Viles, 1959) to augment earlier works by Salmon (1958) and the American Association of School Administrators (1953). Each emphasized the important roles that safety measures and sound plant management practices play in securing economies in the insurance program and also stressed the contribution which they can make to the uninterrupted operation of the schools. The state insurance programs as described by Viles (1956) have not spread to other states even though the programs were considered fundamentally sound.

Linn and others (1956), Linn and Joyner (1952), and Schaerer (1964b) reported that school districts should have adequate financial ability, large enrollments, and sufficient geographical size to spread the risk before they can justify giving consideration to self-insurance programs, and they also suggested that careful study be made of the relative advantages and disadvantages before assuming complete local responsibility for the program. Roe (1961) and Salmon (1958) recommended that local insurance programs be handled in a more efficient manner so that patronage and administrative detail can be reduced. Among the alternatives which have been used is competitive bidding of local insurance programs; Schaerer (1964a) has presented a rather complete treatment of the pros and cons of using this approach.

Management of Capital Outlay Programs. Local school district bonding power and indebtedness programs are subject to state statutory and constitutional limitations. Many of these restrictions impose severe hardships upon local school districts which are faced with enrollment increases and school facility needs. Rates on bond issues have been influenced by a variety of factors; Furno (1965) has classified these into five broad areas: (a) condition of the bond market, (b) amount of the issue, (c) duration of the issue, (d) date of the sale, and (e) credit rating of the local district.

Following his study of bond issues in Indiana over a five-year period Hudson (1966) presented the following suggestions for school districts desiring to secure favorable interest rates: (a) General obligation bonds should be issued in preference to building authority bonds. (b) The term of the issue should be as short as possible without placing undue hardship on the district. (c) Government tax programs should be studied so that bonds will not be issued during peak tax years. (d) Prior to presenting the bond issue for sale or securing the rating from the rating bureau, the total bonded debt for the school district should be reduced as much as possible. (e) The market should be studied to determine the best days of the week on which to offer the bonds for sale. (f) Extreme care should be exercised in preparing the prospectus to assure that the issue and the district are presented in a most favorable fashion. (g) Bond-rating agencies should be contacted to assure that they have full and complete information upon which to base their rating.

An extensive list of the various information items which should be made available to potential purchasers of securities has been prepared by *The Bond Buyer* (1962), a securities trade journal.

Business Affairs in the Local School. Increases in the magnitude of school activity accounting and related problems as summarized by Knezevich and DeKock (1960) have continued, but little definitive research has been conducted. The earlier accounting handbook published by the Association of School Business Officials (1957) has been supplemented by Samuelson and others (1959). In each of these publications the need for adequate controls and placement of responsibility has been emphasized. Voges (1961) in a discussion of trends in activity accounting projected an increase in (a) centralized accounting for local school activities in the school district's administrative offices, (b) coordination between student activity programs and instructional activities with students assuming increased responsibilities, and (c) critical examination of the role that student activities play in the total instructional program. Jones (1967) found a dearth of literature and research which related to sound business practices at the local school level and recommended that local school districts devote attention to pre-service and in-service programs for subprofessional personnel working in the area of business management in local school buildings. Guidelines which can be used by local school districts seeking to study their office management organization and procedures have been developed by Bollinger (1966).

Attention should be given to determining the legal status of activity funds, for the basic question remains concerning whether they are public, quasi-public, or private. Closely related to this question is the power and responsibility which the school board and the central administrative staff have over school activity funds.

K. Forbis Jordan
Indiana University

References

Allen, Clifford H. *School Insurance Administration.* Macmillan, 1965. 133p.

American Association of School Administrators. *Managing the School District Insurance Program.* AASA, 1953. 24p.

Association of School Business Officials. *A Manual of Accounting Principles and Procedures for Student Activity Funds.* The Association, 1957. 65p.

Bates, Austin F. "Availability and Dissemination of Research in School Business Affairs." *Sch Bus Affairs* January:5–8; 1964.

Baum, Milt. "Criteria for Evaluating the School Budget." *Am Sch Bd J* 145:17–8; 1962.

Bloom, Arnold. (Ed.) "Ten Principles for a Good Purchasing Program." *Am Sch and U* March:60–2; 1965.

Bollinger, W. Lynn. "A Survey Instrument For the Self-study of a School Office Management Program." Doctoral dissertation. Indiana U, 1966.

Bond Buyer, The Preparing a Bond Offering of a Local Government for the Market. 1962. 48p.

Bowermaster, Ralph E. "A Study of Current Practices in the Preparation of the Budget in Selected Public Schools in the State of Illinois." Doctoral dissertation. Northwestern U, 1959.

Brock, Dale Eastes, "Survey Instrument for Evaluation of the Economic Efficiency of Public School Purchasing. Doctoral dissertation. Indiana U, 1964.

Burns, H. Spilman. *Purchasing and Supply Management Manual for School Business Officials.* Association of School Business Officials, 1962. 144p.

Casey, Leo M. *School Business Administration.* Center for Applied Research in Education, 1964. 112p.

Caswell, Gordon G. *What Price School Supply Warehousing.* National School Supply and Equipment Association, 1961. 23p.

Cloyd, Helen Smith. "The Practice and Future Use of Cost Accounting in School Districts." *Am Sch Bd J* 148:13–4; 1964.

Conrad, M. J., and Griffith, William. "Organizational Character of Education: Facility Planning and Business Management." *R Ed Res* 34:470–84; 1964.

Cooper, Dan H., and Pound, Clarence A. "Selected References on School Administration." *El Sch J* April:1962, 1963, 1964, 1965.

Cronan, Marion. *The School Lunch.* Charles A. Bennet Co., 1962. 512p.

Denton, J. C., and Prien, Enrich P. "Defining the Perceived Functions of Purchasing Personnel." *J Applied Psychol* Oct:332–8; 1963.

DeYoung, Chris A. *Budgeting in Public Schools.* Doubleday, 1936. 610p.

Educational Research Service. *The Status and Functions of the Local School Business Administrator.* Circular No. 8, NEA, 1966. 56p.

Edwards, L. F. "Coverages Available In School Packaged Insurance." In *Proceedings.* Association of School Business Officials, 1965. p. 218–21.

Endicott, William. "The Business Manager Becomes a Professional." *Am Sch Bd J* 153:20–3; 1966.

Englehardt, N. L., and Englehardt, Fred. *Public School Business Administration.* Teachers Col, Columbia U, 1927. 1068p.

Featherstone, E. G., and Culp, D. P. *Pupil Transportation: State and Local Programs.* Harper, 1965. 263p.

Finchum, R. N. *School Building Maintenance Procedures.* USOE Bulletin No. 17. GPO, 1964. 175p.

Finchum, R. N. *Fire Insurance Economics Through Plant Management.* USOE Bulletin No. 8. GPO, 1965. 81p.

Finchum, R. N., and Boerrigter, Glenn C. *School Fires: Prevention, Control, Protection.* USOE Bulletin No. 6. GPO, 1962. 130p.

Finchum, R. N., and Viles, N. E. *School Insurance, Managing the Local Program.* USOE Bulletin No. 23. GPO, 1959. 97p.

Foster, Charles W. (Ed.). "Cost Accounting Systems." *Sch Bus Affairs* Dec:5; 1964(*a*).

Foster, Charles W. (Ed.). "Professionalization Section." *Sch Bus Affairs* December:6–8; 1964(*b*).

Furno, Orlando. "The Cost of Borrowing Money." *Sch Manag* 9:105–7; 1965.

Furno, Orlando F. *The Cost of Education Index*. Pitman, 1966. 72p.

Garber, Lee O. (Ed.). *Law and The School Business Manager*. Interstate, 1957. 331p.

General Services Administration. *Guide To Specifications and Standards of the Federal Government*. GPO, 1963. 39p.

George, Norvil L., and Heckler, Ruth D. *School Food Centers*. Ronald, 1960. 335p.

Hill, F. W. *The School Business Administrator*. Association of School Business Officials, 1960. 80p.

Hill, F. W., and Colmey, J. W. *School Business Administration in the Smaller Community*. Denison, 1964. 324p.

Hudson, C. C. "An Analysis of Net Interest Costs of Selected Bond Issues for Indiana Schools." Doctoral dissertation. Indiana U, 1966.

Huls, Harry E. "State Limitations on Total Public School Expenditures in The United States." Doctoral dissertation. U Minnesota, 1958.

Johnson, Edwin G. "A New Look at School Insurance Packages." In *Proceedings*. Association of School Business Officials, 1965. p. 109–13.

Jones, James A. "A Study of the Indiana Public Elementary School Secretaryship." Doctoral dissertation. Indiana U, 1967.

Jordan K. F., and Brock, D. E. "Principles of Public School Purchasing." *Am Sch Bd J* 149:13–4; 1964.

Kastman, A. R. "Educational Specifications." *Am Sch U* May:109–10; 1965.

Knezevich, Stephen J. "Managing the School Plant and Business Affairs." *R Ed Res* 31:428–38; 1961.

Knezevich, Stephen J., and DeKock, H. C. "Business Administration—Public Schools." In *Encyclopedia of Educational Research*, rev. ed. Macmillan, 1960. p. 161–73.

Knezevich, Stephen J., and Fowlkes, John G. *Business Management of Local School Systems*. Harper, 1960. 328p.

Lanham, Frank W. *The Meaning of School Accounts*. University Council for Educational Administration, 1964. 120p.

Linn, Henry H., and Joyner, Schuyler C. *Insurance Practices in School Administration*. Ronald, 1952. 437p.

Linn, Henry H., and others. *School Business Administration*. Ronald, 1956. 574p.

Mitchell, Herbert S. *Manual for School Accounting*. Interstate, 1961. 93p.

Mitchell, Herbert S. *School Budget Policies for Financial Control*. Interstate, 1962. 70p.

Moehlman, A. B. *Public School Finance*. Rand McNally, 1927. 508p.

Morrison, H. C. *The Management of the School Money*. U Chicago, 1932. 522p.

National Education Association, Research Division. "Fiscal Authority of City School Boards." *Res B* 24:47–8; 1950.

Novick, David. (Ed.). *Program Budgeting*. Bureau of the Budget. GPO, 1965. 236p.

Ovsiew, Leon, and Castetter, William B. *Budgeting for Better Schools*. Prentice-Hall, 1960. 338p.

Pateros, John J. *Financial Management of Federal-State Education Programs*. USOE Bulletin No. 20. GPO, 1962. p. 4–12.

Reason, Paul L., and Tankard, George G., Jr. *Property Accounting for Local and State School Systems*. USOE Bulletin No. 22. GPO, 1959. 193p.

Reason, Paul L., and White, Alpheus L. *Financial Accounting for Local and State School Systems—Standard Receipt and Expenditure Accounts*. USOE Bulletin No. 4. GPO, 1957. 235p.

Reeder, Ward G. *The Business Administration of a School System*. Ginn, 1929. 454p.

Reuter, George S. *Fiscal Independence Versus Fiscal Dependence of School Boards*. American Federation of Teachers, 1960. 30p.

Roe, William H. *School Business Management*. McGraw-Hill, 1961. 303p.

Salmon, Paul B. *Fire Insurance Principles and Practices In School Districts Employing Nationally Affiliated Business Officials*. Association of School Business Officials, 1958. 89p.

Samuelson, Everett V., and others. *Financial Accounting for School Activities*. USOE Bulletin No. 21. GPO, 1959. 109p.

Schaerer, Robert W. "School Packaged Insurance." In *Proceedings*. Association of School Business Officials, 1963. p. 91–7.

Schaerer, Robert W. "Bidding Insurance." In *Proceedings*. Association of School Business Officials, 1964(a). p. 213–22.

Schaerer, Robert W. "Self Insurance." In *Proceedings*. Association of School Business Officials, 1964(b). p. 384–7.

Schaerer, Robert W. "How Gary, Indiana, Invests Idle Funds and Earns Thousands." *Nation's Sch* 76:78–9; 1965.

Shaw, Archibald. (Ed.) "Next on the Docket: Identical Bids." *Overview* Dec:38–9, 65; 1961.

Singer, H. H., and Micken, C. M. *The Law of Purchasing*. Interstate, 1964. 136p.

Smith, H. P. *Business Administration of Public Schools*. World Bk, 1929. 432p.

Tidwell, S. B. *Public School Fund Accounting*. Harper, 1960. 298p.

Viles, Nelson E. *School Property Insurance Experiences at State Level*. USOE Bulletin No. 7. GPO, 1956. 61p.

Voges, Bernard H. "Activity Funds: New Worry for the Business Head." *Nation's Sch* 68:76–7; 1961.

Wasserman, William. "Education Price and Quantity Indexes." In *The Economics and Politics of Public Education*. Syracuse U Press, 1963. 166p.

Womrath, G. F. *Efficient Business Administration of Public Schools*. Bruce, 1932. 463p.

Yankow, Henry. "Where to Find What Was Written About School Business Practice." *Nation's Sch* 67:96–9; 1966.

Yeager, William A. *Administration of the Noninstructional Personnel and Services*. Harper, 1959. 426p.

SCHOOL HEALTH SERVICES

OBJECTIVES OF SCHOOL HEALTH SERVICES. School health services are primarily designed to assure and enhance the educability of the children of school age. This purpose is implemented through such steps as identifying health problems and health needs among children of school age; encouraging and assisting pupils and parents to obtain the needed health care; maintaining conditions that will promote a healthful environment; increasing pupils' and parents' understanding about health; and adapting school programs to the needs of individual children. School health services include such aspects as appraising the health of pupils; providing health counseling and follow-up for the care of health problems; preventing and controlling communicable disease; promoting and providing a safe environment, including accident prevention; providing care for emergency illness or injury; providing for the special needs of groups such as handicapped children, pregnant teenagers, etc; providing for the health of school personnel; and identifying the gaps in health services for children of school age and assisting in eliminating them.

NEWER LEGISLATION AFFECTING THE HEALTH OF SCHOOL-AGE CHILDREN. Within the last several years, there have been four pieces of major legislation with an impact on the health of children and youth of school age. The first is the Elementary and Secondary Education Act of 1965, administered by the U.S. Office of Education, which makes funds available for health, psychiatric, and psychological services in the schools; supplemental health and food services; special classes for the physically handicapped, the disturbed and for dropouts; special audiovisual aids for disadvantaged children; preschool training programs; and summer school and day camps. The second is the program of grants for Comprehensive Health Services for Children and Youth, administered by the U.S. Childrens Bureau. This program makes it possible to provide comprehensive health services for children in low-income families, including case findings, preventive health service, diagnosis, treatment, correction of defects, and after-care, both medical and dental (U.S. Childrens Bureau, 1965). Third are several of the antipoverty programs, especially Project Head Start, the Neighborhood Youth Corps, the Job Corps, and the neighborhood health center programs. Fourth is the new amendment to the Social Security Act, providing coverage of medical and health care for certain categorical groups, such as Aid to Families with Dependent Children, and for medically indigent families. All of these newer legislative acts should make it possible to assist families in improving the health of children, with special emphasis on those of lower socioeconomic status.

ADMINISTRATION OF SCHOOL HEALTH SERVICES. Wolf and Pritham (1965) have reported the results of a survey of 336 cities in 50 states in the United States made in 1964 and 1965. Of the 230 cities responding, it was found that the Board of Education was responsible for the administration of the school health services in 63 percent, the Health Department in 30 percent, and in 6 percent there was dual administration. A U.S. Public Health Service survey (1963) of health services in 118 school systems in the United States elicited responses from 83 systems in 40 states and the District of Columbia. It was found that the Board of Education was administratively responsible for health services in 62 percent of the reporting systems, the Health Department in 14 percent, and in 24 percent there was joint administration. The reported annual average per pupil expenditure, representing only Board of Education expenditures, varied from $0.10 to $14.02. Over one-half of the communities reported some attempt to coordinate the school health program with other health services available in the area; the most frequent coordinating mechanism was a school or community health council.

MAJOR HEALTH PROBLEMS IN CHILDREN AND YOUTH OF SCHOOL AGE. Mortality. Among children aged 5–14 years, the five leading causes of death in 1962 were accidents, cancer and other malignant diseases, pneumonia and influenza, congenital malformations, and cardiovascular-renal disease. Accidents are by far the most common cause of death in this age group and annually account for the death of 6,000 to 7,000 children. Motor vehicle accidents cause two-fifths of the accidental deaths; drowning accounts for one-fifth; and fire and explosions for about one-eighth. Firearms assume considerable importance as a cause of death in boys. In the age group 15–19 years, accidents, malignant diseases, cardiovascular-renal disease, homicide, and suicide are the major causes of death. Looked at from the viewpoint of preventability, an effective school health service might be expected to influence and reduce mortality due to accidents, heart disease, respiratory infections, homicide, and suicide.

Morbidity. Data from the U.S. National Health Survey in 1960–61 (Schiffer & Hunt, 1963) indicate that children aged 5–14 years have approximately 2.6 acute illnesses per child per year, while youth aged 15–24 years average 1.9 acute illnesses per year. Respiratory diseases, infective and parasitic diseases, and injuries are the most frequent types of acute illness. It is estimated that children aged 6–16 years lost 156,914,000 days from school in the year ending June, 1961—an average of 4 days per child. Eighteen percent of the children under 17 that year were reported to be suffering from at least one chronic condition. The most frequent were allergies (hay fever, asthma, etc.), diseases of the respiratory system (sinusitis, bronchitis, etc.), speech defects, impairment of extremities, and hearing impairment. For 10 percent of the chronic conditions in children under 17, a physician had never been seen, and for another third a physician had not been seen within the previous year. Half of the children under 15 years of age in the United States had never been to a dentist.

National estimates indicate that the number of children of school age with handicapping conditions in the United States is enormous (U.S. Childrens Bureau, 1964). Estimates of the numbers with more common types are children with eye conditions needing specialist care, 10.2 million; the emotionally disturbed, 4 million; children with speech problems, 2.58 million; the mentally retarded, 2.18 million; orthopedically handicapped, 1.925 million; those with hearing loss, 0.36–0.725 million; children with cerebral palsy, 0.37 million; and epileptics, 0.36 million.

On the basis of a recent study of high school children in a middle-class suburb of Pittsburgh, Pennsylvania, Rogers and Reese (1964, 1965) report that approximately 45 percent of the pupils had conditions judged improvable by health care. Almost all defects could be classified in five categories—vision, hearing, dentition, nutrition, and skin. Most absences from high school were due to minor morbidity; respiratory disease of apparent infectious etiology was the illness most commonly associated with absence. Pupils frequently absent had lower academic performance, lower rates of participation in school activities, higher dropout rates, and more frequent visits to the school nurse. Those visiting the health room often were considered to have a higher prevalence of basic social and emotional problems than their classmates.

In a study of children in the second and fourth grades in Onondaga County, New York, Cumming and McCaffrey (1964) found that 7.7 percent were reported as "emotionally disturbed." The percentage was higher in boys than in girls. Two years later one-third of the children originally studied were judged as still having the same symptoms.

Recent antipoverty programs are beginning to reveal the high frequency of health problems among children and youth in this high-risk group. For example, Currie-Frey reported (1966) that in Philadelphia 48 percent of the children examined were found to have defects which were recommended for treatment. In San Francisco, Eisner and others (1966) reported that 60 percent of the enrollees in the Neighborhood Youth Corps were found by two physicians to require medical and/or dental care.

Teen-age pregnancy is another problem requiring increasing attention in schools from school health services (Wallace, 1965). Teen-age marriages are on the increase, and the divorce rate among them is high. Approximately 15 percent, or about 600,000, of all babies born annually in the United States are born to teen-age mothers. Pregnancy has been the most frequent single cause for the adolescent girl to leave school prior to graduation. Each year, there are about a quarter of a million babies born out of wedlock; the figure for 1962 was 245,100. About 92,000 of these babies were born to teen-age girls, of whom 48,300 were under 18 years of age. Teen-age pregnant girls in any community constitute a high risk group needing greatly increased educational, social, psychological and health services.

Venereal disease is also a growing problem among teen-agers (American Social Health Association, 1964). For example, the 10–14-year-old group showed an increase of 15.4 percent in reported infectious syphilis in 1963 over 1962. Seventy-two largest cities reported an increase of 52.9 percent in 1963 over 1962. In the 15–19-year-old group, there was a 5.1 percent increase in 1963 over 1962; in the 72 largest cities, there was a 9.2 percent increase.

Juvenile delinquency is still on the increase in the United States (U.S. Childrens Bureau, 1966). In 1965 about 700,000 juvenile delinquency cases were handled by juvenile courts. Percentage-wise, 2 percent of all children and youth aged 10 through 17 years are involved. The year 1965 showed an increase of 2 percent of delinquency cases over the previous year, outstripping the increase in childhood population.

Still another way of looking at the health needs of the school-age group is through analysis of data from selective service examinations of the younger adult male population. In 1962, 22.7 percent of those called up for military service were rejected for medical reasons, and 24.5 percent for mental reasons (Presidents Task Force . . . , 1964). Major reasons for medical disqualifications were bone and joint diseases, psychiatric disorders, diseases of the circulatory system, eye diseases and defects, and diseases and defects of the ear and mastoid processes.

From the data available there is reason to believe that a more effective school health service might prevent some conditions entirely, might ameliorate the effects of some conditions, might identify some conditions earlier, and might make it possible for some children and youth to secure and maintain necessary health care.

PERSONNEL EMPLOYED IN SCHOOL HEALTH SERVICES. Personnel most frequently employed in school health services are nurses, physicians (both full-time and part-time), dentists, dental hygienists, and audiometrists (U.S. Public Health Service, 1963). In addition, many communities utilize trained volunteers to do some of the routine screening tests as well as nonprofessional activities. Recently, considerable concern has been expressed about the deployment of professional school health personnel. In a report of the U.S. Public Health Service survey (1963), it is stated that "there was no evidence that the school systems had made studies to determine what functions could only be served by medical or nursing personnel, despite national cries of manpower shortages." Benvechio and Dukelon (1961) found that the responsibilities school physicians rated most often in the top ten ranks were: working closely with school nurses to facilitate coordination, belonging to and working with medical organizations, encouraging the use of the family physician for medical examinations, encouraging immunizations, assisting in planning policies and procedures for emergency care, assisting in communicable disease control, promoting and coordinating school and public health programs. Richie (1961) has discussed comparative advantages and disadvantages of separate school nursing services as against having school nursing services combined with the community's public health nursing services. The U.S. Public Health Service survey showed some variation in the utilization of school physicians and more homogeneity in the use of dentists and dental hygenists. The greatest variation was found in the utilization of school nurses.

THE HEALTH APPRAISAL. The health appraisal of the child of school age is a continuation of the health supervision and care which should start from birth and continue throughout the infancy and preschool periods. It begins with the health history, consisting of the careful review of the family history; the mother's pregnancy, labor and delivery; the child's newborn, infant, and preschool course of development; the child's illnesses; and his immunizations (American Academy of Pediatrics, 1966a).

The classroom teacher, except for the child's own family, has the closest contact with the child and represents the best source of information about the child from observation of his daily behavior and condition. In-service education of teachers in health subjects is one method of assisting them in sharpening their observation tools. Upon suspecting that a child is not feeling well or that his condition is not up to par, the teacher needs the opportunity to discuss the child with the school nurse. In addition to this individually timed referral, regular teacher–nurse conferences should be held at least once a year to review each child in the classroom.

Screening procedures constitute another effective method of identifying certain adverse health conditions in school children. Screening of vision may begin well before entry of the child into school through careful observation of the newborn child, and during infancy and the preschool periods for the presence of strabismus. Vision screening and the use of the cover test for strabismus may begin as early as the third year of life and be repeated annually. Annual testing of vision and the use of the cover test are recommended during the child's school life. In addition, any child suspected of having a problem of visual acuity should be screened. In general, the Snellen test is the one most frequently used for this purpose. The "plus lens" is sometimes added to screen for hyperopia. Sometimes a color-vision test is used on males. Children should wear their glasses while being tested. The "screeners" may be trained volunteers or trained nurse assistants, teachers with training or school nurses. Failure at the 20/40 level is the basis for referral of the child for a careful eye examination; failure at the 20/30 level usually necessitates rescreening.

Although attempts have been made to introduce hearing testing in the health care of infants and preschool children, methods have not yet been developed to the easily practical level so that they could be routinely incorporated. Screening of hearing is recommended to be done annually in kindergarten, and grades 1, 2, and 3. Testing can be done less often in subsequent school years, but no child should experience more than a three-year interval between tests from grades 4 through 12 (Darley, 1961). Pure-tone testing is recommended at frequencies of 500, 1000, 2000, 4000, and 6000 cps. Hearing screening is a two-step procedure; the first step is the screening test, mentioned above. The second step consists of a threshold test involving all frequencies. Criteria for failure consist of failure at two of the frequencies tested at 20 db level, or failure at one frequency tested at a level of 30 db. In addition to this routine audiometry, other types of children will require screening for hearing: those new to the school system; those with delayed or defective speech; those who appear to be retarded; those with emotional or behavior problems; and those referred by the classroom teacher. Testing should be done in a quiet room; the instrument needs frequent calibration; and the testing should be done by an audiometrist or another person previously trained (volunteer nurse's assistant, teacher, or nurse). Failure requires that the child be referred for a careful audiologic-otologic examination.

Height and weight measurements are recommended three times a year. It is helpful to record these data on growth charts, for easy visualization of the child's longitudinal course. Deviation from the child's individual pattern is an indication of the desirability of further health appraisal.

Other types of testing of school children will depend on the particular community in which the school health program is located. For example, tuberculin testing might be done in a low-income group where the yield of active cases might be more significant. All positive reactors will require chest X-ray and there will need to be follow-up study of all household and other close contacts. Hemoglobin determination might be done where anemia is prevalent as in children from low-income families or adolescent girls. Stool examinations for ova and parasites might be done in children who are recent arrivals from a developing part of the world. Urine cultures for bacteriuria might be performed routinely on girls. Tape recording of heart sounds might be another screening tool where heart disease in school children is a significant public health problem.

The final portion of the routine health appraisal is the periodic health examination. It has been recommended that this be routinely performed at least three times during the school life of the child: before or at entry into school (kindergarten or first grade), at about the sixth or seventh grade (late childhood and early adolescence), and at about the eleventh grade (adolescence and prior to leaving school) (American Academy of Pediatrics, 1966a). In addition, a child should receive a health examination when a health problem is suspected, when a child is new to the school system, when a child is frequently absent from school, or when required for employment. The content should be complete. In general, it is believed to be advantageous to have the health examination performed by the child's own physician wherever possible, because of the advantages of continued longitudinal observations. In the absence of a personal physician, many school health programs provide school physicians, one of their duties being to perform periodic health examinations.

It is interesting to note in this connection that the Yankauer study in Rochester, New York, has provided evidence that the school medical examination of first-grade children who had been previously examined in kindergarten was valueless from a case-finding standpoint; that periodic school medical examinations during the first four years of elementary school are of little value from a case-finding standpoint; and that the evidence for the educational value of the periodic health examination is not clearcut (Yankauer & Lawrence, 1955, 1956, 1957, 1961). Rogers and Reese (1964, 1965) in Pennsylvania reached the conclusion that "the routine periodic health appraisal appeared to be of limited usefulness as a technique for revealing previously undisclosed health problems in presumably normal high school students."

One of the controversial issues in the health appraisal is that of periodic dental inspection of school children. Some school health services have provided annual dental inspections of school children. Others have taken the position that, with the high frequency of dental caries, emphasis should be placed upon referral of children for a complete dental examination, upon dental care, and upon the use of fluoride as a preventive measure. The author of this article concurs in this latter point of view.

One of the great needs at present is for more accurate methods of detecting incipient signs of emotional difficulty in children and youth of school age. While efforts are being made in this direction, the problem requires much further work and development. Until that has been accomplished, the best and most practical method available is that of teacher observation, together with study of records of school attendance and school performance.

Health appraisal of the school child is of little or no value unless the school health service and the community are in a position to take action with the child's family in regard to adverse health conditions which may be identified. Case findings represent the first step in a sequence to be followed by detailed interpretation to the family (or to the child himself when he is an adolescent), by provisions of follow-up and assistance to the child so that he may be given the necessary work-up and care. The work-up and care should be of the type and quality which the child requires. Health and medical resources of a general nature frequently are not able to provide the kind of specialized services which the child with a special health problem needs. The school health service has the responsibility of acquainting the community with needed health resources and of working with the community to assist in promoting their development.

HEALTH ASPECTS OF PHYSICAL EDUCATION AND ATHLETICS. Physical education, physical activities, and sports activities are of value in providing increased recreational opportunity and emotional outlets for children and youth. The health aspects of physical education include the responsibility for individualizing the amount and type of activity for each child to meet his needs and for establishing policies and procedures in regard to prevention of injury and first aid.

In the field of competitive athletics, certain policies have been recommended (Reichert, 1958; Kansas School Health Advisory Council, n.d.). It is recognized that all children need opportunities to develop skills in a variety of activities, taking into account the age and developmental level of the child. Body contact sports are not recommended for children under the age of 13 years, because of the possibility of bone and joint injury in the growing child. The best available protective equipment should be provided and properly fitted. As a minimum, a pre-season health history and examination should be required and coordinated with what is already known about the individual. These records should be incorporated into the school health service's ongoing program.

COMMUNICABLE DISEASE PREVENTION AND CONTROL. The school health service should take four measures for the prevention and control of communicable diseases among school children. Health education of the child and his family is basic. Provision of safe environmental sanitation is essential, including water, sewage, handwashing facilities, and hygienic food handling. The school must participate in the reporting of communicable diseases required to be reported to the health department.

Immunization against specific communicable diseases is available and needs implementation (American Academy of Pediatrics, 1966b). Begun in infancy with booster injections during the preschool period, the recommended schedule includes the use of smallpox vaccine and diphtheria, and of pertussis and tetanus toxoids upon school entry and every three to five years thereafter. Oral polio trivalent vaccine is recommended on school entry. Measles vaccine should also be used for children entering school who have not been previously immunized. A national survey by Hein and Bauer (1964) revealed that 22 states had laws requiring immunization before entering school—20 for smallpox, 11 for diphtheria, 10 for poliomyelitis, 7 for tetanus, 5 for pertussis, and 2 for typhoid fever.

SAFETY AND ACCIDENT PREVENTION, AND THE CARE OF MEDICAL EMERGENCIES. Accidents represent a major health problem in children and youth of school age. They are the primary cause of death in the age groups 5–19 years; the leading types of accidents playing a role in mortality are motor vehicle, drowning, firearms, fire and explosives, and falls. It has been estimated (National Center for Health Statistics, 1965) that each year about 13 million children between the ages of 6 and 16 years suffer injuries requiring at least one day of restricted activity or medical attention. Based on this survey, the time lost from school annually is 37.3 days per 100 boys and 25.3 days per 100 girls 6 to 16 years of age. Safety and accident prevention measures usually include those directed toward motor vehicle accidents (driver education programs, traffic control measures around schools, the use of seat belts), provision of as safe an environment as possible for playgrounds including playground supervision, provision of safety measures in school laboratories and shops, swimming instruction, and safety precautions in regard to firearms. In many school systems, accidents are reportable and lend themselves to epidemiological studies. Some school systems have an accident insurance system. Safety and accident prevention represents a field where health education can play a major role.

A closely related activity in school health is the establishment of policies and procedures in regard to emergency care, both for illness and accidents. This includes such aspects as prior knowledge of where to reach the child's family and personal physician, the training of school personnel in first aid, providing first aid supplies in each school, and specific instructions for first aid and emergency medical care.

SPECIAL HEALTH PROBLEMS OF ADOLESCENTS. Adolescence is a period of rapid physical growth and development, and for some a period of emotional stress as well. A questionnaire study of 690 adolescents in the state of Washington revealed that 27 percent of them stated that they had health problems (Deisher & Mills, 1963). The ones most frequently reported were concerned with growth and weight; concern related to eyes, ears, nose, and throat; skin problems; and problems of the respiratory tract. Four percent felt their problems were in an emotional area. Chief worries reported by this group were school grades and school activities; financial responsibilities of the future; health, physical abilities, or appearance; interpersonal relationships; and the opposite sex. When asked where they seek help with their worries, about a third named their parents, a fifth named a friend, one percent named a school counselor or teacher, and a fifth named "no one."

It seems clear that adolescents have special health problems and needs. In addition to those cited above, other concerns of adolescents include smoking, drug usage, predelinquent and delinquent behavior, and suicide. Increased attention to the physical and emotional health needs of adolescents should be given by school health personnel in secondary schools. Opportunities for health education are numerous. In an effort to begin to meet these needs, some medical schools and teaching hospitals have developed special health services for teen-agers, primarily on an outpatient basis.

NUTRITIONAL ASPECTS OF SCHOOL HEALTH. Another important aspect of the school health service is nutrition. While malnutrition is much less of a health problem today than formerly, nevertheless for certain school children (those from low-income families, adolescent girls), it may be of considerable significance. Studies indicate that the adolescent girl has the poorest dietary habits of any of the school groups. This finding should be balanced with the knowledge that improvement of teen-age nutrition is one of the forms of preconceptional care. At the other end of the spectrum is the problem of obesity. Increased attention to nutrition can be encouraged through health education. One aspect of the total nutrition program in the school is the school lunch program, which has nutritional, health, educational, social, cultural and sanitation implications (National Education Association & American Medical Association, 1962).

SCHOOL SERVICES FOR HANDICAPPED CHILDREN. According to the American Academy of Pediatrics (1966a), a child with a handicap is any child with a physical, mental, or emotional problem that interferes with normal growth and development. From the standpoint of the school, children with handicaps are those who require special attention beyond that given to other children. The estimated number of handicapped children of school age is large (see earlier section, Major Health Problems in Children and Youth of School Age).

The general trend is for school systems to make provision for handicapped children in as normal a school setting as possible—i.e., in regular classrooms in regular schools—and many handicapped children are able to fit into this pattern. Other types of settings are (1) special day classes in regular schools; (2) special day schools; (3) home instruction; (4) special teachers assigned to hospitals, rehabilitation centers, etc.; (5) special residential schools. One of the essentials is for an interdisciplinary team (composed of special education and health experts) to carefully review and evaluate each child prior to educational placement, periodically (preferably every three months) during placement, and prior to withdrawal from placement.

Modification of the usual school program is essential for many handicapped children. Such modification includes: earlier school admission for some children (i.e., the blind, the deaf, the moderately-to-severely physically handicapped, such as the cerebral palsied); the provision of special transportation and attendant service to and from school for some children (i.e., the blind, the cardiacs, the moderately-to-severely physically handicapped); the provision of ramps, side rails, and elevators for some children (i.e., for those in wheelchairs or walking with crutches or braces); the provision of special equipment such as sound amplification for the deaf and hard of hearing; large-sized print and chalk and blackboards with reduced glare for the partially sighted; and braille and talking books for the blind. Where possible, children may spend most of the day in the regular classroom, and only a part of the day in a special classroom. Other special provisions include therapy services (physical, occupational, and speech) and health specialists (pediatrician, psychologist, nurse, social worker). The teacher trained in special education is essential. For the young teen-ager who is handicapped, early vocational testing and counseling with subsequent training and placement are a necessity.

HEALTH OF SCHOOL PERSONNEL. Health standards have now been established for school employees in many school systems (National Education Association & American Medical Association, 1960). These standards apply to all teaching, administrative, and service personnel under the school's jurisdiction. They include a preemployment examination, an examination at periodic intervals (usually at intervals of one, two, or three years), and examination whenever there is a suspicion of poor health or following frequent or prolonged illness. The health examination includes the health history, the medical and dental examinations, selected laboratory tests (such as blood count, urinalysis, and tuberculin test or chest X-ray). Usually in larger school systems, the cost of the health examination is borne by the Board of Education. The examination may be performed by the employee's own physician, or by physicians designated by the school system. In addition, school systems have established provisions for sick leave and frequently have provisions for group prepaid health insurance. A plan for a comprehensive health program for school personnel is important both for the benefit of the school children to be served and for the maintenance of optimal health for the individual employee.

HEALTH TEACHING. Teaching pupils and their families about health and health practices is one of the key parts of a school health program. The classroom or homeroom teacher carries primary responsibility for the health teaching program. The teacher may look to the members of the school health staff and to the staff of the community's health department and medical society as resources for assistance in the program—for recommending or providing current authoritative health resource materials. Health teaching should be incorporated into other classroom and school activities and opportunities for health teaching in general should be identified and used. Most school systems have established guides for health teaching, providing continuity throughout the child's elementary- and secondary-school life. Concern has been expressed about the quality and effectiveness of health teaching, which prompted the recent School Health Education Study (Sliepcevich, 1964). This study has corroborated the general impression of the need for strengthening the health teaching programs, both in regard to content, and in regard to preparation and supervision of the teachers in health subjects. Of special current interest in the schools is the question of timing, content, and methods of teaching family life education, including sex education.

The Need for Evaluation. One of the greatest needs in school health services at present is to evaluate their effectiveness. Many policies and procedures have been recommended and practiced for considerable periods of time with little or no evidence to indicate that they are effective at all or that they are the most effective methods of assisting pupils to achieve optimal health. A systematic plan for studies of effectiveness of the many component parts of school health services is greatly needed. Funds are needed for the support of carefully designed studies in this area.

Helen M. Wallace
University of California

References

American Academy of Pediatrics. *Report of the Committee on School Health.* The Academy, 1966(*a*). 128p.

American Academy of Pediatrics. *Report of the Committee on the Control of Infectious Disease.* The Academy, 1966(*b*). 185p.

American Social Health Association. *Today's VD Control Problem.* The Association, 1964. 75p.

Bonvechio, R. L., and Dukelon, D. A. "Responsibilities of School Physicians." *J Sch Health* 31:21–30; 1961.

Cumming, J., and McCaffrey, I. *Persistence of Emotional Disturbances Reported Among Second and Fourth Grade Children.* New York State Department of Mental Hygiene, 1964. 13p.

Currie-Frey, M. E. "Health Findings and Follow-through Programs in Head Start in 1965–66." 1966. 9p. (Mimeographed.)

Darley, F. L. (Ed.) "Identification Audiometry." *J Speech Hearing Disorders.* Monogr. Supplement No. 9, 1961.

Deisher, R. W., and Mills, C. A. "The Adolescent Looks at His Health and Medical Care." *Am J Public Health* 53:1928–36; 1963.

Eisner, V., and others. "Health Enrollees in Neighborhood Youth Corps." *Pediatrics* 38:40–3; 1966.

Hein, F. V., and Bauer, W. W. "Legal Requirements for Immunizations." *Archives of Environmental Health* 9:82–5; 1964.

Kansas School Health Advisory Council. *Prevention and Management of Injuries Incurred in School Athletics and Physical Activities.* Kansas State Health Department, n.d. 30p.

National Center for Health Statistics. *Acute Conditions: Incidence and Associated Disibility.* GPO, 1965.

National Education Association and American Medical Association. Joint Committee on Health Problems in Education. *Health Examination of School Personnel.* NEA and AMA, 1960. 22p.

National Education Association and American Medical Association. Joint Committee on Health Problems in Education. *Health Aspects of the School Lunch Program.* 2nd ed. SEA and AMA, 1962. 30p.

Presidents Task Force on Manpower Conservation. *One Third of A Nation.* GPO, 1964. 35p.

Reichert, J. L. "Competitive Athletics for Pre-teenage Children." *J AMA* 166:1701–7; 1958.

Richie, J. "School Nursing: A Generalized Or A Specialized Service?" *Am J Public Health* 51:1251–9; 1961.

Rogers, K. D., and Reese, G. "Health Studies—Presumably Normal High School Students." *Am J Diseases of Children* 108:572–600, 1964; 109:9–27; 42–78, 1965.

Schiffer, C. G., and Hunt, E. P. *Illness Among Children.* GPO, 1963. 107p.

Sliepcevich, E. M. *Summary Report of a Nationwide Study of Health Instruction in the Public Schools.* School Health Education Study, 1964. 74p.

U.S. Childrens Bureau. *Health of Children of School Age.* GPO, 1964. 31p.

U.S. Childrens Bureau. *Grants for Comprehensive Health Services for Children and Youth.* GPO, 1965. 26p.

U.S. Childrens Bureau. *Juvenile Court Statistics—1965.* GPO, 1966. 22p.

U.S. Public Health Service, School Health Section. "A Survey of School Health Services in 83 School Systems in 1963." n.d. 30p. (Mimeographed.)

Wallace, H. M. "Teen-age Pregnancy." *Am J of Obstetrics and Gynecology* 93:1125–31; 1965.

Wolf, J. M., and Pritham, H. C. "Administrative Patterns of School Health Services." *J AMA* 193:195–9; 1965.

Yankauer, A., and Lawrence, R. A. "A Study of Periodic School Medical Examinations." *Am J Public Health* 45:71–8, 1955; 46:1553–62, 1956; 47: 1421–9, 1957; 51:1532–40, 1961.

SCHOOL PERSONNEL ADMINISTRATION

Administration has been defined in various ways. Basic to most definitions is a conception of administration as a function of a social organization or system serving to relate the several elements of the system to the shared goal which provides the *raison d'être* of the system. The essential characteristic is often thought to be the decision process which relates the means of the system (resources—material, human, and social) to the goals of the system. School administration, then, may be seen as the decision process by which the resources of a school system are related to the goals of the system. Employed personnel (they will be referred to as "school personnel" and are to be clearly distinguished from the school's client group, pupil personnel) constitute one of the resources of the system. School personnel administration may thus be conceived as the decision process which serves to relate the services of school personnel to the goals of the school system. This decision process, for analytic purposes, may be seen as having three stages: (1) decisions on bringing people into employed status in the system or, the *hiring* stage, (2) decisions during service as employed personnel or, the *employment* stage, and (3) decisions on withdrawal from employed status or, the *withdrawal* stage.

Functional differentiation of school personnel has taken different forms resulting in such distinctions as instructional and noninstructional, professional and nonprofessional, certificated and noncertificated personnel. Three functional groups of school personnel are considered here: (1) those responsible for the instructional tasks of the school (*instructional service personnel*), including teachers, counselors, etc.; (2) those responsible for the operation of the total school system or its subsystems (*administrative service personnel*), including chief executives, assistants, and heads of units such as principals, deans, etc.; and (3) those who perform tasks which are not directly instructional but support the instructional service tasks (*supporting service personnel*), including cafeteria workers, clerks, custodians, doctors, mechanics, etc. In general, then, school personnel administration is here seen as decision making with respect to the services of various types of school personnel as they move into, serve in, and leave the school system.

Stated in the above general terms, personnel administration is a function of any formal social system, past, present or future, for all involve decisions regarding the services of people related to the system's goals. It appears to be this common human element which prompted Xenophon, in the *Socratic Discourses*, to attribute to Socrates the statement that "over whatever a man may preside, he will, if he knows what he needs, and is able to provide it, be a good president, whether he has the direction of a chorus, a family, a city, or an army." It is presumed, therefore, since all social systems involve the services of people whose individual and group behavior springs from essentially similar psychological and sociological processes, that school personnel administration has much in common (a *g*-factor) with personnel administration in government, industry, and the like. At the same time individuals and schools claim their own special characteristics (an *s*-factor). Some contend that the personnel function in schools is basically different from that of industry because of the very different goals of the two types of systems. Similarly, it is also contended that the personnel function in a college or university is very different from that in an elementary–secondary public school system, in part at least, because of different conceptions that personnel have of their relationships with the systems. Thus it seems reasonable to assume areas of commonality among the several fields of general and personnel administration, *g*-factors, together with areas of dissimilarity and uniqueness, *s*-factors. To date, the literature has dealt with common and unique dimensions, typically on a priori grounds. There is a need for more definitive research. It is not yet clear how propositions concerning general dimensions may be related conceptually, if they may, to propositions concerning *s*-factors.

Development of the personnel function will be considered first from the general point of view and then from the special perspective of schools.

EVOLUTION OF THE PERSONNEL FUNCTION. It has already been pointed out that the personnel function has, by definition, been present in all organized human efforts. As a social system becomes larger and the operations more complex, a division of labor becomes more useful; as the available knowledge and skill in a specialization increases, the activity is likely to take on increased professional status. The rapid growth of professions in the nineteenth and twentieth centuries has been an immediate outgrowth of the growing body of knowledge associated with the Scientific Revolution (Carr-Saunders & Wilson, 1933).

As a result of the expansion of knowledge and a growing commitment to professional expertise in specialized fields, the pharmacist branched off from the grocer and the surgeon from the barber. During the nineteenth century a number of new professional specializations arose, including the engineer, city manager, and skilled civil servants.

At the same time urbanization was resulting in the growth of rather large school systems. Under the dual impact of urbanization and professionalization, together with other social changes, it was natural that a more refined division of labor should emerge in the schools. The superintendency and principalship appeared with the first recorded appointments in 1837–38 (Hunt & Pierce, 1958). The stage was then set for the emergence of other specializations within school systems.

The above trends were supported and, in an important way, made possible by other social tendencies. The role of the employee was changing from the feudal conception of status and traditional authority to a newer view of the employee as another human being with social rights and obligations based upon rationally supportable grounds rather than upon traditional status. An increasingly humanitarian view of the employee at the turn of this century led to employee welfare programs in business and industry.

At the same time many business and industrial plants had grown so large that there was evident need for someone who could take charge of organization–employee relationships and help employees to feel part of a total social unit. The literature of the time reflected considerable concern with employee turnover. On the other hand, employees were achieving greater unified action through the development of unions. The average employee was coming to be better educated.

Under the above circumstances it was quite natural that at the turn of the century administrative concern for relations between the employee and the employing organization was taking an active expression, particularly in the appointment of welfare secretaries to head up welfare programs. The more broadly conceived personnel functions began to take shape early in the present century. Literature on personnel began to emerge (e.g. Vreeland, 1906; Bitner, 1919; Fleisher, 1917). Tead (1934) reports that by 1912 there were at least a dozen corporations in which personnel work was designated as a distinct and separate function. The growing significance of the personnel function is reflected in the fact that the May 1916 issue of *The Annals of the American Academy of Political and Social Science* was devoted to "Personnel and Employment Problems in Industrial Management" (Bloomfield & Willets, 1916). The appearance in 1920 of Tead and Metcalf's *Personnel Administration* provided the first major book in the field.

SCHOOL PERSONNEL ADMINISTRATION IN ELEMENTARY–SECONDARY AND HIGHER INSTITUTIONS. At the end of the second decade of this century, as the above trends were taking shape, school personnel needs of school systems were increasing because of the wartime increase in births. It is not surprising, therefore, to find that the personnel function became incorporated into the school's division of labor at about that time. The first reported appointment of a school personnel administrator at the elementary–secondary level was made at Dallas, Texas, in 1919. Several school systems made similar appointments during the 1920's (National Education Association, 1962; Gibson & Hunt, 1965). At the college level, the University of Pennsylvania appointed a personnel officer in 1921 (Gibson & Freedman, 1966).

The number of such positions did not expand rapidly and the depression served further to restrict development. At the same time other trends were emerging, anticipating future development. Scientific management of the early part of this century had emphasized requirements of a task and ways in which they could be met well and efficiently. It was natural to study fatigue; such studies were undertaken at the General Electric Hawthorn plant. Findings from the Hawthorn experiments (e.g. Mayo, 1933; Roethlisberger, 1941; Homans, 1950) pointed to the importance of the perceptions and attitudes of the employee in task performance. As a result, by the 1940's, greatly increased concern for human relationships within the employing organization had emerged. This development gave new impetus to the emergence of the personnel function and the formulation of expectations for the role of the personnel administrator. These new insights were part of an increasing body of knowledge available from the behavioral sciences. Again, after World War II, as after World War I, school enrollments increased sharply and the personnel function assumed increased importance, particularly because more school personnel had to be recruited from a population depleted by lower births in the 1930's and by war fatalities. Studies indicate that more departments of school personnel administration were opened during the decade of 1950–1960 than had been opened during the three decades from 1920–1950 (National Education Association, 1962; Gibson & Hunt, 1965). It has been estimated that by about 1960 there probably were 200 school districts with school personnel administration (National Education Association, 1962). It may very well be that the number is now closer to 500.

One of the early books to focus upon the school personnel function was Lewis's *Personnel Problems of the Teaching Staff* (1925). Probably the first comprehensive treatment in the periodical literature was the "Educational Personnel Administration Number" of *Education* in 1954 (Mones, 1954). Several other writers have given special attention to school personnel administration (Graves, 1932; Davis, 1939; Elsbree & Reutter, 1954; Weber, 1954; Chandler & Petty, 1955; Moore & Walters, 1955; Keppel, 1961; Castetter, 1962; Steffensen, 1963; Fawcett, 1964; Van Zwoll, 1964; Gibson & Hunt, 1965; Harkness, 1965).

As a field of study or performance takes on professional stature, one of the usual concomitants is the emergence of a professional association. As the number of professions grew during the nineteenth century, the number of professional associations also expanded. Among school personnel administrators in K–12 systems the opportunity for an association arose when the American Council on Education called a meeting in May 1940 of representative teacher examiners to consider teacher selection in large school systems. The new organization was called the "National Conference of Teacher Examiners," reflecting the early emphasis upon the hiring stage. In 1945 the word "National" was changed to "American." In 1950 the title was changed to the "American Association of Examiners and Administrators of Educational Personnel" which, in 1959, was changed to the present "American Association of School Personnel Administrators."

In 1951 the Association published *Principles and Procedures of Teacher Selection* and in 1960, *Standards for School Personnel Administration* (American Association of School Personnel Administrators, 1963).

The professional association of personnel administrators in higher institutions is The College and University Personnel Association. This organization came into existence as a result of a meeting called in April 1946 by Donald Dickason, director of nonacademic personnel, University of Illinois. The first annual meeting was held in May 1947 (Harkness, 1965; Pop, 1965). The Association's publication is *The Journal of the College and University Personnel Association*.

In 1958 full-time personnel officers in colleges and universities were reported to number 67; by 1961–62 the number had increased to 101 and it is now in excess of 150 (Pop, 1965). While the duties of personnel officers in higher education have tended to be limited, with emphasis upon supporting service personnel rather than upon instructional personnel (Whitlow, 1960), it appears that the duties have broadened and that present occupants of positions look forward to more general personnel responsibilities in the future (Gibson & Freedman, 1966).

What are the conditions which result in the school personnel function becoming institutionalized into a school personnel office and department? It has already been suggested that increasing size and complexity would tend to extend the division of labor. Chandler and Petty (1955) have suggested that a school system operating more than 150 classroom units and related services might very well consider establishing a personnel office. Other factors include rate of growth of the school system, priority given to personnel tasks, character of the division of labor in the school organization, and perceptions of staff relationships (National Education Association, 1962). The decision to establish a personnel department in a particular system is, therefore, a result of a number of situational forces, each with its pattern of expectations and priorities.

Public elementary–secondary-school personnel offices tended to start with teacher recruitment, examination, and placement and later extended to all personnel (instructional, administrative, and supporting) in all phases (hiring, employment, and withdrawal), often assuming duties previously held by curriculum and business officers. Thus, these personnel officers have tended to function at the level of administrative policy and decision. On the other hand, in colleges and universities the personnel office regularly serves to centralize the personnel function with respect to supporting service personnel only (clerical, custodial, security, etc.). Consequently, the office is often tied to the department of business affairs. Most often the office began with the need to handle fringe benefits (Whitlow, 1960). Lacking direct educational impact, the personnel officer, at the college level, typically does not function at the level of major policy and decision making. The personnel function for instructional personnel in higher education has tended to be highly decentralized with major decision power lodged at the departmental level. Such policy coordination of the personnel function in the academic sector as has taken place has tended to be through the central administrative officer for academic affairs.

Some contend that the personnel function will never be institutionalized in colleges and universities with anything like the centralization that has occurred in public schools. But there are also forces working at the higher level toward greater organizational rationalization of personnel functions and organizational goals. For example, there are the debates regarding the relative importance of teaching and research. The *Annual Report* of the Carnegie Foundation in 1965 sharply delineated some of the conflicts between goals of professors and universities (Gardner, 1965). These matters involve important personnel policy decisions. Just how these instructional personnel functions in colleges and universities will come to be handled administratively and how they will be coordinated, if they are, with other personnel functions seems to be an open question for the future. The very trends which resulted in emergence of the personnel function within this century, namely, increased specialization in knowledge, professionalization, more elaborate division of labor, and rational articulation of individual and organizational goals, converge in sharper relief in colleges and universities than anywhere else, except, perhaps, in research and development departments of business and industry. The rapid expansion in enrollments at the collegiate level in the years immediately ahead will increase greatly the problems of staff recruitment, appointment, and retention. It seems reasonable to expect that personnel officers will prove useful in coping with these tasks as they did in elementary-secondary schools.

The position of school personnel administrators in K–12 systems has emerged under a number of titles. The most frequent are Assistant Superintendent for Personnel and Director of Personnel. The position is normally placed at a level of responsibility next to that of the chief school officer. As in business and industry, a "staff" relationship with the chief officer is typical, indicating an advisory role in decision making and a cooperative role in implementation. The title Director of Personnel is frequently used in colleges and universities.

NATIONAL PERSONNEL POLICY AND ADMINISTRATION. To this point, the personnel function has been viewed as a relationship between an employee and an employing organization. The personnel function may also be viewed in terms of human resources and national educational goals. From this perspective it becomes important to assess the personnel dimensions of the national educational undertaking, the nature of personnel supply and demand, and mechanisms for national policy decision on the personnel function.

The educational establishment in the United States has been, and remains, highly decentralized. It has been contended that hogs and cattle have been more systematically counted than have pupils and school personnel. Rough estimates of the size of the educational establishment have been prepared (Roucek, 1965; Gibson & Hunt, 1965). It appears that about 3 million people are now employed in nearly 25,000 operating public K–12 school districts, almost 20,000 private schools, and over 2,000 colleges and universities. This number has been interpreted as indicating that school personnel account for about 1 out of every 25 persons in the labor force. The greatest part of that 3 million (about 2.5 million) are instructional personnel. With increased enrollments at all levels (elementary, secondary, and higher) anticipated throughout the rest of this century, personnel needs are expected to increase at all levels. There will be differences in rates of growth, however. Personnel needs in colleges and universities will increase at a rapid rate throughout the period. Elementary and secondary needs will fluctuate depending upon birth rates.

Composition of the staff of a school varies as a result of federal, state, and local policies in such matters as district reorganization, guidance services, and social welfare. Illustrative of such shifts in staff composition is the change which took place nationally in the decade between 1951–52 and 1961–62. During that time, as reported in U.S. Office statistics of state school systems (U.S. Department of Health, Education and Welfare, 1955, 1964) the number of school districts was reduced sharply from 44,791 to 31,197 with the average number of school personnel per school district increasing from 28.0 to 71.8. During that period, according to data from the same reports, the composition of the national body of school personnel changed as follows: the proportion of administrative personnel changed from 4.8 percent to 3.8 percent; that of instructional personnel dropped from 77.6 percent to 67.9 percent; and the proportion of supporting personnel increased from 17.6 percent to 28.2 percent. There was a great absolute increase in all three sectors of the school personnel force. The mix was changing. Such a change could be expected as improved education is sought through larger districts with the concomitant increase in needed services —bus, cafeteria, telephone, clerical, etc. This change suggests an important role of supporting service personnel in the improvement of education.

By far the largest part of the nation's school personnel force is in the professional–technical sector of the labor force. The professional–technical sector is an increasing part of the labor force, rising from 4.3 percent in 1900 to 8.6 percent in 1950, and to an anticipated 14.2 percent in 1975 (Gibson & Hunt, 1965). During the first half of this century teachers, as a percent of the professional–technical group, declined from 35.3 percent in 1900 to 22.6 percent in 1950. Thus the major part of the school personnel staff of the nation's schools is being drawn from an increasingly competitive sector of the labor force. This trend will probably continue in the future. It is not yet clear whether the increasing competition at the professional level will have an adverse or positive effect upon the school personnel function. Unless the schools demonstrate a competitive advantage, the impact can be expected to be adverse.

For some years there was an acute teacher shortage because rapidly expanding school enrollments had to be served by school personnel drawn from a population limited by the low birth rates of the thirties. By 1965 that gap had largely been closed. The problem had shifted from one of overall shortage to one of shortages and overages in different fields. Recently a surplus of elementary teachers has been utilized by preparing them to fill shortages at the secondary level. There has been a continuing excess of male physical education teachers and a shortage of female teachers in this field. While there is typically a surplus of social studies teachers, there is often a shortage of language teachers. At the same time that there is a shortage of secondary-school teachers, they constitute one of the major sources from which new college teachers are being recruited.

The rates of growth of demand in different areas will change. For example, at the elementary level the demand increased sharply during the 1950's, has slowed down during the 1960's, and will increase again during the 1970's. Given such a kaleidoscopic situation, it is not surprising that annual reports continue to show discrepancies between supply and demand.

Most projections of supply and demand are extrapolations of past relationships into the future. Certainly a number of variables may change, thus affecting the size and direction of the supply–demand gap. The federal education legislation of 1965 introduced a major change into the educational scene and served to increase again the excess of demand over supply.

In sum, the short range outlook for staffing the nation's schools includes a variety of imbalances between supply and demand. The long-range trend will probably be of more critical importance and will reflect a society that is becoming more dependent upon knowledge and its application, namely, the rapid expansion of the professional–technical sector of the labor force in both absolute and relative terms. This trend suggests an enhanced role for education in the future. At the same time it suggests that there will be increasingly keen competition for professional personnel. In order to cope with such competition, the rewards for service in schools will have to compare favorably with those available in other sectors of the labor force. Whether the presently increasing shortage of teachers is related to a less favorable competitive position of schools is not at all clear. Continuing research on such economic variables can be most helpful.

With increasing competition in the professional sector, some contend that a more conscious approach to personnel policy and planning to meet staff needs is desirable. One suggestion is a national advisory council that would report annually to the President "pointing up current conditions and trends, surveying the implications for public policy, and outlining the alternatives available that would permit an adequate policy and program of action at state and local levels as well as for the federal government" (Gibson & Hunt, 1965).

SOME TRENDS. Trends already exist which can be expected to make real changes in the personnel function in the future. Others appear to be taking shape. Reference has been made to the rapid development of professionalism within the last century and a half. There has been a concomitant trend toward replacement of respect for traditional authority with a reliance upon policy and action that have a rational base in knowledge. Already many changes reflecting that trend have taken place in society at large with respect to freedom of speech and action. Teachers are now expecting a greater voice in decisions on educational policy in schools. There is increasing use of devices for mutual consideration of differences, including grievance and negotiation procedures. These probably are manifestations of the search for a new balance between public welfare and special interests in a society that is becoming more specialized and expert. This search will present administrators generally, including the school personnel administrator, with many novel and challenging problems in the years ahead.

The nation has apparently passed from a period of gross school personnel shortage to one of selective maladjustment between supply and demand. Long-term trends suggest the possibility of continuing and even of aggravated shortages. In an increasingly competitive situation, it is doubtful that such discrepancies can be afforded; more conscious planning for national staff needs is indicated.

Historically, the hiring phase of the personnel function received primary attention over those of employment and withdrawal. With increasing attention in the public schools to relationships of personnel with the system during employment, the focus of attention can be expected to shift from the hiring to the employment stage. At the college level, because of the rapid increase in faculty needs and traditional acceptance of faculty autonomy, the hiring stage will probably assume greater importance, and, where the personnel officer shows that he can be helpful, he will move increasingly into assistance with the task of employing instructional personnel.

School systems at all levels have been growing in size. This growth, combined with the thrust toward more rational decision processes, will tend to bring about more rationally articulated relations and to increase the extent of formally stated policies. Thus, coordination and control within the personnel function can be expected to reflect increasingly the rational relating of means to professionally significant institutional goals. If these trends are valid, then an increasingly significant partnership between employed school personnel and employing boards and their administrative officers is to be anticipated. It may well be that this changed relationship will involve changed conceptions of the employer–employee relationship, particularly in the public domain. It has already been implied that the change to be expected is one that will move away from traditional, status-based, personalistic power toward rational formulation of ends and the means to their accomplishment. In turn, on the basis of the initial definitions, this trend indicates a thrust that will increase the need for more rational and wise personnel administration. The above trends anticipate more critical importance of the function of school personnel administration in the future and an opportunity for an enhanced role for the school personnel profession.

If the trend in administration is toward more rational relating of means to ends in social systems, then research will become increasingly important to administrative decision making. Research concerned with school personnel relations and administration faces the various problems posed by experimentation with humans. Experimental studies in school settings are few and those conducted on the basis of rigorous experimental design are even more difficult to find. Perhaps more important than the techniques of experimental design and statistical analysis is the formulation of hypotheses that are rooted in conceptualizations that somehow offer heuristic promise for the study of the behavior of people in organizations. As the incidence and reliability of deductively derived hypotheses increase, hopefully, the all too frequent "collection of all the facts" will come to be replaced by selective and deliberate attention to events and collection of data. Without ideas to give them meaning, data are dumb and blind. The critical need is for conceptualizations which can give broader meaning to research and provide a more firm base for rational formulation of courses of action with respect to personnel needs.

R. Oliver Gibson
State University of New York
At Buffalo

References

American Association of School Personnel Administrators. *Standards for School Personnel Administration.* The Association, 1960.

American Association of School Personnel Administrators. *Proceedings of the Twenty-fifth Annual Conference. American Association of School Personnel Administrators.* The Association, 1963.

Bitner, L. S. "Personnel Department Organization." *Ind Manag* 58:502–4; 1919.

Bloomfield, Meyer, and Willits, Joseph H. (Eds.) "Personnel and Employment Problems in Industrial Management." *Annals of the AAPSS* 65: 1916. 326p.

Carr-Saunders, A. M., and Wilson, P. A. *The Professions.* Oxford U Press, 1933.

Castetter, William B. *Administering the School Personnel Program.* Macmillan, 1962.

Chandler, B. J., and Petty, Paul V. *Personnel Management in School Administration.* World Book Company, 1955.

Davis, Hazel. *Personnel Administration.* Teachers Col, Columbia U, 1939.

Elsbree, Willard S., and Reutter, E. Edmund, Jr. *Staff Personnel in the Public Schools.* Prentice-Hall, 1954.

Fawcett, Claude W. *School Personnel Administration.* Macmillan, 1964.

Fleisher, Alexander. "Welfare Service for Employees." *Annals of the AAPSS* 69: 50–7; 1917.

Gardner, John W. "The Antileadership Vaccine." In *Annual Report.* Carnegie, 1965.

Gibson, R. Oliver, and Freedman, Allan. "Performance of Personnel Administrators in Colleges and Universities." 1966. (Mimeographed.)

Gibson, R. Oliver, and Hunt, Herold C. *The School Personnel Administrator.* Houghton, 1965.

Graves, Frank Pierrepont. *The Administration of American Education—With Special Reference to Personnel Factors.* Macmillan, 1932.

Harkness, Charles A. *College Staff Personnel Administration.* College and University Personnel Association, 1965.

Homans, George C. *The Human Group.* Harcourt, 1950.

Hunt, Herold C., and Pierce, Paul R. *The Practice of School Administration.* Houghton, 1958.

Keppel, Francis. *Personnel Policies for Public Education.* U Pittsburgh Press, 1961.

Lewis, Ervin Eugene. *Personnel Problems of the Teaching Staff.* Century, 1925.

Mayo, Elton. *The Human Problems of Industrial Civilization.* Macmillan, 1933.

Mones, Leon. (Ed.) "Educational Personnel Administration Number." *Ed* 75: No. 4; 1954.

Moore, Harold E., and Walters, Newell B. *Personnel Administration in Education.* Harper, 1955.

National Education Association, Research Division. *The Public School Personnel Administrator.* Research Monograph 1962—MI, The Association 1962.

Pop, Daniel William. *Professional Characteristics of The College and University Non-academic Personnel Director.* Doctoral dissertation, U Nebraska, 1965.

Roethlisberger, F. J. *Management and Morale.* Harvard U Press, 1941.

Roucek, Joseph S. "The Role of Educational Institutions with Special Reference to Highly Industrialized Areas." In Bereday, George Z. F., and Lauwerys, Joseph A. *The Education Explosion.* Harcourt. 1965. p. 141.

Steffensen, James P. *Staff Personnel Administration.* HEW, GPO, 1963.

Tead, Ordway. "Personnel Administration." In Seligman, Edwin B. A., and Johnson, Alvin (Eds.) *Encyclopedia of the Social Sciences.* Macmillan, 1934. p. 88.

Tead, Ordway, and Metcalf, Henry C. *Personnel Administration.* McGraw-Hill, 1920.

U.S. Department of Health, Education and Welfare. "Statistics of State School Systems: Organization, Staff, Pupils, and Finances, 1951–52." In *Biennial Survey of Education in the United States, 1951–52.* GPO, 1955.

U.S. Department of Health, Education, and Welfare. *Statistics of State School Systems, 1961–62.* GPO, 1964.

Van Zwoll, James A. *School Personnel Administration.* Appleton, 1964.

Vreeland, H. H. "Relations Between Employer and Employee." *Annals of the AAPSS* 27:507–9; 1906.

Weber, Clarence A. *Personnel Problems of School Administrators.* McGraw-Hill, 1954.

Whitlow, Edward Wesley. *Status of Faculty-Administration Personnel Services in American Higher Education and Its Development in Selected Institutions.* Doctoral dissertation, Cornell U, 1960.

SCIENCE EDUCATION

Smith and Anderson (1960), in a comprehensive survey of benchmarks in science education, point out that the history of science instruction in American schools has proceeded in a relatively unbroken line from the middle of the nineteenth century to the present. It has moved from lonely pleas for toleration and acceptance of science in the curriculum by men such as Herbert Spencer and Thomas Huxley to the currently insistent and widespread demand for an ever-increasing role for science in the schools in order to equip youngsters adequately for life in the late twentieth century. In general, enrollments have reflected this demand. Biology and chemistry registrations (though not physics) continue to rise steeply in secondary schools (Woodburn & Obourn, 1965). Science has become a standard feature of the elementary school curriculum.

PRECOLLEGE SCIENCE EDUCATION. Some Antecedents of Current Research. Until World War II, systematic analysis and research in science education focused primarily on definition of objectives. Hurd's (1949, 1954, 1961) studies reveal that delineation of the purposes for science teaching dominated scholarly discussion in the field for five decades. He infers from this extended period of establishing a conceptual base for science teaching that there was considerable ferment about basic assumptions—a situation not conducive to empirical investigations.

Woodburn and Obourn (1965) and Underhill (1941) describe science education in American schools during the eighteenth and nineteenth centuries by identifying the major distinctive periods and highlighting significant reports. The development of high school science on a broad scale dates from 1872, when Harvard College began accepting science courses for college entrance. The recommendations of the NEA's Committee of Ten (1893) influenced science teaching further by promulgating standards that were accepted until the 1920's. For the elementary grades, a course in nature study, stressing botany and zoology, was advocated. Year-long courses in botany, zoology, physics, and chemistry were suggested for the secondary school. This committee also recommended the teaching of physiology and hygiene.

Later a formal and well-defined pattern based on extensive discussion of the Committee of Ten's report was enunciated for high schools by the NEA's Committee on College Entrance Requirements (1899): physical geography for the first year, biology for the second, physics for the third, and chemistry for the fourth. Nature study was to be the science component for the elementary school grades. At the secondary school level, each course was to meet at least four periods per week. Two "exercises" per week were recommended for the nature study program.

The period from 1900 to 1930 was characterized, then, by a strong college-preparatory emphasis for the secondary school program. This focus was strengthened by reports such as those issued by the NEA's Commission on the Reorganization of Secondary Education (1918) and its Subcommittee on the Teaching of Science (Caldwell & others, 1920). The elementary school curriculum in nature study had as a primary purpose the inculcation of certain aesthetic values and moral commitments. The movement grew largely as a reaction to problems of urbanization and drew its theoretical base from leaders at colleges of agriculture, particularly the one at Cornell University. A study of nature was seen as a means of checking the population flow to the cities. Nature study was to instill a love of plants and animals such that people would want to remain on farms and in small towns. Bailey (1909), the leading spokesman for the movement, emphatically stressed the distinction between science and nature study. "Nature Study is not science. It is not knowledge. It is not facts. It is spirit. It is an attitude of mind."

The influence of the Nature Study movement was widely felt because of its base in agriculture. State of New York appropriations were used to publish and distribute bulletins to teachers. Comstock (1931) describes the New York system, in which the head of the agricultural extension program in the state decreed in the late 1890's that the basis for effective agriculture was nature study. He suggested that children should be instructed in this subject in all communities where farmers' institutes were conducted.

The period from 1925 to 1935 saw a shift in emphasis in the aims for science education at all precollege levels. Objectives related to social utility began to receive attention. In an influential study at the elementary level, Craig (1927) suggested that an understanding of the impact of science on daily life should be a primary purpose of science instruction. Science and technology seemed to be affecting human patterns markedly; the schools should accent the nature of this influence. The study had broad effects on the development of subsequent curricula and textbooks in science.

At about the same time, plans were formulated that resulted in the publication of the thirty-first NSSE yearbook (National Society for the Study of Education, 1932). This yearbook took a strong stance against nature study, which was seen as an overly sentimentalized, anthropomorphic, nonsystematic approach to science. Craig's (1927) ideas were given the status of the sanctioned approach. The document advocated stressing generalizations in science rather than facts. It attempted to sketch an integrated approach to secondary school science, an approach centered around a few dozen pervasive principles identified in studies such as those by Downing (1928) and Robertson (1935). This document crystallized prevalent thought about the field at all instructional levels. Writers of the NSSE yearbook were key individuals in science education who trained the leaders in the field. Their statement stood as the dominant pronouncement until the late 1950's.

The NSSE yearbook was followed by the PEA's (Progressive Education Association, 1938) report of its Committee on the Function of Science in General Education, which further accented the need for a science program based on factors of social utility. However, the report also made a strong plea for stressing science because the techniques of this discipline were thought to be applicable in solving social problems. In fact, a major feature of science instruction of this period began to be a growing commitment to objectives related to "scientific method" and "problem solving." Committee reports and considerable research were directed toward definition of this goal in operational terms and demonstrations of the superiority of "problem solving" over other, more expository, teaching methods. Noll (1939) examined lists of science objectives from a variety of sources and reported that ability to use the scientific method ranked fifth in frequency of mention on a list of twelve sets of objectives.

The concept of scientific method stressed during this period leaned heavily on an interpretation of the writings of Dewey (1933). The concept postulated scientific method as a series of steps: (1) definition of the problem, (2) collection of data, (3) formulation of a hypothesis, (4) testing the hypothesis, (5) drawing a conclusion, and (6) applying the conclusion. Studies during the 1930's and 1940's frequently examined one or all of these steps and selected effects of their implementation in the classroom. A summary of such studies was reported by Barnard (1953).

The stress on problem solving, as well as the teaching of broad principles of science, was reinforced by the forty-sixth NSSE yearbook (National Society for the Study of Education, 1947). This work relied heavily on the above-cited reports of the preceding decade. It may be viewed as a refinement and elaboration of the earlier statements. Objectives were categorized as relating to facts, to concepts, to understanding of principles, to skills, to problem solving, to attitudes, to appreciations, and to interests.

The period from 1930 to about 1955 may be viewed as one of consolidation and refinement of a viewpoint about science education that placed considerable stress on the social utility of the subject. Science should be taught to enable students to utilize the knowledge in daily living. Twentieth-century children are surrounded by manifestations of science and the products of science. The schools should make the world of science and technology comprehensible to them. It was felt that accretion of knowledge was occurring so rapidly as to make it impossible for schools to cope with more than a small fraction of the information. Emphasis was placed, therefore, on unifying principles selected because of their potential for explicating the social utility of the subject and on the methodology of science.

Recent Trends. A negative reaction to the social-utility approach began to be articulated in the early 1950's, first in mathematics then in science. The initial criticism came primarily from academicians, who pointed out that programs based on uses of science in daily life often were accurate but could be characterized by critics as trivial with respect to concepts of science and mathematics considered fundamental by the scientists. The point was made that the ideas taught in school compounded the confusion in the minds of most people between science and the fruits of science, between science and technology. It was suggested that the two endeavors, science and technology, are distinct and that courses carrying a "science" designation should teach science. Beberman (1958), writing about mathematics, was one of the first to enunciate the point of view that began to evolve.

This position with respect to science education was developed first by a group centered in the Boston area, composed largely of physicists from Harvard and the Massachusetts Institute of Technology. This group, the Physical Science Study Committee, began to develop a high school course in physics based upon principles identified by research physicists (Finlay, 1962). By the late 1950's the National Science Foundation (1962) was supporting similar efforts in high school biology, high school chemistry, elementary school science, and several other fields.

A distinguishing characteristic of the wave of curriculum reform in science generated in the late 1950's was the fact that academic scientists were involved centrally in curriculum development activities. Inasmuch as the resulting shift in emphasis was relatively dramatic, the early 1960's represented another period in which empirical research was submerged beneath more global questions. During the closing stages of the social utility emphasis in science education, in the 1950's, research began to appear in increased quantity partly because basic assumptions about the purposes of science teaching were generally accepted. But with the revolution in purposes for teaching science, most academically oriented science educationists became involved in assessing the feasibility of the novel approaches developed in the new programs or in reexamining prevalent theory in the field. Atkin (1961) and Scott (1962), for example, reported evidence indicating the acceptability to teachers and children of the approach taken in the NSF-supported projects. The need for feasibility studies gradually diminished because of the growing acceptance of the new orientation.

The American Association for the Advancement of Science (Hall & others, 1961) sponsored a major study designed to review the status of elementary school science and to formulate a plan for improvements. Conferences were held in three different regions, with each conference being attended by scientists, psychologists, teachers, school supervisors, and science educationists. In addition to advocating the merit of major focus on problems of elementary school science education, this report stressed that "cognitive processes" be given special emphasis at the elementary school level.

Thus the report highlighted an issue in science education which began to assume considerable importance: the relative stress to be given to "content" goals and "process" goals. In one approach, the content of a discipline as it is viewed by academicians is the primary source of innovation. Here the basic principles underlying the field are identified by scientists in an attempt to underscore the conceptual unity of a subject and counteract what has been perceived as the triviality of the content taught previously. An underlying assumption of this viewpoint is that there are a relatively small number of pervasive ideas within any discipline. If one can identify these ideas, one has a basis for developing a stable program for students below the college level.

In the "process" approach, as reported by Gagné (1966), the most basic attribute of science, particularly for young learners, is the method by which scientists engage in their investigations. Scientists observe. They measure. They classify. They infer. "Process skills" are generalizable over many science fields. Major efforts should be given to the identification of these skills and their inclusion in school programs. This viewpoint is close to the one accepted during the 1930's; however, in its more recent form, scientists have played a more prominent role in identification and description of the methods used in scientific investigation. During the 1930's, few scientists displayed interest in curriculum construction below the college level.

Suchman (1961), Atkin and Karplus (1962), Butts (1963), Heathers (1961), and others have reported studies which seem to indicate that content approaches, process approaches, or combinations of the two can serve as the basis for a curriculum program. These divergent points of emphasis, however, are based ultimately on value determinations. Most schools during the 1960's seem to be developing or accepting programs that stress both facets of science—the conceptual aspects and the methodological aspects; it is probably impossible as well as undesirable to separate the two completely.

Research on Teaching Science. Watson (1963) has reported a comprehensive survey of research on classroom instruction in science. He was particularly interested in investigations of possible relationships between the behavior of science teachers and the behavior of science students over an extensive range of outcomes, pointing out that the broad objectives for science teaching are seldom explicated in research conducted in a classroom context. He cited studies such as those by Cogan (1958) and Reed (1961) as two approaches which have made appropriate use of pupils' descriptions of teacher behavior in order to understand relationships between the two and advocated increased use of such research procedures. (Cogan reported that teacher characteristics categorized as "warm or friendly" and "well-organized" seemed to have positive effects on pupil performance.) Watson concluded with an additional plea for a logical and psychological analysis of the behavior of teachers that might be predictable from their personal traits and value systems. Such analyses might be used ultimately to assess some of the resulting effects on children.

Research and systematic analysis in science education seem to be divided between exploratory and speculative examinations of new programs, in which frameworks for inquiry are as yet poorly defined, and complex investigations utilizing highly refined experimental techniques. Studies in the former category are sometimes classified as developmental; they are not yet widely accepted in the field, and their relationship to construction of theory is both unproved and unclear. Studies in the latter category are exemplified by investigators who rely heavily, as Cooley (1961) suggests they do, on procedures developed in the behavioral sciences. Such studies keep apace of current developments in experimental design but are usually highly restricted in their application. They focus on characteristics and events that are most readily measured, but the variables that are most readily measured are not necessarily those most relevant to the total educational context. Belanger (1964) skillfully documents examples of emerging research patterns in science education but, in doing so, also highlights the need for commensurate construction of theory to avoid the risk of testing insignificant hypotheses.

An acceptable style of discourse is needed to broaden and deepen the exploratory and developmental types of analysis in science education. Significant variables must be identified and measured to increase the importance of highly refined experimental studies. Thus the field seems to require major innovations on two distinctive fronts, and at a period in educational research when the relationship between the two approaches remains fuzzy.

COLLEGE-LEVEL SCIENCE EDUCATION. Objectives. The report of the Harvard Committee on Objectives of General Education in a Free Society (1945) analyzed the characteristics of two broad, integrative courses it considered desirable: one in the physical sciences and one in the biological sciences. The objectives proposed were an analysis of science as a method of formal inquiry and a comparison of this with other "modes of thought"; a comparison of the structures and investigative strategies of individual sciences; the relations of science with human society; and the history of science in relation to that of the human being as a social and political animal. The report denied the validity of systematic factual surveys. It emphasized the broad methodological aspects of the scientific enterprise and science as a part of human history and advancement. In short, it proposed an integrative and humanistic bias for college-level general education in science. This 1945 report stimulated a great deal of rethinking of the objectives of science teaching at the college level and added impetus to the development of general education courses.

Objectives as such, however, have not formed a fruitful area of investigation. Objectives represent value judgments and, as such, are beyond the scope of research except in a normative, historical, or philosophical sense. One can count noses to determine what objectives are preferred; or one can determine what is emphasized in instruction and deduce implied objectives from what goes on. Indeed, both have been done, and a representative example is the study of Hopka (1958), in which 45 Lutheran colleges and universities were studied to determine the nature of their physical science offerings to pretheology students. Prevailing practices were compared with practices desired by administrators, instructors, and Lutheran pastors. Thirty-six statements of objectives were studied in terms of desirable emphasis by 67 instructors of physical science, 38 college administrators, and a randomized sample of 183 pastors. There was general agreement on the objectives, with the science instructors leaning more toward emphasis on the understanding of theories and laws, the administrators favoring social implications, and the pastors desiring closer integration of science with Biblical statements. "A feeling of reverence toward the Creator was one attitude rated high by all respondents." This study is of interest for two reasons. One, it typifies a common procedure whereby objectives are determined by the judgment process. Two, it may illustrate the important point that objectives so arrived at are simply representations of the value judgments of a sample population of a universe of men of a particular sort—in this case instructors, administrators, and pastors of one religous denomination. Quite different objectives might conceivably emerge if the population sampled were that of research scientists, say, or engineers. Such studies raise the question of whose judgments are to be sought if our concern is for general education.

A slightly different procedure is to use a jury of "experts" to rank or otherwise determine the importance of individual items from a set of generalizations and principles. Fribourgh (1957) had a jury of biologists study a list of 61 such principles and generalizations in order to determine which were essential for general education and which were essential for a further study of biology. Another jury of junior-college biology teachers judged the appropriateness of each item for junior-college biology courses. This study is essentially no different from that of Hopka just cited, although Fribourgh narrowed his jury's choice to principles of biology. Differences in the nature of the judging groups inevitably result in differences in the objectives valued. For example, principles in such areas as cytology, histology, physiology, reproduction, heredity, and evolution were recommended in the Fribourgh study, which was concluded by the development of a course of study based on 50 principles finally recommended for junior-college biology.

Courses and Programs. The place of general education science courses at the college level has long been and remains a matter of controversy. As was the case for objectives, decisions on whether to offer specially designed courses for general education purposes and on the content and organization of such courses if offered are, fundamentally, value judgments. And, as might be expected, a number of investigations have sought to determine the status of such courses, trends in the number of institutions providing them, and judgments on whether such courses should be offered or whether standard introductory science courses provide a more satisfactory education for the student who does not intend to major in a science field.

One of the earlier studies of the status of general education science courses was conducted by Bullington (1949). Major findings of this investigation were that more than half of the four-year colleges and universities in the United States offered some kind of general education science courses; the most commonly offered program consisted of two separate courses, one in the biological sciences and one in the physical sciences; and that a survey of subject matter was the most common approach, with a block-and-gap approach, a study of selected problems, and a historical approach, respectively, the next most popular methods of organizing the courses. Bullington (1952) conducted another study a few years later and found that an increasing number of institutions were offering survey courses.

On the other hand, Badgley (1956) found that survey courses were far from common. His study utilized a questionnaire to determine the nature of general studies curricula in science and mathematics throughout the United States. His sample involved 140 institutions, and 80 percent of these responded. Many institutions had adopted a two-year general education core, but the great majority required basic introductory courses in specific science fields for specialists and science majors. Most respondents considered that integration was provided by attention to interrelations within a given subject matter and among fields. This was commonly accomplished by means of a prescribed core of liberal arts courses, with 12 semester hours of such work being a common requirement for general education purposes. Although a few integrated courses were used, these were restricted to small basic cores in general studies programs.

The *Advanced Placement Program: Course Descriptions, 1964–66* issued by the College Entrance Examination Board (1966) contains a description designed to reflect what is taught in introductory college biology courses. This description was based on college courses in 1953, however, and was thought to be out-of-date in terms of changing college biology curricula. This led to a detailed survey of 32 leading college introductory courses in biology, sponsored by the CEEB Committee of Examiners for the Advanced Placement Examination in Biology. The survey was conducted through interviews, during which a questionnaire was administered to a sample of instructors of introductory biology courses at the 32 colleges and universities, chosen on the basis of various criteria including geographical spread. One of the criteria was that of securing a wide range of types of programs rather than a random group. Reported by Moore (1965), this survey provides a useful picture of the organization and content of such courses in 1962–63. The major findings of the study included the following: (1) there is great variation of content, with two-thirds of the respondents reporting recent changes with less phylogeny and more physiology and cellular and molecular biology; (2) introductory biology courses throughout the nation are in a state of flux; (3) of the 32 colleges sampled, 15 were giving a single introductory course, 8 were giving two courses, 6 were giving three, 3 were giving four courses, and 28 of the colleges were providing at least one course that combined botany and zoology; (4) the courses are organized around such topics as molecular biology and physiology and use such general themes as evolution and ecology in 29 of the institutions surveyed; and (5) quantitative experimental work is emphasized in the laboratory, and taxonomic work and drawing has been deemphasized.

One approach to the question of whether regular academic introductory courses or specially designed general education courses offer better education is to compare students from each group of courses on some criterion such as test results. The difficulty, of course, is that the objectives of instruction in general education courses may be different from those in standard liberal arts courses. One such study is that of Tuckman and Etkin (1961), who compared the science proficiency of college graduates who had taken a sequence of four one-semester general education courses (physics, chemistry, biology, astronomy and geology) with that of academically matched graduates who had elected the regular department science courses. Scores on the Graduate Record Examination were used as the measure of science proficiency. The results showed no significant difference between the two groups in mean scores for physics, chemistry, and biology. It should be noted, however, that the sample was small, with only 24 matched pairs, and that the general education science sequence was organized by discipline rather than on the basis of integrative elements which cut across subject fields.

Yet another approach is to analyze a course or program against some criterion such as a prestigious report of recommendations. Davis (1962) studied the introductory biology programs in the 30 state-supported junior colleges of Texas and compared them with the *Recommendations on Undergraduate Curricula in the Biological Sciences*, which was developed under the auspices of the National Academy of Science and the National Research Council (n.d.). He found that these introductory programs were typically a botany-zoology combination, that the teaching methods consisted largely of specific descriptions, that the laboratory work involved mainly dissections and drawings of preserved specimens, and that there was a "vast discrepancy between the program found in Texas junior colleges and the one recommended by the National Research Council."

Few studies have been reported in which the investigator undertakes to modify the course with clear aims in mind and then to evaluate the course in terms of these explicit objectives. One such study is that of Moore and Henderson (1957), who used various objective instruments and pre- and posttest Likert-type attitude scales to measure course results and student and staff ratings of a portion of a two-year general education physical science course. The purpose of the study was to evaluate a reorientation of the course in terms of the objective of providing students with an understanding and appreciation of the nature and role of science in American culture. Gain in this main objective was demonstrated at the 5 percent level of confidence by use of the T test. Student and staff anonymous evaluation of the revised course showed general satisfaction.

Sandler (1961) developed an integrated course in physics and mathematics on the basis of physics principles and the related mathematical concepts and skills. He then compared this integrated course with separate courses in the two subjects in terms of knowledge of physics facts and principles, problem-solving ability in the mathematics involved in physics, knowledge of mathematical concepts and terms, and ability to solve new problems in mathematics. A group of 36 freshmen were taught in each course and were tested on the dimensions indicated above. Significant differences in favor of the students in the integrated class were found with respect to knowledge of physics facts and principles and their ability to solve both physics and mathematics problems. No significant difference was found with respect to knowledge of mathematical terms and concepts,

In general, it may be said that research has brought us no nearer than we were twenty years ago to agreement on what courses and programs should serve the purposes of general education in science at the college level. The last two studies cited bear additional witness to this fact.

As a part of a broader study which included science requirements for elementary school and high school science teachers, Raksaboldej (1961) found that there was no general agreement on the objectives and practices of general education science courses among 25 state teachers colleges representing all of the five accrediting regions of the United States. Webster (1958) also found a great diversity of opinion and practices in his study of science in general education at the Oklahoma state colleges. Weaknesses he discerned included a lack of integration both among subject areas and within them. Another weakness reported was a general lack of a philosophy favorable to general education science courses among the instructors teaching such courses. He concluded that these two weaknesses are partly a result of the fact that the instructors were trained as specialists rather than for general education instruction.

Instructional Processes and Strategies. Kruglak has conducted a number of carefully designed investigations of teaching techniques in college physics and has compared the results of instruction employing individual laboratory work with that of instruction by lecture demonstrations and that of instruction with neither demonstrations nor laboratory work (Kruglak, 1951, 1952a, 1952b, 1953, 1954, 1955). In general, these studies show that individual laboratory work does not significantly affect the learning of facts and principles or the ability of students to apply them in terms of the tests that were used. As would be expected, however, individual laboratory work provides manipulatory skills and understanding of the use of laboratory equipment that are not developed by teacher demonstrations or other nonlaboratory strategies. In one of his studies, Kruglak (1952b) included an investigation of the interaction of instructors and the methods (conventional versus demonstration) being analyzed. Analysis of covariance was used to control scholastic ability, previous knowledge of physics, and mathematical ability of the students. Kruglak's studies are technically excellent, and the fact that, as a whole, little difference in learning (except for laboratory skills) seems to result from the instructional approaches used may only indicate the complexity of research into methodology and the probable existence of multiple and uncontrolled variables.

It is probable that well over 100 studies have been made which attempt to compare the results of lecture demonstrations with those of individual laboratory work. Most of these inquiries have been carried out at the secondary level, but a number have been done at the college level. Most have found no significant differences in terms of the instruments and measures used; some have shown a superiority of the lecture demonstration technique, and some have shown individual laboratory work to be superior. Why there have been such variations in results is an open question. It is clear that many of these studies have been poorly designed. It is equally clear that the instruments and evaluative techniques employed have varied in nature and reliability, as well as in what was assessed and with what emphasis. In any event, these studies have left us with little light on the possible superiority of one method over the other even in terms of clearly specified instructional objectives.

The promotion of critical thinking has been the subject of many investigations at the college level. The studies reported below are representative. Rickert (1961) organized a one-semester experimental physical science course designed to emphasize the analysis of problems, the examination of assumptions, the collection and organization of data, and the testing of hypotheses. Study guides and references provided the required information for the course, and class sessions were devoted to analytical activities. Gains in critical thinking ability were determined by pre- and post-course application of the American Council on Education's Test of Critical Thinking, Form G (1952). Twenty-two randomly selected students from the experimental course were compared with the same number of students from a general physics course and also from a survey physical science course. Gains in critical thinking of the experimental group were superior to those in the other two groups, and these gains were significant at the 5 percent level of confidence.

In another study on the development of critical thinking, Montague (1963) utilized a general-education-oriented freshman chemistry course in which nine laboratory sections were experimental and nine served as controls. Both students and instructors were randomly assigned. The experimental sections were provided with problem-solving experiences that involved open-ended experiments over a period of 10 weeks. The control sections performed the customary laboratory manual experiments. Burmester's (1951) test for inductive aspects of scientific thinking was used as a pre- and posttest and Watson and Glaser's (n.d.) *Critical Thinking Appraisal* was given only as a posttest. A laboratory performance test was also used. Montague found that ability to solve problems in an actual laboratory situation was significantly greater for the experimental group; there was no significant difference between the group gains as measured by the Burmester test; and ability to think critically about everyday problems as measured by the Watson-Glaser test was significantly greater for the experimental group.

Mason (1951) investigated the relative effectiveness of a "scientific thinking method" and a descriptive method of teaching biological science in terms of gains in scientific thinking. The scientific-thinking approach was directed toward acquisition of the methods and attitudes of science in both the lecture and the laboratory periods. Only facts and principles were stressed in the descriptive approach, and the laboratory sessions consisted essentially of applications in which the instructor presented facts, performed the demonstrations, and drew the conclusions for the students. Tests were employed which measured factual information, thinking ability, and scientific attitudes. Scores were treated by analysis of variance and covariance with two independent variables. The descriptive-method lectures were found to be the more effective in teaching factual information over spans of one and two terms, but after three terms the two methods were found equally effective. The scientific-thinking-approach lectures were more effective in teaching scientific attitudes. The laboratories of the two methods were equally effective with respect to the acquisition of factual information and the development of scientific attitudes. However, the scientific-method approach in laboratory work was more effective in teaching certain abilities associated with scientific thinking.

Montean (1959) studied the effectiveness of discussion groups as an instructional device for increasing the ability of students to think critically. Subjects of the investigation were students in experimental and control sections of one-semester courses in general chemistry and in general education physical science. Test results showed that students of median and low mental ability in the experimental classes (in which "discussion groups" was the independent variable) achieved a gain significantly greater than that of their intellectual peers in the control classes. High-ability students in the experimental general science group showed significantly greater gains than did students of similar mental ability in the control classes, but no significant differences were found in gains of high-ability students in general chemistry. Among other results of the study, it was found that a significant difference favoring the experimental class in general science existed with regard to "understanding-type" items but that no significant difference existed for "recall-type" items.

Stubbs (1958) found the inductive method of teaching general chemistry to be more effective than the deductive method for training students in the skillful use of scientific method, for developing critical thinking, and in teaching fundamental concepts and general chemical knowledge.

A great deal of attention has been paid to inductive and other heuristic approaches in the teaching of science, but relatively few studies of competence have been carried out to determine if the purported advantages are real and significant. Schefler (1965) compared an inductive laboratory approach to the teaching of genetics in a course in freshman biology with a traditional lecture and illustrative laboratory approach. From the sampling population of some 800 students who were taking the course, 409 students constituted a random sample. These 409 students formed four instructional groups. Two instructors taught two laboratory sections each, one with an inductive and one with a traditional approach. Tested were knowledge of the facts and principles of genetics, understanding of the nature and process of science, interest in science, and attitudes toward science and scientists. Published tests and instruments were employed for all these measures, except for subject-matter knowledge, in which a genetics test developed by the investigator was used. Concepts were introduced to the two experimental groups by a discovery technique, and the lecture periods following the laboratory were used for group discussions of the laboratory data and their implications. The control groups were introduced to the same concepts by lecture, and the laboratory work that followed was illustrative and merely confirmed the concepts and basic facts and principles. All four groups were pretested with the criterion instruments and then were posttested at the end of the 10-week unit. Analysis of covariance was employed. In none of the measures employed was there a significant difference between the experimental and the control groups. Interestingly, the students of one instructor did significantly better than the students of the other instructor, regardless of method, on the test of subject matter. Thus, in this study, as is probable in many studies of this nature, the variable of teacher difference may be of greater moment than method difference. More research is clearly needed on the effect of teacher personality and style, as well as on their control as a variable element in studies of achievement and attitudes.

Perhaps it is the grossness of many studies that precludes the likelihood of dependable results. The classical experimental study which compares a broad experimental approach with a control method involves multiple variables which inevitably intrude and make the results meaningless or uncertain, whatever they may show statistically. Relatively few studies undertake to investigate a single and limited variable in which uncontrolled, and usually unrecognized, other variables have less likelihood of affecting the results. One such study was that of Macri (1963), who tested the effectiveness of the Atomic Orbital Board as a teaching aid. An experimental group of 125 students was taught atomic structure by use of the orbital-board technique in a general physical science course. A control group of 125 was taught through use of the blackboard. A test was constructed and shown to have a reliability coefficient of .82. It purported to measure understanding of the principles of atomic structure, concepts related to atomic structure, and ability to solve problems related to atomic structure. Utilizing the F technique in the analysis of covariance, Macri found a statistically significant difference between the mean gains achieved by each group, which favored three of the Atomic Orbital Board subgroups at the 1 percent level and the fourth subgroup at the 5 percent level of confidence.

Televised instruction and programmed education have been the subjects of several investigations. The three studies cited below are illustrative. Abrams (1961) studied the relative effectiveness of demonstrations, laboratory, demonstrations combined with laboratory, group discussions, lectures, and correspondence work as supplements to a televised course in physics during two semesters. He collected data from 27 colleges that used the course the first semester and from 24 the second semester. None of the methods of supplementation significantly increased the ability to solve problems or knowledge of physics facts and principles over that of students who had received no supplementary treatment. Syrocki and Wallin (1962) compared the results of teaching general biology by closed-circuit television with conventional instruction and found no significant differences among any of their measures. Geller (1963) compared the effectiveness of a linear teaching machine program unassisted by a teacher with the traditional lecture-demonstration procedure. Achievement in facts and principles of organic chemistry in first-year college chemistry was equal for both groups, and an equal percentage of students instructed by each method was interested in further study. However, the students instructed by machine found the subject more superficial and less interesting than did the students in the conventional program, and most of the machine treatment students did not like the method. The investigator demonstrated that students can learn the fundamentals of organic chemistry without a teacher, thus freeing an instructor's time for the "speculative leisurely teaching" desirable for analysis, structural theory, and so forth.

Kuhnen (1960) investigated the field trip in general botany as compared with traditional laboratory work, in terms of gain in knowledge, ability to apply principles, and increase in interest. The experiment ran for a period of three spring sessions of six weeks each, and a rotation technique was employed in which each of the 112 students formed an experimental group for three weeks and a control group for three weeks. Tests of information and application of principles were given as pre- and posttests, and a questionnaire was employed to determine increase in interest and viewpoints on the two methods each student had experienced. Results indicated that neither method contributed importantly to the ability to apply principles; gains in knowledge favored the laboratory group; and the questionnaire responses showed that students felt both methods should be included in a course in general botany, since each approach provided advantages not found in the other. Hatcher (1957) found no statistically significant differences in knowledge and understanding, in ability to understand and interpret scientific information from popular periodicals, or in ability to "apply the scientific approach" in judging statements of purported facts among three groups of students in a general education science class. The experimental treatments were class recitation, group discussion, and individual consultation.

Robinson (1963) studied the effect of using science articles in a physical science course. The experimental group skipped some of the regular text study in favor of 15 articles, mostly from *Scientific American*, and these constituted the basis of class discussions. The control group studied only the text. Robinson found that the use of the articles promoted "science understanding" (how discoveries are made and how they affect people's lives and beliefs), but not "science reasoning" (forming hypotheses and drawing valid conclusions). Dearden (1962) evaluated four methods of teaching a general biology course: (1) individual laboratory work, (2) demonstration laboratory work, (3) the submission by the student of weekly workbook exercises, and (4) a term paper on a selected biological topic. All students attended the same type of lecture sessions. Nine hundred twenty-four students, randomly assigned to these treatments, were given pre- and posttests on biological attitudes, knowledge, and scientific thinking. The

T tests for correlated variances more consistently showed increased final test variances for the individual laboratory groups, suggesting that this method allows more adequately for individual differences in ability. But the results in general showed no significant superiority of any treatment group as measured by the tests employed.

Kruglak has been one of the most careful, persistent, and knowledgeable investigators of teaching strategies and techniques in physical science at the college level. His study of achievement in general physics as a function of the number of laboratory partners working together supports these points and is revealing of the more reflective approach to research. Kruglak and Goodwin (1955) designed and carried out an investigation at the U.S. Naval Academy on the specific question of the influence of the number of laboratory partners on instructional outcomes. They measured achievement by scores on a multiple-choice laboratory test, a performance test, and in terms of the laboratory grade as assigned by the instructors. The data were analyzed by means of the variance and covariance methods and the following results were reported: no significant difference between the means of the two tests could be ascribed to the instructors or the methods (single work in the laboratory, in pairs, and in quartets). Significant differences were found in the means of the laboratory grades in favor of the quartet grouping. Three-fourths of the 16 instructors favored the pair method, with only one instructor choosing the quartet method as the best, despite the fact that the relatively subjective laboratory grades assigned implied instructor belief in the superiority of the quartet method. The investigators concluded that (1) laboratory achievement is independent of the number of students working on an experiment (up to four, the limit investigated in this study); (2) laboratory achievement is not measurably influenced by the instructor; (3) students working in quartets earn better average marks on laboratory reports *written in the laboratory* than do students working singly or in pairs; and (4) laboratory grades based primarily on written laboratory reports vary significantly from instructor to instructor. The investigators point out that this investigation underlines the importance of using several criteria for the measurement of laboratory achievement and that much additional work must be done in defining the objectives of laboratory instruction and in devising more effective evaluation instruments. The same points could well be emphasized for the measurement of achievement in connection with any investigation of teaching techniques.

Teacher Education. Few studies have focused specifically on problems related to preparing instructors of college-level general education science courses. Those which have been made were designed either to determine the training experience of those who are presently instructors, to secure the judgments of instructors and administrators on what training is desirable, or both. Frazier (1956) utilized questionnaires to elicit information from administrators and instructors concerning competencies and areas of content desirable in the general, special, and professional training of instructors of general education biology courses. Additional information was secured from the instructors with respect to their own undergraduate and graduate courses and the nature of the general biology courses they were teaching. Responses were received from 131 administrators of general education programs and from 251 biology instructors. From the judgments expressed, Frazier deduced the competencies and patterns of training desirable. In general, administrators and instructors believed that the general biology instructor should have broad preparation in the biological sciences, along with concentration in some one field (such as genetics or zoology); that this should be buttressed with a broad background of work in the physical sciences, the humanities, and the social sciences; and that professional education courses specifically designed for prospective instructors of general biology should form a part of the training program.

Kinerson (1957) utilized similar techniques in determining what would constitute appropriate training for junior-college physical science instructors. Questionnaire responses were obtained from 104 junior-college administrators, 186 physical science instructors, and 38 nationally known authorities in the field of junior-college education. Results similar to those of the Frazier study were obtained, including the recommendations of a broad major, supporting work in the social sciences and humanities, and work in professional education. In addition, a teaching internship in a junior college and a two-year graduate program oriented toward developing understanding of the technical-industrial applications of physical science and toward developing an interest in teaching rather than research were recommended.

Rankin (1952) studied instructor competencies and the problems of preparing general education physical science teachers for the jobs they do. Comparable in many ways to the two investigations already cited, Rankin's study called attention to the difficulty, within present doctoral programs, of avoiding intense specialization at the expense of desirable breadth of preparation. His study also called attention to the factors of prestige, promotion, and opportunities for appropriate research for those who dedicate their lives to general education science rather than to instruction and research in prestige disciplines of science. Indeed, in some ways Rankin's study encompasses many of the problems besetting general education college science.

Research to date has done little to resolve these problems. There is still no agreement on the objectives of general education science at the college level, nor is it at all clear that special courses designed for general education values are either necessary or desirable. If such courses are offered, it is not apparent whether descriptive surveys, courses integrated on the basis of principles or conceptual schemes, block-and-gap courses with intensive treatment of a limited number of topics, courses emphasizing the "tactics" and "strategies" of science as Conant (1947) suggested, or something different from all these is the most desirable way of organizing content and instruction. There is yet little solid evidence on which to build superior teaching strategies, even if there were agreement on purposes and on the way to organize courses. This being the case, it is impossible to know how to prepare master teachers of such courses. Frazier, Kinerson, and Rankin simply secured the judgments of those who are in the business of general education science teaching. Perhaps that is about all which can be done at the present time.

SCIENCE EDUCATION IN OTHER COUNTRIES. Research in foreign countries varies from sophisticated studies of limited scope that employ modern statistical techniques to broad assessments, status studies, and evaluation of course-improvement projects. The following survey samples each of these types and attempts to illustrate the range and levels of research that has been done. Typical examples are given both for developing nations and for the technically advanced.

Much of the research reported in English and in journals generally available in this country is essentially of three types: (1) comparative studies between the United States and one or more other countries; (2) studies of the status of science education in a foreign country; and (3) general assessments of science education with proposals for modification that are usually based on an examination of national goals, indigenous values, and similar sociological, psychological, and philosophical bases. These have been done most commonly by nationals working on doctoral dissertations in United States universities.

Examples of the first type are a comparative study of high school biology teaching in the U.S.S.R. and in the United States done by Freitag (1955) and a comparison of chemistry courses in selected schools of Canada, Great Britain, New Zealand, and the United States done by Routh (1961). Freitag's study was based primarily on a detailed analysis of four Soviet and two American textbooks, both widely used at the time of his inquiry. He concluded that the Soviet courses provide better preparation in anatomy, physiology, and systematic relationships of plants and animals and that the American courses provide a better understanding of genetics, conservation, health, and hygiene. Freitag also believed that he detected evidence in the texts that Soviet biology teaching is strongly oriented toward fostering support of the communist state. Those familiar with American biology texts of the 1950's may be surprised that he found the American texts (and three American syllabi) to "support the basic principles of the American social and political order as presently constituted."

Routh's study attempted to compare selected schools in terms of concepts of chemistry most frequently taught and in terms of the relative importance of these concepts. He selected 25 schools from each country on the basis of their high reputation for instruction in chemistry. He sent a detailed questionnaire to each school, and his analysis was based on the questionnaire responses as well as on an analysis of the five most widely used textbooks in each country (without reference to the texts actually used in these highly rated schools). His conclusions included the following national ranking of chemistry courses in terms of excellence: Great Britain, New Zealand, Canada, and the United States. There is value in these studies, and they are typical of others of a comparable sort. It is clear, however, that far more comprehensive studies are required if we are to gain much insight from other countries, and they from us.

An example of the second type of study is an analysis of science teaching in grades 6 through 8 in selected Soviet schools by Harmon (1960). Although purely a status study, the bases for the analysis were more comprehensive than those used in the studies cited above. Harmon visited 14 schools in Moscow, Leningrad, Kiev, and Irkutsk, and he interviewed teachers and administrators and visited classrooms. His conclusions include the following: Russian science teachers are well trained; they have a light teaching load (18 hours per week); centrally distributed textbooks and strong central control results in much the same work being done in Irkutsk, Siberia, as in Moscow; only 19 percent of the schools visited had student tables adapted for laboratory use; the strong vertical correlation of science material indicates a standardized schedule of presentation; and the common teaching technique is lecture-demonstration. Extensive use was made of board recitation and copybooks, leading Harmon to the view that rote teaching, memory work, and "training" rather than a comprehensive science education was the probable common result.

Examples of the third type of study are those by Sangalang (1961), Hernandez (1960), Boulos (1960), and Khalid (1954). Sangalang made a comprehensive review of literature on Philippine rural life from which he developed a checklist of rural needs. This was given to the directors of various agencies of the government involved in rural development, with the request that they rate each specified need in terms of its importance. From this and other sources, Sangalang established criteria for the development of science learning experiences. Sangalang's study was based on the explicit assumption that rural science education in the Philippines should directly minister to the more urgent needs of rural life. Health and increase in farm production were, for example, the most urgent needs on his list. His study included four detailed "learning experiences" designed to suggest approaches by which science teaching might help meet the needs disclosed by the study. These included experiments with controls, to be conducted in the school or on local farms, designed to demonstrate the advantages of record keeping and the application of scientific principles. The study by Hernandez was also done in order to determine the direction that science education should take in the Philippines. Hernandez' main assumption was that science education should contribute to the solution of social problems, including the raising of the standard of living. The study was essentially philosophical and intuitive and resulted in conclusions that derived inevitably from the main assumption.

Boulos's study and that by Khalid were similar, in design and purpose, to those just cited. Boulos developed a course of study in biology for Egyptian schools that was based on the "needs of individuals together with the needs of the society. . . ." Khalid stated his central purpose to be a proposal for the reconstruction of Iraqi science education which would foster the improvement of individual and societal conditions. His procedure included an analysis of Iraqi society, including consideration of the major social problems toward the solving of which science education might presumably make a contribution. This was followed by an analysis of the present strengths and weaknesses of science education in Iraq and a proposed scheme for the reconstruction of science education in terms of objectives, content, teaching method, examinations, and the preparation of science teachers. An 11-year integrated science program was outlined.

A study of Soviet schools cited earlier (Harmon, 1960) stressed the dominance of memory work and rote teaching in science classes. It is therefore of interest that a Soviet writer, Lerner (1964), has analyzed various teaching approaches as a means of stimulating independent thinking of Russian students. (His article first appeared in a Russian journal and almost certainly reflected an official point of view. The author is with the Research Institute of General and Polytechnical Education, RSFSR Academy of Pedagogical Sciences.) He analyzed the "research method in teaching" science, pointed out that the method has not been applied broadly, and proposed that this heuristic approach be made an object of serious investigation and analysis.

Few, if any, of the studies already cited bear the marks of careful research design or employ modern statistical procedures. Nonetheless, they represent the styles as well as the emphases typical of most studies of science education in foreign countries.

Science interests and the development of scientific concepts in children have intrigued European just as they have American investigators. In one study of concept development by King (1961), 70 questions on estimation of length, volume, time, and so on, as well as about mechanical principles, living things, and seasons, were given to over 1,800 children aged 5 to 12 in English junior schools. An example of the questions used is this: "When a stone is added to water in a jar, is the level of the water higher, lower, or the same as it was before?" The results were tabulated in terms of percentages for boys and girls with increasing chronological age, and types of questions in terms of age trends. Twenty-four questions showed steady increases in correct responses with age (from about 54 percent at 6 years to 89 percent at 11 years). The author judged that these questions could be answered correctly from experience alone and without formal teaching. Estimations of length, volume, and other quantities showed very little increase with age, and the author assumed that these and other questions require formal instruction to supplement out-of-school experience if gains are to be made.

Rowlands (1961) attempted to study differences between prospective scientists, nonscientists, and early school dropouts in a representative sample of English grammar school boys. He utilized a questionnaire, an attitude test, an interest test, and a vocational choice test on a sample of 654 fifteen-year-old boys and analyzed his results according to father's occupation, economic status, number of books in the home, and so on.

In another English study, Meyer and Penfold (1961) analyzed 150 students in an East London school by use of subjective interest tests. Measured were leisure science interests, interest in school science topics, and interest in scientific method. The unweighted total of these three measures was used as the criterion for measuring "interest in science," which was used as the basis for a ranking of presumably related factors such as the father's interest in science.

There is a certain stylized brittleness in the studies just reported, as there is in a large percentage of American studies. One wonders whether statistical manipulation does not often obscure the fact that the studies hardly answer any question worth asking and whether, indeed, one can generalize from the results or even employ them usefully with the population studied.

With this reservation in mind, an example of a fifth type of study will be reported next. This is operational, loosely designed, and lacking in technical sophistication. It is, however, a long-range attack on a fundamental problem, and it could well be emulated wherever curriculum research and development projects are underway. This study was done in Ghana, and the report on it by Chaplin (1964) is based on six and a half years of analysis and curriculum development. His report describes a major research effort of the University of Ghana that is unusual with respect to course improvement projects in developing countries. The work involved 2,000 children, 42 teachers, and three and a half years of analysis, followed by three years of curriculum development work based upon the analysis. The research included giving identical tests to American and Ghanaian children (such as explaining why a crumpled paper falls more quickly than a flat paper). At nine years of age the Ghanaian children were "equal in all respects to the American children in New York State." But the improvement in scores of American children who had two more years of schooling were *three* times as great as that of Ghanaian children who had *five* more years of schooling. Indeed, the Ghanaian students showed little or no improvement at all in their ability to answer such practical questions and to analyze simple phenomena. This was true even when the study included comparisons of primary school children, secondary school students, and students in training colleges. The latter students had a much larger reservoir of remembered facts and definitions; but this did nothing, apparently, to increase their ability to think about, understand, and explain phenomena. Based upon such analyses and tentative trials of new materials and approaches, Chaplin and his coworkers developed a collection of topics teachable entirely by means of the "physical experience of hand and eye in every step of the explanation."

Chaplin suggests that anxiety to equate Ghanaian syllabi quantitatively with European practice resulted in frantic memoriter learning without understanding. He believes that he has evidence that the experimental topics result in true understanding, even though the newer method takes from five to eight times as long for understanding to develop as is required for students to memorize under the older (and still common) Ghanaian methods. He also found that teachers need not necessarily be specially qualified academically to teach with the new approach. Two years of experimentation showed that teachers acquire understanding by exactly the same sequence of practical experiences as were found useful in educating children.

Such long-range exploratory studies in which analysis precedes and accompanies the development of newer materials and methods can be extremely fruitful for gains in student learning, in the development of sound curricular materials and teaching strategies, and in the development of insights upon which more carefully focused and suitably designed research of promise can be based.

ADDITIONAL SOURCES OF INFORMATION. Course improvement projects incorporating varying degrees of assessment and research are underway in almost every region of the world. The most comprehensive listing of such projects is a joint report of the Commission on Science Education, the American Association for the Advancement of Science, and the Science Teaching Center at the University of Maryland (Lockard, 1966). The first of an annual series of reports from the International Clearinghouse on Science and Mathematics Curricular Developments, this work provides basic data on 54 curriculum and course development projects underway in foreign countries throughout the world. Apparently, however, even the more sophisticated of these projects (the five Nuffield projects in England, for example) engage in little research beyond that of testing materials in the field in ways quite comparable to methods used in similar projects in the United States.

Eells (1959) has provided a listing of the 33 studies in science and mathematics education he located in more than 1,000 doctoral dissertations dealing with education in foreign countries. The first of these studies was done in 1905, and the last in 1959. Four concerned Canada; nineteen, Europe; four, Africa; and six, Asia.

A useful overview of elementary school science and mathematics in Western Europe was a study by McKibben (1961) based on a survey of published reports on the primary schools of Great Britain, West Germany, the Netherlands, Sweden, Denmark, Norway, Switzerland, and France. Subject matter and time allotments were considered, and results support the author's conclusions that science is far from a universal subject in the elementary schools of Western Europe.

J. Myron Atkin
R. Will Burnett
University of Illinois

References

Abrams, Leonard S. "A Comparison of the Teaching Effectiveness of Some Methods of On-Campus Supplementation of the Telecourse 'Atomic Age Physics'." Doctoral dissertation. New York U, 1961.

American Council on Education. *Test of Critical Thinking, Form G.* ACE, 1952. (out of print)

Atkin, J. Myron. "Teaching Concepts of Modern Astronomy to Elementary-School Children." *Sci Ed* 45:54–8; 1961.

Atkin, J. Myron, and Karplus, Robert. "Discovery or Invention?" *Sci Teach* 29:45–51; 1962.

Badgley, Ralph Emerson. "A General Studies Curriculum in Science and Mathematics for Colleges of Education in Oregon." Doctoral dissertation. U Colorado, 1956.

Bailey, Liberty H. *The Nature Study Idea.* Macmillan, 1909. 246p.

Barnard, J. Darrell. "Teaching Scientific Attitudes and Methods in Science." *Nat Assn Sec Sch Prin B* 37:178–83; 1953.

Beberman, Max. *An Emerging Program of Secondary School Mathematics.* Harvard U, 1958.

Belanger, Maurice. "Methodology of Educational Research in Science and Mathematics." *R Ed Res* 34:374–90; 1964.

Boulos, Sami Ibrahim. *A Course in Biology for the Senior High Schools in Egypt.* Doctoral dissertation. U Florida, 1960.

Bullington, Robert A. "A Study of Science for General Education at the College Level." *Sci Ed* 33:235–41; 1949.

Bullington, Robert A. "The Subject-Matter Content of General Education Science Courses." *Sci Ed* 36:285–92; 1952.

Burmester, Mary Alice. "The Construction and Validation of a Test to Measure Some of the Inductive Aspects of Scientific Thinking." Doctoral dissertation. Michigan State U, 1951.

Butts, David P. "The Degree to Which Children Conceptualize from Science Experience." *J Res Sci Teach* 1:135–43; 1963.

Caldwell, Otis W., and others. *Report of the Subcommittee on the Teaching of Science.* B 26. USOE, 1920.

Chaplin, Basil H. G. "The Re-planning of Junior Science Education in West Africa." *Sci Ed* 48:366–70; 1964.

Cogan, M. L. "The Behavior of Teachers and the Productive Behavior of Their Pupils." *J Exp Ed* 27:107–24; 1958.

College Entrance Examination Board. *Advanced Placement Program: Course Descriptions, 1964–66.* 1966. 160p.

Comstock, Anna B. *Handbook of Nature Study.* Comstock Publishing Company, 1931.

Conant, J. B. *On Understanding Science.* Yale U Press, 1947.

Cooley, William W. "Challenges to the Improvement of Science Education Research." *Sci Ed* 45:383–7; 1961.

Craig, Gerald S. *Certain Techniques Used in Developing a Course of Study in Science for the Horace Mann Elementary School.* Teachers Col, Columbia U, 1927.

Davis, Dewey Dale. "A Critical Analysis of the Status of Existing Biology Programs in Texas Junior Colleges Compared with Established Objectives for the Biology Programs in Colleges of the United States." Doctoral dissertation. U Texas, 1962.

Dearden, Douglas M. "A Study of Contrasting Methods in College General Biology Laboratory Instruction." *Sci Ed* 46:399–401; 1962.

Dewey, John. *How We Think.* Heath, 1933.

Downing, Elliott R. "An Analysis of Textbooks in General Science." *Gen Sci Q* 12:509–16; 1928.

Eells, Walter Crosby. "American Doctoral Dissertations on Scientific and Mathematical Education in Foreign Countries." *Sci Ed* 43:274–5; 1959.

Finlay, Gilbert C. "The Physical Science Study Committee." *Sch R* 70:63–81; 1962.

Frazier, Ralph Paul. "The Competencies and Patterns of Training Desirable for Instructors of Biological Science Courses in College General Education Programs." Doctoral dissertation. U Illinois, 1956.

Freitag, Charles Robert. "Biological Science Teaching at the Secondary School Level in the United States of America and the Union of Soviet Socialist Republics: A Comparative Study." Doctoral dissertation. Cornell U, 1955.

Fribourgh, James Henry. "Recommended Principles and Generalizations for an Introductory Biology Course in the Junior College." Doctoral dissertation. State U Iowa, 1957.

Gagné, Robert M. "Elementary Science: A New Scheme of Instruction." *Sci* 151:49–53; 1966.

Geller, Molly. "The Measurement of the Effectiveness of a Teaching Machine Program in the Organic Chemistry Area of First Year College Chemistry." *J Res Sci Teach* 1:154–61; 1963.

Hall, Thomas S., and others. "Science Teaching in Elementary and Junior High Schools." *Sci* 133:2019–24; 1961.

Harmon, John Millard, Jr. "A Study of Science Teaching in Grades Six Through Eight in Selected Ten-Year Schools of the U.S.S.R." Doctoral dissertation. Boston U, 1960.

Harvard Committee on Objectives of General Education in a Free Society. *General Education in a Free Society.* Harvard U, 1945. 267p.

Hatcher, Benjamin Edward. "An Experimental Study of Three Different Patterns of Student Participation in a General-Education Science Course for College Freshmen." Doctoral dissertation. Wayne State U, 1957.

Heathers, Glen. "A Process-Centered Elementary Science Sequence." *Sci Ed* 45:201–6; 1961.

Hernandez, Dolores F. "Developing Needs of Science Education in the Republic of the Philippines." Doctoral dissertation. Indiana U, 1960.

Hopka, Erich. "Objectives of Physical Science Education for Pre-theological Students at Lutheran Colleges." *J Exp Ed* 26:355–66; 1958.

Hurd, Paul Deh. "A Critical Analysis of the Trends in Secondary School Science Teaching from 1895–1948." Doctoral dissertation. Stanford U, 1949.

Hurd, Paul Deh. "The Educational Concepts of Secondary School Science Teachers." *Sch Sci Math* 54:89–96; 1954.

Hurd, Paul Deh. *Biological Education in American Secondary Schools 1890–1960.* American Institute of Biological Sciences, 1961. 263p.

Khalid, Abdulrahman M. "Science Education in the Iraqi Society." Doctoral dissertation. Columbia U, 1954.

Kinerson, Kendall Scott. "A Study of the Academic and Professional Preparation of Junior College Teachers of Physical Science." Doctoral dissertation. Michigan State U, 1957.

King, W. H. "The Development of Scientific Concepts in Children." *Br J Ed Psychol* 31:1–20; 1961.

Kruglak, Haym. "Some Behavior Objectives for Laboratory Instruction." *Am J Physics* 19:223–5; 1951.

Kruglak, Haym. "Experimental Outcomes of Laboratory Instruction in Elementary College Physics." *Am J Physics* 20:136–41; 1952(*a*).

Kruglak, Haym. "A Comparison of the Conventional and Demonstration Methods in the Elementary College Physics Laboratory." *J Exp Ed* 20:293–300; 1952(*b*).

Kruglak, Haym. "Achievement of Physics Students with and Without Laboratory Work." *Am J Physics* 21:14–6; 1953.

Kruglak, Haym. "The Measurement of Laboratory Achievement." *Am J Physics* 22:442–62; 1954.

Kruglak, Haym. "Measurement of Laboratory Achievement." *Am J Physics* 23:82–7; 1955.

Kruglak, H., and Goodwin, R. A. "Laboratory Achievement in Relation to the Number of Partners." *Am J Physics* 23:257–64; 1955.

Kuhnen, Sybil Marie. "The Effectiveness of Field Trips in the Teaching of General Botany." Doctoral dissertation. New York U, 1960.

Lerner, I. I. "Aquainting Pupils with Scientific Methods as a Way of Linking Learning with Life." *Soviet Ed* 6:15–26; 1964.

Lockard, J. David. (Director). *Report of the International Clearinghouse on Science and Mathematics Curricular Developments, 1966.* AAAS and U Maryland, 1966. 291p.

Macri, Alfred Roger. "A Comparison of the Effectiveness of Two Methods on the Competence of College Students to Understand Atomic Structure in a One Semester Course in General Physical Science." Doctoral dissertation. New York U, 1963.

Mason, John Murwyn. "An Experimental Study in

the Teaching of Scientific Thinking in Biological Science at the College Level." Doctoral dissertation. Michigan State U, 1951.

McKibben, Margaret J. "Elementary School Science and Mathematics Education in Western Europe." *Sch Sci Math* 61:404–17; 1961.

Meyer, G. R., and Penfold, D. M. Edwards. "Factors Associated with Interest in Science." *Br J Ed Psychol* 31:33–7; 1961.

Montague, Earl John. "Using the College Chemistry Laboratory to Develop an Understanding of Problem Solving in Chemistry." Doctoral dissertation. Ohio State U, 1963.

Montean, John J. "An Experimental Study of the Use of Discussion Groups in General Chemistry and General Science as a Means of Increasing Group Growth in Critical Thinking." Doctoral dissertation. Syracuse U, 1959.

Moore, Maxine Ruth. "A Survey of College Biology Departments Regarding Introductory Course Curricula and Advanced Placement Practices." *J Res Sci Teach* 3:235–45; 1965.

Moore, William I., and Henderson, Leon N. "A Study in the Development of Attitudes in a General Education Physical Science Course." *Jun Col J* 28:132–6; 1957.

National Academy of Sciences, National Research Council. *Recommendations on Undergraduate Curricula in the Biological Sciences.* n.d.

National Education Association, Commission on the Reorganization of Secondary Education. *Cardinal Principles of Secondary Education.* B 35. USOE, 1918.

National Education Association, Committee on College Entrance Requirements. "Report of the Committee on College Entrance Requirements." *Addresses and Proceedings.* 38:625–30; 1899.

National Education Association, Committee of Ten. *Report of the Committee on Secondary School Studies.* NEA, 1893.

National Science Foundation. *Twelfth Annual Report for the Fiscal Year Ended June 30, 1962.* GPO, 1962. 368p.

National Society for the Study of Education. *A Program for Teaching Science.* 31st Yearbook. Part I. Public School Publishing Co. 1932. 364p.

National Society for the Study of Education. *Science Education in American Schools.* 46th Yearbook. Part I. U Chicago, 1947. 300p.

Noll, Victor H. *The Teaching of Science in Elementary and Secondary Schools.* McKay, 1939. 238p.

Progressive Education Association, Commission on Secondary School Curriculum, Committee on the Function of Science in General Education. *Science in General Education.* Appleton, 1938. 591p.

Raksaboldej, Bitak. "A Survey of Science Programs in Selected State Teachers Colleges." Doctoral dissertation. New York U, 1961.

Rankin, Oren R. "A Study of Competencies Desirable for Instructors of College General Education Courses in the Physical Sciences." *Sci Ed* 36:301–7; 1952.

Reed, H. B., Jr. "Teacher Variables of Warmth, Demand and Utilization of Intrinsic Motivation Related to Pupils' Science Interests." *J Exp Ed* 29:205–29; 1961.

Rickert, Russell Kenneth. "The Critical Thinking Ability of College Freshman Physical Science Students." Doctoral dissertation. New York U, 1961.

Robertson, Martin L. "A Basis for the Selection of Course Content in Elementary Science." *Sci Ed* 19:1–4; 65–70; 1935.

Robinson, Jack H. "Effects of Teaching With Science Articles." *Sci Ed* 47:73–83; 1963.

Routh, Charles Joseph. "A Comparison of the Concepts Taught in Secondary School Chemistry Courses in Selected Schools of Canada, Great Britain, New Zealand, and the United States." Doctoral dissertation. U Pittsburgh, 1961.

Rowlands, R. G. "Some Differences Between Prospective Scientists, Non-scientists and Early Leavers in a Representative Sample of English Grammar School Boys." *Br J Ed Psychol* 31:21–32; 1961.

Sandler, Barney. "A Comparison of an Integrated Course in College Physics and Mathematics of One Semester Duration with Separate Courses in the Two Subjects in a Two-Year Community College." Doctoral dissertation. New York U, 1961.

Sangalang, Luz E. "Some Aspects of Science Education for Rural Philippines and Implications for the Education of Teachers for the Community Schools." Doctoral dissertation. Indiana U, 1961.

Schefler, William C. "A Comparison Between Inductive and Illustrative Laboratories in College Biology." *J Res Sci Teach* 3:218–23; 1965.

Scott, Lloyd. "An Experiment in Teaching Basic Science in the Elementary School." *Sci Ed* 46:105–8; 1962.

Silverstein, Alvin. "The Effectiveness of Student-Constructed Three-Dimensional Models in the Teaching of College General Biology." Doctoral dissertation. New York U, 1962.

Smith, Herbert A., and Anderson, Kenneth E. "Science." In Harris, Chester W. (Ed.) *Encyclopedia of Educational Research,* 3rd ed. Macmillan, 1960. p. 1216–30.

Stubbs, Ulysses Simpson, Jr. "A Comparison of Two Methods of Teaching Certain Quantitative Principles of General Chemistry at the College Level." Doctoral dissertation. New York U, 1958.

Suchman, J. Richard. "Inquiry Training: Building Skills for Autonomous Discovery." *Merrill Palmer Q Behavior Develop* 7:147–69; 1961.

Syrocki, B. John, and Wallin, Russell S. "A Two-Year Study of Teaching Human Biology via Television." *Sci Ed* 46:379–84; 1962.

Tuckman, Jacob, and Etkin, William. "The Relationship Between Science Proficiency and Training Among Liberal Arts Graduates." *J Ed Res* 54:273–5; 1961.

Underhill, Orra E. *The Origins and Development of Elementary-School Science.* Scott, 1941. 347p.

Watson, Fletcher G. "Research on Teaching Science." In Gage, N. L. (Ed.) *Handbook of Research on Teaching.* Rand McNally, 1963. p. 1031–59.

Watson, Goodwin, and Glaser, Edward M. *Critical Thinking Appraisal.* Harcourt, n.d.

Webster, Samuel Omer. "Science in General Education at the Oklahoma State Colleges." Doctoral dissertation. U Oklahoma, 1958.

Woodburn, John H., and Obourn, Ellsworth S. *Teaching the Pursuit of Science.* Macmillan, 1965. 470p.

SCORES AND NORMS

The performance of an examinee on a test of educational achievement, ability, aptitude, personality, or interest is most commonly defined initially as the number of correct or keyed responses, modified in some instances by a weighting factor applied to some or all of the test items, or by the application of a correction for wrong responses. Such a measure of performance, usually termed a *raw score*, typically has little intrinsic significance. Raw scores are affected, for example, by arbitrary features of a test, such as the number of items in it. They are also functions of item difficulty and discrimination values and item intercorrelations, which are usually controlled by the test maker so as to maximize discrimination or improve predictive value, rather than to generate inherent meaning in the score as a direct index of whatever trait or attribute the test purports to measure. Raw scores do indeed serve to order examinees along a continuum presumably reflective of the characteristic being measured, and with repeated use of a test they may acquire meaning almost in their own right for a test user; but in common practice they take on meaning largely through reference to bodies of data that are descriptive of the performance of specified groups on the test in question. These bodies of data, which permit assertions concerning the relative value of a particular score, or, more exactly, the relative standing of the individual obtaining the score with reference to the group whose performance is described, are the "norms" for the test.

To be sure, there has been no lack of recommendations that test constructors design tests whose scores would be intrinsically meaningful. Ebel (1962) proposed that test content be specified and selected in such a fashion that test performance will lend itself to immediate, direct interpretation by means of a *content standard test score*, defined as the "per cent of a systematic sample from a defined domain of tasks which an individual has performed correctly." Somewhat similar proposals had been made earlier by Flanagan (1951) and followed by him in the development of many of the tests used in Project TALENT (Flanagan & others, 1962). Illustrations of such "self-interpreting" tests would be a test of typing, yielding results in terms of words per minute, an intrinsically meaningful unit; or an appropriately designed reading test, results on which may be expressed in terms of the percentage of comprehension or success which an examinee has in reading particular types of material, such as newspaper editorials, popular magazines, etc. While there is much to be said for efforts to develop tests providing such content-related interpretation, few published tests have indeed been designed in this fashion. It is not always possible to define an achievement domain in such a manner as to permit the kind of systematic sample Ebel's scheme requires; nor is the need for descriptive information about the performance of some reference groups obviated by use of content standard scores or their equivalent. It appears likely that major reliance in interpreting test scores will continue to be placed on relating them to bodies of normative data.

It continues to be necessary to distinguish between *norms*, as here defined, and *standards*. A tendency persists on the part of some test users to invest normative data with evaluative connotations: being "below the norm" is equated with inadequate or absolutely poor performance, while "above the norm" status is seen *ipso facto* as commendable or good. It is essential for clarity in test interpretation to recognize that norms are simply "descriptive" data, in themselves devoid of valuative potential. "Standards," on the other hand, do incorporate value judgments of a type permitting qualitative categorization of performance, as "excellent," "satisfactory," "failing," etc.

TYPES OF NORMS. For most tests at the preschool or school (including college) level, the common way of interpreting scores is through reference to the performance of groups of specified age or specified grade placement ("age" or "grade" norms), or of otherwise educationally significant groups—e.g. college-admission candidates, students completing second-level French, etc.—on the test at hand.

The use of age norms has commended itself to makers of tests from the earliest days of psychological and educational measurement. Binet's original intelligence scale was an age scale, composed of a series of tasks chosen in part because they differentiated between subjects of successive age levels. Since most cognitive functions are developmental in character, correlating to some degree with increasing age, at least through the teen years, it seemed sensible to describe performance on tests of such functions in terms of resemblance to the performance of subjects of specified age. Thus, there emerged the concept of the "mental age" corresponding to a score (or "reading age," "arithmetic age," etc., in the case of tests of these functions), defined as the chronological age of examinees for whom the score in question is the typical or average score. It occurred early to test makers that these age values (also termed "age equivalents") could be compared to the actual age of a subject, as by subtracting one from the other or computing a ratio between them, to yield an index of relative standing within an age group. Best known of such ratios is, of course, the IQ, originally defined as the ratio of mental age to chronological age. Growing awareness of statistical deficiencies in these types of comparison, especially those of the ratio type, has led to great curtailment in their use; virtually all recently published intelligence tests, for example, derive IQ's, if at all, by what is essentially a standard score system rather than by the ratio method.

Second in importance to age—indeed equaling or exceeding it in certain respects—in the interpretation of scores on many tests is grade placement. Scores on achievement tests (as well as on some tests of general ability) are so definitely consequent on amount of schooling, or exposure to specific curricular content, that it is almost inevitable that they be interpreted in relation to scores of groups having specified educational experience. Thus, it has become common to express scores on such achievement tests as *grade equivalents* or *grade scores*, defined as the grade placement of pupils for whom the score in question is the typical or median score; a grade equivalent of 5.7 on a reading test, for example, is assigned to the score that is the median score for pupils in the seventh month of the fifth grade in the norm group.

The technique for the establishment of age or grade norms is basically simple. Subjects in the norming group are categorized by age or grade, and the median scores for subjects in these subgroups are computed; these medians for the groups are then plotted on cross-section paper against age or grade, smooth curves (norm lines) fitted, mathematically or judgmentally, to the successive points, and norm values read off relating score to age or grade. Beneath the surface simplicity of this procedure, however, there lurk not a few thorny problems: the establishment of equivalence or comparability among levels when, as is usually the case, several levels of the test are required to cover the entire range of ages or grades; the selection of the optimum time, or times, in the school year at which to test for norming purposes; the proper bases on which to interpolate between obtained medians, or to extrapolate beyond them; treatment of semiannually *vs.* annually promoted groups, to mention some of the more vexing ones. Research attention has been directed to some of these issues. Bernard (1964) and Beggs and Hieronymous (1968) have studied, for example, the appropriateness of straight-line interpolation procedures; but there is still much room in age and grade norming procedures for individual judgment on the part of the test maker, rather than the application of research-validated techniques.

Kelley (1940) drew attention to a property of grade norms as traditionally defined that he considered objectionable—namely, the depressing effect on such norms of the inclusion of substantial numbers of overage, duller children in the typical grade group. He proposed substituting for traditional grade norms what he termed "ridge-route norms," essentially a type of norm based on grade groups from which were excluded pupils greatly deviant in age from the typical or "modal-age" pupil. Many achievement tests published in the past 25 years have provided modal-age or "age-controlled" grade norms, either as defined by Kelley or in some cognate manner, which in effect describe the achievement of pupils who have made normal progress through school. The force of Kelley's original criticism has been blunted somewhat by changes in promotion policies in the intervening years, which have had the effect of making grade populations more homogeneous with respect to age, but the concept of controlling age variance in grade norm groups seems likely to endure.

It is not difficult to explain the popularity, over the years, of age and grade equivalents as ways of interpreting scores on ability and achievement tests. They have a beguiling simplicity or straightforwardness; they appear to the relatively unsophisticated test user as natural, readily comprehended units; and, because they constitute continuous scales over sustained periods of mental or educational development, they give promise of permitting measurement of growth, a prized objective of much testing. Yet, in spite of these features, and their admitted utility for certain purposes, it has become increasingly recognized that age and grade equivalents have serious limitations as interpretive systems. Indeed, writers on measurement in textbooks and elsewhere over the past decade seem to have been approaching a consensus that these units should be relegated to a secondary role in test interpretation.

The reasons for disenchantment with age and grade equivalents are numerous. (1) The relations of the functions measured by various tests to age or grade are by no means uniform, a circumstance which seriously affects or even vitiates attempts to compare relative development in various functions on the basis of results expressed in age or grade terms. (2) Development in the functions measured by most ability or achievement tests for unselected groups tends to become negligible at some point in the teen or high school years; thus, the expression of test scores for examinees whose scores exceed average values at this level must be in terms of an essentially fictitious set of extrapolated or artificial age or grade values. (3) Age and grade scales do not constitute equal-unit scales; a year or a grade at one part of the range is not "equal" to a year or a grade at another part. Therefore, age and grade units are poorly suited for use as measures of growth. (4) While "age" is an unambiguous variable, "grade" has no such universal meaning. Gradedness probably had more significance as an index of educational level in the early days of measurement than it does at present, since promotion policies now tend to give greater weight to factors other than achievement. Moreover, the increasing prevalence of nongraded organizations, particularly at the primary level, has had the effect not only of making it more difficult to develop grade norms but of rendering such norms notably less useful for the interpretation of scores in systems operating on a nongraded basis. (5) Grade equivalents, finally, appear to have been a particularly fertile source of misinterpretation of achievement-test results. Parents have found it difficult to understand why a child whose test performance was interpreted as equivalent to that of a child a grade or two above his actual grade placement could not be considered thereby ready to do the work of the higher grade.

Growing awareness of these shortcomings of age and grade units has resulted in an increased resort to other types of score conversion and interpretation. The most common alternative has been the adoption of a "percentile rank" system, in which a score is assigned a percentile value that denotes the percent of scores of a specified group that are exceeded by the score in question—e.g., a score of 35 on a spelling test is assigned a percentile rank of 48 among grade 5 pupils, if it exceeds the scores of 48 percent of the grade 5 pupils in the norming group. These percentile systems still most often utilize as reference groups examinees classified by grade or age; thus they are subject to some of the limitations of age and grade norms, such as the complications attendant upon the prevalence of nongraded schools. However, since a score is considered in relation only to the scores of a group of examinees similar in age or grade, the likelihood of the erroneous inferences to which age or grade equivalents give rise is greatly diminished. Virtually all of the more widely used achievement and ability measures published during the past five years provide percentile-rank systems for the interpretation of scores. One of the more widely used batteries offers a variant in the form of a *percentile band* system, in which a score is not converted to a single percentile rank but rather is seen as denoting a probable level of performance within a range or band of percentiles, the range being established as a function of the error of measurement of the score.

Percentile ranks are readily comprehended by test users, examinees and the lay public, despite occasional confusion with the time-honored percent system of marking. They do facilitate inter-test comparison for an examinee, though this is properly limited to comparisons among tests normed on the same group. Nevertheless, percentile ranks have certain properties which render them less than ideal for statistical manipulation as well as for the accurate portrayal and interpretation of intra-individual differences. Most serious of these limitations is the fact that percentile ranks constitute a scale of unequal units. Percentile differences near the middle of the range are systematically smaller in "true" terms than numerically equal differences at the extremes: the difference between the 55th and 60th percentile, for example, corresponds to a much smaller true difference in whatever characteristic is measured by a test than does the difference between the 90th and 95th percentile. For this reason, percentile ranks, like age and grade units, are ill-suited for measurement of growth and for measurement of inter-test differences.

Efforts to cope with this problem of inequality of units in interpretive systems have led to adoption of certain transformational schemes. The most popular of such transformational schemes is that giving rise to the so-called *stanine* system, according to which scores are converted to values in a nine-point scale having a mean of five and a standard deviation of two for the scaling group. Conversions are accomplished so that the resulting stanine distribution is a normal distribution; the stanine units may, in a certain sense, be said to be equal units. Stanine systems appear to be growing in use; apart from their technical merits, they are relatively easy to understand, and the single-digit stanine values lend themselves well to various types of statistical manipulation. Since stanine units are almost always coarser than the raw score units to which they correspond, their use frequently involves loss of some of the discrimination and precision present in the original raw scores; such loss needs to be weighed, in particular interpretive situations, against the presumed advantages. There is also a temptation to impose the normal stanine distribution in situations where there may be little psychological or educational warrant for positing it.

Normative data for interest and personality inventories, particularly those used at the adult level, commonly take the form of percentile rank or stanine conversion tables. For the most part, reference groups defined by grade or age are clearly irrelevant for the interpretation of results of such instruments, although in the case of some recently developed instruments for assessing levels of literacy among adult subjects, interpretations are provided that relate scores to supposedly equivalent levels of schooling.

Some tests used for selection or placement purposes at the adult level, as well as some tests used in schools, present normative information in the form of *expectancy charts,* in which scores on the test or tests are graphically related to measures of success on a job, in training programs or in various educational enterprises. Essentially, these expectancy charts permit probability statements concerning the likelihood of success in various undertakings associated with particular levels of test score. Expectancy charts are well regarded by test specialists as ways of presenting normative data and interpreting scores, since in portraying the relationships between test scores and criteria, they in effect display validity information as well as norm data.

NORMS POPULATIONS AND NORMS SAMPLES. The utility or meaningfulness of normative information depends upon the nature of the group or groups—the "norms population"—whose performance is described by the normative data. As a general principle, it may be said that the group with whose performance the score of an individual examinee is to be compared ought to be a group of which the examinee may properly be considered a part—in other words, that the norm group be relevant. The difficulty in applying this principle is that almost always an individual examinee may be thought quite properly to belong to a considerable number of groups, with any or all of whose performance it makes sense to compare his performance. That is to say, there are frequently several reference groups of which an individual may be considered a member, and the identification of the group or groups with which it is most appropriate to compare him in any given context depends on the purposes of the comparison. The meaning of a test score is illumined and expanded by referring it to a variety of sets of normative data; for example, a score on a reading test for a grade 8 pupil may be considered in relation to the scores of grade 8 pupils generally throughout the country, or in relation to the scores of grade 8 pupils of a similar level of scholastic aptitude, or in relation to the scores of other grade 8 pupils in the same school system, or in relation to scores of other pupils who have pursued a similar program of reading instruction, etc., each of these considerations of the score being done by determining its relative standing in a body of normative data for the groups in question.

Advantages exist, on the one hand, in having a norms population as broadly based and comprehensive as possible, in order that there be a common interpretive system with the greatest possible universality. This has generally been taken to imply, for tests intended for fairly general use, the provision of so-called *national norms*. This universality, however, is achieved at the price of maximizing the heterogeneity of the norm group, and thus of introducing into its scores sources of variance that tend to cloud the interpretation and understanding of the score of an individual examinee, or of the average score of a particular class or school, because of their dissimilarity in some essential respects from a national norm population. The desire to relate scores to performance of some more homogeneous group or groups, made up of individuals more similar to the individual whose score is being interpreted, leads to the interest in special norm groups—regional, state, local, ability-differentiated, sex, private school, etc.

The great heterogeneity of a national norm group, and the consequent decreased likelihood that it is an altogether appropriate group to which to relate the score of an individual or of a particular school or system, together with the great practical difficulties in carrying out standardization efforts that will give rise to a norms sample that may be defended as adequately representative of a national population, have prompted some measurement specialists to urge that the whole notion of national norms be abandoned in favor of more specialized and presumably more relevant sets of normative data. This would appear to be a minority viewpoint among test makers; virtually all the major batteries of achievement tests and general ability tests published within the past decade continue to provide norms that are represented as descriptive of national performance. There has, at the same time, been an increasing tendency to furnish more specialized bodies of normative information: for example, achievement-test norms for groups of various levels of ability or scholastic aptitude, norms for large-city school systems, norms differentiated by sex, norms for private vs. public schools, etc., are not uncommon supplements to the basic national normative information.

Interest in specialized normative populations may reflect current educational concerns; for example, the heightened attention paid in recent years to the problems of education of the culturally disadvantaged has prompted some, as in *Guidelines for Testing Minority Youth* (Society for the Psychological Study of Social Issues, 1964), to seek special norms descriptive of the performance of culturally disadvantaged pupils; the emergence of new curricular patterns, such as the so-called "modern mathematics" widely adopted in the 1960's, or the new science programs at the secondary level, has given rise to a need for norms based on pupils involved in such programs. Proponents of such specialized norms do not always appear to have given adequate thought either to the problems of definition or identification of the target groups, or to the problem of whether these specialized populations are in fact differentiated in performance from more universal norming populations.

Test users sometimes wonder which is the "best" set of norms to use—local, regional, or other specialized set. From what has been said above, it should be clear that the several modes of interpretation afforded by various sets of norms should not be seen as mutually exclusive but as complementary. All types of interpretation can be useful. In theory, use of a variety of sets of normative data should enhance understanding of test scores, inasmuch as each set of normative data in effect eliminates or greatly restricts one source of variance in the scores, and thus makes their interpretation less ambiguous. Two practical problems present themselves in the preparation and use of numerous sets of normative data. The first is the cost involved in developing and disseminating multiple bodies of normative information for a test, particularly in view of the fact that each such set of specialized norms is likely to be of interest to a relatively small fraction of the total body of users of the test. The second difficulty has to do with the ability of consumers of test data to digest or make effective use of numerous possible interpretations of a test score. Related to this problem is the complexity of record keeping involved, and the potential confusion and error that arise from use of numerous sets of interpretations of a given score.

Even after the test maker or test user has defined the norms population, or populations, that he deems most appropriate for a test, it is not always possible, practical, or desirable to include the entire population in the normative testing. In developing local norms, or norms for special groups of fairly limited size, or even norms for an entire state, it may be feasible to test the entire norms population; but, in the case of a national norms population, it is clearly impossible to do so. It becomes necessary, therefore, to base the norms on performance of only a sample—the *norms sample*—from the population. The problems of defining, selecting, and reaching such samples are among the most critical in norming technology. It is virtually impossible to reach for testing purposes a random sample of all pupils of given age or grade in the country, for numerous and valid reasons, such as lack of any complete listing of pupils, disruptions of school activities, and negligible usefulness of test results for such a sample for teacher or school administrator. Therefore, alternative sampling designs must be adopted. In recent years these have typically taken the form of stratified cluster sampling designs, or, in a few instances, stratified random cluster sampling. Because the efficiency of sampling (in the sense of minimization of sampling error per examinee tested in a norming program) is increased through stratification of the sample in terms of relevant variables, there has been interest in the identification of characteristics which would be useful as such stratifying variables. A succession of studies, including those of Davenport and Remmers (1950), Thorndike (1951), Lennon (1952), Mollenkopf and Melville (1956), and Flanagan (1962), have contributed knowledge about community and school system characteristics importantly related to scores on achievement and ability tests—e.g., region (South vs. non-South), adult educational level, income, teacher characteristics, etc. It is important to recognize, however, that while such information undeniably contributes to more efficient sampling designs, at best it permits control over only a minor fraction of the sources of variance in the scores; the best combinations of these demographic variables appear to correlate only to the extent of about .60 with test scores.

Lindquist and Hieronymous (1964) and others have repeatedly pointed out that the sampling unit in most norming programs is not the individual examinee but the school. (Oddly, it has much less commonly been noted that in many such norming programs it is, in fact, not even the school but the school system that should be considered the sampling unit.) The consequences of this fact with respect to size of sample, sample-design strategy, estimation of sampling errors, and norms reporting have not always received appropriate attention. Lord (1955, 1956, 1959) has dealt intensively with these and other norming problems. He has provided formulas appropriate for estimating sampling errors under various sampling designs, and has made recommendations as to desirable sample size under various designs for attainment of reasonable stability in norms. Test users sometimes inquire as to the size of a norm group needed to insure dependability or accuracy; from what has been said, it will be seen that size of sample per se is of very limited value as an index to its adequacy in representing population performance; sample design and the relevance of any variables used for stratification purposes are the potent determiners of the goodness of the norms. Norms for most published tests suffer from the fact that participation in their norming programs is voluntary, a circumstance which unavoidably introduces a bias of unknown magnitude and even direction.

COMPARABILITY OF NORMS. As Lennon (1966) has observed, norming practice among major test-making agencies has improved appreciably over the past decade with respect to both sophistication of design and quality of execution. Nevertheless, there remain serious problems, chief among which is the matter of norms comparability across various ability and achievement tests. The norms for various widely used batteries of achievement tests and mental ability tests, even for those that adopt fairly similar definitions of a national norms population, may not be assumed to be comparable; indeed, there are empirical demonstrations of systematic differences of not negligible size among the norms for tests purporting to measure similar functions. Such systematic differences among norms greatly complicate and, in the extreme, invalidate efforts to profile results, to compare or consolidate results from two or more tests, to study changes in a pupil, school or school system over time when various tests are used, or other efforts that depend upon comparability among interpreted scores. Over the years various approaches to this problem have been proposed, as by Toops (1939), Cureton (1941), and Lennon (1966); but none of these approaches has as yet been adopted on a sufficiently broad basis to provide comparability as among tests produced by various test-making agencies. The most feasible approach to the attainment of comparability appears to be the incorporation in every norming program of a common or "anchor" test that will permit definition of various norms groups in terms of a single scale. Even if various norms groups are not brought into conformity with some agreed-on distribution on such an anchor test, there would at least be the possibility of estimating how much of the difference among norms was attributable to differences in the caliber of the norms group.

Angoff (1966) and Lindquist (1964) have considered another approach to providing comparability among norms; namely, that of establishing tables of equivalence or correspondence through direct equating, as by an equi-percentile system. They agree on the general inadequacy of such methods for the development of truly comparable scores except as between tests so similar as to constitute strictly equivalent forms.

Mention should be made of the beneficial influence on norming practice, and more particularly on the level of reporting about norms in test manuals, of *Standards for Educational and Psychological Tests and Manuals* (American Educational Research Association & American Psychological Association, 1966). Manuals for recently published tests such as *Differential Aptitude Tests* (Bennett & others, 1947–1963), *Lorge-Thorndike Intelligence Tests* (Lorge & Thorndike, 1954–1964), *SRA Achievement Tests* (Thorpe & others, 1955–1964), *Iowa Tests of Basic Skills* (Lindquist & Hieronymous, 1964), *Stanford Achievement Test* (Kelley & others, 1964), and *Otis-Lennon Mental Ability Test* (Otis & Lennon, 1967) reflect improvements in definitions of norms populations, in sampling design, in control of normative testing conditions, etc.; and while not all of this improvement may be ascribed to the AERA–APA standards, they surely deserve some of the credit.

It is in the norming practices reflected in published instruments such as those mentioned rather than in norming theory or technology that most notable advances have occurred since the state of the art was reviewed in the last edition of this Encyclopedia.

Roger T. Lennon
Harcourt, Brace & World, Inc.

References

American Educational Research Association and American Psychological Association. *Standards for Educational and Psychological Tests and Manuals.* AERA, APA 1966. 40p.

Angoff, William H. "Can Useful General-Purpose Equivalency Tables Be Prepared for Different College Admissions Tests?" In Anastasi, Anne. (Ed.) *Testing Problems in Perspective.* ACE, 1966. p. 251–64.

Angoff, William H. "Scales, Norms, and Equivalent Scores." In Thorndike, Robert L. (Ed.) *Educational Measurement.* ACE, in press.

Beggs, Donald., and Hieronymous, Albert N. "Uniformity of Growth in the Basic Skills Throughout the School Year and During the Summer." *J Ed Meas* (in press).

Bennett, George K., and others. *Differential Aptitude Tests.* Psychological Corp., 1947–1963.

Bernard, Jack. "A Common Fallacy in Achievement Test Norms." *Psychol Sch* 1:428–31; 1964.

Cureton, Edward E. "Minimum Requirements in Establishing and Reporting Norms on Educational Tests." *Harvard Ed R* 11:287–300; 1941.

Davenport, Kenneth S., and Remmers, Hermann H. "Factors in State Characteristics Related to Average A-12 V-12 Test Scores." *J Ed Psychol* 41:110–5; 1950.

Ebel, Robert L. "Content Standard Test Scores." *Ed Psychol Meas* 22:15–25; 1962.

Flanagan, John C. "Units, Scores, and Norms." In Lindquist, E. F. (Ed.) *Educational Measurement.* ACE, 1951. p. 695–763.

Flanagan, John C. "Symposium: Standard Scores for Achievement Tests." *Ed Psychol Meas* 22:35–9; 1962.

Flanagan, John C., and others. *Studies in the American High School.* Cooperative Research Project No. 226, U Pittsburgh, 1962. 223p.

Kelley, Truman L. "Ridge-route Norms." *Harvard Ed R* 10:309–14; 1940.

Kelley, Truman L., and others. *Stanford Achievement Test.* World Book, 1964.

Lennon, Roger T. *Prediction of Academic Achievement and Intelligence from Community and School System Characteristics.* Doctoral dissertation. Teachers Col, Columbia U, 1952.

Lennon, Roger T. "Norms: 1963." In Anastasi, Anne. (Ed.) *Testing Problems in Perspective.* ACE, 1966. p. 243–50.

Lindquist, E. F. "Equating Scores on Non-parallel Tests." *J Ed Meas* 1:5–18; 1964.

Lindquist, E. F., and Hieronymous, Albert N. *Iowa Tests of Basic Skills.* Houghton, 1964.

Lord, Frederic M. "The Standard Error of Norms and the Standard Error of Measurement." In Research Memorandum 55-16. ETS, 1955.

Lord, Frederic M. "The Measurement of Growth." *Ed Psychol Meas* 16:421–37; 1956.

Lord, Frederic M. "Test Norms and Sampling Theory." *J Exp Ed* 27:247–63; 1959.

Lorge, Irving, and Thorndike, Robert L. *Lorge-Thorndike Intelligence Tests.* Houghton, 1954–1964.

Mollenkopf, William G., and Melville, S. Donald. "A Study of Secondary School Characteristics as Related to Test Scores." In *Research Bulletin 56-6.* ETS, 1956.

Otis, Arthur S., and Lennon, Roger T. *Otis-Lennon Mental Ability Test.* Harcourt, 1967.

Society for the Psychological Study of Social Issues. "Guidelines for Testing Minority Group Children." *J Soc Issues* 20(2):127–45; 1964.

Thorndike, Robert L. "Community Variables as Predictors of Intelligence and Academic Achievement." *J Ed Psychol* 42:321–38; 1951.

Thorpe, Louis P., and others. *SRA Achievement Tests.* SRA, 1955–1964.

Toops, Herbert A. *A Proposal for a Standard Million in Compiling Norms.* Bulletin No. 125. Ohio College Association, c. 1939.

SECONDARY EDUCATION

SCOPE. Education of and for youth, as contrasted with education for children or education for adults, can represent both the wide scope and limitations of modern secondary education. Yet, definitions for census purposes or in statutory provisions for financial support have been confused and are frequently in conflict in official documents. Reference to appropriate tables in recent editions of the GPO publications *Statistical Abstract of the United States* and, in particular, *Current Population Reports* (Series P-20) will serve to illustrate such confusion.

Perhaps the use of grade levels within schools as determinants of the limits of secondary education has too long added to this confusion. The revival of the term "middle school" as a substitute or replacement for the junior high school has more recently aggravated the problem of clarity of definition.

Yet the fluidity of grade organization represented in American public and private schools lends further weight to the argument that grade level in itself is no clear indication of what school one is in, let alone of the distinction between elementary and secondary education. Conant (1960) found that an amazing variety of grade combinations exists among the so-called junior high schools, and the recent reemergence of the designation "middle school" further complicates such classification. This latter, as suggested for New York City by the group known as the "Allen Committee" (Commissioner's Advisory Committee. . . , 1964), confuses elementary and secondary education as the largest city has known them in the past; the middle school in New York City is to involve grades 5 through 8, whereas in the suburbs the school of the same name begins with grade 6 or even with grade 8. It seems that the middle school, then, is a school inserted between elementary and high school. It is for both children and teen-age youth, and its very existence challenges any neat distinction between elementary and secondary education.

At the upper end of the youth range, another source of confusion exists. Much of the post-high school education to be found in the modern community college or junior college is terminal in nature and, in the opinion of some authorities, consists of an upward extension of secondary education for the older adolescent (Medsker, 1960). Further, much that is done in the technical and vocational institutes in which post-high school programs are found may also be logically classified as another aspect of secondary education.

Lacking confidence in determination based on grade levels involved, it seems reasonable to hold to the definition of secondary education as consisting of *organized and systematic education for youth.*

HISTORY. Origins of the present programs of secondary education in America and throughout the world are rooted in prehistorical events and customs. Certainly every known or reconstructed society has been aware of the period of change from childhood to adult status, and means of preparing boys and girls for their changed responsibilities and rights are found in every land and among all peoples. From the Yam culture of primitive New Guinea to the fields of Eaton, from the Navajo tribe of Arizona to the yard at Harvard or the Sather Gate at Berkeley, the stage of youth and its education are respected, acknowledged in ceremony, and viewed with alarm.

Old World to New. The Renaissance was responsible in part for the loosening of systematic education from the *memoriter* practic of the church and for the significant concern for content of learning as well as its form. The Reformation, in turn, brought challenge to established religious authority and a concern for man's own decision regarding his religious belief. There was a further renewal of interest in the classical ideas to be found in Latin and Greek manuscripts (Meyer, 1957). To many historians, Vittorino's work in his court school was the prototype of the modern, and even progressive, schoolmaster in the best sense (Woodward, 1897). Mind, body, and spirit were the focal concern, and education of Vittorino's youth, both boys and girls, was planned so that they should learn to live a moral and purposeful life.

The court schools of Italy were highly influential in determining the eventual form and substance of secondary education in France, England, and the Teutonic lands. In turn, when colonial America established its first formal education, programs that were intended for the favored youth who continued his formal education beyond the primary schools were clearly an import from across the Atlantic. American education per se was typically derived from immediate, basic needs—plus a primitive modification of the English forms of secondary education.

Yet several dilemmas concerning education faced the colonists, for the imported forms of education did not allow for such social changes as had been sought by the dissenting devout who came to the new shores. A common public school system is an anachronism among a people who seek religious freedom, if all education must be religious. Further, a dual system of education based on a social class system prevailed among the very colonies which were reaching for a classless society. Latin grammar schools and colleges were available for the upper classes, and elementary schools and apprenticeships were open to the lower classes. This dual system was almost universal among the colonies (Butts & Cremin, 1953).

The dual system lacked certain elements of practicality. During the latter part of the eighteenth century a contrasting dualism arose; the emergence of a larger merchant and trading class called for education more appropriate to their interests, while the farmer and backwoodsman still sought early release from formal education so that youth could learn their tasks by practicing them. The latter group resented taxes to support education of a useless type, which was how they viewed academic education. Statewide support and control of education was doomed throughout the century; the stress on local control of locally needed education thus emerged. Yet neither the Latin grammar school nor early apprenticeship adequately served the demands of many parents and youth in the eastern states and New England. Academies, including those for "young ladies," came into existence and so expanded in numbers and popularity that it is estimated that by 1850 more than 6,000 such schools existed, and more than a quarter of a million students were enrolled in them (Butts & Cremin, 1953).

These academies were clearly an American invention, but that they owed much of their form and purpose to the English grammar school, the French *collège,* and the German *Gymnasium,* is very clearly established (Meyer, 1957). Yet their survival was not consonant with the needs nor the resources available. The American high school, which appeared in small numbers during the late 1860's, seemed to be more uniquely a segment for all youth in the public school system, in contrast to the usually private academies. The new form not only survived and served, but by about 1890 it had clearly supplanted the academy in the provisions for education of American youth. The phenomenal growth in number of such schools is perhaps among the most dramatic aspects of American educational history. From 1890 to 1930, the number of such schools doubled each decade, and the present peculiarly American provision of free, public education for all American youth is a primary aspect of the remarkable state of educational accomplishment of an affluent people in a free land (Meyer, 1957).

Just as the academy faded, so other forms and means of educating American youth have passed from the scene. Changing social and technical forces have left little room for school-age youth in the world of work; he has slight opportunity to learn the skills of a trade or the requirements of responsible citizenship from practicing them as an independent worker. Rather, the place for youth to be, both because of lack of work opportunity and the demands for more and more formal education, is in school. The formal apprenticeship has become a museum piece, and the chores of farm life are known to fewer and fewer youth. Secondary schools, either public or otherwise, are the center of educational and work effort for nearly all American youth.

Landmarks. Certainly the creation and extension of free public education beyond the elementary school years did not happen without considerable travail. Of the challenges and court cases which were instrumental in the history of such struggles, one that occurred in Michigan, usually referred to as the Kalamazoo Case, was most dramatic. The decision, handed down in 1874 by the supreme court of Michigan, held that the school district had the right to levy taxes for public high schools (Butts & Cremin, 1953).

The reorganization of secondary education, involving a shuffling of the boundaries between elementary and secondary education, began through the efforts of various members and committees of the National Education Association to bring about a reduction in time spent in the elementary schools through the beginning of secondary education after six or seven years of childhood schooling (Eliot, 1888). These committees, of varied composition and purpose, supported the change in boundary age and grade and thus promoted the establishment, probably first in 1910, of the junior high school (Popper, 1967).

No genuine history of the development of secondary education in the United States can overlook the significant emergence of nonpublic schools and school systems. Of those controlled by religious interests, the Roman Catholic schools are most numerous and enroll the largest numbers. Further, the private preparatory schools and present-day academies of New England do influence and affect secondary educational practices and policies to a remarkable degree. Among the present academies, Phillips Andover is a carry-over from the first chartering of such an institution under control of a corporation. This charter was granted in 1778. Along with its sister academy in Exeter, it represents a private form of secondary education most frequently found in the New England and Middle Atlantic states which has served a favored few college-bound young men and led in many of the advances in secondary education. The founding purposes of the two academies were largely concerned with the "promotion of piety and virtue," and these institutions represented from the beginning the persistent concern for moral education which marked the earliest forms of education for youth in this country (Butts & Cremin, 1953). That the role of both the church-related and other forms of nonpublic secondary education is important in terms of sheer numbers is beyond doubt; the variety of influence, on the other hand, is difficult to define because of the varied purposes which they are created to serve and the lack of dependable data.

For the nation as a whole, the best available evidence seems to indicate that in 1964, some 14.2 percent of all secondary schools in the United States were nonpublic in control and sources of support. The regional variations are worthy of note; 29.7 percent of all secondary schools in the six New England states were nonpublic. The figure for four East South Central states was 7.9 percent, and for the eight Mountain states it was 9.5 percent (U.S. Department of Health, Education and Welfare, 1965b). For numbers of students enrolled, population data for October, 1965, indicate that 11.2 percent of high school enrollments were in nonpublic schools for the nation as a whole (U.S. Department of Commerce, 1965).

Another landmark in the history of secondary education was the emergence of nonacademic programs of significance in the majority of secondary schools following the passage of the Smith-Hughes Act in 1917. A series of subsequent bills, through which the Federal government stimulated an increasing program of vocational education in secondary schools, has had major influence on state leadership and local programs which are considered more appropriate than the conventional academic program for a large proportion of enrolled American youth.

Finally, the passage of Public Law 89-10 by the Eighty-ninth Congress was a landmark, but its magnitude is difficult to assess as yet on the basis of only one or two years of experience with its provisions (U.S. Department of Health, Education and Welfare, 1965a). Through this law, Federal aid was extended to elementary and secondary education both for the disadvantaged and for all youth.

PROGRAM. It is probable that no aspect of American education has been the subject of greater controversy among educators and the general public than has the content of education for youth. Attempts to define the nature and task of the secondary school and to study the selection, organization, and methods of presentation of instructional materials have, no doubt, resulted in the production of much heat and some light. National figures have caught the attention of parent, teacher, and generally concerned citizens as they have championed some aspects of secondary education and challenged others (Conant, 1961; Rickover, 1959). Following the launching of Sputnik I in the autumn of 1957, an apparent renewal of interest in educational opportunities and requirements for youth drew the attention of savants and scholars, of parents and priests, of editors and educationists. This has led to a reorganization of secondary education (Alexander, 1967).

Several aspects of this restructuring of secondary education give meaning to its character. A host of national curriculum projects has emerged, largely characterized by a deep interest in a single subject field (Alexander, 1967). Some such projects have by now become regularized and institutionalized (Killiam, 1959). Much of the restructuring has no doubt led to an updating of material long in need of reorganization or replacement. There are very few high schools which have not been encouraged to consider the new math or biology or physics or chemistry; it is clear that here lay the first concern of many who saw a need for increased emphasis in mathematics and science in order that we as a nation might better compete with other nations (Sand & Miller, 1963).

Within the past four or five years, much has been learned about such campaigns and strategies, and questions concerning the effect of monodisciplinary curriculum development on the meaningful learning of youth are very pertinent (Bellack, 1965). The need for more persuasive evidence that knowledge of the live phenomena will be achieved from study of the social sciences is clear to such curricular theorists as Bellack. Because he suggests that the social sciences cannot be sharply separated and that our distinctions between them are man-made approaches to analysis, he searches for a curriculum which leads to understanding of the broad cultural clusters of knowledge, not handicapped by the unrelated development of new knowledge and structures of the separate disciplines.

There is much to suggest that the high school continues to be subject-centered and that the demands of the new reorganization and stress on rigor have encouraged this trend (Conant, 1961). A series of reminders of this trend, as well as of the earlier and peculiar purposes of the American public high school, has appeared in professional journals (Wiles & Patterson, 1959; Wilhelms, 1966; Berman, 1954; Tyler, 1965). That such subject-centered programs may be frustrating to a serious degree for many youth, particularly for those who make up Wilhelm's "society of losers," is perfectly clear. The unsuitability of much of the academically oriented precollege education for a significant proportion of the youth population, particularly in large cities, has been clearly stated (Coleman, 1960; Deutsch, 1963).

Certainly the problems of urban youth and their education are most difficult. As well-informed and socially sensitive a person as Conant (1961) was frankly shocked to discover the dramatic disparity between going to school in Westchester County and merely tolerating school on the Lower East Side of Manhattan. The search for better education, adapted to the various ranges of opportunity and cultural advantage, has prompted more and more studies in which a wider range of scholarly disciplines are bringing their particular modes of inquiry to bear upon the problem (Passow, 1963).

Pedagogy and Learning. In their very essence, attacks on curricular problems have drawn impetus from the remarkably stimulating contributions of Bruner (1960, 1966), who clearly acknowledges a debt to the widely honored and dramatic work of Piaget. The central theme of this approach to the cultural disciplines lies in a discovery of the structures peculiar to each and the stressing of these structures with appropriate degrees of simplicity or complexity for varying age levels.

Another major effort concerning the total curriculum and the teaching-learning activity of the schools was sponsored by the National Education Association, which issued two preliminary volumes entitled *Deciding What to Teach* and *Planning and Organizing for Teaching*, which were followed by a summary volume, *Schools for the 60's* (National Education Association. . . , 1963a, 1963b, 1963c). Background committee work was completed, and then writers were chosen to prepare the three volumes. Here, in summary, are to be found twelve key questions identified by a group of blue-ribbon committees and their final list of 33 recommendations. Many of the questions and most of the recommendations have indirect or direct bearing on the program of secondary education in this decade and after.

That the influence of colleges and universities relative to the program of secondary education is strong has long been clear. The increasing proportion of youth avowedly seeking admission to institutions of higher education, the assumption that programs of higher education will provide broadened opportunity for all who are so favored, the repeated stress on the increasing demands for more education in the technical world of work are some—and a significant part —of the forces determining what youth will study and what the schools will try to teach. Although all this is not new to education for youth in America, the tightening of admissions requirements, as applications overtake and overwhelm the capacity of colleges, plus an increasing variety of screens to assist admissions officers and committees in selecting among applicants, has led to frenetic activity in the homes and schools of aspiring youth.

For two decades or more, appreciable research efforts of a rather low level of sophistication have dealt with the "holding power" of our schools. Through much of the elementary program and, indeed, into the senior high school years, most youth are in school because of the legal requirement to be there. But beyond this age, social pressure and the attractiveness of the program to youth and their parents, as contrasted with other activity which might have appeal, is a multivariable phenomenon. Data assembled by the U.S. Office of Education attest this "holding power" of formal education and the staying power of youth. The latest such data indicate that 37.8 percent of all youth enter college, and 71.0 percent graduate from high school. These figures, for 1965, compare rather markedly with those of the year before. In 1964, 35.7 percent of all youth entered college, and 66.7 percent graduated from high school. This latter year contrasts even more dramatically with 1954, when the corresponding figures were 28.3 percent and 55.3 percent. Two decades earlier, in 1934, the high schools graduated only 33.3 percent of all youth, and only 12.9 percent entered college (U.S. Department of Commerce, 1966). It is quite clear that programs for a wide range of interest and ability are needed in most of our secondary schools, since most American youth do stay in school into their seventeenth and eighteenth years. And here, in the breadth of interest and ability in the youth population, lies the apparent source of greatest difficulty faced by those responsible for developing and improving the programs of secondary education.

ORGANIZATION. Although little change has occurred in the total organization of schools for youth during the past 30 years, clarification of some aspects of internal organization has been studied, and a host of innovative alterations have been championed.

Grade organization has undergone an interesting change; for the first time, data collected by the Office of Education revealed in 1959 that the most common form of secondary school was no longer the traditional four-year high school. Instead, the six-year junior-senior high school had replaced it and represented 41.8 percent of all public secondary schools. Nearly a third of all youth enrolled in all public secondary schools attend schools with six grades included (U.S. Department of Commerce, 1966).

A persistent issue in the field of secondary educational organization is a concern with appropriate organization for providing the skills and knowledge needed in the world of work. In the larger American cities, specialized high schools for this and other purposes are traditional. Yet such a plan has obvious weaknesses, including most notably the matter of social class cleavages, obsolescence of skills taught, and the early career decisions forced upon youth. These considerations, within the context of a confused world of work, has led to restatement of organizational plans. A parallel question has been a concern with the level of skills which should be taught in technical institutes, community colleges, and other post-high school programs. Strong interest has recently been evident in a better melding of the known facts regarding future jobs, the skills needed for them, the welfare of individuals, and the welfare of the nation and its economic life (Draper, 1967).

Middle Years. The history of the junior high school movement has been told and retold. There is frank evidence that not all such schools came into existence because of philosophical or pedagogical advantage; rather, the actual matter of physical facilities has no doubt led to the establishment and subsequent adjustment of the grades and pupils to be accommodated in the "intermediate school," "junior high school," and again, the "middle school" (Briggs, 1920; Van Til & others, 1961). More recently, however, two significant approaches to the early secondary school years have been developed. Popper (1967), drawing on social and behavioral sciences, has developed a rationale for a school that is neither secondary nor elementary in its essential character. Schonhaut (1967), in a skillful piece of literary research, has sought to review all published evidence which might provide a rational answer as to what grades and what children and youth had best be included in the junior high school years.

Other innovative aspects of organization have dealt with such matters as "ungradedness" (Brown, 1963; Beggs & Buffie, 1967), team teaching, independent study, large and small group instruction, and so-called flexible scheduling (Trump & Baynham, 1961). The latter innovations are clustered under what has been called the "Trump plan" and are the result of evidence gathered and interpreted by the Commission on the Experimental Study of the Utilization of the Staff in the Secondary School, appointed by the National Association of Secondary School Principals and supported by The Fund for the Advancement of Education and the Ford Foundation. Certainly the charge that "experimentation never gets into the lifeblood of the schools" has been denied by the very fact of the wide distribution of pamphlets, still films, and television tapes concerned with the Trump plan.

Schedules. The related factors in the employment of teacher talent, time, space, and pupils in order that learning may best be effected must be well coordinated if the secondary school is to survive day by day. The business of making the master schedule is well known to all experienced administrators and to most counselors and teachers. As schools have grown larger and as their offerings have proliferated, while ability groupings and "tracks" have been maintained, the problems of scheduling all pupils for their best possible program has required skill and organizational planning of a high order. The conventional small-school operation, whereby one person had the onerous overall task of "schedule building" and then, usually, had help in the actual scheduling of individual students, has been replaced to a degree with the use of better means of assembling, examining, and relating the necessary data for this procedure. For many schools with rather conventional programs, the use of marginal punch cards in this process has become routine and quite successful. However, in the search for more flexible schedules and the necessary manipulation of masses of data, more sophisticated applications of modern technical resources have been developed. Two examples from several quite complex programs will be mentioned.

At Stanford University, drawing upon the skills of their colleague Oakford of the industrial engineering faculty, Bush and Allen have proposed a newer organization of the curriculum employing various time modules and relating them to general educational requirements and needs for all pupils. This model program would be quite impossible to operate without the use of present-day data-processing equipment, which Oakford has so skillfully adapted to this particular activity (Bush & Allen, 1964).

On the East Coast, the story of GASP (Generalized Academic Simulation Programs) has been written. The problem of scheduling such an unusual and complicated institution as M.I.T. was forced upon the administration by the impending retirement of the one person who had hand-scheduled this increasingly complicated university for some three decades. The registrar, aware of this challenge and the resources of the institution, saw salvation in the computer. After conferring with knowledgeable staff members, the responsibility for extending relevant programming research was turned over to Robert Holz. With the assistance of several younger colleagues and underwritten by the Educational Facilities Laboratories, a means of scheduling the huge M.I.T. program was first developed in 1961 and was followed by its application to other higher and secondary educational programs. Further, from this experience, the staff learned to develop simulated programs for nonexistent schools, involving still more innovative time and substantive relationships. GASP programs employ highly sophisticated combinations of digital computers, but as is the case in the Stanford program, clear analysis of the goals to be accomplished and the interrelationships of priorities is an essential preliminary. In other words, *expertise* on the part of school authorities and those who handle the computers is required (Educational Facilities Laboratories, 1964).

OTHER COUNTRIES. Research dealing with secondary education is not so voluminous nor, with few exceptions, so impressive in other countries as in the United States. In some other nations, however, many of the problems familiar to American educators are clearly manifest and studied. Reorganization of the forms of education for the youth of the land in harmony with political, social, and economic goals and resources is frequent. Attempts to reduce the influence of long-established academic schools such as the public schools of England and to replace them with schools of a more comprehensive character have been made. No doubt, new forms of educational organization will follow. A loss of confidence in the results of the "11 plus" and similar screening devices is even reported in the popular press (Peterson, 1962; Pedley, 1963; King, 1958).

In less developed lands, and particularly in the emerging nations, the status of youth education is ill-defined. In these, as is true of the early history of all nations, formal education for youth is limited to the favored few. This is partly because of the obvious costs involved, the need for more young people in the work force, and the frequent class distinctions which may characterize the social matrix. It is clear, however, that interest in education is great and that an increasingly interdependent, shrinking world will require that among all peoples knowledge must be systematically acquired and applied to the problems confronting the world as a whole.

PROBLEMS. The major and chronic problem which confronts all who are concerned with secondary education is that of the goals to be sought. Much clarification of statements having to do with this problem has occurred in the past decade, and more is needed. Part of the problem lies in our desirable diversity as a people and as youth, and part of it is a by-product of our decentralization of the control (and much of the design) of American education (Krathwohl & Bloom, 1956).

The changing role of teachers in secondary schools has been commented upon in many studies, and a broader understanding of the teacher's relationship to students, parents, administration, and society at large is clearly needed. Further, how this teacher works with other teachers and with students—involving a "team" relationship, new levels of preparation, and continued study—all suggests rich fields of inquiry (Zeigler, 1966).

Mention has been made above of the extension of our knowledge, through studies within and without the classroom, of the act and art of teaching. Piaget and Bruner suggest further extensive studies, most of which call for great resources in intellect, time, and money. The fact that the Federal government increasingly is encouraging research through grants and that foundations large and small are further supporting a wide range of studies, some determined by the foundations themselves and others by applicants for grants, suggests that much more information on knowledge and learning may be a predictable future result.

Second to the matter of goals perhaps, in its insistent demand for the attention of competent researchers, is the role of youth in modern America. His status, his problems, his abilities, and his future are worthy of our best research and our best educational effort.

David B. Austin
Columbia University

References

Alexander, William M. (Ed.) "The Changing Secondary School Curriculum; Readings by Wm. M. Alexander." Holt, 1967. 479p.

Beggs, David W., III, and Buffie, Edward G. *Nongraded Schools in Action.* Indiana U Press, 1967. 270p.

Bellack, Arno A. "What Knowledge Is of Most Worth?" H Sch J 48:318–32; 1965.

Berman, Sidney. "As a Psychiatrist Sees Pressures on Middle Class Teen-agers." NEA J 54:17ff; 1954.

Briggs, Thomas H. *The Junior High School.* Houghton, 1920. 350p.

Brown, B. Frank. *The Nongraded High School.* Prentice-Hall, 1963. 223p.

Bruner, Jerome S. *The Process of Education.* Harvard U Press, 1960. 97p.

Bruner, Jerome S. *Toward a Theory of Instruction.* Belknap Press, 1966. 176p.

Bush, Robert N., and Allen, Dwight W. *A New Design for High School Education, Assuming a Flexible Schedule.* McGraw-Hill, 1964. 197p.

Butts, R. Freeman, and Cremin, Lawrence A. *A History of Education in American Culture.* Holt, 1953. 628p.

Coleman, James S. "The Adolescent Subculture and Academic Achievement." Am J Sociol 65:337–47; 1960.

Commissioner's Advisory Committee on Human Relations and Community Tensions. *Desegregating the Public Schools of New York City.* Office of the State Education Commissioner of New York, 1964. 47p.

Conant, James B. *Education in the Junior High School Years.* ETS, 1960. 46p.

Conant, James B. *Slums and Suburbs*. McGraw-Hill, 1961. 147p.

Deutsch, Martin P. "The Disadvantaged Child and the Learning Process." In Passow, A. Harry. (Ed.) *Education in Depressed Areas*. Teachers Col, Columbia U, 1963. p. 163–79.

Draper, Dale C. *Educating for Work*. National Association of Secondary School Principals, 1967. 115p.

Educational Facilities Laboratories. *School Scheduling by Computer: The Story of GASP*. The Laboratories, 1964. 46p.

Eliot, Charles W. "Can School Programmes Be Shortened and Enriched?" In *Proceedings of the Department of Superintendence of the National Education Association, 1888*. GPO, 1888. p. 101–18.

Killian, James Rhyne. *Education for the Age of Science*. GPO, 1959. 36p.

King, Edmund J. *Other Schools and Ours*. Holt, 1958. 224p.

Krathwohl, David R., and Bloom, Benjamin S. (Eds.) *Taxonomy of Educational Objectives; The Classification of Educational Goals, By a Committee of College and University Examiners*. McKay, 1956.

Medsker, Leland L. *The Junior College*. McGraw-Hill, 1960. 367p.

Meyer, Adolph E. *An Educational History of the American People*. McGraw-Hill, 1957. 444p.

National Education Association, National Committee of the Project on Instruction. *Deciding What to Teach*. NEA, 1963(a). 264p.

National Education Association, National Committee of the Project on Instruction. *Planning and Organizing for Teaching*. NEA, 1963(b). 190p.

National Education Association, National Committee of the Project on Instruction. *Schools for the 60's*. McGraw-Hill, 1963(c). 146p.

Passow, A. Harry. (Ed.). *Education in Depressed Areas*. Teachers Col, Columbia U, 1963.

Pedley, Robin. *The Comprehensive School*. Penguin Books, Ltd., 1963. 222p.

Peterson, A. D. C. *A Hundred Years of Education*. Collier Books, 1962. 320p.

Popper, Samuel H. *The American Middle School*. Blaisdell Publishing Co., 1967. 378p.

Rickover, Hyman George. *Education and Freedom*. Dutton, 1959. 256p.

Sand, Ole, and Miller, Richard I. "Perspectives on National Studies in the Disciplines." *J Sec Ed* 38:27–33; 1963.

Schonhaut, Charles I. *An Examination of Educational Research as it Pertains to the Grade Organization for the Middle Schools*. Teachers Col, Columbia U, 1967.

Trump, J. Lloyd, and Baynham, Dorsey. *Guide to Better Schools*. Rand McNally, 1961. 148p.

Tyler, Ralph W. "The Knowledge Explosion: Implications for Secondary Education." *Ed Forum* 29: 145–53; 1965.

U.S. Department of Commerce, Bureau of the Census. *Current Population Reports*. GPO, 1965.

U.S. Department of Commerce. *Statistical Abstract of the United States*, 87th ed. GPO, 1966. 1039p.

U.S. Department of Health, Education, and Welfare. "P.L. 89–10: The Nation's First Elementary and Secondary Education Act . . ." *Indicators* May, 1965(a). 20p.

U.S. Department of Health, Education, and Welfare, and U.S. Office of Education. *Digest of Educational Statistics*. GPO, 1965(b).

U.S. Department of Health, Education, and Welfare, and U.S. Office of Education. "Fall 1965 Statistics of Public Schools." *Statistical Abstracts*. GPO, 1965(c).

Van Til, William, and others. *Modern Education for the Junior High School Years*. Bobbs-Merrill, 1961. 527p.

Wiles, Kimball, and Patterson, Franklin. "Beliefs About the American High School." In *The High School We Need*. NEA, 1959. p. 2–4.

Wilhelms, Fred T. "Background for Choice-Making." *Nat Assn Sec Sch Prin B* 313:3–74; 1966.

Woodward, W. H. *Vittorino Da Feltre and Other Humanist Educators*. Cambridge U Press, 1897. 261p.

Zeigler, Harmon. *The Political World of the High School Teacher*. U Oregon Press, 1966. 160p.

SEX DIFFERENCES

The subject of differences between the sexes is one of perennial interest both to research workers and to the general public. There are at least two reasons for this interest. The first is that the organization of society requires that men and women play somewhat different roles, and it is desirable that the shaping of these roles be based on dependable knowledge about masculine and feminine characteristics. For example, in the designing of school systems, decisions about coeducation must be made. Should boys and girls go to the same schools, or should they be separated for part or all of their work? Should they begin their schooling at the same age, or do developmental differences suggest an earlier age of entry for girls than for boys?

The second source of continuing interest in sex differences is the desire to promote better relationships between the sexes. If the family is to continue as a basic social institution and if men and women are to work in harmony in all the complex undertakings of a highly developed society, it is important that the special needs and abilities of males and females be understood.

HISTORICAL TRENDS IN RESEARCH. At the time research on sex differences was initiated toward the end of the nineteenth century and the beginning of the twentieth century, the feminist movement was generating a special interest in the question of whether women's intelligence was or was not equal to men's. Generally speaking, what most investigators hoped to find was evidence for equality.

During the second quarter of the twentieth century, partly because of the influence of psychoanalytic theory, the emphasis shifted to the question of personality differences. This was the era in which M-F scales flourished—that is, personality inventories composed of items differentiating significantly between groups of males and females.

Since about 1950, the major emphasis has been on developmental differences. There have been many studies of sex role concepts, identification patterns, and the relationships between personality variables within each sex group.

ABILITY DIFFERENCES. The initial question, Do males and females differ in intelligence? has never been settled and the reasons why it cannot be with our present techniques for measuring intelligence have become clear. Intelligence tests do not measure pure native ability. What their scores represent are differences between individuals in ability developed through a complex interaction between initial endowment and experience in successive learning situations. These learning situations are not alike for boys and girls, even those who grow up in what look like identical environments. Consequently, males are more likely to give good answers to some kinds of questions, females to other kinds. The result is that total scores on a test tend to average higher for males if the test contains a predominance of masculine items, higher for females if feminine items predominate. In constructing tests to be used in assessing the general ability of individuals of both sexes, the different kinds of questions to be included are selected in such a way as to balance the two varieties and produce average scores for males and females that do not differ significantly (McNemar, 1942). But when one does this he rules out any possibility of finding out by means of such a test whether or not the sexes are truly equal. Equality has been built into the test itself.

A problem with more practical implications, in school and in the world at large, is that of the nature and origins of achievement differences between the sexes. It is a well-documented fact that girls do better in school than boys do, at least so far as teacher-rated achievement is concerned (Northby, 1958). It is a fact equally well supported by historical evidence that outstanding life achievements are much rarer in women than in men (Tyler, 1965).

On educational achievement tests sex differences are small but their directions are consistent from one study to another. Girls typically excel in English, spelling, writing, and art, boys in mathematical reasoning, history, geography, and science (Terman & Tyler, 1954).

Special-ability tests typically show feminine superiority on verbal fluency (though not on vocabulary or verbal comprehension), manual dexterity, rote memory, and clerical aptitude, masculine superiority on spatial relationships, problem solving, and mechanical aptitudes (Tyler, 1965).

The variability within each sex group is, in general, so large that the practical significance of the differences between group averages is not great. Some girls, for example, are far above the boys' average in mathematical reasoning; some boys are far above the girls' average in verbal fluency.

PERSONALITY AND MOTIVATIONAL DIFFERENCES. In the realm of personality needs and orientation, differences between average scores for comparable male and female groups have turned out to be much more striking than they are for abilities. Study after study shows that males from preschool to adult levels are more aggressive than females (Oetzel, 1962), whether the trait is assessed by means of observation, ratings, projective techniques, or self-report inventories.

Girls and women tend to score higher on measures of neuroticism or emotional instability (Terman & Tyler, 1954), and a study by Honzik and McKee (1962) suggests that this difference may be in evidence even during the preschool years, if one is willing to accept thumb-sucking as evidence for instability.

Differences in interests also appear at all ages in studies utilizing many different assessment techniques. Males are more interested in adventurous, mechanical, scientific, and leadership activities, females in artistic, musical, literary, clerical, and social service activities (Strong, 1943; Traxler & McCall, 1941). Interests of girls, as measured by the Strong Vocational Interest Blank, appear to be less diversified than those of boys. A large majority of them receive their only high scores on scales for occupations that can be considered typically feminine—e.g., office worker, stenographer, secretary, and housewife.

Children's interests show sex differences even at an early age. Boys express stronger preferences for active games and vigorous physical activities. They like stories or television programs involving adventure and violent action. Girls prefer dolls, paper activities with pencils and crayons, games calling for skillful movements, and sentimental and domestic stories. Tyler's comparison of the interests of English and American children (1956) and Gaier and Collier's comparison of the reading interests of American and Finnish children (1960) suggest that sex differences are greater than nationality differences, at least within Western culture.

One of the most pervasive of these sex differences in orientation has to do with general sensitivity and responsiveness to people. The summary by Oetzel (1962) covers many such research reports using different assessment techniques for different groups. Goodenough (1957) showed that such differences can be observed even in two-year-olds.

Another pervasive sort of difference appears to be related to body image. When asked to make drawings to complete simple figures, females draw closed figures, static objects, flowers, rooms, and household furnishings; males draw open figures, moving objects, vehicles, and projectiles (Franck & Rosen, 1949). Erikson (1951) and Honzik (1951) obtained evidence for the same sort of differences using the technique of having boys and girls construct stage scenes from building-materials and small objects.

Because all the research studies on temperament and motivation show considerable within-sex variability, efforts to construct measuring instruments to assess just how "masculine" or "feminine" an individual is in comparison with others of the same sex have frequently been made. The pioneer effort in this direction was by Terman and Miles (1936). The standard procedure is to select for an M-F scale those items from a personality or interest inventory for which there is a significant difference in the responses of comparable male and female groups. Masculinity-femininity scales have been useful in some kinds of research, but they have not proved to have much practical value in describing individual personality. Scales derived from different item pools give scores that do not correlate to any great extent with one another (Barrows & Zuckerman, 1960). It seems doubtful that *general masculinity-femininity* is a useful descriptive term.

THE ORGANIZATION OF PERSONALITY. The most salient findings from the research on sex differences since about 1950 have been the evidence that personality traits are linked together differently in males and in females and that these differences in personality organization grow out of differences in developmental processes. When factor analyses of either ability or personality measures are carried out separately for the two sex groups, the factor patterns are not alike. Gardner and others (1959) demonstrated this for what they call cognitive control principles—e.g., leveling–sharpening, focusing–scanning. Diggory (1953) presented evidence of differential factor patterns for attitudes, Barratt (1955) for space-visualization, Bereiter (1960) for fluency.

Other kinds of analyses of correlation coefficients have also pointed to the existence of sex differences, although the investigators have often not been able to come up with satisfactory explanations for them. Seashore (1962) brought together a large number of validity coefficients for scholastic aptitude tests and found that groups of girls had typically produced significantly higher coefficients than had groups of boys. Weitz and Colver (1959) reported that having selected a major study before one entered college led to better grades for men but not for women students. Kagan and Moss (1962), investigating the stability of personality traits from childhood to adulthood, found that for some aspects of aggression, correlations between ratings at the two stages of life were higher for boys than for girls, whereas for passive-dependent behavior, correlations over a period of time were higher for girls than for boys.

For some personality characteristics, the direction of the relationship is different for males and females. Beloff (1958) found that on the tendency to neuroticism conforming women tended to be rated lower than the nonconforming, whereas conforming men tended to be more neurotic than the nonconforming. Iscoe and Garden (1961) noted that field dependence is positively related to popularity for girls, negatively related to popularity for boys.

Results cited by Shaw and McCuen (1960) suggest that the origins of underachievement in school are not the same for boys as for girls. For the male underachievers they studied, the behavior pattern began in the first grade. For the female underachievers good achievement during the first five school years had been followed by a sudden slump during the sixth.

A comprehensive research report by Kogan and Wallach (1964) demonstrated that the tendency to take risks, typically more characteristic of males than females, was differently related to anxiety and defensiveness in the two sexes.

RESEARCH ON DEVELOPMENTAL CONCEPTS. Theoretical explanations of many kinds of differences such as those just cited have increasingly been couched in developmental terms. Controversy about whether such differences are hereditary or environmental, biological or social no longer occupies a prominent position in such discussions.

The biological fact that females mature more rapidly than males, so that at least during their first eight or nine years in school girls are farther along in their own growth process than boys are, has been well established. Whether mental growth is related closely enough to physical growth to warrant any kind of differential treatment in school is less certain. Ames and Ilg (1964) compared sex groups made up of 33 boy–girl pairs matched for IQ, age, and socioeconomic status, and they reported that at the kindergarten and first- and second-grade levels, the girls scored significantly higher on four types of tests having to do with aptitude for school learning. However, sex differences did not appear in Clark's analysis (1959) of third-, fifth-, and eighth- grade scores on the California Test of Mental Maturity, and they had not shown up in most previous comparisons.

The theoretical concept around which much of the more sophisticated developmental research has been organized is the concept of sex roles. In every society males and females are assigned somewhat different parts to play, somewhat different tasks to carry out, because of the basic biological fact that childbearing is a female function. Anthropological research such as that of Mead (1949) has testified to this differentiation in sex roles in a wide variety of cultures and has demonstrated at the same time large differences in the way such roles are defined by various groups. Psychologists have concerned themselves with the nature of these sex-role definitions in Western society and with the developmental processes that occur as boys and girls assimilate them.

Several studies based on quite different age groups have pointed out that opinions about behavior appropriate for persons of each sex show a good deal of agreement from one sample of the population to another. Sheriffs and Jarrett (1953) found that male and female college students tend to agree about the ways in which the sexes differ, and McKee and Sherriffs (1957) showed that both boys and girls tend to assume male superiority. Tuddenham (1952), by means of a peer-rating technique, in which elementary school children filled in the names of classmates exhibiting various personality traits, demonstrated that different sets of traits are correlated with popularity ratings for the two sexes.

The most salient finding from the many inquiries into the developmental processes through which sex roles are learned and accepted has been that they begin very early in the individual's life. One favored technique for attaining information from young children has been the "It" test devised by Brown (1956), which asks subjects to make choices for a child pictured in such a way that it can be seen as either a boy or a girl. It is assumed that each child will attribute his own sex to "It," although some results obtained by Brown (1962) suggest that this does not always happen. While Brown (1956) showed that there was a steady increase from kindergarten through the elementary grades in the average number of sex-appropriate choices, such choices predominate even at the kindergarten level, especially for boys. Hartup and Zook (1960) reported that even three-year-olds choose sex-appropriate pictures. Evidence that these choices reflect parental expectations comes from a study by Fauls and Smith (1956), in which it was shown that children's choices tend to agree with choices they think their parents would make for them. Using a standardized doll-play situation to reveal opinions about sex roles, Sears and others (1948) found that boys whose fathers were at home developed the concept of aggressiveness as a masculine trait much earlier than boys whose fathers were absent.

Such findings, suggesting that children somehow learn sex role concepts from their parents in early childhood, have focused attention on the concept of identification. In a series of studies, Mussen and Rutherford (1963) have thrown some light on this process. It seems not to be simply a matter of the child's imitating the specific behavior of the parent of the same sex. In boys the development of masculine characteristics turned out to be related to the closeness of the relationship between the boy and his father rather than to the father's particular personality characteristics. In girls the development of feminine characteristics was related to the mother's scores on power and self-acceptance as well as nurturance (a predominantly feminine trait); it is also related to certain characteristics of the father, his masculinity score and the degree to which he encouraged feminine behavior. Kagan (1964) has produced a comprehensive review of research on sex typing and sex role identity.

IMPLICATIONS FOR EDUCATION. The policy questions most clearly related to the research on sex differences are those having to do with the advisability or inadvisability of coeducation. The issues are complex, and evidence tending to support both sides of the question can be selected from the available research findings. Those who favor separate schools at elementary, secondary, or higher levels can point to the sex differences in needs, interests, and life styles to support their position. Particularly at the primary level, some think that because of the sex differences in rate of development, boys enter school with a disadvantage and would be better off if they did not have to face competition from the more mature girls. The most cogent support for coeducation from the research data is the universal finding that for all traits measured, within-sex differences are greater than between-sex differences. A special curriculum focused on the needs of the "typical" boy or the "typical" girl would still be unsuitable for a sizeable proportion of the individuals in a single-sex school. Generally, American educators have considered that the advantages of coeducation outweigh its disadvantages.

Another implication of the research findings for education is that attention must be paid to subtle as well as obvious influences on development if each individual is to make his maximum contribution to society. Especially in the case of girls, concepts of sex roles can be restrictive and limit individual achievement more effectively than overt discrimination does. Because such concepts develop very early in life, and largely without deliberate instruction, even a coeducational school does not really provide an identical environment for boys and girls. To encourage a larger number of highly intelligent girls to enter scientific occupations, for example, it will probably be necessary to communicate not only the fact that there are opportunities but also the fact that scientific occupations are not inherently inappropriate for women. Drews (1965) has explored various ways of accomplishing this purpose.

The solutions to problems raised for education by sex differences will most likely come through more extensive individualization of the whole educational undertaking. When it becomes possible to recognize a variety of kinds and levels of achievement in students of both sexes, and to plan individual learning experiences directed toward individually planned goals, sex differences, like the many other kinds of differences between persons, will enrich rather than complicate the work of the educator.

Leona E. Tyler
University of Oregon

References

Ames, Louise B., and Ilg, Frances L. "Sex Differences in Test Performance of Matched Girl-boy Pairs in the Five-to-nine-year-old Range." *J Genet Psychol* 104:25–34; 1964.

Barratt, Ernest S. "The Space-visualization Factors Related to Temperament Traits." *J Psychol* 39:279–87; 1955.

Barrows, Gordon A., and Zuckerman, Marvin. "Construct Validity of Three Masculinity-femininity Tests." *J Cons Psychol* 24:441–5; 1960.

Beloff, Halla. "Two Forms of Social Conformity: Acquiescence and Conventionality." *J Abn Social Psychol* 56:104; 1958.

Bereiter, Carl "Verbal and Ideational Fluency in

Superior Tenth Grade Students." *J Ed Psychol* 51:337-45; 1960.

Brown, Daniel G. "Sex-role Preference in Young Children." *Psychol Monogr* 70: No. 14; 1956.

Brown, Daniel G. "Sex-role Preference in Children: Methodological Problems." *Psychol Reports* 11: 477-8; 1962.

Clark, William W. "Boys and Girls—Are There Significant Ability and Achievement Differences?" *Phi Delta Kappan* 41:73-6; 1959.

Diggory, James A. "Sex Differences in the Organization of Attitudes." *J Pers* 22:89-100; 1953.

Drews, Elizabeth M. "Counseling for Selfactualization in Girls and Young Women." *J Couns Psychol* 12:167-75; 1965.

Erikson, Erik H. "Sex Differences in the Play Configurations of Preadolescents." *Am J Orthopsychiatry* 21:667-92; 1951.

Fauls, Lydia B., and Smith, Walter D. "Sex-role Learning of Five-year-olds." *J Genet Psychol* 89: 105-17; 1956.

Franck, Kate, and Rosen, Ephraim. "A Projective Test of Masculinity-femininity." *J Cons Psychol* 13: 247-56; 1949.

Gaier, Eugene L., and Collier, Mary J. "The Latency-stage Story Preferences of American and Finnish Children." *Child Develop* 31:431-51; 1960.

Gardner, Richard W., and others. "Cognitive Control: A Study of Individual Consistencies in Cognitive Behavior." *Psychol Issues* 1: Monogr 4; 1959.

Goodenough, Evelyn W. "Interest in Persons as an Aspect of Sex Difference in the Early Years." *Genet Psychol Monogr* 55:287-323; 1957.

Hartup, Willard W., and Zook, Elsie Z. "Sex-role Preferences in Three- and Four-year-old Children." *J Cons Psychol* 24:420-6; 1960.

Honzik, Marjorie P. "Sex Differences in the Occurrence of Materials in the Play Constructions of Pre-adolescents." *Child Develop* 22:15-35; 1951.

Honzik, Marjorie P., and McKee, John P. "The Sex Difference in Thumb-sucking." *J Pediatrics* 61: 726-32; 1962.

Iscoe, Ira, and Carden, Joyce A. "Field Dependence, Manifest Anxiety, and Sociometric Status in Children." *J Cons Psychol* 25:184; 1961.

Kagan, Jerome "Acquisition and Significance of Sex Typing and Sex Role Identity." In Hoffman, M. L., and Hoffman, L. W. (Eds.) *Review of Child Development Research*. Russell Sage, 1964. p. 137-67.

Kagan, Jerome, and Moss, Howard A. *Birth to Maturity*. Wiley, 1962. 381p.

Kogan, Nathan, and Wallach, Michael A. *Risk-taking: A Study in Cognition and Personality*. Holt, 1964. 278p.

McKee, John P., and Sherriffs, Alex C. "The Differential Evaluation of Males and Females." *J Pers* 25:356-71; 1957.

McNemar, Quinn. *The Revision of the Stanford-Binet Scale*. Houghton, 1942. 185p.

Mead, Margaret. *Male and Female*. Morrow, 1949. 477p.

Mussen, Paul, and Rutherford, Evaretta. "Parent-child Relations and Parental Personality in Relation to Sex-role Preferences." *Child Develop* 34: 589-607; 1963.

Northby, Arwood S. "Sex Differences in High School Scholarship." *Sch Soc* 86:63-4; 1958.

Oetzel, R. M. "Selected Bibliography on Sex Differences." Stanford U, 1962. (Mimeographed.)

Sears, Robert R., and others. "Effect of Father Separation on Pre-school Children's Doll-play Aggression." *Child Develop* 17:219-43; 1948.

Seashore, Harold G. "Women are More Predictable than Men." *J Couns Psychol* 9:261-70; 1962.

Shaw, Merville C., and McCuen, John T. "The Onset of Under-achievement in Bright Children." *J Ed Psychol* 51:103-9; 1960.

Sheriffs, Alex C., and Jarrett, Rheem F. "Sex Differences in Attitudes about Sex Differences." *J Psychol* 35:161-8; 1953.

Strong, Edward K., Jr. *Vocational Interests of Men and Women*. Stanford U Press, 1943. 746p.

Terman, Lewis M., and Miles, Catherine C. *Sex and Personality: Studies in Masculinity and Femininity*. McGraw-Hill, 1936. 600p.

Terman, Lewis M., and Tyler, Leona E. "Psychological Sex Differences." In Carmichael, L. (Ed.) *Manual of Child Psychology*, 2d ed. Wiley, 1954. p. 1064-114.

Traxler, Arthur E., and McCall, William C. "Some Data on the Kuder Preference Record." *Ed Psychol Meas* 1:253-68; 1941.

Tuddenham, Read D. "Studies in Reputation. I: Sex and Grade Differences in School Children's Evaluations of Their Peers." *Psychol Monogr* 66: No. 1; 1952.

Tyler, Leona E. "A Comparison of the Interests of English and American School Children." *J Genet Psychol* 88:175-81; 1956.

Tyler, Leona E. *The Psychology of Human Differences*. Appleton, 1965. 572p.

Weitz, Henry, and Colver, Robert M. "The Relationship Between the Educational Goals and the Academic Performance of Women, a Confirmation." *Ed Psychol Meas* 19:373-80; 1959.

SOCIAL AND EMOTIONAL DEVELOPMENT

The social and emotional development of an individual is a process of interrelated transactions between an organism and its environment. The organism is an open-energy system continuously receiving information and energy from its environment, modifying itself and the environment by the way it processes the information and expends energy. Both heredity and environment are mutually responsible. An open system means development is modifiable throughout life rather than being set and unalterable on the basis of early life experiences only. The importance attached to early experience grows out of the psychoanalytic tradition, the field work of behavioral biologists, and longitudinal studies such as those of Bloom (1964) and Kagan and Moss (1962). However, even these studies, as well as other longitudinal efforts, suggest that change is also a characteristic of development over time (Emmerich, 1966).

The child modifies his behavior so that, although there are consistent aspects of his fundamental personality organization evident through time, there are changes in specific behavior appropriate to internal changes and external demands.

The body contributes not only the original biochemical organization with which to receive and interpret stimuli but also the continuing endocrine triggers of change, which serve as additional stimuli and require reinterpretation of meanings. The social context provides patterns of information which serve as stimuli to which the growing body must respond. The results of these responses are labeled "patterns of behavior," and from these emotion, values, attitudes, and self concepts of children and youth are inferred.

Processes of development may be seen as nearly universal; the particular content of ideas and the way in which emotions are expressed, as well as the conditions which trigger emotional response, are related to the social environment of a child. Further, the emerging pattern of behavior, because of both biological and environmental circumstances, is unique to the individual (Bayley, 1956) yet reflective of a given culture (Havighurst, 1960). Individuality of behavior is observable in the neonate (Kessen & others, 1961).

Certain major categories of development, by no means mutually exclusive, are presented below as examples of this transactional process and of the contributions of family, culture, and individual to his own growth.

EMOTIONS AND THEIR DEVELOPMENT. The area of research into emotions is experiencing an upheaval. In addition to the traditional approaches to the investigation of separate emotions (Ausubel, 1960), new terminology and concepts about emotion as a general state are developing. All behavior is affect-laden, although intensity varies considerably. Emotion has both cognitive and conative aspects; that is, one experiences something, with some degree of intensity, and assigns meaning, usually a label, to the experience. One school of thought suggests the abandonment of traditional labels for separate emotions and the substitution of the notion of arousal, which is inseparable from motivation. Duffy (1957) indicates that arousal breaks down the distinction between drives and emotions, since there is postulated an active organism in differing states of intensity. High-intensity states are what were formerly called "emotions" (Duffy, 1962). The intensity state, or level of activation, is a function of a situation, a stimulus, and the organism. Included within this theory would be levels of activation influenced by drugs such as LSD. The individual's level of activation is usually in keeping with the demands of the situation as seen by the individual and includes past experience with goal-attainment behavior.

As an indication of the cognitive-conative approach to emotion, Schachter and Singer (1962) suggest that emotional states and their labels are functions of the interaction of physiological arousal and appropriate cognitions. Simply stated, if one is told he should be angry, but is not physiologically aroused, he will not state that he is angry. If one is physiologically aroused by ambiguous circumstances (such as by drugs) for which there is no clear label available, the person will be unable to identify his emotions. The interplay of organism and environmental forces in both the intensity and the display of emotion is also illustrated in the longitudinal studies of Jones (1966) and Murphy and others (1962). Jones measured reactivity during early infancy under provocative situations. Research on the same subjects as adolescents and again when in their thirties suggests a continuing individual pattern of reactivity related to external observable measures. For example, those who are low reactives on GSR are more talkative, more animated, more attention-seeking, and more exertive as adolescents. The Murphy study suggests that youngsters who are highly sensitive at birth develop differential modes of coping with emotion as a result of the sensitivity level and emotionality of the mother. Highly sensitive infants with highly emotional mothers develop different patterns from infants with low sensitivity and highly emotional mothers.

Emotional development is seen as the evolution of specific emotions from a general one that is usually labeled "excitement." Plutchik (1962) postulates that there are a small number of pure emotions and that each exists in varying degrees of intensity or levels of arousal. Further, he defines emotion as consisting of patterned organic responses which have goal direction, such as protection or exploration. This concept of emotion as functional to the person is a classical one, going back to ideas of "flight or fight."

Both the psychoanalytic tradition and the general behavior approach deal with specific emotions such as curiosity, aggression, love, fear, and anxiety.

Fear and Anxiety. Sullivan (1953) differentiates between fear and anxiety by defining anxiety as a reflection of internal discomfort, and fear as a means of dealing with external danger. Erickson (1950) indicates that the younger the child the harder it is to distinguish between fear and anxiety. Ausubel (1960) sees fear as related to self-esteem and the cognitive development of the child. He differentiates between fear and anxiety by stating that anxiety is an internal subjective state originating in an internal subjective fashion related to threat to the self-esteem of the child. Anxiety is a more diffuse state; fear is more related to specific environmental objects or people.

Fear and anxiety are seen as learned behaviors growing out of interaction particularly with parents in infancy and early childhood (Sears & others, 1957; Whiting & Child, 1953; Kagan & Moss, 1962). To some degree these are related to dependency patterns and punishment techniques. An example of psychosocial multiple causation of emotional behavior is school phobia, a particular manifestation of anxiety. It is more prevalent in children of above average intelligence, in Jewish families with two children, and in situations in which the mother discourages the development of independent behavior and encourages dependency (Sarason, 1960). The culture not only indicates what objects, events, or people should be feared but also provides vehicles for channeling fear. Henry (1965) analyzes television as a device for instilling appropriate fears, such as fear of death, in preschoolers.

Studies of school-age children indicate that fears of bodily injury and physical punishment are extremely common. Girls seem to report more fears than boys. The girls' fears seem to be more social in nature, whereas the boys are more concerned with bodily injury (Jersild & Holmes, 1935). Children's worries and fears about self do not change in frequency as a function of age from 9 to 17 (Anderson, 1959).

Whether fear established early is predictive of later adjustment is not as yet fully established empirically, although it is a basic assumption in most theories of development. There are correlates between child-rearing practices and adult behavior (Whiting & Child, 1953). Some longitudinal data suggests stability of pattern. For example, social interaction anxiety in the early school years is related to similar patterns of adult behavior (Kagan & Moss, 1962).

Although neither fear nor anxiety were specifically identified, the California Growth Study yields information on such affect-laden behavior categories as friendly, social; bold, irritable, defiant, hostile; happy, positive behavior, calm. Stability of boys' behavior seems to be related to a stable mother-son relationship. Boys' behavior is also more closely associated with maternal behavior than is girls'. Girls appear to go through an earlier adolescent disruption in their behavior but stabilize sooner than do the boys (Bayley, 1964).

Aggression. Aggression has been described in the following ways: reaction to frustration (Dollard & others, 1939); learned through social learning and modeling after the adult (Bandura & Walters, 1963); learned behavior explainable through conditioning in early childhood growing out of a situation of rage (Sears & others, 1957); and instinctual in man (Lorenz, 1960).

Learning to direct rage (either inward or outward) begins within the first year of life. The infant learns to use this emotion to manipulate his mother. During the second year aggression is gratifying in that, at the very least, it relieves tension (Sears & others, 1957). There generally is a positive relation between parental control and the use of power, especially of a punitive sort, and displays of aggression (Becker, 1964). The concept of modeling behavior (Bandura & Walters, 1963; Sears & others, 1957) suggests that when the child sees significant adults engaging in aggression, with a consequent absence of punishment, he tends to become more aggressive. This would imply that children can learn to be aggressive through other means than reinforcement.

Aggression in adolescent boys seems to be related to early childhood experiences particularly in relation to fathers. A retrospective study (Bandura & Walters, 1959) suggests that a poor interpersonal relationship between father and son in the second year of life is a major factor in later aggressive delinquent behavior. Some of the other factors which contribute to adolescent aggression are: rejection, punitiveness, and inconsistent treatment from parent to parent.

Ethologists view aggression as innate, healthy, necessary, and ineradicable (Lorenz, 1960). Further, aggression is seen as not limited to the human species but as operative even on subhuman levels in maintaining control over territory.

Longitudinal studies again indicate predictability, within limits, of adult behavior patterns from childhood aggression.

Positive Emotion. Because of the nature of the destructive emotions, most research has been concentrated upon them. Positive emotions such as affection and curiosity have not been so thoroughly investigated. Berlyne (1960) postulates curiosity as a basic motivational force. In a series of researches Harlow (1958, 1962) has investigated affection in infant monkeys and their later behavior as adults. It is clear that positive emotional development is a complex phenomenon. It seems to stem from the meeting of basic physiological needs, including the need for intimate physical contact with the mother. For example, when placed in fear situations, infant monkeys responded to the surrogate mother, a terry-cloth model which provided tactile stimulation, in preference to the model which provided only food. However, monkeys reared on surrogate mothers experienced considerable difficulty in normal sexual development. When female monkeys so reared become mothers, they do not demonstrate usual maternal behavior.

The research on love has been mostly confined to the effects of its absence on the development of children rather than on its developmental history in children. Prescott (1952) has attempted to define love and describe its role in human development.

Love has been postulated as arising in infancy at the same time as the infant begins to differentiate "self" and "not-self." Its origins represent the need of the infant to elicit response from his environment (Suttie, 1952). The mother or mothering-one is the critical respondent, and a transactional relationship is built. Maternal expression of affection and emotional involvement in the first three years are highly related to daughters' happiness during that period and to sons' positive behavior up to the age of seven (Bayley, 1964).

The establishment of feelings of being loved and being able to give love become clearer as the self concept is developed and become key elements in the structure of the self. With age, love is extended beyond the family circle, to pets and peers and other adults. The sexual component of love, present probably from the beginning, comes into sharp awareness after puberty and often leads to confusion between the terms *sex* and *love*. Love relationships established early in life influence not only development of values but also sex-role identification.

Sex-role Identification. The concept of identification originally stemmed from psychoanalytic theory, but has now been incorporated into general behavior and transactional theories of development. Identification is a major process in socialization. Sex-role identification may be seen as an exemplar of the process, relating to emotions, moral development, and self concept. There are two main questions: (1) When do children identify themselves by sex, and how stable is this identification? (2) How do they learn appropriate roles?

Sex typing is established very early. At one and a half years, kibbutz children select play objects and activities by sex type (Neubauer, 1965), although other research indicates that it is not until the age of three that most children are able to distinguish between the sexes. All typing is probably well established by the age of five or six and remains comparatively stable thereafter (Kagan & Moss, 1962; Bandura & Walters, 1963; Whiting & Child, 1953). The early perceptual awareness that one is boy or girl is probably a key factor. Explanations of identification must rest first upon this perception. Until a child knows his biological sex, he probably cannot interpret the behavior that is directed toward him. Self-labeling probably precedes the process of identification (Kohlberg, 1966). The traditional psychoanalytic notion of the original identification with mother for boys and a switch to identification with father does not seem clearly borne out empirically (Sears & others, 1965; Bandura & Walters, 1963). In the preschool period, high activity is associated with later masculinity for both sexes.

Although role typing is well established early, the process of identification continues throughout the adolescent years. The period of preadolescence, or that period known as "latency," does not seem to be free of sex-role concerns and behavior. Analysis of children's games (Rosenberg & Sutton-Smith, 1960) indicates shifts in acceptable masculine and feminine activities. It may be that in preadolescence the image of the boy is more circumscribed and the girl is freer to play either masculine or feminine roles. The importance of this period is borne out in a longitudinal study which indicates that there is a clear relationship between masculine behavior such as masculine interest, vocations, and competition in ages 6 to 14 and adult male sexuality. Further, failure to identify through behavior in the preschool and early school years is related to high sex anxiety in adulthood (Kagan & Moss, 1962).

The socialization process by which sexual identification is accomplished seems to be a complex process in which learning (reward and punishment), role playing, child-rearing practices, modeling, and general social expectations all play roles. A simple explanation from any one theory does not seem to account for the data.

Social-learning studies indicate that a system of intermittent rewards and punishments is related to sex identification of the self in boys (Mussen & Distler, 1959; Mussen & Rutherford, 1963). Nurturance and demonstrated power to control resources are two major qualifications in adult behavior which lead to imitation of the model by preschoolers (Bandura & others, 1963). Who the child perceives as powerful plays a role in appropriate sex identification.

The joint effects of power and support have been translated into a circumplex socialization model for revealing relationships between them and sex-role identification as well as such personality dimensions as extroversion-introversion and ego strength–ego weakness (Strauss, 1964).

The role of the father is significant in the development of identification for both boys and girls. Lynn (1962) indicates that identification is accomplished in different fashion for boys and girls, owing to the general presence of the mother and absence of the father. The girl has a clear-cut image, whereas the boy learns by indirection. School-age and adolescent boys who are highly masculine perceive their fathers as rewarding and affectionate on one hand and possessing strength and power on the other (Mussen, 1961). The investigation of attitudes of English college women by Wright and Tuska (1966) indicates that feminine women saw their mothers as emotionally satisfying and their fathers as successful, whereas masculine women saw their mothers as unsympathetic and their fathers as emotionally satisfying.

Just as the father influences female sex-role identification, the mother influences the male. Support for the concept of the relationship of maternal behavior to male identification is found in Kagan and Moss (1962), whose data indicate that maternal protection seems to be a feminizing factor for both sexes.

Child-rearing techniques, combined with the emotional climate of the home, contribute to sex-role behavior. Sears and others (1965), in a study of four-year-olds, found that freedom in sexual play (including choice of toys and occupations) is positively related to masculinity. Punishment and nonpermissive behavior is associated with feminine identification. This may relate, in preschool years, to high activity levels being associated with masculinity.

Different studies focus on different variables or label the same variable differently. Thus, we have terms such as "permissive," "protective," and "nurturant." The complexity of causation, the variety of methods used in investigation, and the language used lead to mixed results concerning the influence of punishment. Sears and others (1965) indicate it as feminizing. The research cited earlier would indicate that a punitive male model who is highly nurturant may be related to male sex identification. The problem may be one of measurement difficulties, or it may be resolvable through the power-support model. What is clear is that the family as a transactional situation is the key influence on sex-role identification.

The process of sex-role identification begins early in the home, probably after the child has become physically aware of his biological sex. Boys seem to learn their role under highly permissive and exploratory situations, whereas girls seem to learn more directly from nonpermissive behavior of the mother. Also, girls seem to learn the role sooner. Both parents are important in the process for both boys and girls. Although patterns of sex-role behavior may change with age, early labeling and acceptance of one's sex seem predictive of later behavior. The development of an adequate sex role is intimately related to the more general construct of self concept, in which definition of one's sex is a dimension.

INTERGROUP RELATIONS. Children not only define an appropriate sex role but also identify with particular subgroups within a culture. Attitudes toward one's own group and toward members of other identifiable groups are learned simultaneously through differentiation. Children learn early to identify their particular racial membership. Knowledge of race develops at about two and half years (Allport, 1954). Pasamanick and Knobloch (1955) indicate that testing of Negro children as early as age two by white examiners yields depressed language scores, because of the apparent early awareness of racial difference. There is ethnic group identification at about the age of five or six, and role perceptions comparing group members as early as six to eight (Hartley and others, 1948).

Prejudice has its beginnings at this early age. The initial attitude seems to be in part a result of parental teaching (Allport, 1954) but also is derived from a variety of environmental sources. Contact with the group against which one is prejudiced is not necessary. Attitudes are derived from membership in a group possessing the attitudes and are learned in the general socialization process. Three stages of prejudice have been identified: (1) the child learns to hate certain people; (2) he rejects all aspects of a group; (3) he becomes selective in which members of the group he hates (Allport, 1954). The prejudiced person has been seen as an authoritarian personality. The key assumption is that all prejudice is related to emotional disturbance, which reflects certain home patterns (Adorno, 1950).

Since 1960, research on determination of prejudice has focused upon belief systems. Rokeach and his colleagues have conducted a series of investigations based upon the concept that the crucial factor in prejudice in intergroup relations is the lack of congruence of beliefs (Rokeach & others, 1960; Stein, 1966). Using both laboratory and real-life situations, they conclude that one develops his prejudices from social pressures exerted by members of his own group. One then perceives dissimilarities of belief between himself and members of a given group. Because of this dissimilarity there is a lack of contact, which leads to increased prejudice. From this position, congruence of beliefs is a more critical factor than race in Negro-white prejudice. However, beliefs are learned and may be seen as symptoms rather than causes. Belief systems are not clearly organized in the child at the time he becomes prejudiced.

Conformity, cognitive dissonance, and security are also seen as determinants of social distance (Triandis & Triandis, 1960). The latter factor relates to the authoritarian personality. Triandis and Davis (1965) indicate that there are five factors in intergroup relations: formal social acceptance, subordination, social distance, marital acceptance, and friendship acceptance. For social distance and marital acceptance, race seems to be the most important influence; for formal acceptance and subordination, occupation seems most important.

Competition and frustration may also be seen as determinants of prejudice. Sherif and Sherif (1956) created prejudice by designing competitive and frustrating situations between two groups of boys in camp. Hostility is usually most marked in social classes that are nearest to those toward which the prejudice is directed. This may relate to the concept of self-and-other. If one needs to make some demarcation, he is most threatened by those who in all but one respect resemble him most closely and yet who are in direct competition with him for jobs or living space.

MORAL DEVELOPMENT. A classical study was that of Hartshorne and May (1930), in which they concluded that conscience was not a unitary trait and that many children exhibited little consistency in their moral behavior from one occasion to another. They also separated moral knowledge from moral behavior and indicated that peers as well as the family group determined behavior, while knowledge may be related to intelligence.

The split between moral judgment and moral behavior has been seen as arising from social conditions (Berkowitz, 1964). Children who "know better" will cheat on examinations when they feel that the situation requires it, even though they may feel guilty afterward.

Discrepancy between judgment and behavior may be understood in terms of a self-situation transaction. If the youngster brings a strong self to the situation, he may be able to resist temptation. If he brings a weak self, the situation may be the overriding factor. If the code is ambiguous—that is, if it is unclear to him what is truly expected—then behavior becomes unpredictable.

Piaget (1932) began another approach to moral judgment. His technique consisted of presenting children with short stories and asking them to judge the outcomes. He postulated a developmental sequence in moral judgment as a result of a combination of maturational and environmental forces. Until about age seven or eight, the child responds in terms of a morality constraint in which adults are seen as dominant and omnipotent and rules as being fixed and unchanging. At about the age of nine or ten a child moves to a morality of cooperation; he considers intent in making judgments. The third stage, about age eleven, begins when the child takes equity into consideration. This age sequence is not fixed.

Research based upon this theory suggests that social class (MacRae, 1954; Boehm & Nass, 1962), religion (Boehm, 1962), and nationality (Luria, 1963) influence the age at which children move from stage to stage. Parental occupation, along with parental constraint (Johnson, 1962; Bronfenbrenner, 1962), seem to influence this development. Punitive parents tend to cause immature judgment.

In an application of Piaget's stages to concepts of God and religion, Goldman (1964) found three stages which were analogous to those of Piaget.

Another main stream of work in moral development stresses emotional components rather than the intellectual components investigated by Piaget. Conscience is developed through internalizing the family's value system either through identification or through techniques of shame and guilt (Ausubel, 1955). Love-oriented techniques are usually associated with strong moral values in children (Sears & others, 1957; Rosen, 1964; Bandura & Walters, 1959). Consistent behavior on the part of adults and abundant affection (Bandura & McDonald, 1963) are related to internalization of family values.

There may be different kinds of guilt. Guilt over aggressive behavior may be different from guilt over disobedience to one's parents. The former seems to occur earlier in development, during the first year and a half of life (Allinsmith, 1957). A cross-cultural study indicates that the child attempts to emulate the person who enjoys resources of high value to him. Moral development may be produced by conditional rather than unconditional positive regard (Whiting & Child, 1953).

The model of adults or older children and the general social scene may be very important contributors to value development in which role identification is of the utmost importance. For example, Wortis and others (1963) investigated culturally deprived Negro mothers and found that the physical and familial environment was serving a preparative function for incorporating these children into the lower-lower class.

The Soviet Union's use of the children's collective as the primary socializing agent in all areas except the strictly academic is seen by Bronfenbrenner (1964) as serving the function of preparing the child to fit into Soviet society. The children's house of the Israeli kibbutz serves a similar socialization function. Each society, whether systematically or not, inculcates its value system in its young.

COGNITIVE STYLE. Cognitive style is a person's individual preference for organization and categorization of stimuli in his environment (Gardner, 1953; Kagan & others, 1963; Ausubel, 1963). Although there may be aspects of inherent predisposition, it is usually assumed that cognitive styles are learned patterns of behavior.

Three main classes of styles related to the emotions have been defined. One class of styles reflects psychoanalytic theory, in that it functions as ego defense. The dimensions of this set are leveling and sharpening, field articulation, scanning control, and tolerance of unrealistic experiences (Gardner & others, 1960).

The second class has as its major dimension an analytical versus a global-field approach. These are contrasting ways in which individuals approach a task. A field-dependent person seems unable to overcome the context experienced in the global way. A field-independent or analytical person seems able to abstract data from a welter of stimuli. This dimension is measurable on a variety of physical, perceptual, and cognitive tasks (Witkin & others, 1962).

The third class consists of three categories of style: analytic-descriptive, inferential-categorical, and relational. A person who is analytic focuses on a part of the total stimulus. An inferential-categorical response involves an inference about the stimuli, and a relational response is given by someone who sees functional combinations among the stimuli. These were developed by using a conceptual style test based upon perception and categorization of sets of pictures (Kagan & others, 1963).

The terminology indicates that Gardner's "field articulation," Witkin's "field-independent," and Kagan's "analytical" are similar, but this has yet to be demonstrated.

The relationship between emotion and style is a close one; impulsivity and inability to delay gratification represent meeting points between them, and both reflect family and cultural conditions.

Styles relate to impulsivity. Kagan and others (1963) and Witkin and others (1962) seem to indicate that nonanalytic and field-dependent children may have problems with impulse control; that is, they seem less able to delay responses and handle their impulsivity. Styles also seem to relate to emotional factors which influence intelligence test performance. An analysis of errors made by children yields indications of perseveration related to conceptual or cognitive style (Sigel, 1963).

Styles develop out of life experiences in the family. Dependency conflict, sex typing, punishment patterns, and father absence are some of the variables which relate to cognitive style as measured by academic performance of college students (Nelsen & Maccoby, 1966). Peer interaction patterns are also important in determining analytic or global style (Witkin & others, 1962). With age, children seem to move toward more analytic styles and seem more able to use either an analytic or global response.

There are clear sex differences: men seem to be more analytical than women (Witkin, 1949; Kagan & others, 1963) and seem to have a more concrete approach (Bieri & others, 1958).

Sociological variables also influence style, and style is defined differently from the explanation given above. Lower-class children seem to be oriented to respond more to the visual and kinesthetic environment rather than to oral or written symbols (Reissman, 1962). Their responses tend to be concrete, motoric, and short-time. They seem to be present-time-oriented and unable to delay gratification (Deutsch, 1963). Lack of early sensory experience seems to limit the range of style and strategies available to children (Bruner, 1961).

Cognitive style serves as a bridging concept, reflecting emotional, social, and intellectual processes. As such, it leads into the more generalized unifying construct—the self.

DEVELOPMENT OF THE SELF CONCEPT.

The self concept is a hypothetical construct which allows the integration of the above areas of social and emotional development into a single system. It has been variously defined as "the self as known to the self" (Murphy, 1947), "those aspects of the individual which seem most vital and important to the person" (Combs & Snygg, 1959), and "the sum total of all a person can call his" (Jersild, 1960).

A differentiation can be made between the *self system*, which Sullivan (1953) postulates as being developed early in life to fend off anxiety and which has also been viewed as the child's organized experience at a given moment in time, and the *self concept*, or that portion of the system which is more clearly defined and known to the person. It is a mixture of affect and cognition, action and reflection.

Affect or emotion can be seen as indicative of the self concept at a particular moment. Anxiety has been interpreted as arising from threats to self-esteem (Ausubel, 1960). The concept of defense mechanisms can be understood as defenses of the self concept from stimuli which might create cognitive dissonance and thus require change. Positive emotions of joy and love can be seen as manifestations of self-esteem and reinforcement of positive self-regard.

The general rule that all living systems act to maintain and enhance the already existing organization applies to the self system. Emotion becomes interpretable as a process by which the child accomplishes this activity. It is also a sign that such activity in a given situation has a high level of meaning to the child. The use of the term "self" thus implies an assumption of organization within the child which can be inferred from behavior or other communication and cannot be measured directly.

The self concept emerges from the life experiences of the individual and has its beginnings in the transactions between the family and the culture and the infant's body. Just as the child develops his sexual identity and sense of values, the interpersonal relations between parents and child are significant in developing concepts of self and worth. For example, indifferent parents seem to be positively related to children with the lowest self-esteem (Rosenberg, 1963).

The self concept grows out of a process of evaluation by the infant and child and from the reflected appraisals of significant others. A first step is self-sentience, that is, the experiencing of one's own body (Sullivan, 1953). This is a perceptual step beginning the differentiation of "me" from "not me." A second step is a mixture of this perception with attitudes or feelings about oneself. This is the discovery of self as performer (Jersild, 1960), in which the child begins to attempt to control aspects of his environment. His sense of self is shaped by whether the adults important to him respond in ways which give him a sense of mastery and competence. This relates to the "permissive" attitudes found to be associated with the masculine role.

Perceived parental behavior is relevant to the child's development of self-esteem. It was found that girls perceive themselves as more accepted and intrinsically valued than boys and that boys seek to enhance themselves through ability, whereas girls seek to develop self-esteem through dependency relationships (Ausubel & others, 1954). That this attitude toward one's parents continues beyond childhood is indicated by Jourard and Remy (1955), who found that an individual's attitude as an adult toward his body varied with his belief concerning his parent's attitudes. Body image begun in self-sentience remains a significant variable in self-assessment in adulthood. Perception rather than any objective "truth" is the significant variable. How one perceives his parents, whether accurately or not, is a vital source of influence on the developing self.

Cultural factors compound familial ones in influencing perception and the self concept. Disadvantaged children in American culture, particularly Negroes, seem to have inadequate views of themselves (Kvaraceus, 1965; Deutsch, 1965). This inadequate view is shaped by the reflected appraisals of the society and is learned during the preschool years. Because of impoverished home situations, Negro children of the lower class seem to have few experiences of stability, warmth, and attention. Erikson (1950) postulates that the foundation for all later development consists in acquiring a sense of basic trust. Social factors which do not permit this, such as economic and emotional deprivation or inadequate or incomplete interpersonal relationships, lead to inadequate self concepts. The absence of the father probably inhibits not only the development of appropriate (for the society) concepts of maleness but also the concept of self as able, as an individual. The lack of elaborate language patterns also plays a role, in that all concept development, including self, requires categorization and abstract symbolization. Both emotional and cognitive elements of the self concept are damaged.

Age trends are discernible in self-development. The self concept is not a unified structure but is multidimensional, with different aspects of the self system moving into sharper focus at different age levels. In infancy and early childhood, language pronouns ("me do") and the bodily self seen in an holistic and unclear fashion perhaps are predominant over the role of adult evaluation. At about age three a child centers his view of himself less on his own direct feedback with objects and more on adult views (Murphy, 1947). During this period of preschool development, the youngster learns to take on the role of others through play and games (Mead, 1934). In this fashion he further delineates "me" and "not me" and internalizes the attitudes and values surrounding him.

Entrance into school brings a change in structure from holistic views to a more dimensionalized organization. For example, Coombs and Soper (1963) found one large factor labeled "adequacy" in kindergarten children but the emergence of at least a second factor labeled "peer" in first-graders. In third-graders, the self concept seems organized around two main factors: (1) the quality of interpersonal relationships with peers and adults and (2) highly valued bodily attributes such as strength and bravery (Engel & Raine, 1963). Jersild (1952), using open-ended themes, found that intermediate-grade pupils wrote about various categories such as physical characteristics, home and family, school, character, and social attitudes in relation to the theme "What I like or dislike about myself." Changes in self concept occur between the fourth and the sixth grade. Sixth-graders tend to have greater stability of concepts than do fourth-graders, and the distance between real and ideal views of the self decreases (Perkins, 1957).

Accuracy of self-estimate in the middle-childhood and early adolescent years seems to be a function of teacher and peer appraisal (Gordon & Wood, 1963; Sears & Sherman, 1964), as well as of previous experience with reality testing on specific tasks (Brandt, 1958). Self-esteem develops when self-appraisals are consistent with the appraisals of others. Further, when teacher and pupil tend to agree on evaluation, the child is more able to predict his performance on a scholastic achievement test. Thus reality testing and self-esteem are functions of each other. Realistic self-appraisal may also be related to age. In testing Piaget's postulate that children move from egocentricity toward reality bases for cognitive judgment during the intermediate school years, Phillips (1963) found movement, with increasing age, from distortion to reality in accuracy of self-perception.

Changes in relative importance of aspects of the self with age indicate a shift between elementary and junior high school for girls, with the transcendence of concern for physical appearance emerging in the junior high school years (Gordon, 1966).

Interpersonal relationships, physical appearance, and popularity are critical aspects of self-esteem for adolescent girls, whereas work and skill are the most important factors for adolescent boys (Douvan & Adleson, 1966). The relationship of body to self becomes important for boys in relation to puberty. Late-maturing boys seem to devalue themselves (Mussen & Jones, 1959), whereas early maturers feel adequate.

There appears to be a cyclical pattern in the development of the self concept. First, it is based on the body, followed by the appraisals of significant others. These others are expanded in school to include teachers and peers. The body again moves into a primary position during adolescence, but at this time acceptance of one's body has social implications. This shift in focus in the evolving concepts of self suggests that self-esteem is not fixed and unchanged simply on the basis of infant or preschool experience but undergoes modification, probably throughout life. The question "Who am I?" is a continuous social-emotional one.

IMPLICATIONS FOR EDUCATION. Emotions and values are in a transactional relationship with classroom behavior and learning. Children's self-esteem not only is related to family background variables but also can be modified by the school situation. Positive self-regard, the internalization of values, and the development of a repertoire of cognitive styles begin early but are modifiable through experience in school. The importance of the early years in influencing the pattern of development suggests that society must concern itself with providing optimum settings for growth. Education begins before formal schooling. Knowledge about developmental processes suggests that schooling should begin earlier, in situations which allow young children to see affectionate, somewhat permissive, but clear models of adults of both sexes. This should be continued through the years, so that traditional schooling does not destroy the early pattern. Curricula must take social-emotional factors into account, so that not only the subject field but also the child is considered. Teacher education in understanding the meaning of behavior and ways of modifying it is essential if teachers are to provide settings in which the child can make the most of the information available. Variety of cognitive styles, cues for arousal, and feelings of threat or competence must be considered in the design of teaching materials, be they electronic or print media.

Only when all aspects of the child's development are seen as interrelated and mutually dependent can schools accomplish the valid purpose of self-development, uniting cognitive with affective development.

Ira J. Gordon
University of Florida

References

Adorno, Theodor W., and others. *The Authoritarian Personality.* Harper, 1950. 990p.

Allinsmith, Wesley. "Conscience and Conflict, The Moral Force in Personality." *Child Develop* 28: 469–76; 1957.

Allport, Gordon W. *The Nature of Prejudice.* Addison, 1954. 537p.

Anderson, John E. *A Survey of Children's Adjustments over Time.* Institute for Child Development and Welfare, U Minnesota, 1959. 42p.

Ausubel, David P. "Relationships Between Shame and Guilt in the Socializing Process." *Psychol R* 62: 378–90; 1955.

Ausubel, David. "Emotional Development." In Harris, Chester. (Ed.) *Encyclopedia of Educational Research,* rev. ed. Macmillan, 1960. p. 448–53.

Ausubel, David. *The Psychology of Meaningful Verbal Behavior.* Grune, 1963. 255p.

Ausubel, David, and others. "Perceived Parent Attitudes as Determinants of Children's Ego Structure." *Child Develop* 25:173–83; 1954.

Bandura, Albert, and McDonald, Frederick J. "The Influence of Social Reinforcements and the Behavior of Models in Shaping Children's Moral Judgments." *J Abn Social Psychol* 67:274–82; 1963.

Bandura, Albert, and Walters, Richard H. *Adolescent Aggression.* Ronald, 1959. 475p.

Bandura, Albert, and Walters, Richard H. *Social Learning and Personality Development.* Holt, 1963. 329p.

Bandura, Albert, and others. "A Comparative Test of the Status Envy, Social Power and Secondary Reinforcement Theories of Identification Learning." *J Abn Psychol* 67:527–31; 1963.

Bayley, Nancy. "Individual Patterns of Development." *Child Develop* 27:45–74; 1956.

Bayley, Nancy. "Consistency of Maternal and Child Behavior in the Berkeley Growth Study." *Vita Humana* 7:73–95; 1964.

Becker, Wesley. "Consequences of Parental Discipline." In Hoffman, Martin L., and Hoffman, Lois W. (Eds.) *Review of Child Development Research*. Russell Sage, 1964. p. 169–208.

Berkowitz, Leonard. *The Development of Motives and Values in the Child*. Basic Books, 1964. 114p.

Berlyne, David E. *Conflict, Arousal, and Curiosity*. McGraw-Hill, 1960. 350p.

Bieri, James, and others. "Sex Differences in Perceptual Behavior." *J Pers* 26:1–12; 1958.

Bloom, Benjamin. *Stability and Change in Human Characteristics*. Wiley, 1964. 237p.

Boehm, Leonore. "The Development of Conscience: A Comparison of Students in Catholic Parochial Schools and in Public Schools." *Child Develop* 33:591–602; 1962.

Boehm, Leonore, and Nass, Martin L. "Social Class Differences in Conscience Development." *Child Develop* 33:565–74; 1962.

Brandt, Richard M. "The Accuracy of Self Estimate: A Measure of Self-concept Reality." *Genet Psychol Monogr* 58:55–99; 1958.

Bronfenbrenner, Urie. "The Role of Age, Sex, Class, and Culture in Studies of Moral Development." *Relig Ed—Res Supplement* 57:S3–S17; 1962.

Bronfenbrenner, Urie. "Upbringing in Collective Settings in Switzerland and the Soviet Union." In *Proceedings of the Seventeenth International Congress of Psychology*. North Holland Publishing Company, 1964. p. 159–61.

Bruner, Jerome. "The Cognitive Consequences of Early Sensory Deprivation." In *Sensory Deprivation: A Symposium Held at Harvard Medical School*. Harvard U, 1961. p. 195–207.

Combs, Arthur W., and Snygg, Donald. *Individual Behavior*, rev. ed. Harper, 1959. 522p.

Combs, Arthur W., and Soper, Daniel W. *The Relationship of Child Perceptions to Achievement and Behavior in the Early Years*. USOE Cooperative Research Project No. 814, U Florida, 1963.

Deutsch, Martin. "The Disadvantaged Child and the Learning Process." In Passow, Harry A. (Ed.) *Education in Depressed Areas*. Teachers Col, Columbia U, 1963. p. 163–79.

Deutsch, Martin. "Some Psychosocial Aspects of Learning in the Disadvantaged." In Torrance, Paul E., and Strom, Robert D. (Eds.) *Mental Health and Achievement*. Wiley, 1965. p. 320–6.

Dollard, John, and others. *Frustration and Aggression*. Yale U, 1939. 209p.

Douvan, Elizabeth, and Adelson, Joseph. *The Adolescent Experience*. Wiley, 1966. 471p.

Duffy, Elizabeth. "The Psychological Significance of the Concept of 'Arousal' or 'Activation'." *Psychol R* 64:265–75; 1957.

Duffy, Elizabeth. *Activation and Behavior*. Wiley, 1962. 384p.

Emmerich, Walter. "Stability and Change in Early Personality Development." *Young Children* 21:233–45; 1966.

Engel, Mary, and Raine, Walter J. "A Method for the Measurement of the Self-concept of Children in the 3rd Grade." *Genetic Psychol* 102:125–37; 1963.

Erickson, Erik H. *Childhood and Society*. Norton, 1950. 397p.

Gardner, Riley W. "Cognitive Styles in Categorizing Behavior." *J Pers* 22:214–33; 1953.

Gardner, Riley W., and others. "Personality Organization in Cognitive Controls." *Psychol Issues* 2; 1960. 150p.

Goldman, Ronald. *Religious Thinking from Childhood to Adolescence*. Routledge, 1964. 276p.

Gordon, Ira J. *Studying the Child in School*. Wiley, 1966. 145p.

Gordon, Ira J., and Wood, Patricia C. "The Relationship Between Pupil Self-evaluation, Teacher Evaluation of the Pupil, and Scholastic Achievement." *J Ed Res* 56:440–3; 1963.

Harlow, Harry F. "The Nature of Love." *Am Psychol* 13:673–85; 1958.

Harlow, Harry F. "The Heterosexual Affectional System in Monkeys." *Am Psychol* 17:1–9; 1962.

Hartley, Eugene L., and others. "Children's Perceptions of Ethnic Group Membership." *J Psychol* 26:387–98; 1948.

Hartshorne, Hugh, and May, Mark A. *Studies in the Nature of Character*. 3 vols. Macmillan, 1930. 498p.

Havighurst, Robert. "Social Development." In Harris, Chester. (Ed.) *Encyclopedia of Educational Research*, rev. ed. Macmillan, 1960. p. 1287–90.

Henry, Jules. "Death Fear and Climax in Nursery School Play." In Neubauer, Peter (Ed.) *Concepts of Development in Early Childhood Education*. Thomas, 1965. p. 112–24.

Jersild, Arthur T. *In Search of Self*. Teachers Col, Columbia U, 1952. 141p.

Jersild, Arthur T. *Child Psychology*. Prentice-Hall, 1960. 623p.

Jersild, Arthur T., and Holmes, Frances B. "Children's Fears." *Child Develop Monogr* No. 20, 1935. 356p.

Johnson, Ronald C. "A Study of Children's Moral Judgments." *Child Develop* 33:327–54; 1962.

Jones, Harold E. "The Significance of Patterns of Emotional Expression for Later Adjustment." In Conrad, Herbert S. (Ed.) *Studies in Human Development*. Appleton, 1966. p. 217–26.

Jourard, Sidney M., and Remy, Richard M. "Perceived Parental Attitudes, The Self, and Security." *J Cons Psychol* 19:364–6; 1955.

Kagan, Jerome, and Moss, Howard A. *Birth to Maturity, a Study in Psychological Development*. Wiley, 1962. 381p.

Kagan, Jerome, and others. "Psychological Significance of Styles of Conceptualization." *Soc Res Child Develop Monogr* No. 28:73–112; 1963.

Kessen, William, and others. "Selection and Test of Response Measures in the Study of the Human Newborn." *Child Develop* 32:7–24; 1961.

Kohlberg, Lawrence. "A Cognitive-Developmental Analysis of the Formation of Sex-role Concepts and Attitudes." In Maccoby, Eleanor E. (Ed.) *Sex Differences and Sex Typing.* Stanford U, 1966.

Kvaraceus, William C. (Ed.) *Negro Self Concept.* McGraw-Hill, 1965. 186p.

Lorenz, Konrad. "On Aggression." In Tanner, James M., and Inhelder, Barbel. (Eds.) *Discussion on Child Development* Int U, 1960. 186p.

Luria, Zelda. "Response to Transgression in Stories by Israeli Children." *Child Develop* 34:271–80; 1963.

Lynn, David B. "Sex-role and Parental Identification." *Child Develop* 33:555–64; 1962.

MacRae, Duncan. "A Test of Piaget's Theories of Moral Development." *J Abn Social Psychol* 49:14–8; 1954.

Mead, George H. *Mind, Self and Society.* Chicago U, 1934. 400p.

Murphy, Gardner. *Personality: A Biosocial Approach.* Harper, 1947. 999p.

Murphy, Lois B., and others. *The Widening World of Childhood.* Basic Books, 1962. 399p.

Mussen, Paul. "Some Antecedents and Consequents of Masculine Sex-typing in Adolescent Boys." *Psychol Monogr* No. 75: 1–24; 1961.

Mussen, Paul, and Distler, Luther. "Masculinity, Identification and Father-Son Relationships." *J Abn Social Psychol* 59:350–6; 1959.

Mussen, Paul H., and Jones, Mary C. "Self-conceptions, Motivations, & Interpersonal Attitudes of Late and Early Maturing Boys." *Child Develop* 28:243–56; 1959.

Mussen, Paul, and Rutherford, Eldred. "Parent-Child Relations and Parental Personality in Relation to Young Children's Sex-role Preferences." *Child Develop* 34:589–607; 1963.

Nelsen, Edward A., and Maccoby, Eleanor E. "The Relationship Between Social Development and Differential Abilities on the Scholastic Aptitude Test." *Merrill-Palmer Q* 12:269–84; 1966.

Neubauer, Peter (Ed.) *Children in Collectives.* Thomas, 1965. 383p.

Pasamanick, Benjamin, and Knobloch, Hilda. "Early Language Behavior in Negro Children and Testing of Intelligence." *J Abn Social Psychol* 50:401–2; 1955.

Perkins, Hugh V. "Changing Perceptions of Self." *Child Ed* 34:82–5; 1957.

Phillips, Beeman N. "Age Changes in Accuracy of Self-perceptions." *Child Develop* 34:1041–6; 1963.

Piaget, Jean. *Moral Judgment of the Child.* Harcourt, 1932. 411p.

Plutchik, Robert. *The Emotions; Facts, Theories, and a New Model.* Random, 1962. 204p.

Prescott, Daniel A. "The Role of Love in Human Development." *J Home Econ* 44:173–6; 1952.

Riessman, Frank. *The Culturally Deprived Child.* Harper, 1962. 140p.

Rokeach, Milton, and others. "Two Kinds of Prejudice or One?" in Rokeach, Milton (Ed.) *The Open and Closed Mind.* Basic Books, 1960. p. 132–68.

Rosen, Bernard. "Family Structure and Value Transmission." *Merrill Palmer Q* 10:59–76; 1964.

Rosenberg, Benjamin G., and Sutton-Smith, Brian. "A Revised Conception of Masculine-Feminine Differences in Play Activities." *J Genet Psychol* 96:165–70; 1960.

Rosenberg, Morris. "Parental Interest and Children's Self-conceptions." *Sociometry* 26:35–49; 1963.

Sarason, Herbert, and others. *Anxiety in Elementary School Children.* Wiley, 1960. 351p.

Schachter, Stanley, and Singer, Jerome E. "Cognitive, Social and Physiological Determinants of Emotional State." *Psychol R* 69:379–99; 1962.

Sears, Pauline S., and Sherman, Vivian S. *In Pursuit of Self-esteem.* Wadsworth, 1964. 280p.

Sears, Robert R., and others. *Patterns of Child Rearing.* Harper, 1957. 549p.

Sears, Robert R., and others. *Identification and Child Rearing.* Stanford U, 1965. 383p.

Sherif, Muzafer, and Sherif, Carolyn W. *An Outline of Social Psychology.* Harper, 1956. 792p.

Sigel, Irving E. "How Intelligence Tests Limit Understanding of Intelligence." *Merrill-Palmer Q* 9:39–56; 1963.

Stein, David D. "The Influence of Belief Systems on Interpersonal Preference: A Validation Study of Rokeach's Theory of Prejudice." *Psychol Monogr* No. 80, 1966. 29p.

Strauss, Murray A. "Power and Support Structure of the Family in Relation to Socialization." *J Marriage and the Family* 26:318–26; 1964.

Sullivan, Harry S. *The Interpersonal Theory of Psychiatry.* Norton, 1953. 393p.

Suttie, Ian. *The Origins of Love and Hate.* Julian Press, 1952. 275p.

Triandis, Harry C., and Davis, E. E. "Race and Belief as Determinants of Behavioral Intentions." *J Pers Social Psychol* 2:715–25; 1965.

Triandis, Harry C., and Triandis, Leigh M. "Race, Social Class, Religion, and Nationality as Determinants of Social Distance." *J Abn Social Psychol* 61:110–8; 1960.

Whiting, John, and Child, Irvin L. *Child Training and Personality: A Cross-cultural Study.* Yale U, 1953. 353p.

Witkin, Herman. "Sex Differences in Perception." *Transactions New York Academy Science,* Vol. 12. 1949. p. 22–6.

Witkin, Herman A., and others. *Psychological Differentiation.* Wiley, 1962. 418p.

Wortis, Helen, and others. "Child Rearing Practices in a Low Socioeconomic Group." *Pediatrics* 32:298–307; 1963.

Wright, Benjamin, and Tuska, Shirley. "The Nature and Origin of Feeling Feminine." *Br J Social Clin Psychol* 5:140–9; 1966.

SOCIAL STUDIES EDUCATION

This article seeks to report significant and exemplary research done within the past ten years on the teaching of social studies at the elementary (K–6) and secondary (7–14) levels of American education. Concerned with a study of man and his relationship to his social and physical world, social studies adapts the content and methods of the various social sciences, either in terms of a particular discipline or through a cross-disciplinary approach, often enriched by ideas from the humanities and the natural sciences.

Because of space limitations, research from general areas such as evaluation and individual differences is not reported here unless it has been specifically conducted in a social studies setting. Attention to citizenship is restricted, since there is a separate entry for it elsewhere. The authors believe that this article should report research in the total field, even though some of the studies may not be in the most crucially needed areas.

HISTORY OF THE FIELD. The history of social studies education in the United States can be divided chronologically into five periods. The first period—the period up to 1893—covers the emergence of history as the social studies curriculum, with some inclusion of geography and civil government. The second period, from 1893 to 1916, involves the maturation of history as *the* social studies curriculum under the leadership of important national committees, with peripheral concern for civil government and some physical geography, economics, and sociology. It was during the third period, roughly from 1916 to 1936, that genuine "social studies" came into being, challenging the stranglehold of history and witnessing the inclusion of content from the disciplines of political science, economics, human geography, and sociology as separate or cross-disciplinary subjects. The scientific approach to education, more attention to individual differences, new developments in educational psychology, and concern for the needs of the student encouraged a new and experimental social studies.

The fourth period, encompassing approximately 1936 to 1955, was a period of reaction domestically and internationally to economic and political upheavals, resulting in critical attacks on national committee leadership and social studies programs that had not met the challenge. The call arose for locally determined (and nationally chaotic) curricula, stressing societal needs, citizenship education, and individual adjustment.

The fifth period, from 1955 to 1967, provided a return to many of the advances of the third period, coupled with greater attention to the structure of the social science disciplines. The transition year between complacency and action in social studies education would seem to be 1963. Essentially, the current period takes advantage of technological growth and is attempting to unite concerns of the student, society, and the social sciences in order to produce individuals who, knowing the working methods of the social scientists, will apply inquiry to new problems, make decisions in the light of internalized value complexes, and effectively carry on a changing society of free men.

By 1967 the social studies field has arrived at a point where analytical, scientific methods of inquiry are in vogue on both the elementary and the secondary levels, but whether the content is to be organized along the lines of separate disciplines or with a cross-disciplinary approach seems a moot question. Sound research is needed in this area; perhaps major breakthroughs will result from the some 90 social studies projects cited by Hill and others (1967). Fraser (1965), in appraising current trends in these projects, heavily concerned with materials, points out that although the major efforts are beamed toward the able student and are concerned primarily with the cognitive as opposed to the affective domain, discernible and challenging foci are emerging in conceptual frameworks, sequencing of topics, readiness, the behavioral sciences, depth studies, a comprehensive world view, societal problems, and inquiry amid a climate of experimentation and innovation.

OBJECTIVES. There has been little research done concerning social studies education objectives, although many viewpoints have been expressed. Research by Engle (1964b) presents the best description of the dichotomy that exists between those concerned with designing measurable objectives based on the social sciences and those concerned with designing objectives related to the moral purposes and problems in effective citizenship. A similar dichotomy was resolved by those concerned with the National Assessment of American Education program through the expedient of forming two groups of objectives: one for social studies education and one for citizenship. Indeed, in this volume separate entries exist in the two fields. This may be the sound way to resolve the question of whether social studies education should be discipline- or citizenship-oriented. The answer emerging may well be that it has both content objectives and citizenship goals, as do the community, the school as a whole, and virtually all the separate subject areas.

The results of investigations by Bloom and Krathwohl (1956) into the cognitive domain and by Krathwohl and others (1964) into the affective domain have provided basic general taxonomies of educational objectives which leaders in social studies education have used in developing objectives that can be implemented and evaluated. Among others, Jarolimek (1962) on the elementary level has turned to the cognitive domain, and Fenton (1966) on the secondary level has studied both the cognitive and affective domains. Research still has not provided clear guidelines into which type of content is best used in the cognitive domain: (1) concepts, generalizations, and methodology related to the structure of the social science disciplines or (2) the more vital, but perhaps transient, public-issues approach.

Kurfman (1967) presents one set of overall objectives derived from the National Assessment program's five categories: (1) using analytical, scientific procedures; (2) possessing knowledge relative to major ideas and concerns of social scientists; (3) commitment to the values that sustain a free society; (4) curiosity about human affairs; and (5) sensitivity to creative-intuitive methods of explaining the human condition. The third category tends more toward indoctrination than is suggested by the affective-domain taxonomy, but the above categories might serve as the basis for a possible set of objectives that integrates current concerns without opening the floodgates to broad citizenship generalities, including adjustment to the *status quo*.

SOURCES OF CONTENT. Alternatives for selection of content range from the use of individual disciplines through utilization of concepts from all the social sciences as espoused by Price and others (1965), who identified 18 substantive concepts, 5 value concepts, and 11 aspects of method. A new source or determinant of content is inquiry methodology rather than content itself; certainly, with the expansion of knowledge and with change rapidly becoming the basic constant, this may be one answer.

History. History once held almost complete sway over the social science curriculum. The two major challenges to this tradition are (1) the encroachment upon its time allotment by other social sciences and (2) the use of "postholing" techniques in the remaining time. These would change the "tapestry" approach to either a sampling approach or an area-studies or cultural-concept presentation, which may be more social-science- than history-oriented.

Courses in United States history, perhaps because they are valuable in instilling patriotism and an appreciation of our way of life and because the subject encompasses a shorter and more manageable time span, have not fallen prey to the above challenges in the same degree. Weaver (1962) attempted to identify key generalizations to be stressed in the elementary grades and validated 104 out of an original 1400 which placed stress on a broad understanding of American history, emphasizing social history and the period through the eighteenth century, except for the emergence of the United States as a world power. Devitt (1958) applied the same technique on the secondary level and validated 61 of the original 938 concepts covering the full gamut of United States history. Only about 5 of the 90 current social studies projects listed by Hill and others (1967) center on United States history, with a definite stress on materials.

The teaching of world history has been the object of more creative research in new efforts to upset the *status quo* and to attack head-on the problems resulting from time-allotment cuts in traditional ancient, medieval, and modern history. Massialas (1961) compared a reflectively oriented approach and the traditional narrative-factual approach. He found no significant difference between the two approaches in standardized-content test results and concluded that such tests are not designed to measure adequately the skills of critical thinking, since results from more sophisticated evaluation techniques indicated that the former method produced a significantly higher sensitivity to skills of critical thinking and reflective inquiry, growth in independent thought, and ability to discuss controversial issues in a more systematic fashion. Some 14 projects related to the teaching of world history are currently being conducted, the majority of which are concerned with cultural history and non-Western areas. Engle (1964a) reported significant attention to content, including the teaching of intellectual history and consideration of cultural regions beyond the scope of Western civilization.

Geography. Another traditional bulwark of the social studies curriculum has, one would judge from an examination of recent research, been undergoing critical review similar to that of world history. Centered on the West and long taught factually by public school teachers, the subject of geography is caught between a rising realization of its importance by leaders and the poor preparation of those who are teaching it.

Anderson (1963), after reviewing the history of secondary school geography teaching in the twentieth century, surveyed cities over 10,000 in the North Central region to ascertain current status and trends. He reported that as geography evolved from a descriptive to a physical to a social study it did not attain its rightful place because it did not possess an organizing or unifying concept or a unique body of social content. As an interpretive subject, geography has served too frequently as a basis for the study of other subjects. Mayo (1964) found that, when geography is taught as a separate subject in the secondary school, it is usually global geography; when it is taught with an integrated approach, the stress is usually economic.

At present there are some five social studies projects underway (Hill & others, 1967) concerned with specific aspects of the significant general problem, plus two research efforts centering on conservation. Only the High School Geography Project and the Crabtree Project seem to be looking at the problem with the fresh thought necessary. Helburn (1966) has reported on the former project's experimentation with a topical program involving conceptual objectives, the discovery-learning approach, and a stress on problem solving. Crabtree (1966), identifying area association as the core concept of geographic theory, indicates how sequential learning can be developed in grades 1, 2, and 3, through use of inquiry strategies and appropriate instructional materials. Hanna and others (1966) have provided some additional specific guide lines in their organized presentation of significant concepts and skills relating geography to the newer instructional approaches in elementary and junior high schools. However, unless a great deal more research is activated in this field, geography may continue to flounder.

Economics. Probably no social science discipline has received more attention, financial aid, or organized effort toward furthering its development in the last twenty years than has economics. That such attention continues is attested in nine social studies projects currently devoted to this concern. Perhaps no other subject in social studies education, save United States history, has within the past decade come so close to arriving at a nationally agreed upon body of content. This accord is due in the main to the efforts of the Joint Council on Economic Education and the Council for the Advancement of Secondary Education, as well as to the publication by the Committee for Economic Development (1961) of the volume *Economic Education in the Schools: A Report of the National Task Force on Economic Education*. In this report the American Economic Association spelled out in seven major areas the basic economic concepts essential for a high school graduate to know something about. This does not imply national consensus on method, grade placement, or even whether the content be placed in separate courses or integrated with other content in basic social studies offerings.

Surveys on the status of economic instruction in the schools are abundant. Perhaps the most comprehensive is that described by G. Jones (1965), wherein all secondary schools, public and private, enrolling over 300 students were surveyed. The 69.8 percent that responded enrolled 20 percent of their seniors in separate economics courses or, including courses below the senior level, 6.1 percent of all students in grades 9 through 12. This shows an increase over the 4.7 percent USOE figure of 1948-49. It is interesting to note that 82.4 percent of the teachers of separate economics courses had taken two or more college courses in economics.

One area receiving greater attention in the literature is instruction related to economic concepts in the elementary school. Robinson (1963) revealed what can be done in kindergarten, and in describing the Elkart Project (grades 1-12), Senesh (1960) indicated the need for an organic curriculum beginning in the first grade.

Lovenstein and others (1966) have researched a course for grade 9, and Sperling and Wiggins (1966) developed ECON 12 for a principles course. It would seem that the concern has been to deemphasize personal finance and to develop content competency in institutional economics; but as Wagner and Metcalf (1963) indicate, content too often is descriptive, and rarely are students required to do disciplined, analytical thinking. Additional research is needed on the impact of the instruction being given to students, involving content that is more centrally and better planned.

The Behavioral Sciences and Government. Sources that hold great promise for a "new" content basis are the behavioral sciences and government. These are evolving in similar directions toward an integrated study of human behavior, with individuals and groups seen in interaction with the socioeconomic-political-cultural environment. The disciplines involved most centrally here are cultural anthropology, psychology, social psychology, and sociology. To these has been added government. Economics may be included, but current research efforts do not point in that direction as yet. Each of these disciplines has its more traditional aspect as one of the social sciences, but as social studies education gravitates toward (1) inquiry-centered study and (2) a smaller number of significant concepts, those aspects of the disciplines concerned with the study of modern man and his behavior show signs of being brought together through the above two components. The role of the central behavioral sciences of cultural anthropology, psychology, social psychology, and sociology has received little research attention as a major contributor to social studies education. Kenyon (1965) did make a significant contribution when he found that high school seniors held very positive attitudes toward studying the sciences of human behavior but were deficient in their knowledge of them.

In sociology Nash (1962) listed concepts and generalizations from abstract sociology which would focus content less on social pathology and more on the insights needed to further broad positive goals of social studies education. Feldmesser (1966) points out experimentation that is being conducted by Sociological Resources for Secondary Schools in testing episodes wherein students will gather, classify, manipulate, and interpret important data through instructional models involving laboratory work in various secondary courses. Joyce and Weinberg (1964) found that the use of "guiding" questions in conversations was very helpful in enabling elementary school pupils to observe examples of such sociological concepts as "norms" and "values" in meaningful ways.

In a national survey by Thornton (1965), psychology on the secondary school level was found to be a separate, usually one-semester course in 14.5 percent of the high schools in 49 states. In those schools offering the course, 1.4 percent of the students in grades 9 through 12 were taking it, or 5.4 percent of the total student enrollment in the grade in which the course was given. In analyzing six texts specifically designed for the course, he noted that in accordance with recommendations by authorities major emphases were on personality, interpersonal relationships, mental hygiene, and the biological foundations of behavior. Nebergall (1965) researched the need for presenting materials appropriate to an integrated, problem-solving, and non-text-oriented study of normal people reacting in and adapting to their physical and social environments.

To date, no significant research results are available concerning the content selection from cultural anthropology as a strong component in social studies education (grades K-12), but very soon perhaps some of the materials from the Georgia Project on the elementary school level and the Anthropology Curriculum Study Project on the secondary school level will have been sufficiently tested to provide needed direction for establishing the role of this important discipline in developing a behavioral science approach to the study of man in his cultural setting. These projects bear watching.

In Government, although some research was done in the traditional areas of teacher concern about instruction in governmental structure, it is noteworthy that during the past ten years the stress has been on political socialization and political behavior. Students are being encouraged to generalize about observed phenomena of political behavior on the local, state, national, and international levels and to test these generalizations by using appropriate tools of analysis and empirical investigation. Riddle and Cleary (1966) point up significant areas of the "new content" with suggestions for implementation in social studies education.

A good deal of attention has been given to the degree of political socialization the elementary child possesses, with implications for more sophisticated content and methodology from kindergarten through grade 6. Easton and Hess (1962), Greenstein (1964), and Estvan (1962) are among those leading in this research. Easton and others, who devoted over five years to studying some 12,000 elementary school pupils nationally, found that a child's political world begins to take shape before he enters school and undergoes rapid change from kindergarten through grade 6. By the time the child has completed elementary school many of his basic political attachments, attitudes, and values are firmly established and are not subject to significant change during the secondary school years. The importance of providing more content related to government and political behavior is clear, and the need becomes more evident when related to Estvan's findings on what is being taught by elementary teachers in Wisconsin. Individual responsibility rather than government per se was stressed in the lower grades, and in the intermediate grades governmental organization was emphasized. Analytical skills and critical thinking were neglected. Greenstein found that in children 9 to 13 most significant learning about political behavior occurs outside the formal instructional program of the classroom. Individuals were found to be easier for children to understand than were complex institutions such as the legislature—all of which suggests that political behavior approaches might be substituted at this level for process or legal-institutional approaches.

Shaver (1965) found, much as Estvan had for the elementary school level, that reflective thinking usually is not encouraged on the secondary level; his conclusion was based on a study of 93 texts mostly dealing with American government and civics. Such texts did not provide springboards for (1) evaluating societal issues, (2) systematically conceptualizing a pluralistic society, (3) handling clashes of values, or (4) preparing youth to deal with issues realistically. In reviewing current social studies projects, it is interesting to note that, including international understanding and world affairs, more are concerned with government (some 15) than with any one of the other social sciences.

Values. As the social sciences become more "realistic," with calls for inquiry, analysis of discipline structure, and insights into basic concepts, an emerging source of content is the area of values and value complexes—the affective domain. This includes a study of contemporary values in flux and the establishing of values and value complexes by students in grades K–14, as their total social studies education program combines value content with insights from the social sciences in an effort to meet life's problems. This approach differs from, but does not totally exclude, the purely humanistic and historical study of values which others have held. It does not, however, imply character education or the legalistic-moralistic approach. Brady (1966) advocates a new "discipline of social studies" using value studies as content, organized about a conceptual model involving (1) value systems, (2) sociocultural drifts, (3) historical and geographic factors influencing values and drifts, and (4) social problems as value-drift conflicts.

In defining the content of values for use in schools in the United States, there seems to be two approaches, namely, the direct and the indirect. As a direct approach, Perchlik (1964) identified nine major freedoms, each with subdivisions—of speech, press, petition and demonstration, political action, assembly, education, association, investigation and research, and travel—which he established as contributors to diversity.

The concern for establishing an indirect approach to value study is generated by three considerations: (1) a desire not to engage in moralistic indoctrination, (2) awareness of results from anthropological research that show how one gains in comprehension of his own culture through the study of others, and (3) empirical evidence such as furnished by Horton (1955) that instruction in civics and American government does not correlate positively with attitudinal results on democracy and freedom versus totalitarianism. B. Allen (1965) attempted to meet this problem by establishing an instrument to measure gain in attitudes related to American values and beliefs through instruction in adverse referents. This whole area of content from values, including instruction in and evaluation thereof, presents a genuine research challenge for more effective social studies education.

Area Studies. This "new" area of content suggests possibilities for providing the basis for many of the preceding subtopics; it involves the social science with values, including adverse referents. Walsh (1962) incorporated the above goals in an excellent teaching model for culture studies on the elementary school level, which would also be useful on the secondary level, where such an approach is usually found in the "world block" in grades 9 and 10. Some five social studies projects are concerned with developing content guides and materials in area studies, particularly as related to Sub-Saharan Africa, Asia, and Latin America.

ORGANIZING THE CURRICULUM. The organization of the social studies curriculum (grades K–14) for the past half century has resisted needed change, with that of grades K through 6 based on the expanding-community concept from the individual through the world; grades 7–12, the double three-year cycles of world history and United States history and civics; and the 13–14 level, an "introduction" to world and United States history and the various traditional social science disciplines. No unifying theory seems to exist. However, four areas of agreement are emerging: (1) content drawn from all the social sciences, (2) content introduced earlier and required longer, (3) an inquiry-centered approach, and (4) in-depth study of selected areas, eras, or issues.

Fraser and McCutchen (1965) suggest 15 organizing themes and propose patterns of organization with the above areas of agreement incorporated into two- or three-year articulated blocks. Four social studies projects (Hill & others, 1967) hold some promise for a needed articulation, in grades K through 12. Muessig (1965) provides excellent guide lines for both newer content and curriculum procedures. Adair (1962) establishes a theoretical model to aid curriculum leaders in recognizing readiness for curriculum change in a given school situation.

Elementary School Curriculum (Grades K–6). Significant trends in elementary school curriculum patterns include more emphasis on inquiry, human relationships, contemporary affairs, and cross-disciplinary social science. A comprehensive overview of recent trends, issues, and problems has been presented by Michaelis (1962).

The three-phased Stanford Project, as discussed by Hanna and Lee (1962), is built upon the expanding-community concept. Ten dissertations, each centering on a basic human activity, identified 3,272 basic social science generalizations. The second phase involves selecting and modifying those generalizations deemed highly significant to the study of each of the expanding communities, and the third phase will test the content resulting from the earlier phases.

A growing body of literature indicates a need for revision of the elementary school social studies curriculum, since children's interests, abilities, and needs extend beyond those reflected in current practice. From examination of children's art, writing, oral expression, and selection of reading materials in grades 2, 4, and 6, LaDue (1962) found that pupil interests exceeded the geographic areas of their own environment and included current problems dominating the international scene. Clements (1964) examined how anthropologists, sociologists, and historians engage in inquiry and identified three task stages: (1) clarification of inquiry purposes, (2) conduct of inquiry and (3) report of findings. He concluded that if elementary school students are to use the methods of the social scientists, they must be given the opportunity to do so.

Secondary School Curriculum (Grades 7–14). The secondary curriculum organization still remains sharply divided between junior and senior high school, though some experts advocate a world civilization block for grades 9 and 10 which would bridge the gap between the two levels. Curriculum changes on the secondary level since 1955 have been reported in detail for North Central schools by Sjostrom (1964).

On the junior high school level Hansen (1964) found the prevalent sequence in Wisconsin to be similar to the unchanged national picture, with the leading required course in grade 7 being geography; in grade 8, United States history; and in grade 9, citizenship. Teachers basically were not prepared in the subjects they were teaching. In appraising the use of core material, Phillips (1961) reports no significant differences between students in corelike and noncore situations in their achievement, interest development, or social-adjustment improvement. Students under the noncore approach developed more liberal attitudes Aldrich and others (1967) appraise the social studies curriculum of the junior high school and present five sample programs in detail.

On the senior high school level Moreland (1962) found in a national survey that the most common offerings are world history in grade 10, United States history in grade 11, and problems in grade 12. Moreland concluded that the general practice in curriculum revision is change of subject matter within courses and addition of electives rather than reorganization involving basic course titles. Olmo (1966) found that college entrance requirements influence the senior high school curriculum heavily and that professional reading receives little attention by teachers.

Virtually no significant research has appeared in the past decade on curriculum developments in the junior college or the first two years of general education (13–14). Gross and Maynard (1965), in surveying history and foreign relations offerings, verify the dominance of traditional Western civilization and introductory social science courses needed by students to meet their major requirements. Much will need to be done at this level if newer developments (grades K–12) are to be built upon in meaningful ways.

Instruction. Research in social studies methodology is moving into a new era, with emphasis on investigating the potential in a reflective theory of method. In actual classroom practice, far too little innovation in instructional approach can be found, with the traditional teacher-led discussion based on textbook assignments being the dominant mode. The complex problem of unifying theory and practice must be solved in conjunction with an examination of the nature of the teaching-learning situation—by far the most significant aspect of the social studies classroom. One must agree with Oliver that, considering that this field is at least as complex as problems dealing with the atom, research into social studies methodology is by comparison neither very rich nor very extensive.

Learning Problems. The most common characteristic of the culturally disadvantaged, as is generally agreed by those actually working with them, is a lack of direct or firsthand experience. Student feelings of insecurity, coupled with unsuitable materials and inflexible curricula, contribute to the problem of reaching the disadvantaged. Curry (1962) found, in a study of children in grade 6, that socioeconomic status seems to have no effect upon scholastic achievement when the students have high intellectual ability. However, as intellectual ability decreases, the effect of socioeconomic conditions on scholastic achievement greatly increases. Edgar (1965), in a study involving Negro and Puerto Rican children in deprived areas of New York City, developed fictional and biographical materials which integrated a limited number of social studies concepts with other subjects. Clear goals and a simple teaching methodology were established to help ensure repeated success experiences. The experimental group using the above approach gained more points on the Wechsler Intelligence Scale over a three-year period than did the control group. Those students who fall behind their peers in the application of skills, particularly in reading skills, experience difficulty with the highly verbal and abstract social studies curriculum which is still the major educational fare.

Several studies indicate work is being done to provide for the needs of the fast learner. Bidna (1961), surveying 201 social studies programs for academically talented high school students, found the most frequently reported administrative programs were ability grouping, specialized classes, enrichment within regular classes, and advanced placement. Although only 33 percent of the schools developed a written statement of program objectives and less than 50 percent formally evaluated their specialized programs, they claimed that their programs created a stimulating atmosphere that resulted in high accomplishment.

Teaching Strategies. Lux (1959) found that a wide variety of teaching methods and strategies were employed by social studies teachers rated superior by administrators. The unit method was preferred; teacher-led discussions, as well as emphasis on individual activities, were common. Junior high school teachers used dramatizations, chart and map construction, bulletin board displays, other visual aids, and supplementary texts more than did senior high school teachers. Casteel (1963) investigated whether methods of political science could be translated into activities which would equip students with techniques and skills necessary for making wise decisions. These methods included the generic, descriptive, analytical, case-study, survey, experimental, and mathematical approaches. Casteel found that students of varying abilities in grades 9 through 12 successfully used political science techniques.

R. Jones (1964) compared the problems approach with the main-ideas approach to determine which was more successful in producing conceptual learning among pupils in grade 5. Results showed that children following the main-ideas approach scored higher on concrete concepts, whereas children using the problems approach scored higher on abstract concepts. Oliver and Baker (1959), working with slow students in grades 7 and 11 concluded that the case method challenges the student to make personal decisions about important social problems. Other conclusions were as follows: (1) the listening span was good at both levels, but discussion was more conceptual and wholistic in grade 11; (2) the conceptual experience necessary to understand cases was much lower in grade 7; and (3) both groups made gains in knowledge of facts and in ability to distinguish fact from opinion.

Inquiry Approaches. Although current social studies programs give only minimal attention to conceptual teaching, Metcalf (1963) does present a comprehensive review of the research concerning its theory. Possien (1965) compared the effectiveness of three teaching methodologies: (1) inductive (self-discovery), (2) deductive (telling of facts and generalizations by the teacher and rote learning by the students), and (3) deductive (including detailed explanations of causal relationships underlying concepts). Those students trained in the use of inductive procedures exhibited more characteristics of effective problem-solving behavior than did pupils taught by either of the two deductive methods. Numerous writers in the field of social studies education have indicated that using the reflective theory of method holds the most promise for uniting theory with practice. Although most studies in this area assume reflective thinking can best be improved through the problems approach, McGarry (1961) found that even greater gains were achieved through the process of determining meaning. Much research, not specifically in social studies education, is available in the area of inquiry approaches.

Skills Development. Since skills play such a significant role in social studies achievement no matter which method or strategies are used or regardless of the nature of the student involved, this area warrants separate attention. Research on the development of those skills necessary to acquire, analyze, evaluate, and apply social learning will be presented in this section. Carpenter (1963) has provided a comprehensive source of information on skills development.

Reading. Haffner (1959) analyzed 42 social studies textbooks used in grades 5 and 6 in order to determine and compare vocabulary load, social-concept burden, and reading grade level. Findings indicated that textbooks for grade 6 presented less vocabulary difficulty than did those for grade 5 and that the social-concept burden was greater in texts for grade 6; also, textbooks on both grade levels contained excessive vocabulary loads and concept burdens. Tankersley (1965) compared the direct approach to developing skills in locating information, which utilizes a systematic presentation of lessons, with an indirect approach involving teaching such skills only when needed. Results favored the direct approach. Even with its use, involving social studies class time, content achievement was not affected adversely.

Maps and Globes. The question of at what mental-age levels the various skills in map and globe interpretation can be mastered was investigated by

Sorohan (1962). Eleven interpretive skills were tested, including legends and symbols, scale, grid location, projections, and regional concept. Mastery of each skill was set at 80 percent correct responses, and mental-age placement was set at the point where 75 percent of the group attained mastery. Sorohan concluded that the skills he investigated, although often introduced at earlier grade levels, do not begin to be mastered by the group as a whole until the mental age of 131 months, or approximately in grade 5. Since results indicate the mental age at which each skill is mastered, implications exist for teaching based on individual differences, which are more in line with mental than chronological age or grade placement. Various methods have been employed in developing map and globe skills, including conceptual teaching as reported by Carmichael (1965). Conceptual teaching was defined as an inquiry-discovery approach based upon concept attainment. The problem was to determine the effectiveness of (1) a conceptual method in teaching map reading and geographic understanding and (2) regular classroom teachers using that method without prior training. The experimental group, using a unit of study stressing concepts rather than facts, made far greater improvement in both geographic concepts and in map reading. Reading skills played an important part in understanding geographical concepts, but not in map reading. Teachers had no difficulty in teaching the course without extra training.

Time and Chronology. Numerous studies have dealt with the development of time sense and chronology. Arnsdorf (1959) investigated learning experiences which emphasized activities related to chronology in grade 6, including chronological terms, time lines, and time charts. The major conclusions of this worthwhile study were that planned instruction helped children in the following respects: (1) to comprehend definite and indefinite time terms; (2) to note similarity of time spans with reference to given events; (3) to develop skill in ordering events with dates; and (4) to develop competency in recognizing time absurdities. Children in grade 2 were studied by McAulay (1961) to determine their understanding of time as related to self, their immediate environment, and historical events. The children had more difficulty in associating past and present when related to self or family than if unrelated to self and immediate environment. They seemed to have an appreciably better understanding of time periods if the periods were concerned with events, rather than with places or people. They were capable of comprehending known events of the past related to the present, of associating persons with events, and of connecting historical persons with their accomplishments. Gill (1962) investigated whether significant difficulties and differences existed among various grade levels in interpreting indefinite expressions of time commonly found in textbooks and class discussions. Gill constructed a test of indefinite time expressions and administered it to randomly selected groups of college juniors and seniors, potential teachers, high school juniors and seniors, and students in grades 5 and 8. Terms included "a long time ago," "in colonial times," and "the last decade." Findings indicated that (1) indefinite time expressions were loosely interpreted at all grade levels; (2) the higher grade levels, particularly the college group, demonstrated a superior grasp of indefinite time expressions; and (3) when teachers use indefinite time expressions, a variety of meanings is perceived by the pupils.

Critical Thinking. Critical thinking, a necessary goal of social studies instruction, is perhaps the goal least often satisfied. There is agreement as to the skills needed to be a "critical thinker"; little research exists, however, on how to develop these skills. Fair and Shaftel (1967) discuss the nature of critical thinking, its implementation, and its evaluation.

Cousins (1962), in a noteworthy study involving a theoretical model of reflective thinking, described and analyzed its development in grade 8. Conclusions were that pupils could be taught to think reflectively without jeopardy to factual knowledge and that teachers can develop valid instruments to evaluate instruction designed to further critical thinking.

MATERIALS. Although an increasing amount of material is being published for use in social studies education, much of it fails to take into account research relative to the learning process. In textbooks, changing objectives generally are not reflected, important social issues either are avoided or are treated superficially, and inadequate scholarship is all too prevalent. Supplementary materials, however, seem to be meeting many important needs that textbooks fail to meet.

Textbooks. The treatment of social change in high school history texts was examined by Palmer (1960), who found that 82 percent of the textbooks failed to contribute significantly to building an understanding of the social change process. Kennedy (1960) concluded that in social studies textbooks the treatment of the Moslem nations and of India and Israel was dated and that supplementary materials were needed. Lemmond (1964) investigated the degree to which social studies textbooks provided human value orientation. Wealth and power received most attention, and least was given to affection and rectitude; in general, human values were often ignored or treated lightly.

Programmed and Simulated Materials. During recent years there has been a remarkable growth in self-instruction materials. A challenge to the traditional textbook, programmed materials are Socratic in nature, since they lead the learner to higher levels of understanding through small steps of graduated difficulty. A problem arises in developing such materials for many aspects of social studies; for instance, intuitive and reflective thinking are not easily programmed. Wood (1962) investigated the learning of factual information in grade 9 by a comparison of a programmed-materials and teacher-led instructional combination with a traditional approach. Students using programmed materials learned factual material better. Cherryholmes (1965) adapted a game involving simulation in international relations for use with high school students. Student interest was high, and realistic attitudes resulted. Many problems, both theoretical and practical, are evident; nevertheless, the potential gains from using this type of material merit continued experimentation.

Audiovisual Aids. Research dealing with audiovisual materials in social studies education is limited. While the aids themselves are plentiful, research is needed to determine which type is best for a given situation. Pictures, projected through various means, have been shown to promote vocabulary growth and motivation in social studies (Georgiady, 1959). A comparative study of the effectiveness of a geography course taught via television and one taught in a regular classroom setting was made by Johnson (1960). Material was covered in 33 percent less time on television. Although the mean score on the final examination for students taking the television course was lower, their content retention after three months was greater.

EVALUATION. Substantive research on evaluation done specifically in social studies education over the past decade is limited. This might derive from the fact that social studies educators and teachers of social studies, not being "at home" in this area, are not aware of its potential and, therefore, of the need to utilize that potential effectively. Perhaps the need is acknowledged, but the responsibility is left to professionals in evaluation.

D. Allen (1959) found the lack of sophistication in evaluation among social studies teachers to be disturbing. They did not like evaluation and wished that need for it would disappear. If placing concern for evaluation before objectives is "putting the cart before the horse," some of the research developments discussed in the section on objectives may in essence be basic research in the area of evaluation. That the need to use more sophisticated evaluation procedures is great has been pointed out by Massialas (1961), whose work has been referred to in the previous discussion of sources of content in world history. Some techniques, such as programming and simulation, build in their own unique procedures. Concrete suggestions are to be found in the article of Berg (1965), who spells out the role of evaluation in social studies education and provides specific recommendations for its achievement.

Many instruments have been specially designed by researchers to conduct investigations into other areas of social studies education, and these have been described above under the appropriate headings. Three tests developed to meet particular needs are those by B. Allen (1965), in the area of belief in American values; Figert (1966), on dogmatism or open-and closed-mindedness of children in grades 4 through 6; and Gall (1966), for determining progress of elementary school children in decision-making ability. Oliver and Shaver (1962) have reported on means for more effective evaluation of student statements made in oral discussion. Goolsby (1963) sounds a warning note on utilization of subtest scores in elementary school social studies evaluation when objectives have not been discretely stated or sufficiently sophisticated instruments have not been employed.

TEACHER EDUCATION. Several studies, such as that of Hansen (1964) on secondary school curriculum (grades 7–14), have indicated that social studies teachers are not well prepared. Hart (1960), in analyzing factors related to high and low achievement among high school seniors in understanding basic social concepts, found that teachers in high-ranking schools had had major undergraduate preparation in social studies, whereas teachers in low-ranking schools had their major undergraduate preparation in fields other than social studies. Further, among teachers in high-ranking schools, qualities of teaching effectiveness and methodology were consistently rated more important by students than were personality characteristics.

Black (1963) did research among 400 secondary social studies teachers in grades 7 through 12 in Florida, Georgia, and South Carolina to determine the relationship between undergraduate content preparation and teaching assignments during the first and fifth years. Black found that most had an undergraduate content specialty of 18 or more semester hours in one subject, usually history, with some collateral work in one to three of the other social sciences. This was the pattern preferred by college advisors. When teaching assignments were analyzed, it was found that neither initial nor later responsibilities related to the area of concentration selected during undergraduate work. Most frequently taught social studies courses were history, geography, and civics, in that order, initially at the junior high level and later moving "up" to the senior high. Although teachers had only one or two social studies subjects to teach each year, over a five-year period they had taught in two to five social science content areas. Principals preferred social studies teachers with content preparation in all five of the basic social sciences, plus a 15–18-semester-hour depth in one. Indications were that their desires for content preparation corresponded more with what teachers actually taught. These findings are interesting in light of how closely they correlate with the "Guidelines for the Preparation of Social Studies Teachers" issued by the National Council for the Social Studies (1967), which advocates an undergraduate content major in secondary social studies education involving broad preparation in anthropology, economics, geography, history, political science, psychology, and sociology, with depth study in one of those disciplines. The NCSS also endorsed a graduate program combining further content and professional education study. Elementary teachers should have completed a program consistent with the same philosophy, and social studies educators should be proficient in both the subject matter and teaching methods of social studies. In a study concurring with the later recommendation, Searles (1965), pointed out that, in comparison with 1952, in 1965 42 percent rather than 27 percent of the social studies educators were teaching social science content courses in combination with education classes.

The above research points up needs related to content preparation. Little significant research is available on programs for pre- and in-service education designed for *and actually producing* more effective social studies teachers. Kirk (1964), experimenting with the use of the Minnesota System of Interaction Analysis, found that employing this system significantly modified the amount of discourse by student teachers and resulted in increased pupil discussion participation in intermediate-grades social studies classes. Various systems of classifying and analyzing classroom behavior that are continually being tested in subjects on all levels hold promise for social studies education. In the area of new media in teacher education, Chabe (1962) found that osbervation by closed-circuit television in elementary school social studies methods courses proved almost as effective as guided observation in actual classrooms. Further experimentation with recorded experiences of student and in-service social studies teachers may reveal the potential of using more sophisticated and objective analysis, reexamination, reflection, and criticism based on a conceptual framework of teaching. Some progress in this research area has been reported, but not specifically in social studies education.

One overarching conclusion is warranted: if improvements are to be made in social studies education which relate more effective teaching to developments emerging on both the content and methods fronts, broad research-based and field-tested programs of teacher education need to be conducted and reported nationally. Research will continue to improve if writings such as that of Price (1964), proposing in detail needed research in social studies education, are heeded. Then the results of research as indicated in this article and in Metcalf (1963), McPhie (1964), Massialas and Smith (1965), and others must be thoroughly studied, applied in teacher education programs, and implemented in grades K through 14.

J. R. Skretting
J. E. Sundeen
Florida State University

References

Adair, Charles H. "Predicting Readiness for Social Studies Curriculum Change: A Study of Determining Forces in Secondary Schools." Doctoral dissertation. Florida State U, 1962.

Aldrich, Julian C., and others. (Eds.) *Social Studies for Young Adolescents: Programs for Grades 7, 8 and 9.* National Council for the Social Studies, 1967. 87p.

Allen, Benjamin J. "The Construction of an Instrument Designed to Measure Student Held Attitudes Toward Certain American Values as Related to a Jury of Experts Consensus." Doctoral dissertation. Florida State U, 1965.

Allen, Dwight W. "Evaluation in Social Studies Classrooms: Ideals and practices." Doctoral dissertation. Stanford U, 1959.

Anderson, Randall C. "Geography in Secondary Education." Doctoral dissertation. U Nebraska Teachers Col, 1963.

Arnsdorf, Val E. "An Investigation of Teaching of Chronology in the Sixth Grade." Doctoral dissertation. U Minnesota, 1959.

Berg, Harry D. (Ed.) *Evaluation in Social Studies.* 35th Yearbook. National Council for the Social Studies, 1965. 251p.

Bidna, David B. "Social Studies Programs for Academically Talented High School Students." Doctoral dissertation. U Southern California, 1961.

Black, Watt L. "The Undergraduate Content Background of Secondary Social Studies Teachers: An Evaluation as Related to Teaching Assignments Accepted." Doctoral dissertation. Florida State U, 1963.

Bloom, Benjamin S., and Krathwohl, David R. *Taxonomy of Educational Objectives: Handbook I, The Cognitive Domain.* McKay, 1956. 207p.

Brady, Marion. "A New Social Studies." *Phi Delta Kappan* 48:68–71; 1966.

Carmichael, Dennis R. "Developing Map Reading Skills and Geographic Understanding by Means of Conceptual Teaching Methods." Doctoral dissertation. U California, Berkeley, 1965.

Carpenter, Helen McCracken. (Ed.) *Skill Development in Social Studies.* 33rd Yearbook. National Council for the Social Studies, 1963. 332p.

Casteel, Doyle. "Utilizing the Methods of the Political Scientist in the Social Studies Classroom." *Peabody J Ed* 40:219–27; 1963.

Chabe, A. M. "Experiment with CCTV in Teacher Education." *Peabody J Ed* 40:24–30; 1962.

Cheeryholmes, Cleo. "Developments in Simulation of International Relations in High School Teaching." *Phi Delta Kappan* 46:227–31; 1965.

Clements, Henry M. "An Empirical Study of Inquiry in Three Social Sciences." Doctoral dissertation. Stanford U, 1964.

Committee for Economic Development. *Economic Education in the Schools: A Report of the National Task Force on Economic Education.* The Committee, 1961.

Cousins, Jack E. "The Development of Reflective Thinking in an Eighth Grade Social Studies Class." Doctoral dissertation. Indiana U, 1962.

Crabtree, Charlotte. "Inquiry Approaches to Learning Concepts and Generalizations in Social Studies." *Social Ed* 30:407–11, 14; 1966.

Curry, Robert L. "The Effect of Socio-economic Status on the Scholastic Achievement of Sixth-grade Children." *Br J Ed Psychol* 32:46–9; 1962.

Devitt, Joseph J. "The Relative Importance of United States History Concepts in General Education Programs At the Secondary School Level." Doctoral dissertation. Boston U, 1958.

Easton, David, and Hess, Robert D. "The Child's

Political World." *Midwest J Political Sci* 6:229–46; 1962.

Edgar, Robert W. "History, Reading, and Human Relations: An Integrated Approach." *Social Ed* 29: 155–8; 1965.

Engle, Shirley H. (Ed.) *New Perspectives in World History.* 34th Yearbook. National Council for the Social Studies, 1964(*a*). 667p.

Engle, Shirley H. "Objectives of the Social Studies." *B Sch Ed,* Indiana U 40:1–11; 1964(*b*).

Estvan, Frank J. "Teaching Government in the Elementary chools." *El Sch J* 62:291–7; 1962.

Fair, Jean, and Shaftel, Fannie R. (Eds.) *Effective Thinking in the Social Studies.* 37th Yearbook. National Council for Social Studies, 1967. 258p.

Feldmesser, Robert A. "Sociology in the Secondary Schools." *Sociol Ed* 39:200–1; 1966.

Fenton, Edwin. *Teaching the New Social Studies in Secondary Schools.* Holt, 1966. 526p.

Figert, Russel L. "An Elementary School Form of the Dogmatism Scale: Development of an Instrument for Use in Studies of Belief-Disbelief Systems of Children in Grades Four, Five, and Six." Doctoral dissertation. Ball State U, 1965. 162p.

Fraser, Dorothy McClure. "Status and Expectations of Current Research and Development Projects." *Social Ed* 29:421–34; 1965.

Fraser, Dorothy McClure, and McCutchen, Samuel P. (Eds.) *Social Studies in Transition: Guidelines for Change.* National Council for the Social Studies, 1965. 67p.

Gall, Morris. "Improving Competence in Judgment." *Social Ed* 30:88–90; 1966.

Georgiady, Nicholas P. "Vocabulary Growth in the Elementary Social Studies as Influenced by the Use of Selected Audio-Visual Materials." Doctoral dissertation. U Wisconsin, 1959.

Gill, Clark C. "Interpretations of Indefinite Expressions of Time." *Social Ed* 26:454–6; 1962.

Goolsby, Thomas M. "Interrelationships Among Seven Measures of Competency in Elementary School Social Studies." Doctoral dissertation. State U Iowa, 1963.

Greenstein, Fred L. *Children and Politics.* Yale U Press, 1964. 199p.

Gross, Richard E., and Maynard, David M. "Social Science Offerings in Junior Colleges Reveal Urgent Curricular Problems." *Social Stud* 56:123–7; 1965.

Haffner, Hyman. "A Study of Vocabulary Load and Social-concept Burden of Fifth and Sixth Grade Social Studies, History, and Geography Textbooks." Doctoral dissertation. U Pittsburgh, 1959.

Hanna, Paul R., and Lee, John R. "Content in the Social Studies." In *Social Studies in Elementary Schools.* 32nd Yearbook. National Council for the Social Studies, 1962. p. 62–89.

Hanna, Paul R., and others. *Geography in the Teaching of Social Studies: Concepts and Skills.* Houghton, 1966. 511p.

Hansen, John H. "The Social Studies Program of a Representative Sample of Wisconsin Junior High Schools and the Preparation of Social Studies Teachers." Doctoral dissertation. U Wisconsin, 1964.

Hart, Richard Laverne. "An Analysis of Factors Related to High and Low Achievement in Understanding Basic Social Concepts." Doctoral dissertation. U Nebraska Teachers Col, 1960.

Helburn, Nicholas. "High School Geography and What Is Being Done About It." *Social Ed* 30: 631–2, 645; 1966.

Hill, Wilhelmina, and others. "A Directory of Social Studies Projects." *Social Ed* 31:509–11; 1967.

Horton, Roy E. "American Freedom and the Values of Youth." Doctoral dissertation. Purdue U, 1955.

Jarolimek, John. "The Taxonomy: Guide to Differentiated Instruction." *Social Ed* 26:445–7; 1962.

Johnson, Hildegard B. "A Comparative Study of an Introductory Geography Course on ETV and in the Classroom." Doctoral dissertation. Macalester Col, 1960.

Jones, Galen. "The Current Status of Economics Teaching in the High Schools of the United States." *B Nat Assn Sec Sch Prin* 49:3–26; 1965.

Jones, Rita. "Relationships Between Two Modes of Social Studies Instruction." Doctoral dissertation. U California, Berkeley, 1964.

Joyce, Bruce, and Weinberg, Carl. "Using the Strategies of Sociology in Social Education." *El Sch J* 64:265–72; 1964.

Kennedy, Leonard M. "The Treatment of Moslem Nations, India, and Israel in Social Studies Textbooks Used in Elementary and Junior High Schools of the United States." Doctoral dissertation. Washington State U, 1960.

Kenyon, John G. "Attitudes Toward and Knowledge of the Social Sciences Held by Certain High School Seniors." Doctoral dissertation. Syracuse U, 1965.

Kirk, Jeffery. "Effects of Teaching the Minnesota System of Interaction Analysis to Intermediate Grade Student Teachers." Doctoral dissertation. Temple U, 1964.

Krathwohl, David R., and others. *Taxonomy of Educational Objectives: Handbook II, The Affective Domain.* McKay, 1964. 196p.

Kurfman, Dana. "A National Assessment of Social Studies Education." *Social Ed* 31:209–11; 1967.

Ladue, Donald. "Social Studies Interests of Second, Fourth, and Sixth Grade Children as Evidenced in Their Art, Writing, Oral Expression, and Selection of Reading Materials." Doctoral dissertation. Pennsylvania State U, 1962.

Lemmond, Lewis E. "A Value Analysis of Social Studies Textbooks. Doctoral dissertation. East Texas State Col, 1964.

Lovenstein, Meno, and others. *Development of Economic Curricular Materials for Secondary Schools.* USOE Project HS-082. Ohio State U Research Foundation, 1966. 935p.

Lux, John E. "Teaching Methods and Activities Used by Social Studies Teachers Rated as Superior by Their Administrators." Doctoral dissertation. U Nebraska, 1959.

Massialas, Byron G. "Description and Analysis of a Method of Teaching a High School Course in World History." Doctoral dissertation. Indiana U, 1961.

Massialas, Byron G., and Smith, Frederick R. (Eds.) *New Challenges in the Social Studies, Implications of Research for Teaching.* Wadsworth, 1965. 261p.

Mayo, William L. "The Development of Secondary School Geography as an Independent Subject in the United States and Canada." Doctoral dissertation. U Michigan, 1964.

McAulay, John D. "What Understandings Do Second Grade Children Have of Time Relationships?" *J Ed Res* 54:312–14; 1961.

McGarry, Eugene L. "An Experiment in the Teaching of Reflective Thinking in the Social Studies." Doctoral dissertation. State U Iowa, 1961.

McPhie, Walter E. (Ed.) *Dissertations in Social Studies Education: A Comprehensive Guide.* National Council for the Social Studies, 1964. 99p.

Metcalf, Lawrence E. "Research on Teaching the Social Studies." In Gage, N. L. (Ed.) *Handbook of Research on Teaching.* Rand McNally, 1963. p. 929–65.

Michaelis, John U. (Ed.) *Social Studies in Elementary Schools.* 32nd Yearbook. National Council for the Social Studies, 1962. 334p.

Moreland, Willis, "Curriculum Trends in the Social Studies." *Social Ed* 26:73–6; 1962.

Muessig, Raymond H. (Ed.) *Social Studies Curriculum Improvement, A Guide for Local Committees.* National Council for the Social Studies, 1965. 117p.

Nash, John F. "A Study of the Relevance of Selected Major Concepts and Generalizations from the Field of Sociology to Commonly Accepted Objectives of the Social Studies in the Secondary School." Doctoral dissertation. Syracuse U, 1962.

National Council for the Social Studies. "Guidelines for the Preparation of Social Studies Teachers." *Social Ed* 31:490–1; 1967.

Nebergall, Nelda S. "A Study of the Teaching of High School Psychology and a Proposed Text Plan." Doctoral dissertation. U Oklahoma, 1965.

Oliver, Donald, and Baker, Susan. "The Case Method." *Social Ed* 23:25–8; 1959.

Oliver, Donald W., and Shaver, James P. "Evaluating the Jurisprudential Approach to Social Studies." *H Sch J* 46:55–63; 1962.

Olmo, Barbara M. "A Study to Determine the Status of the Social Studies Curriculum Development in Selected New Jersey Public Secondary Schools." Doctoral dissertation. Rutgers U, 1966.

Palmer, John R. "The Treatment of Social Change in High School History Textbooks," Doctoral dissertation. U Illinois, 1960.

Perchlik, Richard A. "Diversity of Knowledge in a Democracy, and a Classification of the Freedoms of Expression and Knowledge Basic to Its Consideration in the Secondary School Social Studies Curriculum." Doctoral dissertation. U Colorado, 1964.

Phillips, James E. "An Appraisal of Social Studies Instruction in Single and Double Period and in Core-like and Non-core-like Classes in Selected Junior High Schools of St. Paul, Minnesota." Doctoral dissertation. Indiana U, 1961.

Possien, Wilma M. "A Comparison of the Effects of Three Teaching Methodologies on the Development of the Problem Solving Skills of Sixth Grade Children." Doctoral dissertation. U Alabama, 1965.

Price, Roy A. (Ed.) *Needed Research in the Teaching of the Social Studies.* National Council for the Social Studies, 1964. 126p.

Price, Roy A., and others. *Major Concepts for Social Studies.* Social Studies Curriculum Center, Syracuse U, 1965. 62p.

Riddle, Donald H., and Cleary, Robert E. (Eds.) *Political Science in the Social Studies.* 36th Yearbook. National Council for the Social Studies, 1966. 346p.

Robinson, Helen F. "Learning Economic Concepts in the Kindergarten." Doctoral dissertation. Columbia U, 1963.

Searles, John E. "The Teacher of the Teacher of the Social Studies." *J Teach Ed* 16:445–9; 1965.

Senesh, Lawrence. "The Organic Curriculum: A New Experiment in Economic Education." *The Councilor* 21:43–56; 1960.

Shaver, James P. "Reflective Thinking Values and Social Studies Textbooks." *Sch R* 73:226–57; 1965.

Sjostrom, Jack E. "An Appraisal of the Curriculum Status, Trends, and Techniques Used in Social Studies Curriculum Revision in North Central Accredited High Schools." Doctoral dissertation. U Colorado, 1964.

Sorohan, Lawrence Joseph. "The Grade Placement of Map Skills According to the Mental Ages of Elementary School Children." Doctoral dissertation. Ohio State U, 1962.

Sperling, John G., and Wiggins, Suzanne E. "Design and Evaluation of a 12th Grade Course in the Principles of Economics." USOE Project H153. San Jose State Col, 1966. (Mimeographed.)

Tankersley, Gene J. "Development of Selected Study Skills in Social Studies." Doctoral dissertation. U California, Berkeley, 1965.

Thornton, Bobby M. "A National Survey of the Teaching of Psychology in the High School." Doctoral dissertation. Duke U, 1965.

Wagner, Lewis E., and Metcalf, Lawrence E. "Economic Education in Transition." *Teach Col Rec* 64:706–18; 1963.

Walsh, Huber M. "A Teaching Model for Culture Studies." Doctoral dissertation. U California, Los Angeles, 1962.

Weaver, Verner P. "Basic American History Generalizations for the Social Studies Curriculum in the Elementary Grades." Doctoral dissertation. Pennsylvania State U, 1962.

Wood, Leslie A. "Programmed Textual Materials as a Partial Substitute for Teacher-led Classroom Procedures in Geography." Doctoral dissertation. Stanford U, 1962.

SOCIOLOGY OF EDUCATION

The sociological study of education began with modern sociology itself. In 1883 Lester Ward published his *Dynamic Sociology*, a meliorist argument against Spencer, in which education was viewed as the principal agent of human progress (Ward, 1883). By 1887 Emile Durkheim had begun his lectures on pedagogy at Bordeaux, in 1905 transferred to the Sorbonne (Durkheim, 1956, 1961). Max Weber's main contributions to the study of education appeared between 1915 and 1921 (Gerth & Mills, 1946).

Ward's work presaged a voluminous American literature that was essentially reformist and pragmatic. Whatever may have been the influence of these hortative writings on educational practice, they are not analyses of the social institution of education.

It was Durkheim and Weber who founded the sociology of education as an analytical field of study. Serious interest in education, however, has not been typical of sociologists. Nonetheless, Willard Waller (1932) and Florian Znaniecki (1936) presented major theoretical arguments. Karl Mannheim's utopian-reformist program for social education deserves close attention, but as a theoretical statement its value is limited (Mannheim, 1951).

For various reasons, perhaps the most important of which is the centrality of education as an institution of modern societies, the research literature in the sociology of education has grown rapidly since 1955. [For an excellent critical review of the earlier literature, see Floud & Halsey (1958).] The sociology of education now includes a body of empirical findings in the light of which earlier theoretical work may be examined.

CORRELATION OF TYPES OF SOCIETY AND OF EDUCATION. Durkheim and Weber viewed education as a social creation. Durkheim was preoccupied with the problem of social integration in simple as contrasted to complex, industrial societies. Weber ranged more widely, but he too centered on the emergence of industrial society and the major historical processes of which, he said, it is the culmination. Both were led by these interests to consider education in relation to social change.

Durkheim. Durkheim viewed the function of education as "above all the means by which society perpetually recreates the conditions of its very existence" (1956), socializing the young to adult responsibilities. "Its structure, he regarded as the adaptation of a social fact, *sui generis*, to the society's characteristic structural traits and beliefs. In simpler ("mechanical") societies, the social bond was created by kinship and by widely shared and automatically accepted beliefs. Education proceeded without self-conscious design through family and generational relationships. In complex ("organic") societies, solidarity must be renewed continually.

In these societies, which are structures of highly specialized and interdependent parts, cooperative activity is essential. Still, solidarity cannot be maintained by kinship; the family develops a conjugal rather than an extended form, and its power shrinks. Contract replaces kinship obligation. Moreover, social complexity and rational, scientific thought advance together. Social values and the means for attaining them become matters of choice, and traditional sentiment as the basis for social action is replaced by the secular spirit, knowledgeability, and intellectual power.

But, with the decay of kinship and tradition, there is no longer a forceful moral governor restraining the pursuit of self-interest. Scientific analysis may indicate the most rational approach to given ends, but it does not ensure, as did tradition, that men or groups will agree on the ends to be pursued. Nor does structural interdependence promote agreement, for contractual obligations without moral basis are weaker than the calculus of personal advantage. Moreover, men freed from the constraints of tradition, though freer, are prone to demoralization and the personally destructive force of unregulated ambition ("infinite aspiration").

Consequently moral consensus must be created, since it is inconceivable for a state to marshal sufficient power to enforce widespread, enduring compliance with its moral dictates. In each generation must be instilled loyalty to the state (and thus to the society), respect for its moral authority, and the discipline of cooperation. At the same time, the scientific basis of organic society requires thoroughly trained intellects, and the differentiation of its parts requires the balancing of moral agreement with specialized technical and scientific training.

Only the state, said Durkheim, is capable of such education, as an agency sufficiently powerful, universal, and secular to cross-cut the parochial, specialist, and familistic divisions that fragment organic societies. State systems of common education overlaid with advanced, specialized schooling are, in fact, a mark of the organic society.

Each of the other institutions of organic society is in some way educationally incapacitated. The family's resources are too limited. Its parochial and affective atmosphere pulls its members away from broader loyalties and is a source more of self-indulgence than of discipline. The church, historically responsible for formal education, is opposed to the rational spirit; whereas other social units, because of their functional specialization and the complexity of their tasks, are neither organized to teach nor able to temper their exacting requirements for discipline and intellectual skill. The toughness and complexity of organic society does not permit education by direct participation in adult life, as had once occurred in the medieval guilds.

At this point Durkheim's analysis fails. He assumes that the state will identify the basic moral precepts on which common school teaching will center, assuring us that they are "self-evident" (1956). Yet he does not follow through with what he saw clearly in France—namely, that the subcultural divisions which cut through organic societies, mirroring persistent ethnic, religious, and regional cleavages as well as those of class and occupation, generate alternative views of the "moral." He is not clear at all about factors affecting the formation of advanced, specialist schools. State policy on education, in point of fact, is more likely to reflect the distribution of political power among competing interest and status groups than to be a revealed social truth or automatic result of state fiat.

That common schooling is a major instrument of national unification and that specialized training is of great economic importance make state school policy a potent political issue, particularly when the interests or beliefs of a controlling group are challenged by rising strata demanding schooling as a right of citizenship. The appearance in modern societies of national systems of education cannot be understood apart from the political structure and pattern of political action; but Durkheim neglects this issue. More generally, his view of the institutional development of education is severely limited by his failure to consider the interplay of education, national governments, and other social institutions. Yet these linkages presumably set the conditions under which modern forms of education emerge.

Weber. Weber's interest centered on these interrelationships and on education as it responds to the polity, economy, and stratification system. Like Durkheim, he viewed history as the movement of societies toward rationality ("the demystification of the world") and a complex, functional division of labor; but his eye never left the specific historical processes by which this movement has occurred. Weber viewed rationalization, however inevitable, less as a smooth evolutionary sweep than as uneven, halting, and conflict-ridden. The relation of education to social change, while essentially adaptive, is itself one of strain and tension—a fitful, irregular advance toward modern forms.

Weber viewed social change in the light of varying authority ("domination") in society. He postulated three types of authority, three concomitant forms of social organization, and three derivative varieties of education. No one of these "ideal-typical" authority structures—charismatic, traditional, or bureaucratic—has totally pervaded a society; the tension among mixed types of authority is itself an important source of social change.

Charismatic authority and social forms are of least interest here. The charismatic leader (who, like the prophet or heroic warrior, has magical gifts or a "presence" that attracts a following) rules by revelation and must continually prove his worth to his followers. This form of authority is inherently unstable (though it can be welded to other more stable forms), and charismatic education is equally so. Because it seeks only to awaken and test capacities inherent as "gifts of grace," charismatic education is rudimentary in method and content and occurs sporadically, depending upon the occasional appearance of a gifted one to be awakened by an older hero or magician. Although charisma remains, for Weber, an important source of creative disruption in more complex societies, charismatic education has all but disappeared with the heroes and prophets. (It may persist on the margins of educational activity, as in the artistic apprenticeship.)

Traditional authority is based especially upon beliefs about the political prerogatives of elite status groups and results in a patrimonial monopoly on power by this ruling stratum. Patrimonial societies are the direct historical antecedents of modern bureaucratic society, in which authority relations are based on rationality (the appeal to efficiency and predictability) and where social activity (the family excepted) is coordinated through hierarchies of "offices" that are regulated in their interaction by codified rules.

The course of history thus leads from unstable charismatic organization toward the stability of patrimonial forms and, finally, to thoroughgoing "demystification" and bureaucracy. (Weber, however, noted bureaucratic capitalism as one of several elements in earlier periods of European history.) The bureaucratization of society can be seen most clearly, according to Weber, in the rise of science and technology, in the emergence of the national state with its monopoly of the means of violence (in contrast to the feudal pattern of decentralized coercive power), in the growth of organized mass parties and party government, and in the replacement of "political" by "high" capitalism.

As a result, authority moves from the hands of traditional ruling strata, such as gentry or nobility, into the hands of career managers and experts, while government increasingly depends upon mass support mediated by "career" politicians, skilled in party management. Science, technology, management, and politics alike become vocations that can be pursued only in bureaucratic settings (whether of private or "state" capitalism), for neither power nor technical or altruistic aims can be pursued without the concentrated means that these organizations provide. The entire male adult population in a bureaucratic society forms a specialized labor force, stratified primarily according to skill, training, and differing access to high organizational office. Elite and proletarian alike are "alienated from the means of production," for in no one stratum is concentrated both the management and "ownership" of the major sources of economic or political power (in contrast to the total domination of patrimonial societies by a ruling group).

In patrimonial and bureaucratic, as in charismatic, societies are found distinctive forms of education: education that aims at "cultivating the pupil for a conduct of life . . . the conduct of a status group . . ." and that which seeks to "impart specialized training . . ." (Gerth & Mills, 1946). Education for life conduct is usually marked by a steady flow of pupils through organized schools. Such education has often contained an important element of technical training (for example, preparation for statecraft in the Confucian schools of imperial China and Tokugawa Japan), but the curriculum centers on a style of life —the moral norms, tastes, and manners of a status group, "its internal and external deportment in life" (Gerth & Mills, 1946).

The main function of these schools is "differentiating" (Floud & Halsey, 1958), in order to maintain the dominance of the ruling group by strengthening the legitimacy of its authority (and perhaps by recruiting new blood into its ranks). What the student is taught is directly dictated by his social rank (popular versions of the esteemed curriculum may be offered in the interest of social order). Historical variations of "life conduct" education are to be understood by reference to differences of stratification among patrimonial societies. Especially important are the life style and political and economic interests of the "decisive stratum" and, as it affects selective recruitment of children of lower orders, the openness of the stratification system (Gerth & Mills, 1946).

Social unrest arising from the political or economic demands of newly powerful strata may in part be expressed in patrimonial societies as dissent from existing educational arrangements (rights of entry or ability to provide alternative curricula in separate schools). The source of this dissent is to be found not within the institution of education but outside, in altered stratum interests [for instance, demands for the "Dutch learning" by rising commercial groups in late Tokugawa Japan (Dore, 1965)].

In any event, decisions about life conduct education are always made by the decisive stratum in a patrimonial society. This decisive stratum is not always the ruling one, so that decisions about patrimonial education may reflect the political situation existing between the rulers and their immediate dependents. Thus in China the literati, not the imperial family, determined the content and form of education. Nonetheless, the Confucian schools persisted as long as they did not only because they suited the mandarins but also because an educational system in which examinations were tied to future office made the candidates competitive and kept the mandarins from fusing into a "feudal office nobility" (Gerth & Mills, 1946).

In bureaucratic societies, contrary to the claims of Marxian theorists who have described education as a weapon of capitalist exploitation (Floud & Halsey, 1958), it is impossible for any one stratum to be "decisive" about education. The pervasive stress in these societies upon personal merit and rational performance favors a universal recruitment of pupils and undercuts prerogatives of traditional elite strata. More important, education is exposed to the multiple demands of private and state bureaucracies (requiring specialist managers and technicians and scientific knowledge and technique), of disparate clienteles (avidly engaged in the rational calculation of life chances and seeking specialist training that will bring rewarding careers), and of the vocations themselves.

Such education can be mounted only by organized systems of schools that are themselves rationally ordered and affluent and, therefore (for Weber, as for Durkheim) must be provided by the state. Schooling becomes, in Weber's term, a "State capitalist" enterprise (Gerth & Mills, 1946).

Weber thought that the tensions generated by advancing bureaucratization would be especially visible in the universities. Repositories of the Humanist tradition and linked to elite patterns of life conduct education, the universities would nonetheless succumb to state capitalism, the professor to a salaried career (and alienation from the means of scholarly production), and the curriculum to scientific specialization (Gerth & Mills, 1946). Moreover, as the principal agency for specialist training and channel of social mobility [the "selective" function of Floud and Halsey (1958)], the university inevitably would be subject to strong pressures from students—some seeking to advance, others to maintain, social rank through prestigious careers. These pressures would accompany continuing, though outmoded, demands for "cultivation" as traditional status insurance. [Cf. Weber on the Prussian fraternities (Gerth & Mills, 1946) and J. F. Scott (1965) on the sororities in American colleges].

Weber, viewing education as adaptive, did not discuss the knowledge-producing function of the university as a source of strain or, more generally, as a major link of the university to the rest of bureaucratic society. Bureaucratic societies are "knowledgeable" societies (Lane, 1966) in which the universities—through the refinement and alteration of canons of veridical knowledge, through the production of "basic" findings and technological innovation, through sheer concentration of expertise—must amass substantial power and become major centers for social change, more often perhaps through adaptive innovation than through radical transformation. Does this concentration of political and intellectual power tend toward autonomy and domination of the society (Floud & Halsey, 1958), or is it led into closely interdependent combinations with other centers of political power, especially government and capitalist enterprise (Price, 1965)?

CASE STUDIES OF HISTORICAL AND "DEVELOPING" SOCIETIES. Durkheim and Weber raised two broad question. First, what is the general relation between education and social change? Second, how is this relation manifested in specific modern (that is, bureaucratic, organic) societies?

In pursuing these questions, one very important line of work will be to describe analytically the educational systems of historical societies and of the new nations. Such case studies, unlike the trivia that often have passed for comparative education, must be informed by sociological concepts, and their data must be relevant to main issues in the analysis of education and social change (such as levels of bureaucratization in school organization, patterns of student recruitment, and normative content of curricula).

Such work has dual significance. It will provide the elements from which a comparative sociology of education must be built. Without detailed historical knowledge of specific societies, comparisons are likely to be facile and superficial. It also may have theoretical significance in its own right, testing propositions advanced elsewhere and generating propositions to be tested with data from other settings.

A very small number of studies are of this type. Dore (1965), from a detailed description of the organization and curricula of the fief and private venture schools of Tokugawa Japan, has confirmed Weber's notion of the determining role of a decisive stratum in forming life conduct education. But he also has shown how such education promoted social change by helping to prepare for national unification under the Meiji restoration and how rising classes can force changes in the curricula of the traditional schools and loosen the hold of old elites on the educational system.

Foster (1965) has given a detailed picture of the Ghanaian educational system from its beginnings to the present, demonstrating the close dependence of change in the educational system both upon the persistence of traditional tribal bonds and upon shifts in the occupational structure (and thus upon patterns of basic economic organization, such as types of land tenure and capital formation). Kazamias (1965) has provided similar information for Turkey.

Wilkinson (1964) and Weinberg (1967) have analyzed the influence of the English public schools upon the "social character" of the upper classes and, in turn, upon the stability and conservatism of national policy. For the American case, there is only Bailyn's essay (1960), in which he proposes that the instability of family-based apprenticeship in the colonial period fostered the development of town schools and state provision for education.

Many more than these few and rather scattered case studies will be needed before adequately grounded comparative work can begin. The choice of cases can be guided by anticipating the requirements of comparative analysis. Societies may be selected at one historical period or another, either because they possess particularly significant societal attributes (for example, rapid industrialization), the consequences of which may then be traced, or because they display clearly one or another type of education, which can be traced back to its societal antecedents. In either event, one must attend to the deviant cases in which society-education relations take unexpected forms.

EDUCATION AND POLITICS. Despite such work as that of Dore and Foster, sociologists of education have paid little heed to the functions of schooling in social change. Knowledge about political linkages between education and national development is scant indeed.

On the question of national unification, Anderson (1966) has an excellent theoretical discussion of the use by central governments of systems of common education to weaken traditionally based social cleavages. For the United States there is some evidence that, in the years before the Civil War, efforts in the states to counter moral diversity and class distinctions through the common schools for a time exacerbated class, ethnic, and religious antagonisms, while at the same time stimulating the more general integration of these pluralistic elements into the political fabric (Bidwell, 1966; Katz, in press).

Any analysis of the role of education in national unification must proceed from a consideration of the social structures and cultural elements entering into the formation of a national state. In the new nations, the viability of Western-style education and its contribution to modernization depend on such preconditions as the ability of tribal leadership to use to its own ends the skills that education provides, the compatibility of traditional cultures with knowledgeability, some freedom of personal movement, and an economic organization that will permit flexible combinations of free resources (see Foster, 1964; Geertz, 1963).

In the United States the absence of a feudal heritage and the weakness of ethnic and religious divisions in the early national period undoubtedly fostered widespread adoption of common schooling, the success of school "reform," and the rapid solution of questions of citizenship rights, including rights of access to the common schools.

In other Western societies a national polity was imposed on preexisting authority relations and typically on a culturally diverse population. Variations in authority structures and population composition across these societies set distinctive conditions for educational arrangements. In Germany, for example, where national development proceeded from a politically dominant alliance between the landed and industrial-commercial classes (Moore, 1966), the state was able to centralize mass education without popular opposition, despite a diverse population, while fostering rapid industrial growth through a "State capitalist" system of university and institute science. In England, where the bourgeoisie established an independent economic base against the crown and landed interests, even incorporating a large portion of the landed classes into the capitalist advance (Moore, 1966), the role of the state in providing education was less significant. The public schools and Oxford and Cambridge persisted as independent foundations that prepared students for the occupations and "conduct" of the upper strata. The state's educational efforts were limited largely to extending the charitable impulse in common education. These efforts served at once the interests of the upper classes with respect to social order and of the lower in economic and political betterment (a harmony of interest no doubt fostered by cultural homogeneity). Indeed, there was little unrest about education until the Victorian era, when the industrial and commercial leadership became uneasy over the inability of this somewhat disjointed system to produce technology and technicians as rapidly or as flexibly as Germany's "State capitalist" schools (Kazamias, 1966).

What can be said about education and the polity in modern bureaucratic societies? Largely because of the difficulty of gathering data about totalitarian regimes, present knowledge is limited to the Western democracies. In these societies, occupational placement is closely linked to educational attainment (Lipset & Bendix, 1959; Morgan & others, 1962), and there is some evidence that popular demand for access to education focuses on advanced and specialist training as a function of more sophisticated calculation of life chances and of a more stringent popular definition of equity in the distribution of education (Parsons, 1959; Trow, 1962; Davis, 1963).

Questions of access to higher and more specialized levels of education become major party issues. The political parties, as spokesmen for significant sectors of the electorate, thus act as prime movers in the formation of government policy on education, pressing government toward specialist, mobility-relevant training, along with other similar pressures from commercial and industrial interests, from the growing number of organized expert occupations, and from the organized scientific disciplines.

The convergence of these pressures should accelerate the bureaucratization of education, especially of the universities and academic specialities, and in turn foster the political power and autonomy of these sectors of the educational system. The universities and government may then develop a close interdependence, in which higher education enjoys broad government patronage (for example, through urban-renewal legislation, subject-area foundations, and fiscal support) in exchange for academic and technical expertise and knowledge.

The structure of the educational system has important effects upon its political action. In the case of higher education, if policy making and control are gathered into a central government, the response to political pressure presumably can be orderly, integrated, and uniform, with the allocation of specific functions throughout the system. This response is likely to be of a "manpower planning" sort, in which popular pressure is balanced against economic forecasts and demands from other sectors of the society (employers and professional organizations, of course, but also the more powerful of the schools being regulated). Under such circumstances there is a tendency to preserve the extant structure and to limit change to an expansion of "places," rather than to reallocate functions radically or create new kinds of schools. [For an example of policy of this kind, see the recent Robbins report on English higher education (Robbins, 1963).]

In a more decentralized system, as in the United States, individual schools are more immediately vulnerable to student demand, as well as to demands from consumers of knowledge. Thus the system tends to differentiate according to clientele; and the schools, in entrepreneurial fashion, to compete for prestige, funds, and preferred students. Largely because of differences in the resources that they can muster for this competition, the American colleges and universities have stratified according to the quality of their students, faculty, and facilities. But to improve their competitive position, all but the weakest of these schools have sought at least the outward appearance of the most eminent (Riesman, 1956).

The significance of education in democratic politics, particularly in times of social stress, also exposes schools to populistic demands for retrenchment, moral and political conventionality, and "down-to-earth" vocationalism (Lazarsfeld & Thielens, 1958). Decentralization makes schools especially vulnerable to local sources of political pressure, but the way in which they are affected may vary widely from place to place. Minar (1966) has presented data suggesting that political conflict over local schools occurs mainly in lower-class school districts, where the skills of tension management are scarce. In high-status communities, local school officials enjoy substantial autonomy. Moreover, survey data suggest that schools in large or more urban and sophisticated districts are not of direct concern to voters, although the public remains vaguely favorable toward school affairs (Carter, 1960).

One may view the relation of education and the polity from a quite different direction, namely, studying the effect of differing amounts and types of education upon a society's political life. This perspective calls attention especially to the common schools and to Durkheim's notion of moral education.

One important issue involved here is the prevalence of literacy and its consequences for the nature and stability of regimes. Lipset has argued that literacy is an essential precondition of stable democracy (Lipset, 1959). The evidence supporting his contentions, however, is by no means conclusive, and he himself notes literacy drives by totalitarian regimes to make subject populations more accessible for indoctrination (Lipset, 1959). Moreover, it would appear that the effects of literacy on the readiness of individuals for modern politics vary with such factors as the availability of reading material that provides information about political life and issues (Schuman & Inkeles, in press).

From the viewpoint of Durkheim's "moral consensus," schooling may also affect politics by forming sentiments basic to participation in a complex polity. There has been no research on this matter, but in a theoretical discussion Dreeben (1967) extends Durkheim's ideas by arguing that the social organization of the school, in contrast to the structure of family life, accustoms children to placement in social categories, teaches them the meaning of fairness in the distribution of rewards, and adapts them to affective neutrality, universalism, and impersonality in social relations. In Dreeben's view, one cannot accept the legitimacy of modern opposition politics or, more generally, the legal order of the modern state without these sentiments. Dreeben assumes that these effects occur independently of curricular content, in contrast to students of "political socialization" who trace the cognitive outcomes of instruction about politics (Greenstein, 1965; Hess & Torney, 1965).

The aggregate effects on a population of both socialization to political norms and learning of cognitive material about politics need further study. Banfield and Wilson (1965) have argued that extension of "middle class" attitudes in better-educated city populations has led to the decline of the patrimonial style in urban politics and to its replacement by bureaucratic and professional forms. At present, however, such phenomena cannot be traced to one or another form of schooling.

EDUCATION AND THE ECONOMY. Less can be said about the relation between education and the economy. Much of the existing work falls in the area of manpower planning (Harbison & Meyers, 1964). It centers on the demand for labor at a given level of economic development in relation to the labor supply and flow of graduates from the various levels of the educational system. Analysis of this kind, however, takes the labor supply as given, whereas for the sociologist the problem is to discover factors that affect variation in this supply. The question of labor supply may then be viewed in the light of patterns of political control of education, of social factors that condition student performance and aspiration, and of the organization of the educational system with reference to the allocation of students into status groups or occupations (Floud & Halsey, 1958).

An important problem is to determine the particular relation between education and economic activity at varying stages of societal development. Whereas in industrially mature societies variation in the output of highly trained specialists may have fairly direct effects on the economy, in societies that are only beginning industrialization relations between economic growth and increasing literacy appear more problematic (Blaug, 1966).

Another approach to the economy-education relationship is through analysis of allocations of economic resources to education—either as an aggregate of individual decisions to "invest" in one's own education (Schultz, 1963) or as societal allocation to the educational system and its various components. Vaizey (1958) has refined the latter approach. His work raises questions, as yet unanswered, about relations between the political and normative context in which allocations are made. Thus Vaizey's demonstration of British concentration of government grants in the grammar schools is consistent with Banks's (1955) data concerning the high prestige of these schools relative to the secondary modern schools and with Turner's (1960) description of the alleged norm of sponsored mobility in British education.

One might also inquire into the economic productivity, in industrially advanced countries, of the system of higher education—quite apart from its role in training and selecting for a specialized labor force. Machlup (1962), who has made a beginning for the United States, notes the great economic force of "research and development." The specialization of research first noted by Weber has evolved into a complex organizational network that contains many high-level research roles besides that of professor-researcher. This network overflows the universities into the spheres of business and government and presumably heightens their interdependence (such research organizations, for instance, as the Bell Laboratories and the National Institutes of Health).

Finally, there is the question of the place of commercial and industrial enterprises in the control of education. The emergence of a "knowledge industry" suggests that the universities may influence, as much as they are influenced by, economic organizations. But the question must be pursued in societies of differing economic complexity and political structure, with both centralized and decentralized educational systems.

Direct control from the economy, in contrast to that mediated by government, is an interesting problem. There are a few older American studies that purport to show business (or upper or upper-middle class) control of American universities and public school systems (Warner & others, 1944, 1949; Beck, 1947; Hollingshead, 1949), but these studies assume that members of governing boards usually act according to their own economic or class interests—an assumption that is not clearly valid (Charters, 1953).

EDUCATION AND STRATIFICATION. The most popular research topic in the sociology of education is the relation between education and stratification. Study of "life conduct" education is necessarily an analysis of this relation [cf. the work by Dore (1965), Wilkinson (1964), and Weinberg (1967) reviewed earlier], and it will have a prominent place in research on national development [cf. Foster's (1965) monograph]. But nearly all the recent findings center on modern societies.

These findings relate to one of two topics: (1) effects of education on occupational placement and social mobility, and (2) consequences of stratum of origin for students' sentiments and performance. It is usually assumed that as the industrial development and bureaucratization of a society advance, the link between educational attainment and occupational status tightens. But the relevant data are not so extensive as one might wish. Especially to the point is the degree to which access to given occupational levels is restricted by educational attainment. Clark (1964) presents a table for the United States, drawn from U.S. Department of Labor statistics, which shows that, in 1959, 75.0 percent of professional or technical workers had completed some college. In a similar table reported by Foster (1965) for Ghana, in 1961 the analogous figure was 37.3 percent. Among American clerical workers, 75.0 percent had at least completed high school. The Ghanaian proportion was 41.7. Among skilled workers, the proportions completing a minimum of high school were 33.0 and 12.8, respectively, for the two countries.

Thus it would appear that in the United States occupations involving at least a modicum of skill are more restrictive with regard to education than in Ghana. This inference is not clearly supported, however, since the educational level characterizing an occupation may result from many factors other than technical requirements. These factors include general educational upgrading of a population in conjunction with the differential age composition of occupations (Nam, 1965), the occupational preferences of persons at various educational levels, the availability of varieties of specialized training, control of job entry by unions or professional associations, and the distribution of income by occupation (which is not entirely determined by technical requirements or scarcity of labor supply). No one has as yet undertaken a sufficiently refined analysis to sort out these phenomena, thereby pinpointing the consequences of technical specialization and its correlates for the linkage of education to job placement.

With respect to intergenerational occupational

mobility, the evidence is only somewhat clearer. In general, this evidence suggests that in modern societies the importance of educational attainment is increasing, both as a factor intervening between an individual's original stratum and his attained occupation, and independent of social origin (Duncan & Hodge, 1963). But in another way, the occupational structures of these societies appear to be opening to the qualified—operating increasingly on the universalist criterion of schooling completed, less on such ascriptive factors as family status or ethnic or religious membership.

In developing nations, educational attainment is not unimportant in affecting intergenerational mobility (Foster, 1965), but its weight is less and its effects do not seem so uniform across the occupational structure. Indeed, an oversupply of the educated may result in a measure of downward movement. On the other hand, this inference should not be pushed too far. Anderson (1961) has shown that, even in thoroughly industrialized societies, intergenerational mobility is not predicted accurately on the assumption that education determines job placement. Such factors as "luck," persistent ascriptive criteria, and differential knowledge continue to affect intergenerational movement between levels of work.

When one turns to family social status as a determinant of school performance and school-related sentiments, one finds strong family influence, even in modern bureaucratic societies. Because many of the data come from the United States and England, one can examine this influence in a system of comprehensive and a system of specialized schools.

In England, despite major efforts by the Local Education Authorities to select at "eleven-plus" on the basis of intellectual merit, disproportionate grammar school places are allocated to children of higher-status families. This differential is a function of the link between parental social status, on the one hand, and test performance, prior school achievement, available school openings, and parental sophistication and beliefs about alternative forms of secondary education, on the other (Floud & others, 1956; Jackson & Marsden, 1962).

In the United States, the consequences of differential family status are no less clear, though different in kind. Both actual and desired college-going are positively correlated with family social status, although studies show wide differences in the weight of parental rank relative to the student's measured ability. A Boston study showed status to be twice as important as ability (Kahl, 1953); a Wisconsin study gave ability a threefold weight (Sewell & others, 1957). In addition, the strength of achievement motives appears generally to rise with social rank (Rosen, 1956). School dropout is inversely related to family social status (Havighurst & others, 1962).

Stratification has effects beyond the family, as it is reflected in the correspondence of the social composition of schools with that of neighborhoods (Wilson, 1959) and local communities (Rogoff, 1961). But the power of these variables in relation to ability and family status is unclear. The one effort to clarify this point shows that neighborhood status composition has less influence on college-going intentions than does measured ability or family rank (Sewell & Armer, 1966); but the study is the subject of spirited technical debate (*American Sociological Review*, 1966).

Moreover, there is as yet little evidence concerning the mechanisms that produce the effects of school or community contexts or of family status. Campbell and Alexander (1965) have presented data indicating that the social-class composition of high schools determines the probability of having high- or low-status friends and that these friendships determine high or low academic aspirations. Other recent work suggests that norms governing achievement level may intervene between a school's social-class composition and pupil performance (McDill & others, 1966). With regard to effects of status, Kahl (1953) has shown how the vicarious ambitions of mobility-blocked working-class parents press their sons to desire college. Strangely, there are few studies of processes within families of higher social ranks that bear upon academic aspiration or performance.

All the foregoing relationships show up in accentuated form in patterns of educational discrimination against ethnic and racial minorities [that is, with the persistence of educational differentiation along racial or ethnic lines in universalist educational systems (Floud & Halsey, 1958)]. The literature on the Negro American is extensive. As Clark notes (1964), Negroes in the United States have encountered educational discrimination in one of three ways: directly because of race; indirectly because of attending inferior schools in racially segregated neighborhoods; and indirectly because of the combined influence of race and lower-class status on residence and school quality.

A massive national survey recently completed by Coleman and others (1966) supplants much of the previous work on the education of Negroes. It finds that physical facilities, libraries and laboratories, pupil density, and the verbal proficiency of teachers made available to northern metropolitan Negro students, through some or all of the processes Clark lists, are inferior to those available to white students in the same cities. Moreover, remedial programs are fewer for Negroes, and their teachers are more likely to be Negro. [These findings are consistent with another recent study by Herriott and St. John (1966).] Coleman and his associates found that each of these factors is associated with lower school achievement among Negroes.

But the single most powerful effect on achievement is that of pupil composition of the school. In the predominantly Negro schools, prior effects of discrimination result in a distinct concentration of Negro pupils (poor, of lower-class status, and from fatherless homes) for whom there is little stimulus to achievement. These findings confirm the earlier literature, and, significantly, for Negro as for white pupils return to effects of school contexts and to the need to explain them. The difference for the Negro student appears to be not in the processes affecting his aspirations or performance but in the distinctly unfavorable circumstances of his home and school life.

SOCIAL ORGANIZATION OF EDUCATIONAL ACTIVITIES. In material first published between 1903 and 1925, Durkheim delineated a second major topic in the sociology of education: the study of the social organization of schools and classrooms. But his treatment of this issue, like his discussion of society and education, was brief and uneven. It remained for Waller (1932) to make the first systematic theoretical statement.

Durkheim assumed that the school and its classrooms are microcosmic social facts, with their own structural and cultural integrity, although they share the characteristic processes of society itself. Hence they may be studied in their own right as social systems. One aspect of this study is analysis of *la vie scholaire*, that is, the emergent social traits and subcultures which Durkheim assures us are to be found in every school and classroom (1961). Yet he tells us very little about the texture of social relations among students or about the interplay of *la vie scholaire* and the formal structure of the classroom.

Durkheim's preoccupation with moral education led him to center on the instruction of young children and, thus, to identify domination as the prime structural trait of classrooms. The teacher's position is one of indisputable authority. He appears before his students as the "incarnation of duty." The teacher's authority has a dual base: age and vocation. Because the teacher is an adult, he shares the general moral superiority of all adults vis-à-vis children and may benefit from the child's readiness to conform to adult will. But it is the teacher's calling especially that engenders respect for his authority. The child acknowledges in the teacher not personal charisma but impersonal moral authority—higher and more general than the particular classroom relation.

Nonetheless, Durkheim failed to consider how the basis of the teacher's authority might shift in accordance with the age of his pupils and with school level and type. In point of fact, the specialization of education that Durkheim described elsewhere (Durkheim, 1956) provides two important sources of variation in the basis of teacher authority: the scientific-technical content of instruction in the specialties, which raises questions of the teacher's competence, whatever his sense of calling; and mass enrollment beyond the common school, which undercuts "gentlemanly" assumptions about the legitimacy of teacher authority.

Durkheim did suggest that students, even young children, may not always take kindly to teacher domination. Students develop a sense of equity (just how, Durkheim did not say) by which a teacher's acts are judged. To orders or punishments that seem unfair, students may react with individual withdrawal or rebellion, or perhaps with moblike uprisings of demoralization (Durkheim, 1961). But Durkheim, in contrast to Waller, did not expect a student society, emerging as an independent organized force, to come into direct opposition to teacher authority.

Durkheim feared teacher tyranny, fostered by the nature of teaching, the dominative structure of classrooms, and the differentiated quality of modern society. The moral order of the classroom is impersonal, cold, often harsh. It is in fact the teacher's task to introduce his pupils to the "austerity of duty." Unlike the parent, the teacher cannot temper discipline with love, since familial warmth is unsuited to the growth of personal discipline. Moreover, the teacher's students are conscripts, brought into the classroom without regard for their preferences.

In addition, the teacher is imbued with civilization; his students have yet to be "civilized." In close daily contact, "[t]here is the same relation between them as between two populations of unequal culture" (Durkheim, 1961). The teacher's sense of moral and intellectual superiority to his pupils in this situation is likely to produce in the teacher "an exaggerated self-conception, expressed in gesture, attitude, and language . . ." (Durkheim, 1961). Moreover, this feeling is given ". . . to violent expression, for any behavior which offends it easily takes on the character of sacrilege" (Durkheim, 1961).

The teacher himself is not readily subject to external discipline. Durkheim noted the physical isolation of classrooms and the concomitant fragmentation of supervision. Within broad limits and subject to occasional inspection, teachers are free to do as they wish. Pupils are in no position to resist, since they lack access to any form of legitimate power. There is no one to control the teacher but the teacher himself, whose sense of calling is so easily distorted.

What of possible colleague controls? Despite his syndicalist views, Durkheim saw in teachers' associations a further source of teacher tyranny. With the appearance of teaching as an organized occupation comes a collective thrust toward autonomy. Teacher organizations sanctify teachers' moral and intellectual superiority and assert their right to occupational autonomy as specialists and cultivated men. Hence this sense of superiority which in the classroom sets the teacher against his students, in society in general, sets the whole teaching occupation against the force of state supervision and public opinion. The more specialized and vocationally aware the teaching force, the greater the propensity for teachers and schools to enclose themselves within school walls.

Waller. To a point, Waller's analysis of the school society parallels Durkheim's. From the physical and social closeness of the school emerges a distinctive social structure and "separate culture." These emergent trends are in part accounted for by the involuntary recruitment of pupils; schooling and childhood are alien.

Thus the teacher faces two major tasks: to control and discipline the class and to foster achievement. These tasks, said Waller, reinforce each other and press the teacher toward dominative authority. Controlling a class and making its members work both require compliance to impersonal standards, and to enforce compliance the teacher draws on the joint resources of official position and adult status.

At this point the parallel with Durkheim stops. While Durkheim thought that emotion and sympathy are foreign to teaching, Waller saw them as integral, yet contradictory to the dominative side of the teacher's role. To foster learning, the teacher needs a warm, close relation to his pupils. Domination may produce compliance, but compliant students often learn very little and grow resistant to teacher demands. For Durkheim student resistance arrives with the failure of impersonality. For Waller it is the inevitable product of impersonality, that is, of domination unleavened by affect.

But affect brings its own problems, for it particularizes the relation between the teacher and each of his students, while he must at the same time be an evenhanded judge of conduct and accomplishment.

This dilemma, according to Waller, is usually resolved in favor of domination, but not for Durkheim's reasons. Waller noted that teachers tend to form tightly knit colleague groups, eager to defend occupational prerogatives from invasion. But, he said, this group forms from weakness, not strength. (Note that Waller's data come from the small towns of pre-Depression America; Durkheim's observations, from the France of 1900.) In Waller's eyes, teachers' special training and cosmopolitan occupational outlook alienate them from the parochial towns where they teach and at times make them morally threatening to townspeople. But their mobility, ready replaceability, and child clientele render them peculiarly vulnerable to domination by local citizens and school officials. Teachers withdraw for mutual support and common defense into closed circles of fellow teachers.

The solidarity of these circles is strengthened as they confront a student society. Since school attendance is enforced on whole age cohorts, the school becomes a major center for the life of its students. They are involved in the school as total personalities, and within the formally undifferentiated school class emerge varieties of cliques, friendship pairs, and larger peer circles that partially reflect community social structure, but in part are unique to the school. These age-layered groupings become integrated across age and school grades in a school-wide hierarchy of prestige and leadership.

Moreover, every student society forms around its own subculture, transmitted from one student generation to the next. This subculture is rooted, says Waller, in the local child culture, and thus in the culture of the local community as well. From this base, it develops uniquely in every school as a collective solution to the distinctive problems of being a student. None of these problems is more significant than to scale down to manageable proportions teacher demands for good conduct and high performance. The student subculture, therefore, forms in opposition to teachers' achievement and adult-centered standards, and teachers and students are brought into inevitable conflict.

Teachers, in fact, form into a "fighting group" that relies upon domination, mixed with occasional efforts to penetrate the student society with personal warmth and responsiveness. But however a teacher blends official authority and warmth, he dominates the class. He decides when to be warm and when to be cold; he alone judges performance and distributes grades. If matters in class come to a crisis, students know who has the upper hand (and who will be supported by higher officials).

Thus the student society must also form a "fighting group," struggling to preserve its own way of life and to deflect or assimilate teacher demands. School discipline, therefore, is never more than an unstable equilibrium, despite the safety valves of athletics and the extracurriculum, with student unrest threatening learning, order, and the school's local reputation.

Current research on the school society. Since Waller, there have been few comprehensive studies of the small society of the school. Gordon (1957), in a detailed study of social relationships in one public high school, and Coleman (1961), in a comparative analysis of the student societies of ten high schools, essentially confirmed Waller's view of the social structure of student life and the tendency for the reward system of the extracurriculum to shape this structure. The nature of these rewards was differentiated by sex: athletics generated solidarity and cooperation among the boys, whereas the absence of a comparable integrating activity for girls made their social relations more fragmentary, even hostile. This finding reminds one that the solidarity of the student society must not be taken as given, but as a variable related to differing incentive systems of schools and to the interaction of student social types (of which sex typing is only one variety) with these incentives.

Gordon pressed farther than Coleman into the actual structure of student-teacher relations and found substantial evidence that these relations are antagonistic. In the high school that he studied, as in those investigated by Coleman, prestige among students rested in part upon good grades. Gordon found that teachers' expectations derived coercive power from the grading system, because of the instrumental, prestige-enhancing value that students placed upon grades. But the students successfully assimilated teachers' standards, and as the student role was learned, teachers were skillfully manipulated to raise grade averages.

High grades did not always correspond to subject-matter competence, but Gordon did not in fact present evidence that teachers uniformly linked grades to intellectual skill. Thus one might entertain the hypothesis that teacher-student antagonism arose not from a pervasive value cleavage but from emphasis by teachers on grades per se as the criterion of student excellence. If so, the teacher-manipulating behavior of students was more a rational adaptation to the student role than evidence of the subcultural alienation of students from the academic side of school life.

Indeed, in a theoretical essay Znaniecki (1936) argued that in contemporary schools, bound by the subordination of education to specialist ("vocational") training that results from societal bureaucratization, teachers must place the grade-point standard at the center of teaching, whereas students learn only to serve the grade. Moreover, Becker and his colleagues (1961), in a careful participant observation study of medical students (to whom the instrumental value of schooling was presumably clear) found that student norms centered on the sheer problem of surviving an avalanche of subject matter. Wallace (1964) noted a similar phenomenon among the students of a liberal arts college. In these studies, peer norms showed powerful effects in defining "proper" levels of student effort, but these norms may be integrated with teacher demands for good grades, while student-teacher antagonism centers on adjustment of grade standards.

This adjustment may be unstable, as teachers seek to raise and students to lower the level of teacher expectations. In Gordon's study, this continuing contest led teachers to deemphasize official authority and to turn to affect and the force of personality to motivate students. But this teacher adaptation was also the outcome of colleague norms stressing nurturant teaching, of the extracurriculum through which teacher-advisers and students developed particularistic relations, and of a principal loath to support teacher authority. Moreover, the tension between official authority and affective teaching may be less severe at other school levels. In Becker's medical school, where the teaching staff uniformly stressed the technical content of instruction and was relatively inaccessible to students, the student culture defined efficient means of studying rather than ways of influencing teachers' standards.

In the contrasting setting of elementary schools, teachers may define instruction primarily in nurturant, particularistic terms (Parsons, 1959). This need not lessen teachers' power, and Henry (1955, 1957) has described how elementary school teachers dominate their classes not by impersonal moral force but through a manipulative use of affect.

Both Gordon and Coleman have suggested that other aspects of the value systems of high school students, especially emphasis upon dating and its correlates, on "personality," and on extracurricular status, indicate further an encapsulated student subculture. But here, too, one may question the existence of cultural cleavages dividing adolescents from teachers or parents. The difficulty lies in assuming, as did Gordon and Coleman, that adults—whether teachers or parents—want young people to succeed academically to the exclusion of other forms of success in the round of adolescent life. That adults, even teachers, stress academic values so exclusively is a moot point. Neither Gordon nor Coleman presented data about teacher or parent values that would clarify this issue. Nor did they probe far enough into the values of their student subjects to indicate clearly the ordering of values held or the distribution of student agreement about the preeminence of adolescent "fun." Certainly students have a culture, and this culture apparently is shaped to a significant degree by the realities of school life; but that there is a profound cultural division between youth and adults remains unclear.

Again the level of education may be an important variable. In his study of Bennington College, Newcomb (1943) showed how convergent teacher and student norms of political liberalism, supported by social bonds forming students and teachers into a college community, had pervasive effects on student attitudes, even among the initially conservative. Thistlethwaite more recently (1960) has demonstrated the influence of attractive college teachers in recruiting students to their own fields of study. Unfortunately, current work on peer societies and subcultures of college students is more descriptive and taxonomic than analytic. [For reviews of this work, see Sanford (1962) and Newcomb & Wilson (1966).]

Historical circumstance undoubtedly colors the internal structure of schools; an interesting question is the bearing of types of society and of social change upon the social organization of instruction. Almost nothing is known about teacher-student relations in premodern societies. Dore (1965) described in some detail the social structure of Tokugawa fief schools. Elaborate ceremonials of deference bound teacher and student and seemed to liberate day-to-day instruction from reliance on coercion and to give wide latitude to nurturant, even indulgent, teaching. But in the absence of parallel data about "life conduct" education elsewhere, one may suspect that this quality of schooling was more a product of Tokugawa culture than an intrinsic attribute of education in patrimonial societies.

The effects of recent historical change in Western societies are problematic. To illustrate these difficulties, consider the present situation in American high schools and colleges. Since the work of Gordon and Coleman, pressure on high school students for academic success may well have increased in response to widening access to higher education and its linkage to numerous adult occupations. One might follow Znaniecki, arguing that under these conditions teachers and students alike will center on the instrumental question of maintaining good grades, with a decline in the relevance of "fun" and the extracurriculum. High schools then would seem more like medical schools, with teachers better able to enforce their standards and students more compliant to teacher demands. One might follow Znaniecki even farther (1936) and suggest, as a consequence of teacher preoccupation with grade and examination records, the decline of intellectual creativity as an outcome of schooling. (This thesis raises complex questions of the cognitive and motivational effects of national programs of testing for college entrance and scholarships (Goslin, 1963).

Even with more college places available, not every high school student will go to college, nor will college seem relevant to those students whose occupational aspirations are held down by family and peer environments or by realistic perceptions. High school student bodies may then become polarized, as students are differentiated according to their integration into the culture of school success. Students outside this culture may find it less necessary to go to purposive war with teachers, easier to withdraw from school or to engage in hedonistic forms of rebellion. In point of fact, Stinchcombe (1965) has described for one high school how working-class students of low aspiration expressed by diffuse rebellion the irrelevance of the school curriculum.

Unquestioning academic performance need not characterize all students who reasonably expect good jobs. Especially for students from professional and managerial families, the bureaucratization of careers may lead to a heightened assurance of adult success [contrary to Parsons' (1959) dictum about status anxiety] and to a relaxation of tension about academic requirements. Given the link between schooling and career, however, this relaxation may lead neither to "fun" nor to intellectual play, but to a critical examination of school life from the standpoint of personal values. In college and university this critical propensity may be strengthened by the interpenetration of higher education and economic and political institutions. Students' values undoubtedly remain rooted, at least in part, in the family, and it is interesting that current college student movements for academic reform draw their supporters principally from upper-middle-class students who follow their parents in espousing liberal or radical political views (Westby & Braungart, 1966).

As Durkheim and Waller made plain, the teacher colleague group is integral to the school society; yet it has been ignored in research. There is no evidence to bring to bear upon Durkheim's thesis of the strain between societal controls and separatist teacher organizations or upon Waller's description of teacher solidarity as defensive. Durkheim and Waller by no means exhausted the possible forms of teacher colleague relations. Indeed, Lortie (in press) suggests that in American public schools teachers are characterized less by solidarity and viable colleague controls than by isolation from colleagues and sentiments favoring personal autonomy in the classroom. These teachers seem to be caught up in a fragmenting work structure that minimizes formal and informal interaction with fellow teachers.

In more centralized systems (England, France, Germany), at least in the secondary schools, teachers apparently enjoy more viable occupational organization. Such differences, to the extent that they in fact occur, may have many determinants, among these national differences in the structure of educational systems, historical factors in the formation of the teaching occupation, or variation in the recruitment of teachers at different school levels.

As for the characteristics of school administrators and of school administration under varying social conditions, even informed speculation is lacking, despite an extensive literature on the administration of American school systems (Bidwell, 1965). Preoccupation with student life seems to have unduly narrowed the sociological study of schools and schoolteaching.

Charles Bidwell
The University of Chicago

References

American Sociological Review 31:698–712; 1966.

Anderson, C. Arnold. "A Skeptical Note on the Relation of Education and Mobility." *Am J Sociol* 66:560–70; 1961.

Anderson, C. Arnold. "State Education and Cultural Alienation." In *Yearbook of Education*. Evans Brothers, 1966. p. 238–51.

Bailyn, Bernard. *Education in the Forming of American Society*. U North Carolina Press, 1960. 147p.

Banfield, Edward, and Wilson, James Q. *City Politics*. Harvard U Press, 1965. 362p.

Banks, Olive. *Parity and Prestige in English Secondary Education*. Routledge, 1955. 262p.

Beck, Hubert P. *Men Who Control Our Universities*. King's Crown Press, 1947. 229p.

Becker, Howard S., and others. *Boys in White*. U Chicago Press, 1961. 456p.

Bidwell, Charles E. "The School as a Formal Organization." In March, James G. (Ed.) *Handbook of Organizations*. Rand McNally, 1965. p. 972–1022.

Bidwell, Charles E. "The Moral Significance of the Common School." *Hist Ed Q* 6:50–91; 1966.

Blaug, Mark. "Literacy and Economic Development." *Sch R* 74:393–418; 1966.

Campbell, Ernest Q., and Alexander, C. Norman. "Structural Effects and Interpersonal Relations." *Am J Sociol* 71:284–9; 1965.

Carter, Richard F. *Voters and Their Schools*. Stanford U Institute for Communications Research, 1960. 311p.

Charters, W. W., Jr. "Social Class Analysis and Control of Public Education." *Harvard Ed R* 23:268–83; 1953.

Clark, Burton. "Sociology of Education." In Faris, R. E. L. (Ed.) *Handbook of Modern Sociology*. Rand McNally, 1964. p. 734–69.

Coleman, James S. *The Adolescent Society*. Free, 1961. 368p.

Coleman, James S., and others. *Equality of Educational Opportunity*. GPO, 1966. 737p.

Davis, James A. "Higher Education: Selection and Opportunity." *Sch R* 71:249–65; 1963.

Dore, Ronald P. *Education in Tokugawa Japan*. U California Press, 1965. 346p.

Dreeben, Robert. *On What Children Learn in School*. Addison, 1967.

Duncan, Otis D., and Hodge, R. W. "Education and Occupational Mobility: A Regression Analysis." *Am J Sociol* 68:629–44; 1963.

Durkheim, Emile. *Education and Sociology*. Free, 1956. 163p.

Durkheim, Emile. *Moral Education.* Free, 1961. 288p.

Floud, Jean, and Halsey, A. H. "The Sociology of Education." *Current Sociol* 7:165–233; 1958.

Floud, Jean, and others. *Social Class and Educational Opportunity.* Heinemann, 1956. 152p.

Foster, Philip. "Status, Power and Education in a Traditional Community." *Sch R* 72:158–82; 1964.

Foster, Philip. *Education and Social Change in Ghana.* U Chicago Press, 1965. 322p.

Geertz, Clifford. *Peddlers and Princes.* U Chicago Press, 1963. 162p.

Gerth, Hans H., and Mills, C. Wright. *From Max Weber: Essays in Sociology.* Oxford, 1946. 490p.

Gordon, C. Wayne. *The Social System of the High School.* Free, 1957. 184p.

Goslin, David A. *The Search for Ability.* Russell Sage, 1963. 204p.

Greenstein, F. I. *Children and Politics.* Yale U Press, 1965. 199p.

Harbison, Frederick H., and Meyers, Charles A. *Education, Manpower, and Economic Growth.* McGraw-Hill, 1964. 229p.

Havighurst, Robert, and others. *Growing Up in River City.* Wiley, 1962. 189p.

Henry, Jules. "Docility, On Giving The Teacher What She Wants." *J Social Issues* 11:33–41; 1955.

Henry, Jules. "Attitude Organization in Elementary School Classrooms." *Am J Ortho-Psychiatry* 27:117–33; 1957.

Herriott, Robert E., and St. John, Nancy H. *Social Class and the Urban School.* Wiley, 1966. 289p.

Hess, Robert D., and Torney, Judith V. "The Development of Basic Attitudes and Values Toward Government and Citizenship During the Elementary School Years, Part I." USOE Cooperative Research Report No. 1078, 1965.

Hollingshead, August B. *Elmtown's Youth.* Wiley, 1949. 480p.

Jackson, Brian, and Marsden, Dennis. *Education and The Working Class.* Routledge, 1962. 268p.

Kahl, Joseph. "Educational and Occupational Aspirations of 'Common Man' Boys." *Harvard Ed R* 23:186–203; 1953.

Katz, Michael. *The Irony of Urban School Reform.* Harvard U Press, in press.

Kazamias, Andreas. *Social Functions of the Turkish Lise.* U Chicago Press, 1965.

Kazamias, Andreas. *Politics, Society and Secondary Education in England.* U Pennsylvania Press, 1966. 381p.

Lane, Robert E. "The Knowledgeable Society." *Am Sociol R* 31:649–62; 1966.

Lazarsfeld, Paul, and Thielens, Wagner. *The Academic Mind.* Free, 1958. 460p.

Lipset, Seymour M. *Political Man.* Doubleday, 1959. 432p.

Lipset, Seymour M. *The First New Nation.* Basic Books, 1963. 366p.

Lipset, Seymour, and Bendix, Reinhard. *Social Mobility in Industrial Society.* U California Press, 1959. 309p.

Lortie, Dan. "The Balance of Control and Autonomy in Elementary School Teaching." In Etzioni, Amitai. (Ed.) *The Heteronomous Professions.* Free, in press.

Machlup, Fritz. *The Production and Distribution of Knowledge in the United States.* Princeton U Press, 1962. 416p.

Mannheim, Karl. *Freedom, Power, and Democratic Planning.* Routledge, 1951. 384p.

McDill, Edward, and others. "Institutional Effects on the Academic Behavior of High School Students." Paper presented at Annual Meeting, American Sociological Association, 1966.

Minar, David. "The Community Basis of Conflict in School System Politics." *Am Sociol R* 31:822–34; 1966.

Moore, Barrington, Jr. *Social Origins of Dictatorship and Democracy.* Beacon, 1966. 599p.

Morgan, James N., and others. *Income and Welfare in the United States.* McGraw Hill, 1962. 531p.

Nam, Charles B. "Family Patterns of Educational Attainment." *Sociol Ed* 38:393–403; 1965.

Newcomb, Theodore. *Personality and Social Change.* Dryden, 1943. 225p.

Newcomb, Theodore, and Wilson, E. K. *College Peer Groups.* Aldine Publishing Co., 1966. 317p.

Parsons, Talcott. "The School Class as a Social System." *Harvard Ed R* 29:297–318; 1959.

Price, Don K. *The Scientific Estate.* Belknap Press, 1965. 323p.

Riesman, David. *Constraint and Variety in American Education.* U Nebraska Press, 1956. 160p.

Robbins, Lionel Lord. *Higher Education, Report of the Committee Appointed by the Prime Minister Under the Chairmanship of Lord Robbins,* H. M. Stationery Office, 1963. 335p.

Rogoff, Natalie. "Local Social Structure and Educational Selection." In Halsey, A. H., and others. (Ed.) *Education, Economy and Society.* Free, 1961. p. 414–20.

Rosen, Bernard C. "The Achievement Syndrome." *Am Sociol R* 21:203–11; 1956.

Sanford, R. Nevitt. (Ed.) *The American College.* Wiley, 1962. 1084p.

Schultz, Theodore W. *The Economic Value of Education.* Columbia U Press, 1963. 92p.

Schuman, Howard, and Inkeles, Alex. "Some Social Psychological Effects and Non-effects of Literacy in a New Nation." *Econ Develop Social Change.* in press.

Scott, John F. "The American College Sorority: Its Role in Class and Ethnic Endogamy." *Am Sociol R* 30:514–26; 1965.

Sewell, William H., and Armer, J. Michael. "Neighborhood Context and College Plans." *Am Sociol R* 31:159–68; 1966.

Sewell, William H., and others. "Social Status and Educational and Occupational Aspiration." *Am Sociol R* 22:62–73; 1957.

Stinchcombe, Arthur. *Rebellion In a High School.* Quadrangle Books, 1965. 240p.

Thistlethwaite, Donald. "College Press and Changes in Study Plans of Talented Students." *J Ed Psych* 51:222–34; 1960.

Trow, Martin. "The Democratization of Education

in the United States." *Archives European Sociol* 3: 231–62; 1962.
Turner, Ralph. "Sponsored and Contest Mobility and The School System." *Am Sociol R* 25:855–67; 1960.
Vaizey, J. *The Costs of Education.* Allen, 1958. 256p.
Wallace, Walter. "Institutional and Life-cycle Socialization of College Freshmen." *Am J Sociol* 70:303–18; 1964.
Waller, Willard. *The Sociology of Teaching.* Wiley, 1932. 467p.
Ward, Lester F. *Dynamic Sociology.* 2 Vols. Appleton, 1883. 1396p.
Warner, W. Lloyd, and others. *Who Shall Be Educated?* Harper, 1944. 190p.
Warner, W. Lloyd, and others. *Democracy in Jonesville.* Harper, 1949. 313p.
Weinberg, Ian. *English Public Schools.* Atherton Press, 1967. 217p.
Westby, D. L., and Braungart, R. G. "Class and Politics in the Family Backgrounds of Student Political Activists." *Am Sociol R* 31:690–2; 1966.
Wilkinson, Rupert. *Gentlemanly Power.* Oxford, 1964. 243p.
Wilson, Alan B. "Residential Segregation of Social Classes and Aspirations of High School Boys." *Am Sociol R* 24:836–45; 1959.
Znaniecki, Florian. *Social Actions.* Wiley, 1936. 746p.

SPECIAL EDUCATION

HISTORICAL TRENDS. The field of special education for handicapped children had important beginnings in the nineteenth century, as represented in the pioneering work of such persons as Itard, Seguin, Gallaudet, Howe, Montessori, Braille, and many others. Schools which provided full-time care as well as education for handicapped children tended to be the preferred arrangement; thus the many residential schools for deaf, blind, and retarded children which were established during the late nineteenth century set the early pattern for special education in the United States. Early in the twentieth century, local day-school programs for handicapped children began to appear in significant numbers in the form of special classes and special schools. Prototypical special class programs for gifted children began to appear in the 1920's (Hollingworth, 1926). During the first half of the century developments regarding both the handicapped and the gifted were modest at best.

In recent years, a remarkable upturn in the pace of development has been observed. Special-education programs in many states have doubled and redoubled in size in the last two decades, as if an outpouring of energies saved through a long period of neglect were channeled into one large effort. With the perspective provided by these rapid advances and the growing awareness of great, continuing unmet needs, it becomes clear that the history of education for exceptional children has been mainly a story of rejection and denial. Most handicapped children in the United States, even in quite recent years, have suffered a profound educational neglect (Prouty, 1966). The gifted have fared little better and, perhaps, have had less special attention than any other group.

The special needs of atypical children and the large numbers of such children (currently estimated at about one child in ten) were sometimes noted—as in the remarkable 30-volume "Children's Charter" produced by the 1930 White House Conference on Children and Growth (Wilbur, 1931)—but only comparatively few exceptional children received needed special services until quite recently. The colleges and universities, with but few exceptions, had scarcely made a start in preparing teachers for the exceptional child before the 1950's.

In a summary of a series of nationwide surveys conducted by the U.S. Office of Education, Mackie (1965b) reported that 442,000 children were enrolled in special-education programs in 1948. The comparable figure for 1963 was 1,666,000 children, which indicates that special-education enrollments had more than tripled in 15 years. Mackie computed that 27 percent of the estimated 6.1 million school-age exceptional children were receiving special education in 1963, whereas 15 years earlier only about 12 percent of an estimated 3.8 million exceptional children were in special programs. In a recent projection, Mackie (1965a) estimated that, by 1968, 35 percent of the exceptional children would be enrolled in special programs.

In the 1963 survey 5,600 local school districts reported having special-education programs, and 4,000 of these had been organized since 1948. By 1963, about one-half the school systems in the United States were thought to be providing some type of special-education service, either on their own or in cooperation with other districts.

Survey data on special-education programs such as those cited in the above paragraphs, though scarce and somewhat unreliable, are sufficient to document a burst of development in the field over the past two decades—as well as the fact that, despite the recent gains, substantially less than half the exceptional children are yet receiving needed special services.

LEGISLATIVE PROVISIONS. Each of the 50 states now has some form of special legislative provision for special-education programs. In nearly all states, modifications have been made recently in statutes pertaining to special education, and these changes show several clear trends. One of these is to make special-education programs mandatory, rather than permissive, in local school districts for "educable" handicapped children. The term *educable* refers to handicapped children who are able to profit from an academic curriculum and who are expected to be able to function independently in open community life upon completion of schooling. The mandatory feature of these statutes requires school attendance by all the educables and forces school districts to provide suitable education for them. A currently developing trend is to extend the mandatory feature of state legislation to children judged to be below the educable level, such as the "trainable" retarded. These are severely handicapped children with IQ's between about 25 and 35 who are not expected to profit from extensive academic training and who tend to show lifelong dependency patterns. Usually they are employable only in sheltered environments. About 2 to 4 children per 1,000 children of school age are considered to be in this "trainable" category. Special programs for them require extraordinary coordination among the educational and health and welfare agencies of the community.

Another clear trend at the state level is to provide more generous special financial aid to local school districts, either as "incentive" or "excess cost" aids, to help defray the high costs of such specialized programs (Fogarty, 1964).

Since 1956, the U.S. Office of Education has become a strong influence in special education. Indeed, the field of special education has served as a kind of pilot area for the rest of education in showing how Federal, state, and local agencies can combine their efforts and resources to good purpose. For example, the U.S. Office of Education was enabled to start its Cooperative Research Program in 1957 with an appropriation of $1 million—of which $675,000 was earmarked for research relating to education of the retarded. The National Association for Retarded Children (a volunteer organization of parents and friends of the mentally retarded) deserves much credit for urging this beginning research effort. The Cooperative Research Program has since been greatly enlarged through further legislative action (most notably through Title IV of Public Law 89–10) and has come to play a very significant role in the educational research efforts of the Federal government, colleges, universities, and school systems at all levels.

Following Congressional mandate (see Title VI, Public Law 89-10 as amended), the U.S. Office of Education created a new Bureau of Education for the Handicapped in 1967. Within this bureau are three major divisions, one of which is concerned with research and development activities. In 1967 this research division was funded at a level of somewhat over $8 million, and steep increases for future years appear in projections made by various study groups. Virtually all these funds are used to support extramural research and development projects. Thus far, most funds have been used to support individual projects and a network of regional Instructional Materials Centers. Plans call for more emphasis on the creation of major research centers and programmatic research support.

A very significant Federal role has also evolved within the past decade in support of training programs for teachers and other personnel needed to conduct special-education programs. The Eighty-fifth Congress authorized a small support program, beginning in 1957, for training college instructors and educational administrators in the field of mental retardation. In the Eighty-seventh Congress a somewhat broader program in the area of education for the deaf was passed. In the Eighty-eighth Congress a much broader Federal program was developed and was formally established on October 31, 1963, with the signautre of the late President Kennedy on Public Law 88-164. This statute included provisions dealing with many facets of mental health and mental retardation. With later amendments it extended training grants for teachers and other educational pernel to all areas of the handicapped. In 1967 more than $24 million was allocated to various colleges, universities, and state departments of education to support preservice and in-service training of teachers, researchers, and administrators in the field of special education. Even further Federal participation may be expected in future years under the provisions of Title VI of Public Law 89-10, known as the Elementary and Secondary Education Act. All 50 states are currently engaged in planning activities stimulated and supported by Title VI of this important law, and it is anticipated that broad support down to the level of local educational programs will follow the planning period.

In almost none of the above Federal legislation have programs for gifted children been included. Most states have shown a similar tendency to make provisions for special education of handicapped children through so-called categorical legislation, but to withhold similar action relating to gifted children. At least 15 states have taken recent categorical action relating to the gifted, however, and this may foretell similar moves in the remaining states (Bryan, 1963).

CURRENT PROGRAMMATIC TRENDS. In recent developments a number of trends may be noted, among them a movement toward greater use of local day-school programs rather than to enlarge residential (that is, boarding) schools for handicapped children. This is part of a general trend to make as little separation of the handicapped from normal school, home, and community life as possible. Increasingly, for example, blind children are enrolled in regular classrooms for most of the school day, with supplementary education provided in part-time "resource rooms" dealing with such skills as braille, typing, mobility, and orientation. Similarly, many different types of day programs for emotionally disturbed children are being organized, including simple consultation with regular teachers, "crisis teacher" programs, full- and part-time day classes, and special schools. Taken together, these many levels or types of programs make up what are sometimes called "broad cascades" or "hierarchies of services." Exceptional children are accommodated at as nonspecialized a level as possible and are returned to regular programs as soon as feasible.

Another trend is to provide services at earlier age levels for handicapped children and "high risk" children from deprived homes. In many special programs deaf children are enrolled as early as age three or four; in some districts, schools are taking on responsibility for even younger children by working with parents to encourage and improve special home care and education of handicapped toddlers.

Preschool programs designed to compensate disadvantaged children for deprivations in home and community experience are also receiving much attention. It is observed that culturally deprived children, identified according to housing, educational, occupational, and income levels of the family, tend not only to enter school with handicaps but also to show a progressive retardation throughout their school years (Krugman, 1961). Experiments conducted by Gray and others (1966), using intensive summer teaching plus "home visitor" services during the school year as a form of compensatory preschool education for severely disadvantaged children, have shown some positive results in the form of IQ and language-development gains. Similarly, Kirk's (1958) intensive teaching efforts with preschool educable retardates produced encouraging results, particularly for children from psychosocially deprived home situations.

The emphasis on preschool programs has grown, in part, from the new and more "open" interpretations of the nature-nurture problem (Hunt, 1964) and specific work relating to early language development (Hess & Shipman, 1965) as a factor in cognitive development and style. Federal financial support through the Office of Economic Opportunity, which is popularly known as the Antipoverty Program, has strongly influenced development of preschool programs on a nationwide basis.

A third major trend is toward more-specialized school provisions for multiple--handicapped children. It appears that there are relatively more children with multiple handicaps today than in the past—perhaps because of the increasing number of premature babies who are kept alive and diseases such as rubella (Harper & Wiener, 1965). But, in addition, it appears that special educators have become more cognizant of the fact that many handicapped children do indeed have more than one special need. A general tendency to program more flexibly and with less rigorous adherence to traditional "categories" of handicaps is clearly evident.

BRIEF OVERVIEWS IN SPECIAL FIELDS.
Given below are brief statements summarizing program and research developments in several of the special-education areas.

Mental Retardation. After a brief surge of interest in the late nineteenth century, the field of mental retardation was virtually abandoned by the helping professions until about 1950. Sloan (1963) attributes this specific neglect of the retarded in a period of generally enlightened and progressive social action to a pervasive public misinformation concerning genetics and criminal tendencies and a general attitude of hopelessness toward mental retardation. The reversal since 1950, from lethargy to active interest, is very distinct in this field.

A major facet of the changing scene has been a shift to a more open or optimistic view concerning the potentialities of the retarded. The clearest mark of this shift is the official change made by the American Association of Mental Deficiency in 1959 to eliminate the notion of "incurability" as an essential component in the definition of mental retardation (Heber, 1959). The important reviews of psychological, anthropological, and medical studies by Masland and others (1958) and Hunt's (1961) review of studies relating to the genesis of intellect have also stimulated this more optimistic view. Heber's review (1963) of research relating to education of the educable retarded illustrates the way in which nature-nurture studies of the 1920's and 1930's have been revived by education for reinterpretations emphasizing environmental determinants of intelligence.

Several major followers of B. F. Skinner's views on learning have turned their attention to the field of mental retardation and have added to the environmental interpretation. Among them, Ogden Lindsley (1964) would appear to have taken a position near the extreme in saying that it is modern science, rather than the children, which shows retardation by its inability to design appropriate environments for some special children. Impressive practical application of operant principles to the teaching of school subjects to retarded children has been provided by Bijou (1965) and others. These workers tend to define retardation simply in terms of limited behavior repertoire and assume that such limits are a function of unfortunate environmental history or of unusual reinforcement functions. The appropriate social action indicated by the more optimistic view, of course, is to make fuller provision for learning by the retarded.

Several lines of psychological research of great interest and importance to educators suggest that the mentally retarded may suffer specific deficits which impair learning ability. The Ellis volume (1963) provides chapter-length reviews and bibliographies on the several theories proposed in this regard. Included in this work are Ellis's own stimulus-trace theory, Luria's dissociation hypothesis, Zeaman's notions on attentional deficit, and Spitz's theory of cortical satiation. Zigler (1967) neatly contrasts these "defect" theories with a more conservative "general development" theory, which he prefers in accounting for the behavior of garden-variety or familial-cultural types of mental retardation. It is assumed that about three-fourths of the retarded are of familial type, with the remainder admittedly showing definite pathology and varying forms of deficit. Zigler views most mental retardation simply as a condition of attenuated cognitive development, accountable on a normal genetic basis in the same way as for other "normals." This is the more traditional view, except that Zigler urges an educational attack on emotional, social, and motivational aspects of the problems which he believes have been underestimated as components of intelligent behavior.

By far the most frequent administrative arrangement for education of educable mentally retarded pupils has been the "special class," organized in neighborhood schools for groups of about 15 children. Typically, such a class consists of children ranging over not more than about four years in chronological age and ranging in IQ from about 50 to 80. A rash of studies designed to evaluate this special-class format has been observed over the past decade, most involving comparisons of special-class children with retarded children in regular classes. Unfortunately, in most instances comparisons were made for children after they had been assigned to programs and without attention to differences which might have existed prior to their assignment. Thus it has been impossible to separate effects which might have precipitated special-class placement from effects resulting from special placement. Most of these studies, for what it may be worth, reported superior academic achievement by retardates in regular classes and superior personality adjustment by special-class members.

The most definitive of these so-called efficacy studies was a four-year experiment conducted at the University of Illinois by Goldstein and others (1965). The report of this research also includes a review of earlier studies in this field. The Goldstein study involved 126 children with IQs below 85; half were randomly assigned to newly organized, carefully defined special classes and the other half to regular classes. The data on academic achievement at the end of the four-year experiment suggested that a kind of intersection occurred at an IQ of about 80. Below this IQ level, the special class tended to be "superior" for academic learning; for those above 80 in IQ, the regular class tended to be superior. Social and personal adjustment measures tended generally to favor the special-class pupils. The study as a whole requires careful interpretation because, on the basis of repeated measure, a large proportion of the subjects in the study proved not to be retarded. Also, the conditions of placement and of instruction were quite atypical. Perhaps the clearest conclusion is that educational researchers still lack the tools and skills necessary to achieve global evaluations of complex programs.

Along with rapid development of classes for the trainable retarded, there have appeared a variety of studies showing incidence rates, characteristics of such children, and similar matters. The clearest attempt at general evaluation of trainable classes (Cain & Levine, 1961) failed to show differences between trainable children attending community schools and those children living in the community but not attending school. Trainable children remaining in the community did tend to show growth advantages over institutionalized children. Again, it was clear that improved instrumentation is required before this kind of study will yield dependable results.

Education of the Gifted. The portrait of the gifted child drawn from Terman's classic study of high-IQ children has had much influence in American education (Terman & Oden, 1947). The findings of his study suggest that children who possess a lot of "g," or general intelligence, tend also to rank high in virtually all desirable human traits. Recent studies (Smith, 1964) show that in Terman's group of gifted children, identified in 1921–1922, intellectual giftedness was confounded with selective factors regarding social class, nationality, and religion and that when these factors are controlled, the association between desirable traits and giftedness is not nearly so clear.

In the latest follow-up study, conducted in the mid-1950's, on the Terman gifted population, it was shown that, in general, high-IQ children become noteworthy adults. But from the 1,528 gifted children considered, all of whom were identified by using traditional IQ tests, there developed few, if any, preeminently creative adults (Terman & Oden, 1959). It is on this facet of giftedness that many events have turned in the space age—that is, since 1957. Guilford conducted a long series of studies of human intellect using factor-analysis techniques and concluded that the human intellect is far too complex to be represented by a single score. In contrast to Terman and other "g" theorists, he has presented a complex 120-factor model of intellect. The model has three dimensions—operations, products, and content —each of which has several subcategories. Most attention has centered on the five types of intellectual operations, as follows: cognition, memory, convergent production, divergent production, and evaluative thinking. Guilford argues that existing tests and school curricula tend to emphasize only the first three types of intellectual operations and to neglect the latter two, divergent production and evaluative thinking.

Much of the modern work on creativity has its base in Guilford's work, particularly in his emphasis upon divergent thinking and his view of the child as "producer" as well as "learner." Getzels and Jackson (1962), using some of Guilford's tests of creativity, identified highly creative adolescents and compared them with the so-called high-IQ students. Although replete with technical shortcomings, the Getzels-Jackson study has had much influence. It showed that highly creative children achieved as well as high-IQ children, even in traditional subject matter, despite their lower IQs. Getzels and Jackson felt that the cognitive style and related personality characteristics of creative children tended to estrange them from teachers. Torrance's more extensive work on some of the same topics, which was centered mainly at the elementary school level, has tended to confirm the Getzels-Jackson findings. Torrance (1965) has also done much work on measurement of creativity and on curriculum modifications.

Use of ability grouping has tended to come back into favor since the mid-1950's as one method of educational adjustment for the gifted; however, recent research suggests it may be more important to give teachers an arrangement whereby they specialize by subject, even in the elementary school, rather than by ability level (Goldberg & Passow, 1962). Acceleration of programs for gifted students has continued to be viewed favorably if practiced in moderate degree (Reynolds, 1960). Acceleration processes at the point of transition from high school to college, both by early admission to college and by advanced-standing placements in college, have been carefully studied and their results found favorable to both procedures (Fund for the Advancement of Education, 1957).

The expanded concept of intellect proposed by Guilford and the related work it has stimulated stands as perhaps the major contribution of recent years in the field of education for the gifted. In general, however, progress in education of the gifted has not been impressive. Immediately after the launching of Sputnik, a wave of interest in the gifted was evident. More than the usual number of textbooks on the gifted were published, but relatively little substantive development ensued. As compared with interest in handicapped pupils, interest in the gifted continues to be weak and spasmodic.

Visual Impairment. Jones (1963) estimated that in 1963 about 1 child of school age in every 3,000 to 4,000 was blind; this represented a decline in rate from only a few years earlier. Projecting to 1970, he estimated that the rate of blindness among children would be further reduced to about 1 for every 7,000 to 8,000. This sharp reduction in incidence of blindness is attributable mainly to virtual elimination of new instances in the form of blindness called "retrolental fibroplasia." It occurred with high frequency in the 1940's and until about 1954, when the cause—excessive use of oxygen in hospital incubator care of infants—was discovered and corrective action was taken. Many schools currently have relatively large enrollments of so-called RLF children in junior and senior high schools, but none in elementary schools. There is an apparent increase in the number of children with problems of partial vision, often in combination with other handicapping conditions, and a possible "wave" of problems due to rubella is anticipated. Jones's estimate of partial-vision incidence among school-age children in 1963 was 1 in 1,000 to 1,500.

The educational placement of visually impaired children has tended toward integrating them with normal children in regular schools and classes whenever feasible. Even children formally enrolled in residential schools (Jones & Collins, 1965) tend to be placed for part of the day in day schools. Bateman (1963) has shown that some children with visual problems also have definite learning problems and that it is the combination of problems which often precipitates special placements.

Several studies (Nolan, 1964a) have noted that an increasing proportion of legally blind children actually read "clear" print acceptably and thus may not need instruction in braille. Mainly in day schools, but lately also in residential schools, the proportion of print readers is up and that of braille readers is down.

Research relating to education of the blind has progressed quite disappointingly on the whole, but some promising lines of research concerning braille reading (Pick & others, 1966), mobility (Lord & others, 1966), listening techniques (Nolan, 1964b), and use of technological services (American Foundation for the Blind, 1963) are developing. For example, Pick observed that blind braille readers follow the same grapheme-phoneme grouping principles as do sighted print readers. Several workers (Nolan & others, 1966) have reported promising findings concerning the use of listening techniques, having observed that learning efficiency of the blind by listening or "compressed speech listening" techniques far surpasses that in ordinary braille reading. Since World War II strong programs have developed in veterans hospitals for instruction of blind veterans in mobility and orientation techniques. Research in this aspect of education for the visually impaired is at the beginning stages, but practical techniques are being disseminated through several teacher-preparation centers.

Hearing Impairment. The incidence of hearing impairments among children has not shown dramatic change, but steady increase in enrollments in special school programs for such children has been observed. Great concern is developing currently because of an apparent upsurge in incidence of hearing problems at the preschool level, as a consequence of a rubella epidemic in parts of the United States three years ago. Robinson (1964) has cited reasons for expecting increases in genetically determined deafness in future years.

The specialized residential school for the deaf and day classes for the deaf have tended to rise side by side in the United States. Comparing the two administrative arrangements, Quigley and Frisina (1961) concluded that day schooling for the deaf tended to facilitate their use of oral communication—a not unexpected finding in view of the more frequent emphasis on that communication mode in day schools. On the other hand, they found that "adjustment" measures favored resident pupils.

Research in education for hearing-impaired children, which had languished for decades, is beginning to show some signs of development. The major emphasis of such research is on language development. Modeling their research on Piaget's concepts, Oléron and Le Herren (1961), for example, have shown deaf children to be markedly retarded in tasks concerning conservation of weight and volume. Furth's research (1966), which he believes demonstrates that intelligent thinking does not need the support of a conventional symbol system, is a source of much interest. He believes that deaf persons are not inferior to those with normal hearing in their cognitive functioning when the criterion of language is removed. As part of her extensive investigation of vocabulary problems of deaf children, Templin (1966) also concluded that deaf and hearing children were alike in general intellectual ability, but that the deaf were immature in language development.

Watson (1963) reports that preschool training and parent education programs relating to the education of deaf children are developing in wide areas of the world. Methods used in Russia (Morkovin, 1960) which combine finger spelling, natural signs, and speech reading in early education of the deaf are receiving considerable attention.

With increasing availability of individual electronic hearing aids, there has been a wave of optimism concerning regular school placement of children with minor and moderate hearing losses. On the basis of analyses showing marked distortions of some speech signals in the ordinary classroom environment, Watson (1964) has issued a caution against excessive optimism concerning regular class placements.

Emotionally Disturbed and Socially Maladjusted Children. A recent innovation in many states has been to include services for emotionally disturbed and socially maladjusted children as part of the special-education program. The surge of interest and program development in this field is perhaps due to the increasing awareness of the tremendous social cost of neglect plus clear signs that traditional forms of prevention and treatment of emotional disturbance have fallen pitifully short of needs (Joint Commission on Mental Illness & Health, 1961). Attention has tended to shift from a medical orientation, centered on clinics, hospitals, and individual therapy, to schools and the "educational model" and to total community mobilization for dealing with health problems.

The way in which schools have organized to meet problems in this sphere was summarized in a broad study by Morse and others (1964). Their survey covered approximately 160 separate special programs throughout the United States. Site visits and mail questionnaires were used to gather information. Some of their results were as follows:

1. Pupils enrolled in special programs were primarily boys from the upper elementary grades.
2. Pupil reception and discharge tended to be handled somewhat unsystematically.
3. The most frequent classification of pupils was "neurotic," but the basis for this diagnostic judgment was frequently inadequate.
4. Very few "withdrawn" children were involved.
5. About a fourth of the children and their mothers were receiving therapy in addition to the special school program.

The special classes for these children which were studied appeared to differ from regular classes mainly in class size (fewer children per class), which also meant that instruction could be more individualized. Instruction seemed oriented mainly to normal educational development and toward a return to regular classes. Behavior control and motivation were the most frequent problems reported by teachers.

A distinctly innovative project, called "Project Re-Ed," launched by Hobbs (1966) and his associates at Peabody College, was modeled somewhat after the French program of small centers for disturbed children that are staffed mainly by educators. Two five-day-a-week residential schools (one in Tennessee and the other in North Carolina) and a related teacher-counselor Master of Arts level training program have been developed since 1961 as part of the Re-Ed project. The teacher-counselors serve round-the-clock in the schools and related camping facilities. Beginning efforts at evaluation of the project (Weinstein, 1965) have been quite encouraging. A major question concerns the logistics of recruiting, training, placing, and retaining competent teacher-counselors.

Relatively little careful evaluation of teaching strategies has been attempted in this burgeoning new field of education for the disturbed. Haring and Phillips (1962) provided one example of an effort to evaluate and compare three methods of working with emotionally disturbed children. Fifteen emotionally disturbed elementary-age children were randomly distributed to each of three treatment situations:

1. Special class emphasizing structured curriculum methods and ability grouping.
2. Regular classroom plus psychological consultation and other traditional "help."
3. Special class based on interest with less structure.

The experimenters felt that results, on the basis of both achievement and social-adjustment criteria, favored the structured special class. Reviewers have been less convinced that the evidence was conclusive.

Cruickshank and several collaborators reported on a pilot study (1961) of somewhat similar design which involved 20 disturbed children diagnosed as brain-injured and 20 others who showed similar behavior but had no definite neurological evidence of brain injury. Children in these two categories were balanced among four classes of 10 children each. Two experimental classes were conducted, with removal of extraneous stimuli and other adaptive features geared to the so-called Strauss syndrome (Strauss & Lehtinen, 1947). Control teachers used methods of their choice. There was no difference in achievement or social behavior between the experimental and control groups. Similarly, there was no apparent difference between hyperactive disturbed children who *were* and those who *were not* brain-injured.

When one turns to delinquent children, the picture is no more sanguine. For example, Craft and others (1964) were unable to specify any advantage to adolescent psychopaths as a result of having received intensive group therapy as compared with "benevolent authoritarian" treatment. In fact, the group-therapy subjects were slightly worse than the authoritarian-treatment group, as shown in follow-up studies based on criteria of reconviction, readmission, and clinical well-being. Similarly, a long-term experimental study involving individual and group counseling for "potentially delinquent" girls in a New York vocational high school failed to produce noticeable effect, as measured by school dropout rate, truancy, conduct, illegitimate pregnancies, and attitudes toward school (Meyer & others, 1965).

These rather consistently discouraging results, from the viewpoint of support offered for highly specialized interventions, may easily be attributable to major technical problems inherent in evaluative research of global designs. Indeed, the technical problems are so great as to make it doubtful that major innovations in education should be risked in early stages by present evaluative procedures (Reynolds, 1966).

As in other areas of special education, one of the techniques increasingly applied in work with the emotionally disturbed is operant conditioning. The volume by Krasner and Ullman (1965), which presents a variety of individual case studies of deviant children treated by conditioning therapies, has become a basic source book in the education of disturbed children.

An encouraging note is provided in studies by Jones and Gottfried (1962), which suggest that teachers of exceptional children are judged as possessing greater prestige than are regular teachers and that teachers of disturbed children in particular are among those having highest prestige. A rapidly increasing number of colleges and universities have launched training programs for teachers of the emotionally disturbed and socially maladjusted in the past half-dozen years, often with financial support from the National Institute of Mental Health and, since 1964, from the U.S. Office of Education. The teacher-preparation programs are themselves becoming the object of evaluation (Balow, 1966).

Speech Handicapped. In the 15-year interval from 1948 to 1963, the rate of increase in employment of speech correctionists in local public schools was greater than for any other type of specialist serving the handicapped (Mackie, 1965*b*). Since the typical speech correctionist serves approximately 100 children, the increase in numbers of children receiving speech correction services has been very great. Mackie estimates that about half the children needing speech services have programs accessible to them.

The most frequent type of speech problem dealt with is that of articulation disorders. As part of an effort to devise a predictive screening test for children with articulatory defects, Van Riper (1966) found that the demarcation line between normal and defective speech tended to shift during the primary grades. The findings suggest that some children now receiving therapy would probably display normal articulation in a short time *without* therapy. The findings of this study, if replicated and confirmed, will have major implications, mainly in freeing more professional time for the more severe cases.

Stuttering problems also occupy much of the time of correctionists and researchers. A series of summary articles on stuttering by Bloodstein (1961) suggests an interpretation of stuttering as an "anticipatory struggle behavior" consisting of tension and fragmentation in speech.

Speech problems which have obvious origins in anatomical defects rather regularly have less obvious implications as well. For example, Morris (1962) has demonstrated the broad implications for development of communication skills of cleft lips and palates and has made a plea for diagnostic and habilitation efforts which go beyond physical restoration.

Growing interest in language development is evident among speech correctionists as well as among other special educators. Winitz (1966) has cited reasons for this trend, in particular the interest in psycholinguistics. Winitz suggests that language be thought of as a system or a set of subsystems (phonological, morphological, syntactical, and semantic) for which there are rules. These are acquired only gradually. The child's "system" at any point correlates imperfectly with adult systems. Within such a framework, articulation problems may not be strictly an inability to make certain sounds but may involve a more basic language difference having quite different implications for teachers and therapists.

Learning Disabilities. When all the obvious categories of exceptional children have been identified, there remain a significant number of children—more of them boys than girls—who show serious learning problems. Particular concern centers on children who show problems in language skills, such as reading. For decades, teachers, pediatricians, neurologists, and psychologists have struggled in isolated fashion to deal with learning-disabled children. There was little shared practice, research, or literature among the several professions.

Within recent years there has occurred a remarkable confluence which is now bringing a broad range of professions into a collaborative attack on learning disability problems. One of the key events in the history of this trend was the publication of a study entitled *Psychopathology and Education of the Brain Injured Child* by Strauss and Lehtinen (1947). That volume, which owed much to the basic work of Professor Heinz Werner at Clark University, was the joint product of a physician and a teacher. It proposed general classroom procedures and specific techniques for teaching basic school subjects to children who showed hyperactivity, perceptual disorders, motor awkwardness, or easy distractibility—in short, children thought to be brain-injured but whose general intelligence level was average or above. Significant related contributions have been made by Cruickshank and others (1957), Kephart (1960), and Myklebust (1964). Implications for teacher preparation have been summarized in a volume edited by Cruickshank (1966).

Definition problems have plagued the field. Terms such as *dyslexic, minimally neurologically impaired, brain-injured, perceptually disabled,* and at least twenty others have been used in oddly overlapping ways. Whether a definite neurological basis for the learning difficulty *is* or is *not* required in the definition is one of the major stumbling points. Because of indefiniteness on such matters, it is almost meaningless to specify incidence rates for children with learning disabilities.

A promising development in instrumentation at the University of Illinois, the development of the Illinois Test of Psycholinguistic Abilities, has greatly stimulated research in the field (Kirk & McCarthy, 1961). The ITPA has become the most active research instrument not only with children showing specific learning disabilities but with handicapped children in general.

It provides a psychodiagnostic profile showing the relative abilities of children on nine variables representing nine input-output channels and three levels of meaningfulness of language. The assumption is that the diagnostic profile suggests deficiencies in basic functions which can perhaps be remedied, or bypassed, by specific teaching techniques. No assumptions about neurology are involved. The approach is presumably more basic than, for example, simply to drill directly at a word-reading level (McCarthy & Olson, 1964).

A flourishing and exotic diagnostic-remedial program to deal with language problems has been advanced by Delacato (1966). It involves analyses of "neurological organization" of clients in the diagnostic phase. Establishing a definite lateral dominance in neurological organization is presumed to be requisite for adequate language development, and much of the therapy is directed to this end. The theory and methods are highly controversial and have been little researched. Robbins (1966) has reported on one experimental study conducted in a school situation, the results of which were negative with respect to the Delacato methods. Correlational data also showed none of the relationships between level of neurological organization and reading level that were to be expected according to the theory. More extensive studies are required.

The operant conditioners have also applied their techniques to learning disabilities. Staats and Butterfield (1965), for example, reported a case study of a very deprived 14-year-old boy who, with but 40 hours of reading instruction under carefully devised conditions of stimulus control and reinforcement procedure, increased his reading grade level from 0 to 4.3. During the same period, his misbehavior in school was virtually eliminated.

In many ways the work in the field of learning disabilities offers promise to all areas of special education. The focus is quite strictly on learning; the several "helping" professions are working together; basic measurement and research problems are being attacked; and new teaching strategies and instructional procedures are being developed. From a base of learning-disabilities orientation, new concepts of classification and treatment are emerging which extend to far places in special education.

Maynard C. Reynolds[*]
University of Minnesota

[*] The author gratefully acknowledges the assistance of Mrs. Helen Juliar and Mrs. Burnae Marrinan in reviewing the literature used as background for this article.

References

American Foundation for the Blind. *Proceedings of the International Congress on Technology and Blindness.* Vols. 1–4. The Foundation, 1963. 316p.

Balow, Bruce. "A Program of Preparation for Teachers of Disturbed Children." *Excep Child* 32:7, 455–60; 1966.

Bateman, Barbara. "Mild Visual Defect and Learning Problems in Partially Seeing Children." *Sight Saving R* 33:30–3; 1963.

Bijou, Sidney W. "Application of Operant Principles to the Teaching of Reading, Writing, and Arithmetic." In *New Frontiers in Special Education.* Council for Exceptional Children, NEA, 1965. p. 1–5.

Bloodstein, O. "The Development of Stuttering: III Theoretical and Clinical Implications." *J Speech Hearing Disorders* 26:67–81; 1961.

Bryan, J. Ned (Ed.) *Talent: A State's Resource, A State's Responsibility,* Bulletin No. 34. USOE, 1963. 96p.

Cain, Leo F., and Levine, Samuel. *A Study of the Effects of Community and Institutional School Classes for Trainable Mentally Retarded Children.* USOE Cooperative Research Project No. 589. San Francisco State Col, 1961. 244p.

Craft, Michael, and others. "A Controlled Trial of Authoritarian and Self Governing Regimes with Adolescent Psychopaths." *Am J Orthography* 34:543–54; 1964.

Cruickshank, William M. (Ed.) *The Teacher of Brain Injured Children.* Syracuse U Press, 1966. Monogr Series 7. 334p.

Cruickshank, William M., and others. *Perception and Cerebral Palsy.* Syracuse U Press, 1957. 123p.

Cruickshank, William M., and others. *A Teaching Method for Brain Injured and Hyperactive Children: A Demonstration Pilot Study.* Syracuse U Press, 1961. Special Education Monogr Series 6. 576p.

Delacato, Carl H. *Neurological Organization and Reading.* Thomas, 1966. 189p.

Ellis, N. R. (Ed.) *Handbook of Mental Deficiency.* McGraw-Hill, 1963. 722p.

Fogarty, John E. "Stimulating Special Education through Federal Legislation." *Excep Child* 31:1–4; 1964.

Fund for the Advancement of Education. *They Went to College Early.* Ford Foundation, 1957. 117p.

Furth, Hans G. *Thinking Without Language: Psychological Implications of Deafness.* Free, 1966. 236p.

Getzels, J. W., and Jackson, P. W. *Creativity and Intelligence.* Wiley, 1962. 293p.

Goldberg, Miriam L., and Passow, A. Harry. "The Effects of Ability Grouping." *Ed* 82:1–6; 1962.

Goldstein, Herbert, and others. *The Efficacy of Special Class Training on the Development of Mentally Retarded Children.* USOE Cooperative Research Project No. 619. U Illinois, 1965. 23p.

Gray, Susan W., and others. *Before First Grade.* Teachers Col, Columbia U, 1966. 120p.

Guilford, J. P. *The Nature of Human Intelligence.* McGraw Hill, 1967. 538p.

Haring, Norris G., and Phillips, E. Lakin. *Educating Emotionally Disturbed Children.* McGraw-Hill, 1962. 322p.

Harper, P. A., and Wiener, G. "Sequelae of Low Birth Weight." *Annual R Med* 16:405–20; 1965.

Heber, R. F. "A Manual on Terminology and Classification in Mental Retardation." *Am J Mental Deficiency* 64:2; 1959.

Heber, R. F. "The Educable Mentally Retarded." In Kirk, S. A., and Weiner, B. B. (Eds.) *Behavior Research on Exceptional Children.* Council for Exceptional Children, NEA, 1963. p. 54–89.

Hess, R. D., and Shipman, Virginia. "Early Experience and the Socialization of Cognitive Modes in Children." *Child Develop* 36:869–86; 1965.

Hobbs, Nicholas. "Helping Disturbed Children: Psychological and Ecological Strategies." *Am Psychologist* 21:12; 1105–15; 1966.

Hollingworth, Leta S. *Gifted Children: Their Nature and Nurture.* Macmillan, 1926. 374p.

Hunt, J. McVicker. *Intelligence and Experience.* Ronald, 1961. 416p.

Hunt, J. McVicker. "The Psychological Basis for Using Pre-school Enrichment as an Antidote for Cultural Deprivation." *Merrill-Palmer Q* 10:3; 1964.

Joint Commission on Mental Illness and Health. *Action for Mental Health.* Science Editions, 1961.

Jones, John Walker. *The Visually Handicapped Child at Home and School.* Bulletin No. 39. USOE, 1963. 55p.

Jones, John W., and Collins, Anne P. "Trends in Program and Pupil Placement Practices in the Special Education of Visually Handicapped Children." *Int J Ed Blind* 14:79–82; 1965.

Jones, Reginald L., and Gottfried, Nathan W. "Preferences and Configurations of Interest in Special Class Teaching." *Excep Child* 28:371–7; 1962.

Kephart, Newell C. *The Slow Learner in the Classroom.* C. E. Merrill Books, 1960. 292p.

Kirk, Samuel A. *Early Education of the Mentally Retarded.* U Illinois Press, 1958. 216p.

Kirk, Samuel A., and McCarthy, James J. "The Illinois Test of Psycholinguistic Abilities—an Approach to Differential Diagnosis." *Am J Mental Deficiency* 66:3, 399–412; 1961.

Krasner, Leonard, and Ullmann, Leonard P. (Eds.) *Research in Behavior Modification.* Holt, 1965. 403p.

Krugman, Morris. "The Culturally Deprived Child in School." *NEA J* 20:23–5; 1961.

Lindsley, Ogden. "Direct Measurement and Prosthesis of Retarded Behavior." *J Ed* 147:62; 1964.

Lord, F. E., and others. *Project Report.* California State Col, Los Angeles, 1966. 162p.

Mackie, Romaine P. "Converging Circles—Education of the Handicapped and Some General Federal Programs." *Excep Child* 31:5; 250–5; 1965(a).

Mackie, Romaine P. "Spotlighting Advances in Special Education." *Excep Child* 32:77–81; 1965(b).

Masland, R. L., and others. *Mental Subnormality: Biological Psychological and Cultural Factors.* Basic Books, 1958. p. 145–400.

McCarthy, James J., and Olson, James L. *Validity Studies on the Illinois Test of Psycholinguistic Abilities.* U Wisconsin, 1964. 106p.

Meyer, H. J., and others. *Girls at Vocational High: An Experiment in Social Work Intervention.* Russell Sage, 1965. 225p.

Morkovin, Boris. *Through the Barriers of Deafness and Isolation.* Macmillian, 1960.

Morris, H. "Communication Skills of Children with Cleft Lips and Palates." *J Speech Hearing Res* 5:79–90; 1962.

Morse, William C., and others. *Public School Classes for the Emotionally Handicapped: A Research Analysis.* Council for Exceptional Children. NEA, 1964. 142p.

Myklebust, Helmer. *The Psychology of Deafness,* 2nd ed. Greene, 1964. 423p.

Nolan, Carson Y. "Blind Children; Degree of Vision, Mode of Reading: A 1163 Replication." *Inspection and Introspection of Special Education.* NEA, 1964(a). p. 86–94.

Nolan, Carson Y. "Research in Teaching Mathematics to Blind Children." *Int J Ed Blind* 13:97–100; 1964(b).

Nolan, Carson Y., and others. "Annual Report-Fiscal 1966. Department of Educational Research." Am Printing House for the Blind, 1966. 7p. (Mimeographed.)

Oléron, P., and Le Herren, H. "L'acquisition des conservations et le Langage: Etude comparative sur des Enfants Sourds et Entendants." *Enfance* 14:203–19, 1961.

Pick, Anne D., and others. "The Role of Grapheme-phoneme Correspondences in the Perception of Braille." *J Verbal Learning Verbal Behavior* 5:3; 298–300; 1966.

Prouty, Winston L. "Exceptional Children—the Neglected Legion." *NEA J* 53:3; 1966.

Quigley, Stephen, and Frisina, D. Robert. *Institutionalization and Psycho-educational Development of Deaf Children.* Council for Exceptional Children. Research Monogr Series A No. 3, NEA, 1961. 49p.

Reynolds, M. C. "Acceleration." In Torrance, E. P. (Ed.) Talent and Education. U Minnesota Press, 1960. p. 106–25.

Reynolds, M. C. "A Crisis in Evaluation." *Excep Child* 32:585–92; 1966.

Robbins, Melvyn P. "A Study of the Validity of Delacato's Theory of Neurological Organization." *Excep Child* 32:8; 517–24; 1966.

Robinson, Geoffrey C. "Hearing Loss in Infants and Young Pre-school Children." *Volta R* 66:314–6; 1964.

Sloan, William. "Four Score and Seven." *Am J Mental Deficiency* 68:1, 6–14; 1963.

Smith, Donald C. *Personal and Social Adjustment of Gifted Adolescents.* Council for Exceptional Children Research Monogr No. 4, NEA. 1964.

Staats, A. W., and Butterfield, W. H. "Treatment of Non-reading in a Culturally Deprived Juvenile Delinquent: An Application of Reinforcement Principles." *Child Develop* 36:926–42; 1965.

Strauss, Alfred A., and Lehtinen, Laura A. *Psychopathology and Education of the Brain-Injured Child.* Greene, 1947. 206p.

Templin, Mildred C. "Vocabulary Problems of the Deaf Child." *Int Audiology* 5:3, 349–54; 1966.

Terman, L. M., and Oden, Melita H. *The Gifted Child Grows Up. Genetic Studies of Genius,* Vol. 4. Stanford U Press, 1947. 448p.

Terman, L. M., and Oden, Melita H. *The Gifted Group at Mid-life; Thirty-five Years Follow-up of the Superior Child. Genetic Studies of Genius.* Vol. 5 Stanford U Press, 1959. 187p.

Torrance, E. Paul. *Rewarding Creative Behavior.* Prentice-Hall, 1965. 353p.

Van Riper, Charles. "A Predictive Screening Test for Children with Articulatory Speech Defects." Cooperative Research Project No. 1538. Western Michigan U, 1966.

Watson, T. J. "Research in the Education of the Deaf Outside the United States." *Volta R* 65:535–41; 1963.

Watson, T. J. "Use of Hearing Aids by Hearing Impaired Pupils in Ordinary Schools." *Volta R* 66:741–7; 787; 1964.

Weinstein, Laura. "Social Schemata of Emotionally Disturbed Boys." *J Abn Psychol* 70:457–61; 1965.

Wilbur, Roy L., and others. *White House Conference on Children and Youth 1930: Addresses and Abstracts of Committee Reports.* Century, 1931.

Winitz, H. "The Development of Speech and Language in the Normal Child." In Rieber, R., and Brubaker, R. S. (Eds.) *Speech Pathology.* North Holland, 1966.

Zigler, E. "Familial Mental Retardation: A Continuing Dilemma." *Sci* 55:292–8; 1967.

SPEECH

Speech, a form of social behavior manifested by visible bodily action and audible symbols used as signals by a speaker to stir up ideas and affective states desired by the speaker in an audience of one or more listeners, is learned. It is a behavioral code which is verbal when it affects the listener by stimulating his ears; nonverbal, when it affects him by stimulating his eyes. When the verbal and nonverbal signals are combined and synchronized into a unity, speech behavior is complex and capable of unlimited variations in clarifying and intensifying meanings in an infinite number of appeals to the auditory and visual senses.

The initial bodily action of a human infant seems purposeless and is sometimes annoying, but it results, sooner or later, in a response desired by the infant from its mother or some other person. As if the infant notes mentally the specific action which signals the specific desired response, the action is repeated as long as it elicits successfully the same response. Similarly, the child *learns* to use another specific bodily action to signal another desired response and not to use some other bodily action which signals an undesired response. Likewise, the infant learns which of its random bodily actions of cooing and wailing results in rewards and which in penalties by its mother and other persons. The child learns, through many trials, errors, and successes, to manipulate its bodily action to produce rewarding signals, both visible and audible, and to avoid penalizing signals. Later, the child learns to imitate signals it sees and those it hears; later, words; and later, simple sentences. O'Neill and Weaver (1926) suggested theories of the origin of speech, its evolution, and experiences and methods for its development and refinement for purposes of thinking, expression, and communication. Dewey (1933) referred to speech as the great instrument of social adaptation and stated that the development of speech adaptation of a baby's activities to and with those of other persons gives the keynote of mental life.

Listening to a speaker is the act of interpreting his speech behavior and comprehending its meaning. Basic to speech behavior and an integral part of it are both speaking and listening. Basic to speaking are fundamentals of speech which Balcer and Seabury (1965) classified as (1) basic content or ideas, (2) organization of ideas, (3) developmental or supporting details, (4) adjustment to the speech situation, (5) bodily action for purposes of communication, (6) voice usage, (7) enunciation, articulation, and pronunciation, (8) language, (9) adaptation in the speech situation, and (10) listening. The assumption that, because a child or adult is able to make utterances, he needs nothing further is false, as stated by Hockmuth (1948). Speech behavior as a means of expression and communication for purposes of social adaptation, cooperation, and control has long been studied, learned, and taught.

Speech education has many meanings. In its broadest sense, it embraces all experiences through which speech is learned in the home, school, and community. Usually as the term is used by speech educators, it refers to the theories, principles, methods, materials, and activities utilized by students to *learn* and by speech educators and other specialists to *teach* speech. The "speech activities" most frequently encompassed by programs of speech education in American high schools and colleges are identified in divisions of speech education such as language arts, communication skills, rhetoric, public address, dramatic art, oral interpretation, speech correction and audiology, and radio-television-film. In a strict pedagogical sense, speech education is interpreted to mean "*teaching* and *learning to teach* speech."

HISTORY. Although Egyptologists have ascertained few facts to support the belief that drama was written or that plays were produced in Egypt, drama in some form appeared in Egypt by 3200 B.C.—if not as early as 4000 B.C., as indicated by Freedley and Reeves (1941). As early as 2500 B.C., "modern" precepts of speech education were recorded on Egyptian papyrus, known as the oldest "book" in the world. As reported by Gunn (1924), Ptah-ho-tep, a vizier under King Isosi in the Fifth Dynasty of the Old Kingdom of Egypt, advised his son thus:

> If thou find an arguer talking, thy fellow, one that is within thy reach, keep not silence when he saith ought that is evil; so shalt thou be wiser than he. Great will be the applause on the part of the listeners, and thy name shall be good in the knowledge of the princes. If thou find an arguer talking, a poor man, that is to say, not thine equal,

be not scornful toward him because he is lowly. Let him alone; then shall he confound himself; question not to please thine heart, either pour out thy wrath upon him that is before thee, it is shameful to confuse a mean mind. . . . If thou find an arguer talking, one that is well disposed and wiser than thou, let thine arms fall, bend thy back, be not angry with him if he agrees not with thee. Refrain from speaking evilly; oppose him not at any time when he speaketh. . . . If thou be powerful, make thyself to be honored for knowledge and for gentleness. Speak with authority . . . for he that is humble falleth into errors. . . . Be not silent, but beware of interruptions and of answering words with heat. . . . Control thyself. . . . Repeat not extravagant speech. . . . He that obeyeth his heart shall command.

In Ptah-ho-tep's precepts are reflected, with surprising specificity, fundamentals of speech as they are classified in 1967 by American speech educators.

Greece, First Center of Speech Education. Democracy was conceived in the Greek cities. By 348 B.C., a utopian society was visualized by Greek philosophers and statesmen. With a vision of Utopia, Plato (Jowett, 1946) devoted himself to the evolution of an ideal state and a system of state education to serve mankind, as implied in his concept of a democratic state: "A State, I said, arises, as I conceive, out of the needs of mankind; no one is self-sufficing, but all of us have many wants. Can any other origin of a state be imagined? There can be no other."

In the fourth and fifth centuries B.C., Greece was not a unified country under a single authority. The country encompassed various city-states, each with its own government. Sparta had an aristocratic government which sought to establish uniformity. Athens, originally aristocratic and monarchical, had changed to a democratic government. The people of Athens were independent and interested in developing citizens capable of serving the city-state and thereby of serving the people. Each of them was expected to participate in goverment councils, to plead his own cases in the courts of law, and to serve in assemblies and on juries. Since slaves in this incomplete Grecian democracy did much of the menial work, Athenians were free to pursue the education of their bodies, senses and minds. With their ceremonial worship of pagan gods, practiced for centuries, with their newly acquired obligations to participate in their city-state government, and with their desire to develop as citizens, Athenians were motivated to benefit from their system of city-state education.

Aristotle recognized the origins of Grecian drama and dramatic art in the nature of man, as revealed in the translations of his *De Poetica* by Bywater (1924), Cooper (1927), and Twining (1934):

> I propose to speak not only of the art . . . but its specifics. Epic poetry and Tragedy, as also Comedy, Dithyrambic poetry, and most of flute-playing and lyre-playing, are all . . . modes of imitation. But . . . they differ from one another . . . either by a difference of kind in their means, or by differences in the objects, or in the manner of their imitations. . . . Even in dancing . . . such diversities are possible. . . . Man learns first by imitation. And it is also natural for all to delight in works of imitation.

Greek drama began in the hymns sung and danced at the festivals in honor of the god Dionysus. Later, episodes of the story of Dionysus were acted out in public, and drama emerged, as told by Aristotle, out of the storytelling instinct basic to man. With man's desire to feel as others feel and to understand why others act as they do, imitation enables man to learn about his world and acceptable behavior of people in it. Dramas produced and directed by Athenian playwrights such as Aeschylus (525–456 B.C.), Sophocles (496–406 B.C.), Euripides (484–406 B.C), Aristophanes (448–385 B.C.), and Menander (343–291 B.C.) helped Athens to become the educational and cultural center of the ancient world. The city-state itself and the patronage of wealthy citizens provided the theater, financed the productions, remunerated the playwrights who were usually the producers and directors, paid the actors, supervised the judging by secret ballot, and awarded prizes for winning plays and outstanding actors in the festivals and contests during celebrations to which everyone was invited at public expense. These celebrations and the assemblies, councils, and courts of government, in which a greater percentage of Athenians in their city-state could participate than would be possible in a large nation-state with representative democracy, provided the first great center of speech education in the Greek world.

About 467 B.C., the ruling tyrants of Sicily were overthrown and replaced by a democratic government. People thereupon undertook to recover property previously taken from them. Because no trained lawyers were available, each man who sought relief in the courts had to plead his own case. Corax of Syracuse, a Sophist teacher, and his student Tisias were first to give systematic instruction in public speaking to help citizens plead their cases. They taught men basic principles of speech organization and persuasive methods to win favorable court decisions. They, like other Sophist teachers later, emphasized winning a decision, sometimes with inadequate evidence, by appeals to emotion, by skill in using fundamentals of speech delivery, and by language and style.

Gorgias of Leontini (427 B.C.), another student of Corax and Tisias, went to Athens, where he remained and became wealthy as a speaker and a teacher of public speaking. He sought to reject the name "Sophist" because of its implications concerning the ethics of a speaker. Protagoras (481–411 B.C.) and Isocrates (436–338 B.C.) were other successful Sophist teachers in Athens.

Isocrates, a famous teacher of rhetoric of his day, founded a school for young men who wished to train for civic life. They enrolled as early as age fifteen and paid tuition in order to profit from Isocrates' teaching. His concept of general education was that it should be moral, broad, thorough, interdisciplinary, and practical. The core of his program was public speaking, because it sharpened the faculty of judgment and required sound thinking. Although philosophy, mathematics, history, and classical prose and poetry were included in the curriculum of his school, he taught speech and debate largely through the use of models for study, the application of principles of rhetoric, and practice in exercises and contests. He specialized in developing very close teacher-student relationships. For 50 years, his school had great influence on Greek education and leadership. Nearly all successful speakers in the Athens of his day had studied with him. Aristotle called him "the master of all rhetoricians."

Although training in public speaking by the Sophists was much in demand and a lucrative profession, Socrates (470–399 B.C.), often reputed to be the wisest Greek philosopher, and Plato (427–338 B.C.), the philosophical rhetorician and a student of Socrates for 20 years, objected to speech education by the Sophists because it encouraged speakers (1) to seek immediate, superficial ends; (2) to avoid sincere, patient research; (3) to hold too little respect for truth; (4) to seek favorable decisions by deceptive, persuasive appeals rather than by persuasion based on the merits of their cases; (5) to develop glibness of language rather than knowledgeable speech; (6) to become orators skilled in the use of questionable argument, false evidence, and chicanery and, therefore, unethical in their speech practices; and (7) to demonstrate attributes and practices which reflected unfavorably on speech education as a discipline for study. In three of his Socratic dialogues, the *Gorgias*, the *Phaedrus*, and the *Republic*, Plato (Jowett, 1946) expressed objections to the teaching of Sophists, as indicated only briefly here:

> . . . our youth are corrupted by Sophists, or that private teachers of the art corrupt them. . . . When they [young and old, men and women alike] meet together, and the world sits down at an assembly, or in a court of law, or a theatre, or a camp, or in any other popular resort, and there is a great uproar, and they praise some things which are being said or done, and blame other things, equally exaggerating both, shouting, and clapping their hands, and the echo of the rocks and the place in which they are assembled redoubles the sound of the praise or blame—at such a time will not a young man's heart, as they say, leap with him? Will any private training enable him to stand firm against the overwhelming flood of popular opinion? Or will he be carried away by the stream? Will he not have the notions of good and evil which the public in general have—he will do as they do, and as they are, such will he be? . . . Is not the first rule of good speaking that the mind of the speaker should know the truth of what he is going to say? . . . There never is nor ever will be a real art of speaking which is unconnected with the truth. . . . And he who is practiced in the art will make the same thing appear to the same persons to be at one time just and another time unjust, if he has a mind. . . . Skillful speakers they are, and impart their skill to anyone who will consent to worship them as kings and bring them gifts.

Socrates recognized essential social values of oratory, as he stated in the dialogue in Plato's *Phaedrus:* "And this art he will not attain without a great deal of trouble, which a good man ought to undergo, not for the sake of speaking and acting before men, but in order that he may be able to say what is acceptable to God and in all things to act acceptably to Him as far as in him lies."

From approximately 480 to 292 B.C., ten Attic orators (Aeschines, Andocides, Antiphon, Deinarchus, Demosthenes, Hypereides, Isaeus, Isocrates, Lycurgus, and Lysias) exercised significant and lasting influence upon speech education. Antiphon (born about 480 B.C.), the earliest of the ten orators, became well versed in rhetoric, skilled in his use of rigid poetic diction, eminent in the law of homicide, and suspect for his cleverness and austerity as a professional ghost writer of forensic and political speeches. Isaeus (born about 420 B.C.), a student of Isocrates, and later of Lysias, became a teacher of rhetoric, a master of Attic law and forensic dispute, and a career ghost writer of forensic speeches concerned with private claims to property and money by litigants in the law courts. He, like Antiphon, was subjected to public satire for his clever and passionate persuasion, evidenced in forensic oratory by the litigants for whom he wrote speeches during more than 20 years.

Demosthenes (born 384 B.C.) is recognized today as the great Attic orator who overcame his speech debility by such measures as "declaiming to the waves with pebbles in his mouth" and who developed his speech ability and attributes as a fiery forensic orator under the private and paid tutelage of Isaeus. Demosthenes is praised for his use of chains of argument, his intensity and sincerity as a student and speaker, his oratory free of embellishment, his speech "On the Crown," and his "winning a crown" for forensic oratory and service in the public interest.

Although noted for his "purity of style" as a forensic orator, his friendship with Socrates, and his opposition to Aristotle and Plato, Aeschines (389–314 B.C.) was recognized as the Attic orator and forensic opponent of Demosthenes.

Lysias (about 459–380 B.C.) excelled as a teacher of rhetoric and as an orator who became a model of plainness, a master of idiom, of vivid description, and of tactful adaptation of speeches, and a persuader who organized his speeches by the use of partitions recognized today as introduction, narration of facts, proof, and conclusion. Andocides (born about 440 B.C.) gained a measure of success as a speaker by his acceptance of the idiom as used by his teacher Lysias and by his avoidance of the rigid poetic diction as used by Antiphon.

Isocrates, as noted earlier, was the career educator among the Attic orators. In his school at Athens, ". . . the eloquence of all Greece was trained and perfected," including that of Hypereides (390–322 B.C.), called by Jebb (1876) "the Sheridan of Athens," whose strength lay in his perception of issues, subtle arrangement of subject matter, avoidance of pretense, mastery of vocabulary and wit, and simplicity of composition. Although he tended to be redundant and to digress from his topic, the clarity of his utterances and his firm patriotism made a place for him among the Attic orators.

Lycurgus (396–325 B.C.) was probably most noted as a statesman whose public-spirited deeds and patriotism contributed to his stature. In his speechmaking, he had neither elegance nor charm and tended to digress and repeat. He was accepted as an orator whose intellect, intensity and earnestness, clarity of utterance, loyalty to the public welfare (including his support of the Dionysiac theater), severe prosecution of disloyal citizens, and, probably above all, ethos were the sources of his power.

Deinarchus (361–291 B.C.), the latest born of the ten orators, was neither an inventor nor a perfecter as a ghost writer but an imitator of Hypereides, Lysias, and Demosthenes, for whose prosecution Deinarchus later served as a professional speech writer.

These ten Attic orators had a lasting influence on the emerging speech education. After Pericles (490–291 B.C.), they were practitioners of rhetoric in the law courts and state assemblies whose orations were studied as models. They were teachers who emphasized *ideas* as more important than *delivery* in speaking and speechmaking. With them, *thought* was first and *language* second. Their extant speeches and the exposition by Jebb (1876) of their philosophy, speaking, and teaching reveal their rejection of chicanery and their acceptance of mastery of subject matter and its ideas, partitions, language, and audience psychology as important for forcefulness in speaking and speechmaking. From their concepts and practices came foundations of modern speech education.

The great contributions by the Greeks to today's speech education came through the works of Aristotle (384–322 B.C.). His *Rhetoric* and *Poetics* present in systematic and clearly organized treatises most ideas and methodology in speech education worth conserving at the end of his lifetime of experience and thought. As Thonssen and Baird (1948) have stated: "Aristotle is perhaps the most highly esteemed figure in ancient rhetoric. . . . The *Rhetoric* is generally considered the most important single work in the literature of speech-craft." Likewise, the *Poetics* is highly regarded by students concerned with the origin, early concepts, and development of the arts. Although neither Aristotle's *Rhetoric* nor his *Poetics* is complete or scientifically precise, both books remain useful today and the objects of continued study.

Students of rhetoric consider as meaningful Aristotle's definition of persuasion, ". . . the faculty of observing in any given case the available means of persuasion." He advanced three means of persuasion: (1) *ethos*, a speaker's power of evincing personal attributes which make his speech credible; (2) *pathos*, his power of appealing to the emotion of his listeners; and (3) *logos*, his power of proving a truth, or an apparent truth, by means of persuasive arguments. He stressed three principles, still accepted today, essential to the effective speaker, who must (1) understand himself, (2) understand his message, and (3) carefully analyze his audience. He identified three kinds of rhetoric: (1) *forensic* or *legal*, concerned with justice and injustice in the accusation and defense of wrongdoers and their victims; (2) *political* or *deliberative*, concerned with dehortation of "bad" and exhortation of "good" policies and courses of action in the public interest; and (3) *ceremonial* or *epideictic* oratory of display, concerned with praise of honor and virtue and censure of dishonor and vice. Modern textbooks on speech education reflect these and many other concepts expressed by Aristotle in his *Rhetoric* and *Poetics*.

Rome, Second Center of Speech Education. Rome had two outstanding rhetoricians, Cicero (106–43 B.C.) and Quintilian (A.D. 35–100).

Cicero (Sutton, 1959), the great Roman orator and writer on rhetorical theory and practice, gave marked impetus to the functional approach in teaching speech. His 57 extant speeches are considered models of Roman oratory. His *De Oratore* (55 B.C.), written in the form of dialogue between the orator Crassus, who expressed the ideas of Cicero, and the orator Antonius, who countered Cicero's ideas, presents (1) the essential education and qualities of an orator, (2) the subject matter of an oration, and (3) the structure and delivery of an oration. Thus, Cicero advocated thorough general education as essential for effective and "good" speaking and speechmaking. In *De Inventione* (80 B.C.), Cicero (Hubbell, 1949) clarified the five procedures which he advocated and practiced for preparing and delivering any speech: (1) *inventio*, finding valid ideas and developmental or supporting details related to the topic; (2) *dispositio*, planning and arranging the speech with its ideas and details organized clearly for the audience and the speaker; (3) *elocutio*, or style, choosing and using language which serves best to evoke in the audience the meaning intended by the speaker; (4) *memoria*, grasping and retaining the ideas, details, plan, and language of the speech; and (5) *pronuntiatio*, using the body and voice in keeping with the speaker's purpose, the dignity of the subject and occasion, and the meaning effected in the audience as intended by the speaker. He restated and clarified the *exordium*, or introduction; *narration*, or events and facts of the topic; *proof*, or the establishment of the events and facts; and the *peroration*, or conclusion of a speech.

Quintilian (Butler, 1920), a great speech educator in Rome, wrote probably the most famous work on the teaching of speech. His treatise entitled *Institutio Oratoria* (95 A.D.), in twelve books, serves both general and speech educators. Quintilian traced the education of an orator from birth to his adult success on a platform. He emphasized Aristotle's and Cicero's recommendations for thorough training in all kinds of subject matter as education for living every phase of the good life. He expressed concern for training in speech for a child from birth to adulthood and identified the problem of a child's learning in infancy a style of speech which he needs to unlearn before he can learn to speak well. He urged training in speech for fathers and mothers and for nurses for the sake of the speech education of children. He advocated speech education in the curricula of public schools and its application in the communities. In his speaking and writing, he admonished teachers and other adults to develop programs of speech education based on the individual differences and group tendencies in the speech capacities and habits of children. As perhaps the first teacher of speech in a state-supported public school, he insisted on the development of high ethical standards in his students. An orator, he stated, is a "good man trained in speaking." Quintilian's rhetorical principles and methodology offer abundant suggestions useful to contemporary teachers.

With the decline of the Roman Empire and the disappearance of democratic processes in government, interest in original speaking was minimal. Rhetoric was limited to a study of style and delivery. Declamation consisting of practice selections for developing skills in delivery encouraged the demise of other significant facets of speech education.

The Middle Ages and the Renaissance. For nearly a thousand years, the priests, monks, and scholars associated with religious orders kept rhetoric alive. Aristotelian rhetoric was neglected. Writers evidenced understanding of Ciceronian prose and of Cicero's *De Oratore* and *De Inventione*. Saint Augustine (A.D. 354–430) wrote perhaps the most significant work of the epoch, entitled *De Doctrina Christiana* (A.D. 425). He was concerned with the use of rhetorical skill in Christian teaching. He discouraged Sophist artificiality in speaking and, to emphasize the importance of matter and thought over delivery, encouraged the *emulation* and *imitation* of successful speakers to help students to *think the thought* rather than to *think about delivery*. Although he introduced training in reading aloud to effect improvement in the reading of the Scriptures, he insisted on the reader's grasping the full meaning of a passage. Saint Augustine's pedagogical belief on means for improvement of delivery in reading and speaking was reflected by Howell (1951):

> ... a discourse to be persuasive must be simple, natural ... its art must be concealed ... when it appears too elegant, it makes the listener distrustful. ... [He discussed in Ciceronian terms] the arrangement of subject matter; the mixture of diverse styles; the ways to make a discourse forever grow; the necessity to be simple and familiar, even at times in the tones of the voice and in gestures, though what one says be elevated when one preaches of religion; and finally, the way to overpower and move.

Probably Saint Augustine's greatest contribution, as it was explained and documented by Baldwin (1928), was his preservation for posterity of concepts of speech education gained from earlier teaching and writing by the Greeks and Romans.

The Venerable Bede (A.D. 672–735) summed up most of the learning of western Europe in his *Ecclesiastical History of the English Nation* and other works and, at his death, left a coterie of scholars well-grounded in his works. Alcuin (A.D. 735–804), educated in the academic environment of these scholars, was the first Englishman to be recognized in Europe, for his pronouncement of Cicero's five procedures in *De Rhetorica* (A.D. 794). Charles the Great, or Charlemagne (A.D. 742–877), King of the Franks and crowned by Pope Leo III as Emperor of the Romans, invited Alcuin to assist in a revival of learning among the Franks. Although Alcuin carried to the Continent the learning of England, the tradition of learning in England suffered a long eclipse upon his death.

During the Renaissance speech education was revitalized in France, especially in England, and then later in the United States. Most important to this revitalization were Quintilian's *Institutes of Oratory* (1416), Cicero's *De Oratore* (1422), and Aristotle's *Rhetoric* (1508). Leonard Cox, an English schoolmaster, wrote *The Arte of Crafte of Rhetorique* (1529), the first schoolbook written in English and published in London. Also, Thomas Wilson wrote *The Art of Rhetorique* (1533). Both publications were in the Ciceronian tradition. Peter Ramus, a celebrated French educator and antagonist of Aristotle between 1584 and 1642, dominated the teaching of rhetoric in England and influenced its teaching in the American colonies. He recognized that the classical treatments of logic and rhetoric overlapped and proposed that the "liberal arts" be categorized in three diverse areas, to give each area of study and teaching its own special province without infringing on the province of any other area. He suggested that the teaching of invention and arrangement of ideas be assigned to teachers of logic, that the development of ornamental language and effective delivery be assigned to teachers of rhetoric, and that grammar, as it dealt with etymology and syntax, constitute a separate third of the language studies. His *Dialectique* (1555) treated invention and arrangement. Ramus's friend, Audomarus Taleus, limited his *Rhetoric* to a treatment of style and delivery, including gesture and voice. Although Ramus's theory prevailed for many years in the teaching of dialectic and rhetoric in England, his contemporaries, perhaps inevitably, became increasingly interested in more limited specializations; this distressed Ramus, who recognized the close relationships among logic, rhetoric, and grammar. Other English texts, published in considerable number after the invention of printing in 1440, treated rhetoric as an art of developing ideas in ornamental language and figurative speech. Richard Sherry in *The Treatise, Schemes, and Tropes* (1550) and Henry Peacham in the *Garden of Eloquence* (1577) treated speech as an art of expression and exhibition to control the behavior of an audience. Robert Robinson, in his *Art of Pronunciation* (1617), and John Bishver, in his *Chirologia and Chironomia* (1644), were concerned with bodily action, voice, and pronunciation. The limited conception of rhetoric by each of these writers was in keeping with (1) the specialization sought by contemporaries of Peter Ramus, (2) the rejection of rhetoric as a broad discipline by some writers, (3) the elocution movement resulting from adverse criticism of the manner of speaking by English preachers, (4) the expansion of the concept of speech to include reading and acting, and (5) the lack of consensus on the limitation and scope of speech education.

England, the Center of Speech Education in the Eighteenth Century. As early as 1667 the Royal Society of London, reflecting an earlier statement by Francis Bacon, angrily denounced the teaching of rhetoric as an art of ornate language and exhibitionary delivery rather than as a functional means of "everyday" communication. Three principal contributions to rhetoric were forthcoming during the eighteenth century. In 1759, John Ward utilized the works of Cicero and Quintilian in his *System of Oratory*, which helped to break the Ramean limitation of rhetoric to style and delivery. In 1776, George Campbell, a Presbyterian minister, presented the results of his penetrating inquiry into rhetoric. In his *Philosophy of Rhetoric*, he evidenced, in keeping with the psychology of his day, his acceptance of the concept of the human mind as divided into the faculties of *knowing* and *feeling* and his understanding of the purposes and desired outcomes of a speaker as determined by his decision to appeal to one of the faculties in the minds of his audience. In his *Lectures on Systematic Theology and Pulpit Eloquence* (1807), Campbell defined eloquence and its objectives. Together, his two treatises were the most insightful work on rhetoric in the history of the discipline. In 1783, Hugh Blair, in his *Lectures on Rhetoric and Belles Lettres,* in which he emphasized language style and eloquence, expanded the scope of rhetoric to provide a comprehensive treatise on elements of composition in both speaking and writing. This treatise, concerned with both literature and rhetoric, was widely adopted in American colleges.

After 1754, elocutionists pressed forward in their advocacy of improvement in delivery in interpretative reading and in speaking as the most rewarding objective to be served by rhetorical instruction. Their movement started as a result of (1) adverse criticism of delivery by English preachers by men such as Defoe, Dryden, Garrick, Sheridan, and Swift; (2) a developing pride in the English language; (3) a desire to standardize and improve language usage in speaking and writing; (4) proposals to establish an English Academy as an aid to refining and enriching the English language; and (5) perception of speech as a potent means of persuasion in parliament, church, theater, and other social situations. They held that the principles of effective delivery came from nature. The "natural" group permitted freedom and spontaneity in expression, but the "mechanical" group insisted that nature must be controlled by rules within nature. Thus, every aspect of delivery was included in their teaching, based upon understanding by readers and speakers of ideas and emotions to be communicated.

Contributors to the literature of elocution were numerous. John Mason first introduced the key word "elocution" in his book entitled *An Essay on Elocution, or Pronunciation.* Thomas Sheridan left his career as an actor, became a teacher of elocution in 1756, and wrote both his *Dictionary* and *Grammar* (1780). John Walker forsook the stage, turned to teaching and lecturing, and wrote at least six books, including his widely used *Elements of Elocution* (1781). The Reverend Gilbert Austin developed in his *Chironomia* (1806) an elaborate system of precepts and an anthology of quotations on delivery from the writings of ancient and contemporary rhetoricians. His work affected the teaching of speech as late as 1916, when American writers were still drawing from it. Hundreds of manuals, written primarily for the clergy, were in demand in American schools and homes.

SPEECH EDUCATION IN THE UNITED STATES. Speech education, beginning in Egypt no later than 2500 B.C., developed as rhetoric under state education auspices in Grecian democracy, from which concepts and values were inherited by American education. This heritage reached the United States by a circuitous route, along which speech education drew mightily on the works of such men as Corax, Aristotle, Sophocles, the Attic orators, Cicero, Quintilian, and Saint Augustine. Alcuin carried traditional rhetoric through England and to western Europe, where Ramus reduced it to part of the trivium consisting of grammar, logic, and rhetoric. English rhetoricians such as Cox, Wilson, Ward, Campbell, Blair, and Whately and elocutionists such as Sherry, Robinson, Mason, Sheridan, Walker, and Austin carried forward, with conflicting motivations, the classical tradition of speech education.

The democratic values of speech education were recognized in early American schools. Works on grammar and logic which included concepts of invention and arrangement, as recommended by Peter Ramus and endorsed by John Harvard and Cotton Mather, were part of the curriculum of Harvard College established in 1636 primarily for the preparation of lawyers and ministers who served as teachers. Oratory, public address, declamation, and, in 1680, a form of educational dramatics were included in the program of the first college in the American colonies.

Ramean "rhetorical logic" dominated the teaching of speech for the next hundred years in the schools designed primarily to assure preparation of ministers and officials to serve the religious sects and the state. However, the Ramean doctrine was increasingly challenged by demands for forensic disputation, even as interest mounted in widely circulated works such as Anthony Blackwell's *Introduction to the Classics* (1718) and John Mason's *Essay on Elocution.* Benjamin Franklin, in his *Proposals Relating to the Education of Youth in Pennsylvania* (1744), urged a study of model speeches, tenets of logic and rhetoric, and contemporary literature. Cubberley (1920) reported that "algebra, astronomy, botany, . . . declamation, and debating" were taught in the academies. John Ward's *System of Rhetoric* "helped pave the way for the great creative rhetorics of the eighteenth century," stated Ehninger (1951), even after its circulation ceased in 1780. Guthrie (1948) concluded that, after 1785, texts by Blair, Campbell, and Whately based on classical foundations were most influential in American colleges.

Blair's sermons were popular upon reaching the American audience, and his treatment of taste, genius, and sublimity probably gave impetus to studies of criticism and taste in rhetoric, the subject of rhetorical theses in several colleges. Blair's *Lectures on Rhetoric and Belles Lettres* was more popular than Campbell's *Philosophy of Rhetoric* and *Lectures on Systematic Theology and Pulpit Eloquence*, but Campbell offered more original contributions to rhetoric and greater challenge for productive scholarship and teaching in rhetoric—assuming, as seems correct, that Campbell's work inspired achievements by Newman, Porter, and Day. Whately's *Elements of Rhetoric* (1828) became popular immediately for its emphasis on logical proof and invention in the Aristotelian tradition and for its indictment of the elocutionary teaching of delivery, resulting in speakers with an "affected style of spouting, worse, in all respects, than their original mode of delivery."

Dominance by the works of Blair, Campbell, and Whately survived limited competition by the work of Alexander Jamieson and influenced contributions to speech education by famous American educators and statesmen. John Witherspoon, president of Princeton University from 1768 to 1794, seems to have paved the way for British eighteenth-century rhetoric in America. John Quincy Adams, appointed first Boylston Professor of Rhetoric and Oratory at Harvard University in 1806, relied little on English rhetoric or elocution but drew heavily on Aristotelian rhetoric in his lectures, which aided the transition from the prevalent oratory of the clergy to that of American statesmen. Ebenezer Porter, Bartlett Professor of Sacred Rhetoric at Andover (1813–31), reflected Campbell's concepts.

Chauncey Allen Goodrich, Professor of Rhetoric at Yale University (1817–39), made a lasting contribution to America's heritage of speech education by identifying the need in rhetorical criticism for an adequate biographical-historical setting of an orator and his speeches. He demonstrated the value of an adequate setting in his own masterful rhetorical criticism of 20 British orators.

Over a century after Goodrich's work entitled *Select British Eloquence* (Goodrich, 1852) first appeared, scholars in speech education continued to pursue rhetorical studies of actors, educators, ministers, statesmen, and others involved in the various media of communication and expression. Recently reported studies have been devoted to an extensive and varied list of individuals: Brown, Bryson, Darrow, Dewey, Douglas, Eisenhower, Fitzmaurice, Fosdick, Goldwater, Graham, Humphrey, Hutchins, Kennedy, Kerr, King, Lippmann, Lodge, Mann, Reagan, Roosevelt, Sevareid, Shaw, Sinclair, Sockman, Stevenson, Talmage, Truman, Vandeman, Wallace, and Wise. When this method of historical research is applied to speakers in their roles in human endeavor, it serves to record facts, to posit causations and probabilities in phenomena of speaking and speechmaking, and to offer a flexible guide for use in future speech activities and development. Baird (1956) stated that such studies "give us deeper insight into all that comprises our evolving civilization . . . enable us better to frame criteria of effectiveness, and so to apply such tests . . . to our own training and performances [and thereby give us] a clearer view of the principles in practice and a more mature awareness of our own rhetorical problems and practices."

Similar benefits result from applications of the method to human roles as speakers in educational radio and television, voice and speech development, play direction and production, and international negotiation, as historical assessments of earlier efforts at communication and expression are available to students and teachers.

Speech educators gave priority to research in their first professional organization and its first publication. One of five purposes of the new National Association of Academic Teachers of Public Speaking was, O'Neill (1915) stated, "to promote and encourage research work in various parts of the field of public speaking; we wish to encourage and assist individuals and committees who will undertake by scientific investigation to discover the true answer to certain problems. . . ." Blanton (1915), editor of the association's initial publication, announced: "We will give in the pages of the *Quarterly Journal* the right of way over all other material to articles giving the results of research. . . ." Winans (1915) wrote:

. . . by scholarship which is a product of research, the standing of our work in the academic world will be improved. . . . We shall not only stand better but teach better, when we have more scholarship; when we have the better understanding of fundamentals and training in the methods which test and determine truth. . . . Is it not true that as a class we trust too much to limited observation, theorize too quickly from limited data? Finding that a certain method helps in some cases, do we not too often jump to the conclusion that it embodies a great principle? And we repeat our guess until we believe it proved. We need the man of patient research to subject our guesses to rigid observation.

Woolbert (1916) supported the view of the other sixteen founders of the Association:

I stand for a search for the facts; the facts of how speaking is done; of what its various effects are under specified conditions; how these facts can be made into laws and principles; and how other people can best be taught to apply them . . . we need to get together on some common acceptable basis. The only one I know of comes from scientifically conducted investigation and research.

Since the awarding of a master's degree by a department of speech to H. S. Buffum at the University of Iowa in 1902 and the first doctor's degree by a department of speech to Sara Stinchfield [Hawke] at the University of Wisconsin, over 28,000 graduate degrees in speech have been granted by more than 170 universities in the United States; over 17,000 master's thesis titles have been indexed; and over 3,300 doctoral dissertations have been recorded, as reported by Knower (1967). The latter author's report on graduate work (compiled annually in *Speech Monographs*) reveals the titles of 272 doctoral dissertations in speech that were completed during 1966. Based on an examination of the dissertation titles, 41 percent would appear to employ the historical method of research; 31 percent, the descriptive; 26 percent, the experimental; and 2 percent, the creative. Although historical research studies continue to be inviting to scholars, as evidenced in the annual reports, use of the experimental method has increased since 1956, when 15 percent of the dissertations appeared to employ the experimental method, according to Auer (1959).

AUDIENCE BEHAVIOR AND LISTENING. Speech educators have long been interested in studies of audience behavior. Rhetorical studies of speakers have taken into account the attitudes of audience members, as indicated by their reactions to speakers and their messages. Many studies of public address and radio-television communications have involved measurement of audience reactions. Techniques used in radio-audience analysis have been applied to theater audiences. Problems in communicating with mass audiences are also speech problems. Recently, experimenters have attempted to evaluate the effect of some controlled variables upon an audience. A few social psychologists, such as Hovland and others (1953), have studied attitude development and change. Cronkhite (1966) analyzed studies concerned with autonomic correlates of dissonance and attitude change. Other experimental researchers have been concerned with the problem of fear-arousing message appeals dependent upon the interaction of a variety of source, message, and receiver variables. Among these experimenters are Miller and Hewgill (1966), who analyzed the methodology and results of several of these studies.

A number of studies on listening have been done since Nichols (1948) brought the problem of listening to the attention of educators. Studies have revealed varied degrees of relationship between listening and reading skill. These relationships differ, depending upon the test used to measure listening or reading. Brown and Carlson (1951) have produced the most frequently used test of listening. Duker (1964) has prepared the most extensive bibliography on listening yet published.

ATTITUDES AND ADJUSTMENTS OF SPEAKERS. Speakers' attitudes have been studied extensively. Barnes (1940) defined adjustment, stated the objective of adjustment to be achieved by speakers, and specified both positive and negative characteristics of well-adjusted speakers. Knower (1938) studied the speech attitudes and adjustments of high school and college speakers. Gilkinson (1942), Henrikson (1943), Dickens and others (1950), Dickens and Parker (1951), Paulson (1951), and Greenleaf (1952) have done studies designed to measure symptoms and causes of speech fright. Three approaches are evident in these studies: (1) introspective reports by speakers of their speech fright, (2) reports by observers of speakers in speechmaking situations, and (3) reports by qualified medical personnel of the physiological changes in speakers *before, during,* and *after* their speaking. These studies indicate that the problem of speech fright is common, bothersome to speakers, more typical of poor speakers, and subject to solution by developing confidence through training in speech.

SPEECH AND HEARING DISORDERS. Students of speech and hearing disorders are typically concerned with speakers whose speech is defective. The American Speech and Hearing Association Committee on Legislation (1963) reported that 5 percent of school-age children and 1.3 percent of children under five years of age had serious speech defects, and another 5 percent had minor voice and speech defects, or speech which noticeably interfered with their communication. Eisenson and Ogilvie (1963) stated that about 75 percent of the speech defects in a school population are articulatory—one of eight types. Many children with speech and hearing problems of lesser, or even greater, severity are not speech-defective and do not require therapy by a speech correctionist: for example, incorrect formation of audible symbols due to immaturity, substandard language usage and pronunciation, unsatisfactory oral reading, and psychological disturbances reflected in speech. Dysfluencies in the speech of young children are sometimes mistakenly identified by parents and teachers as stuttering. Parental and teacher anxiety about the speech problems of young children can put them in a state of anxiety and result in their developing speech defects. Speech clinicians, with the help of teachers trained to hear symptoms of the various speech defects, use three methods to enable them to determine the extent of children's speech disorders: (1) referral by parents and teachers, (2) survey by the clinicians, and (3) class visits by the clinicians. For descriptions of stages of speech development, speech defects, theories and practices of speech diagnosticians and therapists, and summaries of research, the works of Hahn (1943), Irwin (1953), Van Riper (1954), Johnson and others (1956), West and others (1957), Darley and Winitz (1961), and Eisenson and Ogilvie (1963) can be helpful. Also, the American Speech and Hearing Association publishes regularly the *Journal of Speech and Hearing Disorders* and the *Journal of Speech and Hearing Research.*

Students in this area are concerned with hearing

problems and the relationships between hearing impairment and language and speech learning. Studies of various segments of the school population have resulted in estimates that impaired hearing in school-age children varies from 5 to 10 percent. The variation in the estimate depends on different interpretations of hearing impairment. In testing such problems, speech researchers and clinicians have drawn close to doctors of medicine, partly because a persistent problem in the testing of hearing is one of differential diagnosis of the person with organic defects in contrast with the functionally defective or the malingerer. A hearing impairment, even if very slight and undetected except by periodic audiometric tests, has been found to account for faulty attitudes and behavior of children in social situations. Davis and Silverman (1960) presented the results of surveys and expositions of hearing problems and lucidly explained the research concerning testing instruments and methods used to determine the types, degree, and implications of hearing impairment for language and speech development. More recent studies are reported in *Deafness, Speech and Hearing Abstracts,* published quarterly by the American Speech and Hearing Association and Gallaudet College, and in publications by the American Hearing Society. Much progress is evident in the development of lipreading and hearing aids to compensate for hearing loss in children and adults, as described in the literature of special education.

LANGUAGE AND LINGUISTICS. Scholars in speech as well as those in other areas have used a variety of research methods in studying problems in language and linguistics. Basic to these studies are the works of Scott and others (1935), Hayakawa (1941), and Pei (1949). W. Johnson (1946) and Black and Moore (1955) applied general semantics to speech education. Matthews (1947) studied the effect of loaded language on audience comprehension of speech. Black (1954) and Fairbanks (1954) used concepts of information theory in the study of language. Andersch and Staats (1960) recorded steps for the improvement of language in speaking. Attempts have been made to use readability formulas as indices of language difficulty. Some studies indicate no relation between indices of reading ease and difficulty of language usage in speech. Other studies have indicated that listeners can more easily comprehend and retain material presented in a style graded as easy than material presented in a style graded as difficult. The meaning of language and the differences and similarities between spoken and written language persist as problems, as indicated by Gibson and others (1966). The work of Osgood and others (1965) offers comprehensive surveys and analyses of theory and research in psycholinguistics and prospects for advancement in understanding the processes of encoding and decoding as they relate states of messages to states of communicators transformed into signals and, in turn, transformed into the interpretations of hearers. This whole area is beginning to challenge the efforts of scholars in communications research.

VOICE AND SPEECH RESEARCH. Research in voice reveals conflicts between the findings and the concepts reflected in much of the earlier literature. Gray and Wise (1959) analyzed the results of studies devoted to the testing of hypotheses in this area of study. For example, Huyck and Allen's (1937) investigation of the diaphragmatic action of good and poor speaking voices suggested that the control and direction of respiration were more important than a great quantity of air for sustained voice loudness. They supported the conclusion that a greater quantity of air was required to sustain a voiceless whisper than to sustain voice loudness. Hanley and Thurman (1962) concluded from their study that the ratio of inhalation time to exhalation time is about 1:1 in relaxed life breathing but that the ratio averages about 1:7 in inhalation and exhalation for speech. Fairbanks (1954) and Black (1954) illustrated the value for research of systematic conceptions or models. Recently, interest has been manifested in the use of intelligibility and other testing programs as devices for developing more objective evaluation of voice performance and the practical application of voice skills in speech activities on the telephone, between personnel in aircraft, and between personnel in a variety of military situations. The employment of voice skills between personnel in spacecraft and their control stations has opened a new field of study. Black and others (1967) have cited background research studies in this area in an exposition of their research on a self-administered procedure for altering intelligibility.

Studies in this area suggest a number of conclusions. The optimal rate of speaking appears to be approximately 125 to 150 words per minute, but rate varies considerably about any normative figure. The pitch of female voices exhibits a narrower range in frequency than that of male voices. The efficiency of voice in speaking is increased by predominance of lower pitch levels. The production of various vowel sounds influences some voice qualities. Efficient resonance is associated with enlargement of the pharyngeal cavity. The degree of voice nasality is known to vary with sound-pressure levels. A study of voice rating indicates that vocal quality has little relation to the voice characteristics of the rater. Vocal tones are known to influence understanding. Voice, enunciation, and articulation can be improved through training. Criteria for evaluation of voice and speech usage in speaking are available in much of the literature.

DISCUSSION, DEBATE, AND PARLIAMENTARY PROCEDURE. The subject of discussion has challenged the research efforts of many scholars. Dickens and Heffernan (1949), Auer (1953), and Golembiewski (1962) analyzed much of the research in group discussion. The discussion process seems to be closely allied by most writers with the concept of thinking by an individual as explained in John Dewey's *How We Think* (1933): a felt difficulty, definition and analysis of the problem, citation and consideration of the possible solutions, choice of the most workable and beneficial solution in the situation, consideration of the circumstances, and determination of means by which the best solution can be put into effect. McBurney and Hance (1950), Haiman (1951), and Harnack and Fest (1964) pointed out principles, practices, and types of discussion which are of interest to students of speech. Glaser (1941) and A. Johnson (1943) made available two of the best tests designed to measure problem-solving ability and critical thinking.

Debate has a long history in human endeavor and as a school activity. Such great encounters as the Webster-Hayne and Lincoln-Douglas debates have stimulated research efforts by a number of scholars. Interscholastic and intercollegiate debating has been indicted as a highly competitive enterprise, but it has been staunchly defended by many who deny that any of the alleged evils are inherent in debate. Based on much experience and keen insight, many works on argumentation and debate present information of interest to students of speech. Kruger (1964) compiled a classified bibliography on argumentation and debate which includes citations of earlier bibliographies.

Parliamentary procedure has been subjected to little research analysis. Most of the works on parliamentary procedure reflect close attention of writers to the work by Robert (1915). Gray (1964) stated points of emphasis in teaching parliamentary procedure.

The Speech Association of America publishes many articles on these and other areas of speech in its three publications: *Quarterly Journal of Speech, Speech Monographs,* and *Speech Teacher.*

ORAL INTERPRETATION OF LITERATURE. Oral or interpretative reading attracts a few research scholars and some teachers each year who do a limited number of studies. Theories of reading have been analyzed and developed, and instructional programs have evolved as research projects. A common type of study has involved the analysis for reading of some literary work or the works of some famous literary figure. Little research has been reported on the high school declamation program, which is probably the most widely used form of speech activity in interscholastic festivals and tournaments. Baffling questions provoke conflicts among students and teachers concerned with the meaning of reading aloud, oral interpretation, declamation, acting, play reading, and readers' or interpreters' theater. Other disagreements arise regarding the classification and quality of selections, reading from "the printed page" or from memory, and bodily action appropriate for use by oral interpreters. Some recent studies reported are those of Coger (1963), who presented a definition of readers' theater, a summation of its history, and an analysis of contemporary productions; of Geiger (1963), who analyzed applications of theories of oral interpretation in view of what is known about contemporary literary criticism; and of Kleinau and Kleinau (1965), who analyzed readers' theater as a means of effectively communicating a given piece of literature.

THEATER ARTS. The theater arts have long been most attractive as an area for research in the field of speech. The greatest number of these studies appear to be critical or historical in nature, but an increasing number seem to involve the creative tasks of playwriting and play production. A limited number have involved quantitative and experimental research.

Research topics in theater run a gamut from the history of the theater, extending back to perhaps 4000 B.C., to principles of business management in the modern theater. Playwrights of all ages and from all continents, great actors of the past and present, directors and producers, scenic designers, theater architects, and critics continue to provide abundant subject matter for research designed to develop greater insight into this popular art form. Variations in dramatic art form have been traced with painstaking care. Many studies of theaters as they have developed and are operated in specific communities are completed annually. Specialized forms of theater such as children's theater, radio-television, religious theater, and professional theater receive much attention by scholars in the theater arts. Recently, research in motion pictures seems to have increased, perhaps as a result of increased instruction in cinema and greater respect for the art form and techniques employed in cinema. Research in this area may be encouraged by a growing interest in instruction, programming, production, and research in radio and television dramatics and its real and potential impact on viewers. Detailed consideration of the educational impact of theater experience on both participant and audience has appeared to be of less concern to the theater artist than are the satisfactions derived from seeing the performance of a play. The advent of radio and television theater may cause researchers to develop greater interest in studying the effect a performance has on the audience. Some notice has been taken of developments in creative dramatics and in educational approaches to acting in the lower levels of elementary education through secondary education to higher education.

The Educational Theatre Journal, published by the American Educational Theatre Association, provides a regular channel for publication of research in the theater arts. The most extensive bibliography in theater arts, consisting of 4,063 titles, was compiled and edited by Melnitz (1959), who updated McDowell's bibliography on theater and drama, encompassing the period 1936–46.

RADIO-TELEVISION-FILM. Radio-television-film is a new, rich, and rapidly growing area for research and teaching in speech. Since the beginnings of commercial radio in the early 1920's and the slow development of television in the 1930's and 1940's, broadcasting and broadcasters have been confronted with multifarious demands and expectations by various segments of society. Business and industry have demanded prime time for selling goods and services; educational institutions, an opportunity for extending knowledge and influence for social betterment; financial interests, safe investment opportunities with prospects for lucrative returns; broadcasters, opportunity to gain a livelihood, power, and professional status and to give service; and government, prime time for disseminating information of concern to the general public. The expectations of listeners and viewers have centered on entertainment and information beneficial to them, without cost beyond the price of their receivers and their expenditure of time and without obligation or responsibility on their part.

With an estimated 6,000 radio and 800 television stations on the air and 230 million radio and 75 million television sets in the United States (U.S. Information Agency & Federal Communications Commission, 1967), various forms of public address, including discussion and debate, theatrical performances, school curricula and extraclass activities, religious services, and much of the old New England town meeting, have been channeled into homes and school classrooms. These developments in the mass communications media of radio and television have invited renewed research on many topics long studied in speech, such as audience behavior when confronted by persuasive speaking and subtle persuaders, speaker-message adjustment and impact, voice and speech usage, public address, and theater arts. As Becker and Harshbarger (1958) stated,

> ... speaking on television is not different in kind from any speech situation which has occurred since the dawn of history. Any speech begins with an idea in someone's brain. For television, this idea is translated into aural and visual symbols, transmitted, and received. It is then translated from the aural and visual symbols back into an idea. . . . The message may be distorted if we use the medium improperly.

Use of the medium led to concern with problems of programming in radio broadcasting, which resulted in patterns of organization used later in television. The most numerous studies were of the radio audience and of educational broadcasting, respectively, as listed by Thonssen and Fatherson (1939). The social implications of mass communication by radio made evident a variety of topics for study by students of speech—topics that were related to the art of speaking by announcers, newscasters, advertisers, and political speakers, for example. Radio play production embraced many topics for study. Several rhetorical research studies grew out of radio broadcasts of presidential campaign speeches, such as Brandenburg's (1949) investigation of speech preparation by Franklin D. Roosevelt, Crowell's (1950) study of Franklin D. Roosevelt's audience persuasion, and Bormann's (1957) research on the national radio broadcasts of Senator Huey P. Long. Likewise, the later development of television challenged speech scholars to focus research on speaking in the McCarthy hearings, the Kennedy-Nixon debates, the national political conventions, the United Nations sessions, the speeches of government officials, and the expositions and course offerings of educators. As the number of local television stations and regional and national networks increased, unlimited dramatic performances challenged the research efforts of students in speech in all phases of theater arts. The evolution and use of picture transmission on television stimulated interest in new art forms and techniques in films. In recent annual reports of research in *Speech Monographs*, studies of films refer to critical analyses of advertising, standards of excellence of American feature films, documentary films, South African broadcasting and educational films, and film experience in England. For an understanding of concepts, practices, and background of radio-television-film, many recent works are available, such as those by Baddeley (1963), Becker and Harshbarger (1958), Bluem and Mannell (1967), Fielding (1965), Geduld (1967), Giraud and others (1963), Herdeg (1967), Hilliard (1964), Jones (1965), MacCann (1966), Rubin (1967), Simonson (1966), Steinberg (1966), Summers and Summers (1966), Taylor (1967), Willis (1967), and Zettl (1961).

Publications of the Speech Association of America and *The Journal of Broadcasting* provide outlets for research in this area.

SPEECH TEACHING. Teaching speech occurs with many organizational patterns in homes and in all grade levels, beginning in kindergarten and extending through graduate college and professional education. Huckleberry and Strother (1966) cited and utilized much research by earlier investigators in their exposition of an elementary school curriculum in speech education.

In a high school, the objectives and desired outcomes of teaching speech in the curriculum and in extraclass activities are to be determined by a teacher of speech who possesses the qualifications to develop the program and to gain recognition for its values from students, parents, other teachers, and administrators. Some schools have rich and extensive programs in both curricular and extraclass speech education. States with the most extensive programs have substantial curricular teaching of speech in a large majority of the high schools. All states have speech instruction in extraclass speech activities such as oral interpretation, play production, and debate in high schools and interscholastic speech activities among high schools. Over 90 percent of the states have statewide associations and leagues which sponsor interscholastic debating and which are represented in the annual meetings of the advisory council of the National Committee on Discussion and Debate. The North Central Association of Colleges and Secondary Schools worked in cooperation with the Speech Association of America (McBurney, 1951) in formulating a program basic to the teaching of speech in high schools. The National Association of Secondary School Principals has for a number of years devoted full issues of its *Bulletin* to "Speech Education for All American Youth," "Dramatics in the Secondary School," "Speech and Hearing Problems in the Secondary School," "Public Address in the Secondary School," and "A Speech Program for the Secondary

School." Abundant texts in each area of speech education are available for use in the high school and in programs designed for preparation of teachers of speech in colleges and universities. Several texts on the teaching of speech are available to teachers and potential teachers of speech. Balcer and Seabury's book (1965) includes a selected bibliography of these texts for high school students and teachers.

In adult speech education, concepts and practices of speech, speaking, speechmaking, and listening have been adapted to serve business and professional men and women. Clapp (1920), Hoffman (1923), DuBois (1926), and Carnegie (1926) were some of the early contributors to this special type of speech education. Since Sandford and Yeager (1929) made available a major book on business and professional speaking, innumerable special short courses in adult speech education have been organized and taught to personnel in business, government, industry, labor unions, military services, and professions. The appeal and growth of these special types of programs and course offerings have probably resulted in no small measure from successful efforts by students of speech to analyze the communication needs and abilities of men and women in many kinds of communication situations and to develop programs and courses to serve the personnel involved in these situations.

In colleges and universities, programs in the broad discipline of speech and in the professional preparation of teachers of speech are numerous. Most college speech curricula are in the liberal arts tradition in colleges of arts and sciences. Some specific courses recommended for speech majors on the undergraduate and graduate levels are offered in other colleges. The point is that the curricula for speech majors have no set pattern, and the courses are not confined to the offerings in any one college or in any one department in colleges of arts and sciences. Flexibility in course planning permits students and their advisors to select courses in any college or colleges which hold promise for strengthening the programs of study for the students. The Educational Testing Service provides a Graduate Record Examination in speech. Hargis (1950) provided a comprehensive picture of the undergraduate program for speech majors. Some success has been achieved in determining the background and potential of students as a basis for admission to college speech programs and for the planning of programs for students who gain admission. State requirements for certification of teachers are reflected in the professional requirements and course offerings in programs of professional preparation for teachers of speech. These programs are usually conducted in colleges of education, or in departments of education in small colleges.

The broad academic and professional interests of teachers of speech have led to the development of various types of interdepartmental programs in communication, language arts, and rhetoric. For example, Michigan State University developed a junior-college skills program, as described by Bagwell (1945), and an upper division of communication arts in the university. Other universities have experimented with different kinds of communication programs, courses, methods of teaching, and evaluation of instruction. Programs in senior colleges and graduate colleges lean heavily upon the development of programs of instruction based on insights gained through scholarly and field research. Probably the most helpful guide to research in speech and dramatic art was prepared by Brockett and others (1963).

Hugh F. Seabury
University of Iowa

References

American Speech and Hearing Association Committee on Legislation. "1959 Report." In Eisenson, Jon, and Ogilvie, Mardel. (Eds.) *Speech Correction in the Schools*. Macmillan, 1963. 399p.

Andersch, Elizabeth G., and Staats, Lorin C. *Speech for Everyday Use*. Holt, 1960. 329p.

Auer, J. Jeffery. "Recent Literature in Discussion." *Q J Speech* 39:95–8; 1953.

Auer, J. Jeffery. *An Introduction to Research in Speech*. Harper, 1959. 244p.

Baddeley, Hugh. *The Technique of Documentary Film Production*. Hastings, 1963. 256p.

Bagwell, Paul. "A Composite Course in Speaking and Writing." *Q J Speech* 31:79–87; 1945.

Baird, A. Craig. *American Public Addresses, 1740–1952*. McGraw-Hill, 1956. 331p.

Balcer, Charles L., and Seabury, Hugh F. *Teaching Speech in Today's Secondary Schools*. Holt, 1965. 435p.

Baldwin, Charles S. *Medieval Rhetoric and Poetic*. Macmillan, 1928. 321p.

Barnes, Harry G. "A Philosophy of Speech Education." *Q J Speech* 26:585–8; 1940.

Becker, Samuel L., and Harshbarger, H. Clay. *Television: Techniques for Planning and Performance*. Holt, 1958. 182p.

Black, John W. "Systematic Research in Experimental Phonetics, Signal Reception: Intelligibility and Sidetone." *J Speech Hearing Disorders* 19:140–6; 1954.

Black, John W., and Moore, Wilbur E. *Speech: Code, Meaning, and Communication*. McGraw-Hill, 1955. 430p.

Black, John W., and others. "Altering Intelligibility through a Self-administered Procedure." *Q J Speech* 53:361–4; 1967.

Blanton, Smiley. "Editorial." *Q J Speech* 1:304; 1915.

Bluem, A. William, and Mannell, Roger. (Eds.) *Television: The Creative Experience*. Hastings, 1967. 328p.

Bormann, Ernest J. "A Rhetorical Analysis of the National Radio Broadcasts of Senator Huey Pierce Long." *Speech Monogr* 24:244–57; 1957.

Brandenburg, Ernest. "The Preparation of Franklin D. Roosevelt's Speeches." *Q J Speech* 35:214–21; 1949.

Brembeck, Winston L., and Howell, William S. *Persuasion*. Prentice-Hall, 1952. 488p.

Brigance, William N. (Ed.) *History and Criticism of American Public Address.* 2 Vols. McGraw-Hill, 1943. 1030p.

Brockett, Oscar G., and others. *A Bibliographical Guide to Research in Speech and Dramatic Art.* Scott, 1963. 118p.

Brown, Charles T. "Studies in Listening Comprehension." *Speech Monogr* 26:288–94; 1959.

Brown, James I., and Carlson, G. Robert. *Brown-Carlson Listening Comprehension Test.* Harcourt, 1951.

Butler, H. E. (Trans.) *The Institio Oratoria* (Quintilian). 4 Vols. Putnam, 1920.

Bywater, Ingram. "De Poetica." In Ross, W. D. (Ed.) *The Works of Aristotle.* Clarendon, 1924. p. 1447a–62b.

Carnegie, Dale. *Public Speaking.* 2 Vols. Association Press, 1926.

Clapp, John M. *Talking Business.* Ronald, 1920. 526p.

Cleary, James W. "John Bulwer's Chirologia . . . Chironomia: A Facsimile Ed. with Introduction and Notes." *Speech Monogr* 24:88; 1957.

Coger, Leslie Irene. "Interpreters Theatre: Theatre of the Mind." *Q J Speech* 49:157–64; 1963.

Cooper, Lane. *The Poetics of Aristotle: Its Meaning and Influence.* McKay, 1927. 148p.

Cronkhite, Gary. "Autonomic Correlates of Dissonance and Attitude Change." *Speech Monogr* 33:392–9; 1966.

Crowell, Laura. "Franklin D. Roosevelt's Audience Persuasion in the 1936 Campaign." *Speech Monogr* 17:48–64; 1950.

Cubberley, Ellwood P. *History of Education.* Houghton, 1920. 849p.

Darley, F. L., and Winitz, H. "Age of First Word: Review of Research." *J Speech Hearing Disorders* 26:272–90; 1961.

Davis, Hallowell, and Silverman, S. Richard. (Eds.) *Hearing and Deafness,* rev. ed. Holt, 1960. 573p.

Dewey, John. *How We Think.* Heath, 1933. 310p.

Dickens, Milton, and Hefferman, Marguerite. "Experimental Research in Group Discussion." *Q J Speech* 35:23–9; 1949.

Dickens, Milton, and Parker, William R. "An Experimental Study of Certain Physiological, Introspective, and Rating-scale Techniques for the Measurement of Stage Fright." *Speech Monogr* 18:251–9; 1951.

Dickens, Milton, and others. "An Experimental Study of the Overt Manifestations of Stage Fright." *Speech Monogr* 17:37–47; 1950.

DuBois, Warren C. *Essentials of Public Speaking.* Macmillan, 1926. 268p.

Duker, Sam. *Listening Bibliography.* Scarecrow, 1964. 211p.

Ehninger, Douglas. "John Ward and His Rhetoric." *Speech Monogr* 18:1–16; 1951.

Eisenson, Jon, and Ogilvie, Mardel. *Speech Correction in the Schools,* rev. ed. Macmillan, 1963. 399p.

Evans, Dina R. "The High School State—A Laboratory for Personality Development." *Nat Assn Sec Sch Prin B* 32:74–81; 1948.

Fairbanks, Grant. "Systematic Research in Experimental Phonetics: A Theory of the Speech Mechanism as a Servo-mechanism." *J Speech Hearing Disorders* 19:133–9; 1954.

Fielding, Raymond. *The Technique of Special Effects Cinematography.* Hastings, 1965. 396p.

Fotheringham, Wallace. "Measuring Speech Effectiveness." *Speech Monogr* 23:31–7; 1956.

Freedley, George, and Reeves, John A. *A History of the Theatre.* Crown, 1941. 688p.

Geduld, Harry M. (Ed.) *Film Makers on Film Making.* Indiana U, 1967. 288p.

Geiger, Don. *The Sound, Sense, and Performance of Literature.* Scott, 1963. 115p.

Gibson, James W., and others. "A Quantitative Examination of Differences and Similarities in Written and Spoken Messages." *Speech Monogr* 33:444–51; 1966.

Gilkinson, Howard. "Social Fears as Reported by Students in College Speech Classes." *Speech Monogr* 9:141–60; 1942.

Giraud, Chester, and others. *Television and Radio: An Introduction,* 3rd ed. Appleton, 1963. 659p.

Glaser, Edward M. *An Experiment in the Development of Critical Thinking.* Columbia U, 1941. 212p.

Golembiewski, Robert T. *The Small Group.* U Chicago, 1962. 303p.

Goodrich, Chauncey Allen. *Select British Eloquence.* Harper, 1875. 947p.

Gray, Giles Wilkeson. "Points of Emphasis in Teaching Parliamentary Procedure." *Speech Teach* 13:10–5; 1964.

Gray, Giles W., and Wise, Claude M. *The Bases of Speech,* 3rd ed. Harper, 1959. 562p.

Greenleaf, Floyd I. "An Exploratory Study of Speech Fright." *Q J Speech* 38:326–30; 1952.

Gunn, Battiscombe. "The Instruction of Ptah-ho-tep and the Instruction of Kegemmi: The Oldest Books in the World." In Sylvester, Charles H. (Ed.) *The Writings of Mankind,* Vol. 2. Bellows Reeve, 1924. 748p.

Guthrie, Warren A. "The Development of Rhetorical Theory in America, 1635–1850." *Speech Monogr* 15:61–71; 1948.

Hahn, Eugene F. *Stuttering: Significant Theories and Therapies.* Stanford U, 1943. 177p.

Haiman, Franklyn S. *Group Leadership and Democratic Action.* Houghton, 1951. 309p.

Hanley, Theodore D., and Thurman, Wayne L. *Developing Vocal Skills.* Holt, 1962. 197p.

Hargis, Donald E. "The General Speech Major." *Q J Speech* 36:71–7; 1950.

Harnack, R. Victor, and Fest, Thorrel B. *Group Discussion Theory and Technique.* Appleton, 1964. 456p.

Hayakawa, Samuel I. *Language in Action.* Harcourt, 1941. 345p.

Henrikson, Ernest H. "Some Effects on Stage Fright of a Course in Speech." *Q J Speech* 29:490–1; 1943.

Herdeg, Walter. (Ed.) *Film and TV Graphics.* Hastings, 1967. 200p.

Hilliard, Robert L. (Ed.) *Understanding Television:*

An Introduction to Broadcasting. Hastings, 1964. 256p.

Hockmuth, Marie. "Speech and Society." *Nat Assn Sec Sch Prin B* 32:32; 1948.

Hoffman, William G. *Public Speaking for Business Men.* McGraw-Hill, 1923. 300p.

Hovland, Carl I., and others. *Communication and Persuasion.* Yale U, 1953. 315p.

Howell, Wilbur S. *Fenelon's Dialogues on Eloquence, A Translation with an Introduction and Notes.* Princeton U, 1951. 160p.

Hubbeull, H. M. (Trans.) *De Inventione* (Cicero). Harvard U Press, 1949. 466p.

Huckleberry, Alan W., and Strother, Edward S. *Speech Education for the Elementary Teacher.* Allyn, 1966. 280p.

Huyck, Mary E., and Allen, Kenneth D. A. "Diaphragmatic Action of Good and Poor Speaking Voices." *Speech Monogr* 4:101–9; 1937.

Hyde, Stuart, W. *Television and Radio Announcing.* Houghton, 1959. 451p.

Irwin, Ruth B. *Speech and Hearing Therapy.* Prentice-Hall, 1953. 243p.

Jebb, Richard Claverhouse. *The Attic Orators.* 2 Vols. Macmillan, 1876.

Johnson, Alma. "An Experimental Study in the Analysis and Measurement of Reflective Thinking." *Speech Monogr* 10:83–96; 1943.

Johnson, Wendell. *People in Quandaries.* Harper, 1946. 532p.

Johnson, Wendell, and others. *Speech Handicapped School Children,* rev. ed. Harper, 1956. 575p.

Jones, Peter. *The Technique of the Television Cameraman.* Hastings, 1965. 243p.

Jowett, Benjamin. (Trans.) *The Republic* (Plato). Harcourt, 1946. 383p.

Kleinau, Marion L., and Kleinau, Marvin D. "Scene Location in Readers Theatre: Static or Dynamic?" *Speech Teach* 14:193–9; 1965.

Knower, Franklin H. "A Study of Speech Attitudes and Adjustments." *Speech Monogr* 5:130–1; 1938.

Knower, Franklin H. (Ed.) "Graduate Theses: An Index of Graduate Work in Speech." *Speech Monogr* 34:321–76; 1967.

Kruger, Arthur N. *A Classified Bibliography of Argumentation and Debate.* Scarecrow, 1964. 400p.

Lawton, Sherman P. *The Modern Broadcaster: The Station Book.* Harper, 1961. 350p.

MacCann, Richard D. *Film: A Montage of Theories.* Dutton, 1966. 384p.

Matthews, Jack. "The Effects of Loaded Language on Audience Comprehension of Speeches." *Speech Monogr* 14:176–86; 1947.

McBurney, James H. (Ch.) "A Program of Speech Education." *Q J Speech* 37:347–58; 1951.

McBurney, James H., and Hance, Kenneth G. *Discussion in Human Affairs.* Harper, 1950. 432p.

Melnitz, William W. *Theatre Arts Publications in the United States, 1947–1952.* American Educational Theatre Association, 1959. 91p.

Miller, Gerald R., and Hewgill, Murray A. "Some Recent Research on Fear-arousing Message Appeals." *Speech Monogr* 33:337–91; 1966.

National Education Association and National Association of Secondary School Principals. "Speech Education for All American Youth." *Bulletin* No. 151 1948. 238p.

National Education Association and National Association of Secondary School Principals. "Dramatics in the Secondary School." *Bulletin* No. 166, 1949. 272p.

National Education Association and National Association of Secondary School Principals. "Speech and Hearing Problems in the Secondary School." *Bulletin* No. 173. 1950. 140p.

National Education Association and National Association of Secondary School Principals. "Public Address in the Secondary School." *Bulletin* No. 187, 1952. 318p.

National Education Association and National Association of Secondary School Principals. "A Speech Program for the Secondary School." *Bulletin* No. 199, 1954. 300p.

Nichols, Ralph G. "Factors in Listening Comprehension." *Speech Monogr* 15:154–63; 1948.

O'Neill, James M. "The National Association." *Q J Speech* 1:56–7; 1915.

O'Neill, James M., and Weaver, Andrew T. *The Elements of Speech.* McKay, 1926. 477p.

Oringel, Robert S. *Audio Control Handbook: For Radio and TV Broadcasting,* rev. ed. Hastings, 1963. 160p.

Osgood, Charles E., and others. *Psycholinguistics.* Indiana U, 1965. 307p.

Paulson, Stanley F. "Changes in Confidence during a Period of Speech Training: Transfer of Training and Comparison of Improved and Non-improved Groups on the Bell Adjustment Inventory." *Speech Monogr* 18:260–5; 1951.

Pei, Mario. *The Story of Language.* Lippincott, 1949. 493p.

Robert, Henry M. *Rules of Order Revised.* Scott, 1915. 323p.

Roe, Yale. (Ed.) *Television Station Management.* Hastings, 1964. 251p.

Ross, Rodger J. *Television Film Engineering.* Wiley, 1966. 507p.

Ross, Walter A. (Ed.) *Best TV Commercials of the Year.* Hastings, 1967. 190p.

Rubin, Bernard. *Political Television.* Wadsworth, 1967. 200p.

Sandford, William Phillips, and Yeager, Willard Hayes. *Business and Professional Speaking.* McGraw-Hill, 1929. 374p.

Scott, Harry F., and others. *Language and Its Growth: An Introduction to the History of Language.* Scott, 1935. 389p.

Simonson, Solomon. *Crisis in Television.* Living Books, 1966. 229p.

Steinberg, Charles S. (Ed.) *Mass Media and Communication.* Hastings, 1966. 530p.

Summers, Robert E., and Summers, Harrison B. *Broadcasting and the Public.* Wadsworth, 1966. 416p.

Sutton, E. W. (Trans.) *De Oratore* (Cicero). 2 Vols. Harvard U Press, 1959.

Taylor, Sherril W. *Radio Programming in Action: Realities and Opportunities.* Hastings, 1967. 192p.

Thompson, Wayne N. *Quantitative Research in Public Address and Communication.* Random, 1967. 256p.

Thonssen, Lester, and Baird, A. Craig. *Speech Criticism: The Development of Standards of Rhetorical Appraisal.* Ronald, 1948. 542p.

Thonssen, Lester, and Fatherson, Elizabeth. (Comp.) *Bibliography of Speech Education.* Wilson, 1939. 800p.

Twining, Thomas. "Aristotle's Poetics." In Rhys, Ernest. (Ed.) Everyman's 1934. p. 5–60.

U.S. Information Agency and Federal Communications Commission. *Almanac Yearbook.* Reader's Digest Association, 1967. 1023p.

Van Riper, Charles G. *Speech Correction: Principles and Methods,* 3rd ed. Prentice-Hall, 1954. 582p.

Wallace, Karl R. (Ed.) *History of Speech Education in America: Background Studies.* Appleton, 1954. 687p.

West, Robert W., and others. *The Rehabilitation of Speech.* Harper, 1957. 688p.

Willis, Edgar E. *Writing Television and Radio Programs.* Holt, 1967. 384p.

Winans, James A. "The Need for Research." *Q J Speech* 1:17–8; 1915.

Woolbert, Charles H. "A Problem in Pragmatism." *Q J Speech* 2:264; 1916.

Zettl, Herbert. *Television Production Handbook.* Wadsworth, 1961. 461p.

SPEECH PATHOLOGY AND AUDIOLOGY

Within the past forty years speech pathology and audiology have developed as fields for scientific inquiry and training. However, many years before this period, there had been recognition by society of the needs of the speech and hearing handicapped. Responses by society have varied from rejection of the individual with speech and/or hearing problems to the development of carefully planned programs of rehabilitation. One could point to the Greek Demosthenes, in the fourth century B.C., who is said to have placed pebbles in his mouth to help correct his stuttered speech, as an early recognition that therapeutic measures could be worked out for disordered speech. From the fourth century B.C., too, one could point to the Chinese Chuang Tsu, as one who gave early recognition to the factors important to the development of oral language in children when he emphasized that children learn to talk by hearing others talk, not because they are specially taught. The importance of hearing to speech and language development was commented upon by Aristotle, also in the fourth century B.C., as he observed the absence of speech among those who were deaf (Fay, 1912). In the sixteenth century formalized training of the deaf got underway in Europe. This training was directed toward teaching of speech and language to the hearing handicapped. Such schools were started in Spain, France, Germany, and England. Early in the nineteenth century, an American by the name of Gallaudet studied methods of teaching the deaf in France and thereafter returned to America to establish a school in Hartford, Connecticut (Peet, 1852). By the turn of the century a number of similar schools had been started, and also by then there was growing interest in the approaches employed in the teaching of language communication. Some advocated the oral method, whereas others advocated the manual method, which utilized finger spelling and hand signs.

In the early decades of the twentieth century there was a growing awareness of the speech and hearing mechanisms per se, and also of speech problems not associated with hearing debility. Written contributions included those of Bell (1914), Scripture (1906), and Stetson and Hudgins (1930). These comprised some of the important foundations upon which experimental phonetics, as an area of scientific inquiry, was built. Much of the scientific research in speech pathology has stemmed from the findings of experimental phoneticians, and many of the methodologies employed have been those which have characterized the scientific research in later years in the field of experimental phonetics.

Between the second and fourth decades of the twentieth century, programs of service and training in speech pathology and audiology were initiated in several public schools and colleges in the United States. As early as 1910 the Chicago public school system provided a program of remedial services for children with speech handicaps (Wilson, 1961). Today there are remedial speech and hearing programs in the public schools of all 50 states.

In America, programs of clinical training and research in these fields have been established in colleges of arts and science, schools of education, and other institutions of learning. In Europe, these programs of training and service are most frequently carried out within medical settings.

Some of the most important professional and scholarly societies that deal with problems of speech pathology and audiology are:

The American Speech and Hearing Association
The International Association of Logopedics and Phoniatrics
The Council for Exceptional Children
The International Society for the Rehabilitation of the Disabled
The American Cleft Palate Association
International Society of Audiology

The journals of the American Speech and Hearing Association are *ASHA, Journal of Speech and Hearing Disorders,* and *Journal of Speech and Hearing Research.* This association, which has programs of individual and institutional certification, has a membership of approximately 16,000 and its national headquarters is located in Washington, D.C.

The study of speech pathology and audiology is

multidisciplinary in nature. In order to understand the complexities of these human functions, it is necessary to call upon information from other areas such as anatomy, physiology, neurology, physics, psychology, linguistics, medicine, engineering, and education. Speech pathology and audiology share a common core of information and information collecting procedures. Moreover, a specific vocabulary, concerned with normal and disordered functioning of the human systems of speech and audition has been developed for purposes of communication.

INSTRUCTIONAL AND SERVICE PROGRAMS IN SPEECH AND HEARING. Programs of instruction and service in speech and hearing are carried out at various levels. Although programs of service have been most in evidence for elementary schoolchildren, there has also been considerable activity at the secondary school level. More recently, increased activity in the service area has been noted at preschool and college levels. During the past ten years, such services have been greatly increased for the adult as well. These services are provided mainly in university, hospital, and community clinics. The monitoring of standards for service programs in the schools is carried out by state departments of education or health. Clinical services programs in universities, hospitals, and community centers have the opportunity of applying to the American Speech and Hearing Association for certification by its Professional Service Board.

In the elementary school programs, the aspect of speech most frequently defective is that of articulation (Johnson & others, 1947). Clinicians serving the public schools usually carry a case load of 75 to 100 children. Statistics show that about one-fourth of the speech clinicians in public schools work at all grade levels, approximately one-third work in elementary schools exclusively (kindergarter through grade 6), about one-third in kindergarten through grade 9, and some 2 percent work only at the high school level (Bingham & others, 1961).

The need for speech improvement programs is receiving more attention from educators and parents alike. Speech improvement differs from speech therapy for defective speakers in that it is designed for children with "normal" speech who need help in increasing their communication effectiveness through improvement of speech, voice quality, and language patterns. This type of activity is sometimes a part of language arts programs and, as such, is handled by the classroom teacher. However, since this type of work is closely akin to speech therapy, it sometimes becomes the responsibility of the school speech therapist to develop and conduct these programs. Irwin (1960) suggests that the speech therapist, even though mostly occupied with corrective work, should assume some responsibility for speech improvement problems in order to supplement or enhance his own efforts in the rehabilitation program. She suggests that the role of the therapist should be to:

1. Work with the classroom teacher to correlate speech rehabilitation with work done in the classroom.

2. Conduct in-service speech training insofar as it supplements or aids the speech rehabilitation program (provided that the therapist is trained and experienced).

3. Encourage teachers to take extension or summer courses in voice and diction, speech correction, and speech improvement for the classroom teacher.

4. Provide opportunities for the teacher to observe the therapist teach clinical speech classes.

5. Plan with those teachers who are interested specific lessons which will develop acceptable speech in the classroom.

Garrison (1961), in studying nine representative school systems, shows that there is a paucity of data relative to the organization and supervision of programs of speech improvement, as well as little material concerning preparation of personnel and evaluative criteria. Her study does reveal some other pertinent facts, however: (1) that the training level of persons working in speech improvement varies greatly and (2) that the percentage of persons holding master's degrees is about the same as those who hold no college degree. The greatest number (slightly less than 40 percent) hold bachelor's degrees and have done some graduate work. Speech improvement is concentrated in kindergarten, first, and second grades, with 58 percent of the teachers teaching it at this level. In terms of the effectiveness of speech improvement programs, the study showed that, in the judgment of the speech improvement teachers, 67 percent feel definitely that it helped their students to develop good speech, voice quality, and language patterns; 64 percent definitely felt it helped students correct minor speech and voice problems, and 57 percent felt it helped students express ideas clearly. Several other works give information concerning speech improvement: Lysaght (1960) has reviewed and abstracted the literature on speech improvement between 1946 and 1960; Pronovost (1959), Van Riper and Butler (1955), Ogilvie (1954), Scott and Thompson (1951), and Byrne (1965) have all contributed textual materials for use in speech improvement programs.

The status of education and training programs for speech pathology and audiology is best reflected by the report of Castle and others (1966). They point out that there are 247 known education and training programs and that 180 (73 percent) offer graduate degrees; 49 offer doctor's degrees, and the other 131 offer only the master's degree. The remaining 67 are preprofessional and offer degrees at the bachelor's level. Sixteen institutions offer postdoctoral programs, with a total of 33 postdoctoral students enrolled at the time of the report. In terms of types of training, 85 programs offer speech pathology, audiology, and nonclinical training, whereas 105 offer speech pathology and audiology exclusively. Five programs offer speech pathology and nonclinical training; one offers audiology and nonclinical; 49 offer speech pathology only, and one audiology only. There was but one program that offered only nonclinical training. As shown by the Castle study, the items listed most frequently as the most serious barriers to graduate program development were: (1) lack of financial support for students, (2) lack of financial support for additional faculty, (3) lack of qualified personnel for faculty, and (4) lack of space and facilities. In 1958, of the total number of degrees granted in speech and hearing programs, 76 percent were bachelor's, 21 percent were master's, and 3 percent were doctoral; by 1965, those percenatges had changed to 60, 36, and 4, respectively. This change reflects the growing emphasis on graduate education in the field.

RESEARCH IN SPEECH PATHOLOGY AND AUDIOLOGY. Both speech and hearing have been studied by many persons who vary markedly in interests, training, background, and purpose. Some have studied one without real concern for the other. For example, someone devoting his energies to the understanding of the electrophysiology of the auditory system might have little if any interest in the speed of movement of the velum in effecting velopharyngeal closure, or vice versa. Engineers, physiologists, neurologists, otolaryngologists, psychologists, linguists, physicists, and speech and hearing scientists have all made distinct contributions to the understanding of speech, language, and hearing processes. The speech pathologist and audiologist are centrally concerned with the functioning of the speech and hearing systems as they enhance or impede verbal symbolic communication. It is around this central fact that workers in the field rally, irrespective of the particular focus of their scientific investigations or clinical activities. Methodologies employed in investigations include chiefly the experimental and the descriptive.

PSYCHOACOUSTICS. Audiology. A number of areas of exploration have captured the interest of researchers in experimental audiology. These include automatic audiometry, auditory fatigue and adaptation, objective measurement of hearing through electrophysiologic techniques, and signal detectability. As a result, many studies have been carried out along the lines dictated by these varied interests.

The purpose of exploring and perfecting automatic audiometric techniques is to care for the growing number of individuals who are given audiometric examinations each year. In Stockholm Von Békésy (1947) described a new type of audiometer with a range of frequencies from 100 to 10,000 Hz (cycles per second). This new development permitted taking an audiogram by placing a microswitch in the hands of the subject, who controlled intensity as the instrument swept through the frequency dimension. Throughout the 1950's other automatic devices were developed by Rudmose (Glorig & Harris, 1957), Brogan (1955), Licklider, Ward, and Glorig (Webster, 1957).

Because noise levels are on the increase in the industrial and military spheres, there is growing concern over the threshold shifts that occur from prolonged exposure to noxious auditory stimuli. Ward (1963) summarizes work in this area and concludes that the problem of auditory fatigue is still perplexing, in that so many of the relevant research parameters are interactive. This problem may be clarified further when there are more data relative to the attenuation characteristics of the middle-ear muscles.

Auditory adaptation occurs, just as adaptation occurs in other sensory systems. Such adaptation, which is brought about by the stimulus itself, may vary along the pitch and intensity dimensions. Several techniques of measurement, including (1) alternate binaural balance, (2) delayed balance, (3) intensive and phase localization, (4) moving phantom, (5) simultaneous dichotic balances (varied intensity), and (6) asymtotic localization, are discussed by Small (1963), who concludes that the deterrent to the study of loudness adaptation is lack of a suitable technique of measurement.

Electrophysiological techniques for measurement of auditory function give promise of more objective assessment of hearing acuity. When these are perfected, one will not have to rely upon the overt response of the subject. Responses elicited with this general method are electrodermal responses (EDR) and electroencephalic responses (EER). Derbyshire and others (1956, 1966), Von Békésy (1961a, 1961b, 1962), and Goldstein (1966; Goldstein & Rosenblut, 1965; Goldstein & Derbyshire, 1957) have contributed substantially in this area.

In working toward a more inclusive theory of hearing, some investigators have employed the theory of signal detectability. As Clarke and Bilger (1963) point out, this approach shows promise in that it permits analysis of input information available to the observer and provides a way of analyzing and describing human performance. Moreover, it permits one to distinguish between the detectability of the observer and the observer criterion. Lastly, the measure of detectability obtained does not vary significantly with instructional variables.

Diagnostic Audiometry. Diagnostic or clinical audiology is concerned with the measurement of hearing level among those who have, or are suspected of having, a decrease in auditory function. Refinements have occurred in the testing of both children and adults over the past 15 years. The development of needed apparatus and methods in the field of audiometry reflects in part the scientific era in which we live, with its great emphasis on quantifying various aspects of human behavior (O'Neill & Oyer, 1966). Methods of measuring hearing have been developed over the past 140 years, as represented by the development of the Weber (1834), Rinne (1885), and Schwabach (1890) tests (Bunch, 1946). In 1878, one of the first attempts was made to construct a pure-tone audiometer that was electrically activated. Over the past 25 years, with refinements in electronics, many different types of audiometers have been developed. In addition to the routine air-conduction tests of threshold for pure tones, tests for bone conduction of sound have been constructed. Jerger and Tillman (1960) have referred to their modification of the Rainville (1959) technique for testing bone conduction as the test of Sensorineural Acuity Level (SAL). Earlier, Lightfoot (1960) also constructed a modified Rainville test. The three methods (Rainville, modified Rainville, and SAL) are all attempts at developing bone-conduction tests which are more accurate and which preclude confounding of results from cross-lateralization and masking.

Not only has it been found to be important to determine the air- and bone-conduction thresholds with pure tones, but it is of utmost importance to know how well or how poorly the person with suspected auditory deficit hears and discriminates among speech stimuli. To this end, tests consisting of words and sentences have been constructed by Hirsh and others (1952) and by Haskins (1949). Oyer and Doudna (1959, 1960) have found that the most common type of error response to the Hirsh lists is substitution of other than the correct word, and that the substitution type of error increases as less familiar words (as indicated by Thorndike and Lorge ratings) are presented to hard-of-hearing subjects. Carhart (1965) clarifies the problems involved in the measurement of speech discrimination and cautions against complete acceptance of the prevailing tests of discrimination. He points out that the need is for new tests, the items of which are tested against the kinds of backgrounds actually encountered in everyday listening situations.

Advanced audiometric tests have also been constructed for purposes of determining whether the loss is organic or functional and also of establishing the site of the lesion, if the failure is organic in nature. Jerger (1961) has contributed greatly in this area with the development of categories and refinement of analyses in Békésy audiometry.

Rehabilitative Audiology. Although aural rehabilitation has been engaged in for centuries, it has received far less attention by researchers than has diagnostic audiometry. There is growing concern over this fact, and in 1966 there was established an Academy of Rehabilitative Audiology, the purpose of which, in part, is to stimulate much-needed research in auditory training, lipreading, and language learning processes. Identification of the needs in aural rehabilitation has been accomplished quite thoroughly by several authors, who emphasize the need for additional investigations (O'Neill & Oyer, 1966; Oyer, 1966).

SPEECH AND LANGUAGE. Speech Science. Some scholars in the field of speech have registered interest in the information available in the field of linguistics. This is evident in the work of those desiring to understand more completely the vocal and articulatory systems, as well as in the research activity of those who seek to derive more complete knowledge regarding the development of speech and language patterns in children and of those who are involved in the study of aberrant speech and language patterns associated with central nervous system involvements, such as cerebral palsy and aphasia.

Fairbanks (1954), Black and others (1966), and Peterson and Shoup (1966) have all contributed to the understanding of the speaking system as a servo system; to the comprehension of intelligibility; and to the influence of linguistic and environmental factors on speech flow.

The vocal mechanism has received great attention in relation to the anatomical, physiological, neurological, and acoustic correlates. Hollien (1964, 1962) has shown that laminagraphic X-ray techniques are valid in vocal research. The early work of Negus (1949), Moore (Hollien & Moore, 1960), Russell (1931), and Fletcher (1954) has laid a foundation for current investigations.

Disorders of Speech and Language. The diagnosis and evaluation of speech and language problems comprise a large share of the work to which the speech pathologist devotes his time. Stuttering, functional articulatory disorders, speech disorders associated with cerebral palsy, cleft palate, aphasia, laryngeal speech, and voice problems of varied origins have all provided areas of investigation for research scholars; however, the amount of energy directed toward each of these disorders varies substantially.

Stuttering. Research on stuttering has been approached from several vantage points, which include theoretical considerations of causation and also practical considerations of therapy. There is a lack of agreement as to etiology, and suggestions for the management of the stutterer vary greatly. Some promising research is being conducted at the Ohio State University by Stromsta (1959), who is examining neurological correlates of stuttering. Many have contributed to the study of stuttering; particularly notable are the contributions of Johnson (1955), Van Riper (1954), Williams (1957), Sheehan (1958), and Wischener (1952), who have dealt specifically with theory relative to etiology as well as with therapeutic considerations.

Articulatory Problems. Functional articulatory problems, particularly noticeable among young children, constitute approximately 80 percent of speech problems among schoolchildren. The hope of therapists is to modify faulty articulation through habilitative or rehabilitative procedures. Griffith (1965) has found that she could, through instrumental conditioning (with candy as a reward), significantly improve articulatory performance of young children.

Cerebral Palsy and Cleft Palate. Disorders of speech associated with cerebral palsy and cleft palate are being studied with emphasis mainly upon physiological and intelligibility factors.

Aphasia. Aphasia in adults, a symbolic disorder, is brought about through disease and accidents. This disorder has received considerable attention following World War II, because of the prevalence of head injuries during that period. As an area for research, it has attracted many workers from a variety of disciplines. Tests have been developed by speech pathologists in an attempt to provide the clinician with instruments that provide a diagnostic profile of the language deficit. Schuell (1955) and Wepman and Jones (1961) have developed test instruments for this purpose.

Laryngectomy. Research in the area of laryngectomy has shown that removal of the larynx, because of cancer, has ramifications which go beyond the fact of losing a voice-producing system. Gardner (1964) points out that the number of laryngectomies in industry has increased over the past decade. A survey of these men has shown that 75 percent of them use esophageal speech. Opportunities for learning esophageal speech are available through university speech and hearing centers, as well as at community speech and hearing centers.

Evaluation. Evaluation of efforts expended by clinical workers in speech pathology and audiology presents a continuing problem. Rating scales and tests of intelligibility in speech pathology and audiology, as well as audiometric retest in audiology, comprise the major approaches utilized in determining the success of clinical treatment. Researchers in both speech pathology and audiology are constantly concerned with the development of more objective ways of evaluating the effectiveness of therapy. Since the ultimate goal in speech pathology and audiology is to enhance effectiveness in human communication, the evaluative criteria must continue to be those of degree of success in reception and perception of speech, the intelligibility of speech, and the adjustment of self and society to the handicap of disordered speech and/or hearing.

Herbert J. Oyer
Michigan State University

References

Bell, Alexander. *The Mechanism of Speech*. Funk, 1914.
Bingham, Dale S., and others. "IV Program Organization and Management." *J Speech Hearing Disorders,* Monogr Supplement 8:35; 1961.
Black, John W., and others. "Oral Copying of Heard Phrases." *J Speech Hearing Res* 9:542–5; 1966.
Brogan, F. A. "An Automatic Numerically Recording Audiometer." *J Acoustical Soc Am* 27:200; 1955.
Bunch, C. C. *Clinical Audiometry*. Mosby, 1946.
Byrne, Margaret C. *The Child Speaks*. Harper, 1965.
Carhart, Raymond. "Problems in the Measurement of Speech Discrimination." *Archives Otolaryngology* 82:253–60; 1965.
Castle, William E., and others. "The Status of Education And Training Programs For Speech Pathology And Audiology 1966." *J Am Speech Hearing Assn* 8:447–53; 1966.
Clarke, Frank R., and Bilger, Robert C. "The Theory of Signal Detectability And The Measurement of Hearing." In Jerger, James. (Ed.) *Modern Developments in Audiology*. Academic, 1963. p. 371–408.
Derbyshire, A. J., and others. "Electroencephalography." *J Clin Neurology* 8:467; 1956.
Fairbanks, Grant. "Systematic Research In Experimental Phonetics. 1. A Theory of the Speech Mechanism As A Servosystem." *J Speech Hearing Disorders* 19:133–9; 1954.

Fay, E. A. "What Did Lucretius Say?" *Am Annals Deaf* 57:213; 1912.
Fletcher, W. W. "Vocal Fold Activity and Subglottic Air Pressure In Relation To Vocal Intensity: A Brief Historical Review." *Speech Monogr* 21:73–8; 1954.
Gardner, Warren H. "Laryngectomies in Industry." *Archives Environmental Health* 9:777–89; 1964.
Garrison, Geraldine. "VII Speech Improvement." *J Speech Hearing Disorders* Monogr Supplement 8: 78–92; 1961.
Glorig, Aram, and Harris, J. D. "Audiometric Testing In Industry." In Harris, Cyril. (Ed.) *Handbook of Noise Control*. McGraw-Hill, 1957. p. 6–12.
Goldstein, Robert. "Clinical Use of EEA With An Average Response Computer: A Case Report." *J Speech Hearing Disorders* 31:75–8; 1966.
Goldstein, Robert, and Derbyshire, A. J. "Suggestions For Terms Applied to Electrophysiologic Tests of Hearing." *J Speech Hearing Disorders* 22:696–8; 1957.
Goldstein, Robert, and Rosenblut, B. "Factors Influencing Electrophysiologic Responsivity In Normal Adults." *J Speech Hearing Res* 8:323–47; 1965.
Griffith, J. "The Modification of Functional Articulation Errors Under Principles of Instrumental Conditioning." *Speech Monogr* 32:178–84; 1965.
Haskins, Harriet L. "A Phonetically Balanced Test of Speech Discrimination for Children." Master's thesis. Northwestern U, 1949.
Hirsh, I. J., and others. "Development of Materials for Speech Audiometry," *J Speech Hearing Disorders* 17:321–37; 1952.
Hollien, Harry. "Vocal Fold Thickness And Fundamental Frequency of Phonation." *J Speech Hearing Res* 5:237–43; 1962.
Hollien, Harry. "Laryngeal Research By Means of Laminagraphy." *Archives Otolaryngology* 80:303–8, 1964.
Hollien, Harry, and Moore, G. Paul. "Measurements of the Vocal Folds During Changes In Pitch." *J Speech Hearing Res* 3:157–65; 1960.
Irwin, Ruth B. "The Role of the Speech Therapist In The Speech Improvement Program." *Speech Teach* 9:278; 1960.
Jerger, James, and Tillman, Tom. "A New Method For Clinical Determination of Sensorineural Acuity Level (SAL)." *Archives Otolaryngology* 71:948–55; 1960.
Jerger, James. "Recruitment and Allied Phenomena in Differential Diagnosis." *J Auditory Res* 1:145–51; 1961.
Johnson, Wendell, and others. *Speech Handicapped School Children*. Harper, 1947.
Johnson, Wendell. *Stuttering In Children And Adults*. U Minnesota Press, 1955.
Lightfoot, Charles. "The M-R Test of Bone Conduction Hearing." *Laryngology* 70:1552–9; 1960.
Lysaght, Carol. "An Analysis of Literature Pertaining To Speech Improvement Programs In The Public Schools." Master's thesis. Boston U, 1960.
Negus, V. E. *The Comparative Anatomy and Physiology of the Larynx*. Grune, 1949.

Ogilvie, Mabel. *Speech In The Elementary School.* McGraw-Hill, 1954.

O'Neill, John J., and Oyer, Herbert J. *Visual Communication.* Prentice-Hall, 1961.

O'Neill, John J., and Oyer, Herbert J. *Applied Audiometry.* Dodd, 1966.

Oyer, Herbert J. *Auditory Communication.* Prentice-Hall, 1966.

Oyer, Herbert J., and Doudna, Mark. "Structural Analysis of Word Responses Made by Hard-of-Hearing Subjects on a Discrimination Test." *Archives Otolaryngology* 70:357–64; 1959.

Oyer, Herbert J., and Doudna, Mark. "Word Familiarity as a Factor in Testing Discrimination of Hard-of-Hearing Subjects." *Archives Otolaryngology* 72:351–5; 1960.

Oyer, Herbert J., and others. *Aural Rehabilitation of the Acoustically Handicapped.* Seminar Proceedings, VRA-Contract No. 66–41. Michigan State U SHSLR 266, 1966.

Peet, H. P. "Tribute To The Memory of the Late Thomas Gallaudet." *Am Annals Deaf* 4:65–77; 1852.

Peterson, Gordon, and Shoup, J. "The Elements of an Acoustic Phonetic Theory." *J Speech Hearing Res* 9:68–99; 1966.

Pronovost, Wilbert. *Teaching of Speech And Listenin the Elementary School.* McKay, 1959.

Rainville, M. J. "New Method of Masking for the Determination of Bone Conduction Curves." In Tonndorf, Juergen. (Ed.) *Translations of Beltone Institute for Hearing Research,* No. 11, 1959.

Russell, G. Oscar. "Motion Picture Demonstration of Normal Laryngeal Functions Which Block The View of the Glottal Lips." *Archives Otolaryngology Rhinology and Laryngology* 40:318–20; 1931.

Schuell, Hildred M. *Minnesota Test For Differential Diagnosis of Aphasia.* U Minn, 1955.

Scott, Louise B., and Thompson, J. J. *Talking Time.* Webster, 1951.

Scripture, E. W. *Researches In Experimental Phonetics.* Carnegie Institute of Washington, 1906.

Sheehan, Joseph. "Projective Studies of Stuttering." *J Speech Hearing Disorders* 23:18–24; 1958.

Siedentrop, K. H., and others. "Auditory Threshold Determination." *AMA Archives Otolaryngology* 83: 203–6; 1966.

Small, Arnold Jr. "Auditory Adaptation." In Jerger, James. (Ed.) *Modern Developments In Audiology.* Academic, 1963. p. 287–336.

Stetson, R. H., and Hudgins, C. V. "Functions of the Breathing Movements in the Mechanism of Speech." *Archives Neerlandaises de Phonet Exp* 5:1–30; 1930.

Stromsta, C. "Experimental Blockage of Phonation by Distorted Sidetone." *J Speech Hearing Res* 2: 286–301; 1959.

Van Riper, Charles. *Speech Correction Principles And Methods.* Prentice-Hall, 1954.

Van Riper, Charles, and Butler, Katherine G. *Speech In The Elementary Classroom.* Harper, 1955.

von Békésy, Georg. "A New Audiometer." *Acta Otolaryngology* 35:411–22; 1947.

von Békésy, Georg. "Concerning the Fundamental Component of Periodic Pulse Patterns and Modulated Vibrations Observed on the Cochlear Model with Nerve Supply." *J Acoustical Soc Am* 33:888–96; 1961(*a*).

von Békésy, Georg. "Pitch Sensation And Its Relation to the Periodicity of the Stimulus. Hearing And Skin Vibrations." *J Acoustical Soc Am* 33: 341–8; 1961(*b*).

von Békésy, Georg. "Can We Feel the Nervous Discharges of the End Organs During Vibratory Stimulation of the Skin?" *J Acoustical Soc Am* 34: 850–8; 1962.

Ward, Dixon D. "Auditory Fatigue And Masking." In Jerger, James. (Ed.) *Modern Developments In Audiology.* Academic, 1963. p. 240–286.

Webster, J. C. "Problems In Military Audiometry: A Symposium, 6, Automatic Audiometry." *J Speech Hearing Disorders* 22:748; 1957.

Wepman, Joseph, and Jones, L. V. *Studies In Aphasia: An Approach to Testing.* Ed Ind Service, 1961.

Williams, Dean E. "A Point of View About Stuttering." *J Speech Hearing Disorders* 22:390–7; 1957.

Wilson, Betty A. "I. Introduction: The Problem And The Project Procedure." *J Speech Hearing Disorders* Monogr Supplement 8, 26:1; 1961.

Wischener, George J. "An Experimental Approach To Expectancy And Anxiety in Stuttering Behavior." *J Speech Hearing Disorders* 17:139–54; 1952.

SPELLING

HISTORY. Dissatisfaction with the ability of children and adults to spell correctly has been a persistent concern since at least the thirteenth century (Hodges, 1964*b*; Mulcaster, 1925). Despite the attention devoted by schools to improved spelling, present-day complaints concerning the effectiveness of spelling instruction (Hall, 1964) have early counterparts reported prior to the middle of the nineteenth century (Connecticut Common School Journal, 1840–41) and later (Cornman, 1902; Rice, 1897).

Causes of Difficulty. Difficulties in spelling caused by inconsistencies in English orthography are primarily the result of an alphabet inadequate for the consistent spelling of necessary speech sounds and the historical impact of orthographies of other languages that have contributed to the English lexicon. However, recent views take exception to the approach that writing serves only as a mirror for speech and that deviations from a perfect letter-sound relationship are irregularities (Venezky, 1967).

Continuing complaints concerning the inconsistencies of English orthography may be explained in part by the fact that words of non-Anglo-Saxon origin appear to constitute a majority of the whole English lexicon. Of these words, approximately 80 percent are distributed almost equally between words of French origin and French words, with few exceptions, derived from Latin (Neilson, 1954). The remaining 20 percent of our borrowed words have come largely from Celtic, Latin, Scandinavian, and Norman-French. The spelling of some borrowed words has been retained (e.g., contralto), whereas with others the spelling has been adapted (e.g., religion). Also, many words of Anglo-Saxon origin were respelled as a result of the degradation of the language following the Norman Conquest in 1066.

Other factors contributing to the inconsistencies of English orthography include anglicized pronunciation of borrowed words without a corresponding graphemic change; lack of concern or agreement as to what constituted standard spelling on the part of early writers and printers; pronunciation changes for words of Anglo-Saxon origin with no corresponding graphemic modification; changes in inflections; the persistence of regional dialects, in addition to the more recently defined English social dialects (Shuy, 1964); and the deletion or addition of alphabetical symbols coupled with changes in graphemic values (Clark, 1954; Dobson, 1957; Downing, 1962; Francis, 1958; Fries, 1964; Furness, 1959; Gove, 1963; Kennedy, 1935; Neilson, 1954; Smith, 1965; Sweet, 1888; Thomas, 1947; Wijk, 1959; Wyld, 1953).

Additional factors associated with spelling difficulties include organic disabilities of vision and hearing and speech disorders such as aphasia; pronunciation; auditory and visual discrimination; and various psychological factors (Aaron, 1954; Bradford, 1954; Fairhurst, 1913; E. Horn, 1960; D. Russell, 1955, 1958; Williamson, 1933a, 1933b).

"Then and Now" Studies. The drop in interest and related activity in spelling noted in the 1960's (T. Horn, 1967) may in part explain evidence indicating that spelling achievement in the United States may have declined by mid-century (Doyle, 1950; Fitzgerald, 1951b; Fox & Eaton, 1946). Most words on earlier spelling scales (Ashbaugh, 1922; Ayres, 1915) have lower accuracies for grades 2 through 8 in the *New Iowa Spelling Scale* (Greene, 1954). There is also an apparent decline in the spelling ability of high school and college students (Ayer, 1951; Furness, 1956; Harris, 1948). Nevertheless, there is considerable variation in spelling achievement among schools (Ayer, 1951; Fox & Eaton, 1946), and spelling performance in some schools actually equals or exceeds their past levels (National Education Association, 1951). In addition to the factors of low interest in and concern for spelling mentioned earlier, other possible explanations for the evidence indicating lower spelling achievement include the following (E. Horn, 1960): differences in sampling procedures and the sample populations; lower prestige value of spelling ability of students; differences in the nature and number of words taught; a decline in the systematic teaching of spelling, possibly resulting from erroneous interpretations of the values and limitations of incidental learning; general use of instructional procedures which have been shown to be inferior; reduced emphasis on developing composition skills; confusion resulting from phoneme-grapheme relationships; and absence of systematic appraisal.

Research Design and Analysis. Because of faulty design and analysis, there are continuing problems with reference to interpreting research findings in spelling. Even the more recent studies suffer from one or more of the following limitations (T. Horn, 1967): inadequate description of the experimental and/or traditional methods and materials; difficulty in maintaining control of time allotments for the treatments being compared; effect of instruction in other areas on the treatments being compared either is ignored or is extremely difficult to control or describe; insufficient information concerning the learner variable (e.g., conation level, readiness factors, physical condition, and set toward learning); inadequate attention to cultural factors such as socioeconomic levels, differing values placed on education and bicultural factors such as Spanish- or French-speaking, Negro, and/or disadvantaged pupil populations; unreported description or control of the teacher variable, especially the utilization of volunteer teachers for the experimental method and nonvolunteers with the "traditional" method; provisions for in-service education for the experimental teachers but not for the control teachers; administrative factors such as organization of class with reference to instruction, duration of the study, characteristics of the classroom and school, financial support of the school, supportiveness of the principal, and differences in class size; and instrumentation, particularly in studies concerned with disadvantaged pupils.

THE SPELLING CURRICULUM. Based upon available evidence, major curricular decisions must be made to (1) which words should be studied; (2) how many words should be studied and at what rate words should be introduced; (3) when specific words should be studied, that is, at which grade level or levels; and (4) how much time should be allotted to spelling. The ultimate goal in spelling instruction desired by most schools is to enable students to spell correctly the words needed both in and outside school, in their present student status and later as literate adults. Although there is as yet little tangible evidence concerning the contribution that student writings in other curricular areas make to the development and maintenance of spelling ability, logically such contributions would seem important. Also, little solid evidence is available on the contribution made to spelling by the acquisition of dictionary skills and pupil orientation to dictionary use.

Which Words Should Be Studied. Beyond a central core of 3,000 or 4,000 high-frequency words, it is impossible to predict with confidence the range of words any particular individual will need to know how to spell in his lifetime. After several hundred words have been learned, the law of diminishing returns sets in to a marked degree (Fitzgerald, 1951a; E. Horn, 1939; T. Horn & Otto, 1954). Decisions must be made concerning the criteria to be used in selecting words for the spelling curriculum. These decisions must take into consideration student and adult writing needs; the range in pupil familiarity with words, including the knowledge of affixes; what material other than spelling lists the curriculum should contain; and words that present unusually persistent difficulty, that is, spelling "demons" (Davis, 1954; Fitzgerald, 1951a, 1951b; E. Horn, 1967; T. Horn & Otto, 1954; McKee, 1939; National Education Association, 1927).

Until recently, criteria for word selection were based primarily upon various elements of social utility: (1) frequency of occurrence; (2) difficulty; (3) geographic spread; (4) spread among various types of writings; (5) permanence of value; (6) social acceptability or word quality; and (7) cruciality (E. Horn, 1960). With the increased interest in phoneme-grapheme relationships that arose in the 1950's and the completion of the Stanford studies (Hanna & others, 1966; National Conference on Research in English, 1966; Venezky, 1967), investigations have been made regarding the selection and grade placement of words to be studied according to linguistic principles, with child (Rinsland, 1945) and adult (Buckingham & Dolch, 1936; E. Horn, 1926; Thorndike & Lorge, 1944) writing and reading needs assuming lesser roles. However, no evidence has been reported concerning the effectiveness in actual classrooms of word selection based upon linguistic principles (Hanna & Moore, 1953; E. Horn, 1957; Kenyon & Knott, 1951; Kurath, 1939–41; National Conference on Research in English, 1966). The implications of using linguistic principles in word selection and grade placement will be discussed in more detail below, under METHODS OF INSTRUCTION.

The spelling needs of children have been determined by tabulating samples of children's writings in school, such as themes and letters composed as school assignments and letters written outside the school (Fitzgerald, 1934, 1951a; McKee, 1939; Rinsland, 1945; Seegers, 1939). All studies of children's vocabularies have had to face sampling problems, which have produced inconsistency in the frequencies reported grade by grade in the various studies. It is self-evident that a sampling of children's writing from themes about health will include words which will not be found in themes based on science or social science or in letters written outside the school. On the other hand, the frequencies of common words such as *time, they, to, she, was,* and *when* are listed by Rinsland in all grades among the first 100 words of highest frequency (E. Horn, 1960).

An examination even of Rinsland's extensive analysis of more than 6 million running words from children's writings reveals limited data on the written vocabulary of first-grade children. These limited data may be supplemented by data from the spoken vocabularies of young children (M. Horn, 1928; McCarthy, 1954; Seegers, 1939).

A landmark in the identification of adult writing needs is the precomputer compilation of 10,000 words found in *A Basic Writing Vocabulary* (E. Horn, 1926). Data from the most significant earlier studies were combined with Horn's own more extensive tabulation, resulting in a compilation of over 5 million running words and 36,373 different word forms, excluding the names of persons and places. Sources for the tabulation included business letters, letters of literary men, personal letters, letters of application and recommendation, letters contributed to newspapers and magazines, minutes of meetings, written excuses, letters of a single individual, and a composite list secured from earlier adult vocabulary studies (E. Horn, 1926). Even in a compilation as extensive as *A Basic Writing Vocabulary,* it was not possible to secure writing samples from political or geographical divisions that were commensurate with their populations; nor was an adequate sampling of writings from persons at lower educational levels secured (E. Horn, 1960).

In addition to sampling issues, the question is sometimes raised about the reliability of a vocabulary sample taken at a particular time as compared with vocabulary samples of other kinds and/or writing samples taken thirty or more years before or after the compilation. A comparison was made between *A Basic Writing Vocabulary* and a tabulation of 100,000 running words from the letters of Benjamin Franklin. It was found that 97 percent of the words Franklin used ten or more times and 95 percent of the words used five to nine times appear in *A Basic Writing Vocabulary* (E. Horn, 1939). Also, in a comparison with *The Teacher's Word Book* (Thorndike, 1921), all but 170 of the 5,000 words of highest frequency in Horn's 1926 study occur in the same form or in a base form from which the words could be built by adding suffixes but are not reported separately by Thorndike (E. Horn, 1960). A sampling of over a quarter of a million running words found in letters to the editors of eight periodicals identified 22,485 different words (McCann, 1955). The number of high-frequency new words in the period 1926–56, based upon McCann's summary, was found to be negligible (Browning, 1957).

It is apparent from examination of data reported in studies of adult writing vocabularies and written vocabularies of children that there is considerable overlap between child and adult writing needs (Davis, 1954; Fitzgerald, 1951a). Comparing the 2,999 highest-frequency words of the Rinsland list with Horn's list of 10,000 words and Fitzgerald's list of 2,650 words, a total of 2,392 words were common to all three lists (Davis, 1954). Only 198 words, or 6.6 percent of the 2,999 highest-frequency words of the Rinsland list, did not appear in *A Basic Writing Vocabulary.* Examples of high-frequency words written by children reported by Rinsland and not found in Horn's list are *amendments, bike, confederation, fairies, jacks, kitty, spinach,* and *walrus.* These words illustrate how the criterion of permanence of value operates with words written frequently by children but not by adults, as well as the effect of other curricular areas upon writing samples: that is, *amendments, confederation,* and *walrus* (Davis, 1954; Fitzgerald, 1951a; E. Horn, 1926, 1939). Despite the overlap of high-frequency words between child and adult needs, variability in the use of criteria for selection by various textbook authors has resulted in marked lack of agreement in words selected for inclusion in existing texts, especially when comparisons are made grade by grade (Ames, 1965; Betts, 1949).

Data from the Stanford studies (Hanna & others, 1966; Hodges, 1964a; National Conference on Research in English, 1966; Rudorf, 1965; Venezky, 1967), when field-tested in actual classrooms, should provide useful information about the manner in which words may best be selected for study. The wide range in pupil language development—for instance, differing familiarity with words resulting from sources such as variability in socioeconomic levels and experiential backgrounds—has long been recognized. In making decisions concerning curriculum for the primary grades, consideration should be given words found in reading (Dale & Razik, 1963; Thorndike & Lorge, 1944), in addition to the speaking vocabularies of young children (M. Horn, 1928). Consideration must also be given to the handling of spelling in children's writing; pupil knowledge of linguistic principles and instruction in phonetics; and pupil knowledge of affixation and the extent to which word-building exercises are provided in language instruction (Fitzgerald, 1951b; Thorndike, 1941).

Few educators today, if any, consider the 3,000 to 4,000 words found in most spelling series as anything more than the security segment of the spelling curriculum. Although the role of spelling in practical writing is different from its purpose in creative writing, where the flow of thought is the prime consideration, both of these instructional areas provide the means for greatly expanding students' writing vocabularies. It is very probable that spelling ability is best developed and maintained in the long run through stimulation of, and careful attention to, the writing that children do. On the other hand, there is as yet no field-tested substitute for direct instruction on the basic core of high-frequency words needed in child and adult writing.

How Many Words Should Be Studied. The number of words to be studied and the rate at which they should be introduced depends upon how words are selected for the curriculum, the total number of words selected, the grade level involved, pupil abilities, the extent and distribution of reviews, and the time spent in developing abilities related to spelling, such as reading, composition, handwriting, and speech. The 3,000 to 4,000 words contained in most spelling curricula do not represent the total curriculum and total pupil needs any more than a basal reading series represents the total reading program or total individual pupil reading needs.

It has been shown that, with their repetitions, the 4,001 highest-frequency words in *A Basic Writing Vocabulary* constitute 97.8 percent of the total 5,180,000 running words (Horn and Otto, 1954). If the 6,006 words of next highest frequency are added to these 4,001 core words, the resulting 10,007 words, with their repetitions, represent 99.4 percent of the total running words, or an increase of only 1.6 percent. This illustration of the law of diminishing returns suggests that the security segment of a spelling curriculum may be provided by 3,000 to 4,000 highest-frequency words which are needed in and out of school by children and adults. Nevertheless, this figure does not by any means represent the total writing needs of any particular individual. Concurrent with mastery of the security segment is attention to other pupil writing needs, and pupil habituation to correct spelling, including study habits, proofreading, and use of the dictionary, which hopefully will enable the individual to constantly widen the range of words he can spell correctly.

As yet, satisfactory evidence is not available whether more benefits would accrue from a security segment smaller or larger than 3,000 or 4,000 words. Whereas superior spellers can learn many more words than a segment of this size, the poor spellers, particularly those with limited oral vocabularies, may require fewer words for study. The rate at which words should be introduced also appears to be an individual matter, depending upon pupil capabilities and their writing needs and skills in other curricular areas.

When Specific Words Should Be Studied. Once the decision has been made concerning which words and how many are to be included in the security segment of the spelling curriculum, the next step is to decide at which grade level or levels the words are to be studied. The major factors involved with grade placement of words include: (1) frequency of occurrence in child writing, grade by grade (Rinsland, 1945); (2) permanence of value, as measured by adult usage (E. Horn, 1926); (3) difficulty of the word, as measured by scales (Greene, 1954); and (4) the extent to which words should be graded by combinations of the foregoing factors, or should be grouped according to linguistic principles, or should be grouped according to some common problem.

The data analyzed in the Stanford study (Hanna & others, 1966; National Conference on Research in English, 1966) have been used to suggest word selection and gradation according to linguistic principles in order to make possible, hopefully, an almost unlimited correctly spelled writing vocabulary. Other data are available concerning the application of linguistic principles to the selection and gradation of words in actual instruction, the following plan provides reasonably well for the child's present and future needs (E. Horn, 1960). (1) In each of the first six grades, the basic word list should be chosen from the words which are most important in the writing done by children in that grade and which are also important in the writing of adults. However, in selecting the words for later grades, words previously taught will be omitted unless they are still difficult to spell for students in the later grades. The data on probable difficulty are provided by spelling scales and by counts of errors made in children's writing. (2) Words which are frequently written by children but which are of marginal value to adults should either be placed in supplementary lists or be left to incidental learning. (3) Words which are of great importance in the writing of adults but which are infrequently written by children should be placed toward the end of the period of systematic instruction in spelling. (4) The extent of word reviews within a grade and in subsequent grades should be determined by the degree and persistence of word difficulty.

Time Allotment. Time allotment per se is relatively meaningless unless one considers such other elements as: (1) the number, difficulty, and grade placement of the words selected; (2) pupil abilities; (3) the drive and adroitness with which both the teacher and pupils engage in the learning process; (4) the amount and quality of instruction in other areas that pertains to spelling; and (5) the efficiency of the methods being used. Early studies which indicated little or no increase in spelling achievement for schools with large time allotments as compared with schools with smaller time allotments have been supported by later investigations (Fox & Eaton, 1946; T. Horn, 1947). It appears likely that the time allotted for direct study of spelling in excess of 60 minutes a week may be spent more advantageously in other areas (T. Horn, 1947).

METHODS OF INSTRUCTION. Although spelling instruction has been considered a relatively simple matter in comparison with instruction in such areas as the social sciences and sciences, recurring expressions of dissatisfaction with spelling ability indicate that the attainment of desirable instructional results is not a simple matter. Decisions concerning the kind of instructional methods to be used should be based upon: (1) factors conditioning spelling ability; (2) roles of direct instruction and incidental learning; (3) modes of presentation; (4) the role of spelling in other curricular areas; (5) utility of learning generalizations; and (6) the role of tests (Shane, 1955).

Factors Conditioning Spelling Ability. Although superior intelligence is not a guarantee of superior spelling ability, positive correlations have been consistently reported between spelling ability and intelligence. This is not surprising in the light of the effects language factors have on intelligence scores (Gates, 1926; Guiler & Lease, 1942; Hollingworth, 1918; Knoell & Harris, 1952; McGovney, 1930; Newton, 1960; Oswalt, 1962; D. Russell, 1955).

Motivation in spelling is affected by teacher and pupil attitudes and interests; the educational expectations of parents; the level of pupil motivation; the set to learn and remember; work habits; instructional methods and their utilization; and self-confidence. Intrinsic incentives for learning to spell, such as essentially positive attitudes and interests, are preferred to the extrinsic incentives of school grades and competition (Columba, 1926; Diserens & Vaughn, 1931; Forlano, 1936; E. Horn, 1960, 1967; D. Russell, 1937; Sand, 1938; Thorndike, 1935).

Interaction between pupil and teacher interest in spelling per se and in language arts instruction related to spelling make the difference between excellent results from an enthusiastic use of the most efficient methods and poor results achieved through drab mechanical teaching and learning. The greater interest reported in spelling as compared with composition (Chase, 1949) suggests that instruction in composition may be even less meaningful and lively than efforts in spelling. Probably the most important source of interest and motivation is the child's awareness of progress (Columba, 1926; Diserens & Vaughn, 1931; E. Horn, 1967; McKee, 1939; Thorndike, 1935). Games and special devices would also appear to enhance motivation in spelling (Fitzgerald, 1951b; Gates & Graham, 1934; Hildreth, 1955).

The development and maintenance of desirable attitudes toward spelling may be accomplished by "(1) showing the student that the words taught are those most likely to be needed by him now and in the future; (2) limiting the student's study to those words which tests have shown him to be unable to spell; (3) providing the student with a definite and efficient method of learning; (4) emphasizing individual and class progress; and (5) encouraging in the class the spirit of mutual pride and cooperation in spelling achievement" (E. Horn, 1960).

Closely related to levels of motivation, poor study habits are one of the most common causes of poor spelling achievement (Fitzgerald, 1951b; Gates, 1922; E. Horn, 1967; McKee, 1924; D. Russell, 1937, 1955; Williamson, 1933a, 1933b). The factor of home conditions, reported as being significantly related to spelling achievement (Adkins, 1943), very likely also has an effect on pupil work habits.

The effect of home conditions on school achievement in the case of markedly disadvantaged populations would appear to be self-evident (Macmillan, 1966). Studies reporting relationships between personality and the language arts have been largely motivated by interest focused upon reading and personality development; few have implications for spelling (Adkins, 1943; Gates & others, 1949; D. Russell, 1953).

Physical characteristics which may condition spelling ability (Adkins, 1943) and involve language and/or speech problems and problems of visual and auditory acuity will be discussed below. Sex differences generally favor girls over boys in the whole language arts area, particularly in spelling (Anderson, 1963; Personke, 1966). Although there is earlier evidence indicating a much larger incidence of enlarged tonsils or adenoids in backward as compared with normal spellers (Schonell, 1942), it is not known whether a similar correspondence exists today and, if it does, whether it is merely a reflection of poor socioeconomic conditions such as inadequate diets, housing, and medical care and the resulting effects upon energy levels, hearing, and speech.

Special abilities and disabilities which condition learning to spell may be conveniently categorized as: (1) visual, (2) auditory, (3) oral, and (4) modes of learning. Severe mental and physical disabilities typically dealt with under special-education provisions will not be discussed here.

Spelling ability has been shown to be strongly

related to visual perception, visual discrimination, and visual memory (Aaron, 1954; Adkins, 1943; Comerford, 1954; DeBoer, 1955; Gates, 1926; Gilbert & Gilbert, 1942; Hartmann, 1931; Hudson & Toler, 1949; Mack, 1953; Newton, 1960; Phelan, 1940; D. Russell, 1937, 1943, 1955; Spache, 1940b; Visitation, 1929; Worcester, 1925). Although marked impairment of vision may be an important factor in certain cases, reasonable variation in visual acuity does not appear to distinguish between good and poor spellers (D. Russell, 1937, 1955). Other evidence indicates little relationship, on the average, between defective vision and general school achievement (Dalton, 1943). The evidence reported on eye movements in learning to spell indicates that good spellers have fewer regressions, more regular fixation, shorter time fixation, and more effective methods of analysis. Improvement of perceptual analysis may apparently be achieved through training (Gilbert, 1932, 1940; Gilbert & Gilbert, 1942; Hudson & Toler, 1949).

Significant relationships have also been found between spelling and sound perception and discrimination (Bradford, 1954; Damgaard, 1956; Gates, 1922, 1926; Hudson & Toler, 1949; D. Russell, 1937, 1943, 1955, 1958; Templin, 1954; Zedler, 1956). However, these correlations appear to be lower than those between visual factors and spelling (Newton, 1960; D. Russell, 1958). Despite some controversy as to the effect of auditory acuity upon spelling, good and poor spellers apparently are not markedly differentiated by hearing loss (Aaron, 1954; Damgaard, 1956; Gates, 1922, 1926; Hartmann, 1931; Holmes, 1954; Mack, 1953; D. Russell, 1937, 1953, 1955, 1958; Templin, 1948). Evidence indicating that deaf children make fewer spelling errors than children with normal hearing (Gates & Chase, 1926) has been substantiated by evidence that both deaf and hard-of-hearing children make substantially fewer errors in theme writing than do those with normal hearing (Templin, 1948). Available evidence indicates that sound discriminations can be improved (Hudson & Toler, 1949; Zedler, 1956).

That the ability to produce "standard" American-English speech is related to the ability to discriminate between speech sounds is self-evident. It is also self-evident that a non-English-speaking pupil, say, a French- or Spanish-speaking one or a child whose first dialect differs markedly from that used in school (Shuy, 1964), will have even more difficulty with spelling than did pupils sampled in earlier studies which reported that faulty speech habits, particularly in pronunciation, were frequently found among poor spellers (Bradford, 1954; Carrell & Pendergast, 1954; Gates & Russell, 1937; Hollingworth, 1923; D. Russell, 1937, 1955; Schonell, 1934).

Although research on the speech-language problems of disadvantaged populations has been beset with problems of instrumentation (T. Horn, 1966), interpretations of relationships between language and socioeconomic levels (MacMillan, 1966), and/or differing ethnic groups (McDowell, 1966), some promising beginnings in language instrumentation have been reported (Jameson, 1967; Ott, 1967). Direct instruction to establish a "standard" dialect, using audiolingual techniques developed in modern foreign-language teaching, has appeared relatively recently. Recent data indicate substantial improvement in the quality of oral English as a result of such direct instruction (Ott, 1967).

All learners use varying amounts of visual, auditory, and kinesthetic imagery when attempting to spell correctly. Individuals who are blind or deaf must obviously compensate for their loss by sharpening the sensory modes of learning and perception that are left to them. Indeed, as mentioned earlier, deaf children have been shown to make fewer errors than children with normal hearing. Since the identification of individual imagery types has proved extremely elusive for psychologists, learning experiences which involve all imagery types should be most fruitful (Aaron, 1954; Abbott, 1909; Fairhurst, 1913; M. Fernald, 1912; Hollingworth, 1918; Winch, 1916; Woodworth & Schlosberg, 1954). It may well be that one reason for the efficiency of the corrected test technique (T. Horn, 1947) in learning to spell is that it utilizes all three types of imagery, with emphasis on the visual and auditory during pupil self-correction. In any event, the classroom teacher is not equipped to identify image types as a basis for recommending individual modes of learning.

Of the foregoing factors that condition spelling ability, the following have been shown to be amenable to instruction or remedial measures: motivation; work habits; and special abilities and disabilities in vision, hearing, and speech (Blair, 1956; Brueckner & Melby, 1931). The surge during the 1960's in compensatory education for learners who are environmentally handicapped may prove to have a positive effect on the factors of home conditions and intelligence scores.

The Role of Direct Instruction and of Incidental Learning. Spelling occupies a minor, though important, place in the present-day school curriculum. Early statements of dissatisfaction with spelling methodology at the turn of the century (Cornman, 1902; Rice, 1897) gave rise to the issue of whether or not supplanting direct instruction by incidental methods of learning would be desirable. The controversy persisted through the 1930's and into the World War II years (Gates & others, 1926; E. Horn, 1937, 1944). The post-Sputnik impact on the curriculum, with increasing emphasis upon science, mathematics, and eventually the humanities, forced a new look at the optimum ways in which direct instruction and incidental learning could complement each other. So-called linguistically based reading materials sought to incorporate spelling instruction more closely in reading development. Evidence concerning the contributions to spelling improvement in grades 2 and 3 of varying combinations of direct and incidental (functional) instruction has been inconsistent from grade to grade (Reid, 1966; Reid & Hieronymus, 1963). This suggests that how well a method is implemented may be more crucial than the nature of the methods used in the investigation.

The extent to which the 3,000- to 4,000-word security segment of the spelling curriculum may be learned through activities outside the regular spelling period may be determined by tests using sample words from the security list. Through testing, the pupil knows which, if any, words he needs to study; the teacher is aware of individual pupil progress, including pupils in need of special help; mastery of the security segment is not left to chance; and the individual student is released from unnecessary study of words he has learned through other activities.

Modes of Presentation. The modes of presentation and their relationship to research findings include (Fitzgerald, 1951b; Hildreth, 1955; T. Horn & Otto, 1954): (1) list versus contextual study; (2) individualized self-selective spelling; (3) plans for differentiated instruction that is adapted to individual differences; (4) other elements, such as grouping by linguistic principles, calling attention to specific difficulties, efforts to recall and overlearning, distributed versus mass learning and review, visual-auditory syllabic presentations, use of the dictionary, programmed instruction, kinesthetic techniques; and (5) oral spelling and the role of "games."

The presentation of words in list form is apparently more efficient than their introduction in context, except to the extent to which some context is necessary to identify words in a test presentation, for instance, homonyms (Hawley & Gallup, 1922; E. Horn, 1967; T. Horn & Otto, 1954). Since the words in the security segment of the spelling curriculum are those occurring more frequently in child writing, it is generally a waste of time to review the meanings of all the words being given in a test. In those cases where common meanings of words in the test list are not known to a pupil, of course, the meanings should be briefly considered through oral explanation or use of the dictionary.

With the advent of self-selection in reading, it has been suggested that the same approach be extended to individualized (that is, self-selective) spelling. If self-selection comes from the security segment of the spelling curriculum already identified (Fitzgerald, 1951a; E. Horn, 1926; Rinsland, 1945), and if such self-selection involves the study of misspelled words from the security segment *plus* words from individual lists, the results are very likely to be positive if efficient methods of study are used. On the other hand, those who contend that a locally devised list of words (if based on counts approaching those of Fitzgerald, E. Horn, and Rinsland) will deviate significantly from the high-frequency words already identified are in for disillusionment; evidence has already shown that the high-frequency vocabulary in children's and in adult writing is very similar (Davis, 1954). Over and above the security segment of the spelling curriculum, pupils should be free to pursue their own special writing interests and needs and should be encouraged to do so. Nevertheless, local school districts can better employ staff time in other ways than in attempting to develop a local list of spelling words to be learned (Deacon, 1956; Fitzgerald, 1951a; Gates & others, 1926; E. Horn, 1944, 1967; T. Horn and Otto, 1954).

Prior to, and in addition to, the development of interest in self-selective spelling, plans for differentiated instruction to accommodate individual differences have included the following elements: (1) use of a term test based upon the security segment list as a criterion for excusing from formal spelling instruction those students who spell 90 percent or more of the test words correctly; a new sampling of the security segment may be used as a midterm test to see which students may be excused for the second half of the year; (2) by using the corrected test technique, pupils working in pairs or in varying-sized groups may proceed at their own speed; (3) students who attain 90 percent mastery of the initial term tests are very often those who have greater language facility and should be encouraged in creative writing or some area of personal interest; some students, however, may prefer to continue with the security segment of the curriculum or to pursue more specialized writing vocabularies arising from other areas of study; and (4) the seriously retarded speller is usually, though not always, retarded in other areas of the language arts; such pupils ordinarily may best be accommodated through attention to relevant factors conditioning spelling ability, such as particular disabilities, and by a reduction in the number of words to be studied. In any plan for differentiated instruction, it is important that the teacher conduct periodic progress checks, which may best be accomplished by term tests consisting of words selected from the difficulty level being studied—that is, the level at which the pupil is *studying* rather than the grade level to which he has been chronologically assigned.

Whatever principles are used to group words for spelling must involve very few exceptions, in order to avoid spelling errors due to misapplication of generalizations (Archer, 1930; Carroll, 1930; Hanna & others, 1966; National Conference on Research in English, 1966; Rogness, 1953; Sartorius, 1931). Extensive computer analysis of phoneme-grapheme relationships completed at Stanford suggests that words to be learned might be carefully grouped in a way to allow pupils to arrive inductively at certain sound-letter generalizations (Hanna & others, 1966). This approach was antedated by earlier efforts which explored the feasibility of grouping spelling words according to morphological bases, e.g., affixation (Archer, 1930; Osburn, 1954); phonological bases, e.g., homonyms (Harder, 1937); and orthographic considerations, e.g., certain silent letters, as exemplified in *doubt*. An analysis of the spelling and pronunciation of the 20,000 most commonly used English words that was also completed at Stanford may have implications for grouping. Its purpose was to establish rules for translating from spelling to sound (that is, to read), and it distinguished between rules based primarily upon phonemic and morphemic considerations and rules based primarily upon orthographic considerations (Venezky, 1967). The evidence regarding grouping words for instruction by a homonym system indicates that there is a slight advantage to teaching them separately rather than together, although such advantage is not consistent for all homonyms or from grade to grade (Harder, 1937).

Despite data showing that many words have a particular place at which half or more of the errors are made (Gates, 1937), calling attention to "hard spots" is a doubtful practice (Masters, 1927; Mendenhall, 1930; Rosemeier, 1965) and may even be a harmful one (Tireman, 1930). Very few words contain specific mistakes made by as many as half the pupils in any given class, a fact which suggests that students concern themselves with their particular spelling difficulties as identified by the corrected test procedure.

The practice of recall has been shown to be beneficial in all fields of learning, and the use of recall is built into most spelling methods, for both initial learning and review (Abbott, 1909; E. Horn, 1967; Woodworth & Schlosberg, 1954). Variability of learning set among students generally determines how aggressively individual efforts to recall are made. It is not easy, unfortunately, to get pupils to utilize recall. Each word should be learned beyond the point of one successful recall, although the exact number of successful recalls most effective for mastery varies with individual pupils (Gates & others, 1949; Krueger, 1929).

Distributed learning appears to be more effective than mass learning in the process of word mastery. Although the amount and rate of forgetting varies with the individual, provisions for retention should include a general review of persistently difficult words and additional reviews for students unable to maintain word mastery (Hunter, 1934; Ruch, 1928; Wallin, 1911; Woodworth & Schlosberg, 1954). Reviews should (1) be spaced two or three days apart during initial instruction; (2) focus on words known to present persistent difficulty in general, as well as on individual words which for some reason prove difficult only for certain pupils; and (3) be repeated after a longer lapse of time, such as a month or six weeks (Gates & others, 1949; E. Horn, 1967; McKee, 1939; Ruch, 1928; Woodworth & Schlosberg, 1954).

The visual presentation of words in syllabified form has not demonstrated any advantage over the undivided method of word presentation, and for some words (e.g., purpose, therefore) there is a negative effect (T. Horn, 1949). However, when the words showing negative effects were tested by Humphrey in her syllabified pronunciation study, no significant differences were found between the orally presented syllabified and undivided methods. The data indicate that there is no advantage in presenting words in syllabified form either visually or orally and that the undivided method of word presentation should thus be retained. For purposes of variety or enrichment, visual or oral presentation of words in syllables might occasionally be used (T. Horn, 1949, 1956).

The extent to which dictionaries are used by pupils to secure information on meaning, pronunciation, and spelling usually sets the superior speller apart from poorer ones. Unfortunately, instruction in use of the dictionary does not ensure its habitual use in spelling. Primary factors motivating pupil use of dictionaries include individual drive to spell correctly and to expand one's writing vocabulary. Efficient dictionary use is basic to any spelling program and is crucial for accommodating individual differences.

Programmed instruction in spelling may lend itself to such accommodation of individual differences. Its success is dependent, of course, upon how the program reflects research in learning and curriculum and methods of instruction in spelling. Studies reported between 1962 and 1967 involved for the most part small samples, which may account for their varying conclusions regarding the effectiveness of programmed instruction (Buzby & Mann, 1962; Edgerton & Twombly, 1962). Evidence suggests that programmed instruction in spelling may not function successfully below grade 3 (Friedman, 1967).

Kinesthetic techniques, such as tracing, have proved useful in work with poor spellers and slow learners (G. Fernald, 1922). Actually, Fernald's kinesthetic techniques are combined with both visual and auditory imagery (G. Fernald, 1922; Fitzgerald, 1951b; Hildreth, 1955).

Games have been suggested from time to time as aids to spelling, such as spelling matches and crossword puzzles, and these can make a positive contribution to pupil motivation (Fitzgerald, 1951b; Gates & Graham, 1934; Hildreth, 1955). Although the need for oral spelling is very rare in contrast to the almost continual needs of writing, the spelling bee has been an American institution for generations (Read, 1941). Games are not, however, a substitute for direct instruction in learning to spell, and their major contribution is the stimulation or maintenance of student interest.

Spelling in Other Curricular Areas. Significant relationships have been noted between spelling and other instructional areas such as reading, handwriting, speech, and composition (E. Horn, 1967). The evidence with regard to reading is voluminous, particularly with reference to auditory and visual perception and word-analysis skills. Whereas comprehension is a function of all the language arts—indeed, the essence of reading, writing, speaking, and listening—the encoding of language from sound to written symbols is unique to spelling, and the decoding of language from written symbols to sound is unique to reading.

READING. Correlations reported between reading and spelling have been relatively high (e.g., .48, .51, .61, .63), though not quite so high as those reported between reading and intelligence (e.g., .71, .73, .83) (Bond, 1940; Gates, 1922; Merrill, 1924; Peake, 1940; Phelan, 1940; D. Russell, 1943, 1946; Sparrow, 1951; Townsend, 1947; Visitation, 1929). It is to be expected that students will learn many words through reading (T. Horn & Otto, 1954; Tyler, 1939; Williamson, 1933a, 1933b), and this phenomenon has been described by Standing at the primary level (Hildreth, 1955) as well as at junior high, senior high, and college levels (Gilbert, 1934a, 1934b, 1935). The general status of the contribution of reading to spelling may be described as follows: (1) although a single reading of words in context produces temporary improvement in the reader's spelling of those words, direct study is required for maintenance of this improvement; (2) words encountered repeatedly in reading that are also frequently used in writing are more likely to be learned without direct instruction than are words that appear infrequently in reading; (3) all but 63 of the 222 most persistently misspelled words (Fitzgerald, 1951*b*) are among the 1,000 words of highest frequency in reading, thus indicating that reading alone will not ensure spelling mastery; (4) granting the positive general contributions to spelling by reading, nonetheless, students should not be asked to interrupt, while reading, the flow of thought in order to learn the spelling of words in the text; and (5) the formal spelling period should capitalize on the relationships with reading that are known to be most beneficial to spelling (Beltramo, 1954; Betts, 1945; Groff, 1965; Mason, 1957; D. Russell, 1943, 1946).

Because spelling ability has been shown to be highly related to visual perception, visual discrimination, and visual memory (Aaron, 1954; Adkins, 1943; Comerford, 1954; DeBoer, 1955; Gates, 1926; Gilbert & Gilbert, 1942; Hartmann, 1931; Hudson & Toler, 1949; Mack, 1953; Newton, 1960; Phelan, 1940; D. Russell, 1937, 1943, 1955; Spache, 1940*b*; Visitation, 1929; Worcester, 1925) and since significant relationships have also been found between spelling and sound perception and discrimination (Bradford, 1954; Damgaard, 1956; Gates, 1922, 1926; Hudson & Toler, 1949; D. Russell, 1937, 1943, 1955, 1958; Templin, 1954; Zedler, 1956), it is likely that these factors account for a major portion of the relatively high correlations which have been reported between reading and spelling (Bond, 1940; Gates, 1922; Merrill, 1924; Peake, 1940; Phelan, 1940; D. Russell, 1943, 1946; Sparrow, 1951; Townsend, 1947; Visitation, 1929).

Correspondences between phonic knowledge, reading, and spelling have been shown to be positive (.20 to .70), whether such knowledge has been achieved incidentally or through direct instruction (Rudisill, 1957; Templin, 1954; Zedler, 1956). The evidence concerning word analysis is inconsistent and complicated (Aaron, 1954; Bradford, 1954; Durrell, 1956; Hahn, 1964; Ibeling, 1961; Jackson, 1953; Mack, 1953; Plessas & Dison, 1965; Plessas & Ladley, 1963; K. Russell, 1954), and educators and some linguists have been criticized for naïveté regarding sound-to-letter and letter-to-sound relationships categorized under the overly simplified term "phonics" (Hall, 1964; Venezky, 1967). It is true that (1) more than a third of the words in one dictionary (Kenyon & Knott, 1951) have more than one acceptable pronunciation, often due to regional differences over and above social dialect variations (E. Horn, 1957; Kurath, 1939–41; Shuy, 1964); (2) sounds are spelled in many ways, and exceptions to even the commonest spelling occur (Barnhart, 1953; Hanna & others, 1966; E. Horn, 1929*b*, 1957; Moore, 1951); (3) most letters spell many sounds (E. Horn, 1944, 1957; Neilson, 1954); and (4) over half of the words in a dictionary contain so-called silent letters (Hildreth, 1955; E. Horn, 1957). However, analyses of computer-compiled data at Stanford reveal often-ignored complexities in the orthography (including nonphonetic features). For example, rather than 26 graphemes available for correspondences for phonemes, there are actually more; "th" and "ch," for instance, are spelling units as basic to the orthography as "a" and "b." The inappropriateness of labeling as silent all unpronounced letters may be illustrated by two cases: the words *subtle* and *bomb*. Whereas it is correct to assign silent status to the "b" in *subtle*, it is incorrect to assign unequivocal silent status to the "b" in *bomb* when we have *bombard* and *bombardier* (Venezky, 1967). It would seem desirable to modify a sound-to-spelling algorithm based on phonology alone (Hanna & others, 1966; National Conference on Research in English, 1966) to include morphological and syntactic features of the orthography.

While comprehension is a function of all aspects of language, its role in reading is different as compared with its function in spelling. Whereas, depending upon the purpose of the reader, the comprehension skills required for reading will vary, the spelling problems typically faced by a writer follow the larger problem of encoding his flow of thought in order to communicate with a reader. If the writer knows what he wishes to write and the reasons for writing it, his pertinent immediate considerations of language include syntax, handwriting, and spelling. Under these circumstances, teaching the meanings of spelling words is unnecessary, since their meanings are already known and the primary purpose is to learn correct spellings of the needed words.

HANDWRITING. Speed and legibility in handwriting are factors commonly mentioned as affecting spelling ability, though reported correlations between spelling and handwriting are not very high, with an average of about .20 (Baker, 1929; Gates, 1922; D. Russell, 1937; Spache, 1940*a*). In any spelling test in which time is a factor, a faster writer obviously has an advantage over a slower one (D. Russell, 1943), just as it is obvious that the practice of counting illegible words wrong is advantageous to the student with legible handwriting.

Early studies reported favorable effects, in terms of legibility, of manuscript writing upon spelling (Voorhis, 1931); but there was no evident advantage of manuscript over cursive writing in terms of spelling accuracy (Varty, 1938). In later studies at the third-grade level, evidence indicated no significant difference in the number of spelling errors between groups using cursive and those using manuscript handwriting (Byers, 1963); and there was no significant difference in spelling gains between third-grade pupils who made the transition to cursive writing in October and others who made the transition the following May (Bolen, 1964). Increased speed and improved legibility in handwriting, whether manuscript or cursive, enables students to convey language in written form with greater facility, which in turn helps to expand their written vocabulary and, ultimately, to increase their potential for scoring higher on spelling tests.

SPEECH. Speech aberrations that may be related to spelling disabilities can be caused by (1) inadequate command of American English, proceeding from a primary use of other languages or marked dialects, that is, having standard English as a second language; (2) articulatory defects and mispronunciations which respond to remedial treatment; and (3) speech disorders which do not respond to the usual instructional techniques (Carrell & Pendergast, 1954; Gates & Russell, 1937; Hartmann, 1931; T. Horn & Otto, 1954; Jameson, 1967; Ott, 1967; D. Russell, 1937; Schonell, 1934; Shuy, 1964). Improvement of speech and language patterns should logically improve spelling ability. Although development of good speech habits has been a matter of instructional concern for years, direct instruction (using audiolingual techniques) in English as a second language or a second dialect is a recent development focused largely upon native-born, immigrant, and refugee Spanish-speaking populations, particularly in the Southwest, as well as on Negroes, American Indians, and the French-speaking, among others. Speech problems that affect spelling are varied and complicated and may derive from any of the following causes: (1) inadequate instruction in English as a second language (e.g., saying "eet" for *it,* "chip" for *ship*); (2) bidialectism (e.g., saying "ked" for *carried,* "hep" for *help*); (3) regional differences (e.g., "idear" for *idea,* "bahn" for *barn*); (4) certain speech habits (e.g., "liberry" for *library,* "probly" for *probably*); and (5) "standard" language with built-in problems for spelling, such as unaccented syllables resulting in the *schwa,* or "short i" sound (e.g., arithmetic, Monday) (Barnhart, 1953; E. Horn, 1957; Jameson, 1967; Kenyon & Knott, 1951; Kurath, 1939–41; Ott, 1967; Shuy, 1964).

COMPOSITION AND PROOFREADING. Careful attention to the writing that pupils do in all areas of the curriculum and, particularly, provision for a strong composition and creative writing program should include checking for spelling errors and providing study time for those words important enough to learn. Despite the obvious advantages of developing the ability to proofread and of becoming accustomed to doing so consistently, evidence from earlier studies indicates that students ordinarily are not very good at proofreading (E. Horn, 1937; McKee, 1939; Leyson, 1944). Evidence from two later studies in grade 5 is inconsistent concerning the effect of instruction in proofreading on spelling: (1) proofreading instruction produced significant differences in the improvement of spelling, as measured by a standardized test for males with IQ's of 110 and below; females were significantly better than males in recognizing misspelled words and in correcting these misspellings (Oswalt, 1962); and (2) in comparing a textbook-based spelling program with a program focused on proofreading and a study of both the variant and more regularly spelled sounds of the language, no significant differences in achievement were found between the two groups, as measured by a standardized spelling test, or in the proportion of correct and incorrect spellings of *studied* words on a dictated spelling test prepared by the investigator; significant differences at the 1 percent level were found in favor of classes receiving instruction in proofreading on the posttest of the author-prepared dictated test and in the proportion of correct and incorrect spellings of *unstudied* words on the dictated test (Bishop, 1965).

Utility of Learning Generalizations. The utility of any rule is dependent upon the degree to which it satisfies the following criteria: (1) a rule must have wide application and few exceptions; and (2) student knowledge of the rule must make a positive difference in the ability to learn. Relatively few spelling rules based on morphological or orthographic considerations qualify under these criteria (Archer, 1930; Fitzgerald, 1951b; Gates, 1935; King, 1932; Sartorius, 1931; Thorndike, 1941). The rules that do qualify include these (E. Horn, 1960): (1) the rules for adding suffixes (changing "y" to "i," dropping final silent "e," doubling the final consonant); (2) the letter "q" is followed by "u" in common English words; (3) English words do not end in "v"; (4) proper nouns and most adjectives formed from proper nouns should begin with capital letters; (5) the rules for the use of periods in abbreviations; and (6) rules for the correct use of the apostrophe to show possession or indicate the missing letters in contractions.

Since the 1950's, interest has been steadily rising in the issues involving letter-sound relationships with respect to learning to read (Bailey, 1967; Clymer, 1963; Emans, 1967; Venezky, 1967), as well as in sound-letter correspondences as aids in learning to spell (Hanna & others, 1966; Hodges, 1964a; E. Horn, 1957; Lester, 1964; Moore, 1951; National Conference on Research in English, 1966; Petty, 1955; Rudorf, 1965). The extensive computer analyses at Stanford (Hanna & others, 1966; National Conference on Research in English, 1966) of phoneme-grapheme relationships in 17,310 words were based upon a "standard" (Midwest) pronunciation system of 22 vowel and 30 consonant phonemes. With phonological cues alone, it was found that individual phoneme-grapheme relationships could be predicted with an accuracy of 89.6 percent, but when the algorithm was applied in terms of full words, this accuracy dropped to just under 50 percent. Of the words spelled incorrectly, 6,332 (37.2 percent) were spelled with one error; 1,941 (11.4 percent) had two errors; and 390 (2.3 percent) had three or more errors. A comparison was then made (Solomon & MacNeill, 1966) between computer output based on the phonemic-graphemic algorithm and actual student performance in the elementary grades, on the basis of scores made by pupils who participated in the *New Iowa Spelling Scale* development (Greene, 1954). With a 1,000-word sample selected from the

New Iowa Spelling Scale, the results indicated that student performance exceeded the algorithm performance for high-frequency words, but the algorithm performance greatly exceeded student performance for the words occurring less frequently. Inferences were made that, using simple sound rules, the algorithm spelled as a third-grade pupil; and using a more sophisticated set of rules, it spelled as a fifth-grade pupil. In comparing the algorithm with student spelling performance on a list of spelling "demons," the algorithm was found to be inadequate for those words which students found particularly difficult to spell (Solomon & MacNeill, 1966). Words of such great difficulty must be treated as individual learning tasks.

The promise of the Stanford study for establishing usable generalizations rests upon (1) the validity of the pronunciation system used to establish the regularity of phoneme-grapheme relationships; (2) the reliability of resulting generalizations in terms of regional and social dialects and words with more than one acceptable pronunciation; and (3) the extent to which students can assimilate and effectively use generalizations in learning to spell. Various issues pertaining to all three of the foregoing remain unresolved.

There are differences of opinion among linguists about what represents a "standard" pronunciation and what the best definition of a *phoneme* should be. The effect of generalizations based on "standard" pronunciation upon spelling, when local speech deviates from this so-called standard, has yet to be established. The fact that 313 rules were required for the computer algorithm (Rudorf, 1965) is understandable when it is remembered that as many as 20 separate component "rules" may be required to state a single general rule in computer language. Of the approximately 170 graphic options for the 52 phonemes described in the Stanford study, 40 occurred only once in each of 40 different words in the corpus. Evidence concerning rules that has been reported thus far indicates that, even when very few rules are taught, many students cannot remember them, do not recall them when needed, or misapply them (Archer, 1930; Cook & O'Shea, 1914; Jackson, 1953).

Data have yet to be reported with regard to (1) which phonological generalizations have the greatest potential value for students learning to spell; (2) which generalizations should be taught and which should be left to the student to discover; (3) which generalizations are likely to be misapplied; and (4) what extent students can establish generalizations intuitively (and may yet be unable to state them explicitly) and apply them successfully in writing.

Methods for effectively teaching rules include the following recommendations: (1) with few exceptions, only one rule should be introduced at a time; (2) students should be taught each rule inductively in connection with the words to which each rule applies; (3) both positive and negative aspects of the rule, if any, should be taught; (4) after initial explanation, the rules should be systematically applied and reviewed; and (5) the emphasis should always be on the use of rules rather than on their verbalization (E. Horn, 1960; King, 1932; Sartorius, 1931).

Role of Tests. In addition to the use of tests for motivation, diagnosis, and evaluation, tests administered before related study are basic to the instructional program, in order to show the individual student which words and parts of words he needs to study and to reveal to the teacher individual differences requiring special attention (Fitzgerald, 1951*b;* Gates, 1931; E. Horn, 1967; T. Horn, 1958; Kilzer, 1926; McKee, 1939). For instructional purposes, evidence indicates that the modified sentence-recall form is the most valid and economical test: that is, the teacher pronounces each word, uses it in an oral sentence, and pronounces it again. The students then write the word (Brody, 1944; W. Cook, 1932; Nisbet, 1939). Such preliminary tests are sometimes criticized on the erroneous assumption that initial errors are likely to persist. Evidence indicates that, with a five-periods-per-week plan, a negligible percentage of errors made in the Monday test were duplicated in the Friday test, if they had been immediately corrected on Monday (McKee, 1939). Evidence reported earlier indicated that such tests before study appeared to be less effective in grade 2 than in higher grades (Gates, 1931); later evidence indicates that test-study procedures are equal to or superior to study-test procedures for grade 2 as well as other levels (R. Cook, 1957; Fitzgerald, 1951*b;* T. Horn, 1958, 1960). The corrected-test technique is by far the most efficient single procedure for learning to spell if the students (1) clearly understand the purpose of the pretest; (2) immediately correct their errors with care; and (3) understand that alert correction of the "pretest" contributes greatly to the reduction of errors (Hall, 1964; T. Horn, 1947; Tyson, 1953). There is some evidence that the corrected-test method is more effective with better spellers (Schoephoerster, 1962).

DIAGNOSIS AND EVALUATION. The use of tests to motivate and guide learning and to provide information for accommodating individual differences has been discussed elsewhere. Two other highly important functions of tests are (1) for comparing class or school achievement in spelling with analogous achievement of other classes and schools and (2) as dependent variables in instructional research. The fact that poor tests are often used for both of the foregoing purposes makes careful appraisal of tests imperative, at least to the extent of perusing competent available appraisals before test selection (Buros, 1965).

Paralleling the early scientific study of written vocabularies was the development of scaled lists of words from which teachers could select test words for measuring achievement in spelling (Ashbaugh, 1922; Ayres, 1915; Buckingham, 1913; Hudelson & others, 1920). The *New Iowa Spelling Scale* (Greene, 1954) appeared some 30 years after Ashbaugh's *Iowa Spelling Scales.* The best standardized spelling tests for comparing the status of one school with that of another are found as subtests of achievement batteries. It should be pointed out, however, that most of these tests are of the recognition type: for example, "choose the incorrect spelling out of four words" (*Iowa Tests of Basic Skills,* 1956; *Stanford Achievement Test,* 1964); or some combination such as "mark each key word as capital R (right), capital W (wrong), capital DK (don't know)"; and if capital W, testee writes corrected spelling, (*Metropolitan,* 1964). It is probably worth noting that, although the foregoing techniques represent editorial requirements similar to proofreading, evidence indicates that the subtests may not differentiate between groups who were instructed in proofreading as compared with those given no such instruction (Bishop, 1965; Oswalt, 1962); whereas, in at least one case (Bishop, 1965), significant differences were obtained on a recall-type dictation test. This seems to confirm earlier data at the junior and senior high school levels which suggest that a student's failure to *recognize* a misspelled word does not mean he cannot spell it correctly under other conditions (Kelley, 1934; Leyson, 1944).

Error Studies. A number of error studies have been reported concerning children's misspelling of words by grade level, specific details causing the greatest difficulty within words, and relationships between spelling difficulty, phonetic elements of words, and the serial-position effect on spelling errors (Fitzgerald, 1951*a;* Gates, 1937; Jenson, 1962; Johnson, 1950; Kooi & others, 1965; Lamb, 1964; Ludes, 1955; Petty, 1957; Plessas, 1963; Traxler, 1948). These and other investigations (Fitzgerald, 1951*b;* Masters, 1927; Pollock, 1954; Spache, 1941*a,* 1941*b*) provide data indicating the incidence of errors grade by grade, the persistence of errors word by word throughout the grades, and probable causes of errors.

SPELLING REFORM. The spelling "ghoti" for *fish* ("gh" as in *enough,* "o" as in *women,* "ti" as in *nation*), attributed to George Bernard Shaw, is probably one of the better-known examples of interest in spelling reform. It is also an example of the well-intentioned utterances that exasperate linguists. "It is surely a national disgrace to us to find that the wildest arguments concerning English spelling and etymology are consistently being used even by well-educated persons whose ignorance of early English pronunciation and of modern English phonetics is so complete, that they have no suspicion whatever of the amazing worthlessness of their ludicrous utterances" (Skeat, 1892). Although a detailed history of English spelling is not available in print, useful bibliographies are available (Venezky, 1967; Wijk, 1959). A brief chronology of individuals interested in spelling reform indicates that such interest is not a recent phenomenon: Orm, 1200; Smith, 1568; Hart, 1569; Lantham, 1575; Bullokar, 1580; Mulcaster, 1582; Gill, 1621; Butler, 1634; Howell, 1662; Douglas, 1740; Webster, 1789; Ellis, 1880; Mencken, 1937; Smith, 1965 (Venezky, 1967; Wijk, 1959).

A new era of activity to bring about spelling reform in the United States began in 1906 with establishment of the Simplified Spelling Board, supported in part by funds provided by Andrew Carnegie. This was followed by the formation in 1908 of the Simplified Spelling Society in England, with Skeat as president. A series of bulletins was issued by the Simplified Spelling Board in the United States and pamphlets were printed by the Simplified Spelling Society in England until interrupted by World War I. These activities resumed on both sides of the Atlantic following the war and included joint publications by existing organized groups in 1925 and 1931 (Craigie, 1927; Wijk, 1959). Except for a relatively few minor changes (e.g., "tho" for *though*), none of the proposals for reform achieved general public acceptance.

Since even the less radical proposals for spelling reform would have necessitated the manufacture of new type and the printing of special materials for reading instruction, the factor of publishing costs added an inhibitory effect to that of the widespread public reluctance to change the system of written symbols. Nevertheless, interest in reform again took an upswing following World War II. Beginning in England (Downing, 1962), experimentation with the Initial Teaching Alphabet, or ITA, was conducted in reading instruction to explore its possibilities for alleviating initial reading difficulties. Because the ITA procedures involved a transition to traditional orthography, wholesale revamping of type forms was unnecessary, thus easing the problem of printing costs. The whole movement has been subject to considerable controversy, with significant differences in favor of ITA reported in some instances (Downing, 1965; Mazurkiewicz, 1966, 1967; Tanyzer & Alpert, 1966), whereas others reported nonsignificant differences (Fry, 1966, 1967; H. Hahn, 1966) or had reservations or suggestions concerning research designs (Fry, 1967; Marsh, 1966; Ohanian, 1966). The evidence indicates that the transition from ITA to traditional orthography does not cause negative effects on spelling (Fry, 1967; Mazurkiewicz, 1967; National Foundation for Educational Research in England and Wales, 1967).

In contrast to proposals that English spelling be reformed, the Stanford studies of sound-to-spelling correspondences (Hanna & others, 1966) and spelling-to-sound correspondences (Venezky, 1967) may provide possibilities for alternatives. Venezky has entered the next research phase following his recent studies, that of determining whether or not, given that a general pattern is constructed to account for a spelling-sound relationship, literates actually use this pattern. As suggested in the discussion concerning the utility of learning generalizations, a comparable phase is needed for sound-spelling relationships: namely, whether or not, given a general pattern constructed to account for a sound-spelling relationship, writers actually use this pattern. It appears unlikely that public lethargy will be moved by even a reasonable proposal based upon existing symbols (Wijk, 1959). If so, future evidence from the next phases of the Stanford studies would assume even greater importance.

NEEDED RESEARCH. Necessary additional research has been suggested from time to time throughout this article, but the need to efficiently apply what is already known to classroom instruction is of equal importance. In addition to research needs identified elsewhere, other areas include: (1) replication of studies needing adequate research design and data analyses; (2) extension of recent studies in applied linguistics with particular reference to implications for word selection, generalization, and contributions to learning strategies; (3) identification of the load-carrying elements which improve spelling achievement, such as the language arts, and especially composition; and (4) possible contributions of computer-assisted instruction.

Thomas D. Horn
University of Texas

References

Aaron, Ira E. "The Relationship of Auditory-Visual Discrimination to Spelling Ability." Doctoral dissertation. U Minnesota, 1954.

Abbott, Edwina E. "On the Analysis of the Memory Consciousness in Orthography." In Colvin, Stephen S. (Ed.) *Studies From the Psychological Laboratory of the University of Illinois. Psychol Monogr* 11(1):127–58; 1909.

Adkins, Margaret M. "Relationships Involving Particular Groups of Syndromes; Factors Related to School Success." *Monogr Soc Res Child Develop* 8:503–22, 583–638; 1943.

Ames, Wilbur S. "A Comparison of Spelling Textbooks." *El Engl* 42:146–50, 214; 1965.

Anderson, Irving H. *Comparisons of the Reading and Spelling Achievement and Quality of Handwriting of Groups of English, Scottish, and American Children.* USOE Cooperative Research Project No. 1903. U Michigan, 1963. 305p.

Archer, Clifford P. "Transfer of Training in Spelling." *U Iowa Stud Ed* 5(5):1–63; 1930.

Ashbaugh, Ernest J. *The Iowa Spelling Scales. J Ed Res Monogr*, No. 3. Bobbs-Merrill, 1922. 144p.

Ayer, Fred C. "An Evaluation of High-School Spelling." *Sch R* 59:233–6; 1951.

Ayres, Leonard P. *A Measuring Scale for Ability in Spelling.* Russell Sage, 1915. 58p.

Bailey, Mildred H. "The Utility of Phonic Generalizations in Grades One Through Six." *Reading Teach* 20:413–8; 1967.

Baker, Harry J. *Educational Disability and Case Studies in Remedial Teaching.* Bobbs-Merrill, 1929. 172p.

Barnhart, Clarence L. (Ed.) *American College Dictionary.* Random, 1953. 1432p.

Beltramo, Louise. "An Alphabetical Approach to the Teaching of Reading in Grade One." Doctoral dissertation. State U Iowa, 1954.

Betts, Emmett A. "Inter-relationship of Reading and Spelling." *El Engl R* 22:13–23; 1945.

Betts, Emmett A. *Second Spelling Vocabulary Study.* American, 1949. 36p.

Bishop, Inez E. "The Comparison of a Conventional Method of Teaching Spelling With a Method Emphasizing Proofreading as an Integral Part of Spelling Program." Doctoral dissertation. U Illinois, 1965.

Blair, Glenn M. *Diagnostic and Remedial Teaching.* Macmillan, 1956. 409p.

Bolen, John Emil. "A Study of Manuscript Writing and Spelling Achievement in the Third Grade." Doctoral dissertation. U California, 1964.

Bond, Elden A. *Tenth-Grade Abilities and Achievements.* Teachers Col, Columbia U, 1940. 67p.

Bradford, Henry F. "Oral-Aural Differentiation Among Basic Speech Sounds as a Factor in Spelling Readiness." *El Sch J* 54:354–8; 1954.

Brody, David S. "A Comparative Study of Different Forms of Spelling Tests." *J Ed Psychol* 35:129–44; 1944.

Browning, Julia R. "Writing Vocabularies: A Study of Significant New Words in the United States Since 1926." Master's thesis. U Texas, 1957.

Brueckner, Leo J., and Melby, Ernest O. *Diagnostic and Remedial Teaching.* Houghton, 1931. 598p.

Buckingham, Burdette R. *Buckingham Extension of the Ayres Spelling Scale.* Bobbs-Merrill, 1913. 11p.

Buckingham, Burdette R., and Dolch, Edward W. *A Combined Word List.* Ginn, 1936. 185p.

Buros, Oscar K. (Ed.) *The Third Mental Measurements Yearbook.* Gryphon. 1949. 1047p.

Buros, Oscar K. (Ed.) *The Fourth Mental Measurements Yearbook.* Gryphon, 1953. 1163p.

Buros, Oscar K. (Ed.) *The Fifth Mental Measurements Yearbook.* Gryphon, 1959. 1292p.

Buros, Oscar K. (Ed.) *Tests in Print.* Gryphon, 1961. 479p.

Buros, Oscar K. (Ed.) *The Sixth Mental Measurements Yearbook.* Gryphon, 1965. 1714p.

Buzby, John J., and Mann, Lester. "The TMI Self-tutoring Program in Spelling Compared With Teacher and Flash Card Taught Programs." *J Ed Res* 55:585–6; 1962.

Byers, Loretta. "The Relationship of Manuscript and Cursive Handwriting to Accuracy in Spelling." *J Ed Res* 57:87–9; 1963.

Carrell, James, and Pendergast, Kathleen. "An Experimental Study of the Possible Relation Between Errors of Speech and Spelling." *J Speech Hearing Disorders* 19:327–34; 1954.

Carroll, Herbert A. *Generalizations of Bright and Dull Children.* Teachers Col, Columbia U, 1930. 54p.

Chase, W. Linwood. "Subject Preferences of Fifth-grade Children." *El Sch J* 50:204–11; 1949.

Clark, John W. "American Spelling." In Vallins, George H. *Spelling.* Deutsch, 1954. p. 174–92.

Clymer, Theodore. "The Utility of Phonic Generalizations in the Primary Grades." *Reading Teach* 16:252–8; 1963.

Columba, Sister Mary. *A Study of Interests and Their*

Relations to Other Factors of Achievement in Elementary School Subjects. Catholic U, 1926. 35p.

Comerford, Joseph F. "Perceptual Abilities in Spelling." Doctoral dissertation. Boston U, 1954.

Connecticut Common Sch J 3:34–5; 1840–41.

Cook, Ruth C. "Evaluation of Two Methods of Teaching Spelling." *El Sch J* 59:21–7; 1957.

Cook, Walter W. "The Measurement of General Spelling Ability Involving Controlled Comparisons Between Techniques." *U Iowa Stud Ed* 6(6):1–112; 1932.

Cook, William A., and O'Shea, M. V. *The Child and His Spelling.* Bobbs-Merrill, 1914. 282p.

Cornman, Oliver P. *Spelling in the Elementary School: An Experimental and Statistical Investigation.* Ginn, 1902. 98p.

Craigie, William A. *English Spelling. Its Rules and Reasons.* Croft, 1927. 115p.

Dale, Edgar, and Razik, Taher. *Bibliography of Vocabulary Studies.* 2nd rev. ed. Bureau of Educational Research and Service, Ohio State U, 1963. 257p.

Dalton, M. M. "A Visual Survey of 5000 School Children." *J Ed Res* 37:81–94; 1943.

Damgaard, Thelma L. J. "Auditory Acuity and Discrimination as Factors in Spelling Competence." Doctoral dissertation. Stanford U, 1956.

Davis, Bennie Joe. "A Study of the Vocabulary Overlap Between Words Written by Children and Words Written by Adults." Master's thesis. U Texas, 1954.

Deacon, Lawrence. "The Teaching of Spelling Can Become Too Individualized." *Ed* 76:300–2; 1956.

DeBoer, John J. "Oral and Written Language." *R Ed Res* 25:107–20; 1955.

Diserens, Charles M., and Vaughn, James. "The Experimental Psychology of Motivation." *Psychol B* 28:15–65; 1931.

Dobson, Eric J. *English Pronunciation 1500–1700,* Vol. 1. Clarendon, 1957. 444p.

Downing, John A. "The Relationship Between Reading Attainment and the Inconsistency of English Spelling at the Infants' School Stage." *Br J Ed Psychol* 32:166–77; 1962.

Downing, John A. *The Initial Teaching Alphabet Reading Experiment.* Scott, 1965.

Doyle, Andrew M. "A Study of Spelling Achievement." *Cath Ed R* 48:171–4; 1950.

Durrell, Donald D. *Improving Reading Instruction.* Harcourt, 1956. 402p.

Edgerton, Alice K., and Twombly, Ruth W. "Programmed Course in Spelling." *El Sch J* 62:380–6; 1962.

Emans, Robert. "The Usefulness of Phonic Generalizations Above the Primary Grades." *Reading Teach* 20:419–25; 1967.

Fairhurst, Susie S. "Psychological Analysis and Educational Method in Spelling." In *Report, British Association for the Advancement of Science,* Vol. 83. The Association, 1913. p. 302–4.

Fernald, Grace. "Report of Experimental Work With Poor Spellers and Non-readers, With Applications to Normal Children." In Terman, Lewis M., and others. (Eds.) *Intelligence Tests and School Reorganization.* Harcourt, 1922. p. 103–11.

Fernald, Mabel R. "The Diagnosis of Mental Imagery." *Psychol Monogr* 14(1); 1912. 169p.

Fitzgerald, James A. "Letters Written Outside the School by Children of the Fourth, Fifth, and Sixth Grades: A Study of Vocabulary, Spelling Errors, and Situations." *U Iowa Stud Ed* 9(1):7–50; 1934.

Fitzgerald, James A. *A Basic Life Spelling Vocabulary.* Bruce, 1951(a). 161p.

Fitzgerald, James A. *The Teaching of Spelling.* Bruce, 1951(b). 233p.

Forlano, George. *School Learning With Various Methods of Practice and Rewards.* Teachers Col, Columbia U, 1936. 114p.

Fox, William H., and Eaton, Merrill T. "Analysis of the Spelling Proficiency of 82,833 Pupils in Grades 2 to 8 in 3,547 Teaching Units of the City Schools in Indiana." *Indiana U B Sch Ed* 22(2):3–50; 1946.

Francis, W. Nelson. *The Structure of American English.* Ronald, 1958. 614p.

Friedman, Myles I. "The Effectiveness of Machine Instruction in the Teaching of Second and Third Grade Spelling." *J Ed Res* 60:366–9; 1967.

Fries, Charles C. "Linguistics and the Teaching of Reading." *Reading Teach* 17:594–8; 1964.

Fry, Edward B. "First Grade Reading Instruction Using Diacritical Marking System, Initial Teaching Alphabet, and Basal Reading System." *Reading Teach* 19:666–9; 1966.

Fry, Edward B. "First Grade Reading Instruction Using Diacritical Marking System, Initial Teaching Alphabet, and Basal Reading System—Extended to Second Grade." *Reading Teach* 20:687–93; 1967.

Furness, Edna L. "Pink Pills for a Pale Spelling Situation." *Am Sch Bd J* 133:17–8; 1956.

Furness, Edna L. "Spelling: Illogical and Inconsistent." *Clearing House* 33:330–3; 1959.

Gates, Arthur I. *The Psychology of Reading and Spelling With Special Reference to Disability.* Teachers Col, Columbia U, 1922. 108p.

Gates, Arthur I. "A Study of the Role of Visual Perception, Intelligence, and Certain Associative Processes in Reading and Spelling." *J Ed Psychol* 17:433–45; 1926.

Gates, Arthur I. "An Experimental Comparison of the Study-Test and Test-Study Methods in Spelling." *J Ed Psychol* 22:1–19; 1931.

Gates, Arthur I. *Generalization and Transfer in Spelling.* Teachers Col, Columbia U, 1935. 80p.

Gates, Arthur I. *A List of Spelling Difficulties in 3876 Words.* Teachers Col, Columbia U, 1937. 166p.

Gates, Arthur I., and Chase, Esther H. "Methods and Theories of Learning to Spell Tested by Studies of Deaf Children." *J Ed Psychol* 17:289–300; 1926.

Gates, Arthur I., and Graham, Frederick B. "The Value of Various Games and Activities in Teaching Spelling." *J Ed Res* 28:1–9; 1934.

Gates, Arthur I., and Russell, David H. *Diagnostic and Remedial Spelling Manual.* Teachers Col, Columbia U, 1937. 50p.

Gates, Arthur I., and others. "A Modern Systematic vs. an Opportunistic Method of Teaching." *Teach Col Rec* 27:679–700; 1926.

Gates, Arthur I., and others. *Educational Psychology,* 3rd ed. Macmillan, 1949. 818p.

Gilbert, Luther C. "An Experimental Investigation of Eye Movements in Learning to Spell Words." *Psychol Monogr* 43(3); 1932. 81p.

Gilbert, Luther C. "Effect of Reading on Spelling in the Ninth Grade." *Sch R* 42:197–204; 1934(*a*).

Gilbert, Luther C. "Effect of Reading on Spelling in the Secondary Schools." *California Q Sec Ed* 9: 269–75; 1934(*b*).

Gilbert, Luther C. "A Study of the Effect of Reading on Spelling." *J Ed Res* 28:570–6; 1935.

Gilbert, Luther C. "A Genetic Study of Growth in Perceptual Habits in Spelling." *El Sch J* 40:346–57; 1940.

Gilbert, Luther C., and Gilbert, Doris W. "Training for Speed and Accuracy of Visual Perception in Learning to Spell." *U California Pub Ed* 7:351–426; 1942.

Gove, Philip B. (Ed.) *Webster's Third New International Dictionary.* Merriam, 1963. p. 33a–51a.

Greene, Harry A. *The New Iowa Spelling Scale.* State U Iowa, 1954. 178p.

Groff, Patrick J. "Visual and Auditory Perception Training and Spelling Achievement." *El Engl* 42: 163–4, 168; 1965.

Guiler, Walter S., and Lease, Gilbert A. "An Experimental Study of Methods of Instruction in Spelling." *El Sch J* 43:234–8; 1942.

Hahn, Harry T. "Three Approaches to Beginning Reading Instruction—ITA, Language Arts and Basic Readers." *Reading Teach* 19:590–4; 1966.

Hahn, William P. "Phonics: A Boon to Spelling?" *El Sch J* 64:383–6; 1964.

Hall, Norman. "The Letter Mark-Out Corrected Test." *J Ed Res* 58:148–57; 1964.

Hanna, Paul R., and Moore, James T., Jr. "Spelling—From Spoken Word to Written Symbol." *El Sch J* 53:329–37; 1953.

Hanna, Paul R., and others. *Phoneme-Grapheme Correspondences as Clues to Spelling Improvement.* USOE Cooperative Research Project No. 1991. GPO, 1966. 1715p.

Harder, Keith C. "The Relative Efficiency of the 'Separate' and 'Together' Methods of Teaching Homonyms." *J Exp Ed* 6(September):7–23; 1937.

Harris, Oliver E. "An Investigation of Spelling Achievement of Secondary School Pupils." *Ed Adm Sup* 34:208–19; 1948.

Hartmann, George W. "The Relative Influence of Visual and Auditory Factors in Spelling Ability." *J Ed Psychol* 22:691–9; 1931.

Hawley, W. E., and Gallup, Jackson. "The 'List' vs. the 'Sentence' Method of Teaching Spelling." *J Ed Res* 5:306–10; 1922.

Hildreth, Gertrude. *Teaching Spelling.* Holt, 1955. 346p.

Hodges, Richard E. *An Analysis of the Phonological Structure of American-English Orthography.* Doctoral dissertation. Stanford U, 1964(*a*).

Hodges, Richard E. "A Short History of Spelling Reform in the United States." *Phi Delta Kappan* 45:330–2; 1964(*b*).

Hollingworth, Leta S. *The Psychology of Special Disability in Spelling.* Teachers Col, Columbia U, 1918. 105p.

Hollingworth, Leta S. *Special Talents and Defects.* Macmillan, 1923. 216p.

Holmes, Jack A. "A Substrata Analysis of Spelling Ability for Elements of Auditory Images." *J Exp Ed* 22:329–49; 1954.

Horn, Ernest. *A Basic Writing Vocabulary.* U Iowa Monogr Education, No. 4, 1926. 225p.

Horn, Ernest. "The Influence of Past Experiences Upon Spelling." *J Ed Res* 19:283–8; 1929(*a*).

Horn, Ernest. "A Source of Confusion in Spelling." *J Ed Res* 19:47–55; 1929(*b*).

Horn, Ernest. "The Incidental Teaching of Spelling." *El Engl R* 14:3–5, 21; 1937.

Horn, Ernest. "The Validity and Reliability of Adult Vocabulary Lists." *El Engl R* 16:129–34, 138; 1939.

Horn, Ernest. "Research in Spelling." *El Engl R* 21:6–13; 1944.

Horn, Ernest. "Phonetics and Spelling." *El Sch J* 57:424–32; 1957.

Horn, Ernest. "Spelling." In Harris, Chester W. (Ed.) *Encyclopedia of Educational Research,* 3rd ed. Macmillan, 1960. p. 1337–54.

Horn, Ernest. "Teaching Spelling." In *What Research Says to the Teacher.* NEA, 1967. 32p.

Horn, Madeline D. (Ch.) *A Study of the Vocabulary of Children Before Entering the First Grade.* International Kindergarten Union, 1928. 36p.

Horn, Thomas D. "The Effect of the Corrected Test on Learning to Spell." *El Sch J* 47:277–85; 1947.

Horn, Thomas D. "Learning to Spell as Affected by Syllabic Presentation of Words." *El Sch J* 49: 263–72; 1949.

Horn, Thomas D. "How Syllables Can Help in Spelling." *Ed* 76:291–5; 1956.

Horn, Thomas D. "Some Issues in Learning to Spell." *Ed* 79:229–33; 1958.

Horn, Thomas D. "Spelling and Children's Written Composition." Reprinted from *El Engl.* NCTE, 1960. p. 52–63.

Horn, Thomas D. "Three Methods of Developing Reading Readiness in Spanish-Speaking Children in First Grade." *Reading Teach* 20:38–42; 1966.

Horn, Thomas D. "Handwriting and Spelling." *R Ed Res* 37:168–77; 1967.

Horn, Thomas D., and Otto, Henry J. "Spelling Instruction: A Curriculum-Wide Approach." Bureau of Laboratory School, U Texas, 1954. 160p.

Hudelson, Earl, and others. "Sixteen Spelling Scales." *Teach Col Rec* 21:337–91; 1920.

Hudson, Jess S., and Toler, Lola. "Instruction in Auditory and Visual Discrimination as Means of Improving Spelling." *El Sch J* 49:466–9; 1949.

Hunter, Walter S. "Learning: IV. Experimental

Studies of Learning." In Murchison, Carl. (Ed.) *A Handbook of General Experimental Psychology.* Clark U, 1934. p. 497–570.

Ibeling, Frederick W. "Supplementary Phonics Instruction and Reading and Spelling Ability." *El Sch J* 62:152–6; 1961.

Jackson, Joseph. "The Influence of Word Analysis Upon Spelling Attainment." *J Ed Res* 47:107–15; 1953.

Jameson, Gloria R. "Oral English Language Proficiency Test I: The Development of a Phonemic Analysis for an Oral English Proficiency Test for Spanish-Speaking School Beginners." Doctoral dissertation. U Texas, 1967.

Jenson, Arthur R. "Spelling Errors and the Serial-Position Effect." *J Ed Psychol* 53:105–9; 1962.

Johnson, Leslie W. "One Hundred Words Most Often Misspelled by Children in the Elementary Grades." *J Ed Res* 44:154–5; 1950.

Kelley, Edmund G. "The Relationship Between the Ability to Correct Spelling Errors in a Proofreading Test and the Ability to Spell Dictated Words." Master's thesis. U Iowa, 1934.

Kennedy, Arthur G. *Current English.* Ginn, 1935. 737p.

Kenyon, John S., and Knott, Thomas A. *A Pronouncing Dictionary of American English.* Merriam, 1951. 484p.

Kilzer, Louis R. "The Test-Study Method *vs.* the Study-Test Method in Teaching Spelling." *Sch R* 34:521–5; 1926.

King, Luella M. *Learning and Applying Spelling Rules in Grades Three to Eight.* Teachers Col, Columbia U, 1932. 80p.

Knoell, Dorothy M., and Harris, Chester W. "A Factor Analysis of Spelling Ability." *J Ed Res* 46:95–111; 1952.

Kooi, Beverly J., and others. "Spelling Errors and the Serial-Position Effect." *J Ed Psychol* 56:334–6; 1965.

Krueger, William C. F. "The Effect of Overlearning on Retention." *J Exp Psychol* 12:71–8; 1929.

Kurath, Hans. (Ed.) *Linguistic Atlas of New England.* 3 vols. Brown U, 1939–41.

Lamb, Hazel B. "A Study of the Extent and Nature of Words Misspelled by Tenth Grade Students Enrolled in the Jefferson City, Missouri, High School." Doctoral dissertation. U Missouri, 1964.

Lester, Mark. "Graphemic-Phonemic Correspondences as the Basis for Teaching Spelling." *El Engl* 41:748–52; 1964.

Leyson, Elta L. "A Comparison of the Ability of Seventh-Grade Pupils to Proofread Studied and Unstudied Words When Presented in Different Test Situations." Master's thesis. U Iowa, 1944.

Ludes, Titus H. "A Survey of the Spelling Errors Found in the Undirected Writings of Catholic Elementary and Secondary School Pupils in the United States." Doctoral dissertation. Fordham U, 1955.

Mack, Esther. "An Investigation of the Importance of Various Word Analysis Abilities in Reading and Spelling Achievement." Doctoral dissertation. Boston U, 1953.

MacMillan, Robert W. "A Study of the Effect of Socioeconomic Factors on the School Achievement of Spanish-Speaking School Beginners." Doctoral dissertation. U Texas, 1966.

Marsh, R. W. "Some Cautionary Notes on the Results of the London i.t.a. Experiment." *Reading Res Q* 2(Fall):119–26; 1966.

Mason, Geoffrey P. "Word Discrimination and Spelling." *J Ed Res* 50:617–21; 1957.

Masters, Harry V. "A Study of Spelling Errors." *U Iowa Stud Ed* 4(4):1–80; 1927.

Mazurkiewicz, Albert J. "ITA and TO Reading Achievement When Methodology Is Controlled." *Reading Teach* 19:606–10; 1966.

Mazurkiewicz, Albert J. "ITA and TO Reading Achievement When Methodology Is Controlled—Extended Into Second Grade." *Reading Teach* 20:726–9; 1967.

McCann, Letitia Moerke. "Writing Vocabularies: A Comparison of the Nature, Extent, and Mobility of Child and Adult Writing Needs." Master's thesis. U Texas, 1955.

McCarthy, Dorothea. "Language Development in Children." In Carmichael, Leonard. (Ed.) *Manual of Child Psychology.* Wiley, 1954. p. 492–630.

McDowell, Neil A. "A Study of the Academic Capabilities and Achievements of Three Ethnic Groups: Anglo, Negro, and Spanish Surname, in San Antonio, Texas." Doctoral dissertation. U Texas, 1966.

McGovney, Margarita. "Spelling Deficiency in Children of Superior General Ability." *El Engl R* 7:146–8; 1930.

McKee, Paul G. "Teaching and Testing Spelling by Column and Context Forms." Doctoral dissertation. State U Iowa, 1924.

McKee, Paul G. *Language in the Elementary School,* rev. ed. Houghton, 1939. 500p.

Mendenhall, James E. *An Analysis of Spelling Errors: A Study of Factors Associated With Word Difficulty.* Teachers Col, Columbia U, 1930. 65p.

Merrill, Maud A. "On the Relation of Intelligence to Achievement in the Case of Mentally Retarded Children." *Comp Psychol Monogr* 2(10):1–100; 1924.

Moore, James T., Jr. "Phonetic Elements Appearing in a Three-Thousand Word Spelling Vocabulary." Doctoral dissertation. Stanford U, 1951.

Mulcaster, Richard. *Mulcaster's Elementarie—1582, The First Part of the Elementarie.* Reprint. Clarendon, 1925. 292p.

National Conference on Research in English. *Research on Handwriting and Spelling.* NCTE, 1966. 79p.

National Education Association, Department of Superintendence. "A List of Spelling 'Demons' for the Junior High School." In *Junior High School Curriculum.* 5th Yearbook. NEA, 1927. p. 114–20.

National Education Association, Research Division. *The Three R's Hold Their Own at the Midcentury.* NEA, 1951. 28p.

National Foundation for Educational Research in England and Wales. *The i.t.a. Symposium.* King, Thorne, and Stace, Sussex, England. 1967. 168p.

Neilson, William A. (Ed.) *Webster's New International Dictionary.* 2nd ed. Merriam, 1954. p. xxii–xc.

Newton, Bertha M. "A Study of Certain Factors Related to Achievement in Spelling." Doctoral dissertation. U Missouri, 1960.

Nisbet, Stanley D. "Non-Dictated Spelling Tests." *Br J Ed Psychol* 9:29–44; 1939.

Ohanian, Vera. "Control Populations in i/t/a Experiments." *El Engl* 43:373–80; 1966.

Osburn, Worth J. "Teaching Spelling by Teaching Syllables and Root Words." *El Sch J* 55:32–41; 1954.

Oswalt, William W. "The Effect of Proofreading for Spelling Errors on Spelling Achievement of Fifth Grade Pupils." Doctoral dissertation. Temple U, 1962.

Ott, Elizabeth H. "Oral English Language Proficiency Test II: A Study of Levels of Fluency and Proficiency in Oral English of Spanish-Speaking School Beginners." Doctoral dissertation. U Texas, 1967.

Peake, Nellie L. "Relation Between Spelling Ability and Reading Ability." *J Exp Ed* 9:192–3; 1940.

Personke, Carl R. "Spelling Achievement of Scottish and American Children." *El Sch J* 66:337–43; 1966.

Petty, Walter T. An Analysis of Certain Phonetic Elements in a Selected Test of Persistently Difficult Spelling Words." Doctoral dissertation. State U Iowa, 1955.

Petty, Walter T. "Phonetic Elements as Factors in Spelling Difficulty." *J Ed Res* 51:209–14; 1957.

Phelan, Sister Mary Benedict. *Visual Perception in Relation to Variance in Reading and Spelling.* Catholic U, 1940. 48p.

Plesass, Gus P. "Children's Errors in Spelling Homonyms." *El Sch J* 64:163–8; 1963.

Plesass, Gus P., and Dison, Peggy A. "Spelling Performances of Good Readers." *California J Ed Res* 16:14–22; 1965.

Plessas, Gus P., and Ladley, Dorothea M. "Some Implications of Spelling and Reading Research." *El Engl* 42:142–5; 1963.

Pollock, Thomas C. "Spelling Report." *Col Engl* 16:102–9; 1954.

Read, Allen W. "The Spelling Bee: A Linguistic Institution of the American Folk." *PMLA* 56:495–512; 1941.

Reid, Hale C. "Evaluating Five Methods of Teaching Spelling—Second and Third Grades." *Instructor* 75:77, 82; 1966.

Reid, Hale C., and Hieronymus, A. N. *An Evaluation of Five Methods of Teaching Spelling in the Second and Third Grades.* Cooperative Research Project No. 1869. State U Iowa, 1963. 111p.

Rice, J. M. "The Futility of the Spelling Grind." *Forum* 23:1963–72; 1897.

Rinsland, Henry D. "A Basic Vocabulary of Elementary School Children." Macmillan, 1945. 636p.

Rogness, Alton S. "Grouping Spelling Words According to the Rule." Doctoral dissertation. Colorado State Col, 1953.

Rosemeier, Robert A. "Effectiveness of Forewarning About Errors in Response-Selective Learning." *J Ed Psychol* 56:309–14; 1965.

Ruch, Theodore C. "Factors Influencing the Relative Economy of Massed and Distributed Practice in Learning." *Psychol R* 35:19–45; 1928.

Rudisill, Mabel. "Interrelations of Functional Phonic Knowledge, Reading, Spelling, and Mental Age." *El Sch J* 57:264–7; 1957.

Rudorf, E. Hugh. "The Development of an Algorithm for American-English Spelling. Doctoral dissertation. Stanford U, 1965.

Russell, David H. *Characteristics of Good and Poor Spellers.* Teachers Col, Columbia U, 1937. 103p.

Russell, David H. "A Diagnostic Study of Spelling Readiness." *J Ed Res* 37:276–83; 1943.

Russell, David H. "Spelling Ability in Relation to Reading and Vocabulary Achievement." *El Engl R* 23:32–7; 1946.

Russell, David H. "Interrelationships of the Language Arts and Personality." *El Engl R* 30:167–80; 1953.

Russell, David H. "A Second Study of Characteristics of Good and Poor Spellers." *J Ed Psychol* 46:129–41; 1955.

Russell, David H. "Auditory Abilities and Achievement in Spelling in the Primary Grades." *J Ed Psychol* 49:315–9; 1958.

Russell, Karlene V. "The Effect of Word Analysis on Spelling Ability." Doctoral dissertation. Boston U, 1954.

Sand, Harold J. "An Evaluation of the Effects of Marks as Incentives to Pupil Growth in Spelling Ability and of the Comparative Values of Equated Scales and Informal Tests as Measurements of the Progress." *J Ed Res* 31:678–82; 1938.

Sartorius, Ina C. *Generalization in Spelling.* Teachers Col, Columbia U, 1931. 65p.

Schoephoerster, Hugh. "Research Into Variations of the Test-Study Plan of Teaching Spelling." *El Engl* 39:460–2; 1962.

Schonell, Fred J. "The Relation Between Defective Speech and Disability in Spelling." *Br J Ed Psychol* 4:123–39; 1934.

Schonell, Fred J. *Backwardness in the Basic Subjects.* Oliver, 1942. 560p.

Seegers, J. Conrad. (Ch.) *Vocabulary Problems in the Elementary School.* National Conference on Research in English, 7th Annual Research Bulletin. Scott, 1939. 60p.

Shane, Harold G. *Research Helps in Teaching the Language Arts.* ASCD, 1955. 80p.

Shuy, Roger W. (Ed.) *Social Dialects and Language Learning.* NCTE, 1964. 157p.

Skeat, Walter W. *Principles of English Etymology,* Vol. 1. Clarendon, 1892. 547p.

Smith, Nila B. *American Reading Instruction.* International Reading Association, 1965. p. 25–30, 66.

Solomon, Herbert, and MacNeill, Ian. "Spelling Ability: A Comparison Between Computer Output

Based on a Phonemic-Graphemic Algorithm and Actual Student Performance in Elementary Grades." Stanford U, 1966. 38p.
Spache, George. "A Critical Analysis of Various Methods of Classifying Spelling Errors, I." *J Ed Psychol* 31:111–34; 1940(*a*).
Spache, George. "The Role of Visual Defects in Spelling and Reading Disabilities." *Am J Orthopsychiatry* 10:229–38; 1940(*b*).
Spache, George. "Spelling Disability Correlates I— Factors Probably Causal in Spelling Disability." *J Ed Res* 34:561–86; 1941(*a*).
Spache, George. "Spelling Disability Correlates II— Factors That May Be Related to Spelling Disability." *J Ed Res* 35:119–37; 1941(*b*).
Sparrow, Julia L. A Study of the Relationship Between Spelling Ability and Reading Ability." Doctoral dissertation. State U Iowa, 1951.
Sweet, Henry. *A History of English Sounds From the Earliest Period.* Clarendon, 1888. 409p.
Tanyzer, Harold J., and Alpert, Harvey. "Three Different Basal Reading Systems and First Grade Reading Achievement." *Reading Teach* 19:636–42; 1966.
Templin, Mildred C. "A Comparison of the Spelling Achievement of Normal and Defective Hearing Subjects." *J Ed Psychol* 39:337–46; 1948.
Templin, Mildred C. "Phonic Knowledge and Its Relation to the Spelling and Reading Achievement of Fourth Grade Pupils." *J Ed Res* 47:441–54; 1954.
Thomas, Charles K. *An Introduction to the Phonetics of American English.* Ronald, 1947. 181p.
Thorndike, Edward L. *The Teacher's Word Book.* Teachers Col, Columbia U, 1921. 134p.
Thorndike, Edward L. *The Psychology of Wants, Interests, and Attitudes.* Appleton, 1935. 301p.
Thorndike, Edward L. *The Teaching of English Suffixes.* Teachers Col, Columbia U, 1941. 81p.
Thorndike, Edward L., and Lorge, Irving. *The Teacher's Word Book of 30,000 Words.* Teachers Col, Columbia U, 1944. 274p.
Tireman, Lloyd S. "Value of Marking Hard Spots in Spelling." *U Iowa Stud Ed* 5(4):1–48; 1930.
Townsend, Agatha. "An Investigation of Certain Relationships of Spelling With Reading and Academic Aptitude." *J Ed Res* 40:465–71; 1947.
Traxler, Arthur E. "Spelling in College." *J H Ed* 19:256–9; 1948.
Tyler, I. Keith. *Spelling as a Secondary Learning.* Teachers Col, Columbia U, 1939. 116p.
Tyson, Ivernia M. "Factors Contributing to the Effectiveness of the Corrected Test in Spelling." Doctoral dissertation. State U Iowa, 1953.
Varty, Jonathan W. *Manuscript Writing and Spelling Achievement.* Teachers Col, Columbia U, 1938. 63p.
Venezky, Richard L. "English Orthography: Its Graphical Structure and Its Relation to Sound." *Reading Res Q* 2(3):75–105; 1967.
Visitation, Sister Mary of the. *Visual Perception in Reading and Spelling.* Cath U, 1929. 48p.
Voorhis, Thelma G. *The Relative Merits of Cursive and Manuscript Writing.* Teachers Col, Columbia U, 1931. 58p.
Wallin, John E. W. *Spelling Efficiency in Relation to Age, Grade, and Sex, and the Question of Transfer.* Warwick and York, 1911. 91p.
Wijk, Axel. *Regularized English.* Almqvist and Wiksell, 1959. 361p.
Williamson, Edmund G. "Mental Abilities Related to Learning to Spell." *Psychol B* 30:743–51; 1933(*a*).
Williamson, Edmund G. "The Relation of Learning to Spelling Ability." *J Ed Psychol* 24:257–65; 1933(*b*).
Winch, W. H. "Additional Researches on Learning to Spell: The Questions of 'Transfer' and 'Direct' versus 'Indirect' Methods." *J Ed Psychol* 7:93–110; 1916.
Woodworth, Robert S., and Schlosberg, Harold. *Experimental Psychology.* Holt, 1954. 948p.
Worchester, D. A. "Memory by Visual and by Auditory Presentation." *J Ed Psychol* 16:18–27; 1925.
Wyld, Henry C. "English Language." In *Encyclopaedia Britannica*, Vol. 8. Britannica, 1953. p. 554–62.
Zedler, Empress Y. "Effect of Phonic Training on Speech Sound Discrimination and Spelling Performance." *J Speech Hearing Disorders* 21:245–50; 1956.

STATE REGULATION OF EDUCATION

In the United States education has been established as a state function. Tradition and natural evolutionary processes in the political, social, and economic growth of our nation have accounted for the general acceptance of this educational pattern (Thurston & Roe, 1957).

The premise that education is in a true legal sense a state function may easily be proved. Its roots had been firmly embedded in the past by colonial law that foreshadowed state law (Edwards & Richey, 1947; Martin, 1897). Its pattern was developed through ordinances governing the territories that were later to become the states of the Union (Fitzpatrick, 1933). When the United States became a reality, the structural pattern began to grow through general reservation of power in the Federal constitution, through positive expressions in state constitutions, and through state statutory practice and judicial review (Pierce, 1964).

Delegation of education to the states, or to the people, left to them the job of providing a structure and method of operation. The trend has been to make general reference to educational responsibility in the state constitution and then give the legislature wide powers under constitutional provision to establish an adequate and uniform system of education. Thus, the organizational and regulatory aspects of education have become more or less a legislative responsibility (Garber, 1965).

LEGAL BASIS. The courts historically have played an important part in shaping the pattern of public education and in determining the bounds of power and responsibilities of the various agents and agencies concerned with education (Hamilton & Mort, 1941). The relation of schools to government and society on the one hand, and to the individual on the other, is nowhere so well defined as in the body of decisions rendered by the highest courts of our state and Federal judiciary (Edwards, 1965).

Throughout the history of public education in the United States there has been much questioning of the legality of certain statutes and actions of state and local officials in regard to education. Each state Supreme Court and the U.S. Supreme Court have, without exception, upheld the premise that education is a state function (Thurston & Roe, 1957).

Time after time, the U.S. Supreme Court has stated that the exclusive right of the state to administer, organize, conduct, and manage an education system cannot be questioned. In three famous cases [*Cummings v. Richmond County Board of Education,* 175US528 (1900); *Gong Lum et al. v. Rice* 275US78 (1927); *Berea College v. Kentucky,* 211US45 (1908)] the Supreme Court has ruled that any interference on the part of the Federal authority cannot be justified except in the case of a clear, unmistakable disregard of rights secured by the supreme law of the land. In fact, it was not until 1954 that the U.S. Supreme Court was willing to consider that the rights of the individual as guaranteed by the U.S. Constitution outweighed the right of the individual states to conduct education without question. In its famous decisions in *Brown v. Board of Education* (347US483, 74 S. Ct. 686 and 349US294, 75 S. Ct. 753), the court ruled that the doctrine of separate but equal facilities was in essence unequal and, therefore, that Negro children were deprived of equal protection of the law as guaranteed by the fourteenth amendment. Other court cases have reaffirmed and expanded this decision. Nonetheless, though the court was unanimous in its decision, it was careful to reassert that education is a state function and that the Federal government cannot interfere with its management except in clear-cut cases of practices contrary to Federal law.

The foundation of the state educational system is laid down in the various state constitutions. The state legislature, through statutes and enactments, provides ways and means for the conduct of the educational function (Cubberly & Elliott, 1915). When a state constitution directs the legislature to provide for a system of public education and schools, this imposes upon the legislature the duty of doing so. The establishment, maintenance, and continuance of public schools must be legally accepted as primarily a function of the state as such rather than of the Federal government or any municipality or other local subdivision. Its powers are governmental in nature, so that in a sense they are exclusive and may not be delegated to agencies outside the state. Local boards, viewed in this light, are held to be state, not local officers. They are creatures of the state and have only such powers as the statutes confer upon them and those necessarily implied to enable them to carry out the express powers granted (Hamilton & Mort, 1941).

Although the title to school property is vested in the school district, the property belongs to the state. Being bodies corporate, school districts are authorized to hold and dispose of property in the state's name, provided that all statutory provisions are met (Garber, 1964b).

The legislature may modify or abrogate the powers of school districts as it sees fit, and only such districts exist as are created or provided by statute. Subject to express constitutional limitations, the legislature has full and exclusive power to create, organize, establish, or disband school districts or other local school organizations, or to divide, unite, enlarge, change boundaries of, or otherwise alter existing districts and organizations (Garber, 1963).

The authority of the state is not limited to instruction in the lower grades. The famous Kalamazoo case, *Stuart v. School District No. 1,* Kalamazoo 30 Michigan 69 (1874), also extended the authority of the state over high schools and colleges. By the same token, the power of the state legislature to control curriculum is to all intents and purposes practically unlimited. The legislature generally may enact any legislation, including compulsory attendance, which in its judgment will promote the welfare of the general school community. The only limitation on these powers is that they must not conflict with any constitutional provision, nor can they be arbitrary in action (Garber, 1961).

The control of the state extends to private education. The case of *Pierce et al. v. Society of Sisters,* 268US510, ruled the state cannot prohibit private schools but that it can prohibit the teaching of doctrines which challenge the existence of the state and the well-being of society. It may, moreover, require that children be educated in schools which meet substantially the same standards as the state requires of its own schools, and it has power to provide agencies of inspection to see that these standards are met. In general, the courts have ruled that there is no question concerning the power of the state to regulate all schools: to inspect, supervise, and examine them, their teachers, and their pupils; to require that all children of proper age attend some school, that certain studies plainly essential to good citizenship be taught, and that nothing manifestly inimical to the public welfare be taught. However, to tell parents that their children cannot attend a private school which adheres to qualified procedure and standards is judged an unreasonable interference with the liberty of parents and guardians to direct the upbringing of their children, and thus a violation of the fourteenth amendment (Thurston & Roe, 1957).

The method of financing schools does much to determine the character of education (Munse, 1965). It has been uniformly held by the courts that there is no inherent power in school districts to levy taxes. This special power must be conferred upon them by the legislature if it is to be exercised. School taxes are of a state and not a local nature; a school district may be compelled to establish and maintain schools of a given standard, and the task of financing them according to this standard may be imposed upon the local school district. The generally accepted principle that the wealth of the state may be used to educate children no matter where they reside has been consistently accepted by the courts (Garber, 1963).

It may be seen, then, that through court mandate the states have given their legislatures broad all-inclusive authority in regard to education, which authority has in turn been upheld by the courts. The states have been given wide choice in setting up a system of operating schools (Will, 1964).

STATE EDUCATIONAL AGENCY. The legislature, with the mandate of providing a system of education for the state, could not do its duty without a central state education agency to which it could turn for advice, to expedite procedures and clarify its rules, and to assist in executing many of its statutes. Lacking the technical knowledge and organization to carry on this function, the legislators therefore turn to the state Department of Education when statewide action or interpretation is necessary (Will, 1964). Thus, all states make provisions for a chief state school officer, a state department of education, and some type of state-oriented board of education (Council of Chief State School Officers, 1963). These three components make up what is termed the central state education agency. While the external pattern for carrying out state regulation of education is essentially the same throughout the country, the internal organization may be quite different in each state (Roe, 1961a). Therefore, for all intents and purposes, we have 50 different state systems of education in the United States (Johns, 1967).

State Board of Education. Forty-eight of the fifty states have bona fide state boards of education responsible for coordinating and directing the elementary and secondary education of the state. Although two of the fifty states (Wisconsin and Illinois) do not have a general state board of education, each of these states has boards for specific educational agencies and services. All fifty states, therefore, have some type of state-oriented education board (Johns, 1967).

The methods used in selecting state board members vary. Eight states elect state board members by popular vote; in three states, representatives of the people select the state board members; in thirty-two states, the governor appoints the majority of the members, usually with approval of the legislature; in four states, the majority of the members serve ex-officio; and in one state, the chief state school officer appoints the board (Will, 1964).

Although the functions of the state boards vary greatly, encompassing a range of executive, legislative, and judicial duties, the trend is toward designating the state board as the legislative component of the central education agency, with full responsibility for the legislative policy-making functions (Campbell & others, 1965). Thus, the chief state school officer, assisted by his staff, would be delegated full responsibility for conducting the executive functions of the agency (Pierce, 1964).

The Chief State School Officer. Every state has a chief state school officer who is charged with the general supervision of its public school system. Nomenclature varies; the most common designation of the chief state school officer is superintendent of public instruction, but other titles such as commissioner of education, superintendent of free schools, and state superintendent of schools are also used. The importance of this position relative to state regulation is brought into proper perspective when it is recognized that this officer with his staff has the principal duties and responsibilities of state government in the administration of the state public school system (Thurston & Roe, 1957). The chief state school officer is appointed by the state board of education in 23 states, appointed by the governor in 5 states, and elected directly by the people in 22 states (Johns, 1967). It is now generally recognized that the chief state school officer should be a professionally qualified educator with considerable administrative experience. The growing trend is definitely toward having the state board of education select the chief state school officer on the basis of professional criteria, free of partisan influence. Although many educators believe the chief state school officer should serve at the board's pleasure, a fixed term of office is desirable if a seperation of powers is to be maintained at the administrative level in the central educational agency (Pierce, 1964). Whereas the board enacts rules and regulations pursuant to the laws and makes educational policy at the administrative level of state government, the chief state school officer functions as its executive officer. He directs and controls the staff in doing the work of the agency (Council of Chief State School Officers, 1963).

CONTROLS. While education is legally a state function, the states have seen fit to delegate portions of the schools' operation to local people through local boards of education and local school districts. State control, then, is exercised through legislation and administrative directives of the State Department of Education (Council of State Governments, 1963). As these controls are reviewed, it may be seen that the 50 states could almost be classified according to a continuum, starting with low control and emphasis on local initiative and moving toward a high degree of state control and emphasis on centralization (Hayes, 1963).

Accreditation and Assessment. The most direct method of regulation of local schools is through the accreditation or approval process. The legal authority to approve or accredit schools is delegated by states to the state board of education, the chief state school officer, the state department of education, or a combination of the three. All states have some form of accreditation or approval, but procedures vary widely among the states. The primary purpose of state programs of approval or accreditation is to assist local school officials to better administer and improve their educational programs. Accreditation means that the local schools have met or exceeded the minimum acceptable state standards. Forty-four of the fifty states print or mimeograph statewide standards or criteria for accreditation (Rich, 1960). The state education agency usually has some working relationship with regional accrediting agencies, which have done much to influence better accrediting practices in the various states. However, there is a fair amount of evidence that standards for accreditation or approval, both by state and regional accrediting associations, tend to discourage local school districts from conducting independent research or experimental programs (Teckman, 1962). There are some who advocate having the states turn over their formal accrediting function to duly appointed accrediting agencies (Morphet & Ryan, 1967).

Recently there has been intensive study and discussion of a national assessment of education (Klein, 1967). This possibility has been under study through a grant from the Carnegie Foundation and has been strongly endorsed by the U.S. Office of Education. Some see this as a threat to state control and authority over education and as a movement to fit all schools into some sort of national pattern (Rice, 1966).

Curriculum. Although many educators and board members believe that the program of a school is sacred, in most states it is the legislature that has the final say about what schools will teach. Also, the legislature may determine what not to teach—for example, birth control in Michigan and theory of evolution in Tennessee and Alabama (Garber, 1964a). The state legislature has legal authority for determining what subjects shall be taught in the school. Forty-three of the states require some state authority for approval to establish required courses in local schools; thirty-four states even require approval for nonrequired courses (Cox, 1964). Research shows that there is a constant growth in the number of statutory enactments for public school curriculum and that subject requirements for high school graduation and the number of units of required subjects continue to increase. It is also interesting to note that subjects once adopted by action of a state legislature invariably remain in the statutes and, strangely enough, also find their way into statutes of other states in identical legislative terminology (Artac, 1963).

While legislation relative to curriculum is on the increase, so too is the encouragement of particular voluntary programs through leadership and stimulation of curriculum guides (Cox, 1965). Yet, it may be said that no state legislature has usurped complete control of the curriculum. The movement toward increased requirements appears to come from a need to meet contemporary social problems: for example, vocational education of the handicapped, safety education, driver education (Nihan, 1961; Key, 1959).

Certification. Another important area of control by the state is through the process of certification of those who teach in the local schools. Authority to fix requirements and to issue, reissue, and revoke teachers' certificates is a function of the state which is almost completely vested by legislative authority in the state education agency (Rooney, 1959). Only six states (California, Colorado, Illinois, Indiana, Nebraska, North Dakota) and Puerto Rico report that their legislatures retain some measure of certification authority (Armstrong & Stinnett, 1964). In the laws vesting authority in the state education agencies, specifications are usually established that deal with age, citizenship, health, loyalty oaths, and special course requirements such as state history and study of the Federal and state government. Under the authority of certification, states also have an important influence on teacher training programs and, in a true sense, approve and authorize a college or university, whether public or private, to operate a teacher training program in line with state certification requirements (Farmer, 1965).

One would have to report that the period of the 1960's has been marked by vehement attacks on state certification requirements. Both Koerner (1963) and Conant (1963) have published books which were highly critical of the state legal provisions for certification. Conant calls the specificity of state certification requirements a "bankrupt process" and recommends a housecleaning by reducing specific state prescriptions to a minimum and turning over the details of programs to preparatory institutions. In contrast to these sharply critical points of view, Kinney (1964), has written a thoughtful analysis of state teacher certification philosophy and practice.

Compulsory School Attendance. Although the Federal and state constitutions guarantee certain rights to the individual, parental rights to the care and custody of their children are not regarded as absolute. School attendance is one such area where parental control is subordinate to the control of the state. Therefore, a legal basis is developed for enactment and enforcement of compulsory school attendance laws (Benton, 1965). Attendance laws, however, may not be arbitrary or unreasonable and, by their terms and enforcement, (1) must apply equally to all individuals, (2) must not interfere with constitutional guarantees of religious liberty, and (3) must follow the regular processes of law. The prevalent compulsory age range for public education is seven to sixteen. Only two states, Mississippi and South Carolina, lack compulsory attendance laws. Six states—Alabama, Arkansas, Florida, Louisiana, North Carolina, and Texas—exempt from compulsory attendance any child whose parents object to his attending an integrated school (Steinhilber & Sokolowski, 1967a).

School District Organization. A school district is created by, and derives all its authority from, the state. Early in their history, state legislatures established school districts as local units for the administration of education, and their operation was delegated to local people. Inevitably, under this system schools in America became "peoples'" schools, and their roots became firmly entrenched in the local soils. The small, more personal school districts which served so well with the limited transportation of the nineteenth and early twentieth centuries became a roadblock to educational progress later on in the twentieth century (Masters & others, 1964). As a result, one of the most bitter, yet poignant, struggles taking place in almost every state in the country—but particularly in the Midwest—has been the struggle to reorganize school districts (Thurston & Roe, 1957).

Local people view the loss and expansion of their school districts as loss of local control. The states have been hesitant in exercising their full authority to reorganize school districts because of the strength of local pride and proprietary feeling. The history of district reorganization in the United States has been one of states having control and full authority to change districts but using the velvet glove to create change through study committees, incentive legislation, and other more sensitive means (Wilklow, 1967). From 1956 to 1966 the number of school districts in the United States fell from 55,000 to 23,461—a decline of some 60 percent (National School Public Relations Association, 1967). The high point in numbers of school districts occurred in 1932, with 127,529 (Dawson & Ellena, 1954).

School Finance. Finance is a universal tool of social and institutional control. In the establishment of a state educational system and the maintenance of local schools, finance is always a shaping—and often the governing—factor (National Education Association Committee on Educational Finance, 1966a). Local schools in the United States, on the average, obtain slightly more than 40 percent of their funds from state governments (Gardner and Howe, 1966). States generally establish certain minimum requirements, regulations, and/or fundamental programs as part of their state aid program and use the withholding of state aid as an unspoken threat for compliance with requirements (de Bruin, 1962). Johns and Morphet (1960) contend that an important way of assessing a state's policy toward education is to study its provisions for financing. They assert that money is such a powerful instrument that it may be used to facilitate or retard the development of education. Posey's (1963) study points out that state control over local districts has increased in recent years with a growing relationship between percentage of funds contributed from state sources and the amount of centralized control. In addition, administrators perceive more control being exerted after adoption of basic state programs; at the same time they observe a greater degree of state regulation, there appears to be a lesser degree of genuine leadership. Pateros (1962) and Masters (1965) both predict that, with a greater proportion of spending for education coming from the United States government and being funneled through the state educational agency, state regulation over local units of government will increase.

School Buildings. All states have regulations which affect the construction of school buildings (Parenty, 1966). However, there is a wide range among states in the number of statutes prescribing specific responsibilities for stipulated state agencies in connection with public school construction programs. Many of the regulations are tied to state aid plans either through direct financing of school buildings or by requiring state approval of building plans in order to receive state aid (North, 1959). Cameron (1965) points out that there is a great deal of emphasis by legislatures on fire safety and sanitary conditions. However, the statutes concerned with public school construction in many states have been enacted without due regard for existing statutes relating to responsibilities of other state agencies, which has resulted in apparent conflict of duties in some cases and overlap of responsibilities in others.

Transportation. All states provide statewide regulations relative to transportation for children of local school districts (Murray, 1965). All states have some type of statewide school transportation program, and 85 percent of the states have established some type of financial plan for assisting with this transportation (Burrup & Anderson, 1966). State laws relative to transportation include a wide variety of stipulations, such as the minimum distance pupils must live from school to be eligible for transportation; who may be transported; transportation of non-public school children; use of school buses for extracurricular activities; qualifications for bus drivers; standards for school bus construction and equipment; coordination of state and local traffic laws; accounting regulations; and insurance (Critchfield, 1960).

Textbooks. The most-used teaching tools in the United States, textbooks have been a sensitive item of regulation by the various states. All states have some type of prescribed rules and regulations regarding textbooks. Among the various states, however, there is great variance in such control (Thurston & Roe, 1957). As the general overseer of education within the state, the state education agency has accepted responsibility to see that textbooks are in harmony with democratic ideology, free from selfish group or class propaganda, scholarly in their preparation, and impartial in outlook. In addition, the state agencies have accepted a broader leadership responsibility to guard against rigorous crystallization and outdating of both content and method.

There appears to be a trend toward some type of statewide adoption or approval of textbooks. Slightly more than half of the states adopt textbooks at the state level. In most cases, however, flexibility is provided by establishing a multiple listing of books, with free choice from the list in addition to allowing use of supplementary texts. Four states (Arizona, Arkansas, Nevada, California) adopt on the elementary level only (National Council of Teachers of English, 1966).

Most states have put regulatory controls on the sale and purchasing of textbooks. There is keen competition among textbook publishers, and the purchase of textbooks involves huge sums of money. If such school expenditures were not carefully governed, many unscrupulous practices could result.

Nonpublic Schools. There are few explicit responsibilities delegated to state education agencies in regulating and supervising nonpublic schools. State regulation of nonpublic schools is largely accomplished under laws regulating activities of private individuals and organizations (Wilson, 1966). Will (1958) lists twelve major areas where regulation could take place to varying degree at the state level: (1) establishment and supervision, (2) compulsory education, (3) curriculum, (4) records and reports, (5) teacher certification, (6) pupil transportation, (7) health and safety, (8) textbooks, (9) school lunch, (10) surplus property, (11) scholarships, and (12) miscellaneous.

There is a growing body of regulations relative to providing state financial support and services to nonpublic schools. Steinhilber and Sokolowski (1967b) suggest that recent church-state controversies and confusion are traceable in part to complex legislation within the states.

In all, 20 states prohibit transportation for nonpublic school students and 8 states ban publicly financed textbooks for their use. Four states (Florida, Georgia, Nebraska, South Dakota) have legal policies preventing the furnishing of either. Publicly financed transportation is permitted in 8 states and required in 12; textbooks are permitted in 2 states and required in 4. Louisiana, New Mexico, and Rhode Island are the only states authorizing both textbooks and transportation for nonpublic school students. Four states (Iowa, Kentucky, Massachusetts, Mississippi) have policies permitting either state-financed textbooks or transportation but prohibiting the other.

But the laws say different things in different states: in West Virginia only nonpublic school students classified as "indigents" qualify for textbooks; Ohio permits free transportation at the high school level and requires it at the elementary level; four states have statutory provisions authorizing the state education department to give teachers in public and nonpublic schools books on fire prevention (Garber, 1963).

Professional Conditions of Employment. A new type of state regulation is emerging in the wake of governmental social legislation and regulation of employment conditions for employees of private enterprise (Stinnett & others, 1966). Nationally, teachers have been demanding more participation in negotiations to improve their condition of employment. As the national and state educational associations exert pressure, more state legislation is being written relative to tenure, minimum salaries, types of contracts, vacation periods, and rights and responsibilities of teachers (Steffensen, 1964).

As a major part of this movement, one finds a growing number of states passing legislation requiring or establishing a formalized procedure for resolving certain differences between teachers and the school boards. Prior to 1965, three states had collective bargaining laws applying to all public employees, including teachers: Alaska (1959), New Hampshire (1955), and Wisconsin (1962) (Stinnett & others, 1966). In 1965, six other states signed negotiation bills into law: California, Connecticut, Massachusetts, Michigan, Oregon, and Washington (Lieberman & Moskow, 1966). A snowball effect is apparent in this movement. Based on activity of the state and national education associations, a conservative prediction is that most states will have a professional negotiations law of some type by the early 1970's.

IMPROVING STATE EDUCATION AGENCY LEADERSHIP. The "New Frontier" and "Great Society" programs of the Kennedy-Johnson administrations and the upsurge in educational legislation, particularly the Elementary and Secondary Education Act of 1965, placed new responsibility for leadership on the state departments of education (American Association of School Administrators, 1965). When billions of dollars were allocated to education by the Eighty-ninth Congress, a decision was made to strengthen the authority of state education agencies by funneling a large portion of the money through their hands. At the same time, funds were provided to develop their leadership capacity (Bean, 1965). Thus, in a sense, the Federal government was saying that attainment of the national goals for education depends upon the leadership and character of the state departments of education. With leadership came a new type of regulation, and the state departments of education became responsible for coordination of exemplary and innovative projects of local school districts financed by the U.S. Office of Education. In addition, local districts were allowed to approve, to a certain degree, the disbursement of funds and were requested to account for their expenditure (Keppel, 1966).

Weaknesses of State Education Agencies. As Federal legislation added to the responsibilities of state education agencies, it became obvious that some states were inadequately prepared for this new role. The state education agency generally lacked resources for activities which had not been supported by state law, such as long-range planning, evaluation and assessment, research and development, and stimulation of innovative experiments and practices (Little, Inc., 1964). Consequently, they often were unable to compete with colleges and universities, and even with local districts, for the skilled manpower required for these tasks (Ohio Legislative Service Commission, 1960). In addition, special-purpose state and Federal legislation had often created program imbalances that the state departments of education were helpless to remedy, and resources had to be committed to these special purposes for which public aid moneys were received (Keppel, 1965). Constant (1964) has charged that a major weakness of the state departments of education is their incapacity to respond to forces outside the educational establishment and their unwillingness to examine public school needs with a critical eye. The recent White House education conference suggested that the role and functions of state departments of education needed extensive critical appraisal, because even a cursory examination of the existing patterns of state organization in this area revealed a lack of any clear-cut notion as to what the role and function of these departments should be (White House Conference on Education,

1965). As a result of attention being called to these many weaknesses, Title V of Public Law 89–10 provided grants to assist the states in strengthening the leadership and resources of their departments of education.

A Partnership. With increased Federal aid and the concomitant fears of Federal control, there emerged the concept of local, state, and Federal partnership and a creative federalism (American Association of School Administrators, 1965). Creative federalism conveys the idea that increase in the power of the Federal government to deal with educational problems in turn increases the power of state and local school districts to deal with the same problems (Johns, 1967). This point of view holds that each governmental unit operates as an equal and each assumes responsibility to perform that portion of the educational function which can most effectively be dealt with at that level (Thurston & Roe, 1957).

On the other hand, many see the growing disbursement of Federal funds, even though accomplished through state departments of education, as developing ultimate Federal control over the schools. Arvid J. Burke (1966) predicted that the second half of the twentieth century would be characterized by a shift of control over education from states to the Federal government comparable to the shift from local units to the states which had occurred during the first half of the century. Wayson (1966) saw a political revolution in the making, with a gradual shift of power to Washington but with the ultimate situation depending on the initiative and intelligence of each level of government and on the educators themselves.

A Compact. In an attempt to give the states a base of greater strength and power in educational matters, it was proposed that they join together in a compact of states (Allen, 1966). The feeling was that if they did not band together, if they stood apart, education would be changed by the Federal government without their participation and the states would be bypassed. Some years ago, this idea of a compact was proposed by the National Citizens Commission for Education. It was popularized by Conant (1964) and finally implemented in 1965 by Terry Sanford, former governor of North Carolina (Moskowitz, 1965). The proposed plan was for the political and educational leaders in each state to form a partnership for the betterment of education; members from the various states, in turn, would band together in a legal compact which would enable them to make studies, coordinate their forces, and eventually develop nationwide education policies that would make the states the senior partners in national educational leadership. This movement continues to be active; it remains to be seen whether the compact principle can serve as a focal point for consolidating and maintaining the power and strength of the states in education.

William H. Roe
The University of Connecticut

References

Advisory Council on State Departments of Education. *Improving State Leadership in Education.* GPO, 1966. 145p.

Allen, James E. "The Compact—New Strength For the State." *Ed Rec* 47(1): 113–5; 1966.

American Association of School Administrators. *The Federal Government and Public Schools.* AASA 1965. 71p.

Armstrong, W. Earl, and Stinnett, T. M. *A Manual on Certification Requirements for School Personnel in the United States.* NEA, 1964. p. 9.

Artac, Eugene J. "State Control of the Public Secondary School Curriculum From 1945–1961." Doctoral dissertation. U Pittsburgh, 1963.

Bean, John E. *Research in State Departments of Education,* HEW, 1965.

Benton, Malcolm Thomas. "Legal Aspects of Compulsory School Attendance." Doctoral dissertation. Duke U, 1965.

Berea College v. Kentucky 211 US 45 (1908).

Burke, Arvid J. "U. S. Control of Schools Will Grow." *Am Sch Bd J* 153(5):26–7; 1966.

Burrup, Percy, and Anderson, Norris D. "Should States Pay to Bus Pupils?" *Am Sch Bd J* 152(6): 21–2; 1966.

Cameron, John Lansing. "The Constitutional and Statutory Responsibilities of State Agencies for School Construction." Doctoral dissertation. U North Carolina, 1965.

Campbell, Roald F., and others. *The Organization and Control of American Schools.* Charles E. Merrill Books, Inc., 1965. 553p.

Conant, James B. *The Education of American Teachers.* McGraw-Hill, 1963. 275p.

Conant, James B. *Shaping Educational Policy.* McGraw-Hill, 1964. 139p.

Council of Chief State School Officers. *The State Department of Education.* The Council, 1963. 47p.

Council of Chief State School Officers. *Guidelines for Development and Codification of Policy for State Departments of Education.* The Council, 1965. 23p.

Council of State Governments. *The Book of States 1962–63.* The Council, 1963. 410p.

Council of State Governments. *The Book of States 1964–65.* The Council, 1964. 336p.

Cox, Roy L. "Elective Courses: Gaining State Approval." *Ed Leadership* 22(3):177–81; 1964.

Cox, Roy L. "Developing Instructional Guides." *Ed* 86(4):213–5; 1965.

Critchfield, John Geary. Legislation Affecting Pupil Transportation in the United States. Doctoral dissertation. U Pittsburgh, 1960.

Cubberly, Ellwood P., and Elliott, Edward C. *State and County School Administration.* Macmillan, 1915. p. 12–7.

Cummings V. Richmond County Board of Education. 175 US 528 (1900).

Dawson, Howard A., and Ellena, William J. *The Status of Schools, School Districts and School*

District Reorganization. Department Rural Education, NEA, 1954.

De Bruin, Hendrik Cornelius. "State Regulation of Local School District Financial Administration." Doctoral dissertation. U Arizona, 1962.

Edwards, I. N. "State Educational Policy and the Supreme Court of the United States." In Garber, Lee O. *The Yearbook of School Law 1965.* Interstate, 1965. p. 186–95.

Edwards, Newton, and Richey, Herman A. *The School in the American Social Order.* Houghton, 1947. 880p.

Farmer, Donald E. "The Legal Status of Student Teaching in Forty Selected States." Doctoral dissertation. U Kansas, 1965.

Fitzpatrick, John C. (Ed.) *Journals of the Continental Congress.* XXVIII. GPO, 1933. 410p.

Garber, Lee O. *The Yearbook of School Law 1960.* Interstate, 1960. 184p.

Garber, Lee O. *The Yearbook of School Law 1961.* Interstate, 1961. 249p.

Garber, Lee O. *The Yearbook of School Law 1962.* Interstate, 1962. 234p.

Garber, Lee O. *The Yearbook of School Law 1963.* Interstate, 1963. 266p.

Garber, Lee O. "The State Decides What to Teach." *Nations Sch* 74(6):26; 1964(*a*).

Garber, Lee O. *The Yearbook of School Law 1964.* Interstate, 1964(*b*). 283p.

Garber, Lee O. *The Yearbook of School Law 1965.* Interstate, 1965. 242p.

Gardner, John W., and Howe, Harold, II. *Progress of Education in the U.S.A. 1965–66.* GPO, 1966. 71p.

Gong Lum, et al v. Rice. 275 US 78 (1927).

Hamilton, Robert R., and Mort, Paul R. *The Law and Public Education.* Foundation Press, 1941. 579p.

Hayes, Charles Burnett. "A Taxonomy of Patterns of Control Exercised Over Local School Districts by the Various States." Doctoral dissertation. 1963.

Johns, Roe L. "State Organization and Responsibilities for Education." In Morphet, Edgar L., and Ryan, Charles O. (Eds.) *Implications for Education of Prospective Changes in Society.* Designing Education for the Future: An Eight-state Project, 1967. p. 245–67.

Johns, Roe L., and Morphet, Edgar L. *Financing the Public Schools.* Prentice-Hall, 1960. p. 232.

Keppel, Francis. *Aid to Elementary and Secondary Education, Part I, Hearings on H.R. 2361 and H.R. 2362.* USOE, 1965. p. 104.

Keppel, Francis. *The Necessary Revolution in American Education.* Harper, 1966. 201p.

Key, Norman. *Status of Driver Education in the United States: A Study of Courses as Described by State and Local School Systems in Response to Special Inquiry.* American, 1959. 248p.

Kimbough, Ralph B. *Political Power and Educational Decision-making.* Rand McNally, 1964. 307p.

Kinney, Lucien B. *Certification in Education.* Prentice-Hall, 1964. 178p.

Klein, Frederick C. "Testing the Schools." *Wall Street J* 169(9):1, 12; 1967.

Knight, Edgar W. *Education in the United States.* Ginn, 1934. p. 105.

Koerner, James D. *The Miseducation of American Teachers.* Houghton, 1963. 360p.

Lieberman, Myron, and Moskow, Michael H. *Collective Negotiations for Teachers.* Rand McNally, 1966. 745p.

Little, Arthur D., Inc. *Requirements for Effective Leadership for California Education.* California State Department of Education, 1964. 85p.

Martin, George Henry. *Evolution of the Massachusetts Public School System.* Appleton, 1897. 186p.

Masters, Nicholas A. "The Role of the States." In *Contemporary Issues in American Education.* USOE, 1965. p. 42–57.

Masters, Nicholas A., and others. *State Politics and Public Schools.* Knopf, 1964. p. 319.

Morphet, Edgar L., and Ryan, Charles O. *Implications for Education of Prospective Changes in Society.* Designing Education for the Future: An Eight-State Project, 1967. 323p.

Moskowitz, Ronald. "The Compact for Education." In *Local, State, Federal Partnership in School Finance.* NEA, 1965. p. 27–32.

Munse, Albert R. *State Programs for Public School Support.* HEW, 1965. 113p.

Murray, John B. "An Analysis of State Plans for Financing Pupil Transportation." Doctoral dissertation. Michigan State U, 1965.

National Council of Teachers of English. "Report on Textbook Selection Practices." NCTE, 1966. 53p. (Mimeographed.)

National Education Association, Committee on Educational Finance. *Financial Status of the Public Schools.* NEA, 1966(*a*).

National Education Association, Committee on Educational Finance. *Partnership in School Finance.* NEA, 1966(*b*). 165p.

National School Public Relations Association. *Education U.S.A.* The Association, 1967. p. 122.

Nihan, James Frederick. "A Study of State Laws and State Education Department Regulations for Safety Education in the Public Schools of the United States." Doctoral dissertation. New York U, 1961.

North, Steward Donavan. "Some Characteristics of Programs of State Support for School Plants." Doctoral dissertation. U Wisconsin, 1959.

Ohio Legislative Service Commission. *Organization and Methods of the Ohio Department of Education.* The Commission, 1960. 53p.

Parenty, Patrick. "An Analysis of State Policies for the Provision of Educational Facilities." Doctoral dissertation. Rutgers U, 1966.

Pateros, John J. *Financial Management of Federal–State Education Programs.* GPO, 1962. 11p.

Pierce, Truman M. *Federal State and Local Government in Education.* Center for Applied Research in Education, 1964. 120p.

Posey, Ellis Benton, Jr. "State Education Agency Control of Public School Expenditures in Selected

Foundation Programs." Doctoral dissertation. U Texas, 1963. 656p.

Rice, Arthur H. "Let Cities and States Decide What to Measure!" *Nations Sch* 78(1):8–10; 1966.

Rich, William Edward. *Approval and Accreditation of Public Schools.* HEW, 1960. p. 5.

Roe, William H. "Organizational Patterns: State and Federal." *R Ed Res* 31(4):368–79. 1961(a).

Roe, William H. *School Business Management.* McGraw-Hill, 1961(b). 303p.

Rooney, Patrick Otis. "An Analysis of Legislative Statutes, Judicial Decisions, Policies, and Practices Related to the Revocation of Certification of Public School Personnel." Doctoral dissertation. U Southern California, 1959.

Steffensen, James P. *Teachers Negotiate With Their School Boards.* (O.E. 23036), Bulletin No. 40. USOE, 1964. 84p.

Steinhilber, August W., and Sokolowski, Carl J. *State Law on Compulsory Attendance.* GPO, 1967(a). 103p.

Steinhilber, August W., and Sokolowski, Carl J. *State Laws Related to Transportation and Textbooks for Parochial School Students and Constitutional Protection of Religious Freedom.* GPO, 1967(b). 45p.

Stinnett, T. M., and others. *Professional Negotiations in Public Education.* Macmillan, 1966.

Teckman, Charles Edward. "The Influence of State Departments and Regional Accrediting Associations on Secondary-School Experimentation." Doctoral dissertation. Ohio State U, 1962.

Thurston, Lee M., and Roe, William H. *State School Administration.* Harper, 1957. 427p.

Wayson, William W. "Political Revolution in Education, 1965." *Phi Delta Kappan* 57(7):333–9; 1966.

White House Conference on Education, *A Milestone for Educational Progress.* GPO, 1965. 217p.

Wilklow, Leighton B. "Legislative Practices and Progress in Reorganization in Selected States." Doctoral dissertation. U Connecticut, 1967.

Will, Robert F. "An Analysis of the Legal Responsibilities of State Departments of Education for Nonpublic Schools." Doctoral dissertation. U Maryland, 1958.

Will, Robert F. *State Education, Structure, and Organization.* GPO, 1964. 156p.

Wilson, Robert E. *Educational Administration.* Charles E. Merrill Books, Inc., 1966. p. 305–15.

STATISTICAL METHODS

This article will be concerned with descriptive statistics and inferential statistics, with the latter including treatment of conventional or "classic" procedures for estimation and hypothesis testing as well as some mention of Bayesian statistics. In addition, the article will deal with bivariate and multivariate procedures and will include a section on factor analysis, a set of techniques which may—or may not—be "statistical." It is pertinent to state explicitly that certain topics will not be considered here. Not all quantitative procedures will be regarded as statistical; for example, problems of measurement and scaling (including the concepts of reliability and validity and the problems of their estimation) will not be discussed in this article. Although the processing of data is clearly related to statistics, this topic is given separate treatment elsewhere. Statistical methods associated with survey research methods are also given separate treatment, as are problems of experimental design. Some of the distinctions on which these inclusions and exclusions rest are suggested in selected reviews carried in recent December issues of *Review of Educational Research,* particularly those of 1960, 1963, and 1966.

Short reports of new developments in statistical theory tend to be concentrated in a few journals, such as *Annals of Mathematical Statistics, Journal of the American Statistical Association, Biometrics, Biometrika,* and *Journal of the Royal Statistical Society.* Journals such as *Psychometrika* and *British Journal of Statistical Psychology* report similar developments which are of special interest to those in the field of psychology. A relatively new journal, *Journal of Mathematical Psychology,* occasionally treats problems of statistical theory and application, but goes beyond these to deal with such topics as mathematical learning theory. The standard guides to periodical literature can be consulted to locate such journal material. Over a period of 27 years the *Psychological Bulletin* printed a number of reviews and notes on statistical methods; an index to these was prepared by Andrews (1967). In addition to a large number of articles appearing during any period, there occasionally appear one or more books that constitute original contributions rather than mere summaries or pedagogical arrangements of well-known material, as are most textbooks. Scheffé's *The Analysis of Variance* (1959) probably was one such volume, as was Savage's *The Foundations of Statistics* (1954). Two volumes by Fisher that appeared much earlier undoubtedly are classic examples of volumes which, together with their subsequent editions, have exercised a great influence on the theory and practice of statistics; these are Fisher's *Statistical Methods for Research Workers* (1925) and *The Design of Experiments* (1935). The three volumes by Kendall and Stuart (1961, 1963, 1966) probably constitute the most comprehensive treatment of various topics in statistics available in a single publication. These volumes are an excellent guide to the important literature.

Summaries of new developments and critical reviews of current material that are oriented toward the practitioner appear periodically in such publications as *Annual Review of Psychology* and *Review of Educational Research.* The *Annual Review of Psychology* was converted to a biennial review of statistical theory, beginning with Volume 13 in 1962. Of recent reviews appearing there, one by Binder (1964) is most informative. Some evidence of the quantity of available relevant material is indicated by the fact that Binder discusses 195 references in his review of a two-year period. The December issues of *Review of Educational Research* published in 1960, 1963, and 1966 contain summaries of recent developments and critical assessments of these for several topics related to educational research. These issues differ in organization and in emphasis. The 1960 issue covered many loosely related topics, ranging from the philosophy of science to methods of observing and recording behavior. Michael and Hunka (1960), who treat statistical methods as one of several types of research tools, cover a wide range of topics in their review. The 1963 December issue of the *Review* was devoted entirely to topics in statistics or to very closely related topics. Michael (1963), Moonan and Wolfe (1963), and Clark (1963) wrote reviews that are directly relevant to the topics being discussed here. The 1966 issue contains several relevant chapters; one of these is Meyer's (1966) review of Bayesian statistics.

Sources of information such as these enable the interested reader to discover what appear to be new developments and to receive help in interpreting what these developments may mean for practice. The review by Meyer (1966) is a good example of a pedagogically oriented review that accomplishes its purpose quite well. In addition to these sources of information, the many textbooks in statistics offer both catalogs of techniques and interpretations of their use. The text by Hays (1963) is an unusual one in that it contains a wealth of material not ordinarily mentioned by—and possibly not known by—authors of other texts. It is not an easy introduction to statistical methods, but it is the kind of introduction from which a student who wishes to work can profit immensely.

DESCRIPTIVE STATISTICS. One way to suggest a meaning for statistical methods is to point out that statistical methods concern sets of data and thus imply that some type of replication of observation is necessary if statistical methods are to be relevant. This is merely to say that the single case (single datum) is not of *statistical* interest. A common type of replication consists of making the same type of observation for each of a set of subjects. In educational research, these subjects commonly are persons, such as students in grade 9; however, the subjects might be school districts or regions, buildings, passages in the *Federalist Papers*, trees, and so on. Making the same type of observation for each of a set of subjects and quantifying each observation in some fashion yields a set of data. These data may then be summarized and/or pictured in various ways.

Given a set of data, such as a set of test scores, one may wish to describe certain features of the set of data. For example, one may focus attention on some typical or central value in the set of data; several measures of central tendency—such as the arithmetic mean, the median, and the crude mode—may be employed. Each of these may be regarded as a *statistic*; in the section on inferential procedures, later, the question will be raised of how to develop generalizations about the behavior of such statistics when they are drawn from different samples of data. Another aspect of a set of data is its variability: the extent to which the various observations take on markedly different values. A number of statistics have been invented or developed to measure this aspect of a set of observations; these would include the various ranges (such as the range of the entire distribution or the range of the middle 50 percent) and various average-deviation measures. Of these, the variability index most widely used in connection with inferential statistics appears to be the standard deviation, which is taken as the positive square root of the variance. The variance is a function of the *squared* deviations of the observations from their arithmetic mean and, thus, for a set of real numbers is always nonnegative.

Still other aspects of a set of data may be identified. Skewness, as opposed to bilateral symmetry, is often of interest. There are many types of symmetric distributions: for example, U-shaped, rectangular, the normal. Other distributions have either positive skew (the tail is at the right) or negative skew. Positive skew for a distribution of test scores might occur if the test has a definite "floor" but is characterized by a large number of very difficult items; these difficult items tend to sort out the abler persons taking the test. A test characterized by a marked "ceiling" (a test that does not sort out the abler students) will tend to yield a set of scores characterized by a negative skew. Another aspect of the shape of a distribution is its kurtosis, or degree of peakedness or flatness. A rectangular and a normal distribution are both symmetric, but they differ markedly in kurtosis.

Discussions of descriptive statistics commonly include explanations of two systems of deriving relative measures that have greater interpretability (with respect to the reference distribution) than do the raw data alone. A raw score may not be very meaningful, apart from a relevant distribution of scores to which it may be referred. Thus the raw score of 78 might be either a very good score (e.g., on the Miller Analogies Test) or a relatively poor one (e.g., on an "easy" multiple-choice final examination consisting of 200 items). A percentile system that attaches to each point on the score scale a number describing the percentage of cases in a reference distribution which fall below that point gives a translation of raw scores into directly interpretable numbers, the percentile ranks. It should be emphasized, of course, that the reference group is critical; thus, the 90th percentile for a distribution of heights of 6-year-olds corresponds to a quite different raw score than does the 90th percentile for a similar distribution for 12-year-olds.

A second system of deriving relative measures is the standard score system. This permits giving a raw score an equivalent standard score which describes how far above or below the arithmetic mean that score is in standard deviation units. For some purposes, standard scores with means of zero and standard deviations of unity are commonly used; as tabled in most statistics textbooks, the normal curve is $N(0,1)$, which means that it is tabled in terms of standard scores with a mean of zero and a standard deviation of 1. In this system a standard score of $+2$ indicates a score two standard deviations above the mean; a negative standard score indicates a score below the mean. Other systems may be used: for example, one can form standard scores with a mean of 50 and a standard deviation of 10; in this system, a standard score of 70 is two standard deviations above the mean. This type of standard score has often been called a T score; however, some persons regard T scores as *normalized* standard scores—that is, as nonlinear transformations of the raw scores. Hence one must look carefully at how a particular author defines his T scores.

Descriptive statistical procedures are extremely useful in condensing large masses of data by giving pictorial or numerical representations of them. Descriptive statistical procedures also can be used to focus attention on selected aspects of a set of data. This may lead to misinterpretation; *How to Lie with Statistics* by Darrell Huff (1954) is an amusing book that indicates ways in which descriptive methods can be and have been used to give misleading impressions of data.

Earlier it was noted that some type of replication is necessary in order to generate a set of data, and this was illustrated, rather generally, by describing replication of the same type of observation over a set of individuals. Another type of replication occurs when the same type of observation is made for a given individual over time. An illustration would be the data for a single rat which runs a T maze over a number of trials. The observation might be the time required to run the maze; alternatively, it might be whether or not the rat turns left or right on each trial. This latter is an example of a measurement on a nominal scale. The resulting data can be coded numerically by using 0's and 1's; this set of numbers would then yield as a summary statistic the proportion of trials in which the rat turned right (or left). This proportion is a descriptive statistic and is the analog of the arithmetic mean for such nominal data. An analog of the variance also exists. The variance for nominal data is a function of the proportion; in this situation the mean and the variance are not independent of each other. The data for the various trials might also be arranged in order of time of occurrence and be examined for runs, or repetitions of the same behavior; thus one might find that the proportion of turns to the right shifts markedly after so many trials.

This kind of statement always has as its referent the data in hand, that is, the data for the sample. Our interest, however, often is in statements that can have as a referent not merely the sample but also a population of some sort that includes the sample. Inferential statistics deals with problems of developing such generalizations.

INFERENTIAL STATISTICS. This section will begin with what is a conventional or "classic" view of inference and, later in the discussion, will attempt to suggest what lies behind some of the uneasiness currently associated with tests of hypotheses. It probably is fair to say that very few of the current textbooks written for students in education and/or psychology pay much attention to this uneasiness; the text of Hays (1963) is an exception. Before attempting to document this uneasiness, let us sketch the theory of statistical inference in terms of two main topics: confidence intervals and tests of hypotheses. In order to do this, it will be pertinent to consider statistics as estimators of parameters and to consider the notion of a sampling distribution of a statistic.

An important distinction to be made is that of a population, as opposed to a sample drawn from that population. Parameters describe characteristics of the data for a population, just as statistics describe characteristics of the data for the sample. Thus the mean IQ for a sample of 100 ten-year-olds is a "statistic"; the mean IQ for the population of all such ten-year-olds is a "parameter."

In many situations a statistic, such as the sample mean, is used as an estimator of a parameter, the population mean. This reflects the fact that the parameter is generally regarded as unknown—more explicitly, it is regarded as "unknowable precisely." In the face of this uncertainty, the value of the analogous statistic may be used as a point estimate of the unknown parameter. One might expect that such a procedure would give an accurate estimate very, very seldom; nonetheless, one might be satisfied with such a procedure provided that the estimate is likely to be "close" to the true, but unknown, value and provided that it does not tend, in a disproportionately large number of cases, to fall only on one side of the true value. This second desideratum suggests that one might consider the concept of repeated sampling from a designated population, each time taking a sample of the same size, and then attempt to make statements about the sampling behavior of a given estimator. For example, if the distribution of the statistic under repeated sampling from the same population tends to span or bracket the unknown parameter with the parameter somewhere near the center of this distribution, the second requirement would be met. If this distribution is relatively restricted in range, then the first requirement would also be met.

The question of which estimator should be chosen, when more than one estimator is available, necessarily arises. This can be a fairly realistic question. If one wished to estimate the median of a population, for example, he might choose between the median of a sample and the value that lies halfway between the smallest and largest observation in the sample. This second estimator would have much to recommend it on practical grounds: it is easy to calculate and easy to understand; further, it seems fairly sensible as an estimator of the "middle" of a distribution. Over a period of time, certain criteria for estimators have been developed. Several of these are "large-sample" criteria and thus are regarded by some statisticians as not very important for actual statistical work.

Unbiasedness is one criterion. An unbiased estimator is one that has as the mean of its sampling distribution the population parameter which it estimates. Thus the arithmetic mean is in general an unbiased estimator of the population mean, but the sample variance (when computed by dividing by the sample size n, rather than by the number of degrees of freedom) is a biased estimator of the variance of a normal population. Unbiasedness is of some advantage but probably is not a critical requirement for an estimator. If a biased estimator has other desirable characteristics, it can often be corrected for bias.

Consistency refers to the behavior of the estimator as the sample size increases without limit; if under these conditions the estimator becomes concentrated near the population value, it is said to be consistent. A consistent estimator may be biased for finite sample sizes, even though within the limit it is unbiased. Conversely, it is possible to have unbiased estimators that are not consistent. A consistent estimator guarantees that if a large enough sample is taken, the point estimate is likely to be near the parameter; however, defining "large enough" may be difficult in any particular instance.

Efficiency is a third, and often highly regarded, criterion. This criterion considers the limiting variance of the estimator as the sample size increases; it states that, among estimators of a certain class, those whose sampling distributions have the smallest limiting variance are efficient estimators. (This class of estimators is restricted to those which are normally distributed within the limit as the sample size increases. Not all estimators have this characteristic; of those which do, one or more may be the most efficient.) Thus, the arithmetic mean is an efficient estimator of the center of a normal distribution, but it is less efficient than the median when the population is U shaped.

Sufficiency is a fourth criterion. An estimator satisfies this criterion when no other statistic that can be calculated from the same sample provides any additional information about the parameter which is to be estimated. A sufficient estimator is efficient, and an efficient estimator is necessarily consistent.

Maximum likelihood estimators are sufficient and, consequently, are efficient and consistent. The maximum-likelihood principle chooses as an estimator of the unknown parameter that value which, if it exists, would maximize the probability of having obtained the given set of observations. In other words, the mode of the likelihood distribution is focussed upon. In order to employ the principle of maximum likelihood to choose an estimator, the population distribution and the parameters upon which it depends must be specified. This is relatively easy to do for certain "standard" populations, such as the binomial and the normal. Some of the maximum-likelihood estimators turn out to be very familiar statistics. For example, for a binomial distribution, the maximum-likelihood estimator of the unknown population proportion is simply the sample proportion. For a normally distributed bivariate population, the maximum-likelihood estimator of a population regression coefficient is simply the same regression coefficient. However, some maximum-likelihood estimators are not the analogous sample statistics; for example, the fourth moment about the mean for the sample is not a maximum-likelihood estimator of the fourth moment about the mean for a normal population.

A sampling distribution for a given statistic may be conceived as the distribution that would be formed by the different obtained values of the statistic if the statistic were computed for all the different samples which could be drawn from this population according to a designated sampling plan. If the population distribution is specified precisely and a probability sampling plan chosen, then it may be possible to deduce the exact sampling distribution of a given statistic. Such a distribution depends rather generally upon the statistic of interest, the nature of the population distribution, the method of sampling, and the size of the sample. A number of "models" for sampling distributions have been identified, together with the conditions under which a given model is valid. These include such distributions as the binomial and the normal, the t distribution, and the variance ratio or F distribution.

In statistical inference one recognizes conditions under which a sampling distribution is known exactly and conditions under which it is known only approximately. The importance of the normal distribution as a model for a sampling distribution is linked to a proof that maximum-likelihood estimators have a large-sample distribution that is well approximated by the normal distribution under rather general conditions. Thus, even though the population may not be normally distributed—as when the population consists only of 0's and 1's, or nominal data—still an estimator such as the sample proportion may have a large-sample distribution that is quite well approximated by the normal. This convergence of the binomial distribution on the normal with increasing sample size has been known for many years.

The specification of a sampling distribution answers one kind of question: With what relative frequency will various values of the sample statistic appear under these conditions? This could be interesting information to have, and it could be useful in helping one to know what to expect if the postulated conditions hold. The problem of inference, however, is different. Rather than deducing the relative frequency of possible "events" for a given "state of the world," inference requires that this state of the world be inferred from a known event. Hotelling (1958) has given a very good explanation of the difference between the deductive and the inductive, an explanation that also shows how mathematics is distinguished from, but related to, statistical inference. Mathematics is deductive and develops "if-then" statements that can hold precisely. Probability theory, which is a branch of mathematics, shows how the probabilities of events, such as anticipated observations, can be calculated from known probabilities of antecedent conditions. Statistical inference, in contrast, attempts to solve the inverse problem: reasoning from observations back to the causal relations that are presumed to have led to these observations.

Confidence Intervals. Let us now turn to confidence intervals as an estimation procedure. In addition to point estimates of a parameter, it is possible to make interval estimates. These last-named consist of a range of values which is expected to bracket or enclose the unknown parameter with a preset probability that is labeled a "confidence coefficient." The notion of repeated sampling is relevant here. One may conceive of building a confidence interval (that is, specifying the upper and lower limits) based on each of an indefinitely large number of random samples from the sample population. These intervals would vary from sample to sample, possibly in span, but certainly in the location of the lower and upper limits. The procedure used is designed to make certain that, if this repeated sampling were done, a preset proportion of these confidence intervals would actually enclose or bracket the unknown parameter. A 95 percent confidence interval, then, is one of an indefinitely large number of intervals, 95 percent of which actually bracket the unknown parameter. Thus, when one selects a single sample at random, there is an a priori probability of .95 that one will draw a sample for which the associated interval is "correct," that is, one that encloses the parameter. Actually, of course, this repeated sampling is not done; the variation in confidence intervals is conceived rather than observed. It is interesting but possibly discouraging to note that, having calculated a confidence interval, one does not know whether or not that particular interval is correct; and so long as the parameter is unknown, there is no way of knowing.

Since a confidence interval specifies a range of values, it constitutes an interval rather than a point estimate of a parameter. A rather general criticism of many of the applied textbooks is that they do not give enough prominence to the methods of estimation represented by confidence intervals but prefer instead to emphasize hypothesis testing. This criticism also applies to research workers' choices of methods of presenting their results. For example, Rozeboom (1960) flatly states that the basic statistical report of research results should, whenever possible, be in the form of a confidence interval. Such an interval typically is in effect a subset of alternative hypotheses that are not discounted by the data. Rozeboom criticizes quite severely the null-hypothesis significance test, in part on the grounds that testing a single-valued hypothesis unrealistically limits the outcome of an experiment to two alternatives. Tatsuoka and Tiedeman (1963), writing on statistical methods for the *Handbook of Research on Teaching*, take quite a different stand and emphasize the empirical testing of hypotheses as the proper role of statistics in scientific method. Here is an area of controversy, about which more will be said later.

No attempt is made here to explain how to construct a confidence interval; the procedures for constructing both exact and approximate confidence intervals can be found in appropriate books. In general, it is possible to compute confidence intervals for means, medians, proportions, variances, correlation coefficients, and other values. Some of these procedures may be called "nonparametric"; for example, an exact confidence interval for a population proportion can be computed without making any parametric assumptions. A random selection of a sample of a given size is sufficient to ensure that the binomial distribution is the valid model for the sampling distribution of the observed proportion in samples of that size. By postulating various values of the population proportion, one can then divide the surface of joint occurrences of sample and population proportions into two regions, based on a selected confidence coefficient, and from these regions determine the limits for a confidence interval associated with any observed sample proportion. A relatively old textbook by Walker and Lev (1953) explains the method quite well. As a specific example, one finds that an observed proportion of 13, in a sample of 10 cases, implies the limits of .05 and .65 for a .95 confidence interval. It is important to note that the upper and lower limits are not equidistant from the observed value of .3; students often erroneously believe that the observed statistic must be in the center of a confidence interval. A nonparametric method of developing a confidence interval for the population median would also rely on the binomial distribution as the appropriate model for the sampling distribution, with the further specification that by definition the probability of selecting at random a score above the median of the population is exactly equal to the probability of selecting at random a score below the median.

Siegel (1956) prepared what became a very popular text on nonparametric methods. One interesting fact about this book is that it is oriented entirely toward the testing of hypotheses; however, interval estimation procedures can be constructed to parallel many of the procedures Siegel explains. In the early 1950's, *nonparametric* became a glamorous term for many students of statistics; as interpreted by some, nonparametric statistics promised not only completely assumption-free tests of hypotheses but also minimal calculation. With increased availability of computation aids, the question of the calculation burden becomes relatively unimportant in choosing a statistical method. The question of what assumptions are required, however, remains an important consideration.

Tests of Hypotheses. It has been indicated above that the applied textbooks tend to emphasize hypothesis testing as the major type of statistical inference. In its simplest form, the test of a stated hypothesis, often labeled H_0, consists of deducing the sampling distribution of a given statistic, on the assumption that H_0 is true, and then noting where in this sampling distribution an actual observed value of the statistic falls. In order to interpret the result, that is, to compare the observed statistic with the value postulated in H_0, one specifies a rejection region in the sampling distribution and then rejects H_0 whenever the observed value falls in this region. One has a choice of where to locate this rejection region; the difference between a one-tailed and a two-tailed test is a difference in location. In the "classic" Neyman-Pearson theory, considerations of power also influence the location of the rejection region. One also has a choice of how large this rejection region is to be; by choosing α, or the probability of a type I error, one specifies the size of the rejection region.

As an example, consider testing a hypothesis that some population mean, labeled μ, has a value of zero. Assume that a sample mean is used as our test statistic, computed for a sample of given size, N. If the sampling distribution can be deduced under the condition that H_0 is true, one can specify a range of values of sample means that would be looked upon as highly improbable values to be observed if H_0 actually were true. α specifies this degree of improbability or rareness and thus determines how much of the area of the sampling distribution is to be included in the rejection region. If the test under consideration regards a departure from zero in either direction as evidence that our hypothesis is not true, then the rejection region should be located in the two tails of the sampling distribution; obviously, this is a two-tailed test. If not, one must choose whether a positive or a negative deviation from zero constitutes evidence against the hypothesis and place the rejection region in the corresponding tail. If one knows, or can estimate, the variance of the sampling distribution of the mean for the given sample size, and if he knows that this sampling distribution has (or is well approximated by) a tabled form, such as the t distribution for the proper number of degrees of freedom, then it can be determined whether the observed sample mean falls in the rejection region. If it does, H_0 must be rejected. To a considerable extent, this practice follows Fisher's recommendation that we specify a hypothesis and give Nature the opportunity of refuting it.

A problem may arise when the observed mean does not fall in the rejection region. If this happens, what is to be concluded? Some statisticians would distinguish sharply between "conclusions," in the sense of generalizations that can be added to the store of knowledge, and "decisions," in the sense of rules for acting. Conventional hypothesis testing can be regarded as a decision process in which only two alternatives are possible: accept H_0 or reject H_0. (A third alternative—to continue gathering data—can be introduced, as it is in a sequential test.) If, then, one considers two decisions as the possible outcome of the test, he is led to consider two types of error. If H_0 is in fact true, then one makes an error in rejecting H_0. The magnitude of this error is under control, since this is the type I error, the probability of which is fixed by determining the size of the rejection region. However, if H_0 is in fact false but the outcome of the test is not to reject H_0, a second type of error (type II) is made. The consequences of these two types of error may be quite different. For example, let H_0, which states that $\mu = 0$, be identified with a statement that a specified treatment has no effect; a type I error (falsely rejecting H_0) would lead one to prescribe this treatment when it is actually worthless; such an action would be detrimental to at least some extent. A type II error (falsely failing to reject H_0) differs in that it would lead us to overlook an effective treatment. Again, such an action would be detrimental but probably to a different extent. If one can specify the costs of these two types of error, he can arrive at a decision rule that minimizes this cost or loss.

In much educational and psychological research it does not seem possible to specify cost or loss functions; thus the decision rules adopted for significance tests usually are quite arbitrary and conventional.

The typical practice clearly is to be concerned primarily with type I errors, choosing α as .05 or .01, and to allow the probability of a type II error to be a function of other factors in the experiment. This need not be so, since it is possible to plan a study with some concern for the power of the test against a specified alternative hypothesis. The power of a test is defined as the complement of the probability of a type II error; if β designates this probability of a type II error, then $1 - \beta$ is the power of the test. In general, power increases with increase in sample size; consequently it is theoretically possible to choose a sample size large enough to detect very small deviations from any stated H_0. Because this is so, the student should be aware that in a particular situation he may have been a "victim" of the power of his test, turning up significant differences that are of trivial importance simply because he employed a very large sample. Hays (1963), who gives an excellent discussion of hypothesis testing as a decision process, points out that psychologists practically never use it effectively but rely instead on arbitrary decision rules. In addition, Hays discusses "testmanship," or the interpretation of differences, and shows how the strength of association between the independent and the dependent variable can be assessed as an aid in interpreting significant differences. The inclusion of this kind of material in a widely used textbook should help to improve the statistical training of students. It is unfortunate that the Tatsuoka and Tiedeman chapter (1963), which appeared in the same year as Hays's volume and is addressed directly to persons concerned with research in education, gives such a limited and conventional view of hypothesis testing as compared with the discussion by Hays. Educational research must necessarily suffer if the Tatsuoka and Tiedeman view is regarded as the best current thinking.

Certain aspects of the analysis of variance provide further illustrations of issues and procedures in hypothesis testing. In its simplest form, the one-way analysis of variance is a test of the hypothesis that the means of k populations are equal. The alternative hypothesis is generally stated as follows: At least two populations differ in mean. Independent samples from each of these k populations can be examined in two ways. The variability within each sample can be assessed, and the variability between means of the k samples can be assessed. If the populations are assumed to be homogeneous in variance, then the appropriate pooling of variances within samples can yield an unbiased estimate of the common population variance. If the population means do not differ, then the variability among means of the k samples can be used to develop a second estimate of the common population variance. This latter estimate will, under certain circumstances, be independent of the former. One can then test H_0, which states that the population means are identical, by comparing the two independent estimates of the same variance. This is a variance-ratio test, for which the F distribution is used. Some reflection will suggest that, if the means of the population are the same, then over repeated experiments one would expect the two estimates to have the same average value—an expected value of 1 for the variance ratio. However, if the means of the populations differ, then over repeated experiments the ratio of the variance estimate based on sample means to the variance estimate based on within sample variability would have an expected value greater than 1. In performing this test, a value for α, the probability of a type I error, is chosen; if the observed variance ratio (F value) exceeds the appropriate tabled value for this α, then one rejects H_0.

This is a "shotgun" test in one sense, since a significant result merely indicates a difference in means somewhere. If one gets a significant result with the chosen α, then two additional questions should be raised. The first is the question of the strength of the relationship between the independent and the dependent variables; Hays (1963) shows how this can be done for the analysis of variance. If the estimate of the conditional variance of the dependent variable, given the independent variable, is relatively large, then even though the test was significant, the finding is probably not very important. On the other hand, if the independent variable appears to "explain" or account for a sizable portion of the variance of the dependent variable, then the finding is important in the sense that knowing the independent variable enables one to predict the value of the dependent variable with a reasonable degree of success. If the examination of the strength of relationship convinces one that something of importance has been found, then he may wish to ask a third question: Where is this effect located? When $k = 2$, this question does not arise, since there is only one difference. However, with k greater than 2, the question of which populations or combinations of populations differ in mean does arise. This is the problem of multiple comparisons following an analysis of variance. At one time, there was considerable argument about how these should be made and, in particular, about what the error rate should be. Ryan (1959, 1962), Gaito (1959), and Wilson (1962) battled in print on this issue. The major techniques for making such comparisons are described and critical sources are cited by Hopkins and Chadbourn (1967), who suggest a flow diagram as a guide to various decisions involved in making multiple comparisons.

The interpretation problems dealt with by Hopkins and Chadbourn tend to arise with one-way analysis of variance designs. However, the one-way analysis of variance seems to be used relatively infrequently in educational research. Instead, a more complicated design with two or more effects, each at two or more levels, is more common. In these designs the effects are usually crossed, though nesting is sometimes appropriate. In the crossed designs it is possible to test hypotheses about main effects and about interactions of effects. The proper method of making these tests, that is, of choosing error terms for the F ratio, depends upon the model. Fixed-effect, random-effect, and mixed models exist and differ among themselves in the proper test procedures. At this point a discussion of the analysis of variance becomes as much a discussion of experimental design as it does of statistical methods, if not more so. In practice, except for reliability studies, the completely fixed model appears to be used most often. Special problems exist for studies in which there is only one entry per cell; repeated measurement studies usually are of this character. Winer's text (1962) indicates the complexity of the statistical analysis that is required for certain types of designs.

Randomization tests differ somewhat from the tests discussed so far. Probably the classic example of a randomization test is the Fisher exact test for a set of frequencies arranged in a fourfold table. In this type of test, there is no appeal to a sampling distribution of an estimator; instead, one computes a measure of how extreme or unusual the obtained arrangement of frequencies is in comparison with all the possible arrangements, given fixed marginal frequencies. This type of test, which does not appear to have any associated or equivalent confidence-interval procedure, is of current interest and is studied usually by "Monte Carlo" procedures on computers. A number of the so-called nonparametric tests described by Siegel (1956) are essentially randomization tests, though reading the approximate probabilities from available tables is often recommended under certain conditions. Thus the chi-square test of association in a fourfold table is an approximation to the exact test by randomization; both are commonly called nonparametric tests. The review by Page and Marcotte (1966) indicates that nonparametrics probably have lost the glamor attributed to them in the 1950's and are becoming integrated into the general body of statistical methods.

CRITICISMS OF CONVENTIONAL PROCEDURES. A number of journal articles readily document the fact that there is much current criticism of the conventional procedures such as those described above. Three attacks on the use of null-hypothesis significance tests in psychology give much of the flavor of this criticism. One is the paper by Rozeboom (1960) mentioned above; the other two are by Edwards (1965) and Bakan (1966).

One line of criticism is that hypothesis testing is a decision process that can rarely be used intelligently in psychological research, since it is inappropriate for scientific work. This criticism regards decision theory as an excellent formulation when an acceptable tolerance region can be specified, when both "accept H_0" and "reject H_0" represent appropriate actions, when a loss function can be specified, and when minimizing an overall loss for a series of decisions or actions is a sensible administrative practice. In much scientific work, however, many of these conditions are not met; the problem instead is to describe, possibly rather generally, an effect or a relationship. Meyer (1966) emphasizes this point in his review of Bayesian statistics.

A second criticism is that very sharp null hypotheses are nearly always known, a priori, to be false.

For example, it is quite reasonable to believe that two different treatments will be associated with at least some mean difference in an outcome variable, even though the difference is not large. In other words, it is difficult to believe that treatments which actually differ will not have some differential effect, even though it is not a marked one. Therefore, a test of the hypothesis that the difference is precisely zero is, from this point of view, somewhat unreasonable. If the difference in means for the population is of the magnitude of .007, say, rather than precisely zero, then a failure to reject the hypothesis that the difference in means is zero simply reflects a lack of power. Thus, by stating a null hypothesis that is judged a priori to be a highly unlikely state of affairs, in effect one makes the test of this hypothesis an uninformative exercise. Occasionally in educational research an investigator compares the effects of a preferred treatment with no treatment. Here a sharp null hypothesis is extremely likely to be false, and the associated test suffers. Another, but much more difficult, attack is to identify treatments that can be conceptualized as differing in several ways or "dimensions" and then attempt to determine the relative strength of these conceptualized effects. Somewhat related—but certainly not well implemented for the problems of educational research—is the notion of a response surface methodology which attempts to vary inputs in such a way as to determine the optimum levels of combinations of inputs in the production of the response. Once again a discussion of statistical methods moves into the area of experimental design; for some leads on response surface methodology and an indication of its difficulties, see McLean (1966).

A third criticism of the conventional procedures is that they usually ignore prior information. Typical hypothesis-testing studies begin with the assumption that nothing is known about the effects of the treatments under study; in other words, every such study is assumed to be the pioneer study. In many instances this is a bad assumption, for the same or very similar treatments actually have been studied at other times and places, and it would be prudent to attempt to incorporate the known prior information with the results of the new study. It is easy to agree that this would be desirable; it is not so easy to find means of doing this which will satisfy all the current students of statistical analysis. The so-called Bayesian movement in statistics is at least partly responsible for this concern, though Binder (1964) points out that there is evidence that such concern dates back at least to the 1930's. Today, as then, the question of how such prior information is to be quantified so that it can be incorporated in the analysis remains a critical one. Those who are interested in Bayesian statistics—which, incidentally, is not a unitary concept—could begin their exploration with the review by Binder (1964), who sees the claims of this approach as quite inflated, and the review by Meyer (1966), who is much more sympathetic to the developments represented as part of this point of view. As of late 1967, there existed very few guides to practical applications of Bayesian procedures to problem of interest to educational researchers. This may change in time; if so, important modifications in current text can be anticipated.

BIVARIATE AND MULTIVARIATE PROBLEMS. Textbooks in applied statistics often are written and organized so that the material on regression and correlation could be set aside—or even extirpated from the text—without doing much damage to the student's understanding of the remaining sections of the text. It is true, of course, that references to a "regression model" in the chapter or chapters on the analysis of variance might be more difficult to understand if the material in the separate chapter or chapters on regression were not available, but it would still be possible for the student to pass quite a few test items dealing with the analysis of variance without ever having read about slopes of regression or Karl Pearson. This "separateness" is, of course, quite correct from one point of view. Testing hypotheses about means is obviously different from computing correlation coefficients, and certainly the two activities have no clear hierarchical relationship which demands that one be learned before the other. Related to this separateness is the distinction often made between experimental studies and correlation studies, a distinction which if pursued would lead again into the territory of experimental design. Rather than try to decide what kinds of studies are of most worth, let us suggest a pervasive role that concepts of regression and of association play in statistics and then consider some specific points.

A very useful notion is the distinction between independent and dependent variables, which can be illustrated with a very simple case. Testing the hypothesis that the difference in means of two populations is zero is possibly the simplest case of analysis of variance. This is an example of a one-way analysis of variance, with $k = 2$. Let the two populations be, say, middle-class and lower-class boys of a specified age. If a sample is made appropriately from these two populations separately and then some variable of interest is measured, such as ability to solve certain kinds of problems, one can make an inference about this type of problem-solving performance for the two populations. A naïve person who uses the term *effect* in very loose fashion might entitle such a study "The Effect of Socioeconomic Class on Problem-solving Ability." It would be preferable, however, to call it a study of the *relation* of socioeconomic class to problem-solving ability; such a title would more aptly convey the point that concerns us here. This study postulates "social class" or "socioeconomic class" as an independent (but not necessarily manipulatable) variable and then, in effect, investigates the relation of this independent variable to the dependent variable, problem-solving ability. The fact that the independent variable takes only two values (middle-class and lower-class) is important but does not disqualify it as a variable.

Tatsuoka and Tiedeman (1963) have done something very useful for educational researchers by emphasizing this distinction between independent and dependent variables and then organizing classes of statistical procedures in terms of differences in numbers, kinds, and so on, of these two types of variables. The point to be emphasized is that many statistical procedures do—in one fashion or another—a very simple thing, namely, assess the relation between independent and dependent variables. For example, recall that it was mentioned above that estimating the strength of a relationship between independent and dependent variables may be an important interpretation of the results of tests of hypotheses. In this sense, the concept of association, or relationship, underlies many statistical procedures.

The concept of regression is also a central one in statistics. It has already been stated that the analysis of variance typically is developed from a linear regression model, in which a single dependent variable is being approximated or "predicted" by functions of variables associated with the main effects and their interactions. A constant, often identified with the grand mean, usually is incorporated in the equation also. The analysis of covariance employs regression to "adjust" the observed values of the dependent variable for differences in an independent variable which has not been controlled experimentally but which has been measured. An example is an adjustment for intelligence level in a study of the effect of teaching methods on achievement.

A familiar example of a linear regression equation would be the kind of equation often used to predict college grade point average in the freshman year from a knowledge of aptitude test results. Usually the aptitude test or tests are given to students prior to the beginning of their college studies, and the criterion data (grade point average) are gathered subsequently. Here the independent variable is the prior variable (predictor) and the dependent variable is the subsequent one (criterion); this is typical of prediction studies in education and in industry. If there is a single predictor, the estimated score on the criterion is taken as some constant multiplied by the individual's score on the predictor, plus another constant that adjusts the mean. If there are several predictors, several constants or weights—one for each predictor—are employed; this is called "multiple regression." The equations are linear when only the first power of the predictor variable or variables is employed (and no products of predictor variables are included).

An interesting use of nonlinear or curvilinear regression, or orthogonal polynomials, has been described by Grant (1956). Perhaps the simplest case is one in which repeated measurements are available for a number of individuals; the model permits describing the variance from trial to trial in terms of linear, quadratic, cubic, and other such components. A quadratic component might be prominent, for example, if practice facilitated the response but an inhibiting effect such as fatigue built up during the later trials. The model can be complicated by employing different treatment groups and studying the interaction of these treatments with the various components of trial-to-trial variance. A recent volume by Draper and Smith (1966), which is an excellent guide to applied regression analysis, concludes with a chapter on the nonlinear case.

The number of correlation coefficients or measures of association is extensive. The Pearson product-moment coefficient of correlation is usually what is meant when one speaks of a "correlation." It takes somewhat different forms, depending upon the scale characteristics of the variables being related; for example, our study of two groups of boys would provide data that might be summarized as a point biserial correlation coefficient, which is equivalent to taking as the score on the independent variable (social class) a value of 0 or 1, depending upon which group the boy belonged to. Walker and Lev (1953) are a good source for details, including computation procedures, concerning a large number of correlation coefficients. In contrast, Hays (1963) mentions very little of the material that Walker and Lev discuss. The indicated trend is for the topic of regression to remain important and probably to increase in importance as time goes on; correlation coefficients per se are of less and less interest, except possibly to the factor analyst. This is somewhat ironic, since some lines of development in factor analysis are focusing attention not on correlations strictly defined but on covariances of diverse types.

If one studies the relationship between two variables, he deals with a bivariate surface or distribution. A scatter diagram is a "flat" representation of this surface (for the sample). If the distribution is bivariate normal in the population, then sample data can be used to make inferences concerning the degree of association. In this case the population is characterized by five parameters: the two means, the two variances, and the correlation coefficient. If the bivariate distribution is not normal, then the appropriate inferential procedures may not be known and the use of those based on the assumption of bivariate normality for the population probably gives at best only approximate results. When there are more than two variables, one speaks of a multivariate distribution; if this distribution is multivariate normal in the population, then again a number of exact inferential procedures are available. Let us turn to some of these.

The review of multivariate analysis by Cramer and Bock (1966) is an important addition to the coverage of the *Review of Educational Research* cycle that is devoted to methodology. Going back to the 1930's, Cramer and Bock quite properly make this review rather comprehensive; their reference list is very valuable, since it gives the major books in this area as well as key articles. The volume by Morrison (1967), which appeared too recently to be included in that list, is a new text of medium difficulty.

The questions that can be answered by multivariate techniques (other than factor analysis) are several. Very generally, the multivariate analysis of variance permits multiple dependent variables (as well as multiple independent variables) to be incorporated in the analysis and treated jointly, rather than singly. As Cramer and Bock point out, studies of the effectivenes of teaching methods and/or curricula nearly always should be made with respect to several dependent variables, rather than to only a single dependent variable; in assessing such effects, one can usually conceive of more than one kind of outcome that should be examined. A fairly common practice is to do multiple univariate analyses: that is, to test the significance of the treatment effect separately for each of several types of achievement, attitude, and so on. The problem is that these univariate results are not independent unless the dependent variables have zero correlation (in the population); however, this is quite unlikely since various types of achievement tend to be related rather than independent, attitude tends to be related to achievement, and so forth. Multivariate analysis of variance can deal with this realistic problem in an elegant way.

Two other multivariate procedures are of interest. One is canonical correlation, which includes as special cases both multiple correlation and the simplest case of all—the correlation of two variables. A set of variables may be arbitrarily sorted into two groups; then weights for each group of variables can be determined, such that the two weighted composites have a maximum correlation. For multiple correlation the sorting is into a group of predictor variables and a second group consisting of a single criterion variable. One might have more than one criterion measure, however, and thus have a second group consisting of more than one variable; this would be the general canonical model.

Discriminant or dispersion analysis permits the use of several variables to discriminate among or separate groups of individuals. Let us consider a one-way analysis of variance with a single dependent variable, which in effect is asking to what extent one can reliably discriminate among the various groups of subjects using this single variable. Using several variables, rather than one, requires a change in the arithmetic but permits one to answer a similar question. It is true that the multivariate analysis of variance "includes" both canonical correlation and discriminant analysis; this was evident earlier in the formulation of the conventional univariate analysis of variance as a discrimination problem.

Multivariate procedures often require extensive computation; consequently their use is often dependent upon computation facilities—both machines and programs. Conversely, the growth of computing facilities, including programs, has spurred interest in multivariate procedures and has probably increased their use. In this area the computer program and its available explanation play a crucial role in influencing research. Without good documentation, a program is unlikely to be used. But if the write-up is clear and easy to follow, so that the researcher can introduce his data into the machine easily and with little likelihood of instructional error, and if the output can be readily interpreted by the researcher, then the program is likely to be used—unfortunately, even at times when it should not be.

FACTOR ANALYSIS. It is useful to distinguish between component analysis and factor analysis, though many persons do not do so. Component analysis, concerned with an analysis of the data in hand, may be conceived as transforming the variables being studied into a new set of linear composites. These linear composites of the data in hand may be called "component measurements"; associated with these are weights for the variables, which may be described very generally as coefficients in the linear equations used to estimate the data from the component measurements. Often an orthogonal analysis is made, in which case the coefficients are also correlations of the variables with the components. If enough components are identified (the maximum number being the number of variables), then the data in hand can be perfectly reproduced from the weights and the component measurements; usually only an incomplete component analysis is made, in which case the reproduction is only approximate. It is purely incidental that it is convenient to do a component analysis by working on the matrix of intercorrelations of the variables; the computation procedure tends to obscure the nature of the analysis.

In contrast, factor analysis is concerned not with the data in hand but with the underlying (and generally unobservable) common portions of the data. The methods are designed to identify coefficients (weights) for the variables which, together with an unobservable set of factor measurements, would reproduce these common portions of the data. Note that the factor measurements are not available and, thus, that the actual reproduced common portions of the data are not computed. The degree of fit, however, can be assessed. Again, if one identifies enough factors, the fit can be very good; the interest, however, is usually in getting a moderately good fit with relatively few factors. Thus a number of workers have been interested in using factor analysis procedures to identify relatively few common factors in intelligence test performance. Computation procedures may focus on correlations of the variables, as is done in component analysis, but again this is incidental. Furthermore, some of the current models which have rather good theoretical bases do not focus on correlations of the variables themselves but on certain covariances.

Two reviews (Merrifield & Cliff, 1963; Glass & Taylor, 1966) treat a large number of the recent developments in component and factor analysis. These recent developments are numerous; in fact, the 1960's appear to be an era in which factor analytic theory and methodology has been advanced substantially on several fronts. One such advance has been an improvement of the computational procedures for the Lawley-Rao maximum-likelihood solution; this has been accomplished by Jöreskog (1967). It is now possible to secure with a reasonable amount of computation a maximum-likelihood solution that is quite stable with respect to iterations. Previously, the computing procedures gave solutions which often appeared to be stable but which would change markedly with another 200 or 300 iterations. Since the maximum-likelihood solution is associated with tests of significance for the number of factors, making this method computationally feasible should result in more substantive studies having this kind of inferential rigor.

A second line of development is the construction of fairly new models. Guttman's image theory (1953) has been available—but neglected—for some time; Harris (1962), by showing certain relationships of image theory to factor and component analysis, in effect added image analysis as a type of component analysis to the set of available procedures. Kaiser and Caffrey (1965) developed a new common-factor model, called "α-factor analysis" because of a relationship with coefficient α. This model is genuinely different from those which were available at that time and has several interesting characteristics; for instance, it may be characterized as scale-free. A third example is the multimode model developed and illustrated by Tucker (1963). This model recognizes that one may have variation in several dimensions or modes, including subjects, variables, and occasions. Typical component or factor analysis allows for variation in only two modes, usually subjects and variables.

Still another line of development is that represented by "nonmetric factor analysis." These procedures are concerned with developing spatial arrangements of points, representing variables, with the distances between points consistent with the ordinal information in the data. For nonmetric analysis, the number of dimensions must be specified; this is a problem analogous to the problem of the number of factors in conventional, or metric, factor analysis. Again, the desire usually is to secure a good representation with a minimum number of dimensions, that is, a smallest space. Several persons have been active in this area. Kruskal (1964) has extended the basic work of Shepard. (This earlier work can be identified from Kruskal's references.) Guttman (1965) has given an illustration of the application of nonmetric analysis to data on intelligence test performance; more recently, Lingoes and Guttman (1967) have discussed theoretical aspects of nonmetric factor analysis and have furnished additional examples.

These three lines of development appear to be major ones, in the sense that they are changing our conceptions of the problems to be dealt with and/or are making possible solutions that were not readily available before. Many other specific examples of new ideas and new procedures might be cited; for example, the so-called rotation problem—particularly oblique rotation—has been given new treatment by several different workers. All in all, it appears that there is a lively interest in component and factor analysis, one which is likely to alter the character of these procedures in the future.

Chester W. Harris
University of Wisconsin

References

Andrews, Thomas G. "Statistical Methods and Research Design: Index of Reviews and Notes in the *Psychological Bulletin*, 1940–1966." *Psychol B* 68: 213–20; 1967.

Bakan, David. "The Test of Significance in Psychological Research." *Psychol B* 66:433–7; 1966.

Binder, A. "Statistical Theory." *Annual R Psychol* 15: 277–310; 1964.

Clark, Cherry Ann. "Hypothesis Testing in Relation to Statistical Methodology." *R Ed Res* 33:455–73; 1963.

Cramer, Elliot M., and Bock, R. Darrell. "Multivariate Analysis." *R Ed Res* 36:604–17; 1966.

Draper, Norman, and Smith, Harry. *Applied Regression Analysis.* Wiley, 1966. 407p.

Edwards, Ward. "Tactical Note on the Relation Between Scientific and Statistical Hypotheses." *Psychol B* 63:400–2; 1965.

Fisher, Ronald A. *Statistical Methods for Research Workers.* Oliver, 1925. 175p.

Fisher, Ronald A. *The Design of Experiments.* Hafner, 1935. 252p.

Gaito, J. "Multiple Comparisons in Analysis of Variance." *Psychol B* 56:392–3; 1959.

Glass, Gene V., and Taylor, Peter A. "Factor Analytic Methodology." *R Ed Res* 36:566–87; 1966.

Grant, David A. "Analysis-of-Variance in the Analysis and Comparison of Curves." *Psychol B* 53:141–54; 1956.

Guttman, Louis. "Image Theory for the Structure of Quantitative Variates." *Psychometrika* 18:277–96; 1953.

Guttman, Louis. "The Structure of Interrelations among Intelligence Tests." In *Proceedings of the 1964 Invitational Conference on Testing Problems.* ETS, 1965. p. 25–36.

Harris, Chester W. "Some Rao-Guttman Relationships." *Psychometrika* 27:247–63; 1962.

Hays, William L. *Statistics for Psychologists.* Holt, 1963. 719p.

Hopkins, Kenneth D., and Chadbourn, Russell A. "A Schema for Proper Utilization of Multiple Comparisons in Research and a Case Study." *Am Ed Res J* 4:407–12; 1967.

Hotelling, Harold. "The Statistical Method and the Philosophy of Science." *Am Statistician* 12:9–14; 1958.

Huff, Darrell. *How to Lie with Statistics.* Norton, 1954. 142p.

Jöreskog, K. G. "Some Contributions to Maximum Likelihood Factor Analysis." *Psychometrika* 32: 443–82; 1967.

Kaiser, Henry F., and Caffrey, John. "Alpha Factor Analysis." *Psychometrika* 30:1–14; 1965.

Kendall, Maurice G., and Stuart, Alan. *The Advanced Theory of Statistics,* Vol. 2: "Inference and Relationship." Hafner, 1961. 676p.

Kendall, Maurice G., and Stuart, Alan. *The Advanced Theory of Statistics,* Vol. 1: "Distribution Theory," 2nd ed. Hafner, 1963. 433p.

Kendall, Maurice G., and Stuart, Alan. *The Advanced Theory of Statistics,* Vol. 3: "Design and Analysis and Time-Series." Hafner, 1966. 552p.

Kruskal, J. B. "Multidimensional Scaling by Optimiz-

ing Goodness of Fit to a Nonmetric Hypothesis." *Psychometrika* 29:1–28; 1964.
Lingoes, James C., and Guttman, Louis. "Nonmetric Factor Analysis: A Rank Reducing Alternative to Linear Factor Analysis." *Multivariate Behavioral Res* 2:485–506; 1967.
McLean, Leslie D. "Design and Analysis Methodology —An Overview." *R Ed Res* 36:491–502; 1966.
Merrifield, Philip R., and Cliff, Norman. "Factor Analytic Methodology." *R Ed Res* 33:510–22; 1963.
Meyer, Donald L. "Bayesian Statistics." *R Ed Res* 36:503–16; 1966.
Michael, William B. "Selected Contributions to Parametric and Nonparametric Statistics." *R Ed Res* 33:474–89; 1963.
Michael, William B., and Hunka, Steve. "Research Tools: Statistical Methods." *R Ed Res* 30:440–86; 1960.
Moonan, William J., and Wolfe, John H. "Regression and Correlation." *R Ed Res* 33:501–9; 1963.
Morrison, Donald F. *Multivariate Statistical Methods.* McGraw-Hill, 1967. 338p.
Page, Ellis B., and Marcotte, Donald R. "Nonparametric Statistics." *R Ed Res* 36:517–28; 1966.
Rozeboom, William W. "The Fallacy of the Null-Hypothesis Significance Test." *Psychol B* 57:416–28; 1960.
Ryan, T. A. "Multiple Comparisons in Psychological Research." *Psychol B* 56:26–47; 1959.
Ryan, T. A. "The Experiment as the Unit for Computing Rates of Error." *Psychol B* 59:301–5; 1962.
Savage, L. J. *The Foundations of Statistics.* Wiley, 1954. 294p.
Scheffé, H. *The Analysis of Variance.* Wiley, 1959. 477p.
Siegel, Sidney. *Nonparametric Statistics for the Behavioral Sciences.* McGraw-Hill, 1956. 312p.
Tatsuoka, Maurice M., and Tiedeman, David V. "Statistics as an Aspect of Scientific Method in Research on Teaching." In Gage, N. L. (Ed.) *Handbook of Research on Teaching.* Rand McNally, 1963. p. 142–70.
Tucker, Ledyard R. "Implications of Factor Analysis of Three-way Matrices for Measurement of Change." In Harris, C. W. (Ed.) *Problems in Measuring Change.* U Wisconsin Press, 1963. p. 122–37.
Walker, Helen M., and Lev, Joseph. *Statistical Inference.* Holt, 1953. 510p.
Wilson, W. "A note on the Inconsistency Inherent in the Necessity to Perform Multiple Comparisons." *Psychol B* 59:296–300; 1962.
Winer, B. J. *Statistical Principles in Experimental Design.* McGraw-Hill, 1962. 672p.

STUDENT CHARACTERISTICS: COLLEGE AND UNIVERSITY

The institution of higher education in the United States, although much more diverse in structure and function than its antecedent counterparts on the European continent, seems to have evolved quite similarly, in a gradual transition from earlier programs and practices to those of the present. A discerning appraisal would reveal apparent changes at this advanced level of education, but many of these have been cyclical in nature; problems, issues, and new developments tend to wax and wane. Concern for students, that is, for their characteristics and achievements, as well as research on these topics, has experienced some fluctuation of emphasis. But, along with this cyclical aspect of research on students, there has been a tenor and direction of concern fairly closely related to the development of testing and psychological measurement. The thread of such a history in this country is examined in the work of Anastasi (1954) and McConnell and Heist (1962).

Studies of college student characteristics initially appeared in considerable quantity about the beginning of World War II. Two major examples are represented in the findings of Learned and Wood (1938) and Newcomb (1943). However, comprehensive research on students went through a long period of abatement, except for prediction studies, until the appearance of publications by Sanford (1956), Stern and others (1956), and Jacob (1957). Following this latter period, there has been a fairly continuous increase in publications covering a full range of studies about modern students; many of these are reviewed below. This sequence of research over the past 10 years culminated in a plethora of reports about the activities of alienated and protesting students of the 1960's. A diverse selection of some of the earliest of these studies on activist minorities is presented in the investigations by Somers (1965), Heist (1962), Peterson (1966), and Watts and Whittaker (1966).

ACADEMIC APTITUDE AND ACHIEVEMENT. In the two decades since World War II, assessments of college students' potential for success in the academic world have covered a much wider range of attributes than previously. Prior to 1948, descriptive data were mainly limited to high school and college grades and to the results of tests of academic aptitude and achievement. Recently it has become commonplace to describe an entering class not only by noting their average score on an aptitude test but also by providing biographical data and personality test scores.

Nevertheless, in measuring characteristics presumably most closely related to academic achievement and persistence, academic aptitude continues to be the variable in wide and general usage. An increasing majority of colleges and universities now use one of several well-known tests of academic aptitude as a means of predicting college success. But, because many students with academic ability above the national freshman average fail to achieve at levels commensurate with their measured potential, educators are beginning to recognize that ability scores have limited utility as the chief basis of admission and prediction. The problems and inadequacies of prediction have also led others (Heist & Webster, 1960) to consider and weigh the validity or appropriateness of other performance criteria and of the overall educational process.

There is little, if any, research to invalidate the general importance of ability in forecasting different levels of academic attainment by *large groups of students*. However, prediction in a particular institution or for individual students is imprecise. Because of this and as a result of increased criticism of testing, agencies such as the Educational Testing Service and the College Entrance Examination Board began to encourage a search for improved and more specific ability tests, the measurement of additional facets of the cognitive domain, and the assessment of other behavioral (noncognitive or nonintellective) variables. This general concern and reexamination of ability testing was given impetus via earlier research and critiques by Fishman (1958, 1959, 1962) and Fishman and Pasanella (1960), both of whom were then members of the College Board staff. In addition to showing how little improvement in prediction of academic attainment had been evident over a quarter century, they pointed out that continued research along traditional lines would have minimal return. Fishman (1962) concluded that a more comprehensive approach to prediction, including a wider range of predictive variables and a variety of *performance* criteria —both sets of factors theoretically based—was essential.

In the spring of 1967, a commission on testing was appointed by the College Entrance Examination Board to review and examine the Board's existing program, the emphasis on ability testing, and the possible need for change and to consider and initiate plans for the kinds of tests that might be needed in the future. The appointment of this commission on testing was in part an outgrowth of criticism from outside the testing agencies and in part a result of a continuing interest in the overall impact of mass student testing on students, educational institutions, and society. The latter interest probably was engendered also by the research and critiques of Fishman and Pasanella. However, Yonge pointed out (1965) that it is difficult to determine the effect of Fishman's criticisms and recommendations on the research in the years following, but the later pattern of studies indicates the beginning of a trend away from the innumerable attempts to predict academic performance from intellective predictors and toward a more comprehensive approach to understanding students and their varied behavior in the academic context.

Among such comprehensive studies on achievement reported since 1960, Goodstein and Heilbrun (1962) examined the predictive relevance of personality traits, as measured by the Edwards Personal Preference Schedule, by analyzing the correlations with academic achievement at three levels of ability. Holland and Nichols (1964), using self-report data regarding interests and activities, found they could predict nonintellective attainments as well as intellective achievement when they used both aptitude and self-report information as predictors. French (1965) supplemented the usual mathematical and verbal measures with measures of new variables in the attempt to improve prediction for those students who approach the "ceiling" of the general aptitude subtests. He found a significant correlation between measures of reasoning and information and freshman-year grades.

A continuing stress on high aptitude in the recruitment and selection of bright or capable students has focused even greater attention on other differences among students. McConnell (1961) drew attention to the fact that although institutions have increased their differential selectivity with respect to a variety of student characteristics, as noted above, they have not lessened their attention to aptitude. He examined the question of matching the student and the college, suggesting that a concern for total student development implies that the relationship between student and school is based on a number of characteristics. McConnell and Heist (1962) further pursued the question of "fit" between student and college, chiefly from the standpoint of ability, but with attention to other considerations.

The most thorough analysis of diversity on the ability variable was presented by Darley (1962), whose findings were drawn from a representative sampling of youth in 200 colleges and universities. He demonstrated an astonishing variation in student academic ability among institutions, both nationally and within every major geographical region. Great differences among schools were also found among institutions within all classifications, such as universities, private and public, and four-year colleges.

Holland and Richards (1965) examined the relationship between a variety of test and inventory data and the academic and nonacademic accomplishments of bright students in 24 institutions, and they found that the two types of performance achievement were uncorrelated and could not be predicted by similar "input" measures.

SOCIOECONOMIC BACKGROUND. The realization that biographical and socioeconomic factors play an important part in the recruitment, admission, education, and persistence of college students was strengthened after World War II when it became apparent that students were applying in larger numbers than could be accommodated. As more students entered college from a greater range of economic levels, many colleges and universities became more selective in their clientele, thus discouraging or eliminating students from lower-level economic homes and channeling them into certain types of schools. The two-year colleges became the chief accommodation for youth from the lower economic levels, most of whom had high withdrawal rates, especially in urban settings. In effect, many people from lower-status backgrounds have little choice in the type of continuing education available to them and become concentrated in systems from which they finally withdraw at an early date (Clark, 1960).

Building numerous institutions, two- and four-year colleges as well as universities, has not had the effect of changing the general distribution of students by economic means or ability. The varieties of financial assistance made available since the mid-1950's have probably done most to further the search for talent initiated during those years (C. Cole, 1956), while simultaneously aiding high-ability students to enroll in larger numbers in the most selective institutions (Astin & Holland, 1962). The growing number and variety of scholarships and loans has not been as effective as hoped in accommodating all college-entering youth who need such assistance nor in altering the patterns of choice of those most in need of such help.

In addition to economic background, experiences in the home and in a certain social strata are closely related to, if not determinants of, some of the choices and behavior students exhibit. The social life and values in the home are closely related to the attitudes, values, and personality traits of the student. Sanders (1955) demonstrated this carryover from home background to college in a study of the students matriculating in a large, public university. She found significant variations between students from urban backgrounds and those from rural backgrounds in abilities, skills, and personality traits assessed at the time of entrance. Brown and Bystryn (1956) examined the effect of religious and ethnic background, as shown through a measure on authoritarianism, and selected personality characteristics in a sample of freshmen students enrolled in three quite different institutions of higher education. They found attitude differences at entrance which were associated with certain backgrounds, and also that changes in the degree of authoritarian thinking varied among those from different social-ethnic backgrounds.

The results of a comprehensive exploration of the relationship between the social class of male college students and their opinions and attitudes were reported by N. Miller (1958). His findings, drawn from a large sample enrolled in a number of colleges and universities in the early 1950's, strongly suggested that socioeconomic status of students' families was not so salient a determinant of certain attitudes as were ethnic and religious factors, and he proposed that the background complex of students could be better understood as being composed of all three factors.

A more extensive report, from the context of the same study and sample utilized by Miller, presented some additional information about the relationship between students' backgrounds and certain attitudes (Goldsen & others, 1960). The economic level of the home, as determined by the father's salary, was found to be correlated with attitudes toward economic issues —with students from the homes representing the highest incomes being the most conservative. Financial status also appeared to influence these students' choices of peer associations and choice of campus residence. This same investigation permitted a review of the influence of family background on political attitudes and opinions. The great majority of the males in this large sample espoused the political attitudes of their fathers and subscribed to their party affiliations. But no matter what affiliation the students espoused—Republican, Democrat, or independent— the general political attitudes and beliefs of the majority could only be described as conservative. Young political rebels and radicals, so prominent on many a college campus just 10 years later, were difficult to identify among the males from this diverse sampling of institutions.

A persistent influence of family values in various subcultures was claimed by McArthur (1960) in interpreting the differences in academic performance observed between boys coming from public and private secondary schools. As Harvard students, groups of boys coming from the two different backgrounds exhibited dissimilar cognitive styles and social values. The public school group demonstrated higher achievement as measured by grades and a stronger interest in the sciences; the private school group did not achieve in accordance with measured potential. The private school group showed stronger inclinations toward the humanities and the arts, while also showing more creative impulses.

The results of a longitudinal investigation on a generation of students at Michigan State University revealed differences among students from various backgrounds which substantiate and supplement some previous findings. Lehmann (1962) indicated that entering students coming from parochial high schools, mostly Catholic, were more authoritarian and dogmatic in their thinking than those from public or other private schools. Results similar to those for youths from parochial schools obtained for those whose parents had not attended college, as compared with those having parents who attended college; and for those from rural homes, as compared with those from urban areas. Students of noncollege parents and those from rural areas subscribed more to traditional values. When the students' attitudes and values were reassessed four years later, Dressel and Lehmann (1965) found that the general differences found among religious and status groups as freshmen held true for the seniors.

The results of an extensive survey of large samples of college students in several different states permitted Darley (1962) to analyze the effect of family status in two different geographical regions. He used father's occupational level as an index of high and low socioeconomic status, determining its influence on the type of college attended. Colleges and universities in the states of Minnesota, Wisconsin, and Texas participated in the study. To illustrate with data from one state, for those entering Minnesota institutions in the fall of 1952, a significant relation was found between status and the type of institution entered. For example, both the junior colleges and the state colleges drew their men and women entrants mostly from the low-status groups, the Catholic colleges from somewhat higher status groups, whereas the private coeducational colleges drew a majority of both sexes from high-status homes. At the state university, the proportions were different for men and women, with a majority of women coming from homes of higher occupational status, and with the opposite being true for the men.

Medsker and Trent (1965), reporting from the

context of another large-sample study across several states, analyzed the distribution of high school youths among a variety of institutions in higher education. They found that the status of the students' home background, using father's occupational level as the index, was more important than ability and high school rank in determining college attendance. Approximately three-fourths of the graduates from the top three status categories entered college, as compared with less than one-third from the lowest three, and more students of low ability from high-status homes entered college than did high-ability students from low socioeconomic status homes. The educational attainment of both parents, as well as occupational status and type of religion, were found to be associated with the specific *type* of college entered.

A significant study of Negro education was reported by Gurin and Katz (1966), in which the major analyses were largely confined to the students enrolled in 10 Negro colleges in the South. These students' socioeconomic backgrounds, although considerably varied among the schools, were very dissimilar from what would be found in a national sample of college youth. The authors indicated that 30 percent of the enrollees came from homes that other authorities would define as impoverished, with the proportion approaching 50 percent in one institution. Only 16 percent were from families with incomes of $10,000 or over. From the standpoint of parents' education, both fathers and mothers of these Negro college students had attained higher levels than Southern or national nonwhite adult populations, although differences in the educational levels attained varied greatly among the colleges. Approximately one-fourth had had some college education, but about one-half had not graduated from high school.

The most extensive research relating a variety of background factors to college-going and college attainment has been conducted by Sewell (1964), who initially demonstrated that the percentage of college youth from urban communities increased with the size of the community, with the smallest number coming from the rural areas. However, these differences among the number of urban youth coming from different size communities are not found when the level of intelligence and socioeconomic status are held constant. Thus, rural youth of all ability levels were not proportionally represented. Sewell and Armer (1966) challenged the long-held thesis that the neighborhood status was a major factor in college plans and attendance, by showing that a neighborhood effect could be accounted for largely by sex, family socioeconomic status, and intelligence. This finding, however, applies more to men than to women. Sewell and Shah (1967) resorted to a complex method of analysis to show that socioeconomic status and intelligence together have direct effects on college plans, attendance, and level of attainment. For women the effect of socioeconomic status was relatively greater than that of intelligence, whereas for men this was reversed. For those attending college, intelligence became the most important variable for both sexes in determining the rate of graduation.

ACADEMIC AND VOCATIONAL INTERESTS.

There is an arbitrary aspect to defining interests, since there are a number of different purposes for which the term is employed. When considering students and their education, academic major and vocational choice are frequently viewed as important interest areas. Most of the recent research contributing to the understanding of students' interests and preferences has focused on these topics. Although a number of comprehensive interest tests are available and are widely used, research on specific or measured general interests, especially as they may be important or relevant to the educational process, has not been abundant in recent years.

Besides work on students' preferences for different academic majors and future occupations, studies of those actually majoring or working in particular subject areas also resulted in meaningful findings. Bereiter and Freedman (1962) reviewed the literature from the end of World War II to 1960 on students' general interests in and choices of academic fields of study and on students pursuing different majors. The results from a number of fairly similar investigations led them to conclude that certain behavioral characteristics tend to be more typical of students choosing some fields and quite atypical of students selecting others. Along with differences in nonintellective interests, they drew upon the studies demonstrating differences in the proportions of students from several ability levels who entered certain fields. For example, the natural sciences and engineering generally were found to attract the largest quota of persons who measured high on standard tests of academic ability. Thistlethwaite (1960) reported on the choices of majors of National Merit Scholars, which also demonstrated the overconcentration of high-ability men in the natural and biological sciences, whereas women of high ability distributed themselves more equally among the major discipline areas. Bereiter and Freedman suggested that such results regarding general ability may be related to the status associated with the vocations. They proposed that it was of greater significance, however, that the various majors and disciplines drew dissimilar proportions of students exhibiting liberal or conservative attitudes, inner- or other-directed values, and certain social-emotional adjustment traits, since such differences suggest implications for educating students in the various disciplines.

Beardslee and O'Dowd (1962) speculated on the significance of the findings which show college students, especially the more capable ones, to be interested in only a limited range of the possible occupations. (Most students chose professions demanding advanced education.) The authors examined the extent to which the stated occupational interests and goals are confused with commonly shared stereotypes about the professions or related to the actual knowledge which students possess about the professions. Astin (1965a) examined changes in career interests and choices over the college years for a sample of more than 3,500 male scholarship winners and near-winners enrolled in 73 colleges. He found that students have a greater tendency to shift their choices to different careers if enrolled in an institution where many other students are interested in those careers.

Dunn (1962) reported on the measured interests of a large sample of students who took their majors in the science and liberal arts areas. The students in the various majors differed greatly on 8 out of 10 occupational-interest orientations (scales). Hewer (1965) explored the relationship between the measured interests of college students and the socioeconomic status of their homes and found that, in general, interests were not independent of social origin.

Berdie's (1965) findings lent support to a variety of earlier research evidence which had indicated that the objectively measured interests (SVIB) of students are valid and predictive of future occupational choice. He found that, for a sample of students who finished college and completed advanced training in four different professions, their measured interests as high school seniors related significantly to their chosen occupations.

Holland (1966) examined the development of vocational images in the minds of young people and the rationale of decisions underlying their vocational choices, and he constructed a system of categorizing individuals into six basic types, according to their vocational preferences. Underlying Holland's thinking has been extensive research on large samples of college students over approximately 10 years, resulting in the development of an inventory for measuring, classifying, and describing students from the standpoint of both interests and general personality. A series of reports on the development, as well as the functioning and predictive value, of the inventory is available (Holland, 1962, 1963). Astin (1965b) utilized Holland's system of categorizing students, based on the classification of students' vocational preferences, as a chief means of differentiating among the student bodies of approximately 250 institutions. The student bodies were described according to the personality variables associated with six categorical types.

NONINTELLECTIVE CHARACTERISTICS. The variety of reports and articles within the general and expanding area of student characteristics does not lend itself to easy classification. For example, some publications reviewed under other headings might well have been placed in this section. In fact, a few reports are mentioned or reviewed in part in at least two places. Nonintellective characteristics encompass numerous social and psychological variables and forms of assessment. The available reported work in this area of nonintellective or personality variables is represented by selections which demonstrate some major research concerns and activities in this general area over the past 10 years.

Ludeman's report (1956) on the results of a survey of 500 men and women at all class levels and in different institutions, during the years of the "quiet generation," presented the students' perceptions of an ideal and effective college student. This portrait of the ideal student emerged: good personality, honest, intelligent, cooperative, friendly, sociable, studious and scholarly, with high goals, and participative in activities. This sedate picture of college students 10 years ago provides an interesting contrast to the characterizations of the current student generation, with its sizable minorities expressing concern and demonstrating their commitments on a number of issues.

Brown (1960) reported on the qualities of the ideal student as seen by a college faculty. The faculty concurred in general with the qualities posed as ideal by the students in Ludeman's study but nominated as ideal individuals 40 students who had records of high academic achievement and exhibited to a greater degree than other students the characteristics of intelligence and scholarship, social-emotional maturity, independence, inner direction, sense of morality, sensitivity to others, civic-mindedness, and social responsibility. It is interesting that more recent research has shown many of these traits to be typical of the constructive activist youth (Somers, 1965; Heist, 1962).

The comprehensive study reported by Goldsen and others (1960) represented one of the most extensive surveys of students to date. It drew on a sample of more than 4,000 persons, mostly males, in 11 institutions, who responded to a questionnaire asking about personal objectives, educational goals, kinds of education sought, career aspirations, campus organizations, religious and ethical beliefs, and attitudes toward numerous personal and social concerns and issues. The data, indicating a conservative *status quo* perspective of most of the students, were collected in the early 1950's, when the Cold War, the Korean War, and economic fluctuations did not pose highly disruptive influences in the lives of most college youth.

A number of investigations in the 1950's have been directed to the mental health of college students, with attention given to the characteristics of students exhibiting deviant patterns of adjustment. However, actual data on students' adjustment difficulties were available from only a few such studies. Wedge (1958) edited a composite of reports and case analyses, chiefly of Yale men, which presented a picture of academic, social, and emotional problems, with related personality and background variables. The contributors, mostly members of the Yale clinic, viewed the students' course through college, their achievements, and difficulties as the result of interaction of the characteristics of postadolescent development and the college environment. Johnson (1959) described the results of an investigation which attempted to assess students' adjustment problems through a questionnaire submitted directly to them. Among a sample of 1,000 freshmen in a university setting, researchers found that the admitted problems differed between men and women, urban and rural youths, and among levels of intelligence. The men indicated being more troubled than did the women in relation to problems of social relations, finances, and health and less troubled than women by emotional problems.

The most prominent and consistent research contribution to knowledge about the behavior of college students has come from the staff of the National

Merit Scholarship Research Corporation. Although much of their research has dealt with a highly selective sample of high school graduates who enrolled in college, they have examined a diversity of topics and problems. Two related reports of student characteristics, drawn from the writings of the senior staff in the middle years of this group's productivity, illustrate the complexity of their interests and research methods. Astin (1964a) analyzed information received from a sample of more than 127,000 college freshmen, condensing the data obtained to six factors which he used as distinguishing characteristics for the description of college populations. Sets of scores were computed for the freshmen in 248 institutions. The factor-based characteristics are: intellectualism, estheticism, status, leadership, masculinity, and pragmatism.

In a followup report, Astin (1964b) showed that the characteristics of the students in 243 institutions were related to measurable characteristics of the colleges. He concluded that the aspirations of the students appeared to be well suited to the curriculum offerings of the types of institution they were attending. For example, within this sample of schools, private nonsectarian colleges tended to recruit students with greater potential for a total liberal arts type of academic program, including science and art, than did the other types of institutions.

The American College Testing Program (ACT) began more recently to collect information also on large samples of high school and college youth. A research division within this program has initiated a series of reports, most of which are relevant or directed to the matter of student characteristics. Abe and others (1965) opened the series with general, descriptive analyses of the "typical" college man and woman and also of the variety of students who were freshmen in a representative selection of American colleges and universities in the spring of 1964. The gross analyses of a great variety of data for this large student sample, enrolled in a variety of institutions, chiefly substantiates the astonishing diversity of mankind seeking further education. In two later reports, Abe and Holland (1965a, 1965b) studied and described "subgroups" of first-year students, classified according to their intentions to major in one of 13 subject areas or according to their stated preferences for certain vocations. Probably the real value of such reports is yet to be attained in their providing a foundation for later studies of the students, who act on their initial declarations or change their preferences one or more times.

Dallas (1966) studied random samples of university students drawn from fraternities, dormitories, and off-campus housing. Using objective personality inventories, he found the fraternity males to be more dominant than other students but not independent of their own fraternal groups. In comparison with others, they were also more concerned with social recognition and were less altruistic. These men also differed from the other two groups in the high economic and educational status of their homes. The off-campus students who came from the lowest-status homes were the most concerned with the welfare of others. In a second study on the differences between fraternity and nonfraternity men, Kaludis and Zatkin (1966) studied fraternity pledges, as compared with a matched sample of nonfraternity freshmen, chiefly to determine reasons for the relative constancy of the fraternity population within an undergraduate enrollment which had doubled. Besides finding a number of the expected differences, such as the higher economic and status level of the pledges' homes and families, which may have been related to their choice of residence, the authors concluded that the chief answer to the study's major objective may be that fraternities were failing to draw from the general or total supply of students entering the increasing variety of subject-matter fields.

CHANGE IN NONINTELLECTIVE CHARACTERISTICS. Concern for the impact of a college education on student development in nonintellective characteristics has reached a crescendo in this past decade. The seed of this present concern was planted in early investigations by Nelson (1938), Newcomb (1943), and Arsenian (1943). Their findings, based on studies in single institutions or in limited areas, such as basic values or religious attitudes, indicated that although most students changed over the college years the small extent of the average change restricted the interpretation of amount and quality of change for most.

In the mid-1950's Dressel (1954) found that selected interests of students did change, depending on the experiences intervening between the testing periods, contrary to the general belief about postadolescent stability of interests. But there were some indications that these findings varied according to the type of student and the area he chose to major in. Two years later, Sanford and associates (1956) published the initial report on a long-range, comprehensive study of the women at Vassar. The early findings indicated that these women, considered as a group, changed in a number of ways during four college years. The seniors were described as more mature in behavior and less authoritarian, less religious, more tolerant, truer to their impulses, and somewhat more disturbed.

In 1957, Jacob presented results of a comprehensive survey and review of existing research on college students. His research pointed to the disturbing conclusion that college experiences, by and large, had a limited effect on the values and attitudes of students and that students graduated from college mostly unchanged or, at best, a little less rigid or conservative in their thinking than when they entered. Studies of change in students' thinking and behavior since that date have used the Jacob findings as a basis for numerous research questions and later investigations.

In the years immediately following the Jacob critique and before 1960, several studies, somewhat different in their focus or approach, reported on change in nonintellective traits over varied periods of time. Bender (1958) reported the findings from one of the first longitudinal studies going beyond the span of the college years. Using the Allport-Vernon-Lindzey *Study of Values* (Allport & others, 1951), he retested the religious values of a group of adults of one faith who had been assessed 15 years earlier as students. He found a significant average change denoting a shift to greater interest in religion in the postcollege years. The changes in individuals varied with the amount of church attendance and the extent of other religious-oriented practices.

Except for the Vassar project (Sanford, 1956), the most comprehensive research of the 1950's was reported in two studies by Plant (1958a, 1958b). The first of these was a two-year project which included a sample of students who completed the sophomore year and a control group that did not complete the first two years of college. The college group changed significantly during the two years in the mean scores obtained on a measure of ethnocentrism, scoring in a more liberal direction. The control group did not change on this particular measure. In the second study, conducted over four years, Plant again found significant differences between the freshman and senior scores. Senior students were less accepting of ethnocentric ideology, with women changing to a greater degree than men.

E. Miller (1959) called attention to an important concern in reporting that the students in a small random sample showed some changes as a group on nonintellective variables, but that no two students exhibited the same pattern of change across the several variables. In other words, the average change was not indicative of what happened to individuals. This finding highlights the problem of interpreting all difference scores underlying the assessment of change for groups, a factor that plagues all research on growth and development. Hammond (1959) found that five-year engineering students changed as a group on four nonacademic orientations—materialistic, technical, competitive, and humanitarian—with the latter two (concern for prestige and for people) gaining in importance, and the first two becoming less important.

Research on American college students has proliferated in this decade, with a host of yet unreported studies in many institutions. This increase has been precipitated in part by some major projects conducted prior to 1960 but reported after the beginning of this decade. One example is an extensive study of one class (46 women) of Sarah Lawrence students by Murphy and Raushenbush (1960). They found that changes or growth in academic accomplishment and intellectual qualities were related to personality traits of the students, with the women who were more ready for change as freshmen in turn changing the most. Along with the cognitive changes, the authors concluded that the seniors had also gained in confidence and exhibited greater social responsibility.

A second contribution reported after 1960 from earlier research is found in a chapter in *The American College* (Webster & others, 1962). Giving attention to the topic of change in students' abilities, interests, attitudes, and values, this report represents the most comprehensive review of change studies up to that time. It also includes a fairly extensive résumé of the objective test data from the Mellon Foundation research on Vassar College women (Sanford, 1956). The Mellon research revealed changes in scores over two and four years for a number of personality dimensions, particularly on some developed by the Mellon research staff. Change data on the same scales and over the same years are also presented for one class of Bennington students.

The results drawn from the studies of a generation of Vassar and Bennington women give emphasis to two major findings. First, the significant differences between the women in these two schools, both at the freshman and the senior level, clearly indicated that persons with quite different orientations matriculate on the two campuses. On scales measuring social maturity, developmental status, and impulse expression, the Bennington freshmen scored considerably higher than Vassar seniors. The second finding is that the women on both campuses changed significantly on these scales, a majority in the direction of positive development and greater maturity. Specifically, the seniors were described as less conservative in their approach to religious and political matters, more tolerant of individual differences, and freer to express impulses.

Another study conducted during the 1950's and reported later by Heath (1964) was a long-range, intensive examination of the lives of 36 Princeton men during college and thereafter. A thorough, although rather subjective, analysis of three categorized types of students highlights significant individual differences in the way students learn and the fact that success in college demands varied responses and adaptations for different students in various fields.

Two projects conducted after 1960 are particularly noteworthy for their use of control groups. Lehmann (1963) reported that Michigan State University students improved their critical thinking ability, became more open-minded, more receptive to new ideas, and less authoritarian and ethnocentric. However, he pointed out that, with one exception (flexible versus traditional value orientations), the control group, which was composed of students who first enrolled and then dropped out, changed in the same way as the graduates. Using some of the same scales to measure change in San Jose State students, Plant (1962) reported less dogmatism, ethnocentrism, and authoritarianism for those students who completed four years of college, but also for those who attended for more limited periods. These findings were essentially replicated in a second study of students who attended six junior colleges for varying periods of time (Telford & Plant, 1963). The authors again found that significant test-retest changes occurred for all, unrelated to length of enrollment in the junior colleges. The results of these controlled studies, in seeming contradiction to Plant's pre-1960 findings (1958a, 1958b), encourage a more discerning interpretation of the reasons for the measured changes found in college student groups, with maturation being given increasing credit as part of the explanation.

The results of a somewhat different examination of college impact were reported by Selvin (1963), who presented selected evidence that changes in certain occupational choices (within prominent professions) are associated with certain combinations of students' type of college residence and their fathers' education. One drawback of this selected analysis, fairly typical of almost all change studies, is the tendency to confuse correlation with cause. Possibly, choice of living arrangements (or, in other studies, different colleges or different majors) is dependent on the personality characteristics of the individual. However, results of an earlier study by Thistlethwaite (1960) indicated that other experiences or factors were more potent determinants of changes in career plans than was the influence of student group living. Chief among these were the characteristics, styles of teaching, and general behavior of teachers, which appeared to vary by department. In examining changes in career plans during college among large samples of very bright students, Nichols (1964) discovered cyclical trends that were unrelated to job opportunities and salary differentials. From the work of Selvin, Thistlethwaite, and Nichols, it seems that changes in career plans during college are difficult to explain and do not appear to be related to one or two prominent variables.

STUDENTS IN OTHER COUNTRIES. Reports of the characteristics and attitudes of students in other countries have been drawn from journals and books available in this country and from a few foreign journals printed in English. Without access to non-English journals, one cannot accurately estimate the amount of research on the topic of students nor the variety of information available. It is of interest to note how very few of the available studies of the backgrounds and characteristics of students in other countries were done over a decade ago. More recently, various aspects of students and their lives have been and are being studied in a small but growing number of countries. The results of recent studies to be reviewed here have been drawn as examples of the variety of work in this area.

Some research activity has been initiated from outside the particular countries, and in some instances comparative studies have involved student samples from two or more nations. The direction and type of research reported in English generally appear to follow the trends in the United States, perhaps reflecting interests of an English-speaking audience. For example, increased attention since 1960 has focused on political concerns and activities of students—in the industrially advanced countries, in developing countries, and in underdeveloped countries. The relatively large number of recent studies is commensurate with the apparent prevalence of student unrest throughout much of the world.

Cross-cultural Studies. Two fairly extensive, cross-cultural studies, conducted approximately 15 years apart and directed to quite different concerns, dealt with samples of students from widely separated countries. Gillespie and Allport (1955) surveyed small samples from the United States and 13 nations in Europe, the Middle East, the Far East, the Orient, and elsewhere in North America. They sought to determine how college youths viewed their future and that of their nation a few years after World War II. Among other problems, the size and source of the samples in most of the countries severely limit the interpretations of the differences obtained in a study like this. Another more recent multination study, conducted with a large sample of students from six scattered countries, permitted D. Cole (1966) to examine some of the background experiences underlying the current orientation of students by focusing on the types and amount of parental praise they received as children.

Student protest and political activity have a long history in many foreign countries. The more common manifestations of student unrest and protest and the students involved were examined across international lines in two recent studies. Bereday (1966) surveyed the activities of students in four cities on four different continents. He analyzed the rather different developments in Montreal, Ibadan, Warsaw, and Rangoon in the last 10 years and concluded that there are some characterizations which underlie or apply to varied student aggressions, such as general dissatisfaction with the adult world and intergenerational tensions and conflict. However, he indicated that conflict between age groups is seldom if ever the chief or single reason for the developments witnessed. Chief credit for the instigation of protests and movements is given to small minorities of students, often from either the homes of the elite or the "have-nots" or both, who assume leadership in response to a complex of social and political factors and events.

Soares (1966) directed a thorough inquiry of concerns and problems which were similar to those examined by Bereday. He reviewed data on students' political attitudes and activities from studies in the United States and several Latin American countries. He drew conclusions about visible, participative minorities, both on an institutional and national basis, whose intense behavior is frequently misinterpreted as representing much larger segments of college youth. Recognizing this degree of higher participation of vocal, radical students as compared with conservative groups, he points out that the intensity of involvement and activity gives them a significance beyond their mere numerical strength. Thus, he suggests that the extent of leftist radicalism in student politics in underdeveloped countries is probably overemphasized and not what it appears.

Europe. Educators and social scientists on the European continent have not pursued college students as subjects for research to an extent approaching the rate of research on students in the United States, at least not until very recently. Undoubtedly, the struggle for economic and social recovery during the postwar years and the general orientation of the European social science disciplines toward researchable problems have had some effect. The following reports will illustrate the varied types of interest shown in the areas of student nonacademic behavior.

Simenson and Geis (1955) used a sample of students at the University of Wisconsin as a reference group for studying students at the University of Oslo. They found that the Norwegian students of that period were about two years older than the average college student in this country and were much more independent of the university (with only 10 percent living in organized housing, less than 20 percent belonging to university clubs, and spending an average of only 6 hours per week in class as compared with 16 for Americans, but giving twice as much time to studying). Also, compared with the Wisconsin men and women, the Oslo students attended church in much smaller numbers (5 percent), gave more time to reading, and attended the theater much more frequently.

Hopkins (1958) conducted a study of college success and failure on a large sample of former college students in England. He found that the students who entered but did not graduate from University College, London, differed from the graduates on a small composite of social-psychological factors, which included health, finances, and relations with the opposite sex.

Quite different concerns about the modern European student were represented in two more recent studies. The phenomenon of student trade unionism, which began in France in the postwar period, was studied by Pinner (1964). He traced the histories of the movements in Belgium, Holland, and France and also discussed the reasons given by students for joining. Morrison and McIntyre (1966) surveyed a sample of graduate students in Scotland, who gave their opinions of various countries, political leaders, and the policies of the East and West power blocs. Their attitudes toward the blocs were independent of their views on policies and politicians. The students associated the United States and President Johnson with capitalism, democracy, and military preparedness; but they also associated justice, coexistence, and broad-based education with the Western bloc, whereas they associated disarmament with the communist countries.

Near East. In a study of students in a university in Lebanon, Melikian and Prothro (1957) compared the interests of Lebanese students with a sample of American students. These Near Eastern students were more interested in vocational, academic, and political achievement than were the Americans and were less concerned with world peace and family welfare. In a second study, Prothro (1958) compared several philosophies of life—as measured by an inventory assessing styles or modes of living—held by two samples of Arab students, one sample being Moslem and the other Christian. No differences were found in general value orientations between the two religious groups.

Africa. Two reports on African students have been selected because they are addressed to two of the important problem areas of this diverse continent.

Danziger (1958) surveyed samples of South African college students from African, Indian, and European ethnic backgrounds regarding their personal values and their estimate of the general racial-social situation. The nonwhite students saw "white civilization" as a system of exploitation and oppression, whereas the Europeans or whites saw it as having moral advantages. In the matter of personal values, the nonwhites placed emphasis on political values and the goal of helping their own communities, whereas the whites gave emphasis to the private spheres of their lives. The second African study selected (Wyllie, 1966) represents the results of several surveys of Ghanian students at different times and on two university campuses. The results confirmed earlier findings that the student population was becoming more representative of the general population, but the majority of college entrants were still coming from the cities. The evidence also indicated that Ghanian students were becoming more geographically mobile, both before and after college.

Australia. Two similar studies are representative of a small supply of fairly recent research on college students in Australia. Students in the United States were used as reference groups in both investigations. In the first, Anderson (1960) used a 16-scale inventory to describe the personality traits of Australian university freshmen. Students of both sexes, as compared with the Americans, were found to be less warm and sociable, less adventurous, more suspicious and jealous, and more self-sufficient. The Australian women were also judged to be more intellectual, feminine, and guilt-prone. In the second study, also focusing on personality traits of university freshmen, the relationship between students' traits or needs and academic achievement was analyzed by Gibbs (1965–66). He found that the relationship between psychological needs and achievement differed for men and women, with the results for the Australian women being more similar to those reported for women in the United States. The author suggested that the correlations between achievement and the Deference and Heterosexuality scales for the Australian men might be due to the effect of a male-dominated society.

Far East. A sampling of the interests and concerns of college students in India has been introduced through a series of research findings reported by Sinha and colleagues. The study samples were drawn from the undergraduate and graduate student body at the university at Patna. Among students at both levels, Sinha and Panda (1959) found some understandable differences between the sexes in their expressed occupational preferences, but both men and women in these samples resorted to the same explanations for their occupational choices, listing social prestige and money as the chief motivational factors for them (Sinha and Dash, 1959). A second sample of men and women students at Patna was surveyed by Sinha and Roy (1959) regarding opinions on different aspects of education. Both sexes supported coeducation, the use of examinations, and Hindi as a medium of instruction. However, the women were much more in favor of the first and last than the men were. Sinha and Roy (1960) surveyed another sample of Patna graduate students regarding their extracurricular activities and discovered that the entertainment aspects of their pursuits were highly flavored with esthetic and cultural interests; however, organized university activities—whether academic, athletic, or cultural—were ranked low by the majority.

Another Indian study using United States students as a reference group was conducted by Ghei (1966). In comparing the measured psychological needs of a sample of Indian college women and a similar socioeconomic group in this country, he found the Indian students to be higher as a group on the following scales of the *Personal Preference Schedule* (Edwards, 1959): Achievement, Deference, Order, Dominance, Endurance, and Aggression. They were lower on Exhibition, Affiliation, Intraception, and Heterosexuality. Paul (1966) surveyed a sample of Indian students enrolled in another university to determine variables related to degrees of worldmindedness. The students from higher economic levels were more nationalistic in their thinking than those from lower income brackets. Worldmindedness, and not nationalism, was typical of students inclined toward the Communist party or of those intending to work in the professions or administrative services.

Burma. A large sample of Burmese students, who attended two universities, participated in a survey inquiring into their values, goals, and aspirations. Wohl and Silverstein (1966) noted some conflicts in the students who sought both humanitarian goals and materialistic values or who were caught between the values of their Buddhist backgrounds and those introduced by the cosmopolitan Western world. In general, these college students expressed a desire for more education and a career, in the belief that a degree would automatically bring status, security, and happiness. However, many students expressed their interest in serving others, particularly their families and the nation.

Korea. Two cross-cultural studies, both involving college samples in the United States, were directed to examining existing moral codes among and the personalities of Korean students. Rettig and Pasamanick (1959) studied a large sample of women students at Seoul University and concluded that the Koreans, who were mostly atheists, took a more rigorous stand on all moral issues than did the American girls. Park (1966) reported on a comparison of certain personality traits measured in Korean and American women students. No difference was found between these two nationalities on the masculinity-femininity concept, but Korean women scored lower on a measure of ego strength. Park suggested that the latter score probably was related to the confusion and anxiety resulting from comparatively recent changes in female role in that country.

Paul Heist
University of California

References

Abe, Clifford, and Holland, John L. "A Description of College Freshmen: I. Students with Different Choices of Major Fields." In *ACT Research Report No. 3*. ACT, 1965(a). 53p.

Abe, Clifford, and Holland, John L. "A Description of College Freshmen: II. Students with Different Vocational Choices." In *ACT Research Report No. 4*. ACT, 1965(b). 51p.

Abe, Clifford, and others. "A Description of American College Freshmen." In *ACT Research Report No. 1*. ACT, 1965. 65p.

Allport, G. W., and others. *Study of Values—Manual of Direction.* Houghton, 1951.

Anastasi, Anne. *Psychological Testing.* Macmillan, 1954. 682p.

Anderson, A. W. "Personality Traits of Western Australian University Freshmen." *J Social Psychol* 51:87–91; 1960.

Arsenian, Seth. "Changes in Evaluative Attitudes During Four Years of College." *J Applied Psychol* 27:338–49; 1943.

Astin, Alexander W. "Some Characteristics of Student Bodies Entering Higher Educational Institutions." *J Ed Psychol* 55:267–75; 1964(a).

Astin, Alexander W. "Distribution of Students Among Higher Educational Institutions." *J Ed Psychol* 55:276–87; 1964(b).

Astin, Alexander W. "Effect of Different College Environments on the Vocational Choices of High Aptitude Students." *J Counseling Psychol* 1:28–34; 1965(a).

Astin, Alexander W. *Who Goes Where to College?* SRA, 1965(b). 125p.

Astin, Alexander W., and Holland, John L. "The Distribution of 'Wealth' in Higher Education." *Col U* 37:113–25; 1962.

Barger, B., and Hall, E. "Relation of Expected College Activities to Ability and Achievement." *J Col Student Pers* 6:300–4; 1965.

Beardslee, David C., and O'Dowd, Donald B. "Students and the Occupational World." In Sanford, Nevitt. (Ed.) *The American College.* Wiley, 1962. p. 597–626.

Bender, Irving E. "Changes in Religious Interest—A Retest After 15 Years." *J Abn Social Psychol* 57:41–6; 1958.

Berdie, Ralph. "Strong Vocational Interest Blank Scores of High School Seniors and Their Later Occupational Entry." *J Applied Psychol* 49:188–93; 1965.

Bereday, George Z. "Student Unrest on Four Continents: Montreal, Ibadan, Warsaw and Rangoon." *Comp Ed R* 10:188–204; 1966.

Bereiter, Carl, and Freedman, Mervin B. "Fields of Study and the People in Them." In Sanford, Nevitt. (Ed.) *The American College.* Wiley, 1962. p. 563–96.

Brown, Donald R. "Non-intellective Qualities and the Perception of the Ideal Student by College Faculty." *J Ed Soc* 33:269–78; 1960.

Brown, Donald R., and Bystryn, D. "College Environment, Personality, and Social Ideology of Three Ethnic Groups." *J Social Psychol* 44:279–88; 1956.

Clark, Burton R. *The Open Door College: A Case Study*. McGraw-Hill, 1960. 207p.

Cole, Charles C., Jr. *Encouraging Scientific Talent*. CEEB, 1956. 259p.

Cole, David L. "Intercultural Variations in Recall of Parental Reward Patterns." *Sociol Soc Res* 50:436–47; 1966.

Dallas, Robert J. "Student Characteristics and Choice of Housing." *J Col Student Pers* 7:147–50; 1966.

Danziger, Kurt. "Value Differences Among South African Students." *J Abn Social Psychol* 57:339–46; 1958.

Darley, John G. *Promise and Performance: A Study of Ability and Achievement in Higher Education*. Center for the Study of Higher Education, 1962. 191p.

Dressel, Paul L. "Interests—Stable or Unstable." *J Ed Res* 48:95–102; 1954.

Dressel, Paul L., and Lehmann, Irvin J. "The Impact of Higher Education on Student Attitudes, Values, and Critical Thinking Abilities." *Ed Rec* 46:248–58; 1965.

Dunn, Frances E. "Interest Patterns of College Majors." *J Col Student Pers* 4:79–85; 1962.

Edwards, Allen L. *Personal Preference Schedule*. Psychol Corp., 1959.

Fishman, Joshua A. "Unsolved Criterion Problems in the Selection of College Students." *Harvard Ed R* 28:340–9; 1958.

Fishman, Joshua A. "Non-intellective Factors as Predictors, as Criteria, and as Contingencies in Selection and Guidance." In *Selection and Educational Differentiation*. Center for the Study of Higher Education, U California, 1959. p. 55–73.

Fishman, Joshua A. "Some Social–Psychological Theory for Selecting and Guiding College Students." In Sanford, Nevitt. (Ed.) *The American College*. Wiley, 1962. p. 666–89.

Fishman, Joshua A., and Pasanella, Ann K. "College Admission-Selection Studies." *R Ed Res* 30:298–310; 1960.

French, John W. "New Tests for Predicting the Performance of College Students with High-level Aptitude." *J Ed Psychol* 55:184–94; 1965.

Ghei, S. N. "Needs of Indian and American College Females." *J Social Psychol* 69:3–11; 1966.

Gibbs, D. N. "A Cross-cultural Comparison of Needs and Achievements of University Freshmen." *Pers Guid J* 44:813–6; 1965–66.

Gillespie, James M., and Allport, Gordon W. *Youth's Outlook on the Future*. Doubleday, 1955. 61p.

Goldsen, Rose K., and others. *What College Students Think*. Van Nostrand, 1960. 240p.

Goodstein, Leonard D., and Heilbrun, Alfred, Jr. "Prediction of College Achievement from the Edwards Personal Preference Schedule at Three Levels of Intellectual Ability." *J Applied Psychol* 46:317–20; 1962.

Gurin, Patricia, and Katz, Daniel. *Motivation and Aspiration in the Negro College*. Institute for Social Research, U Michigan, 1966. 346p.

Hammond, Marjorie. "Attitudinal Changes of Successful Students in a College of Engineering." *J Counseling Psychol* 6:69–71; 1959.

Heath, Roy. *The Reasonable Adventurer: A Study of the Development of Thirty-six Undergraduates at Princeton*. U Pittsburgh, 1964. 165p.

Heist, Paul. "Diversity in College Student Characteristics." *J Ed Soc* 33:279–91; 1960.

Heist, Paul. "Intellect and Commitment: The Faces of Discontent." In Knorr, O. A., and Minter, W. J. (Eds.) *Order and Freedom on the Campus*. Western Interstate Commission for Higher Education, 1962. p. 61–9.

Heist, Paul, and Webster, Harold. "A Research Orientation to Selection, Admission, and Differential Education." In Sprague, Hall T. (Ed.) *Research on College Students*. Western Interstate Commission for Higher Education, 1960. p. 21–40.

Hewer, Vivian H. "Vocational Interests of College Freshmen and Their Social Origins." *J Applied Psychol* 49:407–11; 1965.

Holland, John L. "Some Explorations of a Theory of Vocational Choice: I. One- and Two-year Longitudinal Studies." *Psychol Monogr* 76:26 (Whole No. 545); 1962.

Holland, John L. "Some Explorations of a Theory of Vocational Choice and Achievement: II. A Four-year Prediction Study." *Psychol Reports* 12:545–94; 1963.

Holland, John L. *The Psychology of Vocational Choice*. Blaisdell, 1966. 132p.

Holland, John L., and Nichols, Robert C. "Prediction of Academic and Extracurricular Achievement in College." *J Ed Psychol* 55:55–65; 1964.

Holland, John L., and Richards, James M., Jr. "Academic and Non-academic Accomplishment: Correlated or Uncorrelated?" In *ACT Research Report No. 2*. ACT, 1965. 26p.

Hopkins, J. "Some Non-intellectual Correlates of Success and Failure Among University Students." *Br J Ed Psychol* 28:25–36; 1958.

Hoult, Thomas F. "Religion as a Cultural Factor in One Aspect of the Personality of Selected College Students." *J Ed Soc* 33:75–81; 1957.

Jacob, Philip E. *Changing Values in College*. Harper, 1957. 174p.

Johnson, Edward E. "Some Adjustment Problems of College Freshmen." *Col U* 34:305–8; 1959.

Kaludis, George, and Zatkin, Gilbert. "Anatomy of a Pledge Class." *J Col Student Pers* 7:282–4; 1966.

Learned, William S., and Wood, B. D. *The Student and His Knowledge*. Bulletin No. 29. Carnegie, 1938. 167p.

Lehmann, Irvin J. "Some Socio-cultural Differences in Attitudes and Values." *J Ed Soc* 36:1–9; 1962.

Lehmann, Irvin J. "Changes in Critical Thinking, Attitudes, and Values from Freshman to Senior Years." *J Ed Psychol* 54:305–15; 1963.

Ludeman, W. S. "Qualities of the Ideal and Effective College Student: A Study of Student Evaluation." *J Ed Res* 50:151–3; 1956.

McArthur, Charles, "Subculture and Personality During the College Years." *J Ed Soc* 33:260–8; 1960.

McConnell, T. R. "Problems of Distributing Students Among Institutions with Varying Characteristics." *North Cen Assn Q* 35:226–38; 1961.

McConnell, T. R., and Heist, Paul. "The Diverse College Student Population." In Sanford, Nevitt. (Ed.) *The American College*. Wiley, 1962. p. 225–52.

Medsker, Leland L., and Trent, James W. *The Influence of Different Types of Public Higher Institutions on College Attendance from Varying Socioeconomic and Ability Levels.* USOE Cooperative Research Project No. 438. Center for Research and Development in Higher Education, U California, 1965. 110p.

Melikian, Levon H., and Prothro, E. Terry. "Goals Chosen by Arab Students in Response to Hypothetical Situations." *J Social Psychol* 46:3–9; 1957.

Miller, Eleanor O. "Non-academic Changes in College Students." *Ed Rec* 40:118–22; 1959.

Miller, Norman. "Social Class and Value Differences Among American College Students." Doctoral dissertation. Columbia U, 1958. 593p.

Morrison, A., and McIntyre, D. "The Attitudes of Students Toward International Affairs." *Bri J Social Clin Psychol* 5:17–23; 1966.

Murphy, Lois B., and Raushenbush, Esther. (Eds.) *Achievement in the College Years.* Harper, 1960. 240p.

Nelson, Erland. "Radicalism–Conservatism in Student Attitudes." *Psychol Monogr* 50:1–32; 1938.

Newcomb, Theodore M. *Personality and Social Change.* Dryden, 1943. 225p.

Nichols, R. C. "Career Decisions of Very Able Students." *Science* 144:1315–19; 1964.

Park, Soja. "A Cross-cultural Study of Personality as Manifested by American and Korean College Women." Paper read at Midwestern Psychology Association, Chicago; May, 1966.

Paul, Satindu K. "Worldminded Attitudes of Punjab University Students." *J Social Psychol* 69:33–7; 1966.

Peterson, Richard E. *The Scope of Organized Student Protest in 1964–1965.* ETS, 1966. 58p.

Pinner, Frank A. "Student Trade Unionism in France, Belgium, and Holland." *Soc Ed* 37:177–99; 1964.

Plant, Walter T. "Changes in Ethnocentrism Associated With a Four-year College Education." *J Ed Psychol* 49:162–5; 1958(*a*).

Plant, Walter T. "Changes in Ethnocentrism Associated With a Two-year College Experience." *J Gen Psychol* 92:189–97; 1958(*b*).

Plant, Walter T. *Personality Changes Associated With a College Education.* USOE Cooperative Research Project No. 348. San Jose State Col, 1962. 83p.

Prothro, E. Terry. "Arab Students' Choices of Ways to Live." *J Social Psychol* 47:3–7; 1958.

Rettig, Salomon, and Pasamanick, Benjamin. "Moral Codes of American and Korean College Students." *J Social Psychol* 50:65–73; 1959.

Sanders, Wilma B. "Intelligence and Academic Performance of College Students of Urban, Rural, and Mixed Backgrounds." *J Ed Res* 49:185–93; 1955.

Sanford, Nevitt. "Personality Development During the College Years." *J Social Issues* 12:3–72; 1956.

Selvin, Hanan C. "The Impact of University Experiences on Occupational Plans." *Sch R* 71:317–29; 1963.

Sewell, William H. "Community of Residence and College Plans." *Am Sociol R* 29:24–38; 1964.

Sewell, William H., and Armer, J. Michael. "Neighborhood Context and College Plans." *Am Sociol R* 31:159–68; 1966.

Sewell, William H., and Shah, Vimal P. "Socioeconomic Status, Intelligence, and the Attainment of Higher Education." *Soc Ed* 40:1–23; 1967.

Simenson, William, and Geis, Gilbert. "A Cross-cultural Study of University Students." *J H Ed* 26:21–4, 56–7; 1955.

Sinha, A. K. P., and Dash, J. K. "Motivational Factors Underlying Occupational Choice." *Indian J Psychol* 34:197–202; 1959.

Sinha, A. K. P., and Panda, K. C. "A Study of the Occupational Choice of College Students." *Indian J Psychol* 34:135–41; 1959.

Sinha, A. K. P., and Roy, S. K. "Attitudes Toward Controversial Educational Problems." *Indian J Psychol* 34:111–4; 1959.

Sinha, A. K. P., and Roy, S. K. "A Study of Extracurricular Interests of University Students." *Indian J Psychol* 35:125–35; 1960.

Soares, Glancio A. D. "The Active Few: Student Ideology and Participation in Developing Countries." *Comp Ed R* 10:205–19; 1966.

Somers, Robert H. "The Mainsprings of the Rebellion: A Survey of Berkeley Students in November, 1964." In Lipset, Seymour M., and Wolin, Sheldon. (Eds.) *The Berkeley Student Revolt: Facts and Interpretations.* Anchor. 1965. p. 530–57.

Stern, George G., and others. *Methods in Personality Assessment.* Free, 1956. 271p.

Telford, Charles W., and Plant, Walter T. *The Psychological Impact of the Public Two-year College on Certain Non-intellectual Functions.* USOE Cooperative Research Project No. 914. San Jose State Col, 1963. 82p.

Thistlethwaite, Donald L. "College Press and Changes in Study Plans of Talented Students." *J Ed Psychol* 51:222–34; 1960.

Watts, William A., and Whittaker, David N. E. "Free Speech Advocates at Berkeley." *J Applied Behavioral Sci* 2:41–62; 1966.

Webster, Harold, and others. "Personality Changes in College Students." In Sanford, Nevitt. (Ed.) *The American College*, Wiley, 1962. p. 811–46.

Wedge, Bryant M. (Ed.) *Psychosocial Problems of College Men.* Yale U, 1958. 291p.

Wohl, Julian, and Silverstein, J. "The Burmese University Student: An Approach to Personality and Subculture." *Public Opin Q* 30:237–48; 1966.

Wyllie, Robert W. "Ghanian University Students: A Research Note." *Br J Soc* 17:306–11; 1966.

Yonge, George D. "Students." *R Ed Res* 35:253–63; 1965.

STUDENT CHARACTERISTICS: ELEMENTARY AND SECONDARY

At the present time the characteristics of elementary school students are the characteristics of children ages 6 to 14, since approximately 99 percent of the children in these age groups are attending school, according to the U.S. Bureau of the Census (1966). It is clear that the secondary students are also rapidly approaching the time when they will be representative of the total group of young people. Data for autumn of 1966 from the U.S. Office of Education (1966) indicate that enrollment in grades 9 through 12 was equal to about 92 percent of the population of ages 14 through 17 years.

The most descriptive single characteristic of the socioeconomic background of students is provided by father's occupation. Table 1 indicates the reports of twelfth-grade students when asked (Flanagan & others, 1964) to describe the work of their father.

TABLE 1
PERCENTAGE OF TWELFTH-GRADE STUDENTS REPORTING OCCUPATION OF FATHER

Occupation	Males	Females
Farm or ranch owner	9.5	8.2
Farm or ranch foreman	0.7	0.5
Farm or ranch worker	1.6	1.9
Workman or laborer	15.7	17.3
Private household worker	0.2	0.2
Service worker	1.2	1.1
Semiskilled worker	7.9	7.1
Skilled worker or foreman	19.7	20.3
Clerical worker	2.8	2.8
Salesman	4.7	4.2
Manager	7.6	7.1
Official	2.7	2.2
Proprietor or owner	8.5	8.7
Professional	6.1	6.1
Technical	3.0	2.9
Don't know	6.3	7.7

This table indicates that only about 6 percent of the secondary school students' fathers are in professional occupations and only about one-third would be classified as being in white-collar jobs. About an additional one-third are in skilled occupations, with the remaining one-third being occupied in semiskilled and unskilled work.

Their homes, according to a recent study reported by Coleman and others (1966), are described by students in Table 2. It is clear that the large majority of the students come from homes that have many of the advantages of our modern civilization. In a similar study (Flanagan & others, 1964), students in grade 12 reported that 73 percent had a telephone, television set, radio, and phonograph. Another 16 percent reported having three of the four items, and only about 5 percent reported they had none or only one of these conveniences. It is interesting to note that in this study, the twelfth-grade male students reported that 48 percent had a car of their own or one that was mostly for their use. About 20 percent of the twelfth-grade girls answered "yes" to the same question.

TABLE 2
PERCENTAGE OF STUDENTS HAVING "MODERN" ADVANTAGES IN THEIR HOMES

Item in Home	Elementary Students	Secondary Students
Automobile	89	93
Telephone	80	88
Vacuum cleaner	–	85
Daily newspaper	73	85
Encyclopedia	71	80
100 Books or more	–	39

In the national study referred to above (Coleman & others, 1966), elementary school students in the fall of 1965 reported that only 17 percent had been read to often before they started school. In the Project Talent survey, the secondary school students reported (Flanagan & others, 1964) that most of them had started in grade 1 at age six or below: 4 percent reported they were four years old or younger; 35 percent, five years old; 53 percent, six years old; 7 percent, seven years old; and 1 percent, eight years old or older.

In two reports Anderson and others (1956, 1957) presented findings on the age at which children learned to read with individualized instruction in an experimental school enrolling children with superior intelligence. They found that 31 percent of the boys and 19 percent of the girls did not learn to read until after their eighth birthday. Similarly, 37 percent of the boys and 45 percent of the girls learned to read before their seventh birthday. The criterion for having learned to read was achieving a score of 7.0 years in reading age on the Gates Primary Reading Tests. Age at learning to read was found to be substantially related to intelligence as measured by the Stanford-Binet test in grade 1, with correlations of .57 for girls and .54 for boys. The correlation between age at learning to read and reading age in grade 6 was reported to be .67 for girls and .65 for boys.

In the Project Talent survey, twelfth-grade students reported that 10 percent had changed schools five or more times since starting first grade, not counting promotions from one school to another. Another 15 percent had changed schools three or four times. Only 41 percent reported they had never changed schools, and 24 percent indicated they had changed schools only once. About three-fourths of these twelfth-grade students indicated that their families had bought, or were buying, their own homes.

About three-fourths of the twelfth-grade students

reported that they had read at least one book during the previous summer in the 1965 survey referred to above. The details are reported in Table 3. It is significant that about 15 percent of the students reported they had read 11 or more books during the summer.

TABLE 3
BOOKS REPORTED READ DURING THE SUMMER OF 1965 BY TWELFTH-GRADE STUDENTS

Books Read	Percentage of Students
None	24
1–5	45
6–10	14
11–15	6
16–20	4
21 or more	5
No response	2

PHYSICAL CHARACTERISTICS AND GENERAL HEALTH. The heights and weights reported by twelfth-grade students in March, 1960, are shown in Tables 4 and 5, which are taken from the Project Talent report referred to above. The median height for the boys was about 5' 10", and for the girls about 5' 4". The median weight for the boys was 154 pounds, and for the girls 120 pounds.

TABLE 4
PERCENTAGE OF TWELFTH-GRADE STUDENTS REPORTING VARIOUS HEIGHTS

Height	Males	Females
4'5" or less	0.2	2.4
4'6" to 4'8"	0.3	0.5
4'9" to 4'11"	0.4	1.8
5'0" to 5'2"	0.8	22.2
5'3" to 5'5"	3.9	43.1
5'6" to 5'8"	20.0	26.5
5'9" to 5'11"	41.6	3.4
6'0" to 6'2"	28.0	0.2
6'3" to 6'5"	4.4	0.1
6'6" or more	0.5	0.0
Median	**5'10"**	**5'4"**

The health of the students is another point of general interest. Table 6, from the same report, indicates the number of different times students reported they had been sick in bed (as much as a day) during the past year. Nearly 80 percent of the boys and 63 percent of the girls reported they had been sick in bed two times or less; 9 percent of the boys and 18 percent of the girls reported they had been sick in bed five or more times in the past year; 80 percent of the boys reported that their health had been very good or excellent in the past three years, and 72 percent of the girls gave similar reports. Only 1 percent of the boys and 2 percent of the girls reported that their health was poor or very poor. Nearly half of both the boys and girls reported that they had not been treated by a doctor outside school for illness, injury, or accident in the past six months; 14 percent of the boys and 15 percent of the girls reported they had been treated by a doctor three or more times for these reasons during the past six months.

TABLE 5
PERCENTAGE OF TWELFTH-GRADE STUDENTS REPORTING VARIOUS WEIGHTS

Weight in Pounds	Males	Females
74 or less	0.2	0.1
75 to 89	0.2	0.5
90 to 104	0.4	10.9
105 to 119	2.0	37.3
120 to 134	11.0	32.0
135 to 149	25.6	13.3
150 to 164	28.4	3.7
165 to 179	17.9	1.3
180 to 194	8.1	0.5
195 to 209	3.6	0.2
210 to 224	1.5	0.1
225 or more	1.2	0.1
Median	**154**	**120**

With respect to certain other health and physical fitness items, 18 percent of the boys and 19 percent of the girls reported wearing glasses all the time; 23 percent of the boys and 38 percent of the girls reported they had trouble seeing things from a distance, and 20 percent of the boys and 38 percent of the girls reported they wore glasses for special purposes such as reading or television watching. About 8 percent of the boys and 7 percent of the girls

TABLE 6
PERCENTAGE OF TWELFTH-GRADE STUDENTS CONFINED TO BED FOR A DAY OR MORE DURING PAST YEAR

Number of Times	Males	Females
None	36	22
1 or 2	43	41
3 or 4	12	19
5 or 6	5	8
7 or 8	2	4
9 or more	2	6

reported they had had asthma, and about 20 percent of both boys and girls indicated that they suffered from hay fever. About 11 percent of the boys and 24 percent of the girls reported they often get severe headaches. About 44 percent of the boys and girls reported that they got eight hours of sleep each night, and about 88 percent reported an average of seven to nine hours sleep a night.

In concluding this review of the physical characteristics of today's students, it appears that they are getting taller, heavier, and healthier than their parents. Comparative data on the health of their parents are not available, but certainly the general impression is one of greatly improved health.

ABILITY AND ACHIEVEMENT. The abilities of elementary and secondary school students have been a concern of many researchers. A very large and representative sample of secondary school students was given two days of tests in Project Talent in March, 1960. One of the most important abilities acquired by students is the ability to read and understand verbal materials. The results from the Project Talent reading comprehension tests are reported by Flanagan and others (1964) in terms of student ability to read and understand the writings of ten standard authors and also the contents of ten popular American magazines. It is difficult to provide a meaningful and precise description of the students' understanding of these materials. The criterion of 50 percent of the items correct for a particular author was used as a basis for the findings reported here. This would seem appropriate, since each group of items was designed to include the following: a very simple point, a point of average difficulty for the passage, an item measuring general understanding of the passage, an item on the most difficult point in the passage, and an item measuring the student's appreciation, application, or ability to make an inference based on some aspect of the paragraph. Using the 50 percent correct criterion as indicating understanding, it appears that about 60 percent of the ninth-grade students and 85 percent of the twelfth-grade students can read and understand the writings of Louisa May Alcott fairly well. For Robert Louis Stevenson the corresponding figures are 42 percent for ninth-grade students and 72 percent for twelfth-grade students. For Rudyard Kipling they are 17 percent and 44 percent, respectively; for Joseph Conrad, 12 percent and 35 percent. For Thomas Mann, the most difficult author in the set of ten, less than 1 percent of the students in grade 9 showed this level of comprehension, and only 4 percent of the students in grade 12 achieved this standard.

For magazines the findings indicate that, using the same standards, 75 percent of the ninth-grade students and 92 percent of the twelfth-grade students have a reasonably good comprehension of what is in the "movie" magazines. However, for the *Reader's Digest,* only 18 percent of the ninth-grade students and 45 percent of the twelfth-grade students achieve this standard of comprehension, and for *Time* magazine only 7 percent of the ninth-grade students and 25 percent of the twelfth-grade students attain this degree of comprehension. For the *Saturday Review,* less than 1 percent of the ninth-grade students and only 4 percent of the twelfth-grade students achieve what might be considered an acceptable degree of comprehension of typical paragraphs from these sources.

Another important basic ability is the association of known words with new combinations of letters in a different language. The Project Talent results indicated that the average ninth-grade student, when given a list of 24 new words to be associated with familiar words, is able to learn the meaning of 10.4 words in four minutes, or about 2.5 words a minute. The average twelfth-grade student is able to associate the new words with familiar words somewhat more effectively, getting 12.3 right after four minutes of study, or about 3 words per minute.

In the 1960 survey almost all the rules of capitalization were tested, and it was found that the median students in grade 9 knew the answers to at least 80 percent of the items and that the median students in grade 12 knew the answers to at least 87 percent. Another specific area in which a special "domain test" was used is spelling. Here the test was calibrated in terms of a representative sample of 5,000 words used most frequently in published materials. The results show that the average ninth-grade student can spell about 83 percent of the 5,000 most frequently used words correctly, as compared with 93 percent for the average twelfth-grade student.

One of the most striking findings of the study reported by Shaycoft (1967) referred to the overlap in performance of students retested after three years in such variables as reading comprehension, English, social studies information, and most of the basic abilities and aptitudes. The individual differences were very large in relation to the amount of growth for achievement between grades 9 and 12. For English and social studies, it was found that about 30 percent of the students in grade 9 exceeded the average student's performance in grade 12. Only in the test on information regarding literature was the gain by students between grades 9 and 12 more than a standard deviation. For most of the tests, the gains were between 0.4 and 0.8 of a standard deviation. This emphasizes the large amount of overlapping in the distributions of scores for students in grades 9 and 12. It is clear that a substantial fraction of the ninth-grade students have the ability and information of the twelfth-grade students and, also, that a large proportion of the twelfth-grade students are at a level more typical of ninth-grade students. These findings provide further evidence of the need for individualizing instruction in American schools.

This report also provides information regarding the stability of various measures of basic skills for persons tested at the end of grade 9 and again at the end of grade 12. It was found that the Vocabulary Test showed the greatest stability over this period— the ranking of the students retested being essentially the same as the initial ordering, allowing for sampling errors. The next most stable measure over this three-year period was the Arithmetic Reasoning Test. The correlation between the two sets of scores (corrected for attenuation) was about .90. Many of the other measures of ability and aptitude, including reading comprehension, abstract reasoning, visualization in three dimensions, mechanical reasoning, and creativity, had correlation coefficients (corrected for attenuation) on the order of .80. The stabilities of the tests measuring speed and accuracy of arithmetic computation and clerical checking were surprisingly low.

SEX DIFFERENCES IN ABILITY. The conclusion from the study of the extensive testing in Project Talent is that most of the differences between the mean test scores of boys and girls at the secondary school level are fairly small. The larger differences, as reported by Flanagan and others (1964), appear to reflect differences between the sexes in interest. For example, the scores made by boys are much higher than those of the girls in information tests on aeronautics and space, mechanics, electricity and electronics, sports, hunting, and fishing. The scores of boys, as reported in this study, were also better than those of girls in physical science information, but their superiority in this area was not nearly so great as in related nonacademic areas such as electricity and electronics.

The mechanical field provides an interesting series of comparisons. The difference between the scores of the boys and the girls at the grade 9 level on the Mechanical Information Test of Project Talent is just a little more than one standard deviation, as calculated from the combined distribution of scores. The difference between the average scores for boys and girls at the grade 12 level is 1.25 standard deviations when calculated from the scores for the combined group of students. A similar analysis of the scores of boys and girls at these two grade levels on the Mechanical Reasoning Test shows corresponding differences at the grade 9 and 12 levels of 0.8 standard deviation and 1.0 standard deviation, respectively. Moving on to the Test of Visualization in Three Dimensions, which is a well-established measure of mechanical aptitude, the corresponding differences are found to be 0.25 standard deviation and about 0.375 standard deviation. It appears from these results that the differences are much greater on those tests in which activities and experience make the largest contribution to the score. This is especially true when the activities are largely out-of-school and voluntary, as in the case of mechanical information, rather than in-school and required of all students, as in the case of physical science in the first eight grades.

As might be expected, girls make much better scores than boys in such areas of information as music, art, architecture, theater and ballet, foods, etiquette, home economics, and color names. Girls also performed better than boys on the tests of language skills, including the various aspects of English usage, capitalization, punctuation, spelling, and effectiveness of expression.

In a study of sex differences in achievement as related to IQ, Parsley and others (1964) analyzed the California Achievement Test battery results for 3,551 pupils in grades 4 through 8 and found significant differences. The results indicated that girls at these levels excelled in reading achievement and in arithmetic fundamentals, whereas boys tended to excel in arithmetic reasoning. The differences were rather small, however, and seemed of little practical significance. Bradway and Thompson (1962) reported comparisons of Stanford-Binet intelligence scores administered at preschool age and in adolescence with results of Stanford-Binet and Wechsler adult intelligence scales given at about age 30. Based on a sample of 111, they reported a product-moment correlation coefficient between preschool IQ's and adult IQ's of a trifle more than .60, and a correlation between adolescent IQ's and adult IQ's a little higher than .80. Boys showed more improvement in intelligence test performance between the period of adolescence and adulthood than did girls. Analysis of performance on specific Stanford-Binet test items shows more growth after adolescence in abstract reasoning and vocabulary than in rote memory and practical reasoning. The verbal and memory items in the preschool tests are better predictors of both verbal and performance adult intelligence scores than are the nonverbal items.

As a part of Project Talent, some of the students tested in grade 9 in 1960 were tested again as in grade 12 to determine growth in cognitive skills. The results of this retesting were reported by Shaycoft (1967). In tests of four basic skills (creativity, arithmetic reasoning, abstract reasoning, and visualization in three dimensions), the boys showed definitely larger gains than did the girls. Since these are basic skills not usually taught in grades 9 through 12, these findings raise some important questions about the appropriateness of the content of secondary education as now being given to the nation's girls. The girls showed greater gains than did the boys in memory for words.

MOTIVATION AND ACHIEVEMENT. In a comparative study of achieving and underachieving high school boys of the same high intellectual ability, Frankel (1960) determined that achievers at Bronx High School of Science came from better home backgrounds, with higher socioeconomic status and better-educated fathers, than did underachievers. Curry (1964) studied the effect of socioeconomic status on the scholastic achievement of sixth-grade children. He reported that children with above-average intellectual ability usually overcome the effects of a deprived home environment. For students with lower intellectual ability, the deprived social and economic conditions of the home tend to reduce scholastic achievement.

The joint effect of academic ability and socioeconomic background on whether or not male and female students enter college in their first year after graduation from high school was investigated in Project Talent. The results as reported by Flanagan and others (1966) are shown in Tables 7 and 8. The probability of a male student going to college ranged from 0.10 for students in the low socioeconomic and the low-ability quarters to 0.92 for students in the highest quarter on both variables. For females, probabilities ranged from 0.08 to 0.87. As shown in the table, a high socioeconomic score helps to only a slight extent to enable a person in the low-academic-ability quarter to enter college. On the other hand, being in the lowest quarter on the socioeconomic index is a serious handicap for both boys and girls in the high-academic-ability quarter. The

TABLE 7
PROBABILITY OF ELEVENTH-GRADE MALES LATER ENTERING A FOUR-YEAR OR JUNIOR COLLEGE (1960)

Academic ability Quarter	Socioeconomic Quarter			
	Low 1	2	3	High 4
Low 1	.10	.17	.21	.38
2	.19	.22	.34	.52
3	.31	.45	.55	.76
High 4	.61	.77	.81	.92

TABLE 8
PROBABILITY OF ELEVENTH-GRADE FEMALES LATER ENTERING A FOUR-YEAR OR JUNIOR COLLEGE (1960)

Academic ability Quarter	Socioeconomic Quarter			
	Low 1	2	3	High 4
Low 1	.08	.13	.09	.37
2	.13	.13	.26	.43
3	.26	.32	.44	.72
High 4	.42	.75	.75	.87

handicap is a little greater for girls than for boys.

The 1965 survey by Coleman and others (1966) indicated that about 40 percent of all twelfth-grade students were enrolled in a college-preparatory course. That report also indicated that minority groups did not deviate markedly from this figure. That many of those in other courses wished to go to college is clear from the answers of the twelfth-grade students to the question, "How far do you want to go in school?" The answers were as follows: "Does not wish to finish high school," 2 percent; "Wants to finish high school," 13 percent; "Wants to attend technical school," 26 percent; "Wants some college training," 11 percent; "Wants to finish college," 30 percent; "Wants to attend professional or graduate school," 17 percent; and, "No response," 2 percent.

The Project Talent findings from the 1960 survey are shown in Table 9.

PERSONALITY CHARACTERISTICS. The noncognitive characteristics of American youth have also received a large amount of attention from researchers. In reviewing studies of the American adolescent, Douvan and Adelson (1966) reported that there was a tendency for the conflicts of the age and the force of modern mass communication to cast adolescent experience into a uniform pattern greatly influenced by middle-class values. In reporting on a study of 44,756 high school seniors in Minnesota, Berdie and Hood (1964) stated that young people from farms appeared to be less sociable than other young people and that girls rated themselves as more sociable than the boys rated themselves. On the basis of the large

TABLE 9
PERCENTAGE OF TWELFTH-GRADE STUDENTS ENROLLED IN VARIOUS HIGH SCHOOL COURSES

Course	Males	Females
General	25	19
College-preparatory	48	38
Commercial or business	7	37
Vocational	12	3
Agricultural	4	0
Other programs	3	3

sample of twelfth-grade boys and girls in their 1960 survey, Flanagan and others (1964) reported that girls described themselves as having more culture, greater social sensitivity, more tidiness, and a more mature personality than did boys. In this study both boys and girls tended to describe themselves as sociable, showing social sensitivity, more deliberate than impulsive, only moderately vigorous, calm, fairly tidy, more of a follower than a leader, having only a moderate degree of self-confidence, but having a relatively mature personality.

TABLE 10
PERCENTAGES OF TWELFTH-GRADE STUDENTS WHO EXPECT TO HAVE SPECIFIC TYPES OF JOBS AFTER FINISHING THEIR EDUCATION

Type of Job	Percent
Professional	35
Manager	4
Official	2
Technical	7
Farm owner	1
Salesman	1
Skilled worker	7
Semiskilled worker	17
Laborer	1
Farm worker	0
Don't know	17
No response	9

In a study comparing personality characteristics with performance, Kagan (1965) found that primary-grade children with fast response times and high error scores on visual matching tests (that is, impulsive children) made more errors in reading English words than did children with long decision times and low error scores on the matching tests (reflective children). In summarizing a study of approximately

1,000 British boys in grammar school, Astington (1960) found that the boys with the best relative academic achievement received higher ratings on persistence, independence, and interest and considered themselves less extroverted and less sociable than did their fellow students who performed less well academically. Confirming a study done 30 years earlier, Hallworth (1964) analyzed the ratings that housemasters assigned to British pupils for 14 traits. The analysis indicated two factors accounted for most of the variation, and he tentatively labeled these "sociability" (or "social extroversion") and "emotional stability" or ("reliability and conscientiousness").

On the basis of a series of studies of personality traits, Cattell and Coan (1957) concluded that the personality factor structure in younger children does not appear to be noticeably less complex than that for adults. They reported that not only the same number but essentially the same primary personality factors were found in studies of adults, 11-year-old children, and 6- and 7-year-old children.

INTERESTS. Several studies have emphasized the lack of realism in the aspirations of high school students. In studying the vocational maturity of ninth-grade boys, Super and Overstreet (1960) found that more than half wished to enter occupations that appeared inappropriate for them in terms of the intellectual level required. The results of the survey of Coleman and others (1966) are presented in Table 10 for twelfth-grade students. It is clear from these results that far too many twelfth-grade students expected positions in professional occupations and far too few in skilled work and business.

Further information of this type is presented in Tables 11 and 12, based on the Project Talent survey and one-year follow-up results (Flanagan & others, 1966). As shown in Table 11, in both grades 10 and 12, engineering was much the most frequently planned occupation. At the grade 12 level, teacher, businessman, and skilled worker were the next most frequently reported vocational plans. Here again, one finds a lack of realism in the plans of these students, with many more planning occupations which require

TABLE 11
CAREER PLANS OF MALE TENTH- AND TWELFTH-GRADE STUDENTS AND THE STABILITY OF THEIR PLANS FOLLOWING GRADUATION

Occupation	Grade 10 Plans	Plans One Year after Graduation	Percent Stability	Grade 12 Plans	Plans One Year after Graduation	Percent Stability
Mathematician	2	1	4	1	1	17
Physical scientist	4	1	14	3	2	28
Biological scientist	3	1	9	1	1	14
Engineer	19	7	18	17	9	35
Physician	3	2	40	2	3	59
Dentist	2	1	9	2	1	33
Nurse	0	0	2	0	0	5
Pharmacist	2	1	15	2	1	35
Psychologist/Sociologist	0	1	9	1	1	14
Social worker	1	0	0	1	0	6
Clergyman, etc.	2	2	26	2	2	66
Government	0	1	6	0	1	11
Lawyer	4	3	24	3	3	36
Teacher	5	8	28	8	8	49
Accountant	3	4	16	5	4	29
Businessman	4	9	21	8	8	26
Writer	1	1	9	1	1	46
Artist/Entertainer	2	3	36	2	2	39
Engineering/Scientific aide	1	5	10	1	4	9
Aviation	3	1	3	2	1	8
Medical technician	0	1	4	0	1	22
Office worker	0	2	4	0	3	10
Salesman	1	3	12	1	2	22
Armed forces	8	3	6	6	3	12
Protective	2	2	12	2	1	24
Skilled worker	6	10	24	8	8	33
Structural worker	1	6	32	1	5	29
Housewife	0	0	3	0	0	18
Barber	1	2	12	1	2	21
Farmer	5	3	22	4	3	44
Other	16	20	26	14	20	29
Overall Stability			19			31

university graduate and professional training than can possibly be expected to achieve this degree of training. The next column in the table, showing the student's plans one year after graduation from high school, indicates that the trends toward realism noted between grades 10 and 12 are accelerated the year after graduation. For example, the proportion planning a career in engineering drops sharply, the numbers planning careers in business and teaching and as engineering and scientific aides increase significantly, as do the numbers for office worker, salesman, and structural worker. Probably even more dramatic than the changes in the overall proportions is the instability in occupational planning shown in the third column. For example, only 4 percent, or 1 in 25, of the students planning a career as a mathematician in grade 10 still had the same plan one year after graduation. For grade 12, the figure is 17 percent, or about 1 in 6. The students planning careers as physicians show a good deal more stability, with 40 percent of those planning careers as physicians in grade 10 indicating the same plans one year after graduation from high school. The corresponding figure is 59 percent stability for the period between grade 12 and one year later. The overall stability, as shown at the bottom of the table for tenth-grade students, is 19 percent. For the twelfth-grade students, with whom only one year elapses instead of three, the stability is somewhat greater: 31 percent showing the same plans one year later. These findings suggest substantial waste both in terms of false starts in inappropriate courses and also in the substantial loss in motivation, which having confidence in a sound plan can give a student.

The picture for girls is rather similar, except that they are concentrated on a smaller number of occupations. The most frequently mentioned career is housewife. The others most frequently mentioned include: office worker, teacher, nurse, and beautician. Those having the same plans one year after graduation include 29 percent for the tenth-grade girls and 41 percent for the twelfth-grade girls.

Although the match between student abilities and the requirements for specific occupations may not be

TABLE 12
CAREER PLANS OF FEMALE TENTH- AND TWELFTH-GRADE STUDENTS AND THE STABILITY OF THEIR PLANS FOLLOWING GRADUATION

Occupation	Grade 10 Plans	Plans One Year after Graduation	Percent Stability	Grade 12 Plans	Plans One Year after Graduation	Percent Stability
Mathematician	1	0	3	1	0	18
Physical scientist	1	0	3	1	0	22
Biological scientist	1	0	4	0	0	12
Engineer	1	0	1	0	0	21
Physician	1	0	5	1	0	28
Dentist	0	0	1	0	0	2
Nurse	12	6	22	10	6	45
Pharmacist	1	0	3	0	0	17
Psychologist/Sociologist	1	1	7	2	1	16
Social worker	3	1	6	2	1	16
Clergyman, etc.	0	0	9	0	1	33
Government	0	0	5	0	0	37
Lawyer	1	0	5	0	0	26
Teacher	15	17	49	16	16	63
Accountant	2	1	2	2	1	10
Businessman	0	2	5	0	2	8
Writer	1	1	16	1	1	18
Artist/Entertainer	3	2	16	3	2	42
Engineering/Scientific aide	0	0	0	0	0	9
Aviation	0	0	1	0	0	1
Medical technician	2	2	15	2	2	35
Office worker	25	21	38	30	23	45
Salesman	0	1	3	1	1	14
Armed forces	1	0	1	0	0	18
Protective	0	0	3	0	0	15
Skilled worker	0	0	19	0	0	3
Structural worker	0	1	0	0	1	0
Housewife	12	29	50	10	27	59
Beautician	4	6	21	4	5	42
Farmer	0	0	2	0	0	7
Other	10	7	8	10	8	12
Overall Stability			29			41

improving rapidly, a study reported by Nichols (1964) suggests that trends may be correcting some of the disproportionate emphasis on a few occupations. He reported that in the period 1957–63 there was a decrease in interest expressed by National Merit semifinalists in physical sciences and engineering and, during the same period, an increase in interest in the social sciences and humanities. In a study comparing the vocational interests of Negroes and whites, Chansky (1965) found that, when the two groups were matched on aptitude scores, the Negroes in the matched groups scored higher on interpersonal and business interests and the whites on interests relating to mechanical and natural activities. A study reported by Kinnane and Pable (1962), using Super's developmental approach to vocational choice as a theoretical framework, confirmed the hypothesis that family influences are critical in the development of work values of eleventh-grade boys.

The Project Talent study (Flanagan & others, 1964) reported the occupations and activities that the students said they liked or disliked most. It was suggested that they disregard educational requirements, salary, social standing, or other factors. The four occupations most popular with ninth-grade boys were: Air Force officer, aviator, professional athlete, and rancher, in that order. The same four were also most popular with tenth- and eleventh-grade boys, although the order changed slightly. For twelfth-grade boys the top five were: aviator, professional athlete, president of a large company, Air Force officer, and rancher. The most popular activities for the boys at all four grade levels were: swimming, saving money, and becoming a millionaire. The order of the three was reversed in grade 12. The next three most popular in grade 12 were: working for oneself, owning your own business, and hunting. These were also in the second most popular three at the other levels, except that at the grade 11 level, baseball replaced owning your own business. For boys, the most unpopular activities were: washing and ironing clothes, fortune-telling, practicing music all day, and firing a person. Going to art galleries, reading poetry, writing themes and letters, typewriting, and attending symphony concerts were other activities disliked by the boys.

For the twelfth-grade girls, the most liked occupations were: housewife, airline hostess, decorator, social worker, secretary, designer, typist, and elementary school teacher. These likes were shared by girls in grades 10, 11, and 12, except that in the lower grades secretary and typist were placed higher and decorator and social worker lower on the list. The ninth-grade girls also included actress and beautician in their most liked occupations. In terms of activities, the girls at all four grade levels rated saving money, swimming, and helping the poor as the top three activities. At the upper grade levels, the next four activities were: becoming a millionaire, teaching children, helping your parents, and working for yourself. The activities the girls indicated they liked least were: firing someone, working in a steel mill, operating a crane or derrick, working on an auto assembly line, and fortune-telling. Repairing an auto was also near the bottom of the list for the girls in these four grades.

The two items showing the greatest difference between boys' and girls' likes, that is, which are liked by the boys and disliked by the girls are repairing an auto and inventing new tools. The two items showing the greatest discrepancy in being liked by the girls and disliked by the boys are typewriting and teaching children.

Rudman (1955) noted that children had an especially strong interest in science. Sarhan (1950) reported that the interests of Egyptian children are quite similar to those of Americans. Tyler (1956) found a similar degree of correspondence between British and American students' interests.

ACTIVITIES AND VALUES. A survey of the values of students in grades 9, 10, 11, and 12 in 1960 provides an excellent overview of this aspect of their daily living. Although the principal finding as reported by Flanagan and others (1964) is the individuality of the activities of these students, some picture of students in general can be gained by reporting those items they do often or very often. Participating in sports of all kinds is clearly the main activity that twelfth-grade boys indicate they have done very often or often in the past three years. For example, 67 percent report participation in such sports as baseball, football, or basketball; 59 percent participate often or very often in hunting and fishing; 59 percent also report frequent participation in swimming, tennis, or golf; 44 percent check frequent participation in bicycling, skiing, ice skating, canoeing, or horseback riding; and 39 percent in hockey, lacrosse, handball, boxing, wrestling, and track or field events. The next most frequent types of activities are auto repair or mechanical work, in which 37 percent report frequent activity, and raising or caring for animals or pets, for which 36 percent report active participation. Activities such as building model airplanes are reported as having been done often by only 22 percent, and only 19 percent report that they have often made or repaired electrical or electronic equipment.

A typical twelfth-grade boy works for pay several hours each week, not including chores around home; 29 percent report working more than 16 hours per week, and 65 percent report working at least one hour or more for pay. These boys report that such jobs are a primary source of their spending money. Of those studied, 44 percent report that they get 80 percent or more of their spending money from such jobs. The most frequently reported types of jobs are delivering newspapers, mowing lawns, retail-store work, and farmwork. About 30 percent of the boys report having participated in these types of jobs often in the past three years.

For the twelfth-grade girls, the activities reported as having been participated in most frequently are of a household nature. Cooking is reported as having been done often or very often by 75 percent of these girls. Sewing, knitting, and crocheting or embroidering are indicated as having been frequently done by 57 percent of the girls. They report most participation in swimming, tennis, or golf, with 58 percent indicating frequent activity in these. Also, 47 percent of these girls report participating often in bicycling, skiing, ice skating, canoeing, or horseback riding. Baseball, football, or basketball are decidedly less popular with girls, but still are reported as having been done often by 33 percent of the girls. Raising or caring for animals or pets was a little more popular with the girls than the boys, with 44 percent reporting frequent participation. About 30 percent of the girls reported frequent participation in such activities as acting, singing, or dancing for public performance and also attending concerts, lectures, plays, or visiting art galleries or museums. Drawing, painting, sculpting, and decorating were reported as frequent activities by about 26 percent of the girls, and the same percentage reported that they often participated in gardening or raising flowers or vegetables. Although not quite so many of the girls reported working for pay as did the boys, 16 percent reported working 16 or more hours per week for pay outside the regular chores in their home (which, incidentally, exceeded those of the boys). Among the girls, 51 percent worked one or more hours a week for pay; 30 percent of these girls reported that they obtained 80 percent or more of their spending money from such jobs. For girls the most frequent jobs were: babysitting and housework, in which 54 percent reported frequent participation; saleswork was reported by 19 percent; clerical work by 15 percent; and retail-store work by 12 percent of the girls.

Two national surveys included a question on time spent studying. Coleman and others (1966) asked twelfth-grade students how much time they spent studying outside school on the average school day. The students reported as follows: no time, 8 percent; one-half hour, 9 percent; one hour, 18 percent; one and a half hours, 16 percent; two hours, 23 percent; three hours, 16 percent; four or more hours, 7 percent; and no response, 2 percent. The results reported in the Project Talent survey tended to be rather similar. In that study it was reported that 41 percent of the boys and 51 percent of the girls studied 10 or more hours a week, including study periods in school as well as studying done at home.

The survey reported by Flanagan and others (1964) provided further evidence on the wide range of individual differences and the inappropriateness of textbooks for a large portion of the students in terms of their answers to the question: "How often do you read material over and over again without really understanding what you have read?" In response, 16 percent of the boys and 17 percent of the girls reported that this happened to them most of the time. For the same twelfth-grade group, an additional 18 percent of both boys and girls reported that this happened about half the time.

Based on a recent factor analysis of Project Talent data, Lohnes (1966) reported that a large portion of the variance in 38 variables related to activities, interests, and self-description on personal traits could be accounted for by the following 11 factors: conformity needs; business interests; outdoors; shop interests; scholasticism; cultural interests; science interests; activity level; leadership; impulsion; sociability; and introspection.

Cooley and Lohnes (1968) found a lack of stability in the career plans of twelfth-grade boys based on a follow-up study of these students five years after graduation from high school. These data are presented in Table 13. A little more than half of those who in 1960 were planning careers either in technical or nontechnical fields not requiring college training were pursuing similar careers in 1965. The figures were about the same for those planning college careers outside the fields of science. For those planning careers in science, mathematics, or engineering when in grade 12, only 31 percent had

TABLE 13

PERCENTAGE OF TWELFTH-GRADE BOYS IN PROJECT TALENT WITH EACH OF FOUR TYPES OF CAREER PLANS WHO HAD SIMILAR CAREER PLANS. FIVE YEARS LATER IN 1969

Grade 12 Plan (1960)	Five-Year Follow-up Plan (1965)			
	College Science	College Nonscience	Noncollege Technical	Noncollege Nontechnical
College science	31	9	8	5
College nonscience	42	56	9	15
Noncollege technical	10	7	51	29
Noncollege nontechnical	17	29	35	55
Sample sizes	4,217	2,646	3,113	3,955

similar plans in 1965. Many of these had shifted their plans to careers requiring college training in other fields.

It seems clear from the foregoing review that the most striking characteristics of students in the elementary and secondary schools are the very great individual differences in patterns of aptitude and ability and the lack of sound educational planning based on a full understanding of the significance of the unique potential of each student.

John C. Flanagan
American Institutes for Research

References

Anderson, Irving H., and others. "Age of Learning to Read and Its Relation to Sex, Intelligence, and Reading Achievement in the Sixth Grade." *J Ed Res* 49:447–53; 1956.

Anderson, Irving H., and others. "The Rate of Reading Development and Its Relation to Age of Learning to Read, Sex, and Intelligence." *J Ed Res* 50:481–94; 1957.

Astington, E. "Personality, Assessments, and Academic Performance in a Boys Grammar School." *Br J Ed Psychol* 30:225–36; 1960.

Berdie, Ralph F., and Hood, Albert B. "Personal Values and Attitudes as Determinants of Post-highschool Plans." *Personnel Guid J* 42:754–9; 1964.

Bradway, Katherine P., and Thompson, Clare W. "Intelligence at Adulthood: A Twenty-five Year Follow-up." *J Ed Psychol* 53:1–14; 1962.

Cattell, Raymond B., and Coan, Richard W. "Personality Factors in Middle Childhood as Revealed in Parents' Ratings." *Child Develop* 28:439–58; 1957.

Chansky, Norman. "Race, Aptitude, and Vocational Interests." *Personnel Guid J* 43:780–4; 1965.

Coleman, James S., and others. *Equality of Educational Opportunity*. GPO, 1966. 737p.

Cooley, William W., and Lohnes, Paul R. *Predicting the Development of Young Adults*. American Institutes for Research, 1968.

Curry, Robert L. "The Effect of Socioeconomic Status on the Scholastic Achievement of Sixth-grade Children." *Br J Ed Psychol* 32:46–9; 1964.

Douvan, Elizabeth, and Adelson, Joseph. *The Adolescent Experience*. Wiley, 1966. 471p.

Flanagan, John C., and others. *The American Highschool Student*. U Pittsburgh, 1964. 738p.

Flanagan, John C., and others. *One-year Follow-up Studies*. U Pittsburgh, 1966. 346p.

Frankel, Edward. "Comparative Study of Achieving and Underachieving High School Boys of High Intellectual Ability." *J Ed Res* 53:172–80; 1960.

Hallworth, H. J. "Personality Ratings of Adolescents: A Study in a Comprehensive School." *Br J Ed Psychol* 34:171–7; 1964.

Kagan, Jerome. "Reflection-Impulsivity and Reading Ability in Primary Grade Children." *Child Develop* 36:609–28; 1965.

Kinnane, John F., and Pable, Martin W. "Family Background and Work Value Orientations." *J Counseling Psychol* 9:320–5; 1962.

Lohnes, Paul R. *Measuring Adolescent Personality*. U Pittsburgh, 1966. 212p.

Nichols, Robert C. "Career Decisions of Very Able Students." *Sci* 144:1315–9; 1964.

Parsley, Kenneth M., and others. "Further Investigation of Sex Differences in Achievement of Underaverage and Over-achieving Students Within Five IQ Groups in Grades Four through Eight." *J Ed Res* 57:268–70; 1964.

Rudman, Herbert C. "Informational Needs and Reading Interests of Children in Grades IV through VIII." *El Sch J* 55:502–12; 1955.

Sarhan, El-Demerdash. "A Comparison of the Interests of Egyptian and American Children." *Sci Ed* 34:300–6; 1950.

Shaycoft, Marion F. *The High School Years: Growth in Cognitive Skills*. American Institutes for Research and U Pittsburgh, 1967. 376p.

Super, Donald E., and Overstreet, Phoebe L. *The Vocational Maturity of Ninth-grade Boys*. Columbia U, 1960. 212p.

Tyler, Leona E. "A Comparison of the Interests of English and American School Children." *J Genet Psychol* 88:175–81; 1956.

U.S. Bureau of the Census. *Current Population Reports, Population Characteristics*. GPO, 1966.

U.S. Office of Education. *Digest of Educational Statistics*. USOE, 1966.

STUDENT FINANCIAL AID, COLLEGE AND UNIVERSITY

BACKGROUND. When considering student financial aid, which encompasses grants (or scholarships or stipends), employment, and loans, one must bear in mind the essential difference between public and private institutions. Public institutions, although entering the scene of higher education in the United States later than private ones and being fewer in number, enroll two-thirds of the students. They receive 44 percent of their income from state and local government, 33 percent from the Federal government, only 11 percent from tuition and fees and just 3 percent from gifts, grants, and endowment. However, private institutions receive 30 percent of their income from tuition and fees, 51 percent from the Federal government and 16 percent from gifts, grants, and endowment (Simon & Grant, 1966).

A look at the costs facing undergraduates at American universities will help to put the picture in clearer perspective. One-half of all the students at four-year accredited institutions of higher education are enrolled at the 173 public and nonsectarian private universities, each of which has an average total enrollment of about 10,000 students. Tuition and fees at the private universities are nearly five times those at the public universities ($1,210 to $250). At the public universities and at the private universities alike, approximately 10 percent of the undergraduates hold either term-time employment (during the academic year) or receive loans. However, while only 10 percent of the undergraduates at the public universities have grants, 18 percent of those at the private universities do. Furthermore, the average grant held by undergraduates at the private universities is worth nearly three times that held by those at the public universities ($550 compared with $190). The average value of loans at the private universities is nearly 50 percent greater than at the public universities ($380 compared with $260). The average value of term-time employment is about equal at both types of institutions at $200 (Nash & others, 1967). Because private institutions rely more heavily on student fees, extensive financial-aid programs are offered to help the students pay these fees. A large portion of grants are simply discounts to those who cannot pay the full cost. In recent years a large proportion of grant, loan, and employment funds has come from the Federal government. Because of the fundamental differences between public and private institutions, there has been a long-standing division within the higher educational community about the method which the Federal government should employ in aiding higher education. A Federal grant program would help the private institutions more. Funds for operating expenses would be preferred by public institutions.

HISTORY. Rudolph (1962a, 1962b), in recounting the history of student financial aid in the nineteenth century, reports substantial differences in the periods preceding and following the Civil War. Prior to 1860 colleges were underfinanced and manifested many of the aristocratic purposes and customs of the English residential college. The curriculum was far removed from the problems of a developing America. Both to attract more students to an unpopular curriculum and in an attempt to appear to be more democratic, the colleges offered financial aid of a charitable nature which was principally for poorer students. Yale, Princeton, and Brown had dining halls especially for poor students. There were also general financial-aid programs. In the 1830's a manual labor movement flourished, with the aim of enabling students to pay their way through college by working at useful trades. It was not successful. Farms operated by the colleges lost money, and students in colleges in Ohio made so many wooden barrels that they glutted the market. The American Education Society, founded in 1815, supported promising ministerial candidates at a number of colleges. Private colleges have long made a practice of raising money to be used for scholarship funds. In the mid-nineteenth century there was a large increase in the number of private colleges, and although some (such as Columbia and Pennsylvania) received state funds, most did not. Many private colleges authorized their agents to sell at a set price—generally in the neighborhood of $500—a perpetual scholarship to the college, entitling the owner to free tuition for one person in perpetuity. Many established colleges such as Lafayette and Antioch engaged in this practice between 1835 and 1860. This was not a long-range solution, because the funds were soon spent and students continued to come.

After the Civil War, higher education became relevent through the developments in technological and scientific education. The Morrill Act of 1862 put Federal funds into the state development of land-grant colleges. Municipalities also started colleges. Federal, state, and municipal support of higher education was in the form of grants directly to the colleges, rather than to students. Tuition was kept as low as possible. By 1900, state legislatures had restricted their funds primarily to state-affiliated institutions of higher education. Private institutions were forced to depend on student fees and philanthropy. Many of the private colleges founded prior to the Civil War were forced to close.

Federal aid given directly to students, which is now the major portion of student financial aid, was slow to develop (Rivlin, 1961). Some state legislatures provided free tuition to Civil War veterans at state universities, but there were no stipends or traineeships. The Reserve Officer Training Corps was established at a large number of colleges during the academic year 1917–18, but students received only small amounts of money from the program. The first Federally supported student financial-aid program was the Student Work Program of the National Youth Administration, which began in 1933. During World War II some college students received War Loans to complete their training. It was not until the end of World War II that the Federal government became involved in large-scale programs of student financial aid.

One of the fundamental features of student financial aid is its recent emergence as an item of major institutional concern. The founding by the College Entrance Examination Board of the College Scholarship Service in 1955 signaled the awareness of institutions of higher education of the problems of administering financial aid. Long-term loans to students did not become a major factor until the passage of the National Defense Educational Act in 1958. Not until the Higher Education Act of 1965 became law did an integrated Federal program of grants, loans, and employment for undergraduates become a reality.

DEFINITION OF TERMS USED IN STUDENT FINANCIAL AID. The categories of grants, loans, and employment subsume a number of different forms of aid, and there is a lack of generally accepted definitions. This causes problems not only for students attempting to apply for financial aid but also for those who would attempt to compile information about how much financial aid is available. Rauth (1966) has urged adoption of uniform definitions. According to his classification, there are three distinct types of grants: scholarships, by which student's academic potential is rewarded; grants-in-aid, by which the student's performance or potential performance in college programs is rewarded; and benefit awards, for which occupation of the parents (such as members of the clergy) constitutes the basis for granting the award. There is little likelihood that institutions of higher education will accept uniform definitions unless the Office of Education requires them to do so for reporting purposes. The difficulty of compiling accurate statistics is compounded by the fact that institutions of higher education do not administer all forms of financial aid received by their students. One-quarter of the colleges do not attempt to determine the total amount of scholarships awarded to undergraduates from sources outside the college (Nash & others, 1967). Directors of financial aid frequently do not administer term-time jobs on or off the campus and therefore do not know how much their students earn from these sources.

INTERRELATION OF GRANTS, LOANS, AND EMPLOYMENT. The College Scholarship Service has had as one of its principal objectives the combining of grants, loans, and employment into "packaged" awards of financial aid, which are fairer to more students and make aid resources go further. Most colleges now centralize the three forms of financial aid in one administrator (the director of student financial aid), and 86 percent of the colleges report that they package grants, loans, and employment (Nash & Lazarsfeld, 1968). The packaging of financial-aid awards is further helped by the fact that the majority of colleges' financial-aid committees administer both grants and loans. Many colleges use standard formulas to determine the type of financial-aid package a student will be offered. A typical formula at a high-tuition college might specify that the student's first $500 of need be met by a loan, the next $300 by term-time employment, the next $400 via a summer job, and the remaining $300 (if his total need was judged to be $1,500) by a grant. Haven and Smith (1965) found that two-thirds of all institutions packaged at least some aid and that the grant-loan combination was the most frequently used. Nash and others (1967) analyzed the relationship of the various forms of aid to one another and to institutional factors. Institutions usually have either large grant and loan programs or small grant and loan programs. As tuition increases, so does the value of grants and loans and the proportion of students holding each; but the value of employment does not increase, and thus jobs are less important at more expensive schools. Tuition (and therefore the size of the financial-aid program) is strongly associated with admissions selectivity and with the resources (such as the student-faculty ratio) of the institution. Tuition is also moderately related to the wealth of the state in which the institution is located.

GROWTH OF FEDERAL AND STATE UNDERGRADUATE FINANCIAL-AID PROGRAMS. Federal student financial-aid programs are now making nearly $2 billion per year available to students at institutions of higher education. These programs have found wide acceptance among administrators of universities and colleges, and one reason for their growth is that they do not threaten the autonomy of the institutions and they avoid the controversy over the separation of church and state. Although the funds go to students and not to institutions, the major beneficiaries are the institutions, who now find that more students are able to afford higher education. Despite the fact that college costs have been rising steadily in recent years, 92 percent of college-aid administrators agree that "the various increases in financial aid that have occurred in the last six or seven years have meant that a substantial number of students can now attend your college who could not have previously" (Nash & Lazarsfeld, 1968). A number of generalizations can be made about the development of Federal programs. Congress has generally passed more liberal legislation than originally proposed by the Administration. Programs once begun tend to become more liberal than intended, and hence more costly and beneficial. In the past 15 years there has been good cooperation between institutions of higher education and the Federal government.

The first major program, the Student Work Program, was started by the Federal Emergency Relief Administration in 1933 and then taken over by the National Youth Administration (Axt, 1952; Rivlin 1961). A system of loans was rejected on the grounds that the neediest students would be unable to enter college in order to apply and would be unable to provide a satisfactory credit rating. Similarly, grants were turned down because it was felt that most of the funds would go to the brightest students, who might not be most in need of aid. Despite the fact that many educators were concerned about the possibility of Federal control, approximately 1,500 out of the 1,700 eligible colleges participated in the program, which was administered at the state level by Federal officials. The college administered the program, but the students received their paychecks directly from the Federal government. During the period 1933–1943, about 620,000 youths were employed in the Student Work Program, and they earned about $93,000,000. The average number employed per month was about 110,000 at the college level and about 3,000 at the graduate level, and there were more applicants than jobs. Monthly earnings averaged only $12 for undergraduates and $20 for graduate students.

The Student War Loans, although a small program, were important because these were the first Federal loans to college students, and the students proved to be good credit risks. The program ran only from 1942 to 1944, and only $3,000,000 was lent to about 11,000 students in scientific and technical fields. The students were allowed to borrow up to $500 per year and had low interest payments, but they were expected to accept war-related employment upon graduation.

Veteran's benefits from World War II, which eventually aided about 8,000,000 former servicemen under a number of laws, were by far the largest of any student financial-aid program. The benefits were broadened far beyond President Roosevelt's original intentions. At the time that President Roosevelt approved the amendment to the Selective Service Act permitting the induction of 18-year-olds, he appointed a committee of educators to suggest a program of postwar education for veterans. In transmitting the preliminary report of this committee to Congress in 1943, the President made two recommendations. First, all veterans who had served a minimum period in the armed forces should be allowed one calendar year in college, a technical institution, or in industry. Second, a limited number of veterans, selected for their special aptitudes, should be permitted to carry on their general, technical, or professional education for further periods of up to three years. The Servicemen's Readjustment Act, as originally passed in 1944, made education up to one year available for practically every veteran and provided additional education or training for those whose education had been delayed by reason of military service. Shortly after the end of the war Congress liberalized the benefits, which included both vocational rehabilitation and education and training, in order to entitle almost any veteran to pursue any elected course, at any approved institution, for a period equal to his wartime service plus the year authorized by the original law, up to a total of 48 calendar months. Almost 15 million veterans were eligible to receive training, and the peak in enrollment was approximately 1,100,000 in 1947. In 1946 and 1947, approximately one-half of all college level students were veterans, and enrollment was almost double that of a decade earlier (going from 1.3 to 2.6 million), with the increase being almost entirely attributable to what came to be known as the "GI Bill."

Officials in the Veterans Administration, rather than educators, administered the program. There were many problems with the proprietary institutions, which sprung up quickly and were accused of catering to the veterans' every whim. The Federal government paid living allowances directly to students and paid tuition and fees directly to the universities and colleges. Problems arose at public institutions which were subsidized with state or local funds and which charged low tuition that did not cover the increased enrollment. Disagreements arose between administrators of public institutions and the Congress, the General Accounting Office, the Bureau of the Budget, and various courts. Many educators felt that the Veterans Administration was not sympathetic to their problems. By the fiscal year 1950 the Federal government had paid almost $4 billion to or for students in higher education, and of this amount more than $1 billion had gone to colleges and universities for tuition and fees. In 1947 and 1948, Veterans Administration payments to institutions represented about one-half of all student fees and about one-quarter of all educational and general income.

Partly because of the administrative difficulties and also because it was felt that some colleges had raised tuition to profit from the program, Federal payments to institutions were dropped entirely when the GI Bill was extended to Korean War veterans in 1952. Korean War veterans instead received flat monthly payments (adjusted to the number of dependents), which were somewhat higher than the earlier subsistence payments, but they were required to pay tuition and fees personally. This simplified the administration of the program considerably, although it induced veterans to choose institutions that cost less. This program had a much smaller impact, both relatively and absolutely, on institutions of higher education.

The first two major forms of Federal aid to college students—the Student Work Program of the Depression years and the GI Bill of the 1940's and 1950's—differ considerably from the types of aid currently in effect. In neither case did the Federal government give money directly to the institution for it to disburse to students. Although the colleges and universities did decide which students would be eligible for jobs under the Student Work Program, the Veterans Administration determined eligibility under the GI Bill even before a student had applied to college. Neither program required any contribution of funds from the institution of higher education. Although students at a wide range of proprietary and vocational schools were eligible for the GI Bill, the Student Work Program was restricted to the standard lists of universities and colleges. Each of the two programs was intended to solve a specific problem and to last for a limited duration. By contrast, most of today's Federal programs allow the individual college or university to determine who shall or shall not receive aid. The legislation implies that the programs are expected to endure. Most of the programs have excluded proprietary institutions, but there appears to be a good chance that this restriction will be dropped from a number of the programs.

In 1946 President Truman appointed a commission headed by George F. Zook (President of the American Council on Education) to study the role of the government in financing higher education. It has been stated that the commission's six-volume report, issued in 1947 and 1948, was biased in favor of publicly controlled higher education and that this was in part due to the membership of the commission (Axt, 1957). Because the basic recommendations of the commission were that there should be grants to the states for operating expenses (of public higher education), grants for construction, and a scholarship and fellowship program, the main beneficiaries would have been public institutions. Possibly because of the controversy the report engendered within the educational community, the commission's recommendations had little impact. The Office of Education, however, pushed for a Federal fellowship program, and such a proposal was contained in President Eisenhower's message to Congress in 1952. Furthermore, in 1949 Commissioner of Education Earl J. McGrath had urged that the Federal government support a program of guaranteed loans to students. In 1949 the National Education Association polled its members on the recommendations of the Zook Commission and found that there was general support only for the scholarship program. At that time less than half of the colleges and universities favored guaranteed loans to college and university students (Axt, 1952, 1957).

In 1956 President Eisenhower appointed a Committee on Education beyond the High School chaired by Devereux C. Josephs. The Josephs Committee's recommendations had greater acceptance by educators, and many of their suggestions have been acted on by Congress. The committee spoke of an urgent need to do something for teachers and this contributed to passage of the National Defense Education Act in 1958. It was against a Federal scholarship program, but in favor of a work-study program. It spoke of the need for a Federal policy of aid to higher education which would allow for better coordination of the numerous Federal programs affecting higher education. Despite the fact that the Josephs report was well received, and that the House Committee on Education and Labor was holding hearings on possible Federal scholarship and loan programs for college students at the time of Sputnik, it seems unlikely that any substantial Federal legislation would have resulted if it had not been for the technological threat that Russia's Sputnik represented (Rivlin, 1961).

The National Defense Educational Act was passed as an emergency measure designed to counteract serious deficiencies. Undergraduate scholarships were eliminated, but student loans were made a part of the program, and those who went into elementary and secondary teaching were eligible for cancellation of up to one-half of their loans. The program did not really get into operation until the academic year 1959–60. By June, 1960, the loan fund amounted to $80 million, of which the Federal government had contributed approximately 90 percent and the 1,300 institutions of higher education participating in the program the balance. By 1960 the average loan was nearly $500, and 140,000 loans had been made. About one-half of the colleges participating had not had loan programs prior to the passage of the act (Rivlin, 1961). In following years the loan program has been broadened so that almost all students enrolled in institutions of higher education are eligible to borrow. The cancellation feature was broadened so that teachers going into poverty areas could have up to 100 percent of their loans cancelled and college teachers are also eligible for cancellation. By June, 1967, more than one million students had borrowed over $1 billion, and in the academic year 1966–67 nearly 400,000 students borrowed approximately $220 million. The program was intended to help students from poorer families, and approximately 70 percent of the borrowers were from families earning $6,000 a year or less. The National Defense Student Loan Program (the name has been changed to reflect its broadening) has become the first long-term Federal program to aid undergraduates. Despite the fact that college-aid administrators object to the complexity of Federal reports, 78 percent report that they are strongly in favor of National Defense Student Loans being made (Nash & Lazarsfeld, 1968). One-third of the colleges feel that their program is too small, and almost none feel that it is too large. The loyalty oath that was originally required of students making loans was objected to, first by a small number of liberal colleges and then by a larger number. College presidents enlisted the support of Congress, and the law was substantially modified to meet most objections. In 1965 President Johnson wanted to curtail the program, and again the higher educational community rose up and successfully defended its interests.

The next large student financial-aid program was the College Work-Study Program, which was passed by Congress as part of the Economic Opportunity Act of 1964—the beginning of President Johnson's war on poverty. There had been nearly unanimous support in the educational community for the work-study program which was proposed by the Josephs Committee in 1957. The Advisory Committee on National Student Financial Aid Programs (1963) of the College Entrance Examination Board came out in favor of Federal aid for term-time employment, as long as this form of financial aid could be combined with grants and loans. The legislation as originally introduced in Congress called for the Federal government to pay one-half the cost and the educational institution to provide the other half. Legislation as passed found the Federal government paying 90 percent of the costs during the first years and 75 percent in subsequent years. (Perhaps one of the reasons that the work-study program was included in the war on poverty was the fact that President Johnson had been the state youth director for the National Youth Administration in Texas.) The program at first limited aid to students who received virtually no financial help from their parents. Responsibility for the program was transferred from the Office of Economic Opportunity to the Office of Education in 1965, and student eligibility was broadened to include all who needed a job to pay for college expenses. Students may work at their college or in their community. Just as most colleges participated in the National Defense Student Loan Program, almost all participated in the College Work-Study Program, and in the academic year 1966–67 students earned approximately $160 million (Nash & Nash, 1967).

The Educational Opportunity Grants Program, a part of the Higher Education Act of 1965, is specifically for needy students. Each grant is required to be matched by other financial aid from the institution. The efforts to secure a Federal grant program for undergraduates had been long and strenuous, but were always marked by the difference of opinion between public and private institutions. A Federal scholarship program almost became a reality in both 1958 and 1961. It was felt that lack of support from the education community was the principal reason why such legislation was not passed (West, 1956; Lichtenstein, 1961). In the academic year 1966–67, the first of the program, $46 million was awarded in Education Opportunity Grants; the maximum individual award was $800, and 123,000 students were aided.

In 1966 Congress passed a bill, which was again more liberal than that introduced by the Administration, under which all veterans who had served in the Armed Forces since 1955 were eligible for educational benefits. Veterans enrolled in school on a full-time basis receive $100 per month for 36 months if single, and up to $150 per month if they have dependents. During the academic year 1966–67, some 330,000 veterans entered college-level training (four-fifths were on the undergraduate level), and another 120,000 enrolled in vocational and technical training. Although the number of students is approximately one-half as large as the number participating in the World War II GI Bill, the effect on institutions of higher education is less because veterans now constitute a smaller proportion of the total enrollment.

The Higher Education Act of 1965 also authorized the Guaranteed Loan Program, by which the Federal government subsidizes the interest and helps to provide the guarantee on loans obtained by students from banks and other private lenders. Students are allowed lengthy repayment terms and are charged low interest. The first full year that the program was in operation was the academic year 1966–67, when 330,000 students borrowed approximately $250 million. However, the loans were not uniformly available and students in New York state borrowed approximately one-third of the total. In one-third of the states the Guaranteed Loan Program was administered by state student loan agencies that had been in existence prior to 1965 (the establishment of the Federal program). The previous experience of these agencies probably helped them to get the program operating more quickly in their states. The U.S. Commissioner of Education has estimated that by 1972 college students will be borrowing $3 billion per year under this program. The success of individual state loan programs, some of which started in the 1950's, undoubtedly helped to secure passage of the Guaranteed Loan Program, which is administered at the state level either by independent state agencies or by United Student Aid Funds, Inc., a private organization that works with lenders to foster student loans. The Guaranteed Loan Program, which is the largest Federal financial-aid program for college students, is the first to offer substantial aid to students from middle-income families. The modal family income of the Guaranteed Loan borrower was between $9,000 and $12,000 and the average student borrowed $750. The importance of the Guaranteed Loan Program would seem to indicate that Harris (1964) and those who agree with him have been successful in convincing Congress that a most important means of aiding more students to attend college is to allow the student himself to pay part of the cost of his increased productivity from his anticipated increased earnings. There are a number of supporters for programs that would allow students to borrow more liberally and repay their loans out of their entire lifetime earnings. If the Guaranteed Loan Program does become successful in all 50 states, thus allowing college students through borrowing to pay a large proportion of the total cost of their education, it is likely that the more ambitious programs such as the Educational Opportunity Bank will not be put into operation (Panel on Educational Innovation, 1967).

In concert with the growth of Federal programs of student financial aid has been the growth of state scholarship programs, which now exist in 17 states (Ferguson, 1967). Most of the programs began in the mid-1950's but New York's program dates to 1913 and Oregon's to 1935. Most of the states with large numbers of college students, such as California, New York, Michigan, Illinois, and Pennsylvania, have state scholarship programs. Many of the states have conducted comprehensive studies in an attempt to estimate the amount and types of aid that are required (Pearson, 1967; Sanders & Palmer, 1965). Many of the scholarship programs are administered by the state agencies that also administer the Federal Guaranteed Loan Program. There is an association of directors of state scholarship programs which meets regularly. Most of the 17 programs have the following four similarities: they take financial need into account in making awards; they limit awards to tuition alone or tuition and fees; they allow liberal renewal of up to four years; and they confine awards to undergraduate study. The majority do not make awards to allow students to go to college out of state. For the 10 states with such data, the average family income of those awarded scholarships was $6,200. The 16 states for which there are data awarded $98,100,000 in grants to 259,000 students in 1966. The average award received by the student was approximately $380. Two-thirds of the money was awarded in New York state. In some of the states (such as California, Illinois, and New York) most of the money goes to students attending private institutions; however, in others such as Michigan and Oregon, most goes to public institutions. For the 9 states on which there are data, half the money goes to public institutions and half goes to private. In some cases the state scholarship programs have a specific purpose, such as in California, where the program is intended to help private institutions survive in competition with the strong system of public higher education in the state.

FEDERAL AID TO GRADUATE EDUCATION. Federal aid to graduate education began in 1938 in the health sciences, when the National Cancer Institute offered its first fellowships (Rivlin, 1961; Axt, 1952). There are five major Federal agencies which support graduate students through fellowships, traineeships, and training grants. These agencies are the Department of Health, Education and Welfare, The Department of State, the Atomic Energy Commission, the National Aeronautics and Space Administration, and the National Science Foundation. Almost all grants are offered to students in specific disciplines. Students in the life and physical sciences, engineering, the social sciences, and education have received extensive Federal support, whereas students in the arts and humanities have received very little. In some cases the student can decide which institution he wants to attend. Many Federal grants include a cost of education payment for the institution, so that it is difficult to determine exactly how much aid goes to the student and how much to his institution.

TOTAL OF FINANCIAL AID FROM ALL SOURCES. Nash and Nash (1967) have estimated the total amount of student financial-aid funds for the academic year 1966–67. The total amount of funds awarded to students from all Federal programs was $1,699,100,000. Out of this appropriation, the largest amount, or 61 percent, was in the form of grants. The bulk of Federal grants ($730 million) were training grants, fellowships, and traineeships which went to graduate students in the physical, social and life sciences and in education. The next largest amount (or 30 percent) was in loans; 9 percent was in employment through the College Work-Study Program. The amount of Federal financial aid increased by 47 percent between the academic years 1965–66 and 1966–67. The largest proportion of the increase was attributed to the new GI Bill and the growth in the Guaranteed Loan Program. The growth in training grants, fellowships, and traineeships, although substantial, was at a much lower rate.

There was no single source that made it possible to estimate the amount of funds from foundations and business corporations. Four of the largest foundation programs (National Merit, Woodrow Wilson, Rockefeller, and Sloan) contributed approximately $23,500,000 in 1966. The Ford Foundation has been responsible for two innovations: the National Merit Scholarship for undergraduates and the Woodrow Wilson Fellowship, which is awarded only to graduate students. The National Merit program awards grants on the basis of an achievement test administered nationally to about 800,000 high school seniors. The amount of the award varies with the student's financial need. Some who score high on the test get awards from other sources. The Woodrow Wilson program is designed to enable outstanding students to become college teachers. Both programs allow the student to attend the institution of his choice. For the academic year 1960–61, O'Meara (1964) estimated that businesses contributed about $8 million in financial aid to students enrolled in higher education. Nash and Nash estimated the amount of funds from foundations and business corporations at $50 million. R. Moon (1963) estimated this amount to have been $40 million for the academic year 1960–61.

The U.S. Office of Education surveyed the amount that institutions of higher education made available from their own funds for student financial aid for the academic year 1959–60, and it repeated the survey for 1963–64 (McKee, 1965). Projecting forward from the 1963–64 figures, Nash and Nash estimated that institutional grants were $241 million for undergraduates and $30 million for graduate students; institutional employment, $197 million for undergraduates and $10 million for graduate students; and institutional loans, $25 million for undergraduates and $10 million for graduate students in the academic year 1966–67. The total amount of financial aid from all sources for the academic year 1966–67 was approximately $2,241,400,000. Of this, 60 percent was in grants, 24 percent in loans, and 16 percent in employment. Of the total, the programs of the Federal government contributed 71 percent, the institutions contributed 23 percent, state scholarships (which were $98,100,000) amounted to 4 percent, and foun-

TABLE 1
ESTIMATED TOTAL STUDENT FINANCIAL AID AT INSTITUTIONS OF HIGHER EDUCATION FOR ACADEMIC YEAR 1966-67

Type of Aid	Amount in Millions		
	Undergraduate	Graduate	Total
Grants			
Federal grants and fellowships	$ 256.0	$673.6	$ 929.6
State scholarships	83.0	15.0	98.0
Institutional grants and fellowships	241.0	30.0	271.0
Foundation and corporate awards	27.0	23.0	50.0
Subtotal	$ 607.0 (44%)	$741.6 (87%)	$1,348.6 (60%)
Employment			
College Work-Study Program	$ 142.5	$ 7.5	$ 150.0
Institutional employment	197.0	10.0	207.0
Subtotal	$ 339.5 (24%)	$ 17.5 (2%)	$ 357.0 (16%)
Loans			
Federal loan programs	$ 200.6	$ 51.8	$ 252.5
Guaranteed loans (private lenders with interest subsidy)	221.1	27.3	248.4
Institutional loans	25.0	10.0	35.0
Subtotal	$ 446.7 (32%)	$ 89.1 (11%)	$ 535.8 (24%)
TOTAL	$1,393.2 (100%)	$848.2 (100%)	$2,241.4 (100%)

dation and corporative grants were estimated to amount to 2 percent.

Nash and Nash estimated what proportion of the total educational bill was met by student financial-aid funds. Most of the aid programs listed in the $2,241,400,000 total are awarded to full-time students. In the fall of 1966, there were approximately 4,469,800 full-time students enrolled in institutions of higher education. The total cost of tuition and fees for the academic year 1966–67 was estimated at $2,660,000,000, or an average of $595 per student. Students, of course, also have to pay for their living during the course of the academic year and a large portion of student financial-aid funds goes to pay for room and board. The College Entrance Examination Board (1965a) estimated that the cost for room and board, transportation, supplies, and personal expenses for a person living at home for one academic year was $1,150 as of 1965. Adding living expense to the cost of education brought the total for the average student to $1,867. The total bill for all students was $8,344,000,000. Out of this, approximately 26 percent was met through student financial aid. Grants covered 16 percent of the total, employment covered 4 percent, and loans 6 percent. Financial-aid programs of the Federal government met approximately 19 percent of the cost of full-time students enrolled in institutions of higher education. There was approximately $500 of financial aid for each full-time student. The Federal government's financial aid programs contributed about $360 for each full-time student.

For the academic year 1960–61, R. Moon (1963) estimated that total student financial-aid funds were $716 million. The average increase per year since then has been more than 50 percent. Moon estimated that funds for Federal student financial-aid programs were $346,309,000 in 1960–61. The increase since then has averaged more than 80 percent per year. Moon attempted to estimate the total amount of financing that would be needed to provide funds beyond that which students and parents could furnish for undergraduate financial aid. He called this the "national family dollar deficit for undergraduate higher education" (R. Moon, 1964).

OTHER SOURCES OF FINANCIAL AID. O'Meara's (1964) survey of the grant and loan plans of 181 companies disclosed that most of the programs were either for employees or children of employees. The majority allowed the student to attend the college of his choice. Although $8 million was spent on 7,900 grants, loan plans were much less prevalent, amounting to about $1 million. Deverall (1965) surveyed grants offered by the AFL-CIO and concluded that as of 1965 about $1 million aided approximately 1,000 students. He estimated that the amount of aid offered by the union had doubled in a period of several years. The Citizens Scholarship Foundation of America is a movement of community scholarship fund-raising groups which started in Fall River, Massachusetts, as the Fall River Plan. As of 1965 it had 170 chapters in 35 states (the majority being in New England). By 1964 the organization was raising $800,000 per year in awards (*Financial Aid News*, April, 1965). Insurance companies have a large variety of plans, such as the College Education Plan of Prudential Life Insurance. This plan allows the parents to combine savings before college, borrowing during college, and repayment after college. Foundations have also aided loan plans. Starting in 1960 the Ford Foundation made $6,000,000 available for loans to engineers, but the program was terminated when engineers became eligible for National Defense Student Loans.

Many faculty members get a waiver of tuition for their children. Ingraham and King (1965) report that 93 percent of private institutions waived some or all of the tuition for children of their faculty members. Only about 20 percent of public institutions have some form of tuition waiver. Tuition Exchange, Incorporated, is an agreement among institutions to allow the educational exchange of faculty children at no charge. Ingraham reported that the plan had not worked out well because too many children wanted to go to a few prestigious institutions. Some institutions in the same communities allow exchanges for faculty children.

RESEARCH ON FINANCIAL AID AND ATTENDANCE AT COLLEGE. Who pays for undergraduate education? Hollis (1957) studied 15,000 students at 110 colleges in the academic year 1952–53. Parents and relatives were the primary source of funds for college, and they contributed 40 percent of the total. Earnings were the second most important source at 28 percent, savings contributed 20 percent, scholarships 3 percent, veterans benefits 3 percent, and loans only 1 percent. Men and women differed in that women spent less, but their parents contributed more. Men borrowed more, and a higher proportion of them worked. Those with lower family income received larger scholarships, which suggests that financial need was being taken into account even in 1952. Hollis focused on the difficulty of financing living costs.

Lansing and others (1960) surveyed a national random sample of 2,800 families living in private homes. These parents reported that the costs of higher education averaged $1,550 per academic year for their single children. The most important source of financing was again parents, who contributed 61 percent of the total. Half of the parents had drawn on savings, and 44 percent took money out of current income by reducing expenses. To help pay for their children's college, 20 percent of the mothers went to work, and 8 percent of the fathers took on extra work. Only 8 percent of the families borrowed. Among unmarried students in college, 13 percent received no help from their families; 40 percent of the families reported that payment for their children's education had been difficult, but 30 percent felt that they could have given more than they did. The size of the parents' contribution was found to depend upon their income, the number of other dependents, and the education of the parents. Three studies were conducted by the Educational Testing Service on students who applied for financial aid at a group of colleges using the College Scholarship Service's "Parents' Confidential Statement" (Cliff, 1962a, 1963; Cliff & Ekstrom, 1962). A family having trouble paying for a child's college costs establishes certain priorities. First the family reduces the amount to be put away as savings. Then luxury items, such as vacations and home furnishings, are cut. Next, the family having trouble financing higher education considers a change in housing and finally decides that one child's education must be sacrificed for the sake of another. Parents also indicated their willingness to borrow to cover college costs. The most important variable predicting how much a family would provide for college was the parents' income. Sherwood (1957) found that parents' and students' attitudes, not their socioeconomic status, were most important in determining the type of contribution parents would make.

Because student financial aid involves money, there are frequently legal problems. Davis (1965) surveyed the obligations of fathers to pay for children's education in the case of divorce. He found that the trend is to call college education a necessity if social conditions warrant it and if the child has academic ability.

There have been a number of surveys of students' costs both at individual institutions and in selected states. Little (1959) surveyed 40,000 students in 45 Wisconsin colleges and found that 19 percent held some type of scholarship, with 40 percent of the scholarships being awarded by agencies outside the institution itself. Another 19 percent had borrowed money for college expenses, and more than 50 percent planned to work part-time in college. Sanders and Palmer (1965) studied 5,000 students in California and related students' financial backgrounds to the characteristics of their schools. The median family income of students in private universities was $15,100, compared with $8,800 for students at junior colleges. Although 94 percent of students at private universities received support from their families, only 50 percent of those at the junior colleges did. They also compared self-supporting students with those who received money from their parents. Marple and Marple (1967) surveyed middle-income parents and found that they tended to overestimate the amount of financial aid available for college students and that only two out of every five had any savings plan for college. Margolius (1965b) reports that family service agencies throughout the nation say that financing higher education ranks high among the reasons for emotional stress by people seeking professional counseling. What the student himself thinks of the situation is uncertain. Most agree (National Education Association, 1964) that the average student has money troubles. Although he works both over the summer and during the school year, he is still dependent on his parents or relatives. Not only are his earnings limited, but he has a large bill to pay. Proponents of large-scale borrowing on the part of students to finance their higher education argue that the principal benefits would be that the student would be free from dependence upon his parents and would be less bothered by financial problems.

The relation between finances and college attendance is a complex one. Although money emerges as an important factor, it has come to be generally accepted that grant aid alone, offered at the end of the senior year of high school, will have relatively little effect on increasing the number and proportion of students who will attend college. The Project Talent study of a large national sample of high school students concludes that between 80,000 and 100,000 students in the upper one-third of the graduating class of 1960 failed to enter college, at least partly for financial reasons (National Education Association, 1964). Among National Merit Scholar examinees, approximately 40 percent failed to go on to college for financial reasons (National Education Association, 1964). Sanders and Palmer (1965) cite at least four ways in which economic barriers may impede prospective college-bound students: (1) they may actually prevent the first enrollment in college; (2) they may increase the number who drop out before completion of a program; (3) they may delay the completion of the program by limiting the attendance to part-time; or (4) they may force the student to choose a program of studies or an institution which may be inappropriate in terms of his abilities and interests.

There are two ways in which the proportion of students not attending college for financial reasons (or attending college only because of grant aid) can be studied. First, a sample of students enrolled in college can be asked what effect financial aid had. Second, a group of students can be selected while in high school and those who do not attend college can be asked about their reasons for nonattendance. In an example of the first type of research, a study of several thousand veterans enrolled at 16 colleges found that only 10 percent said that they definitely would not have gone to college except for the GI Bill, and another 10 percent said they probably would not have (Frederickson & Schraeder, 1951).

Several studies which have compared scholarship recipients to nonrecipient applicants have shown that scholarship receipt has relatively little impact on college plans. Of 1,600 students who had requested but been denied scholarship aid, 90 percent went on to college (Cole, 1957). Most had managed to secure some form of financial aid, either at the same or another college.

Perhaps the most significant research to demonstrate the importance of motivational factors and the relative unimportance of finances alone was Berdie's study (1954) of 25,000 Minnesota high school seniors. Although only 35 percent of the seniors intended to go on to college (and did in fact go on), 75 percent of the high-ability boys and 62 percent of the high-ability girls intended to go to college. Berdie concluded that only approximately 400 superior students each year from the state of Minnesota might be influenced to go to college through a scholarship program. Most of the high-ability students who did not intend to go to college had other reasons. Many of the girls planned to get married. Only one-third of those who were planning not to go on to college said they would go to college if they had more money. For most of the students, parents' attitudes and factors in the home, as well as their intellectual ability, had been responsible for their decision as to whether or not to attend college. Another study to demonstrate the lack of effect of a scholarship program by itself was a combination action and research program undertaken at the University of New Mexico which concluded that only 1 percent of the state's high school graduates possessed both the competence and the motivation to attend college coupled with the lack of money to do so (Smith & others, 1960). Henry (1965) found that the ability of the family to contribute to college costs had little impact on college-going behavior when other factors were controlled. Herriott (1963) placed the financial factors very low in the scale of determinants. He found that the plans of friends and the educational aspirations of the family were far more decisive than finances. Brazer and others (1963) found that the economic factor should be given a ranking no higher than sixth in a scale of 12 factors affecting the college decision. Sanders and Palmer (1965) pointed out that it should not be concluded that income and socioeconomic status are unimportant in the college decision nor that financial aid should not be used to increase the proportion of students attending college. The conclusion that can be drawn is that a scholarship program without a need factor which is announced only to high school seniors will have little impact on the college-going plans of talented students. A large proportion of less talented, poorer students are not now attending college who could benefit from higher education. To get these students to college requires both counseling and careful liaison between high school and college, in addition to financial aid.

FINANCIAL AID AND ATTENDANCE AT GRADUATE SCHOOL. The finances of graduate students have been studied much more thoroughly than those of undergraduates. This is because graduate students receive much larger awards, there are fewer of them in fewer institutions, and it is important that the maximum yield be obtained from graduate schools in order to overcome manpower shortages in the sciences and professions. The first major comprehensive study of graduate student finances was conducted by J. Davis (1962) for the National Science Foundation in the academic year 1958–59. The major source of income for a random sample of 2,800 graduate students was grants (or stipends), which were reported by 74 percent of the total. Only 22 percent of the graduate students received any support from parents, and thus the major differences between graduate students and undergraduates is that the former are responsible for providing for their own education. Savings, employment, and veteran's benefits were all major sources of funds. Although only 9 percent had taken loans, a surprisingly large 18 percent had full-time jobs. Although graduate students marry later than the rest of the population, the majority of the males older than 25 were married. For married students, the work income of the spouse was a major source of income. The median income for graduate students was $400 per month during the academic year, of which only 15 percent was spent on graduate school. Single students had lower incomes and smaller expenses, and they seldom worked full-time. Most of the students felt that their income was adequate and did not worry about money. Financial need is not a factor in awarding grants in graduate school. The more capable students were more likely to receive grants. Students in public institutions, those in the natural sciences. and those in the advanced stages of graduate study were more likely to hold grants. Even in 1958 Davis felt that a saturation point had been reached, for 85 percent of advanced natural scientists in public institutions held either an assistantship or a grant.

Warkov and others (1965) did a more comprehensive analysis of graduate study, securing questionnaires from 20,000 graduate students at 130 schools in 1963. Their findings were very similar to those of Davis. Two-thirds of all graduate students reported that they held grants (or stipends), and the median value of these was $2,400. In the life and physical sciences three-quarters of the students held grants, but this was the case for slightly less than one-half of the students in the humanities. The value of grants was relatively similar from field to field. The most important predictor of the proportion of students holding grants was the field of study. Full-time employment was found to be an alternative to grant support. The largest single amount of support was the student's own earnings, which averaged $4,000. Approximately one-half of all students held jobs. Only one-quarter of the students received aid from parents, and this averaged only $400. A comparison between grants awarded in 1958 and 1963 revealed relatively little change. The proportion of students reporting grants in the life and behavioral sciences was higher in 1963, while the proportion in the physical sciences and humanities was lower. The rate of full-time study was approximately twice as high for grant holders as for those without grants. Single students were more often enrolled full-time than were those who were married.

J. Davis (1964), in the largest comprehensive survey of college seniors, obtained questionnaires from 34,000 members of the class of 1961 at 135 institutions. About one out of five had held a grant at some time during his undergraduate career. Davis examined the reasons for not going to graduate school and the chances of a prospective graduate student receiving a grant. The largest single reason for not going to graduate school (which was given by one-half of all those not intending to go on) was motivational. Approximately one-fifth of those not intending to go on had both motivational reasons and financial obstacles. A similar proportion had financial obstacles but no motivational reason. The decisions to undertake both graduate and undergraduate education are similar. Although finances are important, motivational factors are more important. Students with low grades were less likely to apply for a grant and less likely to receive one if they did apply. Although women were less likely to apply for grants, those who did apply did just as well as men. A study of the decision to undertake a graduate education by Gropper and Fitzpatrick (1959) found that the influences of faculty members and the college experience were much greater than influence exerted by the graduate student's family. A large proportion of undergraduates planning graduate education would decide against advanced education if it were not feasible because they lacked the necessary money. The large sums of grant support which help the majority of graduate students complete their education are a major factor in attracting students to graduate education. Three of the preceding studies of graduate education and plans were conducted by the National Opinion Research Center at the University of Chicago. Davis's 1961 seniors have been reinterviewed in order to study the transition from college to graduate school. This has led to more detailed studies of those entering the fields of accounting and of law (Warkov & Zelan, 1965; Thielens, 1966). There have also been studies of the role of finances in graduate education in the fields of sociology, education, and medicine, as well as a study of all graduate education in the state of California (Sibley, 1963; Moore & others, 1960; Altenderfer & West, 1965; Sanders & Palmer, 1965). These studies have had a major impact on financial-aid policies in the areas in which they concentrated. For example, the study of medical education demonstrated that medical students had extreme financial problems, and this led to the passage of Federal scholarship and loan programs for medical students.

FINANCIAL AID TO DISADVANTAGED STUDENTS. Plaut (1966) has reviewed the programs specifically aimed at helping disadvantaged students. Among these are the National Scholarship Service and Fund for Negro students, which began in 1949 and which has been supplemented since 1963 by a number of programs sponsored by the Federal government and by foundations. The National Achievement Program (a part of the National Merit Program) awards 200 scholarships yearly on the basis of academic ability. The Independent Schools Talent Search Program recruits and refers students to about 75 member institutions. The College Assistance Program finances visits to high schools by college officials to encourage college enrollment. The GAP Program (which stands for the "gap" between high school and college) of the Carnegie Corporation provides college grants to students who have participated in institutes such as Project Upwardbound. The Higher Education Act of 1965 provided funds for a talent search program by which the Office of Education awards contracts to groups such as Project College Bound in Philadelphia to seek out and motivate disadvantaged high school students on a person-to-person basis. Because most programs designed to aid the disadvantaged operate on the assumption that the decision to enter college is based on more than financial reasons, they offer extensive counseling and tutoring and try to reach the students long before they will be graduating from high school. Morris (1966) describes a $2 million program named Project Opportunity, involving schools and colleges in the South. It starts by selecting seventh graders who have the potential for college and offering them counseling and special help all the way through high school.

Despite all this recent help, in reviewing recent research Kendrick (1967) points out that the public junior college and the predominantly Negro college are the principal hope for higher education for Negroes and other disadvantaged students. Less than 1 percent of the enrollment of private four-year colleges in the Northeast is Negro. Only 1 percent of all Negro college students enrolled in the United States go to school in New England, and it is likely that the great majority of these are from upper- and middle-class backgrounds and hence are not disadvantaged students. Although there are a number of programs to aid Negro students, there are extremely few Negro students in many colleges. Because of poor high school grades and a lack of motivation, very few Negro or Puerto Rican students are able to attend the free New York City colleges. However, most northern institutions of higher education have some Negro students and a large proportion of these receive assistance under the Federal programs designed specifically for students from low-income families. Many northern universities have special programs specifically designed for disadvantaged students (Nash & Nash, 1966). The University of Michigan has the Opportunity Awards Program, which was begun in 1963–64 and is financed largely by the Educational Opportunity Grant Program of the Federal government. In 1966–67 it gave scholarships to 90 students from low-income families, most of whom were Negro. A Negro admissions officer located 350 applicants, of whom 130 were admitted and 90 received awards. The students were identified as a special group by the administration and a number of services were made available to them. They were brought to the campus early for a remedial and indoctrination session. They were allowed to take a reduced course load and to drop a course later in the semester than other students. The Negro administrator in charge of the program explained that, although the disadvantaged could not be graded more leniently, everything else was done to give the students a special break. Despite all the care taken by the university, the dropout rate in the first years of the program was considerably higher than the university-wide attrition rate.

Jaffe and others (1968) surveyed the approximately 100 predominantly Negro colleges in 1965 and found that slightly over one-half of all their students received financial aid from one source or another. They also concluded that a larger proportion of the students in less prestigious Negro colleges received Federal financial assistance than did those in the higher-rated schools. They concluded that the Federal student financial-aid programs were causing the less prestigious Negro colleges to grow at a faster rate. Meeth (1966) surveyed 1,300 predominantly white colleges in the United States in 1964 and found that 114 gave scholarships specifically to Negro students. Gordon and Wilkerson (1966) did an extensive survey of the plans and programs available to help disadvantaged students.

BIBLIOGRAPHIES AND DIRECTORIES OF STUDENT FINANCIAL AID. There has been so much written on student financial aid that the U.S. Office of Education has issued two annotated bibliographies (Mattingly, 1957; Eells & Hollis, 1962). West (1956) and Sanders and Palmer (1965) have summarized much of the research on financial aid. The growth of the field of student financial aid can be seen from the fact that, whereas the 1957 bibliography contained only 121 titles covering a 30-year period, the 1961 bibliography contained 451 titles, 95 percent of which appeared between 1955 and 1961. *College Student Personnel Abstracts* summarizes all studies relating to student financial aid. There are a large number of guides and directories to financial aid. Books for students and parents include Splaver (1964) and Margolius (1965b). Most books about preparation for college include a section on student financial aid. The U.S. Office of Education (1966; U.S. Department of Health, Education and Welfare, 1966) puts out detailed publications describing student financial-aid programs to college administrators and short publications describing the programs to students. However, most student financial aid is administered by individual institutions of higher education. R. Moon (1965) estimated that by 1970 institutions of higher education will be administering, either directly or indirectly, about 85 percent of all student financial-aid funds. This makes communications from the college financial-aid officer and the high school guidance counselor the most important sources of information for the college-bound student. The College Entrance Examination Board (1967) publishes a guide for high school counselors. Nash and Lazarsfeld (1968) found that two-thirds of all institutions of higher education had a brochure on financial aid, other than the catalog, which was available to applicants. Many aid directors were not satisfied with the job done by their college catalogs in describing the financial aid available at their institutions. Only one-quarter of the aid directors said that they felt that their college did a very good job of describing the aid available, and many said they felt that the catalog did a poor job. Nash and others (1967) did a study of college catalogs and found that most college catalogs devoted only one or two pages to financial aid. The college catalog (which is the document most readily available to the high school guidance counselor and high school student) did not do a good job of describing the total amount of aid available or the basis on which it is awarded. Many of the catalogs included long lists of donated scholarships which were of little relevance to the student applying for financial aid. Not only do private publishers, the Federal government, and colleges and universities furnish information on financial aid, but also several states issue publications on the financial aid available in those states (Olsen & Anderson, 1965; Crowell, 1966). There are no magazines devoted exclusively to student financial aid, although magazines and newspapers on higher education now give a substantial amount of space to student financial aid. The College Scholarship Service publishes a newsletter entitled the *Financial Aid News,* which began in 1960. Several of the regional associations of student financial-aid administrators issue newsletters. The College Scholarship Service has held yearly colloquia on student financial aid, dating from 1962. The College Scholarship Service issues and regularly updates a *Manual for Financial Aid Officers* (College Entrance Examination Board, 1965b), which not only describes the use of its Parents' Confidential Statement (a means of assessing the financial need of an applicant) but also gives a great deal of general information on student financial aid. Now that the American College Testing Program has started to compute financial need there will be another source of information on financial aid. Since 1937 the American Council on Education has been holding meetings on college student personnel work, and the brochures it has issued have devoted space to financial-aid activities. The first "how to" manual on student financial-aid policies and practices for colleges and universities was written by Babbidge in 1960.

RESEARCH ON GRANTS AND SCHOLARSHIPS. There has been a considerable amount of research on how scholarship holders differ from non-scholarship holders at the same colleges. A number of studies dating back to 1930 all agree that students with scholarships do better in school than their non-scholarship-holding classmates (G. Moon, 1930; Williamson, 1937; Letson, 1956). Because students from higher-income backgrounds tend to do better in high school, they are more likely to win scholarships when the scholarships are awarded without taking financial need into consideration. West and Gleazer (1964), in studying scholarship offers made by 65 institutions, concluded that scholarships go disproportionately to higher-income students. The Illinois Board of Higher Education in studying scholarships financed by state funds in Illinois found that four-fifths were given without regard to financial need (*Financial Aid News,* April, 1966). However, in New York state financial need is a criterion in awarding state-financed scholarships, and Muirhead (1950) found that scholarship holders were representative of high school graduates of that state. Although Williamson and Feder (1953) also found that scholarship holders did better academically than those who did not receive scholarships, when they controlled for ability as measured before entrance to college, they found that most of the difference disappeared. Colver (1954) and Clark and others (1957) showed that scholarship holders get better grades in college when the renewal of their scholarship is dependent upon their meeting a given minimum grade-point average. Iffert (1957a) studied the records of scholarship holders at 147 institutions and found that 25 percent of all scholarship funds were awarded to students who did not graduate within four years after starting college. Although scholarship holders did better academically than nonscholarship holders, Iffert felt that too much scholarship aid was awarded to students who did not graduate. He suggested that funds to entering students should be reduced and that more funds be made available to students after their performance and need had been studied on the campus.

Newspaper articles frequently state that large amounts of scholarship funds go unused because people do not know about them. This probably was never true of large amounts of student financial-aid funds, and now that colleges and universities have gotten restrictions removed from most of their own funds it is a fairly unusual phenomenon. Probably the only scholarship funds that are unused in large amounts are those for which veterans or their orphans are eligible. A study by the American Legion reported in the *Financial Aid News* (June, 1963) showed that less than one-half of the eligible war orphans were taking advantage of their right to free higher education. A study by Elam (1947) showed that $250,000 in scholarship funds at the Illinois State Teachers Colleges was not being used, but the value of the individual scholarship was small. A study by Burnett (1950) of the use of scholarship funds in California showed that less than 5 percent of available funds were not used because of a lack of qualified applicants.

The most extensive research on who gets what sort of financial aid was an analysis by Schlekat (1967) of 6,500 financial-aid offers made to students during 1964–65. The study concluded that it is not possible to give simple straightforward answers to such questions as whether college financial-aid programs treat the various socioeconomic classes differently. Students from higher socioeconomic backgrounds received preferential treatment because they had better test scores; but students from poorer backgrounds did better because they had more financial need. Colleges and universities are now awarding the majority of aid on the basis of financial need, and upper-middle-class students are less likely to receive aid. Students from more humble backgrounds are less likely to receive grants and more likely to be expected to borrow or accept employment, even when ability was held constant. Of all those who filed applications for financial aid, only one-third received an award. As was the case in graduate education, there was no difference between men and women in the likelihood of receiving financial assistance once it had been applied for.

RESEARCH ON EMPLOYMENT. Seven studies covering the period from 1936 to 1963 have demonstrated that the holding of term-time jobs does not adversely affect grades. Schaffner (1936) compared working to nonworking students matched on ability. The students working from 6 to 21 hours ranked first scholastically; those working longer hours ranked second, and the nonworking students ranked third. Although academically weak students can be harmed by working, the student with ability can work and go to college (Reeder & Newman, 1939; Baker, 1941; Trueblood, 1954; Silver, 1956; Dickinson & Newbegin, 1959; Burke, 1963). A number of institutions have surveyed the employment situation of their students. At Southern Illinois, Adams (1963) has compiled a manual of job titles which describes term-time jobs. At Colorado Southern, Miller and others (1967) found that the proportion of students seeking employment increases steadily from the freshman through the senior year and that upperclassmen want to work longer hours. Burke (1963) has described the Harvard School Agencies, a nonprofit corporation organized to provide capital and organizational facilities to enable students to operate small businesses and earn money with which to meet their college expenses. Yale, Princeton, Columbia, and other schools have similar programs with the students running their own businesses, ranging from selling magazine subscriptions to class rings. Burke also describes a program operated at Harvard (and a number of other institutions) which trains students in marketable skills such as bar-tending, computer programming, and short-order cooking. These programs enable students to increase their earning capacity while in school.

With the advent of the College Work-Study Program, which allows students to work up to 40 hours per week during the summer, colleges have begun to pay more attention to summer employment as a form of financial aid. Many aid officers now require that the student himself meet a portion of his financial need out of his summer earnings. The College Entrance Examination Board (1965a) has estimated the amounts that students should be expected to save from their summer earnings. Male students going into their senior year are expected to save $450, but women entering their freshman year are expected to save only $200. Just how easy it is for college students to get summer employment is not known. Sanders and Palmer (1965) estimated that it is getting more difficult. However, Nash and Nixon (1968) found that most of the students with summer jobs in the Work-Study Program said that they would have been able to get another job.

A different form of student employment is the cooperative work-study program where students go to school full-time for part of the academic year and work full-time (often at a distance far removed from the campus) for the balance of the year. About 60 colleges (Armsby, 1954) operate these programs, and many involve engineering students. Some institutions such as Antioch College, which was a pioneer in the program, are well known for their work-study programs. At Antioch it takes five years for a student to complete his undergraduate work. Wilson and Lyons (1961) did a comprehensive survey of students, faculty, and employers. They traced the inception of the program to one involving engineering students at the University of Cincinnati in 1906. The money earned from cooperative education was a major factor for many students selecting such programs. The students reported that the extra year required in college was not a handicap in starting a career. Another advantage of the program was that it allowed the student to see the relevance of theory to practical situations. The employers involved were found to be very positive about cooperative educational programs. They felt that cooperative work contributes substantially to a student's development of mature judgment.

The Kiplinger Washington Editors (1966) surveyed job opportunities at 250 colleges. They found that, on the average, male students earn about $500 during the academic year and $600 during the summer. Women were reported to make about $400 during the academic year and slightly more during the summer. The range was wide, however, as were the hourly rates paid to students. The best-paying jobs were found to be faculty assistants, tutors, research assistants, recreational assistants, and lifeguards. The average student worker put in 13 hours per week, and the average college recommends 16 hours of work per week as the maximum that should be worked. The most frequently held jobs were clerk typist, library assistant, secretary, and science lab assistant. The average rate for these jobs was about $1.25 per hour. Most colleges felt that term-time employment opportunities were increasing. The College Work-Study Program has brought a minor revolution to the college campus because it requires that most students be paid at least legal minimum hourly rates. Slightly more than one-half the colleges responding to a House Subcommittee on Education questionnaire in 1967 (which was tabulated by the author) said that the College Work-Study Program had significantly increased the pay scale for student employment at their institution.

There have been two Federal student aid programs that have employed undergraduates. Both the Student Work Program of the National Youth Administration and the College Work-Study Program have been criticized on the grounds that some of the student workers were engaged in busy work (Rivlin, 1961). Large-scale studies have been made of the students participating in each of the programs, and in each case it was found that most of the students were doing fairly high-level, interesting work which was both demanding and educational. Of 1,250 students participating in the NYA at Ohio State University, 90 percent felt that the standard of work required of them was higher than private employers would expect (Lindley & Lindley, 1938). A large proportion of the students also indicated that the work was educationally valuable and that their academic work had been helped by their NYA activities. Some 530 projects were surveyed, and only a small proportion were found to be poorly administered or of low social utility. The largest proportion of students was doing some form of clerical work or research, and the next largest number was occupied in community service. However, 20 percent of the students were used in maintenance, construction, or janitorial work. The study also sought to determine whether the money received was really needed. Two-thirds of the students said they definitely could not have continued college without the aid, and most of the rest said their situation would have been doubtful. The City of New York started the Urban Corps with 1,150 college students from 60 colleges working in 60 city agencies as full-time employees for the summer of 1966 (Nash & Nixon, 1968). Ninety percent of their salary was paid by the Federal government under the College Work-Study Program, and the balance was paid by the City of New York. Questionnaires were returned by the majority of students and their city agency supervisors. Most students found their work interesting and challenging. About 20 percent of the students, however, said that their jobs were very dull and that they had nothing to do a substantial part of the time. A number of the students said that they had become more interested in urban and minority problems, and about 20 percent said they felt that they might go to work for a city or state agency or for the Federal government as a result of their summer's experience. Students liked the opportunity to work with people, and they did better when they were assigned to work on an individual basis rather than being given assignments en masse. The supervisors generally rated the students highly, and it was most important to the supervisor that the student really cared about what he was doing. In some agencies the program was far more successful than in others. On the whole, both the students and the supervisors felt that the program was very successful, and as a result in the second summer twice as many students were brought into the program.

RESEARCH ON LOANS. Before the National Defense Student Loan Program started, two studies of college administrators found that they were not in favor of loans to students (Kiplinger Washington Editors, 1956; Axt, 1952). However, once the loan program became operational, college financial-aid officers were strongly in favor of it (Nash & Lazarsfeld, 1968). Surveys of parents by Gallup (*Financial Aid News*, August, 1962) and by Cliff and Ekstrom (1962) demonstrated that parents were strongly in favor of loans to students. The Kiplinger study reported that the largest source of college loan funds was gifts or endowments. Most colleges reported that they had all or more of the loan funds than they needed, and in 1955 nearly one-half of all loan funds were not being utilized. The Kiplinger Washington Editors (1962) secured questionnaires from 800 banks and found that only 14 percent had special loan programs for students, but the majority said that they made loans to students. They found that the interest rate in most programs was fairly reasonable. As student loan programs became more prevalent, Abate (1963a) and Mullins (1962) looked at actual interest costs and recommended caution to student borrowers dealing with private lenders.

Hall and Craige (1962) studied the impact of the National Defense Student Loan Program from 30,000 questionnaires completed by students at 1,000 colleges. The majority of the students were from low-income families. The average student felt that he could safely borrow only $2,000 in total. Nine out of ten said that the availability of a student loan made it possible for them to start or to continue in college on a full-time basis. One-half of the students said that they had been able to reduce the hours that they spent on part-time jobs; and because of their loan, one out of six borrowers had been able to change from part-time to full-time status. One-third of the borrowers got no support from their family.

One of the earliest forces in the student loan field was the Harmon Foundation, which made loans to students from the early 1920's. The Harmon Foundation (1929) concluded from seven years of experience that students were excellent credit risks. Ormes (1957) and Ruegsegger (1956) each analyzed the results of loan programs at their colleges and found that the repayment results had been excellent. Massachusetts, one of the first states to make guaranteed loans to students, also found its repayment record to be excellent (Massachusetts Higher Education Assistance Corporation, 1959). However, the collection experience was not so good for many colleges and universities participating in the National Defense Student Loan Program. The Subcommittee on Education of the House of Representatives (1965) reported that 16 percent of the amount then due was delinquent. The figure was even worse than it appeared, because 47 percent of the amount due was either deferred (because students were in school or in service) or cancelled because the students had gone into teaching. Of $9,500,000 due to the institutions, only $6,500,000 was collected and thus $3,000,000 was delinquent. The U.S. Office of Education drew up a list of the institutions with most delinquencies and tried to have administrative reforms made. Analysis of the delinquencies showed that the college's administrative machinery was often at fault and that most students actually intended to repay. Colleges in the poorer states had poorer repayment records, and the delinquency rate at Negro colleges was several times that at the balance of colleges. Abate (1963b) and Hill (1965) surveyed the administrative practices of colleges and compared their procedures to those of bankers. They found that the colleges often employed inexperienced personnel, who did not advise students of their responsibility to repay and did not keep accurate records with which to trace the students. Hill warned that collection would be an extremely expensive process for the colleges. The Guaranteed Loan Program should solve many of the problems of repayment, since experienced lenders and state loan agencies will be responsible for collection rather than the institutions of higher education. There have been no surveys of the effects of borrowing on students, although many girls now begin married life with a negative dowry and many young men owe several thousand dollars before holding their first full-time job.

FINANCIAL NEED AND DROPPING OUT OF COLLEGE. Cliff (1962a) summarized the literature on college dropouts, which agrees that about 60 percent of all students who enter college do not graduate by the end of a four-year period. Financial reasons are usually given as important for those who drop out. When those who drop out are compared with those who have stayed, the students who stay are found to be happier, with more favorable attitudes toward college, and they are usually more successful. It appears that students cite financial reasons more frequently because they are socially acceptable. The study done by Iffert (1958) on 2,400 students who dropped out of 20 colleges found that 38 percent of the dropouts transferred to other colleges and 48 percent planned to return to some other college. Academic reasons were the reason most frequently given for dropping out; 25 percent dropped out for reasons of health and family, and a large proportion of these were girls getting married or having children; 15 percent of the students dropping out gave financial reasons. Cliff (1962a) studied 1,200 students who had been awarded scholarships, of whom 85 percent were not dropouts. The principal difference between the dropout boys and the controls in Cliff's study was that the former received less scholarship aid. Dropout girls were somewhat lower on socioeconomic variables. Academic reasons would not be of major importance for scholarship dropouts, because the majority would have had to be good students to have been awarded scholarships.

Irvine (1966) studied 145 subjects who withdrew from the University of Georgia in good standing. Three-quarters went on to attend college elsewhere. One-third cited financial reasons for their decision to drop out of college. Astin (1964) studied academically able dropouts and found that girls most frequently cited inability to afford college costs, but boys were more likely to give personal reasons. Only 14 percent of the academically able girls dropped out of college, and only 9 percent of the boys did so. The dropouts came from a lower socioeconomic background and were less likely to be planning graduate or professional study. Approximately 90 percent of those who dropped out said that they planned to return to college. Goetz and Leach (1967) compared freshmen who had dropped out with those who did not and found that financial problems were more pressing for the withdrawals. Esty (1966) notes that dropping out of college is considered to be socially unacceptable behavior, and this results in an overreporting of financial problems which are not in fact the real reason. He cites the increasing practice of colleges granting leaves of absence in good standing to students who seem to be immature or unmotivated.

Just as with the decision to attend college, finances are only one of a number of reasons that cause students to withdraw from college. The financial struggle may not be worth the price if college does not seem sufficiently rewarding. For many girls the attraction of marriage is stronger than that of a college diploma. Many college aid officers have worked out special programs to help students with temporary financial emergencies, so that they can be prevented from dropping out. Some colleges have short-term emergency loan funds. As loans become more important in financing undergraduate education, the dropout becomes more of a problem. Both college aid directors and bankers agree that the dropout is a major source of their delinquent loan accounts (Nash & Nash, 1967).

FINANCIAL NEEDS OF TRANSFER STUDENTS. Knoell and Medsker (1965) studied 7,000 junior college students who transferred to 43 four-year colleges and universities. They estimated that, although at least 75 percent would earn a baccalaureate degree eventually, only 62 percent of the junior college students earned a degree within three years after transfer (or after at least five years of college). The former junior college students were found to be less able scholastically and to have cited a lack of finances as the reason for having attended junior college in the first place. A substantial number who dropped out of the four-year college cited financial reasons. Most colleges were found to be poorly prepared to handle transfer students. Nash and Lazarsfeld (1968) found that either loans or scholarships were at least potentially available to transfers from two-year colleges at 93 percent of all four-year accredited colleges with financial-aid programs. Transfers from four-year colleges fared slightly less well. The large increase in Federal student loan programs should be of special assistance to transfer students.

SOURCES OF INSTITUTIONAL FINANCIAL-AID FUNDS. R. Moon (1958) estimated that by 1958 the major source of institutional grants to students had become general income rather than endowed funds or gifts earmarked specifically for grants or scholarships. This means that the college is not compensated, even on paper, for the increase in grants that is needed to meet increasing tuition. Pollard and Barett's study (1955) of 750 colleges found that 59 percent of grant funds came from general income. An analysis by the American Alumni Council and the Council for Financial Aid to Education (1966) of gifts received by 1,000 colleges showed that 12 percent was earmarked specifically for student financial aid.

ADMINISTRATION OF STUDENT FINANCIAL AID. There have been comprehensive studies of student personnel services by Ayers and others (1966) and by the American Association of Junior Colleges (1965). The latter studied the programs at 49 junior colleges by means of personal visits and questionnaires to all members of the student personnel staff. Generally junior colleges were found to have weak financial-aid programs, but the quality of administration of student financial aid was average when compared with the 20 other student personnel functions. This study attempted to rate the effectiveness of each college's program and found that the level of training of student personnel workers was not associated with the effectiveness of the program. The factors that contributed to effectiveness were the resources of the institution, leadership, and the peer support or cohesion that existed among faculty and staff at the college. The administration at a large number of the junior colleges was found to be in a state of flux.

The first national study of student financial-aid administrators and financial-aid policies and practices was done by Nash and Lazarsfeld (1968). Questionnaires were returned by 849 accredited four-year institutions. One-third were found to have full-time aid directors (that is, a person spending 70 percent or more of his time on financial-aid administration). Whether or not an administrator was full- or part-time in financial aid was found to be the most significant determinant of his satisfaction with aid administration, his level of information, and the amount of communication he had with aid directors of other colleges. Full-time aid directors were found to enjoy the work, and a large proportion regarded student financial administration as a lifetime career. Approximately one-half of the aid administrators had attended school at the institution at which they worked. While a majority held a master's degree, less than one in five had a doctorate. It was found that aid directors spend a large amount of time interviewing students and that this was the type of work they enjoyed doing most. Helping students who would not otherwise be able to attend college and instituting and coordinating new programs were the greatest sources of satisfaction for aid directors. Demanding or uncooperative students and parents and too much work were the major sources of dissatisfaction. The aid director ranked himself about equal in status to the admissions officer. Most colleges had financial-aid committees, and these, along with the aid director, were the principal determinants of financial-aid policy. A large turnover was found among aid administrators, but this was attributed in part to the fact that many institutions had recently appointed full-time aid directors. Financial aid has become a separate and independent function from admissions, but there is close coordination between the two. Most aid directors administered all undergraduate grants and loans, but a substantial proportion did not administer term-time employment. Grants to graduate students are much more likely to involve the student's department in the decision-making process.

Although financial-aid administration is not a profession which requires specific training and licensing in the same fashion as does medicine or law, the size of student financial-aid programs is such that the financial-aid administrator seems to have taken his place as a permanent member of the college administration. College aid administrators in most parts of the nation can now belong to regional associations of aid directors. The first regional association for financial-aid administrators started in the Midwest in 1962. It has been followed by similar associations in the South, the Southwest, and the East. The National Student Financial Aid Council was formed in 1966 to coordinate the activities of the regional associations. Babbidge (1960), Nash and Lazarsfeld (1968), and Gross (1962, 1966) have noted that the aid director is both a counselor and an administrator of funds. Gross has reviewed the development of financial-aid counseling.

INTERCOLLEGE COOPERATION. One of the reasons that the College Scholarship Service was founded by the College Entrance Examination Board in 1955 was to reduce the competition between colleges on scholarship offers. The College Scholarship Service notifies the colleges involved when an applicant applies for financial aid to two or more colleges. About one aid director in six consults regularly with other colleges, so that students who apply to both receive similar awards (Nash & others, 1967). However, approximately one-half of all nonsectarian private colleges engage in this practice. O'Hearne (1966) has described the growth of intercollege comparison of financial-aid offers. There has also been an effort by colleges to agree on the terms and conditions of financial-aid awards. Approximately 75 institutions in the Midwest agreed in 1964 to subscribe to a financial-aid compact that contained such provisions as the right of a student to decline part of a financial-aid award and accept another (*Financial Aid News*, April, 1964).

FINANCIAL AID TO ATHLETES. There has been little research on the amount of financial aid awarded to athletes or the effect on other students of large aid sums being awarded to athletes. Nash and others (1967) found that one-quarter of the aid directors did not agree that their office could effectively monitor financial aid to athletes. This was a particular problem at larger institutions. Hart (1956) studied athletic scholarships at the University of Missouri over a four-year period, during which the University spent $86,000 per year on athletic scholarships. The major part of the money was awarded to football players. The scholarship recipients were found to be average students scholastically. Iffert (1957b) studied the scholarship aid given to athletes. Although the majority of intercollegiate athletes had no scholarship support, one in ten had a grant that covered more than one-half of his expenses. The proportion of students holding athletic scholarships increased with each succeeding year in college, and one-half of all senior athletes held scholarships. The National Collegiate Athletic Association's Committee on Recruiting and Financial Aid (1960) surveyed policies and practices at 250 universities and colleges. Fifty large schools reported that they had 2,100 football players receiving financial assistance, three-quarters of whom were receiving the maximum allowed. Football enrolled by far the largest number of athletes on financial aid, and basketball came in second, with about one-third as many students receiving grants. The fifty largest institutions reported intercollegiate athletic budgets averaging $540,000 each, with financial aid to athletes amounting to about one-quarter of that ($145,000 per institution per year). The National Collegiate Athletic Association administers a code regulating aid to athletes and recruiting practices. In the period from 1952 to 1967 the Association investigated 485 alleged breaches of the athletic code and found 138 institutions guilty of violations. Penalties ranged from a private reprimand to a total ban on the right to compete in intercollegiate athletics. Although the total size and scope of financial aid to athletes is unknown, it is a major factor on the college campus and has been since the late nineteenth century (Rudolph, 1962a).

FOREIGN STUDENTS IN THE UNITED STATES. The Institute of International Education (1967) has estimated that there were approximately 100,000 foreign students in the United States in the academic year 1966–67. The number was about evenly divided between undergraduates and graduate students. About 40 percent of all foreign students were self-supporting, but this was less than the comparable figure of 48 percent in 1950–51. Colleges and universities themselves gave financial aid to the largest proportion of foreign students, and 22 percent of the students got some aid from the college or university. Foundations and private organizations supported 11 percent of the students, and the United States government supported 8 percent. Foreign governments supported only 6 percent of the students. North American students were the most likely to be self-supporting, while African students were the least likely to have their own financial resources. Interviews with 1,500 foreign students (Institute of International Education, 1966) revealed that approximately one-half stated they had no financial problems, but that approximately one student in ten had acute financial problems. About one-quarter of the students indicated that their housing was only fair or poor. The financing of the education of foreign students in the United States has become extremely controversial because of the reputed brain drain from underdeveloped countries. Sasnett (1965) has prepared a guide covering the cost of college and the amount of financial aid available for foreign students in the United States. The Institute of International Education (1965) has issued a directory which describes the programs available and regulations with which foreign students must deal.

FINANCIAL AID IN OTHER COUNTRIES. R. Moon (1960) has contrasted the American, the English, and the German systems of higher education and student financial aid. As Germany started to rebuild its system of higher education after World War II, it relied heavily on student loans to pay the costs. As the economy has improved, grant programs have increased in importance and loans have declined, but they still play an important role. Today the situation in higher education in Germany is similar to that in the United States, because most able students can expect to go to college. A national scholarship program is available to the ablest 20 percent in German universities. Only about 5 percent of all students of university age go to universities in Great Britain, but most of those who do go receive substantial financial support. In England the use of personal credit is virtually nonexistent. There are two contrasting systems. In the United States there is some help for all who are moderately talented and needy, and a large proportion of high school graduates go to college. In England the talented get all their expenses paid, but only a small proportion go. Germany falls between the two poles.

Bowles' (1963) international study of college admissions for UNESCO presents data on financial aid in 64 countries, 11 of which were singled out for intensive study. The problems encountered in data collection were substantial, because in many countries no one agency administers all aid to students. Lack of comparability was also a problem, because there is no universally accepted definition as to what constitutes higher education. In most countries there is no student financial aid in the form of direct cash payment to students; rather, a select group of students receives free or subsidized room, board, and transportation. In many less developed countries a substantial proportion of aid is actually a salary paid during training. The amount of aid per student in higher education was found to be highest in England, followed closely by the amount awarded in Sweden. West Germany, the Netherlands, and the United States are grouped closely in a tie for third. In the United States most aid to graduate education is awarded by discipline. In most other countries student aid is free from such strings or direction. Three different types of aid programs were described: "seedbed," "manpower," and "equalization." The first, which is employed in the countries with the greatest need, attempts to educate educators. The second attempts to meet the needs for skilled manpower other than educators. The third aims to "level up" educational opportunities. It was argued that the level of a country's industrialization was a major determinant of the type of aid program it would have. Countries also varied as to the amount of overall planning, which was characterized as extremely high in France and quite low in the United States. The less developed countries, particularly those attempting to establish planned economies, have usually taken great care to ensure that their aid programs do not simply maintain the established social order. The social structure of a nation usually determines the system of higher education that will prevail. The United States is a pluralistic society with a free-market, primarily private economy. The system of student financial aid that has evolved here represents an attempt to help finance both private and public institutions of higher education and at the same time to fill the country's manpower needs and promote social equality.

George Nash
Columbia University

References

Abate, Robert B. "College on Credit: Be Careful." *J Assn Col Admissions Counselors* 8:14–6; 1963(a).

Abate, Robert B. "How to Collect NDEA Loans." *Col U Bus* 35:34–8; 1963(b).

Adams, Frank C. "A Classification System for Student Employment in State Universities of Illinois." Unpublished doctoral dissertation. Southern Illinois U, 1963.

Advisory Committee on National Student Financial Aid Programs. *The Federal Work-Study Concept: An Analysis.* CEEB, 1963.

Altenderfer, Marion E., and West, Margaret D. *How Medical Students Finance Their Education: Results of a Survey of Medical and Osteopathic Students, 1963–64.* Public Health Service, 1965.

American Alumni Council and Council for Financial Aid to Education. *Voluntary Support of Education, 1965–66.* The Councils, 1966.

American Association of Junior Colleges, National Committee for Appraisal and Development of Junior College Student Personnel Programs. *Junior College Student Personnel Programs—Appraisal and Development.* AAJC, 1965.

Armsby, Henry. *Cooperative Education in the United States.* USOE, 1954.

Astin, Alexander W. "Personal and Environmental Factors Associated with College Dropouts Among High Aptitude Students." *J Ed Psychol* 55:219–27; 1964.

Axt, Richard G. *The Federal Government and Financing Higher Education.* Columbia U Press, 1952.

Axt, Richard G. "The Joseph's Report—Toward a Federal Policy in Higher Education." *Ed Rec* 38:291–9; 1957.

Ayers, Archie R., and others. *Student Services Administration in Higher Education.* USOE, 1966.

Babbidge, Homer D., Jr. *Student Financial Aid—Manual for Colleges and Universities.* APGA, 1960.

Baker, Harold B. "The Working Student and His Grades." *J Ed* 35:28–35; 1941.

Berdie, Ralph F. *After High School What?* U Minnesota Press, 1954.

Bowles, Frank. *Access to Higher Education—The International Study of University Admissions,* Vol 1. UNESCO, 1963.

Brazer, Harvey E., and others. *Income and Welfare in the United States.* McGraw-Hill, 1963.

Burke, Dustin M. "Student Employment—An Underdeveloped Resource." *Financial Aid News* 3:4; 1963.

Burnett, Collins W. "Scholarships Go to Town." *California J Sec Ed* 25:367–8; 1950.

Clark, Selby G., and others. "Do Renewable Scholarships Promote Higher Grades?" *Personnel Guid J* 35:302–6; 1957.

Cliff, Norman. *An Investigation of Factors Associated With Dropout and Transfer by Scholarship Applicants.* ETS, 1962(a).

Cliff, Norman. *Family Characteristics and Parents' Contribution Toward College Expenses.* ETS, 1962(b).

Cliff, Norman. *Student Economic Behavior and Attitudes.* ETS, 1963.

Cliff, Norman, and Ekstrom, Ruth B. *Practices and Attitudes in Paying for College.* ETS, 1962.

Cole, Charles C., Jr. "Scholarship Applicants Today." *Col Bd R* 32:17–20; 1957.

College Entrance Examination Board. *Determining*

Awards Under Federal Student Aid Programs. CEEB, 1965(a).

College Entrance Examination Board. *Manual for Financial Aid Officers.* CEEB, 1965(b).

College Entrance Examination Board. *Financing a College Education—A Guide for Counselors.* CEEB, 1967.

Colver, Robert M. "Scholarship Selection and Administration—An Objective Appraisal of One Program." *Col U* 30:20–7; 1954.

Crowell, Donald P. *Financial Aid for Connecticut Students.* Connecticut State Department of Education, 1966.

Davis, Frampton. "Fathers Who Refuse to Pay for College." *Col Bd R* 56:19–21; 1965.

Davis, James A. *Stipends and Spouses: The Finances of American Arts and Science Graduate Students.* U Chicago, 1962.

Davis, James A. *Great Aspirations: The Graduate School Plans of American College Seniors.* Aldine Publishing Company, 1964.

Deverall, Richard L. G. "AFL-CIO-Sponsored Scholarships and Awards." *Financial Aid News* 5:4; 1965.

Dickinson, C., and Newbegin, Betty. "Can Work and College Mix?" *Personnel Guid J* 38:314–7; 1959.

Eells, Walter C., and Hollis, Ernest V. *Student Financial Aid in Higher Education—An Annotated Bibliography.* USOE, 1962.

Elam, Stanley. "A Quarter of a Million and No Takers." *Illinois Ed* 35:235; 1947.

Esty, John C. Jr. "College Dropouts' Real Problem: What to Drop Into?" *Col Bd R* 62:20–1; 1966.

Ferguson, Josephine L. *Survey of State Scholarship Programs.* State Scholarship Commission of Indiana, 1967.

Frederickson, Norman, and Schraeder, W. B. *Adjustment to College: A Study of 10,000 Veteran and Non-Veteran Students in Sixteen American Colleges.* ETS, 1951.

Goetz, Walter, and Leach, Donald. "The Disappearing Student." *Personnel Guid J* 45:883–7; 1967.

Gordon, Edmund W., and Wilkerson, Doxey A. *Compensatory Education for the Disadvantaged: Programs and Practices: Preschool through College.* CEEB, 1966.

Gropper, George L., and Fitzpatrick, Robert. *Who Goes to Graduate School?* American Institute for Research, 1959.

Gross, Stanley C. "Financial Counseling Reconsidered." *J Col Student Personnel* 8:3; 1962.

Gross, Stanley C. "A Critique of Practice in the Administration of Financial Aid." *J Col Student Personnel* 7:78–85; 1966.

Hall, Robert C., and Craige, Stanton. *Student Borrowers and Their Needs.* USOE, 1962.

Harmon Foundation. *Seven Years' Experience with Student Loans.* The Foundation, 1929.

Harris, Seymour E. *Economic Aspects of Higher Education.* Organization for Economic Cooperation and Development, 1964.

Hart, James Earl. "Administration of Athletic Scholarships at the University of Missouri." *Dissertation Abstracts* 16:2366–7; 1956.

Haven, Elizabeth W., and Smith, Robert E. *Financial Aid to College Students, 1963–64.* ETS, 1965.

Henry, Joe B. "Family Financial Power and College Attendance." *Personnel Guid J* 43:775–9; 1965.

Herriot, Robert E. "Some Social Determinants of Educational Aspiration." *Harvard Ed R* 33:157–77; 1963.

Hill, W. W., Jr. *An Analysis of College Student Loan Programs.* United Student Aid Funds, Inc., 1965.

Hollis, Ernest V. *Costs of Attending College: A Study of Student Expenditures and Sources of Income.* USOE, 1957.

House of Representatives, Sub-committee on Education. *Report on Collection of National Defense Student Loans—Background Material with Related Recommendations.* United States Congress, 1965.

Iffert, Robert E. "College Scholarship Funds—Investment or Speculation." *H Ed* 13:143–6; 1957(a).

Iffert, Robert E. "Scholarship Fund and Extracurricular Activities." *H Ed* 14:51–5; 1957(b).

Iffert, Robert E. *Retention and Withdrawal of College Students.* USOE, 1958.

Ingraham, Mark H., and King, Francis P. *The Outer Fringe: Faculty Benefits Other Than Annuities and Income.* U Wisconsin Press, 1965.

Institute of International Education. *Handbook on International Study for Foreign Nationals.* The Institute, 1965.

Institute of International Education. *Report on International Exchange—Open Doors 1967.* The Institute, 1967.

Institute of International Education. *International Educational and Cultural Exchange.* The Institute, 1966.

Irvine, Donald W. "University Dropouts in Good Standing." *J Assn Col Admissions Counselors* 12:14–9; 1966.

Jaffe, A. J., and others. *Ethnic Higher Education—Negro Colleges in the 1960's.* Praeger, 1968.

Kendrick, S. A. "Notes on the Disadvantaged." CEEB, 1967. (Staff memorandum.)

Kiplinger Washington Editors. *Student Loans—Their Place in Student Aid.* Editors of *Changing Times*, 1956.

Kiplinger Washington Editors. *Commercial Loans for Colleges.* Editors of *Changing Times*, 1962.

Kiplinger Washington Editors. *Colleges with Jobs for Students 1966–67—A Survey of Job Openings in Four-Year and Two-Year Accredited Colleges.* Editors of *Changing Times*, 1966.

Knoell, Dorothy, and Medsker, Leland L. *From Junior to Senior College: A National Study of the Transfer Student.* ACE, 1965.

Lansing, John B., and others. *How People Pay for College.* U Michigan Survey Research Center, 1960.

Letson, Robert J. "A Study of the Curators' Freshman Scholarship and Award Students and Their Success in the University of Missouri, 1950–54." *Dissertation Abstracts* 16:2077; 1956.

Lichtenstein, Gene. "Two Cultures." *Financial Aid News* 2:1; 1961.

Lindley, Betty, and Lindley, Ernest K. *A New Deal for Youth: The Story of the National Youth Administration.* Viking Press, 1938.

Little, J. Kenneth. "College Scholarships in Wisconsin." *Ed Rec* 40:348–52; 1959.

Margolius, Sidney. *Planning for College.* Avon Books, 1965(*a*).

Margolius, Sidney. "The Emotional Problems of Financing College." *Financial Aid News* 5:5; 1965(*b*).

Marple, Betty Lou N., and Marple, Wesley W., Jr. "How Affluent Families Plan to Pay for College." *Col Bd R* 63:11–6; 1967.

Massachusetts Higher Education Assistance Corporation. *Higher Education Loan Plan for Massachusetts Students.* The Corporation, 1959.

Mattingly, Richard C. *Scholarships and Fellowships: A Selected Bibliography.* USOE, 1957.

McKee, Richard C. *Financial Assistance for College Students.* USOE, 1965.

Meeth, L. Richard. "Breaking Racial Barriers, Part III: Scholarships for Negro Students in Predominantly White Colleges and Universities." *J H Ed* 37:246–52; 1966.

Miller, C. Dean, and others. "Student Patterns of Financing Education at a Land-grant University." *Personnel Guid J* 45:687–91; 1967.

Moon, George R. "Records of Students Who Entered the University with Freshman Scholarships." *Sch Soc* 38:443–9; 1930.

Moon, Rexford G., Jr. "Who Should Pay the Bill?" *Col Bd R* 35:21–4; 1958.

Moon, Rexford G., Jr. "German and English Student Aid—and Our Own." *Col Bd R* 40:24–8; 1960.

Moon, Rexford G., Jr. *Student Financial Aid in the United States: Administration and Resources.* CEEB, 1963.

Moon, Rexford G., Jr. "Determining Aid Needs for 1970: a Model." *Col Bd R* 54:11–3; 1964.

Moon, Rexford G., Jr. "Financial Aids, Present and Future." *J Assn Col Admissions Counselors* 11:22–4; 1965.

Moore, Harold E., and others. *The Doctorate in Education: An Inquiry into Conditions Affecting Pursuit of the Doctoral Degree in the Field of Education.* AACTE, 1960.

Morris, Darrell R. "Project Opportunity: A Status Report." *Col Bd R* 61:7–10; 1966.

Muirhead, Peter. "Who Wins University Scholarships?" *State of New York B Sch* 36:293–5; 1950.

Mullins, John M. "What Kind of Education Expense Plan?" *Financial Aid News* 2:2; 1962.

Nash, George, and Lazarsfeld, Paul F. *New Administrator on Campus: A Study of the Director of Student Financial Aid.* CEEB, 1968.

Nash, George, and Nash, Patricia. "Survey of Activities in Urban and Minority Problems at the University of Michigan." Columbia U, 1966. (Mimeographed.)

Nash, George, and Nash, Patricia. *A Report of the Opinions and Practices of Student Financial Aid Administrators and Bankers in the Federal Guaranteed Loan Program.* Columbia U, Bureau of Applied Social Research, 1967.

Nash, George, and Nixon, Julian. *The New York City Urban Corps: A Study of Student Participation in Government.* Praeger, 1968.

Nash, George, and others. *Financial Aid Policies and Practices at Accredited Four-year Universities and Colleges.* Columbia U, Bureau of Applied Social Research, 1967.

National Collegiate Athletic Association. *Special Report of the Committee on Recruiting and Financial Aid.* The Association, 1960.

National Education Association. "College for the Fortunate or the Finest." *The Shape of Education for 1964.* NEA, 1964.

O'Hearne, John J. "Why Not Compare Scholarship Offers?" *Financial Aid News* 7:1; 1966.

Olsen, Andrew L., and Anderson, Robert C. *Source Guide to Financial Aid for Students of Michigan Colleges and Universities.* Michigan State U, Cooperative Extension Service, 1965.

O'Meara, J. Roger. *Company Sponsored Scholarship and Student Loan Programs.* National Industrial Conference Board, 1964.

Ormes, Ferguson R. "Wabash College Finds the Record Good on Repayment of Student Loans." *Col U Bus* 22:23–5; 1957.

Panel on Educational Innovation, President's Science Advisory Committee. *Educational Opportunity Bank.* GPO, 1967.

Pearson, Richard. *The Opening Door: A Review of New York State's Programs of Financial Aid for College Students.* CEEB, 1967.

Plaut, Richard L. "Plans for Assisting Negro Students to Enter and to Remain in College." *J Negro Ed* 35:393–9; 1966.

Pollard, John A., and Barett, Norman W. "The Financial Status of Colleges and Universities in the United States." *H Ed* 11:125–9; 1955.

Rauth, Morton. *Definitions of Terms Used in Student Financial Aids.* Antioch Col, 1966.

Reeder, C. W., and Newman, S. C. "The Relation of Employment to Scholarship." *Ed Res B* 18:203–14; 1939.

Rivlin, Alice. *The Role of the Federal Government in Financing Higher Education.* The Brookings Institution, 1961.

Rudolph, Frederick. *The American College and University: A History.* Knopf, 1962(*a*).

Rudolph, Frederick. "Myths and Realities of Student Aid." *Col Bd R* 48:18–23; 1962(*b*).

Ruegsegger, Lester J. "Pay-as-you-go Plan Really Works: Five Advantages of Policy Whereby Student Finances Own Plan of Installment Paying of Tuition Fees." *Col U Bus* 21:32–3; 1956.

Sanders, J. Edward, and Palmer, Hans. *The Financial Barrier to Higher Education in California.* California State Scholarship Commission, 1965.

Sasnett, Martina. *Financial Planning for Study in the United States: A Guide to Costs, Financial Aid, and Spending for Students from Other Countries.* CEEB, 1965.

Schaffner, Martha. "A Comparison of the Scholastic

Success of Employed and Non-employed College Students." Master's thesis. Kansas State Teachers Col, 1936.

Schlekat, George A. *An Analysis of Selected College Financial Awards as a Function of Socio-economic Class.* ETS, 1967.

Sherwood, Paul M. "Student and Family Attitudes Toward Financing the College Experience." *Dissertation Abstracts* 17:66; 1957.

Sibley, Elbridge. *The Education of Sociologists in the United States.* Russell Sage, 1963.

Silver, Robert Eugene. "The Effect of Self-support upon Student Success in Walla Walla College." *Dissertation Abstracts* 16:1817–20; 1956.

Simon, Kenneth A., and Grant, Vance W. *Digest of Educational Statistics 1966.* USOE, 1966.

Smith, Sherman E., and others. *Are Scholarships the Answer? A Report on a Scholarship Program for Students of Limited Means.* U New Mexico, 1960.

Splaver, Sarah. *Your College Education—How to Pay for It.* Julian Messner, Inc., 1964.

Thielens, Wagner, Jr. *Recruits for Accounting: How the College Class of 1961 Entered the Profession.* Columbia U, Bureau of Applied Social Research, 1966.

Trueblood, D. L. "Academic Achievement of Employed and Non-employed Students in the Indiana School of Business." *Dissertation Abstracts* 14:643–4; 1954.

United States Department of Health, Education, and Welfare. *Grants-in-Aid and Other Financial Assistance Programs.* HEW, 1966.

United States Office of Education. *Aids to Students in Vocational, College and Graduate Programs.* USOE, 1966.

Warkov, Seymour, and Zelan, Joseph. *Lawyers in the Making.* Aldine Publishing Company, 1965.

Warkov, Seymour, and others. *Graduate Student Finances, 1963.* NORC, 1965.

West, Elmer D. *Background for a National Scholarship Policy.* ACE, 1956.

West, Elmer D., and Gleazer, Charlene. "Who Gets the Scholarships?" *Financial Aid News* 4:4; 1964.

Williamson, B. Lois, and Feder, Daniel D. "Scholarship Winners, How They Rate on Campus and in Class." *Personnel Guid J* 31:336–40; 1953.

Williamson, Edmund G. "College Graduates and NYA Scholarships." *Sch Soc* 46:510–2; 1937.

Wilson, James W., and Lyons, Edward H. *Work-Study College Programs—Appraisal and Report of the Study of Cooperative Education.* Harper, 1961.

STUDENT ORGANIZATIONS AND STUDENT ACTIVITIES: COLLEGE AND UNIVERSITY

The pattern of American higher education has changed dynamically in the past several decades. The physical environs of the campus have been drastically altered to keep pace with the tremendous growth in the student population; knowledge and research have been accumulating at an unprecedented rate; and the pressures for societal change have forced American education into the mainstream of American life. America's unsolved urban problems have been imported to the campus both by morally committed students and also by demands and inducements that university facilities be made available for seeking solutions to the problems of twentieth-century urban culture. No doubt, insulated ivory towers can still be found, but in small numbers.

One way to describe the development of student activities might be in terms of the following arbitrary phases:

1. Repression and regimentation of dress, behavior, and piety in the colonial period.
2. Substitution of the "caring" relationship of the family with the father figure as dominant.
3. Revolt against authority figures.
4. Search for relevancy to current societal problems.
5. Excessive rejection of external authority and restraint in an effort to be "free."

Further discussion of these periods will be found below, in the history section of this article.

Student activities (or the extracurriculum) as a contributor to the total educational process have also been notably affected. Their nature and scope have been challenged to adapt to the needs of a changing university mission and the demands of a new student generation. The professional student-activities or student personnel worker, too, has acknowledged the need to search the recent literature of the behavioral sciences and thus reassess his function as an adviser and consultant to student life and, at the same time, to find ways of discharging his responsibilities to the institution for "controlling" and protecting its rights and interests—a most difficult task of balancing the interests of his student "charges" and his obligation to the college.

GENERAL SCOPE. One view of the scope of the extracurriculum and its objectives, especially in relation to general education, was defined in the 1952 yearbook of the National Society for the Study of Education (1953). That relationship was the basis for both organized and informal activities conducted by students in the school, the college, or the surrounding community. The extracurriculum included aesthetic programs, athletic participation, lectures and debates, and membership in various student organizations.

Bloland (1967) has limited this category to only the more formal or organized programs engaged in by students with institutional sanction. Another author, Mueller (1961) uses the terms "extracurriculum," "extracurricular," "cocurricular," "extraclass," or simply "activities" interchangeably. Broadly speaking, these are defined as including everything the student does outside the classroom, during all the hours of the day he does not spend at his desk or in the library. Pruitt (1966), acknowledging the limitations of such a broad definition, defined the area of student activities as those out-of-class experiences, either formally or informally organized, in which students participate as a function of their "citizenship" in the campus community. Stroup (1965) states that activities properly designated as student activities are only those conducted under professional leadership and with the sanction of the university. Usually no academic credit is given for these activities.

The definition to be used in this article includes all the activities and interest of students involved in the following kinds of organizations: governing boards and intergroup councils, student publications, fraternities and sororities, residence-hall, cooperative housing and rooming houses, recognition and honorary societies, and special-interest affiliations such as religious, political, social action, language, music, drama, recreational or hobby, social service, international, and academic departmental and professional groups. Included, thus, are all the active interests of these student organizations either on or off campus, as well as the student union and intramural activities.

Political activist groups not seeking institutional recognition and other groups not formally recognized by the school administrations should also be included.

College officials must recognize that they may have some involvement in the activities of individual students as well as in those of student groups. For example, such off-campus activities as student involvement in civil rights demonstrations, peace marches, or picketing of the House Un-American Activities Committee are not excluded, and certainly the Berkeley incidents (Lipset & Wolin, 1965) both on and off campus, fall within the range of extracurricular interests.

HISTORY. A discussion of the development of student activities cannot be divorced from the unique characteristics of American higher education. Just as American higher education is founded upon diversity in size and institutional purpose, so also has the nature and scope of extracurricular activity been changed in the course of historical trends and transitions. Rudolph (1965), for example, traces the student's infusing of intellectual vigor into the sterile classical curriculum of the eighteenth-century college.

The extracurriculum has been characteristic of higher education since the early colonial period. To be sure, Brubacher and Rudy (1958) noted that under the church-dominated college in early America there existed a unity between curriculum and extracurriculum. The early colleges, influenced by the seventeenth-century English colleges, were organized residential associations for purposes of inculcating specific patterns of religious and social conduct. The college was truly a way of life, in the sense that professors and students lived in the same dormitories and ate in the same dining halls. The professor was the supervisor and "controller" of the students' total life and activities.

In the early 1800's there was evidence of student activities emerging apart from the activities of the faculty. The most popular forms were religious organizations and literary programs and events. The latter also included debates, collecting and maintaining libraries, and student government. These developments heralded the gradual evolution of a total program of student organizational life that has persisted to this day, with the more recent addition of political and other activist movements. Some of the early societies were secret organizations, and others were chartered directly by the student government; some of these were practically beyond faculty control. Leonard (1956) cites a reason frequently given for the emergence of activities apart from the colleges' instructional program as a reaction against the impersonalism and classical formalism of the university.

Other changes were occurring that influenced college aims. Enrollments were increasing with the spread and acceptance of the concept of universal education; moreover, education was thought to be the "right" of every citizen, regardless of sex or vocational aspiration; there was also increased emphasis on vocational education and on preparation for citizenship (for example, the Morrill Land Grant Act of 1862); and Colleges returned to the early emphasis of inculcation of moral values and the molding of the whole character of the student. Along with these changes came a rapid expansion of student activities and an attempt to bridge the gap between student out-of-class life and the objectives of the college.

DeVane (1965) has characterized higher education at the turn of the century as the era of big-time athletics and "real" collegiate life. The most important thing for many students of this era was not the course of study, but cultivation of educated gentlemen in an environment of friendship and social development, fraternity houses, good sportsmanship, and athletic teams. One reason for this emphasis, according to Rudolph (1965), was student expectations beyond graduation. Since the world of business was a world of dealing with people, what better preparation could there be than the collegiate social life outside the classroom? College became a social habit, and the classroom was not the most important part. This "real" collegiate life continued to assert itself following World War I and flourished in the Roaring Twenties until the depression of the 1930's.

The campus during the depression years, which culminated in World War II, reflected the mood of a country plunged into uncertainty and then despair. The spirit of change, social protest, and repudiation of the past was one of the most significant characteristics of the American campus of that era (Rudolph, 1965). Both the campus and classroom were subjected to a critical scrutiny that helped shape a social awareness and a social outlook that the United States had never known before. Student activity for the vocal minority who became seriously concerned included standing in picket lines or organizing leftist activities. Another relevant development during this era was the growth of Dewey's progressivism (Dewey, 1920). Acceptance of the idea that education and experience were compatible led to the exploration of ways of bridging the gap between education and society. In the spirit of innovation, new experimental colleges such as Bennington and Sarah Lawrence were born, schools in which integration of the curriculum and extracurriculum was attempted.

The post-World War II period showed that the revolts and questioning of the prewar student activists did not constitute a permanent condition for college youth. The college student of this era has been described by Eddy (1962) as lethargic and apathetic, and is perhaps best characterized by the GI's who returned to the campus in large numbers to get their rights and reward, a college education. The Jacob (1957) and Eddy (1959) studies of the late 1950's give vivid portrayals of the mixture of apathy and "Joe College" which tended to permeate the types of activities dominating the extracurriculum during the 1950's. Additionally, these studies have provided impetus for realizing the potential impact that the total environmental forces, including the extracurriculum, can have on the college student.

PURPOSES. Student activities, to be compatible with the unique objectives of individual institutions of higher education and relevant to the interests and needs of students and student groups, must serve a variety of purposes. Few institutions can choose to ignore or to disclaim interest in the many facets of student group life. Although some institutions continue to deal with student activities as if they existed only when the student activity causes "trouble," the growing practice among colleges and universities is to foster and encourage student activities to the end that they become educational resources which complement the curriculum in fostering learning and maturity.

For many educators, student activities are viewed as contributing to the general education of the individual, a concept which encompasses moral and aesthetic development as well as intellectual development. General education, says Brubacher (1965), is first concerned with fashioning a man who has been brought to the full utilization of his capabilities and, thus, should be the concern of all facets of the institution. Sanford (1966), a strong advocate of the university as an institution for maximizing student potentialities, recognizes the potential of the extracurriculum as an integral force in accomplishing that end. According to Stroup (1965), the potential of student activities for acceptance in the university community depends upon their contribution to the student's total development.

Landahl (1966) perceives the extracurriculum as an auxiliary academic program. He is not calling for the abolition of all social activities, but rather for attainment of a balance by transforming traditional cocurricular activities into informal educational activities. A crucial aim of such a proposal would be the elevation of the student personnel worker to a stature approaching the role of the faculty member within the educational community.

Other authors have stressed social learning and the development of interpersonal skills as a function of the student activities program. Mueller (1961) sees student activities as an opportunity for gaining experience in group interaction and relationships. Additionally, they provide a favorable continuation of the socialization process of the individual. Stroup (1965) emphasized programs aimed at the development of social maturity and the development of social responsibility. McConnell (1966) stressed the achievement of student identity through diverse groups on the campus.

Koile (1966b) discusses student affairs programs as contributing to student development by providing opportunity to experience freedom, to accept responsibility, to make decisions, and to be confronted with the realistic consequences of such freedom. Gould (1966) offers a similar point of view when he suggests that the total educational program should be committed to the development of student maturity. This objective is to be achieved by giving students the opportunity to learn of the relationships between authority and responsibility, as well as the relationship between action and consequence. Also related is Monypenny's (1965) conception of the extracurriculum as helping students learn to make independent decisions.

Student activities have also been conceived (Mueller, 1961) as facilitating the development of future leaders during the students' years on the college and university campus. Gardner (1965), another proponent of student activities for the development of leadership, has acknowledged the loss of potential leadership because many students, for numerous reasons, have failed to utilize the opportunities offered in the extracurriculum.

Stroup (1965) has delineated a philosophy of student activities which stresses the creative tension between individual growth and the development of social responsibility. He points out that many student activities are related to a never-ending campus dialogue about freedom and order, in which the individual's unrestricted personal expression represents freedom and the responsibility to society is the restricting order.

Since World War II, creative tension among students has focused on restrictive membership policies in student organizations (fraternities and sororities), freedom of the student press, political and religious activities on campus, the sponsorship of controversial speakers (political and other), from off-campus by a student group, civil rights activities (on or off-campus) and the student's right to be involved in institutional decision-making. Activities continue to be also recreational in nature. The pursuit of pleasure is a part of American culture.

Some students believe that out-of-class life should be only social, diverting, and "off-duty" in character, as a sort of balance wheel for the individual against the rigors of study and classroom competition. There will always be some of this "fun" type of activity, but the main emphasis of the college should be directed toward educational activity throughout the whole institution, with the educative purpose not being confined exclusively to the classroom. Part of the emerging student personnel program is the welding together of the intellectual and recreational aspects of college life into an overall educational development program.

ADMINISTRATION. In the colonial period, the college president and faculty were given the responsibility of regulating and supervising the entire student life of the campus. Leonard (1956) suggests that this responsibility grew out of the religious, social, and political life of the early colonists. Early American legislation assumed that the entire personnel of the colleges was responsible for religious training, training in citizenship for participation in government, vocational training, and also instruction in morality and good manners. During the colonial period, instructors were assigned the disciplinary responsibility (as proctors) of enforcing strict rules and regulations—a role and a regimen that prevented the establishment of friendly relationships between faculty and students. The term *in loco parentis* was then used to describe this relationship of teacher and student. Williamson (1964) cites a shift following the Civil War in the nature of the relationship between students and faculty from the harsh regimentation and enforcement of regulation in colonial times to a benign "family model," with its caring relationships—a relationship he designates as "intellectual comradeship."

The "student personnel" point of view that has evolved in the twentieth century arose in conjunction with the express purpose of individualizing education. Wrenn (1951) summarized the movement as a deep concern for the individual, and the goal of education as the total development of the individual student. The outgrowth of this movement has been the creation of a variety of student personnel services, of which student activities is a part and whose primary medium of operation is the extracurriculum. The emergence of the student personnel movement may well be a further blending of the regulatory functions of the previous century and the caring relationship described by Williamson (1964). Some degree of authority and control is essential to preserve the efficient operation of the institution.

The proper relationship between the extracurricular sphere and the faculty and staff has become a highly contested issue in recent years. Many students and faculty have challenged the term *in loco parentis*, as it has been used to describe the traditional colonial relationship of the college as a sort of parental guardian over the moral, intellectual, and social activities of the student. Student leaders at a recent United States National Student Association (1966) convention, for example, condemned the *in loco parentis* concept because they claimed that it permits arbitrary and extensive repression of student pursuits, reinforces immaturity or conformity, and removes responsibility for personal decision-making from the student. Others such as Bakken (1961) and Strickland (1965) admit that, although *in loco parentis* has been used to justify arbitrary rules made by the college, it has also identified a solicitous interest in the growth and development of individual students. It is with this ideal that student personnel workers have identified themselves most recently. Although supervision still enters into their task, student personnel workers now consider themselves essentially as educators, not as proctors or policemen, with respect to the development of students to their full personality and capacity outside the classroom.

Student personnel administrators and educators have recently been examining the nature of the relationship between the institution, themselves, and the extracurriculum. Williamson (1961) suggested the concept of partnership in learning as both an integration of the adviser-supervisor relationship with students and a similar authority status for both students and faculty-staff. This concept combines the regulatory and supervisory functions, an inevitable requirement of the educational institution, with the advisory relationship of a helpful partner. The basis for such a relationship says Bloland (1961) is an honest and continual discussion of roles. Students have a right to know where their power and authority reside, as well as the right to know the rationale for the necessity of supervision. Furthermore, the lines of authority are not static or irreversible, but must be open to continual review and revision.

The student activities worker is often called upon to fulfill a liaison function by relaying student concerns to college and university administrators less directly involved with students. Pruitt (1966) stated that student activity workers should interpret student thought and attitudes to college faculty and administrators, who are less directly involved with students' lives. Likewise, information from faculty and staff should be reported to students. Farnsworth (1958) believes that the student activities worker should be the students' protagonist, a leader in representing their points of view to the institution. At the same time, he also utilizes his role as a teacher to encourage all students to develop attitudes that are consistent with a college education.

The student personnel adviser's relationship with his student organization, says Bloland (1961a), should be active rather than passive. He states that, if the adviser is to be anything more than a custodian or watchdog whose only function is to see that the group "keeps out of trouble," he must deliberately and systematically influence the organizations to move in educationally desirable directions.

The staff advisory role differs from that of the faculty adviser and is unique in certain respects (Bloland, 1961a). The staff adviser is professionally trained and exercises research, counseling, educational, and supervisory responsibilities. Because his concern is the implementation of general educational and institutional objectives to be achieved through both the curriculum and the extracurriculum, he should perceive each group in a broader context than that provided by the group's own program and activities.

A positive and constructive view of the joint adviser-supervisor role includes three aspects: (1) maintenance functions, (2) program development functions, and (3) program content. The overall goal is to make membership in the organization an educationally meaningful experience.

As an aftermath of the Berkeley dispute, newly selected president Roger Heyns described the effective student activities worker as one who achieves a balance between the rights of students and the maintenance of university tradition, has a canny and successful blend of firmness and an open mind, and emphasizes effective and open lines of communication.

PROGRAMS. American colleges are committed to the development of independence and maturity of the individual student. According to Koile (1966b), the function of the student activities program is the accomplishment of that commitment by helping students utilize the campus environment, faculty, peer relationships, living arrangements, and social and cultural opportunities in their own learning and maturing process. Such a program, according to Sanford (1962), must recognize the vast potential of the social-psychological forces operating on the campus and mobilization of these toward maximization of student potentialities. An excellent example of this approach has been the increasing emphasis on extracurricular programs in dormitories and other college housing.

The influence of the peer group and the dynamics of dormitory living upon the development of student attitudes and student behavior has been documented in recent years by Newcomb (1962) and Riker (1966). Recent programming in on-campus residence has been aimed at mobilizing these potentially constructive forces toward educational ends. Primary concern has been with the *total* impact that the residential environment can have upon the educational experience of its residents.

Dormitories and residential units have often served as centers for extraclass activities, with varying degrees of emphasis on social skills, personal standards, and citizenship (Riker, 1965). To incorporate the total educational experience, a more recent interest in a wide range of intellectual matter has been added. Roskens and Hansheimer (1961), for example, have reported increased discussion of the latent potential of residence units as intellectual laboratories. In their frame of reference, residence units would be regarded as informal "classrooms away from the classroom." One experimental program of this nature, the living-learning system of residence halls at Michigan State University, has been reported by Olsen (1964a, 1964b). A recent innovation, devised at the University of California at Santa Cruz, calls for up to 20 semiautonomous residential colleges for undergraduates within the overall administrative framework of the university (Riker, 1966). These are some examples of attempts to minimize the dichotomy between the curriculum and the extracurriculum and the distinction between "life" and learning.

In other areas of the extracurriculum one finds additional examples of new dimensions in programming. Quigley (1966) has discussed the educational value of interesting foreign students and American students into various international programs on an equal basis. One program of this nature has been annual simulated United Nations assemblies. Moore (1966) has recommended both formal and informal means of motivating exchanges on the local campus between American and foreign students. Stark (1966) discussed an organized human relations program that emphasized seminars and forums on civil rights and an active service program among minority groups. Innovations in religious programming have been discussed by Carey (1962) and Buerk (1965). Anderson (1965) and Butler (1965) have written about the contemporary and future prospects of fraternities.

The activities of students representing student government and diverse political and social action groups, which may or may not be formally recognized by the university, have provided the most dramatic events on the campus in recent years. Vocal minorities of student activists have shifted their attention to issues of social and moral concern, as well as to the issue of their rights and freedom as students on the campus. The student activist of this decade has been portrayed by Mallery (1966) as a veteran picket, a militant demonstrator, or one who "sits in" for societal and moral causes. Keniston (1966) has hypothesized about the types of students and type of campus climate most conducive to student activists.

The activities of student dissidents have taken a variety of forms. Kauffman (1966), Cox (1966), and Goldworn (1965) have documented the use and acceptance of sit-ins and nonviolent demonstrations as a means of protest in the student rights movement. The most publicized example of student protest was the Berkeley uprising, which has been well documented by Lipset and Wolin (1965) and by Lunsford (1965). A relevant research study by Heist (1965) has produced information regarding the personal traits and characteristics of the students who took an active part in the Berkeley movement. The consequence of such efforts has been the exertion of pressures by students on college and university administrations for changes whenever they believe their rights or freedoms have been infringed upon.

Other forms of activity have been the teach-in (Greenfield, 1965), a marathon session of speakers and discussions on current issues, and the "free" university (Mathews, 1966), a movement offering courses on contemporary issues such as Vietnam, LSD, extremism in America, civil rights, and sex. "Free" universities, which exist outside the curriculum of any particular college, have operated with varying degrees of success on such campuses as the Universities of New Mexico, Minnesota, and Pennsylvania.

Another movement has been the formation of

extremist political and social action groups such as the Students for a Democratic Society (SDS), the W. E. B. DuBois Clubs, Campus Committee to End the War in Vietnam, Students for Integration, and others. The goals of one such group, the SDS, have been presented in papers by Potter (1965) and Davidson (1966). Essentially this group advocates a participatory democracy in which a union of students decides the kinds of rules they want, without participation by the college faculty or administration.

Student legislation on major issues at both the campus and national levels has been increasing. An example is the position that the United States National Student Association has taken on major issues in recent years (Liebert, 1966). Resolutions calling for educational reform, the evaluation of classroom teachers, and the removal of discriminatory membership clauses exemplify some of the significant measures taken on various campuses.

The issuing of statements by various student organizations and their delineation of desirable freedoms or privileges for students has been another significant trend in recent years. The American Civil Liberties Union (1962) has issued a formulation on rights of privacy, free discussion, and due process involving student discipline. Committee S of the American Association of University Professors (1964) has prepared a similar statement. The United States National Student Association policy declaration (1966) parallels the general policy on academic freedom of the faculty and defines it as the freedom to seek, discover, publish, and teach the truth as they see it. Most of the items on their list of ten rights of students deal with individual rights. Those items related to the extracurriculum call for the right of free speech, the organizing of partisan political groups on campus, absence of membership lists for student groups, and the right to protest and demonstrate for any cause of interest to students.

Another relevant issue has been the demand of student groups that they be permitted to bring any speaker of their choice to the campus. Williamson (1961) and Hoffmann (1965) recount the controversy and trials of testing the principles of academic freedom in speaker invitations. Van Alystyne (1963) has written about the legality of this issue on state university campuses.

An assessment of the campus climate, issues, and topics students would be permitted to discuss, acceptability of certain off-campus speakers, and other dimensions of freedom were the subject of a major research study by Williamson and Cowan (1966). Their findings show that, where students have the widest range of opportunities to hear speakers, to discuss issues, and to express themselves (demonstrations, rallies, etc.), there seems to be the most prevalent academic freedom for students.

The impact of the shift in student concern has not gone unheeded by educators. Even before students began actively exerting pressure for change, some educators were calling for a reexamination of the role of students in the power structure of the university. Klopf (1960) and Bloland (1961b)

advocated and described a student government which called for significant areas of responsibility, such as representation on faculty and administrative committees. A similar point of view has been taken by Schoen (1965), who called for clarification and delineation of the areas of student rights and associated areas of responsibility. A student government based upon a partnership concept similar to that which has been advocated must be a calculated risk, according to Somers (1966). Its leaders will make mistakes as part of the learning and growing process, and no social sanctions should result as a consequence.

Gallagher (1965) and Gould (1966) have written about the need for continual dialogue among faculty, administrators, and students and the need to draw students into the orbit of decision-making. From five alternative methods for establishing student rights, Williamson (1965) has cited the alternative of "continuous conversation" as the most effective method.

The college can no longer exist as an ivory tower separated from society, because the student activist has become a part of the forces that have pulled the college into society (that is, social concerns and action) and society into college life. Questioning of major issues and policies, such as the war in Vietnam and civil rights, has been brought about in a large degree by students. Moreover, colleges recognize that this type of activity is merely beginning.

PARTICIPATION IN STUDENT ACTIVITIES. In addition to previously cited references, there is further evidence of a definite shift in the type of activities in which the contemporary student participates. Roskens and Hansheimer (1961) state that the traditional big football weekends, the crowded social calendars, and the "rah! rah" campus atmosphere are all waning and are being replaced by more intellectual pursuits. Pruitt (1966) cites the opinions of a group of student leaders who define a trend from big group activities to smaller occasions and groups, offering identification with a personalized meaning rather than simply the identity of "belonging to something." Zander (1963) suggests that traditional organized student activities may be becoming less attractive, in favor of more exciting and challenging types of activity.

Several miscellaneous studies have reported the numbers and types of students participating in student activities. Williamson and others (1954) found that, without regard for the form or type of activity, 71 percent of the women and 60 percent of the men participated in one or more organized activities at the University of Minnesota. There was no single organized activity in which an overwhelming number of students tended to participate. Diversity, rather than commonality, seemed to characterize student life at that particular university. Extensive participation in activities was seen as an undergraduate phenomenon which decreased as the student advanced and matured in the academic environment. Wise (1958) noted that activities were most appealing to freshmen and noted the waning interest in activities among upperclassmen. Reich (1961) concluded from a survey of the trends in student oragnizations and activities that there was no conclusive evidence either for or against an increase in interest toward activities. Some indication was given that change might be more apparent on larger campuses. In yet another study, Dressel (1965) found that married students are not so active as participants in extracurricular activities as are single students.

Two studies are relevant to a correlation of student participation and academic ability or achievement. Barger and Hall (1965) found a relationship between the types of activities in which students participated and their scholastic test scores. Students with lower scores turned to social and athletic activity for their satisfaction. In contrast, students with high scores tended to turn to political and preprofessional activities. These trends were similar for both males and females. Hartnett (1965) found no relationship between the extent of extracurricular participation and scholastic performance.

RELATED RESEARCH. Although there has been a dearth of research in the specific area of student activities, educators agree with Koile (1966b), Hardee (1962), and Berdie (1966) that alteration of traditional programs should be based on well-founded premises, including basic knowledge about student characteristics and the institutional climate of learning. This can be done by utilizing related studies in the behavioral sciences and adapting these to on-going programs for satisfying the needs of a particular campus.

In recent years considerable attention has been given to the study of college students, the college environment, and the interaction of student and campus. Studies by Jacob (1957), Eddy (1959), Goldsen and others (1960), in addition to Sanford's (1962) monumental volume on the American college, have added much to our present knowledge of the college student. The most recent contributions edited by Dennis and Kauffman (1966) and Lloyd-Jones and Estrin (1967) are further examples of the stimulating literature currently being written about the contemporary student. Related research using instruments to assess the campus environmental forces (Stern, 1963; Astin, 1965; McConnell & Heist, 1959) provides new methods for measuring the potential as well as the impact of student activities programs on students. Additionally, the identification of campus subcultures reported by Trow (1962), Pace (1966), and Peterson (1966) has provided new insights for explicit program efforts directed toward the needs of specific elements of the student population. In recent reviews of research in guidance and student personnel work, Winfrey and Feder (1965) and Kehas (1966) have cited these systematic investigations of student and environmental characteristics as a significant trend. Yonge (1965) has called these developments a significant breakthrough in the sociopsychological study of the student and of the various institutional forces which have an impact upon the student in higher education.

Even a casual reading of the various stages of a history of the extracurriculum will reveal no uniformity among different colleges or within a single college concerning the content, objectives, or emphasis of such programs. As is true of every other part of American education, student life or activities are changeable in response to the influence of American culture as it has moved from a rural agricultural setting to a predominantly urban industrial complex. Collegiate extracurriculum has changed not only because of increasing affluence, industrialization, and world political leadership but also under the impact of the increased understanding of how to influence human development in the achievement of American ways of living. It will continue to be dynamic as a result of the application of research findings on the learning and developmental processes to college life. It would not overstate our case to predict that the extracurriculum will increase its influence on the socialization, emotional development, and intellectual attainment of more college students.

E. G. Williamson
Donald Zander
University of Minnesota

References

American Association of University Professors. "Statement on Faculty Responsibility for Academic Freedom of Students." *AAUP B* 50:254–7; 1964.

American Civil Liberties Union. "Academic Freedom and Civil Liberties of Students in Colleges and Universities." *AAUP B* 48:110–5; 1962.

Anderson, Gary. "Focus on Fraternities—Postscript or Prologue?" *J Assn Deans Administrators Student Affairs* 3:3–16; 1965.

Astin, Alexander W. *Who Goes Where to College.* SRA, 1965. 125p.

Bakken, Clarence J. "The Legal Basis for Student Personnel Work." APGA, Student Personnel Series No. 2, 1961. 44p.

Barger, Ben, and Hall, Everett. "Relation of Expected College Activities to Ability and Achievement." *J Col Student Personnel* 6:300–4; 1965.

Berdie, Ralph. "Characteristics of Students Today." In *Urbanization and the College Student.* U Minnesota, 1966. 18p.

Bloland, Paul. "The Personnel Worker as a Group Adviser." *J Col Student Personnel* 2:43–7; 1961(a).

Bloland, Paul "A New Concept in Student Government." *J H Ed* 32:94–7; 1961(b).

Bloland, Paul. "Student Group Advising in Higher Education." APGA, Student Personnel Series No. 8, 1967. 32p.

Brubacher, John. *Basis for Policy in Higher Education.* McGraw-Hill, 1965. 144p.

Brubacher, John, and Rudy, Willis. *Higher Education in Transition.* Harper, 1958. 390p.

Buerk, John A. "Changing Role of the Protestant Campus Minister." *J Assn Deans Administrators Student Affairs* 4:29–30; 1965.

Butler, William. "Forces at Work in Development of Fraternities." *J Col Student Personnel*. 6:240–3; 1965.

Butler, William. "Student Revolt for Freedoms." *J Col Student Personnel* 6:324–30; 1965.

Carey, John J. "Jerusalem and Athens: The Religious Worker on the College Campus." *Personnel Guid J* 40:426–31; 1962.

Cox, Archibald. "Can Civil Disobedience be Legally Justified? *Col U Bus* 40:53–8; 1966.

Davidson, Carl. "Toward Student Syndicalism." *New Left Notes* September: 11–2; 1966.

Dennis, Lawrence, and Kauffman, Joseph. (Eds.) *The College and the Student*. ACE, 1966. 390p.

DeVane, William. *Higher Education in Twentieth Century America*. Harvard U Press, 1965. 181p.

Dewey, John. *Reconstruction in Philosophy*. Holt, 1920. 177p.

Dressel, Fred B. "Logic, Research and the Married College Student." *Personnel Guide J* 43:920–4; 1965.

Eddy, Edward D., Jr. *The College Influences on Student Character*. ACE, 1959. 183p.

Eddy, Edward D., Jr. "The New Student in the Old College." *Sch Soc* 90:135–7; 1962.

Farnsworth, Dana. "Who Really Helps Our Students?" In Sutherland, R. L. (Ed.) *Personality Factors on the College Campus*. Hogg Foundation, 1958. p. 93–109.

Gallagher, Buell G. "Student Unrest: What Are the Causes? What Does it Mean?" *Col U Bus* 38:51–5; 1965.

Gardner, John W. "Agenda for College and Universities: Higher Education in an Innovative Society." *J H Ed* 36:359–65; 1965.

Goldsen, Rose K., and others. *What College Students Think*. Van Nostrand, 1960. 208p.

Goldworn, William J. "Student Violations of Criminal Statutes or Ordinance—the Dean's Role." *J Assn Deans Administrators Student Affairs* 2:33–5; 1965.

Gould, Samuel B. "The Role of the Student in the Life of the University." *J Assn Deans Administrators Student Affairs* 4:53–8; 1966.

Greenfield, Jeff. "The Teach-in Lessons." *Am Student* 1:3–5; 1965.

Hardee, Meluena D. "Research on College Students: The Student Personnel Worker's View." *Ed Rec* 43:132–8; 1962.

Hartnett, Rodney T. "Involvement in Extracurricular Activities as a Factor in Academic Performance." *J Col Student Personnel* 6:272–4; 1965.

Heist, Paul A. "Intellect and Commitment: The Faces of Discontent." In Knorr, Owen A., and Minter, W. John. (Eds.) *Order and Freedom on the Campus*. Western Interstate Commission for Higher Education, 1965. p. 61–9.

Hoffman, Randall. "Encounter with Rockwell." *J Assn Deans Administrators Student Affairs* 3:13–8; 1965.

Jacob, Phillip. *Changing Values in College*. Harper, 1957. 174p.

Kauffman, Joseph. "The Time of the Student: Shall We Overcome?" In Dennis, Lawrence E., and Kauffman, Joseph. (Eds.) *The College and the Student*. ACE, 1966. p. 385–90.

Kehas, Chris D. "Theoretical Formulations and Related Research." *R Ed Res* 36:207–18; 1966.

Keniston, Kenneth. "How to Mount a Protest." Paper presented to the APA, September, 1966.

Klopf, Gordon J. *College Student Government*. Harper, 1960. 108p.

Koile, Earl A. "The University Can be a Personal Place." In *Urbanization and the College Student*. U Minnesota, 1966(a). p. 51–73.

Koile, Earl A. "Student Affairs: Forever the Bridesmaid" *J Assn Deans Administrators Student Affairs* 4:65–72; 1966(b).

Koile, Earl A., and others. "Higher Education Programs." *R Ed Res* 36:233–55; 1966.

Landahl, Charles "Toward Campus Enrichment." *J Assn Deans Administrators Student Affairs* 4:29–31; 1966.

Leonard, Eugenie A. *The Origins of Personnel Services in American Education*. U Minnesota Press, 1956. 146p.

Liebert, Roland. (Ed.) *Student Conduct and Social Freedom*. U.S. National Student Association, 1966. 120p.

Lipset, Seymour M., and Wolin, Sheldon S. *The Berkeley Student Revolt*. Anchor, 1965. 585p.

Lloyd-Jones, Esther M., and Estrin, Herman A. (Eds.) *The American Student and His College*. Houghton, 1967. 379p.

Lunsford, Terry F. "The Free Speech Crisis at Berkeley 1964–1965: Some Issues for Social and Legal Research." U California, Berkeley, 1965. 255p. (Mimeographed.)

Mallery, David. *Ferment on the Campus*. Harper, 1966. 147p.

Mathews, Richard. "Society's Just Got to Go—We All Know That." *Saturday R* 49:74–6; 1966.

McConnell, T. R. "The Attainment of Individuality." In *Urbanization and the College Student*, U Minnesota, 1966. p. 35–50.

McConnell, T. R., and Heist, Paul A. "Do Students Make the College?" *Col U* 34:442–52; 1959.

Monypenny, Phillip. "Student Academic Freedom." *J Assn Deans Administrators Student Affairs* 2:3–9; 1965.

Moore, Forrest G. "The International Dimensions of the University—the Years Ahead." In Klopf, G. J. (Ed.) *College Student Personnel Work in the Years Ahead*. American College Personnel Association, Student Personnel Series No. 7. 1966. p. 46–53.

Mueller, Kate M. *Student Personnel Work in Higher Education*. Houghton, 1961. 562p.

National Society for the Study of Education. *Adapting the Secondary School Program to the Needs of Youth*. 52nd Yearbook, Part 1, NSSE. U Chicago Press, 1953. 316p.

Newcomb, Theodore M. "Student Peer Group Influence." In Sanford, N. (Ed.) *The American College*. Wiley, 1962. p. 469–88.

Olsen, LeRoy A. "Living Learning Units." *J H Ed* 35:83–6; 1964(a).

Olsen, LeRoy A. "Students Reactions to Living, Learning Residence Halls." *J Col Student Personnel* 6:29–31; 1964(*b*).

Pace, C. Robert. "Implications of Differences in Campus Atmosphere." In Sutherland, R. L. (Ed.) *Personality Factors on the College Campus.* Hogg Foundation, 1958. p. 43–61.

Pace, C. Robert, "Perspectives on the Student and His College." In Dennis, L. C., and Kauffman, J. P. (Eds.) *The College and the Student.* ACE, 1966. p. 76–100.

Peterson, Richard E. *The Scope of Organized Student Protest in 1964–65.* ETS, 1966. 48p.

Potter, Paul. "Student Discontent and Campus Reform." In Knorr, O. A., and Minter, W. J. (Eds.) *Order and Freedom on the Campus.* Western Interstate Commission for Higher Education, 1965. p. 71–9.

Pruitt, Witton. "College Students, Their Community, and Their Activities." In Klopf, Gordon J. (Ed.) *College Student Personnel Work in the Years Ahead.* American College Personnel Association, Student Personnel Series No. 7, 1966. p. 10–21.

Quigley, Thomas E. "The Campus: Lab for a World Community." *Int Ed and Cultural Exchange* Spring: 43–7; 1966.

Reich, Helen. "A Survey of Student Opinion on Campus Social Life." *J Col Student Personnel* 3:11–6; 1961.

Riker, Harold C. "The Changing Role of Student Housing." In Klopf, G. J. (Ed.) *College Student Personnel Work in the Years Ahead.* American College Personnel Association, Student Personnel Series No. 7, 1966. p. 69–76.

Riker, Harold C. "College Housing as Learning Centers." APGA, Student Personnel Series No. 3. 1965.

Roskens, Ronald W., and Hansheimer, Thomas W. "For Student Personnel Work: Our Desideratum" *J H Ed* 32:402–8; 1961.

Rudolph, Frederick. *The American College and University.* Vintage, 1965. 496p.

Rudolph, Frederick. "Changing Patterns of Authority and Influence." In Knorr, Owen A., and Minter, W. John. (Eds.) *Order and Freedom on the Campus.* Western Interstate Commission for Higher Education, 1956. p. 1–10.

Sanford, Nevitt. (Ed.) *The American College.* Wiley, 1962. 1034p.

Sanford, Nevitt. *Self and Society.* Atherton, 1966. 355p.

Schoen, Walter T. "Clarification and Revelation of Areas of Student and Faculty Responsibility." *J Col Student Personnel* 6:244–6; 1965.

Somers, Eldon K. "Student Government: Points to Ponder." *J Assn Deans Administrators Student Affairs* 4:23–5; 1966.

Stark, Matthew. "Human Relations Programs: Social Reconstruction Through Collegiate Extracurricular Activities." *Nat Assn Women Deans Counselors* 30:82–5; 1966.

Stern, George G. "The Intellectual Climate of College Environments." *Harvard Ed R* 33:5–41; 1963.

Strickland, Donald A. "In Loco Parentis—Legal Mots and Morals." *J Col Student Personnel* 6:335–40; 1965.

Stroup, Herbert. *Toward A Philosophy of Student Activities.* U Minnesota Press, 1965. 175p.

Taylor, Harold. "American Idealism, 1956." *Saturday R* 48:14–6; 1965.

Trow, Martin. "Student Cultures and Administrative Action." In Sutherland, R. L. (Ed.) *Personality Factors on the College Campus.* Hogg Foundation, 1962. p. 203–25.

United States National Student Association. *Codification of Policy, 1966.* The Association, 1966. 200p.

Van Alstyne, William W. "Banning the Campus Speaker." *Nation* 196:267–8; 1963.

Van Alystyne, William W. "Student Academic Freedom and Rule-Making Powers of Public Universities: Some Constitutional Considerations." *Law in Transition Q* 2:1–34; 1965.

Williamson, Edmund G. "Education and the Extracurriculum." In *General Education.* 51st Yearbook, NSSE. U Chicago Press, 1952. p. 230–49.

Williamson, Edmund G. *Student Personnel Services in Colleges and Universities.* McGraw-Hill, 1961. 462p.

Williamson, Edmund G. "Do Students Have Academic Freedom?" *Col U* 39:466–87; 1964.

Williamson, Edmund G. "Establishing Student Freedoms and Rights." *J Assn Deans Administrators Student Affairs* 3:9–13; 1965.

Williamson, Edmund G., and Cowan, John L. "The Role of the President in the Desirable Enactment of Academic Freedom for Students." *Ed Rec* 46: 351–72; 1965.

Williamson, Edmund G., and Cowan, John L. *The American Students Freedom of Expression.* U Minnesota Press, 1966. 170p.

Williamson, Edmund G., and others. *A Study of Participation in College Activities.* U Minnesota Press, 1954. 99p.

Winfrey, James K., and Feder, Daniel D. "Noninstructional Services." *R Ed Res* 35:318–34; 1965.

Wise, W. Max. *They Come for the Best of Reasons.* ACE, 1958. 47p.

Wrenn, C. Gilbert. *Student Personnel Work in College.* Ronald, 1951. 508p.

Yonge, George D. "Students." *R Ed Res* 35:253–63; 1965.

Zander, Donald R. "Are Students Reacting Against Campus Activities?" *J Col Student Personnel* 5: 103–7; 1963.

STUDENT ORGANIZATIONS AND ACTIVITIES: ELEMENTARY AND SECONDARY

Those experiences now commonly called student activities and traditionally known as extracurricular activities are also called extraclass or nonclass activities, school-life activities, and the cocurriculum. Good's *Dictionary of Education* (1959) suggests that the term "extraclass activities" is gaining acceptance in order to establish a contrast with the term "curriculum," which now encompasses what was once considered "extracurricular." Colleges and universities and many secondary schools currently use the term "student activities," whereas elementary schools sometimes use the term "school-life activities." Student-activity enthusiasts usually prefer the term "cocurriculum," which stresses the importance of activities in relation to classroom studies.

Despite the lack of a precise term or definition, everyone agrees that student activities are likely to be more student-centered than classes are. Such activities include athletic programs, clubs, student councils, student publications, debate teams, assemblies, homeroom participation, social events sponsored by classes, and camps, as well as artistic, dramatic, and musical organizations under the guidance of school leaders. Student activities, especially in high schools, are usually extraclass and carry no Carnegie Unit credit. In some junior and senior high schools, however, experience in music, art, drama, and newswriting is now incorporated into the regular school program as courses for which credit may be earned. In elementary schools, pupil activities are generally part of classroom experience.

On all levels, several significant characteristics distinguish student activities—in theory if not always in practice—from formal classwork. In student activities, students assume responsible positions of leadership; pupils' spontaneous interests and immediate needs determine affiliations and experiences; and the teacher-sponsor is a mentor or guide rather than an instructor.

Academicians and the general public sometimes describe student activities, especially athletics, as "play" and classroom studies as "work" (Bush, 1959). Student activities constitute the major ingredient of the organized social life of the school and are analogous to the organized social life of the community. Children and adolescents learn skills, develop understanding, and find outlets for their interests and abilities in student activities, just as adults derive similar benefits from participating in community organizations. As members of such voluntary associations, young people and adults may also be entertained, although entertainment is generally a by-product of membership in an organization rather than a primary purpose.

HISTORY. The early history of student activities is obscure and perhaps unimportant. Student activities in ancient Greece, in medieval European universities, in seventeenth- and eighteenth-century England, and in nineteenth-century America have been cited as forerunners of present-day extracurricular activities in the United States. [For a summary of this history, see the article of Faunce (1960).] The effort to trace the movement to antiquity is an attempt to assign historic roots, which does not minimize the significance of student activities sponsored by schools as a peculiarly twentieth-century American innovation.

Student activities in earlier European schools have not given rise to extensive programs of student activities in present-day European schools. In general, school authorities in Europe today hold graduation exercises, permit occasional class parties, and take student groups on field and camping trips as extensions of classroom studies, but youth organizations are ordinarily sponsored by social agencies other than the schools. Intramural sports have, however, been an important part of schooling in England's public schools since the eighteenth century. Although English schools, both private and public, also sponsor other kinds of student activities, their programs are not nearly so extensive as those of American high schools. Since the Soviet schools are modeled on those of western Europe, the recent sponsorship by a few Soviet schools of what are called student activities in the West, as well as the use of Komsomol and Young Pioneer groups in these activities, is an interesting development (Korotov, 1964).

In the United States, student activities have, however, been an accepted part of the school program for many years. Acceptance of such activities came slowly. At the turn of the century, only a few American schools sponsored athletic teams, musical organizations, and literary societies. This was the *sub rosa* period: athletic teams and other informally organized student groups usually functioned without the sanction or encouragement of school officials. Gradually these groups entered the school "by the back door"—student leaders persuaded principals to give them a place to meet or to keep athletic equipment. Recognizing the need, administrators finally began to provide faculty advisers for student activities. This growing acceptance of school activities is reflected in the 1918 report on the "Cardinal Principles of Secondary Education," which recommended that high school principals appoint a Director of Preparation for Leisure, a title later supplanted by that of Director of Activities.

Prior to 1910, interscholastic athletics seem to have comprised the major part of the student activity program; but from 1910 on, and accelerating rapidly during the 1920's, nonathletic activities increased. In 1933, Reavis and Van Dyke, tracing the development of student activities in four high schools in and around Chicago, found that between 1910 and 1920 nonathletic activities increased by 60 percent and between 1920 and 1930 by 340 percent. Activities for girls increased so markedly that by 1928 participation of girls exceeded that of boys. Studies of student activities since 1930 have also shown that more girls than boys participate in most high schools (Tompkins, 1950).

Student activities attained a status worthy of serious study during the 1920's. The twenty-fifth Yearbook of the National Society for the Study of Education (1926) included Leonard V. Koos' survey *Extra-curricular Activities*. In 1917, Elbert K. Fretwell, sometimes called the "father of extracurricular activities," offered the first course devoted to extra-curricular activities at Columbia University. He also wrote one of the first textbooks on the subject (Fretwell, 1931). In 1921, Harry C. McKown enrolled in Professor Fretwell's course. In subsequent years, McKown became a leader in the activities movement. He edited *School Activities,* a journal founded in 1929, and was the author of many books about various student activities. (Professor Fretwell died in 1962; his admirer and distinguished student, Dr. McKown, died two years later.)

Incorporation of student activities into school schedules is further evidence of the increased acceptance of such activities as an integral part of American education. During the late 1920's many rural schools and a few urban schools began scheduling an activity period as part of the school day. In 1930, reports from 224 high schools indicated that 32.1 percent of them had adopted this practice. Between 1930 and 1945, the number of large schools scheduling activity periods increased slowly. By 1950 a study of 42 high schools in 22 states revealed that 70 percent of them had an activity period (Tompkins, 1950). Expert opinion holds that the incorporation of activities, particularly sessions of the student council, into the school day—sometimes as a class—has spread since 1950 (Van Pool, 1967). The experts recognize that the existence of an activity period does not preclude activities taking place before and after school, but they believe it helps to make the activity program more accessible to some students.

The student activity movement has spread into the junior high school, which tends to emulate the senior high school. This tendency has been facilitated by the diffusion of a "teenage subculture" in recent decades, which includes preadolescents 10 to 12 years old. Dances and interscholastic athletics as well as clubs, Junior Red Cross, student councils, and other activities have become increasingly common in junior high schools. In like manner, the elementary school has been influenced by the activity movement. The lower schools have begun to sponsor student councils, Red Cross councils, and safety patrol councils; some elementary schools have also organized science clubs, camps, and library groups within the last few years.

Student activities have become an accepted part of American schools for many reasons. The rapid urbanization and industrialization of the United States freed youths from home and farm chores and gave them time to engage in outside activities. Until recently, because not many community agencies sponsored youth programs, schools felt obliged to provide them. Progressive educators who accepted John Dewey's concept of educating the "whole child" through "experiences" also encouraged school leaders to sponsor student activities. Dewey's philosophy was reinforced by psychologists' teachings of organismic psychology and by their stress upon the developmental tasks of youth. Many principals and teachers may have seen in student activities a means by which some of the reluctant learners, trapped in school by compulsory education, could have their interest in attending school stimulated. Furthermore, pupils, parents, and the public liked the activity program. Parents saw student activities as being significant to their children's development of "personality" and of social skills needed in a bureaucratic society. Finally, with some reluctance, administrators and teachers agreed that student activities made valuable contributions to learning and to school spirit. In the last decade or so, many educational leaders have also recognized that such activities help to counteract feelings of anonymity and lack of identity in a "mass society."

STATED OBJECTIVES. Writers of textbooks usually state that the general objectives of student activities are essentially the same as those of education as articulated, for example, in the "Seven Cardinal Principles" (Kilzer & others, 1956). By studying authoritative statements written between 1936 and 1948, Tompkins (1950) identified education for leisure as the objective most often mentioned at that time. McKown (1959) said that the primary end of student activities is "good citizenship." One hundred and sixty-nine principals believed that the most valuable contribution of student activities was the opportunities they provided for practicing democratic principles (Miller, 1954). A recent NEA publication cited two similar purposes: to help pupils learn skills of human relationships and to give them practice in behaving democratically (Graham, 1966). Obviously, there are other desirable objectives, such as to educate for international and intergroup understanding, to provide opportunities for adolescents and adults to work together as partners, to increase identification with and loyalty to the school, and to enrich the curriculum.

Critics agree that no activity program sponsored by the schools should be antithetical to the general goals of education, but the schools may regret the failure to identify specific aims which can be more readily achieved in student activities than in the formal program of studies. They argue that general objectives point to an ultimate goal, but because they are so generalized, they do not identify precise aims or suggest ways of measuring outcomes. Crum (1955) has demonstrated a way to express relatively specific aims. The following statements are adapted from his examples:

School Objective: To enable students to develop initiative and assume responsibility.

Pupil Objective(s): To start and to plan their own projects; to assume obligations imposed by activities.

Over a third of a century ago, Tillinghast (1930) suggested that aims be stated specifically in terms of the behavioral qualities desired and that observed actions of participants in student activities be recorded in order to determine the degree of success or failure in achieving the desired behavior. Leaders of a group, for example, can determine objectively the number of members who speak in a group discussion, but they may have difficulty determining whether students are developing initiative (Graham, 1966).

Lack of clear objectives has been a handicap to the evaluation of student activities. Whether a pupil is being successfully educated to use leisure creatively and "wisely" or to be a "good" citizen cannot easily be measured objectively because the goals are distant and the terms are value-laden. Whether a pupil has learned democratic principles and skills of human relations from his opportunities to apply them in student activities also defies evaluation, unless the general objectives are broken down into the specific behavior patterns and skills that pupils are expected to demonstrate in a particular activity. The result of the failure to spell out definitive objectives is that most evaluations have of necessity been limited to overall judgments.

EVALUATIONS. Evaluation provides estimates of the growth and progress made in attaining stated objectives. Few administrators have systematically evaluated their student activity programs. A survey of 421 Indiana high schools revealed that only 3 faculties out of 10 and only 2 student bodies out of 10 had studied their club program in an organized way during the past three years and that three-fourths of the schools had never systematically evaluated it (Jung & Fox, 1952). Of 10 selected Texas schools, only one evaluated its program yearly, and the method used there was simply to require recommendations from sponsors (Hamilton, 1960). A study of Oklahoma schools showed that fewer than one-half of the schools had evaluated their student activity programs during the preceding five years (Mullins, 1962). The report of a New Jersey school, after a study of its activity program from 1929 until 1961, concluded that part of the success of its program was attributable to evaluation which led to dropping or adding activities (Walther, 1962). Where evaluations did occur, evaluators seemed to be concerned with opinions and judgments about the strengths and weaknesses of the local program.

Determining the strengths and weaknesses of a program is important in building a better program. Several instruments have been developed to aid schools in making such evaluations systematic. Section E of the *Evaluative Criteria* (National Study of Secondary School Evaluation, 1960) is divided into 14 aspects of student activities that should be studied. These aspects include all student activities, plus items relating to finances, organization, special characteristics, and general evaluation. Hearn (1966) proposes eight major categories of student activities and a general section. He lists appropriate criteria for each category, followed by evaluative questions.

Frederick (1959) suggests that such overall judgments should be supplemented for supervisory or improvement purposes. He proposes several additional types of evaluations: studies of specific activities, participants with special characteristics, costs, quality of sponsors, load of sponsors, community needs, and specific aims. Useful suggestions and/or instruments for evaluating specific activities are found in McAllester (1955), Warkow (1942), Anderson (1963), and others. The techniques used in several studies reported below (see *Trends in Research*) supply models for evaluations of pupils with special characteristics. Hand's instrument (1949) is useful in evaluating costs. Evaluation techniques to study sponsors and community needs probably are yet to be developed.

Few of the reported studies made at the local level have attempted to measure changes in behavior patterns of participants. An exception is Mayberry's (1931) comparison of pretest and posttest scores of student council members on the Upton-Chassell Citizenship Scale with those of a paired control group. He found that after a period of participation the student council members had gained more in civic values than had the control group. Another exception is Martin's (1961) study of how a junior high school activity program enriches the curriculum. He reports that from 24 to 26 percent of the experiences that pupils had in seventh-grade mathematics and science were reinforced by the activity sponsored by the teacher.

In this neglected area of measurement, observer-participant methods, sociometrics, anecdotal records, open-ended questions, participant reaction forms, and systematic judgments of experts using checklists and rating scales can be useful. A form developed by Erickson (1965) to analyze the extent to which seniors in 30 Minnesota high schools influenced decision-making in student activities may also be helpful.

Many schools that have no systematic evaluations may have outstanding programs and specific activities which are of excellent quality. Nevertheless, evaluations are important not only in refining methods in order to achieve aims but also in persuading skeptical persons of the value of student activities.

TRENDS IN RESEARCH. Much research in this field, especially during the 1930's and 1940's, has tended to be descriptive in nature and unsophisticated in design. Surveys and questionnaires were the chief instruments used, and the results were not usually tested for significance or analyzed in depth.

Many writers simply reported appraisals of student activities given by pupils, parents, teachers, alumni, or principals. For example, Eells (1939) found that 75 percent of 17,000 pupils in 192 high schools throughout the nation said that their participation in activities was valuable. Another survey, reported by Trump (1944), disclosed that 3,525 high school pupils, 435 alumni, 214 sponsors, and 994 parents believed that the chief values derived from participation in activities were related to developing friendships, interest in school, sportsmanship, school loyalty, social graces, better use of leisure, pupil-teacher relations, and tolerance and to acquiring information not gained in classes. Despite their limitations, these surveys and others less extensive in coverage served to convince school leaders and parents of the educational values of student activities.

Other studies have demonstrated the superiority of those who were engaged in student activities over those who were not, in such respects as socioeconomic status, intelligence, school grades, educational aspirations, and leadership (Brown, 1933). In the late 1940's, researchers who rejected the implicit assumption that taking part in student activities accounted for some of the differences between participants and nonparticipants looked to other reasons. Some of them examined the costs of membership in activities (Hand, 1949, 1951); others saw discriminatory practices in the social structure of the high school (Hollingshead, 1949).

Still other early studies attempted to discover whether participation in athletics affected the scholarship of the participant. Several researchers (Cormany, 1935) concluded that the scholarship of athletes did not differ appreciably from that of nonathletes. Cormany used standardized tests as the measure of scholarship; the other investigators used teachers' grades. Many educators refused to accept these findings. Although the methodology used in these studies was open to question on several counts, critics usually attacked teachers' grades as the only criterion of scholarship. They further suggested that teachers might show favoritism in grading and pointed out that the refusal to permit student athletes with low grades to participate in athletics resulted in biased comparisons with nonathletes.

Like these early studies, recent research is concerned with some of the same issues and frequently utilizes questionnaires and rating scales, but methodology has generally been improved. In some of the current research, one finds a significant conceptualization of the role of student activities in the social life of the school. In turn, the social life of the school is viewed as being important to academic learning and educational aspirations, as well as to future success in "real" life. Other recent studies, however, seem to lack this orientation.

In the tradition of earlier studies of values as reported by teachers and students, Hamilton (1960) studied teacher and student ratings of the educational value of student activities in 24 high schools. He found a high correlation (.84) between these ratings. Both groups rated the activity program as being of above-average value in meeting youth needs pertaining to socialization, mental health, reasoning ability, guidance, and preparation for future education. They rated the program as being of "average value" in contributing to physical health, life in the natural and scientific environments, choice of occupation, and leisure. An analysis of variance showed no differences in valuations based on sex and community or interactions of these two variables. Race, however, was a significant influence. Whites consistently rated the school activity program lower than did Negroes. This finding, coupled with studies of dropouts, makes a survey of the extent of participation in 25 Negro high schools in Alabama worthy of note. Howell (1958) found a range of from 20 to 92 percent participation in various Negro high schools.

Studies of the relationship between academic performance and participation in student activities, especially athletics, have continued. Eidsmoe (1963) found that 168 basketball players and 592 football players in Iowa high schools had higher grades than did other members of their classes. Keating (1961) found similar results. Nevertheless, disbelief in the overall benefit of athletics to the academic program is evident in other studies. Coleman (1961a, 1961b) suggests that the rewards given athletes as opposed to those given scholars divert adolescent energies in general—and of the brightest boys in particular—from the pursuit of scholarship.

Although not concerned with the general effects on a student body of rewards to athletes vis à vis scholars, studies by Schafer and Amer (1966) support the contention that athletes get slightly better grades than nonathletes. These researchers matched 152 pairs of athletes and nonathletes on four variables: the fathers' occupational class and the students' intelligence test scores, choices of high school curriculums, and grade-point averages in junior high school. They found that 56.6 percent of the athletes exceeded the matched nonathletes in academic performance and that the median grade-point average of athletes was slightly higher than that of nonathletes. Not only do these data fail to support the hypothesis of athletic participation exerting a negative influence upon scholarship, but they also fail to support the assumption that those who spend a great deal of time in several sports, or in major sports such as football and basketball, earn lower grades. Again, boys who gave a considerable amount of time to various sports or who took part in major sports were found to have slightly higher grades than nonathletes. Although only a few boys from any social group had lower grades than the matched nonathletes and most boys seemed to benefit academically from participation, boys from blue-collar homes who had lower-than-average intelligence test scores and who were enrolled in noncollege preparatory courses exceeded their control counterparts in grade-point averages to a greater extent than did bright, middle-class boys enrolled in college preparatory courses.

Another study, by Rehberg and Schafer (1966), sought to determine whether the extent of participation in interscholastic sports affects the chances that boys will continue their education beyond high school. The authors examined responses to a career-orientation questionnaire of 785 twelfth-grade boys in three public and three parochial high schools in Pennsylvania. After treating the results statistically and holding social status and parental encouragement constant, they concluded that athletes in their sample, when compared with nonathletes, expected to attend college "somewhat more often" and to complete college "considerably more often."

Hauser (1965) was also interested in the relationship of participation in student activities to students' goals. He postulated four theoretical types: "Activists," who had good grades and belonged to one or more student activities; "Students," who had good grades but did not take part in activities; "Joiners," whose grades were average or below and who belonged to one or more activities; and "Uninvolved," who had average or below-average grades and did not belong to student activities. He studied the responses of 154 high school seniors who had completed an Adolescent Survey Questionnaire prior to graduation and a Mail-Back Questionnaire after graduation. After dividing these seniors into the four types on the basis of their school records, he found the Activists more likely and the Uninvolved least likely to be integrated into school life, to hold high self-concepts, to choose college preparatory work in high school, not to be bored in school, to have upper-white-collar occupational aspirations, and to enter college. The Students and Joiners were less likely than the Activists, but more likely than the Uninvolved, to share these attitudes and goals.

Since students who quit school are usually not integrated into the life of the school, their participation, or lack of participation, in student activities is of interest to persons seeking reasons for their leaving school. A four-year study made in the Chicago area (Thomas, 1954), a review of the literature from 1949 to 1956 (Tesseneer & Tesseneer, 1958), studies in Illinois (Livingston, 1966), in Louisiana (Bertrand, 1962), in Oregon (Pierce, 1965), and in Kansas (Bell, 1964) confirm a relationship between lack of participation in student activities and dropping out of school. Schafer and Polk (1967) found that delinquents also participated in student activities less than nondelinquents did. These last-named authors therefore recommended to the President's Commission on Law Enforcement and the Administration of Justice that extracurricular activities be made available to more youth. They urged diversified activities that might appeal to low-income, potential delinquents.

Other researchers, interested in the gifted rather than in dropouts and delinquents, contend that talent is lost if college entrance requirements stress only academic achievement and ignore applicants' achievements in student activities. Holland and Richards (1965), studying the high school records of 7,262 college freshmen in 24 colleges and universities, concluded that the academic and nonacademic dimensions are relatively independent measures of talent. In a similar study, Holland and Nichols (1964) found that records of extracurricular activities of high-scoring Merit Finalists were needed to predict those who would be outstanding. Using 60 items from an activities index that discriminated between high and low achievers at Ripon College, Behring (1966) developed a scale called APAS, which he found predicts college students' grade-point averages ($r = .35$) almost as well as the College Entrance Examination Board verbal test ($r = .36$) and better than the College Entrance Examination Board mathematics test ($r = .13$). As if in anticipation of the day when colleges and employers will ask for a score on student activities similar to the grade-point average, Lawson (1959) developed a method of quantity-quality record keeping of participation that yields a score comparable to a grade-point average.

Finger (1966) found a relationship between achievement in student activities and in occupations other than the professions. He concluded that if colleges are not to exclude those who will become successful businessmen, they must consider applicants' achievements in student activities in college admission policies. A study of aviation cadets' records of participation in student activities, especially in athletics, revealed that these data predicted peer group leadership ratings of these cadets better than chance (Krumboltz & others, 1959).

These studies suggest that student activities deserve more attention than they usually command from educational leaders. Taba (1955) was one of the earliest exponents of the view that student activities constitute, in effect, a practical laboratory of human relations in which pupils learn concepts and attitudes, both good and bad. Mallery (1962) describes a school in which students were learning through student activities to be tolerant, socially sensitive, cooperative, secure, responsible, and self-directing. Gordon (1957) found more bad than good in a high school in which students, dominated by cliques, competed intensely for prestige. In this school, student activities served the function of differentiating the students into a prestige hierarchy. Gordon concluded that the social behavior of the students there was functionally related to the general status they attained in the social structure of the school.

Taba's research, completed in 1948, also demonstrated that the social climate of each school differs. It differs, she states, because the philosophy of school leaders and the nature of the school's population and parental influence differ. Although her book is outdated in some respects, it provides useful suggestions for action researchers and for faculties interested in improving their own program of activities (Taba, 1955).

Despite long-standing interest in adolescence and research on youth "subcultures," few social scientists have recognized the role that student activities play in the lives of young people. Several researchers have found that boys and girls who are liked by their peers come closer to realizing their academic potentials and behave better in classrooms than do boys and girls who are not liked by their peers (Schmuck & others, 1963). But these investigators have not delved into the influence of participation in student activities upon a student's being liked. In this respect, Gordon's study and that of Coleman are different from other studies, for they analyzed, among other things, the relationship of student activities to the adolescent status system (Coleman, 1961b). Some of their assumptions and conclusions are open to question; but their findings, especially Coleman's, which have been widely quoted, praised, and criticized, may direct attention to a neglected area of research.

Possibilities for research are indeed limitless. For example, Barker and Gump's study (1964) is one of the few that suggests a relationship between size of student body and quality and extent of participation. They found that students in small schools (83 to 151 pupils) are more likely than those in a large school (2,287 pupils) to take part in and to hold positions of "importance and responsibility" in student activities. Such findings suggest that the few large schools which have adopted the House Plan, or Oxford Plan, may increase the extent and quality of participation in student activities (*School Management*, 1962). By this plan, a large school is divided into several separate student bodies, each with its own administration, faculty, student activities, and the like.

Another illustration of the variety of approaches open to researchers is a study by Erickson (1965). After examining a representative sample of 30 Minnesota schools, he found that the wealth of the community is an index to participation in speech activities and journalism but not to other activities. He also concluded, from responses of students to questions about their share in making certain decisions, that they had little influence in controlling student activities.

As the number of researchers interested in aspects of the student activity program increases, their findings may suggest ways to improve the extent and quality of participation. But in interpreting these studies, school leaders should not confuse correlation with causation. The research on athletes, dropouts, delinquents, and other groups, for example, does not justify the conclusion that if a nonparticipant can be persuaded to join an organization, his behavior will change in other ways. Hopefully, he may develop his self-concept, improve his relations with his peers, stay in school, and raise his grades and his educational expectations; but he may not.

Many variables influence student behavior. Although sophisticated statistical techniques and improved research designs enable the investigator to find more reliable evidence today than he could even a few years ago, he still cannot control all the variables in a real-life situation. In studies of athletes' grades, for example, in which several such variables have been controlled, the researcher cannot adequately measure what may be the key variable—motivation. Other variables which possibly could have been measured but were not in the studies cited include: Do athletes cheat more than other students? Is the pressure of a grade-point average required for participation one source of motivation that slightly raises their grades? What attitudes and values that differ from those of other students do athletes bring with them into activities? Do athletes have greater physical stamina than other students before as well as after participation? Is this factor important to scholarship? Another variable is the community. Are the results of studies in a few schools typical of results that may be found in other schools? The possibility that such variables as these, rather than those held constant, have influenced results makes a cautious interpretation imperative.

Various benefits now suggested as outcomes of participation in student activities may, in fact, be evident largely because participation is so often limited to youths of above-average talents. The voluntary basis of most student activities creates an element of self-selection. Perhaps students who choose to participate are for some reason more strongly motivated to succeed in general. Nevertheless, all other things being equal, educators agree that those who take part in a genuinely educative student activity are generally better off for having done so.

RECENT DEVELOPMENTS. Since Sputnik, pressures to achieve academic excellence have diverted some pupils from their interest in student activities, but a survey of administrators' opinions shows that interscholastic athletics have not been adversely affected (Campbell, 1964a). The student council has more than held its own. The effects of academic competition upon other nonathletic activities have not been detrimental, however, in this respect; present-day student activities seem to have more serious purposes than heretofore.

One of these purposes is to encourage occupational interests of students. The well-established 4-H Clubs and Future Business Leaders, Future Farmers, Future Homemakers, and Future Teachers groups have been joined by new or recently activated organizations to stimulate vocational and avocational interests: the Future Physicians Club, founded in 1959, which requires students to work in hospitals; the Future Nurses; the Future Scientists of America, founded in 1960; library organizations; aeronautics, aerospace, rocket, astronomy, industrial arts, radio-electronics, and meteorology clubs. Such student groups are often provided with suggested programs by adult organizations.

Recently, however, a number of Soviet schools have begun doing much more to generate occupational interests through after-school activities than do American schools. These Soviet educators, while emphasizing the significance of work, devote three or four hours in the late afternoon to helping pupils learn the skills of the lathe operator, metalsmith, welder, mechanic, carpenter, construction designer, horticulturist, animal breeder, radio and electronics technician, and other occupations. Using extensive equipment, high school adolescents and even upper elementary school pupils, under the supervision of teachers, teach simple skills to children as young as first graders (Sukholinskii, 1963).

Another recent development in student activities in the United States is a concerted effort to improve competencies of students for work in activities. Leadership classes are becoming common. Each year tens of thousands of high school students attend workshops, conferences, and camps to learn more about journalism, music, drama, debating, student council operations, athletics, leadership, safety, and even cheerleading and baton twirling.

Students in activities are demonstrating seriousness of purpose in their commitment to serving others. The relatively new service-oriented Key Club, sponsored by Kiwanis, boasts thousands of high school chapters. Chapters of this club sponsor innumerable projects, from selling apples in order to buy shoes for poor children to attacking vandalism in school and community. Members of the National Honor Society, student councils, Key Clubs, and other groups tutor pupils who need help in their studies. High school students tape stories and comic strips for use in elementary schools and in schools for blind children. The exceptionally active Farmington (New Jersey) Youth Citizenship Building Project attracts adolescents and adults to its service projects for school and community. Adult and youth collaboration as partners in such programs is not very common, but such cooperation between generations represents a desirable new direction.

Student activities designed to further international understanding are also being stressed. Mock UN Assemblies for high school students are statewide affairs; the number of "sister schools" in foreign countries, pen pal clubs, and exchanges of exhibits and taped messages are increasing. Foreign students are studying in American high schools, and American students are studying in secondary schools abroad. Since 1956, the National Association of Student Councils has sponsored summer tours of Europe for selected high school students (Van Pool, 1963).

In addition to inviting foreigners to this country, students in a few schools have initiated "domestic student exchanges." They invite students from other regions of the United States to exchange places with them for about a week.

The number of student clubs involved in enriching the curriculum, particularly those devoted to mathematics and science, has also multiplied. In addition, participation in high school science fairs increased by an estimated twentyfold between 1954 and 1963.

In junior high schools, school leaders have welcomed the growing popularity of science fairs and of Junior Great Books Clubs, but many rue the spread of interscholastic activities into the junior high schools. In 1962, the Colorado State Junior High School Principals' Study Group at its Estes Park retreat made 16 recommendations that in general called for less activity in athletics, especially interscholastic games and drill teams, and in graduation exercises.

Recent changes and developments in specific student activities are these: The student council has gained status to the extent that it rivals athletic teams in conferring prestige to members. Many such councils now have written constitutions, use parliamentary procedures in meetings, and have the power to charter, coordinate, and supervise clubs. A number of councils require annual reports of activities from these clubs. The reports are used to justify extensions or revocations of charters. On the other hand, the idea of a student "government" has been replaced by that of faculty and student cooperation, and student courts are becoming less common. All-school assemblies are held less frequently, sometimes because of lack of facilities. More schools than formerly are introducing diversified assemblies for boys only or girls only, for those interested in specific subjects or for those in a single academic class.

The administration of activity programs has generally improved, partly because of the support given to principals by activities associations in a number of states (Weldy, 1964) and partly because more schools now have directors of activities. Although a principal is generally recognized as a key person in administering the activity program, a director of activities helps to assure improved coordination and supervision. In many schools, administrators have also instituted better financial accounting systems.

Administrators, however, have had to face thorny legal issues in the last decade. A marked increase in teenage marriages has led a number of school boards to forbid married students to take part in activity programs. Such rules have been challenged in court by plaintiffs in Texas, Michigan, Ohio, and Utah.

In each case, the court ruled that the school board, and not the court, has the power to regulate schools and that the court may not interfere unless there is evidence that a board has abused its authority (Bolmeier, 1965). In none of these cases did the court review the wisdom of the rule. From the school administrator's point of view, good arguments can be made for and against allowing married students to take part in student activities (Davis & Lofton, 1964). The decisions in these cases indicate, however, that in most jurisdictions courts tend to regard student activities as a privilege, not a vested right (Clare, 1965). In short, they do not see student activities as part of the regular school curriculum.

Another legal issue that has provoked concern in recent years is that of the liability of teachers and school board members in the event of injuries incurred during participation in both class and out-of-class activities. A teacher may be held liable for another's bodily harm if he is judged to have been negligent and not to have exercised reasonable care. Although parental permissions to participate do not take away an injured minor's right to sue, they help to demonstrate that a teacher planned well and in advance for a particular event. The teacher is further protected if the school board has designated student activities that occur off campus as a part of the school's curriculum (Guerke, 1965). The use of private automobiles to transport students has also led to damage suits when accidents occur. In some instances, insurance companies have refused to pay damages if the owner of the automobile has accepted money for oil and gasoline from guest passengers (Cochrane, 1963).

CONTINUING PROBLEMS. Too many pupils are not participating in activities for school leaders to be content with their programs. The percentage of nonparticipants, as well as the reasons for their not participating, varies from school to school. Many students are eliminated by academic requirements of eligibility, after-school scheduling, prohibitive costs, physical and mental handicaps, or feelings of not being wanted in an activity. Few activity programs provide meaningful organizations serving a wide range of interests. Not many of them meet the needs of newcomers, the underprivileged, and pupils who are not socially well-adjusted. Nevertheless, some schools have been markedly successful in enrolling almost all students in activities. Such evidence suggests that, under enlightened leadership, ways can be found to attract most students to activity programs.

The quality of the leadership of administrators and sponsors is undoubtedly a key factor in developing outstanding activity programs. If school leaders do not provide adequate leadership, they may not have learned how to do so in teacher education programs. Campbell (1946b) reports that only 28 of 69 colleges and universities observed offered courses devoted to the study of the extracurriculum. Schools also rarely provide in-service training for sponsors of student activities.

Another factor which has been detrimental to activity programs is that most school districts do not finance them adequately. Students themselves must pay many costs; teachers are usually expected, without additional remuneration, to add the sponsoring of an activity to their regular teaching loads. Only when teachers are educated to be sponsors and when school systems support student activities financially are the greatest benefits likely to be gained by a substantial proportion of students.

Grace Graham
University of Oregon

References

Anderson, James Carl. "Planning and Evaluating School Activities." *Sch Activities* 34 (January): 131–4; 1963.

Barker, Roger G., and Gump, Paul V. *Big School, Small School*. Stanford U, 1964. 250p.

Behring, Daniel W. "Activities and Academic Achievement." *Personnel Guid J* 44:734–7; 1966.

Bell, James W. "School Dropouts and School Activities." *Sch Activities* 35 (September):4–7; 1964.

Bertrand, Alvin L. "School Attendance and Attainment." *Social Forces* 40:228–33; 1962.

Bolmeier, E. C. "Legal Aspects of the Curriculum and the Extracurriculum." *Nat Assn Sec Sch Prin B* 49 (March):128–42; 1965.

Brown, Marion. *Leadership Among High School Pupils*. Teachers Col, Columbia U, 1933. 166p.

Bush, Robert N. "The Proper Place of the Extracurriculum in High School." *California J Sec Ed* 34: 257–62; 1959.

Campbell, Laurence R. "Emphasis on Academic Achievement and Student Interest in Sports." *Sch Activities* 35 (January):137–8; 1964(a).

Campbell, Laurence R. "School Activity Courses in Colleges." *Sch Activities* 36 (November):3–6; 1964(b).

Clare, James F. "Legal Status and Jurisdiction of State Associations." *Sch Activities* 37 (November): 5–10; 1965.

Cochrane, Maynard. "How to Commit Suicide—Financially." *Sch Activities* 35 (November):80; 1963.

Coleman, James S. "Competition for Adolescent Energies." *Phi Delta Kappan* 42:231–6; 1961(a).

Coleman, James S. *The Adolescent Society*. Free Press, 1961(b). 368p.

Cormany, W. J. B. "High-school Athletics and Scholarship Measured by Achievement Tests." *Sch R* 43: 456–61; 1935.

Crum, Lewis R. "Evaluation of an Activities Program." *Sch Activities* 26 (April):243–7; 1955.

Davis, Lester D., and Lofton, Ray J. "Married High School Students Should Not Participate in Student Activities." *Sch Activities* 36 (October):3–6, 26; 1964.

Eells, Kenneth W. "Evaluating Pupil Activities." *Nations Sch* 23 (January):29–31; 1939.

Eidsmoe, Russell M. "High School Athletes Are Brighter." *Sch Activities* 35 (November):75–7; 1963.

Erickson, Ralph. "Growing Up—Or Growing Older?" *Sch Activities* 36 (April):3–10; 1965.

Faunce, Roland C. "Extracurricular Activities." In Harris, Chester W. (Ed.) *Encyclopedia of Educational Research*, rev. ed. Macmillan, 1960. p. 506–11.

Finger, John A., Jr. "Academic Motivation and Youthculture Involvement." *Sch R* 74:177–95; 1966.

Frederick, Robert W. *The Third Curriculum*. Appleton, 1959. 454p.

Fretwell, Elbert K. *Extra-curricular Activities in Secondary Schools*. Houghton, 1931. 552p.

Gordon, C. Wayne. *The Social System of the High School*. Free, 1957. 184p.

Graham, Grace. *Improving Student Participation*. NASSP, 1966. 50p.

Guerke, Warren E. *School Law*. Center for Applied Research in Education, 1965. 116p.

Hamilton, Homer H. *The Educational Values of Pupil Activities*. Texas Study of Secondary Education, 1960. 36p.

Hand, Harold C. *How to Conduct the Participation in Extra-class Activities Study*. Illinois State Department of Public Instruction, 1949. 66p.

Hand, Harold C. "Do School Costs Drive Out the Youth of the Poor?" *Prog Ed* 28:89–93; 1951.

Hauser, Gary Stuart. "Student Adaptation to High School Academics and Athletics." Master's thesis. U Oregon, 1965. 134p.

Hearn, Arthur C. *Evaluation of Student Activities*. NASSP, 1966. 40p.

Holland, John L., and Nichols, Robert C. "Prediction of Academic and Extracurricular Achievement in College." *J Ed Psychol* 55:55–6; 1964.

Holland, John L., and Richards, James M., Jr. "Academic and Non-academic Accomplishment: Correlated or Uncorrelated?" *J Ed Psychol* 56:165–74; 1965.

Hollingshead, August B. *Elmtown's Youth*. Wiley, 1949. 480p.

Howell, Elva J. "Student Activities in Twenty-five High Schools in Alabama." *J Negro Ed* 27:90–3; 1958.

Jung, Christian W., and Fox, William H. "Extracurricular Activities in Indiana High Schools: The Club Program." *Sch of Ed B*. Indiana U, 1952. 53p.

Keating, Walter T. "Scholarship of Participants in High School Football." *The Athletic J* 41:11; 1961.

Kilzer, Louis, and others. *Allied Activities in the Secondary School*. Harper, 1956. 357p.

Korotov, V. "More on Student Government." *Soviet Ed* 6:20–34; 1964.

Krumboltz, John D., and others. "Predicting Leadership Ratings from High School Activities." *J Ed*

Lawson, John D. "Evaluating Personnel in the Co-curriculum." *Personnel Guid J* 37:513–5; 1959.

Livingston, A. Hugh. "High School Graduates and Dropouts—A New Look at a Persistent Problem." *Sch R* 66:195–203; 1966.

Mallery, David. *High School Students Speak Out.* Harper, 1962. 165p.

Martin, Keith F. "The Educational Process Is Assisted by the Activity Program." *Sch Activities* 33 (September):10–1; 1961.

Mayberry, Burt A. "A Study of High-school Pupils to Determine the Effect of Student Council Participation on the Formation of Certain Habits of Citizenship." *J Ed Res* 24:305–7; 1931.

McAllester, E. S. "Extracurricular Activities of the Senior High Schools of Utah." *Nat Assn Sec Prin B* 39 (November):88–93; 1955.

McKown, Harry C. "Sputnik and Extracurricular Activities." *California J Sec Ed* 34:300–4; 1959.

Miller, Franklin A. "Co-curriculum Activities." *NEA J* 43:408–9; 1954.

Mullins, J. Dale. "Activity Programs in Oklahoma—A Report to the Profession." *Sch Activities* 33 (March):197–9; 1962.

National Society for the Study of Education. *Extracurricular Activities.* 25th Yearbook, Part II. NSSE, 1926. 235p.

National Study of Secondary School Evaluation. *Evaluative Criteria*, 2nd ed., 1960. 376p.

Pierce, Keith A. "Dropouts, Delinquents, and Their Student Peers." Doctoral dissertation. U Oregon, 1965.

Rehberg, Richard A., and Schafer, Walter E. "The Effect of Participation in High School Athletics on Future Educational Expectations." Paper presented at the International Seminar on Leisure Time and Recreation, Havana, Cuba, 1966. 10p. (Mimeographed.)

Schafer, Walter E., and Amer, J. Michael. "Participation in High School Athletics and Academic Achievement." Paper presented at World Congress of Sports and Physical Education, Madrid, Spain, September, 1966. 22p. (Mimeographed.)

Schafer, Walter E., and Polk, Kenneth. *Delinquency and the Schools: Report to the President's Commission on Law Enforcement and the Administration of Justice.* Prentice-Hall, 1967. 262p.

Schmuck, Richard A., and others. "Interpersonal Relations and Mental Health in the Classroom." *Mental Hygiene* 47:289–99; 1963.

School Management Reprint, "How to Make a Big School Little." 1962. 6p.

Sukholinskii, V. A. "Developing Individual Abilities and Inclinations in School Children." *Soviet Ed* 6 (December):44–54; 1963.

Taba, Hilda. *School Culture.* ACE, 1955. 123p.

Tesseneer, R. A., and Tesseneer, L. M. "Review of the Literature on School Dropouts." *Nat Assn Sec Sch Prin B* 42 (May):141–53; 1958.

Thomas, Robert Jay. "An Empirical Study of High School Drop-outs in Regard to Ten Possibly Related Factors." *J Ed Soc* 28:11–8; 1954.

Tillinghast, Charles C. "Can We Measure the Success of Citizenship Training?" *Clearing House* 4:297–300; 1930.

Tompkins, Ellsworth. *Extraclass Activities for ALL Pupils.* USOE, GPO, 1950. 54p.

Trump, J. Lloyd. *High-school Extracurricular Activities.* Chicago U, 1944. 210p.

Van Pool, Gerald M. "What's in the Wind for Student Activities?" *Parent-Teach Assn M* 57 (April):25–7; 1963.

Van Pool, Gerald M. Personal communication. January, 1967.

Walther, Joan. "A Student Activities Program Grows." *Sch Activities.* 33 (April):246–7; 1962.

Warkow, Carl J. "Evaluation—Report Card on Student Council Activities." In *The Student Council in the Secondary Schools.* NASSP, 1942. p. 389–96.

Weldy, Gilbert. "Supervision and Control of Nonathletic Interscholastic Contests and Activities." *Nat Assn Sec Sch Prin B* 48; 60–8; 1964.

STUDENT TEACHING

During the past decade there has been an unprecedented outpouring of publications about student teaching and internship. This massive accumulation of material is dominated by articles and reports describing current practices, expressing opinions or theoretical ideas, and advocating points of view. However, the quantity of research publications has also increased sharply over any previous period. For example, in the period June, 1955–May, 1957, there were 16 research reports in the *Education Index*; between July, 1964, and June, 1966, there were 42. The numerical increase was accompanied by a striking rise in the number of experimental and descriptive studies listed in the *Index*—from 5 in 1955–57 to 24 in 1964–66. The increases can be explained, in part, by the greater attention given by authorities in the field to the need for more emphasis on systematic studies that reflect sophisticated design and statistical analyses and on those which provide evidence for the assessment and improvement of practice (Hamann, 1962; Strom, 1961; Lindsey & others, 1959).

The increased volume and changed nature of research in this field can also be attributed, in part, to availability of funds to support research, particularly the U.S. Office of Education Cooperative Research funds. However, during the period 1956–63, only seven Cooperative Research grants were for studies directly related to student teaching and internships (U.S. Office of Education, 1963).

Most of the literature of the period continues to furnish strong positive support for the importance of student teaching. Conant (1963) cites student teaching as the "one indisputably essential element in professional education." Interview and survey studies of college students and in-service teachers show it to be the most strongly approved portion of teacher preparation (Hermanowicz, 1966).

However, amid the general approval, there is a growing tendency to question the continuation of student teaching in its present form (Andrews, 1964). One joint committee of seven influential national organizations alleges that student teaching is "entangled in a mass of confusion, unmade decisions, and experiences . . . [without] a comprehensive definition and clear-cut statement of goals and purposes. . . ." (National Council for Accreditation of Teacher Education, 1960). Fielder, seeing the functions of student teaching as largely ceremonial, calls for its abandonment (Fielder, 1966). Similarly, Iannaccone and Button (1964) conclude that student teaching is a time of cultural compression, during which prospective teachers learn to get through lessons on time at the expense of engaging children in some significant enterprise.

FORCES INFLUENCING STUDENT TEACHING. Toward the end of the present decade, major changes and forces in education and society have begun to have an impact on student teaching. Although some of these developments are not yet adequately reflected in the literature, they nevertheless deserve the attention of scholars and researchers in the field. A few of the most important are sketched below.

Civil Rights. The civil rights movement and the increasing pace of school integration have not yet produced corresponding changes in teacher preparation programs. Comparatively few Negro or white education students have opportunities to observe or student-teach in integrated classrooms (National Education Association, National Commission on Professional Rights . . . , 1966). There is a growing recognition that the teacher can play a positive role in the transition from racial segregation to racial integration in the schools (Noar, 1966; Haubrich, 1966).

War on Poverty. The "War on Poverty" and the growing concern about the complex social and educational problems in the nation's slums are leading to revisions of traditional teacher education programs, particularly of student teaching and other professional laboratory experiences. Increased time for supervised observation and teaching in schools in disadvantaged neighborhoods is widely recommended (Schueler, 1963; M. Smith, 1966).

Federal Programs. The substantial impact on education of federally financed programs is being felt in student teaching and internships. For example, both the National Teacher Corps and Inexperienced Teacher Fellowship programs authorized in Title V of the Higher Education Act of 1965 provide funds for inducting college graduates into teaching through post-bachelor's degree programs, with a heavy emphasis on practical experience in the schools. Likewise, several of the antipoverty programs have encouraged the employment of college students interested in teaching as aides and assistant teachers in the schools.

State Department Activity. Increasing state department of education activity in the field of teacher education is also having an impact on student teaching. The seven state M-Step programs give major attention to student teaching and internship. For example, the State Department of Education of Maryland is participating in a Model Center for Laboratory Experiences, sponsored jointly by the State Department of Education, the University of Maryland, and the Montgomery County public schools (*Phi Delta Kappan,* 1966).

Strong support is developing for increased state responsibility for student teaching, including the fixing of responsibilities among the various participating agencies and assuming a portion of the cost (Conant, 1963; Allen, 1967; Smith & Cunningham, 1961; Armstrong & Stinnett, 1967).

Militant Teachers. The new militancy of teachers and teacher organizations has an influence on student teaching and internship. Teachers are asking for a greater voice in determining educational policy, including that which governs student teaching. Bargaining and negotiated agreements provide teacher organizations with a vehicle for influencing policies, such as regulations covering the selection and compensation of supervising teachers (Davies, 1966).

Innovation in Education. Innovative practices in elementary and secondary schools are receiving increased attention. Such practices as team teaching, flexible and modular scheduling, the nongraded elementary school, computer-based instruction, the utilization of paid and unpaid auxiliary personnel to free the teacher from routine tasks, new approaches to utilizing the services of specialists, programmed instruction and teaching machines, automated information storage and retrieval, instructional television, and large- and small-group instruction are not yet reflected in any substantial way in the literature about student teaching. Growing concern about exposing student teachers to innovative practices will very likely lead to changes in student-teaching programs.

New Approaches to Induction. Emerging ideas about the induction of new teachers, which tend to blur the traditional lines between preservice and inservice preparation, will undoubtedly influence the purposes and nature of student teaching. In some new and proposed programs, the last years of the baccalaureate period are being planned to coordinate with the early years on the job (Hite, 1967; Bush, 1965; Boyan, 1965).

TERMINOLOGY. Wide diversity in terminology is characteristic of student teaching, just as is diversity in practice. The definitions used in this article are largely consistent with those proposed by Andrews (1964) and adapted by him from the recommended terminology of the Association for Student Teaching and the 1948 publication *School and Community Laboratory Experiences in Teacher Education.*

Professional laboratory experiences are all those contacts with children, youth, and adults in school and community, including observation, participation, teaching, and other leadership activities that make a direct contribution to understanding of basic concepts and principles as well as of individuals and their guidance in the teaching-learning process. Terms such as "clinical experiences," "direct experiences," and "field experiences" are also widely used. "Student teaching" is a period of guided teaching, during which a college student assumes increasing responsibility for directing the learning of a group or groups of learners over a period of consecutive weeks. The old term "practice teaching," vigorously deplored by teacher educators for two decades, is showing signs of revival and makes an occasional appearance in the current literature. The "student teacher" is a college student assigned to student-teaching experience; however, the term is often used to refer to any college student preparing to teach. The "supervising teacher" is a regular teacher of school pupils who also directs the work of a student teacher with these same pupils. "Cooperating teacher," "coordinating teacher," and "master teacher" are other terms still used; "critic teacher" is only rarely seen nowadays. The "college supervisor" is a regular college staff member who has, as all or part of his assigned work load, the supervision of activities of student teachers and the relationships and conditions under which they carry on their work. Other terms in fairly common use, depending on the nature of the student-teaching plan, include "off-campus supervisor," "resident supervisor," and "area supervisor." The "director" or "coordinator of student teaching" is a member of the college staff who has administrative responsibility for the institution's student-teaching program. A laboratory school is a school, either on or off campus, in which the operation, curriculum, functions or selection of staff, or any combination of these are controlled wholly or in part by the college. The term "campus laboratory school" is commonly used to refer to this kind of institution, which is located on a college campus and which is, as a rule, entirely under the control of the college. A "cooperating school" or "cooperating school system" is a school or a system which provides facilities for professional laboratory experiences but which usually is neither controlled nor supported by the college.

The most controversial and diversely used term is "internship." It is sometimes used, as in the state of Florida, as another name for student teaching. *Internship* is also sometimes used to mean an advanced level of student teaching in which the intern teaches a major portion or all of the school day, is a college graduate who has completed an undergraduate teacher education program, and is certificated, paid by the school district, and supervised by both school and college personnel. *Internship* is also commonly used to refer to a period of initial professional experience as a part of a fifth-year program leading to initial certification. It is likely that the term will be increasingly used with a wide variety of meanings. Both readers and writers in this field should proceed with caution to avoid confusion.

The most important new term to appear in student teaching in recent years is "clinical professor." Bush employed the term in 1962 to refer to highly skilled teachers in the schools who are recognized as clinical professors by the preparative institutions and are given responsibility for supervising two or three teachers in training (Bush, 1962). Conant used the same term to mean the professor from the college or university who is to supervise and assess practice teaching. He stipulated that the clinical professor must be an excellent schoolteacher who must return from time to time to the school classroom to teach and who might serve the college either on a part-time or full-time basis (Conant, 1963). It is likely that the term "clinical professor" will be applied increasingly to individuals formerly called "supervising teachers" and "college supervisors," as well as to individuals in newly created and defined positions who supervise prospective teachers and who are jointly responsible to and salaried by a school and a college.

PURPOSES. Despite the enormous quantity of literature on student teaching, there are few careful analyses of the nature and value of the experience (Andrews, 1964); and despite the importance attributed to it, behavioral objectives are seldom identified (Sarason, 1962).

It is reported that student teaching, until after World War I at least, consisted of "imitation and repeated practice of a particular method taught by the normal school professor and demonstrated in a classroom by the model teacher" (Andrews, 1964). After 1920, broadened views of the nature of student teaching developed and became dominant. Student teaching and other direct experiences were seen as ways to illuminate the theory of the college course. As student teaching moved from the campus into the public schools following World War II, major attention was also directed to introducing the neophyte into the full range of responsibilities and activities of the teacher.

The most commonly stated objective of student teaching is to give the student teacher direct, supervised experience with pupils (Watters & Halstead, 1962); and its principal value, that he learn to integrate all aspects of his training (Woodruff, 1960).

Textbooks and handbooks for student teachers, college catalogs, and articles about student teaching —all with lists of purposes of student teaching and other direct experiences—are abundant. The following items, compiled by Andrews (1964), represent a synthesis of such listings of purposes: providing a basis for a personal decision to become or not to become a teacher; developing readiness for professional courses, professional experiences, professional growth, and full-responsibility teaching; developing mature professional purposes and attitudes; strengthening understanding by exposure to reality, which adds feeling and other sensory impressions to verbalized knowledge; providing an opportunity to acquire, use, and test information; developing professional understanding of concepts and theories from professional and related disciplines; developing skill in the use of professional techniques; developing insight and judgment in applying professional knowledge; providing a basis for evaluating professional, social, and personal growth; providing a feeling of significant personal worth—the satisfaction that comes from giving useful professional service.

New concepts about the nature and purposes of student teaching and other direct experiences are growing out of the research on teaching that is reported in detail elsewhere in this volume. The studies by Hughes, Bellack, Flanders, Amidon, and others of teacher and student behavior in the classroom are leading to a reexamination of the student-teaching experience. Shaplin advances the idea that a primary purpose of practice teaching is that the student teacher learn to analyze, criticize, and control his own teaching behavior (Shaplin, 1962).

New concepts about the nature and purposes of student teaching are also developing out of reexaminations of the relationship between preservice and in-service education. The paragraph quoted below states this new concept of student teaching as follows (Joint Committee on State Responsibility for Student Teaching, 1967):

> The new student teaching should be a creative, fulfilling experience and at the same time provide for critical analysis in order to make student teachers and their supervisors scholars of teaching. It should not be confined to a block of time at the end of the senior year. It should range from simple observation to brief exposures with learners, to the development of skills in discrete elements of the teaching act (e.g., through micro-teaching), to analysis of personal skills and insights, all the way to the teaching of regular classes under the analytical eye of a professional mentor. It should be a study of teaching in various clinical situations. This new concept of student teaching demands new arrangements, revised administrative structures, and new systems of control. There needs to be a new order in student teaching.

ADMINISTRATION. Diversity is the most accurate description of practices in the administration of student-teaching programs; it is impossible to draw up many generalizations about their current status in the public schools. The most significant points demonstrated are that most school systems with enrollments of 12,000 or more are engaged in the training of large numbers of prospective teachers and that there is, at present, little uniformity either among the school systems or the teacher training institutions in the procedures or arrangements governing this cooperative enterprise (National Education Association, Research Division, 1964).

Organization. A majority of institutions, regardless of size, use full-time teaching assignments, with half-time assignments a close second (Woodruff, 1960; Nelson, 1963). In the pattern of programs, there is surprising similarity between private liberal arts colleges and state colleges. In fact, differences among the liberal arts colleges are greater than differences between state and liberal arts colleges (Inlow, 1960). Public institutions average slightly larger numbers of off-campus student teachers, supervising teachers, and cooperating schools than do private or church-related institutions (Jones, 1960). Supervising teachers indicate strong preference for all-day, semester-long experiences (Kuhl, 1961). One new program offers all the elements of teacher preparation, including student teaching, in one semester labeled the "acroclinical semester" (McQuigg, 1966). One program for preparing Cuban refugees to become teachers of Spanish utilizes a 14-week student-teaching seminar and half-day assignments for a group of mature, well-educated people (Phillips, 1965).

Admission. Admission practices for student-teaching programs vary. A national survey indicates the need for selective admission to teacher education and repeated evaluation of candidates. The factors most often considered are performance in professional and other courses, physical fitness as determined by the college physician, emotional stability, and ethical and moral fitness. Few institutions use standardized instruments for assessing the student's ability (Stout, 1957).

Assignment. Student teachers are given placements in a variety of ways; there is some evidence to indicate that placement is important to their success. Factors of grade level, school socioeconomic level, and student-teacher preference for an age group exert a significant influence on the student teacher's classroom behavior (Wilk, 1964); the lapse of time between completion of methods courses and a student-teaching assignment does not seem to affect this behavior significantly (Popham, 1965). In view of this, assignment of student teachers on the basis of a theoretical framework of the behavior involved in interaction with others is urged (Chaltas, 1965).

Finance. The colleges and universities are usually responsible for financing student-teaching programs. The majority of institutions do not charge student teachers a fee for the expenses of the field experience (Woodruff, 1960).

Typically, the colleges do not pay the public schools any money for participation in the preparation of teachers, but well over half of them do pay the supervising teachers in amounts ranging from $10 to $300 per student teacher. This money comes from the college budget, although there are a few state departments of education that contribute. There are no significant geographic differences in practice (Woodruff, 1960).

There is increased interest in having the states provide more financial support for student-teaching programs (Andrews, 1964). Need for increased Federal and state aid for teachers in training is supported by the size of the enterprise and the mobility of teachers. Shaplin (1962) and others recommend that efforts be made to provide support for teacher education from the Federal level, as is done in many other countries.

Certification and Accreditation. All states require student teaching for issuance of regular initial certificates for elementary or secondary schoolteachers. In those states which have specific credit requirements rather than an approved-program system, the range is from 3 to 12 semester credits for the elementary schoolteacher certificate and from 2 to 8 for secondary schoolteachers. There has been little significant change in the nature or amount of student teaching required for certification in recent years (Armstrong & Stinnett, 1967).

Most states have a system for state approval or accreditation of teacher education programs. Whenever general or specific standards exist, major attention is given to student teaching. Most states encourage or require a block-scheduling approach to student teaching (Mayor, 1965). The national accrediting agency, the National Council for Accreditation of Teacher Education, devotes one of its seven standards to professional laboratory experience. The NCATE has encouraged programs of professional laboratory experience "designed to make real concepts that are developed through reading, lectures, discussions . . . and to help students acquire skill in applying these concepts in practice. . . . The professional laboratory experience should culminate in a continuous period of student teaching so organized as to provide for a wide range of professional activities in which teachers should engage. . . ." (National Council for Accreditation of Teacher Education, 1960). The influence of the NCATE is strongly directed toward full-time, off-campus student-teaching plans and strongly discourages one- and two-hour-a-day programs (Mayor, 1965).

Conant (1963) recommends that most of the burden in the approved-program approach to teacher certification rest on student teaching. He called on the state "to regulate the conditions under which practice teaching is done and the nature of the methods instruction that accompanies it . . . and to require that the colleges and public school systems involved submit evidence concerning the competence of those appointed as cooperating teachers and clinical professors."

Facilities. The facilities needed for student-teaching programs are determined in part by the number of student teachers to be served from colleges in the area and the number of available qualified resource people to whom students can be assigned. The range of facilities includes campus or laboratory schools; off-campus laboratory schools; off-campus public schools in the local area; off-campus public schools at some distance; off-campus centers, usually at some distance; and combinations of two or more of these (Andrews, 1964).

The campus school was the traditional center for the student-teaching program, but this has changed radically since 1945 under the pressure of increased enrollments and changing needs of teacher education programs (Venable, 1960). The campus schools are changing into learning centers where students may observe, work with children, and participate in programs allied with college courses (Lautenschlager, 1965).

Even though most student teaching is now done in off-campus schools, a majority of campus school officials still see it as an essential function of the campus school; only 42 percent of the campus schools feel that they could justify their program if student-teaching activities were withdrawn (Blackman, 1964). The number of reorganizing and expanding campus-school programs is about equal to the number being phased out. The definite national trend is to discontinue state support for such schools (Kelley, 1964).

INTERNSHIP. New programs for the recruitment, selection, and induction of teachers through a fifth year of work have been labeled "internships." These usually lead to the M.A. or M.A.T. degree. These vary as much in structure and function as do the more traditional student-teaching programs; the major difference from student teaching is that internships are not viewed as the culminating activity but as the critical core around which the program is developed (Stone, 1967).

Internships are viewed by some as a new half-step between student teaching and full-time responsibility in the classroom. In one proposal, the intern would move from student teacher to teacher in successive three-year steps (Rivlin, 1966). Programs that utilize the study–full-time teaching–study sequence leading to the M.A.T. or M.A. degree allow a better concentration of energies for the students than do those which involve classroom teaching and study at the same time (Stone, 1967). Descriptions of new fifth-year programs do not include definite behavioral objectives. There is no evidence that the decision to choose one or another of basic internship patterns results from any particular theoretical commitment (Shaplin & Powell, 1964).

Internship programs for college graduates who have not prepared to teach during their undergraduate years are seen as a way of tapping new sources for teachers. These programs are particularly directed to those not normally attracted to teaching, such as housewives seeking careers, returning military personnel, mature men seeking new careers, and liberal arts graduates of all ages and kinds. The major emphasis is on secondary schoolteaching, although there are some elementary programs. There are twice as many women as men in the programs (Stone, 1967). Studies of the interns find that they were rated more responsible, systematic, and businesslike than regular first-year teachers (Haberman, 1965). The recent graduates of the Ford Foundation-sponsored project on internships were described as high-quality, scholarly people who, because of special recruitment and special care during their internship, feel that both they and the program are quite special (Stone, 1967). Over a three-year period, individuals lacking professional training have been found to perform as well as those trained in traditional programs (Butterweck, 1960).

Some curriculum concepts held to be effective and essential to internship programs are:

1. A four-year liberal arts degree program, with professional education usually reserved for the fifth year and culminating in a M.A.T. degree—preservice for some, in-service for many.

2. Institutional responsibility exercised by supporting faculties in the academic and education disciplines, with subject-matter competence emphasized through general and specialized study coupled with or topped by professional preparation.

3. The paid teaching internship, which has been the means of recruiting high-caliber liberal arts graduates to teaching, has made clinical practice the heart of the training program and has made it pos-

sible for public school systems to fulfill their indispensable clinical role in teacher education.

4. The continuous integration of theory and practice throughout the professional curriculum, embodying institutional–school district cooperation and utilizing a staff team that teaches, supervises, evaluates, and guides a particular group of students throughout the professional sequence.

5. A reorganization of the professional content of education courses along some other lines than compartmentalization of separate courses taught by different instructors separate from clinical practice.

6. The use by the prospective teachers of the newest curricula, the latest materials, the most experimental methods, and the newest techniques and organization for carrying on instruction.

7. High personal, academic, and professional standards for admission to, retention in, and graduation from the program.

8. Multiple pathways to teaching, recognizing the diverse needs of the teaching profession and the varying abilities and backgrounds of those who wish to teach (Stone, 1967).

School-College Relations. The concept of joint responsibility for student teaching by the colleges and public schools is giving some new direction to programs. The problem of size of student-teacher groups needing laboratory facilities has forced the exploration of new approaches. A comprehensive report of thinking in this area was made by Andrews (1964). The concept of teaching centers has developed from growing acceptance of joint responsibility for teacher preparation. Cooperative structures are already operative in New York City, Detroit, Pittsburgh, and Kansas City (E. B. Smith, 1965). The success of such ventures is said to rest on the development of new lines of responsibility and organizational structures that are viable enough not to depend on individual personalities. Barriers of status and differences of outlook between schools and colleges are hindering progress (E. B. Smith, 1964).

Growing acceptance by school systems of responsibility for teacher education is evident (Smith & Cunningham, 1961). A majority of public school systems in the North Central states have student-teaching programs at some time during the school year (Westfall, 1963). Many colleges have developed contractual arrangements with the school systems. An example is the Student Teaching Council developed by St. Cloud State College, in St. Cloud, Minnesota; this is a 43-member council of college faculty, representatives from public school districts, and supervising teachers. The council has been effective in improving communications between school districts and the college (Perry, 1965).

Public relations practices by colleges with regard to student teaching vary greatly, without correspondence to the size of the program. An important conclusion is that the most effective efforts are those which help supervising teachers in directing the student teacher (Van Winkle, 1959). The biggest problem in this area is lack of time to devote to the extra work involved; teachers are seldom released from any of their usual teaching responsibilities in order to have time to supervise (Hullfish, 1957).

The public schools are also becoming increasingly involved in teacher education on the pre-student-teaching level. Opportunities for college students to fill teacher-aide positions offer valuable experience when colleges and public schools share the responsibility. Several colleges have community field work as an integral part of their pre-student-teaching program; one example is the Manhattan Project at New York University (Mills & Williams, 1958).

There is need for more local initiative in the use of available Federal money to improve school-college relations. As a start, colleges could direct their efforts to aiding the schools in improvement of teaching. There is much work yet to be done to make genuine school-college collaboration a reality (Barnes, 1967).

SUPERVISION. The work of guiding, supporting, and teaching the student teacher is known as supervision. This work is done by several people, including the college professor of education, the supervising teacher in the public school to whom the student is assigned, and sometimes by the building principal or head of a department in a secondary school. There is growing involvement of liberal arts professors in this responsibility; however, there is little research about their participation. The major work has been done on college supervision, the supervising teacher, and the student teacher.

College Supervisor. The role of the college supervisor is sometimes defined in terms of a liaison person between the college and the public schools, a counselor of student teachers in the field, teacher of student teachers in the field and on the campus, and an intermediary between the student teacher and the supervising teacher (Inlow, 1956).

There is wide variation in equating the load of the college supervisor of student teachers and that of other faculty members (Evans, 1957). There is no relationship between the size of the institutions and the assignment of load credit hours for supervising one student teacher. The range is from one-fourth of a credit hour to more than one credit hour, with the mode at one-half of a credit hour per student teacher supervised. Fifteen credit hours are considered a typical full teaching load. The college supervisor typically sees the student teacher from three to five times during the assignment (Woodruff, 1960).

One study of a supervisory team composed of a specialist in elementary school curriculum and a specialist in educational psychology resulted in the lessening of student anxieties, more objective and reasoned solutions to student problems, and some positive influence on student-teacher viewpoints about desirable teacher behavior (Grey & Greenblatt, 1963).

The role of the principal in student-teaching programs has been slighted in the literature. He carries the most potential for setting the tone of the experience for student teachers, since certain of his functions cannot be carried out so well by anyone else (Andrews, 1964). These may be described as facilitating functions, such as matching student teachers and supervising teachers, providing adequate conference time for the supervising teacher, introducing the student teacher to other staff, providing status for the student teachers in the building, arranging a wide variety of experiences for student teachers, and conferring with student teachers to ensure that the best possible learning is taking place (Schwartz, 1964).

Supervising Teacher. The supervising teacher is described as having six responsibilities: (1) as friend, adviser, and counselor of the student teacher; (2) as an outstanding teacher of boys and girls; (3) as director of observation; (4) as professional person and desirable model; (5) as evaluator of teaching proficiency; and (6) as innovator and experimenter (Nash, 1965).

The supervising teacher is usually one who has been approved by his principal or supervisor and by the college. Most colleges require a valid certificate, and about one-fifth require a master's degree or equivalent experience (Woodruff, 1960). Forty states report no certification requirements for supervising teachers; eight have specific requirements for supervising teachers and/or state-controlled criteria for approval (Lingren, 1957). The state of Georgia reports a program of internships for supervising teachers as a means of appraising their grasp of materials and techniques considered in a college course in supervision (Whiting, 1957). In view of the assumption that supervision requires many special skills beyond that of good teaching, there is a need for special training for supervising teachers (Shaplin, 1962). Many school districts and colleges are offering courses in supervision for their cooperating teachers (Scrivner, 1966).

The supervising teacher usually works with one student teacher at a time, although the number may vary from one to eight; during the school year, the typical supervising teacher will have two student teachers. The supervising teacher typically completes an evaluation form concerning the student teacher for the college; but in deciding the final grade, he advises the college supervisor as often as he determines the grade alone (Woodruff, 1960).

Follow-up studies of student teachers reveal that supervising teachers do influence their student-teachers' behavior (Price, 1961); this influence is greater if the relationship of the supervising teacher with his student has been a formal one. Student-teaching experiences influence the student teachers more than methods courses do (McAulay, 1960).

Student Teachers. The student-teaching experience helps the student to integrate skills and leads to changes in his self image. The bulk of research centers on the changes in the student teacher's attitudes about himself and about teaching in general.

Although the field experience of one group of pre-student-teaching students did not increase their positive attitudes toward education (Cox, 1960), it did change their attitudes measurably. Student teachers showed a significant decrease in consistency of ideas about education after they had completed student teaching (Newsome & others, 1965). This may be attributed to the development of the student-teachers' individuality, but there is some evidence that various factors in the situation play a part in this attitude change. Sharp positive change in the attitudes of student teachers toward children after their student teaching is associated with interaction with certain college supervisors, placement in lower grades, and a single rather than a multiple student-teaching placement. The changes were less marked for student teachers in upper-grade placements and for those whose undergraduate field was psychology or sociology (Corrigan & Griswold, 1963). Positive changes in Minnesota Teacher Attitudes Inventory scores, indicative of positive feelings toward children, were related to grade placement of student teachers and their choice of school (Wilk, 1964).

The attitudes toward teaching of students who had an alternating program of student teaching and courses in teaching methods and materials were significantly better than attitudes of those who were enrolled in a program providing one to two hours a day of student teaching along with other courses (Nagle, 1959). Students attributed their feelings of increased competency in the classroom directly to their student-teaching experience (Hoover & others, 1965).

The student-teachers' perceptions of themselves and other teachers are also altered by their student-teaching experience; their basic values do not seem to change, but they do seem to feel a need for a greater harmony of ideas. They perceive themselves as being more trustful and accepting of their interpersonal behavior, and they gain new insights into and appreciation of themselves. They perceive other teachers as being more trustful and the ideal teacher as being trusting and somewhat more normal and realistic than they did before student teaching (Lantz, 1964).

A series of experimental studies is under way at the Research and Development Center in Teacher Education, University of Texas. These deal with the characteristics of studies, student teachers, classroom interaction, the use of projective techniques and counseling with student teachers, pupils in relation to student teachers, and supervisory techniques. Preliminary findings in one of these studies indicate that feedback of various kinds does influence student-teacher behavior and responses on projective tests (Menaker & Fuller, 1967).

An analysis of pre- and post-student-teaching behavior on videotapes of teaching sessions during the junior-year participation period and again in senior-year student teaching indicates that a major effect of the two-year period of experimental treatment is to produce an increased proportion of classroom behavior classified as indirect and a decreased proportion of behavior classified as direct. Indirect behavior includes such items as acceptance of children's feelings and ideas, praise, and asking questions; direct behavior is involved in the giving of directions, lecturing, and criticizing (Menaker & Fuller, 1967).

One effort to find student-teacher characteristics predictive of persistence in the profession was futile. It was conceded that no predictive measures for persistence in teaching could be found and that additional measures are needed to form positive conclusions (Lohman, 1966).

Evaluation. Evaluation of the student teacher by the college is usually expressed in a letter grade. This evaluation is based on the observation and judgment of the college supervisor and the supervising teacher as to the effectiveness of student teaching. Supervising teachers, college supervisors, and students tend to differ on what constitutes effective teaching (Getzels & Jackson, 1963). There is need to reappraise the standards and to revise the practices used in evaluations. Marks for laboratory experiences are unrealistic; over an eight-year period in one college, 75 percent of the grades for student teaching were A's (Simmons, 1964).

One of the possible causes of the differences in defining teaching effectiveness is the different frames of reference used by observers. Discrepancies in evaluation are caused by a lack of common understanding of the concepts involved in the specific experience. Rater bias is an important factor affecting evaluation (Wilk & others, 1962). A possible clue to achieving greater success in objectively evaluating student teachers is found in two studies. A survey of supervisor's reports found that they were neglecting specific classroom behavior and were itemizing strengths and weaknesses that did not describe the student teachers adequately (Wilkinson, 1963). Another study showed the feasibility of basing student-teachers' grades on an induced set of specific goals (Witrock, 1962). This study suggests that specific behavioral goals can influence the student-teachers' behavior in the classroom.

The relationships between student-teaching evaluations and securing a position as a teacher have been studied. A survey of over 300 large school systems showed that selection methods focused almost entirely on the overt characteristics of teacher candidates, and not on covert personality characteristics. Most selection procedures are determined by what is easily obtainable rather than what might be important to assess, including the mental health of the prospective teacher (Gilbert, 1966). One state survey showed seven qualities most important in selecting student teachers for teaching positions: emotional poise, health and vitality, courtesy and tact, ability to plan lessons and motivate learners, knowledge of basic skills, development of pupil morale, and attention to individual differences (Rhodes & Peckham, 1960).

TECHNOLOGY. New kinds of audiovisual and electronic equipment and new uses for familiar equipment are having an influence on two aspects of the student-teaching program: (1) evaluation of student teachers and (2) helping student teachers to learn to teach better. Most of the work reported relates to the latter. The interest in utilizing samples of student-teachers' teaching as a means of evaluation is evident, but no actual studies have been reported.

New methods of providing direct experience for preservice teachers include expanding the experience throughout the program via audiovisual media and joining forces with public schools for use of such equipment. Emphasis in general is on the analysis of teaching (Hunter & Amidon, 1966). The use of films and television in conjunction with programmed instruction can help the student teacher to gain prompt feedback on his performance (Briggs, 1964). One study cites the effectiveness of this feedback on the teaching behavior of the student teacher. The student-teacher's rating in student teaching was found to be directly related to improvement in the quality of the questions he prepared after receiving feedback from his pupils (McNeil, 1962).

A progressive system of experiences for neophyte teachers developed at Stanford University involves three distinct phases: (1) tutoring one student; (2) teaching one concept for three weeks; and finally, (3) team planning of a unit for four or five students. The student-teachers' behavior is recorded on videotape for later self-evaluation (Allen & Gross, 1965). The implications of the microteaching technique are probably most useful for more experimenting and innovating in the teaching-learning act by neophyte teachers (Meierhenry, 1966).

Closed-circuit television has been used to give student teachers practice in the skills of observation and to practice in the pre-student-teaching program (Wooley & Smith, 1962). There is less emotional involvement of the observer in the television situation than in live observations; this results in more profitable discussion about the observation (Weiss, 1962). The advantages and disadvantages are discussed at length, but the dominant advantage is the flexibility of the classroom teacher and the availability of the college instructor for consultation on what is happening in the classroom (Rench, 1961; Keller, 1961). When used alone, closed-circuit television is not found to produce greater student gain than does live observation experience (Keller, 1961). Combinations of television and other methods were more positive in results. After training with kinescopes, preservice education students are more able to evaluate classroom incidents than after television observation alone (Stoller & others, 1964). Combinations of closed-circuit television and live observations are just as effective as live observations alone (Woodward, 1964).

Film clips and simulation techniques were found to be effective. The simulation experience gives the student an opportunity to respond to classroom incidents presented on film with a choice of possible behavior (Bushnell, 1963; Painter, 1962).

The use of technology to bring resource lectures and planned classes to schoolrooms via the telephone (known as "telelecture") has been found to improve the work of student teachers (Myers, 1965). Computer programs have proved effective in matching student teachers and supervising teachers (G. Smith, 1962). Whole courses in media-learning techniques have been programmed for student teachers, with a resulting improvement in their work (Knirk & McGoney, 1964).

Colleges have attempted to improve student-teachers' work by developing instructional materials centers for their use during student teaching. Most of these centers are on college campuses, but a few have become decentralized and are located in schools, teaching centers, and libraries. Student teachers favored the decentralized locations as being more functional (Hall, 1964).

URBAN STUDENT TEACHING. One of the newest areas of concern in student teaching is in programs of urban education. Most of the reported work centers on program descriptions and proposals for competencies needed to teach disadvantaged children (Rivlin, 1965). Half of the children in urban areas may be in depressed schools (Arnez, 1966); the special importance of good teachers for these children is clear and suggests the need to match teachers and pupils more effectively (Coleman, 1966).

Two hundred colleges have in operation or in preparation programs related to teaching disadvantaged children; most of these are on the graduate level (Ornstein, 1966). Programs for teachers of the disadvantaged emphasize preparation beyond what is expected of ordinary student teachers and usually operate on a volunteer basis (Haubrich, 1963). It is reported that most colleges hesitate to place student teachers in slum areas because of parental and student objection, but most student teachers who do their student teaching in a slum area subsequently take positions there (Ornstein, 1966).

The urban schools in which the student teachers are placed are using a broad range of teaching materials and show a flexibility of techniques in administrative approaches such as team teaching and flexible scheduling (Baynham, 1963). Extensive use of field experience is a basic part of these programs (Knapp, 1965). The students sometimes form a big-brother relationship to a child for a period of time, tutor him, and then move into a teaching capacity in a school in the community (Ornstein, 1966).

One urban college assigns pre-student-teaching students to after-school centers for disadvantaged children. These students did not differ significantly in student-teaching grades from students not working in such centers, but more of them did stay in the general methods sequences (Downing & others, 1965).

There is need for devising appropriate methods and techniques to prepare teachers for these schools. One program found that it was important to student teachers to overcome their tendency to isolate themselves from the community they serve. There is a tendency to underestimate the idealism of youth. There is more success in these programs with undergraduate student teachers than with teachers in the field. Some urge that all students be involved in such programs (Schueler, 1963); others are sure that such experience should be voluntary (Rivlin, 1965).

Because of the vast quantity of material available, only a very small sampling is included in this summary. Excluded completely are unpublished doctoral and master's theses. Preference in selection was given to studies based on a national rather than a state sample and on those of an experimental nature.

Scholars pursuing further the topic of student teaching will find the following sources particularly helpful: the yearbooks and bulletins of the Association for Student Teaching and of the AACTE; the periodical annotated résumé of research in education published by the Educational Research Information Center, USOE; *The Journal of Teacher Education* and other publications of the National Commission on Teacher Education and Professional Standards; the *Journal of Educational Research;* research reports of the USOE-supported Regional Educational Laboratories and Research and Development Centers, particularly those at Stanford University and the University of Texas.

A review of research in this field leaves one with a great feeling of urgency to expedite the study of student teaching; given its ascribed importance in teacher education, it is alarming to find so little systematic research directly related to it. Discussion and descriptive reports are plentiful, but comprehensive basic study of the process involved is lacking. Studies of what really happens to the student teacher are vital. An explication of the principles and values inherent in or preceding student teaching would be of infinitely more value than is private opinion (Sarason & others, 1962). The models for new approaches have been reported; it would be helpful if work of a substantive nature could evolve from these.

Don Davies
National Education Association
Kathleen Amershek
The University of Maryland

References

Allen, Dwight W., and Gross, Richard E. "Microteaching." *NEA J* 55:25–6; 1965.

Allen, Wendell C. "State Government and Teacher Education—a Different Role for the State Education Agency." In *The Seattle Conference: Role of the State Department of Education in Teacher Education.* Superintendent of Public Instruction, State of Washington, 1967. p. 76–83.

Andrews, L. O. *Student Teaching.* Center for Applied Research in Education, 1964. 116p.

Andrews, L. O. "Theory Underlying Proposed State and Federal Support to Promote High-quality Student Teaching." In *Action for Improvement of Teacher Education.* 18th Yearbook. AACTE, 1965. p. 203–15.

Armstrong, W. Earl, and Stinnett, T. M. *A Manual on Certification Requirements for School Personnel in the United States.* NEA, 1967.

Arnez, Nancy. "Teacher Education for an Urban Environment." *Improving Col and U Teach* 14: 81–6; 1966.

Barnes, Melvin W. "Building School-University Relations in Teacher Education." In Elam, Stanley. (Ed.) *Improving Teacher Education in the United States.* PDK, 1967. p. 137–64.

Baynham, D. "The Great Cities Project." *NEA J* 52: 17–20; 1963.

Blackman, C. Robert. "The Research Functions in College Controlled Laboratory Schools." In *New Development, Research and Experimentation in Professional Laboratory Experiences.* Bulletin No. 22. Association for Student Teaching, 1964. p. 127–9.

Boyan, Norman J. "Improving the Quality of Education: Teacher Education." In *White House Conference on Education.* GPO, 1965. p. 35–44.

Briggs, Leslie J. "The Teacher and Programmed Instruction." *Audiovisual Instruction* 9:273–80; 1964.

Bush, Robert N. "The Formative Years." In *The Real World of the Beginning Teacher.* NEA, 1965. p. 1–14.

Bush, Robert N. "Self-determination and Self-regulation in the Profession of Teaching." In *Professional Imperatives: Expertness and Self-Determination.* NEA, 1962. p. 37–53.

Bushnell, David D. "Computer-based Simulation: A New Technology for Education." *AV Communication R* 11:45–55; 1963.

Butterweck, Joseph S. *Preparing Teachers for Secondary Schools: Pilot Study II of an Experimental Program in Teacher Education.* Temple U, 1960. 200p.

Chaltas, John G. "Student Teaching: Assignment and Misassignment." *J Teach Ed* 16:311–8; 1965.

Coleman, James S. *Summary of Equality of Educational Opportunity.* GPO, 1966. 737p.

Conant, James B. *The Education of American Teachers.* McGraw-Hill, 1963. 275p.

Corrigan, Dean, and Griswold, Kenneth. "Attitude Changes of Student Teachers." *J Teach Ed* 14: 93–5; 1963.

Cox, Dan. "An Objective and Empirical Study of the Factors of Laboratory Experience in a Professional Education Course Prior to Student Teaching." *J Exp Ed* 29:89–94; 1960.

Davies, Don. "An Era of Opportunity in Teacher Education." *Teach Col J* 38:12–5; 1966.

Downing, Gertrude L., and others. *The Preparation of Teachers for Schools in Culturally Deprived Neighborhoods.* Queens Col of The City U of New York, 1965. 19p.

Evans, Howard R. "The Supervision of Student Teaching in the Calculation of Teaching Load." *J Teach Ed* 8:387–92; 1957.

Fielder, William R. "Keynote Address: Albuquerque." In *Remaking the World of the Career Teacher.* NEA, 1966. p. 98–107.

Getzels, J. W., and Jackson, P. W. "The Teacher's Personality and Characteristics." In Gage, N. L. (Ed.). *Handbook of Research on Teaching.* Rand McNally, 1963. p. 506–82.

Gilbert, Harry B. *Teacher Selection Policies and Procedures in Large Public School Systems in the United States.* Cooperative Research Project No. S-334. Board of Education of the City of New York, 1966. 63p.

Grey, Loren, and Greenblatt, Edward L. "An Experiment in Team Supervision." *J Teach Ed* 14: 154–62; 1963.

Haberman, M. "Comparison of Interns with Regular First-year Teachers." *J Ed Res* 59:92–4; 1965.

Hall, Sedley D. "The Instructional Materials Center." *El Sch J* 64:210–3; 1964.

Hamann, J. Stanley. "Educational Research Today." In *Research and Professional Experiences in Teacher Education.* Bulletin No. 20. Association for Student Teaching, 1962. p. 3–8.

Haubrich, Vernon. "The Culturally Different: New Context for Teacher Education." *J Teach Ed* 14: 163–7; 1963.

Haubrich, Vernon. "Philadelphia." In *Remaking the World of the Career Teacher.* NEA, 1966. p. 43–59.

Hazelton, Paul. "Student Teaching: A Hard Look." *J Teach Ed* 11:470–3; 1960.

Hermanowicz, Henry J. "The Pluralistic World of Beginning Teachers: A Summary of Interview Studies." In *The Real World of the Beginning Teacher.* NEA, 1966. p. 15–25.

Hite, Herbert. "An Innovation in Teacher Education and State Leadership." In *The Seattle Conference: The Role of the State Department of Education in Teacher Education.* Superintendent of Public Instruction, Olympia, Washington, 1967.

Hoover, Kenneth H., and others. "A Comparison of Expressed Teaching Strengths Before and After Student Teaching." *J Teach Ed* 16:324–8; 1965.

Hullfish, H. Gordon. "Teaching Aides: An Educational Opportunity." *Ed Leadership* 14:381–3; 1957.

Hunter, Elizabeth, and Amidon, Edmund. "Direct Experience in Teacher Education: Innovation and Experimentation." *J Teach Ed* 17:282–9; 1966.

Iannaccone, Laurence, and Button, H. Warren. *Functions of Student Teaching.* Cooperative Research Project No. 1026. Washington U, 1964. 117p.

Inlow, Gail M. "The Complex Role of the College Supervisor." *Ed Res B* 35:10–7; 1956.

Inlow, Gail M. "A Comparative Study of Student Teaching Practices in Thirty-eight Midwestern Institutions." *J Exp Ed* 28:337–49; 1960.

Joint Committee on State Responsibility for Student Teaching. *A New Order in Student Teaching.* NEA, 1967. 44p.

Jones, Rodney M. "Off-campus Student Teaching Programs: Their Size and Importance." *J Teach Ed* 11:512–9; 1960.

Keller, Robert J. "The Teachers College: Research in Closed Circuit TV." *North Cen Assn Q* 35:312–4; 1961.

Kelley, Evan Hugh. "Some Pertinent Facts Concerning the Campus Laboratory School in the United States." In *New Developments, Research and Experimentation in Professional Laboratory Experiences.* Bulletin No. 22. Association for Student Teaching, 1964. p. 141–4.

Knapp, Dale L. "Preparing Teachers of Disadvantaged Youth: Emerging Trends." *J Teach Ed* 16: 188–92; 1965.

Knirk, Frederick G., and McGoney, Gary L. "Programming Teacher Education in Media." *Audiovisual Instruction* 9:527, 542; 1964.

Kuhl, Raymond E. "Time for Student Teaching." *J Teach Ed* 12:43–7; 1961.

Lantz, Donald W. "Changes in Student Teachers' Concepts of Self and Others." *J Teach Ed* 15:200–3; 1964.

Lautenschlager, Harley. "New Dimensions in the Laboratory School." *Teach Col J* 36:172–3; 1965.

Lindsey, Margaret, and others. *Improving Laboratory Experiences in Teacher Education.* Teachers Col, Columbia U, 1959. 262p.

Lingren, Vernon C. "The Certification of Cooperating Teachers in Student Teaching Programs." *J Teach Ed* 8:403–7; 1957.

Lohman, Maurice A. "Certain Characteristics of Student Teachers Who Stay in Teaching." CRP No. S-332. The City U of New York Research Foundation, 1966. 51p.

Mayor, John R. *Accreditation in Teacher Education —Its Influence on Higher Education.* National Commission on Accrediting, 1965. 311p.

McAulay, J. D. "How Much Influence Has a Cooperating Teacher?" *J Teach Ed* 11:79–83; 1960.

McNeil, John. "An Experimental Effort To Improve Instruction Through Visual Feedback." *J Ed Res* 55:283–5; 1962.

McQuigg, R. Bruce. "The Acroclinical Semester—A Crucial Part of a New Teacher Education Project at Indiana University." *Teach Col J* 37:208–9; 1966.

Meierhenry, Wesley C. "The New Significance of Learning Theory." *Ed Screen Audiovisual Guide* 45:22–3; 1966.

Menaker, S. L., and Fuller, F. F. "A Study of Elementary Teacher Training—Experimental Control Group Comparisons and Changes During the Two-year Training Period." Research and Development Center for Teacher Education, U Texas, 1967.

Mills, Jane, and Williams, Lovelle. "A Community-oriented Teacher Training Program." *J Ed Sociol* 31:194–205; 1958.

Myers, Kent C. "Learning by Telephone." *Clearing House* 39:475–8; 1965.

Nagle, W. Marshall. "Some Effects of Student Teaching Patterns upon Professional Attitudes." *J Ed Res* 52:355–7; 1959.

Nash, Curtis E. "The Role of the Supervising Teacher." *Teach Col J* 37:59, 83–8; 1965.

National Council for Accreditation of Teacher Education. *Standards and Guides.* The Council, 1960. 23p.

National Education Association, National Commission on Professional Rights and Responsibilities, Committee on Civil and Human Rights. *Task Force Survey of Teacher Displacement in Seventeen States.* The Commission, 1966. 61p.

National Education Association, Research Division. *Cooperation in Student Teaching.* Circular No. 4. The Association, 1964. 56p.

Nelson, Horace. "A Survey of Student-teaching Practices in Eight Southeastern States." *J Teach Ed* 14: 188–93; 1963.

Newsome, George L., Jr., and others. "Changes in Consistency of Educational Ideas Attributable to Student-teaching Experiences." *J Teach Ed* 16: 319–23; 1965.

Noar, Gertrude. *The Teacher and Integration.* NEA, 1966. 97p.

Ornstein, Allen C. "Learning To Teach the Disadvantaged." *J Sec Ed* 41:206–13; 1966.

Painter, William I. "New Media in Teacher Education." *Phi Delta Kappan* 43:389–90; 1962.

Perry, Floyd. "The Student Teaching Council Model." In *Cooperative Structures in School-College Relationships for Teacher Education.* AACTE, NEA, 1965. p. 93–100.

Phi Delta Kappan. "For Teacher Education Improvement for Teachers." *Phi Delta Kappan* 43:135; 1966.

Phillips, T. A. "Laboratory Experiences for Cuban Refugees." *Teach Col J* 36:179; 1965.

Popham, W. J. "Student Teachers' Classroom Performance and Recency of Instructional Methods Course Work." *J Exp Ed* 34:85–8; 1965.

Price, Robert D. "The Influence of Supervising Teachers." *J Teach Ed* 12:471–5; 1961.

Rench, Hazel S. "Observing Teaching via Closed-circuit Television." *J Teach Ed* 12:39–42; 1961.

Rhodes, Fred G., and Peckham, Dorothy R. "Evaluative Reports on Student Teachers." *J Teach Ed* 11:520–3; 1960.

Rivlin, Harry N. (Ed.) "Teaching and Teacher Education for Urban Disadvantaged Schools." *J Teach Ed* 16:135–86; 1965.

Rivlin, Harry N. "A New Pattern for Urban Teacher Education." *J Teach Ed* 17:177–84; 1966.

Sarason, S. B., and others. *The Preparation of Teachers: An Unstudied Problem in Education.* Wiley, 1962. 124p.

Schueler, Herbert N. "The Hunter College Program." In *Strength Through Reappraisal.* 16th Yearbook. AACTE, 1963. p. 141–6.

Schwartz, Sheila. "The Role of the Principal in the Student Teaching Program." *New Developments, Research and Experimentation in Professional Laboratory Experiences.* Bulletin No. 22. Association for Student Teaching, 1964.

Scrivner, A. W. "Action Programs of Inservice Education." In *Professional Growth Inservice of the Supervising Teacher.* 45th Yearbook. Association for Student Teaching, 1966. p. 75–100.

Shaplin, Judson T. "Practice in Teaching." In Smith, E. R. (Ed.) *Teacher Education: A Reappraisal.* Harper, 1962. p. 80–124.

Shaplin, Judson T., and Powell, Arthur G. "A Comparison of Internship Programs." *J Teach Ed* 15: 175–83; 1964.

Simmons, Gayle. "A, B (and Lack of) C's in Grading Student Teachers." *Sch Com* 51:27, 44–5; 1964.

Smith, E. Brooks (Ed.) *School-College Relationships in Teacher Education: Report of a National Survey of Cooperative Ventures.* AACTE, 1964. 69p.

Smith, E. Brooks. "Problems and Developments in School-College Cooperation." *NEA J* 54:36; 1965.

Smith, Emmitt D., and Cummingham, Fred J. "Administrative Relationships Between Teacher Education Institutions and Cooperating Public Schools." In *Teacher Education and the Public Schools*. 40th Yearbook. Association for Student Teaching, 1961. p. 3–22.

Smith, Gary R. "A Computer Program for the Placement of Student Teachers." *J Teach Ed* 13: 431–2; 1962.

Smith, Mildred B. "An Internship-Residency Training Program for Teachers of Disadvantaged Children." In *Remaking the World of the Career Teacher*. NEA, 1966. p. 184–5.

Stoller, Nathan, and others. "A Comparison of Methods of Observation in Preservice Teacher Training." *AV Communication R* 12:177–97; 1964.

Stone, James C. "Breakthrough in Teacher Education?" In Elam, Stanley. (Ed.) *Improving Teacher Education in the United States*. PDK, 1967. p. 165–90.

Stout, Ruth A. "Selective Admissions and Retention Practices in Teacher Education." *J Teach Ed* 8: 299–317; 422–32; 1957.

Strom, Ingrid M. *Leadership Through Research*. Research Bulletin No. 4. Association for Student Teaching, 1961. 27p.

U.S. Office of Education. *Cooperative Research Projects: A Seven Year Summary, July 1956 to June 1963*. GPO, 1963. 74p.

Van Winkle, Harold. "Public Relations and Cooperating Teachers." *J Teach Ed* 10:125–8; 1959.

Venable, Tom C. "The Function of the Laboratory School in the Teacher Training Program." *Teach Col J* 32:74–6+; 1960.

Walton, John. "The Study and Practice of Teaching." *Sch R* 69:136–50; 1961.

Watters, Edith, and Halstead, Jessie. "Changes During Relatively Recent Years." 41st Yearbook. Association for Student Teaching, 1962. p. 27–45.

Weiss, David. "Closed Circuit Television and Teacher Education." *Ed Forum* 26:229–31; 1962.

Westfall, Byron E. "Student Teaching Programs in Certain School Systems of the North Central Association Area." *North Cen Assn Q* 37:237–45; 1963.

Whiting, Helen A. "Internship of Supervising Teachers and Its Appraisal." *Ed Adm Sup* 43:23–32; 1957.

Wilk, Roger E. "An Experimental Study of the Effects of Classroom Placement Variables on Student Teacher Performance." *J Ed Psychol* 55: 375–80; 1964.

Wilk, Roger E., and others. *A Study of the Relationship Between Observed Classroom Behaviors of Elementary Student Teachers, Predictors of Those Behaviors and Ratings by Supervisors*. College of Education, U Minnesota, 1962. 60p.

Wilkinson, Rachel D. "Evaluation Based upon Observation of Reports of Supervisors of Student Teachers." *J Ed Res* 56:264–71; 1963.

Witrock, M. C. "Set Applied to Student Teaching." *J Ed Psychol* 53:175–80; 1962.

Woodruff, Asahel D. *Student Teaching Today*. AACTE, 1960. 56p.

Woodward, John C. "The Use of Television in Teacher Education." *J Teach Ed* 15:56–60; 1964.

Wooley, Ethel, and Smith, Ralph L. "Studio Teaching Before Student Teaching." *J Teach Ed* 13: 333–9; 1962.

STUDY

Studying has long been the primary means by which school learning takes place outside the classroom. Through homework assignments, independent study on special projects, and guided study under the supervision of a teacher or counselor, the student organizes his materials, drills on exercises in order to master specific skills, and formulates his own ideas in a way that can be evaluated by his teacher. Frequently he relies upon libraries to obtain specialized information or to take advantage of new learning resources such as listening tapes and filmstrips. Or he may take an entire course by correspondence study, in which he is completely on his own and thus his study habits, motivation to learn, and general attitudes are paramount in determining his success or failure. With the advent of new educational technology based upon television, programmed learning, and computer-assisted instruction, studying has become less distinct from the instructional process itself and more intertwined with the initial presentation of subject matter. In most situations, however, some form of study will continue to be the preferred method of individualized learning outside the classroom.

STUDY HABITS AND ATTITUDES. Wide variations have been universally noted in the methods of studying typically practiced by students. The time of day preferred, the time lapse between study sessions, the degree of noise or music tolerated or invited as background, the physical conditions of study, the extent to which extracurricular activities interfere, and the particular study mechanics employed are but a few of many factors which vary in every conceivable way among individuals. Many study habits appear detrimental to efficient learning, whereas others would seem to facilitate it. This observation has led numerous educators to write manuals on how to study, to develop checklists or inventories of study habits, and to offer courses on study skills.

Until recently, most recommendations on study skills were based on common sense or expert opinion rather than on scientific evidence of their value. Laycock and Russell (1941) analyzed 38 study manuals published between 1926 and 1939, from which they compiled 313 items mentioned four or more times. They noted that few if any were based on research findings; direct disagreement was evident in some areas. These findings verified the work of Cuff (1937), who studied Kentucky schoolchildren in grades 4 through 12. Many of the 75 so-called good study habits which he examined were reportedly being followed more exactly by the inferior students than by the better ones.

A more fruitful approach has been the comparison of good and poor students by questionnaires, interviews, or direct observation. One of the earliest attempts to develop a study habits inventory on an empirical basis of actual discrimination between good and poor students was made by Wrenn. The revised edition of the *Study Habits Inventory* developed by Wrenn and Larsen (1941) is still in use today, although other more comprehensive inventories have been devised. These early questionnaires and checklists placed heavy emphasis upon the mechanics of studying rather than on attitudes or motivation; consequently, they were not very successful in differentiating good and poor students. As Danskin and Burnett (1952) demonstrated, the reported study techniques of superior students are essentially the same as those of other students when a questionnaire approach is used in obtaining information.

An intensive clinical investigation of students at Sarah Lawrence College led Tiebout (1943) to emphasize the "lazy student syndrome" as a primary problem in studying. A number of poor students had four characteristics in common: (1) a need to rely upon strong and immediate motivations to start studying, (2) a tendency to be governed by strong hedonistic principles, (3) a tendency to have interests of a transitory, impermanent nature, and (4) a deep-seated problem in learning. Another way of describing such students is to stress their lack of inquisitiveness, interest, and drive for learning in an academic setting. Rebizov (1961) reported similar findings regarding pupil motivation in the Soviet Union, for which he blamed the schools and family life. Schlesser and Young (1945) found that questionnaire items which significantly differentiated good and poor college students were those which dealt with attitude, set, and motivation rather than study habits as such.

Taking advantage of prior empirical studies, Brown and Holtzman (1955; Holtzman & others, 1954) developed the *Survey of Study Habits and Attitudes* (*SSHA*). A total of 234 items was compiled from group interviews with good and poor students, existing inventories on study habits, studies using observational and interview techniques, and reports on related experiments in the field of learning. After several revisions based upon item analyses using college grades as a criterion, the 75-item *SSHA* was published in 1953. Scoring keys based on validity studies in ten colleges were developed, with one-semester grade averages as a criterion. Average validity coefficients for these widely different colleges were .42 and .45 for men and women, respectively. Low correlations with scholastic aptitude made it possible to increase the accuracy of prediction appreciably for college grades by adding the *SSHA*.

Subsequent studies by Lum (1960), Popham and Moore (1960), and other investigators verify the general finding that inclusion of items dealing with study attitudes and motivation increases appreciably the discrimination of good and poor students as compared with items concerned only with study habits. More recently, a successful adaptation of the *SSHA* in Hindi for use in India has been reported by Pandey (1966), who concluded that scores are not influenced by the self-esteem, self-enhancing, or social-desirability type of response set.

The *SSHA* was successfully modified for junior high school students by McBee and Duke (1960), who found that the kinds of study habits and attitudes covered were more relevant to achievement in reading, arithmetic, and science than in the areas of language functioning and social studies. The presence of several related dimensions in the *SSHA*, the desirability of a standardized version for junior and senior high school students as well as for college students, and the value of subscales for diagnostic and counseling purposes spurred the development of two revised editions, Form C for college (Brown & Holtzman, 1966) and Form S for high school (Brown & Holtzman, 1967). While retaining all previously significant items, both forms were expanded to 100 items grouped into four basic scales: Delay Avoidance, Work Methods, Teacher Approval, and Educational Acceptance. Additional reliability, validity, and normative studies are reported in the *SSHA* manuals, based on national samples of 3,054 college students and over 11,000 junior and senior high school students for Forms C and S, respectively.

Special techniques and environmental factors affecting learning have been investigated extensively, although direct applications to study methods are relatively few. Early investigations on outlining and summarizing, as opposed to rereading and underlining, were reviewed by Woodring and Flemming (1935), who concluded that for most students outlining and summarizing seem to produce superior results. Among Dutch psychology students, the best performers were those who used a more formalized study method, concentrated on the examination requirements rather than simply on following the content, appeared to be more self-critical and independent, and preferred to work alone (Van Parreren & Schutte-Poen, 1964). Confirmation of this last finding comes from a review of social facilitation studies by Zajonc (1965), who has one practical suggestion to offer: A student should study alone, but take his exams in the company of many other students and in the presence of a large audience to achieve the best results.

MANUALS AND COURSES ON HOW TO STUDY. A large number and variety of manuals, pamphlets, study aids, and books have been written for the student interested in improving his study skills. Typical of the better guides is *Effective Study* by Robinson (1961), the originator of the Survey Q3R method of studying. The five steps which are elaborated in this method consist of the following: (1) *Survey.* Glance quickly over the chapter headings, main points, and summary (to grasp the main ideas). (2) *Question.* Turn the first heading into a question (to arouse curiosity). (3) *Read.* Actively search for the answer to your question by reading the text. (4) *Recite.* Look away from the book and try briefly to recite the answer to your question. Then, after repeating steps 2, 3, and 4 on each succeeding headed section, go on to the final step. (5) *Review.* Look over your notes; recall main points first and then the subpoints. Practice exercises are provided, and more attention is given to motivation and higher-level study skills than was found in earlier guides.

Most colleges and many high schools offer courses on how to study. Since there is a dearth of clear-cut research findings on what to include or how to teach such study-skills courses, most rely heavily upon expert opinion and common sense tempered by feedback from students. Entwistle (1960) reviewed 22 research studies in which college study-skills courses were evaluated. Improvement in students' grades ranged from slight to substantial, as compared with control groups who did not take the course. Such courses are most beneficial for students who are highly motivated to take them. Varying in length from seven hours to two semesters, the courses were devoted to reading skills, study habits, individual or group counseling, testing, and occasionally supervised study of regular course material.

As in most research dealing with instruction, few unqualified generalizations can be made about study-skills courses. Berg and Rentel (1966) found that students who are motivated to improve and who voluntarily enroll in study-skills courses raise their grade point averages, whereas those who are similarly motivated but do not enroll fail to make the same gains. Format and content do not seem to be nearly so important as motivation and interest. Instructional methods in such courses can range over a continuum from instructor-centered lectures to student-centered discussions. Krumboltz and Farquhar (1957) compared these two extremes and a third more eclectic method with interesting results. Regardless of actual instruction given, students who originally expressed a preference for cognitive-type instruction showed a marked rise in *SSHA* scores after the course, whereas scores for those who expressed a preference for affective or student-centered instruction dropped significantly. Such interactions between attitude or personality traits and type of instruction are probably more commonplace than is generally realized.

With the greatly increased number of freshmen entering college each fall, it is virtually impossible to reach more than a few of them with the traditional course on study skills. A new approach involving upperclassmen as freshman counselors on study skills has been successfully demonstrated by Brown (1965). Three student-to-student counseling sessions, each lasting two hours, are given in the first few weeks of the fall semester at a critical time when the new student needs help. Survival orientation, test interpretation, and study-skills guidance constitute the substance of the small group meetings. At the end of the year it was found that counseled freshmen earned significantly higher grades than matched control cases. The student counselors are carefully selected and given brief training, and the entire program is under professional supervision.

HOMEWORK AND ASSIGNMENTS. Schools have always demanded some kind and amount of homework. The variety of assignments is almost unlimited and includes everything a student might be expected to learn (Yoakum, 1932). On the basis of preliminary experimental study of techniques in the mastery of high school science, Beauchamp (1923) concluded that definite assignments, regardless of type, result in superior achievement as measured by later test performance. With few exceptions, most of these early studies tried to determine prevailing practices and beliefs concerning homework and assignments rather than to evaluate their effectiveness. A good review of standard procedures in making assignments of homework for elementary and secondary pupils is presented by Burton (1944).

There has been much debate about the relative merits of compulsory versus voluntary homework or none at all. The controversy reached its peak in the mid-1930's, with most educators advocating less compulsory homework and more guided study or individual assignments in the school. The home environment, interest and educational background of parents, nature of the assignment, and follow-through by the teacher are but a few of the more important factors which determine the success or failure of home study. In one of the earliest empirical studies, Brooks (1916) visited the homes of 268 pupils in the fourth, fifth, and sixth grades of a city school system and gathered data on the type of home, amount of homework, amount of assistance, and school grades. As have others after him, Brooks discovered that children generally do well when their parents are capable of guiding the child and are inclined to supervise the home study, and that children with disinterested parents in poor home environments tend to have trouble with their schoolwork. This kind of survey information is a major argument used by advocates of guided study and individual assignments in the school instead of homework, especially in the lower grades.

A major element of this debate was resolved by an experiment involving 1200 children in the fifth and seventh grades of six New York City schools selected as representative of different neighborhoods (Di Napoli, 1937). One-half of the children were required to do regular homework assignments, which were checked and included as part of the grade at the end of the school term. The other half were given only voluntary homework—topics for home study suggested by both the teacher and children—that was not graded. Fifth graders with compulsory homework performed slightly better than their control counterparts, whereas the reverse tended to occur for the seventh graders, testifying once again to the overriding importance of other factors and the need for flexibility in dealing with assignments. As Strang (1955) points out, the current general trend is toward no homework in the primary grades, some in the middle grades, and a regular amount of home study in the high schools.

The type of assignments made by teachers is an important factor in pupil learning. Although there has been general agreement for many years that a variety of interesting assignments employing different techniques is best, Powers (1929) found that the great majority of teachers use only one kind of assignment. Brink (1934) analyzed assignments made by 1,000 high school teachers and found that 90 percent of them were entirely teacher-dominated. In spite of strenuous efforts on the part of educators and supervisors to overcome this teacher-centered style of instruction during the past 30 years, it is likely that the majority of teachers still dictate assignments and in other ways assume a more or less authoritarian manner. On the other hand, it is quite evident from studies of pupil attitudes toward teaching procedures (Doll, 1947) that most students prefer assignments resulting from joint planning by both the teacher and the students. In a study of factors associated with the teaching of mathematics, Schunert (1951) found that students who were given identical (that is, group) assignments did not do so well as students who were given assignments tailored to their specific interests and weaknesses. A good general presentation of criteria for assignments is given by Burton (1950).

GUIDED STUDY IN SCHOOL. The concept of guided or supervised study has undergone several changes in the past half century. The growing realization that assigning homework failed to result in satisfactory learning in many children, partly because of poor conditions in the home, strengthened the movement to provide study periods within the school day, for which teachers would be available to guide the study activity. In reviewing 60 early investigations, Brownell (1925) pointed out that evidence from the few controlled experiments slightly favored guided study over traditional homework or undirected independent study, where the acquisition of information was the goal of learning. Thirteen years later, in another review of guided study, Brownell (1938) found disappointingly few additional investigations involving controlled experiments. While he concluded that the kinds of guided study thus far investigated seemed hardly worth continuance of the programs, he was not ready to abandon the general concept if appropriately implemented. All too frequently, guided study has degenerated into mere maintenance of large study halls in which the primary role of the teacher is keeping order rather than providing professional assistance.

The introduction of students as monitors and the involvement of student councils in developing rules have helped to reduce somewhat the policing duty of the teacher (Strang, 1955). Nevertheless, the atmosphere in large study halls remains much the same. In a national opinion sample, Blumenfeld and Remmer (1966) collected information from 2,000 high school students on their attitudes toward study hall as related to their school grades. The better students disliked study hall, spent less time in study hall and more on homework, and showed a marked preference for serious study at home rather than in school. About one-third of those sampled avoided study hall completely; only 18 percent really preferred to study at school. As Burton (1950) points out, superior students appear to be less effective in study halls than on their own, whereas it does not seem to make a great deal of difference for the average students, and for the weaker ones study hall does have some definite advantages.

Undoubtedly the concept of guided study is changing again and perhaps is again becoming closer to the idealized notion of many years ago, which stressed a tutorial interaction between teacher and pupil. Although it is still too early to make firm predictions, the advent of new educational technology and the strong emphasis upon individualized instruction in mass education show considerable promise of blending formal instruction and study into a single instructional strategy. The concept of a study carrel for each pupil in a responsive learning environment, with audiovisual devices and tutorial interaction under computer control, is a far cry from the indifferent study hall all too prevalent today.

INDEPENDENT STUDY. The highest degree of student-centered instruction takes place when the inquiry is self-directed and the teacher remains in the background, offering assistance in small groups or in individual conferences. Advocates of independent study stress the advantages of working creatively on one's own, gaining in initiative and resourcefulness, studying intensively an area of special interest, developing self-discipline, and learning research techniques in a chosen field. As generally conceived, independent study is more likely to occur in higher education than at the elementary or secondary levels, although it is certainly not limited in this respect. New ways of incorporating the ideas of independent study into the curriculum of childhood education are receiving increased attention (Veatch, 1967).

Traditionally, independent study has been the preferred method of European universities since their inception. The reading or tutorial programs at Oxford are classic examples of such programs; and many American colleges have attempted to follow this pattern of study, at least for their best students. While an occasional seminar course or informal colloquium can be found on nearly every campus, organized programs of independent study for lower-division students are much less common. In a 1954 survey of 1,084 senior colleges, Bonthius and others (1957) discovered that only 26 percent offered a regular independent-study program. The typical college in this sampling enrolled less than a dozen students a year in such programs.

In only a handful of the independent-study programs has there been any systematic evaluation of the method. One of the most recent experimental studies is the Antioch College program, in which a large number of students were followed up to determine their attitudes and retention of subject matter two years after completing either the independent-study program or the regular classroom program in the same courses. Pre- and post-treatment measures were obtained for both the experimental and the control students. Baskin (1962) reported that both groups of students learned equally well in the Antioch experiment, regardless of academic ability. Nor could any differences be detected by objective tests two years afterward. Student dissatisfaction with independent study was fairly general at the beginning of the experiment but diminished considerably at the end of the program. A major problem arose because entering freshmen were poorly prepared for independent study. A similar experiment at the University of South Florida attested to greater learning by independent study than by traditional classes (Hartnett & Stewart, 1966). Usually restricted to students of proven ability, most research, however, shows little or no difference between regular classes and independent study when formal examinations are used.

One of the more unique programs of independent study is that leading to a Bachelor of Liberal Studies Degree at Oklahoma University (Burkett, 1965). Offered entirely on an independent-study basis, the program requires that the student attend a four-week residence seminar in a given area once he has completed the readings. Books are furnished on a long-term rental basis, and the student is informed of programs, telecasts, lectures, and other activities that supplement the readings. The degree is granted after a final interarea seminar and comprehensive examination.

A variety of approaches to independent study have been collected in a single volume by Hatch and Richards (1965). Self-directed study, library research, honors programs, and special experiments at Harvard, Knox, Cornell, Hope, Antioch, and Mount Holyoke are presented as illustrations of successful innovations in independent study. In general, it can be concluded that independent-study programs are on the increase as an opportunity for growth toward intellectual self-reliance.

USE OF LIBRARIES. The rapid growth of public libraries throughout the country early in this century was a major force in the educational development of the nation. After reviewing studies on the use of public libraries, Berelson (1949) estimated that public libraries supply about one-fourth of all books read. The smaller the community, the larger the proportion of library users. About 1 out of every 3 children and 1 out of 10 adults are regular users of the public library. As Waples and Carnovsky (1939) reported in a study of libraries and readers in the state of New York, the public library, together with school and home, is a major source of materials for study.

In most colleges and universities, the library is the center of learning for every discipline, as well as the major archive for scholarly research. In spite of the importance of the library for study, relatively few colleges have a systematic program for instructing students on the use of the library. Josey (1962) reported that in only one out of four colleges did the reference librarian offer a general course on library use. The librarian may give a lecture or two as part of freshman orientation, or an interested faculty member of the English department may provide some guidance on how to use a library. In most colleges, however, learning how to use the library occurs haphazardly and informally through a trial-and-error process of hunting down needed material.

A special effort to overcome the weaknesses and barriers of the typical college library program was made at Monteith College, an experimental college founded in 1959 as part of Wayne State University. The primary goal of the Monteith project was to help the undergraduate attain a high level of competence in the use of the library by special new programs of instruction developed jointly by the library staff and the general faculty. Since about half of the four-year curriculum consists of basic courses required of every student, instruction on use of the library is woven into this core curriculum. A description of the way in which the librarians work with the general faculty at Monteith College and a preliminary summary of results are given by Knapp (1964).

Although nearly everyone agrees that all high school students should receive training in the use of library resources, in reality only a small proportion actually receive it. When properly given, such instruction can significantly increase the student's performance in other courses. Hastings and Tanner (1963) studied two experimental and two control classes of tenth-grade English to determine the importance of library work in improving English language skills. The experimental groups received weekly instruction in the library on the use of a wide variety of reference materials. The control groups drilled in grammar and spelling and used the library only occasionally. Improvement of English language skills was significantly greater for the experimental groups, indicating that library experience enhanced ability to comprehend the meaning of words from their context.

In elementary schools, a major obstacle to the use of libraries is the serious lack of centralized library facilities and an even more acute shortage of trained librarians to run them. Some educators have felt that independent collections of material for each classroom are preferable to the centralized collection. But this concept is rapidly losing ground with the advent of new technology and the expansion of the library into a comprehensive learning-resources center for the elementary school. Gaver (1963) and

Powell (1966) present empirical data bearing upon this issue.

The role of the elementary school librarian in teaching study skills within the library has been emphasized by Henne (1966). In a study of 188 children drawn from 11 elementary schools with a professional librarian and 12 schools without one, Gengler (1966) found marked differences in the extent to which problem-solving skills were developed. Children in the schools with a librarian demonstrated greater ability directly attributable to the kind of instruction received in the library. In a number of the model library programs under development, the introduction of new technology and the transformation of the library into a comprehensive learning center is placing still greater responsibility upon library personnel for teaching study skills. Typical of such forward-looking programs is the learning center at Shaker Heights for the middle grades in two elementary schools (Krohn, 1964). The two-year work-study skills program emphasizes the development of independent-study habits by providing pupils with study carrels, listening areas, and reference facilities. Such trends will accelerate still further within the nongraded school, which places a premium on individualized instruction and new technology.

CORRESPONDENCE STUDY. Instruction by correspondence is as old as written communication. The home-study movement developed rapidly at the turn of the century. The number of students enrolled in the International Correspondence Schools grew from only 80,000 in 1899 to nearly 1 million seven years later (Clarke, 1906). Rising standards and development of accreditation transformed correspondence study into a major extension of high school, university, and adult education in general. Further explosive growth occurred in World War II when the U.S. Armed Forces Institute was formed to provide correspondence study for servicemen (Houle & others, 1947). By 1958, nearly 2 million adults were enrolled in university correspondence courses alone. Home study by correspondence for academic credit has proved successful at every level from first grade to postdoctoral work and has made possible the continued education of otherwise inaccessible people.

At first glance, the student enrolled in correspondence courses would appear to be at a disadvantage when compared with regular classroom students. Personal interaction with the instructor and fellow students is missing, and many of the resources for learning are not readily available. In spite of these differences, correspondence students perform at least as well as classroom students, according to most investigations comparing the two methods. Childs (1954) compared 1,800 high school students and 1,250 correspondence students in fields ranging from mathematics to foreign languages. In most courses the achievement of correspondence students was significantly above that of classroom students of comparable age and ability. Childs (1956) followed up 79 students who took high school mathematics by correspondence and a comparable group who took mathematics in the classroom. Both groups were compared after having taken mathematics at the University of Nebraska. The students with a background in correspondence study actually achieved significantly higher grades in college mathematics than did the regular students. In successfully completing home-study work, many correspondence students apparently develop a level of motivation and self-discipline that is valuable in higher education.

For many years correspondence study was largely restricted to materials that could be mailed back and forth. The availability of educational television opened new possibilities, and by 1957 four schools were integrating television with correspondence study of the more traditional type. Zigerell (1967) reported a follow-up study of 300 students who had completed at least one correspondence course over television in Chicago City College. Nearly all the students maintained that they had learned as much from the television instruction as they had in the classroom and that they had earned comparable grades. Of the 1966 graduates at Chicago City College, 14 students took all their courses by TV correspondence study. With the development of more effective technology, the student enrolled in correspondence courses can look forward to a wider variety of enriched instruction that will closely approximate resident (that is, person-to-person) instruction in the future.

Wayne H. Holtzman
The University of Texas

References

Baskin, Samuel. "Experiment in Independent Study (1956–1960)." *J Exp Ed* 31:183–5; 1962.

Beauchamp, Wilbur I. "A Preliminary Experimental Study of Techniques in the Mastery of Subject Matter in Elementary Physical Science." In *Studies in Secondary Education*, Vol. I. U Chicago, 1923. p. 47–87.

Berelson, Bernard R. *The Library's Public*. Columbia U, 1949. 174p.

Berg, Paul C., and Rentel, Victor M. "Improving Study Skills." *J Reading* 9:343–6; 1966.

Blumenfeld, Warren S., and Remmer, H. H. "Attitudes Toward Study Hall as Related to Grades." *J Ed Res* 59:406–8; 1966.

Bonthius, Robert H., and others. *Independent Study Programs in the United States*. Columbia U, 1957. 259p.

Brink, William G. "Assignment Procedures of 1000 High School Teachers." *Ed Trends* 1:6–14; 1934.

Brooks, E. C. "The Value of Home Study Under Parental Supervision." *El Sch J* 17:187–94; 1916.

Brown, William F. "Student-to-Student Counseling for Academic Adjustment." *Personnel Guid J* 43: 811–7; 1965.

Brown, William F., and Holtzman, Wayne H. "A

Study-Attitudes Questionnaire for Predicting Academic Success." *J Ed Psychol* 46:75–84; 1955.

Brown, William F., and Holtzman, Wayne H. *Survey of Study Habits and Attitudes: Form C.* The Psychological Corporation, 1966.

Brown, William F., and Holtzman, Wayne H. *Survey of Study Habits and Attitudes: Form S.* The Psychological Corporation, 1967.

Brownell, William A. *A Study of Supervised Study.* Bureau of Educational Research, U Illinois, 1925. 48p.

Brownell, William A. "What Has Happened to Supervised Study?" *Ed Meth* 17:373–7; 1938.

Burkett, J. E. "Curriculum Leading to Bachelor of Liberal Studies Degree." *Ed Rec* 46:195–203; 1965.

Burton, William H. *The Guidance of Learning Activities.* Appleton, 1944. 601p.

Burton, William H. "Implications for Organization of Instruction and Instructional Adjuncts." In *Learning and Instruction.* 49th Yearbook. Part I, N S S E, U Chicago, 1950. p. 217–55.

Childs, Gayle B. "A Comparison of Supervised Correspondence Study Pupils and Classroom Pupils in Achievement in School Subjects." *J Ed Res* 47:537–43; 1954.

Childs, Gayle B. "Success in Initial University Mathematics Courses of Students with Correspondence and Non-Correspondence Background in High School Mathematics." *J Ed Res* 49:607–12; 1956.

Clarke, J. J. "The Correspondence School: Its Relation to Technical Education and Some of Its Results." *Sci* 24:327; 1906.

Cuff, Noel B. "Study Habits in Grades Four to Twelve." *J Ed Psychol* 28:295–301; 1937.

Danskin, David G., and Burnett, Collins W. "Study Techniques of Those Superior Students." *Personnel Guid J* 31:181–6; 1952.

Di Napoli, Peter J. *Homework in the New York City Elementary Schools.* Teachers Col, Columbia U, 1937. 60p.

Doll, Donald C. "High School Pupils' Attitudes Toward Teaching Procedures." *Sch R* 55:22–7; 1947.

Entwistle, Doris R. "Evaluations of Study-Skills Courses: A Review." *J Ed Res* 53:243–51; 1960.

Gaver, Mary Virginia. *Effectiveness of Centralized Library Service in Elementary Schools,* 2nd ed. Rutgers, 1963. 268p.

Gengler, Charles R. "Developing Skills for Problem-Solving: A Study." *Sch Lib* 15:31–5; 1966.

Hartnett, Rodney T., and Stewart, Clifford T. "Final Examination Grades of Independent Study Students Compared with Those Students Taught by Traditional Methods." *J Ed Res* 59:356–60; 1966.

Hastings, Dorothy M. H., and Tanner, Daniel. "The Influence of Library Work in Improving English Language Skills at the High School Level." *J Exp Ed* 31:401–5; 1963.

Hatch, Winslow R., and Richards, Alice L. (Eds.) *Approach to Independent Study.* USOE, 1965. 73p.

Henne, Frances. "Learning to Learn in School Libraries." *Sch Lib* 15:15–23; 1966.

Holtzman, Wayne H., and others. "The Survey of Study Habits and Attitudes: A New Instrument for the Prediction of Academic Success." *Ed Psychol Meas* 14:726–32; 1954.

Houle, Cyril O., and others. *The Armed Services and Adult Education.* ACE, 1947. 257p.

Josey, E. J. "The Role of the College Library Staff in Instruction in the Use of the Library." *Res Lib* 23:492–8; 1962.

Knapp, Patricia B. "Methodology and Results of the Monteith Pilot Project." *Lib Trends* 13:84–102; 1964.

Krohn, M. L. "Learning and the Learning Center." *Ed Leadership* 21:217–22; 1964.

Krumboltz, John D., and Farquhar, William W. "The Effect of Three Teaching Methods on Achievement and Motivational Outcomes in a How-to-Study Course." *Psychol Monogr* 71(14); 1957. 25p.

Laycock, S. R., and Russell, D. H. "An Analysis of Thirty-eight How-to-study Manuals." *Sch R* 49:370–9; 1941.

Lum, Mabel K. M. "Comparison of Under- and Overachieving Female College Students." *J Ed Psychol* 51:109–15; 1960.

McBee, George, and Duke, Ralph L. "Relationship between Intelligence, Scholastic Motivation, and Academic Achievement." *Psychol Reports* 6:3–8; 1960.

Pandey, Jagdish. "Response Set on Survey of Study Habits and Attitudes (Hindi Adaptation)." *Psychol Stud* 11:9–14; 1966.

Popham, James and Moore, Mary R. "A Validity Check on the Brown-Holtzman *Survey of Study Habits and Attitudes* and the Borow *College Inventory of Academic Adjustment.*" *Personnel Guid J* 38:552–4; 1960.

Powell, William R. "Classroom Libraries: Their Frequency of Use." *El Engl* 43:395–7; 1966.

Powers, J. Orin. "Analysis of the Use Made of the Recitation Period." In *Scientific Methods in Supervision.* 2nd Yearbook. National Conference of Supervisors and Directors of Instruction. Teachers Col, Columbia U, 1929. p. 145–63.

Rebizov, D. G. "Ob Otnoshinii uchaschikhaya k ucheniyu i trudu." [On the Attitude of Pupils Toward Study and Work.] *Voprosy Psikhologii* 7:19–26; 1961.

Robinson, Francis P. *Effective Study.* Harper, 1961. 278p.

Schlesser, George M., and Young. C. W. "Study and Work Habits." *Sch R* 53:85–95; 1945.

Schunert, J. "The Association of Mathematical Achievement with Certain Factors Resident in the Teacher, in the Teaching, in the Pupil, and in the School." *J Exp Ed* 19:219–38; 1951.

Strang, Ruth. *Guided Study and Homework.* NEA, 1955. 33p.

Tiebout, Harry M. "The Misnamed Lazy Student." *Ed Rec* 24:113–29; 1943.

Van Parreren, C. F., and Schutte-Poen, W. L. "Studiegewoonten van Psychologiestudenten." *Nederlands Tydschrift voor de Psychologie* 19:255–68; 1964.

Veatch, Jeannette. "Improving Independent Study." *Child Ed* 43:284–8; 1967.

Waples, Douglas, and Carnovsky, Leon. *Libraries and Readers in the State of New York.* U Chicago, 1939. 160p.

Woodring, Maxie N., and Flemming, Cecile W. *Directing Study of High School Pupils.* Teachers Col, Columbia U, 1935. 235p.

Wrenn, C. Gilbert, and Larsen, Robert P. *Studying Effectively.* Stanford U Press, 1941. 3 p.

Yoakum, Gerald A. *The Improvement of the Assignment.* Macmillan, 1932. 398p.

Zajonc, Robert B. "Social Facilitation." *Sci* 149:269–74; 1965.

Zigerell, James J. "Chicago's TV College." *AAUP B* 53:49–54; 1967.

SUPERVISION

Instructional supervision has long been regarded as an essential part of school administration. Burton and Brueckner (1955) suggest that supervision was first conceived as a form of inspection. Its earliest beginnings in the United States were probably in Boston, when in 1709 a group of citizens was appointed to inspect the school plant and equipment and the level of achievement of pupils. The town selectmen served as inspectors until other administrative arrangements began to evolve. With the development of the administrative positions of principal and superintendent, inspection was gradually shifted from lay people to professionals. Supervisors of special subjects made their appearance late in the nineteenth century. Gwynn (1965) reports that supervision was carried forward as an inspection role until about 1920. The period since 1920 has been characterized by the added dimension of democratic leadership in the supervisory role. Contempory writers such as Harris (1963), Curtin (1964), Wiles (1967), Crosby (1957), and Heald and Moore (1968) all suggest that the fundamental role of the instructional supervisor is to bring about improved instruction. Burton and Brueckner (1955) and Wiles (1967) stress the involvement of teachers in the process of their own improvement as a goal of supervision. An even broader concept is expressed by Neagley and Evans (1964). They consider that the growth of teachers, administrators, and parents, as well as of the children, is a legitimate concern of the supervisor who works toward improved instruction.

The Dictionary of Education (Good, 1945) defines supervision as "all efforts of designated school officials toward providing leadership to teachers and other educational workers in the improvement of instruction; involves the stimulation and professional growth and development of teachers, a selection and revision of educational objectives, materials of instruction, and methods of teaching, and the evaluation of instruction." Harmes (1959) states that "supervision may be broadly defined as services provided for the improvement of instruction." Harmes further suggests that because the teacher is an agent of instruction, his improvement is also a legitimate goal of supervision. Wiles (1967) adds that "supervision is assistance in the development of a better teaching-learning situation."

While most writers agree that the improvement of instruction should be the main focus of supervision, there remains much disagreement over the means to best effect improvement. Eye and Netzer (1965) assert that, though there is a dichotomy of functions between administration and supervision, supervision is nevertheless a phase of administration. Heald and Moore (1968) propose that lay communities are likely to expect supervision to be done by administrators. Davis (1964) states that "where there is a supervisory principal, he is almost always the chief evaluator of his teachers." Certainly the evaluation aspect of supervision has largely come to reside with the principal's office, for it is from this office more than any other that recommendations must come for reemployment, tenure, salary, and promotions.

Not all authors agree that supervision should come from a line position. Babcock (1965) states the generally held view of the Association for Supervision and the Curriculum Development when he suggests that supervision is a service rather than an administrative function. "We have long recognized that the supervision of instruction in the classroom should be removed from the 'authority' role. It should be removed as far as possible from the 'line-staff' relationship." Supervision would thereby be a staff function to be conducted by supervisory specialists. Gwynn (1965) outlines three additional principles: (1) the supervisor's position should be that of improving instruction through in-service programs; (2) the supervisor's responsibility is for fostering good human relations through effective use of group processes; and (3) supervision is best accomplished when it is related to curriculum revision and curriculum building.

Though disagreement does exist over the manner in which supervision can best be accomplished, reasonable agreement does exist for the goals of supervision. It might be expected that agreement would provide a reasonably strong base for the conduct of research. However, MacDonald (1965) concluded that "in comparison with other aspects of educational concern (e.g., teaching and administering), supervision held less basis in fact." Rather, he suggests that folklore, personal experience, and philosophy are the more normal bases for most supervisory practices. Yet, the goal of supervision is to improve instruction, and it would seem logical to expect that research would center on the effects of various supervisory practices upon instruction.

In his extensive study of 6,000 teachers and 1,700 schools, Ryans (1960) undertook to identify teacher characteristics and to analyze their classroom behavior. Such research is relevant to problems of supervision. In research studies and reviews of research studies, Barr (1961) and Medley and Mitzel

(1959) have diagnosed the problems inherent in evaluating teachers and teaching. They point out that because of the absence of strong, suitable criteria and the paucity of measures of teacher effectiveness, research in the field of supervision has centered on other areas.

LEADERSHIP. If leadership is, as Lipham (1964) suggests, "the initiation of a new structure or procedure for accomplishing an organization's goals and objectives or for changing an organization's goals and objectives," then supervision and leadership are closely allied. The capacity to lead may be related to the skill of the leader in assessing the expectations and interests of his teachers. Chesler and others (1963) report that a staff's propensity to change is closely related to the principal's ability to perceive his faculty's expectations accurately.

In a national study of 501 principals in 41 cities, Gross and Herriot (1965) measured the ability of principals to stimulate improvement in the quality of their staffs' performance. Such behavior, labeled Executive Professional Leadership (EPL), was studied in elementary school principals with measures relying heavily upon teacher responses and principal self-evaluations. EPL was rated highest by teachers for the principal who consistently (1) provided for their involvement in his decisions, (2) kept his interpersonal relationships on an egalitarian rather than a status basis, (3) provided social support, (4) provided managerial support, and (5) supported the authority of his faculty. EPL was also found to be higher for young principals and for those with less professional, formal education in administration. Erickson (1965) provides a thoughtful analysis of the EPL studies.

Leadership style is also of importance to the supervisor. Principals or other evaluators may project their own style of leadership into their perceptions of the staff members with whom they must work. Brown (1966) found that ratings by a system-centered principal of the effectiveness of his teachers differed greatly from the ratings by a principal whose leadership style was more individual-centered.

In a study of over 1,000 teachers, the Council on Administrative Leadership found that teachers perceived administration as largely a leadership position. They expressed a desire for clearer job definitions, and they wanted those in leadership positions to be more knowledgable, to recognize their needs more often and to work toward a meeting of those needs. Many studies, including that of Bradfield (1959), have found that teachers rate as best those procedures which are perceived as democratic and which involve good human relations and group interactions. Luckie (1963) also found that skills in human relations were important in determining the effectiveness of directors of instruction. However, Bradfield (1959) found that the actual assistance received by teachers from supervisors was more often concerned with routine administrative matters than with instructional leadership.

The relationship between authority and leadership has also been studied. Enns (1965) declared that the task of teacher evaluation should not be placed upon a principal who already has operations and development as his full-time concerns. He found that principal behavior which was perceived as highly directive and restrictive as correlated with teacher dissatisfaction. On the other hand, leadership behavior which was perceived as exemplary and which was personally stimulating and professionally motivating correlated much more highly with teacher satisfaction. Principals were rated as most effective when they exhibited the latter characteristics.

The amount of authority which administrators invest in teachers is dependent upon expectations of a return on that investment. Viewing teacher responsibilities and institutional expectations as an exchange system, Anderson (1967) asserts that unreliable measures of performance output, distrust of teacher motivations, and general lack of faith in the return on an authority investment results in reducing the investment because of the perceived risk.

When threat and stress is introduced into the supervisory relationship, it sometimes results in a deterioration in the performance of teachers. Brown (1962) found that pupil-teacher rapport, warmth and understanding, and pupil-teacher interaction suffer from stress induced by the supervisor. The technical aspects of the teaching act were largely unaffected. Stress had its greatest negative impact on the performance of teachers high in neuroticism and in scholastic aptitude. Improved performance followed stress induced in those teachers low in neuroticism and scholastic aptitude. Brown concluded that supervisors would do well to differentiate between those for whom stress would be a positive or negative motivating factor.

In a later study of 1,551 teachers in 170 schools, Brown (1967) found that teacher's descriptive profiles of their principals were much more like their perceptions of community leaders than like their perceptions of corporation presidents. The principal's image was characterized by tolerance and a low productivity drive. Teacher satisfaction and the confidence which teachers placed in principals were influenced by the perceived leadership of the principal. In another study of leadership styles, Vigilante (1964) found that principals and supervisors expected supervisors to be ideographic when confronted with situations involving a status dimension. Supervisors were expected to be transactional in situations involving an authority dimension or a means-end dimension.

The creative administrator has been defined by Antley (1966) as a sensitive, perceptive, flexible, and fluent person with a capacity for novel ideas and the ability to reorganize and to redefine. In a study of 42 superintendents and principals and 800 teachers, he found that such administrators (1) possessed a large store of factual knowledge about administration and supervision, (2) offered more possible solutions to teachers' problems, (3) dealt more often with school-wide problems than with isolated ones, and

(4) involved more persons in the decision-making process.

MORALE. Although it has often been hypothesized that morale has a direct effect on teaching effectiveness, research supporting this contention is largely lacking—again for the reason that measures of teaching effectiveness have not lived up to their promise. The concept of morale has received serious attention. Blocker and Richardson's (1963) summary of morale research calls attention to diverse methods of measuring morale and morale factors. It also describes the many factors which have been found to influence morale. The teacher-supervisor relationship appears as a factor in many of the studies they report. In a later study (Richardson & Blocker, 1966), they reveal that faculty morale can be measured in the dimensions of (1) supervision, (2) self-integration, (3) institutional environment, and (4) employment rewards. The categories subsumed by the instrument under "supervision" were communication with administrators and relations with immediate superiors. Faculty members rated as highly important a reciprocity of communication and a willingness to listen on the part of the superior. In a study of 5,000 teachers in 24 systems, Redefer (1959) found that (1) morale and educational quality were related; (2) morale and supervisor ratings were closely related; (3) salary and salary schedules do not determine morale; (4) morale is not well correlated with "problem" situations; and (5) personal characteristics of teachers are not a large morale factor.

Harap (1959), in a study of 20 school systems, found that the most common causes of poor morale were inadequate salaries, large classes, poor administrative support, lack of free time, unsatisfactory facilities, lack of material and equipment, and other work-related conditions. Although the size of salaries may be a morale factor, Chandler (1959) reports that the type of salary program (merit versus nonmerit) was not a significant morale factor.

Rather than falling along a continuum, factors which determine teacher satisfaction and dissatisfaction may be quite polar. Sergiovanni (1967) reports that archievement, recognition, and responsibility positively affect job satisfaction. Dissatisfaction seems to have roots in interpersonal relations with students and peers, school policy and the manner of its administration, status, and personal life. In general, satisfaction seems to focus on the nature of the work, and dissatisfaction on the conditions surrounding the work.

EVALUATION. Of the many expectations held for supervisors, among the most common is the expectation that the supervisor will evaluate the work of the teacher. Such a position is consistent with the view that supervision is best done from a "line" position. Many kinds of evaluation procedures have been suggested to identify outstanding teachers. Hawkins and Stoops (1966) compared ten methods, which included various objective and subjective means. Concordance among the ten methods was very high. Evaluation reports from personnel files proved to be the least discriminating of the methods. Other methods, using objective data, were also less discriminating than the subjective methods. They found that school-associated groups tend to agree with the evaluating professionals on who the outstanding teachers are. Principals' judgments were found to be no better than those of other persons at discriminating among teachers. It was further found that principals had little influence over the judgments of the teachers by their peers.

Much concern has been expressed over the degree to which an evaluator's personality enters into his evaluation. Guba and Bidwell (1957) have posited that a principal's estimate of a teacher's effectiveness is in reality an estimate of the degree to which a teacher fits the principal's expectation of the teacher role. If personality were a factor in expectations and behavior, then personality similarities or differences might affect teacher ratings made by principals. Andrews and Brown (1959) studied 608 teachers and principals to determine if the principal's ratings of teacher effectiveness were contaminated by similarities or differences in the personality characteristics of attitudes, values, and manifest needs. It was concluded that by and large, principals were capable of keeping their ratings uncontaminated by similarities in personality characteristics. Their findings supported an earlier study by Prince (1957), which tested the congruence of educational values with teacher ratings.

Perhaps the most comprehensive study of evaluation procedures was completed by the National Educational Association (1964). This study involved 600 superintendents, 800 principals, and 1,100 teachers. Although teachers were evaluated in almost every reporting system, only slightly more than one-half of the school systems reported having clearly defined criteria describing good teaching. The building principal was the primary supervisory agent and the person held most accountable for making teacher evaluations. In almost all cases, evaluation reports had the principal as one of the signers. In about 10 percent of the cases he shared accountability with an instructional supervisor other than himself. In larger cities, written evaluation reports were filed with personnel directors, whereas in smaller school systems the superintendent was the major recipient of evaluation reports. The most common kinds of ratings came from lists of criteria which required checking by the evaluator, with additional spaces provided for comments on specified factors. The second most common form of written report was a simple checklist of criteria, with no additional comments required. The most common uses of the evaluations were stated to be improved instruction, reappointment, or tenure. Over one-half of the teachers reported that the written evaluations of their work resulted in no observable changes in their behavior.

The NEA survey repoted many differences in perceptions associated with the evaluation procedure.

For example, superintendents were most confident in the capacity of evaluation programs to improve the quality of teaching, but teachers were the least confident. The percentage of principals who believed that evaluation programs stimulate teachers to improve instruction was nearly twice as high as the percentage of teachers who believed that improvement followed evaluation.

The most common method used to obtain evaluations was the classroom observation. More than 90 percent of the principals reported using this method. Teacher conferences and out-of-class contacts were also reported as common means of evaluating teachers' work. The teachers reported a much smaller number of evaluation observations than did principals, with about one-fourth of the teachers saying they had not been observed during the preceding year. Probationary teachers and experienced teachers apparently were observed at about the same rate.

OTHER ROLES AND PRACTICES. The supervisor spends his time in many ways other than formally evaluating the work of his teachers. His role, if effective, consists of bringing diverse materials and methods to the task of improving instruction. In a study of Michigan teachers and administrators, Goldman (1966) found that the role of the principal, as perceived by teachers, is best fulfilled when the principal is helping to solve teacher problems and when he is providing for teacher participation in the decision-making process. Columbro (1964) adds another dimension to the supervisor's role when she suggests that he should integrate action research into total teacher growth efforts.

Following a study conducted by Louisiana school supervisors, Landry (1959) reported that the most persistent activities of supervisors were visiting the classes, doing clerical work, conferring with principals and teachers, working with lay groups, traveling, and participating in group conferences. At least half of the activities were found to be unrelated to improving instruction. The most commonly reported practices that were perceived as related to improving instruction included working with principals, engaging in classroom visitation, initiating ideas and suggestions, serving as resource persons, and providing individual help to teachers. In a study of Canadian elementary and secondary schools, Riederer (1965) found that elementary principals spent less than two hours per pupil per year in supervisory and administrative activities. Secondary principals spent slightly more than four hours per pupil per year. Teal (1965) found that the time spent in supervisory activities was not a function of personal or personality variables but, rather, was a function of the number of tenured teachers on the supervisor's staff.

Observations and conferences are often used as supervisory techniques. Sandberg (1965) reports that teachers liked conferences best when the supervisor's role was made clear. Teacher observation was found to be effective when used to analyze problems and less effective when used for inspection purposes. However, it should be noted that supervisors felt that observation for inspection purposes was effective. Observation was found to be of particular value when followed by conferences. Teacher expectations of conferences included getting help in planning and problem solving.

In addition to observation and conferences, in-service activities are often planned as aids to improving instruction. In Flanders' (1963) study of the effectiveness of in-service programs, an attempt was made to effect changes in patterns of teacher influence as practiced in the classroom. It was shown that teacher progress following the in-service sessions was related to the consistency between the teacher's initial preferred style of influence and the method utilized in the in-service program. There appear to be substantial differences between the perceptions of teachers and the perceptions of administrators about what constitutes effective orientation and in-service practices. Teachers in Tower's (1956) study rated help from other teachers as the most effective practice, but principals rated it at rank 13. Principals rated their conferences with teachers as the second-best practice, but teachers rated the conferences at rank 14. A limited survey conducted by Cappa and Van Meter (1957) indicated that teachers preferred small group meetings, bulletins, visitations, and conferences to other procedures.

Conflicts and pressures of real situations sometimes reduce the gains made in in-service programs. McNassor (1951) found that workshops could change teachers' attitudes and behaviors, but that the changes were largely temporary, since teachers reverted to their old behavior when they returned to their own classroom. Bowers and Soar (1961) found that some kinds of teachers can effect real changes in their teaching behavior through intensive in-service programs. Those whose personality measures correlated most highly with effective practices were generally the ones who gained most from the in-service programs. Allen (1966) suggested that microteaching, which involves limited concepts taught to small numbers in short periods of time, provides a good framework for building immediate feedback and criticism. Reinforcement and corrections can take place nearer to the moment of the teaching behavior.

Faculty meetings are also a commonly employed technique in the supervisory process. The perceptions of principals about the value and nature of faculty meetings may be very different from the perceptions of teachers. In Amidon and Blumberg's (1966) study, principals saw meetings as attractive, productive situations. Teachers were neutral or negative in their perceptions. Similar differences were noted in the perception of interpersonal problems within the schools.

Coody (1967) suggests that teaching demonstrations can promote changes in teacher behavior. Downing (1964) reports that role effectiveness is best when demonstrations of methodology are conducted in a natural context at appropriate times. She concludes that supervision is most effective when demonstrations are done without diminishing the teacher's role, and when supervisory behavior is characterized by support rather than threat and by evaluation rather than rating.

Self-evaluation also seems to be an important method used by supervisors. Fuller and Richek (1966) report that audio tapes can be used for feedback to a teacher on his performance. Self-evaluation can be furthered through self-study of the tapes. Improved methodology in using and integrating the technique seems to be needed if full benefits are to accrue from this method of self-evaluation. Interaction analysis, such as Flander's system, can be used to study tapes taken from the learning environment. Amidon and others (1966) report that such interaction analysis has been used successfully to assist the development of introspective processes.

SELECTION, TRAINING, AND CERTIFICATION. The selection of supervisors, as suggested by the Georgia Teacher Education Council and reported by Cox (1966), should give consideration to (1) evidence of leadership, (2) ability to get along with others, (3) teaching capacity, (4) tolerance level, and (5) the ability to respect persons with whom differences are known.

In a jointly sponsored experiment in the training of educational supervisors, Berea College and the University of Kentucky provided educational experiences for 30 supervisors. Ogletree and others (1962) disclosed that the effectiveness of the program, as measured by changes in supervisory behavior, was most closely related to interpersonal warmth of relationships developed between trainer and student. Need identification and the prescription of experiences to meet needs were the basis for professional cooperation. Rogers (1967) suggested that intensive group experiences among the membership of school systems are requisite to providing for self-directed change of educational organizations. He suggested that T groups, sensitivity training, and encounter groups are good experiences for preparing the membership of an organization for change. After observing the performance of over 200 principals in a simulated setting, Hemphill and others (1962) concluded that simulation techniques provide an excellent method for teaching the many skills required of administrators.

Although extensive research has not been done in the general area of the certification of supervisors, Hallberg (1966) reports that a 1964 study indicated a great discrepancy in the standards for the certification of supervisory personnel. Seventy-one different certificates were identified in 36 of the 50 states. Some certificates were good for both elementary and secondary levels, and others were limited to one level or to a special subject area.

Concepts of supervision and supervisory practices have undergone much change since their beginnings. The impact of teacher negotiations on the historical role of the building principal and teacher-principal relationships has yet to be fully assessed. New patterns of supervision will undoubtly emerge. The best measure of the efficacy of emerging patterns must wait for new and better measures of assessing instructional improvement.

James E. Heald
Michigan State University

References

Allen, Dwight W. "Micro-Teaching: A New Framework for In-service Education." *H Sch J* 49:355–62; 1966.

Amidon, Edmund, and Blumberg, Arthur. "Principal and Teacher Perceptions of School Faculty Meetings." *Administrator's Notebook* 15 (November); 1966. 4p.

Amidon, Edmund J., and others. "Group Supervision." *Nat El Prin* 45:54–8; 1966.

Anderson, James G. "The Authority Structure of the School: System of Social Exchange." *Ed Adm Q* 3:130–45; 1967.

Andrews, John H. M., and Brown, Alan. "Can Principals Exclude Their Own Personality Characteristics When They Rate Their Teachers?" *Ed Adm Sup* 45:234–42; 1959.

Antley, Elizabeth M. "Creativity in Educational Administration." *J Exp Ed* 34:21–7; 1966.

Babcock, Chester D. "The Emerging Role of the Curriculum Leader." In *Role of the Supervisor and Curriculum Director in a Climate of Change.* Yearbook. ASCD, 1965. p. 50–64.

Barr, A. S. (Ed.) "Wisconsin Studies of Measurement and Prediction of Teacher Effectiveness, Summary of Investigations." *J Exp Ed* 30:5–156; 1961.

Blocker, Clyde E., and Richardson, Richard C. "Twenty-five Years of Morale Research: A Critical Review." *J Ed Sociol* 36:200–10; 1963.

Bowers, N. D., and Soar, R. S. *Studies in Human Relations in the Teaching Learning Process.* Cooperative Research Project No. 469. USOE, 1961.

Bradfield, Luther E. "Elementary School Teachers: Their Problems and Supervisory Assistance." *Ed Adm Sup* 45:102–06; 1959.

Brown, Alan F. "Exploring the Human Element in Supervision." *Canadian Ed R Digest* 2:178–84; 1962.

Brown, Alan F. "A Perceptual Taxonomy of the Effective-rated Teacher." *J Exp Ed* 35:1–10; 1966.

Brown, Alan F. "Reactions to Leadership." *Ed Adm Q* 3:62; 1967.

Burton, William H., and Brueckner, Leo. *Supervision: A Social Process.* Appleton, 1955. 715p.

Cappa, Dan, and Van Meter, Margaret. "Opinions of Teachers Concerning the Most Helpful Supervisory Procedures." *Ed Adm Sup* 43:217–22; 1957.

Chandler, Bobby J. "Salary Policies and Teacher Morale." *Ed Adm Sup* 45:107–10; 1959.

Chesler, Mark, and others. "The Principal's Role in Facilitating Innovation." *Theory into Practice* 2:269–77; 1963.

Columbro, Mary. "Supervision and Action Research." *Ed Leadership* 21:297–300; 1964.

Coody, Betty F. D. "A Study of the Impact of Demonstration Teaching on Experienced and Inexperienced Teachers Under Various Supervisory Conditions." Doctoral dissertation. U Texas, 1967.

Council of Administrative Leadership. *How Teachers View School Administration*. The Council, 1959.

Cox, Johnnye V. "Selection and Recruitment of Supervisors." *Ed Leadership* 24:47–51; 1966.

Crosby, Muriel. *Supervision as Cooperative Action*. Appleton, 1957. 334p.

Curtin, James. *Supervision in Today's Elementary Schools*. Macmillan, 1964. 302p.

Davis, Hazel. "Evolution of Current Practices in Evaluating Teacher Competence." In Biddle, Bruce J., and Elena, William J. (Eds.) *Contemporary Research on Teacher Effectiveness*. Holt, 1964. p. 41–66.

Downing, Gertrude. "A Supervision Experiment with the Disadvantaged." *Ed Leadership* 21:433–5; 1964.

Enns, Frederick. "Rating Teacher Effectiveness: The Function of the Principal." *Ed Adm* 3:81–95; 1965.

Erickson, Donald A. "Some Misgivings Concerning a Study of Leadership." *Ed Adm Q* 1:51–9; 1965.

Eye, Glen G., and Netzer, Lanore. *Supervision of Instruction*. Harper, 1965. 400p.

Flanders, Ned A. "Teacher Behavior and In-service Programs." *Ed Leadership* 21:25–9; 1963.

Fuller, Francis F., and Richek, Ronald G. "Tape Recordings, Feedback, and Prospective Teachers' Self Evaluation." *Alberta J Ed Res* 12:301–07; 1966.

Goldman, Harvey. "A Study of the Teacher-Administrator Relationship and the Influence of Need Patterns." Doctoral dissertation. Michigan State U, 1966.

Good, Carter V. (Ed.) *Dictionary of Education*. McGraw-Hill, 1945. 495p.

Gross, Neal, and Herriot, Robert. *Staff Leadership in Public Schools*. Wiley, 1965.

Guba, E. G., and Bidwell, C. E. *Administrative Relationships: Teacher Effectiveness, Teacher Satisfaction, and Administrative Behavior*. U Chicago, 1957.

Gwynn, J. Minor. *Theory and Practice of Supervision*. Dodd, 1965. 473p.

Hallberg, H. Irene. "Certification Requirements for General Supervisors and/or Curriculum Workers Today-Tomorrow." *Ed Leadership* 23:623–5; 1966.

Harap, Henry. "Many Factors Affect Teacher Morale." *Nations' Sch* 63:55–7; 1959.

Harmes, H. M. "Improving Teaching Through Supervision: How is it Working?" *Ed Adm Sup* 45:169–72; 1959.

Harris, Ben. *Supervisory Behavior in Education*. Prentice-Hall, 1963. 557p.

Hawkins, Edward E., and Stoops, Emery. "Objective and Subjective Identification of Outstanding Elementary Teachers." *J Ed Res* 59:344–6; 1966.

Heald, James E., and Moore, Samuel A., II. *The Teacher and Administrative Relations in School Systems*. Macmillan, 1968. 304p.

Hemphill, J. K., and others. *Administrative Performance and Personality*. Teachers Col, Columbia U, 1962.

Landry, Thomas. "Louisiana Supervisors Examine Their Practices." *Ed Adm Sup* 45:305–11; 1959.

Lipham, James. "Leadership and Administration." In *Behavioral Science and Educational Administration*. 63d Yearbook, Part II, NSSE, 1964. p. 119–141.

Luckie, William R. "Leader Behavior of Directors of Instruction." Doctoral dissertation. U Southern Mississippi, 1963.

MacDonald, James B. "Knowledge about Supervision: Rationalization or Rationale?" *Ed Leadership* 61:161–3; 1965.

McNassor, Donald J. "Conflict in Teachers Who Try to Learn About Children." *California J Ed Res* 2:147–55; 1951.

Medley, Donald M., and Mitzel, Harold E. "Some Behavioral Correlates of Teacher Effectiveness." *J Ed Psychol* 50:239–46; 1959.

National Education Association. *Evaluation of Classroom Teachers*. NEA, 1964.

Neagley, Ross, and Evans, N. Dean. *Handbook for Effective Supervision of Instruction*. Prentice-Hall, 1964. 274p.

Ogletree, James R., and others. "Preparing Educational Supervisors." *Ed Leadership* 20:163–6; 1962.

Prince, R. "Individual Values and Administrative Effectiveness." *Administrators' Notebook* 6:1–4; 1957.

Redefer, Frederick L. "Factors That Affect Teacher Morale." *Nations' Sch* 63:59–62; 1959.

Richardson, Richard C. Jr., and Blocher, Clyde. "An Item Factorization of the Faculty Attitude Survey." *J Exp Ed* 34:89–93; 1966.

Riederer, L. A. "A Time Study of Educational Supervision and Administration of Urban School Districts of Saskatchewan." *Canadian Ed Res Digest* 5:40–7; 1965.

Rogers, Carl R. "A Plan for Self-directed Change in an Educational System." *Ed Leadership* 24:717–31; 1967.

Ryans, David G. *Characteristics of Teachers*. ACE, 1960.

Sandberg, Herbert H. "Beginning Teachers' and Supervisors' Appraisals of Selected Supervisory Techniques." Doctoral dissertation. Pennsylvania State U, 1965.

Sergiovanni, Thomas. "Factors Which Affect Satisfaction and Dissatisfaction of Teachers." *J Ed Adm* 5:66–82; 1967.

Teal, Charles E. "A Study of the Relationship Between Selected Variables and the Amount of Time Devoted to Supervision of Instruction by Elementary School Principals." Doctoral dissertation. Colorado State Col, 1965.

Tower, Melvin. "A Study of Orientation and In-service Education Practices in the Indianapolis Public Schools." *Ed Adm Sup* 42:219–29; 1956.

Vigilante, Nicholas J. "A Role Perception Study of

Elementary Principals and Elementary Supervisors in the State of Ohio." Doctoral dissertation. Ohio State U, 1964.

Wiles, Kimball. *Supervision for Better Schools.* Prentice-Hall, 1967. 399p.

Worth, Walter H. "Can Administrators Rate Teachers?" *Canadian Adm* 1:1–6; 1961.

SURVEY RESEARCH METHOD

The "survey research method" is a form of scientific inquiry which has proved particularly useful in the study of social and social-psychological relationships. It seems unfortunate that this method, which has been used with considerable success by social scientists who study the phenomena of formal education, is held in low esteem by most of those who guide the training of educational researchers. Trow (1967) and Sieber (1968) have examined the treatment of "survey research" in many prominent introductory texts in educational-research methods and have found it to be highly critical. This hostility appears to be the result of the strong psychological and experimental tradition which has dominated educational research, but it may also result from a misunderstanding about the nature of this method *as used by social scientists* and its full power in the investigation of many of the important problems of contemporary American education.

Part of this misunderstanding stems from a confusion between the terms "survey" and "survey research." The hurried preparation of a questionnaire to be administered to a convenient group of pupils or teachers in order to explore some problem of purely local interest (characteristic of so many dissertations in education) may represent "a survey" to educators, but it is not "survey research" as the term is known to social scientists. Survey research utilizes carefully selected samples to make quantitative generalizations. These samples can be selected for two basic reasons, and both reasons may be present in a single study.

In *descriptive survey research* the sample is selected to describe a well-defined population in terms of its characteristics, attitudes, or behavior. Often this description is "differentiated" by the detailed subclassification of the sample on additional variables. Probability theory is utilized to assess the sampling error surrounding these descriptions.

In *explanatory* (sometimes called *analytic*) *survey research*, the sample is selected with the intent of making statements about theoretical relationships and processes within the population. Statistical models are often used to summarize complex relationships. In general, explanatory survey research is similar to traditional experimental research in that it is designed to explore questions of cause and effect (Tiedeman, 1960). Time series and panel designs which are *longitudinal* (time-ordered), in contrast to the more conventional *cross-sectional* (time-bound) designs, facilitate this process, as do procedures which permit the time ordering of variables in time bound designs (Blalock, 1964a; Campbell & Stanley, 1963). However, whereas the experimenter designs his research to remove the effects of extraneous variables *before* collecting his data, the survey researcher must remove them *after* collecting his data, generally through statistical manipulation (Glock, 1967b). Causal inference in survey research is seldom as convincing as it is in experiments, but through sophisticated reasoning, sampling, instrumentation, data collection, data reduction, and data analysis, plausible inferences can be made. We shall consider each of these aspects of the survey research method, then discuss some examples of survey research dealing with educational phenomena.

REASONING. The most basic element in the survey research method is that of "reasoning." Through this process the survey objectives and design are determined. In descriptive studies, reasoning may involve merely the careful identification of the population to be described and of the variables on which this description is to take place.

In explanatory studies this first step is far more complex (Lazarsfeld, 1958). Once the social scientist has carefully outlined his central interest (for example, to study the social determinants of pupil aspiration or the effects of formal education on political behavior), he explores the prior research in that general area. From his interpretation of this research he derives a series of hypotheses (sometimes called predictions or expectations) to guide his own research. Often these hypotheses are not reported explicitly but must be deduced from what the researcher does later. However, many problems of data analysis and of inference can be avoided if such hypotheses are made explicit.

The hypotheses form the bases of the development of a survey research design (Merton, 1957; Zetterberg, 1965). They provide two kinds of guidance. First, they indicate the nature of the data which, in the light of current knowledge and reasonable extrapolations thereof, must be taken into account at the time of data collection. Second, they provide statements about the relations between the theoretical *concepts* against which the data actually collected can be compared.

The empirical test of a set of hypotheses requires the identification or construction of *indicators* to represent the concepts under study. For some concepts (e.g., sex and age) the selection of indicators is relatively simple and is based upon standard practices. However, for many concepts (e.g., aspiration and morale) the selection of appropriate indicators requires many simplifying assumptions which generally need to be made explicit (Hempel, 1952; Zetterberg, 1965). Pretests and validating studies are often used to clarify such concepts and to identify their most appropriate indicators. (More extensive discussions of reasoning in social research are available [Brown, 1963; Direnzo, 1966; Kaplan, 1964; Zetterberg, 1965].)

Although some reasoning takes place throughout the entire process of survey research, it is only after considerable thought has been given to hypotheses, concepts, and indicators that an appropriate survey sample can be designed, an instrument constructed, and data collected.

SAMPLING. The design of a survey sample is determined by the objectives of the survey, but this is generally not a one-way process. Often problems of sample design influence and cause a reformation of survey objectives. Sample design has two steps: a selection process, in which rules and operations are developed by which certain members of the population are included in the sample, and an estimation process, in which the sample statistics, which are sample estimates of population values, are computed.

Inferences from samples to populations always contain some degree of error. Different sample designs result in different errors in estimating population values, and the selection of a design which, for a given unit of cost, minimizes errors of estimation is the major objective of sampling.

The basic units in sampling are the elements of the population. As Kish (1965) has noted, a population is defined jointly with its elements: ". . . the *population* is the aggregate of the elements, and the *elements* are the basic units that [constitute] and define the population" (p. 7). Sampling units are used in selecting specific elements into a sample. In *element sampling* each sampling unit consists of only one element; in *cluster sampling* units called clusters may contain more than one element. For example, a sample of schools (elements) may be selected from a sample of school systems (clusters). In *multistage cluster sampling* a hierarchy of clusters is used. A sample of pupils (elements) may be selected from a sample of classrooms (first clusters), in a sample of schools (second clusters), in a sample of school systems (third clusters). Several stages of selection can often reduce error when sampling from widespread populations, but this introduces many complexities into the process of selection and estimation. For example, most conventional tests of statistical significance assume element samples and require modification when used with cluster samples.

Sampling can be fortuitous, purposive, or random. Although the fields of astronomy, experimental physics, and chemistry have made extensive use of fortuitous sampling, in which little concern is expressed for the representativeness of the selected elements, social scientists generally design either purposive or probability samples. Most descriptive survey research utilizes *probability sampling*, in which each element in the population has a known, nonzero probability of being selected. Although the most sophisticated explanatory survey research also uses probability sampling, many explanatory surveys are conducted on *purposive samples* in which, for example, pupils, schools, or school systems are selected on the assumption that they are typical or representative of some "hypothetical universe." However, an inference from a sample to a hypothetical universe is not very meaningful if the gap between the universe and any real population is very large (Kish, 1965). Replication studies in which an identical inference can be made using data from similar, but independent, purposive samples help to provide greater confidence in such results.

INSTRUMENTATION AND DATA COLLECTION. The design of a data-collection procedure is largely determined by the survey objectives and the sample design, but it can in turn influence both the objectives and the sample; potential problems in instrumentation and data collection can cause a reformulation of both objectives and sample. The data to be collected generally describe the elements of the population. These elements generally are the subjects of the research, and later become the units of analysis. However, data descriptive of individual subjects (e.g., students) can be aggregated to describe the social context in which they are situated (e.g., school). Often several units of analysis (e.g., both students and schools) are used at different times in a single study.

Data are usually collected from respondents. These respondents may be the subjects, or they may be reporting about the subjects. For example, in a study of teachers, the teachers may be asked to report about themselves, or the school principal may be asked to report about them.

In survey research, data are collected primarily by asking questions of respondents. This process can be differentiated in a variety of ways. One basic dimension of differentiation is the degree to which the asking and the answering of questions is "structured." In a highly structured (sometimes called "closed") form of data collection the respondent may be asked a very specific question and be required to choose among only a minimum of alternatives: "yes or no," "agree or disagree," etc. In a highly unstructured (sometimes called "open-ended") situation, the researcher is free to ask different questions (often differentiated in terms of a previous answer) of different respondents and to permit greater latitude in the scope of the response. One advantage of structuring in data collection is that it permits rapid tabulation of results, particularly if the responses are obtained in a form amenable to punch cards or computer-tape records. However, "elite respondents," such as college professors and school-board members, are often greatly antagonized by highly structured questioning. Also, highly structured instruments tend to overabstract phenomena, so that the answers the respondent would like to give are often far more complex than the alternatives available to him. Unstructured procedures of data collection tap this complexity, but they present problems to the researcher as he attempts to summarize diffuse responses into standardized categories amenable to tabulation or analysis. Often unstructured procedures are utilized in *pilot studies* to identify useful categories for subsequent investigations with more structured procedures.

A second basis of differentiation in data-collection procedures is the extent of the researcher's contact with the respondent. Such contact varies from the individual interview to the self-administered mailed questionnaire, with such intermediate procedures as telephone interviews, group interviews, and group-administered questionnaires. The individual interview facilitates unstructured questioning (particularly the asking of complex questions) and permits the researcher to clarify questions which may not be understood by particular respondents. However, it lacks standardization across interviews and requires large expenditures of the interviewer's time, particularly if the sample is widely dispersed geographically. The group-administered questionnaire and the self-administered mailed questionnaire are primarily devices for structured questioning, but both assume a highly literate and compliant respondent. Through extensive pretesting, a high degree of clarity in questions and of comprehensiveness in the response choices can be obtained.

The mailed questionnaire has the major advantage of reaching large numbers of subjects economically. In addition, it permits questions which might be embarrassing to the respondent if asked in an interpersonal situation. The most candid responses to sensitive questions are generally obtained through anonymous, self-administered, mailed questionnaires.

The major weakness of such an approach is the infrequent return of the questionnaire to the researcher. Response rates of less than 50 percent are common. However, in the more sophisticated studies, response rates of 75 percent are usual, and rates as high as 95 percent have been reported. Careful preparation of a cover letter and of the questionnaire itself helps to stimulate a high degree of rapport similar to that of an individual interview. If the questionnaire is not anonymous, several stages of following up, including special-delivery letters and long-distance telephone calls, can be used to increase the response rate.

The problem of nonresponse, although still an important one in survey research, is not as serious as it was once thought to be (Deming, 1960; Kish, 1965; McDonagh & Rosenblum, 1965). The major complication introduced by nonresponse is in the estimation of sampling errors. If some data about the nonrespondents can be obtained from other sources, recent developments in high-speed data processing and statistical inference can be used to assess the extent to which, on a limited number of variables, the obtained sample deviates from the desired one. In some cases the obtained sample can be weighted to approximate the desired sample, and occasionally it can be shown that the results of a survey would not be significantly altered were the nonrespondents to be included.

It should be noted carefully that experienced survey researchers pay particular attention to matters of data collection. The construction and administration of a useful questionnaire or interview schedule is an extremely complex task and can not be approached casually. Many problems of data analysis can be avoided by the careful wording and rewording of questions. Pilot studies to pretest all research instruments are generally required. (More-extensive discussions of data collection in survey research are available [Backstrom & Hursh, 1963; Goode & Hatt, 1952; Hyman & others, 1954; Merton & others, 1956; Oppenheim, 1966; Phillips, 1966; Richardson & others, 1965; Sellitz & others, 1959].)

DATA REDUCTION. In descriptive survey research the variables to be described are often obtained directly from the data-collection instrument. For example, tabulations of the educational level of American adults by sex, age, and color require little reorganization of structured-interview or questionnaire data. However, in most explanatory survey research the investigator faces a complex problem of reducing his data to reliable and valid indexes of the concepts suggested by his reasoning. Since standardized indexes are not available for most social science concepts, the investigator generally must develop his own measures of his key concepts. Although this is often done in an ad hoc manner by assigning assumed numerical weights to different responses chosen in terms of their "face validity" and summing them to form a "total score" for a particular index, many studies utilize *measurement models*.

Coombs (1964), Torgerson (1958), and Edwards (1957) have presented a variety of models which are helpful to the survey researcher. For example, two models which have been found to be particularly useful in the reduction of data to measure *well-defined* concepts are Guttman scaling and principal-components analysis. Both methods have an advantage over the total-score approach in that they provide an empirical basis for separating "good" indicators of a concept from "bad" ones and even further for weighting the good indicators as to their degree of goodness. Where Guttman scaling and principal-components analysis differ is in their assumptions regarding level of measurement and in the criteria used to separate the good from the bad items. In general, the Guttman procedure involves less-stringent assumptions (e.g., ordinal as opposed to interval measures) than does principal-components analysis, whereas the latter is probably more objective. Both procedures can be greatly expedited through the use of high-speed computers (see Dixon, 1965).

DATA ANALYSIS. Although procedures of sampling, instrumentation, data collection, and data reduction are important aspects of the survey research method, the success of the method generally depends on the procedures used to relate well-reasoned and well-measured variables to each other. The analysis of data collected specifically to answer the questions being asked of it is termed "primary analysis." If data collected for one purpose are later examined in terms of new objectives, the term "secondary analysis" is generally used. Often large-scale national surveys make their data available for secondary analyses by other researchers. The Project Talent "data bank" is such a case (Project Talent, 1965). Secondary analysis has the major advantage of generally being less expensive than primary analysis, for it avoids the heavy costs of data collection. However, the scope of most secondary analyses is greatly limited by the fact that the data available to a researcher are often only indirectly related to the research issues he is most anxious to explore. The term "proxy variable" is often used to designate a measure that is substituted for a more relevant, but unavailable, measure of an important concept.

Many forms of data analysis are directed at understanding the relationship between just two variables—a "cause" and its "effect," an "independent" and a "dependent" variable, an "antecedent" and a "consequent" variable, or more generally, a *first* and a *second variable*. However, in survey research few two-variable relationships are unaffected by other variables. What distinguishes data analysis in survey research from data analysis in more traditional forms of scientific inquiry is an emphasis on the *logic* of multivariate analysis and the careful selection and examination of many variables simultaneously (Blalock, 1964a). Those additional variables which are brought into an analysis are spoken of as third variables (sometimes called control variables), while those which are not introduced are referred to as fourth variables (sometimes called unmeasured variables) (Tukey & Wilk, 1966). Although the survey researcher is primarily interested in the interrelation of first, second, and third variables, he must not ignore the possibility that unmeasured variables are confounding his interpretations. One of the key strategies in the reasoning, instrumentation, and data-collection phases of survey research is the recognition and elimination of unmeasured variables which might prove troublesome during data analysis.

Third variables can be introduced in two major major forms. The term "controlling on," applied to a third variable, is generally used to designate the physical separation of data cases in terms of broad categories of the third variables. The term "partialing out," applied to a third variable, designates the addition of third variables to what was originally a bivariate regression equation. Both controlling and partialing have historical roots in social science which go back more than 50 years (Glock, 1967a). They are used extensively in the most sophisticated contemporary survey research.

There are diverse reasons for introducing additional variables into a two-variable analysis, and different a priori reasons logically lead to different expectations about how the data should behave. Terms such as "intervening variable," "invalidating variable," and "conditional variable" characterize the various roles played by third variables. Lazarsfeld (1955) has proposed a general equation for the formalization of the different expectations and outcome involving a single third variable which can be encountered in the analysis of survey data. One advantage of this formula is that it permits the investigator to communicate more effectively how he expects his data to behave. In this way empirical results involving a third variable can be interpreted in terms of explicit expectations. Presented below is an extended example of the Lazarsfeld approach.

A General Three-variable Model. For the purpose of discussion let it be assumed that three variables (X, Y, and Z) are each dichotomous (a and b). The causal relationship of primary interest is that between variables X (what we shall call the first variable) and variable Y (the second variable). The *elaboration* of this two-variable *primary relationship* through the introduction of the third variable (Z) results in four new two-variable relationships:

1. the *marginal relationship* of variable X to variable Y (denoted by ZY),
2. the marginal relationship of variable Z to variable Y (denoted by ZY),
3. the *partial relationship* of variable X to variable Y when variable Z is of state a (denoted by $XY;Z^a$), and
4. the partial relationship of variable X to variable Y when variable Z is of state b (denoted by $XY;Z^b$).

Lazarsfeld (1958, 1961), building on the earlier work of Yule (1911), has shown that the primary relationship can be "decomposed" and expressed as a function of these two marginal and two partial relationships. His discussion is rather technical, but it can be summarized by the following formula:

(1) $[XY] = [XY;Z^a] \oplus [XY;Z^b] \oplus [XZ] \odot [ZY]$.

Stated verbally formula 1 is as follows: the relationship of primary interest (XY) is equal to the sum of the two partial relationships when the population is stratified according to the third variable ($[XY;Z^a] \oplus [XY;Z^b]$) plus an additional term which is the product of the marginal relationships between the third variable and each of the other two ($[XZ] \odot [ZY]$). The symbols "$\oplus$" and "$\odot$" have been used to represent the fact that the summation and multiplication processes are not simple ones. In order to express formula 1 mathematically, one must introduce into each term weights which for reasons of logical simplicity can be ignored; in this sense the expression is best thought of as a *formalizing equation* rather than as a mathematical one (Hyman, 1955).

Subsidiary Three-variable Models. An important property of formula 1 is that the terms to the right of the equal sign can vary independently, thus permitting the equation to take many subsidiary forms. Although, as noted above, it is not essential to the present discussion to symbolize mathematically the magnitude of the four two-variable relationships represented within a given three-variable formula, it is helpful to indicate whether each two-variable relationship is expected to be positive, negative, or zero, and so the symbol "+," "−," or "0" will be prefixed to each relationship to note its direction. A three-variable formula designed to represent the expectation that all two-variable relationships are positive would be written as:

(2) $[+(XY)] = [+(XY;Z^a)] \oplus [+(XY;Z^b)] \oplus [+(XZ)] \odot [+(ZY)]$.

The expectation that all two-variable relationships are negative would appear as:

(3) $[-(XY)] =$
$[-(XY;Z^a)] \oplus [-(XY;Z^b)] \oplus [-(XZ)] \odot [-(ZY)]$.

To express the expectation that all two-variable relationships are zero, the general formula would be written as:

(4) $[0(XY)] =$
$[0(XY;Z^a)] \oplus [0(XY;Z^b)] \oplus [0(XZ)] \odot [0(ZY)]$.

It is, however, the possible combination of positive, negative, and zero terms in formula 1 which permits the survey researcher to communicate a variety of three-variable expectations and outcomes. Such situations are of two types, "specification" and "explanation," and can generally be identified according to the reason for the introduction of the third variable. A further classification of each type of model can be based on the effect which the third variable is thought to have on the relationship between the other two variables.

One general use of third variables is to specify the conditions which differentiate a relationship (Glock, 1967b). For example, one might expect the primary relationship to be positive if the third variable is of state a and zero if it is of state b, or he might expect the primary relationship to be "strong" if the third variable is of state a and "weak" if it is of state b.

Let us first consider the case in which the primary relationship is expected to be stronger in one state of the third variable than in the other. For example, the investigator may assume that the third variable is unrelated to either the first or the second variable *but* not to both and thus affects the strength of the primary relationship. A three-variable model of the form

(5) $[+(XY)] =$
$[+(XY;Z^a)] \oplus [+(XY;Z^b)] \oplus [0(XZ)] \odot [+(ZY)]$

or

(6) $[+(XY)] =$
$[+(XY;Z^a)] \oplus [+(XY;Z^b)] \oplus [+(XZ)] \odot [0(ZY)]$

represents this expectation. The primary relationship is a function solely of the partial terms (Hyman, 1955). After simplification the model can be expressed as:

$[+(XY)] =$
$[+(XY;Z^a)] \oplus [+(XY;Z^b)]$,

where

$[+(XY)] \neq [+(XY;Z^a)] \neq [+(XY;Z^b)]$.

In cases such as these, the third variable is referred to as a *conditional variable*, for it specifies the conditions under which the primary relationship is expected to be different. In the psychological literature such a variable has been referred to as a "predictability variable" (Ghiselli, 1960) or as a "moderator variable" (Saunders, 1956). This general three-variable phenomenon has been termed "interaction."

A second type of specification occurs when the primary relationship is expected to be identical for both states of the third variable. Here the investigator often assumes that the third variable is unrelated to both the first and the second variable. The formalizing equation then takes the form

(7) $[+(XY)] =$
$[+(XY;Z^a)] \oplus [+(XY;Z^b)] \oplus [0(XZ)] \odot [0(ZY)]$,

which, after simplification, becomes

$[+(XY)] = [+(XY;Z^a)] \oplus [+(XY;Z^b)]$,

where

$[+(XY)] = [+(XY;Z^a)] = [+(XY;Z^b)]$.

In this case the third variable is referred to as a *replication variable*, for it has the effect of demonstrating that the primary relationship is identical (i.e., replicated) within both states of the third variable. Replication can also be explored in the case of a third variable that is related to either the first or the second variable or to both variables.

A third type of specification occurs when it is thought that the primary relationship will be zero, not because there is no relationship, but because the partial terms are of opposite signs and thus cancel each other. Here the model can take the form

(8) $[0(XY)] =$
$[-(XY;Z^a)] \oplus [+(XY;Z^b)] \oplus [0(XZ)] \odot [0(ZY)]$,

which, upon simplification, becomes

$[0(XY)] = [-(XY;Z^a)] \oplus [+(XY;Z^b)]$.

In this case the third variable is referred to as a *directional variable*, for it affects the direction of the primary relationship. This, too, is a form of interaction.

A second general use of third variables is to explain theoretically why a primary relationship exists (or does not exist). For example, one might expect that the primary relationship exists because of the spurious effects of an antecedent third variable, or one might expect a third variable to intervene temporally between the first and second variables. In the case of explanation, unlike that of specification discussed above, the investigator generally assumes that the third variable is related to both the first and the second variable; for if it is not related to both variables in the primary relationship, it cannot produce that relationship. Even then the formula can take many forms.

A frequent expectation of investigators is that a third variable is linked temporally in a causal sequence with the first and second variables. To test such a hypothesis one assumes that the relationship of primary interest is produced solely by the marginal terms (Hyman, 1955). Thus, the partial terms are expected to be zero, and the general formula takes the form

(9) $[+(XY)] =$
$[0(XY;Z^a)] \oplus [0(XY;Z^b)] \oplus [+(XZ)] \odot [+(ZY)]$,

which, when simplified, becomes

$[+(XY)] = [+(XZ)] \odot [+(ZY)]$.

In such a model the third variable is referred to as an intervening variable if it is thought to intervene temporally between the first and second variables and as an *antecedent variable* if it is thought to precede the first variable as part of a "developmental sequence." Gold (1962) has considered some of the misinterpretations which can occur in research when the requirements of this model are not adequately understood.

Frequently an investigator desires to demonstrate that the relationship of primary interest is *not* produced by a third variable. In that case he may take the position that although the third variable is related to both the first and second variables that fact will *not* "explain away" the primary relationship (Hyman, 1955). Thus, he expects the partial terms to be nonzero and the formula to take the form

(10) $[+(XY)] =$
$[+(XY;Z^a)] \oplus [+(XY;Z^b)] \oplus [+(XZ)] \odot [+(ZY)]$.

Here the third variable is called a *potentially invalidating variable* if it is thought to be temporally antecedent to the first variable and a *rival explanatory variable* if it is thought to be cotemporal with the first variable. Blalock (1964b) has discussed some of the misunderstandings which can occur in the use of this model.

A third form of explanation occurs when an investigator suspects that the primary relationship is being hidden by the effects of a third variable. One instance in which this can occur is when the third variable has opposite relationships to the first and second variables, thus causing the marginal term of the general formula to be negative and to cancel the sum of the two partial terms. Here the formula can take the form

(11) $[0(XY)] =$
$[+(XY;Z^a)] \oplus [+(XY;Z^b)] \oplus [-(XZ)] \odot [+(ZY)]$

or

(12) $[0(XY)] =$
$[+(XY;Z^a)] \oplus [+(XY;Z^b)] \oplus [+(XZ)] \odot [-(ZY)]$.

In cases such as these, the third variable is referred to as a *suppressor variable*, for it has the effect of "suppressing" the primary relationship.

These selected subsidiary models do not exhaust the possible logical variations of the general model. They do, however, represent some of the most common expectations and outcomes which survey researchers report with respect to the interrelationships of three variables. (A more complete discussion of multivariate logical models for dichotomous variables is presented by Lazarsfeld [1961] and for continuous variables by Blalock [1964a].)

Statistical Procedures. A large number of multivariate *statistical* models are available to assist the survey researcher to summarize his empirical data and to fit them to multivarite *logical* models like those discussed above. Historically, cross-tabulation and nonparametric statistics have been advocated as most appropriate (Coleman, 1964; Phillips, 1966; Zeisel, 1957; Zelditch, 1959). However, such procedures are greatly limited in terms of the number of variables which can be considered simultaneously. Therefore, survey researchers concerned with the complex relationships among many variables have begun to use multivariate linear regression techniques such as those discussed by Anderson (1958), Kendall (1957), and Rao (1952) and programmed for high-speed computers by Cooley and Lohnes (1962) and by Dixon (1965). The introduction of dichotomous "dummy variables" (Suits, 1957) can facilitate the handling of nominal and ordinal measures by such techniques.

It is important to note, however, that whereas the explanation models presented above all assume additive effects on the part of the first and third variables, their effects in the specification models are generally assumed to be multiplicative. Thus, techniques of partial correlation or regression which assume additive effects are inappropriate for use in fitting data to specification models. However, statistical procedures for fitting survey research data to specification models which provide for the extensive examination of interaction effects are available (Morgan & Sonquist, 1963; Sonquist & Morgan, 1964). Morgan and others (1962) have provided many examples of the application of these models in survey research.

One of the most promising recent developments in the statistical analysis of explanatory survey research data is the utilization of "path coefficients" to characterize rather extended causal sequences within cross-sectional designs. Discussions of path coefficients with empirical examples relevant to the sociology of education are available (Duncan, 1966; Blau & Duncan, 1967). Boudon (1965, 1968) has argued that both regression analysis and path analysis are special cases of "dependence analysis."

SOME EXAMPLES OF THE SURVEY RESEARCH METHOD. Many examples of survey research are available in the literature of the social sciences and of education; if studied carefully they provide insights into the utility of this method. The selections which follow consider both descriptive and explanatory surveys relevant to the field of education. However, they deal primarily with monographs, for it is generally in studies of considerable magnitude that the strengths of this method are most apparent.

Governmental agencies and educational organizations have been the major initiators of *descriptive survey research*. In general these descriptions are differentiated to include the simultaneous consideration of many variables. At the federal level the Office of Education and the Bureau of the Census conduct censuses and sample surveys to assist policymakers by describing the characteristics of both individuals and instructions. The Office of Education conducts annual and biennial sample surveys of schools and institutions of higher education to describe the enrollment status of the American population (see Schloss, 1966). Each October the Bureau of the Census obtains similar estimates by sampling households (see Bureau of the Census, 1967). A digest of educational data from several governmental sources is prepared annually by the Office of Education (see Simon & Grant, 1966). A comprehensive analysis of educational trends and relationships, observable within data from a variety of official surveys conducted between 1840 and 1963, has been performed by Folger and Nam (1967).

Although studies conducted by governmental agencies contain valuable data about educational institutions and individuals, they seldom explore questions of cause and effect. Such *explanatory surveys* have been most frequently conducted by academically based social scientists. The work of the nineteenth-century French sociologist Émile Durkheim contains many elements of the survey research method as it is used today in explanatory studies. However, the major impetus for this method as a unique research form came from the work of Lazarsfeld, Stouffer, and their associates during World War II (see Stouffer & others, 1949a, 1949b, 1949c, 1950). Since then a variety of studies, many exploring issues of considerable relevance to the field of education, have utilized and extended the method. These studies relate to education in several ways. Some are designed to examine the effects of formal education, and others to explore its determinants. However, the greatest number of studies have been designed to learn more about educational roles and educational organizations.

Our first exemplar is a study by Stouffer (1955) which explored in part the effects of formal education on attitude formation. In 1955 he published *Communism, Conformity, and Civil Liberties*, a book examining the reactions of a national sample of the American public to the threat of Communism thought to exist at that time.

Stouffer's research design included a multistage probability sample of 4,933 citizens and a purposive sample of 1,533 local community leaders. Data were collected from both samples through an interview schedule (containing both structured and unstructured items) administered individually by 537 skilled interviewers from two nationally prominent survey agencies.

One of the major dependent variables considered by Stouffer was the public's willingness to tolerate a specific group of nonconformists (as measured by a 15-item modified Guttman scale). Through extensive use of two-, three-, and four-variable tables (introducing such first and third variables as geographical region, size of community, sex, church attendance, age, and level of education), Stouffer developed a number of multivariate explanatory models to explore differences in tolerance.

Somewhat typical of Stouffer's approach to data analysis, and a good example of the use of a potentially invalidating variable in studying the effects of formal education, was his method for considering the effects of education (X) on tolerance (Y) with the effects of age (Z) removed. Through two two-variable tables Stouffer had earlier shown that both education and age were related to tolerance: the greater the education, the greater the tolerance; and the greater the age, the less the tolerance. He had also shown that education and age were related: the greater the age, the less the education.

Stouffer then asked whether the observed relationship between education and tolerance could be explained away by the observed relationship between age and tolerance. Subsequently, he organized his data to demonstrate that *in all age groups,* the better-educated tended to be more tolerant than the less well educated. He concluded, therefore, that the positive relationship observed between education and tolerance could not be explained away by age differences in the population under study. Thus his three-variable analysis added weight to his earlier two-variable inference that education produces tolerance.

Lazarsfeld and Thielens' *The Academic Mind* (1958) was similar in many ways to Stouffer's study. The monograph provided detailed information about the social origin, self-image, productivity, and political and intellectual beliefs of American teachers of undergraduate social science courses. Their national multistage probability sample, drawn in 1955, was composed of 2,451 college teachers, stratified by size of institution and type of control. Data were obtained from the teachers through the use of structured and unstructured interview schedules administered by the staffs of two professional survey agencies.

Lazarsfeld and Thielens differed from Stouffer in their method of data reduction. Whereas Stouffer constructed a Guttman scale to measure his key concepts, they used a total-score approach. For example, one of the major dependent variables they used was "permissiveness," a variable defined operationally by the summation of the replies of respondents to four questions designed to tap a conservative orientation (assigned a negative weight) and to two questions tapping a permissive orientation (assigned a positive weight). Not only were these investigators able to classify individuals according to their permissiveness, but, by computing the proportion of faculty at each institution designated as being high in permissiveness, they developed a measure of the permissiveness of each college.

Although much of *The Academic Mind* must be considered primarily as a differentiated description of an occupational group, Lazarsfeld and Thielens were also concerned with the explanation of social processes. For example, a basic hypothesis in sociology predicts the importance of the social context in producing attitudes and behavior. They used this expectation to elaborate the relationship between age (X) and permissiveness (Y)—a relationship which had been shown to be negative. The question then posed was whether this relationship was a function merely of aging (in that an individual's enthusiasm for innovation declines as he grows older) or whether it was also a function of the social context in which he was located (Z). They hypothesized that the social context was a conditional variable and then performed a "contextual analysis."

Acknowledging that a cross-sectional survey does not provide a definitive answer, Lazarsfeld and Thielens were nevertheless able to present rather convincing evidence in support of their expectation. After separating the data in terms of the school permissiveness rate, they showed that the negative relationship between teacher permissiveness and age was weakest in the colleges characterized as being most permissive and strongest in those characterized as being less permissive. Thus, they concluded that the social context within which the teachers worked placed conditions upon the relationship between age and attitudes.

In *The Social Context of Ambition* Turner (1964) presented an outstanding example of the interplay of reasoning and analysis in survey research. His purposive sample (selected to represent a range of nonethnic socioeconomic backgrounds in the Los Angeles area) consisted of 1,352 boys and 1,441 girls in the twelfth grade at ten high schools. To collect his data, Turner and a research assistant personally administered a structured questionnaire to students in approximately 100 "Senior Problems" classes.

The reasoning and analysis presented by Turner are at times difficult to follow, but they provide many examples of the application of the multivariate models of "explanation" and "specification." At one point Turner examined the phenomenon of "anticipatory socialization"—a tendency of upwardly mobile persons to adopt the attitudes and values characteristic of the social stratum to which they aspire. His dependent variable (Y) was a measure of such class-related values. Turner argued that these values are the result of ambition (X) but acknowledged that an individual's socioeconomic background (Z) might also play a part in producing his values.

Basically Turner proposed two alternative three-variable models. In the first, ambition and background were seen as rival explanatory variables, each one independently producing variation in values. In the second, ambition was seen as a variable intervening between background and values as part of a causal sequence. Turner hypothesized that the second model was the more realistic one.

After using nonparametric statistics to consider the relationship between both background and ambition with each of 15 class-value items, Turner used the total score method to combine 9 of these items into a "class-value index" amenable to correlation analysis. Then, using partial correlation, he showed that the relationship between background and values (with the effects of ambition removed) was less than the relationship between ambition and values (with the effects of background removed). On the basis of these results he claimed some support for his intervening-variable model.

Turner then proposed and rejected a series of alternative causal sequences involving these three variables and, after showing an unusual awareness of the limitations of his data and methods, concluded that his theoretically derived intervening-variable hypothesis (that background produces ambition which in turn produces values) received the strongest support from his data.

In a book entitled *Staff Leadership in Public Schools* Gross and Herriott (1965) utilized the survey research method to examine both the determinants and the effects of the leadership behavior of school principals. They performed a secondary analysis of data collected in 1960 from a multistage cluster sample of 175 elementary-school principals in 40 large American cities. Four-hour interviews were held with each principal, and in addition a questionnaire had been mailed to 10 teachers in each school. Both Guttman scaling and principal-components analysis were used to reduce the data from questionnaire and interview items to scales measuring the key variables of the research.

In examining the effects of the principal's leadership, Gross and Herriott performed a series of intervening-variable analyses utilizing correlational statistics. After reasoning, and then observing, that the leadership behavior of the principal (X) is related to teachers' morale (Z_1), teachers' professional performance (Z_2), and pupils' academic performance (Y), they reasoned further that a causal sequence could exist among these four variables. Their subsequent analysis supported this hypothesis, for they showed that the relationship between leadership (the independent variable) and pupils' academic performance (the dependent variable) was reduced to nearly zero as first the effects of the third variables of teachers' morale and then teachers' professional performance were partialed out.

At an earlier point in their analysis Gross and Herriott demonstrated rather vividly the isolation of a suppressor variable. First they reasoned that the leadership behavior of the principal (X) would be related to the academic performance of pupils in their schools (Y). However, upon examining their data they could find no evidence of such a two-variable relationship. This led them to reason that if pupils' academic performance is related positively to pupils' socioeconomic status (an empirical regularity observed previously by other investigators) and if, further, the principals who exhibit the greatest leadership are located in the schools of lowest average pupil socioeconomic status, then school socioeconomic status (Z) could be suppressing the relationship between the principals' leadership and the academic performance of the pupils in their schools. Their subsequent analysis bore this out, for when the effects of school socioeconomic status were removed through partial correlation, the relationship between the principals' leadership and the pupils' performance rose from an insignificant coefficient to one which was statistically significant.

In *Social Class and the Urban School* Herriott and St. John (1966) reported the first extensive use of the survey research method to study the effects of the social context of schools on teachers and principals. They conducted a secondary analysis of data collected in 1960. To characterize the socioeconomic composition of a national sample of 490 elementary and junior high and senior high schools they performed a principal-components analysis on reports of the education, occupation, and income background of the parents of the pupils attending each school.

One of the major analyses of Herriott and St. John is similar to that of Lazarsfeld and Thielens reported above, in that they too utilized a variable measuring social context to place conditions on the relationship between two other variables. Herriott and St. John reasoned that because of certain explicit phenomena affecting schools of different socioeconomic (SES) composition in different ways, the relationship between the principal's performance (X) and that of the teachers (Y) would vary with the SES of the school (Z). They predicted that this relationship would be stronger in the schools of low SES (where a dynamic principal was seen to be more crucial to teacher success) than in the schools of high SES. In examining their data separately for the two types of schools, they found that in the schools of low SES 19 of 23 aspects of the principals' performance were related to a teacher performance score, while in the schools of high SES none of the 23 was related. Thus they were able to demonstrate that, as they had expected, the third variable of school SES placed conditions on the relationship between the other two variables.

Herriott and St. John also provided detailed examples of the use of school level as a replication variable and of school racial composition as a potentially invalidating variable.

One of the most extensive applications of the survey research method to a study of educational phenomena was conducted by Coleman and others (1966). In *Equality of Educational Opportunity* they reported both differentiated descriptions and explanatory analyses using data from 645,000 pupils and 4,000 schools. They characterized school environments in different areas of the United States and examined the effects of both home and school factors on pupil achievement and motivation. Their examination of the relative effects of home (X) and school (Z) on pupil achievement (Y) is particularly noteworthy for its sophisticated use of elaborate multivariate regression models.

These six studies merely give an introduction to the variety of education problems to which the survey research method can be applied. After a comprehensive consideration of the uses and abuses of the survey method in education, Trow (1967) has identified additional studies which can serve as exemplars of the method and has pointed out many untapped areas of inquiry to which this method is particularly applicable.

Robert E. Herriott
Florida State University

References

Anderson, T. W. *An Introduction to Multivariate Statistical Analysis.* Wiley, 1958. 374p.

Backstrom, Charles H., and Hursh, Gerald D. *Survey Research.* Northwestern U Press, 1963. 192p.

Blalock, Hubert M., Jr. *Causal Inference in Nonexperimental Research.* U North Carolina Press, 1964(a). 200p.

Blalock, Hubert M., Jr. "Controlling for Background Factors: Spuriousness Versus Developmental Sequences." *Sociol Inquiry* 34:28–40; 1964(b).

Blau, Peter M., and Duncan, Otis D. *American Occupational Structure.* Wiley, 1967. 520p.

Boudon, Raymond. "A Method of Linear Causal Analysis: Dependence Analysis." *Am Sociol R* 30: 365–74; 1965.

Boudon, Raymond. "A New Look at Correlation Analysis." In Blalock, Hubert M., Jr., and Blalock, Ann B. (Eds.) *Methodology in Social Research.* McGraw-Hill, 1968.

Brown, Robert R. *Explanation in Social Science.* Aldine Publishing Co., 1963. 198p.

Bureau of the Census. *Current Population Reports.* Series P-20, No 162. GPO, 1967. 12p.

Campbell, Donald T., and Stanley, Julian C. "Experimental and Quasi-experimental Designs for Research on Teaching." In Gage, N. L. (Ed.) *Handbook of Research on Teaching.* Rand McNally, 1963. p. 171–246.

Coleman, James S. *Introduction to Mathematical Sociology.* Free, 1964. 554p.

Coleman, James S., and others. *Equality of Educational Opportunity.* GPO, 1966. 737p.

Cooley, William W., and Lohnes, Paul R. *Multivariate Procedures for the Behavioral Sciences.* Wiley, 1962. 211p.

Coombs, Clyde H. *A Theory of Data.* Wiley, 1964. 585p.

Deming, W. Edwards. *Sample Design in Business Research.* Wiley, 1960. 517p.

Direnzo, Gordon J. (Ed.) *Concepts, Theory, and Explanation in the Behavioral Sciences.* Random, 1966. 302p.

Dixon, W. J. (Ed.) *Biomedical Computer Programs.* UCLA Student Store, 1965. 620p.

Duncan, Otis D. "Path Analysis: Sociological Examples." *Am J Sociol* 72:1–16; 1966.

Edwards, Allen L. *Techniques of Attitude Scale Construction.* Appleton, 1957. 256p.

Folger, John K., and Nam, Charles B. *Education of the American Population.* GPO, 1967. 290p.

Ghiselli, Edwin E. "Differentiation of Tests in Terms of the Accuracy with Which They Predict for a Given Individual." *Ed Psychol Meas* 20:675–84; 1960.

Glock, Charles. "Introduction." In Glock, Charles, and others. (Eds.) *The Uses of Survey Research.* Russell Sage, 1967(*a*). p. IX–XXI.

Glock, Charles. "Survey Design and Analysis in Sociology." In Glock, Charles, and others. (Eds.) *The Uses of Survey Research.* Russell Sage, 1967(*b*). p. 1–62.

Gold, David. "Independent Causation in Multivariate Analysis: The Case of Political Alienation and Attitude Toward a School Bond Issue." *Am Sociol R* 27:85–7; 1962.

Goode, William J., and Hatt, Paul K. *Methods in Social Research.* McGraw-Hill, 1952. 386p.

Gross, Neal, and Herriott, Robert E. *Staff Leadership in Public Schools.* Wiley, 1965. 247p.

Hempel, Carl G. "Fundamentals of Concept Formation in Empirical Science." In Neurath, Otto, and others. (Eds.) *International Encyclopedia of Unified Science, Foundations of the Unity of Science.* Vol 2, No. 7. U Chicago Press, 1952. p. 1–93.

Herriott, Robert E., and St. John, Nancy Hoyt. *Social Class and the Urban School.* Wiley, 1966. 289p.

Hyman, Herbert H. *Survey Design and Analysis.* Free, 1955. 425p.

Hyman, Herbert H., and others. *Interviewing in Social Research.* U. Chicago Press, 1954. 415p.

Kaplan, Abraham. *The Conduct of Inquiry: Methodology for Behavioral Science.* Chandler Publishing Company, 1964. 428p.

Kendall, Maurice G. *A Course in Multivariate Analysis.* Griffin, 1957. 185p.

Kish, Leslie. *Survey Sampling.* Wiley, 1965. 643p.

Lazarsfeld, Paul F. "Interpretation of Statistical Relations as a Research Operation." In Lazarsfeld, Paul F., and Rosenberg, Morris. (Eds.) *The Language of Social Research.* Free, 1955. p. 115–25.

Lazarsfeld, Paul F. "Evidence and Inference in Social Research." *Dædalus* 87:99–130; Fall 1958.

Lazarsfeld, Paul F. "The Algebra of Dichotomus Systems." In Solomon, Herbert. (Ed.) *Studies in Item Analysis and Prediction.* Stanford U Press, 1961. p. 111–57.

Lazarsfeld, Paul F., and Thielens, Wagner, Jr. *The Academic Mind.* Free, 1958. 460p.

McDonagh, Edward C., and Rosenblum, A. Leon. "A Comparison of Mailed Questionnaires and Subsequent Structured Interviews." *Public Opin Q* 29:131–6; 1965.

Merton, Robert K. *Social Theory and Social Structure.* Free, 1957. 645p. Chs. 2 and 3.

Merton, Robert K., and others. *The Focused Interview.* Free, 1956. 186p.

Morgan, J. N., and Sonquist, L. "Problems in the Analysis of Survey Data—and a Proposal." *J Am Stat Assn* 58:415–34; 1963.

Morgan, J. N., and others. *Income and Welfare in the United States.* McGraw-Hill, 1962. 531p.

Oppenheim, A. N. *Questionnaire Design and Attitude Measurement.* Basic Books, 1966. 298p.

Phillips, Bernard S. *Social Research.* Macmillan, 1966. 336p.

Project Talent. *The Project Talent Data Bank.* The Project, 1965. 24p.

Rao, C. Radhakrishna. *Advanced Statistical Methods in Biometric Research.* Wiley, 1952. 390p.

Richardson, Stephan A., and others. *Interviewing.* Basic Books, 1965. 380p.

Saunders, David R. "Moderator Variables in Prediction." *Ed Psychol Meas* 16:209–22; 1956.

Schloss, Samuel. *Fall 1965 Statistics of Public Elementary and Secondary Day Schools.* GPO, 1966. 31p.

Sellitz, Claire, and others. *Research Methods in Social Relations,* rev. ed. Holt, 1959. 622p.

Sieber, Sam D. "Survey Research in Education: The Case of the Misconstrued Technique." *Phi Delta Kappan* 49:273–6; 1968.

Simon, Kenneth A., and Grant, W. Vance. *Digest of Educational Statistics.* GPO, 1966. 124p.

Sonquist, John A., and Morgan, James N. *The Detection of Interaction Effects.* Survey Research Center, U Michigan, 1964. 292p.

Stouffer, Samuel A. *Communism, Conformity, and Civil Liberties.* Doubleday, 1955. 278p.

Stouffer, Samuel A., and others. *Studies in Social Psychology in World War II.* Vol. 1. *The American Soldier: Combat and Its Aftermath.* Princeton U Press, 1949(*a*). 675p.

Stouffer, Samuel A., and others. *Studies in Social Psychology in World War II.* Vol. 2. *The American Soldier: Adjustment During Army Life.* Princeton U Press, 1949(*b*). 599p.

Stouffer, Samuel A., and others. *Studies in Social Psychology in World War II.* Vol. 3. *Experiments on Mass Communication.* Princeton U Press, 1949(*c*).

Stouffer, Samuel A., and others. *Studies in Social Psychology in World War II.* Vol. 4. *Measurement and Prediction.* Princeton U Press, 1950. 756p.

Suits, Daniel B. "Use of Dummy Variables in Regression Equations." *J Am Stat Assn* 52:548–51; 1957.

Tiedeman, David V. "Experimental Method." In Harris, Chester W. (Ed.) *Encyclopedia of Educational Research,* 3rd ed. Macmillan, 1960. p. 486–90.

Torgerson, Warren S. *Theory and Methods of Scaling.* Wiley, 1958. 460p.

Trow, Martin. "Education and Survey Research." In Glock, Charles, and others. (Eds.) *The Uses of Survey Research.* Russell Sage, 1967. p. 315–75.

Tukey, J. W., and Wilk, M. B. "Data Analysis and Statistics: An Expository Overview." *AFIPS Conference Proceedings, 1966 Fall Joint Computer Conference.* Spartan Books, 1966. p. 695–709.

Turner, Ralph H. *The Social Context of Ambition.* Chandler Publishing Company, 1964. 269p.

Yule, G. Udney. *An Introduction to the Theory of Statistics.* Griffin, 1911. 516p.

Zeisel, Hans. *Say It with Figures,* 4th ed. Harper, 1957. 257p.

Zelditch, Morris, Jr. *A Basic Course in Sociological Statistics.* Holt, 1959. 370p.

Zetterberg, Hans L. *On Theory and Verification in Sociology,* 3rd. ed. Bedminster Press, 1965. 177p.

TEACHER CERTIFICATION

Teacher certification has been generally defined as the legal evidence of competence or as the legal authorization to receive public funds in payment for teaching. The major purposes of teacher certification, drawn, of course, from the definition, are to protect children from the unqualified, to safeguard public funds, and to protect the competent practitioner against the unfair competition of the substandard or unqualified.

Kinney (1964) has distinguished between licensure and certification. The former, he holds, is evidence of admission to the teaching profession. Legal licensure, in his view, is a civil service procedure, the purpose of which is to control employment and remuneration. According to this view, certification should be the prerogative of professional associations and would, in fact, be based upon evidence of competence and would be a prerequisite to legal licensure. Evidence that licensure may not presently reflect qualification and competence in teaching is the continued practice of the states of issuing upward of 100,000 emergency or substandard licenses each year and the great diversity among the states in minimum requirements for regular certification.

Stinnett (1967) reported a pronounced movement in the direction of certification of competence by professional associations, pointing out that the National Education Association (NEA) instituted in 1964 the prerequisite for membership of completion of the bachelor's degree, and licensure where it is required; and by 1967, a total of 26 state education associations had adopted similar requirements. In addition, the American Association of School Administrators made effective in 1964 the membership prerequisite of two years of graduate work in an institution accredited by NCATE.

EVOLUTION OF STATE CERTIFICATION. Kinney (1964) traced the historical evolution of the legal licensure of teachers in the United States, holding that this practice is peculiarly American. He held that it is unrealistic to search European practices for the beginning of teacher certification.

Other writers have generally found that the early European practices, although largely extralegal, were transplanted to America and evolved in time in governmental licensure.

Edwards and Richey (1963) describe the early "community schools" or "old field schools," in which the teachers, ministers, or lay readers of the Anglican Church held licenses from the bishop of London or from the governor. An early attempt at legal licensure of teachers in Virginia is reported in the action of the General Assembly requiring schoolmasters to attend the assembly and be examined to receive licenses from the governor. Also, the governor-schoolmaster in New England generally was required to hold a certificate signed by the minister of the town in which he was to teach.

According to Stinnett and Huggett (1963) certification of teachers in colonial times was haphazard or nonexistent. The process varied from colony to colony, authority being vested in towns, churches, royal commissioners, or governors, or even the bishop of London. Licenses, such as existed, were valid only in the school of employment. The results of such hit-or-miss processes were that examinations were superficial, standards were intolerably low, and nepotism was prevalent.

Kinney (1964) pointed out that no certification structure worthy of the name existed during the colonial period. He cites the date 1825 as the beginning of the evolution of certification structure, when the emergence of state school systems was imminent. This began in Ohio with the designation of county examining officers in 1825. New York, in 1841, and Vermont, in 1845, followed suit, providing for county superintendents of schools, among whose duties were to examine candidates and issue teaching certificates. By 1860 this office was widely established and became the focus of teacher certification. Between this date and 1900, certification authority was shared by county and state authorities, being almost completely based on the examination system.

An alternative basis for certification (completion of a prescribed teacher-preparing curriculum) began to emerge with the founding of the normal schools. By 1850, of the then 30 states, 28 had established chief state school officers. And this date, according to Stinnett and Huggett (1963), marked the beginning of the shift from local to state control, although local control was to persist in varied forms, but with the diminution of responsibility, for about a century. By 1910 the shift from examination to college credit was in full flow. In 1849, according to LaBue (1960), New York became the first state to prescribe by law that a diploma (from the Albany State Normal School) would be evidence of qualification for teaching. By 1911 a total of 15 states issued all certificates, with 27 sharing the authority with county officials.

Carmen (1961) has stated that the motivating factors in the drive for legal licensure are mixed: public pressure in seeking protection from the unqualified; the urge of professions to create monopolies for the purpose of eliminating competition and raising prices; and the prestige and psychological satisfaction accorded to a group with legal authorization to practice a profession.

Carmen (1961) marks the Civil War as the dividing line between laissez-faire in certification for the professions and the beginning of tighter state controls. Following the end of the war there were public outcries against fraud, quackery, and incompetence and demands for remedial legislation.

First steps toward this end were the efforts of local, state, and national associations to enforce the codes of ethics and standards of competence. In time these efforts were supported by state legislation. With the evolving growth of society's needs for professional services, a partnership began developing between these professional associations and the states in setting and enforcing standards of competence and practice.

Between 1898 and 1940, according to Frazier (1940), the number of states vested with authority for certification grew from 3 to 42. The trend toward centralization of certification in state departments of education was accelerated by the origin and growth of the practice of accepting normal-school diplomas in lieu of written or oral examinations. Legislation in New York state between 1864 and 1894 authorized the state superintendent to issue certificates upon either an examination or a college graduation, to accept normal-school diplomas from other states, and to revoke certificates for cause. An Illinois statute in 1865 vested authority in the state superintendent to issue life certificates, statewide in application, based on examination.

By 1900, local licensure still predominated, with some 3,000 countries or local units still possessing the power to issue certificates. In only 3 states was the certification of teachers completely vested in the state education agency; in 36 states there was a division of the certification authority between counties and states; and in 4 states, exclusive authority still was vested in counties.

But by 1900 there was evidence of a rapid shift both in certification authority and in the basis of issuance. New York originated the normal-school-diploma basis in 1849, California adopted it in 1863; and by 1900 at least one-half the states waived prescribed examinations for normal-school graduates, and 41 states issued certificates to normal-school graduates.

The steady increase in preparation requirements since 1921 for *elementary teachers* has been indicated by LaBue (1960) as follows: In 1921, a total of 30 states had no specified preparation requirements for certification; in 14 states high school graduation was specified; and no state required college graduation. For *secondary-school teachers* (Armstrong & Stinnett, 1964) in 1900 only 2 states were requiring college graduation; by 1920 the number had grown to 10; by 1930 to 23; and by 1940 to 40; and in 1964 all 50 states required college graduation. In 1930 2 states were requiring college graduation for beginning elementary teachers; in 1940, 11 states; in 1950, 21 states; and in 1964, 46 states.

Legal Certification Authority. Armstrong and Stinnett (1951–1964) have reported the steady development of centralization of the authority for setting the requirements for issuance, renewal, and revocation of teachers certificates. Stinnett (1967) reported that in 1967 this authority, except for minor provisions set forth in law, was virtually completely vested in the respective state departments of education. (The state certification practices reported hereinafter, except as otherwise cited, are taken from Stinnett [1967], as the latest data available.) In 10 states some sharing of the authority to issue certificates was reported. The major parts of such sharing were with certain large cities in five states, with authority to issue certificates to their teachers, and with state colleges and universities in two states, with authority to issue certificates to their graduates. In only two states is minor authority retained by county superintendents to issue restricted certificates in certain class schools.

REQUIREMENTS FOR CERTIFICATION. In 1967 all but four states and Puerto Rico required completion of the bachelor's degree for beginning elementary teachers; all states required completion of at least the bachelor's degree for high school teachers, and 2 states and the District of Columbia had adopted the five-year requirement, but the 2 states were not enforcing it fully. Completion of the fifth year of preparation during the period of initial teaching on the bachelor's degree certificate (usually five to seven years) was mandated by 18 states.

Rapid progress toward the minimum requirement of six college years of preparation for professional special or auxiliary school service personnel was reported. In 1967 a total of 20 states required a minimum preparation of six or more years for superintendents; 47 states required five years or more for secondary-school principals; 44 states required five years or more for elementary-school principals.

Personnel Required to Hold State Certificates. All states in 1967 required teachers, administrators, and special school personnel to hold appropriate certificates; in 42 states teachers in public kindergarten schools, and in 19 states teachers in public nursery schools, were required to hold certificates; in 10 states teachers in public junior colleges were required to hold certificates. Teachers in nonpublic elementary and secondary schools, at some school levels or under specified conditions, were required by law or regulation in 18 states to hold state certificates. The typical practices, however, were to require state certification if the school that was involved sought or held state accreditation, or to issue state certificates upon the voluntary request of teachers in nonpublic schools.

Lindner (1966), in a study of state certification practices of teachers in Catholic schools, categorized such practices as follows: mandatory (in 11 states for elementary- and 10 states for secondary-school teachers); mandatory–accreditation (in 16 states for elementary- and 19 states for secondary-school teachers); permissive (in 19 states for elementary- and 17 states for secondary-school teachers); and no provision for certification (in 4 states for both elementary- and secondary-school teachers). Her survey of the reactions of teachers in Catholic schools and of diocesan superintendents to the desirability of state certification reflected favorable attitudes. Almost 90 percent of the certified elementary and secondary teachers in Catholic schools (of a sample of 10,000) favored state certification; among the noncertified teachers the favorable responses were lower (77 and 69 percent, respectively) but still preponderantly in favor. Similar favorable responses from the diocesan superintendents were recorded.

General Requirements. In addition to specific requirements establishing qualifications for certification, according to specialized fields or areas, there are general requirements of states, usually set forth in state laws, applicable to all candidates for certification, such as age, citizenship, health, loyalty oaths, and special courses. Thirty states require U.S. citizenship or declaration of intent; 25 states require a loyalty oath; 43 states require recommendation of the preparing college or of the employing superintendent in the case of experienced teachers; 18 states specify no minimum age, and 34 states specify a minimum age of 18 or above; 21 states require a general health certificate; and the number of states (in 1967) requiring a special course, such as state history or constitution, has dropped to 8, of which only 4 require credit in a formal, special course as a prerequisite to certification.

Number of Teacher Education Institutions. A total of 1,198 colleges and universities were approved for teacher education by the 50 states, the District of Columbia, and Puerto Rico in 1967. Among these, of the once numerous normal schools, teachers colleges, and state colleges of education, only 20 (9 public and 11 private) remain. A total of 808 were general colleges; 601 were private liberal arts colleges; and 207 were public, state, or general colleges; there were 299 universities—153 private and 146 public.

The producers of newly graduated teachers reported in 1964 (National Education Association . . ., 1965) were: teachers colleges, 5.1 percent; general colleges, 53 percent; and universities, 41.9 percent. The production percentages according to institutional controls were: public institutions, 67.9 percent; nonpublic, 32.1 percent.

A growing trend is reflected in the proportion of new teacher graduates produced each year by institutions accredited by NCATE since its establishment. The percentages were: 1955, 60.5 and 59.8 percent of the new supply of elementary- and secondary-school teachers, respectively; in 1958, the percentages were 65.1 and 63.3; in 1961 the percentages were 71.3 and 67.4; and in 1964 they were 74.1 and 73.7 (National Education Association . . ., 1965).

Reciprocity Practices. Efforts to achieve reasonable mobility in teacher certification through regional reciprocity compacts, which began in the 1930's, have diminished, and in 1967 all but one of such compacts had fallen into disuse. The increasing mobility of teachers now requires a workable national plan.

One of the continuing controversies that have involved certification procedures is the use of NCATE accreditation. Stinnett (1967) reported in 1967 that 37 states were basing some degree of reliance upon NCATE accreditation for the acceptance of credentials for certification of in-migrating teachers. Conant (1963) sharply criticized this practice because of the alleged domination of NCATE by NEA units or departments and because of the procedures used in NCATE accrediting. The National Commission on Accrediting, stimulated by protests from its constituent organizations, has conducted searching reviews of NCATE structure and procedures—in 1954, 1956, 1960–61, and again in 1965–66 (Mayor, 1965). The controversies involving Carleton College and the University of Wisconsin were instrumental in initiating a study by Mayor (1965). This study reported that accreditation came into being, as did limiting legislation by government, as the result of excesses under the policies of laissez faire. In general, Mayor supported the need for national accreditation for teacher education, with suggested refinements in the NCATE structure, standards, and procedures.

Armstrong (1961) suggested four steps in achieving the free movement of qualified teachers across state lines: (1) reduction in number of certificates issued by the states; (2) state requirements for certificates stated in terms other than courses and credits; (3) combination of legal and extralegal action by professional groups to control assignment of teachers to their fields of qualification; and (4) national accreditation for certification of migrating teachers. Lieberman (1961) proposed a plan of national certification of teachers (not necessarily federal certification), perhaps through the extralegal setting of standards by extralegal groups.

An effort in this direction was the joint study, by the National Association of State Directors of Teacher Education and Certification and the American Association for the Advancement of Science, of secondary-school science and mathematics. This study was aimed at bringing about a unified approach to teacher education–certification requirements among the states (Viall, 1961).

The New York State Education Department (Lierheimer, 1965) began a study in 1966 of "teacher mobility," under a grant from the U.S. Office of Education.

Examinations in Certification. A growing use of examinations was reported in 1967—especially of the *National Teachers Examination (NTE)*, the *Modern Foreign Language Association Examination,* and the *Graduate Record Examination*—in state certification practices. Six states used the *NTE* as prerequisite for one or more types of certificates, and two used the *NTE* for institutional self study. Nine states used proficiency examinations in lieu of credit in some courses.

In addition, many of the largest school systems used examinations, typically the *NTE,* although some used local examinations, either as a prerequisite to certification—where the state had legal authority to certificate its teachers—or to become eligible for appointment to positions.

Mosier (1961) opposed the use of examinations for certification, while Shuck (1961) advocated flexibility in teacher education and certification through wider use of proficiency examinations. Kurland (1964) predicted that proficiency examinations will become generally accepted in certification procedures among the states.

The Problem of Multiple Certification. A persistent barrier to interstate reciprocity in certification is the large number of separate name certificates. About 1950 the states were issuing over 1,000 separate certificates. Stinnett (1967) reported that this number has declined to 549. The range among the states in the number of separate name certificates issued was from 1 to 57; the median was 7; the mode was 5.

Types of Certificates. The types of certificates issued by the states generally have fallen into well-defined categories, according to term, levels of preparation, field or area of specialization, and substandard. The designations of certificates denoting the length of term or duration were life, permanent, limited, continuing, provisional, and probationary; the designations reflecting levels of preparation were regular, standard, professional, advanced standard, and advanced professional; the designations generally reflecting teaching fields or areas for which the holder is authorized to teach were endorsed, blanket (with the enforcement of assignments left to other means), and special field (with endorsements); the designations reflecting substandard preparation were emergency, temporary, and permit. Of course, there were overlappings in these categories and designations. For example, "limited" and "permanent" in some instances are used also to connote levels of preparation; "probationary" and "provisional" in some instances connote substandard preparation.

NEW DEVELOPMENTS. Relatively new developments in state certification procedures consisted of efforts to decentralize to some degree the process, by placing greater responsibility in the profession and in approved teacher education institutions. These efforts were classified as: advisory councils, the approved-programs approach, and the professional practices acts.

Advisory councils (variously called councils, committees, or commissions on teacher education–certification) began to be established about 1933. In 1967, all but one state, the District of Columbia, and Puerto Rico had advisory groups to the state board of education. Twelve states had such bodies created by law. In the remaining states the bodies were extralegal, having been created by the state boards of education and the constituency appointed by the chief state school officers. The membership was intended to represent the major segments of the teaching profession.

The approved-programs approach is the process by which the proposed programs of a given institution for the preparation of teachers are submitted to the state certification authorities. When once approved, graduates are somewhat automatically certificated, upon recommendation of the preparing institution. This plan avoids the weakness of certification on the basis of checking off course credits against the prescribed requirements of the state. Its strength is the placing of greater responsibility upon the preparing institutions, permitting them to differ widely in programs according to the philosophy, the staff, and the facilities of the various institutions. In 1967, 40 states were using this plan in varying degrees.

The most recent trend toward decentralization and democratization of certification procedures was the passage of professional practices acts. Such acts created professional practices commissions or professional standards boards, consisting of wide representation from the major segments of the teaching profession. The functions of the commissions and boards were the development and enforcement of standards of performance and ethical practice, as well as serving as advisory groups in the application of certification standards in special cases. By 1967, six states had such laws, and in several others proposals were before legislatures for action.

PROPOSALS FOR CHANGE. From the literature on certification, the following changes appeared to be most vigorously advocated: (1) a nationwide procedure to assure the free movement of qualified teachers across state lines; (2) a reduction in the number of separate name certificates to some manageable number—five or fewer; (3) refinement of standards and processes used in NCATE accreditation; (4) strengthening of the standards and procedures for state approval of teacher education institutions; (5) full implementation of the approved programs approach; and (6) greater uses of proficiency and qualifying examinations in certification.

T. M. Stinnett
Texas A&M University

References

Armstrong, W. Earl. "A Basis for Reciprocity in Teacher Certification." In *The Education of Teachers: Certification.* NCTEPS, NEA, 1961. p. 226.

Armstrong, W. Earl, and Stinnett, T. M. *A Manual on Certification Requirements for School Personnel in the United States.* NCTEPS, NEA. See 1951, 1953, 1955, 1957, 1959, 1961, and 1964 editions.

Carmen, Harry J. "The Historical Development of Licensing for the Professions." In *The Education of Teachers: Certification.* NCTEPS, NEA, 1961. p. 145-55.

Conant, James B. *The Education of American Teachers.* McGraw-Hill, 1963. 275p.

Conant, James B. *The Certification of Teachers: The Restricted State Approved Programs Approach.* AACTE, 1964. 28p.

Corey, A. F. "CTA Speaks Out for Higher Standards in Licensure of Teachers." *California Ed* 3:3-6; 1966.

Edwards, Newton, and Richey, Herman G. *The School in the American Social Order.* Houghton, 1963. 694p.

Frazier, Benjamin W. *Education of Teachers as a Function of State Department of Education.* USOE, 1940.

Kinney, Lucien B. *Certification in Education.* Prentice-Hall, 1964. 178p.

Kinney, L. B., and Stone, J. C. "State Certification or Else? Revision of *Certification in Education*." *California Teach Assn J* 60:12–3; 1964.

Koerner, James D. *The Miseducation of American Teachers.* Houghton, 1963. 360p.

Kurland, Norman D. "Proficiency Examinations in Teacher Certification: A New Approach." In *Changes in Teacher Education: An Appraisal.* NCTEPS, NEA, 1964. p. 89–102.

LaBue, Anthony C. "Teacher Certification in the United States: A Brief History." *J Teach Ed* 11:147–72; 1960.

Lieberman, Myron. "Considerations Favoring National Certification of Teachers." In *The Education of Teachers: Certification.* NCTEPS, NEA, 1961. p. 200–10.

Lierheimer, Alvin P. *Interstate Certification of Teachers and Other School Personnel.* New York State Education Department, 1965. 3p. Mimeographed.

Lindner, Sister Mary John, D.C. "State Certification of Teachers in Catholic Elementary and Secondary Schools." Unpublished doctoral dissertation. St. John's U, 1966.

Mayor, John R. *Accreditation in Teacher Education.* Nat Commission on Accrediting, 1965. 311p.

Melaro, Constance L. "Comments on Teacher Certification." *NEA J* 55:18; 1963.

Mosier, Earl E. "Proficiency Examination—A Wise or Unwise Policy?" In *The Education of Teachers: Certification.* NCTEPS, NEA, 1961. p. 232–9.

National Education Association, Research Division. *Teacher Supply and Demand in the Public Schools, 1964–65.* NEA, 1965. 60p.

Shuck, Emerson C. "Flexibility in Certification Programs." In *The Education of Teachers: Certification.* NCTEPS, NEA, 1961. p. 121–9.

Stinnett, T. M. *A Manual on Certification Requirements for School Personnel in the United States.* NCTEPS, NEA, 1967.

Stinnett, T. M., and Huggett, Albert J. *Professional Problems of Teachers*, 2nd ed. Macmillan, 1963. 516p.

Stone, J. C. "Teacher Education by Legislation: The California Story Continued." *Phi Delta Kappan* 47:287–91; 1966.

Viall, William P. "The NASDTEC-AAAS Teacher Preparation-certification Study." In *The Education of Teachers: Certification.* NCTEPS, NEA, 1961. p. 282–5.

Woellner, Elizabeth H., and Wood, M. Aurilla. *Requirements for Certification*, 31st ed. U Chicago Press, 1967. 158p.

TEACHER EDUCATION PROGRAMS

Teacher education programs have been studied more than researched. Innovations have tended to be implanted and imitated with a minimum of evaluation. Practices and procedures have evolved rather than developed through controlled experimentation. The trend, however, is toward more scientific inquiry. Historical, philosophical and normative survey types of studies are being supplemented by analytical and experimental investigations. Established traditions as well as new changes are being challenged to demonstrate their superiority. The past decade has seen programs of teacher education the center of intensive controversy; the prospects are that this will become a field of more concentrated and more objective research in the years ahead.

Early studies of programs of teacher education were status surveys. A classical example, and one of the earliest, was supported by the Commonwealth Fund. It was completed in 1929 under the auspices of the University of Chicago (Charters & others, 1929). An even more extensive nationwide survey, the first and only comprehensive study of teacher education that has been financed by the federal government of the United States, was completed four years later (U.S. Office of Education, 1933). A third early overview type of study had the support of the Julius Rosenwald Fund (Embree, 1938). The historical development of teacher education programs was summarized a year later in a commemorative volume sponsored by the National Education Association (Harper, 1939). These pioneer investigations were historically important not only for the information they provided on the status of teacher education but also for the trends and problems identified. In retrospect it is clear that they mark the beginning of a nationwide concern for the quality of programs to prepare teachers for elementary and secondary schools.

The first comprehensive effort to analyze the impact of various approaches to teacher education was made by the Commission on Teacher Education of the American Council on Education (1939, 1944). The strategy followed was to encourage selected and representative types of institutions to develop innovations in programs for investigational purposes. The scope of the series of studies sponsored by the commission ranged from a definition of cultural and social elements in the education of teachers (Bigelow, 1940) to the use of evaluation in teacher education (Troyer & Pace, 1944). A statement of major issues (P. Smith & others, 1944) charted the direction of subsequent investigations into the nature and effectiveness of teacher education programs.

Program Conceptualizations: General Theory and Rationale. The focus on improving programs to prepare teachers initiated by the Commission on Teacher Education ranged from theory to rationale. It set in motion a series of studies, work conferences, and reports aimed at projecting new conceptualizations for programs of teacher education. One technique employed was that of a jury of experts to judge existing theory and practice and to project the ideal (Stiles, 1945). Another was the analytical conference of selected leaders to define issues and describe and assess practice as well as to project promising developments. The National Commission on Teacher Education and Professional Standards of the National Education Association (NEA) has been the host to a series of annual study conferences of this type dealing with such subjects as new conceptions (National Education Association, 1961), program control and certification (National Education Association, 1960a), and content (National Education Association, 1959).

The most striking new conceptualization in programs to prepare teachers has been the Master of Arts in Teaching (M.A.T.) pattern for graduates of liberal arts colleges. This exclusively graduate-level concentration of professional preparation was pioneered in by Harvard University as early as 1936. Another postbaccalaureate model for a statewide teacher education program was developed in the state of Arkansas with financial assistance from the Fund for the Advancement of Education of the Ford Foundation (Krathwohl & Spalding, 1956). Subsequently, other institutions developed variations of the graduate-level programs. Many of these new ventures originally had help from the Ford Foundation (Woodring, 1957). The new programs varied in length from one to two years. Common characteristics of these M.A.T. programs include admission of candidates at the graduate level, a reduced emphasis on pedagogical studies, the close correlation of professional content with an internship, and increased responsibility of school systems for clinical experience (Woodring, 1957).

Diversity was the most noticeable characteristic of programs of teacher education at mid-twentieth century, with each institution seemingly aspiring to be unique (Stiles & others, 1960). Discontent was the typical reaction of leaders in the field as well as outside observers (Cottrell & others, 1956; Bestor, 1953). Efforts to achieve standardization through national accreditation of teacher education programs produced further controversy (Mayor, 1965). Central concerns that motivated inquiry were such factors as control of programs (Conant, 1963), quality of professional courses (Stiles, 1959), program emphasis (Koerner, 1963), organizational patterns (National Education Association, 1960b), and quality of product (American Association of Colleges for Teacher Education, 1963). The controversies of the 1950's and early 1960's sparked a variety of changes (National Education Association, 1963, 1964) and planned innovations (O'Brien, 1965; Hazard, 1966) that may well provide the models for research on teacher education programs in the future.

Organizational Trends. The extent and nature of interdisciplinary participation and responsibility for programs of teacher education have been the focus of a number of recent studies. Interest in this area has been stimulated by the need to find effective ways for professors of education and those in the liberal arts fields to cooperate in the preparation of teachers. The dimensions of the problem were outlined in three reports by the National Council on Teacher Education and Professional Standards (National Education Association, 1958, 1959). Ways of achieving viable interdisciplinary involvement in policy making and program development were the central focus of a two-year study of teacher education reported by James B. Conant in 1963. A nationwide survey of institutional practices revealed that over half of the institutions preparing teachers in 1966 provided for some form of interdisciplinary cooperation (Stiles & Carver, 1967). The all-institution council was the most common arrangement; a major model was projected for state universities in California (Boyer, 1965).

A new emphasis in programs to prepare for teaching has been the use of educational technology. In an experimental study Woodward (1964) found that prospective teachers learned as much by viewing classes via closed-circuit television, with substantial economies of time, as they did from direct observation. Chabe (1962) found television observations "almost" as effective as classroom visits. A comparison of three methods of observation—kinescope portrayals, closed-circuit viewing, and direct observation—revealed that candidates learned best to evaluate a class critically by studying a kinescope and that none of the techniques proved superior in conveying information (Stoller & others, 1964). Similar results were obtained by Fulton and Rupiper (1962) and in another study by Schueler and Gold (1964). Vlcek (1966) used simulator techniques to prepare candidates for student teaching. The major gain was in the growth in level of confidence of teacher trainees. Attempting to achieve a balanced view, Mars (1966) suggests a systematic program for introducing teacher candidates to the teaching possibilities of educational technology.

Programs especially designed to prepare teachers for inner-city schools represent a growing trend. The need for teachers with unique training to work with educationally deprived students was enunciated by Conant (1963) and analyzed by Pillard (1962). A pioneering program was the Cardozo Project in Urban Teaching (Cuban, 1964). It recruited Peace Corps and VISTA veterans and persons experienced in other types of human service and, later, graduates direct from college to prepare to teach in inner-city schools. Located in the Washington, D.C., schools, the key elements of the program were a supervised internship, related seminars focused on urban teaching problems, the development of instructional materials adapted to educationally deprived students, and direct study of family and community life. Results indicated that such a program can be effective in recruiting able, mature, and dedicated young people, from a variety of socioeconomic backgrounds, to train for and to teach in inner-city schools. Hunter College of the City University of New York demonstrated an 80-percent rate of retention in urban teaching for volunteers who were specially prepared to teach in inner-city schools. It found it impossible to predict the type of person who would volunteer (Schueler, 1963). Mercy College in Detroit (Lofthouse, 1963) and Queens College of the City University of New York (Rivlin, 1966) have developed programs with special emphasis on urban teaching.

A significant development in recent years has been the entry of the federal government into financial sponsorship of programs to prepare teachers for educationally disadvantaged children and youth. In the summer of 1965, 118 colleges and universities trained 29,933 teachers to teach in Project Head Start, a program to prepare particularly needy young children for school entry (Drazek, 1966). The 89th session of the national Congress passed legislation to create the Teacher Corps, the purposes of which would be twofold: (1) to provide concentrated educational services to inner-city type schools and (2) to recruit and to train college graduates for urban teaching (*New York Times*, 1966). Modeled after the Cardozo Project, the Teacher Corps brings into national focus the needs of urban schools for teachers uniquely trained and committed to work with young people in inner-city type schools.

Fifth-year and M.A.T. Programs. Perhaps the most visible trend in programs in teacher education has been the growth of Master of Arts in Teaching (M.A.T.) programs. These programs were designed specifically to prepare liberal arts graduates who had little or no background in education to teach in secondary schools. The first M.A.T. program was begun at Harvard in 1936. Impetus to further M.A.T. programs has been provided by philanthropic organizations, especially the Ford Foundation and its subsidiary, the Fund for the Advancement of Education (Woodring, 1957). A clear analysis and description of the salient features of M.A.T. programs are provided by Cartwright (1961). At Duke University the M.A.T. Cooperative Program enrolls some 40 interns per year who teach under contract in local school systems in teams of four to six (Cartwright, 1961). At Johns Hopkins the intern teaches a full load for one semester a year and in the other semester does full-time graduate work in his subject field; the professional courses are taken in the summer prior to the academic year. The Yale M.A.T. program is typical in its emphasis on subject-area knowledge, carefully supervised practice teaching, and relevant professional courses; in addition, it offers assistance to teachers already in service (Holden, 1959). The programs vary in length from a summer and a year to two full years. The Northwestern M.A.T. program, for instance, requires five quarters of work—two summers with a full year in between. The distinction between practice teaching and internship teaching also varies, as does the salary that interns receive for their teaching. Many other recommendations for graduate degree programs for teachers have been made (Crall & Myers, 1960; Cartwright, 1959). A survey undertaken at Eastern Michigan College categorizes the various patterns of preparation for certification and teaching offered to liberal arts graduates (Woronoff, 1958). All of these graduate-degree programs stress the necessity of interdisciplinary cooperation among university faculties in planning and administering the programs (Lumiansky, 1959).

The new Teacher Intern Program at Stanford emphasizes continuous teaching, in-depth study in the foundation areas, in curriculum and instruction in one's field, and in one's subject field, plus continuous dialogue with a tutor-supervisor. Built into this program is ongoing experimentation in teacher attitudes and behaviors (Allen, 1966). An experimental five-year program at George Peabody College for Teachers has attempted the rapid development of career teachers by incorporating extensive school visitation, in-depth seminars, and a full year of paid internship teaching and granting the M.A. degree at the end of the fifth year (Turney & Stoneking, 1965). The new secondary internship program at the University of California at Los Angeles (UCLA) for postgraduate students involves a summer of practice teaching plus a year of salaried intern teaching, coincidentally with a series of seminars in the foundations of education (Wulk & Miller, 1965). The fifth-year program at Cornell University is one of the few fifth-year programs solely for the preparation of elementary teachers (Mitzel, 1958).

PRESERVICE PROGRAMS: CONTENT AND DESIGN. Liberal Arts Foundation Courses. Although controversy and conflict continue over the place of liberal education and the role of liberal arts colleges in teacher education, little actual research has been done in this area. Arguments are advanced that liberal arts colleges have caused much of the conflict by failing to define their role in teacher education (Stiles, 1964). The vitality, variety, and freedom found in many liberal arts colleges is essential for effective programs of teacher education (Reinert, 1965). Others argue for the necessity of liberal education in teacher education programs as a prerequisite for the good life (Broudy, 1966). Also, strong rationales have been developed for the offering of foundation courses in the history, philosophy, and psychology of education to all liberal arts students, not just those preparing to teach (T. Carter, 1965). A 1961 survey gave evidence that, increasingly, departments of anthropology, sociology, and political science are joining with departments of education in studying educational problems and in developing courses for the preparation of teachers (Quintana & Sexton, 1961). In opposition to this general survey is a more recent study which suggests that social studies teachers generally have little specific background in political science or government (Hahn, 1965). In accordance with the findings of this study is McAulay's survey (1966) of 100 elementary-education programs which suggests that the content of social studies methods courses gives students little opportunity to practice the newer methods of inquiry, stimulation, and experimentation which, hopefully, they will use when they begin teaching. Much controlled research remains to be done in this area.

Professional Sequence. As with the role of the liberal arts in teacher education, controversy continues in regard to the importance, nature, structure, and relevance of professional courses in preparing teachers. Concomitantly, the argument over the question of whether education is or is not a discipline continues. Stanley (1966) argues that education is a *professional* discipline; Walton and Kuethe (1963) also argue for education as a discipline. The predominant trend in the past few years is away from the frequent proliferation of professional courses toward their consolidation into a few more logical and meaningful courses (Harap, 1962). At Northwestern University the Tutorial and Clinical Program requires just 24 quarter hours of work in professional education, out of a total of 192, all done on a tutorial basis (Hazard, 1966). The report of a 1960 conference of Indiana institutions involved in teacher preparation revealed a general consolidation of professional courses and a corresponding expansion of liberal arts requirements (Indiana State University, 1960). A 1960 conference sponsored by the Fund for the Advancement of Education supported the need for such consolidation (E. R. Smith, 1960). A study done at the University of Oregon concluded that their teacher education candidates were not overburdened with education courses, nor were these candidates lacking in subject specialization (Wattles & Osibov, 1960). At San Francisco State College the professional courses are built around a series of laboratory experiences geared toward the personal development of each teacher candidate (Robb, 1965). Tyler and Okumu's work at UCLA in developing a system for the analysis of teacher education programs focuses on the identification of the behavioral objectives of existing courses and the comparison of these objectives with the stated goals and content of the course; such research has considerable import for future efforts in professional course revision. (Tyler & Okumu, 1965). The Teacher Education and Media Project (TEAM) represents an attempt to develop a professional education curriculum on the basis of carefully defined behavioral outcomes and to create guide lines for instructional units which utilize new media to achieve these outcomes (La Grone, 1965). This project has divided professional study into five areas—analytical study of teaching, structure and uses of knowledge, concepts of learning and development, designs for teaching-learning, and demonstration and evaluation of teaching competences—and prepared a series of carefully selected and controlled, direct and simulated experiences in these areas.

Of the professional content courses, educational psychology is one of the most frequently required. Despite this fact the area still suffers from lack of research and adequate standardization of subject matter. Nunney (1964) surveyed 11 major introductory texts to identify the core of educational psychology. Schoben (1964) criticized the triviality and irrelevance of much of the research in educational psychology, claiming that methods are too often substituted for substance.

Studies in group processes have particular relevance to teacher education, because of the teacher's predominant responsibility for educating groups of students. Two experiments done specifically in the area of teacher education deserve consideration. By creating a group-centered, group-planned course for teacher education students, Forst and Matthews (1964) attempted to provide experience in democratic processes, plus the inducement of behavioral changes in the students toward increased autonomy in learning, increased sensitivity to sociopsychological classroom factors, and objectivity toward their role as teachers. They found that the students were frustrated initially but that they slowly gained momentum in planning and initiating their own learning experiences. In a similar experiment with students in the fifth-year program at the University of North Carolina, Davis and Bowers (1961) attempted, through the use of lectures, readings, small-group tasks, sessions in analyzing role playing, and unstructured large-group discussions, to plan a curriculum aimed at developing increased group sensitivity of preservice teachers. They found that the students generally benefited from the experience by developing more realistic perceptions and acceptances of self.

Clinical Experiences. Historically, the student-teaching or practice-teaching experience has been the least criticized, and often the least researched, part of the total teacher education program. Conant, in his recent study of teacher education (1963), focused particular attention on practice teaching when he recommended that the competence of a future teacher be tested by practice teaching under state-determined conditions and supervision. From Conant's study came the term "clinical experience," borrowed from medical education, to denote the various kinds of actual teaching experiences developed for preservice teachers prior to certification. In a recent criticism of the focus of present clinical teaching experiences, Goodlad (1965) suggested that too often these experiences are oriented toward the development of specific teaching, or survival, techniques, rather than, as John Dewey suggested, toward the understanding of the principles of education on which practice is based. He recommends that future research efforts be directed toward the establishment of the vital links between psychology and education and toward the defining of expectancies for the future teacher in terms of behavioral objectives. In a study of student-teaching practices at 38 Midwestern institutions Inlow (1960) discovered considerable variety in the number of hours required; greater uniformity was found in the payment of money to cooperating teachers, the arrangements for pre-student-teaching classroom visits, the lack of screening of student teachers by cooperating school systems, and the general feeling of confidence by university people in the cooperating teachers. E. D. Smith and F. J. Cunningham (1961), surveying the administrative relationships between 75 teacher education institutions and their cooperating public schools, found that only one-third of the respondents had well-organized programs for policy making and only one-fifth used personnel cooperatively; however, two-thirds made some attempt to prepare teachers for their supervisory roles. The growing emphasis on pre-practice-teaching clinical experiences is shown by Northwestern's Tutorial and Clinical Program, which begins in the freshman year with classroom visits and dialogues with teachers and progresses through volunteer work with community agencies, attendance at school-board meetings, teacher-aide experiences in schools, and school-based research work to the actual half-day practice teaching in the senior year (Hazard, 1966). This series of clinical experiences is integrated in small-group tutorials with the professional and liberal study in which each student is engaged. Michigan State's Elementary

Intern Program, originally a five-year program but now, like Northwestern's, a four-year undergraduate program, places each elementary-teacher candidate in a full-time teaching experience in a regular school on a salaried basis (Corman & Olmsted, 1964). The problem of the supervision of practice or intern teachers has also received considerable attention. Northwestern University, following Conant's suggestion, pioneered in establishing the Clinical Professorship in Education (Hazard, 1966). By definition and practice the clinical professor is a master teacher in a public school who devotes half-time to the university, where he works with and supervises the teacher candidates in all levels of their clinical experiences in an attempt to blend theory and continuing practice at a highly meaningful level. Ezer and Lambert (1966) suggest a two-semester "residency in supervision" program to prepare classroom teachers for their roles as supervising teachers.

Many other facets of the practice-teaching experience have recently been researched. An ongoing longitudinal study at the University of Minnesota is attempting to relate data collected on teacher candidates at the time of their admission to the university with their observed behavior as practice teachers (Wilk & Edson, 1963). To date, significant correlation has been found only between the results of the Honor Point Ratio and Minesota Teacher Attitude Inventory (MTAI) tests (administered during the sophomore year) and integrative behavior during practice teaching. In a rather subjective study at Arizona State University, researchers examined the ranking of 25 teaching techniques by teacher candidates before and after practice teaching in terms of their feelings of confidence about using the techniques (Hoover & others, 1965). Newsome and others (1965), using the GNC Scale (a test of logical consistency of ideas about education), examined the changes in consistency of educational ideas attributable to practice-teaching experiences and found that, with the exception of mathematics and elementary teachers, the students' ideas about education were significantly less consistent after practice teaching than they were before. Using the MTAI, Brim (1966), at the University of Denver, found that the clinical experiences of 250 teacher candidates significantly liberalized their attitudes toward children. Shumsky and Murray (1961), using a cartoon situation prepared by the Bank Street College of Education as a projective technique, helped practice teachers explore their attitudes toward discipline; in the process the students came to feel less guilty about establishing and using their authority as adults.

A final important area of research related both to future clinical programs and to the studies in group-sensitivity training reported earlier (Davis & Bowers, 1961; Forst & Matthews, 1964) is the pioneering work in interaction analysis reported recently by Flanders and followed by several other significant studies. Flanders' interaction-analysis instrument (1962) enables a systematic and precise analysis to be made of the interaction between teacher and class, particularly in terms of the emotional climate and verbal behavior of each. Amidon (1966) concluded that as a result of training in the Flanders system of interaction-analysis and the provision of feedback about verbal behavior during practice teaching, teacher candidates became more accepting and less critical and they encouraged more pupil-initiated talk. Moskowitz (1966) trained cooperating teachers in the use of the Flanders system, concluding that it enabled them to form more positive interpersonal relationships with their practice teachers. Nelson (1966) studied the model teaching styles used by different teachers in language-arts programs, using Flanders' system in the discussion prior to writing assignments, followed by an evaluation of the writing itself. A similar interaction-analysis coding system is being used at the University of Chicago and at Manhattanville College of the Sacred Heart to help elementary-teacher candidates analyze teaching behavior and develop a wider, more flexible range of teaching behaviors of their own (Joyce & Hodges, 1966).

Evaluation of Teacher Education Programs. Evaluation of entire teacher education programs, or even of segments of programs, is spotty and inadequate. Ebel (1966) listed four ways in which tests have been or could be used in teacher education programs: (1) in selection of students, (2) in advising and counseling students, (3) in evaluating their achievement in courses, and (4) in helping to certify their competence to teach. In none of these areas does he find that sufficient, meaningful research has been done. In attacking the difficult problem of evaluating an entire teacher education program, Woodruff (1963) proposed that we begin by identifying a basic set of segments or elements common to all teacher education programs. Second, tests should be designed which are appropriate for the various segments and which could be administered in any combination; third, institutions preparing teachers should be assisted in preparing profiles of their own programs so that they could select the tests appropriate to their particular program. Kearney (1958) describes an evaluation instrument developed in Minnesota for teacher education institutions in that state. This instrument, which covers seven basic areas, is used both for self-evaluation and for state certification of teacher education programs. An example of a broad-scale evaluation is Saxe's study (1965) of the efforts of the Fund for the Advancement of Education, later the Ford Foundation's educational division, to bring about particular change in teacher education. He attempted to answer the question of what the Fund for Advancement of Education and the Ford Foundation got for their money, their influence, and their prestige. The results, based on data gathered from the grantee institutions, fund personnel, and others in the profession, suggested that changes did occur in the curricula of the grantee institutions, that the fund was successful in involving the grantee institutions more fully in teacher education but that it was difficult to evaluate whether the fund's attempts to affect teacher education nationally were successful or not. A more recent example of a broad evaluation is Stiles's study (1967) of the Cardozo Project in

Urban Teaching. Using objective data such as undergraduate academic records and National Teacher Examination results, plus thorough reports by qualified observer-judges, Stiles concluded that the kinds of teachers produced by this project are more effective in dealing with the instructional problems unique to the urban environment than teachers prepared in traditional programs.

Assessment of various segments of teacher education programs has received more research attention. Although little of real assistance has as yet been discovered in the examination of teacher personality as a predictor of success in teaching, Cook (1964) suggests the directions which research may best follow. To evaluate English-methods courses in New Hampshire teacher education institutions, Foy (1964) polled their graduates who had taken such courses and who had taught or were still teaching in local school systems. He also polled a sample of junior and senior high school principals to elicit their opinions of these courses. His results showed that the teachers felt that their English-methods course was the best education course that they had taken and that neither the teachers nor the principals favored the elimination of pedagogical courses, either English methods or general methods. Keffer (1964) attempted to use expert judgments in developing a science-methods course. By sending appropriate questionnaires to random samples of secondary-school science teachers and college-level science-methods instructors drawn from a North Central Association of Colleges and Secondary Schools' list, he tried to determine the topics that experts believed could be taught most productively and the relative emphasis which should be given to each topic. The OScAR, developed for identifying and categorizing the emotional climate of a classroom, has proved useful in studying student teaching behavior, both through direct observation and through the use of television (Schueler & others, 1962). Jalbert (1966) demonstrated that training in evaluation of classroom instruction prior to student teaching improved ability in self-evaluation. Again on a broader level, a clear description of the National Teacher Examinations and their relevance to teacher education is given by Fenstermacher and Swineford (1958).

PROMISING RESEARCH DESIGNS. In the past few years many unique and promising teacher education programs have been originated in colleges and universities across the country. Selected from among these programs are five which seem to show in their design unusual potential for preparing teachers of high quality and for conducting ongoing research toward the improvement of teacher education on a broad scale.

Four-year Undergraduate Programs. The Tutorial and Clinical Program at Northwestern University represents a comprehensive and imaginative attempt at innovation in teacher education (Hazard, 1966). The theme of the program is an all-university commitment to the preparation of teachers. The planning was based on three fundamental assumptions: (1) that the program meet the requirements for general education established by the university faculty, (2) that academic majors be planned jointly with the appropriate departments of the college of arts and sciences, and (3) that all professional instruction be given through tutorials and related clinical experiences rather than through formal course work. The key person is the tutorial professor. From his day-by-day contacts with the students, individually and in groups of ten, come the problems and issues that generate for students and staff a spirit of continual inquiry and growth. In the winter quarter of freshman year the students begin a carefully planned series of clinical experiences, culminating with practice teaching in the senior year. Increasingly, the students work jointly with their tutorial professor and with a clinical professor, a master teacher from a local public school who devotes half-time to working with the students in the clinical part of the program. Ongoing research and evaluation are coordinated by the program's Director of Research. Data gathered so far suggest that the students selecting the Tutorial and Clinical program are highly motivated and academically superior to those students who choose the traditional program. Eventually, research will be conducted to determine the percentage of students who complete the program and the number of students who enter and remain in teaching.

The Wisconsin Intern-in-Team program, a part of the overall Wisconsin Improvement Program, offers another promising program design (O'Brien, 1966). Although basically a five-year program, it is possible for students to complete it, including the internship, in four years. Like Northwestern's program, it builds toward the clinical teaching experience as its culmination. Unlike Northwestern, the intern assumes full-time teaching position as a member of a teaching team which may number from two to six people. The internship lasts for one semester, and the major supervision and evaluation of the intern is handled by the team members. Research conducted to date on the Intern-in-Team program suggests several interesting things about team teaching and teacher training. Students taught by the teams do as well on achievement tests as those taught in traditional, self-contained classrooms. Using the "Flanders model" with some modification, researchers discovered that all teachers, including interns, did much more talking than they thought they did. Finally, the interns felt that the value of team planning and team criticism of teaching performance was most beneficial to their growth as mature teachers. The same intern-in-team concept for teaching and for teacher education has been adopted at Claremont (Polos, 1960).

Fifth-year Graduate Programs. One of the most radically new programs is the Cardozo Project in Urban Teaching (Cuban, 1964). This program, which is designed specifically to prepare liberal arts graduates as teachers for inner-city schools, is located in the Cardozo High School in Washington, D.C. This program differs from the usual type in that leadership for it comes from the school system itself. The Cardozo Project is affiliated with Howard University. Some of the foundation courses are taught by Howard professors, and the interns earn credits toward an M.A.T. from Howard. The interns, many of whom have had Peace Corps or VISTA experience, teach partial loads for a full year and are paid salaries slightly below those of first-year teachers. They are closely supervised by subject-matter specialists, who themselves are experienced teachers and who also teach partial loads. During the summer prior to the year of teaching, and while they are teaching, the interns attend a series of seminars in urban sociology, the psychological foundations of learning, the humanities, and teaching methods and curriculum development. Unique to the program are its emphases on the development of instructional units geared to inner-city, disadvantaged students and the commitment to get to know the students and the community in which they live. The interns and subject-matter specialists are assisted by the residents, themselves former interns, who have remained in the program to teach part-time and to work with interns and in developing instructional units. An independent evaluation of the Cardozo Project found it extremely successful in preparing participants to be effective teachers of inner-city youth (Stiles, 1967). Also, the instructional units produced by the project staff and interns were judged to be of high quality and effectiveness. This program, suggestive of the necessity for specialization in preparing teachers for different kinds of schools, offers an excellent model for future experimentation and research.

Stanford University's Teacher Intern Program, a new graduate program of teacher education begun in 1964, serves four important functions: (1) that of a vehicle of research and experimentation for the testing of alternative concepts and procedures, (2) that of a laboratory for the preparation of teacher educators, (3) that of promoting closer university-public school cooperation, and (4) that of identifying and recruiting candidates for careers of leadership in education (Allen, 1966). The program, which lasts 12 months, involves continuity of study in six areas: (1) practice in teaching, first "microteaching" (a series of scaled-down teaching experiences prior to full-fledged practice or intern teaching) and then two classes for the academic year; (2) the scientific, behavioral foundations of education; (3) procedures in curriculum and instruction in major teaching field; (4) secondary education; (5) academic major; and (6) self-criticism and evaluation of teaching with a tutor-supervisor assigned for the 12-month period. The interns are also supervised by a resident supervisor, who is given released time, extra pay, and recognition as a university staff member. Various kinds of ongoing research and experimentation have been incorporated into the program. Along with the microteaching, video recording and 35-mm. time-lapse photography have also been used for studying and modifying teaching behavior. The Stanford Teacher Competence Appraisal Guide has been developed and used in the measurement of teaching effectiveness, and automated data-processing procedures have been used for their analysis and summary. Unlike the Cardozo Project, the Stanford Teacher Intern Program does not attempt to specialize in the training of teachers. However, the two programs do share a spirit of energy and innovation and an open desire for improvement in the quality of their product.

Six-year Undergraduate-graduate Program. The Teacher Education Experimental Program was begun at Wayne State University to prepare career teachers (Bantel, 1966). The first three years of the program are devoted entirely to work in the liberal arts; the second three are devoted to professional study and clinical experience. The fourth year, which begins the professional sequence, involves an integrated series of learning cycles, rather than discrete courses. Lectures, seminars, independent study, field observation, and work with videotape and the perception laboratory make up the bulk of this year's work. The fifth year, or internship, involves 12 weeks of full-time teaching, a 3-week colloquium, and a final 19 weeks of teaching, all supervised by public school teachers who have had special training in supervision at Wayne State. In the sixth year, or externship, the student continues teaching full-time and participating in a research seminar which leads both to self-evaluation and to a research project reported to a faculty examining group. Upon successful completion of the sixth year, the teacher receives an M.A.T. degree.

These programs, ranging from one to six years in length, give evidence of the kinds of imaginative innovations, predicated on sound research evidence and subjected to careful evaluation measures, which have and are coming rapidly about in teacher education. Such programs, as models of and for further fruitful research and experimentation, offer considerable promise for the future of teacher education.

Lindley J. Stiles
Northwestern University
Robert P. Parker, Jr.
Northwestern University

References

American Association of Colleges for Teacher Education. *Strength Through Reappraisal.* AACTE, 1963.

American Council on Education, Commission on Teacher Education. *Cooperation in the Improvement of Teacher Education.* ACE, 1939. 19p.

American Council on Education, Commission on Teacher Education. *The Improvement of Teacher Education.* ACE, 1944.

Allen, Dwight W. "New Design for Teacher Education; The Teacher Intern Program at Stanford University." *J Teach Ed* 17:296–300; 1966.

Amidon, Edward. "Interaction Analyses Applied to Teaching." *Nat Assn Sec Sch Prin B* 50:93–7; 1966.

Association of Student Teachers. *Teacher Education and the Public Schools.* 40th Yearbook. The Association, 1961.

Bantel, Edward A. "Teacher Education Experimental Project; A Design for Preparing Career Teachers." *Childh Ed* 42:417–21; 1966.

Bestor, Arthur. *Educational Wastelands; The Retreat from Learning in Our Public Schools.* U Illinois, 1953. 226p.

Bigelow, Karl W. *Cultural and Social Elements in the Education of Teachers.* ACE and NEA, 1940.

Bigelow, Karl W. "New Directions in Teacher Education Appraised." *Teach Col Rec* 59:350–6; 1958.

Boyer, Ernest L. "Campus-wide Preparation of Teachers." *J Teach Ed* 16:271–4; 1965.

Brim, Burl J. "Attitude Changes in Teacher Education Students." *J Ed Res* 59:441–5; 1966.

Broudy, Harold S. "Role of the Liberal Arts in Professional Study. *J Gen Ed* 18:50–67; 1966.

Carter, Harold J. "The Improvement of Teacher Education at City College." *J Teach Ed* 9:45–50; 1958.

Carter, Thomas M. "Preparation of Teachers in a Liberal Arts College." *Sch Soc* 93:242–4; 1965.

Cartwright, William H. "Graduate Education of Teachers: Proposals for the Future." *Ed Rec* 40:148–54; 1959.

Cartwright, William H. "Fifth-year Programs in Teacher Education." *J H Ed* 32:297–311; 1961.

Chabe, Alexander M. "An Experiment with CCTV in Teacher Education." *Peabody J Ed* 40:24–30; 1962.

Chandler, B. J., and others. (Eds). *Education in Urban Society.* Dodd, 1962. 279p.

Charters, Werrett W., and others. *The Commonwealth Teacher-training Study.* U Chicago Press, 1929. 658p.

Conant, James B. *Slums and Suburbs.* McGraw-Hill, 1961. 147p.

Conant, James B. *The Education of American Teachers.* McGraw-Hill, 1963. 275p.

Cook, Desmond L. "The Personal Data Form as a Predictor of Success in a Teacher Education Program and Entry into Teaching." *J Teach Ed* 15:61–6; 1964.

Corman, Bernard R., and Olmsted, Ann G. *The Internship in the Preparation of Elementary School Teachers.* Michigan State U, 1964. 101p.

Cottrell, Donald P. "Institutional Co-operation in Teacher Education." *Teach Col Rec* 59:45–51; 1957.

Cottrell, Donald P., and others. *Teacher Education for a Free People.* AACTE, 1956. 415p.

Crall, H. William, and Myers, R. Maurice. "Recommendations for Master's Degree Preparation for Teachers of Biological Sciences." *J Teach Ed* 11:506–11; 1960.

Cuban, Larry. "The Cardozo Peace Corps Project: Experiment in Urban Education." *Soc Ed* 28:446–9; 1964.

Davis, O. L., and Bowers, Norman D. "Group Sensitivity Training in a Teacher Education Program; An Initial Attempt." *Peabody J Ed* 39:68–74; 1961.

Drazek, S. J. "Training 30,000 Head Start Teachers." *Sch Soc* 94:130–1; 1966.

Ebel, Robert L. "Measurement Applications in Teacher Education; A Review of Relevant Research." *J Teach Ed* 17:15–25; 1966.

Embree, Edwin R. "The Education of Teachers." In *Review of the Two-year Period, 1936–38.* Julius Rosenwald Fund, 1938. p. 6–19.

Ezer, M., and Lambert, R. "Residency in Supervision: A Unique Role for Laboratory Schools." *J Ed* 44:155–9; 1966.

Fenstermacher, Guy M., and Swineford, Frances. "The National Teacher Examinations and the Appraisal of Teacher Education." *J Teach Ed* 10:429–34; 1958.

Flanders, Ned A. *Teacher Influence, Pupil Attitudes and Achievement.* U Michigan, 1962.

"The Ford Foundation and Teacher Education." *Teach Col Rec* 62:224–31; 1960. (Editorial.)

Forst, Florence, and Matthews, Jack. "Preparing Teachers by Exposure to Group Processes." *J Teach Ed* 15:404–14; 1964.

Foy, Robert J. "Evaluation of English Methods Courses." *Peabody J Ed* 42:131–7; 1964.

Freedman, Florence B. "Teacher Education by CCTV." *J Teach Ed* 10:291–6; 1957.

Fulton, William R., and Rupiper, O. J. "Observation of Teaching: Direct Versus Vicarious Experience." *J Teach Ed* 13:157–64; 1962.

Goodlad, John I. "Analyses of Professional Laboratory Experiences in the Education of Teachers." *J Teach Ed* 16:263–70; 1965.

Hahn, Harlan. "Teacher Preparation in Political Science. *Social Ed* 29:86–9; 1965.

Harap, Henry. *Fifth Year Programs of Classroom Teacher Education: A Digest of the Survey Report.* HEW Bulletin OE 58007. GPO, 1962.

Harper, Charles A. *A Century of Public Teacher Education.* NEA, 1939. 175p.

Hazard, William. *The Tutorial and Clinical Approach to Teacher Education.* Northwestern U, 1966. 109p.

Hershey, L. and others. "Effectiveness of Classroom Observation and Simulated Teaching in an Introductory Educational Psychology Course." *J Ed Res* 58:233–6; 1965.

Holden, William P. "The M.A.T. at Yale, 1951–58." *J Teach Ed* 10:393–400; 1959.

Hoover, Kenneth H., and others. "A Comparison of Expressed Teaching Strengths Before and After Student Teaching." *J Teach Ed* 16:324–8; 1965.

Indiana State University. "Changing Curricula in Teacher Education Programs." *Teach Col J* 32:7–9; 1960.

Inlow, Gail M. "A Comparative Study of Student-Teaching Practices in Thirty-eight Midwest Institutions." *J Exp Ed* 28:337–49; 1960.

Jalbert, Elizabeth L. "Effectiveness of Training in the Evaluation of Classroom Instruction as an Aid to Self-Evaluation in Student Teaching." *J Ed Res* 60:130–5; 1966.

Joyce, Bruce R., and Hodges, Richard E. "Instructional Flexibility Training." *J Teach Ed* 17:409–16; 1966.

Kearney, Nolan C. "Evaluative Criteria for Teacher Education Institutions in Minnesota." *J Teach Ed* 10:395–401; 1958.

Keffer, Eugene R. "Use of Expert Judgments in the Development of a Science Methods Course." *J Exp Ed* 33:55–63; 1964.

Kennedy, Paul C. "Teacher Education at the University of Omaha." *J Teach Ed* 8:415–6; 1957.

Keppel, Francis. *The Necessary Revolution in American Education.* Harper, 1966. 201p.

Koerner, James D. *The Miseducation of American Teachers.* Houghton, 1963. 360p.

Krathwohl, David, and Spalding, Willard B. "Evaluation of the Arkansas Experiment in Teacher Education." *J Teach Ed* 7:233–5; 1956.

La Grone, Herbert F. "Toward a New Curriculum for Professional Teacher Development." *Liberal Ed* 51:70–6; 1965.

Lofthouse, Y. "Teachers for Megalopolis." *AACTE Yearbook* 16:135–49; 1963.

Lumiansky, R. M. "Concerning Graduate Education for Teachers." 40:143–7; 1959.

Mars, Walter J. "Developing Appropriate Media Competencies." *J Teach Ed* 17:430–7; 1966.

Mayor, John R. *Accreditation in Teacher Education: Its Influence on Higher Education.* National Commission on Accrediting, 1965. 311p.

McAulay, J. D. "Preparation of Elementary Teachers in the Social Studies." *J Teach Ed* 17:89–92; 1966.

Mitzel, Harold E. "Comments on the Cornell Experimental Program for the Preparation of Elementary Teachers." *J Teach Ed* 9:383–6; 1958.

Moskowitz, G. "Toward Human Relations in Supervision." *Nat Assn Sec Sch Prin B* 50:98–114; 1966.

National Education Association, National Commission on Teacher Education and Professional Standards. *The Education of Teachers: New Perspectives.* NEA, 1958.

National Education Association, National Commission on Teacher Education and Professional Standards. *The Education of Teachers: Curriculum Programs.* NEA, 1959.

National Education Association, National Commission on Teacher Education and Professional Standards. *The Education of Teachers: Certification.* NEA, 1960(a).

National Education Association, National Commission on Teacher Education and Professional Standards. *The Education of Teachers: Considerations in Planning Institutional Programs.* NEA, 1960(b).

National Education Association, National Commission on Teacher Education and Professional Standards: *New Horizons: The Becoming Journey.* NEA, 1961.

National Education Association, National Commission on Teacher Education and Professional Standards. *Changes in Teacher Education: An Appraisal.* NEA, 1963.

Nelson, Lois Ney. "Teacher Leadership: An Empirical Approach to Analyzing Teacher Behavior in the Classroom." *J Teach Ed* 17:417–25; 1966.

Newsome, George L., and others. "Changes in Consistency of Educational Ideas Attributable to Student-teaching Experiences." *J Teach Ed* 16:319–23; 1965.

New York Times. "National Teacher Corps; Starting This Autumn." *Times Ed Supplement* 2657:1207; 1966.

Nunney, Derek N. "Trends in the Content of Educational Psychology, 1948–63." *J Teach Ed* 15:372–7; 1964.

O'Brien, Dean W. *A School of Education in the Life of Our Time.* U Wisconsin, 1965.

O'Brien, Dean W. *Continued Effort Toward Better Schools.* U Wisconsin, 1966. 48p.

Pillard, Matthew J. "Teachers for Urban Schools." In Chandler, B. J., and others. (Eds.), *Education in Urban Society.* Dodd, 1962. 279p.

Polos, Nicholas C. "Progress in Teacher Education—The Claremont Plan." *J Teach Ed* 11:398–400; 1960.

Quintana, Bertha, and Sexton, Patricia. "Sociology, Anthropology, and Schools of Education." *J Ed Sociol* 35:97–103; 1961.

Rabinowitz, William, and Mitzel, Harold E. "Programming in Education and Teacher Preparation." *Teach Col Rec* 64:128–38; 1962.

Reinert, Paul C., "Liberal Arts and Teacher Education." *Liberal Ed* 51:20–8; 1965.

Rivlin, H. N. "New Pattern for Urban Teacher Education." *J Teach Ed* 17:177–84; 1966.

Robb, Felix C. "The Professional Content of Teacher Education." *Liberal Ed* 51:37–43; 1965.

Saxe, Richard W. "Evaluating the Breakthrough Programs." *J Teach Ed* 16:202–9; 1965.

Schoben, Edward J. "Psychology in the Training of Teachers." *Teach Col Rec* 65:436–40; 1964.

Schueler, Herbert. "Teachers and Resources for Urban Education." In National Committee on Teachers of Education, Professional Standards, *Official Report.* The Committee, 1963. p. 233–7.

Schueler, Herbert, and Gold, Milton J. "Video Recordings of Student Teachers." *J Teach Ed* 15:358–64; 1964.

Schueler, Herbert, and others. *The Use of Television for Teacher Training and for Improving Measures of Student-teaching Performance.* Hunter Col, 1962. 127p.

Shumsky, Abraham, and Murray, Walter I. "Student Teachers Explore Attitudes Toward Discipline." *J Teach Ed* 12:453–7; 1961.

Smith, E. D., and Cunningham, F. J. "Administrative Relationships between Teacher Education Institutions and Cooperating Public Schools." In *Teacher Education and the Public Schools,* 40th Yearbook, Association of Student-Teachers, 1961. p. 3–21.

Smith, Elmer R. (Ed.) *A Re-appraisal of the Professional Aspects of Teacher Education.* Center for Advanced Study in Behavioral Science, 1960. 207p.

Smith, Payson, and others. *Major Issues in Teacher Education.* ACE, 1944.

Stabler, Ernest. *The Education of the Secondary School Teacher.* Wesleyan U, 1962.

Stanley, William O. "The Role of the Social Foundations Subjects in the Professional Training of Teachers." In *Social Foundations of Education: An Essential in the Professional Education of Teachers."* State Col Iowa, 1966. p. 12–30.

Stiles, Lindley J. "Pre-service Education of High

School Teachers in Universities." Doctoral dissertation. U Colorado, 1945. 371p.
Stiles, Lindley J. "All-institution Approach to Teacher Education." *Phi Delta Kappan* 40:121–4; 1958.
Stiles, Lindley J. "Attitudes Toward Education Courses." *J Teach Ed* 10:182–8; 1959.
Stiles, Lindley J. "Role of Liberal Arts Colleges in Teacher Education." *Ed Forum* 28:171–7; 1964.
Stiles, Lindley J. "Interdisciplinary Organization for Teacher Education." *J Gen Ed* 18:6–20; 1966.
Stiles, Lindley J. *Cardozo Project in Urban Teaching: Evaluation and Recommendations.* Washington, D.C., Public Schools, Model School Division, 1967.
Stiles, Lindley J., and Carver, Fred D. "Interdisciplinary Approach to Teacher Education." *Teach Col Rec* October 1967.
Stiles, Lindley J., and others. *Teacher Education in the United States.* Ronald, 1960. 497p.
Stinnett, Timothy M. "Pre-dominant Program of Teacher Education in the United States." *AACTE Yearbook* 16:32–45; 1963.
Stinnett, Timothy M. *The Profession of Teaching.* Center for Applied Research in Education, 1962.
Stoller, Nathan, and others. "A Comparison of Methods of Observation in Pre-service Teacher Training." *AV Communications R* 12:177–85; 1964.
Troyer, Maurice E., and Pace, C. Robert. *Evaluation in Teacher Education.* ACE, 1944. 368p.
Turney, David, and Stoneking, Lewis W. "A Professional Sequence for the Development of Career Teachers." *J Teach Ed* 16:281–5; 1965.
Tyler, Louise, and Okumu, Laura J. "Beginning Step: A System for Analyzing Courses in Teacher Education." *J Teach Ed* 16:438–44; 1965.
U.S. Office of Education. *National Survey of the Education of Teachers.* Vols. 1 and 4. USOE, 1933.
University of Wisconsin. *Experiences in Team Teaching.* The U, 1963.
Vlcek, Charles. "Classroom Simulation in Teacher Education." *A-V Instructor* 11:86–90; 1966.
Walton, John, and Kuethe, J. L. (Eds). *The Discipline of Education.* U Wisconsin, 1963. 190p.
Wattles, Marshall D., and Osibov, Henry. "The Content of Teacher Education." *J Teach Ed* 10:464–9; 1960.
Wilk, Roger E., and Edson, William H. "Predictions and Performance: An Experimental Study of Student Teachers." *J Teach Ed* 14:308–17; 1963.
Woodring, Paul. *New Directions in Teacher Education.* Fund for the Advancement of Education, 1957. 142p.
Woodruff, Asahel D. "Proposed Linkage System for Program Comparison and Test Evaluation." *Am Col Teach Yearbook* 16:178–82; 1963.
Woodward, John C. "The Use of Television in Teacher Education." *J Teach Ed* 15:56–60; 1964.
Woronoff, Israel. "What Programs Are Schools Offering to Prepare Liberal Arts Graduates for Teaching?" *J Teach Ed* 10:359–62; 1958.
Wulk, Jerry E., and Miller, Ralph M. "New Approach at UCLA: Secondary Teaching Internships." *J Teach Ed* 16:300–2; 1965.

TEACHER EFFECTIVENESS

Teacher effectiveness is an area of research which is concerned with *relationships* between the characteristics of teachers, teaching acts, and their effects on the educational outcomes of classroom teaching. The research which is reviewed herein permits cautious optimism and indicates that the tools long needed for the analysis of the teaching-learning process are gradually being developed. This optimism is in contrast with the conclusions reached in past reviews. For example, Morsh and Wilder (1954, p. 4) concluded, after reviewing research on teaching effectiveness published between 1900 and 1952, "No single, specific, observable teacher act has yet been found whose frequency or percent of occurrence is invariably [and] significantly correlated with student achievement."

In the past decade, however, research has begun to relate certain teacher behaviors to specific consequences in the climate of the classroom and in the academic achievement of pupils. The shift has been from subjective evaluations to a more objective counting of teacher-pupil interactions, using more sophisticated observation systems, and handling the larger quantities of data by taking full advantage of computer capability. Further discriminations and additional relationships now seem within reach as future research builds on present progress.

A POINT OF DEPARTURE. The most important single publication with regard to teaching effectiveness since the third edition of the *Encyclopedia of Educational Research* has been the *Handbook of Research on Teaching* (Gage, 1963a). Because this book covers research in this area at least through 1959 far more effectively than can be accomplished in this condensed review, citations dated from 1960 to 1966 are included here. The serious scholar should begin with the Gage *Handbook,* especially chapters 6, 7, and 11, which deal with observation, rating scales, and teacher personality. The present review is a guide to subsequent research.

THE STRUCTURE OF THIS REVIEW. Titles listed in the *Education Index* and *Psychological Abstracts* from 1960 to 1966 which gave promise of including empirical data about teaching effectiveness were recorded. All articles which reported the characteristics of teachers, teacher behavior, or teacher-pupil interaction and then related one or more of these to either pupil achievement or pupil attitudes were nominated for inclusion. Even some of these could not be included in the final writing. The most serious shortcoming of this procedure was an inadequate survey of government publications and an inability to secure such publications within a reasonable length of time. Additional inadequacies may have resulted from the quality of abstracts which graduate students prepared and on which the authors necessarily depended. Productivity of research on teaching effectiveness has increased so rapidly that a review once every ten years is no longer practical for a single, unassisted author.

A REVIEW OF OTHER REVIEWS. The reader may wish to consult the reports of others who have attempted to review research on teaching effectiveness during this same time period. Some of the references which may be most helpful are discussed in this short section.

Anderson and Hunka (1963) spotlight problem areas in research on teacher effectiveness. They discuss studies which have used predictor or criterion variables and conclude that this research has reached a dead end. Attempts to build a theory of teaching from a statistical description of what is happening fail to prescribe what should be happening. Even examples of the best of teaching may not provide the theoretical basis for the most effective teaching.

Gage (1965) considers why researchers continue to search for relationships between teacher characteristics and pupil growth when their rewards are so meager. His tentative answer is that the need for knowledge in this area is pressing. He suggests that the upsurge in the amount and quality of research on teaching in the past ten years may have made the results of research done prior to that time obsolete. He concludes that a review of literature at the present time allows for the selection of five global characteristics which seem to be components of effective teaching. The five he selects are (1) warmth, (2) cognitive organization, (3) orderliness, (4) indirectness, and (5) problem-solving ability.

Medley and Mitzel (1963) substantiate Gage's conclusion that much of the work on teacher effectiveness must be discarded as irrelevant either because the criteria of teaching effectiveness have been invalid or because no objective measures of teacher behavior have been used. After discussing assumptions underlying collections of classroom observational data and limitations of studies utilizing rating scales they note that more powerful statistical methods will help to identify relationships between teaching behaviors and their effects.

Fattu (1962) and Howsam (1960) both reviewed the research on predictor criteria and teacher effectiveness and concluded that such research had failed to substantiate links for such characteristics as intelligence, age, experience, cultural background, socioeconomic background, sex, marital status, scores on aptitude tests, job interest, voice quality, and special aptitudes. There were slight positive correlations shown between scholarship and teaching effectiveness, although no particular course or group of courses has been shown to be a predictor. Professional knowledge has proved to be a more successful predictor, particularly of teaching performance. Howsam reviewed studies using various kinds of rating scales and discusses four kinds used commonly in research: (1) self-ratings, which have proved of little use because there is a consistent bias toward overrating, (2) peer ratings by colleagues, which seem to be based on marginal evidence, (3) student ratings, which seem to be more consistently and favorably treated in the literature than other ratings, and (4) supervisor or administrator ratings, which do not correlate either with ratings of other supervisors or with other external measures. Supervisors' ratings seem to be highly biased and subjective.

Both Biddle (1964) and Soar (1964), after independently reviewing recent research on teacher effectiveness, declare a need for agreement about the effects that the teacher is to produce in order to determine the components of teacher effectiveness. They distinguish between the research component of teacher effectiveness (in which relationships between teacher characteristics and behaviors and pupil output measures are determined) and the criteria component (which is a question of selecting the pupil output components considered to be desirable). Both specify the collection of observational data as the most direct method of learning about teaching, and Biddle discusses the practical limitations of this kind of classroom observation.

Bellack and Huebner (1960) and Amidon and Simon (1965) have reviewed the studies which focus on teaching and present findings which relate to teacher behaviors as measured by various classroom observational techniques, and Barr and others (1961) present a critical overview of 75 doctoral studies on teacher effectiveness.

David G. Ryans (1963) and B. Othand Smith (1962) discuss the need for a conceptual framework for understanding the research findings on teacher effectiveness. Ryans utilizes a system-analysis approach and discusses the general implications of the studies reviewed. This review includes an extensive listing of terms used to describe teachers' behavior patterns as compared with terms used by researchers. Smith reviews four major studies on teacher effectiveness and notes that the value of these studies lies in their describing what the teacher is doing rather than in trying to label the teacher with a global title such as autocratic or dominative. He points out that there are probably no pure types of teacher, and therefore that teacher behaviors should be described so that the particular mixtures of teaching behaviors are not buried under broad category headings.

Popular Topics Excluded from this Review. While research located by the procedures already described is reviewed in this article, certain topics are not included. Readers wishing to locate references about team teaching, teaching for creativity or inquiry, group versus individual instruction, programmed learning materials, class size, the use of teaching space, and class formations must look elsewhere for guidance. The issues that surround "merit pay" are also ignored, since the classification of teachers in such a way that there are social, political, and economic consequences for both the school system and the teacher is more properly assigned to research in the field of educational administration. Finally, research on what is taught and when it is taught has been excluded, since those are matters of curriculum research. The focus of this review has been on research which investigates relationships between classroom behavior and educational outcomes because the analysis of classroom behavior has produced data-collecting innovations and because the relationships found have been stronger and more consistent than has been true in the past.

PROGRESS IN ANALYZING CLASSROOM PROCESSES. Part of the progress in research on teaching effectiveness during the past decade has been owing to the further development of techniques for analyzing verbal communication. Since chapter 6 of the Gage *Handbook* (1963a) deals almost exclusively with this topic, it becomes a basic reference for the serious student. Some of the observation systems which have been developed after chapter 6 was written include those of Bellack and Davitz (1963) and Bellack and others (1965), who describe "moves" made by teachers in the "game" of classroom communication; Miller (1964), who has adapted Hughes's system along a responsive-directive scale; Taba and others (1964), whose categories are based on a model of how children think; Gallagher and Aschner (1963), who became interested in convergent and divergent thinking; Perkins (1964, 1965), who has combined selected logical aspects of communication with the pattern of teacher influence; Openshaw and Cypert (1966), who have developed a taxonomy of teacher behaviors; Parakh (1965), who specialized in a system for biology classrooms; and Hough (1967), who expanded his category system to include both logical and emotional dimensions of classroom interaction. An unusually interesting system for analyzing nonverbal behavior has been developed by Galloway (1962). Many of the earlier as well as the more recent systems are undergoing fairly continuous modification through changes in categories and observation procedures so that the most up-to-date information can best be secured by writing to the researchers. The gap between research and publication remains a problem.

Those readers who do refer to chapter 6 in the *Handbook* may develop reservations about Medley and Mitzel's proposals concerning concepts that refer to reliability. On page 254 they suggest: "The coefficient of observer agreement tells us something about the objectivity of an observational technique; the coefficient of stability tells us something about the consistency of behavior from time to time. But only the reliability coefficient tells us how accurate our measurements are." Definitions are arbitrary conventions, and those above are designed to fit into Medley and Mitzel's statistical paradigm, which they call a "general design for reliability estimation" (starting on p. 310). Their four-way analysis-of-variance model employs between-class, between-observer, between-item, and between-situation variances. This model is a substantial step forward in the field of research on teaching effectiveness.

The point here, however, is that good judgment must be exercised in matching the statistical model with a particular research design. As the model is described, for example, an inexperienced researcher might infer that differences in teaching behavior that occur between visits need not be of concern since they can be handled as an error term. For example, note such formations as "If the scale is supposed to measure differences between classes, and if any and all idiosyncrasies of observers, items, or situations are regarded as sources of distortion or error . . ." (p. 309). Or, later, in discussing a specific application: "Variation from situation to situation within the same class . . . appears greater than variation in average behavior from one class to another. . . . In order to measure differences between classes reliably, therefore, it is necessary to observe each class in a number of situations, so that the fluctuations measured . . . can cancel one another out" (pp. 316–317).

Good judgment in sampling and in conceptualizing the study of teaching behavior must take into account that ineffective and effective teaching behavior, but especially the latter, will vary from one time period to the next according to the purpose and nature of the learning activities. Compare, for example, the role of a teacher during "show and tell" versus "reading instruction" in a self-contained primary-level class. Should the occasions for a visit be selected at random, the differences in teaching behavior between two visits may be so great that between-class (or between-treatment) differences can be masked.

The definitions of reliability suggested by Medley and Mitzel seem to be most appropriate when the purpose of research is to show that certain types of teachers provide certain stable patterns of teaching. In order to accomplish this purpose the number of visits must be sufficiently large to cancel the between-visit differences. Such a purpose is a natural outgrowth of research on "classroom climate" (see chs. 6 and 13 of Gage's *Handbook*). Current research on teaching effectiveness is gradually moving away from this purpose toward the more complex question of why teachers vary their behavior from one teaching episode to the next and whether or not this variation is itself associated with educational outcomes.

To summarize these comments, a reader is advised to make use of the *Handbook of Research on Teaching* as a basic reference in the study of teaching effectiveness. However, given the progress since 1960, the cutting edge of research on teaching effectiveness during the next decade may be more concerned with variation of teaching behavior between visits and with the consequences of this variation compared with the thrust of research that existed when the Gage *Handbook* went to press. New conventions with regard to the definition of reliability may become necessary, and a particular research design may require some logical strategy in sampling teaching episodes, especially if variation in behavior is of interest, so that one episode may be compared with the next.

The organization of this review makes full use of Mitzel's distinction (1960, p. 1482) between presage, process, and product criteria. To measure a teacher's trait of *warmth toward pupils* is to consider a characteristic which existed before the teaching starts; this is a presage variable. The corresponding process variable would be some behaviorally specified measure of warm acts while teaching. The product variable, in this case, would be an educational outcome, such as more learning or a measure of some pupil attitude logically related to teacher warmth. The research reviewed will be presented, whenever possible, in terms of relationships between process and product, presage and process, and presage and product variables.

RESEARCH LINKING PROCESS AND PRODUCT. Pupil Attitudes and Achievement. The early history of relationships between classroom processes and their consequences has been summarized by Withall and Lewis (1963, pp. 687–710), Medley and Mitzel (1963, pp. 254–297) and Remmers (1963, pp. 330–342) in the Gage *Handbook*.

To illustrate progress note that this may be the first review that can marshal a set of widely separated research studies which provide statistically significant support for a particular type of relationship between process and product. The primitive quality of our present knowledge is exemplified by the concepts, methods of quantification, and lack of specificity to be found in the relationship. Nevertheless, it can now be stated with fairly high confidence that *the percentage of teacher statements that make use of ideas and opinions previously expressed by pupils is directly related to average class scores on attitude scales of teacher attractiveness, liking the class, etc., as well as to average achievement scores adjusted for initial ability.* Most of the studies to be reviewed in this section provide either direct or indirect support for this relationship, while only a few fail to provide such support, and none provides counterevidence of a significant but negative finding.

In work started before 1957 but published later by Flanders (1965) the above process-product relationship was supported in four separate studies. In all four studies 51 teachers were observed who had been selected to be representative of a larger sample. The reference population of all four studies exceeded 240 teacher-classroom units in elementary and junior high grade levels located in New Zealand and Minnesota. In the first two studies, measures of constructive pupil attitudes were the only product variables; in the last two, both attitude and achievement measures were included. The process variables in all of these studies were obtained by having a classroom observer code verbal communication into a set of categories at a nearly constant rate. One category was the teacher's use of ideas previously expressed by pupils. In Michigan, Morrison (1966) found significant evidence supporting the same relationship for positive pupil-attitude scores, as well as adjusted achievement gain scores of language usage, social study skills, and arithmetic computation and problem solving. She observed 30 sixth-grade teachers drawn from a sample of 102, located in 15 different school districts. In Pennsylvania, LaShier (1965) found statistically significant support for the same relationship in eighth-grade science classrooms involving 239 pupils and 10 student teachers. Nelson (1964) found similar support in a study of the learning of linguistic skills. In a small study involving 6 high school English teachers near Detroit, Johns (1966) found that pupils exposed to teachers who made more use of their ideas and opinions not only had more positive attitudes but were also more likely to ask thought-provoking questions during class discussions. The incidence of such pupil questions is extremely low, however, accounting for less than 1 percent of all verbal communication, a finding independently supported by Dodl (1966) in California and Parakh (1965, p. 147) in New York. Pankratz (1967) located 5 "high" and 5 "low" teachers of high school physics, from a sample of 30, by using principal ratings, class averages of a pupil-attitude inventory, and a "teacher situation-reaction test" completed by each teacher. These 10 classes were visited for six class periods by an observer who coded verbal interaction by a system developed by Hough who expanded Flanders' ten categories. Among other findings, this study supported the proposition that the 5 teachers determined to be more effective by the three scores indicated above made more use of the ideas and opinions expressed by pupils at the .01 level of confidence than the 5 less effective teachers.

In all of the above studies, treatment differences were created by finding teachers whose natural styles differed. The same process-product relationship mentioned earlier was also supported in a series of experiments in which role-playing teachers learned, then practiced, and finally produced two patterns of teaching behavior in order to create contrasting treatments. In one treatment the ideas and opinions expressed by the pupils were acknowledged and integrated into the classroom discourse, and in the other treatment that pattern was minimized. Systematic coding through interaction analysis verified the existence of the treatment differences. Either random assignment or covariance analysis or both helped to control differences in pupil activity. Amidon and Flanders (1961) used this design to show that not all pupils, but only those classified as "dependent" by their scores on a special scale, learned more principles of geometry when their ideas were made use of. Schantz (1963) showed that similar treatment differences provided support for the relationship in a study of 61 fourth-grade children in which verbal recall was the product variable. Filson (1957) showed that when the behavior patterns of role-playing teachers made more use of pupil ideas and opinions, there was less "dependence on the teacher." The task in the Filson experiment was to make judgments about the form of music being heard. Flanders and others (1963) found similar differences during an in-service training project for classroom teachers. In this study, adult pupils developed perceptions of greater independence and self-direction during the five weeks of a nine-week in-service program, indicating that such perceptions probably develop in a cumulative fashion. Adult pupils exposed to an instructor who reacted more often to their ideas and opinions saw themselves as becoming more independent and had higher measures of work output compared with those having the contrasting treatment.

In all studies cited thus far some form of systematic classroom observation was employed to quantify classroom interaction in order to provide a process variable. Cogan (1963) provided statistically significant support for the same process-product relationship with data from a questionnaire administered to 987 junior high pupils in 33 classes. The questionnaire provided (1) one score for the pupils' perception that their ideas were central to decisions and action taken in the classroom, (2) another score that indicated how much of the regularly assigned work was completed, and (3) a third score that indicated how much extra work, work not regularly assigned, was completed. The positive relationships he found between (1) and (2) and (1) and (3) can be construed as supporting the same process-product relationship provided that one is willing to accept pupils' perceptions as valid measures of teacher behavior. The pupils' perceptions of the teacher's behavior were, in effect, a process variable—although such an interpretation is open to question because teaching behavior itself was not assessed directly. The pupils' reports of how much work they accomplished, which was corroborated by teacher ratings of pupil effort, is more clearly a product variable.

Miller (1964) created controlled experimental treatments on the responsive-directive dimensions suggested originally by the work of Hughes (1959). They found that the junior high pupils in the classes of the responsive teacher had significantly more positive attitudes and used significantly higher levels of thinking than did pupils in classes in which the opposite treatment was used.

Three studies failed to provide support for the notion that the teacher's acceptance and use of pupil ideas is related to product variables as stated. Snider (1965), studying classroom interaction in high school physics classes, did not find supporting evidence. It appeared that his teachers rarely made use of pupils' ideas, and apparently there was little cultivation of inquiry even in laboratory sessions. Thus, it is possible, although not certain, that there was not enough variation among classroom processes within his sample to provide enough treatment contrast to test the process-product relationship. Guggenheim (1961) used the *Wrightstone Teacher-Pupil Rapport Scale* to identify the 11 most "integrative" and the 11 most "dominative" classes among 50 third-grade classes and, in addition, reported observation data to verify the climate differences of the treatment groups. Comparisons of pupil achievement, using matched pupils, failed to show treatment differences. Hoover (1963) created "teacher-centered," "pupil-centered" and "group-centered" classroom climates by having role-playing teachers intentionally adopt different behaviors and by differences in classroom organization. He failed to find significant differences on the *Purdue Rating Scale,* which pupils scored to produce an attitude product variable.

Several researchers investigated the use of teachers' praise statements, a type of teacher behavior which is usually positively correlated with the use of pupil ideas and opinions, and its effect on product variables. Reed (1961, 1962) found statistically significant, positive correlations (+ 0.20 to + 0.40) between certain types of teacher behavior, as perceived by the pupils, such as "warmth," "demand," and "using intrinsic motivation," and a product variable of "pupil interest in science." The sample included 38 classes of ninth-grade general science involving 1,045 pupils. Dollins and others (1960) carried out an experiment involving varying degrees of teacher praise in fourth-grade classrooms and decided that more praise helped pupil adjustment but did not affect arithmetic achievement.

Coats (1966) reanalyzed the relationships between pupils' attitude and achievement scores versus various measures which can be derived from a 10×10 matrix based on Flanders' categories. He completed a stepwise linear regression analysis of the 62 classes reported earlier by Flanders (1965) and Morrison (1966)—that is, 30 sixth-grade classes, 16 seventh-grade core classes, and 16 eighth-grade mathematics classes. In the first phase of his study he showed that 62 class averages in preachievement had a correlation of + 0.92 with postachievement and that the correlation for each group was + 0.99, + 0.80, and + 0.92, respectively. Similar correlations for the pupil-attitude variable were, respectively, + 0.87, + 0.69, and + 0.73. The same correlation was + 0.78 for all 62 classes. Thus, accurate predictions of posttest class averages can be made from pretest averages. However, once pupils are assigned to a class, the initial quality of a class is beyond the control of the teacher, and such predictions fall outside of research on teaching effectiveness.

The second phase of his study was concerned with predicting final class averages from knowledge of process variables derived from the systematic observation of classroom communication, purposely excluding knowledge of initial scores. In each analysis the predictors included several variables which either represent or are correlated with the tendency of the teacher to make use of ideas and opinions expressed by pupils. With regard to achievement, process variables combined to show a correlation of + 0.67 for the sixth grade, + 0.90 for the seventh grade, and + 0.70 for the eighth grade; for all 62 classes this correlation was + 0.45. The variation among the first three correlations may reflect the test used to measure achievement. In the sixth grade parts of a nationally standardized test were used, and performance on the test could have been influenced by experiences outside the classroom such as watching television or living in a home where children are encouraged to read. The highest correlation, in the seventh grade, made use of a test especially designed to measure the objectives of a two-week unit of study about New Zealand. Experiences outside the classroom would be least likely to influence test performance. The two-week unit in the eighth-grade mathematics classes involved material not normally taught before grade nine, but the scores of a few of the brighter pupils might have been influenced by experiences outside the classroom. The lower overall correlation is not unexpected, since the behaviors of the teachers which correlated with achievement would naturally be different in a self-contained sixth-grade elementary class, a two-hour combined English–social studies class, and a single-hour mathematics course taught in a fashion which is more typical of secondary, departmentalized education. In all four correlations, however, evidence to support the process-product relationship was prominent. The same predictions for attitude were sixth grade, $+0.63$; seventh grade, $+0.77$; and eighth grade, $+0.74$. For all 62 classes it was $+0.53$. To the knowledge of the authors, these are the highest prediction coefficients of process-product variables in which achievement and pupil-attitude scores are involved.

One study has analyzed the same classroom discourse by the Flanders categories and the system developed by Bellack and others. Furst (1967) reanalyzed the original data (Bellack & others, 1965) by contrasting the classroom discourse in the high school classes which scored highest and lowest on achievement. The unit of study, the tests, the textbook, and the number of teaching days were the same in all classes. The high-achieving classes differed from the low-achieving classes by having more responsive teacher behavior, less teacher talk, and more extended pupil talk, just as has been found in similar studies which involved the Flanders categories. In terms of the Bellack categories, the same contrast involved more variety of substantive-logical processes, moderate amounts of teacher structure of the learning activities, and moderate pace of teaching cycles. One overall concept which seems to encompass the inferences from both category systems is that teacher influence was more flexible in the high-achieving classes.

As this article is being written, observation systems for quantifying process variables are undergoing rapid and continuous development. For example, papers read at the annual conventions of several different societies in 1966 and 1967 reported changes which had not yet been published; apparently the most current information about an observation system must be obtained from the researchers involved.

In the studies linking process to product variables which have been reviewed thus far, the research design called for the use of a score based on a process variable in order to classify teachers into two or more groups which were then used to make comparisons. For example, in studies making use of Flanders' categories, some teachers were classified as "indirect," in contrast with "direct," in order to make certain comparisons such as adjusted pupil achievement. The net effect of this use of systematic classroom observation, was not to explain teaching behavior but to use the data in order to assign a teacher to a particular experimental-treatment group based on a teaching pattern. Subsequent analysis would then shed some light on the differences in educational outcomes when two types of teaching were compared. The primitive nature of such contrasts is self-evident, since it is obvious that teaching patterns vary from one situation to the next.

In the next section, research is reviewed which is also primitive but which does, at least, attempt to distinguish variations in teaching patterns with the passage of time.

More Differentiated Relationships and Variation with Time. Progress in making fine distinctions in process and product relationships and the availability of ever-more-powerful computer languages are not unrelated; the former cannot take place without the latter.

The possibility that different teaching patterns are more or less effective with different types of pupils or, to take another tack, that different sequences of teaching acts are more or less appropriate to different kinds of teaching situations can provide a logical next step in research linking process and product variables. Types of pupils, for example, can be identified by different patterns of scores on instruments which assess pupil traits, illustrated by Amidon and Flanders' interest in "dependent prone" pupils (1961). Different teaching situations can be illustrated by Flanders' (1965) interest in such time-use periods as "administrative routine," "planning work," and "supervising seatwork." To deal differently with two kinds of pupils or to adjust teaching patterns from one time period to the next is to introduce the concept of *flexibility of teacher influence*. Should such knowledge lead to lawful relationships, then principles of instruction that involve sequence are closer at hand.

Perhaps the most theoretically complete research involving differential effects of process and product variables has been the work of Taba (1964). Starting with a model of how children think, Taba proposed a controlled pattern of teacher behavior for guiding class discussion which was consistent with her model of how children think. Twenty elementary-school teachers were trained to guide class discussions and learning activities in such a way that concepts at higher levels of abstraction in the field of social studies were not reinforced by the teacher until a large proportion of the class was ready for "lifting the level of discourse." Early results indicate that the children in those classrooms in which the teacher was successful in maintaining the desired sequence in teaching strategy did exhibit gains in making inferences. Lack of a control group raises questions about the validity of the results, but these initial efforts were in the form of a pilot project concerned with curriculum innovation. The study stands as an excellent model for the development of teaching patterns which simultaneously are concerned with the cognitive and socioemotional consequences of teaching acts when they occur in different sequences. Her systematic coding by observers required, apparently for the first time, that observation data be displayed along a time line which preserved the sequence of events over periods of one-half hour or longer. Incidently, a similar display of time-line data, making use of Flanders' categories, has been developed by

Urbach (1966) in an effort to investigate recurring patterns of teaching.

Other examples of research on the sequence of classroom events can be found in the observation systems of Bellack and Davitz (1963) and B. Othanel Smith (1962) as well as the early hypotheses of Flanders (1960). There is some evidence to suggest (see Flanders, 1965, pp. 102–110) that in classrooms in which pupils have more positive attitudes and seem to be learning more content there is also greater flexibility and variation in teacher behavior. Another outcome of the Morrison (1966) study cited above was that pupils who scored high on a trait scale of "externality" (that is, who were dependent on reinforcement from sources outside themselves) appeared to be significantly more aware of variation in teaching behavior when it occurred than were those who scored low on the scale.

Another study that illustrates further differential relationships was conducted by Solomon and others (1964), who studied adult education classes. They found that factual gain and comprehension gain were uncorrelated, each associated with different types of teacher behavior. Joyce and Hodges (1966) pointed out that while the teacher is handling information with one teaching pattern he may be using a different pattern for dealing with class organization. Gallagher and Aschner (1963) and Gallagher (1965) alone examined the level of thinking of intellectually superior junior and senior high pupils. They found that the level of thinking of the pupils was related to the level of thinking of the teacher; for example, when the teacher used divergent thinking, the pupils responded on the divergent level more often.

Summarizing Process and Product Research. A careful reading of most of the research thus far reviewed presents a rather dismal picture of the quality, not the quantity, of teacher talk as it occurs in current teaching practice. For example, Bellack and Davitz (1963) and Bellack and others (1965, Part II) observed 15 high school economics teachers for four days and developed their scheme for analyzing pedagogical moves in the classroom game. The point here is that teachers did most of the structuring and soliciting moves while pupils supplied the responding moves. Both Kliebard (1963) and Bellack point out that only 2 teaching cycles, out of a possible 21, account for more than half of the interaction cycles used. Hughes (1959), Travers (1961), Flanders (1965), Parakh (1965), and many others have reported consistently that teachers talk between 65 and 75 percent of the time, on the average, and that this talk is of a quality that pupils' verbal communication occurs is primarily in response to the initiative of the teacher. With a more cognitive orientation, Gallagher (1965) pointed out that pupils more often respond in terms of cognitive memory, taking their cues from rather rigid patterns of teacher stimulation. These results suggest that pupils' initiative and independent thinking are not encouraged in classroom discourse. Most of these studies provided evidence that teachers are more alike than they are different. The less effective teachers are more alike and less flexible (Flanders, 1965, p. 103–104) and probably easier to identify than more effective teachers are.

So far, no study has investigated how far an already flexible, responsive teacher can move toward an even more extreme pattern and still expect an improvement in pupil attitudes and achievement. It would be reasonable to expect a curvilinear relationship which would identify an optimum balance between teacher response and initiation. The preponderance of evidence gathered so far would indicate that most currently practicing teachers could adopt patterns which are more responsive to the ideas and opinions expressed by pupils and realize a gain in both positive pupil attitudes and pupil achievement.

RESEARCH LINKING PRESAGE TO PROCESS VARIABLES. In this section, research is reviewed which attempts to compare some aspect of the teaching process with something that existed before the teaching process started. The topic is presented in two parts: first, studies are discussed which involve teacher traits, such as measures of teacher personality or teacher perception; and, second, studies are discussed which provide some kind of training experience for preservice or in-service teachers.

Teacher Traits and Teaching Behavior. Davies (1961) found only one or two measures among 25 teacher traits to be significantly related to patterns of teaching observed with the ten Flanders categories. For example, teachers' scores on the subscale of "warmth" from the Cattell 16 PF Tests and the total *Minnesota Teacher Attitude Inventory* (*MTAI*) scores were associated with responsive teacher behavior as indicated by statistically significant, low positive correlations. However, the 51 junior high teachers constituting her sample taught in many different subject-matter areas, which might reduce such expected relationships. Ringness and others (1964) compared similar observation scores of 27 first-year teachers with measures of self concept as teachers, measures of security, and measures of anxiety. Although there were significant relationships among the self-perception scores, the measures were not significantly associated with observed overt behavior while teaching. Bowie and Morgan (1962) tested relationships between teachers' values and their verbal behaviors. After confirming some of the relationships but not others, the authors cautioned that common-sense assumptions about the relationships between teacher values and personality factors need to be tested empirically. Wilk and Edson (1963) tested the relationship between such presage variables as sophomore Honor Point Ratio (HPR), the *Miller Analogies*, the *MTAI*, and measures derived from personal interviews, on the one hand, and such process variables as scores from the *OScAR* and the Flanders system of observation, on the other hand. In a sample of 36 female elementary-school student teachers, the strongest relationships existed between a special weighting system of the Flanders categories and the two characteristics of HPR and *MTAI* scores.

Simon (1966) tested the relationship between a teacher's preference for a class and verbal behavior using Flanders' system. More praise statements appeared in the preferred classes, but the vast majority of communication in the two types of classes was similar. M. B. Smith (1965) found significant correlations between positive and encouraging teacher statements and the high-status occupations that the teacher anticipated the pupils would attain and between negative statements and the low-status occupations that pupils were presumably headed toward. This disquieting conclusion involved seven white female teachers over 25 years of age with middle-class backgrounds as they interacted with 40 white boys in the sixth grade. It sheds some light on the problem of the teacher's differential treatment of pupils.

In-service or Preservice Training and Teaching Behavior. After an observer has watched some teaching and wishes to make a suggestion, it is difficult to decide what can be said to the teacher in order to help the teacher act differently during his next performance. How are the observations to be recorded? How can they best be displayed so that the trainee can understand? How much change occurs from one trial to the next? Here the presage variables are one or another kind of training program, kind of feedback, or preteaching experience. The process variables are measures of teaching behavior.

Gage (1963b) developed a questionnaire to be completed by pupils in which they rated their present teacher and also indicated their preferred or ideal teacher. In his study 86 sixth-grade teachers were given the reactions of their pupils once a month for part of the school year, while 90 teachers did not receive the feedback, even though the attitude inventories were administered. On 10 of 12 scales the pupils perceived a shift toward their ideal type of teacher during the course of the study; 4 of these shifts were statistically significant in comparison with the control-group data.

Bowers and Soar (1961) examined the relationships between human-relations training, teacher personality, and teaching behavior for a sample of 54 elementary teachers. The human-relations training was designed to help teachers develop skill in using classroom instructional groups to help pupils work more effectively in such groups. The *OScAR* and the *Russell Sage Social Relations Test* were used to obtain measures of teacher and pupil behaviors. An initial analysis of variance and covariance failed to identify relationships between change in teachers' or pupils' behavior and the training program, but an interesting application of the Johnson-Neyman technique showed that certain relationships achieve statistical significance at extreme positions of deviation; for example, the best adjusted teachers become more effective following training, but the less well adjusted teachers became less effective.

In a second study of the effects of sensitivity training, Soar (1966) tested the effects of training groups of teachers from four schools, while the principals were given similar training separately. The criterion measures employed were factor scores involving both process and change measurements of pupil products including subject matter, creativity, and personality. No evidence of overall increase in teacher effectiveness as a consequence of the experimental procedure was obtained, but there was evidence that better adjusted teachers were more effective and less well adjusted teachers were less effective after training than before. These results cross-validated the same finding in the earlier study.

In a third study by Soar (1966) a set of criterion measures of teacher effectiveness was developed by factor-analyzing process and product measures together. These were related to presage measures from the *Minnesota Multiphasic Personality Inventory* (*MMPI*) and the *National Teacher Examinations* (*NTE*), years of teaching experience, and semester hours in education. The number of significant correlations was approximately that expected by chance. When the same presage measures were related to the product measures of classroom mean residual true gain, however, the number of significant relationships was considerably greater than chance expectancy, and were reasonable: For example, pupils tended to dislike maladjusted teachers, teachers with higher *NTE* scores produced more arithmetic growth in pupils, and more experienced (older) teachers evoked less interest in independent work of pupils. The *MMPI* produced more significant relations with product measures than the three criteria commonly used for evaluating teachers—years of experience, amount of preparation, and scores on the NTE.

Flanders and others (1963) investigated the effects of teaching experienced teachers how to analyze verbal statements so that they could study their own classroom interaction. Two different treatments were created by having the instructor use two different styles by changing his verbal interaction. In one treatment he clarified ideas suggested by teachers more often than he did in the other treatment. One criterion measure reported was the number of experimental observations carried out by teachers. In addition, pretraining and posttraining measures of verbal interaction were analyzed in terms of the two types of in-service training programs. Although there was evidence of contamination between the two treatment programs, one program showed more evidence of change than the other. In a concurrent study of the same data, Storlie (1961) failed to find strong relationships between change in behavior after the in-service training and 25 personality variables measured before the training began.

Allen and others (1966) have developed a preservice training procedure called "microteaching" which involves intensive feedback and have analyzed the effects of such a program on the subsequent teaching behavior of three or four generations of college students who have completed the Stanford Teacher Intern Program. The procedure involves a simulation of teaching in which an intern teaches three to five high school pupils for five minutes while a magnetic audio and video recording is made. This is followed by the analysis of the recording in order to set new goals for the next session; this leads to another five minutes of teaching with different pupils, followed by more analysis, and so on. The pupils in each session as well as the supervisor complete a questionnaire which provides an assessment of the intern's performance. Statistically significant relationships between training assessment measures and subsequent ratings of teaching performance during the first year indicate that the intense behavioral training involving frequent and immediate feedback, in combination with attention to instructional theory, does affect subsequent teaching performance constructively.

In a study in which 20 preservice teachers were taught the Flanders system of interaction analysis and a control group took a traditional student teaching seminar, Hough and Amidon (1964) found that student teachers in the experimental course were given significantly higher ratings by their supervisors, made significantly more positive responsive on a teaching-attitudes test, and found the course significantly more challenging, interesting, and professionally meaningful than did students in conventional sections. In a series of doctoral studies testing the interaction between certain measures of personality, attitude, and training on the verbal behaviors of teachers in simulated teaching conditions (Hanny, 1966), in student teaching (Ober, 1966; Kirk, 1963) and among elementary-school teachers (Hill, 1966), it was found that training in interaction analysis did have an effect in each case which allowed the trained teacher to increase his use of some indirect behaviors or decrease his use of some direct behaviors. In no case was a significant difference reported in a direction contrary to the hypothesized direction. Although the student teachers in the experimental group in Ober's study were observed 4 to 12 months after instruction, there were significant differences in the hypothesized direction between those who had been taught the Flanders system and those who had not.

Summary of Presage-Process Research. Progress in presage-process research adds up to "sweet and sour." The sour is the continued difficulty of relating teacher traits to performance variables. In no study has sufficient attention been given to the methodological problems of keeping the conditions constant in the performance setting so that correlations with possible traits are maximized. Under the best of conditions reported, the correlations are still too low to give promise of utility; for example, errors in selecting prospective teachers by a predictor test would be too high except in the most extreme and obvious cases.

The sweet is the remarkable progress, from 1960 to 1966, in developing training experiences which do hold promise of providing a foundation upon which new preservice and in-service programs can be built. A program of such experiences may include simulating teacher-pupil interaction by using adult-to-adult social-skill training exercises. It may also include quasi simulated microteaching programs which make use of "live teacher-pupil interaction" under highly focused and controlled conditions which permit intensive feedback, ending with carefully programmed experiments involving a teacher's working with a full-sized class. Much work still remains, but the early results give reason for some optimism.

RESEARCH ON PRESAGE, SETTING, AND PRODUCT VARIABLES. In this section some characteristic of a teacher, such as a trait or some training experience, is compared to some outcome variable, such as measures of pupil learning or attitude, in an attempt to establish a relationship which has utility in the field of education. Also included are projects which seem to be concerned with the classroom setting, factors outside of the classroom, and the effects of these variables on the teaching-learning processes.

Research in this area is least productive when it lacks careful explanation or theory and merely seeks to establish a correlation between an outcome and some other situational variable. In many cases the correlations are statistically significant but have no utility beyond meeting the needs of the researcher. Research is more productive when some model or theory is involved and when long-term research programs permit the careful verification of results in different settings.

Long-term Research Programs. One example of a long-term research program is the work of Turner and Fattu, whose published reports extend from 1960 to 1967. They start with four propositions (Turner & Fattu, 1960, 1961): (1) that teaching is a form of problem-solving behavior, (2) that the problem-solving skills of the teacher are acquired through training and experience, (3) that these problem-solving skills may be measured by teacher performance on simulated teaching tasks, and (4) that the teaching-task performance of teachers is associated with teacher success.

Evidence bearing on the tenability of these propositions has been drawn wholly from experience and prospective elementary teachers. An initial set of studies (Turner, 1960, 1961; Wade, 1961) examined the apparent effects of training and experience on the performance of simulated problem tasks in arithmetic and reading. The results indicated a significant advance in performance among prospective teachers between the beginning of the methods courses and the end of student teaching. Collaterally, teachers with one to three years of experience showed performance significantly superior to that of prospective teachers at the end of student teaching. The performance of experienced teachers leveled off after the third year of experience. The performance of experienced teachers showed significant effects attributable to type of school-system setting. A second set of studies (Turner & others, 1963) showed that performance on simulated tasks in arithmetic among experienced elementary teachers was significantly associated with supervisory ratings of skill in teaching arithmetic, with pupil gains in arithmetic achievement, and with teacher efficiency and success in performing abstract problems (modified Kohs block design). Task performance in reading, and to a lesser degree in arithmetic, together with *MTAI* scores, was also shown to be predictive of teacher mobility at the end of the first year of experience, such that permissive poor problem solvers were most likely to be mobile.

Subsequently, Turner modified the earlier propositions by adding (1) that teaching involves the performance of a body of work tasks the precise nature of which is contingent on the setting in which teaching occurs, (2) that both the personal-social and problem-solving characteristics of teachers are relevant to the performance of these tasks, and (3) that the relationship between teacher problem-solving performance, the personal-social characteristics of the teacher, and teacher success are mediated by the school setting (Turner, 1965a).

Working on the basis of the modified position, Turner (1965b) examined the effects of school setting and (1) changes in problem-task performance during the first two years of teaching and (2) the relationships among task performance, personal-social characteristics (as measured by Ryans's *Teacher Characteristics Schedule*), teacher success, and teacher classroom problems. The results indicated that increases in task performance in arithmetic were associated almost wholly with school settings characterized by a predominance of working-class pupils. Within these settings increases were directly associated with the amount of supervision received by the beginning teachers. Increases in task performance in reading were similarly influenced by setting and supervision, but an additional effect directly attributable to experience in teaching reading was also isolated. The level of task performance in reading and arithmetic was found to increase rapidly during the first year of teaching experience and to level off during the second year. Examination of the relationship between task performance and the personal-social characteristics of the teachers indicated that these two sets of variables were orthogonal but that each set was related to teacher success, as perceived by supervisory personnel, depending on the setting. In settings in which pupils of working-class background predominated, the task-performance characteristics of teachers were predictive of success, but personal-social characteristics were nonpredictive. In settings in which middle-class pupils predominated, the personal-social characteristics of the teachers were positive predictors of success, but task-performance characteristics were negative predictors. Analysis of the relationships between beginning teachers' problems and teacher personal-social and task-performance characteristics (Turner, 1967) indicated that discipline problems and problems in setting correct expectations for pupils were associated with both sets of characteristics. Teachers with discipline problems were aloof, unbusinesslike, and poor problem solvers, while teachers with problems in setting expectations for pupils were teacher-centered, cool, and poor problem solvers.

The weight of the evidence from the studies reviewed suggests that problem-solving performance is a measurable characteristic of teachers and that this characteristic changes under teacher preparation and experience but that its importance to teacher success is largely contingent on the type of setting within which the teacher does his work.

As a second example of longitudinal research, Koskenniemi (1965) reports on his efforts to locate predictors of teaching success from a study of 48 male and 24 female students in elementary education in Finland. The project started with entrance to teacher preparation and followed the subjects through their first three years of teaching. Data-gathering techniques were influenced by the work of Ryans and the Cook-Leeds *MTAI* and included a special rating instrument which was employed during two full days of observation. Although Koskenniemi found it necessary to report to the Finnish government, which sponsored the research, that his results did not justify selecting and rejecting teacher applicants on the basis of scores on the instruments used, he did report a number of relationships. For example, (1) positive educational attitudes increase with training; (2) the same attitudes correlated with social class at the beginning, but not at the end, of training and are not correlated with academic success; (3) the predictive efficiency of profiles based on the entrance examinations showed no simple correspondence with measures of teaching success; and (4) no relationship was found between adjustment to and cooperation with the supervisor of student teaching and success in practice teaching. He also reported that teachers with exceptionally poor in-service records have a larger number of traits which they hold in common but which are not shared by teachers who do exceptionally well. One consequence is that negative development is easier to predict than positive development. Most of the unsuccessful teachers appeared to lack sensitivity to and understanding of children's thinking and attitudes and to exhibit low capacity for effective structuring of instructional situations, whereas no corresponding similarities between the most efficient teachers were discernible.

Measures of Teachers' Personality and Effectiveness. The research on teachers' personality and effectiveness reviewed in this section merely illustrates typical findings. For each study reported, three or four others with similar results could also have been included, were it not for space limitations.

The notion that certain types of teachers might be more effective with certain types of pupils attracted the attention of Heil and Washburne (1962). By using a variety of tests in 55 classrooms, some for the teachers and others for the pupils, as well as ratings of teachers from classroom observation, teachers were classified into three types: (A) turbulent, impulsive, and variable; (B) self-controlling, orderly, and work-oriented; and (C) fearful. The pupils were divided into four types: (1) conformers; (2) opposers; (3) waverers; and (4) strivers. Most pupils made the most progress in mathematics and science under type-A teachers and in language arts under type-B teachers. Type-C teachers seemed most effective in social studies. Certain differences in progress among pupil types were also reported; for example, waverers grew in "friendliness" most with type-C teachers but did not grow with type-A teachers. Confidence in the utility of such "in-the-field" correlations will be much higher when a true experiment is conducted and when an explanation of the dynamics of such relationships can be explored.

Medley (1961) administered the Edwards *Personal Preference Schedule* to 91 female student teachers. Several months later pupil reactions were collected and used as a measure of pupil-teacher rapport. There were no relationships between personality and rapport scores when the data from all teachers were analyzed. When the scores of all but 25 teachers were discarded on the basis that they scored high on the "consistent" scale suggesting insincere responses, certain correlations became significant. Those teachers with the best rapport scores expressed a greater need to understand others, to analyze their own motives, to be successful, to feel guilty and accept blame when wrong, to attack contrary points of view, to blame others when things go badly, and to be timid in the presence of superiors. Just what can be interpreted from a −.22 correlation between rapport scores and the teachers' heterosexual scores would depend, probably, on the reader's inclinations.

Burkhard (1962) administered *Thematic Apperception Tests (TAT)* to 300 female teachers in a parochial school system, spread through grades 4 to 12, with *TAT* evaluations processed by sequence analysis and 95 percent agreement among three judges. A total of 10,720 pupils completed ratings of their teachers on various dimensions including "liking for the teacher" and "ability to explain." Fifty pairs of classes, matched for age and IQ, were selected from the highest and lowest centiles of all classes based on average pupil ratings. High-ranking teachers appear to be more active, to recognize their own limitations, to be more objective, and to have higher scores on similar virtues.

Flanagan (1961) compared *MMPI* scores of 147 female teachers with ratings made in four categories of teaching effectiveness by supervisors. A high coding on Hy (hysteria) was positively related to supervisor ratings of effectiveness. Bowers and Soar (1962) also found Hy to be a useful predictor of a teaching effectiveness measure, when using the MMPI, and in addition, the scales Pd (psychopathic deviate), Sc (schizophrenia) and Pt (psychasthenia). Flanagan concluded that ". . . the *MMPI* has potential usefulness in aiding in the prediction of the success of [teachers]" (1961, p. 353). In this same area of research can be placed studies which made use of the MTAI test of teacher attitudes. Ellis (1961) and Munro (1964) both compared MTAI scores with ratings by either principals or supervisors. Although some correlations were statistically significant, Munro stated: "The magnitude of the coefficients . . . suggests that making predictions based on *MTAI* scores would be an extremely hazardous undertaking" (1961, 139). Ellis concluded: ". . . none of the factors herein considered are determinative in predicting outstanding teachers of the social studies" (1964, p. 28). To these conclusions Lawler (1964) added, after comparing principals' ratings with pupil achievement, "Principals were not good raters of teacher efficiency" (p. 86). Lawler's conclusion was reached after comparing the academic progress of 294 fifth-grade classes who were taught by 98 teachers. However, Lawler raised some questions about his use of academic progress as a criterion of teaching effectiveness, because he was able to document cases of variability in progress of classes under the same teacher.

At this point the work of Gowan (1961), Christensen (1960), Yamamoto (1963), Dixon and Morse (1961), Dugan (1961), Morman (1965), and many others could be cited. However, such studies tend most often to show that some aspect of teaching, either observed by an adult educator or estimated from pupil judgments, can be shown to be correlated with dogmatism as measured by the F-scale, scores on the *MTAI*, or scores from some scale on the *MMPI* at levels that exceed chance. However, most of these studies were not replicated. Many simply reported negative results. The possibility of finding a predictor of teaching effectiveness through such field correlational studies appears to be most unrewarding and not likely to contribute to our knowledge of effective teaching.

Years of Experience and Qualifications. The notion that experience in teaching and completion or noncompletion of the requirements for certification ought to be related to measures of teaching performance was also investigated by a number of researchers. By and large the results are not very encouraging.

LuPone (1961, p. 62) stated, after studying 240 elementary teachers, ". . . the permanently certified [versus provisionally certified] received higher ratings in: the ability to translate subject matter into living experience, the proficiency in using effectively related materials in classroom instruction, an understanding and more sympathetic attitude toward the child, . . ." and similar characteristics. The ratings were made during the first, second, and third years of teaching experience. Hawkins and Stoops (1966), on the other hand, concluded that "training and years of experience appear to have no significant advantage or disadvantage over either formal or informal evaluation for measuring teacher competence . . . except that of greater objectivity." Hall (1964) concluded that fully certified teachers were more effective when pupils' achievement scores were used as an effectiveness criterion. Positive results were also reported by Beery (1962) and Collins (1964), who analyzed the same relationships.

Others have investigated different aspects of training in an effort to establish correlations. Freehill (1963, p. 311) concluded that "the quality of teaching beyond the crucial minimum of failure is related to ability as measured by college entrance scores and academic success. It is at least as closely related to records of social participation and attitude. The best predictor was from a scale measuring democratic attitudes." Fielstra (1963) compared the top and bottom quartiles of 200 secondary-level student teachers given a composite rating scale on teaching performance and discovered that measures which best discriminated the excellent from the poor were adaptability to a variety of teaching situations, skill in planning, success in carrying out plans, resourcefulness in teaching, and effective teacher-pupil relationships. Simun and Asher (1964) found relatively low correlations ($r = .2$ or $.3$) between ratings by administrators and a variety of measures. The most consistent predictors were academic average and student-teaching reports.

RESEARCH TRENDS. Certain characteristics of research are discernible when work in the decade of the 1960's is compared with previous efforts. Perhaps the most significant is the development of more-powerful observation techniques which help in the analysis of what takes place in the classroom. Systems of interaction analysis are likely to become more flexible, and when they are integrated into shared-time computer systems much of the tedious clerical and tabulation chores will be eliminated. Clusters of categories may be developed which will permit a trained observer to select a particular dimension of the interaction to be recorded and automatically tabulated into a display which emphasizes this aspect of the teacher-pupil interchange. When such tools have been developed there will be new possibilities for assisting a teacher to develop and make use of particular patterns of teacher influence. In turn, these patterns can be evaluated in terms of learning outcomes.

A second characteristic is the lack of development of teaching units which can be used to evaluate educational outcomes. The emphasis on nationally standardized tests has much to commend it, but such assessment tools may be less related to what takes place in the classroom than some kind of instructional package in which instructional materials for any pattern of teaching are carefully matched with tests which evaluate pupil performance. It will be unfortunate if the techniques for assessing patterns of interaction develop without a concurrent development of tests of pupil attitude and achievement for the various grade levels and subject-matter areas.

The third characteristic, which may grow out of the current activities of Taba, Turner, Biddle, Ballack, and others, is a more active interest in the development of models which can be used to conceptualize classroom interaction and, in turn, help to specify and to suggest methods of quantifying research variables more systematically. Too little is known about classroom interaction. It would, therefore, be premature to advocate any particular approach to the conceptualization of classroom teaching-learning activities. Yet a large proportion of research on teaching appears to be almost randomly empirical with little or no coordination or comparison of studies.

A fourth characteristic is a decrease in research activity which has been so unrewarding for so many years. Research energy is still being expended at rates far in excess of expected progress by relating teacher personality variables to educational outcomes without due regard for the analysis of the teacher-pupil interaction. Curiosity among researchers which drives them to explain *why* relationships of one sort or another exist seems as rarely present as ever. Certain types of rating forms are still in use in spite of their known inadequacies. Consistent, long-range research programs are still few in number and single-shot correlational studies much too frequent.

Ned A Flanders
The University of Michigan
Anita Simon
Temple University

References

Allen, Dwight W., and others. *Micro-teaching: A Description.* School of Education, Stanford U, 1966.

Amidon, Edmund J., and Flanders, Ned A. "The Effects of Direct and Indirect Teacher Influence on Dependent-prone Students Learning Geometry." *J Ed Psychol* 52:286–91; 1961.

Amidon, Edmund J., and Simon, Anita. "Teacher-Pupil Interaction." *R Ed Res* 35:135–6; 1965.

Anderson, C. C., and Hunka, S. M. "Teacher Evaluation: Some Problems and a Proposal." *Harvard Ed R* 33:74–95; 1963.

Barr, A. S., and others. *Wisconsin Studies of the Measurement and Prediction of Teacher Effectiveness: A Summary of Investigations.* Dembar, 1961. 156p.

Beery, J. R. "Does Professional Preparation Make a Difference?" *J Teach Ed* 13:386–95; 1962.

Bellack, Arno A., and Davitz, Joel. *The Language of the Classroom: Meanings Communicated in High School Teaching.* USOE Cooperative Research Project No. 1497, Institute of Psychological Research, Teachers Col, Columbia U, 1963. 200p.

Bellack, Arno A., and Huebner, D. "Teaching." *R Ed Res* 30:246–57; 1960.

Bellack, Arno A., and others. *The Language of the Classroom: Meanings Communicated in High School Teaching.* USOE Cooperative Research Project No. 2023, Institute of Psychological Research, Teachers Col, Columbia U, 1965. 260p.

Biddle, Bruce J., and Ellena, William J. (Eds.) *Contemporary Research on Teacher Effectiveness.* Holt, 1964. 352p.

Bowers, N. D., and Soar, Robert S. *Studies of Human Relations in the Teaching-learning Process.* Part V: *Final Report.* USOE Cooperative Research Project No. 469, 1961. 210p.

Bowers, N. D., and Soar, Robert S. "The Influence of Teacher Personality on Classroom Interaction." *J Exp Ed* 30:309–11; 1962.

Bowie, B. L., and Morgan, H. G. "Personal Values and Verbal Behavior of Teachers." *J Exp Ed* 30:337–45; 1962.

Burkhard, M. I. "Discernment of Teacher Characteristics by TAT Sequence Analysis." *J Ed Psychol* 53:279–87; 1962.

Christensen, C. M. "Relationship Between Pupil Achievement, Pupil Affect-need, Teacher Warmth, and Teacher Permissiveness." *J Ed Psychol* 51:169–74; 1960.

Coats, W. D. "Investigation and Simulation of the Relationships Among Selected Classroom Variables." Doctoral dissertation. USOE Cooperative Research Project No. 6-8330. U Michigan, 1966. 183p.

Cogan, M. L. "Research on the Behavior of Teachers: A New Phase." *Teach Ed* 14:238-43; 1963.

Collins, M. "Untrained and Trained Graduate Teachers: A Comparison of Their Experiences During the Probationary Year." *Br J Ed Psychol* 34:75-84; 1964.

Davies, Lillian S. "Some Relationships Between Attitudes, Personality Characteristics, and Verbal Behavior of Selected Teachers." Doctoral dissertation. U Minnesota, 1961. 225p.

Dixon, W. R., and Morse, W. C. "The Prediction of Teaching Performance: Empathic Potential." *J Teach Ed* 12:322-9; 1961.

Dodl, Norman R. "Pupil Questioning Behavior in the Context of Classroom Interaction." *Dissertation Abstracts* 26:644-2; 1966.

Dollins, Joseph G., and others. "With Words of Praise." *El Sch J* 60:446-50; 1960.

Dugan, R. R. "Personality and the Effective Teacher." *J Teach Ed* 12:355-7; 1961.

Ellis, J. R. "Relationships Between Aspects of Preparation and Measures of Performance of Secondary Teachers of the Social Studies. *J Ed Res* 55:24-8; 1961.

Fattu, Nicholas A. "Effectiveness—An Elusive Quality." *Ed Digest* 27:24-6; 1962.

Fielstra, C. "Discriminative and Predictive Values of Rating Given to UCLA Student Teachers on the Secondary School Level." *California J Ed Res* 14:11-8; 1963.

Filson, T. N. "Factors Influencing the Level of Dependence in the Classroom." Doctoral dissertation. U Minnesota, 1957.

Flanagan, D. E. "A Study of the Relationship of Scores on the MMPI to Success in Teaching as Indicated by Supervisory Ratings." *J Exp Ed* 29:329-54; 1961.

Flanders, Ned A. "Diagnosing and Utilizing Social Structures in Classroom Learning." In Henry, Nelson B. (Ed.) *The Dynamics of Instructional Groups*, 59th Yearbook, NSSE. U Chicago Press, 1960. p. 187-217.

Flanders, Ned A. *Teacher Influence, Pupil Attitudes and Achievement*. Monograph No. 12. USOE, CRP 397, U Minnesota, 1960. 126p.

Flanders, Ned A., and others. *Helping Teachers Change Their Behavior*. USOE Project Nos. 1721012 and 7-32-0560-171.0, U Michigan, 1963. 154p.

Freehill, M. F. "The Prediction of Teaching Competence." *J Exp Ed* 31:307-11; 1963.

Furst, N. F. "The Multiple Languages of the Classroom: A Further Analysis and a Synthesis of Meanings Communicated in High School Teaching." Doctoral dissertation. Temple U, 1967.

Gage, N. L. (Ed.) *Handbook of Research on Teaching*. Rand McNally, 1963(a). 1218p.

Gage, N. L. "A Method for Improving Teacher Behavior." *J Teach Ed* 14:261-6; 1963(b).

Gage, N. L. "Desirable Behaviors of Teachers." *Urban Ed* 1:85-95; 1965.

Gallagher, James J. "Expressive Thought by Gifted Children in the Classroom." *El Engl* 42:559-68; 1965.

Gallagher, James J., and Aschner, M. J. "A Preliminary Report on Analyses of Classroom Interaction." *Merrill-Palmer Q* 9:183-94; 1963.

Galloway, Charles. "An Exploratory Study of Observational Procedures for Determining Teacher Nonverbal Communication." Doctoral dissertation. U Florida, 1962.

Gowan, J. C. "A Follow-up Study of Teaching Candidates." *J Ed Res* 54:353-5; 1961.

Guggenheim, F. "Classroom Climate and the Learning of Mathematics." *Arithmetic Teach* 8:363-7; 1961.

Hall, H. O. "Professional Preparation and Teacher Effectiveness." *J Teach Ed* 15:72-6; 1964.

Hanny, Robert Joseph. "The Relationship Between Selected Personality Characteristics and Teacher Verbal Behavior." Doctoral dissertation. Ohio State U, 1966.

Hawkins, E. E., and Stoops, E. "Objective and Subjective Identification of Outstanding Elementary Teachers." *J Ed Res* 59:344-6; 1966.

Heil, L. M., and Washburne, C. "Characteristics of Teachers Related to Children's Progress." *J Teach Ed* 12:401-6; 1961.

Heil, L. M., and Washburne, C. "Brooklyn College Research in Teacher Effectiveness." *J Ed Res* 55:347-51; 1962.

Hill, William Morris. "The Effects on Verbal Teaching Behavior of Learning Interaction Analysis as an In-service Education Activity." Doctoral dissertation. Ohio State U, 1966.

Hoover, Kenneth H. "Degree of Teacher Domination in Group Processes and Student Attitude Toward Instruction in Secondary Methods Classes." *J Ed Res* 56:379-81; 1963.

Hough, John B. "An Observational System for the Analysis of Classroom Instruction." In Amidon, Edmund J., and Hough, John B. (Eds.) *Interaction Analysis: Theory, Research and Application*. Addison, 1967, 402p.

Hough, John B., and Amidon, Edmund J. "Behavioral Change in Pre-service Teacher Preparation: An Experimental Study." College of Education, Temple U, 1964.

Howsam, R. B. *Who's a Good Teacher? Problems and Progress in Teacher Evaluation*. California Teachers Association, 1960. 48p.

Hughes, Marie M. *Development of the Means for the Assessment of the Quality of Teaching in Elementary Schools*. USOE Cooperative Research Project No. 353, U Utah, 1959. 314p.

Johns, Joseph P. "The Relationship Between Teacher Behaviors and the Incidence of Thought-provoking Questions by Students in Secondary Schools." Doctoral dissertation. U Michigan, 1966. 103p.

Joyce, Bruce R., and Hodges, Richard E. "A Rationale for Teacher Education." *El Sch J* 66:254-66; 1966.

Kirk, Jeffrey, "Effects of Teaching the Minnesota

System of Interaction Analysis to Intermediate Grade Student Teachers." Doctoral dissertation. Temple U, 1963.

Kliebard, H. M. "Teacher Cycles: A Study of the Pattern and Flow of Classroom Discourse." Ed. D. Project Report, Teachers Col, Columbia U, 1963.

Koskenniemi, Matti. *The Development of Young Elementary School Teachers: A Follow-up Study.* Suomalaisen Teideakatemian Toimituksia Annales Academiae Scientiarum Fennicae, Sarja-ser. B Nidetom. 138. Helsinki, 1965. 635p.

LaShier, William S., Jr. "An Analysis of Certain Aspects of the Verbal Behavior of Student Teachers of Eighth Grade Students Participating in a BSCS Laboratory Block." Doctoral dissertation. U Texas, 1965.

Lawler, E. S. "Differing Rates of Progress of Classes Under the Same and Different Teachers." *J Ed Res* 58:84–6; 1964.

LuPone, O. J. "A Comparison of Provisionally Certified and Permanently Certified Elementary School Teachers in Selected School Districts in New York State." *J Ed Res* 55:53–63; 1961.

Medley, Donald M. "Teacher Personality and Teacher-Pupil Rapport." *J Teach Ed* 12:152–6; 1961.

Medley, Donald M., and Mitzel, Harold E. "Measuring Classroom Behavior by Systematic Observation." In Gage, N. L. (Ed.) *Handbook of Research on Teaching.* Rand McNally, 1963. p. 247–328.

Miller, George L. "An Investigation of Teaching Behavior and Pupil Thinking." Department of Education, U Utah, 1964.

Mitzel, Harold E. "Teacher Effectiveness." In Harris, Chester W. (Ed.) *Encyclopedia of Educational Research,* 3rd ed. Macmillan, 1960. p. 1481–6.

Morman, R. R., and others. "High School Teaching Effectiveness." *J Sec Ed* 40:270–4; 1965.

Morrison, B. M. "The Reactions of Internal and External Children to Patterns of Teaching Behavior." Doctoral dissertation. U Michigan, 1966. 149p.

Morsh, J. E., and Wilder, E. W. "Identifying the Effective Instructor: A Review of Quantitative Studies, 1900–1952." Research Bulletin No. AFPTRC-TR-54-44. USAF Personnel Training Research Center (San Antonio, Texas), 1954.

Munro, B. C. "Minnesota Teacher Attitude Inventory as a Predictor of Teaching Success." *J Ed Res* 58:138–9; 1964.

Nelson, Lois Ney. "The Effect of Classroom Interaction on Pupil Linguistic Performance." *Dissertation Abstracts* 25:789; 1964.

Ober, Richard. "Predicting Student Teacher Verbal Behavior." Doctoral dissertation. Ohio State U, 1966.

Openshaw, M. Karl, and Cypert, Frederick R. "The Development of a Taxonomy for the Classification of Teacher Classroom Behavior." Ohio State U Research Foundation, 1966.

Pankratz, Roger. "Verbal Interaction Patterns in the Classrooms of Selected Physics Teachers." In Amidon, Edmund J., and Hough, John B. (Eds.) *Interaction Analysis: Theory, Research and Application.* Addison, 1967. 402p.

Parakh, J. S. *To Develop a System for Analyzing the Reactions of Teachers and Students in Biology Classes.* USOE Cooperative Research Project No. S-269, Cornell U, 1965. 188p.

Perkins, Hugh V. "A Procedure for Assessing the Classroom Behavior of Students and Teachers." *Am Ed Res J* 1:249–60; 1964.

Perkins, Hugh V. "Classroom Behavior and Underachievement." *Am Ed Res J* 2:1–12; 1965.

Pfeiffer, I. L. "Teaching in Ability Grouped English Classes: A Study of Verbal Interaction and Cognitive Goals." Doctoral dissertation. Kent State U, 1966. 194p.

Reed, H. B. "Effect of Teacher Warmth." *J Teach Ed* 12:330–4; 1961.

Reed, H. B. "Implications for Science Education of A Teacher Competence Research." *Sci Ed* 46:473–86; 1962.

Remmers, H. H. "Rating Methods in Research on Teaching." In Gage, N. L. (Ed.) *Handbook of Research on Teaching.* Rand McNally, 1963. p. 329–78.

Ringness, Thomas A. and others. "Self-role Conflict, Personality Variables, and Classroom Interaction." Extension Research and Services in Education, U Wisconsin, 1964.

Ryans, David G. "Teacher Behavior Theory and Research: Implications for Teacher Education." *J Teach Ed* 14:274–93; 1963.

Schantz, Betty M. B. "An Experimental Study Comparing the Effects of Verbal Recall by Children in Direct and Indirect Teaching Methods as a Tool of Measurement." Doctoral dissertation. Pennsylvania State U, 1963.

Simon, Anita. "The Effects of Training in Interaction Analysis on the Teaching Patterns of Student Teachers in Favored and Non-Favored Classes." Doctoral dissertation. Temple U, 1966.

Simun, P. B., and Asher, J. W. "The Relationships of Variables in Undergraduate School and School Administrators' Ratings of First-Year Teachers." *J Teach Ed* 15:293–302; 1964.

Smith, B. Othanel. "Conceptual Frameworks for Analysis of Classroom Social Interaction: Comments on Four Papers." *J Exp Ed* 30:325–6; 1962.

Smith, B. Othanel, and others. "A Tentative Report on the Strategies of Teaching." Bureau of Educational Research, U Illinois, 1964. 103p.

Smith, M. B. "Interpersonal Relationships in the Classroom Based on the Expected Socioeconomic Status of Sixth Grade Boys." *Teach Col J* 36:200–6; 1965.

Snider, Ray M. *A Project to Study the Nature of Effective Physics Teaching.* USOE Cooperative Research Project No. S-280, Cornell U, 1965.

Soar, Robert S. "Methodological Problems in Predicting Teacher Effectiveness." *J Exp Ed* 32:287–91; 1964.

Soar, Robert S. "Research in the Teaching Processes: Four Studies with the OScAR Technique." National Society of Colleges for Teacher Education, 1966.

Solomon, D., and others. "Teacher Behavior and Student Learning." *J Ed Psychol* 55:23–30; 1964.

Storlie, T. R. "Selected Characteristics of Teachers Whose Verbal Behavior Is Influenced by an Inservice Course in Interaction Analysis." Doctoral dissertation. U Minnesota, 1961. 209p.

Taba, Hilda, and others. *Thinking in Elementary School Children.* USOE Cooperative Research Project No. 1574, San Francisco State Col, 1964. 207p.

Travers, Robert M. and others. *Measured Needs of Teachers and Their Behavior in the Classroom.* USOE Cooperative Research Project No. 444, U Utah, 1961.

Turner, R. L. *Problem Solving Proficiency Among Elementary School Teachers.* Part II: *Further Investigations of Teachers of Arithmetic, Grades 3–6.* Institute of Educational Research, Mono., Indiana U, 1960.

Turner, R. L. *Problem Solving Proficiency Among Elementary School Teachers.* Part IV: *Further Investigations of Teachers of Arithmetic, Grades 3–6. Institute of Educational Research,* Mono., Indiana U, 1961.

Turner, R. L. "Acquisition of Teaching Skills in Elementary School Settings; A Research Report." *Indiana U Sch Ed B* 41:1–94; 1965(*a*).

Turner, R. L. "Characteristics of Beginning Teachers: Their Differential Linkage With School-system Types." *Sch R* 73:48–58; 1965(*b*).

Turner, R. L. "Some Predictors of Problems of Beginning Teachers." *El Sch J* 67:251–6; 1967.

Turner, R. L., and Fattu, Nicholas A. "Skill in Teaching, A Reappraisal of the Concepts and Strategies in Teacher Effectiveness Research." *Indiana U Sch Ed B* 36(No. 3); 1960.

Turner, R. L., and Fattu, Nicholas A. "Skill in Teaching, Assessed on the Criterion of Problem Solving." *Indiana U Sch Ed B* 37:1–32; 1961.

Turner, R. L., and others. "Skill in Teaching Assessed on the Criterion of Problem Solving: Three Studies." *Indiana U Sch Ed B* 39:1–32; 1963.

Urbach, Floyd D. "A Study of Recurring Patterns of Teaching." Doctoral dissertation. Nebraska, 1966.

Wade, E. W. *Problem Solving Proficiency Among Elementary School Teachers III: Teachers of Reading, Grades 2–5.* Institute of Educational Research, Mono., Indiana U, 1961.

Wilk, Roger E., and Edson, William H. "Predictions and Performance: An Experimental Study of Student Teachers." *J Teach Ed* 14:308–17; 1963.

Withall, John, and Lewis, W. W. "Social Interaction in the Classroom." In Gage, N. L. (Ed.) *Handbook of Research on Teaching.* Rand McNally, 1963. p. 683–714.

Yamamoto, Kaoru. "Relationships Between Creative Thinking Abilities of Teachers and Achievement and Adjustment of Pupils." *J Exp Ed* 32:2–25; 1963.

TEACHER ROLES

The role of the teacher involves two broad fields of research. On the one hand, "role" refers to behavior; thus, studies of teacher-role performance are those in which the actual behavior of teachers is observed. On the other hand, "role" refers to expectations of behavior; thus, studies of teacher-role expectations are those in which expectations maintained for teachers by teachers and others are investigated. In general, these are two distinct fields of research investigation and are summarized separately here.

STUDIES OF TEACHER-ROLE EXPECTATIONS. As is suggested by Biddle and Thomas (1966), the role field is characterized by some terminological and conceptual confusion. This is particularly evident in research published on teacher-role expectations, where a wide variety of terms are often used to describe common methods and where the same term may be applied to quite different techniques. In general, for purposes of this review terms similar to those proposed by Biddle and Thomas are used.

Subject Persons. Teacher-role expectations may be held by a variety of persons who are usually identified by the social positions which they hold. Thus, expectations held by parents may be contrasted with those held by teachers themselves, principals, school-board members, and so on. Among the criteria used by investigators to differentiate groups of subjects were the subjects' ethnic, religious, or racial backgrounds (Fishburn, 1962; Mays, 1963; Terrien, 1955, 1953); the school level (e.g., Merrill & Jex, 1964; T. Smith, 1965; D. Smith & Cooper, 1965; Yamamoto & Dizney, 1966); the number of years within the school (e.g., Champlin, 1931; Clinton, 1930; Davis, 1933; Haggard, 1943; Tiedeman, 1942); the school type, such as religious, public, or independent (e.g., Allen & Seaberg, 1964; Becker, 1953; Hatfield, 1961; Seidman & Knapp, 1953; Yourglich, 1955); the training received (Arkoff & Shears, 1961; Brenner & others, 1962); the subjects' life conditions, such as socioeconomic level (e.g., Cheong & DeVault, 1966; Collins & Smith, 1965; Hart, 1965; Phillips, 1955); their occupations (Koopman, 1946; Trabue, 1953); the community ecology (e.g., Chilcott, 1961; Jordan, 1929; Mays, 1963; Reitz & others, 1965); and the subject matter taught by teacher respondents (e.g., Brookover, 1943; Dunlop, 1965; Fishburn, 1962; Lacognata, 1965). Given the wide range of subject persons whose expectations were to be differentiated, it is not surprising to discover that a variety of limiting criteria were also applied by investigators to enable them to sample a limited group of subjects. Of the 74 studies dealing with role expectations, 17 limited coverage to the primary level, 25 to the secondary level, and 30 to the tertiary level. Of these same studies 48 reported data from teacher-subjects, 43 had pupil- or student-subjects, 12 had administrator-subjects, 4 dealt with guidance counselors (Dunlop, 1965; Schmidt, 1962; Warman, 1960; Watley, 1965)—but none with janitors, secretaries, school nurses, or dieticians!—and 13 dealt with members of the family or the community in general. In the last group, it is interesting that to date no study has appeared in which a random sample of public opinion concerning teacher-role expectations has yet been published, although an early study did report data from a national sample of teachers (Charters & Waples, 1929).

Object Persons. Expectations for the role of the teacher may be held, of course, for teachers in general or may refer to any subgroup of teachers, such as primary teachers, male teachers, track coaches, and experienced teachers. Among the 74 studies reviewed, 50 asked for expectations pertaining to teachers in general, thus exhibiting a widespread reification of the general designating term "teacher." However, a wide variety of subpositional investigations were also conducted: of male and female teachers (Lantz, 1965; Mason & others, 1959), of inexperienced and experienced teachers (Lantz, 1965; Mason & others, 1959; T. Smith, 1965; Trabue, 1953), of special-education teachers (Collins & Smith, 1965), of student teachers (Bradley, 1966; Lantz, 1965), of guidance counselors (Dunlop, 1965; Rippee & others, 1965; Warman, 1960; Watley, 1965), of administrators (Arkoff & Shears, 1961; Bidwell, 1955; Carson & Schultz, 1964; Story, 1950), and of the school as a reified entity (Lacognata, 1965; Musgrove, 1961). In addition, either by advertence or by inadvertence, many investigators limited their study to the teacher's role within a specific, institutional context: in 16 cases to the primary level, 21 cases to the secondary, 21 cases to the tertiary, etc. Another type of limitation also appeared in that some studies asked respondents to consider the role of a specific person—themselves in 13 studies concerned with teachers' own self-expectations, and another individual teacher in 10 other studies where subjects were asked to give expectations for a specific teacher.

Persons Referred to. Whereas subject persons are actually contacted by the investigator, object persons are only referred to—their performances are only spoken of, not actually observed. Persons referred to may also appear in a second capacity within the teacher-role expectation—expectations may be assigned to them by the subject. For example, a teacher may speak of the expectations held by his principal or the parents of his pupils. Usually such attributed expectations are thought to be a source of role conflict—for instance, when the teacher reveals that the expectations he attributes to another are at variance with his own. Among the 74 studies reviewed, 5 asked subjects to attribute expectations to sentient others, including teachers in general (Biddle & others, 1962), pupils in general (Brenner & others, 1962; Fausti & Moore, 1966), extension students (Brenner & others, 1962), administrators (Biddle & others, 1962), the community (Hanson & Umstattd, 1937; Manwiller, 1958; Phillips, 1955), and the school (Biddle & others, 1962).

Modality. Expectations may appear in a variety of modalities. For example, a subject may prescribe or proscribe a teacher characteristic, in which case we say that he is expressing a *norm*. He may also state that a teacher characteristic is or is not likely of occurrence, in which case he expresses an *anticipation*. Or he may personally approve or disapprove a teacher characteristic, in which case a *value* is given. (Interestingly, investigators of teachers' roles have adopted no uniform vocabulary to express these distinctions, nor do the majority of authors appear even to understand that there are modalities other than the one being reported in the published study!) Of the studies reviewed, 40 were confined to the normative mode, 21 appeared to use the anticipatory mode, and 13 were clearly valuational. One study (Biddle & others, 1962) used more than a single mode, but in that work the investigators took pains to contrast findings for the various modes. In several cases it was difficult to assess whether the normative or valuational mode was used, and investigators appeared to confuse these two modes more readily than they confused either with the anticipatory mode. The majority of both normative and valuational studies asked for positively valued characteristics (those prescribed or approved), although a sizable group asked for both positive and negative characteristics. Only two studies (Haer, 1953; Phillips, 1955) were confined to the negative case. Among anticipatory studies, the majority dealt with anticipations that were laid in the "timeless present," although six dealt with reports of past activities (e.g., Ryan, 1966; Very & Dye, 1966) and two with future events (Allen & Seaberg, 1964; Mason & others, 1959). Among the five studies in which expectations were attributed to sentient persons, the majority of the expectations attributed were normative, although one study (Fausti & Moore, 1966) dealt with attributed anticipations.

Object Characteristics. It is also possible for teacher-role expectations to deal with a wide variety of teacher characteristics. Studies reported have, indeed, represented a broad range of interests, from physical features of the teaching population (Jones & Gottfried, 1966) through backgrounds teachers are presumed to exhibit (Bogen, 1954; Hart, 1965; Ryan, 1966) to traits of teacher behavior (e.g. Becker, 1953; Keighin, 1948; Richey & Fox, 1948; Rogers, 1950; Yamamoto & Dizney, 1966; Yourglich, 1955). However, the majority of studies reviewed have concerned themselves with teachers' performances. Since the realm of performances is largely unbounded, investigators have been constrained to limit coverage by a variety of strategies for contextualization. For 9 studies teachers' performances were laid within a specific physical location such as the classroom, home, or "community" (e.g., Allen & Seaberg, 1964; Bogen, 1954; McGill, 1931; Twyman & Biddle, 1963); 2 studies used academic schedules as contexts (Washburne, 1957; Watley, 1965); 7 utilized the contextualizing properties of activities such as "lessons" or "field trips" (e.g. Greenhoe, 1940; Hanson & Umstattd, 1937; Story, 1950; Yamamoto & Dizney, 1966); and 4 studies dealt with teachers' responses to teachers' problems (Bidwell, 1955; Lacognata, 1964; Ryan, 1966; Warman, 1960). A single study used the context of teachers' plans for the future (Mason & others, 1959), while 16 studies used one or more types of *functional* categorizations to apply to teachers' roles (Biddle & others, 1962; Colombotos,

1963; Furst, 1965; D. Smith & Cooper, 1965). As used by this last group of investigators, functional contexts are prechosen end-states presumed by either the investigator himself or some stated theorist to define the domain of impact of the teaching occupation. Examples given have included the teacher as an instructor, counselor, representative of community values, referrer (to other professionals), and member of a profession. To date there has appeared no apparent agreement on such a basic list of functions for the teaching profession, although a number of functions (particularly that of instructor) appear in most lists. It appears to the reviewer that agreement on a minimal list of functions is prerequisite for the devising of instruments that may be used for the assessment of teacher role in various communities, regions, or nations.

Instruments Used. Given a general lack of agreement concerning either the functions presumed to integrate the teacher's role or other forms of contextualization, it comes as no surprise to discover that a wide range of instruments has been used for the measurement of teacher-role expectations. The range of instruments used may be indicated by the listing of but a few of those adopted from other sources for the study of teachers' roles. The list includes the Teacher Practices Questionnaire (Sorenson & others, 1963), Medley and Mitzel's OScAR (Lantz, 1965), The Leadership Opinion Questionnaire (Arkoff & Shears, 1961), Wrightstone's Pupil-Teacher Rapport Scale (Bogen, 1954), and Fiedler's Modified Ideal Patient-Therapist Relationship Scale (Reitz & others, 1965; Soper & Combs, 1962). However, most investigators have in fact developed their own instruments in the studies reported and in so doing have used a wide variety of techniques for the measurement of role expectations. Most studies have made use of Likert scaling techniques, which call for subjects to select from a range of ranked alternatives that response or those responses which most clearly correspond to their norm, anticipation, or value. For example, subjects might be asked whether they "highly approved of," "moderately approved of," "felt neutral about," "moderately disapproved of," or "highly disapproved of" a selected teacher performance, such as using corporal punishment on pupils. However, 6 studies reported the use of Q-sort methods (e.g., Bradley, 1966; Hatfield, 1961; Reitz & others, 1965; Strong & Insel, 1965), 1 used the Osgood semantic differential (T. Smith, 1965), 3 reported the use of ranking techniques (Champlin, 1931; Collins & Smith, 1965; Taylor, 1962), and in 24 studies respondents were asked to reply to open-ended questions (e.g., Cobb, 1952; Dallolio, 1955; Demos & Belok, 1963; Koopman, 1946; Lamson, 1942; T. Smith, 1963). Interestingly, no study that has been reported made use of the powerful methods based on Guttman scale analysis. In view of the fact that most investigators devised their own instruments and made use of prescaled questions, the methods used for selection of items—thus determining the content—of the instruments devised was clearly an issue. The majority of studies reported the use of items that were preselected from content that was generated by the earlier interviewing of informants. However, several studies reported the use of more sophisticated item-selection techniques, including the use of preexisting (mostly functional) theory (Fausti & Moore, 1966; Getzels & Guba, 1955; Soper & Combs, 1962; Watley, 1965; Yamamoto & Dizney, 1966), the observation of teachers' behavior (Bogen, 1954; Gordon, 1955; Hatfield, 1961; Terrien, 1955), the use of preexisting records (Babchuck & Bates, 1962; Gordon, 1955), and even the use of factor analyses of items taken from a larger pool (e.g. Bidwell, 1955; Furst, 1965; Sorenson & others, 1963; Very & Dye, 1966).

Findings. Although most of the studies reviewed have dealt with specific problems, such as role conflict for public school teachers, differences in expectations held for teachers by various groups of persons, effects of teacher training on teacher-held role expectations, and the like, nevertheless a number of findings or stereotypes have been repeated in various studies. For example, teachers generally felt that their position is held in low esteem by members of the community at large and that they do not receive appropriate rewards for their efforts (Brenner & others, 1962; Collins & Smith, 1965; Terrien, 1955; Washburne, 1957). Teachers were generally felt by others to be nonaggressive and acquiescent and to sin primarily by omission rather than by commission. In addition, both teachers and other subjects expressed concern over the fact that in many (especially in small) communities teachers are expected to maintain their professional roles during off-duty hours and in settings outside of the school. Among findings that were reported for differences among subject positions, there appeared to be generally high consensus among students in their expectations of teachers' characteristics (Dallolio, 1955; Demos & Belok, 1963; Tiedeman, 1942). However, differences appeared in expectations depending upon subjects' year at the university, sex, personality characteristics, school activities, attitudes toward school, and social acceptability (Cheong & DeVault, 1966). In addition, varying expectations were held for teacher role within various types of communities (Champlin, 1931; Clinton, 1930; Getzels & Guba, 1955). When disparities appeared between expectations held for teachers by teachers, school officials, parents, and pupils they usually centered on behaviors involving teachers' self-indulgence, participation in community affairs, and maintenance of discipline (Twyman & Biddle, 1963).

Research in Other Countries. As is true of most fields of educational research, the bulk of the studies reviewed were American in origin, the exceptions being those of Musgrove (1961); Taylor (1962), and the Organization for Comparative Social Research, reported by Jacobson and Schacter (1954). This is unfortunate, because good reasons exist for presuming that expectations for teacher role vary as a result of different educational values, goals, and procedures. For example, teachers in many other countries are educated in training colleges that are outside of the university system, and, again, in many other Western countries the primary and secondary schools are operated by the state within a system of centralized control. The reviewer is aware of only two comparative studies of teacher role, in which data were actually collected from subjects representing more than one country; one is the brief study by Anderson and Anderson (1961) and the other the somewhat longer but unfortunately never adequately reported investigation sponsored by the Organization of Comparative Social Research (Jacobson & Schachter, 1954). Studies of teacher role are presently under way, however, in Britain, Italy, Australia, and elsewhere, and a comparative study will shortly be reported by the reviewer and others in which teacher roles in the major Anglo-American countries are compared.

Comment. It has often been assumed (see, for instance, Soles, 1964; Sorenson & others, 1963; Getzels, 1958) that the study of teacher-role expectations leads to knowledge about teacher-role performance—that expectations and performance are linked either through behavioral conformity to expectations or through expectational accuracy. That this assumption is questionable has been suggested by Biddle and others (1968), who point out that both theory and evidence from other fields suggest independence of the role-performance and role-expectation fields. However, they also observe that so far *no* study has appeared in which teacher-role expectations were measured and corresponding teacher-role performances were observed directly. This startling lack of information leaves us somewhat in the dark about the true meaning of findings for teacher-role expectations. It is reasonable to presume that expectations have "some" effect on behavior; certainly teachers report being aware of the expectations of others, and studies of role conflict in teachers (see, for example, Twyman & Biddle, 1963) are based on the assumption that disparities between expectations held by various groups (or attributed to various groups) lead to problems and unhappiness for the teachers involved. It is also reasonable to presume that "some" expectations are used to plan social behavior, while others may in fact reflect only rationalization, prejudice, or stereotype. Thus, although the behavioral implications of teacher-role information may not be clear at present, the phenomena of teacher-role expectations may be presumed to hold continued interest for teachers and others, and research on this subject will continue to expand because of its own intrinsic interest.

STUDIES OF TEACHER-ROLE PERFORMANCE. In contrast with expectational studies, studies of teacher-role performance have been fewer in number but generally more systematic in their approach. Presumably this reflects the greater cost of investigations of overt behavior. Studies of teacher behavior have also been laid primarily within the classroom context. That is unfortunate; as suggested earlier, studies of teacher-role expectations cover a broader range of contexts than simply the classroom, and patently teachers—especially secondary-school teachers—often exhibit unique and job-related performances in other settings than classrooms, both within the school and in the community. However, majority interest in teacher role-performance research has appeared to stem from concern with the direct effects of teacher behavior on pupil learning, and for such a concern the observation of the classroom would appear to be more relevant. (Besides, classrooms are easier to observe in than is the school lunchroom or playground.) It should also be pointed out that for most investigators, teachers' classroom performance is but an integrated part of the behavioral system of the classroom; thus, many studies have dealt with other behavioral properties of the classroom system in addition to teachers' performance.

Coverage. Generally speaking, investigators of teacher performance to date have attempted to examine only a small range of classroom types. Various criteria have been used to specify the type of classroom to which the investigation was limited, including grade level (Gump, 1967; Hughes, 1959; Meux & Smith, 1964; Nuthall & Lawrence, 1966; B. Smith & others, 1964; Taba & others, 1964), subject matter (Bellack & others, 1963; Biddle & Adams, 1967; Flanders, 1960), social class of pupils (Jackson, 1965; Perkins, 1965; L. Smith & Geoffrey, 1965), pupil achievement (Perkins, 1965; Taba & others, 1964), and pupil adjustment (Kounin & others, 1966). Again, where various classroom structural conditions have been investigated as independent variables, the range of variables chosen has been limited. Studies have dealt with variations in the age and sex of the teacher (Biddle & Adams, 1967), subject matter (Biddle & Adams, 1967; Flanders, 1960; Hughes, 1959), teacher training (Flanders, 1960; Taba & others, 1964; Waimon & Hermanowicz, 1965), nationality differences (Flanders, 1960), and phases of the school year (L. Smith & Geoffrey, 1965). These limitations on coverage and variability of the classroom-situations studies have had effects on the fruitfulness of teacher performance research. First, studies have appeared to be expressions of concepts, methods, and outlook unique to the particular type of classroom investigated. Second, results of studies done so far represent but a restricted range of classroom (let alone of educational) events; for example, of those studies reviewed only that of Louis M. Smith and William Geoffrey (1965) have dealt explicitly with the lower-class school. Finally, the restriction of independent variables limits the possibility of discovering interaction among independent-variable conditions that may determine teachers' classroom performances. It is reasonable to presume, for example, that both teacher-held role expectations and other classroom events help to determine teachers' classroom behavior; but the specific part played by each variable cannot be determined until both are examined within a single study.

Methods of Data Collection. Research on teacher performance has exhibited a wide variety of methodological approaches. These may, however, be classified under three headings: nonparticipant observation, observer rating, and behavioral recording.

In nonparticipant observation (exemplified by studies of Jackson, 1965, and L. Smith & Geoffrey, 1965) the behavioral scientist enters a new social system unobtrusively to take detailed, nonsystematic notes and to develop insights about the culture of the system. Recording, encoding, data analysis, and synthesis all take place in the mind of the observer. This method has its greatest utility in its ability to generate insights and hypotheses; it is not useful for the controlled testing of hypotheses.

In observer rating a human observer enters the classroom to make systematic records of behavioral events. Studies using such techniques exhibit replicable methods of encoding behavior; however, they suffer from an overwhelming difficulty in that a single observer can pick up only a fraction of the events happening concurrently within the classroom. Should the observer focus on the teacher's performance, for instance, he will miss cues that are emitted by the pupils; if he judges behavior for warmth, he will have difficulty also encoding for logic or emphasis or topic. Various forms of observer rating have appeared, including postsession rating, where the behavioral observer is asked to delay rating until after the lesson is over (see Ryans, 1960), sign observation, where the observer is given a list of possible events that might occur in the classroom and asked to check off those that actually occur (see Medley & Mitzel, 1958), and categorical observation, where the observer is provided with a list of categories or scales into which events are to be coded (see, for example, Kowatrakul, 1959; Flanders, 1964; or Perkins, 1964). Of these three forms, categorical observation is the only form of observer rating that provides a sequential record of behavioral events, and it is therefore to be preferred to the other two forms.

A number of recent investigations, however, are based on the use of behavioral recordings, which appear to avoid the limitations of ratings by the live behavioral observer. In behavioral recordings the actual performances of classroom participants are "frozen" by some technological means and may thereafter be replayed over and again until they are adequately coded. Various means of behavior recording have also appeared, including the use of specimen records based on investigator dictation (see Hughes, 1959; Gump & Kounin, 1960; Barker, 1963; Gump, 1967), sound—usually tape—recordings (Bellack & others, 1963; Nuthall & Lawrence, 1966; B. Smith & others, 1964; Taba & others, 1964; Waimon & Hermanowicz, 1965), visual recordings (Gump, 1967), and audiovisual recordings using motion picture film (Kounin & others, 1966) and videotape (Biddle & Adams, 1967; Schueler & others, 1962). Of these various techniques, videotaping offers flexibility, the most complete record, and the least chance of investigator bias. It is, however, an expensive method of collecting data, although a number of additional studies are now under way using videotape as a medium.

Unit of Time. Apart from those who study the lesson as a whole, the investigator of teacher performance, or other classroom phenomena, is faced with the problem of stating a unit of analysis which will then be coded or rated in some fashion. Various units have been suggested for this task. A number of investigators (see Flanders, 1960; Kowatrakul, 1959; Medley & Mitzel, 1963) have made use of arbitrary units of time—for example, a three-second interval at the end of which a rating or code must be given. Other studies (Kounin & others, 1966; Schoggen, 1963; Dyck, 1963; Gump, 1967) report the use of phenomenal units, gross breakdowns in the classroom day that will presumably be recognized by teachers and others, such as "arithmetic lesson," "milk-money time," and "show and tell." Finally, still other investigators have made use of analytic units that are defined in terms of a theoretical system of concepts stated by the investigator. Analytic units may vary widely in size and reflect various conceptual assumptions. For example, one comprehensive set of units is provided by investigators who have focused on direct exchanges between teachers and target pupils. The smallest of these units is the unit act, generally termed a "move." A sequence of moves consisting of a set of exchanges between the teacher and an individual pupil on a single subject matter is called a "reciprocating episode" by B. Othanel Smith and others (1964). A somewhat longer sequence which may involve several target pupils is termed by Smith and others a "coordinate episode, by Nuthall and Lawrence (1966) an "incident," by Waimon and Hermanowicz (1965) a "teaching episode." Two still longer units are also suggested by Smith and others: the "strategy," a set of verbal actions that serves to attain certain results and to guard against others, and the "venture," a segment of discourse consisting of a set of utterances dealing with a single topic and having a single overarching content objective.

Generally speaking, arbitrary units of time have an advantage for observer rating because of their mechanical character. However, they cannot in fact reflect actual behavioral events, and their boundaries may or may not coincide with the boundaries of events we are interested in studying. Phenomenal units are certainly useful for partitioning the primary classroom day. However, our common vocabulary for discussing characteristics of classroom events is not great, and it is unreasonable to assert that smaller phenomenal units are perceived by either the teacher or the pupils. Indeed, when teachers are interviewed about what "went on" in their classroom, they are likely to make their initial description in terms of educational ideology rather than in operational terms. Thus, although there are difficulties with the recognition and formulation of analytic units, which are due in no small part to investigators' own lack of familiarity with or fuzziness about new concepts proposed for the study of classroom events, for serious investigations of teacher performance analytic units appear to be indispensable.

Concepts Used for Teacher Performance. In general, investigators studying the classroom have adopted three distinct postures for coding teacher performance. In some studies, reviewed in this paragraph, the performance of the teacher is abstracted out of the classroom context and is dealt with as a subject of direct investigation. Among the studies in which this posture is adopted, a wide variety of concepts have been proposed for teacher performance. However, in actuality only three basic teacher characteristics appear to have been dealt with. The first of these is teacher's actions, or concepts describing the performances of teachers considered in active or 'verbal' form. Codes for teacher action may be found in studies by Flanders (1960), Hughes (1959), Jackson (1965), and Perkins (1964). A second focus is that of teacher manners, the passive or 'adverbial' ways in which teachers are presumed to conduct their performances. Studies of teacher manners may be found in the studies by Ryans (1960) and Kounin and others (1966). Finally, still another group of investigators has studied the characteristic roles of teachers, that is, the relatively stable patterns of behavior that may be exhibited by teachers in various classroom situations. Investigations exemplifying that approach are those of Perkins (1964) and Gump (1967). Considerable difficulty will be experienced by those who seek to compare lists of items proposed by various investigators for the coding of teachers' actions, manners, and characteristic roles. Most lists appear to offer little more than ad hoc assemblage of items drawn from various theories or insights, to offer little or no theoretical rationale for their unity, and to be innocent of any knowledge that other, overlapping lists were available. In short, of the lists of items that have so far appeared for coding teachers' performances, only a few comprise one or more carefully discriminated analytic *facets*. Thus, research using this first approach has generally violated one of the basic canons of good behavioral research (see Guttman, 1954; Foa, 1965). Whether this violation is simply sloppiness on the part of investigators or reflects an inherent weakness in the posture is not yet clear.

Concepts Used in Studying Teacher-Pupil Interaction. A second approach for studying teacher performance has been through teacher-pupil interaction. In this approach, sequences of interaction between the teacher and one or more target pupils have been recognized, and codes have been devised to reflect the joint characteristics of the sequence. In such cases, teacher performance is embedded within a common, interactive framework, and the teacher's skill is manifested not so much as that of an orator but rather as that of an interaction supervisor. Studies of this nature have been somewhat more theoretically sophisticated than those of the first approach and have generally reflected one or more models.

Language models have appeared in the work of Othanel Smith and others (1964), Nuthall and Lawrence (1966), and Taba and others (1964). Sequences of such a model generally begin with an initiating move by the teacher. They are then continued by the target pupil, may or may not contain additional teacher-target interaction, and are terminated by teacher comment or by a change in the subject matter.

Learning models have been suggested by Nuthall and Lawrence (1966) and are studied more extensively in the research of Waimon and Hermanowicz (1965). In this contrasting model the investigators examined a sequence which begins with behavior by the target pupil which is then acted upon by the teacher's performance as a stimulus. The effectiveness of the stimulus is then judged by changes in the target pupil's behavior.

Decision-making models have not yet been applied directly to the encoding of teacher-target interaction, although L. Smith and Geoffrey (1965) suggested that such a model is probably more adequate than either the language or the learning model. In such a model, concepts are available to express problems that teachers and pupils must overcome in dealing with their collective, classroom world, and Smith and Geoffrey suggest a branching model for interactive sequences in which each move opens up new possibilities for continued interaction.

Flexible models are those in which interactive sequences may be analyzed to check any of a variety of sequence models, the best example of which appears in the work of Bellack and others (1963). It would appear that the analysis of teacher-pupil interaction holds considerable promise and is bound to generate additional research during the next decade.

Concepts of the Classroom as a Social System. Finally a third group of investigators has dealt with teacher behavior as but one component of an analysis of the classroom as an integrated social system. Using this third approach the classroom as a whole is reified, and behavioral characteristics of the total classroom complex are coded; the teacher is viewed neither as an orator nor as an interaction supervisor but rather as the stage manager of a social enterprise, an orchestral conductor. Again, a variety of models have been proposed for examining the classroom. The first of these, communication structure, is built on the fact that classrooms may be broken into one, more than one, or indeed no communicating groups. The integrated lecture is but one aspect of classroom activity; at other times the classroom may exhibit seatwork, a whispered conversation between two deviants in the back of the room, or two or more work groups. Those who have studied communication structure include Gump (1967), Kounin and others (1966), and Biddle and Adams (1967).

Ecological structure deals with the relationships among the bodies of classroom participants and their proximity to and use of the physical properties that are found in the classroom. Among those dealing with ecology are Kounin and others (1966), Biddle and Adams (1967), and Bellack and others (1963). It should be pointed out, however, that the study of classroom ecology is just nascent, and no investigator is known to have systematically studied the effects of chalk, pencils, model airplanes, or carpeting on classroom events.

Activity structure concerns the characteristic modes of activity that may occur in the classroom. Although words for classroom-activity structures are common enough (lecture, discussion, etc.), these concepts have rarely been applied to classroom observation studies. Apparently they simply do not apply reliably to observable patterns of classroom activity. Instead, analytic vocabularies have been devised for the purpose by such investigators as B. Smith and others (1964), Flanders (1960), and Perkins (1964, 1965).

Finally, it is also possible to observe the social functions of the classroom activity, in the end-states or products that are induced by classroom behavior. Functions may be recognized from a variety of theoretical perspectives, including those of instruction, system maintenance, pupil support, teacher self-expression, and classroom culture. Those suggesting codes for social functions include Bellack and others (1963, 1965, 1966), Jackson (1965), Gump (1967), L. Smith and Geoffrey (1965), and Biddle and Adams (1967). The idea of observing joint, social properties of the classroom has appeared only recently in the research literature, and once again it is reasonable to presume that this posture will also generate additional research during the next decade.

Findings. Because of the wide variety of methods, units, and concepts that have been used in studies of teacher-role performance, it is extraordinarily difficult to summarize their collective findings. In addition, as was pointed out earlier, but a small range of classrooms have been studied to date, and with the exception of the study by L. Smith and Geoffrey (1965) no investigation has reported data from a lower-class setting. However, some generalizations may be worthy of note. Several investigators (notably Jackson, 1968) have commented on the rapid pace of classroom exchange. Teachers may be expected to generate several thousand acts or moves or exchanges during the classroom day. The teacher is also a "ringmaster" (Biddle & Adams, 1967). He tends to occupy the center of the classroom much of the time, to engage in formation dissemination within the context of a single, integrated, communication structure, and to communicate with pupils in the physical center of the group. For the pupils the classroom appears to be a setting of some boredom. For one thing, there are many pupils encapsulated into a small area; for another, the teacher's disciplinary control over the classroom is generally quite successful, and pupils have learned to sit in solemn silence rather than to interrupt in other than prescribed ways; and, for still another, the classroom tends to be "an affectional desert" (Flanders, 1960) with but little warmth or indeed any other emotional display on the part of either the teacher or the pupils. These observations point to a classroom that is "traditional" in its orientation. To the extent that these findings may indeed be applied to contemporary role behavior by teachers, the teacher of today has been little affected by a progressive ideology or the concepts of an activity-centered education.

Research in Other Countries. Of the studies reviewed, only that of Nuthall and Lawrence (1966) clearly represents data gathered in another country (New Zealand), while only one study, that of Flanders (1960), compared teaching practices of American teachers with teachers from another country (again New Zealand). There is considerable interest in classroom research in other countries, however, and studies of teacher performance are presently under way in England, Sweden, Australia, New Zealand, and other countries.

Comment. Whereas studies of teacher-role expectations date back at least forty years, serious studies of teacher-role behavior are much more recent. It can be argued, in fact, that the serious study of behavioral phenomena was impossible before the invention of modern techniques for behavioral recording. However that may be, studies of teacher-role behavior are bound to proliferate. They are of relevance to teachers, administrators, teacher trainees, and others who are concerned with the teaching profession. In addition, the study of actual educational behavior bears the promise of the eventual development of an empirically based theory of education.

Bruce J. Biddle
University of Missouri

References

Allen, A. T., and Seaberg, D. I. "Teachers-in-the-Becoming." *El Sch J* 64:332–8; 1964.

Anderson, H. H., and Anderson, Gladys L. "Image of the Teacher by Adolescent Children in Seven Countries." *Am J Orthopsychiatry* 31:481–92; 1961.

Arkoff, A., and Shears, Loyda. "Conceptions of 'Ideal' Leadership in Accepted and Rejected Principal Training Candidates." *J Ed Res* 55:71–4; 1961.

Babchuck, N., and Bates, A. P. "Professor or Producer: The Two Faces of Academic Man." *Soc Forces* 40:341–8; 1962.

Barker, Roger G. *The Stream of Behavior: Exploration of Its Structure and Content.* Appleton, 1963. 352p.

Becker, H. S. "The Teacher in the Authority System of the Public School." *J Ed Sociol* 27:128–41; 1953.

Bellack, Arno A., and others. *The Language of the Classroom: Meanings Communicated in High School Teaching,* USOE Cooperative Research Project No. 1497, Institute of Psychological Research, Teachers Col, Columbia U, 1963. 200p.

Bellack, Arno A., and others. *The Language of the Classroom: Meanings Communicated in High School Teaching,* Part II. USOE Cooperative Research Project, No. 2023, Institute of Psychological

Research, Teachers Col, Columbia U, 1965. 260p.
Bellack, Arno A., and others. *The Language of the Classroom*. Institute of Psychological Research, Teachers Col, Columbia U, 1966. 274p.
Biddle, Bruce J., and Adams, Raymond S. *An Analysis of Classroom Activities*. Missouri U, 1967. 715p.
Biddle, Bruce J., and Thomas, Edwin J. (Eds.) *Role Theory: Concepts and Research*. Wiley, 1966. 453p.
Biddle, Bruce J., and others. "The Role of the Teacher and Occupational Choice." *Sch R* 70:191–206; 1962.
Biddle, Bruce J., and others. "Teacher Role: Conceptions and Behavior." In Biddle, Bruce J. (Ed.) *Essays on the Social Systems of Education*. Holt, 1968.
Bidwell, C. E. "The Administrative Role and Satisfaction in Teaching." *J Ed Sociol* 29:41–7; 1955.
Bogen, I. "Pupil-Teacher Rapport and the Teacher's Awareness of Status Structures Within the Group." *J Ed Sociol* 28:104–14; 1954.
Bradley, R. C. "Clarifying the Supervising Teacher's Role." *Teach Col J* 38:92–4; 1966.
Brenner, D. J., and others. "Views of Prospective Teachers and Non-teachers in a Journalism Graduate Class Toward Teaching." *Journalism Q* 41:253–8; 1962.
Brookover, W. B. "The Social Roles of Teachers and Pupil Achievement." *Am Sociol R* 8:389–93; 1943.
Carson, J. O., Jr., and Schultz, R. E. "A Comparative Analysis of the Junior College Dean's Leadership Behavior." *J Exp Ed* 32:355–62; 1964.
Champlin, C. D. "Attributes Desired in College Instructior." *Sch Soc* 33:89–90; 1931.
Charters, W. W., and Waples, D. *The Commonwealth Teacher-training Study*. U Chicago Press, 1929.
Cheong, G. S., and DeVault, M. V. "Pupils Perceptions of Teachers." *J Ed Res* 59:446–9; 1966.
Chilcott, J. H. "The School Teacher Stereotype: 'A New Look.'" *J Ed Sociol* 34:389–90; 1961.
Clinton, R. J. "Qualities College Students Desire in College Instructors." *Sch Soc* 32:702; 1930.
Cobb, P. R. "High School Seniors' Attitudes Toward Teachers and the Teaching Profession." Nat Assn Sec Sch Prin B 36:140–4; 1952.
Collins, H. A., and Smith, A. C. "The Vocational Values of Special Education Teachers." *Excep Child* 31:487; 1965.
Colombotos, J. "Sex-role Area Professionalism: A Study of High-school Teachers." *Sch R* 71:27–40; 1963.
Dallolil, Helen C. "Teachers on Trial: Group of Pupils Tell What They Like in Teachers." *Clearing House* 29:497–9; 1955.
Davies, J. E. "What Are the Traits of the Good Teacher from the Standpoint of Junior High School Pupils?" *Sch Soc* 38:649–52; 1933.
Demos, G. D., and Belok, M. V. "The Professional Image." *Voc Guid Q* 12:46–9; 1963.
Dunlop, R. S. "Professional Educators, Parents, and Students Assess the Counselor's Role." *Personnel Guid J* 43:1024–8; 1965.

Dyck, Arthur J. "The Social Contracts of Some Midwest Children with Their Parents and Teachers." In Barker, Roger E. (Ed.) *The Stream of Behavior: Exploration of Its Structure and Content*. Appleton, 1963. p. 78–98.
Fausti, R. P., and Moore, N. J. "The Affiliative Relationship Between the Student and the Teacher." *Speech Teach* 15:197–9; 1966.
Fishburn, C. E. "Teacher Role Perception in the Secondary School." *J Teach Ed* 13:55–9; 1962.
Flanders, Ned A. *Teacher Influence, Pupil Attitudes, and Achievement: Studies in Interaction Analysis*. Minnesota, 1960. 121p.
Flanders, Ned A. "Some Relationships Among Teacher Influence, Pupil Attitudes, and Achievement." In Biddle, Bruce J., and Ellena, William J. (Eds.) *Contemporary Research on Teacher Effectiveness*. Holt, 1964. p. 196–231.
Foa, Uriel G. "New Developments in Facet Design and Analysis." *Psychol R* 72:262–74; 1965.
Furst, E. J. "A Factor Analysis of Preferences in Teacher Role Behavior." *J Exp Ed* 33:379–82; 1965.
Getzels, J. W. "Administration as a Social Process." In Halpin, A. W. (Ed.) *Administrative Theory in Education*. U Chicago, 1958. p. 150–65.
Getzels, J. W., and Guba, E. G. "The Structure of Roles and Role Conflict in the Teaching Situation." *J Ed Sociol* 29:30–40; 1955.
Gordon, C. W. "The Role of the Teacher in the Social Structure of the High School." *J Ed Sociol* 29:21–9; 1955.
Greenhoe, Florence. "Community Contacts of Public-school Teachers." *El Sch J* 40:497–506; 1940.
Gump, Paul V. *Setting Variables and the Prediction of Teacher Behavior*. U Kansas, 1967. 11p.
Gump, Paul V., and Kounin, Jacob S. "Issues Raised by Ecological and 'Classical' Research Efforts." *Merrill Palmer Q* 6:145–52; 1960.
Gutman, Louis P. "A New Approach to Factor Analysis: The Radex." In Lazarsfeld, Paul F. (Ed.) *Mathematical Thinking in the Social Sciences*. Free, 1954. p. 258–348.
Haer, J. L. "The Public Views the Teacher." *J Teach Ed* 4:202–4; 1953.
Haggard, W. W. "Some Freshmen Describe the Desirable College Teacher." *Sch Soc* 58:238–40; 1943.
Hanson, E. M., and Umstattd, J. G. "Mores and Teacher Selection in Minnesota." *Sch Soc* 45:579–82; 1937.
Hart, J. W. "Socially Mobile Teachers and Classroom Atmosphere." *J Ed Res* 59:166–8; 1965.
Hatfield, Agnes B. "An Experimental Study of the Self-concept of Student Teachers." *J Ed Res* 55:87–9; 1961.
Hughes, Marie M. *Development of the Means for the Assessment of the Quality of Teaching in Elementary Schools*. USOE Cooperative Research Project No. 353, U Utah, 1959. 314p.
Jackson, Philip W. *Teacher-Pupil Communication in the Elementary Classroom: An Observational Study*. Chicago, 1965. 17p.

Jackson, Philip W. *Life in Classrooms.* Holt, 1968.
Jacobson, Eugene, and Schachter, Stanley (Eds.) "Cross-national Research: A Case Study." *J Social Issues* 10:4–70; 1954.
Jones, R. L., and Gottfried, N. W. "The Prestige of Special Education Teaching." *Excep Child* 32:465–8; 1966.
Jordan, F. "A Study of Personal and Social Traits in Relation to High-school Teaching," *J Ed Sociol* 3:27–43; 1929.
Keighin, Mary A. "Thornburn Teachers Rated on Their Own Terms." *Clearing House* 23:82–3; 1948.
Koopman, Margaret O. "What One Midwestern Community Thinks of Its Teachers." *Ed Res B* 25:34–41; 1946.
Kounin, Jacob S., and others. "Managing Emotionally Disturbed Children in Regular Classrooms." *J Ed Psychol* 57:1–13; 1966.
Kowatrakul, Surang. "Some Behaviors of Elementary School Children Related to Classroom Activities and Subject Areas." *J Ed Psychol* 50:121–8; 1959.
Lacognata, A. A. "University Extension Faculty and Student Role Expectations: An Empirical Analysis." *J Exp Ed* 33:107–20; 1964.
Lacognata, A. A. "Faculty Academic Role Expectations." *J Social Psychol* 66:337–44; 1965.
Lamson, Edna E. "Some College Students Describe the Desirable College Teacher." *Sch Soc* 56:615; 1942.
Lantz, D. L. "Relationship Between Classroom Emotional Climate and Concepts of Self, Others, and Ideal Among Elementary Student Teachers." *J Ed Res* 59:80–3; 1965.
Manwiller, L. V. "Expectations Regarding Teachers." *J Exp Ed* 26:315–54; 1958.
Mason, W. S., and others. "Sex Role and the Career Orientations of Beginning Teachers." *Harvard Ed R* 29:370–83; 1959.
Mays, N. "Behavioral Expectations of Negro and White Teachers on Recently Desegregated Public School Facilities." *J Negro Ed* 32:218–26; 1963.
McGill, K. H. "The School-teacher Stereotype." *J Ed Sociol* 4:642–50; 1931.
Medley, Donald M., and Mitzel, Harold E. "A Technique for Measuring Classroom Behavior." *J Ed Psychol* 49:86–92; 1958.
Medley, Donald M., and Mitzel, Harold E. "Measuring Classroom Behavior by Systematic Observation." In Gage, N. L. (Ed.) *Handbook of Research on Teaching.* Rand McNally, 1963. p. 247–328.
Merrill, M. R., and Jex, F. B. "Role Conflict in Successful Science Teachers." *J Ed Res* 58:72–4; 1964.
Meus, Milton, and Smith, B. Othanel. "Logical Dimensions of Teaching Behavior." In Biddle, Bruce J., and Ellena, William J. (Eds.) *Contemporary Research on Teacher Effectiveness.* Holt, 1964. p. 127–64.
Musgrove, S. "Parents' Expectations of the Junior School." *Sociol R* 9:167–80; 1961.
Nuthall, Graham A., and Lawrence, P. J. *Thinking in the Classroom.* New Zealand Council for Educational Research, 1966. 60p.

Perkins, Hugh V. "A Procedure for Assessing the Classroom Behavior of Students and Teachers." *Am Ed Res J* 1:249–60; 1964.
Perkins, Hugh V. "Classroom Behavior and Underachievement." *Am Ed Res J* 2:1–12; 1965.
Phillips, B. N. "Community Control of Teacher Behavior." *J Teach Ed* 6:293–300; 1955.
Reitz, W. E., and others. "Experience, Expertness, and Ideal Teaching Relationships." *Ed Psychol Meas* 25:1051–60; 1965.
Richey, R. W., and Fox, W. H. "How Do Teachers Compare with Other Community Members?" *Ed Res B* 27:238–41, 247–8; 1948.
Rippee, B. D., and others. "The Influence of Counseling on the Perception of Counselor Role." *Personnel Guid J* 43:696–701; 1965.
Rogers, Dorothy. "Implications of Views Concerning the 'typical' School Teacher." *J Ed Sociol* 23:482–7; 1950.
Ryan, K. "Teaching Intern: A Sociological Stranger." *J Teach Ed* 17:185–91; 1966.
Ryans, David G. *Characteristics of Teachers: Their Description, Comparison, and Appraisal.* ACE, 1960. 416p.
Schmidt, L. D. "Concepts of the Role of Secondary School Counselors." *Personnel Guid J* 40:600–5; 1962.
Schoggen, Phil. "Environmental Forces in the Everyday Lives of Children." In Barker, Roger G. (Ed.) *The Stream of Behavior: Exploration of Its Structure and Content.* Appleton, 1963. p. 42–69.
Schueler, Herbert, and others. *The Use of Television for Improving Teacher Training and for Improving Measures of Student-teacher Performance.* Phase I: *Improvement of Student Teaching.* New York, 1962. 127p.
Seidman, J. M., and Knapp, Leda B. "Teacher Likes and Dislikes of Student Behavior and Student Perceptions of These Attitudes." *J Ed Res* 47:143–9; 1953.
Smith, A. A. "What Is Good College Teaching?" *J H Ed* 15:216–8; 1944.
Smith, B. Othanel, and others. "A Tentative Report on the Strategies of Teaching." Bureau of Educational Research, U Illinois, 1964. 103p.
Smith, D. M., and Cooper, Bernice. "An Analysis of Certain Aspects of Teacher-Pupil and Parent Opinions." *J Social Psychol* 66:191–9; 1965.
Smith, Louis M., and Geoffrey, William. *Toward a Model of Teacher Decision-making in an Urban Classroom.* Washington U, 1965. 245p.
Smith, T. E. "The Image of High-school Teachers: Self and Other, Real and Ideal (Should Teachers Be Seen and Not Heard?)" *J Ed Res* 59:99–104; 1965.
Soles, S. "Teacher Role Expectations and the Internal Organization of Secondary Schools." *J Ed Res* 57:227–38; 1964.
Soper, D. W., and Combs, A. W. "The Helping Relationship as Seen by Teachers and Therapists." *J Cons Psychol* 26:288; 1962.
Sorenson, A. G., and others. "Divergent Concepts of Teacher Role: An Approach to the Measurement

of Teacher Effectiveness." *J Ed Psychol* 54:287–94; 1963.

Story, M. L. "Public Attitude Is Changing Toward the Teacher's Personal Freedom." *Nation's Sch* 45:69–70; 1950.

Strong, D. J., and Insel, S. A. "Perceptions of the Counselor Role Among a Variety of Rehabilitation Counseling Supervisors." *J Counseling Psychol* 12:141–7; 1965.

Taba, Hilda, and others. *Thinking in Elementary School Children*. USOE Cooperative Research Project No. 1574, San Francisco State Col, 1964. 207p.

Taylor, P. H. "Children's Evaluations of the Characteristics of a Good Teacher." *Br J Ed Psychol* 32:258–66; 1962.

Terrien, F. W. "Who Thinks What About Educators?" *Am J Sociol* 59:150–8; 1953.

Terrien, F. W. "The Occupational Roles of Teachers." *J Ed Sociol* 29:14–20; 1955.

Tiedeman, S. C. "A Study of Pupil-teacher Relationship." *J Ed Res* 35:657–64; 1942.

Trabue, M. R. "Judgments by 820 College Executives of Traits Desirable in Lower-Division College Teachers." *J Exp Ed* 21:337–41; 1953.

Twyman, J. P., and Biddle, Bruce J. "Role Conflict of Public School Teachers." *J Psychol* 55:183–98; 1963.

Very, P. S., and Dye, N. W. "Conceptualizations of the College Teacher." *Perceptual Motor Skills* 22:889–90; 1966.

Waimon, Morton D., and Hermanowicz, Henry J. *A Conceptual System for Prospective Teachers to Study Teaching Behavior*. Illinois State U, 1965. 18p.

Warman, R. E. "Differential Perceptions of Counseling Role." *J Counseling Psychol* 7:269–74; 1960.

Washburne, C. "The Teacher in the Authority System." *J Ed Sociol* 30:390–4; 1957.

Watley, D. J. "How Do Counselors Perceive Their Ideal Roles?" *J Counseling Psychol* 12:102; 1965.

Yamamoto, Kaoru, and Dizney, Henry F. "Eight Professors: A Study on College Students' Preferences Among Their Teachers." *J Ed Psychol* 57:146–50; 1966.

Yourglich, Anita. "Study on Correlations Between College Teachers' and Students' Concepts of 'Ideal-student' and 'Ideal-teacher.'" *J Ed Res* 49:59–64; 1955.

TEACHING METHODS

Teaching methods inevitably constitute significant aspects of the human effort to educate. Along with the questions of who shall be educated and for what ends, the question of how to teach is perennial. This article deals with the definition, history, and dimensionalization of teaching methods; with the relationships of teaching method to educational objectives and other factors; and with some of the currently recognized "methods," namely, classroom discourse, the lecture method, the discussion method, and the discovery method. Other reviews of research on teaching methods have been provided by Wallen and Travers (1963), who also presented a general learning model for analyzing teaching methods; by McKeachie (1967), who focused on teaching methods in higher education; by Withall and Lewis (1963), who dealt with social interaction in the classroom; and by authors of chapters in the *Handbook of Research on Teaching* (Gage, 1963) on teaching at two levels (nursery school and college) and in various subject matters (reading, social studies, composition and literature, secondary school mathematics, science, foreign languages, and the visual arts).

DEFINITION. Teaching methods are patterns of teacher behavior that are recurrent, applicable to various subject matters, characteristic of more than one teacher, and relevant to learning. Teaching methods so defined refer to a human teacher and may be considered a subcategory of educational methods, which also include instructional devices (educational methods that employ nonhuman media), such as teaching machines, conventional and programmed textbooks, simulators, films, and the like. (See articles on PROGRAMMED INSTRUCTION and EDUCATIONAL COMMUNICATIONS MEDIA.)

A pattern of teacher behaviors is a set of behaviors that occurs either simultaneously or in sequence in a unified way. In the lecture method, for example, the pattern consists of an uninterrupted sequence of oral statements by the teacher; in classroom discourse, Bellack and others (1966) found that "The fundamental pedagogical pattern of discourse consisted of a teacher's solicitation followed by a pupil's response; this sequence was frequently followed by a teacher's reaction." Here the component behaviors are the teacher's asking a question, the pupil's response, and the teacher's reaction to or rating of the pupil's response; their occurrence in a given sequence constitutes the pattern, and the recurrence of the pattern constitutes a teaching method.

By recurrence is meant the repetition of the pattern of teacher behavior over intervals measured in minutes or weeks. The interval depends on the duration of the behavior pattern and the frequency of the occasions on which it is used. Some patterns recur frequently, that is, every few minutes or every hour. But a pattern may be used as infrequently as once a year, as when certain methods are used for teaching subtraction or the meaning of allegory.

A teaching method is typically applicable to more than one topic or specific objective. At one extreme, a special teaching method may be applicable to only one objective, such as demonstration of a proof in teaching ability to recall the Pythagorean theorem. A general teaching method can also be applied to a whole course of study, such as the discovery method in secondary school mathematics or the lecture method in introductory sociology. In its most general sense, a teaching method, such as the lecture method or the discussion method, is applicable to all subjects. This article deals with such general teaching methods; for teaching methods relevant only to a single subject or grade level (such as reading or mathematics, the nursery school or college), the reader should examine the various articles in this work relating to those subjects or levels. Within the literature of those subjects will also be found treatments of teaching methods related to specific objectives, such as word recognition in reading or computational skills in arithmetic.

A teaching method must be usable by more than one teacher. If a pattern of behavior is unique to one teacher and unavailable, for whatever reason, to other teachers, it is not regarded as a teaching method. In this respect, a teaching method is comparable to a "role" as defined by social psychologists. That is, it involves a relatively uniform set of behaviors expected of persons occupying a given position, such as lecturer or discussion leader. Variations of behavior within the teaching method, or role, are then attributed to the "personality" of the teachers (cf. Getzels and Jackson, 1963).

The term "teaching method" is sometimes used to refer not to teacher behavior patterns but to curricular materials of some kind. Such use of the term reflects the indistinctness of the boundary between curriculum and teaching method. Typically, these terms refer to what is taught and how it is taught, respectively, but their referents may interact and fuse. Thus, the issue of meaningful versus rote methods of teaching subtraction (Brownell and Moser, 1949) may be regarded as a matter of either curriculum or teaching method. Similarly, the concept of teaching method is frequently used to embrace such things as the initial teaching alphabet, the color phonics system, the chemical bond approach, and the chronological versus topical methods of teaching music appreciation. The present article, however, does not deal with teaching methods in this sense, despite their influence on teacher behavior. For discussion of these aspects of method, see CURRICULUM.

Some writers have found that teaching methods do not account for significant variance in educational outcomes. Thus, Wallen and Travers (1963) concluded that "teaching methods do not seem to make much difference" and that "there is hardly any direct evidence to favor one method over another." Siegel and Siegel (1967) stated, ". . . it is generally discovered that students learn about as much when exposed to one kind of instructional environment as they do when exposed to another. The absence of significant differences is reported with monotonous regularity." Stephens (1967) concluded that practically no "administrative device," including teaching methods, makes much difference in what the school accomplishes, after background factors (such as maturational tendencies and home and community environment) and spontaneous tendencies of teachers and learners have had their overall effect. Summary statements of this kind were used by Stephens as one basis for his "theory of spontaneous schooling," which relegates teaching method to a minor role among the factors that determine attainment of the objectives of schooling.

These broad generalizations need to be tempered by consideration of more specific questions. The present article deals with a sample of such issues. Although positive results remain hard to come by, some can be cited to indicate that, depending on which teaching methods are considered, they can make a difference in educational outcomes.

HISTORY. First, however, this article deals with the history of teaching methods. It is possible to see many precursors of contemporary research issues in that history. Hedegard (1967) reviewed historical formulations of theories of instruction in terms of nine dimensions: structure of the learning process, modeling and identification, learner behavior vis-à-vis the teacher, reward and punishment, moral development, learner motives and emotions, relationship between school and home, adaptability as an instructional outcome, and ego development as an instructional outcome. The theories considered included those of the ancient Greeks, the Jesuits, Comenius, Pestalozzi, Froebel, Herbart, Montessori, James, Dewey, Neill, and Ashton-Warner.

Saettler (1968) described many of the same figures as background for an account of the development of school museums, instructional films, the audio-visual movement, instructional radio and television, programmed instruction, and the systems approach. He also dealt with the Lancasterian and Montessori methods and drew E. L. Thorndike, John Dewey, Carleton Washburne, Helen Parkhurst, Henry C. Morrison, Kurt Lewin, and B. F. Skinner into the historical narrative. McDonald (1964) reviewed the influence of learning theories on education; he gave particular attention to the influences of William James, G. Stanley Hall, E. L. Thorndike, John Dewey, Boyd Bode, the Gestaltists, the Freudians, and the functionalists.

In their account, organized in terms of 11 major "exemplars," Broudy and Palmer (1965) covered the centuries from ancient Greece to Deweyan progressivism. The following sketches are based on their description.

1. The Rhetoricians used the method of systematized imitation to teach young men of ancient Athens to speak effectively.

2. Socrates used exhortation to induce the learner to become concerned about achieving the good, true, and beautiful and engaged the learner in dialectical self-examination. He also used a kind of conditioning to discipline appetites. His method culminated in intellectual training in dialectics by means of the Socratic dialogue, whereby deductive relations were discovered to exist in reality, definitions were clarified, and the relations between them were tested. His first step, creating anxiety in the learner about his own knowledge, required much of the teacher, especially an ability to combine the tragic and the comic, logic and myth.

3. Alcuin, aiming largely at inculcating literacy in Latin in the eighth century A.D., made use of riddles,

poems, puzzles, and witty exchanges but also emphasized drill and repetition.

4. Abelard, in the twelfth century, used the lecture method, structured materials logically, and argued theological and philosophical issues by the method of reconciliation between affirmative and negative sides of a question. Such reconciliation entailed exploring contexts, disproving textual corruptions, judging real meanings of texts, ensuring that no retractions were on record, and searching out the circumstances that led up to an enactment or decision. In addition to lectures, he used disputation with doctrinal opponents to train and certify teachers. St. Thomas Aquinas further developed the method of logical demonstration by requiring the lecturer to formulate the question, consider the authorities, offer his own solution, and refute counterarguments. Students learned to give lectures modeled after the master's. In the disputation —a kind of logical sparring—two opponents sharpened their skills in using the rules of deduction, induction, and evidence.

5. Ascham, in the sixteenth century, taught the classics by the tutorial method (that is, one teacher working with one student) and also used the method of double translation in teaching languages. The curriculum was based on the theory of imitation, whereby one studied how a model (e.g., Cicero) had himself imitated others (e.g., certain Greeks). First, the student translated from Latin to English and then, after an interval, he tried to translate his English into the original Latin. Syntax was thus to be learned by imitating the best writers. Discipline was to be maintained by the teacher's cheerfulness, praise, love, and gentleness, rather than by their opposites. Individual differences were also noted: children of "hard" wit, that is, who were low in pliability and suggestibility, might prove more valuable products of education in the long run than those of "quick" wit, and should be recognized and treated appropriately.

6. The Jesuits, in the sixteenth century, systematized materials, methods, and teacher training in order to standardize procedures for motivation, presentation, practice, and testing. Individual and team rivalry was used to motivate and also to instruct pupils, since rivals would try to catch and correct every mistake. Even more important was teacher approval and disapproval. Corporal punishment was to be inflicted not by the teacher but by a Corrector, and misdeeds were to be overlooked when possible. To present material, teachers used prelection, or studying the assignment aloud. To ensure overlapping review, every segment of instruction—the day's lecture, the week's work, the term's course—was reviewed soon after its completion. Written assignments, handed in regularly, were corrected by the teacher or fellow pupils or by the pupil himself.

7. Comenius, in the seventeenth century, advocated the principle of proceeding from the universal, or most general, to the particular, or most detailed, with the broad topics being covered at an appropriate level at every stage of the learner's development. He urged understanding rather than mere memorization, explaining the purpose of tasks, learning through teaching others, correlating words with things, and relating amusement to serious study. In teaching the arts, the method should be that of eliciting imitation of a model and providing immediate correction.

8. Pestalozzi (1746–1827) advocated showing pupils that they were loved and thereby sought to release their powers, spirit, and efficiency. He gave pupils freedom of physical movement and respected their interests and abilities. Subject matter was to be adjusted to capacity. Instruction, like intellectual development, was to proceed from simple to complex, from concrete to abstract, from particular to universal. Instruction must use number, form, and language, each analyzed into simple and concrete units that were later to be combined into more complex and abstract ones. The pupil was given images, models, or criteria of the desirable patterns of responses. In object lessons, real objects were discussed in a progression from sense impressions to formal definitions, that is, in an inductive process of concept formation.

9. Froebel (1782–1852) invented the kindergarten out of a concern for the laws of human development, which he regarded as entailing "opposition," or a swing between opposites. The law of converse influence, whereby one looks for causes in what is radically different from what is being caused, implied that teaching should be "simultaneously double-sided— giving and taking, uniting and dividing, prescribing and following, active and passive, positive yet giving scope, firm and yielding. . . ." The whole process was to be guided by a third something: namely, the right, the best, the ideal. A recapitulation theory of development—the individual develops through the same stages as the race has gone through—should guide curriculum development. In the kindergarten, the curriculum emphasized drawing, rhythm, manipulation of materials, and play.

10. Herbart (1776–1841) formulated ideas used by his followers to identify steps in teaching: preparation, presentation, association, systematization, and application. In his view, cognition was basic to both feeling and willing, and human experience was derived from presentations, received through the nervous system, that are compared, abstracted, and generalized in developing concepts. The child's experience and social intercourse have given him basic elementary ideas and sympathies of which he quickly becomes conscious. Instruction is a process of building the apperceptive mass out of clusters of ideas. Preparation has two aspects, motivational and cognitive. Motivation can take extrinsic or intrinsic forms. Cognitive preparation entails recalling similar, analogous, opposite, antecedent, consequent, or other materials relevant to the learning task. If the available ideas are inadequate, the teacher must clarify or reorganize them. Some preparation precedes the class meeting; the rest comes from inducing pupils to talk about matters related to the lesson. Intrinsic interests may be irrelevant, but apperception is itself rewarding and produces new interests that facilitate learning. Presentation, aimed at engendering clear awareness of an object or unit, is aided by vividness, clarity of perception, verbalization, and the learner's possession

of organizing principles appropriate to the subject matter. Association, or comparison and contrast of instances, builds concepts. Systematization puts facts and generalizations together in appropriate groupings. Teaching is to be aimed at finding the ways of organizing ideas that will facilitate their recall when needed. The intellectual disciplines provide such organization for classifying ideas. Finally, application is needed to test the new learning—its firmness, its connection with interests, its availability for future learning, and its transferability to new materials.

11. Kilpatrick (1871–1965), John Dewey's foremost disciple, advocated the project method. Teachers should involve learners in wholehearted activity aimed at solving problems that are real to the learners and related to their genuine concerns. Having involved the pupils, the teacher should help them plan, execute, and evaluate their work on the problems identified and selected. In this process, the teacher's own mastery of intellectual disciplines may be less important than his interpersonal sensitivities and skills. Even skills like reading and multiplication could best be developed through the activities entailed in projects, such as putting together a bulletin board or determining the proper number of sheets of paper for a publication.

In these sketches of teaching methods advocated by historic figures, anticipations of the following contemporary ideas and issues may be discerned: the learner's developmental stages; theories of cognitive development; categories of educational objectives; types of motivation; social arrangements, ranging from independent study through tutoring and dialogues to competitions and lectures; issues in cognitive structuring, such as the inductive versus the deductive arrangement of learning experiences and the use of drill and games; the interaction of teaching methods with learner characteristics, so that optimal outcomes are attainable only through some individualization; the standardization of materials; and the systematization of experiences. All these concerns of the historic exemplars have counterparts in the research and developmental work of the 1960's.

THE OBJECTIVES-METHODS MATRIX. Teaching methods are means toward ends—the latter being educational, or instructional, objectives. No method is best in any absolute sense; its value depends on its causal relationship to the learner's achievement of one or more objectives of education. Any valid evaluation of a teaching method must be related to some objective or goal. Hence, it is useful to envision an "objectives-methods matrix," in which the rows represent various objectives and the columns represent various teaching methods. Into the cells of such a matrix would be inserted a measure of the suitability of the method for promoting achievement of the objective. For example, in considering the lecture method, one should in all logic have clearly identified the objectives for which it will be used. In one view (Buxton, 1956), lectures in college courses should not be highly similar to the reading material or merely repeat it; nor should the lecture material be completely unrelated to what has been read. Rather, the lectures should reinforce, supplement, and illuminate what the students have been asked to read. In another view, set forth in a "matrix of goals and tools" (Walker and McKeachie, 1967), lectures should be used primarily for presenting the newest developments in the field and for communicating the intrinsic interest of the subject matter; secondarily, for introducing the full range of subject matter and providing an identification model; and not at all for communicating elementary concepts, providing facts in support of the concepts, integrating the course material, communicating the basic attitudes of the discipline, providing individual guidance and monitoring, or developing selected intellectual skills.

The matrix would need additional dimensions if other relevant parameters, such as learner characteristics, were taken into account. That is, if some methods are optimal for certain objectives only for pupils with certain aptitudes (Cronbach, 1957), then the matrix would need a third dimension referring to pupil aptitudes. Similarly, if objectives are defined in terms specific to subject matters, then a fourth dimension must be assigned to subject matters, such as reading or mathematics.

Such a "multivariate paradigm" has been set forth by Siegel and Siegel (1967). Beyond instructor variables, their paradigm includes: (1) as independent variables, the learning environment, learner variables, and course variables; and (2) as dependent variables, factual and conceptual achievement, thought processes, attitude, and extraclass behavior.

This article does not focus on these several kinds of variables, other than teaching method, that are extremely influential in determining educational outcomes. Among these are the various characteristics of the learner, such as his intelligence, prior knowledge, and motivation, and the various characteristics of the subject matter, such as the ways in which it is structured, its content, and its level in relation to the preparation of the student. In view of the focus of this article, such variables, and their interactions with teaching methods, are not considered here. Furthermore, the choice of teaching method must inevitably be influenced by various administrative factors over which a teacher may have no control, such as the size of the group to be taught, the size of the room, the time available, the seating and other physical arrangements, and the communications media available (film projectors, record players, and so on).

THE PROBLEM OF DIMENSIONALIZATION. Throughout the history of the study of teaching methods, the problems of classification and dimensionalization have received much attention. Educators have distinguished methods from one another on many different bases. Wallen and Travers (1963), for example, classified teaching methods on the basis of their origins in teaching traditions, social learnings in the teacher's background, philosophical traditions, the teacher's own needs, conditions existing in the school and community, and scientific research on learning. Monroe and Marks (1938) simply distinguished and described the "general" methods—those applicable in two or more subject-matter fields—that were current at the time they wrote: lecture method, recitation method, object teaching, development methods, laboratory method, project method, problem method, socialized recitation, and the Morrison unit-mastery plan. More recently, this kind of categorization has given way, for the most part, to a few much broader categories: lecture, discussion, and discovery. Probably the most widely used "method" nowadays is what may be called the "classroom discourse," discussed below.

Before discussing these categories, it is appropriate to consider the general problem of dimensionalization—the problem of finding ways to compare methods along basic underlying dimensions so that the differences between them can be more clearly identified and their effects can be more closely associated with those differences. Just how does the lecture method differ from the discussion method? Just how does classroom discourse differ from discussion? Just how does one teacher's classroom discourse differ from another's? To answer such questions in scientifically useful terms requires identifying a set of basic dimensions, locating the methods on these dimensions, and specifying the differences in terms of these locations. Then it will become possible to attribute the differences in effects of the methods more clearly to the specifiable differences in the methods conceived as independent variables. In short, it is necessary to penetrate beneath the global terminology referring to "methods" to the specifics of teacher and learner behavior for which the terms stand.

Such a program of dimensionalization has been sketched by Medley (1967) as one aimed at defining a "teacher behavior space," whose axes would represent dimensions along which teacher behaviors vary. Any teacher's behavior would be plotted as a point in the space of N dimensions. Actual and ideal behavior, pre- and post-training behavior, effective and ineffective behavior—all these could be represented by pairs of points in the space.

CLASSROOM DISCOURSE. Because most efforts at dimensionalization of teacher behavior have been directed at the study of classroom discourse, the problem will be considered here in that framework. Classroom discourse is the most prevalent and the most loosely defined teaching method. It consists of a mixture of brief and informal lectures with discussions and recitations. The nature of the mixture has been studied by many observers and recorders of classroom behavior and interaction. It consists in large part of the recitation method, in which teachers ask questions based on reading assignments, but it ranges more freely into teacher explanations, free discussions, and questions aimed at provoking the learner's discovery of ideas on his own. Despite its prevalence, it has not frequently been considered a "method" and has been subjected to detailed description and analysis only in the last two decades.

Logical Approaches. To define the dimensions of classroom discourse requires a variety of logical and empirical approaches. A logical approach, entailing analysis of teaching into "technical skills," has been developed as part of the microteaching procedure in teacher education (Bush, 1966). Microteaching consists of a small segment of teaching, performed in five to ten minutes, in a class of about five pupils, to practice a single technical skill. To define a technical skill requires an analysis of teaching, and thus far analyses have yielded such skills as "higher-order questioning," "the use of silence and nonverbal cues to promote and guide discussion," "reinforcement," and "set induction." Five categories, each embracing several skills, have been identified: initiating, presenting, consolidating, monitoring, and evaluating.

A second logical approach is that exemplified in an anthology of 26 classroom observation instruments (Simon and Boyer, 1967), whose editors were able to classify the systems successively according to the following sets of dimensions for their foci: (1) affective, cognitive, work process, or behavioral events; (2) verbal or nonverbal behavior, or both; and (3) teacher, students, or both. Further, they classified all the affective categories, or teachers' positive-negative reactions, into four dimensions dealing with pupil ideas or cognitive output, feelings or emotional output, attempts to manage classroom procedure and set standards, and nonverbal behavior. The cognitive systems were classified according to processes (data recall, data processing, and evaluation) and categories of verbal behavior (for example, stating, explaining, quoting, interpreting, and elaborating).

Empirical Approaches. Among empirical approaches, factor analysis has obvious potential. The behaviors of a large sample of teachers would be measured on many variables of the kinds that have been specified by Flanders (1964), Smith and others (1967), Bellack and others (1966), Spaulding (1965), Medley and Mitzel (1959), and others. Then the intercorrelations of the scores on the variables would be subjected to factor analysis. The resulting factors would define the dimensions in relatively parsimonious, or "simple structure," terms. One difficulty with this approach, as Meux (1967) has pointed out, is that the number of variables tends to become too large for the number of teachers or classrooms feasibly measured—a condition that tends to invalidate the assumptions of the factor analytic method.

Another approach (Miller and others, 1965) to the problem of dimensions proceeds by developing statements descriptive of classroom actions or behaviors, getting sorters to put these statements into categories that impress each sorter as dealing with a given aspect of the teaching task, and then applying categorical factor analysis to determine the "latent structure" of the categorical statements. This kind of factor analysis begins with a matrix whose cells indicate the extent to which the sorters agreed in placing any pair of actions or behaviors in the same category; it yields a matrix of loadings for each action on a set of latent categories, which represents a composite of the sorters' conceptualizations, or dimensionalizations, of teaching. In their study of interview data on elementary school teachers' behaviors, Miller and others (1965) labeled the resultant latent categories as follows: maintaining control and order, maintaining climate for learning, stimulating learning receptivity, using real resources, initial orientation, gauging pupil receptivity, pupil involvement, knowing pupils, pupil differences, instructional tactics. The meaning of these categories resides not in labels, of course, but in the terms that have substantial loadings on them. The same technique could, of course, be applied to items concerning teacher behavior derived not from interviews with teachers but from classroom observation instruments.

Conceptual Problems. Beyond such logical and empirical contributions, conceptual metatheoretical problems arise. In dealing with dementionalization, one such issue is that of whether the teacher behaviors should be coded in terms of intentions, objective characteristics, or effects; Biddle's analysis (1967) led him to recommend that "greatest emphasis should be given to objective characteristics."

Another problem is that of making categories of teacher behavior mutually exclusive and yet reasonably exhaustive of the domain of significant teacher behaviors. A promising approach to this problem, suggested by Biddle (1967), is that of facet design and analysis (Foa, 1965), whereby variables are defined in terms of their component elements. Then a set of the elements becomes a "facet" (Guttman, 1954). Thus, one facet of classroom behavior might be the person behaving, that is, the teacher or a pupil; a second might be the modality of the behavior, verbal or nonverbal; a third might be the affect of the behavior, that is, its positive or negative emotional significance. Combining these three merely illustrative facets would yield eight (that is, $2 \times 2 \times 2$) variables, or types of classroom events, as the Cartesian product of the facets; that is, the variables would be teacher's positive verbal behavior, . . . , teacher's negative nonverbal behavior, . . . , pupil's positive nonverbal behavior, and pupil's negative nonverbal behavior. Such a scheme has indeed been developed by Fowler (Soar, 1966), who developed a "hostility-affection schedule" with these eight categories, each elaborated in several more specific activities such as "teases," "frowns," "smiles," and "praises."

Facet design would help systematize the dimensionalization of classroom behavior, but it would not determine which facets should be used, that being "a substantive rather than a methodological problem" (Foa, 1965). Beyond formalizing and organizing the definition of variables so that they do not overlap and are exhaustive of a defined domain, facet analysis can suggest empirically testable hypotheses about relationships between variables. Thus, variables that have more facets, or more important facets, in common should be more highly correlated.

Another path out of the welter of classroom behavior dimensions may be obtained by clarification of the purposes for which such dimensions are formulated or selected. In any classroom, an undeterminate number of events occurs in any hour or year. To which one should scientific and educational attention be directed? The answer clearly depends on one's purpose. If that purpose is to understand and improve, say, cognitive achievement, then one set of events becomes most relevant; if achievement of affective objectives is one's concern, then other events demand attention. More specific purposes, such as improved achievement of critical thinking ability on social issues, would dictate more specific foci.

Once purposes, criteria, or dependent variables have been identified, choices among dimensions can be made according to their demonstrated empirical relevance to those purposes. To determine such relevance has, of course, been the aim of the studies made to determine correlations between observed aspects of teacher behavior and various educational outcomes. It was the generally low and inconsistent character of such correlations that led writers to draw the negative conclusions, quoted above, about the importance of teaching methods. Recently, however, more sanguine conclusions have been drawn about the trend of results in studies of correlations between teaching method variables and educational outcomes. Thus, Gage (1968) saw "warmth" as an aspect of teaching method, measured in various ways, that had been found relevant to pupil achievement and attitudes in a number of studies. Similarly, Simon and Boyer (1967) refer to the fact that "measures of the teacher's *affective* response to pupil response predict subsequent pupil *cognitive* outputs such as achievement in subject matter. . . ." Finally, Flanders (see TEACHER EFFECTIVENESS) refers to the consistent finding of a positive relationship between the degree to which teachers' statements make use of ideas and feelings previously expressed by pupils and the average class scores for attitudes (toward the teacher and the class) and achievement.

The diffuse character of present concerns may be seen in the review by Biddle (1967), who found that recent studies of classrooms have dealt with teacher performance (including actions, manners, and characteristic roles), audience performance, target performance, teacher-target interaction, externally imposed structure (e.g., subject matter, administrative regulations), and internal structures (e.g., communication structure, ecological structure or spatial arrangements, activity structure, characteristic roles, and social functions). Meux (1967) suggested that a new multiaspect system for classroom observation should include topic-objective units, initiating-reacting cycles, within-the-topic units, content-substantive and instructional facets, group processes, and thinking processes. Such approaches to teaching method and classroom events seem to assume that some all-inclusive conceptualization is desirable and feasible. A more fruitful approach may be that of selecting from the enormous number of possible dimensions those relatively few which appear, on various grounds, to be relevant to some relatively specific purpose.

Nonetheless, attempts at universal and all-embracing dimensionalizations can have value as storehouses from which relevant dimensions may be chosen, and facet design can help in insuring some orderliness in the definition and selection of dimensions. Such a generalized taxonomy has been initiated by Dwight Allen and Richard Snow (Stanford Center for Research and Development in Teaching 1968), and computers have been used for the storage and retrieval of data referring to teacher and learner behavior. More than 1,000 such items have been stored; these can be retrieved and printed by the computer in a form ready for use by observers, raters, and content analysts. The items to be retrieved can be specified according to many different dimensions. Data generated by observers or content analysts concerning the frequency, intensity, or correlates of behaviors denoted by these items can be stored in the computer along with the items. Thus, experience relevant to the reliability and validity of the items with different kinds of teachers, observers, subject matters, criteria of effectiveness, and the like, can become cumulative. In short, the ideal of a universal taxonomy of classroom behaviors useful for many alternative purposes may become attainable through a computer-based system like that being developed at Stanford. If so, the problems of dimensionalizing and describing teaching methods will become substantially more manageable.

One methodological aspect of the dimensionalization problem, namely, the amount of inference that the observer or analyst of teaching behavior is required to engage in, has substantive implications. Some phenomena require relatively little inference; examples of these are the number of rule-example-rule sequences and the frequency of gestures and lateral movements (Rosenshine, 1968) exhibited by the teacher during a given period. Other phenomena require a considerable inference from what is seen or heard in the classroom; examples are the degree to which the teacher is partial versus fair, autocratic versus democratic, aloof versus responsive, or the degree to which the pupils are apathetic versus alert, or obstructive versus responsible (Ryans, 1960). Low-inference dimensions have a major advantage in that findings concerning such dimensions lend themselves much more readily to practical use in teacher education. By definition, it is easier to translate such dimensions into specific ways of behaving; it is more difficult to determine exactly what a teacher should do in order to behave more "fairly," "democratically," or "responsively."

The advent of audio- and videotape recording in research on teaching has improved the feasibility of studying phenomena at all points on the degree-of-inference continuum. Half of the 26 systems collected and described by Simon and Boyer (1967) have been used with such recordings. As Cogan (1963) and Biddle (1967) have noted, such devices make possible a new phase in research on teaching methods. More reliable, replicable, complete, unbiased, complex, analytic, and synthetic studies of teaching method can be made with videotape recordings than with live observation, audiotape recording, or handwritten notes.

Computers are being exploited for the analysis of recorded data, such as for summarizing the thousands of tallies in matrices obtained with Flanders's system for classroom interaction analysis (Simon and Boyer, 1967). Furthermore, computers have been used for content analysis of lectures (Dell, 1968; Hiller, 1968); counts have been made of the frequencies of hundreds of different words specified in various "dictionaries," such as "vagueness" and "explaining links," and these frequencies have then been correlated against learner-achievement criteria.

In the following sections, three additional major categories of contemporary teaching methods are considered: the lecture method, the discussion method, and the discovery method. These form a series ranging from greater to less domination by the teacher. In the lecture, the teacher predominates, exercising close and continuous control over what the learners receive. In the discussion, the teacher shares control to some degree with the learners. In the discovery method, the teacher withholds control to a still greater degree and induces the learners to discover, with varying degrees of guidance, the concepts and principles to be learned.

THE LECTURE METHOD. No discussion of teaching methods can ignore the lecture method, which appeals to everyone as the prototype of what is meant by a teaching method. The lecture method is, of course, that in which the teacher communicates orally—in one direction, for the most part—the knowledge and ways of behaving to be acquired. The major research question is not that of whether the lecture method is effective, or whether it is more or less effective than the discussion method or other methods. Rather, the question should be: For what objectives is the lecture method, used in what ways, more or less effective than other methods?

The lecture can do more than transmit knowledge. It can be used in teaching higher cognitive processes and affective processes, such as attitudes. Further, it can be used to provide a model of "man thinking." Thus, John Dewey as lecturer ". . . seemed to be saying whatever came into his head next. . . . It was then a remarkable discovery to . . . find that what had seemed so casual, so rambling, so unexciting, was of an extraordinary coherence, texture, and brilliance. I had been listening to a man actually *thinking* in the presence of a class" (Irwin Edman, as quoted in Highet, 1955).

That learning results from listening to lectures may seem inconsistent with reinforcement conceptions of learning. How can the passive listener, making no overt responses and apparently receiving no reinforcements, nonetheless learn? Perhaps reinforcement theory can be satisfied by postulating implicit predictive responses by the listener; the anticipatory response is then reinforced if the lecturer's next idea or two confirms the prediction. In this view, learning from listening consists in active participation through anticipating, or covertly predicting, the flow of the lecturer's discourse or argument. When these implicit responses are confirmed—that is, when the listener "comprehends"—he is reinforced, and the probability of his behaving in certain ways increases (Skinner, 1968).

The lecture method has long been condemned. Boswell quoted Johnson as saying: "Lectures were once useful; but now, when all can read, and books are so numerous, lectures are unnecessary. If your attention fails, and you miss a part of a lecture, it is lost; you cannot go back as you do upon a book" (Boswell, 1953). Despite centuries of such criticism, the lecture method persists. Many administrative considerations apparently prevail: (1) economy, in that the learner-teacher ratio can be extremely large; (2) flexibility, in that the lecture can easily be adapted to the audience, subject matter, available time, and equipment; and (3) spontaneity and adaptability to the teacher's schedule, in that teachers cannot always plan ahead sufficiently to have materials reproduced, and sometimes sheer inefficiency, of an all too human kind, prevents teachers from putting on paper exactly the selection of ideas from many sources, in a hitherto unprinted form, that they wish to present. No teaching method so adaptable will disappear in favor of methods requiring more rigorous planning and usable only with certain kinds of groups, subject matter, time intervals, or equipment (projectors, books, audio or video record players, or computers). Furthermore, "social facilitation" may occur, in that lectures make many people simultaneously concern themselves with the same ideas, and each member of the audience may be stimulated by awareness that many others are responding to the lecturer at the same moment. Hence, even the severest critics of the lecture method often find themselves lecturing.

Research on the lecture method has typically compared lectures with other methods, usually the discussion method, or lectures of one kind with those of another. McKeachie (1967) summarized as follows:

> What can we say about lecture versus discussion? Since discussion offers the opportunity for a good deal of student activity and feedback, it could be (according to theory) and is (according to research results) more effective than typical lectures in developing concepts and problem-solving skills. However, because the rate of transmission of information is slow in discussion classes, we would expect the lecture classes to be superior in attaining the objective of teaching knowledge. Research results tend to support this generalization and probably are not more convincing largely because the knowledge tested on course examinations usually can be learned by reading the textbook.

As for the possibility of combining the lecture and discussion methods, McKeachie's summary indicated that "a combination of large lecture and small discussion sections is preferable to the common arrangement of several sections of unwieldy medium size."

Methods of lecturing are studied by comparing effects of lectures that differ along one dimension or another. Much of what is said about good lecturing (Brown and Thornton, 1963) appeals strongly to common sense: lectures should be well introduced, organized, delivered in a clear and confident voice, varied in emphasis and intonation, aptly illustrated with cogent examples, accompanied by abundant "eye-contact" with the listeners, appropriately summarized, and so on. But these admonitions have not been adequately tested empirically. Such empirical tests have at least two values: operational definitions and validation. Operational definitions make the advice more usable; thus, the nature of good examples becomes more carefully defined when this aspect of lectures is measured for research purposes. Validation of presumed desiderata determines whether they actually have desired effects. To illustrate such research, this discussion focuses on two aspects of lecturing that have been studied empirically.

One example is empirical testing of the homily that the lecturer should "communicate enthusiasm for the subject of the lecture" (Brown and Thornton, 1963). Do students indeed learn more from lectures delivered dynamically and enthusiastically? Coats and Smidchens (1966) used two ten-minute lessons, each presented by two teachers in two ways: (1) statically ("The static speaker read the entire speech from a manuscript. He made no gestures or direct eye contact and held vocal inflection to a minimum. However, he did speak with good diction and sufficient volume.") and (2) dynamically ("The dynamic speeches were delivered from memory, with much vocal inflection, gesturing, eye contact, and animation on the part of the speaker."). A test immediately after the lecture indicated that "students did remember much more from the dynamic lecture than from the static one." Similarly, Mastin (1963) had 20 sixth- and seventh-grade teachers present lectures on two different topics a week apart. For one randomly chosen lesson, the teacher behaved so as to convey to the group "a feeling that he had an indifferent attitude toward the ideas and pictures being presented, and toward the subject of the lesson"; for the other lesson, the same teacher conveyed the impression "that he was enthusiastic about the ideas and illustrative materials of the lesson and the subject covered by the lesson." In 19 of the 20 classes, mean achievement was higher for the lesson taught enthusiastically.

A second example of a variable highly touted in advice to lecturers is "organization." Apart from its general plausibility, the importance of organization could be derived from Gestalt theory, developed in the field of perception, whereby the laws of similarity, proximity, closure, and good continuation determine how we perceive the world. Cognitive materials organized in accordance with these laws should presumably be better understood, retained, and transferred. Just what is good organization is not, of course, always clear. Even so, ideas presented according to what the communicator considers a sensible organization ought to be better understood than the same ideas presented in random order. As Buxton (1956) put it, ". . . the goal of lecturing is after all communication, and it is likely to be the more effective if there is an evident order or sequence. . . ." Or, as Skinner (1968) put it, "Material which is well organized is also, of course, easier to learn."

Yet the importance of organization seems hard to demonstrate experimentally. Thompson (1967) summarized many studies as follows: "Disorganization appears to affect comprehension in written communication, but effects upon comprehension and effectiveness in oral communication are doubtful." In a typical study (Beighley, 1954), disorganization was introduced by shifting paragraphs in a controlled random method; comprehension among listeners was not significantly reduced. The plausibility of these surprising results is increased by studies of programmed instruction. Schramm's comprehensive review was summarized as follows (Hilgard and Bower, 1966): "Of five studies comparing the immediate and delayed post-test results of an ordered sequence with a random ordering, three showed no difference, one showed an immediate advantage for the ordered sequence, but none on a delayed test, and only one showed clear advantage for the ordered sequence!" Lack of organization in oral communication may be compensated by cues provided by the delivery; also, the slower rate of listening as compared with reading may permit the listener to compensate for the disorganization (Thompson, 1967). In any case, research on organization in lectures fails to support common-sense expectations.

The significance of many other variables in "informative speaking" has been summarized by Petrie (1963). Of those he dealt with, the ones italicized in the following list appeared to make a generally consistent difference in the many studies he reviewed: (1) the message's *meaningfulness, informality in style,* reading difficulty, *verbal emphasis, development of main ideas,* and organization; (2) the speaker's credibility and delivery, including general quality, formality, vocal quality, rate, various ways of emphasizing important points, *visible action,* and *eye contact;* (3) the listener's *sex,* hearing acuity and auditory discrimination, personality attributes, *intelligence, scholastic achievement,* note-taking, and motivation, including interest in the subject measured before or during or after the presentation, *expectation of a test or monetary reward,* emotional attitudes, anticipatory set, and organizational ability; and (4) the physical environment. Thompson (1967), in a similar review of research in speech, dealt with the ways in which arrangement, style, nonverbal communication, and delivery affect listeners.

THE DISCUSSION METHOD. The discussion method may be defined as that whereby a teacher engages with two or more learners in a cooperative examination and comparison of views in order to illuminate an issue and contribute to the learners' understanding. It is characterized by much more teacher-student and student-student interaction than is the lecture method, but the range in such interaction varies from those instances in which the teacher does most of the talking to others when he is almost completely silent. The variable of teacher domination is reflected also in the degree to which the teacher provides the agenda, procedure, method of attack, and evaluation of contributions or delegates these functions to the students. The continuum from "teacher-centered" to "learner-centered" embraces this variable in all its many ramifications. (Other terms for this continuum are authoritarian-permissive, directive-nondirective, autocratic-democratic, teacher controlled–pupil planned, and dominative-integrative.)

The main argument for the discussion method is the obverse of that against the lecture method. That is, mere one-way communication can better be achieved through printed materials and other media, and the chief justification for bringing teacher and students together is to make possible the two-way communication that cannot be attained through printed and other media. Learners seem passive in lecture classes, whereas they participate when being taught by the discussion method, and learning is considered to be promoted by active participation. In a discussion, the learner has an opportunity to make his own contributions, attempt to solve problems, make applications, evaluate others' ideas, receive confirmation and feedback, and so on. The discussion method should produce different and, for many purposes, superior kinds of learning. It is argued that the desirability of these other types of achievement and their unattainability through lectures, reading, films, independent study, and so on justify the relatively low learner-teacher ratios and correspondingly high cost of the discussion method.

At first glance, the discussion method seems so uncontrollable, in view of the participation of a number of relatively autonomous individuals, that any generalizations concerning its processes or outcomes are well-nigh impossible. Teacher-dominated instruction is difficult enough to control because the live teacher's behavior cannot be "edited" in detail in accordance with any complex research findings, as can printed, filmed, and programmed instructional media. Teaching by the discussion method, where students participate much more freely, would seem to be even less amenable to scientific understanding and control.

Yet an enormous literature on small-group research has been produced. McGrath and Altman (1966) classified, annotated, and catalogued the relationships found in the thousands of items in the bibliography of this field, and Berelson and Steiner (1964) included a substantial chapter on "face-to-face relations in small groups" in their inventory of scientific findings on human behavior. Educators have used the conceptions and findings of social psychologists to gain understanding of processes in instructional groups (National Society for the Study of Education, 1960; Withall and Lewis, 1963). Manuals such as that by McKeachie (1965) contain suggestions for teaching through discussions. Leypoldt (1967) assembled his *40 Ways to Teach in Groups,* describing each approach briefly in terms of its purposes, the activities of the leader and group members, and a diagram showing the pattern of communication between them.

The most frequently studied relationships, by far, have been those relevant to the continuum from teacher-centered to student-centered teaching. Summaries of the results of dozens of studies of this variable have been reported by Anderson (1959), Stern (1963), and McKeachie (1963, 1967). In general, students in student-centered classes participate more and have greater responsibility for the determination of the purposes, content, procedure, and course of the discussion. Generally, no consistent differences occur in knowledge outcomes, but the student-centered class yields greater gains in higher cognitive processes and in affective outcomes (changes in attitude). Thus, McKeachie (1967) summarized as follows:

> In eleven studies, significant differences in ability to apply concepts, in attitudes, in motivation, and in group membership skills have been found between discussion techniques emphasizing freer student participation compared with discussion with greater instructor dominance. In ten of these the differences favored the student-centered method. The eleventh had mixed results.

Underlying this broad generalization, based on studies varying widely in terms of subject matter and details of procedure, are some basic phenomena related to the acquisition of knowledge, higher-level cognitive processes, and attitudes. The lack of difference between teacher- and student-centered discussions in the degree to which students acquire knowledge may be attributable to the availability of many sources of knowledge, such as reading and independent study, other than those provided by the teacher's verbal behavior in the classroom. The superiority of student-centered discussions in promoting higher-level cognitive skills, such as the ability to think critically or make applications, probably stems from the greater opportunity to practice such skills in student-centered discussions, where students have more freedom to try alternatives, covertly or overtly, and receive feedback from the group concerning their validity. Thus Bloom (1953) found that college students' thoughts were more often relevant to the subject matter in discussion than in lecture sessions. And the superiority of student-centered discussions in promoting favorable attitudes toward the subject matter as a whole and in influencing attitudes on specific issues within the subject matter probably arises from the greater degree to which group cohesiveness, norms, interpersonal perceptions, and similar forces can operate in such discussion groups.

But many criticisms (Anderson, 1959) have been made of the research and reasoning on which these conclusions are based. First, the independent variable, student- *versus* teacher-centered discussions, is inadequately defined and probably should be supplanted by more specific variables in the realms of leadership and teaching style to which it refers. Thus directive teaching need not be characterized by harshness, coldness, or other kinds of negative affect; although this ingredient has often been mixed into the teacher-centered style. Second, the two styles need to be further differentiated as to their effectiveness for different kinds of subject matter. Teacher-centered discussion may be more fruitful than student-centered teaching in fields that possess substantial agreement on major concepts, principles, and methods—in mathematics, the natural sciences, and engineering, as against the social sciences and humanities. The latter do not have and, in principle, may never have such high degrees of consensus. Student-centered discussions may well be found to be superior for the objectives of the low-consensus areas, whereas the teacher-centered approach may be better for the objectives of the high-consensus fields. Third, research on teaching by the discussion method needs to look underneath the labels at the details of what goes on in the teaching sessions. Comparing their outcomes without looking at the specifics of process is similar to comparing the merits of two drugs of unknown but varying composition that are being used for the same or different purposes.

THE DISCOVERY METHOD. The discovery method refers to teaching in which the teacher withholds from pupils the concepts and principles they are to learn but gives them the instances, exemplars, and problems from which they can induce these concepts and principles. In a conference on learning by discovery, "there was general agreement . . . that the degree of guidance by the teacher varies from time to time along a continuum, with almost complete direction of what the pupil must do at one extreme to practically no direction at the other" (Shulman and Keislar, 1966). The range from complete guidance (expository teaching) to complete lack of guidance (unguided discovery) can be seen in four treatments used by Wittrock (1963): rule and answer given, rule given and answer not given, rule not given and answer given, and rule and answer not given.

Such teaching is based on the so-called learning-by-discovery hypothesis, that "practice in discovering for one's self teaches one to acquire information in a way that makes that information more readily viable in problem solving" (Bruner, 1961). Bruner also proposed that discovery learning would improve intrinsic motivation, techniques of discovery, and the learner's retrieval of information, or memory. Ausubel (1968) reviewed and questioned many of the arguments for such teaching.

The discovery method has not resided merely in the research laboratory. Major curriculum improvement programs—those of the University of Illinois Committee on School Mathematics, the School Mathematics Study Group, the Chemical Education Materials Study, and the American Institute of Biological Sciences project in the teaching of biology, among others—have adopted the method as a major component of their approaches to teaching (Wittrock, 1966). Individual curriculum workers have also attributed much hope on the method; Suchman (1966) developed materials and procedures for use in "inquiry training" in elementary school science, and

Taba (1966) emphasized "inductive development of basic ideas" in a program of research and development on teaching strategies in elementary school social studies.

Heuristic Teaching. The discovery method is to be contrasted with expository teaching, in which pupils are presented with all the facts, concepts, and principles they are to learn. The same distinction resides in the terms "heuristic" and "didactic" teaching. Many writers regard the expository, presentational, and didactic modes as kinds of teaching that increasingly can be taken over by programmed instruction, television, films, and other media. Thus, Ausubel (1968) concluded that ". . . programmed instruction . . . is potentially the most effective method for transmitting the established content of most subject-matter fields." Advocates of programmed instruction see the traditional classroom as a major obstacle to effective instruction. Thus, according to Skinner (1961), ". . . holding students together in a class is probably the greatest source of inefficiency in education."

Such propositions about the value of programmed instruction for the didactic modes of teaching, and the corresponding deficiencies of classroom discourse for those purposes, raise these questions: What function can teaching in the classroom serve? Is such teaching obsolescent? Although programmed instruction, in its several varieties, can provide some guided discovery, it will not in the near future make possible any genuine dialogue between teachers and learners (Suppes, 1966). Accordingly, it is to the live teacher engaged in such a dialogue, or discourse, with a group of learners, that we must look for any thoroughgoing exploitation of the promise of teaching by the heuristic mode.

In some interpretations (Stanford Center for Research and Development in Teaching, 1968), the concept of heuristic teaching has broader aspects than those connoted by the term "discovery method," despite the similarity of the two terms. For want of a better label, "heuristic teaching" is used to refer to teaching aimed at promoting a broad range of active, process-oriented, self-directed, inquiring, and reflective modes of learning; it includes the discovery method as one component. Such teaching provides one answer to the challenge of programmed instruction and its derivatives, such systems as "individually prescribed instruction" (Lindvall and Bolvin, 1967), and Project PLAN (Flanagan, 1967). The latter systems engage the learner in work on tasks designed for his individual needs and abilities; the learner proceeds at his own rate, independent of others, with carefully organized and sequenced segments. His progress is closely monitored through frequent evaluations, and his subsequent tasks, designed to serve thoroughly explicated objectives, are adjusted accordingly. Such systems will radically alter the teacher's role—relieving him of didactic burdens and freeing him for the uniquely human functions embraced by the concept of heuristic teaching.

Empirical Studies. Ausubel (1968) and Wittrock (1966) reviewed long-term and short-term studies of the heuristic method and concluded that most of these studies were irrelevant, faultily designed, or negative in their findings. The conclusions about negative results may apply, however, only to contrasts between the extremes of completely independent discovery, on the one hand, and complete presentation, on the other. An intermediate method, namely, guided discovery, which provides information about underlying principles, usually does facilitate learning, retention, and possibly transfer more than does less guidance or the furnishing of specific rules (Ausubel, 1968).

A review of the arguments and evidence on teaching by discovery leads one to suspect that much of the opposition stems from construing the learning-by-discovery hypothesis in an extreme form: that learners should be deprived of all cues and left completely unguided in their search for a concept or principle, or that teaching by discovery should be used always for all aspects of all subjects. A more reasonable position, supported by considerable evidence, is that guided discovery—giving the learner only some of the cues he needs—can be used in teaching some aspects of some subjects with advantages for learning, retention, and transfer. Such a moderate position, both on the nature of the discovery method and the extent to which it should be used, seems to be supported by both research and common sense.

Such a position also refutes the powerful argument that the discovery method is impracticable in view of how much there is to be learned. The discovery method is relatively time-consuming, and straight-forward presentation of ideas—without waiting for the learner to discover them—is therefore necessary in many situations. But, if guided-discovery methods are used only occasionally, on strategic occasions, their advantages in increasing interest, involvement, retention, transfer, and problem-solving ability can be gained at a reasonable cost in time.

N. L. Gage
Stanford University

References

Anderson, Richard C. "Learning in Discussions: A Resumé of the Authoritarian-Democratic Studies." *Harvard Ed R* 29:201–15; 1959.

Ausubel, David P. *Educational Psychology: A Cognitive View.* Holt, 1968. 685p.

Beighley, K. C. "An Experimental Study of the Effect of Three Speech Variables on Listener Comprehension." *Speech Monogr* 21:248–53; 1954.

Bellack, Arno A., and others. *The Language of the Classroom.* TC, 1966. 273p.

Berelson, Bernard, and Steiner, Gary A. *Human Behavior: An Inventory of Scientific Findings.* Harcourt, 1964. 712p.

Biddle, Bruce J. "Methods and Concepts in Classroom Research." *R Ed Res* 37:337–57; 1967.

Bloom, Benjamin S. "Thought Processes in Lectures and Discussions." *J Gen Ed* 7:160–9; 1953.

Boswell, James. *Life of Johnson* (1799). 3rd ed. Oxford U Press, 1953.

Broudy, Harry S., and Palmer, John R. *Exemplars of Teaching Method.* Rand McNally, 1965. 172p.

Brown, James W., and Thornton, James W., Jr. *College Teaching: Perspectives and Guidelines.* McGraw-Hill, 1963. 260p.

Brownell, William A., and Moser, Harold E. "Meaningful versus Mechanical Learning: A Study in Grade III Subtraction." *Duke U Res Stud Ed,* No. 8, 1949.

Bruner, Jerome S. "The Act of Discovery." *Harvard Ed R* 31:21–36; 1961.

Bush, Robert N. "The Science and Art of Educating Teachers." In Elam, Stanley (Ed.) *Improving Teacher Education in the United States.* PDK, 1966. p. 35–62.

Buxton, Claude E. *College Teaching: A Psychologist's View.* Harcourt, 1956. 404p.

Coats, William D., and Smidchens, Uldis. "Audience Recall as a Function of Speaker Dynamism." *J Ed Psychol* 57:189–91; 1966.

Cogan, Morris L. "Research on the Behavior of Teachers." *J Teach Ed* 14:238–43; 1963.

Cronbach, Lee J. "The Two Disciplines of Scientific Psychology." *Am Psychologist* 12:671–84; 1957.

DeCecco, John P. *The Psychology of Learning and Instruction: Educational Psychology.* Prentice-Hall, 1968. 800p.

Dell, Daryl L. "Computer Analysis of Teachers' Explanations." Paper presented at the annual meeting of AERA, Feb 1968. 12p. (Mimeo).

Flanagan, John C. "Functional Education for the Seventies." *Phi Delta Kappan* 49:27–32; 1967. *Evaluation, and Distribution of a New System of Education.* American Institute for Research, 1967. (Unpublished manuscript.)

Flanders, Ned A. "Some Relationships among Teacher Influence, Pupil Attitudes, and Achievement." In Biddle, Bruce J., and Ellena, William J. (Eds.) *Contemporary Research on Teacher Effectiveness.* Holt, 1964. p. 196–231.

Foa, Uriel G. "New Developments in Facet Design and Analysis." *Psychol R* 72:262–74; 1965.

Gage, N. L. (Ed.) *Handbook of Research on Teaching.* Rand McNally, 1963. 1218p.

Gage, N. L. "Can Science Contribute to the Art of Teaching?" *Phi Delta Kappan* 49:399–403; 1968.

Getzels, J. W., and Jackson, P. W. "The Teacher's Personality and Characteristics." In Gage, N. L. (Ed.) *Handbook of Research on Teaching.* Rand McNally, 1963. p. 506–82.

Guttman, Louis. "A New Approach to Factor Analysis: The Radex." In Lazarsfeld, P. R. (Ed.) *Mathematical Thinking in the Social Sciences.* Free Press, 1954.

Hedegard, James M. "An Overview of Historical Formulations." In Siegel, Laurence (Ed.) *Instruction: Some Contemporary Viewpoints.* Chandler, 1967. p. 3–23.

Highet, Gilbert. *The Art of Teaching.* Vintage, 1955. 259p.

Hilgard, Ernest R., and Bower, Gordon H. *Theories of Learning.* 3rd ed. Appleton, 1966. 661p.

Hiller, Jack E. *An Experimental Investigation of the Effects of Conceptual Vagueness on Speaking Behavior.* Doctoral dissertation. U Connecticut, 1958.

Leypoldt, Martha M. *40 Ways to Teach in Groups.* Judson Press, 1967. 123p.

Lindvall, C. M., and Bolvin, John O. "Programed Instruction in the Schools: An Application of Programing Principles in 'Individually Prescribed Instruction.'" In *Programed Instruction.* 66th Yearbook, Part II, NSSE. U Chicago Press, 1967. p. 217–54.

Mastin, Victor E. "Teacher Enthusiasm." *J Ed Res* 56:385–6; 1963.

McDonald, Frederick J. "The Influence of Learning Theories on Education." In *Theories of Learning and Instruction.* 63rd Yearbook, Part I, NSSE. U. Chicago, 1964. p. 1–26.

McGrath, Joseph E., and Altman, Irwin. *Small Group Research: A Synthesis and Critique of the Field.* Holt, 1966. 601p.

McKeachie, Wilbert J. "Research on Teaching at the College and University Level." In Gage, N. L. (Ed.) *Handbook of Research on Teaching.* Rand McNally, 1963. p. 1118–72.

McKeachie, Wilbert, J. *Teaching Tips: A Guide-Book for the Beginning College Teacher.* 5th ed. George Wahr, 208p.

McKeachie, Wilbert J. "Research in Teaching: The Gap between Theory and Practice." In Lee, Calvin B. T. (Ed.) *Improving College Teaching.* ACE, 1967. p. 211–39.

Medley, Donald M. "The Language of Teacher Behavior: Communicating the Results of Structured Observations to Teachers." Paper presented at the annual meeting of AERA, Feb 1967. 19p. (Mimeo).

Medley, Donald M., and Mitzel, Harold E. "Some Behavioral Correlates of Teacher Effectiveness." *J Ed Psychol* 50:239–46; 1959.

Meux, Milton O. "Studies of Learning in the School Setting." *R Ed Res* 37:539–62; 1967.

Miller, Donald M., and others. "A Substantive Study of Empirically Defined Categorizations of Teaching Behavior." Paper presented at the annual meeting of AERA, Feb 1965. 24p. (Mimeo).

Monroe, Walter S., and Marks, Arlyn. "General Methods of Teaching." *Ed Adm Sup* 24:497–512; 1938.

National Society for the Study of Education. *The Dynamics of Instructional Groups: Socio-psychological Aspects of Teaching and Learning.* 59th Yearbook, Part II. U Chicago Press, 1960. 286p.

Petrie, Charles R., Jr. "Informative Speaking: A Summary and Bibliography of Related Research." *Speech Monogr* 30:79–91; 1963.

Rosenshine, V. Barak. *Behavioral Predictors of Effectiveness in Explaining Social Studies Material.* Doctoral dissertation. Stanford U, 1968.

Ryans, David G. *Characteristics of Teachers.* ACE, 1960. 416p.

Saettler, Paul. *A History of Instructional Technology.* McGraw-Hill, 1968. 339p.

Shulman, Lee S., and Keislar, Evan R. (Eds.) *Learning by Discovery: A Critical Appraisal.* Rand McNally, 1966. 224p.

Siegel, Laurence, and Siegel, Lila C. "A Multivariate Paradigm for Educational Research." *Psychol B* 68:306–26; 1967.

Simon, Anita, and Boyer, E. Gil. *Mirrors for Behavior: An Anthology of Classroom Observation Instruments.* 6 vols. Research for Better Schools and the Center for the Study of Teaching, Temple U, 1967.

Skinner, B. F. "Why We Need Teaching Machines." *Harvard Ed R* 31:377–98; 1968.

Skinner, B. F. *The Technology of Teaching.* Appleton, 1968. 271p.

Smith, B. Othanel, and others. *A Study of the Strategies of Teaching.* CRP No. 1640. U Illinois, 1967. 321p.

Soar, Robert S. *An Integrative Approach to Classroom Learning.* Temple U, 1966. 326p.

Spaulding, Robert L. *Achievement, Creativity, and Self-Concept Correlates of Teacher-Pupil Transactions in Elementary School Classrooms.* CRP No. 1352. Hofstra U, 1965. 126p. + appendices.

Stanford Center for Research and Development in Teaching. *Second Annual Report.* Stanford U, 1968. 256p.

Stephens, J. M. *The Process of Schooling: A Psychological Examination.* Holt, 1967. 168p.

Stern, George G. "Measuring Noncognitive Variables in Research on Teaching." In Gage, N. L. (Ed.) *Handbook of Research on Teaching.* Rand McNally, 1963. p. 398–447.

Suchman, J. Richard. "A Model for the Analysis of Inquiry." In Klausmeier, H. J., and Harris, Chester W. (Eds.) *Analyses of Concept Learning.* Academic, 1966.

Suppes, Patrick. "The Uses of Computers in Education." *Sci Am* 215:206–20; 1966.

Taba, Hilda. *Teaching Strategies and Cognitive Functioning in Elementary School Children.* CRP No. 2404. San Francisco State Col, 1966. 275p.

Thompson, Wayne N. *Quantitative Research in Public Address and Communication.* Random, 1967. 239p.

Walker, Edward L., and McKeachie, Wilbert J. *Some Thoughts about Teaching the Beginning Course in Psychology.* Brooks/Cole, 1967. 84p.

Wallen, Norman E., and Travers, Robert M. W. "Analysis and Investigation of Teaching Methods." In Gage, N. L. (Ed.) *Handbook of Research on Teaching.* Rand McNally, 1963. p. 448–505.

Withall, John, and Lewis, W. W. "Social Interaction in the Classroom." In Gage, N. L. (Ed.) *Handbook of Research on Teaching.* Rand McNally, 1963. p. 683–714.

Wittrock, Merlin C. "Verbal Stimuli in Concept Formation: Learning by Discovery." *J Ed Psychol* 54:183–90; 1963.

Wittrock, Merlin C. "The Learning by Discovery Hypothesis." In Shulman, Lee S., and Keislar, Evan R. (Eds.) *Learning by Discovery: A Critical Appraisal.* Rand McNally, 1966. p. 33–75.

TENURE OF TEACHERS

Tenure of teachers, or the right of teachers to their positions, from which they can be removed only for good cause, in the public school field is deeply rooted in the general common-law concepts of this country (Fellman, 1961). In public education below the university level, tenure is most likely to be provided by statute. The principles of tenure or of fair-dismissal laws as put forth by various professional organizations seem to be much the same. The National Education Association (NEA) defines a tenure law as one which (1) provides for continuing employment of teachers who have acquired permanent or tenure status and (2) requires employing boards to follow procedural provisions of notice, statement of charges, and right to a hearing before dismissing a tenured teacher.

The NEA has also defined continuing-contract laws of the spring-notification type and annual or long-term contracts and has summarized and categorized the various laws in effect in the several states (National Education Association, Research Division, 1965b). The difference between continuing contracts and tenure is that under continuing-contract provisions the teacher may be dismissed at the end of the school year regardless of cause and without a stated reason being given (Gaurke, 1965).

The American Association of University Professors (AAUP) has established principles of tenure for faculties in colleges and universities (American Association of University Professors, 1964).

Many publications review the court decisions on tenure in some regular way (National Education Association, Research Division, 1958, 1965a; Garber, 1958–1965). Most texts on school law are incomplete without a chapter on tenure which usually defines it and discusses the types of laws and court cases interpreting them which have arisen (Drury & Ray, 1965; Garber & Edwards, 1962; Nolte & Linn, 1963; Remmlein, 1962).

An understanding of tenure laws and the cases interpreting them would help dispel the views of some that they do not protect teachers enough and of others that it is impossible to remove inefficient teachers under them. A review of cases, designed to promote understanding, has been made (Garber, 1956b).

The profession still must do more to inform the public that tenure is "not a crutch for the incompetent," but a right only if deserved. The profession needs to do more to police its own ranks to remove the incompetents (Hummel, 1960). But it is noted that actions of professional associations and the existence of tenure laws have "tended to put a brake on some flagrant abuses of academic freedom" (Reutter, 1965).

As far as higher education is concerned, the decisional law on tenure is "formless and almost rudimentary" (Fellman, 1961). There are four ways in which tenure can become established: by law, by contract, by moral commitment to an accepted academic code, and by "courtesy, kindness, community, or inertia" (Machlup, 1964).

The general meaning of tenure as opposed to the technical, legal meaning is found in the research on teacher turnover, length of service statistics, and mobility studies.

Technical, legal, and the more general types of tenure studies just discussed are included in this review.

TEACHERS. An anomaly of teacher dismissal is that greater liberality is often displayed by parents and jury members, when cases reach the court stage, toward idiosyncratic teacher behavior than that shown by school boards and even the courts. It is the view of some that the protection-of-children theory, which has often been used in the past in upholding the dismissal of teachers who are nonconformists, is a protection which may be unrealistic and unwarranted in today's world (Geis & Huston, 1962). Nevertheless, the view that upholding the rights of individual teachers through tenure protection improves school systems is still vigorously supported (Ligtenburg, 1958).

Many argue that tenure prohibits or minimizes the appointment of employees for selfish motives, including nepotism, and protects against unwarranted dismissals (Stover, 1961). Tenure laws also protect teachers from unjustified reductions in salary (Reutter, 1957). Tenure is also a protection for teachers caught in the merger of districts which are being reorganized (Nolte, 1964).

Many problems can be overcome if the appropriate procedures for dismissing a teacher are followed. A review of many tenure cases shows the causes and procedures which are effective. From these cases, 10 propositions emerge which, if followed, would decrease court cases. In summary, school boards should deal with personnel in good faith, follow statutory procedures for dismissal, provide due-process procedures, and use the services of an attorney in securing advice regarding tenure law (Garber, 1956a).

Despite all of the suggestions and advice to avoid it, tenure cases do get to court each year in the various states. The courts have considered not only specific provisions of tenure laws but also the question of the power of state legislatures to amend or repeal tenure laws. The question is whether the tenure law has established a contractual right which, under article I, section X, of the U.S. constitution may not be impaired (Hamilton & Mort, 1959).

ADMINISTRATORS. Two districts, Spokane, Washington, and Covina, California, recommend rotating principals every few years rather than having them sit out their tenure in one place. To be effective, it is recommended that (1) the school board be informed of details of the plan, (2) a committee of board members and principals investigate the rotation plans of other districts, (3) salary safeguards be established, (4) administrators and the board agree on what the plan is and what it is expected to accomplish, and (5) the plan be gradually implemented by reassigning only a few principals each year and gradually adding more to the program each year (Fox & Jones, 1964). Rotation of principals seems more a topic for debate than a common practice (American Association of School Administrators, 1967).

Defining tenure as length of service rather than as a fair dismissal procedure, one study reported that long tenure of Georgia principals during the decade was associated with women principals, large schools, schools increasing in size, and schools in urban districts with gradually increasing populations. Older principals and a small percentage of low incomes in the district were also associated with long tenure (Bledsoe, 1957).

It has been suggested that state associations of school administrators should become aware of the difficulties and unknown factros regarding tenure and school principals. School codes of most states make no reference to the school principal with respect to tenure. At the minimum, the principal attains tenure as a teacher rather than as a principal. Thus, a principal could be removed from his principalship and given a teaching assignment. In the majority of states however, the principal attains tenure as a certified administrator and does not retain his tenure rights as a teacher after he leaves teaching (Hageny, 1961).

It should be noted that few tenure laws cover the superintendent of schools. It has been suggested that because of the difference in interpretation of state tenure laws by the courts, the legislative body enacting the laws should make an unequivocal statement if it desires to include the superintendent in the coverage provided by the law. There is a view that superintendents should not be protected by tenure laws but should be more susceptible to dismissal by the board of education than are other school personnel, although in one state, New Jersey, tenure is granted to superintendents for six years in cities of 250,000 or more (Seitz, 1958).

Although estimates vary, tenure of superintendents is short. The power structure of a community has an effect on tenure of superintendents, and tenure is shorter in factionalized communities. Effective measures which boards of education could take to protect the superintendent would be to strengthen the superintendent's recommending prerogative and to provide the superintendent with a term contract of three to five years, renewable annually (McCarty, 1964).

Superintendents have been polled to determine whether or not they felt they should receive tenure. In answer to the question "Should superintendents have tenure as teachers guaranteed by law?" 65 percent of the respondents answered yes, 32 percent answered no, and 3 percent had no opinion. Of those answering that tenure as teachers should be granted to administrators, 68 percent felt that a probationary period should be involved. One percent thought it should not, and 31 percent had no opinion. When asked whether or not administrators should have tenure as administrators rather than as teachers, 51 percent said they should not, and 33 percent said they should, while 16 percent expressed no opinion. This was a nationwide sample of superintendents conducted by a national magazine (*Nation's Schools*, 1958).

HIGHER EDUCATION. Faculties employed in higher education in public and private institutions are often employed under contract rather than under tenure laws. So they are governed by the general law of contract, unless it has been modified by tenure regulations which specify under which conditions the contract of an indefinite duration may be terminated. Reviews of cases since 1950 under both the general contract law and tenure provisions in higher education indicate that there is a division of judicial opinion and some uncertainty regarding the effect of tenure regulations established by governing boards (instead of by statute), particularly in the case of state institutions in states where the *statutes* do not provide for tenure. It is noted that often the tenure rights established by the institution are in conflict with the statutes granting the governing board the right to hire and fire, and the statutes will usually govern. The conclusion is that the principles of contract law are not everywhere widely and well understood (Chambers, 1964).

The tenure policies of 31 major U.S. universities have been summarized. There is a variety in reported practices which suggests that an ideal tenure policy has not been found in any university (Dressel, 1963). Somewhat the same situation exists in Canadian universities (Read, 1960). One of the principal areas of litigation in higher education is that of contracts and tenure (Murphy, 1963).

After an extensive review of the plans and practices in higher education regarding tenure, it was concluded that (1) all institutions of higher education should adopt tenure regulations; (2) institutions should consider faculty participation in the adoption of the regulations and the use of advice of the AAUP consultant service; (3) the regulation should be specific and in writing; (4) the regulation should remove any impediments to sound judicial and legal enforcement; (5) the courts should include in remedies for infringement an order for reinstatement; (6) faculty members should recognize their obligations (i.e., give sufficient notice of intent to resign, not give the impression of speaking for the institution, and the like); (7) tenure should be applicable to educational institutions conducted by religious groups, although the regulations must recognize reasonable limitations imposed by the religious objectives of the institution, if those regulations have been agreed to by the faculty member and the institution at appointment; (8) tenure should be granted after a specified probationary period; (9) tenure should be required after a specified probationary period; and (10) there should be provisions for appeal (Byse & Joughin, 1959).

Professional organizations in higher education such as the AAUP usually equate academic freedom with tenure provisions and frequently survey the problems which get into litigation in the tenure area and higher education (Murphy, 1963). A committee of the AAUP reports annually on censures in the *Statement of Principles on Academic Freedom and Tenure* (American Association of University Professors, 1966).

Cases showing the effect of loyalty oaths on tenure as well as the relation of academic freedom to tenure have been reviewed, with emphasis on the issues in tax-supported institutions of higher education (Blackwell, 1961).

NEGOTIATION. It is quite likely that during the next few years a form of tenure will arise from the comprehensive group contracts being negotiated in various cities in the United States by teacher organizations and school boards. In states where tenure laws do not exist or where they are not as protective as teachers might wish them to be, the negotiation agreements will probably contain provisions dealing with the employment and dismissal of teachers. Undoubtedly many of these provisions will provide protection similar to tenure laws now in existence (Lieberman & Moskow, 1966; National Education Association, Office of Professional Development and Welfare, 1965; Stinnett & others, 1966).

Martha L. Ware
National Education Association

References

American Association of School Administrators. *The Right Principal for the Right School.* AASA, 1967. 48p.

American Association of University Professors. "Academic Freedom and Tenure: 1940 Statements of Principles." *Am Assn U Prof B* 50:151–2; Fall: 1964.

American Association of University Professors. "Report of Committee A, 1965–66." *Am Assn U Prof B* 52:115–30; June 1966.

Blackwell, Thomas Edward. *College Law: A Guide For Administrators.* ACE, 1961. p. 58–73.

Bledsoe, Joseph C. "Factors Related to the Tenure of Public School Principals in Georgia During the Decade from 1946 Through 1956." *Ed Adm Sup* 43:193–203; April 1957.

Byse, Clark, and Joughin, Louis. *Tenure in American Higher Education: Plans, Practices and the Law.* Cornell U Press, 1959. 212p.

Chambers, Merritt M. *The Colleges and the Courts Since 1950.* Interstate, 1964. 415p.

Dressel, Paul L. "A Review of the Tenure Policies of Thirty-one Major Universities." *Ed Rec* 44:248–53; July 1963.

Drury, Robert L., and Ray, Kenneth C. *Principles of School Law.* Appleton, 1965. p. 61–5.

Fellman, David. "Academic Freedom in American Public Law." *Teach Col Rec* 62:368–86; February 1961.

Fox, Willard, and Jones, Ronald D. "Don't Let Principals Sit Out Tenure in One Place, Say Two Districts." *Nation's Sch* 74:31; July 1964.

Garber, Lee O. "Causes and Procedures for Dismissing a Tenure Teacher." *Nation's Sch* 58:73–4; December 1956(*a*).

Garber, Lee O. "Making Teacher Tenure Laws Work." *Nation's Sch* 58:63–4; November 1956(*b*).

Garber, Lee O. "Tenure." In *Yearbook of School Law*, 7 vols. Interstate, 1958–1965. (1958: 106–113; 1959: 111–114; 1960: 108–115; 1961: 130–9; 1962: 130–141; 1963: 149–160; 1964: 140–149; 1965: 129–136.)

Garber, Lee O., and Edwards, Newton. *The Law Governing Teaching Personnel.* School Law Casebook No. 4. Interstate, 1962.

Gauerke, Warren E. *School Law.* Center for Applied Research in Education, 1965. 116p.

Geis, Gilbert, and Huston, Robley. "Trends in the Dismissal of Tenure Teachers." *Yearbook of School Law.* Interstate, 1962. p. 199–209.

Hageny, William J. "The Principal and Tenure Laws." In Seitz, Reynolds C. (Ed.) *Law and the School Principal.* W. H. Anderson, 1961. p. 227–34.

Hamilton, Robert R., and Mort, Paul R. *The Law and Public Education*, 2nd ed. Foundation Press, 1959. 302p.

Hummel, Charlton G. "A Right Only If Deserved." *NEA J* 49:67–8; January 1960.

Lieberman, Myron, and Moskow, Michael. *Collective Negotiations For Teachers: An Approach to School Administration.* Rand McNally, 1966. 745p.

Ligtenberg, John. "Courts Hold Tenure Improves School System." *Am Teach M* 43:13–4; October 1958.

Machlup, Fritz. "In Defense of Academic Tenure." *Am Assn U Prof B* 50:112–24; June 1964.

McCarty, Donald J. "How Community Power Structures Influence Administrative Tenure." *Am Sch Bd J* 148:11–3; May 1964.

Murphy, William P. "Educational Freedom in the Courts." *Am Assn U Prof B* 49:309–27; March, 1963.

National Education Association, Office of Professional Development and Welfare. *Guidelines for Professional Negotiation*, rev. ed. NEA 1965. 55p.

National Education Association, Research Division. "Plaintiffs and Defendants—School Teachers in Court." *Res B* 36:58–60; April 1958.

National Education Association, Research Division. *Teacher's Day in Court: Review of 1964.* Research Report 1965-R8. NEA 1965(*a*). 63p.

National Education Association, Research Division. *Tenure and Contracts*, rev. ed. NEA, 1965(*b*).

Nation's Schools. "Tenure for Superintendents . . . Opinion Poll." *Nation's Sch* 62:6; August 1958.

Nolte, M. Chester. "Tenure Teacher Entitled to Hearing When District Merges with Another." *Am Sch Bd J* 148:11–2; March 1964.

Nolte, M. Chester, and Linn, John Phillip. *School Law For Teachers.* Interstate, 1963. p. 111–36.

Read, L. M. "The Crowe Case: Its History and Implications." *Sch Soc* 88:285–9; Summer 1960.

Remmlein, Madaline Kinter. *School Law*, 2nd ed. Interstate, 1962. p. 23–57.

Reutter, E. Edmund, Jr. "Personnel Administration." In Garber, Lee O. (Ed.) *Law and the School Business Manager.* Interstate, 1957. p. 258–64.

Reutter, E. Edmund, Jr. "Legal Aspects of Academic Freedom." In Garber, Lee O. (Ed.) *Current Legal Concepts in Education.* U Pennsylvania Press, 1965. p. 253–68.

Seitz, Reynolds C. "Duration and Determination of Tenure." In Drury, Robert L. (Ed.) *Law and The School Superintendent.* W. H. Anderson, 1958. p. 65–80.

Stinnett, T. M., and others. *Professional Negotiation in Public Education.* Macmillan, 1966. 309p.

Stover, William R. "The What and Why of Tenure." *NEA J* 50:47–8; March 1961.

TEST USE

Test use has taken second place to test development in the interests of professional educators in measurement and research. Most of the prominent measurement specialists have been and are authors of tests or statisticians or researchers. The great majority of the research reported in professional journals deals with the tests themselves and with their contributions to educational and psychological research, rather than with the actual administration and scoring of the tests, with test-program development, or with the use and interpretation of the resulting scores. This is not to say that there is any paucity of written how-to-do-it statements on test administration or test-program development or test interpretation. There are many, but not all of them are supported by relevant research evidence. Experientially based or even speculatively based statements on test use are not necessarily without merit. However, they should be evaluated for what they are without the assumption that they have been tested in controlled situations.

Many general treatises have been prepared to help students understand tests, how to approach them, and what the results may mean (Anderson & others, 1963). Parents and the public in general are the audience of both professional educators (Karmel, 1966) and professional writers (Hawes, 1964) who attempt to give an overview of standardized testing and the utilization of test results. Teachers and counselors have not been ignored (Lyman, 1963; Goldman, 1961) in the deluge of articles, pamphlets, and books seeking to instruct teachers, counselors, and administrators in proper test interpretation. Abuses and misuses and criticisms of tests and test use have been cited both by those within the profession (Womer, 1961) and by those without (Hoffman,

1961). Some of these publications have relied upon research findings to substantiate their suggestions; many have not. In many areas research evidence is not available to substantiate either claims made for or criticisms made of test use.

Some criticisms aimed at standardized tests have been concerned with test development, but most have been concerned with how the results have been or may be used to exclude students from something (rather than to help place students appropriately), to categorize students (rather than to improve understanding), to criticize educational attainments (rather than to aid in educational evaluation), or to pry into personal matters (rather than to understand the whole personality). A comprehensive survey of American adults has shown that about 40 percent have never taken a standardized ability test (Brim & others, 1965). Yet respondents had definite attitudes about ability tests, about how they are used, and about how they should be used. In general they approved of conventional uses of tests (such as for selection purposes) and disapproved of unconventional uses (such as for voting eligibility). The same study investigated attitudes toward testing that are related to the respondent's sex, age, race, and social class. All of these concerns fall within the general area of test use, an area with a certain body of substantive research but also one with large research gaps in it.

TEST-PROGRAM DEVELOPMENT. Research on test-program development is almost nonexistent. However, articles and pamphlets on test-program development are numerous, and there is one general textbook on testing that is aimed specifically at building a testing program (Bauernfeind, 1963). One of the most comprehensive lists of specific suggestions has been drawn up by Traxler and North (1963):

1. Provide for both group and individual needs in testing.
2. Develop a comprehensive and coordinated testing program.
3. Select supplementary tests to meet special needs.
4. Have a representative committee select the tests.
5. Relate test selection to a school's objectives.
6. Relate test selections to test quality (validity, reliability, etc.).
7. Consider the potential utility of any available state or national testing program.
8. Secure a director of testing.
9. Introduce a new testing program gradually.
10. Plan for test administration in detail.
11. Arrange for prompt scoring.
12. Report test results meaningfully to faculty.
13. Provide for evaluation of achievement in relation to tested ability.
14. Record results on individual forms that are available to faculty.
15. Provide in-service education for faculty on test interpretation.
16. Pay special attention to interpretation of aptitude, interest, and personality tests.
17. Formulate a school policy on releasing test results to parents and other nonfaculty.

Many writers in the area of test-program development stress the importance of fitting tests to instructional and guidance purposes. The testing program is seen as a vehicle for securing information that can be useful to teachers and counselors and administrators in their instructional and guidance roles. The testing program is seen as a tool, not as an end in itself.

TEST ADMINISTRATION. Perhaps the best overall treatment of the topic of test administration was done by Traxler (Lindquist, 1951) in a summary and exposition of major concerns, such as timing, clarity of directions, guessing, and physical conditions. Research in this area may be categorized as centering on the examiner, on the examinee, or on the testing situation. The testing situation might be considered to be an interaction among the examiner, the examinee, and the examination. In recent years more attention has been given to the potential influence of the examiner on test results than formerly had been the case. For example, the sex of the examiner has been demonstrated to have an effect on test performance. Three- and four-year-olds of both sexes have been shown to have received higher test scores when the examiner was a woman (Stevenson, 1961). At ages six and seven boys tested higher than girls when the examiner was a woman. The same study showed no effects at ages nine and ten. A later study (Cieutat, 1965) showed that in general female examiners elicited higher IQ's than male examiners did and showed, further, that an examiner of the opposite sex elicited better results. Another study (Stevenson & Allen, 1964) also showed better test performance with examiners of the opposite sex. Results of this sort have particular import for individual testing, but even with group testing it may suggest that both men and women should serve as examiners within a given school.

In the broader field of data collection it has been shown that an experimenter may have a modeling effect on the subject (Rosenthal, 1963b). Personal attributes such as sex, religion, race, status, likability, acquaintanceship, warmth, professional skill, and trust are experimenter variables that influence a subject's response patterns (Rosenthal, 1963a). These attributes have particular relevance for individual testing. They also have implications for the testing of minority-group members, whether a minority group is based on race or socioeconomic level or religion or any other pertinent variable that may apply to one subgroup of students.

The research of the 1960's suggests that previous concern with adequate physical conditions for testing, with accuracy of reading directions and accuracy of timing, and with examinee motivation may have unduly ignored the important variable of the examiner in influencing the test results of students either positively or negatively. Apparently nothing relating to testing can be ignored as inconsequential, any more than it can be ignored in the classroom.

Affective characteristics of examinees have not been overlooked by the researcher seeking to identify potential sources of variance in test scores. Test anxiety was reported to be negatively correlated with aptitude-test scores by Grooms and Endler (1960) and also by Walter and others (1964). The latter study showed no significant correlations between test anxiety and grade-point averages, however. In addition, no significant correlations were found when a relationship between manifest anxiety and achievement on an arithmetic test was sought (Reese, 1961). Related to these findings is a study which showed that stressful situations interfered with performance on a complex task for highly anxious subjects but facilitated simple tasks (Wrightsman, 1962). The same study showed a negative relationship between anxiety and performance on an intelligence test when the examinee perceived the test as important to himself but not when he perceived it as unimportant. A point that is not clear in these various studies is whether test anxiety affects all examinees or whether the group differences are accounted for primarily by a subpopulation for which test anxiety produces substantial individual effects.

The research relating test anxiety to performance on standardized tests is something of a by-product of the greater body of research on anxiety and other personality characteristics. More directly aimed at examinees' characteristics as they affect test performance is the area of response sets. Cronbach (1946, 1950) reviewed the early literature on this topic. Stricker (1965) reviewed more recent studies while doing an important piece of research himself. The early research indicated such response sets as a tendency toward choosing the true response with two-choice items (Cronbach, 1942) and a tendency toward choosing alternatives located in a middle position with multiple-choice items (Rapaport & Berg, 1955) and indicated that these tendencies are elicited by the relatively difficult test items. Stricker (1965), however, did not find item difficulty a significant variable in his study of the response style of criticality. In addition, item reliability was not related to criticality. A critical response style is one which tends toward seeing ambiguities or differences. These findings led Stricker to speculate that certain response sets may be strong enough to be unaffected by item characteristics such as difficulty or content, while others are not. He did find some evidence that criticality was related to item location—the later an item appeared in a test, the more susceptible it was to a critical response style.

In addition to the various personality characteristics that may influence test scores it has been suggested that many students develop specific skills in test taking, skills that enable them to analyze choice-type items on the basis of clues which are built into the items and which are not related to knowledge of item content. This is referred to as test wiseness. An analysis of test wiseness including an outline of test-wiseness principles has been developed (Millman & others, 1965) with the hope that it will serve as a framework for research in the topic. Millman secured student responses to an open-ended question that asked them to suggest things that a student should do when taking a test. The most frequent responses were to read directions carefully, to refrain from spending too much time on any one question, to re-check answers, to guess, and to eliminate obvious foils. Many students seem to have good perceptions of how to take choice-type tests.

When tests are used for selection purposes, questions about the effect of coaching and of practice are raised. In general, the studies indicate that coaching, or practice, or both, on other tests does have a positive effect on subsequent test results. The magnitude of the effect, however, varies considerably. On the *Scholastic Aptitude Test* (*SAT*) one study showed that coaching produced a positive effect of 20 points for the verbal score and 30 points for the mathematics score (French & Dear, 1959). These gains were statistically significant but were less than the standard errors of the tests. Another study showed smaller gains, 8 points and 9 points, respectively, for the coached group (Frankel, 1960). These gains were not significant. The SAT-score scale runs from 200 to 800. Many test technicians have suggested that general maintenance of skills and knowledges in a subject area makes specific coaching for test taking a waste of time.

A third study (Jacobs, 1966) indicated that the effect of coaching varied from no mean difference in one school to 73 points in another school on the College Entrance Examination Board (CEEB) *English Composition Test*. This suggests the specificity of the effect of coaching from school to school. An interesting additional point in this study was the disappearance of the increments favoring coached schools after a 10-month interval.

The practice effect of taking a test on subsequent performance on a different form of that test has been investigated rather thoroughly. Frankel (1960) showed gains from junior-year SAT scores to senior-year scores of 30 points on the verbal test and 50 points on mathematics. This reflects a year of study, however, and really is practice plus educational development. Two studies of the practice effect on the *Miller Analogies Test* showed that 81 percent and 75 percent of groups of college students taking two forms of the test made higher scores on the second form (Spielberger, 1959; Colver & Spielberger, 1961). An investigation of the practice effect of taking an achievement test on an intelligence test and vice versa showed that for seventh graders scores on the *California Test of Mental Maturity* (*CTMM*) were greater when it was administered after the *California Achievement Tests* (*CAT*), whereas *CAT* scores were lower when it was administered after the *CTMM*. In some fashion the *CAT* facilitated *CTMM* performance while the *CTMM* interfered with *CAT* performance (Dizney & Yamamoto, 1965). These order effects did not appear at the fourth-grade level. Several studies of practice effect on personality instruments have indicated a significant difference between first and second administrations of the same instrument whereas subsequent administrations produced results like the second one (Fiske, 1957; Howard, 1964).

Statistically significant differences in test scores from one administration of a test to another often are small numerically and not of great import for counselors 'or teachers' use of test results, although they may be important in research studies. The large number of tests administered to elementary and secondary students suggests that they are receiving considerable practice in taking standardized tests and that specific coaching or practice may not be worth the necessary time and effort.

The subject of examinee guessing as a variable in test performance has received considerable attention. At one time formulas that corrected for guessing were widely used with standardized tests. The past decade has seen an almost complete abandonment of the use of scoring formulas other than the simple number of right responses. The problem of guessing seems to be confounded by the evidence that guessing sometimes is completely random and sometimes is based on partial knowledge (Coombs & others, 1956). There is evidence that while some students do refrain from answering some questions when told not to do random guessing, others do guess and mark all questions (Sheriffs & Boomer, 1954; Swineford & Miller, 1953). In addition, there is evidence that instructing all examinees to guess does not necessarily lower test reliability but may improve it (Michael & others, 1963). Undoubtedly the practical advantages of telling all examinees to answer all items has been an important consideration in the increased reliance on scoring right responses only.

A common concern of many examinees is to have what is felt to be sufficient time to work on a test. Some students are more deliberate workers than others and feel constrained by time limits. Most standardized tests, except for speeded tests, have time limits that allow 90 percent or more of a typical group of examinees to finish. In spite of the fact that some examinees do not finish, studies generally show that unlimited time to work on a test does not change a student's rank order substantially (Boag & Neild, 1962). The same study suggests that the changes that do take place with unlimited time are primarily with average students rather than with high- or low-scoring students.

TEST SCORING. Test scoring has become primarily a machine process in the past decade. There still are schools that hand score their standardized tests, particularly in the elementary grades (Womer, 1963), but the overwhelming trend is toward machine scoring. The introduction of the IBM 805 in the late 1930's was followed some twenty years later by the development of Midwest Research Center (MRC) test-scoring machines that used a different scoring principle and multiplied scoring efficiency manyfold. Whereas machine scoring at one time meant the IBM 805, it now may mean MRC, IBM 1230, Digitek, Docutran, Scribe, or any one of several other electronic machines that are not identified by specific names. There are a number of researchable problems associated with the use of machines for test scoring. Many of them focus upon the accuracy of machine scoring and the compatability of results when using different answer media appropriate to the different machines.

A problem common to all machine operations is that of the lack of accuracy of the marks made by students on the answer sheets. Durost (1954) reported that it was necessary to erase or darken marks on from 10 to 50 percent of student-marked answer sheets before they could be put through an IBM 805. Most machine operations are still hampered by the fact that answer sheets must be scanned by an individual, by hand, before they can be inserted into the machine.

A series of studies has been made to check the accuracy of scoring for the *Strong Vocational Interest Blank* (*SVIB*). Burack (1961) reported sending a series of *SVIB* answer sheets for rescoring five weeks after they were initially scored by a scoring agency. Ninety-six percent of the sheets showed some change: 42 percent showed a change of at least one level, and 12 percent showed a change of two levels. This study led to a check of machine-scoring accuracy, and some changes were made by the agency involved. A follow-up study (Weigel & others, 1965) found only 13 percent of the *SVIB* scores changing one level and found no changes of two levels. Errors, however, had not been eliminated. Another follow-up study (Merwin & others, 1965) again showed some errors, but few variations were large enough to affect profile interpretation. A recent study of the accuracy of Digitek scoring (Spencer, 1966) suggests that one user of that machine has achieved very reliable scoring accuracy. The author reports that for a large set of answer sheets scored both by machine and by hand, only 11 differences were found. An additional point was that all of the errors were in hand scoring; the Digitek scoring was 100 percent accurate. It is questionable whether a user of that machine or any other should count on 100 percent accuracy, however.

The reports of test-scoring accuracy that are given in the literature must account for only a minute portion of the accuracy checks that have been made and are made regularly with machine scoring. Each machine has had to go through a shakedown period, a time of pain for the test user as well as for the scoring agency.

A more important concern to the test user than the transient problems associated with machine accuracy is the problem of answer-media format and its influence on test norms. Each differently scoring machine requires a different answer sheet or card. The spacing of response positions is different on different media, the answer-space sizes are different, and the shapes are different. Some users have assumed that an answer sheet is an answer sheet is an answer sheet and that norms developed on one type of answer sheet are automatically satisfactory for any other type. Fortunately many test users and many test publishers have not been willing to make this assumption, for there are examples of different norms being prepared for different answer media. The *Lorge-Thorndike Intelligence Tests' Examiner's Manual* (Lorge & Thorndike, 1957) has a correction factor that must be applied to raw scores before entering the regular norm tables whenever the Consumable Edition of the tests for grades 4, 5, and 6 is used rather than the separate answer-sheet edition. This correction does not appear at higher grade levels. The *Differential Aptitude Tests (DAT) manual* (Bennett & others, 1966) presents different norms for the Clerical Speed and Accuracy Test for IBM 805, MRC, IBM 1230, and Digitek answer sheets. This points up the particular susceptibility of a speeded test to answer-media format. Presumably the norms of the other tests of the *DAT* were not affected appreciably by the use of different answer sheets.

Other researchers have been concerned with answer-media format and its effect on test scores. A comparison of the IBM 805 with the IBM 1230 showed no significant differences in test scores (Dizney & others, 1966) in spite of the fact that more students expressed difficulty in using the 1230 answer sheets. Another study showed no mean IQ differences between the use of the IBM answer sheets and the IBM mark-sense cards (Slater, 1964), but the author added that 10 percent of the sample showed IQ differences of 10 points or more. The individual differences that appeared were not consistently in one direction or the other.

A comparison of a new answer format for the *Lorge-Thorndike Intelligence Tests* with the previous one showed no appreciable differences for eighth graders (Miller, 1965). A change in color had no significant effect on test performance. The same study reported inconclusive evidence at grade 4. A study of different answer sheets available for use with the *General Aptitude Test Battery (GATB)* showed significant differences between the different types of sheets (Bell & Hoff, 1964). No one design seemed to be better. The short time limits for many of the *GATB* tests may have influenced these results, if the *DAT* example holds true in general.

Still another approach to testing the effect of answer-media format on norms was to design answer sheets in a variety of patterns that are not standard—e.g., by putting answer spaces in vertical order rather than horizontal, and to compare them with the standard IBM 805 answer sheet (Miller & Minor, 1963). This study showed significant differences between four experimental forms and the IBM 805 and showed differences between the experimental forms. Allied to this was a comparison of IBM 805 answer sheets with a write-in type of sheet. The means of the tests using the IBM sheets were significantly lower than for the write-in sheets (Whitcomb, 1958). This result was obtained with highly speeded tests and reaffirms the importance of the type of answer media in such tests.

The evidence at hand is rather conclusive that the answer media can make a difference but in many instances do not. This suggests that test publishers or test users, or both, must not use an answer medium different from the one on which a test has been standardized without evidence of the comparability of the norms.

TEST USE AND TEST INTERPRETATION. It is very possible that the major consumers of standardized test results today are counselors, particularly at the secondary-school level. And, if that is not so, test results certainly are widely used in the counseling process, and much of the recent research on test use has been done by and for counselors. Nevertheless, the results apply to the use of test information by anyone working with students. Although there is an expanding body of research in the area of test use, it hardly can be considered sufficient to enable a test user to approach test interpretation with great confidence that his actions are well grounded on research findings. Perhaps the most comprehensive coverage of test interpretation, including a review of the research as well as an exposition of theory and procedures, has been done by Goldman (1961). He devotes about two-thirds of his text to this topic. Ohlsen (1963) includes a review of the research in test interpretation in his chapter on test interpretation in the 62nd yearbook of the National Society for the Study of Education. On the basis of research findings on test interpretation, Lister and McKenzie (1966) have formulated a set of conditions that they consider to be essential if one posits that test interpretation is designed to improve student self-understanding: (1) The student should have a felt need for information, (2) students' questions should be put into specific operational terms, usually of a probability nature, (3) there should be empirical evidence of the relationship between test scores and criterion measures, and (4) the information should be clearly communicated to the student.

A number of studies have dealt with the specific effects of test interpretation in counseling. In general, they show significant increases in accuracy of self-estimates of test scores after pretesting orientation as well as increased interest in seeking information about results of tests (Lister & Ohlsen, 1962). Counseling was shown to increase the accuracy of self-estimates of achievement, intelligence, and interest scores with students from four different grade levels (Lister & Ohlsen, 1965). The latter study suggests that the counselor's role is more a facilitating one than an information-giving one. In contrast to this, Hills and Williams (1965) found that communication of test results had no significant effect in influencing positive changes in self-perceptions.

Other studies, which were designed to test differential effects of different methods of test interpretation, have shown overall improvement in recall of test information resulting from various methods of counseling (Holmes, 1964; Wright, 1963; Lallas, 1956; Folds & Gazda, 1966). A study of college freshmen indicated that test results conveyed in any one of four different methods produced an awareness of a need to improve in areas in which test results were low (Holmes, 1961).

The evidence on the differential effects of directive versus nondirective counseling in improving self-knowledge of test results is conflicting. Lane (1952) obtained results in favor of a more permissive technique over a traditional authoritarian technique. A comparison of the self-evaluative interview with the test-centered interview, for retention of knowledge of test results (Rogers, 1954), showed no statistically significant differences although the test-centered interview seemed to work better with high-intelligence students while the self-evaluative interview seemed best for the student who participates actively in the interview. A study of three methods for introducing a test and four methods of test interpretation with varying degrees of counselor responsibility, from great to little, showed no significant differences in client learning about self (Gustad & Tuma, 1957). A more recent study compared a written, mailed resume of test results with two counselor-dominant methods and one student-dominant method (Holmes, 1964). While each method improved recall of test information, the only difference between groups was that the students receiving a written mailed report considered the test information of least value. This confirms Lister and Ohlsen's contention (1965) that the counselor's role is more in the affective than the cognitive domain.

There have been a number of studies evaluating the relative effectiveness of individual versus group methods of test interpretation. The evidence is quite consistent in showing that both individual and group methods of test interpretation do increase the accuracy of self-estimates of test scores. The evidence, however, does not show either the individual or the group approach to be better. One study by Walker (1965) supports the individual approach as producing better student acceptance of measured abilities. A study by Folds and Gazda (1966) supports the individual approach as increasing student satisfaction with test interpretation. This study also showed significant gains in self concepts for all three methods of test interpretation that were used, individual, small group, and written records.

In contrast to these two studies Wright (1963) found no significant differences between individual and group counseling in degree of accuracy of self-ratings, acquisition of information about tests, feasibility of vocational choice, or counselee satisfaction. Lallas (1956) found that a combination of group and individual counseling was better than either one alone for improving the agreement between test estimates and self-estimate. Adamek (1961) found no significant difference between individual and group methods for the same criteria.

The research evidence strongly supports the view that test interpretation of various types improves self-estimates of test scores. The differential effects are not as clear-cut; the superiority of neither the directive nor the nondirective method is clearly supported by research, and the superiority of neither the group nor the individual approach is clearly supported by research. The question of the import of test information in a student's own decision making has not been investigated.

A very common complaint among school administrators is that the teachers don't use the standardized test results. There seems to be a general feeling that although the information gained from standardized test results gets into the cumulative record, too often it does not get into the classroom. In spite of such complaints one study indicated that while counselors were primarily responsible for test interpretation in the secondary grades, teachers had that responsibility in the elementary grades (Womer, 1963). Having responsibility and exercising it may be two different things.

There is a real paucity of research on how teachers or administrators do or should use test results. Typical of the articles on using test results in the classroom or the school in general are (1) those that outline areas in which tests can be helpful (e.g., Traxler, 1960), (2) those that suggest how standardized test interpretation should take place (e.g., Seashore, 1958), (3) those that suggest how teacher-made tests should be used (e.g., Ebel, 1965), and (4) those that make specific suggestions or investigate some one aspect of test use (Putt & Ray, 1965).

Traxler (1960) listed ten ways to use the results from a school testing program, paraphrased as follows:

1. Assessing abilities and aptitudes.
2. Comparing achievement with scholastic aptitude.
3. Judging the level of ability or achievement in a classroom.
4. Improving self-understanding in counseling.
5. Diagnosing strengths and weaknesses both of individual students and of classes.
6. Discovering special abilities.
7. Identifying students' interests.
8. Guiding students toward educational and vocational goals.
9. Helping students with adjustment problems.
10. Doing research in education and guidance.

Others might arrange or word the list differently, but most such listings cover the same areas.

Seashore (1958) offered specific suggestions for teachers' interpretations of standardized tests:

1. Help the students understand what a standardized test is, and help him regard his performance on such a test as a check on his own progress.
2. Be able to interpret group-test results properly (a) in comparisons of one class group with others, local and national, and (b) in comparisons of an individual student's performances with that of his class.
3. Help a student to understand each test that was used and the degree of accuracy (and error) in test scores.

Ebel (1965) has suggestions for interpreting a teacher's own tests to his students: (1) prepare a frequency distribution, with its mean and standard deviation; (2) record test scores rather than letter grades; (3) estimate test reliability and standard error of measurement; and (4) report all this information to students when scored tests are returned.

Putt and Ray (1965) investigated the use of

three standardized reading tests in a fifth-grade in a demonstration that both standardized tests and a teacher's own informal tests contributed to a complete diagnosis of classroom achievement.

Hastings (1966) points out the great need for studies of *how* decisions are made when test results are used. In the case of test use in the classroom, maxims rather than proofs are the rule.

TEST NORMS. The consumers of standardized tests must be and are concerned with the adequacy of the development of test norms. But they are particularly concerned with the interpretation of test norms, with the comparability of norms from test to test, with sex differences in test norms, with the use of local norms, and so on. Womer (1965) has written a monograph on test norms and their use aimed at the consumer of standardized tests, particularly the school administrator. He treats the development of norms from a nontechnical point of view and stresses those aspects of test norms that bear most directly upon proper test interpretation.

One of the bugaboos of the test user is the adequacy of test norms. Are norms of test X reasonable yardsticks of achievement, as contrasted to those of test Y? The publisher of test X claims to have developed truly national norms; the publisher of test Y claims to have developed truly national norms. Yet the two tests may not yield directly comparable scores. Many a director of school testing has wrestled with this problem, often by trying out a set of new or revised tests to get a "feeling" for the adequacy of the norms. Only a few studies of the comparability of test norms have been reported in the literature. One study compared five widely used series of achievement tests at the third-grade level in Nebraska (Stake, 1961). The results showed one test, the *California Achievement Tests* (*CAT*), yielding grade equivalents about a half year above the mean of the other four. A later study compared the California tests with two other achievement series and found that while the 1957 *CAT* norms were significantly higher than those of the Iowa and Metropolitan series, the 1963 *CAT* norms were only slightly higher (Millman & Lindlof, 1964). These illustrative studies suggest the importance of using a single, standardized test series normed on the same population or of using local norms when different test series are used.

Of specific interest to some test users are comparisons between different schools or different types of schools on test norms. Large-scale research studies such as Project Talent and that of the Exploratory Committee on Assessing the Progress of Education have taken elaborate precautions to avoid the possibility of comparisons between schools. In contrast to this was a study by Bauernfeind and Blumenfeld (1963) which showed that Catholic-school pupils scored higher on achievement tests (*SRA High School Placement Test*) when matched with public school pupils on reasoning ability, sex, and geographic location. Such studies often raise more questions than they answer, relating to school objectives, selection of student body, and so on. Nevertheless, they do provide information of a census nature, the status quo on selected elements of achievement.

Still another area of major concern in interpreting test norms is the area of sex differences. Many studies have demonstrated that sex differences do exist in test norms, and some widely used tests prepare different norm tables for boys and girls (Bennett & others, 1966). One recent study showed differences for certain parts of the *Stanford Achievement Tests*, generally favoring girls in the third and sixth grades (Wozencraft, 1963). Similar results have been reported for the *CAT*, with girls generally excelling in reading and arithmetic fundamentals whereas boys excelled in arithmetic reasoning (Parsley & others, 1964). Results like these have been found for years. In a comprehensive report of Project Talent results the following points were made, all applying to grades 9 through 12 (Flanagan & others, 1964):

1. Girls finish more items than boys on a test of information.

2. Differences in subtest reliability between the sexes related to sex differences in interest in the subject area.

3. There were no appreciable sex differences in factorial composition of the tests.

4. Little sex difference was shown in reading at the middle or higher comprehension levels.

5. Girls exceeded boys in arithmetic computation at grade 9 but not at grade 12.

6. No significant sex differences were shown in arithmetic reasoning, though boys were higher by grade 12.

7. Boys scored higher in vocabulary tests at all levels.

The Project Talent results suggest that boys catch up and in some areas surpass girls on standardized achievement tests as they move into the secondary grades. Teachers using standardized test results in the elementary and secondary grades need to keep these potential differences in mind as they interpret standardized test scores.

Frank B. Womer
The University of Michigan
N. Kishor Wahi
The University of Michigan

References

Adamek, Edward G. "The Effects of Testing and Test Interpretation on Selected Self Perception." Doctoral dissertation. U Illinois, 1961.

Anderson, Scarvia B., and others. *Meeting the Test.* Scholastic, 1963. 185p.

Bauernfeind, Robert H. *Building a School Testing Program.* Houghton, 1963. 343p.

Bauernfeind, Robert H., and Blumenfeld, Warren S. "A Comparison of Achievement Scores of Public-

school and Catholic-school Pupils." *Ed Psychol Meas* 23:331–6; 1963.
Bell, Forest O., and Hoff, Alvin L. "Answer Sheets Do Make a Difference." *Personnel Psychol* 17:65–71; 1964.
Bennett, George K., and others. *Manual for the Differential Aptitude Tests*, 4th ed. Psych Corp, 1966. 178p.
Boag, Audrey K., and Neild, Margaret. "The Influence of the Time Factor on the Scores of the Triggs Diagnostic Reading Test as Reflected in the Performance of Secondary School Pupils Grouped According to Ability." *J Ed Res* 55:181–3; 1962.
Brim, Orville G., Jr., and others. *Experiences and Attitudes of American Adults Concerning Standardized Intelligence Tests*. Russell Sage, 1965. 194p.
Burack, B. "Have You Checked Machine Scoring Error Lately?" *Voc Guid Q* 9:191–3; 1961.
Cieutat, Victor J. "Examiner Differences With the Stanford-Binet IQ." *Perceptual Motor Skills* 20:317–8; 1965.
Colver, Robert M., and Spielberger, Charles D. "Further Evidence of a Practice Effect on the Miller Analogies Test." *J Applied Psychol* 45:126–7; 1961.
Coombs, Clyde H., and others. "The Assessment of Partial Knowledge." *Ed Psychol Meas* 16:13–37; 1956.
Cronbach, Lee J. "Studies of Acquiescence as a Factor in the True-False Test." *J Ed Psychol* 33:401–15; 1942.
Cronbach, Lee J. "Response Sets and Test Validity." *Ed Psychol Meas* 6:475–94; 1946.
Cronbach, Lee J. "Further Evidence on Response Sets and Test Design." *Ed Psychol Meas* 10:3–31; 1950.
Dizney, Henry F., and Yamamoto, Kaoru. "Note on Effects of Practice and Fatigue in Group Testing of Intelligence and Achievement." *Psychol Reports* 16:537–8; 1965.
Dizney, Henry F., and others. "Effects of Answer-sheet Format on Arithmetic Test Scores." *Ed Psychol Meas* 26:491–3; 1966.
Durost, Walter N. "Present Progress and Needed Improvements in School Evaluation Programs." *Ed Psychol Meas* 14:247–54; 1954.
Ebel, Robert L. "Using the Results of Measurement." In *Evaluation in Social Studies*. NEA, 1965. p. 202–17.
Fiske, Donald W. "An Intensive Study of Variability Scores." *Ed Psychol Meas* 17:453–65; 1957.
Flanagan, John C., and others. *The Identification, Development, and Utilization of Human Talents: The American High School Student*. USOE Cooperative Research Project No. 635, U Pittsburgh, 1964. 700p.
Folds, Jonell H., and Gazda, George M. "A Comparison of the Effectiveness and Efficiency of Three Methods of Test Interpretation." *J Counseling Psychol* 13:318–24; 1966.
Frankel, Edward. "Effects of Growth, Practice, and Coaching on Scholastic Aptitude Test Scores." *Personnel Guid J* 38:713–9; 1960.
French, John W., and Dear, Robert E. "Effect of Coaching on an Aptitude Test." *Ed Psychol Meas* 19:319–30; 1959.
Goldman, Leo. *Using Tests in Counseling*. Appleton, 1961. 434p.
Grooms, Robert R., and Endler, Norman S. "The Effect of Anxiety on Academic Achievement." *J Ed Psychol* 51:299–304; 1960.
Gustad, John W., and Tuma, Abdul H. "The Effects of Different Methods of Test Introduction and Interpretation on Client Learning in Counseling." *J Counseling Psychol* 4:313–7; 1957.
Hastings, J. Thomas. "How Teachers Use Intelligence Tests." In *Proceedings of the 1965 Invitational Conference on Testing Problems*. ETS, 1966. p. 12–8.
Hawes, Gene R. *Educational Testing for the Millions*. McGraw-Hill, 1964. 290p.
Hills, David A., and Williams, John E. "Effects of Test Information Upon Self-evaluation in Brief Educational-Vocational Counseling." *J Counseling Psychol* 12:275–81; 1965.
Hoffmann, Banesh. "The Tyranny of Multiple-choice Tests." *Harper's* 222:37–44; 1961.
Holmes, June E. "The Comparison of Four Techniques Used in Presenting Information to Freshmen Students." Doctoral dissertation. Boston U, 1961.
Holmes, June E. "The Presentation of Test Information to College Freshmen." *J Counseling Psychol* 11:54–8; 1964.
Howard, Kenneth I. "Differentiation of Individuals as a Function of Repeated Testing." *Ed Psychol Meas* 24:875–94; 1964.
Jacobs, Paul I. "Effects of Coaching on the College Board English Composition Test." *Ed Psychol Meas* 26:55–67; 1966.
Karmel, Louis J. *Testing in Our Schools*. Macmillan, 1966. 112p.
Lallas, John E. "A Comparison of Three Methods of Interpretation of the Results of Achievement Tests to Pupils." Doctoral dissertation. Stanford U, 1956.
Lane, David. "A Comparison of Two Techniques of Interpreting Test Results to Clients in Vocational Counseling." Doctoral dissertation. Columbia U, 1952.
Lindquist, E. F. (Ed.) *Educational Measurement*. ACE, 1951. 810p.
Lister, James L., and McKenzie, Donald H. "A Framework for the Improvement of Test Interpretation in Counseling." *Personnel Guid J* 45:61–6; 1966.
Lister, James L., and Ohlsen, Merle M. *The Effects of Orientation to Testing on Motivation for and Outcomes of Test Interpretation*. USOE Cooperative Research Project No. 1344, U Illinois, 1962. 149p.
Lister, James L., and Ohlsen, Merle M. "The Improvement of Self-understanding Through Test Interpretation." *Personnel Guid J* 43:804–10; 1965.
Lorge, Irving, and Thorndike, Robert L. *The Lorge-*

Thorndike Intelligence Tests, Examiner's Manual. Houghton, 1957. 32p.

Lyman, Howard B. *Test Scores and What They Mean.* Prentice-Hall, 1963. 223p.

Merwin, Jack C., and others. "SVIB Machine Scoring Provided by a Test Scoring Agency." *Personnel Guid J* 43:665–8; 1965.

Michael, William B., and others. "An Experimental Determination of the Optimal Scoring Formula for a Highly-speeded Test Under Different Instructions Regarding Scoring Penalties." *Ed Psychol Meas* 23:83–99; 1963.

Miller, Irwin, and Minor, Frank J. "Influence of Multiple-choice Answer Form Design on Answer Marking Preference." *J Applied Psychol* 47:374–9; 1963.

Miller, Irwin. "A Note on the Evaluation of a New Answer Form." *J Applied Psychol* 49:199–201; 1965.

Millman, Jason, and Lindlof, John. "The Comparability of Fifth-grade Norms of the California, Iowa and Metropolitan Achievement Tests." *J Ed Meas* 1:135–7; 1964.

Millman, Jason, and Others. "An Analysis of Test-wiseness." *Ed Psychol Meas* 25:707–26; 1965.

Ohlsen, Merle M. "Interpretation of Test Scores." In *The Impact and Improvement of School Testing Programs,* 62nd Yearbook, Part II, NSSE. U Chicago Press, 1963. p. 254–94.

Parsley, Kenneth M., Jr., and Others. "Further Investigation of Sex Differences in Achievement of Under-, Average-, and Over-Achieving Students Within Five IQ Groups in Grades Four Through Eight." *J Ed Res* 57:268–70; 1964.

Putt, Robert C., and Ray, Darrel D. "Putting Test Results to Work." *El Sch J* 65:439–44; 1965.

Rapaport, Gerald M., and Berg, Irwin A. "Response Sets in a Multiple-choice Test." *Ed Psychol Meas* 15:58–62; 1955.

Reese, Hayne W. "Manifest Anxiety and Achievement Test Performance." *J Ed Psychol* 52:132–5; 1961.

Rogers, Lyle B. "A Comparison of Two Kinds of Test Interpretation Interview." *J Counseling Psychol* 1:224–31; 1954.

Rosenthal, Robert. "Experimenter Attributes as Determinants of Subjects' Responses." *J Projective Techniques* 27:324–31; 1963(*a*).

Rosenthal, Robert. "Experimenter Modeling Effects as Determinants of Subject's Responses." *J Projective Techniques* 27:467–71; 1963(*b*).

Seashore, Harold. "How Can the Results of a Testing Program Be Used Most Effectively?" *B Nat Assn Sec Sch Prin* 42:64–8; 1958.

Sherriffs, Alex C., and Boomer, Donald S. "Who Is Penalized by the Penalty for Guessing?" *J Ed Psychol* 45:81–90; 1954.

Slater, Richard D. "The Equivalency of IBM Marksense Answer Cards and IBM Answer Sheets When Used as Answer Formats for a Precisely-timed Test of Mental Ability." *J Ed Res* 57:545–7; 1964.

Spencer, Richard E. "Reliability and Validity of the Digitek Optical Scanner in Test Scoring Operations." *Ed Psychol Meas* 26:719–23; 1966.

Spielberger, Charles D. "Evidence of a Practice Effect on the Miller Analogies Test." *J Applied Psychol* 43:259–63; 1959.

Stake, Robert E. "Overestimation of Achievement with the California Achievement Test." *Ed Psychol Meas* 21:59–62; 1961.

Stevenson, Harold W. "Social Reinforcement with Children as a Function of CA, Sex of Examiner, and Sex of Subject." *J Abn Social Psychol* 63:147–54; 1961.

Stevenson, Harold W., and Allen, Sara. "Adult Performance as a Function of Sex of Experimenter and Sex of Subject." *J Abn Social Psychol* 68:214–6; 1964.

Stricker, Lawrence J. "Difficulty and Other Correlates of Criticalness Response Style at the Item Level." *Ed Psychol Meas* 25:683–706; 1965.

Swineford, Frances, and Miller, Peter M. "Effects of Directions Regarding Guessing on Item Statistics of a Multiple-choice Vocabulary Test." *J Ed Psychol* 44:129–39; 1953.

Traxler, Arthur E. "Use of Results of Large-scale Testing Programs in Instruction and Guidance." *J Ed Res* 54:59–62; 1960.

Traxler, Arthur E., and North, Robert D. "The Selection and Use of Tests in a School Testing Program." In *The Impact and Improvement of School Testing Programs,* 62nd Yearbook, Part II, NSSE. U Chicago Press, 1963. p. 211–31.

Walker, Joseph L. "Four Methods of Interpreting Test Scores Compared." *Personnel Guid J* 44:402–4; 1965.

Walter, Dean, and others. "Anxiety and the Intellectual Performance of High School Students." *Child Develop* 35:917–26; 1964.

Weigel, Richard, and others. "Re-evaluating Machine Scoring Consistency." *Voc Guid Q* 13:209–11; 1965.

Whitcomb, Milton A. "The IBM Answer Sheet as a Major Source of Variance on Highly Speeded Tests." *Ed Psychol Meas* 18:757–9; 1958.

Womer, Frank B. "Testing Programs—Misconceptions, Misuse, Overuse." *Michigan J Sec Ed* 2:153–61; 1961.

Womer, Frank B. *Testing Programs in Michigan Schools, 1963.* U Michigan, 1963. 64p.

Womer, Frank B. *Test Norms: Their Use and Interpretation.* National Association of Secondary School Principals, 1965. 56p.

Wozencraft, Marian. "Sex Comparisons of Certain Abilities." *J Ed Res* 57:21–7; 1963.

Wright, E. Wayne. "A Comparison of Individual and Multiple Counseling for Test Interpretation Interviews." *J Counseling Psychol* 10:126–35; 1963.

Wrightsman, Lawrence S., Jr. "The Effects of Anxiety, Achievement Motivation, and Task Importance upon Performance on an Intelligence Test." *J Ed Psychol* 53:150–6; 1962.

TEXTBOOKS

School textbooks have commanded a great deal of attention in the years just past, on the part of the general public and governmental agencies as well as educators. All that attention to textbooks has been natural—indeed inevitable—because during those years education became one of the great national concerns. Yet there has been little research. Cronbach (1955) noted that fact and added that what work had been done was "scattered, inconclusive, and often trivial." That is, unfortunately, still true.

HISTORY OF THE TEXTBOOK. The history of the textbook must be viewed in the context of national purposes and character. The U.S. state systems of free, tax-supported schools were established and took shape in the past century in response to social and political needs. Literacy was clearly a requirement for responsible participation in representative government. A welcome to masses of immigrants from all nations could be maintained only by supporting agencies for assimilating them into the culture. Belief in equality of social and economic opportunity, however imperfectly conceived, required that there be equal access to at least the first steps in education.

In the early schools the textbook was an indispensable tool. It provided serviceable answers to the hard questions of what to teach, of the order in which to teach it, and—at least in some measure—of how to teach it. Its role in the schools was reinforced by the rise of cities, which forced the development of the graded school system with a standard, uniform curriculum. Professional organizations of educators were formed, and they, too, advanced the development of an educational system with national, rather than local, characteristics. Textbook publishing thus found a predictable market, and expanded.

The question of the relationship of the textbook to curriculum uniformity is both an old and a current one. In his comprehensive book on publishing, Jovanovich (1964, p. 56) says: "The schools inscribed a pattern, the publishers issued books to fit it, and in that gradual transmutation that became usual over the past half-century, the books that made the course as often as the course made the books."

Developments in the early decades of the present century reinforced curriculum uniformity. Standardized achievement tests were developed; obviously, such tests assumed some standardization of curriculum. High school education was made available to all, as elementary education had been before, and accreditation agencies and college admission requirements made for uniformity of secondary-school courses. Textbooks continued to play a central role in curriculum practice.

Not all educators have agreed that the role of the textbook should be so central; indeed, the phrase "textbook teaching" has long carried a derogatory meaning. This attitude was perhaps most strongly expressed during the progressive education movement. The progressive philosophy opposed reliance on the textbook on several grounds, notably because of the conviction that learning must proceed from personal experience. Had the progressive movement come to full expression in the schools, textbooks might have largely been displaced by printed materials shaped to use as reference, or resource, reading carried out in relation to activities. However, it did not. It may be added, however, that the progressive education movement did influence curriculum practice, and therefore textbooks. It emphasized the use of supplementary materials which took the learner beyond the textbook, and itemized procedures to adapt learning experiences to the varying needs and interests of children. Both ideas continue to influence textbook publishing and use.

To point to the Russian launching of Sputnik as the starting signal for contemporary curriculum change is to oversimplify matters somewhat; there were signs of change before 1957. Yet the past decade has been one of sweeping curriculum change. The mathematics curriculum serves as a useful example. The reform dealt with both subject matter and method and with the whole range of elementary and secondary education. The wellsprings of reform were the mathematics departments, not of schools of education, but rather of the universities. The reform efforts, notably the School Mathematics Study Group (SMSG), were supported by federal funds. Finally, the SMSG textbooks were developed for use chiefly in trial situations. There was no intent to make finally approved, elaborately produced textbooks available to the schools. Instead, the announced policy encouraged textbook authors to improve, expand on, and draw from the materials.

There have been major curriculum reforms in other subjects, notably in science and modern languages, supported by federal funds. Unlike SMSG, the most important of the science-curriculum groups did develop textbooks which have been made available through publishing houses under contractual arrangements. The same is true of textbooks (with supporting materials, such as tapes) in modern languages. Other projects are proceeding with federal support. Thus, a new dimension has been added to the history of textbooks in American education; but it is, at the same time, a development which continues to assert the importance of the textbook.

THE EVOLUTION OF THE TEXTBOOK. Textbooks change in response to changes in educational purposes, in psychology and method, in subject matter, and in printing technology.

One striking development is that most recent textbooks include pictures of children and adults of all the races making up the American people. Moreover, they picture racially integrated groups. This new policy with respect to illustration is matched by a concern that the content reflect the pluralistic character of our society and give full, fair, and balanced treatment to minority groups. These concerns are expressed in the report "New Look in School Books" in the *Wilson Library Bulletin* (1963). Niemeyer (1965) says that in the traditional reading textbook there is nothing for the disadvantaged child to identify with; "he simply isn't there." He adds that the advantaged urban child is little better off. Huck (1965) notes that basic readers representative of the multiethnic background of this country have been prepared. Two such series—those prepared by the Detroit schools and the Bank Street readers—are cited in the *Wilson Library Bulletin* report noted above.

The same concern prompted a careful study of the treatment of the Negro in the leading junior and senior high school history textbooks by Sloan (1966), under a grant from the American Federation of Teachers. He notes improvement in recent years.

Textbooks also change as the subject matter of given subjects changes. The reform in the mathematics curriculum has been referred to above, but it should be noted that Feynman (1966) says the content of mathematics had, largely, been developed before 1920, and that the new mathematics involved a new approach. Science textbooks have changed to incorporate new subject matter and new methodological emphases (American Association for the Advancement of Science, 1962; BSCS, 1963). The same is true of textbooks in modern foreign languages. Research and study projects now going forward in other subjects are concerned with both subject matter and method, and as useful reports appear, textbooks will reflect them. This is notably true of the current interest in exploring what changes in English subjects should be made on the basis of linguistic studies.

It is worth noting that textbooks seeking to incorporate new subject matter or method sometimes go to extremes. Fenman (1966) points to the use of unnecessary technical jargon and the introduction of topics without adequate explanation or apparent purpose in some arithmetic textbooks.

Another development relates to the interest in programmed instruction. The aim of programmed instruction, whether carried forward by use of a teaching machine or by use of a programmed textbook without any machine, is to individualize instruction. The subject matter is presented in small, carefully sequenced steps; the learner responds, and the program tells him if his response is correct. The book by Lumsdaine and Glaser (1960) is a useful one. Though early developments in programming text materials relied on machines (often referred to as "hardware," the programs being called the "software" —both terms being unfortunate ones), it became clear that practical, versatile machines were not available, and a good many programmed textbooks were offered. Some dealt with limited topics; a few presented whole courses. The presentation of subject matter in programmed format requires space, a matter of some practical importance.

There have been a number of studies of the use of programmed text materials. Those by Fincher and Fillmer (1965), Reed and Hayman (1962), and Bradley (1964) are examples.

No sweeping conclusions about programmed textbooks are supportable, even when all available studies are considered. It is plain that there has been a decline of interest in programmed instruction, and few programmed textbooks are now being offered. However, the basic premises of programmed instruction touch on important concerns; notably, of course, the need to provide for individual differences, and to shape learning experiences so they are more self-directed.

A study of nineteenth-century textbooks by Elson (1964) sheds an interesting light on another aspect of textbook change. The study notes that the early textbooks made little, if any, pretense of neutrality with respect to what may be called the traditional values. Rather, authors assumed a moral nature in the universe and sought forthrightly to inculcate values—for example, industry and thrift—in the learner. Some critics of modern life and education seem to favor a return to such textbooks as models.

There is as yet apparently little research on changes in textbooks developed for use in church-related schools, though important changes in religious thought and practice have taken place. LaNoue (1962) found the use of religious symbols and subjects to be general in science, mathematics, and language textbooks and also found the espousal of specific sectarian views to be common in textbooks in those subjects. The evolution of textbooks for church-related schools seems to offer particularly interesting research possibilities.

Basal reading textbooks have long been under attack on several grounds. It is charged by some that those most widely used rely too much on the whole-word method ("see and say"); that the vocabulary is too limited and too rigidly controlled. Strickland (1962) has pointed out that although children in the early grades use a wide range and variety of language patterns in their speech, those patterns are not found in the reading textbooks. Burrows and Mayer (1962), in reviewing Strickland's research, question whether the implied criticism of reading textbooks is sound.

Basal reading textbooks are changing, but there is little research to support general statements about how they are changing. Huck (1965) reports that vocabulary controls have been lifted or eased at a considerably earlier level in those published since 1960 and that readers try to reflect the natural language patterns of children—for example, contractions are used—and there is more use of nonliterary selections. Another trend seems to be increased attention to what may be called decoding skills, expressed in some readers in the old, familiar emphasis on phonics and in others in ways more consistent with linguistic knowledge. It must be noted, however, that none of the several attempts to develop basal reading programs based on linguistic principles has, to this date, proved very successful.

FUNCTIONS AND USE OF THE TEXTBOOK. A revolution in communications is perhaps the hallmark of our time. Yet, it remains true that it is books which give man a permanently available store of knowledge. The textbook is, of course, a special kind of book. It seldom expresses new knowledge, for that is not its function. Its essential function is, rather, to make the knowledge which does exist available to the student in a selected, ordered way. Indeed, Cronbach (1955) points out that the textbook is a textbook by virtue of the principles which control its organization of subject matter, and states those principles: It is organized in relation to the organized discipline; thus, it is a textbook in grammar, or geography, or some other "subject." Since any one textbook obviously cannot present all knowledge of its subject, it is selective. Being addressed to immature learners, the subject matter is appropriately simplified. It is ordered; any chapter typically presupposes study of earlier chapters.

Those principles of organization suggest the textbook's function: it presents organized knowledge in a selected, simplified, ordered way. And it is always available; unlike the teaching film or a television program, it can be returned to, reread, studied.

The ways in which textbooks are used reflect differing points of view about the functions they serve. The traditional, and today still the usual, way is to use a textbook as the basis for a given course or subject. There will be supplementary experiences of various kinds, but the textbook plays the central role. In some measure—and in substantial measure if the teacher follows the teacher's guide or manual or teacher's edition—the author also shapes the method. Moreover, the modern textbook is usually accompanied by other publications. Thus, a workbook may be used for varied purposes—to provide additional practice or drill, to extend the topics developed in the textbook, or to guide the learner in independent or semiindependent, related activities. There are often test booklets, for periodic checking of achievement. There may be a related book of supplementary readings.

As noted above, "textbook teaching" is condemned by many educators, who urge teachers to develop procedures and materials particularly suited to local needs, even to their particular classroom and to the special needs of individual learners. Others urge the use of textbooks in varied ways. In this vein, Phillips (1965) urges a different approach to textbooks. He recommends that several copies of the "best" of several textbooks in a given subject be used, rather than a "basal" textbook. Lourie (1960) urges the development of critical reading skills in connection with textbook use. McGoldrick (1961) suggests procedures for developing research skills, starting from the textbook.

It may be observed, however, that "nontextbook teaching" is not necessarily good teaching. There are sensible reasons for basing instruction on a common textbook.

In recent years there has been very considerable interest in the use of paperback books. It was reported at a conference on the role of paperback books in education in 1965 (*Publishers' Weekly*, 1965) that while "educational paperbacks" made up 13 percent of the paperback market in 1961 the percentage jumped to 30 percent by 1965. It is not clear what part of the increase is explained by college use, but it is clear that more paperbacks are being used in the public schools. Flayderman (1965) notes some of the advantages they offer, as does Klingmeyer (1960). Among them are low initial cost, flexibility of use, and convenience.

There is no doubt that paperbacks serve useful purposes in classrooms; for example, literature courses can be extended by having at hand paperback editions of the works of many authors. They will continue to be used widely and in varied ways both in relation to the basal textbook and independently of it. Moreover, a number of paperback textbooks—as distinct from both general trade books and workbooks—have been published, and more will be. For economic and other reasons, however, it seems clear that most basal textbooks will continue to be hardbound.

With textbooks in use in every classroom every day, it would seem reasonable to expect many studies of specific, practical problems. Only a few are reported, however. Olson (1965) reports a study of the vocabulary of seven primary-reading series and questions the wisdom of having first-grade pupils read preprimers, primers, and first readers as "co-basal," with the idea that by so doing the pupil is reexposed to the vocabulary of the basal series.

The use of basal readers has been challenged by some who favor "individualized reading," making use of juvenile trade books. More advocacy than research has supported this recommendation, and the idea has not been widely adopted. Johnson (1965) found that pupils in individualized reading classes can achieve as well as, and perhaps even better than, pupils in basal reading programs. More research is needed, and Duker (1966) suggests questions which need answering. There are also important and difficult practical problems to be considered in reaching any decision to abandon reliance on basal readers.

Davis and Hunkins (1966) analyzed end-of-chapter questions in several fifth-grade social studies textbooks, to determine what thinking processes they encouraged. Using categories (or levels) of cognitive thought as defined by Bloom, they concluded that from 86 to 89 percent of the questions focused primarily on acquisition of knowledge and that there were almost no questions which called for analysis, synthesis, and evaluation.

INFLUENCE OF THE TEXTBOOK. It remains true that the textbook is one of the dominant influences in education. It is precisely because its influence is so great that it is so often criticized; were it of little influence, there would be far less criticism. Criticisms directed at its influence take many forms. Some are trivial, but there are substantive issues. These seem to be expressed in three charges: that by and large the textbook exerts too strongly a conservative influence, that it somehow blocks creativity in teaching or in learning, and—in words reminiscent of progressive education—that it is a woefully inadequate substitute for direct experience.

In one sense, textbooks are by definition conservative. Indeed, this is true of the school as a social institution; certainly one of its functions is to *pass on the past*. At the same time, the school—and the textbook, as one of the tools it uses—must serve as an agency of change and by so doing helps to shape the future. That the textbook is often a liberalizing influence is demonstrably true. As noted above, many new textbooks reflect the multiethnic nature of American society; they are (some more effectively than others, of course) asserting the need for change in social institutions. Reforms in subject matter and in method are presented through the textbook; witness the reforms in mathematics and in modern foreign languages.

The charge that the textbook blocks creativity is more difficult of analysis, if for no other reason than that it is often quite unclear what is meant by "creativity." In this connection, it is often said that textbooks are authoritative. Again, the meaning is not wholly clear. A good textbook should be authoritative, in one sense. Its presentation of subject matter should be reliable, accurate, and true to scholarship. But the textbook, if it is well written and carefully edited, can invite creative response. It can be a guide to discovery. Moreover, the textbook's influence is modified by how the teacher uses it and by the opportunities the school creates for experiences to supplement it.

To say that the textbook is an inadequate substitute for direct experience as a basis for learning is, again, to invite questions about meaning. It is clear that any child must learn a great deal about things he cannot experience directly, and one way he can do so is by reading. And experience is of many kinds; there is such a thing as intellectual experience. Yet it should be said that the textbook writer and editor must always bear in mind that the learner apprehends meaning in terms of his experiences and that he is prone to test the relevance of what he reads against his ongoing experience.

The influence of the textbook will continue to be very strong; conflicting views on the nature of its influence will continue to be expressed. The extent to which its influence is conservative or reformative will vary in different periods. There will be—as there have been and are now—differences in textbooks. Some will be more tuned to the past, some more to an emerging future. Teachers will continue to use the textbook in different ways, some more creatively than others. The textbook will continue to be a source of knowledge for learners—knowledge they could never build from direct experience—and good schools will continue to supplement the textbook with other types of experience.

SELECTION AND ADOPTION OF TEXTBOOKS. Textbook adoption procedures in the different states vary, but in general any state is either a "state adoption" or an "open territory" state. The former implies that some state authority adopts one or more textbooks—or series of textbooks—for a given period of time. All schools within that state then must use that textbook, if it is a single adoption; or, if it is a multiple adoption, then one of those on the adopted list. The length of the adoption period varies. "Open territory" states, as the term implies, do not adopt textbooks, and each local school unit therefore can choose from all those available.

To be more specific, there are 25 "state adoption" states. Six states adopt textbooks only for the elementary schools, leaving the high school free to choose as in "open territory" states. Nineteen states adopt textbooks for both elementary and high schools. Adoption practices vary; most adopt a multiple list, but again there is variation. Some list three, four, or five textbooks or series in a given subject; others will list a good many more so that they become almost "open territory." North Carolina, by contrast, typically makes a single adoption; so does California, though in both states there have been examples of "co-basal" adoptions. California, alone among the states, prints the state-adopted textbooks in its state-owned printing plant, leasing plates from the publisher of the adopted books. Though long under attack by many California educators, the practice persists, and because it is expressly provided for in the state constitution it will not easily be changed.

Information bearing on adoptions is reported in a survey of textbook purchasing practice by *School Management* (1966). Over the years 1959–1966 the amount spent for textbooks remained steady at about 1.1 percent of the overall educational budget. But the amount spent for "teaching materials" rose from 2.9 percent of the budget to 3.9 percent. The schools are, in short, allocating about the same part of their budgets for textbooks purchase while spending more for other teaching materials. It may be noted that this trend was encouraged by federal aid programs; presumably the availability of such aid will also spur textbook purchase. In 1959 about 70 percent of the high schools provided free textbooks; in 1966 fewer —some 60 percent—did. In 1959, 19 percent of all districts used the textbook rental system; in 1966 29 percent did. (Again, it should be noted that with the new flow of federal funds into public education, patterns of textbook purchasing and management are subject to change.)

In all adoptions, legal responsibility rests with boards of education. In practice the selection is made by professional educators. The selection process is not easily described. Spalding's discussion (1955), though published over a decade ago, is comprehensive. More recent discussions by James (1964) and Eibling (1964), and in a general report in *School Management* (1964), suggest that procedures have not changed much. It is general practice to assign responsibility to a committee representative of the interests concerned—for example, different grade levels, when a series is to be selected. The weight of an administrator's or supervisor's views varies; some exercise stronger leadership than others do. The use of the textbook rating scale as a tool for objectifying evaluation is less widespread than was true some years ago. Appraisal is, rather, made in more general terms stated as criteria.

When all is said and done the selective process is heavily subjective. Even in the best of schools, adoptions are sometimes made in an atmosphere of uncertainty. Any break with the past—and adoption of a new textbook is a break with the past—gives rise to some anxieties. Members of adoption committees are aware that teacher training lags behind curriculum innovation. They must choose not what may seem "best" in an abstract sense but what seems best for their situation. The task is not an easy one. The whole textbook selection process invites research. For example, to what extent is there concern for sequence bridging the elementary and secondary grades?

A word must be said about attacks on textbooks. The book by Nelson and Roberts (1963) is enlightening. The authors note that it is the ultraconservatives who are most militant in attacking textbooks and in pressuring school boards. Nelson (1963), in a general review of attacks on textbooks, notes that textbooks are frequently attacked in state legislatures. Not all attacks on textbooks focus on the social studies. For example, Lisonbee (1965) reports an attack on the BSCS biology textbooks in Arizona by those opposed to teaching the theory of evolution.

READABILITY OF TEXTBOOKS. From the viewpoint of those selecting textbooks, it is obviously of importance that there be some way of measuring (or predicting) their readability by the learners who will use them. It is equally clear that the textbook writer and editor need guides to control reading difficulty. Evidence of continuing interest in the problem is found in a number of studies. Smith and Heddens (1964a) studied, first, the readability of certain experimental mathematics materials, finding them considerably above their assigned grade levels. A similar study of five commercially published arithmetic textbook series was reported by the same authors (1964b). The commercially published textbooks were less difficult than the experimental materials but had a considerable range of readability. Reports on readability of science textbooks are given by Brown (1965) and Newport (1965); Aukerman (1965) reports on a study of high school literature anthologies. Mills and Richardson (1963) "graded" a variety of elementary textbooks, using the Spache and the Dale-Chall formulas, and compared results with publishers' lists, noting rather wide disagreement.

Bormuth (1966) notes that much of the important research in readability was done some years ago and suggests that lack of progress in recent years had two causes: lack of valid methods for measuring the comprehension difficulties of written language and lack of an organized body of basic research and theory upon which readability research could draw. He suggests that development of the cloze test solved the first problem and organization of psycholinguistics as a discipline the second. His study—reported very fully—questions the value of existing readability formulas and reports his own research on five problems. In summary, he suggests that nonlinear correlation techniques will have to be used in some readability formulas, that the validity of readability formulas based on linguistic variables can be greatly improved, that readability formulas can be developed which make "usefully valid" predictions of the difficulty of words, independent clauses, and sentences, and that formulas can be made to predict difficulty for different levels of ability.

Klare's book *The Measurement of Readability* (1963) is the third of a series of which the earlier volume "Legibility of Print" by Tinker (1962) was the second. Klare's book has the usefulness of a kind of handbook: it discusses practical applications, reviews the development of all of the important readability formulas, discusses their applications, reviews studies of their reliability and validity, and offers an extensive bibliography.

It is reasonable to hope that new research techniques and the rising influence of linguistic scholarship may lead to significant progress in dealing with problems of readability.

AUTHORS OF TEXTBOOKS. Given the general agreement on the importance of textbooks, it is surprising that there has been so little research on textbook authors. Bierstedt's discussion (1955) remains the most comprehensive, but he wrote, necessarily, without information based on research. Jovanovich, in his book on publishing (1964), also discusses textbook writers and writing.

One trend of recent years can be stated with confidence. The number of university scholars writing elementary and secondary textbooks has increased. This is noted in the report of the American Association for the Advancement of Science (1962) on the new science programs. The discussion makes some interesting points: the projects (the Physical Science Study Committee and like efforts in chemistry and biology) have prestige, organizational strength, and financial support (federal funds). Thus, and importantly, scholars were able to give full time to the writing of textbooks and text-related materials such as teachers' manuals and laboratory manuals. A study by Brownson and Schwab (1963) compared authorship of science textbooks published in 1955 with those published in 1915 and showed, in general, that the scholarly standing of 1955 authors was lower than that of 1915 authors. Therefore it may be at last partly true that the recent involvement of scholars in textbook writing is a return to an earlier practice.

For most textbook authors, however, the elements of prestige, organizational strength, and financial backing are absent. Who are they, then, and how and why do they write textbooks? Research does not supply adequate answers. Lynch and Evans (1963) compiled information on authors and "editors" of high school English textbooks. (In their usage "editors" refers to those who put together literary anthologies, not to editors in publishing houses.) They found, in every instance, more than a single author; rather, authorship was by a "team." Most teams included both high school and college-level teachers. Most—indeed there were very few exceptions—authors were currently engaged in teaching or in related work such as supervision; thus, textbook writing was something they did in addition to other, regular duties.

Textbook authors are not, primarily and by profession, authors; they are teachers or supervisors or college or university faculty members. If they are college or university faculty members, they tend to be identified with teacher education, though, as noted above, there is increasing participation by some in the academic disciplines. But they are all, at least initially, amateurs at writing textbooks. They find that the work demands a very great deal of time, extending over two, three, four, or more years. They find themselves working with one, two, or more other authors on a work which must in final form exhibit unity and coherence. All this is particularly true of the author who is involved in writing a textbook series, and less so if the effort is a single textbook. A textbook series—say a mathematics series for grades 1–8 or a high school literature series—will include a basic textbook for each year and many related publications. Even the single textbook—say, in chemistry—will have a teacher's manual, a laboratory manual, and a testing program. Authorship is often multiple because of the amount of work to be done and because those who are engaged in it are at the same time engaged in other work.

The work involves, too, a relationship with one or more editors in the publishing house. Having written, the author often finds he must rewrite.

Why, then, does the author become an author? The obvious answer is that textbook authorship—assuming success of the textbook in a highly competitive market—is financially rewarding. It is, and it is right that it should be, given the need for good textbooks. Yet it must be noted that good textbook authors do have motives other than financial gain. The good textbook author is first of all a good teacher. He (or she, for many textbook authors are women) is a teacher—a good one, one who enjoys teaching. Through a textbook he extends the reach of his interest and his competence. It is also true that textbook writing is a skill, even with some claim to being an art. Once the skill is learned, its exercise is in some measure self-rewarding. The great textbook authors—and there have been and are great authors—engage in their skill or art as others do, perhaps, in golf or in painting.

TEXTBOOK PUBLISHING. Through the first half of the century, textbook publishing proceeded in established and therefore reasonably predictable and describable ways. A period of sweeping change began in the 1950's and continued at an accelerated pace in the 1960's. Educational publishing is today a very complex business, a business in transition moving toward new patterns not as yet clear. These concerns will be sketched later. First, what are the dimensions of the business, and how does the business proceed?

In 1966 there were 96 member companies of the American Textbook Publishers Institute (ATPI) plus nine map companies. Those companies are not all of a kind; some are solely educational publishers, others are general publishers who also publish textbooks. There are also some textbook publishers not members of ATPI. Together the publishers issue textbooks to serve the schools, in which there were enrolled 35,976,000 elementary and 13,018,000 secondary pupils in 1965, a total of 48,994,000. Elementary and high school textbook sales were reported to total $347,255,000 in 1965; the per-pupil expenditure for elementary textbooks was $5.97 and for secondary textbooks $10.19.

As to how the business proceeds, it first must be said that it does so in various ways. There are useful statements of the general patterns of educational publishing. Schramm's chapter (1955) is perhaps the most complete, especially his explanation of the textbook editor's role. Jovanovich's book (1964), mentioned several times before, is an informed, insightful report in publishing in general, including textbook publishing.

How does a textbook—or, as is more usually the case, a textbook series—come to publication? The initiative is almost always taken by the publisher, who must always be engaged in editorial planning as well as in current publishing. Planning proceeds as a search for opportunities in relation to the list the publisher already has and to the market as it exists and as it is emerging. Usually the publisher seeks the author or authors. Exploratory discussion and planning leads to a publishing contract. There follow some three, four, or five years of cooperative work, with the textbook editor—who is always finally anonymous—helping to give the work its final form and character. Sometimes the publisher advances funds to enable authors to devote full time to the work. (But this is helpful only if the employing school or college agrees, and textbook writing is not always applauded by administrators.)

The dimensions of the task are, of course, greatest for a textbook series, which will include from twenty to forty separate titles. (One recent development in elementary textbook publishing is the appearance of more textbooks for grades 1, 2, and even some for kindergarten.)

Finally, it must be said that it does sometimes happen that an author decides to write a textbook, does so, and offers it to a publisher, who accepts it, publishes it, and sells it.

What changes have taken place in textbook publishing, and what changes are likely in the years ahead? Some are relatively minor, simply evolutionary steps. The use of color in books has increased markedly; today many secondary textbooks are printed by offset printing and use full color throughout. Almost never, today, is a textbook offered without related ("satellite") publications; the full-scale "teacher's edition" has even appeared for secondary textbooks. Textbooks for groups of differing ability are being published; there is of course, particular concern for books to serve needs in the inner-city schools. More supplementary books are being published. Costs have increased, as indeed they have for things other than books. But there are other and more fundamental changes.

(1) Most publishing companies have, to use the vernacular, "gone public" in ownership. The shift

from private ownership to listing on the stock exchanges has accented the business aim of publishing. (It does, after all, have other aims.) The shift has had interesting consequences, not the least of which is that publishing has become much more visible.

(2) There have been many mergers of publishing houses. Rice (1960) notes this fact. In general, mergers were prompted by the need to expand, which called for capital and for larger resources, including staff, and for greater volume and diversity of business.

(3) There has recently begun a trend toward the merging of publishing companies and other businesses—makers of electronic equipment, makers of copying machines and, as Keppel (1967) notes, "above all, makers of money." (A comprehensive discussion of this whole matter is offered in the issue of *Phi Delta Kappan* in which Keppel's article appears.) Neither the reasons for this development nor the consequences which will flow from it are as yet wholly clear. There is, obviously, an interest on the part of what may be termed Big Business (publishing has never yet been that) in the growing educational market. Moreover, business mergers and acquisitions seem to be widespread. Still, there is more here; there is the conviction that somehow there can be developed *systems* of teaching-learning materials in which electronic technology will play an important part. There is, indeed, already a term in general use which may signal the future: computer-assisted instruction, or CAI. No one can doubt that the results of serious research now underway are potentially revolutionary.

(4) Electronic technology has the promise of effecting changes in book-publishing procedures. Computer composition is a reality, though it still has limitations. The uses of the computer in manuscript editing are being explored.

(5) The active participation of the federal government in public education touches on textbook publishing. As noted above, federally financed study groups have developed new textbooks in several subjects, textbooks made available through commercial publishers. The present policy of the United States Office of Education places federally supported project materials in the public domain, but some authors have "revised" their works and offered them to publishers. Future roles of the project groups and the publishers are not clear, and this lack of clarity may well continue for some years. Rice, in the study referred to above, suggests that local school units should develop textbooks, a view others have also expressed, and some actual examples in which they did so can be cited.

(6) There is, finally, the copyright problem. A good discussion by Heilprin (1967) points to the developments which make the problem so difficult of analysis and solution. The old copyright law (the law is at the time of this writing being revised by Congress) dealt with "reproduction" at a time when the only serious means of reproducing was the printing press. There have been, it is true, the mimeograph and other rather awkward duplicating machines in the schools, not always used in ways that squared with the law. But these have not been a major concern.

Today there are many ways to reproduce; reproduction is very rapid, very easy, and relatively inexpensive. There is increasing use of microfilm, of tape, and of video recorders. The nature of the copyright problem is radically changed.

Moreover, organized teacher groups have asserted their interest in a liberalized copyright law, to cover what they see as "fair use" of materials in the classroom. Teachers' definitions of what is fair may differ widely from definitions authors would give. The problem of accommodating competing or conflicting interests is never an easy one.

TEXTBOOKS IN OTHER COUNTRIES. There have been a number of interesting reports on textbooks in other countries. Hahn (1959) reviewed 71 textbooks in use in England, France, and both East and West Germany. He found that they showed little concern for student interest, stressed factual knowledge, gave little attention to recent times, made limited use of color, and generally did not suggest additional reading. Krug (1961) found that history textbooks published in East and West Germany in 1959, 1960, and 1961 often gave biased and distorted pictures of German and European history. A Russian report on Soviet social science textbooks frankly notes the role of those books in the party program (*Soviet Education,* 1963) and states that the "method of induction" is increasingly popular. Dominy (1963) compared American arithmetic textbooks with those of England, France, West Germany, and Russia.

Interest in international cooperation in textbook work continues. Pillsbury (1966) describes the International Textbook Institute. The institute reviews textbooks from many nations, under agreements with both governments and professional associations. A report from the International Bureau of Education (1959) reports data from 69 nations on primary-school textbooks, their preparation, selection, and use.

UNESCO continues to give attention to textbooks. Abraham (1964) discusses UNESCO activities, suggesting that the organization has found critical analysis of textbooks (in its concern that textbooks avoid prejudiced treatment of topics) not the most fruitful of ventures and is turning its efforts more to the development of background materials for teachers and supplementary materials for students. However, research workers still find the analyses of textbooks useful. For example: *The Treatment of Asia in Western Textbooks and Teaching Materials,* a UNESCO report in November 1956; and *The Treatment of the West in Textbooks and Teaching Materials of South and East Asia,* issued in November 1958.

Many other UNESCO efforts deserve attention—more, really, than can be given here. It has sponsored several international conferences of educational publishers and has established special missions to new nations on the writing and printing of textbooks.

An Alliance for Progress project, financed by the Agency for International Development (AID), has provided textbooks for use in Central American schools as a help to standardizing primary education.

Mention must be made, too, of the work being done by Franklin Book Programs, Inc., a private, nonprofit organization that works to strengthen, and where necessary to help create, local book-publishing industries in the developing nations of Asia, Africa, and Latin America. Its activities range over all of book publishing, but textbooks have a high priority. The 1966 annual report shows the range of its efforts (Franklin Books Programs, 1966).

Ernest Hilton
Harcourt, Brace & World, Inc.

References

Abraham, Herbert J. "The Role of the United Nations Organizations in Education for International Understanding." In Bereday, George Z., and Lauwerys, Joseph A. (Eds.) *Education and International Life.* Harcourt, 1964. p. 365–79.

American Association for the Advancement of Science. *The New School Science: A Report to School Administrators On Regional Orientation Conferences in Science.* AAAS, 1962.

Aukerman, Robert C. "Readability of Secondary School Literature Textbooks: A First Report." *Engl J* 54: 533–40; 1965.

Bierstedt, Robert. "The Writers of Textbooks." In Cronbach, Lee J. (Ed.) *Text Materials in Modern Education.* U Illinois, 1955. Ch. 5.

Biological Sciences Curriculum Study. *Biology Teachers' Handbook.* Wiley, 1963. 585p.

Bormuth, John R. "Readability: A New Approach." *Reading Res Q* 1:79–132; 1966.

Bradley, Philip A. "Individualized Instruction Through Cooperative Teaching and a Programmed Text." *Nat El Sch Prin* 43:46–9; 1964.

Brown, Walter R. "Science Textbook Selection and the Dale-Chall Formula." *Sch Sci Math* 65:164–7; 1965.

Brownson, William E., and Schwab, Joseph J. "American Science Textbooks and Their Authors." *Sch R* 71:170–80; 1963.

Burrows, Alvina, and Mayer, Edgar. Review of "Language of Elementary School Children" by Ruth Strickland. *El Engl* 41:532–6; 1962.

Cronbach, Lee J. (Ed.) *Text Materials in Modern Education.* U Illinois Press, 1955. 216p.

Davis, O. L., and Hunkins, Francis P. "Textbook Questions: What Thinking Processes Do They Foster?" *Peabody J Ed* 43:285–92; 1966.

Dominy, Mildred M. "A Comparison: Textbooks, Domestic and Foreign." *Arithmetic Teach* 10:428–34; 1963.

Duker, Sam. "Needed Research on Individualized Reading." *El Engl* 43:220–5; 1966.

Eibling, Harold H. "Textbook Selection: How to Be Sure the Right Ones Are Picked." *Sch Manag* 8:81–6; 1964.

Elson, Ruth M. *Guardians of Tradition: American Schoolbooks of the Nineteenth Century.* U Nebraska Press, 1964. 424p.

Feynman, Richard P. "New Textbooks for the New Mathematics." *California Ed* 3:8–14; 1966.

Fincher, Glen E., and Fillmer, H. T. "Programmed Instruction in Elementary Arithmetic." *Arithmetic Teach* 12:19–23; 1965.

Flayderman, Phillip C. "A Frank Query: Paperback vs. Hardcovers." *Clearing House* 39:410; 1965.

Franklin Books Programs. *Annual Report for the Year Ending 30 June 1966.* Franklin, 1966.

Hahn, Walter. "Textbooks in European High Schools." *Clearing House* 33:396–400; 1959.

Heilprin, Laurence B. "Technology and the Future of the Copyright Principle." *Phi Delta Kappan* 48:220–5; 1967.

Huck, Charlotte S. "The Changing Character of Basic Reading Materials." *Ed Leadership* 22:377–81; 1965.

International Bureau of Education. *"Primary School Textbooks: Preparation, Selection, Use.* The Bureau (Geneva), 1959. 245p.

James, William H. "Textbook Selection: How to Get Rid of the Weak Ones." *Sch Manag* 8:81–4; 1964.

Johnson, Rodney H. "Individualized and Basal Primary Reading Programs." *El Engl* 42:902–4; 1965.

Jovanovich, William. *Now, Barabbas.* Harper, 1964. 228p.

Keppel, Francis. "The Business Interest in Education." *Phi Delta Kappan* 48:186–90; 1967.

Klare, George R. *The Measurement of Readability.* Iowa State U Press, 1963. 328p.

Klingmeyer, Faye M. "Paperbacks and Hardbacks." *Clearing House* 34:415–6; 1960.

Krug, Mark M. "The Teaching of History at the Center of the Cold War—History Textbooks in East and West Germany." *Sch R* 69:561–87; 1961.

LaNoue, George. "The National Defense Education Act and 'Secular' Subjects." *Phi Delta Kappan* 43:380–7; 1962.

Lisonbee, Lorenzo. "Thwarting the Anti-evolution Movement in Arizona." *Sci Teach* 32:35–7; 1965.

Lourie, Samuel. "Breaking the Textbook Strait-jacket." *Clearing House* 34:417–8; 1960.

Lumsdaine, A. A., and Glaser, Robert. *Teaching Machines and Programmed Learning.* NEA, 1960. 724p.

Lynch, James J., and Evans, Bertrand. *High School English Textbooks: A Critical Examination.* Little, 1963. 526p.

McGoldrick, James H. "Research Starting with the Textbook." *Clearing House* 35:31–2; 1961.

Mills, Robert E., and Richardson, Jean R. "What Do Publishers Mean by 'Grade Level'?" *Reading Teach* 16:359–62; 1963.

Nelson, Jack. "What Is the Problem?" *NEA J* 52:19–21; 1963.

Nelson, Jack, and Roberts, Gene. *The Censors and the Schools.* Little, 1963. 208p.

Newport, John F. "A Look at the University of

Illinois Astronomy Materials." *Sch Sci Math* 65:145–7; 1965.

Niemeyer, John J. "The Bank Street Readers: Support for Movement Toward an Integrated Society." *Reading Teach* 18:542–5; 1965.

Olson, Arthur V. "An Analysis of the Vocabulary of Seven Primary Reading Series." *El Engl* 42:261–4; 1965.

Phillips, Howard F. "A Different Approach to Textbooks." *Clearing House* 39:529; 1965.

Pillsbury, Kent. "International Cooperation in Textbook Evaluation: The Braunschweig Institute." *Compar Ed R* 10:48–52; 1966.

Publishers' Weekly. "The Role of Paperback Books in Education Examined in Depth." 188:13–27; 1965. (A report on a conference.)

Reed, Jerry E., and Hayman, John L. "An Experiment Involving Use of English 2600, An Automated Instruction Text." *J Ed Res* 55:476–84; 1962.

Rice, Arthur H. "A New Outlook for Textbooks." *Nation's Sch* 65:55–6; 1960.

School Management. "Textbook Selection: Whose Job?" 8:74–8; 1964.

School Management. "A Survey of Textbook Purchasing Practices." 10:137–66; 1966.

Schramm, Wilbur. "The Publishing Process." In Cronbach, Lee J. (Ed.) *Text Materials in Modern Education.* U Illinois Press, 1955. Ch. 6.

Sloan, Irving. *The Negro in Modern American History Textbooks.* American Federation of Teachers, 1966. 47p.

Smith, Kenneth J., and Heddens, James W. "The Readability of Experimental Mathematics Materials." *Arithmetic Teach* 11:391–4; 1964(*a*).

Smith, Kenneth J., and Heddens, James W. "The Readability of Elementary Mathematics Books." *Arithmetic Teach* 11:466–8; 1964(*b*).

Soviet Education. "The Social Science Textbook." 5:12–9; 1963.

Spalding, Willard B. "The Selection and Distribution of Printed Materials." In Cronbach, Lee J. (Ed.) *Text Materials in Modern Education.* U Illinois Press, 1955. Ch. 7.

Strickland, Ruth. "The Language of Elementary School Children: Its Relationship to the Language of Reading Textbooks and the Quality of Reading of Selected Children." *B Sch Ed Indiana U* 38(4):1–131; 1962.

Tinker, Miles A. *Legibility of Print.* Iowa State U Press, 1962. 329p.

Wilson Library Bulletin. "New Look in School Books." 33:376; 1963.

TRAINING RESEARCH WORKERS

EDUCATIONAL RESEARCH IN THE UNITED STATES. Increased research attention has been focused recently upon the organization and structure of educational research and the educational researchers who participate in this activity. Buswell and others (1966) studied a number of the characteristics of 1954 and 1964 doctoral graduates in education. Sieber (1966) analyzed the organization of educational research and researchers. Bargar and others (1965) surveyed some characteristics of the educational-research community, and later Bargar & Okorodudu (1968) proceeded to draw together a "conceptual map" of variables relating to educational researchers. Clark and Hopkins (1968) projected some dimensions of the educational-research community of the near future and described new research and research-related roles which appeared to be emerging.

Using these and other data, Guba and Horvat (1967) characterized American educational research as being (1) loosely organized, with no central organization or coordination; (2) university-based; (3) directed according to the interests of individual researchers; (4) related to the theories of social and behavioral disciplines such as psychology and sociology rather than to the solution of existing educational problems; (5) committed to experimental approaches; (6) conducted by persons trained in educational psychology, statistics, and measurement theory; (7) the part-time pursuit of persons with other demanding duties; (8) funded primarily by the federal government; (9) insufficiently staffed; and, (10) inadequately funded to perform its functions effectively. Bargar and others (1965) added that most researchers neither (11) received their primary training in research nor (12) identify themselves professionally in areas primarily oriented toward research. These generalizations form the warp of educational research through which the following paragraphs should be woven.

INSTITUTIONAL CHARACTERIZATION. The preparation of educational researchers in the United States is performed traditionally by the universities, and Buswell and others (1966) discovered that approximately 60 percent of the active researchers in their study were produced by the eight state universities of Minnesota, Illinois, Michigan, California (Berkeley), Texas, Wisconsin, Indiana, and Oregon and the privately maintained Columbia and New York universities.

The contribution to research preparation of most of the remaining graduate schools has been small. Although there were 107 graduate schools of education which awarded the doctorate in 1963–64, exclusive of tecnological schools, Sieber (1966) found that during a three-year period 30 percent of the graduate schools of education did not produce *any* doctoral recipients in education who then entered positions where research was a primary responsibility. Only 17 percent of the graduate schools of education emphasized research preparation and provided some form of program (most frequently the regular degree program) for students who wanted to make research a career. As for the quality of these programs, almost half the deans of education surveyed cited the research preparation being conducted in schools of education as a major *hindrance* to the advancement of educational research. The graduates believed themselves trained when they were not trained to engage in research on real problems of critical importance to education.

Buswell and others (1966) found that only 1 in 20 doctoral graduates in education became an active researcher. Ten years after receiving the doctorate nearly 75 percent of the education graduates had published no research, and only 12 percent had two or more research publications to their credit. In sum, the annual addition to the body of active educational researchers from all colleges and universities approximates 150 to 200 qualified persons.

Organizational Arrangements for Research. Some schools provide a research unit, such as a bureau of educational research, in which their doctoral candidates are exposed to systematic efforts to prepare them for independent research. Lazarsfeld and Sieber (1964) reported that research-unit experiences provided no guarantee that research assistants or students working on dissertations would adopt research careers. Where faculty resources were of fairly low quality or were mainly devoted to field services, these experiences contributed nothing to the preparation of researchers.

Only 27 percent of the schools which participated in the Sieber study (1966) had separate divisions for research preparation. Further, only a minor portion of educational research in the universities was carried out in research units. These units affected the preparation of only 2.4 percent of all doctoral candidates in education in schools where there were research bureaus. Fewer than a third of all the bureaus had preparation programs, and fewer than half of *those* bureaus had any funds allocated specifically to their preparation programs.

Faculty Research. Research productivity among members of the faculty has been reported in most studies as conducive to the establishment of a favorable "institutional climate" for the development of researchers. Where members of the faculty are productive in research, students currently and retrospectively report that they have or have had visible models and a warmer reception for their research proclivities and that they were more likely to become involved in a research project which was related to their interests than if the faculty had not been so productive. Heiss (1966) reported that most of the graduate faculty in the institutions which produced her sample of outstanding scholars were engaged in ongoing research in which their students participated.

Faculty Interaction with Students. The interaction which occurs between professors and their students has been found to influence students' decisions to embark upon research careers. Brown and Slater (1960) and Thistlethwaite (1962) found that former undergraduate and early graduate professors exerted a dominant influence upon students who decided to go on to take advanced graduate work. This influence was exercised through (1) discussion with the student regarding his goals, (2) help given to students having difficulty, (3) aid in seeking redress of grievances, and (4) encouragement of individual students' initiative and creativity.

PROGRAM CHARACTERIZATION. For discussion purposes, the course-work and experience components of preparation programs in educational research have been separated, but they are typically integrated in the institutions offering the preparation programs.

Course Work. The courses taken by a doctoral student in educational research were found by Krathwohl (1965) to vary according to the student's desire to (1) create new methodology, (2) teach methodology to others, or (3) be able competently to use the methodology. The common core of course work included a single research-method course; two courses in statistics, including factor and multivariate analysis; a course in experimental design; and three courses in educational and psychological measurement and scaling.

The extent to which programs leading toward the three objectives differed may be judged by the variation in the type and amount of statistics and experimental design in each. The program of those who wished to create new methodology usually included advanced calculus, matrix theory, numerical analysis, finite differences and measurement theory, and, frequently, computer programming. The program of those who wished to teach methodology to others was exemplified by an approach based on probability, but without calculus. The program for users of research methodology generally began with descriptive statistics and extended through analysis of variance.

In addition to the common core, courses in philosophy of science, research methods, basic mathematics, and computer coding appeared in a large number of programs. Most also required enough education courses for the student to be able to communicate with his professional colleagues.

A variety of special features were provided for trainees. These included courses in methods of teaching at the college level, consultant experiences, special courses with visiting staff, summer training programs, and courses at the undergraduate level.

Sieber (1966) found an average of 9.5 courses in research available in the 107 universities in which the graduate schools of education offered doctorates, but these were usually scattered throughout several departments and were specialized according to the students' field of concentration. He found, further, that the availability of research courses in schools of education was *unrelated* to the production of researchers (except for seminars offered in a research-bureau setting). Even when course-work opportunities outside the school of education were considered, opportunities for course-work in research did not seem to promote the adoption of research as a career.

Wherever the courses were located, their contents were quite similar if the use of standard texts is any measure. According to Krathwohl (1965) over half the courses in educational-research methods used as their basic text that of either Van Dalen (1962),

Travers (1964), or Mouly (1963). The leading text in statistics was that of Garrett (1958), followed by those of Guilford (1956), Blommers and Lindquist (1960), and Ferguson (1959). Those of Lindquist (1953) and Edwards (1960) were used almost equally and exclusively in courses in experimental design.

The data from studies on the preparation of researchers indicate that while there may be some uniformity in the content of preparation programs among institutions, it is undesirable to seek conformity among students within institutions in taking the courses offered. Clark (1957), for example, reported that psychologists who experienced less supervision during graduate preparation showed greater independence in their research than those who experienced more supervision.

Drevdahl (1961) concluded that conformity is detrimental to creativity—a primary characteristic of the productive researcher. The necessary conditions for nurturing creativity within a preparation program appear to be a nondirective, relatively unstructured curriculum which has few required courses, considerably more research activity than formal courses, and freedom of student choice with respect to the "mix" of courses and research experiences.

Experiences. The bulk of those who have written about research preparation indicate that doing research constitutes the most critical training variable affecting later research productivity. Sieber (1966) noted, for example, that preparation programs that did not provide apprenticeships produced many fewer researchers than preparation programs that did. Sibley (1948) found that natural scientists considered practical experience in the preparation program to be indispensable to the production of researchers in their fields and went on to draw a parallel with apprenticeship experience in preparation programs in the social sciences. Nevertheless, as many as one-half of the institutions which offer the doctorate in education require no more than the dissertation experience. Provision of research experiences has been quite rare in education even though a number of patterns of clinical experience are possible. Some patterns which Guba (1965) enumerated were:

1. The collaborator pattern, in which students are attached to professors and collaborate with them on research problems.

2. The participant training pattern, which attaches students to ongoing projects where they participate to the extent of their abilities. The students may also be permitted to carve out areas of interest of their own.

3. The consortium pattern, where each institutional consortium provides a graduate student of ability for staff service on a specific project. This pattern opens the possibility of exchange of students among institutions for special experiences.

4. The training-team pattern, which brings researchers together with a variety of experts and consultants to pool their knowledge for the solution of a problem.

5. The research-institute pattern, in which students are associated with entire programs of research (as contrasted with a single research project) so that they can move from one type of experience to another, as and when it seems necessary or desirable.

TRAINEE CHARACTERIZATION. The student pool from which research trainees presently are drawn is largely composed of persons who are not best suited for research careers, if the experience of the natural and social sciences is any measure. Taylor and Barron (1963) abstracted from a number of studies a list of characteristics of the productive scientist. They found him to be self-sufficient, interested in intellectual rather than social challenges and pursuits, highly organized, emotionally stable, lacking in impulsiveness, and of superior general intelligence. Cooley (1963) and Drevdahl (1961) reported further that the research student in the natural or social sciences was more interested in ideas, in discovery, and in observing and reasoning than was the college student not interested in research.

Doctoral students in education, on the other hand, typically are successful practitioners who hope to change their roles (e.g., from teacher to administrator) or the level at which they work (e.g., from secondary to higher education). Davis (1964) described seniors anticipating graduate work in education as low on the Academic Performance Index (a measure of intellectual achievement), low in the ratio of males to females, from small home towns, high in their orientation toward people, low in their orientation toward money, and highly conventional. In short, (research trainees in education are drawn from a pool of students whose characteristics are so widely divergent from the characteristics of researchers and research trainees in the natural and social sciences that undoubtedly many, if not most, research trainees in education are not temperamentally suited for a productive lifetime career in research.

Recruitment. The dissimilarity between characteristics of researchers and graduate students in education indicates that both attention and resources are needed to attract to educational research a type and caliber of graduate student rarely found among education doctoral students. Yet few universities engage in active recruitment. Moore and others (1960) found that 30 percent of the 80 schools in their study engaged in no recruitment activities whatsoever. Among those who did recruit, the most common activity was the encouragement of better master's-degree students to take advanced graduate studies. Other recruiting avenues found were (1) faculty and other personal contacts, (2) publications, (3) scholarships, fellowships, and assistantships, (4) personal letters, and (5) reliance on reputation and alumni.

The higher the reputation of the intellectual or research quality of the institution, the greater its attraction for students. Berelson's data (1960) showed that the better-known universities had more applicants than less well-known ones, especially among the most capable, and therefore had the greatest opportunity to select elite students.

The dissimilarity between the characteristics of researchers and the pool of typical education graduate students has already been noted. Continued mining of this human resource pool is warranted, but Clark (1966) pointed out other manpower pools of equal or greater potential for supplying the type and caliber of students suitable for a career in educational research. Students prepared in graduate departments other than education could be attracted to education. Undergraduate programs in education could open up, rather than close, research careers to young educationists if they provided an opportunity for early successful experiences in research. And more diverse pools of talent could be tapped more appropriately if program planners would specify the roles for which they were preparing students.

Selection. It is at the point of trainee selection that the most critical decisions are made with regard to the production of primary researchers. The intellectual quality and interest of the persons selected are more important predictors of eventual productivity than any institutional or program factor (Sieber, 1966).

Stanley (1962) has long maintained that if we are to improve educational research we must select bright, young persons having such characteristics as (1) a cum laude undergraduate record or better, (2) excellent verbal and quantitative performance, and (3) a willingness to pursue a three-year program which leads to a doctorate in educational psychology before age thirty.

Buswell and others (1966) suggested as additional researcher characteristics which may be used for selection (1) an early decision to pursue graduate work, (2) undergraduate work taken at an institution which offers doctoral programs, and (3) fewer than the average number of undergraduate courses in education.

Gardner (1967) and Bidwell (1967) were among a number of authors who maintained that many of these bright young recruits should be selected for discipline-based educational research from a field other than educational psychology. Sociology, anthropology, economics, political science, and social psychology were suggested as other fertile fields from which to select students who have been attracted to education.

However, the demand for trained researchers may become so great that even an expanded recruitment effort will not be able to keep pace, and some of these selection criteria will have to be relaxed. In that case, Clark (1966) suggested that some criteria which systematically exclude likely research and development candidates—e.g., undergraduate major in education or prior teaching experience—will have to be reexamined. A teaching experience requirement defers graduation and, hence, research production during the most creative years.

Ph.D. or Ed.D. Degree. Although both Ph.D. and Ed.D. programs are offered in many institutions, the trainees in these institutions appear to suffer from close conjunction. Ed.D. candidates appear to believe that their training in research is inferior to that of Ph.D. candidates and they therefore tend to shy away from research involvement. However, Sieber (1966) found that the research-preparation standards for Ph.D. students tended to become similar to the Ed.D. standards. Where that happened the research preparation of Ph.D. students was only slightly more advanced than that of Ed.D. students. It was clear, however, that many more Ph.D. students became active researchers than did Ed.D. students.

Interdisciplinary experience. Griffiths (1967) suggested that since there is no discipline of education, professors in schools of education must be drawn from the several disciplines which contribute knowledge to the solution of educational problems. These professors would do their major research and teaching in education but maintain some activity in their basic disciplines. Bidwell (1967) would have educational researchers secure their preparation in research methods from arts and sciences departments in order to be better able to apply the knowledge of the disciplines to education.

The relationship, if any, between interdisciplinary experiences and research productivity is unclear. In some high-prestige schools that have professors with joint appointments there does seem to be some benefit, but the caliber of the students at these institutions is so high that this factor alone could account for the differences discovered (Sieber, 1966).

Education doctoral students take a substantial number of courses outside the school of education. Fully half of the schools require this of their students. But research has yet to show any relationship either between the number of noneducation courses taken and research productivity or the proportion of faculty securing their degrees outside of education and the number or quality of researchers produced.

Nevertheless, Sieber (1967) pointed out that interdisciplinary experiences must be encouraged because education's isolation from the disciplines has resulted in the accumulation of numbers of unresearched areas of educational structure and process. He also pointed out the distorted view of the world which must result from the predominance of psychologically oriented behavioral scientists in education.

THE FUTURE TRAINING OF RESEARCHERS.

The field of education was profoundly affected by the passage of the Elementary and Secondary Education Act of 1965. As an officially proclaimed instrument of national policy, educational improvement became essential, rather than merely desirable. National progress was openly linked to the improvement of educational practice. The nature, role, and composition of educational research was similarly affected by this turn of events. Some of the changes which may be expected to occur in research preparation as a result of this new federal involvement appear below.

Federal Support of Research Preparation. Title IV of the Elementary and Secondary Education Act provided federal funds for the development of research-preparation programs and for the support of functioning programs. Stipends were provided for trainees at the undergraduate, graduate, and postdoctoral levels. Support was also offered to persons for attending short-term institute programs in order to sharpen their skills.

The first effect of this program was to shift a portion of the base of support for extant programs from the institution to the government. Program expansion and redirection have been slow since then, but as the federal government determines the objectives it wishes to attain it will be in a position to influence virtually all research preparation toward these objectives. A possible future effect is that preparation programs for educational researchers will be oriented toward the development of knowledge which has direct application to improved educational practice at the classroom level.

Broadening of Roles. Federal administrators are interested in the extent to which research will "pay off" in improved practice. Research results most effectively influence practice when they are incorporated into a textbook, teaching method, or teaching device which classroom teachers can use. Therefore, Clark (1967) suggested that increased attention and support are likely to be given to the preparation of "development" persons who can serve as members of a team which (1) seeks out basic research with possible application to education, (2) carries the research one or two steps further in order to secure results which have operational applicability, (3) invents a device or method based on the principles that the research suggests are relevant, and (4) engineers this device or method for the use of many teachers in a wide variety of settings. Still other roles may be created to disseminate information to local education agencies about educational innovations and the conditions under which they are effective.

The Research Utilization Committee of the American Educational Research Association (1966) documented the need for roles they identified as (1) development specialist, (2) field tester, (3) quality controller, (4) change agent, and (5) "county agent." Demand from the field for such persons, and the simultaneous development of institutional programs to prepare them, may create a condition in which new approaches to the preparation task will become essential.

Preparation-program Content. The emergence of new research and development roles will create a demand for content which simply does not now exist in education. Take, for example, the necessity of testing and evaluating proposed programs in local school districts. Old conceptions of evaluation and measurement are nearly hopeless as the institutional researcher grapples with the problem of developing an operations-research or quality-control program in a local school district. But such new roles and new content will be needed, and the institutions which must build preparation programs for this purpose will have to turn to allied fields, such as industrial engineering, for assistance in developing new courses and new content.

Shortage of Personnel. A developing shortage of qualified persons may also act to mandate new approaches to the preparation task. According to Clark and Hopkins (1968) the gap between the number of available research and development *positions* and the number of qualified research and development *persons* will number in the tens of thousands by 1972. The pressures which will develop from this gap between demand and supply will probably be sufficient in themselves to create such changes as (1) a reduction in the length of preparation programs, (2) increased specialization among the roles toward which a given program is directed, and (3) increased emphasis on self-instruction and instruction through experience.

Interdisciplinary Involvement. Significant changes may be brought about in existing preparation programs through the involvement in educational research of persons from other disciplines. Numbers of persons from other disciplines have been attracted to the field by the availability of funds, and they will undoubtedly bring with them a different perspective on appropriate ways of preparing researchers.

John E. Hopkins
Indiana University
David L. Clark
Indiana University

References

American Educational Research Association, Research Utilization Committee. "Training for Research Utilization." AERA, 1966.

Bargar, Robert, and Okorodudu, Corahann. *An Investigation of Factors Influencing the Training of Educational Researchers.* Ohio State U Research Foundation, 1968.

Bargar, Robert, and others. *Development of a National Register of Educational Researchers.* USOE Cooperative Research Project No. E-014, Ohio State U, Research Foundation, 1965.

Berelson, Bernard. *Graduate Education in the United States.* McGraw-Hill, 1960.

Bidwell, Charles. "Effect of the Socialization Process on Decisions Related to the Training of Educational Researchers." In Clark, David L., and Worthen, Blaine R. (Eds.) *Preparing Research Personnel for Education.* PDK, 1967. p. 45–51.

Blommers, Paul J., and Lindquist, E. F. *Elementary Statistical Methods in Psychology and Education.* Houghton, 1960.

Brown, L. D., and Slater, J. M. *The Graduates.* Vol. 1: *The Doctorate in Education.* AACTE, 1960.

Buswell, Guy T., and others. *Training for Educational Research.* USOE Cooperative Research Project No. 51074, Center for the Study of Higher Education, University of California, 1966.

Clark, David L. "The Training of Educational Researchers." In *Report of the Fourth Canadian Con-*

ference on Educational Research. Canadian Council for Research in Education, U Toronto, 1966. p. 73–91.
Clark, David L. "Educational Research and Development: The Next Decade." In Morphet, Edgar L., and Ryan, Charles O. (Eds.) Implications for Education of Prospective Changes in Society. Designing Education for the Future: An Eight-State Project, Denver, 1967. p. 156–76.
Clark, David L., and Hopkins, John E. Study of Roles for Researchers in Education. USOE Cooperative Research Project No. X-022, Indiana U Research Foundation, 1968.
Clark, Kenneth E. America's Psychologists: A Survey of a Growing Profession. APA, 1957.
Cooley, W. W. "Predicting Choice of a Career in Scientific Research." Personnel Guid J 42:21–8; 1963.
Davis, J. A. Great Aspirations: The Graduate Plans of America's College Seniors. Aldine Publishing Co., 1964.
Drevdahl, J. E. A Study of the Etiology and Development of the Creative Personality. USOE Cooperative Research Project No. 664, U Miami, 1961.
Edwards, Allen L. Experimental Design in Psychological Research. Rinehart, 1960.
Ferguson, George A. Statistical Analysis in Psychology and Education. McGraw-Hill, 1959.
Gardner, Eric F. "The Single Discipline Approach to the Training of Educational Researchers." In Clark, David L., and Worthen, Blaine R. (Eds.) Preparing Research Personnel for Education. PDK, 1967. p. 51–6.
Garrett, Henry E. Statistics in Psychology and Education. McKay, 1958.
Griffiths, Daniel E. "An Inter-disciplinary Staffing Plan for Schools of Education: A New Approach to Training Researchers for Education." In Clark, David L., and Worthen, Blaine R. (Eds.) Preparing Research Personnel for Education. PDK, 1967. p. 22–7.
Guba, Egon G. "An Overview of the Symposium." In Guba, Egon G., and Elam, Stanley. (Eds.) The Training and Nurture of Educational Researchers. PDK, 1965.
Guba, Egon G., and Horvat, John J. "Concluding Note." In Guba, Egon G. (Ed.) The Role of Educational Research in Educational Change. UNESCO Institute for Education (Hamburg, Germany), 1967.
Guilford, J. Paul. Fundamental Statistics in Psychology and Education. McGraw-Hill, 1956.
Heiss, Ann M. "A Study of Outstanding Scholars and Their Training for Research." In Buswell, Guy T., and others. (Eds.) Training for Educational Research. USOE Cooperative Research Project No. 51074, Center for the Study of Higher Education, U California, 1966. p. 71–113.
Krathwohl, David R. "Current Formal Patterns of Educating Empirically Oriented Researchers and Methodologists." In Guba, Egon G., and Elam, Stanley. (Eds.) The Training and Nurture of Educational Researchers. PDK, 1965. p. 73–93.
Lazarsfeld, Paul F. and Sieber, Sam D. Organizing Educational Research. Prentice-Hall, 1964.
Lindquist, E. F. Design and Analysis of Experiments in Psychology and Education. Houghton, 1953.
Moore, H. E., and others. The Institution. Vol. 2: The Doctorate in Education. AACTE, 1960.
Mouly, George J. The Science of Educational Research. American, 1963.
Sibley, E. The Recruitment, Selection, and Training of Social Scientists. Bulletin No. 8. Social Science Research Council, 1948.
Sieber, Sam D. The Organization of Educational Research. USOE Cooperative Research Project No. 1974, Bureau of Applied Social Research, Columbia U, 1966.
Sieber, Sam D. "Proposals for a Radical Revision of Research Training in Schools of Education." In Clark, David L., and Worthen, Blaine R. (Eds.) Preparing Research Personnel for Education. PDK, 1967. p. 27–34.
Stanley, Julian C. "Helping Doctoral Students in Educational Psychology Become Excellent Researchers." U Wisconsin, 1962. (AERA symposium paper.)
Taylor, C. W., and Barron, F. "A Look Ahead: Reflections of the Conference Participants and the Editors." In Taylor, C. W., and Barron, F. (Eds.) Scientific Creativity: Its Recognition and Development. Wiley, 1963. p. 372–91.
Travers, Robert M. W. An Introduction to Educational Research. Macmillan, 1964.
Thistlethwaite, D. L. "Fields of Study and Development of Motivation to Seek Advanced Training." J Ed Psychol 53:53–64; 1962.
Van Dalen, Deobold B. Understanding Educational Research: An Introduction. McGraw, 1962.

TRANSFER OF LEARNING

Psychologists are concerned with determining functional relationships among variables which influence transfer of learning. Increasingly, the concern is with determining the precise variables which influence transfer between tasks and not merely with determining whether transfer occurs. School and other training personnel desire instructional programs and methods that maximize positive transfer and minimize negative transfer. Both groups are interested in the influence of practice in one task upon the performance of other tasks. One kind of influence, called lateral or horizontal transfer, may be a generalizing from one task that facilitates performance on another task of about the same level of complexity. For example, the study of American literature may facilitate the learning of American history or English literature. Another influence may be that knowledge and abilities acquired in performing one task facilitate the learning of higher-order tasks of the same broad class. This is vertical or cumulative transfer. As an example, the ability to add, subtract, and multiply facilitates the subsequent mastery of division. Although schooling is directed toward securing positive transfer of both the horizontal and vertical type, the attention given to vertical transfer during the past decade has increased sharply.

Transfer of learning occupies a central position in Harlow's learning-set and error-factor theory (1959) and a lesser position in Neal Miller's liberalized S-R theory (1959). Deese and Hulse (1967) give transfer of training a prominent place in the psychology of learning, pointing out three ways in which tasks can be related. First, a current task may consist largely of common components or capabilities learned earlier with other tasks; second, one task may be related to another by common underlying principles which may be extended to the second task; third, tasks may be related by similar, rather than common, components and principles. Recently, Ellis (1965) devoted an entire volume to transfer; Stolurow (1966) developed a taxonomic system for studies of transfer and reported over 200 principles based on a review of 1,700 articles; and Wittrock (1967) sketched three subtheories of transfer which emphasize transfer as a foremost concern in educational psychology.

More directly related to education are the curriculum reforms of the past two decades, which reflect increasing interest in vertical transfer within the various subject fields (Heath, 1964). The major concepts of the disciplines, rather than specific factual information, are emphasized in the new textbooks. As vertical transfer receives greater emphasis in the new curricula, there is a corresponding decline of interest in transfer across subject fields and from in-school to out-of-school situations.

The high interest of educators and psychologists in the transfer of learning is reflected in the subsequent treatment of four main topics: definition and measurement of transfer, theoretical viewpoints about transfer, determinants of transfer, and securing positive transfer.

DEFINITION AND MEASUREMENT OF TRANSFER. Definition. Many agree that "transfer" refers, in a general sense, to the influence of prior learning upon later learning. This point of view is prevalent even though various researchers approach the topic differently in both laboratory and educational settings. The influence of prior learning may be such that (1) the learning of one task facilitates the learning of some subsequent task (positive transfer), (2) subsequent learning is impaired or inhibited as a result of prior learning (negative transfer), or (3) prior learning results in no measurable influence upon subsequent learning (zero transfer).

The phenomenon of transfer is so pervasive that it is difficult to distinguish between research on transfer specifically and on learning in general. For example, Schultz (1960) applies some of the fundamental principles of transfer to the analysis of problem-solving tasks. Similarly, Underwood (1966b) indicates that the analytic approach to the study of transfer is relevant to the study of concept learning and that many of the paradigms employed in transfer situations can be used to represent concept learning in pure form. In connection with this close relationship between learning and transfer, studies selected for inclusion in this article emphasize performance on a second task rather than initial acquisition or mastery of a first task.

Measurement: Paradigms for Transfer. Although many paradigms are used in studying transfer, there is one basic design having many variations. In the basic design the transfer group learns task I and then task II, while the control group learns only task II. This experimental paradigm is illustrated below:

Transfer Group:	Learn task I	Learn task II
Control Group:	Rest	Learn task II

The emphasis in this situation is on the learning of task II rather than on the retention of either task I or task II. It should be noted, however, that the study of retention after the transfer task may help to clarify the process of transfer (Barnes & Underwood, 1959). More detailed discussions of the various paradigms employed in transfer situations are to be found in the works by Ellis (1965), Stolurow (1966), and Underwood (1966a).

Variations from this basic paradigm typically employ more than one transfer or experimental group and one or two control groups to permit more precise clarification of the independent variables. When only a gross measure of transfer is sufficient, the control condition as illustrated above is adequate. In this situation, however, any difference between the experimental group and the control group might be accounted for as practice effects which carry over from task I learning. These practice effects are referred to as nonspecific sources of transfer (Ellis, 1965) or as nonassociative components (Underwood, 1966a). When a more specific source of transfer is to be studied, a different control condition is necessary. In that case the control group is required to learn a task which has no formal similarities to the transfer task but which should eliminate possible differences between the groups related to warm-up or learning to learn.

Usually a specific source of transfer such as similarity of the stimuli or responses is the primary concern of an experiment and constitutes the independent variable. Nonspecific sources of transfer, on the other hand, are usually present in the transfer situation but, for the most part, are task-independent. Practice effects such as warm-up and learning to learn are sources of nonspecific transfer.

"Warm-up" refers to the general enhancement of performance on a second task as a result of some preliminary practice. Presumably this preliminary practice enables a subject to develop "attentional" and "postural" adjustments which allow him to perform at a more efficient level than would have been possible without preliminary practice. Learning to learn is inferred from improved performance on subsequent tasks as a function of prior practice on a series of related tasks. Presumably this practice enables a subject to develop skills, strategies, or modes of attack which facilitate subsequent performance.

Both learning-to-learn and warm-up effects were demonstrated in a study by Thune (1951). Subjects learned three successive lists of paired adjectives each day for five days. Thune found that performance improved more rapidly within days than between days and suggested that the within-session facilitation was a function of warm-up while the between session facilitation was a function of learning to learn. Furthermore, the facilitation associated with warm-up dissipated over relatively short time periods (Hamilton, 1950; Thune, 1951). This transitory nature of warm-up is often used as a characteristic for distinguishing it from learning to learn.

More recently learning to learn has been studied through experiments in verbal learning. Primary consideration is given to the conditions of prior learning that contribute to learning to learn. The conditions of prior learning which have received attention are the type or class of verbal materials (trigrams or words), the method of practice (paired-associate or serial), and the type or variety of transfer paradigm (A–B, A–B'; A–B, A–C; A–B, A–Br or A–B, C–D).

Postman and Schwartz (1964) demonstrated that both the method of practice and the class of verbal materials employed in prior practice influenced learning to learn. They found that learning to learn was maximal when the same method of practice and the same class of materials were employed in the initial and subsequent task. Postman (1964) demonstrated that learning to learn increased as a function of practice but that the rate of learning to learn was a function of the particular paradigm employed. Subsequently, Keppel and Postman (1966) found that the skills acquired during practice on a particular paradigm readily generalized to new paradigms.

Measurement. In transfer studies raw scores on tests or scaled scores of performance are frequently used. Several formulas have been devised for expressing the amount and direction of transfer as a percentage, based on the obtained raw scores. The formula considered to be best by Ellis (1965) and Deese and Hulse (1967) will clarify this type of measurement. This formula, outlined in detail by Murdock (1957), is symmetrical and ranges in value from 100 percent positive transfer to 100 percent negative transfer. It is a ratio of the difference between the mean performance of the transfer group (T) and the mean performance of the control group (C) to the sum of the mean performance of the two groups:

$$\text{percentage of transfer} = \frac{T - C}{T + C} \times 100.$$

This formula is employed in a transfer study when the dependent variable is expressed in terms of the number of correct responses. However, if the magnitude of the dependent variable reflects poor performances, such as errors, trials, or time, then the formula becomes:

$$\text{percentage of transfer} = \frac{C - T}{T + C} \times 100.$$

The preceding formula enables comparison of the results of studies in which the basic paradigm is used and ordinal scores are obtained. It has merit for the researcher planning a single experiment or a series of experiments using the basic paradigm. At the same time, the formula is not being applied and may not be relevant to the study of learning to learn and other nonspecific sources of transfer or to the study of vertical transfer on a longitudinal basis in school settings. For example, Thune (1951) and Postman (1964), previously cited, and Gagné and others (1962), did not use the formula.

More important than the formula is precise measurement of the independent and dependent variables in transfer experiments. Especially needed are better systems for scaling or measuring the similarity components of the stimuli and responses of two or more tasks. Knowledge about transfer would be extended by better measurement techniques. The information about specific and nonspecific sources of transfer must be more analytical in order to develop general laws and to design instructional programs that maximize positive transfer and minimize negative transfer.

THEORETICAL VIEWPOINTS ABOUT TRANSFER. Viewpoints about transfer set forth in early global stimulus-response, functionalist, and cognitive theories of learning varied markedly among individuals who proposed one or another of these theories. However, each theory made methodological and substantive contributions to knowledge about transfer. The current trend is away from global theories that attempt to account for all learning and transfer phenomena under all conditions. The categories of human learning outlined in Melton's book (1964) are indicative of the tendency to deal more precisely and thoroughly with various human learning processes, such as classical and operant conditioning, verbal learning, rote learning, perceptual-skill learning, concept learning, and problem solving.

Objectives of education which for decades have been classified in the cognitive and psychomotor domains are also being defined more precisely. Differentiations of the content and abilities to be learned and used by the students have been made in the various domains—for example, among different psychomotor skills in football, typing, and music and among the concepts of science, mathematics, and English. Considerable correspondence has been shown between the categories of learning as outlined in Melton's book (1964) and instructional models, or systems, designed to achieve the more specific objectives of education (Klausmeier & Goodwin, 1966).

As the interests of more psychologists, educators, and scholars in the subject disciplines merge, serious attempts are being made to relate learning and instruction (Bruner, 1966b). In connection with transfer, the experimental psychologists continue to deal primarily with task factors stated in terms of stimulus and response similarities while the educational researcher is more concerned with subject-matter content and sequence (task variables), organismic factors, and instructional methods. These three categories of variables, or factors, have direct relevance to education and should also be considered by the psychologist in validating his laboratory-based viewpoints.

Most historical and many contemporary viewpoints about transfer deal with only a small number of variables within one or more of the preceding categories. Early theoretical viewpoints about transfer were based on the analysis of task relationships. The study of stimulus relationships, mostly intertask, is represented historically in the viewpoints about identical elements (Thorndike & Woodworth, 1901), generalization (Judd, 1908), and transposition (Köhler, 1925; Kuenne, 1946). According to the identical-elements viewpoint the more specific facts, skills, or attitudes transfer; according to the generalization viewpoint it is the principles; and according to transposition it is the broader pattern of relationships between the tasks. Not well accounted for in these viewpoints are learning to learn, abilities, and other organismic factors.

Learning set and instructions are posited by Gagné (1962, 1965) as the principal categories of variables essential to explaining and facilitating transfer. Since the instructions variables have not been related to learning sets directly by Gagné, they are not discussed further. Gagné uses the terms "learning sets" and "capabilities" synonymously in various writings to partially account for positive transfer. Learning sets are inferred from observations of the performances of subjects, including their performances on achievement tests.

In a study important for its design and theory as well as for its substance directly related to school learning, Gagné and others (1962) hypothesized that a class of tasks to be learned—for example solving linear equations—could be organized into a hierarchical structure of learning sets. These learning sets were assumed to mediate transfer of learning in a unidirectional fashion from one to another and ultimately to final performance. The hypothesis was supported with a high degree of regularity. The acquisition of knowledge of increasingly higher complexity was markedly facilitated by the acquisition of relevant prior learning sets or capabilities. Although one might consider the facilitating effects as a function of practice of the successive subordinate skills, Gagné and his colleagues (1962), like Harlow (1949) and Postman (1964), suggest that there is also a nonspecific source of transfer, a learning to learn, that is acquired as the student learns the subordinate capabilities. The facilitation thus is partly a function of learning to learn as well as of the practice and mastery of the more specific similar task components.

The present reviewers classify abilities as organismic factors. An ability is a union of a content and a process and is measurable. Learning to learn also may be treated as a nonspecific ability. An ability, such as arithmetic comprehension, is a union of at least one type of content, mathematical, and of one process, comprehension. Also the level or quality of the ability, though relatively invariant over a short period of time, changes with maturation and learning. In the cognitive domain abilities vary not only on the many possible unions of mental processes and contents but also on a specificity–generality continuum. The more general abilities are most invariant according to time. Abilities are acquired through practice or experience; and it is the ability, such as syllogistic reasoning, rather than knowledge of the specific content, or syllogisms, that facilitates subsequent performance of a broad number of tasks.

Efforts of a few investigators during recent years to relate abilities and learning, including transfer, are now of central concern. Ferguson (1956) outlined three different contexts in which to view human abilities. He proposed that positive transfer between tasks not having identifiable similar stimulus or response components is a function of specifiable abilities. Continuing to identify and classify human abilities related to various contents and products, Guilford and his associates have recently completed the analysis for concepts (Dunham & others, 1966). Stolurow (1966) also has given attention to abilities, aptitudes, and learning to learn in a generalized-process view of transfer of training. Klausmeier (1961) defined the central theme of educational psychology as the study of the relationships between learning and human abilities, emphasizing that the main job of education is to nurture emerging intellectual and psychomotor abilities through careful selection and sequencing of learning tasks.

DETERMINANTS OF TRANSFER. As noted in the preceding section, systematic attempts to account for the amount and direction of transfer have emphasized task characteristics. Similarity between the stimulus and response components of tasks is still the most widely studied transfer phenomenon. A second set of determinants of transfer is associated with learning or practice in the initial task. Since the emphasis in this article is on transfer rather than initial learning or retention, only those conditions of initial learning clearly related to transfer are treated. Organismic factors, both cognitive and affective, although not fully established in their explanatory value of transfer, are of interest in predicting differential school achievements in many subject fields.

Task Considerations. In some studies gross similarities between the initial and the subsequent tasks are pointed to as the basis of transfer. Analytic approaches deal with the more precise characteristics of the stimuli and of the responses related to the tasks. The amount and direction of transfer are also reported occasionally as a function of task similarity, variety, and meaningfulness.

Task Similarity. Similarity between the initial task and transfer task is one significant determinant of transfer, and similarity has been operationally defined in many different ways (Ellis & Feuge, 1966; Posner, 1964; Shepard & Chang, 1963). Despite the operational definitions, the measurement of similarity of tasks, per se, is exceedingly difficult. Ellis (1967) presented a detailed discussion of the problem of measurement of the similarity relationships in the study of transfer. The specification and measurement of gross task similarity are practically impossible and are highly complex when one is dealing specifically with stimuli or response characteristics.

Stimulus Similarity. Although not measured precisely, greater stimulus similarity between initial and transfer tasks is associated with an increasing amount of positive transfer (Deese & Hulse, 1967; Ellis, 1965). Studies by Yum (1931) demonstrated the positive relationship between stimulus similarity and transfer when three different types of stimulus material were varied systematically—nonsense syllables, geometric figures, and word meanings. Also, Ryan (1960) found that high similarity in connotative meanings was associated with positive transfer relative to control words which were low in connotative similarity. Also, words which were common associates (high verbal associations—e.g., slow-fast or square-round) were equally, if not more, important in facilitating learning of a transfer list. The same results were also reported by Jenkins and Brown (1965). Duncan (1953) also found that transfer increased as the amount of stimulus similarity increased in a motor-skills task.

Similarity of stimuli is associated with negative transfer when different responses are required on the transfer task. Gibson (1941) required subjects to associate nonsense syllables with geometric figures in the initial task and identical or similar nonsense syllables with different responses in the transfer task. When different responses were required on the transfer task, negative transfer increased as the similarity of the stimuli between the initial and transfer task increased. In summary, when the responses are identical in the initial and transfer tasks, an increase in stimulus similarity results in greater positive transfer; however, when the responses are different, an increase in stimulus similarity results in negative transfer.

Response Similarity. There is some support for the generalization that holding the stimuli identical in the initial and transfer tasks but varying the responses produces negative transfer (Ellis, 1965). Results of studies of response similarity as a determinant of transfer, however, have not been as consistent as those dealing with stimulus similarity. Underwood (1951), for example, reported increasing amounts of positive transfer with corresponding increases in response similarity.

There is, however, one condition of response similarity which consistently leads to negative transfer. Besch and Reynolds (1958) had subjects successively learn two lists of paired adjectives. Three conditions were then utilized in the transfer test: (1) one group learned a list composed of stimuli from the first list with new and unrelated responses (A–B; A–C); (2) another group learned a list composed of stimulus and response items from the first list, but the responses were re-paired with different stimulus items (A–B; A–Br); and (3) a third group, a control, learned a new list consisting of new stimulus and response items (A–B; C–D). In comparison to the control group, both experimental groups demonstrated negative transfer, with the re-paired response condition showing the greatest amount. The finding that the greatest amount of negative transfer occurs with rearrangement of old responses has been consistently demonstrated (Merikle & Battig, 1963; Porter & Duncan, 1953; Postman, 1962).

Transfer Surface. As early as 1927, Robinson (1927) attempted to specify a systematic relationship between intertask similarity and transfer. However, he did not differentiate stimulus and response similarity, nor did he specify the dimensions or the amount of intertask similarity (Battig, 1966). Osgood (1949) more precisely specified the relationship between intertask similarity and transfer, taking into account the stimulus and response components and also the amount of transfer. He stated the functional relationships in three principles: (1) As the similarity among stimulus components increases, corresponding increases in positive transfer occur when the response components are functionally identical. (2) As the similarity among response components increases, corresponding decreases in negative transfer occur when the stimulus components are functionally identical. (3) As the similarity among stimulus components increases, negative transfer increases when both stimulus and response components are simultaneously varied. Osgood incorporated these three principles graphically in his classic three-dimensional transfer surface in which the relative amount and direction of transfer was represented along one dimension, the similarity of response components along a second dimension, and the similarity of stimulus components along the third dimension.

Subsequently many researchers attempted to test or extend Osgood's transfer surface, but the results are inconsistent (Bugelski & Cadwallader, 1956; Dallett, 1962, 1965; Houston, 1964; Martin, 1965; Wimer, 1964). Battig (1966) stated that the resolution of this "similarity paradox" awaited the development of several necessary methodological prerequisites. This somewhat discouraging state of affairs demonstrates the complexity of the problem of functionally relating task similarity and transfer.

It also suggests that factors related to the organism, such as abilities and motivation, and experimental conditions, such as instructions, should simultaneously be considered. Ellis (1967), however, feels that other variables must be considered as secondary because their influences are also determined by similarities between components of initial and subsequent tasks.

Task Variety. Harlow (1949) demonstrated that monkeys given extended training on numerous discrimination problems improved in the rate at which they learned successive discrimination problems; further, performance on a given problem became virtually errorless after the first trial when the subject had been given sufficient practice on a number of related problems. Adams (1954) hypothesized that the same facilitating effect could be produced in human subjects by giving them extended practice on the same problem rather than on a variety of problems. As hypothesized, performance on the transfer task was superior for subjects trained on one problem rather than for subjects trained on a variety of problems. The apparent discrepancy between the findings of Harlow and Adams was in part resolved by Duncan (1958), who varied independently both the amount of training and the variety of training. Both variables were significant determinants of transfer; transfer was greater under the varied training conditions than under the condition in which the subjects received an equal amount of constant training. Thus, the findings of Adams may be accounted for in terms of lack of sufficient training in the varied training condition.

Callantine and Warren (1955) provided further evidence concerning the facilitating effects of training on initial tasks in a concept-learning situation, as did Morrisett and Hovland (1959) in a problem-solving situation. Thus, practice on a variety of related initial tasks results in greater transfer than does constant practice on one type of task, provided a sufficient amount of practice is given on each problem.

Task Meaningfulness. Underwood (1966a) has shown meaningfulness to have a powerful effect on verbal learning. Here meaningfulness is defined operationally as a set of highly correlated attributes, including number of associates, pronounceability, familiarity, and others.

Ausubel (1963) presented a cognitive point of view and pointed to concepts of logical meaning and psychological meaning. "Logical meaning" refers to attributes of the subject matter, or substantive material. For example, according to Ausubel, m-o-n-e-t-a-r-y is potentially more meaningful in our culture than is z-w-f-h-x-b-n-c. Also, 1-2-3-4-5-6-7-8 is more meaningful than 5-1-9-2-4-7-3-8. The second set in each pair of letters and numbers is less logical, less meaningful in the sense that it does not relate well to other ordered and consistent elements of our language and mathematical systems. According to Ausubel, psychological meaning is determined by the individual's already developed knowledge and skills, or cognitive structure, which enable him to relate new material to what he already knows. This definitional account of meaning does not indicate precisely how relationships among ideas develop in the first place or how the knowledge and skills are initially learned. Nevertheless, Ausubel presents a substantial amount of evidence, based on early studies of transfer in school subjects, that subject matter, logically ordered by the rules of our language and mathematics and related to what the child already knows, yields positive transfer. Ausubel cites as additional evidence the idea that concepts and generalizations, once acquired, facilitate transfer through their mediational properties.

Transfer and Initial Learning. The preceding discussion indicated that practice on a variety of problems rather than on a single problem resulted in positive transfer, provided that sufficient practice was given on each problem in varied training. Therefore, the amount of practice is an important determinant of transfer.

Negative transfer is observed when relatively small amounts of practice are given on the initial task (Underwood, 1949). Postman (1962) and Jung (1962) demonstrated that under conditions designed to produce negative transfer, as the amount of first task practice increases beyond relatively low degrees of training, the amount of negative transfer either increases (when the A–B, A–Br paradigm is employed) or decreases (when the A–B, A–C paradigm is employed). In those situations designed to produce positive transfer (A–B, A–C or A–B, A–B') higher first-task mastery results in increases in the amount of positive transfer (Duncan, 1953; Underwood, 1951).

Mandler (1962) suggested that the function which best describes the relationship between amount of first task practice and transfer is U-shaped; at relatively low levels of first-task practice negative transfer occurs, which is followed by a return to zero transfer and then is superseded by positive transfer effects as the amount of practice is increased. Postman (1962), however, observed that increases in the degree of first-task practice resulted in positive transfer only when the response components of the initial and transfer tasks are similar and when nonspecific sources of transfer are not controlled.

If learning the initial task involves preliminary experience with only the stimulus components which are employed in subsequent learning, then this preliminary experience is referred to as stimulus predifferentiation. Presumably this preliminary experience provides the opportunity for a subject to "predifferentiate" the stimulus elements so that the subsequent learning is facilitated. Consequently stimulus predifferentiation is considered as a special type of transfer situation. Ellis (1965) suggested that the principle of stimulus predifferentiation is employed in many educational situations. Audiovisual aids, for example, may be used to provide a student with preliminary experiences which facilitate the subsequent learning of complex skills and concepts.

Organismic Factors. When attempting to develop a parsimonious set of principles the theorist is not greatly concerned with individual differences. This point of view is reflected in the fact that organismic variables are often not treated in research on transfer. In the present section, however, a small amount of information is presented to indicate that organismic factors should be taken into account. Brief statements are made relating transfer to abilities and level of cognitive development.

Ferguson (1965) sketched the direction of research during the past quarter century in ascertaining the relation between human abilities and learning. Early studies focused on the relations between abilities and performance on tasks such as adding numbers and solving anagrams. Later studies attempted to identify and clarify the abilities involved at different stages in the learning of various tasks. Recently, abilities and the amount of transfer have become a primary concern. Ferguson reviewed a number of studies and concluded that some abilities can be measured quite reliably, that they can be dealt with in the basic transfer research paradigm previously outlined and also in other paradigms, and that they are useful in accounting for both horizontal and vertical transfer.

The relationship between the level of cognitive development, reflecting the work of Piaget, and transfer has been summarized succinctly by Lovell (1966). Transfer may occur at any level of cognitive development—for example, intuitive thought, concrete operations, or logical operations. The amount of transfer is dependent upon the quality and flexibility of an individual's cognitive structure. Thus, transfer at the level of intuitive thought may reflect gross generalization based primarily upon perceptual similarities, but at the level of logical operations highly abstract generalizations may transfer to mathematical and other tasks that are no longer bound to perceptual experiences. A related viewpoint concerning developmental differences in transfer is that of the Kendlers (T. Kendler, 1963; T. Kendler & others, 1960). They find that a child's level of cognitive development influences transfer from an initial to a subsequent discrimination. Their results imply that young children respond on the basis of a relatively primitive perceptual process and that with increasing maturity, corresponding to concrete operations, performance is determined by a mediating process.

SECURING POSITIVE TRANSFER. In designing an educational system the characteristics of the students are assessed; objectives are specified; an instructional program, incorporating content, materials, and methods of instruction, is organized; and measurement and evaluation are carried out to assess student progress, to provide the essential feedback for executing the program, and to evaluate the program in relation to the objectives. In line with this approach to educational planning, positive transfer can best be assured through two closely related activities: selecting or designing appropriate learning tasks and properly managing instruction. Textbook writers and others participate in the selection of content and the designing of learning tasks.

Task Selection and Design. The knowledge constituting the content of many subject fields may be organized on a continuum of specificity to generality —arbitrary associations, specific factual information, concepts, principles, and theoretical statements (Klausmeier & Goodwin, 1966). Mental abilities, or skills, may be arranged in a hierarchical order from simple to complex—comprehension, application, analysis, synthesis, evaluation (Bloom, 1956). Combinations of abilities are involved in a broad class of supraordinate abilities designated by such terms as "learning to learn," "strategies of learning," (Bruner & others, 1956), and "plans of learning" (G. Miller & others, 1960). In the previous sections, transfer was shown to be associated with similarity of stimuli, analogous to subject-matter content, and nonspecific factors such as learning to learn. In this section additional research is presented regarding various types of content and possible educational applications are given.

The high transfer value of principles has a long history. Recently Wittrock (1963) and Klausmeier and others (1964) showed that the rules or principles taught to the subjects facilitated the attainment of successive concepts of the same class. Also, McDougall (1958) demonstrated that concepts based on a relatively large number of facts were retained better than the facts per se and showed greater possibility of transfer. The conclusion is quite clear that presenting information about a principle underlying two tasks facilitates transfer. Also, concepts, more than specific information, facilitate transfer. Concepts and principles that are similar or identical in two successive tasks show higher positive transfer after a considerable time interval than do arbitrary associations and specific factual information, apparently because there is less likelihood of similarity between the specific than the general components of two tasks and therefore less transfer and because concepts facilitate the recall and retrieval of more specific information when it is needed.

Abilities of varying levels of complexity facilitate transfer, as shown previously (Ferguson, 1965). A complex conservative focusing strategy as outlined by Bruner and others (1956) was taught to college students and markedly facilitated the attainment of successive concepts of the same class (Klausmeier & others, 1964). Children of ages eight to nine were taught to use a strategy of testing one hypothesis at a time that facilitated concept attainment; a more efficient multiple-hypothesis testing strategy can be taught to more mentally mature children (Stern & Keislar, 1967). That strategies can be incorporated in instructions, can be learned by students, and can facilitate subsequent learning is clear. The extent to which strategies can be described, related to various school tasks, and taught to children of varying developmental levels is a promising area of study for those who design instructional materials as well as for those who teach.

Work-study skills, similar to strategies, can be taught. Leggitt (1934) instructed ninth-grade students in the use of reference books, interpretation of charts, and construction of outlines and summaries. Positive transfer occurred from the initial tasks to later tasks in the same course. Howell (1950) also noted steadily improving work-study skills, grades 4–8, and better performance in various school subjects that he judged were related to the work-study skills. Although work-study skills received initial attention long ago, little research has been done recently regarding them. Some might prefer to class work-study skills as information-securing and information-processing skills. These also have not received the attention they deserve from the standpoint of facilitating transfer.

In summary, the major concepts and principles in a subject field show greater positive transfer to later tasks than does specific information. Abilities, including strategies and learning to learn, facilitate positive transfer to subsequent tasks of the same class and to other classes of tasks.

Instructional Processes. Capabilities acquired in

speaking a second language may not be utilized efficiently in learning to write the language later, and the study of mathematics does not produce automatically better understanding of electrical circuits. Further, initial learning may be incomplete, with rapid loss thereafter through forgetting, thereby assuring little or no transfer. After learning tasks are carefully selected in terms of their potential transfer value, the probability of positive transfer is increased through proper guidance during initial learning, providing for a variety of experiences, arranging sequential cumulative experiences, and evaluating the student's ability to transfer. Although not directly related to instructional processes, learning by discovery, programmed instruction, and motor skills require consideration in relation to transfer.

Initial Learning. Conditions of initial learning are related to the amount and direction of subsequent transfer. Three related principles clarify the relationship but are not exhaustive: point out or emphasize the information—concepts or generalizations—and abilities that are expected to transfer; make certain the information is understood; and make the initial learning thorough. Information as used here includes all subject-matter content.

The teacher and designer of instructional material, more than the student, are expected to know the learning tasks that will be encountered in the future and the information and abilities acquired now that will be most useful later. Emphasizing the knowledge and abilities requisite for performing subsequent tasks facilitates transfer. Giving assistance in identifying the rules (Wittrock & others, 1964); presenting information concerning how stimulus material was organized (Klausmeier & others, 1964); having the students verbalize a principle while solving training problems (Gagné & Smith, 1962); and having the students verbalize a generalization after completing an initial task (Overing & Travers, 1966) exemplify procedures that facilitate transfer.

Making certain that students initially understand the concepts or other information has been shown repeatedly to facilitate transfer related to various school subjects (Ausubel, 1963). The same conclusion is drawn in some experiments (Ausubel, 1962; Ausubel & Fitzgerald, 1962) in which advance organizers were used. However, Stolurow (1966) did not obtain facilitating effects with advance organizers. Relevant early instruction that clarifies the subject-matter organization, the responses to be made, or the information facilitates transfer.

A principal deterrent to securing positive transfer is incomplete initial learning, as shown in the preceding section. Individuals whose initial mastery of the task is low quickly forget and fail to achieve transfer. However, educable mentally retarded children who mastered arithmetic tasks initially to the same criterion as average and high-ability children also performed equally well on transfer tasks (Klausmeier & Check, 1962). A primary weakness of some textbooks and teaching procedures appears to be related to the presentation of much information in a superficial manner.

Variety of Experiences. Negative transfer to a second task, associated with repeated use of the same tool in performing a first task, was observed by Birch and Rabinowitz (1951). Subsequently, positive transfer effects have been demonstrated in connection with the use of a variety of experiences. For example, practice on a variety of initial problems facilitated transfer on problems of the same class (Lloyd, 1960; Morrisett & Hovland, 1959); practice on several classes of problems in the initial situation produced more transfer than did practice on the same class (Wittrock & Twelker, 1964); and training in alternative methods of solving one class of problems facilitated performance on another class (Ackerman & Levin, 1958). An increase in positive transfer tends to occur with only a small increase in the number of initial tasks (Stolurow, 1966). Apparently a variety of methods or experiences facilitates transfer through encouraging an experimental attitude and higher motivation or attention to the task. Further, there is a greater likelihood of commonality of the method or process components of the two tasks when several methods are used on the initial task.

Cumulative Experiences. Motor skills, concepts, and cognitive abilities are not learned completely during a week or year; rather they are learned cumulatively through distributed practice and use over a period of years. The nature of vertical transfer suggests that relatively complete outlines of content and skills related to the various subject fields should be organized to achieve the favorable results previously reported by Gagné and others (1962) in mathematics instruction. Cronbach (1963) has attempted to relate Piaget's stages, sensorimotor through logical operations, to vertical transfer; that is, the child's concepts and intellectual operations at each stage lay the basis for the next stage. Klausmeier and Goodwin (1966) emphasize continuity in learning throughout the school years. Continuous examination of the sequencing of instruction within the various school levels and of the continuity between school levels is essential. Studying American history in grade 8 and not again until grade 11, discontinuing French at the end of grade 6 and not starting it again until grade 9, and discontinuing instruction in reading, handwriting, and spelling at the end of the elementary-school years are a few of many widespread practices that impede vertical transfer.

Evaluation of Student Performance. A principal reason for developing a taxonomy of objectives in the cognitive domain (Bloom, 1956) was to provide a basis for assessing the student's intellectual abilities other than memory and comprehension of factual information. Despite this, there is still a tendency not to assess the student's ability to utilize or apply newly acquired knowledge and skills. However, students tend to learn what they are tested on. Therefore, testing their ability to apply and use knowledge and skills in new situations should facilitate vertical transfer in the various subject fields and horizontal transfer across subject fields and to out-of-school situations.

Transfer and Discovery. The concept of discovery

Inter-task Similarity." *J Exp Psychol* 45:1–11; 1953.

Duncan, Carl P. "Transfer After Training with Single Versus Multiple Tasks." *J Exp Psychol* 55:63–72; 1958.

Dunham, Jack L., and others. *Abilities Pertaining to Classes and the Learning of Concepts.* Psychological Laboratory Reports 39. U Southern California, 1966.

Ellis, Henry C. *The Transfer of Learning.* Macmillan, 1965. 200p.

Ellis, Henry C. "Transfer and Retention." In Marx, Melvin H. (Ed.) *Learning: Processes.* Macmillan, 1967. Chs. 1–4.

Ellis, Henry C., and Feuge, Robert L. "Transfer of Predifferentiation Training to Gradients of Generalization in Shape Recognition." *J Exp Psychol* 71:539–42; 1966.

Ferguson, George A. "On Transfer and the Abilities of Man." *Canadian J Psychol* 10:121–31; 1956.

Ferguson, George A. "Human Abilities." In Farnsworth, Paul A. (Ed.) *Annual Review of Psychology.* Annual Reviews, 1965. p. 39–62.

Fitts, Paul M. "Perceptual-motor Skill Learning." In Melton, Arthur W. (Ed.) *Categories of Human Learning.* Academic, 1964. p. 243–85.

Gagné, Robert M. "The Acquisition of Knowledge." *Psychol R* 69:355–65; 1962.

Gagné, Robert M. *The Conditions of Learning.* Holt, 1965. 308p.

Gagné Robert M., and Smith, E. C. "A Study of the Effects of Verbalization on Problem Solving." *J Exp Psychol* 63:12–8; 1962.

Gagné, Robert M., and others. "Factors in Acquiring Knowledge of a Mathematical Task." *Psychol Monogr* No. 526; 1962. 21p.

Gibson, E. J. "Retroactive Inhibition as a Function of the Degree of Generalization between Tasks." *J Exp Psychol* 28:93–115; 1941.

Hamilton, C. E. "The Relationship Between Length of Interval Separating Two Tasks and Performance on the Second Task." *J Exp Psychol* 40:613–21; 1950.

Harlow, Harry F. "The Formation of Learning Sets." *Psychol R* 56:51–65; 1949.

Harlow, Harry F. "Learning Set and Error Factor Theory." In Koch, Sigmund. (Ed.) *Psychology: A Study of a Science.* Study 1: *Conceptual and Systematic;* Vol. 2: *General Systematic Formulations, Learning, and Special Processes.* McGraw-Hill, 1959. p. 492–537.

Haslerud, G. M., and Meyers, Shirley. "The Transfer Value of Given and Individual Derived Principles." *J Ed Psychol* 49:293–8; 1958.

Heath, Robert W. (Ed.) *New Curricula.* Harper, 1964. 284p.

Houston, J. P. "Verbal Transfer and Interlist Similarities." *Psychol R* 71:412–4; 1964.

Howell, Wallace J. "Work-study Skills of Children in Grades IV to VIII." *El Sch J* 50:384–9; 1950.

Jenkins, James J., and Brown, Lynn K. "The Use of Interspersed Test Items in Measuring Mediated Response Transfer." *J Verbal Learning Verbal Behavior* 4:425–9; 1965.

Judd, C. H. "The Relation of Special Training to General Intelligence." *Ed R* 36:28–42; 1908.

Jung, J. "Transfer of Training as a Function of Degree of First-list Learning." *J Verbal Learning Verbal Behavior* 1:197–9; 1962.

Kendler, Howard H. "Reflections on the Conference." In Shulman, Lee S., and Keislar, Evan R. (Eds.) *Learning by Discovery: A Critical Appraisal.* Rand McNally, 1966. p. 171–6.

Kendler, Tracy S. "Development of Mediating Responses in Children." *Monogr Soc Res Child Develop* 28(No. 2, Serial No. 86):33–48; 1963.

Kendler, Tracy S., and others. "Reversal and Nonreversal Shifts in Nursery School Children." *J Comp Physiol Psychol* 53:83–7; 1960.

Keppel, Geoffrey, and Postman, Leo. "Studies of Learning to Learn. III: Conditions of Improvement in Successive Transfer Tasks." *J Verbal Learning Verbal Behavior* 5:260–7; 1966.

Klausmeier, Herbert J. *Learning and Human Abilities: Educational Psychology.* Harper, 1961. 562p.

Klausmeier, Herbert J., and Check, John. "Retention and Transfer in Children of Low, Average, and High Intelligence." *J Ed Res* 55:319–22; 1962.

Klausmeier, Herbert J., and Goodwin, William L. *Learning and Human Abilities: Educational Psychology,* and ed. Harper, 1966. 720p.

Klausmeier, Herbert J., and others. *Strategies of Learning and Efficiency of Concept Attainment by Individuals and Groups.* USOE Project No. 1442, U Wisconsin, 1964. 124p.

Köhler, Wolfgang. *The Mentality of Apes.* Harcourt, 1925. 336p.

Kuenne, M. R. "Experimental Investigation of the Relation of Language to Transposition Behavior in Young Children." *J Exp Psychol* 36:471–90; 1946.

Leggitt, Dorothy. "Measuring Progress in Working Skills in Ninth-grade Civics." *Sch R* 42:676–87; 1934.

Lloyd, Kenneth E. "Supplementary Report: Retention and Transfer of Responses to Stimulus Classes." *J Exp Psychol* 59:206–7; 1960.

Lovell, Kenneth. "Concepts in Mathematics." In Klausmeier, Herbert J., and Harris, Chester W. (Eds.) *Analyses of Concept Learning.* Academic, 1966. p. 207–22.

Mandler, George. "From Association to Structure." *Psychol R* 69:415–27; 1962.

Martin, Edwin. "Transfer of Verbal Paired Associates." *Psychol R* 72:327–43; 1965.

McDougall, W. P. "Differential Retention of Course Outcomes in Educational Psychology." *J Ed Psychol* 49:53–60; 1958.

Melton, Arthur W. (Ed.) *Categories of Human Learning.* Academic, 1964. 356p.

Merikle, P. M., and Battig, W. F. "Transfer of Training as a Function of Experimental Paradigms and Meaningfulness." *J Verbal Learning Verbal Behavior* 2:485–8; 1963.

Miller, George A., and others. *Plans and the Structure of Behavior.* Holt, 1960. 226p.

Miller, Neal E. "Liberalization of Basic S-R Concepts: Extensions to Conflict Behavior, Motivation,

is ambiguous, according to Howard Kendler (1966), and Bruner (1966a) urged caution in talking about discovery as the principal vehicle of education. Caution is warranted in terms of prior research about the relationships between transfer and guided learning, guided learning being defined as arriving at a problem solution, concept, or principle with guidance but not being told the solution or concept. Giving students some information, the amount not clearly specified, has had a uniform history of securing better results than providing no information. Although this is the case, there is limited evidence to suggest that a principle arrived at with a minimum amount of guidance may produce more positive transfer than a principle told to the student (Haslerud & Meyers, 1958). In order to have some assurance of securing positive transfer, the following minimum instructional conditions seem to be relevant: set up a problem situation that the students accept as important, define the limits within which solutions and methods varying from correct or conventional usage will be accepted, guide the student in securing and interpreting information, and provide informative feedback so that the students can ascertain the adequacy of their methods and responses.

Transfer and Programmed Instruction. Programmed instruction has received much attention during the past decade. Programs are being developed in many subject fields that are intended to facilitate student achievement, defined in terms of an acquisition test upon completion of the program or in terms of gains between pretest and posttest scores. Despite this rational approach, the issue of transfer has been almost completely ignored in research with programmed instruction (Ellis, 1965). Stolurow (1966) projected a ten-year research program with the focus on studying transfer phenomena in the medium of programmed instruction. If programmed instruction is to contribute to the scientific foundation of educational psychology as enthusiasts have hoped, others will join Stolurow.

Perceptual-motor Skills. The previous generalizations regarding task selection and instructional processes may be relevant for motor skills; however, very little research was done on transfer and motor skills during the past decade. Battig (1966), in reviewing transfer related to motor skills, indicated a preference for discussing interference and facilitation rather than negative and positive transfer. Fitts (1964) likewise described the learning of motor skills in terms of early, middle, and late acquisition stages. Adams (1964) emphasized intertask learning to learn. Although this direction for research methodology in motor skills is stressed, systematic experimentation dealing with the facilitation of motor-skill learning is not being reported. Rather, analogies are being drawn with verbal learning. Caution is thus justified concerning the facilitation of motor-skill learning.

Herbert J. Klausmeier
The University of Wisconsin
J. Kent Davis
The University of Wisconsin

References

Ackerman, W. I., and Levin, H. "Effects of Training in Alternative Solutions on Subsequent Problem Solving." *J Ed Psychol* 49:239–44; 1958.

Adams, Jack A. "Multiple Versus Single Problem Training in Human Problem Solving." *J Exp Psychol* 48:15–8; 1954.

Adams, Jack A. "Motor Skills." In Farnsworth, Paul R. (Ed.) *Annual Review of Psychology.* Annual Reviews, 1964. p. 181–202.

Ausubel, David P. "A Transfer of Training Approach to Improving the Functional Retention of Medical Knowledge." *J Med Ed* 37:647–55; 1962.

Ausubel, David P. *The Psychology of Meaningful Verbal Learning.* Grune, 1963. 255p.

Ausubel, David P., and Fitzgerald, D. "Organizer, General Background, and Antecedent Learning Variables in Sequential Verbal Learning." *J Ed Psychol* 53:243–9; 1962.

Barnes, Jean M., and Underwood, Benton J. "'Fate' of First-list Associations in Transfer Theory." *J Exp Psychol* 58:97–105; 1959.

Battig, William F. "Facilitation and Interference." In Bilodeau, Edward A. (Ed.) *Acquisition of Skill.* Academic, 1966. p. 215–44.

Besch, Norma F., and Reynolds, William F. "Associative Interference in Verbal Paired-associate Learning." *J Exp Psychol* 55:554–7; 1958.

Birch, H. G., and Rabinowitz, H. S. "The Negative Effect of Previous Experience on Productive Thinking." *J Exp Psychol* 41:121–5; 1951.

Bloom, Benjamin S. (Ed.) *Taxonomy of Educational Objectives: The Classification of Educational Goals.* Handbook I: *Cognitive Domain.* McKay, 1956. 207p.

Bruner, Jerome S. "Some Elements of Discovery." In Shulman, Lee S., and Keislar, Evan R. (Eds.) *Learning by Discovery: A Critical Appraisal.* Rand McNally, 1966(a). p. 101–13.

Bruner, Jerome S. *Toward a Theory of Instruction.* Harvard U Press, 1966(b). 176p.

Bruner, Jerome S., and others. *A Study of Thinking.* Wiley, 1956. 330p.

Bugelski, B. R., and Cadwallader, T. C. "A Reappraisal of the Transfer and Retroaction Surface." *J Exp Psychol* 52:360–6; 1956.

Callantine, M. F., and Warren, J. M. "Learning Sets in Human Concept Formation." *Psychol Reports* 1:363–7; 1955.

Cronbach, Lee J. *Educational Psychology*, 2nd ed. Harcourt, 1963. 706p.

Dallett, K. M. "The Transfer Surface Re-examined." *J Verbal Learning Verbal Behavior* 1:91–4; 1962.

Dallett, K. M. "A Transfer Surface for Paradigms in which Second-list S-R Pairings Do Not Correspond to First-list Pairings." *J Verbal Learning Verbal Behavior* 4:528–34; 1965.

Deese, James, and Hulse, Stewart H. *The Psychology of Learning*, 3rd ed. McGraw-Hill, 1967. 514p.

Duncan, Carl P. "Transfer in Motor Learning as a Function of Degree of First-task Learning and

and Social Learning." In Koch, Sigmund. (Ed.) *Psychology: A Study of a Science.* Study I: *Conceptual and Systematic;* Vol. 2: *General Systematic Formulations, Learning, and Special Processes.* McGraw-Hill, 1959. p. 196–292.

Morrisett, Lloyd, and Hovland, Carl I. "A Comparison of Three Varieties of Training in Human Problem Solving." *J Exp Psychol* 58:52–5; 1959.

Murdock, Bennet B., Jr. "Transfer Designs and Formulas." *Psychol B* 54:313–26; 1957.

Osgood, Charles E. "The Similarity Paradox in Human Learning: A Resolution." *Psychol R* 56:132–43; 1949.

Overing, Robert L. R., and Travers, Robert M. W. "Effect upon Transfer of Variations in Training Conditions." *J Ed Psychol* 57:179–88; 1966.

Porter, Lyman W., and Duncan, Carl P. "Negative Transfer in Verbal Learning." *J Exp Psychol* 46:61–4; 1953.

Posner, M. I. "Uncertainty as a Predictor of Similarity in the Study of Generalization." *J Exp Psychol* 68:113–8; 1964.

Postman, Leo. "Transfer of Training as a Function of Experimental Paradigm and Degree of First-list Learning." *J Verbal Learning Verbal Behavior* 1:109–18; 1962.

Postman, Leo. "Studies of Learning to Learn. II: Changes in Transfer as a Function of Practice." *J Verbal Learning Verbal Behavior* 3:437–47; 1964.

Postman, Leo, and Schwartz, Marian. "Studies of Learning to Learn. I: Transfer as a Function of Method of Practice and Class of Verbal Materials." *J Verbal Learning Verbal Behavior* 3:37–49; 1964.

Robinson, E. S. "The 'Similarity' Factor in Retroaction." *Am J Psychol* 39:297–312; 1927.

Ryan, James J. "Comparison of Verbal Response Transfer Mediated by Meaningfully Similar and Associated Stimuli." *J Exp Psychol* 60:408–15; 1960.

Schultz, Rudolph W. "Problem Solving Behavior and Transfer." *Harvard Ed R* 30:61–77; 1960.

Shepard, Roger N., and Chang, J. J. "Stimulus Generalization in the Learning of Classifications." *J Exp Psychol* 65:94–102; 1963.

Stern, Carolyn, and Keislar, Evan R. "Acquisition of Problem Solving Strategies by Young Children, and Its Relation to Mental Age." *Am Ed Res J* 4:1–12; 1967.

Stolurow, Lawrence M. *Psychological and Educational Factors in Transfer of Training: Section 1.* Final Report. Training Research Laboratory (Urbana, Illinois), 1966. 312p.

Thorndike, E. L., and Woodworth, R. S. "The Influence of Improvement in One Mental Function upon the Efficiency of Other Functions (I). II: The Estimation of Magnitudes. III: Functions Involving Attention, Observation, and Discrimination." *Psychol R* 8:247–61, 384–95, 553–64; 1901.

Thune, Leland E. "Warm-up Effect as a Function of Level of Practice in Verbal Learning." *J Exp Psychol* 42:250–6; 1951.

Underwood, Benton J. "Proactive Inhibition as a Function of Time and Degree of Prior Learning." *J Exp Psychol* 39:24–34; 1949.

Underwood, Benton J. "Associative Transfer in Verbal Learning as a Function of Response Similarity and Degree of First-list Learning." *J Exp Psychol* 42:44–53; 1951.

Underwood, Benton J. *Experimental Psychology.* Appleton, 1966(*a*). 678p.

Underwood, Benton J. "Some Relationships Between Concept Learning and Verbal Learning." In Klausmeier, Herbert J., and Harris, Chester W. (Eds.) *Analysis of Concept Learning Academic,* 1966(*b*). p. 51–63.

Wimer, R. "Osgood's Transfer Surface: Extension and Test." *J Verbal Learning Verbal Behavior* 3:274–9; 1964.

Wittrock, Merle C. "Verbal Stimuli in Concept Formation; Learning by Discovery." *J Ed Psychol* 54:183–90; 1963.

Wittrock, Merle C. "Three Conceptual Approaches to Research on Transfer of Training." In Gagné, Robert M. (Ed.) *Research Approaches to School-subject Learning.* Rand McNally, 1967.

Wittrock, Merle C., and Twelker, P. A. "Verbal Cues and Variety of Classes of Problems in Transfer of Training." *Psychol Reports* 14:827–30; 1964.

Wittrock, Merle C., and others. "Verbal Cues in Concept Identification." *J Ed Psychol* 55:195–200; 1964.

Yum, K. W. "An Experimental Test of the Law of Assimilation." *J Exp Psychol* 14:68–82; 1931.

TRANSPORTATION OF STUDENTS

Transporting students to and from the school they attend as a function of school operation has a history now spread over a full century. The expenditure of public funds for transporting students was first legalized by the Massachusetts legislature in 1869. But the concept of public involvement in transporting students developed slowly. Its origin was at a time when the major means of transportation available was horseback or horse-drawn conveyances. It was also at a time when the tendency was to establish and operate a large number of small schools and to situate a school within walking distance of any child who wished to attend. Any child not within such range was free to make some kind of boarding arrangement that permitted his attendance or to simply not bother to attend school at all.

The reluctance to follow the lead of Massachusetts is illustrated by the fact that by 1900 only slightly more than one-third of the states had authorized the use of public funds to pay for or support the cost of transporting students. It was not until the advent and practical use of motor vehicles and the development of a network of hard-surface roads that programs for transporting students became an important part of public education in the United States.

Noble (1940) has documented the early history and rapid growth of student transportation. For the school year 1919–20, the first year for which national totals were estimated, the U.S. Office of Education (USOE) reported that 356,000 students, approximately 1.7 percent of the public elementary- and secondary-school students enrolled that year, were transported at public expense. By 1925–26 the number had more than tripled, with about 1,100,000 students being transported. This rapid growth has continued with substantial increases in the number transported each year. By the 1966–67 school year approximately 17.1 million students were daily school bus passengers, nearly two of every five enrolled in school.

The basis for transporting students, both for the earliest efforts and at present, is the belief that all children, regardless of where they live, should have access to adequate and appropriate educational opportunities. While the major developmental stage of the transportation of students was limited almost exclusively to rural areas, the provision of programs and transportation for handicapped children and those involved in other special programs has resulted in its extension into even the largest cities. Virtually all school systems, rural or urban, are now providing transportation for some proportion of their students.

SCHOOL-BOARD RESPONSIBILITY. In spite of the necessity for providing transportation, there are wide variations among the states with regard to legal authorization and responsibility. In most states local school boards are required to transport all students living farther than a specified distance from school, although in some this mandate applies only to certain ages or grades. In others the law is permissive, and school boards may but are not legally required to provide transportation. Featherston and Culp (1965) have described these variations, pointing out that Delaware is the only state which has no legal authorization in which transportation is mentioned. The specific permissive and mandatory provisions in state laws have been reported by Featherston and Murray (1960).

Whether transportation of students is legally required or is merely permitted on the part of school systems electing to provide it, major responsibility for what is done resides with each local school district board of education. Other than what is specifically provided for or required by state law, how the transportation needed will be provided, the specific characteristics of the operation, and the specific circumstances in which it will be furnished or denied are to a large extent matters which local school boards must decide. Garber (1960) has provided a legal documentation of local school-board authority and the broad range of discretion they have with respect to who shall be transported, school bus routes, walking distance requirements, discipline, and liability.

Type of Operation. School boards have two options open to them in providing transportation for those of their students in need of it. They may contract with one or more private individuals or business organizations and thus purchase transportation service, or they may decide to purchase their own school buses, employ drivers, and furnish the transportation needed as a regular part of the school operation. Both methods are in wide use.

During the early history of student transportation, when the transportation provided was by horse-drawn conveyance, it was much more practical for a school district to pay a farmer living within the school area to transport children than to build a barn, buy horses and carriages, and employ someone to care for and drive them. When motor vehicles came into use, the practice of contracting with private individuals was continued, partly because of precedent and partly because many schools either did not have sufficient funds to purchase buses or because legal barriers within the state discouraged or prevented such expenditures.

Gradually, however, school systems began to purchase vehicles and to provide transportation as a public enterprise in all respects. This approach was stimulated during the economic depression of the 1930's, and Noble (1940) reports that by 1936–37 slightly more than one-third of all the school buses in use were publicly owned. A number of studies comparing the relative cost of providing transportation by contract and with publicly owned fleets were completed during the years following Noble's study with almost overwhelming evidence of substantial savings through public ownership. Although the findings of these studies were later found by Pope (1950) to be not nearly as overwhelming as had been believed, they were sufficient to give impetus to public ownership. By 1949–50 the proportions had been almost completely reversed, with nearly two-thirds of all buses in use publicly owned. This trend toward public ownership has continued as transportation operations have grown larger. Approximately 70 percent of all school buses now in use for transporting students are publicly owned and operated.

While this trend toward public ownership must be recognized as one of the major characteristics of the development of student transportation programs, many students continue to be transported by buses owned by private contractors. In some states the number of privately owned vehicles far exceeds the number publicly owned. Many school systems prefer to purchase transportation service rather than take on the detailed responsibilities of purchasing and maintaining buses, employing drivers and mechanics, and all else a public transportation operation requires (*School Management,* 1962). And as Pope (1950) points out, under certain circumstances contracting may be the less expensive of the two methods. Factors other than cost are sometimes considered, however. Henry (1964) has emphasized the flexibility and control possible with a publicly owned school bus fleet and the necessity of these characteristics when school buses are used for supporting the instructional program.

Transporting Students to Nonpublic Schools. Another area of school-board responsibility relates to providing transportation for students who attend nonpublic schools. While such service is prohibited in some states, it is required in others. Still other states permit transporting nonpublic school students provided the school bus does not deviate from its regular route, or other stipulations are made. This whole area of activity has been widely debated and in some states contested in the courts. Garber (1958) has considered certain legal questions involved in such transportation, and a comprehensive background work has been prepared by Powell (1960). The variations among the states and the specific provisions in state law have been reported by Steinhilber and Sokolowski (1966). Because of differing requirements and prohibitions among the states and a considerable latitude for local school-board decision, no uniform nationwide practices can be described.

SAFETY IN STUDENT TRANSPORTATION. School systems take on a greater responsibility for students who are transported than they do for non-transported students. Their responsibility for their conduct, general supervision, and safety begins at the time they board the school bus, often many miles from the school they attend, and continues both while they are at school and until they are delivered to their homes at the end of the school day. Added to this longer period of responsibility is the recognition that students riding in a school bus are exposed to all the ordinary hazards of highway travel. With its continuous start-and-stop type of operation, the school bus can be considered exposed to more than ordinary traffic hazards. It is for these reasons that safety—safe school buses, safe drivers, safe operating procedures, and safe student passengers—is given major consideration in every program for transporting students (Featherston & Culp, 1965; National Education Association, 1965a).

Concern for ensuring the highest possible degree of safety has led to the adoption of specific state laws designed to control motor vehicle traffic when school buses are stopped for loading or unloading students. Every state except Hawaii has such a law, although there are variations in the types of signaling devices used on school buses to warn other vehicles that they are stopped or about to stop, in the way these signaling devices are used, and in what other vehicles are required or permitted to do when they overtake a bus that has stopped (National Committee on Uniform Traffic Laws and Ordinances, 1964). States differ, for example, in whether or not all motor vehicle traffic must stop when they meet or overtake a stopped school bus from either direction and whether these same provisions apply to dual-lane highways, in business and residential areas, and in other particular circumstances. This lack of national uniformity creates some confusion for motorists and represents a potential safety hazard (Edgren, 1960). National groups are continuously working for the development of uniform laws and procedures, and, with but minor exceptions, most state laws now conform or are in substantial conformity with the recommendations of the National Committee on Uniform Traffic Laws and Ordinances and included in the Uniform Vehicle Code.

In addition to requiring motorists to stop for a school bus in the process of loading or discharging passengers, many other procedures for assuring student safety have been developed. Some are also included in state law. All students who must cross a roadway before boarding or after alighting from a school bus, for example, uniformly must do so in front of the bus. The bus is required to remain in its stopped position with its signals activated to warn other motorists until all students have safely reached the other side of the road. Only then may the school bus proceed to its next stop. The use of student patrols, well-marked school bus loading zones, continuous training programs for school bus drivers, and other techniques have also been developed to assure student safety. The result of all these efforts is reflected in the fact that school buses have a remarkable record for safe operation.

School Bus Accidents and Passenger Protection. In spite of the precautions taken to assure safe operation, school buses do get involved in accidents, and injury and fatalities to students sometimes result. Of special concern is evidence indicating that the incidence of accidents involving school buses has been increasing steadily since 1960 with a percentage increase nearly double the increase in the number of students transported (Stewart, 1966). Any such increase is cause for alarm. As a result, several state groups are now making a careful analysis of all accidents involving school buses—their nature and causes and the ways by which they might have been prevented. Accident reporting and accident records are in the process of being refined and upgraded.

Substantial and perhaps even innovative developments may come from such studies. For example, a particular and troublesome problem identified in New Jersey was the fact that many motorists were passing stopped school buses even though their signal lights were flashing their warning. A study of this problem led Parrish to the discovery that when a school bus stopped in a position other than completely parallel with the direction of the highway, there was the actual possibility of a "blind spot" in which the flashing lights were not visible to an approaching vehicle until it had almost overtaken the bus (*School Bus Transportation*, 1962b). From this discovery came the development of a broad-beam warning light now in common use in all states. The arc of light refraction is such that the warning signals are observable to approaching motorists even though the bus may be parked at a substantial angle to the road direction.

A second innovative development in New Jersey also is related to the warning lights. In that state the law is specific that the alternately flashing red warning lamps will be activated only when the school bus is stopped. This led to experimentation with and ultimate state adoption of alternately flashing amber lights for prewarning other vehicles that the school bus was about to stop. During the first year this system of prewarning was in use, the number of accidents at school bus stops decreased approximately 72 percent. There was also a decrease of more than 10 percent in the number of arrests for passing a stopped school bus (*School Bus Trans-*

portation, 1963). Subsequent experience shows an even greater improvement. Front and rear-end accidents have virtually been eliminated throughout the state.

Without doubt the most scientific study yet undertaken in relation to school bus accidents was conducted by the University of California at Los Angeles' Institute of Transportation and Traffic Engineering (Severy & others, 1967). Rather than being directed toward accident prevention, the focus of this study was on how school bus passengers might be better protected when accidents do occur. Using research techniques and engineering methodology designed to provide realistic and objective findings relating to school bus passenger safety, three full-scale collision experiments involving a school bus were made. The head-on, side, and rear-end type collisions of the study represent the majority of all accidents in which a school bus is involved. Highly sophisticated and electronically instrumented anthropometric dummy passengers and high-speed photography together with various types of passenger-restraining devices were all part of the tests conducted. The study's findings may well influence the type of seat to be provided on school buses in the future as well as many other details regarding specific dimensions and specification details. The school bus seat on which student passengers ride was determined to have the possibility of offering the greatest passenger protection of any component in the passenger compartment of the bus. Current production-model seats were found inadequate. The study could also do more than any previous effort to press for an elimination of overcrowded buses. The results demonstrate clearly that students standing in a bus aisle have virtually no protection when the bus is involved in a collision.

THE SCHOOL BUS. Today's school bus is far different from the horse-drawn wagons and carriages, the canvas-curtained motor trucks, and the vehicles with steel panels secured to wooden frames from which it has evolved. The early history of vehicles used for transporting students has been recorded by Belknap (1950) along with an accounting of the gradual development of state requirements and specifications for their construction. This developmental period was characterized by rapid advances in the quality of vehicles used as school buses, but variations among the states in what was required had the effect of eliminating the possibility of mass-production methods by manufacturers and of adding substantially to vehicle cost.

In an effort to attain some degree of uniformity in school bus design and construction, official representatives of the states met together in 1939 at the invitation of the Council of Chief State School Officers. From this conference came a series of specific recommendations or minimum standards for school buses consistent with safety and economy. All-steel school bus bodies and a uniform yellow color (national school bus chrome) were among the recommendations advanced. While all of these national standards were little more than agreed-upon recommendations requiring state-by-state adoption, the results desired in terms of uniformity were largely achieved. State standards and construction requirements—those adopted on the basis of the recommendations of the 1939 conference and from the revisions recommended by the subsequent national conferences held in 1945, 1948, 1951 (an interim and limited conference), 1954, 1959, and 1964—have been closely related to the national recommendations (National Education Association, 1965a). Because the emphasis of all of the national recommendations has been on basic minimums, the standards of some states exceed but do not conflict with those developed by the national conferences.

While the initial efforts for developing standards were specifically directed to the conventional school bus, the standards recommendations now also cover small vehicles used to transport students, transit and metropolitan type buses, and vehicles used for transporting the physically handicapped (National Education Association, 1965a).

During the past decade a definite trend toward the purchase of heavier school bus equipment has been observable. This is a sharp contrast to the general pattern of the low-cost school bus characteristic of former years. Heavier axles, more powerful engines, air brakes, automatic transmissions, interlock differentials, power steering, higher capacity generators (alternators), and other improvements are now commonly written into the purchaser's specifications. As yet limited but definitely on the increase is the use of diesel-powered school buses. While all of these components add to the initial cost of the vehicle, lower maintenance costs and improved operation may prove them to be long-range economies (*Nation's Schools*, 1966).

SCHOOL BUS MAINTENANCE. School bus fleet operations have almost universally adopted a philosophy and program of preventive maintenance, the regular inspection of vehicles and immediate correction of any mechanical defects identified. Daily, weekly, monthly, and annual inspection guided by a check sheet, regular lubrication, the availability of spare buses to permit any vehicle in need of maintenance or repair to be taken out of service until the needed work has been completed, and a maintenance record for each bus in the fleet are essentials for an effective preventive maintenance program. Where school buses are school system owned, a preventive maintenance program also requires ready access to a maintenance garage and school-employed mechanics and servicemen committed to the philosophy of prevention (Featherston & Culp, 1965).

In addition to the regular local inspection of vehicles, state inspections ranging from annual to monthly are also general practice. In some states the state department of education has responsibility for this inspection of vehicles, while in others it is given to or shared with the state highway patrol, department of motor vehicles, public service commission, department of public safety, or other appropriate state agency. Murray (1963b) has made a state-by-state inventory of these inspection requirements.

A recent development is the experimental use of data processing procedures for school bus maintenance records by the Ohio State Department of Education. The system has contributed both to the development of uniformity in the type of maintenance records kept by separate school systems and to the availability of valuable information regarding the frequency of specific mechanical deficiencies. Without machine records procedures, the recurrence of these mechanical problems, documentation of such trouble, and rapid detection among scattered school bus fleets would not be possible. The same state agency has been carrying on a pilot program in which an inventory of school bus parts is maintained by a machine record system. The approach has proved itself. A computer can quickly locate a specific part needed to repair a school bus when delivery delays through normal distribution channels are encountered. The system has enabled buses in need of mechanical attention to be back in service in a matter of hours or days rather than weeks. Both of these experiments offer much promise for further development.

ADMINISTERING THE STUDENT TRANSPORTATION PROGRAM. Like most educational functions, the administration of the program of student transportation has become highly complex. Developing specifications for the purchase of school buses, planning school bus routes and schedules, selecting, training, and supervising school bus drivers and the mechanics assigned to vehicle maintenance, keeping careful records of purchases, inventories, and vehicle maintenance, coordinating the transportation operation with the instructional and other needs of individual schools as well as with new housing developments and new school buildings, and interpreting all of these highly specialized aspects of the program to the board of education and the public has become more than the general administrator of a school system can effectively manage without specialized assistance. As transporting students has developed and matured, it has become a field of specialization in its own right.

While many school systems operating a fleet of school buses have yet to employ an administrator specifically assigned to directing and supervising student transportation, the number of systems having such a position in the administrative branch is growing rapidly. As a result, state associations of transportation directors and a national association have come into being. These organizations provide opportunities for these administrators to learn about new developments, to share experiences, and to plan studies and action designed to bring about program improvement.

Training and Supervising School Bus Drivers. The key position in any student transportation system is that of the school bus driver. His ability to operate a heavy vehicle in a safe manner, to maintain discipline on the bus, to meet rigorous time schedules, and to report any mechanical malfunctions so they can be corrected without delay are determiners of program efficiency. The driver's responsibilities are such that a specific program of training has become an important necessity. Not only are such driver-training programs required of beginning drivers, but in most operations a continuing program for experienced drivers is also carried on. In some instances, detailed curriculum content for school bus driver-training programs has been developed (National Education Association, 1965b).

Traditionally, school bus drivers have been adult males, and this group continues to constitute a majority of all school bus drivers. In a few states some of those employed as school bus drivers are high school students. The major development of the past decade, however, has been the increased use of women as school bus drivers. In many operations women make up a majority of all those driving buses. Women have displayed a readiness for training and superior relationships with students and tend to be less abusive of school bus equipment than their male counterparts. Because very few women are likely to have had previous experience as drivers of heavy equipment, training is a most important part of any program which employs them as drivers.

Routing and Scheduling Buses. One of the major achievements in the transportation of students has been increased use of equipment. Only in areas of extreme population sparsity and long routes are buses now generally limited to one load of students in the morning and one in the afternoon. In most instances buses are now used for two, three, and four separate trips each morning and afternoon. Generally this type of procedure involves operating the elementary, junior high, and senior high school programs on separate schedules or having the schools in different parts of the school district on different schedules. After planning a number of multiple-route transportation operations, Wolfe (1964) has documented the possibilities of this approach for reducing the number of school buses required and the annual operating cost of transportation.

In an early stage of development but nevertheless significant is computer application to planning school bus routing patterns. Boyer (1961) did some pioneering work as he experimented with the application of mathematical models to the problems of routing. This approach proved unproductive and was abandoned, but it suggested ways by which a computer could be used to explore all possible combinations of predetermined school bus stops and identify those having greatest promise (Boyer, 1964). Although such computer application in planning school bus routes and schedules is not yet fully perfected, the progress made and the local operations independently attempting to refine the procedures used in these early efforts indicate that a breakthrough is imminent (Boyer & others, 1967).

FINANCING. The cost of student transportation is now commonly shared by state and local school systems. Although it was financed almost completely from local resources in its early years, state finance plans have generally recognized that those school systems required to transport a large proportion of their students have a financial burden over and above the cost of providing an educational program.

The specific provisions of state participation in the financing of transportation varies considerably, although most plans clearly identify on a distance-from-school or another basis those who can be included in computing the state's share of the cost, the formula or other method by which the state share is determined, any ceilings applicable, and any other limitations which might apply. In some states the proportion of state support is related to the basic foundation program for financing the total educational program.

The actual costs incurred in operating a student transportation program vary greatly from one type of area to another. While some studies have tended to compare these costs on the assumption that lower costs reflect greater efficiency, there are too many variables to permit direct cost comparisons. Obviously the transportation cost will be greater where students must be transported a long distance than where the distance is significantly less. Population density is another obvious factor. Henry (1964) identified a combination of the number of students per mile and the number of miles of route as the most valid predictive measure of transportation costs. He also documented the fact that the cost of transporting physically or mentally handicapped students is much greater than that of transporting regular students.

Although the capital cost of school buses is totally a local responsibility in most states, there is increasing state assistance in this area as in support for operating costs. In some instances financial assistance is provided by the inclusion of a depreciation-allowance factor or some other such provision in the formula used in computing the amount of state support to be provided. Murray (1963a) has summarized the various state plans related to the purchase of school buses.

ENRICHING EDUCATIONAL PROGRAMS. The development of student transportation has been a major factor in broadening and enriching the kind of educational programs available to communities throughout the United States. Many of the educational developments could not have come about without provision for transporting large numbers of students. Universal access to public secondary education is dependent on it. School district reorganization and school consolidation could not otherwise have been undertaken. Many of the special programs for the handicapped could not have been developed. Transportation from its beginning has had equalizing educational opportunity as a basic objective. And it has contributed greatly to the realization of this goal.

There are many additional educational activities requiring the use of school buses. Athletic programs, musical organizations, drama groups, and many other activities are dependent on the kind of mobility a school bus can provide. The range of possibilities for instructional trips is limitless. A zoo, dairy, music hall, museum, court, park, factory, or any other facility can be made an extension of the classroom (*School Bus Transportation,* 1962a). Buses are now widely used in summer recreation programs, in programs operated for educationally disadvantaged children, in transporting students to area vocational and technical schools and other types of supplementary educational centers, for outdoor-education programs, in orientation programs for teachers, and in countless other ways. The adaptability of the school bus for instructional field trips and various other educational purposes is sufficiently broad that Isenberg (1960) described it as one of the major tools available to the instructional programs. Its utilization for instructional purposes is increasing markedly year by year.

There are indications of even further extensions of school bus use in the future. Beginnings have already been made to employ buses for shuttling students about college and university campuses (*American School and University,* 1964). Experimental programs taking central-city slum children to suburban schools are being attempted. Plans for educational parks are being developed. These special programs as well as many of the other innovative ideas for enriching educational programs involve some method of transporting groups of students. The ultimate potential of the school bus as an instrument for equalizing educational opportunity undoubtedly extends well beyond what can now be conceived.

Robert M. Isenberg
National Education Association

References

American School and University. "The School Bus Goes to College." 36:32–3; 1964.

Belknap, Burton H. *The School Bus.* Educational Publishers, 1950. 212p.

Boyer, Roscoe A. *The Use of Mathematical Programming to Solve Certain Problems in Public School Transportation.* Cooperative Research Project No. 783. USOE, 1961. 74p.

Boyer, Roscoe A. *The Use of a Computer to Design School Bus Routes.* Cooperative Research Project No. 1605. USOE, 1964. 31p. + 84 (figs.)

Boyer, Roscoe A., and others. *The Use of a Computer to Design School Bus Routes: A Status Report.* U Mississippi, 1967. 11p.

Edgren, W. T. "Need for Uniform Operating Procedures, Laws." *Nation's Sch* 65:82–3; 1960.

Featherston, E. Glenn, and Culp, D. P. *Pupil Transportation: State and Local Programs.* Harper, 1965. 263p.

Featherston, E. Glenn, and Murray, John B. *State Provisions for Transporting Pupils,* rev. ed. Circular No. 453. USOE, 1960. 15p.

Garber, Lee O. "School Bus Standards Can Vary." *Nation's Sch* 62:68–9; 1958.

Garber, Lee O. "In School Transportation, Boards Have Much Discretionary Authority." *Nation's Sch* 65:92, 114, 116; 1960.

Henry, Paul Albert. "A Study of Factors Related to State Reimbursement of Pupil Transportation Costs in the Twenty-four Local School Systems of Maryland." Doctoral dissertation. American U, 1964. 188p.

Isenberg, Robert M. "The Bus Can Be an Instructional Facility." *Nation's Sch* 65:80–1; 1960.

Murray, John B. *Summary of State Plans and Procedures for Purchasing School Buses.* USOE, 1963(a). 5p.

Murray, John B. *Summary of State Provisions for School Bus Inspections.* USOE, 1963(b). 4p.

National Committee on Uniform Traffic Laws and Ordinances. *Motorists' Duties Toward School Children.* Traffic Laws Commentary No. 64–3. The Committee, 1964. 15p.

Nation's Schools. "Dual-wheel Traction Gets School Buses Over the Hills." 78:48; 1966.

National Educational Association, National Commission on Safety Education. *Minimum Standards for School Buses,* rev. ed. NEA, 1965(a). 100p.

National Educational Association, National Commission on Safety Education. *Selection, Instruction, and Supervision of School Bus Drivers: Recommended Policies and Practices.* NEA, 1965(b). 24p.

Noble, M. C. S., Jr. *Pupil Transportation in the United States.* Int Textbook, 1940. 541p.

Pope, Farnham G. "A Comparison of Pupil Transportation Costs Under District-owned and Contract Systems." *J Exp Ed* 19:95–100; 1950.

Powell, Theodore. *The School Bus Law.* Wesleyan U Press, 1960. 334p.

School Bus Transportation. "Diversified Use of School Buses." 7:20–6; 1962(a).

School Bus Transportation. "New Warning Lights for New Jersey School Buses." 7:29–31; 1962(b).

School Bus Transportation. "New Warning Lights Reduce Passing Accidents 72 Percent." 8:41–2; 1963.

School Management. "The Pros and Cons of Contract Buses." 6:46–50, 90, 92, 95, 97; 1962.

Severy, Derwyn M., and others. *School Bus Passenger Protection.* Monogr 670040. Society of Automotive Engineers, 1967. 165p.

Steinhilber, August W., and Sokolowski, Carl J. *Transportation and Textbooks for Parochial School Students and Constitutional Protection of Religious Freedom.* Circular No. 795. USOE, 1966. 45p.

Stewart, Paul T. *Types, Causes and Results of School Bus Accidents.* National Safety Council, Motor Transportation Department, 1966. 9p.

Wolfe, William. "Dual Scheduling Saves One Bus in 15." *Sch Bus Transportation* 9:18–9; 1964.

URBAN EDUCATIONAL PROBLEMS

Although the percentage of the United States population which is urban has increased steadily since 1790, the uniqueness of urban educational problems was not generally recognized until the middle of the twentieth century (Conant, 1961; Chandler & others, 1962). This essay focuses upon these problems as they have developed and been studied in the largest cities of the nation. It is important to note, however, that the same problems are becoming increasingly apparent in smaller cities. Large cities had educational problems before 1960, but few researchers addressed themselves to them. Their attention was usually devoted to lighthouse suburban districts where programs appeared more innovative and research was more readily managed. Few outsiders noticed when in 1956 superintendents and board of education members from ten major cities began the Great Cities Program for School Improvement. These people organized the program in 1956 for the purpose of studying educational problems of special interest to cities with populations over 600,000.

The first concern of the Research Council was with vocational education. In 1958 the group began to study the educational needs of culturally deprived children, in 1960 they examined teacher education, in 1964 they began work on instructional materials to meet the needs of urban youth, and in 1965 they undertook studies associated with school housing. These activities do not represent the totality of problems associated with urban education, but they do indicate the areas of greatest concern to city school officials (Research Council of the Great Cities Program for School Improvement, 1966).

Since 1960 scholars from many fields have shown increasing interest in problems of urban education. Work in the early part of the 1960's concentrated upon defining those problems and making their character explicit to the broader society. The best example of that trend is the work that has been done on the problem of the culturally deprived. Sexton (1961) pointed out that educational opportunities for city children were highly correlated with their parents' income and thus distributed inequitably. Riessman (1962) identified the special characteristics of underprivileged children which impeded educational achievement. In an important statement issued in 1962, the Educational Policies Commission of the National Education Association (1962) described the challenges which disadvantaged youth present to schools. The collective impact of these works was such that by 1963 persons of national stature were attending numerous workshops and seminars addressed to problems of educating the culturally deprived. Illustrative of the conclusions reached by these groups were the reports issued by Passow (1963) and the Bank Street College of Education (1965).

Workshop reports such as these marked a turning point in the literature on urban problems in that the national focus shifted from the definition of problems to the advancement of strategies for their solution. Continuing the example of works dealing with the culturally deprived, the research of Deutsch (1964) and Bloom (1964) suggested the need to educate young children prior to their entrance to the elementary school. Other documents which emphasized positive practices in new directions dealt with improving English skills of culturally different youth (Jewett & others, 1964), encouraging school–home partnerships (Fusco, 1964), and restructuring language patterns (Corbin & Crosby, 1965).

THE SETTING FOR URBAN EDUCATIONAL PROBLEMS. Urban school problems have their basis in population shifts. In the decade and a half following 1950, the school systems of large cities experienced amazing increases in enrollments. Consider as examples the changes in enrollments in the public schools of the 12 largest cities in the United States. During that period the enrollment in one of these cities increased over 100 percent, in another the increase was over 90 percent, in 3 more the increase was over 50 percent, in 2 others the increase was over 40 percent, and in the remaining 5 the increase was greater than 20 percent (Research Council of the Great Cities Program for School Improvement, 1964c, 1965). One city in the latter group was New York City. Although New York's total percentage increase was only slightly more than 20 percent, it represented a gain of 183,155 pupils. Only 7 other cities in the United States have total enrollments of more than 183,000 students. As another example, the total increase in public school enrollment in Los Angeles during this 15-year period was 296,560 pupils.

A fact sometimes overlooked is that while this great increase in pupil enrollment was occurring, the total population of the same cities was either decreasing or increasing at a much slower rate. Again, referring to the 12 largest cities in the United States, in the decade from 1950 to 1960, 4 cities—Baltimore, Chicago, Cleveland, and Washington—each decreased in total population while their public school enrollment increased over 30 percent. Even in the fastest growing cities, Houston and Los Angeles, city population increased only 57 percent and 26 percent, respectively, while public school enrollment increased 85 percent and 70 percent, respectively (U.S. Bureau of the Census, 1962; Research Council. . . , 1964d, 1965).

The increase in urban pupil population is a result of the post-World War II baby boom and, more recently, of the migration of many relatively large, low-income families to major American cities. The Chicago Commission on Human Relations reported an annual average of more than 12,000 newcomers—or more than 1,000 each month—to Chicago between 1953 and 1963. This figure represents a leveling off of in-migration from the peak years during the 1950's, when the average rate was 30,000 families per year.

Once the migrant family arrives in a large city, however, its movement does not always stop. Rather, a continued pattern of residential shifting often occurs. For example, over 50 percent of the non-white population in Houston, Los Angeles, Milwaukee, Baltimore, Cleveland, Washington, and Chicago moved within the city between 1950 and 1960 (Research Council . . . , 1964). Moreover, 40 percent of the white population in those cities moved during the same period. Many in the latter group moved from the cities to surrounding suburbs.

These population shifts have obvious implications for school-enrollment patterns. For example, the general superintendent of the Chicago public schools pointed out in his annual report of 1961 that all of Chicago's 20 administrative districts had sizable enrollment changes (Willis, 1962). In the 5 districts that had the highest record of pupil mobility, almost 40,000 pupils transferred in and out during just two school months, September and October. This represented an average of 1,000 children moving every day of those 40 days in one-fifth of the entire city. In these 5 districts one school alone accounted for almost 1,000 transfers in and out during the two-month period. It is not uncommon for records of individual students in such districts to indicate enrollment in as many as 10 or 12 schools. Moreover, these schools must accept students who come from a wide variety of backgrounds. For example, one school during a four-month period showed new enrollments from 52 Chicago public schools, 19 private schools, 18 other states, and 5 other countries. Pupil-enrollment statistics from other large systems reflect similar increases in enrollment and pupil mobility within the city.

This dramatic increase in student population has required city school systems to expand programs and build facilities at rapid rates. For example, in the decade from 1952 to 1963 Chicago added a total of 4,801 new classrooms in 236 new buildings or additions (Willis, 1964). Yet the cities have by no means caught up with school building needs. A 1964 study by the U.S. Office of Education (Collins & Stormer, 1965) indicated that the cities belonging to the Great Cities Research Council would require an additional 15,485 classrooms in order to house elementary and secondary pupils in classrooms with a ratio of 30 pupils to 1 teacher. The study indicated that an additional 50,800 classrooms would be required to meet this standard of pupil housing for the entire nation. By the 30-to-1 criterion, 30 percent of the nationwide need for additional classrooms existed within 15 cities.

Growth in student populations has been accompanied by shifts in urban resources and the emergence of new demands upon urban tax dollars. These changes have worked to the disadvantage of public school financing in large cities. The main support of public schools in the nation's major cities comes from local property taxes. Yet the per-pupil taxable assessed valuation in most of these cities has decreased in recent years. It is also known that large cities require greater expenditures than suburbs or smaller communities for police and fire protection, sanitation services, welfare programs, maintenance of streets and expressways, and other welfare and culture-oriented services. City schools, therefore, get a smaller part of the property-tax dollars than do their rural and suburban counterparts.

The situation of Pittsburgh is illustrative (Research Council. . . , 1964a). Pittsburgh residents contribute 61 cents of each tax dollar to nonschool governmental units. The average Pennsylvania community requires only 22 percent of the property-tax dollar for such services. Thus, the people of Pittsburgh contribute 39 percent of their total property-tax payments for services that smaller cities do not provide. This municipal overburden represents a major limitation upon efforts to support city school programs.

Several researchers have acknowledged the special financial problems which confront big-city school systems. James and others (1966) studied the determinants of educational expenditures in 107 of the largest American school districts in 1960 and concluded that "the prognosis will remain pessimistic until social policy for education in our cities is determined on grounds other than the availability of resources under tax structures designed decades ago." The Conference of Large City Boards of Education of New York State (1964) pointed out that the costs of building sites in large urban school districts is far greater than the cost of such sites in nonurban school districts. They noted that average per-acre cost in urban districts was $87,195, while that in nonurban districts was $1,355. Similar findings were reported by the Research Council of the Great Cities Program for School Improvement (1964a).

Proposals to take into account the special financial needs of the urban school systems have made headway in some states. New York State has introduced a correction factor for pupil density in the allocation of state aid to school districts. McClure (1966) recommended that state aid in Illinois take account of density corrections for all districts with enrollments of more than 20,000 students. The corrections suggested by McClure range from 3 percent for districts with enrollments of 20,000 to 24,999 students to 16 percent for districts of enrollments of over 300,000 students.

ORGANIZATIONAL PATTERNS IN BIG-CITY SCHOOLS. Large cities, like their smaller counterparts, place the responsibility for making school policy with lay boards of education. Cronin (1966) studied the development of boards of education in large cities from a historical standpoint. He noted that city school boards in the nineteenth century were very large and that they often were dominated by ward politicians. Reforms have reduced the size of school boards. Today most boards range in membership from 5 to 15 individuals and are considered beyond the pale of partisan politics.

A modern question of considerable importance involves the extent to which boards of education in large cities represent lay citizens. The methods of selecting board members range from public election to appointment by the mayor on the recommendation of a select committee to the practice in Washington, D.C., by which boards of education are appointed by district-court judges. While there is little evidence to suggest that methods of selecting board members have differential impact upon a school system's behavior, neither is there much literature which discusses the extent to which school boards represent citizens' views. The extent to which big-city school boards actually govern the affairs of school systems has been the subject of some inquiries. There have been suggestions that school boards are limited by organized constraints in the extent to which they can effect school policy. As Dykes (1965) and James and others (1966) have pointed out, what appears to be policy making may in fact be ritual or the legitimation of decisions made either outside the school system by state and federal officials or within the school system by administrators. For example, state legislatures have traditionally passed laws which apply only to big-city school systems in the state. Indeed, James noted that among the 14 major cities he studied, 7 had state-imposed restrictions upon budget making which were more severe than the conditions applicable to other, smaller cities in their states. A common restriction of this type is one which requires the city council to approve the annual school budget. In a case study of the Chicago Board of Education, Pois (1964) pointed out that the increasing legal requirements calling for "open" meetings force the Board of Education to deal with highly delicate and controversial issues under intense public scrutiny.

City school systems are large bureaucratic organizations. For example, the Research Division of the National Education Association (1962) reported that in 1962 New York employed 42,624 professionals, Chicago 19,543 professionals, Philadelphia 9,588, and Houston 7,089. A large number of those people are involved in staff activities, such as developing curriculum guides, planning the budget, maintaining attendance and transportation records, conducting research, recruiting and dealing with personnel, and providing other supportive services. What may be considered the line organization of urban school systems is often arranged on five or six levels. There is a superintendent of schools, a group of associate or assistant superintendents, a group of district superintendents each responsible for the schools within a particular regional area, principals, assistant principals, and teachers.

The size of city-school-system bureaucracies contributes to several organizational problems. One of these is determining the hierarchical level at which staff services should be provided. Havighurst (1964) pointed out the dysfunctions that result from concentrating curriculum services at the central-office level.

A second problem is that of coordinating activities on a district-wide basis and ensuring that lines of communication exist, both vertically and horizontally, between individual schools. In their study of Chicago, Janowitz and Street (1965) pointed out that principals have great autonomy because the central office lacks control devices other than universal directives. Thus, while city school systems may be highly centralized in the development of curriculum materials, the recruitment of teachers, the provision of pupil services, the processing of records, and the articulation of policy on a universalistic level, these systems may make few provisions for dealing directly with problems of individual schools. Operational decentralization encourages teachers and principals to seek ways to "beat the system" and evade the universalistic policy pronouncements which come from the central office. Griffiths and others (1963) documented this tendency with regard to the transfer and promotion policies toward personnel in the New York public schools.

A third problem related to the size of school bureaucracies and augmented by the low articulation among building and district units is the difficulty which outsiders have in approaching and dealing with the system. Thus, citizens or agencies with problems or questions to be addressed to the schools often do not know how to approach the system. Many times what are essentially building matters are taken directly to the central-office level, while problems which demand central-office attention are thrown in the lap of a school principal.

Perhaps the most controversial organizational problem of the 1960's involved strategies for assigning pupils and teachers to particular school buildings. In the past, assignments were made according to students' propinquity to school buildings and according to teachers' preferences. Beliefs that children should attend a school in their neighborhood and that teachers should be able to choose their places of employment were cherished in most communities. However, the shifts in residential patterns discussed before resulted in vast neighborhoods of homogeneous racial and socioeconomic character, and educators and others began to question the wisdom of continuing to assign pupils and teachers to schools on the basis of the traditional criteria. Studies such as those by Sexton (1961) and Riessman (1962) pointed to the educational disadvantages which some children suffer because of the neighborhoods in which they live.

Many segments of society support racially integrated educational experiences, both as an end in themselves and as means of assuring good instruction. Several researchers documented the problems associated with segregation in the public school. Among the studies were those by Hauser (1964) in Chicago, Swanson (1966) in New York, Crain (1966) in eight Northern cities, the U.S. Commission on Civil Rights (1967) and the nationwide survey conducted by the U.S. Office of Education under the direction of James S. Coleman (Coleman & others, 1966). Coleman's report noted that the great majority of American children attend schools that are largely segregated and that schools across the country offer unequal educational opportunities.

Steps which schools have taken to ameliorate problems associated with racial segregation include:

1. The development of open-enrollment plans.
2. Redrawing of district boundaries.
3. Pairing of predominantly white and Negro schools.
4. Institution of public-transfer policies.
5. New plans for teacher assignment and transfers.
6. Grade-level reorganizations which draw students from a broader geographical area into particular schools.

Among the most popular proposals to reorganize schools have been plans to develop middle schools and educational parks. A middle school is a school for grades 4–6 or 5–8 or perhaps 4–8 which serves a broad geographical area and draws students from several primary schools. An educational park is planned as a large institution that houses perhaps as many as 12,000–15,000 students on a single campus. The report of the U.S. Commission on Civil Rights (1967) gave strong endorsement to the development of educational parks because of their potential for contributing to improved education and desegregated schools.

Still another proposal for decreasing school segregation calls for central cities to cooperate with their surrounding suburbs in busing children back and forth across district boundaries (Center for Field Studies, 1965). This suggestion, if adopted, would mark a significant step toward the reorganization of city schools on a metropolitan basis.

Metropolitan reorganization also should help mitigate the financial problems which burden urban schools. Toronto, Ontario (Goldenberg, 1965), is one city which has already moved toward the establishment of metropolitan government for education, and Louisville, Kentucky, is in the preliminary stages of such development (Cunningham & others, 1966). The possibilities inherent in a shift toward metropolitan educational government were discussed at length in the 1968 yearbook of the National Society for the Study of Education (Havighurst, 1968).

STUDENTS AND LEARNING EXPERIENCES. The teacher moving into a school in an impacted and disadvantaged area of a city meets a unique situation. He is faced with a concentration of unfamiliar behavior and learning problems. Different bases of motivation and aspiration often exist for the educationally disadvantaged child. In his world there is a lack of experiences appropriate for school learning and little reinforcement of school experiences in the home. Parents are sometimes indifferent toward or distrustful of the schools and often not knowledgeable about what to do when they are interested. Many teachers find that their training courses and experiences have not prepared them for this confrontation. They are at a loss in trying to reach pupils and parents and fail to secure satisfaction from their efforts. They often become frustrated and request transfers to schools in middle-class neighborhoods, or they may leave teaching for some other occupation.

The disadvantaged child is handicapped by cultural experiences which are frequently limited to those of his immediate community. He may never have been to a museum, the public library, a concert, a play, the zoo, a downtown department store, or a large office building. His neighborhood will reveal in many instances few supporting community agencies, no library, few yards, little grass, and few or no flowers and trees. Persons who operate businesses in the neighborhood, agency personnel, teachers, and clergymen frequently live outside of the community.

Many disadvantaged youth are newcomers to the city, who have had limited opportunities for intellectual, social, and physical development. Many are oblivious to the opportunities which surround them or have rejected these opportunities because of feelings of insecurity, differing values and aspirations, or lack of familial encouragement. Staff members from several large cities (Great Cities School Improvement Studies, 1958) characterized disadvantaged children as follows: They are overage for the grade they attend, their school attendance is poor, they have a high rate of failure and a high drop-out rate, their aspiration level is low, they are without kindergarten experience, they have low achievement in reading and arithmetic, their participation in cultural activities is negligible, and their potential appears to exceed their achievement-test scores.

A decade ago many of the schools attended by the disadvantaged were characterized by large enrollments, large classes, half-day sessions, inadequate gymnasium, lunchroom, and auditorium facilities, an unattractive and uninviting appearance, inexperienced teachers, mobile pupil populations, difficult day-to-day maintenance problems, and rapid consumption of instructional materials.

City schools have moved to overcome some of these shortcomings, but their success has been by no means complete. As early as 1957, with the introduction of the Demonstration Guidance Project (Hillson & Myers, 1963) in New York City, followed by the Higher Horizons Program (Landers, 1963), a new era for the disadvantaged was initiated. Then, under the aegis of the Great Cities Program for School Improvement, a proposal was drawn outlining the problem and ways in which it could be approached. Eleven cities developed individual projects based on some phase of the central proposal and received grants to help pay for these programs. The programs developed in the great cities (Research Council . . . , 1964b, 1964c) did three things:

1. They modified or replaced traditional teaching methods where these had proved inadequate in teaching the disadvantaged child.

2. They provided compensatory services which enhanced learning and made more effective teaching possible.

3. They extended and augmented the role of the school in areas critical to the child's successful development—areas where family and out-of-school support, as normally provided, had had insufficient or negative effects.

Since 1964 programs and literature dealing with the educational problems of disadvantaged youth have proliferated at a rapid rate. Among the most noteworthy of the publications are those by Bloom and others (1965), Wattenberg (1966), and Witty (1967). Gordon and Wilderson (1966) compiled a directory of sample programs in compensatory education across the United States. Further development of these programs has been encouraged by the monies available under provisions of the Economic Opportunity Act of 1964 and the Elementary and Secondary Education Act of 1965.

PROBLEMS ASSOCIATED WITH TEACHERS IN BIG CITIES. The quality of the school staff is an important determinant in the success of educational programs. The most clearly articulated educational goals and the most carefully delineated instructional programs depend on the ability and skill of teachers, supervisors, and supporting personnel for effective implementation. Before the series of experimental programs for the culturally deprived was completed, members of the Great Cities Research Council reported that care had to be exercised in selecting staff participants, since teachers graduating from colleges of education were often not prepared to teach in the inner city. As the cities began to spread "promising practices" from the experimental or pilot stages to the large-scale demonstration programs, the need for large numbers of teachers whose personal qualities and specific preparation qualified them to help disadvantaged children learn became apparent (Chandler & Bertolaet, 1967).

Compounding the problem of finding specially prepared teachers for the disadvantaged has been the overall need for teachers in large cities. In one short decade, large cities found that their former surplus of teachers had disappeared. In Chicago in 1950, certificated teachers awaiting placement acted as day-to-day substitutes because of the lack of regular openings. But by 1961, of 21,000 teachers in the Chicago public schools, over 4,000 had some temporary classification. In March of 1962, while launching a teacher education project, superintendents from Cleveland and New York (Research Council . . . , 1962) indicated, respectively, that approximately 50 percent of the Cleveland teaching staff was on limited contract with less than four years of training and that of 42,000 teachers in New York City 9,000 were substitutes (although holding bachelor's degrees).

Teachers with temporary classifications typically have been found in inner-city schools. The traditional career pattern of big-city teachers has been one of transferring from initial assignment in the inner city to the outer fringes. In 1960–61 the number of transfers in urban school districts (city population 500,000 or more) was 6.6 percent of all teachers employed, while middle-sized cities (30,000–99,999) reported a transfer rate of less than half that proportion (National Education Association, Research Division, 1963). Becker (1952) investigated this horizontal movement of teachers as it existed in Chicago during the late 1940's, and over a decade later Boykin (1964) found it still was operative.

In spite of large-scale recruitment efforts, the shortage of teachers for urban schools remains great. Such schools continue to open their doors in the fall with classrooms uncovered by even temporary help. City salaries are competitive with those offered elsewhere, but the substantial advantage once enjoyed by urban districts has virtually disappeared. Furthermore, the elaborate mechanisms of written and oral examinations, developed as quality-control devices in the days when long eligibility lists were the rule, continue to exist. Another deterrent to recruitment of teachers for urban schools is the image of the city and its schools. The image of the city as a cultural and intellectual center sometimes is overshadowed by descriptions of crime, violence, vice, and decay.

Recognizing the need to prepare more teachers for the city, members of the Great Cities Research Council cooperated with metropolitan colleges and universities to develop preservice and in-service programs that would equip prospective teachers to teach disadvantaged children and overcome the "reality shock" of embarking on a teaching career in impacted, economically depressed areas. Chandler and others (1963) conducted a research seminar on teacher education which stimulated intercity communication and dialogue between teacher education institutions in metropolitan areas and large-city school systems. As an outgrowth of this seminar, Usdan and Bertolaet (1966) reported on the envisioned establishment of cooperatively operated school-university centers in disadvantaged areas that would serve as the focal point for the professional and field experiences for teacher education. The program cores of these centers would include (1) the teaching-learning situation of the school in the disadvantaged neighborhood; (2) the social-psychological characteristics of the pupils, teachers, parents, and community; and (3) continuing self-study and self-evaluation as a teacher of the disadvantaged. The public school systems in New York, Pittsburgh, Philadelphia, and Detroit are developing prototype center programs, and other large cities have begun to apply various facets of the center concepts.

The recent militancy of teachers' organizations has added a new dimension to personnel administration in urban school systems. With the legitimation of collective bargaining in the public sector, most large-city school systems have conducted determining elections and proceeded to write master contracts with an acknowledged bargaining agent. Occasional work disruptions, public protests, prolonged negotiation sessions, modifications in teachers' working conditions, and increasing limitations upon administrative jurisdiction have followed in the wake of teachers' protests and demonstrations.

New York City's public schools set a pattern for collective relationships followed, to a considerable extent, by many large school systems (Lieberman & Moscow, 1966). Following the determining election in the fall of 1961, the designated exclusive bargaining agent, the United Federation of Teachers, commenced negotiations with the Board of Education. In February 1962 an interim agreement was reached, and a budget proposal was submitted to the city. When the board was advised in April that its operating budget would be somewhat less than that which the February agreement called for, negotiations were resumed, interrupted by a one-day strike on April 11. Negotiations continued until early May, when general agreement was reached on salaries and working conditions requiring budgetary allotment. Other, nonbudgetary items were then considered, and final agreement was reached with ratification of the contract by union membership and its adoption by the board of education on October 11, 1962. The original New York agreement contained 15 articles dealing with such matters as union recognition, salaries, working conditions, grievance procedures, and union dues check off. It also included a comprehensive no-strike pledge.

The most significant feature of arrangements consummated by both American Federation of Teachers and National Education Association affiliates has been the range of matters regarded as negotiable. Virtually everything within the dimensions of the teachers' interest, including programs for the disadvantaged, the dropout problem, standardized testing, and student-teacher ratios, has been subjected to negotiations in one or more cities. It is apparent that teachers are just now beginning to do what administrators and college professors have exhorted them to do all along. They are insisting upon sharing in the making of educational decisions as is discussed below.

FORCES FOR CHANGE IN URBAN EDUCATION. Several factors which promise to alter the present shape of urban education can be identified. Changing public expectations for education are not the least of these. Increased public awareness of the importance of cognitive skills has developed as a result of recent proliferation of professional and technological occupations. Some individuals sensing the problems associated with poverty and racial segregation have viewed the schools as potential agencies for social change. The desire to increase the effectiveness of schools in both the cognitive and affective domains has stimulated a variety of efforts to introduce new curricular programs, utilize advanced technology, implement new organizational patterns, and increase the amount of money available to urban schools.

A second important force for change in urban education is the increasing militancy of teachers that was noted above. The effect of teachers' organizations' collective negotiations for salary increases and changes in work rules has been to increase the amount of teacher participation in school decision making, increase the specificity of teacher assignments, and introduce new ambiguities into school-personnel role relationships. The access of teachers to school boards at the bargaining table has suggested the need to think anew about the proper relations between teachers and principals and the responsibility of superintendents to represent the teachers, the boards of education, or both. While past negotiations have emphasized salary and work conditions, it is apparent that future deliberations will focus more directly upon the shape of school curricula. An open question in that area is the extent to which teacher militancy will aid or hinder efforts to attract individuals of high capability into teaching roles. Perhaps this is the most crucial question in assessing the future of urban education in light of teacher militancy.

The third and most recent force for change in urban education is the concentrated effort of the federal government in this direction. The Vocational Education Act of 1963, The Economic Opportunity Act of 1964, The Elementary and Secondary Education Act of 1965, and the Demonstration Cities and Metropolitan Development Act of 1966 offer encouragement to innovations in urban education. Under provisions of the Civil Rights Act of 1964, urban school systems have been encouraged to take steps to reduce problems of de facto segregation. Given continued public interest in ameliorating urban education problems, it is realistic to expect the federal government to maintain or even increase its efforts with regard to these problems.

Frederick W. Bertolaet
The University of Michigan
Raphael O. Nystrand
Ohio State University

References

Bank Street College of Education. *Education of the Deprived and Segregated.* USOE Cooperative Research Project No. G-021, Bank Street Col of Education, 1965. 69p.

Becker, Howard S. "The Career of the Chicago Public School Teacher." *Am J Sociol* 57:470-7; 1952.

Bloom, Benjamin S. *Stability and Change in Human Characteristics.* Wiley, 1964. 237p.

Bloom, Benjamin S., and others. *Compensatory Education for Cultural Deprivation.* Holt, 1965. 179p.

Boykin, Arsene Ogenius. "Demographic Factors Associated with Intra-system Teacher Mobility in an Urban School System." Doctoral dissertation. U Illinois, 1964. 128p. (Abstract in *Dissertation Abstracts* 24, No. 12, Part I):51111-2; 1964.

Center for Field Studies, Harvard Graduate School of Education. *Schools for Hartford.* Harvard Graduate School of Education, 1965. 52p.

Chandler, B. J., and Bertolaet, Frederick. "Administrative Problems and Procedures in Compensatory Education." In Witty, Paul A. (Ed.) *The Educationally Retarded and Disadvantaged,* 66th Yearbook, Part I, NSSE. U Chicago, 1967. Ch. 14, p. 306-27.

Chandler, B. J., and others. *Education in Urban Society.* Dodd, 1962. 279p.

Chandler, B. J., and others. *Research Seminar on Teacher Education.* USOE Cooperative Research Project No. G-011, Research Council of the Great Cities Program for School Improvement, 1963. 171p.

Coleman, James S., and others. *Equality of Educational Opportunity,* Vol 1 USOE, GPO, 1966. 737p.

Collins, George J., and Stormer, William L. *Condition of Public School Plants, 1964-65.* Miscellaneous Publication No. 50, OE-21033. USOE, GPO, 1965. 38p.

Conant, James Bryant. *Slums and Suburbs.* McGraw-Hill, 1961. 147p.

Conference of Large City Boards of Education of New York State. *An Analysis of the Educational and Financial Needs of Large Cities in New York State with Recommendations for Revision of the State Aid Formulas.* The Conference, 1964. 18p.

Corbin, Richard, and Crosby, Muriel. *Language Programs for the Disadvantaged.* NCTE, 1965. 327p.

Crain, Robert L. *School Desegregation in the North: Eight Comparative Case Studies of Community Structure and Policy Making.* USOE Project No. 5-0641-2-12-1. National Opinion Research Center, 1966. 331p.

Cronin, Joseph M. "The Selection of School Board Members in 'Great Cities.'" *Administrator's Notebook* 14(No. 6):1-4; 1966.

Cunningham, Luvern L. and others. *Report on the School Merger Issue.* Louisville and Jefferson County Public Schools, 1966. 100p.

Deutsch, Martin. "Facilitating Development in the Pre-school Child: Social and Psychological Perspectives." *Merrill-Palmer Q* 10:249-63; July 1964.

Dykes, Archie R. "Of School Boards and Superintendents." *Teach Col Rec* 66:399-404; February 1965.

Fusco, Gene C. *School-Home Partnership.* Bulletin 1964, No. 20, OE-31008. GPO, 1964. 74p.

Goldenberg, H. Carl. *Report of the Royal Commission on Metropolitan Toronto.* The Commission, 1965. 213p.

Gordon, Edmund W., and Wilderson, Doxey A. *Compensatory Education for The Disadvantaged.* CEEB, 1966. 299p.

Great Cities School Improvement Studies. *A Cooperative Program to Improve the Education of Culturally Deprived Children.* Great Cities School Improvement Program, 1958. 26p.

Griffiths, Daniel E., and others. *Teacher Mobility in New York City.* Center for School Services, New York U, 1963. 267p.

Hauser, Philip M. *Integration of the Public Schools—Chicago.* Board of Education of the City of Chicago, 1964. 86p.

Havighurst, Robert J. *The Public Schools of Chicago.* Chicago Board of Education of the City of Chicago, 1964. 502p.

Havighurst, Robert F. (Ed.) *Metropolitanism: Its Challenge to Education.* 67th Yearbook, NSSE. U Chicago Press, 1968 (in press).

Hillson, Henry T., and Myers, Florence C. *The Demonstration Guidance Project 1957-1962.* Board of Education of the City of New York, 1963. 31p.

James, H. Thomas, and others. *Determinants of Educational Expenditures in Large Cities in the United States.* USOE Cooperative Research Project No. 2389, School of Education, Stanford U, 1966. 198p.

Janowitz, Morris, and Street, David. "Innovation in the Public School System of the Inner City: A Policy Perspective." In Street, David. (Ed.) *Innovation in Mass Education.* U Chicago Press, 1965.

Jewett, Arno, and others. (Eds.) *Improving English Skills of Culturally Different Youth in Large Cities.* USOE Bulletin 1964, No. 5, OE–30012. GPO, 1964. 216p.

Landers, Jacob. *Higher Horizons.* Board of Education of the City of New York, 1963. 109p.

Lieberman, Myron, and Moskow, Michael H. *Collective Negotiations for Teachers.* Rand McNally, 1966. 745p.

McClure, William P. *Education for the Future of Illinois.* State of Illinois, 1966. 220p.

National Education Association, Educational Policies Commission. *Education and the Disadvantaged American.* NEA, 1962. 39p.

National Education Association, Research Division. *Urban Research Series. Professional Staffing Ratios 1961–62.* NEA, 1962. 34p.

National Education Association, Research Division. "Teacher Transfer." *NEA Res B* 41:62–3; 1963.

Passow, A. Harry. (Ed.) *Education in Depressed Areas.* Teachers Col, Columbia U, 1963. 359p.

Pois, Joseph. *The School Board Crisis.* Ed Meth, 1964. 309p.

Research Council of the Great Cities Program for School Improvement. "Minutes of the Meeting of the Research Council March 23–25, 1962." The Council, 1962. 15p. (Mimeographed.)

Research Council of the Great Cities Program for School Improvement. *The Challenge of Financing Public Schools in Great Cities.* The Council, 1964(a). 16p.

Research Council of the Great Cities Program for School Improvement. *The Culturally Deprived.* The Council, 1964(b). 32p.

Research Council of the Great Cities Program for School Improvement. *Promising Practices from the Projects for the Culturally Deprived.* The Council, 1964(c). 81p.

Research Council of the Great Cities Program for School Improvement. *Social and Economic Profiles of the Great Cities.* The Council, 1964(d). 104p.

Research Council of the Great Cities Program for School Improvement. *Sources of Revenue for the Public Schools of the Great Cities.* The Council, 1965. 16p. (Mimeographed.)

Research Council of the Great Cities Program for School Improvement. *The Past Is Prologue.* The Council, 1966. 18p.

Riessman, Frank. *The Culturally Deprived Child.* Harper, 1962. 140p.

Sexton, Patricia Cayo. *Education and Income.* Viking, 1961. 298p.

Swanson, Bert E. *The Struggle for Equality.* Hobbs, Dorman, and Company, 1966. 146p.

U.S. Bureau of the Census. *U.S. Census of Population and Housing: 1960. Census Tracts.* GPO, 1962. 180p.

U.S. Commission on Civil Rights. *Racial Isolation in the Public Schools.* GPO, 1967. 276p.

Usdan, Michael D., and Bertolaet, Frederick. *Teachers for the Disadvantaged.* Follett, 1966. 240p.

Wattenberg, William W. (Ed.) *Social Deviancy Among Youth.* 65th Yearbook, Part I. NSSE. U Chicago Press, 1966. 434p.

Willis, Benjamin C. *Annual Report of the General Superintendent, 1961.* Board of Education of the City of Chicago, 1962.

Willis, Benjamin C. *Ten Years of Growing.* Board of Education of the City of Chicago, 1964. 52p.

Witty, Paul A. (Ed.) *The Educationally Retarded and Disadvantaged.* 66th Yearbook, Part I. NSSE. U Chicago Press, 1967. 384p.

VOCATIONAL AND TECHNICAL EDUCATION

Our concern with change—adapting to it, anticipating it, fearing it or being secure in it, making it happen—is inextricably entangled with our interest in our own, and society's, future. The function of educational research in our preparation for the future is generally accepted as crucial and, in the long run, indispensable. In few bands of the educational spectrum have new knowledge, research, and development occurred more dramatically and explosively than in the vocational subjects, if one generously accepts the term "vocational" as the umbrella under which may be included all education and preparation for occupations, professions, and careers in the sphere of work. Few areas of formal education have contributed more to the advent and development of the technologies (or, conversely, have been more affected by them) than have the various subjects dealt with in this article of the encyclopedia. Some writers indicate that the technologies are products of knowledge, and it may be speculated that one of the most important aspects of technological change itself is in the area of social invention. The economist Kenneth Boulding (1966), in his treatise investigating the uncertain future of knowledge and technology, "Expecting the Unexpected," places a finger on the subtle problem of the role of the educational system in providing a new moral identity in an era of technological displacement of skills, in the race of intelligence against machines, in the recognition of educational frills, and in the production of men (and people) rather than manpower. This explicit purpose of education, the treating of people as ends and not as means, has outwardly been obscured for vocationalists, whose pronouncements, at least in much of the literature, seem concerned with the overriding objectives of the production and full utilization of trained manpower, the needs of industry and employers, and the composition of the labor force. Hopefully, the vocationalist has an implicit human purpose in the recognition of the value of people. Unfortunately, he has not said so.

Boulding's predictions about technological change, social invention, and the role of the schools find a great deal of reinforcement in the comparison of the "missing community" and the "great society" made by Newmann and others (1967). Technological change accelerates the breakdown of conditions which support human dignity; the "missing community" is characterized by a fragmentation of life and an exponential rate of social change, a bankruptcy of aesthetics and ideals, the depersonalization of experience that results from automation, and, finally, the loss of control over one's destiny—powerlessness. By contrast, the idea of the great society, based in bright optimism, holds that new and satisfying forms of self-realization are in the offing. The suggested reform of education in the conflict between the missing community and the great society should be perceived as an active pushing out of the walls of the school (and therefore the environments of education) in three enlarged contexts: the "school" context, the "laboratory-studio-work" context, and the "community seminar" context.

At least the social and technological spirit of the times, then, disregarding the economical and political, suggests a future role of educational research which is crucial and dynamic rather than barely adequate, as our traditional job-analysis techniques have been. Generally, research must reckon with a concept of curriculum and a psychology of learning which have at their hearts the functional behavior and perpetual adjustment of individuals in their vocations and the intimate manner in which individuals' vocations are related to their welfare and to the demands of daily living. In the democratic view of our society the ultimate benefactors of educational research, and consequently of education itself, must not be a chosen few at the highest level of intelligence in a vertical hierarchy of vocations.

This article primarily attempts to show the scope and nature of research activity in vocational and technical education, as they are described and delimited below. It goes beyond the descriptive and attempts to make clear the various trends, influences, and resources which promise an exciting future. There is a strong, and, hopefully, a clear, line of demarcation that limits its treatment of vocational and technical education to that available in the public secondary and postsecondary schools, with references to higher education because research, teacher education, and curriculum development are most active at the college and university level. No serious attempt is made to cover or exhaustively treat the research performed or under way in the various formal specializations of vocational education, such as agricultural, business and distributive, home economics, industrial, and technical education, which are usually considered to be affiliated with vocational and technical education in the public schools. If specialized research and study in one of these areas has critical significance for the group as a whole, an attempt is made to describe it within the space limitations of the article.

In general, research activity in vocational and technical education is in limbo. Possibly a far greater amount of research is under way than is completed and whose implications are disseminated; this article focuses on what are thought to be evolutionary elements in that development. Very closely bound up with this condition and critical to it is the problem of research administration and organization, and that problem is outlined below. Finally, some of the persistent problems which generally plague educational research—preparation of researchers, personnel supply and demand, resources, and restrictions—are investigated particularly with respect to their influences on vocational and technical education.

CHANGING NATURE AND ROLE OF VOCATIONAL AND TECHNICAL EDUCATION. The vocational and technical education embodied in the work of the secondary schools, as well as postsecondary aspects of such education, in the United States for roughly the past half-century is adequately treated by Byram and Wenrich (1956) and, in the third edition of this encyclopedia, by Wenrich (1960). A different and more detailed description by Henry and others is given in one of the yearbooks of the National Society for the Study of Education (1943—NSSE). The NSSE yearbook, in describing the myriad programs, activities, relationships, types, agencies, institutions, etc., provides ample evidence that vocational and technical education may be found in many forms and on many educational levels. Some specialists, reviewing the change and development in vocational and technical education since 1917, when federal support began, describe it as bending with the varying winds of social, economic, and political change. Their observations are well documented, since the program has changed—or has had change thrust upon it—over the period in which there have been two major wars, a few minor ones, a depression, varying recessions, and a dramatic period of technological development. Emerson (1962a), writing for the report of the President's Panel of Consultants on Vocational Education, *Education for a Changing World of Work*, describes achievements and limitations of the program as they are related to national crises and emergencies.

Omnibus educational legislation, to forget for a moment the impact of science and technology, made an almost spectacular appearance in 1958. Such legislation was held to be necessary to the nation's welfare and security, and as a result education was given a powerful shot in the arm, and vocational and technical education (particularly for the preparation of technicians) received another transfusion of federal funds. Optimism about the new provision of resources was well founded, but business could not be conducted "as usual": technicians were to be *highly skilled*—necessary for the national defense, to be trained in area schools, and to have functional knowledge of mathematics and science. The implementation of criteria of this nature, the resultant tremors to the educational system, and the initial rumblings of jurisdictional disputes, all of these and many others brought focus to a new role of vocational and technical education on the American scene.

A TRANSFIGURATION AND A NEW CHALLENGE. Vocational education of the reimbursed kind commemorated its semicentennial in 1967. Its desire to commit itself to a new and more vital role is inspired by far more than nostalgia and a half-century of service which cannot be evaluated. To a sizable degree the concept of a new role is motivated, or propelled, by the staggering dimensions of the overall legislative complex and its provisions supporting many forms of occupational education on many levels. Generally, the profession of vocational education is facing up to the task as it is reported by the American Vocational Association (1967). The impact of federal legislation alone is explained by Mobley and Barlow (1965), and Barlow (1965) outlines a new platform for the future, in the 64th yearbook of the National Society for the Study of Education. Much more important and motivating to the new role, however, than the generous provisions of contemporary legislation are the basic social, political, and economic changes which, when all are combined, make up a new way of life for persons at all levels of the world of work and for institutions which are educating them for it.

An avalanche of literature of the past decade has described the world of work. A great deal of it has attempted to indicate the advancement of science, technology, and automation and its implications. National commissions have studied and made recommendations concerning the preparation and, to a possibly greater degree, the use, of the scientist, the engineer, the technician, the craftsman, the operator, and others in the work force. Specialized economists and sociologists have contributed research, study, and publications. Manpower experts of many talents have analyzed the occupations, projected quantitative demand and supply, and prophesied the general nature of work in moving from a goods-producing work force to one which will supply services to people, institutions, and organizations. There is unmistakable evidence of the accuracy of their predictions in observations of the nature of work today, but the business of making a comparable *qualifications* analysis of people presently in the work force (and those who will be in it in the years ahead) is a more difficult, if not an impossible, task. The education and preparation of people and the role of the schools are crucial aspects of the total problem. A synthesis of ideas related to this general condition by a group of vocational educators is portrayed by Brandon and others (1957) in *Vocational Education in a Robot Revolution*.

Stage I—Technicians and Technical Education. Historically, the preparation of many types of technicians has occurred within the general organization of vocational education. Many excellent programs in technical high schools, technical institutes, and colleges and universities had been in operation long before the National Defense Education Act of 1958. Little attention was paid to occupation "technician" other than to classify it as subprofessional in the occupational hierarchy. With the explosion of science and technology and the resultant impact upon the preparation of scientific and engineering personnel, particularly at the professional level, the technician became almost at once the man of the hour and the subject of debated definitions, none of which was acceptable. Obviously, not all ranks of subprofessional technical personnel could be accepted as technicians; under the influence of some professional groups in the search for talented manpower some technicians were grouped as engineering technicians, others as industrial technicians, others as components of a team, others as super-technicians in research and development, and others, in final desperation, within a category of "technical employments." Emerson (1962b), who is one of many troubled observers, made a careful analysis and numerous recommendations in "Technical Training in the United States." Brandon (1958) interviewed numerous engineers in industry and discovered that old craft titles prevailed, little prescription could be laid down for functional learning, and technician job titles were being compounded with other, more descriptive terms. His study, *Twin City Technicians,* supplied what became a popular survey methodology in several communities and states and was a prelude to Title VIII of the National Defense Education Act and its subsequent regulations. The technical institute and its status and role were studied in great detail by Henninger (1959).

But while Title VIII provoked an intensive search for the meaning of "technician," it also ushered in a more powerful concern and reawakened an old antagonism in public education in general—the struggle to break down the barriers of school consolidation and hardening of the high school curriculum. The "area school" concept of education was formalized in Title VIII, but its broadening influence was reserved for the education of technicians. It is an educational paradox that Title VIII introduced both a revitalization of the area-school concept and an elitism in the preparation of technicians. A generous background of resources in the literature and research and study activities is consolidated in a bibliography prepared by the Center for Vocational and Technical Education (1966). A description of the many technical and scientific societies related to technical education appears in a recent bulletin by the U.S. Office of Education, Division of Vocational and Technical Education (1966d).

Stage II—Redirection. At the start of the present decade a number of powerful forces were combining to demand reshaping of education in general and of vocational and technical education in particular. The problems, on the whole, were not new: the manpower shortage, the scarcity of trained scientific and technical workers, people out of work amid job vacancies which demanded new skills, school dropouts and "pushouts," juvenile delinquency, racial and sexual discrimination in employment, unequal opportunity in education, etc. Professionals in vocational education were investigating trends and planning alleviations for the decade ahead, described in a publication of the U.S. Office of Education, Division of Vocational and Technical Education (1961). One of the few cooperative research projects in vocational education, that by Woerdehoff and others (1960), was an attempt to study social, economic, and technical trends as they were related to vocational education in the public schools. The investigators synthesized 55 trends which were subsequently rank-ordered by a jury which included 430 economists, sociologists, educational philosophers, vocational-teacher educators, and labor and management personnel. A review by Karnes (1962) of the literature for a six-year period in technical education indicates that the study and fact-finding activity was quite intense, but "the literature is nebulous and the terminology is confusing."

The most positive redirection of the vocational and technical education program was launched by President John F. Kennedy's message on American education to Congress in 1961 and the subsequent appointment of the President's Panel of Consultants on Vocational Education. Two of the panel's primary reports (sometimes called the Willis Reports after Benjamin C. Willis, the panel chairman), three appendixes, and a number of unpublished studies and reports had strong influence on the design of the Vocational Education Act of 1963. The panel's recommendations for redirection of the vocational program are detailed in *Education for a Changing World of Work*, a publication of the U.S. Department of Health, Education, and Welfare (1963).

Generally, the panel's suggestions made a sharp break with the past, but perhaps not as sharp a break as some would have recommended. The old theme, vocational education solely for employment and as preparation for entering the world of work, is still quite discernible. Refreshingly new was the panel's basic concern for the needs of people—the recognition of their need for access to vocational education, the planned enrichment of curriculum both in nature and number of offerings, a new awareness of supply and demand in the occupations, the recognition of the needs of persons with special requirements or disadvantages, and the translation of the nature of the world of work into realistic new patterns and programs of preparation. These concerns and others were placed into categories for four general groups of people—in-school youth, post-high school youth, out-of-school youth and adults, and youth with special needs. The ancillary services—teacher education, instructional materials, expanded research, and supervisory services—were bolstered to make it possible for the program to follow its new directions. Unmistakably, the panel report, while it certainly lacked the foundation of sophisticated research data for precision in its recommendations, cast the die for vocational education legislation and the rash of professional literature which followed. Levitan (1963) summarized federal policy for vocational education in introducing provisions of the Perkins Bill, which ultimately became the Vocational Education Act of 1963. Appendix III of the panel report describes four studies under contract: (1) Clark's "Economic and Social Background of Vocational Education," (2) Brookover and Nosow's "Sociological Analysis of Vocational Education," (3) Moore's "Case for Education for Home and Family Living," and (4) Hoyt's "Contribution to the National Economy of the Use of Resources Within and by the Family." Numerous other reports, position papers, studies, and results of committee discussions were sponsored by the panel, but for the most part these were not formally published.

Many states, running true to precedent, made state studies and attempted to follow the panel's format in describing their needs. Smith (1963) made an atypical descriptive report of a program for the state of Michigan based upon a comparison of the programs of ten other states. In the national literature, Venn (1964), Kourmadas and others (1965), and Gordon Swanson and others (1965) contributed to an effort to add realism and meaning to the image of vocational and technical education, which was newly in the public eye.

Stage III—Competition in the Vocational Marketplace. Currently, many forms of occupational education are supported by generous provisions of massive federal legislation and by the efforts of many states to participate in the programs. Contemporary legislation of major consequence began with Title VIII of the National Defense Education Act and progressed chronologically through the Area Redevelopment Act, the Manpower Training and Development Act, the Vocational Education Act, the Economic Opportunity Act, and, although it has not been exploited to any degree in an occupational sense, the Elementary and Secondary Education Act. It is interesting to speculate with Gordon Swanson and others (1965) that this legislative complex has resulted from a "massive social protest movement." Proponents of the various acts risk making overgeneralizations, but they tend to believe that (1) the American high school has failed in its democratic purpose, that of serving all Americans, (2) secondary and higher education persist in clinging to an aristocracy of learning, a cleavage of general versus vocational education, a built-in casualty risk for dropouts, (3) occupational programs take an unnecessarily long time to complete, (4) for many Americans the curriculum is an impoverished one, (5) the basic role of vocational education should be more than the training of persons for employment, and, finally, (6) numerous Americans are unemployed because of lack of preparation or lack of opportunity for preparation.

Provisions of the legislative complex have produced, and will continue to produce, competition for the funds to support vocational and technical education and the research which should accompany it. The professional community has mixed feelings about whether the competition is a healthful development; the resources are being put to varied use in supporting occupational education (and research) within and outside of the public schools, in private business and industry, and among numerous disciplines. The tug for administrative control is most evident in public education itself. Here may be seen the *institutional* conflict between the comprehensive high school, the vocational and technical school, the area school, the technical institute, the community junior college, the university branch campus, and colleges and universities. Generally, with the *amount* of occupational education needed by youth and adults, the efforts, if they are sincere and not exploitative, can be handled by all of the institutions. Nevertheless, the mounting costs of occupational education must be reconciled with resources which, however rich, are limited and which, as a matter of fact, have not increased proportionately with resources supporting education in general. The establishment of institutional jurisdictions has a way of producing duplication and, in the final analysis, a lack of overall service to the public need. This pitfall is particularly hazardous in vocational and technical education and to its perception in educational institutions: general studies and vocational studies are conceived of as separate "tracks" leading to separate life objectives; vocational education is used to train delinquents; and the "vocational track" is now used for taking over the education of students who have been rejected by the general program. Feldman (1966) describes this condition and some alternatives in *Making Education Relevant.*

The competition for human and physical research resources is producing mixed benefits. Administrators and legislators are dissatisfied with research efforts, the nature of planned activity, and the dissemination and application processes. Researchers, themselves in short supply and insisting upon a measure of freedom, are not attracted to earmarked research priorities, to commitments to applications, or to solving social problems outside their scholarly areas. Most seriously, researchers and research administrators have strong distastes for proposal making, gamesmanship, and grantsmanship, which have become critical attributes in tapping the average $6-billion yearly expenditure of the federal government for education and educational research, as reported in "Grantsmanship" (1966).

CURRENT NATURE AND SUPPORT OF RESEARCH. Notwithstanding the presence of historical and legal provisions to support study and research in vocational and technical education, the inquiry process has not been productive until recent years, despite annual and periodic attempts by the Congress to evaluate and suggest improvements in the vocational program. The Russell Report (Russell & others, 1938) and the report of the Panel of Consultants (U.S. Department of Health, Education, and Welfare, 1963) indicated this traditional weakness and the lack of data on the program.

Vocational administrators have generally used provisions for ongoing program activities in keeping with the legislative intent to promote and encourage vocational education. Numerous local communities and states and occasionally the federal government have conducted surveys of the need for vocational education and its support for many years. The influences of the promotion and encouragement motivation can be informally traced through many theses and dissertations. Business and industrial organizations and state agencies affiliated with labor and the employment services occasionally have cooperated in this type of research activity. Studies of student placement and follow-up studies have frequently been made by individual schools, individual states, and several states in a regional form of cooperation. Considerable discussion and study, not of a research nature, have taken place for many years in curriculum study as appropriate to the development of programs and instructional materials in several laboratories across the country. Unfortunately, through lack of communication and coordination, much duplication in course offerings and materials has occurred, and far too little effort has been devoted to the exploration of new occupations and the changing nature of work.

Colleges and universities with programs of vocational-teacher education have traditionally conducted most of the research in the broad field. For the most part, this activity is the product of graduate students in the various specializations of vocational and technical education, guidance, and counseling, and occasionally in educational administration. Little basic research has been done, and few staff studies by teacher educators, who are largely committed to conducting classes, have added new knowledge or improved techniques. Commensurately, the preparation of researchers has also received only incidental attention. Notably, some of the teacher educators in agricultural education and home economics education have cooperated for many years in their respective specializations in regional research efforts.

For most of the half-century of reimbursed vocational education, the federal government, particularly the U.S. Office of Education (USOE), has been weak in research activity, in employing research personnel, in disseminating research results, and in encouraging and coordinating research in the states. This condition is difficult to reconcile with the traditional purpose of the federal agency and its commission to collect educational data and statistics to describe the state of education in the nation at large.

Fortunately, however—and particularly since the passage of the Vocational Education Act of 1963 and other legislation affecting occupational education—research activity in all aspects of vocational and technical education has been increasing at an accelerated pace. Burgener (1967) reports the formation of a new organization for research personnel in vocational education. Cooperative efforts to prepare research personnel, particularly through research seminars, have taken place during the past five years as a result of planning on the part of the Research Committee of the American Vocational Association, the USOE, and many universities throughout the nation.

Suggested Nature of Research. Particularly since

1960 there have been numerous theories about the nature of research in vocational and technical education. Basically, the theories are not antithetical, but because of the limited research which has been conducted, many of the suggestions will not be implemented for a decade or longer. Despite the apparent lack of vocational research, vocational education has pioneered in the use of community occupational surveys, recommendations of local advisory committees, and occupational analyses; it is unlikely that those responsible for any other aspect of the secondary-education program have planned their program on as sound a research basis as that of vocational education. Brandon and Evans (1965) use a paradigm developed by Clark and others (1962) and make some adaptations for vocational research. Evans in particular emphasizes the categories of (1) investigation of educationally oriented problems, (2) classroom experimentation, (3) field testing, and (4) demonstration and dissemination, but with the reservation that unless the results of research in basic scientific investigation (content-indifferent and content-relevant) are known to researchers their work will be seriously handicapped or completely worthless. He also indicates a need for "social bookkeeping" with respect to the supply and demand of trained workers, both quantitative and qualitative aspects.

In another context, that of reporting research performed in vocational, technical, and practical arts education, Wenrich and others (1962) point out that research is highly compartmentalized, that industrial sociologists and psychologists are not aware of work done in vocational and practical arts education, and that there are glaring deficiencies in the treatment of principles of teaching and learning and curricular experimentation. They further indicate the need for research dealing with the sociological and psychological implications of work, specific information about the kind and character of community manpower needs, and the organization and administration of the vocational education program. Their article and bibliography are important, brief indicators of the research up to 1962.

There are numerous other suggestions about needed research. A great many of these are concerned with funded research and have categories or priorities which the funders will recognize. This practice is quite typical of the federal agencies, as made necessary by controlling legislation, the recommendations of advisory committees, or ultimate decisions of administrative officers. Private foundations also tend to support research of a particular viewpoint or orientation. It is likely that state educational agencies with research coordination units (RCU) recently acquired under Title IV C of the Vocational Education Act of 1963 or set up under ancillary provisions of the same law will frame priority lists in compliance with the federal agency or their own designs and purposes. These priorities and categories are indicated in this article in the discussion of the function and activity of the agency or foundation being treated.

Practitioners (teachers, administrators, supervisors, etc.) these days wish to see more of the applied and action-type research. This attitude suggests that more practitioners should be conducting or directing the research; research results, accordingly, should be quickly interpreted, disseminated, applied, and evaluated. Professional researchers, however, should teach practitioners research design and the other elements of the action-type project. This attitude also suggests in this context that instruction in research, while popular and considered good use of provisions, should not be too theoretical or sophisticated. Thus, in research and development there is a strong tendency for the stress to be laid on development, and the practitioners can influence the funders to make it so.

At the other end of the continuum, professional and scholarly researchers advocate more basic research related to the psychological and social foundations of education. They indicate a need for much more freedom, fewer earmarks and priorities, more long-term grants, investment in an idea and a chief investigator, and fewer obligations to interpret and apply research findings. Research instruction should accordingly be theoretical and find great implementation in undergraduate and graduate programs for the preparation of teachers, research personnel, and other educational specialists.

A smaller voice, not necessarily a weaker one, is heard from the advocate of interdisciplinary research. Such an approach would demand the involvement of educators, economists, sociologists, engineers, and specialized others in vocational and technical educational research. It would also involve numerous research methodologies. It is quite clearly illustrated in the research related to the economics of education in general and to vocational education in particular. Current efforts in costs-benefits analysis fall into this category. Systems analysis, operations analysis, and management analysis for decision making are all related to this trend in research and research administration.

Obviously, research activities with the three positions approaches that have been outlined and others will continue. That their extreme positions must be reconciled is quite clear if research and study are to contribute to the meaningful education of youth and adults for the occupational world.

The New Focus on Research Centers. A research center at a major university or in a unit of government is a contemporary development. In vocational and technical education an organizational unit of this nature has been proposed for many years but chiefly for purposes of the coordination of instructional materials in the teaching of occupations in the public schools. The proposal was never implemented, but recently several research centers were established in vocational and technical education. The impetus for at least two of the centers was the reevaluation of vocational education by the Panel of Consultants, its perception of the importance and need for research, and the opportunity it afforded the profession to present position papers. Brandon and Evans (1965) presented the position of the Research Committee of the American Vocational Association in favor of a center which resembled a miniature of the National Science Foundation with research functions particularly in coordination, implementation, and dissemination. Another proposal which indicated a need for a center to concentrate on research, training, and leadership development was drawn up by a group in professional agricultural education (C. Swanson, 1961).

Taylor (1967) describes the philosophy, purposes, organization, and relationships of the Center for Research and Leadership Development in Vocational and Technical Education at Ohio State University. The center's seven purposes include three objectives related to research, plus the study of the role of vocational and technical education, the improvement of leadership, foreign assistance, and retrieval of information. The center cooperates with the Education Research Information Center (ERIC) of the USOE. It is the official clearinghouse for vocational and technical education, although at the present time its abstracting service has not been assimilated into ERIC Central. The center is organized as a separate unit of the university and has an extensive advisory committee to help formulate its direction and activities. It has numerous relationships with professional groups in the field, many of which are represented on its advisory body, and it is also related to the Committee of Institutional Cooperation of the universities of the Big Ten and the University of Chicago. Staff at the center represent a wide range of specialties in the vocational areas and related disciplines of psychology, sociology, and economics. In this early stage of its development the center has been very active in sponsoring numerous professional seminars and conferences in the various areas of vocational education, has taken an active part in evaluation, and has consolidated a great deal of the literature and research information for its abstracting relationship with ERIC.

An active center effort at the University of Wisconsin includes three focuses of research intimately related to vocational and technical education. In the order of their establishment they are the Industrial Relations Research Institute, the Center for Studies in Vocational and Technical Education, and the Institute for Research on Poverty. Brief statements of their functions and official affiliations are made by Somers (1967) on the cover pages of a joint quarterly publication, *The Journal of Human Resources*. Annual reports of the vocational center for 1965 and 1966 by Little and Somers (1966) indicate titles and descriptions of completed or current research projects and of their purposes, staff, conference efforts, and publications. Somers and Little (1966) have published the *Irri Report* dealing with news of the center and the industrial relations institute, research in progress, publications of the faculty, and literature of the field.

At first blush, numerous purposes, functions, and activities of the centers at Ohio State University and the University of Wisconsin appear almost identical. The composition of advisory committees is quite similar in terms of the disciplinary affiliations of members. The Wisconsin staff, which includes many university faculty members, however, shows much stronger ties with economics and sociology than is the case at Ohio State. Wisconsin is not linked with ERIC Central as a primary clearinghouse, but it is active in collecting and disseminating information. Mimeographed newsletters and bibliography under the masthead "Vocational-Technical Report" are distributed by Little and Somers (1967). The Vocational Center and the Poverty Institute at Wisconsin are primarily affiliated with the Ford Foundation and the U.S. Office of Economic Opportunity, respectively, but the center at Ohio State is more formally related to the USOE's Division of Adult and Vocational Research (DAVR).

Another center in vocational and technical education has recently been established at North Carolina State University. A description of its purposes and activities has not been published in the current literature.

Undoubtedly, there are many organizations which are now devoting or which have in the past devoted research efforts to the broad field of occupational education. Numerous colleges and universities have for many years centralized study and research activities in institutes of labor, management, industrial relations, business, and other interests which are intimately related to the various areas of specialization in vocational and technical education. Increased resources from private and public sectors of the economy may allow an expansion of such activity.

There are several centers on the international level which are active in vocational and technical education. There are also current efforts on the part of the United States within the International Education Act to provide for the development of a center of this nature. Wellens (1966) devotes considerable editorial space in a new British periodical, *Industrial Training International*, to a discussion of the establishment of a national center for industrial training in England. He indicates that one difficulty is that such a center would have to show great qualities of leadership and give industrial training a perception of academic and practical study while simultaneously serving as an experimental cross between a government department and an academic or quasi-academic body in a socially oriented field.

The International Labour Organisation (ILO) with headquarters at Geneva, Switzerland, maintains centers for vocational training and research. The center at Geneva distributes a training periodical and a continuing abstract service which are available on a subscription basis directly from ILO Geneva or its Washington, D.C., office. The ILO has been active since 1919, and its machinery consists of (1) the International Labour Conference (world forum), (2) the Governing Body (executive council), and (3) the International Labour Office (world information center and publisher). The ILO's Report of the Director-General (International Labour Conference, 1960), *Youth and Work*, its Bulletin Number 1, *Automation: A Discussion of Research Methods* (International Labour Office, 1964), and its Bulletin Number 2, *A Tabulation of Case Studies on Techno-*

logical Change (International Labour Office, 1965) should be of considerable interest to vocational and technical educators and persons interested in the broad field of manpower.

A more recent establishment of the ILO is the International Centre for Advanced Technical and Vocational Training, at Turin, Italy, which began its operation in 1965. It is a forum for study and research on two levels: (1) by the fellows in the center in the form of their study and its evaluation, and (2) by various organizations interested in the different aspects of economic development, be it sociological, psychological, or pedagogical. Languages of instruction are English, French, and Spanish.

The extensive literature of the ILO and its two centers is readily available from ILO Geneva. It is more accessible at many libraries of major United States colleges and universities.

In 1964, 21 countries and 25 international organizations made up the Organisation for Economic Cooperation and Development (OECD), whose headquarters are in Paris and which has a publication unit with McGraw-Hill Book Company, New York. Although there is not at present a center within OECD, its activities, publications, and interests in economic growth, manpower, and social affairs, development aid, and science and education make it an important organization with respect to vocational and technical education. Its organization and purposes are briefly described in its publication *The OECD at Work* (Organisation for Economic Cooperation and Development, 1964).

There are other international organizations with centralized offices which are active although without formally established centers of research. UNESCO (headquarters are at Place de Fontenoy, Paris), in its Division of Educational Studies and Research and its Department of Application of Sciences to Development, conducts research related to vocational and technical education. The International Bureau of Education (at Palais Wilson, Geneva, Switzerland) records research in comparative education and publishes status reports of the educational levels and types of education of the majority of countries of the world. The United Nations Food and Agriculture Organization (FAO) at Rome, Italy (via delle Terme di Caracalla), carries out a number of functions in technical education and training in food and agriculture.

Federal and Private Support of Research. There are no data which indicate the *total* federal support of research in the broad field of vocational and technical education. Only by inference from the total amounts which are spent for education and training by 10 cabinet departments and more than 15 other agencies is it possible to conclude that the support of research is sizable. A report of the U.S. Bureau of the Budget (1966) estimates an expenditure of $8.4-billion in budget and trust-fund expenditures for education, training, and related programs in 1967. In 1967 the Department of Health, Education, and Welfare used 45 percent ($3.8-billion) of the total, compared with the Department of Defense's 25 percent ($2.1-billion) share, and the remainder of 30 percent ($2.5-billion) will go to all of the remaining agencies of the federal government. More recent data for fiscal year 1967 of federal money for programs administered by the USOE is reported in *American Education* (U.S. Department of Health, Education and Welfare, 1967b).

An October 1966 report of the Division of Adult and Vocational Research (DAVR) of the USOE indicates that a total of 365 projects were approved and funded over the two-year period of 1964–1966 (U.S. Office of Education, Division of Adult and Vocational Research, 1966). By type, there were 139 projects in research, 74 in training, 106 in experimental (including developmental and pilot) studies, 2 in research centers, and 44 in research coordinating units (RCU). The 365 projects were distributed over eight priority areas as follows:

Priority area	Number of projects
Program evaluation	21
Curriculum experimentation	90
Personal and social significance of work	44
Personnel recruitment and development	77
Program organization and administration	75
Adult and continuing education	14
Occupational information and career choice	28
Miscellaneous	16
Total:	365

Most (215) of the projects were approved by the Educational Resources Branch of DAVR. Only 54 projects were approved in the Employment Opportunities Branch. The Human Resources Branch accounted for 96 of the total. The total expenditure for the two years is reported at $28-million, $11-million in 1965 and $17-million in 1966. Annual, unpublished statements of projects funded over the two years of operation are put out by DAVR along with guide lines for proposals, small-project research, and other descriptive materials. The program is also described by the Bureau of Research (U.S. Department of Health, Education, and Welfare, 1967a), in *Office of Education Support for Research and Related Activities*, and by the Management Evaluation Branch (U.S. Office of Education, 1967), in *Fact Book: Office of Education Programs*. Several abstracts of the projects funded by DAVR appear in monthly copies of *Research in Education*, a new publication of the Division of Research Training and Dissemination of the USDE, which is primarily responsible for the operation of ERIC. A helpful, explanatory mimeographed paper of DAVR, "Vocational, Technical, and Adult Education Research for 1967–68" (U.S. Office of Education, Division of Adult and Vocational Research, 1966), indicates the purposes, activities, and research and training priorities of the division.

As previously described in this article, DAVR supports the establishment of two research centers at Ohio State University and North Carolina State University. DAVR also has cooperated with state education agencies to form 44 research coordinating units in as many states whose purpose is to stimulate, encourage, and coordinate research activities among state departments of education, universities, local school districts, and others with an interest in vocational and technical education. The division also supports teacher-administrator in-service training institutes.

The five priority areas in the support of individual projects, which represent the largest share of DAVR's efforts, are (1) program evaluation, (2) vocational education curricula, (3) vocational education resources development, (4) vocational guidance and career-choice processes, and (5) adult and continuing education.

Traditionally, another federal division of the USOE has guided the vocational and technical education program since its inception. Its current designation is the Division of Vocational and Technical Education (DVTE), and it is part of the Bureau of Adult and Vocational Education. In its history it has undergone numerous organizational changes, several of which have occurred in recent years. This division has had a profound effect upon vocational and technical education in the states because it has been the administrative office and the headquarters of specialized personnel of the various vocational and technical categories or subject-matter areas. Since this office has administered the various forms of federal legislation which have supported vocational education through formal channels and relationships with state-agency personnel, many states have emulated many aspects of the federal pattern for a half-century. Current decentralization of the USOE into nine federal regions throughout the United States will have a pronounced effect upon vocational and technical education and the research which should support it. According to a preliminary draft of a memorandum of the Bureau of Research (U.S. Office of Education, 1966c) concerning small-project research, the regional or district offices, when they have been fully staffed, will be highly tied to DAVR.

DVTE's operation is intimately involved with study and research. Currently these may be best seen in its publications list (U.S. Office of Education, Division of Vocational and Technical Education, 1966e). It engages in numerous curriculum studies, professional conferences, a great deal of planning and consultation, and many other activities in addition to its administrative and regulatory functions. It is very active in the broad area of facilities planning in connection with the rapid growth and development of the area vocational-technical school since 1963. Russo and others (1966) have produced a basic planning guide for vocational and technical education; the bulletin includes a bibliography of program and facility planning resources, although it does not include the numerous publications of the Educational Facilities Laboratories, a sample of which is provided by Judith Murphy (1966), and which has high potential interest to researchers in facilities, equipment, and program planning.

DVTE specialists in technical education have a number of publications in process which may be of considerable value to researchers and program planners. In connection with the USOE's Cooperative Project for Standardization of Terminology in Instructional Programs of Local and State School Systems, sometimes referred to as the taxonomy, the Ad Hoc Committee for Technical Education (U.S. Office of Education, Division of Vocational and Technical Education, 1966b) developed a draft of terms to identify and describe items of information about subject-matter content in elementary, secondary, junior-college, and adult instructional programs. Also in development are the mimeographed guides "Criteria for Technician Education" (U.S. Office of Education, Division of Vocational and Technical Education, 1966a) and "Pretechnical Post High School Programs" (U.S. Office of Education, Division of Vocational and Technical Education, 1966c). Roney (1962) prepared an important bulletin designed to utilize research results specifically keyed to the preparation of personnel for technical occupations. As illustrated in the curriculum guide, *Electronic Technology* (U.S. Office of Education, Division of Vocational and Technical Education, 1960), numerous technology curricula have been published including chemical and metallurgical, civil and highway, electrical, electronic data processing, instrumentation, and mechanical technology guides. Basically the guides have utilized a matrix as a framework for determining instructional units that are appropriate to various clusters or families of occupations within a technical group.

Many specialists in the division have periodically published research and study reports in agricultural education, home economics education, and industrial education. These reports of graduate research, staff studies, and bibliographies generally reflect activity since 1960; they are listed in the division's publications list (U.S. Office of Education, Division of Vocational and Technical Education 1966e), which also includes materials in administration, food service, health occupations, manpower and training, office occupations, teacher education, and trade and industrial education.

The traditional digests of annual reports of state boards for vocational education to the USOE now appear as *A Review of Activities in Federally Aided Programs* . . . (U.S. Office of Education, 1966b). The review is compiled from financial, statistical, and descriptive state reports and also includes data related to occupational training for the unemployed under the Area Redevelopment Act and the Manpower Development and Training Act of 1962, as amended.

The many study and research activities of the U.S. Department of Labor as they are related to vocational and technical education require treatment which is not possible here; the major efforts and research publications are therefore very briefly summarized. An outgrowth of a research effort initiated in 1934 has produced three indispensable volumes to vocationalists and others interested in manpower, its changing nature, and its importance to the nation's welfare and security. In 1965 the third edition of the *Dictionary of Occupational Titles* was produced by the U.S. Department of Labor (U.S. Department of Labor, Bureau of Employment Security, 1965). The three volumes of the third edition are *Definitions of Titles, Occupational Classification,* and the *Supplement* "Selected Characteristics of Occupations (Physical Demands, Working Conditions, Training Time)." The research involved over 45,000 individual job studies to verify the content of the definitions; over 75,000 job observations were made. The information was mostly obtained by job analyses which involved direct observations of and interviews with workers and consultations with supervisory personnel and the use of data from employers, trade associations, labor organizations, professional societies, and public employment offices. The third edition includes and defines 21,741 separate job titles, which are known by 13,809 additional titles, making a total of 35,550 defined titles. This edition contains 6,432 jobs new to the *Dictionary*. Numerous new features are present. New relationships of job requirements in terms of *data, people,* and *things* is indicated in the six-digit code which identifies each occupation.

Although the *Dictionary* seems to be the most ambitious product of the U.S. Employment Service, particularly of the Division of Technical Development, Heinz, in an unpublished paper written in 1966 reporting the contribution of occupational analysis to vocational education, describes other services which are available: (1) the nationwide network of eight field centers and five special project states observe and analyze jobs in all industries on a cyclical basis, identify new and emerging occupations, and publish the information, (2) pamphlets and brochures are published covering jobs in a selected industry or groups of occupations and trades, and (3) individual job-analysis studies are made by the field centers which contain more detailed information than that found in the *Dictionary,* and changes in jobs and in staffing patterns resulting from the installation of highly mechanized equipment also are identified and charted. A new relationship of the state public employment system and vocational education represented by state boards of education was provided by the Vocational Education Act of 1963. New arrangements should make possible the exchange of information and cooperative working relationships between the organizations.

Two recent publications of the U.S. Department of Labor that should be of great interest to vocational and technical educators are the Employment Service's *Health Careers Guidebook* (U.S. Department of Labor, Employment Service, and National Health Council, 1965) and an entire issue of the periodical *Employment Service Review* (U.S. Department of Labor, Employment Service, 1966), which are both devoted to an emerging new vocational area in health services. In prior issues of the *Review,* Howard (1965) described the work-training provision of the Economic Opportunity Act of 1964 and its relationship to the Neighborhood Youth Corps, and Levine (1965) examined the overall function of the Employment Service in the antipoverty program. Freeberg of the Educational Testing Service is reported to be conducting a study for the Neighborhood Youth Corps and has also reviewed the literature on vocational techniques (tests of interest, social orientation, job-getting and job-holding skills, etc.).

The Bureau of Labor Statistics of the Department of Labor is the primary indicator of the *demand* for workers for the nation's economy. The Occupational Outlook Service, which grew out of a recommendation of the President's Advisory Committee on Education in 1938, began operation in 1941 to supply occupational literature to vocational educators, particularly to guidance and counseling personnel. Typical of manpower status and forecasts is the Bureau of Labor Statistics' *America's Industrial and Occupational Manpower Requirements, 1964–75* (U.S. Department of Labor, Bureau of Labor Statistics, 1966). This publication was the result of a study requested by the National Commission on Technology, Automation, and Economic Progress (1966), which has produced seven voluminous publications concerned with the next decade, *Technology and the American Economy*. The Occupational Outlook Service's *Occupational Outlook Handbook* (U.S. Department of Labor, Bureau of Labor Statistics, 1965) is revised every two years and represents a cooperative effort of several federal agencies and organizations to depict the American world of work to a very diversified readership. The November 1964 issue of the *Occupational Outlook Quarterly* presents an annotated bibliography by Lafayette (1964) of occupational and other manpower information, including a "basic manpower bookshelf" of government publications on manpower. Salt (1966) estimates the need for skilled workers for the decade 1965–1975 in the *Monthly Labor Review,* another publication of the Bureau of Labor Statistics. Of prime interest to technical education is the report, prepared for the bureau, by Rosenthal (1966) on technician manpower requirements, resources, and training needs.

At least three current publications of the Women's Bureau of the U.S. Department of Labor are related to the employment of women as technicians: (1) *Careers for Women as Technicians* (U.S. Department of Labor, Women's Bureau, 1961), (2) the *Handbook on Women Workers* (U.S. Department of Labor, Women's Bureau, 1965), and (3) *Future Jobs for High School Girls,* Pamphlet 7 (U.S. Department of Labor, Women's Bureau, 1966a). Leaflet 10, a list of currently available *Publications of the Women's Bureau* (U.S. Department of Labor, Women's Bureau, 1966b), indicates a dozen classifications of reports which are especially important for information on the status, employment, and education of women in the work force and on legislation affecting them. Considerable information is brought together from other publications of the department, particularly from the Occupational Outlook Service and the Employment Service.

Annual reports of the U.S. Department of Labor's Office of Manpower Policy, Evaluation, and Research (1966—OMR) as illustrated in *Manpower Research Projects* are required reading for researchers in vocational and technical education. In an informal, unpublished statement Rosen indicates that OMR's research program has covered the social, cultural, educational, and economic aspects of unemployment and the underutilization of manpower and that research has centered on the excessive unemployment or underutilization of the young, the nonwhite, the poorly educated, the handicapped, the older worker, and others. Investigations are also made of employment in chronically depressed communities, regions, and industries, and skill shortages. OMR's four years of sponsored research have led to at least five amendments to the Manpower Development and Training Act. There is evidence of the application of OMR research in education and industry and in the publication of three recent books: Sheppard and Belitsky's *The Job Hunt* (1966), Greenfield's *Manpower and the Growth of Producer Services* (1966), and Kuhn's *Scientific and Managerial Manpower in Nuclear Industry* (1966). OMR, in addition to serving as a coordinator of research in the Department of Labor, was instrumental in the passage of an amendment which authorized the secretary of labor to make grants to strengthen manpower programs in colleges and universities and to stimulate the study of manpower problems by individual students and scholars. This action has been implemented through the small-grants program and an institutional-grants program, the latter to support long-term programs of research, to provide technical assistance to organizations interested in manpower policies and programs, to recruit and train needed research personnel, and to develop interdisciplinary research concerned with the utilization of human resources. Currently 40 doctoral students are receiving support from the small-grants program; 45 scholars are being supported in innovative and exploratory studies.

OMR is optimistic about its program in 1967–68, when studies currently under way will be completed and others initiated with two primary emphases: people in the world of work, and the economy and its manpower institutions. Promising studies of people in the world of work are (1) The Ohio State University's longitudinal study of labor-force behavior, (2) a study by the Bureau of Social Science Research of in-migrants and their occupational adjustment, and (3) a study by the New York City chapter of the Association for the Help of Retarded Children on the employment of mentally retarded adults. Studies concerned with the economy and manpower institutions are (1) the Purdue Research Foundation's study of needed educational and training adjustment of apprenticeship program (2) the Milwaukee State Employment Service's development of a model system of occupational and employment information under the Vocational Education Act of 1963, (3) Harvard University's study of internal adjustments in manufacturing to tightening labor markets and skill shortages, (4) the University of Illinois' study (under W. H. Franke) of training and recruitment problems for selected technical occupations with labor shortages, (5) Youth Corps Program studies at George Washington University and by National Analysts (Philadelphia), and (6) other action-oriented projects. OMR is also interested in initiating research concerning the adequacy, extent, and quality of training in the United States.

The National Science Foundation's interest in the education of scientific and engineering personnel has led to some research activities on its part and to its cooperation with others in studies that relate to the engineering technician. It cooperated with the U.S. Employment Service (U.S. Department of Labor, Employment Service, 1961) in examining technical occupations in research, design, and development. Its grant and contract studies are usually reported in the literature and in its *Publications of the National Science Foundation* (National Science Foundation, 1966), in "Manpower and Education Studies."

The various military services are very active in research which is invaluable to vocational and technical education. Training, testing, curriculum construction, personnel research and analysis, and many other activities are being conducted on an almost inconceivable scale in various branches of the military. Despite the fact that the activities are carried on in a military environment and that much information is classified, military occupations and their civilian counterparts have many similarities in function and in the vocational and technical education they require. In the past the most difficult problem for researchers has been that of securing information easily on a systematic basis for study and reference. Under grants, numerous private and public persons, organizations, colleges, and universities conduct research for the military services that is in addition to research and study performed by each service in its central office and field branches.

Ready access to military research information is now possible. Wiersteiner (1967), in an unpublished description written for this article, indicates the presence of a primary information-retrieval system used by the federal government (and which includes almost all research done under government auspices) under the clearinghouse term Defense Documentation Center (DDC). The computerized DDC, formerly Armed Forces Technical Information Agency, ASTIA, is based on identification (AD) numbers. DDC's periodical manual, *Technical Abstract Bulletin* (*TAB*), contains brief research descriptions and AD numbers by which copies of research reports may be ordered. Quarterly summaries of *TAB* are published and also a thesaurus of DDC descriptions by which research reports can be identified when AD numbers or exact titles are not known. Classified materials are indicated. The Defense Supply Agency distributes these publications in connection with DDC.

In addition to DDC, another government agency, Clearinghouse for Federal, Scientific, and Technical

Information (CFSTI), provides information retrieval. This system, formerly the Office of Technical Services, provides service and AD numbers similar to DDC's. Its semimonthly journal, *U.S. Government Research and Development Reports,* is available from the U.S. Department of Commerce. It consists of machine-usable records from the Atomic Energy Commission, the National Aeronautics and Space Administration, the Defense Documentation Center, and the Clearinghouse for Federal, Scientific, and Technical Information.

In 1963 the Ford Foundation and its Fund for the Advancement of Education became interested in vocational and technical education in the United States. They are currently assisting numerous experiments and pilot programs which have application for the improvement of the program. The status of its support program is reported in *Ford Foundation Grants in Vocational Education* (Ford Foundation, 1965). The report indicates that grants are supporting work in principally four categories in secondary schools, technical institutes, community colleges, research organizations, universities, and teacher education institutions: (1) curriculum improvement, (2) research, development, and information, (3) vocational-technical teacher education, and (4) cooperative work-study education. The foundation supports work at the University of Wisconsin and at the American Institute for Research. A one-year study by the W. E. Upjohn Institute for Employment Research financed by a grant from the Ford Foundation concentrated on the study of industrial advisory committees and their relationships, influences on programs, selection of students for job placement, and financial support. Portions of this study are reported by Burt (1966).

Selected Research in Colleges and Universities. Funds recently made available for research and development under the Vocational Education Act, the Manpower Development and Training Act, the Elementary and Secondary Education Act, the Economic Opportunity Act, and other legislation have greatly stimulated research acitvity in higher education. There is no federal coordination and evaluation of this total effort, and there are precedents that suggest that Congress will assess the value of the expenditure or cut back the funds, or perhaps do both. Current vocational-research funds have already received the Congressional axe.

The research products of graduate students include few studies which are related to the total field of vocational and technical education. The subject matter of graduate education is not structured to produce research of this nature. Wiersteiner (1967), in an abstract search and report prepared for this article for the period 1958–1966, found a total of 2,416 masters' and doctoral studies (including 18 staff studies) in the whole field. Approximately two-thirds of these were reported as studies for the master's degree. It is probably safe to conclude that the availability of research funds has not greatly influenced the amount of research activity in vocational and technical education on the part of graduate students up to the present time. If special research provisions in forms of fellowships, scholarships, small grants, etc., for graduate students are made, there could be an upsurge in interest and productivity which might have a more pronounced effect upon educational theory and practice such activity now has. The efforts of experienced scholars and investigators which are now supported by research funds are fruitful. Acknowledged weaknesses are in dissemination, application, and evaluation. Numerous completed projects and others currently in progress are worthy of examination.

Borosage (1963) completed a four-year, inter-university study in cooperation with the Michigan State Board of Control for Vocational Education. Actually, the evaluation study and report is a compilation of 25 substudies by many individuals who made separate reports. As illustrated in a study of high school principals' perceptions of assistance needed for vocational programs, Wenrich and Ollenburger (1963) made a series of the substudies. The overall study has several distinctions: (1) it is unique as a state evaluation study of vocational education, (2) it involved numerous individuals and groups in the evaluation process, (3) it brought under close scrutiny for a fresh attack a series of traditional practices, and (4) its recommendations for program adjustment were made at an opportune time for influencing the new vocational legislation of 1963. Subsequently, Wenrich and Hodges (1966) concentrated on the study of administrative and supervisory leadership for the local schools' vocational programs. Silvius and Laws (1966), also of Michigan, used a task-force approach in studying the relationship of mathematics to technicians' preparation and functions. With continued support of the Michigan Department of Public Instruction for evaluation, Byram (1965) developed a manual as a result of two years of work with three local schools to determine the feasibility of appraisal on a smaller scale with less involvement.

Since 1958 studies of technicians and technologies have been frequent. Previous to 1960, as may be expected, study concentrated for the most part on the need for and utilization of technicians, on the analysis of technicians' activities on the job, and occasionally on the educational needs of technicians. Since 1960 much greater interest has been shown in curriculum planning in technical education, particularly in relation to its relationships to mathematics and science. Brandon (1960) attempted to develop a research design or methodology for curriculum construction on a matrix scheme. Barlow and Schill (1962) examined the role of mathematics in electrical-electronic technology with data from technical workers and instructors on the basis of interviews and Q-sorts which determined concepts or skills needed in job performance. Roney and Fribance (1966) designed a two-year post-high school curriculum for electromechanical technology with emphasis on the interrelationship of electronic and mechanical phenomena and their basic relationship to mathematics and science. Bjorkquist (1966) is currently experimenting with a retraining research project using two mechanical-design programs, each one of which is shortened to one year instead of having the traditional two-year organization. Extensive follow-up treatment of graduates is being conducted. In a move to minimize extraneous and repetitious content, Schill and Arnold (1967) are studying basic curriculum similarities in six technologies and their common relationship to communication, numerical control, data processing, projection and graphic representation, and machine elements and calculations. Whitney (1966), in cooperation with the American Technical Education Association, has completed a pilot project in the development and testing of instruments and procedures for a study of student-selection practices in technical education. Baysinger (1966), working with the Fluid Power Society, has produced an extensive report concerned with the introduction of emerging technologies as explored in seven institutes and with the development of new instructional materials heretofore unavailable to schools. Mitzel and Brandon (1966) are in the second year of experimentation with teaching strategies which employ computer-assisted instruction in mathematics, engineering mechanics, and communications teleprocessed from a campus laboratory to a branch campus and an area community college. Impellitteri is using Mitzel's computer hardware at Pennsylvania State University to develop a workable counseling tool to provide students with current occupational information that is relevant to their capabilities and interests.

Industrial and community surveys of the need and nature of technician employments are very frequent; several of the outstanding examples are quite extensive. McClure and Mann (1960), assisted by a research committee, made a very comprehensive study of vocational and technical education for the state of Illinois. The specific target of the study was the projection of a ten-year goal of educational development; organizational and financial plans for the program were analyzed, and proposals were made. In a more limited Illinois study of technician need, Christy A. Murphy and others (1964) surveyed Vermilion County for the number of practicing technicians, their job functions, educational qualifications, material for curriculum development, and a refined method of making technician studies. Dobrovolny (1965) developed several new curricula in electronic and machine-design technologies in cooperation with the Illinois Board of Vocational Education.

Adequate research and study is not being devoted to new and emerging occupations and their educational implications. Undue emphasis upon the industrial and engineering technician and relatively little study of occupations in agriculture, business and distribution, and health and medicine generally indicate that public school curriculum planners may be content to develop existing programs in depth at the expense of at least experimental programs to train people for promising new occupations and to awaken student interest. Rarer still is research on the occupational education of persons who are disadvantaged, who certainly are educable and potentially productive, who are assets in a tight labor market, and who should not become delinquents or institutional cases. Included in this large group are those who leave school early and the dropouts from the general and the occupational education programs.

Fullerton's study of the identification of common courses in paramedical education (1966) is related to an emerging new field of occupational education. His objective was to design curricula based on changing requirements of medical care. Consequently the project gathered curriculum materials for 20 paramedical careers from 126 programs in 110 separate institutions. A recent study of the Bureau of Occupational Research of New York *Education for Occupations* (1967), is an interesting analysis of grass-roots opinion and a summary of the multicounty area studies.

Somewhat akin to the emphasis of the work of the research center at the University of Wisconsin is Kaufman's summary (1967), unpublished, of the status of four current projects of the Institute for Research on Human Resources at the Pennsylvania State University: (1) "The Role of the Secondary Schools in Preparing Youth for Employment," (2) "A Cost-Benefit Study of Vocational Education," (3) "A Comparison of the Effect of Skilled Training Versus Academic Programs on Young School Dropouts," and (4) "A Developmental Program for the Evaluation of Vocational Education in Pennsylvania." Stormsdorfer (1967) made a preliminary study of evaluation for the institute during 1966.

A tentative schema consisting of (1) perception, (2) set, (3) guided response, (4) mechanism, and (5) complex overt response characterized Simpson's research (1966) in the classification of educational objectives in the psychomotor domain. The study is atypical of the nature of research conducted by vocational educators.

Depth study of the administration and organization of vocational and technical education at state levels has not been undertaken very frequently. The nationwide study in progress by Swanson and others should show preliminary reports by 1967 of the administrative aspect and its relationship to all of the 50 states. Four other studies are presently in progress at the School of Education of the University of California at Berkeley.

Research in State Agencies and Consortiums. The nature, amount, and effects of research at the state level at this time are not known. Several interesting new features have become prominent: (1) the effects of the new federal regions of education, (2) the regional consortiums of educational laboratories of state agencies and universities whose primary reasons for existence, according to the legislation that supports them, are related to ameliorating or abolishing low income (and therefore to increasing employment and improving vocational education), (3) the efforts and products of the research coordinating units which are now established in almost all the states and which represent a network centralized in federal funding, and (4) the new compact, the Educational Commission of the States, which establishes a sounding board for educational discussion and an inquiry base for the improvement of education. Unique in federal subsidy of many activities, state agencies have administered the vocational program for fifty years; this condition is strenuously challenged by higher education, by labor and poverty legislation, and by the entry of private industry into the educational fields traditionally reserved for the public schools.

Numerous state studies of the past and those currently being made attest to considerable activity. This activity has principally been by nature a form of social bookkeeping or needs assessment. If it is done well and with some degree of regularity, its importance cannot be denied. Its limitation, and one which is likely to continue, is the fact that it is not basic research in the sense that the learning process is investigated and more adequately understood.

Research on the International Level. Vocational and technical education as a general endeavor has been, and will continue to be, very active in other countries. Research in the field has been far less actively undertaken than has instruction itself. The establishment and efforts of the research centers previously described indicate that interest and expectations are running high for the tasks of research and study. This attitude is not reserved to the developed countries of western Europe, the Soviet Union, Japan, or the few countries which have received the bulk of foreign assistance; the developing countries in Latin America and Southeastern Asia are also interested in research in vocational and technical education. The Agency for International Development (AID) of the U.S. Department of State (1966) reports numerous studies and surveys in Africa, the Middle East, South Asia, Latin America, and the Far East. The report shows AID assistance going to 182 active projects in 59 developing countries for a total dollar expenditure of $98,608,000, plus another $11,030,000 in loans in fiscal year 1965.

Special facsimile pages from a UNESCO report made for this article show a planned expenditure of $18,638,500 for technical and technological education and training for 1967–68. Projects seem to involve teacher education, curriculum development, literacy, and access of women to education. Programs in agricultural education and science will use an expenditure of $2,390,000.

In Western Europe, Scandinavia, Russia, and Italy quite drastic reorganizations of education, including vocational and technical education, have taken place during the past decade. The first issue of *CIRF Training for Progress,* a periodical of the International Labour Organisation (1961), devoted a section to research and development in technical education in France, Italy, and the European Coal and Steel Community. The modernization of apprenticeship, a system and an institution which has not tolerated many changes since the Middle Ages, is occurring in the developed countries of Europe. Hopefully, the medium of research may provide a channel of communication and a mutual understanding that has not been too successfully achieved by other vehicles in the past.

CONTINUING ADMINISTRATIVE PROBLEMS IN RESEARCH. The general problems of research administration manifest themselves with considerable difference in the vocational and technical areas. This is not to say that sound principles of administration will not work. To begin with, vocational and technical administrators are not "research prone," and that simply means that research may have to justify itself in some ways which may not be palatable to research personnel. Possibly this sensitivity between researcher and administrator is always present, because the former wishes to study what he pleases, and the latter wishes to direct the attention and study to justifiable or demonstrable ends. Evans and Brandon (1965), in the 64th yearbook of the NSSE, suggest that a delicate balance must prevail. There is also the further problem that many administrators are not experienced in problems of research administration; the heavy support of research during the past few years has brought on, inopportunely, the many problems of organizing, operating, and evaluating a research program of sizable dimensions.

Research in vocational and technical education is a recent undertaking, and before some degree of sophistication could be achieved in and among the various specializations of this field, considerable research had become interdisciplinary. Regardless of the desirability of the interdisciplinary involvement, communication and understanding are highly problematical. Research techniques, methodology, and the jargon and terminology of any one discipline are not always well understood or readily acceptable to workers in another discipline. This condition is clearly reflected in research in the area of the economics of education, and more particularly in the economics of vocational education, which is being actively pursued at the present time. No doubt, the economist has justifiable interest in the analysis of expenditures and benefits if they are related to the decision-making process. The educator, on the other hand, cannot tolerate the hanging of a price tag on the many intangible purposes of educational programs or a monetary assessment of their contributions to the welfare of the benefactors of the programs. Obviously, if research is to be interdisciplinary in nature it will have to be accompanied by education at many levels and not restricted to any one of the disciplines, even if the necessity of such education is not immediately evident to those who are counting the costs.

The ratio of supply to demand of research personnel and its imbalance may not be unique as a problem of administration. It is severe and critical in the vocational and technical education areas. Little alleviation is promised from teacher education at the undergraduate level if teaching and teacher education persist in being the royal road to all areas of professional specialization and career objectives. At the master's level the condition is little better. Hopefully the advent of funds for programs to prepare research personnel is a step in a promising direction. Funding alone will not correct the situation or supply the numbers of dedicated personnel with the curiosity and intellectual capacity to attack the research problems which must be confronted in the years ahead.

George L. Brandon
Pennsylvania State University

References

American Vocational Association. "Program of Work—Focus 1967." *Am Voc Assn Washington Desk* 1:2–3; 1967.

Barlow, Melvin L. "A Platform for Vocational Education in the Future." In Barlow, Melvin L. (Ed.) *Vocational Education,* 64th Yearbook, Part I, NSSE. U Chicago Press, 1965. p. 280–93.

Barlow, Melvin L., and Schill, William J. *The Role of Mathematics in Electrical-electronic Technology.* U California, 1962. 132p.

Baysinger, Gerald. *The Fluid Power Institutes—A Pilot Program for Introducing Emerging Technologies.* Fluid Power Society, 1966. 290p.

Bjorkquist, David C. "Selection, Performance, and Placement of Trainees in Two Technical Programs Under the Manpower Development and Training Act." Paper presented at the 60th Annual Convention of the American Vocational Association, Pennsylvania State U, 1966. 7p. (Mimeographed.)

Borosage, Lawrence. *Vocational Education in Michigan.* Final Report of the Michigan Vocational Evaluation Project. Michigan State U, 1963. 252p.

Boulding, Kenneth E. "Expecting the Unexpected: The Uncertain Future of Knowledge and Technology." In Morphet, E. L. (Ed.) *Prospective Changes in Society by 1980.* Colorado Department of Education, 1966. p. 199–213.

Brandon, George L. *Twin Cities Technicians.* Michigan State U, 1958. 70p.

Brandon, George L. *Explorations in Research Design: Curricula for Technicians.* USOE Cooperative Research Project No. 629, Michigan State U, 1960. 75p.

Brandon, George L., and Evans, Rupert N. "Research in Vocational Education." In Barlow, Melvin L. (Ed.) *Vocational Education,* 64th Yearbook, Part I, NSSE. U Chicago, 1965. p. 263–80.

Brandon, George L., and others. *Vocational Education in a Robot Revolution.* Michigan State U, 1957. 37p.

Burgener, V. E. "AVERA Officially Organized." *Am Voc J* 42:64; 1967.

Burt, Samuel M. "Industry Participation in Local Public School Vocational and Technical Education." In *Dimensions of Manpower Policy: Programs and Research.* Johns Hopkins Press, 1966. p. 181–99.

Byram, Harold M. *Evaluation of Local Vocational Education Programs.* Michigan State U, 1965. 81p.

Byram, Harold M., and Wenrich, Ralph C. *Vocational Education and Practical Arts in the Community School.* Macmillan, 1956. 512p.

Center for Vocational and Technical Education. *A Bibliography on Technical Education.* Ohio State U, 1966. 16p.

Clark, David, and others. "The Behavioral Sciences in Education." In Goldhammer, Keith, and Elam, Stanley (Eds.) *Dissemination and Implementation: Third Annual Phi Delta Kappa Symposium on Educational Research.* PDK, 1962. p. 107.

Clark, Harold F., and others. In Willis, Benjamin C. (Ed.) *Education for a Changing World of Work,* Appendix III. GPO, 1963. 91p.

Dobrovolny, Jerry S. *Machine Design Technology.* U Illinois, 1965. 65p.

Emerson, Lynn A. "Achievements and Limitations." In Willis, Benjamin C. (Ed.) *Education for a Changing World of Work.* GPO, 1962(*a*). p. 100–10.

Emerson, Lynn A. "Technical Training in the United States." In Willis, Benjamin C. (Ed.) *Education for a Changing World of Work,* Appendix I. GPO, 1962(*b*).

Evans, Rupert N., and Brandon, George L. "Research in Vocational Education." In Barlow, Melvin L. (Ed.) *Vocational Education* 64th Yearbook, NSSE. U Chicago Press, 1965. p. 276.

Feldman, Marvin J. *Making Education Relevant.* Ford Foundation, 1966. 14p.

Ford Foundation. *Ford Foundation Grants in Vocational Education.* The Foundation, 1965. 28p.

Fullerton, Bill J. *The Identification of Common Courses in Paramedical Education.* Arizona State U, 1966. 158p.

"Grantsmanship." *Ed Age* 3:44–5; 1966.

Greenfield, Harry I. *Manpower and the Growth of Producer Services.* Columbia U Press, 1966. 144p.

Henninger, G. Ross. *The Technical Institute in America.* McGraw-Hill, 1959. 276p.

Howard, Jack. "The Neighborhood Youth Corps." *Employment Service R* 2:37–40; 1965.

International Labour Conference. *Youth and Work.* Report of the Director-general. International Labour Office, 1960. 119p.

International Labour Office. *Automation: A Discussion of Research Methods.* Labour and Automation. International Labour Organization, 1964. 276p.

International Labour Office. *A Tabulation of Case Studies on Technological Change.* Labour and Automation. International Labour Organization, 1965. 87p.

International Labour Organisation. "Research and Development." Centre Internationale d'Information et de Recherche sur la Formation Professionelle: *Training for Progress* 1:31–3; 1961.

Karnes, M. Ray. "Technical Education." *R Ed Res* 32:423–32; 1962.

Kaufman, Jacob J. "Summary Statement of the Activities of the Institute for Research on Human Resources." Pennsylvania State U, February 20, 1967. (Letter to the author.)

Kourmadas, John F., and others. "Vocational Education: Time for Decision." *B Nat Assn Sec Sch Prin* 49:3–153; 1965.

Kuhn, James W. *Scientific and Managerial Manpower in Nuclear Industry*. Columbia U Press, 1966. 209p.

Lafayette, David P. "Counselor's Guide to Occupational and Other Manpower Information." *Occupational Outlook Q* November 1964. 87p.

Levine, Louis. "The Employment Service Retools for the Antipoverty Program." *Employment Service R* 2:1–4; 1965.

Levitan, Sar A. *Vocational Education and Federal Policy*. W. E. Upjohn Institute for Employment Research, 1963. 29p.

Little, J. Kenneth, and Somers, Gerald G. "Annual Report, November 1966." Center for Studies in Vocational and Technical Education, U Wisconsin, 1966. 65p. (Mimeographed.)

Little, J. Kenneth, and Somers, Gerald G. "Newsletter." *Voc-Technical Report* 1:1–5; 1967. (Mimeographed.)

McClure, William P., and Mann, George C. *Vocational and Technical Education in Illinois: Tomorrow's Challenge*. U Illinois, 1960. 163p.

Mitzel, Harold E., and Brandon, George L. *Experimentation with Computer-assisted Instruction in Technical Education*. Semi-annual Progress Report. Pennsylvania State U, 1966. 127p.

Mobley, Mayor D., and Barlow, Melvin L. "Impact of Federal Legislation and Policies upon Vocational Education." In Barlow, Melvin L. (Ed.) *Vocational Education*, 64th Yearbook, Part I, NSSE. U Chicago, 1965. p. 186–203.

Murphy, Christy A., and others. *Technician Need Study: Vermilion County, Illinois*. U Illinois, 1964. 78p.

Murphy, Judith. *Middle Schools*. Educational Facilities Laboratories, Inc., 1966. 64p.

National Commission on Technology, Automation, and Economic Progress. *Technology and the American Economy*. Vol. 1. GPO, 1966. 115p. (Series of appendix vols: 1: *The Outlook for Technological Change and Employment*. 373p.; 2: *The Employment Impact of Technological Change*, 397p.; 3: *Adjusting to Change*, 275p.; 4: *Educational Implications of Technological Change*, 151p.; 5: *Applying Technology to Unmet Needs*, 291p.; 6: *Statements Relating to the Impact of Technological Change*, 309p.)

National Science Foundation. *Publications of the National Science Foundation*. The Foundation, 1966. 8p.

National Society for the Study of Education. *Vocational Education*. 42nd Yearbook, Part I. U Chicago, 1943. 494p.

Newmann, Fred M., and others. "Education and Community." *Harvard Ed R* 37:61–106; 1967.

Organisation for Economic Co-operation and Development. *The OECD at Work*. The Organization, 1964. 137p.

Roney, Maurice W. *Occupational Criteria and Preparatory Curriculum Patterns in Technical Education Programs*. OE-80015, Vocational Division Bulletin No. 296. GPO, 1962. 26p.

Roney, Maurice W., and Fribance, Austin E. *Electromechanical Technology: A Post-high School Technical Curriculum*. Oklahoma State U, 1966. 34p.

Rosenthal, Neal H. *Technician Manpower: Requirements, Resources, and Training Needs*. GPO, 1966. 111p.

Russell, John D., and others. *Vocational Education*. GPO, 1938. 325p.

Russo, Michael, and others. *Basic Planning Guide for Vocational and Technical Education Facilities*. USOE, GPO, 1966. 32p.

Salt, Allan F. "Estimated Need for Skilled Workers." *Mon Labor R* April: 365–71; 1966.

Shill, William J., and Arnold, John P. "Researchers Developing Core Program for Six Major Technical Occupations." *Sch Shop* 26:12; 1967.

Sheppard, Harold L., and Belitsky, A. Harvey. *The Job Hunt*. W. E. Upjohn Institute for Employment Research. Johns Hopkins Press, 1966. 270p.

Silvius, G. Harold, and Laws, Norman G. *Mathematical Expectations of Technicians in Michigan Industries*. Wayne State U, 1966. 58p.

Simpson, Elizabeth Jane. *The Classification of Educational Objectives, Psychomotor Domain*. U Illinois, 1966. 35p.

Smith, Harold T. *Education and Training for the World of Work*. W. E. Upjohn Institute for Employment Research, 1963. 165p.

Somers, Gerald G. (Ed.) "Education, Manpower, and Welfare Policies." *J Hum Resources* 2:1–130; 1967.

Somers, Gerald G., and Little, J. Kenneth. *Irri Report*. U Wisconsin, 1966. 14p.

Stormsdorfer, Ernest W. "A Developmental Program for an Economic Evaluation of Vocational Education in Pennsylvania." Unpublished report, Pennsylvania State U, June 30, 1967.

Swanson, Chester. "Panel of Consultants on Vocational Education; Summary of Activities." August 8, 1961. 9p. (Mimeographed.)

Swanson, Gordon, and others. "The Swing to Vocational-Technical Education." *Phi Delta Kappan* 46:353–412; 1965.

Taylor, Robert E. "Information on the Center for Research and Leadership Development in Vocational and Technical Education." Ohio State U, 1967. 6p. (Mimeographed.)

University of the State of New York, Bureau of Occupational Education Research. *Education for Occupations*. U State New York, 1967. 82p.

U.S. Bureau of the Budget. *Federal Education, Training, and Related Programs*. The Bureau, 1966. p. 82–101.

U.S. Department of Health, Education, and Welfare. *Education for a Changing World of Work*. GPO, 1963. 296p.

U.S. Department of Health, Education, and Welfare. *Office of Education Support for Research and Related Activities*. GPO, 1967(*a*). 22p.

U.S. Department of Health, Education, and Welfare. "Where the Money Is." *Am Ed* 3:14–7; 1967(*b*).

U.S. Department of Labor, Bureau of Employment Security. *Dictionary of Occupational Titles*, 3rd ed. Vol. 1: *Definitions of Titles*, 809p.; Vol. 2: *Oc-*

cupational Classification, 656p.; Supplement, 280p. GPO, 1965.

U.S. Department of Labor, Bureau of Labor Statistics. Occupational Outlook Handbook. 1966–1967 edition. GPO, 1965. 858p.

U.S. Department of Labor, Bureau of Labor Statistics. America's Industrial and Occupational Manpower Requirement, 1964–75. GPO, 1966. 181p.

U.S. Department of Labor, Employment Service. Technical Occupations in Research Design and Development. GPO, 1961. 113p.

U.S. Department of Labor, Employment Service. "Health Manpower." Employment Service R 3:1–94; 1966.

U.S. Department of Labor, Employment Service, and National Health Council. Health Careers Guidebook. GPO, 1965. 251p.

U.S. Department of Labor, Office of Manpower Policy, Evaluation, and Research. Manpower Research Projects. GPO, 1966. 129p.

U.S. Department of Labor, Women's Bureau. Careers for Women as Technicians. Bulletin No. 282. GPO, 1961. 28p.

U.S. Department of Labor, Women's Bureau. Handbook on Women Workers. Bulletin 290. GPO, 1965. 321p.

U.S. Department of Labor, Women's Bureau. Future Jobs for High School Girls. Pamphlet 7. GPO, 1966(a). 67p.

U.S. Department of Labor, Women's Bureau. Publications of the Women's Bureau. GPO, 1966(b). 10p.

U.S. Department of State, Agency for International Development. A Survey of A.I.D. Educational Cooperation with Developing Countries. USOE, Bureau of Higher Education, 1966. 271p.

U.S. Office of Education. Res Ed. 2; 1966(a). 57p.

U.S. Office of Education. A Review of Activities in Federally Aided Programs of Vocational and Technical Education, Fiscal Year 1964. GPO. 1966(b). 74p.

U.S. Office of Education. "Small Project Research." USOE, 1966(c). 11p. (Mimeographed.)

U.S. Office of Education. Fact Book: Office of Education Programs. GPO, 1967. 85p.

U.S. Office of Education. Division of Adult and Vocational Research. "Vocational, Technical, and Adult Education Research for 1967–68." USOE, 1966. 12p. (Mimeographed.)

U.S. Office of Education, Division of Vocational and Technical Education. Electronic Technology. GPO, 1960. 97p.

U.S. Office of Education, Division of Vocational and Technical Education. Vocational Education in the Next Decade: Proposals for Discussion. GPO, 1961. 197p.

U.S. Office of Education, Division of Vocational and Technical Education. "Criteria for Technician Education: A Suggested Guide." USOE, 1966(a). 147p. (Mimeographed.)

U.S. Office of Education, Division of Vocational and Technical Education. Ad Hoc Committee on Technical Education. "Preliminary Draft Materials on Taxonomy of Terminology of Technical Education." USOE, 1966(b). 24p. (Mimeographed.)

U.S. Office of Education, Division of Vocational and Technical Education. "Pretechnical Post-high School Programs: A Suggested Guide." USOE, 1966(c). 75p. (Mimeographed.)

U.S. Office of Education, Division of Vocational and Technical Education. Scientific and Technical Societies Pertinent to the Education of Technicians. OE-80037. GPO, 1966(d). 48p.

U.S. Office of Education, Division of Vocational Technical Education. "Vocational and Technical Education Publications List." USOE, 1966(e). 15p. (Mimeographed.)

Venn, Grant. Man, Education and Work. ACE, 1964. 184p.

Wellens, John. "Editorial." Ind Train Int 1:329; 1966.

Wenrich, Ralph C. "Vocational Education." In Harris, Chester W. (Ed.) Encyclopedia of Educational Research, 3rd ed. Macmillan, 1960. p. 1555–64.

Wenrich, Ralph C., and Hodges, Lewis H. Experimental Program for the Identification, Selection, and Development of Persons for Leadership Roles in the Administration and Supervision of Vocational and Technical Education. U Michigan, 1966. 82p.

Wenrich, Ralph C., and Ollenburger, Alvin. High School Principals' Perceptions of Assistance Needed in Order to Develop More Adequate Programs for Employment-bound Youth. U Michigan, 1963. 27p.

Wenrich, Ralph C., and others. "Vocational, Technical and Practical Arts Education." R Ed Res 32:363–432; 1962.

Whitney, George. "The Development and Testing of Instruments and Procedures for a Study of Student Selection Practices in Technical Education Programs." American Technical Education Association, 1966. 3p. (Mimeographed.)

Wiersteiner, S. R. "Government Information Retrieval Systems." Pennsylvania State U, March 31, 1967. (Typewritten.)

Woerdehoff, Frank J., and others. Vocational Education in Public Schools as Related to Social, Economic, and Technical Trends. Purdue U, 1960. 116p.